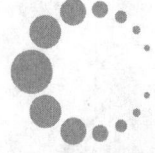

Collins
Russian Dictionary

Collins
Russian Dictionary

HarperCollins Publishers
Westerhill Road
Bishopbriggs
Glasgow
G64 2QT
Great Britain

Second Edition 2000

Latest Reprint 2005

ISBN 0-00-718382-8

www.collins.co.uk

A catalogue record for this book is available from the British Library

HarperCollins Publishers, Inc.
10 East 53rd Street, New York, NY 10022

ISBN 0-06-095661-5

Library of Congress Cataloging-in-Publication Data has been applied for

www.harpercollins.com

First HarperCollins edition published 1995

HarperCollins books may be purchased for educational, business, or sales promotional use. For information, please write to: Special Markets Department, HarperCollins Publishers Inc., 10 East 53rd Street, New York, NY 10022

Dictionary text typeset by Tradespools Ltd, Frome, Somerset

Printed in Italy by Legoprint S.P.A.

Acknowledgements
We would like to thank those authors and publishers who kindly gave permission for copyright material to be used in the Collins Word Web. We would also like to thank Times Newspapers Ltd for providing valuable data.

АВТОРСКИЙ КОЛЛЕКТИВ/MAIN CONTRIBUTORS

Albina Ozieva • Olga Stott • Marina Hepburn • Katya Butler
Maria Marquise • Elena Cook • Irina Moore • Dr Lara Ryazanova
Dr Natasha Vasilyeva McGrath • Tanya Herries • Fatima Eloyeva
Daniel Brennan • Rose France • Rebecca Brown
Michael Cowan-Young • Sheila Bentley
Professor D. Ward

РЕДАКТОР СЕРИИ/SERIES EDITOR

Lorna Sinclair Knight

ЗАВЕДУЮЩИЙ РЕДАКЦИЕЙ/EDITORIAL MANAGEMENT

Jeremy Butterfield

ВЕДУЩИЙ РЕДАКТОР/EDITOR

Maree Airlie

РЕДАКТОРЫ/EDITORIAL STAFF

Judith Turtle • Andrew Knox • Isobel Gordon
Sandra Harper • Elspeth Anderson
Mary Steele • Merle Read

КОМПЬЮТЕРНОЕ ОБСЛУЖИВАНИЕ/COMPUTING

André Gautier • Colette Clenaghan

Содержание

Contents

ВВЕДЕНИЕ

Мы рады, что Вы выбрали словарь, подготовленный издательством Коллинз. Мы надеемся, что он окажется Вам полезен, где бы Вы им ни пользовались – дома, на отдыхе или на работе.

В настоящем введении излагаются некоторые советы по эффективному использованию данного издания: его обширного словника и сведений, содержащихся в каждой словарной статье. Правильное и максимально полное использование приводимой информации поможет Вам не только читать и понимать современный английский, но также овладеть устной речью.

В начале словаря Коллинз помещён список условных сокращений, используемых в корпусе словаря. Далее следуют произносительные таблицы для русского и английского языков. Между двумя частями словаря помещён раздел, посвящённый русской грамматике. В конце англо-русской части даётся список английских неправильных глаголов а также таблицы русских неправильных форм. Некоторые словарные статьи отсылают читателя к данным таблицам для получения нужной грамматической информации. Числительные и фразы, обозначающие даты и время, находятся в самом конце словаря.

INTRODUCTION

We are delighted that you have decided to use the Collins Russian Dictionary and hope that you will enjoy it and benefit from using it at home, on holiday or at work.

This introduction gives you a few tips on how to get the most out of your dictionary – not simply from its comprehensive wordlist but also from the information provided in each entry. This will help you to read and understand modern Russian, as well as communicate and express yourself in the language.

The Collins Russian Dictionary begins by listing the abbreviations used in the text, followed by a guide to Russian and English pronunciation. Between the two sides of the dictionary you will find a section on Russian grammar, and at the end of the English-Russian text are listed English irregular verbs, plus the tables of irregular Russian forms to which entries in the text are referred. Numbers and expressions using time and date are situated at the very back of the dictionary.

О Пользовании Словарём

Заглавные слова

Заглавными называются слова, начинающие словарную статью. Они напечатаны жирным шрифтом и расположены в строго алфавитном порядке. При многих из них приводятся словосочетания и сращения, частью которых выступает данное заглавное слово. Они напечатаны жирным шрифтом меньшего размера. Два заглавных слова в верхней части страницы указывают на первое и последнее слово, отрезка словника, представленного на данной странице.

Перевод

Перевод заглавных слов напечатан обычным шрифтом. Как правило, варианты перевода рассматриваемого слова разделяются запятой, если они синонимичны и взаимозаменяемы в значении, обозначенном пометой. Различные значения многозначного слова разделены точкой с запятой. Более подробно о пометах см. ниже.

Переводы для различных значений многозначных производных слов часто разделены только точкой с запятой и перед ними даётся одна помета типа (*см прил*). Это означает, что последовательное разделение значений рассматриваемого слова и их переводов даётся при слове, от которого данное производное слово образовано. Например, **annul/annulment**.

В некоторых случаях точный эквивалент перевода невозможен, например, когда английское слово обозначает явление или учреждение, не существующие в России, или же существующие в несколько иной форме. Если возможен приблизительный эквивалент перевода, то он обозначается знаком (≈). Если же культурный эквивалент в языке перевода отсутствует, то вместо него приводится толкование.

Пометы

Пометы, служат для разделения значений многозначного слова. Они приводятся на языке-источнике. Их цель – помочь читателю выбрать перевод, наиболее подходящий в том или ином контексте. Пометы являют собой либо синоним, либо слово, указывающее на характерную для данного значения слова лексическую сочетаемость. Пометы также обозначают переносные значения. Пометы напечатаны курсивом и заключены в круглые скобки.

При многих заглавных словах даны необходимые стилистические пометы, обозначающие разговорное или просторечное использование этих слов. Эмоционально – стилистическая окраска перевода обычно совпадает с окраской переводимого слова. Нецензурные или грубые слова помечены восклицательным знаком (!).

Произношение

В англо-русской части словаря все заглавные слова снабжены фонетической транскрипцией, которая заключена в квадратные скобки. В тех случаях, где в роли заглавного слова выступает словосочетание, состоящее из двух или более слов, которые, в свою очередь, приводятся в словаре по отдельности, их произношение указывается только там, где они даны как одиночные слова в алфавитном порядке. Список фонетических знаков приводится на страницах xxix–xxx.

В русско-английской части словаря все русские слова снабжены знаком ударения, поскольку их произношение большей частью достаточно ясно, если указано место ударения. В тех словах, где возможно двоякое ударение, обычно указывается только одно, наиболее часто употребляющееся. Омографы (слова, имеющие одинаковое написание, но различное ударение и значение) приводятся как самостоятельные заглавные слова в том порядке, в котором в них проставлено ударение, например, первым даётся слово **за́мок**, затем - **замо́к.** Более подробную информацию о принципах русского произношения читатель может найти в разделе на страницах xxiv-xxviii.

Служебные слова

В словаре уделяется особое внимание тем русским и английским словам, которые обладают сложной грамматической или семантической структурой. Таковыми являются в первую очередь служебные слова, вспомогательные глаголы, местоимения, частицы итп. Они обозначены пометой KEYWORD.

Английские фразовые глаголы

Фразовыми глаголами называются устойчивые сочетания глагола с элементами **in**, **out**, **up** итп, типа **blow up**, **cut down** итп. Они приводятся в словарной статье базовых глаголов, таких как **blow**, **cut**, и сгруппированы в алфавитном порядке.

Аббревиатуры и собственные имена существительные

Аббревиатуры, сложносокращённые слова и собственные имена существительные включены в общий словник словаря в алфавитном порядке.

Употребление "Вы/ты" при переводе "You"

При переводе на русский язык английских фраз, содержащих местоимения "you/your", даются две формы местоимения:одна в ед. числе, а другая во мн. числе --» "ты/твой", "Вы/Ваш". Если в состав фразы входит глагол в форме повелительного наклонения, то он также переводится двумя формами: 2-го лица ед. числа / 2-го лица мн. числа. В тех случаях, где эмоционально-стилистическая окраска фразы является явно неформальной, для местоимения даётся только форма "ты/твой", а для глаголов в повелительном наклонении форма 2-го лица ед. числа, например, "get lost!" переводится как "отстань!"

Употребление or/или, косой черты и скобок

В англо-русской части словаря между взаимозаменяемыми вариантами перевода, а также частями фразы на языке-источнике употребляется союз "*or*". В русско-английской части словаря ему соответствует союз "*или*". Косая черта (/) означает, что приведённые варианты перевода или фразы в языке-источнике не являются взаимозаменяемыми. В круглые скобки заключаются необязательные но возможные в данном выражении слова, как в переводе, так и во фразе на языке-источнике.

Употребление тильды (~)

Тильда в англо-русской части заменяет заглавное слово в словосочетаниях. Например, если в качестве заглавного выступает слово “**order**”, то фраза “**out of order**” будет представлена следующим образом: **out of ~**. В русско-английской части тильда заменяет: 1) целое заглавное слово: например, в статье “**до́бр|ый**” фраза “**до́брый день**” показана следующим образом: **~ день**. 2) тильда заменяет часть заглавного слова, предшествующую вертикальной черте: например, в статье “**до́бр|ый**” фраза “**до́брое у́тро**” показана следующим образом: **~ое у́тро**.

Употребление звёздочки (*)

При переводе звёздочкой (*) отмечаются те существительные, в склонении которых наблюдаются те или иные отклонения от нормы. В русско-английской части даётся дополнительная информация относительно отклонений от правил склонения и спряжения.

Using the Dictionary

Headwords

The **headword** is the word you look up in a dictionary. Headwords are listed in alphabetical order, and printed in bold type so that they stand out on the page. Each headword may contain other references such as **phrases** and **compounds**, which are in smaller bold type. The two headwords appearing at the top of each page indicate the first and last word dealt with on the page in question.

Translations

The translations of the headword are printed in ordinary roman type. As a rule, translations separated by a comma can be regarded as interchangeable for the meaning indicated. Translations separated by a semi-colon are not interchangeable, though the different meaning splits are generally marked by an indicator (see below). Where a semi-colon separates translations and the indicator refers to a different part of speech eg. (*see adj*), the translations mirror the splits shown at the other part of speech eg. **annul/annulment**.

It is not always possible to give an exact translation equivalent, for instance when the English word denotes an object or institution which does not exist or exists in a different form in Russia or in the Republics. If an approximate equivalent exists, it is given preceded by ≈. If there is no cultural equivalent, a *gloss* is given to explain the source item.

Indicators

An *indicator* is a piece of information in the source language about the usage of the headword to guide you to the most appropriate translation. Indicators give some idea of the contexts in which the headword might appear, or they provide synonyms for the headword. They are printed in italic type and shown in brackets.

Colloquial and informal language in the dictionary is marked at the headword. You should assume that the translations will match the source language in register, and rude or offensive translations are also marked with (!).

Pronunciation

On the English-Russian side of the dictionary you will find the phonetic spelling of the word in square brackets after the headword. Where the entry is composed of two or more unhyphenated words, each of which is given elsewhere in this dictionary, you will find the pronunication of each word in its alphabetical position. A list of the symbols used is given on pages xxix-xxx.

For Russian-English, stress is given on all Russian words as a guide to pronunciation. Where stress can be placed over either of two vowels, the most common or correct stress position is shown for the purpose of this dictionary. Words which are spelt in the same way, but have different stress positions are treated as separate entries, the order following the order of the stress eg. **за́мок** comes before **замо́к**. The section on pages xxiv-xxviii explains Russian pronunciation in more detail.

Keywords

In this dictionary we have given special status to "key" Russian and English words. As these words can be grammatically complex and often have many different usages, they have been given special attention in the dictionary, and are labelled with KEYWORD.

Abbreviations and proper names

Abbreviations, acronyms and proper names have been included in the word list in alphabetical order.

"You" in phrases

In translations of English phrases containing "you/your" or the imperative, "Вы/Ваш" and the formal form is given, unless the phrase is very colloquial eg. "get lost!" where it would be more natural to give the familiar form of the imperative.

Use of or/или, oblique and brackets

The words "*or*" on the English-Russian side, and "*или*" on the Russian-English side are used between interchangeable parts of a translation or source phrase. The oblique (/) is used between non-interchangeable alternatives in the translation or source phrase. Round brackets are used to show optional parts of the translation or source phrase.

Use of the swung dash (~)

The swung dash (~) is used on the English-Russian side of the dictionary to stand for the headword in phrases eg. at "order" the phrase "**out of order**" is shown as "**out of** ~". On the Russian- English side of the dictionary the swung dash can either stand for the full headword eg. at "**до́бр|ый**" the phrase "**до́брый день**" is shown as "~ **день**", or it can stand for the part of the word before the hairline eg. at "**до́брый**" the phrase "**до́брое у́тро**" appears as "**~ое у́тро**".

Use of the superior asterisk (*)

The asterisk (*) is used to mark translations which are in some way irregular in their declension. The Russian-English side of the dictionary contains further information on irregularities.

American variants

American spelling variants are generally shown at the British headword eg. **colour/color** and also as a separate entry if they are not alphabetically adjacent to the British form. Variant forms are generally shown as headwords in their own right eg. **trousers/pants**, unless the British and American forms are alphabetically adjacent, in which case the American form is only shown separately if phonetics are required eg. **jump leads/jumper cables**.

Russian reflexive verbs

Russian reflexive verbs eg. **мы́ться, кра́ситься** are listed under the basic verb eg. **мыть, кра́сить**.

Style and Layout of the Dictionary

RUSSIAN-ENGLISH

Inflectional and grammatical information

Inflectional information is shown in the dictionary in brackets immediately after the headword and before the part of speech eg. **стол (-á)** *м*.

Grammatical information is shown after the part of speech and refers to the whole entry eg. **завид|овать (-ую;** *perf* **позави́довать)** *несов неперех* (*+dat*).

Where grammatical information eg. *no perf* is given in the middle of the entry, it then governs all the following senses.

Use of hairline (|)

The hairline is used in headwords to show where the inflection adds on eg. **книг|а (-и)**. It is also used for swung dash relacement where the swung dash stands for the part of the word before the hairline in phrases.

Stress

Stress changes are shown where they occur, the last form given being indicative of the rest of the pattern eg. **игр|á (-ы́;** *nom pl* **-ы)**. In this example the stress is on the last syllable for the singular declension, moves to the first syllable for the plural and remains there for the rest of the plural declension.

Tables

Some headwords which have particularly irregular inflections are declined in full in tables at the back of the dictionary. Shown in these tables are a small group of nouns, verbs, all cardinal and collective numerals, and personal, interrogative and negative pronouns.

Nouns

In order to help you determine the declension and stress pattern of nouns, we have shown the genitive singular for all singular nouns, and the genitive plural for all plural nouns. This is given as the first piece of information after the headword and is not labelled eg. **стол (-á)**.

Where the noun has further irregularities in declension such as irregular plural forms, partitive genitive, locative singular in "у/ю" or change in stress throughout the declension these are shown at the headword and labelled eg. **яблок|о (-а;** *nom pl* **-и)**.

Adjectives

As the declension of a large number of adjectives in the long form is governed by regular rules, we have not shown the long form endings for these adjectives.

Long form endings have been shown for adjectives which may cause problems in declension in the long form such as adjectives ending in **-ий**, where you might be unsure whether the adjective is "soft" or not, and adjectives ending in **-ин** and **-ов**.

Short form endings have been shown for all adjectives where they exist.

Numerals and pronouns

The genitive has been shown for all numerals and pronouns.

Verbs

Where to look:

The majority of verbs are dealt with in aspectual pairs, and we have chosen to show the translation of the verb at the base form of the pair.

Where the perfective is formed by adding a prefix to the imperfective, the imperfective is considered to be the base form and the translation is shown there. The corresponding perfective aspect can also be found in the dictionary in its alphabetical position, cross-referred to the imperfective aspect.

Where the aspect to be cross-referred is alphabetically adjacent to the aspect to which it will be referred, it is not shown separately unless there is some irregularity in its declension. With the pair **зави́нчивать/завинти́ть, зави́нчивать** is not shown separately.

Where the imperfective is formed by adding a suffix to the perfective, the perfective is considered to be the base form and the translation is shown there. The corresponding imperfective aspect can also be found in the dictionary in its alphabetical position, cross-referred to the perfective aspect.

Verbs which do not occur in aspectual pairs are dealt with at their individual headwords.

In phrases both aspects are shown if both work in the context.

To help you see how a verb conjugates, inflections are shown immediately after the verb headword for all verbs according to the following rules:

– for regular 1st conjugation verbs the 1st person singular only is shown eg. **работа|ть (-ю)**

– for 1st conjugation verbs which contain vowel/consonant mutation the 1st and 2nd person singular are shown eg. **жд|ать (-у, -ёшь)**
пи|са́ть (-шу́, -шешь)

– for regular 2nd conjugation verbs the 1st and 2nd person singular are shown eg. **говор|и́ть (-ю́, -и́шь)**

– for 2nd conjugation verbs which contain vowel/consonant mutation, insert "л", or where the stress changes throughout the declension the 1st and 2nd person singular are shown eg. **люб|и́ть (-лю́, -ишь)**

– for verbs where the verb form changes more than once throughout the conjugation, the 1st, 2nd person singular and 3rd person plural are shown. *umn* is inserted after the 2nd person singular to show that the pattern continues until the next form shown eg. **тол|о́чь (-ку́, -чёшь** *umn*, **-ку́т)**

– for verbs which are not used in the 1st person singular, the inflections are shown for their usual usage eg. **темне|ть** (*3sg* **-ет**) Where the restriction applies to one of the senses, the inflections are shown at the sense itself only if they are irregular.

The imperative mood is shown at the headword where it is irregularly formed.

The past tense is shown at the headword where it is irregularly formed or contains a change in stress.

Inflections given as separate entries

Irregular inflected forms are also shown at their alphabetical position and cross-referred to the base headword. In places an inflected form appears as a separate entry and is followed by *umn*, meaning that there are other inflected forms of the same headword which follow the same pattern eg. **отцá** *umn* means that the other inflections of **отéц** follow the same pattern by dropping a vowel in oblique cases.

Spelling rules

Russian has the following spelling rules which we have not taken as irregular when showing inflection information:

- after ж,ч,ш,щ,г,к and х, ы is replaced by и, я by а and ю by у.
- after ж,ч,ш,щ and ц, е replaces an unstressed о.
- the letter и is replaced by ы following a prefix ending in a consonant.

ENGLISH-RUSSIAN

Gender

The gender of Russian nouns given as translations is not shown for:

- masculine nouns which end in a hard consonant eg. труд, in -й eg. музéй or in a hard or soft sibilant eg. нож, плащ
- feminine nouns which end in -а eg. странá or in -я eg. землѧ́
- neuter nouns which end in -о eg. окнó, in -е eg. мóре or in -ё eg. ружьё.

Nouns for which the gender is shown are:

- those ending in -ь which can be either masculine or feminine eg. дождь
- neuter nouns ending in -я
- masculine nouns ending in -а eg. пáпа or -я eg. дя́дя

Nouns which have a common gender eg. сиротá are labelled *m/f*.

Indeclinable nouns are labelled with gender followed by the abbreviation *ind* eg. кинó *nt ind*.

Adjectives used as nouns are labelled with gender followed by the abbreviation *adj* eg. столóвая *f adj*.

Where the feminine form of a masculine noun is also given as a translation, and the gender of the masculine noun is shown according to the guidelines given above, the gender of the feminine is shown as follows: учи́тель(ница) *m(f)*.

Plural noun translations are always labelled with the abbreviation *pl*, eg. кани́кулы *pl*, and the gender is shown if a singular form exists.

Noun translations are only marked with *sg* where a plural noun headword has a singular translation.

The label *no pl* is used for nouns which do not have a plural form and are only used in the singular eg. лу́ковица, unless the English is also not used in the plural.

Feminine forms

The following conventions are used in this dictionary to show feminine forms of masculine nouns.

- If the feminine ending adds on to the masculine form, the feminine ending is bracketed eg. учи́тель(ница).
- If the feminine ending substitutes part of the masculine form, the last common letter of the masculine and feminine form is shown before the feminine ending, preceded by a dash and enclosed in brackets eg. актёр(-три́са). Where an adjective is used as a noun and has a feminine form, the last common letter does not have to be given eg. безрабо́тный(- ая).
- If the feminine form is given in full, it is bracketed and separated from the masculine form by a character space eg. чех (че́шка).

Adjectives

Russian translations of adjectives are always given in the masculine, unless the adjective relates only to a feminine noun eg. бере́менная.

The masculine short form (or feminine if the adjective only applies to a feminine noun) is also given where it is appropriate.

Verbs

In translation of the headword, imperfective and perfective aspects are shown in full where they both apply eg. **to do** делать (сделать *perf*). If only one aspect is shown, it means that only one aspect works for this sense.

In infinitve phrases, if the two aspects apply they are shown and labelled eg. **to buy sth** покупа́ть (купи́ть *perf*) что-н.

Where the English phrase contains the construction "to do" standing for any verb, it has been replaced by *+infin/+impf infin/+perf infin* in the Russian translation, depending on which aspects of the Russian verb work in the given context.

Where the English phrase contains the past tense of a verb in the 1st person singular, the Russian translation gives only the masculine form eg. **I was glad** я был рад

Where both the present tense and the past tense of the verb "to be" are given in a phrase, eg. **he is/was** ..., it means that the Russian translation will govern the nominative case in either tense. If, however, only the present tense is shown, it can be assumed that the past tense of the Russian translation will govern the instrumental case.

Prepositions

Unless they are bracketed, prepositions and cases which follow verbs, adjectives etc are obligatory as part of the translation eg. **to inundate with** зава́ливать (завали́ть *perf*) *+instr*

Where they are separated by *or* they are interchangeable.

An oblique (/) is used to separate prepositions when the preposition depends on the following noun rather than on the preceding verb eg. идти в/на.

Условные Сокращения в Англо-Русской Части

сокращение	***abbr***	abbreviation
винительный падеж	***acc***	accusative
прилагательное	***adj***	adjective
администрация	***ADMIN***	administration
наречие	***adv***	adverb
сельское хозяйство	***AGR***	agriculture
анатомия	***ANAT***	anatomy
архитектура	***ARCHIT***	architecture
автомобильное дело	***AUT***	automobiles
вспомогательный глагол	***aux vb***	auxiliary verb
авиация	***AVIAT***	aviation
биология	***BIO***	biology
ботаника	***BOT***	botany
британский английский	***BRIT***	British English
химия	***CHEM***	chemistry
коммерция	***COMM***	commerce
компьютер	***COMPUT***	computing
союз	***conj***	conjunction
строительство	***CONSTR***	construction
сращение	***cpd***	compound
кулинария	***CULIN***	culinary
дательный падеж	***dat***	dative
склоняется	***decl***	declines
определённый артикль	***def art***	definite article
уменьшительное	***dimin***	diminutive
экономика	***ECON***	economics
электроника	***ELEC***	electricity
особенно	***esp***	especially
и тому подобное	***etc***	et cetera
междометие	***excl***	exclamation
женский род	***f***	feminine
в переносном значении	***fig***	figurative
родительный падеж	***gen***	genitive
география	***GEO***	geography
геометрия	***GEOM***	geometry
безличный	***impers***	impersonal
несовершенный вид	***impf***	imperfective verb
несклоняемое	***ind***	indeclinable
неопределённый артикль	***indef art***	indefinite article
разговорное	***inf***	informal
грубо	***infl***	offensive
инфинитив	***infin***	infinitive
творительный падеж	***instr***	instrumental
неизменяемое	***inv***	invariable
неправильный	***irreg***	irregular
лингвистика	***LING***	linguistics

Условные Сокращения в Англо-Русской Части

местный падеж	***loc***	locative
мужской род	***m***	masculine
субстантивированное прилагательное	***m/f/nt adj***	adjectival noun
математика	***MATH***	mathematics
медицина	***MED***	medicine
военный термин	***MIL***	military
музыка	***MUS***	music
имя существительное	***n***	noun
морской термин	***NAUT***	nautical
именительный падеж	***nom***	nominative
существительное во множественном числе	***npl***	plural noun
средний род	***nt***	neuter
числительное	***num***	numeral
себя	***o.s.***	oneself
разделительный	***part***	partitive
пренебрежительное	***pej***	pejorative
совершенный вид	***perf***	perfective verb
фотография	***PHOT***	photography
физика	***PHYS***	physics
физиология	***PHYSIOL***	physiology
множественное число	***pl***	plural
политика	***POL***	politics
страдательное причастие	***pp***	past participle
предлог	***prep***	preposition
местоимение	***pron***	pronoun
предложный падеж	***prp***	prepositional
психология	***PSYCH***	psychiatry
прошедшее время	***pt***	past tense
железнодорожный термин	***RAIL***	railways
религия	***REL***	religion
кто-нибудь	***sb***	somebody
просвещение	***SCOL***	school
единственное число	***sg***	singular
что-нибудь	***sth***	something
подлежащее	***subj***	subject
превосходная степень	***superl***	superlative
техника	***TECH***	technology
теле(связь)	***TEL***	telecommunications
театр	***THEAT***	theatre
телевидение	***TV***	television
типографский термин	***TYP***	printing

Условные Сокращения в Англо-Русской Части

американский английский	***US***	American English
обычно	***usu***	usually
глагол	***vb***	verb
непереходный глагол	***vi***	intransitive verb
глагольное слобосочетание	***vt fus***	inseparable verb
переходный глагол	***vt***	transitive verb
зоология	***ZOOL***	zoology
зарегистрированный товарный знак	®	registered trademark
вводит культурный эквивалент	≈	introduces a cultural equivalent

ABBREVIATIONS USED IN RUSSIAN-ENGLISH

aviation	***АВИА***	авиация
automobiles	***АВТ***	автомобильное дело
administration	***АДМИН***	администрация
anatomy	***АНАТ***	анатомия
architecture	***АРХИТ***	архитектура
impersonal	***безл***	безличный
biology	***БИО***	биология
botany	***БОТ***	ботаника
parenthesis	***вводн сл***	вводное слово
military	***ВОЕН***	военный термин
reflexive	***возв***	возвратный глагол
geography	***ГЕО***	география
geometry	***ГЕОМ***	геометрия
verb	***глаг***	глагол
offensive	***груб!***	грубо
singular	***ед***	единственное число
feminine	***ж***	женский род
zoology	***ЗООЛ***	зоология
history	***ИСТ***	история
et cetera	***итп***	и тому подобное
predicate	***как сказ***	как сказуемое
commercial	***КОММ***	коммерция
computing	***КОМП***	компьютер
somebody	***кто-н***	кто-нибудь
culinary	***КУЛИН***	кулинария
linguistics	***ЛИНГ***	лингвистика
masculine	***м***	мужской род
mathematics	***МАТ***	математика
medicine	***МЕД***	медицина
exclamation	***межд***	междометие
pronoun	***мест***	местоимение
plural	***мн***	множественное число
nautical	***МОР***	морской термин
music	***МУЗ***	музыка
adverb	***нареч***	наречие
invariable	***неизм***	неизменяемое
intransitive	***неперех***	непереходный глагол
indeclinable	***нескл***	несклоняемое
imperfective	***несов***	несовершенный вид
attributive	***опред***	определение
figurative	***перен***	в переносном значении
transitive	***перех***	переходный
subject	***подлеж***	подлежащее
politics	***ПОЛИТ***	политика
superlative	***превос***	превосходная степень
preposition	***предл***	предлог

ABBREVIATIONS USED IN RUSSIAN-ENGLISH

pejorative	***пренебр***	пренебрежительное
adjective	***прил***	имя прилагательное
possessive	***притяж***	притяжательный
school	***ПРОСВЕЩ***	просвещение
psychology	***ПСИХОЛ***	психология
informal	***разг***	разговорное
religion	***РЕЛ***	религия
see	***см***	смотри
collective	***собир***	собирательное
perfective	***сов***	совершенный вид
abbreviation	***сокр***	сокращение
neuter	***ср***	средний род
comparative	***сравн***	сравнительная степень
construction	***СТРОИТ***	строительство
noun	***сущ***	имя существительное
agriculture	***С.-Х.***	сельское хозяйство
television	***ТЕЛ***	телевидение
technology	***ТЕХ***	техника
printing	***ТИПОГ***	типографский термин
diminutive	***уменьш***	уменьшительное
physics	***ФИЗ***	физика
photography	***ФОТО***	фотография
chemistry	***ХИМ***	химия
particle	***част***	частица
somebody's	***чей-н***	чей-нибудь
numeral	***чис***	числительное
something	***что-н***	что-нибудь
economics	***ЭКОН***	экономика
eletricity	***ЭЛЕК***	электроника
law	***ЮР***	юридический термин
registered trademark	®	зарегистрированный товарный знак
introduces a cultural equivalent	≈	вводит культурный эквивалент

Guide to Russian Pronunciation

Vowels

1. Russian vowels are inherently short, whereas in English some vowels are inherently long (eg. **beat**) while others are inherently short (eg. **bit**). Russian stressed vowels, however, tend to be slightly longer than unstressed vowels. In unstressed positions all vowels are "reduced" ie. their individual characteristics are not as definite as those of their stressed counterparts.

2. In unstressed positions the letter **o** has the same value as the letter **a** eg. **городá** [gərʌ'da]. Some loanwords and acronyms are exceptions eg. **рáдио** ['raḑio], **госбáнк** [goz'bank].

3. In unstressed positions the letter **e** is pronounced like **bit** eg. **селó** [şi'lo]. The same is true of **я** before stressed syllables eg. **пятѝ** [pi'ţi], and of **a** when it follows **ч** or **щ** eg. **щадѝть** [ʃʃi'ḑiţ]. After **ж**, **ц** and **ш** unstressed **e** is pronounced as [ɨ] eg. **женá** [ʒɨ'na].

4. All Russian diphthongs end in [j], which in diphthongs is pronounced as [i] (eg. **sheet**) with the tongue very close to the roof of the mouth.

N.B. The letter **ё**, always stressed, is not an independent letter of the alphabet, being used only in grammar books, dictionaries etc. to avoid ambiguity eg. **нéбо** and **нёбо**.

Consonants

1. The consonants **п, б, м, ф, в, т, д, н, с, з, л, р, к, г, х** have "soft" or "palatalised" consonants, which are indicated by a "softening" vowel letter **е, ё, и, ю, я** or the soft sign **ь** following the consonant letter: **те** [ţɛ], **нѝва** ['ņivə], **сяду** ['şadu], **мать** [maţ]. Consonants preceding a "soft" consonant may also be pronounced soft, usually if they are pronounced in the same place in the mouth (ie. are "homorganic") eg. **стих** [şţix], though this is not always the case eg. **свет** [şɣɛt].

2. The "soft" consonants **п, б, м, ф, в, г** are pronounced like their "hard" counterparts with simultaneous [j] (as in **yet**).

3. In pronouncing "soft" **т, д, н** the tip of the tongue is drawn back slightly from the position for **т, д, н** and in these "soft" consonants, togther with "soft" **с, з**, the front of the tongue is arched up towards the [j] position.

4. "Soft" **л** is very different from **л**. The front of the tongue is raised to the [j] position, while the back of the tongue must not be raised at all, cf. **лот** [lot] and **лёт** [ļot], **пóлка** ['polkə] and **пóлька** ['poļkə].

5. In "soft" **к, г, х** the back of the tongue is raised somewhat further forward in the mouth than in **к, г, х** and a good portion of the middle of the tongue touches or approaches the roof of the mouth eg. **рукѝ** [ru'ķi], **ногѝ** [nʌ'ģi].

6. The consonants **т, д, н** eg. **ток** [tok], **дом** [dom], **нас** [nas] are pronounced with the tongue-tip slightly further forward in the mouth than in the English counterparts.

7. The consonants **п, т, к** eg. **пасть** [paşţ], **ток** [tok] and **кот** [kot] are pronounced without the slight puff of air which follows them in English before stressed vowels.

8. **л** eg. **лóдка** ['lotkə] is pronounced with the tongue-tip in the same position as in English [l], but the back of the tongue is raised as if one were pronouncing [u], while the middle of the

tongue is depressed. The result is an **л** which is even "darker" than that at the end of English **wall**.

9. There are pairs of voiced and voiceless consonants –

Voiced: **б**, **в**, **д**, **з**, **г** and their "soft" counterparts
Voiceless: **п**, **ф**, **т**, **с**, **к** and their "soft" counterparts

a) At the end of a word a voiced consonant is replaced by the corresponding voiceless consonant eg. **го́род** ['gorət] (cf. **го́рода** ['gorədə]).

b) When a voiced consonant occurs before a voiceless consonant in the same word or at the close juncture of two words it is replaced by the corresponding voiceless consonant eg. **городка́** [gərʌt'ka], **из того́** [is tʌ'vo] (cf. **из э́того** [l'zɛtəvə]).

c) When a voiceless consonant occurs before one of the voiced members of the pairs (except **в** and its "soft" counterpart), the converse happens, and the voicless consonant is replaced by a voiced consonant eg. **сдава́ть** [zd 'vaţ] (cf. **сойти́** [śʌj'ţi]), but **свой** [svoj], **свет** [şγɛt].

N.B. The spelling does not reflect these consonant changes except that the prefixes **воз-/вз-**, **из-**, **(с)низ-** and **раз-/роз-** change to **вос-/вс-**, **ис-**, **(с)нис-** and **рас-/рос-** respectively in the appropriate circumstances eg. **изойти́** [ɪzʌj'ţi] to **исходи́ть** [isxʌ'ḑiţ].

RUSSIAN PRONUNCIATION

Vowels and Diphthongs

Symbol	*Russian Example*	*English Example/Explanation*
[ɑ]	д***а***ть	pronounced like the beginning of diphthong in "eye"
[æ]	ч***а***сть	c***a***t
[ʌ]	д***а***ва́л, ***а***двока́т	c***u***p
[ə]	сту́л***а***	***a***long
[ɪ]	ч***а***сы́, щ***а***ди́ть	b***i***t
[ɛ]	с***е***л	g***e***t
[e]	се́***е***ли	pronounced like the beginning of diphthong in "eight"
[jɛ]	***е***л	***ye***t
[je]	***е***сть	only before "soft" consonants
[ɪ]	с***е***ло́	b***i***t
[ji]	***е***го́	***yi***p
[ɨ]	ж***е***на́	*see note 3 under Vowels*
[o]	д***ё***сны, ч***ё***рный	***aw***e
[jo]	***ё***лка, мо***ё***	***yaw***n
[i]	***и***х, н***и́***ва	sh***ee***t
[ɪ]	***и***гра́	b***i***t
[ɨ]	ж***и***ть	after "ж, ц, ш"
[j]	***й***од, мо***й***	***y***ield
[o]	к***о***т	***aw***e
[ʌ]	***но***га́, ***о***ткрыва́ть	c***u***p
[ə]	к***о***лбаса́, я́бл***о***к***о***	***a***long
[u]	***у***м	sh***oo***t
[ɨ]	с***ы***н	pronounced like "ee", but with the tongue arched further back in the mouth
[ɛ]	***э́***то	g***e***t
[e]	***э́***то	pronounced like the beginning of diphthong in "eight"
[ɨ]	съ***э***коно́мить	not after "soft" consonants
[u]	ут***ю́***г	n***oo***n
[ju]	***ю***г, обо***ю***дный	***you***, ***you***th
[a]	т***я́***жкий	pronounced like the beginning of diphthong in "eye"

[ja]	**я́**сно	initially and after vowels
[æ]	с**я**дь	c**a**t
[jæ]	**я́**сень	**ya**k
[ɪ]	п**я**ти́	b**i**t
[jɪ]	**я**зы́к, по**я**са́	**yi**p
[ə]	ды́н**я**	**a**long
[jə]	сча́сть**я**	"y" + **a**long

Consonants

Symbol	*Russian Example*	*English Example/Explanation*
[b]	**б**анк	**b**ut
[b̦]	о**бе́**д	*see note 2 under Consonants*
[p]	зу**б**, ю́**б**ка	**p**ut
[p̦]	го́лу**бь**	*see note 2 under Consonants*
[v]	**в**от	**v**at
[v̦]	**ве́**тка	*see note 2 under Consonants*
[f]	ле**в**	**f**at
[f̦]	бро**вь**	*see note 2 under Consonants*
[g]	**г**од	**g**ot
[g̦]	но**ги́**	*see note 5 under Consonants*
[k]	но**г**, но́**г**ти	**c**at
[d]	**д**ом	**d**og
[d̦]	**де́**вушка	*see note 3 under Consonants*
[t]	са**д**	**t**op
[ț]	ло́ша**дь**	*see note 3 under Consonants*
[ʒ]	**ж**ена́	mea**s**ure
[ʃ]	ё**ж**, ло́**ж**ка	**sh**oot
[z]	**з**а́втра	do**z**e
[z̦]	га**зе́**та	*see note 3 under Consonants*
[s]	га**з**	ga**s**
[ş]	гря**зь**	at end of word or before voiceless consonant
[ʒ]	и**з**жо́га	mea**s**ure
[k]	**к**от	**c**ot
[k̦]	ру**ки́**	*see note 5 under Consonants*

[ʃ]	и***з*** шёлка	***sh***oot
[ᶋ]	и***з*** чегó	***sh***eet
[l]	***л***óдка	wa***ll***
[ᶅ]	***л***ес	*see note 4 under Consonants*
[m]	***м***ать	***m***at
[ᶆ]	***м***ять	*see note 2 under Consonants*
[n]	***н***ас	***n***o
[ᶇ]	***н***ет	*see note 3 under Consonants*
[p]	***п***асть	***p***ut
[ᶈ]	***п***еть	*see note 2 under Consonants*
[b]	ослé***п***	***b***ut
[r]	***р***от	pronounced like rolled Scots "r"
[ᶉ]	***р***яд	*see note 2 under Consonants*
[s]	***с***ад	***s***at
[ᶊ]	***с***ел	*see note 3 under Consonants*
[z]	***с***давáть	do***z***e
[ᶎ]	***с***дéлать	before some voiced consonants
[ᶋ]	***с***шить	***sh***oot
[ʒ]	***с***жать	mea***s***ure
[ᶋ]	***с***чи́стить	***sh***eet
[t]	***т***ок	***t***op
[ƫ]	***т***е	*see note 3 under Consonants*
[d]	о***т***говори́ть	***d***og
[ᶁ]	о***т***дéлать	before "soft" "д"
[f]	***ф***óрма	***f***at
[ᶂ]	бу***ф***éт	*see note 2 under Consonants*
[v]	а***ф***гáнец	***v***at
[x]	***х***од	pronounced like Scots "ch" in "loch"
[ᶍ]	***х***и́мик	*see note 5 under Consonants*
[ts]	***ц***ель	bi***ts***
[dz]	отé***ц*** ***б***ы	a***dz***e
[tʃ]	***ч***áсто	***ch***ip
[dʒ]	до***ч***ь ***б***ы	***j***ig
[ʃ]	***ш***ýтка	***sh***oot
[ᶋᶋ]	***щ***ит	fre***sh sh***eets

Английское Произношение

Гласные и дифтонги

Знак	*Английский Пример*	*Русское Соответствие/Описание*
[ɑ:]	f**a**ther	м**á**ма
[ʌ]	b**u**t, c**o**me	**а**льянс
[æ]	m**a**n, c**a**t	**э́**тот
[ə]	fath**e**r, **a**go	ра́н**а**, п**а**рохо́д
[ə:]	b**i**rd, h**ea**rd	ф**ё**дор
[ɛ]	g**e**t, b**e**d	ж**е**ст
[ɪ]	**i**t, b**i**g	к**и**т
[i:]	t**ea**, s**ea**	**и́**ва
[ɔ]	h**o**t, w**a**sh	х**о**д
[ɔ:]	s**a**w, **a**ll	**о́**чень
[u]	p**u**t, b**oo**k	б**у**к
[u:]	t**oo**, y**ou**	**у́**лица
[aɪ]	fl**y**, h**igh**	л**а́й**
[au]	h**ow**, h**ou**se	**а́у**т
[ɛə]	th**ere**, b**ear**	произно́сится как сочета́ние зву́ков "э" и кра́ткого "а"
[eɪ]	d**ay**, ob**ey**	**эй**
[ɪə]	h**ere**, h**ear**	произно́сится как сочета́ние зву́ков "и" и кра́ткого "а"
[əu]	g**o**, n**o**te	**о́у**
[ɔɪ]	b**oy**, **oi**l	б**ой**
[uə]	p**oo**r, s**ure**	произно́сится как сочета́ние зву́ков "у" и кра́ткого "а"
[juə]	p**ure**	произно́ситься как сочета́ние зву́ков "ю" и кра́ткого "а"

Согласные

Знак	*Английский Пример*	*Русское Соответствие/Описание*
[b]	**_b_**ut	**_б_**ал
[d]	men**_ded_**	аре́н**_д_**а
[g]	**_g_**o, **_g_**et, bi**_g_**	**_г_**ол, ми**_г_**
[dʒ]	**_g_**in, **_j_**ud**_ge_**	**_дж_**и́нсы, и́ми**_дж_**
[ŋ]	si**_ng_**	произно́сится как ру́сский "н", но не ко́нчиком языка́, а за́дней ча́стью его́ спи́нки
[h]	**_h_**ouse, **_h_**e	**_х_**а́ос, **_х_**и́мия
[j]	**_y_**oung, **_y_**es	**_й_**од, **_й_**емен
[k]	**_c_**ome, mo**_ck_**	**_к_**а́мень, ро**_к_**
[r]	**_r_**ed, t**_r_**ead	**_р_**от, т**_р_**ава́
[s]	**_s_**and, ye**_s_**	**_с_**ад, ри**_с_**
[z]	ro**_s_**e, **_z_**ebra	ро́**_з_**а, **_з_**е́бра
[ʃ]	**_sh_**e, ma**_ch_**ine	**_ш_**и́на, ма**_ш_**и́на
[tʃ]	**_ch_**in, ri**_ch_**	**_ч_**ин, кули́**_ч_**
[v]	**_v_**alley	**_в_**альс
[w]	**_w_**ater, **_wh_**ich	**_уо́_**тергейт, **_уи_**к-э́нд
[ʒ]	vi**_s_**ion	ва́**_ж_**ный
[θ]	**_th_**ink, my**_th_**	произно́сится как ру́сский "с", но ко́нчик языка́ нахо́дится ме́жду зуба́ми
[ð]	**_th_**is, **_th_**e	произно́сится как ру́сский "з", но ко́нчик языка́ нахо́дится ме́жду зуба́ми
[f]	**_f_**ace	**_ф_**акт
[l]	**_l_**ake, **_l_**ick	**_л_**ай, **_л_**ом
[m]	**_m_**ust	**_м_**ат
[n]	**_n_**ut	**_н_**ет
[p]	**_p_**at, **_p_**ond	**_п_**арохо́д
[t]	**_t_**ake, ha**_t_**	э́**_том_**, не**_м_**
[x]	lo**_ch_**	**_х_**од

[aʒ]	А, а
[be]	Б, б
[ve]	В, в
[ge]	Г, г
[de]	Д, д
[je]	Е, е
[jɔ]	Ё, ё
[ʒe]	Ж, ж
[ze]	З, з
[i]	И, и
[iˈkratkɔje]	Й, й
[ka]	К, к
[ɛl]	Л, л
[ɛm]	М, м
[ɛn]	Н, н
[ɔ]	О, о
[pe]	П, п
[ɛr]	Р, р
[ɛs]	С, с
[te]	Т, т
[u]	У, у
[ɛf]	Ф, ф
[xa]	Х, х
[tse]	Ц, ц
[tʃe]	Ч, ч
[ʃa]	Ш, ш
[ʃta]	Щ, щ
[ˈtyɔrdɨ znak]	Ъ, ъ
[ɨ]	Ы, ы
[ˈɱakkɨ znak]	Ь, ь
[ɛ]	Э, э
[ju]	Ю, ю
[ja]	Я, я

A, a [eɪ]
B, b [bi:]
C, c [si:]
D, d [di:]
E, e [i:]
F, f [ɛf]
G, g [dʒi:]
H, h [eɪtʃ]
I, i [aɪ]
J, j [dʒeɪ]
K, k [keɪ]
L, l [ɛl]
M, m [ɛm]
N, n [ɛn]
O, o [əu]
P, p [pi:]
Q, q [kju:]
R, r [ɑ:*]
S, s [ɛs]
T, t [ti:]
U, u [ju:]
V, v [vi:]
W, w ['dʌblju]
X, x [ɛks]
Y, y [waɪ]
Z, z [zɛd, (*US*) zi:]

~ А, а ~

А, а *сущ нескл* (*буква*) *the 1st letter of the Russian alphabet*; **от ~ до я** from A to Z.

KEYWORD

а *союз* **1** (*выражает противопоставление*) but; **он согласи́лся, а я отказа́лся** he agreed, but I refused; **я чита́л, а он рисова́л** I was reading and he was drawing
2 (*выражает присоединение*) and; **снача́ла говори́л он, а пото́м мы** first he spoke, and then we did
3 (*перед перечислением*) namely; (*перед уточнением*) to be exact *или* precise; **пришли́ дво́е, а и́менно: Ивано́в и Петро́в** two people came, namely Ivanov and Petrov; **я должен встать ра́но, а и́менно в 6 утра́** I have to get up early, at 6 am to be exact *или* precise
4 (*во фразах*): **а (не) то** or (else); **спеши́, а (не) то опозда́ешь** hurry, or (else) you'll be late; **а и́менно** (*то есть*) that is; **а вот** but
◆ *част* **1** (*усиливает обращение*) hey; **Ма́ша, а́ Ма́ша!** hey, Masha!
2 (*обозначает отклик*): **иди́ сюда́! – а, что тако́е!** come here! – yes? what is it?; **а как же** (*разг*) of course; **ты обеда́л? а как же** have you had lunch? of course
◆ *межд* (*выражает припоминание, догадку*) ah; (*выражает ужас, боль*) oh; **а ну** (*разг*) go on; **а ну, беги́ в дом!** go on, run along in!; **а ну́ его!** (*разг*) stuff him!

А- *сокр*: **~72, ~76** *different grades of petrol.*
абажу́р (**-а**) *м* lampshade.
абба́т (**-а**) *м* (*в монастыре*) abbot.
аббати́с|а (**-ы**) *ж* abbess.
абба́тств|о (**-а**) *ср* abbey.
аббревиату́р|а (**-ы**) *ж* abbreviation.
Аберди́н (**-а**) *м* Aberdeen.
абза́ц (**-а**) *м* paragraph.
абитурие́нт (**-а**) *м entrant to university, college etc.*
абитурие́нт|ка (**-ки**; *gen pl* **-ок**) *ж см* **абитурие́нт.**
абонеме́нт (**-а**) *м* season ticket.
абонеме́нтный *прил* (*концерт, лекция*) for season-ticket holders.
абоне́нт (**-а**) *м* subscriber.
абориге́н (**-а**) *м* aborigine.
або́рт (**-а**) *м* abortion; **де́лать (сде́лать** *perf*) **~** to have an abortion.
абрази́в (**-а**) *м* abrasive.
абракада́бр|а (**-ы**) *ж* gobbledegook.
абрико́с (**-а**) *м* (*плод*) apricot; (*дерево*) apricot tree.
абсолю́тен *прил см* **абсолю́тный.**
абсолюти́зм (**-а**) *м* absolutism.
абсолю́тно *нареч* absolutely.
абсолю́т|ный (**-ен, -на, -но**) *прил* absolute; **~ная монопо́лия** absolute monopoly; **абсолю́тный слух** perfect pitch.
абсорби́р|овать (**-ую**) (*не*)*сов перех* to absorb.
абстраги́р|оваться (**-уюсь**) (*не*)*сов возв*: **~ (от** *+gen*) to detach o.s. (from).
абстра́кт|ный (**-ен, -на, -но**) *прил* abstract; **абстра́ктное (и́мя) существи́тельное** abstract noun.
абстра́кци|я (**-и**) *ж* abstraction.
абсу́рд (**-а**) *м* absurdity; **доводи́ть (довести́** *perf*) **что-н до ~а** to take sth to the point of absurdity.
абсу́рд|ный (**-ен, -на, -но**) *прил* absurd.
абсце́сс (**-а**) *м* abscess.
аванга́рд (**-а**) *м* (*также ВОЕН*) vanguard; (*ИСКУССТВО*) avant-garde; **в ~е** (*+gen*) in the vanguard (of).
авангарди́зм (**-а**) *м* the avant-garde.
ава́нс (**-а**) *м* (*КОММ*) advance; **~ в счёт платеже́й** advance against payments.
аванси́р|овать (**-ую**) (*не*)*сов перех*: **~ что-н кому́-н** to advance sb sth; (*КОММ*) to make sb an advance payment of sth.
ава́нсом *нареч* in advance.
авансце́н|а (**-ы**) *ж* proscenium.
авантю́р|а (**-ы**) *ж* adventurism; **втя́гивать (втяну́ть** *perf*) **кого́-н в ~у** to involve sb in a risky undertaking.
авантюри́ст (**-а**) *м* adventurist.
авантюри́ст|ка (**-ки**; *gen pl* **-ок**) *ж см* **авантюри́ст.**
авари́йный *прил* (*служба, машина*) emergency *опред*; (*дом, состояние техники*) unsafe; **авари́йный сигна́л** alarm signal.
ава́ри|я (**-и**) *ж* accident; (*повреждение*:

The spelling rules for Russian are shown on page xvii.

механизма, аппаратуры) breakdown; **терпе́ть (потерпе́ть** *perf*) **~ю** (*машина, самолёт итп*) to crash; **попа́сть** (*perf*) **в ~ю** to have an accident.
а́вгуст (-а) *м* August; *см также* **октя́брь**.
а́вгустовск|ий (-ая, -ое, -ие) *прил* August *опред*.
а́виа *нескл* (*авиапочта*) air mail.
авиали́ни|я (-и) *ж* flight path.
авиано́с|ец (-ца) *м* aircraft carrier.
авиацио́нный *прил* aviation *опред*.
авиа́ци|я (-и) *ж* aviation; **гражда́нская ~** civil aviation.
ави́зо *ср нескл* (*КОММ*) advice note.
авитамино́з (-а) *м* vitamin deficiency, avitaminosis.
аво́сек *сущ см* **аво́ська**.
аво́сь *част* (*разг*) perhaps; **на ~** (*разг*) on the off chance; (: *наугад*) by guesswork; **наде́яться** (*impf*) **на ~** to trust to luck.
аво́с|ька (-ьки; *gen pl* -ек) *ж* (*разг*) (string) bag.
авра́л (-а) *м* (*МОР*) emergency task; (*перен*: *разг*) rush job.
австрали́ек *сущ см* **австрали́йка**.
австрали́|ец (-йца) *м* Australian.
австрали́|йка (-йки; *gen pl* -ек) *ж см* **австрали́ец**.
австрали́йск|ий (-ая, -ое, -ие) *прил* Australian.
австрали́йца *итп сущ см* **австрали́ец**.
Австра́ли|я (-и) *ж* Australia.
австри́ек *сущ см* **австри́йка**.
австри́|ец (-йца) *м* Austrian.
австри́|йка (-йки; *gen pl* -ек) *ж см* **австри́ец**.
австри́йск|ий (-ая, -ое, -ие) *прил* Austrian.
австри́йца *итп сущ см* **австри́ец**.
А́встри|я (-и) *ж* Austria.
авт. *сокр* (= *автомоби́льный*) auto. (= *automobile*); = **автоно́мный, а́вторский, а́втор**.
авто- *часть сложных слов* (*со значением автоматический*) *indicating sth done automatically eg*. *автопило́т*; (*со значением автомобильный*) *indicating a connection with vehicles eg*. *автозаво́д*; (*со значением свой, само-*) *self- or auto-, indicating a connection with oneself eg*. *автобиогра́фия*.
автоба́з|а (-ы) *ж* depot (*where a company's vehicles are kept and maintained*).
автобиографи́ческ|ий (-ая, -ое, -ие) *прил* autobiographical.
автобиогра́фи|я (-и) *ж* autobiography.
авто́бус (-а) *м* bus; (*на дальние расстояния*) coach (*BRIT*), bus (*US*).
авто́бусный *прил* (*см сущ*) bus *опред*; coach *опред* (*BRIT*).
автовокза́л (-а) *м* bus *или* coach (*BRIT*) station.
авто́граф (-а) *м* autograph.
автодоро́жный *прил* (*происшествие*) road *опред*; (*инспекция*) traffic *опред*.
автозаво́д (-а) *м* car (*BRIT*) *или* automobile (*US*) plant.
автозапра́вочн|ая (-ой; *decl like adj*) *ж* (*также*: **~ ста́нция**) filling station.
автока́р (-а) *м* fork-lift truck.
автола́в|ка (-ки; *gen pl* -ок) *ж* mobile shop.
автомагистра́л|ь (-и) *ж* motorway (*BRIT*), expressway (*US*).
автома́т (-а) *м* automatic machine; (*ВОЕН*) sub-machine-gun.
автоматиза́ци|я (-и) *ж* automation.
автоматизи́р|овать (-ую) (*не*)*сов перех* to automate.
автома́тик|а (-и) *ж* automatic equipment.
автомати́ческ|ий (-ая, -ое, -ие) *прил* automatic.
автомаши́н|а (-ы) *ж* (motor)car, automobile (*US*).
автомоби́л|ь (-я) *м* (motor)car, automobile (*US*); **легково́й ~** (passenger) car.
автоно́мен *прил см* **автоно́мный**.
автоно́ми|я (-и) *ж* autonomy.
автоно́м|ный (-ен, -на, -но) *прил* autonomous; (*ТЕХ*) independent; (*КОМП*) off-line, stand-alone.
автоотве́тчик (-а) *м* answering machine.
автопило́т (-а) *м* automatic pilot.
автопортре́т (-а) *м* self-portrait.
а́втор (-а) *м* author.
автореферáт (-а) *м* abstract (*of dissertation*).
авторизова́ть (-у́ю) (*не*)*сов перех* to authorize.
авторита́р|ный (-ен, -на, -но) *прил* authoritarian.
авторите́т (-а) *м* authority; **по́льзоваться** (*impf*) **~ом** to enjoy authority; **завоёвывать (завоева́ть** *perf*) **~** to gain authority.
авторите́т|ный (-ен, -на, -но) *прил* authoritative.
а́вторск|ий (-ая, -ое, -ие) *прил* author's; **а́вторский ве́чер** (*поэта итп*) reading; (*композитора*) recital (*given by the composer*); **а́вторское пра́во** copyright; **а́вторское свиде́тельство** patent.
автору́ч|ка (-ки; *gen pl* -ек) *ж* fountain pen.
автосто́п (-а) *м* (*способ путешествия*) hitchhiking.
автостра́д|а (-ы) *ж* motorway (*BRIT*), expressway (*US*).
автотра́нспорт (-а) *м* road transport.
авуа́р|ы (-ов) *мн* (*КОММ*) assets *мн*.
ага́ *межд* aha ◆ *част* (*разг*: *выражает согласие*) uh huh.
ага́т (-а) *м* agate.
аге́нт (-а) *м* agent.
аге́нтств|о (-а) *ср* agency; **телегра́фное ~** news agency; **аге́нтство печа́ти** press agency.
агенту́р|а (-ы) *ж* intelligence service ◆ *собир* agents *мн*.
агита́тор (-а) *м* (political) campaigner; (*на выборах*) canvasser.
агитацио́нный *прил* (political) promotional.
агита́ци|я (-и) *ж* campaigning.
агити́р|овать (-ую) *несов неперех*: **~ (за** *+acc*) to campaign (for).
аго́ни|я (-и) *ж* death throes *мн*.

агра́рный *прил* agrarian.
агрега́т (-а) *м* machine; (*узел*) unit (*of machine*).
агресси́в|ный (-ен, -на, -но) *прил* aggressive.
агре́сси|я (-и) *ж* aggression.
агроно́м (-а) *м* agronomist.
агрономи́ческ|ий (-ая, -ое, -ие) *прил* agronomic.
агроно́ми|я (-и) *ж* agronomy.
ад (-а) *м* hell.
ада́жио *ср нескл, нареч* adagio.
ада́мово *прил*: **А~ я́блоко** Adam's apple.
адапта́ци|я (-и) *ж* adaptation.
ада́птер (-а) *м* adaptor.
адапти́р|овать (-ую) *(не)сов перех* to adapt
▸ **адапти́роваться** *(не)сов возв* to adapt.
адвока́т (-а) *м* (*ЮР*) ≈ barrister (*BRIT*), ≈ attorney (*US*); (*консультант*) solicitor; **колле́гия ~ов** ≈ the Bar (*BRIT*).
адвокату́р|а (-ы) *ж собир* ≈ the Bar (*BRIT*).
АДД *м сокр* (= *авторефера́т диссерта́ции на соиска́ние учёной сте́пени до́ктора нау́к*) abstract of doctoral thesis.
Адди́с-Абе́б|а (-ы) *ж* Addis Ababa.
адеква́т|ный (-ен, -на, -но) *прил* adequate; (*совпадающий*) identical.
адено́ид|ы (-ов) *мн* (*МЕД*) adenoids *мн*.
адм. *сокр* (= **администра́ция**) admin (= *administration*).
администрати́вн|ый *прил* administrative; (*способности*) managerial, management *опред*; **в ~ом поря́дке** by authority; **~ тон** an official tone of voice.
администра́тор (-а) *м* administrator; (*в театре, гостинице, кино*) manager.
администра́ци|я (-и) *ж, собир* administration; (*гостиницы*) management.
администри́р|овать (-ую) *несов неперех* (*+instr*) to administrate.
адмира́л (-а) *м* admiral.
АДМП *ж сокр* = *Агра́рно-демократи́ческая па́ртия*.
а́дрес (-а; *nom pl* -а́) *м* address; **в ~** *+gen* (addressed) to; **Ва́ше обвине́ние не по ~у** (*разг*) you've got the wrong person; **по ~у кого́-н** concerning *или* about sb; **абсолю́тный/относи́тельный ~** (*КОМП*) absolute/relative address.
а́дресный *прил*: **~ стол** address bureau.
адрес|ова́ть (-у́ю) *(не)сов перех*: **~ что-н кому́-н** to address sth to sb; (*критику*) to direct sth at sb.
адриати́ческ|ий (-ая, -ое, -ие) *прил*: **А~ое мо́ре** the Adriatic (Sea).
а́дск|ий (-ая, -ое, -ие) *прил* (*РЕЛ*) infernal; (*разг*: *холод, условия*) diabolical; (: *терпение, выносливость*) fantastic; (*замысел*) cunning.
адъюта́нт (-а) *м* aide-de-camp.
аж *част, союз* (*разг*) even; **он ~ вскри́кнул от удивле́ния** he even cried out in surprise.
ажиота́ж (-а) *м* (*перен*) commotion; (*КОММ*) stockjobbing.
ажу́р (-а) *м keeping of books up to date*; **в ~е** (*разг*) in cracking order.
ажу́рный *прил* lace; **ажу́рная рабо́та** fine *или* delicate work.
АЗС *ж сокр* (= *автозапра́вочная ста́нция*) filling station.
аз|ы́ (-о́в) *мн* (*перен*) basics *мн*; **начина́ть (нача́ть** *perf*) **с ~о́в** to start from scratch.
аза́ли|я (-и) *м* azalea.
аза́рт (-а) *м* ardour (*BRIT*), ardor (*US*); **с ~ом** with zest; **входи́ть (войти́** *perf*) **в ~** to get carried away.
аза́рт|ный (-ен, -на, -но) *прил* ardent; **аза́ртная игра́** game of chance.
а́збук|а (-и) *м* alphabet; (*букварь*) first reading book; (*перен*: *основные начала*) rudiments *мн*; **но́тная ~** *the system of musical notation*; **а́збука Мо́рзе** Morse code.
а́збучный *прил* alphabetical; **а́збучная и́стина** truism.
Азербайджа́н (-а) *м* Azerbaijan.
азербайджа́н|ец (-ца) *м* Azerbaijani.
азербайджа́н|ка (-ки; *gen pl* -ок) *ж см* **азербайджа́нец**.
азербайджа́нск|ий (-ая, -ое, -ие) *прил* Azerbaijani.
азербайджа́нца *итп сущ см* **азербайджа́нец**.
азиа́т (-а) *м* Asian.
азиа́т|ка (-ки; *gen pl* -ок) *ж см* **азиа́т**.
азиа́тск|ий (-ая, -ое, -ие) *прил* Asian.
а́зимут (-а) *м* azimuth.
А́зи|я (-и) *ж* Asia.
азо́вск|ий (-ая, -ое, -ие) *прил*: **А~ое мо́ре** the Sea of Azov.
азо́рск|ий (-ая, -ое, -ие) *прил*: **А~ие острова́** the Azores.
азо́т (-а) *м* nitrogen.
азо́тный *прил* nitric.
а́ист (-а) *м* stork.
ай *межд* (*выражает боль*) ow, ouch; (*выражает испуг, страх*) oh; **~ да Мари́я!** good for Maria!
айв|а́ (-ы́) *м* (*плод*) quince; (*дерево*) quince tree.
айда́ *межд* (*разг*) let's go; **~ купа́ться!** let's go for a swim!
а́йсберг (-а) *м* iceberg.
акад. *сокр* = **акаде́мик**.
акаде́мик (-а) *м* academician.
академи́ческ|ий (-ая, -ое, -ие) *прил* (*также перен*) academic; **академи́ческий теа́тр** *honorary title given to theatres*.
акаде́ми|я (-и) *ж* academy; **акаде́мия нау́к** the Academy of Sciences; **акаде́мия худо́жеств** the Academy of Arts.
а́ка|ть (-ю) *несов неперех to pronounce unstressed "o" as "a" in Russian.*

акáци|я (-и) *ж* acacia.
акваланг (-а) *м* aqualung.
аквамари́н (-а) *м* aquamarine.
аквамари́новый *прил* aquamarine.
акварéл|ь (-и) *ж* watercolours *мн* (*BRIT*), watercolors *мн* (*US*); (*картина*) watercolo(u)r.
акварéльный *прил* watercolour *опред* (*BRIT*), watercolor *опред* (*US*).
аквáриум (-а) *м* aquarium, fish tank.
акватóри|я (-и) *ж*: ~ **пóрта** area of water near the port.
акведýк (-а) *м* aqueduct.
АКД *м сокр* (= *автореферáт диссертáции на соискáние учёной стéпени кандидáта наýк*) *abstract of dissertation for first level of postgraduate degree*.
акклиматизáци|я (-и) *м* acclimatization, acclimation (*US*).
акклиматизи́р|оваться (-уюсь) *(не)сов возв* to acclimatize, acclimate (*US*).
аккомпанемéнт (-а) *м* (*муз, перен*) accompaniment.
аккомпани́р|овать (-ую) *несов неперех* (*+dat*; *муз*) to accompany.
аккóрд (-а) *м* chord; **брать (взять** *perf***)** ~ to play a chord; **заключи́тельный** ~ (*перен*) climax.
аккордеóн (-а) *м* accordion.
аккóрдн|ый *прил*: **~ая рабóта** piecework; **он на ~ой оплáте** he is on piecework.
аккредити́в (-а) *м* letter of credit.
аккредити́вный *прил* credit *опред*.
аккредитóванный *прил*: ~ **агéнт** accredited agent.
аккредит|овáть (-ýю) *(не)сов перех* to accredit.
аккумули́р|овать (-ую) *(не)сов перех* (*ТЕХ*, *перен*) to accumulate.
аккумуля́тор (-а) *м* accumulator.
аккурáтен *прил см* **аккурáтный**.
аккурáтно *нареч* (*регулярно*) regularly; (*старательно*) carefully; (*опрятно*) neatly.
аккурáтност|ь (-и) *ж* (*см прил*) regularity; meticulousness; accuracy; neatness.
аккурáт|ный (-ен, -на, -но) *прил* (*посещение*) regular; (*работник*) meticulous; (*работа*) accurate; (*костюм*) neat.
акр (-а) *м* acre.
акри́л (-а) *м* acrylic.
акри́ловый *прил* acrylic.
акробáт (-а) *м* acrobat.
акробáтик|а (-и) *ж* acrobatics.
акселерáт (-а) *м* early developer (*physically*).
акселерáтор (-а) *м* accelerator.
акселерáци|я (-и) *ж* early physical maturity.
аксессуáр (-а) *м* (*одежды*) accessory; *см также* **аксессуáры**.
аксессуáр|ы (-ов) *мн* (*перен: в живописи итп*) details *мн*; (: *в театре*) props *мн* (= *properties*).
аксиóм|а (-ы) *ж* axiom.
акт (-а) *м* act; (*торжественное собрание*) ceremony; **составля́ть (состáвить** *perf***)** ~ to draw up a formal document; **áкты граждáнского состоя́ния** register (*of births, marriages, deaths*).
актёр (-а) *м* actor.
акти́в (-а) *м* activists *мн* (*in organization*); (*КОММ*) assets *мн*; **запи́сывать (записáть** *perf***) что-н в** ~ to count sth as an asset; **заморóженные ~ы** (*КОММ*) frozen assets.
акти́вен *прил см* **акти́вный**.
активизи́р|овать (-ую) *(не)сов перех* to enliven.
акти́вно *нареч* (*участвовать*) actively; (*работать*) energetically.
акти́в|ный (-ен, -на, -но) *прил* active; **акти́вный балáнс** balance of assets; **акти́вный словáрь** *или* **запáс слов** active vocabulary.
актри́с|а (-ы) *ж* actress.
актуáлен *прил см* **актуáльный**.
актуáльност|ь (-и) *ж* topicality.
актуáл|ьный (-ен, -ьна, -ьно) *прил* topical.
акýл|а (-ы) *ж* shark.
акупунктýр|а (-ы) *ж* acupuncture.
акýстик|а (-и) *ж* acoustics *ед*; (*в зале, в студии*) acoustics *мн*.
акусти́ческ|ий (-ая, -ое, -ие) *прил* acoustic(al); ~ **соедини́тель** (*КОМП*) acoustic coupler.
акушéр (-а) *м* obstetrician.
акушéр|ка (-ки; *gen pl* -ок) *ж* midwife.
акушéрск|ий (-ая, -ое, -ие) *прил* obstetric(al).
акцéнт (-а) *м* accent; **дéлать (сдéлать** *perf***)** ~ **на** *+prp* (*перен*) to emphasize; **расставля́ть (расстáвить** *perf***) все ~ы** (*перен*) to draw attention to the most important things.
акценти́р|овать (-ую) *(не)сов перех* (*перен*) to accentuate.
акцéпт (-а) *м* (*КОММ, ЮР*) acceptance.
акцéптный *прил* (*КОММ*): ~ **банк** accepting house.
акцепт|овáть (-ýю) *(не)сов перех* (*КОММ*) to accept.
акци́з (-а) *м* (*КОММ*) excise (tax).
акци́зный *прил* (*КОММ*) excise *опред*.
акционéр (-а) *м* shareholder.
акционéрный *прил* joint-stock *опред*; **акционéрное óбщество** joint-stock company; **акционéрный капитáл** share capital.
акционéрск|ий (-ая, -ое, -ие) *прил* (*права, доля*) shareholders'.
áкци|я (-и) *ж* (*КОММ*) share; (*действие*) action; **именнáя/обыкновéнная** ~ registered/ordinary share; **пакéт ~й** block of shares; **пóлностью оплáченная** ~ fully-paid share; **~и без прáва гóлоса** non-voting shares; **дипломати́ческая** ~ diplomatic move.
албáн|ец (-ца) *м* Albanian.
Албáни|я (-и) *ж* Albania.
албáн|ка (-ки; *gen pl* -ок) *ж см* **албáнец**.
албáнск|ий (-ая, -ое, -ие) *прил* Albanian.
албáнца *итп сущ см* **албáнец**.
áлгебр|а (-ы) *ж* algebra.
алгори́тм (-а) *м* algorithm.

алеба́стр (-а) *м* alabaster.
алеба́стровый *прил* alabaster *опред*.
александри́т (-а) *м* (*ГЕО*) alexandrite.
Александри́|я (-и) *ж* Alexandria.
але́|ть (-ю) *несов неперех* (*флаг, мак*) to show scarlet; (*закат*) to glow scarlet; (*perf* **зале́ть**; *закат, небо*) to turn scarlet.
Алжи́р (-а) *м* Algeria.
алжи́р|ец (-ца) *м* Algerian.
алжи́р|ка (-ки; *gen pl* -ок) *ж см* **алжи́рец**.
алжи́рск|ий (-ая, -ое, -ие) *прил* Algerian.
алжи́рца *итп сущ см* **алжи́рец**.
а́либи *ср нескл* alibi.
алиме́нтщик (-а) *м* (*разг: пренебр*) *man paying alimony or maintenance*.
алиме́нт|ы (-ов) *мн* alimony *ед*, maintenance *ед*.
алка́ш (-а́) *м* (*разг: пренебр*) alky.
алкоголи́зм (-а) *м* alcoholism.
алкого́лик (-а) *м* alcoholic.
алкоголи́ч|ка (-ки; *gen pl* -ек) *ж* (*разг*) *см* **алкого́лик**.
алкого́л|ь (-я) *м* alcohol.
Алла́х (-а) *м* Allah.
аллего́ри|я (-и) *ж* allegory.
алле́гро *ср нескл, нареч* allegro.
аллерге́н (-а) *м* allergen.
аллерги́ческ|ий (-ая, -ое, -ие) *прил* allergic.
аллерги́|я (-и) *ж* allergy.
алле́|я (-и) *ж* alley.
аллига́тор (-а) *м* alligator.
аллилу́йя *межд* hallelujah.
алло́ *межд* hello (*on answering phone*).
аллю́р (-а) *м* gait (*of horses*).
А́лма-Ат|а́ (-ы́) *ж* Alma-Ata.
алма́з (-а) *м* diamond.
алма́зный *прил* diamond *опред*; (*инструмент*) diamond-tipped.
ало́э *ср нескл* aloe.
алта́р|ь (-я́) *м* (*в церкви*) chancel; (*жертвенник*) altar; **возлага́ть (возложи́ть** *perf*) **что-н на ~ чего́-н** to sacrifice sth on the altar of sth.
алфави́т (-а) *м* alphabet; **по ~у** in alphabetical order.
а́лчен *прил см* **а́лчный**.
а́лчност|ь (-и) *ж* greed.
а́лч|ный (-ен, -на, -но) *прил* greedy.
а́л|ый (-, -а, -о) *прил* scarlet.
алыч|а́ (-и́) *ж* cherry plum.
альбо́м (-а) *м* album; (*по искусству*) *book of art reproductions*.
альмана́х (-а) *м* anthology.
альпи́йск|ий (-ая, -ое, -ие) *прил* alpine; (*в Альпах*) Alpine.
альпини́зм (-а) *м* mountaineering.
А́льп|ы (-) *мн* the Alps.
альт (-а́) *м* (*голос*) alto; (*инструмент*) viola.
альтернати́в|а (-ы) *ж* alternative.
альтернати́вный *прил* alternative.
альтруи́зм (-а) *м* altruism.
алья́нс (-а) *м* alliance.
Аля́ск|а (-и) *ж* Alaska.
алюми́ниевый *прил* aluminium *опред* (*BRIT*), aluminum *опред* (*US*).
алюми́ни|й (-я) *м* aluminium (*BRIT*), aluminum (*US*).
аляповат|ый (-, -а, -о) *прил* gaudy.
амазо́н|ка (-ки; *gen pl* -ок) *ж* (*всадница*) horsewoman (*мн* horsewomen); (*платье*) riding habit.
амальга́м|а (-ы) *ж* (*ХИМ, перен*) amalgam.
амба́р (-а) *м* barn.
амбицио́з|ный (-ен, -на, -но) *прил* (*человек*) arrogant; (*планы*) presumptuous.
амби́ци|я (-и) *ж* (*самолюбие*) pride, arrogance; (*обычно мн: притязания*) ambition; **ударя́ться (уда́риться** *perf*) **в ~ю** (*разг*) to go into a huff.
амбулато́ри|я (-и) *ж* doctor's surgery (*BRIT*) *или* office (*US*).
амво́н (-а) *м* (*РЕЛ*) ≈ pulpit.
амёб|а (-ы) *ж* amoeba (*BRIT*), ameba (*US*).
Аме́рик|а (-и) *ж* America.
америка́н|ец (-ца) *м* American.
американиза́ци|я (-и) *ж* Americanization.
американизи́р|овать (-ую) *(не)сов перех* to Americanize.
америка́н|ка (-ки; *gen pl* -ок) *ж см* **америка́нец**.
америка́нск|ий (-ая, -ое, -ие) *прил* American.
америка́нца *итп сущ см* **америка́нец**.
амети́ст (-а) *м* amethyst.
аминокисл|ота́ (-оты́; *nom pl* -о́ты) *ж* amino acid.
ами́нь *част* (*РЕЛ*) amen.
аммиа́к (-а) *м* ammonia.
АМН *ж сокр* (= *Акаде́мия медици́нских нау́к*) Academy of Medical Sciences.
амнисти́р|овать (-ую) *(не)сов перех* to grant (an) amnesty to.
амни́сти|я (-и) *ж* amnesty; **попада́ть (попа́сть** *perf*) **под ~ю** to be granted (an) amnesty.
амора́лен *прил см* **амора́льный**.
амора́льност|ь (-и) *ж* (*см прил*) immorality; amorality.
амора́л|ьный (-ен, -ьна, -ьно) *прил* (*поступок*) immoral; (*человек*) amoral.
амортиза́тор (-а) *м* (*ТЕХ*) shock absorber.
амортизацио́нный *прил* (*ТЕХ*) shock-absorbing; (*ЭКОН*) depreciation *опред*; **амортизацио́нные отчисле́ния** (*ЭКОН*) depreciation deductions *мн*; **амортизацио́нный срок** (*ЭКОН*) period of depreciation.
амортиза́ци|я (-и) *ж* (*ТЕХ*) shock absorption; (*ЭКОН*) depreciation; (*КОММ*) amortization.
амо́рф|ный (-ен, -на, -но) *прил* amorphous.
ампе́р (-а) *м* amp (= *ampère*).
амплиту́д|а (-ы) *ж* amplitude.
амплуа́ *ср нескл* (*актёра*) speciality; **э́то не**

моё ~ *(разг)* that's not (in) my line.
а́мпул|а (-ы) *ж* ampoule (*BRIT*), ampule (*US*).
ампута́ци|я (-и) *ж* amputation.
ампути́р|овать (-ую) *(не)сов перех* to amputate.
АМТС *ж сокр (= автомати́ческая междугоро́дная телефо́нная связь)* ≈ STD (*BRIT*)) (= *subscriber trunk dialling*).
амуни́ци|я (-и) *ж собир* ammunition.
Аму́р (-а) *м* Cupid; *см также* **аму́ры**.
аму́р|ы (-ов) *мн (разг: любовные дела)* intrigues *мн*, love affairs *мн*.
амфи́би|я (-и) *ж* amphibian.
амфитеа́тр (-а) *м* amphitheatre (*BRIT*), amphitheater (*US*).
АН *ж сокр (= Акаде́мия нау́к)* Academy of Sciences ◆ *м сокр = самолёт констру́кции О. К. Анто́нова.*
Ан *м сокр* = **АН**.
ана́лиз (-а) *м* analysis; **сдава́ть (сдать** *perf***) кровь/мочу́ на** ~ to give a blood/urine sample; **подверга́ть (подве́ргнуть** *perf***) ~у** to analyse (*BRIT*), analyze (*US*); ~ **изде́ржек и при́былы** (*КОММ*) cost-benefit analysis; ~ **эффекти́вности рабо́ты** time and motion study; **ана́лиз кро́ви** blood test.
анализи́р|овать (-ую; *perf* **проанализи́ровать)** *несов перех* to analyse (*BRIT*), analyze (*US*).
анали́тик (-а) *м (специалист)* analyst; **он хоро́ший** ~ *(склонный к анализу)* he has a very analytical mind.
ана́лог (-а) *м* analogue (*BRIT*), analog (*US*).
аналоги́ч|ный (-ен, -на, -но) *прил* analogous.
анало́ги|я (-и) *ж* analogy; **по ~и (с** *+instr***)** in a similar way (to); **проводи́ть (провести́** *perf***) ~ю ме́жду** *+instr* to draw an analogy between.
анало́|й (-я) *м* lectern.
ана́мнез (-а) *м (МЕД)* case history.
анана́с (-а) *м* pineapple.
анархи́зм (-а) *м* anarchism.
анархи́стск|ий (-ая, -ое, -ие) *прил* anarchist *опред*.
ана́рхи|я (-и) *ж* anarchy.
анато́ми|я (-и) *ж* anatomy.
ана́фем|а (-ы) *ж* anathema; **предава́ть (преда́ть** *perf***) ~е** to anathematize.
анахрони́зм (-а) *м* anachronism.
анахрони́ч|ный (-ен, -на, -но) *прил* anachronistic.
анга́р (-а) *м* hangar.
а́нгел (-а) *м (также разг)* angel.
а́нгельск|ий (-ая, -ое, -ие) *прил* angelic; **а́нгельское терпе́ние** the patience of a saint.
анги́н|а (-ы) *ж* tonsillitis, quinsy.
англи́йск|ий (-ая, -ое, -ие) *прил* English; *(британский)* British; ~ **язы́к** English; **англи́йская була́вка** safety pin; **англи́йский газо́н** lawn.
англика́нск|ий (-ая, -ое, -ие) *прил* Anglican; **англика́нская це́рковь** the Anglican church.
англича́н|ин (-ина; *nom pl* **-е,** *gen pl* **-)** *м* Englishman (*мн* Englishmen).
англича́н|ка (-ки; *gen pl* **-ок)** *ж* Englishwoman (*мн* Englishwomen).
А́нгли|я (-и) *ж* England.
Анго́л|а (-ы) *ж* Angola.
анго́л|ец (-ьца) *м* Angolan.
анго́л|ка (-ки; *gen pl* **-ок)** *ж см* **анго́лец**.
анго́льск|ий (-ая, -ое, -ие) *прил* Angolan.
анго́льца *итп сущ см* **анго́лец**.
анго́рск|ий (-ая, -ое, -ие) *прил* angora *опред*; **анго́рская шерсть** angora (wool).
А́нд|ы (-) *мн* the Andes.
анекдо́т (-а) *м* joke; **со мной случи́лся** ~ *(разг)* something funny happened to me.
анекдоти́ч|ный (-ен, -на, -но) *прил (смешной и странный)* funny.
анеми́ч|ный (-ен, -на, -но) *прил* anaemic (*BRIT*), anemic (*US*).
анеми́|я (-и) *ж* anaemia (*BRIT*), anemia (*US*).
анестезио́лог (-а) *м* anaesthetist (*BRIT*), anesthesiologist (*US*).
анестези́р|овать (-ую) *(не)сов перех* to anaesthetize (*BRIT*), anesthetize (*US*).
анестези́|я (-и) *ж* anaesthesia (*BRIT*), anesthesia (*US*); **ме́стная/о́бщая** ~ local/general ana(e)sthesia.
анили́н (-а) *м* aniline.
анили́новый *прил* aniline *опред*.
ани́совый *прил* aniseed *опред*; **ани́совая во́дка** aniseed vodka.
АНК *м сокр (= Африка́нский национа́льный конгре́сс)* ANC (= *African National Congress*).
Анкар|а́ (-ы́) *ж* Ankara.
анке́т|а (-ы) *ж (опросный лист)* questionnaire; *(бланк для сведений)* form; *(сбор сведений)* survey; **проводи́ть (провести́** *perf***) ~у** to carry out a survey.
анке́тн|ый *прил*: **~ые да́нные** personal details *мн*; **анке́тный лист** questionnaire.
анна́л|ы (-ов) *мн* annals *мн*; **в ~ах исто́рии** in the annals of history.
анне́кси|я (-и) *ж* annexation.
аннота́ци|я (-и) *ж* précis.
аннoти́р|овать (-ую; *perf* **проаннoти́ровать)** *несов перех* to summarize.
аннуите́т (-а) *м (КОММ)* annuity; **пожи́зненный** ~ life annuity.
аннули́ровани|е (-я) *ср (см глаг)* annulment; repeal; cancellation.
аннули́р|овать (-ую) *(не)сов перех (брак, договор)* to annul; *(закон)* to repeal; *(долг)* to cancel.
ано́д (-а) *м* anode.
анома́л|ьный (-ен, -ьна, -ьно) *прил* anomalous.
анони́м (-а) *м* anonymous author.
анони́мен *прил см* **анони́мный**.
анони́м|ка (-ки; *gen pl* **-ок)** *ж (разг: пренебр)* poison-pen letter.
анони́м|ный (-ен, -на, -но) *прил* anonymous.
анони́мок *сущ см* **анони́мка**.
ано́нс (-а) *м* announcement.

анорéкси|я (**-и**) *ж* anorexia; **онá страдáет ~ей** she is anorexic.
ансáмбл|ь (**-я**) *м* ensemble; (*танцоров*) troupe; (*эстрадный*) group.
АНТ *м сокр* = *самолёт констрýкции А. Н Туполева.*
антагонúзм (**-а**) *м* antagonism.
Антарктúд|а (**-ы**) *ж* Antarctica.
Антáрктик|а (**-и**) *ж* Antarctica, the Antarctic.
антарктúческ|ий (**-ая, -ое, -ие**) *прил* Antarctic.
Антвéрпен (**-а**) *ж* Antwerp.
антéнн|а (**-ы**) *ж* aerial (*BRIT*), antenna (*US*); **~ космúческой свя́зи** satellite dish.
антибиóтик (**-а**) *м* antibiotic.
антивоéнный *прил* antiwar.
антидемократúческ|ий (**-ая, -ое, -ие**) *прил* antidemocratic.
антиквáр (**-а**) *м* antiquary.
антиквариáт (**-а**) *м собир* antiques *мн.*
антиквáр|ный *прил* antique *опред*; **антиквáрный магазúн** antique shop.
антилóп|а (**-ы**) *ж* antelope.
антинаýч|ный (**-ен, -на, -но**) *прил* antiscientific.
антипатúч|ный (**-ен, -на, -но**) *прил* unlikable.
антипáти|я (**-и**) *ж* antipathy.
антипóд (**-а**) *м* antithesis.
антирелигиóзный *прил* antireligious.
антисанитáрен *прил см* **антисанитáрный**.
антисанитарú|я (**-и**) *ж* unhygienic *или* insanitary conditions *мн.*
антисанитáр|ный (**-ен, -на, -но**) *прил* unhygienic, insanitary.
антисемúт (**-а**) *м* anti-Semite.
антисемитúзм (**-а**) *м* anti-Semitism.
антисемúт|ка (**-ки**; *gen pl* **-ок**) *ж см* **антисемúт**.
антисемúток *сущ см* **антисемúтка**.
антисемúтск|ий (**-ая, -ое, -ие**) *прил* anti-Semitic.
антисéптик (**-а**) *м* antiseptic.
антисептúческ|ий (**-ая, -ое, -ие**) *прил* antiseptic.
антитéз|а (**-ы**) *ж* antithesis.
антитéл|о (**-а**; *nom pl* **-á**) *ср* (*обычно мн*) antibody.
антифашúстск|ий (**-ая, -ое, -ие**) *прил* antifascist.
антифрúз (**-а**) *м* antifreeze.
антúхрист (**-а**) *м* Antichrist.
антициклóн (**-а**) *м* anticyclone.
антúчност|ь (**-и**) *ж* antiquity.
антúчный *прил* classical; **антúчный мир** the Ancient World.
антолóги|я (**-и**) *ж* anthology.
антóним (**-а**) *м* antonym.
антóнов|ка (**-ки**; *gen pl* **-ок**) *ж* antonovka (*apple*).
антрáкт (**-а**) *м* interval.
антрацúт (**-а**) *м* anthracite.
антрекóт (**-а**) *м* entrecôte.
антрепренёр (**-а**) *м* impresario.
антресóл|и (**-ей**) *мн* (*полуэтаж*) mezzanine *ед*; (*балкон*) gallery *ед*; (*под потолком*) cupboard *ед.*
антропológи|я (**-и**) *ж* anthropology.
анфáс *нареч* full face.
анфилáд|а (**-ы**) *ж* suite (*of rooms*).
анчóус (**-а**) *м* anchovy.
аншлáг (**-а**) *м* (*объявление*) sellout; (*заголовок*) banner headline; **проходúть** (**пройтú** *perf*) **с ~ом** to be a sellout.
анютины *прил*: **~ глáзки** pansy *ед.*
АО *ж сокр* = *автонóмная óбласть* ◆ *м сокр* = *автонóмный óкруг.*
А/О *ср сокр* (= *акционéрное óбщество*) joint-stock company.
аóрт|а (**-ы**) *ж* aorta.
АП *м сокр* (= *Ассóшиэйтед пресс*) AP (= *Associated Press*).
апартеид (**-а**) *м* apartheid.
апатúч|ный (**-ен, -на, -но**) *прил* apathetic.
апáти|я (**-и**) *ж* apathy.
апеллúр|овать (**-ую**) *(не)сов неперех* (*ЮР*) to appeal; ~ *(impf/perf)* **к** *+dat* to appeal to.
апелляциóнный *прил* (*ЮР*) appeal *опред*; **апелляциóнный суд** court of appeal.
апеллáци|я (**-и**) *ж* (*ЮР*) appeal; ~ **к** *+dat* appeal to.
апельсúн (**-а**) *м* orange.
апельсúнный *прил* = **апельсúновый**.
апельсúновый *прил* orange.
аперитúв (**-а**) *м* aperitif.
АПК *м сокр* = *агрáрно-промышленный кóмплекс.*
аплодúр|овать (**-ую**) *несов неперех* (*+dat*) to applaud.
аплодисмéнт|ы (**-ов**) *мн* applause *ед.*
аплóмб (**-а**) *м* assurance; **с ~ом** with aplomb.
АПН *ср сокр* (= *агéнтство печáти „Нóвости"*) "Novosti" Press Agency ◆ *ж сокр* (= *Акадéмия педагогúческих наýк*) Academy of Pedagogical Sciences.
апогé|й (**-я**) *м* (*также перен*) apogee; **он в ~е слáвы** he is at the height of his fame.
апокáлипсис (**-а**) *м* (*РЕЛ*) (the Book of) Revelation, the Apocalypse.
аполитúч|ный (**-ен, -на, -но**) *прил* apolitical.
апологéт (**-а**) *м* apologist.
апóстол (**-а**) *м* apostle; (*книга*) the Acts of the Apostles and the Epistles.
апóстольск|ий (**-ая, -ое, -ие**) *прил* apostolic.
апострóф (**-а**) *м* apostrophe.
апофеóз (**-а**) *м* (*восхваление*) apotheosis; (*ТЕАТР*) grand finale.
аппарáт (**-а**) *м* apparatus; (*ФИЗИОЛОГИЯ*) system; (*штат*) staff; **телефóнный ~** telephone; **госудáрственный ~** state apparatus.
аппарáтн|ая (**-ой**; *decl like adj*) *ж* equipment room.
аппаратýр|а (**-ы**) *ж собир* apparatus, equipment;

(*приборы*) instruments *мн*.
аппара́тчик (-а) *м* operative; (*разг: работник аппарата*) apparatchik.
аппе́ндикс (-а) *м* appendix.
аппендици́т (-а) *м* appendicitis.
аппети́т (-а) *м* appetite; (*обычно мн: перен: разг*) craving; **прия́тного ~а!** bon appétit!; **перебива́ть (переби́ть** *perf*) ~ to spoil one's appetite; **во́лчий** ~ a voracious appetite.
аппети́т|ный (-ен, -на, -но) *прил* appetizing.
аппликáци|я (-и) *ж* appliqué.
апре́л|ь (-я) *м* April; *см также* **октя́брь**.
апроби́р|овать (-ую) *(не)сов перех* to approve.
апте́к|а (-и) *ж* dispensing chemist's (*BRIT*), pharmacy.
апте́карск|ий (-ая, -ое, -ие) *прил* (*товары*) pharmaceutical.
апте́кар|ь (-я) *м* chemist (*BRIT*), pharmacist.
апте́ч|ка (-ки; *gen pl* -ек) *ж* medicine chest; (*первой помощи*) first-aid kit.
апте́чный *прил* chemist's.
апчхи́ *межд*: ~! atishoo!
ара́б (-а) *м* Arab.
арабе́с|ка (-ки; *gen pl* -ок) *ж* arabesque (*ART*).
ара́б|ка (-ки; *gen pl* -ок) *ж см* **ара́б**.
ара́бск|ий (-ая, -ое, -ие) *прил* (*страны*) Arab; ~ **язы́к** Arabic; **ара́бские ци́фры** Arabic numerals.
арави́ек *сущ см* **арави́йка**.
арави́|ец (-йца) *м* Arabian.
арави́й|ка (-йки; *gen pl* -ек) *ж см* **арави́ец**.
арави́йск|ий (-ая, -ое, -ие) *прил* Arabian *опред*.
арави́йца *итп сущ см* **арави́ец**.
Ара́ви|я (-и) *ж* Arabia.
ара́льск|ий (-ая, -ое, -ие) *прил*: **А~ое мо́ре** Aral Sea.
аранжи́р|овать (-ую) *(не)сов перех* to arrange.
аранжиро́в|ка (-ки; *gen pl* -ок) *ж* arrangement.
ара́хис (-а) *м* peanut.
ара́хисовый *прил* peanut *опред*.
АРБ *ж сокр* (= *Ассоциа́ция росси́йских ба́нков*) *association of Russian banks*.
арби́тр (-а) *м* (*в спорах*) arbitrator; (*в футболе*) referee; (*в бейсболе, теннисе*) umpire.
арбитра́ж (-а) *м* arbitration; (*орган*) arbitration service.
арбитра́жный *прил* arbitration *опред*.
арбу́з (-а) *м* watermelon.
Аргенти́н|а (-ы) *ж* Argentina.
аргенти́н|ец (-ца) *м* Argentinian.
аргенти́н|ка (-ки; *gen pl* -ок) *ж см* **аргенти́нец**.
аргенти́нск|ий (-ая, -ое, -ие) *прил* Argentinian.
аргенти́нца *итп сущ см* **аргенти́нец**.
арго́н (-а) *м* argon.
аргуме́нт (-а) *м* (*также МАТ*) argument.
аргумента́ци|я (-и) *ж* argument.
аргументи́р|овать (-ую) *(не)сов перех* to argue.
аре́н|а (-ы) *ж* (*в цирке*) ring; (*часть стадиона, перен*) arena.
аре́нд|а (-ы) *ж* (*наём*) lease; (*плата*) rent; **сдава́ть (сдать** *perf*) **в ~у** to lease.
аренда́тор (-а) *м* leaseholder.
аре́нд|ный *прил* lease *опред*; **на ~ых нача́лах** on a rental basis; **аре́ндная пла́та** rent; **аре́ндный подря́д** rental agreement, lease.
аренд|ова́ть (-у́ю) *(не)сов перех* to lease.
аре́ст (-а) *м* (*преступника*) arrest; (*имущества*) sequestration; **брать (взять** *perf*) **кого́-н под ~** to place sb under arrest; **налага́ть (наложи́ть** *perf*) **~ на** *+acc* to sequester; **находи́ться** *(impf)* **под ~ом** to be under arrest.
аресто́ванн|ая (-ой; *decl like adj*) *ж см* **аресто́ванный**.
аресто́ванн|ый (-ого; *decl like adj*) *м person held in custody*.
арест|ова́ть (-у́ю; *impf* **аресто́вывать**) *сов перех* (*преступника*) to arrest; (*имущество*) to sequestrate.
аристокра́т (-а) *м* aristocrat.
аристократи́ческ|ий (-ая, -ое, -ие) *прил* aristocratic.
аристокра́ти|я (-и) *ж* aristocracy.
аритми́|я (-и) *ж* arrhythmia (*irregular heartbeat*).
арифме́тик|а (-и) *ж* arithmetic.
арифмети́ческ|ий (-ая, -ое, -ие) *прил* arithmetic(al).
а́ри|я (-и) *ж* aria.
АРКА *м сокр* (= *Америка́но-Росси́йский комме́рческий алья́нс*) *American-Russian commercial alliance*.
а́р|ка (-ки; *gen pl* -ок) *ж* arch.
арка́д|а (-ы) *ж* (*АРХИТ*) arcade.
арка́н (-а) *м* lasso.
арка́н|ить (-ю, -ишь; *perf* **заарка́нить**) *несов перех* to lasso.
А́рктик|а (-и) *ж* the Arctic.
аркти́ческ|ий (-ая, -ое, -ие) *прил* Arctic.
арлеки́н (-а) *м* harlequin.
армату́р|а (-ы) *ж собир* (*СТРОИТ*) steel framework; (*вспомогательные устройства*) fittings *мн*.
арме́йск|ий (-ая, -ое, -ие) *прил* army *опред*.
Арме́ни|я (-и) *ж* Armenia.
а́рми|я (-и) *ж* army; (*перен*): ~ *+gen* (*помощников, читателей*) army of.
армяни́н (-а; *nom pl* **армя́не**, *gen pl* **армя́н**) *м* Armenian.
армя́н|ка (-ки; *gen pl* -ок) *ж см* **армяни́н**.
армя́нск|ий (-ая, -ое, -ие) *прил* Armenian *опред*; ~ **язы́к** Armenian.
а́рок *сущ см* **а́рка**.
арома́т (-а) *м* (*цветов*) fragrance; (*кофе итп*) aroma; (*перен: молодости*) spirit.
арома́тен *прил см* **арома́тный**.
ароматичéск|ий (-ая, -ое, -ие) *прил* aromatic.
арома́т|ный (-ен, -на, -но) *прил* fragrant.
арсена́л (-а) *м* (*склад*) arsenal; (*завод*) munitions factory; **в ~е** (*перен*) at one's disposal.
арта́ч|иться (-усь, -ишься) *несов возв* (*разг*) to be pig-headed.

артезиа́нск|ий (-ая, -ое, -ие) *прил* artesian.
арте́л|ь (-и) *ж worker's or peasant's cooperative.*
арте́льн|ый *прил* collective *опред*; **на ~ых нача́лах** on a collective basis.
артериа́льн|ый *прил*: **~ое давле́ние** blood pressure.
арте́ри|я (-и) *ж* (*также перен*) artery; **со́нная ~** carotid artery.
арти́кл|ь (-я) *м* (*линг*) article.
артиллери́йск|ий (-ая, -ое, -ие) *прил* artillery *опред*.
артиллери́ст (-а) *м* artilleryman (*мн* artillerymen), gunner (*BRIT*).
артилле́ри|я (-и) *ж* artillery.
арти́ст (-а) *м* artist(e); (*кино*) actor; **он ~ расска́зывать исто́рии** he's ace at telling stories.
артисти́ческ|ий (-ая, -ое, -ие) *прил* artistic; **~ая убо́рная** dressing room.
арти́ст|ка (-ки; *gen pl* **-ок)** *ж* (*см м*) artist(e); actress.
артишо́к (-а) *м* (globe) artichoke.
артри́т (-а) *м* arthritis.
а́рф|а (-ы) *ж* harp.
арфи́ст (-а) *м* harpist.
арфи́ст|ка (-ки; *gen pl* **-ок)** *ж см* **арфи́ст**.
архаи́зм (-а) *м* archaism.
архаи́ч|ный (-ен, -на, -но) *прил* archaic.
арха́нгел (-а) *м* archangel.
Арха́нгельск (-а) *м* Archangel.
архео́лог (-а) *м* archaeologist (*BRIT*), archeologist.
археологи́ческ|ий (-ая, -ое, -ие) *прил* archaeological.
археоло́ги|я (-и) *ж* archaeology.
архи́в (-а) *м* (*учреждение, отдел*) archive; (*собрание рукописей итп*) archives *мн*; **сдава́ть (сдать** *perf*) **что-н в ~** (*перен*) to consign sth to history.
архива́риус (-а) *м* archivist.
архи́вный *прил* archival; **~ файл** (*комп*) archive file.
архиепи́скоп (-а) *м* archbishop.
архиере́|й (-я) *м general term for upper orders of the church.*
архимандри́т (-а) *м* archimandrite.
архипела́г (-а) *м* archipelago.
архите́ктор (-а) *м* architect.
архитекту́р|а (-ы) *ж* architecture.
архитекту́рный *прил* architectural.
арши́н (-а; *gen pl* **- или -ов)** *м* (*устаревший*) arshin (*unit of measurement equal to 0.71 m*); **ме́рить** (*impf*) **кого́-н на свой ~** (*перен*) to judge sb by one's own standards.
арши́нный *прил* (*разг*) *very big, tall, high or long.*
ас (-а) *м* (*лётчик*) ace; (*перен*) expert.
асбе́ст (-а) *м* asbestos.
АСЕАН *ж сокр* ASEAN (= *Association of South-East Asian Nations*).
асепти́ческ|ий (-ая, -ое, -ие) *прил* aseptic.
асимметри́ч|ный (-ен, -на, -но) *прил* asymmetric(al).
асимме́три|я (-и) *ж* asymmetry.
аске́т (-а) *м* ascetic.
аскети́зм (-а) *м* asceticism.
аскети́ческ|ий (-ая, -ое, -ие) *прил* ascetic *опред*.
аскорби́нов|ый *прил*: **~ая кислота́** ascorbic acid.
аспе́кт (-а) *м* aspect; **в ~е** + *gen* in (the) light of.
аспира́нт (-а) *м* postgraduate (*doing a PhD*).
аспиранту́р|а (-ы) *ж* postgraduate studies *мн* (*leading to a PhD*).
аспири́н (-а) *м* aspirin.
ассамбле́|я (-и) *ж* assembly; **Генера́льная А~ Организа́ции Объединённых На́ций** General Assembly of the United Nations.
ассе́мблер (-а) *м* (*комп*) assembler.
ассениза́ци|я (-и) *ж* sewage disposal system.
ассигнова́ни|е (-я) *ср* allocation.
ассигн|ова́ть (-у́ю) *(не)сов перех* to allocate.
ассимили́р|овать (-ую) *(не)сов перех* to assimilate
▸ **ассимили́роваться** *(не)сов возв* to become assimilated.
ассимиля́ци|я (-и) *ж* assimilation.
ассисте́нт (-а) *м* assistant; (*в вузе*) assistant lecturer.
ассисти́р|овать (-ую) *несов неперех* (+*dat*) to assist.
ассорти́ *ср нескл* assortment.
ассортиме́нт (-а) *м* assortment.
ассоциати́в|ный (-ен, -на, -но) *прил* based on association.
ассоциа́ци|я (-и) *ж* association.
ассоции́р|овать (-ую) *(не)сов перех*: **~ что-н с кем-н/чем-н** to associate sth with sb/sth
▸ **ассоции́роваться** *(не)сов возв*: **~ся с** +*instr* to be associated with.
АССР *ж сокр* (*ист*: = *автоно́мная сове́тская социалисти́ческая респу́блика*) ASSR (= *Autonomous Soviet Socialist Republic*).
астеро́ид (-а) *м* asteroid.
астигмати́зм (-а) *м* astigmatism.
а́стм|а (-ы) *ж* asthma.
астма́тик (-а) *м* asthmatic.
астмати́ческ|ий (-ая, -ое, -ие) *прил* asthmatic.
а́стр|а (-ы) *ж* aster.
астро́лог (-а) *м* astrologist.
астроло́ги|я (-и) *ж* astrology.
астрона́вт (-а) *м* astronaut.
астрона́втик|а (-и) *ж* astronautics.
астроно́м (-а) *м* astronomer.
астрономи́ческ|ий (-ая, -ое, -ие) *прил* (*также перен*) astronomic(al).
астроно́ми|я (-и) *ж* astronomy.

АСУ *ж сокр* (= *автоматизи́рованная систе́ма управле́ния*) *automatic control system.*
асфа́льт (-а) *м* asphalt.
асфальти́р|овать (-ую; *perf* **заасфальти́ровать**) *(не)сов перех* to asphalt.
асфикси́|я (-и) *ж* asphyxia.
ата́к|а (-и) *ж* (*также перен*) attack; **идти́ (пойти́** *perf*) **в ~у** to launch an attack; **~ на кого́-н/что-н** an attack on sb/sth.
атак|ова́ть (-у́ю) *(не)сов перех* (*также перен*) to attack.
атама́н (-а) *м* ataman (*Cossack leader*); (*перен: банды*) leader.
атеи́зм (-а) *м* atheism.
атеи́ст (-а) *м* atheist.
атеи́ст|ка (-ки; *gen pl* **-ок**) *ж см* **атеи́ст.**
атеисти́ческ|ий (-ая, -ое, -ие) *прил* atheist *опред.*
атеи́сток *сущ см* **атеи́стка.**
ателье́ *ср нескл* (*художника, фотографа*) studio; (*мод*) tailor's shop; **телевизио́нное ~** television repair shop; **ателье́ прока́та** rental shop.
атланти́ческ|ий (-ая, -ое, -ие) *прил*: **А~ океа́н** Atlantic Ocean.
а́тлас (-а) *м* atlas.
атла́с (-а) *м* satin.
атла́сный *прил* satin; (*шелковистый*) satiny; **атла́сная ко́жа** (*перен*) skin like satin.
атле́т (-а) *м* athlete; (*крепкий человек*) muscleman.
атлети́зм (-а) *м* (*телосложение*) athletic build; (*культуризм*) body building.
атле́тик|а (-и) *ж* athletics; **лёгкая ~** track and field events; **тяжёлая ~** weightlifting.
атлети́ческ|ий (-ая, -ое, -ие) *прил* athletic.
АТМ *ж сокр* (= *автомати́ческая ка́ссовая маши́на*) ATM (= *automated telling machine*).
атмосфе́р|а (-ы) *ж* (*также перен*) atmosphere.
атмосфе́рный *прил* atmospheric.
а́том (-а) *м* atom.
а́томный *прил* atomic; **а́томный вес** atomic weight.
а́томщик (-а) *м* (*разг*) atomic scientist.
атрибу́т (-а) *м* attribute.
атрибути́вный *прил* (*линг*) attributive.
атрофи́рованный *прил* atrophied.
атрофи́р|оваться (*3sg* **-уется**, *3pl* **-уются**) *(не)сов возв* to atrophy.
атрофи́|я (-и) *ж* atrophy.
АТС *ж сокр* (= *автомати́ческая телефо́нная ста́нция*) automatic telephone exchange.
атташе́ *м нескл* attaché.
аттеста́т (-а) *м* certificate; **аттеста́т зре́лости** *certificate attained for passing school-leaving examinations.*
аттеста́ци|я (-и) *ж* certification; (*отзыв*) recommendation.
аттест|ова́ть (-у́ю) *(не)сов перех* (*давать характеристику*) to recommend; (*оценивать знания*) to give a mark.
аттракцио́н (-а) *м* (*цирковой номер*) attraction; (*качели, карусель итп*) amusement.
ау́ *межд* hallo (*cry for attention*).
аудие́нци|я (-и) *ж* (*приём*) audience.
ауди́т (-а) *м* (*комм*) audit; **о́бщий ~** general audit.
аудито́ри|я (-и) *ж* (*помещение*) lecture hall ♦ *собир* (*слушатели*) audience.
аукцио́н (-а) *м* auction; **продава́ть (прода́ть** *perf*) **что-н с ~а** to sell sth by auction; **покупа́ть (купи́ть** *perf*) **что-н на ~е** to buy sth at an auction.
аукционе́р (-а) *м* person attending an auction.
аукциони́ст (-а) *м* auctioneer.
ау́л (-а) *м* aul (*mountain village in the Caucasus and Middle Asia*).
а́ут (-а) *м* (*в теннисе*) out; (*в футболе*): **мяч в а́уте** the ball is out of play; (*в боксе*): **~!** knockout!
аутенти́ч|ный (-ен, -на, -но) *прил* authentic.
аутоге́нн|ый *прил*: **~ая трениро́вка** autogenic training.
аутса́йдер (-а) *м* outsider.
афга́н|ец (-ца) *м* Afghan; (*ветеран*) Afghan war veteran.
Афганиста́н (-а) *м* Afghanistan.
афга́н|ка (-ки; *gen pl* **-ок**) *ж см* **афга́нец.**
афга́нца *итп сущ см* **афга́нец.**
афе́р|а (-ы) *ж* swindle.
афери́ст (-а) *м* swindler.
афери́ст|ка (-ки; *gen pl* **-ок**) *ж см* **афери́ст.**
Афи́н|ы (-) *мн* Athens.
афи́ш|а (-и) *ж* poster.
афиши́р|овать (-ую) *(не)сов перех* to parade.
афори́зм (-а) *м* aphorism.
А́фрик|а (-и) *ж* Africa.
африка́н|ец (-ца) *м* African.
африка́н|ка (-ки; *gen pl* **-ок**) *ж см* **африка́нец.**
африка́нск|ий (-ая, -ое, -ие) *прил* African.
африка́нца *итп сущ см* **африка́нец.**
аффе́кт (-а) *м* fit of passion.
ах *межд*: **~!** oh!, ah!; **~ да!** (*разг*) ah yes!; **не ~** (*разг*) not up to much.
а́ха|ть (-ю; *perf* **а́хнуть**) *несов неперех* (*разг*) *to express surprise, regret etc.*
ахиле́сова *прил*: **~ пята́** Achilles' heel.
ахине́|я (-и) *ж* (*разг*) rubbish; **нести́** (*impf*) **~ю** to talk rubbish.
а́хн|уть (-у, -ешь) *сов от* **а́хать** ♦ *неперех* (*разг: орудие итп*) to bang ♦ *перех* (*разг: сломать*) to smash; (*: выпить*) to knock back; **он и ~ не успе́л, как они́ убежа́ли** (*разг*) before he could get a word out, they ran away.
АХО *м сокр* (= *администрати́вно-хозя́йственный отде́л*) *department concerned with property and maintenance.*
ахти́ *межд* (*разг*): **не ~ как** not specially; **не ~ (како́й)** (*разг*) not specially good.
ацето́н (-а) *м* acetone.
Ашхаба́д (-а) *м* Ashkhabad.
аэро́бик|а (-и) *ж* aerobics.
аэро́бус (-а) *м* airbus.

аэровокза́л (-а) *м* air terminal (*BRIT*).
аэродина́мик|а (-и) *ж* aerodynamics.
аэродинами́ческ|ий (-ая, -ое, -ие) *прил* aerodynamic; **аэродинами́ческая труба́** wind tunnel.
аэродро́м (-а) *м* aerodrome.
аэрозо́л|ь (-я) *м* aerosol.
аэро́н (-а) *м* air-sickness tablets *мн*.
аэропла́н (-а) *м* aeroplane (*BRIT*), airplane (*US*).
аэропо́рт (-а; *loc sg* -у́) *м* airport.
аэроста́т (-а) *м* aerostat.
аэрофотосъё́м|ка (-ки; *gen pl* -ок) *ж* aerial photography.
АЭС *ж сокр* (= *а́томная электроста́нция*) atomic power station.
аятолл|а́ (-ы́) *м* ayatollah.

~ Б, б ~

Б, б *сущ нескл* (*буква*) *the 2nd letter of the Russian alphabet.*
б *част см* **бы.**
ба *межд* well, well!; **~! когó я вúжу!** gosh! look who it is!
бáб|а (-ы) *ж* (*разг*) woman; (: *пренебр*: *мужчина*) old woman.
бáб|а-яг|á (-ы, -й) *ж* Baba Yaga (*old witch in Russian folk-tales*); (*разг*) old witch (*fig*).
бáб|ий (-ья, -ье, -ьи) *прил* (*разг*: *пренебр*) womanish; **бáбье лéто** Indian summer; **бáбьи разговóры** women's talk; **бáбьи скáзки** old wives' tales.
бáб|ка (-ки; *gen pl* **-ок)** *ж* (*бабушка*) grandmother; (*разг*: *старуха*) old woman.
бáбоч|ка (-ки; *gen pl* **-ек)** *ж* butterfly; (*галстук*) bow tie.
бáбуш|ка (-ки; *gen pl* **-ек)** *ж* grandma, granny; (*разг*) old woman; **~ нáдвое сказáла** we shall see (what we shall see).
Бавáри|я (-и) *ж* Bavaria.
бавáрск|ий (-ая, -ое, -ие) *прил* Bavarian.
багáж (-á) *м* luggage (*BRIT*), baggage (*US*); **сдавáть (сдать** *perf*) **вéщи в ~** to check in one's luggage (*BRIT*) *или* bags (*US*); **отправлять (отпрáвить** *perf*) **багажóм** to send as unaccompanied baggage; **багáж знáний** knowledge.
багáжник (-а) *м* (*в автомобиле*) boot (*BRIT*), trunk (*US*); (*на крыше автомобиля*) roof rack; (*на велосипеде*) carrier.
багáжный *прил* luggage *опред* (*BRIT*), baggage *опред* (*US*).
багáмск|ий (-ая, -ое, -ие) *прил*: **Б~ие островá** Bahama Islands, Bahamas.
Багдáд (-а) *м* Baghdad.
багровé|ть (-ю; *perf* **побагровéть)** *несов неперех* to turn crimson; (*no perf*, *цветы*) to show crimson.
багрóв|ый (-, -а, -о) *прил* crimson.
багря́н|ый (-, -а, -о) *прил* crimson.
бадминтóн (-а) *м* badminton.
бадминтонúст (-а) *м* badminton player.
бадминтонúст|ка (-ки; *gen pl* **-ок)** *ж см* **бадминтонúст.**
бáз|а (-ы) *ж* basis; (*ВОЕН, АРХИТ*) base; (*для туристов, спортсменов*) centre (*BRIT*), center (*US*); (*продовольствия, товаров*) warehouse; **на ~е** *+gen* on the basis of; **бáза дáнных** database.
базáльт (-а) *м* basalt.
базáр (-а) *м* market; (*новогодний, книжный итп*) fair; (*перен*: *разг*) racket; **птúчий ~** bird colony.
базáрный *прил* market *опред*; **базáрная бáба** (*разг*) fishwife.
базилúк|а (-и) *ж* basilica.
базúр|овать (-ую) *несов перех*: **~ что-н на** *+prp* to base sth on
▸ **базúроваться** *несов возв* to be based; **~ся** (*impf*) **на** *+prp* (*на фактах итп*) to be based on.
бáзис (-а) *м* basis.
байдáр|ка (-ки; *gen pl* **-ок)** *ж* canoe.
бáйк|а (-и) *ж* flannelette.
Байкáл (-а) *м* Lake Baikal.
бáйковый *прил* flannelette.
байт (-а; *gen pl* **-)** *м* byte.
бак (-а) *м* tank; (*МОР*) forecastle, fo'c'sle.
бакалéйн|ый *прил*: **~ магазúн** grocer's shop (*BRIT*), grocery store (*US*); **~ые товáры** groceries.
бакалé|я (-и) *ж* (*в магазине*) grocery section; (*товары*) groceries *мн*.
бáкен (-а) *м* buoy.
бакенбáрд|ы (-) *мн* sideburns *мн*.
баклажáн (-а; *gen pl* **- или -ов)** *м* aubergine (*BRIT*), eggplant (*US*).
баклýши *мн*: **бить ~** (*разг*) to idle away one's time.
бактериологúческ|ий (-ая, -ое, -ие) *прил* bacteriological; **бактериологúческая войнá** germ *или* bacteriological warfare.
бактерицúдный *прил* bactericidal, germicidal.
бактéри|я (-и) *ж* bacterium (*мн* bacteria).
Бакý *м нескл* Baku.
бал (-а; *loc sg* **-ý,** *nom pl* **-ы́)** *м* (*вечер*) ball.
балагáн (-а) *м* (*перен*: *разг*) farce.
балалá|йка (-йки; *gen pl* **-ек)** *ж* balalaika.
балáнс (-а) *м* (*также КОММ*) balance; (*ведомость*) balance sheet; **расчётный ~** balance of claims and liabilities; **бухгáлтерский ~** balance sheet; **платёжный/торгóвый ~** balance of payments/trade.
балансúр|овать (-ую) *несов неперех*: **~ (на** *+prp*) to balance (on) ◆ (*perf* **сбалансúровать**) *перех* (*КОММ*) to balance; **~** (*impf*) **на грáни чегó-н** (*перен*) to be poised on the verge *или* brink of sth.
балáнсовый *прил* balance *опред*; **балáнсовый**

отчёт balance sheet.
балахо́н (**-а**) *м* (*разг*) sack (*baggy garment*).
балд|а́ (**-ы́**) *м/ж* chump.
балери́н|а (**-ы**) *ж* ballerina.
бале́т (**-а**) *м* ballet.
балетме́йстер (**-а**) *м* ballet master.
ба́л|ка (**-ки**; *gen pl* **-ок**) *ж* (*железобетонная, деревянная*) beam; (*металлическая*) girder; (*овраг*) gully.
Балка́н|ы (**-**) *мн* the Balkans.
балко́н (**-а**) *м* (*АРХИТ*) balcony; (*ТЕАТР*) circle (*BRIT*), balcony (*US*).
балл (**-а**) *м* (*на экзамене*) mark; (*на соревновании*) point; **проходно́й** ~ pass mark; **ве́тер си́лой в 5 ба́ллов** a force 5 wind.
балла́д|а (**-ы**) *ж* ballad.
балла́ст (**-а**) *м* ballast; (*перен*) dead weight.
балли́стик|а (**-и**) *ж* ballistics.
баллисти́ческ|ий (**-ая, -ое, -ие**) *прил* ballistic *опред*; **баллисти́ческая раке́та** ballistic missile.
балло́н (**-а**) *м* (*газовый*) cylinder; (*с жидкостью*) jar; (*с кислотой, щёлочью*) carboy; (*АВТ*) balloon tyre.
баллоти́р|овать (**-ую**) *несов перех* to vote for
▸ **баллоти́роваться** *несов возв*: **~ся в** *+acc* *или* **на пост** *+gen* to stand (*BRIT*) *или* run (*US*) for.
баллотиро́вочный *прил*: ~ **бюллете́нь** ballot paper.
ба́л|овать (**-ую**; *perf* **изба́ловать**) *несов перех* to spoil
▸ **ба́ловаться** *несов возв* to fool around.
ба́лок *сущ см* **ба́лка**.
балти́йск|ий (**-ая, -ое, -ие**) *прил*: **Б~ое мо́ре** the Baltic (Sea).
бальза́м (**-а**) *м* balsam; (*перен*) balm.
бальзами́р|овать (**-ую**) (*не*)*сов перех* to embalm.
ба́льн|ый *прил*: **~ое пла́тье** ball gown; **ба́льные та́нцы** ballroom dancing.
балюстра́д|а (**-ы**) *ж* balustrade.
БАМ (**-а**) *м сокр* (= *Байка́ло-Аму́рская* (*железнодоро́жная*) *магистра́ль*) Baikal-Amur Railway.
бамбу́к (**-а**) *м* bamboo.
ба́мпер (**-а**) *м* bumper.
БАН *м сокр* (= *Библиоте́ка Акаде́мии нау́к*) *library of the Academy of Sciences.*
бана́лен *прил см* **бана́льный**.
бана́льност|ь (**-и**) *ж* banality, platitude.
бана́л|ьный (**-ен, -ьна, -ьно**) *прил* banal, trite.
бана́н (**-а**) *м* banana.
Бангладе́ш (**-а**) *м* Bangladesh.
бангладе́шск|ий (**-ая, -ое, -ие**) *прил* Bangladeshi.
ба́нд|а (**-ы**) *ж* gang.
банда́ж (**-а́**) *м* support bandage.
бандеро́л|ь (**-и**) *ж* package; **я посла́л кни́гу ~ю** I packaged the book and sent it.
банди́т (**-а**) *м* bandit.
банк (**-а**) *м* bank; **сберега́тельный** ~ savings bank; **акционе́рный** ~ joint-stock bank; **э́кспортно-и́мпортный** ~ export-import bank.
ба́н|ка (**-ки**; *gen pl* **-ок**) *ж* (*стеклянная*) jar; (*жестяная*) tin (*BRIT*), can (*US*); (*обычно мн*: *МЕД*) cupping glass.
банке́т (**-а**) *м* banquet.
банки́р (**-а**) *м* banker.
банкно́т (**-а**; *gen pl* **-**) *м* banknote.
ба́нковск|ий (**-ая, -ое, -ие**) *прил* bank *опред*.
банкома́т (**-а**) *м* cash machine.
банкро́т (**-а**) *м* bankrupt; **объявля́ть** (**объяви́ть** *perf*) **кого́-н ~ом** to declare sb bankrupt.
банкро́тств|о (**-а**) *ср* bankruptcy.
ба́нный *прил* bath *опред*.
ба́нок *сущ см* **ба́нка**.
бант (**-а**) *м* bow.
ба́н|я (**-и**; *gen pl* **-ь**) *ж* bathhouse; (*разг*: *мытьё*) bath; **фи́нская** ~ sauna; **ру́сская/туре́цкая** ~ Russian/Turkish baths; **задава́ть** (**зада́ть** *perf*) **кому́-н ~ю** (*разг*) to give sb what for.
бапти́зм (**-а**) *м* baptism.
бапти́ст (**-а**) *м* Baptist.
бар (**-а**) *м* bar; (*gen pl* **-**; *ФИЗ*) bar.
бараба́н (**-а**) *м* drum.
бараба́н|ить (**-ю, -ишь**) *несов неперех* to drum.
бараба́нн|ый *прил*: **~ая перепо́нка** eardrum.
бара́к (**-а**) *м* barracks *мн*.
бара́н (**-а**) *м* sheep; **смотре́ть** (*impf*) **на кого́-н/что-н как ~ на но́вые воро́та** (*разг*) to gawk at sb/sth; **ста́до ~ов** (*также перен*: *пренебр*) flock of sheep.
бара́н|ий (**-ья, -ье, -ьи**) *прил* (*суп, котлета*) lamb; (*тулуп*) sheepskin.
бара́нин|а (**-ы**) *ж* mutton; (*молодая*) lamb.
бара́н|ка (**-ки**; *gen pl* **-ок**) *ж small, hard bread ring*; (*перен*: *разг*) wheel.
барахл|о́ (**-а́**) *ср собир* junk; (*разг*: *человек, вещь*) trash.
барахо́л|ка (**-ки**; *gen pl* **-ок**) *ж* flea market.
бара́хта|ться (**-юсь**) *несов возв* (*разг*) to flounder; (*играя*) to wallow.
бара́ш|ек (**-ка**) *м* (*разг*) lamb; (*шкура*) lambskin; *см также* **бара́шки**.
бара́шк|и (**-ов**) *мн* (*облака*) fleecy clouds *мн*; (*волны*) white horses *мн*, whitecaps *мн*.
барбари́с (**-а**) *м* barberry.
бард (**-а**) *м* singer-songwriter.
барда́к (**-а́**) *м* (*груб!*: *беспорядок*) hell broke loose (*!*)
барелье́ф (**-а**) *м* bas-relief.
ба́ренцев (**-а, -о, -ы**) *прил*: **Б~о мо́ре** Barents Sea.
ба́рж|а (**-и**) *ж* barge.
ба́рин (**-а**; *nom pl* **господа́**, *gen pl* **госпо́д**) *м* (*ИСТ*) ≈ lord (*member of the landowning gentry*);

жить *(impf)* **как** ~ to live like a king.
барито́н (-а) *м* baritone.
ба́рмен (-а) *м* barman (*мн* barmen), bartender (*US*).
бaрока́мер|а (-ы) *ж* pressure chamber.
баро́кко *ср нескл* baroque.
баро́метр (-а) *м* barometer.
барре́л|ь (-я) *м* barrel (*unit of measurement*).
баррика́д|а (-ы) *ж* barricade; **быть** *(impf)* **по ра́зные сто́роны баррика́д** to be on opposite sides of the fence.
баррикади́р|овать (-ую; *perf* **забаррикади́ровать**) *несов перех* to barricade.
барс (-а) *м* snow leopard.
Барсело́н|а (-ы) *ж* Barcelona.
ба́рск|ий (-ая, -ое, -ие) *прил* (*перен*) lordly, haughty; **ба́рская уса́дьба** manor house.
барсу́к (-а́) *м* badger.
ба́ртер (-а) *м* barter; **по** ~**у** on a barter basis.
ба́ртерн|ый *прил*: ~**ая торго́вля** goods *мн* for barter; **на** ~**ой осно́ве** on a barter basis.
ба́рхат (-а) *м* velvet.
ба́рхатный *прил* velvet; (*перен*: *кожа, голос*) velvety; **ба́рхатный сезо́н** *warm autumn days by the sea*.
барье́р (-а) *м* (*в беге*) hurdle; (*на скачках*) fence; (*перен*) barrier; **тари́фный** ~ tariff barrier.
бас (-а; *nom pl* -ы) *м* bass.
ба́сен *сущ см* **ба́сня**.
баскетбо́л (-а) *м* basketball.
баскетболи́ст (-а) *м* basketball player.
баскетболи́ст|ка (-ки; *gen pl* -ок) *ж см* **баскетболи́ст**.
баснoсло́в|ный (-ен, -на, -но) *прил* fabulous.
ба́с|ня (-ни; *gen pl* -ен) *ж* fable; (*обычно мн*: *перен*: *разг*) fairy story.
басо́вый *прил* bass *опред*.
бассе́йн (-а) *м* (swimming) pool; (*реки, озера итп*) basin; **каменноуго́льный** ~ coalfield.
баст|ова́ть (-у́ю) *несов неперех* to be on strike.
баталь́он (-а) *м* battalion.
батаре́|йка (-йки; *gen pl* -ек) *ж* (*ЭЛЕК*) battery.
батаре́|я (-и) *ж* (*отопительная*) radiator; (*ВОЕН, ЭЛЕК*) battery.
бати́ст (-а) *м* cambric, lawn.
бато́н (-а) *м* (white) loaf (*long or oval*).
батра́к (-а́) *м* farm hand.
батра́ч|ка (-ки; *gen pl* -ек) *ж см* **батра́к**.
баттерфля́|й (-я) *м* butterfly (stroke).
ба́тюш|ка (-ки; *gen pl* -ек) *м* (*также РЕЛ*) father; *см также* **ба́тюшки**.
ба́тюшки *межд*: ~ **(мой)!** good heavens!
бах *межд* bang.
ба́хн|уть (-у, -ешь; *impf* **ба́хать**) *сов (не)перех* to bang.
Бахре́йн (-а) *м* Bahrain.
бахром|а́ (-ы́) *ж* fringe.
бахч|а́ (-и́) *ж melon or pumpkin patch*.
бахчевы́е *прил*: ~ **культу́ры** *melons or pumpkins*.
баци́лл|а (-ы) *ж* bacillus (*мн* bacilli).
ба́шен *сущ см* **ба́шня**.
башк|а́ (-и́) *ж* (*разг*) head.
башма́к (-а́) *м* (*туфля*) shoe; (*ботинок*) boot; **деревя́нный** ~ clog; **быть** *(impf)* **под башмако́м у кого́-н** to be under sb's thumb.
ба́ш|ня (-ни; *gen pl* -ен) *ж* tower; (*ВОЕН*) gun turret; (*разг*) tower block.
баю-ба́й *межд* refrain (*in lullaby*).
баю́ка|ть (-ю) *несов перех* to lull to sleep.
ба́юшки-баю́ *межд см* **баю-ба́й**.
бая́н (-а) *м* bayan (*kind of concertina*).
БВЛ *ж сокр* (= *Библиоте́ка всеми́рной литерату́ры*) *series of books on world literature*.
бди́тел|ьный (-ен, -ьна, -ьно) *прил* vigilant.
бег (-а) *м* running; (*СПОРТ*) race; ~ **на дли́нные диста́нции** long-distance race; ~ **на коро́ткие диста́нции** sprint; *см также* **бега́**.
бег|а́ (-о́в) *мн* the races *мн*; **быть** *(impf)* **в** ~**х** (*разг*) to be on the run *или* go.
бе́га|ть (-ю) *несов неперех* to run; (*челнок*) to fly to and fro; ~ *(impf)* **от** +*gen* (*разг*) to avoid; ~ *(impf)* **за кем-н** (*разг*) to chase *или* run after sb; **у него́ глаза́** ~**ли** he looked shifty.
бегемо́т (-а) *м* hippopotamus.
беги́(те) *несов см* **бежа́ть**.
бегле́ц (-а́) *м* fugitive.
бе́гло *нареч* (*читать, говорить*) fluently; (*просмотреть, ознакомиться*) cursorily.
бе́глый *прил* (*каторжник, преступник*) escaped; (*крепостной*) runaway *опред*; (*речь, чтение*) fluent; (*обзор*) cursory; **бе́глые гла́сные** fleeting vowels; **бе́глый ого́нь** (*ВОЕН*) rapid fire.
бегля́н|ка (-ки; *gen pl* -ок) *ж см* **бегле́ц**.
бегов|о́й *прил* (*лошадь*) race *опред*; (*лыжи*) racing; ~**а́я доро́жка** running track.
бего́м *нареч* quickly; (*перен*: *разг*) in a rush; **бежа́ть** *(impf)* ~ to race, fly.
бего́ни|я (-и) *ж* begonia.
бе́гств|о (-а) *ср* (*из плена*) escape; (*из дома*) flight; (*с поля боя*) rout; **обраща́ть (обрати́ть** *perf*) **в** ~ to rout; **спаса́ться (спасти́сь** *perf*) ~**м** to escape.
бегу́ *итп несов см* **бежа́ть**.
бегу́н (-а́) *м* runner.
бегу́нь|я (-и) *ж см* **бегу́н**.
бед|а́ (-ы́; *nom pl* -ы) *ж* tragedy; (*личная*) misfortune; **про́сто** ~! it's just awful!; **попада́ть (попа́сть** *perf*) **в** ~**у́** to get into trouble; **быть** *(impf)* **в** ~**е́** to be in trouble; ~ **в том, что** ... the trouble is (that) ...; ~ **(мне) с ним** (*разг*) he's nothing but trouble (to me); **на** ~**у́** (*разг*) unfortunately; **не** ~! (*разг*) (it's) nothing!; **лиха́** ~ **нача́ло** (*разг*) the first step is always the hardest.
бе́ден *прил см* **бе́дный**.
бёдер *сущ см* **бедро́**.
бедне́|ть (-ю; *perf* **обедне́ть**) *несов неперех* to become poor.
бе́дност|ь (-и) *ж* (*также перен*) poverty.

бе́д|ный (-ен, -на́, -но) *прил* poor.
бедня́г|а (-и) *м/ж* (*разг*) poor thing.
бедня́к (-а́) *м* poor man.
бе́дренный *прил* (*см сущ*) thigh *опред*; hip *опред*.
бедр|о́ (-а́; *nom pl* **бёдра**, *gen pl* **бёдер)** *ср* (*верхняя часть ноги*) thigh; (*таз*) hip.
бе́дствен|ный (-, -на, -но) *прил* disastrous.
бе́дстви|е (-я) *ср* disaster.
бе́дств|овать (-ую) *несов неперех* to live in poverty.
бе|жа́ть (*см* **Table 20**) *несов неперех* to run; (*время*) to fly; (*облака*) to scud ◆ (*не*)*сов* (*из плена, из тюрьмы*) to escape.
бе́жевый *прил* beige.
бе́жен|ец (-ца) *м* refugee.
бе́жен|ка (-ки; *gen pl* **-ок)** *ж см* **бе́женец**.
бе́женца *итп сущ см* **бе́женец**.
бежи́шь *итп несов см* **бежа́ть**.
без *предл* (+*gen*) without; **~ пяти́/десяти́ мину́т шесть** five to/ten to six; **не ~** +*gen* (*труда, осложнений*) not without; **и ~ того́** (*и так уже*) already; **не ~ того́** (*разг*) sort of; **~ у́стали** tirelessly; **~ тебя́ пробле́м хвата́ет** there are enough problems without you adding to them *.
безавари́йный *прил* accident-free.
безала́бер|ный (-ен, -на, -но) *прил* (*разг*) sloppy.
безалкого́льный *прил* nonalcoholic, alcohol-free; **безалкого́льный напи́ток** soft drink.
безапелляцио́н|ный (-ен, -на, -но) *прил* (*тон, ответ*) peremptory; (*юр*: *решение*) final; **~ый пригово́р** *a sentence without the right of appeal*.
безбе́д|ный (-ен, -на, -но) *прил* comfortable.
безбиле́тник (-а) *м* (*разг*: *пассажир*) fare dodger.
безбиле́тниц|а (-ы) *ж см* **безбиле́тник**.
безбо́жен *прил см* **безбо́жный**.
безбо́жник (-а) *м* (*разг*) heathen.
безбо́жно *нареч* (*разг*) shamelessly.
безбо́ж|ный (-ен, -на, -но) *прил* (*разг*) shameless.
безболе́знен|ный (-, -на, -но) *прил* (*также перен*) painless.
безбоя́знен|ный (-, -на, -но) *прил* fearless.
безбра́чи|е (-я) *ср* celibacy.
безбре́ж|ный (-ен, -на, -но) *прил* (*также перен*) boundless.
безве́ст|ный (-ен, -на, -но) *прил* unknown.
безве́трен|ный (-, -на, -но) *прил* calm.
безвку́сен *прил см* **безвку́сный**.
безвку́сиц|а (-ы) *ж* bad taste.
безвку́с|ный (-ен, -на, -но) *прил* tasteless.
безвла́сти|е (-я) *ср* anarchy.
безво́д|ный (-ен, -на, -но) *прил* (*среда, почва*) arid.
безвозвра́т|ный (-ен, -на, -но) *прил* irretrievable; **безвозвра́тная ссу́да** nonrepayable subsidy.
безвозме́здно *нареч* for free.
безвозме́здный *прил* free.
безво́л|ьный (-ен, -ьна, -ьно) *прил* weak-willed.
безвре́д|ный (-ен, -на, -но) *прил* harmless.
безвре́мен|ный (-ен, -на, -но) *прил* untimely.
безвы́ездно *нареч* continuously.
безвы́ход|ный (-ен, -на, -но) *прил* hopeless.
безгла́сный *прил* (*перен*) silent.
безголо́в|ый (-, -а, -о) *прил* (*перен*: *разг*) brainless.
безголо́с|ый (-, -а, -о) *прил*: **~ пе́вец** singer with a weak voice.
безгра́мот|ный (-ен, -на, -но) *прил* illiterate; (*работник*) incompetent.
безграни́ч|ный (-ен, -на, -но) *прил* (*также перен*) boundless.
безгре́ш|ный (-ен, -на, -но) *прил* sinless.
безда́р|ный (-ен, -на, -но) *прил* (*писатель, музыкант*) talentless; (*произведение, роман*) mediocre.
бе́здар|ь (-и) *ж* (*разг*) nobody.
безде́йств|овать (-ую) *несов неперех* (*машина, предприятие*) to be out of action; (*человек*) to take no action.
безделу́ш|ка (-ки; *gen pl* **-ек)** *ж* (*разг*) trinket, knick-knack.
безде́ль|е (-я) *ср* idleness.
безде́льник (-а) *м* (*разг*) loafer.
безде́льниц|а (-ы) *ж см* **безде́льник**.
безде́льнича|ть (-ю) *несов неперех* (*разг*) to loaf *или* lounge about.
безде́нежный *прил* (*расчёт, перевод*) noncash; (*разг*: *человек*) hard up.
безде́т|ный (-ен, -на, -но) *прил* childless.
безде́ятел|ьный (-ен, -ьна, -ьно) *прил* inactive.
бе́здн|а (-ы) *ж* abyss; **у меня́ ~ дел** (*разг*) I've got heaps of things to do.
бездоказа́тел|ьный (-ен, -ьна, -ьно) *прил* unsubstantiated.
бездо́м|ный (-ен, -на, -но) *прил* (*человек*) homeless; (*собака*) stray *опред*.
бездо́н|ный (-ен, -на, -но) *прил* bottomless; **бездо́нная бо́чка** (*разг*) bottomless pit; (: *человек*) (old) soak.
безду́м|ный (-ен, -на, -но) *прил* thoughtless.
безду́ш|ный (-ен, -на, -но) *прил* (*человек*) heartless; (*игра актёра*) soulless.
безе́ *ср нескл* meringue.
безжа́лост|ный (-ен, -на, -но) *прил* ruthless.
безжи́знен|ный (-, -на, -но) *прил* lifeless; (*взгляд, лицо*) expressionless.
беззабо́т|ный (-ен, -на, -но) *прил* carefree.
беззако́нен *прил см* **беззако́нный**.
беззако́ни|е (-я) *ср* lawlessness; (*поступок*) unlawful act.

беззако́н|ный (-ен, -на, -но) *прил* unlawful.
беззасте́нчив|ый (-, -а, -о) *прил* shameless; **~ лгун** barefaced liar.
беззащи́т|ный (-ен, -на, -но) *прил* defenceless (*BRIT*), defenseless (*US*).
беззву́ч|ный (-ен, -на, -но) *прил* inaudible.
беззло́б|ный (-ен, -на, -но) *прил* good-natured.
беззу́б|ый (-, -а, -о) *прил* toothless; (*перен*) feeble.
безли́к|ий (-ая, -ое, -ие; -, -а, -о) *прил* nondescript.
безли́чный *прил* (*лингв*) impersonal.
безлю́д|ный (-ен, -на, -но) *прил* (*улица, место*) deserted, empty; **безлю́дная техноло́гия** automated technology; **безлю́дный фонд** *funds for employees not on regular staff*.
безме́р|ный (-ен, -на, -но) *прил* (*счастье, любовь*) boundless; (*требования*) unlimited.
безмо́зглый *прил* (*разг*) brainless.
безмо́лв|ный (-ен, -на, -но) *прил* (*также перен*) silent; **~ное согла́сие** tacit agreement.
безмяте́ж|ный (-ен, -на, -но) *прил* tranquil.
безнадёж|ный (-ен, -на, -но) *прил* hopeless; **~ больно́й** hopeless case (*MED*).
безнака́зан|ный (-, -на, -но) *прил* unpunished.
безнали́чный *прил* noncash; **безнали́чный расчёт** clearing settlement.
безно́г|ий (-ая, -ое, -ие) *прил* one-legged; (*без двух ног*) legless.
безнра́вствен|ный (-, -на, -но) *прил* immoral.
безо *предл см* **без**.
безоби́д|ный (-ен, -на, -но) *прил* harmless; (*шутка, высказывание*) inoffensive, innocuous.
безо́блач|ный (-ен, -на, -но) *прил* cloudless; (*перен: жизнь, детство*) carefree; (*: счастье*) unclouded.
безобра́зен *прил см* **безобра́зный**.
безобра́зи|е (-я) *ср* (*физическое уродство*) ugliness; (*поступок*) outrage; **~!** it's outrageous!, it's a disgrace!
безобра́зник (-а) *м* (*разг*) (little) horror.
безобра́зница (-ы) *ж см* **безобра́зник**.
безобра́знича|ть (-ю; *perf* **набезобра́зничать**) *несов неперех* (*разг*) to carry on.
безобра́з|ный (-ен, -на, -но) *прил* ugly; (*поступок, действие*) outrageous, disgraceful.
безоговоро́ч|ный (-ен, -на, -но) *прил* unconditional.
безопа́сен *прил см* **безопа́сный**.
безопа́сност|ь (-и) *ж* safety; (*международная*) security; **в ~и** out of danger; **Сове́т Б~и** Security Council; **те́хника ~и** health and safety; **безопа́сность движе́ния** road safety.
безопа́с|ный (-ен, -на, -но) *прил* safe.
безору́ж|ный (-ен, -на, -но) *прил* unarmed; (*перен: в споре*) defenceless (*BRIT*), defenseless (*US*).
безостано́вочно *нареч* incessantly.
безотве́т|ный (-ен, -на, -но) *прил* (*любовь*) unrequited; (*существо*) meek.
безотве́тственност|ь (-и) *ж* irresponsibility.
безотве́тствен|ный (-, -на, -но) *прил* irresponsible.
безотка́з|ный (-ен, -на, -но) *прил* reliable.
безотлага́тел|ьный (-ен, -ьна, -ьно) *прил* urgent.
безотноси́тельно *нареч*: **~ к** *+dat* irrespective of.
безотра́д|ный (-ен, -на, -но) *прил* (*жизнь*) dreary; (*положение*) bleak.
безотхо́д|ный (-ен, -на, -но) *прил*: **~ное произво́дство** *production process which recycles waste*.
безотчёт|ный (-ен, -на, -но) *прил* (*чувство*) irrational; (*поведение*) unaccountable.
безоши́боч|ный (-ен, -на, -но) *прил* (*решение, догадка*) correct; (*судья, ценитель*) infallible.
безрабо́тица (-ы) *ж* unemployment.
безрабо́тн|ая (-ой; *decl like adj*) *ж см* **безрабо́тный**.
безрабо́тн|ый *прил* unemployed ◆ (-ого; *decl like adj*) *м* unemployed person; **~ые** the unemployed.
безра́дост|ный (-ен, -на, -но) *прил* (*жизнь, детство*) cheerless, joyless; (*голос, взгляд*) dull.
безразде́л|ьный (-ен, -ьна, -ьно) *прил* (*господство, владение*) absolute; (*внимание*) undivided.
безразли́чен *прил см* **безразли́чный**.
безразли́чно *нареч* indifferently ◆ *как сказ*: **мне ~** it doesn't matter to me, it makes no difference to me; **~, придёт он или нет** it makes no difference whether he comes or not; **~ кто/что** no matter who/what.
безразли́ч|ный (-ен, -на, -но) *прил* indifferent.
безразме́рн|ый *прил*: **~ые носки́/чулки́** one-size socks/stockings.
безрассу́д|ный (-ен, -на, -но) *прил* (*поведение*) reckless; (*любовь*) impulsive.
безрезульта́т|ный (-ен, -на, -но) *прил* fruitless.
безро́пот|ный (-ен, -на, -но) *прил* uncomplaining.
безрука́в|ка (-ки; *gen pl* -ок) *ж* (*кофта*) sleeveless top; (*куртка*) sleeveless jacket.
безру́к|ий (-ая, -ое, -ие; -, -а, -о) *прил* one-armed; (*без двух рук*) with no arms; (*перен: разг*) ham-fisted.
безры́бь|е (-я) *ср*: **на ~ и рак ры́ба** something is better than nothing.
безубы́точ|ный (-ен, -на, -но) *прил*: **~ное предприя́тие** *business which is not making a loss*.
безуда́р|ный (-ен, -на, -но) *прил* (*лингв*) unstressed.
безукори́знен|ный (-, -на, -но) *прил* (*поведение, человек*) irreproachable; (*работа*) flawless.
безу́мен *прил см* **безу́мный**.
безу́м|ец (-ца) *м* madman (*мн* madmen).
безу́ми|е (-я) *ср* madness; **до ~я** madly.

безу́мно *нареч* (*любить*) madly; (*устать*) terribly.
безу́м|ный (**-ен, -на, -но**) *прил* (*план, намерение*) mad; (*счастье, ярость итп*) wild; **он зараба́тывает ~ные де́ньги** (*разг*) he earns crazy money; **~ная ро́скошь** unbelievable luxury.
безу́мца *итп сущ см* **безу́мец**.
безупре́ч|ный (**-ен, -на, -но**) *прил* (*поведение, человек*) irreproachable; (*работа*) flawless.
безусло́вен *прил см* **безусло́вный**.
безусло́вно *нареч* (*повиноваться, доверить*) unconditionally ♦ *част* (*несомненно*) without a doubt; **~, я бу́ду рад помо́чь Вам** naturally, I'll be happy to help you.
безусло́в|ный (**-ен, -на, -но**) *прил* (*повиновение, доверие*) unconditional, absolute; (*успех, превосходство*) indisputable.
безуспе́ш|ный (**-ен, -на, -но**) *прил* unsuccessful.
безуча́ст|ный (**-ен, -на, -но**) *прил* disinterested.
безъя́дерный *прил* nuclear-free.
безымя́н|ный (**-ен, -на, -но**) *прил* (*река, гора*) unnamed; (*герой, автор*) anonymous; **безымя́нный па́лец** ring finger.
безысхо́д|ный (**-ен, -на, -но**) *прил* hopeless.
бей(ся) *несов см* **би́ть(ся)**.
Бейру́т (**-а**) *м* Beirut.
бе́йте(сь) *несов см* **би́ть(ся)**.
беко́н (**-а**) *м* bacon.
БелА́З (**-а**) *м сокр* = *Белору́сский автомоби́льный заво́д*; (*автомобиль*) *vehicle manufactured at the Belorussian car factory*.
Белару́с|ь (**-и**) *ж* Belarus.
Белгра́д (**-а**) *м* Belgrade.
беле́|ть (**-ю**; *perf* **побеле́ть**) *несов неперех* (*лицо*) to go *или* turn white; (*no perf*; *цветы*) to show white.
белиберд|а́ (**-ы́**) *ж* (*разг*) gobbledegook.
Бели́з (**-а**) *м* Belize.
бели́л|а (**-**) *мн* emulsion *ед*.
бел|и́ть (**-ю́, -ишь**; *perf* **побели́ть**) *несов перех* to whitewash.
бе́лич|ий (**-ья, -ье, -ьи**) *прил* squirrel's; (*шуба*) squirrel (fur).
бе́л|ка (**-ки**; *gen pl* **-ок**) *ж* squirrel; **верте́ться** (*impf*) **как ~ в колесе́** to run round in circles.
белка́ *итп сущ см* **бело́к**.
белко́вый *прил* proteinous.
беллетри́стик|а (**-и**) *ж* fiction; (*лёгкое чтение*) light reading.
белови́к (**-а́**) *м* fair copy.
белогварде́|ец (**-йца**) *м* (*ист*) White Guardsman (*мн* Guardsmen).
бе́лок *сущ см* **бе́лка**.
бел|о́к (**-ка́**) *м* protein; (*яйца*) (egg) white; (*анат*) white (of the eye).
белокро́ви|е (**-я**) *ср* (*мед*) leukaemia (*BRIT*), leukemia (*US*).
белоку́р|ый (**-, -а, -о**) *прил* (*человек*) fair(-haired); (*волосы*) fair.
белору́с (**-а**) *м* Belorussian.
белору́с|ка (**-ки**; *gen pl* **-ок**) *ж см* **белору́с**.
белору́сск|ий (**-ая, -ое, -ие**) *прил* Belorussian.
белору́ч|ка (**-ки**; *gen pl* **-ек**) *м/ж* (*разг*: *пренебр*) shirker.
белосне́ж|ный (**-ен, -на, -но**) *прил* snow-white.
белу́г|а (**-и**) *ж* beluga (*sturgeon*).
белу́ж|ий (**-ья, -ье, -ьи**) *прил* beluga *опред*.
Бе́лфаст (**-а**) *м* Belfast.
бе́л|ые (**-ых**; *decl like adj*) *мн* (*шахматы*) white *ед*.
бе́л|ый (**-, -а́, -о**) *прил* white; (*гриб*) cep ♦ (**-ого**; *decl like adj*) *м* (*человек*) white (person); **средь ~а дня** (*разг*) in broad daylight; **бе́лая воро́на** the odd one out; **бе́лая гва́рдия** (*ист*) the White Guard; **бе́лая горя́чка** the DT's (= *delirium tremens*); **бе́лое духове́нство** secular clergy; **бе́лый медве́дь** polar bear; *см также* **бе́лые**.
бельги́ек *сущ см* **бельги́йка**.
бельги́|ец (**-йца**) *м* Belgian.
бельги́|йка (**-йки**; *gen pl* **-ек**) *ж см* **бельги́ец**.
бельги́йск|ий (**-ая, -ое, -ие**) *прил* Belgian.
бельги́йца *итп сущ см* **бельги́ец**.
Бе́льги|я (**-и**) *ж* Belgium.
бель|ё (**-я́**) *ср собир* linen; (*стиранное*) washing; **ни́жнее ~** underwear; **посте́льное ~** bedclothes, bed linen.
бельэта́ж (**-а**) *м* (*театр*) dress circle; (*архит*) first floor, second floor (*US*).
беля́ш (**-а́**) *м* meat pie.
бемо́л|ь (**-я**) *м* (*муз*) flat.
бенефи́с (**-а**) *м performance commemorating and featuring an actor*.
бензи́н (**-а**) *м* petrol (*BRIT*), gas (*US*).
бензи́новый *прил* petrol (*BRIT*), gas (*US*); **~ дви́гатель** petrol engine.
бензоба́к (**-а**) *м* petrol (*BRIT*) *или* gas (*US*) tank.
бензоколо́н|ка (**-ки**; *gen pl* **-ок**) *ж* petrol (*BRIT*) *или* gas (*US*) pump.
Бенилю́кс (**-а**) *м* Benelux.
бенуа́р (**-а**) *м* (*театр*) boxes *мн*.
бе́рег (**-а**; *loc sg* **-у́**, *nom pl* **-а́**) *м* (*моря, озера*) shore; (*реки*) bank.
берёг(ся) *итп несов см* **бере́чь(ся)**.
берегов|о́й *прил* (*см сущ*) coastal; riverside; **берегова́я ли́ния** coastline; **берегова́я слу́жба** coastguard.
берегу́(сь) *итп несов см* **бере́чь(ся)**.
бе́режен *прил см* **бе́режный**.
бережёшь(ся) *итп несов см* **бере́чь(ся)**.
бережли́вост|ь (**-и**) *ж* economy, thrift.
бережли́в|ый (**-, -а, -о**) *прил* economical, thrifty.
бе́режност|ь (**-и**) *ж* care.
бе́реж|ный (**-ен, -на, -но**) *прил* (*заботливый*)

caring; (*осторожный*) careful.
берёз|а (**-ы**) *ж* birch (tree).
Берёз|ка (**-ки**; *gen pl* **-ок**) *ж* Beriozka (*hard-currency shop in the USSR*).
берёзовый *прил* birch.
Берёзок *сущ см* **Берёзка**.
берём *несов см* **брать**.
бере́мене|ть (**-ю**; *perf* **забере́менеть**) *сов неперех* to get pregnant.
бере́менн|ая (**-а**) *прил* pregnant ◆ (**-ой**; *decl like adj*) *ж* pregnant woman.
бере́менност|ь (**-и**) *ж* pregnancy.
бере́т (**-а**) *м* beret.
берёт *итп несов см* **брать**.
бер|е́чь (**-егу́, -ежёшь** *итп*, **-егу́т**; *pt* **-ёг, -егла́, -егло́**) *несов перех* (*документы*) to keep; (*деньги*) to be careful with; (*время*) to make good use of; (*здоровье, детей*) to look after, take care of; ~ (*impf*) **как зени́цу о́ка** to guard with one's life
▸ **бере́чься** (*perf* **поберéчься**) *несов возв* (*+gen*) to watch out for; **~еги́тесь просту́ды** take care you don't catch a cold; **~еги́тесь!** watch out!
бе́рингов (**-а, -о, -ы**) *прил*: **Б~ проли́в** Bering Strait.
Берли́н (**-а**) *м* Berlin.
берму́дск|ий (**-ая, -ое, -ие**) *прил*: **Б~ие острова́** Bermuda, the Bermudas.
Берн (**-а**) *м* Berne.
беру́(сь) *итп несов см* **брать(ся)**.
берцо́в|ый *прил*: **~ая кость** shinbone.
бес (**-а**) *м* demon, devil; (*перен*) devil.
бесе́д|а (**-ы**) *ж* conversation; (*не официальная*) chat; (*популярный доклад*) discussion.
бесе́д|ка (**-ки**; *gen pl* **-ок**) *ж* pavilion.
бесе́довать (**-ую**) *несов неперех*: ~ (**с** *+instr*) to talk (to); (*не официально*) to chat (to).
бесе́док *сущ см* **бесе́дка**.
бе|си́ть (**-шу́, -сишь**; *perf* **взбеси́ть**) *несов перех* to infuriate
▸ **беси́ться** *несов возв* (*разг*) to run wild; (*perf* **взбеси́ться**; *раздражаться*) to become furious; **с жи́ру ~ся** (*impf*) (*разг*) to become spoilt and fussy.
бескла́ссовый *прил* classless.
бескомпроми́сс|ный (**-ен, -на, -но**) *прил* uncompromising.
бесконе́чен *прил см* **бесконе́чный**.
бесконе́чно *нареч* (*очень долго*) endlessly; (*чрезвычайно*) infinitely.
бесконе́чност|ь (**-и**) *ж* infinity; **до ~и** (*очень долго*) endlessly; (*очень сильно*) infinitely.
бесконе́ч|ный (**-ен, -на, -но**) *прил* (*пространство, дорога*) endless; (*время, удовольствие*) endless, infinite; (*число*) infinite; (*вечер, песня*) interminable; (*любовь, ненависть*) undying.
бесконтро́л|ьный (**-ен, -ьна, -ьно**) *прил* uncontrolled.
бескоры́стен *прил см* **бескоры́стный**.
бескоры́сти|е (**-я**) *ср* unselfishness.
бескоры́ст|ный (**-ен, -на, -но**) *прил* unselfish.
бескро́в|ный (**-ен, -на, -но**) *прил* bloodless.
беспардо́н|ный (**-ен, -на, -но**) *прил* shameless, brazen.
бесперебо́|йный (**-ен, -йна, -йно**) *прил* uninterrupted.
бесперспекти́в|ный (**-ен, -на, -но**) *прил* (*работа*) without prospects; (*отношения*) with no future.
беспе́чен *прил см* **беспе́чный**.
беспе́чност|ь (**-и**) *ж* carefreeness.
беспе́ч|ный (**-ен, -на, -но**) *прил* carefree.
беспла́т|ный (**-ен, -на, -но**) *прил* free.
беспло́ден *прил см* **беспло́дный**.
беспло́ди|е (**-я**) *ср* (*женщины*) infertility; (*земли*) barrenness, infertility.
беспло́д|ный (**-ен, -на, -но**) *прил* (*женщина*) infertile; (*брак*) childless; (*почва*) barren, infertile; (*попытки, дискуссии*) fruitless.
бесповоро́т|ный (**-ен, -на, -но**) *прил* irrevocable.
бесподо́б|ный (**-ен, -на, -но**) *прил* (*разг*) fantastic.
беспоко́ен *прил см* **беспоко́йный**.
беспоко́|ить (**-ю, -ишь**) *несов перех* (*причинять боль*) to trouble; (*perf* **побеспоко́ить**; *мешать*) to disturb; (*perf* **обеспоко́ить**; *тревожить*) to bother, worry
▸ **беспоко́иться** *несов возв* (*утруждать себя*) to put o.s. out, trouble o.s.; (*тревожиться*): **~ся о** *+prp* *или* **за** *+acc* to worry about; **не ~йтесь, я сде́лаю всё сам** don't put yourself out, I'll do it myself.
беспоко́|йный (**-ен, -йна, -йно**) *прил* (*человек*) anxious; (*взгляд*) uneasy, anxious; (*поездка*) uncomfortable; (*ребёнок*) fidgety, restless; (*море, сон, время*) troubled; **э́то о́чень ~йная рабо́та** it's a very stressful job.
беспоко́йств|о (**-а**) *ср* anxiety, unease; (*заботы, хлопоты*) trouble; **прости́те за ~!** sorry to trouble you!
бесполе́з|ный (**-ен, -на, -но**) *прил* useless.
беспо́мощен *прил см* **беспо́мощный**.
беспо́мощност|ь (**-и**) *ж* (*см прил*) helplessness; weakness.
беспо́мощ|ный (**-ен, -на, -но**) *прил* helpless; (*перен*) weak.
беспоря́дк|и (**-ов**) *мн* disturbances *мн*.
беспоря́д|ок (**-ка**) *м* disorder; **в ~ке** (*комната, дела*) in a mess; *см также* **беспоря́дки**.
беспоря́доч|ный (**-ен, -на, -но**) *прил* (*груда бумаг*) disorderly, untidy; (*рассказ, записи*) confused.
беспоса́дочный *прил* nonstop.
беспо́чвен|ный (**-, -на, -но**) *прил* groundless.
беспо́шлинный *прил* duty-free.
беспоща́д|ный (**-ен, -на, -но**) *прил* (*наказание, удар*) merciless; (*критика, сатира*) ruthless; ~ **к** *+dat* ruthless *или* merciless towards.
беспра́вен *прил см* **беспра́вный**.

беспра́ви|е (-я) *ср* (*беззаконие*) lawlessness.
бесправ|ный (-ен, -на, -но) *прил* without rights.
беспреде́л (-а) *м* lawlessness.
беспреде́л|ьный (-ен, -ьна, -ьно) *прил* (*пространство, море*) boundless; (*любовь, ненависть*) immeasurable.
беспрекосло́в|ный (-ен, -на, -но) *прил* unquestioning.
беспрепя́тственно *нареч* without difficulty.
беспрепя́тствен|ный (-, -на, -но) *прил* unimpeded.
беспрецеде́нт|ный (-ен, -на, -но) *прил* unprecedented.
бесприбыл|ьный (-ен, -ьна, -ьно) *прил* unprofitable.
беспризо́рен *прил см* **беспризо́рный**.
беспризо́рник (-а) *м* (street) urchin.
беспризо́рниц|а (-ы) *ж см* **беспризо́рник**.
беспризо́р|ный (-ен, -на, -но) *прил* (*ребёнок*) homeless; (*дом, хозяйство*) neglected.
беспринци́п|ный (-ен, -на, -но) *прил* unscrupulous.
беспристра́ст|ный (-ен, -на, -но) *прил* unbias(s)ed.
беспричи́н|ный (-ен, -на, -но) *прил* irrational.
беспросве́т|ный (-ен, -на, -но) *прил* (*нужда*) desperate; (*грусть*) hopeless; (*ночь, мгла*) impenetrable.
беспроце́нтный *прил* interest-free.
Бессара́би|я (-и) *ж* Bessarabia.
бессвя́з|ный (-ен, -на, -но) *прил* disjointed.
бессерде́чен *прил см* **бессерде́чный**.
бессерде́чност|ь (-и) *ж* heartlessness.
бессерде́ч|ный (-ен, -на, -но) *прил* heartless.
бесси́лен *прил см* **бесси́льный**.
бесси́ли|е (-я) *ср* (*больного, старика*) debility; (*чувства*) impotence.
бесси́л|ьный (-ен, -ьна, -ьно) *прил* (*больной, старик*) feeble, weak; (*гнев, ненависть*) impotent; **он/президе́нт ~ен (измени́ть ситуа́цию)** he/the president is powerless (to change the situation).
бессме́ртен *прил см* **бессме́ртный**.
бессме́рти|е (-я) *ср* immortality.
бессме́рт|ный (-ен, -на, -но) *прил* immortal.
бессмы́сленност|ь (-и) *ж* (*слов*) meaninglessness; (*поступка*) senselessness, pointlessness.
бессмы́слен|ный (-, -на, -но) *прил* (*слова*) meaningless; (*поступок*) senseless, pointless; (*взгляд, улыбка*) inane.
бессо́вест|ный (-ен, -на, -но) *прил* (*нечестный*) unscrupulous; (*наглый*) shameless.
бессодержа́тел|ьный (-ен, -ьна, -ьно) *прил* (*слова*) empty; (*статья*) thin.
бессозна́тел|ьный (-ен, -ьна, -ьно) *прил* (*страх, действия*) instinctive; **быть** (*impf*) **в ~ьном состоя́нии** to be unconscious.
бессо́нниц|а (-ы) *ж* insomnia.
бессо́нный *прил* (*ночь*) sleepless; (*страж, сиделка*) wakeful.
бесспо́рен *прил см* **бесспо́рный**.
бесспо́рно *нареч* indisputably ◆ *част* (*несомненно*) absolutely; **он, ~, умён** he is indisputably clever.
бесспо́р|ный (-ен, -на, -но) *прил* indisputable.
бессро́ч|ный (-ен, -на, -но) *прил* indefinite.
бесстра́ш|ный (-ен, -на, -но) *прил* fearless.
бессты́д|ный (-ен, -на, -но) *прил* shameless, brazen; (*ложь*) barefaced.
беста́кт|ный (-ен, -на, -но) *прил* tactless.
бе́сти|я (-и) *м/ж* (*разг*) rogue.
бестолко́в|ый (-, -а, -о) *прил* (*глупый*) stupid; (*невразумительный*) incoherent.
бестсе́ллер (-а) *м* best seller.
бесхи́трост|ный (-ен, -на, -но) *прил* simple.
бесхо́зный *прил* ownerless.
бесхозя́йствен|ный (-, -на, -но) *прил* (*руководитель*) inefficient; (*политика*) uneconomic; **~ная же́нщина** a bad housekeeper.
бесцве́т|ный (-ен, -на, -но) *прил* colourless (*BRIT*), colorless (*US*).
бесце́л|ьный (-ен, -ьна, -ьно) *прил* pointless, futile.
бесце́н|ный (-ен, -на, -но) *прил* (*коллекция, сокровища*) priceless; (*друг, жена*) invaluable.
бесце́нок *м*: **за ~** dirt cheap, for next to nothing.
бесцеремо́н|ный (-ен, -на, -но) *прил* unceremonious, familiar.
бесчелове́ч|ный (-ен, -на, -но) *прил* inhuman.
бесче́|стить (-щу, -стишь; *perf* **обесче́стить**) *несов перех* (*девушку*) to violate.
бесчи́слен|ный (-, -на, -но) *прил* numerous.
бесчу́вствен|ный (-, -на, -но) *прил* (*жестокий*) unfeeling; (*лишённый сознания*) senseless.
бето́н (-а; *part gen* -у) *м* concrete.
бетони́р|овать (-ую; *perf* **забетони́ровать**) *несов перех* to concrete.
бефстро́ганов *м нескл* boeuf *или* beef stroganoff.
бе́шенств|о (-а) *ср* (*перен*) rage; (*МЕД*) rabies; **приходи́ть (прийти́** *perf*) **в ~** to fly into a rage.
бе́шен|ый *прил* (*взгляд*) furious; (*характер, темперамент, ураган*) violent; (*МЕД*) rabid; (*разг: деньги, цены*) crazy; **э́то сто́ит ~ых де́нег** (*разг*) it costs a bomb.
бешу́(сь) *несов см* **беси́ть(ся)**.
биатло́н (-а) *м* biathlon.
биатлони́ст (-а) *м* biathlete.
биатлони́ст|ка (-ки; *gen pl* -ок) *ж см* **биатлони́ст**.
Би-би-си *ж сокр* (= *Брита́нская радиовеща́тельная корпора́ция*) BBC (=

British Broadcasting Corporation).
библе́йск|ий (-ая, -ое, -ие) *прил* biblical.
библиографи́ческ|ий (-ая, -ое, -ие) *прил* bibliographical; **библиографи́ческая ре́дкость** rare edition.
библиогра́фи|я (-и) *ж* bibliography.
библиоте́к|а (-и) *ж* library.
библиоте́кар|ь (-я) *м* librarian.
библиоте́чный *прил* library *опред*.
Би́бли|я (-и) *ж* the Bible.
бигуди́ *ср/мн нескл* curlers *мн*; **накру́чивать (накрути́ть** *perf*) **во́лосы на** ~ to put one's hair in curlers.
бидо́н (-а) *м* (*для молока*) churn; (*маленький*) can.
бижуте́ри|я (-и) *ж* costume jewellery.
би́знес (-а) *м* business; **де́лать (сде́лать** *perf*) ~ **на** *+prp* to make a living from.
бизнесме́н (-а) *м* businessman (*мн* businessmen).
бики́ни *ср нескл* bikini.
биле́т (-а) *м* ticket; (*члена организации*) (membership) card; **обра́тный** ~ return (*BRIT*) *или* roundtrip (*US*) ticket; **казначе́йский** ~ banknote; **входно́й** ~ ticket (*for standing room*).
биллио́н (-а) *м* billion (*one thousand million*).
билья́рд (-а) *м* (*игра*) billiards; (*стол*) billiard table.
бино́кл|ь (-я) *м* binoculars *мн*.
бинт (-а́) *м* bandage; **накла́дывать (наложи́ть** *perf*) **~ы на** *+acc* to put a bandage on.
бинт|ова́ть (-у́ю; *perf* **забинтова́ть**) *несов перех* to bandage.
био́граф (-а) *м* biographer.
биогра́фи|я (-и) *ж* biography.
био́лог (-а) *м* biologist.
биоло́ги|я (-и) *ж* biology.
би́рж|а (-и) *ж* (*КОММ*) exchange; **валю́тная** ~ exchange market; ~ **це́нных бума́г** securities exchange; **това́рная** ~ commodity exchange; **фо́ндовая** ~ stock exchange *или* market; **игра́ть** (*impf*) **на ~е** to play the stock exchange.
биржеви́к (-а́) *м* stockbroker.
биржево́й *прил* (*сделка*) stock-exchange; **биржево́й бро́кер** stockbroker.
би́р|ка (-ки; *gen pl* **-ок)** *ж* tag.
Бирминге́м (-а) *м* Birmingham.
би́рок *сущ см* **би́рка**.
бирюз|а́ (-ы) *ж* (*ГЕО*) turquoise.
бис *межд*: **Б~!** encore!; **исполня́ть (испо́лнить** *perf*) **что-н на** ~ to do sth as an encore.
би́сер (-а; *part gen* **-у)** *м собир* glass beads *мн*; **мета́ть** (*impf*) ~ **пе́ред сви́ньями** to cast pearls before swine.
бискви́т (-а) *м* sponge (cake).
бистро́ *ср нескл* bistro.
бит (-а) *м* (*КОМП*) bit.
би́тв|а (-ы) *ж* battle.
битко́м *нареч*: ~ **(наби́т)** (*разг*) chock-a-block, jam-packed.
би́тый *прил* broken; **би́тый час** (*разг*) a good hour.
бить (бью, бьёшь; *imper* **бей(те)**, *perf* **поби́ть**) *несов перех* (*также перен*) to beat; (*стёкла*) to break ◆ (*perf* **проби́ть**) *неперех* (*часы*) to strike; ~ (*impf*) **в** *+acc* (*в дверь*) to bang at; (*дождь, ветер*) to beat against; (*орудие*) to hit; ~ (*impf*) **на** *+acc* (*стремиться к*) to aim for; ~ (*impf*) **по столу́** to bang on the table; ~ (*impf*) **в бараба́н** to beat a drum; **свет бьёт мне в глаза́** the light is blinding me; ~ (*impf*) **по чьим-н недоста́ткам** to severely criticize sb's failings; ~ (*impf*) **по карма́ну** to hit one's pocket; **э́то бьёт по мои́м интере́сам** it conflicts with my interests; **его́ бьёт озно́б** he's got a fit of the shivers
▸ **би́ться** *несов возв* (*сердце, пульс*) to beat; (*стекло, фарфор*) to be breakable; (*сражаться*) to fight; **би́ться** (*impf*) **о** *+acc* to bang against; **би́ться** (*impf*) **над** *+instr* (*над задачей, над решением*) to struggle with; **хоть голово́й об сте́ну бе́йся** you might as well bang your head against a brick wall.
бифште́кс (-а) *м* steak.
бич (-а́) *м* (*плеть*) whip; (*перен*) scourge.
Бишке́к (-а) *м* Bishkek.
б-ка *сокр* = **библиоте́ка.**
бла́г|а (-) *мн* rewards *мн*; **всех благ!** all the best!
бла́г|о (-а) *ср* benefit; **на** ~ *+gen* for the benefit of; *см также* **бла́га**.
благови́д|ный (-ен, -на, -но) *прил* (*предлог*) plausible; (*стремления, поступки*) seemingly well-intentioned.
благодар|и́ть (-ю́, -и́шь; *perf* **поблагодари́ть**) *несов перех* to thank.
благода́рност|ь (-и) *ж* gratitude, thanks; **приноси́ть (принести́** *perf*) ~ **кому́-н** to express one's gratitude to sb.
благодаря́ *предл* (*+dat*) thanks to ◆ *союз*: ~ **тому́, что** owing to the fact that; **здоро́в,** ~ **тому́, что занима́юсь спо́ртом** I'm healthy thanks to *или* owing to the fact that I play sport.
благоде́тел|ь (-я) *м* benefactor.
благоде́тельниц|а (-ы) *ж* benefactress.
благ|о́й *прил*: **~и́е наме́рения** good intentions *мн*; **крича́ть** (*impf*) **~и́м ма́том** (*разг*) to shout at the top of one's voice.
благонадёж|ный (-ен, -на, -но) *прил* trustworthy.
благополу́чи|е (-я) *ср* (*в семье, в отношениях*) wellbeing; (*материальная обеспеченность*) prosperity; **жела́ю Вам вся́кого ~я** I wish you all the very best.
благополу́ч|ный (-ен, -на, -но) *прил* successful.
благоприя́т|ный (-ен, -на, -но) *прил* favourable (*BRIT*), favorable (*US*).
благоприя́тствовани|е (-я) *ср*: **усло́вия/поли́тика наибо́льшего ~я** the most favourable (*BRIT*) *или* favorable (*US*) conditions/policy.
благоразу́ми|е (-я) *ср* prudence.

благоразу́м|ный (-ен, -на, -но) *прил* prudent.
благоро́д|ный (-ен, -на, -но) *прил* noble; **он ~ного происхожде́ния** he is of noble birth; **благоро́дные га́зы** the noble gases; **благоро́дные мета́ллы** precious metals.
благоро́дств|о (-а) *ср* nobility.
благослов|и́ть (-лю́, -и́шь; *impf* **благословля́ть)** *сов перех* to bless; **~** *(perf)* **кого́-н (на что-н)** to give sb one's blessing (for sth).
благосостоя́ни|е (-я) *ср* wellbeing.
благотвори́тел|ь (-я) *м* philanthropist.
благотвори́тельниц|а (-ы) *ж см* **благотвори́тель.**
благотвори́тельност|ь (-и) *ж* charity.
благотвори́тельн|ый *прил* charitable; **~ая организа́ция** charity (organization); **~ конце́рт** charity concert.
благоустро́ен|ный (-, -на, -но) *прил* (*квартира, дом*) *with all modern conveniences*; **~ го́род** a city with every amenity; **~ная ку́хня** a well-equipped kitchen.
блаже́н|ный (-, -на, -но) *прил* blissful; (*no short form*; *РЕЛ*) Blessed.
блаже́нств|о (-а) *ср* bliss; **быть** *(impf)* **на верху́ ~а** to be in seventh heaven.
бланк (-а) *м* form.
блат (-а) *м* (*разг*) connections *мн*; **по бла́ту** (*разг*) through (one's) connections.
блатно́й *прил* criminal.
бле́ден *прил см* **бле́дный.**
бледне́|ть (-ю; *perf* **побледне́ть)** *несов неперех* to (grow) pale; (*перен*): **~ (пе́ред** *+instr***)** to pale (beside).
бле́дност|ь (-и) *ж* (*см прил*) pallor, paleness; dullness.
бле́д|ный (-ен, -на́, -но) *прил* pale; (*перен*) dull.
блёкн|уть (-у, -ешь; *perf* **поблёкнуть)** *несов неперех* to fade.
блеск (-а; *part gen* **-у)** *м* (*огней, молнии*) brilliance, brightness; (*металла*) shine; (*перен*) brilliance; **во всём бле́ске** in full splendour (*BRIT*) *или* splendor (*US*); **с бле́ском** brilliantly; **сдать** *(perf)* **экза́мен с бле́ском** to pass an exam with flying colours.
блесн|у́ть (-у́, -ёшь) *сов неперех* to flash; **у него́ ~у́ла мысль** a thought flashed through his mind; **~у́ла наде́жда** there was a ray of hope.
бле|сте́ть (-щу́, -сти́шь *или*, **-щешь)** *несов неперех* (*звёзды, металл*) to shine; (*камни, глаза*) to sparkle; **она́ бле́щет красото́й** she is dazzling; **он бле́щет умо́м** he shines intellectually.
блестя́ще *нареч* brilliantly; **дела́ иду́т ~** everything's going brilliantly.
блестя́щ|ий (-ая, -ее, -ие; -, -а, -е) *прил* (*звезда*) bright; (*металл*) shining; (*глаза*) sparkling; (*перен*) brilliant.
блещу *итп несов см* **блесте́ть.**
бле́|ять (-ю) *несов неперех* to bleat.
ближа́йш|ий (-ая, -ее, -ие) *прил* (*город, дом*) the nearest; (*год*) the next; (*планы*) immediate; (*друг*) closest; **в ~ем бу́дущем** in the near future; **при ~ем уча́стии** *+gen* with the close cooperation of; **при ~ем рассмотре́нии** on closer inspection; **ближа́йший ро́дственник** next of kin.
бли́же *сравн прил от* **бли́зкий.**
бли́жн|ий (-яя, -ее, -ие) *прил* (*город, деревня*) neighbouring (*BRIT*), neighboring (*US*); **е́хать (пое́хать** *perf***) ~им путём** to take the shortest route; **Б~ Восто́к** Middle East.
бли́зк|ие (-их; *decl like adj***)** *мн* (*родственники*) relatives *мн*.
бли́з|кий (-кая, -кое, -кие; -ок, -ка́, -ко) *прил* (*город*) nearby; (*конец*) imminent; (*друг, отношения*) close; **~** *+dat* (*интересы, тема*) similar *или* close to; **~ по** *+dat* (*по содержанию, по цели*) similar *или* close in; **они́ близки́ во мне́ниях** they think alike; **бли́зкий ро́дственник** close relative.
бли́зко *нареч* near *или* close by ◆ *как сказ* not far off; **~ от** *+gen* near, close to; **го́род ~** the town isn't far off; **~ узна́ть** *(perf)* **кого́-н** to get to know sb well; **принима́ть (приня́ть** *perf***) что-н ~ к се́рдцу** to take sth to heart.
близне́ц (-а́) *м* (*обычно мн*) twin; **бра́тья/сёстры-близнецы́** twin brothers/sisters; *см также* **Близнецы́.**
Близнец|ы́ (-о́в) *мн* (*созвездие*) Gemini.
бли́зок *прил см* **бли́зкий.**
близору́к|ий (-ая, -ое, -ие; -, -а, -о) *прил* short-sighted (*BRIT*), nearsighted (*US*).
близору́кост|ь (-и) *ж* (*см прил*) short-sightedness, nearsightedness.
бли́зост|ь (-и) *ж* proximity; (*интересов, мнений*) closeness; (*близкие отношения*) intimacy.
блин (-а́) *м* pancake.
бли́нчик (-а) *м уменьш от* **блин.**
блок (-а) *м* (*ПОЛИТ*) bloc; (*ТЕХ*) unit.
блока́д|а (-ы) *ж* (*ВОЕН*) siege; (*ЭКОН*) blockade; **устана́вливать (установи́ть** *perf***)/снима́ть (снять** *perf***) ~у** to impose/lift a blockade.
блоки́р|овать (-ую) *(не)сов перех* to blockade; (*СПОРТ, КОМП*) to block.
блокно́т (-а) *м* notebook.
блонди́н (-а) *м*: **он – ~** he is blond.
блонди́н|ка (-ки; *gen pl* **-ок)** *ж* blonde.
блох|а́ (-и́; *nom pl* **-и)** *ж* flea.
блужда́|ть (-ю) *несов неперех* to wander *или* roam (around); (*перен: мысли*) to wander; (*: взгляд*) to rove.
блу́з|ка (-ки; *gen pl* **-ок)** *ж* blouse.
блю́д|о (-а) *ср* dish.
блю|сти́ (-ду́, -дёшь; *pt* **-л, -ла́-ло́,** *perf*

соблюсти́) *несов перех* (*интересы*) to guard; (*чистоту*) to maintain.
блядь (-и) *ж* (*груб!*: *проститутка*) whore (*!*) ◆ *м/ж* (*груб!*: *женщина*) bitch (*!*); (: *мужчина*) bastard (*!*)
бля́х|а (-и) *ж* (*на форме*) badge; (*на ремне*) buckle.
БМП *ж сокр* (= *боева́я маши́на пехо́ты*) *armoured car for infantry*.
БМР *м сокр* (= *Банк междунаро́дных расчётов*) BIS (= *Bank for International Settlements*).
боб (-а́) *м* bean; **на ~а́х оста́ться** (*perf*) to be left high and dry.
бобр (-а́) *м* beaver.
Бог (-а; *voc* **Бо́же)** *м* God; **ве́рить** (*impf*) **в Бо́га** to believe in God; **~ зна́ет** *или* **весть что** God knows what; **благослови́ Вас ~!** God bless you!; **не дай ~!** God forbid!; **ра́ди Бо́га!** for God's sake!; **сла́ва Бо́гу** (*к счастью*) thank God.
богате́|ть (-ю; *perf* **разбогате́ть)** *несов неперех* to become rich.
бога́тств|а (-) *мн* resources *мн*.
бога́тств|о (-а) *ср* wealth, riches *мн*; (*обстановки, одежды*) richness; *см также* **бога́тства**.
бога́т|ый (-, -а, -о) *прил* rich; **~ урожа́й** bumper harvest; **~** *+instr* (*ископаемыми, событиями*) rich in; **чем ~ы, тем и ра́ды** what's ours is yours.
богаты́р|ь (-я́) *м warrior hero of Russian folk epics*; (*перен*) Hercules.
бога́ч (-а́) *м* rich man (*мн* men).
бога́че *сравн прил от* **бога́тый**.
боге́м|а (-ы) *ж собир* bohemians *мн*; (*образ жизни*) bohemian lifestyle.
боги́н|я (-и) *ж* goddess.
богоро́диц|а (-ы) *ж* the Virgin Mary.
богосло́ви|е (-я) *ср* theology.
богослуже́ни|е (-я) *ср* service; **соверша́ть (соверши́ть** *perf*) **~** to take a service.
боготвор|и́ть (-ю́, -и́шь) *несов перех* to worship, idolize.
богоуго́дн|ый *прил*: **~ое заведе́ние** *charitable institution*.
богоху́льный *прил* blasphemous.
бод (-а) *м* (*КОМП*) baud.
бода́|ть (-ю; *perf* **забода́ть)** *несов перех* to butt.
бо́дрост|ь (-и) *ж* (*см прил*) energy, liveliness; cheerfulness.
бо́др|ый (-, -а́, -о) *прил* (*человек, походка*) energetic, lively; (*настроение, музыка*) cheerful.
боеви́к (-а́) *м* (*солдат*) fighter; (*фильм*) action movie.
боево́й *прил* military; (*настроение, дух*) fighting; **боевы́е иску́сства** martial arts *мн*.
боеголо́в|ка (-ки; *gen pl* **-ок)** *ж* warhead.
бо́ек *прил см* **бо́йкий**.
бо́ен *сущ см* **бо́йня**.
боеприпа́с|ы (-ов) *мн* ammunition *ед*.
бо|е́ц (-йца́) *м* (*солдат*) soldier; (*участник боя*) fighter.
Бо́же *сущ см* **Бог** ◆ *межд*: **~ (ты мой)!** good Lord *или* God!; **~! кака́я красота́!** God, it's beautiful!; **~ сохрани́** *или* **упаси́** *или* **изба́ви** (*разг*) God forbid.
бо́жеск|ий (-ая, -ое, -ие) *прил* (*РЕЛ*) divine; (*разг*: *цены, условия*) half-decent; **приводи́ть (привести́** *perf*) **кого́-н/что-н в ~ вид** to make sb/sth look decent.
боже́ствен|ный (-ен, -на, -но) *прил* divine.
бо́ж|ий (-ья, -ье, -ьи) *прил* God's; **ка́ждый ~ день** every single day; **бо́жий дар** God-given talent; **бо́жья коро́вка** ladybird.
бо|й (-я; *loc sg* **-ю́**, *nom pl* **-и́**, *gen pl* **-ёв)** *м* battle; (*боксёров, быков*) fight; (*барабанов*) beating; (*часов*) striking.
бо́|йкий (-йкая, -йкое, -йкие; -ек, -йка́, -йко) *прил* (*распорядитель, продавец*) smart; (*движения*) brisk; (*речь, ответ*) quick; (*no short form*; *место, базар*) busy.
бойко́т (-а) *м* boycott.
бойкоти́р|овать (-ую) (*не*)*сов перех* to boycott.
бо́йлер (-а) *м* boiler.
бо́|йня (-йни; *gen pl* **-ен)** *ж* slaughterhouse, abattoir.
бойца́ *итп сущ см* **бое́ц**.
бо́йче *сравн прил от* **бо́йкий**.
бок (-а; *part gen* **-у**, *loc sg* **-у́**, *nom pl* **-а́)** *м* side; **под бо́ком** (*разг*) right nearby; **~ о́ ~** side by side.
бока́л (-а) *м* (wine)glass, goblet; **поднима́ть (подня́ть** *perf*) **~ за кого́-н/что-н** to raise one's glass to sb/sth.
бо́ком *нареч* (*выйти, пройти*) sideways; **э́то ему́ ~ вы́шло** (*разг*) it was all screwed up for him.
бокс (-а) *м* (*СПОРТ*) boxing; (*МЕД*) cubicle.
боксёр (-а) *м* boxer.
болва́н (-а) *м* (*разг*) blockhead.
болга́р|ин (-ина; *nom pl* **-ы**, *gen pl* **-)** *м* Bulgarian.
Болга́ри|я (-и) *ж* Bulgaria.
болга́р|ка (-ки; *gen pl* **-ок)** *ж см* **болга́рин**.
болга́рск|ий (-ая, -ое, -ие) *прил* Bulgarian; **~ язы́к** Bulgarian.
бо́лее *нареч* more; **~ или ме́нее** more or less; **~ того́** what's more; **тем ~** all the more so; **~ чем** more than.
боле́знен|ный (-, -на, -но) *прил* sickly; (*укол, перевязка*) painful; (*перен*: *подозрительность*) unhealthy; **у него́ ~ное самолю́бие** he's ultra-sensitive.
боле́зн|ь (-и) *ж* illness; (*заразная*) disease; **~и ро́ста** growing pains.
боле́льщик (-а) *м* fan.
боле́льщиц|а (-ы) *ж см* **боле́льщик**.
бо́лен *прил см* **больно́й**.
бол|е́ть (-е́ю) *несов неперех*: **~** (*+instr*) to be ill (with); (*3sg* **-и́т**, *3pl* **-я́т**; *подлеж*: *руки итп*) to ache; **~** (*impf*) **за** *+acc* to be a fan of; **у меня́ душа́ ~и́т за них** (*перен*) I'm very worried about them.

болеутоля́ющ|ий (**-ая, -ее, -ие**) *прил*: **~ее сре́дство** painkiller.
боло́н|ка (**-ки**; *gen pl* **-ок**) *ж* lapdog.
боло́нь|я (**-и**) *ж* (*ткань*) *lightweight waterproof material.*
боло́т|о (**-а**) *ср* marsh, bog; (*перен*) backwater.
болт (**-а́**) *м* bolt.
болта́|ть (**-ю**) *несов перех* (*разг*) to talk ◆ *неперех* (*разговаривать*) to chat; (*: много*) to chatter; (*без толку*) to drivel; (*лишнее*) to blab; ~ *(impf)* **по-англи́йски** to chatter away in English; ~ *(impf)* **нога́ми** to dangle one's legs ▸ **болта́ться** *несов возв* (*разг*) to dangle; **~ся** *(impf)* **без де́ла** to hang around with nothing to do.
болтовн|я́ (**-и́**) *ж* (*разг*) waffle.
болту́н (**-а́**) *м* chatterbox.
болту́ш|ка (**-ки**; *gen pl* **-ек**) *ж см* **болту́н**.
бол|ь (**-и**) *ж* pain, ache; **зубна́я** ~ toothache; **головна́я** ~ headache; ~ **в груди́/живо́те** chest/abdominal pain.
больни́ц|а (**-ы**) *ж* hospital; **ложи́ться** (**лечь** *perf*) **в ~у** to go into hospital; **выпи́сываться** (**вы́писаться** *perf*) **из ~ы** to be discharged from hospital.
больни́чный *прил* hospital *опред*; **больни́чный лист** medical certificate.
бо́льно *нареч* (*удариться, упасть*) badly, painfully; (*обидеть*) deeply; **~!** that hurts!; **мне** ~ I am in pain; **де́лать** (**сде́лать** *perf*) ~ **кому́-н** to hurt sb; **мне ~ поду́мать об э́том** it hurts me to think about it.
бол|ьно́й *прил* (*рука итп*) sore; (*воображение*) unhealthy; (**-ен, -ьна́, -ьно́**; *нездоров*) ill, sick ◆ (**-ьно́го**; *decl like adj*) *м* (*тот, кто болеет*) sick person; (*пациент*) patient; **у неё ~ вид** she doesn't look very well; **де́ти ~ьны** the children are ill *или* sick; **больно́е се́рдце** a bad heart; **больно́й вопро́с** a sore point.
бо́льше *сравн прил от* **большо́й** ◆ *сравн нареч от* **мно́го** ◆ *нареч*: ~ *+gen* (*часа, килограмма итп*) more than; ~ **не бу́ду** (*разг*) I won't do it again; ~ **так не де́лай** don't do that again; ~ **того́** what's more; ~ **всего́** most of all; **ни ~ ни ме́ньше** (**чем** *или* **как**) no more, no less (than); **она́ здесь ~ не живёт** she doesn't live here any more.
большеви́к (**-а́**) *м* Bolshevik.
большинств|о́ (**-а́**) *ср* majority; **в ~е́** (**слу́чаев**) in most cases; **подавля́ющее** ~ an overwhelming majority.
больш|о́й *прил* (*дом, река, дерево*) big, large; (*радость*) great; (*дети*) grown-up; **бо́льшей ча́стью, по бо́льшей ча́сти** for the most part; **я не ~ люби́тель бале́та** I'm not a great ballet fan; **я не ~ знато́к э́того де́ла** I'm no expert in this matter; **больша́я бу́ква** capital letter; **большо́й па́лец** (*руки*) thumb; (*ноги*) big toe.

боля́ч|ка (**-ки**; *gen pl* **-ек**) *ж* sore.
бо́мб|а (**-ы**) *ж* bomb.
бомб|и́ть (**-лю́, -и́шь**) *несов перех* to bomb.
бомбоубе́жищ|е (**-а**) *ср* bomb shelter.
бо́н|а (**-ы**) *ж* (*обычно мн: КОММ*) bond; (*временные деньги*) voucher.
бордо́вый *прил* dark red.
бордю́р (**-а**) *м* border; (*тротуара*) kerb (*BRIT*), curb (*US*).
бор|е́ц (**-ца́**) *м* (*за свободу итп*) fighter; (*СПОРТ*) wrestler.
бормо|та́ть (**-чу́, -чешь**) *несов перех* to mutter.
бо́рн|ый *прил*: **~ая кислота́** boric acid.
борови́к (**-а́**) *м* cep.
бор|ода́ (*acc sg* **-оду**, *gen sg* **-оды́**, *nom pl* **-оды**, *gen pl* **-о́д**, *dat pl* **-ода́м**) *ж* beard; **отпуска́ть** (**отпусти́ть** *perf*) **бо́роду** to grow a beard; **с ~одо́й** (*перен: разг*) ancient; **анекдо́т с ~одо́й** an old chestnut.
борода́в|ка (**-ки**; *gen pl* **-ок**) *ж* (*на пальцах итп*) wart.
борозд|и́ть (**-жу́, -ди́шь**; *perf* **избородзи́ть**) *несов перех* to furrow; (*корабль*) to leave a wake.
бор|о́ться (**-ю́сь, -ешься**) *несов возв* (*СПОРТ*) to wrestle; ~ *(impf)* (**с** *+instr*) to fight (with *или* against); ~ *(impf)* **с** *+instr или* **про́тив** *+gen* (*с конкурентами*) to compete with *или* against; (*с предрассудками, с наркотиками*) to fight (against); ~ *(impf)* **за** *+acc* (*за мир*) to fight for.
борт (**-а**; *acc sg* **за́ борт** *или* **за бо́рт**, *instr sg* **за бо́ртом** *или* **за борто́м**, *loc sg* **-у́**, *nom pl* **-а́**) *м* side; **на ~у́** *или* ~ on board, aboard; **челове́к за ~о́м!** man overboard!; **остава́ться** (**оста́ться** *perf*) **за ~о́м** (*перен*) to be left behind.
бортпроводни́к (**-а́**) *м* steward (*on plane*).
бортпроводни́ц|а (**-ы**) *ж* air hostess, stewardess (*on plane*).
борца́ *итп сущ см* **бо́рец**.
борщ (**-а́**) *м* borsch (*beetroot-based soup*).
борьб|а́ (**-ы́**) *ж* fight; (*СПОРТ*) wrestling.
босико́м *нареч* barefoot.
бос|о́й (**-, -а́, -о**) *прил* barefoot.
босоно́жк|а (**-и**) *ж* (*обычно мн*) sandal; (*: закрытым носом*) slingback.
босс (**-а**) *м* boss.
Босфо́р (**-а**) *м* Bosphorus.
бося́к (**-а́**) *м* tramp.
бося́ч|ка (**-ки**; *gen pl* **-ек**) *ж см* **бося́к**.
бота́ник|а (**-и**) *ж* botany.
боти́н|ок (**-ка**) *м* (*обычно мн*) ankle boot.
бо́цман (**-а**) *м* boatswain, bosun.
бо́ч|ка (**-ки**; *gen pl* **-ек**) *ж* (*сосуд*) barrel.
бо|я́ться (**-ю́сь, -и́шься**) *несов возв*: ~ (*+gen*) to be afraid (of); ~ *(impf) +infin* to be afraid of doing *или* to do; **я ~ю́сь ходи́ть** *(impf)* **но́чью** I'm afraid of being out *или* to be out at night; **~ю́сь сказа́ть** I wouldn't like to say.

бра́во *межд* bravo.
брази́л|ец (-ьца) *м* Brazilian.
Брази́ли|я (-и) *ж* Brazil.
брази́льск|ий (-ая, -ое, -ие) *прил* Brazilian.
брази́льца *итп сущ см* **брази́лец**.
бразилья́н|ка (-ки; *gen pl* **-ок)** *ж см* **брази́лец**.
бразды́ *мн*: ~ **правле́ния** the reins of power *или* government.
брак (-а) *м* (*супружество*) marriage; (*продукция*) rejects *мн*; (*дефект*) flaw; **вступа́ть (вступи́ть** *perf*) **в** ~ to get married; **расторга́ть (расто́ргнуть** *perf*) ~ to dissolve a marriage.
брако́ванн|ый *прил* reject *опред*.
брак|ова́ть (-у́ю; *perf* **забракова́ть)** *несов перех* to reject.
браконье́р (-а) *м* poacher.
браконье́рств|о (-а) *ср* poaching.
бракосочета́ни|е (-я) *ср* marriage ceremony.
брасле́т (-а) *м* bracelet; (*кольцо из металла, кости итп*) bangle.
брасс (-а) *м* breaststroke.
брат (-а; *nom pl* **-ья,** *gen pl* **-ьев)** *м* brother; **сво́дный** ~ stepbrother; **двою́родный** ~ cousin.
Братисла́в|а (-ы) *ж* Bratislava.
бра́ти|я (-и) *ср* brotherhood.
бра́тск|ий (-ая, -ое, -ие) *прил* brotherly, fraternal; **бра́тская моги́ла** communal grave.
бра́тств|о (-а) *ср* (*содружество*) brotherhood.
бра|ть (беру́, берёшь; *pt* **-л, -ла́, -ло́,** *perf* **взять)** *несов перех* to take; (*билет*) to get; (*няню*) to take on; (*крепость, город*) to take, seize; (*высоту*) to conquer; (*барьер*) to clear; ~ *(impf)* **нало́г у кого́-н/за что-н** to tax sb/sth; ~ **(взять** *perf*) **что-н в расчёт** *или* **во внима́ние** to take sth into account *или* consideration
▸ **бра́ться** (*perf* **взя́ться)** *несов возв*: **бра́ться за** *+acc* (*дотронуться*) to touch; (*хватать рукой*) to take hold of; (*за чтение, за работу*) to get down to; (*за перо*) to take up; (*за книгу*) to begin; (*решение проблемы*) to take on, undertake; **отку́да у тебя́ вре́мя берётся?** where do you find the time?; **отку́да у него́ де́ньги беру́тся?** where does he get the money?; **бра́ться (взя́ться** *perf*) **за ум** to come to one's senses.
бра́тья *итп сущ см* **брат**.
бра́чный *прил* (*контракт*) marriage *опред*; (*союз*) conjugal.
бревн|о́ (-а́; *nom pl* **брёвна,** *gen pl* **брёвен)** *ср* log; (*СПОРТ*) the beam; (*перен*) oaf.
бред (-а; *loc pl* **-у́)** *м* delirium; (*перен*) nonsense; ~ **сумасше́дшего** the ravings of a madman.
бре́|дить (-жу, -дишь) *несов неперех* to be delirious; ~ *(impf)* **кем-н/чем-н** to be mad about sb/sth.
бредо́вый *прил* (*разг*) crazy.
бреду́ *итп несов см* **брести́**.
бре́жу *несов см* **бре́дить**.
бре́зга|ть (-ю) *несов* = **бре́зговать**.
брезгли́в|ый (-, -а, -о) *прил* (*человек*) fastidious; (*взгляд*) disgusted.
бре́зг|овать (-ую; *perf* **побре́зговать)** *несов неперех* (*+instr*) to be fastidious about.
брезе́нт (-а; *part gen* **-у)** *м* tarpaulin.
брёл *итп несов см* **брести́**.
бре́м|я (-ени; *как* **вре́мя**; *см* **Table 4)** *ср* burden.
бр|ести́ (-еду́, -едёшь; *pt* **-ёл, -ела́, -ело́)** *несов неперех* (*человек*) to trudge; (*лошадь*) to plod.
брета́нск|ий (-ая, -ое, -ие) *прил* Breton.
Брета́н|ь (-и) *ж* Brittany.
брето́нск|ий (-ая, -ое, -ие) *прил* = **брета́нский**.
Брето́н|ь (-и) *ж* = **Брета́нь**.
бреш|ь (-и) *ж* (*пролом*) breach.
бре́ю(сь) *итп несов см* **брить(ся)**.
брига́д|а (-ы) *ж* (*ВОЕН*) brigade; (*в поезде*) crew; (*на производстве*) (work) team.
бригади́р (-а) *м* (*в поезде*) ≈ chief guard (*BRIT*), ≈ senior conductor (*US*); (*на производстве*) team leader.
бриз (-а) *м* sea breeze.
бриллиа́нт (-а) *м* (cut) diamond.
бриллиа́нтовый *прил* diamond *опред*.
брита́н|ец (-ца) *м* Briton; **~цы** the British.
Брита́ни|я (-и) *ж* Britain.
брита́н|ка (-ки; *gen pl* **-ок)** *ж см* **брита́нец**.
брита́нск|ий (-ая, -ое, -ие) *прил* British.
брита́нца *итп сущ см* **брита́нец**.
бри́тв|а (-ы) *ж* razor; **безопа́сная** ~ safety razor.
бр|ить (-е́ю, -е́ешь; *perf* **побри́ть)** *несов перех* (*человека*) to shave; (*бороду*) to shave off
▸ **бри́ться** (*perf* **побри́ться)** *несов возв* to shave.
бри́финг (-а) *м* briefing.
бров|ь (-и; *gen pl* **-е́й)** *ж* eyebrow; **попа́сть** (*perf*) **не в** ~**, а в глаз** to hit the nail on the head; **он и бро́вью не повёл** he didn't bat an eyelid.
бро|ди́ть (-жу́, -дишь) *несов неперех* to wander; (*perf* **выброди́ть**; *вино, пиво*) to ferment.
бродя́г|а (-и) *м/ж* tramp; (*любящий странствовать*) drifter.
броже́ни|е (-я) *ср* fermentation; (*перен*) ferment.
брожу́ *несов см* **броди́ть**.
бро́йлер (-а) *м* broiler.
бро́кер (-а) *м* broker; **биржево́й** ~ stockbroker.
бро́керск|ий (-ая, -ое, -ие) *прил* broker's.
бром (-а) *м* bromine.
бронемаши́н|а (-ы) *ж* armoured (*BRIT*) *или* armored (*US*) car.
бронетранспортёр (-а) *м* armoured (*BRIT*) *или* armored (*US*) personnel carrier.
бро́нз|а (-ы) *ж* bronze.
бро́нзовый *прил* bronze; **бро́нзовый век** the Bronze Age; **бро́нзовый призёр** bronze medallist (*BRIT*) *или* medalist (*US*).
брони́ровани|е (-я) *ср* reservation.
брони́р|овать (-ую; *perf* **заброни́ровать)** (*не*)*сов перех* to reserve.
бронх (-а) *м* (*обычно мн*) bronchial tube.
бронхи́т (-а) *м* bronchitis.
брон|ь (-и) *ж* (*разг*) reservation.

бро́н|я (**-и**) *ж* reservation.
брон|я́ (**-и́**) *ж* armour (*BRIT*) *или* armor (*US*) plating.
броса́|ть (**-ю**) *несов от* **бро́сить**
▸ **броса́ться** *несов от* **бро́ситься** ◆ *возв*: **~ся снежка́ми/камня́ми** to throw snowballs/stones at each other; **~ся** *(impf)* **деньга́ми** to throw one's money around; **~ся** *(impf)* **друзья́ми** to abandon one's friends.
бро́|сить (**-шу, -сишь**; *impf* **броса́ть**) *сов перех* (*камень, мяч итп*) to throw; (*якорь*) to drop, cast; (*сети*) to cast; (*семью, друга*) to abandon; (*войска, отряд*) to dispatch; (*спорт*) to give up; **броса́ть** (**~** *perf*) **замеча́ние** to pass comment; **меня́ ~сило в жар** I broke out in a (cold) sweat; **броса́ть** (**~** *perf*) *+infin* to give up doing; **~сьте!** stop it!
▸ **бро́ситься** (*impf* **броса́ться**) *сов возв*: **~ся на** *+acc* (*на врага, на обидчика*) to throw o.s. at; **броса́ться** (**~ся** *perf*) **в дра́ку/ата́ку** to rush into the fray/to the attack; **броса́ться** (**~ся** *perf*) **кому́-н на по́мощь** to rush to sb's aid; **~ся** *(perf)* **по ле́стнице вниз** to rush downstairs; **~ся** *(perf)* **кому́-н в объя́тия** to fall into sb's arms; **кра́ска ~силась ему́ в лицо́** the colour rushed to his face.
бро́совый *прил* (*разг*) trashy; **бро́совая цена́** *giveaway price*; **бро́совый э́кспорт** (*КОММ*) dumping.
бро́ш|ка (**-ки**; *gen pl* **-ек**) *ж* brooch.
бро́шу(сь) *сов см* **бро́сить(ся)**.
брош|ь (**-и**) *ж см* **бро́шка**.
брошю́р|а (**-ы**) *ж* (*небольшая книжка*) pamphlet; (*рекламный буклет*) brochure.
брус (**-а**; *nom pl* **-ья**, *gen pl* **-ьев**) *м* beam; *см также* **бру́сья**.
бруска́ *итп сущ см* **бруско́к**.
брусни́к|а (**-и**) *ж* cowberry.
брус|о́к (**-ка́**) *м* (*камень для точки*) whetstone; (*мыла*) bar.
бру́сь|я (**-ев**) *мн* parallel bars *мн*.
бру́тто *прил неизм* gross *опред*.
бры́з|гать (**-жу, -жешь**) *несов неперех* (*фонтан, грязь*) to splash; (**-гаю**; *опрыскивать*): **~ на** *+acc* to splash.
бры́зг|и (**-**) *мн* splashes *мн*; (*мелкие*) spray *ед*; (*стекла, камня*) fragments *мн*, splinters *мн*.
бры́зжу *итп несов см* **бры́згать**.
бры́нз|а (**-ы**) *ж* brynza (*sheep's milk cheese*).
брысь *межд* shoo.
брю́кв|а (**-ы**) *ж* swede.
брю́к|и (**-**) *мн* trousers *мн*, pants *мн* (*US*).
брюне́т (**-а**) *м*: **он ~** he has dark hair.
брюне́т|ка (**-ки**; *gen pl* **-ок**) *ж* brunette.
Брюссе́л|ь (**-я**) *м* Brussels.
брю́х|о (**-а**) *ср* (*также разг*) belly; (*разг*: *толстое*) pot.
брюшно́й *прил* abdominal; **брюшно́й тиф** typhoid fever.
БСЭ *ж сокр* = *Больша́я Сове́тская Энциклопе́дия*.
бубён *сущ см* **бу́бны**.
бу́блик (**-а**) *м* ≈ bagel.
бу́б|ны (**-ён**; *dat pl* **-нам**) *мн* (*КАРТЫ*) diamonds *мн*.
буг|о́р (**-ра́**) *м* mound; (*на коже*) lump.
Будапе́шт (**-а**) *м* Budapest.
будди́зм (**-а**) *м* Buddhism.
будди́ст (**-а**) *м* Buddhist.
будди́ст|ка (**-ки**; *gen pl* **-ок**) *ж см* **будди́ст**.
бу́дем *несов см* **быть**.
бу́дет *несов см* **быть** ◆ *част* that's enough; **попла́кали и ~** that's enough crying; **~ тебе́!** that's enough from you!
бу́дешь *итп несов см* **быть**.
буди́льник (**-а**) *м* alarm clock; **заводи́ть** (**завести́** *perf*) **~ на** *+acc* to set the alarm (clock) for.
бу|ди́ть (**-жу́, -дишь**; *perf* **разбуди́ть**) *несов перех* to wake (up), awaken; (*perf* **пробуди́ть**; *перен*) to awaken.
бу́д|ка (**-ки**; *gen pl* **-ок**) *ж* (*сторожа*) hut; (*для собаки*) kennel; **часова́я ~** sentry box; **телефо́нная ~** telephone booth *или* box.
бу́дн|и (**-ей**) *мн* working *или* week days *мн*; (*перен*: *обыденная жизнь*) routine *ед*.
бу́док *сущ см* **бу́дка**.
будора́ж|ить (**-у, -ишь**) *несов от* **взбудора́жить**.
бу́дто *союз* (*якобы*) apparently; (*словно*): (**как**) **~** (**бы**) as if; **уверя́ет, ~ сам её ви́дел** he claims to have seen her himself; **он ~ бы до́лжен е́хать в Москву́** apparently he has to go to Moscow; **он улыба́лся, ~** (**бы**) **был рад ви́деть нас** he smiled as if he were glad to see us.
бу́ду *итп несов см* **быть**.
бу́дущ|ее (**-его**; *decl like adj*) *ср* the future; **в ~ем** in the future; **на ~** for the future; **не де́лайте э́того в ~ем** don't do it in future.
бу́дущ|ий (**-ая, -ее, -ие**) *прил* (*следующий*) next; (*предстоящий*) future; **бу́дущее вре́мя** future tense.
бу́дь(те) *несов см* **быть** ◆ *союз*: **будь то** be it.
бу́ен *прил см* **бу́йный**.
бужени́н|а (**-ы**) *ж cold cooked and seasoned pork* .
бужу́ *несов см* **буди́ть**.
бу|й (**-я**; *nom pl* **-и́**) *м* buoy.
бу́йвол (**-а**) *м* buffalo.
бу́йволиц|а (**-ы**) *ж см* **бу́йвол**.
бу́|йный (**-ен, -йна́, -йно**) *прил* wild; (*обильный*: *растительность*) luxuriant, lush.
бук (**-а**) *м* beech.
бу́кв|а (**-ы**) *ж* letter; (*перен*): **~** *+gen* (*закона, документа*) the letter of; **прописна́я/строчна́я**

~ capital/small letter; **~ в бу́кву** word for word.
буква́льно *нареч* literally.
буква́льный *прил* literal.
буква́р|ь **(-я́)** *м* first reading book.
буке́т **(-а)** *м* (*цветов, вина*) bouquet; (*перен*: *разг*: *болезней, недостатков*) range.
букини́ст **(-а)** *м second-hand bookseller*.
букинисти́ческ|ий **(-ая, -ое, -ие)** *прил*: **~ магази́н** second-hand bookshop.
букле́т **(-а)** *м* booklet.
букси́р **(-а)** *м* tug; (*трос*) towrope; **тяну́ть** *(impf)* *или* **вести́** *(impf)* **на ~е** to give sb a tow.
була́в|ка **(-ки**; *gen pl* **-ок)** *ж* pin; **англи́йская ~** safety pin.
була́н|ый **(-ого**; *decl like adj)* *м* dun.
була́т **(-а)** *м* Damascus *или* damask steel.
бу́л|ка **(-ки**; *gen pl* **-ок)** *ж* roll; (*белый хлеб*) loaf.
бу́лоч|ка **(-ки**; *gen pl* **-ек)** *ж см* **бу́лка**.
бу́лочн|ая **(-ой**; *decl like adj*) *ж* baker, baker's (shop).
булы́жник **(-а)** *м* cobblestone.
булы́жн|ый *прил*: **~ая мостова́я** cobbled street.
бульва́р **(-а)** *м* boulevard.
бульва́рный *прил* boulevard *опред*; **~ рома́н** trashy novel; **бульва́рная пре́сса** gutter press.
бульдо́г **(-а)** *м* bulldog.
бульдо́зер **(-а)** *м* bulldozer.
бульо́н **(-а**; *part gen* **-у)** *м* stock.
бум **(-а)** *м* (*оживление*) boom.
бума́г|а **(-и)** *ж* paper; **~ за по́дписью кого́-н** a document signed by sb; **це́нные ~и** securities; **ге́рбовая ~** headed paper; *см также* **бума́ги**.
бума́г|и **(-)** *мн* papers *мн*.
бума́ж|ка **(-ки**; *gen pl* **-ек)** *ж* piece of paper.
бума́жник **(-а)** *м* wallet, pocketbook (*US*).
бума́жный *прил* paper; (*бюрократический*) bureaucratic; **бума́жная волоки́та** red tape.
бумера́нг **(-а)** *м* boomerang.
бу́нгало *ср нескл* bungalow.
бу́нкер **(-а)** *м* bunker.
бунт **(-а)** *м* (*мятеж*) riot; (: *на корабле*) mutiny.
бунт|ова́ть **(-у́ю)** *несов неперех* (*см сущ*) to riot; to mutiny.
бура́в|ить **(-лю, -ишь**; *perf* **пробура́вить)** *несов перех* to drill.
бура́к **(-а́)** *м* beetroot.
бура́н **(-а)** *м* blizzard, snowstorm.
бу́ргер **(-а)** *м* burger.
бургоми́стр **(-а)** *м* ≈ mayor.
бурд|а́ **(-ы́)** *ж* (*разг*): **э́тот чай про́сто ~** the tea is just like dishwater.
бу́рен *прил см* **бу́рный**.
буре́ни|е **(-я)** *ср* boring, drilling.
буржуази́|я **(-и)** *ж* bourgeoisie; **ме́лкая ~** petty bourgeoisie.
буржуа́зный *прил* bourgeois.
буржу́|й **(-я)** *м* (*разг*) bourgeois.
бур|и́ть **(-ю́, -и́шь**; *perf* **пробури́ть)** *несов перех* to bore, drill.
бу́ркн|уть **(-у, -ешь)** *сов перех* (*разг*) to grunt.
бурл|и́ть **(-ю́, -и́шь)** *несов неперех* (*вода*) to boil; (*ручей*) to bubble; (*толпа*) to seethe (*with excitement*).
бу́р|ный **(-ен, -на́, -но)** *прил* (*погода, океан*) stormy, rough; (*река*) turbulent; (*чувство, порыв*) wild; (*спор*) heated; (*рост*) rapid.
бурови́к **(-а́)** *м* driller.
буро́вой *прил* boring, drilling; **бурова́я вы́шка** derrick; **бурова́я сква́жина** bore(hole).
бурч|а́ть **(-у́, -и́шь**; *perf* **пробурча́ть)** *несов неперех* (*разг*: *ворчать*) to mutter; **~ (пробурча́ть** *perf***) себе́ под нос** to mutter *или* grumble to o.s.
бу́р|ый **(-, -а́, -о)** *прил* brown; **бу́рый у́голь** (*ГЕО*) brown coal, lignite.
бу́р|я **(-и)** *ж* storm; (*перен*) burst; **~ в стака́не воды́** storm in a teacup.
буря́т **(-а**; *gen pl* **-)** *м* Buryat.
Буря́ти|я **(-и)** *ж* Buryatia.
буря́т|ка **(-ки**; *gen pl* **-ок)** *ж см* **буря́т**.
бу́с|ы **(-)** *мн* beads *мн*.
бутафо́ри|я **(-и)** *ж* (*ТЕАТР*) props *мн*) (= *properties*;) (*перен*) sham.
бутербро́д **(-а)** *м* sandwich.
буто́н **(-а)** *м* bud.
бу́тс|а **(-ы)** *ж* (*обычно мн*) football boot.
буты́л|ка **(-ки**; *gen pl* **-ок)** *ж* bottle.
буты́лочный *прил* bottle *опред*; (*цвет*) bottle-green.
бу́фер **(-а**; *nom pl* **-а́)** *м* (*также перен, КОМП*) buffer.
буфериза́ци|я **(-и)** *ж* (*КОМП*) buffering.
бу́ферный *прил* (*также перен*) buffer *опред*.
буфе́т **(-а)** *м* (*для продажи закусок*) snack bar; (*шкаф*) sideboard.
буфе́тчик **(-а)** *м* assistant (*in snack bar*).
буфе́тчиц|а **(-ы)** *ж см* **буфе́тчик**.
бух *межд*: ~! bang!; (*разг*: *упал*) whoops!
буха́н|ка **(-ки**; *gen pl* **-ок)** *ж* loaf.
Бухаре́ст **(-а)** *м* Bucharest.
бу́ха|ть **(-ю)** *несов от* **бу́хнуть**.
бухга́лтер **(-а)** *м* accountant, book-keeper; **~-ревизо́р** auditor.
бухгалте́ри|я **(-и)** *ж* accountancy, book-keeping; (*отдел*) accounts office.
бухга́лтерск|ий **(-ая, -ое, -ие)** *прил* book-keeping *опред*, accountancy *опред*; **бухга́лтерские кни́ги** books; **бухга́лтерский учёт** book-keeping, accountancy.
бу́хн|уть **(-у, -ешь**; *impf* **бу́хать)** *сов неперех* (*дверь*) to bang; (*пушка*) to thunder ◆ *несов неперех* to swell.
бу́хт|а **(-ы)** *ж* bay.
бу́хты-бара́хты *нареч*: **с ~** just like that; (*внезапно*) out of the blue.
буш|ева́ть **(-у́ю)** *несов неперех* (*пожар, ураган*) to rage.
Буэ́нос-А́йрес **(-а)** *м* Buenos Aires.
БЦЖ *ж сокр* BCG (= *Bacillus Calmette-Guérin*).

KEYWORD

бы *част* **1** (*выражает предположительную возможность*): **купи́л бы, е́сли бы бы́ли де́ньги** I would buy it if I had the money; **я бы**

давнó ужé купи́л э́ту кни́гу, éсли бы у меня́ бы́ли дéньги I would have bought this book long ago if I had had the money
2 (*выражает пожелание*): **я бы хотéл поговори́ть с тобóй** I would like to speak to you; **я бы не хотéл об э́том говори́ть** I would rather not talk about it; **чáю бы** I could do with some tea
3 (*выражает совет*): **ты бы написáл ей** you should write to her
4 (*выражает опасение*): **не захвати́л бы нас дождь** I hope we don't get caught in the rain; **отдохну́ть/погуля́ть бы** it would be nice to have a rest/walk; **не опоздáть бы** better not be late.

бывáло *част expresses a repeated action in the past*; **~ сиди́м и разговáриваем** we used to *или* would sit and talk.
бывá|ть (-ю) *несов неперех* (*приходить, посещать*) to be; (*случаться, происходить*) to happen, take place; **он ~ет у нас чáсто** he often comes to see us; **~ют стрáнные слу́чаи** strange things happen; **как не ~ло** (*разг*) as if it had never been; **как ни в чём не ~ло** (*разг*) as if nothing had happened; **с кем не ~ет** it happens to the best of us.
бы́вш|ий (-ая, -ее, -ие) *прил* former; (*жена, муж*) ex-, former.
бык (-á) *м* bull; (*рабочий*) ox; **брать (взять** *perf*) **~á за рогá** to take the bull by the horns.
был *итп несов см* **быть**.
были́н|а (-ы) *ж* bylina (*Russian folk epic*).
бы́ло *част expresses non-fulfilment of an intended action*; **он нáчал ~ говори́ть, но останови́лся** he was about to say something, but stopped; **мы нáчали ~ уходи́ть, но пошёл дождь** we were about to leave, but it began to rain.
был|ь (-и) *ж* (*рассказ*) true story.
бы́стро *нареч* quickly.
быстрот|á (-ы́) *ж* speed; (*ума, рук*) quickness.
быстрохóд|ный (-ен, -на, -но) *прил* fast.
бы́стр|ый (-, á, -о) *прил* fast; (*лошадь*) swift, fast; (*проворный, беглый*) quick.
быт (-а; *loc sg* -у́) *м* life; (*повседневная жизнь*) everyday life; **э́то вошлó в ~** this has become a part of our everyday life; **слу́жба бы́та** consumer services *мн*.
бытовóй *прил* everyday *опред*; **бытовáя жи́вопись** genre painting; **бытовóе обслу́живание населéния** consumer services *мн*; **бытовóе явлéние** everyday occurrence.

KEYWORD

быть (*см* **Table 21**) *несов* ***1*** (*omitted in present tense*) to be; **кни́га на столé** the book is on the table; **зáвтра я бу́ду в шкóле** I will be at school tomorrow; **дом был на краю́ гóрода** the house stood on the edge of the town; **на ней краси́вое плáтье** she is wearing a beautiful dress; **вчерá был дождь** it rained yesterday
2 (*часть составного сказ*) to be; **я хочу́ быть учи́телем** I want to be a teacher; **я был рад ви́деть тебя́** I was happy to see you; **так и быть!** so be it!; **как быть?** what is to be done?; **э́того не мóжет быть** that's impossible; **кто/какóй бы то ни́ был** whoever/whatever it might be; **бу́дьте добры́!** excuse me, please!; **бу́дьте добры́ – позови́те егó!** would you be so good *или* kind as to call him?; **бу́дьте здорóвы!** take care!
3 (*образует будущее время*: +*impf vb*): **вéчером я бу́ду писáть пи́сьма** I'll be writing letters this evening; **я бу́ду люби́ть тебя́ всегдá** I'll love you forever.

бью(сь) *итп несов см* **бить(ся)**.
Бэ́йсик (-а) *м* (*КОМП*) BASIC.
бюджéт (-а) *м* budget; **дохóдный ~** income, revenue; **расхóдный ~** expenditure.
бюджéтный *прил* budgetary.
бюллетéн|ь (-я) *м* bulletin; (*листок*: *для голосования*) ballot paper; (: *нетрудоспособности*) medical certificate; **быть** (*impf*) **на ~е** to be off sick (*from work*).
бюрó *ср нескл* office, agency; **спрáвочное ~** inquiry office; **бюрó (дóбрых) услу́г** domestic help agency; **бюрó нахóдок** lost property office; **бюрó по трудоустрóйству** employment agency.
бюрокрáт (-а) *м* bureaucrat.
бюрократи́зм (-а) *м* bureaucracy.
бюрократи́ческ|ий (-ая, -ое, -ие) *прил* bureaucratic.
бюрокрáти|я (-и) *ж* bureaucracy.
бюст (-а) *м* bust.
бюстгáльтер (-а) *м* bra (= *brassiere*).
бяз|ь (-и) *ж* calico.

~ В, в ~

В, в *сущ нескл* (*буква*) *the 3rd letter of the Russian alphabet.*

В *сокр* (= *вольт*) v. (= *volt*).

KEYWORD

в *предл* (*+acc*) ***1*** (*о месте направления*) in(to); **я положи́л кни́гу в портфе́ль** I put the book in(to) my briefcase; **я сел в маши́ну** I got in(to) the car

2 (*уехать, пойти*) to; **он уе́хал в Москву́** he went to Moscow; **идти́ (пойти́** *perf*) **в учителя́** to become a teacher; **выбира́ть (вы́брать** *perf*) **кого́-н в комите́т** to elect sb to a committee

3 (*об изменении состояния*): **погружа́ться в рабо́ту** to be absorbed in one's work; **погружа́ться** (*impf*) **в разду́мье** to be deep in thought

4 (*об объекте физического действия*): **он постуча́л в дверь** he knocked on the door; **он посмотре́л мне в глаза́/в лицо́** he looked me in the eyes/face; **мать поцелова́ла меня́ в щёку** mother kissed me on the cheek

5 (*обозначает форму, вид*): **брю́ки в кле́тку** checked trousers; **лека́рство в табле́тках** medicine in tablet form; **разрыва́ть (разорва́ть** *perf*) **что-н в кло́чья** to tear sth to shreds; **растира́ть (растере́ть** *perf*) **что-н в порошо́к** to grind sth to a powder

6 (*о размере, количестве*): **ве́сом в 3 то́нны** 3 tons *или* tonnes in weight; (: *+prp*): **дра́ма в трёх частя́х** a drama in three acts; **отря́д в де́сять челове́к** a detachment of ten men; **в пяти́ ме́трах от доро́ги** five metres (*BRIT*) *или* meters (*US*) from the road

7 (*о соотношении величин*): **в два раза́ бо́льше/длинне́е/то́лще** twice as big/long/thick; **во мно́го раз лу́чше/умне́е** much better/cleverer; **во мно́го раз поле́знее/краси́вее** much more useful/beautiful

8 (*о времени совершения чего-н*): **он пришёл в понеде́льник** he came on Monday; **я ви́дел его́ в про́шлом году́** I saw him last year; **я встре́тил его́ в два часа́** I met him at two o'clock; **э́то случи́лось в ма́рте/в двадца́том ве́ке** it happened in March/in the twentieth century

9 (*+prp*; *о месте*) in; **ко́шка сиди́т в корзи́не** the cat is sitting in the basket; **я живу́ в дере́вне** I live in the country; **сын у́чится в шко́ле/университе́те** my son is at school/university; **в отдале́нии/сосе́дстве** in the distance/the neighbourhood

10 (*о чём-н облегающем, покрывающем*): **ру́ки в кра́ске/са́же** hands covered in paint/soot; **това́р в упако́вке** packaged goods; **не́бо в ту́чах** the sky is overcast

11 (*об одежде*) in; **мужчи́на в очка́х/в ша́пке** a man in *или* wearing glasses/a hat

12 (*о состоянии*): **быть в у́жасе/негодова́нии** to be terrified/indignant.

в. *сокр* (= **век**) c (= *century*); (= **восто́к**) E (= *East*); (= **восто́чный**) E (= *East*).

ва-ба́нк *нареч* (*также перен*): **идти́ ~** to stake everything.

ваго́н (-а) *м* (*пассажирский*) carriage (*BRIT*), coach (*BRIT*), car (*US*); (*товарный*) wagon (*BRIT*), truck; **спа́льный ~** couchette car; **мя́гкий ~** ≈ sleeping car; **ваго́н-рестора́н** dining (*BRIT*) *или* club (*US*) car.

ваго́не́т|ка (-ки; *gen pl* **-ок)** *ж* trolley (*RAIL*).

ваго́нный *прил* carriage *опред* (*BRIT*), car *опред* (*US*); **ваго́нный парк** train depot.

вагоноремо́нтный *прил* (*завод*) coach (*BRIT*) *или* car (*US*) reparation *опред.*

вагоностро́ительный *прил* (*завод*) coach (*BRIT*) *или* car (*US*) building *опред.*

ва́жен *прил см* **ва́жный**.

ва́жнича|ть (-ю) *несов неперех* to act in a self-important manner.

ва́жност|ь (-и) *ж* importance; (*надменность*) self-importance; **(не) велика́ ~** what does it matter.

ва́жный (-ен, -на́, -но) *прил* important; (*гордый*) pompous.

ВАЗ (-а) *м сокр* = *Во́лжский автомоби́льный заво́д*; (*автомобиль*) *vehicle manufactured at the Volga car factory.*

ва́з|а (-ы) *ж* vase.

вазели́н (-а; *part gen* **-у)** *м* Vaseline®.

вака́нси|я (-и) *ж* vacancy; **откры́лась ~ в бухгалте́рии** a vacancy has now arisen in accounts.

вака́нт|ный (-ен, -на, -но) *прил* vacant; **~ная до́лжность** vacancy.

ва́кс|а (-ы) *ж* black shoe polish.

ва́куум (-а) *м* (*также перен*) vacuum.

вакци́н|а (-ы) *ж* vaccine.

вакцини́р|овать (-ую) *(не)сов перех* to vaccinate.
вал (-а; *loc sg* **-у́**, *nom pl* **-ы́)** *м (насыпь)* bank; (: *крепости*) rampart; (*стержень*) shaft; (*волна*) breaker; (*ЭКОН*) gross product.
валё́жник (-а) *м собир* dead wood.
ва́лен|ок (-ка) *м (обычно мн)* felt boot.
валериа́н|а (-ы) *ж* valerian.
валериа́нк|а (-и) *ж* valerian drops *мн*.
валериа́нов|ый *прил*: **~ые ка́пли** valerian drops.
валерья́н|а (-ы) *ж* = **валериа́на**.
вале́т (-а) *м (КАРТЫ)* jack.
валидо́л (-а) *м type of mild sedative*.
ва́лик (-а) *м (в механизме)* cylinder; (*для краски*) roller; (*подушка*) bolster.
вал|и́ть (-ю́, -ишь; *perf* **свали́ть** *или* **повали́ть)** *несов перех (заставить падать)* to knock over; (*рубить*) to fell; (*perf* **свали́ть**; *разг: бросать*) to dump ◆ *неперех (no perf; народ)* to flock; (*дым, пар*) to pour out; **~ (свали́ть** *perf*) **вину́ на** *+acc (разг)* to point the finger at; **ва́лит снег** it's snowing heavily; **толпа́ ~и́ла на конце́рт** the crowd flocked to the concert
▸ **вали́ться** (*perf* **свали́ться** *или* **повали́ться)** *несов возв (падать)* to fall; (*разг: опускаться*) to flake out; **все бе́ды ва́лятся на него́** he attracts misfortune; **у него́ всё ва́лится из рук** everything he does fails; **~ся** *(impf)* **с ног** (*разг*) to be dead on one's feet.
валово́й *прил (доход)* gross *опред*; **валово́й вну́тренний проду́кт** gross domestic product; **валово́й национа́льный проду́кт** gross national product; **валова́я при́быль** gross profit; **~ объём прода́жи** gross sales *мн*.
ва́лом *нареч*: **~ вали́ть** (*разг: народ*) to flock.
валто́рн|а (-ы) *ж* French horn.
валу́н (-а́) *м* boulder.
вальс (-а) *м* waltz.
вальц|ева́ть (-у́ю) *несов перех* to roll.
вальц|ы́ (-о́в) *мн (станок)* rolling press *ед*.
валю́т|а (-ы) *ж* currency ◆ *собир* foreign currency; **твёрдая ~** hard currency.
валю́тно-фина́нсовый *прил* monetary.
валю́тный *прил* currency *опред*; **~ контро́ль** exchange control; **валю́тный курс** rate of exchange; **валю́тный фонд** currency reserves *мн*.
валю́тчик (-а) *м (разг) person illegally dealing in foreign currency*.
валю́тчиц|а (-ы) *ж см* **валю́тчик**.
валя́|ть (-ю) *несов перех (катать)* to roll; (*perf* **сваля́ть**; *скатывать*) to shape
▸ **валя́ться** *несов возв (кататься)* to roll about; (*разг: человек, бумаги итп*) to lie about; (: *с гриппом итп*) to be laid up; **де́ньги на земле́** *или* **на доро́ге не ~ются** (*разг*) money doesn't grow on trees.
вам *итп мест см* **вы**.
вампи́р (-а) *м* vampire.
ВАН *м сокр (= Ве́стник Акаде́мии нау́к Росси́и)* Bulletin of the Russian Academy of Science.
вандали́зм (-а) *м* vandalism.
ванили́н (-а; *part gen* **-у)** *м* vanillin.
вани́л|ь (-и) *ж* vanilla.
ва́нн|а (-ы) *ж* bath; **принима́ть (приня́ть** *perf*) **~у** to take *или* have a bath.
ва́нн|ая (-ой; *decl like adj*) *ж* bathroom.
ва́рвар (-а) *м* barbarian.
ва́рварск|ий (-ая, -ое, -ие) *прил* barbaric.
ва́рварств|о (-а) *ср (бескультурие)* barbarism; (*жестокость*) barbarity.
ва́реж|ка (-ки; *gen pl* **-ек)** *ж (обычно мн)* mitten.
варе́ник (-а) *м (обычно мн)* sweet dumpling (*with curd or fruit filling*).
варё́ный *прил* boiled.
варе́нь|е (-я) *ср* jam.
вариа́нт (-а) *м* version; (*возможность*) option; (*разновидность*) variant.
вариа́ци|я (-и) *ж* variation.
вар|и́ть (-ю́, -ишь; *perf* **свари́ть)** *несов перех* (*обед*) to cook; (*суп, кофе*) to make; (*картофель, мясо*) to boil; (*ТЕХ*) to weld; (*сталь*) to found; **у него́ голова́** *или* **котело́к ва́рит** (*разг*) he has a good head on his shoulders
▸ **вари́ться** (*perf* **свари́ться)** *несов возв* (*приготовляться*) to be cooking; **~ся** *(impf)* **в со́бственном соку́** (*перен*) to live in a world of one's own; **до́лго/бы́стро ~ся** *(impf)* to cook slowly/quickly.
Варша́в|а (-ы) *ж* Warsaw.
варьете́ *ср нескл* variety show.
варьи́р|овать (-ую) *несов (не)перех* to vary.
вас *мест см* **вы**.
василё́к (-ька́) *м* cornflower.
ВАТА *ж сокр (= Всеми́рная ассоциа́ция туристи́ческих аге́нтств)* IATA (= *International Association of Travel Agencies*).
ва́т|а (-ы) *ж* cotton wool (*BRIT*), (absorbent) cotton (*US*).
вата́г|а (-и) *ж (ребят)* gang.
ватерли́ни|я (-и) *ж* water line.
ватерпа́с (-а) *м* spirit level.
ватерполи́ст (-а) *м* water-polo player.
ватерпо́ло *ср нескл* water polo.
вати́н (-а) *м* padding.
ва́тк|а (-и) *ж* cotton wool ball.
ва́тман (-а) *м heavy paper for drawing etc.*
ва́тник (-а) *м* quilted jacket.
ва́тный *прил* cotton-wool (*BRIT*), absorbent cotton *опред* (*US*); **ва́тное одея́ло** quilt.
ватру́ш|ка (-ки; *gen pl* **-ек)** *ж* curd tart.
ватт (-а) *м* watt.
ва́учер (-а) *м* voucher.
ва́фельный *прил*: **~ торт** waffle.
ва́фл|я (-ли; *gen pl* **-ель)** *ж* wafer.

ва́хт|а (-ы) *ж* watch; **стоя́ть** *(impf)* **на ~е** to keep watch.
ва́хтенный *прил* (*служба*) watch *опред*; **ва́хтенный журна́л** log(book).
вахтёр (-а) *м* caretaker, janitor.
Ваш *мест см* **ваш**.
ваш (-его; *f* -а, *nt* -е, *pl* -и; *как* **наш**; *см* **Table 9**) *притяж мест* your; **э́то ва́ше** this is yours; **наш дом бо́льше ва́шего** our house is bigger than yours; *см также* **ва́ши**.
ва́ш|и (-их; *decl like adj*) *мн* your nearest and dearest *мн*; **и на́шим и ~м** (*разг: пренебр*) all things to all people.
Вашингто́н (-а) *м* Washington.
вбе|жа́ть (*как* **бежа́ть**; *см* **Table 20**; *impf* **вбега́ть**) *сов неперех*: **~ (в** *+acc*) to run in(to).
вберу́ *итп сов см* **вобра́ть**.
вбива́|ть (-ю) *несов от* **вбить**.
вбира́|ть (-ю) *несов от* **вобра́ть**.
вбить (**вобью́, вобьёшь**; *impf* **вбива́ть**) *сов перех*: **~ (в** *+acc*) to drive *или* hammer in(to); **я не могу́ ~ э́то ей в го́лову** (*разг*) I can't seem to get it into her thick skull.
вблизи́ *нареч* nearby ◆ *предл*: **~** *+gen или* **от** *+gen* near (to).
вбок *нареч* sideways.
вбра́сыва|ть (-ю) *несов от* **вбро́сить**.
вброд *нареч*: **переходи́ть (перейти́** *perf*) **~** to ford.
вбро́|сить (-шу, -сишь; *impf* **вбра́сывать**) *сов перех* to throw in; **вбра́сывать (~** *perf*) **мяч** (*СПОРТ*) to take a throw-in.
ввал|и́ться (-ю́сь, -ишься; *impf* **вва́ливаться**) *сов возв* (*разг*): **~ (в** *+acc*) to burst in(to); (*щеки, глаза*) to become sunken.
введе́ни|е (-я) *ср* introduction; (*войск*) sending in; (*данных*) input.
ввез|ти́ (-у́, -ёшь; *pt* **ввёз, -ла́, -ло́**, *impf* **ввози́ть**) *сов перех* (*в дом итп*) to take in; (*в страну*) to import.
вве́ргн|уть (-у, -ешь; *impf* **вверга́ть**) *сов перех* (*перен*): **~ в** *+acc* to reduce to; **он вверга́ет меня́ в тоску́** he depresses me.
вверн|у́ть (-у́, -ёшь; *impf* **ввёртывать**) *сов перех* to screw in; (*перен: разг: слово*) to put in.
вверх *нареч* up ◆ *предл*: **~ по** *+dat* up; **~ по тече́нию** upstream; **всё в до́ме/в ко́мнате ~ дном** (*разг*) everything in the house/room is topsy-turvy; **~ нога́ми** (*разг*) upside down.
вверху́ *нареч* up ◆ *предл* (*+gen*) at the top of.
вв|ести́ (-еду́, -едёшь; *pt* -ёл, -ела́, -ело́, *impf* **вводи́ть**) *сов перех* to take in; (*машину: в гараж*) to put in; (*иглу: в вену итп*) to slip in; (*лекарство, раствор*) to inject; (*в компьютер*) to enter; (*установить: закон, пошлины итп*) to introduce; (*сделать действующим*): **~ что-н в** *+acc* to put sth into; **вводи́ть (~** *perf*) **кого́-н в заблужде́ние/искуше́ние** to mislead/tempt sb; **вводи́ть (~** *perf*) **кого́-н в расхо́ды** to cause sb expense; **вводи́ть (~** *perf*) **что-н в мо́ду** to bring sth into fashion; **вводи́ть (~** *perf*) **кого́-н в курс собы́тий** to bring sb up-to-date with events.
ввиду́ *предл* (*+gen*) in view of ◆ *союз*: **~ того́, что** in view of the fact that; **~ плохо́й пого́ды рейс отло́жен** the flight has been delayed because of the bad weather.
ввин|ти́ть (-чу́, -ти́шь; *impf* **вви́нчивать**) *сов перех* to screw in.
ввод (-а) *м* bringing in; (*данных*) input, feeding in; (*электрический, телефонный*) lead-in.
вво|ди́ть (-жу́, -дишь) *несов от* **ввести́**.
вво́дн|ый *прил* (*статья*) introductory; (*устройство*) lead-in *опред*; **вво́дное отве́рстие** input; **вво́дное сло́во** parenthesis.
ввожу́ *несов см* **ввози́ть**.
ввоз (-а) *м* (*процесс*) importation; (*импорт*) imports *мн*; **беспо́шлинный ~** duty-free imports.
вво|зи́ть (-жу́, -зишь) *несов от* **ввезти́**.
ввозн|о́й *прил* imported; **ввозны́е по́шлины** import duty *ед*.
вво́лю *нареч* to one's heart's content.
ввосьмеро́м *нареч* in a group of eight; **они́ живу́т там ~** there are eight of them living there.
ВВП *м сокр* (= *валово́й вну́тренний проду́кт*) GDP (= *gross domestic product*).
ВВС *мн сокр* (= *воє́нно-возду́шные си́лы*) ≈ RAF (= *Royal Air Force ед*).
ВВФ *м сокр* (= *Вое́нно-возду́шный флот*) ≈ RAF (= *Royal Air Force*).
ввысь *нареч* upwards.
ввя|за́ться (-жу́сь, -жешься; *impf* **ввя́зываться**) *сов возв* (*разг*) to get involved.
вгиба́|ть (-ю) *несов от* **вогну́ть**.
вглубь *нареч* (down) into the depths ◆ *предл* (*+gen*; *вниз*) into the depths of; (*внутрь*) into the heart of.
вгля|де́ться (-жу́сь, -ди́шься; *impf* **вгля́дываться**) *сов возв*: **~ в** *+acc* to peer at.
вгоню́ *итп сов см* **вогна́ть**.
вгоня́|ть (-ю) *несов от* **вогна́ть**.
вда|ва́ться (-ю́сь) *несов от* **вда́ться**.
вдав|и́ть (-лю́, -ишь; *impf* **вда́вливать**) *сов перех*: **~ (в** *+acc*) to press in(to).
вдади́мся *итп сов см* **вда́ться**.
вдалеке́ *нареч* in the distance; **~ от** *+gen* a long way from.
вдали́ *нареч* = **вдалеке́**.
вдаль *нареч* into the distance.
вда́ться (*как* **дать**; *см* **Table 14**; *impf* **вдава́ться**) *сов возв*: **~ в** *+acc* to jut out into; (*перен: в рассуждения*) to get caught up in; **вдава́ться** *(impf)* **в подро́бности** to go into details.
вдво́е *нареч* (*сложить*) in two; **~ сильне́е/умне́е** twice as strong/clever.
вдвоём *нареч*: **они́ живу́т/рабо́тают ~** the two of them live/work together.
вдвойне́ *нареч* (*получить, заплатить*) double (the amount).
вде́ла|ть (-ю; *impf* **вде́лывать**) *сов перех*: **~ в** *+acc* (*вставить*) to set into.

вде|ть (**-ну, -нешь**; *impf* **вдева́ть**) *сов перех* to put in; **вдева́ть** (~ *perf*) **ни́тку в иго́лку** to thread a needle.
ВДНХ *ж сокр* (= *Вы́ставка достиже́ний наро́дного хозя́йства СССР*) *exhibition of economic achievements of the USSR.*
вдоба́вок *нареч* (*разг*) in addition ◆ *предл*: ~ **к** *+dat* in addition to.
вдов|а́ (**-ы́**; *nom pl* **-ы**) *ж* widow.
вдов|е́ц (**-ца́**) *м* widower.
вдо́воль *нареч* to one's heart's content; **(в до́ме) всего́** ~ there is plenty of everything (in the house).
вдовца́ *итп сущ см* **вдове́ц**.
вдо́вый *прил* widowed.
вдого́нку *нареч* (*бежать*) behind ◆ *предл*: ~ **за** *+instr* after.
вдоль *нареч* (*сломаться, расколоться*) lengthways ◆ *предл* (*+gen*) along; ~ **и поперёк** here, there and everywhere; (*перен*) inside out.
вдох (**-а**) *м*: **де́лать (сде́лать** *perf*) ~ to breathe in.
вдохнове́ни|е (**-я**) *ср* inspiration.
вдохнове́н|ный (**-ен, -на, -но**) *прил* inspired.
вдохнов|и́ть (**-лю́, -и́шь**; *impf* **вдохновля́ть**) *сов перех* to inspire; ~ *(perf)* **кого́-н на что-н** to inspire sb to sth
▸ **вдохнови́ться** (*impf* **вдохновля́ться**) *сов возв* (*+instr*) to be inspired by.
вдохн|у́ть (**-у́, -ёшь**; *impf* **вдыха́ть**) *сов перех* (*воздух*) to breathe in; (*дым, лекарство*) to inhale; **вдыха́ть** (~ *perf*) **уве́ренность/ве́ру в кого́-н** to inspire confidence/faith in sb.
вдре́безги *нареч* to smithereens.
вдруг *нареч* suddenly; (*а если*) what if; ~ **он не придёт** what if he doesn't come.
вду́ма|ться (**-юсь**; *impf* **вду́мываться**) *сов возв*: ~ **в** *+acc* to think over.
вду́мчив|ый (**-, -а, -о**) *прил* contemplative.
вду́мыва|ться (**-юсь**) *несов от* **вду́маться**.
вдыха́ни|е (**-я**) *ср* inhalation.
вдыха́|ть (**-ю**) *несов от* **вдохну́ть**.
веб (**-а**) *м* the (World Wide) Web.
вегетариа́н|ец (**-ца**) *м* vegetarian.
вегетариа́н|ка (**-ки**; *gen pl* **-ок**) *ж см* **вегетариа́нец**.
вегетариа́нск|ий (**-ая, -ое, -ие**) *прил* vegetarian.
вегетариа́нца *сущ см* **вегетариа́нец**.
вегета́ци|я (**-и**) *ж* vegetation.
ве́да|ть (**-ю**) *несов перех* (*знать*) to know ◆ *неперех*: ~ *+instr* (*делами*) to be in charge of.
ведём *несов см* **вести́**.
ве́дени|е (**-я**) *ср* authority; **принима́ть (приня́ть** *perf*) **в своё** ~ to take charge of; **быть** *(impf)* **в** ~**и кого́-н** to be under sb's authority.
веде́ни|е (**-я**) *ср* (*урока, следствия*) conducting; (*войны*) waging; ~ **хозя́йства** housekeeping.
вёдер *сущ см* **ведро́**.
ведёт(ся) *итп несов см* **вести́(сь)**.
ве́домо *ср*: **с/без ве́дома кого́-н** (*согласие*) with/without sb's consent; (*уведомление*) with/without sb's knowledge.
ве́домост|и (**-ей**) *мн* gazette *ед*.
ве́домост|ь (**-и**; *gen pl* **-е́й**) *ж* register; **расчётная** *или* **платёжная** ~ payroll; *см также* **ве́домости**.
ве́домственный *прил* departmental; (*подход*) narrow-minded.
ве́домств|о (**-а**) *ср* department.
ведр|о́ (**-а́**; *nom pl* **вёдра**, *gen pl* **вёдер**) *ср* bucket, pail; **(дождь) льёт, как из** ~**а́** it's pouring *или* bucketing (with rain).
веду́(сь) *итп несов см* **вести́(сь)**.
веду́щая (**-ей**; *decl like adj*) *ж см* **веду́щий**.
веду́щий (**-ая, -ее, -ие**) *прил* leading ◆ (**-его**; *decl like adj*) *м* presenter.
ведь *нареч* (*в вопросе*): ~ **ты хо́чешь пое́хать?** you do want to go, don't you?; (*в утверждении*): ~ **она́ не спра́вится одна́!** she surely can't manage alone! ◆ *союз* (*указывает на причину*) seeing as; ~ **она́ ра́да?** she is glad, isn't she?; **пое́шь,** ~ **ты го́лоден** you should eat, seeing as you're hungry; ~ **я проси́л тебя́!** I asked YOU!
ве́дьм|а (**-ы**) *ж* (*также перен*) witch; **охо́та за** ~**ми** *или* **на ведьм** witch-hunt.
ве́ер (**-а**; *nom pl* **-а́**) *м* fan.
ве́жливо *нареч* politely.
ве́жливост|ь (**-и**) *ж* politeness.
ве́жлив|ый (**-, -а, -о**) *прил* polite.
вёз *итп несов см* **везти́**.
везде́ *нареч* everywhere; ~ **и всю́ду** everywhere you go.
вездесу́щий (**-ая, -ее, -ие**; **-, -а, -е**) *прил* (*Бог*) omnipresent; (*человек*) ubiquitous.
вездехо́д (**-а**) *м* ≈ Landrover®.
везе́ни|е (**-я**) *ср* luck.
вез|ти́ (**-у́, -ёшь**; *pt* **вёз, -ла́, -ло́**) *несов перех* to transport, take; (*двигать: за собой*) to pull; (: *перед собой*) to push ◆ (*perf* **повезти́**) *безл* (*+dat*; *разг*) to be lucky; **ему́ (ча́сто)** ~**ёт** he is (often) lucky.
Везу́ви|й (**-я**) *м* Vesuvius.
везу́ч|ий (**-ая, -ее, -ие**; **-, -а, -е**) *прил* lucky.
ве́й(те) *несов см* **вить**.
век (**-а**; *loc sg* **-у́**, *nom pl* **-а́**) *м* century; (*исторический период*) age; (*чья-н жизнь*) lifetime; **це́лый** ~ **тебя́ не ви́дел** I haven't seen you for ages; **на** ~**а́** forever; **в ко́и-то ве́ки** (*разг*) for the first time in ages; **жить** *(impf)* **в** ~**а́х** to live on forever; **во ве́ки** ~**о́в** forever.
ве́к|о (**-а**) *ср* eyelid.
векова́й *прил* (*традиция, дерево*) ancient.
ве́ксел|ь (**-я**; *nom pl* **-я́**) *м* promissory note; **переводно́й** ~ bill of exchange; **казначе́йский**

~ treasury bill; **плати́ть (заплати́ть** *perf*) **по ~ю** to settle an account.
вёл(ся) *итп несов см* **вести́(сь)**.
вел|е́ть (-ю́, -и́шь) *(не)сов неперех* (*+dat*) to order; **он ~е́л мне прийти́, он ~е́л, что́бы я пришёл** he ordered me to come.
велика́н (-а) *м* giant.
вели́к|ий (-ая, -ое, -ие; -, -а́, -о́) *прил* great; (*no full form*; *обувь, одежда*) too big; **сапоги́ велики́** the boots are too big; **вели́кие держа́вы** the Great Powers.
Великобрита́ни|я (-и) *ж* Great Britain.
великоду́ш|ный (-ен, -на, -но) *прил* magnanimous, big-hearted.
великоле́п|ный (-ен, -на, -но) *прил* (*роскошный*) magnificent, splendid; (*разг*) fantastic.
великому́ченик (-а) *м* holy martyr.
великоро́сс (-а) *м* (*ИСТ*: *обычно мн*) Great Russian (*old name for a Russian*).
вели́чествен|ный (-, -на, -но) *прил* majestic.
вели́честв|о (-а) *ср*: **Ва́ше** *итп* ~ Your *итп* Majesty.
вели́чи|е (-я) *ср* grandeur.
величин|а́ (-ы́) *ж* size; (*МАТ*) quantity; (*КОМП*: *значение*) value.
вело́(сь) *несов см* **вести́(сь)**.
велого́н|ка (-ки; *gen pl* **-ок)** *ж* (*СПОРТ*: *обычно мн*) cycle race.
велодро́м (-а) *м* velodrome.
велосипе́д (-а) *м* bicycle; **го́ночный ~** racing bicycle, racer.
велосипеди́ст (-а) *м* cyclist.
велосипеди́ст|ка (-ки; *gen pl* **-ок)** *ж см* **велосипеди́ст**.
вельве́т (-а) *м* corduroy.
вельмо́ж|а (-и) *м* dignitary.
велю́р (-а) *м* velours.
Ве́н|а (-ы) *ж* Vienna.
ве́н|а (-ы) *ж* vein.
венге́р|ка (-ки; *gen pl* **-ок)** *ж см* **венгр**.
венге́рск|ий (-ая, -ое, -ие) *прил* Hungarian; ~ **язы́к** Hungarian.
венгр (-а) *м* Hungarian.
Ве́нгри|я (-и) *ж* Hungary.
Вене́р|а (-ы) *ж* Venus.
венери́ческ|ий (-ая, -ое, -ие) *прил*: **~ая боле́знь** venereal disease.
венероло́ги|я (-и) *ж* venereology.
Венесуэ́л|а (-ы) *ж* Venezuela.
венесуэ́л|ец (-ьца) *м* Venezuelan.
венесуэ́л|ка (-ки; *gen pl* **-ок)** *ж см* **венесуэ́лец**.
венесуэ́льск|ий (-ая, -ое, -ие) *прил* Venezuelan.
венесуэ́льца *итп сущ см* **венесуэ́лец**.
вен|е́ц (-ца́) *м* crown; (*АСТРОНОМИЯ*) corona; **идти́ (пойти́** *perf*) **под ~ с кем-н** to walk down the aisle with sb.
венециа́нск|ий (-ая, -ое, -ие) *прил* Venetian.
Вене́ци|я (-и) *ж* Venice.
ве́нзел|ь (-я; *nom pl* **-я́)** *м* monogram.
ве́ник (-а) *м* broom, besom.
венка́ *итп сущ см* **вено́к**.
вено́зный *прил* venous.
вен|о́к (-ка́) *м* wreath.
вентили́р|овать (-ую; *perf* **провентили́ровать**) *несов перех* (*помещение*) to ventilate.
ве́нтил|ь (-я) *м* valve.
вентиля́тор (-а) *м* (ventilator) fan.
вентиля́ци|я (-и) *ж* ventilation.
венца́ *итп сущ см* **вене́ц**.
венча́ни|е (-я) *ср* (*коронование*) coronation; (*бракосочетание*) church wedding.
венча́|ть (-ю; *perf* **обвенча́ть** *или* **повенча́ть**) *несов перех* (*соединять браком*) to marry; (*находиться наверху*) to crown; ~ *(impf)* **на ца́рство кого́-н** to crown sb
▸ **венча́ться** (*perf* **обвенча́ться**) *несов возв* to be married (*in church*).
ве́нчик (-а) *м* (*БОТ*) corolla.
венчу́рн|ый *прил*: **~ое предприя́тие** venture; ~ **капита́л** venture capital.
ве́р|а (-ы) *ж* faith; (*в бога*) belief; ~ **в кого́-н/что-н** faith in sb/sth; **~ой и пра́вдой служи́ть** *(impf)* **кому́-н/чему́-н** to serve sb/sth faithfully; **на ~у принима́ть (приня́ть** *perf*) **что-н** to take sth on trust.
вера́нд|а (-ы) *ж* verandah.
ве́рб|а (-ы) *ж* pussy willow.
верба́льный *прил* verbal.
верблю́д (-а) *м* camel.
верблю́диц|а (-ы) *ж см* **верблю́д**.
ве́рбн|ый *прил*: **~ое воскресе́нье** ≈ Palm Sunday.
верб|ова́ть (-у́ю; *perf* **завербова́ть**) *несов перех* to recruit.
вербо́в|ка (-ки; *gen pl* **-ок)** *ж* recruitment.
верди́кт (-а) *м* verdict; **выноси́ть (вы́нести** *perf*) **обвини́тельный/оправда́тельный ~** to pronounce a verdict of guilty/not guilty.
верёв|ка (-ки; *gen pl* **-ок)** *ж* (*толстая*) rope; (*тонкая*) string; (*для белья*) line; **вить** *(impf)* **~ки из кого́-н** to twist sb round one's little finger.
ве́рен *прил см* **ве́рный**.
верени́ц|а (-ы) *ж* (*предметов*) line; (*людей*) file; (*перен*: *мыслей итп*) series.
ве́реск (-а) *м* heather.
верет|ено́ (-ена́; *nom pl* **-ёна)** *ср* spindle.
верещ|а́ть (-у́, -и́шь) *несов неперех* (*женщина*) to chatter.
верзи́л|а (-ы) *м/ж* (*разг*) beanpole.
вери́г|а (-и) *ж* (*обычно мн*) chain (*worn for religious reasons*).
вери́тельн|ый *прил*: **~ая гра́мота** credentials *мн*.
ве́р|ить (-ю, -ишь; *perf* **пове́рить**) *несов неперех* (*+dat*) to believe; (*доверять*) to trust; ~ **(пове́рить** *perf*) **в кого́-н/что-н** to believe *или* have faith in sb/sth; ~ *(impf)* **(в Бо́га)** to believe (in God); ~ **(пове́рить** *perf*) **на́ слово кому́-н** to take sb at his *итп* word; **я не ~ю свои́м**

глазам/ушам I don't believe my eyes/ears
▸ **вериться** *несов безл*: **не ~ится, что это правда** it's hard to believe it's true.
вермишел|ь (-и) *ж* vermicelli.
вермут (-а) *м* vermouth.
вернее *вводн сл* or rather; ~ **всего** most likely.
вернисаж (-а) *м* private view (*of art exhibition etc*).
верно *нареч* (*преданно*) faithfully; (*правильно*) correctly ◆ *как сказ* that's right ◆ *вводн сл* probably; **она, ~, больна** she must be *или* is probably ill.
вернопо́данн|ая (-ой; *decl like adj*) *ж см* **верноподанный**.
верноподанн|ый (-ого; *decl like adj*) *м* loyal subject.
верност|ь (-и) *ж* (*преданность*) faithfulness, loyalty; (*правильность*) correctness; **для ~и** just to make sure.
верн|уть (-у, -ёшь) *сов перех* to return, give back; (*долг*) to pay back; (*здоровье, надежду итп*) to restore; ~ (*perf*) **кого-н к действительности** to bring sb back (down) to earth; ~ (*perf*) **кого-н прошлому** to take sb back
▸ **вернуться** *сов возв*: **~ся (к** +*dat*) to return (to).
вер|ный (-ен, -на, -но) *прил* (*преданный*) faithful; (*надёжный*) sure; (*правильный*) correct; (*no short form*; *неизбежный*) certain; ~ **слову** true to one's word; **она верна самой себе** she acts true to form.
веровани|е (-я) *ср* (*обычно мн*) belief.
вер|овать (-ую) *несов неперех* to believe (in God).
вероисповедани|е (-я) *ср* faith.
веролом|ный (-ен, -на, -но) *прил* (*друг*) treacherous; (*нападение*) deceitful.
вероотступник (-а) *м* apostate.
веротерпимост|ь (-и) *ж* (*РЕЛ*) tolerance.
вероучени|е (-я) *ср* teachings *мн*.
вероятен *прил см* **вероятный**.
вероятно *как сказ* it is likely *или* probable ◆ *вводн сл* probably.
вероятност|ь (-и) *ж* probability; **по всей ~и** in all probability.
вероят|ный (-ен, -на, -но) *прил* likely, probable; **~нее всего** most likely *или* probably.
верси|я (-и) *ж* version.
верст|а (-ы; *nom pl* **вёрсты**) *ж* verst (*former Russian unit of measurement equal to 1.06 km*); **видно за ~у** it is visible from a long way away.
верстак (-а) *м* (*ТЕХ*) (work)bench.
верста|ть (-ю; *perf* **сверстать**) *несов перех* to set.
вёрстк|а (-и) *ж* (page)proof.
вертел (-а; *nom pl* -а) *м* spit (*for roasting*).
вер|теть (-чу, -ишь) *несов перех* (*руль*) to turn; ~ (*impf*) +*instr* (*зонтиком, тростью*) to twirl; **как ни ~ти, а он прав** (*разг*) no matter which way you look at it, he's right; ~ (*impf*) **в руках что-н** to fiddle with sth
▸ **вертеться** *несов возв* (*колесо*) to spin; (*человек*) to fidget; (: *хлопотать*) to be kept busy; **~ся** (*impf*) **в голове** (*разг*: *мысль*) to go round and round in one's head; **его имя вертится у меня на языке** his name is on the tip of my tongue; **~ся** (*impf*) **под ногами** (*разг*) to get *или* be under one's feet.
вертика́л|ьный (-ен, -ьна, -ьно) *прил* vertical.
вертихвост|ка (-ки; *gen pl* -ок) *ж* flirt.
вертолёт (-а) *м* helicopter.
вертолётчик (-а) *м* helicopter pilot.
верту́ш|ка (-ки; *gen pl* -ек) *ж* revolving object; (*разг*: *о человеке*) featherbrain; **дверь-~** revolving door.
верующ|ая (-ей; *decl like adj*) *ж см* **верующий**.
верующ|ий (-его; *decl like adj*) *м* believer.
верф|ь (-и) *ж* shipyard; (*военная*) dockyard.
верх (-а; *loc sg* -у, *nom pl* -и) *м* (*дома, стола*) top; (*экипажа, коляски*) hood; (*шубы*) outer layer; (*обуви*) upper; ~ **совершенства/глупости** the height of perfection/stupidity; **одерживать (одержать** *perf*) *или* **брать (взять** *perf*) **~ над кем-н** to get the upper hand over sb; *см также* **верхи**.
верх|и (-ов) *мн*: **в ~ах** at the top; **встреча/переговоры в ~ах** summit meeting/talks.
верхн|ий (-яя, -ее, -ие) *прил* top; **верхняя одежда** outer clothing *или* garments *мн*.
верховный *прил* (*главный*) supreme; **Верховный Совет** Supreme Soviet; **Верховный Суд** High Court (*BRIT*), Supreme Court (*US*).
верхов|ой *прил*: **~ая езда** riding, horseback riding (*US*); **~ая лошадь** mount.
верховь|е (-я) *ср* upper reaches *мн*.
верхолаз (-а) *м* steeplejack.
верхом *нареч* astride; ~ **на лошади** on horseback.
верху́ш|ка (-ки; *gen pl* -ек) *ж* (*дерева, насыпи*) top; (*перен*: *правящая*) elite.
верчу(сь) *несов см* **вертеть(ся)**.
вершин|а (-ы) *ж* (*холма, дерева*) top; (*горы*) summit, peak; **на ~е славы** at the height of his *итп* fame; **на ~е счастья** in seventh heaven.
верш|ить (-у, -ишь) *несов перех* (*суд*) to conduct ◆ *неперех*: ~ +*instr* (*судьбами*) to control.
вес (-а; *part gen* -у, *nom pl* -а) *м* weight; (*перен*: *влияние*) authority; **весом в 5 килограмм** weighing 5 kilogrammes; **закреплять (закрепить** *perf*) **что-н на ~у** to suspend sth; **прибавлять (прибавить** *perf*) **в весе** to put on weight; **борец лёгкого/тяжёлого веса** light-/heavyweight wrestler; **цениться** (*impf*) *или* **быть** (*impf*) **на ~ золота** to be worth one's weight in

gold.
весел *прил см* **весёлый**.
вёсел *сущ см* **весло**.
веселе́|ть (-ю; *perf* **повеселе́ть)** *несов неперех* to cheer up.
весел|и́ть (-ю́, -и́шь; *perf* **развесели́ть)** *несов перех* to amuse
▸ **весели́ться** *несов возв* to have fun.
ве́село *нареч* (*сказать*) cheerfully ◆ *как сказ*: **здесь** ~ it's fun here; **мне** ~ I'm having fun.
вес|ёлый (-ел, -ла́, -ло) *прил* cheerful.
весе́ль|е (-я) *ср* (*настроение*) cheerfulness; (*времяпровождение*) merriment.
весе́нн|ий (-яя, -ее, -ие) *прил* spring *опред*.
ве́|сить (-шу, -сишь) *несов неперех* to weigh.
ве́с|кий (-кая, -кое, -кие; -ок, -ка, -ко) *прил*: ~ **аргуме́нт** an argument that carries a lot of weight.
весл|о́ (-а́; *nom pl* **вёсла,** *gen pl* **вёсел)** *ср* oar.
весн|а́ (-ы́; *nom pl* **вёсны,** *gen pl* **вёсен)** *ж* spring.
весно́й *нареч* in (the) spring.
весно́ю *нареч* = **весно́й**.
весну́ш|ка (-ки; *gen pl* **-ек)** *ж* (*обычно мн*) freckle.
весово́й *прил* (*хлеб, конфеты итп*) *sold or bought by weight*; **весова́я катего́рия** (weight) category (*in boxing etc*).
ве́сок *прил см* **ве́ский**.
весо́м|ый (-, -а, -о) *прил* (*перен*) substantial.
вест (-а) *м* (*МОР*) west; (*ветер*) west wind.
ве́стерн (-а) *м* western.
ве|сти́ (-ду́, -дёшь; *pt* **вёл, -ла́, -ло́)** *несов перех* to take; (*машину, поезд*) to drive; (*корабль*) to navigate; (*войско, отряд*) to lead; (*собрание, заседание*) to chair; (*работу, исследования*) to conduct; (*хозяйство*) to run; (*дневник, записи*) to keep ◆ (*perf* **привести́**) *неперех*: ~ **к** *+dat* to lead to; ~ *(impf)* **себя́** to behave; ~ *(impf)* **речь о** *+prp* to talk about; ~ *(impf)* **нача́ло от** *+gen* to originate from
▸ **вести́сь** *несов возв* (*расследование*) to be carried out; (*переговоры*) to go on.
вестибю́л|ь (-я) *м* (*в гостинице*) lobby; (*в метро*) entrance hall.
ве́стник (-а) *м* messenger; (*перен*) herald; (*издание*) bulletin.
вест|ь (-и) *ж* news; **пропада́ть (пропа́сть** *perf***) бе́з ~и** (*ВОЕН*) to go missing; **бе́з ~и пропа́вший** (*ВОЕН*) missing feared dead; **Бог ~ кто/что** (*разг*) God knows who/what; **пье́са была́ не Бог ~ кака́я** (*разг*) the play wasn't up to much.
вес|ы́ (-о́в) *мн* scales *мн*; (*созвездие*): **В~** Libra.
весь (всего́; *см* **Table 13;** *f* **вся,** *nt* **всё,** *pl* **все)** *мест* (*целый, полностью*) all; ~ **день** all day; **я стара́лась изо всех сил** I tried with all my might; **он появи́лся ~ мо́крый/гря́зный** he appeared all wet/dirty; **при всём жела́нии я не смогу́ тебе́ помо́чь** with the best will in the world, I can't help you; **всего́ хоро́шего** *или* **до́брого!** all the best!; **без всего́** with nothing; **по всему́** (*по всем признакам*) by all the signs.
весьма́ *нареч* quite; ~ **непло́хо** not bad.
ветв|ь (-и; *gen pl* **-е́й)** *ж* branch.
ве́т|ер (-ра) *м* wind; **каки́м ~ром его́ сюда́ занесло́?** (*разг*) what brought him here?; **у него́ ~ в голове́** (*разг*) he hasn't a serious thought in his head.
ветера́н (-а) *м* veteran.
ветерина́р (-а) *м* vet (*inf*)) (= *veterinary surgeon,*) veterinarian (*US*).
ве́т|ка (-ки; *gen pl* **-ок)** *ж* branch; **железнодоро́жная ве́тка** branch line.
ве́то *ср нескл* veto; **накла́дывать (наложи́ть** *perf***)** ~ **на что-н** to veto sth.
ве́ток *сущ см* **ве́тка**.
ве́тра *сущ см* **ве́тер**.
ве́треный *прил* windy; (*девушка*) empty-headed.
ветро́в|ка (-и) *ж* windcheater.
ветрово́й *прил* wind *опред*; **ветрово́е стекло́** windscreen (*BRIT*), windshield (*US*).
ветря́н|ка (-ки) *ж* (*МЕД*) chickenpox.
ветрян|о́й *прил* (*двигатель*) wind-powered; **~а́я ме́льница** windmill.
ве́тх|ий (-ая, -ое, -ие; -, -а́, -о) *прил* (*старик*) decrepit; (*дом*) dilapidated; (*одежда*) shabby; **Ве́тхий Заве́т** the Old Testament.
ветхозаве́тный *прил* Old Testament *опред*; (*перен*) antediluvian.
ветч|ина́ (-ины́; *nom pl* **-и́ны)** *ж* ham.
ве́х|а (-и) *ж* (*обычно мн*) landmark.
ве́ч|е (-а) *ср* (*ИСТ*) *town assembly in medieval Russia*.
ве́чен *прил см* **ве́чный**.
ве́чер (-а; *nom pl* **-а́)** *м* evening; (*праздник*) party; **на ~е** at a party.
вечере́|ть (*3sg* **-ет)** *несов безл* to grow dark.
вечери́н|ка (-ки; *gen pl* **-ок)** *ж* party.
вече́рн|ий (-яя, -ее, -ие) *прил* evening *опред*; **~ие ку́рсы** evening classes.
вече́рник (-а) *м* (*разг*) part-timer (*studying in the evening*).
ве́чером *нареч* in the evening.
ве́чно *нареч* eternally; (*разг: жаловаться*) perpetually.
вечнозелёный *прил* evergreen.
ве́чност|ь (-и) *ж* eternity; **не ви́дел тебя́ це́лую** ~ (*разг*) I haven't seen you for ages.
ве́ч|ный (-ен, -на, -но) *прил* eternal, everlasting; (*бессрочный*) indefinite; (*no short form; разг: непрестанный*) perpetual; **ве́чная мерзлота́** permafrost; **ве́чные снега́** everlasting snows.
ве́шал|ка (-ки; *gen pl* **-ок)** *ж* (*планка*) rack; (*стойка*) hatstand; (*плечики*) coat hanger; (*гардероб*) cloakroom; (*петля*) loop.
ве́ша|ть (-ю; *perf* **пове́сить)** *несов перех* to hang; (*perf* **све́шать**; *товар*) to weigh; ~ **(пове́сить** *perf***) го́лову** to look downcast
▸ **ве́шаться** (*perf* **пове́ситься**) *несов возв* to hang o.s.; **~ся** *(impf)* **на ше́ю кому́-н** (*разг: пренебр*) to throw o.s. at sb.

ве́шу *несов см* **ве́сить.**
веща́|ть (*3sg* **-ет**, *3pl* **-ют**) *несов неперех* to broadcast; ~ *(impf)* **на Москву́** to broadcast to Moscow.
веще́ственный *прил* material; **веще́ственное доказа́тельство** material evidence.
веществ|о́ (**-а́**) *ср* substance.
ве́щ|ий (**-ая, -ее, -ие**) *прил* prophetic.
вещ|ь (**-и**; *gen pl* **-е́й**) *ж* thing; (*книга, фильм*) piece; **она́ оста́вила ве́щи в маши́не** she left her things in the car; **называ́ть (назва́ть** *perf*) **ве́щи свои́ми имена́ми** to call a spade a spade.
ве́яни|е (**-я**) *ср* breath; (*перен: в искусстве*) trend.
ве́|ять (**-ю, -ешь**) *несов неперех* (*ветер*) to blow lightly; (*флаг, парус*) to flutter; **в во́здухе ~ет весно́й** spring is in the air.
вжи́|ться (**-ву́сь, -вёшься**; *pt* **-лся, -ла́сь, -ло́сь**, *impf* **вжива́ться**) *сов возв*: ~ **в роль** to get into a role.
взад *нареч*: **~-вперёд** (*разг*) back and forth; **он не дви́гался ни ~ ни вперёд** he didn't budge (an inch).
взаи́мен *прил см* **взаи́мный.**
взаи́мност|ь (**-и**) *ж* mutual feeling; **любо́вь без ~и** unrequited love; **отвеча́ть** *(impf)* **кому́-н ~ю** to reciprocate sb's feelings; **по́льзоваться** *(impf)* **~ю** to be loved in return.
взаи́м|ный (**-ен, -на, -но**) *прил* mutual.
взаимовы́руч|ка (**-ки**; *gen pl* **-ек**) *ж* team spirit.
взаимоде́йстви|е (**-я**) *ср* (*связь*) interaction; (*поддержка*) cooperation.
взаимообусло́вленност|ь (**-и**) *ж* interdependence.
взаимоотноше́ни|е (**-я**) *ср* (*обычно мн*) (inter) relationship.
взаимопо́мощ|ь (**-и**) *ж* mutual assistance *или* aid.
взаимопонима́ни|е (**-я**) *ср* mutual understanding; **достига́ть (дости́гнуть** *или* **дости́чь** *perf*) **~я** to come to *или* reach a mutual understanding.
взаимосвя́з|ь (**-и**) *ж* interconnection.
взаймы́ *нареч*: **дава́ть/брать де́ньги ~** to lend/ borrow money.
взаме́н *нареч* in exchange ◆ *предл* (*+gen*; *вместо*) instead of; (*в обмен*) in exchange for; **он ничего́ не про́сит ~** he doesn't want anything in return.
взаперти́ *нареч* under lock and key; **сиде́ть** *(impf)* ~ (*перен*) to stay indoors.
взахлёб *нареч* (*разг*) eagerly; ~ **хвали́ть** *(impf)* **что-н** to gush over sth.
взба́дрива|ть (**-ю**) *несов от* **взбодри́ть.**
взба́лмош|ный (**-ен, -на, -но**) *прил* (*разг*) hysterical.
взба́лтыва|ть (**-ю**) *несов перех от* **взболта́ть.**
взбе́й(те) *сов см* **взбить.**
взберу́сь *сов см* **взобра́ться.**
взбе|си́ть(ся) (**-шу́(сь), -си́шь(ся)**) *сов от* **беси́ть(ся).**
взбива́|ть (**-ю**) *несов от* **взбить.**
взбира́|ться (**-юсь**) *несов от* **взобра́ться.**
взбить (**взобью́, взобьёшь**; *imper* **взбе́й(те)**) *сов перех* (*яйца*) to beat; (*сливки*) to whip; (*волосы*) to fluff up; (*подушки*) to plump up.
взбодр|и́ть (**-ю́, -и́шь**; *impf* **взба́дривать**) *сов перех* (*эмоционально*) to hearten, cheer; (*физически*) to invigorate.
взболта́|ть (**-ю**; *impf* **взба́лтывать**) *сов перех* to shake.
взбре|сти́ (**-ду́, -дёшь**; *pt* **взбрёл, -ла́, -ло́**) *сов неперех*: ~ **на́ гору** to slog up a hill; **ему́ ~ло́ в го́лову** *+infin* ... (*разг*) he took it into his head to ....
взбудора́ж|ить (**-у, -ишь**; *impf* **взбудора́живать** *или* **будора́жить**) *сов перех* to agitate.
взбунт|ова́ться (**-ую(сь)**) *сов возв* to rebel.
взбу́ч|ка (**-ки**; *gen pl* **-ек**) *ж* (*разг*) dressing-down.
взвал|и́ть (**-ю́, -ишь**; *impf* **взва́ливать**) *сов перех*: ~ **что-н на** *+acc* to haul sth up onto; **взва́ливать (~** *perf*) **отве́тственность на кого́-н** (*перен: разг*) to burden sb with responsibility.
взведу́ *итп сов см* **взвести́.**
взвёл *сов см* **взвести́.**
взве́|сить (**-шу, -сишь**; *impf* **взве́шивать**) *сов перех* (*товар*) to weigh; (*перен: факты*) to weigh up, consider.
взве|сти́ (**-ду́, -дёшь**; *pt* **взвёл, -ла́, -ло́**, *impf* **взводи́ть**) *сов перех*: **взводи́ть куро́к** to cock a gun.
взве́шен|ный (**-, -на, -но**) *прил* (*обдуманный*) considered; **во ~ном состоя́нии** (*перен: разг*) in suspense.
взве́шива|ть (**-ю**) *несов от* **взве́сить.**
взве́шу *сов см* **взве́сить.**
взвива́|ться (**-юсь**) *несов от* **взви́ться.**
взви́згн|уть (**-у, -ешь**; *impf* **взви́згивать**) *сов неперех* to let out a squeal.
взвин|ти́ть (**-чу́, -ти́шь**; *impf* **взви́нчивать**) *сов перех* (*разг: цены*) to jack up.
взви́нчен|ный (**-, -на, -но**) *прил* (*состояние*) agitated; **он взви́нчен** he is worked up.
вз|ви́ться (**-овью́сь, -овьёшься**; *impf* **взвива́ться**) *сов возв* to shoot up; (*перен*) to fly off the handle.
взвод (**-а**) *м* platoon; **на взво́де** (*курок*) cocked; (*разг: человек*) on edge.
взво|ди́ть (**-жу́, -ди́шь**) *несов от* **взвести́.**
взволно́ван|ный (**-, -на, -но**) *прил* (*в тревоге*) agitated; (*радостный*) excited.
взволн|ова́ть(ся) (**-у́ю(сь)**) *сов от* **волнова́ть(ся).**
взв|ыть (**-о́ю, -о́ешь**) *сов неперех* (*животное*,

человек) to howl; (*сирена*) to wail; ~ (*perf*) **от бо́ли** to howl in *или* with pain.
взгляд (-а) *м* glance; (*выражение*) look; (*перен*: *мнение*) view; **с пе́рвого взгля́да, на пе́рвый** ~ at first sight *или* glance; **обме́ниваться (обменя́ться** *perf*) **взгля́дами** to exchange glances; **на мой/твой** ~ in my/your view; **остана́вливать (останови́ть** *perf*) ~ **на** *+acc* to rest one's gaze on.
взгляну́ть (-у́, -ешь; *impf* **взгля́дывать**) *сов неперех*: ~ **на** *+acc* to look at; (*кратко*) to glance at; (*no impf*; *обратить внимание*) to look at.
взгромозди́ть (-жу́, -ди́шь; *impf* **взгроможда́ть**) *сов перех*: ~ (**на** *+prp*) to haul up (onto).
взгрустну́ться (*3sg* **-ётся**) *сов безл* (*+dat*; *разг*) to feel sad.
вздёрнуть (-у, -ешь; *impf* **вздёргивать**) *сов перех* to jerk up; (*руку*) to throw up; ~ (*perf*) **кого́-н на ви́селицу** (*разг*) to string sb up.
вздор (-а) *м* (*разг*) rubbish; **нести́** (*impf*) *или* **моло́ть** (*impf*) ~ (*разг*) to talk rubbish.
вздо́рен *прил см* **вздо́рный**.
вздо́рить (-ю, -ишь; *perf* **повздо́рить**) *несов неперех* to squabble.
вздо́рный (-ен, -на, -но) *прил* (*нелепый*) absurd; (*сварливый*) crotchety.
вздорожа́ть (-ю) *сов от* **дорожа́ть**.
вздох (-а) *м* (*облегчения итп*) sigh; (*ужаса*) gasp.
вздохну́ть (-у́, -нёшь) *сов неперех* to sigh; (*разг*: *отдохнуть*) to have a breather; **мне** ~ **не́когда** I'm rushed off my feet.
вздра́гивать (-ю) *несов от* **вздро́гнуть**.
вздремну́ть (-у́, -ёшь) *сов неперех* (*разг*) to have a nap *или* snooze.
вздро́гнуть (-у, -ешь) *сов неперех* to shudder.
вздува́ться (-юсь) *несов от* **взду́ться**.
взду́мать (-ю) *сов неперех* (*разг*): **он ~л заня́ться ру́сским языко́м** he took it into his head to learn Russian; **не ~йте лгать!** don't even think of lying!
вздуть (-ю, -ешь) *сов перех* (*разг*: *цены*) to inflate; **у него́ взду́ло живо́т** his stomach became bloated
▸ **взду́ться** (*impf* **вздува́ться**) *сов возв* (*щека, живот*) to swell up; (*разг*: *цены*) to shoot up.
вздыма́ться (*3sg* **-ется**, *3pl* **-ются**) *несов возв* (*грудь*) to heave; (*волны*) to rise.
вздыха́ть (-ю) *несов неперех* to sigh; (*тосковать*): ~ **о** *+prp* (*о молодости*) to yearn for; ~ (*impf*) **по** *+dat* to pine for.
взима́ние (-я) *ср* collecting.
взима́ть (-ю) *несов перех* to collect.
взла́мывать (-ю) *несов от* **взлома́ть**.
взлеле́ять (-ю) *сов от* **леле́ять**.
взлёт (-а) *м* (*самолёта*) takeoff; (*перен*: *мысли*) flight.
взлете́ть (-чу́, -ти́шь; *impf* **взлета́ть**) *сов неперех* (*птица*) to soar; (*самолёт*) to take off; **взлета́ть** (~ *perf*) **на во́здух** to explode.
взлётно-поса́дочный *прил*: **взлётно-поса́дочная полоса́** runway.
взлётный *прил*: **~ая полоса́** *или* **доро́жка** runway, airstrip.
взлечу́ *сов см* **взлете́ть**.
взлома́ть (-ю; *impf* **взла́мывать**) *сов перех* to break open, force.
взло́мщик (-а) *м* burglar.
взлохма́тить (-чу, -тишь) *сов от* **лохма́тить**.
взма́ливаться (-юсь) *несов от* **взмоли́ться**.
взмахну́ть (-у́, -ёшь; *impf* **взма́хивать**) *сов неперех* (*+instr*; *рукой*) to wave; (*крылом*) to flap.
взметну́ться (-у́сь, -ёшься) *сов возв* (*пыль, искры*) to fly up; (*пламя, конь*) to leap up.
взмоли́ться (-ю́сь, -ишься; *impf* **взма́ливаться**) *сов возв* to beg.
взмо́рье (-я) *ср* seashore.
взмути́ть (-чу́, -ти́шь) *сов от* **мути́ть**.
взмыть (-о́ю, -о́ешь; *impf* **взмыва́ть**) *сов неперех* to soar.
взнос (-а) *м* (*страховой*) payment; (*в фонд*) contribution; (*членский, вступительный*) fee; **ежеме́сячный** ~ monthly instalment.
взобра́ться (**взберу́сь, взберёшься**; *pt* **-лся, -ла́сь, -ло́сь**, *impf* **взбира́ться**) *сов возв*: ~ **на** *+acc* to climb (up) onto; **взбира́ться** (~ *perf*) **на́ гору** to climb (up) a hill.
взобью́ *итп сов см* **взбить**.
взовью́сь *итп сов см* **взви́ться**.
взойти́ (*как* **идти́**; *см* **Table 18**; *impf* **всходи́ть** *или* **восходи́ть**) *сов неперех* (*солнце, луна*) to rise; (*семена*) to come up; (*на гору, на престол*) to ascend.
взор (-а) *м* glance; (*выражение*) look.
взорва́ть (-у́, -ёшь; *pt* **-ал, -ала́, -а́ло**, *impf* **взрыва́ть**) *сов перех* (*бомбу*) to detonate; (*дом, мост*) to blow up
▸ **взорва́ться** (*impf* **взрыва́ться**) *сов возв* (*граната, бомба*) to explode; (*мост, дом*) to be blown up; (*разг*: *не сдержаться*) to blow up.
взошёл *итп сов см* **взойти́**.
взрасти́ть (-щу́, -сти́шь; *impf* **взра́щивать**) *сов перех* to cultivate, grow; (*перен*) to nurture.
взреве́ть (-у́, -ёшь) *сов неперех* to roar.
взро́слая (-ой; *decl like adj*) *ж см* **взро́слый**.
взросле́ть (-ю; *perf* **повзросле́ть**) *несов неперех* to grow up; (*духовно*) to mature.
взро́слый *прил* (*человек*) grown-up *опред*; (*фильм, билет, животное*) adult *опред* ◆ (**-ого**; *decl like adj*) *м* adult.
взрыв (-а) *м* explosion; (*дома*) blowing up; (*+gen*; *возмущения*) outburst of; **разда́лся** ~ there was an explosion; ~ **сме́ха** a burst of laughter.
взрыва́ть(ся) (-ю(сь)) *несов от* **взорва́ть(ся)**.
взрывно́й *прил*: **~а́я волна́** blast.
взрывоопа́сный (-ен, -на, -но) *прил* (*также перен*) explosive.
взрывча́тка (-ки; *gen pl* **-ок**) *ж* explosive

(substance); **закладывать (заложить** *perf*) **~ку** to plant an explosive.

взрывчатый *прил* explosive.

взрыхл|ить (-ю, -ишь) *сов от* **рыхлить** ◆ (*impf* **взрыхлять**) *перех* to break up.

взъерош|ить (-ю, -ишь) *сов от* **ерошить**.

взыва|ть (-ю; *perf* **воззвать**) *несов неперех*: **~ к кому-н о** *+prp* to appeal to sb for; **~ (воззвать** *perf*) **к чьему-н милосердию/разуму** to appeal to sb's sense of compassion/reason.

взыскани|е (-я) *ср* (*долга*) recovery; (*штрафа*) exaction; (*выговор*) reprimand; **накладывать (наложить** *perf*) **~ на кого-н** to reprimand sb.

взыскател|ьный (-ен, -ьна, -ьно) *прил* (*публика*) demanding; (*начальник*) exacting; (*критика*) severe.

взы|скать (-щу, -щешь; *impf* **взыскивать**) *сов перех* (*долг*) to recover; (*штраф*) to exact ◆ *неперех*: **~ с кого-н** to call sb to account; **не ~щите!** I'm sorry!

взяти|е (-я) *ср* (*власти, территории*) seizure; (*города, крепости*) capture.

взят|ка (-ки; *gen pl* **-ок**) *ж* (*подкуп*) bribe; (*КАРТЫ*) trick; **давать (дать** *perf*) **кому-н ~ку** to bribe sb; **брать** (*impf*) **~ку** to take a bribe.

взяточник (-а) *м* bribe-taker.

взяточниц|а (-ы) *ж см* **взяточник**.

взя|ть (возьму, возьмёшь; *pt* **-л, -ла, -ло**) *сов от* **брать** ◆ *перех* (*разг*) to nick; **возьму и** *или* **да и откажусь** (*разг*) I could refuse just like that; **~л да и поехал** (*разг*) he upped and left; **~** *или* **возьмите хотя бы такой пример** let's take this example; **с чего** *или* **откуда ты ~л** (*разг*: *пренебр*) whatever gave you that idea?

▸ **взяться** *сов от* **браться** ◆ *возв*: **откуда ни возьмись, появилась Маша** Masha appeared from out of the blue *или* as if from nowhere.

вибрир|овать (-ую) *несов неперех* to vibrate.

вивисекци|я (-и) *ж* vivisection.

вид (-а; *part gen* **-у**, *loc sg* **-у**) *м* (*внешность*) appearance; (*состояние*: *предмета*) form; (*панорама*) view; (*разновидность*: *растений, животных*) species; (: *спорта*) type; (: *искусства*) form; (*линг*) aspect; (*состояние*): **у него больной/сердитый ~** he looks ill/angry; **в виде** *+gen* in the form of; **на ~у у** *+gen* in full view of; **под видом** *+gen* in the guise of; **~ на озеро/горы/площадь** a view of the lake/hills/square; **в виде шутки** as a joke; **иметь** (*impf*) **в ~у** to mean; (*учитывать*) to bear in mind; **скрываться (скрыться** *perf*)**/исчезать (исчезнуть** *perf*) **из вида** to hide/disappear from view; **делать (сделать** *perf*) **~** to pretend; **упускать (упустить** *perf*) **из виду что-н** (*перен*) to lose sight of sth; **терять (потерять** *perf*) **кого-н из виду** to lose sight of sb; **вид на жительство** residence permit; *см также* **виды**.

вида|ть (-ю; *perf* **повидать**) *несов перех* to see; (*испытать*) to know ◆ *вводн сл* obviously; **где это видано!** (*разг*) whatever next!

▸ **видаться** (*perf* **повидаться**) *несов возв* (*разг*) to see each other.

виден *прил см* **видный**.

видени|е (-я) *ср* vision.

видени|е (-я) *ср* (*во сне*) vision; (*призрак*) apparition.

видеозапис|ь (-и) *ж* video (recording).

видеоигр|а (-ы; *nom pl* **-ы**) *ж* video game.

видеокамер|а (-ы) *ж* camcorder, videocamera.

видеокассет|а (-ы) *ж* video cassette.

видеомагнитофон (-а) *м* video (recorder).

видеоплён|ка (-ки; *gen pl* **-ок**) *ж* (video) tape.

видеофильм (-а) *м* video (film).

ви|деть (-жу, -дишь) *несов неперех* to see ◆ (*perf* **увидеть**) *перех* to see; (*испытать*) to know; **рад Вас ~** it's good to see you; **~дите ли** you see; **(там) увидим** (*разг*) we'll see

▸ **видеться** *несов от* **привидеться** ◆ (*perf* **увидеться**) *возв* to see each other; **выход ~дится в экономии средств** economizing is viewed as the solution; **мы с ним часто ~димся** we see a lot of each other.

видимо *вводн сл* it looks like; **он, ~, не придёт** it looks like he's not coming.

видимо-невидимо *нареч* (*разг*): **народу на площади ~** there are masses of people in the square.

видимост|ь (-и) *ж* visibility; (*подобие*) outward appearance; **по всей ~и** seemingly; **для ~и** for the sake of appearances.

видим|ый (-, -а, -о) *прил* visible; (*no short form*; *кажущийся*) superficial; **~ экспорт/импорт** visible exports/imports *мн*.

видне|ться (*3sg* **-ется**, *3pl* **-ются**) *несов возв* to be visible.

видно *как сказ* (*можно видеть*) one can see; (*можно понять*) clearly ◆ *вводн сл* probably; **из окна ~ горы** you can see the hills from the window; **~, что он волнуется** clearly he is worried; **~, он устал** he is probably tired; **тебе виднее** you know best; **как ~** as it happens; **там ~ будет** we'll see.

вид|ный (-ен, -на, -но, -ны) *прил* (*заметный*) visible; (*no short form*; *известный*) prominent; (*привлекательный*): **он ~ мужчина** he's a fine figure of a man; **~ен успех** success is in sight.

видоизмен|ить (-ю, -ишь; *impf* **видоизменять**) *сов перех* to modify

▸ **видоизмениться** (*impf* **видоизменяться**) *сов возв* to alter.

вид|ы (-ов) *мн* prospects *мн*; **иметь** (*impf*) **~ на что-н** to have one's sights set on sth.

вижу(сь) *несов см* **видеть(ся)**.

виз|а (-ы) *ж* visa; (*директора, редактора*) official stamp.

византийск|ий (-ая, -ое, -ие) *ж* Byzantine.

Византи|я (-и) *ж* Byzantine Empire.
визг (-а) *м* (*собаки*) yelp; (*ребёнка, поросенка*) squeal; (*человека*) shriek; (*металла, тормозов итп*) screech.
визж|áть (-ý, -ишь) *несов неперех* (*см сущ*) to yelp; to squeal; to shriek; to screech.
визи́р|овать (-ую; *perf* **завизи́ровать**) *несов перех* (*документ*) to stamp; **емý ~овали пáспорт** he was issued with a visa.
визи́т (-а) *м* visit; **прибывáть (прибыть** *perf*) **с ~ом** to arrive on an official visit; **дéлать (сдéлать** *perf*) *или* **наноси́ть (нанести́** *perf*) **~ комý-н** to visit sb.
визи́тн|ый *прил*: **~ая кáрточка** (business) card.
визуáл|ьный (-ен, -ьна, -ьно) *прил* visual.
викáри|й (-я) *м* vicar.
виктори́н|а (-ы) *ж* quiz game.
ви́л|ка (-ки; *gen pl* -ок) *ж* fork; **штéпсельная ~** two-pin plug.
ви́лл|а (-ы) *ж* villa.
ви́лок *сущ см* **ви́лка**.
ви́л|ы (-) *мн* pitchfork *ед*; **~ами на водé пи́сано** (*разг*) it's pie in the sky.
вильн|ýть (-ý, -ёшь) *сов неперех*: **~** *+instr* (*хвостом*) to wag; (*бёдрами*) to wiggle; (*дорога, река итп*) to bend sharply.
Ви́льнюс (-а) *м* Vilnius.
виля́|ть (-ю) *несов неперех*: **~** *+instr* (*хвостом*) to wag; (*бёдрами*) to wiggle; (*дорога, река итп*) to wind (along); (*перен: разг: человек*) to be shifty.
вин|á (-ы́; *nom pl* -ы) *м* (*чувство*) guilt; (*ответственность*) blame; **возлагáть (возложи́ть** *perf*) **~ý на** *+acc* to place the blame on; **авáрия произошлá по егó ~é** the accident was his fault, he was to blame for the accident.
винегрéт (-а) *м* beetroot salad.
вини́тельный *прил*: **~ падéж** accusative (case).
вин|и́ть (-ю́, -и́шь) *несов перех*: **~ когó-н в** *+prp* to blame sb for; (*упрекать*): **~ когó-н за** *+acc* to accuse sb of.
вин|ó (-á; *nom pl* -а) *ср* wine.
виновáт|ый *прил* (*взгляд итп*) guilty; (-, -а, -о): **~ (в** *+prp*) (*в проигрыше, неудаче*) responsible (for), to blame (for); **~!** sorry!, excuse me!; **чýвствовать** (*impf*) **себя́ ~ым** to feel guilty; **он виновáт пéред дрýгом** he has failed his friend; **он виновáт в том, что ...** it is his fault that ....
винóвен *прил см* **винóвный**.
винóвн|ая (-ой; *decl like adj*) *ж см* **винóвный**.
винóвник (-а) *м* culprit; **он – ~ трагéдии** he is to blame for the tragedy.
винóвниц|а (-ы) *ж см* **винóвник**.
винóвност|ь (-и) *ж* guilt; **устанáвливать (установи́ть** *perf*) **~** to establish guilt.
винóв|ный (-ен, -на, -но) *прил* guilty ♦ (-ного; *decl like adj*) *м* guilty party; **признавáть (признáть** *perf*) **себя́ ~ным** to plead guilty.
виногрáд (-а) *м* (*растение*) (grape)vine; (*ягоды*) grapes *мн*.
виногрáдник (-а) *м* vineyard.
винодéли|е (-я) *ср* wine-making.
винт (-á) *м* screw; (*самолёта*) propeller.
ви́нтик (-а) *м* screw.
винтóв|ка (-ки; *gen pl* -ок) *ж* rifle.
виньéт|ка (-ки; *gen pl* -ок) *ж* vignette.
виóл|а (-ы) *ж* (*муз*) viol.
виолончели́ст (-а) *м* cellist.
виолончели́ст|ка (-ки; *gen pl* -ок) *ж см* **виолончели́ст**.
виолончéл|ь (-и) *ж* cello.
ви́ра *межд*: **~!** lift!
вирáж (-á) *м* (*поворот*) turn; (*СПОРТ*) bend.
виртуáльный *прил* (*КОМП*) virtual.
виртуóз (-а) *м* virtuoso.
виртуóз|ный (-ен, -на, -но) *прил* masterly; **~ное исполнéние** a virtuoso performance.
ви́рус (-а) *м* virus.
вис *итп несов см* **ви́снуть**.
ви́селиц|а (-ы) *ж* gallows *ед*.
ви|сéть (-шý, -си́шь) *несов неперех* to hang; (*угрожать*): **~ над** *+instr* to hang over; **~** (*impf*) **в вóздухе** (*перен*) to be up in the air; **у негó на шéе ~ся́т рóдственники жены́** (*разг*) his wife's relatives are a burden to him; **~** (*impf*) **на телефóне** (*разг*) to spend ages on the phone.
вискá *сущ см* **висóк**.
ви́ски *ср нескл* whisky (*BRIT*), whiskey (*US, IRELAND*).
вискóз|а (-ы) *ж* viscose.
Ви́сл|а (-ы) *ж* Vistula (*river*).
ви́с|нуть (-ну, -нешь; *pt* -, -ла, -ло, *perf* **пови́снуть**) *несов неперех* (*цветы*) to droop; (*волосы*) to hang limply; **~** (*impf*) **у когó-н на шéе** (*перен*) to cling to sb.
вис|óк (-кá) *м* (*АНАТ*) temple.
високóсный *прил*: **~ год** leap year.
ви́ст (-а) *м* whist.
вися́ч|ий (-ая, -ее, -ие) *прил*: **~ мост** suspension bridge; **закрепля́ть (закрепи́ть** *perf*) **что-н в ~ем положéнии** to suspend sth.
витами́н (-а) *м* vitamin.
витá|ть (-ю) *несов неперех* (*запах*) to hang in the air; **~** *perf* **над** *+instr* (*опасность, смерть*) to hang *или* hover over; **~** (*impf*) **в облакáх** (*перен*) to have one's head in the clouds.
витиевáт|ый (-, -а, -о) *прил* flowery.
виткá *сущ см* **витóк**.
витóй *прил* twisted; (*лестница*) spiral.
вит|óк (-кá) *м* (*спирали*) twist; (*перен: этап*) stage.
витрáж (-á) *м* stained-glass window.
витри́н|а (-ы) *ж* (*в магазине*) shop window; (*в музее*) display case.
витри́но-вы́ставочн|ый *прил*: **~ая реклáма** display advertising.
ви|ть (вью, вьёшь; *pt* -л, -лá, -ло, *imper* **вей(те)**, *perf* **свить**) *несов перех* (*венок, веревку*) to weave; (*гнездо*) to build
▸ **ви́ться** *несов возв* (*растения*) to trail; (*волосы*) to curl; (*флаг, лента*) to flutter; (*дым*) to spiral up.
вих|óр (-рá) *м* forelock.

вихр|ь (-я) *м* whirlwind; (*перен*: *революции*) maelstrom; (: *развлечений*) whirl.
ви́це-председа́тел|ь (-я) *м* vice-chairman.
ви́це-президе́нт (-а) *м* vice president.
ВИЧ *м сокр* (= *ви́рус иммунодефици́та челове́ка*) HIV (= *human immunodeficiency virus*); **~инфици́рованный** HIV-positive.
ви́шен *сущ см* **ви́шня**.
вишнёвый *прил* cherry.
ви́ш|ня (-ни; *gen pl* **-ен)** *ж* (*дерево*) cherry (tree); (*плод*) cherry.
вишу́ *несов см* **висе́ть**.
вишь *част* (*разг*) (just) look (*used sarcastically*); **~ (ты), како́й он сме́лый** look how brave he is, what a hero.
вка́лыва|ть (-ю) *несов от* **вколо́ть** ♦ *неперех* (*no perf*; *разг*) to slog.
вка́пыва|ть (-ю) *несов от* **вкопа́ть**.
вка|ти́ть (-чу́, -тишь; *impf* **вка́тывать)** *сов перех* (*тачку, коляску*) to wheel in; (*бочку*) to roll in; (*перен*: *разг*): **~ кому́-н пощёчину/вы́говор** to give sb a slap across the face/a dressing-down.
вклад (-а) *м* (*действие*) investment; (*в банке*) deposit; (*в науку, в литературу*) contribution; **вноси́ть (внести́** *perf*) **~ в** *+acc* to make a contribution to.
вкла́дчик (-а) *м* investor.
вкла́дчиц|а (-ы) *ж см* **вкла́дчик**.
вкла́дыва|ть (-ю) *несов от* **вложи́ть**.
вкла́дыш (-а) *м* (*в книге, в альбоме*) insert; (*в детали*) inlay.
включа́|ть (-ю) *несов от* **включи́ть** ♦ *перех*: **~ (в себя́)** to include
▸ **включа́ться** *несов от* **включи́ться**.
включа́я *предл* (*+acc*) including; **пришли́ все ~ дире́ктора** everybody came including the director.
включи́тельно *нареч* inclusive; **с 1-го по 5-ое ма́я ~** from (the) 1st to (the) 5th of May inclusive.
включ|и́ть (-у́, -и́шь; *impf* **включа́ть)** *сов перех* to turn *или* switch on; **включа́ть (~** *perf*) **кого́-н в что-н** to include sb in sth
▸ **включи́ться** (*impf* **включа́ться**) *сов возв* to come on; (*присоединиться*): **~ся в** *+acc* to join in.
вкол|о́ть (-ю́, -ёшь; *impf* **вка́лывать)** *сов перех* to stick in.
вконе́ц *нареч* completely and utterly.
вкопа́|ть (-ю; *impf* **вка́пывать)** *сов перех*: **~ что-н в** *+acc* to sink sth into.
вкось *нареч* at an angle; **смотре́ть (посмотре́ть** *perf*) **~ на кого́-н** to look at sb out of the corner of one's eye.
вкраду́сь *итп сов см* **вкра́сться**.
вкра́дчив|ый (-, -а, -о) *прил* ingratiating.
вкра́дыва|ться (-юсь) *несов от* **вкра́сться**.
вкрапле́ни|е (-я) *ср* (*обычно мн*: *в горных породах*) fragment; (*в тексте*) interspersion.
вкра́|сться (-ду́сь, -дёшься; *impf* **вкра́дываться)** *сов возв* to creep in; **вкра́дываться (~** *perf*) **в дове́рие к кому́-н** to worm one's way into sb's confidence.
вкра́тце *нареч* briefly.
вкривь *нареч*: **~ и вкось** (*разг*) squint.
вкругову́ю *нареч*: **ходи́ть ~** to go the long way round.
вкру|ти́ть (-чу́, -ти́шь; *impf* **вкру́чивать)** *сов перех* to screw in.
вкруту́ю *нареч* hard-boiled; **вари́ть (свари́ть** *perf*) **яйцо́ ~** to hard-boil an egg.
вкру́чива|ть (-ю) *несов от* **вкрути́ть**.
вкручу́ *сов см* **вкрути́ть**.
вку́пе *нареч*: **~ с** *+instr* together with.
вкус (-а; *part gen* **-у)** *м* taste; **про́бовать (попро́бовать** *perf*) **что-н на ~** (*еду*) to taste sth; **на чей-н ~, в чьём-н вку́се** to sb's taste; **приходи́ться (прийти́сь** *perf*) **кому́-н по вку́су** to be to sb's taste *или* liking; **она́ оде́та со вку́сом** she is tastefully dressed; **входи́ть (войти́** *perf*) **во ~** to start to enjoy o.s.; **о вку́сах не спо́рят** there is no accounting for taste.
вку́сен *прил см* **вку́сный**.
вку́сно *нареч* tastily ♦ *как сказ*: **о́чень ~** it's delicious; **она́ ~ гото́вит** she is a good cook; **здесь ~ ко́рмят** the food here is very good.
вку́с|ный (-ен, -на́, -но) *прил* tasty; **обе́д был о́чень ~** the lunch was delicious.
вла́г|а (-и) *ж* moisture.
влага́лищ|е (-а) *ср* vagina.
владе́л|ец (-ьца) *м* (*магазина, завода*) owner, proprietor; (*книги, картины*) owner.
владе́лиц|а (-ы) *ж см* **владе́лец**.
владе́льца *сущ см* **владе́лец**.
владе́ни|е (-я) *ср* estate; (*заводом*) ownership; (*обычно мн*: *британские итп*) possession; **вступа́ть (вступи́ть** *perf*) **во ~ чем-н** to assume ownership *или* possession of sth.
владе́|ть (-ю) *несов неперех* (*+instr*; *обладать*) to own, possess; (*уметь пользоваться*): **хорошо́ ~ шпа́гой** to be a proficient *или* skilful swordsman; **~** (*impf*) **собо́й** to control o.s.; **~** (*impf*) **рука́ми/нога́ми** to have the use of one's arms/legs; **она́ в соверше́нстве ~ет англи́йским** she has a perfect command of English.
Владивосто́к (-а) *м* Vladivostok.
Владикавка́з (-а) *м* Vladikavkaz.
вла́жность (-и) *ж* humidity.
вла́ж|ный (-ен, -на́, -но) *прил* (*земля, воздух*) damp; (*глаза, кожа*) moist.
вла́ств|овать (-ую) *несов неперех*: **~ над** *+instr* to rule; (*перен*) to hold sway over.
вла́стен *прил см* **вла́стный**.
вла́ст|и (-е́й) *мн* authorities *мн*.
вла́ст|ный (-ен, -на, -но) *прил* (*человек*,

характер) imperious; **он не ~ен** *+infin* ... it's not within his power to ....

власт|ь (-и; *gen pl* **-е́й**) *ж* (*политическая*) power; (*родительская*) authority; **быть** *(impf)* **у вла́сти** to be in power; **приходи́ть (прийти́** *perf*) **к вла́сти** to come to power; **теря́ть (потеря́ть** *perf*) **~ над собо́й** to lose one's self-control; *см также* **вла́сти.**

вле́во *нареч* (to the) left; **~ от доро́ги** to the left of the road.

влез|ть (-у, -ешь; *pt* -, -ла, -ло, *impf* **влеза́ть**) *сов неперех*: **~ на** *+acc* (*на дерево*) to climb (up); (*на крышу, на стул итп*) to climb onto; **влеза́ть** (~ *perf*) **в** *+acc* (*забраться*) to climb into; (*разг*: *в трамвай, в автобус итп*) to get on; (*пренебр*: *в разговор*) to butt in on; (: *в дело*) to meddle in; **ешь ско́лько вле́зет** (*разг*) eat as much as you want *или* like.

вле́й(те) *сов см* **влить.**

влёк *итп несов см* **влечь.**

влеку́ *итп несов см* **влечь.**

вле|те́ть (-чу́, -ти́шь; *impf* **влета́ть**) *сов неперех*: **~ в** *+acc* to fly into ◆ *безл* (*+dat*; *разг*) to be told off; **ему́ ~те́ло от учи́теля за опозда́ние** he was told off by his teacher for being late.

влече́ни|е (-я) *ср*: **~ (к** *+dat*) (*к человеку*) attraction (to); (*к искусству итп*) liking (for); (*к науке, к политике*) interest (in).

влечу́ *сов см* **влете́ть.**

вле|чь (-ку́, -чёшь *итп*, -ку́т; *pt* **влёк, -кла́, -кло́,** *perf* **повле́чь**) *несов перех*: **~ за собо́й** to lead to; (*no perf*): **его́ ~чёт нау́ка** he is drawn to science.

влива́ни|е (-я) *ср* injection.

влива́|ть (-ю) *несов от* **влить.**

вли́п|нуть (-ну, -нешь; *pt* -, -ла, -ло) *сов неперех* (*в мёд*) to get stuck; (*перен*: *разг*) to get into a mess.

вли|ть (волью, вольёшь; *pt* -л, -ла́, -ло, *imper* **вле́й(те)**, *impf* **влива́ть**) *сов перех* to pour in; (*перен*: *средства*) to inject

▸ **вли́ться** *сов возв*: **вли́ться в** *+acc* to flow into.

влия́ни|е (-я) *ср* influence; **ока́зывать (оказа́ть** *perf*) **~ на** *+acc* to influence, have an influence on; **под ~м** *+gen* under the influence of.

влия́тел|ьный (-ен, -ьна, -ьно) *прил* influential.

влия́|ть (-ю) *несов неперех*: **~ на** *+acc* (*на людей, на события*) to influence; (*на организм, на климат*) to affect; **хорошо́/пло́хо ~** *(impf)* **на** *+acc* to have a good/bad influence on.

ВЛКСМ *м сокр* (*ист*: = *Всесою́зный Ле́нинский Коммунисти́ческий Сою́з Молодёжи*) Leninist Communist Youth League.

вложе́ни|е (-я) *ср* (*обычно мн*: *ЭКОН*) investment.

влож|и́ть (-у́, -ишь; *impf* **вкла́дывать**) *сов перех* (*средства, деньги*) to invest; (*положить внутрь*) to insert.

влюб|и́ться (-лю́сь, -ишься; *impf* **влюбля́ться**) *сов возв*: **~ в** *+acc* to fall in love with; **влюбля́ться** (~ *perf*) **в кого́-н с пе́рвого взгля́да** to fall in love with sb at first sight.

влюблён|ный (-, -а́, -о) *прил* in love; (*no short form*; *взгляд, глаза*) loving ◆ (-ного; *decl like adj*) *м*: **~ные** lovers; **смотре́ть** *(impf)* **на кого́-н ~ными глаза́ми** to look lovingly at sb.

влюблю́сь *сов см* **влюби́ться.**

влюбля́|ться (-юсь) *несов от* **влюби́ться.**

вмен|и́ть (-ю́, -и́шь; *impf* **вменя́ть**) *несов перех*: **~ что-н кому́-н в вину́** to lay the blame for sth on sb; **вменя́ть** (~ *perf*) **кому́-н в обя́занность** *+infin* to charge sb to do.

вменя́ем|ый (-, -а, -о) *прил* (*ЮР*) of sound mind.

вменя́|ть (-ю) *несов от* **вмени́ть.**

вме́сте *нареч* together; **~ с** *+instr* together with; **~ с тем** at the same time.

вмести́тел|ьный (-ен, -ьна, -ьно) *прил* (*помещение, автобус*) spacious; **э́тот чемода́н о́чень ~** this suitcase holds a lot.

вме|сти́ть (-щу́, -сти́шь; *impf* **вмеща́ть**) *сов перех* (*подлеж*: *зал*) to hold; (: *гостиница*) to accommodate; (*уместить*): **~ что-н/кого́-н в** *+acc* to fit sth/sb into

▸ **вмести́ться** (*impf* **вмеща́ться**) *несов возв* to fit in.

вме́сто *предл* (*+gen*; *взамен*) instead of; (*замещая*) in place *или* instead of ◆ *союз*: **~ того́ что́бы** instead of, rather than; **пошли́ в теа́тр ~ конце́рта** let's go to the theatre instead of the concert; **он рабо́тает ~ отца́** he's standing in for his father; **~ того́ что́бы критикова́ть, постара́йтесь поня́ть** try and understand instead of just criticizing.

вмеша́тельств|о (-а) *ср* (*в разговор, в спор*) interference; (*ВОЕН, ЭКОН*) intervention.

вмеша́|ть (-ю; *impf* **вме́шивать**) *сов перех* (*добавить*) to mix in; (*перен*): **~ кого́-н в** *+acc* to get sb mixed up in

▸ **вмеша́ться** (*impf* **вме́шиваться**) *сов возв* (*вторгнуться*) to interfere; (*присоединиться*: *в переговоры итп*) to intervene.

вмеща́|ть(ся) (-ю(сь)) *несов от* **вмести́ть(ся).**

вмещу́(сь) *сов см* **вмести́ть(ся).**

вмиг *нареч* instantly.

вмонти́р|овать (-ую) *сов перех*: **~ что-н в** *+acc* to fix sth to.

вмя́тин|а (-ы) *ж* dent.

внаём *нареч*: **отдава́ть ~** to let, rent out; **«сдаётся ~»** (*объявление*) "to let (*BRIT*) *или* rent (*US*)".

внаймы́ *нареч* = **внаём.**

внакла́де *как сказ* (*разг*): **остава́ться ~** to come out worse off.

внача́ле *нареч* at first; **~ она́ испуга́лась** at first she was scared.

вне *предл* (*+gen*) outside; (*чьих-н обязанностей*) outwith; (*сверх*: *плана*) over and above; **~ о́череди** out of turn; **он был ~ себя́** he was beside himself; **э́то ~ вся́кого сомне́ния** that is beyond any doubt.

внебра́чный *прил* (*отношения*) extramarital;

(*ребёнок*) illegitimate.
внедоро́жник (**-а**) *м* four-wheel drive.
внедре́ни|е (**-я**) *ср* introduction.
внедр|и́ть (**-ю́, -и́шь**; *impf* **внедря́ть**) *сов перех* (*ввести*) to introduce
▸ **внедри́ться** (*impf* **внедря́ться**) *сов возв* (*методы*) to become established; (*идеи, традиции*) to take root.
внеза́п|ный (**-ен, -на, -но**) *прил* sudden.
внекла́ссный *прил* extracurricular.
внема́точ|ный *прил*: **~ная бере́менность** ectopic pregnancy.
внеочередно́й *прил* unscheduled; (*заседание*) extraordinary.
внес|ти́ (**-у́, -ёшь**; *pt* **внёс, -сла́, -сло́**, *impf* **вноси́ть**) *сов перех* (*вещи, мебель итп*) to carry *или* bring in; (*взнос, сумму*) to pay; (*законопроект*) to bring in; (*поправку, параграф*) to insert; (*раздор, путаницу*) to cause; **вноси́ть** (**~** *perf*) **предложе́ние/пла́ту** to make a proposal/payment; **он внёс оживле́ние в вечери́нку** he livened up the party; **вноси́ть** (**~** *perf*) **я́сность в де́ло** to shed light on the proceedings.
внешко́льный *прил* extracurricular.
вне́шне *нареч* outwardly.
внешнеполити́ческ|ий (**-ая, -ое, -ие**) *прил* foreign-policy.
внешнеторго́в|ый *прил* (*связи, оборот*) foreign-trade.
вне́шн|ий (**-яя, -ее, -ие**) *прил* (*стена*) exterior *опред*; (*спокойствие*) outward; (*связи*) external; **~яя охра́на** outer guard; **~ мир** outside world; **~яя сторона́** *+gen* the outside of; **вне́шний вид** appearance; **вне́шняя поли́тика** foreign policy; **вне́шняя торго́вля** foreign trade.
вне́шност|ь (**-и**) *ж* appearance; **у неё прия́тная ~** she is good-looking.
вешта́тный *прил* freelance.
Внешторгба́нк (**-а**) *м сокр* (= *Банк для вне́шней торго́вли*) foreign trade bank.
вниз *нареч*; **~** (**по** *+dat*) down; **~ по тече́нию** downstream.
внизу́ *нареч* below; (*в здании*) downstairs ◆ *предл* (*+gen*): **~ страни́цы** at the foot *или* bottom of the page; **доро́га прохо́дит ~** the road runs down below; **~ магази́н нахо́дится** there is a shop on the ground (*BRIT*) *или* first (*US*) floor.
вни́к|нуть (**-ну, -нешь**; *pt* **-, -ла, -ло**, *impf* **вника́ть**) *сов неперех*: **~ в** *+acc* to understand.
внима́ни|е (**-я**) *ср* attention; **~ю покупа́телей/пассажи́ров!** attention all shoppers/passengers!; **привлека́ть** (**привле́чь** *perf*) **~ к** *+dat* to draw attention to; **принима́ть** (**приня́ть** *perf*) **во ~ что-н** to take sth into account *или* consideration; **ока́зывать** (**оказа́ть** *perf*) **~ кому́-н** to pay attention to sb.
внима́тельност|ь (**-и**) *ж* (*в работе*) care; (*заботливость*) attentiveness.
внима́тел|ьный (**-ен, -ьна, -ьно**) *прил* (*сосредоточенный*) attentive; (*тщательный*) careful; (*заботливый*): **~ к** *+dat* attentive to.
внима́|ть (**-ю**) *несов от* **внять**.
вничью́ *нареч* (*СПОРТ*): **сыгра́ть ~** to draw.
вновь *нареч* again.
вно|си́ть (**-шу́, -сишь**) *несов от* **внести́**.
ВНП *м сокр* (= *валово́й национа́льный проду́кт*) GNP (= *gross national product*).
вну|к (**-ка**; *nom pl* **-ки** *или* **-ча́та**) *м* grandson; *см также* **вну́ки**.
вну́к|и (**-ов**) *мн* grandchildren *мн*.
вну́тренне *нареч* inwardly.
вну́тренн|ий (**-яя, -ее, -ие**) *прил* (*поверхность, стенка*) interior; (*побуждение, голос*) inner; (*политика, рынок*) domestic; (*рана, кровотечение*) internal; **Министе́рство вну́тренних дел** ≈ the Home Office (*BRIT*), ≈ the Department of the Interior (*US*); **вну́тренние о́рганы** internal organs *мн*.
вну́тренност|и (**-ей**) *мн* (*АНАТ*) insides *мн*; (*КУЛИН*) offal *ед*.
вну́тренност|ь (**-и**) *ж*: **~** (*+gen*) interior (of); *см также* **вну́тренности**.
внутри́ *нареч* inside; (*в пределах, в рамках*) within ◆ *предл*: **~** *+gen* (*дома, ящика*) inside; (*организации*) within.
внутриве́нный *прил* intravenous.
внутриполити́ческ|ий (**-ая, -ое, -ие**) *прил* (*кризис*) internal political *опред*; **~ая борьба́** political infighting.
внутрь *нареч* inside ◆ *предл* (*+gen*) inside; **принима́ть** (*impf*) **лека́рство ~** to be taken internally.
внуча́та *сущ см* **внук**.
внуча́т(н)ый *прил*: **~ племя́нник** great-nephew.
вну́ч|ка (**-ки**; *gen pl* **-ек**) *ж* granddaughter.
внуша́|ть (**-ю**) *несов от* **внуши́ть**.
внуши́тел|ьный (**-ен, -ьна, -ьно**) *прил* (*внешность*) imposing; (*сумма, успех*) impressive.
внуш|и́ть (**-у́, -и́шь**; *impf* **внуша́ть**) *сов перех* (*вызвать*) to inspire; **внуша́ть** (**~** *perf*) **что-н кому́-н** to instil (*BRIT*) *или* instill (*US*) sth in sb.
вня́т|ный (**-ен, -на, -но**) *прил* (*отчётливый*) clear; (*вразумительный*) intelligible.
вня|ть (*pt* **-л, -ла́, -ло**, *impf* **внима́ть**) *сов неперех* (*+dat*; *просьбам*) to heed.
В.О. *м сокр* = *Васи́льевский о́стров (Петербу́рг)*.
ВО *м сокр* = *вое́нный о́круг*.
во *предл см* **в** ◆ *част* (*разг*: *вот*) there; (*: выражает согласие*) that's it; (*: выражает оценку*) great.
во́бл|а (**-ы**) *ж* Caspian roach.

The spelling rules for Russian are shown on page xvii.

вобрá|ть (вберý, вберёшь; *pt* **-л, -лá, -ло**, *impf* **вбирáть)** *сов перех* (*воздух, воду*) to take in; **вбирáть** (~ *perf*) **в себя** to incorporate; **вбирáть** (~ *perf*) **гóлову в плéчи** to hunch one's shoulders.

вовéк(и) *нареч* (*навек*) forever; (*никогда*) never; ~ **егó не прощý** I will never forgive him.

вовл|éчь (-екý, -ечёшь *итп* **-екýт**; *pt* **-ёк, -еклá, -еклó**, *impf* **вовлекáть)** *сов перех*: ~ **когó-н в** *+acc* (*в разговор, в спор*) to draw sb into; (*в работу*) to involve sb in.

вóвремя *нареч* on time.

вóвсе *нареч* (*разг*) completely; ~ **нет** not at all; **онá на тебя ~ не сéрдится** she's not angry with you at all.

вовсю *нареч* (*разг*): **бежáть/гнать (машйну)** ~ to run/drive as fast as one can; **он старáется** ~ he is giving it his all.

во-вторы́х *вводн сл* secondly, in the second place.

вогнá|ть (вгоню, вгóнишь; *pt* **-л, -лá, -ло**, *impf* **вгонять)** *сов перех*: ~ **(во что-н)** to drive in(to sth); **вгонять** (~ *perf*) **когó-н в отчáяние** to drive sb to despair; **вгонять** (~ *perf*) **в крáску когó-н** to make sb blush.

вóгнут|ый (-, -а, -о) *прил* concave.

вогн|ýть (-ý, -ёшь; *impf* **вгибáть)** *сов перех* to bend *или* curve inwards.

вод|á (*acc sg* **-у**, *gen sg* **-ы́**, *nom pl* **-ы**) *ж* water; (*no pl*; *перен*: *в докладе*) padding; **что ты как ~ы́ в рот набрáл?** (*разг*) has the cat got your tongue?; **как в вóду опýщенный** (*разг*) down in the dumps; **похóжи как две кáпли ~ы́** as like as two peas in a pod; **выходи́ть (вы́йти** *perf*) **сухи́м из ~ы́** (*разг*) to get off scot-free; **выводи́ть (вы́вести** *perf*) **на чи́стую вóду когó-н** (*разг*) to force sb to come clean; *см также* **вóды**.

водвор|и́ть (-ю, -и́шь) *сов перех* (*поселить*) to settle; (*тишину*) to establish

▶ **водвори́ться** *возв* (*тишина*) to be established.

водеви́л|ь (-и) *ж* musical comedy.

води́тел|ь (-я) *м* driver.

води́тельск|ий (-ая, -ое, -ие) *прил*: **~ие правá** driving licence (*BRIT*), driver's license (*US*).

во|ди́ть (-жý, -дишь) *несов перех* (*ребёнка, собаку*) to take; (*лошадь, войско*) to lead; (*машину, поезд*) to drive; (*самолёт*) to fly; (*корабль*) to sail; ~ (*impf*) **дрýжбу/знакóмство с кем-н** to be friends/acquainted with sb; ~ (*impf*) **зá нос когó-н** to lead sb on

▶ **води́ться** *несов возв* (*рыба итп*) to be (found); **~ся** (*impf*) **с** *+instr* (*разг*) to be pals with; **у негó вóдятся дéньги** (*разг*) he's got money; **как вóдится** (*разг*) as is usually the way.

вóдк|а (-и) *ж* vodka.

вóдный *прил* water *опред*; **вóдные лы́жи** water-skiing; **вóдное пóло** water polo; **вóдные процедýры** hydrotherapy.

водоворóт (-а) *м* whirlpool; (*перен*) whirlpool, maelstrom.

водоём (-а) *м* reservoir.

водоизмещéни|е (-я) *ср* displacement; **сýдно ~м в 10 ты́сяч тонн** a vessel of 10 thousand tons displacement.

водокáчк|а (-ки; *gen pl* **-ек)** *ж* (*ТЕХ*) waterworks.

водолáз (-а) *м* (*человек*) diver.

Водолé|й (-я) *м* (*созвездие*) Aquarius.

водолечéбница (-ы) *ж* hydrotherapy clinic.

водолюби́вый *прил* (*растение*) water-loving.

водонапóрн|ый *прил*: **~ая бáшня** water tower.

водонепроницáемый *прил* waterproof.

водоотта́лкивающ|ий (-ая, -ее, -ие) *прил* water-repellent.

водоочистнóй *прил* water-purifying.

водопáд (-а) *м* waterfall.

водопó|й (-я) *м* (*для животных*) (water) trough.

водопровóд (-а) *м* water supply system; **у них в дóме ~** their house has running water.

водопровóдный *прил* (*труба, кран*) water *опред*; (*система*) plumbing *опред*.

водопровóдчик (-а) *м* plumber.

водораздéл (-а) *м* (*также перен*) watershed.

водорóд (-а) *м* hydrogen.

водорóдный *прил* hydrogen *опред*; **водорóдная бóмба** hydrogen bomb.

вóдоросл|ь (-и) *ж* (*обычно мн*) algae *мн*; (*разг*: *в реке*) waterweed; (*в море*) seaweed.

водосбрóс (-а) *м* floodgate.

водостóчн|ый *прил*: **~ая трубá** drainpipe; **~ая канáва** gutter.

водохрани́лищ|е (-а) *ср* reservoir.

водру|зи́ть (-жý, -зи́шь; *impf* **водружáть)** *сов перех* to raise.

вóд|ы (-) *мн* (*государственные, нейтральные*) waters *мн*; (*минеральные источники*) spa *ед*.

водяни́стый *прил* watery.

водянóй *прил* water *опред*; **водянóй знак** watermark; **водянóй пар** steam.

во|евáть (-юю) *несов неперех* (*страна*) to be at war; (*человек*) to fight; ~ (*impf*) **с бюрокрáтами** *или* **прóтив бюрокрáтов** (*перен*) to wage war on *или* against bureaucracy.

воеди́но *нареч* together.

военачáльник (-а) *м* (military) commander.

военизи́р|овать (-ую) *(не)сов перех* to militarize.

военкомáт (-а) *м сокр* (= *воéнный комиссариáт*) ministry for war.

воéнно-воздýшн|ый *прил*: **воéнно-воздýшные си́лы** (the) air force.

воéнно-морскóй *прил*: ~ **флот** (the) navy.

военнообя́занн|ый (-ого; *decl like adj*) *м* *person eligible for compulsory military service*.

военноплéнн|ый (-ого; *decl like adj*) *м* prisoner of war.

воéнно-полевóй *прил* (*госпиталь*) field *опред*; **воéнно-полевóй суд** court martial.

воéнно-промы́шленный *прил*: ~ **кóмплекс** military-industrial complex.

военнослýжащ|ий (-его; *decl like adj*) *м*

serviceman (*мн* servicemen).
во́енн|ые (-ых; *decl like adj*) *мн собир* the military.
во́енн|ый *прил* military; (*врач*) army *опред* ◆ (**-ого**; *decl like adj*) *м* serviceman (*мн* servicemen); **во́енное положе́ние** martial law; **во́енная промы́шленность** military-related industry; *см также* **во́енные**.
во́енщин|а (-ы) *ж собир* (*пренебр*) warmongers *мн*.
вожа́к (-а́) *м* leader.
вожа́т|ый (-ого; *decl like adj*) *м* (*в горах*) guide.
вожделе́ни|е (-я) *ср* (*к женщине*) lust; (*к власти, к пище*) craving.
вожде́ни|е (-я) *ср* (*машины, поезда*) driving; (*судна*) steering; (*яхты*) sailing; (*самолёта*) flying.
вожд|ь (-я́) *м* (*племени*) chief, chieftain; (*движения, партии*) leader.
вожж|а́ (-и́; *nom pl* **-и**, *gen pl* **-е́й**) *ж* (*обычно мн*) rein.
вожу́(сь) *несов см* **води́ть(ся)**, **вози́ть(ся)**.
ВОЗ *м сокр* (= *Всеми́рная организа́ция здравоохране́ния*) WHO (= *World Health Organization*).
воз (-а; *loc sg* **-у́**, *nom pl* **-ы́**) *м* loaded cart; (*перен*: *разг*) loads *мн*, heaps *мн*.
возбраня́|ться (*3sg* **-ется**, *3pl* **-ются**) *несов возв* (*запрещается*) to be prohibited.
возбуди́м|ый (-, -а, -о) *прил* excitable.
возбуди́тел|ь (-я) *м* (*МЕД*) pathogen.
возб|уди́ть (-ужу́, -у́дишь; *impf* **возбужда́ть**) *сов перех* (*вызвать*) to arouse; (*взволновать*) to excite; **возбужда́ть (~** *perf*) **де́ло** *или* **проце́сс про́тив** *+gen* to bring a case *или* institute proceedings against; **возбужда́ть (~** *perf*) **иск** to begin legal proceedings; **возбужда́ть (~** *perf*) **хода́тайство о** *+prp* to submit a petition for; **возбужда́ть (~** *perf*) **не́нависть** to incite hatred
▸ **возбуди́ться** *сов возв* (*возникнуть*) to be aroused; (*взволноваться*) to become excited.
возбужда́ющ|ий (-ая, -ее, -ие) *прил*: **~ее сре́дство** stimulant.
возбужде́ни|е (-я) *ср* (*волнение*) agitation; (: *радостное*) excitement.
возбуждённый *прил* (*см сущ*) agitated; excited.
возбужу́(сь) *сов см* **возбуди́ть(ся)**.
возведе́ни|е (-я) *ср* (*здания, стены итп*) elevation.
возвели́ч|ить (-у, -ишь; *impf* **возвели́чивать**) *сов перех* to extol.
возве|сти́ (-ду́, -дёшь; *pt* **возвёл, -ла́, -ло́**, *impf* **возводи́ть**) *сов перех* to erect; **возводи́ть (~** *perf*) **что-н в при́нцип** to adopt sth as a fundamental principle; **э́то бы́ло ~дено́ в зако́н** it was enshrined in law; **возводи́ть (~** *perf*) **обвине́ние на кого́-н** to level an accusation against sb; **возводи́ть (~** *perf*) **клевету́ на кого́-н** to slander sb; **возводи́ть (~** *perf*) **что-н к** *+dat* to trace sth back to.
возве|сти́ть (-щу́, -сти́шь; *impf* **возвеща́ть**) *сов перех* to proclaim.
возво|ди́ть (-жу́, -дишь) *несов от* **возвести́**.
возвра́т (-а) *м* return; (*долга, займа*) repayment; **без ~а** irrevocably; **подлежа́щий ~у** returnable; **не подлежа́щий ~у** nonreturnable; **возвра́т нало́га** tax refund.
возвра|ти́ть (-щу́, -ти́шь; *impf* **возвраща́ть**) *сов перех* (*книгу, покупку*) to return; (*долг, ссуду*) to repay; (*свободу, здоровье, счастье*) to restore; **возвраща́ть (~** *perf*) **кого́-н к жи́зни** (*больного*) to bring sb back from the brink of death
▸ **возврати́ться** (*impf* **возвраща́ться**) *сов возв*: **~ся (к** *+dat*) to return *или* come back (to).
возвра́тный *прил* (*КОММ*) repayable; (*ЛИНГ*) reflexive.
возвраща́|ть(ся) (-ю(сь)) *несов от* **возврати́ть(ся)**.
возвраще́ни|е (-я) *ср* return.
возвращу́(сь) *сов см* **возврати́ть(ся)**.
возвы́|сить (-шу, -сишь; *impf* **возвыша́ть**) *сов перех* (*работника итп*) to elevate; **возвыша́ть (~** *perf*) **кого́-н в чьих-н глаза́х** to raise sb in sb's estimation
▸ **возвы́ситься** (*impf* **возвыша́ться**) *сов возв* to be elevated.
возвыша́|ться (-юсь) *несов возв* to tower.
возвыше́ни|е (-я) *ср* elevation.
возвы́шен|ный (-, -на, -но) *прил* (*перен*: *идея, цель*) lofty; (*натура, музыка*) sublime; (*берег*) high.
возвы́шу(сь) *сов см* **возвы́сить(ся)**.
возгла́в|ить (-лю, -ишь; *impf* **возглавля́ть**) *сов перех* to head.
во́зглас (-а) *м* exclamation.
возда|ва́ть (-ю́) *несов от* **возда́ть**.
возда́ть (*как* **дать**; *см* **Table 14**; *impf* **воздава́ть**) *сов перех*: **~ хвалу́** *или* **по́чести кому́-н** to eulogize sb, pay homage to sb; **воздава́ть (~** *perf*) **кому́-н по заслу́гам** (*в награду*) to reward sb for their services; (*в наказание*) to give sb what they deserve; **воздава́ть (~** *perf*) **до́лжное кому́-н** to give sb their due.
воздви́г *итп сов см* **воздви́гнуть**.
воздвига́|ть (-ю; *perf* **воздви́гнуть**) *несов перех* to erect.
воздви́г|нуть (-ну, -нешь; *pt* **-, -ла, -ло**) *несов от* **воздвига́ть**.
возде́йстви|е (-я) *ср* effect; (*идеологическое, педагогическое*) influence; **ока́зывать (оказа́ть** *perf*) **~ на** *+acc* to influence; **под ~м** *+gen* under the influence of.
возде́йств|овать (-ую) (*не*)*сов неперех*: **~ на**

+acc (*(по)влиять*) to have an effect on; (*оказать действие*) to influence.

возде́ла|ть (**-ю**; *impf* **возде́лывать**) *сов перех* (*обрабатывать*) to cultivate; (*растить*) to grow.

воздержа́вш|аяся (**-ейся**; *decl like adj*) *ж см* **воздержа́вшийся**.

воздержа́вш|ийся (**-егося**; *decl like adj*) *м* (*полит*) abstainer.

возде́ржан|ный (**-, -на, -но**) *прил* frugal; (*в напитках, еде*) abstemious; **он возде́ржан в оце́нках/в сужде́ниях** he is cautious in his evaluations/judgements.

возд|ержа́ться (**-ержу́сь, -е́ржишься**; *impf* **возде́рживаться**) *сов возв*: **~ от** *+gen* (*от комментариев, от курения*) to refrain from; (*от голосования*) to abstain from; **~ержа́лось 10 челове́к** there were 10 abstentions.

во́здух (**-а**) *м* air; (*перен*) atmosphere; **на (откры́том) ~е** outside, outdoors; **в ~е но́сится опа́сность** there is danger in the air.

возду́шн|ый *прил* air *опред*; (*десант*) airborne; **посыла́ть (посла́ть** *perf*) **кому́-н ~ поцелу́й** to blow sb a kiss; **возду́шная трево́га** air-raid warning; **возду́шная я́ма** air pocket; **возду́шный флот** air force.

воззва́ни|е (**-я**) *ср* appeal.

возз|ва́ть (**-ову́, -вёшь**) *сов от* **взыва́ть**.

воззре́ни|е (**-я**) *ср* view.

во|зи́ть (**-жу́, -зишь**) *несов перех* to take; **нас ~зи́ли по Ло́ндону на авто́бусе** we were taken round London on a bus; **ка́ждый день она́ во́зит дете́й в шко́лу на маши́не** every day she takes *или* drives the children to school; **~** *(impf)* **во́ду на ком-н** (*разг*) to work sb into the ground

▸ **вози́ться** *несов возв* to potter about; (*дети*) to romp around *или* about; **~ся** *(impf)* **с** *+instr* (*разг*: *с работой итп*) to make heavy weather of; (*с детьми итп*) to spend a lot of time with.

возлага́|ть (**-ю**) *несов от* **возложи́ть**.

во́зле *нареч* nearby ◆ *предл* (*+gen*) near; **де́ти игра́ли ~** the children were playing nearby; **дом был ~ реки́** the house stood near the river.

возлож|и́ть (**-у́, -ишь**; *impf* **возлага́ть**) *сов перех* (*положить*) to lay, place; (*поручить*) to entrust; **возлага́ть (~** *perf*) **вину́ на кого́-н** to lay the blame on sb; **возлага́ть (~** *perf*) **отве́тственность на кого́-н** to hold sb responsible; **возлага́ть (~** *perf*) **наде́жды на кого́-н** to pin one's hopes on sb.

возлю́бленн|ая (**-ой**) *ж см* **возлю́бленный**.

возлю́бленн|ый (**-ого**; *decl like adj*) *м* beloved.

возме́зди|е (**-я**) *ср* retribution.

возме|сти́ть (**-щу́, -сти́шь**; *impf* **возмеща́ть**) *сов перех* (*ущерб, убытки*) to compensate for; (*затраты*) to refund, reimburse.

возмеще́ни|е (**-я**) *ср*: **~ убы́тков** compensation; **~ затра́т** reimbursement; **изде́ржки ~я** replacement cost; **сто́имость страхово́го ~я** (*комм*) replacement value.

возмещу́ *сов см* **возмести́ть**.

возмо́жен *прил см* **возмо́жный**.

возмо́жно *как сказ* it is possible ◆ *вводн сл* (*может быть*) possibly ◆ *нареч*: **~ лу́чше/ бы́стрее** as well/quickly as possible; **~ ему́ помо́чь** it is possible to help him; **~, он согласи́тся** he may possibly agree.

возмо́жност|и (**-ей**) *мн* (*творческие*) potential; **фина́нсовые** *или* **материа́льные ~** financial resources.

возмо́жност|ь (**-и**) *ж* opportunity; (*допустимость*) possibility; **по (ме́ре) ~и** as far as possible; **име́ть** *(impf)* **~** *+infin* to be able to do; **при пе́рвой ~и** at the first opportunity; *см также* **возмо́жности**.

возмо́ж|ный (**-ен, -на, -но**) *прил* possible.

возмужа́|ть (**-ю**) *сов от* **мужа́ть**.

возмути́тел|ьный (**-ен, -ьна, -ьно**) *прил* appalling.

возму|ти́ть (**-щу́, -ти́шь**; *impf* **возмуща́ть**) *сов перех* to appal (*BRIT*), appall (*US*)

▸ **возмути́ться** (*impf* **возмуща́ться**) *сов возв* to be appalled.

возмуще́ни|е (**-я**) *ср* indignation.

возмущённо *нареч* indignantly.

возмущённый *прил* indignant.

возмущу́(сь) *сов см* **возмути́ть(ся)**.

вознагра|ди́ть (**-жу́, -ди́шь**; *impf* **вознагражда́ть**) *сов перех* to reward; (*комм*) to remunerate.

вознагражде́ни|е (**-я**) *ср* reward.

вознагражу́ *сов см* **вознагради́ть**.

возненави́|деть (**-жу, -дишь**) *сов перех* to come to hate.

Вознесе́ни|е (**-я**) *ср* Ascension Day.

вознес|ти́ (**-у́, -ёшь**; *pt* **вознёс, -ла́, -ло́**, *impf* **возноси́ть**) *сов перех* (*хвалить*) to exalt; **возноси́ть (~** *perf*) **чьи-н досто́инства** to extol (*BRIT*) *или* extoll (*US*) sb's virtues

▸ **вознести́сь** (*impf* **возноси́ться**) *сов возв* to rise (up).

возни́к *итп сов см* **возни́кнуть**.

возника́|ть (**-ю**) *несов от* **возни́кнуть**.

возникнове́ни|е (**-я**) *ср* emergence.

возни́к|нуть (**-ну, -нешь**; *pt* **-, -ла, -ло**, *impf* **возника́ть**) *сов неперех* to arise.

возно|си́ть (**-шу́, -сишь**) *несов от* **вознести́**.

возн|я́ (**-и́**) *ж* (*при игре*) frolicking; (*перен*: *интриги*) intrigue; **~ с** *+instr* (*хлопоты*) bother with; **мыши́ная ~** (*перен*) a lot of fuss about nothing.

возоблада́|ть (*3sg* **-ет**, *3pl* **-ют**) *сов неперех*: **~ над** *+instr* to prevail over.

возобнов|и́ть (**-лю́, -и́шь**; *impf* **возобновля́ть**) *сов перех* (*начать снова*) to resume; **возобновля́ть (~** *perf*) **контра́кт** to renew a contract

▸ **возобнови́ться** (*impf* **возобновля́ться**) *сов возв* to resume.

возомн|и́ть (**-ю́, -и́шь**) *сов перех*: **~ себя́ ге́нием/поэ́том** to consider o.s. a genius/poet.

возража́|ть (**-ю**) *несов от* **возрази́ть**.

возраже́ни|е (**-я**) *ср* objection; **предложе́ние встре́тило ~я** the proposal met with opposition.
возра|зи́ть (**-жу́, -зи́шь**; *impf* **возража́ть**) *сов неперех*: ~ (*+dat*) to object (to); **возража́ть** (~ *perf*) **на замеча́ние/обвине́ние** to object to a remark/an allegation.
во́зраст (**-а**) *м* age; **ребёнок в ~е десяти́ лет** a ten-year-old child; **он был уже́ в ~е** he was getting on in years; **вы́йти** *(perf)* **из ~а** to be over the age limit.
возр|асти́ (*3sg* **-астёт**, *3pl* **-асту́т**, *pt* **-о́с, -осла́, -осло́**, *impf* **возраста́ть**) *сов неперех* to grow.
возрастно́й *прил* age *опред*.
возро|ди́ть (**-жу́, -ди́шь**; *impf* **возрожда́ть**) *сов перех* to revive
▸ **возроди́ться** (*impf* **возрожда́ться**) *сов возв* to revive.
возрожде́ни|е (**-я**) *ср* (*хозяйства, традиции*) revival; (*нации, веры*) rebirth; (*территории, демократии*) regeneration; **В~** Renaissance.
возро́с *итп сов см* **возрасти́**.
возыме́|ть (**-ю**) *сов перех*: ~ **де́йствие** to take effect.
возьму́(сь) *итп сов см* **взять(ся)**.
во́ин (**-а**) *м* warrior.
во́инск|ий (**-ая, -ое, -ие**) *прил* military; **во́инская пови́нность** conscription.
вои́нствен|ный (**-ен, -на, -но**) *прил* (*племена*) warlike; (*вид, тон, намерения*) belligerent; (*воинствующий*) militant.
вои́стину *нареч* in truth.
во|й (**-я**) *м* howl.
войду́ *итп сов см* **войти́**.
во́йлок (**-а**) *м* felt.
войн|а́ (**-ы́**; *nom pl* **-ы**) *ж* war; **вести́** *(impf)* **~у́** to wage war; **идти́ (пойти́** *perf*) **на ~у́** to go to war.
во́йск|о (**-а**; *nom pl* **-а́**) *ср* (*обычно мн*) (the) forces *мн*.
войти́ (*как* **идти́**; *см* **Table 18**; *impf* **входи́ть**) *сов неперех*: ~ (**в** *+acc*) to enter, go in(to); (*включиться*) to become a member (of); (*уместиться*) to fit in(to); **в шкаф вхо́дит мно́го книг** the cupboard holds a lot of books; **э́та статья́ не вошла́ в сбо́рник** this article was not included in the collection; **входи́ть** (~ *perf*) **в спи́сок** to be added to the list; **входи́ть** (~ *perf*) **в систе́му** (*комп*) to log in.
вокали́ст (**-а**) *м* vocalist.
вока́льн|ый *прил* vocal; (*конкурс*) singing *опред*; **она́ у́чится на ~ом отделе́нии** she is studying singing.
вокза́л (**-а**) *м* station.
вокру́г *нареч* around, round ◆ *предл*: ~ *+gen* (*кругом*) around, round; (*по поводу*) about, over; ~ **го́рода лес** the town is surrounded by a forest; ~ **рефо́рмы бы́ло мно́го спо́ров** there was a lot of controversy surrounding *или* over the reforms; **ходи́ть** *(impf)* ~ **да о́коло** (*разг*) to beat about the bush.

The spelling rules for Russian are shown on page xvii.

вол (**-а́**) *м* ox (*мн* oxen), bullock.
вола́н (**-а**) *м* (*на одежде*) flounce; (*в бадминтоне*) shuttlecock.
Во́лг|а (**-и**) *ж* Volga.
Волгогра́д (**-а**) *м* Volgograd.
волды́р|ь (**-я́**) *м* blister.
волево́й *прил* (*человек, характер*) strong-willed; (*усилие, натура*) determined.
волейбо́л (**-а**) *м* volleyball.
волейболи́ст (**-а**) *м* volleyball player.
волейболи́ст|ка (**-ки**; *gen pl* **-ок**) *ж см* **волейболи́ст**.
во́лей-нево́лей *нареч* (*без желания*) like it or not; **ему́ ~ пришло́сь э́то сде́лать** he had no choice but to do it.
во́лен *прил см* **во́льный**.
во́лжск|ий (**-ая, -ое, -ие**) *прил* Volga *опред*, of the Volga.
волк (**-а**; *gen pl* **-о́в**) *м* wolf (*мн* wolves); **во́лком смотре́ть** *(impf)* **на кого́-н** to look daggers at sb.
волкода́в (**-а**) *м* wolfhound.
волн|а́ (**-ы́**; *nom pl* **во́лны**) *ж* (*также перен*) wave; **на коро́тких/сре́дних/дли́нных во́лнах** on short/medium/long wave.
волне́ни|е (**-я**) *ср* (*на море*) choppiness; (*человека*: *радостное*) excitement; (: *нервное*) agitation; (*обычно мн*: *в массах*) disturbance, unrest *ед*.
волни́ст|ый (**-, -а, -о**) *прил* (*волосы*) wavy.
волн|ова́ть (**-у́ю**; *perf* **взволнова́ть**) *несов перех* (*общество, человека*) to be concerned about ; (*море*) to agitate
▸ **волнова́ться** (*perf* **взволнова́ться**) *несов возв* (*море*) to be rough *или* choppy; (*человек*) to worry.
волоки́т|а (**-ы**) *ж* red tape.
вол|окно́ (**-окна́**; *nom pl* **-о́кна**, *gen pl* **-о́кон**) *ср* fibre (*BRIT*), fiber (*US*).
волонтёр (**-а**) *м* volunteer.
во́лос (**-а**; *gen pl* **воло́с**, *dat pl* **-а́м**) *м* hair *только ед*; **~ы рвать** *(impf)* **на себе́** (*перен*) to kick o.s.; **э́то притя́нуто за́ волосы** that's a bit far-fetched.
волоса́т|ый (**-, -а, -о**) *прил* (*грудь*) hairy.
волос|о́к (**-ка́**) *м* hair; (*лампочки*) filament; **быть** *(impf) или* **находи́ться** *(impf)* **на ~** *или* **на волоске́ от** *+gen* to be within a hair's-breadth of; **висе́ть** *(impf) или* **держа́ться** *(impf)* **на ~ке́** to hang by a thread.
во́лост|ь (**-и**) *ж* volost (*administrative division*).
волосяно́й *прил* (*покров*) hair *опред*.
волоч|и́ть (**-у́, -и́шь**) *несов перех* to drag; **едва́** *или* **е́ле но́ги ~** *(impf)* to drag o.s. along.
волча́та *итп сущ см* **волчо́нок**.
во́лч|ий (**-ья, -ье, -ьи**) *прил* wolf *опред*; ~ **зако́н** the law of the jungle; ~ **аппети́т** voracious appetite.
волчи́ц|а (**-ы**) *ж* she-wolf.

волч|óнок (**-óнка**; *nom pl* **-áта**, *gen pl* **-áт**) *м* wolf cub.
волшéбник (**-а**) *м* wizard.
волшéбниц|а (**-ы**) *ж* (good *или* white) witch.
волшéбный *прил* magic *опред*; (*перен*: *чарующий*) magical.
волшебств|ó (**-á**) *ср* (*также перен*) magic.
волы́н|ка (**-ки**; *gen pl* **-ок**) *ж* bagpipes *мн*; (*разг*: *канитель*) palaver.
вольгóт|ный (**-ен, -на, -но**) *прил* free and easy.
вольéр (**-а**) *м* enclosure.
вольничá|ть (**-ю**) *несов неперех* (*разг*) to take liberties.
вóльно *нареч* freely; **~!** (*ВОЕН*) at ease!; **~ или невóльно** willing or not.
вольнодýм|ец (**-ца**) *м* freethinker.
вольнолюби́в|ый (**-, -а, -о**) *прил* freedom-loving.
вольнонаёмный *прил* (*рабочий, труд*) casual.
вóльност|ь (**-и**) *ж* (*нескромность*) licence (*BRIT*), license (*US*).
вóл|ьный (**-ен, -ьнá, -ьно**) *прил* (*свободный*) free; (*нескромный*) familiar ◆ *как сказ* (*no full form*): **~ен** *+infin* he is free to do; **вóльная борьбá** freestyle wrestling; **вóльные упражнéния** free floor routine; **вóльный перевóд** free translation.
вольт (**-а**; *gen pl* **-**) *м* volt.
вольтмéтр (**-а**) *м* voltmeter.
волью́ *итп сов см* **влить**.
вóл|я (**-и**) *ж* will; (*стремление*): **~ к побéде/ достижéнию чегó-н** the will to win/to achieve sth; **давáть (дать** *perf***) ~ю слезáм/языкý** to cry/speak without restraint; **давáть (дать** *perf***) ~ю чýвствам** to give free rein to one's feelings; **дéлать (сдéлать** *perf***) что-н по своéй ~е** to do sth of one's own volition *или* free will; **э́то не в моéй ~е** it's not in *или* within my power.
вон *нареч* (*разг*: *прочь*) out; (: *там*) (over) there ◆ *част*: **~ тудá иди́те** you need to go THAT way; **~ отсю́да!** get lost!; **вы́йди ~!** get out!; **~ онá идёт** look, there she is; **~ (онó) что** so that's it!
вон|зи́ть (**-жý, -зи́шь**; *impf* **вонзáть**) *сов перех*: **~ (в** *+acc*) (*иголка, кинжал*) to stick in(to); (*зубы, когти*) to sink in(to)
▸ **вонзи́ться** (*impf* **вонзáться**) *сов возв* (*иголка, кинжал*) to stick out; (*когти, зубы*) to sink in.
вон|ь (**-и**) *ж* (*разг*) pong.
воню́ч|ий (**-ая, -ее, -ие; -, -а, -е**) *прил* (*разг*) pongy.
воня́|ть (**-ю**) *несов неперех* (*разг*) to pong.
воображá|ть (**-ю**) *несов от* **вообрази́ть** ◆ *неперех* (*разг*: *гордиться*) to think a lot of o.s.
вообра|зи́ть (**-жý, -зи́шь**; *impf* **воображáть**) *сов перех* to imagine; **он ~зи́л, что все прóтив негó** he imagined that everyone was against him; **он ~зи́л себя́ гéнием** he fancied himself as a genius; **~зи́те!** (just) imagine!

KEYWORD

вообщé *нареч* **1** (*в общем*) on the whole; **онá вообщé дóбрая** on the whole she is kind
2 (*при любых обстоятельствах*) absolutely; **ходи́ть в кинó он вообщé запрети́л** he absolutely forbade us to go to the cinema; **э́то нам вообщé не подхóдит** that does not suit us at all
3 (*+noun*; *не касаясь частностей*) in general; **мы говори́ли о поли́тике вообщé** we talked about politics in general; **вообщé говоря́** generally speaking.

воодушев|и́ть (**-лю́, -и́шь**; *impf* **воодушевля́ть**) *сов перех* to inspire; **~** (*perf*) **когó-н на то, чтóбы** *+infin* to inspire sb to do
▸ **воодушеви́ться** *сов возв* (*+instr*) to be inspired by.
воодушевлéни|е (**-я**) *ср* enthusiasm.
воодушевлю́ *сов см* **воодушеви́ть**.
воодушевля́|ть (**-ю**) *несов от* **воодушеви́ть**.
вооружá|ть(ся) (**-ю(сь)**) *сов см* **вооружи́ть(ся)**.
вооружéни|е (**-я**) *ср* (*процесс*) arming; (*оружие*) arms *мн*; (*техника*) armament equipment; **брать (взять** *perf***) на ~** (*перен*) to make use of.
вооружённост|ь (**-и**) *ж* (*оснащённость*) armed capability; **техни́ческая ~** technical capability.
вооружённый *прил* armed; **вооружённые си́лы** (the) armed forces.
вооруж|и́ть (**-ý, -и́шь**; *impf* **вооружáть**) *сов перех* to arm; (*перен*) to equip
▸ **вооружи́ться** (*impf* **вооружáться**) *сов возв* (*человек, полиция*) to arm o.s.; (*население*) to take up arms; **вооружáться (~ся** *perf***) терпéнием** to arm o.s. with patience.
вoóчию *нареч* with one's own eyes.
во-пéрвых *нареч* firstly, first of all.
воп|и́ть (**-лю́, -и́шь**) *несов неперех* (*разг*: *кричать*) to shriek; (*громко плакать*) to keen.
вопию́щ|ий (**-ая, -ее, -ие**) *прил* (*ошибка, несправедливость*) glaring; (*безобразие, обман*) brazen ◆ (**-его**; *decl like adj*) *м*: **глас ~его в пусты́не** a voice in the wilderness.
вопло|ти́ть (**-щý, -ти́шь**; *impf* **воплощáть**) *сов перех* to embody; **воплощáть (~** *perf***) в себé** to be the embodiment of; **воплощáть (~** *perf***) в жизнь** to realize
▸ **воплоти́ться** (*impf* **воплощáться**) *сов возв*: **~ся в** *+prp* to be embodied in; **воплощáться (~ся** *perf***) в жизнь** to be realized.
воплощéни|е (**-я**) *ср* embodiment.
воплощý *сов см* **воплоти́ть**.
вопл|ь (**-я**) *м* scream.
воплю́ *несов см* **вопи́ть**.
вопреки́ *предл* (*+dat*; *ожиданию, прогнозу*) contrary to; (*желанию, приказу*) against.
вопрóс (**-а**) *м* question; (*проблема*) question, issue; **задавáть (задáть** *perf***) ~** to ask a question; **стáвить (постáвить** *perf***) под ~** to call into question; **быть** (*impf*) *или* **находи́ться**

(impf) **под ~ом** to be in question; **поднима́ть (подня́ть** *perf*) ~ to raise an issue; **э́то – ~ де́нег/вре́мени** it's a question of money/time; **~ по поря́дку веде́ния** (*ЮР*) point of order.
вопроси́тельный *прил* (*взгляд, интонация*) questioning; (*ЛИНГ*) interrogative; **вопроси́тельный знак** question mark.
впью́сь *итп сов см* **впи́ться.**
вор (**-а**; *gen pl* **-о́в**) *м* thief.
ворв|а́ться (**-у́сь, -ёшься**; *pt* **-а́лся, -ала́сь, -а́лось**, *impf* **врыва́ться**) *сов возв* to burst in; (*звуки*) to flood in.
ворк|ова́ть (**-у́ю**) *несов неперех* (*также перен*) to coo.
вороб|е́й (**-ья́**) *м* sparrow.
воро́ванный *прил* stolen.
вор|ова́ть (**-у́ю**) *несов перех* to steal.
воро́в|ка (**-ки**; *gen pl* **-ок**) *ж см* **вор.**
воровств|о́ (**-а́**) *ср* theft.
во́рон (**-а**) *м* raven.
воро́н|а (**-ы**) *ж* crow; (*перен: разг*) scatterbrain.
воро́н|ить (**-ю, -ишь**; *perf* **проворо́нить**) *сов перех* (*разг*) to miss.
воро́н|ка (**-ки**; *gen pl* **-ок**) *ж* (*для переливания*) funnel; (*после взрыва*) crater.
ворон|о́й *прил* black ◆ (**-о́го**; *decl like adj*) *м* black horse.
воро́нок *сущ см* **воро́нка.**
во́рот (**-а**) *м* neck (*of clothes*).
воро́т|а (**-**) *мн* gates *мн*; (*вход*) gateway *ед*; (*СПОРТ*) goal *ед*; **э́то ни в каки́е ~ не ле́зет** (*разг*) this is daft.
вороти́л|а (**-ы**) *м* (*разг*) big shot.
воротни́к (**-а́**) *м* collar.
во́рох (**-а**; *nom pl* **-а́**) *м* heap.
воро́ча|ть (**-ю**) *несов перех* to shift ◆ *неперех* (*+instr*; *разг*) to have control of
▸ **воро́чаться** *несов возв* to toss and turn.
ворош|и́ть (**-у́, -и́шь**) *несов перех* (*листья, пепел*) to stir up; ~ *(impf)* **се́но** to toss hay; ~ *(impf)* **про́шлое** to stir up the past.
ворс (**-а**) *м* (*на ткани*) nap.
ворча́ни|е (**-я**) *ср* (*животного*) growling; (*человека*) grumbling.
ворч|а́ть (**-у́, -и́шь**) *несов неперех* (*см сущ*) to growl; to grumble.
ворчли́в|ый (**-, -а, -о**) *прил* querulous.
ворчу́н (**-а́**) *м* (*разг*) whinger.
восемна́дцати *чис см* **восемна́дцать.**
восемна́дцат|ый (**-ая, -ое, -ые**) *чис* eighteenth; *см также* **пя́тый.**
восемна́дцат|ь (**-и**; *как* **пять**; *см* **Table 27**) *чис* eighteen; *см также* **пять.**
во́с|емь (**-ьми́**; *как* **пять**; *см* **Table 27**) *чис* eight; *см также* **пять.**
во́с|емьдесят (**-ьми́десяти**; *как* **пятьдеся́т**; *см* **Table 29**) *чис* eighty; *см также* **пятьдеся́т.**
вос|емьсо́т (**-ьмисо́т**; *как* **пятьсо́т**; *см* **Table 34**) *чис* eight hundred; *см также* **сто.**
воск (**-а**; *part gen* **-у**) *м* wax.
воскли́кн|уть (**-у, -ешь**; *impf* **восклица́ть**) *сов неперех* to exclaim.
восклица́ни|е (**-я**) *ср* exclamation.
восклица́тельный *прил* (*интонация*) exclamatory; **восклица́тельный знак** exclamation mark (*BRIT*) *или* point (*US*).
восклица́|ть (**-ю**) *несов от* **воскли́кнуть.**
восков|о́й *прил* wax; (*цвет*) waxen.
воскре́с *итп сов см* **воскре́снуть.**
воскреса́|ть (**-ю**) *несов от* **воскре́снуть.**
воскресе́ни|е (**-я**) *ср* (*РЕЛ*) resurrection; (*перен: обновление*) regeneration; (*: идеи, движения*) revival.
воскресе́нь|е (**-я**) *ср* Sunday; **в ~** on Sunday; **по ~ям** on Sundays; **в сле́дующее/про́шлое ~** next/last Sunday; **сего́дня ~ деся́тое ма́я** today is Sunday (the) 10th (of) May.
воскре|си́ть (**-шу́, -си́шь**; *impf* **воскреша́ть**) *сов перех* to resurrect, raise from the dead; (*перен*) to revive.
воскре́с|нуть (**-ну, -нешь**; *pt* **-, -ла, -ло**, *impf* **воскреса́ть**) *сов неперех* to be resurrected, rise from the dead; (*перен*) to be revived.
воскре́сный *прил* Sunday *опред.*
воскреша́|ть (**-ю**) *несов от* **воскреси́ть.**
воскреше́ни|е (**-я**) *ср* resurrection.
воскрешу́ *сов см* **воскреси́ть.**
воспале́ни|е (**-я**) *ср* inflammation; **воспале́ние лёгких** pneumonia.
воспал|и́ться (**-ю́сь, -и́шься**; *impf* **воспаля́ться**) *сов возв* to become inflamed.
восп|е́ть (**-ою́, -оёшь**; *impf* **воспева́ть**) *сов перех* to extol (*BRIT*), extoll (*US*).
воспита́ни|е (**-я**) *ср* upbringing; (*школьников, граждан*) education; **~ че́стности** instilling of honesty; **брать (взять** *perf*) **на ~** to adopt.
воспи́танник (**-а**) *м* (*учителя, тренера*) pupil; (*вуза*) student; (*приёмный ребёнок*) adopted child.
воспи́танниц|а (**-ы**) *ж см* **воспи́танник.**
воспи́тан|ный (**-, -на, -но**) *прил* well-brought-up.
воспита́тел|ь (**-я**) *м* teacher; (*в лагере, в колонии*) instructor.
воспита́|ть (**-ю**; *impf* **воспи́тывать**) *сов перех* (*ребёнка*) to bring up; (*трудолюбие, честность итп*) to foster, cultivate; **воспи́тывать (~** *perf*) **из кого́-н специали́ста/спортсме́на** to make a specialist/sportsman of sb.
воспламен|и́ться (**-ю́сь, -и́шься**; *impf* **воспламеня́ться**) *сов возв* to ignite.
воспо́лн|ить (**-ю, -ишь**; *impf* **восполня́ть**) *сов перех* (*недостатки*) to make up *или* compensate for; (*пробелы*) to fill in.
воспо́льз|оваться (**-уюсь**) *сов от*

по́льзоваться.
воспомина́ни|е (-я) *ср* memory, recollection; *см также* **воспомина́ния.**
воспомина́ни|я (-й) *мн* memoirs *мн*, reminiscences *мн*.
воспою́ *итп сов см* **воспе́ть.**
воспрепя́тств|овать (-ую) *сов от* **препя́тствовать.**
воспре|ти́ть (-щу́, -ти́шь; *impf* **воспреща́ть)** *сов перех* to forbid.
воспреща́|ться (*3sg* **-ется,** *3pl* **-ются)** *несов возв* to be forbidden; **посторо́нним вход ~ется** no entry to unauthorized persons.
воспрещу́ *сов см* **воспрети́ть.**
восприи́мчив|ый (-, -а, -о) *прил* (*легко усваивающий*) receptive; (*подверженный*) susceptible.
воспр|иня́ть (-иму́, -и́мешь; *impf* **воспринима́ть)** *сов перех* to perceive; (*идею, смысл*) to comprehend.
восприя́ти|е (-я) *ср* perception.
воспроизведе́ни|е (-я) *ср* (*звука, мелодии*) reproduction; (*событий, пейзажа*) re-creation.
воспроизв|ести́ (-еду́, -едёшь; *pt* **-ёл, -ла́, -ло́,** *impf* **воспроизводи́ть)** *сов перех* to reproduce; (*капитал*) to restore.
воспроизв|оди́ть (-ожу́, -о́дишь) *несов от* **воспроизвести́.**
воспроти́в|иться (-люсь, -ишься) *сов от* **проти́виться.**
воспря́н|уть (-у, -ешь) *сов неперех*: **~ ду́хом** to take heart.
воссозда|ва́ть (-ю́) *несов от* **воссозда́ть.**
воссозда́ть (*как* **дать;** *см* **Table 14;** *impf* **воссоздава́ть)** *сов перех* (*образ, события*) to re-create.
восста|ва́ть (-ю́, -ёшь) *несов от* **восста́ть.**
восстана́влива|ть(ся) (-ю(сь)) *несов от* **восстанови́ть(ся).**
восста́ни|е (-я) *ср* uprising.
восстанови́тельный *прил* (*работы*) restoration *опред*; **~ пери́од** period of restoration.
восстан|ови́ть (-овлю́, -о́вишь; *impf* **восстана́вливать)** *сов перех* to restore; **восстана́вливать (~** *perf***) кого́-н в до́лжности** to reinstate sb; **восстана́вливать (~** *perf***) кого́-н в права́х** to restore sb's rights; **восстана́вливать (~** *perf***) кого́-н про́тив кого́-н/чего́-н** to turn *или* set sb against sb/sth
▸ **восстанови́ться** (*impf* **восстана́вливаться)** *сов возв* to be restored.
восста́|ть (-ну, -нешь; *impf* **восстава́ть)** *сов неперех*: **~ (про́тив** *+gen***)** to rise up (against); (*перен*) to take a stand (against).
восто́к (-а) *м* east; **В~** the East, the Orient; **е́хать** *(impf)* **на ~** to travel east; **лежа́ть** *(impf)***/ находи́ться** *(impf)* **к ~у от** *+gen* to lie/be situated to the east of.
восто́рг (-а) *м* rapture; **быть** *(impf)* **в ~е от** *+gen* to be enraptured by; **приходи́ть (прийти́** *perf***) в ~ от** *+gen* to be thrilled by.
восторга́|ть (-ю) *несов перех* to delight, enrapture
▸ **восторга́ться** *несов возв* (*+instr*) to be delighted *или* enraptured by.
восто́ржен|ный (-, -на, -но) *прил* (*зритель, поклонник итп*) ecstatic; (*слова, похвала*) rapturous.
восторжеств|ова́ть (-у́ю) *сов неперех*: **~ (над** *+instr***)** to triumph (over).
восто́чный *прил* eastern; **~ ве́тер** east wind.
востре́бовани|е (-я) *ср* (*багажа, груза*) claim; **письмо́ до ~я** a letter sent poste restante (*BRIT*) *или* general delivery (*US*).
востре́б|овать (-ую) *сов перех* to claim.
востро́ *нареч*: **держа́ть у́хо ~** (*разг*) to keep an ear to the ground.
восхити́тел|ьный (-ен, -на, -но) *прил* (*музыка, стихи итп*) delightful; (*красавица*) ravishing.
восхи|ти́ть (-щу́, -ти́шь; *impf* **восхища́ть)** *сов перех*: **меня́ ~ща́ет он/его́ хра́брость** I admire him/his courage
▸ **восхити́ться** (*impf* **восхища́ться)** *сов возв* (*+instr*) to be delighted with.
восхище́ни|е (-я) *ср* admiration; (*восторг*) delight; **приходи́ть (прийти́** *perf***) в ~ от** *+gen* to be enraptured *или* delighted by; **приводи́ть (привести́** *perf***) в ~ кого́-н** to delight sb.
восхищу́(сь) *сов см* **восхити́ть(ся).**
восхо́д (-а) *м*: **~ со́лнца** sunrise; **~ луны́** moonrise.
вос|ходи́ть (-ожу́, -о́дишь) *несов от* **взойти́** ◆ *неперех*: **~ к** *+dat* (*к периоду времени*) to date back to; (*к традиции*) to be based on.
восходя́щ|ий (-ая, -ее, -ие) *прил* rising.
восхожу́ *несов см* **восходи́ть.**
восьм|а́я (-о́й; *decl like adj***)** *ж*: **одна́ ~** one eighth.
восьмёр|ка (-ки; *gen pl* **-ок)** *ж* (*разг: цифра*) eight; (*группа из восьми*) group of eight; (*разг: автобус, трамвай итп*) (number) eight (*bus, tram etc*); **ло́дка-~** eight (*ROWING*).
во́сьмер|о (-ы́х; *как* **че́тверо;** *см* **Table 36a)** *чис* eight; *см также* **дво́е.**
восьми́ *чис см* **во́семь.**
восьми́десяти *чис см* **во́семьдесят.**
восьмидесятиле́ти|е (-я) *ср* (*срок*) eighty years *мн*; (*годовщина*) eightieth anniversary; (*день рождения*) eightieth birthday.
восьмидесятиле́тн|ий (-яя, -ее, -ие) *прил* (*период*) eighty-year; (*старик*) eighty-year-old.
восьмидеся́т|ый (-ая, -ое, -ые) *чис* eightieth; *см также* **пятидеся́тый.**
восьмидне́вный *прил* eight-day.
восьмикла́ссник (-а) *м pupil in eighth year at school (usually 14 years old).*
восьмикла́ссниц|а (-ы) *ж см* **восьмикла́ссник.**
восьмикра́тн|ый *прил*: **~ чемпио́н** eight-times champion; **в ~ом разме́ре** eightfold.
восьмиле́ти|е (-я) *ср* (*срок*) eight years; (*годовщина*) eighth anniversary.

восьмиле́тн|ий (**-яя, -ее, -ие**) *прил* (*период*) eight-year; (*ребёнок*) eight-year-old.
восьмиме́сячный *прил* eight-month; (*ребёнок*) eight-month-old.
восьминеде́льный *прил* eight-week; (*ребёнок*) eight-week-old.
восьмисо́т *чис см* **восемьсо́т**.
восьмисотле́ти|е (**-я**) *ср* (*срок*) eight hundred years *мн*; (*годовщина*) eight-hundredth anniversary, octocentenary.
восьмисотле́тн|ий (**-яя, -ее, -ие**) *прил* (*период*) eight hundred-year; (*дерево*) eight hundred-year-old.
восьмисо́т|ый (**-ая, -ое, -ые**) *чис* eight-hundredth.
восьмиуго́льник (**-а**) *м* octagon.
восьмичасово́й *прил* (*рабочий день*) eight-hour; (*поезд*) eight-o'clock.
восьм|о́й (**-а́я, -о́е, -ы́е**) *чис* eighth; *см также* **пя́тый**.

KEYWORD

вот *част* ***1*** (*при указании*): **вот моя́ ма́ма** there is my mother; **вот мои́ де́ти** here are my children; **вот он идёт** here he comes
2 (*выражает указание*) this; **вот в чём де́ло** this is what it's about; **вот где ну́жно иска́ть** this is where we need to look
3 (*при эмфатике*): **вот посмотри́, како́е безобра́зие** just look at the mess; **вот ты и сде́лай э́то** YOU do this; **вот негодя́й!** what a rascal!
4 (*как часть сказ*): **но́вая кни́га – вот моя́ цель** a new book – that's my goal; **вот-во́т** (*разг*: *вот именно*) you've got it; **он вот-во́т ля́жет спать** he is just about to go to bed; **вот ещё!** (*разг*) not likely!; **вот (оно́) как** *или* **что!** is that so *или* right?; **вот тебе́ (и) погуля́ли!** (*разг*) so much for the walk!; **вот тебе́ и на** *или* **те раз!** (*разг*) well I never!

воткн|у́ть (**-у́, -ёшь**; *impf* **втыка́ть**) *сов перех* (*иголку, нож*) to stick in; **втыка́ть** (~ *perf*) **кол в зе́млю** to drive a stake into the ground.
вотру́(сь) *итп сов см* **втере́ть(ся)**.
во́тум (**-а**) *м*: ~ **дове́рия/недове́рия** vote of confidence/no confidence.
вошёл *итп сов см* **войти́**.
вошь (**вши**; *instr sg* **во́шью**, *nom pl* **вши**) *ж* louse (*мн* lice).
вошью́ *итп сов см* **вшить**.
вощёный *прил* waxed.
во́ю *итп несов см* **выть**.
впада́|ть (**-ю**) *несов от* **впасть** ◆ *неперех*: ~ **в** *+acc* to flow into.
впа́дин|а (**-ы**) *ж* (*в земле*) gully; (*на дне моря*) trench; **глазна́я** ~ eye socket.
впа|сть (**-ду́, -дёшь**; *impf* **впада́ть**) *сов неперех* (*щёки, глаза*) to become sunken; **впада́ть** (~ *perf*) **в отча́яние** to fall into despair; **впада́ть** (~ *perf*) **в исте́рику** to go into hysterics; **впада́ть** (~ *perf*) **в па́нику** to get into a panic; **впада́ть** (~ *perf*) **в оши́бку** to err; **впада́ть** (~ *perf*) **в кра́йность** to go to extremes; **впада́ть** (~ *perf*) **в заблужде́ние** to be deluded.
впервы́е *нареч* for the first time.
вперёд *нареч* (*идти, смотреть итп*) (straight) ahead, forward; (*заплатить, требовать*) in advance.
впереди́ *нареч* in front; (*в будущем*) ahead ◆ *предл* (*+gen*) in front of; **у Вас вся жизнь** ~ you have your whole life in front of you.
вперемёшку *нареч* higgledy-piggledy.
впечатле́ни|е (**-я**) *ср* impression; **находи́ться** (*impf*) **под ~м чего́-н** to be impressed by sth; **производи́ть** (**произвести́** *perf*) ~ **на** *+acc* to make an impression on; **тако́е** ~, **что** *или* **бу́дто** it looks as if.
впечатли́тел|ьный (**-ен, -ьна, -ьно**) *прил* impressionable.
впечатля́|ть (**-ю**) *несов неперех* to be impressive.
впива́|ться (**-юсь**) *несов от* **впи́ться**.
впи|са́ть (**-шу́, -шешь**; *impf* **впи́сывать**) *сов перех* to insert, include
▸ **вписа́ться** (*impf* **впи́сываться**) *сов возв* (*перен*) to fit in well.
впита́|ть (**-ю**; *impf* **впи́тывать**) *сов перех* to absorb; (*перен*) to absorb, take in
▸ **впита́ться** *сов возв* to be absorbed.
впи́ться (**вопью́сь, вопьёшься**; *impf* **впива́ться**) *сов возв*: ~ **в** *+acc* (*комар*) to bite; **впива́ться** (~ *perf*) **глаза́ми в** *+acc* to fix *или* fasten one's eyes on; **впива́ться** (~ *perf*) **когтя́ми/зуба́ми в** *+acc* to sink one's claws/teeth into.
впишу́(сь) *итп сов см* **вписа́ть(ся)**.
ВПК *сокр* (*= вое́нно-промы́шленный ко́мплекс*) ≈ military-industrial complex.
вплавь *нареч* by swimming.
вплотну́ю *нареч* (*близко*) close (by) ◆ *предл*: ~ **к** *+dat* (*близко*: *к городу*) right up close to; (: *к стене*) right up against; **занима́ться** (**заня́ться** *perf*) **чем-н** *или* **бра́ться** (**взя́ться** *perf*) **за что-н** ~ to get down to sth in earnest.
вплоть *предл*: ~ **до** *+gen* (*вечера, зимы*) right up till; (*включая*) right up to; ~ **до того́, что ...** to the extent that ....
вполго́лоса *нареч* (*говорить, спросить*) in hushed tones; (*петь*) softly.
впо́ру *как сказ*: ~ *+infin* there is nothing for it but to do; **пла́тье/шля́па** ~ the dress/hat fits nicely.
впосле́дствии *нареч* subsequently.
впотьма́х *нареч* in the dark.
ВПП *ж сокр* (*= взлётно-поса́дочная полоса́*) landing strip.
впра́ве *как сказ*: ~ *+infin* to do rightly *или* justly;

он не ~ так поступа́ть he's got no right to behave like that.
впра́в|ить (**-лю, -ишь**; *impf* **вправля́ть**) *сов перех* to set.
впра́во *нареч* to the right; **~ от до́ма** to the right of the house.
впредь *нареч* in future ◆ *предл*: **~ до** *+gen* pending.
вприты́к *нареч* (*разг*) right up close.
впро́голодь *нареч*: **жить ~** to live from hand to mouth.
впрок *нареч* for future use ◆ *как сказ*: **идти́ ~ кому́-н** to do sb good.
впроса́к *нареч*: **попа́сть(ся) ~** (*разг*) to get (o.s.) into a fix.
впро́чем *союз* however, though ◆ *вводн сл* but then again; **пого́да здесь хоро́шая, ~ не всегда́** the weather's good here, though not always; **~, я не уве́рен** but then again, I'm not sure.
впряг *umn сов см* **впрячь.**
впряга́|ть (**-ю**) *несов от* **впрячь.**
впрягу́ *umn сов см* **впрячь.**
впрямь *част*: **и ~** (*разг*) really; **он и ~ испуга́лся** he really got a fright.
впря|чь (**-гу́, -жёшь** *umn*, **-гут**; *pt* **-г, -гла́, -гло́**, *impf* **впряга́ть**) *сов перех* to harness.
впу|сти́ть (**-щу́, -стишь**; *impf* **впуска́ть**) *сов перех* (*в дом, в зал*) to admit, let in.
впу́та|ть (**-ю**) *сов от* **пу́тать** ◆ (*impf* **впу́тывать**) *перех* (*разг*): **~ кого́-н** (**в** *+acc*) to get sb mixed up (in)
▸ **впу́таться** *сов от* **пу́таться** ◆ (*impf* **впу́тываться**) *возв* to get involved.
впущу́ *сов см* **впусти́ть.**
впя́теро *нареч* (*больше, меньше*) five times; (*увеличить*) fivefold.
впятеро́м *нареч* in a group of five.
в-пя́тых *вводн сл* fifthly, in the fifth place.
враг (**-а́**) *м* enemy ◆ *собир* (*ВОЕН*) the enemy.
вражд|а́ (**-ы́**) *ж* enmity, hostility; **пита́ть** (*impf*) **~у́ к** *+dat* to harbour enmity towards.
вражде́б|ный (**-ен, -на, -но**) *прил* (*отношение, тон*) hostile; (*лагерь, сторона*) enemy *опред*.
вражд|ова́ть (**-у́ю**) *несов неперех*: **~** (**с** *+instr*) to be on hostile terms (with).
враз *нареч* (*разг*) at once.
вразбро́д *нареч* separately.
вразбро́с *нареч* (*разг*) scattered about.
вразва́лку *нареч* (*разг*): **ходи́ть ~** to waddle.
вразнобо́й *нареч* (*разг*) in a muddled way.
вразно́с *нареч*: **торгова́ть ~** to peddle.
вразре́з *нареч*: **~ с** *+instr* in contravention of.
вразуми́тел|ьный (**-ен, -ьна, -ьно**) *прил* comprehensible.
вразум|и́ть (**-лю́, -и́шь**; *impf* **вразумля́ть**) *сов перех*: **~ кого́-н** to make sb understand.
вран|ьё (**-я́**) *ср* (*разг*) lies *мн*.
враспло́х *нареч* unawares.
врассыпну́ю *нареч* in all directions.
врата́р|ь (**-я́**) *м* goalkeeper.
вр|ать (**-у́, -ёшь**; *pt* **-ал, -ла́, -ло**, *perf* **навра́ть** *или* **совра́ть**) *несов неперех* (*разг*: *человек*) to fib; (: *часы*) to be wrong.
врач (**-а́**) *м* doctor.
враче́бный *прил* medical.
враща́|ть (**-ю**) *несов перех* (*колесо*) to turn
▸ **враща́ться** *несов возв* (*колесо, планета*) to revolve, rotate; **~ся** (*impf*) **в полити́ческих круга́х** to move in political circles; **разгово́р ~лся вокру́г теа́тра** the conversation revolved around the theatre.
враще́ни|е (**-я**) *ср* revolution, rotation.
вред (**-а́**) *м* (*делу, здоровью*) damage; (*человеку*) harm, injury ◆ *предл*: **во ~** *+dat* to the detriment of; **его́ де́йствия бы́ли во ~ интере́сам фи́рмы** his actions were against the company's interests; **причиня́ть (причини́ть** *perf*) *или* **приноси́ть (принести́** *perf*) **~ кому́-н** to harm sb, do sb harm; **причиня́ть (причини́ть** *perf*) *или* **приноси́ть (принести́** *perf*) **~ чему́-н** to damage *или* cause damage to sth.
вре́ден *прил см* **вре́дный.**
вреди́тел|ь (**-я**) *м* (*насекомое*) pest; (*человек*) saboteur.
вре|ди́ть (**-жу́, -ди́шь**; *perf* **навреди́ть**) *несов неперех* (*+dat*) to harm, hurt; (*здоровью*) to damage; (*врагу*) to inflict damage on.
вре́дно *нареч*: **~ влия́ть на** *+acc* to have a harmful effect on ◆ *как сказ*: **кури́ть ~** smoking is bad for you; **ему́ ~ есть жи́рное** fatty foods are bad for him.
вре́д|ный (**-ен, -на́, -но**) *прил* harmful; (*no short form*; *разг*) nasty.
вре́|зать (**-жу, -жешь**) *сов перех* (*замок*) to fit ◆ *неперех* (*разг*: *ударить*): **~ кому́-н** to bash sb.
врежу́ *несов см* **вреди́ть.**
вре́|заться (**-жусь, -жешься**; *impf* **вреза́ться**) *сов возв*: **~ в** *+acc* (*пила, веревка*) to cut into; (*ворваться*) to plough (*BRIT*) *или* plow (*US*) into; (*в сердце, в память*) to engrave itself on.
врем|ена́ (**-ён**; *dat pl* **-ена́м**) *мн* (*эпоха*) the time *ед*; **~ Петра́ Пе́рвого** the time of Peter the First.
времена́ми *нареч* at times.
вре́мени *umn сущ см* **вре́мя.**
вре́мен|ный (**-ен, -на, -но**) *прил* temporary.
вре́м|я (**-ени**; *см* **Table 4**) *ср* time; (*ЛИНГ*) tense ◆ *предл*: **во ~** *+gen* during ◆ *союз*: **в то ~ как** *или* **когда́** while; **(а) в то же ~** (but) at the same time; **во вре́мя** during; **~ от вре́мени** from time to time; **в после́днее ~** recently; **в своё ~** (*когда необходимо*) in due course; **в своё ~ она́ была́ краса́вицей** she was a real beauty in her day; **на ~** for a while; **со ~енем** with *или* in time; **тем ~енем** meanwhile; **ско́лько ~ени?** what time is it?; **в 8 часо́в по моско́вскому ~ени** at 8 o'clock (by) Moscow time; **~ до́ступа** (*КОМП*) access time; **~ реализа́ции зака́за** (*КОММ*) lead time; **лу́чшее эфи́рное ~** prime time; **хорошо́ проводи́ть (провести́** *perf*) **~** to have a good time; **вре́мя го́да** season; *см также* **времена́.**

времяисчисле́ни|е (-я) *ср* calendar.
времяпрепровожде́ни|е (-я) *ср* way of spending time.
время́н|ка (-ки; *gen pl* -ок) *ж* (*печка*) makeshift stove; (*жилище*) makeshift hut (*next to new rural dwelling*).
вро́вень *нареч*: ~ **с** +*instr* level with.
вро́де *предл* (+*gen*) like ◆ *част* it looks as if; **он у меня́ ~ сове́тника** he's like an advisor to me; **он ~ уе́хал** it looks as if he's gone.
врождённый *прил* (*способности*) innate; (*уродство, болезнь*) congenital.
врозь *нареч* (*жить*) apart; (*работать, ехать*) separately ◆ *предл*: ~ **с** +*instr* или **от** +*gen* (*разг*) separate from.
вро́ю *итп сов см* **врыть**.
вру *несов см* **врать**.
вруб|и́ть (-лю́, -ишь; *impf* **вруба́ть**) *сов перех* (*разг: включить*) to turn on.
врун (-а́) *м* (*разг*) fibber.
вру́нь|я (-и) *ж см* **врун**.
вруч|и́ть (-у́, -и́шь; *impf* **вруча́ть**) *сов перех*: ~ **что-н кому́-н** to hand sth (over) to sb; (*орден, премию*) to present sb with sth.
вручну́ю *нареч* (*разг*) by hand.
врыва́|ться (-юсь) *несов от* **ворва́ться**.
вр|ыть (-о́ю, -о́ешь; *impf* **врыва́ть**) *сов перех* (*столб*) to sink in; (*дерево*) to plant firmly.
вряд *част*: ~ **ли** hardly; ~ **ли он согласи́тся** he's hardly likely to agree.
ВС *мн сокр* (= *Вооружённые Си́лы*) armed forces *мн*; (= *Верхо́вный Сове́т*) Supreme Soviet.
вса|ди́ть (-жу́, -дишь; *impf* **вса́живать**) *сов перех*: ~ **в** +*acc* (*нож, стрелу*) to sink into; **вса́живать** (~ *perf*) **пу́лю в лоб кому́-н** (*разг*) to put a bullet in sb's head.
вса́дник (-а) *м* rider, horseman (*мн* horsemen).
вса́дниц|а (-ы) *ж* rider, horsewoman (*мн* horsewomen).
вса́жива|ть (-ю) *несов от* **всади́ть**.
всажу́ *сов см* **всади́ть**.
вса́сыва|ть (-ю) *несов от* **всоса́ть**.
все *мест см* **весь**.

KEYWORD

всё (**всего́**) *мест см* **весь**
◆ *ср* (*как сущ: без исключения*) everything; **вот и всё, э́то всё** that's all; **ча́ще всего́** most often; **лу́чше всего́ написа́ть ей письмо́** it would be best to write to her; **меня́ э́то волну́ет ме́ньше всего́** that is the least of my worries; **мне всё равно́** it's all the same to me; **Вы хоти́те чай или ко́фе? – всё равно́** do you want tea or coffee? – I don't mind; **я всё равно́ пойду́ туда́** I'll go there all the same
◆ *нареч* **1** (*разг: всё время*) all the time
2 (*разг: до сих пор*) still
3 (*только*) all; **э́то всё он винова́т** it's all his fault
4 (*о нарастании признака*): **шум всё уси́ливается** the noise keeps getting louder
5 (*о постоянстве признака*): **всё так же** still the same; **всё там же** still there; **всё же** all the same; **всё ещё** still.

всевла́сти|е (-я) *ср* absolute power.
всевозмо́жный (-ен, -на, -но) *прил* all sorts of.
всегда́ *нареч* always.
всего́ *мест см* **весь, всё** ◆ *нареч* in all ◆ *част* only; ~ **лишь** (*разг*) only; ~-**на́всего** (*разг*) all in all.
вселе́нн|ая (-ой; *decl like adj*) *ж* the whole world; **В~** universe.
вsel|и́ть (-ю́, -и́шь; *impf* **вселя́ть**) *сов перех* (*жильцов*) to install; (*перен*) to instil (*BRIT*), instill (*US*)
▸ **всели́ться** (*impf* **вселя́ться**) *сов возв* (*жильцы*) to move in; (*перен*) to be instilled.
всем *мест см* **весь, всё, все**.
всеме́рный *прил* (*помощь*) all possible.
всемеро́м *нареч* in a group of seven.
все́ми *мест см* **все**.
всеми́рный *прил* worldwide; (*конгресс*) world *опред*.
всемогу́щ|ий (-ая, -ее, -ие; -, -а, -е) *прил* omnipotent, all-powerful.
всему́ *мест см* **весь, всё**.
всенаро́ден *прил см* **всенаро́дный**.
всенаро́дно *нареч* publicly.
всенаро́д|ный (-ен, -на, -но) *прил* national.
все́нощн|ая (-ой; *decl like adj*) *ж* (*РЕЛ*) vespers.
всеобу́ч (-а) *м сокр* (= *всео́бщее обуче́ние*) general education.
всео́бщ|ий (-ая, -ее, -ие; -, -а, -е) *прил* universal; **всео́бщая забасто́вка/пе́репись** general strike/census.
всеобъе́млющ|ий (-ая, -ее, -ие; -, -а, -о) *прил* comprehensive.
всеору́жи|е (-я) *ср*: **во ~и зна́ний** armed with knowledge; **встреча́ть** (**встре́тить** *perf*) **врага́ во ~и** to be primed for battle.
всеросси́йск|ий (-ая, -ое, -ие) *прил* All-Russia.
всерьёз *нареч* in earnest; **ты э́то говори́шь ~?** are you serious?
всеси́ль|ный (-ен, -ьна, -ьно) *прил* all-powerful.
всесторо́н|ний (-няя, -нее, -ние; -ен, -ня, -не) *прил* comprehensive.
всё-таки *част* still, all the same ◆ *союз*: **а ~** all the same, nevertheless; **мо́жет, ~ пое́дем?** can we not still go?; **бы́ло ску́чно, и ~ я не ушёл** I was bored, but all the same I didn't leave.
всеуслы́шание *ср*: **во ~** publicly.
всех *мест см* **все**.
всеце́ло *нареч* completely.
всея́дный *прил* omnivorous.
вска́кива|ть (-ю) *несов от* **вскочи́ть**.
вска́пыва|ть (-ю) *несов от* **вскопа́ть**.

вскара́бка|ться (-юсь) *сов от* **кара́бкаться.**
вскачь *нареч* at a gallop; **пуска́ть (пусти́ть** *perf***) коня́** ~ to break into a gallop.
вски́н|уть (-у, -ешь; *impf* **вски́дывать)** *сов перех* (*на плечи*) to shoulder; (*голову*) to jerk up; (*руки*) to throw up; **вски́дывать (**~ *perf***) что-н на что-н** to throw sth on(to) sth; **вски́дывать (**~ *perf***) глаза́ на кого́-н** to glance up at sb.
вскип|е́ть (-лю́, -и́шь; *impf* **кипе́ть)** *сов неперех* to boil; (*перен*) to flare up; ~ *(perf)* **от гне́ва** to fly into a rage.
вскипя|ти́ть(ся) (-чу́(сь), -ти́шь(ся)) *сов от* **кипяти́ть(ся).**
всклоко́ченный *прил* (*разг*) tousled.
всколыхн|у́ть (-у́, -ёшь) *сов перех* (*подлеж: ветер*) to stir; (*перен: массы*) to stir up
▸ **всколыхну́ться** *сов возв* (*перен*) to become stirred up.
вскользь *нареч* in passing.
вскопа́|ть (-ю; *impf* **вска́пывать)** *сов перех* to dig (over).
вско́ре *нареч* soon ◆ *предл*: ~ **по́сле** *+gen* soon *или* shortly after.
вскоч|и́ть (-у́, -ишь; *impf* **вска́кивать)** *сов неперех*: ~ **в/на** *+acc* (*на коня, в седло*) to leap up onto; **вска́кивать (**~ *perf***) (на́ ноги)** to leap to one's feet.
вскри́кн|уть (-у, -ешь; *impf* **вскри́кивать)** *сов неперех* to cry out.
вскро́ю(сь) *итп сов см* **вскры́ть(ся).**
вскруж|и́ть (-у́, -ишь) *сов перех*: ~ **го́лову кому́-н** to turn sb's head (*fig*).
вскрыва́|ть (-ю) *несов от* **вскрыть.**
вскры́ти|е (-я) *ср* (*трупа*) postmortem (examination); (*сейфа итп*) opening.
вскр|ыть (-о́ю, -о́ешь; *impf* **вскрыва́ть)** *сов перех* (*открыть*) to open; (: *с силой*) to force open; (*выявить*) to reveal; (*нарыв*) to lance; (*труп*) to carry out a postmortem on
▸ **вскры́ться** *сов возв* (*перен: выявиться*) to come to light, be revealed; **река́ ~ылась** the ice on the river cracked.
всласть *нареч* to one's heart's content.
вслед *нареч* (*бежать*) behind ◆ *предл*: ~ **(за** *+instr***)** after; ~ *+dat* (*другу, поезду*) after.
всле́дствие *предл* (*+gen*) as a result of, because of ◆ *союз*: ~ **того́ что** because; ~ **чего́** as a result of which.
вслепу́ю *нареч* blindly; **печа́тать** *(impf)* **на маши́нке** ~ to touch-type.
вслух *нареч* aloud; **сказа́ть** *(perf)* **что-н** ~ to say sth out loud.
вслу́ша|ться (-юсь; *impf* **вслу́шиваться)** *сов возв*: ~ **в** *+acc* to listen carefully to.
ВСМ *м сокр* (*= Всеми́рный Сове́т Ми́ра*) World Peace Council.
всмотр|е́ться (-ю́сь, -ишься; *impf* **всма́триваться)** *сов возв*: ~ **в** *+acc* to peer at.
всмя́тку *нареч*: **яйцо́** ~ soft-boiled egg.
всо́выва|ть (-ю) *несов от* **всу́нуть.**
всос|а́ть (-у́, -ёшь; *impf* **вса́сывать)** *сов перех* (*втянуть*) to suck; (*впитать*) to absorb.
вспа́рхива|ть (-ю) *несов от* **вспорхну́ть.**
вспа|ха́ть (-шу́, -шешь) *сов от* **паха́ть.**
вспе́н|иться (-юсь, -ишься) *сов от* **пе́ниться.**
всплеск (-а) *м* (*волны*) splash.
всплесн|у́ть (-у́, -ёшь; *impf* **всплёскивать)** *сов неперех* (*рыба, пловец*) to splash; ~ *(perf)* **рука́ми** to throw up one's hands.
всплыва́|ть (-ю) *несов от* **всплыть.**
всплыву́ *итп сов см* **всплыть.**
всплы́ти|е (-я) *ср* surfacing.
всплы|ть (-ву́, -вёшь; *pt* **-л, -ла́, -ло,** *impf* **всплыва́ть)** *сов неперех* to surface, come to the surface; (*перен*) to come to light; **всплыва́ть (**~ *perf***) в па́мяти** to pop into one's head; **всплыва́ть (**~ *perf***) в созна́нии** to appear before one.
всполош|и́ть(ся) (-у́(сь), -и́шь(ся)) *сов от* **полоши́ть(ся).**
вспо́мн|ить (-ю, -ишь; *impf* **вспомина́ть)** *сов перех* to remember ◆ *неперех*: ~ **о** *+prp* to remember about.
вспомога́тельный *прил* (*материал, литература*) supplementary; (*судно, отряд*) auxiliary; **вспомога́тельный глаго́л** auxiliary verb.
вспорхн|у́ть (-у́, -ёшь; *impf* **вспа́рхивать)** *сов неперех* to fly off.
вспоте́|ть (-ю) *сов от* **поте́ть.**
вспры́сн|уть (-у, -ешь; *impf* **вспры́скивать)** *сов перех* to spray.
вспугн|у́ть (-у́, -ёшь; *impf* **вспу́гивать)** *сов перех* to scare away *или* off.
вспу́хн|уть (-у, -ешь) *сов от* **пу́хнуть** ◆ *(impf* **вспуха́ть)** *неперех* to swell up.
вспу́ч|иться (*3sg* **-ится,** *3pl* **-атся)** *несов от* **пучи́ться.**
вспыл|и́ть (-ю́, -и́шь) *сов неперех* to lose one's temper.
вспы́льчивост|ь (-и) *ж* short-temperedness.
вспы́льчив|ый (-, -а, -о) *прил* short-tempered.
вспы́хн|уть (-у, -ешь; *impf* **вспы́хивать)** *сов неперех* (*солома, бумага*) to burst into flames; (*спичка, конфликт, страсть*) to flare up; (*покраснеть: человек*) to blush; **в окне́ ~ул свет** the window lit up.
вспы́ш|ка (-ки; *gen pl* **-ек)** *ж* flash; (*энтузиазма*) burst; (*гнева*) outburst; (*болезни*) outbreak.
вспять *нареч* back.
ВСРФ *мн сокр = вооружённые си́лы росси́йской федера́ции.*
вста|ва́ть (-ю́; *imper* **-ва́й(те))** *несов от* **встать** ◆ *неперех*: **рабо́тать/писа́ть не ~ва́я** to work/ write without a break.
вста́в|ить (-лю, -ишь; *impf* **вставля́ть)** *сов перех* to insert, put in; **вставля́ть (**~ *perf***) зу́бы** to have a set of dentures *или* false teeth made; **вставля́ть (**~ *perf***) ка́мень в опра́ву** to set a stone.
вста́в|ка (-ки; *gen pl* **-ок)** *ж* insertion; (*в одежде*)

inset.
вста́влю *сов см* **вста́вить.**
вставля́|ть (-ю) *несов от* **вста́вить.**
вставн|о́й *прил* (*рамы*) removable; **~ы́е зу́бы** dentures, false teeth.
вста́вок *сущ см* **вста́вка.**
вста|ть (-ну, -нешь; *impf* **встава́ть)** *сов неперех* (*на ноги*) to stand up; (*с постели*) to get up; (*солнце*) to rise; (*трудности, вопрос*) to arise; (*no impf; разг: часы, мотор*) to stop; **пе́ред на́ми вста́ли но́вые тру́дности** we were faced with new difficulties.
встопо́рщ|ить(ся) (-ю(сь), -ишь(ся)) *сов от* **топо́рщить(ся).**
встрева́|ть (-ю) *несов неперех* (*разг: вмешиваться*) to stick one's oar in.
встрево́жен|ный (-, -а, -о) *прил* anxious.
встрево́ж|ить(ся) (-у(сь), -ишь(ся)) *несов от* **трево́жить(ся).**
встрепен|у́ться (-у́сь, -ёшься) *сов возв* to give a start.
встре́|тить (-чу, -тишь; *impf* **встреча́ть)** *сов перех* to meet; (*гостей, делегацию итп*) to meet, welcome; (*обнаружить: слово, цитату*) to come across; (*оппозицию, сопротивление*) to meet with, encounter; (*праздник итп*) to celebrate
▸ **встре́титься** (*impf* **встреча́ться**) *сов возв*: **~ся с** *+instr* to meet; (*перен: с сопротивлением итп*) to meet with, encounter; **мне ~тились друзья́/интере́сные фа́кты** I came across some friends/interesting facts.
встре́ч|а (-и) *ж* meeting; (*поединок*) match.
встреча́|ть (-ю) *несов от* **встре́тить**
▸ **встреча́ться** *несов от* **встре́титься** ◆ *возв* (*регулярно видеться*) to meet; (*попадаться*) to be found.
встре́чн|ый *прил* (*машина, поезд итп*) oncoming; (*мера*) counter *опред* ◆ **(-ого;** *decl like adj*) *м someone coming from the opposite direction*; **~ ве́тер** head wind; **пе́рвый ~** (*разг*) anyone; **встре́чная ата́ка** counterattack; **встре́чный иск** counterclaim.
встре́чу(сь) *сов см* **встре́тить(ся).**
встря́с|ка (-ки; *gen pl* **-ок)** *ж* (*потрясение*) shock; (*системы*) upheaval.
встряхн|у́ть (-у́, -ёшь; *impf* **встря́хивать)** *сов перех* to shake (out); (*перен: общество*) to shake (up).
вступа́|ть(ся) (-ю(сь)) *несов от* **вступи́ть(ся).**
вступи́тельный *прил* (*речь, статья*) introductory; **вступи́тельный взнос** subscription fee; **вступи́тельный экза́мен** entrance exam.
вступ|и́ть (-лю́, -ишь; *impf* **вступа́ть)** *сов неперех*: **~ в** *+acc* to enter; (*в партию, в общество*) to join; (*в спор, в переговоры*) to enter into; **вступа́ть (~** *perf*) **на** *+acc* to mount; **вступа́ть (~** *perf*) **в бой** to join battle
▸ **вступи́ться** (*impf* **вступа́ться**) *сов возв*: **~ся за** *+acc* to stand up for.
вступле́ни|е (-я) *ср* (*войск: в город*) entry; (*в партию*) joining; (*в стадию*) entering; (*в книге, в статье*) introduction; (*в беседе*) preamble.
вступлю́ *сов см* **вступи́ть.**
всу́н|уть (-у, -ешь; *impf* **всо́вывать)** *сов перех*: **~ (в** *+acc*) to stick *или* put in(to).
всухомя́тку *нареч*: **пита́ться ~** *to live off cold snacks*; **есть** (*impf*) **хлеб ~** to eat dry bread.
всуч|и́ть (-у́, -ишь; *impf* **всу́чивать)** *сов перех* (*навязать*) to palm off.
всхлип (-а) *м* sob.
всхли́пыва|ть (-ю) *несов неперех* to sob.
всхо|ди́ть (-жу́, -дишь) *несов от* **взойти́.**
всхо́д|ы (-ов) *мн* shoots *мн*.
всхожу́ *сов см* **всходи́ть.**
всып|ать (-лю, -лешь; *impf* **всыпа́ть)** *сов перех*: **~ в** *+acc* to pour into ◆ *неперех*: **~ кому́-н** (*разг: отчитать*) to give sb what for.
всю *мест см* **вся.**
всю́ду *нареч* everywhere.
вс|я (-ей) *мест см* **весь.**
вся́к|ий (-ая, -ое, -ие) *мест* (*каждый*) every; (*разнообразный*) all kinds of; (*любой*) any ◆ **(-ого;** *decl like adj*) *м* (*любой*) anyone; (*каждый*) everyone; **здесь продаю́т ~ие това́ры** all kinds of goods are sold here; **у меня́ пропа́ло ~ое жела́ние помо́чь** I have lost all desire to help; **без ~ого сомне́ния/интере́са/жела́ния** without the slightest doubt/interest/desire; **безо ~ого** *или* **~их согласи́ться** (*perf*)**/приня́ть** (*perf*) (*разг*) to agree/accept without a second thought.
вся́ко *нареч* (*разг*) all sorts of things.
вся́чески *нареч* in every possible way.
вся́ческ|ий (-ая, -ое, -ие) *мест* (*поддержка, сопротивление*) all possible; (*товары*) all kinds of.
вся́чин|а (-ы) *ж* (*разг*): **вся́кая ~** all sorts of things.
Вт *сокр* (= *ватт*) W (= *watt*).
вта́йне *нареч* secretly, in secret.
вта́лкива|ть (-ю) *несов от* **втолкну́ть.**
вта́птыва|ть (-ю) *несов от* **втопта́ть.**
втащ|и́ть (-у́, -ишь; *impf* **вта́скивать)** *сов перех*: **~ (в** *+acc*) to drag in(to).
втёк *итп сов см* **втечь.**
втека́|ть (*3sg* **-ет,** *3pl* **-ют)** *несов от* **втечь.**
втеку́т *сов см* **втечь.**
втере́ть (вотру́, вотрёшь; *pt* **втёр, втёрла, втёрло,** *impf* **втира́ть)** *сов перех*: **~ (в** *+acc*) to rub in(to)
▸ **втере́ться** (*impf* **втира́ться**) *сов возв* to be absorbed; (*разг: пренебр*) to worm one's way in; **~ся** (*perf*) **в дове́рие кому́-н** to worm one's way into sb's confidence.

вте|чь (*3sg* **-чёт**, *3pl* **-кýт**, *pt* **втёк, -клá, -клó**, *impf* **втекáть**) *сов неперех*: ~ **в** *+acc* to flow into.
втирá|ть(ся) (**-ю(сь)**) *несов от* **втерéть(ся)**.
втúсн|уть (**-у, -ешь**; *impf* **втúскивать**) *сов перех*: ~ (**в** *+acc*) to cram in(to)
▸ **втúснуться** *сов возв* (*разг*) (*impf* **втúскиваться**): **~ся** (**в** *+acc*) (*человек*) to squeeze in(to).
втихомóлку *нареч* (*разг*) on the quiet.
втолкн|ýть (**-ý, -ёшь**; *impf* **втáлкивать**) *сов перех*: ~ (**в** *+acc*) to push in(to).
втолк|овáть (**-ýю**; *impf* **втолкóвывать**) *сов перех* (*разг*): ~ **что-н комý-н** to get sth through to sb.
втоп|тáть (**-чý, -чешь**; *impf* **втáптывать**) *сов перех*: ~ (**в** *+acc*) to trample in(to); **втáптывать** (~ *perf*) **когó-н в грязь** (*перен*) to humiliate sb.
втор|áя (**-óй**; *decl like adj*) *ж*: **однá** ~ one half.
втóргн|уться (**-усь, -ешься**; *impf* **вторгáться**) *сов возв*: ~ **в** *+acc* (*в страну*) to invade; (*вмешаться*) to interfere with *или* in.
втóр|ить (**-ю, -ишь**) *несов неперех* (*+dat*; *петь*) to sing the second part to; (*разг*: *поддакивать*) to parrot.
вторúчный *прил* (*повторный*) second; (*второстепенный*) secondary; **вторúчное сырьё** recyclable materials.
втóрник (**-а**) *м* Tuesday; **во** ~ on Tuesday; **по ~ам** on Tuesdays; **в слéдующий/прóшлый** ~ next/last Tuesday; **сегóдня ~, десятое мáя** today is Tuesday (the) 10th (of) May.
второгóдник (**-а**) *м pupil repeating a year at school.*
второгóдница (**-ы**) *ж см* **второгóдник**.
втор|óе (**-óго**; *decl like adj*) *ср* main course; **на ~ – бифштéкс** the main course is steak.
втор|óй (**-áя, -óе, -ые**) *прил* second; (*роль*) secondary; **быть** (*impf*) **на ~óм плáне** to stay in the background; **сейчáс ~ час** it's after one; **сейчáс половúна ~óго** it's half past one; **вторóе дыхáние** second wind; **вторáя мóлодость** second wind; **вторóй сорт** second class; *см также* **пятый**.
второклáссник (**-а**) *м pupil in second year at school (usually eight years old).*
второклáссница (**-ы**) *ж см* **второклáссник**.
второпях *нареч* in a hurry.
второсóрт|ный (**-ен, -на, -но**) *прил* second-class; (*посредственный*) second-rate.
второстепéн|ный (**-ен, -на, -но**) *прил* secondary.
в-трéтьих *вводн сл* thirdly, in the third place.
втрúдорога *нареч* (*разг*): **платúть** ~ to pay a mint *или* bomb.
втрóе *нареч* (*больше, меньше*) three times; (*увеличить*) threefold.
втроём *нареч* in a group of three.
втройнé *нареч* three times as much.
втýл|ка (**-ки**; *gen pl* **-ок**) *ж* (*пробка*) plug; (*ТЕХ*) bush.
втыкá|ть (**-ю**) *несов от* **воткнýть**.
втян|ýть (**-ý, -ешь**; *impf* **втягивать**) *сов перех* (*втащить*) to pull in; (*вобрать*) to take in; **втягивать** (~ *perf*) **когó-н в** *+acc* (*перен*: *в дело*) to involve sb in; (: *в конфликт итп*) to draw sb into
▸ **втянýться** (*impf* **втягиваться**) *сов возв*: **~ся в** *+acc* to get involved in; (*привыкнуть*) to settle into.
вуалúр|овать (**-ую**; *perf* **завуалúровать**) *несов перех* to veil.
вуáл|ь (**-и**) *ж* veil.
вуз (**-а**) *м сокр* (= *высшее учéбное заведéние*) institution of higher education.
вýзовск|ий (**-ая, -ое, -ие**) *прил* university *опред*; **~ая системá** higher education system.
вулкáн (**-а**) *м* volcano; **дéйствующий/потýхший** ~ active/extinct volcano.
вульгáрен *прил см* **вульгáрный**.
вульгáрност|ь (**-и**) *ж* vulgarity.
вульгáр|ный (**-ен, -на, -но**) *прил* (*человек, слова*) vulgar.
вундеркúнд (**-а**) *м* child prodigy.
вход (**-а**) *м* (*движение*) entry; (*место*) entrance; (*ТЕХ*) inlet; (*КОМП*) input.
вхо|дúть (**-жý, -дишь**) *несов от* **войтú**.
входнóй *прил* (*дверь*) entrance *опред*; (*КОМП*) input *опред*; **входнóй билéт** entrance ticket.
входящ|ий (**-ая, -ее, -ие**) *прил* incoming.
вхожý *сов см* **входúть**.
вхолостýю *нареч*: **рабóтать** ~ to idle.
вцеп|úться (**-лю́сь, -ишься**; *impf* **вцепляться**) *сов возв*: ~ **в** *+acc* to seize.
ВЦСПС *м сокр* (= *Всероссúйский Центрáльный Совéт профессионáльных союзов*) *central trade-union council.*
ВЧ *ж сокр* (= *высóкая частотá*) HF (= *high frequency*) ◆ *прил* (*высокочастóтный*) HF (= *high-frequency*).
вчерá *нареч, м нескл* yesterday.
вчерáшн|ий (**-яя, -ее, -ие**) *прил* (*также перен*) yesterday's; **жить** (*impf*) **~им днём** to live in the past.
вчернé *нареч* in rough.
вчéтверо *нареч* (*больше, меньше*) four times; (*увеличить*) fourfold.
вчетверóм *нареч* in a group of four.
в-четвёртых *нареч* fourthly, in the fourth place.
вчитá|ться (**-юсь**; *impf* **вчитываться**) *сов возв*: ~ (**в** *+acc*) to get the gist (of).
вшéй(те) *сов см* **вшить**.
вшéстеро *нареч* (*больше, меньше*) six times; (*увеличить*) sixfold.
вшестерóм *нареч* in a group of six.
вши *итп сущ см* **вошь**.
вшивá|ть (**-ю**) *несов от* **вшить**.
вшúве|ть (**-ю**; *perf* **завшúветь**) *несов неперех* to become lice-ridden.
вшúвый *прил* lice-ridden.
вширь *нареч* in breadth; **раздавáться** (**раздáться** *perf*) ~ to put on weight.
вшить (**вошью, вошьёшь**; *imper* **вшéй(те)**, *impf*

вшивáть) *сов перех* to sew in.
въедá|ться (**-юсь**) *несов от* **въéсться**.
въéдешь *итп сов см* **въéхать**.
въéдлив|ый (**-, -а, -о**) *прил* meticulous.
въéду *итп сов см* **въéхать**.
въедя́тся *сов см* **въéсться**.
въезд (**-а**) *м* (*движение*) entry; (*место*) entrance.
въезднóй *прил* entry *опред*.
въезжá|ть (**-ю**) *несов от* **въéхать**.
въé|сться (*3sg* **-стся**, *3pl* **-дя́тся**, *impf* **въедáться**) *сов возв*: ~ **в** *+acc* (*кислота, ржавчина*) to eat into; (*краска, грязь*) to become ingrained in.
въé|хать (*как* **éхать**; *см* **Table 19**; *impf* **въезжáть**) *сов неперех* to enter; (*в новый дом*) to move in; (*наверх: на машине*) to drive up; (*: на коне, велосипеде*) to ride up.
вы- *префикс* (*in verbs*; *об исчерпанности действия*) *indicating completion of action eg. вы́яснить, вы́спаться*; (*о движении иаружи*) *indicating movement outwards eg. вы́бежать*.
Вы (**Вас**; *см* **Table 5b**) *мест* you; **быть** *(impf)* **на ~ с кем-н** to be on formal terms with sb.
вы (**вас**; *см* **Table 5b**) *мест* you (*plural*).
вы́бе|жать (*как* **бежáть**; *см* **Table 20**; *impf* **выбегáть**) *сов неперех* to run out.
вы́бей(те) *сов см* **вы́бить**.
вы́бел|ить (**-ю, -ишь**) *сов от* **бели́ть**.
вы́беру(сь) *итп сов см* **вы́брать(ся)**.
выбивá|ть(ся) (**-ю(сь)**) *несов от* **вы́бить(ся)**.
выбирá|ть (**-ю**) *несов от* **вы́брать** ◆ *перех*: ~ **словá** to choose one's words
▸ **выбирáться** *несов от* **вы́браться**.
вы́би|ть (**-ью, -ьешь**; *imper* **вы́бей(те)**, *impf* **выбивáть**) *сов перех* to knock out; (*противника*) to oust; (*ковер*) to beat; (*надпись*) to carve; (*разг: деньги, контракт*) to manage to get; **выбивáть (~** *perf*) **чек** (*кассир*) to ring up the total; **выбивáть (~** *perf*) **чек в кáссе** (*покупатель*) to get a ticket from the cashier (*to claim purchase*)
▸ **вы́биться** (*impf* **выбивáться**) *сов возв*: **~ся из** *+gen* (*освободиться*) to get out of; **выбивáться (~ся** *perf*) **из сил** to wear o.s. out; **выбивáться (~ся** *perf*) **из грáфика** to fall behind schedule; **~ся** *(perf)* **в лю́ди** to make one's way up in the world.
вы́боин|а (**-ы**) *ж* (*на дороге*) pothole; (*на металле, в стене*) dent.
вы́бор (**-а**) *м* choice; (*ассортимент*) choice, selection; **предлагáть (предложи́ть** *perf*) **что-н на** ~ to offer a selection of sth; **по чьему́-н ~у** of sb's choice.
вы́бор|ка (**-ки**; *gen pl* **-ок**) *ж* (*обычно мн: из текста*) extract; (*статистическая*) sample.
вы́борный *прил* (*собрание, кампания*) election *опред*; (*бюллетень*) ballot *опред*; (*должность, орган*) elective.
вы́борок *сущ см* **вы́борка**.
вы́бороч|ный (**-ен, -на, -но**) *прил* selective.
вы́борщик (**-а**) *м* (*полит*) ≈ elector (*US*), *elected representative taking part in elections on a higher level*.
вы́бор|ы (**-ов**) *мн* election *ед*.
выбрáсыва|ть(ся) (**-ю(сь)**) *несов от* **вы́бросить(ся)**.
вы́б|рать (**-еру, -ерешь**; *impf* **выбирáть**) *сов перех* to choose; (*отобрать*) to pick; (*голосованием*) to elect
▸ **вы́браться** (*impf* **выбирáться**) *сов возв* to manage to get out; (*разг: в театр*) to find time to go.
вы́бр|ить (**-ею, -еешь**; *impf* **выбривáть**) *сов перех* to shave.
выбро|ди́ть (**-жу́, -дишь**) *сов от* **броди́ть**.
вы́брос (**-а**) *м* (*газа, радиации*) emission; (*отходов*) discharge; (*нефти*) spillage; (*десанта*) landing.
вы́бро|сить (**-шу, -сишь**; *impf* **выбрáсывать**) *сов перех* to throw out; (*разг: с работы*) to sack; (*отходы*) to discharge; (*газы*) to emit; (*десант*) to land; **выбрáсывать (~** *perf*) **на ры́нок** to bring onto the market
▸ **вы́броситься** (*impf* **выбрáсываться**) *сов возв* (*из окна*) to throw o.s. out; **выбрáсываться (~ся** *perf*) **с балкóна** to throw o.s. off the balcony; **выбрáсываться (~ся** *perf*) **с парашю́том** to bale out.
вы́б|ыть (*как* **быть**; *см* **Table 21**; *impf* **выбывáть**) *сов неперех*: ~ **из** *+gen* to leave.
вы́бью *итп сов см* **вы́бить**.
вы́вал|ить (**-ю, -ишь**; *impf* **вывáливать**) *сов перех*: ~ (**из** *+gen*) to empty (out of)
▸ **вы́валиться** (*impf* **вывáливаться**) *сов возв* (*выпасть*) to fall out; (*разг: толпа*) to pour out.
выведéни|е (**-я**) *ср* (*формулы*) deduction; (*цыплят, птенцов*) hatching; (*сорта, породы*) breeding; (*вредителей*) extermination.
вы́веду(сь) *итп сов см* **вы́вести(сь)**.
вы́вез|ти (**-у, -ешь**; *impf* **вывози́ть**) *сов перех* to take; (*товар: из страны*) to take out.
вы́вер|ить (**-ю, -ишь**; *impf* **выверя́ть**) *сов перех* to check; (*часы*) to set (*to the right time*).
вы́верн|уть (**-у, -ешь**; *impf* **вывёртывать** *или* **вывора́чивать**) *сов перех* (*винт, лампу*) to unscrew; (*пробку*) to pull out; (*карманы, рукава*) to turn inside out
▸ **вы́вернуться** (*impf* **вывёртываться** *или* **вывора́чиваться**) *сов возв* (*винт, лампа*) to come unscrewed; (*пробка*) to come out; (*человек: из беды*) to get out.
выверя́|ть (**-ю**) *несов от* **вы́верить**.
вы́ве|сить (**-шу, -сишь**; *impf* **вывéшивать**) *сов перех* (*флаг, лозунг*) to put up; (*бельё*) to hang

out; (*объявление*) to post (up).
вы́вес|ка (**-ки**; *gen pl* **-ок**) *ж* sign; (*перен*) front; **под ~кой чего́-н** under the guise of sth.
вы́ве|сти (**-ду, -дешь**; *impf* **выводи́ть**) *сов перех* to take out; (*войска: из города*) to pull out; (*: на парад*) to bring out; (*формулу*) to deduce; (*заключение*) to draw; (*птенцов*) to hatch; (*сорт, породу*) to breed; (*вредителей*) to exterminate; (*КОМП*) to output; (*изобразить*) to portray; (*исключить*): **~ кого́-н из** *+gen* (*из партии, из комитета*) to expel sb from; (*из игры*) to take sb off; **выводи́ть (~** *perf*) **кого́-н из шо́ка/из тра́нса** to bring sb out of a shock/ trance; **выводи́ть (~** *perf*) **кого́-н из терпе́ния** to exasperate sb; **выводи́ть (~** *perf*) **кого́-н из равнове́сия** to disturb sb's equilibrium; **выводи́ть (~** *perf*) **кого́-н в лю́ди** to help sb on in life; **выводи́ть (~** *perf*) **кого́-н из себя́** to drive sb mad
▸ **вы́вестись** (*impf* **выводи́ться**) *сов возв* (*цыплята*) to hatch (out); (*исчезнуть*) to be eradicated.
вы́ветр|иться (*3sg* **-ится**, *3pl* **-ятся**, *impf* **выве́триваться**) *сов возв* (*запах, дым*) to disperse; (*берег, горные породы*) to weather.
выве́шива|ть (**-ю**) *несов от* **вы́весить**.
вы́вешу *сов см* **вы́весить**.
вы́вих (**-а**) *м* dislocation.
вы́вихн|уть (**-у, -ешь**; *impf* **выви́хивать**) *сов перех* to dislocate.
вы́вод (**-а**) *м* (*войск: из города*) withdrawal; (*формулы*) deduction; (*умозаключение*) conclusion; (*ЭЛЕК*) outlet; (*КОМП*) output; **приходи́ть (прийти́** *perf*) **к ~у** to come to a conclusion.
вы|води́ть(ся) (**-вожу́(сь), -во́дишь(ся)**) *несов от* **вы́вести(сь)**.
вы́вод|ок (**-ка**) *м* brood.
вывожу́(сь) *несов см* **выводи́ть(ся)**, **вывози́ть**.
вы́воз (**-а**) *м* removal; (*детей: на дачу*) taking out; (*товаров*) export.
вы|вози́ть (**-вожу́, -во́зишь**) *несов от* **вы́везти**.
вывозно́й *прил* export *опред*.
вывора́чива|ть(ся) (**-ю(сь)**) *несов от* **вы́вернуть(ся)**.
вы́гада|ть (**-ю**; *impf* **выга́дывать**) *сов перех* (*получить преимущество*) to gain; (*сэкономить*) to save.
вы́гиб (**-а**) *м* curve.
выгиба́|ть (**-ю**) *несов от* **вы́гнуть**.
вы́гла|дить (**-жу, -дишь**) *сов от* **гла́дить**.
вы́гля|деть (**-жу, -дишь**) *несов неперех* to look; **она хорошо́ ~дит сего́дня** she looks nice today; **он ~дит печа́льным** he looks sad.
выгля́дыва|ть (**-ю**) *несов от* **вы́глянуть**.
вы́гляжу *несов см* **вы́глядеть**.
вы́глян|уть (**-у, -ешь**; *impf* **выгля́дывать**) *сов неперех* to look out.
вы́г|нать (**-оню, -онишь**; *impf* **выгоня́ть**) *сов перех* to throw out; (*из страны*) to banish; (*разг: с работы*) to sack; (*стадо, табун*) to drive out.
вы́гн|уть (**-у, -ешь**; *impf* **выгиба́ть**) *сов перех* to bend; (*спину*) to arch.
выгова́рива|ть (**-ю**) *несов от* **вы́говорить**.
вы́говор (**-а**) *м* (*произношение*) accent; (*за провинность*) reprimand; **де́лать (сде́лать** *perf*) **~ кому́-н за что-н** to tell sb off for sth; **выноси́ть (вы́нести** *perf*) **~ кому́-н** to issue sb with a reprimand.
вы́говор|ить (**-ю, -ишь**; *impf* **выгова́ривать**) *сов перех* (*произнести*) to pronounce; (*сказать*) to say
▸ **вы́говориться** *сов возв* (*разг*) to say what's on one's mind.
вы́год|а (**-ы**) *ж* advantage, benefit; (*прибыль*) profit; **кака́я ему́ от э́того ~?** what does he hope to gain from this?
вы́годно *нареч* (*продать*) at a profit ◆ *как сказ* it is profitable; **мне э́то ~** this is to my advantage; (*финансово*) this is profitable for me.
вы́год|ный (**-ен, -на, -но**) *прил* (*сделка*) profitable; (*условия*) advantageous; (*впечатление*) favourable (*BRIT*), favorable (*US*); **выставля́ть (вы́ставить** *perf*) *или* **представля́ть (предста́вить** *perf*) **что-н в ~ном све́те** to show sth to (the) best advantage.
вы́гоню *итп сов см* **вы́гнать**.
выгоня́|ть (**-ю**) *несов от* **вы́гнать**.
вы́гор|еть (*3sg* **-ит**, *3pl* **-ят**, *impf* **выгора́ть**) *сов неперех* (*сгореть*) to burn down; (*высохнуть*) to be scorched; (*выцвести*) to fade; (*разг: удаваться*) to come off.
вы́горо|дить (**-жу, -дишь**; *impf* **выгора́живать**) *сов перех* (*разг*) to fence off.
вы́гравир|овать (**-ую**) *несов от* **гравирова́ть**.
вы́гре|сти (**-бу, -бешь**; *pt* **-б, -ла, -ло**, *impf* **выгреба́ть**) *сов перех* to rake out.
вы́гру|зить (**-жу, -зишь**; *impf* **выгружа́ть**) *сов перех* to unload; (*КОМП*) to dump
▸ **вы́грузиться** (*impf* **выгружа́ться**) *сов возв* to unload; (*высадиться*) to disembark; (*: из поезда*) to get off.
выда|ва́ть (**-ю́**) *несов от* **вы́дать**
▸ **выдава́ться** *несов от* **вы́даться** ◆ *возв*: **~ся чем-н** to stand out by virtue of sth.
вы́дав|ить (**-лю, -ишь**; *impf* **выда́вливать**) *сов перех* (*лимон*) to squeeze; (*ягоды*) to press; (*дверь*) to break down; **выда́вливать (~** *perf*) **что-н из чего́-н** to squeeze sth out of sth.
вы́да|ть (*как* **дать**; *см* **Table 14**; *impf* **выдава́ть**) *сов перех* to give out; (*свидетельство, патент итп*) to issue; (*продукцию*) to produce; (*тайну, сообщников*) to give away; **выдава́ть (~** *perf*) **кого́-н/что-н за** *+acc* to pass sb/sth off as; **выдава́ть (~** *perf*) **де́вушку за́муж** to marry a girl off
▸ **вы́даться** (*impf* **выдава́ться**) *сов возв* (*берег*) to jut out; **сего́дня ~лся хоро́ший день** (*разг*) it's turned out fine today.

вы́дач|а (-и) *ж* (*справки*) issue; (*зарплаты*) payment; (*продукции*) output; (*заложников*) release.
вы́дашь(ся) *сов см* **вы́дать(ся)**.
выдаю́щ|ийся (-аяся, -ееся, -иеся) *прил* outstanding.
выдвига́|ть(ся) (-ю(сь)) *несов от* **вы́двинуть(ся)**.
выдвиже́ни|е (-я) *ср* (*кандидата*) nomination; (*предложения*) proposal.
выдвижно́й *прил* sliding.
вы́двин|уть (-у, -ешь; *impf* **выдвига́ть**) *сов перех* to pull out; (*предложение, гипотезу, человека*) to put forward; (*обвинение*) to level
▸ **вы́двинуться** (*impf* **выдвига́ться**) *сов возв* to slide out; (*работник*) to get ahead, advance; **выдвига́ться** (**~ся** *perf*) **на руководя́щую рабо́ту** to be promoted to a management position.
вы́двор|ить (-ю, -ишь; *impf* **выдворя́ть**) *сов перех* (*разг*) to kick out.
вы́дела|ть (-ю; *impf* **выде́лывать**) *сов перех* to treat.
выделе́ни|е (-я) *ср* (*средств*) allocation; (*ФИЗИОЛОГИЯ*) secretion; (*обычно мн*: *в гинекологии*) discharge.
вы́дел|ить (-ю, -ишь; *impf* **выделя́ть**) *сов перех* to assign, allocate; (*время*) to allot; (*отличить*: *ученика, цитату*) to pick out; (*пот*) to secrete; (*газы, вредные вещества*) to emit
▸ **вы́делиться** (*impf* **выделя́ться**) *сов возв* (*в отдельное предприятие*) to split off; (*пот*) to be secreted; (*газ, вредные вещества*) to be emitted; **выделя́ться** (**~ся** *perf*) **чем-н** to stand out by virtue of sth.
вы́делк|а (-и) *ж* treatment.
выде́лыва|ть (-ю) *несов от* **вы́делать** ◆ *перех* (*разг*: *вытворять*) to get up to; **что э́то он там ~ет?** what is he up to?
выделя́|ть(ся) (-ю(сь)) *несов от* **вы́делить(ся)**.
выдёргива|ть (-ю) *несов от* **вы́дернуть**.
вы́держан|ный (-, -на, -но) *прил* (*человек*) self-possessed; (*no short form*; *изложение, теория*) consistent; (*вино, сыр*) mature; (*древесина*) seasoned.
вы́держ|ать (-у, -ишь; *impf* **выде́рживать**) *сов перех* (*давление, тяжесть*) to withstand; (*боль*) to bear; (*экзамен, испытание*) to get through; (*график, параметры*) to keep to; (*вино, сыр*) to let mature; (*древесину*) to season ◆ *неперех*: **он не ~ал и рассмея́лся** he couldn't contain his laughter; **кни́га ~ала мно́го изда́ний** the book has been published in several editions; **выде́рживать** (~ *perf*) **хара́ктер** to hold one's ground.
вы́держек *сущ см* **вы́держка**.
выде́ржива|ть (-ю) *несов от* **вы́держать**.
вы́держ|ка (-ки; *gen pl* -ек) *ж* (*самообладание*) self-control; (*из текста*) excerpt; (*вина*) maturing; (*древесины*) seasoning; (*ФОТО*) exposure.
вы́дерн|уть (-у, -ешь; *impf* **выдёргивать**) *сов перех* to pull out.
вы́деру *итп сов см* **вы́драть**.
выдира́|ть (-ю) *несов от* **вы́драть**.
вы́долб|ить (-лю, -ишь) *сов от* **долби́ть**.
вы́дох (-а) *м* exhalation; **де́лать** (**сде́лать** *perf*) **~** to breathe out.
вы́дохн|уть (-у, -ешь; *impf* **выдыха́ть**) *сов перех* to exhale, breathe out
▸ **вы́дохнуться** (*impf* **выдыха́ться**) *сов возв* (*вино, духи*) to lose all smell; (*разг*) to be washed out.
вы́др|а (-ы) *ж* otter.
вы́дра|ить (-ю, -ишь) *сов от* **дра́ить**.
вы́д|рать (-еру, -ерешь) *сов от* **драть** ◆ (*impf* **выдира́ть**) *перех* (*разг*: *вырвать*) to tear out.
вы́дрессир|овать (-ую) *сов от* **дрессирова́ть**.
вы́дуб|ить (-лю, -ишь) *несов от* **дуби́ть**.
выдува́|ть (-ю) *несов от* **вы́дуть**.
вы́думанный *прил* made-up.
вы́дума|ть (-ю; *impf* **выду́мывать**) *сов перех* (*историю*) to make up, invent; (*игру*) to invent.
вы́дум|ка (-ки; *gen pl* -ок) *ж* invention.
выду́мыва|ть (-ю) *несов от* **вы́думать**.
вы́ду|ть (-ю; *impf* **выдува́ть**) *сов перех* to blow out; (*разг*: *водку итп*) to knock back; (*impf* **выдува́ть** *или* **дуть**; *ТЕХ*) to blow.
выдыха́ни|е (-я) *ср* exhalation.
выдыха́|ть(ся) (-ю(сь)) *несов от* **вы́дохнуть(ся)**.
выеда́|ть (-ю) *несов от* **вы́есть**.
вы́еду *итп сов см* **вы́ехать**.
вы́езд (-а) *м* (*отъезд*) departure; (*место*) way out.
вы́ез|дить (-жу, -дишь; *impf* **выезжа́ть**) *сов перех* (*лошадь*) to break in.
вы́ездк|а (-и) *ж* (*СПОРТ*) dressage.
выездно́й *прил* (*виза, документ*) exit *опред*; (*сессия суда*) in temporary premises; (*спектакль*) travelling (*BRIT*), traveling (*US*); **~ матч** away match.
выезжа́|ть (-ю) *несов от* **вы́ехать**.
вы́езжу *сов см* **вы́ездить**.
вы́ем|ка (-ки; *gen pl* -ок) *ж* (*писем*) collection; (*грунта*) excavation; (*углубление*) hollow.
вы́есть (*как* **есть**; *см* **Table 15**; *impf* **выеда́ть**) *сов перех* (*съесть*) to eat; (*испортить*) to eat through.
вы́е|хать (*как* **е́хать**; *см* **Table 19**; *impf* **выезжа́ть**) *сов неперех* (*уехать*) to leave; (*машина, танк*) to drive out; (*всадник*) to ride out; **выезжа́ть** (~ *perf*) **на ком-н/чём-н** (*перен*: *разг*) to use sb/sth.

вы́ж|ать (**-му, -мешь**; *impf* **выжима́ть**) *сов перех* (*лимон*) to squeeze; (*ягоды*) to press; (*бельё*) to wring (out); **выжима́ть** (~ *perf*) **что-н из чего́-н** to squeeze sth out of sth; **выжима́ть** (~ *perf*) **что-н из кого́-н** (*перен*) to wring sth out of sb.

вы́жгу *итп сов см* **вы́жечь.**

вы́жд|ать (**-у, -ёшь**; *impf* **выжида́ть**) *сов перех*: ~ **подходя́щий моме́нт** to pick one's moment.

вы́ж|ечь (**-гу, -жешь** *итп* **-гут**; *pt* **-ег, -гла, -гло**, *impf* **выжига́ть**) *сов перех* to burn; (*подлеж: солнце*) to scorch; **выжига́ть** (~ *perf*) **клеймо** to brand; **выжига́ть** *(impf)* **по де́реву** to do pokerwork.

выжива́ни|е (**-я**) *ср* survival.

выжива́|ть (**-ю**) *несов от* **вы́жить.**

вы́живу *итп сов см* **вы́жить.**

выжига́|ть (**-ю**) *несов от* **вы́жечь.**

выжида́тел|ьный (**-ен, -ьна, -ьно**) *прил* (*тактика, политика*) delaying; **занима́ть** (**заня́ть** *perf*) ~**ьную пози́цию** to play a waiting game.

выжида́|ть (**-ю**) *несов от* **вы́ждать.**

выжима́|ть (**-ю**) *несов от* **вы́жать.**

вы́жи|ть (**-ву, -вешь**; *impf* **выжива́ть**) *сов неперех* to survive ◆ *перех* (*разг*) to drive out; ~ *(perf)* **из ума́** to become senile.

вы́жму *итп сов см* **вы́жать.**

вы́з|вать (**-ову, -овешь**; *impf* **вызыва́ть**) *сов перех* to call; (*гнев, критику*) to provoke; (*восторг*) to arouse; (*пожар*) to cause; **вызыва́ть** (~ *perf*) **кого́-н на что-н** to challenge sb to sth; **вызыва́ть** (~ *perf*) **что-н к жи́зни** to give rise to sth; **вызыва́ть** (~ *perf*) **врача́ на́ дом** to call out a doctor

▸ **вы́зваться** (*impf* **вызыва́ться**) *сов возв*: ~**ся** *+infin* to volunteer to do.

вы́звол|ить (**-ю, -ишь**; *impf* **вызволя́ть**) *сов перех* (*разг*) to bale out.

вы́здоров|еть (**-лю, -ишь**; *impf* **выздора́вливать**) *сов неперех* to recover.

вы́зов (**-а**) *м* call; (*в суд, к директору*) summons; ~ *+dat* (*обществу, родителям итп*) challenge to; **броса́ть** (**бро́сить** *perf*) ~ **кому́-н/чему́-н** to challenge sb/sth.

вы́зову(сь) *сов см* **вы́звать(ся).**

вы́зубр|ить (**-ю, -ишь**) *сов от* **зубри́ть.**

вызыва́|ть(ся) (**-ю(сь)**) *несов от* **вы́звать(ся).**

вызыва́ющий (**-ая, -ее, -ие**) *прил* provocative.

вы́игра|ть (**-ю**; *impf* **выи́грывать**) *сов перех* to win ◆ *неперех* (*получить выгоду*) to gain, benefit.

вы́игрыш (**-а**) *м* (*матча*) winning; (*крупный, денежный*) winnings *мн*; (*выгода*) advantage; ~ **пал на но́мер 10** number 10 wins.

вы́игрыш|ный (**-ен, -на, -но**) *прил* (*выгодный*) advantageous; ~ **вклад** ≈ premium bonds.

вы́|йти (*как* **идти́**; *см* **Table 18**; *impf* **выходи́ть**) *сов неперех* to leave; (*из игры*) to drop out; (*сойти*) to get off; (*появиться*) to come out; (*случиться*) to ensue; (*комп*) to exit; (*иссякнуть*) to run out; (*оказаться*): ~ *+instr* to come out; **выходи́ть** (~ *perf*) **из** *+gen* (*из затруднения*) to get out of; (*из употребления, из моды*) to go out of; (*из крестьян*) to be descended from; (*из графика, из расписания*) to fall behind; **выходи́ть** (~ *perf*) **на** *+acc* (*разг*) to get in with; **выходи́ть** (~ *perf*) **за́муж за** *+acc* to marry (*of woman*), get married to; **выходи́ть** (~ *perf*) **из больни́цы** to leave hospital; **выходи́ть** (~ *perf*) **из себя́** to lose one's temper; **выходи́ть** (~ *perf*) **из систе́мы** (*комп*) to log off; **из него́** ~**шел хоро́ший врач** he has turned out to be a good doctor; **из э́того ничего́ не** ~**шло** nothing came of it.

выка́лыва|ть (**-ю**) *несов от* **вы́колоть.**

выка́пыва|ть (**-ю**) *несов от* **вы́копать.**

вы́карабка|ться (**-юсь**; *impf* **выкара́бкиваться**) *сов возв*: ~ (**из** *+gen*) to clamber out (of); (*разг: из трудностей*) to get o.s. out (of); (: *из болезни*) to pull through.

выка́рмлива|ть (**-ю**) *несов от* **вы́кормить.**

вы́ка|тить (**-чу, -тишь**; *impf* **выка́тывать**) *сов перех* (*что-н круглое*) to roll out; (*что-н на колесах*) to wheel out; **выка́тывать** (~ *perf*) **глаза́** (*разг*) to open one's eyes wide.

вы́кача|ть (**-ю**; *impf* **выка́чивать**) *сов перех* to pump out; (*перен: разг: деньги*) to squeeze *или* wring out.

вы́качу *сов см* **вы́катить.**

выка́шива|ть (**-ю**) *несов от* **вы́косить.**

выки́дыва|ть (**-ю**) *несов от* **вы́кинуть.**

вы́кидыш (**-а**) *м* miscarriage.

вы́кин|уть (**-у, -ешь**; *impf* **выки́дывать**) *сов перех* (*мусор*) to throw out; (*пропустить*) to omit; (*разг: товар*) to put on sale; **выки́дывать** (~ *perf*) **шу́тку** *или* **фо́кус** (*разг*) to play a trick.

вы́кип|еть (*3sg* **-ит**, *3pl* **-ят**, *impf* **выкипа́ть**) *сов неперех* to boil away.

вы́клад|ка (**-ки**; *gen pl* **-ок**) *ж* (*облицовка*) facing; (*обычно мн: расчёты*) calculation.

выкла́дыва|ть(ся) (**-ю(сь)**) *несов от* **вы́ложить(ся).**

выключа́тел|ь (**-я**) *м* switch.

вы́ключ|ить (**-у, -ишь**; *impf* **выключа́ть**) *сов перех* to turn off; (*исключить*) to expel

▸ **вы́ключиться** (*impf* **выключа́ться**) *сов возв* (*мотор, телевизор итп*) to go off; (*свет*) to go out; (*перен*) to switch off.

вы́клянч|ить (**-у, -ишь**) *сов от* **кля́нчить.**

вы́к|овать (**-ую**; *impf* **выко́вывать**) *сов перех* (*металл*) to forge.

выкола́чива|ть (**-ю**) *несов от* **вы́колотить.**

вы́коло|тить (**-чу, -тишь**; *impf* **выкола́чивать**) *сов перех* (*ковёр*) to beat; (*налоги*) to wring out.

вы́кол|оть (**-ю, -ешь**; *impf* **выка́лывать**) *сов перех* to poke out.

вы́колочу *сов см* **вы́колотить.**

вы́копа|ть (**-ю**; *impf* **выка́пывать** *или* **копа́ть**) *сов перех* (*яму*) to dig; (*колодец*) to sink; (*овощи*) to dig up.

вы́корм|ить (**-лю, -ишь**; *impf* **выка́рмливать**) *сов перех* to rear.

вы́корч|евать (**-ую**; *impf* **выкорчёвывать** *или* **корчева́ть**) *сов перех* to uproot; (*перен*) to root out.
вы́ко|сить (**-шу, -сишь**; *impf* **выка́шивать**) *сов перех* to mow.
выкра́дыва|ть (**-ю**) *несов от* **вы́красть**.
выкра́ива|ть (**-ю**) *несов перех* to cut out.
вы́кра|сить(ся) (**-шу(сь), -сишь(ся)**) *сов от* **кра́сить(ся)**.
вы́кра|сть (**-ду, -дешь**; *impf* **выкра́дывать**) *сов перех* to steal.
вы́крик (**-а**) *м* shout.
вы́крикн|уть (**-у, -ешь**; *impf* **выкри́кивать**) *сов перех* to shout *или* cry out.
вы́кристаллиз|оваться (*3sg* **-уется**, *3pl* **-уются**) *сов от* **кристаллизова́ться**.
вы́кроек *сущ см* **вы́кройка**.
вы́кро|ить (**-ю, -ишь**) *сов от* **крои́ть** ♦ (*impf* **выкра́ивать**) *перех* (*перен*): ~ **вре́мя на** *+acc* to find time for; ~ (*perf*) **де́ньги на** *+acc* to scrape together money for.
вы́кро|йка (**-йки**; *gen pl* **-ек**) *ж* pattern.
выкрута́с|ы (**-ов**) *мн* (*разг*: *в танце*) fancy footwork *ед*; (*перен*: *в речи*) fancy turns *мн* of phrase; (: *в поведении*) foibles *мн*.
вы́кру|тить (**-чу, -тишь**; *impf* **выкру́чивать**) *сов перех* to unscrew; **выкру́чивать** (~ *perf*) **ру́ки кому́-н** (*также перен*) to twist sb's arm
▸ **вы́крутиться** *сов возв* to come unscrewed; (*перен*) to get o.s. out.
вы́куп (**-а**) *м* (*действие*: *заложника*) ransoming; (: *вещей*) redemption; (*плата*) ransom.
вы́купа|ть(ся) (**-ю(сь)**) *несов от* **купа́ть(ся)**.
вы́куп|ить (**-лю, -ишь**; *impf* **выкупа́ть**) *сов перех* (*заложника*) to ransom; (*вещи*) to redeem.
вы́кур|ить (**-ю, -ишь**; *impf* **выку́ривать**) *сов перех* (*трубку*) to smoke; (*зверя*) to smoke out.
выла́влива|ть (**-ю**) *несов от* **вы́ловить**.
вы́лаз|ка (**-ки**; *gen pl* **-ок**) *ж* (*ВОЕН*) sortie.
выла́мыва|ть (**-ю**) *несов от* **вы́ломать**.
вылеза́|ть (**-ю**) *несов от* **вы́лезти**.
вы́лез|ти (**-у, -ешь**; *pt* **-, -ла, -ло**, *impf* **вылеза́ть**) *сов неперех* (*волосы, шерсть*) to fall out; **вылеза́ть** (~ *perf*) (**из** *+gen*) to climb out (of); (*разг*: *из долгов*) to get o.s. out (of); (: *из болезней*) to pull through; (: *рубашка*) to hang out.
вы́леп|ить (**-лю, -ишь**) *сов от* **лепи́ть**.
вы́лет (**-а**) *м* departure.
вы́ле|теть (**-чу, -тишь**; *impf* **вылета́ть**) *сов неперех* to fly out; (*машина*) to hurtle out; **его́ и́мя ~тело у меня́ из головы́** his name has slipped my mind.
вы́леч|ить (**-у, -ишь**; *impf* **выле́чивать** *или* **лечи́ть**) *сов перех* to cure
▸ **вы́лечиться** (*impf* **выле́чиваться** *или* **лечи́ться**) *несов возв* to be cured.
вы́лечу *сов см* **вы́лететь**.

вылива́|ть(ся) (**-ю(сь)**) *несов от* **вы́лить(ся)**.
вы́ли|зать (**-жу, -жешь**; *impf* **выли́зывать**) *сов перех* (*тарелку*) to lick clean; (*разг*: *дом*) to spring-clean.
вы́л|ить (**-ью, -ьешь**; *impf* **вылива́ть**) *сов перех* to pour out; (*impf* **лить**; *деталь, статую*) to cast
▸ **вы́литься** (*impf* **вылива́ться**) *сов возв* (*также перен*) to pour out; **вылива́ться** (~**ся** *perf*) **в** *+acc* to turn into.
вы́лов|ить (**-лю, -ишь**; *impf* **выла́вливать**) *сов перех* to catch.
вы́лож|ить (**-у, -ишь**; *impf* **выкла́дывать**) *сов перех* to lay out; (*перен*: *правду*) to lay bare; **выкла́дывать** (~ *perf*) **что-н чем-н** (*кирпичом, плиткой*) to face sth with sth
▸ **вы́ложиться** (*impf* **выкла́дываться**) *сов возв* to apply o.s.
вы́лома|ть (**-ю**; *impf* **выла́мывать**) *сов перех* to break open.
вы́луп|иться (*3sg* **-ится**, *3pl* **-ятся**, *impf* **вылу́пливаться**) *сов возв* (*птенцы*) to hatch (out).
вы́лью(сь) *итп сов см* **вы́лить(ся)**.
вы́ма|зать (**-жу, -жешь**) *сов от* **ма́зать** ♦ (*impf* **выма́зывать**) *перех* (*покрыть*) to coat; (*разг*: *запачкать*) to smear
▸ **вы́мазаться** *сов от* **ма́заться**.
выма́лива|ть (**-ю**) *несов от* **вы́молить**.
вы́ман|ить (**-ю, -ишь**; *impf* **выма́нивать**) *сов перех* (*зверя*) to lure out; **выма́нивать** (~ *perf*) **что-н у кого́-н** to cheat sb out of sth.
вы́мара|ть(ся) (**-ю(сь)**) *сов от* **мара́ть(ся)**.
выма́чива|ть (**-ю**) *несов от* **вы́мочить**.
вы́мени *итп сущ см* **вы́мя**.
вы́м|ереть (*3sg* **-рет**, *3pl* **-рут**, *impf* **вымира́ть**) *сов неперех* (*динозавры*) to die out, become extinct; (*город, селение*) to be dead.
вы́ме|сти (**-ту, -тешь**; *pt* **-л, -ла, -ло**, *impf* **вымета́ть**) *сов перех* to sweep out.
вы́ме|стить (**-щу, -стишь**; *impf* **вымеща́ть**) *сов перех*: ~ **что-н на ком-н** to take sth out on sb.
вымета́|ть (**-ю**) *несов от* **вы́мести**.
вы́мету *итп сов см* **вы́мести**.
вымеща́|ть (**-ю**) *несов от* **вы́местить**.
вы́мещу *сов см* **вы́местить**.
вымира́|ть (*3sg* **-ет**, *3pl* **-ют**) *несов от* **вы́мереть**.
вымога́тел|ь (**-я**) *м* extortionist.
вымога́тельств|о (**-а**) *ср* extortion.
вымога́|ть (**-ю**) *несов перех* to extort.
вы́мок|нуть (**-ну, -нешь**; *pt* **-, -ла, -ло**) *сов неперех* to get soaked through.
вы́молв|ить (**-лю, -ишь**) *сов перех* to utter.
вы́мол|ить (**-ю, -ишь**; *impf* **выма́ливать**) *сов перех* to successfully plead for.
вы́мо|стить (**-щу, -стишь**) *сов от* **мости́ть**.
вы́моч|ить (**-у, -ишь**; *impf* **выма́чивать**) *сов*

перех to soak.
вымощу *сов см* **вымостить.**
вымою *итп сов см* **вымыть.**
вымпел (-а) *м* (*на мачте корабля*) pennant; (*награда*) award (*in the form of a pennant*).
вымрет *итп сов см* **вымереть.**
вымуштр|овать (-ую) *сов от* **муштровать.**
вымыва|ть (-ю) *несов от* **вымыть.**
вымыс|ел (-ла) *м* fantasy; (*ложь*) fabrication.
вым|ыть (-ою, -оешь; *impf* **мыть**) *сов перех* to wash; (*impf* **вымывать**; *яму*) to hollow out; (*русло*) to channel out.
вымышлен|ный (-, -на, -но) *прил* fictitious.
вым|я (-ени; *как* **время**; *см* **Table 4**) *ср* udder.
вынашива|ть (-ю) *несов от* **выносить.**
вынес|ти (-у, -ешь; *pt* -, -ла, -ло, *impf* **выносить**) *сов перех* to carry *или* take out; (*приговор, вердикт*) to pass, pronounce; (*впечатления, знания*) to gain; (*боль, оскорбление*) to bear; **выносить** (~ *perf*) **кому-н благодарность** to officially thank sb; **выносить** (~ *perf*) **кому-н выговор** to issue sb with a reprimand
▸ **вынестись** (*impf* **выноситься**) *сов возв* to fly *или* rush out.
вынима|ть (-ю) *несов от* **вынуть.**
вынос (-а) *м* (*тела*) bearing out (*of coffin*); **продавать** *(impf)* **на** ~ to do take-aways.
выно|сить (-шу, -сишь; *impf* **вынашивать**) *сов перех* (*перен*) to nurture; (*младенца*) to carry to term.
вын|осить (-ошу, -осишь) *несов от* **вынести** ◆ *перех*: **я его не ~ошу** I can't bear *или* stand him
▸ **выноситься** *несов от* **вынестись.**
вынослив|ый (-, -а, -о) *прил* hardy.
выношу *сов см* **выносить.**
выношу(сь) *несов см* **выносить(ся).**
выну|дить (-жу, -дишь; *impf* **вынуждать**) *сов перех*: ~ **кого-н/что-н к чему-н** to force sb/sth into sth; **вынуждать** (~ *perf*) **кого-н/что-н** *+infin* to force sb/sth into doing.
вынужденный *прил* forced; **вынужденная посадка** emergency landing.
вынужу *сов см* **вынудить.**
вын|уть (-у, -ешь; *impf* **вынимать**) *сов перех* to take out.
вынырн|уть (-у, -ешь; *impf* **выныривать**) *сов неперех* (*из воды*) to surface; (*разг*: *из-за угла*) to pop up.
выпад (-а) *м* (*враждебное действие*) attack; (*СПОРТ*) lunge (*in fencing*).
выпада|ть (-ю) *несов от* **выпасть.**
выпадени|е (-я) *ср* (*осадков*) fall; (*зубов, волос*) falling out.
выпаду *итп сов см* **выпасть.**
выпал|ить (-ю, -ишь) *сов от* **палить** ◆ (*impf* **выпаливать**) *перех* (*перен*: *разг*) to blurt out.
выпар|иться (*3sg* **-ится**, *3pl* **-ятся**, *impf* **выпариваться**) *сов возв* to evaporate.
выпа|сть (-ду, -дешь; *impf* **выпадать**) *сов неперех* to fall out; (*осадки*) to fall; (*+dat*; *задание, задача итп*) to fall to; **мне ~л случай/счастье встретить его** I chanced to/had the luck to meet him.
выпачка|ть(ся) (-ю(сь)) *сов от* **пачкать(ся).**
выпей(те) *сов см* **выпить.**
выпека|ть (-ю) *несов от* **выпечь.**
выпеку *итп сов см* **выпечь.**
вып|ереть (-ру, -решь; *pt* **-ер, -ерла, -ерло**, *impf* **выпирать**) *сов перех* (*разг*) to chuck out.
выпест|овать (-ую) *сов от* **пестовать.**
выпечк|а (-и) *ж* baking.
выпечн|ой *прил*: **~ые изделия** bakery products *мн*.
выпе|чь (-ку, -чешь *итп*, **-кут**; *impf* **выпекать**) *сов перех* to bake.
выпивк|а (-и) *ж* (*разг*: *попойка*) boozing ◆ *собир* (*спиртное*) booze.
выпира|ть (-ю) *несов от* **выпереть** ◆ *неперех* (*разг*: *выпячиваться*) to stick out.
выпи|сать (-шу, -шешь; *impf* **выписывать**) *сов перех* (*цитату, данные*) to copy *или* write out; (*пропуск, счёт, рецепт*) to make out; (*газету, журнал*) to subscribe to; (*пациента*) to discharge; (*с местопроживания*) to change sb's residence permit
▸ **выписаться** (*impf* **выписываться**) *несов возв* (*из больницы*) to be discharged; (*с местопроживания*) to change one's residence permit.
выпис|ка (-ки; *gen pl* **-ок**) *ж* (*действие*) copying *или* writing out; (*цитата*) extract; ~ **с банковского счёта** bank statement.
выписыва|ть(ся) (-ю(сь)) *несов от* **выписать(ся).**
вып|ить (-ью, -ьешь; *imper* **-ей(те)**) *сов от* **пить.**
выпишу(сь) *итп сов см* **выписать(ся).**
выплав|ить (-лю, -ишь; *impf* **выплавлять**) *сов перех* to smelt.
выплав|ка (-ки; *gen pl* **-ок**) *ж* (*действие*) smelting; (*продукция*) smelted metal.
выплавлю *сов см* **выплавить.**
выплавля|ть (-ю) *несов от* **выплавить.**
выплавок *сущ см* **выплавка.**
выплат|а (-ы) *ж* payment.
выпла|тить (-чу, -тишь; *impf* **выплачивать**) *сов перех* to pay; (*долг*) to pay off.
выплёвыва|ть (-ю) *несов от* **выплюнуть.**
выплесн|уть (-у, -ешь; *impf* **выплёскивать**) *сов перех* to pour out.
выплы|ть (-ву, -вешь; *impf* **выплывать**) *сов неперех* to swim out; (*всплыть*) to surface; (*перен*) to emerge, come to light.
выплюн|уть (-у, -ешь; *impf* **выплёвывать**) *сов перех* to spit out.
выполз|ти (-у, -ешь; *pt* -, **-ла, -ло**, *impf* **выползать**) *сов неперех* to crawl out.
выполним|ый (-, -а, -о) *прил* practicable, feasible.
выполн|ить (-ю, -ишь; *impf* **выполнять**) *сов перех* (*задание, заказ*) to carry out; (*план, условие*) to fulfil (*BRIT*), fulfill (*US*); (*рисунок,*

чертёж) to execute; (*КОМП*) to run.
вы́полоска|ть (**-ю**) *сов от* **полоска́ть**.
вы́пол|оть (**-ю, -ешь**) *сов от* **поло́ть**.
вы́пор|оть (**-ю, -ешь**) *сов от* **поро́ть**.
вы́порхн|уть (**-у, -ешь**) *сов неперех* to dart out.
вы́потрош|ить (**-у, -ишь**) *сов от* **потроши́ть**.
вы́прав|ить (**-лю, -ишь**; *impf* **выправля́ть**) *сов перех* (*расспрямить*) to straighten (up); (*текст, чертёж*) to correct; (*положение, ситуацию*) to rectify, put right
▸ **вы́правиться** (*impf* **выправля́ться**) *несов возв* (*что-н кривое*) to straighten (out); (*положение, ситуация*) to be rectified.
вы́прав|ка (**-ки**; *gen pl* **-ок**) *ж* bearing.
вы́правлю(сь) *сов см* **вы́править(ся)**.
выправля́|ть(ся) (**-ю(сь)**) *несов от* **вы́править(ся)**.
вы́правок *сущ см* **вы́правка**.
выпра́шива|ть (**-ю**) *несов перех* to beg for.
вы́про|сить (**-шу, -сишь**) *сов перех*: **он ~сил у отца́ маши́ну** he persuaded his father to give him the car.
вы́пру *итп сов см* **вы́переть**.
вы́прыгн|уть (**-у, -ешь**; *impf* **выпры́гивать**) *сов неперех* to jump out.
вы́прям|ить (**-лю, -ишь**; *impf* **выпрямля́ть**) *сов перех* to straighten (out)
▸ **вы́прямиться** (*impf* **выпрямля́ться**) *несов возв* to straighten (up).
выпрямля́|ть(ся) (**-ю(сь)**) *несов от* **вы́прямить(ся)**.
вы́пуклый *прил* (*лоб, глаза итп*) bulging; (*стекло, линза*) convex; (*буква*) embossed.
вы́пуск (**-а**) *м* (*продукции*) output; (*газа, воздуха*) emission, release; (*книги*) instalment (*BRIT*), installment (*US*); (*денег, марок, акций*) issue; (*учащиеся*) school leavers *мн* (*BRIT*), graduates *мн* (*US*).
выпуска́|ть (**-ю**) *несов от* **вы́пустить**.
выпускни́к (**-а́**) *м* final-year student; (*окончивший вуз*) graduate.
выпускни́ц|а (**-ы**) *ж см* **выпускни́к**.
выпускн|о́й *прил* (*класс*) final-year; (*ТЕХ*): **~ кла́пан** exhaust valve; **~о́е отве́рстие** outlet; **выпускно́й ве́чер** graduation; **выпускно́й экза́мен** final exam, finals *мн*.
вы́пу|стить (**-щу, -стишь**; *impf* **выпуска́ть**) *сов перех* to let out; (*дым*) to exhale; (*заключённого, заложника*) to release; (*специалистов*) to turn out; (*продукцию*) to produce; (*книгу, газету итп*) to publish; (*заём, марки*) to issue; (*деньги*) to put into circulation; (*исключить: часть текста, параграф*) to omit; **выпуска́ть** (**~** *perf*) **(из рук)** to let go of; **выпуска́ть** (**~** *perf*) **в свет** (*книгу, журнал*) to publish; **выпуска́ть** (**~** *perf*) **из рук возмо́жность/шанс** to miss an opportunity/a chance; **выпуска́ть** (**~** *perf*) **кого́-н/что-н из ви́ду** to let sb/sth out of sight.
вы́пута|ться (**-юсь**; *impf* **выпу́тываться**) *сов возв* (*также перен*) to extricate o.s.
выпу́тыва|ться (**-юсь**) *несов от* **вы́путаться**.
вы́пущу *сов см* **вы́пустить**.
вы́пью *итп сов см* **вы́пить**.
вы́пя|тить (**-чу, -тишь**; *impf* **выпя́чивать**) *сов перех* (*разг: грудь*) to stick out; **выпя́чивать** (**~** *perf*) **губу́** to pout.
вы́работа|ть (**-ю**; *impf* **выраба́тывать**) *сов перех* to produce; (*план*) to work out; (*характер, стиль, привычку*) to develop.
вы́работ|ка (**-ки**; *gen pl* **-ок**) *ж* (*действие*) production; (*годовая, промышленная*) output, production; (*продукты*) yield.
выра́внива|ть(ся) (**-ю(сь)**) *несов от* **вы́ровнять(ся)**.
выража́|ть (**-ю**) *несов от* **вы́разить**
▸ **выража́ться** *несов от* **вы́разиться** ♦ *возв* (*разг*) to swear.
выраже́ни|е (**-я**) *ср* expression.
выражу(сь) *сов см* **вы́разить(ся)**.
вырази́тельно *нареч* (*читать*) expressively.
вырази́тел|ьный (**-ен, -ьна, -ьно**) *прил* expressive.
вы́ра|зить (**-жу, -зишь**; *impf* **выража́ть**) *сов перех* to express
▸ **вы́разиться** (*impf* **выража́ться**) *сов возв* (*чувство, состояние*) to manifest *или* express itself; (*человек*) to express o.s.
выраста́|ть (**-ю**) *несов от* **вы́расти**.
вы́р|асти (**-асту, -астешь**; *pt* **-ос, -осла, -осли**) *сов от* **расти́** ♦ (*impf* **выраста́ть**) *неперех* (*горы, башня*) to rise up; **выраста́ть** (**~** *perf*) **в** *+acc* to become; **выраста́ть** (**~** *perf*) **из оде́жды** to grow out of one's clothes.
вы́раст|ить (**-у, -ишь**; *impf* **выра́щивать**) *сов перех* (*детей*) to raise; (*растение*) to grow; (*животных*) to rear.
выра́щивани|е (**-я**) *ср* (*растений*) cultivation; (*животных*) rearing.
выра́щива|ть (**-ю**) *несов от* **вы́растить**.
вы́ращу *сов см* **вы́растить**.
вы́рв|ать (**-у, -ешь**; *impf* **вырыва́ть**) *сов перех* to pull out; (*отнять*): **~ что-н у кого́-н** to snatch sth from sb; (*перен*) to wring sth from sb ♦ (*impf* **рвать**) *безл* (*разг*): **её ~ало** she threw up; **ему́ ~али зуб** he had his tooth taken out
▸ **вы́рваться** (*impf* **вырыва́ться**) *сов возв* (*из объятий*) to free o.s.; (*из рук, из пут*) to break free, escape; (*из тюрьмы*) to make a break; (*перен: в театр, на концерт*) to manage to get away; (*пламя*) to shoot out; (*дым*) to pour out.
вы́режу *итп сов см* **вы́резать**.
вы́рез (**-а**) *м*: **пла́тье с больши́м ~ом** a low-cut dress.
вы́ре|зать (**-жу, -жешь**; *impf* **выреза́ть**) *сов перех* (*фотографию итп*) to cut out; (*опухоль,*

гнойник) to remove; (*из дерева, из кости итп*) to carve; (*на камне, на металле итп*) to engrave; (*население, животных*) to slaughter.
вы́рез|ка (**-ки**; *gen pl* **-ок**) *ж* (*газетная*) cutting, clipping; (*мясная*) fillet.
вы́рис|оваться (*3sg* **-уется**, *3pl* **-уются**, *impf* **вырисо́вываться**) *сов возв* (*стать видным*) to stand out; (*стать явным*) to appear; (*перен*: *ситуация*) to emerge.
вы́ровня|ть (**-ю**) *сов от* **ровня́ть** ◆ (*impf* **выра́внивать**) *перех* to level
▸ **вы́ровняться** (*impf* **выра́вниваться**) *сов возв* (*отряд*) to form ranks; (*перен*: *характер*) to improve.
вы́род|иться (*3sg* **-ится**, *3pl* **-ятся**, *impf* **вырожда́ться**) *сов возв* (*также перен*) to degenerate.
вы́род|ок (**-ка**) *м* (*разг*) degenerate.
вырожда́|ться (**-юсь**) *несов от* **вы́родиться**.
вырожде́ни|е (**-я**) *ср* degeneration.
вы́рон|ить (**-ю, -ишь**) *сов перех* to drop.
вы́рос *итп сов см* **вы́расти**.
вы́рост (**-а**) *м*: **покупа́ть оде́жду на ~** (*разг*) *to buy clothes with room for growth*.
вы́рою *итп сов см* **вы́рыть**.
выруба́|ть (**-ю**) *несов от* **вы́рубить**.
вы́руб|ить (**-лю, -ишь**; *impf* **выруба́ть**) *сов перех* (*лес, деревья*) to cut down; (*яму, углубление*) to hew out; (*свет, сигнализацию*) to cut off.
вы́руга|ть(ся) (**-ю(сь)**) *сов от* **руга́ть(ся)**.
вы́руч|ить (**-у, -ишь**; *impf* **выруча́ть**) *сов перех* to rescue, help out; (*деньги*) to make; **выруча́ть** (*~ perf*) **кого́-н из беды́** to help sb out of trouble.
вы́ручк|а (**-и**) *ж* rescue; (*деньги*) takings *мн*; **приходи́ть (прийти́** *perf*) **на ~у кому́-н** to come to sb's rescue.
вырыва́|ть(ся) (**-ю(сь)**) *несов от* **вы́рвать(ся)**, **вы́рыть**.
вы́р|ыть (**-ою, -оешь**) *сов от* **рыть** ◆ (*impf* **вырыва́ть**) *перех* (*картофель, камень итп*) to dig up.
вы́са|дить (**-жу, -дишь**; *impf* **выса́живать**) *сов перех* (*растение*) to plant out; (*пассажира*: *дать выйти*) to drop off; (: *заставить выйти*) to throw out; (*войска, отряд*) to land; *~ (perf)* **деса́нт** to make a landing
▸ **вы́садиться** (*impf* **выса́живаться**) *сов возв*: **~ся (из** *+gen*) to get off.
выса́сыва|ть (**-ю**) *несов от* **вы́сосать**.
высве́тлива|ть (**-ю**; *perf* **вы́светлить**) *несов перех (также комп)* to highlight.
высве́чивани|е (**-я**) *ср* (*комп*) highlighting.
вы́свобо|дить (**-жу, -дишь**; *impf* **высвобожда́ть**) *сов перех* (*ногу, руку*) to free; (*рабочую силу, средства*) to release; (*время*) to set aside.
вы́сек *итп сов см* **вы́сечь**.
высека́|ть (**-ю**) *несов от* **вы́сечь**.
вы́секу *итп сов см* **вы́сечь**.
вы́сел|ить (**-ю, -ишь**; *impf* **выселя́ть**) *сов перех* to evict.
вы́се|чь (**-ку, -чешь** *итп*, **-кут**; *pt* **-к, -кла, -кло**) *сов от* **сечь** ◆ (*impf* **высека́ть**) *перех* (*фигуру*) to carve, sculpt; (*надпись*) to engrave.
вы́си|деть (**-жу, -дишь**; *impf* **выси́живать**) *сов перех* to hatch; (*перен*: *лекцию*) to sit out.
вы́с|иться (*3sg* **-ится**, *3pl* **-ятся**) *несов возв* to tower.
выска́блива|ть (**-ю**) *несов от* **вы́скоблить**.
вы́ска|зать (**-жу, -жешь**; *impf* **выска́зывать**) *сов перех* to express; **я ему́ всё ~зал** I told him exactly what I thought
▸ **вы́сказаться** (*impf* **выска́зываться**) *сов возв* to speak one's mind; **выска́зываться (~ся** *perf*) **про́тив** *+gen*/**за** *+acc* to speak out against/in favour of.
выска́зывани|е (**-я**) *ср* (*мнения*) expression; (*суждение*) statement.
выска́зыва|ть(ся) (**-ю(сь)**) *несов от* **вы́сказать(ся)**.
выска́кива|ть (**-ю**) *несов от* **вы́скочить**.
выска́льзыва|ть (**-ю**) *несов от* **вы́скользнуть**.
вы́скобл|ить (**-ю, -ишь**; *impf* **выска́бливать**) *сов перех* (*очистить*) to scrape; (*удалить скоблением*) to remove.
вы́скользн|уть (**-у, -ешь**; *impf* **выска́льзывать**) *сов неперех* (*также перен*) to slip out.
вы́скоч|ить (**-у, -ишь**; *impf* **выска́кивать**) *сов неперех* to jump out; **его́ и́мя ~ило у меня́ из головы́** (*разг*) his name has slipped my mind.
вы́скоч|ка (**-ки**; *gen pl* **-ек**) *м/ж* (*разг*: *пренебр*) upstart.
вы́|слать (**-шлю, -шлешь**; *impf* **высыла́ть**) *сов перех* (*посылку, деньги*) to send off; (*полит*) to exile; (*шпиона*) to deport.
вы́сле|дить (**-жу, -дишь**; *impf* **высле́живать**) *сов перех* to track down.
вы́слуг|а (**-и**) *ж*: **за ~у лет** for long service.
вы́служ|ить (**-у, -ишь**; *impf* **выслу́живать**) *сов перех* (*пенсию, повышение*) to qualify for; (*орден, награду*) to earn
▸ **вы́служиться** *сов возв* to work one's way up.
вы́слуша|ть (**-ю**; *impf* **выслу́шивать**) *сов перех* to hear out.
вы́сме|ять (**-ю**; *impf* **высме́ивать**) *сов перех* to ridicule.
вы́сморка|ть (**-ю**) *сов от* **сморка́ть** ◆ *перех*: **~ нос** to blow one's nose
▸ **вы́сморкаться** *сов от* **сморка́ться**.
высо́выва|ть(ся) (**-ю(сь)**) *несов от* **вы́сунуть(ся)**.
высо́к|ий (**-ая, -ое, -ие**; **-, -а́, -о́**) *прил* high; (*человек*) tall; (*честь, ответственность*) great; (*гость*) distinguished; **быть** *(impf)* **~ого мне́ния о** *+prp* to have a high opinion of; **высо́кая вода́** high tide.
высоко́ *нареч* high (up) ◆ *как сказ* it's high (up), it's a long way up; **до верши́ны** ~ it is a long way to the top.
высокого́рный *прил* alpine.

высокока́чественный *прил* high-quality.
высококвалифици́рованный *прил* (*учитель, юрист*) highly qualified; (*слесарь, токарь*) highly skilled.
высокоме́рен *прил см* **высокоме́рный**.
высокоме́ри|е (**-я**) *ср* haughtiness, arrogance.
высокоме́р|ный (**-ен, -на, -но**) *прил* haughty, arrogant.
высокоопла́чиваемый *прил* highly paid.
высокопа́р|ный (**-ен, -на, -но**) *прил* (*речь*) high-flown, pompous.
высокопоста́вленный *прил* high-ranking.
высокопроизводи́тел|ьный (**-ен, -ьна, -ьно**) *прил* highly productive.
вы́сос|ать (**-у, -ешь**; *impf* **выса́сывать**) *сов перех* to suck out; (*насосом*) to pump out.
выс|ота́ (**-оты́**; *nom pl* **-о́ты**) *ж* height; (*ГЕО*) altitude; (*звука*) pitch; (*давления, температуры*) level; **набира́ть** (**набра́ть** *perf*) **~оту́** to climb, gain height; **на большо́й ~оте́** at a high altitude *или* great height; **быть** *(impf) или* **оказа́ться** *(perf)* **на ~оте́ (положе́ния)** to be equal to the occasion.
высо́тный *прил* (*полёт*) high-altitude; (*здание*) high-rise.
вы́сох|нуть (**-ну, -нешь**; *pt* **-, -ла, -ло**) *сов от* **со́хнуть** ◆ (*impf* **высыха́ть**) *неперех* (*бельё, дрова*) to dry out; (*лужа, река*) to dry up.
высо́честв|о (**-а**) *ср*: **Ва́ше** *итп* **В~** Your *итп* Highness.
вы́сп|аться (**-люсь, -ишься**; *impf* **высыпа́ться**) *сов возв* to sleep well.
вы́став|ить (**-лю, -ишь**; *impf* **выставля́ть**) *сов перех* (*поставить наружу*) to put out; (*грудь*) to stick out; (*кандидатуру*) to put forward; (*требования*) to lay down; (*картину*) to exhibit; (*товар*) to display; (*часовых, охрану*) to post; (*разг*: *выгнать*) to chuck out; **выставля́ть** (**~** *perf*) **кого́-н в дурно́м све́те** to show sb in an unfavourable light
▸ **вы́ставиться** (*impf* **выставля́ться**) *сов возв* (*на выставке*) to exhibit.
вы́став|ка (**-ки**; *gen pl* **-ок**) *ж* exhibition, show; **~-прода́жа книг** book fair.
вы́ставлю(сь) *сов см* **вы́ставить(ся)**.
выставля́|ть(ся) (**-ю(сь)**) *несов от* **вы́ставить(ся)**.
вы́ставок *сущ см* **вы́ставка**.
выста́ива|ть (**-ю**) *несов от* **вы́стоять**.
вы́стега|ть (**-ю**) *сов от* **стега́ть**.
вы́ст|лать (**-елю, -елешь**; *impf* **выстила́ть**) *сов перех*: **~ что-н чем-н** to line sth with sth.
вы́сто|ять (**-ю, -ишь**; *impf* **выста́ивать**) *сов неперех* (*долго простоять*) to stand; (*удержаться*) to remain standing; (*не сдаться*) to stand one's ground.
вы́страда|ть (**-ю**) *сов перех* to suffer; (*счастье, свободу*) *to achieve through much suffering*.
выстра́ива|ть(ся) (**-ю(сь)**) *несов* = **стро́ить(ся)**.
вы́стрел (**-а**) *м* shot; **разда́лся ~** a shot rang out.
вы́стрел|ить (**-ю, -ишь**) *сов неперех* to fire; **~** *(perf)* **из ружья́/из пу́шки** to fire a gun/cannon.
вы́строга|ть (**-ю**) *сов от* **строга́ть**.
вы́стро|ить(ся) (**-ю(сь), -ишь(ся)**) *сов от* **стро́ить(ся)**.
вы́ступ (**-а**) *м* ledge.
выступа́|ть (**-ю**) *несов от* **вы́ступить** ◆ *неперех* (*берег*) to jut out; (*скулы*) to protrude.
вы́ступ|ить (**-лю, -ишь**; *impf* **выступа́ть**) *сов неперех* (*против закона, в защиту друга*) to come out; (*из толпы, из рядов*) to step out; (*оркестр, актёр*) to perform; (*пот, сыпь*) to break out; (*в поход, на поиски*) to set off *или* out; **выступа́ть** (**~** *perf*) **с ре́чью** to make a speech.
выступле́ни|е (**-я**) *ср* (*МУЗ*) performance; (*в поход*) departure; (*в печати*) article; (*речь*) speech.
вы́ступлю *сов см* **вы́ступить**.
вы́сун|уть (**-у, -ешь**; *impf* **высо́вывать**) *сов перех* to stick out; **бежа́ть** *(impf)*, **~ув язы́к** (*перен*: *разг*) to run flat out
▸ **вы́сунуться** (*impf* **высо́вываться**) *сов возв* to lean out; (*рука, нога*) to stick out; (*перен*: *разг*): **~ся с** *+instr* to come out with.
вы́суш|ить(ся) (**-у(сь), -ишь(ся)**) *сов от* **суши́ть(ся)**.
вы́счита|ть (**-ю**; *impf* **высчи́тывать**) *сов перех* to calculate.
вы́сш|ий (**-ая, -ее, -ие**) *прил* (*орган власти, начальство*) highest, supreme; **в ~ей сте́пени** extremely; **това́ры ~его со́рта** goods of the highest quality; **вы́сшая ме́ра наказа́ния** capital punishment; **вы́сшая шко́ла** higher education; **вы́сшее образова́ние** higher education; **вы́сшее уче́бное заведе́ние** higher education establishment.
высыла́|ть (**-ю**) *несов от* **вы́слать**.
вы́сыл|ка (**-ки**; *gen pl* **-ок**) *ж* (*посылки, денег*) sending; (*осуждённого*) exile; (*шпиона*) deportation.
вы́сып|ать (**-лю, -лешь**; *impf* **высыпа́ть**) *сов перех* to pour out ◆ *неперех* (*сыпь, прыщи*) to break out; (*разг*: *толпа, народ итп*) to pour out
▸ **вы́сыпаться** (*impf* **высыпа́ться**) *сов возв* to pour out.
высыха́|ть (**-ю**) *несов от* **вы́сохнуть**.
выс|ь (**-и**) *ж* height.
выта́лкива|ть (**-ю**) *несов от* **вы́толкнуть**.
выта́птыва|ть (**-ю**) *несов от* **вы́топтать**.
вы́таращ|ить(ся) (**-у(сь), -ишь(ся)**) *сов от* **тара́щить(ся)**.
выта́скива|ть (**-ю**) *несов см* **вы́тащить**.
вы́тащ|ить (**-у, -ишь**) *сов от* **тащи́ть** ◆ (*impf* **выта́скивать**) *перех* (*мебель*) to drag out.

вы́твер|дить (**-жу, -дишь**) *сов от* **тверди́ть.**
вытворя́|ть (**-ю**) *сов перех* (*разг*) to get up to.
вы́тек *итп сов см* **вы́течь.**
вытека́|ть (*3sg* **-ет**, *3pl* **-ют**) *несов от* **вы́течь** ◆ *неперех* (*вывод*) to follow; (*река*) to flow out.
вы́т|ереть (**-ру, -решь**; *pt* **-ер, -ерла, -ерло**, *impf* **вытира́ть**) *сов перех* (*грязь, лужу*) to wipe up; (*посуду*) to dry (up); (*руки, глаза*) to wipe; **вытира́ть** (~ *perf*) **пыль** to dust
▸ **вы́тереться** (*impf* **вытира́ться**) *сов возв* (*человек*) to dry o.s.
вы́терп|еть (**-лю, -ишь**) *сов перех* to bear, endure.
вы́тесн|ить (**-ю, -ишь**; *impf* **вытесня́ть**) *сов перех* (*удалить*) to oust; (*заменить собой*) to supplant.
вы́те|чь (*3sg* **-чет**, *3pl* **-кут**, *pt* **-к, -кла, -кло**, *impf* **вытека́ть**) *сов неперех* to flow out.
вытира́|ть(ся) (**-ю(сь)**) *несов от* **вы́тереть(ся).**
вы́тк|ать (**-у, -ешь**) *сов перех* to weave.
вы́толкн|уть (**-у, -ешь**; *impf* **выта́лкивать**) *сов перех* to push out.
вы́топ|тать (**-чу, -чешь**; *impf* **выта́птывать**) *сов перех* to trample down.
вы́точ|ить (**-у, -ишь**) *сов от* **точи́ть.**
вы́трав|ить (**-лю, -ишь**; *impf* **вытра́вливать**) *сов перех* (*пятно*) to remove; (*крыс, тараканов*) to exterminate; (*рисунок*) to etch.
вытрезви́тел|ь (**-я**) *м overnight police cell for drunks*.
вы́тру(сь) *итп сов см* **вы́тереть(ся).**
вы́тряс|ти (**-у, -ешь**; *pt* **-, -ла, -ло**) *сов от* **трясти́.**
вы́тряхн|уть (**-у, -ешь**; *impf* **вытря́хивать**) *сов перех* to shake out.
выть (**во́ю, во́ешь**) *несов неперех* (*зверь, ветер, вьюга*) to howl; (*сирена*) to wail; (*разг: плакать*) to howl, wail.
вытя́гива|ть(ся) (**-ю(сь)**) *несов от* **вы́тянуть(ся).**
вы́тяж|ка (**-ки**; *gen pl* **-ек**) *ж* (*действие: дыма, вредных частиц*) extraction; (*экстракт*) extract.
вы́тян|уть (**-у, -ешь**; *impf* **вытя́гивать**) *сов перех* to pull out; (*дым, вредные вещества*) to extract; (*руки, ноги, ткань*) to stretch ◆ *неперех* (*разг: выдержать*) to last out; ~ *(perf)* **(всю) ду́шу из кого́-н** (*разг*) to wear sb out; **из него́ сло́ва не ~ешь** (*разг*) you won't get a word out of him
▸ **вы́тянуться** (*impf* **вытя́гиваться**) *сов возв* (*дым, газ*) to escape; (*одежда*) to stretch; (*на диване, вдоль берега*) to stretch out; (*разг: вырасти*) to shoot up; (*встать смирно*) to stand at attention; **у него́ ~улось лицо́** (*перен*) his face fell.
вы́у|дить (**-жу, -дишь**; *impf* **выу́живать**) *сов перех* (*рыбу*) to catch; (*перен: разг: сведения*) to wheedle out.
вы́утюж|ить (**-у, -ишь**) *сов от* **утю́жить.**
выучива́|ть (**-ю**) *несов* to learn.
вы́уч|ить(ся) (**-у(сь), -ишь(сь)**) *сов от* **учи́ть(ся).**
выха́жива|ть (**-ю**) *несов от* **вы́ходить.**
вы́хва|тить (**-чу, -тишь**; *impf* **выхва́тывать**) *сов перех* (*вырвать*) to snatch; (*пистолет*) to draw.
выхлопно́й *прил* exhaust *опред*; **выхлопны́е га́зы** exhaust fumes.
вы́ход (**-а**) *м* (*войск*) withdrawal; (*из партии, из комиссии*) departure; (*из кризиса*) way out; (*на сцену*) appearance; (*в море*) sailing; (*книги*) publication; (*на экран*) showing; (*место,* КОМП) exit; **дава́ть (дать** *perf*) **~ чему́-н** to give vent to sth.
вы́ходе|ц (**-ца**) *м*: **он ~ из Росси́и** he is of Russian origin *или* is Russian by birth.
выхо́дит *вводн сл* (*разг*) it turns out.
вы́хо|дить (**-жу, -дишь**; *impf* **выха́живать**) *сов перех* (*больного*) to nurse (back to health).
вых|оди́ть (**-ожу́, -о́дишь**) *несов от* **вы́йти** ◆ *неперех*: **~ на** *+acc* (*юг, север*) to face; **окно́ ~о́дит в парк** the window looks out onto the park; **дверь ~о́дит в коридо́р** the door opens onto the corridor.
вы́ходк|а (**-ки**) *ж* prank.
выходн|о́й *прил* exit *опред*; (*платье, костюм*) best ◆ (**-о́го**; *decl like adj*) *м* (*также:* **~ день**) day off (work); **~о́е отве́рстие** outlet; **сего́дня ~** (*разг*) today is a holiday; **я сего́дня ~** (*разг*) I have a day off today; **~ы́е** weekend *ед*; **выходна́я дверь** exit; **выходно́е посо́бие** redundancy payment; **выходны́е да́нные** imprint.
вы́ходца *итп сущ см* **вы́ходец.**
вы́хожу *сов см* **вы́ходить.**
выхожу́ *несов см* **выходи́ть.**
вы́царапа|ть (**-ю**; *impf* **выцара́пывать**) *сов перех* to scratch out; (*перен: деньги, путёвку*) to wring out.
вы́цве|сти (*3sg* **-тет**, *3pl* **-тут**, *impf* **выцвета́ть**) *сов неперех* to fade.
вы́черкн|уть (**-у, -ешь**; *impf* **вычёркивать**) *сов перех* to cross *или* score out.
вы́черпа|ть (**-ю**; *impf* **вычёрпывать**) *сов перех* (*извлечь*) to scoop out; (*опорожнить*) to drain; **вычёрпывать** (~ *perf*) **во́ду из ло́дки** to bail out a boat.
вы́ч|есть (**-ту, -тешь**; *impf* **вычита́ть**) *сов перех* (МАТ) to subtract; (*долг, налог*) to deduct.
вы́чет (**-а**) *м* deduction ◆ *предл*: **за ~ом** *+gen* minus; **до ~а нало́гов** pre-tax.
вычисле́ни|е (**-я**) *ср* calculation.
вычисли́тельный *прил* (*операция, функция*) computing; **вычисли́тельная маши́на** computer; **вычисли́тельная те́хника** computers *мн*; **вычисли́тельный центр** computer centre (BRIT) *или* center (US).
вы́числ|ить (**-ю, -ишь**; *impf* **вычисля́ть**) *сов перех* to calculate.
вы́чи|стить (**-щу, -стишь**) *сов от* **чи́стить.**

вычита́ни|е (**-я**) *ср* subtraction.
вы́чита|ть (**-ю**; *impf* **вычи́тывать**) *сов перех* (*разг*: *узнать*) to find out (*by reading*).
вычита́|ть (**-ю**) *несов от* **вы́честь**.
вы́чту *сов см* **вы́честь**.
вычи́тыва|ть (**-ю**) *несов от* **вы́читать**.
вы́чур|ный (**-ен, -на, -но**) *прил* elaborate.
вы́швырн|уть (**-у, -ешь**; *impf* **вышвы́ривать**) *сов перех* (*также перен*: *разг*) to chuck out.
вы́ше *сравн прил от* **высо́кий** ◆ *нареч* higher; (*в тексте*) above ◆ *предл* (*+gen*) above; **мы подняли́сь ~** we went further up, we climbed higher; **~ мы привели́ но́вые да́нные** we have cited new data above; **самолёт лете́л ~ облако́в** the plane was flying above the clouds; **э́то ~ моего́ понима́ния** it is beyond me *или* my comprehension.
вы́шек *сущ см* **вы́шка**.
вы́шел *сов см* **вы́йти**.
вышестоя́щ|ий (**-ая, -ее, -ие**) *прил* higher; **~ее лицо́** superior.
вы́шиб|ить (**-у, -ешь**; *pt* **-, -ла, -ло**, *impf* **вышиба́ть**) *сов перех* (*выбить*) to knock out; (*разг*: *прогнать*) to chuck out.
вышива́ни|е (**-я**) *ср* needlework.
вышива́|ть (**-ю**) *несов от* **вы́шить**.
вы́шив|ка (**-ки**; *gen pl* **-ок**) *ж* embroidery.
вышин|а́ (**-ы́**) *ж* (*высота*) height.
вы́ш|ить (**-ью, -ьешь**; *impf* **вышива́ть**) *сов перех* to embroider.
вы́ш|ка (**-ки**; *gen pl* **-ек**) *ж* (*высокое строение*) tower; (*разг*: *преступнику*) death penalty; (*СПОРТ*) diving board; **бурова́я** *или* **нефтяна́я ~** derrick; **прыжки́ в во́ду с ~ки** high diving.
вы́школ|ить (**-ю, -ишь**) *сов перех* to train.
вы́шла *итп сов см* **вы́йти**.
вы́шлю *итп сов см* **вы́слать**.
вы́шью *итп сов см* **вы́шить**.
вы́щипа|ть (**-ю**; *impf* **выщи́пывать**) *сов перех* to pluck.
вы́яв|ить (**-лю, -ишь**; *impf* **выявля́ть**) *сов перех* (*талант*) to discover; (*недостатки*) to expose
▸ **вы́явиться** (*impf* **выявля́ться**) *сов возв* to come to light, be revealed.
вы́ясн|ить (**-ю, -ишь**; *impf* **выясня́ть**) *сов перех* (*обнаружить*) to find out; (*сделать ясным*) to clarify; **нам ну́жно ~ отноше́ния** we have to sort things out between us
▸ **вы́ясниться** (*impf* **выясня́ться**) *сов возв* to become clear.
Вьетна́м (**-а**) *м* Vietnam.
вьетна́м|ец (**-ца**) *м* Vietnamese.
вьетна́м|ка (**-ки**; *gen pl* **-ок**) *ж см* **вьетна́мец**.
вьетна́мск|ий (**-ая, -ое, -ие**) *прил* Vietnamese.
вьетна́мца *итп сущ см* **вьетна́мец**.
вью́г|а (**-и**) *ж* snowstorm, blizzard.
вью́чн|ый *прил*: **~ое живо́тное** beast of burden.
вяжу́ *сов см* **вяза́ть**.
вя́жущ|ий (**-ая, -ее, -ие**) *прил* (*вкус*) acerbic; (*материал, состав*) binding, cementing.
вяз *итп несов см* **вя́знуть** ◆ (**-а**) *м* elm.
вяза́ни|е (**-я**) *ср* (*снопов*) tying, binding; (*рукоделие*) knitting.
вя́заный *прил* knitted.
вя|за́ть (**-жу́, -жешь**; *perf* **связа́ть**) *несов перех* to tie up, bind; (*кофту, носки*) to knit ◆ *безл* (*no perf*): **э́то лека́рство вя́жет во рту** this medicine burns the inside of your mouth.
вя́з|кий (**-кая, -кое, -кие; -ок, -ка́, -ко**) *прил* (*тягучий*) viscous; (*топкий*) boggy.
вя́з|нуть (**-ну, -нешь**; *pt* **-, -ла, -ло**, *perf* **завя́знуть** *или* **увя́знуть**) *несов неперех*: **~ (в** *+prp*) to get stuck (in).
вя́зок *прил см* **вя́зкий**.
вя́леный *прил* dried.
вя́л|ить (**-ю, -ишь**) *несов перех* to dry.
вя́ло *нареч* (*говорить*) dully.
вя́лост|ь (**-и**) *ж* sluggishness.
вя́л|ый (**-, -а, -о**) *прил* (*листья, цветы*) wilted, withered; (*человек, речь*) sluggish.
вя́|нуть (**-ну, -нешь**; *perf* **завя́нуть** *или* **увя́нуть**) *несов неперех* (*цветы*) to wilt, wither; (*перен*: *красота*) to fade; **его́ слу́шать – у́ши ~нут** (*разг*) it makes you sick to listen to him.

~ Г, г ~

Г, г *сущ нескл (буква) the 4th letter of the Russian alphabet.*
г *сокр* (= **грамм**) g, gm (= *gram*).
г. *сокр* = **год, го́род.**
га *м сокр* (= **гекта́р**) ha (= *hectare*).
Гаа́г|а (-и) *ж* The Hague.
габари́т (-а) *м (обычно мн: ТЕХ)* dimension; *см также* **габари́ты.**
габари́т|ы (-ов) *мн (разг: человека)* size *ед*.
ГАБТ (-а) *м сокр (= Госуда́рственный академи́ческий Большо́й теа́тр)* (State Academic) Bolshoi Theatre (*BRIT*) *или* Theater (*US*).
Гава́йи *м нескл* Hawaii.
Гава́н|а (-ы) *ж* Havana.
га́вань (-и) *ж* harbour (*BRIT*), harbor (*US*).
га́вка|ть (-ю) *несов неперех (разг: также перен)* to yap.
гага́р|а (-ы) *ж* diver (*BRIT*), loon (*US*).
гага́т (-а) *м (ГЕО)* jet.
гад (-а) *м (разг)* rat.
гада́л|ка (-ки; *gen pl* **-ок)** *ж* fortune-teller.
гада́|ть (-ю) *несов неперех (строить предположения)* to guess; (*perf* **погада́ть**): ~ **кому́-н** to tell sb's fortune; ~ **(погада́ть** *perf*) **на ка́ртах** to read the cards; ~ *(impf)* **на кофе́йной гу́ще** ≈ to read the tea leaves.
га́дин|а (-ы) *ж (разг)* rat.
га́|дить (-жу, -дишь; *perf* **нага́дить)** *несов неперех (разг: животное)* to defecate; ~ **(нага́дить** *perf*) *+dat (разг)* to do the dirty on.
га́д|кий (-кая, -кое, -кие; -ок, -ка́, -ко) *прил* loathsome.
га́дко *нареч (поступить)* terribly ◆ *как сказ*: **э́то** ~ it's disgusting.
га́дост|ь (-и) *ж (поступка, слов)* nastiness; (*разг*) filth; **де́лать (сде́лать** *perf*)**/говори́ть (сказа́ть** *perf*) **~и** to do/say nasty things; **э́то** ~ it's disgusting.
гадю́к|а (-и) *ж* viper.
га́ек *сущ см* **га́йка.**
га́ечный *прил*: ~ **ключ** spanner.
га́же *сравн прил от* **га́дкий** ◆ *сравн нареч от* **га́дко.**
га́жу *несов см* **га́дить.**
ГАЗ (-а) *м сокр (автомобиль) vehicle manufactured at the Gorky car factory.*
газ (-а; *part gen* **-у)** *м* gas; **гото́вить (пригото́вить** *perf*) **на га́зе** to cook with gas; **дава́ть (дать** *perf*) ~ (*разг*) to put one's foot down (*BRIT*), step on the gas (*US*); *см также* **га́зы.**
газе́т|а (-ы) *ж* newspaper.
газе́тный *прил* newspaper *опред*.
газе́тчик (-а) *м (разг: сотрудник)* journalist; (*продавец*) newspaper vendor.
га́зик (-а) *м (разг) car manufactured at the Gorky car plant.*
газиро́ванн|ый *прил*: **~ая вода́** carbonated water.
газиро́в|ка (-ки; *gen pl* **-ок)** *ж (разг)* soda.
газовщи́к (-а́) *м (разг)* gasman (*мн* gasmen).
га́зов|ый *прил* gas; **га́зовая ка́мера** gas chamber.
газо́н (-а) *м* lawn.
газопрово́д (-а) *м* gas pipeline.
га́з|ы (-ов) *мн (МЕД)* wind *ед*.
ГАИ *ж сокр (= Госуда́рственная автомоби́льная инспе́кция) state motor vehicle inspectorate.*
Гаити *м нескл* Haiti.
гаитя́нск|ий (-ая, -ое, -ие) *прил* Haitian.
гаи́шник (-а) *м (разг)* ≈ traffic cop.
га́|йка (-йки; *gen pl* **-ек)** *ж* nut; **закру́чивать (закрути́ть** *perf*) **~йки** (*разг*) to put the screws on.
гаймори́т (-а) *м* sinusitis.
гала́ *прил неизм* gala *опред*.
гала́ктик|а (-и) *ж* galaxy; **На́ша Г~** the Galaxy.
гала́нтен *прил см* **гала́нтный.**
галантере́|я (-и) *ж* haberdashery (*BRIT*), notions store (*US*).
гала́нт|ный (-ен, -на, -но) *прил* gallant.
галере́|я (-и) *ж* gallery.
гале́т|а (-ы) *ж sort of biscuit.*
галимать|я́ (-и́) *ж (разг)* gobbledygook.
галифе́ *мн/ср нескл* riding breeches *мн* ◆ *прил неизм*: **брю́ки** ~ jodphurs.
га́л|ка (-ки; *gen pl* **-ок)** *ж* jackdaw.
галло́н (-а) *м* gallon.
галлюцина́ци|я (-и) *ж* hallucination.
га́лок *сущ см* **га́лка.**
гало́п (-а) *м (бег лошади)* gallop; (*танец*) galop.
гало́пом *нареч* at a gallop; **я прочита́л кни́гу** ~ (*разг*) I raced through the book.
га́лоч|ка (-ки; *gen pl* **-ек)** *ж (в тексте)* tick, check (*US*).
гало́ш|а (-и) *ж (обычно мн: обувь)* galosh; **сажа́ть (посади́ть** *perf*) **кого́-н в ~у** (*разг*) to

put sb on the spot; **сади́ться (сесть** *perf*) **в ~у** (*разг*) to get into a jam.
га́лстук (-а) *м* tie, necktie (*US*); **завя́зывать (завяза́ть** *perf*) ~ to tie a tie.
гальваниза́ци|я (-и) *ж* galvanization.
гальванизи́р|овать (-ую) *(не)сов перех* to galvanize.
га́льк|а (-и) *ж, собир* pebble.
гам (-а) *м* uproar.
гама́к (-а́) *м* hammock.
гама́ш|а (-и) *ж* (*обычно мн*) gaiter.
Га́мбург (-а) *м* Hamburg.
га́мбургер (-а) *м* hamburger.
га́мм|а (-ы) *ж* (*муз*) scale; (*чувств, красок*) range.
га́мма-глобули́н (-а) *м* gamma globulin.
га́мма-излуче́ни|е (-я) *ср* gamma radiation.
Га́н|а (-ы) *ж* Ghana.
гангре́н|а (-ы) *ж* gangrene.
га́нгстер (-а) *м* gangster.
гандбо́л (-а) *м* handball.
гандболи́ст (-а) *м* handball player.
гандболи́ст|ка (-ки; *gen pl* **-ок**) *ж см* **гандболи́ст**.
ганте́л|ь (-и) *ж* dumbbell.
гара́ж (-а́) *м* garage.
гара́нт (-а) *м* guarantor.
гаранти́йный *прил* guarantee *опред*, warranty *опред*; **гаранти́йное письмо́** letter of guarantee.
гаранти́р|овать (-ую) *(не)сов перех* to guarantee; ~ *(impf/perf)* **кого́-н от** *+gen* to protect sb against.
гара́нти|я (-и) *ж* guarantee; **~ от убы́тков** guarantee against damage; **това́р с ~ей** item under guarantee; **ба́нковская** ~ bank's letter of guarantee; **авари́йная** ~ warranty; **~ за́нятости** job security.
гардеро́б (-а) *м* wardrobe; (*в общественном здании*) cloakroom.
гардеро́бщик (-а) *м* cloakroom attendant.
гардеро́бщиц|а (-ы) *ж см* **гардеро́бщик**.
гарди́н|а (-ы) *ж* curtain.
га́рев|ый *прил*: **~ая доро́жка** cinder track.
гаре́м (-а) *м* harem.
гармо́ник|а (-и) *ж* concertina; **губна́я** ~ mouth organ.
гармони́р|овать (-ую) *несов неперех*: **~ с** *+instr* (*со средой*) to be in harmony with; (*одежда*) to go with.
гармони́ст (-а) *м* concertina player.
гармони́ч|ный (-ен, -на, -но) *прил* harmonious.
гармо́ни|я (-и) *ж* harmony.
гармо́ш|ка (-ки; *gen pl* **-ек**) *ж* (*разг*) ≈ squeeze-box; (*одежда*): **в ~ку** creased; **при уда́ре маши́на смя́лась в ~ку** the car concertinaed on impact.
гарнизо́н (-а) *м* garrison.
гарни́р (-а) *м* side dish.
гарниту́р (-а) *м* (*одежды*) outfit; (*украшения*) set; (*мебели*) suite.
гарпу́н (-а́) *м* harpoon.
гар|ь (-и) *ж* (*угля*) cinders *мн*; **па́хнет га́рью** there's a smell of burning.
гас *итп несов см* **га́снуть**.
га|си́ть (-шу́, -сишь; *perf* **погаси́ть**) *несов перех* (*лампу, свет*) to put out; (*пожар*) to extinguish, put out; (*скорость*) to reduce; (*звук*) to deaden; (*марку*) to frank; (*no perf; перен: инициативу*) to stifle, suppress; ~ **(погаси́ть** *perf*) **задо́лженность** to settle one's debts; ~ **(погаси́ть** *perf*) **и́звесть** to slake lime.
га́с|нуть (-ну, -нешь; *pt* **-** *или* **-нул, -ла, -ло**, *perf* **пога́снуть** *или* **уга́снуть**) *несов неперех* (*огни*) to go out; (*звезды, чувства, надежда*) to fade.
гастри́т (-а) *м* gastritis.
гастро́л|и (-ей) *мн* *performances of a touring company*; **е́здить/е́хать (пое́хать** *perf*) **на** ~ to go on tour.
гастроли́р|овать (-ую) *несов неперех* to be on tour.
гастроно́м (-а) *м* food store.
гастрономи́ческ|ий (-ая, -ое, ие) *прил*: ~ **магази́н = гастроно́м**.
гастроно́ми|я (-и) *ж* delicatessen.
ГАТТ *м сокр* (= *Генера́льное соглаше́ние о тари́фах и торго́вле*) GATT (= *General Agreement on Tariffs and Trade*).
гауптва́хт|а (-ы) *ж* (*ВОЕН*) guardroom (*as a place of detention*); **сажа́ть (посади́ть** *perf*) **кого́-н на ~у** to confine sb to the guardroom.
гашён|ый *прил* (*марка*) franked; **~ая и́звесть** slaked lime.
гаши́ш (-а) *м* hashish.
гашу́ *несов см* **гаси́ть**.
ГБ *ж сокр* = **госбезопа́сность**.
гвалт (-а) *м* (*разг*) row.
гварде́|ец (-йца) *м* (*ВОЕН*) guardsman (*мн* guardsmen).
гва́рди|я (-и) *ж* (*ВОЕН*) Guards *мн*; **Кра́сная/Бе́лая** ~ (*ИСТ*) the Red/White Guard.
Гватема́л|а (-ы) *ж* Guatemala.
Гвине́|я (-и) *ж* Guinea.
гвозди́к|а (-и) *ж* (*цветок*) carnation; (*пряность*) cloves *мн*.
гвозд|ь (-я́; *nom pl* **-и**, *gen pl* **-е́й**) *м* nail; ~ **програ́ммы** the highlight of the show; **и никаки́х ~е́й!** (*разг*) and that's that!
гг *сокр* = **го́ды**; (= **господа́**) Messrs (= *messieurs*).
ГД *ж сокр* = **Госуда́рственная Ду́ма**.
Гда́ньск (-а) *м* Gdansk.
где *нареч* where; (*разг: где-нибудь*) somewhere, anywhere ◆ *союз* where; ~ **Вы живёте?** where do you live?; **поду́майте, не забы́ли ли** ~ try and think whether you left it anywhere *или* somewhere; **го́род, ~ я жил** the town where I lived; **ты ско́ро бу́дешь бога́тым – ~ уж там!**

(*разг*) you'll soon be rich – hardly!
где́-либо *нареч* = **где́-нибудь.**
где́-нибудь *нареч* somewhere; (*в вопросе*) anywhere.
где́-то *нареч* somewhere.
ГДР *ж сокр* (*ИСТ*: = *Герма́нская Демократи́ческая Респу́блика*) GDR (= *German Democratic Republic*).
гегемони́зм (**-а**) *м* hegemony.
ге́йзер (**-а**) *м* geyser.
гейм (**-а**) *м* (*СПОРТ*) game.
гекта́р (**-а**) *м* hectare.
гел|ь (**-я**) *м* gel (*for hair*).
гемоглоби́н (**-а**) *м* haemoglobin (*BRIT*), hemoglobin (*US*).
геморро́|й (**-я**) *м* haemorrhoids *мн* (*BRIT*), hemorrhoids *мн* (*US*), piles *мн*.
гемофили́|я (**-и**) *ж* haemophilia (*BRIT*), hemophilia (*US*).
ген (**-а**) *м* gene.
ге́ндерный *прил* (*проблема*) gender *опред*.
генеалоги́ческ|ий (**-ая, -ое, -ие**) *прил*: **~ое де́рево** genealogical chart; (*семьи*) family tree.
генеало́ги|я (**-и**) *ж* genealogy.
ге́незис (**-а**) *м* genesis.
генера́л (**-а**) *м* (*ВОЕН*) general.
генера́льн|ый *прил* general; (*главный*) main; **~ая убо́рка** spring-clean; **генера́льная репети́ция** dress rehearsal; **генера́льное сраже́ние** decisive battle; **генера́льный штаб** chief headquarters.
генера́тор (**-а**) *м* generator.
гене́тик (**-а**) *м* geneticist.
гене́тик|а (**-и**) *ж* genetics.
генети́чески *нареч*: **~ модифици́рованный** genetically modified.
генети́ческ|ий (**-ая, -ое, -ие**) *прил* genetic.
гениа́льно *нареч* (*написанный*) superbly ◆ *как сказ* it's great.
гениа́л|ьный (**-ен, -ьна, -ьно**) *прил* great.
ге́ни|й (**-я**) *м* genius.
ге́нный *прил* genetic; **ге́нная инжене́рия** genetic engineering.
геноци́д (**-а**) *м* genocide.
генсе́к (**-а**) *м сокр* = *генера́льный секрета́рь*; General Secretary (*of the Communist Party*).
Ге́ну|я (**-и**) *ж* Genoa.
гео́граф (**-а**) *м* geographer.
геогра́фи|я (**-и**) *ж* geography.
геоде́зи|я (**-и**) *ж* geodesy.
гео́лог (**-а**) *м* geologist.
геоло́ги|я (**-и**) *ж* geology.
геоме́три|я (**-и**) *ж* geometry.
геополи́тик|а (**-и**) *ж* geopolitics.
георги́н (**-а**) *м* dahlia.
георги́н|а (**-ы**) *ж* = **георги́н.**
гепа́рд (**-а**) *м* cheetah.
гепати́т (**-а**) *м* hepatitis.
гера́льдик|а (**-и**) *ж* heraldry.
гера́н|ь (**-и**) *ж* geranium.
герб (**-а́**) *м* coat of arms; **госуда́рственный ~** national emblem.
герба́ри|й (**-я**) *м* herbarium.
гербици́д (**-а**) *м* herbicide.
ге́рбов|ый *прил* heraldic; (*с гербом*) bearing a coat of arms; **ге́рбовая бума́га** headed paper; **ге́рбовая ма́рка** official stamp (*relating to stamp duty*); **ге́рбовый сбор** stamp duty.
геркуле́с (**-а**) *м* (*человек*) Hercules; (*КУЛИН*) porridge oats *мн*.
герма́н|ец (**-ца**) *м* (*обычно мн*: *ИСТ*) Teuton.
Герма́ни|я (**-и**) *ж* Germany.
герма́нск|ий (**-ая, -ое, -ие**) *прил* German.
герметизи́р|овать (**-ую**; *perf* **загермети-зи́ровать**) *несов неперех* to make airtight.
термети́ч|ный (**-ен, -на, -но**) *прил* hermetic.
герои́зм (**-а**) *м* heroism.
геро́ин (**-а**) *м* heroin.
герои́н|я (**-и**) *ж* heroine.
герои́ческ|ий (**-ая, -ое, -ие**) *прил* heroic; **герои́ческий э́пос** heroic epic.
геро́|й (**-я**) *м* hero.
герц (**-а**) *м* hertz.
ге́рцог (**-а**) *м* duke.
герцоги́н|я (**-и**) *ж* duchess.
геста́по *ср нескл* the Gestapo.
геста́пов|ец (**-ца**) *м* member of the Gestapo.
гетероге́нный *прил* heterogeneous.
ге́тр|а (**-ы**) *ж* (*обычно мн*) legwarmer.
ге́тто *ср нескл* ghetto.
г-жа *м сокр* = **госпожа́.**
гжел|ь (**-и**) *ж type of ceramic made in Gzhel.*
гиаци́нт (**-а**) *м* hyacinth.
гиб *итп несов см* **ги́бнуть.**
ги́белен *прил см* **ги́бельный.**
ги́бел|ь (**-и**) *ж* (*человека*) death; (*армии*) destruction; (*самолета, надежды, ценностей*) loss; (*карьеры*) ruin; **они́ бы́ли обречены́ на ~** they were doomed; **на краю́ ~и** (*дело*) on the brink of disaster; (*человек*) on the verge of death.
ги́бел|ьный (**-ен, -ьна, -ьно**) *прил* disastrous.
ги́бк|ий (**-кая, -кое, -кие; -ок, -ка́, -ко**) *прил* flexible; **ги́бкий диск** (*КОМП*) floppy disk; **ги́бкое произво́дство** (*ТЕХ*) flexible production methods.
ги́бкост|ь (**-и**) *ж* flexibility.
ги́б|нуть (**-ну, -нешь**; *pt* **-, ла, -ло**, *perf* **погибнуть**) *несов неперех* to perish; (*растения*) to die; (*перен*) to come to nothing; **~** (**поги́бнуть** *perf*) **от** *+gen* to die of.
ги́бок *прил см* **ги́бкий.**
Гибралта́р (**-а**) *м* Gibraltar.
гибри́д (**-а**) *м* hybrid.
ги́бче *сравн прил от* **ги́бкий.**
гига́нт (**-а**) *м* giant; **пласти́нка-~, диск-~** twelve-inch record.
гига́нтск|ий (**-ая, -ое, -ие**) *прил* gigantic.
гигие́н|а (**-ы**) *ж* hygiene.
гигиени́ческ|ий (**-ая, -ое, -ие**) *прил* sanitary; **гигиени́ческий тампо́н** tampon.
гигиени́ч|ный (**-ен, -на, -но**) *прил* hygienic.
гигроскопи́чный *прил* absorbent.
гид (**-а**) *м* guide.
гидравли́ческ|ий (**-ая, -ое, -ие**) *прил*

hydraulic.
гидрокостю́м (-а) *м* diving suit.
гидрометце́нтр (-а) *м сокр* = *Гидрометеорологи́ческий центр*.
гидроста́нци|я (-и) *ж см* **гидроэлектроста́нция**.
гидроэлектроста́нци|я (-и) *ж* hydroelectric power station.
гие́н|а (-ы) *ж* hyena.
ги́льди|я (-и) *ж* guild.
ги́льз|а (-ы) *ж* cartridge case.
гильоти́н|а (-ы) *ж* guillotine.
Гимала́|и (-ев) *мн* the Himalayas.
гимн (-а) *м* (*госуда́рственный*) anthem; (*хвале́бная пе́сня*) hymn.
гимнази́ст (-а) *м* ≈ grammar school student.
гимнази́ст|ка (-ки; *gen pl* **-ок**) *ж см* **гимнази́ст**.
гимна́зи|я (-и) *ж* ≈ grammar school.
гимна́ст (-а) *м* gymnast.
гимнастёр|ка (-ки; *gen pl* **-ок**) *ж* soldier's blouse.
гимна́стик|а (-и) *ж* exercises *мн*; **(спорти́вная)** ~ gymnastics *мн*; **худо́жественная** ~ modern rhythmic gymnastics; **де́лать (сде́лать** *perf*) **~у** to do one's exercises.
гимна́ст|ка (-ки; *gen pl* **-ок**) *ж см* **гимна́ст**.
гинеко́лог (-а) *м* gynaecologist (*BRIT*), gynecologist (*US*).
гинеколо́ги|я (-и) *ж* gynaecology (*BRIT*), gynecology (*US*).
гипе́рбол|а (-ы) *ж* hyperbole.
гиперто́ник (-а) *м* *person suffering from high blood pressure*.
гипертони́|я (-и) *ж* high blood pressure.
гипертрофи́рованный *прил* (*МЕД*) hypertrophied; (*перен*) excessive.
гипно́з (-а) *м* hypnosis.
гипнотизи́р|овать (-ую; *perf* **загипнотизи́ровать**) *несов перех* to hypnotize.
гипо́тез|а (-ы) *ж* hypothesis; **выдвига́ть (вы́двинуть** *perf*) **~у** to put forward a hypothesis.
гипотети́ческ|ий (-ая, -ое, -ие) *прил* hypothetical.
гипото́ник (-а) *м* *person suffering from low blood pressure*.
гипотони́|я (-и) *ж* low blood pressure.
гиппопота́м (-а) *м* hippopotamus.
гипс (-а) *м* (*ГЕО*) gypsum; (*ИСКУССТВО*) plaster of Paris; (*МЕД*) plaster; **накла́дывать (наложи́ть** *perf*) **~ на что-н** to put sth in plaster.
гипю́р (-а) *м* (guipure) lace.
гирля́нд|а (-ы) *ж* garland.
ги́р|я (-и) *ж* (*весо́в*) weight; (*СПОРТ*) dumbbell.
гита́р|а (-ы) *ж* guitar.
гитари́ст (-а) *м* guitarist.
гитари́ст|ка (-ки; *gen pl* **-ок**) *ж см* **гитари́ст**.
ГК *м сокр* (= *Гражда́нский Ко́декс*) civil code.
гл. *сокр* (= *глава́*) ch. (= *chapter*).
глав|а́ (-ы́; *nom pl* **-ы**) *ж* (*делега́ции, семьи́*) head; (*це́ркви*) dome; (*кни́ги, статьи́*) chapter; **во ~е́ с** *+instr* headed by; **во ~е́** *+gen* at the head of; **во ~у́ угла́ ста́вить (поста́вить** *perf*) **что-н** to give top priority to sth.
глава́р|ь (-я́) *м* (*ба́нды*) leader.
главе́нств|о (-а) *ср* leading role.
главе́нств|овать (-ую) *несов неперех*: **~ над** *+instr* to hold sway over.
главк (-а) *м сокр* (= *гла́вный комите́т*) *chief administrative body within a ministry*.
гла́вное *вводн сл* the main thing; **он, ~, все отрица́ет** the main thing is, he denies everything.
главнокома́ндующ|ий (-его; *decl like adj*) *м* commander in chief.
гла́вн|ый *прил* main; (*ста́рший по положе́нию*) senior, head *опред*; **~ым о́бразом** chiefly, mainly; **гла́вная кни́га** (*КОММ*) general ledger.
глаго́л (-а) *м* verb.
глади́л|ьный (-ен, -ьна, -ьно) *прил*: **~ьная доска́** ironing board.
гладио́лус (-а) *м* gladiolus.
гла́|дить (-жу, -дишь; *perf* **погла́дить**) *несов перех* to iron; (*во́лосы*) to stroke; **они́ тебя́ не погла́дят по голо́вке за э́то** they won't be best pleased with you for this.
гла́д|кий (-кая, -кое, -кие; -ок, -ка́, -ко) *прил* (*ро́вный*) smooth; (*одноцве́тный*) plain, unpatterned; (*пла́вный*) flowing; (*прямо́й*) straight.
гла́дко *нареч* (*ро́вно*) smoothly; (*причёсанный*) tightly; **~ вы́бритый** clean-shaven.
гла́же *сравн прил от* **гла́дкий** ◆ *сравн нареч от* **гла́дко**.
гла́жу *несов см* **гла́дить**.
глаз (-а; *loc sg* **-у́**, *nom pl* **-а́**, *gen pl* **-**) *м* (*та́кже перен*) eye; (*зре́ние*) eyesight; **в ~а́х** *+gen* in the eyes of; **на ~а́х у кого́-н** before sb's eyes; **с гла́зу на́ ~** tête à tête; **на ~** roughly; **она́ всегда́ говори́т о нём за ~а́** (*разг*) she is always talking about him behind his back; **за ним ну́жен ~ да ~** you need to keep your eye on him; **куда́ ~а́ глядя́т идти́ (пойти́** *perf*) (*разг*) to go where one's fancy takes one; **де́лать (сде́лать** *perf*) **больши́е ~а́** to look amazed.
глаза́стый *прил* (*разг*) with big eyes; (*зо́ркий*) sharp-eyed.
Гла́зго *м нескл* Glasgow.
глазе́|ть (-ю) *несов неперех*: **~ на** *+acc* to stare at.
глазир|ова́ть (-у́ю) *(не)сов перех* (*та́кже ТЕХ*) to glaze; (*торт*) to ice, frost (*US*).
глазка́ *сущ см* **глазо́к**.
глазни́к (-а́) *м* (*разг*) eye doctor.
глазни́ц|а (-ы) *ж* eyeball.
глазно́й *прил* eye *опред*.
глаз|о́к (-ка́) *м* peephole.

глазомéр (-а) *м*: **у негó хорóший ~** he has a good eye.
глазýнь|я (-и) *ж* fried egg.
глазýр|ь (-и) *ж* (*на керамике итп*) glaze; (*на торте*) icing, frosting (*US*).
глáнд|а (-ы) *ж* (*обычно мн*) tonsil.
глас|ить (*3sg* **-ит**, *3pl* **-ят**) *несов перех* to state; **закóн/прáвило ~ит, что ...** the law/rule states that ...; **устáв ~ит, что** the regulations stipulate that.
глáсност|ь (-и) *ж* openness; (*ИСТ*) glasnost; **предавáть (предáть** *perf*) **~и** to make public.
глáсн|ый *прил* (*суд, процесс*) public; (*ЛИНГ*) voiced ◆ **(-ого**; *decl like adj*) *м* vowel.
глаукóм|а (-ы) *ж* glaucoma.
глин|а (-ы) *ж* clay.
глинтвéйн (-а; *part gen* **-у)** *м* mulled wine.
глиняный *прил* clay.
глист (-á) *м* (*обычно мн*) (intestinal) worm.
глицерин (-а) *м* glycerin(e).
глицини|я (-и) *ж* wisteria.
глобáл|ьный (-ен, -ьна, -ьно) *прил* (*перен*) thorough; (*no short form*; *климат, политика*) global.
глóбус (-а) *м* globe.
глодá|ть (-ю) *несов перех* to gnaw at.
глотá|ть (-ю; *perf* **проглотить)** *несов перех* to swallow; (*разг*: *обед*) to scoff; (*перен*: *книгу*) to devour; **~ (проглотить** *perf*) **слёзы** to choke back one's tears.
глóт|ка (-ки; *gen pl* **-ок)** *ж* gullet.
глот|óк (-кá) *м* gulp, swallow; (*воды, чая*) drop.
глóх|нуть (-ну, -нешь; *pt* **-, -ла, -ло**, *perf* **оглóхнуть)** *несов неперех* to grow deaf; (*perf* **заглóхнуть**; *шум*) to die away; (*мотор*) to stall.
глýбже *сравн прил от* **глубóкий** ◆ *сравн нареч от* **глубокó**.
глуб|инá (-ины́; *nom pl* **-и́ны)** *ж* depth; (*дно*) depths *мн*; (*леса*) heart; (*зала, сада*) middle; (*перен*): **~** *+gen* (*идеи итп*) profundity of; **на ~инé 10 мéтров** at a depth of 10 metres (*BRIT*) *или* meters (*US*); **в ~инé души́** in one's heart of hearts; **до ~ины́ души́ трóнут** deeply moved; **до ~ины́ души́ удивлён** astounded; **до ~ины́ души́ огорчён** cut to the quick.
глубóк|ий (-ая, -ое, -ие; -, -á, -ó) *прил* deep; (*провинция*) remote; (*мысль, интерес*) profound; (*зима, осень*) late; **~ая стáрость** ripe old age; **~ая ночь** the dead of night; **~ снег** deep snow; **~ поклóн** deep bow; **~ая тáйна** deep secret.
глубокó *нареч* deeply ◆ *как сказ*: **здесь ~** it's deep here.
глубоковóд|ный (-ен, -на, -но) *прил* deep; (*no short form*; *исследования*) deep-sea.
глубокомы́слен|ный (-, -на, -но) *прил* (*речь, замечание*) profound; (*взгляд, вид*) thoughtful.
глубокоуважáемый *прил* dear.
глуб|ь (-и́) *ж* (*леса*) heart; (*океана*) depths *мн*.
глуми́|ться (-лю́сь, -и́шься) *несов возв*: **~ над** *+instr* to mock.
глупé|ть (-ю; *perf* **поглупéть)** *несов неперех* to grow stupid.
глуп|и́ть (-лю́, -и́шь; *perf* **сглупи́ть)** *несов неперех* to be silly *или* stupid.
глýпо *нареч* stupidly ◆ *как сказ* it's stupid *или* silly.
глýпост|ь (-и) *ж* stupidity, silliness; (*поступок*) stupid *или* silly thing; (*слова*) nonsense; **дéлать** (*impf*) **~и** to do silly things; **написáть ей письмó бы́ло ~ю** it was foolish *или* stupid to write to her; **имéть** (*impf*) **~** *+infin* to be foolish enough to do; **~и! никудá не пойдёшь** nonsense! you're not going anywhere.
глýп|ый (-, -á, -о) *прил* stupid, silly.
глухáр|ь (-я́) *м* (*ЗООЛ*) capercaillie.
глух|óй (-, -á, -о) *прил* deaf; (*волнение, недовольство*) suppressed, pent-up; (*звук*) muffled; (*no short form*; *пора*) dead; **~ лес** dense forest; **~áя стенá** blank wall; **он глух к прóсьбам/жáлобам** he is deaf to requests/ complaints.
глухонем|óй *прил* deaf-and-dumb ◆ **(-óго**; *decl like adj*) *м* deaf-mute; **áзбука для ~ы́х** deaf-and-dumb alphabet.
глухот|á (-ы́) *ж* deafness.
глуши́тел|ь (-я) *м* (*ТЕХ*) silencer; (*АВТ*) silencer (*BRIT*), muffler (*US*); (*перен*) suppressor.
глуш|и́ть (-ý, -ишь; *perf* **заглуши́ть)** *несов перех* (*звуки, шум итп*) to muffle; (*мотор*) to turn off; (*перен*: *инициативу*) to stifle, suppress; (*perf* **оглуши́ть**; *рыбу*) to stun; **~** (*impf*) **вóдку/винó** to hit the vodka/wine.
глуш|ь (-и́; *instr sg* **-ью**, *loc sg* **-и́)** *ж* wilderness; (*леса*) deepest part; (*перен*) backwoods *мн*.
глы́б|а (-ы) *ж* (*ледяная*) block; **кáменная ~** boulder.
глюкóз|а (-ы) *ж* glucose.
гля|дéть (-жý, -ди́шь; *perf* **поглядéть)** *несов неперех* to look; (*заботиться*): **~ за** *+instr* to look after; (*оценивать*): **~ на** *+acc* to look at; **нá ночь гля́дя** (so) late at night; **нá зиму гля́дя** just before winter; **я захотéл есть, гля́дя на тебя́** seeing you eat has made me hungry; **тогó и ~ди́ дождь пойдёт** (*разг*) it looks like it could rain any minute; **тогó и ~ди́ дéньги закóнчатся** the money might run out at any time; **там погляди́м** (*разг*) we'll see
▸ **глядéться** *несов возв*: **~ся в** *+acc* to look at o.s. in.
гля́н|ец (-ца) *м* lustre (*BRIT*), luster (*US*), sheen; **наводи́ть (навести́** *perf*) **~ на что-н** (*перен*) to add the finishing touches to sth.
гля́нцевый *прил* glossy.
гм *межд* h'm.
гна|ть (гоню́, гóнишь; *pt* **-л, -лá, -лó)** *несов перех* (*стадо*) to drive; (*зверя*) to chase; (*удалять*: *человека*) to throw out; (*лошадь*) to drive *или* urge on; (*машину*) to drive fast; (*водку итп*) to distil (*BRIT*), distill (*US*); (*разг*: *продукцию*) to churn out; **~** (*impf*) **от себя́** to drive off *или* away; **~** (*impf*) **когó-н с** *+instr* to

rush sb with; **гони́те де́ньги/еду́!** *(разг)* give us your money/some food!
▸ **гна́ться** *несов возв*: **гна́ться за** *+instr* *(преследовать)* to pursue; *(добиваться)* to strive after.
гнев (-а) *м* wrath; **быть** *(impf)* **в гне́ве** to be in a rage.
гне́ва|ться (-юсь) *несов возв* to be angry.
гне́вен *прил см* **гне́вный**.
гнев|и́ть (-лю́, -и́шь) *несов перех* to anger; **не ~и́ Бо́га!** ≈ you should count your blessings!
гне́в|ный (-ен, -на́, -но) *прил* wrathful.
гнедо́й *прил* *(масть лошади)* bay.
гнезд|и́ться *(3sg* **-и́тся**, *3pl* **-я́тся)** *несов возв* *(птицы)* to nest; *(мысль, чувство)* to take root.
гнезд|о́ (-а́; *nom pl* **гнёзда**, *gen pl* **гнёзд)** *ср* *(у птиц)* nest; *(для патронов)* socket, pocket; *(для посуды)* compartment; *(линг)* word family; **вить (свить** *perf*) **~** to build a nest.
гнездо́вь|е (-я) *ср* nesting.
гне|сти́ (-ту́, -тёшь) *несов перех* to gnaw.
гнёт (-а) *м* *(бедности итп)* yoke; **под ~ом** under the yoke.
гнету́щ|ий (-ая, -ее, -ие) *прил* depressing.
гни́д|а (-ы) *ж* nit; *(разг: пренебр)* louse.
гнил|о́й (-, -а́, -о) *прил* *(продукты, ткань итп)* rotten; *(климат)* unhealthy; *(перен: настроения, теория)* decadent.
гнил|ь (-и) *ж* rotten stuff.
гни|ть (-ю́, -ёшь; *perf* **сгнить)** *несов неперех* to rot.
гно|и́ть (-ю́, -и́шь; *perf* **сгнои́ть)** *несов перех* to let rot
▸ **гнои́ться** *несов возв* *(рана)* to discharge.
гно|й (-я) *м* pus.
гнойни́к (-а́) *м* boil.
гном (-а) *м* gnome.
гнуса́в|ить (-лю, -ишь) *несов неперех* to talk through one's nose.
гнуса́в|ый (-, -а, -о) *прил* *(голос, тон)* affected and nasal.
гну́сен *прил см* **гну́сный**.
гну́сност|ь (-и) *ж* *(клеветы, поведения)* vileness; *(поступок)* vile thing.
гну́с|ный (-ен, -на́, -но) *прил* vile.
гн|уть (-у, -ёшь; *perf* **согну́ть)** *несов перех* to bend; **~** *(impf)* **свою́ ли́нию** *(разг)* to have things one's own way; **куда́** *или* **к чему́ он ~ёт?** *(разг)* what's he driving at?; **~** *(impf)* **спи́ну на кого́-н** to slave away for sb
▸ **гну́ться** *несов возв* *(ветка, полка)* to bend.
гнуша́|ться (-юсь; *perf* **погнуша́ться)** *несов возв* (*+gen*) to abhor; **ниче́м не ~** *(impf)* to have no scruples whatsoever.
гобеле́н (-а) *м* tapestry.
гобо́|й (-я) *м* oboe.
гове́|ть (-ю) *несов неперех* *to fast and attend church in preparation for confession and Communion.*
говн|о́ (-а́) *ср* *(груб!)* shit (*!*)
го́вор (-а) *м* *(линг)* dialect; *(звуки разговора)* voices *мн*.
говор|и́ть (-ю́, -и́шь; *perf* **сказа́ть)** *несов перех* to say; *(правду)* to tell ◆ *неперех* to speak, talk; *(обсуждать)*: **~ о** *+prp* to discuss, talk about; *(общаться)*: **~ с** *+instr* to talk to *или* with; **~я́т** it's said, they say; **~** *(impf)* **по-ру́сски** to speak Russian; **что вы ~и́те?** you don't say!, really?; **не ~я́ (уже́) о** *+prp* not to mention; **что и ~!** *(разг)* what else is there to say?; **что ни ~и́!** *(разг)* say what you like!; **коро́че** *или* **ко́ротко ~я́** in short; **стро́го ~я́** strictly speaking; **открове́нно ~я́** to be frank; **по пра́вде ~я́** to tell (you) the truth; **ина́че ~я́** in other words
▸ **говори́ться** *несов возв* *(произноситься)* to be said; **как ~и́тся** as they say.
говорли́в|ый (-, -а, -о) *прил* talkative.
говя́дин|а (-ы) *ж* beef.
го́гот (-а) *м* *(гусей)* honking; *(разг: пренебр)* guffaw.
гого|та́ть (-чу́, -чешь; *perf* **прогогота́ть)** *несов неперех* *(см сущ)* to honk; to guffaw.
год (-а; *part gen* **-у**, *loc sg* **-у́**, *nom pl* **-ы**, *gen pl* **-о́в/лет)** *м* year; **прошло́ 3 го́да/5 лет** 3/5 years passed; **из го́да в ~** year in year out; **кру́глый ~** all year round; **с ~а́ми** with the years; **~ от го́да** from year to year; *см также* **го́ды**.
года́ми *нареч* for years.
го́ден *прил см* **го́дный**.
го|ди́ться (-жу́сь, -ди́шься) *несов возв* (*+dat*) to suit; **~** *(impf)* **в** *+nom pl* to be (well) suited to be; **~** *(impf)* **для** *+gen* to be suitable for; **куда́ э́то ~ди́тся?** *(разг)* what good is this?; **~** *(impf)* **в отцы́/в ма́тери кому́-н** to be old enough to be sb's father/mother; **~** *(impf)* **в сыновья́ кому́-н** to be young enough to be sb's son.
го́дност|ь (-и) *ж* suitability; *(билета)* validity; **срок ~и** shelf life.
го́д|ный (-ен, -на́, -но) *прил*: **~ к** *+dat* *или* **для** *+gen* fit *или* suitable for; **биле́т ~ен до ...** the ticket is valid until ....
годовщи́н|а (-ы) *ж* anniversary; **~ со дня́ сме́рти кого́-н** the anniversary of sb's death.
го́д|ы (-о́в) *мн*: **де́тские/вое́нные ~** childhood/war years; **он уже́ в года́х** he's getting on (in years) now; **пятидеся́тые ~** the Fifties *или* 1950s.
гожу́сь *несов см* **годи́ться**.
Гозна́к (-а) *м сокр* = *Гла́вное управле́ние произво́дством госуда́рственных зна́ков, моне́т и ордено́в.*
гол (-а; *nom pl* **-ы́)** *м* goal; **забива́ть (заби́ть** *perf*) **~** to score a goal.
голеносто́пный *прил*: **~ суста́в** ankle.
го́лен|ь (-и) *ж* shin; *(у животного)* shank.
голки́пер (-а) *м* goalkeeper.

голла́нд|ец (-ца) *м* Dutchman (*мн* Dutchmen).
Голла́нди|я (-и) *ж* Holland.
голла́нд|ка (-ки; *gen pl* **-ок**) *ж* Dutchwoman (*мн* Dutchwomen).
голла́ндск|ий (**-ая, -ое, -ие**) *прил* Dutch; ~ **язы́к** Dutch; **„Г~ аукцио́н"** (*КОММ*) Dutch auction.
голла́ндца *итп сущ см* **голла́ндец.**
Голливу́д (-а) *м* Hollywood.
гол|ова́ (**-овы́**; *acc sg* **-ову**, *dat sg* **-ове́**, *nom pl* **-овы**, *gen pl* **-о́в**, *dat pl* **-ова́м**) *ж* head; **с ~овы́ до ног** from head to foot; **его́ имя́ вы́летало у меня́ из ~овы́** his name slipped my mind; **на́ ~ову вы́ше кого́-н** head and shoulders above sb; **де́лать (сде́лать** *perf*) **что-н на свою́/чью-н го́лову** (*разг*) to make matters worse for o.s./sb; **они́ де́йствовали че́рез мою́/его́ го́лову** they acted over my/his head.
голове́ш|ка (**-ки**; *gen pl* **-ок**) *ж* smouldering (*BRIT*) *или* smoldering (*US*) log.
голо́в|ка (**-ки**; *gen pl* **-ок**) *ж* (*гвоздя*) head; (*чеснока*) bulb; ~ **лу́ка** onion.
головно́й *прил* (*платок итп*) head *опред*; (*отряд*) front *опред*; (*предприятие*) main; **головно́й мозг** brain.
голо́вок *сущ см* **голо́вка.**
головокруже́ни|е (-я) *ср* giddiness.
головокружи́тельный *прил* (*высота*) dizzy; (*карьера*) breath-taking.
головоло́м|ка (**-ки**; *gen pl* **-ок**) *ж* (*также перен*) puzzle; **задава́ть (зада́ть** *perf*) **(кому́-н) ~ку** (*перен*) to pose a problem (to sb).
головомо́й|ка (-и) *ж* (*разг*) telling off.
головоре́з (-а) *м* (*бандит*) cutthroat.
го́лод (-а) *м* hunger; (*длительное недоедание*) starvation; (*массовое бедствие*) famine; (*перен*): **кни́жный/бума́жный** ~ severe shortage of books/paper; **умира́ть (умере́ть** *perf*) **с ~у** *или* **от ~а** to die of hunger.
голода́ни|е (-я) *ср* starvation; (*воздержание*) fasting; **кислоро́дное** ~ oxygen deficiency.
голода́|ть (-ю) *несов неперех* to starve; (*воздерживаться от пищи*) to fast.
гол|о́дный (**-оден, -одна́, -одно**) *прил* hungry; (*год, время*) hunger-stricken; (*край*) barren; **~о́дные бо́ли** hunger pangs; **~о́дная смерть** death from starvation.
голодо́в|ка (**-ки**; *gen pl* **-ок**) *ж* hunger strike; (*разг*) famine; **объявля́ть (объяви́ть** *perf*) **~ку** to go on hunger strike.
гололёд (-а) *м* (*на дорогах*) black ice.
гололе́дица (-ы) *ж* (*на деревьях*) ice; (*на дорогах*) black ice.
го́лос (**-а**; *part gen* **-у**, *nom pl* **-а́**) *м* voice; (*в хоре*) part; (*крови*) the call; (*ПОЛИТ*) vote; ~ **рассу́дка/со́вести** the voice of reason/ conscience; **подава́ть (пода́ть** *perf*) ~ to vote; **пра́во ~а** the right to vote; **в оди́н** ~ with one voice; **во весь** ~ at the top of one's voice; *см также* **голоса́.**
голос|а́ (**-о́в**) *мн foreign-controlled radio stations broadcasting to the Soviet Union.*
голоси́ст|ый (**-, -а, -о**) *прил* loud.
голосло́в|ный (**-ен, -на, -но**) *прил* unsubstantiated.
голосова́ни|е (-я) *ср* ballot, vote; **откры́тое/та́йное** ~ open/secret ballot; **манда́тное** *или* **представи́тельское** ~ card *или* block vote.
голос|ова́ть (**-у́ю**; *perf* **проголосова́ть**) *несов неперех* to vote; (*разг*) to hitch (a lift); ~ **(проголосова́ть** *perf*) **за** *+acc*/**про́тив** *+gen* to vote for/against.
голосов|о́й *прил* vocal; **~ы́е свя́зки** vocal chords.
голубе́|ть (-ю) *несов неперех* to show blue; (*perf* **поголубе́ть**) to turn blue.
голуб|е́ц (**-ца́**) *м* (*обычно мн*) stuffed cabbage leaf.
голуби́к|а (-и) *ж* great bilberry.
голу́бк|а (-и) *ж* (*обращение*) pet.
голуб|о́й *прил* light blue ◆ (**-о́го**; *decl like adj*) *м* (*разг: гомосексуалист*) gay; **голуба́я мечта́** pipe dream; **голубо́й экра́н** small screen.
голу́бушк|а (-и) *ж см* **голу́бчик.**
голубца́ *итп сущ см* **голубе́ц.**
голу́бчик (-а) *м* (*разг*) (my) dear.
го́луб|ь (**-я**; *gen pl* **-е́й**) *м* pigeon; dove; ~ **ми́ра** dove of peace.
голубя́т|ня (**-ни**; *gen pl* **-ен**) *ж* pigeon loft; dovecot.
го́л|ый (**-, -а́, -о**) *прил* (*человек*) naked; (*череп*) bald; (*дерево, стены*) bare; (*no short form*; *правда*) naked; (*цифры, факты*) bare; **~ыми рука́ми** with one's bare hands; **его́ ~ыми рука́ми не возьмёшь** (*перен*) he's a slippery character; **го́лый про́вод** bare wire.
голышо́м *нареч* starkers.
гол|ь (-и) *ж собир* rabble; ~ **на вы́думки хитра́** ≈ necessity is the mother of invention.
гольф (-а) *м* golf; (*обычно мн*: *чулки*) knee sock; *см также* **го́льфы.**
го́льф|ы (**-ов**) *мн* (*брюки*) plus-fours *мн.*
гомеопа́т (-а) *м* homoeopath (*BRIT*), homeopath (*US*).
гомеопати́ческ|ий (**-ая, -ое, -ие**) *прил* homoeopathic (*BRIT*), homeopathic (*US*); **~ая до́за** (*перен*) tiny amount.
гомеопа́ти|я (-и) *ж* homoeopathy (*BRIT*), homeopathy (*US*).
гомери́ческ|ий (**-ая, -ое, -ие**) *прил*: ~ **смех** *или* **хо́хот** roar of laughter.
гомоге́нный *прил* homogenous.
го́мон (-а) *м* (*толпы*) hubbub; **пти́чий** ~ chorus of birdsong; **поднима́ть (подня́ть** *perf*) ~ to make a din.
гомосексуали́зм (-а) *м* homosexuality.
гомосексуали́ст (-а) *м* homosexual.
гонг (-а) *м* gong; **уда́рить** (*perf*) **в** ~ to beat a gong.
гондо́л|а (-ы) *ж* gondola; (*дирижабля*) car (*of airship*).

Гондура́с (-а) *м* Honduras.
гоне́ни|е (-я) *ср* persecution; **подверга́ться (подве́ргнуться** *perf*) **~ям** to be persecuted; **~я на кого́-н/что-н** persecution of sb/sth.
гон|е́ц (-ца́) *м* messenger.
го́н|ка (-ки; *gen pl* -ок) *ж* (*разг*: *спешка*) rush; (*обычно мн*: *соревнования*) racing; **го́нка вооруже́ний** arms race.
Гонко́нг (-а) *м* Hong Kong.
го́нок *итп сущ см* **го́нка**.
го́нор (-а) *м* arrogance.
гонора́р (-а) *м* fee; **а́вторский ~** royalty.
гоноре́|я (-и) *ж* gonorrhoea (*BRIT*), gonorrhea (*US*).
го́ночный *прил* racing *опред*; **го́ночный велосипе́д** racer.
гонт (-а) *м* (*СТРОИТ*) shingles *мн*.
гонца́ *итп сущ см* **гоне́ц**.
гонча́р (-а́) *м* potter.
го́нч|ая (-ей; *decl like adj*) *ж* hound.
го́нщик (-а) *м* (*автомобиля*) racing (*BRIT*) *или* race car (*US*) driver; (*велосипеда*) racing cyclist.
гоню́(сь) *итп несов см* **гнать(ся)**.
гоня́|ть (-ю, -ешь) *несов перех* (*стадо*) to drive; (*птиц, поклонников*) to chase off *или* away; (*разг*: *курьера*) to keep on the go; (: *мяч*) to knock about; (: *ученика*) to grill ◆ *неперех* to race; **~** (*impf*) **голубе́й** (*СПОРТ*) to race pigeons; (*перен*: *разг*) to loaf around; **~** (*impf*) **чай** (*разг*) to lounge around drinking tea
▸ **гоня́ться** *несов возв*: **~ся за** *+instr* (*преследовать*) to chase (after); (*перен*) to pursue.
гоп-компа́ни|я (-и) *ж* (*разг*) rowdy bunch.
гор. *сокр* = **го́род, городско́й**.
гор|а́ (*acc sg* -у, *gen sg* -ы́, *nom pl* -ы, *dat pl* -а́м) *ж* mountain; (*небольшая*) hill; (*перен*: *разг*) heap; **идти́ (пойти́** *perf*) **в го́ру** to go uphill; (*перен*: *разг*: *улучшаться*) to be looking up; (: *делать карьеру*) to go up in the world; **идти́ (пойти́** *perf*) **по́д ~у** (*также перен*: *разг*) to go downhill; **у меня́ ~ с плеч свали́лась** (*разг*) that's a weight off my mind; **обеща́ть** (*impf*) **золоты́е го́ры** to promise the earth; **стоя́ть** (*impf*) **~о́й за кого́-н** (*разг*) to stand up for sb; **пир ~о́й** (*разг*) celebratory blowout; *см также* **го́ры**.
гора́зд (-а, -о) *как сказ* (*разг*): **~ на что-н/**+*infin* very good at sth/at doing; **кто во что ~** (*разг*: *пренебр*) everyone doing his own thing.
гора́здо *нареч* much.
горб (-а́; *loc sg* -у́) *м* hump; **тащи́ть** (*impf*) **всё на ~у́** (*перен*: *разг*) to take everything upon o.s.; **испы́тывать (испыта́ть** *perf*) **что-н на своём ~у́** (*разг*) to learn sth the hard way; **он зарабо́тал всё свои́м ~о́м** (*разг*) he earned everything through his own hard graft.
горба́т|ый (-, -а, -о) *прил* (*человек*) hunchbacked; (*нос*) hooked; **~ого моги́ла испра́вит** he *umn* will never change, ≈ a leopard can't change his spots.
горби́н|ка (-ки; *gen pl* -ок) *ж*: **нос с ~кой** Roman nose.
го́рб|ить (-лю, -ишь; *perf* **сго́рбить**) *несов перех*: **~ спи́ну** to stoop
▸ **го́рбиться** (*perf* **сго́рбиться**) *несов возв* to stoop; (*от старости*) to develop a stoop.
горбоно́с|ый (-, -а, -о) *прил* hooknosed.
горбу́н (-а́) *м* hunchback.
горбу́нь|я (-и) *ж см* **горбу́н**.
горбу́ш|а (-и) *ж* (hunchback) salmon.
горбу́ш|ка (-ки; *gen pl* -ек) *ж* crust.
горде́ли́в|ый (-, -а, -о) *прил* proud.
гор|ди́ться (-жу́сь, -ди́шься) *несов возв* (*+instr*) to be proud of.
го́рдост|ь (-и) *ж* pride; (*+instr*; *победой, успехами*) pride in; **он – ~ на́шей семьи́** he's the pride and joy of the family.
го́рд|ый (-, -а́, -о, -ы) *прил* proud; (*+instr*; *победой, успехами*) proud of.
го́р|е (-я) *ср* (*скорбь*) grief, sorrow; (*несчастье*) misfortune; **хлебну́ть** (*perf*) **~я** (*разг*) to suffer one's share of misfortune; **помога́ть (помо́чь** *perf*) **~ю** to help out in times of trouble; **с ~я** with *или* from grief; **в ~** in (one's) grief; **как на ~** (*разг*) as ill luck would have it; **~ ты моё!** you'll be the death of me!; **ему́ и ~я ма́ло** (*разг*) he couldn't care less.
гор|ева́ть (-ю́ю) *несов неперех* to grieve; **~** (*impf*) **о** *+prp* to grieve for; **не ~ю́й!** cheer up!
го́рек *прил см* **го́рький**.
горе́л|ка (-ки; *gen pl* -ок) *ж* burner; **пая́льная ~** blowtorch.
горе́лый *прил* burnt.
горелье́ф (-а) *м* high relief.
горемы́к|а (-и) *м/ж* (*разг*) poor soul.
го́рест|ный (-ен, -на, -но) *прил* sorrowful.
го́рест|ь (-и) *ж* grief, sorrow; (*обычно мн*: *несчастье*) trouble.
гор|е́ть (-ю́, -и́шь; *perf* **сгоре́ть**) *несов неперех* to burn; (*no perf*; *дом, лес*) to be on fire; (*больной, лоб*) to be burning hot; (*рана*) to smart; (*глаза*) to shine; (*+instr*; *ненавистью, нетерпением*) to burn with; **зака́т ~е́л** there was a blazing sunset; **~** (*impf*) **от стыда́/любопы́тства** to burn with shame/curiosity; **он ~и́т на рабо́те** he puts everything into his work; **план/спекта́кль ~и́т!** the plan/play is in danger of being a complete failure!; **~и́ всё си́ним огнём** *или* **пла́менем!** (*разг*) to hell with it!; **не ~и́т** (*разг*) there's no hurry; **у меня́ душа́ ~и́т** I'm bursting with enthusiasm.
го́р|ец (-ца) *м* mountain dweller.
го́реч|ь (-и) *ж* bitter taste; (*потери*) bitterness.
горже́т|ка (-ки; *gen pl* -ок) *ж* boa.
горжу́сь *несов см* **горди́ться**.

горизо́нт (**-а**) *м* horizon; **появля́ться** (**появи́ться** *perf*) **на чьём-н ~е** to come into sb's life.
горизонта́лен *прил см* **горизонта́льный.**
горизонта́л|ь (**-и**) *ж* horizontal; (*на карте*) contour; (*на шахматной доске*) rank.
горизонта́л|ьный (**-ен, -ьна, -ьно**) *прил* horizontal.
гори́лл|а (**-ы**) *ж* gorilla.
горисполко́м (**-а**) *м сокр* (*ист*: = *городско́й исполни́тельный комите́т*) town *или* city executive committee.
гори́стый *прил* mountainous.
го́р|ка (**-ки**; *gen pl* **-ок**) *ж* hill; (*склон*) slope; (*шкаф*) cabinet; (*кучка*) small pile; (*АВИА*) steep climb.
го́ркн|уть (*3sg* **-ет**, *perf* **прого́ркнуть**) *несов неперех* (*масло*) to go rancid.
горко́м (**-а**) *м сокр* (*ист*: = *городско́й комите́т*) town *или* city committee.
горла́н|ить (**-ю, -ишь**) *несов неперех* (*разг*) to bawl.
горла́ст|ый (**-, -а, -о**) *прил* (*разг*) noisy.
го́рлиц|а (**-ы**) *ж* turtledove.
го́рл|о (**-а**) *ср* throat; (*у сосуда*) neck; **стать** *(perf)* **поперёк ~а кому́-н** (*перен*: *разг*) to stick in sb's throat; **во всё ~** (*разг*) at the top of one's voice; **пристава́ть** (**приста́ть** *perf*) **к кому́-н с ножо́м к ~у** (*разг: пренебр*) to pester the life out of sb; **у меня́ рабо́ты по ~** (*разг*) I'm up to my ears in work; **я сыт по ~** (*разг*) I'm stuffed; (: *перен*: *обещаниями, упрёками*) I've had it up to here.
го́рлыш|ко (**-ка**; *nom pl* **-ки**, *gen pl* **-ек**) *ср* (*бутылки, сосуда*) neck.
гормо́н (**-а**) *м* hormone.
гормона́льный *прил* hormonal.
горн (**-а**) *м* (*для переплавки*) furnace; (*для обжига*) kiln; (*МУЗ*) bugle.
горни́ст (**-а**) *м* bugler.
го́рничн|ая (**-ой**; *decl like adj*) *ж* chambermaid.
горно-бурово́й *прил* mining *опред*, mine-excavation *опред*.
горнодобыва́ющ|ий (**-ая, -ее, -ие**) *прил* mining *опред*.
горнозаво́дск|ий (**-ая, -ое, -ие**) *прил* mining *опред*.
горнолы́жный *прил* ski *опред*.
горнопромы́шленный *прил* = **горнозаво́дский.**
горнопрохо́дческ|ий (**-ая, -ое, -ие**) *прил*: **~ие рабо́ты** tunnelling work *ед*.
горнорабо́ч|ий (**-его**; *decl like adj*) *м* miner.
горноспаса́тельный *прил* mountain-rescue *опред*.
горноста́|й (**-я**) *м* stoat; (*мех*) ermine.
го́рн|ый *прил* mountain *опред*; (*лыжи*) downhill *опред*; (*страна*) mountainous; (*богатства*) mineral *опред*; (*промышленность*) mining *опред*; **~ые поро́ды** rocks; **~ хруста́ль** rock crystal; **го́рная боле́знь** altitude sickness; **го́рный хребе́т** mountain range.
горня́к (**-а́**) *м* (*рабочий*) miner; (*инженер*) mining engineer.
го́род (**-а**; *nom pl* **-а́**) *м* (*большой*) city; (*небольшой*) town; **е́хать** (**пое́хать** *perf*) **за́ город** to go out of town; **жить** *(impf)* **за́ городом** to live out of town.
горо|ди́ть (**-жу́, -ди́шь**) *несов перех*: **~ ерунду́** *или* **вздор** *или* **чушь** (*разг: пренебр*) to talk rubbish.
городо́|к (**-ка́**) *м* small town; **спорти́вный ~** sports complex; **вое́нный ~** military settlement; **университе́тский ~** (university) campus; **де́тский ~** playground.
городско́й *прил* urban; (*сад*) municipal; **~ жи́тель** town dweller; (*большого города*) city dweller.
горожа́н|ин (**-ина**; *nom pl* **-е**, *gen pl* **-**) *м* city dweller.
горожа́н|ка (**-ки**; *gen pl* **-ок**) *ж см* **горожа́нин.**
горожу́ *несов см* **городи́ть.**
го́рок *сущ см* **го́рка.**
гороско́п (**-а**) *м* horoscope.
горо́х (**-а**; *part gen* **-у**) *м собир* peas *мн*; (*на платье итп*) polka dots *мн*; **как об сте́ну ~** like talking to a brick wall.
горо́ховый *прил* (*суп*) pea; **шут ~** (*разг: пренебр*) buffoon.
горо́ш|ек (**-ка**) *м собир* peas *мн*; (*на платье итп*) polka dots *мн*; **ткань в ~** spotted material; **зелёный ~** garden peas *мн*; **души́стый ~** sweet pea.
горо́шин|а (**-ы**) *ж* pea.
горо́шка *итп сущ см* **горо́шек.**
горсове́т (**-а**) *м сокр* (= *городско́й сове́т*) ≈ town *или* city council.
го́рст|ка (**-ки**; *gen pl* **-ок**) *ж* (*также перен*) handful.
горст|ь (**-и**; *gen pl* **-е́й**) *ж* (*руки*) cupped hand; (*также перен*) handful.
горта́нный *прил* guttural.
горта́н|ь (**-и**) *ж* larynx.
горте́нзи|я (**-и**) *ж* hydrangea.
го́рца *итп сущ см* **го́рец.**
го́рче *сравн прил от* **го́рький** ◆ *сравн нареч от* **го́рько.**
горч|и́ть (*3sg* **-ит**, *3pl* **-ат**) *несов неперех* to taste bitter.
горчи́ц|а (**-ы**) *ж* mustard.
горчи́чник (**-а**) *м* mustard plaster.
горчи́чный *прил* mustard.
го́рше *сравн прил от* **го́рький** ◆ *сравн нареч от* **го́рько.**
горш|о́к (**-ка́**) *м* pot; (*также*: **ночно́й ~**) chamber pot; **цвето́чный ~** flowerpot.
го́р|ы (**-**; *dat pl* **-а́м**) *мн* mountains *мн*.
го́р|ький (**-ькая, -ькое, -ькие; -ек, -ька́, -ько**) *прил* (*вкус, разочарование*) bitter; (*обида, событие*) painful; **го́рькая и́стина** the painful truth; **го́рький пья́ница** (*разг*) a hopeless drunkard; **го́рькие слёзы** bitter tears; **го́рький**

смех bitter laughter.
го́рько *нареч* (*плакать*) bitterly ♦ *как сказ*: **во рту** ~ I have a bitter taste in my mouth; **мне** ~, **что меня́ не понима́ют** I feel bitter that nobody understands me.
горю́ч|ее (**-его**; *decl like adj*) *ср* fuel.
горю́ч|ий (**-ая, -ее, -ие**) *прил* flammable; **~ие слёзы** bitter tears.
горя́чек *сущ см* **горя́чка**.
горя́ч|ий (**-ая, -ее, -ие; -, -а́, -о́**) *прил* hot; (*перен*: *любовь*) passionate; (: *спор*) heated; (: *желание*) burning; (: *человек*) hot-tempered; (*день итп*) hectic; ~ **хара́ктер** hot temper; **де́лать** (**сде́лать** *perf*) **что-н по ~им следа́м** to do sth without delay; **я попа́л ему́ под ~ую ру́ку** I caught him while he was in a bad mood; **горя́чая то́чка** trouble spot.
горяч|и́ться (**-у́сь, -и́шься**; *perf* **разгорячи́ться**) *несов возв* to get worked up.
горя́ч|ка (**-ки**; *gen pl* **-ек**) *ж* (*разг*) frenzy; **поро́ть** *(impf)* **~ку** to rush.
горя́чност|ь (**-и**) *ж* irascibility.
горячо́ *нареч* (*спорить, любить*) passionately ♦ *как сказ* it's hot.
Госба́нк (**-а**) *м сокр* (= *госуда́рственный банк*) state bank.
госбезопа́сност|ь (**-и**) *ж сокр* (*ИСТ*: = *госуда́рственная безопа́сность*) national security.
госбюдже́т (**-а**) *м сокр* (= *госуда́рственный бюдже́т*) state budget.
госдепарта́мент (**-а**) *м сокр* (= *госуда́рственный департа́мент*) State Department.
Госкомизда́т *м сокр* = *Госуда́рственный комите́т Сове́та Мини́стров по дела́м изда́тельства полигра́фии и кни́жной торго́вли*.
госкомите́т (**-а**) *м сокр* (= *госуда́рственный комите́т*) state committee.
госкреди́т (**-а**) *м сокр* (= *госуда́рственный креди́т*) state credit.
госпитализи́р|овать (**-ую**) *(не)сов перех* to hospitalize.
го́спитал|ь (**-я**) *м* army hospital.
Госпла́н *м сокр* (*ИСТ*: = *Госуда́рственная пла́новая коми́ссия*) state planning committee.
господа́ *итп сущ см* **господи́н**.
го́споди *межд*: **Г~!** good Lord!
госп|оди́н (**-оди́на**; *nom pl* **-ода́**, *gen pl* **-о́д**) *м* gentleman (*мн* gentlemen); (*хозяин*) master; (*при обращении*) sir; (*при фамилии, звании*) Mr (= *Mister*).
госпо́дств|о (**-а**) *ср* supremacy; (*над страной*) dominion; (*идей*) predominance.
госпо́дств|овать (**-ую**) *несов неперех* to rule; (*мнение*) to prevail; ~ *(impf)* **на мо́ре** to rule the seas; ~ *(impf)* **над** *+instr* (*местностью*) to tower above, dominate.
госпо́дствующ|ий (**-ая, -ее, -ие**) *прил* (*партия, класс*) ruling; (*взгляды*) prevailing; (*гора, башня итп*) imposing.
Госпо́дь (**Го́спода**; *voc* **Го́споди**) *м* (*также*: ~ **Бог**) the Lord; **не дай Го́споди!** God forbid!; **сла́ва тебе́ Го́споди!** Glory be to God!; (*разг*) thank God!
госпож|а́ (**-и́**) *ж* lady; (*хозяйка*) mistress; (*при обращении, звании*) Madam; (*при фамилии*: *замужняя*) Mrs; (: *незамужняя*) Miss; (: *замужняя или незамужняя*) Ms.
Госстра́х (**-а**) *м сокр* (= *Гла́вное управле́ние госуда́рственного страхова́ния Министе́рства фина́нсов России*) *department dealing with national insurance*.
госстра́х (**-а**) *м сокр* (= *госуда́рственное страхова́ние*) ≈ national insurance.
ГОСТ (**-а**) *м сокр* (= *госуда́рственный общесою́зный станда́рт*) *standard manufacturing specifications under the Soviet system*.
гост (**-а**) *м сокр* = **ГОСТ**.
гостеприи́м|ный (**-ен, -на, -но**) *прил* hospitable.
гости́н|ая (**-ой**; *decl like adj*) *ж* living *или* sitting room, lounge (*BRIT*); (*мебель*) living-room suite.
гости́ниц|а (**-ы**) *ж* hotel.
го|сти́ть (**-щу́, -сти́шь**) *несов неперех* to stay.
гост|ь (**-я**; *gen pl* **-е́й**) *м* guest; **идти́** (**пойти́** *perf*) **в го́сти к кому́-н** to go to see sb; **быть** *(impf)* **в ~я́х у кого́-н** to be at sb's house; **в ~я́х хорошо́, а до́ма лу́чше** there's no place like home.
го́ст|ья (**-ьи**; *gen pl* **-ий**) *ж см* **гость**.
госуда́рственн|ый *прил* state *опред*; ~ **язы́к** official language; ~ **строй** government system; **госуда́рственное пра́во** public law; **госуда́рственный экза́мен** Finals *мн*.
госэкза́мен (**-а**) *м сокр* (= *госуда́рственный экза́мен*) ≈ finals *мн*.
госуда́рств|о (**-а**) *ср* state.
госуда́рын|я (**-и**; *gen pl* **-ь**) *ж* sovereign; (*при обращении*) Your Majesty; **ми́лостивая** ~ Madam.
госуда́р|ь (**-я**) *м* sovereign; (*при обращении*) Your Majesty; **ми́лостивый** ~ Sir.
го́тик|а (**-и**) *ж* Gothic.
готи́ческ|ий (**-ая, -ое, -ие**) *прил* Gothic.
готова́л|ьня (**-ьни**; *gen pl* **-ен**) *ж* (*архитектора*) drawing instruments *мн*; (*школьника*) geometry set.
гото́в|ить (**-лю, -ишь**; *perf* **пригото́вить**) *несов перех* to get ready; (*уроки*) to prepare; (*обед*) to prepare, make; (*perf* **подгото́вить**; *специалиста*) to train; (*ученика*) to coach ♦ *неперех* to cook; **она́ хорошо́ ~ит** she's a good cook

▸ **гото́виться** (*perf* **пригото́виться**) *несов возв*: **~ся к** *+dat* (*к отъезду*) to get ready for; **~ся (подгото́виться** *perf*) **к** *+dat* (*к экзамену*) to prepare for; **~ятся больши́е собы́тия/измене́ния** great events/changes are in the offing.
гото́вност|ь (**-и**) *ж* readiness; ~ *+infin* readiness *или* willingness to do; **в боево́й ~и** ready for action.
гото́во *как сказ* that's it.
гото́в|ый (**-, -а, -о**) *прил* (*обед*) ready; (*no short form*; *изделие*) ready-made; ~ **к** *+dat*/*+infin* prepared for/to do; ~ **на перегово́ры** prepared *или* willing to negotiate; ~ **на всё** ready for anything; **она́ живёт на всём ~ом** her every need is catered for; **гото́вое пла́тье** off-the-peg (*BRIT*) *или* off-the -rack (*US*) dress.
гофриро́ванный *прил* (*юбка*) pleated; (*жесть*) corrugated.
гофрир|ова́ть (**-у́ю**) *несов перех* (*см прил*) to pleat; to corrugate.
гощу́ *несов см* **гости́ть**.
ГПТУ *ср сокр* (= *городско́е профессиона́льно-техни́ческое учи́лище*) ≈ CTC (= city technology college).
гр. *сокр* (= **гра́дус**) d. (= *degree*); (= **граждани́н**) Mr (= *Mister*); (= **гражда́нка**) Mrs; = **гру́ппа**.
граб (**-а**) *м* hornbeam.
граб|ёж (**-ежа́**) *м* (*также перен*) robbery; (*дома*) burglary; ~ **среди́ бе́ла дня** (*разг*) daylight robbery.
гра́бель *сущ см* **гра́бли**.
граби́тел|ь (**-я**) *м* (*см сущ*) robber; burglar.
граби́тельск|ий (**-ая, -ое, -ие**) *прил* (*война*) predatory; (*цены*) extortionate; **~ое нападе́ние** (*на дом*) burglary; (*на банк*) robbery; (*на страну*) pillage.
гра́б|ить (**-лю, -ишь**; *perf* **огра́бить**) *несов перех* (*также перен*: *человека*) to rob; (*дом*) to burgle; (*город*) to pillage.
гра́б|ли (**-ель** *или* **-лей**) *мн* rake *ед*.
гра́блю *несов см* **гра́бить**.
гравёр (**-а**) *м* engraver.
гра́ви|й (**-я**) *м* gravel.
гравир|ова́ть (**-у́ю**; *perf* **вы́гравировать**) *несов перех* to engrave ◆ *неперех* to etch.
гравита́ци|я (**-и**) *ж* gravitation.
гравю́р|а (**-ы**) *ж* (*оттиск*) engraving; (*офорт*) etching.
град (**-а**) *м* (*также перен*) hail; (*перен*): ~ *+gen* (*пуль*) hail of; (*упрёков*) stream of.
града́ци|я (**-и**) *ж* gradation.
гра́дин|а (**-ы**) *ж* hailstone.
гради́р|ня (**-ни**; *gen pl* **-ен**) *ж* cooling tower.
гра́дом *нареч* thick and fast; **кати́ться** (*impf*) ~ (*слёзы*) to stream down.
градострои́тел|ь (**-я**) *м* town (*BRIT*) *или* city (*US*) planner.
градострои́тельств|о (**-а**) *ср* town (*BRIT*) *или* city (*US*) planning.
гра́дус (**-а**) *м* degree; **под ~ом** (*разг*) tiddly.
гра́дусник (**-а**) *м* thermometer.
граждани́н (**-а**; *nom pl* **гра́ждане**, *gen pl* **гра́ждан**) *м* citizen.
гражда́н|ка (**-ки**; *gen pl* **-ок**) *ж см* **граждани́н**.
гражда́нск|ий (**-ая, -ое, -ие**) *прил* civil; (*долг*) civic; (*платье*) civilian; **гражда́нская война́** civil war; **гражда́нская панихи́да** civil funeral service; **гражда́нский ко́декс** civil code.
гражда́нств|о (**-а**) *ср* citizenship; **получа́ть (получи́ть** *perf*) ~ *или* **права́ гражда́нства** to be granted citizenship.
грамза́пис|ь (**-и**) *ж* recording; **о́пера в ~и** recording of an opera.
грамм (**-а**; *gen pl* **-** *или* **-ов**) *м* gramme (*BRIT*), gram (*US*); **у него́ (нет) ни гра́мма со́вести** (*разг*) he doesn't have an ounce of conscience.
грамма́тик|а (**-и**) *ж* grammar.
граммати́ческ|ий (**-ая, -ое, -ие**) *прил* (*ошибка*) grammatical; (*упражнение*) grammar *опред*.
гра́мот|а (**-ы**) *ж* reading and writing; (*документ*) certificate; **для меня́ э́то кита́йская** ~ (*разг*) it's Greek *или* double Dutch (*BRIT*) to me; **почётная** ~ certificate of merit.
гра́мот|ный (**-ен, -на, -но**) *прил* (*человек*) literate; (*текст*) properly *или* correctly written; (*специалист, план*) competent.
грампласти́нк|а (**-и**) *ж* gramophone (*BRIT*) *или* phonograph (*US*) record.
грана́т (**-а**) *м* (*плод*) pomegranate; (*дерево*) pomegranate (tree); (*минерал*) garnet.
грана́т|а (**-ы**) *ж* grenade.
грана́товый *прил* (*сок*) pomegranate *опред*; (*браслет*) garnet *опред*; (*цвет*) deep red.
гранатомёт (**-а**) *м* grenade launcher.
грандио́з|ный (**-ен, -на, -но**) *прил* (*сооружение*) grand; (*масштабы, планы*) grandiose.
гранёный *прил* (*стакан*) cut-glass *опред*; (*алмаз*) cut *опред*.
грани́т (**-а**) *м* granite.
грани́тный *прил* (*плита*) granite.
гран|и́ть (**-ю́, -и́шь**) *несов перех* to cut.
грани́ц|а (**-ы**) *ж* (*государства*) border; (*участка*) boundary; (*обычно мн*: *перен*) limit; **е́хать (пое́хать** *perf*) **за ~у** to go abroad; **жить** (*impf*) **за ~ей** to live abroad; **из-за ~ы** from abroad; **в ~х прили́чия/зако́на** within the bounds of decency/the law; **его́ поведе́ние перехо́дит все ~ы!** he's gone too far!
грани́ч|ить (**-у, -ишь**) *несов неперех*: ~ **с** *+instr* to border on; (*перен*) to verge on.
гра́н|ка (**-ки**; *gen pl* **-ок**) *ж* (*ТИПОГ*) proof.
грант (**-а**) *м* grant.
гра́нул|а (**-ы**) *ж* granule.
гран|ь (**-и**) *ж* (*ГЕОМ*) face; (*алмаза*) facet; (*перен*) bounds *мн*; **переступа́ть (переступи́ть** *perf*) ~ to overstep the mark; **на гра́ни** *+gen* on the brink *или* verge of.
граф (**-а**) *м* count, earl (*BRIT*).
граф|а́ (**-ы́**) *ж* column.
гра́фик (**-а**) *м* (*МАТ*) graph; (*план*) schedule,

timetable; (*художник*) graphic artist; **рабо́тать** *(impf)* **по ~у** to work to schedule; **по́езд идёт по ~у** the train is running to time; **~ расчёта то́чки „нулево́й" при́были** (*комм*) break-even chart.
гра́фик|а (**-и**) *ж* graphic art; (*буквы*) script ◆ *собир* (*рисунки*) graphics *мн*.
графи́н (**-а**) *м* (*для воды*) water jug; (*для вина*) decanter; (: *открытый*) carafe.
графи́н|я (**-и**) *ж* countess.
графи́т (**-а**) *м* (*минерал*) graphite; (*грифель*) (pencil) lead.
граф|и́ть (**-лю́, -и́шь**; *perf* **разграфи́ть**) *несов перех* to rule (*lines*).
графи́ческ|ий (**-ая, -ое, -ие**) *прил* graphic.
графлю́ *несов см* **графи́ть**.
гра́фств|о (**-а**) *ср* county.
граццио́з|ный (**-ен, -на, -но**) *прил* graceful.
гра́ци|я (**-и**) *ж* grace; (*корсет*) corset.
грач (**-а́**) *м* rook.
грёб *итп несов см* **грести́**.
гребён|ка (**-ки**; *gen pl* **-ок**) *ж* (*также ТЕХ*) comb; **стричь** *(impf)* **всех под одну́ ~ку** to lump everyone together.
гре́б|ень (**-ня**) *м* comb; (*волны, горы*) crest.
греб|е́ц (**-ца́**) *м* oarsman (*мн* oarsmen), rower.
гребеш|о́к (**-ка́**) *м* comb; (*также:* **морско́й ~**) scallop.
гре́бл|я (**-и**) *ж* rowing.
гребно́й *прил*: **~ спорт** rowing.
гре́бня *итп сущ см* **гре́бень**.
греб|о́к (**-ка**) *м* stroke.
гребу́ *итп несов см* **грести́**.
гребца́ *итп сущ см* **гребе́ц**.
гре́жу(сь) *несов см* **гре́зить(ся)**.
грёз|а (**-ы**) *ж* (*обычно мн*) daydream.
гре́|зить (**-жу, -зишь**) *несов неперех* to (day) dream, fantasize
▸ **гре́зиться** (*perf* **пригре́зиться**) *несов возв*: **ему́ ~зится...** he dreams of ....
гре́йдер (**-а**) *м* grader; (*разг*: *дорога*) dirt road.
гре́йпфрут (**-а**) *м* grapefruit.
грек (**-а**) *м* Greek (man) (*мн* men).
гре́л|ка (**-ки**; *gen pl* **-ок**) *ж* hot-water bottle; **электри́ческая ~** electric blanket.
грем|е́ть (**-лю́, -и́шь**; *perf* **прогреме́ть**) *несов неперех* (*поезд*) to thunder by; (*выстрелы*) to thunder out; (*гром*) to rumble; (*перен*) to resound; **~** (**прогреме́ть** *perf*) *+instr* (*ведром, кастрюлями*) to clatter; (*ключами*) to jangle.
грему́ч|ий (**-ая, -ее, -ие**) *прил*: **~ая змея́** rattlesnake; **~ газ** firedamp.
Грена́д|а (**-ы**) *ж* Grenada.
гренадёр (**-а**; *gen pl* **-** *или* **-ов**) *м* (*солдат*) grenadier; **он настоя́щий ~** (*разг*) he's a real hulk.
гренка́ *итп сущ см* **грено́к**.
Гренла́нди|я (**-и**) *ж* Greenland.
гренла́ндск|ий (**-ая, -ое, -ие**) *прил* Greenlandic.
грен|о́к (**-ка́**; *nom pl* **-ки́**) *м* (*обычно мн*) crouton.
гре|сти́ (**-бу́, -бёшь**; *pt* **грёб, -бла́, -бло́**) *несов неперех* to row; (*веслом, руками*) to paddle ◆ *перех* to rake.
гре|ть (**-ю**) *несов перех* (*подлеж*: *солнце, печь*) to heat, warm; (: *шуба*) to keep warm; (*воду*) to heat (up); (*руки*) to warm; **~** *(impf)* **ру́ки на чём-н** (*разг*) to line one's pockets with sth
▸ **гре́ться** *несов возв* (*человек*) to warm o.s.; (*вода*) to warm *или* heat up.
грех (**-а́**) *м* sin ◆ *как сказ*: **~** *+infin* (*разг*) it's a sin to do; **как на ~** (*разг*) as ill luck would have it; **от ~а́ пода́льше** just to be on the safe side; **уйди́ от ~а́ пода́льше!** go away and stay out of trouble!; **с ~о́м попола́м** (*разг*) by a hair('s breadth).
грехо́в|ный (**-ен, -на, -но**) *прил* sinful.
грехопаде́ни|е (**-я**) *ж* the Fall.
Гре́ци|я (**-и**) *ж* Greece.
гре́цк|ий (**-ая, -ое, -ие**) *прил*: **~ оре́х** walnut.
греча́н|ка (**-ки**; *gen pl* **-ок**) *ж* Greek (woman) (*мн* women).
гре́ческ|ий (**-ая, -ое, -ие**) *прил* Greek; (*культура*) (Ancient) Greek; **~ язы́к** Greek.
гречи́х|а (**-и**) *ж* buckwheat.
гре́чк|а (**-и**) *ж* buckwheat.
гре́чневый *прил* buckwheat.
гре́шен *прил см* **гре́шный**.
греш|и́ть (**-у́, -и́шь**; *perf* **согреши́ть**) *несов неперех* to sin; (*perf* **погреши́ть**; *противоречить*): **~ про́тив** *+gen* to sin against.
гре́шник (**-а**) *м* sinner.
гре́шница (**-ы**) *ж см* **гре́шник**.
гре́ш|ный (**-ен, -на́, -но**) *прил* sinful.
гриб (**-а́**) *м* fungus (*мн* fungi); (*съедобный*) (edible) mushroom; **несъедо́бный ~** toadstool.
грибка́ *итп сущ см* **грибо́к**.
грибни́к (**-а́**) *м* mushroom picker.
грибни́ца (**-ы**) *ж* mushroom spore.
грибн|о́й *прил* (*суп*) mushroom; **~о́е ме́сто** a good place for mushrooms; **грибно́й дождь** *rain during sunshine*.
гриб|о́к (**-ка́**) *м* (*на коже*) fungal infection; (*на дереве*) fungus; (*на хлебе итп*) mould; (*укрытие*) *mushroom-shaped shelter in a playground, on the beach etc*.
гри́в|а (**-ы**) *ж* mane.
гри́венник (**-а**) *м* (*разг*) ten-kopeck piece.
грим (**-а**) *м* stage make-up, greasepaint.
грима́с|а (**-ы**) *ж* grimace; **стро́ить** (**состро́ить** *perf*) *или* **ко́рчить** (**ско́рчить** *perf*) **~ы** to make *или* pull faces.
грима́снича|ть (**-ю**) *несов неперех* to make *или* pull faces.
гримёр (**-а**) *м* make-up artist.
гримёрн|ая (**-ой**; *decl like adj*) *ж* dressing room.
гримир|ова́ть (**-у́ю**; *perf* **загримирова́ть**) *несов перех*: **~ кого́-н** to make sb up

▸ **гримирова́ться** (*perf* **загримирова́ться** *или* **нагримирова́ться**) *несов возв* to put on one's make-up.
грипп (-а) *м* flu.
гриппо́зн|ый *прил* flu *опред*; **у больно́го ~ое состоя́ние** the patient has influenza.
гриф (-а) *м* (*зоол*) vulture; (*мифология*) griffin; (*муз*) fingerboard; (*штемпель*) stamp.
гри́фел|ь (-я) *м* (pencil)lead.
гроб (-а; *loc sg* **-у́**, *nom pl* **-ы́**) *м* coffin; **вгоня́ть** (**вогна́ть** *perf*) **кого́-н в ~** (*разг*) to drive sb to their grave; **в ~у́ я э́то ви́дел!** (*разг*) I don't give a damn about it!
гро́б|ить (-лю, -ишь; *perf* **угро́бить**) *несов перех* (*разг*) to screw up.
гробни́ц|а (-ы) *ж* tomb.
гробов|о́й *прил*: **~ го́лос** sepulchral tones *мн*; **гробово́е молча́ние** deathly silence; **гробова́я тишина́** deathly hush.
грог (-а; *part gen* **-у**) *м* grog.
грожу́(сь) *несов см* **грози́ть(ся)**.
гр|оза́ (-озы́; *nom pl* **-о́зы**) *ж* thunderstorm; (*перен*): **~** *+gen* (*садов, зверей*) threat to.
гроздь (-и; *gen pl* **-е́й**) *ж* (*винограда*) bunch; (*сирени*) cluster.
гро́зен *прил см* **гро́зный**.
гро|зи́ть (-жу́, -зи́шь) *несов неперех* (*no perf*; *опасность*) to loom; (*+instr*; *катастрофой*) to be threatened by; (*perf* **погрози́ть**): **~ кому́-н чем-н** to threaten sb with sth; **~** (**пригрози́ть** *perf*) **кому́-н разво́дом** to threaten sb with divorce; **он пригрози́л нача́льнику уйти́** he threatened the boss that he would resign
▸ **грози́ться** (*perf* **пригрози́ться**) *несов возв* to threaten.
гро́з|ный (-ен, -на́, -но) *прил* (*взгляд, письмо*) threatening; (*противник, оружие*) formidable; (*царь*) severe, harsh; (*учитель*) strict.
грозов|о́й *прил*: **~а́я ту́ча** storm cloud.
гром (-а; *gen pl* **-о́в**) *м* thunder; (*перен*) din; **пока́ ~ не гря́нет** (*разг*) until it's too late; **мета́ть** (*impf*) **гро́мы и мо́лнии** (*перен*: *разг*) to rant and rave.
грома́д|а (-ы) *ж* bulk.
грома́ден *прил см* **грома́дный**.
грома́дин|а (-ы) *ж* (*разг*) whopper, monster.
грома́дный *прил* enormous, huge.
гром|и́ть (-лю́, -и́шь) *несов перех* to destroy; (*перен*: *разг*) to slag (off).
гро́м|кий (-кая, -кое, -кие; -ок, -ка́, -ко) *прил* (*голос*) loud; (*no short form*; *скандал*) big; (*имя, дело*) famous; (*слова*) high-flown.
гро́мко *нареч* loudly.
громкоговори́тел|ь (-я) *м* (loud)speaker.
громлю́ *несов см* **громи́ть**.
громов|о́й *прил* (*голос*) thunderous; **~ы́е раска́ты** thunderclaps *мн*.
громогла́с|ный (-ен, -на, -но) *прил* very loud; **~ное заявле́ние** public announcement.
громоз|ди́ть (-жу́, -ди́шь; *perf* **нагромозди́ть**) *несов перех* to pile up
▸ **громозди́ться** (*perf* **нагромозди́ться**) *несов возв* (*скалы*) to loom; **~ся** (**взгромозди́ться** *perf*) **на** *+acc* (*разг*) to clamber up onto.
громо́зд|кий (-кая, -кое, -кие; -ок, -ка, -ко) *прил* cumbersome; (*перен*) clumsy.
громозжу́(сь) *несов см* **громозди́ть(ся)**.
гро́мок *прил см* **гро́мкий**.
громоотво́д (-а) *м* lightning conductor.
гро́мче *сравн прил от* **гро́мкий** ◆ *сравн нареч от* **гро́мко**.
громыха́|ть (-ю; *perf* **прогромыха́ть**) *несов неперех* (*разг*: *гром*) to rumble; (*колёса*) to rattle; **~** (**прогромыха́ть** *perf*) *+instr* (*кастрюлями, ведром*) to clatter.
гроссме́йстер (-а) *м* grandmaster.
грот (-а) *м* (*пещера*) grotto; (*парус*) mainsail.
гроте́ск (-а) *м* grotesque.
гро́хн|уть (-у, -ешь) *сов неперех* (*разг*: *выстрел*) to ring out; (: *рассмеяться*) to go into stitches ◆ *перех* (*разг*: *вазу итп*) to smash; (: *мешок*) to bang down
▸ **гро́хнуться** (*impf* **гро́хаться**) *сов возв* (*разг*) to come crashing down.
гро́хот (-а) *м* racket.
грох|ота́ть (-очу́, -о́чешь; *perf* **прогрохота́ть**) *несов неперех* to rumble.
грош (-а́) *м* half-kopeck coin; **э́то сто́ит ~и́** it costs next to nothing; **у меня́ нет ни ~а́** (*разг*) I'm stony broke; **~а́ ло́маного не сто́ит** (*разг*) it's not worth a brass farthing (*BRIT*) *или* a plugged nickel (*US*).
грошо́вый *прил* (*разг*: *вещь*) dirt-cheap; (*сумма*) paltry; (*расчёты*) petty.
грубе́|ть (-ю; *perf* **огрубе́ть**) *несов неперех* (*человек*) to grow rude; (*душа*) to grow hard; (*perf* **загрубе́ть**; *кожа*) to become rough; (*perf* **погрубе́ть**; *черты*) to harden.
груб|и́ть (-лю́, -и́шь; *perf* **нагруби́ть**) *несов неперех* (*+dat*) to be rude to.
грубия́н (-а) *м* rude person (*мн* people).
грубия́н|ка (-ки; *gen pl* **-ок**) *ж см* **грубия́н**.
грублю́ *несов см* **груби́ть**.
гру́бо *нареч* (*отвечать*) rudely; (*разговаривать*) crudely; (*обточить, подсчитать*) roughly; **~ говоря́** roughly speaking.
гру́бост|ь (-и) *ж* (*выражение*) crudeness, coarseness; (*поступок*) rudeness.
гру́б|ый (-, -а́, -о) *прил* (*человек, поведение*) rude; (*ткань, пища*) coarse; (*кожа, подсчёт*) rough; (*голос*) gruff; (*ошибка, шутка*) crude; (*нарушение правил*) gross.
гру́д|а (-ы) *ж* pile, heap.
груди́нк|а (-и) *ж* (*говядина*) brisket; (*копченая свинина*) bacon; **бара́нья ~** breast of lamb; **свина́я ~** pork fillet.
грудни́ц|а (-ы) *ж* mastitis.
грудн|о́й *прил* (*молоко*) breast *опред*; (*кашель*) chest *опред*; (*младенец*): **~ ребёнок** baby; **грудно́й го́лос** chest voice; **грудны́е же́лезы** mammary glands *мн*; **грудна́я кле́тка** thorax;

грудно́е кормле́ние breast-feeding.
гр|удь (**-уди́**; *instr sg* **-у́дью**, *nom pl* **-у́ди**) *ж* (*АНАТ*) chest; (: *женщины*) breasts *мн*; ~ **руба́шки** shirt front; **встава́ть (встать** *perf*) **~у́дью на защи́ту кого́-н/чего́-н** to stake one's life in defence (*BRIT*) *или* defense (*US*) of sb/sth; **корми́ть** (*impf*) **~у́дью** to breast-feed.
гружёный *прил* loaded.
гружу́(сь) *несов см* **грузи́ть(ся)**.
груз (**-а**) *м* (*тяжесть*) weight; (*товар*) cargo, freight.
груздь (**-я**) *м* milk agaric.
гру́зен *прил см* **гру́зный**.
грузи́л|о (**-а**) *ср* sinker, weight.
грузи́н (**-а**) *м* Georgian.
грузи́н|ка (**-ки**; *gen pl* **-ок**) *ж см* **грузи́н**.
грузи́нск|ий (**-ая, -ое, -ие**) *прил* Georgian.
гр|узи́ть (**-ужу́, -у́зишь**; *perf* **загрузи́ть** *или* **нагрузи́ть**) *несов перех* (*корабль итп*) to load (up); ~ (**погрузи́ть** *perf*) (**в/на** *+acc*) (*товар*) to load (onto)
▸ **грузи́ться** (*perf* **погрузи́ться**) *несов возв* (*люди*) to board; (*судно*) to take on cargo; (*машина*) to be loaded up.
Гру́зи|я (**-и**) *ж* Georgia.
гру́з|ный (**-ен, -на́, -но**) *прил* (*человек*) hefty; (*походка*) lumbering.
грузови́к (**-а́**) *м* lorry (*BRIT*), truck (*US*).
грузов|о́й *прил* (*судно, самолёт*) cargo *опред*; **грузова́я маши́на** goods vehicle; **грузово́е такси́** removal (*BRIT*) *или* moving (*US*) van.
грузооборо́т (**-а**) *м* turnover of goods.
грузоотправи́тел|ь (**-я**) *м* consignor of goods.
грузоподъёмност|ь (**и**) *ж* freight *или* cargo capacity.
грузополуча́тел|ь (**-я**) *м* consignee.
гру́зчик (**-а**) *м* (*на складе*) warehouse porter; (*в магазине*) stockroom worker; (*в порту*) docker (*BRIT*), stevedore (*US*); (*на вокзале*) porter.
грунт (**-а**) *м* soil, earth; (*дно водоёма*) bottom; (*краска*) primer.
грунт|ова́ть (**-у́ю**; *perf* **загрунтова́ть**) *несов перех* to prime.
грунто́вк|а (**-и**) *ж* undercoat.
грунтов|о́й *прил*: **~а́я доро́га** dirt road; **~а́я кра́ска** primer.
гру́пп|а (**-ы**) *ж* group; **гру́ппа кро́ви** blood group.
группир|ова́ть (**-у́ю**; *perf* **сгруппирова́ть**) *несов перех* (*людей*) to group; (*отдел*) to establish, set up; (*данные, цифры*) to group, classify
▸ **группирова́ться** (*perf* **сгруппирова́ться**) *несов возв* (*объединяться*) to form groups; (*классифицироваться*) to be grouped *или* classified.
группиро́в|ка (**-ки**; *gen pl* **-ок**) *ж* grouping; (*религиозная*) group.
группово́й *прил* group *опред*.
гру́стен *прил см* **гру́стный**.
гру|сти́ть (**-щу́, -сти́шь**) *несов неперех* to be melancholy, feel very sad; ~ (*impf*) **по** *+dat* *или* **о** *+prp* (*семье, дому*) to pine for.
гру́стно *нареч* sadly ◆ *как сказ* (*+dat*): **мне** ~ I feel sad.
гру́ст|ный (**-ен, -на́, -но**) *прил* (*настроение*) sad, melancholy; (*no short form*; *конец*) sad.
груст|ь (**-и**) *ж* sadness, melancholy.
гру́ш|а (**-и**) *ж* (*плод*) pear; (*дерево*) pear (tree).
грущу́ *несов см* **грусти́ть**.
гры́ж|а (**-и**) *ж* hernia.
грыз *итп несов см* **грызть**.
грызн|я́ (**-и**) *ж* (*разг*: *собак итп*) scrap; (*перен*: *пренебр*) squabble.
грыз|ть (**-у́, -ёшь**; *pt* **-, -ла, -ло**) *несов перех* (*печенье, яблоки*) to nibble (at); (*perf* **разгры́зть**; *кость*) to gnaw (on); (*орехи*) to nibble; (*перен*: *разг*: *человека*) to get at; ~ (*impf*) **но́гти** to bite one's nails; **меня́ гры́зло раска́яние/сомне́ние** I was consumed by remorse/doubt
▸ **гры́зться** *несов возв* (*собаки итп*) to fight; (*перен*: *разг*) to squabble.
грызу́н (**-а́**) *м* rodent.
гряд|а́ (**-ы́**; *nom pl* **-ы**) *ж* row (*of flowers, vegetables*); (*гор*) range; (*волн*) series; ~ **облако́в** bank of cloud.
грядёт *итп несов см* **грясти́**.
гря́д|ка (**-ки**; *gen pl* **-ок**) *ж* row.
гряду́щее (**-его**; *decl like adj*) *ср* the future.
гряду́щ|ий (**-ая, -ее, -ие**) *прил* (*год*) coming; **на сон** ~ before going to bed.
грязелече́ни|е (**-я**) *ср* mud cure.
гря́зен *прил см* **гря́зный**.
гря́з|и (**-ей**) *мн* mud cure; (*место*) mud baths *мн*.
грязн|и́ть (**-ю́, -и́шь**; *perf* **загрязни́ть**) *несов перех* (*платье*) to get dirty; (*пол*) to make dirty; (*перен*: *репутацию*) to tarnish ◆ (*perf* **нагрязни́ть**) *неперех* (*в доме*) to make a mess; (*на улице*) to drop litter
▸ **грязни́ться** (*perf* **загрязни́ться**) *несов возв* to become dirty.
гря́зно *как сказ безл*: **до́ма/на у́лице** ~ the street/house is filthy.
грязну́л|я (**-и**) *м/ж* (*разг*) pig; (: *ребёнок*) mucky kid.
гря́з|ный (**-ен, -на́, -но**) *прил* dirty; (*ребёнок, платье*) dirty, grubby; (*перен*: *анекдот, личность*) sordid; (*цвет*) murky; **~ное де́ло** dirty business; **~ная война́** dirty war.
гряз|ь (**-и**; *loc sg* **-и́**) *ж* dirt; (*на дороге*) mud; (*перен*) filth; **облива́ть (обли́ть** *perf*) **кого́-н гря́зью, меша́ть (смеша́ть** *perf*) **кого́-н с гря́зью** (*перен*) to sling mud at sb; *см также* **гря́зи**.
гря́н|уть (**-у, -ешь**) *сов перех* (*марш*) to strike up ◆ *неперех* (*выстрел*) to ring out; (*война*) to

break out; ~ *(perf)* **пе́сню** to burst into song; **~ул гром** there was a clap of thunder.
гря|сти́ *(3sg* **-дёт**, *3pl* **-ду́т**) *несов неперех* to draw near.
гуа́ш|ь (**-и**) *ж* gouache.
губ|а́ (**-ы́**; *nom pl* **-ы**, *dat pl* **-а́м**) *ж* lip; (*обычно мн*: *тисков*) jaw (*of pliers etc*); (*залив*) bay (*in North Russia*); **дуть (наду́ть** *perf*) **гу́бы** (*перен*: *разг*) to be in a huff; **у него́ ~ не ду́ра** (*разг*) he knows what's good for him.
губе́рни|я (**-и**) *ж* gubernia (*administrative region*).
губерна́тор (**-а**) *м* governor.
губе́рнск|ий (**-ая, -ое, -ие**) *прил* gubernia, regional.
губи́тел|ьный (**-ен, -ьна, -ьно**) *прил* (*климат*) unhealthy; (*влияние*) pernicious; (*последствия*) ruinous; (*привычка*) harmful; (*мороз*): **~ (для** *+gen*) disastrous (for).
губ|и́ть (**-лю́, -ишь**; *perf* **погуби́ть**) *несов перех* to kill; (*урожай, здоровье*) to ruin; **он её погу́бит** he'll be the ruin of her.
гу́б|ка (**-ки**; *gen pl* **-ок**) *ж* sponge.
гублю́ *несов см* **губи́ть**.
губн|о́й *прил*: **~а́я пома́да** lipstick; **~а́я гармо́шка** harmonica.
гу́бок *сущ см* **гу́бка**.
ГУВД *сокр* (= *Гла́вное управле́ние вну́тренних дел*) ≈ police headquarters.
гуверна́нт|ка (**-ки**; *gen pl* **-ок**) *ж* governess.
гувернёр (**-а**) *м* (private) tutor.
гугу́ *как сказ*: **она́ ни** ~ (*разг*) she doesn't say a word; **ни ~!** (*разг*) not a word!
гуде́ни|е (**-я**) *ср* (*жуков*) drone; (*проводов*) hum; (*ветра*) moan.
гу|де́ть (**-жу́, -ди́шь**) *несов неперех* (*шмель, провода*) to hum; (*ветер*) to moan; (*толпа*) to murmur; (*машина*) to hoot; (*разг*: *ноги итп*) to throb.
гуд|о́к (**-ка́**) *м* (*устройство*: *автомобиля*) horn; (: *парохода, завода*) siren; (*звук*) hoot.
гудро́н (**-а**) *м* tar.
гужу́ *несов см* **гуде́ть**.
гул (**-а**) *м* (*машин, голосов*) drone; (*море*) murmur.
гу́л|кий (**-кая, -кое, -кие**; **-ок, -ка́, -ко**) *прил* (*удар, шаги*) resounding; (*свод*) echoing.
гу́лькин *прил*: **с ~ нос** (*разг*) next to nothing.
гуля́н|ье (**-ья**; *nom pl* **-ий**) *ср*: **наро́дное ~** *outdoor merrymaking on a public holiday*.
гуля́|ть (**-ю**; *perf* **погуля́ть**) *несов неперех* (*прогуливаться*) to stroll; (*быть на улице*) to be out; (*на свадьбе*) to have a good time, enjoy o.s.; **идти́ (пойти́** *perf*) ~ to go for a walk; **я сего́дня ~ю** (*разг*) I am taking the day off today.
гуля́ш (**-а́**) *м* goulash.
ГУМ (**-а**) *м сокр* (= *Госуда́рственный универса́льный магази́н*) *state department store*.
гуманита́рн|ый *прил* (*помощь*) humanitarian; (*образование, факультет*) arts *опред*; **гуманита́рные нау́ки** the humanities *или* arts.
гума́нност|ь (**-и**) *ж* humaneness, humanity.
гума́н|ный (**-ен, -на, -но**) *прил* humane.
гумн|о́ (**-а́**) *ср* (*сарай*) barn; (*площадка*) threshing floor.
гурма́н (**-а**) *м* gourmet.
гурт (**-а́**) *м* (*коров*) herd.
гурто́м *нареч* (*разг*: *отправиться*) en masse; (: *продать, купить*) in bulk.
гурьб|а́ (**-ы́**) *ж* crowd; **ходи́ть** *(impf) или* **гуля́ть** *(impf)* **~о́й** to go about in a gang.
гуса́к (**-а́**) *м* gander.
гу́сениц|а (**-ы**) *ж* caterpillar; (*трактора*) caterpillar track.
гус|ёнок (**-ёнка**; *nom pl* **-я́та**, *gen pl* **-я́т**) *м* gosling.
гуси́н|ый *прил* (*яйцо*) goose; **~ое ста́до** gaggle of geese; **~ая ко́жа** goose flesh, goose pimples (*BRIT*) *или* bumps (*US*).
густе́|ть (*3sg* **-ет**, *3pl* **-ют**, *perf* **погусте́ть**) *несов неперех* (*туман*) to grow *или* become denser; (*perf* **загусте́ть**; *каша*) to thicken.
густ|о́й (**-, -а́, -о**) *прил* (*лес, облака*) dense; (*брови*) bushy; (*суп, волосы*) thick; (*цвет, бас*) deep, rich.
густонаселённый *прил* densely-populated.
густот|а́ (**-ы́**) *ж* (*волос, каши*) thickness; (*зарослей, дыма*) density; (*голоса, цвета*) richness, deepness.
гусы́н|я (**-и**) *ж* goose (*female*).
гус|ь (**-я**; *gen pl* **-е́й**) *м* goose; **как с гу́ся вода́** (*разг*) like water off a duck's back; **хоро́ш ~!** (*разг. пренебр*) a fine one!
гусько́м *нареч* in single file.
гуся́та *итп сущ см* **гусёнок**.
гуся́тниц|а (**-ы**) *ж* casserole (dish).
гутали́н (**-а**) *м* shoe polish.
гу́щ|а (**-и**) *ж* (*кофейная*) grounds *мн*; (*пивная*) lees *мн*, dregs *мн*; (*супа*) solids (*in soup etc*); (*леса*) thicket; **в ~е собы́тий/толпы́** in the thick of things/the crowd.
гу́ще *сравн прил от* **густо́й**.
Гц *сокр* (= *герц*) Hz (= *hertz*).
ГЭС *ж сокр* (= *гидроэлектроста́нция*) hydroelectric power station.

~Д, д~

Д, д *сущ нескл* (*буква*) *the 5th letter of the Russian alphabet.*

д. *сокр* = **дере́вня, дом.**

KEYWORD

да *част* **1** (*выражает утверждение, согласие*) yes
2 (*не так ли*): **ты придёшь, да?** you're coming, aren't you?; **ты меня́ лю́бишь, да?** you love me, don't you?; **я получи́л письмо́ от ма́мы – да?** I got a letter from my mum – really?
3 (*при воспоминании, размышлении*) oh, yes
4 (*пусть: в лозунгах, призывах*): **да – ми́ру!** yes to peace!; **да здра́вствует демокра́тия!** long live democracy!; **вот э́то да!** (*разг*) cool!; **ну да!** (*разг*) sure!; (*выражает недоверие*) I'll bet!; **да ну́!** (*разг*) no way!
◆ *союз* (*и*) and; (*но, однако*) but; **помога́ет ма́ло, да и то неохо́тно** he doesn't help much, and then only unwillingly; **у неё то́лько одно́ пла́тье, да и то ста́рое** she only has one dress and even that's old; **пла́чет, да и то́лько** he does nothing but cry.

да́бы *союз*: ~ *+infin* in order to do; **он спря́тал де́ньги, ~ никто́ не нашёл** he hid the money in order that it wouldn't be found.

дава́й(те) *несов см* **дава́ть** ◆ *част* let's; ~ **пить чай** let's have some tea; ~ **помоги́(те) мне!** come on, give me a hand!; **дава́й-дава́й!** (*разг*) come on!, get on with it!

да|ва́ть (**-ю́**; *imper* **дава́й(те)**) *несов от* **дать** ◆ *перех* (*no perf*; *разг*: *продавать*) to sell; **вот (во) ~ёт!** (*разг*) that's incredible!; **в магази́не ~ю́т мя́со** (*разг*) they sell meat in the shop
▸ **дава́ться** *несов от* **да́ться** ◆ *возв* (*иметь место*) to take place.

дав|и́ть (**-лю́, -ишь**) *несов перех* (*подлеж*: *обувь*) to pinch; (*perf* **задави́ть**; *калечить*) to crush, trample; (*подлеж*: *машина*) to run over; (*perf* **раздави́ть**; *насекомых*) to squash; (*подлеж*: *чувства*) to oppress; ~ *(impf)* **на** *+acc* (*налегать тяжестью*) to press *или* weigh down on; ~ *(impf)* **кого́-н свои́м авторите́том** (*разг*) to intimidate sb; **воротни́к да́вит** the collar feels tight
▸ **дави́ться** *несов возв* (*разг*: *в автобусе, в тесной комнате*) to be crushed *или* squashed; **~ся (подави́ться** *perf*) *+instr* (*ко́стью, слова́ми*) to choke on.

да́в|ка (**-ки**; *gen pl* **-ок**) *ж* crush.

давле́ни|е (**-я**) *ср* (*газа, жидкости, воздуха*) pressure; **кровяно́е** ~ blood pressure; **атмосфе́рное** ~ atmospheric pressure; **под ~м** *+gen* under the pressure of; **ока́зывать (оказа́ть** *perf*) ~ **на** *+acc* to put pressure on.

давлю́(сь) *несов см* **дави́ть(ся).**

да́вн|ий (**-яя, -ее, -ие**) *прил*: **в ~ие времена́** a long time ago; **с ~их пор** for a long time; **э́то ~ слу́чай** it happened a long time ago.

давно́ *нареч* (*случиться, встретиться*) a long time ago; (*ждать*) for a long time; ~ **бы так!** about time too!

да́вност|ь (**-и**) *ж* (*юр*: *срок*) prescription; (*длительное существование*): **дру́жба/вражда́ име́ет большу́ю** ~ the friendship/feud is of long standing; **за ~ю лет** due to the number of years which have elapsed.

давны́м-давно́ *нареч* (*разг*) ages ago.

да́вок *сущ см* **да́вка.**

дади́м(ся) *итп сов см* **дать(ся).**

да́же *част* even; **так испуга́лся, ~ вскри́кнул** I was so frightened, I even screamed; ~ **я согласи́лся** even I agreed.

да́йджест (**-а**) *м* newspaper rubric.

да́й(те) *сов см* **дать** ◆ *част* (*разг*): ~ **я поду́маю** let me think.

дактилоскопи́|я (**-и**) *ж* fingerprinting.

дал *итп сов см* **дать.**

да́лее *нареч* further; **и так ~** and so on; **не ~ как** *или* **чем вчера́** only yesterday.

далёк|ий (**-ая, -ое, -ие; -, -а́, -о́**) *прил* (*страна, звуки*) distant, far-off; (*прошлое, будущее*) distant; (*путь, путешествие*) long; **в ~ие го́ды** in the distant past; **они́ далеки́ друг от дру́га** they have nothing in common; ~ **от реа́льности** far removed from reality; **она́ – челове́к ~ от нау́ки** she's far from being an expert when it comes to science.

далеко́ *нареч* (*о расстоянии*) far (away); (*о времени*) a long way off ◆ *как сказ* (*располагаться*) it's a long way away; **до го́рода ещё ~** the town is still a long way off; **до ле́та ~**

The spelling rules for Russian are shown on page xvii.

summer is a long way off; ~ **от** *+gen* far (away) from; ~ **за** *+acc* long after; **ему́ ~ за 50** he's well over 50; ~ **не** far from, by no means; ~ **пойти́** *(perf)* *(перен)* to go far; **мне ~ до него́** I'm no match for him.

да́ло *итп сов см* **дать**.

дал|ь (**-и**; *loc sg* **-и́**) *ж* faraway place; **э́то така́я ~** (*разг*) it's such a long way (away).

дальне́йш|ий (**-ая, -ее, -ие**) *прил* further; **в ~ем** in the future.

да́льн|ий (**-яя, -ее, -ие**) *прил* distant; **Д~ Восто́к** the Far East; **раке́та ~его де́йствия** long-range missile; **по́езд/авто́бус ~его сле́дования** long-distance train/bus.

дальнобо́йный *прил* (*ВОЕН*) long-range.

дальнови́д|ный (**-ен, -на, -но**) *прил* far-sighted.

дальнозо́р|кий (**-кая, -кое, -кие; -ок, -ка, -ко**) *прил* long-sighted (*BRIT*), far-sighted (*US*); (*дальновидный*) far-sighted.

да́льше *сравн прил от* **далёкий** ◆ *сравн нареч от* **далеко́** ◆ *нареч* next; **так пло́хо, ~ не́куда** (*разг*) things couldn't be any worse; **не ~ как** *или* **чем вчера́/у́тром** only yesterday/this morning.

дам(ся) *сов см* **дать(ся)**.

да́м|а (**-ы**) *ж* lady; (*КАРТЫ*) queen.

Дама́ск (**-а**) *м* Damascus.

дама́сск|ий (**-ая, -ое, -ие**) *прил*: **~ая сталь** Damascus steel, damask.

да́мб|а (**-ы**) *ж* dam.

да́м|ка (**-ки**; *gen pl* **-ок**) *ж* king (*in draughts or checkers*).

да́мск|ий (**-ая, -ое, -ие**) *прил* ladylike; (*одежда, парикмахер*) ladies'.

Да́ни|я (**-и**) *ж* Denmark.

да́нност|ь (**-и**) *ж* actuality.

да́нн|ые (**-ых**; *decl like adj*) *мн* (*сведения*) data *ед*, information *ед*; (*способности*) talent *ед*.

да́нн|ый *прил* this, the given; **в ~ом слу́чае** in this case; **в ~ моме́нт** at present.

дан|ь (**-и**) *ж* tribute; (*перен*: *моде, традиции*) concession; **отдава́ть (отда́ть** *perf***) ~ кому́-н/чему́-н** to pay tribute to sb/sth.

дар (**-а**; *nom pl* **-ы́**) *м* (*также перен*) gift; **получа́ть (получи́ть** *perf***) что-н в ~** to be given sth as a present.

дар|и́ть (**-ю́, -ишь**; *perf* **подари́ть**) *несов перех* to give; ~ *(impf)* **что-н кому́-н** to give sb sth as a present.

дармов|о́й (**-а́я, -о́е, -ы́е**) *прил* (*разг*) free.

дармое́д (**-а**) *м* (*разг*) sponger.

дарова́ни|е (**-я**) *ср* gift.

дарови́т|ый (**-, -а, -о**) *прил* gifted.

да́ром *нареч* (*бесплатно*) free, for nothing; (*бесполезно*) in vain; **теря́ть (потеря́ть** *perf***) вре́мя ~** to waste time; **э́то ему́ ~ не пройдёт** he'll pay for this; **~ пропада́ть (пропа́сть** *perf***)** to be wasted, go to waste.

да́рственн|ый *прил*: **~ая на́дпись** dedication.

даст(ся) *сов см* **дать(ся)**.

да́т|а (**-ы**) *ж* date; **кру́глая ~** *anniversary which is a multiple of ten years*; **~ вступле́ния в си́лу** effective date.

да́тельный *прил*: **~ паде́ж** dative case.

дати́р|овать (**-ую**) *(не)сов перех* to date.

да́тск|ий (**-ая, -ое, -ие**) *прил* Danish; **~ язы́к** Danish.

датча́н|ин (**-ина**; *nom pl* **-е**, *gen pl* **-**) *м* Dane.

датча́н|ка (**-ки**; *gen pl* **-ок**) *ж см* **датча́нин**.

да́тчик (**-а**) *м* sensor.

дать (*см* **Table 14**; *impf* **дава́ть**) *сов* to give; (*разг*: *ударить*) to clout; (*устроить*: *концерт, спектакль*) to put on; (*позволить*): **~ кому́-н** *+infin* to allow sb to do, let sb do; **дава́ть (~** *perf***) кому́-н что-н** to give sb sth, give sth to sb; **дава́ть (~** *perf***) себя́ знать** to make itself felt; **зима́ даёт себя́ знать** winter is making its presence felt; **ни ~ ни взять** (*разг*) no more, no less; **я тебе́ дам!** (*угроза*) I'll get you!; **~ (дава́ть** *impf***) кому́-н знать о чём-н** (*сообщить*) to let sb know about sth

▸ **да́ться** (*impf* **дава́ться**) *сов возв* (*разг*): **я не да́мся им в ру́ки** I won't let them catch me; **ей легко́ даю́тся языки́** languages come easily to her; **дала́сь тебе́ э́та те́ма!** (*разг*) you're obsessed with the subject!

да́ч|а (**-и**) *ж* (*дом*) dacha (*holiday cottage in the country*); (*корма*) portion; (*показаний, консультаций*) provision; **они́ всё ле́то живу́т на ~е** they are spending the whole of the summer at their dacha.

да́чник (**-а**) *м person who spends time at his or her dacha*.

да́чниц|а (**-ы**) *ж см* **да́чник**.

дашь(ся) *сов см* **дать(ся)**.

ДВ *сокр* (*= длинные волны*) LW= *long wave ед* ◆ *прил сокр* (*= длинноволновой*) LW (*= long-wave*).

дв|а (**-ух**; *см* **Table 23**; *f* **две**, *nt* **два**) *м чис* two ◆ *м нескл* (*ПРОСВЕЩ*) ≈ poor (*school mark*); **ей ~ года́** she is two (years old); **они́ живу́т в до́ме но́мер ~** they live at number two; **о́коло ~ух** about two; **кни́га сто́ит ~ рубля́** the book costs two roubles; **~ с полови́ной часа́** two and a half hours; **~е с полови́ной мину́ты** two and a half minutes; **сейча́с ~ часа́** it's two o'clock; **я́блоки продаю́тся по ~е шту́ки** the apples are sold in twos; **дели́ть (раздели́ть** *perf***) что-н на ~** to divide sth into two; **в ~ух шага́х (от** *+gen***)** within a stone's throw (of *или* from); **в ~ух слова́х** in a few words; **в ~ счёта** (*разг*) in a jiffy.

двадцати́ *чис см* **два́дцать**.

двадцатиле́ти|е (**-я**) *ср* (*срок*) twenty years; (*годовщина*) twentieth anniversary.

двадцатиле́тн|ий (**-яя, -ее, -ие**) *прил* (*период*) twenty-year; (*человек*) twenty-year-old.

двадцатипятиле́ти|е (**-я**) *ср* (*срок*) twenty-five years; (*годовщина*) twenty-fifth anniversary.

двадца́т|ый (**-ая, -ое, -ые**) *чис* twentieth; *см также* **пятидеся́тый**.

два́дцат|ь (-и́; *как* **пять**; *см* **Table 27**) *чис* twenty; *см также* **пятьдеся́т**.
два́жды *нареч* twice; **он приходи́л сюда́ ~** he has come here twice; **~ три – шесть** two times three is six; **я́сно как ~ два** (*разг*) as plain as day.
две *ж чис см* **два**.
двена́дцати *чис см* **двена́дцать**.
двенадцатипе́рстн|ый *прил*: **~ая кишка́** duodenum.
двенадцатичасово́й *прил* (*рабочий день*) twelve-hour; (*отправление*) twelve-o'clock.
двена́дцат|ый (-ая, -ое, -ые) *чис* twelfth; *см также* **пя́тый**.
двена́дцат|ь (-и; *как* **пять**; *см* **Table 27**) *чис* twelve; *см также* **пять**.
две́р|ца (-цы; *gen pl* -ец) *ж* door.
двер|ь (-и; *loc sg* -и́, *gen pl* -е́й) *ж* door; **при закры́тых ~я́х** behind closed doors; **стоя́ть** (*impf*) **в ~я́х** to stand in the doorway; **показа́ть** (*perf*) **на ~ кому́-н** (*перен*) to show sb the door; **день откры́тых ~е́й** open day.
дв|е́сти (-ухсо́т; *см* **Table 31**) *чис* two hundred; *см также* **сто**.
дви́гател|ь (-я) *м* engine, motor; (*перен*) driving force; **~ вну́треннего сгора́ния** internal-combustion engine.
дви́|гать (-гаю; *perf* **дви́нуть**) *несов перех* to move; (*3sg* -жет, *3pl* -жут; *перен*) to further; (*no perf*; *механизм*) to drive; **им ~жет за́висть/любо́вь** he is motivated by envy/love; **~ (дви́нуть** *perf*) **па́льцами/руко́й** to move one's fingers/hand
▸ **дви́гаться** (*perf* **дви́нуться**) *несов возв* to move; (*отправляться*): **~ся в/на** *+acc* to set off *или* start out for; **~ся (дви́нуться** *perf*) **в путь** to set off on a journey; **де́ло не ~гается** we are making no progress.
движе́ни|е (-я) *ср* movement; (*дорожное*) traffic; (*перен*) impulse; **приводи́ть (привести́** *perf*) **что-н в ~** to set sth in motion; **пра́вила доро́жного** *или* **у́личного ~я** ≈ the Highway Code; **~ в защи́ту ми́ра** the peace movement.
дви́жимост|ь (-и) *ж* movables *мн*.
дви́жим|ый (-, -а, -о) *прил*: **~** *+instr* motivated by; **дви́жимое иму́щество** movables.
движ|о́к (-ка́) *м* (*ТЕХ*) *sliding part of a mechanism*.
дви́н|уть(ся) (-у(сь), -ешь(ся)) *сов от* **дви́гать(ся)**.
дво́|е (-и́х; *см* **Table 36a**) *м чис* two; **~ часо́в/сане́й** two watches/sledges; **~ брюк/но́жниц** two pairs of trousers/scissors; **их бы́ло ~** there were two of them; **он не спал ~ су́ток** he didn't sleep for forty-eight hours; **есть** (*impf*) **за двои́х** to eat enough for two; **на свои́х двои́х** (*разг*) on foot.
двоебо́рь|е (-я) *ср* biathlon.
двоебра́чи|е (-я) *ср* bigamy.
двоевла́сти|е (-я) *ср* dual power, diarchy.
дво́ек *сущ см* **дво́йка**.
дво́ен *сущ см* **дво́йня**.
двоето́чи|е (-я) *ср* (*ЛИНГ*) colon.
дво́ечник (-а) *м* (*разг*) dimwit.
дво́ечница (-ы) *ж см* **дво́ечник**.
двои́м *итп чис см* **дво́е**.
дво|и́ться (*3sg* -и́тся) *несов возв*: **у него́ в глаза́х ~и́тся** he is seeing double.
двои́х *чис см* **дво́е**.
двои́чный *прил* binary.
дво́|йка (-йки; *gen pl* -ек) *ж* (*цифра, карта*) two; (*ПРОСВЕЩ*) ≈ D (*school mark*); (*разг*: *автобус, трамвай итп*) (number) two (*bus, tram etc*).
двойн|о́й (-а́я, -о́е, -ы́е) *прил* double; **двойна́я игра́** double-dealing.
дво́|йня (-йни; *gen pl* -ен) *ж* twins *мн*.
дво́йствен|ный (-, -на, -но) *прил* ambiguous.
двор (-а́) *м* (*между домами*) courtyard, yard; (*при отдельном доме*) yard; (*крестьянское хозяйство*) homestead; (*королевский*) court; **моне́тный ~** mint; **при ~е́** at court; **на ~е́ темно́** (*разг*) it's dark outside; **не ко ~у́ оказа́ться** (*perf*) *или* **прийти́сь** (*perf*) (*разг*) to be like a fish out of water.
двор|е́ц (-ца́) *м* palace; **дворе́ц бракосочета́ния** wedding palace (*venue for wedding ceremonies*), ≈ registry office (*BRIT*); **дворе́ц спо́рта** sports centre (*BRIT*) *или* center (*US*).
дво́рник (-а) *м* (*работник*) road sweeper; (*АВТ*) windscreen (*BRIT*) *или* windshield (*US*) wiper.
дворня́г|а (-и) *ж* mongrel.
дворня́ж|ка (-ки; *gen pl* -ек) *ж* = **дворня́га**.
дворца́ *сущ см* **дворе́ц**.
дворцо́вый *прил* palace *опред*.
двор|яни́н (-яни́на; *nom pl* -я́не, *gen pl* -я́н) *м* nobleman (*мн* noblemen).
дворя́н|ка (-ки; *gen pl* -ок) *ж* noblewoman (*мн* noblewomen).
дворя́нств|о (-а) *ср* nobility.
двоюро́дн|ый *прил*: **~ брат** (first) cousin (*male*); **~ая сестра́** (first) cousin (*female*).
двоя́к|ий (-ая, -ое, -ие; -, -ка, -ко) *прил* dual.
двубо́ртный *прил* double-breasted.
двузна́чный *прил* (*число*) two-digit; (*слово, выражение*) ambiguous.
двукра́тн|ый *прил*: **~ чемпио́н** two-times champion; **в ~ом разме́ре** twofold.
двули́ч|ный (-ен, -на, -но) *прил* two-faced.
двум *итп чис см* **два**.
двумста́м *итп чис см* **две́сти**.
двунапра́вленный *прил* (*КОМП*) bidirectional.
двуно́г|ий (-ая, -ое, -ие) *прил* two-legged.
двусло́жный *прил* two-syllable.
двусмы́слен|ный (-, -на, -но) *прил* ambiguous; **~ная шу́тка** double entendre.
двуспа́льн|ый *прил*: **~ая крова́ть** double bed;

двуспальная палатка two-person tent.
двуствольн|ый *прил*: **~ое ружьё** double-barrelled (*BRIT*) *или* double-barreled (*US*) shotgun.
двусторон|ний (-няя, -нее, -ние; -ен, -ня, -не) *прил* (*движение*) two-way; (*соглашение, переговоры*) bilateral; **~нее воспаление лёгких** double pneumonia.
двух *чис см* **два**.
двухгодичный *прил* two-year.
двухдневный *прил* two-day.
двухкопееч|ный *прил*: **~ная монета** two-kopeck coin.
двухлети|е (-я) *ср* (*срок*) two years; (*годовщина*) second anniversary.
двухлетн|ий (-яя, -ее, -ие) *прил* (*период*) two-year; (*ребёнок*) two-year-old; (*БОТ*) biennial.
двухместный *прил* (*номер*) double; (*купе, каюта*) two-berth.
двухмесячный *прил* two-month; (*ребёнок*) two-month-old; (*издание*) bimonthly.
двухнедельный *прил* two-week; (*ребёнок*) two-week-old; (*издание*) fortnightly.
двухпалатный *прил* (*ПОЛИТ*) two-chamber.
двухсмен|ка (-ки; *gen pl* **-ок)** *ж* (*разг*) *two shift working pattern*.
двухсот *чис см* **двести**.
двухсотлетие (-я) *ср* (*срок*) two hundred years; (*годовщина*) bicentenary (*BRIT*), bicentennial (*US*).
двухсотлетн|ий (-яя, -ее, -ие) *прил* (*период*) two-hundred-year; (*дерево*) two-hundred-year-old.
двухсот|ый (-ая, -ое, -ые) *чис* two hundredth.
двухстах *чис см* **двести**.
двухтомник (-а) *м* two-volume edition.
двухцветный *прил* two-coloured (*BRIT*), two-colored (*US*).
двухчасов|ой (-ая, -ое, -ые) *прил* (*фильм*) two-hour; (*отправление*) two-o'clock.
двухэтажный *прил* two-storey (*BRIT*), two-story (*US*).
двушк|ка (-ки; *gen pl* **-ек)** *ж* (*разг*) two-kopeck coin.
двуязыч|ный (-ен, -на, -но) *прил* bilingual.
дебаркадер (-а) *м* landing stage.
дебатир|овать (-ую) *несов перех* to debate.
дебат|ы (-ов) *мн* debate *ед*.
дебет (-а) *м* debit; **заносить (занести** *perf***) что-н в ~** to debit sth.
дебетовани|е (-я) *ср*: **прямое ~** direct debit.
дебет|овать (-ую) *(не)сов перех* to debit.
дебетовый *прил*: **~ остаток** debit balance; **дебетовое авизо** debit note.
дебил (-а) *м* (*разг: пренебр*) moron.
дебитор (-а) *м* debtor.
дебр|и (-ей) *мн* (*в лесу*) thicket *ед*; (*перен*): **~** *+gen* (*науки, техники*) maze of.
дебют (-а) *м* debut; (*в шахматах*) opening.
дебютант (-а) *м* *person making his debut*.
дебютант|ка (-ки; *gen pl* **-ок)** *ж см* **дебютант**.
дев|а (-ы) *ж*: **старая ~** spinster; (*созвездие*): **Д~** Virgo.
девальваци|я (-и) *ж* devaluation.
девальвир|овать (-ую) *(не)сов перех* to devalue.
дева|ть (-ю) *несов от* **деть** ♦ *сов перех* (*разг*) to put; **мне некуда ~ деньги/время** I've got more money/time than I know what to do with
▸ **деваться** *несов от* **деться** ♦ *сов возв* (*разг*): **куда она ~лась?** where has she got to?; **куда ~ся** it can't be helped.
девер|ь (-я) *м* brother-in-law (*wife's brother*).
девиз (-а) *м* motto.
девица (-ы) *ж* (*ФОЛЬКЛОР*) maiden.
девица (-ы) *ж* (*девушка*) girl.
девичеств|о (-а) *ср* (*до замужества*) girlhood; **в ~е Петрова** née Petrova.
девич|ий (-ья, -ье, -ьи) *прил*: **~ья фамилия** maiden name.
дев|ка (-ки; *gen pl* **-ок)** *ж* (*разг: девушка*) girl.
девоч|ка (-ки; *gen pl* **-ек)** *ж* (*ребёнок*) little girl; (*разг: девушка*) girl.
девуш|ка (-ки; *gen pl* **-ек)** *ж* girl; (*разг: обращение*) miss.
девчон|ка (-ки; *gen pl* **-ок)** *ж* (*разг: девочка*) little girl, kid.
девяност|о (-а; *как* **сто**; *см* **Table 30)** *чис* ninety; *см также* **пятьдесят**.
девяностолети|е (-я) *ср* (*срок*) ninety years; (*годовщина*) ninetieth anniversary.
девяностолетн|ий (-яя, -ее, -ие) *прил* (*период*) ninety-year; (*человек*) ninety-year-old.
девяност|ый (-ая, -ое, -ые) *чис* ninetieth; *см также* **пятидесятый**.
девят|ая (-ой; *decl like adj*) *ж*: **одна ~** one ninth.
девятер|о (-ых; *как* **четверо**; *см* **Table 36a)** *чис* nine; (*ботинок, перчаток*) nine pairs; *см также* **двое**.
девяти *чис см* **девять**.
девятидневный *прил* nine-day.
девятиклассник (-а) *м* *pupil in ninth year at school (usually 15 years old)*.
девятиклассница (-ы) *ж см* **девятиклассник**.
девятикратн|ый *прил*: **~ чемпион** nine-times champion; **в ~ом размере** ninefold.
девятилети|е (-я) *ср* (*срок*) nine years; (*годовщина*) ninth anniversary.
девятилетн|ий (-яя, -ее, -ие) *прил* (*период*) nine-year; (*ребёнок*) nine-year-old.
девятимесячный *прил* nine-month; (*ребёнок*) nine-month-old.
девятинедельный *прил* nine-week; (*ребёнок*) nine-week-old.
девятисот *чис см* **девятьсот**.
девятисотлети|е (-я) *ср* (*срок*) nine hundred years *мн*; (*годовщина*) nine-hundredth anniversary.
девятисотлетн|ий (-яя, -ее, -ие) *прил* (*период*) nine hundred-year; (*дерево*) nine hundred-year-old.
девятисот|ый (-ая, -ое, -ые) *чис* nine-

hundredth.
девятистáм *итп чис см* **девятьсóт**.
девятичасов|óй (-áя, -óе, -ые) *прил* (*операция*) nine-hour; (*отправление*) nine o'clock.
девя́т|ка (-ки; *gen pl* **-ок)** *ж* (*цифра, карта*) nine; (*группа из девяти*) group of nine; (*разг*: *автобус, трамвай итп*) (number) nine (*bus, tram etc*).
девятнáдцати *чис см* **девятнáдцать**.
девятнáдцат|ый (-ая, -ое, -ые) *чис* nineteenth; *см также* **пя́тый**.
девятнáдцат|ь (-и; *как* **пять**; *см* **Table 27)** *чис* nineteen; *см также* **пять**.
девя́ток *сущ см* **девя́тка**.
девя́т|ый (-ая, -ое, -ые) *чис* ninth; *см также* **пя́тый**.
дéвят|ь (-и́; *как* **пять**; *см* **Table 27)** *чис* nine; *см также* **пять**.
девят|ьсóт (-исот; *как* **пятьсóт**; *см* **Table 34)** *чис* nine hundred; *см также* **сто**.
девятью́ *чис см* **дéвять** ◆ *нареч* nine times; ~ **пять – сóрок пять** nine times five is forty-five.
девятьюстáми *чис см* **девятьсóт**.
дегенерати́в|ный (-ен, -на, -но) *прил* degenerate.
дегенерáци|я (-и) *ж* degeneration.
дёг|оть (-тя) *м* tar.
деградúр|овать (-ую) *(не)сов неперех* to degenerate.
дёгтя *сущ см* **дёготь**.
дегусти́р|овать (-ую) *(не)сов перех* to taste, sample.
дед (-а) *м* grandfather; (*разг*) old man; **Дед Морóз** ≈ Father Christmas; *см также* **деды́**.
дéдовск|ий (-ая, -ое, -ие) *прил* grandfather's; (*перен*) old-fashioned.
дедовщи́н|а (-ы) *ж the abuse of new conscripts by older soldiers*.
дедýкци|я (-и) *ж* deduction.
дед|ы́ (-óв) *мн* (*разг*) *final-year conscripts*.
деепричáсти|е (-я) *ср* gerund.
дееспосóб|ный (-ен, -на, -но) *прил* (*войска*) functional; (*ЮР*) responsible.
дежýр|ить (-ю, -ишь) *несов неперех* (*в порядке очереди*) to be on duty; ~ *(impf)* **у чегó-н** to guard sth; ~ *(impf)* **у постéли больнóго** to sit at a patient's bedside.
дежýрн|ая (-ой; *decl like adj)* *ж см* **дежýрный**.
дежýрн|ый *прил* (*пренебр*: *цитаты, остроты*) hackneyed; ~ **врач/милиционéр** doctor/(police) officer on duty ◆ **(-ого**; *decl like adj)* *м* person on duty; (*по станции*) assistant station master; **дежýрный магази́н** late-night shop; **дежýрное блю́до** dish of the day.
дезерти́р (-а) *м* deserter.
дезерти́р|овать (-ую) *(не)сов неперех* to desert.

дезинсéкци|я (-и) *ж* pest control (*of insects*).
дезинфéкци|я (-и) *ж* disinfection.
дезинфици́р|овать (-ую) *(не)сов перех* to disinfect.
дезинформáци|я (-и) *ж* misinformation.
дезинформи́р|овать (-ую) *(не)сов перех* to misinform.
дезодорáнт (-а) *м* antiperspirant.
дезорганизáци|я (-и) *ж* disorganization.
дезорганиз|овáть (-ýю) *(не)сов перех* to disorganize.
дезориенти́р|овать (-ую) *(не)сов перех* to disorientate.
дéйствен|ный (-, -на, -но) *прил* effective.
дéйстви|е (-я) *ср* (*механизма, закона*) functioning; (*романа итп*) action; (*часть пьесы*) act; (*лекарства, предупреждения*) effect; **вводи́ть (ввести́** *perf*) **в** ~ (*фабрику*) to open; (*турбину*) to activate; (*закон*) to introduce; **приводи́ть (привести́** *perf*) **в** ~ to carry out, implement; **под ~м** *+gen* under the influence of; *см также* **дéйствия**.
действи́телен *прил см* **действи́тельный**.
действи́тельно *нареч, вводн сл* really; **онá ~ краси́ва** she is really beautiful; **~, ужé порá идти́** it really is time to go.
действи́тельност|ь (-и) *ж* reality; **в ~и** in reality.
действи́тел|ьный *прил* (*факт, польза*) real, actual; **(-ен, -ьна, -ьно**; *пропуск, удостоверение*) valid; **действи́тельный залóг** active voice; **действи́тельная (воéнная) слýжба** active service (*BRIT*) *или* duty (*esp US*).
дéйстви|я (-й) *мн* (*поступки*) actions *мн*; (*ВОЕН*) operations *мн*.
дéйств|овать (-ую) *несов неперех* (*человек*) to act; (*механизмы, закон*) to operate, work; (*perf* **подéйствовать**; *влиять*): ~ **на** *+acc* (*лекарство, уговоры*) to have an effect on.
дéйствующ|ий (-ая, -ее, -ие) *прил*: **~ие ли́ца** (*персонажи*) characters *мн*; (*участники событий*) protagonists *мн*; **дéйствующая áрмия** standing army; **дéйствующий вулкáн** active volcano.
декабри́ст (-а) *м* (*ИСТ*) Decembrist.
декáбр|ь (-я́) *м* December; *см также* **октя́брь**.
декáд|а (-ы) *ж* ten-day period; ~ **францýзского кинó** ten-day festival of French cinema.
декадéнт (-а) *м* decadent.
декадéнтск|ий (-ая, -ое, -ие) *прил* decadent.
декадентств|о (-а) *ср* decadence.
декáн (-а) *м* dean.
деканáт (-а) *м* faculty office.
деклами́р|овать (-ую; *perf* **продеклами́ровать)** *несов перех* to recite.
декларáци|я (-и) *ж* declaration; **тамóженная ~** customs declaration; ~ **судовóго грýза** ship's manifest.

деклари́р|овать (-ую) *(не)сов перех* to declare.
деклассированн|ый *прил*: **~ые элеме́нты** social outcasts.
деко́дер (-а) *м* (*КОМП*) decoder.
декоди́р|овать (-ую) *(не)сов перех* to decode.
декольте́ *ср нескл, прил неизм* décolleté.
декорати́вный *прил* (*растения*) ornamental; (*искусство*) decorative.
декора́ци|я (-и) *ж* (*ТЕАТР*) set.
декре́т (-а) *м* (*постановление*) decree; (*разг*: *отпуск*) maternity leave; **издава́ть (изда́ть** *perf*) **~ о** *+prp* to issue a decree on; **уходи́ть (уйти** *perf*) **в ~** (*разг*) to take maternity leave.
декре́тный *прил*: **~ о́тпуск** maternity leave.
де́ланный *прил* (*смех*) false.
де́ла|ть (-ю; *perf* **сде́лать)** *сов перех* to make; (*упражнения, опыты, подлость итп*) to do; **~ (сде́лать** *perf*) **уро́ки** to do one's homework; **~ (сде́лать** *perf*) **прыжо́к** to jump; **~ (сде́лать** *perf*) **из кого́-н что-н** to make sth out of sb; **~** (*impf*) **не́чего ~** there is nothing to be done; **от не́чего ~** for want of something better to do; **что ~?** what can be done?
▸ **де́латься** (*perf* **сде́латься)** *несов возв* (*происходить*) to happen; **~ся (сде́латься** *perf*) *+instr* to become.
делега́т (-а) *м* delegate.
делега́т|ка (-ки; *gen pl* **-ок)** *ж см* **делега́т**.
делега́ци|я (-и) *ж* delegation.
де́лен *прил см* **де́льный**.
деле́ни|е (-я) *ср* division; (*на линейке, в термометре*) point.
дел|е́ц (-ьца́) *м* dealer.
Де́ли *м нескл* Delhi.
деликате́с (-а) *м* delicacy.
делика́тно *нареч* tactfully.
делика́тный *прил* delicate.
дел|и́ть (-ю́, -ишь; *perf* **подели́ть** *или* **раздели́ть)** *несов перех* (*также МАТ*) to divide; **~ (раздели́ть** *perf*) **что-н на** *+acc* to divide sth by; **~ (раздели́ть** *perf*) **что-н с** *+instr* to share sth with; **~ (раздели́ть** *perf*) **ра́дость/го́ре (с кем-н)** to share one's joy/grief (with sb)
▸ **дели́ться** (*perf* **раздели́ться)** *несов возв*: **~ся (на** *+acc*) (*отряд*) to divide *или* split up (into); **~ся** (*impf*) **на** *+acc* (*книга, статья*) to be divided into; (*МАТ*) to be divisible by; **~ся (подели́ться** *perf*) **чем-н с кем-н** to share sth with sb.
де́л|о (-а) *ср* matter; (*надобность, также КОММ*) business; (*положение*) situation; (*поступок*) act; (*ЮР*) case; (*АДМИН*) file; **э́то моё ~** that's my business; **э́то не твоё ~** it's none of your business; **я пришёл по ~у** I've come on business; **у меня́ к Вам ~** I have something to discuss with you; **как дела́?** how are things?; **в чём ~?** what's wrong?; **~ в том, что ...** the thing is that ...; **не в э́том ~** this isn't the issue; **на (са́мом) ~е** in (actual) fact; **на ~е** in practise; **пе́рвым ~м** in the first case *или* instance; **за ~** fairly; **ме́жду ~м** in between times; **то и ~** every now and then.
делови́тост|ь (-и) *ж* businesslike manner.
делови́т|ый (-, -а, -о) *прил* businesslike.
делов|о́й (-а́я, -о́е, -ы́е) *прил* (*встреча, круги*) business *опред*; (*человек*) efficient; (*вид, тон*) businesslike.
делопроизводи́тел|ь (-я) *м* clerk.
делопроизво́дств|о (-а) *ср* clerical work.
де́л|ьный (-ен, -ьна, -ьно) *прил* (*человек*) businesslike, efficient; (*совет, предложение*) practical.
де́льт|а (-ы) *ж* delta.
дельтапла́н (-а) *м* hang-glider.
дельфи́н (-а) *м* dolphin.
дельца́ *итп сущ см* **деле́ц**.
деля́г|а (-и) *м* (*разг*: *пренебр*) wheeler-dealer.
демаго́г (-а) *м* demagogue.
демаго́ги|я (-и) *ж* demagogy; **разводи́ть (развести́** *perf*) **~ю** (*разг*) to talk a lot of hot air.
демаркацио́нн|ый *прил*: **~ая ли́ния** demarcation line.
демилитариза́ци|я (-и) *ж* demilitarization.
демисезо́нн|ый *прил*: **~ое пальто́** *coat for spring and autumn wear*.
демобилиза́ци|я (-и) *ж* demobilization.
демобилиз|ова́ться (-у́юсь) *(не)сов возв* to be demobilized.
демографи́ческ|ий (-ая, -ое, -ие) *прил* (*исследование*) population *опред*, demographic; **демографи́ческий взрыв** population explosion.
демогра́фи|я (-и) *ж* demography.
демокра́т (-а) *м* democrat.
демократи́зм (-а) *м* democracy.
демократи́ческ|ий (-ая, -ое, -ие) *прил* democratic.
демокра́ти|я (-и) *ж* democracy.
де́мон (-а) *м* demon.
демонстра́нт (-а) *м* demonstrator.
демонстра́нт|ка (-ки; *gen pl* **-ок)** *ж см* **демонстра́нт**.
демонстрати́в|ный (-ен, -на, -но) *прил* (*поведение, уход*) theatrical.
демонстра́ци|я (-и) *ж* demonstration; (*показ: фильма*) showing; (*: экспонатов*) show.
демонстри́р|овать (-ую) *(не)сов неперех* (*ПОЛИТ*) to demonstrate ◆ *несов перех* to show.
демонти́р|овать (-ую) *(не)сов перех* to dismantle.
деморализа́ци|я (-и) *ж* demoralization.
де́мпинг (-а) *м* (*КОММ*) dumping.
де́мпингов|ый *прил*: **~ые це́ны** artificially lowered prices.
денатура́т (-а) *м* meths.
денационализа́ци|я (-и) *ж* denationalization.
денационализи́р|овать (-ую) *(не)сов перех* to denationalize.
дендра́ри|й (-я) *м* arboretum.
де́нег *сущ см* **де́ньги**.
де́нежный *прил* (*реформа*) monetary; (*рынок*) money *опред*; (*разг*) well-off; **де́нежный знак**

banknote; **дéнежный штраф** fine.
деноминáци|я (**-и**) *ж* (*ЭКОН*) denomination.
дéну(сь) *итп сов см* **деть(ся)**.
день (**дня**) *м* day; **Д~ Побéды** ≈ V-E Day, Victory Day (*the anniversary of the USSR's victory over Germany in World War 2*): **световóй** ~ daylight; ~ **ото дня** day by day; **изо дня в** ~ day in, day out; **чéрез** ~ every other day; **со дня нá** ~ (*постепенно*) from one day to the next; (*скоро*) in the next few days; **на другóй** ~ the next day; **на днях** (*скоро*) in the next few days; (*недавно*) the other day; **день рождéния** birthday.
дéн|ьги (**-ег**; *dat pl* **-ьгáм**) *мн* money *ед*; **бросáть** (*impf*) *или* **швырять** (*impf*) ~ **на вéтер** to throw money down the drain; **бумáжные** ~ paper money, banknotes; **налúчные** ~ (ready) cash.
департáмент (**-а**) *м* department.
депéш|а (**-и**) *ж* dispatch.
депó *ср нескл* depot.
депозúт (**-а**) *м* deposit.
депозúтный *прил* deposit *опред*.
депозúтор (**-а**) *м* depositor.
депонéнт (**-а**) *м* = **депозúтор**.
депонúр|овать (**-ую**) (*не*)*сов перех* to deposit.
депортáци|я (**-и**) *ж* deportation.
депортúр|овать (**-ую**) (*не*)*сов перех* to deport.
депрéсси|я (**-и**) *ж* depression.
депутáт (**-а**) *м* deputy (*POL*).
депутáтск|ий (**-ая, -ое, -ие**) *прил* deputies'.
дёрга|ть (**-ю**) *несов перех* to tug *или* pull (at); (*перен: разг*) to hassle ◆ *неперех* (*+instr*; *плечом, головой*) to jerk
▸ **дёргаться** *несов возв* (*машина, лошадь*) to jerk; (*лицо, губы*) to twitch; (*перен: разг*) to (make a) fuss.
деревенé|ть (**-ю**; *perf* **одеревенéть**) *несов неперех* to grow *или* go numb.
деревéнск|ий (**-ая, -ое, -ие**) *прил* (*дом, житель*) country *опред*; (*тишина, пейзаж*) rural; (*площадь, колодец*) village *опред*.
дерéв|ня (**-ни**; *gen pl* **-éнь**, *dat* **-ням**) *ж* (*селение*) village; (*местность*) the country; **олимпúйская** ~ Olympic Village.
дéр|ево (**-ева**; *nom pl* **-éвья**, *gen pl* **-éвьев**) *ср* tree; (*древесина*) wood; **родослóвное** ~ family tree; **крáсное** ~ mahogany.
деревообрабóт|ка (**-ки**; *gen pl* **-ок**) *ж* timber processing.
дерéвья *итп сущ см* **дéрево**.
деревянный *прил* (*также перен*) wooden.
держáв|а (**-ы**) *ж* (*государство*) power; (*эмблема*) orb; **велúкие ~ы** The Great (World) Powers.
держáтел|ь (**-я**) *м* holder.
держ|áть (**-ý, -ишь**) *сов перех* to keep; (*в руках, во рту, в зубах*) to hold; (*не отпускать*) to keep hold of; (*поддерживать*) to hold up; (*нанимать*) to take on; ~ (*impf*) **речь** to make a speech; ~ (*impf*) **экзáмен** to sit an exam; ~ (*impf*) **отвéт** to be responsible; ~ (*impf*) **слóво** to keep one's word; ~ (*impf*) **себя прóсто/высокомéрно** to behave simply/haughtily; ~ (*impf*) **себя в рукáх** to keep one's head
▸ **держáться** *несов возв* to stay; (*на колоннах, на сваях*) to be supported; (*иметь осанку*) to stand; (*вести себя*) to behave; **~ся** (*impf*) *+gen* (*берега, стены итп*) to keep to; (*перен*) to adhere to; **~ся** (*impf*) **за** *+acc* (*за сумку, за стену*) to hold onto; **~ся** (*impf*) **за гóлову** to hold one's head.
дерз|úть (*2sg* **-úшь**, *3sg* **-úт**) *несов неперех*: ~ **комý-н** to be rude to sb.
дéрз|кий (**-кая, -кое, -кие**; **-ок, -кá, -ко**) *прил* (*грубый*) impertinent; (*смелый*) audacious.
дéрзост|ь (**-и**) *ж* (*см прил*) impertinence; audacity; **говорúть** (**сказáть** *perf*) **~и** to be impertinent; **имéть** (*impf*) ~ *+infin* to have the cheek to do.
деривáт (**-а**) *м* (*ЛИНГ*) derivative.
дерматúн (**-а**) *м* leatherette.
дерматолóги|я (**-и**) *ж* dermatology.
дёрн (**-а**) *м* turf.
дёрн|уть (**-у, -ешь**) *несов перех* to tug (at) ◆ *неперех* (*+instr*; *плечом, головой*) to jerk; **~уло меня** *или* **чёрт ~ул меня сдéлать это** (*разг*) I don't know what possessed me to do it
▸ **дёрнуться** *несов возв* (*машина*) to start with a jerk; (*лошадь*) to shy; (*лицо, губы*) to twitch.
дерý(сь) *несов перех см* **дрáть(ся)**.
дерьм|ó (**-á**) *ср* (*груб!*: *также перен*) shit (*!*), crap (*!*)
десáнт (**-а**) *м* landing troops *мн*; (*высадка войск*) landing; **высáживать** (**вы́садить** *perf*) ~ to make a landing.
десáнтник (**-а**) *м* (*ВОЕН*) paratrooper.
дёсен *сущ см* **деснá**.
десéрт (**-а**) *м* dessert.
дéскать *част*: **онá, ~, ничегó не знáет** she claims she doesn't know anything.
десн|á (**-ы́**; *nom pl* **дёсны**, *gen pl* **дёсен**) *ж* (*АНАТ*) gum.
деспотúческ|ий (**-ая, -ое, -ие**) *прил* despotic.
десят|ая (**-ой**; *decl like adj*) *ж*: **однá** ~ one tenth.
дéсятер|о (**-ы́х**; *как* **чéтверо**; *см* **Table 36a**) *чис* ten; (*десять пар*) ten pairs; *см также* **двóе**.
десятú *сущ см* **дéсять**.
десятибóр|ец (**-ца**) *м* decathlete.
десятибóрь|е (**-я**) *ср* decathlon.
десятиднéвный *прил* ten-day.
десятиклáссник (**-а**) *м* *pupil in tenth year at school (usually 17 years old)*.
десятиклáссниц|а (**-ы**) *ж см* **десятиклáссник**.
десятикопéечн|ый *прил*: **~ая монéта** ten-kopeck coin.
десятикрáтн|ый *прил*: ~ **чемпиóн** ten-times

champion; **в ~ом разме́ре** tenfold.
десятиле́ти|е (-я) *ср* (*срок*) decade; (*годовщина*) tenth anniversary.
десятиле́т|ка (-ки; *gen pl* -ок) *ж* (*разг*) ≈ secondary school (*BRIT*), ≈ high school (*US*).
десятиле́тн|ий (-яя, -ее, -ие) *прил* (*период*) ten-year; (*ребёнок*) ten-year-old.
десятиле́ток *сущ см* **десятиле́тка**.
десятиме́сячный *прил* ten-month; (*ребёнок*) ten-month-old.
десяти́н|а (-ы) *ж old unit of measurement approximately equal to 2.7 acres.*
десятинеде́льный *прил* ten-week; (*ребёнок*) ten-week-old.
десятирублёв|ка (-ки; *gen pl* -ок) *ж* (*разг*) ten-rouble note.
десятичасов|о́й (-а́я, -о́е, -ы́е) *прил* (*операция*) ten-hour; (*отправление*) ten o'clock *опред*.
десяти́чный *прил* decimal.
деся́т|ка (-ки; *gen pl* -ок) *ж* (*цифра*) ten; (*группа из десяти*) group of ten; (*разг*: *денежный знак*) tenner; (: *автобус, трамвай итп*) (number) ten (*bus, tram etc*).
деся́тк|и (-ов) *мн*: ~ **люде́й/книг** scores of people/books.
деся́т|ок (-ка) *м* ten; **он не ро́бкого ~ка** he's not afraid of anything; **ему́ пошёл шесто́й ~** he has turned fifty; *см также* **деся́тки**.
деся́т|ый (-ая, -ое, -ые) *прил* tenth; *см также* **пя́тый**.
де́сят|ь (-и́; *как* **пять**; *см* **Table 27**) *чис* ten; *см также* **пять**.
дета́лен *прил см* **дета́льный**.
детализи́р|овать (-ую) *(не)сов перех* to work out in detail.
дета́л|ь (-и) *ж* detail; (*механизма, прибора*) component, part.
дета́льно *нареч* (*обсудить*) in detail.
дета́л|ьный (-ен, -ьна, -ьно) *прил* detailed.
детвор|а́ (-ы) *ж собир* little children *мн*.
детдо́м (-а; *nom pl* -а́) *м сокр* (= *де́тский дом*) children's home.
детдо́мов|ец (-ца) *м child in care*.
детдо́мов|ка (-ки; *gen pl* -ок) *ж см* **детдо́мовец**.
детдо́мовца *сущ см* **детдо́мовец**.
детекти́в (-а) *м* (*следователь*) detective; (*фильм*) detective film; (*книга*) detective novel.
детекти́вный *прил* detective *опред*.
дете́ктор (-а) *м* detector.
детёныш (-а) *м* cub.
де́т|и (-е́й; *dat pl* -ям, *instr pl* -ьми́, *prp pl* -ях, *nom sg* **ребёнок**) *мн* children *мн*.
дети́н|а (-ы) *м* (*разг*) hulk.
де́тищ|е (-а) *ср* creation.
де́тка (-и) *ж* (*в обращении*) sweetheart.
детона́тор (-а) *м* detonator.
детса́д (-а; *nom pl* -ы) *м сокр* (= *де́тский сад*) kindergarten.
де́тск|ая (-ой; *decl like adj*) *ж* nursery.
де́тск|ий (-ая, -ое, -ие) *прил* (*годы, болезнь*) childhood; (*книга, игра*) children's; (*рассуждение, затея*) childish; **де́тская площа́дка** playground; **де́тский дом** children's home; **де́тский сад** kindergarten.
де́тств|о (-а) *ср* childhood; **впада́ть (впасть** *perf*) **в ~** to go senile.
де|ть (-ну, -нешь; *impf* **дева́ть**) *сов перех* (*разг*) to put; (*время, деньги*) to do with; **куда́ же я ~л э́ту кни́гу?** what on earth have I done with that book?; **э́того никуда́ не де́нешь** there's no arguing with that
▸ **де́ться** (*impf* **дева́ться**) *сов возв* (*разг*) to get to; **куда́ она́/кни́га де́лась?** where has she/the book got to?; **не́куда ~ва́ться** (*impf*) (*разг*) there's nothing else for it.
де-фа́кто *нареч* de facto.
дефе́кт (-а) *м* defect.
дефекти́в|ный (-ен, -на, -но) *прил* (*умственно*) mentally defective; (*физически*) physically handicapped.
дефе́ктный *прил* defective.
дефектоскопи́|я (-и) *ж* (*ТЕХ*) detection of flaws.
дефи́с (-а) *м* hyphen.
дефици́т (-а) *м* (*ЭКОН*) deficit; (*нехватка*): ~ *+gen или* **в** *+prp* shortage of; ~ **платёжного бала́нса** (*ЭКОН*) balance of payments deficit.
дефици́тный *прил* (*предприятие, производство*) unprofitable; (*товар, сырьё*) scarce, in short supply.
дефля́ци|я (-и) *ж* (*ЭКОН*) deflation.
деформа́ци|я (-и) *ж* deformation.
деформи́р|овать (-ую) *(не)сов перех* to deform
▸ **деформи́роваться** *(не)сов возв* to be deformed.
децентрализа́ци|я (-и) *ж* decentralization.
децентрализ|ова́ть (-у́ю) *(не)сов перех* to decentralize.
децибе́л (-а) *м* decibel.
децимéтр (-а) *м* decimetre (*BRIT*), decimeter (*US*).
дешеве́|ть (*3sg* -ет, *3pl* -ют, *perf* **подешеве́ть**) *несов неперех* to go down in price.
дешёв|ка (-ки; *gen pl* -ок) *ж* (*перен: пренебр*): **э́та карти́на ~** this picture is tacky; **купи́ть** (*perf*)/**прода́ть** (*perf*) **что-н по ~ке** to buy/sell sth dirt-cheap.
деше́вле *сравн прил от* **дешёвый** ◆ *сравн нареч от* **дёшево**.
дёшево *нареч* (*купить*) cheaply.
дешёвок *сущ см* **дешёвка**.
дешёвый (**дёшев, дешева́, дёшево**) *прил* (*также разг*) cheap.
дешифр|ова́ть (-у́ю) *(не)сов перех* to decipher.
де-ю́ре *нареч* de jure.
де́ятелен *прил см* **де́ятельный**.
де́ятел|ь (-я) *м*: **госуда́рственный ~** statesman; **полити́ческий ~** politician; **~ культу́ры** *person involved in the arts.*
де́ятельност|ь (-и) *ж* (*научная, педагогическая*) work, activity; (*сердца, мозга*)

activity.
де́ятел|ьный (-ен, -ьна, -ьно) *прил* active, energetic.
джаз (-а) *м* jazz.
джем (-а) *м* jam.
дже́мпер (-а) *м* jumper.
джентльме́н (-а) *м* gentleman (*мн* gentlemen).
джин (-а) *м* gin.
джи́нсов|ый *прил* denim; **джи́нсовая ткань** denim.
джи́нс|ы (-ов) *мн* jeans *мн*.
джо́йстик (-а) *м* (*комп*) joystick.
джо́кер (-а) *м* (*карты*) joker.
джу́нгл|и (-ей) *мн* jungle *ед*.
джут (-а) *м* jute.
дзюдо́ *ср нескл* judo.
дзюдои́ст (-а) *м* judoist.
диабе́т (-а) *м*: **са́харный ~** diabetes.
диабе́тик (-а) *м* diabetic.
диа́гноз (-а) *м* diagnosis; **ста́вить (поста́вить** *perf***) ~** to make a diagnosis.
диагности́р|овать (-ую) *(не)сов перех* (*мед*) to diagnose; (*тех*) to check.
диагона́л|ь (-и) *ж* diagonal.
диагра́мм|а (-ы) *ж* diagram.
диакрити́ческ|ий (-ая, -ое, -ие) *прил*: **~ знак** diacritical mark.
диале́кт (-а) *м* dialect.
диале́ктик|а (-и) *ж* dialectics; (*событий, процесса*) dialectic.
диало́г (-а) *м* dialogue.
диало́говый *прил* (*комп*) conversational.
диа́метр (-а) *м* diameter.
диапазо́н (-а) *м* range; (*частот*) waveband; (*голоса, звука*) range, diapason.
диапозити́в (-а) *м* (*фото*) slide.
диате́з (-а) *м* diathesis.
диафи́льм (-а) *м* (*фото*) slide film.
диафра́гм|а (-ы) *ж* diaphragm.
дива́н (-а) *м* sofa.
дива́н-крова́т|ь (-и) *ж* sofa bed.
ди́вен *прил см* **ди́вный**.
диверса́нт (-а) *м* saboteur.
диверсифика́ци|я (-и) *ж* diversification.
диве́рси|я (-и) *ж* sabotage; **соверша́ть (соверши́ть** *perf***) ~ю** to commit sabotage.
дивертисме́нт (-а) *м* divertissement.
дивиде́нд (-а) *м* dividend; **приноси́ть (принести́** *perf***) ~ы** to pay dividends.
дивизио́н (-а) *м* unit; (*военных кораблей*) division.
диви́зи|я (-и) *ж* division.
ди́в|ный (-ен, -на, -но) *прил* marvellous.
дидакти́ческ|ий (-ая, -ое, -ие) *прил* didactic.
дие́з (-а) *м* (*муз*) sharp.
дие́т|а (-ы) *ж* diet; **быть** *(impf)* **на ~е** to be on a diet; **соблюда́ть** *(impf)* **~у** to keep to a diet.
диети́ческ|ий (-ая, -ое, -ие) *прил* dietetic.
диза́йн (-а) *м* design.
диза́йнер (-а) *м* designer.
ди́зел|ь (-я) *м* diesel engine.
дизентери́|я (-и) *ж* dysentery.
дика́р|ка (-ки; *gen pl* **-ок)** *ж* savage; (*перен*) *shy, unsociable woman or girl*.
дика́р|ь (-я́) *м* savage; (*перен*) *shy, unsociable man or boy*; (: *разг*) independent holidaymaker; **е́хать (пое́хать** *perf***) дикарём на юг/на мо́ре** to go off on spec to the South/the seaside.
ди́к|ий (-ая, -ое, -ие; -, -а́, -о) *прил* wild; (*человек*) savage; (*ребёнок*) shy and unsociable; (*голод, холод*) terrible.
дикобра́з (-а) *м* porcupine.
дико́вин|а (-ы) *ж* (*разг*) marvel; **э́то мне в ~у** this is all too new.
дико́вин|ка (-ки; *gen pl* **-ок)** *ж* = **дико́вина**.
дикорасту́щ|ий (-ая, -ее, -ие) *прил* wild.
ди́кост|ь (-и) *ж* wildness; (*поступка, мысли*) absurdity.
дикта́нт (-а) *м* dictation.
дикта́тор (-а) *м* dictator.
диктату́р|а (-ы) *ж* dictatorship.
дикт|ова́ть (-у́ю; *perf* **продиктова́ть)** *несов перех* to dictate.
дикто́в|ка (-ки; *gen pl* **-ок)** *ж* dictation; **под чью-н ~ку** (*записывать*) from sb's dictation; (*действовать*) at sb's bidding.
ди́ктор (-а) *м* announcer; (*читающий новости*) newsreader.
диктофо́н (-а) *м* Dictaphone®.
ди́кци|я (-и) *ж* diction.
диле́мм|а (-ы) *ж* dilemma.
ди́лер (-а) *м*: **~ (по** *+prp***)** dealer (in).
дина́мик (-а) *м* (loud)speaker.
дина́мик|а (-и) *ж* (*физ*) dynamics; (*развития, процесса*) dynamics *мн*.
динами́т (-а) *м* dynamite.
динами́ч|ный (-ен, -на, -но) *прил* dynamic.
дина́сти|я (-и) *ж* dynasty.
диноза́вр (-а) *м* dinosaur.
дио́д (-а) *м* diode.
дио́птри|я (-и) *ж* dioptre (*BRIT*), diopter (*US*).
дипко́рпус (-а) *м сокр* (= *дипломати́ческий ко́рпус*) CD (= *Corps Diplomatique*).
дипло́м (-а) *м* (*просвещ: свидетельство*) degree certificate; (: *на конкурсе*) certificate, diploma; (*научная работа*) dissertation (*for undergraduate degree*); **защища́ть (защити́ть** *perf***) ~** to have a viva (*for undergraduate degree*).
диплома́нт (-а) *м* award winner.
диплома́т (-а) *м* diplomat; (*разг: портфель*) briefcase.
дипломати́ческ|ий (-ая, -ое, -ие) *прил* diplomatic.
диплома́ти|я (-и) *ж* diplomacy.
дипломи́рованный *прил* qualified.
дир. *сокр* (= **дире́ктор**) dir. (= *director*).

директи́в|а (-ы) *ж* directive.
дире́ктор (-а; *nom pl* -á) *м* director; **~ шко́лы** headmaster; **~-распоряди́тель** managing director; **гла́вный исполни́тельный ~** chief executive.
дире́кци|я (-и) *ж* (*завода, фабрики*) management; (*школы*) ≈ board (of governors); (*фирмы*) board (of directors).
дирижа́бл|ь (-я) *м* airship, dirigible.
дирижёр (-а) *м* (*МУЗ*) conductor.
дирижёрск|ий (-ая, -ое, -ие) *прил*: **~ая па́лочка** (conductor's) baton.
дирижи́р|овать (-ую) *несов неперех* (+*instr*) to conduct.
дисгармо́ни|я (-и) *ж* discord.
диск (-а) *м* (*также КОМП*) disk; (*СПОРТ*) discus; (*МУЗ*) record; **ги́бкий/жёсткий ~** floppy/hard disk; **~ с удво́енной пло́тностью** double-density floppy disk.
дисквалифици́р|овать (-ую) *(не)сов перех* (*врача, юриста*) to strike off; (*спортсмена*) to disqualify.
диске́т (-а) *м* diskette.
диске́т|а (-ы) *ж* = **диске́т**.
диск-жоке́|й (-я) *м* disc jockey.
ди́ско *ср нескл* disco.
диско́нт (-а) *м* (*КОММ*) discount.
дискоте́к|а (-и) *ж* (*собрание пластинок*) record collection; (*танцы*) discotheque.
дискредити́р|овать (-ую) *(не)сов перех* to discredit.
дискримина́ци|я (-и) *ж* discrimination.
дискримини́р|овать (-ую) *(не)сов перех* to discriminate against.
дискуссио́нный *прил* (*спорный*) debat(e)able.
диску́сси|я (-и) *ж* discussion.
дискути́р|овать (-ую) *несов перех* to discuss.
дислока́ци|я (-и) *ж* (*ВОЕН*) deployment; (*МЕД*) dislocation.
дислоци́р|овать (-ую) *(не)сов перех* (*ВОЕН*) to deploy.
диспансе́р (-а) *м* dispensary.
диспе́тчер (-а) *м* controller; **авиацио́нный ~** air-traffic controller.
диспе́тчерск|ая (-ой; *decl like adj*) *ж* controller's office; (*АВИА*) control tower.
диспе́тчерск|ий (-ая, -ое, -ие) *прил*: **~ая слу́жба** control section; **~ая вы́шка** control tower.
диспле́|й (-я) *м* (*КОМП*) display.
диспропо́рци|я (-и) *ж* disproportion.
ди́спут (-а) *м* debate.
диссерта́нт (-а) *м* *(post-graduate) student defending a PhD thesis*.
диссерта́ци|я (-и) *ж* ≈ PhD thesis; **защища́ть** *(impf)* **~ю** to be examined on one's thesis; **защити́ть** *(perf)* **~ю** to pass a viva.
диссиде́нт (-а) *м* dissident.
диссона́нс (-а) *м* (*МУЗ*) dissonance; (*перен*) discord; **вноси́ть (внести́** *perf*) **~ во что-н** (*перен*) to bring a note of discord into sth.
дистанцио́нн|ый *прил*: **~ое управле́ние** remote control.
диста́нци|я (-и) *ж* distance; **сохраня́ть (сохрани́ть** *perf*) **~ю** (*перен*) to keep one's distance; **он сошёл с ~и** (*СПОРТ*) he didn't last the distance.
дистилли́р|овать (-ую) *(не)сов перех* to distil (*BRIT*), distill (*US*).
дистрибью́тор (-а) *м* distributor.
дистрофи́|я (-и) *ж* dystrophy.
дисципли́н|а (-ы) *ж* discipline.
дисциплини́рован|ный (-, -на, -но) *прил* disciplined.
дит|я́ (-и́; *nom pl* **де́ти**) *ср* child; *см также* **де́ти**.
дифтери́т (-а) *м* diphtheria.
дифто́нг (-а) *м* diphthong.
дифференциа́льный *прил* (*ЭКОН*) differential *опред*.
дифференци́рованн|ый *прил*: **~ая зарпла́та** differential.
дифференци́р|овать (-ую) *(не)сов перех* to differentiate.
дича́|ть (-ю; *perf* **одича́ть**) *несов неперех* to grow wild.
дич|ь (-и) *ж собир* game; (*разг*) rubbish.
диэле́ктрик (-а) *м* dielectric.
ДК *м сокр* (= *Дворе́ц культу́ры, Дом культу́ры*) *centre for social and cultural activities*.
длин|а́ (-ы́) *ж* length; **в ~у́** lengthways; **~о́й 10 ме́тров** 10 metres (*BRIT*) *или* meters (*US*) long; **~ тка́ни – 10 метро́в** the cloth is 10 metres long.
дли́нен *прил см* **дли́нный**.
длинноволново́й *прил* long-wave.
длинноволо́сый *прил* long-haired.
длинноно́г|ий (-ая, -ое, -ие) *прил* long-legged.
длиннору́к|ий (-ая, -ое, -ие) *прил* with long arms.
дли́нно *нареч* (*рассуждать*) at length ◆ *как сказ*: **пла́тье мне ~** the dress is too long for me.
дли́н|ный (-ен, -на́, -но) *прил* long; (*разг*: *человек*) tall; **у него́ ~ язы́к** (*разг*) he's got a big mouth; **дли́нный рубль** (*разг*) easy money.
дли́тельност|ь (-и) *ж* length.
дли́тельный *прил* lengthy.
дл|и́ться (*3sg* **-и́тся**, *3pl* **-я́тся**, *perf* **продли́ться**) *несов возв* (*урок, беседа*) to last.

KEYWORD

для *предл* (+*gen*) ***1*** for; **для о́бщего бла́га** for the general good; **ме́сто для по́дписи** space for a signature; **крем для лица́** face cream; **альбо́м для рисова́ния** sketch pad
2 (*в отношении кого-н/чего-н*): **для меня́ э́то име́ет большо́е значе́ние** this is very important to me; **для того́ что́бы** in order to; **для него́ э́то про́сто рабо́та** this is just work to him; **э́то поле́зно для здоро́вья** this is good for one's health; **для своего́ во́зраста он о́чень развито́й** he is very advanced for his age

дм *сокр* (= **дециме́тр**) dm= *decimetre* (*BRIT*) *или decimeter* (*US*).
дн|ева́ть (-ю́ю, -ю́ешь) *несов неперех*: **~ и**

ночева́ть где́-нибудь (*разг*) to be somewhere day and night.
дневни́к (-á) *м* diary; (*ПРОСВЕЩ*) register; **вести́** (*impf*) ~ to keep a diary.
дневн|о́й *прил* (*выработка, заработок*) daily; **~а́я фо́рма обуче́ния** full-time education; **~ свет** daylight; **~о́е вре́мя** daytime; **дневно́й спекта́кль** matinee.
днём *сущ см* **день** ◆ *нареч*: ~ in the daytime; (*после обеда*) in the afternoon; **его́ ~ с огнём не найти́** he is absolutely nowhere to be found.
Днепр (-а) *м* Dnieper.
Днестр (-а) *м* Dniester.
дни *итп сущ см* **день**.
дни́щ|е (-а) *ср* bottom.
ДНК *ж сокр* (= *дезоксирибонуклейновая кислота́*) DNA (= *deoxyribonucleic acid*).
дн|о (-а) *ср* (*моря, реки*) bottom, bed; (*ямы, оврага*) bottom; (*nom pl* **до́нья**, *gen pl* **до́ньев**; *бочки, ящика*) bottom; **идти́ (пойти́** *perf*) **ко ~у** to sink to the bottom; (*перен*: *предприятие*) to go under; (: *человек*) to sink.
дня *итп сущ см* **день**.

KEYWORD

до *предл* (+*gen*) ***1*** (*о пределе движения*) as far as, to; **мы доéхали до реки́** we went as far as *или* to the river; **я проводи́л его́ до ста́нции** I saw him off at the station
2 (*о расстоянии*) to; **до го́рода 3 киломе́тра** it is 3 kilometres (*BRIT*) *или* kilometers (*US*) to the town
3 (*о временном пределе*) till, until; **я отложи́л заседа́ние до утра́** I postponed the meeting till *или* until morning; **я рабо́таю с восьми́ до пяти́** I work from eight to five; **до свида́ния!** goodbye!
4 (*перед*) before; **мы зако́нчили до переры́ва** we finished before the break
5 (*о пределе состояния*): **мне бы́ло оби́дно до слёз** I was so hurt I cried; **он крича́л до хрипоты́** he shouted himself hoarse; **на́до нагре́ть во́ду до кипе́ния** the water must be heated until it boils
6 (*полностью*): **я отда́л ей всё до копе́йки** I gave her everything down to my last kopeck; **он вы́пил буты́лку до дна́** he drank the bottle dry
7 (*направление действия*): **ребёнок дотро́нулся до игру́шки** the child touched the toy; **мне до него́ нет никако́го де́ла** (*разг*) I have no truck with him
◆ *ср нескл* (*МУЗ*) doh.

до- *префикс* (*in verbs*; *доведеине действия до конца*) *indicating completion of action eg.* *добежа́ть*; (*о достижении какого-нибудь результата*) *indicating achievement of a certain goal eg.* *дозвони́ться*; (*in adverbs*; *доведение качества до какого-нибудь предела*) *indicating attainment of a quality to a certain degree eg.* *докрасна́*; (*о дополнительном действии*) *indicating supplement to an action eg.* *дода́ть*; (*in adjectives*; *бывший прежде чего-н*) pre-.
доба́в|ить (-лю, -ишь; *impf* **добавля́ть**) *сов перех* to add.
доба́в|ка (-ки; *gen pl* -ок) *ж* (*к обеду*) additional helping; (*пищевая, бетонная*) additive.
добавле́ни|е (-я) *ср* addition; **де́лать (сде́лать** *perf*) **~я к** +*dat* to make an addition to; **в ~ к** +*dat* in addition to.
доба́влю *сов см* **доба́вить**.
добавля́|ть (-ю) *несов от* **доба́вить**.
доба́вок *сущ см* **доба́вка**.
доба́вочн|ый *прил* additional ◆ (-ого; *decl like adj*) *м* (*также*: **~ телефо́н**) extension number.
добе|жа́ть (*как* **бежа́ть**; *см* **Table 20**; *impf* **добега́ть**) *сов неперех*: **~ до** +*gen* to run to *или* as far as; (*звуки, волны*) to reach.
добела́ *нареч*: **отмы́ть что-н ~** to wash sth clean; **раскали́ть** (*perf*) **что-н ~** to heat sth until it's white-hot.
доберу́сь *итп сов см* **добра́ться**.
добива́|ть(ся) (-ю(сь)) *несов от* **доби́ть(ся)**.
добира́|ться (-юсь) *несов от* **добра́ться**.
доб|и́ть (-ью́, -ьёшь; *impf* **добива́ть**) *сов перех* (*убить*) to finish off; (*разбить*) to break
▸ **доби́ться** (*impf* **добива́ться**) *сов возв* (+*gen*) to achieve; **добива́ться (~ся** *perf*) **своего́** to get what one wants.
до́блест|ный (-ен, -на, -но) *прил* valiant.
до́блест|ь (-и) *ж* valour (*BRIT*), valor (*US*).
доб|ра́ться (-еру́сь, -ерёшься; *impf* **добира́ться**) *сов возв*: **~ до** +*gen* to get to, reach; (*решения*) to reach; **добира́ться (~** *perf*) **до су́ти (де́ла)** to get to the heart of the matter; **я до тебя́ ~еру́сь!** (*разг*) I'll get you!
добре́|ть (-ю; *perf* **подобре́ть**) *несов неперех* to become kinder; (*perf* **раздобре́ть**; *разг*) to fill out.
добр|о́ (-á) *ср* good; (*разг*: *имущество*) things *мн* ◆ *част* (*разг*: *ладно*) fine; **жела́ть (пожела́ть** *perf*) **кому́-н ~а́** to wish sb well; **~ пожа́ловать (в Москву́)!** welcome (to Moscow)!; **дава́ть (дать** *perf*) **кому́-н ~ на что-н** to give sb the go-ahead for sth; **получа́ть (получи́ть** *perf*) **~ (на что-н)** to get the go-ahead (for sth).
доброво́л|ец (-ьца) *м* volunteer; **идти́ (пойти́** *perf*) **~ьцем** to volunteer.
доброво́л|ьный (-ен, -ьна, -ьно) *прил* voluntary; **на ~ьных нача́лах** on a voluntary basis.
доброво́льца *итп сущ см* **доброво́лец**.
доброде́тел|ь (-и) *ж* virtue.
доброде́тельный *прил* virtuous.

добродýш|ный (**-ен, -на, -но**) *прил* good-natured.
доброжелáтельност|ь (**-и**) *ж* benevolence.
доброжелáтельный *прил* benevolent.
доброкáчествен|ный (**-, -на, -но**) *прил* (*продукт, изделие*) quality *опред*; (*no short form*; *опухоль*) benign.
добропорядоч|ный (**-ен, -на, -но**) *прил* respectable.
добросердéч|ный (**-ен, -на, -но**) *прил* (*человек*) kind-hearted; (*слова*) kind.
добросóвест|ный (**-ен, -на, -но**) *прил* conscientious.
добрососéдств|о (**-а**) *ср* neighbourliness (*BRIT*), neighborliness (*US*).
доброт|á (**-ы́**) *ж* kindness.
добрóт|ный (**-ен, -на, -но**) *прил* good-quality.
дóбр|ый (**-, -á, -о, -ы́**) *прил* kind; (*совет, имя*) good; (*милый*: *друг итп*) dear; **бýдьте добры́!** excuse me!; **бýдьте добры́, позвони́те нам зáвтра!** would you be so good as to phone us tomorrow?; **всегó ~ого!** all the best!; **~ого здорóвья!** take care!; **~ день/вéчер!** good afternoon/evening!; **~ое ýтро!** good morning!; **по ~ой вóле** of one's own free will; **чегó ~ого** (*разг*) it's not impossible.
добýду *итп сов см* **добы́ть**.
добывá|ть (**-ю**) *несов от* **добы́ть**.
добывáющ|ий (**-ая, -ее, -ие**) *прил*: **~ая промы́шленность** *mining, gas and oil industries*.
добы́тчик (**-а**) *м* (*золота*) miner; (*нефти*) oil worker.
добы́ть (*как* **быть**; *см* **Table 21**; *impf* **добывáть**) *сов перех* (*денег, машину*) to get; (*нефть*) to extract; (*руду, золото*) to mine.
добы́ч|а (**-и**) *ж* (*процесс*: *нефти*) extraction; (: *руды*) mining, extraction; (*то, что добыто*) output; (: *на охоте, ловле*) catch.
добью́(сь) *итп сов см* **доби́ть(ся)**.
доведý(сь) *итп сов см* **довести́(сь)**.
довез|ти́ (**-ý**; *pt* **довёз, -лá, -лó**, *impf* **довози́ть**) *сов перех*: **~ когó-н до** *+gen* to take sb to *или* as far as.
довёл(ся) *итп сов см* **довести́(сь)**.
довéренност|ь (**-и**) *ж* power of attorney; **дéйствовать** *(impf)* **по ~и** to act by proxy.
довéренн|ый (**-ого**; *decl like adj*) *м* (*также*: **~ое лицó**) proxy.
довéри|е (**-я**) *ср* confidence, trust; **пóльзоваться** *(impf)* **чьим-н ~м** to enjoy sb's confidence; **входи́ть (войти́** *perf***) в чьё-н ~** to gain sb's confidence; **выходи́ть (вы́йти** *perf***) из чьегó-н ~я** to lose sb's confidence.
довери́телен *прил см* **довери́тельный**.
довери́тел|ь (**-я**) *м* *person who empowers another to act on his or her behalf*.
довери́тель|ный (**-ен, -ьна, -ьно**) *прил* trusting.
довéр|ить (**-ю, -ишь**; *impf* **доверя́ть**) *сов перех*: **~ что-н комý-н** to entrust sb with sth
▸ **довéриться** (*impf* **доверя́ться**) *сов возв*: **~ся** *+dat* to confide in; (*положиться*) to trust.
дóверху *нареч* (up) to the top; **напóлненный ~** full to the brim.
довéрчивост|ь (**-и**) *ж* trustingness.
довéрчив|ый (**-, -а, -о**) *прил* trusting.
доверша́|ть (**-ю**) *несов от* **доверши́ть**.
довершéни|е (**-я**) *ср* completion; **в ~** *или* **к довершéнию всегó** on top of everything else.
доверш|и́ть (**-ý, -и́шь**; *impf* **доверша́ть**) *сов перех* to complete.
доверя́|ть (**-ю**) *несов от* **довéрить** ◆ *неперех*: **~** *+dat* to trust.
дове|сти́ (**-дý, -дёшь**; *pt* **довёл, -лá, -лó**, *impf* **доводи́ть**) *сов перех*: **~ когó-н/что-н до** *+gen* to take sb/sth to *или* as far as; **доводи́ть (~** *perf***) что-н до концá** to see sth through to the end; **доводи́ть (~** *perf***) когó-н до слёз** to reduce sb to tears; **доводи́ть (~** *perf***) когó-н до отчáяния** to drive sb to despair; **доводи́ть (~** *perf***) что-н до совершéнства** to perfect sth; **доводи́ть (~** *perf***) скóрость до предéла** to reach the speed limit; **доводи́ть (~** *perf***) что-н до свéдения когó-н** to inform sb of sth
▸ **довести́сь** *сов безл*: **мне не ~дётся вернýться тудá** I won't get the opportunity *или* chance to go back there; **передáйте привéт, éсли Вам ~дётся встрéтить её** say hello if you happen to see her.
дóвод (**-а**) *м* argument; **приводи́ть (привести́** *perf***) ~** to put forward an argument.
дово|ди́ть (**-жý, -дишь**) *несов от* **довести́**
▸ **доводи́ться** *несов от* **довести́сь** ◆ *возв*: **он довóдится ей брáтом/внýком** (*разг*) he is her brother/grandson.
довоéнный *прил* prewar.
довожý(сь) *несов см* **доводи́ть(ся)**.
дово|зи́ть (**-жý, -зишь**) *несов от* **довезти́**.
довóлен *прил см* **довóльный**.
довóльно *нареч* (*известный, сильный*) quite; (*улыбаться, сказать*) with satisfaction ◆ *как сказ* it's enough; **~ спóров** *или* **спóрить!** that's enough arguing!
довóл|ьный (**-ен, -ьна, -ьно**) *прил* satisfied, contented; **он ~ен рабóтой/жи́знью** he's satisfied *или* happy with his work/life.
довóльств|оваться (**-уюсь**) *несов возв*: **~** *+instr* to be happy *или* content with; **он ~уется мáлым** *или* **немнóгим** it doesn't take much to make him happy.
довооруж|и́ть (**-ý, -и́шь**; *impf* **довооружáть**) *сов перех* (*окончательно*) to arm; (*дополнительно*) to provide with additional arms.
довы́бор|ы (**-ов**) *мн* ≈ by-election *ед*.
дог (**-а**) *м* (*ЗООЛ*) Great Dane.
догадá|ться (**-юсь**; *impf* **догáдываться**) *сов возв* to guess.
догáд|ка (**-ки**; *gen pl* **-ок**) *ж* guess; **стрóить** *(impf)* **~ки о** *+prp* to speculate about; **терáться** *(impf)* **в ~х** to be baffled *или* at a loss.

догáдлив|ый (-, -а, -о) *прил* quick-witted.
догáдок *сущ см* **догáдка**.
догáдыва|ться (-юсь) *несов от* **догадáться**.
дóгм|а (-ы) *ж* dogma.
догмáт (-а) *м* (*РЕЛ*) dogma.
догматúческ|ий (-ая, -ое, -ие) *прил* dogmatic.
дог|нáть (-оню, -óнишь; *impf* **догонять**) *сов перех* to catch up with; ~ *(perf)* **когó-н/что-н до** *+gen* to drive sb/sth to.
договáрива|ться (-юсь) *несов от* **договорúться**.
договóр (-а) *м* (*ПОЛИТ*) treaty; (*КОММ*) agreement; ~ **о** *+prp*/**на** *+acc* agreement on *или* about; **заключáть (заключúть** *perf*)/**расторгáть (растóргнуть** *perf*) ~ to sign/annul a treaty.
договорённост|ь (-и) *ж* agreement; **достигáть (достúгнуть** *perf*) **~и в чём-н** to reach an agreement on *или* about sth; **по ~и** by agreement.
договоренó *как сказ*: ~ **о** *+prp* ... there's been an agreement on ....
договор|úться (-ю́сь, -úшься; *impf* **договáриваться**) *сов возв*: ~ **с кем-н о чём-н** (*о встрече*) to arrange sth with sb; (*о цене*) to agree sth with sb; **мы ~úлись до глýпостей/грýбостей** we ended up talking nonsense/insulting each other; **мы ~úлись встрéтиться** we agreed to meet.
договóрник (-а) *м* (*разг*) contract worker.
договóрн|ый *прил* (*цена*) agreed; (*обязательство*) contractual; **на ~ых начáлах** on a contractual basis.
доголá *нареч*: **раздéться** ~ to strip bare; **постричься** *(perf)* ~ to have all one's hair cut off.
догоню́ *итп сов см* **догнáть**.
догоня́|ть (-ю) *несов от* **догнáть**.
догор|éть (-ю́, -úшь; *impf* **догорáть**) *сов неперех* to burn out.
догру|зúть (-жý, -зишь) *сов перех* to finish loading.
додáть (*как* **дать**; *см* **Table 14**; *impf* **додавáть**) *сов перех*: ~ **комý-н 10 рýблей** to give sb an extra 10 roubles.
додéла|ть (-ю; *impf* **додéлывать**) *сов перех* to finish.
додýма|ться (-юсь; *impf* **додýмываться**) *сов возв*: ~ **до** *+gen* to hit on; **как ты мог до такóго ~?** what on earth gave you that idea?
доедá|ть (-ю) *несов от* **доéсть**.
доéдешь *итп сов см* **доéхать**.
доедúм *итп сов см* **доéсть**.
доéду *итп сов см* **доéхать**.
доезжáй(те) *сов см* **доéхать**.
доезжá|ть (-ю) *несов от* **доéхать**.
доéсть (*как* **есть**; *см* **Table 15**; *impf* **доедáть**) *сов перех* to finish off, eat up.
доéхать (*как* **éхать**; *см* **Table 19**; *impf* **доезжáть**) *сов неперех*: ~ **до** *+gen* to reach.
доéшь *сов см* **доéсть**.
дожд|áться (-ýсь, -ёшься; *pt* **-áлся, -алáсь, -алóсь**, *imper* **-ú(те)сь**) *сов неперех*: ~ **когó-н/чегó-н** to wait until sb/sth comes; ~ *(perf)* **пóезда** to wait until the train arrives; **он ~ётся вы́говора** (*разг*) he'll end up getting told off; **ты у меня́ ~ёшься!** (*разг*) just you wait!; **он ждёт не ~ётся** (*разг*) he can't wait.
дождлúв|ый (-, -а, -о) *прил* rainy.
дожд|ь (-я́) *м* rain; (*перен*) cascade; **гуля́ть** *(impf)* **в** ~ to go for a walk in the rain; ~ **идёт** it's raining; ~ **пошёл** it has started to rain; **попадáть (попáсть** *perf*) **под** ~ to get caught in the rain; ~ **льёт как из ведрá** it's bucketing (with rain).
доживá|ть (-ю) *несов от* **дожúть** ◆ *неперех* (*жизнь, годы*) to live out.
дожидá|ться (-юсь) *несов возв* (*+gen*) to wait for.
дожú|ть (-вý, -вёшь; *impf* **доживáть**) *несов неперех*: ~ **до** *+gen* (*до старости*) to live to; (*до конца года*) to live until.
дóз|а (-ы) *ж* dose; ~ **облучéния** dose of radiation.
дозвáнива|ться (-юсь) *несов от* **дозвонúться**.
дозвóленный *прил* permitted.
дозвон|úться (-ю́сь, -úшься; *impf* **дозвáниваться**) *сов возв* to get through.
дозúметр (-а) *м* dosimetre (*BRIT*), dosimeter (*US*).
дозúр|овать (-ую) *(не)сов перех* to measure out.
дозóр (-а) *м* patrol; **быть** *(impf)* **в ~е** to be on patrol.
доигрá|ть (-ю; *impf* **доигрывать**) *сов перех* to finish (playing).
доúгрывани|е (-я) *ср* (*СПОРТ*) playing to a finish.
доúгрыва|ть (-ю) *несов от* **доигрáть**.
доисторúческ|ий (-ая, -ое, -ие) *прил* prehistoric.
до|úть (-ю́, -ишь; *perf* **подоúть**) *несов перех* to milk.
дóйн|ый *прил*: **~ая корóва** dairy cow.
доймý *итп сов см* **доня́ть**.
дойтú (*как* **идтú**; *см* **Table 18**; *impf* **доходúть**) *сов неперех*: ~ **до** *+gen* to reach; (*традиции, предания*) to be passed down to; (*слова, смысл*) to get through to; **доходúть (~** *perf*) **до отчáяния/истощéния** to reach the point of desperation/exhaustion; **до моегó свéдения дошлó, что ...** it has been brought to my attention that ....
док (-а) *м* dock.
докажý *итп сов см* **доказáть**.

доказа́тельств|о (-а) *ср* (*правоты, дружбы*) proof, evidence; (*теории*) demonstration; **служи́ть (послужи́ть** *perf*) **~м** *+gen* to be evidence of.
дока|за́ть (**-жу́, -жешь**; *impf* **дока́зывать**) *сов перех* (*правду, виновность*) to prove; (*теорему*) to demonstrate.
дока́нчива|ть (-ю) *несов от* **доко́нчить**.
дока́нывa|ть (-ю) *несов от* **докона́ть**.
дока́пыва|ться (-юсь) *несов от* **докопа́ться**.
дока|ти́ться (**-чу́сь, -тишься**; *impf* **дока́тываться**) *сов возв* (*звуки, шум*) to reach; **дока́тываться (~** *perf*) **до** *+gen* (*мяч, волны*) to roll in to; **дока́тываться (~** *perf*) **до преступле́ния** to stoop to crime.
до́кер (-а) *м* docker.
докла́д (-а) *м* (*на съезде итп*) paper; (*директору итп*) report.
докладн|а́я (**-о́й**; *decl like adj*) *ж* (*также:* **~ запи́ска**) memo.
докла́дчик (-а) *м* speaker.
докла́дчиц|а (-ы) *ж см* **докла́дчик**.
докла́дыва|ть (-ю) *несов от* **доложи́ть**.
докона́|ть (-ю; *impf* **дока́нывать**) *сов перех* (*разг*): **~ кого́-н** to do sb in.
доко́нч|ить (**-у, -ишь**; *impf* **дока́нчивать**) *сов перех* to finish off.
докопа́|ться (**-юсь**; *impf* **дока́пываться**) *сов возв*: **~ до** *+gen* (*перен: разг: до фактов, истины*) to dig up; (*до клада, воды*) to dig down to.
до́ктор (**-а**; *nom pl* **-а́**) *м* doctor; **~ нау́к** Doctor of Sciences (*postdoctoral research degree in Russia*).
до́кторск|ий (**-ая, -ое, -ие**) *прил* (*МЕД*) doctor's; (*ПРОСВЕЩ*) postdoctoral.
докт ри́н|а (-ы) *ж* doctrine.
докуме́нт (-а) *м* document.
докуча́|ть (-ю) *несов неперех*: **~ кому́-н чем-н** to pester sb with sth.
документа́л|ьный (**-ен, -ьна, -ьно**) *прил* documentary; **документа́льный фильм** documentary.
документа́ци|я (-и) *ж собир* documentation.
документи́р|овать (-ую) *(не)сов перех* to document.
долб|и́ть (**-лю́, -и́шь**; *perf* **продолби́ть**) *несов перех* to hollow out; (*no perf; разг: зубрить*) to learn by rote; **~** *(impf)* **в дверь** (*разг*) to hammer on the door.
долг (**-а**; *loc sg* **-у́**, *nom pl* **-и́**) *м* debt; **вне́шний/ госуда́рственный ~** (*ЭКОН*) foreign/national debt; **дава́ть (дать** *perf*)**/брать (взять** *perf*) **что-н в ~** to lend/borrow sth; **входи́ть (войти́** *perf*)**/залеза́ть (зале́зть** *perf*) **в ~и́** to get/fall into debt; **быть** *(impf)* **в ~у́ пе́ред кем-н** *или* **у кого́-н** to be indebted to sb; **по до́лгу слу́жбы** in the course of duty; **пе́рвым до́лгом** (*разг*) first of all.
до́л|гий (**-гая, -гое, -гие; -ог, -га́, -го**) *прил* long; **в ~ я́щик откла́дывать (отложи́ть** *perf*) **что-н** to put sth off, postpone sth; **до́лгий гла́сный** long vowel.
до́лго *нареч* for a long time; **как ~ продли́тся фильм?** how long will the film last?
долгове́ч|ный (**-ен, -на, -но**) *прил* (*материал*) durable, long-lasting; (*дружба*) lasting.
долгов|о́й *прил*: **~а́я расписка** IOU; **~о́е обяза́тельство** promissory note.
долговре́менный *прил* prolonged.
долгожда́нный *прил* long-awaited.
долгожи́тел|ь (-я) *м* long-lived person.
долгожи́тельниц|а (-ы) *ж см* **долгожи́тель**.
долгоигра́ющ|ий (**-ая, -ее, -ие**) *прил*: **~ая пласти́нка** L.P. (*= long-playing record*).
долголе́тн|ий (**-яя, -ее, -ие**) *прил*: **~ее сотру́дничество** long-standing cooperation.
долгосро́чный *прил* long-term.
долгот|а́ (-ы) *ж* length; (*ГЕО*) longitude.
до́лее *сравн прил от* **до́лгий** ◆ *сравн нареч от* **до́лго**.
до́лек *сущ см* **до́лька**.
доле|те́ть (**-чу́, -ти́шь**; *impf* **долета́ть**) *сов неперех*: **~ до** *+gen* to fly to, reach; (*звук, слухи*) to reach.

KEYWORD

до́лж|ен (**-на́, -но́, -ны́**) *часть сказуемого* (*+infin*) ***1*** (*обязан*): **я до́лжен уйти́** I must go; **я до́лжен бу́ду уйти́** I will have to go; **она́ должна́ была́ уйти́** she had to go
2 (*выражает предположение*): **он до́лжен ско́ро прийти́** he should arrive soon
3 (*+dat; о долге*): **ты до́лжен мне 5 рубле́й** you owe me 5 roubles
4: **должно́ быть** (*вероятно*) probably; **кто́-то, должно́ быть сто́рож, закры́л дверь** somebody, probably the night watchman, closed the door; **должно́ быть, она́ о́чень уста́ла** she must have been very tired.

должни́к (-а́) *м* debtor.
должни́ц|а (-ы) *ж см* **должни́к**.
до́лжн|ое (**-ого**; *decl like adj*) *ср* due; **отдава́ть (отда́ть** *perf*) *или* **воздава́ть (возда́ть** *perf*) **~ кому́-н** to give sb his *umn* due.
должностн|о́й *прил* official; **~о́е преступле́ние** malfeasance; **должностно́е лицо́** official.
до́лжност|ь (**-и**; *gen pl* **-е́й**) *ж* (*пост*) post; (*обязанность*) duties *мн*; **вступа́ть (вступи́ть** *perf*) **в ~ кого́-н** to assume sb's post; **по ~и** ex officio.
до́лжн|ый *прил* (*уровень*) required; (*внимание*) sufficient.
доли́н|а (-ы) *ж* valley.
до́ллар (-а) *м* dollar.
до́лларов|ый *прил* dollar *опред*; **~ счёт** dollar account.
долож|и́ть (**-у́, -ишь**; *impf* **докла́дывать**) *сов перех* to report ◆ *неперех*: **~ о** *+prp* to give a report on; **~** *(perf)* **о прихо́де кого́-н** to announce sb.
доло́й *нареч* away with; **~ апарте́йд!** down

with apartheid!
дол|ото́ (-ота́; *nom pl* **-о́та)** *ср* chisel; (*для бурения*) drill.
до́льше *сравн прил от* **до́лгий ♦** *сравн нареч от* **до́лго.**
до́л|ька (-ьки; *gen pl* **-ек)** *ж* (*апельсина*) segment.
до́л|я (-и; *gen pl* **-е́й)** *ж* share; (*пирога*) portion; (*судьба*) lot, fate; ~ **секу́нды/сантиме́тра** a fraction of a second/centimetre (*BRIT*) *или* centimeter (*US*); **входи́ть (войти́** *perf*) **в ~ю с кем-н** to go shares with sb; **выпада́ть (вы́пасть** *perf*) **на чью-н ~ю** to fall to sb's lot.
дом (-а; *nom pl* **-а́)** *м* house; (*многоэтажный*) block of flats (*BRIT*), apartment building (*US*); (*свое жильё*) home; (*семья*) household; ~ **Рома́новых** the house of Romanov; ~ **культу́ры** *centre for social and cultural activities*; **рабо́тать** *(impf)* **на ~у́** to work from home; **рабо́тать** *(impf)* **по до́му** to do the housework; **дом моде́лей** fashion house; **дом о́тдыха** ≈ holiday centre (*BRIT*) *или* center (*US*).
до́ма *нареч* at home; **быть** *(impf) или* **чу́вствовать** *(impf)* **себя́ как** ~ to feel at home; **его́ нет** ~ he's out *или* not at home; **сиде́ть** *(impf)* ~ to stay in *или* at home; **у него́ не все** ~ (*разг*) he's not all there.
дома́шн|ий (-яя, -ее, -ие) *прил* (*адрес, телефон*) home *опред*; (*еда*) home-made; (*животное*) domestic; **~ие ту́фли** (carpet) slippers; **~ее пла́тье** housecoat; **дома́шняя хозя́йка** housewife; **дома́шняя рабо́тница** domestic help (*BRIT*), maid (*US*); **дома́шнее зада́ние** homework.
до́менн|ый *прил* (*цех*) smelting *опред*; **~ая печь** blast furnace.
доминика́нск|ий (-ая, -ое, -ие) *прил*: **Д~ая Респу́блика** Dominican Republic.
доминио́н (-а) *м* dominion.
домини́р|овать (-ую) *несов неперех* (*идея, мелодия*) to predominate; ~ *(impf)* **над** *+instr* to dominate.
домино́ *ср нескл* (*игра*) dominoes *ед*; (*фишка, костюм*) domino.
домко́м (-а) *м сокр* (= *домово́й комите́т*) ≈ residents' association.
домкра́т (-а) *м* (*ТЕХ*) jack.
домовладе́л|ец (-ьца) *м* home owner.
домовладе́ни|е (-я) *ср* (*дом с участком*) *house with grounds attached*; (*владение домом*) home ownership.
домово́дств|о (-а) *ср* home economics.
домов|о́й (о́го; *decl like adj*) *м* (*ФОЛЬКЛОР*) house spirit.
домо́вый *прил* (*ворота*) house *опред*; **домо́вая кни́га** property register.
домога́|ться (-юсь) *несов возв*: ~ *+gen* (*власти*) to strive for; ~ *(impf)* **чьей-н руки́** to court *или* woo sb.
домо́й *нареч* home; **мне пора́** ~ it's time for me to go home.
доморо́щенный *прил* (*разг*: *пренебр*) homespun.
домосе́д (-а) *м* stay-at-home.
домоуправле́ни|е (-я) *ср* ≈ housing department.
домофо́н (-а) *м* intercom.
домохозя́|йка (-йки; *gen pl* **-ек)** *ж* (= *дома́шняя хозя́йка*) housewife.
домоча́д|ец (-ца) *м* (*обычно мн*) member of the household.
домрабо́тниц|а (-ы) *ж* (= *дома́шняя рабо́тница*) domestic help (*BRIT*), maid (*US*).
домч|а́ться (-у́сь, -и́шься) *сов возв*: ~ **(до** *+gen*) to rush (to).
до́мыс|ел (-ла) *м* conjecture.
донага́ *нареч*: **разде́ть кого́-н** ~ to strip sb naked.
дона́шива|ть (-ю) *несов от* **доноси́ть.**
доне́льзя *нареч* (*разг*) terribly.
донёс *итп сов см* **донести́.**
донесе́ни|е (-я) *ср* report.
донес|ти́ (-у́, -ёшь; *pt* **донёс, -ла́, -ло́**, *impf* **доноси́ть)** *сов перех* to carry ♦ *неперех*: ~ **на** *+acc* to inform on; ~ *(perf)* **о** *+prp* to report on
▸ **донести́сь** (*impf* **доноси́ться)** *сов возв*: **~сь до** *+gen* to reach.
до́низу *нареч* to the bottom; **све́рху** ~ from top to bottom.
донима́|ть (-ю) *несов от* **доня́ть.**
до́нор (-а) *м* donor.
до́норск|ий (-ая, -ое, -ие) *прил* donor *опред*.
доно́с (-а) *м*: ~ **(на** *+acc*) denunciation (of); **де́лать (сде́лать** *perf*) ~ **на кого́-н** to inform on sb.
доно|си́ть (-шу́, -сишь) *несов от* **донести́ ♦** (*impf* **дона́шивать)** *сов перех* (*одежду*) to wear out; (*ребёнка*) to carry to term; **дона́шивать (~** *perf*) **ве́щи за кем-н** to wear sb's hand-me-downs
▸ **доноси́ться** *несов от* **донести́сь.**
доно́счик (-а) *м* informer.
доно́счиц|а (-ы) *ж см* **доно́счик.**
доношу́(сь) *сов см* **доноси́ть(ся).**
до́нья *итп сущ см* **дно.**
до|ня́ть (-йму́, -ймёшь; *impf* **донима́ть)** *сов перех* (*разг*) to exasperate.
доп. *сокр* = **дополни́тельный.**
допе́й(те) *сов см* **допи́ть.**
допива́|ть (-ю) *несов от* **допи́ть.**
до́пинг (-а) *м* drugs *мн*.
допис|а́ть (-шу́, -шешь; *impf* **допи́сывать)** *сов перех* (*письмо*) to finish (writing); (*картину*) to finish (painting); (*написать дополнительно*) to add.
допи́|ть (допью́, допьёшь; *pt* **-, -ла́, -ло**, *imper* **допе́й(те)**, *impf* **допива́ть)** *сов перех* to drink

up.
допишу́ *итп сов см* **дописа́ть.**
допла́т|а (-ы) *ж* additional payment; ~ **за бага́ж** excess baggage (charge).
допл|ы́ть (**-ву́, -вёшь**; *pt* **-л, -ла́, -ло**, *impf* **доплыва́ть**) *сов неперех*: ~ **до** *+gen* (*на корабле*) to sail to; (*вплавь*) to swim to.
допо́длинно *нареч*: ~ **изве́стно** for certain.
допоздна́ *нареч* (*разг*) till late.
дополне́ни|е (**-я**) *ср* supplement; (*линг*) object; **в** ~ (**к** *+dat*) in addition (to); **прямо́е/ко́свенное** ~ direct/indirect object.
дополни́тельно *нареч* in addition.
дополни́тельный *прил* additional.
допо́лн|ить (**-ю, -ишь**; *impf* **дополня́ть**) *сов перех* to supplement; **дополня́ть** (~ *perf*) **кого́-н** to add to what sb has said; **дополня́ть** (*impf*) **друг дру́га** to complement one another.
допото́пный *прил* (*разг*) ancient.
допра́шива|ть (**-ю**) *несов от* **допроси́ть.**
допро́с (**-а**) *м* interrogation; **подверга́ть** (**подве́ргнуть** *perf*) **кого́-н** ~**у** to subject sb to an interrogation.
допро|си́ть (**-шу́, -сишь**; *impf* **допра́шивать**) *сов перех* to interrogate, question.
до́пуск (**-а**) *м* (*к зданию*) admittance; (*к документам*) access; (*ТЕХ*) tolerance.
допуска́|ть (**-ю**; *perf* **допусти́ть**) *несов перех* to admit, allow in; (*предположить*) to assume; ~ (**допусти́ть** *perf*) **оши́бку** (*делать*) to make a mistake; (*позволять*) to allow for a mistake; ~ (**допусти́ть** *perf*) **кого́-н до уча́стия/соревнова́ния** to allow sb to participate/compete.
допу́стим *вводн сл* let us assume.
допусти́м|ый (**-, -а, -о**) *прил* permissible, acceptable; (*мысль*) feasible.
допу|сти́ть (**-щу́, -стишь**) *несов от* **допуска́ть.**
допуще́ни|е (**-я**) *ср* (*см глаг*) admittance; assumption.
допущу́ *сов см* **допусти́ть.**
допью́ *итп сов см* **допи́ть.**
дорабо́та|ть (**-ю**; *impf* **дораба́тывать**) *сов неперех*: ~ **до** *+gen* to work until ◆ *перех* to finish.
дораст|и́ (**-у́, -ёшь**; *pt* **доро́с, доросла́, доросло́**, *impf* **дораста́ть**) *сов неперех*: ~ **до** *+gen* (*до потолка*) to grow to; (*до какого-н возраста*) to reach; **он доро́с до дире́ктора** he rose to become a director.
дорв|а́ться (**-у́сь, -ёшься**; *pt* **-а́лся, -ала́сь, -ало́сь**, *impf* **дорыва́ться**) *сов неперех*: ~ **до** *+gen* (*разг*: *до власти*) to grab; (: *до еды*) to fall (up)on.
дореволюцио́нный *прил* pre-revolutionary.
доро́г|а (**-и**) *ж* way; (*путь сообщения*) road; **по** ~**е** on the way; **мне с тобо́й** *или* **нам по** ~**е** we're going the same way; **сбива́ться** (**сби́ться** *perf*) **с** ~**и** (*также перен*) to lose one's way; **желе́зная** ~ railway (*BRIT*), railroad (*US*).
до́рого *нареч* (*купить, продать*) at a high price ◆ *как сказ* it's expensive; **заплати́ть** (*perf*) ~ **за что-н** (*перен*) to pay dearly for sth; ~ **бы дал** *или* **заплати́л** I *итп* would give anything; **э́то** ~ **сто́ит** it's expensive.
дорогови́зн|а (**-ы**) *ж* high prices *мн*.
доро́гой *нареч* on the way.
дор|ого́й (**-ог, -ога́, -ого**) *прил* (*книга, дом*) expensive; (*цена*) high; (*no short form*; *друг, мать*) dear; (*no full form*; *воспоминания, подарок*) cherished ◆ (**-ого́го**; *decl like adj*) *м* dear, darling; ~ **цено́й плати́ть** (**заплати́ть** *perf*) **за что-н** (*перен*) to pay dearly for sth.
дорожа́|ть (*3sg* **-ет**, *3pl* **-ют**, *perf* **вздорожа́ть** *или* **подорожа́ть**) *несов неперех* to rise *или* go up in price.
доро́же *сравн прил от* **дорого́й** ◆ *сравн нареч от* **до́рого.**
доро́жек *сущ см* **доро́жка.**
дорож|и́ть (**-у́, -и́шь**) *несов неперех*: ~ *+instr* to value.
доро́ж|ка (**-ки**; *gen pl* **-ек**) *ж* pathway; (*для плавания*) lane; (*для бега, на магнитофоне*) track; (*ковёр*) runner; (*в аэропорту*) runway.
доро́жный *прил* (*знак, строительство*) road *опред*; (*костюм, расходы*) travelling (*BRIT*), traveling (*US*); (*сумка*) travel; **доро́жный чек** traveller's cheque (*BRIT*), traveler's check (*US*).
доро́с *итп сов см* **дорасти́.**
дорыва́|ться (**-юсь**) *несов от* **дорва́ться.**
ДОС *ж сокр* (= *ди́сковая операцио́нная систе́ма*) DOS (= *disk operating system*).
ДОСАА́Ф *м сокр* = *Доброво́льное о́бщество соде́йствия а́рмии, авиа́ции и фло́ту*.
Досаа́ф *м сокр* = **ДОСАА́Ф.**
доса́д|а (**-ы**) *ж* annoyance; **с** ~**ы** out of annoyance; ~ **берёт меня́** I am annoyed.
доса́дный (**-ен, -на, -но**) *прил* annoying.
дос|ка́ (**-ки́**; *nom pl* **-ки**, *gen pl* **-ок**) *ж* board; (*мраморная*) slab; (*чугунная*) plate; **их нельзя́ ста́вить на одну́ до́ску** they're not in the same league; **доска́ объявле́ний** notice (*BRIT*) *или* bulletin (*US*) board.
доска|за́ть (**-жу́, -жешь**; *impf* **доска́зывать**) *сов перех* to finish (telling).
доскона́л|ьный (**-ен, -ьна, -ьно**) *прил* thorough.
иссле́довани|е (**-я**) *ср* (*ЮР*) further examination *или* inquiry.
дословно́ *нареч* verbatim, word for word.
досло́вный *прил* literal, word-for-word.
дослуж|и́ться (**-у́сь, -ишься**; *impf* **дослу́живаться**) *сов возв*: ~ **до** *+gen* to rise to the rank of.
дослу́ша|ть (**-ю**; *impf* **дослу́шивать**) *сов перех* to listen to.
досма́трива|ть (**-ю**) *несов от* **досмотре́ть.**
досмо́тр (**-а**) *м*: **тамо́женный** ~ customs examination.
досмотр|е́ть (**-ю́, -ишь**; *impf* **досма́тривать**) *сов перех* to watch the end of; (*багаж*) to check; ~ (*perf*) **до** *+gen* to watch until.

досóк *сущ см* **доскá**.
доспéх|и (-ов) *мн* (*рыцаря*) armour *ед* (*BRIT*), armor *ед* (*US*); (*перен: разг*) gear *ед*.
досрóчно *нареч* early, ahead of time.
досрóчный *прил* early.
достa|вáть(ся) (-ю́(сь)) *несов от* **достáть(ся)**.
достáв|ить (-лю, -ишь; *impf* **доставля́ть)** *сов перех* (*груз*) to deliver; (*пассажиров*) to carry, transport; (*удовольствие, возможность*) to give; (*трудности*) to cause.
достáв|ка (-ки; *gen pl* **-ок)** *ж* delivery; **с ~кой нá дом** ≈ recorded delivery (*BRIT*), ≈ certified mail (*US*).
достáвлю *сов см* **достáвить**.
доставля́|ть (-ю) *несов от* **достáвить**.
достáвок *сущ см* **достáвка**.
достáну(сь) *итп сов см* **достáть(ся)**.
достáнь(те) *сов см* **достáть**.
достáт|ок (-ка) *м*: **жить в ~ке** to be well provided for.
достáточно *нареч*: **~ хорошó/подрóбно** good/detailed enough ♦ *как сказ* that's enough; **~ дéнег/хлéба** enough money/bread; **~ шептáться/болтáть!** that's enough whispering/ chattering!; **~ уви́деть, чтóбы поня́ть** one only has to see to understand; **~ сказáть, что ...** suffice it to say, that ....
достá|ть (-ну, -нешь; *imper* **достáнь(те)**, *impf* **доставáть)** *сов перех* to take; (*раздобыть*) to get ♦ *неперех*: **~ до** *+gen* to reach
▸ **достáться** (*impf* **доставáться)** *сов возв* (*+dat*; *при разделе*): **мне ~лся дом** I got the house; **мнóго забóт емý ~лось** he was burdened down with a lot of worries; **мне ~лось** (*разг*) I got it in the neck.
дости́г *итп сов см* **дости́чь**.
достигá|ть (-ю) *несов от* **дости́гнуть, дости́чь**.
дости́гну *итп сов см* **дости́чь**.
дости́гн|уть (-у, -ешь) *сов см* **дости́чь**.
достижéни|е (-я) *ср* achievement; (*предела, возраста*) reaching.
достижи́м|ый (-, -а, -о) *прил* achievable, attainable.
дости́|чь (-гну, -гнешь; *pt* **-г, -гла, -гло**, *impf* **достигáть)** *сов неперех* (*+gen*) to reach; (*результата, цели*) to achieve; (*положения*) to attain.
достовéр|ный (-ен, -на, -но) *прил* reliable; **из ~ных истóчников** from reliable sources.
достóен *прил см* **достóйный**.
достóинств|о (-а) *ср* (*книги, плана*) merit; (*моральные качества*) virtue; (*уважение к себе*) dignity; (*КОММ*) value; **чýвство сóбственного ~а** self-respect; **считáть (посчитáть** *perf*) **что-н ни́же своегó ~а** to consider sth beneath one's dignity; **бáнковский билéт ~м в 100 рублéй** a banknote to the value of 100 roubles; **оцéнивать (оцени́ть** *perf*) **по ~у когó-н/что-н** to judge sb/sth on his/its merits.
достóйно *нареч* with dignity.
достó|йный *прил* (*награда, кара*) fitting; (*человек*) worthy; (**-ен, -йна, -йно**; *+gen*): **~ любви́/уважéния** worthy of love/respect.
достопримечáтельност|ь (-и) *ж* sight; (*музея*) interesting exhibit; **осмáтривать (осмотрéть** *perf*) **~и** to go sightseeing.
достопримечáтел|ьный (-ен, -ьна, -ьно) *прил* noteworthy.
достоя́ни|е (-я) *ср* property; **стать** (*perf*) *или* **сдéлаться** (*perf*) **~м нарóда** to become public property.
дóступ (-а) *м* admittance; (*к документам итп*) access; **открывáть (откры́ть** *perf*) **~ комý-н кудá-нибудь** to give sb access to somewhere; **нет ~а вóздуха/кислорóда** there is no way for air/oxygen to get in.
достýп|ный (-ен, -на, -но) *прил* (*место*) accessible; (*цены*) affordable; (*объяснение, изложение*) comprehensible; (*человек*) approachable.
досýг (-а) *м* leisure (time); **на ~е** in one's spare *или* free time.
дóсуха *нареч*: **вы́тереть ~** to dry.
дóсыта *нареч*; **их накорми́ли ~** they were fed until they could eat no more.
досьé *ср нескл* dossier, file; **заводи́ть (завести́** *perf*) **~ на когó-н** to open a file on sb.
досягáемост|ь (-и) *ж*: **вне ~и** unattainable; **в предéлах ~и** attainable.
досягáем|ый (-, -а, -о) *прил* (*задача, цель*) attainable; (*место*) accessible.
дотáскива|ть(ся) (-ю(сь)) *несов от* **дотащи́ть(ся)**.
дотáци|я (-и) *ж* subsidy.
дотащ|и́ть (-ý, -ишь; *impf* **дотáскивать)** *сов перех* to lug; **éле дотáскивать (~** *perf*) **нóги** to drag one's feet
▸ **дотащи́ться** (*impf* **дотáскиваться)** *сов возв* (*разг*): **~ся до** *+gen* to drag o.s. to.
дотемнá *нареч* until dark.
дотлá *нареч*: **сгорéть ~** to burn down (to the ground).
дотóш|ный (-ен, -на, -но) *прил* (*разг*) meticulous.
дотрóн|уться (-усь, -ешься; *impf* **дотрáгиваться)** *сов возв*: **~ до** *+gen* to touch.
дотянýть (-ý, -ешь; *impf* **дотя́гивать)** *сов перех*: **~ что-н до** *+gen* to extend sth as far as; **он ~ýл рабóту до вéчера** he dragged the work out until the evening
▸ **дотянýться** (*impf* **дотя́гиваться)** *сов возв*: **~ся до** *+gen* to reach.
доуч|и́ться (-ýсь, -ишься; *impf* **доýчиваться)** *сов возв* to complete one's education; **~** (*perf*) **до концá гóда/пя́того клáсса** to study up until the

end of the year/of fifth form.
до́хл|ый *прил* dead; (*разг*: *слабосильный*) wimpish.
до́х|нуть (**-ну, -нешь**; *pt* **-, -ла, -ло**, *perf* **подо́хнуть**) *несов неперех* (*животное*) to die; (*разг*: *человек*) to snuff it.
дохн|у́ть (**-у́, -ёшь**) *сов неперех* (*разг*: *человек*) to breathe; **мне ~ не́когда** (*разг*) I don't get a moment's rest.
дохо́д (**-а**) *м* (*предприятия*) income, revenue; (*человека*) income; **национа́льный ~** the national income; **дава́ть (дать** *perf*) *или* **приноси́ть (принести́** *perf*) **~** to generate income; **извлека́ть (извле́чь** *perf*) **~ из чего́-н** to make a profit from sth.
дохо́ден *прил см* **дохо́дный**.
доходи́ть *несов от* **дойти́**.
дохо́д|ный (**-ен, -на, -но**) *прил* profitable.
дохо́дчив|ый (**-, -а, -о**) *прил* clear, easy to understand.
доце́нт (**-а**) *м* ≈ reader (*BRIT*), ≈ associate professor (*US*).
до́чек *сущ см* **до́чка**.
до́чери *итп сущ см* **дочь**.
доче́рн|ий (**-яя, -ее, -ие**) *прил* daughter's; **~яя компа́ния/фи́рма** subsidiary company/firm.
до́черью *итп сущ см* **дочь**.
до́чиста *нареч* clean.
дочита́|ть (**-ю**; *impf* **дочи́тывать**) *сов перех* to finish (reading); **~** (*perf*) **до** *+gen* to read until.
до́ч|ка (**-ки**; *gen pl* **-ек**) *ж* daughter.
доч|ь (**-ери**; *см* **Table 2**) *ж* daughter.
дошёл *сов см* **дойти́**.
дошко́льник (**-а**) *м* preschool child.
дошко́льниц|а (**-ы**) *ж см* **дошко́льник**.
дошко́льный *прил* preschool.
дошла́ *сов см* **дойти́**.
доща́тый *прил* made of boards.
доя́р|ка (**-ки**; *gen pl* **-ок**) *ж* milkmaid.
ДПР *ж сокр* = *Демократи́ческая па́ртия Росси́и*.
др. *сокр* = **друго́й, други́е**.
драгоце́нност|ь (**-и**) *ж* jewel; (*перен*) gem, treasure.
драгоце́нный *прил* (*камень, металл*) precious; (*время, сведения, мех*) valuable.
драже́ *ср нескл* dragée.
дразн|и́ть (**-ю́, -ишь**) *несов перех* to tease; (*аппетит, воображение*) to stimulate.
дра́|ить (**-ю, -ишь**; *perf* **надра́ить**) *несов перех* to scrub.
дра́к|а (**-и**) *ж* fight; (*битва*) battle; **лезть (поле́зть** *perf*) *или* **вя́зываться (ввяза́ться** *perf*) **в ~у** to get into a fight.
драко́н (**-а**) *м* dragon; (*зоол*) draco *или* flying lizard.
драко́новск|ий (**-ая, -ое, -ие**) *прил*: **~ие ме́ры** Draconian measures.
дра́м|а (**-ы**) *ж* drama; (*событие*) crisis; **пережива́ть (пережи́ть** *perf*) **тяжёлую ~у** to go through a crisis.
драматизи́р|овать (**-ую**) (*не*)*сов перех* to dramatize.
драмати́ческ|ий (**-ая, -ое, -ие**) *прил* dramatic; (*актёр*) stage *опред*; **драмати́ческий кружо́к** drama group; **драмати́ческий теа́тр** theatre, theater (*US*).
драмату́рг (**-а**) *м* playwright.
драматурги́|я (**-и**) *ж* drama ◆ *собир* plays.
драмкружо́к (**-ка́**) *м сокр* (= *драмати́ческий кружо́к*) drama group.
дра́ный *прил* (*разг*) ragged.
драп (**-а**) *м thick woollen cloth*.
драпир|ова́ть (**-у́ю**; *perf* **задрапирова́ть**) *несов перех*: **~ (чем-н)** to drape (with sth).
драпиро́в|ка (**-ки**; *gen pl* **-ок**) *ж* drapery.
драть (**деру́, дерёшь**; *perf* **разодра́ть**) *несов перех* (*бумагу, одежду*) to tear *или* rip up; (*perf* **задра́ть**; *подлеж*: *волк, лиса*) to tear to pieces; (*perf* **вы́драть**; *разг*: *побить*) to thrash; (*perf* **содра́ть**; *кору, обои*) to strip; **~ (содра́ть** *perf*) **шку́ру с живо́тного** to skin an animal; **~ (содра́ть** *perf*) **де́ньги с кого́-н** (*разг*) to rip sb off; **он с меня́ шку́ру сдерёт** (*разг*) he'll have my guts for garters; **~** (*impf*) **го́рло** (*разг*) to bawl
▸ **дра́ться** *несов возв*: **дра́ться (с** *+instr*) to fight (with); (*perf* **подра́ться**; *дети*) to fight.
дребеде́н|ь (**-и**) *ж* (*разг*) rubbish.
дре́безг (**-а**) *м*: **разби́ться с ~ом** to shatter; **разбива́ть (разби́ть** *perf*) **в ме́лкие ~и** to smash to smithereens.
дребезж|а́ть (*3sg* **-и́т**, *3pl* **-а́т**) *несов неперех* to jingle.
древеси́н|а (**-ы**) *ж собир* wood.
древе́сный *прил* wood; **древе́сные поро́ды** species of tree; **древе́сный у́голь** charcoal.
дре́вк|о (**-а**) *ср* (*копья*) shaft; **~ фла́га** flagpole.
дре́вн|ий (**-яя, -ее, -ие**) *прил* ancient; **дре́вняя исто́рия** ancient history.
дре́вност|ь (**-и**) *ж* antiquity.
дрези́н|а (**-ы**) *ж* trolley (*BRIT*), handcar (*US*).
дрейф (**-а**) *м* drift; **снима́ться (сня́ться** *perf*) **с дре́йфа** to regain course; **лежа́ть** (*impf*) **в дре́йфе** to heave to.
дрейф|ова́ть (**-у́ю**) *несов неперех* to drift.
дрел|ь (**-и**) *ж* drill.
дрем|а́ть (**-лю́, -лешь**) *несов неперех* to doze; **враг не дре́млет** (*перен*) the enemy never sleeps.
дремот|а́ (**-ы́**) *ж* drowsiness.
дрему́ч|ий (**-ая, -ее, -ие**; **-, -а, -е**) *прил* dense; (*перен*: *невежда*) absolute.
дрена́ж (**-а́**) *м* (*почвы*) drainage; (*раны*) draining.
дрессир|ова́ть (**-у́ю**; *perf* **вы́дрессировать**) *несов перех* to train.
дро́бен *прил см* **дро́бный**.
дроб|и́ть (**-лю́, -и́шь**; *perf* **раздроби́ть**) *несов перех* (*камень, кость*) to crush; (*силы, отряд*) to divide.
дроблёный *прил* (*орехи*) crushed.
дро́б|ный (**-ен, -на, -но**) *прил* (*перечень*,

список) itemized; (*стук, шаг*) staccato; (*no short form; МАТ*) fractional.
дроб|ь (**-и**; *gen pl* **-е́й**) *ж* fraction; (*дождя, шагов*) patter; (*барабана*) beat.
дров|а́ (**-**; *dat pl* **-а́м**) *мн* firewood *ед*; **он наломал ~!** (*перен: разг*) he made a hash of it!; **кто в лес, кто по ~** at sixes and sevens.
дро́гн|уть (**-у, -ешь**) *сов неперех* (*стёкла, руки, голос*) to shake, tremble; (*лицо*) to quiver; (*свет, огонь*) to flicker; (*человек*) to waver; **у меня́ рука́ не ~ет** *+infin* ... I won't hesitate to ....
дрожа́ни|е (**-я**) *ср* (*стёкол*) vibration; (*колен, голоса*) trembling; (*лица*) quivering; (*света, огня*) flickering.
дрож|а́ть (**-у́, -и́шь**) *несов неперех* (*стёкла*) to vibrate; (*руки, голос*) to shake, tremble; (*лицо*) to quiver; (*свет, огонь*) to flicker; *~ (impf)* **за** *+acc или* **над** *+instr* (*разг*) to fuss over; *~ (impf)* **над (ка́ждой) копе́йкой** to grudge every penny; *~ (impf)* **пе́ред кем-н** to tremble before sb.
дро́жж|и (**-е́й**) *мн* yeast *ед*.
дрож|ь (**-и**) *ж* (*от холода*) shiver; (*от страха*) shudder; **его́ броса́ет в ~** he is shuddering.
дрозд (**-а́**) *м* thrush; **чёрный ~** blackbird.
дру|г (**-га**; *nom pl* **-зья́**, *gen pl* **-зе́й**) *м* friend; (*разг: обращение*) mate; **~ дру́га** one another, each other; **~ дру́гу** (*говорить*) to one another *или* each other; **~ за дру́гом** one after another; **~ о дру́ге** (*говорить*) about one another *или* each other.
друг|и́е (**-и́х**; *decl like adj*) *мн* others *мн*.
друг|о́й *прил* (*иной*) another; (*второй*) the other; (*не такой, как этот*) different ◆ (**-о́го**; *decl like adj*) *м* (*кто-то иной*) another (person); (*второй*) the other (one); **~о́е мне́ние** different opinion; **в ~ раз** another time; **и тот и ~** both; **что́-то ~о́е** something else; **~и́ми слова́ми** in other words; **на ~ день** the next day; **э́то ~о́е де́ло** that's a different matter; *см также* **други́е**.
дру́жб|а (**-ы**) *ж* friendship.
дружелю́би|е (**-я**) *ср* friendliness.
дружелю́б|ный (**-ен, -на, -но**) *прил* friendly, amicable.
дру́жен *прил см* **дру́жный**.
дру́жески *нареч* in a friendly manner, amicably.
дру́жеск|ий (**-ая, -ое, -ие**) *прил* friendly.
дру́жествен|ный (**-ен, -на, -но**) *прил* friendly.
дружи́н|а (**-ы**) *ж* (*ИСТ. ВОЕН*) host.
друж|и́ть (**-у́, -ишь**) *несов неперех*: **~ с** *+instr* to be friends with
▸ **дружи́ться** (*perf* **подружи́ться**) *несов возв*: **~ся с** *+instr* to make friends with.
дружи́щ|е (**-а**) *м* (*разг*) mate.
дру́ж|ный (**-ен, -на́, -но, -ны́**) *прил* (*семья, коллектив*) close-knit; (*аплодисменты, смех*) general; (*усилия*) concerted.
друж|о́к (**-ка́**) *м* (*друг*) friend; (*разг: пренебр*) crony; (*обращение*) love.

друзья́ *итп сущ см* **друг**.
дры́га|ть (**-ю**) *несов неперех*: **~ нога́ми** to kick.
дры́хн|уть (**-у, -ешь**) *несов неперех* (*разг*) to kip, sleep.
дря́бл|ый (**-, -а́, -о**) *прил* (*кожа*) sagging; (*человек, тело*) flabby.
дря́зг|и (**-**) *мн* (*разг*) squabbles *мн*.
дрянно́й *прил* (*разг: товар, работа*) trashy; (*: характер*) rotten.
дрян|ь (**-и**) *ж* (*разг*) rubbish (*BRIT*), trash (*US*).
дряхле́|ть (**-ю**; *perf* **одряхле́ть**) *несов неперех* to become infirm.
дря́хл|ый (**-, -а́, -о**) *прил* (*человек*) infirm; (*здание*) dilapidated, decrepit.
ДСО *ср сокр* (= *доброво́льное спорти́вное о́бщество*) amateur sports association.
ДТП *сокр* (= *доро́жно-тра́нспортное происше́ствие*) RTA (= *road traffic accident*).
дуб (**-а**; *loc sg* **-у́**, *nom pl* **-ы́**) *м* (*БОТ*) oak (tree); (*древесина*) oak; (*перен: разг*) blockhead.
дуби́н|а (**-ы**) *ж* club ◆ *м/ж* (*разг*) blockhead.
дуби́н|ка (**-ки**; *gen pl* **-ок**) *ж* cudgel; **рези́новая ~** truncheon.
дуб|и́ть (**-лю́, -и́шь**; *perf* **вы́дубить**) *несов перех* to tan.
дублён|ка (**-ки**; *gen pl* **-ок**) *ж* sheepskin coat.
дублёный *прил* (*мех*) tanned.
дублёр (**-а**) *м* backup; (*ТЕАТР*) understudy; (*КИНО*) double.
дублика́т (**-а**) *м* duplicate.
Ду́блин (**-а**) *м* Dublin.
дубли́р|овать (**-ую**) *несов перех* (*деятельность*) to duplicate; (*ТЕАТР*) to understudy; (*КИНО*) to dub; (*КОМП*) to back up.
дубл|ь (**-я**) *м* (*КИНО*) take.
дубо́вый *прил* oak; (*перен: стиль, язык*) ponderous.
дуг|а́ (**-и́**; *nom pl* **-и**) *ж* (*ГЕОМ*) arc.
дуд|е́ть (*2sg* **-и́шь**, *3sg* **-и́т**) *несов неперех* to play the pipe.
ду́д|ка (**-ки**; *gen pl* **-ок**) *ж* (*МУЗ*) pipe; **пляса́ть** *(impf)* **под чью-н ~ку** (*перен*) to dance to sb's tune.
ду́ж|ка (**-ки**; *gen pl* **-ек**) *ж* (*серёг*) hoop; (*ведра*) handle.
ду́л|о (**-а**) *ср* (*отверстие ствола*) muzzle; (*сам ствол*) barrel.
ду́м|а (**-ы**) *ж* (*размышление*) meditation, thought; **Д~** (*ПОЛИТ*) the Duma (*lower house of the Russian parliament*); **Госуда́рственная Д~** the State Duma.
ду́ма|ть (**-ю**) *несов неперех*: **~ (о чём-н)** to think (about sth); *~ (impf)* **над чем-н** to think sth over; **он ~ет купи́ть маши́ну** he is thinking of buying a car; **я ~ю, что да/нет** I think/don't think so; **и не ~йте!** (*разг*) don't even think of it!
▸ **ду́маться** (*perf* **поду́маться**) *несов безл* (*+dat*) to seem; **мне ~ется, он прав** I think he's

right.
Дунá|й (-я) *м* Danube.
дуновéни|е (-я) *ср* breath.
дýн|уть (-у, -ешь) *сов неперех* to blow.
дуп|лó (-лá; *nom pl* -ла, *gen pl* -ел) *ср* (*дерева*) hollow; (*зуба*) cavity.
дýр|а (-ы) *ж* (*разг*) fool, idiot.
дурáк (-á) *м* (*разг*) fool, idiot; **игрáть** *(impf)* **в дуракá** to play "durak" (*Russian card game*); **он не ~ вы́пить/поéсть** (*разг*) he loves his drink/food; **дуракá валя́ть** *(impf)* (*разг*: *дурачиться*) to clown about, play the fool; (: *бездельничать*) to lounge about; **оставáться (остáться** *perf*) **в дуракáх** (*перен*: *разг*) to be made a fool of.
дурáцк|ий (-ая, -ое, -ие) *прил* (*разг*) stupid, idiotic.
дурáчеств|о (-а) *ср* stupidity, idiocy.
дурáч|ить (-у, -ишь; *perf* **одурáчить**) *несов перех* (*разг*) to con
▸ **дурáчиться** *несов возв* (*разг*) to play the fool.
дурачь|ё (-я́) *ср собир* (*разг*) bunch of idiots.
дурён *сущ см* **дурнóй**.
дýр|ень (-ня) *м* (*разг*) dimwit, fool.
дурé|ть (-ю; *perf* **одурéть**) *несов неперех* (*разг*): **~ от** +*gen* to grow stupid from.
дýр|ий (-ья, -ье, -ьи) *прил*: **~ья головá** *или* **башкá** (*разг*) dope, fool.
дур|úть (-ю́, -ишь) *несов неперех* (*разг*: *человек*) to fool around; (*животное*) to be stubborn; **~ (задурúть** *perf*) **гóлову комý-н** (*разг*) to mix sb up.
дурмáн (-а) *м* thorn apple, jimson weed (*US*); (*опьяняюще средство*) intoxicant; (: *перен*) drug.
дурмáн|ить (-ю, -ишь; *perf* **одурмáнить**) *несов перех* to intoxicate.
дурнé|ть (-ю; *perf* **подурнéть**) *несов неперех* to lose one's looks.
дýрно *нареч* (*пахнуть, выглядеть*) bad; (*вести себя*) badly ◆ *как сказ*: **мне ~** I don't feel well; **емý сдéлалось ~** he felt faint.
дур|нóй (-ён, -нá, -но) *прил* nasty; (*питание*) bad; **онá ~нá собóй** she is very plain; **дурнóй прúзнак** bad omen.
дурнот|á (-ы́) *ж* faintness.
дýрня *итп сущ см* **дýрень**.
дýроч|ка (-ки; *gen pl* -ек) *ж* (*разг*) silly girl.
дуршлáг (-а) *м* colander.
дур|ь (-и) *ж* (*разг*) rubbish, nonsense; **вы́брось э́ту ~ из головы́!** (*разг*) get that foolish idea out of your head!; **дýрью мáяться** *(impf)* *или* **мýчиться** *(impf)* (*разг*) to muck around.
дýтый *прил* hollow; (*перен*) exaggerated, inflated.
ду|ть (-ю, -ешь) *несов неперех* to blow ◆ (*perf* **вы́дуть**) *перех* to blow; **здесь дýет** it's draughty (*BRIT*) *или* drafty (*US*) in here.
дух (-а; *part gen* -у) *м* spirit; (*разг*): **перевестú ~** to get one's breath back; **в дýхе** +*gen* in the spirit of; **пáдать** *(impf)* **дýхом** to lose heart; **быть** *(impf)* **в дýхе/не в дýхе** to be in high/low spirits; **сохраня́ть (сохранúть** *perf*) **присýтствие дýха** to retain one's presence of mind; **у меня́ не хвáтит дýху на э́то** (*разг*) I don't have the heart to do this; **во весь ~** (*разг*) at full *или* top speed; **чтоб дýху твоегó здесь нé было!** (*разг*) get out of my sight!
дух|ú (-óв) *мн* perfume *ед*, scent *ед*.
духовéнств|о (-а) *ср собир* clergy; (*православное, католическое*) priesthood.
духóвк|а (-и) *ж* oven.
духóвник (-а) *м* confessor.
духóвност|ь (-и) *ж* spirituality.
духóвный *прил* (*интересы, запросы*) spiritual; (*сила, мир, жизнь*) inner; (*музыка*) sacred, church *опред*; **духóвная акадéмия** seminary; **духóвное звáние** ecclesiastical rank; **духóвное лицó** ecclesiastic, cleric; **духóвный сан** holy orders *мн*.
духовóй *прил* (*муз*) wind *опред*.
духот|á (-ы́) *ж* stuffiness; (*жара*) closeness.
душ (-а) *м* shower; **принимáть (приня́ть** *perf*) **~** to have *или* take a shower.
душ|á (-ú; *nom pl* -и) *ж* soul; (*ист*: *крестьянин*) serf; **дóбрая ~** kind heart; **нúзкая/пóдлая ~** mean/ignoble spirit; **~ моя́** my dear; **рабóтать** *(impf)* **с ~óй** to put one's heart into one's work; **в ~é** at heart; **на дýшу (населéния)** per head (of the population); **он в ней ~и не чáет** she's the apple of his eye; **быть** *(impf)* **~óй** +*gen* (*общества, дела*) to be the life and soul of; **не имéть** *(impf)* **грошá за ~óй** to be without a penny to one's name; **говорúть** *(impf)*/**бесéдовать** *(impf)* **по ~м** to have a heart-to-heart talk/chat; **отводúть (отвестú** *perf*) **дýшу** to pour out one's heart; **как Бог нá ~у полóжит** (*разг*) any old way; **у меня́ ~ в пя́тки ушлá** (*разг*) I was scared to death; **от всей ~и** from the bottom of one's heart; **в глубинé ~и** in one's heart of hearts.
Душанбé *м нескл* Dushanbe.
душевнобольн|áя (-óй; *decl like adj*) *ж см* **душевнобольнóй**.
душевнобольн|óй (-óго; *decl like adj*) *м* mentally-ill person.
душéвн|ый *прил* (*силы, подъём*) inner; (*разговор*) sincere, heartfelt; (*человек*) kindly; **~ое потрясéние** shock.
душегрéйк|а (-и; *разг*) *ж* body warmer.
душегýб (-а) *ж* (*разг*) butcher.
душегýб|ка (-ки; *gen pl* -ок) *ж см* **душегýб**; (*автомашина*) *mobile gas chamber*.
дýшен *сущ см* **дýшный**.
душераздирáющ|ий (-ая, -ее, -ие; -, -а, -е) *прил* (*крик*) bloodcurdling; (*плач*) heart-rending.
душúстый *прил* (*цветок*) fragrant; (*мыло*) perfumed.
душúтел|ь (-я) *м* (*перен*) suppressor.
душ|úть (-ý, -ишь; *perf* **задушúть** *или* **удушúть**) *несов перех* to strangle; (*свободу, прогресс*) to stifle, suppress; (*perf* **надушúть**; *платок*) to scent; **егó дýшит смех** he is choking with

laughter; ~ *(impf)* **в объятиях кого-н** to smother sb in one's embrace.

души́ц|а (-ы) *ж* marjoram.

ду́шно *как сказ* it's stuffy *или* close; **в ко́мнате** ~ the room is very stuffy; **мне ~, откро́йте окно́** I find it very stuffy *или* close, open the window.

ду́ш|ный (-ен, -на́, -но) *прил* stuffy; (*жаркий*) sultry.

дуэ́л|ь (-и) *ж* duel; **вызыва́ть (вы́звать** *perf*) **кого-н на** ~ to challenge sb to a duel.

дуэ́т (-а) *м* (*произведение*) duet, duo; (*исполнители*) duo.

ды́бом *нареч*: **встава́ть** ~ (*волосы, шерсть*) to stand on end.

дыб|ы́ (-о́в) *мн*: **на ~ станови́ться** (*лошадь*) to rear up; (*перен*: *разг*) to kick up a fuss.

дым (-а; *part gen* -у, *loc sg* -у́, *nom pl* -ы) *м* smoke; **поруга́ться** *(perf)* **в** ~ to fall out completely.

дым|и́ть (-лю́, -и́шь; *perf* **надыми́ть**) *несов неперех* (*печь, дрова*) to smoulder (*BRIT*), smolder (*US*); (*разг*): ~ *+instr* to puff on

► **дыми́ться** *несов возв* (*труба*) to be smoking.

ды́мк|а (-и) *ж* haze.

ды́мно *как сказ*; **(здесь)** ~ it's smoky (in here).

ды́мный *прил* (*дрова, головешка*) smouldering (*BRIT*), smoldering (*US*); (*комната, помещение*) smoky, smoke-filled.

дымохо́д (-а) *м* flue.

ды́мчатый *прил* (*кот*) smoky; **ды́мчатые очки́** tinted glasses.

ды́н|я (-и) *ж* melon.

дыр|а́ (-ы́; *nom pl* -ы) *ж* hole; **в ды́рах** full of holes.

ды́р|ка (-ки; *gen pl* -ок) *ж* hole.

дыроко́л (-а) *м* punch.

дыря́в|ый (-, -а, -о) *прил* (*разг*) holey; **у него́ ~ая голова́** (*разг*) he has a head like a sieve.

дыха́ни|е (-я) *ср* breathing, respiration; ~ **весны́** a breath of spring; **с затаённым ~м** with bated breath; **второ́е** ~ second wind; **иску́сственное** ~ artificial respiration.

дыха́тельный *прил* (*упражнения*) breathing *опред*; (*процесс*) respiratory; **дыха́тельное го́рло** windpipe; **дыха́тельные пути́** respiratory tract *ед*.

дыш|а́ть (-у́, -ишь) *несов неперех* to breathe; ~ *(impf) +instr* (*ненавистью*) to exude; (*любовью*) to radiate

► **дыша́ться** *несов возв* (*+dat*): **мне здесь ле́гче ды́шится** I can breathe more easily here.

дья́вол (-а) *м* devil; **за каки́м ~ом я до́лжен идти́ туда́!** (*разг*) why the devil should I go there!; **како́го ~а ...!** what the devil ...!

дья́вольск|ий (-ая, -ое, -ие) *прил* diabolic(al); (*разг*: *холод*) devilish; **~ое терпе́ние** ≈ the patience of Job.

дья́кон (-а) *м* deacon.

дю́жин|а (-ы) *ж* dozen; **чёртова** ~ baker's dozen.

дюйм (-а) *м* inch.

дю́н|а (-ы; *gen pl* -) *ж* (*обычно мн*) dune.

дюралюми́ни|й (-я) *м* Duralumin®.

дюше́с (-а) *м* (*БОТ*) Duchess pear.

дя́гил|ь (-я) *м* angelica.

дя́д|ька (-ьки; *gen pl* -ек) *м* uncle; (*разг*) guy.

дя́д|я (-и) *м* uncle; (*разг*) man; (: *обращение*) mister.

дя́т|ел (-ла) *м* woodpecker.

~ Е, е ~

Е, е *сущ нескл (буква) the 6th letter of the Russian alphabet.*
ЕАСТ *ж сокр (= Европéйская ассоциáция свобóдной торгóвли)* EFTA (= *European Free Trade Association*).
ЕБРР *м сокр (= Европéйский банк реконстрýкции и развúтия)* EBRD (= *European Bank for Reconstruction and Development*).
евáнгели|е (-я) *ср* the Gospels *мн*; (*однá из книг*) gospel.
евангелúст (-а) *м* evangelist.
евангелúческ|ий (-ая, -ое, -ие) *прил* evangelical.
евáнгельск|ий (-ая, -ое, -ие) *прил*: **~ текст** gospel.
éвнух (-а) *м* eunuch.
Еврáзи|я (-и) *ж* Eurasia.
еврéек *сущ см* **еврéйка.**
еврé|й (-я) *м* Jew.
еврé|йка (-йки; *gen pl* **-ек)** *ж* Jewess.
еврéйск|ий (-ая, -ое, -ие) *прил (нарóд, обычаи)* Jewish; **~ язык** Hebrew.
евроазиáтск|ий (-ая, -ое, -ие) *прил* Eurasian.
Евровúдени|е (-я) *ср* Eurovision.
Еврóп|а (-ы) *ж* Europe.
европé|ец (-йца) *м* European.
европéйк|а (-и) *ж см* **европéец.**
европéйск|ий (-ая, -ое, -ие) *прил* European; **европéйский совéт** Council of Europe; **европéйский суд** European Court of Justice; **европéйское сообщество** European Community.
европéйца *итп сущ см* **европéец.**
ЕВС *ж сокр (= Европéйская валютная систéма)* EMS (= *European Monetary System*).
ЕВФ *м сокр (= Европéйский валютный фонд)* (= *European monetary fund*).
éгер|ь (-я) *м (на охóте)* huntsman (*мн* huntsmen).
Егúп|ет (-та) *м* Egypt.
егúпетск|ий (-ая, -ое, -ие) *прил* Egyptian.
Егúпта *итп сущ см* **Егúпет.**
египтя́н|ин (-ина; *nom pl* **-е,** *gen pl* **-)** *м* Egyptian.
египтя́н|ка (-ки; *gen pl* **-ок)** *ж см* **египтя́нин.**
егó *мест см* **он, онó** ◆ *притяж мест (относительно мужчины итп)* his; (*относительно предмета итп*) its.
егожý *несов см* **егозúть.**
егоз|á (-ы) *м/ж (разг)* fidget.
его|зúть (-жý, -зúшь) *несов неперех (разг)* to fidget; **~** *(impf)* **пéред** *+instr (перен)* to fawn on.
едá (-ы) *ж (пища)* food; (*процесс*): **за ~óй, во врéмя ~ы** at mealtimes; **мóйте рýки пéред ~óй** wash your hands before eating.

KEYWORD

едвá *нареч* **1** (*с трудом: нашёл, достал, доехал итп*) only just
2 (*тóлько, немнóго*) barely, hardly; **больнóй едвá дышит** the patient is barely *или* hardly breathing; **едвá созрéвший плод** a barely ripe fruit
3 (*тóлько что*) just; **емý едвá испóлнилось 20 лет** he has just turned 20
◆ *союз (как тóлько)* as soon as; **едвá он пришёл, начáл рабóтать** as soon as he arrived, he set to work; **едвá ли** hardly; **ужé пóздно, едвá ли он придёт** it's late, he's hardly likely to come now; **едвá ли не** almost; **он едвá ли не сáмый лýчший ученúк** he is almost the best pupil.

éдем *итп сов см* **éхать.**
едúм *несов см* **есть.**
единéни|е (-я) *ср* unity.
единúц|а (-ы) *ж (цифра)* one; (*изображéние*) the figure 1; (*ПРОСВЕЩ*) ≈ very poor (*school mark*); (*измерения, часть целого*) unit; **дéнежная ~** monetary unit; **штáтная ~** member of staff; *см также* **единúцы.**
единúц|ы (-) *мн* a few; **остáлись в живых ~** only a few people survived.
единúч|ный (-ен, -на, -но) *прил (рéдкий: экземпляр)* single; (*случай*) isolated.
единобóрств|о (-а) *ср* single combat; **вступáть (вступúть** *perf*) **в ~ с** *+instr* to enter into combat with.
единобрáчи|е (-я) *ср* monogamy.
единовлáстен *прил см* **единовлáстный.**
единовлáсти|е (-я) *ср* autocracy.
единовлáст|ный (-ен, -на, -но) *прил* autocratic.
единоврéмен|ный (-ен, -на, -но) *прил* one-off; **~ное пособие** one-off benefit payment.
единоглáсен *прил см* **единоглáсный.**
единоглáси|е (-я) *ср* unanimity.
единоглáсно *нареч* unanimously; **прúнято ~** carried unanimously.

единогла́с|ный (-ен, -на, -но) *прил* unanimous.
единоду́ши|е (-я) *ср* unanimity.
единоду́шно *нареч* unanimously.
единоду́шный *прил* unanimous.
единокро́вный *прил*: ~ **брат** half-brother (*with the same father*).
единоли́чник (-а) *м* (*ист*) peasant smallholder; (*пренебр*) maverick.
единоли́чный *прил* (*индивидуальный*: *власть, решение*) individual.
единомы́сли|е (-я) *ср* like-mindedness.
единомы́шленник (-а) *м* like-minded person; (*сообщник*) confederate.
единонача́ли|е (-я) *ср* one-man rule.
единообра́з|ный (-ен, -на, -но) *прил* unified.
единоро́г (-а) *м* unicorn.
единоутро́бный *прил*: ~ **брат** half-brother (*with the same mother*).
еди́нственен *прил см* **еди́нственный**.
еди́нственно *част* (*только*) only ◆ *нареч*: ~ **пра́вильный/возмо́жный путь** the only correct/possible way; ~, **о чём я прошу́** the only thing I ask.
еди́нствен|ный (-ен, -на, -но) *прил* (the) only; ~ **в своём ро́де** one of a kind; ~**ная наде́жда** the only hope; **он – ~ ребёнок** he is an only child; **еди́нственное число́** (*линг*) singular.
еди́нств|о (-а) *ср* unity.
еди́н|ый *прил* (*цельный*) united; (*общий*) common; (*только один*) one, single; ~**ое це́лое** a unified whole; **все до ~ого** to a man; **еди́ный (проездно́й) биле́т** travel pass (*for use on all forms of transport*).
еди́те *несов см* **есть**.
е́д|кий (-кая, -кое, -кие; -ок, -ка́, -ко) *прил* (*также перен*) caustic; (*запах, дым*) acrid.
е́дкост|ь (-и) *ж* (*хим*) causticity; (*перен*) acerbity.
е́док *прил см* **е́дкий**.
едо́к (-а́) *м*: **у него́ в семье́ пять едоко́в** he has five mouths to feed.
е́ду *итп несов см* **е́хать**.
едя́т *несов см* **есть**.
её *мест от* **она́** ◆ *притяж мест* (*относительно женщины итп*) her; (*относительно предмета итп*) its.
ёж (-а́) *м* hedgehog; **морско́й** ~ sea urchin; **ежу́ поня́тно** (*разг*) it's as plain as the nose on your face.
ежеви́к|а (-и) *ж* (*растение*) bramble; (*ягода*) blackberry; (*собир*) blackberries *мн*, brambles *мн*.
ежеви́чный *прил* (*варенье, куст*) blackberry *опред*, bramble *опред*.
ежего́дник (-а) *м* annual (publication).
ежего́дно *нареч* annually.
ежего́дный *прил* annual *опред*.
ежедне́вен *прил см* **ежедне́вный**.
ежедне́вник (-а) *м* (*блокнот-дневник*) diary.
ежедне́вно *нареч* daily, every day.
ежедне́в|ный (-ен, -на, -но) *прил* daily; (*повседневный*) everyday.
ежеме́сячник (-а) *м* (*периодическое издание*) monthly.
ежеме́сячно *нареч* monthly.
ежеме́сячный *прил* monthly *опред*.
ежеминý́тен *прил см* **ежеминý́тный**.
ежеминý́тно *нареч* every minute; (*постоянно*) constantly.
ежеминý́т|ный (-ен, -на, -но) *прил*: ~**ная прове́рка** checks at one-minute intervals; (*очень частый*) constant.
еженеде́льник (-а) *м* weekly.
еженеде́льно *нареч* weekly.
еженеде́льный *прил* weekly *опред*.
ежесекý́нд|ный (-ен, -на, -но) *прил* occurring every second; (*чрезвычайно частый*) incessant.
ёжик (-а) *м* hedgehog; (*причёска*) crew cut; **стри́чься (постри́чься** *perf*) ~**ом** to have a crew cut.
ёж|иться (-усь, -ишься; *perf* **съёжиться**) *несов возв*: ~ **от** +*gen* (*от холода*) to huddle up from; (*от страха, от стыда*) to cringe with.
ежо́вый *прил*: **держа́ть кого́-н в ежо́вых рукави́цах** to rule sb with a rod of iron.
езд|а́ (-ы́) *ж* (*перемещение*: *на велосипеде, верхом*) riding; (: *на машине*) driving; (*мера*: *на машине*) drive; **в двадцати́ мину́тах ~ы́ от** +*gen* a twenty-minute drive from.
е́здить (-жу, -дишь) *несов неперех* to go; ~ (*impf*) **на** +*prp* (*на лошади, на велосипеде*) to ride; (*на поезде, на автобусе итп*) to travel *или* go by; (*разг*: *эксплуатировать*) to make use of.
ездово́й *прил*: **ездова́я соба́ка** sled dog; **ездова́я ло́шадь** draught horse.
ездо́к (-а́) *м* rider; **туда́ я бо́льше не** ~ I'm not going there again.
е́зжу *несов см* **е́здить**.
ей *мест см* **она́**.
ей-бо́гу *межд* (*разг*) really, truly.
ЕКА *ср сокр* (= *Европе́йское косми́ческое аге́нство*) ESA (= *European Space Agency*).
Екатеринбý́рг (-а) *м* Ekaterinburg.
ёка|ть (*3sg* **-ет**, *3pl* **-ют**, *perf* **ёкнуть**) *несов неперех* (*сердце*) to miss a beat.
ёкн|уть (*3sg* **-ет**, *3pl* **-ут**) *сов от* **ёкать**.
ел *итп несов см* **есть**.
е́ле *нареч* (*с трудом*) only just; (*едва*) barely, hardly.
е́ле-е́ле *нареч*: **он ~ спа́сся** he had a narrow escape; **ло́шадь ~ плетётся** the horse is on its last legs.
еле́|йный (-ен, -йна, -йно) *прил* (*перен*: *слащавый*) unctuous.
ёлк|а (-ки; *gen pl* **-ок**) *ж* fir (tree); (*БОТ*) spruce; (*праздник*) *New Year party for children*;

(рождéственская *или* **новогóдняя) ~** ≈ Christmas tree.

елóвый *прил* fir; (*БОТ*) spruce.

ёлок *сущ см* **ёлка.**

ёлочн|ый *прил*: **~ые украшéния** *или* **игрýшки** Christmas-tree decorations *мн.*

ел|ь (-и) *ж* fir (tree); (*БОТ*) spruce.

éльник (-а) *м* (*лес*) fir grove; (*плантация*) fir plantation; (*ветки*) fir branches *мн.*

ем *несов см* **есть.**

ём|кий (-кая, -кое, -кие; -ок, -ка, -ко) *прил* (*вместительный*) capacious; (*перен*: *содержательный*) meaningful.

ёмкост|ь (-и) *ж* (*вместимость*) capacity; (*вместилище*) container; **мéры ~и** units of volume.

ёмок *прил см* **ёмкий.**

емý *мест см* **он, онó.**

енóт (-а) *м* raccoon.

енóтовый *прил* raccoon.

епáрхи|я (-и) *ж* diocese; (*в православной церкви*) eparchy.

епúскоп (-а) *м* bishop.

ералáш (-а) *м* (*разг*: *беспорядок*) mess.

Еревáн (-а) *м* Yerevan.

éрес|ь (-и) *ж* heresy; (*перен*) nonsense.

еретúк (-á) *м* heretic.

еретúческ|ий (-ая, -ое, -ие) *прил* heretical.

ёрза|ть (-ю) *несов неперех* (*разг*: *беспокойно сидеть*) to fidget.

ерóш|ить (-у, -ишь; *perf* **взъерóшить)** *несов перех* (*разг*: *волосы*) to ruffle.

ерунд|á (-ы́) *ж* (*разг*: *чепуха*) rubbish, nonsense; **э́то ~** (*пустяк*) it's a mere trifle, it's nothing.

ёрш (-á) *м* (*рыба*) ruff(e); (*щётка*) brush.

ерш|úться (-ýсь, -úшься) *несов возв* (*о волосах*) to stick up; (*разг*: *горячиться*) to fly off the handle.

ЕС *ср сокр* (= *Европéйское сообщество или союз*) EC (= *European Community*) ◆ *м сокр* (= *Европéйский совéт*) Council of Europe.

есаýл (-а) *м* esaul (*rank equivalent to captain in Cossack army*).

KEYWORD

éсли *союз* ***1*** (*в том случае когда*) if; **éсли онá придёт, дай ей э́то письмó** if she comes, give her this letter; **éсли ..., то ...** (*если*) if ..., then ...; **éсли он опоздáет, то идú одúн** if he is late, (then) go alone

2 (*об условном действии*): **éсли бы(, то/ тогдá)** if; **éсли бы я мог, (то) помóг бы тебé** if I could, I would help you

3 (*выражает сильное желание*): **(ах** *или* **о) éсли бы** if only; **ах éсли бы он позвонúл!** oh, if only he would phone (*BRIT*) *или* call (*US*)!

4 (*выражает противопоставление*) if; **éсли с мáмой я чáсто спóрю, то с óтцом мне легкó** if I argue with Mum, I get on all the better with Dad; **éсли не ..., то ...** if not ..., then ...; **éсли не кáждый день, то чáсто** often, if not every day; **éсли уж на то пошлó** if it comes to it; **éсли хотúте** *или* **угóдно** (*возможно*) perhaps; **что éсли...?** (*а вдруг*) what if...?

ест *несов см* **есть.**

естéственен *прил см* **естéственный.**

естéственно *нареч* naturally ◆ *вводн сл* (*конечно*) of course.

естéственност|ь (-и) *ж* (*нормальность*) naturalness; (*непринуждённость*) spontaneity.

естéствен|ный (-ен, -на, -но) *прил* natural; **~ные наýки** natural sciences; **~ная смерть** death from natural causes.

естествознáни|е (-я) *ср* natural sciences *мн.*

естествоиспытáтел|ь (-я) *м* (natural) scientist.

есть (*см* **Table 15;** *perf* **поéсть** *или* **съесть)** *несов перех* (*питаться*) to eat; (*perf* **съесть;** *разрушать химически*: *металл*) to corrode; (*no perf*; *раздражать*) to sting, irritate; **мне хóчется ~** I'm hungry; **~** (*impf*) **когó-н глазáми** (*разг*) to gaze at sb.

есть *несов* (*один предмет*) there is; (*много предметов*) there are ◆ *межд*: **~!** (*ВОЕН*) yes, sir!; **~ мнóго возмóжностей** there are many possibilities; **на столé ~ я́блоки** there are apples on the table; **у меня́ ~ друг** I have a friend.

ЕФР *м сокр* (= *Европéйский фонд развúтия*) EDF (= *European Development Fund*).

ефрéйтор (-а) *м* (*ВОЕН*) lance corporal.

éхать (*см* **Table 19)** *несов неперех* to go; (*поезд, автомобиль*: *приближаться*) to come; (: *двигаться*) to go, travel; (*разг*: *скользить*) to slide; **~** (*impf*) **на** *+prp* (*на лошади, на велосипеде*) to ride; **~** (*impf*) *+instr* *или* **на** *+prp* (*на поезде, на автобусом*) to travel *или* go by.

ехúден *прил см* **ехúдный.**

ехúдн|а (-ы) *ж* echidna, spiny anteater.

ехúднича|ть (-ю; *perf* **съехúдничать)** *несов неперех* (*разг*: *язвить*) to make spiteful remarks.

ехúд|ный (-ен, -на, -но) *прил* malicious, spiteful.

ехúдств|о (-а) *ср* (*язвительность*) spite.

ешь *несов см* **есть.**

KEYWORD

ещё *нареч* ***1*** (*дополнительно*) more; **хочý ещё кóфе** I want more coffee; **купú ещё 3 кнúги** buy 3 more books; **нáдо ёще порабóтать** we must do some more work

2 (*опять*: *приеду, позвоню итп*) again; **позвоню́ ещё зáвтра** I'll phone again tomorrow

3 (*до сих пор*) still; **ты ещё не знáешь, что случúлось?** do you still not know what happened?; **нет ещё** not yet

4 (*уже*): **он закóнчил рабóту ещё вчерá** he had already finished the work the day before; **онá уéхала ещё три гóда назáд** she left as long as three years ago; **ещё студéнтом он сдéлал вáжное открытие** while still a student he made an important discovery

5 (*о наличии возможности*) still; **ещё успéю на самолёт** I can still catch the plane
6 (*+comparative*; *лучше, красивее итп*) even; **в результáте он стал ёще богáче** as a result he became even richer
◆ *част* (*усиливает выразительность*): **ещё как рассердúлся/испугáлся** boy, did he get angry/frightened; **дай мне кнúгу! какýю ещё кнúгу!** give me the book! what book for goodness sake!; **всё ещё** still; **онú всё ещё не помирúлись** they still haven't made up; **ещё бы!** (*разг*) you bet!; **вот ещё!** (*разг*) not likely!; **ещё чегó!** (*разг*) not likely!

ЭС *ср сокр* (= *Европéйское экономúческое соóбщество*) EEC (= *European Economic Community*).

éю *мест см* **онá**.

~ Ж, ж ~

Ж, ж *сущ нескл* (*буква*) *the 7th letter of the Russian alphabet.*
ж *союз, част см* **же**.
жа́б|а (-ы) *ж* (*зоол*) toad.
жабо́ *ср нескл* jabot.
жа́бр|а (-ы) *ж* (*зоол*: *обычно мн*) gill; **брать (взять** *perf*) **за ~ы кого́-н** (*разг*) to twist sb's arm.
жа́ворон|ок (-ка) *м* (*зоол*) lark.
жа́ден *прил см* **жа́дный**.
жа́дин|а (-ы) *м/ж* (*разг: пренебр*) meanie.
жа́днича|ть (-ю; *perf* **пожа́дничать**) *несов неперех* (*разг*) to be mingy.
жа́дност|ь (-и) *ж*: ~ (**к** +*dat*) (*к вещам, к деньгам*) greed (for); (*к жизни*) lust (for); (*к развлечениям*) desire (for); ~ **к еде́** greed; **с ~ю** (*есть*) greedily; (*слушать, смотреть*) avidly.
жа́д|ный (-ен, -на́, -но) *прил* greedy; (*на работу*) eager.
жа́жд|а (-ы) *ж* thirst; ~ **зна́ний** (*перен*) thirst for knowledge; ~ +*infin* eagerness to do; **утоля́ть (утоли́ть** *perf*) **~у** to quench one's thirst.
жа́жд|ать (-у, -ешь) *несов неперех*: ~ +*gen* (*перен*: *мира*) to long for; ~ (*impf*) +*infin* (*познавать*) to long to do.
жаке́т (-а) *м* (woman's) jacket.
жал(ся) *итп несов см* **жать(ся)**.
жале́|ть (-ю; *perf* **пожале́ть**) *несов перех* to feel sorry for; (*скупиться*) to grudge ◆ *неперех*: ~ **о** +*prp* to regret; **не ~я сил** sparing no effort; ~ **(пожале́ть** *perf*), **что ...** to regret that ....
жа́л|ить (-ю, -ишь; *perf* **ужа́лить**) *несов перех* (*подлеж*: *оса*) to sting; (: *змея*) to bite.
жа́л|кий (-кая, -кое, -кие; -ок, -ка, -ко) *прил* (*вид*) pitiful, pathetic; (*одежда*) shabby; (*трус*) abject.
жа́лко *как сказ* = **жаль**.
жа́л|о (-а) *ср* (*пчелы*) sting; (*змеи*) forked tongue.
жа́лоб|а (-ы) *ж* complaint; **подава́ть (пода́ть** *perf*) **~у на кого́-н** to lodge a complaint against sb.
жа́лоб|ный (-ен, -на, -но) *прил* (*голос, песня*) plaintive; (*лицо*) sorrowful; **жа́лобная кни́га** complaints book (*in shop, post office etc*).
жалова́нь|е (-я) *ср* salary.
жа́л|овать (-ую) *несов перех* (*разг*): **колле́ги его́ не ~уют** he is not very popular with his colleagues
▸ **жа́ловаться** (*perf* **пожа́ловаться**) *несов возв*: **~ся на** +*acc* to complain about; (*разг*: *ябедничать*) to tell on.
жа́лок *прил см* **жа́лкий**.
жа́лостен *прил см* **жа́лостный**.
жа́лостлив|ый (-, -а, -о) *прил* sympathetic.
жа́лост|ный (-ен, -на, -но) *прил* mournful; ~ **фильм** tear-jerker.
жа́лост|ь (-и) *ж*: ~ **к** +*dat* sympathy for; **кака́я ~** what a shame; **де́лать (сде́лать** *perf*) **что-н из ~и** to do sth out of pity.

KEYWORD

жаль *как сказ* ***1*** (+*acc*; *о сострадании*): **(мне) жаль дру́га** I am sorry for my friend
2 (+*acc или* +*gen*; *о сожалении, о досаде*): **(мне) жаль вре́мени/де́нег** I grudge the time/money
3 (+*infin*): **жаль уезжа́ть так бы́стро** it's a pity *или* shame to leave so soon; **жаль, что ты меня́ не понима́ешь** it's a pity *или* shame you don't understand me
◆ *вводн сл* (*к сожалению*) unfortunately; **хоте́л пое́хать в Ло́ндон, да, жаль, нет вре́мени** I wanted to go to London, but unfortunately I didn't have time.

жанр (-а) *м* (*лирический*) genre; (*перен*) style.
жар (-а; *part gen* **-у**, *loc sg* **-у́**) *м* (*тепло*) heat; (*перен*) fervour (*BRIT*), fervor (*US*); (*МЕД*) fever; **его́ бро́сило в ~** (*перен*) he broke out in a sweat.
жар|а́ (-ы́) *ж* heat.
жарго́н (-а) *м* slang; (*профессиональный*) jargon.
жа́реный *прил* (*на сковороде*) fried; (*в духовке*) roast.
жа́р|ить (-ю, -ишь; *perf* **зажа́рить**) *несов перех* (*на сковороде*) to fry; (*в духовке*) to roast
▸ **жа́риться** (*perf* **зажа́риться**) *несов возв* to fry; **~ся** (*impf*) **на со́лнце** (*разг*) to bask in the sun.
жа́рк|а (-и) *ж* frying.
жа́р|кий (-кая, -кое, -кие; -ок, -ка́, -ко) *прил* hot; (*перен*) heated; **жа́ркие стра́ны** tropical countries.
жа́рко *нареч* (*спорить*) heatedly; (*целовать*) passionately ◆ *как сказ* it's hot; **мне́ ~** I'm hot; **ему́ ни хо́лодно ни ~** (*разг*) it's all the same to him.
жарк|о́е (-о́го; *decl like adj*) *ср* meat (*fried*).
жа́рок *прил см* **жа́ркий**.
жаропонижа́ющ|ий (-ая, -ее, -ие) *прил* febrifugal.

жаропрóч|ный (-ен, -на, -но) *прил* (*материал*) heat-resistant; (*посуда*) ovenproof.
жар-птúц|а (-ы) *ж* Firebird.
жáрче *сравн прил от* **жáркий**.
жасмúн (-а) *м* jasmine.
жáтв|а (-ы) *ж* harvest.
жать (жму, жмёшь) *несов перех* (*руку*) to shake; (*лимон, сок*) to squeeze; **(жну, жнёшь;** *perf* **сжать**; to harvest; **сапогú мне жмут**; my boots are pinching (my feet); **э́то плáтье жмёт в тáлии**; this dress is too tight at the waist;
▸ **жáться; жмусь, жмёшься)** ◆ *несов возв* (*от холода*) to huddle up; (*разг: колебаться*) to dither; (: *скупиться*) to be stingy.
жвáч|ка (-ки; *gen pl* **-ек)** *ж* cud; (*разг: жевательная резинка*) chewing gum.
жгу(сь) *итп несов см* **жечь(ся)**.
жгут (-á) *м* (*из соломы*) rope; (*МЕД*) tourniquet.
жгýч|ий (-ая, -ее, -ие; -, -а, -е) *прил* (*также перен*) burning; (*мороз*) biting; **жгýчий брюнéт** *man with jet-black hair*.
ж.д. *сокр* **(= желéзная дорóга)** R., r. (= *railway*), RR (*US*) (= *railroad*).
ж/д *сокр* = **ж.д.**
ж.-д. *сокр* = **ж.д.**
жд|ать (-у, -ёшь; *pt* **-ал, -алá, -áло)** *несов перех* (*also +gen*; *письмо, дождя, гостей*) to expect; (*друга, поезда*) to wait for; (*надеяться: награды, пощады*) to hope for; **что нас ~ёт?** what's in store for us?; **~áли, что он извинúтся** they hoped that he would apologize; **врéмя не ~ёт** there's no time to lose; **я ~у не дождýсь канúкул** (*разг*) I can't wait for the holidays.

KEYWORD

же *союз* **1** (*при противопоставлении*) but; **я не люблю́ матемáтику, литератýру же обожáю** I don't like mathematics, but I love literature
2 (*вводит дополнительные сведения*) and; **успéх зáвисит от налúчия ресýрсов, ресýрсов же мáло** success depends on the presence of resources, and the resources are insufficient
◆ *част* **1** (*ведь*): **вы́пей ещё чáю, хóчешь же!** have more tea, you want some, don't you?
2 (*именно*): **придý сейчáс же** I'll come right now; **когдá же ты уйдёшь?** when will you go then?
3 (*выражает сходство*): **такóй же** the same; **такóй же дом** the same (kind of) house; **в э́том же годý** this very year; **те же лю́ди** the same (kind of) people.

жевáть (-ую́) *несов перех* to chew.
жёг(ся) *итп несов см* **жечь(ся)**.
жезл (-а) *м* baton.
желáнен *прил см* **желáнный**.
желáни|е (-я) *ср* (*просьба*) request; **~** *+gen/+infin* desire for/to do; **горéть** *(impf)* **~м** *+infin* to be eager to do.
желáн|ный (-ен, -на, -но) *прил* (*гость, весть*) welcome.
желáтелен *прил см* **желáтельный**.
желáтельно *как сказ*: **~** *+infin* it is desirable to do; **~, чтóбы Вы пришлú** it would be preferable if you could come.
желáтел|ьный (-ен, -ьна, -ьно) *прил* desirable.
желá|ть (-ю; *perf* **пожелáть)** *несов неперех* (*+gen*) to desire; **~ (пожелáть** *perf***)** *+infin* to wish *или* want to do; **~ (пожелáть** *perf***) комý-н счáстья/всегó хорóшего** to wish sb happiness/all the best; **Вáша рабóта оставляéт ~ лýчшего** your work leaves much to be desired.
желáющ|ий (-его; *decl like adj***)** *м* (*обычно мн*): **~ие поéхать/порабóтать** those interested in going/working; **~ие есть?** is anybody interested?
желвáк (-á) *м* (*разг*) lump.
желé *ср нескл* jelly.
жел|езá (-ы́; *nom pl* **-езы**, *gen pl* **-ёз**, *dat pl* **-езáм)** *ж* gland.
железнодорóжник (-а) *м* rail(way) (*BRIT*) *или* railroad (*US*) worker.
железнодорóжный *прил* (*вокзал*) railway *опред* (*BRIT*), railroad *опред* (*US*); (*транспорт*) rail *опред*.
желéзн|ый *прил* (*также перен*) iron; (: *логика*) cast-iron; **~ые нéрвы** nerves of steel; **желéзная дорóга** railway (*BRIT*), railroad (*US*).
желéз|о (-а) *ср* iron.
железобетóн (-а) *м* reinforced concrete.
жёлоб (-а; *nom pl* **-á)** *м* (*водосточный*) gutter.
желтé|ть (-ю; *perf* **пожелтéть)** *несов неперех* to turn yellow; (*no perf*; *виднеться*) to show yellow.
желт|óк (-кá) *м* yolk.
желторóт|ый (-, -а, -о) *прил* yellow-beaked (*of young birds*); (*разг: пренебр*): **он ещё ~ юнéц** he's still wet behind the ears.
желтýх|а (-и) *ж* jaundice.
жёлт|ый (-, -á, -о) *прил* yellow; **жёлтая прéсса** the gutter press.
желýд|ок (-ка) *м* (*АНАТ*) stomach; **расстрóйство ~ка** stomach upset.
желýдочный *прил* (*боль*) stomach *опред*; (*сок*) gastric.
жёлуд|ь (-я) *м* acorn.
жёлч|ный *прил*: **~ пузы́рь** gall bladder; **(-ен, -на, -но;** *перен***)** bilious.
жёлч|ь (-и) *ж* (*также перен*) bile.
жемáн|ный (-ен, -на, -но) *прил* affected.
жéмчуг (-а; *nom pl* **-á)** *м* pearls *мн*; **бýсы из ~а** pearl necklace.
жемчýжин|а (-ы) *ж* pearl; (*перен*) treasure.
жемчýжный *прил* pearl; (*перен: зубы*) pearly.
жен|á (-ы́; *nom pl* **жёны**, *gen pl* **жён)** *ж* wife.
женáт|ый (-, -ы) *прил* married (*of man*); **он**

женат на *+prp* he is married to; **они ~ы** they are married.
Женев|а (**-ы**) *ж* Geneva.
жен|ить (**-ю, -ишь**) *(не)сов перех* (*сына, внука*): **~ (на** *+prp***)** to marry (off) (to); (*perf* **поженить**; *разг*) to marry
▸ **жениться** *(не)сов возв*: **~ся на** *+prp* to marry (*of man*); (*perf* **пожениться**; *разг*) to get hitched.
жених (**-а**) *м* (*до свадьбы*) fiancé; (*на свадьбе*) (bride)groom.
женоненавистник (**-а**) *м* misogynist, woman-hater.
женоподоб|ный (**-ен**) *прил* effeminate.
женск|ий (**-ая, -ое, -ие**) *прил* (*одежда, раздевалка*) women's; (*логика, органы*) female; **женская консультация** ≈ gynaecological and antenatal (*BRIT*) *или* gynecological and prenatal (*US*) clinic; **женский пол** the female sex; **женский род** feminine gender.
женственный *прил* feminine.
женщин|а (**-ы**) *ж* woman.
женьшен|ь (**-я**) *м* ginseng.
жерд|ь (**-и**; *gen pl* **-ей**) *ж* pole.
жереб|ёнок (**-ёнка**; *nom pl* **-ята**, *gen pl* **-ят**) *м* foal.
жереб|ец (**-ца**) *м* stallion.
жереб|иться (*3sg* **-ится**, *3pl* **-ятся**, *perf* **ожеребиться**) *несов возв* to foal.
жеребца *итп сущ см* **жеребец**.
жеребьёв|ка (**-ки**; *gen pl* **-ок**) *ж* casting *или* drawing of lots.
жеребята *итп сущ см* **жеребёнок**.
жерл|о (**-а**; *nom pl* **-а**) *ср* (*пушки, вулкана*) mouth.
жёрнов (**-а**; *nom pl* **-а**) *м* millstone.
жертв|а (**-ы**) *ж* victim; (*РЕЛ*) sacrifice; **приносить (принести** *perf***) кого-н/что-н в ~у кому-н/чему-н** to sacrifice sb/sth for sb/sth; **человеческие ~ы** casualties; **пасть** *(perf)* **~ой чего-н** to fall victim to sth.
жертв|овать (**-ую**; *perf* **пожертвовать**) *несов неперех* (*+instr*) to sacrifice ◆ *перех* to donate.
жертвоприношени|е (**-я**) *ср* (*РЕЛ*) sacrifice; **совершать (совершить** *perf***) ~** to offer up a sacrifice.
жест (**-а**) *м* gesture; **язык жестов** sign language.
жестикулир|овать (**-ую**) *несов неперех* to gesticulate.
жёст|кий (**-кая, -кое, -кие**; **-ок, -ка, -ко**) *прил* (*кровать, человек*) hard; (*мясо*) tough; (*волосы*) coarse; (*условия*) strict; **жёсткий вагон** *railway carriage with hard seats*; **жёсткая вода** hard water; **жёсткий диск** hard disk.
жесток|ий (**-ая, -ое, -ие**; **-, -а, -о**) *прил* cruel; (*перен*) severe; **~ая необходимость** cruel necessity.
жестоко *нареч* (*расправиться*) cruelly.
жестокост|ь (**-и**) *ж* cruelty.
жёстче *сравн прил от* **жёсткий**.
жест|ь (**-и**) *ж* *tin-plated sheet metal*.
жестян|ка (**-ки**; *gen pl* **-ок**) *ж* tin box.
жетон (**-а**) *м* tag; (*в метро*) token.
жечь (**жгу, жжёшь** *итп*, **жгут**; *pt* **жёг, жгла, жгло**, *perf* **сжечь**) *несов перех* to burn
▸ **жечься** *несов возв* (*утюг*) to be very hot; (*крапива*) to sting; (*perf* **обжечься**; *разг*) to burn o.s.
жжени|е (**-я**) *ср* burning sensation.
жжёшь(ся) *итп несов см* **жечь(ся)**.
живител|ьный (**-ен, -ьна, -ьно**) *прил* (*воздух*) invigorating.
живо *нареч* (*представить себе*) vividly; (*откликнуться*) animatedly.
жив|ой (**-, -а, -о**) *прил* alive; (*no short form*; *организм*) living; (*животное*) live; (*человек*: *энергичный*) lively; (*выразительный*) vivid; **~ пример** a living example; **он ~ надеждой/воспоминаниями** he lives in hope/for his memories; **он ещё ~?** is he still alive?; **жив – здоров** (*разг*) alive and well; **в нем ещё ~а обида** the insult still rankles with him; **ни жив ни мёртв** (*разг*) petrified; **задевать (задеть** *perf***) кого-н за ~ое** to cut sb to the quick; **остаться** *(perf)* **в ~ых** to survive; **живая изгородь** hedge; **живой уголок** *area in school where pets are kept for pupils to look after*; **живой язык** living language; **живые цветы** fresh flowers.
живописен *прил см* **живописный**.
живопис|ец (**-ца**) *м* painter.
живопис|ный (**-ен, -на, -но**) *прил* picturesque.
живописца *итп сущ см* **живописец**.
живопис|ь (**-и**) *ж* (*искусство*) painting.
живот (**-а**) *м* stomach, abdomen; (*разг*) belly, tummy.
животновод (**-а**) *м* *farmer specializing in animal husbandry*.
животноводств|о (**-а**) *ср* animal husbandry.
животн|ое (**-ого**; *decl like adj*) *ср* (*также перен*) animal.
животный *прил* animal *опред*; (*перен*) bestial.
животрепещущ|ий (**-ая, -ее, -ие**) *прил* topical.
живу *итп несов см* **жить**.
живуч|ий (**-ая, -ее, -ие**; **-, -а, -е**) *прил* hardy; (*обычай, представление*) enduring; (*предрассудки*) deep-rooted; **он ~ как кошка** he has nine lives.
живьём *нареч* alive.
жид|кий (**-кая, -кое, -кие**) *прил* liquid; (**-ок, -ка, -ко**; *молоко, суп*) watery; (*состояние, мускулы, голос*) weak; (*волосы*) sparse, thin; **жидкое топливо** liquid fuel.
жидкост|ь (**-и**) *ж* liquid.
жидок *прил см* **жидкий**.
жиж|а (**-и**) *ж* slurry.
жиже *сравн прил от* **жидкий**.
жизнедеятельност|ь (**-и**) *ж* (*организма, клетки*) (vital) activity.
жизнен|ный (**-, -на, -но**) *прил* (*вопрос, интересы*) vital; (*необходимость*) basic; **~ уровень** standard of living; **~ опыт** experience;

~ **путь** journey through life.
жизнера́дост|ный (**-ен, -на, -но**) *прил* cheerful.
жизнеспосо́б|ный (**-ен, -на, -но**) *прил* (*также перен*) viable.
жизн|ь (**-и**) *ж* life; **о́браз жи́зни** way of life; **у́ровень жи́зни** standard of living; **как ~?** (*разг*) how's life?
жи́л|а (**-ы**) *ж* (*также ГЕО*) vein; (*сухожилие*) tendon, sinew; **золота́я ~** (*перен: разг*) gold mine.
жиле́т (**-а**) *м* waistcoat (*BRIT*), vest (*US*); **спаса́тельный ~** life jacket.
жил|е́ц (**-ьца́**) *м* (*квартиросъёмщик*) tenant; (*квартирант*) lodger; **он не ~** (*разг*) he's not long for this world.
жи́листый (**-, -а, -о**) *прил* (*мясо*) stringy; (*старик*) sinewy; (*рука*) veiny.
жили́щ|е (**-а**) *ср* (*дом*) dwelling.
жили́щный *прил* housing *опред*.
жи́л|ка (**-ки**; *gen pl* **-ок**) *ж* vein; (*перен: склонность*) streak.
жило́й *прил* (*дом, здание*) residential; (*комната, помещение*) inhabited; **жила́я пло́щадь** accommodation.
жи́лок *сущ см* **жи́лка**.
жилпло́щад|ь (**-и**) *ж сокр* = **жила́я пло́щадь**.
жиль|ё (**-я́**) *ср* (*человеческое*) habitation; (*жилище*) accommodation (*BRIT*), lodgings *мн*.
жильца́ *итп сущ см* **жиле́ц**.
жи́молост|ь (**-и**) *ж* honeysuckle.
жир (**-а**; *part gen* **-у**, *loc sg* **-у́**, *nom pl* **-ы́**) *м* (*животный*) fat; (*растительный*) oil; **с жи́ру беси́ться** (*impf*) (*разг*) to become spoilt; **ры́бий ~** (*МЕД*) cod-liver oil.
жира́ф (**-а**) *м* giraffe.
жи́рен *прил см* **жи́рный**.
жире́|ть (**-ю**; *perf* **разжире́ть** *или* **ожире́ть**) *несов неперех* to grow fat.
жи́р|ный (**-ен, -на́, -но**) *прил* (*пища*) fatty; (*человек*) fat; (*no short form*; *волосы*) greasy; (*чернозём, известь*) rich; **жи́рный шрифт** bold type.
жирови́к (**-а́**) *м* lipoma.
жирорасчёт (**-а**) *м* Giro.
жите́йск|ий (**-ая, -ое, -ие**) *прил* (*мудрость*) worldly; (*проблемы*) everyday; **де́ло ~ое!** (*разг*) that's nothing unusual!
жи́тел|ь (**-я**) *м* resident; **городско́й ~** city dweller.
жи́тельниц|а (**-ы**) *ж см* **жи́тель**.
жи́тельств|о (**-а**) *ср* residence; **ме́сто постоя́нного ~а** permanent place of residence.
жи́тниц|а (**-ы**) *ж* (*перен*) breadbasket.
жи|ть (**-ву́, -вёшь**; *pt* **-л, -ла́, -ло**) *несов неперех* to live; (*также перен*): **~ в** *+prp* to live in; **~** (*impf*) *+instr* (*детьми, наукой*) to live for; **~** (*impf*) **на** *+acc*/**с** *+instr* to live on/with; **~** (*impf*) **на свои́ сре́дства** to support o.s.; **~л-был** there once was, once upon a time there was
▸ **жи́ться** *несов безл* (*разг*): **ему́ ве́село/тоскли́во ~вётся** he's having a good/miserable time; **как Вам ~вётся?** how's life?
жмот (**-а**) *м* (*разг*) skinflint.
жму(сь) *итп несов см* **жа́ть(ся)**.
жму́р|ить (**-ю, -ишь**; *perf* **зажму́рить**) *несов неперех*: **~ глаза́** to screw up one's eyes
▸ **жму́риться** (*perf* **зажму́риться**) *несов возв* to squint; **~ся (зажму́риться** *perf*) **от све́та** to squint in the light.
жму́р|ки (**-ок**) *мн* blind man's buff *ед*; **игра́ть** (*impf*) **в ~** to play blind man's buff.
жнец (**-а́**) *м* reaper.
жни́ц|а (**-ы**) *ж см* **жнец**.
жну *итп несов см* **жать**.
жоке́|й (**-я**) *м* jockey.
жонглёр (**-а**) *м* juggler.
жонгли́р|овать (**-ую**) *несов неперех*: **~** *+instr* to juggle (with).
жо́п|а (**-ы**) *ж* (*груб!*) arse (*BRIT*) (*!*), ass (*US*) (*!*)
жр|ать (**-у, -ёшь**; *pt* **-ал, -ала́, -а́ло**, *perf* **сожра́ть**) *несов перех* (*разг*) to scoff.
жре́би|й (**-я**) *м*: **броса́ть ~** to cast lots.
жрец (**-а́**) *м* (*РЕЛ*) (pagan) priest; (*перен*) devotee.
жри́ц|а (**-ы**) *ж* (*РЕЛ*) (pagan) priestess.
ЖСК *м сокр* (= *жили́щно-строи́тельный кооперати́в*) *housing cooperative*.
жу́желиц|а (**-ы**) *ж* ground beetle.
жужж|а́ть (**-у́, -и́шь**) *несов неперех* to buzz.
жук (**-а́**) *м* beetle.
жу́лик (**-а**) *м* swindler; (*в игре*) cheat.
жу́льнича|ть (**-ю**; *perf* **сжу́льничать**) *несов неперех* (*разг*) to cheat.
жу́льничеств|о (**-а**) *ср* underhandedness; (*в игре*) cheating.
жура́вл|ь (**-я́**) *м* crane.
жур|и́ть (**-ю́, -и́шь**) *несов перех* (*разг*) to chide.
журна́л (**-а**) *м* magazine; (*судовой*) journal; (*классный*) register; (*КИНО*) short; **~ протоко́лов** minute book.
журнали́ст (**-а**) *м* journalist.
журнали́ст|ка (**-ки**; *gen pl* **-ок**) *ж см* **журнали́ст**.
журнали́стик|а (**-и**) *ж* journalism.
журнали́сток *сущ см* **журнали́стка**.
журч|а́ть (**-у́, -и́шь**) *несов неперех* (*ручей итп*) to babble, murmur.
жу́т|кий (**-кая, -кое, -кие; -ок, -ка́, -ко**) *прил* terrible.
жу́тко *нареч* (*неприятный*) terribly ◆ *как сказ*: **здесь ~** it's terrifying here; **мне ~** I am terrified.
жу́ток *прил см* **жу́ткий**.
жут|ь (**-и**) *ж* (*разг*) terror ◆ *как сказ* it's terrible; **кака́я ~!** (*разг*) how terrible!
жу́хлый *прил* faded.
ЖЭК (**-а**) *м сокр* (= *жили́щно-эксплуатацио́нная конто́ра*) ≈ housing office.
жюри́ *ср нескл* panel of judges.

~З, з~

З, з *сущ нескл (буква) the 8th letter of the Russian alphabet.*

з. *сокр* (= **за́пад**) W (= *West*); (= **за́падный**) W (= *West*).

KEYWORD

за *предл (+acc)* ***1*** out (of); **вы́йти** *(perf)* **за дверь** to go out (of) the door
2 *(позади)* behind; **спря́таться** *(perf)* **за де́рево** to hide behind a tree
3 *(около: сесть, встать)* at; **сесть** *(perf)* **за стол** to sit down at the table
4 *(свыше какого-н предела)* over; **ему́ за со́рок** he is over forty; **моро́з за два́дцать гра́дусов** over twenty degrees of frost
5 *(при указании на расстояние, на время)*: **за пять киломе́тров отсю́да** five kilometres (*BRIT*) *или* kilometers (*US*) from here; **за три часа́ до нача́ла спекта́кля** three hours before the beginning of the show; **за э́ти де́сять лет он постаре́л** he has aged over the last ten years
6 *(при указании объекта действия)*: **держа́ться за** *+acc* to hold onto; **ухвати́ться** *(perf)* **за** *+acc* to take hold of; **взять** *(perf)* **кого́-н за́ руку** to take sb by the hand; **взя́ться** *(perf)* **за рабо́ту** to start work
7 *(об объекте чувств)* for; **ра́доваться** *(impf)* **за сы́на** to be happy for one's son; **отвеча́ть** *(impf)* **за успе́х предприя́тия** to be responsible for the success of an enterprise; **беспоко́иться** *(impf)* **за му́жа** to worry about one's husband
8 *(о цели)* for; **сража́ться** *(impf)* **за побе́ду** to fight for victory
9 *(в пользу)* for, in favour (*BRIT*) *или* favor (*US*) of; **голосова́ть** *(impf)* **за предложе́ние** to vote for *или* in favour (*BRIT*) *или* favor (*US*) of a proposal
10 *(по причине, в обмен)* for; **благодарю́ Вас за по́мощь** thank you for your help; **плати́ть (заплати́ть** *perf*) **за что-н** to pay for sth; **быть** *(impf)* **нака́занным за воровство́** to be punished for stealing; **я сде́лал э́то за де́ньги** I did it for money
11 *(вместо кого-н)* for; **рабо́тать** *(impf)* **за дру́га** to fill in for a friend
◆ *предл (+instr)* ***1*** *(по другую сторону)* on the other side of; **жить** *(impf)* **за реко́й** to live on the other side of the river
2 *(вне)* outside; **жить** *(impf)* **за́ го́родом** to live outside the town; **за грани́цей** abroad
3 *(позади)* behind; **стоя́ть** *(impf)* **за две́рью** to stand behind the door; **я шёл за ним** I walked behind him; **бежа́ть** *(impf/perf)* **за престу́пником** to run after a criminal
4 *(около: стоять, сидеть)* at; **сиде́ть** *(impf)* **за столо́м** to sit at the table
5 *(о смене событий)* after; **год за го́дом** year after year; **за зимо́й идёт весна́** spring comes after winter
6 *(во время чего-н)* over; **поговори́ть** *(perf)* **за за́втраком** to talk over breakfast
7 *(о объекте внимания)*: **смотре́ть** *или* **уха́живать за** *+instr* to look after; **моя́ сестра́ за́мужем за врачо́м** my sister is married to a doctor
8 *(с целью получить, достать что-н)* for; **я посла́л его́ за газе́той** I sent him out for a paper; **он пошёл за врачо́м** he went to fetch the doctor
9 *(по причине)* owing to; **за отсу́тствием доказа́тельств** in the absence of proof
◆ *как сказ (согласен)* in favour (*BRIT*) *или* favor (*US*); **кто за?** who is in favour (*BRIT*) *или* favor (*US*)?
◆ *ср нескл* pro; **взве́сить** *(perf)* **все за и про́тив** to weigh up all the pros and cons.

за- *префикс (in verbs; о начале действия) indicating beginning of an action eg.* *зааплоди́ровать*; *(о доведении действия до крайней степени) indicating taking sth to an extreme degree eg.* *завра́ться*; *(образует совершенный вид) used in the formation of some perfective aspects eg.* *заасфальти́ровать*; *(in nouns and adjectives; находящийся по ту сторону чего-н)* trans-.

заале́|ть *(3sg* **-ет**, *3pl* **-ют**) *сов неперех* to turn scarlet.

заарка́н|ить (-ю, -ишь; *impf* **заарка́нивать**) *сов неперех* to lasso.

заарта́ч|иться (-усь, -ишься) *сов возв (разг)* to become obstinate.

заасфальти́р|овать (-ую) *сов от* **асфальти́ровать.**

заба́в|а (-ы) *ж* amusement.

заба́вен *прил см* **заба́вный.**

забавля́|ть (-ю) *несов перех* to amuse
▸ **забавля́ться** *несов возв* to amuse o.s.

забáвно *нареч* (*рассказывать*) in an amusing way ◆ *как сказ* it's funny.
забáв|ный (**-ен, -на, -но**) *прил* amusing.
заба ллотир|овать (**-ую**) *сов перех* to reject.
забальзамир|овать (**-ую**) *сов от* **бальзамировать**.
забарахл|и́ть (*3sg* **-и́т**, *3pl* **-я́т**) *сов неперех* (*разг*: *мотор, компьютер итп*) to go on the blink.
забаррикадир|овать (**-ую**) *сов от* **баррикадировать**.
забаст|овáть (**-ýю**) *сов неперех* to go on strike.
забастóв|ка (**-ки**; *gen pl* **-ок**) *ж* strike; **всеобщая** ~ general strike; **сидя́чая** ~ sit-in.
забастóвочный *прил* strike *опред*.
забастóвщик (**-а**) *м* striker.
забастóвщиц|а (**-ы**) *ж см* **забастóвщик**.
забвéни|е (**-я**) *ср* (*забытьё*) oblivion; **предавáть (предáть** *perf*) **что-н ~ю** to consign sth to oblivion.
забéг (**-а**) *м* (*СПОРТ*) race; **предварительный** ~ preliminary heat; ~ **на сто мéтров** the hundred metres.
забéга|ть (**-ю**) *сов неперех* (*люди*) to start running; (*глаза*) to roam about.
забе|жáть (*как* **бежáть**; *см* **Table 20**; *impf* **забегáть**) *сов неперех*: ~ (**в** *+acc*) (*в дом, в деревню*) to run in(to); (*разг*: *в музей*) to drop in(to); **забегáть** (~ *perf*) **к знакóмым** (*разг*) to drop in on one's friends; **забегáть** (~ *perf*) **со стороны́** (*разг*) to come up from the side; **забегáть** (~ *perf*) **вперёд** to run ahead; (*перен*) to race ahead.
заберéмене|ть (**-ю**) *сов от* **берéменеть**.
заберу́(сь) *итп сов см* **забрáть(ся)**.
забеспокó|иться (**-юсь, -ишься**) *сов возв* to start to worry.
забетонир|овать (**-ую**) *сов от* **бетонировать**.
забивá|ть(ся) (**-ю(сь)**) *несов от* **заби́ть(ся)**.
забинт|овáть (**-ýю**; *impf* **бинтовáть** *или* **забинтóвывать**) *сов перех* to bandage.
забирá|ть(ся) (**-ю(сь)**) *несов от* **забрáть(ся)**.
заби́т|ый (**-, -а, -о**) *прил* cowed.
заб|и́ть (**-ью́, -ьёшь**) *сов неперех* (*часы*) to begin to strike; (*орудие, пушка*) to start firing; (*озноб, лихорадка*) to begin to spread; (*вода*) to begin to flow; (*фонтан*) to start up ◆ (*impf* **забивáть**) *перех* (*гвоздь, сваю*) to drive in; (*СПОРТ*: *гол*) to score; (: *мяч, шар*) to drive home; (*окно, дом*) to board up; (*наполнить*: *склад, холодильник*) to overfill; (*засорить*: *трубу, сток*) to clog (up); (*скот, зверя*) to slaughter; (*перен*: *человека*) to knock flat; ~ (*perf*) **в барабáн/кóлокол** to start drumming/ ringing a bell; **забивáть** (~ *perf*) **гóлову чем-н** to fill one's head with sth
▸ **заби́ться** *сов возв* (*сердце, пульс*) to start beating; (*impf* **забивáться**; *спрятаться*) to hide (away); (*засориться*: *труба, сток*) to clog up; **~ся** (*perf*) **в сýдорогах** to have a fit; **~ся** (*perf*) **в истéрике** to have a fit of hysterics.
забия́к|а (**-и**) *м/ж* (*разг*) bully.
заблаговрéменно *нареч* in good time.
заблагорассу́д|иться (*3sg* **-ится**) *сов безл* (*вздуматься*): **поступáйте, как Вам ~ится** act as you see fit.
забле|стéть (**-щу́, -сти́шь**) *сов неперех* (*река, слёзы*) to glisten; (*глаза*) to light up; (*металл*) to gleam.
забл|уди́ться (**-ужу́сь, -у́дишься**) *сов возв* to get lost.
заблу́дш|ий (**-ая, -ее, -ие**) *прил*: ~ **человéк** *person who has lost his or her way*; **заблу́дшая овцá** (*перен*) a lost sheep.
заблуждá|ться (**-юсь**) *несов возв* to be mistaken.
заблуждéни|е (**-я**) *ср* error, delusion; **вводи́ть (ввести́** *perf*) **когó-н в** ~ to delude sb; **выводи́ть (вы́вести** *perf*) **когó-н из ~я** to open sb's eyes.
заблужу́сь *сов см* **заблуди́ться**.
забодá|ть (*3sg* **-ет**, *3pl* **-ют**) *сов от* **бодáть**.
забó|й (**-я**) *м* (*ГЕО*) (working) face; (*действие*: *скота*) slaughtering.
забóйщик (**-а**) *м* face worker.
заболевáемост|ь (**-и**) *ж* (*по стране*) incidence (*of illness*).
заболевáни|е (**-я**) *ср* illness.
заболé|ть (**-ю**; *impf* **заболевáть**) *сов неперех*: ~ *+instr* (*ветрянкой, гриппом*) to fall ill with; (*разг*: *компьютерами, театром итп*) to get hooked on; (*нога, горло*) to begin to hurt.
заболóчен|ный (**-, -а, -о**) *прил* marshy, boggy.
забóр (**-а**) *м* fence.
забóт|а (**-ы**) *ж* (*беспокойство*) worry; (*уход*) concern; (*обычно мн*: *хлопоты*) trouble.
забó|тить (**-чу, -тишь**) *несов перех* to worry, trouble
▸ **забóтиться** (*perf* **позабóтиться**) *несов возв*: **~ся о** *+prp* to take care of.
забóтлив|ый (**-, -а, -о**) *прил* (*человек*) caring, thoughtful.
забóчу(сь) *несов см* **забóтить(ся)**.
забрак|овáть (**-ýю**; *impf* **браковáть** *или* **забракóвывать**) *сов перех* to reject.
забрáл|о (**-а**) *ср* (*у шлема*) visor; (*ТЕХ*) screen.
забрáсыва|ть (**-ю**) *несов от* **забросáть, забрóсить**.
заб|рáть (**-еру́, -ерёшь**; *pt* **-рáл, -рáлá, -рáло**, *impf* **забирáть**) *сов перех* to take; (*разг*: *захватить*) to nick; (*перен*: *подлеж*: *страх, тоска*) to grip; **забирáть** (~ *perf*) **впрáво/ влéво** to veer off to the right/left
▸ **забрáться** (*impf* **забирáться**) *сов возв* (*спрятаться*) to hide (o.s.) away; (*разг*: *уехать*) to go off; **забирáться** (**~ся** *perf*) **в/на**

+acc (*в шкаф, в дом*) to get inside *или* into; (*на дерево*) to climb up; (*в скважину*) to go down; **забира́ться (~ся** *perf*) **под одея́ло** to crawl under the blanket; **забира́ться (~ся** *perf*) **внутрь/наве́рх** to get inside/to the top.
забреда́|ть (**-ю**) *несов от* **забрести́**.
забреду́ *umn cов см* **забрести́**.
забре́зж|ить (*3sg* **-ит**) *сов неперех* (*огонь*) to flicker; (*рассвет, утро*) to break.
забр|ести́ (**-еду́, -едёшь**; *pt* **-ёл, -ела́, -ело́**, *impf* **забреда́ть**) *сов неперех* (*разг*: *в лес*) to saunter off; (: *в гости*) to drop in.
заброни́р|овать (**-ую**) *сов от* **брони́ровать**.
заброса́|ть (**-ю**; *impf* **забра́сывать**) *сов перех*: ~ **что-н чем-н** (*канаву, яму*) to fill with; (*камнями*) to pelt with; (*цветами*) to shower with; (*перен*: *фактами, вопросами*) to bombard with.
забро́|сить (**-шу, -сишь**; *impf* **забра́сывать**) *сов перех* (*мяч, камень*) to fling; (*десант*) to drop; (*шпиона*) to plant; (*разг*: *доставить*) to drop off; (*не заниматься*) to neglect.
забро́шен|ный (**-, -а, -о**) *прил* (*дом*) derelict; (*шахта*) disused; (*вид, сад, ребёнок*) neglected.
забро́шу *сов см* **забро́сить**.
забры́зга|ть (**-ю**; *impf* **забры́згивать**) *сов перех* to splash.
забу́ду(сь) *umn cов см* **забы́ть(ся)**.
забыва́|ть(ся) (**-ю(сь)**) *несов от* **забы́ть(ся)**.
забы́вчив|ый (**-, -а, -о**) *прил* forgetful.
заб|ы́ть (*как* **быть**; *см* **Table 21**; *impf* **забыва́ть**) *сов перех* to forget; **~у́дь туда́/сюда́ доро́гу!** don't go there/come here any more!; **себя́ не забыва́ть** (~ *perf*) to look out for o.s.
▸ **забы́ться** (*impf* **забыва́ться**) *сов возв* (*задремать*) to doze off; (*в мечтах*) to lose o.s.; (*сорваться*) to forget o.s.; (*события, факты*) to be forgotten.
забыть|ё (**-я́**) *ср* (*беспамятство*) oblivion; (*полусон*) drowsiness; (*задумчивость*) pensiveness; **впа́дать (впасть** *perf*) **в** ~ to lose consciousness; (*уснуть*) to doze off.
забью́(сь) *umn cов см* **заби́ть(ся)**.
зав (**-а**) *м сокр* (*разг*: = *заве́дующий*) boss.
зав. *сокр* = **заве́дующий**.
зава́л (**-а**) *м* obstruction; (*искусственный*) barrier; **у нас сейча́с ~ с рабо́той** we have a backlog of work.
зав|али́ть (**-алю́, -а́лишь**; *impf* **зава́ливать**) *сов перех* (*вход, дверь*) to block off; (*дом, стену*) to knock down; (*разг*: *экзамен, мероприятие*) to mess up; **зава́ливать** (~ *perf*) *+instr* (*дорогу*: *снегом*) to cover with; (*яму*: *землёй*) to fill with; (*разг*: *магазины*: *товарами*) to cram with; (*перен*: *разг*: *поручениями*) to saddle with
▸ **завали́ться** (*impf* **зава́ливаться**) *сов возв* (*упасть*) to fall; (*стена, забор*) to collapse; (*разг*: *дело*) to go to the wall; (: *на экзамене*) to come a cropper; **зава́ливаться (~ся** *perf*) **в го́сти к кому́-н** (*разг*) to turn up on sb's doorstep; **(хоть) ~али́сь!** (*разг*: *очень много*) you can't move for them!
заваля́|ться (*3sg* **-ется**, *3pl* **-ются**) *сов возв* (*разг*) to be kicking about.
зав|ари́ть (**-арю́, -а́ришь**; *impf* **зава́ривать**) *сов перех* (*чай, кофе*) to brew; (*ТЕХ*) to weld; **зава́ривать** (~ *perf*) **ка́шу** (*разг*) to stir up trouble
▸ **завари́ться** (*impf* **зава́риваться**) *сов возв* (*чай, кофе*) to brew; (*разг*: *дело, кутерьма*) to start.
зава́рк|а (**-и**) *ж* (*действие*: *чая, кофе*) brewing; (*разг*: *сухой чай*) char; (*заваренный чай*) brew.
заварн|о́й *прил* (*КУЛИН*): **~о́е те́сто** choux pastry; ~ **крем** custard filling.
заведе́ни|е (**-я**) *ср* (*учреждение*) establishment; **учёбное** ~ educational establishment.
заве́д|овать (**-ую**) *несов неперех* (*+instr*) to be in charge of.
заве́домый *прил* (*обманщик, лжец*) notorious; (*обман, ложь*) blatant.
заведу́(сь) *umn cов см* **завести́(сь)**.
заве́дующ|ая (**-ей**) *ж см* **заве́дующий**.
заве́дующ|ий (**-его**; *decl like adj*) *м* (*складом, редакцией*) manager; (*лабораторией, кафедрой*) head.
зав|езти́ (**-езу́, -езёшь**; *pt* **-ёз, -езла́, -езло́**, *impf* **завози́ть**) *сов перех* to drop off; (*увезти*) to take.
заверб|ова́ть (**-у́ю**) *сов от* **вербова́ть**.
завере́ни|е (**-я**) *ср* assurance.
заве́ренный *прил* (*копия, подпись*) authenticated, certified.
завери́тел|ь (**-я**) *м* (*документа, копии*) witness, attestant.
заве́р|ить (**-ю, -ишь**; *impf* **заверя́ть**) *сов перех* (*копию, подпись*) to witness; **заверя́ть** (~ *perf*) **кого́-н в чём-н** to assure sb of sth.
заверн|у́ть (**-у́, -ёшь**; *impf* **завёртывать** *или* **завора́чивать**) *сов перех* (*рукав*) to roll up; (*кран*) to turn up; (*гайку*) to tighten up; (*налево, направо, за угол*) to turn; (*разг*: *в гости, к другу*) to drop by *или* round; **завёртывать** *или* **завора́чивать** (~ *perf*) (**в** *+acc*) (*посылку, книгу, ребёнка*) to wrap (in)
▸ **заверну́ться** (*impf* **завёртываться** *или* **завора́чиваться**) *сов возв* (*рукав*) to roll up; **завёртываться** *или* **завора́чиваться (~ся** *perf*) **в** *+acc* (*в полотенце, в плед*) to wrap o.s. up in.
зав|ерте́ть (**-ерчу́, -е́ртишь**) *сов неперех* (*+instr*; *верёвкой*) to twirl; (*глазами*) to roll
▸ **заверте́ться** *сов возв* (*колесо, карусель*) to start turning; (*разг*: *захлопотаться*) to be run off one's feet.
завёртыва|ть(ся) (**-ю(сь)**) *несов см* **заверну́ть(ся)**.
заверчу́(сь) *сов см* **заверте́ть(ся)**.
заверша́|ть(ся) (**-ю(сь)**) *несов от* **заверши́ть(ся)**.
заверша́ющ|ий (**-ая, -ее, -ие**) *прил* final.
заверше́ни|е (**-я**) *ср* (*работы*) completion;

(*разговора, лекции*) conclusion; **в ~** *+gen* at the conclusion of.
заверш|ить (**-у́, -ишь**; *impf* **заверша́ть**) *сов перех* to complete; (*разговор*) to end
▸ **заверши́ться** (*impf* **заверша́ться**) *сов возв* to be completed; (*разговор*) to end.
заверя́|ть (**-ю**) *несов от* **заве́рить**.
заве́с|а (**-ы**) *ж* (*перен*) veil; **дымова́я ~** (*перен*) smoke screen.
заве́|сить (**-шу, -сишь**; *impf* **заве́шивать**) *сов перех* (*окно*) to curtain; (*картину, лампу*) to cover.
зав|ести́ (**-еду́, -едёшь**; *pt* **-ёл, -ела́, -ело́**, *impf* **заводи́ть**) *сов перех* to take; (*увести далеко*) to lead; (*приобрести*) to get; (*установить*) to introduce; (*переписку, разговор*) to initiate; (*часы*) to wind up; (*машину*) to start; (*разг*: *разозлить*): **~ кого́-н** to wind sb up
▸ **завести́сь** (*impf* **заводи́ться**) *сов возв* (*появиться*) to appear; (*мотор, часы*) to start working; (*разг*: *разозлиться*) to get (all) wound up.
заве́т (**-а**) *м* (*наставление*) precept; (*РЕЛ*): **Ве́тхий/Но́вый ~** the Old/New Testament.
заве́т|ный (**-ен, -на, -но**) *прил* treasured.
заве́ша|ть (**-ю**; *impf* **заве́шивать**) *сов перех* to hang; **заве́шивать (~** *perf*) **сте́ны карти́нами** to hang pictures on the walls.
заве́шива|ть (**-ю**) *несов от* **заве́сить**, **заве́шать**.
заве́шу *сов см* **заве́сить**.
завеща́ни|е (**-я**) *ср* (*документ*) will; (*наставление*) precept.
завеща́|ть (**-ю**) *(не)сов перех*: **~ что-н кому́-н** (*наследство*) to bequeath sth to sb; **~** *(impf/perf)* **кому́-н** *+infin* to call upon sb to do.
завзя́тый *прил* (*разг*: *курильщик*) inveterate; **он ~ футболи́ст/охо́тник** he is a football/hunting fanatic.
завива́|ть(ся) (**-ю(сь)**) *несов от* **зави́ть(ся)**.
зави́вк|а (**-и**) *ж* (*волос*) curling; (*причёска*) curly hair.
зави́ден *прил см* **зави́дный**.
зави́дно *нареч*: **он ~ краси́в/умён** he has enviable good looks/intelligence ◆ *как сказ*: **~ как она́ говори́т по-англи́йски** her English is enviable; **ему́ ~** he feels envious.
зави́д|ный (**-ен, -на, -но**) *прил* enviable.
зави́д|овать (**-ую**; *perf* **позави́довать**) *несов неперех* (*+dat*) to envy, be jealous of.
завизж|а́ть (**-у́, -и́шь**) *сов неперех* to begin to yelp.
завизи́р|овать (**-ую**) *сов от* **визи́ровать**.
завин|ти́ть (**-чу́, -ти́шь**; *impf* **зави́нчивать**) *сов перех* to tighten (up).
завира́|ться (**-юсь**) *несов от* **завра́ться**.
зави́|сеть (**-шу, -сишь**) *несов неперех*: **~ от** *+gen* to depend on.
зави́симост|ь (**-и**) *ж* (*отношение*) correlation; **~ (от** *+gen*) dependence (on); **в ~и от** *+gen* depending on.
зави́сим|ый (**-, -а, -о**) *прил* (*человек, страна*) dependent; **~ от** *+gen* (*погоды, обстоятельств*) dependent on.
зави́стлив|ый (**-, -а, -о**) *прил* envious.
за́вист|ь (**-и**) *ж* envy, jealousy; **она́ вы́глядит на ~ хорошо́** (*разг*) it makes you sick how well she looks.
завитка́ *сущ см* **завито́к**.
завито́й *прил* (*волосы*) curly; (*девушка*) curly-haired; (*проволока, шнур*) coiled.
завит|о́к (**-ка́**) *м* (*локон*) curl; (*спирали*) twist; (*орнамента*) flourish, whorl.
зав|и́ть (**-ью, -ьёшь**; *pt* **-и́л, -ила́, -ило́**, *impf* **завива́ть**) *сов перех* (*волосы, усы*) to curl; (*проволоку, шнур*) to twist
▸ **зави́ться** (*impf* **завива́ться**) *сов возв* (*волосы, усы*) to curl; (*проволока, шнур*) to get twisted; (*сделать завивку*) to curl one's hair.
завихре́ни|е (**-я**) *ср* whirl; (*перен*) peculiarity.
зави́шу *несов см* **зави́сеть**.
завладе́|ть (**-ю**; *impf* **завладева́ть**) *сов неперех* (*+instr*; *имуществом*) to take possession of; (*ВОЕН, вниманием*) to capture.
завл|е́чь (**-еку́, -ечёшь** *итп*, **-еку́т**; *pt* **-ёк, -екла́, -екло́**, *impf* **завлека́ть**) *сов перех* (*зверя, врага*) to lure; (*перен*) to captivate.
заво́д (**-а**) *м* factory; (*в часах, у игрушки*) clockwork; (*действие*) winding up; **ко́нный ~** stud farm.
зав|оди́ть(ся) (**-ожу́(сь), -о́дишь(ся)**) *несов от* **завести́(сь)**.
заводно́й *прил* (*механизм, игрушка*) clockwork *опред*; (*ключ, ручка*) winding *опред*; (*разг*: *человек*) easily excitable.
заводско́й *прил* factory *опред*.
за́водь (**-и**) *ж* backwater.
завоева́ни|е (**-я**) *ср* (*земель, страны*) conquest; (*обычно мн*: *достижения*) achievement.
завоева́тел|ь (**-я**) *м* conqueror.
завоева́тельн|ый *прил* (*политика*) aggressive; (*набеги*) offensive; **~ые во́йны** wars of conquest.
заво|ева́ть (**-ю́ю**; *impf* **завоёвывать**) *сов перех* to conquer; (*перен*: *доверие*) to win.
завожу́ *несов см* **заводи́ть**, **завози́ть**.
завожу́сь *несов см* **заводи́ться**.
заво́з (**-а**) *м* delivery.
зав|ози́ть (**-ожу́, -о́зишь**) *несов от* **завезти́**.
заволн|ова́ться (**-у́юсь**) *сов возв* to become agitated.
завора́чива|ть(ся) (**-ю(сь)**) *несов от* **заверну́ть(ся)**.
за́ворот (**-а**) *м*: **~ кишо́к** (*МЕД*) acute intestinal illness.
заворо́т (**-а**) *м* (*реки, дороги*) bend; (*движение*)

turn.
заворч|а́ть (**-у́, -и́шь**) *сов неперех* to start grumbling.
заво́ю *итп сов см* **завы́ть**.
завр|а́ться (**-у́сь, -ёшься**; *pt* **-а́лся, -ала́сь, -а́лось**, *impf* **завира́ться**) *сов возв* (*разг*) to get tied (up) in knots (*by lying*).
завсегда́та|й (**-я**) *м* (*разг*) regular.
за́втра *нареч, ср нескл* tomorrow; **до ~!** see you tomorrow!; **откла́дывать (отложи́ть** *perf*) **что-н на** *или* **до ~** to put sth off until tomorrow.
за́втрак (**-а**) *м* breakfast.
за́втрака|ть (**-ю**; *impf* **поза́втракать**) *несов неперех* to have breakfast.
за́втрашн|ий (**-яя, -ее, -ие**) *прил* tomorrow's; **за́втрашний день** tomorrow.
завуали́р|овать (**-ую**) *сов от* **вуали́ровать**.
за́вуч (**-а**) *м сокр* = *заве́дующий уче́бной ча́стью*; (*в школе, в училище*) ≈ deputy head.
завхо́з (**-а**) *м сокр* = *заве́дующий хозя́йством*; (*в школе, в институте*) bursar; (*на заводе*) *person in charge of supplies*.
завши́ве|ть (**-ю**) *сов от* **вши́веть**.
завыва́ни|е (**-я**) *ср* (*собак, метели*) howling; (*сирены*) wail; (*самолёта*) shriek.
завыва́|ть (**-ю**) *несов неперех* (*собака, метель*) to howl; (*сирена*) to wail; (*самолёт*) to shriek.
завы́|сить (**-шу, -сишь**; *impf* **завыша́ть**) *сов перех* (*нормы, цены*) to increase excessively; **~** (*perf*) **план** to set unreasonable targets.
зав|ы́ть (**-о́ю, -о́ешь**) *сов неперех* (*собака*) to begin to howl; (*сирена*) to start to wail.
завыша́|ть (**-ю**) *несов от* **завы́сить**.
завыше́ни|е (**-я**) *ср* excessive increase.
завы́шен|ный (**-, -а, -о**) *прил* excessively increased.
завы́шу *сов см* **завы́сить**.
завью́(сь) *итп сов см* **зави́ть(ся)**.
зав|яза́ть (**-яза́ю, -яза́ешь**) *несов от* **завя́знуть** ♦ (**-яжу́, -я́жешь**; *impf* **завя́зывать**) *сов перех* (*верёвку, ленту*) to tie; (*руку, посылку*) to bind; (*разговор*) to start (up); (*дружбу*) to form; (*отношение*) to establish; (*разг: пить, воровать*) to quit; **завя́зывать (~** *perf*) **глаза́ кому́-н** to blindfold sb
▸ **завяза́ться** (*impf* **завя́зываться**) *сов возв* (*шнурки, бант*) to be tied; (*разговор*) to start (up); (*дружба*) to form; (*отношения*) to become established; (*БОТ*) to set.
завя́з|ка (**-ки**; *gen pl* **-ок**) *ж* (*тесьма*) band; (*лента*) ribbon; (*разговора, событий*) beginning; (*боя*) onset; (*романа, рассказа*) opening.
завя́зн|уть (**-у, -ешь**; *impf* **завяза́ть** *или* **вя́знуть**) *сов неперех* (*в снегу, в грязи*) to get stuck; (*перен: разг*): **~ в** *+prp* (*в трудностях, в долгах*) to be up to one's neck in.
завя́зок *сущ см* **завя́зка**.
завя́зыва|ть(ся) (**-ю(сь)**) *несов от* **завяза́ть(ся)**.
завя́н|уть (**-у, -ешь**) *сов от* **вя́нуть**.
загада́|ть (**-ю**; *impf* **зага́дывать**) *сов перех* (*загадку*) to set; (*шараду*) to act out; (*число, слово*) to think of; (*желание*) to make ♦ *неперех* (*разг*) to guess.
зага́|дить (**-жу, -дишь**) *сов перех* (*разг*) to mess up.
зага́д|ка (**-ки**; *gen pl* **-ок**) *ж* riddle; (*перен*) puzzle, mystery.
зага́доч|ный (**-ен, -на, -но**) *прил* (*явление, событие*) puzzling, mysterious; (*выражение лица, слова*) enigmatic.
зага́дыва|ть (**-ю**) *несов от* **загада́ть**.
зага́жу *сов см* **зага́дить**.
загазо́ван|ный (**-, -а, -о**) *прил* (*атмосфера*) polluted.
зага́р (**-а**) *м* (sun)tan.
загво́зд|ка (**-и**) *ж* (*разг*) obstacle; **в э́том вся ~** (*разг*) that's the whole problem.
загерметизи́р|овать (**-ую**) *сов от* **герметизи́ровать**.
заги́б (**-а**) *м* (*на бумаге*) crease; (*перен: разг*) twist.
загиба́|ть(ся) (**-ю(сь)**) *несов от* **загну́ть(ся)**.
загипнотизи́р|овать (**-ую**) *сов от* **гипнотизи́ровать**.
загла́ви|е (**-я**) *ср* title.
загла́вн|ый *прил*: **~ая бу́ква** capital letter; **загла́вная роль** title role.
загла́|дить (**-жу, -дишь**; *impf* **загла́живать**) *сов перех* (*складки*) to iron; (*лист*) to fold; (*сгиб*) to make; (*перен: ошибки*) to put right; (*: обиду*) to make up for; **загла́живать (~** *perf*) **вину́** to make amends.
загло́хн|уть (**-у, -ешь**) *сов от* **гло́хнуть** ♦ *неперех* (*сад, тропинка*) to become overgrown; (*перен: разг: стройка, дело*) to die a death.
загло́хш|ий (**-ая, -ее, -ие**) *прил* overgrown.
заглуша́|ть (**-ю**; *perf* **заглуши́ть**) *несов перех* = **глуши́ть**.
загл|уши́ть (**-ушу́, -у́шишь**) *сов от* **глуши́ть, заглуша́ть**.
загляде́нь|е (**-я**) *ср* (*разг*) feast for the eyes.
загля|де́ться (**-жу́сь, -ди́шься**; *impf* **загля́дываться**) *сов возв* to gaze.
загл|яну́ть (**-яну́, -я́нешь**; *impf* **загля́дывать**) *сов неперех* (*в окно, в спальню*) to peep; (*в книгу, в словарь*) to glance; (*разг: к соседу, к друзьям*) to pop in; **загля́дывать (~** *perf*) **вперёд** to take a brief look ahead.
загна́ива|ться (**-юсь**) *несов от* **загнои́ться**.
заг|на́ть (**-оню́, -о́нишь**; *pt* **-на́л, -нала́, -на́ло**, *impf* **загоня́ть**) *сов перех* (*коров, детей*) to drive; (*разг: гвоздь, нож*) to ram in; (*: продать*) to flog (*BRIT*), sell; (*изнурить: лошадь*) to ride too hard; (*: рабочих*) to drive into the ground.
загн|и́ть (**-ию́, -иёшь**; *pt* **-и́л, -ила́, -и́ло**, *impf* **загнива́ть**) *сов неперех* to begin to rot.
загно|и́ться (**-ю́сь, -и́шься**; *impf* **загна́иваться**) *сов возв* (*рана*) to fester; (*глаз*) to become inflamed.
за́гнут|ый (**-, -а, -о**) *прил* bent.

загн|у́ть (**-у́, -ёшь**; *impf* **загиба́ть**) *сов перех* (*гвоздь*) to bend; (*край*) to fold; (*страницу*) to dog-ear; (*разг*: *сказать*) to spout; **загиба́ть** (**~** *perf*) **рука́в вверх/вниз** to pull a sleeve up/down
▸ **загну́ться** (*impf* **загиба́ться**) *сов возв* (*гвоздь*) to bend; (*край*) to fold; (*страница*) to become dog-eared; (*воротник*) to twist; (*разг*: *умереть*) to kick the bucket.
загова́рива|ть (**-ю**) *несов от* **заговори́ть** ◆ *неперех*: **зу́бы ~ кому́-н** (*разг*) to steer sb off a subject
▸ **загова́риваться** *несов возв* (*говорить бессвязно*) to rave.
за́говень|е (**-я**) *ср* (*РЕЛ*) eve of fast, ≈ Shrove Tuesday.
за́говор (**-а**) *м* conspiracy; (*от болезни*) spell.
заговор|и́ть (**-ю́, -и́шь**) *сов неперех* (*начать говорить*) to begin to speak; (*по-английски, по-русски*) to be able to speak; (*перен*: *совесть, гордость итп*) to stir ◆ (*impf* **загова́ривать**) *перех* (*болезнь, боль*) to magic away; **загова́ривать** (**~** *perf*) **кого́-н** to wear sb out through constant talk; **в нём ~и́ла со́весть** his conscience stirred in him.
загово́рщик (**-а**) *м* conspirator.
загово́рщиц|а (**-ы**) *ж см* **загово́рщик**.
заголо́в|ок (**-ка**) *м* headline.
заго́н (**-а**) *м* (*скота, овец*) driving in; (*для скота*) enclosure; (*для овец*) pen; **быть** (*impf*) **в ~е** (*разг*) to be pushed to one side.
загоню́ *итп сов см* **загна́ть**.
загоня́|ть (**-ю**) *несов от* **загна́ть**.
загора́жива|ть(ся) (**-ю(сь)**) *несов от* **загороди́ть(ся)**.
загора́|ть(ся) (**-ю(сь)**) *несов от* **загоре́ть(ся)**.
загоре́л|ый (**-, -а, -о**) *прил* tanned.
загор|е́ть (**-ю́, -и́шь**; *impf* **загора́ть**) *сов неперех* to go brown, get a tan
▸ **загоре́ться** (*impf* **загора́ться**) *сов возв* (*дрова, костёр*) to light; (*здание итп*) to catch fire; (*лампочка, глаза*) to light up; **загора́ться** (**~ся** *perf*) **жела́нием** +*infin* to have a burning desire to do; **он ~е́лся э́той иде́ей** the idea fired his imagination.
за́город (**-а**) *м* (*разг*) the country.
загор|оди́ть (**-ожу́, -о́дишь**; *impf* **загора́живать**) *сов перех* (*улицу, вход*) to block off; (*свет*) to block out; **загора́живать** (**~** *perf*) **кого́-н собо́й** to shield sb; **загора́живать** (**~** *perf*) **кому́-н доро́гу** (*перен*) to stand on sb's way
▸ **загороди́ться** (*impf* **загора́живаться**) *сов возв*: **~ся** (**от** +*gen*) (*от солнца, от удара*) to shield o.s. (from).
загоро́д|ка (**-ки**; *gen pl* **-ок**) *ж* barrier; (*в комнате*) partition.
за́городн|ый *прил* (*экскурсия*) out-of-town; (*дом*) country *опред*; **~ая пое́здка** a trip out of town *или* into the country.
загоро́док *сущ см* **загоро́дка**.
загорожу́(сь) *сов см* **загороди́ть(ся)**.
загота́влива|ть (**-ю**) *несов от* **загото́вить**.
заготови́тел|ь (**-я**) *м person responsible for state procurements of timber, grain etc.*
заготови́тельный *прил*: **~ пункт** collection point; **заготови́тельная цена́** state procurement price.
загото́в|ить (**-лю, -ишь**; *impf* **загота́вливать** *или* **заготовля́ть**) *сов перех* (*сено, корм итп*) to lay in; (*билеты, документы итп*) to prepare.
загото́в|ка (**-ки**; *gen pl* **-ок**) *ж* (*действие*: *кормов, леса итп*) laying in; (*закупка государством*) procurement; (*полуфабрикат*) component; (: *для туфель*) upper.
загото́влю *сов см* **загото́вить**.
заготовля́|ть (**-ю**) *несов от* **загото́вить**.
загото́вок *сущ см* **загото́вка**.
загради́тельн|ый *прил*: **~ое сооруже́ние** barrier; **загради́тельный ого́нь** (*ВОЕН*) defensive fire; **загради́тельный патру́ль** roadblock.
загра|ди́ть (**-жу́, -ди́шь**; *impf* **загражда́ть**) *сов перех* to obstruct.
огражде́ни|е (**-я**) *ср* barrier.
загражу́ *сов см* **загради́ть**.
грани́ц|а (**-ы**) *ж* (*разг*) foreign countries *мн*.
заграни́чный *прил* foreign; **заграни́чный па́спорт** passport (*issued specifically for travel abroad*).
За́греб (**-а**) *м* Zagreb.
загрёб *итп сов см* **загрести́**.
загреба́|ть (**-ю**) *несов от* **загрести́** ◆ *неперех* (*вёслами*) to row; (*руками, лапами*) to paddle ◆ *перех*: **~ де́ньги** (*разг*) to rake in the money.
загребу́ *итп сов см* **загрести́**.
загрем|е́ть (**-лю́, -и́шь**) *сов неперех* (*гром*) to crash out; (*голос*) to thunder; (*тарелки итп*) to start to rattle.
загр|ести́ (**-ебу́, -ебёшь**; *pt* **-ёб, -ебла́, -ебло́**, *impf* **загреба́ть**) *сов перех* (*мусор, листья итп*) to rake up.
загри́в|ок (**-ка**) *м* (*у лошади*) withers *мн*; **взять** (*perf*) **кого́-н за ~** (*разг*) to grab sb by the scruff of the neck.
загримир|ова́ть (**-у́ю**; *impf* **загримиро́вывать** *или* **гримирова́ть**) *сов перех* to make up
▸ **загримирова́ться** (*impf* **загримиро́вываться** *или* **гримирова́ться**) *сов возв* to make o.s. up.
загро́бный *прил*: **~ мир** the next world; (*перен*: *голос*) gloomy; **загро́бная жизнь** the afterlife.
загромоз|ди́ть (**-жу́, -ди́шь**; *impf* **загроможда́ть**) *сов перех* to clutter (up).
загрубе́л|ый (**-, -а, -о**) *прил* (*кожа, руки*) calloused, rough; (*лицо*) coarse; (*голос*) gruff; (*перен*: *человек, душа*) hardened.

загрубе́|ть (-ю) *сов от* **грубе́ть**.
загр|узи́ть (-ужу́, -у́зишь) *сов от* **грузи́ть** ◆ (*impf* **загружа́ть**) *перех* (*машину, судно*) to load up; (*КОМП*) to boot, load up; (*перен*: *сотрудников, учеников*) to load with work; (: *день*) to fill up; (: *печь, домну*) to load.
загру́зк|а (-и) *ж* (*машины, судна*) loading; (*предприятия, станка*) capacity.
загрунт|ова́ть (-у́ю; *impf* **загрунто́вывать** *или* **грунтова́ть**) *сов перех* to prime.
загру|сти́ть (-щу́, -сти́шь) *сов неперех* to become sad; ~ *(perf)* **по до́му** to start to feel homesick.
загр|ы́зть (-ызу́, -ызёшь; *impf* **загрыза́ть**) *сов перех* (*овцу, петуха*) to kill; (*no impf*; *перен*: *разг*: *замучить*) to nag to death; **её ~ы́зла со́весть** she was tormented by her conscience.
загрязне́ни|е (-я) *ср* pollution; **загрязне́ние окружа́ющей среды́** (environmental) pollution.
загрязн|ённый (-ён, -ена́, -ено́) *прил* polluted.
загрязн|и́ть (-ю́, -и́шь) *сов от* **грязни́ть** ◆ (*impf* **загрязня́ть**) *перех* (*воздух, водоём*) to pollute; **загрязня́ть** (~ *perf*) **что-н** (*сапоги, платье итп*) to get sth dirty
▸ **загрязни́ться** *сов от* **грязни́ться** ◆ (*impf* **загрязня́ться**) *возв* (*см перех*) to become polluted; to get dirty.
ЗАГС (-а) *м сокр* (= *за́пись а́ктов гражда́нского состоя́ния*) ≈ registry office.
заг|уби́ть (-ублю́, -у́бишь) *сов от* **губи́ть** ◆ *перех* (*человека*) to destroy; (*растение*) to kill; (*жизнь, вечер*) to ruin; (*разг*: *деньги, средства*) to waste.
загу|де́ть (-жу́, -ди́шь) *сов неперех* (*машина*) to honk; (*гудок*) to sound.
загу́л (-а) *м* (*разг*) drinking session; **уда́риться** *(perf)* **в** ~ to go on a bender.
загуля́|ть (-ю; *impf* **загу́ливать**) *сов неперех* (*разг*: *кутить*) to booze.
загусте́|ть (*3sg* **-ет**, *3pl* **-ют**) *сов от* **густе́ть**.
зад (-а; *part gen* **-у**, *loc sg* **-у́**, *nom pl* **-ы́**, *gen pl* **-о́в**) *м* (*человека*) behind, rear; (*животного*) rump; (*машины, дома*) rear.
зада́брива|ть (-ю) *несов от* **задо́брить**.
зада|ва́ть (-ю́, -ёшь) *несов от* **зада́ть**
▸ **задава́ться** *несов от* **зада́ться** ◆ *возв* (*разг*: *важничать*) to be cocky.
зад|ави́ть (-авлю́, -а́вишь) *сов от* **дави́ть** ◆ *перех* to crush; **её ~ави́ло де́ревом** she was crushed under a tree; **его́ ~ави́ла маши́на** he was run over by a car.
зада́м(ся) *итп сов см* **зада́ть(ся)**.
зада́ни|е (-я) *ср* (*поручение*) task; (*упражнение*) exercise; (*ВОЕН*) mission; **дома́шнее** ~ homework.
зад|ари́ть (-арю́, -а́ришь; *impf* **зада́ривать**) *сов перех*: ~ **кого́-н пода́рками** to shower sb with presents.
зада́ром *нареч* (*разг*: *дёшево*) for next to nothing; (: *зря*) for nothing.
зада́ст(ся) *сов см* **зада́ть(ся)**.
зада́тка *сущ см* **зада́ток**.
зада́тк|и (-ов) *мн* (*о способностях*) ability *ед*.
зада́т|ок (-ка) *м* deposit; **дава́ть (дать** *perf*) ~ to put down a deposit; *см также* **зада́тки**.
зад|а́ть (*как* **дать**; *см* **Table 14**; *impf* **задава́ть**) *сов перех* to set; **задава́ть (**~ *perf*) **кому́-н вопро́с** to ask sb a question; **задава́ть (**~ *perf*) **пир** (*разг*) to lay on a spread; **я тебе́ ~а́м!** (*разг*) just you wait!
▸ **зада́ться** (*impf* **задава́ться**) *сов возв*: **~ся це́лью** +*infin* (*сделать, написать итп*) to set o.s. the task of doing; **~ся** *(perf)* **вопро́сом** to ask o.s.
зада́ч|а (-и) *ж* task; (*МАТ*) problem; **ста́вить (поста́вить** *perf*) **пе́ред собо́й ~у** to set o.s. a task; **реша́ть (реши́ть** *perf*) **~у** to solve a problem.
зада́чник (-а) *м* book of problems.
зада́шь(ся) *сов см* **зада́ть(ся)**.
задви́га|ть (-ю) *сов неперех* (+*instr*) to begin to move
▸ **задви́гаться** *сов возв* to begin to move.
задвига́|ть(ся) (-ю(сь)) *несов от* **задви́нуть(ся)**.
задви́жк|а (-и) *ж* bolt; **закрыва́ть (закры́ть** *perf*) **дверь на ~у** to bolt the door.
задвижн|о́й *прил*: **~а́я дверь** sliding door.
задви́н|уть (-у, -ешь; *impf* **задвига́ть**) *сов перех* to push; (*ящик, занавески*) to close
▸ **задви́нуться** (*impf* **задвига́ться**) *сов возв* to close.
задво́р|ки (-ок) *мн* backyard *ед*; **на ~ках о́бщества** (*перен*) on the margins of society; **на ~ках исто́рии** (*перен*) in the footnotes of history.
задева́|ть (-ю) *несов от* **заде́ть** ◆ *сов перех* (*разг*: *положить*) to put; **куда́ ты ~л мою́ су́мку?** where have you put my bag?
▸ **задева́ться** *сов возв* (*разг*) to go missing; **куда́ ~лась моя́ ру́чка?** what's happened to my pen?
заде́йств|овать (-ую) *сов перех* (*оборудование*) to render operational; (*полк, дивизию*) to mobilize ◆ *неперех* (*взяться за дело*) to get busy.
заде́л (-а) *м* groundwork; **создава́ть (созда́ть** *perf*) ~ **на бу́дущее** to create foundations for the future.
заде́ла|ть (-ю; *impf* **заде́лывать**) *сов перех* to seal up.
заде́ну *итп сов см* **заде́ть**.
задёрга|ть (-ю) *сов неперех* (+*instr*; *ногой, вожжами*) to jerk ◆ *перех* (*разг*: *измучить*) to wear out
▸ **задёргаться** *сов возв* (*тело, глаз, губы*) to twitch; (*начать нервничать*) to become twitchy; (*разг*: *измучиться*) to reach the end of one's tether.
задёргива|ть (-ю) *несов от* **задёрнуть**.
задеревене́|ть (-ю) *сов неперех* to go stiff.
задержа́ни|е (-я) *ср* (*ЮР*) detention.

зад|ержа́ть (-ержу́, -е́ржишь; *impf* **заде́рживать**) *сов перех* (*самолёт, поезд итп*) to delay, hold up; (*зарплату, уплату долгов*) to withhold; (*преступника*) to detain; (*школьников*) to keep back; **я не хочу́ Вас ~е́рживать** I don't want to hold you back; **заде́рживать (~** *perf*) **дыха́ние** to hold one's breath; **заде́рживать (~** *perf*) **взгляд на** *+prp* to stare at; **заде́рживать (~** *perf*) **шаг** to slow up

▸ **задержа́ться** (*impf* **заде́рживаться**) *сов возв* to be delayed *или* held up; (*у двери, перед домом итп*) to pause; **заде́рживаться (~ся** *perf*) **с отве́том/рабо́той** to be late in answering/finishing the work.

заде́рж|ка (-ки; *gen pl* **-ек**) *ж* delay, hold-up; **без ~ек** without further delay.

задёрн|уть (-у, -ешь; *impf* **задёргивать**) *сов перех* (*шторы*) to pull shut; **задёргивать (~** *perf*) **окно́ занаве́ской/што́рой** to shut the curtains/blind.

задеру́(сь) *итп сов см* **задра́ть(ся)**.

заде́|ть (-ну, -нешь; *impf* **задева́ть**) *сов перех*: **~ (за** *+acc*) (*стол итп*) to brush against; (*кость, лёгкое*) to graze; (*перен: самолюбие, человека*) to wound; **его́ тон меня́ ~л** I found his tone offensive; **~** (*perf*) **кого́-н за живо́е** to cut sb to the quick.

зади́р|а (-ы) *м/ж* (*разг*) troublemaker.

задира́|ть(ся) (-ю(сь)) *несов от* **задра́ть(ся)**.

задири́ст|ый (-, -а, -о) *прил* quarrelsome.

за́дн|ий (-яя, -ее, -ие) *прил* back *опред*; **помеча́ть (поме́тить** *perf*) **~им число́м** to backdate; **опла́чивать (оплати́ть** *perf*) **~им число́м** to make a back payment; **она́ ~им умо́м крепка́** she's simply being wise after the event; **он был без ~их ног** (*разг*) he was dead on his feet; **~яя мысль** ulterior motive; **~ие но́ги** hind legs; **за́дний прохо́д** (*АНАТ*) rectum; **за́дний ход** back entrance.

за́дник (-а) *м* (*ботинка*) back; (*ТЕАТР*) backdrop.

за́дница (-ы) *ж* (*разг*) backside.

задо́бр|ить (-ю, -ишь; *impf* **зада́бривать**) *сов перех* to soften up.

задо́лго *нареч*: **~ до** *+gen* long before.

задолжа́|ть (-ю) *сов перех* to owe.

задо́лженност|ь (-и) *ж* debts *мн*; (*по работе, в учёбе*) work outstanding.

за́дом *нареч* backwards; **~ наперёд** back to front; **повора́чиваться (поверну́ться** *perf*) **~ к кому́-н** to turn one's back to sb; **стоя́ть** (*impf*) **~ к кому́-н** to stand with one's back to sb.

задо́р (-а) *м* enthusiasm.

задо́р|ный (-ен, -на, -но) *прил* lively.

задохн|у́ться (-у́сь, -ёшься; *impf* **задыха́ться**) *сов возв* (*в дыму*) to suffocate; (*от бега, при ходьбе*) to be out of breath; (*от злости, от смеха*) to choke.

задра́|ить (-ю, -ишь; *impf* **задра́ивать**) *сов перех* (*МОР*) to batten down.

задрапир|ова́ть (-у́ю) *сов от* **драпирова́ть**.

зад|ра́ть (-еру́, -ерёшь; *pt* **-ра́л, -рала́, -ра́ло**, *impf* **драть** *или* **задира́ть**) *сов перех* (*платье, юбка*) to hitch *или* hike up; (*растерзать*) to savage; **задира́ть (~** *perf*) **го́лову** to tip one's head back; **задира́ть (~** *perf*) **нос** (*разг*) to be stuck-up

▸ **задра́ться** (*impf* **задира́ться**) *сов возв* (*разг: платье, рубашка*) to hitch itself up; (*рукав*) to ruck.

задр|ема́ть (-емлю́, -е́млешь) *сов неперех* to doze off.

задрож|а́ть (-у́, -и́шь) *сов неперех* (*человек, голос*) to begin to tremble; (*здание, стекло*) to begin to shake.

задува́|ть (-ю) *несов от* **заду́ть**.

заду́ма|ть (-ю; *impf* **заду́мывать**) *сов перех* (*повесть, план*) to think up; (*карту, число*) to think of; (*+infin; уехать итп*) to think of doing

▸ **заду́маться** (*impf* **заду́мываться**) *сов возв* (*погрузиться в раздумье*) to be deep in thought; **заду́мываться (~ся** *perf*) **над** *+instr***/о** *+prp* (*над задачей, над жизнью*) to ponder; **о чём Вы ~лись?** what are you thinking about?; **он отве́тил, не заду́мываясь** he answered without hesitation; **она́ на мину́ту ~лась** she reflected for a moment.

заду́мчивост|ь (-и) *ж* pensiveness; **быть** (*impf*) **в глубо́кой ~и** to be deep in thought.

заду́мчив|ый (-, -а, -о) *прил* pensive, thoughtful.

заду́мыва|ть(ся) (-ю(сь)) *несов от* **заду́мать(ся)**.

заду́|ть (-ю, -ешь; *impf* **задува́ть**) *сов перех* (*огонь, свечу итп*) to blow out ◆ *неперех* (*ветер*) to get up; **ве́тром ~ло песо́к в ко́мнату** the wind blew sand into the room.

задуше́в|ный (-ен, -на, -но) *прил* (*мысли, тайна, разговор*) intimate; (*песня, рассказ*) soulful; (*друг, человек*) genial.

зад|уши́ть (-ушу́, -у́шишь) *сов от* **души́ть**.

задым|и́ть (-лю́, -и́шь) *сов неперех* to begin to smoulder (*BRIT*) *или* smolder (*US*)

▸ **задыми́ться** *сов возв* to begin to give off smoke.

задыха́|ться (-юсь) *несов от* **задохну́ться**.

заеда́|ть (-ю) *несов от* **зае́сть**.

зае́дешь *итп сов см* **зае́хать**.

заеди́м *итп сов см* **зае́сть**.

зае́ду *итп сов см* **зае́хать**.

заедя́т *сов см* **зае́сть**.

зае́зд (-а) *м* (*СПОРТ*) race (*in horse-racing, motor-racing*); (: *отборочный*) heat; (*туристов, отдыхающих*) arrival; **с ~ом/без зае́зда в Москву́** with/without a stopoff in Moscow.

зае́з|дить (-жу, -дишь) *сов перех* (*перен: разг*):

~ **кого-н** to drive sb too hard.

заезжа|ть (-ю) *несов от* **заехать.**

заезжу *сов см* **заездить.**

заел *итп сов см* **заесть.**

заем *итп сов см* **заесть.**

заём (займа) *м* loan.

заёмщик (-а) *м* borrower.

заесть (*как* **есть**; *см* **Table 15**; *impf* **заедать**) *сов перех* (*подлеж: комары*) to eat; (*разг: подлеж: жена, начальник, среда*) to get to ◆ *безл* (*разг: ружьё*) to jam; **пластинку заело** (*разг*) the record is stuck; **заедать (~ *perf*) лекарство/водку чем-н** to eat sth to take away the taste of the medicine/vodka.

заехать (*как* **ехать**; *см* **Table 19**; *impf* **заезжать**) *сов неперех*: ~ **за кем-н** to go to fetch sb; **заезжать (~ *perf*) в** *+acc* (*в канаву, во двор*) to drive into; (*в Москву, в магазин итп*) to stop off at; ~ (*perf*) **к друзьям** to stop off at friends; ~ (*perf*) **кому-н в лицо** (*разг*) to smash sb in the face.

зажар|ить (-ю, -ишь) *сов от* **жарить** ◆ (*impf* **зажаривать**) *перех* (*на сковородке*) to fry; (*в духовке*) to roast

▸ **зажариться** *сов от* **жариться** ◆ (*impf* **зажариваться**) *возв* (*см перех*) to fry; to roast.

заж|ать (-му, -мёшь; *impf* **зажимать**) *сов перех* to squeeze; (*рот, уши*) to cover; (*перен: инициативу, проект*) to stifle, suppress; (*разг: деньги*) to pocket; **зажимать (~ *perf*) нос** to hold one's nose; **зажимать (~ *perf*) рот кому-н** (*перен*) to silence sb.

зажгу(сь) *итп сов см* **зажечь(ся).**

зажд|аться (-усь, -ёшься) *сов возв* (*+gen*; *разг*) to be sick of waiting for.

заж|ечь (-гу, -жёшь *итп*, **-гут**; *pt* **-ёг, -гла, -гло**, *impf* **зажигать**) *сов перех* (*свечу, спичку итп*) to light; (*свет*) to turn on; (*перен: аудиторию*) to inflame; (: *интерес, любовь*) to spark (off)

▸ **зажечься** (*impf* **зажигаться**) *сов возв* (*свеча, спичка итп*) to light; (*свет*) to go on; (*перен: интерес, любовь*) to be sparked off.

зажива|ть (-ю) *несов от* **зажить.**

заживу *итп сов от* **зажить.**

зажигалк|а (-и) *ж* (cigarette) lighter; (*разг: бомба*) firebomb.

зажигани|е (-я) *ср* (*действие*) lighting; (*АВТ*) ignition; **включать (включить *perf*)** ~ to turn on the ignition.

зажигател|ьный (-ен, -ьна, -ьно) *прил* (*также перен*) inflammatory; (*снаряд*) incendiary; **зажигательный шнур** fuse wire.

зажига|ть(ся) (-ю(сь)) *несов от* **зажечь(ся).**

зажим (-а) *м* (*ТЕХ*) clamp; (*ЭЛЕК*) terminal; (*инициативы, критики*) stifling, suppression.

зажима|ть (-ю) *несов от* **зажать.**

зажиточ|ный (-ен, -на, -но) *прил* prosperous.

заж|ить (-иву, -ивёшь; *pt* **-ил, -ила, -ило**, *impf* **заживать**) *сов неперех* (*рана*) to heal (up); (*no impf*; *начать жить*) to start to live; ~ (*perf*) **по-новому** to change one's lifestyle.

зажму *итп сов см* **зажать.**

зажмур|ить (-ю, -ишь) *сов от* **жмурить** ◆ (*impf* **зажмуривать**) *перех*: ~ **глаза** to screw up one's eyes

▸ **зажмуриться** *сов от* **жмуриться** ◆ (*impf* **зажмуриваться**) *возв* to screw up one's eyes.

зажужж|ать (-у, -ишь) *сов неперех* to start buzzing.

заз|вать (-ову, -овёшь; *pt* **-вал, -вала, -вало**, *impf* **зазывать**) *сов перех* (*разг*): ~ **кого-н в гости** to invite sb over.

зазвен|еть (-ю, -ишь) *сов неперех* to start ringing; **у меня ~ело в ушах** my ears started ringing.

зазвон|ить (-ю, -ишь) *сов неперех* to start ringing.

зазвуч|ать (*3sg* **-ит**, *3pl* **-ат**) *сов неперех* to be heard.

заздравный *прил* congratulatory.

зазелене|ть (*3sg* **-ет**) *сов неперех* to turn green.

заземлени|е (-я) *ср* (*ЭЛЕК: действие*) earthing (*BRIT*), grounding (*US*); (: *устройство*) earth (*BRIT*), ground (*US*).

заземл|ить (-ю, -ишь; *impf* **заземлять**) *сов перех* to earth (*BRIT*), ground (*US*).

зазн|аваться (-аюсь) *несов от* **зазнаться.**

зазна|йка (-йки; *gen pl* **-ек**) *м/ж* (*разг*) bighead.

зазна|ться (-юсь; *impf* **зазнаваться**) *сов возв* (*разг*) to think a lot of o.s.

зазову *итп сов см* **зазвать.**

зазор (-а) *м* gap.

зазрени|е (-я) *ср*: **без ~я совести** without a twinge of conscience.

зазубрен|ный (-, -а, -о) *прил* serrated, jagged.

зазубрива|ть (-ю) *несов от* **зазубрить.**

зазубрин|а (-ы) *ж* serration.

зазубр|ить (-ю, -ишь; *impf* **зазубривать**) *сов перех* (*разг*): ~ **что-н** to learn sth parrot-fashion.

зазыва|ть (-ю) *несов от* **зазвать.**

заигра|ть (-ю) *сов (не)перех* (*музыкант, оркестр*) to begin to play ◆ *неперех* (*музыка*) to begin ◆ (*impf* **заигрывать**) *перех* (*пластинку, колоду карт*) to wear out

▸ **заиграться** (*impf* **заигрываться**) *сов возв* to be absorbed in one's games.

заигрыва|ть (-ю) *несов от* **заиграть** ◆ *неперех*: ~ **с** *+instr* (*разг: любезничать*) to flirt with; (: *заискивать*) to suck up to

▸ **заигрываться** *несов от* **заиграться.**

заик|а (-и) *м/ж* stutterer.

заикани|е (-я) *ср* (*действие*) stuttering; (*порок речи*) stutter.

заика|ться (-юсь) *несов возв* to have a stutter; (*разг: от испуга, от волнения*) to stammer; (*perf* **заикнуться**): ~ **о** *+prp* (*поездке, приглашении*) to drop hints about.

заимодав|ец (-ьца) moneylender; (*пренебр*) loan shark.

заимообразно *нареч* on loan.

заимствовани|е (-я) *ср* borrowing.

заимств|овать (-ую; *impf* **позаимствовать**)

(не)сов перех *(слова, сюжет)* to borrow; *(опыт)* to benefit from.

заиндевéвш|ий (-ая, -ее, -ие) *прил* frost-covered.

заи́ндеве|ть (-ю) *сов от* **и́ндеветь**.

заинтересóван|ный (-, -а, -о) *прил* interested; **я заинтересóван в э́том дéле** I have an interest in the matter; **заинтересóванная сторонá** interested party.

заинтерес|овáть (-ýю; *impf* **заинтерес-óвывать)** *сов перех* to interest

▸ **заинтересовáться** *(impf* **заинтерес-óвываться)** *сов возв (+instr)* to become interested in.

заинтриг|овáть (-ýю; *impf* **заинтригóвывать)** *сов перех* to intrigue.

Заи́р (-а) *м* Zaire.

заи́рск|ий (-ая, -ое, -ие) *прил* Zairean.

заи́скива|ть (-ю) *несов неперех*: ~ **пéред** *+instr* to ingratiate o.s. with.

заи́скивающ|ий (-ая, -ее, -ие) *прил* ingratiating.

зайдý *итп сов см* **зайти́**.

зáйма *сущ см* **заём**.

зáймов|ый *прил*: **~ая операция** loan transaction; ~ **процéнт** interest *(on loan)*.

займý(сь) *итп сов см* **заня́ть(ся)**.

зайти́ *(как* **идти́**; *см* **Table 18**; *impf* **заходи́ть)** *сов неперех (солнце, луна)* to go down; *(спор, разговор)* to start up; *(посетить)*: ~ **(в/на** *+acc***/к** *+dat***)** to call in (at); *(попасть)*: ~ **в/на** *+acc* to stray into; **заходи́ть (~** *perf***) за кем-н** to go to fetch sb; **заходи́ть (~** *perf***) за хлéбом/молокóм** to pop in for bread/milk; **заходи́ть (~** *perf***) на рабóту/к дрýгу** to call in at work/a friend's; **заходи́ть (~** *perf***) спрáва/слéва** to come in from the right/left; **мы зашли́ в незнакóмую часть гóрода** we strayed into an unfamiliar part of town; **заходи́ть (~** *perf***) в тупи́к** *(перен)* to reach a dead end; **дéло зашлó сли́шком далекó** things have gone too far.

зáйца *сущ см* **зáяц**.

зайчáта *итп сущ см* **зайчóнок**.

зáйчик (-а) *м уменьш от* **зáяц**; *(разг: также:* **сóлнечный** ~*)* reflection of the sun.

зайчи́х|а (-и) *ж* doe, female hare.

зайч|óнок (-óнка; *nom pl* **-áта**, *gen pl* **-áт)** *м* leveret.

закабал|и́ть (-ю́, -и́шь; *impf* **закабаля́ть)** *сов перех* to enslave.

закавкáзск|ий (-ая, -ое, -ие) *прил* Transcaucasian.

закады́чный *прил*: ~ **друг** bosom friend.

закажý *итп сов от* **заказáть**.

закáз (-а) *м (действие: платья, обеда итп)* ordering; *(: телефонного разговора)* booking; *(: портрета)* commissioning; *(заказанный предмет)* order; **дéлать (сдéлать** *perf***) что-н на** ~ to make sth to order; **по ~у** *(также перен)* to order.

зак|азáть (-ажý, -áжешь; *impf* **закáзывать)** *сов перех (см сущ)* to order; to book; to commission.

заказн|óй *прил*: **~óе письмó** registered letter.

закáзчик (-а) *м* customer.

закáзчиц|а (-ы) *ж см* **закáзчик**.

закáзыва|ть (-ю) *несов от* **заказáть**.

закал|ённый (-ён, -енá, -енó) *прил (физически)* resistant; *(нравственно)* resilient.

закáливани|е (-я) *ср (ребёнка, организма)* toughening up.

закал|и́ть (-ю́, -и́шь; *impf* **закáливать** *или* **закаля́ть)** *сов перех (сталь)* to harden, temper; *(ребёнка, организм)* to toughen up; *(волю, характер)* to toughen

▸ **закали́ться** *(impf* **закáливаться** *или* **закаля́ться)** *сов возв (сталь)* to be hardened *или* tempered; *(ребёнок, организм)* to build up one's resistance; *(воля, характер)* to toughen.

закáлк|а (-и) *ж (см глаг)* hardening, tempering; toughening up; toughening; *(стойкость)* toughness.

закáлыва|ть (-ю) *несов от* **заколóть**.

закаля́|ть(ся) (-ю(сь)) *несов от* **закали́ть(ся)**.

закамуфли́р|овать (-ую) *сов от* **камуфли́ровать**.

закáнчива|ть(ся) (-ю(сь)) *несов от* **закóнчить(ся)**.

закáпа|ть (-ю; *impf* **закáпывать)** *сов перех (платье, тетрадь итп)* to splatter; *(лекарство, капли)* to apply ◆ *неперех (no impf)*: **дождь ~л** it started spitting (with rain).

закáпыва|ть (-ю) *несов от* **закáпать, закопáть**

▸ **закáпываться** *несов от* **закопáться**.

закáт (-а) *м*: ~ **(сóлнца)** sunset; *(перен: жизни, карьеры)* twilight; **на ~е дней** in the twilight of one's years.

закатá|ть (-ю; *impf* **закáтывать)** *сов перех* to roll up.

зак|ати́ть (-ачý, -áтишь; *impf* **закáтывать)** *сов перех* to roll; **закáтывать (~** *perf***) скандáл** *(разг)* to create a scandal; **закáтывать (~** *perf***) истéрику** *(разг)* to get hysterical; **закáтывать (~** *perf***) глазá** to roll one's eyes

▸ **закати́ться** *(impf* **закáтываться)** *сов возв* to roll; *(солнце)* to set.

закачá|ться (-юсь) *сов возв* to begin to sway.

закачý(сь) *сов см* **закати́ть(ся)**.

закáшля|ть (-ю) *сов неперех* to start coughing

▸ **закáшляться** *сов возв* to have a coughing fit.

заквá|сить (-шу, -сишь; *impf* **заквáшивать)** *сов перех (капусту)* to pickle; *(молоко)* to sour

▸ **заквáситься** *(impf* **заквáшиваться)** *сов возв (см перех)* to be pickled; to be soured.

заквáск|а (-и) *ж (для теста)* leaven; *(для кефира)* culture.

заква́шива|ть(ся) (**-ю(сь)**) *несов от* **заква́сить(ся)**.

заква́шу(сь) *сов см* **заква́сить(ся)**.

закида́|ть (**-ю**; *impf* **заки́дывать**) *сов перех* = **заброса́ть**.

заки́н|уть (**-у, -ешь**; *impf* **заки́дывать**) *сов перех* to throw; **судьба́ ~ула меня́ в Шотла́ндию** fate has brought me to Scotland; **заки́дывать** (**~** *perf*) **у́дочку** to cast a line; (*перен*: *разг*) to put out feelers.

закип|е́ть (*3sg* **-и́т**, *3pl* **-я́т**, *impf* **закипа́ть**) *сов неперех* to start to boil; (*перен*: *работа*) to increase.

заки́с|нуть (**-ну, -нешь**; *pt* **-, -ла, -ло**, *impf* **закиса́ть**) *сов неперех* (*тесто, квас*) to turn sour; (*перен*) to stagnate.

за́кис|ь (**-и**) *ж* oxide.

закла́д (**-а**) *м*: **в ~е** in pawn; **би́ться** (*impf*) **об ~** (*разг*) to bet.

закла́дк|а (**-и**) *ж* (*сада, фундамента*) laying; (*в книге*) bookmark.

закладн|а́я (**-ой**; *decl like adj*) *ж* mortgage deed.

закла́дыва|ть (**-ю**) *несов от* **заложи́ть**.

закл|ева́ть (**-юю́, -юёшь**; *impf* **заклёвывать**) *сов перех* to peck at; (*перен*: *разг*) to harass.

закле́|ить (**-ю, -ишь**; *impf* **закле́ивать**) *сов перех* to seal (up)

▸ **закле́иться** (*impf* **закле́иваться**) *сов возв* to seal.

заклейм|и́ть (**-лю́, -и́шь**) *сов от* **клейми́ть**.

заклепа́|ть (**-ю**; *impf* **заклёпывать**) *сов перех* to rivet.

заклёпк|а (**-и**) *ж* (*стержень*) rivet.

заклёпыва|ть (**-ю**) *несов от* **заклепа́ть**.

заклина́ни|е (**-я**) *ср* (*магические слова*) incantation; (*перен*: *мольба*) plea.

заклина́|ть (**-ю**) *несов перех* (*духов, змея*) to charm; (*перен*: *умолять*) to plead with.

закли́н|ить (**-ю, -ишь**; *impf* **закли́нивать**) *сов перех* (*дверь итп*) to jam; **руль ~ило** the wheel has jammed.

заключа́|ть (**-ю**) *несов от* **заключи́ть**.

заключа́|ться (*3sg* **-ется**, *3pl* **-ются**) *несов возв*: **~ в** *+prp* (*состоять в*) to lie in; (*содержаться в*) to be contained in; (*заканчиваться*): **~** *+instr* to conclude with; **дело́/пробле́ма ~ется в том, что** ... the point/problem is that ...; **на́ша цель ~ется в том, что́бы привле́чь инвести́ции в го́род** our aim is to attract investment into the city.

заключе́ни|е (**-я**) *ср* conclusion; (*в тюрьме*) imprisonment, confinement; **в ~** in conclusion; **тюре́мное ~** imprisonment; **находи́ться** (*impf*) **в ~и** to be held in confinement.

заключённ|ая (**-ой**; *decl like adj*) *ж см* **заключённый**.

заключённ|ый (**-ого**; *decl like adj*) *м* prisoner.

заключи́тельный *прил* concluding, final.

заключ|и́ть (**-у́, -и́шь**; *impf* **заключа́ть**) *сов перех* (*соглашение, договор, сделку*) to conclude, seal; **заключа́ть** (**~** *perf*) **в себе́** to comprise; **заключа́ть** (**~** *perf*) **контра́кт** to conclude a contract; **заключа́ть** (**~** *perf*) **кого́-н в тюрьму́** to put sb in prison; **заключа́ть** (**~** *perf*) **кого́-н под стра́жу** to take sb into custody; **заключа́ть** (**~** *perf*) **кого́-н в объя́тия** to embrace sb.

закля́тый *прил*: **~ враг** sworn enemy.

зак|ова́ть (**-ую́**; *impf* **зако́вывать**) *сов перех* to chain up; (*подлеж*: *лёд*) to cover.

закоди́р|овать (**-ую**) *сов от* **коди́ровать**.

закола́чива|ть (**-ю**) *несов от* **заколоти́ть**.

заколдо́ван|ный (**-, -а, -о**) *прил* enchanted; **заколдо́ванный круг** vicious circle.

заколд|ова́ть (**-у́ю**; *impf* **заколдо́вывать**) *сов перех* to bewitch.

зако́лк|а (**-и**) *ж* (*для волос*) hairpin, hairclip.

закол|оти́ть (**-очу́, -о́тишь**; *impf* **закола́чивать**) *сов перех* (*окна, дом*) to board up; (*ящик*) to nail up.

зак|оло́ть (**-олю́, -о́лешь**) *сов от* **коло́ть** ◆ (*impf* **зака́лывать**) *перех* (*свинью, индейку*) to slaughter; (*волосы*) to pin up; (*галстук, воротник*) to pin back; **у меня́ ~оло́ло в боку́** I've got a stitch.

заколочу́ *сов см* **заколоти́ть**.

закомпости́р|овать (**-ую**) *сов от* **компости́ровать**.

зако́н (**-а**) *м* law; **вне ~а** outside the law; **объявля́ть** (**объяви́ть** *perf*) **кого́-н вне ~а** to outlaw sb; **Зако́н Бо́жий** religious education.

зако́нен *прил см* **зако́нный**.

зако́нност|ь (**-и**) *ж* (*документа, завещания*) legality; (*в стране*) law and order.

зако́н|ный (**-ен, -на, -но**) *прил* legitimate, lawful; (*право, приём*) legal; (*документ*) valid; **на ~ном основа́нии** on a legal basis; **~ным о́бразом** legally, lawfully; **зако́нный брак/муж** lawful wedlock/wedded husband.

законода́тел|ь (**-я**) *м* legislator; (*перен*: *вкусов, мнений*) arbiter; **~ мод** trendsetter.

законода́тельниц|а (**-ы**) *ж см* **законода́тель**.

законода́тельный *прил* legislative.

законода́тельств|о (**-а**) *ср* legislation.

закономе́р|ный (**-ен, -на, -но**) *прил* (*результат, явление*) predictable; (*понятный*) legitimate.

законоп|а́тить (**-а́чу, -а́тишь**; *impf* **законопа́чивать**) *сов перех* to patch up.

законоположе́ни|е (**-я**) *ср* statute.

законопрое́кт (**-а**) *м* (*полит*) bill.

законсерви́р|овать (**-ую**) *сов от* **консерви́ровать**.

законспекти́р|овать (**-ую**) *сов от* **конспекти́ровать**.

законтракт|ова́ть (**-у́ю**; *impf* **законтракто́вывать**) *сов перех* to sign a contract for.

зако́нчен|ный (**-, -на, -но**) *прил* (*мысль, рассказ*) complete; (*негодяй, мерзавец*) utter.

зако́нч|ить (**-у, -ишь**; *impf* **зака́нчивать**) *сов перех* to finish, end

▸ **закóнчиться** (*impf* **закáнчиваться**) *сов возв* to finish, end.
закопá|ть (**-ю**; *impf* **закáпывать**) *сов перех* (*деньги, золото итп*) to bury; (*канаву, яму*) to fill in
▸ **закопáться** (*impf* **закáпываться**) *сов возв* (*в землю итп*) to bury o.s.
закоп|ти́ть (**-чý, -ти́шь**) *сов от* **копти́ть**
▸ **закопти́ться** *сов возв* to be covered in smoke.
закопчённый *прил* (*чайник итп*) charred; (*потолок*) smoke-stained.
закопчý(сь) *сов см* **закопти́ть(ся)**.
закоренéлый *прил* (*традиции, предрассудки итп*) deep-rooted; (*дурак, кокетка итп*) incorrigible; **~ престýпник** hardened criminal.
закоренé|ть (**-ю**) *сов неперех*: **~ в** *+prp* (*мнении, предрассудках*) to be entrenched in.
закóр|ки (**-ок**) *мн* (*разг*): **посади́ть когó-н на ~** to lift sb onto one's back; **нести́** (*impf*) **когó-н на ~ках** to give sb a piggyback.
закорю́ч|ка (**-ки**; *gen pl* **-ек**) *ж* squiggle.
закоснé|ть (**-ю**) *сов от* **коснéть**.
закостенéлый *прил* stiff.
закостенé|ть (**-ю**) *сов от* **костенéть**.
закоýл|ок (**-ка**) *м* (*города*) back street *или* alley; (*дома, замка, двора*) nook; **обы́скивать** (**обыскáть** *perf*) **все ~ки** to look in all the nooks and crannies.
закоченéлый *прил* numb.
закоченé|ть (**-ю**) *сов неперех* to go numb.
закрадётся *итп сов см* **закрáсться**.
закрáдыва|ться (*3sg* **-ется**, *3pl* **-ются**) *несов от* **закрáсться**.
закрá|сить (**-шу, -сишь**; *impf* **закрáшивать**) *сов перех* to paint over.
закр|áсться (*3sg* **-адётся**, *3pl* **-адýтся**, *pt* **-áлся, -áлась, -áлось**, *impf* **закрáдываться**) *сов возв* to creep in.
закрáшива|ть (**-ю**) *несов от* **закрáсить**.
закрáшу *сов см* **закрáсить**.
закрепи́тел|ь (**-я**) *м* (*ФОТО*) fixative.
закреп|и́ть (**-лю́, -и́шь**; *impf* **закрепля́ть**) *сов перех* (*деталь, грунт*) to fasten; (*победу, позицию*) to consolidate; (*ФОТО*) to fix; **закрепля́ть** (**~** *perf*) **что-н за кем-н** to secure sth for sb; **закрепля́ть** (**~** *perf*) **когó-н за кем-н** to assign sb to sb
▸ **закрепи́ться** (*impf* **закрепля́ться**) *сов возв* (*деталь, грунт*) to be fastened; (*победа, успехи*) to be consolidated; (*слово, привычка*) to become established; (*ВОЕН*): **~ся на** *+acc* (*на высоте*) to consolidate one's position on.
закрéпк|а (**-и**) *ж* fastener.
закреплю́(сь) *сов см* **закрепи́ть(ся)**.
закрепля́|ть(ся) (**-ю(сь)**) *несов от* **закрепи́ть(ся)**.
закрепо|сти́ть (**-щý, -сти́шь**; *impf* **закрепощáть**) *сов перех* to enslave.
закрепощéни|е (**-я**) *ср* enslavement.
закрепощý *сов см* **закрепости́ть**.
закрич|áть (**-ý, -и́шь**) *сов неперех* to start shouting.
закрóйщик (**-а**) *м* cutter (*DRESSMAKING*).
закрóйщиц|а (**-ы**) *ж см* **закрóйщик**.
зáкром (**-а**; *nom pl* **-á**) *м* (*в амбаре*) grain store; *см также* **закромá**.
закром|á (**-óв**) *мн* (*перен*) breadbasket *ед* (*esp US*), granary *ед*.
закрóю(сь) *итп сов см* **закры́ть(ся)**.
закруглéни|е (**-я**) *ср* curve.
закруглён|ный (**-, -на, -но**) *прил* curved, rounded.
закругл|и́ть (**-ю́, -и́шь**; *impf* **закругля́ть**) *сов перех* (*край*) to round off; (*поверхность*) to make round
▸ **закругли́ться** (*impf* **закругля́ться**) *сов возв* to become rounded; (*перен*: *разг*: *закончить*) to round off.
закр|ужи́ть (**-ужý, -ýжишь**) *сов перех*: **~ когó-н** (*начать кружить*) (to start) to spin sb round; (*довести до головокружения*) to make sb dizzy
▸ **закружи́ться** *сов возв* (*начать кружиться*) to start spinning; (*ослабеть*) to start to feel dizzy; (*перен*: *разг*: *захлопотаться*) to get o.s. into a tizzy; **у меня́ ~ужи́лась головá** my head has started spinning.
закр|ути́ть (**-учý, -ýтишь**; *impf* **закрýчивать**) *сов перех* (*волосы, усы*) to twist; (*верёвку, ленту*) to wind; (*кран*) to turn off; (*гайку*) to screw in
▸ **закрути́ться** (*impf* **закрýчиваться**) *сов возв* (*верёвка, лента*) to wind up; (*перен*: *разг*: *захлопотаться*) to get o.s. into a flap.
закрывá|ть(ся) (**-ю(сь)**) *несов от* **закры́ть(ся)**.
закры́ти|е (**-я**) *ср* (*магазина итп*) closing (time); (*сезона, конкурса*) close.
закры́т|ый (**-, -а, -о**) *прил* shut, closed; (*no short form*; *терраса, машина*) enclosed; (*стадион, бассейн*) indoor; (*собрание, заседание*) closed, private; (*перелом, рана*) internal; **в ~ом помещéнии** indoors; **при ~ых дверя́х** behind closed doors; **вопрóс закры́т** the matter is closed; **закры́тое голосовáние** secret vote *или* ballot; **закры́тое мóре** inland sea; **закры́тое плáтье** dress with a high neck; **закры́тый кóнкурс** closed competition.
закр|ы́ть (**-óю, -óешь**; *impf* **закрывáть**) *сов перех* to close, shut; (*заслонить, накрыть*) to cover (up); (*проход, проезд, границу*) to close (off); (*воду, газ итп*) to shut off; **закрывáть** (**~** *perf*) **когó-н в кóмнате** to shut sb in a room; **закрывáть** (**~** *perf*) **счёт** to close an account; **закрывáть** (**~** *perf*) **глазá на что-н** to close one's eyes to sth
▸ **закры́ться** (*impf* **закрывáться**) *сов возв* to close, shut; (*магазин, предприятие*) to close

или shut down; (*накрыться*) to cover o.s. up; (*запереться*: *в доме итп*) to shut o.s. up; (*рана*) to close up.
закули́сн|ый *прил* backstage *опред*; (*перен*: *интриги, борьба*) behind-the-scenes; **~ая жизнь** off-stage life.
зак|упи́ть (-уплю́, -у́пишь; *impf* **закупа́ть**) *сов перех* (*купить оптом*) to buy up; (*запастись*) to stock up with.
заку́пк|а (-и) *ж* purchase.
закуплю́ *сов см* **закупи́ть**.
заку́пор|ить (-ю, -ишь; *impf* **заку́поривать**) *сов перех* (*бутылку*) to cork (up); (*бочку*) to seal up.
заку́порк|а (-и) *ж* (*см перех*) corking; sealing; (*МЕД*: *кишечника, сосудов*) blockage; **заку́порка вен** (*МЕД*) embolism.
заку́почн|ый *прил*: **~ая цена́** purchase price.
заку́пщик (-а) *м* buyer.
зак|ури́ть (-урю́, -у́ришь; *impf* **заку́ривать**) *сов перех* to light (up) ◆ *неперех* to start smoking.
закуса́|ть (-ю) *сов перех* (*разг*) to bite; **меня́ ~ли комары́** I've been bitten to death by mosquitoes.
зак|уси́ть (-ушу́, -у́сишь; *impf* **заку́сывать**) *сов неперех* (*поесть*) to have a bite to eat ◆ *перех*: **~ во́дку/лека́рство** *umn* to have sth to eat with the vodka/medicine; **заку́сывать (~ *perf*) губу́** to bite one's lip; **заку́сывать (~ *perf*) удила́** (*перен*) to take the bit between one's teeth.
заку́ск|а (-и) *ж* snack; (*обычно мн*: *для водки*) zakuska (*мн* zakuski), nibbles *мн*; (*в начале обеда*) hors d'oeuvre; **на ~у** (*перен*: *разг*) for the finale.
заку́сочн|ая (-ой; *decl like adj*) *ж* snack bar.
заку́сыва|ть (-ю) *несов от* **закуси́ть**.
заку́та|ть (-ю) *сов от* **ку́тать** ◆ (*impf* **заку́тывать**) *перех* (*ребёнка*) to wrap up; (*ноги umn*) to cover
▸ **заку́таться** *сов от* **ку́таться** ◆ (*impf* **заку́тываться**) *возв* to wrap (o.s.) up.
закут|о́к (-ка́) *м* (*разг*) dark corner.
заку́тыва|ть(ся) (-ю(сь)) *несов от* **заку́тать(ся)**.
закушу́ *сов см* **закуси́ть**.
зал (-а) *м* hall; (*в музее, в библиотеке*) room; **зал ожида́ния** waiting room.
зала́|дить (-жу, -дишь) *сов (не)перех* (*разг*) to harp on (about); (*+infin*) to take to doing.
зала́мыва|ть (-ю) *несов от* **заломи́ть**.
залата́|ть (-ю) *сов от* **лата́ть**.
зала́|ять (-ю) *сов неперех* to start barking, start to bark.
залёг *umn сов см* **зале́чь**.
залега́|ть (-ю) *несов от* **зале́чь**.
заледене́лый *прил* covered in ice; (*пальцы, руки*) icy.
заледене́|ть (-ю) *сов неперех* (*дорога*) to ice over; (*перен*: *пальцы, руки*) to freeze.
залежа́л|ый (-, -а, -о) *прил* (*разг*) old.
залеж|а́ться (-у́сь, -и́шься; *impf* **залёживаться**) *сов возв*: **~ в магази́не/в посте́ли** to lie in the shop/in bed for too long.
за́леж|ь (-и) *ж* (*угля, золота*) seam; (*С-Х*) fallow land.
зале́з|ть (-у, -ешь; *impf* **залеза́ть**) *сов неперех*: **~ на** *+acc* (*на крышу*) to climb onto; (*на дерево, на лестницу*) to climb (up); (*разг*): **~ в** *+acc* (*в квартиру, в магазин*) to break into; **залеза́ть (~ *perf*) кому́-н в карма́н** to pick sb's pockets; **залеза́ть (~ *perf*) в долги́** to get into debt.
зал|епи́ть (-еплю́, -е́пишь; *impf* **залепля́ть**) *сов перех* (*дыру, трещину*) to plaster up; (*подлеж*: *снег, грязь*) to plaster; **~ (*perf*) кому́-н пощёчину** (*разг*) to give sb a slap round the face.
зале|те́ть (-чу́, -ти́шь; *impf* **залета́ть**) *сов неперех*: **~ (в +*acc*)** to fly in(to); **залета́ть (~ *perf*) за** *+acc* (*за море, за облака umn*) to fly over; **залета́ть (~ *perf*) далеко́** to fly a long way; (*перен*) to go far; **самолёт ~те́л в Москву́ за горю́чим** the plane stopped off in Moscow for refuelling.
зал|ечи́ть (-ечу́, -е́чишь; *impf* **зале́чивать**) *сов перех* (*язву, рану*) to heal; **~ (*perf*) кого́-н** (*разг*) to make sb feel worse (*by excessive medication*)
▸ **залечи́ться** (*impf* **зале́чиваться**) *сов возв* to heal (up).
залечу́ *сов см* **залете́ть**.
зал|е́чь (-я́гу, -я́жешь *umn*, **-я́гут**; *pt* **-ёг, -егла́, -егло́**, *impf* **залега́ть**) *сов неперех* (*в постель*) to lie down; (*в нору*) to retreat; (*укрыться*) to lie low; (*ГЕО*: *уголь, золото*) to be deposited; **залега́ть (~ *perf*) в заса́де** to lie in wait.
зали́в (-а) *м* bay; (*длинный*) gulf.
залива́|ть(ся) (-ю(сь)) *несов от* **зали́ть(ся)**.
заливн|о́е (-о́го; *decl like adj*) *ср* (*КУЛИН*) *fish or meat in aspic*.
заливно́й *прил* (*рыба, мясо*) jellied; **заливно́й луг** water meadow.
зал|и́ть (-ью́, -ьёшь; *pt* **-и́л, -ила́, -и́ло**, *impf* **залива́ть**) *сов перех* to flood; (*костёр, огонь*) to extinguish; **залива́ть (~ *perf*) руба́шку пи́вом** to spill beer on one's shirt; **залива́ть (~ *perf*) бензи́н в маши́ну** to fill a car with petrol; **залива́ть (~ *perf*) доро́гу асфа́льтом** to cover a road with asphalt; **залива́ть (~ *perf*) го́ре** to drown one's sorrows; **слёзы ~и́ли его́ лицо́** the tears poured down her face
▸ **зали́ться** (*impf* **залива́ться**) *сов возв* (*луг, пол*) to be flooded; (*вода*) to seep; **залива́ться (~ся *perf*) слеза́ми/сме́хом** to burst into tears/out laughing; **её лицо́ ~и́лось румя́нцем** the colour flooded into her cheeks.
зало́г (-а) *м* (*действие*: *вещей*) pawning; (: *квартиры*) mortgaging; (*заложенная вещь*) security; (*ЛИНГ*: *активный, пассивный*) voice; (*перен*: *знак*) token.
зал|ожи́ть (-ожу́, -о́жишь; *impf* **закла́дывать**) *сов перех* (*покрыть*) to clutter up; (*отметить*) to mark; (*отдать в залог*: *кольцо, шубу*) to pawn; (: *дом*) to mortgage; (*заполнить*: *трубу, дыру*) to block up; **закла́дывать (~ *perf*) что-н**

за что-н to put sth behind sth; **закла́дывать (~** *perf***) го́род** to lay the foundations of a city; **у меня́ ~ожи́ло нос/го́рло** (*разг*) my nose/throat is all bunged up.
зало́жник (-а) *м* hostage.
зало́жниц|а (-ы) *ж см* **зало́жник.**
зал|оми́ть (-омлю́, -о́мишь; *impf* **зала́мывать)** *сов перех* to tear off; **зала́мывать (~** *perf***) ру́ки** to throw up one's hands; **зала́мывать (~** *perf***) высо́кую це́ну** to ask too high a price.
залп (-а) *м* salvo (*мн* salvoes), volley.
за́лпом *нареч* (*разг: проглотить, проговорить*) all in one go; **вы́стрелить** *(perf)* ~ to fire a volley *или* salvo of bullets.
залы́син|а (-ы) *ж* bald patch.
залью́(сь) *umn сов см* **зали́ть(ся).**
залюб|ова́ться (-у́юсь) *сов возв* (*+instr; картиной, девушкой*) to be transfixed by.
заля́гу *umn сов см* **зале́чь.**
заля́жешь *umn сов см* **зале́чь.**
заля́па|ть (-ю; *impf* **заля́пывать)** *сов перех* (*разг*) to mess up.
зам (-а) *м сокр* (*разг: = замести́тель*) number two.
зам. *м сокр* (= **замести́тель**) dep. (= *deputy*).
зам- *префикс* deputy.
зама́|зать (-жу, -жешь; *impf* **зама́зывать)** *сов перех* (*пятно, рисунок*) to paint over; (*окна, щели*) to fill with putty; (*запачкать*) to smear
▸ **зама́заться** (*impf* **зама́зываться**) *сов возв*: **~ся** (*+instr*) to become smeared (with).
зама́зк|а (-и) *ж* putty.
зама́зыва|ть(ся) (-ю(сь)) *несов от* **зама́зать(ся).**
зама́лчива|ть (-ю) *несов от* **замолча́ть.**
зам|ани́ть (-аню́, -а́нишь; *impf* **зама́нивать)** *сов перех* to lure, entice.
зама́нчив|ый (-, -а, -о) *прил* tempting.
замара́|ть(ся) (-ю(сь)) *сов от* **мара́ть(ся).**
замарин|ова́ть (-у́ю) *сов от* **маринова́ть.**
замаскиро́ван|ный (-, -а, -о) *прил* disguised; (*намёк, угроза*) veiled.
замаскир|ова́ть (-у́ю; *impf* **замаскиро́вывать** *или* **маскирова́ть)** *сов перех* to disguise; (*самолёт, танк*) to camouflage
▸ **замаскирова́ться** (*impf* **замаскиро́вываться** *или* **маскирова́ться**) *сов возв* to disguise o.s.; (*солдаты*) to camouflage o.s.
зама́тыва|ть(ся) (-ю(сь)) *несов от* **замота́ть(ся).**
зам|аха́ть (-ашу́, -а́шешь) *сов неперех* (*+instr; палкой, газетой umn*) to brandish; ~ *(perf)* **руко́й** to start waving.
замахну́ться (-у́сь, -ёшься; *impf* **зама́хиваться**) *сов возв*: ~ **на** *+acc* (*на собаку, на ребёнка*) to raise one's hand to; (*перен*) to set one's sights on; **он ~у́лся на бо́льшее** he has set his sights on bigger and better things.
зама́чива|ть (-ю) *несов от* **замочи́ть.**
зама́шк|и (-ек) *мн* manners *мн*.
замбийск|ий (-ая, -ое, -ие) *прил* Zambian.
За́мби|я (-и) *ж* Zambia.
замедле́ни|е (-я) *ср* slowing down; **без ~я** without delay.
заме́дленный *прил* retarded; ~ **ход** reduced speed.
заме́дл|ить (-ю, -ишь; *impf* **замедля́ть)** *сов перех* to slow down; (*no impf; задержаться*): ~ **с** *+instr* to be slow with; **не** ~ *(perf) +infin* to be quick to do
▸ **заме́длиться** (*impf* **замедля́ться**) *сов возв* to slow down.
замёл *umn сов см* **замести́.**
заме́н|а (-ы) *ж* replacement; (*СПОРТ*) substitution.
замени́м|ый (-, -а, -о) *прил* replaceable.
замени́тел|ь (-я) *м* (*суррогат*) substitute.
зам|ени́ть (-еню́, -е́нишь; *impf* **заменя́ть)** *сов перех* to replace; **она́ ~ени́ла им мать** she was like a mother to them.
зам|ере́ть (-ру́, -рёшь; *pt* **-ер, -ерла́, -ерло,** *impf* **замира́ть)** *сов неперех* (*человек, животное*) to stop dead; (*перен: душа, сердце*) to stand still; (*: работа, страна*) to come to a standstill; (*звук*) to die away; (*шум, стрельба*) to die down; ~ *(perf)* **на ме́сте** to stop dead in one's tracks.
замерза́ни|е (-я) *ср* freezing; **то́чка ~я** freezing point.
замёрз|нуть (-ну, -нешь; *pt* **-, -ла, -ло,** *impf* **замерза́ть)** *сов неперех* to freeze; (*река*) to freeze (up); (*окно*) to ice up; **я совсе́м замёрз** I'm completely frozen.
заме́р|ить (-ю, -ишь; *impf* **замеря́ть)** *сов перех* to measure.
за́мертво *нареч*: **упа́сть** *или* **ру́хнуть** ~ to collapse in a heap.
замеря́|ть (-ю) *несов от* **заме́рить.**
зам|еси́ть (-ешу́, -е́сишь; *impf* **заме́шивать)** *сов перех* (*бетон, глину*) to mix up; (*тесто*) to knead.
зам|ести́ (-ету́, -етёшь; *pt* **-ёл, -ела́, -ело́,** *impf* **замета́ть)** *сов перех* (*мусор, листья*) to sweep up; (*подлеж: метель: дорогу umn*) to cover; **замета́ть (~** *perf***) следы́** (*также перен*) to cover one's tracks.
замести́тел|ь (-я) *м* replacement; (*должность*) deputy; ~ **дире́ктора/премье́р-мини́стра** deputy director/prime minister.
замести́тельниц|а (-ы) *ж см* **замести́тель.**
заме|сти́ть (-щу́, -сти́шь) *сов от* **замеща́ть.**
замета́|ть (-ю) *несов от* **замести́.**
заме|та́ться (-чу́сь, -чешься) *сов возв* (*в кровати, в бреду*) to start tossing and turning; (*в отчаянии*) to get into a state; **он ~та́лся по**

ко́мнате he began to rush about the room.
заме́тен *прил см* **заме́тный.**
заме́|тить (**-чу, -тишь**; *impf* **замеча́ть**) *сов перех* to notice; (*запомнить*) to take note of; (*сказать*) to remark.
заме́т|ка (**-ки**; *gen pl* **-ок**) *ж* (*на дереве итп*) mark, notch; (*в записной книжке итп*) note; (*в газете итп*) short piece *или* article; **брать** (**взять** *perf*) **что-н на ~ку** to make a (mental) note of sth; **он на ~ке у мили́ции** (*разг*) the police have got their eye on him.
заме́тно *нареч* noticeably ◆ *как сказ* (*видно*) it is obvious.
заме́т|ный (**-ен, -на, -но**) *прил* noticeable; (*личность, человек*) prominent.
замету́ *итп сов см* **замести́.**
замеча́ни|е (**-я**) *ср* comment, remark; (*выговор*) reprimand.
замеча́телен *прил см* **замеча́тельный.**
замеча́тельно *нареч* (*красив, умён*) extremely; (*писать*) wonderfully, brilliantly ◆ *как сказ*: **~!** that's brilliant *или* wonderful!
замеча́тел|ьный (**-ен, -ьна, -ьно**) *прил* (*очень хороший*) wonderful, brilliant; (*необыкновенный*) remarkable; (*выдающийся*) outstanding.
замеча́|ть (**-ю**) *несов от* **заме́тить.**
замечта́|ться (**-юсь**) *сов возв* to start daydreaming.
заме́чу *сов см* **заме́тить.**
замечу́сь *итп сов см* **замета́ться.**
замеша́тельств|о (**-а**) *ср* confusion; **приводи́ть** (**привести́** *perf*) **кого́-н в ~** to throw sb into confusion; **приходи́ть** (**прийти́** *perf*) **в ~** to become confused.
замеша́|ть (**-ю**; *impf* **заме́шивать**) *сов перех*: **~ кого́-н во что-н** to get sb mixed up in sth
▸ **замеша́ться** (*impf* **заме́шиваться**) *сов возв*: **~ся в** *+acc* (*в историю, в преступление*) to get mixed up in; (*скрыться: в толпе*) to mingle with.
заме́шива|ть (**-ю**) *несов от* **замеси́ть, замеша́ть**
▸ **заме́шиваться** *несов от* **замеша́ться.**
заме́шка|ть (**-ю**) *сов от* **ме́шкать**
▸ **заме́шкаться** *сов возв* (*разг: с работой, с ответом*) to drag one's heels; (*: пробыть дольше*) to faff about.
замешу́ *сов см* **замеси́ть.**
замеща́|ть (**-ю**) *несов перех* (*начальника итп*) to stand in *или* deputize for; (*perf* **замести́ть**; *заменять: работника*) to replace; (*: игрока*) to substitute; (*вакантную должность*) to fill.
замеще́ни|е (**-я**) *ср* (*работника, директора*) replacement; (*игрока*) substitution; **~ вака́нтной до́лжности** filling of a vacancy.
замещу́ *сов см* **замести́ть.**
замина́|ть(ся) (**-ю(сь)**) *несов от* **замя́ть(ся).**
замини́р|овать (**-ую**) *сов от* **мини́ровать.**
зами́нк|а (**-и**) *ж* (*в работе*) hitch; (*в речи*) stumble.
замира́|ть (**-ю**) *несов от* **замере́ть.**
замире́ни|е (**-я**) *ср* appeasement.
за́мка *сущ см* **за́мок.**
замка́ *сущ см* **замо́к.**
за́мкнут|ый (**-, -а, -о**) *прил* (*среда, жизнь*) cloistered; (*человек, характер*) reclusive; **за́мкнутая цепь** (*ЭЛЕК*) closed circuit; **за́мкнутый круг** vicious circle.
замкн|у́ть (**-у́, -ёшь**; *impf* **замыка́ть**) *сов перех* to close
▸ **замкну́ться** (*impf* **замыка́ться**) *сов возв* to close; (*перен: обособиться*) to shut o.s. off; **замыка́ться** (**~ся** *perf*) **в себе́** to withdraw into o.s.
замну́(сь) *итп сов см* **замя́ть(ся).**
замоги́льный *прил*: **~ го́лос** ghostly voice.
за́м|ок (**-ка**) *м* castle.
зам|о́к (**-ка́**) *м* lock; (*также:* **вися́чий ~**) padlock; (*браслета, цепочки*) clasp; **на ~ке́** locked; **под ~ко́м** under lock and key; **храни́ть** (*impf*) **что-н за семью́ ~ка́ми** to keep sth very closely guarded.
замо́к|нуть (*3sg* **-нет**, *pt* **-, -ла, -ло**, *impf* **замока́ть**) *сов неперех* to get soaked.
замо́лв|ить (**-лю, -ишь**) *сов перех*: **~ сло́во за кого́-н** (**пе́ред кем-н**) (*разг*) to put in a word for sb (with sb).
замо́лк|нуть (**-ну, -нешь**; *pt* **-, -ла, -ло**, *impf* **замолка́ть**) *сов неперех* to fall silent; (*звук, песня, спор итп*) to stop.
замолч|а́ть (**-у́, -и́шь**) *сов неперех* (*человек*) to go quiet; (*перестать писать*): **он ~а́л ещё два го́да наза́д** I haven't heard from him for two years ◆ (*impf* **зама́лчивать**) *перех* (*разг: факты, происшествие*) to hush up; **~и́!** be quiet!, shut up!
замора́живани|е (**-я**) *ср* (*продуктов, овощей*) refrigeration; **замора́живание цен/за́работной пла́ты** price/wage freeze.
замора́жива|ть (**-ю**) *несов от* **заморо́зить.**
замор|и́ть (**-ю́, -и́шь**) *сов от* **мори́ть.**
заморо́|зить (**-жу, -зишь**; *impf* **замора́живать**) *сов перех* (*продукты, овощи*) to freeze; (*десну, палец*) to freeze, numb; (*перен: строительство*) to put on hold; **замора́живать** (**~** *perf*) **це́ны/зарпла́ту/счёт** to freeze prices/wages/an account.
за́морозк|и (**-ов**) *мн* frosts *мн.*
заморо́ч|ить (**-у, -ишь**) *сов от* **моро́чить.**
замо́рск|ий (**-ая, -ое, -ие**) *прил* (*разг*) foreign.
замо́рыш (**-а**) *м* (*разг*) weed, wimp.
замо|сти́ть (**-щу́, -сти́шь**) *сов от* **мости́ть.**
замо́тан|ный (**-, -а, -о**) *прил* (*разг*) knackered, whacked.
замота́|ть (**-ю**; *impf* **зама́тывать**) *сов перех* (*разг: утомить*) to knacker out; (*верёвку, канат*): **~ что-н во что-н** to wind sth around sth
▸ **замота́ться** (*impf* **зама́тываться**) *сов возв* (*в платок, шарфом*) to bundle o.s. up; (*разг: утомиться*) to be knackered (out).
замощу́ *сов см* **замости́ть.**

зам|очи́ть (**-очу́, -о́чишь**; *impf* **зама́чивать**) *сов перех*: ~ **кого́-н/что-н** to get sb/sth wet; (*бельё, кожу*) to soak.
замру́ *итп сов см* **замере́ть**.
за́муж *нареч*: **выходи́ть** ~ (**за** *+acc*) to get married (to), marry; **выдава́ть** (**вы́дать** *perf*) **кого́-н** ~ (**за** *+acc*) to marry sb off (to).
за́мужем *нареч* married; **быть** (*impf*) ~ **за кем-н** to be married to sb.
заму́жеств|о (**-а**) *ср* marriage.
заму́жн|яя *прил* married ◆ (**-ей**; *decl like adj*) *ж* married woman (*мн* women).
замур|ова́ть (**-у́ю**; *impf* **замуро́вывать**) *сов перех* (*отверстие, окно*) to brick up; (*человека, ценности*) to brick in.
заму|ти́ть(ся) (**-чу́(сь), -ти́шь(ся)**) *сов от* **мути́ть(ся)**.
заму́ч|ить (**-у, -ишь**) *сов от* **му́чить** ◆ *перех* (*заставить страдать*) to torment; (*утомить*) to exhaust; (*до смерти*) to torture to death
▸ **заму́читься** *сов от* **му́читься** ◆ *возв* (*утомиться*) to exhaust o.s.
замучу́(сь) *сов см* **замути́ть(ся)**.
за́мш|а (**-и**) *ж* suede.
за́мшевый *прил* suede.
замше́лый *прил* mossy, moss-covered.
замыва́|ть (**-ю**) *несов от* **замы́ть**.
замыка́ни|е (**-я**) *ср* (*также*: **коро́ткое** ~) short circuit.
замыка́|ть (**-ю**) *несов от* **замкну́ть** ◆ *перех* (*колонну, шествие*) to bring up the rear of
▸ **замыка́ться** *несов от* **замкну́ться**.
за́мыс|ел (**-ла**) *м* (*человека, правительства*) scheme; (*картины, произведения*) idea.
замы́сл|ить (**-ю, -ишь**; *impf* **замышля́ть**) *сов перех* (*план, побег*) to think up; (*+infin*) to think about doing; **он ~ил купи́ть себе́ дом** he is thinking about buying a house.
замыслова́т|ый (**-, -а, -о**) *прил* intricate.
зам|ы́ть (**-о́ю, -о́ешь**; *impf* **замыва́ть**) *сов перех* to wash out.
замышля́|ть (**-ю**) *несов от* **замы́слить**.
зам|я́ть (**-ну́, -нёшь**; *impf* **замина́ть**) *сов перех* (*разг*: *сделать незаметным*: *вопрос*) to hush up; (: *приостановить*: *разговор*) to put an end *или* a stop to
▸ **замя́ться** (*impf* **замина́ться**) *сов возв* to clam up; (*разг*: *замолчать*) to stop short.
за́навес (**-а**) *м* (*ТЕАТР*) curtain; **желе́зный** ~ (*ИСТ*) the Iron Curtain.
занаве́|сить (**-шу, -сишь**; *impf* **занаве́шивать**) *сов перех* to hang a curtain over.
занаве́с|ка (**-ки**; *gen pl* **-ок**) *ж* curtain.
занаве́шива|ть (**-ю**) *несов от* **занаве́сить**.
занаве́шу *сов см* **занаве́сить**.
зана́шива|ть (**-ю**) *несов от* **заноси́ть**.
зан|ести́ (**-есу́, -есёшь**; *pt* **-ёс, -есла́, -есло́**, *impf* **заноси́ть**) *сов перех* (*принести*) to bring; (*поднять*: *ногу, руку*) to lift; (*записать*) to take down; (*доставить*): ~ **что-н кому́-н** to drop sth off to sb; (*отнести*): ~ **за** *+acc* to take behind; **доро́гу ~есло́ сне́гом** the road is covered over with snow; **судьба́ ~есла́ меня́ сюда́ мно́го лет наза́д** fate brought me here many years ago.
зани́|зить (**-жу, -зишь**; *impf* **занижа́ть**) *сов перех* to lower; **занижа́ть** (**зани́зить** *perf*) **отме́тки кому́-н** to undermark sb.
занима́тел|ьный (**-ен, -ьна, -ьно**) *прил* engaging.
занима́|ть (**-ю**) *несов от* **заня́ть**
▸ **занима́ться** *несов возв*: **~ся** (*+instr*) (*учиться*) to study; (*работать*) to work (in); (*на рояле итп*) to practise (*BRIT*), practice (*US*); **~ся** (*impf*) **англи́йским** (**языко́м**) to study English; **~ся** (*impf*) **спо́ртом/му́зыкой** to play sports/music; **чем ~ется Ваш оте́ц?** what does your father do (for a living)?; **он ~ется би́знесом/поли́тикой** he's a businessman/politician; **чем ты сейча́с ~ешься?** what are you doing at the moment?
за́ново *нареч* again.
заножу́ *сов см* **занози́ть**.
зано́з|а (**-ы**) *ж* splinter.
зано|зи́ть (**-жу́, -зи́шь**) *сов перех* to get a splinter in.
зано́с (**-а**) *м* (*обычно мн*) drift; **сне́жные ~ы** snowdrift.
зан|оси́ть (**-ошу́, -о́сишь**) *несов от* **занести́** ◆ (*impf* **зана́шивать**) *сов перех* (*платье, пальто итп*) to wear out.
зано́счив|ый (**-, -а, -о**) *прил* arrogant.
заноч|ева́ть (**-у́ю**) *сов неперех* to spend the night.
заношу́ (*не*)*сов см* **заноси́ть**.
зану́д|а (**-ы**) *м/ж* bore.
зану́д|ный (**-ен, -на, -но**) *прил* tiresome, tedious.
зан|ы́ть (**-о́ю, -о́ешь**) *сов неперех* (*ребёнок*) to start whinging; (*сердце, зуб*) to begin to ache.
за́нят (**-, -а́, -о**) *прил* busy; **он был о́чень** ~ he was very busy; **телефо́н** ~ the phone *или* line is engaged.
заня́тен *прил см* **заня́тный**.
заня́ти|е (**-я**) *ср* occupation; (*обычно мн*: *в школе, в институте*) lesson, class; (*времяпрепровождение*) pastime, pursuit; **нача́ло шко́льных ~й** (*начало учебного года*) the beginning of the school year; (*утром*) the beginning of the school day.
заня́т|ный (**-ен, -на, -но**) *прил* entertaining.
занято́й *прил* busy; **он –** ~ **челове́к** he is a busy man.
за́нятост|ь (**-и**) *ж* (*ЭКОН*) employment; **по́лная** ~ full employment.
зан|я́ть (**займу́, займёшь**; *pt* **-ял, -яла́, -яло**, *impf* **занима́ть**) *сов перех* (*квартиру, город*) to occupy; (*должность, позицию*) to take up;

(*деньги*) to borrow; (*время*) to take; (*развлечь*) to occupy; ~ *(perf)* **ме́сто кому́-н** to keep a place for sb; **все ~яли́ свои́ места́** everyone took their places; ~ *(perf)* **пе́рвое/второ́е ме́сто** to take first/second place; **э́та рабо́та ~яла́ (у меня́) два часа́** the work took (me) two hours; **э́то займёт всего́ одну́ мину́тку** it will only take a minute

▸ **заня́ться** *сов возв*: **~ся** *+instr* (*языком, предметом, спортом*) to take up; (*бизнесом, политикой*) to go into; (*помочь*): **~ся с кем-н (чем-н)** to assist sb with sth; **~ся** *(perf)* **собо́й/детьми́** to devote time to o.s./one's children; **~ся** *(perf)* **убо́ркой** to do the cleaning; **ему́ пора́ ~ся де́лом** it's time that he did something serious with his life.

зао́блачный *прил* lofty.

заодно́ *нареч* (*вместе*) as one; (*попутно*) at the same time; **де́йствовать** *(impf)* ~ to act as one *или* with one accord; **мы с ни́ми** ~ we are in total accord.

заостр|и́ть (-ю́, -и́шь; *impf* **заостря́ть)** *сов перех* (*копьё, карандаш*) to sharpen; (*перен*: *мысль, вопрос*) to define; **заостря́ть (~** *perf***) внима́ние на чём-н** to focus one's attention on sth

▸ **заостри́ться** (*impf* **заостря́ться**) *сов возв* (*черты лица*) to become more pointed.

зао́чник (-а) *м* part-time student (*studying by correspondence*).

зао́чниц|а (-ы) *ж см* **зао́чник.**

зао́чно *нареч*: **учи́ться** ~ to study part-time (*by correspondence*); **обсужда́ть** *(impf)* **кого́-н** ~ to discuss sb in his *итп* absence.

зао́чный *прил* part-time; **зао́чное обуче́ние** distance learning; **зао́чный институ́т** correspondence school.

за́пад (-а) *м* west; **З~** (*ПОЛИТ*) the West.

запада́|ть (*3sg* **-ет**, *3pl* **-ют**) *несов от* **запа́сть.**

западёт *итп сов см* **запа́сть.**

за́падник (-а) *м* westernizer.

западноевропе́йск|ий (-ая, -ое, -ие) *прил* West European.

за́падный *прил* western; (*ветер*) westerly.

западн|я́ (-и́) *ж* snare; (*перен*) trap.

запа́ива|ть (-ю) *несов от* **запая́ть.**

запак|ова́ть (-у́ю) *сов от* **пакова́ть ◆** (*impf* **запако́вывать**) *перех* to wrap up.

запа́ко|стить (-щу, -стишь) *сов от* **па́костить.**

запа́л (-а) *м* (*заряда*) fuse; (*разг*: *пыл*) fire (*fig*).

запа́льчив|ый (-, -а, -о) *прил* (*человек, характер*) quick-tempered; (*ответ, тон*) impatient.

запанибра́та *нареч* (*разг*): **обраща́ться ~ с кем-н** to be overly familiar with sb.

запаник|ова́ть (-у́ю) *сов неперех* (*разг*) to panic.

запа́рк|а (-и) *ж* (*разг*) mad rush.

запа́рыва|ть (-ю) *несов от* **запоро́ть.**

запа́с (-а) *м* (*продуктов, топлива итп*) store, supply; (*руды, полезных ископаемых*) deposit; (*перен*: *знаний*) store; (*на брюках, на платье*) hem; (*ВОЕН*) the reserves *мн*; **у меня́ два часа́ в ~е** I've got two hours to spare; **оставля́ть (оста́вить** *perf***) себе́ что-н про ~** to put sth by; **золото́й ~** gold reserves *мн*; **запа́с слов** vocabulary.

запаса́|ть(ся) (-ю(сь)) *несов от* **запасти́(сь).**

запа́слив|ый (-, -а, -о) *прил* thrifty.

запа́сник (-а) *м* (*в музее*) storage room; (*разг*: *ВОЕН*) reserve.

запасн|о́й *прил* spare ◆ **(-о́го;** *decl like adj***)** *м* (*СПОРТ*: *также*: **~ игро́к**) substitute; (*ВОЕН*) reservist; **запасно́й вы́ход** emergency exit; **запасно́й путь** siding; **запасно́й соста́в** (*ВОЕН*) the reserves.

запа́сный *прил* = **запасно́й.**

зап|асти́ (-асу́, -асёшь; *pt* **-а́с, -асла́, -асло́,** *impf* **запаса́ть)** *сов перех* (*дрова, топливо*) to lay in

▸ **запасти́сь** (*impf* **запаса́ться**) *сов возв*: **~сь (**+*instr***)** (*хлебом, молоком*) to stock up (on); **запаса́ться (~сь** *perf***) терпе́нием** to arm o.s. with patience.

запа́|сть (*3sg* **-дёт**, *3pl* **-ду́т**, *pt* **-л, -ла, -ло**, *impf* **запада́ть**) *сов неперех* (*глаза, щёки*) to become sunken; (*перен*: *фраза, слова*) to be imprinted; **его́ слова́ ~ли мне в па́мять** his words remain imprinted on my memory.

запатент|ова́ть (-у́ю) *сов от* **патентова́ть ◆** (*impf* **запатенто́вывать**) *перех* to patent.

за́пах (-а; *part gen* **-у)** *м* smell.

запа́х (-а) *м* (*халата, пальто*) fold.

запа́хива|ть (-ю) *несов от* **запахну́ть.**

запа́х|нуть (-ну, -нешь; *pt* **-, -ла, -ло)** *сов неперех*: **~ (**+*instr***)** to start to smell (of).

запахн|у́ть (-у́, -ёшь; *impf* **запа́хивать)** *сов перех* to wrap round.

запа́чка|ть (-ю) *сов от* **па́чкать ◆** *перех* to soil, dirty; (*перен*: *совесть, имя*) to tarnish, sully

▸ **запа́чкаться** *сов от* **па́чкаться ◆** *возв* to get dirty.

запая́|ть (-ю; *impf* **запа́ивать)** *сов перех* to solder.

запева́л|а (-ы) *м/ж* (*МУЗ*) leader (*of a song*).

запева́|ть (-ю) *несов неперех* to lead off ◆ *перех*: **~ пе́сню** to start up a song.

запе́й(те) *сов см* **запи́ть.**

запёк(ся) *итп сов см* **запе́чь(ся).**

запека́нк|а (-и) *ж* (*картофельная итп*) bake; (*сладкая*) baked pudding.

запека́|ть(ся) (-ю(сь)) *несов от* **запе́чь(ся).**

запеку́(сь) *итп сов см* **запе́чь(ся).**

запелена́|ть (-ю) *сов от* **пелена́ть.**

запеленг|ова́ть (у́ю) *сов от* **пеленгова́ть.**

зап|ере́ть (-ру́, -рёшь; *pt* **-ер, -ерла́, -ерло,** *impf* **запира́ть)** *сов перех* (*дверь, шкаф, замок*) to lock; (*дом, человека, деньги*) to lock up

▸ **запере́ться** (*impf* **запира́ться**) *сов возв* (*дверь, шкаф, замок*) to lock; (*человек*) to lock o.s. up; (*разг*: *не признаться*) to clam up.

зап|е́ть (-ою́, -оёшь) *сов перех*: **~ пе́сню** to start singing a song.

запеча́та|ть (**-ю**; *impf* **запеча́тывать**) *сов перех* to seal up.
запечатле́|ть (**-ю**; *impf* **запечатлева́ть**) *сов перех* (*на картине, в повести итп*) to capture; (*в памяти*) to impress
▸ **запечатле́ться** (*impf* **запечатлева́ться**) *сов возв*: **~ся в па́мяти** to be imprinted on one's memory.
запеча́тыва|ть (**-ю**) *несов от* **запеча́тать**.
зап|е́чь (**-еку́, -ечёшь** *итп*, **-еку́т**; *pt* **-ёк, -екла́, -екло́**, *impf* **запека́ть**) *сов перех* to bake
▸ **запе́чься** (*impf* **запека́ться**) *сов возв* to bake; (*кровь*) to congeal; (*губы, рот*) to become parched.
запива́|ть (**-ю**) *несов от* **запи́ть**.
запина́|ться (**-юсь**) *несов от* **запну́ться**.
запи́н|ка (**-ки**; *gen pl* **-ок**) *ж* hesitation; **без ~ки** smoothly.
запира́тельств|о (**-а**) *ср* obstinacy.
запира́|ть(ся) (**-ю(сь)**) *несов от* **запере́ть(ся)**.
зап|иса́ть (**-ишу́, -и́шешь**; *impf* **запи́сывать**) *сов перех* (*адрес, имя итп*) to write down; (*концерт, пластинку*) to record; (*в кружок, на курсы*) to enrol; **запи́сывать** (**~** *perf*) **ле́кцию** to take notes (*in a lecture*); **~** (*perf*) **кого́-н** (**на приём**) **к врачу́** to make a doctor's appointment for sb
▸ **записа́ться** (*impf* **запи́сываться**) *сов возв* (*в кружок, на курсы*) to enrol (o.s.); (*музыкант*: *на плёнку*) to make a recording; **~ся** (*perf*) (**на приём**) **к врачу́** to make a doctor's appointment.
за́пис|и (**-ей**) *мн* (*лекции итп*) notes *мн*.
запи́ск|а (**-и**) *ж* note; (*служебная*) memo; *см также* **записки**.
запи́с|ки (**-ок**) *мн* (*короткие записи*) jottings *мн*; (*ЛИТЕРАТУРА*) notes *мн*, sketches *мн*.
записн|о́й *прил*: **~а́я кни́жка** notebook.
запи́сок *сущ см* **записки**.
запи́сыва|ть(ся) (**-ю(сь)**) *несов от* **записа́ть(ся)**.
за́пис|ь (**-и**) *ж* (*событий, КОМП*) record; (*в дневнике*) entry; (*МУЗ*) recording; (*в кружок, на курсы*) enrolment (*BRIT*), enrollment (*US*); (*на приём к врачу*) registration; *см также* **за́писи**.
зап|и́ть (**-ью́, -ьёшь**; *pt* **-и́л, -ила́, -и́ло**, *imper* **-е́й(те)**, *impf* **запива́ть**) *сов перех* (*лекарство, обед*): **~ что-н** (**чем-н**) to wash sth down (with sth) ◆ (*pt* **-ил, -ила́, -ило**) *неперех* (*начать пить*) to take to drink.
запиха́|ть (**-ю**; *impf* **запи́хивать**) *сов перех*: **~ что-н в** *+acc* (*разг*) to stuff sth into.
запихну́ть (**-у́, -ёшь**) *сов* = **запиха́ть**.
запишу́(сь) *итп сов см* **записа́ть(ся)**.
запла́кан|ный (**-, -а, -о**) *прил* tearful; (*глаза*) puffy.
запла́|кать (**-чу, -чешь**) *сов неперех* to start crying *или* to cry.
запланир|ова́ть (**-ую**) *сов перех* to plan.
запла́т|а (**-ы**) *ж* patch.
запл|ати́ть (**-ачу́, -а́тишь**) *сов от* **плати́ть**.
запла́т|ка (**-ки**; *gen pl* **-ок**) *ж* = **запла́та**.
запла́чу *итп сов см* **запла́кать**.
заплачу́ *сов см* **заплати́ть**.
запл|ева́ть (**-юю́**; *impf* **заплёвывать**) *сов перех* (*пол итп*) to spit on; (*человека*) to spit at.
заплёл *итп сов см* **заплести́**.
заплесневе́лый *прил* mouldy (*BRIT*), moldy (*US*).
запле́сневе|ть (*3sg* **-ет**, *3pl* **-ют**) *сов от* **пле́сневеть**.
запл|ести́ (**-ету́, -етёшь**; *pt* **-ёл, -ела́, -ело́**, *impf* **заплета́ть**) *сов перех* (*волосы, косу*) to plait.
заплета́|ться (*3sg* **-ется**, *3pl* **-ются**) *несов возв*: **у него́ но́ги ~ются** he keeps tripping over his feet; **у неё язы́к ~ется** she is muddling her words.
заплету́ *итп сов см* **заплести́**.
запломбир|ова́ть (**-у́ю**) *сов от* **пломбирова́ть**.
заплы́в (**-а**) *м* (*СПОРТ*) race (*in swimming*); (: *отборочный*) heat.
запл|ы́ть (**-ыву́, -ывёшь**; *impf* **заплыва́ть**) *сов неперех* (*человек*) to swim off; (*корабль*) to sail off; (*бревно*) to float off; (*глаза*) to become swollen.
запн|у́ться (**-у́сь, -ёшься**; *impf* **запина́ться**) *сов возв* to falter, stumble.
запове́дник (**-а**) *м* (*природный*) nature reserve; **пти́чий ~** bird reserve.
запове́дный *прил* (*лес, территория*) protected.
за́поведь (**-и**) *ж* (*РЕЛ*) commandment; (*перен*) cardinal rule; **де́сять ~ей** the Ten Commandments.
заподо́зр|ить (**-ю, -ишь**) *сов перех* to suspect; **~** (*perf*) **кого́-н в** *+acc* to suspect sb of.
запо́ем *нареч*: **пить ~** to drink heavily; **он чита́ет ~** (*разг*) he's an avid reader.
запозда́лый *прил* (*помощь, тревога итп*) belated; (*гость, весна*) late.
запо́|й (**-я**) *м* binge.
заполз|ти́ (**-у́, -ёшь**; *impf* **заполза́ть**) *сов неперех* to crawl.
заполне́ни|е (**-я**) *ср* (*бака, резервуара*) filling; (*анкеты, бланка*) completion.
запо́лн|ить (**-ю, -ишь**; *impf* **заполня́ть**) *сов перех* (*бак, комнату*) to fill (up); (*анкету, бланк*) to fill in *или* out
▸ **запо́лниться** (*impf* **заполня́ться**) *сов возв* to fill up.
заполя́рный *прил* polar.
запомина́|ть (**-ю**) *несов от* **запо́мнить**
▸ **запомина́ться** *несов от* **запо́мниться**; **легко́/тру́дно ~ся** (*impf*) to be easy/difficult to remember.
запомина́ющ|ий (**-ая, -ее, -ие**) *прил* (*КОМП*):

~ее устрóйство memory; **~ее устрóйство с произвóльной выборкой** random access memory.
запóмн|ить (**-ю, -ишь**; *impf* **запоминáть**) *сов перех* to remember
▸ **запóмниться** (*impf* **запоминáться**) *сов возв*: **мне ~ились егó словá** I remembered his words.
зáпонк|а (**-и**) *ж* cuff link.
запóр (**-а**) *м* (*МЕД*) constipation; (*замок*) lock; **быть** (*impf*) **на ~е** to be locked.
зап|орóть (**-орю́, -óрешь**; *impf* **запáрывать**) *сов перех* (*разг*: *испортить*) to botch up.
запорош|и́ть (*3sg* **-и́т**) *сов перех безл* to sprinkle; **дорóгу ~и́ло снéгом** a sprinkling of snow covered the road.
запотевá|ть (**-ю**) *несов от* **запотéть**.
запотéвш|ий (**-ая, -ее, -ие**) *прил* misty.
запотé|ть (**-ю**; *impf* **запотевáть**) *сов неперех* to steam up.
запою́ *итп сов см* **запéть**.
заправ|ить (**-лю, -ишь**; *impf* **заправля́ть**) *сов перех* (*рубашку*) to tuck in; (*лампу*) to fill; (*салат*) to dress; **заправля́ть** (**~** *perf*) **маши́ну** to fill up the engine
▸ **запрáвиться** (*impf* **заправля́ться**) *сов возв* (*разг*: *горючим*) to tank up; (: *поесть*) to fuel up.
запрáв|ка (**-ки**; *gen pl* **-ок**) *ж* (*машины, самолёта итп*) refuelling; (*КУЛИН*) dressing; (*разг*: *также*: **~очная стáнция**) filling station.
запрáвлю(сь) *сов см* **запрáвить(ся)**.
заправля́|ть (**-ю**) *несов от* **запрáвить** ◆ *неперех*: **~** (**+*instr***) (*разг*: *делами итп*) to be in charge (of)
▸ **заправля́ться** *несов от* **запрáвиться**.
запрáвок *сущ см* **запрáвка**.
запрáвск|ий (**-ая, -ое, -ие**) *прил* true, real.
запрáшива|ть (**-ю**) *несов от* **запроси́ть**.
запрéт (**-а**) *м*: **~** (**на** *+acc*/*+infin*) ban (on/on doing); **быть** (*impf*) **под ~ом** to be banned.
запрéтен *прил см* **запрéтный**.
запре|ти́ть (**-щý, -ти́шь**; *impf* **запрещáть**) *сов перех* to ban.
запрéт|ный (**-ен, -на, -но**) *прил* forbidden; **~ная тéма** taboo subject; **запрéтная зóна** restricted area *или* zone; **запрéтный плод** forbidden fruit.
запрещá|ть (**-ю**) *несов от* **запрети́ть**
▸ **запрещáться** *несов возв* to be forbidden *или* prohibited.
запрещéни|е (**-я**) *ср* banning.
запрещён|ный (**-, -а, -о**) *прил* banned; **запрещённый приём** (*СПОРТ*) foul; (*перен*) underhand tactic.
запрещý *сов см* **запрети́ть**.
запрограмми́р|овать (**-ую**) *сов от* **программи́ровать**.
запроекти́р|овать (**-ую**) *сов от* **проекти́ровать**.
запроки́н|уть (**-у, -ешь**; *impf* **запроки́дывать**) *сов перех*: **~ гóлову** to throw one's head back
▸ **запроки́нуться** (*impf* **запроки́дываться**) *сов возв* to jerk backwards.
запропа|сти́ться (**-щýсь, -сти́шься**) *сов неперех* (*разг*) to disappear.
запрóс (**-а**) *м* inquiry; (*обычно мн*: *требования*) need, requirement; (*стремления*) expectation.
запр|оси́ть (**-ошý, -óсишь**; *impf* **запрáшивать**) *сов перех* (*мнение, ответ итп*) to request; (*цену*) to ask.
зáпросто *нареч* (*разг*: *без усилий*) easily; (*без церемоний*) without making a fuss; **он обы́чно захóдит к нам ~** he usually just drops in.
запротест|овáть (**-ýю**) *сов неперех* to start protesting.
запротоколи́р|овать (**-ую**) *сов от* **протоколи́ровать**.
запрошý *сов см* **запроси́ть**.
запрý(сь) *итп сов см* **заперéть(ся)**.
запрýд|а (**-ы**) *ж* (*плотина*) weir; (*водоём*) millpond.
запр|уди́ть (**-ужý, -ýдишь**; *impf* **запрýживать** *или* **пруди́ть**) *сов перех* (*реку, ручей*) to dam; (*impf* **запрýживать**; *перен*: *площадь итп*) to pack.
запры́га|ть (**-ю**) *сов неперех* to start jumping.
запр|я́чь (**-ягý, -яжёшь** *итп*, **-ягýт**; *pt* **-я́г, -яглá, -ягló**, *impf* **запрягáть**) *сов перех* (*лошадь*) to harness, hitch up; (*разг*: *нагрузить работой*) to weigh down.
запýган|ный (**-, -на, -но**) *прил* frightened, scared.
запугá|ть (**-ю**; *impf* **запýгивать**) *сов перех* to frighten, scare.
зáпуск (**-а**) *м* (*мотора, станка*) starting; (*ракеты, спутника*) launch.
запускá|ть (**-ю**) *несов от* **запусти́ть**.
запустéни|е (**-я**) *ср* neglect.
зап|усти́ть (**-ущý, -ýстишь**; *impf* **запускáть**) *сов перех* (*бросить*) to hurl; (*мотор, станок*) to start (up); (*ракету, спутник*) to launch; (*хозяйство, работу, болезнь*) to neglect; (*разг*: *руку, когти*) to plunge; (: *впустить*) to let in ◆ *неперех*: **~ чем-н в когó-н** to hurl sth at sb; **запускáть** (**~** *perf*) **что-н в произвóдство** to launch production of sth.
запýтан|ный (**-, -на, -но**) *прил* (*нитки, волосы*) tangled, entangled; (*дело, вопрос*) confused; (*фраза*) muddled.
запýта|ть (**-ю**) *сов от* **пýтать** ◆ (*impf* **запýтывать**) *перех* (*нитки, волосы*) to tangle; (*вопрос, человека*) to confuse
▸ **запýтаться** *сов от* **пýтаться** ◆ (*impf* **запýтываться**) *возв* (*нитки, волосы*) to become tangled (up); (*человек*: *в верёвках*) to get tangled *или* caught up; (*дело, вопрос*) to become confused; (*разг*: *сбиться с толку*) to get o.s. in a tangle; (: *сбиться с пути*) to get lost; **запýтываться** (**~ся** *perf*) **в долгáх** to become trapped in debt; **запýтываться** (**~ся** *perf*) **в отвéте** to get muddled up.
запýщен|ный (**-, -на, -но**) *прил* neglected.

запущу́ *сов см* **запусти́ть**.
запча́ст|ь (**-и**) *ж сокр* = *запасна́я часть*; (*обычно мн*) spare (part).
запыла́|ть (**-ю**) *сов неперех* (*костёр, камин*) to flare up; (*щёки, человек*) to flush.
запыл|и́ть(ся) (**-ю́(сь), -и́шь(ся)**) *сов от* **пыли́ть(ся)**.
запыха́|ться (**-юсь**) *сов возв* to be out of breath.
запью́ *итп сов см* **запи́ть**.
запя́ст|ье (**-ья**; *gen pl* **-ий**) *ср* wrist.
запят|а́я (**-о́й**; *decl like adj*) *ж* comma.
запятна́|ть (**-ю**) *сов от* **пятна́ть**.
зарабо́та|ть (**-ю**; *impf* **зараба́тывать**) *сов перех* to earn ♦ *неперех* (*no impf*; *начать работать*) to start up
▸ **зарабо́таться** (*impf* **зараба́тываться**) *сов возв* (*разг*) to work o.s. into the ground.
за́работка *сущ см* **за́работок**.
за́работн|ый *прил*: **~ая пла́та** pay, wages *мн*.
за́работ|ок (**-ка**) *м* earnings *мн*.
зара́внива|ть (**-ю**) *несов от* **заровня́ть**.
заража́|ть(ся) (**-ю(сь)**) *несов от* **зарази́ть(ся)**.
зараже́ни|е (**-я**) *ср* (*организма, крови итп*) infection; (*местности, водоёма итп*) contamination.
заражён|ный (**-, -а, -о**) *прил* (*см сущ*) infected; contaminated.
заражу́(сь) *сов см* **зарази́ть(ся)**.
зара́з|а (**-ы**) *ж* infection ♦ *м/ж* (*разг*: *мерзавец*) pain, pest.
зара́зен *прил см* **зара́зный**.
заразител|ьный (**-ен, -ьна, -ьно**) *прил* (*перен*) infectious.
зара|зи́ть (**-жу́, -зи́шь**; *impf* **заража́ть**) *сов перех* (*человека*: *также перен*) to infect; (*воду, местность*) to contaminate
▸ **зарази́ться** (*impf* **заража́ться**) *сов возв* (*+instr*; *гриппом, корью итп*) to catch; (*перен*: *страхом, весельем*) to be infected by.
зара́з|ный (**-ен, -на, -но**) *прил* infectious.
зара́нее *нареч* in advance.
зар|асти́ (**-асту́, -астёшь**; *pt* **-о́с, -осла́, -осло́**, *impf* **зараста́ть**) *сов неперех* (*зажить*: *рана, порез*) to close up; **зараста́ть** (**~** *perf*) (*+instr*) (*травой итп*) to be overgrown (with); **он ~о́с щети́ной** he has let his beard grow.
зарв|а́ться (**-у́сь, -ёшься**; *impf* **зарыва́ться**) *сов неперех* (*разг*) to go too far; **зарыва́ться** (**~** *perf*) **в тре́бованиях** to demand too much.
зарёван|ный (**-, -а, -о**) *прил* (*разг*) = **запла́канный**.
зарев|е́ть (**-у́, -ёшь**) *сов неперех* (*медведь, лев*) to start roaring; (*бык*) to start bellowing; (*разг*: *заплакать*) to start bawling.
за́рев|о (**-а**) *ср* glow.
зарегистри́рованный *прил* registered; **~ торго́вый знак** registered trademark.
зарегистри́р|овать (**-ую**) *сов от* **регистри́ровать**.
заре́жу(сь) *итп сов см* **заре́зать(ся)**.
заре́з (**-а**) *м*: **по ~, до ~у** (*разг*) badly; **мне по ~ нужна́ твоя́ по́мощь** I badly need your help.
заре́|зать (**-жу, -жешь**) *сов от* **ре́зать** ♦ *перех* (*человека*) to knife; (*impf* **ре́зать**; *козу, поросёнка*) to slaughter; (*разг*: *книгу, проект*) to axe (*BRIT*), ax (*US*)
▸ **заре́заться** *сов возв* (*разг*) to knife o.s.
зарека́|ться (**-юсь**) *несов от* **заре́чься**.
зарекоменд|ова́ть (**-у́ю**; *impf* **зарекомендо́вывать**) *сов перех*: **~ себя́** *+instr* to prove *или* show o.s. to be; **он хорошо́ себя́ ~ова́л** he proved to be good.
зар|е́чься (**-еку́сь, -ечёшься** *итп*, **-еку́тся**; *pt* **-ёкся, -екла́сь, -екло́сь**, *impf* **зарека́ться**) *сов возв* (*+infin*) to swear *или* vow never to do; **она́ ~екла́сь ходи́ть туда́** she vowed never to go there.
заржа́ве|ть (*3sg* **-ет**) *сов от* **ржа́веть**.
заржа́влен|ный (**-, -а, -о**) *прил* rusty.
зарж|а́ть (**-у́, -ёшь**) *сов неперех* (*лошадь*) to neigh; (*разг*: *человек*) to roar with laughter.
зарис|ова́ть (**-у́ю**; *impf* **зарисо́вывать**) *сов перех* (*дом, лодку*) to sketch; **они́ ~ова́ли всю стéну** (*разг*) they drew all over the wall.
зарисо́в|ка (**-ки**; *gen pl* **-ок**) *ж* (*действие*) sketching; (*обычно мн*: *рисунок*) sketch.
зарисо́выва|ть (**-ю**) *несов от* **зарисова́ть**.
зарни́ц|а (**-ы**) *ж* sheet lightning.
заровня́|ть (**-ю**; *impf* **зара́внивать**) *сов перех* (*поверхность*) to level; (*яму, канаву*) to fill up.
зарод|и́ться (*3sg* **-и́тся**, *3pl* **-я́тся**, *impf* **зарожда́ться**) *сов возв* (*явление*) to emerge; (*перен*: *идея*) to be born; (: *чувство, сомнения*) to arise.
заро́дыш (**-а**) *м* (*БИО*) embryo; (*растения, также перен*) germ; **в ~е** (*перен*) in embryo; **подавля́ть** (**подави́ть** *perf*) **что-н в ~е** to nip sth in the bud.
зарожда́|ться (*3sg* **-ется**, *3pl* **-ются**) *несов от* **зароди́ться**.
зарожде́ни|е (**-я**) *ср* (*жизни*) emergence; (*идеи, чувства*) conception.
заро́к (**-а**) *м* pledge, vow.
заро́с *итп сов см* **зарасти́**.
за́росл|ь (**-и**) *ж* (*обычно мн*) thicket.
зарпла́т|а (**-а**) *ж* pay.
заруба́|ть (**-ю**) *несов от* **заруби́ть**.
зарубе́жный *прил* foreign.
зарубе́жь|е (**-я**) *ср* overseas; **стра́ны бли́жнего ~я** "near abroad" (*the republics of the former USSR*).
зар|уби́ть (**-ублю́, -у́бишь**; *impf* **заруба́ть**) *сов перех* to hack down; **~уби́ себе́ на носу́** *или* **лбу** (*разг*) mark my words.
зару́бк|а (**-и**) *ж* notch.
зарублю́ *сов см* **заруби́ть**.

зарубц|ева́ться (*3sg* **-у́ется**, *3pl* **-у́ются**) *сов от* **рубцева́ться ◆** (*impf* **зарубцо́вываться**) *возв* to cicatrize.
зарумя́н|иться (**-юсь, -ишься**; *impf* **зарумя́ниваться**) *сов возв* (*лицо, щёки*) to colour (*BRIT*), color (*US*); (*пирог, мясо*) to brown.
заруч|и́ться (**-у́сь, -и́шься**; *impf* **заруча́ться**) *сов возв* (*+instr*; *помощью, согласием*) to secure.
зарыва́|ть (**-ю**) *несов от* **зары́ть**
▸ **зарыва́ться** *несов от* **зары́ться, зарва́ться**.
зарыда́|ть (**-ю**) *сов неперех* to begin to weep.
зар|ы́ть (**-о́ю, -о́ешь**; *impf* **зарыва́ть**) *сов перех* to bury; (*яму, канаву*) to fill
▸ **зары́ться** (*impf* **зарыва́ться**) *сов возв*: **~ся в** *+acc* (*в землю, в песок*) to bury o.s. in; **зарыва́ться** (**~ся** *perf*) **в рабо́ту/учёбу** to bury o.s. in one's work/books; **она́ ~ы́лась голово́й в поду́шку** she buried her head in the pillow.
зар|я́ (**-и́**; *nom pl* **зо́ри**, *gen pl* **зорь**, *dat pl* **зо́рям**) *ж* (*утренняя, также перен*) dawn; (*вечерняя*) sundown; (*ВОЕН*) reveille; **ни свет ни ~** at the crack of dawn; **от ~и́ до ~и́** from dawn to dusk.
заря́д (**-а**) *м* (*ВОЕН, ЭЛЕК*) charge; (*перен*: *бодрости, энергии*) charge, boost.
заря|ди́ть (**-жу́, -ди́шь**; *impf* **заряжа́ть**) *сов перех* (*пистолет, пушку, фотоаппарат*) to load; (*батарейку, аккумулятор*) to charge; **он ~ди́л одно́ и то же** (*разг*) he keeps going on about it; **дождь ~ди́л** (*разг*) it started pouring
▸ **заряди́ться** (*impf* **заряжа́ться**) *сов возв* (*батарейка, аккумулятор*) to recharge; **заряжа́ться** (**~ся** *perf*) **эне́ргией** (*перен*) to recharge one's batteries.
заря́дк|а (**-и**) *ж* (*упражнения*) exercises *мн*.
заряжа́|ть(ся) (**-ю(сь)**) *несов от* **заряди́ть(ся)**.
заряжу́(сь) *сов см* **заряди́ть(ся)**.
заса́д|а (**-ы**) *ж* ambush; (*отряд*) ambush party; **устра́ивать** (**устро́ить** *perf*) **~у** to set up an ambush; **сиде́ть** (*impf*) **в ~е** to lie in ambush.
зас|ади́ть (**-ажу́, -а́дишь**; *impf* **заса́живать**) *сов перех* (*грядку, клумбу*): **~** (*+instr*) to plant (with); (*разг*: *нож, топор*): **~ в** *+acc* to sink into; **~** (*perf*) **кого́-н за решётку** (*разг*) to stick sb behind bars; **заса́живать** (**~** *perf*) **кого́-н за рабо́ту** to set sb to work.
заса́ленный *прил* greasy.
заса́лива|ть (**-ю**) *несов от* **засоли́ть, заса́лить**
▸ **заса́ливаться** *несов от* **заса́литься**.
заса́л|ить (**-ю, -ишь**; *impf* **заса́ливать**) *сов перех* to soil
▸ **заса́литься** (*impf* **заса́ливаться**) *сов возв* to get greasy.
заса́сыва|ть (*3sg* **-ет**, *3pl* **-ют**) *несов от* **засоса́ть**.
заса́харенн|ый *прил*: **~ые фру́кты** crystallized fruits *мн*.
заса́хар|ить (**-ю, -ишь**; *impf* **заса́харивать**) *сов перех* to crystallize
▸ **заса́хариться** (*impf* **заса́хариваться**) *сов возв* (*мёд, варенье*) to crystallize.
засверка́|ть (**-ю**) *сов неперех* (*молния, глаза*) to flash.
засв|ети́ть (**-ечу́, -е́тишь**; *impf* **засве́чивать**) *сов перех* (*ФОТО*) to expose
▸ **засвети́ться** (*impf* **засве́чиваться**) *сов возв* to be exposed.
за́светло *нареч* before nightfall *или* dark.
засве́чива|ть(ся) (**-ю(сь)**) *несов от* **засвети́ть(ся)**.
засвечу́(сь) *сов см* **засвети́ть(ся)**.
засвиде́тельств|овать (**-ую**) *сов перех* (*факт*) to testify to; (*документ, копию*) to certify.
засева́|ть (**-ю**) *несов от* **засе́ять**.
заседа́ни|е (**-я**) *ср* (*собрание*) meeting; (*парламента, суда*) session, sitting.
заседа́тел|ь (**-я**) *м*: **прися́жный ~** member of the jury.
заседа́|ть (**-ю**) *несов неперех* (*на совещании*) to meet; (*в парламенте, в суде*) to sit; (*парламент, суд*) to be in session.
засе́ива|ть (**-ю**) *несов от* **засе́ять**.
засёк *итп сов см* **засе́чь**.
засека́|ть (**-ю**) *несов от* **засе́чь**.
засекре́|тить (**-чу, -тишь**; *impf* **засекре́чивать**) *сов перех* (*сведения, документы*) to restrict access to.
засекре́ченный *прил* (*сведения, документы*) classified; (*завод итп*) secret.
засекре́чива|ть (**-ю**) *несов от* **засекре́тить**.
засекре́чу *сов см* **засекре́тить**.
засеку́ *итп сов см* **засе́чь**.
засе́л *итп сов см* **засе́сть**.
заселе́ни|е (**-я**) *ср* (*земель*) settlement; (*дома*) occupation.
заселённый (**-ён, -ена́, -ено́**) *прил* (*область, район*) settled; (*дом, квартира*) occupied.
засел|и́ть (**-ю́, -и́шь**; *impf* **заселя́ть**) *сов перех* (*земли*) to settle; (*дом*) to take up occupancy of.
зас|е́сть (**-я́ду, -я́дешь**; *pt* **-е́л, -е́ла, -е́ло**) *сов неперех* (*надолго остаться*: *дома*) to ensconce o.s.; (*спрятаться*) to sit tight; (*застрять*) to lodge; **~** (*perf*) **за что-н/** *+infin* to get down to sth/down to doing.
засе́чк|а (**-ки**; *gen pl* **-ек**) *ж* notch.
зас|е́чь (**-еку́, -ечёшь** *итп*, **-еку́т**; *pt* **-ёк, -екла́, -екло́**, *impf* **засека́ть**) *сов перех* (*место*) to locate; (*разг*: *заметить*) to nail down; (*выпороть*) to flog; **засека́ть** (**~** *perf*) **вре́мя** to record the time.
засе́|ять (**-ю**; *impf* **засева́ть** *или* **засе́ивать**) *сов перех* to sow.
заси|де́ться (**-жу́сь, -ди́шься**; *impf* **заси́живаться**) *сов неперех* to stay for a long time; **мы вчера́ ~де́лись в гостя́х** we stayed late at friends yesterday.
заси́ль|е (**-я**) *ср* dominance.
засия́|ть (**-ю**) *сов неперех* to begin to shine.
засо́к (**-а**) *м* (*разг*: *в мыслях*) peculiarity.
заскору́зл|ый (**-, -а, -о**) *прил* (*кожа, руки*)

calloused.
заск|очи́ть (-очу́, -о́чишь) *сов неперех* (*разг: в гости*) to drop in.
заскреж|ета́ть (-ещу́, -е́щешь) *сов неперех*: **~ зуба́ми** to grind one's teeth.
заскуча́|ть (-ю) *сов неперех* to get bored; **~** (*perf*) **по кому́-н/чему́-н** to start to miss sb/sth.
за|сла́ть (-шлю́, -шлёшь; *impf* **засыла́ть)** *сов перех* to send out.
засло́н (-а) *м* screen, shield.
заслон|и́ть (-ю́, -и́шь; *impf* **заслоня́ть)** *сов перех* to block out; (*от ветра, от пули*) to shield, screen.
засло́н|ка (-ки; *gen pl* **-ок)** *ж* (*печи*) vent; (*шлюза*) gate.
заслоня́|ть (-ю) *несов от* **заслони́ть.**
заслу́г|а (-и) *ж* (*обычно мн*) service; **~и пе́ред страно́й** services to one's country; **награди́ть** (*perf*) **кого́-н по ~м** to fully reward sb; **его́ наказа́ли по ~м** he got what he deserved.
заслу́женный *прил* well-deserved, well-merited; (*врач, учёный итп*) renowned; **Заслу́женный арти́ст России/ма́стер спо́рта** *title awarded by the state in honour of cultural/sporting achievement.*
заслу́жива|ть (-ю) *несов от* **заслужи́ть ◆** *перех* (*доверия, внимания итп*) to deserve.
засл|ужи́ть (-ужу́, -у́жишь; *impf* **заслу́живать)** *сов перех* to earn.
заслу́ша|ть (-ю; *impf* **заслу́шивать)** *сов перех* to listen to
▸ **заслу́шаться** (*impf* **заслу́шиваться)** *сов возв*: **~ся (**+*instr***)** (*музыкой, рассказом*) to be captivated (by).
засма́трива|ться (-юсь) *несов от* **засмотре́ться.**
засме|я́ть (-ю́, -ёшь; *impf* **засме́ивать)** *сов перех* to taunt
▸ **засмея́ться** *сов возв* to start laughing.
засм|отре́ться (-отрю́сь, -о́тришься; *impf* **засма́триваться)** *сов неперех*: **~ на** +*acc* to be transfixed by.
засне́жен|ный (-, -а, -о) *прил* snow-covered.
засн|у́ть (-у́, -ёшь; *impf* **засыпа́ть)** *сов неперех* to go to sleep, fall asleep.
засо́в (-а) *м* bolt.
засо́выва|ть (-ю) *несов от* **засу́нуть.**
засо́л (-а) *м* (*рыбы*) salting.
зас|оли́ть (-олю́, -о́лишь; *impf* **заса́ливать)** *сов перех* to salt.
засоре́ни|е (-я) *ср* (*рек*) pollution; (*раковины, туалета*) blockage; **засоре́ние желу́дка** stomach upset.
засор|и́ть (-ю́, -и́шь; *impf* **засоря́ть)** *сов перех* (*комнату, поляну*) to litter; (*раковину, туалет*) to block *или* clog up; (*перен: мысли, речь*) to contaminate; **~** (*perf*) **глаза́** to get grit in one's eyes; **~** (*perf*) **желу́док** to get a stomach upset
▸ **засори́ться** (*impf* **засоря́ться)** *сов возв* (*раковина, туалет*) to become clogged up.
засос|а́ть (-у́, -ёшь; *impf* **заса́сывать)** *сов перех* to suck in **◆** *неперех* (*no impf; подлеж: младенец*) to start feeding.
засо́хн|уть (-у, -ешь) *сов от* **со́хнуть ◆** (*impf* **засыха́ть)** *неперех* (*грязь*) to dry up; (*растение*) to wither.
за́спан|ный (-, -на, -но) *прил* sleepy.
заспо́р|ить (-ю, -ишь) *сов неперех* to start arguing.
заста́в|а (-ы) *ж* (*также:* **пограни́чная ~**) frontier post; (*ВОЕН: отряд*) party, detachment.
заста|ва́ть (-ю́, -ёшь) *несов от* **заста́ть.**
заста́в|ить (-лю, -ишь; *impf* **заставля́ть)** *сов перех* (*занять*) to clutter up; (*закрыть*) to block off; **заставля́ть (~** *perf***) кого́-н** +*infin* to force sb to do, make sb do; **он ~ил меня́ помо́чь ему́** he made me help him.
заста́ива|ться (*3sg* **-ется,** *3pl* **-ются)** *несов от* **застоя́ться.**
заста́ну *итп сов см* **заста́ть.**
застаре́лый *прил* old.
заста́|ть (-ну, -нешь; *impf* **застава́ть)** *сов перех* to catch, find; **я его́ не ~л до́ма** I didn't manage to catch him at home; **я ~л её за рабо́той** I found her at work.
застегн|у́ть (-у́, -ёшь; *impf* **застёгивать)** *сов перех* to do up
▸ **застегну́ться** (*impf* **застёгиваться)** *сов возв* (*человек: на пуговицы*) to button o.s. up; (*: на молнию*) to zip o.s. up; (*пуговицы, молния*) to do up.
застёж|ка (-ки; *gen pl* **-ек)** *ж* fastener.
застекл|и́ть (-ю́, -и́шь; *impf* **застекля́ть)** *сов перех* to glaze.
застел|и́ть (-ю́, -ишь; *impf* **застила́ть)** *сов перех* (*кровать*) to make up; (*стол, пол*) to cover.
застелю́ *итп сов см* **застла́ть.**
засте́нка *сущ см* **засте́нок.**
застенографи́р|овать (-ую) *сов от* **стенографи́ровать.**
засте́н|ок (-ка; *nom pl* **-ки)** *м* torture chamber.
засте́нчив|ый (-, -а, -о) *прил* shy.
застесня́|ться (-юсь) *сов возв* (*разг*) to go all shy.
засти́г *итп сов см* **засти́чь.**
застига́|ть (-ю) *несов от* **засти́гнуть, засти́чь.**
засти́гну *итп сов см* **засти́чь.**
засти́г|нуть (-ну, -нешь; *pt -* *или* **-нул, -ла, -ло,** *impf* **застига́ть)** *сов* = **засти́чь.**
застила́|ть (-ю) *несов от* **застели́ть, застла́ть.**
застира́|ть (-ю; *impf* **засти́рывать)** *сов перех* (*бельё, одежду*) to overwash; (*пятно*) to wash off *или* out.
засти́|чь (-гну, -гнешь; *pt* **-г, -гла, -гло,** *impf* **застига́ть)** *сов перех* to catch.

заст|ла́ть (-елю́, -е́лешь; *impf* **застила́ть)** *сов перех* (*подлеж: облака, туман*) to cover; (: *слёзы, дым*) to blur.
засто́|й (-я) *м* (*в делах, в работе*) standstill; (*в жизни, в мыслях*) stagnation.
засто́йный *прил* (*также перен*) stagnant.
засто́льн|ый *прил*: **~ые разгово́ры** table talk; **~ая пе́сня** drinking song.
заст|она́ть (-ону́, -о́нешь) *сов неперех* to groan.
засто́пор|ить (-ю, -ишь) *сов от* **сто́порить**
▸ **засто́пориться** *сов возв* (*машина, станок*) to come to a halt; (*дело, работа*) to be held up.
засто|я́ться (*3sg* **-и́тся,** *3pl* **-я́ться,** *impf* **заста́иваться)** *сов перех* (*вода*) to go stagnant.
застра́ива|ть (-ю) *несов от* **застро́ить.**
застрахо́ван|ный (-, -а, -о) *прил* insured.
застрах|ова́ть (-у́ю; *impf* **застрахо́вывать)** *сов перех*: **~ (от** *+gen*) (*также перен*) to insure (against)
▸ **застрахова́ться** (*impf* **застрахо́вываться)** *сов возв*: **~ся (от** *+gen*) to insure o.s. (against).
застра́чива|ть (-ю) *несов от* **застрочи́ть.**
застрева́|ть (-ю) *несов от* **застря́ть.**
застр|ели́ть (-елю́, -е́лишь; *impf* **застре́ливать)** *сов перех* to shoot
▸ **застрели́ться** (*impf* **застре́ливаться)** *сов возв* to shoot o.s.
застро́енный *прил* built-up.
застро́|ить (-ю, -ишь; *impf* **застра́ивать)** *сов перех* to build on, develop.
застро́йк|а (-и) *ж* development.
застроч|и́ть (-у́, -и́шь; *impf* **застра́чивать)** *сов перех* (*вытачки, складки*) to stitch ◆ *неперех* (*no impf*; *пулемёт*) to spray bullets; (*начать писать*) to start scribbling away.
застря́|ть (-ну, -нешь; *impf* **застрева́ть)** *сов неперех* to get stuck.
заст|уди́ть (-ужу́, -у́дишь; *impf* **засту́живать)** *сов перех* (*разг*): **~ го́рло/у́ши** to get a sore throat/sore ears.
заст|упи́ться (-уплю́сь, -у́пишься; *impf* **заступа́ться)** *сов возв*: **~ за** *+acc* to stand up for.
засту́пник (-а) *м* defender.
засту́пниц|а (-ы) *ж см* **засту́пник.**
застыва́|ть (-ю) *несов от* **засты́ть.**
засты́вш|ий (-ая, -ее, -ие) *прил* (*также перен*) frozen; (*лава*) solidified; (*цемент, желе*) set.
засты́|ть (-ну, -нешь; *impf* **застыва́ть)** *сов неперех* to freeze; (*лава*) to solidify; (*цемент*) to set; **застыва́ть (~** *perf*) **на ме́сте** to freeze, stop dead; **~** (*perf*) **от стра́ха** to be paralysed with fear.
засуе|ти́ться (-чу́сь, -ти́шься) *сов возв* to start bustling about.
засу́н|уть (-у, -ешь; *impf* **засо́вывать)** *сов перех*: **~ что-н в** *+acc* to thrust sth into.
за́сух|а (-и) *ж* drought.
засухоусто́йчив|ый (-, -а, -о) *прил* drought-resistant.
зас|учи́ть (-учу́, -у́чишь; *impf* **засу́чивать)** *сов перех* (*штанину, рукав*) to roll up; **~учи́в рукава́** (*перен*) in earnest.
зас|уши́ть (-ушу́, -у́шишь; *impf* **засу́шивать)** *сов перех* to dry up.
засу́шлив|ый (-, -а, -о) *прил* dry.
засчита́|ть (-ю; *impf* **засчи́тывать)** *сов перех* to take into account; (*гол, результат*) to allow (to stand).
засыла́|ть (-ю) *несов от* **засла́ть.**
засы́п|ать (-лю, -лешь; *impf* **засыпа́ть)** *сов перех* (*яму, канаву*) to fill (up); (*покрыть*) to cover; (*разг: студента*) to flunk; (*муку, крупу итп*) to pour; **засыпа́ть (~** *perf*) **кого́-н вопро́сами/пода́рками** to bombard sb with questions/gifts; **его́ ~ало песко́м** he was buried under the sand
▸ **засы́паться** (*impf* **засыпа́ться)** *сов возв*: **~ся** *+instr* (*песком, землёй*) to be covered with; (*разг: попасться*) to cock up; (: *на экзамене*) to flunk; **засыпа́ться (~ся** *perf*) **в** *+acc* **/за** *+acc* to get into/behind.
засыпа́|ть (-ю) *несов от* **засну́ть, засы́пать**
▸ **засыпа́ться** *несов от* **засы́паться.**
засы́плю(сь) *итп сов см* **засы́пать(ся).**
засыха́|ть (-ю) *несов от* **засо́хнуть.**
car ся́ду *итп сов см* **засе́сть.**
зата|и́ть (-ю́, -и́шь; *impf* **зата́ивать)** *сов перех* (*неприязнь, мечту*) to harbour (*BRIT*), harbor (*US*); **зата́ивать (~** *perf*) **оби́ду** to harbour a grudge; **зата́ивать (~** *perf*) **дыха́ние** to hold one's breath
▸ **затаи́ться** *сов возв* to hide.
зата́лкива|ть (-ю) *несов от* **затолка́ть, затолкну́ть.**
зата́плива|ть (-ю) *несов от* **затопи́ть.**
зата́птыва|ть (-ю) *несов от* **затопта́ть.**
зата́скан|ный (-, -на, -но) *прил* worn-out.
затаска́|ть (-ю; *impf* **зата́скивать)** *сов перех* (*разг: одежду, шутку*) to wear out; **зата́скивать (~** *perf*) **кого́-н по магази́нам** (*разг*) to drag sb round the shops; **~** (*perf*) **кого́-н по суда́м** (*разг*) to drag sb through the courts.
зата́скива|ть (-ю) *несов от* **затаска́ть, затащи́ть.**
зата́чива|ть (-ю) *несов от* **заточи́ть.**
зат|ащи́ть (-ащу́, -а́щишь; *impf* **зата́скивать)** *сов перех* to drag; **~** (*perf*) **кого́-н в кино́** (*разг*) to drag sb off to the cinema.
затвердева́|ть (*3sg* **-ет,** *3pl* **-ют)** *несов от* **затверде́ть.**
затверде́лый *прил* hardened.
затверде́ни|е (-я) *ср* (*МЕД*) callus.
затверде́|ть (*3sg* **-ет,** *3pl* **-ют,** *impf* **затвердева́ть)** *сов неперех* (*земля, цемент*) to harden; (*жидкость*) to solidify.
затвер|ди́ть (-жу́, -ди́шь) *сов от* **тверди́ть** ◆ (*impf* **затве́рживать)** *перех* to learn by rote.
затво́р (-а) *м* (*плотины*) floodgate; (*фотоаппарата*) shutter; (*винтовки*) breech.
затво́рник *м* (*РЕЛ*) hermit; (*перен*) hermit, recluse.

затво́рниц|а (-ы) *ж см* **затво́рник**.
затева́|ть (-ю) *несов от* **зате́ять**.
зате́йлив|ый (-, -а, -о) *прил* intricate.
зате́йник (-а) *м* entertainer.
затёк *итп сов см* **зате́чь**.
затека́|ть (-ю) *несов от* **зате́чь**.
затеку́т *сов см* **зате́чь**.
зате́м *нареч* (*потом*) then; (*для того*) for that reason; ~ **что́бы** in order to.
затемне́ни|е (-я) *ср* (*перен*: *рассудка*) obscuring; (*ВОЕН*) blackout.
затемнённый *прил* (*очки, стекло*) tinted.
затемн|и́ть (-ю́, -и́шь; *impf* **затемня́ть**) *сов перех* to darken; (*перен*: *рассудок*) to obscure; (*город, окна*) to black out.
за́темно *нареч* (*разг*: *до рассвета*) before light; (: *когда стемнело*) after dark.
затемня́|ть (-ю) *несов от* **затемни́ть**.
затен|и́ть (-ю́, -и́шь; *impf* **затеня́ть**) *сов перех* to shade; (*комнату*) to darken.
зате́пл|иться (*3sg* **-ится**, *3pl* **-ятся**) *сов неперех* (*огонёк*) to begin to flicker; (*надежда*) to appear.
зат|ере́ть (-ру́, -рёшь; *pt* **-ёр, -ёрла, -ёрло**, *impf* **затира́ть**) *сов перех* (*пятно, надпись*) to rub out; (*перен*: *разг*: *работника*) to shackle; **её ~ёрли в толпе́** she got caught up in the crowd; **кора́бль ~ёрло льда́ми** the ship was icebound.
зате́рянный *прил* (*человек*) forgotten; (*место, дом*) forsaken.
затеря́|ться (-юсь) *сов от* **теря́ться** ♦ *возв* (*разг*) to go missing, disappear; (*в дали, в толпе*) to disappear.
зат|е́чь (*3sg* **-ечёт**, *3pl* **-еку́т**, *pt* **-ёк, -екла́, -екло́**, *impf* **затека́ть**) *сов неперех* (*опухнуть*) to swell up; (*онеметь*) to go numb; (*вода*): ~ **за** *+acc*/**в** *+acc* to seep behind/into.
затещу́сь *итп сов см* **затеса́ться**.
зате́|я (-и) *ж* (*замысел*) idea, scheme; (*забава*) escapade; **без ~й** without frills.
зате́|ять (-ю; *impf* **затева́ть**) *сов перех* (*разговор, игру*) to start (up); **он, ка́жется, что́-то затева́ет** (*разг*) he's got something up his sleeve.
затира́|ть (-ю) *несов от* **затере́ть**.
зати́х|нуть (-ну, -нешь; *pt* **-, -ла, -ло**, *impf* **затиха́ть**) *сов неперех* (*люди, место*) to quieten (*BRIT*) *или* quiet (*US*) down; (*шум, ветер, буря*) to die down.
зати́шь|е (-я) *ср* lull.
заткн|у́ть (-у́, -ёшь; *impf* **затыка́ть**) *сов перех* to stop up, plug; ~ (*perf*) **что-н за** *+acc*/**в** *+acc* to stuff sth behind/into; **затыка́ть** (~ *perf*) **кого́-н** *или* **рот кому́-н** (*разг*) to shut sb up; **затыка́ть** (~ *perf*) **кого́-н за по́яс** (*перен*: *разг*) to outdo sb
▸ **заткну́ться** (*impf* **затыка́ться**) *сов возв* (*разг*: *замолчать*) to shut up; **~и́сь!** (*разг*: *пренебр*) shut it!
затмева́|ть (-ю) *несов от* **затми́ть**.
затме́ни|е (-я) *ср* (*солнца, луны*) eclipse; (*разг*: *ума*) blackout; **на меня́ нашло́** ~ my mind went blank.
затм|и́ть (-и́шь; *impf* **затмева́ть**) *сов перех* (*также перен*) to eclipse.
зато́ *союз* (*также*: **но** ~: *однако*) but then (again); (*поэтому*) but (to make up for it); **кварти́ра ма́ленькая, (но) ~ в хоро́шем райо́не** the flat is small, but then again it's in a nice district.
затова́ривани|е (-я) *ср* (*КОММ*: *скопление товаров*) stockpiling; (*склада, магазина*) overstocking.
затова́р|ить (-ю, -ишь; *impf* **затова́ривать**) *сов перех* (*см сущ*) to stockpile; to overstock.
затолка́|ть (-ю; *impf* **зата́лкивать**) *сов перех* (*разг*) to shove; (*в автобусе, в толпе*) to squash.
затолкн|у́ть (-у́, -ёшь; *impf* **зата́лкивать**) *сов перех* to shove.
зат|ону́ть (-ону́, -о́нешь) *сов неперех* to sink.
зат|опи́ть (-оплю́, -о́пишь; *impf* **зата́пливать**) *сов перех* (*печь, камин*) to light; (*impf* **затопля́ть**; *остров, деревню*) to flood; (*судно*) to sink.
зат|опта́ть (-опчу́, -о́пчешь; *impf* **зата́птывать**) *сов перех* (*цветы, газон*) to trample on; (*огонь, следы*) to stamp out; (*убить*) to trample to death.
зато́р (-а) *м* congestion; (*на улице*) traffic jam; (*на реке*) log jam.
затормо|зи́ть(ся) (-жу́, -зи́шь) *сов от* **тормози́ть(ся)**.
затор|опи́ться (-оплю́сь, -о́пишься) *сов возв* to hasten.
затоск|ова́ть (-у́ю) *сов неперех* to begin to feel melancholic; ~ (*perf*) **по** *+dat* to start to miss.
затача́|ть (-ю) *несов от* **заточи́ть**.
заточе́ни|е (-я) *ср* incarceration.
зат|очи́ть (-очу́, -о́чишь; *impf* **зата́чивать**) *сов перех* to sharpen; (*impf* **заточа́ть**; *в тюрьму*) to incarcerate.
затошн|и́ть (*3sg* **-и́т**) *сов безл*: **меня́ ~и́ло** I began to feel sick.
затр|ави́ть (-влю́, -а́вишь) *сов от* **трави́ть** ♦ (*impf* **затра́вливать**) *перех* (*зайца, утку*) to hunt; (*перен*: *человека*) to harass.
затра́гива|ть (-ю) *несов от* **затро́нуть**.
затрапе́з|ный (-ен, -на, -но) *прил* (*разг*) shabby.
затра́т|а (-ы) *ж* expenditure.
затра́|тить (-чу, -тишь; *impf* **затра́чивать**) *сов перех* to expend.
затре́б|овать (-ую) *сов перех* to request.
затреп|ета́ть (-ещу́, -е́щешь) *сов неперех* to begin to tremble.
затрещ|а́ть (-у́, -и́шь) *сов неперех* (*стул, дерево*) to start to split.

затре́щин|а (-ы) *ж* whack.
затро́н|уть (-у, -ешь; *impf* **затра́гивать**) *сов перех* (*подлеж*: *пуля*) to graze; (*перен*: *вопрос, тему*) to touch on; (: *душу, человека*) to affect; **затра́гивать** (~ *perf*) **чьё-н самолю́бие** to dent sb's ego.
затру́ *итп сов см* **затере́ть**.
затрудне́ни|е (-я) *ср* difficulty.
затрудн|ённый (-ён, -ена́, -ено́) *прил* laboured (*BRIT*), labored (*US*).
затрудни́тел|ьный (-ен, -ьна, -ьно) *прил* difficult, awkward.
затрудн|и́ть (-ю́, -и́шь; *impf* **затрудня́ть**) *сов перех*: ~ **что-н** to make sth difficult; **если Вас не ~и́т** if it isn't too much trouble
▸ **затрудни́ться** (*impf* **затрудня́ться**) *сов возв*: **~ся с** *+instr*/*+infin* to have difficulty with/doing; **я ~я́юсь (Вам) сказа́ть** that is difficult to say.
затр|ясти́сь (-ясу́сь, -ясёшься; *pt* **-я́сся, -ясла́сь, -ясло́сь**) *сов возв* (to start) to shake.
затума́н|ить (-ю, -ишь) *сов от* **тума́нить**
▸ **затума́ниться** *сов от* **тума́ниться** ◆ (*impf* **затума́ниваться**) *возв* (*небо*) to cloud over; (*глаза*) to mist over; (*перен*: *сознание*) to become blurred.
зат|упи́ть (-уплю́, -у́пишь) *сов от* **тупи́ть** ◆ (*impf* **затупля́ть**) *перех* to blunt
▸ **затупи́ться** *сов от* **тупи́ться** ◆ (*impf* **затупля́ться**) *возв* to become blunt.
зату́х|нуть (*3sg* **-нет**, *3pl* **-нут**, *pt* **-, -ла, -ло**, *impf* **затуха́ть**) *сов неперех* (*огонь*) to die out; (*сигнал*) to die away; (*колебания*) to die down.
затуш|ева́ть (-у́ю; *impf* **затушёвывать**) *сов перех* to shade (in); (*перен*: *сгладить*) to brush over.
зат|уши́ть (-ушу́, -у́шишь) *сов от* **туши́ть**.
за́тхл|ый (-, -а, -о) *прил* stale; (*запах*) musty.
затыка́|ть(ся) (-ю(сь)) *несов от* **заткну́ть(ся)**.
заты́л|ок (-ка) *м* the back of the head.
заты́ч|ка (-ки; *gen pl* -ек) *ж* (*разг*) stopper.
затю́ка|ть (-ю) *сов перех* (*разг*) to bug.
затя́гива|ть(ся) (-ю(сь)) *несов от* **затяну́ть(ся)**.
затя́ж|ка (-ки; *gen pl* -ек) *ж* (*промедление*) delay; (*при курении*) drag, puff.
затяжно́й *прил* protracted, prolonged; **затяжны́е дожди́** long periods of rain; **затяжно́й прыжо́к** delayed drop.
зат|яну́ть (-яну́, -я́нешь; *impf* **затя́гивать**) *сов перех* (*шнурки, гайку*) to tighten; (*замедлить*) to drag out; (*вовлечь*): ~ **кого́-н в** *+acc* to drag sb into; **она́ ~яну́ла та́лию по́ясом** she pulled the belt tight around her waist; **не́бо ~яну́ло ту́чами** storm clouds gathered in the sky; **затя́гивать** (~ *perf*) **пе́сню** to strike up a song
▸ **затяну́ться** (*impf* **затя́гиваться**) *сов возв* (*петля, узел*) to tighten; (*рана*) to close up; (*дело, переговоры итп*) to drag on; (*при курении*) to inhale; **затя́гиваться (~ся** *perf*) *+instr* (*поясом, корсетом*) to tighten.
зау́м|ный (-ен, -на, -но) *прил* unintelligible.
заун́ыв|ный (-ен, -на, -но) *прил* mournful.
заупоко́йн|ый *прил*: **~ая моли́тва** prayer for the dead; **заупоко́йная слу́жба** funeral service.
заупря́м|иться (-люсь, -ишься) *сов возв* to become stubborn.
заура́д|ный (-ен, -на, -но) *прил* unexceptional, mediocre.
заусе́н|ец (-ца; *nom pl* -цы) *м* (*на металле*) burr; (*у ногтя*) hangnail.
зау́трен|я (-и) *ж* (*РЕЛ*) dawn mass, ≈ matins.
зау́чен|ный (-, -на, -но) *прил* (*ответ, жест*) (pre)rehearsed.
за|учи́ть (-учу́, -у́чишь; *impf* **зау́чивать**) *сов перех* to memorize, learn
▸ **заучи́ться** (*impf* **зау́чиваться**) *сов возв* (*разг*) to study too hard.
зафарши́р|ова́ть (-у́ю) *сов от* **фарширова́ть**.
зафикси́р|овать (-ую) *сов от* **фикси́ровать**.
зафрахт|ова́ть (-у́ю; *impf* **зафрахто́вывать** *или* **фрахтова́ть**) *сов перех* to charter.
захвал|и́ть (-ю, -ишь; *impf* **захва́ливать**) *сов перех* to overpraise.
захва́т (-а) *м* seizure, capture; (*СПОРТ*) hold; (*ТЕХ*) clamp.
захв|ати́ть (-ачу́, -а́тишь; *impf* **захва́тывать**) *сов перех* to seize, capture; (*взять с собой*) to take; (*подлеж*: *музыка, работа*) to captivate; (*болезнь, пожар*) to catch (in time); **дух ~а́тывает** it takes your breath away; **у меня́ дух ~ати́ло от волне́ния** I was breathless with excitement.
захва́тническ|ий (-ая, -ое, -ие) *прил* (*намерения, политика*) aggressive; **~ая война́** war of aggression.
захва́тчик (-а) *м* invader.
захва́тывающ|ий (-ая, -ее, -ие) *прил* (*книга, занятие*) gripping, absorbing; (*вид*) breathtaking.
захва́тыва|ть (-ю) *несов от* **захвати́ть**.
захвачу́ *итп сов см* **захвати́ть**.
захвора́|ть (-ю) *сов неперех* (*разг*) to be taken ill.
захире́|ть (-ю) *сов от* **хире́ть**.
захлам|и́ть (-лю́, -и́шь; *impf* **захламля́ть**) *сов перех* to clutter up.
захламл|ённый (-ён, -ена́, -ено́) *прил* cluttered.
захламлю́ *сов см* **захлами́ть**.
захламля́|ть (-ю) *несов от* **захлами́ть**.
захлебн|у́ться (-у́сь, -ёшься; *impf* **захлёбываться**) *сов возв* to choke; (*перен*: *атака, наступление*) to be stopped in its tracks; (: *мотор*) to fail to start; **захлёбываться (~** *perf*) **от сме́ха/слёз** to choke with laughter/on one's tears; **захлёбываться (~** *perf*) **от сча́стья/восто́рга** to gasp in joy/elation.
захлестн|у́ть (-у́, -ёшь; *impf* **захлёстывать**) *сов перех* (*подлеж*: *волна*) to swallow; (*перен*: *подлеж*: *чувство*) to overwhelm ◆ *неперех* (*вода*) to wash over.
захло́па|ть (-ю) *сов неперех* (*двери*) to slam;

(*выстрелы*) to crash out; (*слушатели, зрители*): ~ **(в ладо́ши)** to start clapping.
захло́пн|уть (**-у, -ешь**; *impf* **захло́пывать**) *сов перех*: ~ **что-н** to slam sth shut
▸ **захло́пнуться** (*impf* **захло́пываться**) *сов возв* to slam shut.
захо́д (**-а**) *м* (*также:* ~ **со́лнца**) sundown; (*в порт*) call; (*попытка*) go; **с пе́рвого/второ́го ~а** at the first/second attempt; **с ~ом/без захо́да в** *+acc* stopping off/without stopping off at.
зах|оди́ть (**-ожу́, -о́дишь**) *несов от* **зайти́** ◆ *сов неперех* to start pacing.
захолу́сть|е (**-я**) *ср* provincial backwater.
захороне́ни|е (**-я**) *ср* (*действие*) burial; (*могила, могильник*) burial ground.
захор|они́ть (**-оню́, -о́нишь**) *сов перех* to bury.
зах|оте́ть (*как* **хоте́ть**; *см* **Table 16**) *сов (не)перех* to want
▸ **захоте́ться** *сов безл* (*+dat*): **мне ~оте́лось есть/пить** I started to feel hungry/thirsty.
захуда́лый *прил* wretched.
зацв|ести́ (*3sg* **-етёт**, *3pl* **-ету́т**, *pt* **-ёл, -ела́, -ело́**, *impf* **зацвета́ть**) *сов неперех* (*цветы*) to blossom, bloom; (*разг*: *сыр, хлеб*) to go mouldy (*BRIT*) *или* moldy (*US*).
зацел|ова́ть (**-у́ю**) *сов перех*: ~ **кого́-н** to smother sb with kisses.
зацементи́р|овать (**-ую**) *сов от* **цементи́ровать**.
зац|епи́ть (**-еплю́, -е́пишь**; *impf* **зацепля́ть**) *сов перех* (*поддеть*) to hook up; (*разг*: *случайно задеть*) to catch against
▸ **зацепи́ться** (*impf* **зацепля́ться**) *сов возв*: **~ся за** *+acc* (*задеть за*) to catch *или* get caught on; (*ухватиться за*) to grab hold of; **я ~епи́лся рука́вом за гвоздь** I caught my sleeve on a nail.
заце́п|ка (**-ки**; *gen pl* **-ок**) *ж* (*перен*) pretext.
зацеплю́(сь) *сов см* **зацепи́ть(ся)**.
зацепля́|ть(ся) (**-ю(сь)**) *несов от* **зацепи́ть(ся)**.
заци́кл|иться (**-юсь, -ишься**; *impf* **заци́кливаться**) *сов возв*: ~ **на** *+acc* (*разг*) to be crazy about.
зачар|ова́ть (**-у́ю**; *impf* **зачаро́вывать**) *сов перех* to enthral (*BRIT*), enthrall (*US*).
зача|сти́ть (**-щу́, -сти́шь**) *сов неперех* to come more often; **дождь ~сти́л** the rain got heavier.
зачасту́ю *нареч* often.
зача́ти|е (**-я**) *ср* conception.
зача́т|ок (**-ка**; *nom pl* **-ки**) *м* (*обычно мн*: *любви, идеи итп*) beginning, germ *только ед*; **в ~ке** (*перен*) in embryo.
зача́точ|ный (**-ен, -на, -но**) *прил* (*также перен*) embryonic; **в ~ном состоя́нии** in an embryonic state.
зач|а́ть (**-ну́, -нёшь**; *pt* **-а́л, -ала́, -а́ло**, *impf* **зачина́ть**) *сов (не)перех* to conceive.
зача́х|нуть (**-ну, -нешь**; *pt* **-, -ла, -ло**) *сов от* **ча́хнуть**.
зачащу́ *сов см* **зачасти́ть**.
заче́м *нареч* why; ~ **он э́то сде́лал?** why did he do it?; **ей ста́ло поня́тно, ~ он э́то сде́лал** it became clear to her why he had done it.
заче́м-нибудь *нареч* for any reason.
заче́м-то *нареч* for some reason.
зачеркн|у́ть (**-у́, -ёшь**; *impf* **зачёркивать**) *сов перех* to cross out; (*перен*: *прошлое*) to blot out.
зачерпн|у́ть (**-у́, -ёшь**; *impf* **заче́рпывать**) *сов перех* to scoop up.
зачерстве́|ть (**-ю**) *сов от* **черстве́ть**.
зач|еса́ть (**-ешу́, -е́шешь**; *impf* **зачёсывать**) *сов перех* to comb.
зач|е́сть (**-ту́, -тёшь**; *pt* **-ёл, -ла́, -ло́**, *impf* **зачи́тывать**) *сов перех* (*одобрить*) to pass; (*засчитать*: *диплом, опыт*) to take into account; **ему́ ~ли́ отрабо́танные дни в счёт о́тпуска** he was given time off in lieu
▸ **заче́сться** (*impf* **зачи́тываться**) *сов возв* to be taken into account.
зачёсыва|ть (**-ю**) *несов от* **зачеса́ть**.
зачёт (**-а**) *м* (ПРОСВЕЩ) test; **сдава́ть** *(impf)***/сдать** *(perf)* ~ **по фи́зике** to sit (*BRIT*) *или* take/pass a physics test.
зачётный *прил*: **зачётная рабо́та** assessed essay (*BRIT*), term paper (*US*); **зачётная кни́жка** assessment record book.
зачешу́ *итп сов см* **зачеса́ть**.
зачина́тел|ь (**-я**) *м* originator.
зачина́|ть (**-ю**) *несов от* **зача́ть**.
зачи́нщик (**-а**) *м* instigator.
зачи́сл|ить (**-ю, -ишь**; *impf* **зачисля́ть**) *сов перех* (*в институт*) to enrol; (*на работу*) to take on; (*на счёт*) to enter; **зачисля́ть** (~ *perf*) **расхо́ды** to keep a record of expenditure
▸ **зачи́слиться** (*impf* **зачисля́ться**) *сов возв* (*в институт*) to enrol; (*на работу*) to be taken on.
зачита́|ть (**-ю**; *impf* **зачи́тывать**) *сов перех* (*прочесть вслух*) to read out; ~ *(perf)* **у кого́-н кни́гу** to borrow a book from sb and not give it back
▸ **зачита́ться** (*impf* **зачи́тываться**) *сов возв*: **~ся** *+instr* (*книгой*) to be engrossed in; **я ~лся до утра́** I read until morning.
зачи́тыва|ть(ся) (**-ю(сь)**) *несов от* **заче́сть(ся), зачита́ть(ся)**.
зачну́ *итп сов см* **зача́ть**.
зачту́(сь) *итп сов см* **заче́сть(ся)**.
зашага́|ть (**-ю**) *сов неперех* to start walking.
зашата́|ться (**-юсь**) *сов возв* (*здание*) to start to shake; (*дерево, пьяница*) to begin to sway.
зашвырн|у́ть (**-ну́, -нёшь**; *impf* **зашвы́ривать**) *сов перех* to hurl.
зашвыря́|ть (**-ю**) *сов перех*: ~ **кого́-н чем-н** to pelt sb with sth.

зашевел|и́ть (-ю́, -и́шь) *сов неперех* (*+instr*) to move
▸ **зашевели́ться** *сов возв* to move.
зашёл *сов см* **зайти́.**
заш|и́ть (-ью́, -ьёшь; *impf* **зашива́ть)** *сов перех* (*дырку, носки*) to mend; (*шов, рану*) to stitch.
зашифр|ова́ть (-у́ю; *impf* **зашифро́вывать)** *сов перех* to encode, put into code.
зашла́ *итп сов см* **зайти́.**
зашлю́ *итп сов см* **засла́ть.**
зашнур|ова́ть (-у́ю; *impf* **зашнуро́вывать)** *сов перех* to lace up.
зашпакл|ева́ть (-ю́ю) *сов от* **шпаклева́ть.**
зашто́па|ть (-ю; *impf* **што́пать)** *сов перех* to darn.
заштрих|ова́ть (-у́ю; *impf* **заштрихо́вывать)** *сов перех* to shade (in).
зашум|е́ть (-лю́, -и́шь) *сов неперех* (*люди, толпа*) to become noisy; **внизу́ ~е́ли голоса́** from downstairs came the sound of voices.
зашью́ *итп сов см* **заши́ть.**
защёлк|а (-и) *ж* (*на двери*) latch; (*на шкатулке, у замка*) catch.
защёлкн|уть (-у, -ешь; *impf* **защёлкивать)** *сов перех* to shut
▸ **защёлкнуться** (*impf* **защёлкиваться)** *сов возв* to click shut.
защем|и́ть (-лю́, -и́шь; *impf* **защемля́ть)** *сов перех* to clamp.
защи́т|а (-ы) *ж* (*также ЮР, СПОРТ*) defence (*BRIT*), defense (*US*); (*от комаров, пыли*) protection; (*диплома, диссертации*) viva (*open to the public*); **брать (взять** *perf***) под ~у** to defend.
защи|ти́ть (-щу́, -ти́шь; *impf* **защища́ть)** *сов перех* to defend; (*от солнца, от комаров итп*) to protect; **защища́ть (~** *perf***) диссерта́цию** to defend one's thesis (*at public viva*)
▸ **защити́ться** (*impf* **защища́ться)** *сов возв* to defend o.s.; (*диссертант, студент*) to defend one's thesis.
защи́тник (-а) *м* (*также СПОРТ*) defender; (*ЮР*) defence counsel (*BRIT*), defense attorney (*US*); **ле́вый/пра́вый ~** (*футбол*) left/right back.
защи́тный *прил* protective; **защи́тный цвет** khaki.
защища́|ть (-ю) *несов от* **защити́ть** ◆ *перех* (*подсудимого, преступника*) to defend
▸ **защища́ться** *несов от* **защити́ться.**
защищу́(сь) *сов см* **защити́ть(ся).**
за|яви́ть (-явлю́, -я́вишь; *impf* **заявля́ть)** *сов перех* (*претензию, протест*) to declare ◆ *неперех*: **~ о** *+prp* to announce; **заявля́ть (~** *perf***) о свои́х права́х (на** *+acc***)** to claim one's rights (to); **заявля́ть (~** *perf***) на кого́-н в мили́цию** to report sb to the police
▸ **заяви́ться** (*impf* **заявля́ться)** *сов возв* (*разг*) to turn up.
зая́в|ка (-ки; *gen pl* **-ок)** *ж*: **~ (на** *+acc***)** application (for); (*на билеты*) order (for); **~ на изобрете́ние** patent application; **присыла́йте ва́ши ~ки по а́дресу** ... please apply to the following address ....
заявле́ни|е (-я) *ср* (*правительства*) statement; (*просьба*): **~ (о** *+prp***)** application (for); **де́лать (сде́лать** *perf***) ~** to make a statement; **подава́ть (пода́ть** *perf***) ~ на рабо́ту/об о́тпуске** to apply for a job/leave.
заявлю́(сь) *сов см* **заяви́ть(ся).**
заявля́|ть(ся) (-ю(сь)) *несов от* **заяви́ть(ся).**
зая́длый *прил* (*разг: курильщик*) inveterate; **он ~ футболи́ст/охо́тник** he is a football/hunting fanatic.
за́|яц (-йца) *м* (*ЗООЛ*) hare; (*разг: безбилетник*) fare dodger.
за́яч|ий (-ья, -ье, -ьи) *прил* (*мех, хвост*) hare's; **за́ячья губа́** harelip.
зва́ни|е (-я) *ср* (*воинское*) rank; (*учёное, почётное*) title; **присва́ивать (присво́ить** *perf***) кому́ ~** to award sb a title.
зва́ный *прил*: **~ гость** welcome guest; **зва́ный обе́д** dinner party.
зв|ать (зову́, зовёшь; *pt* **-ал, -ала́, -а́ло,** *perf* **позва́ть)** *несов перех* to call; (*приглашать*) to ask; (*no perf; +instr; называть*): **~ кого́-н кем-н** to call sb sth; **как Вас зову́т?** what is your name?; **меня́/его́ зову́т Алекса́ндр** my/his name is Alexander; **~ (позва́ть** *perf***) кого́-н в го́сти/в кино́** to ask sb over/to the cinema
▸ **зва́ться** *несов возв* (*+instr*) to be called.
звезд|а́ (-ы́; *nom pl* **звёзды)** *ж* (*также перен*) star; **морска́я ~** starfish.
звёздный *прил* (*ночь, небо*) starry, starlit; **это был его́ ~ час** that was his finest hour; **звёздные во́йны** Star Wars; **Звёздный городо́к** Star City (*training centre for Russian cosmonauts*).
звёздоч|ка (-ки; *gen pl* **-ек)** *ж уменьш от* **звезда́;** (*ТИПОГ*) asterisk.
звен|е́ть (-ю́, -и́шь) *несов неперех* (*звонок*) to ring; (*колокольчик*) to jingle; (*голос*) to chime; (*стаканы*) to clink; (*монеты*) to jangle.
звен|о́ (-а́; *nom pl* **-ья,** *gen pl* **-ьев)** *ср* (*цепи, также перен*) link; (*конструкции*) section; (*ВОЕН: самолётов*) flight; (*в школе*) group; (*на работе*) team.
звере́|ть (-ю; *perf* **озвере́ть)** *несов неперех* to go wild.
звери́н|ец (-ца) *м* menagerie.
звери́ный *прил* (*вой, тропа, шкура*) (wild) animal *опред*; (*перен: законы*) bestial; (*: страх, инстинкт*) animal *опред*.
звероводств|о (-а) *ср breeding of animals for their fur*.
зверолов (-а) *м* trapper.
звéрск|ий (-ая, -ое, -ие) *прил* (*убийство, поступок*) brutal, savage; (*разг: жара, аппетит*) wicked; (*: скука*) severe.
зве́рств|о (-а) *ср* (*жестокость*) brutality; (*обычно мн: ужас*) atrocity.
зве́рств|овать (-ую) *несов неперех* to commit atrocities.

звер|ь (-я; *gen pl* **-ей**) *м* beast, wild animal; (*перен*) beast, animal.
звон (-а) *м* clinking; (*колокола*) peal, chime.
звона́р|ь (-я) *м* bell-ringer.
звон|и́ть (-ю́, -и́шь; *perf* **позвони́ть**) *несов неперех* to ring; (*по телефону*): ~ **кому́** to ring *или* phone *или* call (*US*) sb; ~ *(impf)* **в звоно́к** to ring the bell.
звонка́ *сущ см* **звоно́к**.
зв|о́нкий (-о́нок, -онка́, -о́нко) *прил* (*голос, песня*) sonorous; (*дно, свод*) resonant; **зво́нкий согла́сный** (*линг*) voiced consonant.
звон|о́к (-ка́; *nom pl* **-ки́**) *м* (*на двери, на велосипеде*) bell; (*звук*) ring; (*по телефону*) (telephone) call; **отсиде́ть** *(perf)* **от ~ка́ до ~ка́** ≈ to work from nine to five.
зво́нче *сравн прил от* **зво́нкий**.
звук (-а) *м* sound; **он не произнёс ни зву́ка** he didn't utter a sound; **без зву́ка** (*сделать, согласиться*) without so much as a word.
звуково́й *прил* sound *опред*, audio; **звукова́я волна́** sound wave; **звукова́я доро́жка** track (*on audio tape*); **звукова́я аппарату́ра** hi-fi equipment.
звукоза́пис|ь (-и) *ж* sound recording; **сту́дия ~и** recording studio.
звукоизоля́ци|я (-и) *ж* soundproofing.
звуконепроница́ем|ый (-, -а, -о) *прил* soundproof.
звукоопера́тор (-а) *м* sound technician.
звукоподража́ни|е (-я) *ср* onomatopoeia.
звукоподража́тельн|ый *прил*: **~ое сло́во** onomatopoeic word.
звукопрово́дност|ь (-и) *ж* conductivity (*of sound*).
звукопроводя́щ|ий (-ая, -ее, -ие) *прил* conductive (*of sound*).
звукорежиссёр (-а) *м* sound engineer.
звукоснима́тел|ь (-я) *м* pick-up.
звуча́ни|е (-я) *ср* sound; (*перен*: *политическое итп*) resonance.
звуч|а́ть (*3sg* **-и́т**, *3pl* **-а́т**) *несов неперех* (*издавать звуки*) to sound; (*раздаваться*) to be heard; **~и́т убеди́тельно** it sounds convincing; **в её го́лосе ~а́ла оби́да** she sounded hurt.
зв|у́чный (-у́чен, -учна́, -у́чно) *прил* (*смех, голос*) deep, resounding; (*инструмент*) rich-sounding.
звя́кн|уть (-у, -ешь; *impf* **звя́кать**) *сов неперех* (*звонок*) to ring; (*стакан*) to clink; (*стекло*) to tinkle; (*+instr*; *стаканами*) to clink; (*ключами*) to jangle.
зги: **ни ~ не ви́дно** it's pitch-black.
з-д *сокр* = **заво́д**.
зда́ни|е (-я) *ср* building.
здесь *нареч* here; **есть ~ кто́-нибудь?** is (there) anyone here?; ~ **нет ничего́ смешно́го** there's nothing funny about it.
зде́шн|ий (-яя, -ее, -ие) *прил* (*разг*) local.
здоро́ва|ться (-юсь; *perf* **поздоро́ваться**) *несов возв*: ~ **с** *+instr* to say hello to; ~ **(поздоро́ваться** *perf***) друг с дру́гом** to greet each other; ~ **(поздоро́ваться** *perf***) за́ руку** to shake hands.
здо́рово *нареч* (*разг*: *отлично*) really well; (: *очень сильно*) terribly ◆ *как сказ* (*разг*) it's great.
здор|о́вый (-о́в, -о́ва, -о́во) *прил* healthy; (*питание*) wholesome; (*перен*: *идея*) sound; (**-о́в, -ова́, -ово́**; *разг*: *большой*) hefty; **бу́дьте ~о́вы!** (*при прощании*) take care!; (*при чихании*) bless you!
здоро́вь|е (-я) *ср* health; **как Ва́ше ~?** how are you keeping?; **за Ва́ше ~!** (to) your good health!; **на ~!** enjoy it!
здра́вниц|а (-ы) *ж* convalescent home.
здра́во *нареч* sensibly.
здравомы́слящ|ий (-ая, -ее, -ие) *прил* sensible.
здравоохране́ни|е (-я) *ср* health care; **систе́ма ~я** ≈ the Health Service (*BRIT*), ≈ Medicaid (*US*); **министе́рство ~я** ≈ Department of Health.
здравоохрани́тельный *прил* health-care.
здра́вств|овать (-ую) *несов неперех* to thrive; **~уйте** hello; **да ~ует...!** long live ...!
здра́в|ый (-, -а, -о) *прил* (*политика, мысль*) sound.
зе́бр|а (-ы) *ж* zebra; (*пешеходный переход*) zebra crossing (*BRIT*).
зев (-а) *м* pharynx.
зева́к|а (-и) *м/ж* (*разг*) idler.
зева́|ть (-ю) *несов неперех* to yawn; (*разг*: *глазеть*) to gawp; (*perf* **прозева́ть**; *разг*) to miss out; **не ~й!** (*разг*) keep your wits about you!
зевка́ *итп сущ см* **зево́к**.
зевн|у́ть (-у́, -ёшь) *сов неперех* to yawn.
зев|о́к (-ка́; *nom pl* **-ки**) *м* yawn.
зево́т|а (-ы) *ж* yawning.
зелене́|ть (-ю; *perf* **позелене́ть**) *несов неперех* to go *или* turn green; **на горизо́нте ~л лес** the green of the forest could be seen on the horizon.
зелён|ый (**зе́лен, зелена́, зе́лено**) *прил* (*также перен*) green; **„З~ые"** (*полит*) the Greens; **дать** *(perf)* **чему́-н ~ую у́лицу** to give sth the green light; **зелёные насажде́ния** trees and shrubs; **зелёный лук** spring onion.
зе́лен|ь (-и) *ж* (*цвет*) green ◆ *собир* (*растительность*) greenery; (*овощи и травы*) greens *мн*.
земе́ль *сущ см* **земля́**.
земе́льн|ый *прил* land *опред*; ~ **наде́л** *или* **уча́сток** plot of land.
землевладе́л|ец (-ьца) *м* landowner.
землевладе́ни|е (-я) *ср* landownership.

земледе́л|ец (-ьца) *м* arable farmer.
земледе́ли|е (-я) *ср (возделывание земли)* arable farming.
земледе́льца *сущ см* **земледе́лец.**
земледе́льческ|ий (-ая, -ое, -ие) *прил (район)* agricultural; *(машины)* farming *опред.*
землеме́рный *прил* surveying *опред.*
землепо́льзовани|е (-я) *ср* land tenure.
землеро́йн|ый *прил*: **~ые рабо́ты** dredging; **~ая маши́на** dredger.
землетрясе́ни|е (-я) *ср* earthquake.
землечерпа́лк|а (-и) *ж* dredger.
земли́ст|ый (-, -а, -о) *прил (цвет лица)* sallow; *(песок, торф)* earthy.
зем|ля́ (-ли́; *acc sg* **-лю,** *nom pl* **-ли,** *gen pl* **-е́ль)** *ж* land; *(планета)* earth; *(поверхность)* ground; *(почва)* earth, soil.
земля́к (-а́) *м* compatriot.
земля́н|е (-) *мн* earth dwellers *мн.*
земляни́к|а (-и) *ж (растение)* wild strawberry; *(собир: ягоды)* wild stawberries *мн.*
земля́нк|а (-ки; *gen pl* **-ок)** *ж* dugout *(shelter)*.
землян|о́й *прил (вал, пол)* earthen; **~ы́е рабо́ты** excavations; **земляно́й червь** earthworm.
земля́чк|а (-ки; *gen pl* **-ек)** *ж см* **земля́к.**
земново́дн|ые (-ых; *decl like adj)* *мн* amphibians *мн.*
земново́дный *прил* amphibious.
земно́й *прил (поверхность, кора)* earth's; *(перен: блага, желания)* earthly; **земно́й шар** the globe.
зени́т (-а) *м (также перен)* zenith.
зени́тк|а (-ки; *gen pl* **-ок)** *ж* anti-aircraft gun.
зени́тный *прил (АСТРОНОМИЯ)* zenithal; *(ВОЕН)* anti-aircraft.
зёрен *сущ см* **зерно́.**
зерка́лен *прил см* **зерка́льный.**
зе́рк|ало (-ала; *nom pl* **-ала́,** *gen pl* **-а́л,** *dat pl* **-ала́м)** *ср* mirror; *(перен: воды, залива)* glassy surface.
зерка́л|ьный (-ен, -ьна, -ьно) *прил (производство)* mirror *опред*; *(поверхность)* glassy; **его́ пье́са – э́то ~ьное отображе́ние действи́тельности** his play is a true reflection of real life; **~ шкаф** mirror wardrobe; **зерка́льный карп** mirror carp.
зерни́ст|ый (-, -а, -о) *прил (масса, снег)* granular; *(поверхность)* grainy; **зерни́стая икра́** unpressed caviar.
зерно́ (зерна́; *nom pl* **зёрна,** *gen pl* **зёрен)** *ср (пшеницы)* grain; *(кофе)* bean; *(мака)* seed; *(пороха)* granule ◆ *собир (семенное, на хлеб)* grain; **~ и́стины** a grain of truth; **жемчу́жное ~** pearl.
зернов|о́й *прил (торговля, запас)* grain *опред*; **зерновы́е культу́ры** cereals *мн.*
зернов|ы́е (-ы́х; *decl like adj)* *мн* cereals *мн.*
зерносуши́лк|а (-и) *ж* grain drier.
зерноубо́рочный *прил* harvesting *опред*; **~ комба́йн** combine harvester.
зернохрани́лищ|е (-а) *ср* granary.
зефи́р (-а) *м* ≈ marshmallow.
зигза́г (-а) *м* zigzag.
зи́жд|иться (*3sg* **-ится,** *3pl* **-утся)** *несов возв*: **~ на** *+prp* to be based on.
ЗИЛ *м сокр* = *Моско́вский автомоби́льный заво́д и́мени И.А. Лихачёва*; *(автомобиль)* *vehicle manufactured at the Moscow car factory.*
зим|а́ (-ы́; *acc sg* **-у,** *dat sg* **-е́,** *nom pl* **-ы)** *ж* winter.
Зимба́бве *ср нескл* Zimbabwe.
зимбабви́йск|ий (-ая, -ое, -ие) *прил* Zimbabwean.
зи́мн|ий (-яя, -ее, -ие) *прил (день)* winter's; *(погода)* wintry; *(лес, одежда)* winter *опред.*
зим|ова́ть (-у́ю; *perf* **прозимова́ть)** *несов неперех (человек)* to spend the winter; *(птицы)* to winter.
зимо́вк|а (-ки; *gen pl* **-ок)** *ж* wintering place; *(для птиц)* wintering ground; **остава́ться (оста́ться** *perf)* **на ~ку** to spend the winter.
зимо́вь|е (-я) *ср (для людей)* winter hut; *(зверей, птиц)* wintering ground.
зимо́й *нареч* in the winter.
зия́|ть (*3sg* **-ет,** *3pl* **-ют)** *несов неперех* to gape.
злак (-а) *м* grass; **зерново́й ~** cereal.
зла́чн|ый *прил*: **~ое ме́сто** *(разг)* den of iniquity.
зле́йш|ий (-ая, -ее, -ие) *превос прил*: **~ враг** worst enemy.
зл|ить (-ю, -ишь; *perf* **разозли́ть)** *несов перех* to annoy
▸ **зли́ться** *(perf* **разозли́ться)** *несов возв* to get angry.
зло (зла; *gen pl* **зол)** *ср* evil; *(неприятность)* harm ◆ *нареч (посмотреть, сказать)* spitefully; **со зла** out of spite; **причиня́ть (причини́ть** *perf)* **кому́-н ~** to cause sb harm; **меня́ ~ берёт** *(разг)* it makes me angry; **у меня́ на неё зла не хвата́ет** *(разг)* she annoys me no end; **из двух зол выбира́ть (вы́брать** *perf)* **ме́ньшее** to choose the lesser of two evils.
зло́б|а (-ы) *ж* malice; **статья́ на ~у дня** an article tackling the burning issue of the moment.
зло́б|ный (-ен, -на, -но) *прил (характер, человек)* mean; *(улыбка)* hateful, wicked; *(тон, голос)* nasty.
злободне́в|ный (-ен, -на, -но) *прил* topical.
зло́бств|овать (-ую) *несов неперех* to rage.
злове́щ|ий (-ая, -ее, -ие; -, -а, -е) *прил (улыбка, вид, слухи)* sinister; *(тишина)* ominous.
злово́нен *прил см* **злово́нный.**
злово́ни|е (-я) *ср* noxious odour *(BRIT)* *или* odor *(US)*.
злово́н|ный (-ен, -на, -но) *прил* rank, fetid.
зловре́дный (-ен, -на, -но) *прил* mean, horrid.
злоде́|й (-я) *м* villain.
злоде́йк|а (-и) *ж см* **злоде́й.**
злоде́йск|ий (-ая, -ое, -ие) *прил* wicked.
злоде́йств|о (-а) *ср* act of evil.
злодея́ни|е (-я) *ср* evil deed, crime.
злой (зол, зла, зло) *прил (человек, жена)* mean,

bad-tempered; (*собака*) vicious; (*глаза, лицо*) mean; (*мысли*) evil; (*карикатура, замечание*) scathing; (*перен: разг: мороз*) cruel; (: *перец, горчица*) lethal; **я зол на тебя́** I'm angry with you; **без зло́го у́мысла** no harm meant; **зла́я судьба́** cruel fate; **злы́е языки́** malicious talk.
злока́чествен|ный (-, -на, -но) *прил* malignant.
злоключе́ни|е (-я) *ср* misadventure.
злонаме́рен|ный (-, -на, -но) *прил* ill-intentioned.
злопа́мят|ный (-ен, -на, -но) *прил* (*человек*) unforgiving.
злополу́ч|ный (-ен, -на, -но) *прил* (*охотник*) ill-fated; (*день, час*) fateful.
злопыха́тел|ь (-я) *м* malevolent person (*мн* people).
злопыха́|ть (-ю) *несов неперех* to rant.
злора́д|ный (-ен, -на, -но) *прил* gloating.
злора́дств|о (-а) *ср* malicious pleasure.
злора́дств|овать (-ую) *несов неперех* to gloat.
злосло́ви|е (-я) *ср* abuse, ridicule.
злосло́в|ить (-лю, -ишь) *несов неперех* to indulge in ridicule.
зло́ст|ный (-ен, -на, -но) *прил* (*намерение*) malicious; (*правонарушитель*) persistent.
злост|ь (-и) *ж* malice; **сказа́ть** *(perf)* **что-н со зло́стью** to say sth angrily.
злосча́ст|ный (-ен, -на, -но) *прил* ill-fated.
злоумы́шленник (-а) *м* conspirator.
злоумы́шленный *прил* (*поступок*) malicious.
злоупотреб|и́ть (-лю́, -и́шь; *impf* **злоупотребля́ть**) *сов неперех* (+*instr*) to abuse; (*доверием*) to breach; (*сладким*) to indulge in.
злоупотребле́ни|е (-я) *ср* (+*instr*) abuse of; (*обычно мн: незаконные действия*) malpractise; ~ **дове́рием** breach of confidence.
злоупотреблю́ *сов см* **злоупотреби́ть**.
злоупотребля́|ть (-ю) *несов от* **злоупотреби́ть**.
злю́к|а (-и) *м/ж* crosspatch.
змееви́к (-а́) *м* coil.
змеёныш (-а) *м* (*перен*) little sneak.
змеи́ный *прил* (*кожа*) snake *опред*; (*нора, питомник*) snake's; (*перен: улыбка, усмешка*) venomous; ~ **яд** venom.
зме|й (-я; *gen pl* **-ев**) *м* serpent; (*также:* **возду́шный** ~) kite; **змей-горы́ныч** many-headed dragon.
зм|ея́ (-ей; *nom pl* **-е́и**, *gen pl* **-е́й**) *ж* (*также перен*) snake; **змея́ подколо́дная** (*разг*) snake in the grass.
знак (-а) *м* sign; (*МАТ, МУЗ, ТИПОГ*) symbol; (*КОМП*) character; **в** ~ +*gen* as a sign of; **под зна́ком** +*gen* in an atmosphere of; **знак ра́венства** equals sign; **зна́ки препина́ния** punctuation marks; **зна́ки разли́чия** (*ВОЕН*) stripes; **зна́ки отли́чия** decorations; **зна́ки зодиа́ка** signs of the Zodiac.
знако́м|ая (-ой; *decl like adj*) *ж см* **знако́мый**.
знако́м|ить (-лю, -ишь; *perf* **познако́мить**) *несов перех*: ~ **кого́-н с** +*instr* to introduce sb to; (*perf* **ознако́мить**; *с приказом, с документом*) to acquaint sb with
▸ **знако́миться** (*perf* **познако́миться**) *несов возв*: ~**ся с** +*instr* (*с человеком*) to meet; (*perf* **ознако́миться**; *с приказом, с документом*) to acquaint o.s. with.
знако́мств|о (-а) *ср* (*отношения*) acquaintance; ~**а** (*круг знакомых*) acquaintances; ~ **с** +*instr* acquaintance with; **пе́рвое** ~ **с** +*instr* first introduction to; **завя́зывать (завяза́ть** *perf*) ~ **с кем-н** to make sb's acquaintance.
знако́м|ый (-, -а, -о) *прил*: ~ **(с** +*instr*) familiar (with) ◆ **(-ого**; *decl like adj*) *м* acquaintance.
знамена́телен *прил см* **знамена́тельный**.
знамена́тел|ь (-я) *м* denominator; **приводи́ть (привести́** *perf*) **к о́бщему** ~**ю** to reduce to a common denominator.
знамена́тел|ьный (-ен, -ьна, -ьно) *прил* momentous.
зна́мени *итп сущ см* **зна́мя**.
зна́мени|е (-я) *ср* (*предзнаменование*) omen; **зна́мение вре́мени** sign of the times.
знамени́тост|ь (-и) *ж* celebrity.
знамени́т|ый (-, -а, -о) *прил* famous.
знамен|ова́ть (-у́ю) *несов перех* to mark.
знамено́с|ец (-ца) *м* standard-bearer.
зна́м|я (-ени; *как* **вре́мя**; *см* **Table 4**) *ср* banner; (*перен: руководящая идея*) flag; **под** ~**енем** +*gen* (*перен*) under the banner of.
зна́ни|е (-я) *ср* knowledge *только ед*; **со** ~**м де́ла** knowledgeably.
зн|а́тный (-а́тен, -атна́, -а́тно) *прил* (*род, человек*) noble; (*учёный*) prominent.
знато́к (-а́) *м* (*литературы*) expert; (*вина*) connoisseur.
зна|ть (-ти) *ж* nobility; ◆ (-ю) *несов перех* to know; **она́ не зна́ет ме́ры** she doesn't know when to stop; ~ *(impf)* **своё ме́сто** to know one's place; **кто (его́) зна́ет?** (*разг*) who knows?; **так и** ~**й** (*разг*) mark my words; ~ *(impf)* **це́ну** +*dat* to appreciate; **дава́ть (дать** *perf*) **себя́** ~ to make itself known; **как** ~ maybe; **как зна́ешь** as you wish; **он не** ~**л пораже́ний** he had never known defeat; **он не зна́ет уста́лости** he never tires; **я не зна́ю поко́я** I don't have a moment's peace
▸ **зна́ться** *несов возв*: **зна́ться с** +*instr* (*разг*) to associate with.
значе́ни|е (-я) *ср* (*слова, взгляда*) meaning; (*решения, победы*) importance; **э́то не име́ет** ~**я** it's not important; **придава́ть (прида́ть** *perf*) **осо́бое/большо́е** ~ **чему́-н** to attach special/great importance to sth.
зна́чимост|ь (-и) *ж* (*важность*) significance; (*наличие смысла*) meaningfulness.
зна́чим|ый (-, -а, -о) *прил* important; ~**ая часть**

сло́ва unit of meaning.
зна́чит *вводн сл* (*разг*) so ◆ *союз* (*следовательно*) that means; **~, ты не зна́ешь** so, you don't know then; **идёт снег, ~, сего́дня бу́дет хо́лодно** it's snowing, that means it's going to be cold today.
значи́тел|ьный (-ен, -ьна, -ьно) *прил* significant; (*вид, взгляд*) meaningful; **в ~ьной сте́пени** to a significant degree.
зна́ч|ить (-у, -ишь) *несов* (*не*)*перех* to mean; **что э́то ~ит?** what does it mean?; **э́то ничего́ не ~ит** it doesn't mean anything
▸ **зна́читься** *несов возв* (*состоять*) to appear; (*числиться*): **~ся больны́м** to be considered ill; **его́ и́мя ~ится в спи́ске** his name appears on the list.
знач|о́к (-ка́) *м* badge; (*пометка*) mark.
зна́ющ|ий (-ая, -ее, -ие; -, -а, -е) *прил* competent.
зноб|и́ть (*3sg* **-и́т**) *несов безл*: **его́ ~и́т** he's shivery.
зно́ен *прил см* **зно́йный**.
зно|й (-я) *м* intense heat.
зно́|йный (-ен, -йна, -йно) *прил* (*день, лето*) scorching; (*перен*: *взгляд*) intense; (: *чувство*) burning.
зоб (-а; *loc sg* **-у́**, *nom pl* **-ы́)** *м* (*у птицы*) crop; (*МЕД*) goitre (*BRIT*), goiter (*US*).
зов (-а) *м* (*о помощи, громкий*) call; **приходи́ть (прийти́** *perf*) **по пе́рвому зо́ву** to come at the first call.
зову́ *итп несов см* **звать**.
зодиа́к (-а) *м* zodiac.
зо́дчеств|о (-а) *ср* architecture.
зо́дч|ий (-его; *decl like adj*) *м* architect.
зол *сущ см* **зло** ◆ *прил см* **злой**.
зол|а́ (-ы́) *ж* cinders *мн*.
золо́в|ка (-ки; *gen pl* **-ок)** *ж* sister-in-law, husband's sister.
золоти́ст|ый (-, -а, -о) *прил* golden.
золо|ти́ть (-чу́, -ти́шь; *perf* **позолоти́ть)** *несов перех* to gild; **со́лнце позолоти́ло верху́шки дере́вьев** the sun cast a golden light over the tree tops.
золотни́к (-а) *м* slide valve.
зо́лот|о (-а) *ср* gold; (*золотые нити*) gold thread; **она́ про́сто ~** (*перен*) she's a real gem.
золотоиска́тел|ь (-я) *м* gold-digger.
золот|о́й *прил* gold; (*рубль, локоны, лучи солнца итп*) golden; (*перен*: *человек, время*) wonderful; (: *работник*) priceless ◆ **(-о́го;** *decl like adj*) *м* gold coin; (*дорогой*) precious; **золота́я сва́дьба** golden wedding *или* anniversary; **золота́я середи́на** the golden mean; **золото́е дно** gold mine; **золото́е се́рдце** heart of gold; **золото́е пра́вило** golden rule; **золото́й век** golden age; **золото́й фонд** gold reserves.
золотоно́с|ный (-ен, -на, -но) *прил*: **~ райо́н** goldfield.
золотопромы́шленност|ь (-и) *ж* gold-mining.
золочёный *прил* gilt.
золочу́ *несов см* **золоти́ть**.
Зо́лушк|а (-и) *ж* Cinderella.
зо́н|а (-ы) *ж* zone; (*лесная*) area; (*для заключённых*) prison; **при́городная ~** suburb; **~ о́тдыха** holiday area; **~ обстре́ла** field of fire.
зона́л|ьный (-ен, -ьна, -ьно) *прил* (*граница, деление*) zone *опред*; (*особенности, соревнование*) regional.
зонд (-а) *м* (*МЕД, ТЕХ*) probe.
зонди́р|овать (-ую; *perf* **прозонди́ровать)** *несов перех* to probe; **~ (прозонди́ровать** *perf*) **по́чву** *или* **обстано́вку** (*перен*) to test the water.
зонт (-а́) *м* (*от дождя*) umbrella; (*от солнца*) parasol; (*над дверью, над ветриной*) awning.
зо́нтик (-а) *м* (*от дождя*) umbrella; (*от солнца*) parasol.
зоо́лог (-а) *м* zoologist.
зоологи́ческ|ий (-ая, -ое, -ие) *прил* zoological.
зооло́ги|я (-и) *ж* zoology.
зоомагази́н (-а) *м* pet shop.
зоопа́рк (-а) *м* zoo.
зооте́хник (-а) *м* animal geneticist.
зо́ри *итп сущ см* **заря́**.
зо́р|кий (-кая, -кое, -кие; -ок, -ка, -ко) *прил* (*человек*) sharp-eyed; (*глаза, ум*) sharp; (*перен*: *наблюдатель*) observant.
зрач|о́к (-ка́) *м* (*АНАТ*) pupil.
зре́лищ|е (-а) *ср* (*предмет обозрения*) sight, spectacle; (*представление*) show.
зре́лищн|ый *прил*: **~ые предприя́тия** entertainment venues *мн*.
зре́лост|ь (-и) *ж* (*плода, яблока*) ripeness; (*организма, человека*) maturity.
зре́л|ый (-, -а, -о) *прил* mature; (*плод, зерно*) ripe.
зре́ни|е (-я) *ср* (eye)sight.
зре|ть (-ю; *perf* **созре́ть)** *несов неперех* to mature; (*плод, яблоко*) to ripen; (*решение, мысль*) to develop; (*обида*) to grow.
зри́тел|ь (-я) *м* (*в театре, в кино*) member of the audience; (*на стадионе*) spectator; (*наблюдатель*) onlooker.
зри́тельный *прил* (*память, восприятие*) visual; **зри́тельный зал** auditorium; **зри́тельный нерв** optic nerve.
зря *нареч* (*разг*: *без пользы*) for nothing, in vain; **~ тра́тить** (*impf*) **де́ньги/вре́мя** to waste money/time; **~ ты ему́ э́то сказа́л** you shouldn't have told him about it; **ты ~ купи́л э́ту кни́гу** there was no need to buy this book.
зря́ч|ий (-ая, -ее, -ие) *прил* sighted.
зуб (-а; *nom pl* **-ы**, *gen pl* **-о́в)** *м* tooth (*мн* teeth); (*nom pl* **-ья**, *gen pl* **-ьев**; *пилы, шестерни*) tooth (*мн* teeth); (*грабель, вилки*) prong; **у неё ~ на́ ~ не попада́ет** her teeth are chattering; **говори́ть** (*impf*) **сквозь зу́бы** (*разг*) to talk through one's teeth; **э́то мне не по ~а́м** (*перен*) it's too much for me; **он вооружён до ~о́в** he's armed to the

teeth; **она́ на него́ ~ име́ет** (*разг*) she bears a grudge against him; **ни в ~ ного́й** (*разг*) he *umn* doesn't have a clue; **зуб му́дрости** wisdom tooth.
зуба́ст|ый (-, -а, -о) *прил* (*разг*: *щука, собака*) with big sharp teeth; (*перен*: *разг*) sharp-tongued.
зуб|е́ц (-ца́; *nom pl* -цы́) *м* (*пилы, шестерни*) tooth (*мн* teeth); (*грабель, вилки*) prong.
зуби́л|о (-а) *ср* chisel.
зубка́ *umn сущ см* **зубо́к**.
зубно́й *прил* dental; **зубна́я боль** toothache; **зубна́я па́ста** toothpaste; **зубна́я щётка** toothbrush; **зубно́й врач** dentist; **зубно́й проте́з** dentures.
зубовраче́бный *прил*: **~ кабине́т** dental surgery (*BRIT*), dentist's office (*US*).
зубоска́л (-а) *м* (*разг*) scoffer.
зубоска́л|ить (-ю, -ишь) *несов неперех* (*разг*) to scoff.
зубочи́ст|ка (-ки; *gen pl* -ок) *ж* toothpick.
зубр (-а) *м* bison; (*перен*: *ретроград*) die-hard; (*разг*: *опытный специалист*) boffin.
зубри́л|а (-ы) *м/ж* (*разг*) swot (*BRIT*), grind (*US*).
зубр|и́ть (-ю́, -и́шь; *impf* **вы́зубрить**) *несов перех* (*разг*) to swot (*BRIT*), grind (*US*).
зубца́ *umn сущ см* **зубе́ц**.
зубча́т|ый *прил* (*стена, башня*) castellated; **~ое колесо́** cog(wheel); **~ая переда́ча** toothed gear; **~ край** serrated edge.
зуд (-а) *м* (*также перен*) itch.
зу|де́ть (*3sg* -**ди́т**, *3pl* -**дя́т**) *несов неперех* (*разг*: *чесаться*) to itch; (-**жу́, -ди́шь**; *комар, пчела*) to buzz; (*перен*: *нудиться*) to nag.
ЗУПВ *сокр* (= *запомина́ющее устро́йство с произво́льной вы́боркой*) RAM (= *random access memory*).
зыб|кий (-кая, -кое, -кие; -ок, -ка, -ко) *прил* (*поверхность озера*) ripply; (*грунт, болото*) swampy; (*основание*) shaky; (*перен*: *положение*) unstable.
зыбу́ч|ий (-ая, -ее, -ие; -, -а, -е) *прил*: **~ие пески́** quicksands *мн*.
зыб|ь (-и) *ж* ripple.
зыч|ный (-ен, -на, -но) *прил* (*голос*) booming; (*хохот*) thunderous.
зя́бко *как сказ* (*разг*: *холодно*): **мне ~** I feel chilly.
зя́блик (-а) *м* chaffinch.
зя́бн|уть (-у, -ешь; *perf* **озя́бнуть**) *несов неперех* to be cold.
зяб|ь (-и) *ж field ploughed in autumn ready for sowing in the spring*.
зят|ь (-я) *м* (*муж дочери*) son-in-law; (*муж сестры*) brother-in-law, sister's husband; (*муж золовки*) brother-in-law (*husband's sister's husband*).

~ И, и ~

И, и *сущ нескл (буква) the 9th letter of the Russian alphabet.*

KEYWORD

и *союз* ***1*** and; **я и мой друг** my friend and I; **и вот показа́лся лес** and then a forest appeared

2 *(тоже)*: **и он пошёл в теа́тр** he went to the theatre too; **и он не пришёл** he didn't come either

3 *(даже)* even; **и сам не рад** even he himself is not pleased

4 *(именно)*: **о том и речь!** that's just it!

5 *(во фразах)*: **ну и наглёц же ты!** what a cheek you have!; **туда́ и сюда́** here and there; **и ... и ...** both ... and ....

и́бо *союз (так как)* for, because.

и́в|а (-ы) *ж* willow.

ива́н-ча́|й (-я) *м (no pl)* rosebay willowherb.

и́вовый *прил* willow.

и́вол|га (-ги; *gen pl* -) *ж* oriole.

игл|а́ (-ы́; *nom pl* -ы) *ж* needle; *(у ежа)* spine; *(проигрывателя)* needle, stylus.

иглодержа́тел|ь (-я) *м (МЕД)* needleholder; *(проигрывателя)* cartridge.

иглоука́лывани|е (-я) *ср* acupuncture.

игнори́р|овать (-ую; *perf* **игнори́ровать** *или* **проигнори́ровать**) *несов перех* to ignore.

и́г|о (-а) *ср (рабства итп)* yoke.

иго́л|ка (-ки; *gen pl* -ок) *ж* = **игла́**; **сиде́ть** *(impf)* **как на ~х** to be on tenterhooks.

иго́льн|ый *прил*: **~ое у́шко** eye of a needle.

иго́льчатый *прил (мех)* spiky; *(подшипник)* needle *опред*.

иго́рный *прил*: **~ дом** gaming club.

игр|а́ (-ы́; *nom pl* -ы) *ж* game; *(на скрипке итп)* playing; *(актёра)* performance; **~ воображе́ния** fantasy; **~ слов** play on words.

игра́льн|ый *прил*: **~ые ка́рты** playing cards *мн*.

игра́|ть (-ю) *несов неперех* to play ◆ *(perf* **сыгра́ть***) перех* to play; *(пьесу)* to perform; **~ (сыгра́ть** *perf***) в** *+acc (СПОРТ)* to play; **~** *(impf)* **в пря́тки** to play hide-and-seek *(BRIT) или* hide-and-go-seek *(US)*; **~** *(impf)* **людьми́/в демокра́тию** *(перен)* to play with people/at democracy; **~** *(impf)* **на** *+prp (МУЗ)* to play; **~ (сыгра́ть** *perf***) конём/королём** to play one's knight/king; **~ (сыгра́ть** *perf***) на чьих-н сла́бостях** to play on sb's weaknesses; **~** *(impf)* **на чьих-н не́рвах** to irritate sb; **~ (сыгра́ть** *perf***) сва́дьбу** to celebrate a wedding; **вино́ ~ло в бока́ле** the wine sparkled in the glass.

игра́ючи *нареч (разг: легко)* with one's eyes closed.

игри́в|ый (-, -а, -о) *прил* playful.

игри́стый *прил* sparkling.

игров|о́й *прил*: **~а́я ко́мната** playroom; **~ы́е ви́ды спо́рта** team sports; **игрово́й автома́т** fruit machine.

игро́к (-а́) *м* player; *(в азартные игры)* gambler.

игроте́к|а (-и) *ж (собрание игр)* compendium *(BRIT)*; *(комната)* games room.

игру́шек *сущ см* **игру́шка**.

игру́шечный *прил* toy *опред*; *(перен)* tiny.

игру́ш|ка (-ки; *gen pl* -ек) *ж* toy; *(перен)* puppet; **ёлочные ~ки** Christmas tree decorations.

идеа́л (-а) *м* ideal; **~ демокра́тии** democratic ideal; **он – мой ~** he's someone I look up to.

идеа́лен *прил см* **идеа́льный**.

идеализи́р|овать (-ую) *(не)сов перех* to idealize.

идеали́зм (-а) *м* idealism.

идеали́ст (-а) *м* idealist.

идеалисти́ческ|ий (-ая, -ое, -ие) *прил* idealistic.

идеалисти́чный *прил* idealistic.

идеа́л|ьный (-ен, -ьна, -ьно) *прил* ideal.

иде́|йный (-ен, -йна, -йно) *прил (идеологический)* ideological; *(прогрессивный)* radical; **~йная осно́ва рома́на** the main theme of the novel.

идём *несов см* **идти́**.

идентифици́р|овать (-ую) *(не)сов перех* to identify.

иденти́ч|ный (-ен, -на, -но) *прил* identical.

идео́лог (-а) *м* ideologist.

идеологи́ческ|ий (-ая, -ое, -ие) *прил* ideological.

идеоло́ги|я (-и) *ж* ideology.

идёшь *итп несов см* **идти́**.

иде́|я (-и) *ж* idea; **по ~е** *(разг)* supposedly; **по ~е** *+gen* in accordance with; **подава́ть (пода́ть** *perf***) кому́-н ~ю** to give sb an idea.

идилли́ческ|ий (-ая, -ое, -ие) *прил* idyllic.

иди́лли|я (-и) *ж* idyll.

идио́м|а (-ы) *ж* idiom.

идио́т (-а) *м (также МЕД)* idiot.

идиоти́зм (-а) *м (МЕД)* mental retardation; *(разг: глупость)* idiocy.

идиóтск|ий (-ая, -ое, -ие) *прил* idiotic.
и́дол (-а) *м* idol.
идти́ (*см* **Table 18**) *несов неперех* to go; (*пешком*) to walk; (*дни, годы*) to go by; (*фильм, спектакль итп*) to be on; (*часы*) to work; (*товар*) to sell; (*подходить: одежда*): **~ к** *+dat* to go with; **~ (пойти́** *perf*) **(в/на** *+acc*) to go (to); **~ (пойти́** *perf*) *+instr* (*конём, тузом итп*) to play; **я шёл 3 часá** I walked for 3 hours; **иди́ сюдá!** come here!; **иду́!** (I'm) coming!; **идёт пóезд/автóбус** the train/bus is coming; **пóезд идёт до Москвы́** the train goes as far as Moscow; **маши́на идёт со скóростью 100км в час** the car is going at *или* doing 100km per hour; **идёт дождь/снег** it's raining/snowing; **идёт зимá** winter is coming; **идёт грозá** there is a storm coming; **делá иду́т хорошó/плóхо** things are going well/badly; **сейчáс иду́т переговóры/экзáмены** the talks/exams are in progress; **что сейчáс идёт в кинó?** what's on at the cinema just now?; **спектáкль идёт 2 часá** the play goes on for 2 hours; **мои́ часы́ иду́т мéдленно/бы́стро** my watch is slow/fast; **Вам идёт э́та шля́па** the hat suits you; **из трубы́ идёт дым** there is smoke coming from the chimney; **у меня́ идёт кровь из нóса** my nose is bleeding; **емý идёт пя́тый год** he was four on his last birthday; **~ (пойти́** *perf*) **пешкóм** to walk, go on foot; **~ (пойти́** *perf*) **на рабóту/в теáтр** to go to work/the theatre; **~ (пойти́** *perf*) **на э́кспорт/продáжу** to be for export/sale; **э́ти я́блоки пойду́т на варéнье** these apples will do for making jam; **~ (пойти́** *perf*) **на у́быль** to decrease; **~ (пойти́** *perf*) **на снижéние** to descend; **~ (пойти́** *perf*) **на риск** to take a risk; **~ (пойти́** *perf*) **на компроми́сс** to go for a compromise; **~ (пойти́** *perf*) **на хи́трость/обмáн** to resort to cunning/deception; **идёт!** (*разг*) fine!
иезуи́т (-а) *м* Jesuit.
иéн|а (-ы) *ж* yen.
иерáрхи|я (-и) *ж* hierarchy.
иерóглиф (-а) *м* (*китайский, японский*) character; (*египетский*) hieroglyph (*мн* hieroglyphics).
Иерусали́м (-а) *м* Jerusalem.
ИЖ *м сокр* = *Ижéвский мотоциклéтный завóд*; (*мотоцикл*) *motorcycle manufactured at the Izhevsk motorcycle factory*.
иждивéн|ец (-ца) *м* (*ребёнок, престарелые*) dependant; (*бездельник*) sponger.
иждивéни|е (-я) *ср* maintenance; **состоя́ть** (*impf*) *или* **быть** (*impf*) **на ~и у** *+gen* to be dependent on.
иждивéнца *итп сущ см* **иждивéнец**.
иждивéнчеств|о (-а) *ср* dependence.

KEYWORD

из *предл* (*+gen*) **1** (*о направлении действия откуда-нибудь*) out of; **он вы́шел из кóмнаты** he went out of the room; **онá достáла из кармáна платóк** she took a handkerchief out of her pocket
2 (*при обозначении происхождения, источника*) from; **свéдения из кни́ги** information from a book; **из достовéрных истóчников** from reliable sources; **я из Москвы́** I am from Moscow
3 (*при выделении части из целого*) of; **вот оди́н из примéров** here is one of the examples
4 (*при обозначении компонентов целого*) made of; **э́тот стол сдéлан из сосны́** this table is made of pine; **вáза из стеклá** a glass vase; **варéнье из я́блок** apple jam; **блу́за из нейлóна** nylon blouse
5 (*при указании причины*) out of; **из осторóжности/зáвисти** out of wariness/envy; **из эконóмии** in order to save money
6 (*во фразах*): **из гóда в год** year in, year out; **я бежáл изо всех сил** I ran at top speed.

изб|á (-ы́; *nom pl* **-ы)** *ж* hut.
избави́тел|ь (-я) *м* saviour.
избави́тельниц|а (-ы) *ж см* **избави́тель**.
избáв|ить (-лю, -ишь; *impf* **избавля́ть)** *сов перех*: **~ когó-н от** *+gen* (*от проблем, от забот*) to relieve sb of; (*от врагов*) to deliver sb from
▸ **избáвиться** (*impf* **избавля́ться**) *сов возв*: **~ся от** *+gen* (*от проблем, от посетителей*) to get rid of; (*от страха, от предрассудков*) to get over.
избалóван|ный (-, -на, -но) *прил* spoilt.
избál|овать (-у́ю) *сов от* **бáловать**.
избал|овáться (-у́юсь; *impf* **избалóвываться)** *сов возв* (*разг*) to become spoilt.
избéга|ть (-ю) *сов перех* (*разг*) to run around.
избегá|ть (-ю) *несов от* **избежáть, избéгнуть** ◆ *неперех*: **~ чегó-н/***+infin* to avoid sth/doing.
избéг|нуть (-ну, -нешь; *pt* **-, -ла, -ло,** *impf* **избегáть)** *сов неперех* = **избежáть**.
избегу́ *итп сов см* **избежáть**.
избежáни|е (-я) *ср*: **во ~** *+gen* (in order) to avoid.
избежáть (*как* **бежáть**; *см* **Table 20**; *impf* **избегáть)** *сов неперех*: **~** *+gen* to avoid.
изберу́ *итп сов см* **избрáть**.
избивá|ть (-ю) *несов от* **изби́ть**.
избиéни|е (-я) *ср* beating; (*массовое убийство*) massacre.
избирáтелен *прил см* **избирáтельный**.
избирáтел|ь (-я) *м* voter.
избирáтельниц|а (-ы) *ж см* **избирáтель**.
избирáтел|ьный *прил* (*система*) electoral; **(-ен, -ьна, -ьно;** *эффект*) selective; **~ьная кампáния** election campaign; **избирáтельный**

уча́сток polling station; **избира́тельный бюллете́нь** ballot paper.
избира́|ть (-ю) *несов от* **избра́ть** ◆ *перех* to elect.
изби́т|ый (-, -а, -о) *прил* clichéd, hackneyed.
из|би́ть (-обью́, -обьёшь; *impf* **избива́ть**) *сов перех* (*человека*) to beat; (*обувь*) to wear out.
избороз|ди́ть (-жу́, -ди́шь) *сов от* **борозди́ть**.
избра́ни|е (-я) *ср* election.
избра́нник (-а) *м* chosen one; ~ **судьбы́** fate's darling; **наро́дные ~и** deputies.
избра́нниц|а (-ы) *ж см* **избра́нник**.
и́збранн|ые (-ых; *decl like adj*) *мн* select *или* chosen few *мн*.
и́збранный *прил* (*рассказы, стихи*) selected; (*люди, круг*) select; *см также* **и́збранные**.
изб|ра́ть (-еру́, -ерёшь; *pt* **-ра́л, -рала́, -ра́ло**, *impf* **избира́ть**) *сов перех* (*профессию*) to choose; (*президента*) to elect; **избира́ть (~** *perf*) **кого́-н в парла́мент** to elect sb to parliament.
избы́т|ок (-ка) *м* (*излишек*) surplus; (*обилие*) excess; **име́ть** (*impf*) **что-н в ~ке** to have plenty of sth; **э́того хва́тит с ~ком** it is more than enough; **она́ запла́кала от ~ка чувств** overwhelmed by emotion, she burst into tears.
избы́точ|ный (-ен, -на, -но) *прил* (*вес, влага*) excess *опред*; (*информация*) abundant; **~ное предложе́ние** (*ЭКОН*) excess supply.
извая́ни|е (-я) *ср* effigy.
изве́да|ть (-ю; *impf* **изве́дывать**) *сов перех* to come to know.
изведу́(сь) *итп сов см* **извести́(сь)**.
изве́дыва|ть (-ю) *несов от* **изве́дать**.
и́зверг (-а) *м* monster (*fig*).
изве́ргн|уть (-у, -ешь; *impf* **изверга́ть**) *сов перех* to spew (out).
изверже́ни|е (-я) *ср* eruption.
изве́р|иться (-юсь, -ишься) *сов возв*: ~ **в** +*prp* to lose faith in.
изверн|у́ться (-у́сь, -ёшься; *impf* **извёртываться** *или* **извора́чиваться**) *сов возв* to twist around; (*перен*) to pull through.
изве́стен *прил см* **изве́стный**.
изв|ести́ (-еду́, -едёшь; *pt* **-ёл, -ела́, -ело́**, *impf* **изводи́ть**) *сов перех* (*разг*: *истратить*) to fritter away; (: *измучить*) to exasperate; (*истребить*) to exterminate
▸ **извести́сь** (*impf* **изводи́ться**) *сов возв* to torment o.s.
изве́сти|е (-я) *ср* news; *см также* **изве́стия**.
изве|сти́ть (-щу́, -сти́шь; *impf* **извеща́ть**) *сов перех*: ~ **кого́-н о** +*prp* to inform sb of.
изве́сти|я (-й) *мн* (*издание*) bulletin *ед*.
извёстк|а (-и) *ж* slaked lime.
изве́стно *как сказ*: **~, что** ... it is well known that ...; **мне э́то** ~ I know about it; **наско́лько мне** ~ as far as I know; **как** ~ as is well known.
изве́стност|ь (-и) *ж* fame; **по́льзоваться** (*impf*) **~ю** to be well known; **ста́вить (поста́вить** *perf*) **кого́-н в** ~ to inform sb.
изве́ст|ный (-ен, -на, -но) *прил* famous, well-known; (*no short form*; *разг*: *лентяй, бабник*) notorious; (*условия*) certain; ~ +*instr* famous *или* well-known for; **он ~ен как тала́нтливый руководи́тель** he is known to be a talented leader; **~ное де́ло!** (*разг*) that's no surprise!
известня́к (-а́) *м* limestone.
и́звест|ь (-и) *ж* lime.
изве́ч|ный (-ен, -на, -но) *прил* (*проблема, спор*) perpetual.
извеща́|ть (-ю) *несов от* **извести́ть**.
извеще́ни|е (-я) *ср* notification; (*КОММ*) advice note; **почто́вое** ~ signed receipt of delivery.
извещу́ *сов см* **извести́ть**.
извива́|ться (-юсь) *несов возв* (*змея*) to slither; (*человек*) to writhe; (*дорога, река*) to wind.
изви́лин|а (-ы) *ж* bend; ~ **мо́зга** convolution.
изви́лист|ый (-, -а, -о) *прил* winding, twisting.
извине́ни|е (-я) *ср* apology; (*оправдание*) excuse; **проси́ть (попроси́ть** *perf*) **~я (у кого́-н)** to apologize (to sb).
извини́тел|ьный *прил* (*тон, улыбка*) apologetic; (-ен, -ьна, -ьно; *ошибка, слабость*) excusable, forgivable.
извин|и́ть (-ю́, -и́шь; *impf* **извиня́ть**) *сов перех* (*простить*): **~ что-н (кому́-н)** to excuse (sb for) sth; **~и́те!** excuse me!; **~и́те, Вы не ска́жете где вокза́л?** excuse me, could you tell me where the station is?; **в э́том, ~и́те, я с Ва́ми не согла́сен** sorry, but I cannot agree with you on that
▸ **извини́ться** (*impf* **извиня́ться**) *сов возв*: **~ся (за** +*acc*) to apologize (for); **он ~и́лся, что не позвони́л** he apologized for not phoning (*BRIT*) *или* calling (*US*).
извиня́ющ|ийся (-аяся, -ееся, -иеся) *прил* apologetic.
извлёк *итп сов см* **извле́чь**.
извлека́|ть (-ю) *несов от* **извле́чь**.
извлеку́ *итп сов см* **извле́чь**.
извлече́ни|е (-я) *ср* (*золота, пользы итп*) extraction; (*из документа*) extract, excerpt.
извл|е́чь (-еку́, -ечёшь *итп*, **-еку́т**; *pt* **-ёк, -екла́, -екло́**, *impf* **извлека́ть**) *сов перех* (*занозу, осколок*) to remove, take out; (*золото*) to extract; (*перен*: *пользу, выгоду итп*) to derive; **извлека́ть (~** *perf*) **уро́к** to learn a lesson; **извлека́ть (~** *perf*) **ко́рень** (*МАТ*) to find the root.
извне́ *нареч* from outside.
изв|оди́ть(ся) (-ожу́(сь), -о́дишь(ся)) *несов от* **извести́(сь)**.
изво́зчик (-а) *м* (*кучер*) coachman (*мн* coachmen); (*экипаж*) cab (*coach*).
изво́л|ить (-ю, -ишь) *несов неперех*: ~ +*infin* to condescend to do; **~ьте не крича́ть** would you mind not shouting.
извора́чива|ться (-юсь) *несов от* **изверну́ться**.
изворо́тлив|ый (-, -а, -о) *прил* (*человек*) wily; (*ум, делец*) shrewd.

извра|ти́ть (-щу́, -ти́шь; *impf* **извраща́ть**) *сов перех* to distort.
извраще́ни|е (-я) *ср* distortion; **полово́е ~** sexual perversion.
извращённ|ый (-, -на, -но) *прил* perverted.
извращу́ *сов см* **изврати́ть.**
изга́|дить (-жу, -дишь) *сов перех (разг)* to mess up.
изги́б (-а) *м* bend.
изгиба́|ть(ся) (-ю(сь)) *несов от* **изогну́ть(ся).**
изгла́|дить (-жу, -дишь; *impf* **изгла́живать)** *сов перех*: **~ что-н из па́мяти** to blot sth out of one's memory
▸ **изгла́диться** (*impf* **изгла́живаться**) *сов возв* to be blotted out.
изгна́ни|е (-я) *ср (ссылка)* exile; *(врага)* expulsion; *(злых духов)* exorcism.
изгна́нник (-а) *м* exile.
изгна́нниц|а (-ы) *ж см* **изгна́нник.**
изг|на́ть (-оню́, -о́нишь; *pt* **-на́л, -нала́, -на́ло,** *impf* **изгоня́ть)** *сов перех* to drive out; *(сослать)* to exile.
изго́|й (-я) *м* outcast.
изголо́вь|е (-я) *ср*: **у ~я** at the head of the bed.
изголода́|ться (-юсь) *сов возв* to be starving; *(перен)*: **~ по** *+dat (по книгам)* to long *или* yearn for; **~** *(perf)* **по ла́ске** to crave affection.
изгоню́ *итп сов см* **изгна́ть.**
изгоня́|ть (-ю) *несов от* **изгна́ть.**
и́згород|ь (-и) *ж* fence; **жива́я ~** hedge.
изгото́в|ить (-лю, -ишь; *impf* **изготовля́ть)** *сов перех* to manufacture.
изготовле́ни|е (-я) *ср* manufacture.
изгото́влю *сов см* **изгото́вить.**
изготовля́|ть (-ю) *несов от* **изгото́вить.**
изгры́з|ть (-у́, -ёшь; *pt* **-, -ла, -ло)** *сов перех* to gnaw (away) at.
изд. *сокр* (= **изда́ние**) ed. (= *edition*).
изда|ва́ть (-ю́, -ёшь) *несов от* **изда́ть.**
и́здавна *нареч* for a long time.
издади́м *итп сов см* **изда́ть.**
издалека́ *нареч* from a long way off *или* away; **начина́ть (нача́ть** *perf***) разгово́р ~** *(перен)* to start a conversation in a roundabout way.
и́здали *нареч* = **издалека́.**
изда́м *итп сов см* **изда́ть.**
изда́ни|е (-я) *ср (действие)* publication; *(изданная вещь)* edition.
изда́ст *сов см* **изда́ть.**
изда́тел|ь (-я) *м* publisher.
изда́тельск|ий (-ая, -ое, -ие) *прил* publishing *опред.*
изда́тельств|о (-а) *ср* publisher, publishing house.
изда́ть (*как* **дать**; *см* **Table 14**; *impf* **издава́ть)** *сов перех (книгу)* to publish; *(закон, постановление)* to issue; *(крик, стон)* to let out; *(запах)* to give off.

изд-во *сокр* (= **изда́тельство**) pub(l). (= *publisher*).
издева́тельск|ий (-ая, -ое, -ие) *прил (насмешливый)* mocking, scoffing; *(оскорбительный)* abusive.
издева́тельств|о (-а) *ср* mockery; *(наглое)* jibe; *(жестокое)* abuse.
издева́|ться (-юсь) *несов возв*: **~ над** *+instr (над подчинёнными)* to make a mockery of; *(над книгой)* to pour scorn on; *(над чьей-н одеждой)* to mock, ridicule.
издёв|ка (-ки; *gen pl* **-ок)** *ж (разг)* jibe.
изде́ли|е (-я) *ср (товар)* article; **ювели́рные ~я** jewellery (*BRIT*), jewelery (*US*); **стекля́нные ~я** glassware; **игру́шка куста́рного ~я** handmade toy.
издёрган|ный (-, -на, -но) *прил (разг)* edgy.
издёрга|ть (-ю) *сов перех (разг)* to put on edge
▸ **издёргаться** *сов возв (разг)* to become edgy.
изд|ержа́ть (-ержу́, -е́ржишь; *impf* **изде́рживать)** *сов перех (деньги)* to use up; *(ресурсы)* to exhaust.
изде́рж|ки (-ек) *мн (производственные)* expenses *мн*; **суде́бные ~** legal costs; **э́то всё – ~ плохо́го воспита́ния** it's all the result of bad upbringing.
издеру́ *итп сов см* **изодра́ть.**
издыха́ни|е (-я) *ср*: **при после́днем ~и** on one's deathbed.
изжи́|ть (-ву́, -вёшь; *pt* **-л, -ла́, -ло,** *impf* **изжива́ть)** *сов перех (плохую привычку)* to overcome; *(преступность)* to eliminate; **изжива́ть (~** *perf***) себя́** to outlive its usefulness.
изжо́г|а (-и) *ж* heartburn.
из-за *предл*: **~** *+gen (занавески)* from behind; *(угла)* from around; *(по вине)* because of; **встава́ть (встать** *perf***) ~ стола́** to get up from the table; **~ того́ что** because; **~ тебя́ мы пропусти́ли по́езд** we missed the train because of you.
иззя́б|нуть (-ну, -нешь; *pt* **-, -ла, -ло)** *сов неперех (разг)* to be frozen stiff.
излага́|ть (-ю) *несов от* **изложи́ть.**
изла́мыва|ть (-ю) *несов от* **излома́ть.**
излече́ни|е (-я) *ср (лечение)* treatment; *(выздоровление)* recovery; **быть** *(impf)* **на ~и** to undergo treatment.
изле́чива|ть (-ю) *несов от* **излечить**
▸ **изле́чиваться** *несов от* **излечи́ться** ◆ *возв (болезнь)* to be curable.
излечи́м|ый (-, -а, -о) *прил* curable.
изл|ечи́ть (-ечу́, -е́чишь; *impf* **изле́чивать)** *сов перех*: **~ кого́-н (от** *+gen***)** to cure sb (of)
▸ **излечи́ться** *сов возв*: **~ся от** *+gen (от болезни)* to recover from; *(от наркомании, от алкоголизма)* to be cured of.
изли́|ть (изолью́, изольёшь; *pt* **-л, -ла́, -ло,** *impf* **излива́ть)** *сов перех (перен: тоску)* to pour

out; **изливáть (~ *perf*) дýшу** to pour one's heart out; **изливáть (~ *perf*) гнев** to vent one's anger
▸ **излúться** (*impf* **изливáться**) *сов возв* to pour one's heart out; **изливáться** *(impf)* **в благодáрностях** to express one's great appreciation.
излúш|ек (-ка) *м* (*остаток*) remainder; ~ *+gen* (*влаги, веса*) excess of.
излúшеств|о (-а) *ср* overindulgence.
излúшка *итп сущ см* **излúшек.**
излúш|ний (-няя, -нее, -ние; -ен, -ня, -не) *прил* unnecessary; **комментáрии ~ни** there is nothing to add.
излияни|е (-я) *ср* (*чувств*) gush; (*обычно мн: дружеские, любовные*) outburst.
изловч|úться (-ýсь, -úшься) *сов возв* (*приспособиться*) to manage.
изложéни|е (-я) *ср* presentation.
изл|ожúть (-ожý, -óжишь; *impf* **излагáть)** *сов перех* (*события*) to recount; (*просьбу, решение итп*) to state.
излóман|ный (-, -на, -но) *прил* (*судьба, жизнь*) ruined; (*характер*) unbalanced.
изломá|ть (-ю; *impf* **изламывать)** *сов перех* (*забор, игрушку*) to smash; (*перен: жизнь*) to ruin; (*: характер*) to unbalance.
излучá|ть (-ю) *несов перех* (*также перен*) to radiate
▸ **излучáться** *несов возв* to radiate.
излучéни|е (-я) *ср* radiation.
излýчин|а (-ы) *ж* bend.
излюбленный *прил* favourite (*BRIT*), favorite (*US*).
измá|зать(ся) (-жу(сь), -жешь(ся)) *сов от* **мáзать(ся).**
измарá|ть(ся) (-ю(сь)) *сов от* **марáть(ся).**
измáтыва|ть(ся) (-ю(сь)) *несов от* **измотáть(ся).**
измельчá|ть (-ю) *сов от* **мельчáть.**
измельч|úть (-ý, -úшь) *сов от* **мельчúть**
▸ **измельчúться** *сов возв* to crumble.
измéн|а (-ы) *ж* (*родине*) treason; (*другу*) betrayal; **государственная** ~ high treason; **супрýжеская** ~ adultery.
изменéни|е (-я) *ср* change; (*поправка*) alteration.
изм|енúть (-еню, -éнишь; *impf* **изменять)** *сов перех* to change ◆ *неперех:* ~ *+dat* (*родине, другу*) to betray; (*супругу*) to be unfaithful to; (*память*) to fail; **силы емý ~енúли** his strength failed him
▸ **измениться** (*impf* **изменяться**) *сов возв* to change.
измéнник (-а) *м* (*родине*) traitor.
измéнница (-ы) *ж см* **измéнник.**
измéнчив|ый (-, -а, -о) *прил* changeable.
изменяем|ый (-, -а, -о) *прил* (*линг*): **~ое окончáние** variable ending.
изменя|ть(ся) (-ю(сь)) *несов от* **изменúть(ся).**
измерéни|е (-я) *ср* (*действие: площади*) measurement; (*величина*) dimension.
измерúтельный *прил* measuring *опред.*
измéр|ить (-ю, -ишь; *impf* **измерять)** *сов перех* to measure; **измерять (~ *perf*) температýру комý-н** to take sb's temperature; ~ *(perf)* **когó-н взглядом** to look sb up and down.
измерá|ться (*3sg* **-ется,** *3pl* **-ются)** *несов возв* (*+instr*): **~ килогрáммами/мéтрами** to be measured in kilogrammes/metres (*BRIT*) *или* meters (*US*).
измождéни|е (-я) *ср* exhaustion.
измождён|ный (-, -á, -ó) *прил* (*человек*) worn out; (**-, -на, -но;** *вид, лицо*) haggard.
измóк|нуть (-ну, -нешь; *pt* **-, -ла, -ло)** *сов неперех* to get soaked.
измóр (-а) *м*: **взять когó-н/что-н ~ом** (*горóд*) to wage a war of attrition against sb/sth; (*перен: разг*) to wear down.
ú́зморозь (-и) *ж* hoarfrost.
ú́змoрос|ь (-и) *ж* drizzle.
измотá|ть (-ю; *impf* **измáтывать)** *сов перех* to wear out
▸ **измотáться** (*impf* **измáтываться**) *сов возв* (*разг*) to be worn out.
измýчен|ный (-, -а, -о) *прил* (*человек*) worn out; (**-, -на, -но;** *лицо*) haggard.
измýч|ить (-у, -ишь) *сов от* **мýчить.**
измывá|ться (-юсь) *несов возв*: **~ над** *+instr* (*разг*) to taunt.
измышлéни|е (-я) *ср* fabrication.
из|мять(ся) (-омнý(сь), -омнёшь(ся)) *сов от* **мять(ся).**
изнáнк|а (-и) *ж* (*одежды*) inside; (*ткани*) wrong side; (*перен: жизни, событий*) dark side.
изнасúл|овать (-ую) *сов от* **насúловать.**
изначáл|ьный (-ен, -ьна, -ьно) *прил* initial.
изнáшива|ть(ся) (-ю(сь)) *несов от* **износúть(ся).**
изнéжен|ный (-, -а, -о) *прил* pampered.
изнéж|ить (-у, -ишь) *сов перех* to pamper
▸ **изнéжиться** *сов возв* to be pampered.
изнемóг *итп сов см* **изнемóчь.**
изнемогá|ть (-ю) *несов от* **изнемóчь.**
изнемогý *итп сов см* **изнемóчь.**
изнеможéни|е (-я) *ср* exhaustion; **до ~я** to the point of exhaustion.
изнеможён|ный (-, -á, -ó) *прил* (*человек*) worn out; (**-, -на, -но;** *вид, лицо*) haggard.
изнемó|чь (-гý, -жешь *итп*, **-гýт;** *pt* **-г, -глá, -глó,** *impf* **изнемогáть)** *сов неперех* to be exhausted.
изнóс (-а) *м* (*механизмов*) wear; (*перен: организма*) ageing; **рабóтать** *(impf)* **на ~** (*перен*) to work o.s. into the ground.
изн|осúть (-ошý, -óсишь; *impf* **изнáшивать)** *сов перех* to wear out
▸ **износúться** (*impf* **изнáшиваться**) *сов возв* to wear out.
изнóшен|ный (-, -а, -о) *прил* worn-out.
изношý(сь) *сов см* **износúть(ся).**
изнурён|ный (-, -á, -ó) *прил* (*человек*) exhausted; (**-, -на, -но;** *лицо, вид*) haggard.
изнурúтел|ьный (-ен, -ьна, -ьно) *прил*

exhausting.
изнур|и́ть (**-ю́, -и́шь**; *impf* **изнуря́ть**) *сов перех* to exhaust.
изнутри́ *нареч* from inside.
изныва́|ть (**-ю**) *несов неперех* to languish.
изо *предл* = **из**.
изоби́ли|е (**-я**) *ср* abundance; **в ~и** in abundance.
изоби́л|овать (*3sg* **-ует**, *3pl* **-уют**) *несов неперех* (*+instr*) to abound in.
изоби́л|ьный (**-ен, -ьна, -ьно**) *прил* abundant.
изоблича́|ть (**-ю**) *несов от* **изобличи́ть** ◆ *перех* (*обнаружить*): **~ кого́-н в** *+prp* (*подлеж*: *одежда, акцент итп*) to give sb away as.
изоблич|и́ть (**-у́, -и́шь**; *impf* **изоблича́ть**) *сов перех* (*шпиона, взяточника итп*) to expose; **изоблича́ть (~ *perf*) кого́-н во лжи/в моше́нничестве** to expose sb's lies/deception.
изобража́|ть(ся) (**-ю(сь)**) *несов от* **изобрази́ть(ся)**.
изображе́ни|е (**-я**) *ср* image; (*действие*: *событий*) depiction, representation.
изображу́(сь) *сов см* **изобрази́ть(ся)**.
изобрази́тел|ьный (**-ен, -ьна, -ьно**) *прил* descriptive; **изобрази́тельное иску́сство** fine art.
изобра|зи́ть (**-жу́, -зи́шь**; *impf* **изобража́ть**) *сов перех* (*на картине, в романе итп*) to depict, portray; (*подлеж*: *лицо*) to show; (*копировать*) to impersonate; **изобража́ть (~ *perf*) из себя́ наи́вного/знатока́** to make o.s. out to be naive/an expert
▸ **изобрази́ться** (*impf* **изобража́ться**) *сов возв* to show; **на его́ лице́ ~зи́лся у́жас** a look of horror came over his face.
изобр|ести́ (**-ету́, -етёшь**; *pt* **-ёл, -ела́, -ело́**, *impf* **изобрета́ть**) *сов перех* to invent.
изобрета́тел|ь (**-я**) *м* inventor.
изобрета́тельниц|а (**-ы**) *ж см* **изобрета́тель**.
изобрета́тельност|ь (**-и**) *ж* inventiveness.
изобрета́тельств|о (**-а**) *ср* innovation.
изобрета́|ть (**-ю**) *несов от* **изобрести́**.
изобрете́ни|е (**-я**) *ср* invention.
изобью́ *итп сов см* **изби́ть**.
изогн|у́ть (**-у́, -ёшь**; *impf* **изгиба́ть**) *сов перех* to bend
▸ **изогну́ться** (*impf* **изгиба́ться**) *сов возв* to bend.
из|одра́ть (**-деру́, -дерёшь**; *pt* **-одра́л, -одрала́, -одра́ло**) *сов перех* (*разг*) to rip to shreds.
изо|йти́ (*как* **идти́**; *см* **Table 18**; *impf* **исходи́ть**) *сов неперех*: **~ слеза́ми** to cry one's eyes out; **она́ ~шла́ го́рем** she was completely grief-stricken.
изоли́рованный *прил* (*случай, явление итп*) isolated; (*комната, провод*) insulated.
изоли́р|овать (**-ую**) *(не)сов перех* (*больного, преступника*) to isolate; (*вход*) to cut off; (*ТЕХ, ЭЛЕК*) to insulate
▸ **изоли́роваться** *(не)сов возв* (*челове́к*) to isolate o.s.
изолью́(сь) *итп сов см* **изли́ть(ся)**.
изоля́тор (**-а**) *м* (*ТЕХ, ЭЛЕК*) insulator; (*в больнице*) isolation unit; (*в тюрьме*) solitary confinement.
изоляцио́нн|ый *прил*: **~ая ле́нта** insulating tape.
изоля́ци|я (**-и**) *ж* (*см глаг*) isolation; insulation; **жить** *(impf)* **в ~и** to live in isolation.
изомну́(сь) *итп сов см* **измя́ть(ся)**.
изопью́ *итп сов см* **испи́ть**.
изорв|а́ть (**-у́, -ёшь**; *pt* **-а́л, -ала́, -а́ло**) *сов перех* to rip up; **~** *(perf)* **в кло́чья** to tear to shreds.
изото́п (**-а**) *м* isotope.
изотрётся *итп сов см* **истере́ться**.
изошёл *итп сов см* **изойти́**.
изощрён|ный (**-, -на, -но**) *прил* sophisticated.
изощр|и́ться (**-ю́сь, -и́шься**; *impf* **изощря́ться**) *сов возв* (*отличиться*) to surpass o.s.; (*вкус, ум*) to become sophisticated.
изощря́|ться (**-юсь**) *несов от* **изощри́ться** ◆ *неперех*: **~ в** *+prp* to excel in.
из-под *предл* (*+gen*) from under(neath); (*около*) from outside; **~ стола́ вы́ползла ко́шка** a cat crawled from under the table; **он прие́хал ~ Ки́ева** he comes from outside Kiev; **выходи́ть (вы́йти *perf*) ~ чьего́-н влия́ния** to free o.s. from sb's influence; **бежа́ть** *(impf)* **~ стра́жи** to escape from custody; **ба́нка ~ варе́нья** jam jar; **буты́лка ~ во́дки** vodka bottle.
изразе|ц (**-ца́**) *м* tile.
изразцо́вый *прил* tiled.
Изра́ил|ь (**-я**) *м* Israel.
изра́ильск|ий (**-ая, -ое, -ие**) *прил* Israeli.
израильтя́н|ин (**-ина**; *nom pl* **-е**, *gen pl* **-**) *м* Israeli.
израильтя́н|ка (**-ки**; *gen pl* **-ок**) *ж см* **израильтя́нин**.
изра́н|ить (**-ю, -ишь**) *сов перех* to injure badly.
израсхо́д|овать (**-ую**) *сов от* **расхо́довать**.
и́зредка *нареч* now and then *или* again.
изре́|зать (**-жу, -жешь**; *impf* **изреза́ть**) *сов перех* to cut up; (*подлеж*: *дороги, каналы*) to crisscross.
изрёк *итп сов см* **изре́чь**.
изрека́|ть (**-ю**) *несов от* **изре́чь**.
изреку́ *итп сов см* **изре́чь**.
изрече́ни|е (**-я**) *ср* utterance.
изр|е́чь (**-еку́, -ечёшь** *итп*, **-еку́т**; *pt* **-ёк, -екла́, -екло́**, *impf* **изрека́ть**) *сов перех* to utter.
изреше|ти́ть (**-чу́, -ти́шь**) *сов перех*: **~ кого́-н пу́лями** to pepper sb with bullets.
изр|уби́ть (**-ублю́, -у́бишь**; *impf* **изруба́ть**) *сов перех* (*убить*) to hack to pieces.
изрыга́|ть (**-ю**) *несов перех* (*лаву*) to spew (out); (*перен*: *проклятия*) to let out a torrent of.

изры́т|ый (-, -а, -о) *прил* (*поверхность*) pitted; ~ **о́спой** pockmarked.
изр|ы́ть (-о́ю, -о́ешь) *сов перех* to riddle.
изря́д|ный (-ен, -на, -но) *прил* (*сумма, доход*) fair; (*разг*: *мошенник, пьяница итп*) real.
изуве́р (-а) *м* monster.
изуве́рск|ий (-ая, -ое, -ие) *прил* monstrous.
изуве́рств|о (-а) *ср* monstrosity.
изуве́ч|ить (-у, -ишь; *impf* **изуве́чивать**) *сов перех* to maim
▸ **изуве́читься** (*impf* **изуве́чиваться**) *сов возв* to be maimed.
изукра́|сить (-шу, -сишь; *impf* **изукра́шивать**) *сов перех* to adorn; (*разг*: *избить*) to beat black and blue.
изуми́тел|ьный (-ен, -ьна, -ьно) *прил* marvellous (*BRIT*), marvelous (*US*), wonderful.
изум|и́ть (-лю́, -и́шь; *impf* **изумля́ть**) *сов перех* to amaze, astound
▸ **изуми́ться** (*impf* **изумля́ться**) *сов возв* to be amazed.
изумле́ни|е (-я) *ср* amazement; **приходи́ть (прийти́** *perf*) **в** ~ to be amazed; **с** ~**м** (*слушать, рассматривать*) in amazement; **я с** ~**м обнару́жил, что** ... to my great amazement I discovered that ....
изумлю́(сь) *сов см* **изуми́ть(ся)**.
изумля́|ть(ся) (-ю(сь)) *несов от* **изуми́ть(ся)**.
изумру́д (-а) *м* emerald.
изумру́дный *прил* (*кольцо итп*) emerald; (*цвет*) emerald-green.
изуро́д|овать (-ую) *сов от* **уро́довать**.
изуча́|ть (-ю) *несов от* **изучи́ть** ◆ *перех* (*о процессе*) to study.
изуче́ни|е (-я) *ср* study.
из|учи́ть (-учу́, -у́чишь; *impf* **изуча́ть**) *сов перех* (*язык, предмет*) to learn; (*понять*) to get to know; (*исследовать*) to study.
изъеда́|ть (*3sg* **-ет**, *3pl* **-ют**) *несов от* **изъе́сть**.
изъе́ден|ный (-, -а, -о) *прил*: ~ **мо́лью** moth-eaten; ~ **кислото́й** eaten away by acid.
изъеди́м *итп сов см* **изъе́сть**.
изъе́з|дить (-жу, -дишь) *сов перех* to travel (round).
изъ|е́сть (*как* **есть**; *см* **Table 15**; *impf* **изъеда́ть**) *сов перех* (*мех, ткань*) to eat away; (*металл*) to corrode.
изъяви́тельн|ый *прил* (*лингв*): ~**ое наклоне́ние** the indicative mood.
изъ|яви́ть (-явлю́, -я́вишь; *impf* **изъявля́ть**) *сов перех* to indicate.
изъя́н (-а) *м* flaw.
изъясн|и́ть (-ю́, -и́шь; *impf* **изъясня́ть**) *сов перех* to clarify.
изъя́ти|е (-я) *ср* (*см глаг*) withdrawal; removal.
изъя́ть (**изыму́, изы́мешь**; *impf* **изыма́ть**) *сов перех* (*из обращения, из продажи*) to withdraw; (*отобрать*) to remove.
изыска́ни|е (-я) *ср* investigation; (*геологические*) exploration.
изы́сканност|ь (-и) *ж* refinement.
изы́скан|ный (-, -на, -но) *прил* refined.
изыска́тел|ь (-я) *м* surveyor.
изыска́тельск|ий (-ая, -ое, -ие) *прил* exploratory.
из|ыска́ть (-ыщу́, -ы́щешь; *impf* **изы́скивать**) *сов перех* to find.
изы́скива|ть (-ю) *несов от* **изыска́ть** ◆ *перех* (*искать*) to seek out.
изыщу́ *итп сов см* **изыска́ть**.
изю́м (-а) *м собир* raisins *мн*.
изю́мин|а (-ы) *ж* raisin.
изю́мин|ка (-ки; *gen pl* **-ок**) *ж уменьш от* **изю́мина**; (*перен*) highlight; **без** ~**ки** lacklustre.
изя́щен *прил см* **изя́щный**.
изя́ществ|о (-а) *ср* elegance.
изя́щ|ный (-ен, -на, -но) *прил* elegant.
ика́|ть (-ю) *несов неперех* to hiccup.
икн|у́ть (-у́, -ёшь) *сов неперех* to hiccup.
ико́н|а (-ы) *ж* (*РЕЛ*) icon.
иконопи́с|ец (-ца) *м* icon painter.
и́конопис|ь (-и) *ж* icon painting.
иконоста́с (-а) *м* iconostasis.
ико́т|а (-ы) *ж* hiccups *мн*.
икр|а́ (-ы́) *ж* (*рыбы*) roe; (*чёрная, красная*) caviar; (*кабачковая, баклажанная*) pâté; (*nom pl* **-ы**; *АНАТ*) calf (*мн* calves).
икри́н|ка (-ки; *gen pl* **-ок**) *ж* grain of caviar.
икс (-а) *м* (*МАТ*) X; **ми́стер И**~ Mr X.
ИЛ (-а) *м сокр* = *самолёт констру́кции С.В. Илью́шина*.
ил (-а) *м* silt.
и́ли *союз* or; **чай** ~ **ко́фе** tea or coffee; ~ ... ~ ... either ... or ...; ~ **ты не понима́ешь?** (*разг*) don't you understand or something?
и́лист|ый (-, -а, -о) *прил* silt *опред*.
иллюзиони́ст (-а) *м* conjurer.
иллю́зи|я (-и) *ж* (*также перен*) illusion.
иллюзо́р|ный (-ен, -на, -но) *прил* illusory.
иллюмина́тор (-а) *м* (*корабля*) porthole; (*самолёта*) window.
иллюмина́ци|я (-и) *ж* illuminations *мн*.
иллюстра́тор (-а) *м* illustrator.
иллюстра́ци|я (-и) *ж* illustration.
иллюстри́р|овать (-ую; *perf* **иллюстри́ровать** *или* **проиллюстри́ровать**) *несов перех* to illustrate.
ильм (-а) *м* elm.
им *мест см* **он, оно́, они́**.
им. *сокр* = *и́мени*.
имби́р|ь (-я) *м* ginger.
и́мени *итп сущ см* **и́мя**.
име́ни|е (-я) *ср* estate.
имени́нник (-а) *м person who is celebrating his name day or birthday*.
имени́нниц|а (-ы) *ж см* **имени́нник**.
имени́н|ы (-) *мн* (*РЕЛ*) name day *ед*.
имени́тельный *прил* (*лингв*): ~ **паде́ж** the nominative case.
имени́т|ый (-, -а, -о) *прил* renowned.
и́менно *част* exactly, precisely ◆ *союз* (*перед перечислением*): **а** ~ namely; **э́то на́до сде́лать** ~ **сего́дня** it has to be done today; ~ **в**

этом дóме я родился it was in this house that I was born; ~ **так я и поступил** that is exactly what I did; **вот** ~! exactly!, precisely!; **на собрáнии присýтствовало 6 человéк а** ~: **Ивановó, Петрóв ...** there were 6 people present at the meeting, namely Ivanov, Petrov ....
именнóй *прил* (*оружие, часы*) personalized; (*акции, чек*) nontransferable; **именнóй прóпуск** pass (*issued in somebody's name*); **именнóй спúсок** nominal roll.
имен|овáть (-ýю; *perf* **наименовáть)** *несов перех* to name.
имé|ть (-ю) *несов перех* to have; ~ *(impf)* **мéсто** (*совершаться*) to take place; ~ *(impf)* **дéло с** *+instr* to deal with; **я не хочý** ~ **с ним дéло** I don't want anything to do with him; ~ *(impf)* **в видý** to bear in mind; (*подразумевать*) to mean; **я** ~**ю задáчу/цель** *или* **задáчей/цéлью** *+infin* my task/aim is to do; ~ *(impf)* **что-нибудь прóтив** *+gen* to have something against; **ничегó не** ~ *(impf)* **прóтив** *+gen* to have nothing against
▸ **имéться** *несов возв* (*сведения, средства*) to be available; **у нас** ~**ются нýжные срéдства** we have the necessary resources available.
úми *мест см* **онú**.
úмидж (-а) *м* image.
úмиджмéйкер (-а) *м* image-maker.
имитáци|я (-и) *ж* imitation.
имитúр|овать (-ую; *perf* **сымитúровать)** *несов перех* to imitate.
иммигрáнт (-а) *м* immigrant.
иммигрáнт|ка (-ки; *gen pl* **-ок)** *ж см* **иммигрáнт**.
иммиграциóнный *прил* immigration.
иммигрáци|я (-и) *ж* immigration ◆ *собир* immigrants *мн*.
иммигрúр|овать (-ую) *(не)сов неперех* to immigrate.
иммунитéт (-а) *м* (*МЕД, перен*): ~ **(к** *+dat*) immunity (to); **вырабáтывать (вы́работать** *perf*) ~ **к** *+dat* to develop an immunity to; **у меня** ~ **к шýму/крúтике** I'm immune to noise/ criticism; **дипломатúческий** ~ diplomatic immunity.
иммýнн|ый *прил* (*МЕД*): ~**ая систéма** immune system.
иммунолóги|я (-и) *ж* immunology.
императúв (-а) *м* (*также ЛИНГ*) imperative.
императóр (-а) *м* emperor.
импераtóрск|ий (-ая, -ое, -ие) *прил* imperial.
императрúц|а (-ы) *ж* empress.
империалúзм (-а) *м* imperialism.
империалúст (-а) *м* imperialist.
империалистúческ|ий (-ая, -ое, -ие) *прил* imperialistic.
импéри|я (-и) *ж* empire.
импéрск|ий (-ая, -ое, -ие) *прил* imperial.
импúчмент (-а) *м* (*ПОЛИТ*) impeachment.
имплантáт (-а) *м* (*МЕД*) implant.
имплантáци|я (-и) *ж* implantation.
имплантúр|овать (-ую) *(не)сов перех* to implant.
импонúр|овать (-ую) *несов неперех* (*+dat*) to appeal to.
úмпорт (-а) *м* (*ввоз*) importation ◆ *собир* (*товары*) imports *мн*; (*разг: о заграничных товарах*) foreign goods *мн*; **пóшлины/налóг на** ~ import duty/tax; **úмпорт капитáла** capital investment from abroad.
импортёр (-а) *м* importer.
импортúр|овать (-ую) *(не)сов перех* to import.
úмпортный *прил* imported; **úмпортная квóта** import quota.
импотéнт (-а) *м* impotent male.
импотéнт|ный (-ен, -на, -но) *прил* impotent.
импотéнци|я (-и) *ж* (*МЕД*) impotence.
импресáрио *м нескл* (*музыканта*) agent; (*устроитель концертов итп*) impresario.
импрессионúзм (-а) *м* impressionism.
импрессионистúческ|ий (-ая, -ое, -ие) *прил* impressionist.
импровизáтор (-а) *м* improviser.
импровизáци|я (-и) *ж* improvisation.
импровизúр|овать (-ую; *perf* **импровизúровать** *или* **сымпровизúровать)** *(не)сов перех* to improvise.
úмпульс (-а) *м* (*ФИЗ, БИО*) impulse; (*перен*): ~ **(к** *+dat*) (*к работе, к реформам итп*) impetus (for).
импульсúв|ный (-ен, -на, -но) *прил* impulsive.
имýщественный *прил* property *опред*.
имýществ|о (-а) *ср* property; (*принадлежности*) belongings *мн*; **двúжимое** ~ (*ЮР*) movables; **недвúжимое** ~ (*ЮР*) property.
имýщ|ий (-ая, -ее, -ие) *прил* (*классы*) propertied; **власть** ~**ие** the powers that be.
úм|я (-ени; *как* **время**; *см* **Table 4)** *ср* (*также перен*) name; (*также:* **личное** ~) first *или* Christian name; (*знаменитый человек*) famous name; **во** ~ *+gen* (*ради*) in the name of; **на** ~ *+gen* (*письмо*) addressed to; **билéты остáвлены на Вáше** ~ the tickets have been left under your name; **от** ~**ени** *+gen* on behalf of; **моё** ~ **– Марúя** my name is Maria; **Теáтр** ~**ени Чéхова** the Chekhov Theatre; ~**енем закóна** in the name of the law; **называ́ть** *(impf)* **вéщи своúми именáми** to call a spade a spade; **úмя прилагáтельное** adjective; **úмя существúтельное** noun.
инакомы́слящ|ий (-его; *decl like adj*) *м* dissident.
инáче *нареч* (*по-другому*) differently ◆ *союз* otherwise, or else; **вы́глядеть** *(impf)* ~ to look different; **так úли** ~ one way or another; **а как же** ~? how else?
инвалúд (-а) *м* disabled person (*мн* people).

инвали́дн|ый *прил*: **~ая коля́ска** wheelchair; **инвали́дный дом** home for the disabled.
инвали́дност|ь (**-и**) *ж* disability; **пе́нсия по ~и** disablement benefit; **получа́ть (получи́ть** *perf*) ~ to be registered as disabled.
инвалю́т|а (**-ы**) *ж сокр* (= *иностра́нная валю́та*) foreign currency.
инвалю́тный *прил* (*поступления, счёт*) foreign-currency.
инвентариза́ци|я (**-и**) *ж* stocktaking.
инвента́р|ь (**-я́**) *м* (*предметы*) equipment; (*опись*) inventory.
инве́рси|я (**-и**) *ж* (*линг*) inversion.
инвести́р|овать (**-ую**) (*не*)*сов* (*не*)*перех* (*экон*) to invest.
инвестицио́нный *прил* investment *опред*; **инвестицио́нный банк** investment bank.
инвести́ци|я (**-и**) *ж* (*обычно мн*) investment; **иностра́нные ~и** foreign investment; **дохо́д от ~й** investment income.
инве́стор (**-а**) *м* investor.
ингаля́тор (**-а**) *м* (*мед*) inhaler.
ингаля́ци|я (**-и**) *ж* inhalation.
ингредие́нт (**-а**) *м* ingredient.
ингу́ш (**-а́**) *м* Ingush.
Ингуше́ти|я (**-и**) *ж* Ingushetia.
ингу́ш|ка (**-ки**; *gen pl* **-ек**) *ж см* **ингу́ш**.
и́ндеве|ть (**-ю**; *perf* **заи́ндеветь**) *несов неперех* to become covered in frost.
инде́ек *сущ см* **инде́йка**.
инде́|ец (**-йца**) *м* Native American, North American Indian.
инде́|йка (**-йки**; *gen pl* **-ек**) *ж* turkey.
инде́йца *итп сущ см* **инде́ец**.
и́ндекс (**-а**) *м* (*цен, книг*) index (*мн* indexes); (*также*: **почто́вый ~**) post (*BRIT*) *или* zip (*US*) code; **фо́ндовый ~** share index; **и́ндекс (ро́зничных/потреби́тельных) цен** (retail/ consumer) price index.
индекса́ци|я (**и**) *ж* (*экон*) index-linking (*BRIT*), indexing (*US*).
индекси́р|овать (**-ую**) *несов перех* (*экон*: *зарплату*) to index, index-link (*BRIT*).
индиа́н|ка (**-ки**; *gen pl* **-ок**) *ж см* **инди́ец, инде́ец**.
индиви́д (**-а**) *м* individual.
индивидуа́лен *прил см* **индивидуа́льный**.
индивидуали́зм (**-а**) *м* individualism.
индивидуали́ст (**-а**) *м* individualist.
индивидуа́льност|ь (**-и**) *ж* (*совокупность черт*) individuality; (*личность*) individual.
индивидуа́л|ьный (**-ен, -ьна, -ьно**) *прил* individual.
индиви́дуум (**-а**) *м* individual.
инди́го *ср нескл* indigo.
инди́|ец (**-йца**) *м* Indian.
инди́йск|ий (**-ая, -ое, -ие**) *прил* Indian; **Инди́йский океа́н** the Indian Ocean.
инди́йца *итп сущ см* **инди́ец**.
И́нди|я (**-и**) *ж* India.
индонези́ек *сущ см* **индонези́йка**.
индонези́|ец (**-йца**) *м* Indonesian.
индонези́|йка (**-йки**; *gen pl* **-ек**) *ж см* **индонези́ец**.
индонези́йск|ий (**-ая, -ое, -ие**) *прил* Indonesian.
индонези́йца *итп сущ см* **индонези́ец**.
Индоне́зи|я (**-и**) *ж* Indonesia.
индосса́нт (**-а**) *м* (*комм*) endorser.
индосса́т (**-а**) *м* (*комм*) endorsee.
индуи́зм (**-а**) *м* Hinduism.
инду́кци|я (**-и**) *ж* (*физ*) induction.
инду́с (**-а**) *м* Hindu.
индустриализа́ци|я (**-и**) *ж* industrialization.
индустриализи́р|овать (**-ую**) (*не*)*сов перех* to industrialize.
индустриа́льный *прил* industrial.
индустри́|я (**-и**) *ж* industry; **~ мо́ды/ кино́/тури́зма** the fashion/film/tourist industry.
индю́к (**-а́**) *м* turkey cock.
индю́ш|ка (**-ки**; *gen pl* **-ек**) *ж* (*разг*) = **инде́йка**.
и́не|й (**-я**) *м* hoarfrost.
ине́рт|ный (**-ен, -на, -но**) *прил* (*физ, хим*) inert; (*перен*) inactive.
ине́рци|я (**-и**) *ж* (*физ, перен*) inertia; **дви́гаться** (*impf*) **по ~и** (*физ*) to move by inertia; **де́лать** (*impf*) **что-н по ~и** to do sth out of habit; **я по ~и дал ему́ ста́рый телефо́н** I gave him my old telephone number automatically.
инжене́р (**-а**) *м* engineer; **~ по те́хнике безопа́сности** health and safety officer; **инжене́р-меха́ник/-констру́ктор/-строи́тель** mechanical/design/construction engineer.
инжене́рн|ый *прил*: **~ая нау́ка** engineering (*science*); **~ое де́ло** engineering (*profession*).
инжи́р (**-а**) *м* (*дерево*) fig ◆ *собир* (*плоды*) figs *мн*.
ИНИО́Н (**-а**) *м сокр* = *Институ́т нау́чной информа́ции по обще́ственным нау́кам*.
инициализи́р|овать (**-ую**) (*не*)*сов перех* (*комп*) to initialize.
инициа́л|ы (**-ов**) *мн* initials *мн*.
инициати́в|а (**-ы**) *ж* initiative; **по со́бственной ~е** on one's own initiative.
инициати́в|ный (**-ен, -на, -но**) *прил* enterprising; **он о́чень ~ челове́к** he has a lot of initiative; **инициати́вная гру́ппа** action group.
инициа́тор (**-а**) *м* initiator.
инкасса́тор (**-а**) *м* security guard (*employed to collect and deliver money*).
инкасси́р|овать (**-ую**) (*не*)*сов перех* (*комм*) to encash.
инка́ссо *ср нескл* (*комм*) encashment.
инквизи́тор (**-а**) *м* (*перен*) inquisitor.
инквизи́ци|я (**-и**) *ж* (*перен*) inquisition.
инко́гнито *нареч, м/ж нескл* incognito.
Инкомба́нк (**-а**) *м сокр* (= *Иностра́нный комме́рческий банк*) foreign commercial bank.
инкримини́р|овать (**-ую**) (*не*)*сов перех*: **~ что-н кому́-н** to accuse sb of sth.
инкруста́ци|я (**-и**) *ж* inlay.
инкрусти́р|овать (**-ую**) (*не*)*сов перех* to inlay.
инкуба́тор (**-а**) *м* incubator.

инкубацио́нный *прил*: **~ пери́од** (*БИО, МЕД*) incubation period.
инкуба́ци|я (**-и**) *ж* incubation.
иногда́ *нареч* sometimes.
иногоро́дн|ий (**-яя, -ее, -ие**) *прил* from another town ◆ (**-его**; *decl like adj*) *м person from another town.*
инозе́мный *прил* foreign.
ин|о́й *прил* different ◆ *мест* (*некоторый*) some (people); **~ раз** at times; **~ы́ми слова́ми** in other words; **не что ~о́е, как ..., не кто ~, как ...** none other than ...; **~ы́е счита́ют, что ...** some (people) think (that) ....
и́нок (**-а**) *м* monk (*in the Orthodox Church*).
инопланетя́н|ин (**-ина**; *nom pl* **-е**, *gen pl* **-**) *м* alien.
иноро́д|ный (**-ен, -на, -но**) *прил* alien; **иноро́дное те́ло** (*МЕД*) foreign body.
иносказа́ни|е (**-я**) *ср* allegory.
иносказа́тел|ьный (**-ен, -ьна, -ьно**) *прил* allegorical.
иностра́н|ец (**-ца**) *м* foreigner.
иностра́н|ка (**-ки**; *gen pl* **-ок**) *ж см* **иностра́нец**.
иностра́нн|ый *прил* foreign; **Министе́рство ~ых дел** Ministry of Foreign Affairs, ≈ Foreign Office (*BRIT*), ≈ State Department (*US*).
иностра́нок *сущ см* **иностра́нка**.
иностра́нца *итп сущ см* **иностра́нец**.
иноязы́чн|ый *прил* (*слово*) foreign; **~ое населе́ние** foreign-language-speaking population.
инсинуа́ци|я (**-и**) *ж* insinuation.
инспекти́р|овать (**-ую**; *perf* **проинспекти́ровать**) *несов перех* to inspect.
инспе́ктор (**-а**) *м* inspector.
инспе́кци|я (**-и**) *ж* inspection; (*организация*) inspectorate.
инста́нци|я (**-и**) *ж* (*ПОЛИТ*) body, authority.
инсти́нкт (**-а**) *м* instinct.
инстинкти́в|ный (**-ен, -на, -но**) *прил* instinctive.
институ́т (**-а**) *м* institute; (*семьи, брака*) institution.
институ́тск|ий (**-ая, -ое, -ие**) *прил* institute *опред*.
инструкти́р|овать (**-ую**; *perf* **проинструкти́ровать**) (*не*)*сов перех* to instruct.
инстру́ктор (**-а**) *м* instructor; **~ по пла́ванию/лы́жам** swimming/ski instructor.
инстру́кци|я (**-и**) *ж* instructions *мн*; (*также:* **~ по эксплуата́ции**) instructions (for use).
инструме́нт (**-а**) *м* (*МУЗ, ТЕХ, перен*) instrument ◆ *собир* instruments *мн*.
инструмента́льный *прил* (*МУЗ*) instrumental; **инструмента́льная му́зыка** instrumental music; **инструмента́льный анса́мбль** instrumental ensemble; **инструмента́льный цех** tool workshop.
инсули́н (**-а**) *м* insulin.
инсу́льт (**-а**) *м* (*МЕД*) stroke.
инсцени́р|овать (**-ую**) (*не*)*сов перех* (*перен*: *обморок, ограбление*) to stage; (*роман*) to adapt.
инсцениро́вк|а (**-и**) *ж* adaptation.
ин-т *сокр* **= институ́т**.
интегра́л (**-а**) *м* (*МАТ*) integral.
интегра́льн|ый *прил*: **~ое исчисле́ние** integral calculus.
интегри́р|овать (**-ую**) (*не*)*сов перех* (*также МАТ*) to integrate.
интегра́ци|я (**-и**) *ж* (*также МАТ*) integration.
интелле́кт (**-а**) *м* intellect.
интеллектуа́л (**-а**) *м* intellectual.
интеллектуа́л|ьный (**-ен, -ьна, -ьно**) *прил* intellectual; **интеллектуа́льная со́бственность** intellectual property.
интеллиге́нт (**-а**) *м* member of the intelligentsia.
интеллиге́нт|ный (**-ен, -на, -но**) *прил* cultured and educated.
интеллиге́нци|я (**-и**) *ж собир* the intelligentsia; **техни́ческая/тво́рческая ~** the science/arts community.
интенда́нт (**-а**) *м* (*ВОЕН*) quartermaster.
интенси́в|ный (**-ен, -на, -но**) *прил* intensive; (*окраска*) intense.
интенсифика́ци|я (**-и**) *ж* intensification.
интенсифици́р|овать (**-ую**) (*не*)*сов перех* to intensify.
интеракти́вный *прил* (*КОМП*) interactive.
интерва́л (**-а**) *м* interval; (*ТИПОГ*) spacing; **с ~ом в 10 мину́т** with a 10 minute interval.
интерве́нт (**-а**) *м* interventionist.
интерве́нци|я (**-и**) *ж* intervention.
интервью́ *ср нескл* interview; **брать (взять** *perf***)/дава́ть (дать** *perf***) ~** to do/give an interview.
интервьюи́р|овать (**-ую**; *perf* **проинтервьюи́ровать**) (*не*)*сов перех* to interview.
интере́с (**-а**) *м*: **~ (к** *+dat***)** interest (in); **представля́ть (предста́вить** *perf***) ~ (для** *+gen***)** to be of interest (to); *см также* **интере́сы**.
интере́сен *прил см* **интере́сный**.
интере́сно *нареч*: **он о́чень ~ расска́зывает** he is very interesting to listen to ◆ *как сказ*: **~(, что ...)** it's interesting (that ...); **мне э́то о́чень ~** I find it very interesting; **э́то никому́ не ~** that is of no interest to anyone; **~, где он э́то нашёл** I wonder where he found that; **~ знать, где он был** I'd be interested to know where he was; **как ~!** that's really interesting!; **~!** (*разг*: *выражает недовольство, возражение*) so!; **она́ ~ мы́слит** she has an interesting way of thinking.

интере́с|ный (-ен, -на, -но) *прил* interesting; (*внешность, женщина*) attractive.
интерес|ова́ть (-у́ю) *несов перех* to interest
▸ **интересова́ться** *несов возв* (+*instr*) to be interested in; (*осведомляться*) to inquire after; **он ~ова́лся, когда́ ты приезжа́ешь/где ты бу́дешь жить** he was asking when you would be arriving/where you would be living.
интере́с|ы (-ов) *мн* (*государства, фирмы итп*) interests *мн*; (*духовные*) concerns *мн*; **в ~ах** +*gen* in the interests of; **затра́гивать (затро́нуть** *perf***)** *или* **задева́ть (заде́ть** *perf***) чьи-н ~** to touch on sb's interests.
интерлю́ди|я (-и) *ж* (*МУЗ*) interlude.
интерме́ди|я (-и) *ж* (*ТЕАТР*) interlude.
инте́рн (-а) *м* (*МЕД*) ≈ houseman (*BRIT*) (*мн* housemen), ≈ intern (*US*).
интерна́т (-а) *м* boarding school.
Интернациона́л (-а) *м* (*ИСТ*) the International.
интернационализа́ци|я (-и) *ж* internationalization.
интернационали́зм (-а) *м* internationalism.
интернационали́ст (-а) *м* internationalist.
интернациона́льный *прил* international.
Интерне́т (-а) *м* Internet.
ИНТЕРПО́Л (-а) *м сокр* (= *Междунаро́дная организа́ция уголо́вной поли́ции*) Interpol (= *International Criminal Police Organization*).
интерпрета́тор (-а) *м* interpreter.
интерпрета́ци|я (-и) *ж* interpretation.
интерпрети́р|овать (-ую) *(не)сов перех* to interpret.
интерфе́йс (-а) *м* (*КОМП*) interface.
интерье́р (-а) *м* (*здания*) interior.
инти́м|ный (-ен, -на, -но) *прил* intimate.
интоксика́ци|я (-и) *ж* intoxication.
интона́ци|я (-и) *ж* (*ЛИНГ, МУЗ*) intonation; (*недовольная, тревожная итп*) note.
интри́г|а (-и) *ж* (*политическая*) intrigue; (*любовная*) affair; (*романа*) plot.
интрига́н (-а) *м* intriguer.
интрига́н|ка (-ки; *gen pl* **-ок)** *ж см* **интрига́н**.
интриг|ова́ть (-у́ю; *perf* **заинтригова́ть)** *несов перех* to intrigue ◆ *несов неперех* (*no perf*): **~ про́тив** +*gen* to intrigue against.
интрове́рт (-а) *м* introvert.
интуити́в|ный (-ен, -на, -но) *прил* intuitive.
интуи́ци|я (-и) *ж* intuition.
Интури́ст (-а) *м сокр* (= *Гла́вное управле́ние по иностра́нному тури́зму*) *Russian tourist agency dealing with foreign tourism*.
инфа́ркт (-а) *м* (*также:* **~ миока́рда**) heart attack; **обши́рный ~ (миока́рда)** massive heart attack.
инфекцио́нный *прил* infectious; **инфекцио́нная больни́ца** hospital for infectious diseases.
инфе́кци|я (-и) *ж* infection.
инфинити́в (-а) *м* infinitive.
инфици́рован|ный (-, -на, -но) *прил* infected.
инфля́ци|я (-и) *ж* (*ЭКОН*) inflation.
инфляцио́нный *прил* inflationary.
информати́в|ный (-ен, -на, -но) *прил* informative.
информа́тик|а (-и) *ж* information technology.
информа́тор (-а) *м* informant.
информацио́нный *прил* information *опред*; **информацио́нная програ́мма** news programme (*BRIT*) *или* program (*US*).
информа́ци|я (-и) *ж* information.
информи́рованный *прил* well-informed.
информи́р|овать (-ую; *perf* **информи́ровать** *или* **проинформи́ровать)** *несов перех* to inform.
инфракра́сный *прил* infrared.
инфраструкту́р|а (-ы) *ж* infrastructure.
инциде́нт (-а) *м* incident.
инъе́кци|я (-и) *ж* injection.
иня́з (-а) *м сокр* = *институ́т иностра́нных языко́в; факульте́т иностра́нных языко́в*.
и.о. *сокр* (= *исполня́ющий обя́занности*) acting.
ио́н (-а) *м* ion.
иорда́н|ец (-ца) *м* Jordanian.
Иорда́ни|я (-и) *ж* Jordan.
иорда́н|ка (-ки; *gen pl* **-ок)** *ж см* **иорда́нец**.
иорда́нск|ий (-ая, -ое, -ие) *прил* Jordanian.
иорда́нца *сущ см* **иорда́нец**.
ипоста́с|ь (-и) *ж* (*РЕЛ*) hypostasis; **в ~и** +*gen* (*перен*) in the role of.
ипоте́к|а (-и) *ж* (*КОММ*) mortgage.
ипоте́чн|ый *прил* mortgage; **~ая ссу́да** mortgage; **~ банк** ≈ building society.
ипохо́ндрик (-а) *м* hypochondriac.
ипохо́ндри|я (-и) *ж* hypochondria.
ипподро́м (-а) *м* racecourse (*BRIT*), racetrack (*US*).
ипри́т (-а) *м* mustard gas.
Ира́к (-а) *м* Iraq.
ира́к|ец (-ца) *м* Iraqi.
ира́кск|ий (-ая, -ое, -ие) *прил* Iraqi.
ира́кца *итп сущ см* **ира́кец**.
Ира́н (-а) *м* Iran.
ира́н|ец (-ца) *м* Iranian.
ира́н|ка (-ки; *gen pl* **-ок)** *ж см* **ира́нец**.
ира́нск|ий (-ая, -ое, -ие) *прил* Iranian.
ира́нца *итп сущ см* **ира́нец**.
и́рис (-а) *м* (*БОТ*) iris; (*нитки*) thread (*for embroidery etc*).
ири́с (-а) *м* (*конфета*) toffee.
ири́с|ка (-ки; *gen pl* **-ок)** *ж* (*разг*) toffee.
ирла́нд|ец (-ца) *м* Irishman (*мн* Irishmen).
Ирла́нди|я (-и) *ж* Ireland.
ирла́нд|ка (-ки; *gen pl* **-ок)** *ж* Irishwoman (*мн* Irishwomen).
ирла́ндск|ий (-ая, -ое, -ие) *прил* Irish.
ирла́ндца *итп сущ см* **ирла́ндец**.
ИРЛИ *м сокр* = *Институ́т ру́сской литерату́ры*.
иронизи́р|овать (-ую) *несов неперех*: **~ (над** +*instr***)** to be ironic (about).
ирони́ч|ный (-ен, -на, -но) *прил* ironic.
иро́ни|я (-и) *ж* irony; **~ судьбы́** the irony of fate.
иррациона́л|ьный (-ен, -ьна, -ьно) *прил* irrational.

иррегуля́рн|ый *прил*: **~ые войска́** irregular forces *мн*, irregulars *мн*.
ирригáци|я (-и) *ж* irrigation.
иск (-а) *м* lawsuit; **встре́чный ~** counterclaim; **де́нежный ~** damages; **предъявля́ть (предъяви́ть** *perf***) кому́-н ~** to take legal action against sb.
искажа́|ть(ся) (-ю(сь)) *несов от* **искази́ть(ся)**.
искаже́ни|е (-я) *ср* (*фактов*) distortion; (*в тексте*) error.
иска|зи́ть (-жу́, -зи́шь; *impf* **искажа́ть)** *сов перех* (*факты, смысл*) to distort; (*лицо*) to contort; (*КОМП*) to corrupt; **зло́ба ~зи́ла его́ лицо́** his face contorted with malice
▸ **искази́ться** (*impf* **искажа́ться)** *сов возв* (*изображение, смысл*) to be distorted; (*выражение лица, голос*) to contort.
искале́ч|ить (-у, -ишь) *сов от* **кале́чить**.
иска́ни|е (-я) *ср* (*обычно мн*: *творческие, научные*) quest.
иска́тел|ь (-я) *м* (*золота*) prospector; (*стремящийся к новому*) explorer; **~ приключе́ний** adventure seeker.
иска́тельниц|а (-ы) *ж см* **иска́тель**.
иска́ть (ищу́, и́щешь) *несов перех* to look *или* search for.
исключа́|ть (-ю) *несов от* **исключи́ть**.
исключа́я *предл* (*+acc*) excluding; **не ~** *+gen* including.
исключе́ни|е (-я) *ср* (*из списка, из очереди*) exclusion; (*из института*) expulsion; (*отклонение от нормы*) exception; **~ из пра́вила** exception to the rule; **за ~м** *+gen* with the exception of; **де́лать (сде́лать** *perf***) что-н в ви́де ~я** to make an exception of sth.
исключи́телен *прил см* **исключи́тельный**.
исключи́тельно *нареч* (*особенно*) exceptionally; (*только*) exclusively.
исключи́тел|ьный (-ен, -ьна, -ьно) *прил* exceptional; (*no short form*; *право*) exclusive.
исключ|и́ть (-у́, -и́шь; *impf* **исключа́ть)** *сов перех* (*удалить*: *из списка*) to exclude; (: *из института*) to expel; (*ошибку, случайность*) to exclude the possibility of; **э́то ~ено́** that is out of the question; **компроми́сс ~ён** a compromise is out of the question.
исkове́ркa|ть (-ю) *сов от* **кове́ркать**.
исколе|си́ть (-шу́, -си́шь) *сов перех* (*разг*) to travel; **он ~си́л весь мир** he's been all over the world.
иско́мка|ть (-ю) *сов от* **ко́мкать**.
иско́м|ый *прил* (*МАТ*): **~ая величина́** unknown value ◆ **(-ого;** *decl like adj***)** *ср* (*МАТ*) unknown.
иско́н|ный (-ен, -на, -но) *прил* (*население*) original; (*право*) intrinsic; **~ язы́к** the vernacular.
ископа́ем|ое (-ого; *decl like adj***)** *ср* fossil; (*также*: **поле́зное ~**: *обычно мн*) mineral.
ископа́емый *прил* (*животное, растение*) fossilized.
искоре́ж|ить (-у, -ишь) *сов от* **коре́жить**.
искорен|и́ть (-ю́, -и́шь; *impf* **искореня́ть)** *сов перех* to eradicate.
и́скоса *нареч* (*взглянуть, смотреть*) sideways; **смотре́ть** (*impf*) **~ на кого́-н** (*перен*) to look askance at sb.
и́скр|а (-ы) *ж* (*огня, также перен*) spark; (*снега, бриллианта*) glint, glistening; **у меня́ ~ы из глаз посы́пались** I began to see stars; **засрони́ть** (*perf*) **в ком-н ~у наде́жды** to give sb a glimmer of hope.
и́скренне *нареч* sincerely; **~ Ваш** Yours sincerely.
и́скрен|ний (-няя, -нее, -ние; -ен, -на, -но *или* **-не)** *прил* sincere.
и́скренност|ь (-и) *ж* sincerity.
искрив|и́ть (-лю́, -и́шь; *impf* **искривля́ть)** *сов перех* to bend.
искривле́ни|е (-я) *ср* bend; **искривле́ние позвоно́чника** (*МЕД*) curvature of the spine.
искривлю́ *сов см* **искриви́ть**.
искривля́|ть (-ю) *несов от* **искриви́ть**.
искри́ст|ый (-, -а, -о) *прил* glistening, sparkling.
искр|и́ться (-ю́сь, -и́шься) *несов возв* to glisten, sparkle.
искроме́т|ный (-ен, -на, -но) *прил* (*перен*: *взгляд*) fiery; (: *остроумие*) sparkling.
искромса́|ть (-ю) *сов от* **кромса́ть**.
искрош|и́ть (-у́, -и́шь) *сов от* **кроши́ть**.
искупа́|ть(ся) (-ю(сь)) *сов от* **купа́ть(ся)**.
иск|упи́ть (-уплю́, -у́пишь; *impf* **искупа́ть)** *сов перех* (*перен*: *вину, проступок*) to atone for, expiate; (*возмещать, также РЕЛ*) to redeem.
искупле́ни|е (-я) *ср* (*вины, проступка*) atonement, expiation; (*РЕЛ*) redemption.
искуплю́ *сов см* **искупи́ть**.
искуса́|ть (-ю; *impf* **иску́сывать)** *сов перех* (*подлеж*: *комары*) to bite all over; (: *пчёлы*) to sting all over.
иску́сен *прил см* **иску́сный**.
искуси́тел|ь (-я) *м* tempter.
иску́сник (-а) *м* master.
иску́сниц|а (-ы) *ж см* **иску́сник**.
иску́с|ный (-ен, -на, -но) *прил* (*работник*) skilful (*BRIT*), skillful (*US*); (*работа*) fine.
иску́сственник (-а) *м* bottle-fed baby.
иску́сственниц|а (-ы) *ж см* **иску́сственник**.
иску́сствен|ный *прил* artificial; (*волокно, ткань, камин*) synthetic; (*мех*) fake; **(-, -на, -но**; *притворный*: *смех*) faked; **иску́сственное дыха́ние** artificial respiration; **иску́сственный интелле́кт** artificial intelligence; **иску́сственный спу́тник Земли́** artificial satellite.
иску́сств|о (-а) *ср* art; **де́лать** (*impf*) **что-н из любви́ к ~у** (*разг*) to do sth for its own sake.

искусствове́д (-а) *м* art historian.
искусствове́дени|е (-я) *ср* art history.
иску́сыва|ть (-ю) *несов от* **искуса́ть**.
искуша́|ть (-ю) *несов перех* to tempt; ~ *(impf)* **судьбу́** to tempt fate.
искуше́ни|е (-я) *ср* temptation; **поддава́ться (подда́ться** *perf*) **~ю** to give in to temptation.
искушё́н|ный (-, -а́, -о́) *прил* (*зритель, публика*) sophisticated; (*политик*) seasoned; (*женщина*) worldly; **он искушён в таки́х дела́х** he is well versed in such matters.
исла́м (-а) *м* Islam.
исла́мск|ий (-ая, -ое, -ие) *прил* Islamic.
исла́нд|ец (-ца) *м* Icelander.
Исла́нди|я (-и) *ж* Iceland.
исла́нд|ка (-ки; *gen pl* -ок) *ж см* **исла́ндец**.
исла́ндск|ий (-ая, -ое, -ие) *прил* Icelandic; ~ **язы́к** Icelandic.
исла́ндца *итп сущ см* **исла́ндец**.
испа́ко|стить (-щу, -стишь) *сов от* **па́костить**.
испа́н|ец (-ца) *м* Spaniard.
Испа́ни|я (-и) *ж* Spain.
испа́н|ка (-ки; *gen pl* -ок) *ж см* **испа́нец**.
испа́нск|ий (-ая, -ое, -ие) *прил* Spanish; ~ **язы́к** Spanish.
испа́нца *итп сущ см* **испа́нец**.
испаре́ни|е (-я) *ср* (*действие: воды*) evaporation; (*обычно мн: продукт*) vapour (*BRIT*), vapor (*US*).
испа́рин|а (-ы) *ж* perspiration.
испар|и́ть (-ю́, -и́шь; *impf* **испаря́ть**) *сов перех* to evaporate
▸ **испари́ться** (*impf* **испаря́ться**) *сов возв* (*также перен*) to evaporate.
испа́чка|ть(ся) (-ю(сь)) *сов от* **па́чкать(ся)**.
испеку́(сь) *итп сов см* **испе́чь(ся)**.
испепел|и́ть (-ю́, -и́шь; *impf* **испепеля́ть**) *сов перех* to reduce to ashes; **испепеля́ть** (~ *perf*) **кого́-н взгля́дом** to give sb a withering look.
испе́|чь(ся) (-ку́(сь), -чё́шь(ся) *итп*, -ку́т(ся)) *сов от* **пе́чь(ся)**.
испещр|и́ть (-ю́, -и́шь; *impf* **испещря́ть**) *сов перех* to speckle.
исп|иса́ть (-ишу́, -и́шешь; *impf* **испи́сывать**) *сов перех* (*тетрадь, дневник*) to fill up; (*карандаш, ручку*) to wear out; (*бумагу*) to use up
▸ **исписа́ться** (*impf* **испи́сываться**) *несов возв* (*карандаш*) to wear out; (*ручка*) to run out; (*разг: писатель*) to lose one's touch.
испи́|ть (изопью́, изопьё́шь; *pt* -л, -ла́, -ло) *сов неперех* (*+gen; перен: горя, разочарований*) to suffer; (*воды*) to sup.
испишу́(сь) *итп сов см* **исписа́ть(ся)**.
исповеда́л|ьня (-ьни; *gen pl* -ен) *ж* (*РЕЛ*) confessional.
испове́дани|е (-я) *ср* denomination.
испове́да|ть(ся) (-ю(сь)) *(не)сов* = **испове́довать(ся)**.
испове́дник (-а) *м* (*РЕЛ*) confessor.
испове́д|овать (-ую) *несов перех* (*религию, мораль, идею*) to profess ◆ *(не)сов перех* (*РЕЛ*): ~ **кого́-н** to hear sb's confession
▸ **испове́доваться** *(не)сов возв*: **~ся кому́-н** *или* **у кого́-н** to confess to sb.
и́сповед|ь (-и) *ж* (*РЕЛ, перен*) confession.
и́сподволь *нареч* unbeknown to all.
исподло́бья *нареч*: **гляде́ть на кого́-н** ~ to look at sb with mistrust.
исподтишка́ *нареч* (*разг: действовать*) on the sly *или* quiet.
испоко́н *предл*: ~ **веко́в** from time immemorial.
исполи́н (-а) *м* giant.
исполи́нск|ий (-ая, -ое, -ие) *прил* gargantuan.
исполко́м (-а) *м сокр* (= *исполни́тельный комите́т*) executive committee.
исполне́ни|е (-я) *ср* (*приказа, указа*) execution; (*обещания, желания*) fulfilment (*BRIT*), fulfillment (*US*); (*симфонии, роли итп*) performance; **в ~и** *+gen* performed by; **приводи́ть (привести́** *perf*) **что-н в** ~ to carry sth out; **э́кспортное** ~ (*КОММ*) export version.
испо́лнен|ный (-, -а, -о) *прил* (*+gen*) full of, filled with.
исполни́м|ый (-, -а, -о) *прил* (*просьба, желание*) realizable.
исполни́телен *прил см* **исполни́тельный**.
исполни́тел|ь (-я) *м* (*пьесы, роли*) performer; (*приказа, политики*) executive; **суде́бный** ~ bailiff.
исполни́тельница (-ы) *ж см* **исполни́тель**.
исполни́тел|ьный *прил* (*комитет, власть*) executive; (-ен, -ьна, -ьно; *старательный*) efficient; **исполни́тельный дире́ктор** executive director; **исполни́тельный лист** (*ЮР*) court order.
испо́лн|ить (-ю, -ишь; *impf* **исполня́ть**) *сов перех* (*приказ*) to carry out; (*обещание, долг, желание*) to fulfil (*BRIT*), fulfill (*US*); (*танец, симфонию, роль итп*) to perform; ~ *(perf)* **кого́-н наде́ждой/ра́достью** *итп* to fill sb with hope/joy *итп*
▸ **испо́лниться** (*impf* **исполня́ться**) *сов возв* (*желание*) to be fulfilled; (*+instr; надеждой, радостью итп*) to be filled with; **ему́ ~илось 10 лет** he is 10.
испо́льзовани|е (-я) *ср* use.
испо́льз|овать (-ую) *(не)сов перех* to use.
испо́р|тить(ся) (-чу(сь), -тишь(ся)) *сов от* **по́ртить(ся)**.
испо́рченный *прил* (*замок*) broken; (*настроение*) bad; (*ребёнок*) spoilt; (*КОМП*) corrupt.
испра́вен *прил см* **испра́вный**.
исправи́м|ый (-, -а, -о) *прил* correctable.
исправи́тельный *прил* (*меры*) corrective; **исправи́тельные рабо́ты** (*ЮР*) corrective labour.
исправи́тельно-трудов|о́й *прил*: **исправи́тельно-трудова́я коло́ния** labour (*BRIT*) *или* labor (*US*) colony.
испра́в|ить (-лю, -ишь; *impf* **исправля́ть**) *сов**

перех (*повреждение, телефон*) to repair; (*ошибку*) to correct; (*характер, дисциплину*) to improve
▸ **испра́виться** (*impf* **исправля́ться**) *сов возв* (*характер, человек*) to change (for the better).
исправле́ни|е (**-я**) *ср* (*повреждения*) repairing; (: *характера*) reforming; (*текста, преступника*) correction; **вноси́ть (внести́** *perf*) **~я в** *+acc* to make corrections to.
испра́влю(сь) *сов см* **испра́вить(ся)**.
исправля́|ть(ся) (**-ю(сь)**) *несов от* **испра́вить(ся)**.
испра́вност|ь (**-и**) *ж*: **в (по́лной) ~и** in (full) working order; **всё в ~и** everything's in order.
испра́в|ный (**-ен, -на, -но**) *прил* (*механизм*) in good working order; (*работник*) diligent.
испражне́ни|е (**-я**) *ср* faeces *мн*.
испражня́|ться (**-юсь**) *несов возв* to defecate.
испро́б|овать (**-ую**) *сов от* **про́бовать**.
испу́г (**-а**; *part gen* **-у**) *м* fright; **в ~е, с ~у** in *или* with fright.
испу́ган|ный (**-, -а, -о**) *прил* (*человек*) frightened; (**-, -на, -но**; *вид, взгляд*) frightened.
испуга́|ть(ся) (**-ю(сь)**) *сов от* **пуга́ть(ся)**.
исп|усти́ть (**-ущу́, -у́стишь**; *impf* **испуска́ть**) *сов перех* (*крик, стон*) to let out; (*свет*) to give off, emit.
испыта́ни|е (**-я**) *ср* (*машины, прибора итп*) testing; (*нового работника*) trial; (*обычно мн*: *экзамен*) test; (*несчастье*) ordeal.
испы́тан|ный (**-, -на, -но**) *прил* (*приём*) tried and tested; (*друг*) proven.
испыта́тел|ь (**-я**) *м* tester; **лётчик-испыта́тель** test pilot.
испыта́тельный *прил*: **~ срок** trial period, probation; **испыта́тельная тра́сса** test circuit; **испыта́тельный полёт** test flight.
испыта́|ть (**-ю**; *impf* **испы́тывать**) *сов перех* (*механизм*) to test; (*работника*) to try out; (*нужду, трудности, радость итп*) to experience.
испыту́ющ|ий (**-ая, -ее, -ие**; **-, -а, -е**) *прил*: **~ взгляд** searching look.
испы́тыва|ть (**-ю**) *несов от* **испыта́ть**.
исс|е́чь (**-еку́, -ечёшь** *итп*, **-еку́т**; *pt* **-ёк, -екла́, -екло́**) *сов перех* (*кнутом*) to flog.
и́ссиня- *префикс*: **~чёрный** blue-black.
иссле́довани|е (**-я**) *ср* (*см глаг*) research; examination; (*научный труд*) study; **занима́ться** (*impf*) **~ями в о́бласти** *+gen* to conduct research into.
иссле́довател|ь (**-я**) *м* researcher.
иссле́довательск|ий (**-ая, -ое, -ие**) *прил*: **~ая рабо́та** research; **~ институ́т** research institute.
иссле́д|овать (**-ую**) (*не*)*сов перех* to research; (*больного*) to examine.
иссо́х|нуть (**-ну, -нешь**; *pt* **-, -ла, -ло**, *impf* **иссыха́ть**) *сов неперех* (*водоём*) to dry up; (*трава*) to dry out; (*исхудать*) to wither away.
и́сстари *нареч* since days of old.
исстрада́|ться (**-юсь**) *сов возв* to suffer a great deal.
исстреля́|ть (**-ю**; *impf* **исстре́ливать**) *сов перех* (*патроны*) to use up.
исступле́ни|е (**-я**) *ср* frenzy; **приходи́ть (прийти́** *perf*) **в ~** to go into a frenzy.
исступлён|ный (**-, -на, -но**) *прил* frenzied.
иссыха́|ть (**-ю**) *несов от* **иссо́хнуть**.
исся́к|нуть (*3sg* **-нет**, *3pl* **-нут**, *pt* **-, -ла, -ло**, *impf* **иссяка́ть**) *сов неперех* (*источник, запасы*) to run dry; (*перен*: *терпение, силы*) to run out.
иста́плива|ть (**-ю**) *несов от* **истопи́ть**.
иста́птыва|ть (**-ю**) *несов от* **истопта́ть**.
иста́скан|ный (**-, -на, -но**) *прил* (*разг*: *вид*) bedraggled.
истаска́|ть (**-ю**; *impf* **иста́скивать**) *сов перех* (*разг*) to wear out
▸ **истаска́ться** (*impf* **иста́скиваться**) *сов возв* (*разг*) to wear out.
исте́блишмент (**-а**) *м* the Establishment.
истёк *итп сов см* **исте́чь**.
истека́|ть (**-ю**) *несов от* **исте́чь**.
истеку́т *итп сов см* **исте́чь**.
исте́кш|ий (**-ая, -ее, -ие**) *прил* past, previous.
ист|ере́ться (*3sg* **изотрётся**, *3pl* **изотру́тся**, *pt* **-ёрся, -ёрлась, -ёрлось**, *impf* **истира́ться**) *сов возв* (*подошвы, канат*) to wear down.
истёрзан|ный (**-, -на, -но**) *прил* (*душа, вид*) tortured.
истерза́|ть (**-ю**) *сов от* **терза́ть**.
исте́рик (**-а**) *м* hysterical man (*мн* men).
исте́рик|а (**-и**) *ж* hysterics *мн*; **устра́ивать (устро́ить** *perf*) *или* **зака́тывать (закати́ть** *perf*) **~у** to become hysterical.
истери́чек *сущ см* **истери́чка**.
истери́чен *прил см* **истери́чный**.
истери́ческ|ий (**-ая, -ое, -ие**) *прил* (*больной, смех, плач*) hysterical; **~ припа́док** a fit of hysterics.
истери́ч|ка (**-ка**; *gen pl* **-ек**) *ж* hysterical woman (*мн* women).
истери́ч|ный (**-ен, -на, -но**) *прил* hysterical.
истери́|я (**-и**) *ж* (*МЕД, перен*) hysteria.
ист|е́ц (**-ца́**) *м* plaintiff.
истече́ни|е (**-я**) *ср*: **по ~и** *+gen* (*года, месяца итп*) after a period of; **по ~и э́того сро́ка** once this period has elapsed; **за ~м сро́ка Ва́шего па́спорта** due to expiry of your passport.
ист|е́чь (*3sg* **-ечёт**, *3pl* **-еку́т**, *pt* **-ёк, -екла́, -екло́**, *impf* **истека́ть**) *сов неперех* (*срок*) to expire; (*время*) to run out; **истека́ть (~** *perf*) **кро́вью** to bleed.
и́стин|а (**-ы**) *ж* truth.
и́стинен *прил см* **и́стинный**.
и́стинност|ь (**-и**) *ж* truthfulness.
и́стин|ный (**-ен, -на, -но**) *прил* true.

истира́|ться (*3sg* **-ется**, *3pl* **-ются**) *несов от* **истере́ться**.
истле́|ть (**-ю**; *impf* **истлева́ть**) *сов неперех* (*сгнить*) to decompose; (*сгореть*) to turn to ash.
исто́к (**-а**) *м* (*обычно мн*: *реки*) source *только ед*; (: *перен*) source.
истолк|ова́ть (**-у́ю**; *impf* **истолко́вывать**) *сов перех* to interpret.
истол|о́чь (**-ку́, -чёшь** *итп*, **-ку́т**; *pt* **-о́к, -кла́, -кло́**) *сов от* **толо́чь**.
исто́м|а (**-ы**) *ж* languor.
истом|и́ть(ся) (**-лю́(сь), -и́шь(ся)**) *сов от* **томи́ть(ся)**.
ист|опи́ть (**-оплю́, -о́пишь**; *impf* **иста́пливать**) *сов перех* to heat up.
ист|опта́ть (**-опчу́, -о́пчешь**; *impf* **istáптывать**) *сов перех* to trample all over; (*разг*: *обувь*) to wear out.
исто́рик (**-а**) *м* historian.
истори́ческ|ий (**-ая, -ое, -ие**) *прил* historical; (*важный*: *событие, решение итп*) historic.
исто́ри|я (**-и**) *ж* (*наука, предмет*) history; (*рассказ, происшествие*) story; **попада́ть (попа́сть** *perf*) **в ~ю** (*разг*) to get into a tricky situation; **со мной произошла́ стра́нная/заба́вная ~** a strange/funny thing happened to me; **ве́чная ~!** (*разг*) it's the same old story!; **исто́рия боле́зни** (*МЕД*) case history.
истоск|ова́ться (**-у́юсь**) *сов возв*: **~ по** *+dat* to yearn for.
источа́|ть (**-ю**) *несов перех* (*аромат, свет, тепло*) to emit; (*ненависть, доброту итп*) to exude.
исто́чник (**-а**) *м* (*водный*) source, spring.
исто́щ|ный (**-ен, -на, -но**) *прил* (*крик*) desperate.
истоща́|ть(ся) (**-ю(сь)**) *несов от* **истощи́ть(ся)**.
истоще́ни|е (**-я**) *ср* (*организма*) depletion; (*средств, запасов*) exhaustion; **~ не́рвной систе́мы** nervous exhaustion; **доводи́ть (довести́** *perf*) **себя́ до по́лного ~я** to run o.s. into the ground.
истощённый (**-ён, -ена́, -ено́**) *прил* (*человек*) malnourished; (**-ён, -ённа, -ённо**; *вид, лицо*) drained.
истощ|и́ть (**-у́, -и́шь**; *impf* **истоща́ть**) *сов перех* (*организм*) to run down; (*почву, ресурсы*) to deplete
▸ **истощи́ться** (*impf* **истоща́ться**) *сов возв* (*силы, организм, почва*) to become depleted; (*запасы, терпение*) to run out.
истра́|тить(ся) (**-чу(сь), -тишь(ся)**) *сов от* **тра́тить(ся)**.
истреби́тел|ь (**-я**) *м* (*ВОЕН*: *самолёт*) fighter (plane); (: *лётчик*) fighter pilot; (*тараканов, мышей итп*) exterminator.
истреби́тельн|ый *прил* (*огонь*) destructive; **~ая война́** war of destruction; **~ая авиа́ция** fighter planes.
истреб|и́ть (**-лю́, -и́шь**; *impf* **истребля́ть**) *сов перех* (*лес, посевы итп*) to destroy; (*крыс, тараканов*) to exterminate.
истребле́ни|е (**-я**) *ср* (*см глаг*) destruction; extermination.
истреблю́ *сов см* **истреби́ть**.
истребля́|ть (**-ю**) *несов от* **истреби́ть**.
истр|епа́ть(ся) (**-еплю́(сь), -е́плешь(ся)**) *сов от* **трепа́ть(ся)**.
истре́ска|ться (*3sg* **-ется**, *3pl* **-ются**, *impf* **истре́скиваться**) *сов возв* to crack.
истука́н (**-а**) *м* idol.
истца́ *итп сущ см* **исте́ц**.
и́стый *прил* genuine.
истяза́ни|е (**-я**) *ср* torture.
истяза́|ть (**-ю**) *несов перех* to torture.
исхл|еста́ть (**-ещу́, -е́щешь**; *impf* **исхлёстывать**) *сов перех* to whip.
исхо́д (**-а**) *м* outcome; **у меня́ де́ньги/терпе́ние на ~е** my money/patience is running out; **на ~е дня** at the end of the day; **с лета́льным ~ом** resulting in death.
исх|оди́ть (**-ожу́, -о́дишь**) *несов от* **изойти́** ◆ *сов перех* (*обойти*) to walk all over ◆ *несов неперех*: **~ из** *+gen* (*сведения, слухи*) to emanate from; (*основываться*: *из данных*) to be derived from; **~одя́ из/от** *+gen* on the basis of; **я ~ожу́ из того́, что...** I am working on the premise that ....
исхо́дный *прил* (*идея, данные*) primary; **~ те́зис** premise; **исхо́дное положе́ние** (*СПОРТ*) starting position; **исхо́дный пункт** starting point.
исходя́щ|ий (**-ая, -ее, -ие**) *прил* (*корреспонденция*) outgoing; **исходя́щий но́мер** (*АДМИН*) reference number.
исхожу́ *(не)сов см* **исходи́ть**.
исхуда́лый *прил* emaciated.
исхуда́|ть (**-ю**) *сов неперех* to become emaciated.
исцара́па|ть (**-ю**; *impf* **исцара́пывать**) *сов перех* to scratch all over.
исцеле́ни|е (**-я**) *ср* healing.
исцел|и́ть (**-ю́, -и́шь**; *impf* **исцеля́ть**) *сов перех* to heal
▸ **исцели́ться** (*impf* **исцеля́ться**) *сов возв* to recover.
исча́ди|е (**-я**) *ср*: **~ а́да** the devil incarnate.
исчеза́|ть (**-ю**) *несов от* **исче́знуть**.
исчезнове́ни|е (**-я**) *ср* disappearance.
исче́з|нуть (**-ну, -нешь**; *pt* **-, -ла, -ло**, *impf* **исчеза́ть**) *сов неперех* to disappear.
исчёрка|ть (**-ю**; *impf* **исчёркивать**) *сов перех* to scribble over.
исче́рпа|ть (**-ю**; *impf* **исче́рпывать**) *сов перех* to exhaust; **инциде́нт ~н** the matter is closed
▸ **исчерпа́ться** (*impf* **исче́рпываться**) *несов возв* (*запасы, терпение*) to be exhausted.
исче́рпыва|ться (*3sg* **-ется**, *3pl* **-ются**) *несов от* **исчерпа́ться** ◆ *возв* (*разрешаться*) to end; **э́тим де́ло не ~ется** the matter does not end here.

исчёрпывающ|ий (**-ая, -ее, -ие**; **-, -а, -е**) *прил* exhaustive.

исчислéни|е (**-я**) *ср* (*расходов, стоимости итп*) calculation; (*MAT*) calculus.

исчи́сл|ить (**-ю, -ишь**; *impf* **исчисля́ть**) *сов перех* to calculate.

исчисля́|ться (*3pl* **-ются**) *несов возв* (*+instr*; *тысячами*) to amount to.

ита́к *союз* thus, hence; **~, мо́жно заключи́ть, что** ... thus it can be concluded that ....

Ита́ли|я (**-и**) *ж* Italy.

италья́н|ец (**-ца**) *м* Italian.

италья́н|ка (**-ки**; *gen pl* **-ок**) *ж см* **италья́нец**.

италья́нск|ий (**-ая, -ое, -ие**) *прил* Italian; **~ язы́к** Italian.

италья́нца *итп сущ см* **италья́нец**.

ИТАР *м сокр* (= *Информацио́нное телегра́фное аге́нтство Росси́и*) *Russian telegraph agency*.

и т.д. *сокр* (= **и так да́лее**) etc. (= *et cetera*).

ИТК *м сокр* (= *исправи́тельно-трудова́я коло́ния*) labour (*BRIT*) *или* labor (*US*) colony.

ито́г (**-а**) *м* (*работы, переговоров итп*) result; (*общая сумма*) total; **в ~е** (*при подсчёте*) in total; **в (коне́чном) ~е** in the end; **подводи́ть (подвести́** *perf*) **~и** to sum up.

итого́ *нареч* in total, altogether; **~, мы зарабо́тали 100 рубле́й** in total *или* altogether we made 100 roubles.

ито́говый *прил* (*сумма, цифры*) total; (*результат*) final; **ито́говый отчёт** (*КОММ*) financial report.

и т.п. *сокр* (= **и тому́ подо́бное**) etc. (= *et cetera*).

иудаи́зм (**-а**) *м* Judaism.

их *мест см* **они́** ♦ *притяж мест* their; **~ дом бо́льше на́шего** their house is bigger than ours; **чья э́та маши́на? – ~** whose car is this? – it's theirs.

и́хн|ий (**-яя, -ее, -ие**) *притяж мест* (*разг*) = **их**.

иша́к (**-а́**) *м* (*ЗООЛ*) donkey; (*перен*: *работяга*) dogsbody.

иша́ч|ить (**-у, -ишь**) *несов неперех* (*разг*) to slog away.

и́шиас (**-а**) *м* sciatica.

ишь *част* (*разг*): **~ чего́ захоте́л!** you're asking a lot, aren't you?; **~ како́й он на́глый!** how cheeky can he get!

ище́|йка (**-йки**; *gen pl* **-ек**) *ж* bloodhound; **полице́йская ~** sniffer dog.

ищу́ *итп несов см* **иска́ть**.

ию́л|ь (**-я**) *м* July; *см также* **октя́брь**.

ию́льск|ий (**-ая, -ое, -ие**) *прил* July *опред*.

ию́н|ь (**-я**) *м* June; *см также* **октя́брь**.

ию́ньск|ий (**-ая, -ое, -ие**) *прил* June *опред*.

~ Й, й ~

Й, й *сущ нескл* (*буква*) *the 10th letter of the Russian alphabet*.
Йе́мен (-а) *м* Yemen.
йе́мен|ец (-ца) *м* Yemeni.
йе́мен|ка (-ки; *gen pl* **-ок)** *ж см* **йе́менец**.
йе́менск|ий (-ая, -ое, -ие) *прил* Yemeni.
йог (-и) *ж* yogi.
йо́г|а (-и) *ж* yoga; **занима́ться** *(impf)* **~ой** to do yoga.
йо́гурт (-а) *м* yoghurt.
йод (-а) *м* iodine.
йо́дистый *прил* = **йо́дный**.
йо́дный *прил* iodine *опред*.
Йорк (-а) *м* York.
йо́т|а (-ы) *ж*: **ни на ~у** not one iota.
йота́ци|я (-и) *ж* vowel softening.
Йоха́ннесбург (-а) *м* Johannesburg.

~К, к~

К, к *сущ нескл* (*буква*) *the 11th letter of the Russian alphabet.*

KEYWORD

к *предл* (*+dat*) **1** (*обозначает направление*) towards; **я пошёл к до́му/вокза́лу** I went towards the house/station; **звать (позва́ть** *perf*) **кого́-н к телефо́ну** to call sb to the phone; **мы пое́хали к друзья́м** we went to see friends; **поста́вь ле́стницу к стене́** put the ladder against the wall
2 (*обозначает добавление, включение*) to; **к уже́ существу́ющим пробле́мам приба́вились но́вые осложне́ния** new complications were added to the existing problems; **э́та ба́бочка отно́сится к о́чень ре́дкому ви́ду** this butterfly belongs to a very rare species
3 (*обозначает отношение*) of; **любо́вь к му́зыке/поря́дку** love of music/order; **он привы́к к хоро́шей еде́** he is used to good food; **к моему́ удивле́нию** to my surprise
4 (*обозначает назначение*) with; **Вы хоти́те пече́нья к ча́ю?** would you like biscuits (*BRIT*) *или* cookies (*US*) with your tea?; **припра́вы к мя́су** seasonings for meat.

к. *сокр* = **копе́йка**.
-ка *част* (*разг*) *used to moderate imperative or indicate indecision*; **иди́-ка сюда́** could you come here; **пойду́-ка я домо́й** I think I'll maybe be off home.
каба́к (**-а́**) *м* tavern; (*разг*) pub.
кабал|а́ (**-ы́**) *ж* (*перен*) slavery; **быть** (*impf*) **в ~е́ у кого́-н** to be at sb's mercy.
каба́льн|ый *прил*: **~ труд** slave labour (*BRIT*) *или* labor (*US*); **~ая зави́симость** slavery (*fig*).
каба́н (**-а́**) *м* boar; (*дикий*) wild boar.
кабаре́ *ср нескл* cabaret.
кабачі|о́к (**-ка́**) *м уменьш от* **каба́к**; (*БОТ, КУЛИН*) marrow (*BRIT*), squash (*US*).
ка́бел|ь (**-я**) *м* cable.
ка́бельный *прил* cable *опред*; **ка́бельное телеви́дение** cable television.
каби́н|а (**-ы**) *ж* (*телефонная*) booth; (*грузовика*) cab; (*самолёта*) cabin; (*лифта*) cage; (*для голосования*) voting booth; **пля́жная ~** beach hut.
кабине́т (**-а**) *м* (*в доме*) study; (*на работе*) office; (*ПРОСВЕЩ*) classroom; (*врача*) surgery (*BRIT*), office (*US*); (*ПОЛИТ*: *также*: **~ мини́стров**) cabinet.
каблогра́мм|а (**-ы**) *ж* cablegram.
каблу́к (**-а́**) *м* heel; **быть** (*impf*) **под каблуко́м у кого́-н** (*разг*) to be under sb's thumb.
кабота́ж (**-а**) *м* coastal shipping.
Кабу́л (**-а**) *м* Kabul.
кавале́р (**-а**) *м* (*в танце*) partner; (*поклонник*) suitor; (*награждённый орденом*): **~** *+gen* knight of; **Гео́ргиевский ~** knight of St George.
кавалери́йск|ий (**-ая, -ое, -ие**) *прил* cavalry *опред*.
кавалери́ст (**-а**) *м* cavalryman (*мн* cavalrymen).
кавале́ри|я (**-и**) *ж* cavalry.
кавальіка́д|а (**-ы**) *ж* cavalcade.
каварда́к (**-а́**) *м* (*разг*) mess.
ка́верз|а (**-ы**) *ж* dirty trick; **подстро́ить** (*perf*) **кому́-н ~у** to play a dirty trick on sb.
ка́верз|ный (**-ен, -на, -но**) *прил* tricky.
Кавка́з (**-а**) *м* Caucasus.
кавка́зск|ий (**-ая, -ое, -ие**) *прил* Caucasian.
кавы́ч|ки (**-ек**; *dat pl* **-ка́м**) *мн* inverted commas *мн*, quotation marks *мн*; **открыва́ть (откры́ть** *perf*)**/закрыва́ть (закры́ть** *perf*) **~** to open/close inverted commas; **в ~ках** (*также перен*) in inverted commas.
каго́р (**-а**) *м* red dessert wine.
каде́нци|я (**-и**) *ж* cadence.
каде́т (**-а**) *м* (*ВОЕН*) cadet; (*ИСТ*: = *конституцио́нный демокра́т*) Cadet (*Constitutional Democrat*).
каде́тск|ий (**-ая, -ое, -ие**) *прил* (*форма*) cadet's; **каде́тский ко́рпус** officer training corps.
кади́л|о (**-а**) *ср* (*РЕЛ*) censer.
ка|ди́ть (**-жу́, -ди́шь**) *несов неперех* (*РЕЛ*) to burn incense.
ка́д|ка (**-ки**; *gen pl* **-ок**) *ж* vat.
ка́дми|й (**-я**) *м* cadmium.
ка́док *сущ см* **ка́дка**.
ка́дочный *прил* (*огурцы, капуста итп*) preserved in vats.
кадр (**-а**) *м* (*ФОТО, КИНО*) shot; (*разг*: *работник*) worker; *см также* **ка́дры**.

The spelling rules for Russian are shown on page xvii.

ка́дров|ый *прил* (*офицер, войска*) regular *опред*; (*АДМИН*): **~ая поли́тика** staffing policy.
ка́др|ы (**-ов**) *мн* (*работники*) personnel *ед*, staff *ед*; (*ВОЕН*) regular army personnel *ед*; (*партийные*) cadres *мн*; **отде́л ~ов** personnel department.
кады́к (**-а́**) *м* Adam's apple.
каём *сущ см* **кайма́**.
каём|ка (**-ки**; *gen pl* **-ок**) *ж* = **кайма́**.
каждодне́вный *прил* daily.
ка́ждый *прил* each, every.
кажу́ *несов см* **кади́ть**.
кажу́сь *итп несов см* **каза́ться**.
каза́к (**-а́**; *nom pl* **каза́ки**) *м* Cossack.
каза́н (**-а́**) *м* *large round copper cooking vessel.*
Каза́н|ь (**-и**) *ж* Kazan.
каза́рм|а (**-ы**) *ж* barracks *мн*.
каза́рменный *прил*: **~ поря́док** barracks regime; **каза́рменное положе́ние** confinement to barracks.
ка|за́ться (**-жу́сь, -жешься**; *perf* **показа́ться**) *несов возв* (*+instr*) to look; **(мне) ка́жется/ каза́лось, что ...** it seems/seemed (to me) that ...; **он ~за́лся ста́рше свои́х лет** he looked older than his years.
каза́х (**-а**) *м* Kazakh.
каза́хск|ий (**-ая, -ое, -ие**) *прил* Kazakh.
Казахста́н (**-а**) *м* Kazakhstan.
каза́цк|ий (**-ая, -ое, -ие**) *прил* = **каза́чий**.
каза́чек *сущ см* **каза́чка**.
каза́честв|о (**-а**) *ср собир* the Cossacks *мн*.
каза́ч|ий (**-ья, -ье, -ьи**) *прил* Cossack.
каза́ч|ка (**-ки**; *gen pl* **-ек**) *ж см* **каза́к**.
казема́т (**-а**) *м* cell.
казённый *прил* public; (*отношение, язык*) officious; **на ~ счёт** at public expense; **казённая кварти́ра** tied accommodation; **казённое иму́щество** government property.
казино́ *ср нескл* casino.
казн|а́ (**-ы́**) *ж* treasury.
казначе́|й (**-я**) *м* treasurer.
казн|и́ть (**-ю́, -и́шь**) *несов перех* to execute; (*перен*) to punish
▸ **казни́ться** *несов возв* (*разг*) to torture o.s.
казн|ь (**-и**) *ж* execution; **сме́ртная ~** the death penalty; **приговори́ть** *(perf)* **кого́-н к сме́ртной ка́зни** to sentence sb to death.
Каи́р (**-а**) *м* Cairo.
ка|йма́ (**-ймы́**; *nom pl* **-ймы́**, *gen pl* **-ём**) *ж* hem.
кайф (**-а**) *м* (*разг*) high, kick.
кайф|ова́ть (**-у́ю**) *несов неперех* (*разг*: *на пляже, в отпуске итп*) to chill out; (: *от наркотиков, от вина*) to get high.

KEYWORD

как *местоимённое нареч* **1** (*вопросительное*) how; **как Вы себя́ чу́вствуете?** how do you feel?; **как дела́/де́ти?** how are things/the children?; **как тебя́ зову́т?** what's your name?
2 (*относительное*): **я сде́лал, как ты проси́ла** I did as you asked; **я не зна́ю, как э́то могло́ случи́ться** I don't know how that could have happened
3 (*насколько*): **как бы́стро/то́чно/давно́** how quickly/accurately/long ago
4 (*до какой степени*): **как краси́во/по́дло!** how beautiful/mean!; **как жаль!** what a pity *или* shame!
5 (*выражает возмущение*) what; **как! он опя́ть напи́лся!** what! he's drunk again!
6 (*о внезапном действии*): **она́ как закричи́т/запла́чет** she suddenly cried out/ burst into tears
◆ *союз* **1** (*подобно*) as; **мя́гкий, как ва́та** as soft as cotton wool; **как мо́жно скоре́е/гро́мче** as soon/loud as possible; **он оде́т, как бродя́га** he is dressed like a tramp
2 (*в качестве*) as; **как консульта́нт он о́чень поле́зен** as a consultant he is very useful
3 (*о временных отношениях*: *о будущем, об одновременности*) when; (: *о прошлом*) since; **как зако́нчишь, позвони́ мне** phone (*BRIT*) *или* call (*US*) me when you finish; **как вспо́мню об э́том, хо́чется пла́кать** when I remember it I feel like crying; **прошло́ два го́да, как она́ исче́зла** two years have passed since she disappeared:
4: **как бу́дто, как бы** as if; **он согласи́лся как бы не́хотя** he agreed as if unwillingly; **как же** of course; **как говоря́т** *или* **говори́тся** as it were; **как ни** however; **как ника́к** after all; **как раз во́время/то, что на́до** just in time/what we need; **э́то пла́тье/пальто́ мне как раз** this dress/coat is just my size; **как ..., так и ...** both ... and ...; **как то́лько** as soon as.

какаду́ *м нескл* cockatoo.
кака́о *ср нескл* cocoa.
ка́ка|ть (**-ю**; *perf* **пока́кать**) *несов неперех* (*разг*) to do a pooh.
ка́к-либо *нареч* = **ка́к-нибудь**.
ка́к-нибудь *нареч* (*так или иначе*) somehow; (*когда-нибудь*) sometime; (*кое-как*) anyhow; **уговори́те его́ ~** try to convince him somehow; **зайди́ ~** pop in sometime; **ты всё де́лаешь ~** you're doing everything just anyhow.
како́в (**-а́, -о́, -ы́**) *мест* what; **~ нагле́ц!** what a cheek!; **~ он собо́й?** what does he look like?

KEYWORD

как|о́й (**-а́я, -о́е, -и́е**) *мест* **1** (*вопросительное*) what; **како́й тебе́ нра́вится цвет?** what colour do you like?; **кака́я сего́дня пого́да?** what's the weather like today?; **в како́м году́ э́то бы́ло?** in what year was that?
2 (*относительное*) which; **скажи́, кака́я кни́га интере́снее** tell me which book is more interesting; **скажи́, в како́м го́роде нахо́дится Колизе́й** tell me in which city the Coliseum is
3 (*выражает оценку*) what; **како́й подле́ц!** what a rascal!; **кака́я неожи́данность!** what a surprise!
4 (*в риторических вопросах*: *совсем не*) what kind of; **како́й он дире́ктор?** what kind of

director is he?
5 (*разг*: *неопределённое*) any; **нет ли каки́х вопро́сов?** are there any questions?; **како́й ни на есть** any you like; **ни в каку́ю** not for anything; **каки́м о́бразом** in what way; **како́е там!** no way!

как|о́й-либо (-а́я, -о́е, -и́е) *мест* = **како́й-нибудь.**
как|о́й-нибудь (-а́я, -о́е, -и́е) *мест* (*тот или иной*) any; (*приблизительно*) some; **он и́щет ~ рабо́ты** he's looking for any kind of work; **~и́х-нибудь два-три ме́сяца** in some two or three months.
как|о́й-то (-а́я, -о́е, -и́е) *мест*: **Вам ~о́е-то письмо́** there's a letter for you; (*напоминающий*): **она́ ~а́я-то стра́нная сего́дня** she's acting a bit oddly today; **э́то не ко́мната, а свина́рник ~** it's more like a pigsty than a room.
какофони́ческ|ий (-ая, -ое, -ие) *прил* cacophonous.
какофо́ни|я (-и) *ж* cacophony.
ка́к-то *мест* (*каким-то образом*) somehow; (*в некоторой степени*) somewhat; (*разг*): **~ (раз)** once; **мне бы́ло ~ не по себе́** I was feeling somewhat *или* a little out of sorts; **я ~ встре́тил его́ на у́лице** I bumped into him once in the street.
ка́ктус (-а) *м* cactus (*мн* cacti).
кал (-а) *м* excrement.
каламбу́р (-а) *м* pun.
каламбу́р|ить (-ю, -ишь; *perf* **скаламбу́рить)** *несов неперех* to pun, make puns.
каланч|а́ (-и́; *gen pl* **-е́й)** *ж* watchtower; (*разг*: *человек*) beanpole.
кала́ч (-а́) *м* ≈ cottage loaf; **его́ калачо́м не зама́нишь** nothing will persuade him.
кала́чиком *нареч*: **сверну́ться ~** to curl up in a ball.
калейдоско́п (-а) *м* (*также перен*) kaleidoscope.
ка́лек *сущ см* **ка́лька.**
кале́к|а (-и) *м/ж* cripple.
календа́рный *прил*: **~ ме́сяц/год** calendar month/year.
календа́р|ь (-я́) *м* calendar.
кале́ни|е (-я) *ср* incandescence; **довести́** *(perf)* **кого́-н до бе́лого ~я** to send sb into a blind rage.
калён|ый *прил* red-hot; **выжига́ть (вы́жечь** *perf***) ~ым желе́зом** to brand.
кале́ч|ить (-у, -ишь; *perf* **покале́чить** *или* **искале́чить)** *несов перех* to cripple.
кали́бр (-а) *м* (*ВОЕН, перен*) calibre (*BRIT*), caliber (*US*); (*ТЕХ*) gauge.
калибр|ова́ть (-у́ю) *(не)сов перех* to calibrate.
калибро́вк|а (-и) *ж* calibration.
ка́ли|й (-я) *м* potassium.
кали́н|а (-ы) *ж* guelder-rose.
кали́т|ка (-ки; *gen pl* **-ок)** *ж* gate.
Califо́рни|я (-и) *ж* California.
каллиграфи́ческ|ий (-ая, -ое, -ие) *прил*: **~ по́черк** beautiful handwriting.
каллигра́фи|я (-и) *ж* calligraphy.
калмы́к (-а) *м* Kalmyk.
Калмы́ки|я (-и) *ж* Kalmykia.
калмы́ч|ка (-ки; *gen pl* **-ек)** *ж см* **калмы́к.**
калори́йност|ь (-и) *ж* (*пищи*) calorie content; (*ФИЗ*) calorific value.
кало́ри|я (-и) *ж* calorie.
ка́л|ька (-ьки; *gen pl* **-ек)** *ж* (*бумага*) tracing paper; (*копия*) traced copy; (*ЛИНГ*) calque.
кальки́р|овать (-ую; *perf* **скальки́ровать)** *несов перех* (*чертёж*) to trace.
калькуля́тор (-а) *м* calculator.
кальма́р (-а) *м* squid.
кальсо́н|ы (-) *мн* long johns *мн.*
ка́льци|й (-я) *м* calcium.
КамА́З (-а) *м сокр* = *Ка́мский автомоби́льный заво́д*; (*автомобиль*) *vehicle manufactured at the Kamskiy car factory.*
ка́мбал|а (-ы) *ж* flatfish.
Камбо́дж|а (-и) *ж* Cambodia.
камбоджи́йск|ий (-ая, -ое, -ие) *прил* Cambodian.
ка́мбуз (-а) *м* galley.
каме́ли|я (-и) *ж* camelia.
камене́|ть (-ю) *несов от* **окамене́ть.**
камени́ст|ый (-, -а, -о) *прил* (*почва*) stony.
каменноу́гольный *прил* coal *опред*; **~ бассе́йн** coalfield.
ка́менн|ый *прил* stone; (*перен*) stony; **у неё ~ое се́рдце** she has a heart of stone; **ка́менный век** the Stone Age.
каменоло́м|ня (-ни; *gen pl* **-ен)** *ж* quarry.
каменотёс (-а) *м* stonemason.
ка́менщик (-а) *м* bricklayer; **во́льный ~** Freemason.
ка́м|ень (-ня; *gen pl* **-не́й)** *м* stone; **драгоце́нный ~** precious stone; **краеуго́льный ~** (*перен*) cornerstone; **~ в по́чках** kidney stone; **~ преткнове́ния** stumbling block; **у него́ ~ на се́рдце лежи́т** there's a weight lying heavy on his heart; **у меня́ ~ с души́ свали́лся** it was a great weight off my mind; **держа́ть** *(impf)* **~ за па́зухой** to bear a grudge.
ка́мер|а (-ы) *ж* (*тюремная*) cell; (*АВТ*) inner tube; (*также:* **телека́мера, кинока́мера**) camera; (*ТЕХ, АНАТ*) chamber; **снима́ть (снять** *perf***) что-н скры́той ~ой** to film sth secretly; **ка́мера хране́ния** (*на вокзале*) left-luggage office (*BRIT*), checkroom (*US*); (*в музее*) cloakroom.
камерди́нер (-а) *м* (*ИСТ*) valet.
ка́мерный *прил* (*обстановка*) cosy; **ка́мерная му́зыка** chamber music; **ка́мерный орке́стр** chamber orchestra.

камертóн (-а) *м* tuning fork.
кáмеш|ек (-ка; *nom pl* **-ки**, *gen pl* **-ков**) *м* stone.
камé|я (-и) *ж* cameo (*in jewellery*).
камзóл (-а) *м* frock coat.
ками́н (-а) *м* fireplace.
камнепáд (-а) *м* avalanche (*of rocks, stones*).
кáмня *итп сущ см* **кáмень.**
камóрк|а (-и) *ж* (*разг*) cubbyhole.
кампáни|я (-и) *ж* campaign.
кампучи́йск|ий (**-ая, -ое, -ие**) *прил* Kampuchean.
Кампучи́|я (-и) *ж* Kampuchea.
камуфли́р|овать (**-ую**; *perf* **закамуфли́ровать**) *несов перех* to camouflage.
камуфля́ж (-а) *м* camouflage.
кáмфор|а (-ы) *ж* camphor.
кáмфорн|ый *прил*: **~ое мáсло** camphorated oil.
камы́ш (-á) *м* rushes *мн*.
канáв|а (-ы) *ж* ditch; **стóчная ~** gutter.
Канáд|а (-ы) *ж* Canada.
канáд|ец (**-ца**) *м* Canadian.
канáд|ка (**-ки**; *gen pl* **-ок**) *ж см* **канáдец.**
канáдск|ий (**-ая, -ое, -ие**) *прил* Canadian.
канáдца *итп сущ см* **канáдец.**
канáл (-а) *м* (*также* АНАТ) canal; (СВЯЗЬ, ТЕЛ, *перен*) channel; **я бýду дéйствовать по своим ~ам** I shall use the means available to me.
канализациóнн|ый *прил*: **~ая трубá** sewer pipe; **канализациóнная сеть** the sewers.
канализáци|я (-и) *ж* sewerage.
канáл|ья (**-ьи**; *gen pl* **-ий**) *м/ж* rogue.
канарé|йка (**-йки**; *gen pl* **-ек**) *ж* canary.
канáрск|ий (**-ая, -ое, -ие**) *прил*: **К~ие островá** the Canary Islands, the Canaries.
канáт (-а) *м* cable.
канáтн|ый *прил*: **~ая дорóга** cable car.
канатохóд|ец (**-ца**) *м* tightrope walker.
канв|á (-ы́) *ж* (*в вышивании*) sampler; (*перен: рассказа*) outline.
кандал|ы́ (**-óв**) *мн* shackles *мн*.
канделя́бр (-а) *м* candelabra (*мн* candelabra).
кандидáт (-а) *м* candidate; (ПРОСВЕЩ): **~ наýк** ≈ Doctor.
кандидáтск|ий (**-ая, -ое, -ие**) *прил* candidate's; **кандидáтская диссертáция** ≈ doctoral thesis; **кандидáтский экзáмен** *entrance exam for postgraduate study*.
кандидатýр|а (-ы) *ж* candidacy; **выставля́ть** (**вы́ставить** *perf*) **чью-н ~у** to nominate sb.
кани́кул|ы (-) *мн* holidays *мн* (BRIT), vacation *ед* (US); **парлáментские ~** parliamentary recess.
каникуля́рный *прил* holiday *опред* (BRIT), vacation *опред* (US).
кани́стр|а (-ы) *ж* jerry can.
канитéл|иться (**-юсь, -ишься**) *несов возв* (*разг*): **~** (**с** +*instr*) to waste one's time (over).
канитéл|ь (-и) *ж* (*золотая итп*) thread; (*перен*) bore, drag; **тянýть** (*impf*) **~** (*перен: разг*) to drag things out.
канифóл|ь (-и) *ж* (ХИМ) resin; (МУЗ) rosin.
канкáн (-а) *м* cancan.
каннибáл (-а) *м* cannibal.
каннибали́зм (-а) *м* cannibalism.
канои́ст (-а) *м* canoeist.
канóн (-а) *м* canon.
канонáд|а (-ы) *ж* cannonade.
канонизáци|я (-и) *ж* (*также перен*) canonization.
канонизи́р|овать (**-ую**) *(не)сов перех* (*также перен*) to canonize.
канóник (-а) *м* canon (REL).
канони́ческ|ий (**-ая, -ое, -ие**) *прил* (РЕЛ) canonical; (*перен: правила, образец*) definitive; **~ое прáво** canon law.
канóэ *ср нескл* canoe.
кантáт|а (-ы) *ж* cantata.
кант|овáть (**-ýю**; *perf* **окантовáть**) *несов перех* (*окаймлять*) to mount; (*no perf; переворачивать*) to tilt; **„не ~!"** "keep upright!"
канýн (-а) *м* eve; **в ~** +*gen* on the eve of; **~ Нóвого гóда** New Year's Eve.
кáн|уть (**-у, -ешь**) *сов неперех* (*исчезнуть*) to vanish; **~** *(perf)* **в Лéту** *или* **вéчность** to fade into obscurity; **он слóвно в вóду ~ул** he vanished into thin air.
канцеляри́зм (-а) *м* official jargon.
канцеля́ри|я (-и) *ж* office.
канцеля́рск|ий (**-ая, -ое, -ие**) *прил* office *опред*; **~ слог** *или* **язы́к** officialese.
канцеля́рщин|а (-ы) *ж* (*формализм*) red tape.
кáнцлер (-а) *м* (*глава государства*) chancellor.
каньóн (-а) *м* canyon.
каню́к (-á) *м* buzzard.
каню́ч|ить (**-у, -ишь**) *несов неперех* (*разг*) to whinge.
каоли́н (-а) *м* kaolin.
кáпа|ть (**-ю**) *несов неперех* (*вода*) to drip ◆ (*perf* **накáпать**) *перех* (*микстуру*) to pour out drop by drop; **дождь ~ет** it's spotting with rain.
кáпелек *сущ см* **кáпелька.**
капéлл|а (-ы) *ж* (МУЗ) choir; (РЕЛ) chapel.
капеллáн (-а) *м* chaplain.
кáпель *сущ см* **кáпля.**
капéл|ь (-и) *ж* thaw.
кáпель|ка (**-ьки**; *gen pl* **-ек**) *ж* droplet; **~** +*gen* (*молока итп*) a drop of; (*счастя, правды*) a grain of; **всё до послéдней ~ьки** every last little bit.
кáпельку *нареч* (*разг*) a tad *или* touch; **ну ещё ~** a little bit more; **почитáй хоть ~** read for just a little while at least.
капельмéйстер (-а) *м* bandmaster.
капéльниц|а (-ы) *ж* (МЕД) drip(-feed); **стáвить** (**постáвить** *perf*) **комý-н ~у** to put sb on a drip.
кáперс|ы (**-ов**) *мн* (КУЛИН) capers *мн*.
капилля́р (-а) *м* capillary.
капитáл (-а) *м* (КОММ) capital; (*перен: политический*) power; **вы́пущенный акционéрный ~** (КОММ) issued capital.
капитáлен *прил см* **капитáльный.**
капитализáци|я (-и) *ж* capitalization.
капитализи́р|овать (**-ую**) *(не)сов перех* (КОММ) to capitalize.

капитали́зм (-а) *м* capitalism.
капитали́ст (-а) *м* capitalist.
капиталисти́ческ|ий (-ая, -ое, -ие) *прил* capitalist.
капиталовложе́ни|я (-й) *мн* capital investment *ед*.
капита́л|ьный *прил* (*ЭКОН, КОММ*) capital *опред*; (-ен, -ьна, -ьно; *сооружение, труд*) main; (*вопрос, покупка*) major; **капита́льная стена́** supporting wall; **капита́льное строи́тельство** major construction work; **капита́льные расхо́ды** capital expenditure; **капита́льный ремо́нт** major repairs; **капита́льные това́ры** capital goods.
капита́н (-а) *м* captain.
капита́нск|ий (-ая, -ое, -ие) *прил* captain's; **капита́нский мо́стик** (*МОР*) bridge.
капите́л|ь (-и) *ж* (*АРХИТ*) capital.
капитули́р|овать (-ую) *(не)сов неперех* to capitulate.
капитуля́ци|я (-и) *ж* capitulation.
капка́н (-а) *м* trap.
ка́п|ли (-ель) *мн* (*МЕД*) drops *мн*.
ка́п|ля (-ли; *gen pl* -ель) *ж* (*также перен*) drop; **ни ~ли** not a bit; **вы́пить** *(perf)* **всё до ~ли** to drink every last drop; **подожди́те хоть ~лю** (*разг*) wait just one second; **они́ похо́жи как две ~ли воды́** they're like two peas in a pod; **~ в мо́ре** a drop in the ocean; *см также* **ка́пли**.
капо́т (-а) *м* (*АВТ*) bonnet (*BRIT*), hood (*US*); (*халат*) housecoat.
капра́л (-а) *м* corporal.
капремо́нт (-а) *м сокр* = **капита́льный ремо́нт**.
капри́з (-а) *ж* caprice, whim.
капри́зен *прил см* **капри́зный**.
капри́знича|ть (-ю; *perf* **покапри́зничать**) *несов неперех* to behave capriciously.
капри́з|ный (-ен, -на, -но) *прил* (*человек, характер*) capricious; (*мода, погода итп*) fickle.
капро́н (-а) *м* synthetic thread.
ка́псул|а (-ы) *ж* (*МЕД, ТЕХ*) capsule.
капу́ст|а (-ы) *ж* cabbage; **брюссе́льская ~** Brussels sprouts *мн*; **цветна́я ~** cauliflower.
капу́стник (-а) *м* amateur revue.
капу́стный *прил* cabbage.
капу́т *м нескл*: **магнитофо́ну ~** (*разг*) the tape recorder's kaput; **ему́ ~** he's finished.
капюшо́н (-а) *м* hood.
ка́р|а (-ы) *ж* retribution.
караби́н (-а) *м* (*ВОЕН*) carbine; (*ТЕХ*) karabiner.
кара́бка|ться (-юсь; *perf* **вскара́бкаться**) *несов возв*: **~ на** *+acc* (*человек*) to clamber up; (*растение*) to creep up.
карава́|й (-я) *м* cob (*loaf*).
карава́н (-а) *м* (*судов*) convoy; (*верблюдов*) caravan.
карава́н-сара́|й (-я) *м* caravanserai.
карака́тиц|а (-ы) *ж* (*ЗООЛ*) cuttlefish; (*перен: разг*) clodhopper.
кара́кулевый *прил* astrakhan.
кара́кул|и (-ей) *мн* (*разг*) scrawl *ед*.
кара́кул|ь (-я) *м* astrakhan; *см также* **кара́кули**.
караме́л|ь (-и) *ж собир* (*леденцы*) caramels *мн*; (*жжёный сахар*) caramel.
каранда́ш (-а́; *gen pl* -е́й) *м* pencil.
каранти́н (-а) *м* quarantine.
карапу́з (-а) *м* (*разг*) fatty.
кара́с|ь (-я́) *м* crucian (*type of carp*).
кара́т (-а) *м* carat (*BRIT*), karat (*US*).
кара́тельный *прил* punitive; **~ отря́д** death squad.
кара́|ть (-ю; *perf* **покара́ть**) *несов перех* to punish.
каратэ́ *ср нескл* karate.
карау́л (-а) *м* guard; **выставля́ть (вы́ставить** *perf*) **~** to post a guard; **стоя́ть** *(impf)* **в ~е** to stand guard; **~!** help!
карау́л|ить (-ю, -ишь) *несов перех* to guard; (*разг: ожидать*) to lie in wait for.
карбо́ван|ец (-ца) *м* karbovanets (*Ukrainian currency unit*).
карбо́лов|ый *прил*: **~ая кислота́** carbolic acid.
карбу́нкул (-а) *м* (*ГЕО, МЕД*) carbuncle.
карбюра́тор (-а) *м* carburettor (*BRIT*), carburetor (*US*).
карг|а́ (-и́) *ж* (*разг*) hag.
кардамо́н (-а; *no pl*) *м* cardamom.
кардина́л (-а) *м* (*РЕЛ*) cardinal.
кардина́льно *нареч* (*изменить*) drastically.
кардина́л|ьный (-ен, -ьна, -ьно) *прил* cardinal *опред*, of cardinal importance.
кардио́лог (-а) *м* cardiologist, heart specialist.
кардиологи́ческ|ий (-ая, -ое, -ие) *прил* (*отделение*) cardiac.
кардиоло́ги|я (-и) *ж* cardiology.
каре́ *ср нескл* (*ВОЕН*) square formation; (*КАРТЫ*) four of a kind.
каре́т|а (-ы) *ж* carriage.
каре́т|ка (-ки; *gen pl* -ок) *ж* carriage.
ка́р|ий (-яя, -ее, -ие) *прил* (*глаза*) hazel; (*масть*) chestnut.
карикату́р|а (-ы) *ж* caricature.
карикату́рен *прил см* **карикату́рный**.
карикатури́ст (-а) *м* caricaturist.
карикату́р|ный (-ен, -на, -но) *прил* caricatured.
карка́с (-а) *м* shell (*of a building*).
ка́рка|ть (-ю) *несов неперех* (*ворона*) to caw; (*perf* **нака́ркать**; *перен: разг*) to predict the worst.
ка́рлик (-а) *м* dwarf.
ка́рликовый *прил* (*племена*) pygmy *опред*; (*растения*) dwarf *опред*.
ка́рлиц|а (-ы) *ж см* **ка́рлик**.
карма́н (-а) *м* pocket; **набива́ть (наби́ть** *perf*) **~** (*пренебр*) to line one's pockets; **э́то мне не по ~у** I can't afford it; **нало́ги уда́рили по ~у** the

taxes have hit the population hard; **держи́ ~ ши́ре!** fat chance!; **он не поле́зет за сло́вом в ~** he's never short of something to say.

карма́нн|ый *прил*: **~ые де́ньги/часы́** pocket money/watch; **карма́нный вор** pickpocket; **карма́нный нож** pocketknife; **карма́нные расхо́ды** petty expenses.

карма́ш|ек (-ка) *м уменьш от* **карма́н**; (*мешочек*) pouch.

карнава́л (-а) *м* carnival.

карнава́льный *прил* carnival *опред*.

карни́з (-а) *м* (*под крышей здания*) cornice; (*над дверью*) lintel.

карп (-а) *м* carp.

Карпа́т|ы (-) *мн* Carpathians, Carpathian Mountains.

карт (-а) *м* go-cart.

ка́рт|а (-ы) *ж* (*ГЕО*) map; (*также*: **игра́льная ~**) (playing) card; **ста́вить (поста́вить** *perf*) **на ~у что-н** (*перен*) to put sth at stake; *см также* **ка́рты**.

карта́в|ый (-, -а, -о) *прил*: **он ~** he can't pronounce the letter "r" properly.

картёжник (-а) *м* card player.

картёжниц|а (-ы) *ж см* **картёжник**.

карте́л|ь (-и) *ж* (*ЭКОН*) cartel.

карти́н|а (-ы) *ж* (*также КИНО, перен*) picture; (*ТЕАТР*) scene; (*обычно мн*: *прошлого, природы*) image.

карти́н|ка (-ки; *gen pl* -ок) *ж уменьш от* **карти́на**; (*иллюстрация*) picture (*in book etc*); **кни́га с ~ми** picture book; **пря́мо как ~!** it's beautiful!

карти́нн|ый *прил* picture *опред*; (-ен, -на, -но; *красивый*) picturesque.

карто́граф (-а) *м* cartographer.

картографи́р|овать (-ую) (*не*)*сов перех* to map.

картографи́ческ|ий (-ая, -ое, -ие) *прил* cartographic.

картогра́фи|я (-и) *ж* cartography.

карто́н (-а) *м* cardboard.

карто́нный *прил* cardboard.

картоте́к|а (-и) *ж* card index.

карто́фелин|а (-ы) *ж* potato (*мн* potatoes).

карто́фел|ь (-я) *м* (*растение*) potato plant; (*плод*) potatoes *мн*; **~ в мунди́ре** baked *или* jacket potatoes.

карто́фельный *прил* potato; **карто́фельное пюре́** mashed potato.

ка́рточ|ка (-ки; *gen pl* -ек) *ж* card; (*также*: **фотока́рточка**) photo; **хле́бная/визи́тная ~** ration/business card.

ка́рточн|ый *прил*: **~ая игра́** card game; **~ая систе́ма** rationing; **~ долг** gambling debt; **~ до́мик** (*также перен*) house of cards.

карто́шк|а (-и) *ж собир* potatoes *мн*; **нос ~ой** bulbous nose.

ка́ртридж (-а) *м* cartridge.

карту́з (-а́) *м* peaked cap.

ка́рт|ы (-) *мн* cards *мн*; **игра́ть** (*impf*) **в ~** to play cards; **раскрыва́ть (раскры́ть** *perf*) **свой ~** (*перен*) to show one's hand.

карусе́л|ь (-и) *ж* merry-go-round (*BRIT*), carousel (*US*).

ка́рцер (-а) *м* isolation cell.

карье́р (-а) *м* (*ТЕХ*) quarry; (*галоп*) full gallop; **пуска́ться (пусти́ться** *perf*) **с ме́ста в ~** (*перен*) to rush straight in.

карье́р|а (-ы) *ж* career; **де́лать (сде́лать** *perf*) **~у** to build a career for o.s.

карьери́зм (-а) *м* careerism.

карьери́ст (-а) *м* careerist.

карьери́стск|ий (-ая, -ое, -ие) *прил* careerist *опред*.

каса́ни|е (-я) *ср* contact.

каса́|ться (-юсь; *perf* **косну́ться**) *несов возв*: **~** *+gen* (*дотрагиваться*) to touch; (*затрагивать*) to touch on; **э́то тебя́ не ~ется** it doesn't concern you; **что ~ется Вас, то** ... as far as you are concerned ....

ка́с|ка (-ки; *gen pl* -ок) *ж* helmet.

каска́д (-а) *м* cascade; (*трюк*) stunt; (*перен*) flood.

каскадёр (-а) *м* stunt man (*мн* men).

ка́сок *сущ см* **ка́ска**.

каспи́йск|ий (-ая, -ое, -ие) *прил*: **К~ое мо́ре** Caspian Sea.

ка́сс|а (-ы) *ж* (*ТЕАТР, КИНО*) box office; (*железнодорожная*) ticket office; (*в магазине*) cash desk; (*аппарат*) cash register; (*ящик*) cash box; (*деньги*) cash; (*ТИПОГ*) case.

кассацио́нный *прил*: **~ суд** court of appeal.

касса́ци|я (-и) *ж* (*ЮР*) cassation, annulment; **подава́ть (пода́ть** *perf*) **на ~ю** to lodge an appeal.

кассе́т|а (-ы) *ж* (*магнитофонная*) cassette; (*ФОТО*) cartridge.

касси́р (-а) *м* cashier.

ка́ст|а (-ы) *ж* caste.

кастеля́нш|а (-и) *ж* laundrywoman (*мн* laundrywomen).

касте́т (-а) *м* knuckle-duster.

касто́рк|а (-и) *ж* (*разг*) = **касто́ровое ма́сло**.

касто́ров|ый *прил*: **~ое ма́сло** castor oil.

кастри́р|овать (-ую) (*не*)*сов перех* to castrate.

кастрю́л|я (-и) *ж* saucepan.

катава́си|я (-и) *ж* (*разг*) mayhem.

катакли́зм (-а) *м* cataclysm.

катако́мб|ы (-) *мн* catacombs *мн*.

катализа́тор (-а) *м* catalyst.

катало́г (-а) *м* catalogue (*BRIT*), catalog (*US*).

каталогизи́р|овать (-ую) (*не*)*сов перех* (*книги*) to catalogue (*BRIT*), catalog (*US*).

ката́ни|е (-я) *ср*: **~ на маши́не** driving; **~ на велосипе́де** cycling; **~ на конька́х** skating; **~ на ло́шади** horse (*BRIT*) *или* horseback (*US*) riding; **~ на лы́жах** skiing.

катапу́льт|а (-ы) *ж* (*ТЕХ*) catapult.

катапульти́р|оваться (-уюсь) (*не*)*сов возв* to eject.

ката́р (-а) *м* catarrh.

катара́кт|а (-ы) *ж* (*МЕД*) cataract.
катастро́ф|а (-ы) *ж* (*авиационная, железнодорожная*) disaster; (*перен*) catastrophe.
катастрофи́ческ|ий (-ая, -ое, -ие) *прил* catastrophic, disastrous.
ката́|ть (-ю) *несов перех* (*что-н круглое*) to roll; (*что-н на колёсах*) to wheel; ~ *(impf)* **кого́-н на маши́не** to take sb for a drive
▸ **ката́ться** *несов возв*: **~ся на маши́не/велосипе́де** to go for a drive/cycle; **~ся** *(impf)* **на конька́х/ло́шади** to go skating/horse (*BRIT*) *или* horseback (*US*) riding; **~ся** *(impf)* **от бо́ли** to roll about in pain; **~ся** *(impf)* **со́ смеху** to fall about laughing; **как сыр в ма́сле ~ся** *(impf)* to be in clover.
катафа́лк (-а) *м* hearse.
категори́чен *прил см* **категори́чный**.
категори́ческ|ий (-ая, -ое, -ие) *прил* categoric.
категори́ч|ный (-ен, -на, -но) *прил* categorical.
категори́|я (-и) *ж* category.
ка́тер (-а) *м* boat; **сторожево́й/торпе́дный ~** patrol/torpedo boat.
катехи́зис (-а) *м* catechism.
ка|ти́ть (-чу́, -тишь) *несов перех* (*что-н круглое*) to roll; (*что-н на колёсах*) to wheel ◆ *неперех* (*разг: в автомобиле*) to bomb along; ~ *(impf)* **бо́чки на кого́-н** (*перен*) to snipe at sb.
катка́ *сущ см* **като́к**.
като́д (-а) *м* cathode.
кат|о́к (-ка́) *м* ice *или* skating rink; (*ТЕХ: также:* **асфа́льтовый ~**) steamroller.
като́лик (-а) *м* Catholic.
католици́зм (-а) *м* Catholicism.
католи́чек *сущ см* **католи́чка**.
католи́ческ|ий (-ая, -ое, -ие) *прил* Catholic.
католи́ч|ка (-ки; *gen pl* **-ек)** *ж см* **като́лик**.
ка́торг|а (-и) *ж* hard labour (*BRIT*) *или* labor (*US*).
каторжа́н|ин (-ина; *nom pl* **-е**, *gen pl* **-)** *м* convict (*in a labour camp*).
каторжа́нк|а (-и) *ж см* **каторжа́нин**.
ка́торжник (-а) *м см* **каторжа́нин**.
кату́ш|ка (-ки; *gen pl* **-ек)** *ж* spool.
каучу́к (-а) *м* rubber.
каучу́ковый *прил* rubber.
КАФ *м сокр* CAF (= *cost and freight*).
кафе́ *ср нескл* café.
ка́федр|а (-ы) *ж* (*ПРОСВЕЩ*) department; (*РЕЛ*) pulpit; (*лекторская*) rostrum; **заве́дующий ~ой** chair; **он получи́л ~у** he obtained a chair.
кафедра́льный *прил*: ~ **собо́р** cathedral.
ка́фел|ь (-я) *м собир* tiles *мн*.
ка́фельный *прил* tiled.
кафете́ри|й (-я) *м* cafeteria.
кафта́н (-а) *м* caftan.
кача́л|ка (-ки; *gen pl* **-ок)** *ж* rocking chair.
кача́ни|е (-я) *ср* (*на качелях*) swinging; (*на волнах*) rocking, roll.
кача́|ть (-ю) *несов перех* (*колыбель*) to rock; (*подбрасывать*) to throw into the air; (*нефть*) to pump; ~ *(impf)* **голово́й** to shake one's head; **кора́бль си́льно ~ло** the ship was rocking violently
▸ **кача́ться** *несов возв* to swing; (*на волнах*) to rock, roll; (*от усталости*) to sway.
каче́л|и (-ей) *мн* swing *ед*.
ка́чественно *нареч* (*другой*) essentially; (*делать, работать*) to a high standard.
ка́чествен|ный *прил* qualitative; **(-, -на, -но**; *товар, изделие*) high-quality; **ка́чественное прилага́тельное** qualitative adjective.
ка́честв|о (-а) *ср* quality ◆ *предл*: **в ~е** +*gen* as; **в ~е приме́ра** by way of example; **я рабо́таю в ~е меха́ника** I work as a mechanic.
ка́чк|а (-и) *ж*: **бортова́я ~** rolling; **килева́я ~** pitching.
качн|у́ть (-у́, -ёшь) *сов перех* to swing
▸ **качну́ться** *сов возв* to swing.
ка́ш|а (-и) *ж* ≈ porridge; **у него́ в голове́ ~** he's totally mixed up.
кашало́т (-а) *м* sperm whale.
ка́ш|ель (-ля) *м* cough.
кашеми́р (-а) *м* cashmere.
ка́шля *сущ см* **ка́шель**.
ка́шлян|уть (-у, -ешь) *сов неперех* to cough.
ка́шля|ть (-ю) *несов неперех* to cough.
Кашми́р (-а) *м* Kashmir.
кашне́ *ср нескл* *narrow scarf, usually worn under a coat*.
кашта́н (-а) *м* (*дерево*) chestnut (tree); (*плод*) chestnut; (: *несъедобный*) conker; **таска́ть** *(impf)* **~ы из огня́** to do the dirty work; **ко́нский ~** horse chestnut.
кашта́новый *прил* (*аллея, волосы*) chestnut.
каю́к (-а) *как сказ* (*разг*): **ему́ ~** he's finished.
каю́т|а (-ы) *ж* (*МОР*) cabin.
каю́т-компа́ни|я (-и) *ж* *naval officers' lounge*.
ка́|яться (-юсь; *perf* **пока́яться)** *несов возв*: **~ (в чём-н пе́ред кем-н)** to confess (sth to sb); **я хочу́ тебе́ пока́яться в чём-то** I must tell you something; **до́лжен пока́яться, я никогда́ не люби́л её** I must confess, I never loved her.
кБт *сокр* (= **килоба́йт**) KB, kbyte (= *kilobyte*); = *килоби́т*.
КВ *мн сокр* (= *коро́ткие во́лны*) SW= *short wave ед*.
кв. *сокр* (= **квадра́тный**) sq. (= *square*); (= **кварти́ра**) Apt. (= *apartment*).
квадра́т (-а) *м* square; **возводи́ть (возвести́** *perf*) **что-н в ~** to square sth.
квадра́т|ный (-ен, -на, -но) *прил* square; **~ ко́рень** square root; **квадра́тные ско́бки** square brackets.
ква́кань|е (-я) *ср* croaking.
ква́кн|уть (*3sg* **-ет**, *3pl* **-ут**) *сов неперех* to croak.
квалификацио́нный *прил*: **~ экза́мен**

professional exam.
квалификáци|я (-и) *ж* qualification; (*профессия*) profession.
квалифицúрованно *нареч* competently.
квалифицúрован|ный (-, -на, -но) *прил* (*работник*) qualified; (*труд*) skilled.
квалифицúр|овать (-ую) *(не)сов перех* (*спортсмена*) to rank; (*преступление, поведение*) to categorize.
квант (-а) *м* quantum.
квáнтов|ый *прил*: **~ая механика/физика** quantum mechanics/physics.
квартáл (-а) *м* quarter.
квартáльный *прил* (*отчёт, план*) quarterly.
квартéт (-а) *м* quartet.
квартúр|а (-ы) *ж* flat (*BRIT*), apartment (*US*); (*снимаемое жильё*) lodgings *мн*; **жить** *(impf)* **на ~е** to rent a flat *или* apartment; **съезжáть (съéхать** *perf*) **с ~ы** to move out of lodgings.
квартирáнт (-а) *м* lodger.
квартирáнт|ка (-ки; *gen pl* -ок) *ж см* **квартирáнт**.
квартир|овáть (-ýю) *несов неперех* (*разг*: *снимать жильё*) to rent a flat (*BRIT*) *или* apartment (*US*).
квартиросъёмщик (-а) *м* leaseholder.
квартплáт|а (-ы) *ж сокр* (= *квартúрная плáта*) rent (*for a flat*).
кварц (-а) *м* quartz.
квáрцев|ый *прил* (*порода, руда*) quartz; **~ая лáмпа** quartz lamp.
квас (-а; *nom pl* -ы́) *м* kvass (*mildly alcoholic drink made from fermented rye bread, yeast or berries*).
квá|сить (-шу, -сишь; *perf* **заквáсить**) *несов перех* to pickle; (*молоко*) to sour.
квáшен|ый *прил* (*молоко*) sour; **~ая капýста** sauerkraut, pickled cabbage.
квашн|я́ (-и́; *gen pl* -éй) *ж* (*кадушка*) fermenting bucket (*for dough*); (*разг*: *человек*) clodhopper.
квáшу *несов см* **квáсить**.
Квебéк (-а) *м* Quebec.
квинтéт (-а) *м* quintet.
квинтэссéнци|я (-и) *ж* quintessence.
квитáнци|я (-и) *ж* receipt.
квúты *как сказ* (*разг*): **мы ~** we're quits.
КВН *м сокр* (= *клуб весёлых и находчивых*) *contest in which teams compete in various activities.*
квóрум (-а) *м* quorum.
квóт|а (-ы) *ж* quota; **úмпортная ~** import quota.
кВт *сокр* (= **киловáтт**) kW (= *kilowatt*).
кг *сокр* (= **килогрáмм**) kg (= *kilogram(me)*).
КГБ *м сокр* (*ист*: = *Комитéт государственной безопáсности*) KGB.
кéгл|и (-ей) *мн* skittles *мн*; (*игра*) skittles *ед*.
кедр (-а) *м* cedar (tree).
кéд|ы (-) *мн* pumps *мн*.
Кейптáун (-а) *м* Cape Town.
кейф (-а) *м* = **кайф**.
кейф|овáть (-ýю) *несов* = **кайфовáть**.
кекс (-а) *м* (fruit)cake.
келéен *прил см* **келéйный**.
келéйно *нареч* secretly.
келé|йный *прил* (*жизнь*) reclusive; (*тишина*) sublime; (**-ен, -йна, -йно**; *перен*: *переговоры, совещания*) secret.
Кёльн (-а) *м* Cologne.
кельт (-а) *м* Celt.
кéльтск|ий (-ая, -ое, -ие) *прил* Celtic.
кéл|ья (-ьи; *gen pl* -ий) *ж* (*монашеская*) cell.
кем *мест см* **кто**.
Кéмбридж (-а) *м* Cambridge.
кéмпинг (-а) *м* camping site, campsite.
кенгурý *ср нескл* kangaroo.
кенийск|ий (-ая, -ое, -ие) *прил* Kenyan.
Кéни|я (-и) *ж* Kenya.
кéпи *ср нескл* peaked cap.
кéп|ка (-ки; *gen pl* -ок) *ж* cap.
керáмик|а (-и) *ж собир* ceramics *мн*.
керамúческ|ий (-ая, -ое, -ие) *прил* ceramic.
керосúн (-а) *м* paraffin, kerosene (*US*).
керосúн|ка (-ки; *gen pl* -ок) *ж* paraffin stove.
кéсарев *прил*: **~о сечéние** Caesarean (*BRIT*) *или* Cesarean (*US*) section.
кессóнн|ый *прил*: **~ая болéзнь** decompression sickness, the bends *мн*.
кéт|а (-ы) *ж* Keta salmon.
кефáл|ь (-и) *ж* grey mullet.
кефúр (-а) *м* kefir (*yoghurt drink*).
кибернéтик (-а) *м* specialist in cybernetics.
кибернéтик|а (-и) *ж* cybernetics.
кибернетúческ|ий (-ая, -ое, -ие) *прил* cybernetic.
кибúтк|а (-и) *ж* carriage.
кивá|ть (-ю) *несов неперех* (*+dat*) to nod; **~** *(impf)* **на когó-н** (*разг*) to pin the blame on sb.
кивкá *сущ см* **кивóк**.
кивн|ýть (-ý, -ёшь) *сов неперех* to nod.
кив|óк (-кá) *м* nod.
кидá|ть (-ю) *несов от* **кúнуть**
▸ **кидáться** *несов от* **кúнуться** ◆ *возв*: **~ся камнями** to throw stones at each other; **~ся** *(impf)* **деньгáми** to throw money around.
Кúев (-а) *м* Kiev.
кизúл (-а) *м* cornel.
кизúловый *прил* cornel *опред*.
ки|й (-я; *nom pl* -и́, *gen pl* -ёв) *м* (*СПОРТ*) cue.
кикúмор|а (-ы) *ж female goblin in Russian mythology*; (*пренебр*: *человек*) fright.
килобáйт (-а) *м* kilobyte.
киловáтт (-а) *м* kilowatt.
килогрáмм (-а) *м* kilogram(me).
килограммóвый *прил* of one kilogram(me).
киломéтр (-а) *м* kilometre (*BRIT*), kilometer (*US*).
километрóвый *прил* (*расстояние*) of one kilometre (*BRIT*) *или* kilometer (*US*); (*гонка*) one-kilometre.
кил|ь (-я) *м* keel.
кильвáтер (-а) *м* wake.
кúльк|а (-и) *ж* sprat.
кимонó *ср нескл* kimono.

кинематóграф (-а) *м* (*киноиндустрия*) cinematography; (*кинотеатр*) cinema.
кинематографи́ст (-а) *м* cinematographer.
кинематографи́ческ|ий (-ая, -ое, -ие) *прил* cinematographic.
кинематогрáфи|я (-и) *ж* cinematography.
кинéтик|а (-и) *ж* kinetics.
кинети́ческ|ий (-ая, -ое, -ие) *прил* kinetic.
кинжáл (-а) *м* dagger.
кинó *ср нескл* cinema; (*разг*: *фильм*) film, movie (*US*); **идти́ (пойти́** *perf*) **в ~** (*разг*) to go to the pictures (*BRIT*) *или* movies (*US*); **э́то прóсто ~** (*разг*) it's an absolute joke.
киноактёр (-а) *м* (film) actor.
киноактри́с|а (-ы) *ж* (film) actress.
киноарти́ст (-а) *м* = **киноактёр**.
киноарти́ст|ка (-ки; *gen pl* -ок) *ж* = **киноактри́са**.
кинокарти́н|а (-ы) *ж* film.
кинооперáтор (-а) *м* cameraman.
кинорежиссёр (-а) *м* (film) director.
киностýди|я (-и) *ж* film studio.
киносъёмк|а (-и) *ж* filming, shooting.
кинотеáтр (-а) *м* cinema.
кинофи́льм (-а) *м* film.
ки́н|уть (-у, -ешь; *impf* **кидáть**) *сов перех* (*дрова, камень*) to throw; (*взгляд*) to cast; (*друзей*) to desert; (*силы, ресурсы*) to channel; (*разг*: *обмануть*) to swindle
▸ **ки́нуться** (*impf* **кидáться**) *сов возв*: **~ся на** *+acc* (*на врага*) to attack; (*на еду*) to fall upon; **кидáться (~ся** *perf*) **комý-н на шéю** to fall on sb; **кидáться (~ся** *perf*) **к комý-н** to throw o.s. at sb; **кидáться (~ся** *perf*) **со скáлы** to throw o.s. off a cliff.
киóск (-а) *м* kiosk.
киóт (-а) *м* icon case.
ки́п|а (-ы) *ж* bundle.
кипари́с (-а) *м* cypress.
кипари́совый *прил* cypress *опред*.
кипéни|е (-я) *ср* boiling; **температýра** *или* **тóчка ~я** boiling point.
кип|éть (-лю́, -и́шь; *perf* **вскипéть**) *несов неперех* (*вода, чайник*) to boil; **рабóта ~и́т** work is in full swing; **жизнь ~и́т** life is busy; **~ (вскипéть** *perf*) **негодовáнием/злóбой** to seethe with indignation/anger.
Кипр (-а) *м* Cyprus.
киприóт (-а) *м* Cypriot.
киприóт|ка (-ки; *gen pl* -ок) *ж см* **киприóт**.
кипýч|ий (-ая, -ее, -ие; -, -а, -о) *прил* bubbling; (*перен*) busy.
кипяти́льник (-а) *м* element (*for heating water*).
кипя|ти́ть (-чý, -ти́шь; *perf* **вскипяти́ть**) *несов перех* to boil
▸ **кипяти́ться** *несов возв* (*овощи*) to boil; (*шприцы, бельё*) to be boiled; (*перен*: *разг*: *горячиться*) to get shirty.
кипят|óк (-кá) *м* boiling water.
кипячёный *прил* boiled.
кипячý(сь) *несов см* **кипяти́ть(ся)**.
кирги́з (-а) *м* Kirghiz.
Кирги́зи|я (-и) *ж* Kirghizia.
кирги́з|ка (-ки; *gen pl* -ок) *ж см* **кирги́з**.
кирги́зск|ий (-ая, -ое, -ие) *прил* Kirghiz.
кири́ллиц|а (-ы) *ж* the Cyrillic alphabet.
кирк|á (-и́) *ж* pick(axe).
кирпи́ч (-á) *м* (*СТРОИТ*) brick.
кирпи́чный *прил* brick; **кирпи́чный завóд** brickworks.
кисéйн|ый *прил* muslin; **~ая бáрышня** *prim young miss*.
ки́сел *прил см* **ки́слый**.
кисéл|ь (-я́) *м* fruit jelly; **седьмáя водá на киселé** distant relative.
кисéт (-а) *м* tobacco pouch.
кисе|я́ (-и́) *ж* muslin.
кисли́нк|а (-и) *ж* sour taste.
кислорóд (-а) *м* oxygen.
ки́сло-слáдк|ий (-кая, -кое, -кие; -ок, -ка, -ко) *прил* (*хлеб*) *sweet with a bitter aftertaste*; (*ягоды*) bittersweet.
кисл|отá (-оты́; *nom pl* -óты) *ж* acid.
кислóтност|ь (-и) *ж* acidity.
кислóтный *прил* acid; **~ дождь** acid rain.
ки́с|лый (-ел, -лá, -ло) *прил* (*также перен*) sour; **ки́слая капýста** sauerkraut; **ки́слое молокó** soured milk.
ки́с|нуть (-ну, -нешь; *pt* -, -ла, -ло, *perf* **прокѝснуть** *или* **ски́снуть**) *несов неперех* to go off; (*no perf*; *перен*: *разг*) to mope (about).
кист|á (-ы́) *ж* cyst.
ки́сточ|ка (-ки; *gen pl* -ек) *ж* (paint)brush; (*винограда*) bunch; (*на берете, на скатерти итп*) tassel.
кист|ь (-и) *ж* (*АНАТ*) hand; (*гроздь*: *рябины*) cluster; (: *винограда*) bunch; (*на скатерти, на одежде итп*) tassel; (*художника, маляра*) (paint) brush; **он хорошó владéет ки́стью** he's a good painter; **полотнó ки́сти Мати́сса** painting by Matisse.
кит (-á) *м* whale.
китá|ец (-йца) *м* Chinese.
Китá|й (-я) *м* China.
китáйск|ий (-ая, -ое, -ие) *прил* Chinese; **~ язы́к** Chinese; **~ая грáмота** double Dutch.
китáйца *итп сущ см* **китáец**.
китая́н|ка (-ки; *gen pl* -ок) *ж см* **китáец**.
ки́тел|ь (-я; *nom pl* -и, *gen pl* -ей) *м military jacket*.
китобóйный *прил* whaling *опред*.
китóвый *прил* whale *опред*.
кич|и́ться (-ýсь, -и́шься) *несов возв*: ~ *+instr* to preen o.s. on.
кичли́в|ый (-, -а, -о) *прил* conceited.
киш|éть (*3sg* -и́т, *3pl* -áт) *несов неперех* (*мошкара, черви*) to swarm; **~** (*impf*) *+instr* (*людьми, рыбой*) to teem with.

кише́чник (-а) *м* intestines *мн*.
кише́чный *прил* intestinal.
Кишинёв (-а) *м* Kishinev.
кишк|а́ (-**и́**; *gen pl* -**о́к**, *dat pl* -**ка́м**) *ж* gut, intestine; **пряма́я** ~ rectum; **то́лстая** ~ large intestine.
кишла́к (-**а́**) *м village in Central Asia*.
кишми́ш (-а) *м собир* seedless grapes *мн*; (*изюм*) currants *мн*.
кишмя́ *нареч* (*разг*): ~ **кише́ть** to swarm.
кишо́к *сущ см* **кишка́**.
кл. *сокр* = **класс**.
клавеси́н (-а) *м* harpsichord.
клавиату́р|а (-ы) *ж* keyboard; **(ма́лая)** ~ (*комп*) keypad.
кла́виш|а (-и) *ж* key; ~ **„возвра́т каре́тки"/вы́хода** (*комп*) return/escape key.
кла́вишный *прил*: ~ **инструме́нт** keyboard instrument.
клад (-а) *м* treasure.
кла́дбищ|е (-а) *ср* cemetery; (*возле церкви*) graveyard.
кладби́щенск|ий (-ая, -ое, -ие) *прил* (*см сущ*) cemetery *опред*; graveyard *опред*; ~ **сто́рож** sexton.
кла́дез|ь (-я) *м* (*перен*): ~ **зна́ний** *или* **прему́дрости** mine of information.
кла́дк|а (-и) *ж* (*действие*) laying; **кирпи́чная** ~ brickwork; **ка́менная** ~ masonry.
кладов|а́я (-**о́й**; *decl like adj*) *ж* store.
кладо́в|ка (-ки; *gen pl* -ок) *ж* (*разг*) cubby-hole.
кладовщи́к (-**а́**) *м* storeman (*мн* storemen).
кладовщи́ца (-ы) *ж* storewoman (*мн* storewomen).
кладу́ *итп несов см* **класть**.
клад|ь (-и) *ж* load; **ручна́я** ~ hand luggage.
кла́ксон (-а) *м* horn.
клан (-а) *м* clan.
кла́ня|ться (-юсь; *perf* **поклони́ться**) *несов возв* to bow; (*свидетельствовать уважение*) to send one's regards; (*перен*: *униженно просить*) to beg.
кла́пан (-а) *м* valve.
кларне́т (-а) *м* clarinet.
кларнети́ст (-а) *м* clarinetist.
класс (-а) *м* class; (*комната*) classroom ◆ *как сказ* (*выражает восхищение*) it's great; **он вёл** ~ **фортепья́но в консервато́рии** he taught the piano at the conservatory; **специали́ст высо́кого кла́сса** highly-qualified specialist; **пока́зывать (показа́ть** *perf***)** ~ (*разг*) to show one's class.
кла́ссен *прил см* **кла́ссный**.
кла́ссик (-а) *м* (*литературы, музыки*) classic; (*учёный*) classical scholar.
кла́ссик|а (-и) *ж* classics *мн*.
классификацио́нный *прил* (*экзамен*) assessment *опред*; (*таблица*) classification *опред*.
классифика́ци|я (-и) *ж* classification.
классифици́р|овать (-ую) *(не)сов перех* to classify.
классици́зм (-а) *м* classicism.
класси́ческ|ий (-ая, -ое, -ие) *прил* (*пример, работа*) classic; (*музыка, литература*) classical; (*разг*: *жулик, политикан итп*) typical; ~**ая гимна́зия** *grammar school specializing in Latin and Ancient Greek*; ~**ое образова́ние** classical education.
кла́сс|ный *прил* (*сочинение, собрание*) class *опред*; (-ен, -на, -но; *разг*: *водитель, обед*) great; **кла́ссный руководи́тель** form teacher.
кла́ссовый *прил* class *опред*.
кла|сть (-**ду́**, -**дёшь**; *pt* -л, -ла, -ло, *perf* **положи́ть**) *несов перех* to put; (*perf* **сложи́ть**; *фундамент*) to lay; ~ **(положи́ть** *perf***) основа́ние** to lay down the foundations; ~ **(положи́ть** *perf***) жизнь за кого́-н/что-н** to lay down one's life for sb/sth; ~ **(положи́ть** *perf***) что-н на му́зыку** to put sth to music; ~ *(impf)* **я́йца** to lay eggs.
кла́цань|е (-я) *ср* (*разг*) chattering.
кла́ца|ть (-ю) *несов неперех* (*разг*) to chatter.
клёв (-а) *м* bite; **сего́дня хоро́ший** ~ the fish are biting today.
кл|ева́ть (-**юю́**) *несов перех* (*подлеж*: *птица*) to peck ◆ *неперех* (*рыба*) to bite; ~ *(impf)* **но́сом** to nod; **у меня́** ~**юёт** I've got a bite
▸ **клева́ться** *несов возв* to peck.
кле́вер (-а) *м* clover.
клевет|а́ (-**ы́**) *ж* (*устная*) slander; (*письменная*) libel.
клев|ета́ть (-**ещу́**, -**е́щешь**; *perf* **наклевета́ть**) *несов неперех*: ~ **на** *+acc* (*см сущ*) to slander; to libel.
клеветни́к (-**а́**) *м* slanderer.
клеветни́ческ|ий (-ая, -ое, -ие) *прил* (*см сущ*) slanderous; libellous.
клевещу́ *итп несов см* **клевета́ть**.
клёек *прил см* **кле́йкий**.
клеён|ка (-ки; *gen pl* -ок) *ж* oilcloth.
клеёнчатый *прил* oilskin *опред*.
кле́|ить (-ю, -ишь; *perf* **скле́ить**) *несов перех* to glue
▸ **кле́иться** *несов возв* to stick; (*перен*: *работа*) to come together; (: *разговор*) to go smoothly.
кле|й (-я) *м* glue.
кле́|йкий (-йкая, -йкое, -йкие; -ек, -йка, -йко) *прил* sticky; **кле́йкая ле́нта** sticky tape.
клеймёный *прил* (*товар*) stamped; (*скот*) branded.
клейм|и́ть (-лю́, -и́шь; *perf* **заклейми́ть**) *несов перех* (*товар, груз*) to stamp; (*скот, преступника*) to brand; (*перен*: *человека, поведение*) to stigmatize; ~ **(заклейми́ть** *perf***) кого́-н позо́ром** to hold sb up to shame; **его́ заклейми́ли преда́телем** he was branded a traitor.
клейм|о́ (-**а́**; *nom pl* -а, *gen pl* -) *ср* stamp; (*на теле скота, осуждённого*) brand; ~ **позо́ра** stigma.
кле́йстер (-а; *part gen* -у) *м* paste.

кле́мм|а (**-ы**) *ж* (*ЭЛЕК*) terminal.
клён (**-а**) *м* maple.
клено́вый *прил* maple.
клеп|а́ть (**-а́ю**; *perf* **склепа́ть**) *несов перех* to rivet; ◆ (**-лю́, -лешь**; *perf* **наклепа́ть**) *неперех* (*разг*): ~ **на** *+acc* to snitch on.
клептома́н (**-а**) *м* kleptomaniac.
клептома́ни|я (**-и**) *ж* kleptomania.
клептома́н|ка (**-ки**; *gen pl* **-ок**) *ж см* **клептома́н**.
клерк (**-а**) *м* clerk.
кле́т|ка (**-ки**; *gen pl* **-ок**) *ж* (*для птиц, животных*) cage; (*на ткани*) check; (*на бумаге*) square; (*БИО*) cell; **бума́га в ~ку** squared paper; **ткань в ~ку** checked material; **грудна́я ~** chest; **ле́стничная ~** landing.
кле́точный *прил* (*БИО*) cell *опред*.
клетча́тк|а (**-и**) *ж* (*no pl*; *БОТ*) cellulose; (*АНАТ*) cell tissue.
кле́тчатый *прил* (*ткань, шарф итп*) chequered, checked.
клё|цка (**-ки**; *gen pl* **-ек**) *ж* (*обычно мн*) dumpling.
клёш (**-а**) *м* flare ◆ *прил неизм*: **брю́ки ~** flares; **ю́бка ~** flared skirt.
клешн|я́ (**-и́**; *gen pl* **-е́й**) *ж* claw, pincer.
клещ (**-а́**) *м* (*ЗООЛ*) tick.
кле́щ|и (**-е́й**) *мн* tongs *мн*.
клие́нт (**-а**) *м* client.
клие́нт|ка (**-ки**; *gen pl* **-ок**) *ж см* **клие́нт**.
клиенту́р|а (**-ы**) *ж собир* clientèle.
кли́зм|а (**-ы**) *ж* enema.
клик (**-а**) *м* (*человека*) cry; (*птицы*) call.
кли́к|а (**-и**) *ж* clique.
клику́ш|а (**-и**) *ж* hysterical woman (*мн* women) ◆ *м/ж* panicmonger.
кли́макс (**-а**) *м* (*БИО*) menopause.
климактери́ческ|ий (**-ая, -ое, -ие**) *прил* menopausal; **климактери́ческий пери́од** menopause.
кли́мат (**-а**) *м* (*также перен*) climate.
климати́ческ|ий (**-ая, -ое, -ие**) *прил* climactic.
клин (**-а**; *nom pl* **-ья** *или* **-ы**, *gen pl* **-ьев** *или* **-о́в**) *м* wedge; (*солдат, журавлей*) V-formation; **борода́ кли́ном** goatee; ~ **кли́ном вышиба́ть** (*impf*) to fight fire with fire.
кли́ник|а (**-и**) *ж* clinic.
клини́ческ|ий (**-ая, -ое, -ие**) *прил* clinical; **клини́ческая больни́ца** training hospital; **клини́ческая смерть** (*МЕД*) clinical death.
клин|о́к (**-ка́**) *м* blade.
кли́пс|ы (**-ов**) *мн* clip-on earrings *мн*.
клир (**-а**) *м собир* (*РЕЛ*) the clergy.
кли́рик (**-а**) *м* clergyman (*мн* clergymen).
кли́ринг (**-а**) *м* (*КОММ*) clearing.
кли́рос (**-а**) *м* choir (*part of church*).
клич (**-а**) *м* cry; **боево́й ~** battle cry.
кли́ч|ка (**-ки**; *gen pl* **-ек**) *ж* (*собаки, кошки итп*) name; (*человека*) nickname.
клише́ *ср нескл* (*перен*) cliché; (*ТИПОГ*) plate.
клоа́к|а (**-и**) *ж* (*перен*: *загрязнённое место*) cesspit; (: *безнравственная среда*) cesspool.
клобу́к (**-а́**) *м* (*РЕЛ*) cowl.
кло|к (**-ка́**; *nom pl* **-чья**, *gen pl* **-чьев**) *м* (*волос*) tuft; (*ваты*) wad.
клокота́ни|е (**-я**) *ср* (*воды*) gurgling.
клок|ота́ть (**-очу́, -о́чешь**) *несов неперех* (*вода, поток*) to gurgle; (*перен*: *негодовать*) to seethe.
клон|и́ть (**-ю́, -ишь**) *несов перех* to bow, bend ◆ *неперех*: ~ **к** *+dat* to drive at; **его́ ~и́ло ко сну** he was drifting off (to sleep); **ло́дку кло́нит на́ бок** the boat is tilting; **к чему́ ты кло́нишь?** what are you getting *или* driving at?
▸ **клони́ться** *несов возв* (*пригибаться*) to bend; (*близиться*): **~ся к** *+dat* to approach; **день ~и́лся к ве́черу** evening was drawing near.
клоп (**-а́**) *м* bedbug.
кло́ун (**-а**) *м* clown.
кло́унск|ий (**-ая, -ое, -ие**) *прил* clown's; (*перен*) clownish.
клоч|о́к (**-ка́**) *м уменьш от* **клок**; (*земли*) plot; (*бумаги*) scrap.
кло́чья *итп сущ см* **клок**.
клуб (**-а**) *м* (*общество, здание*) club; (*обычно мн*: *дыма, пыли*) cloud.
клу́б|ень (**-ня**) *м* (*картофеля*) tuber.
клуб|и́ться (*3sg* **-и́тся**, *3pl* **-я́тся**) *несов возв* to swirl.
клубка́ *сущ см* **клубо́к**.
клубни́к|а (**-и**) *ж* strawberry ◆ *собир* strawberries *мн*.
клубни́чный *прил* strawberry.
клуб|о́к (**-ка́**) *м* (*ниток, шерсти*) ball; (*перен*: *противоречий*) tangle, knot; **сверну́ться** (*perf*) **~ко́м** to curl up in a ball.
клу́мб|а (**-ы**) *ж* flowerbed.
клу́ш|а (**-и**) *ж* (*разг*: *пренебр*) clumsy woman.
клык (**-а́**) *м* (*человека*) canine (tooth); (*животного*) fang.
клюв (**-а**) *м* beak.
клюк|а́ (**-и́**) *ж* walking stick.
клю́кв|а (**-ы**) *ж* cranberry ◆ *собир* cranberries *мн*; **разве́систая ~** tall story.
клю́квенный *прил*: ~ **морс/кисе́ль** cranberry juice/jelly.
клю́н|уть (**-у, -ешь**) *сов перех* to peck.
ключ (**-а́**) *м* (*также перен*) key; (*родник*) spring; (*МУЗ*): **скрипи́чный/басо́вый ~** treble/bass clef; **га́ечный ~** spanner; **~ от входно́й две́ри** front-door key; **бить** (*impf*) *или* **кипе́ть** (*impf*) **~о́м** (*вода*) to jet, spout; **жизнь бьёт** *или* **кипи́т ~о́м** life is really buzzing; **в пре́жнем ~е́** (*перен*) as before; **сдава́ть (сдать** *perf*) **что-н под ~** (*здание*) to offer sth ready for immediate entry; **ключ зажига́ния** ignition key.
ключево́й *прил* (*позиция, проблемы итп*) key *опред*; **ключева́я вода́** spring water.
ключи́ц|а (**-ы**) *ж* collarbone.

клю́ш|ка (**-ки**; *gen pl* **-ек**) *ж* (*ХОККЕЙ*) hockey stick; (*ГОЛЬФ*) club.
кля́кс|а (**-ы**) *ж* smudge.
кляну́(сь) *итп несов см* **кля́сть(ся)**.
кля́нч|ить (**-у, -ишь**; *perf* **вы́клянчить**) *несов перех* (*разг*): ~ **что-н у кого́-н** to pester sb for sth.
кляп (**-а**) *м* gag; **засу́нуть** (*perf*) **кому́-н ~ в рот** to gag sb.
кля|сть (**-ну́, -нёшь**; *pt* **-л, -ла́, -ло**) *несов перех* to curse
▸ **кля́сться** (*perf* **покля́сться**) *несов возв* to swear; **кля́сться (покля́сться** *perf*) **в ве́чной любви́** to swear eternal love; **кля́сться (покля́сться** *perf*) **жи́знью/Бо́гу** to swear on one's life/to God.
кля́тв|а (**-ы**) *ж* oath; **дава́ть (дать** *perf*)/ **сде́рживать (сдержа́ть** *perf*) **~у** to take *или* swear/keep an oath; **наруша́ть (нару́шить** *perf*) **~у** to break one's oath.
кля́уз|а (**-ы**) *ж* backbiting.
кля́узен *прил см* **кля́узный**.
кля́узник (**-а**) *м* (*пренебр*) scandalmonger.
кля́узнича|ть (**-ю**; *perf* **накля́узничать**) *несов неперех*: ~ (**на** *+acc*) to spread gossip (about).
кля́уз|ный (**-ен, -на, -но**) *прил*: **~ное письмо́** slanderous letter.
кля́ч|а (**-и**) *ж* (*разг*: *пренебр*: *лошадь*) old nag.
км. *сокр* (= **киломе́тр**) km (= *kilometre* (*BRIT*) *или kilometer* (*US*)).
км/ч *сокр* (= *киломе́тров в час*) km/h (= *kilometres per hour*).
КНДР *ж сокр* (= *Коре́йская Наро́дно-Демократи́ческая Респу́блика*) DPRK (= *Democratic People's Republic of Korea*).
кне́л|и (**-ей**) *мн* quenelles *мн*.
кни́г|а (**-и**) *ж* book; **ка́ссовая** ~ cash-book; **телефо́нная** ~ telephone book *или* directory; ~ **зака́зов** order book; ~ **учёта** day book; **кни́га жа́лоб и предложе́ний** suggestions book.
книголю́б (**-а**) *м* book-lover.
книгопеча́тани|е (**-я**) *ср* book printing.
кни́ж|ка (**-ки**; *gen pl* **-ек**) *ж* book; **записна́я** ~ notebook; **зачётная** ~ (*ПРОСВЕЩ*) register; **трудова́я** ~ employment record book; **че́ковая** ~ chequebook (*BRIT*), checkbook (*US*).
кни́жник (**-а**) *м* (*знаток книг*) bibliophile.
кни́жный *прил* (*перен*: *знания, стиль*) bookish; **кни́жный магази́н** bookshop; **кни́жный шкаф** bookcase; **кни́жный червь** bookworm.
кни́зу *нареч* downwards.
кно́п|ка (**-ки**; *gen pl* **-ок**) *ж* (*звонка, лифта*) button; (*канцелярская*) drawing pin (*BRIT*), thumbtack (*US*); (*застёжка*) press stud, popper (*BRIT*).
КНР *ж сокр* (= *Кита́йская Наро́дная Респу́блика*) PRC (= *People's Republic of China*).
кнут (**-а́**) *м* whip; **поли́тика ~а́ и пря́ника** the carrot and the stick policy.
княги́н|я (**-и**) *ж* princess (*wife of a prince*).
кня́ж|ить (**-у, -ишь**) *несов неперех* to reign.
княж|на́ (**-ны́**; *gen pl* **-о́н**) *ж* princess (*daughter of a prince*).
княз|ь (**-я**; *nom pl* **-ья́**, *gen pl* **-е́й**) *м* prince (*in Russia*); **вели́кий** ~ (*ИСТ*) grand prince (*son or brother of the tsar*).
ко *предл см* **к**.
коагули́р|овать (*3sg* **-ует**, *3pl* **-уют**) *несов перех* to coagulate.
коагуля́ци|я (**-и**) *ж* coagulation.
коа́л|а (**-ы**) *ж* koala (bear).
коалицио́нн|ый *прил*: **~ое прави́тельство** coalition government; ~ **догово́р** coalition pact.
коали́ци|я (**-и**) *ж* coalition.
ко́бальт (**-а**) *м* cobalt.
кобе́л|ь (**-я́**) *м* dog (*male*).
ко́бр|а (**-ы**) *ж* cobra.
кобур|а́ (**-ы́**) *ж* holster.
кобы́л|а (**-ы**) *ж* mare; (*перен*: *разг*) strapping lass.
ко́ван|ый (**-, -а, -о**) *прил* (*меч, решётка итп*) forged; (*обитый железом*) metal-bound.
кова́рен *прил см* **кова́рный**.
кова́рност|ь (**-и**) *ж* treachery.
кова́р|ный (**-ен, -на, -но**) *прил* devious.
кова́рств|о (**-а**) *ср* deviousness.
кова́ть (**кую́, куёшь**; *imper* **куй(те)**, *perf* **скова́ть**) *несов перех* to forge; **куй желе́зо пока́ горячо́** strike while the iron's hot.
ковбо́|й (**-я**) *м* cowboy.
ков|ёр (**-ра́**) *м* carpet; **вызыва́ть (вы́звать** *perf*) **на ~ кого́-н** to call sb to account.
кове́ркань|е (**-я**) *ср* mangling.
кове́рка|ть (**-ю**; *perf* **искове́ркать**) *несов перех* (*произношение, слова*) to mangle; (*язык*) to butcher; (*душу*) to twist; **коверка́ть (исковерка́ть** *perf*) **чью-н мысль/чьи-н слова́** to twist sb's ideas/words.
ко́вк|а (**-и**) *ж* forging.
ковра́ *итп сущ см* **ковёр**.
коври́г|а (**-и**) *ж* loaf (*мн* loaves).
коври́ж|ка (**-ки**; *gen pl* **-ек**) *ж* ≈ gingerbread.
ко́врик (**-а**) *м* rug; (*дверной*) mat; **~ для мы́шки** mouse pad.
ковро́в|ый *прил*: **~ая доро́жка** runner.
коврodéли|е (**-я**) *ср* carpet weaving.
ковче́г (**-а**) *м*: **Но́ев ~** Noah's Ark.
ковш (**-а́**) *м* ladle; (*экскаватора*) shovel.
ковы́л|ь (**-я́**) *м* (*БОТ*) feather grass.
ковыля́|ть (**-ю**) *несов неперех* to hobble.
ковыря́|ть (**-ю**) *несов перех* to dig up; ~ (*impf*) **в зуба́х/носу́** to pick one's teeth/nose
▸ **ковыря́ться** *несов возв* (*медлить*) to faff about; **~ся** (*impf*) (**в** *+prp*) (*копаться*: *в земле*) to root *или* poke about (in).
когда́ *нареч* when; (*иногда*) sometimes; **~ ты зако́нчишь?** when will you finish?; **мы не зна́ем, ~ э́то произошло́** we don't know when it happened; **~ пью ко́фе, ~ чай** sometimes I drink coffee, sometimes tea.
когда́-либо *нареч* = **когда́-нибудь**.
когда́-нибудь *нареч* (*в вопросительных предложениях*) ever; (*в утвердительных

предложениях) some *или* one day; **Вы ~ там были?** have you ever been there?; **я ~ туда́ пое́ду** I'll go there some *или* one day.
когда́-то *нареч* once; **он был ~ бога́т** he was once a rich man; **~ ещё я туда́ пое́ду** just when will I have another chance to go there?
кого́ *мест от* **кто.**
когópт|a (-ы) *ж* (*перен*) cohort.
кóг|оть (-тя; *gen pl* **-те́й)** *м* (*кошки, льва итп*) claw; (*орла*) talon; **пока́зывать (показа́ть** *perf*) **~ти** (*перен*) to bare one's teeth.
код (-а) *м* code; **передава́ть (переда́ть** *perf*) **сообще́ние по ко́ду** to send a message in code; **~ си́мвола** (*КОМП*) character code.
кодеин (-а) *м* codeine.
ко́декс (-а) *м* code; **гражда́нский/уголо́вный ~** (*ЮР*) civil/criminal code.
коди́р|овать (-ую; *perf* **закоди́ровать)** *несов перех* to encode, code.
кодиро́вк|а (-и) *ж* coding.
кодиро́вщик (-а) *м* coder.
коди́рующ|ий (-ая, -ее, -ие) *прил*: **~ее устро́йство** (*КОМП*) encoder.
кодифика́ци|я (-и) *ж* (*ЮР*) codification.
кодифици́р|овать (-ую) *(не)сов перех* (*ЮР*) to codify.
ко́дов|ый *прил*: **~ые зна́ки** code symbols *мн*; **ко́довое назва́ние** codename.
ко́е-где́ *нареч* here and there.
ко́ек *сущ см* **ко́йка.**
ко́е-ка́к *нареч* (*небрежно*) any old how; (*с трудом*) somehow.
ко́е-како́й (ко́е-како́го) *мест* some; **нам нужна́ ко́е-кака́я по́мощь** we need some sort of help.
ко́е-когда́ *нареч* now and then, now and again.
ко́е-кто́ (ко́е-кого́) *мест* (*некоторые*) some (people).
ко́е-куда́ *нареч* (*разг*) this place and that.
ко́е-что́ (ко́е-чего́) *мест* (*нечто*) something; (*немногое*) a little.
ко́ж|а (-и) *ж* skin; (*материал*) leather; (*апельсина, яблока*) peel; **гуси́ная ~** goose bumps *мн или* pimples *мн*; **~ да ко́сти** (*разг*) all skin and bone; **из ~и вон лезть** *(impf)* to sweat blood.
ко́жаный *прил* leather.
коже́венный *прил* leather; **коже́венный заво́д** tannery.
ко́жник (-а) *м* (*МЕД*) dermatologist.
ко́жн|ый *прил*: **~ые боле́зни** skin diseases; **ко́жный врач** dermatologist; **ко́жный покро́в** skin.
кожур|а́ (-ы́) *ж* (*апельсина*) peel; (*ореха*) skin.
коз|а́ (-ы́; *nom pl* **-ы)** *ж* (nanny) goat.
ко́зел *сущ см* **ко́злы.**
коз|ёл (-ла́; *nom pl* **-лы́)** *м* (billy) goat; (*в гимнастике*) horse; (*разг: игра*) dominoes; **от него́ как от ~ла́ молока́** (*разг*) he's worse than useless; **забива́ть** *(impf)* **~ла́** to play dominoes; **козёл отпуще́ния** scapegoat.
Козеро́г (-а) *м* (*созвездие*) Capricorn.
ко́з|ий (-ья, -ье, -ьи) *прил* goat *опред*; **~ье молоко́** goat's milk.
козла́ *итп сущ см* **козёл.**
козлёнок (-ёнка; *nom pl* **-я́та,** *gen pl* **-я́т)** *м* (*ЗООЛ*) kid.
козли́н|ый *прил* (*голос*) reedy; **~ая боро́дка** goatee.
ко́зл|ы (-ел) *мн* (*сиденье*) coach box *ед*; (*опора*) trestle *ед*.
козля́та *итп сущ см* **козлёнок.**
ко́зн|и (-ей) *мн* intrigues *мн*; **стро́ить** *(impf)* **~** to scheme.
козырёк (-ька́) *м* (*картуза, фуражки*) peak; (*навес*) lintel; **брать (взять** *perf*) **под ~** to salute.
козырн|о́й *прил*: **~а́я ка́рта** trump.
козыр|ну́ть (-ну́, -нёшь) *сов от* **козыря́ть.**
ко́зыр|ь (-я) *м* (*КАРТЫ*) trump; (*перен*) trump card.
козырька́ *сущ см* **козырёк.**
козыря́|ть (-ю; *perf* **козырну́ть)** *несов неперех* (*разг: в картах*) to play a trump; (*хвастаться*): **~** *+instr* to show off about; (*: отдавать честь*): **~ть** *+dat* to salute.
козя́в|ка (-ки; *gen pl* **-ок)** *ж* (*разг: букашка*) bug; (*: пренебр: человек*) small fry *только ед*.
ко́|йка (-йки; *gen pl* **-ек)** *ж* (*на судне*) berth; (*в казарме*) bunk; (*в больнице, общежитии*) bed.
кок (-а) *м* (*повар*) ship's cook; (*вихор*) quiff.
кокаин (-а) *м* cocaine.
кокаини́ст (-а) *м* cocaine addict.
кокаини́ст|ка (-ки; *gen pl* **-ок)** *ж см* **кокаини́ст.**
кока́рд|а (-ы) *ж* cockade.
коке́т|ка (-ки; *gen pl* **-ок)** *ж* flirt, coquette.
коке́тливост|ь (-и) *ж* flirtatiousness.
коке́тлив|ый (-, -а, -о) *прил* (*девушка, взгляд, смех*) flirtatious; (*шапочка, платье итп*) pretty.
коке́тнича|ть (-ю) *несов неперех* to flirt.
коке́ток *сущ см* **коке́тка.**
коке́тств|о (-а) *ср* flirting.
коклю́ш (-а) *м* whooping cough.
КОКОМ *сокр* COCOM.
ко́кон (-а) *м* cocoon.
коко́с (-а) *м* coconut.
коко́сов|ый *прил*: **~ая па́льма** coconut palm; **коко́совое молоко́** coconut milk; **коко́совый оре́х** coconut.
кокс (-а) *м* coke.
коксов|а́ть (-у́ю) *несов перех* (*ТЕХ*) to coke.
кокте́йл|ь (-я) *м* cocktail.
кол (-а́; *loc sg* **-у́,** *nom pl* **-ья,** *gen pl* **-ьев)** *м* stake; (*nom pl* **-ы́**; *разг: ПРОСВЕЩ*) ≈ E (*school mark*); **у меня́ нет ни ~а́ ни двора́** I don't have a thing to my name; **(ему́** *итп*) **хоть ~ на голове́ чеши** it's like talking to a brick wall.

ко́лб|а (-ы) *ж (ХИМ)* flask.
колбас|а́ (-ы́) *ж* sausage.
кол-во *сокр (= количество)* amt (= *amount*).
колго́т|ки (-ок) *мн* tights *мн (BRIT)*, panty hose *мн (US)*.
колдо́бин|а (-ы) *ж (на дороге)* pothole.
колд|ова́ть (-у́ю) *несов неперех* to practise (*BRIT*) *или* practice (*US*) witchcraft; *(перен)*: ~ **над** *+instr (над картиной, над ужином итп)* to conjure up.
колдовско́й *прил* magical; *(перен)* bewitching.
колдовств|о́ (-а́) *ср* sorcery, witchcraft.
колду́н (-а́) *м* wizard, sorcerer.
колду́н|ья (-ьи; *gen pl* **-ий,** *dat pl* **-ьям)** *ж* sorceress.
колеба́ни|е (-я) *ср (ФИЗ)* oscillation; *(маятника)* swing; *(почвы, здания)* vibration; *(перен: цен, температуры)* fluctuation; (: *обычно мн: нерешительность*) wavering, vacillation.
колеба́тельный *прил (ФИЗ)* oscillatory.
кол|еба́ть (-е́блю, -е́блешь) *несов перех* to rock, swing; *(perf* **поколеба́ть**; *авторитет)* to shake
▸ **колеба́ться** *(perf* **поколеба́ться***) несов возв (ФИЗ)* to oscillate; *(листья, пламя итп)* to flicker; *(цены, погода)* to fluctuate; *(сомневаться)* to waver, vacillate.
коле́блющ|ийся (-аяся, -ееся, -иеся) *прил (свет, тени)* flickering; *(человек)* vacillating.
коленко́р (-а) *м* calico.
коленко́ровый *прил* calico.
коле́нн|ый *прил*: **~ая ча́шка** kneecap.
коле́н|о (-а; *nom pl* **-и,** *gen pl* **-ей)** *ср* knee; *(nom pl* **-а**; *трубы)* joint; *(разг: МУЗ)* phrase; *(поколение)* generation; **встава́ть (встать** *perf)* **на ~и** to kneel (down); **стоя́ть** *(impf)* **на ~ях** to be kneeling (down); **опуска́ться (опусти́ться** *perf)* **на ~и** to go down on one's knees; **сиде́ть** *(impf)* **у кого́-н на ~ях** to sit on sb's knee *или* lap; **поста́вить** *(perf)* **кого́-н на ~и** *(перен)* to bring sb to his *итп* knees; **ей мо́ре по ~** everything washes straight over her.
коленопреклонённый *прил* kneeling.
коле́нчатый *прил*: **~ вал** crankshaft.
ко́лер (-а) *м* colour (*BRIT*), color (*US*).
колёсик|о (-а) *ср уменьш от* **колесо́**; *(часовое)* wheel.
коле|си́ть (-шу́, -си́шь) *несов неперех* to get around; **я ~си́л по всему́ го́роду** I've been all over town.
колесни́ц|а (-ы) *ж* chariot.
кол|есо́ (-еса́; *nom pl* **-ёса)** *ср* wheel; **пя́тое ~** *(перен)* fifth wheel (*fig*); **жизнь на ~ёсах** life on the road; **жить** *(impf)* **на ~ёсах** to live out of a suitcase.
коле́ц *сущ см* **кольцо́**.
колешу́ *несов см* **колеси́ть**.
коле|я́ (-и́) *ж (на дороге)* rut; *(для поездов)* track; *(перен)* routine; **выбива́ть (вы́бить** *perf)* **из ~и́** to get out of a rut.
ко́лик|и (-) *мн* colic *ед*.
коли́чественный *прил* quantitative.
коли́честв|о (-а) *ср* quantity.
ко́лк|а (-и) *ж (дров)* chopping; *(льда)* breaking up.
ко́л|кий (-кая, -кое, -кие; -ок, -ка́, -ко) *прил (хвоя, трава)* prickly; *(перен: шутка, замечания)* biting.
ко́лкост|ь (-и) *ж (нрава, замечаний)* abrasiveness; *(насмешка)* biting remark.
коллаборациони́зм (-а) *м* collaborationism.
коллаборациони́ст (-а) *м* collaborator.
колла́ж (-а) *м* collage.
колле́г|а (-и) *м/ж* colleague.
коллегиа́лен *прил см* **коллегиа́льный**.
коллегиа́льност|ь (-и) *ж*: **при́нцип ~и** collective responsibility.
коллегиа́л|ьный (-ен, -ьна, -ьно) *прил* collective.
колле́ги|я (-и) *ж (ПОЛИТ)* collegium (*executive body in charge of government ministry*); **адвока́тская ~** ≈ the Bar; **редакцио́нная ~** editorial board.
ко́лледж (-а) *м* college.
коллекти́в (-а) *м* collective; **а́вторский ~** (team of) contributors.
коллекти́вен *прил см* **коллекти́вный**.
коллективиза́ци|я (-и) *ж (ИСТ)* collectivization (*creation of collective farms in the late 1920's and 1930's*).
коллекти́в|ный (-ен, -на, -но) *прил* collective.
колле́ктор (-а) *м (библиотечный)* book depository; *(канализационный)* manifold; *(ЭЛЕК)* collector.
коллекционе́р (-а) *м* collector.
коллекциони́ровани|е (-я) *ср* collecting.
коллекциони́р|овать (-ую) *несов перех* to collect.
коллекцио́нный *прил* collectable.
колле́кци|я (-и) *ж* collection.
ко́лли *ж нескл* collie.
колли́зи|я (-и) *ж* clash.
колло́квиум (-а) *м (ПРОСВЕЩ)* seminar; *(совещание специалистов)* colloquium.
коловоро́т (-а) *м (водоворот)* eddy; *(ТЕХ)* ice drill; *(перен: столпотворение)* hurly-burly; **~ собы́тий** the vortex of events.
коло́д|а (-ы) *ж (бревно)* block; *(карт)* pack, deck; **че́рез пень ~у** half-heartedly.
коло́дезн|ый *прил*: **~ая вода́** water from the well.
коло́д|ец (-ца) *м* well; *(в шахте)* shaft.
коло́д|ка (-ки; *gen pl* **-ок)** *ж (обувная)* shoetree; *(орденская)* strip.
коло́дца *итп сущ см* **коло́дец**.
ко́лок *прил см* **ко́лкий**.
ко́локол (-а; *nom pl* **-а́)** *м* bell; **звони́ть** *(impf)* **в ~** to ring a bell.
колоко́л|ьня (-ьни; *gen pl* **-ен)** *ж* bell tower; **смотре́ть** *(impf)* **со свое́й ~ьни на что-н** to take a narrow view of sth.
колоко́льчик (-а) *м* bell; *(БОТ)* bluebell.

колониали́зм (-а) *м* colonialism.
колониа́льный *прил* colonial.
колониза́тор (-а) *м* colonizer.
колонизи́р|овать (-ую) *(не)сов перех* to colonize.
колониз|ова́ть (-у́ю) *(не)сов* = **колонизи́ровать.**
колони́ст (-а) *м* colonist.
колони́ст|ка (-ки; *gen pl* -ок) *ж см* **колони́ст.**
коло́ни|я (-и) *ж* colony; **исправи́тельно-трудова́я** ~ penal colony; ~ **для малоле́тних престу́пников** *или* **несовершенноле́тних** young offenders' institution.
коло́н|ка (-ки; *gen pl* -ок) *ж* column; (*газовая*) geyser (*BRIT*), water heater; (*для воды, для бензина*) pump.
колонка́ *сущ см* **колоно́к.**
колонко́вый *прил* polecat *опред.*
коло́нн|а (-ы) *ж* (*АРХИТ*) column; (*ряд*): ~ **солда́т/демонстра́нтов** column of soldiers/ demonstrators.
колонна́д|а (-ы) *ж* colonnade.
коло́нок *сущ см* **коло́нка.**
колон|о́к (-ка́) *м* polecat.
колорату́рн|ый *прил*: ~**ое сопра́но** coloratura (*soprano*).
колори́т (-а) *м* (*перен*: *эпохи, страны итп*) colour (*BRIT*), color (*US*); (*ИСКУССТВО*) use of colour; **ме́стный** ~ local colour.
колори́т|ный (-ен, -на, -но) *прил* colourful (*BRIT*), colorful (*US*).
ко́л|ос (-оса; *nom pl* -о́сья, *gen pl* -о́сьев) *м* ear (*of corn, wheat*).
коло́сс (-а) *м* (*также перен*) colossus; ~ **на гли́няных нога́х** a giant with feet of clay.
колосса́л|ьный (-ен, -ьна, -ьно) *прил* colossal; ~**ьно!** that's fantastic!
кол|оти́ть (-очу́, -о́тишь) *несов неперех* (*по столу, в дверь*) to thump ◆ *перех* (*разг*: *бить*) to whack; **меня́** ~**о́тит (дрожь)** I'm shaking all over
▸ **колоти́ться** *несов возв* (*сердце*) to thump; ~**ся** *(impf)* **в дверь** to thump on the door.
ко́лот|ый *прил*: ~ **са́хар** lump sugar; ~**ая ра́на** stab wound.
кол|о́ть (-ю́, -ешь; *perf* **расколо́ть**) *несов перех* (*дрова*) to chop (up); (*орехи*) to crack; (*perf* **заколо́ть**; *штыком итп*) to spear; (*perf* **уколо́ть**; *иголкой*) to prick; (*разг*: *делать укол*): ~ **кого́-н** to give sb an injection; ~ *(impf)* **кому́-н что-н** (*разг*) to inject sb with sth; **у меня́ ко́лет в боку́** I've got a stitch; **пра́вда глаза́ ко́лет** the truth is hard to swallow
▸ **коло́ться** *несов возв* (*ёж, шиповник*) to be prickly; (*орех*) to crack; (*наркоман*) to be on drugs.
колочу́(сь) *несов см* **колоти́ть(ся).**
колпа́к (-а́) *м* (*шутовской, поварской*) hat; (*лампы*) lampshade.
колпач|о́к (-ка́) *м уменьш от* **колпа́к**; (*контрацептив*) (Dutch) cap.
колумби́йск|ий (-ая, -ое, -ие) *прил* Columbian.
Колу́мби|я (-и) *ж* Columbia.
колупа́|ть (-ю) *несов перех* (*разг*) to scratch.
колхо́з (-а) *м* kolkhoz, collective farm.
колхо́зник (-а) *м* kolkhoznik, collective farmer.
колхо́зный *прил* kolkhoz *опред*, collective farm *опред.*
колча́н (-а) *м* quiver.
колчеда́н (-а) *м* pyrite.
колыбе́л|ь (-и) *ж* (*также перен*) cradle; **с** ~**и** (*перен*) from the cradle.
колыбе́льн|ая (-ой; *decl like adj*) *ж* (*также:* ~ **пе́сня**) lullaby.
колыма́г|а (-и) *ж* (*разг*: *машина*) old banger.
колыха́ни|е (-я) *ср* rocking, swaying.
кол|ыха́ть (-ы́шу, -ы́шешь) *несов перех* to rock
▸ **колыха́ться** *несов возв* (*море, грудь*) to heave; (*трава, дерево*) to sway.
ко́лыш|ек (-ка) *м уменьш от* **кол**; (*для палатки*) (tent) peg.
колы́шу(сь) *итп несов см* **колыха́ть(ся).**
колье́ *ср нескл* necklace.
кольн|у́ть (-у́, -ёшь) *сов перех* (*иголькой*) to prick; (*перен*: *обидным намёком*) to sting; **у меня́** ~**у́ло в спине́** a pain shot up my back.
кольра́би *ж нескл* kohlrabi.
кольт (-а) *м* automatic (revolver).
кольцева́ть (-у́ю) *несов перех* to ring.
кольцево́й *прил* round, circular; **кольцева́я доро́га** ring road; **кольцева́я ли́ния** circle line.
кол|ьцо́ (-ьца́; *nom pl* -ьца, *gen pl* -е́ц) *ср* ring; (*в маршруте автобуса итп*) circle.
кольчу́г|а (-и) *ж* (*ИСТ*) chain-mail shirt.
ко́лья *сущ см* **кол.**
колю́чек *сущ см* **колю́чка.**
колю́ч|ий (-ая, -ее, -ие; -, -а, -е) *прил* (*куст, усы, мороз*) prickly; (*перен*: *насмешка, замечание, юмор*) barbed; **колю́чая про́волока** barbed wire.
колю́ч|ка (-ки; *gen pl* -ек) *ж* (*чертополоха, розы*) thorn; (*проволоки*) barb.
коля́д|ка (-ки; *gen pl* -ок) *ж* ≈ Christmas carol (*sung in rural Russia*).
колядова́ть (-у́ю) *несов неперех* ≈ to go carol singing.
коля́док *сущ см* **коля́дка.**
коля́с|ка (-ки; *gen pl* -ок) *ж* (*экипаж*) carriage; (*детская*) pram (*BRIT*), baby carriage (*US*); (*инвалидная*) wheelchair.
ком *мест см* **кто** ◆ (-а; *nom pl* -ья, *gen pl* -ьев) *м* lump; **у меня́** ~ **к го́рлу подкати́л** I felt a lump in my throat; **пе́рвый блин ко́мом** ... (*перен*) ≈ if at first you don't succeed ....
ко́м|а (-ы) *ж* coma.

The spelling rules for Russian are shown on page xvii.

кома́нд|а (-ы) *ж* command; (*судна*) crew; (*СПОРТ*) team; **пожа́рная ~** fire brigade; **~ президе́нта** presidential team; **быть** *(impf)* **под ~ой кого́-н** to be under sb.

команди́р (-а) *м* commander, commanding officer.

командиро́ванн|ый (-ого; *decl like adj*) *м* = **командиро́вочный**.

командир|ова́ть (-у́ю) *(не)сов перех* to post; **его́ ~ова́ли в Москву́** he has been posted to Moscow.

командиро́в|ка (-ки; *gen pl* -ок) *ж* (*короткая*) business trip; (*длительная*) secondment (*BRIT*), posting; **е́хать (пое́хать** *perf***) в ~ку** to go away on business; **получа́ть (получи́ть** *perf***) ~ку** to be seconded (*BRIT*) *или* posted.

командиро́вочн|ые (-ых; *decl like adj*) *мн* (*деньги*) subsistence allowance *ед*.

командиро́вочн|ый *прил*: **~ое удостовере́ние** *permit issued to employee travelling on official business* ◆ (-ого; *decl like adj*) *м* person on business.

кома́ндн|ый *прил* command *опред*; (*должность*) managerial; (*СПОРТ*): **~ое состяза́ние** team event; **~ые высо́ты** (*ВОЕН, перен*) key positions; **кома́ндный соста́в** (*ВОЕН*) command personnel.

кома́ндовани|е (-я) *ср*: **~** (*+instr*) (*судном, войском*) command (of) ◆ *собир* (*ВОЕН*) command.

кома́нд|овать (-ую; *perf* **скома́ндовать**) *несов неперех* to give orders; (*no perf*; *+instr*; *армией*) to command; (*мужем*) to order around.

кома́ндующ|ий (-его; *decl like adj*) *м* commanding officer, commander.

кома́р (-а́) *м* mosquito (*мн* mosquitoes); **~ но́са не подто́чит** you can't fault it.

комато́зный *прил* comatose.

комба́йн (-а) *м* (*С-Х*) combine (harvester); **ку́хонный ~** food processor.

комбайнёр (-а) *м* combine operator.

комбико́рм (-а) *м сокр* (= *комбини́рованный корм*) mixed fodder.

комбина́т (-а) *м* plant; **моло́чный/пищево́й ~** dairy-/food-processing plant.

комбина́ци|я (-и) *ж* combination; (*разг: план*) scheme; (*ШАХМАТЫ*) position; (*женское бельё*) slip.

комбинезо́н (-а) *м* overalls *мн*; (*детский*) dungarees *мн*.

комбини́рованный *прил* (*метод, подход*) integrated.

комбини́р|овать (-ую; *perf* **скомбини́ровать**) *несов перех* (*блюда*) to combine; (*одежду*) to match up ◆ *неперех* (*разг*) to scheme.

комедиа́нт (-а) *м* (*также перен*) comedian.

комедиа́нт|ка (-ки; *gen pl* -ок) *ж* comedienne.

комеди́|йный (-ен, -йна, -йно) *прил* comic; (*актёр*) comedy *опред*.

коме́ди|я (-и) *ж* comedy; (*перен: смешное событие*) farce; **лома́ть** *(impf)* **~ю** to play-act.

коменда́нт (-а) *м* (*общежития, тюрьмы*) warden; (*ВОЕН*) commandant.

коменда́нтск|ий (-ая, -ое, -ие) *прил*: **~ час** curfew.

комендату́р|а (-ы) *ж* (*ВОЕН*) commandant's office.

коме́т|а (-ы) *ж* comet.

коми́зм (-а) *м* comedy; **~ ситуа́ции** the funny side of the situation.

ко́мик (-а) *м* (*актёр*) comedian, comic; (*разг: смешной человек*) comedian.

Коминте́рн (-а) *м сокр* (*ИСТ*: = *Коммунисти́ческий Интернациона́л*) Comintern.

комисса́р (-а) *м* (*ИСТ*: *также:* **Наро́дный К~**) People's Commissar; (*милиции ООН*) commissioner.

комиссионе́р (-а) *м* agent.

комиссио́н|ка (-ки; *gen pl* -ок) *ж* (*разг*) *second-hand shop which sells goods on a commission basis*.

комиссио́нн|ые (-ых; *decl like adj*) *мн* commission.

комиссио́нный *прил*: **~ магази́н** = **комиссио́нка**.

комиссио́нок *сущ см* **комиссио́нка**.

коми́сси|я (-и) *ж* (*ПОЛИТ, КОММ*) commission; **брать (взять** *perf***) что-н на ~ю** to take sth on commission; **постоя́нная ~** standing committee.

комите́т (-а) *м* committee; **Комите́т Госуда́рственной Безопа́сности** (*ИСТ*) the KGB.

коми́чен *прил см* **коми́чный**.

коми́ческ|ий (-ая, -ое, -ие) *прил* comic; **~ актёр** comic actor.

коми́ч|ный (-ен, -на, -но) *прил* comical.

комка́ *сущ см* **комо́к**.

ко́мка|ть (-ю; *perf* **ско́мкать**) *несов перех* (*письмо, бельё итп*) to crumple; (*перен: лекцию итп*) to make a mess of.

коммента́ри|й (-я) *м* (*пояснение, репортаж*) commentary; **дава́ть (дать** *perf***) ~ к чему́-н** to provide a commentary on sth; **~и изли́шни** it speaks for itself.

коммента́тор (-а) *м* commentator.

комменти́р|овать (-ую) *(не)сов перех* (*текст*) to comment on; (*события, матч*) to commentate on.

коммерса́нт (-а) *м* businessman (*мн* businessmen).

комме́рческ|ий (-ая, -ое, -ие) *прил* commercial; **комме́рческий банк** commercial bank; **комме́рческий дире́ктор** sales and finance director; **комме́рческий магази́н** privately-run shop.

коммивояжёр (-а) *м* travelling (*BRIT*) *или* traveling (*US*) salesman (*мн* salesmen).

комму́н|а (-ы) *ж* commune.

коммуна́л|ка (-ки; *gen pl* -ек) *ж* (*разг*) communal flat (*BRIT*) *или* apartment (*US*).

коммуна́льный *прил* communal; **коммуна́льная кварти́ра** communal flat (*BRIT*) *или* apartment (*US*); **коммуна́льные платежи́** bills; **коммуна́льные услу́ги** utilities.
коммуна́р (-а) *м* (*ИСТ*) member of a commune.
коммуни́зм (-а) *м* communism.
коммуника́бел|ьный (-ен, -ьна, -ьно) *прил* sociable.
коммуникати́вный *прил* (*методы*) communicative.
коммуникацио́нн|ый *прил*: **~ая ли́ния** line of communication.
коммуника́ци|я (-и) *ж* communication.
коммуни́ст (-а) *м* communist.
коммунисти́ческ|ий (-ая, -ое, -ие) *прил* communist.
коммуни́ст|ка (-ки; *gen pl* **-ок)** *ж см* **коммуни́ст.**
коммута́тор (-а) *м* (*ТЕЛ*) switchboard; (*ЭЛЕК*) commutator.
коммутацио́нн|ый *прил*: **~ая доска́** switchboard.
коммута́ци|я (-и) *ж*: **~ паке́тов/сообще́ний** (*КОМП*) packet/message switching.
коммюнике́ *ср нескл* communiqué.
ко́мнат|а (-ы) *ж* room; **ко́мната ма́тери и ребёнка** *room for mothers with young children.*
ко́мнатный *прил* indoor *опред*; **ко́мнатная температу́ра** room temperature; **ко́мнатное расте́ние** house plant.
комо́д (-а) *м* chest of drawers.
ком|о́к (-ка́) *м уменьш от* **ком**; (*ваты*) wad; **~ бума́ги** crumpled-up piece of paper; **он – ~ не́рвов** he's a bag *или* bundle of nerves.
компа́кт-диск (-а) *м* compact disc.
компа́кт|ный (-ен, -на, -но) *прил* compact; (*изложение, доклад*) concise.
компане́йск|ий (-ая, -ое, -ие) *прил* (*разг*): **он ~ па́рень** he's good company.
компа́ни|я (-и) *ж* (*друзья*) group of friends; (*КОММ*) company; **вы́пей со мной за ~ю** have a drink, to keep me company; **он тебе́ не ~** he's not the right company for you.
компаньо́н (-а) *м* companion; (*КОММ*) partner.
компаньо́н|ка (-ки; *gen pl* **-ок)** *ж* (*старой дамы*) companion.
компа́рти|я (-и) *ж* Communist party.
ко́мпас (-а) *м* compass.
компенсацио́нный *прил* compensatory.
компенса́ци|я (-и) *ж* compensation.
компенси́р|овать (-ую) *(не)сов перех* to compensate.
компете́нтен *прил см* **компете́нтный.**
компете́нтност|ь (-и) *ж* competence.
компете́нт|ный (-ен, -на, -но) *прил* competent; (*соответствующий*) appropriate.
компете́нци|я (-и) *ж* jurisdiction; **э́то не вхо́дит в на́шу ~ю** that is outside our jurisdiction.
компили́р|овать (-ую; *perf* **скомпили́ровать)** *несов перех* (*пренебр*) to cobble together.
компиляти́в|ный (-ен, -на, -но) *прил*: **~ труд** compilation.
компиля́тор (-а) *м* hack (writer).
компиля́ци|я (-и) *ж* rehash.
ко́мплекс (-а) *м* (*упражнений, мер, знаний итп*) range; **спорти́вный ~** sports complex; **ко́мплекс неполноце́нности** inferiority complex.
ко́мплексный *прил* integrated; (*соединение, число*) complex.
компле́кт (-а) *м* set.
комплекта́ци|я (-и) *ж* assembly; **отде́л ~и** (*в библиотеке*) acquisitions (department).
комплект|ова́ть (-у́ю; *perf* **укомплектова́ть)** *несов перех* to build up.
компле́кци|я (-и) *ж* build (*of person*).
комплиме́нт (-а) *м* compliment; **де́лать (сде́лать** *perf*) **кому́-н ~** to pay sb a compliment; **говори́ть** *(impf)* **~ы (кому́-н)** to pay (sb) compliments.
компози́тор (-а) *м* composer.
композицио́нный *прил* compositional.
компози́ци|я (-и) *ж* composition.
компоне́нт (-а) *м* component.
компон|ова́ть (-у́ю; *perf* **скомпонова́ть)** *несов перех* to arrange, set out.
компоно́вк|а (-и) *ж* (*материалов*) arranging.
компо́ст (-а) *м* compost.
компо́стер (-а) *м* ticket punch.
компости́р|овать (-ую; *perf* **закомпости́ровать)** *сов перех* to punch *или* clip (*ticket*).
компо́стн|ый *прил*: **~ая я́ма** compost pit.
компо́т (-а) *м* compote.
компре́сс (-а) *м* (*МЕД*) compress.
компре́ссор (-а) *м* (*ТЕХ*) compressor.
компромети́р|овать (-ую; *perf* **скомпромети́ровать)** *несов перех* to compromise.
компромети́рующ|ий (-ая, -ое, -ие) *прил* (*поступок, слова*) damaging.
компроми́сс (-а) *м* (*соглашение*) compromise; **идти́ (пойти́** *perf*) **на ~** to (make a) compromise; **приходи́ть (прийти́** *perf*) **к ~у** to come to a compromise.
компроми́ссный *прил* compromise *опред.*
компью́тер (-а) *м* computer.
компью́терный *прил* computer *опред.*
комсомо́л (-а) *м* Komsomol (*communist youth organization*).
комсомо́л|ец (-ьца) *м* komsomol member.
комсомо́л|ка (-ки; *gen pl* **-ок)** *ж см* **комсомо́лец.**
комсомо́льск|ий (-ая, -ое, -ие) *прил* komsomol *опред.*
комсомо́льца *сущ см* **комсомо́лец.**
кому́ *мест см* **кто.**

комфóрт (-а) *м* comfort.
комфортáбел|ьный (-ен, -ьна, -ьно) *прил* comfortable.
комьёв *итп сущ см* **ком.**
кон (-а; *nom pl* **-ы**, *gen pl* **-óв**) *м* (*партия*) round; (*для ставки*) kitty; (*место*: *в городках*) wicket.
конвéйер (-а) *м* conveyor (belt); **постáвить** (*perf*) **что-н на** ~ to mass-produce sth; (*перен*) to churn sth out.
конвéйерн|ый *прил*: **~ая лéнта** conveyor belt.
конвéнци|я (-и) *ж* convention.
конвергéнци|я (-и) *ж* convergence.
конвéрси|я (-и) *ж* conversion.
конвéрт (-а) *м* (*почтовый*) envelope; (*для младенца*) baby nest.
конверти́р|овать (**-ую**) (*не*)*сов перех* to convert.
конверти́руемый *прил* convertible.
конвóир (-а) *м* escort.
конвои́р|овать (**-ую**) *несов перех* to escort.
конвó|й (-я) *м* escort; **под ~ем** under escort.
конвóйн|ый *прил* escort *опред* ◆ (**-ого**; *decl like adj*) *м* escort.
конвýльси|я (-и) *ж* convulsion.
конгломерáт (-а) *м* conglomerate.
Кóнго *ср нескл* Congo (*river and state*).
конголéзск|ий (**-ая, -ое, -ие**) *прил* Congolese.
конгрéсс (-а) *м* (*съезд*) congress; (**в** *США*) Congress.
конгрессмéн (-а) *м* Congressman (*мн* Congressmen).
конденсáтор (-а) *м* condenser.
конденсáци|я (-и) *ж* condensation.
конденси́р|оваться (*3sg* **-уется**, *3pl* **-уются**) (*не*)*сов возв* to condense.
конди́тер (-а) *м* confectioner.
конди́терск|ая (**-ой**; *decl like adj*) *ж* confectioner's.
конди́терск|ий (**-ая, -ое, -ие**) *прил* confectionery *опред*; **конди́терский магази́н** confectioner's.
кондиционéр (-а) *м* air conditioner.
кондициóнный *прил* (*условия поставки*) conditional; (*продукт, овощи итп*) up to standard.
конди́ци|я (-и) *ж* standard; **я сейчáс не в ~и** (*разг*) I'm not in good shape at the moment; **доводи́ть (довести́** *perf*) **что-н до ~и** to bring sth up to scratch.
кондóвый *прил* diehard *опред*.
кондрáшк|а (-и) *ж*: **егó хвати́ла** ~ (*разг*) he had a fit.
кондýктор (-а) *м* (*автобуса*) conductor; (*поезда*) guard.
коневóд (-а) *м* horse-breeder.
коневóдств|о (-а) *ср* horse-breeding.
кон|ёк (**-ькá**) *м уменьш от* **конь**; (*обычно мн*: *СПОРТ*) skate; (*перен*: *любимая тема*) hobbyhorse; **катáться** (*impf*) **на ~ькáх** to skate; **сади́ться** (*impf*) **на своегó ~ькá** to get on(to) one's hobbyhorse; **морскóй** ~ sea horse; *см также* **коньки́**.
кон|éц (**-цá**) *м* end; **без ~цá** endlessly; **из концá в** ~ from end to end; **и дéло с ~цóм** (*разг*) and that's the end of it; **в ~цé концóв** in the end; **билéт в оди́н** ~ single (*BRIT*) *или* one-way ticket; **мне** ~ (*разг*) I'm done for; **своди́ть** (*impf*) **~цы́ с ~цáми** to make ends meet; **на худóй** ~ (*разг*) if the worst comes to the worst; **под** ~ towards the end; **отдáть** (*perf*) **~цы́** (*разг*) to kick the bucket.
конéчно *вводн сл* of course, certainly; **мне мóжно закури́ть? – ~** may I smoke? – of course.
конéчност|ь (-и) *ж* (*обычно мн*) limb.
конéч|ный (**-ен, -на, -но**) *прил* (*цель, итог*) final; (*станция, остановка*) last; **в ~ном счёте** *или* **итóге** in the final analysis; **конéчный пóльзователь** (*КОМП*) end user.
кони́н|а (-ы) *ж* horse meat.
кони́ческ|ий (**-ая, -ое, -ие**) *прил* conical.
конкрéтен *прил см* **конкрéтный.**
конкретизи́р|овать (**-ую**) (*не*)*сов перех*: ~ **что-н** to make sth more concrete.
конкрéтно *нареч* (*говорить*) specifically.
конкрéт|ный (**-ен, -на, -но**) *прил* (*реальный*) concrete; (*факт*) actual.
конкурéнт (-а) *м* competitor.
конкурéнтк|а (-и) *ж см* **конкурéнт.**
конкурéнтн|ый *прил*: **~ая борьбá** competition.
конкурентоспосóб|ный (**-ен, -на, -но**) *прил* competitive.
конкурéнци|я (-и) *ж* competition; **наш товáр вне ~и** our product is in a class of its own.
конкури́р|овать (**-ую**) *несов неперех*: ~ **с** *+instr* to compete with.
кóнкурс (-а) *м* competition; **проходи́ть (пройти́** *perf*) **вне ~а** *to be admitted to university etc under special provisions*; **проходи́ть (пройти́** *perf*) **по ~у** to attain the pass mark.
кóнкурсн|ый *прил* competition *опред*; **~ая коми́ссия** (*в университете*) examining committee; (*в состязании*) judging panel; **кóнкурсный экзáмен** entrance examination.
кóнниц|а (-ы) *ж* cavalry.
конногвардé|ец (**-йца**) *м* cavalryman (*мн* cavalrymen).
коннозавóдчик (-а) *м* stud-farm owner.
кóнный *прил* (*двор, сбруя*) horse *опред*; **кóнная áрмия** cavalry; **кóнный завóд** stud farm; **кóнная мили́ция** mounted police.
конопá|тить (**-чу, -тишь**; *perf* **законопáтить**) *несов перех* (*сруб, лодку, пол итп*) to patch up.
конопáт|ый (**-, -а, -о**) *прил* (*разг*: *веснушчатый*) freckled.
конопáчу *несов см* **конопáтить.**
конопл|я́ (**-и́**) *ж* hemp.
конопля́ный *прил* hemp.
коносáмент (-а) *м* bill of lading.
консервати́вност|ь (-и) *ж* conservatism.
консервати́в|ный (**-ен, -на, -но**) *прил* conservative.

консервáтор (-а) *м* conservative; (*полит*) Conservative.
консерватóри|я (-и) *ж* (*муз*) conservatoire (*BRIT*), conservatory (*US*).
консервáци|я (-и) *ж* (*стройки*) suspension; (*продуктов, здания*) preservation.
консервúровани|е (-я) *ср* (*в жестяных банках*) canning; (*в стеклянных банках*) bottling.
консервúрованный *прил* (*см сущ*) canned; bottled.
консервúр|овать (-ую) *(не)сов перех* to preserve; (*в жестяных банках*) to can; (*в стеклянных банках*) to bottle; (*стройку*) to suspend.
консéрвный *прил*: ~ **завóд** canned-food factory; **консéрвная бáнка** can.
консéрв|ы (-ов) *мн* canned food *ед*.
консúлиум (-а) *м consultation between doctors about a patient*.
консистéнци|я (-и) *ж* consistency.
кóнск|ий (-ая, -ое, -ие) *прил* horse's.
консолидáци|я (-и) *ж* consolidation.
консолидúр|овать (-ую) *(не)сов перех* to consolidate.
консóл|ь (-и) *ж* cantilever.
консóрциум (-а) *м* consortium.
конспéкт (-а) *м* notes *мн*.
конспектúв|ный (-ен, -на, -но) *прил*: **в ~ной фóрме** in note form.
конспектúр|овать (-ую; *perf* **законспектúровать**) *несов перех* to take notes on.
конспиратúвный *прил* conspiratorial; **конспиратúвная квартúра** safe house.
конспирáтор (-а) *м* conspirator.
конспирáци|я (-и) *ж* conspiracy.
констатáци|я (-и) *ж*: ~ **фáктов** stating of the facts.
констатúр|овать (-ую) *(не)сов перех* to certify; (*факты*) to state.
конституциóнный *прил* constitutional.
конститýци|я (-и) *ж* constitution.
конструúр|овать (-ую; *perf* **сконструúровать**) *несов перех* to construct.
конструктúвен *прил см* **конструктúвный**.
конструктúвност|ь (-и) *ж* constructiveness.
конструктúв|ный *прил* construction *опред*; (-ен, -на, -но; *замысл, идея*) constructive.
констрýктор (-а) *м* designer; (*детская игра*) construction set; **инженéр-~** mechanical engineer.
констрýкторск|ий (-ая, -ое, -ие) *прил*: **~ое бюрó** design studio.
констрýкци|я (-и) *ж* construction.
кóнсул (-а) *м* consul.
кóнсульск|ий (-ая, -ое, -ие) *прил* consular.
кóнсульств|о (-а) *ср* consulate.
консультáнт (-а) *м* consultant.
консультациóнный *прил* consultative.
консультáци|я (-и) *ж* (*у врача, у юриста*) consultation; (*учреждение*) consultancy; **жéнская ~** ≈ gynaecological and antenatal (*BRIT*) *или* gynecological and prenatal (*US*) clinic; **давáть (дать** *perf*) **~ю комý-н** to give professional advice to sb.
консультúр|овать (-ую; *perf* **проконсультúровать**) *несов перех* to give professional advice to
▸ **консультúроваться** (*impf* **проконсультúроваться**) *несов возв*: **~ся с кем-н** to consult sb.
контáкт (-а) *м* contact.
контáкт|ный (-ен, -на, -но) *прил* (*человек*) approachable; **контáктные лúнзы** contact lenses; **контáктный телефóн** contact number.
контéйнер (-а) *м* container.
контéкст (-а) *м* context; **в ~е** *+gen* in the context of.
контингéнт (-а) *м* contingent.
континéнт (-а) *м* continent.
континентáльный *прил* continental.
контóр|а (-ы) *ж* office.
контóрск|ий (-ая, -ое, -ие) *прил* office *опред*; **контóрская кнúга** account book.
кóнтр|а (-ы) *ж* (*разг*): **быть в ~х с кем-н** to be at odds with sb.
контрабáнд|а (-ы) *ж* smuggling; (*товары*) contraband.
контрабандúст (-а) *м* smuggler.
контрабандúст|ка (-ки; *gen pl* -ок) *ж см* **контрабандúст**.
контрабáндный *прил* contraband.
контрабáс (-а) *м* double bass.
контрабасúст (-а) *м* double-bass player.
контрадмирáл (-а) *м* rear admiral.
контрáкт (-а) *м* contract; **фóрвардный ~** (*КОММ*) forward contract.
контрáльто *ср нескл* contralto.
контрамáр|ка (-ки; *gen pl* -ок) *ж* ≈ complimentary ticket.
контрапýнкт (-а) *м* counterpoint.
контрáст (-а) *м* contrast.
контрáстен *прил см* **контрáстный**.
контрастúр|овать (-ую) *несов неперех*: ~ **с** *+instr* to contrast with.
контрáст|ный (-ен, -на, -но) *прил* contrasting.
контратáк|а (-и) *ж* counterattack.
контрацептúв (-а) *м* contraceptive.
контрацептúвный *прил* contraceptive *опред*.
контрибýци|я (-и) *ж* reparations *мн*; **налагáть (наложúть** *perf*) **~ю** to exact reparations.
контрнаступлéни|е (-я) *ср* counteroffensive.
контролёр (-а) *м* (*железнодорожный*) (ticket) inspector; (*театральный*) ≈ usher; (*сберкассы*) cashier.

контроли́р|овать (-ую) *несов перех* to control.
контро́л|ь (-я) *м* (*наблюдение*) monitoring; (*проверка*) testing, checking; (*в транспорте*) ticket inspection; (*в магазине*) checkout ◆ *собир* (*проверяющие*) inspectors *мн*; **па́спортный ~** passport control; **~ за це́нами** price control; **~ ка́чества** quality control.
контро́льн|ая (-ой; *decl like adj*) *ж* (*также*: **~ рабо́та**) class test.
контро́льн|ый *прил*: **~ая коми́ссия** inspection team; **~ая рабо́та по** *+prp* class test in; **контро́льные ци́фры** control figures.
контрразве́дк|а (-и) *ж* counterespionage.
контрреволюционе́р (-а) *м* counter-revolutionary.
контрреволю́ци|я (-и) *ж* counter-revolution.
контрфо́рс (-а) *м* buttress.
конту́|зить (-жу, -зишь) *сов безл*: **его́ ~зило** he was contused.
конту́зи|я (-и) *ж* (*МЕД*) contusion.
ко́нтур (-а) *м* contour.
ко́нтурный *прил* contour *опред*; **ко́нтурная ка́рта** contour map.
конур|а́ (-ы́) *ж* (*собачья*) kennel; (*перен*: *комната*) shoe box.
ко́нус (-а) *м* cone.
конусообра́з|ный (-ен, -на, -но) *прил* conical.
конферансье́ *ср нескл* compère.
конфере́нц-за́л (-а) *м* conference room.
конфере́нци|я (-и) *ж* conference.
конфе́т|а (-ы) *ж* sweet.
конфетти́ *ср нескл* confetti.
конфигура́ци|я (-и) *ж* configuration.
конфиденциа́л|ьный (-ен, -ьна, -ьно) *прил* confidential.
конфиска́ци|я (-и) *ж* confiscation.
конфиск|ова́ть (-у́ю) *(не)сов перех* to confiscate.
конфли́кт (-а) *м* (*военный*) conflict; (*в семье, на работе*) tension.
конфли́ктный *прил* (*ситуация*) conflict *опред*.
конфликт|ова́ть (-у́ю) *несов неперех*: **~ с** *+instr* (*разг*) to be at loggerheads with.
конфо́р|ка (-ки; *gen pl* **-ок)** *ж* ring (*on cooker*).
конфронта́ци|я (-и) *ж* confrontation.
конфу́жу(сь) *несов см* **конфу́зить(ся)**.
конфу́з (-а) *м* embarrassment.
конфу́|зить (-жу, -зишь; *perf* **сконфу́зить)** *несов перех* to embarrass
▸ **конфу́зиться** (*perf* **сконфу́зиться**) *несов возв* to get embarrassed.
конца́ *итп сущ см* **коне́ц**.
концентра́т (-а) *м* (*о корме*) concentrate; (*о руде*) concentration.
концентрацио́нный *прил*: **~ ла́герь** concentration camp.
концентра́ци|я (-и) *ж* concentration.
концентри́рованный *прил* concentrated.
концентри́р|овать (-ую; *perf* **сконцентри́ровать)** *несов перех* to concentrate
▸ **концентри́роваться** (*perf* **сконцентри́роваться**) *несов возв* (*капитал*) to be concentrated; (*ученик*) to concentrate.
концентри́ческ|ий (-ая, -ое, -ие) *прил* concentric.
конце́пци|я (-и) *ж* concept.
конце́рн (-а) *м* (*ЭКОН*) concern.
конце́рт (-а) *м* concert; **дава́ть (дать** *perf***) ~** to give a concert; **~ для фортепья́но с орке́стром** piano concerto.
концерти́р|овать (-ую) *несов неперех* to give concerts.
концертме́йстер (-а) *м* (*МУЗ*) leader, concertmaster (*US*); (*аккомпаниатор*) accompanist.
конце́ртный *прил* concert *опред*.
конце́сси|я (-и) *ж* concession; **отдава́ть (отда́ть** *perf***) что-н на ~ю** to grant sth as a concession.
концла́гер|ь (-я; *nom pl* **-я́)** *м сокр* concentration camp.
концо́в|ка (-ки; *gen pl* **-ок)** *ж* ending.
конча́|ть (-ю) *несов от* **ко́нчить**
▸ **конча́ться** *несов от* **ко́нчиться** ◆ *возв*: **~ся на** *+acc* to end in; **всё хорошо́, что хорошо́ ~ется** all's well that ends well.
конча́я *предл* (*+instr*) to; **начина́я с кого́-н/чего́-н и ~ кем-н/чем-н** from sb/sth to sb/sth; **яви́лись все, ~ са́мыми да́льними ро́дственниками** everyone turned up, including the most distant relatives.
ко́нченый *прил*: **он ~ челове́к** he's a lost cause.
ко́нчик (-а) *м* tip.
кончи́н|а (-ы) *ж* end.
ко́нч|ить (-у, -ишь; *impf* **конча́ть)** *сов перех* (*жизнь, представление, отношения*) to end; (*университет, игру, книгу, работу*) to finish; **конча́ть (~** *perf***)** *+instr* (*бандитом*) to end up as; (*пьесой, словами*) to finish with; **конча́ть (~** *perf***) рабо́ту** *или* **рабо́тать** to finish work; **он пло́хо ~ил** he ended up in a bad way
▸ **ко́нчиться** (*impf* **конча́ться**) *сов возв* (*разговор, книга, игра*) to end, finish; (*запасы, деньги*) to run out; (*пустыня, лес итп*) to end.
конъюнктиви́т (-а) *м* conjunctivitis.
конъюнкту́р|а (-ы) *ж* climate; **~ ры́нка** state of the market; **понижа́тельная ры́ночная ~** (*КОММ*) falling market; **пониже́ние/повыше́ние ~ы** downturn/upturn of the market; **он хорошо́ чу́вствует ~у** he is good at gauging the climate.
конъюнкту́рн|ый *прил* (*соображения*) tactical; **~ые це́ны** market prices *мн*.
конъюнкту́рщик (-а) *м* opportunist.
кон|ь (-я́; *nom pl* **-и**, *gen pl* **-е́й)** *м* (*лошадь*) horse; (*ШАХМАТЫ*) knight; **быть** *(impf)* **на ~е́** to be on the ball.
конька́ *итп сущ см* **конёк**.
коньк|и́ (-о́в) *мн* skates *мн*; (*разг*: *вид спорта*) skating *ед*.
конькобе́ж|ец (-ца) *м* speed skater.
конькобе́жный *прил* speed-skating; **конькобе́жный спорт** speed skating.

конькобе́жца *итп сущ см* **конькобе́жец**.
конья́к (-á) *м* brandy, cognac.
ко́нюх (-а) *м* groom (*at stable*).
коню́ш|ня (-ни; *gen pl* **-ен)** *ж* stable.
кооперати́в (-а) *м* cooperative; (*разг: квартира*) *flat in housing cooperative*; **жили́щный** ~ *form of house or flat ownership*.
кооперати́вный *прил* cooperative; ~ **магази́н** *или* **ларёк** co-op; ~ **дом** cooperative (*form of house or flat ownership*).
коопера́тор (-а) *м member of a private enterprise*.
коопера́ци|я (-и) *ж* cooperative enterprise; (*труда*) co-operation; **потреби́тельская** ~ cooperative (society).
кооперир́|овать (-ую) *(не)сов перех* (*труд. средства*) to organize through a cooperative.
кооптир́|овать (-ую) *(не)сов перех* to coopt.
координа́т|а (-ы) *ж* (*ГЕОМ: обычно мн*) coordinate; (*разг: местонахождение*) number (and address).
координа́ци|я (-и) *ж* (*усилий*) coordination.
координир́|овать (-ую) *(не)сов перех* (*действия, усилия, движения*) to coordinate; ~ *(impf/perf)* **произво́дство с тре́бованиями ры́нка** to adjust production to meet the demands of the market.
коп. *сокр* = **копе́йка**.
копа́|ть (-ю) *несов от* **вы́копать** ◆ *перех* to dig; (*выкапывать*) to dig up; ~ *(impf)* **под** *+acc* (*разг*) to cook up a scheme against
▸ **копа́ться** *несов возв* (*в огороде*) to potter about; (*в чужих вещах*) to snoop about; (*разг: в душе*) to search; (*: долго возиться*) to dawdle.
копе́ек *сущ см* **копе́йка**.
копе́ечк|а (-и) *ж*: **э́то тебе́ вста́нет в ~у** it'll cost you a pretty penny.
копе́|йка (-йки; *gen pl* **-ек)** *ж* kopeck; **остава́ться (оста́ться** *perf*) **без ~йки** to be left without a penny.
Копенга́ген (-а) *м* Copenhagen.
копи́л|ка (-ки; *gen pl* **-ок)** *ж* piggy bank.
копира́йт (-а) *м* copyright.
копира́йтный *прил* copyrighted.
копи́рк|а (-и) *ж* (*разг*) carbon paper; **писа́ть** *(impf)* **под ~у** to make a carbon copy of.
копирова́льно-мно́жительный *прил* copying *опред*.
копирова́льн|ый *прил*: **~ая маши́на** photocopying machine, photocopier; **копирова́льная бума́га** carbon paper.
копи́р|овать (-ую; *perf* **скопи́ровать)** *несов перех* to copy.
коп|и́ть (-лю́, -ишь; *perf* **накопи́ть** *или* **скопи́ть)** *несов перех* to save; (*перен: обиды*) to harbour (*BRIT*), harbor (*US*)
▸ **копи́ться** (*perf* **накопи́ться** *или* **скопи́ться)** *несов возв* to accumulate.
ко́пи|я (-и) *ж* copy; (*перен*) spitting image; **он – ~ своего́ отца́!** he's the spitting image of his father; **снима́ть (снять** *perf*) **~ю с чего́-н** to make a copy of sth.
коплю́(сь) *несов см* **копи́ть(ся)**.
копн|а́ (-ы́; *nom pl* **-ы)** *ж* (*сена*) stack; (*волос*) thatch.
копн|у́ть (-у́, -ёшь) *несов перех* to dig; (*перен*): **е́сли ~ поглу́бже** ... if you dig deeper ....
ко́пот|ь (-и) *ж* layer of soot.
копош|и́ться (-у́сь, -и́шься) *несов возв* (*мышь*) to busy itself; (*перен: подозрения*) to stir; (*возиться*) to dawdle.
коп|те́ть (-чу́, -ти́шь) *несов неперех* to give off black smoke; (*корпеть*): ~ **над** *+instr* to pore over.
коп|ти́ть (-чу́, -ти́шь) *несов неперех* (*лампа*) to give off soot ◆ (*perf* **закопти́ть**) *перех* (*мясо, рыбу*) to smoke; ~ *(impf)* **не́бо** to fritter one's life away.
копу́ш|а (-и) *м/ж* (*разг*) slowcoach (*BRIT*), slowpoke (*US*).
копче́ни|е (-я) *ср* (*ветчины*) smoking; **ры́ба горя́чего/холо́дного ~я** *fish smoked at a high/low temperature*; *см также* **копче́нья**.
копчёност|и (-ей) *мн* smoked food *ед*.
копчёный *прил* smoked.
копче́н|ья (-ий) *мн* = **копчёности**.
ко́пчик (-а) *м* coccyx (*мн* coccyxes).
копы́т|о (-а) *ср* hoof (*мн* hooves).
коп|ьё (-ья́; *nom pl* **-ья,** *gen pl* **-ий)** *ср* spear; (*СПОРТ*) javelin; **мета́ние ~ья́** javelin.
кор. *сокр* (= **корреспонде́нт**) corr. (= *correspondent*).
кор|а́ (-ы́) *ж* (*дерева*) bark; (*АНАТ*) cortex; **земна́я** ~ the earth's crust; ~ **головно́го мо́зга** cerebral cortex.
корабе́льный *прил* ship's.
кораблестрое́ни|е (-я) *ср* shipbuilding.
кораблестро́ител|ь (-я) *м* shipbuilder.
кораблестро́ительный *прил* shipbuilding.
кора́бл|ь (-я́) *м* ship; **сжига́ть (сжечь** *perf*) **свои́ корабли́** to burn one's boats.
кора́лл (-а) *м* coral.
кора́лловый *прил* (*также цвет*) coral; **кора́лловый риф** coral reef.
Кора́н (-а) *м* the Koran.
кордебале́т (-а) *м* corps de ballet.
кордо́н (-а) *м* cordon; **за ~ом** (*разг*) abroad.
коре́|ец (-йца) *м* Korean.
корёж|ить (-у, -ишь; *perf* **искорёжить** *или* **покорёжить)** *несов перех* (*разг*) to twist; (*no perf; перен*): **его́ поведе́ние меня́ ~ит** his behaviour makes me cringe.
коре́йк|а (-и) *ж* smoked brisket of pork.
коре́йск|ий (-ая, -ое, -ие) *прил* Korean.
корена́ст|ый (-, -а, -о) *прил* stocky.
корен|и́ться (*3sg* **-и́тся,** *3pl* **-я́тся)** *несов возв*: ~

в *+prp* to be rooted in.
коренн|о́й *прил* (*население, традиции*) indigenous; (*вопрос, преобразования*) fundamental; **~ы́м о́бразом** fundamentally; **коренно́й зуб** molar.
ко́р|ень (-ня; *nom pl* **-ни,** *gen pl* **-не́й)** *м* root; **в ~не** fundamentally; **пресека́ть (пресе́чь** *perf*) **что-н в ~не** to nip sth in the bud; **пуска́ть (пусти́ть** *perf*) **~ни** to put down roots; **подруба́ть (подруби́ть** *perf*) **под ~** to uproot; **смотре́ть** *(impf)* **в ~ вопро́са/де́ла** to examine the root of the problem/matter.
коре́нь|я (-ев) *мн* (*БОТ*) roots *мн*.
ко́реш (-а) *м* (*разг*) mate, pal.
корешо́|к (-ка́) *м уменьш от* **ко́рень**; (*чековой книжки*) counterfoil; (*переплёта*) spine.
коре́йца *итп сущ см* **коре́ец.**
Коре́|я (-и) *ж* Korea.
корея́н|ка (-ки; *gen pl* **-ок)** *ж см* **коре́ец.**
корж (-а́) *м* layer (*of a cake*).
ко́ржик (-а) *м уменьш от* **корж**; (*пряник*) ≈ shortbread.
корзи́н|а (-ы) *ж* basket; **валю́тная ~** (*ЭКОН*) basket of currencies.
корзи́н|ка (-ки; *gen pl* **-ок)** *ж* (small) basket.
корзи́ноч|ка (-ки; *gen pl* **-ек)** *ж* (*КУЛИН*) tart.
корзи́нщик (-а) *м* basket weaver.
кориа́ндр (-а) *м* coriander.
коридо́р (-а) *м* corridor.
коридо́рн|ая (-ой; *decl like adj*) *ж* chambermaid.
коридо́рн|ый (-ого; *decl like adj*) *м* room attendant (*in hotel*).
кор|и́ть (-ю́, -и́шь) *несов перех* to chastise.
корифе́|й (-я) *м* luminary.
кори́ц|а (-ы) *ж* cinnamon.
кори́чневый *прил* brown.
ко́р|ка (-ки; *gen pl* **-ок)** *ж уменьш от* **кора́**; (*апельсинная*) peel; (*на коже*) scab; **прочита́ть** *(perf)* **что-н от ~ки до ~ки** to read sth from cover to cover.
корм (-а; *nom pl* **-а́)** *м* (*для скота*) fodder, feed; (*диких животных*) food.
корм|а́ (-ы́) *ж* stern.
кормёжк|а (-и) *ж* (*разг*: *скота*) feeding; (: *еда*) grub.
корми́л|ец (-ьца) *м* breadwinner.
корми́лиц|а (-ы) *ж* breadwinner; (*грудного ребёнка*) wet nurse.
корми́л|о (-а) *ср*: **стоя́ть** *или* **быть у ~а вла́сти** to be at the helm.
корми́льца *сущ см* **корми́лец.**
корм|и́ть (-лю́, -ишь) *несов перех* to feed; (*perf* **прокорми́ть**; *содержать*) to feed, keep; (*perf* **накорми́ть**): **~ кого́-н (чем-н)** to feed sb (sth); **~** *(impf)* **гру́дью** to breast-feed; **его́ хле́бом не ~и́, то́лько дай в футбо́л поигра́ть** he's never happier than when he's playing football
▸ **корми́ться** (*perf* **прокорми́ться**) *несов возв* (*животное*) to feed; (*+instr*; *человек*) to live on.
кормле́ни|е (-я) *ср* feeding.
кормлю́(сь) *несов см* **корми́ть(ся).**
кормов|о́й *прил* (*С-Х*): **~ы́е сорта́** fodder crops; **кормова́я свёкла** beet; **кормово́е весло́** rudder.
корму́шк|а (-и) *ж* (*для скота*) trough; (*для птиц*) bird table; (*перен*: *разг*) slush fund.
корневи́щ|е (-а) *ср* rhizome.
корнепло́д (-а) *м* root vegetable.
корнепло́дн|ый *прил*: **~ое расте́ние** root plant.
корне́т (-а) *м* cornet.
ко́рня *итп сущ см* **ко́рень.**
ко́роб (-а) *м* rectangular basket; **с три ~а наговори́ть** *(perf)* to talk through one's hat; **с три ~а наобеща́ть** *(perf)* **кому́-н** to promise sb the earth.
коро́б|ить (-лю, -ишь; *perf* **покоро́бить)** *несов перех* to warp; **меня́ ~ит от его́ шу́ток** his jokes make me cringe
▸ **коро́биться** (*perf* **покоро́биться**) *несов возв* to warp.
коро́б|ка (-ки; *gen pl* **-ок)** *ж* box; (*остов дома*) frame; **коро́бка скоросте́й** gearbox.
коробка́ *сущ см* **коробо́к.**
коро́блю(сь) *несов см* **коро́бить(ся).**
коро́бок *сущ см* **коро́бка.**
коробо́|к (-ка́) *м*: **~ спи́чек** box of matches.
коро́боч|ка (-ки; *gen pl* **-ек)** *ж уменьш от* **коро́бка**; (*БОТ*) boll.
коро́в|а (-ы) *ж* cow; (*разг*: *пренебр*) silly cow; **до́йная ~** dairy cow.
коро́в|ий (-ья, -ье, -ьи) *прил*: **~ье молоко́** cow's milk.
коро́вник (-а) *м* cowshed.
коро́вниц|а (-ы) *ж* milkmaid.
ко́рок *сущ см* **ко́рка.**
короле́в|а (-ы) *ж* (*также ШАХМАТЫ, перен*) queen; **короле́ва красоты́** beauty queen.
короле́вск|ий (-ая, -ое, -ие) *прил* royal.
короле́вств|о (-а) *ср* kingdom.
корол|ёк (-ька́) *м* (*апельсин*) blood orange; (*хурма*) sharon fruit; (*ЗООЛ*) goldcrest.
коро́л|ь (-я) *м* (*также ШАХМАТЫ, КАРТЫ*) king.
королька́ *сущ см* **королёк.**
коро́н|а (-ы) *ж* crown.
корона́рный *прил* coronary *опред*.
корона́ци|я (-и) *ж* coronation.
коро́нный *прил* (*разг*) best, favourite; **~ но́мер** party piece.
коронова́ни|е (-я) *ср* crowning.
корон|ова́ть (-у́ю) *(не)сов перех* to crown.
коро́ст|а (-ы) *ж* scab.
коросте́л|ь (-я́) *м* corncrake.
корота́|ть (-ю; *perf* **скорота́ть)** *несов перех* (*вечер, время итп*) to while away; (*свои дни, жизнь*) to live out.
коро́тк|ий (-ая, -ое, -ие; ко́роток, коротка́, ко́ротко, ко́ротки) *прил* short; (*отношения*) close; **у него́ ~ая па́мять** he has a short memory; **у него́ ру́ки ко́ротки** he's not up to it; **мы с ним на ~ой ноге́** we're on good terms; **коро́ткие во́лны** short wave; **коро́ткое**

замыка́ние short circuit.
ко́ротко *нареч* briefly; (*стричься*) short; (*узнать*) intimately ◆ *как сказ*: **э́то пла́тье мне ~** this dress is too short for me.
коротково́лновый *прил* short-wave *опред.*
короткометра́жный *прил*: **~ фильм** short (film).
коротконо́г|ий (-ая, -ое, -ие) *прил* short-legged.
ко́роток *прил см* **коро́ткий.**
коротыш (-а́) *м* (*разг*) shorty.
коро́че *сравн прил от* **коро́ткий** ◆ *сравн нареч от* **ко́ротко**; **~ говоря́** to put it briefly.
ко́рочк|а (-и) *ж уменьш от* **ко́рка**; (*на пироге итп*) crust.
корп|е́ть (-лю́, -и́шь) *несов неперех*: **~ над** *+instr* to slave away at.
корпорати́вный *прил* corporate.
корпора́ци|я (-и) *ж* corporation.
ко́рпус (-а; *nom pl* **-ы)** *м* body; (*самолёта*) fuselage; (*nom pl* **-а́**; *остов*: *судна, здания*) frame; (*здание*) block; (*ист*: *учебное заведение*) academy; (*дипломатический, офицерский*) corps.
корре́ктен *прил см* **корре́ктный.**
корректи́в (-а) *м* (*поправка*: *обычно мн*) amendment; **вноси́ть (внести́** *perf*) **~ы в план** to amend a plan.
корректи́р|овать (-ую; *perf* **скорректи́ровать**) *несов перех* (*ошибку*) to correct; (*perf* **откорректи́ровать**; *рукопись, статью*) to proofread.
корректиро́в|ка (-ки; *gen pl* **-ок)** *ж* (*комп*: *обновление*) update.
корре́кт|ный (-ен, -на, -но) *прил* correct.
корре́ктор (-а) *м* proofreader.
корректу́р|а (-ы) *ж* (*исправление ошибок*) proofreading; (*оттиск с набора*) proofs *мн.*
корре́кци|я (-и) *ж* correction.
корреля́ци|я (-и) *ж* correlation.
корреспонде́нт (-а) *м* correspondent.
корреспонде́нт|ка (-ки; *gen pl* **-ок)** *ж см* **корреспонде́нт.**
корреспонде́нци|я (-и) *ж* correspondence.
корри́д|а (-ы) *ж* bullfight.
корроди́р|овать (*3sg* **-ует**, *3pl* **-уют**) (*не*)*сов неперех* to corrode.
коррози́йный *прил* corrosive.
корро́зи|я (-и) *ж* corrosion.
коррумпи́рован|ный (-, -а, -о) *прил* corrupt.
корру́пци|я (-и) *ж* corruption.
корса́ж (-а) *м* bodice.
корсе́т (-а) *м* corset.
корт (-а) *м* (tennis) court.
корте́ж (-а) *м* (*траурный*) cortege; (*свадебный*) procession.
ко́ртик (-а) *м* dagger, knife (*мн* knives).
ко́рточ|ки (-ек) *мн*: **присе́сть на ~** to squat down; **сиде́ть** (*impf*) **на ~ках** to squat.
корч|ева́ть (-у́ю) *несов от* **вы́корчевать** ◆ *перех* to uproot.
ко́рч|ить (-у, -ишь; *perf* **ско́рчить**) *несов перех* to contort ◆ *безл*: **его́ всего́ ~ило от бо́ли** he was doubled up in pain; **~ (ско́рчить** *perf*) **ро́жу** to pull a face; **~** (*impf*) **из себя́ дурака́/свято́го** (*разг*) to act the fool/saint
▸ **ко́рчиться** (*perf* **ско́рчиться**) *несов возв* (*от боли, от смеха*) to writhe about.
ко́ршун (-а) *м* (*зоол*) kite.
коры́ст|ный (-ен, -на, -но) *прил* (*интерес, цель*) mercenary; (*любовь*) selfish.
корыстолюби́в|ый (-, -а, -о) *прил* mercenary.
корыстолю́би|е (-я) *ср* greed.
коры́ст|ь (-и) *ж* (*выгода*) gain; (*корыстолюбие*) greed.
коры́т|о (-а) *ср* tub; **оста́ться** (*perf*) **у разби́того ~а** to end up with nothing.
кор|ь (-и) *ж* measles *мн.*
ко́рюш|ка (-ки; *gen pl* **-ек)** *ж* smelt (*fish*).
коря́в|ый (-, -а, -о) *прил* (*дерево, пальцы*) gnarled; (*почерк*) squiggly; (*перен*: *фразы, стиль*) clumsy.
коря́г|а (-и) *ж* dead branch (*мн* branches).
кос|а́ (-ы́; *acc sg* **-у**, *dat sg* **-е́**, *nom pl* **-ы)** *ж* (*волосы*) plait; (*орудие*) scythe; **заплета́ть** (*perf*) **ко́сы кому́-н** to plait sb's hair; **носи́ть** (*impf*) **ко́сы** to wear one's hair in plaits; **нашла́ ~ на ка́мень** they are an equal match for each other.
коса́р|ь (-я́) *м* mower (*person*).
коса́тк|а (-и) *ж* killer whale.
ко́свенный *прил* indirect; (*дополнение, падеж*) oblique; **ко́свенная речь** indirect speech.
ко́сен *прил см* **ко́сный.**
коси́л|ка (-ки; *gen pl* **-ок)** *ж* mower (*machine*).
ко́синус (-а) *м* cosine.
ко|си́ть (-шу́, -сишь; *perf* **скоси́ть**) *несов перех* (*газон, сено*) to mow; (*перен*: *подлеж*: *эпидемия, болезнь*) to wipe out; (*рот, глаза*) to twist; (*глаза*) to slant; **у него́ ~ся́т глаза́** he has a slight squint; **~** (*impf*) **под** *+acc* (*разг*) to pretend to be
▸ **коси́ться** (*perf* **скоси́ться**) *несов возв* (*здание*) to lean to one side; **~ся** (*impf*) **на кого́-н** (*смотреть искоса*) to give sb a sidelong glance; (*перен*) to look askance at sb.
коси́ч|ка (-ки; *gen pl* **-ек)** *ж* pigtail.
косма́т|ый (-, -а, -о) *прил* shaggy.
косме́тик|а (-и) *ж* make-up ◆ *собир* cosmetics *мн.*
космети́чек *сущ см* **космети́чка.**
космети́ческ|ий (-ая, -ое, -ие) *прил* cosmetic; **~ ремо́нт** decorating; **космети́ческий кабине́т** beauty salon.
космети́ч|ка (-ки; *gen pl* **-ек)** *ж* (*человек*) beautician; (*сумочка*) make-up bag.
космето́лог (-а) *м* (*также*: **врач-~**) beautician.
космето́логи|я (-и) *ж* cosmeticology.

косми́ческ|ий (-ая, -ое, -ие) *прил* (*полёт, ракета*) space *опред*; (*теория*) cosmic; **~ая ско́рость** (*перен*) terrific speed; **косми́ческий кора́бль** spaceship; **косми́ческое простра́нство** (outer) space.
космодро́м (-а) *м* spaceport.
космоло́ги|я (-и) *ж* cosmology.
космона́вт (-а) *м* cosmonaut; (*в США итп*) astronaut.
космона́втик|а (-и) *ж* space technology and exploration.
космополи́т (-а) *м* cosmopolitan.
космополити́зм (-а) *м* cosmopolitanism.
ко́смос (-а) *м* the cosmos.
ко́см|ы (-) *мн* (*разг*) tousled locks *мн*.
косне́ть (-ю; *perf* **закосне́ть)** *несов неперех*: **~ (в** *+prp*) to stagnate (in).
ко́сност|ь (-и) *ж* intransigence.
косн|у́ться (-у́сь, -ёшься) *сов от* **каса́ться**.
ко́с|ный (-ен, -на, -но) *прил* (*ум, человек*) inflexible; (*среда, общество*) stagnant.
ко́со *нареч* (*расположить*) squint; **~ смотре́ть** *(impf)* **на** *+acc* (*перен*) to look askance at.
кособо́к|ий (-ая, -ое, -ие; -, -а, -о) *прил* lopsided.
косоворо́т|ка (-ки; *gen pl* **-ок)** *ж traditional Russian shirt with a collar fastening at the side*.
косогла́зи|е (-я) *ср* squint.
косогла́з|ый (-, -а, -о) *прил* cross-eyed.
косого́р (-а) *м* hillside.
кос|о́й (-, -а́, -о) *прил* (*глаза*) squinty; (*дождь, лучи*) slanting; **броса́ть** *(impf)* **~ы́е взгля́ды (на** *+acc*) to look askance (at); **у него́ ~а́я са́жень в плеча́х** (*разг*) he's built like an ox.
косола́п|ый (-, -а, -о) *прил* (*человек*) pigeon-toed.
костене́|ть (-ю; *perf* **закостене́ть)** *несов неперех* to go stiff.
кост|ёр (-ра́) *м* campfire.
кости́ст|ый (-, -а, -о) *прил* bony.
костля́в|ый (-, -а, -о) *прил* bony.
ко́стный *прил* (*АНАТ*): **~ мозг** (bone) marrow.
ко́сточ|ка (-ки; *gen pl* **-ек)** *ж уменьш от* **кость**; (*абрикосовая, вишнёвая*) stone; (*винограда*) seed; (*лимона*) pip; **перемыва́ть** *(impf)* **~ки кому́-н** (*разг*) to bitch about sb.
костра́ *сущ см* **костёр**.
косты́л|ь (-я́) *м* (*инвалида*) crutch (*мн* crutches); (*гвоздь*) spike.
кост|ь (-и; *prp sg* **-и́,** *gen pl* **-е́й)** *ж* bone; (*игральная*) dice (*мн* die); **лечь** *(perf)* **~ми́** (*погибнуть*) to lay down one's life; (*перен*) to do everything possible; **промока́ть (промо́кнуть** *perf*) **до ~е́й** to get soaked to the skin.
костю́м (-а) *м* outfit; (*маскарадный, на сцене*) costume; (*пиджак и брюки/юбка*) suit; **брю́чный ~** trouser (*BRIT*) *или* pant (*US*) suit.
костюме́р (-а) *м* wardrobe assistant.
костюми́рованный *прил*: **~ бал** costume ball.
костя́к (-а́) *м* skeleton; (*перен*) backbone.
костян|о́й *прил* (*нож, украшение*) bone; **~а́я му́ка** bone meal.
костя́ш|ка (-ки; *gen pl* **-ек)** *ж* (*пальцев*) knuckle; (*на счётах*) bead; (*домино*) domino.
косу́л|я (-и) *ж* (*ЗООЛ*) roe deer.
косы́н|ка (-ки; *gen pl* **-ок)** *ж* (triangular) scarf.
кося́к (-а́) *м* (*двери*) jamb; (*рыб*) school, shoal; (*птиц*) flock.
кот (-а́) *м* tomcat; **там хле́ба ~ напла́кал** (*разг*) there's hardly any bread left; **вся рабо́та пошла́ ко́ту под хвост** (*разг*) all the work has gone down the plughole; **~ в мешке́** a pig in a poke.
кот|ёл (-ла́) *м* (*сосуд*) pot; (*паровой*) boiler; **о́бщий ~** kitty; **вари́ться** *(impf)* **в одно́м ~ле́** to live in each other's pockets.
котел|о́к (-ка́) *м уменьш от* **котёл**; (*походная кастрюля*) billycan; (*шляпа*) bowler (hat) (*BRIT*), derby (*US*).
коте́льн|ая (-ой; *decl like adj*) *ж* boilerhouse.
кот|ёнок (-ёнка; *nom pl* **-я́та,** *gen pl* **-я́т)** *м* kitten.
ко́тик (-а) *м уменьш от* **кот**; (*тюлень*) fur seal; (*мех*) sealskin.
ко́тиковый *прил* sealskin.
коти́р|овать (-ую) *(не)сов перех* (*КОММ*) to quote
▸ **коти́роваться** *несов возв* (*КОММ*): **~ся (в** *+acc*) to be quoted (at); (*также перен*) to have a high value.
котиро́вк|а (-и) *ж* (*КОММ*) quotation.
кот|и́ться (*3sg* **-и́тся,** *perf* **окоти́ться**) *несов возв* (*кошка*) to have kittens; (*зайцы, кролики итп*) to give birth.
котла́ *сущ см* **котёл**.
котле́т|а (-ы) *ж* rissole; (*также:* **отбивна́я ~**) chop.
котлова́н (-а) *м* pit.
котлови́н|а (-ы) *ж* (*ГЕО*) basin.
кото́м|ка (-ки; *gen pl* **-ок)** *ж* knapsack; (*разг*) bag.

KEYWORD

кото́р|ый (-ая, -ое, -ые) *мест* ***1*** (*вопросительное*) which; **в кото́рый день он пришёл?** which day did he come?; **кото́рый час?** what time is it?
2 (*относительное*: *о предмете*) which; (: *о человеке*) who; **собы́тие, кото́рое нас потрясло́** an event which shook us; **ребёнок, у кото́рого моро́женое** the child who has the ice-cream; **челове́к, с кото́рым я говори́л** the person with whom I was speaking; **же́нщина, сы́на кото́рой я зна́ю** the woman whose son I know; **же́нщина, кото́рую я люблю́** the woman I love
3 (*не первый*): **кото́рый день/год мы не ви́делись** we haven't seen each other for many days/years.

котте́дж (-а) *м* cottage.
котя́та *итп сущ см* **котёнок**.
ко́фе *м нескл* coffee; **~ в зёрнах** coffee beans.
кофева́р|ка (-ки; *gen pl* **-ок)** *ж* percolator.
кофе́ен *сущ см* **кофе́йня**.
кофеи́н (-а) *м* caffeine.
кофе́йник (-а) *м* coffeepot.

кофе́йн|ый *прил* coffee *мн*; **~ого цве́та** coffee-coloured; **кофе́йный серви́з** coffee service.
кофе́|йня (**-йни**; *gen pl* **-ен**) *ж* coffee shop.
кофемо́л|ка (**-ки**; *gen pl* **-ок**) *ж* coffee grinder.
ко́фт|а (**-ы**) *ж* blouse; (*шерстяная*) cardigan.
коча́н (**-а́**) *м*: **~ капу́сты** cabbage.
коч|ева́ть (**-у́ю**) *несов неперех* (*также перен*) to lead a nomadic life; (*животные*) to roam.
коче́вник (**-а**) *м* nomad.
кочево́й *прил* nomadic.
коче́в|ье (**-ья**; *gen pl* **-ий**) *ср* nomad camp.
кочега́р (**-а**) *м* stoker.
кочега́р|ка (**-ки**; *gen pl* **-ок**) *ж* furnace room.
ко́чек *сущ см* **ко́чка**.
кочене́|ть (**-ю**; *perf* **окочене́ть**) *несов неперех* (*руки, труп*) to go stiff; (*человек*) to get stiff.
кочер|га́ (**-ги́**; *gen pl* **-ёг**) *ж* poker.
кочеры́ж|ка (**-ки**; *gen pl* **-ек**) *ж* heart (*of cabbage*).
ко́ч|ка (**-ки**; *gen pl* **-ек**) *ж* tussock.
коша́р|а (**-ы**) *ж* sheepfold.
коша́тник (**-а**) *м* cat-lover.
коша́тниц|а (**-ы**) *ж см* **коша́тник**.
коша́ч|ий (**-ья, -ье, -ьи**) *прил* (*также перен*) feline; (*мех, лапа*) cat's.
ко́шек *сущ см* **ко́шка**.
кошел|ёк (**-ька́**) *м* purse.
кошёл|ка (**-ки**; *gen pl* **-ок**) *ж* basket.
кошелька́ *сущ см* **кошелёк**.
ко́ш|ка (**-ки**; *gen pl* **-ек**) *ж* cat; (*скалолаза: обычно мн*) crampon; **~ки-мы́шки** (*игра*) tag; **игра́ть** *(impf)* **в ~ки-мы́шки с кем-н** (*перен*) to play cat and mouse with sb.
кошма́р (**-а**) *м* (*также перен*) nightmare.
кошма́р|ный (**-ен, -на, -но**) *прил* (*сон*) nightmarish; (*перен*) dreadful, nightmarish.
кошу́(сь) *несов см* **коси́ть(ся)**.
коще́|й (**-я**) *м*: **~ бессме́ртный** *evil spirit in Russian fairytales*.
кощу́нствен|ный (**-, -на, -но**) *прил* blasphemous.
кощу́нств|о (**-а**) *ср* blasphemy.
кощу́нств|овать (**-ую**) *несов неперех* to blaspheme.
коэффицие́нт (**-а**) *м* coefficient; **коэффицие́нт поле́зного де́йствия** efficiency.
КПСС *ж сокр* (*ИСТ*: = *Коммунисти́ческая па́ртия Сове́тского Сою́за*) CPSU (= *Communist Party of the Soviet Union*).
краб (**-а**) *м* crab.
кра́деный *прил* stolen.
краду́(сь) *итп несов см* **кра́сть(ся)**.
кра́дучись *нареч* stealthily.
краеве́д (**-а**) *м* local historian.
краеве́дени|е (**-я**) *ср* local studies *мн*.
краеве́дческ|ий (**-ая, -ое, -ие**) *прил*: **~ музе́й** local-history museum.
краево́й *прил* regional.
краеуго́льный *прил* fundamental; **краеуго́льный ка́мень** cornerstone.
кра́ж|а (**-и**) *ж* theft; **~ со взло́мом** burglary.
кра|й (**-я**; *loc sg* **-ю́**, *nom pl* **-я́**, *gen pl* **-ёв**) *м* edge; (*чашки, коробки*) rim; (*местность*) region; (*ПОЛИТ*) krai (*regional administrative unit*); **непоча́тый ~ рабо́ты** an endless amount of work; **на ~ све́та** to the ends of the earth; **на ~ю́ све́та** at the ends of the earth; **да́льние/тёплые ~я́** far-off/warm climes; **родно́й ~** native country; **находи́ться** *(impf)* **на ~ю́ ги́бели** to be on the verge of disaster; **кра́ем у́ха слу́шать** *(impf)* to half listen; **кра́ем у́ха слы́шать** *(impf)* to overhear; **хвати́ть** *(perf)* **че́рез ~** to go too far; **бить** *(impf)* **че́рез ~** to overflow.
кра́йне *нареч* extremely.
кра́йн|ий (**-яя, -ее, -ие**) *прил* extreme; (*дом*) end *опред*; (*пункт, маршрута*) last, final; **в ~ем слу́чае** as a last resort; **по ~ей ме́ре** at least; **крайний напада́ющий** winger; **Кра́йний Се́вер** the Arctic; **кра́йний срок** (final) deadline.
кра́йност|ь (**-и**) *ж* (*крайняя степень*) extremity; (*противоположное*) extreme; **броса́ться** *(impf)* **в ~и** to go from one extreme to the other; **твоё поведе́ние надое́ло мне до ~и** I find your behaviour tedious in the extreme.
кра́л|я (**-и**) *ж* (*разг*: *подруга*) chick; (: *красотка*) queen bee.
крамо́л|а (**-ы**) *ж* subversion; **говори́ть** *(impf)***/писа́ть** *(impf)* **~у** to say/write subversive things.
крамо́льный *прил* subversive.
кран (**-а**) *м* tap, faucet (*US*); (*СТРОИТ*) crane.
крановщи́к (**-а́**) *м* crane operator.
крановщи́ц|а (**-ы**) *ж см* **крановщи́к**.
крапи́в|а (**-ы**) *ж* nettle.
крапи́вниц|а (**-ы**) *ж* (*МЕД*) nettle rash.
крапи́вный *прил*: **~ щи** nettle soup.
кра́пин|а (**-ы**) *ж* = **кра́пинка**.
кра́пин|ка (**-ки**; *gen pl* **-ок**) *ж* fleck, speck.
краплёный *прил* (*карты*) marked.
кра́пчат|ый (**-, -а, -о**) *прил* speckled.
крас|а́ (**-ы́**) *ж* beauty; (*перен*): **~** *+gen* (*школы итп*) the pride of.
краса́в|ец (**-ца**) *м* handsome *или* good-looking man (*мн* men).
краса́виц|а (**-ы**) *ж* beautiful woman (*мн* women).
краса́вк|а (**-и**) *ж* deadly nightshade.
краса́вца *итп сущ см* **краса́вец**.
кра́сен *прил см* **кра́сный**.
краси́вост|ь (**-и**) *ж* superficial beauty.
краси́в|ый (**-, -а, -о**) *прил* beautiful; (*мужчина*) handsome; (*решение, фраза, слова*) fine.
краси́льный *прил* dye *опред*; **краси́льные вещества́** dyestuffs.
краси́тел|ь (**-я**) *м* dye.
кра́|сить (**-шу, -сишь**; *perf* **покра́сить**) *несов перех* to paint; (*волосы*) to dye; (*perf* **накра́сить**; *щёки, губы итп*) to paint; (*no perf*;

перен: украшать) to adorn; **тако́е поведе́ние тебя́ не ~сит** such behaviour does not become you

▸ **кра́ситься** (*perf* **покра́ситься**) *несов возв* to be covered in paint; (*разг: пачкать*) to run; (*perf* **накра́ситься**) to wear make-up.

кра́с|ка (**-ки**; *gen pl* **-ок**) *ж* paint; (*обычно мн: нежные, весенние итп*) colour (BRIT), color (US); (*стыда*) blush; **опи́сывать (описа́ть** *perf*) **что-н чёрными ~ми** to paint a gloomy picture of sth.

красне́|ть (**-ю**; *perf* **покрасне́ть**) *несов неперех* to turn red; (*от стыда*) to blush, flush; (*от гнева*) to go red; (*перен*): **~ пе́ред кем-н за кого́-н** to be ashamed of sb in front of sb; **~** (*impf*) **до корне́й воло́с** to blush to the roots of one's hair.

красноарме́|ец (**-йца**) *м* (ИСТ) Red-Army soldier.

краснобá|й (**-я**) *м* (*разг*) waffler.

красногварде́|ец (**-йца**) *м* (ИСТ) Red Guardsman (*мн* Guardsmen).

краснодере́вщик (**-а**) *м* cabinet-maker.

красноречи́в|ый (**-, -а, -о**) *прил* (*оратор, письмо*) eloquent; (*взгляд, жест*) expressive; (*цифры, факты*) revealing.

красноре́чи|е (**-я**) *ср* eloquence.

краснот|а́ (**-ы́**) *ж* (*лица*) redness; (*в горле*) inflammation.

краснощёк|ий (**-ая, -ое, -ие**) *прил* rosy-cheeked.

красну́х|а (**-и**) *ж* German measles.

кра́с|ный (**-ен, -на́, -но**) *прил* red; **проходи́ть** (*impf*) **~ной ни́тью** *или* **ли́нией** to run through; **кра́сная а́рмия** Red Army; **кра́сная ры́ба** salmon; **кра́сная строка́** new paragraph; **кра́сное вино́** red wine; **кра́сное де́рево** mahogany; **кра́сный пе́рец** paprika.

крас|ова́ться (**-у́юсь**) *несов возв* (*перед зеркалом, людьми*) to parade.

кра́сок *сущ см* **кра́ска.**

крас|ота́ (**-оты́**; *nom pl* **-о́ты**) *ж* beauty; **~!** wonderful!; *см также* **красо́ты.**

красо́тк|а (**-и**) *ж* pretty girl.

красо́т|ы (**-**) *мн* (*природы*) beautiful scenery *ед.*

кра́соч|ный (**-ен, -на, -но**) *прил* (*язык, расцветка*) colourful (BRIT), colorful (US).

кра|сть (**-ду́, -дёшь**; *perf* **укра́сть**) *несов перех* to steal

▸ **кра́сться** *несов возв* (*человек*) to creep, steal.

кра́сящ|ий (**-ая, -ее, -ие**) *прил*: **~ее вещество́** dye.

крат *нареч*: **во́ сто ~** a hundred times.

кра́тер (**-а**) *м* crater.

кра́т|кий (**-кая, -кое, -кие; -ок, -ка́, -ко**) *прил* short; (*беседа*) brief, short; (*словарь, отчёт*) concise; **~кое прилага́тельное** short-form adjective; **„и" ~кое** *the 10th letter of the Russian alphabet*

кратковре́мен|ный (**-ен, -на, -но**) *прил* short.

краткосро́ч|ный (**-ен, -на, -но**) *прил* (*отпуск, командировка*) short; (*заём, ссуда*) short-term.

кра́ткост|ь (**-и**) *ж* brevity.

кра́тный *прил* divisible.

кра́ток *прил см* **кра́ткий.**

кра́тче *сравн прил см* **кра́ткий.**

крах (**-а**) *м* collapse; (*перен*) destruction.

крахма́л (**-а**) *м* starch.

крахма́л|ить (**-ю, -ишь**; *perf* **накрахма́лить**) *несов перех* to starch.

крахма́льный *прил* starched.

кра́ше *сравн прил от* **краси́вый.**

краше́ни|е (**-я**) *ср* dyeing.

кра́шен|ый *прил* (*мех, ткань*) dyed; (*стол, дверь*) painted; **~ая блонди́нка** (*разг*) peroxide blonde.

крашу́(сь) *несов см* **кра́сить(ся).**

краю́х|а (**-и**) *ж* (*разг: хлеба*) doorstep.

креве́тк|а (**-и**) *ж* shrimp.

креди́т (**-а**) *м* credit; (*политический*) credibility; **в ~** on credit; **превыша́ть (превы́сить** *perf*) **~** to overdraw; **брать (взять** *perf*) **~ в ба́нке** to arrange an overdraft.

креди́тный *прил* credit *опред*; **~ оста́ток на счёте** credit balance; **креди́тная ка́рточка** credit card; **креди́тный счёт** credit account.

кредит|ова́ть (**-у́ю**) *(не)сов перех* to grant credit to.

кредито́р (**-а**) *м* creditor; **незастрахо́ванный ~** unsecured creditor.

кредито́рск|ий (**-ая, -ое, -ие**) *прил* creditor's.

кредитоспосо́бност|ь (**-и**) *ж* solvency.

кредитоспосо́бный *прил* solvent.

кре́до *ср нескл* credo.

кре́йсер (**-а**) *м* (ВОЕН) battleship, cruiser.

крейси́р|овать (**-ую**) *несов неперех* to sail (*along a specific route*); (ВОЕН) to patrol.

кре́кинг (**-а**) *м* (*нефти*) cracking.

крем (**-а**) *м* cream; **сапо́жный ~** shoe polish.

кремато́ри|й (**-я**) *м* crematorium.

крема́ци|я (**-и**) *ж* cremation.

крем|е́нь (**-ня́**) *м* flint.

креми́р|овать (**-ую**) *(не)сов перех* to cremate.

кремл|ь (**-я́**) *м* citadel; **К~** the Kremlin.

кремнёвый *прил* flint.

кре́мни|й (**-я**) *м* silicon.

кремня́ *итп сущ см* **креме́нь.**

кре́мовый *прил* cream.

крен (**-а**) *м* (*судна*) list; (*самолёта*) bank; **~ в сто́рону чего́-н** (*перен*) a move towards sth.

кре́ндел|ь (**-я**; *nom pl* **-я́**) *м* krendel (*sweet pastry*).

крен|и́ть (**-ю́, -и́шь**; *perf* **накрени́ть**) *несов перех* (*су́дно*) to list; (*самолёт*) to bank

▸ **крени́ться** (*perf* **накрени́ться**) *несов возв* (*судно*) to list; (*самолёт*) to bank.

креозо́т (**-а**) *м* creosote.

креп (**-а**) *м* crêpe.

крепдеши́н (**-а**) *м* crêpe de chine.

крепёжный *прил* reinforcing *опред.*

крепи́тельн|ый *прил* (ТЕХ) reinforcing *опред*; **~ое сре́дство** anti-diarrhoea tablets.

креп|и́ть (**-лю́, -и́шь**) *несов перех* to fix;

(*делать прочным*) to reinforce; **меня́ ~и́т** I'm constipated.
кре́п|кий (-кая, -кое, -кие; -ок, -ка́, -ко) *прил* strong; (*мороз, удар*) hard; **~ оре́шек** (*перен*) tough nut; **кре́пкие напи́тки** spirits.
кре́пко *нареч* strongly; (*спать, любить*) deeply; (*завязать*) tightly.
кре́пко-на́крепко *нареч* (*связать, закрыть*) as tightly as possible.
крепле́ни|е (-я) *ср* (*свай*) reinforcement; (*обычно мн: лыжные*) binding.
креплён|ый *прил*: **~ое вино́** fortified wine.
креплю́ *несов см* **крепи́ть.**
кре́п|нуть (-ну, -нешь; *pt* **-, -ла, -ло,** *perf* **окре́пнуть)** *несов неперех* to get stronger; (*уверенность*) to grow.
кре́пок *прил см* **кре́пкий.**
крепостни́к (-а́) *м* (*ИСТ*) serf owner.
крепостни́честв|о (-а) *ср* (*ИСТ*) serfdom.
крепостн|о́й *прил* (*ИСТ: отношения*) serf *опред*; (*башня, сооружение*) fortress *опред* ◆ **(-о́го;** *decl like adj*) *м* (*ИСТ: также:* **~ крестья́нин**) serf; **крепостно́е пра́во** (*ИСТ*) serfdom.
кре́пост|ь (-и) *ж* strength; (*ВОЕН*) fortress.
крепча́|ть (*3sg* **-ет,** *3pl* **-ют**) *несов неперех* (*мороз*) to harden; (*ветер*) to get stronger.
кре́пче *сравн прил от* **кре́пкий** ◆ *сравн нареч от* **кре́пко.**
крепы́ш (-а) *м* (*разг: ребёнок*) chubby chops.
кре́с|ло (-ла; *gen pl* **-ел)** *ср* armchair; (*в театре*) seat.
кре́сл|о-крова́т|ь (-а, -и) *ж* ≈ sofa bed.
крест (-а́) *м* cross; **поста́вить** (*perf*) **~ на ком-н/чём-н** to give sb/sth up for lost.
крест|е́ц (-ца́) *м* sacrum.
кре́ст|и (-) *мн* (*разг: КАРТЫ*) clubs *мн.*
крести́н|ы (-) *мн* christening *ед*, baptism *ед.*
кре|сти́ть (-щу́, -сти́шь; *perf* **окрести́ть)** *несов перех* to christen, baptize; **~ (перекрести́ть** *perf*) **кого́-н** to make the sign of the cross over sb; **~ (окрести́ть** *perf*) **кого́-н кем-н** to christen sb sth
▸ **крести́ться** (*не*)*сов возв* to be christened *или* baptized; (*perf* **перекрести́ться**; *крестить себя*) to cross o.s.
крест-на́крест *нареч* crosswise.
кре́стник (-а) *м* godson.
кре́стниц|а (-ы) *ж* goddaughter.
кре́стн|ый *прил*: **~ое зна́мение** sign of the cross; **~ ход** religious procession.
крёстн|ый *прил*: **~ая мать** godmother; **~ оте́ц** godfather.
кресто́в|ый *прил*: **~ похо́д** crusade; **~ая да́ма/деся́тка** (*разг*) the queen/ten of clubs.
крестоно́с|ец (-ца) *м* crusader.
крестца́ *итп сущ см* **кресте́ц.**
крестья́н|ин (-ина; *nom pl* **-е,** *gen pl* **-)** *м* peasant.
крестья́н|ка (-ки; *gen pl* **-ок)** *ж см* **крестья́нин.**
крестья́нск|ий (-ая, -ое, -ие) *прил* peasant *опред.*
крестья́нств|о (-а) *ср* peasantry.
крети́н (-а) *м* imbecile.
кре́чет (-а) *м* gerfalcon.
креще́ндо *нареч, ср нескл* crescendo.
креще́ни|е (-я) *ср* (*обряд*) christening, baptism; (*праздник*) ≈ the Epiphany; **он получи́л боево́е ~** (*перен*) he fought his first battle.
креще́нск|ий (-ая, -ое, -ие) *прил*: **~ пра́здник** the Epiphany; **~ие моро́зы** *coldest time of the year, traditionally following the Epiphany.*
крещу́(сь) (*не*)*сов см* **крести́ть(ся).**
крив|а́я (-о́й; *decl like adj*) *ж* (*МАТ*) curve.
криве́|ть (-ю; *perf* **окриве́ть)** *несов неперех* to become cockeyed.
кривизн|а́ (-ы́) *ж* (*пола, потолка*) unevenness; (*линии, позвоночника*) curvature.
крив|и́ть (-лю́, -и́шь; *perf* **скриви́ть** *или* **покриви́ть)** *несов перех* to curve; (*лицо, губы*) to twist; **~ (покриви́ть** *perf*) **душо́й** to be insincere
▸ **криви́ться** (*perf* **скриви́ться**) *несов возв* (*забор, стена итп*) to lean; (*лицо, губы*) to twist; (*человек*) to slouch.
кривля́|ться (-юсь) *несов возв* (*гримасничать*) to squirm; (*манерничать*) to show off.
крив|о́й (-, -а́, -о) *прил* (*линия, палка, улыбка*) crooked; (*ноги*) bandy; (*разг: человек*) cockeyed; **~о́е зе́ркало** (*перен*) distorting mirror.
криволине́йный *прил* (*движение*) curvilinear.
кривоно́г|ий (-ая, -ое, -ие) *прил* bow-legged.
кривото́лк|и (-ов) *мн* gossip *ед.*
кри́зис (-а) *м* crisis; (*болезни*) critical point, crisis.
кри́зисный *прил* crisis *опред.*
крик (-а; *part gen* **-у)** *м* cry; (*человека*) shout, cry; (*птиц*) call, cry; **после́дний ~ мо́ды** (*разг*) the last word in fashion.
кри́кет (-а) *м* (*СПОРТ*) cricket.
крикли́в|ый (-, -а, -о) *прил* (*женщина, платье*) loud; (*голос*) yapping.
кри́кн|уть (-у, -ешь) *сов неперех* to shout.
кріку́н (-а́) *м* (*разг*) bawler.
крику́н|ья (-ьи; *gen pl* **-ий)** *ж см* **крику́н.**
кримина́л (-а) *м* (*разг*) criminal case; **я не ви́жу здесь ~а** I don't see anything criminal in it.
криминали́ст (-а) *м* specialist in crime detection.
криминали́стик|а (-и) *ж* crime detection.
кримина́льный *прил* (*случай*) criminal; (*история, хроника*) crime *опред.*
кримино́лог (-а) *м* criminologist.
криминоло́ги|я (-и) *ж* criminology.
кри́н|ка (-ки; *gen pl* **-ок)** *ж ceramic container for milk.*

кристáлен *прил см* **кристáльный.**
кристáлл (-а) *м* crystal.
кристаллизáци|я (-и) *ж* crystallization.
кристаллиз|овáться (*3sg* **-ýется**, *3pl* **-ýются**, *perf* **вы́кристаллизоваться)** *(не)сов возв* to crystallize.
кристáл|ьный (-ен, -ьна, -ьно) *прил* (*светлый*) crystal-clear; (*безупречный*) pure.
Крит (-а) *м* Crete.
критéри|й (-я) *м* criterion (*мн* criteria).
кри́тик (-а) *м* critic.
кри́тик|а (-и) *ж* criticism; **литератýрная ~** literary criticism; **э́то не вы́держивает никакóй ~и** it doesn't stand up to criticism; **подвергáть (подвéргнуть** *perf*) **когó-н/что-н ~е** to subject sb/sth to criticism.
критикáн (-а) *м* (*разг*: *пренебр*) nit-picker.
критик|овáть (-ýю) *несов перех* to criticize.
крити́цизм (-а) *м* criticism.
крити́чен *прил см* **крити́чный.**
крити́ческ|ий (-ая, -ое, -ие) *прил* critical; **~ отдéл** review section; **~ая статья́** critique.
крити́ч|ный (-ен, -на, -но) *прил* critical.
крич|áть (-ý, -и́шь) *несов неперех* (*птица*) to cry; (*человек*: *от боли, от гнева*) to cry (out); (: *говорить громко*) to shout; **~** *(impf)* **на** *+acc* (*бранить*) to shout at.
кричáщ|ий (-ая, -ее, -ие) *прил* (*перен*: *наряды*) loud; (: *реклама*) eye-catching.
кров (-а) *м* shelter; **оставáться (остáться** *perf*) **без крóва** to have no roof over one's head.
кровáв|ый *прил* (*руки, одежда*) bloodied; (*нож*) bloodstained; (*рана, битва*) bloody; (*диктатура*) ruthless; **~ая бáня** blood bath; **~ бифштéкс** rare steak.
кровáт|ка (-ки; *gen pl* **-ок**) *ж* cot (*BRIT*), crib (*US*).
кровáт|ь (-и) *ж* bed.
крóвель *сущ см* **крóвля.**
крóвельный *прил* roofing *опред*.
крóвельщик (-а) *м* roofer.
кровенóсный *прил* blood *опред*.
крóв|ля (-ли; *gen pl* **-ель**) *ж* roof; **жить** *(impf)* **под однóй ~лей** to live under one roof.
крóвн|ый *прил* (*родство*) blood *опред*; (*обида*) grave; **~ые интерéсы** vested interests; **~ враг** deadly enemy; **~ые дéньги** blood money; **крóвная месть** blood feud.
кровожáден *прил см* **кровожáдный.**
кровожáдност|ь (-и) *ж* bloodthirstiness.
кровожáд|ный (-ен, -на, -но) *прил* bloodthirsty.
кровоизлия́ни|е (-я) *ср* haemorrhage (*BRIT*), hemorrhage (*US*).
кровообращéни|е (-я) *ср* (*МЕД*) circulation.
кровоостанáвливающ|ий (-ая, -ее, -ие) *прил* (*средства*) clotting *опред*.
кровопи́йц|а (-ы) *м/ж* bloodsucker.
кровоподтёк (-а) *м* blood blister.
кровопроли́тен *прил см* **кровопроли́тный.**
кровопроли́ти|е (-я) *ср* bloodshed.
кровопроли́т|ный (-ен, -на, -но) *прил* bloody.
кровопускáни|е (-я) *ср* (*также МЕД*) blood-letting.
кровосмешéни|е (-я) *ср* incest.
кровотечéни|е (-я) *ср* bleeding.
кровоточ|и́ть (*3sg* **-и́т**, *3pl* **-áт**) *несов неперех* to bleed.
кров|ь (-и; *loc sg* **-и́**) *ж* blood; **гóлос крóви** call of the blood; **пóртить** *(impf)* **~ комý-н** (*разг*) to make sb's blood boil; **проливáть (проли́ть** *perf*) **(своĸ) ~ за когó-н/что-н** to sacrifice o.s. for sb/sth; **проливáть (проли́ть** *perf*) **чью-н ~** to spill sb's blood; **пить** *(impf)* **чью-н ~** to suck the lifeblood out of sb; **~ с молокóм** *about a healthy, ruddy-faced person*; **плоть и ~ (чья)** (sb's) flesh and blood; **у меня́ сéрдце крóвью обливáется** my heart bleeds.
кровян|óй *прил* blood *опред*; **кровянáя колбасá** black pudding; **кровянóе давлéние** blood pressure.
кро|и́ть (-ю́, -и́шь) *несов перех* to cut out.
крокоди́л (-а) *м* crocodile.
крокоди́лов (-а, -о, -ы) *прил*: **~ы слёзы** crocodile tears *мн*.
крокоди́ловый *прил* crocodile *опред*.
крóлик (-а) *м* rabbit; (*мех*) rabbit fur; **шáпка из ~а** rabbit-fur hat.
крóлич|ий (-ья, -ье, -ьи) *прил* rabbit *опред*.
крольчáтник (-а) *м* rabbit hutch.
крольчи́х|а (-и) *ж* doe (*rabbit*).
крóме *предл*: **~** *+gen* (*за исключением*) except; (*сверх чего-н*) as well as; **~ тогó** besides; **~ негó я никогó не ви́дел** I haven't seen anyone except for *или* apart from him; **~ собáки у них есть ещё и кóшка** as well as a dog, they also have a cat; **~ шýток** (*разг*) joking apart; **емý ничегó остáлось ~ как уйти́** (*разг*) he had no choice but to leave; **~ как от тебя́, ни от когó нé было пи́сем** I didn't get a letter from anyone except (for) you; **~ тогó, мне нáдо идти́ на собрáние** apart from that *или* besides I have to go to a meeting.
кромéшн|ый *прил*: **ад ~** hell on earth; **здесь тьма ~ая** it's pitch-black in here.
крóмк|а (-и) *ж* (*ткани*) trim; (*льда, поля*) edge.
кромсá|ть (-ю; *perf* **искромсáть)** *несов перех* (*хлеб, материал*) to hack off; (*перен*: *рукопись, пьесу*) to chop.
крóн|а (-ы) *ж* (*дерева*) crown; (*деньги*) krona.
кронштéйн (-а) *м* (*балкона*) support; (*лампы, полки*) bracket.
кропá|ть (-ю; *perf* **нáкропать)** *несов перех* (*разг*) to scribble.
кроп|и́ть (-лю́, -и́шь; *perf* **окропи́ть)** *несов перех* (*РЕЛ*) to sprinkle (*with holy water*).
кропотли́в|ый (-, -а, -о) *прил* (*работа*) painstaking; (*человек*) fastidious.
кросс (-а) *м* (*бег*) cross-country; (*гонки*) cross-country race.
кроссвóрд (-а) *м* crossword.
кроссóв|ка (-ки; *gen pl* **-ок**) *ж* (*обычно мн*) trainer.
крот (-á) *м* mole.
крóт|кий (-кая, -кое, -кие; -ок, -кá, -ко) *прил*

meek.
кротóвый *прил* moleskin.
крóток *прил см* **крóткий**.
крóтост|ь (**-и**) *ж* meekness.
крóх|а (**-и**) *ж* (*обычно мн*) scrap ◆ *м/ж* (*ребёнок*) little one.
крохобóр (**-а**) *м* miser.
крохобóрств|о (**-а**) *ср* (*пренебр*) stinginess.
крóхот|ный (**-ен, -на, -но**) *прил* tiny.
крóшек *сущ см* **крóшка**.
крóшеч|ный (**-ек, -на, -но**) *прил* (*разг*) teeny-weeny, tiny.
крош|ить (**-ý, -ишь**) *несов перех* (*хлеб*) to crumble; (*КУЛИН*) to dice ◆ *неперех* (*сорить*) to drop crumbs
▸ **крошиться** *несов возв* (*хлеб, мел*) to crumble.
крóш|ка (**-ки**; *gen pl* **-ек**) *ж* (*кусочек*) crumb; (*малютка*) little one.
крóю(сь) *итп несов см* **крыть(ся)**.
круг (**-а**; *nom pl* **-и́**) *м* circle; (*СПОРТ*) lap; (*сыра, хлеба*) round; (*loc sg* **-ý**; *перен*: *знакомых*) circle; (: *обязанностей, интересов, вопросов*) range; **у меня́ головá крýгом идёт** my head is spinning; **ходи́ть** *(impf)* **по крýгу** to go round and round; **беговóй** ~ racing track; **поля́рный** ~ polar circle; *см также* **круги́**.
круг|и́ (**-óв**) *мн* (*литературные, политические*) circles *мн*.
круглé|ть (**-ю**; *perf* **округлéть**) *несов неперех* (*полнеть*) to fill out; (*становиться круглым*) to become round.
круглогоди́чный *прил* all-year-round.
круглоли́ц|ый (**-, -а, -о**) *прил* round-faced.
круглосýточный *прил* (*работа*) round-the-clock; (*детский сад*) twenty-four-hour.
крýгл|ый (**-, -á, -о**) *прил* round; (*no short form*; *идиот, дурак*) complete, total; (*цифра*) round; ~ **год** all year (round); **~ые сýтки** twenty-four hours; **~ая сýмма** hefty sum.
кругов|óй *прил* circular; **кругова́я порýка** mutual dependence; (*у преступников*) mutual cover-up.
круговорóт (**-а**) *м* cycle; (*событий*) turmoil.
кругозóр (**-а**) *м*: **он человéк ширóкого ~а** he is knowledgeable.
кругóм *нареч* around; (*разг*: *совершенно*) entirely; **идти́ (пойти́** *perf***)** ~ to make a detour; ~! about turn! (*BRIT*), about face! (*US*).
кругооборóт (**-а**) *м* (*КОММ*) turnover.
кругосвéтный *прил* round-the-world.
кружевни́ц|а (**-ы**) *ж* lace-maker.
кружевнóй *прил* lace.
крýжев|о (**-а**; *nom pl* **-á**, *gen pl* **-**) *ср* lace.
крýжек *сущ см* **крýжка**.
круж|и́ть (**-ý, -ишь**) *несов перех* to spin ◆ *неперех* (*птица*) to circle; (*по лесу итп*) to go round in circles
▸ **кружи́ться** *несов возв* (*в хороводе*) to move in a circle; (*в танце*) to spin (around); **у меня́ головá крýжится** my head's spinning.
крýж|ка (**-ки**; *gen pl* **-ек**) *ж* (*жестяная, глиняная*) mug; (*для пожертвований*) collection box.
кружкá *сущ см* **кружóк**.
кружкóв|ый *прил*: **~ые заня́тия** extracurricular activities.
круж|óк (**-кá**) *м* circle; (*организация*) club.
круи́з (**-а**) *м* cruise.
круп (**-а**) *м* (*лошади*) crupper; (*МЕД*) croup.
круп|á (**-ы́**; *nom pl* **-ы**) *ж* grain.
крýпен *прил см* **крýпный**.
крупи́н|ка (**-ки**; *gen pl* **-ок**) *ж* (*разг*) grain.
крупи́ц|а (**-ы**) *ж* (*таланта, здравого смысла*) ounce; (*истины*) grain.
крупнé|ть (**-ю**; *perf* **покрупнéть**) *несов неперех* to grow larger.
крýпно *нареч* (*нарезать*) coarsely; **писáть (написáть** *perf***)** ~ to write in big letters; ~ **поссóриться** *(perf)* **с кем-н** to have a big row with sb.
крупномасштáбный *прил* large-scale.
крýп|ный (**-ен, -нá, -но**) *прил* (*песок, соль*) coarse; (*размеры, ребёнок, фирма*) large; (*талант*) great; (*учёный, дело, фабрикант*) prominent; (*ссора, событие, успех*) major; **у меня́ бýдут ~ные неприя́тности** I'll be in serious trouble; **~ разговóр** (*разг*) serious talk; **крýпный гóрод** major city; **крýпный план** close-up; **крýпный рогáтый скот** (*С-Х*) cattle.
крупóзн|ый *прил*: **~ое воспалéние лёгких** pneumonia with croup.
крутизн|á (**-ы́**) *ж* steepness.
кру|ти́ть (**-чý, -тишь**) *несов перех* (*руль*) to turn; (*perf* **скрути́ть**; *руки*) to twist; (*верёвку*) to splice; (*папиросу*) to roll; ~ *(impf)* **кем-н** (*разг*) to manipulate sb; ~ *(impf)* **ромáн с кем-н** (*разг*) to have an affair with sb; **как ни ~ти́, нам придётся** .. (*разг*) we've no choice but to ...
▸ **крути́ться** *несов возв* (*вертеться*) to turn around; (: *колесо*) to spin; (: *дети*) to fidget; (*перен*: *хлопотать*) to be kept busy.
крýто *нареч* (*подниматься*) steeply; (*поворачивать*) sharply; **~ обходи́ться (обойти́сь** *perf***) с кем-н** to give sb a hard time.
крут|óй (**-, -á, -о**) *прил* (*берег, подъём*) steep; (*поворот, перемены*) sharp; (*нрав, меры*) harsh; (*no short form*; *тесто*) stiff; (*каша*) thick; ~ **кипятóк** fiercely boiling water; ~ **пáрень** (*разг*) cool guy; **крутóе яйцó** hard-boiled egg.
крýч|а (**-и**) *ж* steep slope.
крýче *сравн прил от* **крутóй** ◆ *сравн нареч от* **крýто**.
кручёный *прил* (*нитки*) twisted; **кручёный удáр** (*в теннисе*) spin shot.
кручý(сь) *несов см* **крути́ть(ся)**.
крушéни|е (**-я**) *ср* (*поезда*) crash; (*перен*: *надежд, планов*) shattering; **терпéть**

(потерпеть *perf***)** ~ *(корабль)* to be wrecked; *(поезд)* to crash.
крушин|а (-ы) *ж* buckthorn *(used as a laxative)*.
круш|ить (-у, -ишь) *несов перех (врагов)* to crush; *(деревья, дома)* to wreck.
крыжовник (-а) *м (кустарник)* gooseberry (bush); *(ягода)* gooseberry.
крылат|ый *прил (насекомые)* winged; **~ые слова** proverbial expressions; **крылатая ракета** *(ВОЕН)* cruise missile.
крыл|о (-а; *nom pl* **-ья,** *gen pl* **-ьев)** *ср* wing; *(ветряной мельницы)* sail; **подрезать (подрезать** *perf***) крылья кому-н** *(перен)* to clip sb's wings; **расправлять (расправить** *perf***) крылья** *(перен)* to spread one's wings.
крылышк|о (-а) *ср* wing; **под ~м у кого-н** under sb's wing.
крыльц|о (-а) *ср* porch.
Крым (-а) *м* Crimea.
крымск|ий (-ая, -ое, -ие) *прил* Crimean.
крын|ка (-ки; *gen pl* **-ок)** *ж* = **крынка**.
крыс|а (-ы) *ж* rat.
крысиный *прил (нора, хвост)* rat's; **~ яд** rat poison.
крытый *прил* covered.
кр|ыть (-ою, -оешь; *perf* **покрыть)** *несов перех* to cover; *(карту)* to trump; ~ *(impf)* **матом** *(разг)* to turn the air blue *(with bad language)*
▸ **крыться** *несов возв*: **~ыться в** *+prp* *(причина)* to lie; **в расчётах ~ылась ошибка** the calculations contained a mistake; **причина этого явления ~оется в том, что ...** the reason for this lies in the fact that ....
крыш|а (-и) *ж* roof.
крышк|а (-ки; *gen pl* **-ек)** *ж (ящика, чайника)* lid; **тут ему и ~** *(разг)* that was the end of him.
крэк (-а) *м* crack *(drug)*.
крю|к (-ка; *nom pl* **-чья,** *gen pl* **-чьев)** *м (в стене)* hook; *(разг: лишнее расстояние)* detour.
крюч|ить *(3sg* **-ит,** *perf* **скрючить)** *несов безл*: **его ~ит от боли** he is bent double in pain
▸ **крючиться** *(perf* **скрючиться)** *несов возв* to be bent double.
крючка *итп сущ см* **крючок**.
крючковат|ый (-, -а, -о) *прил* hooked.
крюч|ок (-ка) *м* hook; **~ для вязания** crochet hook.
крючья *итп сущ см* **крюк**.
крюшон (-а) *м (КУЛИН)* punch.
кряду *нареч*: **дождь шёл пять дней ~** it rained for five whole days.
кряж (-а) *м (горный)* ridge.
кряжист|ый (-, -а, -о) *прил (также перен)* stumpy.
кряканы|е (-я) *ср* quacking.
крякa|ть (-ю) *несов от* **крякнуть**.
крякн|уть (-у, -ешь) *сов неперех (утка)* to quack; *(перен: человек)* to grunt.
крях|теть (-чу, -тишь) *несов неперех* to groan.
ксерокопи|я (-и) *ж* photocopy, Xerox®.
ксерокс (-а) *м (автомат)* photocopier; *(копия)* photocopy, Xerox®.
ксилофон (-а) *м* xylophone.
ксилографи|я (-и) *ж (образец работы)* woodcut; *(процесс)* wood engraving.
кстати *вводн сл (между прочим)* incidentally, by the way; *(случайно)* by any chance ◆ *нареч (к месту)* relevant; **~, ты слышал, что ...?** by the way, did you hear that ...?; **Вы, ~, не знаете, что случилось?** you don't, by any chance, know what happened?; **деньги пришлись как нельзя ~** the money came just at the right time.

KEYWORD

кто (кого; *см* **Table 6)** *мест* ***1*** *(вопросительное, относительное)* who; **кто там?** who is there?; **надо узнать, кто приходил** we must find out who has come
2 *(разг: кто-нибудь)* anyone; **если кто позвонит, позови меня** if anyone phones, please call me
***3*: мало ли кто** many (people); **мало кто** few (people); **мало кто пошёл в кино** only a few of us went to the cinema; **кто-кто, а он всегда правду говорит** I don't know about anyone else, but he always tells the truth; **кто из вас ...** which of you ...; **кто (его) знает!** who knows!

кто-либо (кого-либо; *как* **кто;** *см* **Table 6)** *мест* = **кто-нибудь**.
кто-нибудь (кого-нибудь; *как* **кто;** *см* **Table 6)** *мест (в вопросительных предложениях)* anybody, anyone; *(в утвердительных предложениях)* somebody, someone; **мне ~ звонил?** did anybody *или* anyone phone for me?; **~ должен ему помочь** somebody *или* someone should help him.
кто-то (кого-то; *как* **кто;** *см* **Table 6)** *мест* somebody, someone; **~ Вам звонил** somebody *или* someone phoned for you.
куб (-а) *м (ГЕОМ, МАТ)* cube; **3 в кубе** 3 cubed.
куб. *сокр (= кубический)* cu. *(= cubic)*.
Куб|а (-ы) *ж* Cuba.
кубарем *нареч (разг)* headfirst.
кубизм (-а) *м* cubism.
кубик (-а) *м (игрушка)* building brick *или* block.
кубин|ец (-ца) *м* Cuban.
кубин|ка (-ки; *gen pl* **-ок)** *ж см* **кубинец**.
кубинск|ий (-ая, -ое, -ие) *прил* Cuban.
кубинца *итп сущ см* **кубинец**.
кубист (-а) *м* cubist.
кубическ|ий (-ая, -ое, -ие) *прил* cubic; **кубический корень** cube root.
куб|ок (-ка) *м* goblet; *(СПОРТ)* cup.
кубометр (-а) *м* cubic metre *(BRIT) или* meter *(US)*.
кубрик (-а) *м* crew's quarters *мн*.
кувалд|а (-ы) *ж* sledgehammer.
Кувейт (-а) *м* Kuwait.
кувшин (-а) *м* jug *(BRIT)*, pitcher *(US)*.
кувшинк|а (-и) *ж* water lily.
кувырка|ться (-юсь) *несов возв* to somersault.
кувыркн|уться (-усь, -ёшься) *сов возв* to turn a somersault.

кувыркóм *нареч* head over heels; **жизнь у меня́ пошлá ~** my life has been turned on its head.
кувыр|óк (**-кá**) *м* somersault.

KEYWORD

кудá *нареч* **1** (*вопросительное, относительное*) where; **кудá ты положи́л мою́ рýчку?** where did you put my pen?; **скажи́, кудá ты идёшь** tell me where you are going **2** (*разг: для чего*) why; **кудá мне стóлько дéнег?** why would I want so much money? **3** (*+dat; разг: о невозможности чего-н*): **кудá мне с ни́ми состязáться?** how can I compare with them? **4** (*+comparative; разг: гораздо*) much; **мой дом кудá бóльше** my house is much bigger.

кудá-либо *нареч* = **кудá-нибудь**.
кудá-нибудь *нареч* (*в вопросительных предложениях*) anywhere; (*в утвердительных предложениях*) somewhere; **Вы ~ съéздили лéтом?** did you go anywhere in the summer?; **давáй ~ пойдём** let's go somewhere.
кудá-то *нареч* somewhere; **он ~ ушёл** he has gone off somewhere.
кудáхтань|е (**-я**) *ср* clucking.
кудáх|тать (**-чу, -чешь**) *несов неперех* to cluck.
кудéсник (**-а**) *м* sorcerer.
кýдр|и (**-éй**) *мн* curls *мн*.
кудря́в|ый (**-, -а, -о**) *прил* (*волосы*) curly; (*человек*) curly-haired; (*дерево*) bushy; (*перен: слог*) flowery.
кузнéц (**-á**) *м* blacksmith.
кузнéчик (**-а**) *м* grasshopper.
кузнéчный *прил* blacksmith's; **кузнéчные мехá** bellows *мн*.
кýзниц|а (**-ы**) *ж* smithy, forge.
кýзов (**-а**; *nom pl* **-á**) *м* (*АВТ*) back (*of a van, lorry etc*).
куй(те) *несов см* **ковáть**.
кукарéка|ть (**-ю**) *несов неперех* to crow.
кукарекý *межд* (*крик петуха*) cock-a-doodle-doo.
кýкиш (**-а**) *м* fig; **он показáл мне ~** (*перен: разг*) ≈ he told me to get lost.
кýк|ла (**-лы**; *gen pl* **-ол**) *ж* (*также перен*) doll; (*в театре*) puppet; **теáтр ~ол** puppet theatre (*BRIT*) *или* theater (*US*).
кук|овáть (**-ýю**) *несов неперех* to cuckoo; (*перен: разг*) to twiddle one's thumbs.
кýкол *сущ см* **кýкла**.
кýкол|ка (**-ки**; *gen pl* **-ок**) *ж уменьш от* **кýкла**; (*ЗООЛ*) pupa (*мн* pupae).
кýкольный *прил* (*игрушечный*): **~ дóмик** doll's house; **кýкольный теáтр** puppet theatre (*BRIT*) *или* theater (*US*).
кýк|ситься (**-шусь, -сишься**) *несов возв* (*разг*) to sulk.
кукурýз|а (**-ы**) *ж* (*БОТ*) maize; (*КУЛИН*) (sweet) corn.
кукурýзный *прил* (*см сущ*) maize; corn.
кукýшк|а (**-и**) *ж* cuckoo.
кýкшусь *несов см* **кýкситься**.
кулáк (**-á**) *м* fist; (*ИСТ*) kulak (*member of the land-owning peasant class, eradicated during collectivization*).
кулáчный *прил*: **~ бой** fist fight.
кулебя́к|а (**-и**) *ж pie made with meat, fish or rice.*
кул|ёк (**-ькá**) *м* paper bag.
кули́к (**-á**) *м* (*ЗООЛ*) wader.
кулинáр (**-а**) *м* master chef.
кулинари́|я (**-и**) *ж* (*приготовление пищи*) cookery; (*магазин*) ≈ delicatessen ◆ *собир* (*продукты*) *cooked foods and groceries*.
кулинáрный *прил* (*искусство*) culinary.
кули́с|а (**-ы**) *ж* (*обычно мн: ТЕАТР*) wing; **за ~ми** (*также перен*) backstage, behind the scenes.
кули́ч (**-á**) *м* kulich (*Easter cake*).
кули́чки *нареч* (*разг*): **у чёрта на кули́чках** in the middle of nowhere; **к чёрту на ~** to the back of beyond.
кулóн (**-а**) *м* (*украшение*) pendant; (*ФИЗ*) coulomb.
кулуáрный *прил* (*встречи, сделки*) backstage.
кулуáр|ы (**-ов**) *мн* (*ПОЛИТ*) lobby *ед*; **в ~ах бесéды идýт** behind-the-scene talks are currently in progress.
кул|ь (**-я́**) *м* sack.
кулькá *итп сущ см* **кулёк**.
кульминациóнный *прил* climactic.
кульминáци|я (**-и**) *ж* (*АСТРОНОМИЯ*) culmination; (*перен*) high point, climax.
культ (**-а**) *м* (*служение божеству*) cult; (*совокупность обрядов: православный*) religion; (*перен: красоты, денег*) cult worship; **служи́тели кýльта** church officials; **культ ли́чности** personality cult.
культиви́ровани|е (**-я**) *ср* cultivation.
культиви́р|овать (**-ую**) *несов перех* to cultivate.
кýльтовый *прил* religious.
культýр|а (**-ы**) *ж* (*также С.-Х, БИО*) culture; (*разведение: льна итп*) cultivation, culture; (*быта*) high quality; **~ трудá** work ethic.
культýрен *прил см* **культýрный**.
культури́зм (**-а**) *м* body building.
культури́ст (**-а**) *м* body builder.
культýр|ный (**-ен, -на, -но**) *прил* cultural; (*no short form; растение*) cultivated.
кум (**-а**; *nom pl* **-овья́**, *gen pl* **-овьёв**) *м* godfather.
кум|á (**-ы́**) *ж* godmother.
кумачóвый *прил* calico.
куми́р (**-а**) *м* (*также перен*) idol.
кумовств|ó (**-а**) *ср* nepotism.
кумовь|я́ (**-ёв**) *мн от* **кум**.
кумы́с (**-а**) *м* fermented horse's milk.
куни́ц|а (**-ы**) *ж* marten.
купáльник (**-а**) *м* swimming *или* bathing costume (*BRIT*), bathing suit (*US*).

купа́льный *прил*: ~ **костю́м** swimming *или* bathing costume (*BRIT*), bathing suit (*US*); ~ **сезо́н** swimming season.
купа́нь|е (**-я**) *ср* bathing; (*плавание*) swimming.
купа́|ть (**-ю**; *perf* **вы́купать** *или* **искупа́ть**) *несов перех* to bath
▸ **купа́ться** (*perf* **вы́купаться** *или* **искупа́ться**) *несов возв* to bathe; (*плавать*) to swim; (*в ванне*) to have a bath; **~ся** *(impf)* **в зо́лоте** to be rolling in money.
купе́ *ср нескл* compartment (*in railway carriage*).
купе́йный *прил*: ~ **ваго́н** Pullman (car).
купе́л|ь (**-и**) *ж* (*РЕЛ*) font.
куп|е́ц (**-ца́**) *м* merchant.
купе́ческ|ий (**-ая, -ое, -ие**) *прил* (*сословие*) merchant *опред*; (*перен*: *нравы*) vulgar.
купе́честв|о (**-а**) *ср собир* the merchants *мн*.
купи́рованный *прил* = **купе́йный**.
куп|и́ть (**-лю́, -ишь**; *impf* **покупа́ть**) *сов перех* to buy.
купле́т (**-а**) *м* couplet; *см также* **купле́ты**.
купле́т|ы (**-ов**) *мн satirical song in couplet form*.
куплю́ *сов см* **купи́ть**.
ку́пл|я (**-и**) *ж* purchase; **~-прода́жа** buying and selling.
ку́пол (**-а**; *nom pl* **-а́**) *м* cupola.
купо́н (**-а**) *м* (*ценных бумаг*) ticket; (*денежный знак*) coupon (*used as the Ukrainian currency*); **стричь** *(impf)* **~ы** to make easy money; **пода́рочный** ~ gift voucher.
купца́ *итп сущ см* **купе́ц**.
ку́пч|ий (**-ая, -ее, -ие**) *прил* (*также*: **~ая кре́пость**: *ЮР*) deed of purchase.
купчи́х|а (**-и**) *ж см* **купе́ц**.
купю́р|а (**-ы**) *ж* (*сокращение*) cut; (*ЭКОН*) denomination; **статья́ печа́тается без купю́р** the article is printed in full.
ку́р|а (**-ы**) *ж* (*разг*) chicken.
кураг|а́ (**-и́**) *ж собир* dried apricots *мн*.
кура́ж|иться (**-усь, -ишься**) *несов возв*: ~ **над кем-н** to bully sb.
кура́нт|ы (**-ов**) *мн* chiming clock *ед*.
кура́тор (**-а**) *м* supervisor.
курга́н (**-а**) *м* (*могильник*) (burial) mound.
ку́рев|о (**-а**) *ср* (*разг*) smokes *мн*, fags *мн*.
куре́ни|е (**-я**) *ср* smoking.
кури́л|ка (**-ки**; *gen pl* **-ок**) *ж* (*разг*) smoking room.
кури́льщик (**-а**) *м* smoker.
кури́льщиц|а (**-ы**) *ж см* **кури́льщик**.
кури́ный *прил* (*яйцо*) hen's; (*бульон, перья*) chicken; **кури́ная слепота́** (*МЕД*) night blindness.
кури́тельный *прил*: ~ **таба́к** rolling tobacco; **кури́тельная ко́мната** smoking room.
кур|и́ть (**-ю́, -ишь**) *несов* (*не*)*перех* to smoke; **„~ запреща́ется", „не ~"** "no smoking"; **„у нас не ку́рят"** "kindly refrain from smoking"
▸ **кури́ться** *несов возв* (*вулкан*) to smoke; (*вершины гор*) to be shrouded in mist.
ку́р|ица (**-ицы**; *nom pl* **ку́ры**) *ж* hen, chicken; (*мясо*) chicken; **~ам на смех** (*разг*) it's a complete joke; **де́нег у неё ~ы не клю́ют** (*разг*) she's absolutely loaded.
курка́ *сущ см* **куро́к**.
курно́с|ый (**-, -а, -о**) *прил* snub-nosed.
кур|о́к (**-ка́**) *м* hammer (*on gun*); **взводи́ть** (**взвести́** *perf*) ~ to cock a gun.
куроле́|сить (**-шу, -сишь**) *несов неперех* to play up.
куропа́т|ка (**-ки**; *gen pl* **-ок**) *ж* grouse.
куро́рт (**-а**) *м* (holiday) resort.
куро́ртный *прил* (*зона, город*) resort *опред*; **куро́ртный сезо́н** the holiday season.
курс (**-а**) *м* course; (*ПОЛИТ*) policy; (*КОММ*) exchange rate; (*ПРОСВЕЩ*) year (*of university studies*); **брать** (**взять** *perf*) ~ **на** *+acc* to set a course for; **идти́** *(impf)* **по ку́рсу** to be on (the right) course; **переходи́ть** (**перейти́** *perf*) **на четвёртый** ~ to go into the fourth year (*of university*); **быть** *(impf)* **в ку́рсе де́ла** to be up on what's going on; **входи́ть** (**войти́** *perf*) **в ~ чего́-н** to put o.s. in the picture about sth; **вводи́ть** (**ввести́** *perf*) **кого́-н в ~** (**чего́-н**) to put sb in the picture (about sth).
курса́нт (**-а**) *м* (*ВОЕН*) cadet.
курси́в (**-а**) *м* italics *мн*; **„~ мой"** "the italics are mine".
курси́вный *прил*: ~ **шрифт** italic font.
курси́р|овать (**-ую**) *несов неперех*: ~ **ме́жду** *+instr* ... **и** *+instr* ... (*самолёт, автобус*) to shuttle between ... and ...; (*судно*) to sail between ... and ....
курсов|о́й *прил*: **~а́я рабо́та** project; **~о́е собра́ние** student's year meeting; **~а́я ра́зница** (*КОММ*) difference in exchange rates.
ку́рсор (**-а**) *м* cursor.
ку́рт|ка (**-ки**; *gen pl* **-ок**) *ж* jacket.
курча́в|ый (**-, -а, -о**) *прил* (*волосы*) curly; (*человек, животное*) curly-haired.
ку́р|ы (-) *мн от* **ку́рица**.
курьёз (**-а**) *м* curious thing.
курьёз|ный (**-ен, -на, -но**) *прил* curious.
курье́р (**-а**) *м* messenger; (*дипломатический*) courier.
курье́рск|ий (**-ая, -ое, -ие**) *прил*: ~ **отде́л** dispatch department; **курье́рский по́езд** express train.
куря́тин|а (**-ы**) *ж* chicken (*meat*).
куря́тник (**-а**) *м* chicken coop.
куса́|ть (**-ю**) *несов перех* to bite; (*сахар, конфеты*) to crunch
▸ **куса́ться** *несов возв* (*животное*) to bite; (*растение*) to sting; (*разг*: *цены, налоги*) to hurt.
куса́ч|ки (**-ек**) *мн* wire cutters *мн*.
куска́ *итп сущ см* **кусо́к**.
кусково́й *прил*: ~ **са́хар** lump sugar.
кус|о́к (**-ка́**) *м* piece; ~ **са́хара** sugar lump; ~ **мы́ла** bar of soap; ~ **хле́ба** (*перен*) daily bread.
куст (**-а́**) *м* (*БОТ*) bush; **пря́таться** (**спря́таться** *perf*) **в ~ы́** (*перен*) to run for cover.
куста́рник (**-а**) *м* shrubbery ◆ *собир* bushes *мн*.

кустáрный *прил* handicraft *опред*; (*перен*: *методы, оборудование*) crude, primitive; **~ труд** craftwork; **кустáрные издéлия** handicrafts.
кустáр|ь (**-я́**) *м* craftsman (*мн* craftsmen).
кусти́ст|ый (**-, -а, -о**) *прил* bushy.
кýта|ть (**-ю**; *perf* **закýтать**) *несов перех* (*плечи, ноги итп*) to cover up; (*ребёнка*) to bundle up
▸ **кýтаться** (*perf* **закýтаться**) *несов возв*: **~ся в** *+acc* to wrap o.s. up in.
кутёж (**-á**) *м* drinking spree.
кутерьм|á (**-ы́**) *ж* (*разг*) mayhem, chaos.
ку|ти́ть (**-чý, -тишь**) *несов неперех* to go on a drinking spree.
кутýз|ка (**-ки**; *gen pl* **-ок**) *ж* (*разг*) the slammer, the clink (*BRIT*).
кухáр|ка (**-ки**; *gen pl* **-ок**) *ж* cook.
кýх|ня (**-ни**; *gen pl* **-онь**) *ж* (*помещение*) kitchen; (*еда*) cooking; **рýсская ~** Russian cuisine.
кухóнный *прил* kitchen *опред*.
кýхонь *сущ см* **кýхня**.
кýц|ый (**-, -а, -о**) *прил* (*собака*) with no tail; (*перен*: *программа, права*) limited.
кýч|а (**-и**) *ж* (*песка, листьев*) pile, heap; (*+gen*; *разг*: *денег, проблем*) heaps *или* loads of; **вали́ть** *(impf)* **всё в однý ~у** to lump everything together.
кучев|óй *прил*: **~ы́е облакá** cumulus (clouds *мн*).
кýчер (**-а**; *nom pl* **-á**) *м* coachman (*мн* coachmen).
кучý *несов см* **кути́ть**.
куш (**-а**) *м* jackpot; **срывáть (сорвáть** *perf*) **~** to hit the jackpot.
кушáк (**-á**) *м* sash.
кýшан|ье (**-ья**; *gen pl* **-ий**) *ср* food.
кýша|ть (**-ю**; *perf* **покýшать** *или* **скýшать**) *несов перех* to eat; **~йте, пожáлуйста** have something to eat.
кушéт|ка (**-ки**; *gen pl* **-ок**) *ж* couch.
кювéт (**-а**) *м* gutter.

~ Л, л ~

Л, л *сущ нескл (буква) the 12th letter of the Russian alphabet.*
л. *сокр* (= **лист**) f. (= *folio*).
лабири́нт (-а) *м* maze; (*перен*) labyrinth.
лабора́нт (-а) *м* (*в лаборатории*) lab technician; (*на кафедре*) secretary.
лабора́нт|ка (-ки; *gen pl* **-ок)** *ж см* **лабора́нт.**
лаборато́ри|я (-и) *ж* laboratory.
ла́в|а (-ы) *ж* lava; (*забой*) drift.
лава́нд|а (-ы) *ж* lavender.
лава́ш (-а) *м* lavash (*Caucasian flat bread*).
лави́н|а (-ы) *ж* (*также перен*) avalanche.
лави́р|овать (-ую; *perf* **слави́ровать)** *несов неперех* (*МОР*) to tack; (*перен*) to manoeuvre (*BRIT*), maneuver (*US*).
ла́в|ка (-ки; *gen pl* **-ок)** *ж* (*скамья*) bench; (*магазин*) shop.
ла́воч|ка (-ки; *gen pl* **-ек)** *ж уменьш от* **ла́вка**; (*перен: разг*) shady business.
ла́вочник (-а) *м* shopkeeper.
лавр (-а) *м* laurel; *см также* **ла́вры.**
ла́вр|а (-ы) *ж* monastery.
лавро́вый *прил* laurel; **лавро́вый лист** bay leaf.
ла́вр|ы (-ов) *мн* (*венок*) laurels *мн*; **пожина́ть** *(impf)* ~ to be crowned with laurels; **почи́ть** *(perf)* **на ~ах** to rest on one's laurels.
лавса́н (-а) *м* lavsan (*synthetic polyester fibre or fabric*).
ЛАГ *м сокр* (= *Ли́га ара́бских госуда́рств*) Arab League.
ла́герный *прил* camp *опред.*
ла́гер|ь (-я; *nom pl* **-я́)** *м* camp; (*nom pl* **-и**; *перен*) camp.
лагу́н|а (-ы) *ж* lagoon.
лад (-а; *loc sg* **-у́**, *nom pl* **-ы́)** *м* (*разг: гармония*) harmony; (*МУЗ: обычно мн: деление на грифе*) fret; (: *клавиша*) key; (: *строй*) mode; **быть** *(impf)* **не в ~а́х с** *+instr* to be at odds with; **на свой** ~ in one's own way; **на все ~ы́** in all sorts of ways, every which way (*US*); **руга́ть** *(impf)* **кого́-н на все ~ы́** to call sb every name under the sun; **де́ло идёт на** ~ things are getting better.
ла́дан (-а) *м* incense; **дыша́ть** *(impf)* **на** ~ (*разг*) to be on one's last legs.
ла́ден *прил см* **ла́дный.**
ла́|дить (-жу, -дишь; *perf* **пола́дить)** *несов неперех*: ~ **с** *+instr* to get on (well) with
▸ **ла́диться** *несов возв* to go well.
ла́дно *част* (*разг*) O.K., all right; **пойдём в кино́ – ~** let's go to the cinema – O.K. *или* all right; **~ тебе́!** (*разг: не стоит, не надо*) don't be silly!; **~ тебе́ жа́ловаться/крича́ть** that's enough of your complaining/shouting; **да ~!** you don't say!
ла́д|ный (-ен, -на́, -но) *прил* (*разг: хорошо сложенный*) well-built; **у него́ ~ная фигу́ра** he's a fine figure of a man.
ла́дожск|ий (-ая, -ое, -ие) *прил*: **Л~ое о́зеро** Lake Ladoga.
ладо́н|ь (-и) *ж* (*АНАТ*) palm; **отсю́да Москва́ видна́ как на ~и** from here you can see Moscow clearly.
ладо́ш|и (-) *мн*: **бить в** ~ to clap one's hands; **хло́пать** *(impf)* **в** ~ to clap.
лад|ья́ (-ьи́; *gen pl* **-е́й)** *ж* (*ШАХМАТЫ*) rook, castle.
ЛАЗ (-а) *м сокр* = *Льво́вский авто́бусный заво́д*; (*автобус*) *bus manufactured at the Lvov bus factory.*
лаз (-а) *м* gap.
лазаре́т (-а) *м* (*ВОЕН*) field hospital.
ла́за|ть (-ю) *несов* = **ла́зить.**
лазе́|йка (-йки; *gen pl* **-ек)** *ж* gap; (*перен: в правилах*) loophole.
ла́зер (-а) *м* laser.
ла́зерный *прил* laser *опред*; **ла́зерный при́нтер** laser printer.
ла́|зить (-жу, -зишь) *несов неперех* to climb; (*под стол, под кровать итп*) to crawl.
лазури́т (-а) *м* lapis lazuli.
лазу́рный *прил* azure, sky-blue.
лазу́р|ь (-и) *ж* azure.
ла|й (-я) *м* barking.
ла́йк|а (-и) *ж* husky; (*кожа*) kid.
ла́йковый *прил* kid *опред.*
ла́йнер (-а) *м* liner.
лак (-а) *м* (*для ногтей, для пола*) varnish; (*для волос*) lacquer; **покрыва́ть (покры́ть** *perf*) **что-н ла́ком** to varnish sth.
лака́|ть (-ю) *несов перех* to lap up.
лаке́|й (-я) *м* (*слуга*) footman (*мн* footmen); (*подхалим*) lackey.
лакиро́ванный *прил* (*шкатулка*) lacquered; (*туфли*) patent-leather.
лакир|ова́ть (-у́ю; *perf* **отлакирова́ть)** *несов перех* (*изделие*) to lacquer; (*кожу*) to patent.
лакиро́вк|а (-и) *ж* (*изделия*) lacquer.

ла́кмусов|ый *прил*: **~ая бума́га** litmus paper.
ла́ковый *прил* (*изделия*) lacquered; (*раствор, краски*) lacquer *опред*; **ла́ковая ко́жа** patent leather.
ла́ком|иться (**-люсь, -ишься**; *perf* **пола́комиться**) *несов неперех* (*+instr*) to feast on.
ла́ком|ка (**-ки**; *gen pl* **-ок**) *м/ж* (*любящий вкусное*) gourmet; **она́ настоя́щая ~** (*сладкоежка*) she has a sweet tooth.
ла́комлюсь *несов см* **ла́комиться.**
ла́комок *сущ см* **ла́комка.**
ла́комый *прил* delicious; **ла́комый кусо́к** titbit (*BRIT*), tidbit (*US*).
лакони́зм (**-а**) *м* succinctness.
лакони́чно *нареч* laconically, succinctly.
лакони́чный *прил* (*речь*) laconic, succinct; (*формы здания, рисунок*) spare, austere.
лакто́з|а (**-ы**) *ж* lactose.
ла́м|а (**-ы**) *ж* (*ЗООЛ*) llama ◆ *м* (*РЕЛ*) lama.
Ла-Ма́нш (**-а**) *м* the (English) Channel.
ла́мп|а (**-ы**) *ж* (*осветительная, керосиновая*) lamp; (*ТЕХ*) tube; **ла́мпа дневно́го све́та** fluorescent light.
лампа́д|а (**-ы**) *ж* icon lamp.
лампа́с (**-а**) *м* (*обычно мн*) stripe (*down trouser leg*).
ла́мпоч|ка (**-ки**; *gen pl* **-ек**) *ж* lamp; (*для освещения*) light bulb; **ему́ всё до ~ки** (*разг*) he couldn't care less.
ланге́т (**-а**) *м* fillet steak.
ландша́фт (**-а**) *м* landscape.
ла́ндыш (**-а**) *м* lily of the valley.
ланoли́н (**-а**) *м* lanolin.
ланце́т (**-а**) *м* (*МЕД*) lancet.
лан|ь (**-и**) *ж* fallow deer.
Лао́с (**-а**) *м* Laos.
лао́сск|ий (**-ая, -ое, -ие**) *прил* Laotian.
ла́п|а (**-ы**) *ж* (*зверя*) paw; (*птицы*) foot; (*сосны, ёлки*) bough; (*якоря*) fluke; **попада́ть (попа́сть** *perf*) **кому́-н в ~ы** (*разг*) to fall into sb's clutches; **дава́ть (дать** *perf*) **кому́ в ~у** (*разг*) to give sb a backhander; **ходи́ть** (*impf*) **на за́дних ~х пе́ред кем-н** (*перен*: *разг*) to dance attendance on sb.
ла́п|оть (**-тя**; *nom pl* **-ти**, *gen pl* **-те́й**) *м* (*обычно мн*) bast shoe.
ла́поч|ка (**-ки**; *gen pl* **-ек**) *м/ж* (*разг*) dear, darling.
лапт|а́ (**-ы́**) *ж* lapta (*traditional Russian ball game*).
ла́птя *итп сущ см* **ла́поть.**
ла́пушк|а (**-и**) *ж* dear, darling.
лапш|а́ (**-и́**) *ж* noodles *мн*; (*суп*) noodle soup.
лар|ёк (**-ька́**) *м* stall.
лар|е́ц (**-ца́**) *м* (*шкатулка*) casket.
ларинги́т (**-а**) *м* laryngitis.
ларинголо́ги|я (**-и**) *ж* laryngology.
ларца́ *итп сущ см* **ларе́ц.**
лар|ь (**-я́**) *м* bin.
ларька́ *итп сущ см* **ларёк.**
ла́с|ка (**-ки**) *ж* tenderness; (*gen pl* **-ок**; *ЗООЛ*) weasel.
ласка́тельный *прил*: **~ су́ффикс** (*ЛИНГ*) diminutive suffix (*denoting affection*).
ласка́|ть (**-ю**) *несов перех* (*ребёнка, девушку*) to caress; (*собаку*) to pet; **~** (*impf*) **слух/взор** to be pleasing to the ear/eye
▸ **ласка́ться** (*perf* **приласка́ться**) *несов возв*: **~ся к** *+dat* (*ребёнок*) to snuggle up to; (*кошка*) to rub up against; (*собака*) to fawn on.
ла́сков|ый (**-, -а, -о**) *прил* affectionate; (*перен*: *ветер, солнце итп*) gentle.
ла́сок *сущ см* **ла́ска.**
ласт (**-а**) *м* (*ЗООЛ, СПОРТ*: *обычно мн*) flipper.
ла́стик (**-а**) *м* (*разг*) rubber (*BRIT*), eraser.
ла́сточ|ка (**-ки**; *gen pl* **-ек**) *ж* swallow; **городска́я/берегова́я ~** house/sand martin.
лат (**-а**) *м* lat (*Latvian currency unit*).
лата́|ть (**-ю**; *perf* **залата́ть**) *несов перех* to patch.
латви́йск|ий (**-ая, -ое, -ие**) *прил* Latvian.
Ла́тви|я (**-и**) *ж* Latvia.
лати́нск|ий (**-ая, -ое, -ие**) *прил* Latin; **~ язы́к** Latin.
ла́т|ка (**-ки**; *gen pl* **-ок**) *ж* (*разг*) patch.
лату́н|ь (**-и**) *ж* brass.
ла́т|ы (**-**) *мн* armour *ед* (*BRIT*), armor *ед* (*US*).
латы́н|ь (**-и**) *ж* Latin.
латы́ш (**-а́**) *м* Latvian.
латы́ш|ка (**-ки**; *gen pl* **-ек**) *ж см* **латы́ш.**
латышск|ий (**-ая, -ое, -ие**) *прил* Latvian; **~ язы́к** Latvian.
лауреа́т (**-а**) *м* winner (*of an award*).
лафа́ *как сказ* (*разг*): **нам здесь ~** we've got it easy here.
ла́цкан (**-а**) *м* lapel.
лачу́г|а (**-и**) *ж* hovel.
ла́|ять (**-ю**; *perf* **пролаять**) *несов неперех* to bark.
лба *итп сущ см* **лоб.**
ЛГ *ж сокр* (= *«Литерату́рная газе́та»*) "Literary Gazette".
лгать (**лгу, лжёшь** *итп*, **лгут**; *perf* **солга́ть** *или* **налга́ть**) *несов неперех* to lie.
лгун (**-а́**) *м* liar.
лгу́н|ья (**-ьи**; *gen pl* **-ий**) *ж см* **лгун.**
ЛДПР *ж сокр* = *Либера́льно-демократи́ческая па́ртия России.*
лебед|а́ (**-ы́**) *ж* (*БОТ*) orache.
лебедёнок (**-ёнка**; *nom pl* **-я́та**, *gen pl* **-я́т**) *м* cygnet.
лебеди́н|ый *прил* swan *опред*; (*перен*: *шея*) swanlike; (: *поступь*) graceful; **~ая ста́я** flock of swans; **лебеди́ная пе́сня** swan song.
лебёд|ка (**-ки**; *gen pl* **-ок**) *ж* winch.
ле́бед|ь (**-я**; *gen pl* **-е́й**) *м* swan.
лебедя́та *итп сущ см* **лебедёнок.**
лебе|зи́ть (**-жу́, -зи́шь**) *несов неперех*: **~ (пе́ред**

+*instr*) (*разг*) to fawn (on).
лебя́ж|ий (-ья, -ье, -ьи) *прил*: **~ пух** swan's-down.
лев (льва) *м* lion; (*созвездие*): **Л~** Leo.
левко́|й (-я) *м* (*БОТ*) stock.
левосторо́нн|ий (-яя, -ее, -ие) *прил* on the left; **в Великобрита́нии ~ее движе́ние** in Britain they drive on the left.
левш|а́ (-и́; *gen pl* **-е́й)** *м/ж* left-handed person; **он/она́ ~** he/she is left-handed.
ле́в|ый *прил* left, left-hand; (*партия, взгляды*) left-wing; **~ая рабо́та** (*разг*) moonlighting.
лёг *итп сов см* **лечь**.
лега́в|ый (-ого; *decl like adj*) *м type of gun dog*.
лега́лен *прил см* **лега́льный**.
легализи́р|овать (-ую) (*не*)*сов перех* to legalize.
лега́л|ьный (-ен, -ьна, -ьно) *прил* legal.
леге́нд|а (-ы) *ж* legend; (*перен*) fairy story.
легенда́р|ный (-ен, -на, -но) *прил* legendary.
легио́н (-а) *м* legion.
леги́рованн|ый *прил*: **~ая сталь** steel alloy.
лёг|кий (-кая, -кое, -кие; -ок, -ка́, -ко́) *прил* (*нетяжёлый*) light; (*нетрудный, несерьёзный*) easy; (*боль, насморк*) slight; (*фигура*) graceful; (*характер, человек*) easy-going; **у него́ сли́шком ~кое отноше́ние к жи́зни** he doesn't take life seriously enough; **у него́ ~кая рука́** he brings good luck; **он нашёл рабо́ту с мое́й ~кой руки́** he found work thanks to me; **он ~ок на подъём** (*разг*) he doesn't take much persuading; **~ок на поми́не!** (*разг*) talk of the devil!; **лёгкая атле́тика** athletics (*BRIT*), track-and-field (*US*); **лёгкая промы́шленность** light industry.
легко́ *нареч* easily; **~ сказа́ть** (*разг*) easier said than done; **мне здесь ~** I feel at ease here; **э́то ~** it's easy.
легкоатле́т (-а) *м* athlete (*in track and field events*).
легкоатле́т|ка (-ки; *gen pl* **-ок)** *ж см* **легкоатле́т**.
легкове́р|ный (-ен, -на, -но) *прил* gullible, credulous.
легкове́с|ный (-ен, -на, -но) *прил* superficial.
легков|о́й *прил*: **~а́я маши́на, ~ автомоби́ль** car, automobile (*US*).
легкову́ш|ка (-ки; *gen pl* **-ек)** *ж* (*разг*) motor (*BRIT*), auto (*US*).
лёгк|ое (-ого; *decl like adj*) *ср* (*обычно мн*) lung.
легкомы́слен|ный (-, -на, -но) *прил* (*человек*) frivolous; (*поступок*) thoughtless; (*отношение*) frivolous, flippant.
легкомы́сли|е (-я) *ср* (*человека*) frivolity; (*поступка*) thoughtlessness.
легкопла́в|кий (-кая, -кое, -кие; -ок, -ка, -ко) *прил* fusible.
лёгкост|ь (-и) *ж* (*походки, веса*) lightness; (*задания*) simplicity, easiness; (*характера*) easy-going nature; **у него́ мно́го друзе́й благодаря́ ~и его́ хара́ктера** he has many friends thanks to his easy-going nature.
лёгок *прил см* **лёгкий**.
лёгочный *прил* pulmonary, lung *опред*; **~ больно́й** patient with a pulmonary *или* lung condition.
ле́гче *сравн прил от* **лёгкий** ◆ *сравн нареч от* **легко́** ◆ *как сказ*: **больно́му сего́дня ~** the patient is feeling better today.
лёд (льда; *loc sg* **льду)** *м* ice; **~ тро́нулся** (*перен*) things are moving now.
ледене́|ть (-ю; *perf* **заледене́ть** *или* **оледене́ть**) *несов неперех* to freeze; (*человек, руки*) to be freezing; **он оледене́л от стра́ха** fear made his blood run cold.
ледене́|ц (-ца́) *м* fruit drop.
леден|и́ть (*3sg* **-и́т,** *3pl* **-я́т**) *несов перех* to freeze; **у́жас ~и́т (его́) кровь** terror makes his blood run cold.
леденца́ *итп сущ см* **леденец**.
леденя́щ|ий (-ая, -ее, -ие) *прил* (*ветер, вода*) icy; (*перен*: *ужас, страх*) chilling.
ле́ди *ж нескл* lady.
ледни́к (-а́) *м* glacier.
леднико́вый *прил* glacial.
ледо́вый *прил* ice *опред*.
ледоко́л (-а) *м* icebreaker.
ледору́б (-а) *м* ice axe.
ледохо́д (-а) *м breaking up and drifting of ice on rivers in spring*.
ледяно́й *прил* (*глыба, покров*) ice *опред*; (*ветер, вода, взгляд*) icy.
ле́ек *сущ см* **ле́йка**.
лежа́к (-а́) *м* lounger.
лежа́лый *прил* (*хлеб*) stale; (*товар*) old.
лежа́|ть (-у́, -и́шь) *несов неперех* (*человек, животное*) to lie; (*предмет, вещи*: *на столе, на полке*) to be (lying); (: *в ящике, в шкафу итп*) to be; **~** (*impf*) **в больни́це** to be in hospital; **на нём ~ат забо́ты о семье́** he is responsible for looking after his family; **(у меня́) душа́ не ~и́т к э́той рабо́те** my heart's not in this work; **(у меня́) душа́ не ~и́т к нему́** I don't feel very well disposed towards him.
лежа́ч|ий (-ая, -ее, -ие) *прил* lying; **~ больно́й** bedridden patient; **рабо́та – не бей ~его** (*разг*) it's a cushy job.
ле́жбищ|е (-а) *ср* rookery (*of seals etc*).
лежебо́к|а (-и) *м/ж* (*разг*) couch potato.
лез *итп несов см* **лезть**.
ле́зви|е (-я) *ср* blade.
лез|ть (-у, -ешь; *pt* **-, -ла, -ло)** *несов неперех* (*выпадать*: *волосы, шерсть*) to fall out; (*проникать куда-н*): **~ в** +*acc* to climb in(to); **~** (*impf*) **на** +*acc* to climb (up); **~** (*impf*) **в карма́н** (*разг*) to reach into one's pocket; **~** (*impf*) **в чужи́е дела́** (*разг*) to poke one's nose into other people's business; **~** (*impf*) **в разгово́р** (*разг*) to butt into a conversation; **~** (*impf*) **кому́-н на глаза́** (*разг*) to hang around sb.
лей *несов см* **лить** ◆ **(ле́я)** *м* lay (*Moldavian currency unit*).
лейбори́ст (-а) *м* Labour party member.

лейбори́стск|ий (-ая, -ое, -ие) *прил* Labour.
ле́|йка (-йки; *gen pl* **-ек)** *ж* watering can.
лейко́з (-а) *м* leukaemia (*BRIT*), leukemia (*US*).
лейкопла́стыр|ь (-я) *м* sticking plaster (*BRIT*), adhesive tape (*US*).
лейкоци́т (-а) *м* (*обычно мн*) leucocyte.
Ле́йпциг (-а) *м* Leipzig.
ле́йте *несов см* **лить.**
лейтена́нт (-а) *м* lieutenant.
лейтмоти́в (-а) *м* (*также перен*) leitmotif.
лека́л|о (-а) *ср* French curve.
лека́рственный *прил* medicinal; **лека́рственная фо́рма** medicine.
лека́рств|о (-а) *ср* medicine; ~ **от** *+gen* medicine for; ~ **от ка́шля** cough medicine; **принима́ть (приня́ть** *perf***)/пропи́сывать (прописа́ть** *perf***)** ~ to take/prescribe medicine.
ле́ксик|а (-и) *ж* vocabulary.
лексико́граф (-а) *м* lexicographer.
лексикографи́ческ|ий (-ая, -ое, -ие) *прил* lexicographical.
лексикогра́фи|я (-и) *ж* lexicography.
лексиколо́ги|я (-и) *ж* lexicology.
лексико́н (-а) *м* vocabulary.
ле́ктор (-а) *м* lecturer; (*в клубе*) speaker.
лекцио́нный *прил* lecture *опред*; ~ **курс** course of lectures.
ле́кци|я (-и) *ж* lecture.
леле́ять (-ю; *perf* **взлеле́ять)** *несов перех* (*также перен*) to cherish.
ле́мех (-а) *м* ploughshare (*BRIT*), plowshare (*US*).
лему́р (-а) *м* lemur.
лён (льна) *м* (*БОТ*) flax; (*ткань*) linen.
лени́в|ый (-, -а, -о) *прил* lazy.
Ленингра́д (-а) *м* Leningrad.
ленини́зм (-а) *м* Leninism.
лен|и́ться (-ю́сь, -ишься; *perf* **полени́ться)** *несов возв* to be lazy; ~ **(полени́ться** *perf***)** *+infin* to be too lazy to do.
ле́нт|а (-ы) *ж* (*в косе, на шляпе*) ribbon; (*изоляционная, магнитная*) tape; (*фильм*) film.
ле́нточный *прил*: ~ **червь** tapeworm; ~ **транспортёр** conveyor belt.
лентя́ек *сущ см* **лентя́йка.**
лентя́|й (-я) *м* lazybones.
лентя́|йка (-йки; *gen pl* **-ек)** *ж см* **лентя́й.**
лентя́йнича|ть (-ю) *несов неперех* (*разг*) to lounge about.
лен|ь (-и) *ж* laziness ◆ *как сказ*: **ему́ ~ учи́ться/рабо́тать** he can't be bothered studying/working; **(все) кому́ не** ~ (*разг*) anyone who feels like it.
леопа́рд (-а) *м* leopard.
лепест|о́к (-ка́) *м* petal.
ле́пет (-а) *м* babble; **де́тский** ~ (*перен*) drivel.
лепёш|ка (-ки; *gen pl* **-ек)** *ж* flat bread.
леп|и́ть (-лю́, -ишь; *perf* **вы́лепить)** *несов перех* (*из глины, из пластилина*) to model; (*perf* **слепи́ть**; *соты, гнёзда*) to build
▸ **лепи́ться** *несов возв* (*на деревьях, на склонах*) to cling.
ле́пк|а (-и) *ж* modelling (*BRIT*), modeling (*US*).
леплю́(сь) *несов см* **лепи́ть(ся).**
лепно́й *прил* modelled (*BRIT*), modeled (*US*); (*потолок*) moulded (*BRIT*), molded (*US*).
ле́пт|а (-ы) *ж* contribution; **вноси́ть (внести́** *perf***) свою́ ~у (во что-н)** to do one's bit (for sth); (*внести деньги*) to make a contribution (to sth).
лес (-а; *loc sg* **-у́**, *nom pl* **-а́)** *м* (*большой*) forest; (*небольшой*) wood ◆ *собир* (*материал*) timber (*BRIT*), lumber (*US*); **кто в ~, кто по дрова́** at sixes and sevens; *см также* **леса́.**
лес|а́ (-о́в) *мн* (*СТРОИТ*) scaffolding *ед.*
лесбия́н|ка (-ки; *gen pl* **-ок)** *ж* lesbian.
леси́ст|ый (-, -а, -о) *прил* wooded.
ле́ск|а (-и) *ж* fishing line.
лесни́к (-а́) *м* forester.
лесни́честв|о (-а) *ср* (*участок леса*) area of forest; (*учреждение*) ≈ forestry commission.
лесни́ч|ий (-его; *decl like adj***)** *м* forest ranger.
лесно́й *прил* (*см сущ*) forest *опред*; woodland *опред.*
лесово́дств|о (-а) *ср* forestry.
лесозаготó́в|ка (-ки; *gen pl* **-ок)** *ж* (*обычно мн*) logging *ед.*
лесозащи́тн|ый *прил*: **~ая зо́на** shelter belt (*of trees*).
лесоматериа́л (-а) *м* (*обычно мн*) timber *только ед* (*BRIT*), lumber *только ед* (*US*).
лесонасажде́ни|е (-я) *ср* (*искусственный лес*) plantation: (*разведение леса*) afforestation.
лесопа́рк (-а) *м* woodland park.
лесопи́лк|а (-и) *ж* (*разг*) sawmill.
лесопромы́шленност|ь (-и) *ж сокр* (= *лесна́я промы́шленность*) timber (*BRIT*) *или* lumber (*US*) industry.
лесопромы́шленный *прил* timber-industry *опред* (*BRIT*), lumber-industry *орпед* (*US*).
лесоразрабо́т|ки (-ок) *мн* timber (*BRIT*) *или* lumber (*US*) processing.
лесору́б (-а) *м* lumberjack.
лесосе́к|а (-и) *ж* felling area.
лесоспла́в (-а) *м* timber rafting.
лесосте́п|ь (-и) *ж* forest-steppe (*area in which forest and steppe are mixed*).
ле́стен *прил см* **ле́стный.**
ле́стниц|а (-ы) *ж* (*лестничная клетка*) staircase; (*ступени*) stairs *мн*; (*переносная*) ladder; (*стремянка*) stepladder; **служе́бная** ~ career ladder.
ле́стничн|ый *прил*: **~ая площа́дка** landing; ~ **пролёт** stairway; **~ая кле́тка** stairwell.
ле́ст|ный (-ен, -на, -но) *прил* flattering.
лест|ь (-и) *ж* flattery.
лёт (-а) *м*: **на лету́** in flight; (*перен*: *понимать, усваивать*) very quickly; **он по́нял всё с ~у** (*разг*) he understood everything in a flash.

лета́ (лет) *мн см* **год**; (*возраст*): **ско́лько Вам лет?** how old are you?; **ему́ 16 лет** he is 16 (years old); **он в ~х** he is getting on; **он одни́х лет со мной** he is the same age as me.
лета́л|ьный (-ен, -ьна, -ьно) *прил* fatal; **~ьная до́за** lethal dose.
летарги́ческ|ий (-ая, -ое, -ие) *прил* lethargic.
лета́тельный *прил* flying *опред*.
лета́|ть (-ю) *несов неперех* to fly.
ле|те́ть (-чу́, -ти́шь) *несов неперех* to fly; (*перен*: *мчаться*) to fly, rush; (*perf* **полете́ть**; *разг*): **~ с** *+gen* (*со стула*) to fall off; (*с лестницы*) to fall down; **вре́мя ~ти́т** time flies; **все на́ши пла́ны полете́ли** (*разг*) all our plans were dashed.
ле́тн|ий (-яя, -ее, -ие) *прил* summer *опред*.
лётн|ый *прил*: **~ая пого́да** good weather for flying; **лётное по́ле** airfield; **лётная шко́ла** flying school.
ле́т|о (-а) *ср* summer; **ско́лько лет, ско́лько зим!** it's been ages!
летопи́с|ец (-ца) *м* chronicler.
ле́топис|ь (-и) *ж* chronicle.
летосчисле́ни|е (-я) *ср* calendar.
лету́чек *сущ см* **лету́чка**.
лету́ч|ий (-ая, -ее, -ие) *прил* (*газ, масло*) volatile; (*семена*) winged; (*песок*) shifting; (*перен*: *собрание, разговор*) brief; **лету́чая мышь** bat.
лету́ч|ка (-ки; *gen pl* **-ек)** *ж* (*разг*: *собрание*) brief meeting; (: *листок*) leaflet.
лётчик (-а) *м* pilot; **~-испыта́тель** test pilot; **~-истреби́тель** fighter pilot.
лётчиц|а (-ы) *ж см* **лётчик**.
ле́чащ|ий (-ая, -ее, -ие) *прил*: **~ врач** ≈ consultant-in-charge (*BRIT*), ≈ attending physician (*US*).
лече́бниц|а (-ы) *ж* clinic.
лече́бн|ый *прил* (*учреждение*) medical; (*свойства, трава*) medicinal; (*ванна*) medicated; **у него́ бога́тая ~ая пра́ктика** he has extensive clinical experience; **~ая гимна́стика** therapeutic exercise; **лече́бное сре́дство** medication.
лече́ни|е (-я) *ср* (*раненных, детей*) treatment; (*от простуды, от туберкулёза итп*) cure.
леч|и́ть (-у́, -ишь) *несов от* **вы́лечить** ◆ *перех* to treat; (*больного*): **~ кого́-н от** *+gen* to treat sb for
▸ **лечи́ться** *несов от* **вы́лечиться** ◆ *возв* to undergo treatment.
лечу́ *несов см* **лете́ть**.
лечь (ля́гу, ля́жешь *итп*, **ля́гут**; *pt* **лёг, легла́, легло́**, *imper* **ля́г(те)**, *impf* **ложи́ться)** *сов неперех* (*на землю, на диван итп*) to lie down; (*пойти спать*) to go to bed; (*снег*) to fall; (*перен*): **~ на** *+acc* (*ответственность, заботы*) to fall on; **ложи́ться (~** *perf*) **в больни́цу** to be in hospital; **ложи́ться (~** *perf*) **в дрейф** to drift.
ле́ш|ий (-его; *decl like adj*) *м* wood goblin.
лещ (-а́) *м* bream.
лженау́к|а (-и) *ж* pseudoscience.
лжесвиде́тел|ь (-я) *м* perjurer.
лжесвиде́тельниц|а (-ы) *ж см* **лжесвиде́тель**.
лжесвиде́тельств|о (-а) *ср* perjury.
лжесвиде́тельств|овать (-ую) *несов неперех* to commit perjury.
лжец (-а́) *м* liar.
лжи *итп сущ см* **ложь**.
лжи́вост|ь (-и) *ж* falseness.
лжи́в|ый (-, -а, -о) *прил* (*человек*) deceitful; (*улыбка, заверения*) false.
ли *част* (*в вопросе*): **зна́ешь ~ ты, что ...** do you know that ...; (*в косвенном вопросе*): **спроси́, смо́жет ~ он нам помо́чь** ask if he can help us ◆ *союз*: **придёт ~, не придёт, не ва́жно** it's not important if he comes or not; **она́ краси́ва, не так ~?** she's beautiful, isn't she?; **они́ бы́ли пра́вы, не так ~?** they were right, weren't they?
лиа́н|а (-ы) *ж* (*БОТ*: *растение*) liana.
либера́л (-а) *м* Liberal; (*о терпимом человеке*) liberal.
либера́лен *прил см* **либера́льный**.
либерализа́ци|я (-и) *ж* liberalization.
либерали́зм (-а) *м* liberalism; (*с бездельниками, с подчинёнными итп*) tolerance.
либера́льнича|ть (-ю) *несов неперех*: **~ с** *+instr* (*с подчинёнными*) to fraternize with; (*с бездельниками*) to connive at.
либера́л|ьный (-ен, -ьна, -ьно) *прил* liberal; (*no short form*; *партия*) Liberal.
ли́бо *союз* (*или*) or; **~ я, ~ он** it's either me or him.
либретти́ст (-а) *м* librettist.
либре́тто *ср нескл* libretto.
Лива́н (-а) *м* (the) Lebanon.
лива́нск|ий (-ая, -ое, -ие) *прил* Lebanese.
ли́в|ень (-ня) *м* (*дождь*) downpour; (*перен*: *огня, свинца*) shower.
ли́вер (-а) *м* offal.
ли́верн|ый *прил*: **~ая колбаса́** *sausage made with offal*.
Ливерпу́л|ь (-я) *м* Liverpool.
ли́внев|ый *прил*: **~ дождь** downpour; **~ые во́ды** rainwater.
ли́вня *итп сущ см* **ли́вень**.
ливре́|я (-и) *ж* livery.
ли́г|а (-и) *ж* (*ПОЛИТ, СПОРТ*) league.
лигату́р|а (-ы) *ж* (*МЕД, ЛИНГ*) ligature.
ли́дер (-а) *м* leader.
ли́дерств|о (-а) *ср* leadership.
лиди́р|овать (-ую) *несов неперех* to be in the lead, lead.
ли|за́ть (-жу́, -жешь) *несов перех* (*тарелку, мороженое*) to lick; (*подлеж*: *пламя, волны*) to lap.
ли́зинг (-а) *м* leasing.
лизн|у́ть (-у́, -ёшь) *сов перех* to lick.
лик (-а) *м* countenance.
ликбе́з (-а) *м сокр* (*ИСТ*: *= ликвида́ция*

безгра́мотности) campaign against illiteracy; (*перен*: *обучение элементарному*) basic teaching.
ликвида́тор (**-а**) *м* (*пожара, последствий аварии*) relief worker; (*КОММ*) liquidator.
ликвида́ци|я (**-и**) *ж* (*также ЭКОН*) liquidation; (*оружия*) destruction; **доброво́льная** ~ (*ЭКОН*) voluntary liquidation.
ликвиди́р|овать (**-ую**) *(не)сов перех* (*оружие*) to destroy; (*фирму, дела*) to liquidate
▸ **ликвиди́роваться** *(не)сов возв* (*ЭКОН*: *фирма, трест итп*) to be liquidated.
ликви́дност|ь (**-и**) *ж* liquidity.
ликви́дн|ый *прил*: **~ые акти́вы** *или* **сре́дства** liquid assets.
ликви́д|ы (**-ов**) *мн* liquid assets *мн*.
ликёр (**-а**) *м* liqueur.
ликёро-во́дочный *прил*: ~ **заво́д** distillery.
ликова́ни|е (**-я**) *ср* rejoicing.
лик|ова́ть (**-у́ю**) *несов неперех* to be elated.
лилипу́т (**-а**) *м* midget.
лилипу́т|ка (**-ки**; *gen pl* **-ок**) *ж см* **лилипу́т**.
ли́ли|я (**-и**) *ж* lily.
лило́вый *прил* purple.
лима́н (**-а**) *м* mud flats *мн*.
лими́т (**-а**) *м* (*на электроэнергию, на бензин*) quota; (*цен*) limit.
лимити́р|овать (**-ую**) *(не)сов перех* (*потребление, импорт*) to limit; (*цены*) to cap.
лими́тчик (**-а**) *м* (*разг*) *person who holds a temporary residence permit issued in connection with work*.
лимо́н (**-а**) *м* (*дерево*) lemon tree; (*плод*) lemon; **он как вы́жатый** ~ he's completely washed out.
лимона́д (**-а**) *м* lemonade; (*разг*: *любой газированный напиток*) fizzy drink.
лимо́нный *прил* lemon; **лимо́нная кислота́** citric acid.
лимузи́н (**-а**) *м* limousine.
лимфати́ческ|ий (**-ая, -ое, -ие**) *прил* lymphatic.
лингафо́нный *прил*: ~ **кабине́т** language laboratory.
лингви́ст (**-а**) *м* linguist.
лингви́стик|а (**-и**) *ж* linguistics.
лингвисти́ческ|ий (**-ая, -ое, -ие**) *прил* linguistic.
лине́|йка (**-йки**; *gen pl* **-ек**) *ж* (*линия*) line; (*инструмент*) ruler; (*шеренга*) ≈ assembly; **тетра́дь в ~йку** lined notebook.
лине́йн|ый *прил* (*расположение, построение*) linear; ~ **солда́т** soldier of the line; **~ые ме́ры** linear measures; **лине́йные войска́** regular forces; **лине́йный кре́йсер** battle cruiser.
ли́нз|а (**-ы**) *ж* lens.
ли́ни|я (**-и**) *ж* line; (*перен*: *партийная, профсоюзная*) policy, line; **по ~и** *+gen* in the line of; **вести́** *(impf) или* **проводи́ть** *(impf)* **~ю на** *+acc* to pursue a policy of; **проводи́ть** (**провести́** *perf*) **~ю** to draw a line; **вести́** *(impf) или* **гнуть** *(impf)* **свою́ ~ю** (*разг*) to have one's own way; **желе́знодорожная** ~ railway (*BRIT*) *или* railroad (*US*) track; **возду́шная** ~ airway; **морска́я** ~ sea route; **трамва́йная** ~ tramway; **ли́ния фро́нта** (*ВОЕН*) front line; **ли́ния воро́т** goal line.
линко́р (**-а**) *м сокр* (= *лине́йный кора́бль*) destroyer.
лино́ванный *прил* lined, ruled.
лин|ова́ть (**-у́ю**; *perf* **разлинова́ть**) *несов перех* to rule.
лино́леум (**-а**) *м* linoleum.
линч|ева́ть (**-у́ю**) *(не)сов перех* to lynch.
линя́лый *прил* discoloured (*BRIT*), discolored (*US*).
линя́|ть (*3sg* **-ет**, *3pl* **-ют**, *perf* **полиня́ть**) *несов неперех* to run (*colour*); (*perf* **облиня́ть**; *животные*) to moult (*BRIT*), molt (*US*).
Лио́н (**-а**) *м* Lyon.
ли́п|а (**-ы**) *ж* (*дерево*) lime (tree); (*разг*: *фальшивка*) fake.
ли́п|кий (**-кая, -кое, -кие; -ок, -ка́, -ко**) *прил* sticky.
ли́п|нуть (**-ну, -нешь**; *pt* **-, ла, -ло**, *perf* **прили́пнуть**) *несов неперех* (*грязь, тесто*) to stick; (*перен*: *человек*) to cling.
ли́повый *прил* (*цвет, лист*) lime; (*из липы*) lime-blossom *опред*; (*разг*: *фальшивый*) forged.
ли́пок *прил см* **ли́пкий**.
липу́ч|ка (**-ки**; *gen pl* **-ек**) *ж* (*разг*: *липкая лента*) sticky tape; (: *застёжка*) Velcro® fastening.
ли́р|а (**-ы**) *ж* (*МУЗ*) lyre; (*денежная единица*) lira.
лири́зм (**-а**) *м* lyricism.
ли́рик (**-а**) *м* lyric poet.
ли́рик|а (**-и**) *ж* lyric poetry.
лири́чен *прил см* **лири́чный**.
лири́ческ|ий (**-ая, -ое, -ие**) *прил* lyrical.
лири́ч|ный (**-ен, -на, -но**) *прил* lyrical.
лис (**-а**) *м* (male) fox, dog fox.
лис|а́ (**-ы́**; *nom pl* **-ы**) *ж* fox; (*перен*: *хитрый человек*) sly fox.
лис|ёнок (**-ёнка**; *nom pl* **-я́та**, *gen pl* **-я́т**) *м* fox cub.
ли́с|ий (**-ья, -ье, -ьи**) *прил* (*след, нора*) fox's; (*шуба, воротник, горжетка*) fox-fur.
лиси́ц|а (**-ы**) *ж* vixen.
лиси́ч|ка (**-ки**; *gen pl* **-ек**) *ж уменьш от* **лиса́**; (*гриб*) chanterelle.
лист (**-а́**; *nom pl* **-ья**) *м* (*растения, дерева*) leaf; (*nom pl* **-ы́**; *бумаги, железа*) sheet; **исполни́тельный** ~ writ of execution; **опро́сный** ~ questionnaire.
листа́|ть (**-ю**) *несов перех* (*страницы*) to turn; ~ *(impf)* **кни́гу** to leaf through a book.
листв|а́ (**-ы́**) *ж собир* foliage, leaves *мн*.

ли́ственниц|а (-ы) *ж* larch.
ли́ственный *прил* deciduous.
листка́ *итп сущ см* **листо́к.**
листо́в|ка (-ки; *gen pl* **-ок)** *ж* leaflet.
листово́й *прил* (*сталь, железо*) sheet *опред*; (*табак*) leaf *опред*.
листо́вок *сущ см* **листо́вка.**
лист|о́к (-ка́) *м* (*бумаги*) sheet; (*бланк: контрольный, техосмотра*) certificate; **листо́к нетрудоспосо́бности** disability certificate.
листопа́д (-а) *м* fall of leaves.
ли́стья *итп сущ см* **лист.**
лися́та *итп сущ см* **лисёнок.**
лит (-а) *м* lit (*Lithuanian currency unit*).
лита́вр|ы (-) *мн* kettledrum *ед*; **бить** (*impf*) **в ~** (*перен: торжествовать*) to sound the trumpets.
Литв|а́ (-ы́) *ж* Lithuania.
лите́йный *прил*: **~ цех** foundry.
лите́йщик (-а) *м* foundry worker.
ли́тер|а (-ы) *ж* (*ТИПОГ*) type.
литера́тор (-а) *м* literary man.
литерату́р|а (-ы) *ж* literature; (*также:* **худо́жественная ~**) fiction.
литерату́рный *прил* literary; **литерату́рный язы́к** literary language.
литературове́д (-а) *м* literary critic.
литературове́дени|е (-я) *ср* literary criticism.
литературове́дческ|ий (-ая, -ое, -ие) *прил* literary.
ли́терный *прил* (*с цифрой*) lettered; **~ набо́р** typesetting.
ли́ти|й (-я) *м* lithium.
лито́в|ец (-ца) *м* Lithuanian.
лито́в|ка (-ки; *gen pl* **-ок)** *ж см* **лито́вец.**
лито́вск|ий (-ая, -ое, -ие) *прил* Lithuanian; **~ язы́к** Lithuanian.
лито́вца *итп сущ см* **лито́вец.**
литографи́ческ|ий (-ая, -ое, -ие) *прил* lithographic.
литогра́фи|я (-и) *ж* (*ИСКУССТВО*) lithograph; (*ТИПОГ*) lithography.
лито́й *прил* (*ТЕХ*) moulded (*BRIT*), molded (*US*), cast; **лито́е изде́лие** cast.
литр (-а) *м* litre (*BRIT*), liter (*US*).
литро́вый *прил* (*бутылка, фляга итп*) (one-)litre (*BRIT*), (one-)liter (*US*).
литурги́|я (-и) *ж* liturgy.
лить (лью, льёшь; *pt* **лил, лила́, ли́ло)** *несов перех* (*воду*) to pour; (*слёзы*) to shed; (*ТЕХ: детали, изделия*) to cast, mould (*BRIT*), mold (*US*) ◆ *неперех* (*вода, дождь*) to pour; **дождь льёт как из ведра́** it's pouring (down)
▸ **ли́ться** *несов возв* (*вода*) to pour; (*перен: звуки*) to float; (*: свет*) to flood.
лить|ё (-я́) *ср* (*действие: деталей*) casting, moulding (*BRIT*), molding (*US*) ◆ *собир* (*литые изделия*) casts *мн*.
лиф (-а) *м* bodice.
лифт (-а) *м* lift.
лифтёр (-а) *м* lift operator.
лифтёрш|а (-и) *ж см* **лифтёр.**
ли́фчик (-а) *м* bra.
лиха́ч (-а́) *м* (*разг*) reckless driver.
лиха́честв|о (-а) *ср* (*при вождении*) reckless driving; (*в поведении*) recklessness.
лихв|а́ (-ы́) *ж*: **он отплати́л мне с ~о́й за мою́ доброту́** he more than repaid me for my kindness; **тебе́ вре́мени/де́нег хва́тит с ~о́й** you've got more than enough time/money.
ли́х|о (-а) *ср*: **не помина́й(те) ~м** (*разг*) remember me kindly.
лих|о́й (-, -а́, -о) *прил* (*наездник*) dashing; (*скакун*) swift; (*пора, враг*) evil; **~а́ беда́ нача́ло** the first step is the hardest.
лихора́д|ить (*3sg* **-ит**) *несов безл*: **меня́ ~ит** I feel feverish; **эконо́мику ~ит** the economy is ailing.
лихора́дк|а (-и) *ж* (*МЕД, также перен*) fever; (*: на губах*) cold sore; **золота́я ~** gold fever.
лихора́доч|ный (-ен, -на, -но) *прил* (*также перен*) feverish.
Лихтенште́йн (-а) *м* Liechtenstein.
лицев|о́й *прил* (*нерв*) facial; **~а́я сторона́ мате́рии** the right side of the material; **лицево́й счёт** personal account.
лицезр|е́ть (-ю́, -и́шь) *несов перех* to behold.
лицеи́ст (-а) *м* lycée pupil, ≈ secondary school pupil.
лице́|й (-я) *м* lycée, ≈ secondary school.
лицеме́р (-а) *м* hypocrite.
лицеме́рен *прил см* **лицеме́рный.**
лицеме́ри|е (-я) *ср* hypocrisy.
лицеме́р|ить (-ю, -ишь) *несов неперех* to be hypocritical *или* a hypocrite.
лицеме́р|ный (-ен, -на, -но) *прил* hypocritical.
лицензи́ровани|е (-я) *ср* licensing.
лице́нзи|я (-и) *ж* licence (*BRIT*), license (*US*).
ли|цо́ (-ца́; *nom pl* **-ца)** *ср* face; (*перен: индивидуальность*) image; (*ткани итп*) right side; (*ЛИНГ*) person; **от ~ца́** *+gen* in the name of, on behalf of; **пе́ред ~м** *+gen* in the face of; **э́та блу́за тебе́ к ~цу́** that blouse suits you; **тебе́ не к ~цу́ безде́льничать** shame on you for being so lazy; **знать** (*impf*) **кого́-н в ~** to know sb's face; **на ней ~ца́ нет** she looks dreadful; **они́ не уда́рили в грязь ~м** they didn't disgrace themselves; **стира́ть (стере́ть** *perf*) **с ~ца́ земли́** to wipe from *или* off the face of the earth; **пе́рвое/тре́тье ~** (*ЛИНГ*) first/third person; **показа́ть** (*perf*) **това́р ~м** to show sth to advantage; **~м к лицу́** face to face; **официа́льное ~** official; **физи́ческое ~** (*ЮР*) natural person, individual.
личи́н|а (-ы) *ж* mask; **под ~ой** *+gen* under the guise of.
личи́н|ка (-ки; *gen pl* **-ок)** *ж* maggot.
ли́чно *нареч* (*знать*) personally; (*встретить*) in person; **~ я ...** (*разг*) as for me ...; **~ мне всё равно́** (*разг*) personally, I don't care; **он всё проверя́ет ~** he checks everything personally *или* himself.
ли́чност|ь (-и) *ж* (*выдающаяся, загадочная*)

individual; (*обычно мн*: *обидные замечания*) personal remark; **устана́вливать (установи́ть** *perf*) **чью-н** ~ to establish sb's identity.

ли́чный *прил* (*персональный*) personal; (*частный*) private; **ли́чная ссу́да** (*КОММ*) personal loan; **ли́чное де́ло** personal records; **ли́чный соста́в** staff.

лиша́|й (**-я́**) *м* herpes.

лиша́йник (**-а**) *м* lichen.

лиша́|ть (**-ю**) *несов от* **лиши́ть**.

лишён (**-а́, -о́, -ы́**) *как сказ*: **он ~ та́кта/чу́вства ю́мора** he is devoid of tact/a sense of humour; **э́то не лишено́ основа́ния/смы́сла** this is not totally lacking in reason/sense.

лише́ни|е (**-я**) *ср* (*прав, привилегий*) deprivation; (*большое, горькое*) loss; (*обычно мн*: *нужда*) privation; **~ свобо́ды** imprisonment; **терпе́ть** (*impf*) **~я** to suffer privation; **~ пра́ва со́бственности** (*ЮР*) foreclosure.

лиш|и́ть (**-у́, -и́шь**; *impf* **лиша́ть**) *сов перех*: **~ кого́-н/что-н** *+gen* (*отнять*: *прав, привилегий*) to deprive sb/sth of; (*покоя, счастья*) to rob sb/sth of; **лиша́ть (~** *perf*) **кого́-н насле́дства** to disinherit sb; **лиша́ть (~** *perf*) **жи́зни кого́-н** to take sb's life; **лиша́ть (~** *perf*) **кого́-н сло́ва** to deny sb the right to speak.

ли́шн|ий (**-яя, -ее, -ие**) *прил* (*вес*) extra; (*деньги, билет*) spare; (*расходы, вещи*) unnecessary; **~ раз** once again *или* more; **не ~ее** *или* **~е** *+infin* ... it would not be a bad idea to ...; **сказа́ть** (*perf*) **~ее** to say the wrong thing; **три килогра́мма с ~им** over three kilogrammes; **тре́тий ~** three's a crowd.

лишь *част* (*только*) only ◆ *союз* (*как только*) as soon as; **~ бы она́ согласи́лась!** if only she would agree!; **ему́ не ва́жно что де́лать, ~ бы не рабо́тать** he doesn't care what he does, as long as he doesn't have to work; **ему́ ~ бы уйти́** he just wants to leave.

лоб (**лба**; *loc sg* **лбу**) *м* forehead; **сказа́ть** (*perf*) **кому́-н в ~** (*перен*) to tell sb straight; **у него́ на лбу напи́сано, что он врёт** (*разг*) it's written all over his face that he's lying.

ло́бби *ср нескл* lobby.

лобби́ст (**-а**) *м* lobbyist.

ло́бзик (**-а**) *м* fret saw.

ло́бный *прил* (*АНАТ*) frontal.

лобово́й *прил* frontal; **лобово́е стекло́** windscreen (*BRIT*), windshield (*US*).

лоботря́с (**-а**) *м* (*разг*) lazybones.

лов (**-а**) *м* catching.

лов|е́ц (**-ца́**) *м* catcher; **~ же́мчуга** pearl diver.

лов|и́ть (**-лю́, -ишь**; *perf* **пойма́ть**) *несов перех* to catch; (*случай, момент*) to seize; **~** (*impf*) **ры́бу** to fish; **~** (*impf*) **кого́-н на лжи** to catch sb out; **пойма́ть** (*perf*) **кого́-н на сло́ве** to take sb at their word; **~ (пойма́ть** *perf*) **на себе́ чей-н взгляд** to catch sb's eye; **~ (пойма́ть** *perf*) **себя́ на мы́сли, что** ... to catch o.s. thinking that ....

ловка́ч (**-а́**) *м* (*разг*) dodgy character.

ло́в|кий (**-кая, -кое, -кие; -ок, -ка́, -ко**) *прил* (*человек*) agile; (*прыжок, движение*) nimble; (*удар*) swift; (*разг*: *торговец*) sharp.

ло́вко *нареч* (*прыгнуть*) nimbly; (*придумать*) smartly; (*придумано, сделано*) smartly ◆ *как сказ* that's smart.

ловлю́ *несов см* **лови́ть**.

ло́вл|я (**-и**) *ж* (*действие*) catching; **ры́бная ~** fishing.

ло́вок *прил см* **ло́вкий**.

лову́ш|ка (**-ки**; *gen pl* **-ек**) *ж* (*также перен*) trap.

ловца́ *итп сущ см* **лове́ц**.

логари́фм (**-а**) *м* logarithm.

логарифми́ческ|ий (**-ая, -ое, -ие**) *прил*: **~ая лине́йка** slide rule.

ло́гик|а (**-и**) *ж* logic.

логи́чен *прил см* **логи́чный**.

логи́ческ|ий (**-ая, -ое, -ие**) *прил* logical.

логи́ч|ный (**-ен, -на, -но**) *прил* logical.

ло́говище (**-а**) *ср* (*также перен*) den, lair.

ло́гов|о (**-а**) *ср* = **ло́говище**.

ло́джи|я (**-и**) *ж* recess balcony.

ло́д|ка (**-ки**; *gen pl* **-ок**) *ж* boat; **подво́дная ~** submarine.

ло́доч|ка (**-ки**; *gen pl* **-ек**) *ж уменьш от* **ло́дка**; (*обычно мн*: *открытые туфли*) court shoe.

ло́дочный *прил* (*вёсла*) boat's; **ло́дочная ста́нция** boat-hire place.

лоды́ж|ка (**-ки**; *gen pl* **-ек**) *ж* ankle.

ло́дырнича|ть (**-ю**) *несов неперех* (*разг*) to idle.

ло́дыр|ь (**-я**) *м* (*разг*) idler.

ло́ж|а (**-и**) *ж* (*в театре, в зале*) box; (*массонская*) lodge; **ло́жа пре́ссы** press gallery.

ложби́н|а (**-ы**) *ж* dip (*in the ground*).

ло́ж|е (**-а**) *ср* bed.

ло́жек *сущ см* **ло́жка**.

ло́жен *прил см* **ло́жный**.

лож|и́ться (**-у́сь, -и́шься**) *несов от* **лечь**.

ло́ж|ка (**-ки**; *gen pl* **-ек**) *ж* spoon.

ло́ж|ный (**-ен, -на, -но**) *прил* false; (*вывод*) wrong; **представля́ть (предста́вить** *perf*) **что-н в ~ном све́те** to show sth in a false light; **ло́жные показа́ния** false evidence; **ло́жная трево́га** false alarm.

ложь (**лжи**; *instr sg* **ло́жью**) *ж* lie.

лоз|а́ (**-ы́**; *nom pl* **-ы**) *ж* (*ивы итп*) cane; (*винограда*) vine.

ло́зунг (**-а**) *м* (*призыв*) slogan; (*плакат*) banner.

лока́лен *прил см* **лока́льный**.

локализа́ци|я (**-и**) *ж* localization.

локализ|ова́ть (**-у́ю**) (*не*)*сов перех* to localize.

лока́л|ьный (**-ен, -ьна, -ьно**) *прил* local.

лока́тор (**-а**) *м*: **опти́ческий ~** radar; **звуково́й ~** sonar.

локоти́в (**-а**) *м* locomotive.
ло́кон (**-а**) *м* singlet.
ло́к|оть (**-тя**; *gen pl* **-те́й**, *dat pl* **-тя́м**) *м* elbow; **куса́ть** *(impf)* **~ти** (*разг*) to kick o.s.; **чу́вство ~тя** team spirit.
ло́ктя *итп сущ см* **ло́коть.**
лом (**-а**) *м* crowbar ◆ *собир* (*для переработки*) scrap; **металлический ~** scrap metal.
ло́ман|ый *прил* broken; **~ая ли́ния** zigzag.
лома́|ть (**-ю**; *perf* **слома́ть** *или* **разлома́ть**) *несов перех* (*разделять на куски*) to break; (*perf* **слома́ть** *или* **полома́ть**; *приводить в негодность*) to break; (*perf* **полома́ть**; *устои, традиции*) to challenge; (*планы*) to frustrate; ~ *(impf)* **го́лову над чем-то** to rack one's brains over sth; ~ *(impf)* **привы́чки** to force o.s. to change one's habits; **жизнь слома́ла его́** life dealt him a cruel blow
▸ **лома́ться** (*perf* **полома́ться** *или* **слома́ться**) *несов возв* to break; (*no perf*; *перен*: *обычаи, устои*) to be challenged; (: *человек*) to show off; (: *заставлять себя просить*) to be fussy.
ломба́рд (**-а**) *м* pawnshop; **закла́дывать (заложи́ть** *perf***) что-н в ~** to pawn sth.
ломба́рдный *прил* pawn *опред.*
лом|и́ть (**-лю́, -ишь**) *несов безл*: **у меня́ ло́мит ко́сти** my bones are aching; **наро́д ло́мит туда́** (*разг*) the people are flocking there
▸ **ломи́ться** *несов возв* (*ветви, деревья*) to groan; (*разг*: *идти насильно*) to pour in; **стол ~и́лся от еды́** (*перен*) the table groaned under the food.
ло́мк|а (**-и**) *ж* breaking; (*разг*) cold turkey.
ло́м|кий (**-кая, -кое, -кие; -ок, -ка́, -ко**) *прил* (*хрупкий*: *стекло*) fragile; (: *лёд*) brittle.
ломлю́(сь) *несов см* **ломи́ть(ся)**.
ломов|о́й *прил*: **~а́я ло́шадь** carthorse; (*перен*: *разг*) dogsbody.
ло́мок *прил см* **ло́мкий.**
ломо́т|а (**-ы**) *ж* ache.
лом|о́ть (**-тя́**) *м* slice.
ло́мтик (**-а**) *м* = **ломо́ть.**
ломтя́ *итп сущ см* **ломо́ть.**
Ло́ндон (**-а**) *м* London.
ло́ндон|ец (**-ца**) *м* Londoner.
ло́ндон|ка (**-ки**; *gen pl* **-ок**) *ж см* **ло́ндонец.**
ло́ндонца *итп сущ см* **ло́ндонец.**
ло́н|о (**-а**) *ср* (*женщины*) bosom; (*перен*): **на ~е приро́ды** in the open air.
ло́паст|ь (**-и**; *gen pl* **-е́й**) *ж* (*также* ТЕХ) blade.
лопа́т|а (**-ы**) *ж* spade.
лопа́т|ка (**-ки**; *gen pl* **-ок**) *ж уменьш от* **лопа́та**; (АНАТ) shoulder blade; **класть (положи́ть** *perf***) кого́-н на обе ~ки** (*перен*) to beat sb hands down.
ло́па|ть (**-ю**; *perf* **сло́пать**) *несов перех* (*разг*) to gobble (up).
ло́па|ться (**-юсь**) *сов от* **ло́пнуть.**
ло́пн|уть (**-ну, -нешь**; *perf* **ло́паться**) *сов неперех* (*разрываться*: *шар*) to burst; (*стекло*) to shatter; (*верёвка, струна*) to snap; (*разг*: *банк, предприятие*) to go bust; **у меня́ терпе́ние ~уло** (*разг*) I've run out of patience.
лопу́х (**-а́**) *м* burdock; (*перен*: *разг*: *простак*) simpleton.
ЛОР (**-а**) *м сокр* (= *оториноларинголо́гия*) ORL (= *otorhinolaryngology*), ENT (= *ear-nose-throat*).
лорд (**-а**) *м* lord.
лорне́т (**-а**) *ж* lorgnette.
Лос-А́нджелес (**-а**) *м* Los Angeles.
лоси́н|а (**-ы**) *ж* (*кожа лося*) elkskin; (*мясо лося*) elk (meat); *см также* **лоси́ны.**
лоси́н|ы (**-**) *мн* leggings *мн.*
лоси́х|а (**-и**) *ж* female elk *или* moose (*мн* moose).
лоск (**-а**) *м* (*глянец*) shine; (*перен*: *в доме*) spotlessness; (: *в одежде*) flair; **наводи́ть (навести́** *perf***) ~ на что-н** to give sth a polish.
лоску́т (**-а́**) *м* (*материи, кожи*) scrap.
лоску́тн|ый *прил*: **~ое одея́ло** patchwork quilt.
лосн|и́ться (**-ю́сь, -и́шься**) *несов возв* (*от жира, от крема*) to shine.
лососёвый *прил* salmon.
лососи́н|а (**-ы**) *ж* salmon (*meat*).
лосо́с|ь (**-я**) *м* salmon.
лос|ь (**-я**; *gen pl* **-е́й**) *м* elk, moose (*мн* moose).
лосьо́н (**-а**) *м* lotion.
лот (**-а**) *м* (МОР) lead line; (КОММ: *на аукционе, на торгах*) lot.
лотере́йный *прил* lottery *опред.*
лотере́|я (**-и**) *ж* lottery.
лотка́ *итп сущ см* **лото́к.**
лото́ *ср нескл* lotto.
лот|о́к (**-ка́**) *м* (*прилавок*) stall; (*ящик для торговли*) trader's tray; (*жёлоб*) trough.
ло́тос (**-а**) *м* lotus.
лото́чник (**-а**) *м* stallholder.
лохма́|тить (**-чу, -тишь**; *perf* **взлохма́тить**) *несов перех* to fluff up.
лохма́т|ый (**-, -а, -о**) *прил* (*животное*) shaggy; (*волосы*) straggly; (*человек*) dishevelled.
лохма́чу *сов см* **лохма́тить.**
лохмо́ть|я (**-ев**) *мн* rags *мн.*
ло́цман (**-а**) *м* pilot (*on ship*).
лошади́ный *прил* (*седло, упряжь*) horse's; (*лицо*) equine; **лошади́ная си́ла** horsepower.
лоша́дник (**-а**) *м* (*разг*: *любитель лошадей*) horse-lover; (*торговец лошадьми*) horse-trader.
ло́шад|ь (**-и**; *gen pl* **-е́й**) *ж* horse.
лощёный *прил* (*бумага*) glossy; (*перен*: *человек, внешность*) polished.
лощи́н|а (**-ы**) *ж* dell.
лоя́л|ьный (**-ен, -ьна, -ьно**) *прил* loyal (*to the state*).
л.с. *сокр* (= *лошади́ная си́ла*) h.p. (= *horsepower*).
ЛСД *м сокр* LSD (= *lysergic acid diethylamide*).
Луа́р|а (**-ы**) *ж* the Loire.
луб|о́к (**-ка́**) *м* (*кора*) bast; (*повязка*) splint; **ру́сский ~** (ФОЛЬКЛОР) lubok (*popular colour print*).

лубрика́тор (-а) *м* lubricant.
луг (-а; *loc sg* **-у́,** *nom pl* **-а́)** *м* meadow.
лу|ди́ть (-жу́, -ди́шь) *несов перех* to tin.
лу́ж|а (-и) *ж* (*на улице, на дороге*) puddle; (*на полу, на столе*) pool; **сади́ться (сесть** *perf*) **в ~у** (*перен: разг*) to get o.s. into a mess.
лужа́|йка (-йки; *gen pl* **-ек)** *ж* (*полянка*) glade; (*газон*) lawn.
лужён|ый *прил* (*самовар, чайник итп*) tin-plated; **у него́ ~ая гло́тка** (*перен: разг*) he has iron lungs.
лужу́ *несов см* **луди́ть.**
лу́з|а (-ы) *ж* pocket (*on a billiard table*).
лук (-а) *м собир* onions *мн* ◆ *м* (*оружие*) bow; **зелёный ~** spring onion (*BRIT*), scallion; **ре́пчатый ~** onion bulbs.
лука́в|ить (-лю, -ишь; *perf* **слука́вить)** *несов неперех* to be deceitful; **ты, ка́жется, ~ишь** you're being a bit vague.
лука́в|ый (-, -а, -о) *прил* (*человек, поступок*) crafty; (*взгляд, улыбка*) sly; (*девушка*) coquettish.
лу́ковиц|а (-ы) *ж* bulb; (*волоса*) follicle.
луко́ш|ко (-ка; *gen pl* **-ек)** *ср* basket.
лун|а́ (-ы́) *ж* moon; **ты что, с ~ы́ свали́лся?** where've you been all this time?
лу́на-парк (-а) *м* funfair (*BRIT*), amusement park (*US*).
луна́тик (-а) *м* sleepwalker.
лу́н|ка (-ки; *gen pl* **-ок)** *ж* hole.
лу́нн|ый *прил*: **~ые фа́зы** phases of the moon; **лу́нный свет** moonlight.
лу́нок *сущ см* **лу́нка.**
лунохо́д (-а) *м* lunar research module.
лун|ь (-я́) *м* harrier.
лу́п|а (-ы) *ж* magnifying glass.
луп|и́ть (-лю́, -ишь; *perf* **облупи́ть)** *несов перех* (*яйцо*) to shell; (*perf* **отлупи́ть**; *разг: бить*) to thrash; (*no perf; разг: сильно ударять*) to hammer on
▸ **лупи́ться** (*perf* **облупи́ться**) *несов возв* (*шелушиться*) to peel (off).
луч (-а́) *м* ray; (*прожектора, фонаря*) beam; **ре́нтгеновские ~и́** X-ray; **~ наде́жды** a ray of hope; **ла́зерный ~** laser beam.
лучев|о́й *прил* (*физ: энергия*) beamed; **~а́я кость** radius (*bone*); **лучева́я боле́знь** radiation sickness.
лучеза́р|ный (-ен, -на, -но) *прил* (*будущее*) glorious; (*улыбка*) radiant.
лучи́н|а (-ы) *ж* (*щепка*) splinter ◆ *собир* (*щепки*) kindling wood *собир.*
лучи́ст|ый (-, -а, -о) *прил* (*улыбка, лицо*) beaming; (*глаза*) shining.
лу́чник (-а) *м* archer.
лу́чниц|а (-ы) *ж см* **лу́чник.**
лу́чше *сравн прил от* **хоро́ший** ◆ *сравн нареч от* **хорошо́** ◆ *как сказ*: **больно́му ~** the patient is feeling better ◆ *част*: **~ не опра́вдывайся** don't try and justify yourself ◆ *вводн сл*: **~ (всего́) е́сли ты позвони́шь ве́чером** it would be better if you phone in the evening; **от э́того никому́ не ~** it doesn't do anyone any good; **нам ~ чем им** we're better off than them; **будь осторо́жен или, ~, вообще́ не ходи́ туда́** take care, or better still, don't go there at all; **~ возьми́ маши́ну** you'd better take the car; **как нельзя́ ~** couldn't be better; **~ не спра́шивай** don't ask.
лу́чш|ий (-ая, -ее, -ие) *прил* (*самый хороший*) best; **э́то ~ая рабо́та в кла́ссе** it's the best work in the class; **в ~ем слу́чае нам уда́стся зако́нчить рабо́ту за́втра** if we're lucky we'll finish the work tomorrow; **за неиме́нием ~его** for want of something better; **э́то (всё) к ~ему** it's (all) for the best.
лущ|и́ть (-у́, -и́шь; *perf* **облущи́ть)** *несов перех* (*семечки, орехи*) to crack (open); (*горох*) to shell.
лы́ж|а (-и) *ж* (*обычно мн*) ski; *см также* **лы́жи.**
лы́ж|и (-) *мн* (*вид спорта*) skiing; **во́дные ~** (*сами лыжи*) water-skis; (*вид спорта*) water-skiing; **го́рные ~** downhill skis; **ходи́ть** (*impf*) **на ~ах** to go cross-country skiing.
лы́жник (-а) *м* skier.
лы́жниц|а (-ы) *ж см* **лы́жник.**
лы́жный *прил* (*крепления, мазь итп*) ski *опред*; (*соревнования*) skiing *опред*; **лы́жный костю́м** ski suit; **лы́жные па́лки** ski poles.
лыжн|я́ (-и́) *ж* ski track.
лы́к|о (-а) *ср* (*липы, ивы*) bast; **он ~а не вя́жет** (*разг*) he's roaring drunk; **он не ~м шит** (*разг*) he's someone to be reckoned with.
лысе́|ть (-ю; *perf* **облысе́ть** *или* **полысе́ть)** *несов неперех* to go bald.
лы́син|а (-ы) *ж* bald patch.
лы́с|ый (-, -а́, -о) *прил* (*голова, человек*) bald; (*гора, холм*) bare.
ль *част* **= ли.**
львён|ок (-ёнка; *nom pl* **-я́та,** *gen pl* **-я́т)** *м* lion cub.
льви́н|ый *прил* (*шкура, грива итп*) lion's; **~ая ста́я** pride of lions; **~ая до́ля** the lion's share; **льви́ный зев** (*БОТ*) snapdragon.
льви́ц|а (-ы) *ж* lioness.
Львов (-а) *м* Lvov.
львя́та *итп сущ см* **львёнок.**
льго́т|а (-ы) *ж* (*инвалидам, беременным итп*) benefit; (*обычно мн: предприятиям, экспортёрам*) special term; (*элите, ветеранам*) privilege; **нало́говые ~ы** tax relief.
льго́тный *прил* (*тариф*) concessionary; (*условия*) privileged; (*заём*) special-rate; **льго́тный биле́т** concessionary ticket.
льда *итп сущ см* **лёд.**
льди́н|а (-ы) *ж* ice floe.

льди́н|ка (**-ки**; *gen pl* **-ок**) *ж* piece of ice.
льна *итп сущ см* **лён**.
льново́дств|о (**-а**) *ср* flax-growing.
льн|уть (**-у́, -ёшь**; *perf* **прильну́ть**) *несов неперех*: ~ **к** *+dat* (*к матери*) to cling to; (*перен: к богачам, к влиятельным людям*) to try to get in with.
льнян|о́й *прил* (*полотенце, платье*) linen; (*цвет*) flaxen; **~о́е полотно́** linen; **льняно́е ма́сло** linseed oil.
льстец (**-а́**) *м* flatterer.
льсти́в|ый (**-, -а, -о**) *прил* (*человек*) smarmy; (*улыбка*) unctuous; (*заверения, речь*) flattering.
ль|стить (**-щу, -стишь**; *perf* **польсти́ть**) *несов неперех* (*+dat; хвалить из корысти*) to flatter; (*доставлять удовлетворение*) to gratify; ~ *(impf)* **себя́ наде́ждой** to live in hope.
лью(сь) *итп несов см* **лить(ся)**.
любвеоби́л|ьный (**-ен, -ьна, -ьно**) *прил* loving.
любви́ *итп сущ см* **любо́вь**.
любе́зен *прил см* **любе́зный**.
любе́знича|ть (**-ю**) *несов неперех*: ~ **с** *+instr* (*разг*) to pay compliments to.
любе́зност|ь (**-и**) *ж* (*одолжение*) favour (*BRIT*), favor (*US*); (*комплимент*) compliment; (*в поведении*) courtesy; **ока́зывать** (**оказа́ть** *perf*) **~ кому́-н** to do sb a favour; **не откажи́те в ~и?** would you do me a favour?
любе́з|ный (**-ен, -на, -но**) *прил* polite; **бу́дьте ~ны!** excuse me, please!; **бу́дьте ~ны, принеси́те нам ко́фе?** could you be so kind as to bring us some coffee?
люби́м|ая (**-ой**; *decl like adj*) *ж* beloved.
люби́м|ец (**-ца**) *м* (*человек, животное*) favourite (*BRIT*), favorite (*US*).
люби́мица|а (**-ы**) *ж см* **люби́мец**.
люби́мца *итп сущ см* **люби́мец**.
люби́мчик (**-а**) *м* (*разг*) pet; **быть** *(impf)* **в ~ах у кого́-н** to be sb's pet.
люби́м|ый (**-, -а, -о**) *прил* (*женщина, брат*) beloved; (*писатель, занятие итп*) favourite (*BRIT*), favorite (*US*) ◆ (**-ого**; *decl like adj*) *м* beloved.
люби́тел|ь (**-я**) *м* (*непрофессионал*) amateur; ~ **му́зыки/спо́рта** music-/sports-lover.
люби́тельница|а (**-ы**) *ж*: ~ **му́зыки/чте́ния** music-/book-lover.
люби́тельск|ий (**-ая, -ое, -ие**) *прил* (*спорт, театр итп*) amateur; **люби́тельские права́** driving licence (*BRIT*) *или* driver's license (*US*).
люб|и́ть (**-лю́, -ишь**) *несов перех* (*родину, мать, мужа итп*) to love; (*музыку, спорт итп*) to like; **я ~лю́ его́ всем се́рдцем** I love him with all my heart; **цветы́ лю́бят тепло́** plants like the warmth; **я ~лю́, когда́ мне говоря́т комплиме́нты** I like it when people pay me compliments; **я ~лю́, когда́ лю́ди прихо́дят во́время** I like it when people come on time.
любо|ва́ться (**-у́юсь**; *perf* **полюбова́ться**) *несов возв* (*+instr*) to admire; **полюбу́йтесь на него́!** take a look at him!
любо́вник (**-а**) *м* lover.
любо́вница|а (**-ы**) *ж см* **любо́вник**.
любо́вный *прил* (*дела, похождения*) lover's; (*песня, письмо*) love *опред*; (*отношение, подход*) loving.
люб|о́вь (**-ви́**) *ж* love; (*привязанность*): ~ **к** *+dat* (*к родине, к матери итп*) love for; (*к чтению, к искусству итп*) love of; **занима́ться** *(impf)* **~ю** to make love.
любозна́телен *прил см* **любозна́тельный**.
любозна́тельност|ь (**-и**) *ж* inquisitiveness.
любозна́тел|ьный (**-ен, -ьна, -ьно**) *прил* inquisitive.
люб|о́й *мест* (*всякий*) any ◆ (**-о́го**; *decl like adj*) *м* (*любой человек*) anyone; **в ~о́е вре́мя** at any time; **~ цено́й** at any price.
любопы́тен *прил см* **любопы́тный**.
любопы́тно *нареч* curiously ◆ *как сказ*: **~!** that's interesting!; (**мне**) **~ узна́ть** I'm intrigued *или* curious to know.
любопы́т|ный (**-ен, -на, -но**) *прил* (*пример, книга итп*) interesting; (*человек, толпа*) curious.
любопы́тств|о (**-а**) *ср* curiosity; **из ~а** out of curiosity.
лю́бящ|ий (**-ая, -ее, -ие**) *прил* loving.
люд (**-а**) *м собир* (*разг*) folk.
лю́ден *прил см* **лю́дный**.
лю́д|и (**-е́й**; *dat pl* **-ям**, *instr pl* **-ьми́**, *prp pl* **-ях**) *мн* people *мн*; (*солдаты и офицеры*) men *мн*; (*кадры*) staff *ед*; **выходи́ть** (**вы́йти** *perf*) **в ~** to get on in life; **на ~ях** (*разг*) in public; **молоды́е ~** young men; (*молодёжь*) young people; *см также* **челове́к**.
лю́д|ный (**-ен, -на, -но**) *прил* (*улица итп*) busy; (*город*) lively; (*сборище*) crowded.
людое́д (**-а**) *м* (*человек*) cannibal; (*животное*) man-eater; (*в сказке*) ogre.
людое́дств|о (**-а**) *ср* cannibalism.
людско́й *прил* human; **род ~** humankind.
люк (**-а**) *м* (*танка, самолёта*) hatch; (*на дороге*) manhole; (*на сцене*) trap door.
люкс (**-а**) *м* (*о вагоне*) first-class carriage; (*о каюте*) first-class cabin ◆ *прил неизм* (*высшего класса*) first-class; **мы живём в лю́ксе** we've got a luxury suite.
Люксембу́рг (**-а**) *м* Luxemburg.
лю́л|ька (**-ьки**; *gen pl* **-ек**) *ж* (*также СТРОИТ*) cradle; (*мотоцикла*) sidecar.
лю́мпен (**-а**) *м* member of the lumpen proletariat.
люпи́н (**-а**) *м* lupin.
лю́рекс (**-а**) *м* lurex.
лю́стр|а (**-ы**) *ж* chandelier.
лю́тен *сущ см* **лю́тня**.
лютера́н|ин (**-ина**; *nom pl* **-е**, *gen pl* **-**) *м* Lutheran.
лютера́н|ка (**-ки**; *gen pl* **-ок**) *ж см* **лютера́нин**.
лютера́нск|ий (**-ая, -ое, -ие**) *прил* Lutheran.
лю́тик (**-а**) *м* buttercup.
лю́т|ня (**-ни**; *gen pl* **-ен**) *ж* lute.
лю́т|ый (**-, -а́, -о**) *прил* (*враг, зверь*) fierce;

(*ненависть, горе*) intense; (*мороз*) severe.

люце́рн|а (**-ы**) *ж* lucerne.

ля *ср нескл* (*муз*) lah.

ляга́|ть (**-ю**) *несов перех* (*подлеж*: *лошадь, корова*) to kick

▸ **ляга́ться** *несов возв* (*лошадь, корова*) to kick.

лягн|у́ть (**-у́, -ёшь**) *сов перех* to kick.

ля́г(те) *сов см* **лечь**.

ля́гу *итп сов см* **лечь**.

лягуша́та *итп сущ см* **лягушо́нок**.

лягуша́тник (**-а**) *м* (*разг*) shallow end.

лягу́ш|ка (**-ки**; *gen pl* **-ек**) *ж* frog.

лягуш|о́нок (**-о́нка**; *nom pl* **-а́та**, *gen pl* **-а́т**) *м* young frog.

ля́жек *сущ см* **ля́жка**.

ля́жешь *итп сов см* **лечь**.

ля́ж|ка (**-ки**; *gen pl* **-ек**) *ж* thigh.

лязг (**-а**) *м* (*звук*: *цепей, оружия*) clanging; (: *зубов*) gnash; (: *подков*) clatter.

ля́зга|ть (**-ю**) *несов неперех* (*засов, цепь*) to clang; (*+instr*; *зубами*) to gnash; (*ключами*) to rattle.

ля́м|ка (**-ки**; *gen pl* **-ок**) *ж* strap; **тяну́ть** *(impf)* **~ку** (*разг*) to toil away.

ля́па|ть (**-ю**) *несов от* **ля́пнуть** ◆ (*perf* **сля́пать**) *перех* (*разг*: *делать наспех*) to slap together ◆ (*perf* **наля́пать**) *перех* to make a mess of ◆ *неперех* to make a mess.

ля́пн|уть (**-у, -ешь**; *impf* **ля́пать**) *сов перех*: ~ **глу́пость** to make a blunder.

ля́псус (**-а**) *м* blunder.

~ М, м ~

М, м *сущ нескл (буква) the 13th letter of the Russian alphabet.*
М *сокр* = **метро́**; (= *мегабайт*) MB (= *megabyte*).
м *сокр* (= **метр**) m= *metre* (*BRIT*) *или* meter (*US*); (= **мину́та**) m (= *minute*).
мавзоле́|й (**-я**) *м* mausoleum.
маг (**-а**) *м* magician, wizard; (*разг*) tape recorder.
магази́н (**-а**) *м* shop; (*ружья*) magazine.
МАГАТЭ *ср сокр* (= *Междунаро́дное аге́нтство по а́томной эне́ргии*) IAEA (= *International Atomic Energy Agency*).
маги́стр (**-а**) *м* (*учёная степень*) master's degree; ~ **гуманита́рных нау́к** Master of Arts.
магистра́л|ь (**-и**) *ж* (*железнодорожная*) main line; (*дорожная*) arterial road; **во́дная** ~ main waterway.
магистра́льный *прил* main.
маги́ческ|ий (**-ая, -ое, -ие**) *прил* (*перен*) magic *опред*.
ма́ги|я (**-и**) *ж* magic.
магна́т (**-а**) *м* magnate.
магне́зи|я (**-и**) *ж* magnesia.
магнети́зм (**-а**) *м* magnetism.
ма́гни|й (**-я**) *м* magnesium.
магни́т (**-а**) *м* magnet.
магни́тный *прил* magnetic; ~ **диск** (*КОМП*) magnetic disk.
магнито́л|а (**-ы**) *ж* radio cassette player.
магнитофо́н (**-а**) *м* tape recorder; (*кассетный*) tape *или* cassette recorder.
магнитофо́нн|ый *прил*: **~ая за́пись** tape recording; **~ая кассе́та** (audio)cassette.
магно́ли|я (**-и**) *ж* magnolia.
Мадагаска́р (**-а**) *м* Madagascar.
мада́м *ж нескл* madame.
мадемуазе́л|ь (**-и**) *ж* mademoiselle.
мадо́нн|а (**-ы**) *ж* madonna.
Мадри́д (**-а**) *м* Madrid.
ма́ек *сущ см* **ма́йка**.
мает|а́ (**-ы́**) *ж* (*разг*) bother.
мажо́р (**-а**) *м* (*МУЗ*) major key.
мажорита́рн|ый *прил*: **~ая систе́ма** (*ПОЛИТ*) system of majority rule.
мажо́рный *прил* (*МУЗ*) major; (*перен: настроение*) cheerful.
МАЗ (**-а**) *м сокр* = *Ми́нский автомоби́льный заво́д*; (*автомобиль*) *vehicle manufactured at the Minsk car factory.*
ма́|зать (**-жу, -жешь**; *perf* **нама́зать** *или* **пома́зать**) *несов перех* to spread; (*perf* **изма́зать**; *разг*: *пачкать*) to get dirty; (: *рисовать*) to daub ◆ (*perf* **прома́зать**) *неперех* (*разг*) to miss; ~ (**нама́зать** *perf*) **чем-н что-н** to spread sth with sth; ~ (**нама́зать** *perf*) **гу́бы пома́дой** to put on lipstick
▸ **ма́заться** (*perf* **нама́заться**) *несов возв* (*разг: делать макияж*) to put on make-up; (*perf* **вы́мазаться** *или* **изма́заться**; *разг: пачкаться*) to get dirty; **~ся** (**нама́заться** *perf*) **кре́мом/ма́зью** to apply cream/ointment.
мазка́ *сущ см* **мазо́к**.
мазн|я́ (**-и́**) *ж* (*разг: о рисовании*) daub; (: *о письме*) scribble.
маз|о́к (**-ка́**) *м* (*кисти*) stroke; (*МЕД*) smear.
мазу́рк|а (**-и**) *ж* mazurka.
мазу́т (**-а**) *м* fuel oil.
маз|ь (**-и**) *ж* (*МЕД*) ointment; (*лыжная*) wax; (*колёсная*) grease; **де́ло на ~и́** (*разг*) things are going smoothly.
маи́с (**-а**) *м* maize (*BRIT*), corn (*US*).
маи́совый *прил* maize (*BRIT*), corn (*US*).
ма|й (**-я**) *м* May; *см также* **октя́брь**.
ма́|йка (**-йки**; *gen pl* **-ек**) *ж* vest (*BRIT*), sleeveless undershirt (*US*).
майо́лик|а (**-и**) *ж собир* majolica.
майоне́з (**-а**) *м* mayonnaise.
майо́р (**-а**) *м* (*ВОЕН*) major.
ма́йск|ий (**-ая, -ое, -ие**) *прил* May *опред*; **ма́йский жук** May beetle, cockchafer.
мак (**-а**) *м* poppy; (*КУЛИН*) poppy seeds *мн*.
мака́к|а (**-и**) *ж* macaque.
макаро́нник (**-а**) *м* pasta bake.
макаро́н|ы (**-**) *мн* pasta *ед*.
макаро́нный *прил* (*КУЛИН*) pasta *опред*; **макаро́нные изде́лия** pasta.
мака́|ть (**-ю**) *несов перех* to dip.
македо́н|ец (**-ца**) *м* Macedonian.
Македо́ни|я (**-и**) *ж* Macedonia.
македо́н|ка (**-ки**; *gen pl* **-ок**) *ж см* **македо́нец**.
македо́нск|ий (**-ая, -ое, -ие**) *прил* Macedonian.
македо́нца *сущ см* **македо́нец**.
маке́т (**-а**) *м* (*модель*) model; (*КОМП*) breadboard.
макинто́ш (**-а**) *м* mackintosh.
ма́клер (**-а**) *м* (*КОММ*) broker.
макн|у́ть (**-у́, -ёшь**) *сов перех* (*перо, кисть*) to dip.
ма́ковк|а (**-и**) *ж* poppyhead; (*разг: купол церкви*) (onion) dome.

ма́ков|ый (-, -а, -о) *прил* poppy-seed *опред*; **с ~о зёрнышко** as small as a pinhead; **у него́ с утра́ во рту́ ~ой роси́нки не было́** he hasn't had a bite to eat since morning.
макраме́ *ср нескл* macramé.
макре́л|ь (-и) *ж* mackerel.
макроэконо́мик|а (-и) *ж* macroeconomics *мн*.
ма́кси *ср нескл* maxi ◆ *прил неизм* maxi *опред*.
макс(им). *сокр* (= *максима́льный*) max. (= *maximum*).
максима́лен *прил см* **максима́льный**.
максимали́ст (-а) *м* maximalist.
максима́л|ьный (-ен, -ьна, -ьно) *прил* maximum *опред*.
ма́ксимум (-а) *м* maximum ◆ *нареч* at most, maximum.
макулату́р|а (-ы) *ж собир* wastepaper (*for recycling*); (*перен*: *пренебр*) pulp literature.
маку́ш|ка (-ки; *gen pl* -ек) *ж* (*разг*: *дерева, горы*) top; (*головы*) crown; **у него́ у́шки на ~ке** he's keeping his ear to the ground.
Мала́ви *ср нескл* Malawi.
мала́г|а (-и) *ж* (*вино*) Malaga (wine).
мала́|ец (-йца) *м* Malay.
Мала́йзи|я (-и) *ж* Malaysia.
мала́|йка (-йки; *gen pl* -ек) *ж см* **мала́ец**.
мала́йск|ий (-ая, -ое, -ие) *прил* Malaysian.
мала́йца *сущ см* **мала́ец**.
малахи́т (-а) *м* malachite.
мал|ева́ть (-ю́ю, -ю́ешь; *perf* **намалева́ть**) *несов перех* (*разг*) to daub.
мале́йш|ий (-ая, -ее, -ие) *прил* (*ошибка, промах*) the slightest; **не име́ть** (*impf*) **ни ~его представле́ния о чём-н** to not have the slightest idea about sth.
мал|ёк (-ька́) *м* young (fish), fry.
ма́леньк|ий (-ая, -ое, -ие) *прил* small, little; (*незначительный*) slight; (*малолетний*) little ◆ (-ого; *decl like adj*) *м* little one; **моё де́ло ~ое** (*разг*) it's none of my business; **ма́ленькая бу́ква** small letter.
Мали́ *ср нескл* Mali.
мали́н|а (-ы) *ж* (*кустарник*) raspberry cane *или* bush; (*ягода*) raspberries *мн*; **не жизнь, а ~!** (*разг*) it's a cushy life!
мали́нник (-а) *м собир* raspberry canes *мн*.
мали́новк|а (-и) *ж* robin (redbreast).
мали́новый *прил* (*варенье, куст*) raspberry; (*цвет*) crimson.

KEYWORD

ма́ло *чис* (+*gen*; *друзей, книг*) only a few; (*работы, денег*) not much; **нам да́ли ма́ло книг** they only gave us a few books; **я ви́дел ма́ло друзе́й** I only saw a few friends; **у меня́ ма́ло де́нег** I don't have much money; **ма́ло ра́дости** little joy
◆ *нареч* not much; **она́ ма́ло измени́лась** she hasn't changed much; **они́ ма́ло рабо́тают** they don't work much
◆ *как сказ*: **критикова́ть ма́ло, на́до помо́чь** it's not enough to criticize, you have to help; **мне э́того ма́ло** this is not enough for me; **ему́ всё ма́ло** it is impossible to satisfy him; **ма́ло ли что** so what?; **ма́ло ли кто/где/когда́** it doesn't matter who/where/when; **ма́ло того́** (and) what's more; **ма́ло того́, она́ ещё груби́ла** (and) what's more, she was rude; **ма́ло того́ что** not only; **ма́ло того́ что бы́ло хо́лодно, нам ещё не да́ли у́жин** not only was it cold, but they didn't give us any supper.

малова́ж|ный (-ен, -на, -но) *прил* of little importance.
малова́т *как сказ* (*разг*: *о размере*) on the small side.
малова́то *нареч* (*разг*) not quite enough.
малове́р (-а) *м* sceptic.
маловероя́т|ный (-ен, -на, -но) *прил* improbable.
маловоо́дье (-ья; *gen pl* -ий) *ср* low water level; (*недостаток воды*) drought.
маловы́год|ный (-ен, -на, -но) *прил* unprofitable.
малогабари́т|ный (-ен, -на, -но) *прил* small.
малоговоря́щ|ий (-ая, -ее, -ие) *прил* unimpressive.
малогра́мот|ный (-ен, -на, -но) *прил* semiliterate; (*руководитель*) incompetent.
малодосту́п|ный (-ен, -на, -но) *прил* (*место*) inaccessible.
малоду́шен *прил см* **малоду́шный**.
малоду́шнича|ть (-ю; *perf* **смалоду́шничать**) *несов неперех* (*разг*) to be yellow (*fig*).
малоду́ш|ный (-ен, -на, -но) *прил* cowardly.
малозаме́т|ный (-ен, -на, -но) *прил* (*пятно, окраска*) hardly noticeable; (*человек, событие*) insignificant.
малознако́м|ый (-, -а, -о) *прил* unfamiliar.
малокали́берный *прил* small-bore, small-calibre (*BRIT*), small-caliber (*US*).
малокро́ви|е (-я) *ср* (sickle-cell) anaemia (*BRIT*) *или* anemia (*US*).
малоле́тк|а (-и) *м/ж* (*разг*) kid.
малоле́тн|ий (-яя, -ее, -ие) *прил* young.
малолитра́жк|а (-ки; *gen pl* -ек) *ж* (*разг*) small car (*with small cylinder capacity*).
малолитра́жный *прил*: **~ автомоби́ль** small car (*with small cylinder capacity*).
малолю́д|ный (-ен, -на, -но) *прил* (*улица*) unfrequented; (*район, село*) sparsely populated.
ма́ло-ма́льски *нареч* (*разг*) quite.
маloма́льск|ий (-ая, -ое, ие) *прил* (*разг*) the slightest.
маломо́щ|ный (-ен, -на, -но) *прил* weak.
малонаселён|ный *прил* sparsely populated.
малообеспе́ченный *прил* disadvantaged.
малоо́блач|ный (-ен, -на, -но) *прил* (*небо*,

погода) slightly cloudy.
малообразо́ван|ный (-, -на, -но) *прил* undereducated.
малоподви́ж|ный (-ен, -на, -но) *прил* (*образ жизни*) sedentary.
ма́ло-пома́лу *нареч* (*разг*) little by little.
малора́звит|ый (-, -а, -о) *прил* underdeveloped.
малоро́слый *прил* undersized.
малосеме́|йный (-ен, -йна, -йно) *прил* with a small family.
малоси́л|ьный (-ен, -ьна, -ьно) *прил* (*двигатель*) low-powered; (*лошадь*) weak.
малосо́л|ьный (-ен, -ьна, -ьно) *прил* pickled (*in weak brine*).
ма́лост|ь (-и) *ж* (*разг*) trifle ◆ *нареч* (*разг*) a bit.
малотира́жный *прил* (*газета, журнал*) with a low circulation; (*книга*) *published in a small edition*.
малочи́слен|ный (-, -на, -но) *прил* small; (*поселения*) scarce.
ма́л|ый (-, -а́, -о́) *прил* small, little; (*доход, скорость*) low ◆ **(-ого;** *decl like adj*) *м* (*разг*) chap; (*молодой человек*) lad ◆ *как сказ* (*no full form*): **пла́тье/пальто́ мало́** the dress/coat is too small; **дово́льствоваться** *(impf)* **~ым** to have modest needs; **с ~ых лет** from childhood; **у него́ семья́ мал мала́ ме́ньше** he has a very large family of small children; **он мал да уда́л** (*разг*) he's a smart little guy; **без ~ого два часа́** (*разг*) just before two o'clock; **са́мое ~ое** at the very least; **Ма́лая А́зия** Asia Minor.
малы́ш (-а́) *м* little boy.
малы́ш|ка (-ки; *gen pl* **-ек)** *ж* little girl.
малышня́ (-и́) *ж собир* (*разг*) little kids *мн*.
ма́льв|а (-ы) *ж* mallow.
мальди́вск|ий (-ая, -ое, -ие) *прил*: **М~ие острова́** Maldives, Maldive Islands.
малька́ *сущ см* **малёк**.
Ма́льт|а (-ы) *ж* Malta.
мальти́|ец (-йца) *м* Maltese.
мальти́|йка (-йки; *gen pl* **-ек)** *ж см* **мальти́ец**.
мальти́йск|ий (-ая, -ое, -ие) *прил* Maltese.
мальти́йца *сущ см* **мальти́ец**.
ма́льчик (-а) *м* boy.
мальчи́шек *сущ см* **мальчи́шка**.
мальчи́шеск|ий (-ая, -ое, -ие) *прил* (*задор, вид*) boyish; (*несерьёзный*) childish, puerile.
мальчи́шеств|о (-а) *ср* childishness.
мальчи́ш|ка (-ки; *gen pl* **-ек)** *м* (*разг*) boy; (*неопытный мужчина*) child.
мальчи́шник (-а) *м* stag night *или* party (*BRIT*), stag (*US*).
малю́сеньк|ий (-ая, -ое, -ие) *прил* (*разг*) tiny, wee (*esp SCOTTISH*).
малю́т|ка (-ки; *gen pl* **-ок)** *м/ж* baby; **кни́жка/фотоаппара́т-~** miniature book/camera.
маля́в|ка (-ки; *gen pl* **-ок)** *ж* small fish ◆ *м/ж* (*разг*: *пренебр*) shrimp.
маля́р (-а́) *м* painter (and decorator).
маляри́йный *прил* malarial.
маляри́|я (-и) *ж* malaria.
маля́р|ный *прил* painter's; **~ая кисть** paintbrush.
ма́м|а (-ы) *ж* mummy (*BRIT*), mommy (*US*).
мамалы́г|а (-и) *ж* polenta, maize porridge.
мама́ш|а (-и) *ж* (*разг*: *мать*) mummy (*BRIT*), mommy (*US*); (*: обращение к пожилой женщине*) missus.
ма́менькин (-а, -о, -ы) *прил*: **~ сыно́к** (*разг*: *пренебр*) mummy's boy; **~а до́чка** (*разг*) mummy's girl.
ма́монт (-а) *м* mammoth.
мана́т|ки (-ок) *мн* (*разг*) stuff *ед*.
ма́нго *ср нескл* mango.
мангу́ст|а (-ы) *ж* mongoose.
мандари́н (-а) *м* tangerine.
мандари́новый *прил* tangerine.
манда́т (-а) *м* mandate.
мандоли́н|а (-ы) *ж* mandoline.
манёвр (-а) *м* (*также перен*) manoevre (*BRIT*), maneuver (*US*); *см также* **манёвры**.
маневри́р|овать (-ую; *perf* **сманеври́ровать)** *несов неперех* (*войска, дипломат итп*) to manoeuvre (*BRIT*), maneuver (*US*); (*перен*): **~** *+instr* (*ресурсами, финансами*) to make full use of.
манёвр|ы (-ов) *мн* manoeuvres *мн* (*BRIT*), maneuvers *мн* (*US*); (*на железной дороге*) shunting *ед*.
мане́ж (-а) *м* (*для верховой езды*) manège; (*цирка*) ring; (*для младенцев*) playpen; (*также: легкоатлети́ческий ~*) indoor stadium (*мн* stadia).
манеке́н (-а) *м* (*портного*) dummy; (*в витрине*) dummy, mannequin.
манеке́нщик (-а) *м* model.
манеке́нщиц|а (-ы) *ж см* **манеке́нщик**.
мане́р (-а) *м* (*разг*): **таки́м ~ом** like this ◆ *предл*: **на ~** *+gen* like.
мане́р|а (-ы) *ж* manner; (*художника, поэта*) style; *см также* **мане́ры**.
мане́рен *прил см* **мане́рный**.
мане́рнича|ть (-ю) *несов неперех* to put on airs.
мане́р|ный (-ен, -на, -но) *прил* affected.
мане́р|ы (-) *мн* manners *мн*.
манже́т|а (-ы) *ж* cuff.
маниака́льный *прил* maniacal.
маникю́р (-а) *м* manicure.
маникю́рный *прил* manicure *опред*.
маникю́рш|а (-и) *ж* manicurist.
Мани́л|а (-ы) *ж* Manila.
манипули́р|овать (-ую) *несов неперех* (*+instr*; *также перен*) to manipulate.
манипуля́ци|я (-и) *ж* (*также перен*) manipulation.
ман|и́ть (-ю́, -ишь; *perf* **помани́ть)** *несов перех* to beckon; (*no perf*; *перен*: *привлекать*) to attract.
манифе́ст (-а) *м* manifesto.
манифеста́ци|я (-и) *ж* demonstration.
мани́ш|ка (-ки; *gen pl* **-ек)** *ж* (*часть рубашки*) shirt front; (*нагрудник*) dicky.

ма́ни|я (**-и**) *ж* mania.
ма́нк|а (**-и**) *ж* (*разг*) semolina.
ма́нн|а (**-ы**) *ж* manna; **ждать** *(impf)* **как ~ы небе́сной** to await impatiently.
ма́нн|ый *прил*: **~ая ка́ша, ~ая крупа́** semolina.
мано́метр (**-а**) *м* manometer.
манса́рд|а (**-ы**) *ж* garret.
ма́нти|я (**-и**) *ж* robe.
манто́ *ср нескл* (ladies') fur coat.
мануфакту́р|а (**-ы**) *ж* (*ИСТ*: *фабрика*) (textile) mill.
Манче́стер (**-а**) *м* Manchester.
Маньчжу́ри|я (**-и**) *ж* Manchuria.
манья́к (**-а**) *м* maniac.
мара́зм (**-а**) *м* (*МЕД*) dementia; (*перен*: *разг*) idiocy; **ста́рческий ~** senility, senile dementia.
мара́л (**-а**) *м* Siberian deer.
мара́|ть (**-ю**; *perf* **вы́марать** *или* **измара́ть**) *несов перех* (*разг*: *пачкать*) to get dirty; (*perf* **замара́ть**; *перен*: *разг*) to drag through the dirt; (*perf* **намара́ть**; *разг*: *рисовать, писать*) to scribble; **~** *(impf)* **ру́ки** (*перен*: *разг*) to get one's hands dirty
▸ **мара́ться** (*perf* **вы́мараться** *или* **измара́ться**) *несов возв* (*разг*: *пачкаться*) to get dirty; (*perf* **замара́ться**; *разг*: *портить репутацию*) to ruin one's reputation.
марафе́т (**-а**) *м* (*разг*): **навести́ ~** to tidy up; (: *прихорашиваться*) to smarten (o.s.) up.
марафо́н (**-а**) *м* marathon.
марафо́н|ец (**-ца**) *м* marathon runner.
ма́рган|ец (**-ца**) *м* manganese.
марганцо́вк|а (**-и**) *ж* (*разг*) potassium permanganate.
маргари́н (**-а**) *м* margarine.
маргари́т|ка (**-ки**; *gen pl* **-ок**) *ж* daisy.
маргина́льный *прил* marginal.
ма́рж|а (**-и**) *ж* (*КОММ*) margin.
марина́д (**-а**) *м* (*соус*) marinade; (*обычно мн*: *маринованные овощи*) pickle.
марин|ова́ть (**-у́ю**; *perf* **замаринова́ть**) *несов перех* (*грибы, овощи*) to pickle; (*мясо, рыбу*) to marinate, marinade; (*no perf*; *разг*: *дело*) to put off.
марионе́т|ка (**-ки**; *gen pl* **-ок**) *ж* (*также перен*) puppet.
марионе́точный *прил* (*также перен*) puppet *опред*.
Мариу́пол|ь (**-я**) *м* Mariupol.
ма́р|ка (**-ки**; *gen pl* **-ок**) *ж* (*почтовая*) stamp; (*торговая*) trademark; (*сорт*) brand; (*качество*) grade; (*модель*) make; (*денежная единица*) mark; **держа́ть** *(impf)* **~ку** to keep up one's reputation; **держи́те ~ку шко́лы/фи́рмы** don't let your school/the firm down.
ма́ркетинг (**-а**) *м* marketing.
ма́р|кий (**-кая, -кое, -кие**; **-ок, -ка, -ко**) *прил*: **э́то пальто́ о́чень ~кое** this coat shows the dirt easily.
марки|рова́ть (**-у́ю**) *несов перех* (*продукцию*) to trademark.
маркси́зм (**-а**) *м* Marxism.
маркси́ст (**-а**) *м* Marxist.
ма́рлевый *прил* gauze.
ма́рл|я (**-и**) *ж* gauze.
мармела́д (**-а**; *part gen* **-у**) *м* fruit jellies *мн*.
мародёр (**-а**) *м* looter; (*разг*: *спекулянт*) profiteer.
мародёрств|о (**-а**) *ср* looting.
ма́рок *сущ см* **ма́рка** ◆ *прил см* **ма́ркий**.
Маро́кко *ср нескл* Morocco.
ма́рочный *прил* (*изделие*) branded; (*вино*) vintage.
Марс (**-а**) *м* Mars.
Марсе́л|ь (**-я**) *м* Marseilles.
март (**-а**) *м* March; *см также* **октя́брь**.
марты́шк|а (**-и**) *ж* marmoset ◆ *м/ж* (*перен*: *разг*) monkey.
марципа́н (**-а**) *м* marzipan.
марш (**-а**) *м* (*также перен*) march ◆ *межд* (*ВОЕН*): **~!** forward march!; **ле́стничный ~** flight of stairs; **~ домо́й!** (*разг*) off you go home!
ма́ршал (**-а**) *м* marshal.
марши|рова́ть (**-у́ю**; *perf* **промарширова́ть**) *несов неперех* to march.
маршру́т (**-а**) *м* route.
маршру́т|ка (**-ки**; *gen pl* **-ок**) *ж* (*разг*) fixed-route taxi.
маршру́тн|ый *прил*: **~ое такси́** fixed-route taxi.
маршру́ток *сущ см* **маршру́тка**.
ма́сел *сущ см* **ма́сло**.
ма́с|ка (**-ки**; *gen pl* **-ок**) *ж* (*также перен*) mask; (*косметическая*) face pack.
маскара́д (**-а**) *м* masked ball; (*перен*) masquerade.
маски|рова́ть (**-у́ю**; *perf* **замаскирова́ть**) *несов перех* (*также перен*) to camouflage
▸ **маскирова́ться** (*perf* **замаскирова́ться**) *несов возв* to camouflage o.s.
маскиро́вк|а (**-и**) *ж* (*ВОЕН*) camouflage; (*перен*) disguise.
маскиро́вочный *прил* camouflage *опред*.
ма́слениц|а (**-ы**) *ж* ≈ Shrovetide.
маслён|ка (**-ки**; *gen pl* **-ок**) *ж* butter dish; (*ТЕХ*) oilcan.
маслёнок (**-ёнка**; *nom pl* **-я́та**, *gen pl* **-я́т**) *м* annulated *или* yellow boletus (*edible mushroom*).
ма́сленый *прил* (*в масле*) buttery; (*запачканный маслом*) oily; (*перен*: *разг*: *льстивый*) slick; (: *сластолюбивый*) voluptuous; **ма́сленая неде́ля** ≈ Shrovetide.
масли́н|а (**-ы**) *ж* (*дерево*) olive (tree); (*плод*) olive.
ма́сл|ить (**-ю, -ишь**; *perf* **нама́слить** *или*

пома́слить) *несов перех* to butter.
ма́сличный *прил* oil-yielding.
ма́с|ло (**-ла**; *nom pl* **-ла́**, *gen pl* **-ел**) *ср* (*сливочное*) butter; (*растительное, смазочное*) oil; (*ИСКУССТВО*) oils *мн*; **де́ло идёт как по ~лу** (*разг*) things are going smoothly; **подлива́ть** (**подли́ть** *perf*) **~ла в ого́нь** to add fuel to the fire; **~ ма́сляное** (*разг*) tautology.
маслобо́|йня (**-йни**; *gen pl* **-ен**) *ж* creamery.
маслозаво́д (**-а**) *м* creamery.
маслянист|ый (**-, -а, -о**) *прил* oily.
ма́сляный *прил* (*краска, фильтр*) oil *опред*; (*пятно*) oily.
масля́та *итп сущ см* **маслёнок.**
ма́сок *прил см* **ма́ска.**
масо́н (**-а**) *м* Freemason, Mason.
масо́нск|ий (**-ая, -ое, -ие**) *прил* Masonic.
ма́сс|а (**-ы**) *ж* (*также ФИЗ*) mass; (*керамическая*) paste; (*древесная*) pulp; (*no pl*; *много*) loads *мн*; **де́нежная ~** money supply; *см также* **ма́ссы.**
масса́ж (**-а**) *м* massage; **~ се́рдца** cardiac massage.
массажи́ст (**-а**) *м* masseur.
массажи́ст|ка (**-ки**; *gen pl* **-ок**) *ж* masseuse.
масси́в (**-а**) *м* (*водный*) expanse; (*земельный, лесной*) tract; (*КОМП*) array; **го́рный ~** massif; **жило́й** *или* **жили́щный ~** housing estate (*BRIT*) *или* project (*US*).
масси́в|ный (**-ен, -на, -но**) *прил* massive.
масси́рованный *прил* (*атака*) all-out.
масси́р|овать (**-ую**) *несов перех* to massage.
массови́к (**-а́**) *м* *organizer of group activities.*
массо́в|ка (**-ки**; *gen pl* **-ок**) *ж* (*КИНО, ТЕАТР*: *массовая сцена*) crowd scene; (: *статисты*) extras *мн*; (*разг*) group outing.
ма́ссов|ый *прил* mass *опред*; (*поставка*) bulk *опред*; **това́ры ~ого спро́са** mass-market goods; **ма́ссовое произво́дство** (*ЭКОН*) mass production.
ма́сс|ы (-) *мн* (*народ*) the masses *мн*.
маста́к (**-а́**) *м* (*разг*): **~ на** *+acc***/в** *+prp* a dab hand at.
ма́стер (**-а**; *nom pl* **-а́**) *м* master; (*на производстве*) foreman (*мн* foremen); (*ремесленник*) craftsman (*мн* craftsmen); **часово́й ~** watchmaker; **~ на** *+acc* expert at; **~ на все ру́ки** handyman (*мн* handymen); **ма́стер спо́рта** master sportsman (*title awarded to sportsmen*).
мастер|и́ть (**-ю́, -и́шь**; *perf* **смастери́ть**) *несов перех* to make (by hand).
мастер|о́к (**-ка́**) *м* trowel.
мастерск|а́я (**-о́й**; *decl like adj*) *ж* (*часовая, столярная*) workshop; (*художника, скульптора*) studio; (*на заводе*) shop.
мастерств|о́ (**-а́**) *ср* (*квалификация*) skill; (*ремесло*) trade.
масти́к|а (**-и**) *ж* mastic; (*для натирания полов*) floor polish.
масти́т (**-а**) *м* mastitis.
масти́т|ый (**-, -а, -о**) *прил* eminent.
маст|ь (**-и**; *gen pl* **-е́й**) *ж* (*лошади*) colour (*BRIT*), color (*US*); (*КАРТЫ*) suit.
масшта́б (**-а**) *м* scale.
масшта́б|ный *прил* scale *опред*; (**-ен, -на, -но**; *произведение, стройка*) large-scale; **масшта́бная лине́йка** scale.
мат (**-а**) *м* (*ШАХМАТЫ*) checkmate; (*половик, также СПОРТ*) mat; (*ругательства*) bad language; **руга́ться** *(impf)* **ма́том** (*разг*) to use bad language.
матадо́р (**-а**) *м* matador.
матема́тик (**-а**) *м* mathematician.
матема́тик|а (**-и**) *ж* mathematics.
математи́ческ|ий (**-ая, -ое, -ие**) *прил* mathematical; (*факультет*) mathematics *опред.*
ма́тери *итп сущ см* **мать.**
материа́л (**-а**) *м* material; (*обычно мн*: *служебные, следствия*) document.
материа́лен *прил см* **материа́льный.**
материали́зм (**-а**) *м* materialism.
материали́ст (**-а**) *м* materialist.
материа́л|ьный (**-ен, -ьна, -ьно**) *прил* material *опред*; (*no short form*; *финансовый*) financial, material *опред*; **~ уще́рб** material damage; **материа́льная по́мощь** financial assistance.
матери́к (**-а́**) *м* continent; (*суша*) mainland.
материко́вый *прил* mainland *опред.*
матери́нск|ий (**-ая, -ое, -ие**) *прил* maternal; (*БИО, БОТ*) parent *опред.*
матери́нств|о (**-а**) *ср* maternity, motherhood; (*чувство*) motherliness.
матер|и́ться (**-ю́сь, -и́шься**) *несов возв* (*разг*) to swear.
мате́ри|я (**-и**) *ж* matter; (*разг*: *ткань*) cloth; **говори́ть** *(impf)* **о высо́ких ~х** to speak about elevated matters.
ма́терный *прил* (*разг*) obscene.
мате́рчатый *прил* cloth.
матёрый *прил* (*волк, медведь*) mature, full-grown; (*перен*: *преступник*) hardened.
ма́тер|ь (**-и**) *ж*: **М~ Бо́жья** Mother of God.
ма́терью *итп сущ см* **мать.**
ма́т|ка (**-ки**; *gen pl* **-ок**) *ж* uterus, womb; (*ЗООЛ*: *также*: **пчели́ная ~**) queen bee.
ма́тов|ый (**-, -а, -о**) *прил* (*без блеска*) mat(t); **ма́товое стекло́** frosted glass.
ма́ток *сущ см* **ма́тка.**
матра́с (**-а**) *м* mattress.
матра́ц (**-а**) *м* **= матра́с.**
матрёш|ка (**-ки**; *gen pl* **-ек**) *ж* Russian doll.
матриарха́т (**-а**) *м* (*ИСТ*) matriarchy.
ма́тричный *прил*: **~ при́нтер** (*КОМП*) dot-matrix printer.
матро́с (**-а**) *м* sailor.
матро́ск|а (**-и**) *ж* sailor top *или* shirt.
матро́сск|ий (**-ая, -ое, -ие**) *прил* sailor's.
ма́туш|ка (**-ки**; *gen pl* **-ек**) *ж* (*мать*) mother; (*РЕЛ*) *priest's wife.*
матч (**-а**) *м* (*СПОРТ*) match.
мат|ь (**-ери**; *см* **Table 1**) *ж* mother; (*разг*: *как обращение*) missus; **в чём ~ родила́** (*разг*) in

one's birthday suit; **мать-одинóчка** single mother.
мать-и-мáчех|а (-и) *ж* coltsfoot.
мафиóзи *м нескл* mafioso.
мафиóзный *прил* mafia *опред*.
мáфи|я (-и) *ж* the Mafia; (*перен*) Mafia.
мах (-а; *part gen* -у) *м* (*крыла*) flap; (*колеса*) turn; (*ногой*) swing; (*рукой*) swing, stroke; **дать** *(perf)* **мáху** (*разг*: *ошибиться*) to boob.
ма|хáть (-шý, -шешь) *несов неперех* (+*instr*) to wave; (*крыльями*) to flap; ~ *(impf)* **комý-н рукой** to wave to sb.
махúн|а (-ы) *ж* (*разг*) monster (*fig*).
махинáтор (-а) *м* machinator, schemer.
махинáци|я (-и) *ж* machination, scheme.
махн|ýть (-ý, -ёшь) *сов неперех* to give a wave; (*разг*: *поехать*) to go; (*через забор*) to jump; ~ *(perf)* **на когó-н/что-н рукóй** to give sb/sth up as a bad job
▸ **махнýться** *сов возв* (*разг*: +*instr*) to swap.
махóрк|а (-и) *ж* ≈ shag, coarse tobacco.
махрóв|ый *прил* (*халат*) towelling; (*цветок*) double; (*перен*: *отъявленный*) out-and-out; **~ая ткань** terry towelling.
мáчех|а (-и) *ж* stepmother.
мáчт|а (-ы) *ж* mast.
машбюрó *ср нескл сокр* (= *машинописное бюрó*) typing pool.
машúн|а (-ы) *ж* (*также перен*) machine; (*автомобиль*) car.
машинáлен *прил см* **машинáльный**.
машинáльно *нареч* mechanically.
машинáл|ьный (-ен, -ьна, -ьно) *прил* mechanical.
машинúст (-а) *м* (*комбайна, экскаватора*) driver, operator; ~ **локомотúва** engine driver (*esp* BRIT), engineer (US).
машинúст|ка (-ки; *gen pl* -ок) *ж* typist.
машúн|ка (-ки; *gen pl* -ок) *ж* machine; **пúшущая** ~ typewriter.
машúнный *прил* (*производство, части, масло*) machine *опред*; (*счёт, обработка*) mechanical; **машúнное отделéние** engine room; **машúнный код/язык** (КОМП) machine code/ language.
машúнок *сущ см* **машúнка**.
машинопúсный *прил* (*текст*) typewritten; **машинопúсное бюрó** typing pool.
машúнопис|ь (-и) *ж* (*печатание*) typing; (*текст*) typescript.
машиностроéни|е (-я) *ср* mechanical engineering.
машý *итп несов см* **махáть**.
маяк (-á) *м* lighthouse.
мáятник (-а) *м* (*часов*) pendulum.
мá|яться (-юсь; *perf* **умáяться**) *несов возв* (*разг*: *томиться*) to suffer.
маяч|ить (-у, -ишь) *несов неперех* (*разг*: *виднеться*) to be visible; (: *надоедливо возникать*) to hang around.
МБ *м сокр* (= *Министéрство безопáсности*) *ministry for security*.
МБР *м сокр* (= *Министéрство безопáсности Россúи*) *Russian Ministry for security*; (= *межконтинентáльная баллистúческая ракéта*) ICBM (= *intercontinental ballistic missile*).
МБРР *м сокр* (= *Междунарóдный банк реконстрýкции и развúтия*) IBRD (= *International Bank for Reconstruction and Development*).
МВД *ср сокр* (= *Министéрство внýтренних дел*) ≈ the Home Office (BRIT), ≈ the Department of the Interior (US).
МВК *м сокр* (= *механúзм валютных кýрсов*) ERM (= *Exchange Rate Mechanism*).
МВФ *м сокр* (= *Междунарóдный валютный фонд*) IMF (= *International Monetary Fund*).
МВЭС *ср сокр* (= *Министéрство внешнеэкономúческих связей*) *ministry of foreign economic links*.
мг. *сокр* (= *миллигрáмм*) mg (= *milligram(me)*).
мгл|а (-ы) *ж* haze; (*вечерняя*) gloom.
мгновéнен *прил см* **мгновéнный**.
мгновéни|е (-я) *ср* moment; **в однó** ~ right away.
мгновéн|ный (-ен, -на, -но) *прил* (*решение, реакция, фотография*) instant; (*смерть*) instantaneous; (*злость, раздражение*) momentary; (*вспышка*) lightning *опред*.
МГУ *м сокр* (= *Москóвский государственный университéт*) Moscow State University.
МГц *сокр* (= *мегагéрц*) MHz (= *megahertz*).
мéбел|ь (-и) *ж собир* furniture; **мягкая** ~ three-piece suite.
мéбельный *прил* furniture *опред*.
мéбельщик (-а) *м* furniture-maker.
мегабáйт (-а) *м* megabyte.
мегавáтт (-а) *м* megawatt.
мегафóн (-а) *м* megaphone.
мегéр|а (-ы) *ж* (*разг*) dragon.
мёд (-а; *part gen* -у, *loc sg* -ý, *nom pl* -ы) *м* honey.
медалúст (-а) *м* (*человек*) medallist (BRIT), medalist (US).
медалúст|ка (-ки; *gen pl* -ок) *ж* medallist (BRIT), medalist (US).
медáл|ь (-и) *ж* medal; **оборóтная сторонá ~и** (*перен*) the other side of the coin.
медальóн (-а) *м* medallion.
медбрáт (-а) *м сокр* (= *медицúнский брат*) nurse (*male*).
медвéдиц|а (-ы) *ж* she-bear; **Большáя М~** the Great Bear.
медвéд|ь (-я) *м* (*также перен*) bear.
медвежáта *итп сущ см* **медвежóнок**.
медвéж|ий (-ья, -ье, -ьи) *прил* bear *опред*; **медвéжья услýга** ≈ more of a hindrance than a

help.
медвеж|онок (-онка; *nom pl* **-ата,** *gen pl* **-ат)** *м* bear cub.
медик (-а) *м* medic.
медикамент (-а) *м (обычно мн)* medicine.
медицин|а (-ы) *ж* medicine.
медицинск|ий (-ая, -ое, -ие) *прил* medical.
меди|я (-и) *ж* media *мн.*
медленно *нареч* slowly.
медленный *прил* slow.
медлител|ьный (-ен, -ьна, -ьно) *прил* slow.
медл|ить (-ю, -ишь) *несов неперех* to delay; ~ *(impf)* **с решением/ответом** to be slow in deciding/answering.
медный *прил* copper; *(муз)* brass.
медовый *прил* honey *опред;* ~ **вкус/аромат** taste/smell of honey; **медовый месяц** honeymoon.
медпункт (-а) *м сокр (= медицинский пункт)* ≈ first-aid post.
медсестр|а (-ы) *ж сокр (= медицинская сестра)* nurse.
медуз|а (-ы) *ж* jellyfish.
мед|ь (-и) *ж* copper ◆ *собир* coppers *мн.*
медяк (-а) *м (разг)* copper (*coin*).
меж|а (-и; *nom pl* **-и)** *ж* boundary.
междомети|е (-я) *ср* interjection.

KEYWORD

между *предл (+instr)* **1** between; **между домами/городами** between the houses/towns; **между заседаниями/лекциями** between the meetings/lectures; **дорога между Москвой и Петербургом** the road between Moscow and St. Petersburg
2: **они договорились между собой** they agreed among themselves; **между нами (говоря)** between ourselves
3 *(+gen; в окружении)* amongst; **между домов росло большое дерево** a big tree grew in amongst the houses
4: **между прочим** *(попутно)* in passing; *(кстати)* by the way; **между прочим, мы видели Машу** by the way, we saw Masha; **между тем** meanwhile; **между тем как** while.

междуведомственный *прил* interdepartmental.
междугородный *прил* intercity.
международный *прил* international.
мезонин (-а) *м* attic.
Мекк|а (-и) *ж* Mecca.
Мексик|а (-и) *ж* Mexico.
мексикан|ец (-ца) *м* Mexican.
мексикан|ка (-ки; *gen pl* **-ок)** *ж см* **мексиканец.**
мексиканск|ий (-ая, -ое, -ие) *прил* Mexican.
мексиканца *сущ см* **мексиканец.**
мел (-а; *part gen* **-у,** *loc sg* **-у)** *м* chalk.
меланхолик (-а) *м* melancholic.
меланхоличный *прил* melancholic *опред.*
меланхоли|я (-и) *ж* melancholy.
мелет|ь *(3sg* **-ет,** *3pl* **-ют,** *perf* **обмелеть)** *несов неперех* to become shallower.
мелиораци|я (-и) *ж* soil improvement.
мелка *сущ см* **мелок.**
мел|кий (-кая, -кое, -кие; -лок, -лка, -лко) *прил (почерк)* small; *(песок, дождь)* fine; *(неглубокий)* shallow; *(малозначительный)* petty; *(no short form; собственник)* small; *(несущественный)* minor; **~кие деньги** *(мелочь)* small change; **мелкая буржуазия** petty bourgeoisie.
мелко *нареч (резать, дробить)* finely; *(писать)* small ◆ *как сказ (у берега итп)* it's shallow.
мелкобуржуаз|ный (-ен, -на, -но) *прил* petty-bourgeois.
мелковод|ный (-ен, -на, -но) *прил* shallow.
мелкокалиберный *прил* small-bore, small-calibre (*BRIT*), small-caliber (*US*).
мелодич|ный (-ен, -на, -но) *прил* melodious.
мелоди|я (-и) *ж* tune, melody.
мелодрам|а (-ы) *ж (также перен)* melodrama.
мелок *прил см* **мелкий.**
мел|ок (-ка) *м* piece of chalk.
меломан (-а) *м* music-lover.
мелоч|иться (-усь, -ишься) *несов возв (разг)* to be petty.
мелоч|ный (-ен, -на, -но) *прил* petty; *(человек)* small-minded, petty.
мелоч|ь (-и; *gen pl* **-ей)** *ж (пустяк)* triviality; *(подробность)* detail ◆ *ж собир* little things *мн;* *(мелкие монеты)* small change; **«Тысяча мелочей»** *name of shops selling household goods;* **размениваться** *(impf)* **по мелочам** to waste one's talents.
мел|ь (-и; *loc sg* **-и)** *ж* shallows *мн,* shoal; **садиться (сесть** *perf)* **на ~** *(МОР)* to run aground; **быть** *(impf)* **на мели** *(перен: разг)* to be (stony (*BRIT*) *или* stone (*US*)) broke.
Мельбурн (-а) *м* Melbourne.
мелька|ть (-ю) *несов неперех (появиться и исчезнуть)* to flash past; *(мерцать)* to twinkle; ~ *(impf)* **в уме** *или* **голове** to flash through one's mind.
мелькн|уть (-у, -ёшь) *сов неперех* to flash.
мельком *нареч* in passing.
мельник (-а) *м* miller.
мельниц|а (-ы) *ж* mill.
мельничный *прил* mill *опред.*
мельхиор (-а) *м* nickel silver.
мельча|ть (-ю; *perf* **измельчать)** *несов неперех (река, залив)* to get shallower; *(интересы, люди)* to become petty; *(хозяйство итп)* to become smaller.
мельче *сравн прил от* **мелкий** ◆ *сравн нареч от* **мелко.**
мельч|ить (-у, -ишь; *perf* **измельчить** *или* **размельчить)** *несов перех (ножом)* to cut up small; *(в ступке)* to crush.
мелю *итп несов см* **молоть.**
мелюзга (-и) *ж собир (разг: пренебр)* small fry.
мембран|а (-ы) *ж (ТЕХ)* diaphragm.
меморандум (-а) *м* memorandum.

мемориа́л (**-а**) *м* memorial.
мемориа́льный *прил* memorial *опред*.
мемуа́р|ы (**-ов**) *мн* memoirs *мн*.
ме́неджер (**-а**) *м* manager; ~ **по ма́ркетингу** marketing manager.
менеджме́нт (**-а**) *м* management.
ме́нее *сравн нареч от* **ма́ло** ◆ *нареч* less; **тем не** ~ nevertheless; ~ **всего́** least of all; ~ **всего́ удо́бный** least convenient of all.
мензу́р|ка (**-ки**; *gen pl* **-ок**) *ж* measuring glass.
менинги́т (**-а**) *м* meningitis.
менструа́ци|я (**-и**) *ж* menstruation.
ментóл (**-а**) *м* menthol.
ме́ньше *сравн прил от* **ма́лый, ма́ленький** ◆ *сравн нареч от* **ма́ло** ◆ *нареч* less than; ~ **всего́** least of all.
ме́ньш|ий (**-ая, -ее, -ие**) *сравн прил от* **ма́лый, ма́ленький** ◆ *прил* (*младший*) younger; **по ~ей ме́ре** at least; **са́мое ~ее** no less than.
меньшинств|о́ (**-а́**) *ср собир* minority; **национа́льное** ~ ethnic minority.
меню́ *ср нескл* menu.
меня́ *мест см* **я**.
меня́|ть (**-ю**; *perf* **поменя́ть**) *несов перех* to change; ~ (**поменя́ть** *perf*) **что-н на** *+acc* to exchange sth for
▸ **меня́ться** (*perf* **поменя́ться**) *несов возв* to change; (*жилплощадью*) to swap; (*perf* **измени́ться**; *погода, вкусы*) to change; **~ся** (**поменя́ться** *perf*) **чем-н с кем-н** to exchange sth with sb.
ме́р|а (**-ы**) *ж* measure; (*предел*) limit; **без ~ы** extremely; **сверх ~ы** excessively; **в по́лной ~е** fully; **по ~е** *+gen* with; **по ~е того́ как** as; **по ~е сил** as much as one can; **по ~е возмо́жности** as far as possible; **принима́ть** (**приня́ть** *perf*) **~ы по** *+prp* to take measures as regards; **вы́сшая** ~ **наказа́ния** capital punishment.
ме́рен *прил см* **ме́рный**.
мер|е́ть (*3sg* **мрёт**, *3pl* **мрут**, *pt* **мёр, -ла, -ло**) *несов неперех* (*разг*: *умирать*) to snuff it.
мере́щиться (**-усь, -ишься**; *perf* **помере́щиться**) *несов возв* (*+dat*) to appear; **ему́ ~ился о́браз** he thought he saw a figure.
мёрз *итп несов см* **мёрзнуть**.
мерза́в|ец (**-ца**) *м* (*разг*) nasty piece of work.
мерза́в|ка (**-ки**; *gen pl* **-ок**) *ж см* **мерза́вец**.
мерза́вца *сущ см* **мерза́вец**.
ме́рз|кий (**-кая, -кое, -кие**; **-ок, -ка́, -ко**) *прил* (*слова, личность, поступок*) disgusting; (*погода, настроение*) foul.
мерзлот|а́ (**-ы́**) *ж*: **ве́чная** ~ permafrost.
мёрзлый *прил* (*земля*) frozen; (*овощи*) frost-damaged.
мёрз|нуть (**-ну, -нешь**; *pt* **-, -ла, -ло**, *perf* **замё рзнуть**) *несов неперех* to freeze.
ме́рзок *прил см* **ме́рзкий**.
ме́рзост|ь (**-и**) *ж* disgusting thing; (*поступка*) baseness; **кака́я** ~! how disgusting!
меридиа́н (**-а**) *м* meridian.
мери́л|о (**-а**) *ср* criterion (*мн* criteria).
ме́рин (**-а**) *м* gelding.
ме́р|ить (**-ю, -ишь**; *perf* **сме́рить** *или* **изме́рить**) *несов перех* to measure; (*perf* **поме́рить**; *примерять*) to try on; ~ (**сме́рить** *perf*) **взгля́дом кого́-н** (*перен*) to look sb up and down
▸ **ме́риться** (*perf* **поме́риться**) *несов возв* (*+instr*): **~ся зна́ниями/си́лами с кем-н** to measure one's knowledge/strengths against sb.
мерк *итп несов см* **ме́ркнуть**.
ме́р|ка (**-ки**; *gen pl* **-ок**) *ж* measurements *мн*; (*перен*: *критерий*) standard; (*мерило*) measure; **снима́ть** (**снять** *perf*) **~ку с кого́-н** to take sb's measurements.
ме́рк|нуть (*3sg* **-нет**, *3pl* **-нут**, *pt* **-, -ла, -ло**, *perf* **поме́ркнуть**) *несов неперех* (*также перен*) to fade.
Ме́ркури|й (**-я**) *м* Mercury.
ме́р|ный (**-ен, -на, -но**) *прил* (*размеренный*) measured; (*no short form*; *ТЕХ*) measuring.
ме́рок *сущ см* **ме́рка**.
мероприя́ти|е (**-я**) *ср* measure; **культу́рное** ~ cultural event.
мертве́|ть (**-ю**; *perf* **омертве́ть**) *несов неперех* (*от холода*) to go numb; (*perf* **помертве́ть**; *от страха, от горя*) to be numb.
мертве́ц (**-а́**) *м* dead person (*мн* people).
мёртв|ый (**-, -а́, -о́**) *прил* dead; (*взгляд, улица*) lifeless; **спать** (*impf*) **~ым сном** to sleep the sleep of the dead; **лежа́ть** (*impf*) **~ым гру́зом** to lie unused; **мёртвый сезо́н** dead season; **мёртвая хва́тка** mortal grip; **мёртвый язы́к** dead language.
мертвя́щ|ий (**ая, -ое, -ие**) *прил* (*обстановка*) lifeless.
мерца́|ть (*3sg* **-ет**, *3pl* **-ют**) *несов неперех* to glimmer, flicker; (*звёзды*) to twinkle.
ме́сив|о (**-а**) *ср* mush; (*на дороге*) slush.
ме|си́ть (**-шу́, -сишь**; *perf* **смеси́ть**) *несов перех* (*тесто, глину*) to knead; ~ (*impf*) **грязь** (*перен*) to wade through the mud.
ме́сс|а (**-ы**) *ж* (*РЕЛ*) Mass.
мест|а́ (**-**) *мн* provinces *мн*.
места́ми *нареч* in places.
ме|сти́ (**-ту́, -тёшь**; *pt* **мёл, -ла́, -ло́**, *perf* **подмести́**) *несов перех* (*пол, комнату итп*) to sweep; (*мусор, листья итп*) to sweep up; (*подлеж*: *метель*) to whirl; **на дворе́ ~тёт** it's a blizzard outside.
местко́м (**-а**) *м сокр* (= *ме́стный комите́т*) *local trade-union committee*.
ме́стност|ь (**-и**) *ж* (*холмистая, ровная*) terrain; (*сельская, дачная*) area, district.
ме́стн|ый *прил* local ◆ (**-ого**; *decl like adj*) *м* local (inhabitant); **ме́стные вла́сти** local authorities

мн; **мéстный наркóз** (*МЕД*) local anaesthetic (*BRIT*) *или* anesthetic (*US*).
мéст|о (-а; *nom pl* -á) *ср* place; (*для постройки*) site; (*действия, происшествия*) scene; (*работа*) job; (: *вакантное*) post; (*в театре, поезде итп*) seat; (*багажа, груза*) item; (*в книге, в пьесе*) part; **слáбое ~** weak spot; **здесь не ~ говорúть о деньгáх** this is not the place to talk about money; **решúть** (*perf*) **на ~е** to decide on the spot; **~а себé не находúть** (*impf*) to worry; **к ~у** to the point; **спáльное ~** berth; **на Вáшем ~е я бы ...** in your place *или* if I were you, I would ...; **ни с ~а!** don't move!; **у меня душá** *или* **сéрдце не на ~е** I'm worried; *см также* **местá**.
местожúтельств|о (-а) *ср* place of residence.
местоимéни|е (-я) *ср* pronoun.
местонахождéни|е (-я) *ср* location.
местопребывáни|е (-я) *ср* residence.
месторождéни|е (-я) *ср* (*скопление*) deposit; (*угля, нефти, золота*) field.
мест|ь (-и) *ж* vengeance, revenge.
мéсяц (-а; *nom pl* -ы) *м* month; (*часть луны*) crescent moon; (*диск луны*) moon.
мéсячн|ые (-ых; *decl like adj*) *мн* (*разг*) (menstrual) period *ед*.
мéсячный *прил* monthly.
метáлл (-а) *м* metal.
металлúческ|ий (-ая, -ое, -ие) *прил* metal; (*блеск, скрежет*) metallic.
металлолóм (-а) *м* scrap metal.
металлýрги|я (-и) *ж* metallurgy.
метаморфóз|а (-ы) *ж* metamorphosis.
метáтел|ь (-я) *м* thrower; **~ дúска** discus thrower.
ме|тáть (-чý, -чешь) *несов перех* (*гранату, диск итп*) to throw; (*perf* **наметáть**; *шов*) to tack, baste; (*perf* **прометáть** *или* **сметáть**; *для примерки*) to tack; **~** (*impf*) **жрéбий** to draw lots; **~ (сметáть** *perf*) **стог сéна** to stack hay; **~ (вы́метать** *perf*) **икрý** to spawn; **рвать** (*impf*) **и ~** (*impf*) (*разг*) to storm and rage
▸ **метáться** *несов возв* (*в постели, в бреду*) to toss and turn; (*по комнате*) to rush about.
метáфор|а (-ы) *ж* metaphor.
мётел *сущ см* **метлá**.
метéл|ь (-и) *ж* snowstorm, blizzard.
метеóр (-а) *м* meteor.
метеорúт (-а) *м* meteorite.
метеорóлог (-а) *м* meteorologist.
метеоролóги|я (-и) *ж* meteorology.
метеосвóд|ка (-ки; *gen pl* -ок) *ж сокр* (= *метеорологúческая свóдка*) weather forecast *или* report.
метеостáнци|я (-и) *ж сокр* (= *метеорологúческая стáнция*) weather station.
мé|тить (-чу, -тишь; *perf* **помéтить**) *несов перех* to mark ♦ *неперех*: **~ в** +*acc* (*в противника, в цель*) to aim at; **он ~тил в профессорá/ начáльники** his ambition was to become a professor/manager
▸ **мéтиться** (*perf* **намéтиться**) *несов возв*: **~ся в** +*acc* to aim at.
мéт|ка (-ки; *gen pl* -ок) *ж* mark.
мéт|кий (-кая, -кое, -кие; -ок, -кá, -ко) *прил* (*точный*) accurate; (*перен*) apt; **имéть** (*impf*) **~ глаз** to have a good aim.
метл|á (-ы́; *nom pl* **мётлы**, *gen pl* **мётел**) *ж* broom; **нóвая ~** (*разг*) new broom (*fig*).
метн|ýть (-ý, -ёшь) *сов перех* (*диск, камень*) to throw
▸ **метнýться** *сов возв* (*разг*: *устремиться*) to rush.
мéтод (-а) *м* method.
метóдик|а (-и) *ж* (*преподавания*) teaching methodology; (*исследований, работы*) methods *мн*.
методúческ|ий (-ая, -ое, -ие) *прил* systematic.
мéток *прил см* **мéткий**.
метр (-а) *м* metre (*BRIT*), meter (*US*); (*линейка*) measure.
метрáж (-á) *м* (*квартиры, помещения*) (metric) area; (*ткани*) length.
метрдотéл|ь (-я) *м* head waiter.
мéтрик|а (-и) *ж* birth certificate.
метрúческ|ий (-ая, -ое, -ие) *прил* metric; **~ая систéма мер** metric system; **~ая тóнна** metric ton.
метрó *ср нескл* metro, tube (*BRIT*).
метý *итп несов см* **мести́**.
мех (-а; *loc sg* -ý, *nom pl* -á) *м* fur; *см также* **мехá**.
мех|á (-óв) *мн* (*кузнечный, аккордеона*) bellows *мн*.
механизáтор (-а) *м* (*с.-х.*) machine operator.
механизúр|овать (-ую) (*не*)*сов перех* to mechanize.
механúзм (-а) *м* mechanism; (*перен*: *бюрократический*) machinery.
механик (-а) *м* mechanic.
механик|а (-и) *ж* mechanics.
механúческ|ий (-ая, -ое, -ие) *прил* mechanical; (*цех*) machine *опред*.
Мéхико (нескл) *м* Mexico City.
меховóй *прил* fur; **~ магазúн** furrier's.
меч (-á) *м* sword.
мéченый *прил* marked.
мечéт|ь (-и) *ж* mosque.
мечт|á (-ы́; *gen pl* -áний) *ж* dream; **не óтдых, а ~!** (*разг*) it's a dream holiday!
мечтáни|е (-я) *ср* (*обычно мн*) daydream; **предéл ~й** ultimate dream.
мечтáтельный *прил* dreamy.
мечтáтел|ь (-я) *м* dreamer.
мечтáтельниц|а (-ы) *ж см* **мечтáтель**.
мечтá|ть (-ю) *несов неперех*: **~ (о** +*prp*) to dream (of); **~** (*impf*) **стать врачóм/учúться** to dream of becoming a doctor/studying.
мéчу(сь) *сов см* **мéтить(ся)**.
мечý(сь) *итп несов см* **метáть(ся)**.
мешанúн|а (-ы) *ж* (*разг*) jumble.
мешá|ть (-ю; *perf* **помешáть**) *несов перех* (*суп, чай*) to stir; (*perf* **смешáть**; *напитки, краски*) to

mix ◆ *неперех* (*+dat*; *быть помехой*) to disturb, bother; (*создавать затруднения*) to hinder; **не ~ло бы пое́сть** (*разг*) it wouldn't hurt to eat; ~ **(помеша́ть** *perf***) кому́-н** *+infin* (*препятствовать*) to make it difficult for sb to do

▸ **меша́ться** *несов возв* (*разг*: *ребёнок, вещи*) to be a pain; (*perf* **смеша́ться**; *путаться*) to get mixed up; **~ся** (*impf*) **в** *+acc* (*вмешиваться*) to meddle *или* interfere in.

мешка́ *сущ см* **мешо́к**.

ме́шка|ть (-ю; *perf* **заме́шкать)** *несов неперех* (*разг*) to dawdle; ~ **(заме́шкать** *perf***) с отве́том/отъе́здом** to be slow in answering/leaving.

мешкова́т|ый (-, -а, -о) *прил* (*пальто, платье*) baggy; (*фигура*) clumsy.

мешкови́н|а (-ы) *ж* sacking.

меш|о́к (-ка́) *м* sack; (*спальный, вещевой*) bag; (*разг*: *человек*) lump; ~ *+gen* sack(ful) of; **де́нежный ~** moneybags; **у него́ ~ки́ под глаза́ми** he has bags under his eyes; **костю́м сиди́т на нём ~ко́м** his suit hangs like a sack on him.

мешо́ч|ек (-ка) *м*: **в ~** (*яйцо*) soft-boiled.

мешу́ *несов см* **меси́ть**.

мещ|ани́н (-ани́на; *nom pl* **-а́не**, *gen pl* **-а́н)** *м* petty bourgeois.

меща́нк|а (-и) *ж см* **мещани́н**.

меща́нск|ий (-ая, -ое, -ие) *прил* (*взгляды*) petty-bourgeois; (*вкусы*) philistine.

меща́нств|о (-а) *ср* petty-bourgeois mentality; (*вкусы*) vulgarity; (*сословие*) petty bourgeoisie.

ми *ср нескл* (*муз*) mi.

МИГ (-а) *м сокр = самолёт констру́кции А.И. Микоя́на и М.И. Гуре́вича*.

миг (-а) *м* moment.

мига́|ть (-ю) *несов неперех* to wink; (*перен*) to twinkle.

мигн|у́ть (-у́, -ёшь) *сов неперех* to wink.

ми́гом *нареч* (*разг*) as quick as a flash; **приду́ ~!** I'll be there in a jiffy!

мигра́ци|я (-и) *ж* migration.

мигре́н|ь (-и) *ж* migraine.

МИД (-а) *м сокр* (= *Мини́стерство иностра́нных дел*) ≈ the Foreign Office (*BRIT*), ≈ the State Department (*US*).

ми́ди *ср нескл* midi ◆ *прил неизм* midi *опред*.

ми́ди|я (-и) *ж* mussel.

ми́зер|ный (-ен, -на, -но) *прил* meagre (*BRIT*), meager (*US*).

мизи́н|ец (-ца) *м* (*на руке*) little finger; (*на ноге*) little toe.

микроавто́бус (-а) *м* minibus.

микро́б (-а) *м* microbe.

микробио́лог (-а) *м* microbiologist.

микробиоло́ги|я (-и) *ж* microbiology.

микрокли́мат (-а) *м* microclimate; (*перен*) atmosphere.

микро́н (-а) *м* micron.

микроорганизм (-а) *м* microorganism.

микропроце́ссор (-а) *м* microprocessor.

микрорайо́н (-а) *м* ≈ catchment area (*administrative subdivision of urban region in Russia*).

микроско́п (-а) *м* microscope.

микроскопи́ческ|ий (-ая, -ое, -ие) *прил* (*также перен*) microscopic.

микросхе́м|а (-ы) *ж* (micro)chip.

микрофи́льм (-а) *м* microfilm.

микрофи́ш|а (-и) *ж* microfiche.

микрофо́н (-а) *м* microphone.

микрохирурги́|я (-и) *ж* microsurgery.

микроэконо́мик|а (-и) *ж* microeconomics *мн*.

ми́ксер (-а) *м* mixer.

миксту́р|а (-ы) *ж* mixture; **~ от ка́шля** cough mixture *или* linctus.

Мила́н (-а) *м* Milan.

ми́леньк|ий (-ая, -ое, -ие) *прил* (*хорошенький*) pretty *или* sweet little; (: *любимый*) darling; **он сде́лает э́то как ~** he'll do it or else.

милитари́зм (-а) *м* militarism.

милитариз|ова́ть (-ую) *(не)сов перех* to militarize.

милитари́ст (-а) *м* militarist.

милицио́не́р (-а) *м* policeman (*in Russia*) (*мн* policemen).

мили́ци|я (-и) *ж, собир* police (*in Russia*); (*разг*: *участок*) police station.

миллиа́рд (-а) *м* billion.

миллиарде́р (-а) *м* billionaire.

миллигра́мм (-а) *м* milligram(me).

миллиме́тр (-а) *м* millimetre (*BRIT*), millimeter (*US*).

миллиметро́вк|а (-и) *ж* (*разг*) graph paper.

миллио́н (-а) *м* million.

миллионе́р (-а) *м* millionaire.

миллио́нн|ый (-ая, -ое, -ые) *чис* (*посетитель, автомобиль итп*) millionth; (*исчисляемый миллионами*) million-strong; **у него́ ~ое состоя́ние** he is worth millions.

ми́ло *нареч* (*улыбнуться*) sweetly ◆ *как сказ*: **как ~!** how sweet!

ми́л|овать (-ую; *perf* **поми́ловать)** *несов перех* to have mercy on.

милови́д|ный (-ен, -на, -но) *прил* pleasing; **она́ ~на** she has a pleasing appearance.

милосе́рден *прил см* **милосе́рдный**.

милосе́рди|е (-я) *ср* compassion; **сестра́ ~я** nurse.

милосе́рд|ный (-ен, -на, -но) *прил* compassionate.

ми́лостын|я (-и) *ж* alms.

ми́лост|ь (-и) *ж* (*доброта*) kind-heartedness; **де́лать (сде́лать** *perf***) что-н из ~и** to do sth out of the kindness of one's heart; **~и про́сим!**

welcome!; **по твое́й ~и опозда́ли** thanks to you we are late; **скажи́те на ~** you don't say.

ми́лочк|а (-и) *ж* (*разг*: *обращение*) dearest.

ми́л|ый (-, -á, -о) *прил* (*симпатичный*) pleasant, nice; (*дорогой*) dear ◆ (**-ого**; *decl like adj*) *м* (*возлюбленный*) darling.

ми́л|я (-и) *ж* mile; **морска́я ~** nautical mile.

мим (-а) *м* mime (artist).

ми́мик|а (-и) *ж* expression.

ми́мо *нареч* past ◆ *предл* (+*gen*) past.

мимо́з|а (-ы) *ж* (*БОТ*) mimosa.

мимолётн|ый (-ен, -на, -но) *прил* fleeting.

мимохо́дом *нареч* on the way; (*перен*: *упомянуть*) in passing.

мин. *сокр* (= **мину́та**) min. (= *minute*); (= *минима́льный*) min. (= *minimum*).

ми́н|а (-ы) *ж* (*ВОЕН*) mine; (*выражение лица*) expression.

минаре́т (-а) *м* minaret.

миндалеви́дный *прил* almond-shaped; **у него́ миндалеви́дные глаза́** he is almond-eyed.

минда́лин|а (-ы) *ж* (*МЕД*: *обычно мн*) tonsil.

минда́л|ь (-я́) *м* almond.

минда́льный *прил* almond.

минёр (-а) *м* (*ВОЕН*) *person who lays mines*.

минера́л (-а) *м* mineral.

минера́лк|а (-и) *ж* (*разг*) mineral water.

минера́льный *прил* mineral.

минздра́в (-а) *м сокр* (= *министе́рство здравоохране́ния*) Ministry of Health.

ми́ни *ср нескл* mini; **~ ю́бка** miniskirt; **~ пла́тье** minidress.

миниатю́р|а (-ы) *ж* (*ИСКУССТВО*) miniature; (*ТЕАТР*) short play; **в ~е** in miniature.

миниатю́рн|ый (-ен, -на, -но) *прил* (*статуэтка*) miniature *опред*; (*перен*: *женщина*) dainty.

минима́льн|ый (-ен, -ьна, -ьно) *прил* minimum *опред*.

ми́нимум (-а) *м* minimum ◆ *нареч* minimum; **прожи́точный ми́нимум** minimum living wage.

мини́р|овать (-ую; *perf* **замини́ровать**) (*не*)*сов перех* (*ВОЕН*) to mine.

минисериа́л (-а) *м* mini-series.

министе́рск|ий (-ая, -ое, -ие) *прил* ministerial.

министе́рств|о (-а) *ср* ministry.

мини́стр (-а) *м* (*ПОЛИТ*) minister.

мин|ова́ть (-у́ю) (*не*)*сов перех* to pass; (*no impf*; +*gen*; *избежать*) to escape, avoid ◆ *неперех* to pass, be over.

мино́г|а (-и) *ж* lamprey.

миноиска́тел|ь (-я) *м* mine detector.

миномёт (-а) *м* mortar.

минонос|ец (-ца) *м* destroyer.

мино́р (-а) *м* minor key.

мино́рный *прил* (*МУЗ*) minor; (*перен*) subdued.

Минск (-а) *м* Minsk.

мину́вш|ее (-его; *decl like adj*) *ср* the past.

мину́вш|ий (-ая, -ее, -ие) *прил* past.

ми́нус (-а) *м* (*также МАТ*) minus; (*перен*: *недостаток*) drawback ◆ *м нескл* minus; **пять ~ два – три** five minus two equals three.

ми́нусовый *прил* (*температура*) subzero.

мину́т|а (-ы) *ж* minute; **(одну́) ~у!** (*просьба подождать*) just a minute!; **~ в мину́ту** to the minute; **он без пяти́ мину́т врач/юри́ст** (*разг*) he's a step away from qualifying as a doctor/lawyer; **она́ придёт с ~ы на ~у** she will be here any minute.

мину́тный *прил* (*стрелка*) minute *опред*; (*дело, разговор*) brief; (*порыв, увлечение*) momentary.

ми́н|уть (*3sg* **-ет**, *3pl* **-ут**) *сов неперех* (+*dat*; *исполниться*): **ей ~уло 16 лет** she has turned 16.

мин|у́ть (-у́, -ёшь) *сов* (*не*)*перех* to pass.

мир (-а; *nom pl* **-ы́**) *м* world; (*Вселенная*) universe; (*loc sg* **-у́**; *РЕЛ*) (secular) world; (*состояние без войны*) peace; **~ тéсен** it's a small world; **он не от ми́ра сего́** he has his head in the clouds; **заключа́ть (заключи́ть** *perf*) **~** to make peace; **чемпио́н ми́ра** world champion.

мира́ж (-а́) *м* (*также перен*) mirage.

ми́рен *прил см* **ми́рный**.

мир|и́ть (-ю́, -и́шь; *perf* **помири́ть** *или* **примири́ть**) *несов перех* to reconcile

▸ **мири́ться** (*perf* **помири́ться**) *несов возв*: **~ся с** +*instr* to make up *или* be reconciled with; (*perf* **примири́ться**; *с недостатками, с положением*) to come to terms with, reconcile o.s to.

ми́рн|ый (-ен, -на, -но) *прил* peaceful; **ми́рное вре́мя** peacetime; **ми́рное населе́ние** civilian population; **ми́рные перегово́ры** peace talks *или* negotiations.

мировоззре́ни|е (-я) *ср* (*писателя, общества*) philosophy of life.

миров|о́й *прил* world *опред*; (*перен*: *разг*: *хороший*) fantastic.

мирозда́ни|е (-я) *ср* universe.

миролюби́в|ый (-, -а, -о) *прил* peaceable.

миропонима́ни|е (-я) *ср* conception of the world.

миротво́р|ец (-ца) *м* peacemaker.

миротво́рческ|ий (-ая, -ое, -ие) *прил* peacemaking; **миротво́рческие войска́** peacekeeping force *ед*.

мирско́й *прил* (*РЕЛ*) worldly.

ми́с|ка (-ки; *gen pl* **-ок**) *ж* bowl.

мисс *ж нескл* Miss.

миссионе́р (-а) *м* missionary.

ми́ссис *ж нескл* Mrs.

Миссиси́пи *ср нескл* Mississippi.

ми́сси|я (-и) *ж* mission.

ми́стер (-а) *м* Mr.

ми́стик|а (-и) *ж* mysticism; (*разг*: *о чём-н загадочном*) mystery.

мистифика́ци|я (-и) *ж* hoax.

мисти́ческ|ий (-ая, -ое, -ие) *прил* mystical.

ми́тинг (-а) *м* mass meeting, rally.

митинг|ова́ть (-у́ю) *несов неперех* to hold a mass meeting *или* rally.

митрополи́т (-а) *м* (*РЕЛ*) metropolitan.

миф (**-а**) *м* (*также перен*) myth.
мифи́ческ|ий (**-ая, -ое, -ие**) *прил* mythical.
мифоло́ги|я (**-и**) *ж* mythology.
мише́н|ь (**-и**) *ж* (*также перен*) target.
ми́шк|а (**-и**) *м* (*разг*) bear; (*игрушка*) teddy (bear).
мишур|а́ (**-ы́**) *м* tinsel.
МКК *м сокр* (= *Междунаро́дный Кра́сный Крест*) IRC (= *International Red Cross*).
мл. *сокр* (= **мла́дший**) Junr (= *junior*).
младе́н|ец (**-ца**) *м* infant, baby.
младе́ническ|ий (**-ая, -ое, -ие**) *прил*: **~ие го́ды** infancy.
младе́нчеств|о (**-а**) *ср* infancy, babyhood.
мла́дше *сравн прил от* **молодо́й**.
мла́дш|ий (**-ая, -ее, -ие**) *прил* younger; (*самый младший*) (the) youngest; (*сотрудник, класс*) junior; **~ лейтена́нт** second lieutenant.
млекопита́ющ|ее (**-его**; *decl like adj*) *ср* mammal.
мле|ть (**-ю**) *несов неперех*: **~ (от** *+gen*) (*от счастья, от любви*) to be overcome (with).
мле́чный *прил* milky; **М~ Путь** the Milky Way; **мле́чный сок** latex.
млн. *сокр* = **миллио́н**.
мм *сокр* (= *миллиме́тр*) mm= *millimetre* (*BRIT*) *или millimeter* (*US*).
мне *мест см* **я**.
мне́ни|е (**-я**) *ср* opinion.
мни́мый *прил* (*кажущийся*) imaginary; (*ложный*) fake.
мни́телен *прил см* **мни́тельный**.
мни́тельност|ь (**-и**) *ж* suspiciousness.
мни́тел|ьный (**-ен, -ьна, -ьно**) *прил* suspicious.
мно́г|ие *прил* many ◆ (**-их**; *decl like adj*) *мн* (*много людей*) many (people).

KEYWORD

мно́го *чис* (*+gen*) a lot of; **они́ созда́ли нам мно́го пробле́м** they created a lot of problems for us; **мно́го книг тебе́ да́ли?** did they give you many *или* a lot of books?; **мно́го рабо́ты тебе́ да́ли?** did they give you much *или* a lot of work?
◆ *нареч* **1** (*разговаривать, пить итп*) a lot; **он мно́го рабо́тает** he works a lot
2 (*+comparative*; *гораздо*) much
◆ *как сказ*: **у него́ мно́го враго́в** he has a lot of enemies; **у него́ мно́го друзе́й?** does he have many friends?; **по мно́гу** *+gen* many; **они́ приходи́ли по мно́гу раз** they came many times.

многобо́р|ец (**-ца**) *м competitor in multi-event competition*.
многобо́рь|е (**-я**) *ср multi-event competition*.
многогра́нен *прил см* **многогра́нный**.
многогра́нник (**-а**) *м* polyhedron.
многогра́н|ный (**-ен, -на, -но**) *прил* (*талант, камень, личность*) multifaceted; (*фигура*) polyhedral.
многоде́т|ный (**-ен, -на, -но**) *прил* with many children.
мно́г|ое (**-ого**; *decl like adj*) *ср* a great deal.
многожёнств|о (**-а**) *ср* polygamy.
многозна́чен *прил см* **многозна́чный**.
многозначи́тел|ьный (**-ен, -ьна, -ьно**) *прил* significant.
многозна́ч|ный (**-ен, -на, -но**) *прил* (*число, номер*) multi-digit; (*слово, глагол*) polysemantic.
многокра́т|ный (**-ен, -на, -но**) *прил* (*визиты*) repeated; (*виза*) multiple(-entry); **~ чемпио́н/призёр** many-times champion/prizewinner.
многоле́тн|ий (**-яя, -ее, -ие**) *прил* (*планы*) long-term; (*труд, усилия*) of many years; (*растения*) perennial.
многолю́д|ный (**-ен, -на, -но**) *прил* (*улица*) crowded; (*митинг*) well-attended.
многонациона́л|ьный (**-ен, -ьна, -ьно**) *прил* multinational.
многопо́льзовательск|ий (**-ая, -ое, -ие**) *прил* (*КОМП*) multiaccess.
многообеща́ющ|ий (**-ая, -ее, -ие**) *прил* promising.
многообра́зен *прил см* **многообра́зный**.
многообра́зи|е (**-я**) *ср* (*жизни*) variety; (*растений, животных*) diversity.
многообра́з|ный (**-ен, -на, -но**) *прил* diverse, varied.
многосеме́|йный (**-ен, -йна, -йно**) *прил* with a large family.
многосло́в|ный (**-ен, -на, -но**) *прил* verbose, long-winded.
многосло́жный *прил* polysyllabic.
многосторо́н|ний (**-няя, -нее, -ние**) *прил* (*ГЕОМ*) polygonal; (*переговоры, встреча*) multilateral; (*вопрос, личность*) many-sided; (**-ен, -ня, -не**; *интересы*) diverse.
многотира́жк|а (**-и**) *ж* (*разг*) factory news sheet.
многотира́жный *прил* with a large circulation.
многото́чи|е (**-я**) *ср* (*ЛИНГ*) ellipsis.
многоуважа́емый *прил* esteemed; (*в письме*) Dear.
многоуго́льник (**-а**) *м* polygon.
многочи́слен|ный (**-, -на, -но**) *прил* numerous.
многочле́н (**-а**) *м* (*МАТ*) multinomial.
многоэта́жный *прил* multistorey (*BRIT*), multistory (*US*).
мно́жествен|ный *прил*: **~ое число́** (*ЛИНГ*) the plural (number).
мно́жеств|о (**-а**) *ср* (*МАТ*) set; **~** *+gen* a great number of.
мно́жител|ьный *прил*: **~ая те́хника** photocopying equipment.
мно́ж|ить (**-у, -ишь**; *perf* **умно́жить**) *несов перех* (*увеличивать*) to multiply; (*perf* **помно́жить**;

МАТ): ~ **(на** *+acc*) to multiply (by)
▸ **мно́житься** (*perf* **умно́житься**) *несов возв* to multiply.
мной *мест см* **я**.
мнс *м сокр* (= *мла́дший нау́чный сотру́дник*) junior researcher.
мну́ (сь) *итп несов см* **мя́ть(ся)**.
моби́лен *прил см* **моби́льный**.
мобилиза́ци|я (-и) *ж* mobilization.
мобилиз|ова́ть (-у́ю) *(не)сов перех* to mobilize; ~ *(impf/perf)* **кого́-н на что-н** to mobilize sb for sth.
моби́л|ьный (-ен, -ьна, -ьно) *прил* (*войска, дом*) mobile; (*ум, руководство*) active.
мог *несов см* **мочь**.
моги́л|а (-ы) *ж* grave; **стоя́ть** *(impf)* **одно́й ного́й в ~е** (*разг*) to have one foot in the grave.
моги́льник (-а) *м* burial ground; (*для радиоактивных отходов*) dumping ground.
моги́льный *прил* (*плита*) grave *опред*; (*холм, участок*) burial *опред*.
моги́льщик (-а) *м* grave digger.
могла́ *итп несов см* **мочь**.
могу́ *итп несов см* **мочь**.
могу́ч|ий (-ая, -ее, -ие; -, -а, -е) *прил* mighty; (*талант, ум*) great.
могу́ществен|ный (-, -на, -но) *прил* mighty, powerful.
могу́ществ|о (-а) *ср* might, power.
мо́д|а (-ы) *ж* fashion; (*разг: манера поведения*) habit; **по ~е** fashionably; **быть** *(impf)* **в ~е** to be in fashion; **входи́ть (войти́** *perf*) **в ~у** to come into fashion; **выходи́ть (вы́йти** *perf*) **из ~ы** to go out of fashion; *см также* **мо́ды**.
модели́р|овать (-ую) *(не)сов перех* (*одежду*) to design; (*perf* **смодели́ровать**; *процесс, поведение*) to simulate.
моде́л|ь (-и) *ж* model.
моделье́р (-а) *м* fashion designer.
моде́льный *прил* (*обувь, одежда*) high-fashion.
моде́м (-а) *м* (*КОМП*) modem.
мо́ден *прил см* **мо́дный**.
модерниза́ци|я (-и) *ж* modernization.
моде́рн (-а) *м* (*ИСКУССТВО*) art nouveau.
модернизи́р|овать (-ую) *(не)сов перех* to modernize.
модифика́ци|я (-и) *ж* modification.
мо́дник (-а) *м* (*разг*) snappy dresser.
мо́дница (-ы) *ж см* **мо́дник**.
мо́днича|ть (-ю) *несов неперех* (*разг*) to be a snappy dresser.
мо́дно *нареч* (*одеваться, стричься*) fashionably ♦ *как сказ*: **~ носи́ть ми́ни** miniskirts are in fashion.
мо́д|ный (-ен, -на, -но) *прил* fashionable; (*no short form*; *журнал*) fashion *опред*.
мо́д|ы (-) *мн* fashions *мн*; **журна́л мод** fashion magazine.
мо|ё (-его́) *притяж мест см* **мой**.
мо́жет *несов см* **мочь** ♦ *вводн сл* (*разг*) maybe, perhaps.
мо́жешь *итп несов см* **мочь**.
можжеве́льник (-а) *м* juniper.
мо́жно *как сказ* (*возможно*): ~ *+infin* it is possible to do; **~ кури́ть** smoking is allowed *или* permitted; **~ (войти́)?** may I (come in)?; **как ~** (*разг: выражает осуждение*) how could he *итп*; **как ~ лу́чше/быстре́е** as well/quickly as possible.
моза́ик|а (-и) *ж* (*узор*) mosaic; (*искусство*) mosaic work.
моза́ич|ный (-ен, -на, -но) *прил* mosaic.
Мозамби́к (-а) *м* Mozambique.
мозг (-а; *loc sg* **-у́**, *nom sg* **-и́)** *м* brain; (*перен: центр*) nerve centre (*BRIT*) *или* center (*US*); **спинно́й ~** spinal cord; **ко́стный ~** (bone) marrow; **до мо́зга косте́й** through and through; **шевели́ть (пошевели́ть** *perf*) **~а́ми** (*разг*) to use one's head; *см также* **мозги́**.
мозг|и́ (-о́в) *мн* (*КУЛИН*) brains *мн*.
мозг|ова́ть (-у́ю) *несов неперех* (*разг*) to think.
мозгови́тый *прил* (*разг*) brainy.
мозгово́й *прил* cerebral; (*интеллектуальный*) intellectual; **~ центр** nerve centre (*BRIT*) *или* center (*US*).
мозо́лист|ый (-, -а, -о) *прил* calloused.
мозо́л|ить (-ю, -ишь) *несов перех*: **~ глаза́ кому́-н** (*разг*) to bug sb by one's very presence.
мозо́л|ь (-и) *ж* corn, callus.
мозо́льный *прил*: **~ пла́стырь** corn plaster.
мой (моего́; *см* **Table 8**; *f* **моя́**, *nt* **моё**, *pl* **мои́)** *притяж мест* my; **по-мо́ему** my way; (*по моему мнению*) in my opinion.
мо́йк|а (-и) *ж* (*мытьё*) washing; (*раковина*) sink.
МОК (-а) *м сокр* (= *Междунаро́дный олимпи́йский комите́т*) IOC (= *International Olympic Committee*).
мо́к|нуть (-ну, -нешь; *pt* **-, -ла, -ло)** *несов неперех* to get wet; (*лежать в воде*) to be soaking.
мо́кро *как сказ* it's wet.
мокро́т|а (-ы) *ж* phlegm.
мокрот|а́ (-ы́) *ж* (*разг*) dampness.
мо́кр|ый (-, -а́, -о) *прил* wet.
мол (-а; *loc sg* **-у́)** *м* breakwater, mole ♦ *част* (*разг*): **он, ~, ничего́ не зна́ет** he says he knows nothing.
молв|а́ (-ы́) *ж* rumour (*BRIT*), rumor (*US*).
молда́вск|ий (-ая, -ое, -ие) *прил* Moldavian.
Молдо́в|а (-ы) *ж* Moldova.
молдова́н|ин (-ина; *nom pl* **-е)** *м* Moldavian.
молдова́нк|а (-ки; *gen pl* **-ок)** *ж см* **молдова́нин**.
моле́б|ен (-на) *м* (*РЕЛ*) service.
моле́кул|а (-ы) *ж* molecule.
молекуля́рный *прил* molecular.
моле́ни|е (-я) *ср* praying; (*мольба*) entreaty.
моли́тв|а (-ы) *ж* prayer.
моли́твенник (-а) *м* prayer book.
мол|и́ться (-ю́сь, -ишься; *perf* **помоли́ться)** *несов возв*: ~ *+dat* to pray to; (*no perf*; *перен*): ~ **на** *+acc* to idolize.

моллю́ск (-а) *м* mollusc.
молниено́с|ный (-ен, -на, -но) *прил* lightning *опред.*
мо́лни|я (-и) *ж* lightning; (*застёжка*) zip (fastener) (*BRIT*), zipper (*US*); **телегра́мма-~** express telegram.
молодёжный *прил* (*клуб, театр*) youth *опред*; (*мода, газета*) for young people.
молодёж|ь (-и) *ж собир* young people *мн.*
молоде́|ть (-ю; *perf* **помолоде́ть**) *несов неперех* (*выглядеть моложе*) to look younger; (*чувствовать себя моложе*) to feel younger; (*население*) to become younger.
мо́лоде|ц (-ца) *м* (*ФОЛЬКЛОР*) brave lad, fine young man.
молоде́|ц (-ца́) *м* strong fellow; ~! (*разг*) well done!; **она́/он** ~! (*разг*) she/he has done well!; **держа́ться** *(impf)* **~цо́м** to put up a good show.
молоде́цк|ий (-ая, -ое, -ие) *прил* (*вид*) dashing; (*поступок*) valiant.
моло|ди́ть (-жу́, -ди́шь) *несов перех*: **~ кого́-н** to make sb look younger
▸ **молоди́ться** *несов возв* to try to look younger.
молодня́к (-а́) *м собир* (*ЗООЛ*) young (*of animals*); (*БОТ*) saplings *мн.*
молодожён (-а) *м* (*обычно мн*) newlywed.
молодо́й (**мо́лод, молода́, мо́лодо**) *прил* young; (*картофель, листва*) new; (*задор, отвага*) youthful; (*no short form*; *вино, пиво*) young; (*сыр*) unripe.
мо́лодост|ь (-и) *ж* youth; **он не пе́рвой ~и** he's getting on in years.
мо́лодца *итп сущ см* **мо́лодец.**
молодца́ *итп сущ см* **молоде́ц.**
молодцева́тый *прил* sprightly.
моло́дчик (-а) *м* thug.
моложа́в|ый (-, -а, -о) *прил* (*человек*) young-looking; (*вид, лицо*) youthful.
моло́же *сравн прил от* **молодо́й.**
моложу́(сь) *несов см* **молоди́ть(ся).**
молок|о́ (-а́) *ср* milk.
молокосо́с (-а) *м* (*разг: пренебр*) greenhorn.
мо́лот (-а) *м* hammer.
молоти́л|ка (-ки; *gen pl* -ок) *ж* threshing machine.
мол|оти́ть (-очу́, -о́тишь) *несов перех* (*пшеницу*) to thresh; (*разг: колотить*) to hammer.
молот|о́к (-ка́) *м* hammer; **продава́ть (прода́ть** *perf*) **что-н с ~ка́** to sell sth by auction, auction sth.
мо́лотый *прил* (*кофе, перец*) ground.
моло́ть (**мелю́, ме́лешь**; *perf* **смоло́ть** *или* **помоло́ть**) *несов перех* (*зерно, кофе*) to grind; ~ *(impf)* **вздор** *или* **чепуху́** (*разг*) to talk rubbish.
молочк|о́ (-а́) *ср* (*жидкий крем*) lotion.
моло́чник (-а) *м* (*посуда*) milk jug; (*разносчик молока*) milkman (*мн* milkmen).
моло́чница (-ы) *ж* milklady.
моло́чный *прил* (*продукты, скот*) dairy *опред*; (*каша, коктейль*) milk *опред*; (*поросёнок, телёнок*) sucking; (*железа*) mammary; (*ХИМ*) lactic; **моло́чная ку́хня** *place where baby food is prepared*; **моло́чная сестра́** foster sister; **моло́чный брат** foster brother; **моло́чный зуб** milk tooth.
молочу́ *несов см* **молоти́ть.**
мо́лча *нареч* (*кивнуть, уйти*) silently; (*согласиться*) tacitly.
молчали́в|ый (-, -а, -о) *прил* silent; (*no short form*; *согласие, одобрение*) tacit; **~ мужчи́на** a man of few words.
молча́ни|е (-я) *ср* (*безмолвие*) silence; **~ – знак согла́сия** silence can be taken to mean approval.
молч|а́ть (-у́, -и́шь) *несов неперех* to be silent; ~ *(impf)* **о** *+prp* to keep silent *или* quiet about.
мол|ь (-и) *ж* moth.
мольб|а́ (-ы́) *ж* entreaty.
мольбе́рт (-а) *м* easel.
моме́нт (-а) *м* moment; (*в фильме*) episode; (*доклада, исследования*) point; **теку́щий ~** the current situation.
момента́лен *прил см* **момента́льный.**
момента́льно *нареч* instantly.
момента́л|ьный (-ен, -ьна, -ьно) *прил* instant.
мона́рх (-а) *м* monarch.
мона́рхи|я (-и) *ж* monarchy.
монасты́р|ь (-я́) *м* (*мужской*) monastery; (*женский*) convent.
мона́х (-а) *м* monk.
мона́хин|я (-и; *gen pl* -ь) *ж* nun.
мона́шеск|ий (-ая, -ое, -ие) *прил* (*также перен*) monastic.
мона́шеств|о (-а) *ср* monastic life.
Монбла́н (-а) *м* Mont Blanc.
монго́л (-а) *м* Mongol, Mongolian.
монго́л|ка (-ки; *gen pl* -ок) *ж см* **монго́л.**
монго́льск|ий (-ая, -ое, -ие) *прил* Mongolian.
Монго́ли|я (-и) *ж* Mongolia.
моне́т|а (-ы) *ж* coin; **плати́ть (отплати́ть** *perf*) **кому́-н той же ~ой** (*отомстить*) to pay sb back in kind; **принима́ть (приня́ть** *perf*) **что-н за чи́стую ~у** to take sth at face value.
монетари́ст (-а) *м* monetarist.
монета́рный *прил* monetary.
моне́тный *прил*: **~ двор** mint.
монито́р (-а) *м* monitor.
моногра́мм|а (-ы) *ж* monogram.
моногра́фи|я (-и) *ж* monograph.
моноли́т (-а) *м* monolith.
моноли́т|ный (-ен, -на, -но) *прил* (*глыба, колонна*) monolithic; (*перен*) united.
моноло́г (-а) *м* monologue.
монополиза́ци|я (-и) *ж* monopolization.
монополизи́р|овать (-ую) *(не)сов перех* to

monopolize.
монополи́ст (-а) *м* monopolist.
монопо́ли|я (-и) *ж* monopoly.
монопо́льный *прил* monopoly *опред.*
моното́н|ный (-ен, -на, -но) *прил* (*также перен*) monotonous.
монохро́мный *прил* (*КОМП*) monochrome.
Монреа́л|ь (-я) *м* Montreal.
монта́ж (-а́) *ж* (*сооружения*) erection; (*оборудования*) mounting, assembly; (*кадров, фильма*) editing.
монта́жник (-а) *м* (*на стройке*) rigger; (*на фабрике*) fitter.
монта́жниц|а (-ы) *ж см* **монта́жник.**
монтёр (-а) *м* fitter; (*электромонтёр*) electrician.
монти́р|овать (-ую; *perf* **смонти́ровать**) *несов перех* (*оборудование, схему*) to assemble; (*фильм, передачу*) to edit.
монуме́нт (-а) *м* monument.
монумента́л|ьный (-ен, -ьна, -ьно) *прил* monumental.
мопе́д (-а) *м* moped (*with movable pedals*).
мор (-а) *м* pestilence, plague.
мора́лен *прил см* **мора́льный.**
морализи́р|овать (-ую) *несов неперех* to moralize.
мора́л|ь (-и) *ж* (*этика поведения*) morals *мн*, ethics *мн*; (*басни, сказки*) moral; (*разг: нравоучение*) moralizing.
мора́л|ьный (-ен, -ьна, -ьно) *прил* moral; (*no short form*; *кодекс, нормы*) moral, ethical; **мора́льный изно́с, мора́льное устарева́ние** obsolescence.
морато́ри|й (-я) *м* moratorium.
морг (-а) *м* morgue.
морга́|ть (-ю) *несов неперех* to blink; (*подмигивать*): ~ (*+dat*) to wink (at).
моргн|у́ть (-у́, -ёшь) *сов неперех* to blink; (*подмигнуть*): ~ (*+dat*) to wink (at); **не ~у́в гла́зом** (*разг*) without batting an eyelid.
мо́рд|а (-ы) *ж* (*животного*) muzzle; (*разг: лицо*) mug.
мордви́н (-а) *м* Mordvin.
мордви́н|ка (-ки; *gen pl* -ок) *ж см* **мордви́н.**
Мо́рдви|я (-и) *ж* Mordvia.
мо́р|е (-я; *nom pl* -я́, *gen pl* -е́й) *ср* (*также перен*) sea; **откры́тое ~** open sea; **ему́ ~ по коле́но** (*разг*) he's afraid of nothing.
морепла́вани|е (-я) *ср* (*плавание*) seafaring; (*вождение судов*) navigation.
морепла́вател|ь (-я) *м* seafarer.
морехо́дк|а (-и) *ж* (*разг*) naval college.
морехо́дный *прил* (*училище, испытания*) naval; (*инструменты*) navigational.
морж (-а́) *м* walrus; (*перен*) *wintertime open-air bather.*
моржи́х|а (-и) *ж см* **морж.**
моржо́вый *прил* walrus *опред.*
мори́лк|а (-и) *ж* (*разг: краска*) stain; (*от насекомых*) insecticide.
мор|и́ть (-ю́, -и́шь; *perf* **помори́ть**) *несов перех* (*насекомых*) to exterminate; (*дерево*) to stain; (*дуб*) to fume; (*perf* **разморить**; *подлеж: сон, жара*) to exhaust, drain; **~ (заморить** *perf*) **го́лодом кого́-н** to starve sb; **~ (уморить** *perf*) **шу́тками кого́-н** (*разг*) to have sb in stitches with one's jokes.
морко́в|ка (-ки; *gen pl* -ок) *ж* (*разг: одна штука*) carrot; (*морковь*) carrots *мн.*
морко́вный *прил* carrot *опред.*
морко́в|ь (-и) *ж* carrots *мн.*
моро́жениц|а (-ы) *ж* (*аппарат*) ice-cream maker; (*кафе*) ice-cream parlour (*BRIT*) *или* parlor (*US*).
моро́жен|ое (-ого; *decl like adj*) *ср* ice cream.
моро́женый *прил* frozen; (*испорченный морозом*) frost-damaged.
моро́жу *несов см* **моро́зить.**
моро́з (-а) *м* frost; **у нас стоя́т ~ы** we're having a spell of freezing (cold) weather; **Дед М~** ≈ Father Christmas.
моро́зен *прил см* **моро́зный.**
морози́льник (-а) *м* freezer.
морози́льный *прил* freezing; **морози́льная ка́мера** deepfreeze.
моро́|зить (-жу, -зишь) *несов перех* to freeze ◆ *безл*; **на у́лице ~зит** it's freezing outside.
моро́з|ный (-ен, -на, -но) *прил* frosty.
морозосто́|йкий (-йкая, -йкое, -йкие; -ек, -йка, -йко) *прил* frost-resistant.
морос|и́ть (*3sg* -и́т, *3pl* -я́т) *несов неперех* to drizzle.
моро́ч|ить (-у, -ишь; *perf* **заморо́чить**) *несов перех* (*разг*) to fool; **~ (заморо́чить** *perf*) **го́лову кому́-н** (*разг*) to pull sb's leg.
моро́шк|а (-и) *ж* cloudberry.
морс (-а; *part gen* -у) *м* (fruit) drink.
морск|о́й (-а́я, -о́е, -и́е) *прил* sea *опред*; (*БИО, ВОЕН*) marine; (*курорт, лечебница*) seaside *опред*; **~о́е страхова́ние** marine insurance; **~о́е пра́во** maritime law; **морска́я боле́знь** seasickness; **морско́й волк** sea dog; **морска́я сви́нка** guinea pig.
мо́рфи|й (-я) *м* morphine, morphia.
морфоло́ги|я (-и) *ж* morphology.
морщи́н|а (-ы) *ж* (*на лице*) wrinkle; (*на ткани*) crease.
морщи́нист|ый (-, -а, -о) *прил* (*лицо*) wrinkled.
мо́рщ|ить (-у, -ишь; *perf* **намо́рщить**) *несов перех* (*брови*) to knit; (*perf* **смо́рщить**; *нос, лоб*) to wrinkle; (*лицо*) to screw up
▸ **мо́рщиться** (*perf* **намо́рщиться**) *несов возв* to screw up one's face; (*одежда, ткань*) to crease; **~ся (смо́рщиться** *perf*) **от** *+gen* (*от старости, от солнца*) to become wrinkled from; (*от боли*) to wince in.
морщ|и́ть (*3sg* -и́т, *3pl* -а́т) *несов неперех* (*разг*) to be wrinkled.
моря́к (-а́) *м* sailor.
Москв|а́ (-ы́) *ж* Moscow.
москви́ч (-а́) *м* Muscovite.

москви́ч|ка (-ки; *gen pl* **-ек)** *ж см* **москви́ч.**
мост (-á; *loc sg* **-ý)** *м* bridge; (*телевизионный, космический*) link; (*АВТ*) axle.
мóстик (-а) *м* bridge; **капитáнский ~** bridge (*NAUT*).
мо|сти́ть (-щý, -сти́шь; *perf* **вы́мостить)** *несов перех* (*площадь, улицу*) to pave; (*perf* **намости́ть;** *пол*) to lay.
мостк|и́ (-óв) *мн* (*через лужу*) duckboard *ед*; (*у реки, у пруда*) wooden platform *ед*.
мостов|áя (-óй; *decl like adj*) *ж* road.
МОТ *ж сокр* (= *междунарóдная организáция трудá*) ILO (= *International Labour Organization*).
мотá|ть (-ю; *perf* **намотáть)** *несов перех* (*нитки*) to wind ◆ (*perf* **умотáть)** *неперех* (*разг: уехать*) to go off; (*perf* **помотáть)**: ~ *+instr* (*головой*) to shake; **~й отсю́да!** get lost!; ~ (*impf*) **комý-н нéрвы** (*разг*) to get on sb's nerves
▸ **мотáться** *несов возв* to swing; (*разг: хлопотать*) to rush about.
мотéл|ь (-я) *м* motel.
моти́в (-а) *м* (*преступления*) motive; (*для развода*) grounds *мн*; (*мелодия*) motif.
мотиви́р|овать (-ую) (*не*)*сов перех* to justify.
мотка́ *сущ см* **мотóк.**
мотогóн|ка (-ки; *gen pl* **-ок)** *ж* (*обычно мн*) motorcycle race.
мотогóнщик (-а) *м* motorcycle racer.
мот|óк (-кá) *м* skein.
мотóр (-а) *м* motor; (*автомобиля, лодки*) engine.
морори́ст (-а) *м* motor mechanic.
мотóрный *прил* motor *опред*; **мотóрная лóдка** motorboat.
моторóллер (-а) *м* (motor) scooter.
мотоци́кл (-а) *м* motorcycle.
моты́г|а (-и) *ж* hoe.
мотыл|ёк (-ькá) *м* moth.
м|ох (мха; *loc sg* **мху,** *nom pl* **мхи)** *м* moss.
мохéр (-а) *м* mohair.
мохéровый *прил* mohair.
мохнáт|ый (-, -а, -о) *прил* (*животное*) shaggy; (*ель, сосна*) bushy; (*no short form; плед, шапка*) fluffy.
мохови́к (-á) *м* (*БОТ*) variegated boletus.
моциóн (-а) *м* (*прогулка*) constitutional.
мочá (-и́) *ж* urine.
мочáл|ка (-ки; *gen pl* **-ок)** *ж* sponge.
мочевóй *прил*: **~ пузы́рь** bladder.
мочегóнный *прил* diuretic.
мóчек *сущ см* **мóчка.**
мочёный *прил* (*яблоко, брусника*) preserved (*in sugar solution*).
моч|и́ть (-ý, -ишь; *perf* **намочи́ть)** *несов перех* (*ноги, волосы, одежду*) to wet; (*perf* **замочи́ть**; *бельё*) to soak; (*яблоки*) to preserve
▸ **мочи́ться** (*perf* **помочи́ться)** *несов возв* to urinate.
мóч|ка (-ки; *gen pl* **-ек)** *ж* ear lobe.
мо|чь (-гý, -жешь *итп*, **-гут;** *pt* **-г, -глá, -глó,** *perf* **смочь)** *несов неперех*: ~ *+infin* to be able to do ◆ **(-чи)** *ж*: **изо всей мóчи** with all one's might; **я ~гý игрáть на гитáре/говори́ть по-англи́йски** I can play the guitar/talk English; **он мóжет прийти́** he can come *или* is able to come; **онá не ~глá купи́ть дом** she couldn't buy *или* wasn't able to buy the house; **я сдéлаю всё, что ~гý** I will do all I can; **зáвтра мóжешь не приходи́ть** you don't have to come tomorrow; **он мóжет оби́деться** he may well be offended; **не ~гý поня́ть э́того** I can't understand this; **мóжешь бóльше не извиня́ться** don't bother apologising any more; **мóжет быть** maybe; **не мóжет быть!** (*выражение сомнения*) it's impossible!
мóшек *сущ см* **мóшка.**
мошéнник (-а) *м* swindler, crook.
мошéннича|ть (-ю; *perf* **смошéнничать)** *несов неперех* to swindle.
мошéнническ|ий (-ая, -ое, -ие) *прил* devious.
мошéнничеств|о (-а) *ср* deviousness.
мóш|ка (-ки; *gen pl* **-ек)** *ж* midge.
мошкар|á (-ы́) *ж собир* midges *мн*.
мóщен *прил см* **мóщный.**
мощёный *прил* paved.
мóщност|и (-ей) *мн* facilities *мн*.
мóщност|ь (-и) *ж* power; (*воздействие*) force; **неиспóльзуемая произвóдственная ~** idle capacity; *см также* **мóщности.**
мóщ|ный (-ен, -нá, -но) *прил* (*взрыв, выступление*) powerful; (*организм, дуб*) mighty; (*рост, подъем*) vigorous; (*массивный*) massive; (*no short form; двигатель, агрегат*) powerful.
мощý *несов см* **мости́ть.**
мощ|ь (-и) *ж* power, might.
мóю(сь) *итп несов см* **мы́ть(ся).**
мо|я́ (-éй) *притяж мест см* **мой.**
м.п. *сокр* = *мéсто печáти*.
МП *м сокр* (= *маши́нный перевóд*) MT (= *machine translation*).
мрак (-а) *м* (*темнота*) darkness; (*перен*) gloom.
мракобéс (-а) *м* obscurantist.
мрáмор (-а) *м* marble.
мрáморный *прил* (*также перен*) marble; (*узор, линолеум*) marbled; **Мрáморное мóре** Sea of Marmara.
мрáчен *прил см* **мрáчный.**
мрачнé|ть (-ю; *perf* **помрачнéть)** *несов неперех* (*небо, горизонт*) to grow dark; (*взгляд, лицо*) to darken.
мрáч|ный (-ен, -нá, -но) *прил* (*небо, мысли, взгляд*) gloomy; (*времена, годы, период*) dark.
мсти́тел|ь (-я) *м* avenger.
мсти́тельниц|а (-ы) *ж см* **мсти́тель.**

мсти́тел|ьный (-ен, -ьна, -ьно) *прил* vindictive.
мстить (мщу, мстишь; *perf* **отомсти́ть)** *несов неперех*: **~ кому́-н** to take revenge on sb.
МТП *ж сокр* (= *междунаро́дная торго́вая пала́та*) ICC (= *International Chamber of Commerce*).
МТС *ж сокр* (= *междугоро́дная телефо́нная ста́нция*) ≈ intercity telephone exchange.
мудр|ёный (-ён, -ена́, -ено́) *прил* (*непонятный*) strange; (*сложный*) tricky, complicated; **не ~ено́, что** ... it's no wonder that ....
мудре́ц (-а́) *м* wise man (*мн* men).
мудр|и́ть (-ю́, -и́шь; *perf* **намудри́ть)** *несов неперех* to try to be clever.
му́дрост|ь (-и) *ж* wisdom; **зуб ~и** wisdom tooth.
му́др|ый (-, -а́, -о) *прил* wise.
муж (-а; *nom pl* **-ья́,** *gen pl* **-е́й)** *м* husband; (*nom pl* **-и́**): **госуда́рственный ~** elder statesman (*мн* statesmen); **учёный ~** man of science.
мужа́|ть (-ю; *perf* **возмужа́ть)** *несов неперех* to mature
▸ **мужа́ться** *несов возв* to take heart, have courage.
мужеподо́б|ный (-ен, -на, -но) *прил* masculine.
му́жествен|ный (-, -на, -но) *прил* (*лицо, натура*) strong; (*поступок, шаг*) courageous.
му́жеств|о (-а) *ср* courage.
мужи́к (-а́) *м* (*разг*: *мужчина*) man (*мн* men); (*крестьянин*) muzhik.
мужикова́тый *прил* boorish.
мужск|о́й (-а́я, -о́е, -и́е) *прил* (*ботинки, туалет, парикмахер*) men's; (*характер, рукопожатие*) masculine; (*органы, клетка*) male; **мужско́й пол** male sex; **мужско́й род** masculine gender.
мужчи́н|а (-ы) *м* man (*мн* men).
мужья́ *сущ см* **муж**.
му́з|а (-ы) *ж* muse.
музе́|й (-я) *м* museum.
музе́йный *прил* museum *опред*.
му́зык|а (-и) *ж* (*также перен*) music.
музыка́л|ьный (-ен, -ьна, -ьно) *прил* musical; **музыка́льная шко́ла** music school.
музыка́нт (-а) *м* musician.
му́к|а (-и) *ж* torment.
мук|а́ (-и́) *ж* flour; (*грубого помола*) meal; **ко́стная ~** bone meal; **карто́фельная ~** (*крахмал*) potato starch.
мул (-а) *м* mule.
мулл|а́ (-ы́) *м* mullah.
му́льтик (-а) *м* (*разг*) cartoon.
мультиплика́тор (-а) *м* animator.
мультипликацио́нный *прил*: **~ фильм** cartoon.
мультиплика́ци|я (-и) *ж* cartoon.
мультфи́льм (-а) *м сокр* (= *мультипликацио́нный фильм*) cartoon, animation film.
му́ми|я (-и) *ж* mummy.
мунди́р (-а) *м* uniform; **карто́фель в ~е** jacket potatoes.
мундшту́к (-а́) *м* cigarette holder; (*муз*) mouthpiece.
муниципалите́т (-а) *м* municipality, city council.
муниципа́льный *прил* municipal.
МУР (-а) *м сокр* (= *Моско́вский уголо́вный ро́зыск*) Moscow Criminal Investigation Department.
мур|а́ (-ы́) *ж* (*разг*) rubbish.
мурав|е́й (-ья́) *м* ant.
мураве́йник (-а) *м* ant hill.
муравья́ *итп сущ см* **мураве́й**.
мура́ш|ки (-ек) *мн*: **у меня́ ~ по спине́ бе́гают** shivers are running down my spine; **покрыва́ться (покры́ться** *perf*) **~ками** to come out in goose pimples (*BRIT*) *или* goose bumps (*US*).
мурлы́|кать (-чу, -чешь) *несов неперех* to purr ◆ (*perf* **промурлы́кать**) *перех* to hum.
муска́т (-а) *м* (*орех*) nutmeg; (*сорт винограда*) muscat; (*сорт вина*) muscat(el).
му́скул (-а) *м* muscle.
мускулату́р|а (-ы) *ж собир* musculature.
мускули́ст|ый (-, -а, -о) *прил* muscular.
му́сор (-а) *м* rubbish (*BRIT*), garbage (*US*).
му́сор|ить (-ю, -ишь; *perf* **наму́сорить)** *несов неперех* to make a mess.
му́сорный *прил* rubbish *опред* (*BRIT*), garbage *опред* (*US*); **му́сорное ведро́** dustbin.
мусоропрово́д (-а) *м* refuse *или* garbage (*US*) chute.
мусс (-а) *м* (*кулин*) mousse.
мусульма́нин (-а) *м* Muslim.
мусульма́н|ка (-ки; *gen pl* **-ок)** *ж см* **мусульма́нин**.
мусульма́нск|ий (-ая, -ое, -ие) *прил* Muslim.
мусульма́нств|о (-а) *ср* Islam.
му́тен *прил см* **му́тный**.
му|ти́ть (-чу́, -ти́шь; *perf* **взмути́ть** *или* **замути́ть)** *несов перех* (*жидкость*) to muddy; (*perf* **помути́ть**; *перен*: *рассудок*) to cloud; (*no perf*; *разг*: *народ, толпу*) to work up ◆ *несов безл* (*разг*): **меня́ му́тит** I feel sick
▸ **мути́ться** (*perf* **замути́ться**) *несов возв* (*вода, раствор*) to become cloudy; (*perf* **помути́ться**; *перен*: *рассудок*) to become clouded ◆ *безл* (*разг*): **у меня́ в глаза́х** *или* **в голове́ помути́лось** I felt giddy.
мутне́|ть (*3sg* **-ет**, *3pl* **-ют**, *perf* **помутне́ть**) *несов неперех* (*жидкость*) to become cloudy; (*взор, глаза*) to grow dull; **он так уста́л, что у него́ созна́ние ~ет** he is so tired, he can't think straight.
му́т|ный (-ен, -на́, -но) *прил* (*жидкость*) cloudy; (*стекло, взор, глаза*) dull; (*взор, глаза*) glazed; (*перен*: *голова, рассудок*) confused.
мут|ь (-и) *ж* sediment; (*разг*: *фильм, книга итп*) rubbish; (*перен*: *на душе*) ache.
му́фт|а (-ы) *ж* (*TEX*) sleeve; (*женская одежда*) muff.
му́х|а (-и) *ж* fly; **де́лать (сде́лать** *perf*) **из ~и**

слона́ ≈ to make a mountain out of a molehill; **под ~ой** (*разг*) legless.
мухомо́р (**-а**) *м* (*БОТ*) fly agaric.
муче́ни|е (**-я**) *ср* torment, torture.
му́ченик (**-а**) *м* martyr.
му́ченица (**-ы**) *ж см* **му́ченик**.
мучи́телен *прил см* **мучи́тельный**.
мучи́тел|ь (**-я**) *м* tormentor.
мучи́тельниц|а (**-ы**) *ж см* **мучи́тель**.
мучи́тел|ьный (**-ен, -ьна, -ьно**) *прил* agonizing.
му́ч|ить (**-у, -ишь**; *perf* **заму́чить** *или* **изму́чить**) *несов перех* to torment
▸ **му́читься** (*perf* **заму́читься**) *несов возв*: **~ся** *+instr* (*сомнениями, угрызениями совести*) to be tormented by; **~ся** (**заму́читься** *perf*) **от** *+gen* (*от болей, от приступов*) to suffer from; **~ся** (**заму́читься** *perf*) **с** *+instr* (*разг*) to have a lot of hassle with; **~ся** (*impf*) **над** *+instr* to agonize over.
мучн|о́е (**-о́го**; *decl like adj*) *ср* starchy foods *мн*.
му́шк|а (**-ки**; *gen pl* **-ек**) *ж* (*для прицела*) sight; (*на лице*) beauty spot; **брать** (**взять** *perf*) **кого́-н/что-н на ~ку** (*прицелиться*) to take aim at sb/sth; (*перен*) to keep a close eye on sb/sth.
муштр|ова́ть (**-у́ю**; *perf* **вымуштровать**) *несов перех* (*солдат*) to drill.
мха *итп сущ см* **мох**.
МХАТ (**-а**) *м сокр* (= *Моско́вский Худо́жественный академи́ческий теа́тр*) Moscow Arts Theatre (*BRIT*) *или* Theater (*US*).
мч|ать (**-у, -ишь**) *несов неперех* (*поезд, автомобиль*) to speed along; (*лошадь*) to race along ◆ *перех* to rush
▸ **мча́ться** *несов возв* (*поезд, автомобиль*) to speed along; (*лошадь*) to race along; (*перен: годы, время*) to fly past.
мще́ни|е (**-я**) *ср* revenge, vengeance.
мщу *несов см* **мстить**.
мы (**нас**; *см* **Table 5b**) *мест* we; **~ с тобо́й/жено́й** you/my wife and I; **кто зако́нчил рабо́ту? – ~** who finished the job? – we did; **кто винова́т? – ~** who is to blame? – we are.
мы́л|ить (**-ю, -ишь**; *perf* **намы́лить**) *несов перех* to soap
▸ **мы́литься** (*perf* **намы́литься**) *несов возв* to soap o.s.; (*мыло, шампунь*) to lather.
мы́л|о (**-а**) *ср* soap; **он весь в ~е** (*перен: разг: в поту*) he's in a lather.
мы́льниц|а (**-ы**) *ж* soap dish.
мы́льный *прил* soap *опред*.
мыс (**-а**; *loc sg* **-у́**, *nom pl* **-ы**) *м* cape, promontory.
мы́сленно *нареч* mentally.
мы́сленный *прил* mental.
мысли́тел|ь (**-я**) *м* thinker.
мысли́тельный *прил* (*процесс*) thought *опред*; (*способности, уровень*) intellectual.
мы́сл|ить (**-ю, -ишь**) *несов неперех* to think, reason ◆ *перех* to imagine; **я не ~ю жи́зни без рабо́ты** I can't imagine life without work.
мысл|ь (**-и**) *ж* thought; (*идея*) idea: **за́дняя ~** ulterior motive; **о́браз мы́слей** way of thinking; **собира́ться** (**собра́ться** *perf*) **с мы́слями** to collect one's thoughts; **э́то ~!** that's a thought!
мысля́щ|ий (**-ая, -ее, -ие**) *прил* thinking *опред*.
мыть (**мо́ю, мо́ешь**; *perf* **вы́мыть** *или* **помы́ть**) *несов перех* to wash; **рука́ ру́ку мо́ет** *partners in crime will always cover for each other*
▸ **мы́ться** (*perf* **вы́мыться** *или* **помы́ться**) *несов возв* to wash o.s.
мыч|а́ть (**-у́, -и́шь**; *perf* **промыча́ть**) *несов неперех* (*корова*) to moo; (*бык*) to bellow; (*разг: человек*) to mumble.
мы́шек *сущ см* **мы́шка**.
мышело́в|ка (**-ки**; *gen pl* **-ок**) *ж* mousetrap.
мы́шечный *прил* muscular.
мыши́н|ый *прил* (*цвет*) grey (*BRIT*), gray (*US*); **~ая нора́** mouse hole; **мыши́ная возня́** (*перен*) intrigue.
мы́шк|а (**-ки**; *gen pl* **-ек**) *ж уменьш от* **мышь**; **под ~кой** under one's arm.
мышле́ни|е (**-я**) *ср* thought, thinking.
мы́шц|а (**-ы**) *ж* muscle.
мыш|ь (**-и**) *ж* (*ЗООЛ, КОМП*) mouse.
мышья́к (**-а́**; *part gen* **-у́**) *м* arsenic.
мэр (**-а**) *м* mayor.
мэ́ри|я (**-и**) *ж* city hall.
мя́г|кий (**-кая, -кое, -кие**; **-ок, -ка́, -ко**) *прил* soft; (*движения, походка*) smooth; (*характер, человек*) mild, gentle; (*приговор, выговор, наказание*) lenient; (*климат, зима, погода*) mild; **мя́гкий ваго́н** *railway carriage with soft seats*; **мя́гкий знак** soft sign (*Russian letter*).
мя́гко *нареч* gently; (*отругать*) mildly; **~ выража́ясь** to put it mildly.
мягкосерде́ч|ный (**-ен, -на, -но**) *прил* kind-hearted.
мя́гок *прил см* **мя́гкий**.
мя́гче *сравн прил от* **мя́гкий** ◆ *сравн нареч от* **мя́гко**.
мя́киш (**-а**) *м* crumb.
мя́кот|ь (**-и**) *ж* flesh; (*мясо без костей*) meat off the bone.
мя́мл|ить (**-ю, -ишь**; *perf* **промя́млить**) *несов перех* (*разг*) to mumble.
мяси́ст|ый (**-, -а, -о**) *прил* meaty; (*плечи, лицо, плод*) fleshy.
мясни́к (**-а́**) *м* butcher.
мясн|о́й *прил* (*из мяса*) meat; (*корова, скот*) beef; (*отдел, магазин*) butcher's; **~ы́е консе́рвы** tinned meat.
мя́с|о (**-а**) *ср* meat; (*разг: говядина*) beef.
мясору́б|ка (**-ки**; *gen pl* **-ок**) *ж* mincer (*BRIT*), grinder (*US*).
мя́т|а (**-ы**) *ж* mint.
мяте́ж (**-а́**) *м* revolt.
мяте́жный *прил* rebellious; (*душа, характер*)

restless.

мя́тный *прил* mint.

мя́тый *прил* (*одежда*) creased; (*бумага*) crumpled.

мять (**мну, мнёшь**; *perf* **размя́ть**) *несов перех* (*глину*) to knead; (*кожу*) to work; (*perf* **измя́ть** *или* **смять**; *одежду*) to crease; (*бумагу*) to rumple; (*волосы*) to ruffle

▸ **мя́ться** *несов возв* (*разг*: *человек*) to shilly-shally; (*perf* **измя́ться** *или* **помя́ться** *или* **смя́ться**; *одежда*) to get creased; (*бумага*) to get rumpled.

мяу́ка|ть (**-ю**; *perf* **промяу́кать**) *несов неперех* to miaow, mew.

мяч (**-а́**) *м* ball; **ручно́й** ~ (*спорт*) handball; **футбо́льный** ~ football.

~ Н, н ~

Н, н *сущ нескл (буква) the 14th letter of the Russian alphabet.*

KEYWORD

на *предл (+acc)* ***1*** *(направление на поверхность)* on; **положи тарелку на стол** put the plate on the table; **я повесил картину на стену** I hung the picture on the wall; **надо наклеить марку на конверт** you need to stick the stamp on the envelope
2 *(направление в какое-н место)* to; **на Юг/Украину** to the South/Ukraine; **ездить** *(impf)* **на море/работу/конференции** to go to the seaside/to work/to a conference; **сесть** *(perf)* **на поезд** to get on(to) the train
3 *(об объекте воздействия)*: **обрати внимание на этого человека** pay attention to this man; **нажми на педаль/кнопку** press the pedal/button; **я люблю смотреть на детей/на звёзды** I love watching the children/the stars
4 *(о времени, сроке)* for; **назначать (назначить** *perf*) **на завтра/на 5 часов** to arrange sth for tomorrow/for 5 o'clock; **он уехал на час/месяц** he has gone away for an hour/a month
5 *(о цели, о назначении)* for; **деньги на книги** money for books; **ткань на платье** material for a dress; **на написание доклада ушло много времени** much time was spent writing the report; **проверка на сообразительность** intelligence test
6 *(о мере)* into; **делить** *(impf)* **что-н на части/параграфы** to divide sth into parts/paragraphs
7 *(при сравнении)*: **я получаю на сто рублей меньше** I get one hundred roubles less
8 *(об изменении состояния)* into; **надо перевести текст на английский** the text must be translated into English; **мы перешли на русский язык** we switched (in)to Russian; **я обменял машину на яхту** I exchanged the car for a yacht ♦ *предл (+prp)* ***1*** *(нахождение на поверхности)* on; **книга на полке** the book is on the shelf; **я сижу на диване** I am sitting on the sofa; **на девочке шапка/шуба** the girl has a hat/fur coat on
2 *(о пребывании где-н)* in; **на Украине/Кавказе** in the Ukraine/Caucasus; **на улице** in the street; **быть** *(impf)* **на работе/заседании** to be at work/at a meeting
3 *(о времени осуществления чего-н)*: **встретимся на следующей неделе** let's meet next week; **на первых порах** at first; **на ходу** *(сказать, бросить итп)* in passing; *(поймать)* without stopping
4 *(об объекте воздействия)* on; **сосредоточиться** *(perf)***/остановиться** *(perf)* **на чём-н** to concentrate/dwell on sth; **сойти** *(perf)* **с ума на чём-н** to go mad about sth
5 *(о средстве осуществления чего-н)*: **ездить на поезде/велосипеде** to travel by train/bicycle; **играть** *(impf)* **на рояле/скрипке** to play the piano/violin; **кататься** *(impf)* **на лыжах/коньках** to go skiing/skating; **говорить** *(impf)* **на русском/английском языке** to speak (in) English/Russian
6 *(о составной части предмета)*: **раствор на йоде** iodine solution; **каша на воде** porridge made with water
7 *(разг: о большом количестве чего-н)*: **ошибка на ошибке** mistake upon mistake.

на (нате) *част (разг)* here (you are).
наб. *сокр* = **набережная.**
набав|ить (-лю, -ишь; *impf* **набавлять)** *сов перех* to increase.
набалдашник (-а) *м* knob (*of walking stick*).
набалтыва|ть (-ю) *несов от* **наболтать.**
набат (-а) *м* alarm bell; **бить** *(impf)* **в ~** *(перен)* to sound the alarm.
набег (-а) *м* raid.
набега|ть (-ю) *сов перех (километра итп)* to run; **~** *(perf)* **инфаркт** *(разг)* to give o.s. a heart attack (*by running*).
набега|ть (-ю) *несов от* **набежать.**
набега|ться (-юсь) *сов возв* to wear o.s. out running.
набегу *итп сов см* **набежать.**
набедренн|ый *прил*: **~ая повязка** loincloth.
набежать (*как* **бежать;** *см* **Table 20;** *impf* **набегать)** *сов неперех (разг: тучи)* to gather; *(: толпа, букашки)* to come running; *(: вода)* to well up; *(проценты, выходные итп)* to mount up; *(наскочить)*: **~ на** *+acc* to run into; *(волны: на берег)* to lap against.

The spelling rules for Russian are shown on page xvii.

набезобра́знича|ть (-ю) *сов от* **безобра́зничать**.

набекре́нь *нареч* (*шапка*) tilted to one side; **у него́ мозги́** ~ (*разг*) he's not with it.

на́бело *нареч*: **переписа́ть что-н** ~ to write sth out in neat.

на́бережн|ая (-ой; *decl like adj*) *ж* embankment.

наберу́(сь) *umn сов см* **набра́ть(ся)**.

набива́|ть(ся) (-ю(сь)) *несов от* **наби́ть(ся)**.

наби́вк|а (-и) *ж* stuffing.

набивно́й *прил* (*матрас, подушка*) stuffed; (*ткань*) printed.

набира́|ть(ся) (-ю(сь)) *несов от* **набра́ть(ся)**.

наб|и́ть (-ью́, -ьёшь; *impf* **набива́ть**) *сов перех* (*прикрепить гвоздями*) to nail; (*полотно, ситец*) to print; (*разг*: *тарелок, чашек*) to smash; (: *настрелять*) to bag; **набива́ть** (~ *perf*) (+*instr*) (*матрас, чемодан итп*) to stuff (with); ~ (*perf*) **ши́шку/синя́к** (*разг*) to get a bump/bruise; ~ (*perf*) **оско́мину** (*перен*) to reach saturation point; ~ (*perf*) **ру́ку** (**на** +*prp*) (*разг*) to get the knack (of); **набива́ть** (~ *perf*) **це́ну** (*разг*) to talk up the price

▸ **наби́ться** (*impf* **набива́ться**) *сов возв* (*разг*): **~ся в** +*acc* (*в комнату, в автобус*) to pack; **она́ всё вре́мя ~ива́ется к нам в го́сти** she's always inviting herself round.

наблюда́телен *прил см* **наблюда́тельный**.

наблюда́тел|ь (-я) *м* observer.

наблюда́тел|ьный (-ен, -ьна, -ьно) *прил* (*человек*) observant; ~ **пункт** observation point.

наблюда́|ть (-ю) *несов перех* to observe; (*пациента*) to treat ◆ *неперех*: ~ **за** +*instr* to monitor; (*за порядком, за детьми*) to watch over

▸ **наблюда́ться** *несов возв* (*случаться*) to be; **~ся** (*impf*) **у** +*gen* (*лечиться*) to be treated by; **в стране́ ~ется рост престу́пности** there has been an increase in crime across the country.

на́бож|ный (-ен, -на, -но) *прил* devout.

набо́|йка (-йки; *gen pl* -ек) *ж* (*ткани, узора*) printing; (*ткань*) printed fabric; (*на каблуке*) heel.

на́бок *нареч* to one side.

наболева́|ть (*3sg* -ет) *несов от* **наболе́ть**.

наболе́вш|ий (-ая, -ее, -ие) *прил* (*перен*: *проблема, тема*) sensitive; ~ **вопро́с** sore point.

наболе́|ть (*3sg* -ет, *impf* **наболева́ть**) *сов неперех* to become sore; (*проблема*) to become acute; **у неё ~ло на душе́** she has suffered a great deal.

наболта́|ть (-ю; *impf* **наба́лтывать**) *сов перех* (*разг*): ~ **глу́постей** to talk a lot of rubbish ◆ *неперех*: ~ **кому́-н про кого́-н** to tell sb stories about sb.

набо́р (-а) *м* (*совокупность*) set; (*студентов*) selection; (*армии, штата*) recruitment; (*типог*) typesetting. ~ **слов** (*перен*) gibberish.

набо́рный *прил* (*типог*): ~ **цех** typesetter's; **набо́рный стано́к** galley.

набо́рщик (-а) *м* (*типог*) typesetter.

набо́рщиц|а (-ы) *ж см* **набо́рщик**.

набра́сыва|ть (-ю) *несов от* **наброса́ть, набро́сить**

▸ **набра́сываться** *несов от* **набро́ситься**.

наб|ра́ть (-еру́, -ерёшь; *pt* -ра́л, -рала́, -ра́ло, *impf* **набира́ть**) *сов (не)перех* (+*acc или* +*gen*; *грибов, цветов*) to pick; (*воды*) to fetch; (*работы, студентов, работников*) to take on; (*армию, труппу*) to assemble; (*скорость, высоту, баллы*) to gain; (*код, номер телефона*) to dial; (*статью, текст*) to typeset; **набира́ть** (~ *perf*) **о́пыт** to gain experience

▸ **набра́ться** (*impf* **набира́ться**) *сов возв* (+*gen*; *много народу*) to gather; (*сумма денег*) to accumulate; (*разг*: *напиться*) to get sloshed; **~ся** (*perf*) +*gen* (*предрассудков итп*) to acquire; **набира́ться** (**~ся** *perf*) **сил** to build up one's strength; **набира́ться** (**~ся** *perf*) **хра́брости** to muster up courage; **набира́ться** (**~ся** *perf*) **терпе́ния** to arm o.s. with patience.

набр|ести́ (-еду́, -едёшь; *pt* -ёл, -ела́, -ело́, *impf* **набреда́ть**) *сов неперех* (*разг*): ~ **на** +*acc* (*перен*) to come across; ~ (*perf*) **на мысль** (*перен*) to hit upon an idea.

наброса́|ть (-ю; *impf* **набра́сывать**) *сов перех* (*план, текст*) to sketch out ◆ (*не*)*перех* (+*acc или* +*gen*; *вещей, окурков*) to throw about.

набро́|сить (-шу, -сишь; *impf* **набра́сывать**) *сов перех* (*пальто, платок*) to throw on; (*покрывало*) to throw over

▸ **набро́ситься** (*impf* **набра́сываться**) *сов возв*: **~ся на** +*acc* (*на добычу, на жертву*) to fall upon; (*разг*: *на еду, на работу*) to get stuck into; **~ся** (*perf*) **на кого́-н** (*разг*: *с упрёками*) to lay into sb.

набро́с|ок (-ка) *м* (*плана*) sketch; (*статьи, письма*) draft.

набро́шу(сь) *сов см* **набро́сить(ся)**.

набры́зга|ть (-ю) *сов (не)перех*: ~ +*acc или* +*gen или* +*instr* to splash.

набу́х|нуть (*3sg* -нет, *3pl* -нут, *pt* -, -ла, -ло, *impf* **набуха́ть**) *сов неперех* to swell up.

набью́(сь) *umn сов см* **наби́ть(ся)**.

нава́г|а (-и) *ж* (*зоол*) *type of cod*.

наважде́ни|е (-я) *ср* apparition.

нав|али́ть (-алю́, -а́лишь; *impf* **нава́ливать**) *сов (не)перех* (+*acc или* +*gen*; *мусору, кирпичей итп*) to pile up ◆ *неперех* (*no impf*; *толпа*) to flock; **нава́ливать** (~ *perf*) (**на** +*acc*) to pile on(to); **нава́ливать** (~ *perf*) **на кого́-н рабо́ту/обя́занности** to load sb with work/ responsibilities; **в э́том году́ ~али́ло мно́го сне́гу** there was a lot of snow this year

▸ **навали́ться** (*impf* **нава́ливаться**) *сов возв*: **~ся на** +*acc* (*на дверь итп*) to lean into; (*насыпаться*: *земля*) to pile up on; (*разг*: *наброситься*: *на еду*) to get stuck into; **на меня́ ~али́лось мно́го рабо́ты** (*разг*) I'm swamped with work.

навáлом *нареч*: **грузи́ть ~** to pile up ◆ *как сказ*: ~ *+gen* (*разг*: *фруктов, денег итп*) there's loads of.
навáр (-а) *м* (*бульон*) broth; (*жир*) fat; (*разг*: *прибыль*) take-in.
навáрива|ть (-ю) *несов от* **навари́ть**.
навáрист|ый (-, -а, -о) *прил* rich.
нав|ари́ть (-арю́, -áришь; *impf* **навáривать**) *сов перех* (*ТЕХ*: *стали*) to weld; (: *кусок металла*) to weld on ◆ *(не)перех* (*+acc или +gen*; *супа, варенья*) to make a lot of.
навевá|ть (-ю) *несов от* **навéять**.
навéда|ться (-юсь; *impf* **навéдываться**) *сов возв* (*разг*): ~ **к** *+dat* to call in on.
наведéни|е (-я) *ср* (*порядка*) establishment; (*справок*) making; (*орудия*) aiming.
наведу́ *итп сов см* **навести́**.
навéдыва|ться (-юсь) *несов от* **навéдаться**.
нав|езти́ (-езу́, -езёшь; *pt* -ёз, -езлá, -езлó, *impf* **навози́ть**) *сов перех* to bring a lot of.
навéк *нареч* (*навсегда*) for good, forever.
навéки *нареч* = **навéк**.
навёл *итп сов см* **навести́**.
навéрно *вводн сл* probably ◆ *нареч* (*точно*) for sure.
навéрное *нареч* = **навéрно**.
наверн|у́ть (-у, -ёшь; *impf* **навёртывать**) *сов перех*: ~ **(на** *+acc*) (*навинтить*) to screw on(to); (*намотать*) to wrap (around)
▸ **наверну́ться** (*impf* **навёртываться**) *сов возв* (*слёзы*) to well up.
наверня́ка́ *вводн сл* (*конечно*) certainly ◆ *нареч* (*несомненно*) definitely, for sure; **он дéйствует ~** he doesn't take any chances.
наверстá|ть (-ю; *impf* **навёрстывать**) *сов перех* (*ТИПОГ*) to typeset; **навёрстывать (~** *perf*) **упу́щенное** *или* **потéрянное врéмя** to make up for lost time.
нав|ертéть (-ерчу́, -éртишь; *impf* **навёртывать**) *сов перех*: ~ **(на** *+acc*) to twist (around).
навёртыва|ть (-ю) *несов от* **наверну́ть, навертéть**
▸ **навёртываться** *несов от* **наверну́ться**.
навéрх *нареч* up; (*на верхний этаж*) upstairs; (*на поверхность*) to the top; **посмотрéть** (*perf*) ~ to look up; **обращáться (обрати́ться** *perf*) ~ (*перен*: *разг*) to go to the top.
наверху́ *нареч* (*также перен*) at the top; (*в верхнем этаже*) upstairs; (*на поверхности*) on (the) top ◆ *предл* (*+gen*) at the top of.
наверчу́ *сов см* **навертéть**.
навéс (-а) *м* (*над прилавком, у подъезда*) canopy; (*скалы, берега*) overhang.
навеселé *нареч* (*разг*): **быть ~** to be merry *или* tipsy.
навé|сить (-шу, -сишь; *impf* **навéшивать**) *сов перех* (*дверь, замок*) to hang; (*разг*: *картин, плакатов*) to hang up; (*СПОРТ*) to lob.
нав|ести́ (-еду́, -едёшь; *pt* ёл, -елá, -елó, *impf* **наводи́ть**) *сов перех* (*вызвать*: *ужас, грусть итп*) to cause; (*бинокль, объектив*) to focus; (*орудие*) to aim; (*мост*) to lay; (*лак, краску*) to apply; (*разг*: *гостей, приятелей, друзей*) to bring; (*порядок*) to establish; **наводи́ть (~** *perf*) **когó-н на** *+acc* (*на место, на след*) to lead sb to; **наводи́ть (~** *perf*) **спрáвки** to make inquiries; **наводи́ть (~** *perf*) **чистоту́** to clean up; **наводи́ть (~** *perf*) **красоту́** (*разг*) to tart o.s. up; **э́та му́зыка ~óдит на меня́ тоску́** this music makes me sad; **наводи́ть (~** *perf*) **когó-н на мысль** to give sb an idea; **егó расскáз ~ёл меня́ на размышлéния** his story started me thinking.
наве|сти́ть (-щу́, -сти́шь; *impf* **навещáть**) *сов перех* to visit.
навéчно *нареч* for evermore.
навéша|ть (-ю; *impf* **навéшивать**) *сов (не)перех* (*+acc или +gen*; *белья, картин, украшения*) to hang up; (*муки, печений*) to weigh out.
навéшива|ть (-ю) *несов от* **навéсить, навéшать**.
навéшу *сов см* **навéсить**.
навещá|ть (-ю) *несов от* **навести́ть**.
навещу́ *сов см* **навести́ть**.
навé|ять (-ю, -ешь; *impf* **навевáть**) *сов перех* (*перен*: *тоску итп*) to evoke.
нáвзничь *нареч* on one's back.
навзры́д *нареч*: **плáкать ~** to sob loudly.
навигáтор (-а) *м* navigator.
навигáци|я (-и) *ж* navigation.
навин|ти́ть (-чу́, -ти́шь; *impf* **нави́нчивать**) *сов перех* (*гайку, пробку*) to screw in; (*крышку*) to screw on.
нави́с|нуть (-ну, -нешь; *pt* -, -ла, -ло, *impf* **нависáть**) *сов неперех*: ~ **на** *+acc* (*волосы*: *на лоб*) to hang down over; **нависáть (~** *perf*) **на** *+prp* (*сосульки*: *на ветках*) to hang from; **нависáть (~** *perf*) **над** *+instr* (*скалы*) to overhang; (*тучи, опасность*) to loom over.
нави́сш|ий (-ая, -ее, -ие) *прил* (*берег, скала*) overhanging.
навл|éчь (-еку́, -ечёшь *итп*, -еку́т; *pt* -ёк, -еклá, -еклó, *impf* **навлекáть**) *сов перех* (*подозрения, несчастье*) to attract; **навлекáть (~** *perf*) **на когó-н беду́** to bring sb bad luck; **навлекáть (~** *perf*) **на себя́ чей-н гнев** to incur sb's wrath.
нав|оди́ть (-ожу́, -óдишь) *несов от* **навести́**.
навóдк|а (-и) *ж* (*объектива*) focusing; (*оружия*) aiming.
наводнéни|е (-я) *ср* flood; (*рынков товаром*) flooding.
наводн|и́ть (-ю́, -и́шь; *impf* **наводня́ть**) *сов перех*: ~ **что-н** *+instr* (*товарами, продуктами*) to flood sth with.
навóдчик (-а) *м* (*сообщник*) *informant who tips*

thieves off.
наводя́щ|ий (-ая, -ее, -ие) *прил*: **~ вопро́с** pointer, hint.
наво́жу *несов см* **наво́зить.**
навожу́ *несов см* **наводи́ть, навози́ть.**
наво́з (-а) *м* manure.
наво́зить (-жу, -зишь; *perf* **унаво́зить**) *несов перех* to fertilize.
нав|ози́ть (-ожу́, -о́зишь) *несов от* **навезти́.**
на́волоч|ка (-ки; *gen pl* -ек) *ж* pillowcase.
навостр|и́ть (-ю́, -и́шь) *сов перех* (*разг*): **~ у́ши** to prick up one's ears; **~** (*perf*) **лы́жи** (*разг*) to be ready to shoot off.
навр|а́ть (-у́, -ёшь; *pt* -а́л, -ала́, -а́ло) *сов от* **врать.**
навр|еди́ть (-жу́, -ди́шь) *сов от* **вреди́ть.**
навсегда́ *нареч* forever; **раз и ~** once and for all.
навстре́чу *предл* (*+dat*) towards ◆ *нареч*: **бежа́ть ~ к кому́-н** to run towards sb; **она́ вы́шла ~ гостя́м** she came out to meet the guests; **идти́ (пойти́** *perf*) **~ кому́-н** (*перен*) to give sb a hand.
навы́ворот *нареч* (*разг*: *наизнанку*) inside out; (*перен*: *наоборот*) the wrong way round.
на́вык (-а) *м* skill.
навы́кат(е) *нареч*: **глаза́ ~** bulging eyes.
навы́лет *нареч* right through; **его́ ра́нило пуле́й ~** the bullet went right through him.
навы́нос *нареч* to take away (*BRIT*), to go (*US*); **мы не продаём ~** we don't do takeaways (*BRIT*) *или* takeouts (*US*).
навы́пуск *нареч* outside, over; **он но́сит руба́шку ~** he wears his shirt outside his trousers.
навы́тяжку *нареч*: **стоя́ть ~** to stand to attention.
навью́ч|ить (-у, -ишь; *impf* **навью́чивать**) *сов перех* to load.
нав|яза́ть (-яжу́, -я́жешь; *impf* **навя́зывать**) *сов перех*: **~ (на** *+acc*) (*на шею, на удочку*) to tie on(to); **навя́зывать (~** *perf*) *+gen* (*связать*) to knit a lot of; (*снопов, веников*) to tie a lot of; (*венков*) to weave a lot of; **навя́зывать (~** *perf*) **что-н кому́-н** (*перен*) to impose sth on sb
▸ **навяза́ться** (*impf* **навя́зываться**) *сов возв* (*разг*): **~ся кому́-н в друзья́** to impose o.s. on sb; **~ся** (*perf*) **в го́сти** to invite o.s. round.
навя́зчив|ый (-, -а, -о) *прил* (*мысль*) persistent; (*человек*) bothersome; **она́ ужа́сно ~ая** she's a real pest.
навя́зыва|ть(ся) (-ю(сь)) *несов от* **навяза́ть(ся).**
нагада́|ть (-ю; *impf* **нага́дывать**) *сов перех* (*разг*) to predict.
нага́|дить (-жу, -дишь) *сов от* **га́дить.**
нага́дыва|ть (-ю) *несов от* **нагада́ть.**
нага́жу *сов см* **нага́дить.**
нага́|йка (-йки; *gen pl* -ек) *ж* whip.
нага́н (-а) *м* revolver.
нага́р (-а) *м* snuff (*of candle*).
нагиба́|ть(ся) (-ю(сь)) *несов от* **нагну́ть(ся).**
нагишо́м *нареч* (*разг*) stark-naked.
нагла́|дить (-жу, -дишь; *impf* **нагла́живать**) *сов перех* to iron.
нагле́|ть (-ю; *perf* **обнагле́ть**) *несов неперех* to get impudent.
нагле́ц (-а́) *м* impudent upstart.
на́гло *нареч* impudently.
на́глост|ь (-и) *ж* impudence, impertinence.
наглота́|ться (-юсь) *сов возв* (*+gen*) to swallow.
на́глухо *нареч* tight, securely; **застёгиваться (застегну́ться** *perf*) **~** to do one's coat right up.
на́гл|ый (-, -а́, -о) *прил* insolent, impudent; **~ая ложь** brazen lie.
нагля́ден *прил см* **нагля́дный.**
нагляде́ться (-жу́сь, -ди́шься) *сов возв*: **~ на** *+acc* to tire of looking at; **дай мне на тебя́ ~** let me take a good look at you.
нагля́дный (-ен, -на, -но) *прил* (*пример, случай*) clear; (*no short form*; *метод обучения*) visual; **нагля́дные посо́бия** visual aids.
нагляжу́сь *сов см* **нагляде́ться.**
наг|на́ть (-оню́, -о́нишь; *pt* -на́л, -нала́, -на́ло, *impf* **нагоня́ть**) *сов перех* (*беглеца*) to catch up with; (*упущенное, пройденное*) to make up for; (*подлеж*: *ветер*: *грозу, тучи*) to blow; (*спирта, самогона*) to distil (*BRIT*), distill (*US*); **нагоня́ть (~** *perf*) **страх на кого́-н** to strike fear into sb; **нагоня́ть (~** *perf*) **тоску́ на кого́-н** to fill sb with sadness.
нагне|сти́ (-ту́, -тёшь; *impf* **нагнета́ть**) *сов перех* to pump.
нагнета́|ть (-ю) *несов от* **нагнести́** ◆ *перех* (*перен*: *напряжение*) to heighten.
нагное́ни|е (-я) *ср* festering.
нагно|и́ться (*3sg* -и́тся, *3pl* -я́тся) *сов возв* to fester.
нагн|у́ть (-у́, -ёшь; *impf* **нагиба́ть**) *сов перех* (*ветку, человека*) to pull down; (*шею, голову*) to bend
▸ **нагну́ться** (*impf* **нагиба́ться**) *сов возв* to bend down.
награ́рива|ть(ся) (-ю(сь)) *несов от* **наговори́ть(ся).**
наговор (-а) *м* (*разг*: *клевета*) slander; (*колдовской*) spell.
наговор|и́ть (-ю́, -и́шь; *impf* **нагова́ривать**) *сов перех* (*текст*: *на плёнку*) to record ◆ *неперех* (*разг*: *наклеветать*): **~ на** *+acc* to slander; **~** (*perf*) **чепухи́** to talk a lot of nonsense; **~** (*perf*) **кому́-н комплиме́нтов** to shower sb with compliments
▸ **наговори́ться** (*impf* **нагова́риваться**) *сов возв* to talk one's fill.
наг|о́й (-, -а́, -о) *прил* (*человек*) naked, nude; (*руки, ноги, лес*) bare.
на́голо *нареч*: **остри́чься ~** to shave one's head; **обри́ть** (*perf*) **кого́-н ~** to shave sb's head.
наголо́ *нареч*: **ша́шки ~** drawn swords.
на́голову *нареч*: **разби́ть** *или* **разгроми́ть ~** to rout.

нагоню́ *итп сов см* **нагна́ть.**
нагоня́|й **(-я)** *м* (*разг*): **получи́ть ~ (от кого́-н)** to get a ticking off (from sb).
нагоня́|ть (-ю) *несов от* **нагна́ть.**
нагор|е́ть (*3sg* **-и́т,** *impf* **нагора́ть)** *сов безл* (*+gen*; *израсходоваться*) to be used up.
наго́рный *прил* (*пастбище, растительность*) alpine, mountain *опред*; (*гористый*) hilly.
нагор|оди́ть (-ожу́, -о́дишь) *сов (не)перех* (*+acc или +gen*; *разг*: *построек*) to put up; **он ~оди́л ерунды́** (*разг*) he came out with a load of nonsense.
наго́рь|е (-я) *ср* plateau.
нагот|а́ (-ы́) *ж* nudity, nakedness.
нагота́влива|ть (-ю) *несов от* **нагото́вить.**
нагото́ве *нареч* at the ready.
нагото́в|ить (-лю, -ишь; *impf* **нагота́вливать)** *сов перех* (*запасти*) to stock up with; (*сварить*) to cook.
награ́б|ить (-лю, -ишь) *сов перех* to plunder.
награ́д|а (-ы) *ж* reward; (*за учёбу, за работу*) prize; (*ВОЕН*) decoration; **дать** *(perf)* **что-н кому́-н в ~у** to give sb sth as a reward.
награ|ди́ть (-жу́, -ди́шь; *impf* **награжда́ть)** *сов перех*: **~ кого́-н чем-н** (*орденом*) to award sb sth, award sth to sb; (*перен*: *способностями*) to endow sb with sth; (: *поцелуем, улыбкой*) to reward sb with sth.
награжде́ни|е (-я) *ср* awards ceremony.
награжу́ *сов см* **награди́ть.**
нагреба́|ть (-ю) *несов от* **нагрести́.**
нагребу́ *итп сов см* **нагрести́.**
нагрева́ни|е (-я) *ср* heating.
нагрева́тельный *прил*: **~ прибо́р** heating appliance.
нагрева́|ть(ся) (-ю(сь)) *несов от* **нагре́ть(ся).**
нагр|ести́ (-ебу́, -ебёшь; *pt* **-ёб, -ебла́, -ебло́,** *impf* **нагреба́ть)** *сов перех* to rake together.
нагре́|ть (-ю; *impf* **нагрева́ть)** *сов перех* to heat, warm; **~** *(perf)* **ру́ки (на** *+prp*) (*перен*) to line one's pockets (with)
▸ **нагре́ться** (*impf* **нагрева́ться)** *сов возв* to warm up.
нагримир|ова́ться (-у́юсь) *сов от* **гримирова́ться.**
нагроможда́|ть (-ю) *несов от* **громозди́ть.**
нагроможде́ни|е (-я) *ср* (*предметов*) pile; (*фактов*) mound.
нагромоз|ди́ть (-жу́, -ди́шь) *сов от* **громозди́ть.**
нагруб|и́ть (-лю́, -и́шь) *сов от* **груби́ть.**
нагру́дник (-а) *м* bib; (*рыцарский*) breastplate.
нагру́дный *прил*: **~ карма́н** breast pocket.
нагр|узи́ть (-ужу́, -у́зишь) *сов от* **грузи́ть ◆** (*impf* **нагружа́ть)** *перех* to load up; **нагружа́ть (~** *perf*) **кого́-н рабо́той** to load sb with work.
нагру́зк|а (-и) *ж* (*действие*) loading; (*груз, также ЭЛЕК, ТЕХ*) load; (*занятость*) workload; (*общественная*) responsibilities *мн*.
нагрязн|и́ть (-ю́, -и́шь) *сов от* **грязни́ть.**
нагря́н|уть (-у, -ешь) *сов неперех* (*гости, полиция*) to descend on; (*холода*) to set in; **~ула беда́** tragedy struck.
нагуля́|ть (-ю; *impf* **нагу́ливать)** *сов перех* (*разг*): **~ аппети́т** to work up an appetite; **нагу́ливать (~** *perf*) **румя́нец** to get some colour in one's cheeks
▸ **нагуля́ться** *сов возв* to have a good walk.
над *предл* (*+instr*) above; **рабо́тать** *(impf)* **~ прое́ктом** to work on a project; **ду́мать** *(impf)* **~ зада́чей** to think about a problem; **смея́ться** *(impf)* **~ ребёнком** to laugh at a child; **сиде́ть** *(impf)* **~ кни́гой** to sit over a book.
над- *префикс* (*in verbs*; *об увеличении чего-н*) *indicating an increase in sth eg. надстро́ить*; (*о неполном действии*) *indicating an incomplete action eg. надкуси́ть*; (*in nouns and adjectives*; *поверх чего-н*) *indicating position above sth eg. надзе́мный.*
нада|ва́ть (-ю́, -ёшь) *сов перех* (*разг*): **~ кому́-н чего́-н** (*подарков, советов, обещаний*) to give sb lots of sth **◆** *неперех*: **~ кому́-н** (*разг*) to thrash sb.
над|ави́ть (-авлю, -а́вишь; *impf* **нада́вливать)** *сов (не)перех* (*+acc или +gen*; *соку*) to squeeze; (*разг*: *тараканов итп*) to squash **◆** *неперех*: **~ на** *+acc* (*на дверь итп*) to lean against; (*на кнопку*) to press.
нада́ива|ть (-ю) *несов от* **надои́ть.**
надар|и́ть (-ю́, -ишь; *impf* **нада́ривать)** *сов перех* (*разг*): **~ кому́-н пода́рков** to give sb lots of presents.
надба́в|ить (-лю, -ишь; *impf* **надбавля́ть)** *сов перех* (*разг*) = **наба́вить.**
надба́вк|а (-и) *ж* (*к зарплате*) rise; (*к пенсии*) supplement; (*к цене*) surcharge; **надба́вка за вре́дность** danger money (*BRIT*), hazard pay (*US*).
надба́влю *сов см* **надба́вить.**
надбавля́|ть (-ю) *несов от* **надба́вить.**
надви́н|уть (-у, -ешь; *impf* **надвига́ть)** *сов перех*: **~ что-н (на** *+acc*) to pull sth down (over)
▸ **надви́нуться** (*impf* **надвига́ться)** *сов возв* (*гроза, опасность, старость*) to approach; **надвига́ться (~ся** *perf*) **(на** *+acc*) (*на лоб, на уши*) to slide down (over).
надво́дный *прил* above water; (*корабль*) surface *опред*.
на́двое *нареч* in(to) two.
надво́рн|ый *прил*: **~ые постро́йки** outbuildings *мн*.
надв|яза́ть (-яжу́, -я́жешь; *impf* **надвя́зывать)** *сов перех* (*свитер, рукава*) to lengthen (*knitted garment*); (*верёвку, нитку*) to tie on.
надгро́би|е (-я) *ср* gravestone, tombstone.
надгро́бный *прил* (*речь*) at the graveside;

(*надпись*) gravestone *опред*; **надгробный камень** headstone; **надгробный памятник** memorial.
надёванный *прил* (*разг*) worn.
надева|ть (-ю) *несов от* **надеть**.
надежд|а (-ы) *ж* hope; **в ~е на** *+acc* in the hope of; **питать** *(impf)* **~у на что-н** to hope for sth; **подавать** *(impf)* **~ы** to show promise.
надёжен *прил см* **надёжный**.
надёжно *нареч* securely.
надёжност|ь (-и) *ж* reliability.
надёж|ный (-ен, -на, -но) *прил* reliable; (*дверь, механизм*) secure; (*средство, путь*) safe.
надела|ть (-ю) *сов (не)перех (+acc или +gen; ошибок, салатов)* to make lots of; (*неприятностей, вреда*) to cause a lot of; **не ~й глупостей** don't do anything stupid; **что ты ~л?** what have you done?
надел|ить (-ю, -ишь; *impf* **наделять**) *сов перех*: **~ кого-н чем-н** (*землёй, участком*) to grant sb sth; (*перен: талантом, умом*) to endow sb with sth.
надену *итп сов см* **надеть**.
надёрга|ть (-ю; *impf* **надёргивать**) *сов (не)перех (+acc или +gen; перьев, сорняков)* to pull out; (*разг: цитат, примеров*) to choose carefully.
надёрн|уть (-у, -ешь; *impf* **надёргивать**) *сов перех* to pull over.
наде|ть (-ну, -нешь; *impf* **надевать**) *сов перех* to put on.
надея|ться (-юсь) *несов возв*: **~** *+infin* (*отдохнуть, успеть итп*) to hope to do; (*perf* **понадеяться**): **~ на** *+acc* (*на друга, на семью*) to rely on; (*на улучшение*) to hope for; **я надеюсь, что ...** I hope that ....
надземный *прил* (*сооружение*) overground; (*часть растения*) above ground.
надзирател|ь (-я) *м* guard.
надзор (-а) *м* control.
надира|ться (-юсь) *несов от* **надраться**.
надк|усить (-ушу, -усишь; *impf* **надкусывать**) *сов перех* to take a bite of.
надламыва|ть(ся) (-ю(сь)) *несов от* **надломить(ся)**.
надлежащ|ий (-ая, -ее, -ие) *прил* appropriate, suitable; **~им образом** in the appropriate manner.
надлеж|ит (*pt* -ало) *несов безл*: **ему ~ явиться в 9 часов** he is required to make an appearance at 9 o'clock.
надлом (-а) *м* (*на ветке*) crack; (*угнетение*) breakdown.
надл|омить (-омлю, -омишь; *impf* **надламывать**) *сов перех* (*также перен*) to break; (*здоровье, психику*) to damage
▶ **надломиться** (*impf* **надламываться**) *сов возв* to break; (*перен: здоровье*) to suffer; (*: человек*) to damage one's health.
надмен|ный (-ен, -на, -но) *прил* haughty.

KEYWORD

надо *как сказ* **1** (*о долженствовании*): **надо ему помочь** it is necessary to help him; **надо, чтобы он пришёл вовремя** he must come on time; **надо всегда говорить правду** one must always speak the truth; **мне/ему надо закончить работу** I/he must finish the job; **помочь тебе? – не надо!** can I help you? – there's no need!; **не надо!** (*не делай этого*) don't!
2 (*о потребности*): **надо много лет** it takes many years; **на варенье надо много сахара** you need a lot of sugar to make jam; **им надо 5 рублей** they need 5 roubles; **мне надо спать** I need to sleep; **что тебе надо?** what do you want?; **так ему/ей и надо** (*разг*) it serves him/her right; **надо же!** (*разг*) of all things!; **надо думать** (*вероятно*) probably; (*конечно*) of course; **что надо** (*разг*) excellent; **фильм что надо!** it's an excellent film!

надо *предл см* **над**.
надобност|ь (-и) *ж* necessity.
надоеда|ть (-ю) *несов от* **надоесть**.
надоедим *итп сов см* **надоесть**.
надоедлив|ый (-, -а, -о) *прил* tedious, tiresome.
надое|сть (*как есть*; *см* **Table 15**; *impf* **надоедать**) *сов неперех*: **~ кому-н** (*+instr*) (*разговорами, упрёками*) to bore sb (with); **мне ~ло ждать** I'm tired of waiting; **он мне ~л** I've had enough of him; **перестань мне надоедать!** stop bothering me!
надо|ить (-ю, -ишь; *impf* **надаивать**) *сов (не)перех (+acc или +gen; молока)* to get.
надолго *нареч* for a long time; **Вы здесь ~?** are you here for long?
надомник (-а) *м* homeworker.
надомниц|а (-ы) *ж см* **надомник**.
надорв|ать (-у, -ёшь; *impf* **надрывать**) *сов перех* (*лист, материю*) to make a tear in; (*пакет*) to start to tear open; (*перен: голос*) to strain; (*: силы, здоровье*) to tax
▶ **надорваться** (*impf* **надрываться**) *сов возв* (*конверт, воротник*) to tear slightly; (*перенапрячься*) to do o.s. an injury; (*перен*) to overexhaust o.s.
надоум|ить (-лю, -ишь) *сов перех*: **~ кого-н** *+infin* (*разг*) to advise sb to do; **это он меня ~ил** he was the one who gave me the idea.
надп|исать (-ишу, -ишешь; *impf* **надписывать**) *сов перех* (*книгу, фотографию*) to inscribe; (*посылку, конверт*) to address; **надписывать** (**~** *perf*) **адрес на** *+acc* to address.
надпис|ь (-и) *ж* inscription.
надпишу *итп сов см* **надписать**.
надра|ить (-ю, -ишь) *сов от* **драить**.
над|раться (-ерусь, -ерёшься; *impf* **надираться**) *сов возв* (*разг*) to get sozzled.
надрежу *итп сов см* **надрезать**.
надрез (-а) *м* cut.
надр|езать (-ежу, -ежешь; *impf* **надрезать**) *сов перех* to cut into.

надруга́тельств|о (-а) *ср*: ~ **(над** *+instr*) (*над памятью, над честью*) violation (of); (*над человеком*) abuse (of).
надруга́|ться (-юсь) *(не)сов возв*: ~ **над** *+instr* to abuse.
надры́в (-а) *м* (*надорванное место*) tear, rip; (*перен*: *физический*) strain; (: *в пении итп*) hysterical streak; **с ~ом в го́лосе** with a trembling voice.
надрыва́|ть (-ю) *несов от* **надорва́ть**
▸ **надрыва́ться** *несов от* **надорва́ться** ◆ *возв* (*кричать*) to scream away; (*разг*): **~ся (над** *+instr*) to break one's back (over) (*fig*); **у меня́ се́рдце** *или* **душа́ ~ется** my heart bleeds.
надры́в|ный (-ен, -на, -но) *прил* hysterical.
надсмо́трщик (-а) *м* (*тюремный*) warden; (*на плантации*) overseer.
надсмо́трщиц|а (-ы) *ж см* **надсмо́трщик.**
надста́в|ить (-лю, -ишь; *impf* **надставля́ть**) *сов перех* to lengthen (*by adding extra material*).
надстра́ива|ть (-ю) *несов от* **надстро́ить.**
надстро́ек *сущ см* **надстро́йка.**
надстро́|ить (-ю, -ишь; *impf* **надстра́ивать**) *сов перех* (*стену, дом*) to build onto; (*этаж*) to add.
надстро́|йка (-йки; *gen pl* **-ек**) *ж* (*здания*) additional floor; (*ФИЛОСОФИЯ*) superstructure.
надува́тельств|о (-а) *ср* (*разг*) con.
надува́|ть(ся) (-ю(сь)) *несов от* **наду́ть(ся).**
надувно́й *прил* inflatable.
наду́манный *прил* contrived.
наду́ма|ть (-ю; *impf* **наду́мывать**) *сов неперех* (*+infin*; *разг*) to take it into one's head to do.
наду́т|ый (-, -а, -о) *прил* (*почки, вена*) swollen; (*разг*: *высокомерный*) puffed-up; (: *обиженный*) sulky.
наду́|ть (-ю, -ешь; *impf* **надува́ть**) *сов перех* (*мяч, колесо*) to inflate, blow up; (*разг*: *обмануть*) to con ◆ *безл* (*+gen*; *пыли, холоду итп*) to blow; (*в ухо, в шею итп*) to catch a chill; **мне ~ло в грудь** I've caught a chill (on my chest)
▸ **наду́ться** (*impf* **надува́ться**) *сов возв* (*матрас, мяч*) to inflate; (*парус*) to billow; (*почка, вена, река*) to swell; (*перен*: *от важности*) to swell up; (: *разг*: *обидеться*) to sulk; ~ *(perf)* **гу́бы** (*разг*) to go into a sulk.
надым|и́ть (-лю́, -и́шь) *сов от* **дыми́ть.**
надыш|а́ть (-у́, -ишь) *сов неперех* (*в комнате, в купе*) to get warm (*from body heat*); ~ *(perf)* **на** *+acc* (*на стекло, на очки*) to breathe on
▸ **надыша́ться** *сов возв* (*+instr*; *дымом, газом*) to breathe in; **~ся** *(perf)* **во́здухом** to get plenty of fresh air; **пе́ред сме́ртью не надышишься** it's too late to do anything about it now.
наеда́|ться (-юсь) *несов от* **нае́сться.**
нае́дешь *итп сов см* **нае́хать.**
наеди́мся *сов см* **нае́сться.**
наедине́ *нареч*: ~ **(с** *+instr*) alone (with); **они́ оста́лись ~** they were left on their own; **я до́лжен оста́ться ~ с собо́й** I need time to be by myself.
наеди́те(сь) *сов см* **нае́сть(ся).**
нае́ду *сов см* **нае́хать.**
наедя́тся *сов см* **нае́сться.**
нае́зд (-а) *м* (*визит*) visit.
нае́|здить (-зжу, -здишь; *impf* **наезжа́ть**) *сов перех* (*сто километров*) to clock up; (*дорогу*) to flatten; (*лошадь*) to break in
▸ **нае́здиться** *сов возв* to travel a lot; **я ~здился в командиро́вки** I'm tired of going away on business.
нае́здник (-а) *м* rider.
нае́здниц|а (-ы) *ж см* **нае́здник.**
наезжа́|ть (-ю) *несов от* **нае́здить, нае́хать** ◆ *неперех*: ~ **(в го́сти) к кому́-н** to pay sb visits.
нае́зженный *прил* well-used.
нае́зжу(сь) *сов см* **нае́здить(ся).**
нае́лся *итп сов см* **нае́сться.**
нае́мся *сов см* **нае́сться.**
на|ём (-йма) *м* hiring; (*квартиры*) renting.
наёмник (-а) *м* (*ВОЕН, также перен*) mercenary; (*наёмный работник*) casual worker.
наёмный *прил* (*труд, работник*) hired; (*помещение*) rented, leased; (*земля*) leased; ~ **уби́йца** hitman.
нае́сться (*как* **есть**; *см* **Table 15**; *impf* **наеда́ться**) *сов возв* (*+gen*; *сладкого, овощей*) to eat a lot of; (*+instr*; *супом*) to fill o.s. up on; **я нае́лся** I'm full.
нае́|хать (*как* **е́хать**; *см* **Table 19**; *impf* **наезжа́ть**) *сов неперех* (*разг*: *туристы, гости*) to arrive in droves; **наезжа́ть (~** *perf*) **на** *+acc* to drive into; (*угрожать*) to harass.
нае́шься *сов см* **нае́сться.**
нажа́л|оваться (-уюсь) *сов возв* (*разг*): ~ **(кому́-н на** *+acc*) to complain (to sb about).
нажа́р|ить (-ю, -ишь; *impf* **нажа́ривать**) *сов перех* to fry.
наж|а́ть (-му́, -мёшь; *impf* **нажима́ть**) *сов (не)перех* (*+acc или +gen*; *соку*) to squeeze; (*снопов, хлеба*) to reap ◆ *неперех* (*перен*): ~ **на** *+acc* (*на работников, на руководство*) to put pressure on; (*разг*: *на работу, на учёбу*) to get moving with; **нажима́ть (~** *perf*) **на** *+acc* (*на кнопку*) to press; (*на рычаг*) to press (down).
нажгу́ *итп сов см* **наже́чь.**
нажда́к (-а) *м* emery.
нажда́чн|ый *прил*: **~ая бума́га** emery paper.
наж|е́чь (-гу́, -жёшь *итп*, -гу́т; *pt* -ёг, -гла́, -гло́, *impf* **нажига́ть**) *сов (не)перех* (*+acc или +gen*; *дров, угля, керосина*) to burn a lot of; (*разг*: *лицо, спину итп*) to burn.
нажи́в|а (-ы) *ж* gain.
нажива́|ть(ся) (-ю(сь)) *несов от* **нажи́ть(ся).**
нажив|и́ть (-лю́, -и́шь; *impf* **наживля́ть**) *сов перех* to bait.

нажи́вк|а (-и) *ж* bait.
наживлю́ *сов см* **наживи́ть.**
наживля́|ть (-ю) *несов от* **наживи́ть.**
наживн|о́й *прил*: **де́ньги – де́ло ~о́е** money will start to roll in given time.
наживу́(сь) *итп сов см* **нажи́ть.**
нажига́|ть (-ю) *несов от* **нажéчь.**
нажи́м (-а) *м* (*также перен*) pressure; **сде́лать** *(perf)* **что-н под ~ом** to do sth under pressure.
нажима́|ть (-ю) *несов от* **нажа́ть.**
нажира́|ться (-юсь) *несов от* **нажра́ться.**
нажи́|ть (-ву́, -вёшь; *impf* **нажива́ть)** *сов перех* (*состояние, миллионы*) to acquire; *~ (perf)* **(себе́) враго́в** to make enemies; *~ (perf)* **(себе́) неприя́тность** to get o.s. into trouble; **наживёшь себе́ радикули́т** you'll end up with backache
▸ **нажи́ться** (*impf* **нажива́ться)** *сов возв*: **~ся (на** *+prp*) (*на войне, на спекуляции*) to gain (from).
нажму́ *итп сов см* **нажа́ть.**
нажр|а́ться (-у́сь, -ёшься; *impf* **нажира́ться)** *сов возв* (*животное*) to eat its fill; (*разг: человек*) to stuff o.s.; (*: напиться*) to get plastered.
наза́втра *нареч* (*разг*) next day.
наза́д *нареч* back; (*нагнуться, катиться итп*) backwards; **(тому́) ~** ago; **де́сять лет/неде́лю (тому́) ~** ten years/one week ago.
назва́нива|ть (-ю) *несов неперех* (*разг*) to keep ringing.
назва́ни|е (-я) *ср* name; (*отдельное издание*) title; **под ~м** *+gen* named, called; **э́то не велосипе́д, а одно́ ~** you can hardly call it a proper bicycle; **торго́вое ~** trade name.
наз|ва́ть (-ову́, -овёшь; *pt* **-ва́л, -вала́, -ва́ло,** *impf* **называ́ть)** *сов перех* to call; (*ребёнка, собаку*) to name, call; (*назначить: кандидатов, день, цену*) to name; **называ́ть (~** *perf*) **ве́щи свои́ми имена́ми** to call a spade a spade
▸ **назва́ться** (*impf* **называ́ться)** *сов возв* (*+instr*; *представиться*) to call o.s.
назе́мный *прил* surface *опред*; **назе́мные войска́** ground troops.
на́земь *нареч* (*упасть, бросить*) to the ground.
назида́ни|е (-я) *ср* edification.
назида́тел|ьный (-ен, -ьна, -ьно) *прил* edifying.
назло́ *нареч* out of spite; **~ кому́-н** to spite sb; **как ~** to make things worse.
назнача́|ть (-ю) *несов от* **назна́чить.**
назначе́ни|е (-я) *ср* (*времени, цены итп*) setting; (*на работу*) appointment; (*лекарства*) prescription; (*функция*) function; **пункт** *или* **ме́сто ~я** destination.
назна́ч|ить (-у, -ишь; *impf* **назнача́ть)** *сов перех* (*начальником*) to appoint; (*время, цену*) to set; (*встречу*) to arrange; (*лекарство, курс лечения*) to prescribe; **он ~ил ей свида́ние** he asked her to meet him.
назову́(сь) *итп сов см* **назва́ть(ся).**
назо́йлив|ый (-, -а, -о) *прил* (*человек*) tiresome; (*вопрос, мысль*) persistent.
назре́|ть (*3sg* **-ет,** *3pl* **-ют,** *impf* **назрева́ть)** *сов неперех* to come to a head; (*перен: вопрос, разговор*) to become unavoidable.
назубо́к *нареч* (*разг*): **вы́учить/знать ~** to learn/know off by heart.
называ́емый *прил*: **так ~** so-called.
называ́|ть (-ю) *несов от* **назва́ть**
▸ **называ́ться** *несов от* **назва́ться** ◆ *возв* (*носить название*) to be called; **как ~ется э́то ме́сто?** what is this place called?; **ситуа́ция, что ~ется, крити́ческая** the situation is what you might call critical.
наибо́лее *нареч*: **~ интере́сный/краси́вый** the most interesting/beautiful.
наибо́льш|ий (-ая, -ее, -ие) *прил* the greatest.
наи́в|ный (-ен, -на, -но) *прил* naive.
наивы́сш|ий (-ая, -ее, -ие) *прил* the highest.
наи́гранный *прил* artificial, false.
наигра́|ть (-ю; *impf* **наи́грывать)** *сов перех* (*мелодию*) to play; (*для записи*) to record
▸ **наигра́ться** *сов возв* to play for a long time.
наи́грыва|ть (-ю) *несов от* **наигра́ть** ◆ *неперех*: **~ на** *+prp* (*на флейте*) to play quietly on.
на́игрыш (-а) *м* tune.
наизна́нку *нареч* inside out.
наизу́сть *нареч*: **знать/вы́учить ~** to know/learn by heart.
наилу́чш|ий (-ая, -ее, -ие) *прил* the best.
наиме́нее *нареч*: **~ уда́чный/спосо́бный** the least successful/capable.
наименова́ни|е (-я) *ср* name; (*проекта, книги*) title, name.
наимен|ова́ть (-ую) *сов от* **именова́ть.**
наиме́ньш|ий (-ая, -ее, -ие) *прил* (*длина, высота итп*) the smallest; (*усилие*) the least.
наискосо́к *нареч* (*разг: разрезать*) crosswise; (*: идти*) diagonally.
на́искось *нареч* diagonally.
наиху́дш|ий (-ая, -ее, -ие) *прил* the worst.
найдёныш (-а) *м* foundling.
найду́(сь) *итп сов см* **найти́(сь).**
на́йма *итп сущ см* **наём.**
наймит (-а) *м* hireling.
найму́(сь) *итп сов см* **наня́ть(ся).**
на|йти́ (-йду́, -йдёшь; *pt* **-шёл, -шла́, -шло́,** *impf* **находи́ть)** *сов перех* to find ◆ *неперех* (*толпа, гости, тучи*) to gather; (*натолкнуться*): **~ на** *+acc* to stumble into; **на него́ ~шла́ тоска́** he was overcome with sadness; **на меня́ ~шёл смех** I couldn't help laughing; **~шёл чем горди́ться!** (*разг*) is that all you've got to be proud of?; **находи́ть (~** *perf*) **о́бщий язы́к** to find a common language; *~ (perf)* **себя́** to find o.s.
▸ **найти́сь** (*impf* **находи́ться)** *сов возв* (*ключи, ребёнок итп*) to turn up; (*добровольцы, желающие*) to come forward; (*не растеряться*) to come up with an answer.

накажу́ *итп сов см* **наказа́ть**.
нака́з (**-а**) *м* (*полит*) mandate (*to govern*); (*наставление*) wish.
наказа́ни|е (**-я**) *ср* punishment; (*перен*: *разг*) pain, hassle.
нак|аза́ть (**-ажу́, -а́жешь**; *impf* **нака́зывать**) *сов перех* (*за проступок итп*) to punish; (*приказать*) to order.
нака́л (**-а**) *м* (*борьбы*) heat.
накал|и́ть (**-ю́, -и́шь**; *impf* **нака́ливать** *или* **накаля́ть**) *сов перех* to heat up; (*перен*: *обстановку*) to hot up
▸ **накали́ться** (*impf* **нака́ливаться** *или* **накаля́ться**) *сов возв* to heat; (*перен*: *обстановка*) to become heated; (: *страсти*) to become inflamed; **~ся** *(perf)* **докрасна́/добела́** to become red-/white-hot.
нака́лыва|ть(ся) (**-ю(сь)**) *несов от* **наколо́ть(ся)**.
накаля́|ть(ся) (**-ю(сь)**) *несов от* **накали́ть(ся)**.
накану́не *нареч* the day before, the previous day ◆ *предл* (*+gen*) on the eve of.
нака́па|ть (**-ю**) *сов от* **ка́пать**.
нака́плива|ть(ся) (**-ю(сь)**) *несов от* **накопи́ть(ся)**.
нака́пыва|ть (**-ю**) *несов от* **накопа́ть**.
нака́рка|ть (**-ю**) *сов от* **ка́ркать** ◆ *перех* (*разг*): **~ кому́-н беду́** to bring sb bad luck.
наката́|ть (**-ю**; *impf* **нака́тывать**) *сов перех* to roll; (*дорогу, колею*) to flatten out; (*разг*: *написать*) to rattle off
▸ **наката́ться** *сов возв* (*на коньках*) to have a good time skating; (*на лыжах*) to have a good time skiing.
нак|ати́ть (**-ачу́, -а́тишь**; *impf* **нака́тывать**) *сов неперех* (*разг*: *толпа, гости*) to surge forward; (*тоска*) to be overwhelming ◆ *перех*: **~ что-н на** *+acc* to roll sth onto; **нака́тывать** (**~** *perf*) (**на** *+acc*) (*волна*) to roll up (onto)
▸ **накати́ться** (*impf* **нака́тываться**) *сов возв*: **~ся на** *+acc* (*волна, лавина*) to roll up onto.
нака́тыва|ть (**-ю**) *несов от* **наката́ть, накати́ть**
▸ **нака́тываться** *несов от* **накати́ться**.
накача́|ть (**-ю**; *impf* **нака́чивать**) *сов (не)перех* (*+acc или +gen*; *воды, воздуха*) to pump; (*камеру, шину*) to pump up.
накида́|ть (**-ю**; *impf* **наки́дывать**) *сов перех* to throw.
наки́д|ка (**-ки**; *gen pl* **-ок**) *ж* (*одежда*) wrap; (*покрывало*) bedspread, thrower.
наки́дыва|ть (**-ю**) *несов от* **накида́ть, наки́нуть**
▸ **наки́дываться** *несов от* **наки́нуться**.
наки́н|уть (**-у, -ешь**; *impf* **наки́дывать**) *сов перех* (*платок*) to throw on; (*разг*: *набавить*) to add on
▸ **наки́нуться** (*impf* **наки́дываться**) *сов возв*: **~ся на** *+acc* (*на человека*) to hurl o.s. at; (*разг*: *на еду, на книгу*) to get stuck into; **наки́дываться** (**~ся** *perf*) **на кого́-н с вопро́сами/жа́лобами** (*разг*) to bombard sb with questions/complaints.
накип|е́ть (*3sg* **-и́т**, *impf* **накипа́ть**) *сов неперех* (*накипь, пена*) to form ◆ *безл* (*перен*: *злоба, обида*) to build up.
на́кип|ь (**-и**) *ж* (*на бульоне*) scum; (*в чайнике*) fur (*BRIT*), scale (*US*).
накла́д|ка (**-ки**; *gen pl* **-ок**) *ж* (*шиньон*) hairpiece; (*разг*: *недоразумение*) mix-up.
накладн|а́я (**-о́й**; *decl like adj*) *ж* (*КОММ*) bill of lading (*BRIT*), waybill (*US*); **грузова́я ~** consignment note.
накладно́й *прил* (*волосы, борода*) false; (*карман*) sewn-on; **накладно́е зо́лото** rolled gold; **накладны́е расхо́ды** (*ЭКОН*) overheads *мн* (*BRIT*), overhead (*US*).
накла́док *сущ см* **накла́дка**.
накла́дыва|ть (**-ю**) *несов от* **наложи́ть**.
наклев|ета́ть (**-ещу́, -е́щешь**) *сов от* **клевета́ть**.
наклёвыва|ться (*3sg* **-ется**, *3pl* **-ются**) *несов от* **наклю́нуться**.
накле́ек *сущ см* **накле́йка**.
накле́|ить (**-ю, -ишь**; *impf* **накле́ивать**) *сов перех* (*афишу, марку итп*) to stick on; (*фонариков, украшений итп*) to make (*with glue and paper*).
накле́|йка (**-йка**; *gen pl* **-ек**) *ж* label.
наклепа́|ть (**-ю**) *сов от* **клепа́ть** ◆ (*impf* **наклёпывать**) *перех* to rivet on.
наклёпк|а (**-и**) *ж* stud.
наклёпыва|ть (**-ю**) *несов от* **наклепа́ть**.
накли́|кать (**-чу, -чешь**; *impf* **накли́ка́ть**) *сов перех*: **~ кому́-н несча́стье** to bring misfortune on sb.
накло́н (**-а**) *м* incline, slope; (*головы*) tilt; (*почерка*) slope.
наклоне́ни|е (**-я**) *ср* (*ЛИНГ*) mood.
накл|они́ть (**-оню́, -о́нишь**; *impf* **наклоня́ть**) *сов перех* to tilt
▸ **наклони́ться** (*impf* **наклоня́ться**) *сов возв* to bend down.
накло́нност|ь (**-и**) *ж*: **~ к** *+dat* (*к музыке итп*) aptitude for; (*к меланхолии итп*) tendency toward; **дурны́е/хоро́шие накло́нности** bad/good habits.
накло́нный *прил* slanting.
наклоня́|ть(ся) (**-ю(сь)**) *несов от* **наклони́ть(ся)**.
наклю́н|уться (*3sg* **-ется**, *3pl* **-утся**, *impf* **наклёвываться**) *сов возв* (*цыплёнок*) to peck its way out of the shell; (*перен*: *почки, росток*) to form; (: *выгодное дело*) to turn up.
накля́узнича|ть (**-ю**) *сов от* **кля́узничать**.
накова́л|ьня (**-ьни**; *gen pl* **-ен**) *ж* anvil.
нако́жный *прил* skin *опред*.

наколе́нник (-а) *м* (*СПОРТ*) kneepad.
нако́лк|а (-и) *ж* (*разг*: *татуировка*) tattoo.
нак|оло́ть (-олю́, -о́лешь; *impf* **нака́лывать**) *сов перех* (*руку, палец*) to prick; (*татуировку*) to apply; (*прикрепить*): ~ (**на** +*acc*) (*на шляпу, на дверь*) to pin on(to) ◆ (*не*)*перех* (+*acc* или +*gen*; *дров*) to chop; (*сахару*) to break up
▸ **наколо́ться** (*impf* **нака́лываться**) *сов возв*: ~**ся** (**на** +*acc*) to prick o.s. (on).
наконе́ц *нареч* at last, finally ◆ *вводн сл* after all; ~**-то!** at long last!; **он ~ по́нял** he finally understood; **ты мог бы, ~, позвони́ть** if nothing else, you could have phoned; **ну, иди́ же ~!** come on, it really is time for you to go!
наконе́чник (-а) *м* tip, end.
накопа́|ть (-ю; *impf* **нака́пывать**) *сов перех* to dig up.
накопи́тельств|о (-а) *ср* acquisitiveness.
накоп|и́ть (-лю́, -ишь) *сов от* **копи́ть** ◆ (*impf* **нака́пливать**) *перех* (*силы, информацию*) to store up; (*средства*) to accumulate
▸ **накопи́ться** *сов от* **копи́ться** ◆ (*impf* **нака́пливаться**) *возв* (*силы, толпа*) to build up; (*средства*) to accumulate; (*раздражение*) to mount.
накопле́ни|е (-я) *ср* (*действие*) accumulation; ~ **да́нных** (*КОМП*) data storage; *см также* **накопле́ния**.
накопле́ни|я (-й) *мн* (*сбережения*) savings *мн*.
накоплю́(сь) *сов см* **накопи́ть(ся)**.
накоп|ти́ть (-чу́, -ти́шь) *сов от* **копти́ть** ◆ *перех* (*рыбы, колбасы*) to smoke.
накорм|и́ть (-лю́, -ишь) *сов от* **корми́ть**.
накра́пыва|ть (*3sg* **-ет**) *несов неперех* to drizzle.
накра́|сить (-шу, -сишь) *сов от* **кра́сить** ◆ (*impf* **накра́шивать**) *перех* to paint
▸ **накра́ситься** *сов от* **кра́ситься** ◆ (*impf* **накра́шиваться**) *возв* to put on make-up.
накрахма́л|ить (-ю, -ишь) *сов от* **крахма́лить**.
накра́шива|ть(ся) (-ю(сь)) *несов от* **накра́сить(ся)**.
накра́шу(сь) *сов см* **накра́сить(ся)**.
накрен|и́ть(ся) (-ю́(сь), -и́шь(ся)) *сов от* **крени́ть(ся)**.
на́крепко *нареч* (*запереть, забить*) tight; (*также*: **кре́пко-~**: *запретить, наказать*) strictly; **запо́мни ~** be sure to remember.
на́крест *нареч* (*также*: **крест-~**) crosswise.
накрич|а́ть (-у́, -и́шь) *сов неперех*: ~ **на** +*acc* (*на ребёнка, на подчинённого*) to shout at
▸ **накрича́ться** *сов возв* (*разг*) to shout a lot; **ну что, ~а́лся?** are you through shouting?
накропа́|ть (-ю) *сов от* **кропа́ть**.
накрош|и́ть (-у́, -и́шь) *сов от* **кроши́ть**.
накро́ю(сь) *итп сов см* **накры́ть(ся)**.
накр|ути́ть (-учу́, -у́тишь; *impf* **накру́чивать**) *сов перех* (*веревок, пряжи*) to twist; (*разг*: *ерунды, небылиц*) to spin; **накру́чивать** (~ *perf*) (**на** +*acc*) (*гайку*: *на болт*) to screw on(to); (*канат*: *на столб*) to wind (round)
▸ **накрути́ться** (*impf* **накру́чиваться**) *сов возв* (*разг*: *завить*) to put one's hair in rollers; **накру́чиваться** (~**ся** *perf*) **на** +*acc* to wind around.
накр|ы́ть (-о́ю, -о́ешь; *impf* **накрыва́ть**) *сов перех* to cover; (*разг*: *преступника, вора*) to nail, nab; **накрыва́ть** (~ *perf*) (**на**) **стол** to lay the table
▸ **накры́ться** (*impf* **накрыва́ться**) *сов возв* (*разг*: *мероприятие, прогулка*) to fall through; **накрыва́ться** (~**ся** *perf*) (+*instr*) (*пледом, одеялом*) to cover o.s. up (with).
накуп|и́ть (-лю́, -ишь; *impf* **накупа́ть**) *сов перех* to buy lots of.
наку́ренный *прил* (*помещение, вагон*) smoke-filled; (*воздух*) smoky.
нак|ури́ть (-урю́, -у́ришь; *impf* **наку́ривать**) *сов неперех*: ~ **в ко́мнате** to fill a room with smoke
▸ **накури́ться** (*impf* **наку́риваться**) *сов возв* to smoke too much.
налага́|ть (-ю) *несов от* **наложи́ть**.
нала́|дить (-жу, -дишь; *impf* **нала́живать**) *сов перех* (*мотор, станок*) to repair, fix; (*сотрудничество*) to initiate; (*хозяйство*) to sort out; (*порядок*) to establish; (*разг*: *гитару, рояль*) to tune
▸ **нала́диться** (*impf* **нала́живаться**) *сов возв* (*работа*) to go well; (*отношения, здоровье*) to improve.
нала́мыва|ть (-ю) *несов от* **налома́ть**.
нал|га́ть (-гу́, -жёшь) *сов от* **лгать**.
нале́во *нареч* (*повернуть, посмотреть*) (to the) left; (*разг*: *продать, сбыть*) on the side.
налёг *итп сов см* **нале́чь**.
налега́|ть (-ю) *несов от* **нале́чь**.
налегке́ *нареч* (*ехать*) without luggage; (*в лёгкой одежде*) lightly-clad; **путеше́ствовать** (*impf*) ~ to travel light.
налез|ть (-у, -ешь; *impf* **налеза́ть**) *сов неперех* (*разг*: *насекомые, дети*) to accumulate; (*надеться*) to fit; (*шапка*): ~ **на** +*acc* (*на глаза*) to slide over.
налеп|и́ть (-лю́, -ишь) *сов от* **лепи́ть** ◆ (*не*) *перех* (+*acc* или +*gen*; *фигурок, птиц*) to model.
налёт (-а) *м* (*птиц, авиации*) flying in, approach; (*на врага, на город*) raid; (*на банк, на квартиру*) robbery; (*пыли, плесени*) thin layer; (*МЕД*) spot, patch; **с ~а(-у)** (*на полном ходу*) at full pelt; (*перен*: *сразу*) in a flash.
нале|те́ть (-чу́, -ти́шь; *impf* **налета́ть**) *сов неперех*: ~ **на** +*acc* (*натолкнуться*) to fly against; (*перен*: *разг*: *на приятеля, на столб*) to run into; (*напасть*) to swoop down on; (*перен*: *разг*: *с бранью, с упрёками*) to lay into; (*буря, ветер*) to spring up; (*саранча, стая*) to fly in; (*пыль, листва*) to drift in.
налётчик (-а) *м* burglar.
налечу́ *сов см* **налете́ть**.
нал|е́чь (-я́гу, -я́жешь *итп*, -я́гут; *pt* -ёг, -егла́, -егло́, *impf* **налега́ть**) *сов неперех*: ~ **на** +*acc*

(*на стол*) to lean on; (*плечом: на дверь*) to press against; (*перен: на работников*) to exert pressure on; (: *на учёбу, на работу*) to apply o.s. to; (*роса, снег*) to settle on; **налега́ть** (~ *perf*) **на вёсла** to ply one's oars.

налива́|ть(ся) (**-ю(сь)**) *несов от* **нали́ть(ся)**.

нали́в|ка (**-ки**; *gen pl* **-ок**) *ж* fruit liquor.

наливн|о́й *прил*: **~о́е су́дно** tanker; (*яблоко, хлеба*) ripe.

нали́вок *сущ см* **нали́вка**.

нали́пн|уть (*3sg* **-ет**, *3pl* **-ут**, *impf* **налипа́ть**) *сов неперех*: ~ **на** +*acc* to stick to.

налито́й *прил* (*колос, яблоко*) ripe; (*мускулы, щёки итп*) fleshy.

нал|и́ть (**-ью́, -ьёшь**; *impf* **налива́ть**) *сов перех* to pour (out); **налива́ть** (~ *perf*) **стака́н вина́** to pour a glass of wine

▸ **нали́ться** (*impf* **налива́ться**) *сов возв* (*натечь во что-н*): **~ся в** +*acc* to pour into; (*наполниться*): **~ся** +*instr* to fill with; (*рожь, плоды*) to ripen; (*перен: злобой*) to brim over; **~ся** (*perf*) **кро́вью** to turn red.

налицо́ *как сказ*: **фа́кты** ~ the facts are obvious; **доказа́тельство** ~ there is proof; **свиде́тели** ~ there are witnesses on hand.

нали́чи|е (**-я**) *ср* presence.

нали́чник (**-а**) *м* casing, jambs and lintel (*of door or window*).

нали́чност|ь (**-и**) *ж* cash.

нали́чн|ые (**-ых**; *decl like adj*) *мн* cash *ед*; **платёж ~ыми при доста́вке гру́за** cash on delivery.

нали́чн|ый *прил*: **~ые де́ньги** cash; ~ **расчёт** cash payment; ~ **счёт** cash account.

наловч|и́ться (**-у́сь, -и́шься**) *сов возв* (*разг*: +*infin*) to get the hang of doing.

нало́г (**-а**) *м* (*ЭКОН*) tax; **подохо́дный** ~ income tax; **поиму́щественный** ~ property tax; ~ **на ввоз** +*gen* import duty on; ~ **на при́быль** profits tax; ~ **на предме́ты ро́скоши** luxury tax; ~ **на перево́д капита́ла** capital transfer tax; **ко́свенный** ~ hidden tax.

нало́говик (**-а**) *м* taxman.

нало́говый *прил* tax *опред*.

налогоплате́льщик (**-а**) *м* taxpayer.

налогоплате́льщиц|а (**-ы**) *ж см* **налогоплате́льщик**.

нало́женн|ый *прил*: **~ым платежо́м** cash on delivery.

нал|ожи́ть (**-ожу́, -о́жишь**; *impf* **накла́дывать**) *сов перех* to put *или* place on; (*кальку*) to superimpose; (*МЕД: шину*) to fasten; (: *компресс, бинт*) to apply; (*лак, позолоту*) to apply; (*печать*) to affix; (*резолюцию*) to append; (*кашу итп*) to dish up; (*дров: в печку*) to put on; (*impf* **налага́ть**; *штраф*) to impose; (*запрет*) to place.

налома́|ть (**-ю**; *impf* **нала́мывать**) *сов перех* (+*gen*) to break; ~ (*perf*) **дров** (*разг*) to do something stupid.

налью́(сь) *итп сов см* **нали́ть(ся)**.

налюб|ова́ться (**-у́юсь**) *сов возв* to gaze one's fill; **не могу́** ~ **са́дом** I am lost in admiration for the garden.

наля́гу *итп сов см* **нале́чь**.

наля́па|ть (**-ю**) *сов от* **ля́пать**.

нам *мест см* **мы**.

нама́жу(сь) *итп сов см* **нама́зать(ся)**.

нама́з (**-а**) *м* (*РЕЛ*) (*Mohammedan*) *prayer*.

нама́|зать(ся) (**-жу(сь), -жешь(ся)**) *сов от* **ма́зать(ся)**.

намалева́|ть (**-ю**) *сов от* **малева́ть**.

нама́лыва|ть (**-ю**) *несов от* **намоло́ть**.

намара́|ть (**-ю**) *сов от* **мара́ть**.

нама́сл|ить (**-ю, -ишь**) *сов от* **ма́слить**.

нама́тыва|ть(ся) (**-ю(сь)**) *несов от* **намота́ть(ся)**.

намёк (**-а**) *м* (*также перен*) hint.

намека́|ть (**-ю**; *perf* **намекну́ть**) *несов неперех*: ~ **на** +*acc* to hint at.

намелю́ *итп сов см* **намоло́ть**.

наменя́|ть (**-ю**) *сов* (*не*)*перех* (+*acc или* +*gen*; *денег, марок, значков*) to get *или* obtain by exchange.

намерева́|ться (**-юсь**) *несов возв*: ~ +*infin* to intend to do.

наме́рен (**-а, -о**) *как сказ*: **он** ~ **уе́хать** he intends to leave.

наме́рени|е (**-я**) *ср* intention.

наме́рен|ный (**-, -на, -но**) *прил* intentional, deliberate.

на́мертво *нареч* (*разг*) tightly, fast.

намётанный *прил*: ~ **глаз** trained eye; **у него́ глаз намётан** he has a good eye.

намета́|ть (**-ю**) *сов от* **мета́ть**.

наме́|тить (**-чу, -тишь**) *сов от* **ме́тить** ◆ (*impf* **намеча́ть**) *перех* to plan; (*план*) to project; (*контуры*) to outline

▸ **наме́титься** *сов от* **ме́титься** ◆ (*impf* **намеча́ться**) *возв* (*маршрут*) to take shape; (*разногласия, усы*) to begin to show.

намётк|а (**-и**) *ж* (*юбки, платья*) tacking (*BRIT*), basting; (*нитка*) tacking (*BRIT*) *или* basting thread; (*плана*) rough draft; (*маршрута*) preliminary outline.

намеча́|ть(ся) (**-ю(сь)**) *несов от* **наме́тить(ся)**.

наме́чу(сь) *сов см* **наме́тить(ся)**.

на́ми *мест см* **мы**.

намина́|ть (**-ю**) *несов от* **намя́ть**.

намно́го *нареч* much, far; ~ **ху́же/интере́снее** much worse/more interesting.

намну́ *итп сов см* **намя́ть**.

намо́кн|уть (**-у, -ешь**; *impf* **намока́ть**) *сов неперех* to get wet.

нам|оло́ть (**-елю́, -е́лешь**; *impf* **нама́лывать**) *сов перех* to grind, mill.

намо́рдник (**-а**) *м* muzzle.

намо́рщ|ить(ся) (**-у(сь)**, **-ишь(ся)**) *сов от* **мо́рщить(ся)**.
намо|сти́ть (**-щу́**, **-сти́шь**) *сов от* **мости́ть**.
намота́|ть (**-ю**) *сов от* **мота́ть** ◆ (*impf* **нама́тывать**) *перех* to wind
▸ **намота́ться** (*impf* **нама́тываться**) *сов возв* (*нитка на шпульку*) to be wound; (*разг: устать*) to run o.s. ragged.
нам|очи́ть (**-очу́**, **-о́чишь**) *сов от* **мочи́ть**.
намощу́ *сов см* **намости́ть**.
намо́ю *итп сов см* **намы́ть**.
намудр|и́ть (**-ю́**, **-и́шь**) *сов от* **мудри́ть**.
наму́сор|ить (**-ю**, **-ишь**) *сов от* **му́сорить**.
наму́ч|иться (**-усь**, **-ишься**) *сов возв* (*разг*) to wear o.s. out.
намы́лива|ть (**-ю**; *perf* **намы́лить**) *несов перех* = **мы́лить**.
намы́л|ить(ся) (**-ю(сь)**, **-ишь(ся)**) *сов от* **мы́лить(ся)**.
нам|ы́ть (**-о́ю**, **-о́ешь**) *сов перех* to wash; (*плотину*) to deposit; (*золота*) to pan out.
нам|я́ть (**-ну́**, **-нёшь**; *impf* **намина́ть**) *сов (не)перех* (*+acc или +gen*; *льна, кож, глины*) to mash; (*траву, солому*) to trample.
нан|ести́ (**-есу́**, **-есёшь**; *pt* **-ёс**, **-есла́**, **-есло́**, *impf* **наноси́ть**) *сов (не)перех* (*+acc или +gen*; *подарков, продуктов*) to bring; (*снегу, песку*) to heap, pile up ◆ *перех* (*лак, мазь, краску*) to apply; (*узор, рисунок, резьбу*) to draw; (*на карту, на схему*) to plot; (*удар*) to deliver; (*урон*) to inflict; **наноси́ть** (~ *perf*) **кому́-н оскорбле́ние** to insult; **наноси́ть** (~ *perf*) **кому́-н пораже́ние** to defeat sb; ~ (*perf*) **кому́-н визи́т** to pay sb a visit.
нани́зыва|ть (**-ю**) *несов перех* (*жемчуг, бусинки*) to string, thread; (*перен: слова, фразы*) to string.
нанима́тел|ь (**-я**) *м* tenant; (*рабочей силы*) employer.
нанима́тельниц|а (**-ы**) *ж см* **нанима́тель**.
нанима́|ть(ся) (**-ю(сь)**) *несов от* **наня́ть(ся)**.
нано́с (**-а**) *м* (*речной*) alluvium; (*ледниковый, снежный*) drift.
нан|оси́ть (**-ошу́**, **-о́сишь**) *сов от* **нанести́** ◆ *перех* (*воды, песку, камней*) to bring.
нано́сный *прил* (*ил*) alluvial; (*перен: увлечения*) alien.
на|ня́ть (**-йму**, **-ймёшь**; *pt* **-нял**, **-няла́**, **-няло**, *impf* **нанима́ть**) *сов перех* (*работника*) to hire; (*лодку, машину*) to hire, rent
▸ **наня́ться** (*impf* **нанима́ться**) *сов возв* to get a job; **нанима́ться** (**~ся** *perf*) **секретарём/реда́ктором** to get a job as a secretary/editor.
наоборо́т *нареч* (*прочитать слово*) backwards; (*поступать, делать*) the wrong way (round) ◆ *вводн сл, част* (*при противопоставлении*) on the contrary.
наобу́м *нареч* (*разг: делать, отвечать*) without thinking; (*стрелять*) at random.
нао́тмашь *нареч* with a bold swipe.
наотре́з *нареч* flatly, point-blank.
напада́|ть (**-ю**) *несов от* **напа́сть**.
напада́ющ|ий (**-его**; *decl like adj*) *м* (*СПОРТ*) forward.
нападе́ни|е (**-я**) *ср* attack; (*СПОРТ*) forwards *мн*.
напа́дк|и (**-ок**) *мн* attacks *мн*.
нападу́ *итп сов см* **напа́сть**.
напа́ко|стить (**-щу**, **-стишь**) *сов от* **па́костить**.
напа́лм (**-а**) *м* napalm.
напа́рник (**-а**) *м* fellow worker.
напа́рниц|а (**-ы**) *ж см* **напа́рник**.
напа́рыва|ться (**-юсь**) *несов от* **напоро́ться**.
напас|ти́сь (**-у́сь**, **-ёшься**) *сов возв*: **на тебя́ са́хара не ~ёшься** you haven't got in enough sugar.
нап|а́сть (**-а́сти**) *ж* (*разг: беда*) calamity; ◆ (**-аду́**, **-адёшь**; *pt* **-а́л**, **-а́ла**, **-а́ло**, *impf* **напада́ть**) *сов неперех*: ~ **на** *+acc* to attack; (*на золотую жилу*) to come across, stumble (up)on; (*перен: на идею*) to have; (*тоска, грусть, страх*) to grip, seize.
напе́в (**-а**) *м* tune, melody.
напева́|ть (**-ю**) *несов от* **напе́ть** ◆ *перех* (*песенку*) to hum.
напе́в|ный (**-ен**, **-на**, **-но**) *прил* melodious.
напёк *итп сов см* **напе́чь**.
напека́|ть (**-ю**) *несов от* **напе́чь**.
напеку́ *итп сов см* **напе́чь**.
наперебо́й *нареч* vying with each other.
наперево́с *нареч*: **держа́ть ружьё** ~ to hold one's gun at the ready.
наперего́нки *нареч* (*разг*) racing each other.
наперёд *нареч* (*знать, угадать*) in advance; **за́дом** ~ back to front.
наперекор *нареч* (*говорить, поступать, идти*) defiantly ◆ *предл* (*+dat*; *судьбе, врагу, здравому смыслу*) in defiance of.
наперере́з *нареч* (*бежать, идти, плыть итп*) in order to intercept.
нап|ере́ть (**-ру́**, **-рёшь**; *pt* **-ёр**, **-ёрла**, **-ёрло**, *impf* **напира́ть**) *сов неперех*: ~ **на** *+acc* (*разг: на дверь*) to push against.
наперечёт *нареч* (*знать, помнить*) without exception.
напёрст|ок (**-ка**) *м* thimble.
наперч|и́ть (**-у́**, **-и́шь**) *сов от* **перчи́ть**.
нап|е́ть (**-ою́**, **-оёшь**; *impf* **напева́ть**) *сов перех* (*мотив, песню, мелодию*) to sing; **напева́ть** (~ *perf*) **пласти́нку** to make a recording of one's singing.
напеча́та|ть(ся) (**-ю(сь)**) *сов от* **печа́тать(ся)**.
нап|е́чь (**-еку́**, **-ечёшь** *итп*, **-еку́т**; *pt* **-ёк**, **-екла́**, **-екло́**, *impf* **напека́ть**) *сов перех* (*блинов, пирогов*) to bake ◆ *безл* (*разг: голову, плечи*) to burn.
напива́|ться (**-юсь**) *несов от* **напи́ться**.
напи́льник (**-а**) *м* file.
напира́|ть (**-ю**) *несов от* **напере́ть** ◆ *неперех*: ~ **на** *+acc* (*теснить*) to push against; (*перен*) to stress.
написа́ни|е (**-я**) *ср* writing; (*буквы*) spelling.
напи|са́ть (**-шу́**, **-шешь**) *сов от* **писа́ть**.

напи́т|ок (-ка) *м* drink.
нап|и́ться (-ью́сь, -ьёшься; *impf* **напива́ться)** *сов возв* (*воды, сока, чаю*) to have a drink; (*квасом, лимонадом*) to quench one's thirst; (*разг: опьянеть*) to get drunk.
напиха́|ть (-ю; *impf* **напи́хивать)** *сов перех* (*разг*): ~ **в** *+acc* to stuff into.
напи́чка|ть (-ю) *сов от* **пи́чкать.**
напишу́ *итп сов см* **написа́ть.**
напла́кать *сов перех*: **кот напла́кал** (*разг*) very little; **у нас де́нег – кот напла́кал** we have very little money
▸ **напла́|каться ◆ (-чусь, -чешься)** *сов возв* (*ребёнок*) to cry one's eyes out; **напла́чешься ты с ней** (*перен*) you'll have nothing but problems with her.
наплева́тельск|ий (-ая, -ое, -ие) *прил* (*разг: отношение*) harum-scarum.
напл|ева́ть (-юю) *сов от* **плева́ть ◆** *неперех* to spit; ~! (*разг*) to hell with it!
наплы́в (-а) *м* (*перен: туристов*) influx; (: *заявлений, чувств*) flood.
наплы́|ть (-ву́, -вёшь; *impf* **наплыва́ть)** *сов неперех*: ~ **на** *+acc* (*на мель, на камень*) to run against; (*облако, туча*) to drift over *или* in front of; (*тина, водоросли*) to be washed up; (*перен: воспоминания*) to come flooding back.
напова́л *нареч* outright.
наподо́бие *предл* (*+gen*) like, resembling.
нап|ои́ть (-ою́, -о́ишь) *сов от* **пои́ть.**
напока́з *нареч* for show.
наполз|ти́ (-у́, -ёшь; *impf* **наполза́ть)** *сов неперех*: ~ **на** *+acc* (*на преграду*) to crawl onto; (*туча*) to creep up; (*муравьи*) to crawl in.
напо́лн|ить (-ю, -ишь; *impf* **наполня́ть)** *сов перех*: ~ *+instr* to fill with
▸ **напо́лниться** (*impf* **наполня́ться)** *сов возв*: **~ся** *+instr* to fill with.
наполови́ну *нареч* (*уменьшить, увеличить*) by half; (*наполнить, налить*) half.
напо́льн|ый *прил* floor *опред*; **~ые часы́** grandfather clock.
напомина́ни|е (-я) *ср* reminder.
напомина́|ть (-ю) *несов от* **напо́мнить ◆** *перех* (*иметь сходство*) to resemble; **он ~ет мне моего́ отца́** he resembles my father.
напо́мн|ить (-ю, -ишь; *impf* **напомина́ть)** *сов перех*: ~ *+acc или* **о** *+prp* to remind of.
напо́р (-а) *м* (*воды, воздуха*) pressure; (*ветра*) force; (*войск*) onslaught; (*разг: настойчивость*) push, go.
напо́рист|ый (-, -а, -о) *прил* forceful.
напор|о́ть (-ю́, -ешь) *сов от* **поро́ть ◆** *перех* (*разг: руку, ногу*) to cut
▸ **напоро́ться** (*impf* **напа́рываться)** *сов возв*: **~ся на** *+acc* (*разг: на гвоздь, на сучок*) to cut o.s. on; (: *на беду, на скандал*) to run up against.
напо́р|тить (-чу, -тишь) *сов (не)перех* (*+acc или +gen; бумаги, материала*) to spoil ◆ *неперех* (*+dat; разг: делу*) to wreck; (: *другу*) to harm.
напосле́док *нареч* (*разг*) in the end, finally.
напою́ *итп сов см* **напе́ть.**
напра́в|ить (-лю, -ишь; *impf* **направля́ть)** *сов перех* (*взгляд, внимание, разговор*) to direct; (*в госпиталь, к врачу*) to refer; (*на завод*) to assign; (*телеграмму, послание*) to send; **направля́ть (~** *perf*) **свой путь куда́-нибудь** to make one's way somewhere
▸ **напра́виться** (*impf* **направля́ться)** *сов возв*: **~ся в** *+acc***/к** *+dat* (*в город, к острову*) to make for.
направле́ни|е (-я) *ср* direction; (*специалистов*) sending; (*деятельности, также* ВОЕН) line; (*политики*) orientation; (*течение*) school; (*документ: в больницу*) referral; (: *на работу, на учёбу*) directive; **по ~ю к** *+dat* towards.
напра́вленност|ь (-и) *ж* focus.
напра́влю(сь) *сов см* **напра́вить(ся).**
направля́|ть(ся) (-ю(сь)) *несов от* **напра́вить(ся).**
напра́во *нареч* (*идти, повернуть*) (to the) right; (*от дороги, от дома*) to the right.
напра́сен *прил см* **напра́сный.**
напра́сно *нареч* in vain.
напра́с|ный (-ен, -на, -но) *прил* (*труд, усилия*) vain; (*тревога, страх*) unfounded.
напра́шива|ться (-юсь) *несов от* **напроси́ться.**
наприме́р *вводн сл* for example *или* instance.
напрока́знича|ть (-ю) *сов от* **прока́зничать.**
напрока́т *нареч*: **взять ~** to hire; **отдава́ть (отда́ть** *perf*) ~ to hire out.
напролёт *нареч* without a break.
напроло́м *нареч* stopping at nothing.
напроро́ч|ить (-у, -ишь) *сов от* **проро́чить.**
напр|оси́ться (-ошу́сь, -о́сишься; *impf* **напра́шиваться)** *сов возв* (*разг: в гости, на должность*) to force o.s.; **напра́шиваться (~** *perf*) **на** *+acc* (*на комплимент, на оскорбление*) to invite.
напро́тив *нареч* opposite ◆ *вводн сл* on the contrary ◆ *предл* (*+gen*) opposite.
на́прочь *нареч* (*разг*) completely.
напрошу́сь *сов см* **напроси́ться.**
напря́г(ся) *итп сов см* **напря́чь(ся).**
напряга́|ть(ся) (-ю(сь)) *несов от* **напря́чь(ся).**
напрягу́(сь) *итп сов см* **напря́чь(ся).**
напряже́ни|е (-я) *ср* tension; (*внимания, с ресурсами*) strain; (*физ: механическое*) strain, stress; (: *электрическое*) voltage.
напряжён|ный (-, -на, -но) *прил* tense; (*отношения, голос, встреча*) strained.
напрями́к *нареч* (*идти, ехать*) straight; (*перен: сказать*) straight out.
напр|я́чь (-ягу́, -яжёшь *итп*, **-ягу́т;** *pt* **-я́г, -ягла́,**

-ягло́, *impf* **напряга́ть**) *сов перех* to strain
▸ **напря́чься** (*impf* **напряга́ться**) *сов возв* (*мускулы, леска*) to become tense; (*внутренне*) to strain o.s.
напуга́|ть(ся) (**-ю(сь)**) *сов от* **пуга́ть(ся)**.
напу́др|ить(ся) (**-ю(сь), -ишь(ся)**) *сов от* **пу́дрить(ся)**.
напуска́|ть(ся) (**-ю(сь)**) *несов от* **напусти́ть(ся)**.
напускно́й *прил* (*грубость*) affected; (*спокойствие*) feigned.
нап|усти́ть (**-ущу́, -у́стишь**; *impf* **напуска́ть**) *сов перех*: ~ *+gen* (*дыму, воды*) to fill with; (*разг*): ~ **на** *+acc* to put on; (*разг: собак*) to set on; **напуска́ть** (~ *perf*) **на себя́ что-н** to assume sth
▸ **напусти́ться** (*impf* **напуска́ться**) *сов возв* (*разг*): ~**ся на** *+acc* to attack.
напу́та|ть (**-ю**; *impf* **напу́тывать**) *сов (не)перех* (*+acc или +gen*; *ниток, пряжи*) to tangle; **напу́тывать** (~ *perf*) **в** *+prp* (*в делах итп*) to make a mess of.
напу́тственн|ый *прил* (*речь*) farewell *опред*; ~**ое сло́во** parting words *мн*.
напу́тстви|е (**-я**) *ср* parting words *мн или* wishes *мн*, farewell speech.
напу́тыва|ть (**-ю**) *несов от* **напу́тать**.
напущу́(сь) *сов см* **напусти́ть(ся)**.
напы́ж|иться (**-усь, -ишься**) *сов от* **пы́житься**.
напыл|и́ть (**-ю́, -и́шь**) *сов от* **пыли́ть**.
напы́щен|ный (**-, -на, -но**) *прил* (*вид, человек*) pompous; (*речь, рассказ*) high-flown, bombastic.
напью́сь *итп сов см* **напи́ться**.
наравне́ *нареч*: ~ **с** *+instr* on an equal footing with; (*по одной линии*) on a level with.
нара́д|оваться (**-у́юсь**) *сов возв*: ~ **на** *+acc* to fully enjoy.
нараспа́шку *нареч* (*разг: одежда*) unbuttoned; **душа́ ~ у неё** she is very open.
нараспе́в *нареч* drawlingly.
нарас|ти́ (*3sg* **-тёт**, *3pl* **-ту́т**, *impf* **нараста́ть**) *сов неперех* (*много грибов, трава*) to spring up; (*долги, проценты*) to accumulate; (*волнение, сопротивление*) to grow; **нараста́ть** (~ *perf*) **на** *+prp* (*мох*) to grow on; (*плесень*) to form on; (*водоросли*) to build up on.
нара|сти́ть (**-щу́, -сти́шь**; *impf* **нара́щивать**) *сов перех* (*мускулы*) to develop; (*канат, трубу*) to lengthen.
нарасхва́т *нареч* (*продаваться, покупаться*) like hot cakes; **таки́е специали́сты сейча́с ~** such specialists are in great demand nowadays.
нара́щива|ть (**-ю**) *несов от* **нарасти́ть** ♦ *перех* (*темпы, объём итп*) to increase.
наращу́ *сов см* **нарасти́ть**.
нарв|а́ть (**-у́, -ёшь**; *impf* **нарыва́ть**) *сов (не)перех* (*+acc или +gen*; *травы, цветов, земляники*) to pick; (*бумаги*) to tear
▸ **нарва́ться** (*impf* **нарыва́ться**) *сов возв* (*разг*): ~**ся на** *+acc* (*на хулигана, грубияна*) to run up against; (*на оскорбление*) to have to take *или* swallow; **нарыва́ться** (~**ся** *perf*) **на неприя́тность** to run into some trouble.
наре́|зать (**-жу, -жешь**; *impf* **нареза́ть**) *сов (не)перех* (*+acc или +gen*; *колбасы, хлеба, сыр*) to slice, cut; (*веток, цветов*) to cut; (*земли, участки*) to allot (*ТЕХ*) to thread.
наре́зк|а (**-и**) *ж* (*винта*) thread.
нарека́ни|е (**-я**) *ср* reprimand, censure.
наре́чи|е (**-я**) *ср* (*ЛИНГ: говоры*) dialect; (: *часть речи*) adverb.
нарза́н (**-а**) *м* Narzan (*kind of mineral water*).
нарис|ова́ть (**-у́ю**) *сов от* **рисова́ть**.
нарица́тельн|ый *прил*: **и́мя ~ое** (*ЛИНГ*) common noun; ~**ая сто́имость** (*ЭКОН*) nominal cost.
наркоби́знес (**-а**) *м* drug dealing.
наркодел|е́ц (**-ьца́**) *м* drug dealer.
нарко́з (**-а**) *м* (*МЕД*) narcosis, anaesthesia (*BRIT*), anesthesia (*US*).
наркокурье́р (**-а**) *м* drug trafficker.
нарко́лог (**-а**) *м* (*МЕД*) expert in narcotics.
наркологи́ческ|ий (**-ая, -ое, -ие**) *прил*: ~ **диспансе́р** drug-abuse clinic.
наркома́н (**-а**) *м* drug addict *или* abuser.
наркома́ни|я (**-и**) *ж* drug addiction *или* abuse.
наркома́н|ка (**-ки**; *gen pl* **-ок**) *ж см* **наркома́н**.
нарко́тик (**-а**) *м* narcotic, drug.
наро́д (**-а**; *part gen* **-у**) *м* people *мн*, nation; **ру́сский ~** the Russian people; **мно́го ~у** many people.
наро́ден *прил см* **наро́дный**.
наро́дност|ь (**-и**) *ж* nation; (*литературы*) national character.
наро́д|ный (**-ен, -на, -но**) *прил* national; (*фронт*) popular; (*искусство*) folk *опред*; ~ **поэ́т** national poet *или bard*; ~ **худо́жник/арти́ст** *artist/actor who has received an official honour from the state*.
народонаселе́ни|е (**-я**) *ср* population.
нарожа́|ть (**-ю**) *сов перех* (*разг*) to give birth to.
наро́ст (**-а**) *м* (*наслоение*) covering; (*утолщение: на дереве*) outgrowth; (: *на суставах*) growth.
наро́чит|ый (**-, -а, -о**) *прил* deliberate, intentional.
наро́чно *нареч* (*опоздать, отвернуться*) purposely, on purpose; (*разг: сказать, заплакать*) for fun; **как ~** (*разг*) to make things worse; ~ **не приду́маешь!** (*разг*) this is quite something!
на́рочн|ый (**-ого**; *decl like adj*) *м* courier.
на́рт|а (**-ы**) *ж* sledge (*BRIT*) *или* sled (*US*) (*drawn by reindeer or dogs*).
наруб|и́ть (**-лю́, -ишь**; *impf* **наруба́ть**) *сов (не)перех* (*+acc или +gen*; *дров, капусты*) to chop.
нару́жен *прил см* **нару́жный**.
нару́жност|ь (**-и**) *ж* exterior; (*строения, города*) outward appearance.
нару́ж|ный (**-ен, -на, -но**) *прил* (*дверь, стена*) exterior; (*лекарство*) for external application; (*спокойствие, сдержанность*) outward.

нарýжу *нареч* out.
нарумя́н|ить(ся) (**-ю(сь), -ишь(ся)**) *сов от* **румя́нить(ся)**.
нарýчник (**-а**) *м* (*обычно мн*) handcuff.
нарýчн|ый *прил*: **~ые часы́** wristwatch.
наруша́|ть(ся) (**-ю(сь)**) *несов от* **нарýшить(ся)**.
наруши́тел|ь (**-я**) *м* (*закона*) transgressor, infringer; (*границы*) trespasser; (*ЮР*: *порядка*) offender; **~ дисципли́ны** troublemaker.
наруши́тельница (**-ы**) *ж см* **наруши́тель**.
нарýш|ить (**-у, -ишь**; *impf* **наруша́ть**) *сов перех* (*покой, тишину*) to break, disturb; (*связь*) to break; (*правила, договор*) to break, violate; (*дисциплину*) to breach; **наруша́ть** (**~** *perf*) **грани́цу** to illegally cross a border
▸ **нарýшиться** (*impf* **наруша́ться**) *сов возв* to be broken *или* disturbed.
нарци́сс (**-а**) *м* daffodil, narcissus.
на́р|ы (**-**) *мн* plank bed *ед*.
нары́в (**-а**) *м* (*МЕД*) abscess, boil.
нарыва́|ть (**-ю**) *несов от* **нарва́ть** ◆ *неперех* (*рана*) to fester; **у меня́ па́лец ~ет** I have a boil on my finger
▸ **нарыва́ться** *несов от* **нарва́ться**.
наря́д (**-а**) *м* (*одежда*) outfit; (*красивая одежда*) attire; (*распоряжение*) directive; (*КОММ*) order; (*ВОЕН*: *подразделение*) division; (: *задание*) assignment.
наря́ден *прил см* **наря́дный**.
нар|яди́ть (**-яжý, -я́дишь**; *impf* **наряжа́ть**) *сов перех* (*невесту итп*) to dress; (*в караул, на кухню итп*) to assign; **наряжа́ть** (**~** *perf*) **ёлку** ≈ to decorate (*BRIT*) *или* trim (*US*) the Christmas tree; **наря́жать** (**~** *perf*) **кого́-н** *+instr***/в** *+acc* to dress sb as/in
▸ **наряди́ться** (*impf* **наряжа́ться**) *сов возв*: **~ся** (**в** *+acc*) to dress o.s. (in).
наря́д|ный (**-ен, -на, -но**) *прил* (*человек*) well-dressed; (*комната, улица*) well-decorated; (*шляпа, платье*) fancy.
нарядý *нареч*: **~ с** *+instr* at the same time as; (*наравне*) on an equal footing with.
наряжа́|ть(ся) (**-ю(сь)**) *несов от* **наряди́ть(ся)**.
наряжý(сь) *сов см* **наряди́ть(ся)**.
нас *мест см* **мы**.
НАСА *ср сокр* NASA (= *National Aeronautics and Space Administration*).
нас|ади́ть (**-ажý, -а́дишь**; *impf* **наса́живать**) *сов перех* (*надеть*) to put.
наса́д|ка (**-ки**; *gen pl* **-ок**) *ж* (*для рыбы*) bait; (*ТЕХ*) nozzle.
насажде́ни|е (**-я**) *ср* (*БОТ*) plantation.
наса́жива|ть (**-ю**) *несов от* **насади́ть**.
насажý *сов см* **насади́ть**.
насви́стыва|ть (**-ю**) *несов перех*: **~ мело́дию** to whistle a tune under one's breath.
наседа́|ть (**-ю**) *несов от* **насе́сть** ◆ *неперех* (*разг*: *толпа*) to press forward.
насе́д|ка (**-ки**; *gen pl* **-ок**) *ж* broody hen.
насеко́м|ое (**-ого**; *decl like adj*) *ср* insect.
населе́ни|е (**-я**) *ср* population.
населённый *прил* (*район, область*) populated, inhabited; (*квартира*) inhabited; **~ пункт** locality.
насел|и́ть (**-ю́, -и́шь**; *impf* **населя́ть**) *сов перех* (*край*) to settle; (*дом*) to move into.
населя́|ть (**-ю**) *несов от* **насели́ть** ◆ *перех* (*лес, страну*) to inhabit.
насе́ст (**-а**) *м* (*для кур итп*) roost.
нас|е́сть (**-я́ду, -я́дешь**; *impf* **наседа́ть**) *сов неперех* (*пыль, копоть*) to settle; **наседа́ть** (**~** *perf*) **на** *+acc* (*перен*: *разг*: *с просьбами, в вопросами*) to pester; (*на противника*) to fall upon.
насе́ч|ка (**-ки**; *gen pl* **-ек**) *ж* notch.
наси́женн|ый *прил*: **~ое ме́сто** (*разг*) familiar surroundings *мн*.
наси́ли|е (**-я**) *ср* (*физическое*) violence; (*над личностью*) suppression.
наси́л|овать (**-ую**; *perf* **изнаси́ловать**) *несов перех* (*женщину, девушку*) to rape; (*no perf*; *личность*) to suppress.
наси́лу *нареч* (*разг*: *успеть, догнать*) only just.
наси́льник (**-а**) *м person who commits an act of violence*; (*над женщиной*) rapist.
наси́льно *нареч* forcibly; **~ заста́вить** (*perf*) **кого́-н** *+infin* to force sb to do.
наси́льственный *прил* (*меры*) violent; **наси́льственная смерть** violent death.
наска́кива|ть (**-ю**) *несов от* **наскочи́ть**.
насквóзь *нареч* through; **ви́деть** (*impf*) **~ кого́-н** to see (right) through sb.
наскóк (**-а**) *м* (*разг*) slagging; **с ~а** (*разг*) impromptu.
наскóлько *нареч* so much.
на́скоро *нареч* (*разг*) on the double.
наск|очи́ть (**-очý, -о́чишь**; *impf* **наска́кивать**) *сов неперех*: **~ на** *+acc* to run into; (*перен*: *разг*: *на обидчика, на оппонента*) to attack; (: *на неприятность*) to get into.
наскр|ести́ (**-ебý, -ебёшь**; *pt* **-ёб, -ебла́, -ебло́**, *impf* **наскреба́ть**) *сов перех* (*крошек, муки*) to collect; (*перен*: *мелочи, денег*) to scrape together.
наскýч|ить (**-у, -ишь**) *сов неперех*: **~ комý-н** to bore sb.
насла|ди́ться (**-жýсь, -ди́шься**; *impf* **наслажда́ться**) *сов возв*: **~** *+instr* to enjoy.
наслажде́ни|е (**-я**) *ср* enjoyment.
наслажýсь *сов см* **наслади́ться**.
насла́ива|ться (*3sg* **-ется**, *3pl* **-ются**) *несов от* **насло́йться**.
насле́ди|е (**-я**) *ср* (*культурное*) heritage; (*идеологическое*) legacy.
насле|ди́ть (**-жý, -ди́шь**) *сов от* **следи́ть**.

наслéдник (-а) *м (престола, состояния)* heir; (*перен: преемник*) inheritor.
наслéдниц|а (-ы) *ж (см м)* heiress; inheritor.
наслéдный *прил*: **~ принц** prince next in line (to the throne).
наслéдовани|е (-я) *ср* inheritance; (*престола*) succession.
наслéд|овать (-ую) *(не)сов перех* to inherit; (*престол*) to succeed.
наслéдственный *прил* inherited; (*черты, болезнь*) hereditary.
наслéдств|о (-а) *ср (имущество)* inheritance; (*культурное*) heritage; (*идеологическое*) legacy; **получáть (получи́ть** *perf*) **что-н в ~** to inherit sth.
наслежу́ *сов см* **наследи́ть.**
наслоéни|е (-я) *ср (ГЕО)* stratification.
насло|и́ться (*3sg* **-и́тся**, *3pl* **-я́тся**, *impf* **наслáиваться**) *сов возв*: **~ на** *+acc* to settle on; (*перен*) to add to.
наслу́ша|ться (-юсь) *сов возв*: **~** *+gen* to hear a lot of; (*вдоволь послушать*) to hear enough of.
наслы́шан *как сказ*: **я ~ об э́том/о нём** I have heard a lot about it/him.
наслы́ш|аться (-усь, -ишься) *сов возв (разг)*: **~ о** *+prp* to hear a lot about.
насмáрку *нареч (разг)*: **идти́ ~** to be wasted.
нáсмерть *нареч (сражаться)* to the death; (*разбиться, ранить*) fatally; (*перен: разг: перепугаться*) to death; (*: поругаться*) strongly.
насмехá|ться (-юсь) *несов возв*: **~ над** *+instr* to mock.
насмéшек *сущ см* **насмéшка.**
насмеш|и́ть (-у́, -и́шь) *сов от* **смеши́ть.**
насмéш|ка (-ки; *gen pl* **-ек)** *ж (обидная шутка)* jibe; **сказáть** *(perf)* **что-н в ~ку** to say sth mockingly.
насмéшлив|ый (-, -а, -о) *прил* mocking.
насмея́|ться (-юсь) *сов возв*: **~ над** *+instr* to offend.
нáсморк (-а) *м* runny nose.
насм|отрéться (-отрю́сь, -óтришься) *сов возв*: **~ (на** *+acc*) to see enough (of); (*+gen; чудес, людей*) to see a lot of.
насовсéм *нареч (разг)* for good.
насол|и́ть (-ю́, -и́шь) *сов перех* to preserve (*in brine*) ◆ *неперех (+dat; перен: разг: сделать неприятность)* to be nasty to.
насор|и́ть (-ю́, -и́шь) *сов от* **сори́ть.**
насóс (-а) *м* pump.
нáспех *нареч* hurriedly.
наста|вáть (*3sg* **-ёт**, *3pl* **-ю́т**) *несов от* **настáть.**
наставúтел|ьный (-ен, -ьна, -ьно) *прил (тон)* preaching.
настáв|ить (-лю, -ишь) *сов неперех (+gen; поставить)* to put; (*синяков, шишек*) to cause ◆ (*impf* **наставля́ть**) *перех (платье, рукав)* to lengthen; (*револьвер, ружьё*) to aim; **наставля́ть (~** *perf*) **когó-н на путь и́стинный** to set sb on the right path.
наставлéни|е (-я) *ср (поучение)* lecture; (*руководство*) instructions *мн*.
настáвлю *сов см* **настáвить.**
наставля́|ть (-ю) *несов от* **настáвить** ◆ *перех (учеников)* to teach.
настáвник (-а) *м* mentor.
настáива|ть(ся) (-ю(сь)) *несов от* **настоя́ть(ся).**
настá|ть (*3sg* **-нет**, *3pl* **-нут**, *impf* **наставáть**) *сов неперех (лето)* to begin; (*молчание, ночь*) to fall; (*день отъезда*) to come.
нáстежь *нареч (открыть)* wide; (*окно, дверь итп*) wide open; **распахну́ть** *(perf)* **~** to fling wide open.
наст|ели́ть (-елю́, -éлишь) *сов от* **стели́ть.**
настéнный *прил* wall *опред*.
настигá|ть (-ю) *несов от* **насти́чь.**
насти́гн|уть (-у, -ешь; *impf* **настигáть)** *сов перех* = **насти́чь.**
насти́л (-а) *м (из сена)* bedding; (*деревянный*) boarding.
насти́|чь (-гну, -гнешь; *pt* **-г, -гла, -гло,** *impf* **настигáть)** *сов перех* to catch up with.
настóек *сущ см* **настóйка.**
настó|й (-я) *м* infusion.
настó|йка (-йки; *gen pl* **-ек)** *ж (экстракт)* tincture; (*алкоголь*) liqueur.
настóйчив|ый (-, -а, -о) *прил (человек, характер)* persistent; (*просьба, взгляд итп*) insistent.
настóлько *нареч* so.
настóльн|ый *прил (лампа, часы)* table *опред*; (*календарь*) desk *опред*; **~ая кни́га** (*перен*) bible; **настóльный тéннис** table tennis.
насторáжива|ть(ся) (-ю(сь)) *несов от* **насторожи́ть(ся).**
настороже́ *нареч* on the alert ◆ *как сказ*: **он всегдá ~** he is always on the alert.
насторóженно *нареч* intently.
насторóжен|ный (-, -на, -но) *прил* alert.
насторожён|ный (-, -на, -но) *прил* = **насторóженный.**
насторож|и́ть (-у́, -и́шь; *impf* **насторáживать)** *сов перех* to alert
▸ **насторожи́ться** (*impf* **насторáживаться**) *сов возв* to become more alert.
настоя́ни|е (-я) *ср*: **по ~ю когó-н** on sb's insistence.
настоя́тел|ьный (-ен, -ьна, -ьно) *прил* (*просьба*) persistent; (*задача*) urgent.
насто|я́ть (-ю́, -и́шь; *impf* **настáивать)** *сов неперех*: **~ на** *+prp* to insist on ◆ *перех (ромашку)* to infuse; **настáивать (~** *perf*) **на своём** to insist on having one's own way
▸ **настоя́ться** (*impf* **настáиваться**) *сов возв (чай, ромашка)* to infuse.
настоя́щее (-его; *decl like adj*) *ср* the present.
настоя́щ|ий (-ая, -ее, -ие) *прил* real; (*момент, время*) present; (*данный: статья*) this; **по-~ему** (*как надо*) properly; (*преданный*) really; **настоя́щее врéмя** (*линг*) the present

tense.

настрада́|ться (**-юсь**) *сов возв* to suffer a lot.

настра́ива|ть(ся) (**-ю(сь)**) *несов от* **настро́ить(ся)**.

на́строго *нареч* (*разг*) strictly.

настрое́ни|е (**-я**) *ср* mood; (*антивоенное*) feeling; **не в ~и** in a bad mood; **обще́ственное ~** the mood in society.

настро́|ить (**-ю, -ишь**; *impf* **настра́ивать**) *сов* (*не*)*перех* (*+acc или +gen*; *домов, мостов, больниц*) to build ◆ *перех* (*гитару, пианино итп*) to tune; (*приёмник*) to tune in; (*механизм*) to adjust; **настра́ивать** (**~** *perf*) **кого́-н на** *+acc* to put sb in the right frame of mind for; **настра́ивать** (**~** *perf*) **кого́-н про́тив** *+gen* to incite sb against

▸ **настро́иться** (*impf* **настра́иваться**) *сов возв* (*приёмник*) to be tuned in; (*дружелюбно, враждебно*) to be disposed; **~ся** (*perf*) *+infin* to be disposed to do.

настро́|й (**-я**) *м* mood.

настро́йщик (**-а**) *м*: **~ роя́ля** piano tuner.

наступа́тел|ьный (**-ен, -ьна, -ьно**) *прил* (*бой, действие*) offensive.

наступа́|ть (**-ю**) *несов от* **наступи́ть** ◆ *неперех* (*ВОЕН*) to go on the offensive.

наст|упи́ть (**-уплю́, -у́пишь**; *impf* **наступа́ть**) *сов неперех*: **~ на** *+acc* (*на камень, на ногу итп*) to step on; (*ночь, тишина*) to fall; (*утро, лето*) to begin; (*день отъезда*) to come.

наступле́ни|е (**-я**) *ср* (*ВОЕН*) offensive; (*весны, старости*) beginning; (*темноты*) fall; **с ~м зимы́** at the beginning of winter; **с ~м темноты́** at nightfall.

наступлю́ *сов см* **наступи́ть**.

насту́рци|я (**-и**) *ж* nasturtium.

насты́р|ный (**ен, -на, -но**) *прил* (*разг*) persistent.

насу́п|иться (**-люсь, -ишься**) *сов возв* (*разг*) to frown.

на́сухо *нареч*: **вы́тереть что-н ~** to dry sth thoroughly.

насу́щ|ный (**-ен, -на, -но**) *прил* vital.

насчёт *предл* (*+gen*) regarding.

насчита́|ть (**-ю**; *impf* **насчи́тывать**) *сов перех* to count.

насчи́тыва|ть (**-ю**) *несов от* **насчита́ть** ◆ *неперех* to have; **дере́вня ~ет ты́сячу жи́телей** the village has a thousand inhabitants

▸ **насчи́тываться** *несов возв безл* to have.

насы́п|ать (**-лю, -лешь**; *impf* **насыпа́ть**) *сов перех* to pour; (*набросать*) to strew.

на́сып|ь (**-и**) *ж* embankment.

насы́|тить (**-щу, -тишь**; *impf* **насыща́ть**) *сов перех* (*голодного, ребёнка*) to satiate; (*запахом, водой, радостью*) to fill; (*раствор, рынок*) to saturate

▸ **насы́титься** (*impf* **насыща́ться**) *сов возв* (*наесться*) to eat one's fill; (*земля*) to be saturated.

насы́щенный *прил* (*ХИМ*) saturated; (*перен*: *жизнь*) rich.

насы́щу(сь) *сов см* **насы́тить(ся)**.

нася́ду *итп сов см* **насе́сть**.

ната́лкива|ть(ся) (**-ю(сь)**) *несов от* **натолкну́ть(ся)**.

натаска́|ть (**-ю**; *impf* **ната́скивать**) *сов* (*не*)*перех* (*+acc или +gen*; *дров, сучьев итп*) to bring; (*разг*: *перен*: *цитат, отрывков*) to fish out; (: *студента, ученика*) to coach (*for examination*).

натащ|и́ть (**-у́, -ишь**) *сов* (*не*)*перех* (*+acc или +gen*; *разг*: *камней, сучьев, грязи*) to bring in.

натвор|и́ть (**-ю́, -и́шь**) *сов* (*не*)*перех* (*+acc или +gen*; *разг*) to get up to.

нат|ере́ть (**-ру́, -рёшь**; *pt* **-ёр, -ёрла, -ёрло**, *impf* **натира́ть**) *сов перех* (*ботинки, полы*) to polish; (*руку, шею итп*) to chafe; (*морковь, сыр итп*) to grate; **натира́ть** (**~** *perf*) **что-н чем-н** (*руки итп*: *мазью, кремом*) to rub sth into sth; **натира́ть** (**~** *perf*) **себе́ мозо́ли** to get a callus

▸ **натере́ться** (*impf* **натира́ться**) *сов возв*: **~ся** (*+instr*) (*мазью, кремом*) to rub o.s. (with).

натерп|е́ться (**-лю́сь, -ишься**) *сов возв*: **~** *+gen* (*разг*: *горя, беды*) to experience a lot of.

натира́|ть(ся) (**-ю(сь)**) *несов от* **натере́ть(ся)**.

на́тиск (**-а**) *м* pressure.

наткн|у́ться (**-у́сь, -ёшься**; *impf* **натыка́ться**) *сов возв*: **~уться на** *+acc* (*разг*: *на пень, на преграду*) to bump into; (*перен*: *на непонимание, на сопротивление*) to come up against.

НАТО *ср сокр* NATO (= *North Atlantic Treaty Organization*).

натолкн|у́ть (**-у́, -ёшь**; *impf* **ната́лкивать**) *сов перех*: **~ кого́-н на** *+acc* (*разг*: *на идею*) to lead sb to; **ната́лкивать** (**~** *perf*) **кого́-н на мысль** to put a thought into sb's head

▸ **натолкну́ться** (*impf* **ната́лкиваться**) *сов возв*: **~ся на** *+acc* (*также перен*) to bump into.

натоп|и́ть (**-лю́, -ишь**) *сов перех* (*избу, печь*) to heat; (*жир, воск*) to melt.

натоп|та́ть (**-чу́, -чешь**) *сов перех* (*разг*) to make dirty footmarks across.

нат|очи́ть (**-очу́, -о́чишь**) *сов от* **точи́ть**.

натоща́к *нареч* on an empty stomach.

натрав|и́ть (**-лю́, -ишь**; *impf* **натра́вливать**) *сов перех*: **~ кого́-н на** *+acc* to set sb on; (*перен*) to incite sb against.

натрениро́ван|ный (**-, -а, -о**) *прил* trained.

натрениро|ва́ть(ся) (**-у́ю(сь)**) *сов от* **тренирова́ть(ся)**.

на́три|й (**-я**) *м* sodium.

на́трое *нареч* in(to) three.

натру́(сь) *итп сов см* **натере́ть(ся)**.

натр|уди́ться (**-ужу́сь, -у́дишься**) *сов возв* (*разг*) to work hard.

натýг|а (**-и**) *ж* (*разг*) effort.
нáтуго *нареч* (*разг*) tightly.
натýж|иться (**-усь, -ишься**; *impf* **натýживаться**) *сов возв* (*разг*) to strain.
натýр|а (**-ы**) *ж* (*характер*) nature; (*натурщик*) model (*ART*); **увидéть** *(perf)* **что-н/когó-н ~е** to see sth/sb in real life; **рисовáть** *(impf)* **с ~ы** to paint from nature; **~ой, в ~е** (*ЭКОН*) in kind.
натурáлен *прил см* **натурáльный**.
натурализáци|я (**-и**) *ж* naturalization.
натуралúзм (**-а**) *м* naturalism.
натуралúст (**-а**) *м* naturalist.
натурáл|ьный (**-ен, -ьна, -ьно**) *прил* natural; (*мех, кожа, слёзы*) real; (*обмен, доходы, налог*) in kind; **~ьная величинá** life-sized.
натýрщик (**-а**) *м* model (*ART*).
натýрщиц|а (**-ы**) *ж см* **натýрщик**.
натыкá|ться (**-юсь**) *несов от* **наткнýться**.
натюрмóрт (**-а**) *м* still life.
натягивá|ть(ся) (**-ю(сь)**) *несов от* **натянýть(ся)**.
натя́ж|ка (**-ки**; *gen pl* **-ек**) *ж* (*в аргументах*) distortion; **с ~кой** at a pinch.
натя́нут|ый (**-, -а, -о**) *прил* strained.
натян|ýть (**-ý, -ешь**; *impf* **натя́гивать**) *сов перех* (*струны, вожжи, холст*) to pull tight; (*разг*: *сапоги, перчатки*) to pull on; (: *одеяло*) to pull over; **он ~ýл емý пятёрку** (*разг*) he stretched his mark to an A
▸ **натянýться** (*impf* **натя́гиваться**) *сов возв* to tighten.
наугáд *нареч* (*идти, взять*) at random; **отвечáть** *(impf)* **~** to guess.
наýк|а (**-и**) *ж* science; (*разг*: *урок*) lesson; **естéственные ~и** science; **гуманитáрные ~и** arts.
наутёк *нареч* (*разг*: *пуститься, броситься*) at full tilt.
наýтро *нареч* next morning.
наýчен *прил см* **наýчный**.
на|учúть(ся) (**-учý(сь), -ýчишь(ся)**) *сов от* **учúть(ся)**.
наýчно-популя́рный *прил* (*программа*) science *опред*; (*литература*) scientific.
наýчно-технúческ|ий (**-ая, -ое, -ие**) *прил* scientific.
наýч|ный (**-ен, -на, -но**) *прил* scientific; **наýчная фантáстика** science fiction.
наýшник (**-а**) *м* (*обычно мн*: *на шапке*) earflap; **магнитофóнные ~и** headphones.
нафталúн (**-а**; *part gen* **-у**) *м* naphthalene.
нахáл (**-а**) *м* (*разг*) cheeky beggar.
нахáлен *прил см* **нахáльный**.
нахáлк|а (**-и**) *ж см* **нахáл**.
нахáл|ьный (**-ен, -ьна, -ьно**) *прил* cheeky.
нахáльств|о (**-а**) *ср* cheek.
нахам|úть (**-лю́, -úшь**) *сов от* **хамúть**.
нахватá|ть (**-ю**) *сов неперех* (*+gen*; *разг*: *товаров, знаний*) to pick up
▸ **нахватáться** *сов возв* (*+gen*; *разг*: *знаний, привычек*) to pick up; (: *воды*) to gulp.
нахлéбник (**-а**) *м* (*разг*) sponger.
нахлобýч|ить (**-у, -ишь**; *impf* **нахлобýчивать**) *сов перех* (*разг*) to pull down.
нахлы́н|уть (*3sg* **-ет**, *3pl* **-ут**) *сов неперех* (*поток*) to surge; (*перен*: *толпа*) to surge forward; (: *мысли*) to surge up; **~ули воспоминáния** memories came flooding back.
нахмýр|ить(ся) (**-ю(сь), -ишь(ся)**) *несов от* **хмýрить(ся)**.
нах|одúть (**-ожý, -óдишь**) *несов от* **найтú**
▸ **находúться** *несов от* **найтúсь** ◆ *возв* (*дом, город*) to be situated; (*человек*) to be.
нахóд|ка (**-ки**; *gen pl* **-ок**) *ж* (*потерянного*) discovery; (*приём*: *писателя, актёра*) innovation; **он – ~ для нас** he is a real find for us; **Бюрó ~ок** lost property office (*BRIT*), lost and found (*US*).
нахóдчив|ый (**-, -а, -о**) *прил* (*человек*) resourceful; (*ответ*) apt.
нахождéни|е (**-я**) *ср* (*преступника*) whereabouts.
нахóжен|ный (**-, -а, -о**) *прил* (*тропа*) well-trodden.
нахожý(сь) *несов см* **находúть(ся)**.
нахох|отáться (**-очýсь, -óчешься**) *сов возв* to have a good laugh.
нахрáпист|ый (**-, -а, -о**) *прил* (*разг*: *продавец, посетитель*) pushy.
нахрáпом *нареч* (*разг*): **дéйствовать ~** to be pushy.
нахулигáн|ить (**-ю, -ишь**) *сов от* **хулигáнить**.
нацарáпа|ть (**-ю**) *сов от* **царáпать**.
нацедúть (**-ежý, -éдишь**; *impf* **нацéживать**) *сов перех* to strain.
нацéлен|ный (**-, -а, -о**) *прил*: **~ на** *+acc* (*на победу*) aiming for.
нацéл|ить (**-ю, -ишь**) *сов от* **цéлить** ◆ (*impf* **нацéливать**) *перех*: **~ когó-н на** *+acc* to push sb towards
▸ **нацéлиться** *сов от* **цéлиться**.
нацéн|ка (**-ки**; *gen pl* **-ок**) *ж* (*на товар*) surcharge; (*ресторанная*) cover charge.
нацеп|úть (**-лю́, -ишь**; *impf* **нацепля́ть**) *сов перех* (*повесить*) to hang on; (*разг*: *украшения, шляпу*) to doll o.s. up in.
нацúзм (**-а**) *м* Nazism.
национализáци|я (**-и**) *ж* nationalization.
национализúр|овать (**-ую**) *(не)сов перех* to nationalize.
националúзм (**-а**) *м* nationalism.
националúст (**-а**) *м* nationalist.
националúст|ка (**-ки**; *gen pl* **-ок**) *ж см* **националúст**.
националúстск|ий (**-ая, -ое, -ие**) *прил* (*политика, лозунг*) nationalistic.
национáльност|ь (**-и**) *ж* (*нация*) nation; (*принадлежность к нации*) nationality.
национáльный *прил* national; **национáльный óкруг** *administrative division of minor nationalities*.
нацúст (**-а**) *м* Nazi.

наци́стск|ий (**-ая, -ое, -ие**) *прил* Nazi.
на́ци|я (**-и**) *ж* nation; **Организа́ция Объединённых Н~й** United Nations Organization.
нацме́н (**-а**) *м сокр* = *представи́тель национа́льного меньшинства́.*
нач. *сокр* = **нача́льник**.
нача|ди́ть (**-жу́, -ди́шь**) *сов от* **чади́ть**.
нача́л|а (-) *мн* (*методы*) basis *ед*; (*принципы*) fundamentals *мн*; **на коллекти́вных/комме́рческих ~х** on a collective/commercial basis.
нача́л|о (**-а**) *ср* beginning, start; (*основа: организующее, сдерживающее*) foundation; (*: волевое, поэтическое*) nature; **быть** *(impf)* **под ~м кого́-н** *или* **у кого́-н** to be under sb; **брать** *(impf)* ~ to start; **вести́** *(impf)* **своё ~ от** *+gen* to have its origins in; **положи́ть** *(perf) или* **дать** *(perf)* **~ чему́-н** to make a start on sth; *см также* **нача́ла**.
нача́льник (**-а**) *м* (*цеха*) floor manager; (*управления*) head; (*экспедиции*) leader.
нача́льническ|ий (**-ая, -ое, -ие**) *прил* (*тон*) authoritative.
нача́льный *прил* (*период, этап*) initial; (*глава книги*) first; (*первоначальный: сведения, уроки*) very first; **нача́льная шко́ла** (*ПРОСВЕЩ*) primary (*BRIT*) *или* elementary (*US*) school; **нача́льное образова́ние** (*ПРОСВЕЩ*) primary (*BRIT*) *или* elementary (*US*) education; **нача́льные кла́ссы** (*ПРОСВЕЩ*) *the first three classes of primary school*.
нача́льственный *прил* superior.
нача́льств|о (**-а**) *ср* (*власть*) authority ◆ *собир* (*руководители*) management; **под ~м кого́-н** (*служить, находиться*) under sb.
нача́льствующ|ий (**-ая, -ее, -ие**) *прил* managing *опред*.
нача́тк|и (**-ов**) *мн* fundamentals *мн*.
нач|а́ть (**-ну́, -нёшь**; *pt* **-ал, -ала́, -ало**, *impf* **начина́ть**) *сов перех* to begin, start; (*начать использовать*) to start; **начина́ть** (*~ perf*) *+infin* to start doing
▸ **нача́ться** (*impf* **начина́ться**) *сов возв* to begin, start.
начеку́ *нареч*: **быть** ~ to be on one's guard.
начерка́|ть (**-ю**) *сов от* **черка́ть** ◆ *перех* (*разг: линии, штрихи итп*) to draw (*randomly*); (*записку*) to scribble.
начерн|и́ть (**-ю́, -и́шь**) *сов от* **черни́ть**.
на́черно *нареч* (*написать, подготовить*) roughly.
начерта́ни|е (**-я**) *ср* (*букв*) outline.
нач|ерти́ть (**-ерчу́, -е́ртишь**) *сов от* **черти́ть**.
начёс (**-а**) *м* (*на шерсти, на ткани*) nap; (*вид причёски*) bouffant.
начёт (**-а**) *м* (*денежное взыскание*) penalty.
начина́ни|е (**-я**) *ср* initiative.
начина́тел|ь (**-я**) *м* initiator.
начина́|ть(ся) (**-ю(сь)**) *несов от* **нача́ть(ся)**.
начина́ющ|ая (**-ей**; *decl like adj*) *ж см* **начина́ющий**.
начина́ющ|ий (**-ая, -ее, -ие**) *прил* (*писатель, учитель*) novice *опред* ◆ (**-его**; *decl like adj*) *м* beginner.
начина́я *предл* (*+instr*) including; **~ с** *+gen* from; **~ от** *+gen или* **с** *+gen* (*включая*) including.
начин|и́ть (**-ю́, -и́шь**; *impf* **начиня́ть**) *сов перех* (*пирог*) to fill.
начи́н|ка (**-ки**; *gen pl* **-ок**) *ж* filling.
начиня́|ть (**-ю**) *несов от* **начини́ть**.
начисле́ни|е (**-я**) *ср* (*действие*) addition; (*начисленная сумма*) surcharge.
начи́сл|ить (**-ю, -ишь**; *impf* **начисля́ть**) *сов перех* (*проценты*) to add on.
начи́|стить (**-щу, -стишь**; *impf* **начища́ть**) *сов перех* (*туфли*) to clean ◆ *неперех* (*+gen; картошки*) to peel.
на́чисто *нареч* (*набело*) cleanly; (*разг: совершенно*) absolutely.
начистоту́ *нареч* (*разг*) straight.
начи́тан|ный (**-, -на, -но**) *прил* well-read.
начита́|ть (**-ю**; *impf* **начи́тывать**) *сов перех* to read
▸ **начита́ться** *сов возв* (*+gen*) to read a lot of.
начи́тыва|ть (**-ю**) *несов от* **начита́ть**.
начиха́|ть (**-ю**) *сов неперех* (*перен: разг*): **ему́ ~ на сове́ты** he doesn't give a toss about taking people's advice.
начища́|ть (**-ю**) *несов от* **начи́стить**.
начи́щу *сов см* **начи́стить**.
начме́д (**-а**) *м сокр* SG (= *Surgeon General*).
начну́(сь) *итп сов см* **нача́ть(ся)**.
наш (**-его**; *см* **Table 9**; *f* **-а**, *nt* **-е**, *pl* **-и**) *притяж мест* our; **~ го́род о́чень ста́рый** our city is very old; **чей э́то дом? – ~** whose is this house? – ours; **чьи э́то кни́ги? – на́ши** whose are these books? – ours; **по-на́шему** our way; (*по нашему мнению*) in our opinion; **на́ша взяла́!** (*разг*) we won!; *см также* **на́ши**.
нашаты́рный *прил*: **~ спирт** (*МЕД*) liquid ammonia.
нашаты́р|ь (**-я́**) *м* (*ХИМ*) ammonium chloride; (*разг: нашатырный спирт*) liquid ammonia.
на́ше (**-го**) *притяж мест см* **наш**.
наше́стви|е (**-я**) *ср* invasion.
на́ш|и (**-их**) *притяж мест см* **наш**; ◆ *decl like adj мн* (*о членах семьи*) relatives *мн*; (*о соотечественниках*) compatriots *мн*; **и ~м и ва́шим** (*разг*) all things to all people; **~ вы́играли** we won.
нашива́|ть (**-ю**) *несов от* **наши́ть**.
наши́в|ка (**-ки**; *gen pl* **-ок**) *ж* (*на погонах*) stripe (*showing rank*).
на́шим *притяж мест см* **наш, на́ше, на́ши**.
на́шими *притяж мест см* **на́ши**.

нашинк|ова́ть (**-у́ю**) *сов от* **шинкова́ть**.
наш|и́ть (**-ью́, -ьёшь**; *impf* **нашива́ть**) *сов перех* (*тесьму, эмблему*) to sew on ◆ *неперех* (*no perf*): ~ *+gen* (*нарядов*) to sew.
на́ших *притяж мест см* **наш**.
нашлёпа|ть (**-ю**) *сов перех* (*разг*) to smack.
нашпиг|ова́ть (**-у́ю**) *сов от* **шпигова́ть**.
нашум|е́ть (**-лю́, -и́шь**) *сов неперех* to make a lot of noise; (*фильм, книга*) to cause a stir.
нашью́ *итп сов см* **наши́ть**.
нащу́па|ть (**-ю**; *impf* **нащу́пывать**) *сов перех* (*также перен*) to find.
наэлектриз|ова́ть (**-у́ю**) *сов от* **электризова́ть**.
ная́бедничa|ть (**-ю**) *сов от* **я́бедничать**.
наяву́ *нареч* in reality; **как** ~ distinctly.
НДС *м сокр* (= *нало́г на доба́вленную сто́имость*) VAT (= *value-added tax*).
не *част* not; ~ **я написа́л э́то письмо́** I didn't write this letter; **я** ~ **рабо́таю** I don't work; ~ **пла́чьте/опозда́йте** don't cry/be late; ~ **могу́** ~ **согласи́ться/не возрази́ть** I can't help agreeing/objecting; ~ **мне на́до помо́чь, а ему́** I am not the one who needs help, he is; **слу́шаю** ~ **без удово́льствия/удивле́ния** I listen not without pleasure/surprise; ~ **до** *+gen* no time for; **мне** ~ **до тебя́** I have no time for you; ~ **без того́** (*разг*: *в положительных ответах*) that's about it; ~ **то** (*разг*: *в противном случае*) or else; **откро́й дверь,** ~ **то я её слома́ю** open the door or else I'll break it down.
неадеква́т|ный (**-ен, -на, -но**) *прил* inadequate.
неаккура́т|ный (**-ен, -на, -но**) *прил* (*человек*) untidy; (*подсчёт*) inaccurate; (*работа*) sloppy.
неактуа́л|ьный (**-ен, -ьна, -ьно**) *прил* irrelevant.
неаполита́нск|ий (**-ая, -ое, -ие**) *прил* Neapolitan.
Неа́пол|ь (**-я**) *м* Naples.
небезопа́с|ный (**-ен, -на, -но**) *прил* somewhat dangerous.
небезоснова́тел|ьный (**-ен, -ьна, -ьно**) *прил* not unreasonable.
небезызве́ст|ный (**-ен, -на, -но**) *прил* (*факты*) reasonably well-known; (*сплетник, интриган*) notorious.
небезынтере́с|ный (**-ен, -на, -но**) *прил* reasonably interesting.
небеса́ *итп сущ см* **не́бо**.
небе́сный *прил* (*небосвод, сфера*) celestial; (*перен*) heavenly; **небе́сные тела́** heavenly bodies; **небе́сные си́лы** (*РЕЛ*) the heavenly host; **небе́сный цвет** sky blue.
небесполе́з|ный (**-ен, -на, -но**) *прил* reasonably useful.
неблагови́д|ный (**-ен, -на, -но**) *прил* unseemly.
неблагода́рен *прил см* **неблагода́рный**.
неблагода́рност|ь (**-и**) *ж* ingratitude.
неблагода́р|ный (**-ен, -на, -но**) *прил* (*человек*) ungrateful; (*занятие, работа*) thankless.
неблагозву́ч|ный (**-ен, -на, -но**) *прил* dissonant.
неблагополу́ч|ный (**-ен, -на, -но**) *прил* unsuccessful.
не́б|о (**-а**; *nom pl* **небеса́**, *gen pl* **небе́с**) *ср* sky; (*РЕЛ*) Heaven; **на седьмо́м** ~**е** in seventh heaven; **под откры́тым** ~**м** out in the open; **с** ~**а свали́ться** *(perf)* (*разг*: *неожиданно появиться*) to appear out of nowhere; **я был ме́жду** ~**м и землёй** I didn't know whether I was coming or going; **превозноси́ть** *(impf)* **кого́-н до небе́с** to praise sb to the skies.
нёб|о (**-а**) *ср* (*АНАТ*) palate.
небога́т|ый (**-, -а, -о**) *прил* (*страна*) not wealthy; (*выбор, улов*) fairly poor; **он челове́к** ~ he has a modest income.
небольш|о́й *прил* small; (*расстояние, промежуток времени*) short; (*должность, звание*) minor; (*польза, авторитет*) limited; **на** ~ **глубине́/высоте́** not very deep/high; **ей три́дцать (лет) с** ~**и́м** she is a little over thirty.
небосво́д (**-а**) *м* the heavens *мн*.
небоскрёб (**-а**) *м* skyscraper.
небо́сь *вводн сл* (*разг*) I dare say.
небре́жен *прил см* **небре́жный**.
небре́жност|ь (**-и**) *ж* (*в работе, подсчётов*) carelessness; (*родителей, работников*) negligence; (*тона, в обращении*) offhandedness.
небре́ж|ный (**-ен, -на, -но**) *прил* (*человек, работа, подсчёт*) careless; (*причёска, почерк*) untidy; (*тон, отношение*) offhand(ed).
небыва́л|ый (**-, -а, -о**) *прил* (*чувство, ощущение*) unknown; (*случай*) unprecedented.
небыли́ц|а (**-ы**) *ж* tall story.
небыти|е́ (**-я́**) *ср* nonexistence.
Нев|а́ (**-ы́**) *ж* the Neva.
нева́жен *прил см* **нева́жный**.
нева́жно *нареч* (*работать, делать что-н*) not very well ◆ *как сказ* it's not important; **я чу́вствую себя́** ~ I'm not feeling too good; **он** ~ **у́чится в шко́ле** he isn't doing very well at school.
нева́ж|ный (**-ен, -на, -но**) *прил* unimportant; (*не очень хороший*) poor; **обе́д был нава́жный** dinner wasn't great; **у неё** ~**ное здоро́вье** her health isn't very good.
невдалеке́ *нареч* (*слышаться, видеться*) not far off; ~ **от** *+gen* not far from.
невдомёк *как сказ* (*+dat*): **ей** ~, **что ...** (*разг*) she doesn't realize that ....
неве́дени|е (**-я**) *ср* ignorance; **сде́лать** *(perf)*/**сказа́ть** *(perf)* **что-н по** ~**ю** to do/say sth out of ignorance; **он пребыва́ет в по́лном** ~**и** he doesn't know anything (about it).
неве́домо *нареч*: ~ **кто/что/как** *итп* (*разг*) God knows who/what/how *итп*.
неве́дом|ый (**-, -а, -о**) *прил* unknown.
неве́ж|а (**-и**) *м/ж* boor.
неве́жд|а (**-ы**) *м/ж* ignoramus.
неве́жествен|ный (**-, -на, -но**) *прил* ignorant.
неве́жеств|о (**-а**) *ср* ignorance.

невéжлив|ый (-, -а, -о) *прил* impolite.
невезéни|е (-я) *ср* (*разг*) bad luck.
невели́к|ий (-ая, -ое, -ие; -, -á, -ó) *прил* (*по размеру*) small; (*по длине*) short; (*убытки, ущерб*) minor; **он рóстом невели́к** he's not very tall; **невеликá бедá!** (*разг*) it's no big deal!
невéрен *прил см* **невéрный**.
невéри|е (-я) *ср* lack of faith.
невéрно *нареч* incorrectly ◆ *как сказ*: **(э́то)** ~ that's not right.
невéрност|ь (-и) *ж* (*рассуждений, понятия*) incorrectness; (*друга, союзника*) disloyalty; (*жены, мужа*) infidelity.
невéр|ный (-ен, -на, -но) *прил* (*см сущ*) incorrect; disloyal; unfaithful; (*шаги, движения*) unsteady; (*голос, звук*) faltering; (*нота*) false.
невероя́тен *прил см* **невероя́тный**.
невероя́тно *нареч* incredibly ◆ *как сказ* it's incredible.
невероя́тност|ь (-и) *ж* (*сообщения, результатов*) improbability; **до ~и** incredibly.
невероя́т|ный (-ен, -на, -но) *прил* (*неправдоподобный*) improbable; (*чрезвычайный*) incredible.
невéрующ|ий (-ая, -ее, -ие) *прил* (*РЕЛ*) faithless ◆ **(-его**; *decl like adj*) *м* unbeliever.
нев|есёлый (-éсел, -еселá, -éсело) *прил* gloomy.
невесóмост|ь (-и) *ж* (*ФИЗ*) weightlessness.
невесóм|ый (-, -а, -о) *прил* weightless; (*перен*: *преимущество, превосходство*) negligible.
невéст|а (-ы) *ж* (*после помолвки*) fiancée; (*на свадьбе*) bride.
невéст|ка (-ки; *gen pl* **-ок**) *ж* (*жена сына*) daughter-in-law; (*жена брата*) sister-in-law.
невéсть *нареч*: ~ **кто/что/кудá** *итп* (*разг*) goodness knows who/what/where *итп*.
невзгóд|а (-ы) *ж* (*обычно мн*) adversity.
невзирáя *предл*: ~ **на** +*acc* in spite of.
невзл|юби́ть (-юблю́, -ю́бишь) *сов перех* to take a dislike to.
невзначáй *нареч* (*разг*) by accident.
невзрáч|ный (-ен, -на, -но) *прил* ordinary-looking.
невзыскáтел|ьный (-ен, -ьна, -ьно) *прил* undemanding.
нéвидал|ь (-и) *ж* (*разг*) oddity; ~ **какáя!** now there's a surprise!
неви́дан|ный (-, -на, -но) *прил* unprecedented.
невиди́м|ка (-ки; *gen pl* **-ок**) *м/ж* (*человек*) invisible being ◆ *ж* (*шпилька*) hairpin.
неви́дим|ый (-, -а, -о) *прил* invisible.
неви́дящ|ий (-ая, -ее, -ие) *прил* unseeing.
неви́нен *прил см* **неви́нный**.
неви́нност|ь (-и) *ж* innocence.
неви́н|ный (-ен, -на, -но) *прил* innocent.
невинóвен *прил см* **невинóвный**.
невинóвност|ь (-и) *ж* innocence.
невинóв|ный (-ен, -на, -но) *прил* innocent.
невкýсен *прил см* **невкýсный**.
невкýсно *нареч*: **онá ~ готóвит** she is a bad cook; **здесь ~ кóрмят** the food here is not very nice.
невкýс|ный (-ен, -нá, -но) *прил* (*суп, салат, пища*) tasteless.
невменя́емост|ь (-и) *ж* derangement; **в состоя́нии ~и** (*ЮР*) non compos mentis.
невменя́ем|ый (-, -а, -о) *прил* deranged.
невмешáтельств|о (-а) *ср* non interference; (*ЭКОН*) laissez faire.
невнимáни|е (-я) *ср* (*невнимательность*) lack of attention; (*равнодушие*) lack of concern.
невнимáтелен *прил см* **невнимáтельный**.
невнимáтельност|ь (-и) *ж* (*см прил*) inattention; lack of consideration; carelessness.
невнимáтел|ьный (-ен, -ьна, -ьно) *прил* (*ученик, слушатель*) inattentive; (*незаботливый*: *сын, дочь*) inconsiderate; (: *отношение, обращение*) careless.
невня́т|ный (-ен, -на, -но) *прил* muffled.
нéвод (-а) *м* fishing net.
невозврáтен *прил см* **невозврáтный**.
невозврати́м|ый (-, -а, -о) *прил* irretrievable.
невозврáт|ный (-ен, на, -но) *прил* = **невозврати́мый**.
невозвращéн|ец (-ца) *м* defector.
невозвращéн|ка (-ки; *gen pl* **-ок**) *ж см* **невозвращéнец**.
невозвращéнца *итп сущ см* **невозвращéнец**.
невоздéржан|ный (-, -на, -но) *прил* highly strung (*BRIT*), high-strung (*US*).
невозмóжен *прил см* **невозмóжный**.
невозмóжно *как сказ*: ~ +*infin* (*сделать, найти итп*) it is impossible to do ◆ *нареч* (*большой, трудный*) impossibly; **(э́то)** ~ that's impossible.
невозмóжност|ь (-и) *ж*: **до ~и** exceedingly.
невозмóж|ный (-ен, -на, -но) *прил* impossible; (*боль, жара*) unbearable; (*тон, поведение, вид*) insufferable.
невозмути́м|ый (-, -а, -о) *прил* (*человек*) unflappable; (*тон, ответ*) unruffled; (*тишина, спокойствие*) undisturbed.
невóлен *прил см* **невóльный**.
невóл|ить (-ю, -ишь) *несов перех* (*разг*): ~ **когó-н** +*infin* (*согласиться, отказаться итп*) to force sb to do.
невóльник (-а) *м* slave.
невóльниц|а (-ы) *ж см* **невóльник**.
невóл|ьный (-ен, -ьна, -ьно) *прил* (*ложь, вина*) unintentional; (*движение, улыбка, свидетель*) involuntary.
невóл|я (-и) *ж* captivity; **в ~е** in captivity.
невообрази́м|ый (-, -а, -о) *прил* unimaginable.
невооружённ|ый *прил* unarmed; **~ым глáзом**

(*без оптических приборов*) with the naked eye; **это ви́дно ~ым глазо́м** (*перен*) it's plain for all to see.
невоспи́тан|ный (-, -на, -но) *прил* ill-bred.
невосприи́мчив|ый (-, -а, -о) *прил*: ~ (**к** +*dat*) (*к знаниям*) unreceptive (to); (*к болезням*) immune (to).
невостре́бованный *прил* unclaimed.
невпопа́д *нареч* (*разг*) out of turn.
невразуми́тел|ьный (-ен, -ьна, -ьно) *прил* unintelligible.
невралги́ческ|ий (-ая, -ое, -ие) *прил* neuralgic.
невралги́|я (-и) *ж* neuralgia.
неврасте́ник (-а) *м* neurotic.
неврастени́ч|ный (-ен, -на, -но) *прил* neurotic.
неврастени́|я (-и) *ж* (*МЕД*) nervous tension.
невреди́м|ый (-, -а, -о) *прил* (*лодка, машина*) undamaged; (*человек*) unharmed.
невро́з (-а) *м* neurosis (*мн* neuroses).
невропато́лог (-а) *м* neurologist.
невтерпёж *как сказ* (+*dat*): **ей ~ пойти́/узна́ть** she can't wait to go/find out; **ему́ всё ~** he is always in a hurry.
невы́год|ный (-ен, -на, -но) *прил* unprofitable; (*условия, ситуация, впечатление*) unfavourable (*BRIT*), unfavorable (*US*); (*внешность*) unattractive.
невы́держан|ный (-, -на, -но) *прил* (*человек, поведение*) uncontrolled; (*стиль*) erratic.
невыноси́м|ый (-, -а, -о) *прил* unbearable, intolerable.
невыполне́ни|е (-я) *ср* (*обязательства, плана*) failure to carry out; (*обещания*) failure to keep.
невыполни́м|ый (-, -а, -о) *прил* not feasible.
невырази́м|ый (-, -а, -о) *прил* inexpressible.
невырази́тел|ьный (-ен, -ьна, -ьно) *прил* (*лицо, глаза*) expressionless; (*рассказ, исполнение*) bland.
невысо́к|ий (-ая, -ое, -ие; -, -а́, -о) *прил* low; (*человек*) short.
не́г|а (-и) *ж* bliss.
негати́в (-а) *м* (*ФОТО*) negative.
негати́в|ный (-ен, -на, -но) *прил* negative.
негашёный *прил*: **негашёная ма́рка** unused stamp; **негашёная и́звесть** quicklime.
не́где *как сказ* (+*infin*) there is nowhere to do; **мне ~ жить** I don't have anywhere to live; **здесь ~ купи́ть еды́** there is nowhere to buy food around here.
неги́бк|ий (-кая, -кое, -кие; -ок, -ка́, -ко) *прил* (*также перен*) inflexible.
негла́с|ный (-ен, -на, -но) *прил* secret.
неглубо́к|ий (-ая, -ое, -ие; -, -а́, -о́) *прил* (*яма, река*) shallow; (*знания, человек, чувство*) superficial; (*сон*) light.
неглу́п|ый (-, -а́, -о) *прил* fairly clever; **он о́чень неглу́п** he's by no means stupid.
него́ *мест от* **он, оно́**.
него́ден *прил см* **него́дный**.
него́дност|ь (-и) *ж* worthlessness; **приходи́ть (прийти́** *perf*) **в ~** (*оборудование*) to become defunct; (*одежда*) to be worn out.
него́д|ный (-ен, -на, -но) *прил* (*непригодный*) unusable; (*скверный*) good-for-nothing.
негодова́ни|е (-я) *ср* indignation.
негод|ова́ть (-у́ю) *несов неперех* to be indignant.
негоду́ющ|ий (-ая, -ее, -ие) *прил* indignant.
негодя́|й (-я) *м* scoundrel.
негр (-а) *м* black man (*мн* men).
негра́мот|ный (-ен, -на, -но) *прил* (*человек, ученик*) illiterate; (*содержащий ошибки: речь*) ungrammatical; (*специалист, работа*) incompetent.
негритёнок (-ёнка; *nom pl* **-я́та**, *gen pl* **-я́т**) *м* black child (*мн* children).
негритя́н|ка (-ки; *gen pl* **-ок**) *ж* black woman (*мн* women).
негритя́нск|ий (-ая, -ое, -ие) *прил* black.
негритя́та *итп сущ см* **негритёнок**.
негро́м|кий (-кая, -кое, -кие; -ок, -ка́, -ко) *прил* quiet.
не́гр|ы (-ов) *мн* black people *мн*.
неда́вн|ий (-яя, -ее, -ие) *прил* recent; **до ~его вре́мени** until recently.
неда́вно *нареч* recently.
недалёк|ий (-ая, -ое, -ие; -, -а́, -о́) *прил* (*место*) nearby; (*расстояние, путь*) short; (*недавний*) near; (-, -а, -о; *перен*: *человек, ум*) limited; **в ~ом бу́дущем** in the near future; **она́ недалека́ от и́стины** she is not far from the truth.
недалеко́ *нареч* (*жить, находиться*) nearby; (*идти, ехать*) not far ◆ *как сказ*: **~ (до** +*gen*) it isn't far (to); **~ от** +*gen* not far from; **до утра́ ~** it will soon be morning.
недальнови́д|ный (-ен, -на, -но) *прил* short-sighted.
неда́ром *нареч* (*не напрасно*) not in vain; (*не без цели*) for a reason; **я ~ сто́лько учи́лся** all of that studying has paid off; **я ~ прие́хал сего́дня** I do have a reason for coming today.
недви́жимост|ь (-и) *ж* property.
недви́жимый *прил*: **недви́жимое иму́щество = недви́жимость**.
недвижи́м|ый (-, -а, -о) *прил* (*неподвижный*) motionless; (*не способный двигаться: больной*) immobile.
недвусмы́слен|ный (-, -на, -но) *прил* unambiguous.
недееспосо́б|ный (-ен, -на, -но) *прил* (*ЮР*: *человек*) incapacitated; (: *организация, структура*) impotent, ineffective.
недействи́тел|ьный (-ен, -ьна, -ьно) *прил* invalid.
неделика́т|ный (-ен, -на, -но) *прил* (*человек*) tactless; (*замечание, вопрос*) indelicate, tactless.
недели́м|ый (-, -а, -о) *прил* indivisible; **недели́мое число́** prime number.
неде́льный *прил* (*срок, отпуск*) one-week; (*запас, заработок итп*) a *или* one week's.

неде́л|я (-и) *ж* week; **че́рез ~ю** in a week; **на про́шлой/э́той/сле́дующей ~е** last/this/next week.
недобо́р (-а) *м* shortage.
недоброжела́тел|ьный (-ен, -ьна, -ьно) *прил* hostile.
недоброка́чествен|ный (-, -на, -но) *прил* poor-quality.
недобросо́вест|ный (-ен, -на, -но) *прил* (*небрежный*) unconscientious; (*нечестный*) unscrupulous.
недо́бр|ый (-, -а́, -о) *прил* unkind; (*чувства, намерения*) ill; (*время, сон, предчувствие*) bad; **~ые ве́сти** ill tidings.
недова|ри́ть (-арю́, -а́ришь; *impf* **недова́ривать**) *сов перех* to undercook.
недове́ри|е (-я) *ср* mistrust, distrust; **относи́ться (отнести́сь** *perf*) **к кому́-н/чему́-н с ~м** to be mistrustful *или* distrustful of sb/sth.
недове́рчивост|ь (-и) *ж* mistrust, distrust.
недове́рчив|ый (-, -а, -о) *прил* mistrustful, distrustful.
недове́с (-а) *м* shortfall (*in weight*).
недове́|сить (-шу, -сишь; *impf* **недове́шивать**) *сов перех*: **~ кому́-н чего́-н** to give sb too little of sth.
недово́л|ьный (-ен, -ьна, -ьно) *прил* discontented, dissatisfied; **она́ всем ~ьна** she is never satisfied.
недово́льств|о (-а) *ср*: **~** (+*instr*) dissatisfaction (with).
недога́длив|ый (-, -а, -о) *прил* inscrutable.
недогля|де́ть (-жу́, -ди́шь) *сов перех* (*ошибки, опечатки*) to overlook ◆ *неперех*: **~ за** +*acc* to fail to keep an eye on.
недоговор|и́ть (-ю́, -и́шь; *impf* **недогова́ривать**) *сов перех* to leave unsaid; **он что́-то недогова́ривает** there is something that he's not saying.
недоде́лан|ный (-, -на, -но) *прил* unfinished.
недоде́л|ка (-ки; *gen pl* -ок) *ж* loose end.
недоеда́|ть *несов неперех* to eat badly; **они́ постоя́нно ~ют** they never eat enough.
недозре́лый *прил* unripe.
недоим|ка (-ки; *gen pl* -ок) *ж* arrears *мн*.
недока́зан|ный (-, -на, -но) *прил* unproven.
недо́л|гий (-гая, -гое, -гие; -ог, -га́, -го) *прил* short.
недо́лго *нареч* for a short time, not for long ◆ *как сказ* (*разг*): **мне ~ э́то сде́лать** it won't take me long (to do); **~ по́сле** +*gen* not long after; **я там бу́ду ~** I won't be there for long; **ему́ оста́лось ~ (жить)** he hasn't got long (to live).
недолгове́ч|ный (-ен, -на, -но) *прил* short-lived.
недо́лог *прил см* **недо́лгий**.
недолю́блива|ть (-ю) *несов перех* to dislike.
недомога́ни|е (-я) *ср* queasiness; **чу́вствовать** (*impf*) **~** to feel queasy.
недомога́|ть (-ю) *несов неперех* to feel unwell.
недомо́лв|ка (-ки; *gen pl* -ок) *ж* indirect reference; **говори́ть** (*impf*) **о чём-н ~ми** to refer to sth indirectly.
недомы́сли|е (-я) *ср*: **по ~ю** without thinking.
недоно́шен|ный (-, -а, -о) *прил*: **~ ребёнок** premature baby.
недооцени́ть (-еню́, -е́нишь; *impf* **недооце́нивать**) *сов перех* to underestimate.
недооце́нк|а (-и) *ж* underestimation.
недопусти́м|ый (-, -а, -о) *прил* not permissible.
недорабо́тк|а (-и) *ж* = **недоде́лка**.
недора́звит|ый (-, -а, -о) *прил* underdeveloped; (*разг*) dumb.
недоразуме́ни|е (-я) *ср* misunderstanding.
недо́рого *нареч* cheaply.
недорог|о́й (-, -а́, -о) *прил* inexpensive.
недоса́лива|ть (-ю) *несов от* **недосоли́ть**.
недосмо́тр (-а) *м* oversight; **по ~у** through lack of attention.
недосм|отре́ть (-отрю́, -о́тришь) *сов неперех* = **недогляде́ть**.
недос|оли́ть (-олю́, -о́лишь; *impf* **недоса́ливать**) *сов перех*: **ты ~оли́л суп** you haven't put enough salt in the soup.
недосп|а́ть (-лю́, -и́шь; *impf* **недосыпа́ть**) *сов неперех* to not get enough sleep.
недоста|ва́ть (*3sg* -ёт) *несов безл* (+*gen*; *не хватать*) to lack; (*быть нужным*) to need; **ей ~ёт терпе́ния** she lacks patience; **нам о́чень тебя́ ~ва́ло** we really needed you; **э́того ещё ~ва́ло!** as if that were not enough!
недоста́т|ок (-ка; *nom pl* -ки) *м* shortage, lack; (*в характере, в работе*) shortcoming.
недоста́точен *прил см* **недоста́точный**.
недоста́точно *нареч* insufficiently ◆ *как сказ* (+*gen*): **у нас ~ еды́/де́нег** we don't have enough food/money; **я ~ зна́ю об э́том** I don't know enough about it; **~ критикова́ть, на́до помо́чь** it's not enough to criticize, you need to help.
недоста́точност|ь (-и) *ж* inadequacy; **серде́чная ~** heart failure.
недоста́точ|ный (-ен, -на, -но) *прил* insufficient.
недоста́ч|а (-и) *ж* (*разг*: *материалов, оборудования*) lack; (*денег*: *при проверке*) shortfall; **у нас в ка́ссе ~ де́нег** the till is short.
недостаю́щ|ий (-ая, -ое, -ие) *прил* missing.
недостижи́м|ый (-, -а, -о) *прил* (*высота, уровень*) unreachable; (*мечта, идеал*) unattainable.
недостове́р|ный (-ен, -на, -но) *прил* unreliable.
недосто́|йный (-ен, -йна, -йно) *прил*: **~** (+*gen*) unworthy (of).

недосту́п|ный (-ен, -на, -но) *прил (также перен)* inaccessible; (*цена*) unaffordable; (*человек*) unapproachable; **э́то ~но моему́ понима́нию** it is beyond my understanding.
недосу́г *как сказ*: **ему́ ~ (+*infin* ...)** (*разг*) he can never find the time (to ...).
недосчита́|ться (-юсь; *impf* **недосчи́тываться)** *сов возв* (+*gen*) to be short; **я ~лся пяти́ до́лларов** I'm five dollars short; **мы ~лись двух челове́к** we are missing two people.
недосыпа́|ть (-ю) *несов от* **недоспа́ть.**
недосяга́ем|ый (-, -а, -о) *прил* unattainable.
недотро́г|а (-и) *м/ж* (*разг*): **он тако́й ~** he's very touchy.
недоумева́|ть (-ю) *несов неперех* to be perplexed *или* bewildered.
недоумева́ющ|ий (-ая, -ее, -ие) *прил* perplexed, bewildered.
недоуме́ни|е (-я) *ср* perplexity, bewilderment.
недоуме́нный *прил* perplexed, bewildered.
недоу́ч|ка (-ки; *gen pl* **-ек)** *м/ж* (*разг*): **он/она́ ~** he/she is badly educated.
недочёт (-а) *м* (*в подсчётах*) shortfall; (*обычно мн*: *в работе*) deficiency.
не́др|а (-) *мн* depths *мн*; **в ~х земли́** in the bowels of the earth; **в ~х души́** in the depths of one's soul; **в ~х о́бщества** at the heart of society.
недре́млющ|ий (-ая, -ее, -ие) *прил* vigilant.
не́друг (-а) *м* foe.
недружелю́б|ный (-ен, -на, -но) *прил* unfriendly.
неду́г (-а) *м* ailment.
неду́рно *нареч* not badly.
недур|но́й (-ён, -на́, -но) *прил* not bad; **он ~ён собо́й** he's not bad-looking.
неё *мест см* **она́.**
естéствен|ный (-, -на, -но) *прил* unnatural.
нежда́н|ный (-ен, -на, -но) *прил* unexpected.
нежела́ни|е (-я) *ср* unwillingness.
нежела́тел|ьный (-ен, -ьна, -ьно) *прил* undesirable.
не́жен *прил см* **не́жный.**
нежена́т|ый *прил* unmarried.
не́жен|ка (-ки; *gen pl* **-ок)** *м/ж* (*разг*) softy.
неживо́й *прил* dead; (*природа, мир*) inorganic; (*перен*: *взгляд, голос*) lifeless.
нежизнеспосо́б|ный (-ен, -на, -но) *прил* (*организм, растение*) incapable of surviving; (*перен*: *теория*) impractical.
нежило́й *прил* nonresidential.
не́ж|иться (-усь, -ишься) *несов возв* to laze about; **~ (*impf*) на со́лнце** to bask in the sun.
не́жнича|ть (-ю) *несов неперех* (*разг*): **~ с** +*instr* to make a fuss of.
не́жност|ь (-и) *ж* tenderness; **шепта́ть (*impf*) ~и кому́-н на́ ухо** to whisper sweet nothings in sb's ear.
не́жно *нареч* gently.
не́ж|ный (-ен, -на́, -но) *прил* tender, gentle; (*кожа, пух*) soft; (*запах*) subtle; (*сложение, здоровье*) fragile.
незабве́н|ный (-ен, -на, -но) *прил* beloved.
незабу́д|ка (-ки; *gen pl* **-ок)** *ж* forget-me-not.
незабыва́ем|ый (-, -а, -о) *прил* unforgettable.
незави́д|ный (-ен, -на, -но) *прил* unenviable.
незави́симо *нареч* independently; **~ от** +*gen* (*условий, времени*) regardless of.
незави́симост|ь (-и) *ж* independence.
незави́сим|ый (-, -а, -о) *прил* independent.
незави́сящ|ий (-ая, -ее, -ие) *прил*: **по ~им от нас обстоя́тельствам** due to circumstances beyond our control.
незада́ч|а (-и) *ж* (*разг*) pain.
незада́члив|ый (-, -а, -о) *прил* (*разг*) unlucky.
незадо́лго *нареч*: **~ до** +*gen или* **пе́ред** +*instr* shortly before.
незаинтересо́ван|ный (-, -на, -но) *прил* (*ученик, слушатели итп*) indifferent; (*лицо, сторона*) disinterested.
незако́нност|ь (-и) *ж* illegality.
незако́н|ный (-ен, -на, -но) *прил* illegal; (*ребёнок*) illegitimate.
незако́нчен|ный (-, -на, -но) *прил* unfinished, incomplete.
незамедли́тел|ьный (-ен, -ьна, -ьно) *прил* immediate.
незамени́м|ый (-, -а, -о) *прил* irreplaceable.
незаме́тен *прил см* **незаме́тный.**
незаме́тно *нареч* (*изменяться*) imperceptibly ◆ *как сказ* it isn't noticeable; **он ~ подошёл/ушёл** he approached/left unnoticed; **~, что ты всю ночь не спал** you may not have slept all night, but it doesn't show.
незаме́т|ный (-ен, -на, -но) *прил* not noticeable; (*перемены, изменения*) imperceptible; (*перен*: *человек, внешность*) unremarkable.
незаме́чен|ный (-, -на, -но) *прил* unnoticed.
незаму́жняя *прил* unmarried.
незамыслова́т|ый (-, -а, -о) *прил* uncomplicated.
неза́нят|ый *прил* (*дом, помещение*) unoccupied; (*человек, работник*) not occupied; (*вечер, утро*) free; **~ая часть населе́ния** the non-working population.
незапа́мятн|ый *прил*: **с ~ых времён** from time immemorial; **в ~ые времена́** in the days of yore.
незара́з|ный (-ен, -на, -но) *прил* noncontagious.
незаслу́жен|ный (-, -на, -но) *прил* undeserved.
незауря́д|ный (-ен, -на, -но) *прил* exceptional.
не́зачем *как сказ* (*разг*): **~ ходи́ть/э́то де́лать** there's no reason to go/do it.
незва́ный *прил* uninvited.
нездоро́в|иться (*3sg* -ится) *несов безл*: **мне ~ится** I feel unwell, I don't feel well.
нездоро́в|ый (-, -а, -о) *прил* unhealthy; **он нездоро́в** he isn't well; **у него́ ~ цвет лица́** his face is an unhealthy colour; **у неё ~ вид** she doesn't look well.
неземно́й *прил* (*тело, объект итп*) alien;

(*силы, красота*) unearthly.
незнако́м|ец (-ца) *м* stranger.
незнако́м|ка (-ки; *gen pl* **-ок)** *ж см* **незнако́мец.**
незнако́мца *итп сущ см* **незнако́мец.**
незнако́м|ый (-, -а, -о) *прил* unfamiliar; **я незнако́м с ним** I am not acquainted with him; **я незнако́м с э́тими фа́ктами** I am not familiar with these facts.
незна́ни|е (-я) *ср* ignorance.
незна́чащ|ий (-ая, -ее, -ие) *прил* meaningless.
незначи́тел|ьный (-ен, -ьна, -ьно) *прил* (*небольшой*) insignificant; (*несущественный*) trivial.
незре́л|ый (-, -а, -о) *прил* (*яблоко итп*) unripe; (*человек, книга*) immature; (*мысль*) half-formed.
незри́м|ый (-, -а, -о) *прил* anonymous; (*бой*) hidden.
незы́блем|ый (-, -а, -о) *прил* unshakable.
неизбе́жен *прил см* **неизбе́жный.**
неизбе́жно *как сказ*: **э́то ~** it's inevitable.
неизбе́ж|ный (-ен, -на, -но) *прил* inescapable, inevitable.
неизве́дан|ный (-, -на, -но) *прил* (*путь, пространство*) unexplored; (*счастье, чувство*) new.
неизве́стен *прил см* **неизве́стный.**
неизве́стно *как сказ* it's not known; **никому́ ~** nobody knows; **~ кто/что/почему́** Heaven (only) knows who/what/why.
неизве́стн|ое (-ого; *decl like adj*) *ср* (*МАТ*) unknown.
неизве́стност|ь (-и) *ж* uncertainty; (*незаметное существование*) obscurity.
неизве́ст|ный (-ен, -на, -но) *прил* unknown ◆ **(-ного;** *decl like adj*) *м* stranger.
неизглади́м|ый (-, -а, -о) *прил* indelible.
неизлечи́м|ый (-, -а, -о) *прил* (*болезнь*) incurable; (*больной*) terminally ill.
неизме́н|ный (-ен, -на, -но) *прил* (*постоянный*) unchanging; (*верный*) steadfast.
неизменяе́м|ый (-, -а, -о) *прил* invariable.
неизмери́мо *нареч* immeasurably.
неизмери́м|ый (-, -а, -о) *прил* immeasurable.
неизу́ченный *прил* (*вопрос, проблема*) unexplored.
неиме́ни|е (-я) *ср*: **за ~м** *+gen* for want of; **за ~м лу́чшего** for want of something better.
неимове́р|ный (-ен, -на, -но) *прил* extreme.
неиму́щ|ий (-ая, -ее, -ие) *прил* deprived.
неинтере́с|ный (-ен, -на, -но) *прил* boring, uninteresting; (*некрасивый*) plain.
неискорени́м|ый (-, -а, -о) *прил* deep-rooted.
нейскрен|ний (-няя, -нее, -ние; -ен, -на, -но *или* **не)** *прил* insincere.
неискушённый *прил* unsophisticated.
неисполне́ни|е (-я) *ср* failure to carry out.
неисполни́м|ый (-, -а, -о) *прил* unrealizable.
неиспо́льзованный *прил* unused.
неиспо́рченный *прил* (*человек*) innocent.
неиспра́вен *прил см* **неиспра́вный.**
неисправи́м|ый (-, -а, -о) *прил* (*ошибка*) irreversible; (*пьяница*) incorrigible.
неиспра́вност|ь (-и) *ж* (*механизма, станка*) fault.
неиспра́в|ный (-ен, -на, -но) *прил* (*механизм, станок*) faulty; (*плательщик, поставщик*) unreliable.
неиспы́танный *прил* (*самолёт, машина*) untested; (*чувство, счастье*) unexperienced.
неиссле́дованный *прил* (*вопрос, район*) unexplored.
неиссяка́ем|ый (-, -а, -о) *прил* inexhaustible.
неи́стовств|о (-а) *ср* (*исступление*) frenzy; (*жестокость*) atrocity; **приходи́ть (прийти́** *perf*) **в ~** to go into a frenzy.
неи́стовств|овать (-ую) *несов неперех* to be in a frenzy; (*перен: буря, метель*) to rage; (: *каратели*) to commit atrocities.
неи́стов|ый (-, -а, -о) *прил* (*ужас, радость*) intense; (*крики*) frenzied; (*аплодисменты, буря*) wild; (*грохот*) crashing.
неистощи́м|ый (-, -а, -о) *прил* inexhaustible.
неисчерпа́ем|ый (-, -а, -о) *прил* inexhaustible.
неисчисли́м|ый (-, -а, -о) *прил* (*силы*) countless; (*неприятности*) innumerable.
ней *мест см* **она́.**
нейло́н (-а) *м* nylon.
нейло́новый *прил* nylon *опред.*
нейрохиру́рг (-а) *м* neurosurgeon.
нейрохирурги́|я (-и) *ж* neurosurgery.
нейтра́лен *прил см* **нейтра́льный.**
нейтрализа́ци|я (-и) *ж* neutrality.
нейтрализ|ова́ть (-у́ю) (*не*)*сов перех* to neutralize.
нейтралите́т (-а) *м* neutrality.
нейтра́л|ьный (-ен, -ьна, -ьно) *прил* neutral.
нейтро́н (-а) *м* neutron.
неказ́ист|ый (-, -а, -о) *прил* unsightly.
нека́чественно *нареч*: **~ сде́ланный** badly made.
нека́чествен|ный (-ен, -на, -но) *прил* poor-quality.
неквалифици́рован|ный (-, -на, -но) *прил* (*работник*) unqualified, unskilled; (*работа*) unskilled.
не́кем *мест см* **не́кого.**
не́к|ий (-ого; *f* **-ая,** *nt* **-ое,** *pl* **-ие)** *мест* a certain; (*момент, время*) some.
не́когда *как сказ* (*читать, гулять*) there is no time; **ей ~** she is busy; **ей ~** *+infin* ... she has no time to ....
не́кого (*как* **кто**; *см* **Table 6**) *мест*: **~ спроси́ть/позва́ть** there is nobody to ask/call.
некомпете́нт|ный (-ен, -на, -но) *прил* (*человек*) incompetent; (*суждение*)

inappropriate.
не́кому *мест см* **не́кого.**
не́котор|ые (-ых) *мест* (*отдельные*) several.
не́котор|ый (-ого; *f* -ая, *nt* -ое, *pl* -ые) *мест* some; **с ~ых пор** for some time; **в ~ой сте́пени** to a certain degree; **в ~ом ро́де** somewhat; **~ым о́бразом** somehow; *см также* **не́которые.**
некраси́в|ый (-, -а, -о) *прил* (*человек, лицо*) unattractive, ugly; (*поступок, поведение*) ugly.
некроло́г (-а) *м* obituary.
некста́ти *нареч* (*сказать, явиться итп*) at the wrong time ♦ *как сказ*: **э́то ~** this is untimely.
некта́р (-а) *м* nectar.
не́кто *мест* a certain person (*мн* certain people).
не́куда *как сказ* (*идти, поехать*) there is nowhere; **да́льше** *или* **хуже́/лу́чше ~** (*разг*) it can't get any worse/better.
некульту́р|ный (-ен, -на, -но) *прил* (*растение*) uncultivated; (*человек, поведение*) uncivilized.
некуря́щ|ий (-его; *decl like adj*) *м* non-smoker; ♦ (-ая, -ее, -ие) *прил*: **~ мужчи́на, некуря́щая же́нщина** non-smoker.
нела́дно *как сказ* (*в семье, на душе*) there's unease.
нелад|ы́ (-о́в) *мн* (*разг*: *в семье, в коллективе*) tension *ед*; (: *с учёбой, с работой*) problems *мн*.
нелега́л|ьный (-ен, -ьна, -ьно) *прил* (*газета, въезд*) illegal.
нелегити́м|ный (-ен, -на, -но) *прил* illegitimate.
нелёг|кий (-кая, -кое, -кие; -ок, -ка́, -ко́) *прил* (*ноша, груз*) heavy; (*задание, работа*) difficult.
нелегко́ *как сказ* it's not easy; **мне нелегко́ согласи́ться на э́то** it's not easy for me to agree to this.
неле́пост|ь (-и) *ж* stupidity; **говори́ть** (*impf*)**/де́лать** (*impf*) **~и** to say/do stupid things.
неле́п|ый (-, -а, -о) *прил* stupid.
нeléст|ный (-ен, -на, -но) *прил* (*высказывание, характеристика*) unflattering.
нелётн|ый *прил*: **~ая пого́да** poor weather for flying; **~ое вре́мя** not a good time to fly.
нело́в|кий (-кая, -кое, -кие; -ок, -ка́, -ко) *прил* awkward; **нело́вкое положе́ние** awkward situation.
нело́вко *нареч* awkwardly ♦ *как сказ* (*говорить, просить*) it's awkward; **мне ~ (перед ней)** I feel awkward (with her).
нело́вкост|ь (-и) *ж* awkwardness; **чу́вствовать (почу́вствовать** *perf*) **~** to feel awkward.
нело́вок *прил см* **нело́вкий.**
нелоги́ч|ный (-ен, -на, -но) *прил* (*довод, доказательство*) illogical.
нельзя́ *как сказ* (*невозможно*) it is impossible; (*не разрешается*) it is forbidden; **~ ли?** would it be possible?; **~ сказа́ть, что она́ умна́** she can hardly be described as clever; **как ~ лу́чше** as well as could be expected.
нелюби́м|ый (-, -а, -о) *прил* unloved.
нелюди́м|ый (-, -а, -о) *прил* (*человек, сосед*) unsociable.
нём *мест см* **он, оно́.**
нема́ло *нареч* (+*gen*; *денег*) a good deal of; (*идей, людей, книг*) a good few.
немалова́ж|ный (-ен, -на, -но) *прил* significant.
нема́л|ый *прил* (*доход*) reasonable; (*труд*) much; (*успех*) considerable; (*чин, должность*) important; **~ые де́ньги** a sizeable sum of money.
неме́дленен *прил см* **неме́дленный.**
неме́дленно *нареч* immediately.
неме́длен|ный (-ен, -на, -но) *прил* immediate.
неме́ркнущ|ий (-ая, -ее, -ие) *прил* (*также перен*) unfading.
немета́лл (-а) *м* (*хим*) nonmetal.
неме́|ть (-ю; *perf* **онеме́ть**) *несов неперех* (*от ужаса, от восторга*) to be struck dumb; (*нога, руки*) to go numb.
не́м|ец (-ца) *м* German.
неме́цк|ий (-ая, -ое, -ие) *прил* German; **~ язы́к** German.
неми́лост|ь (-и) *ж* disfavour; **впада́ть (впасть** *perf*) **в ~** to fall out of favour (*BRIT*) *или* favor (*US*).
немину́ем|ый (-, -а, -о) *прил* (*беда, события*) unavoidable.
не́м|ка (-ки; *gen pl* -ок) *ж см* **не́мец.**
немно́г|ие (-их; *decl like adj*) *мн* few.
немно́г|ий (-ая, -ое, -ие) *прил* (*части, слова, люди*) a few; **~им ху́же/лу́чше/бо́льше/ ме́ньше** a little worse/better/more/less; **за ~им исключе́нием** with few exceptions.
немно́го *нареч* (*отдохнуть, старше*) a little, a bit; (*друзей, слов*) a few.
немно́г|ое (-ого; *decl like adj*) *ср* (*можно сказать, увидеть*) little.
немногосло́в|ный (-ен, -на, -но) *прил* (*отзыв, изложение*) brief; (*человек*) laconic.
немногочислен|ный (-, -на, -но) *прил* (*ошибки*) few; **на дипломати́ческом приёме бы́ло ~ное о́бщество** there weren't many (people present) at the diplomatic reception.
немно́жко *нареч* (*разг*) = **немно́го.**
немну́щ|ийся (-аяся, -ееся, -иеся) *прил* (*брюки, материя, юбка*) crease-resistant.
нем|о́й (-, -а́, -о) *прил* (*человек*) dumb; (*перен*: *ночь, лес, глубина*) silent; (: *вопрос, упрёк*) implied ♦ (-о́го; *decl like adj*) *м* mute; **нема́я сце́на** *situation in which somebody freezes in surprise, shock etc*; **немо́й фильм** silent film.
нем|олодо́й (-о́лод, -олода́, -о́лодо) *прил* old.
немот|а́ (-ы́) *ж* (*ребёнка, мужчины*) dumbness.
не́мощ|ный (-ен, -на, -но) *прил* (*старик, человек*) sick, ailing.
нему́ *мест от* **он, оно́.**
немудрён|ый (-, -а, -о) *прил* (*разг*) simple.
не́мца *итп сущ см* **не́мец.**
немы́слим|ый (-, -а, -о) *прил* unthinkable.
ненави́|деть (-жу, -дишь) *несов перех* to hate.
ненави́ст|ный (-ен, -на, -но) *прил* (*человек, работа*) hateful.

не́нависть|ь (-и) *ж* hatred.
ненагля́дный *прил* (*разг*) beloved.
ненадёж|ный (-ен, -на, -но) *прил* (*человек, сведения*) unreliable; (*механизм*) unsafe.
нена́добност|ь (-и) *ж*: **вы́бросить что-н за ~ю** to throw sth out *или* away because it is not needed.
ненадо́лго *нареч* for a short while.
ненападе́ни|е (-я) *ср* nonaggression.
ненаро́ком *нареч* (*разг*: *случайно*) without meaning to.
нена́ст|ный (-ен, -на, -но) *прил* (*день, осень*) wet and dismal.
ненастоя́щ|ий (-ая, -ее, -ие) *прил* (*мех, золото*) artificial; (*дружба, любовь*) contrived.
нена́стье|е (-я) *ср* awful weather.
ненасы́т|ный (-ен, -на, -но) *прил* (*также перен*) insatiable.
ненатура́л|ьный (-ен, -ьна, -ьно) *прил* (*мех, свет*) artificial; (*смех*) forced; (*поведение*) affected.
ненорма́лен *прил см* **ненорма́льный**.
ненорма́льност|ь (-и) *ж* abnormality.
ненорма́л|ьный (-ен, -ьна, -ьно) *прил* abnormal; (*разг*: *сумасшедший*) mad ◆ (-ьного; *decl like adj*) *м* (*разг*) crackpot.
нену́ж|ный (-ен, -на́, -но) *прил* (*осторожность*) unnecessary; (*человек*) dispensable; (*инструмент*) inessential.
необду́манно *нареч* (*поступить*) rashly.
необду́ман|ный (-, -на, -но) *прил* ill-considered.
необеспе́ченный *прил* poor.
необита́ем|ый (-, -а, -о) *прил* (*место*) uninhabited; **~ о́стров** desert island.
необозри́м|ый (-, -а, -о) *прил* (*просторы, дали*) vast.
необосно́ван|ный (-, -на, -но) *прил* unfounded.
необрабо́танный *прил* (*земля*) uncultivated; (*деталь*) unfinished; (*металл, дерево*) untreated.
необразо́ван|ный (-, -на, -но) *прил* uneducated.
необу́здан|ный (-, -на, -но) *прил* (*страсть*) unbridled; (*человек, характер*) ungovernable.
необходи́мо *как сказ* it is necessary; **мне ~ с Ва́ми поговори́ть** I really need to talk to you.
необходи́мост|ь (-и) *ж* (*увидеть, сделать*) need, necessity; **~ в** *+prp* need for; **по ме́ре ~и** as (far as is) necessary; **по ~и** out of necessity; **предме́ты пе́рвой ~и** bare essentials.
необходи́м|ый (-, -а, -о) *прил* necessary.
необщи́тел|ьный (-ен, -ьна, -ьно) *прил* unsociable.
необъекти́в|ный (-ен, -на, -но) *прил* (*отношение, критика*) not objective, bias(s)ed.
необъясни́м|ый (-, -а, -о) *прил* inexplicable.
необъя́т|ный (-ен, -на, -но) *прил* (*просторы, дали, познания*) vast.
необыкнове́н|ный (-ен, -на, -но) *прил* exceptional.
необыча́|йный (-ен, -йна, -йно) *прил* = **необыкнове́нный**.
необы́ч|ный (-ен, -на, -но) *прил* (*человек, явление*) unusual.
необяза́тел|ьный (-ен, -ьна, -ьно) *прил* (*предмет, лекция*) optional; (*факты*) nonessential; (*человек*) unreliable.
неограни́чен|ный (-, -на, -но) *прил* unlimited; **неограни́ченная мона́рхия** absolute monarchy.
неодина́ков|ый (-, -а, -о) *прил* (*размер*) different.
неоднокра́тен *прил см* **неоднокра́тный**.
неоднокра́тно *нареч* (*говорить*) repeatedly; (*повторять*) time after time.
неоднокра́т|ный (-ен, -на, -но) *прил* repeated.
неодноро́д|ный (-ен, -на, -но) *прил* (*масса*) heterogeneous; (*тесто*) mixed; (*явления*) dissimilar.
неодобре́ни|е (-я) *ср* disapproval.
неодобри́тел|ьный (-ен, -ьна, -ьно) *прил* disapproving.
неодоли́м|ый (-, -а, -о) *прил* (*упорство, страх*) insurmountable; (*сила*) invincible.
неодушевлённый *прил* inanimate.
неожи́данно *нареч* unexpectedly.
неожи́данност|ь (-и) *ж* (*атаки*) unexpectedness; (*приятная, большая*) surprise; **вздра́гивать (вздро́гнуть** *perf*) **от ~и** to start in surprise.
неожи́дан|ный (-, -на, -но) *прил* unexpected.
неоконча́тел|ьный (-ен, -ьна, -ьно) *прил* (*вариант, решение*) not final.
неоко́нченный *прил* unfinished.
неоли́т (-а) *м* Neolithic.
неологи́зм (-а) *м* neologism.
нео́н (-а) *м* (*хим*) neon.
неонаци́зм (-а) *м* Neo-Nazism.
нео́новый *прил* neon *опред*.
неопа́сен *прил см* **неопа́сный**.
неопа́сно *нареч* safely ◆ *как сказ* it's safe, it's not dangerous.
неопа́с|ный (-ен, -на, -но) *прил* (*путешествие, место*) safe; (*противник, заболевание*) harmless.
неопису́ем|ый (-, -а, -о) *прил* indescribable.
неопла́т|ный (-ен, -на, -но) *прил*: **~ долг** debt that cannot be repaid; **я твой ~ должни́к** I'm greatly indebted to you.
неопла́ченный *прил* unpaid.
неопо́знан|ный (-, -на, -но) *прил* unidentified.
неопра́вданный *прил* (*вывод, обвинение*) unjustified; (*траты, потери*) unwarranted.
неопределённост|ь (-и) *ж* uncertainty.

неопределён|ный (-, -на, -но) *прил* (*время, срок*) indefinite; (*путь*) undecided; (*ответ, выражение, жест*) vague; (*звук*) indistinct.
неопровержи́м|ый (-, -а, -о) *прил* irrefutable.
неопря́т|ный (-ен, -на, -но) *прил* untidy.
неопублико́ванный *прил* unpublished.
нео́пытен *прил см* **нео́пытный.**
нео́пытност|ь (-и) *ж* inexperience.
нео́пыт|ный (-ен, -на, -но) *прил* inexperienced.
неорганизо́ванный *прил* disorganized; (*массы*) unorganized.
неоргани́ческ|ий (-ая, -ое, -ие) *прил* inorganic.
неосведомлённый *прил* ill-informed.
неосла́б|ный (-ен, -на, -но) *прил* (*надзор*) constant; (*контроль*) unrelenting.
неосмотри́тел|ьный (-ен, -ьна, -ьно) *прил* (*человек*) careless; (*поступок*) imprudent.
неоспори́м|ый (-, -а, -о) *прил* (*преимущество*) unquestionable; (*доказательство*) incontrovertible.
неосторо́жен *прил см* **неосторо́жный.**
неосторо́жност|ь (-и) *ж* carelessness.
неосторо́ж|ный (-ен, -на, -но) *прил* (*поступок*) careless; (*поведение, высказывание*) imprudent.
неосуществи́м|ый (-, -а, -о) *прил* unrealizable, unattainable.
неотврати́м|ый (-, -а, -о) *прил* inevitable.
неотдели́м|ый (-, -а, -о) *прил*: **~ (от** *+gen***)** inseparable (from).
неотёсан|ный (-, -а, -о) *прил* unpolished; (*перен*: *разг*) crude.
не́откуда *как сказ*: **мне** *итп* **де́нег взять ~** I *итп* can't get money from anywhere.
неотло́жен *прил см* **неотло́жный.**
неотло́жк|а (-и) *ж* (*разг*: *учреждение*) ambulance service; (: *машина*) emergency medical care.
неотло́ж|ный (-ен, -на, -но) *прил* urgent; **неотло́жная медици́нская по́мощь** emergency medical service.
неотрази́м|ый (-, -а, -о) *прил* (*атака, красота*) irresistible; (*перен*: *довод*) compelling; (*удар, впечатление*) powerful.
неотсту́п|ный (-ен, -на, -но) *прил* (*мечта, мысль*) constant; (*преследование*) relentless.
неотъе́млем|ый (-, -а, -о) *прил* (*право*) inalienable; (*часть*) integral.
неофаши́зм (-а) *м* Neo-fascism.
неофаши́ст (-а) *м* Neo-fascist.
неофаши́стск|ий (-ая, -ое, -ие) *прил* Neo-fascist.
неофициа́л|ьный (-ен, -ьна, -ьно) *прил* unofficial.
неохо́т|а (-ы) *ж* (*разг*: *нежелание*) reluctance ◆ *как сказ*: **мне ~ спо́рить** I don't feel like arguing.
неохо́тно *нареч* reluctantly.
неохо́тный *прил* reluctant.
неоцени́м|ый (-, -а, -о) *прил* invaluable.
неощути́м|ый (-, -а, -о) *прил* (*незаметный*) imperceptible.
Непа́л (-а) *м* Nepal.
непа́льск|ий (-ая, -ое, -ие) *прил* Nepalese.
непа́рный *прил* (*перчатки, ботинки*) odd.
непереводи́м|ый (-, -а, -о) *прил* untranslatable.
непередава́ем|ый (-, -а, -о) *прил* (*страх, впечатление*) inexpressible.
неперехо́дный *прил*: **~ глаго́л** (*лингв*) intransitive verb.
непеча́тный *прил* (*разг*) unprintable.
непи́саный *прил* unwritten.
неплат|ёж (-ежа́) *м* nonpayment.
неплатёжеспосо́б|ный (-ен, -на, -но) *прил* (*человек*) unable to pay; (*предприятие*) insolvent.
неплате́льщик (-а) *м* (*налогов, алиментов*) defaulter.
неплате́льщиц|а (-ы) *ж см* **неплате́льщик.**
неплодоро́д|ный (-ен, -на, -но) *прил* infertile, barren.
непло́тно *нареч* not tightly *или* firmly.
непло́хо *нареч* not badly, quite well ◆ *как сказ* it's not bad.
непл|охо́й (-о́х, -оха́, -о́хо) *прил* not bad, quite good.
непобеди́м|ый (-, -а, -о) *прил* invincible.
неповинове́ни|е (-я) *ср* disobedience, insubordination.
неповоро́тлив|ый (-, -а, -о) *прил* (*неуклюжий*) clumsy; (*медлительный*) slow.
неповтори́м|ый (-, -а, -о) *прил* unique.
непого́д|а (-ы) *ж* bad weather.
непогреши́м|ый (-, -а, -о) *прил* infallible.
неподалёку *нареч* (*разг*) not far off ◆ *предл*: **~ от** *+gen* not far from.
неподви́жен *прил см* **неподви́жный.**
неподви́жно *нареч* without moving.
неподви́ж|ный (-ен, -на, -но) *прил* (*больной, рука, туман*) motionless; (*взгляд*) fixed; (*лицо*) rigid; (*медлительный*) slow.
неподдающ|ийся (-аяся, -ееся, -иеся) *прил* (*разг*: *перевоспитанию, лечению*) resistant, unresponsive.
неподде́л|ьный (-ен, -ьна, -ьно) *прил* (*также перен*) genuine.
неподку́п|ный (-ен, -на, -но) *прил* (*человек, ревизор*) incorruptible; (*совесть, принципы*) honourable (*BRIT*), honorable (*US*).
неподража́ем|ый (-, -а, -о) *прил* inimitable.
неподходя́щ|ий (-ая, -ее, -ие) *прил* (*место*) unsuitable; (*время*) inappropriate.
неподчине́ни|е (-я) *ср* (*закону, властям*) insubordination.
неподъём|ный (-ен, -на, -но) *прил* (*разг*) very heavy.
непозволи́тел|ьный (-ен, -ьна, -ьно) *прил* inadmissible.
непоколеби́м|ый (-, -а, -о) *прил* unshakable.
непоко́р|ный (-ен, -на, -но) *прил* (*конь, слуга*) recalcitrant; (*характер, нрав*) rebellious.
непокры́т|ый *прил*: **с ~ой голово́й**

bareheaded.
непола́д|ки (-ок) *мн* fault *ед*, defect *ед*; (*разг: в семье*) quarrel *ед*.
неполнопра́в|ный (-ен, -на, -но) *прил* not possessing full rights.
неполнот|а́ (-ы́) *ж* incompleteness.
неполноце́нност|ь (-и) *ж* lack; **ко́мплекс ~и** inferiority complex.
неполноце́н|ный (-ен, -на, -но) *прил* insufficient.
непо́л|ный (-он, -на́, -но) *прил* (*чашка, мешок*) not full; (*список, перечень, данные*) incomplete.
непоме́р|ный (-ен, -на, -но) *прил* excessive.
непонима́ни|е (-я) *ср* (*задачи, происходящее*) incomprehension; (*равнодушие*) indifference.
непоня́тен *прил см* **непоня́тный**.
непоня́тлив|ый (-, -а, -о) *прил* (*ученик, студент*) slow on the uptake, dull.
непоня́тно *нареч* incomprehensibly ◆ *как сказ* it is incomprehensible; **мне ~, что происхо́дит** I cannot understand what is going on.
непоня́т|ный (-ен, -на, -но) *прил* incomprehensible.
непоправи́м|ый (-, -а, -о) *прил* (*ошибка*) irreparable; (*шаг, несчастье*) irreversible.
непоро́ч|ный (-ен, -на, -но) *прил* pure, chaste.
непоря́д|ок (-ка; *nom pl* -ки) *м* disorder.
непоря́доч|ный (-ен, -на, -но) *прил* (*человек, поведение*) dishonourable (*BRIT*), dishonorable (*US*).
непосе́д|а (-ы) *м/ж* (*разг*) fidget.
непосе́длив|ый (-, -а, -о) *прил* restless.
непоси́л|ьный (-ен, -ьна, -ьно) *прил* (*труд, задача*) beyond one's strength.
непосле́довательност|ь (-и) *ж* inconsistency.
непосле́довател|ьный (-ен, -ьна, -ьно) *прил* inconsistent.
непослуша́ни|е (-я) *ср* (*детей, подчинённых*) disobedience.
непослу́ш|ный (-ен, -на, -но) *прил* (*ребёнок, собака*) disobedient; (*перен: волосы, кудри*) unmanageable.
непосре́дственност|ь (-и) *ж* spontaneity.
непосре́дствен|ный *прил* (*начальник*) immediate; (*результат, свидетель, участник*) direct; (-ен, -на, -но; *натура, тон*) spontaneous.
непостижи́м|ый (-, -а, -о) *прил* (*загадка, сила*) incomprehensible; **уму́ ~о** it's incomprehensible.
непостоя́н|ный (-ен, -на, -но) *прил* changeable.
непостоя́нств|о (-а) *ж* inconstancy, changeability.
непотре́б|ный (-ен, -на, -но) *прил* (*разг*) indecent.
непохо́ж|ий (-ая, -ее, -ие; -, -а, -е) *прил* dissimilar.
непоча́т|ый (-, -а, -о) *прил* (*бутылка, пачка*) unopened; (*чашка кофе*) full, untouched; (*перен: силы*) unused; (*: запас, энергии*) untapped; **непоча́тый край** no end, a great deal.
непочте́ни|е (-я) *ср* disrespect.
непочти́тельно *нареч* disrespectfully.
непра́в (-а́, -о, -ы) *как сказ:* **ты ~** you are wrong.
непра́вд|а (-ы) *ж* lie, untruth ◆ *как сказ* it's not true; **э́то ~!** it's *или* this is a lie!
неправдоподо́б|ный (-ен, -на, -но) *прил* (*история, рассказ*) improbable, implausible.
непра́вилен *прил см* **непра́вильный**.
непра́вильно *нареч* (*решить*) incorrectly, wrongly ◆ *как сказ:* **э́то ~** it's wrong; **~ ду́мать, что ...** it's wrong to think that ...; **~ понима́ть** (**поня́ть** *perf*) to misunderstand; **~ написа́ть** (*perf*) to misspell.
непра́вил|ьный (-ен, -ьна, -ьно) *прил* (*решение, произношение, идея*) wrong; (*черты лица, форма*) irregular; **непра́вильная дробь** (*МАТ*) improper fraction.
неправоме́р|ный (-ен, -на, -но) *прил* unjustifiable.
неправомо́ч|ный (-ен, -на, -но) *прил* (*неправомо́чная организа́ция*) *organization without legal authority*.
непревзойдён|ный (-, -на, -но) *прил* (*рекорд, мастерство*) unsurpassed; (*тупость, жестокость*) unprecedented.
непредви́денный *прил* unforeseen.
непреднаме́рен|ный (-, -на, -но) *прил* unpremeditated.
непредсказу́ем|ый (-, -а, -о) *прил* unpredictable.
непредубеждённый *прил* unbias(s)ed.
непредусмо́тренный *прил* unforeseen, unanticipated.
непредусмотри́тел|ьный (-ен, -ьна, -ьно) *прил* short-sighted.
непреклó|нный (-ен, -на, -но) *прил* (*человек*) unbending; (*противник*) uncompromising; (*воля*) unshakable; (*характер*) strong, firm; (*решение*) firm.
непрекраща́ющ|ийся (-аяся, -ееся, -иеся) *прил* (*дождь*) persistent; (*ссора*) endless; (*стрельба*) continuous.
непрело́ж|ный (-ен, -на, -но) *прил* (*правило, закон*) immutable; **непрело́жная и́стина** unquestionable truth.
непреме́нен *прил см* **непреме́нный**.
непреме́нно *нареч* (*обязательно*) by all means.
непреме́н|ный (-ен, -на, -но) *прил* (*условие*) necessary; (*следствие*) unavoidable; (*деталь, черта*) indispensable.
непреодоли́м|ый (-, -а, -о) *прил* (*препятствие*) insurmountable; (*желание, смущение*) overwhelming.
непререка́ем|ый (-, -а, -о) *прил* (*авторитет*) unquestionable; (*интонация*) peremptory.
непреры́вен *прил см* **непреры́вный**.

непреры́вно *нареч* (*спрашивать, меняться*) uninterruptedly, continuously.
непреры́в|ный (**-ен, -на, -но**) *прил* uninterrupted, continuous.
неприве́тлив|ый (**-, -а, -о**) *прил* (*человек, тон*) unfriendly; (*перен*: *лес, место*) bleak.
непривлека́тел|ьный (**-ен, -ьна, -ьно**) *прил* unattractive.
непривы́чен *прил см* **непривы́чный**.
непривы́чк|а (**-и**) *ж*: **с ~и к физи́ческому труду́ он бы́стро уста́л** (*разг*) not being used to physical work, he got tired quickly.
непривы́чно *как сказ*: **мне** ~ *+infin* I'm not used to doing.
непривы́ч|ный (**-ен, -на, -но**) *прил* (*мысль*) unusual; (*обстановка*) not the usual; (*человек*) unaccustomed.
неприглядн|ный (**-ен, -на, -но**) *прил* (*вид, внешность*) unsightly, unattractive; (*поступок, поведение*) unseemly.
неприго́д|ный (**-ен, -на, -но**) *прил* unsuitable.
неприе́млем|ый (**-, -а, -о**) *прил* unacceptable.
непри́знанный *прил* (*писатель, художник*) unrecognized, unacknowledged.
неприка́ян|ный (**-, -на, -но**) *прил* (*разг*) restless and drifting.
неприкоснове́нност|ь (**-и**) *ж* inviolability; **дипломати́ческая** ~ diplomatic immunity.
неприкоснове́н|ный (**-ен, -на, -но**) *прил* (*фонд*) reserve *опред*; (*ценность*) inviolable; (*лицо, личность*) protected by law; **неприкоснове́нный запа́с** emergency ration.
неприкра́шенный *прил* (*действительность*) plain, unvarnished; (*вид*) plain.
неприкры́т|ый (**-, -а, -о**) *прил* (*дверь*) open; (*отряд, батальон*) open, exposed; (*перен*: *правда*) plain; (: *ложь*) barefaced, blatant; (: *грубость*) undisguised.
неприли́чен *прил см* **неприли́чный**.
неприли́чи|е (**-я**) *ср*: **до ~я** extremely.
неприли́чно *нареч* indecently, improperly.
неприли́ч|ный (**-ен, -на, -но**) *прил* (*вид, анекдот, рисунок*) indecent; (*платье*) outrageous.
неприме́т|ный (**-ен, -на, -но**) *прил* (*незаметный*) imperceptible; (*непримечательный*) unremarkable.
непримири́м|ый (**-, -а, -о**) *прил* (*спорщики, противоречия*) irreconcilable; (*характер*) uncompromising.
непринуждённост|ь (**-и**) *ж* (*беседы*) informality; (*движений*) freeness, casualness.
непринуждён|ный (**-, -на, -но**) *прил* informal, relaxed.
неприсоедине́ни|е (**-я**) *ср* (*полит*) nonalignment.
непристо́ен *прил см* **непристо́йный**.
непристо́йност|ь (**-и**) *ж* obscenity.
непристо́|йный (**-ен, -йна, -йно**) *прил* obscene.
непристу́п|ный (**-ен, -на, -но**) *прил* (*крепость*) impregnable; (*высота*) inaccessible; (*человек*) unapproachable; (*характер, вид*) unfriendly.
непритво́р|ный (**-ен, -на, -но**) *прил* unfeigned.
непритяза́тел|ьный (**-ен, -ьна, -ьно**) *прил* (*читатель, зритель, вкус*) undiscriminating; (*острота, стихи*) unsubtle.
неприхотли́в|ый (**-, -а, -о**) *прил* (*человек, студент*) unpretentious; (*вкус, требования*) modest; (*растение, цветок*) undemanding; (*простой*: *пища*) frugal; (: *рисунок*) simple.
неприя́знен|ный (**-ен, -на, -но**) *прил* hostile.
неприя́зн|ь (**-и**) *ж* hostility.
неприя́тел|ь (**-я**) *м собир* the enemy.
неприя́тен *прил см* **неприя́тный**.
неприя́ти|е (**-я**) *ср* rejection.
неприя́тно *как сказ*: ~ *+infin* (*думать, слушать*) it's unpleasant *или* disagreeable to do; **мне ~ говори́ть об э́том** I don't enjoy talking about it.
неприя́тност|ь (**-и**) *ж* (*обычно мн*: *на работе, в семье*) trouble.
неприя́т|ный (**-ен, -на, -но**) *прил* unpleasant, disagreeable.
непробива́ем|ый (**-, -а, -о**) *прил* (*броня, борт*) impregnable; (*перен*: *спокойствие*) imperturbable; (: *разг*: *дурак*) utter.
непробу́д|ный (**-ен, -на, -но**) *прил* (*пьяница*) inveterate; **~ сон** deep sleep; **~ное пья́нство** drunken stupor.
непроводни́к (**-а́**) *м* (*физ*) nonconductor, dielectric.
непрогля́д|ный (**-ен, -на, -но**) *прил* (*ночь*) pitch-dark; (*тьма*) impenetrable.
непродолжи́тел|ьный (**-ен, -ьна, -ьно**) *прил* short.
непродукти́в|ный (**-ен, -на, -но**) *прил* unproductive.
непроду́манный *прил* ill-considered.
непрое́зж|ий (**-ая, -ее, -ие**) *прил* impassable.
непрозра́ч|ный (**-ен, -на, -но**) *прил* opaque.
непроизводи́тел|ьный (**-ен, -ьна, -ьно**) *прил* (*труд*) unproductive; (*расходы*) wasteful.
непроизво́л|ьный (**-ен, -ьна, -ьно**) *прил* involuntary.
непроло́з|ный (**-ен, -на, -но**) *прил* (*разг*) impassable.
непромока́ем|ый (**-, -а, -о**) *прил* (*куртка, сапоги*) waterproof.
непроница́ем|ый (**-, -а, -о**) *прил* (*мрак, туман*) impenetrable; (*перен*: *вид, лицо*) inscrutable; ~ **для** *+gen* impervious to.
непропорциона́л|ьный (**-ен, -ьна, -ьно**) *прил* disproportionate.
непрости́тел|ьный (**-ен, -ьна, -ьно**) *прил* unforgivable, inexcusable.
непроходи́мост|ь (**-и**) *ж* (*мед*) blockage.
непроходи́м|ый (**-, -а, -о**) *прил* (*чаща, болото*) impassable; (*no short form*; *перен*: *разг*: *дурак*) utter.
непро́ч|ный (**-ен, -на́, -но**) *прил* (*дом*) unstable; (*материал*) flimsy; (*перен*: *чувства*) questionable; (: *привязанность*) precarious.

непро́шеный *прил* (*разг*) uninvited.
непрямо́й *прил* (*путь*) indirect; (*ответ*) evasive.
Непту́н (-а) *м* Neptune.
непью́щ|ий (-ая, -ее, -ие) *прил* (*человек*) teetotal.
неработоспосо́б|ный (-ен, -на, -но) *прил* unable to work.
нерабо́ч|ий (-ая, -ее, -ие) *прил*: **~ее вре́мя** time off; **~ая обстано́вка** atmosphere which is not conducive to work.
нера́вен *прил см* **нера́вный**.
нера́венств|о (-а) *ср* inequality; **знак ~а** (*МАТ*) inequality sign.
неравноду́ш|ный (-ен, -на, -но) *прил*: **~** (**к** *+dat*) not indifferent (to); **он к ней ~ен** he finds her attractive.
неравноме́р|ный (-ен, -на, -но) *прил* (*развитие, глубина*) uneven; (*движения*) irregular.
неравнопра́вен *прил см* **неравнопра́вный**.
неравнопра́ви|е (-я) *ср* inequality (of rights).
неравнопра́в|ный (-ен, -на, -но) *прил* unequal.
нера́в|ный (-ен, -на́, -но) *прил* unequal.
неради́в|ый (-, -а, -о) *прил* careless, negligent.
неразбери́х|а (-и) *ж* (*разг*) muddle.
неразбо́рчив|ый (-, -а, -о) *прил* (*буквы, почерк*) illegible; (*читатель, вкус*) undiscriminating; **~ в сре́дствах** unscrupulous.
неразвит|о́й (-, -а, -о) *прил* undeveloped.
неразга́данный *прил* unsolved.
неразгово́рчив|ый (-, -а, -о) *прил* taciturn.
неразде́л|ьный (-ен, -ьна, -ьно) *прил* inseparable, indivisible.
неразличи́м|ый (-, -а, -о) *прил* (*схожий*) indistinguishable; (*и́здали, в темноте*) indiscernible.
неразлу́ч|ный (-ен, -на, -но) *прил* inseparable.
неразрешённый *прил* (*запрещённый*) prohibited; (*оставшийся неясным*) unsolved.
неразреши́м|ый (-, -а, -о) *прил* insoluble.
неразры́в|ный (-ен, -на, -но) *прил* indissoluble.
неразу́м|ный (-ен, -на, -но) *прил* (*поведение, поступок*) foolish; (*разг*: *малыш, ребёнок*) silly.
нераспростране́ни|е (-я) *ср* nonproliferation; **~ я́дерного ору́жия** nonproliferation of nuclear weapons.
нерассуди́тел|ьный (-ен, -ьна, -ьно) *прил* lacking (in) common sense.
нерасторжи́м|ый (-, -а, -о) *прил* indissoluble.
нерасторо́п|ный (-ен, -на, -но) *прил* slow, sluggish.
нерасчётлив|ый (-, -а, -о) *прил* wasteful.
нерв (-а) *м* (*АНАТ*) nerve; **больны́е не́рвы** nervous disorder; **он всем де́йствует на не́рвы** he gets on everyone's nerves; **переста́нь трепа́ть мне не́рвы!** (*разг*) stop getting on my nerves!
нерви́р|овать (-ую) *несов перех* to make nervous.
не́рвнича|ть (-ю) *несов неперех* to fret.
не́рвно *нареч* nervously.
нервнобольн|о́й (-о́го; *decl like adj*) *м person suffering from a nervous disorder*.
не́рвный *прил* nervous; (*работа, занятие*) nerve-racking; (*окончания, клетки*) nerve *опред*; **не́рвная систе́ма** the nervous system.
нерво́зен *прил см* **нерво́зный**.
нерво́зност|ь (-и) *ж* nervousness.
нерво́з|ный (-ен, -на, -но) *прил* (*человек*) nervous, highly (*BRIT*) *или* high (*US*) strung; (*тон, характер*) nervous; (*обстановка*) nerve-racking.
нервотрёпк|а (-и) *ж* (*разг*) hassle.
нереа́лен *прил см* **нереа́льный**.
нереа́льност|ь (-и) *ж* (*событий, обстановки*) unreality; (*неосуществимость*) impracticality.
нереа́л|ьный (-ен, -ьна, -ьно) *прил* (*мир, события*) unreal; (*неосуществимый*) impractical.
нерегуля́р|ный (-ен, -на, -но) *прил* irregular.
нере́дко *нареч* (*часто*) not infrequently, quite often.
нерента́белен *прил см* **нерента́бельный**.
нерента́бельност|ь (-и) *ж* unprofitability.
нерента́бел|ьный (-ен, -на, -но) *прил* unprofitable.
не́рест (-а) *м* spawning.
нереши́мост|ь (-и) *ж* indecision.
нереши́телен *прил см* **нереши́тельный**.
нереши́тельно *нареч* indecisively.
нереши́тельност|ь (-и) *ж* indecision, indecisiveness; **быть** (*impf*) **в ~и** to be undecided.
нереши́тел|ьный (-ен, -ьна, -ьно) *прил* indecisive.
нержаве́|йка (-йки; *gen pl* -ек) *ж* (*разг*) stainless steel.
нержаве́ющ|ий (-ая, -ее, -ие) *прил* (*крыша, бочка*) rustproof; **нержаве́ющая ста́ль** stainless steel.
неро́вно *нареч* (*порезать*) unevenly.
неро́вный *прил* (*поверхность, край*) uneven; (*местность*) rough, rugged; (*линия*) crooked; (*пульс*) irregular; (*характер, поведение*) unbalanced.
не́рп|а (-ы) *ж* (*ЗООЛ*) seal.
неруши́мый *прил* (*союз*) indestructible.
неря́х|а (-и) *м/ж* (*разг*) scruff.
неря́шлив|ый (-, -а, -о-) *прил* (*человек, одежда*) scruffy; (*работа*) careless.
несамостоя́тел|ьный (-ен, -ьна, -ьно) *прил* dependent; **Ва́ша рабо́та ~ьна** this is not all your own work.
несбы́точ|ный (-ен, -на, -но) *прил* unrealizable;

~**ные ме́чты** pipe dreams.
несваре́ни|е (**-я**) *ср*: ~ **желу́дка** indigestion.
несве́дущ|ий (**-ая, -ее, -ие**; **-, -а, -е, -и**) *прил* ignorant.
несве́ж|ий (**-ая, -ее, -ие**; **-, -а́, -о**) *прил* (*рубашка*) dirty; **о́вощи ~ие** the vegetables are not very fresh; **у тебя́ ~ вид** you look weary.
несвоевре́мен|ный (**-ен, -на, -но**) *прил* untimely.
несвя́зный *прил* disjointed.
несгиба́емый *прил* staunch.
несгово́рчив|ый (**-, -а, -о**) *прил* pig-headed.
несгора́емый *прил* fireproof.
несде́ржанност|ь (**-и**) *ж* fieriness.
несде́ржан|ный (**-, -на, -но**) *прил* (*характер, человек*) fiery; (*тон, поведение*) passionate.
несдоброва́ть *как сказ*: **ему́ ~** (*разг*) he's in trouble.
несе́ни|е (**-я**) *ср* (*охраны, службы*) carrying out; (*наказания*) taking.
несери́йный *прил* (*изделие*) custom-made.
несерьёз|ный (**-ен, -на, -но**) *прил* (*человек*) frivolous; (*предложение*) flippant; (*болезнь*) mild; **~ная ра́на** flesh wound.
несимметри́ч|ный (**-ен, -на, -но**) *прил* asymmetrical.
несказа́н|ный (**-ен, -на, -но**) *прил* inexpressive.
нескла́д|ный (**-ен, -на, -но**) *прил* (*рассказ, жизнь*) disjointed; (*человек, фигура*) ungainly.
несклоня́емый *прил* (*линг*) indeclinable.
не́скольк|о (**-их**) *чис* (*+gen*) a few ◆ *нареч* (*немного: обидеться*) somewhat; **в ~их слова́х** in a few words, briefly.
несконча́ем|ый (**-, -а, -о**) *прил* unending.
нескро́м|ный (**-ен, -на, -но**) *прил* (*человек, поведение*) immodest; (*вопрос*) indelicate; (*жест, предложение*) brazen.
нескрыва́ем|ый (**-, -а, -о**) *прил* undisguised.
несло́ж|ный (**-ен, -на́, -но**) *прил* simple.
неслы́хан|ный (**-, -на, -но**) *прил* unheard of.
неслы́шно *нареч* (*сказать, проехать*) quietly ◆ *как сказ*: **мне ~** I can't hear.
неслы́ш|ный (**-ен, -на, -но**) *прил* inaudible.
несме́т|ный (**-ен, -на, -но**) *прил* infinite.
несмолка́ем|ый (**-, -а, -о**) *прил* unceasing.
несмотря́ *предл*: **~ на** *+acc* (*трудности, усталость*) in spite of, despite; **~ на то что ...** in spite of *или* despite the fact that ...; **~ ни на что** no matter what.
несмыва́емый *прил* (*пятно*) indelible; (*позор*) ineradicable.
несмышлёный *прил* (*ребёнок*) innocent.
несно́с|ный (**-ен, -на, -но**) *прил* (*человек, поведение итп*) insufferable; (*жара, холод*) unbearable.
несоблюде́ни|е (**-я**) *ср* nonobservance.
несоверше́нен *прил см* **несоверше́нный**.
несовершенноле́тн|ий (**-его**; *decl like adj*) *м* minor; ◆ (**-яя, -ее, -ие**) *прил*: **~ ребёнок** minor.
несовершенноле́тн|яя (**-ей**; *decl like adj*) *ж см* **несовершенноле́тний**.
несоверше́н|ный (**-ен, -на, -но**) *прил* flawed; **несоверше́нный вид** (*лингв*) imperfective (aspect).
несоверше́нств|о (**-а**) *ср* (*общества, системы*) imperfect nature.
несовмести́мост|ь (**-и**) *ж* incompatibility; **несовмести́мость тка́ней** (*МЕД*) antagonism.
несовмести́м|ый (**-, -а, -о**) *прил* incompatible.
несогла́си|е (**-я**) *ср* (*отказ*) refusal; (*в семье*) disagreement.
несогласо́ванност|ь (**-и**) *ж* lack of coordination.
несогласо́ван|ный (**-, -на, -но**) *прил* (*действия*) uncoordinated.
несозна́телен *прил см* **несозна́тельный**.
несозна́тельност|ь (**-и**) *ж* irresponsibility.
несозна́тел|ьный (**-ен, -ьна, -ьно**) *прил* irresponsible.
несоизмери́м|ый (**-, -а, -о**) *прил* (*понятия*) disproportionate.
несокруши́м|ый (**-, -а, -о**) *прил* indestructible.
несомне́нен *прил см* **несомне́нный**.
несомне́нно *нареч* (*правильный, хороший итп*) indisputably ◆ *вводн сл* without a doubt ◆ *как сказ*: **э́то ~** this is indisputable; **~, что он придёт** there is no doubt that he will come.
несомне́нност|ь (**-и**) *ж* indisputability.
несомне́н|ный (**-ен, -на, -но**) *прил* (*факт, успех*) indisputable.
несообра́зен *прил см* **несообра́зный**.
несообрази́тел|ьный (**-ен, -ьна, -ьно**) *прил* (*человек*) slow, thick.
несообра́зност|ь (**-и**) *ж* (*поведения*) foolishness; **говори́ть** *(impf)*/**де́лать** *(impf)* **~и** to say/do foolish things.
несообра́з|ный (**-ен, -на, -но**) *прил* (*поведение*) foolish; **~ с** *+instr* (*с возможностями, с обстоятельствами*) out of line with.
несоотве́тстви|е (**-я**) *ср*: **~** *+dat* (*правилам, закону*) nonconformity with; (*возможностям, обстоятельствам*) discrepancy with.
несоразме́р|ный (**-ен, -на, -но**) *прил* unbalanced.
несостоя́телен *прил см* **несостоя́тельный**.
несостоя́тельност|ь (**-и**) *ж* (*довода*) lack of substantiation; (*КОММ*) insolvency; **обнару́живать** (**обнару́жить** *perf*) **свою́ ~** to prove to be worthless.
несостоя́тел|ьный (**-ен, -на, -но**) *прил* (*довод*) unsubstantiated; (*КОММ: компания, должник*) insolvent; (*руководитель*) incompetent.
неспе́ш|ный (**-ен, -на, -но**) *прил* unhurried.
несподру́чно *как сказ* (*разг*) it is inconvenient; **мне ~ де́лать э́то** it's inconvenient for me to do this.
несподру́чный *прил* (*разг*) inconvenient.
неспоко́ен *прил см* **неспоко́йный**.
неспоко́йно *как сказ* (*в доме, в стране*) there's unease; **у меня́ на душе́ ~** I feel uneasy.
неспоко́|йный (**-ен, -йна, -йно**) *прил* (*сон*)

uneasy; (*жизнь*) troubled.
неспосо́бен *прил см* **неспосо́бный.**
неспосо́бност|ь (**-и**) *ж* inability; **~ на** *+acc* (*на жертвы, на уступки итп*) inability to make.
неспосо́б|ный (**-ен, -на, -но**) *прил*: **~ к** *+dat* incapable of; **~ к языка́м/матема́тике** incapable of learning languages/doing maths; **~ на** *+acc* (*на жертвы, на уступки*) incapable of making.
несправедли́во *нареч* unfairly, unjustly ◆ *как сказ*: **э́то ~** this is unfair *или* unjust.
несправедли́вост|ь (**-и**) *ж* injustice.
несправедли́в|ый (**-, -а, -о**) *прил* (*человек, суд, упрёк*) unfair, unjust; (*сообщение*) unfounded.
неспроста́ *нареч* (*разг*) for a reason.
неспряга́емый *прил* (*линг*) inconjugable.
несрабо́танност|ь (**-и**) *ж* lack of harmony at work.
несравне́нен *прил см* **несравне́нный.**
несравне́нно *нареч* (*лучшее, красивее итп*) incomparably.
несравне́н|ный (**-ен, -на, -но**) *прил* incomparable.
несравни́мый (**-, -а, -о**) *прил* incomparable.
нестанда́рт|ный (**-ен, -на, -но**) *прил* (*подход*) original; (*товар*) substandard.
нестерпи́м|ый (**-, -а, -о**) *прил* intolerable.
нес|ти́ (**-у́, -ёшь**; *pt* **нёс, -ла́, -ло́**) *несов перех* to carry; (*влечь*: *хаос, разруху, неприятности*) to bring; (*разг*: *чепуху, вздор*) to spout; (*perf* **понести́**; *службу, охрану*) to carry out; (*perf* **снести́**; *яйцо*) to lay ◆ *безл*: **~ёт бензи́ном/во́дкой** there's a smell of petrol (*BRIT*) *или* gas (*US*)/of vodka; **с мо́ря ~ёт прохла́дой** coolness wafted in from the sea; **~ (понести́** *perf***) наказа́ние** to take punishment; **~ (понести́** *perf***) поте́ри** to suffer losses; **~ (понести́** *perf***) уще́рб** to be damaged; **куда́ тебя́ ~ёт?** (*разг*) where on earth are you going?; **кого́ э́то ~ёт?** (*разг*) who on earth is that?
▸ **нести́сь** *несов возв* (*человек, машина*) to race; (*перен*: *сплетни*) to spread; (: *музыка*) to carry; (*perf* **снести́сь**; *курица*) to lay eggs.
несто́ящ|ий (**-ая, -ее, -ие**) *прил* (*человек*) worthless; (*дело*) valueless.
нестро́|йный (**-ен, -йна, -йно**) *прил* shapeless; (*ряды*) ragged.
несудохо́дный *прил* not navigable.
несура́зен *прил см* **несура́зный.**
несура́зност|ь (**-и**) *ж* silliness; **говори́ть** *(impf)***/де́лать** *(impf)* **~и** to say/do silly things.
несура́з|ный (**-ен, -на, -но**) *прил* silly; (*характер*) idiotic.
несуще́ственный *прил* inconsequential.
несхо́д|ный (**-ен, -на, -но**) *прил* dissimilar.
несча́стен *прил см* **несча́стный.**
несчастли́вый (**несча́стлив, несча́стлива, несча́стливо**) *прил* (*человек*) unhappy; (*попытка*) unfortunate.
несча́ст|ный (**-ен, -на, -но**) *прил* (*человек, лицо*) unhappy; (*день*) sad; (*no short form*; *разг*: *жалкий*) wretched; **у него́ о́чень ~ вид** he looks very unhappy; **несча́стная любо́вь** unrequited love; **несча́стный слу́чай** accident.
несча́сть|е (**-я**) *ср* (*беда*) misfortune; **к ~ю** unfortunately.
несчётный *прил* incalculable.
несъедо́б|ный (**-ен, -на, -но**) *прил* inedible.

KEYWORD

нет *част* ***1*** (*при отрицании, несогласии*) no; **ты согла́сен? – нет** do you agree? – no; **нет, э́то не то** no, that's not right; **тебе́ не нра́вится мой суп? – нет, нра́вится** don't you like my soup? – yes, I do
2 (*для привлечения внимания*): **нет, ты то́лько посмотри́ на него́!** would you just look at him!
3 (*выражает недоверие*): **нет, ты действи́тельно не се́рдишься?** so you are really not angry?
◆ *как сказ* (*+gen*; *не имеется*: *об одном предмете*) there is no; (: *о нескольких предметах*) there are no; **нет вре́мени** there is no time; **нет биле́тов** *или* **биле́тов нет** there are no tickets; **у меня́ нет де́нег** I have no money; **его́ нет в го́роде** he is not in town
◆ *союз*: ***1***: **(так) нет (же)** (*разг*: *однако*) but; **я помога́л ему́ три дня, (так) нет (же) ему́ всё ма́ло** I helped him for three days, but it still wasn't enough; **своди́ть (свести́** *perf***) что-н на нет** to bring sth to nothing; **сойти́** *(perf)* **на нет** to come to nothing
2 (*во фразах*): **нет – так нет** it can't be helped; **нет-нет да и зайдёт/ска́жет** every now and then he called in/said; **чего́ то́лько нет?** what don't they have?; **нет что́бы извини́ться/сказа́ть пра́вду** (*разг*) instead of saying sorry/telling the truth.

нетакти́чен *прил см* **нетакти́чный.**
нетакти́чност|ь (**-и**) *ж* tactlessness.
нетакти́ч|ный (**-ен, -на, -но**) *прил* tactless.
нетвёрдый *прил* (*походка*) unsteady; (*решение*) shaky.
нетерпели́во *нареч* impatiently.
нетерпели́в|ый (**-, -а, -о**) *прил* impatient.
нетерпе́ни|е (**-я**) *ср* impatience; **с ~м ждать** *(impf)***/слу́шать** *(impf)* to wait/listen impatiently.
нетерпи́мост|ь (**-и**) *ж* intolerance.
нетерпи́м|ый (**-, -а, -о**) *прил* (*недопустимый*) intolerant; (*непримиримый*): **~ к** *+dat* (*ко лжи*) intolerant of.
нетороплúво *нареч* unhurriedly.
нетороплúв|ый (**-, -а, -о**) *прил* unhurried.
нето́чност|ь (**-и**) *ж* (*данных, описания*) inexactness; (*в работе, в описании*)

inexactitude.
нетóч|ный (-ен, -но, -на) *прил* inexact.
нетрéбовател|ьный (-ен, -ьна, -ьно) *прил* (*начальник*) undemanding; (*вкус, публика*) unsophisticated; (*человек*) unassuming.
нетрéзвый *прил* drunk; **в нетрéзвом состоя́нии** drunk.
нетрóнут|ый (-, -а, -о) *прил* (*снег*) virgin; (*обед*) untouched.
нетру́ден *прил см* **нетру́дный**.
нетру́дно *как сказ*: **э́то** ~ it's easy *или* not difficult; ~ **поня́ть** it's easy *или* not difficult to understand.
нетру́д|ный (-ен, -но, -на) *прил* easy.
нетрудовóй *прил*: ~ **дохóд** unearned income.
нетрудоспосóбен *прил см* **нетрудоспосóбный**.
нетрудоспосóбност|ь (-и) *ж* disability; **посóбие по ~и** disability living allowance.
нетрудоспосóб|ный (-ен, -на, -но) *прил* *unable to work through disability*.
нéтто *прил неизм* (*о весе*) net *опред*; **вес** ~ net weight; **~-акти́вы** (*КОММ*) net assets.
неубеди́тел|ьный (-ен, -ьна, -ьно) *прил* unconvincing.
неу́бранный *прил* (*урожай*) ungathered; (*поля*) unharvested; (*постель*) unmade; (*комната*) untidy.
неуважéни|е (-я) *ср* disrespect.
неувéренно *нареч* uncertainly.
неувéренный *прил* (*человек*) unsure; (*тон*) uncertain; ~ **в себé** unsure of o.s.
неувядáем|ый (-, -а, -о) *прил* (*талант, слава*) enduring; (*красота*) unfading.
неувя́з|ка (-ки; *gen pl* **-ок)** *ж* (*разг: в описании, в аргументации*) discrepancy; (*недоразумение*) misunderstanding.
неугаси́м|ый (-, -а, -о) *прил* inextinguishable.
неугомóн|ный (-ен, -на, -но) *прил* unruly.
неудáч|а (-и) *ж* (*в делах*) failure; **терпéть (потерпéть** *perf*) **~у** to meet with failure.
неудáчен *прил см* **неудáчный**.
неудáчлив|ый (-, -а, -о) *прил* (*человек*) unlucky.
неудáчно *нареч* unsuccessfully; **её жизнь сложи́лась** ~ her life was a failure.
неудáч|ный (-ен, -на, -но) *прил* (*попытка*) unsuccessful; (*фильм, стихи*) bad.
неудержи́м|ый (-, -а, -о) *прил* (*поток, бег*) uncontrollable; (*слёзы, радость*) unrestrained.
неудиви́тельно *как сказ* it's not surprising.
неудóбен *прил см* **неудóбный**.
неудóбно *нареч* (*расположенный, сидеть*) uncomfortably ♦ *как сказ* it's uncomfortable; (*неприлично*) it's awkward; **мне** ~ I am uncomfortable; ~ **задавáть лю́дям таки́е вопрóсы** it's awkward to ask people such questions; **(мне)** ~ **сказáть емý об э́том** I feel uncomfortable telling him that.
неудóб|ный (-ен, -на, -но) *прил* uncomfortable.
неудобовари́м|ый (-, -а, -о) *прил* (*также перен*) indigestible.
неудóбств|о (-а) *ср* (*неловкость*) discomfort; (*в поезде итп*) lack of comfort.
неудовлетворённост|ь (-и) *ж*: ~ *+instr* (*работой, жизнью*) dissatisfaction with.
неудовлетворённый *прил* (*любопытство*) unsatisfied; (*читатель, зритель*) dissatisfied.
неудовлетвори́телен *прил см* **неудовлетвори́тельный**.
неудовлетвори́тельно *нареч* (*сделать*) unsatisfactorily ♦ *ср нескл* (*ПРОСВЕЩ*) ≈ D (*school mark*).
неудовлетвори́тел|ьный (-ен, -ьна, -ьно) *прил* unsatisfactory.
неудовóльстви|е (-я) *ср* dissatisfaction.
неуём|ный (-ен, -на, -но) *прил* (*энергия*) irrepressible; (*тоска*) unrestrained.
неужéли *част* really; ~ **онá так ду́мает?** does she really think that?
неужи́вчив|ый (-, -а, -о) *прил* unaccommodating.
неузнавáемост|ь (-и) *ж*: **до ~и** beyond (all) recognition.
неузнавáем|ый (-, -а, -о) *прил* unrecognizable.
неуклóнно *нареч* steadily.
неуклóн|ный (-ен, -на, -но) *прил* steady.
неуклю́ж|ий (-ая, -ее, -ие; -, -а, -е) *прил* clumsy.
неукоси́телен *прил см* **неукоси́тельный**.
неукоси́тельно *нареч* strictly.
неукоси́тел|ьный (-ен, -ьна, -ьно) *прил* strict.
неукроти́м|ый (-, -а, -о) *прил* (*гнев*) unrestrained; (*энергия*) irrepressible.
неулови́м|ый (-, -а, -о) *прил* imperceptible; (*человек*) elusive.
неумéлый *прил* inept.
неумéни|е (-я) *ср* incapability.
неумéрен|ный (-, -на, -но) *прил* (*восторг*) boundless; (*потребности*) unlimited.
неумéст|ный (-ен, -на, -но) *прил* inappropriate; **шу́тка былá совершéнно ~на** the joke was completely out of place.
неу́мный *прил* (*политика*) unintelligent.
неумоли́м|ый (-, -а, -о) *прил* (*мститель*) relentless; (*закон*) stringent.
неумóлч|ный (-ен, -на, -но) *прил* unremitting.
неумы́шленный *прил* (*поступок*) unintentional; (*убийство*) unpremeditated.
неуплáт|а (-ы) *ж* nonpayment.
неупоря́доченный *прил* disorderly.
неупотреби́тел|ьный (-ен, -ьна, -ьно) *прил*: **э́то слóво сейчáс ~ьно** this word is not in use any more.
неуправля́ем|ый (-, -а, -о) *прил* (*недисциплинированный*) unruly.
неуравновéшенност|ь (-и) *ж* irascibility.
неуравновéшен|ный (-, -на, -но) *прил* unbalanced.
неурожá|й (-я) *м* poor harvest.
неурожáйный *прил*: ~ **год** year with a poor harvest.
неурóчный *прил* (*время, час*) unearthly.

неуря́диц|а (-ы) *ж* (*разг*: *обычно мн*: *в семье, на работе*) squabble.
неуспева́емост|ь (-и) *ж* poor performance.
неуспева́ющ|ий (-ая, -ее, -ие) *прил* (*ученик*) poor.
неуста́нен *прил см* **неуста́нный**.
неуста́нно *нареч* indefatigably.
неуста́н|ный (-ен, -на, -но) *прил* indefatigable.
неусто́|йка (-йки; *gen pl* -ек) *ж* (*комм*) penalty; (*разг*: *неудача*) flop.
неусто́йчивост|ь (-и) *ж* (*цен*) instability.
неусто́йчив|ый (-, -а, -о) *прил* (*стул, цены*) unstable; (*погода*) unsettled.
неустрани́м|ый (-, -а, -о) *прил* insurmountable.
неустраши́м|ый (-, -а, -о) *прил* fearless.
неустро́ен|ный (-, -на, -но) *прил* (*жизнь, быт*) uncomfortable.
неусы́п|ный (-ен, -на, -но) *прил* vigilant.
неуте́шен *прил см* **неуте́шный**.
неутеши́тел|ьный (-ен, -ьна, -ьно) *прил* upsetting.
неуте́ш|ный (-ен, -на, -но) *прил* inconsolable.
неутоли́м|ый (-, -а, -о) *прил* (*жажда*) unquenchable; (*голод, также перен*) insatiable.
неутоми́м|ый (-, -а, -о) *прил* untiring.
не́уч (-а) *м* (*разг*) dunce.
неучти́вост|ь (-и) *ж* lack of civility; **говори́ть** (*impf*) **~и** to be uncivil.
неучти́в|ый (-, -а, -о) *прил* uncivil.
неую́тно *нареч* (*сидеть*) uncomfortably ◆ *как сказ* it's uncomfortable; **мне ~ с чужи́ми людьми́** I don't feel at ease with strangers.
неуязви́м|ый (-, -а, -о) *прил* (*противник, позиция*) impregnable; (*аргумент*) unassailable.
неформа́л (-а) *м* (*разг*) *member of a nonconformist organization.*
неформа́льный *прил* (*отношение*) relaxed; (*организация*) nonconformist.
нефри́т (-а) *м* (*мед*) nephritis; (*гео*) jade.
нефтедобыва́ющ|ий (-ая, -ее, -ие) *прил* (*промышленность*) oil *опред*.
нефтедобы́ч|а (-и) *ж* drilling for oil.
нефтедо́ллар|ы (-ов) *мн* petrodollars *мн*.
нефтено́сный *прил*: **~ пласт** oilfield.
нефтеперерабо́тк|а (-и) *ж* oil-processing plant.
нефтепрово́д (-а) *м* oil pipeline.
нефтепроду́кт (-а) *м* (*обычно мн*) oil product.
нефтехрани́лищ|е (-а) *ср* oil storage tank.
нефт|ь (-и) *ж* oil, petroleum.
нефтя́ник (-а) *м* *worker in the oil industry.*
нефтян|о́й *прил*: **~а́я платфо́рма** oil rig; **нефтяна́я вы́шка** (oil) derrick.
нехва́тк|а (-и) *ж*: **~** +*gen* (*разг*) shortage of.
нехи́трый *прил* (*простой*) simple.
нехо́жен|ый (-, -а, -о) *прил* little-used.
нехоро́ш|ий (-ая, -ее, -ие) *прил* bad.
нехорошо́ *нареч* (*поступить*) badly ◆ *как сказ* it's bad; **мне ~** I'm not well; **~ на душе́** I feel uneasy; **он нехоро́ш собо́й** he isn't good-looking.
не́хотя *нареч* unwillingly.
нецензу́р|ный (-ен, -на, -но) *прил* unprintable; **~ное сло́во** swearword.
неча́янно *нареч* unintentionally.
неча́ян|ный (-на, -но) *прил* (*неумышленный*) unintentional; (*неожиданный*) chance *опред*.
не́чего *как сказ*: **~ рассказа́ть** there is nothing to tell; (*разг*: *не следует*) there's no need to do; **не́ для чего стара́ться** there is nothing to try for; **не́ к чему придра́ться** there is nothing to find fault with; **мне не́ с чем идти́** I have nothing to take; **не́ о чем говори́ть** there is nothing to talk about; **не́чему серди́ться** there is nothing to be angry about; **не́ за что!** (*в ответ на благодарность*) not at all!, you're welcome! (*US*); **~ (и) говори́ть** (*разг*: *конечно*) no buts about it; **~ сказа́ть!** (*разг*) would you credit it!; **от ~ де́лать** (*разг*) for want of something better to do; **де́лать ~** there's nothing else to be done.
нечелове́ческ|ий (-ая, -ое, -ие) *прил* inhuman; (*колоссальный*: *усилия*) superhuman.
нечёсаный *прил* unkempt.
нече́стен *прил см* **нече́стный**.
нече́стно *нареч* dishonestly ◆ *как сказ*: **э́то ~** this is dishonest.
нече́стност|ь (-и) *ж* dishonesty.
нече́ст|ный (-ен, -на, -но) *прил* dishonest.
нечётный *прил* (*число*) odd.
нечи́сто *как сказ*: **в ко́мнате ~** the room is untidy; **здесь что́-то ~** (*разг*) there's something fishy here.
нечистопло́т|ный (-ен, -на, -но) *прил* (*неопрятный*) untidy; (*неразборчивый*) unscrupulous.
нечисто́т|ы (-) *мн* sewage *ед*; (*отбросы*) waste *ед*.
нечи́ст|ый (-, -а, -о) *прил* (*одежда, комната*) dirty; (*произношение*) indistinct; (*приёмы, игра*) unscrupulous; **у него́ ~ая со́весть** he has a guilty conscience; **он нечи́ст на́ руку** (*нечестен*) he is dishonest; (*ворует*) he is light-fingered; **нечи́стая си́ла** evil spirit.
не́чист|ь (-и) *ж собир* (*нечистая сила*) evil spirit; (*перен*: *преступная, нацистская*) scum.
нечленоразде́л|ьный (-ен, -ьна, -ьно) *прил* inarticulate.
не́что *мест* something.
нечувстви́телен *прил см* **нечувстви́тельный**.
нечувстви́тельност|ь (-и) *ж* insensitivity.
нечувстви́тел|ьный (-ен, -ьна, -ьно) *прил* insensitive.
нечу́тк|ий (-ая, -ое, -ие) *прил* (*человек*) unsympathetic.
нешу́точ|ный (-ен, -на, -но) *прил* (*серьёзный*)

serious; (*значительный*) large; **это ~ное дéло** it's no laughing matter.

нещáден *прил см* **нещáдный.**

нещáдно *нареч* unmercifully.

нещáд|ный (**-ен, -на, -но**) *прил* (*критика, наказание*) merciless; (*перен*: *жара*) relentless.

неэкономúчен *прил см* **неэкономúчный.**

неэкономúчност|ь (**-и**) *ж* (*методов, технологии*) inefficiency.

неэкономúч|ный (**-ен, -на, -но**) *прил* (*технология, отрасль*) inefficient; (*мотор*) uneconomical.

неэтúчный *прил* (*поведение*) unethical.

неэффектúв|ный (**-ен, -на, -но**) *прил* ineffective.

неяв|ка (**-ки**; *gen pl* **-ок**) *ж* (*на работу*) absence; (*на суд*) failure to appear; **за ~кой, по ~ке** by default.

неясен *прил см* **неясный.**

неясно *нареч*: **он ~ объяснúл положéние** he didn't explain the situation clearly ◆ *как сказ* it's not clear; **мне ~, почемý он отказáлся** I'm not clear *или* it's not clear to me why he refused.

неясност|ь (**-и**) *ж* vagueness; (*в тексте*) ambiguity.

неяс|ный (**-ен, -на, -но**) *прил* (*очертания, звук*) indistinct; (*мысль, вопрос*) vague.

НЗ *м сокр* = **неприкосновéнный запáс.**

KEYWORD

ни *част* **1** (*усиливает отрицание*) not a; **ни одúн** not one, not a single; **онá не произнеслá ни слóва** she didn't say a word; **онá ни рáзу не пришлá** she didn't come once; **у меня не остáлось ни рубля** I don't have a single rouble left:

2: **кто/что/как ни** who/what/however; **скóлько ни** however much; **что ни говорú, а ей прихóдится трýдно** whatever you say, it is hard for her; **как ни старáйся, не убедúшь егó** however hard you try, you will not convince him; **кудá ни посмотрú, вездé бéдность** wherever you look, there is poverty

◆ *союз* (*in negative sentences*; *при перечислении*): **ни ..., ни ...** neither ... nor ...; **ни дéнег, ни еды у неё нет** she has neither money nor food; **ни за что** no way; **ни за какúе дéньги** not for any money; **ни-ни!** (*разг*) no way!

нúв|а (**-ы**) *ж* field (*of crops*).

нивелúр|овать (**-ую**) (*не*)*сов перех* (*перен*) to even out.

нигдé *нареч* nowhere; **егó ~ нé было** he was nowhere to be found; **~ нет моéй кнúги** I can't find my book anywhere, my book is nowhere to be found; **~ не мог поéсть** I couldn't find anywhere to get something to eat.

нигерúйск|ий (**-ая, -ое, -ие**) *ж* Nigerian.

Нигéри|я (**-и**) *ж* Nigeria.

нигилúзм (**-а**) *м* nihilism.

нигилúст (**-а**) *м* nihilist.

нидерлáндск|ий (**-ая, -ое, -ие**) *прил* Dutch.

Нидерлáнд|ы (**-ов**) *мн* the Netherlands.

нúже *сравн прил от* **нúзкий** ◆ *сравн нареч от* **нúзко** ◆ *нареч* (*далее*) later on ◆ *предл* (*+gen*) below; **~ речь пойдёт о** *+prp* ... later (on) we will deal with ...; **он выступил ~ своúх возмóжностей** he performed below his capabilities.

нижеизлóженн|ый *прил*: **~ые дáнные/аргумéнты** the facts/arguments given below.

нижеподписáвш|ийся (**-аяся, -ееся, -иеся**) *прил* undersigned.

нижескáзанн|ое (**-ого**; *decl like adj*) *ср* what has been said below.

нижестоящ|ий (**-ая, -ее, -ие**) *прил* lower.

нижеукáзанный *прил* undermentioned.

нижеупомянутый *прил* = **нижеукáзанный.**

нúжн|ий (**-яя, -ее, -ие**) *прил* (*ступенька, ящик*) bottom; (*течение реки*) lower reaches *мн*; (*регистр*) low; **~ этáж** ground (*BRIT*) *или* first (*US*) floor; **Н~ Нóвгород** Nizhni Novgorod; **нúжнее бельё** underwear; **нúжняя юбка** underskirt.

низ (**-а**; *loc sg* **-ý**, *nom pl* **-ы**) *м* (*стола, ящика итп*) bottom; (*дома*) ground (*BRIT*) *или* first (*US*) floor; **пó ~у** along the bottom; *см также* **низы.**

низвéргн|уть (**-у, -ешь**; *impf* **низвергáть**) *сов перех* to overthrow

▸ **низвéргнуться** *сов возв* to hurtle down.

низúн|а (**-ы**) *ж* low-lying land.

нúзк|ий (**-кая, -кое, -кие**; **-ок, -кá, -ко**) *прил* low; (*no short form*; *происхождение*) lowly; **этот стол мне ~ок** this table is too low for me; **~ лоб** narrow forehead; **~кое мéсто** (*низменность*) low-lying area; **~ поклóн** low bow; (*перен*) forelock tugging.

нúзко *нареч* low.

низкооплáчиваемый *прил* low-paid.

низкопоклóнник (**-а**) *м* sycophant.

низкопоклóнств|о (**-а**) *ср* sycophancy.

низкопрóб|ный (**-ен, -на, -но**) *прил* (*золото, серебро*) low-grade; (*книга, газета*) trashy; (*делец*) amoral.

низкорóслый *прил* (*человек*) small; (*дерево, кустарник*) stunted.

низкосóрт|ный (**-ен, -на, -но**) *прил* low-quality.

низкокáчественный *прил* low-quality.

низл|ожúть (**-ожý, -óжишь**; *impf* **низлагáть**) *сов перех* to depose.

нúзменност|ь (**-и**) *ж* (*ГЕО*) low-lying area; (*интересов*) baseness.

нúзмен|ный *прил* (*местность, болота*) low-lying; (**-, -на, -но**; *интересы, мысли*) base; (*инстинкты*) basic.

низовóй *прил* (*организация*) grass-roots; **низовые рабóтники** the grass roots.

низóв|ье (**-ья**; *gen pl* **-ьев**) *ср* lower reaches *мн*.

нúзок *прил см* **нúзкий.**

нúзом *нареч* along the bottom.

нúзост|ь (**-и**) *ж* baseness; **говорúть** (*impf*) **~и** to say base things; **дéлать** (*impf*) **~и** to behave basely.

ни́зш|ий (**-ая, -ее, -ие**) *сравн прил от* **ни́зкий**; (*звание*) junior; **~ие чины́** the lowest ranks.

низ|ы́ (**-о́в**) *мн* (*низший классы*) lowest classes *мн*; (*широкие массы*) masses *мн*; **он вы́шел из ~о́в** he came from the lowest classes of society; **опира́ться** *(impf)* **на ~** to rely for support on the masses.

ника́к *нареч* (*никаким образом*) no way; **~ не могу́ запо́мнить э́то сло́во** I can't remember this word at all; **дверь ~ не открыва́лась** the door just wouldn't open; **ему́ ~ не удава́лось её встре́тить** there's no way he could have managed to meet her; **~ нельзя́** *+infin* ... one can't do ....

никак|о́й (**-а́я, -о́е, -и́е**) *мест*: **~и́е де́ньги не помогли́** no amount of money would have helped; (*разг*): **~ он не врач** he's not a doctor at all; (: *плохой*): **писа́тель он ~** he can't be called a writer; **ни у како́го челове́ка не бу́дет сомне́ния** nobody will have any doubt about it; **ни к како́му де́лу он не спосо́бен** he is not capable of anything; **он не соглаша́лся ни с каки́м аргуме́нтом** he didn't agree with any of the arguments; **нет ~о́го сомне́ния** there is absolutely no doubt (at all); **у меня́ нет ~о́го сомне́ния** I have absolutely no doubts; **и ~и́х!** and that's that!

Никара́гуа *ж нескл* Nicaragua.

никарагуа́нск|ий (**-ая, -ое, -ие**) *прил* Nicaraguan.

никелир|ова́ть (**-у́ю**; *perf* **отникелирова́ть**) *несов перех* to nickel.

никелиро́вк|а (**-и**) *ж* (*действие*) nickelling (*BRIT*), nickeling (*US*); (*покрытие*) nickel plate.

ни́кел|ь (**-я**) *м* (*ХИМ*) nickel.

ни́кн|уть (**-у, -ешь**) *несов от* **пони́кнуть** ◆ *неперех* (*трава, цветы*) to droop.

никогда́ *нареч* never; **как ~** as never before.

никого́ *мест см* **никто́**.

нико́й *нареч*: **нико́им о́бразом** not at all; **ни в ко́ем слу́чае** under no circumstances.

ни|кто́ (**-кого́**; *как* **кто**; *см* **Table 6**) *мест* nobody ◆ *м*: **она́ мне ~** (*разг*: *не родственник*) she's not a relative of mine; (*не друг*) she's nothing to me; **ни у кого́ нет сомне́ний** nobody has any doubts; **ни к кому́ не подходи́л** I didn't approach anyone; **ни с кем не говори́л** I didn't speak to anyone; **ни о ком не зна́ю** I don't know anything about anyone.

никуда́ *местоимённое нареч* nowhere ◆ *как сказ* (*разг*): **обслу́живание здесь – ~** the service here is terrible; **я ~ не пое́ду** I'm not going anywhere; **~ я не пое́ду** I'm going nowhere; **э́то ~ не годи́тся** that just won't do.

никуды́ш|ный (**-ен, -на, -но**) *прил* (*разг*) good-for-nothing.

никчём|ный (**-ен, -на, -но**) *прил* no good for anything.

Нил (**-а**) *м* the Nile.

НИИ *м сокр* (= *нау́чно-иссле́довательский институ́т*) scientific research institute.

нимб (**-а**) *м* nimbus.

ниотку́да *местоимённое нареч* from nowhere; **~ нет по́мощи** I get no help from anywhere.

нипочём *как сказ*: **бе́дность ему́ ~** (*разг*) being poor doesn't bother him; **ему́ всё ~** (*разг*) nothing hassles him.

ни́ппел|ь (**-я**) *м* (*ТЕХ*) nipple.

ниско́лько *местоимённое нареч* not at all; (*не лучше, не полезнее*) no; (*не рад, не удивлён*) at all; **ты рад? – ~** are you pleased? – not at all *или* in the slightest.

ниспада́|ть (*3sg* **-ет**, *3pl* **-ют**) *несов неперех* to fall.

ниспрове́рг|нуть (**-ну, -нешь**; *pt* **-, -ла, -ло**, *impf* **ниспроверга́ть**) *сов перех* to overthrow.

нисходя́щ|ий (**-ая, -ее, -ие**) *прил* (*линия*) descending; (*интонация*) falling.

нитеви́д|ный (**-ен, -на, -но**) *прил* long and thin.

ни́т|ка (**-ки**; *gen pl* **-ок**) *ж* (*обычно мн*: *для шитья*) thread *ед*; (*для вязания*) yarn; **~ же́мчуга** string of pearls; **~ газопрово́да** gas pipeline; **промо́кнуть** *(perf)* **до ~ки** to get soaked right through; **вдева́ть (вдеть** *perf*) **~ку в иго́лку** to thread a needle.

нитра́т (**-а**) *м* nitrate.

нит|ь (**-и**) *ж* thread; (*для вязания*) yarn; (*+gen*; *повествования, воспоминаний*) thread of; **ни́ти за́говора** strands of a plot; **ни́ти дру́жбы** threads of friendship.

них *мест см* **они́**.

ниц *м*: **па́дать ~** to prostrate o.s.

Ни́цц|а (**-ы**) *ж* Nice.

ничего́ *мест см* **ничто́** ◆ *нареч* fairly well; **(э́то) ~, что ...** it's all right that ...; **извини́те, я Вас побеспоко́ю – ~!** sorry to disturb you – it's all right!; **как живёшь? – ~** how are you? – all right; **~ себе́** (*сносно*) fairly well; **~ себе́!** (*выражает удивление*) well, I never!

нич|е́й (**-ьего́**; *f* **-ья́**, *nt* **-ьё**, *pl* **-ьи́**; *как* **чей**; *см* **Table 7**) *мест* nobody's; **он не слу́шает ~ьи́х сове́тов** he doesn't follow anybody's advice; **ни к чьему́ сове́ту не прислу́шивается** he doesn't listen to anybody's advice; **ни с чьим мне́нием не счита́ется** he doesn't consider anyone's views; **ни о чьём благополу́чии не беспоко́ится** he doesn't worry about anyone's wellbeing.

ниче́йн|ый *прил* (*полоса, зона*) no man's; **~ая земля́** no-man's-land; **~ результа́т, ниче́йная па́ртия** draw.

ничко́м *нареч* face down.

нич|то́ (**-его́**; *как* **что**; *см* **Table 6**) *мест, ср* nothing; **ни для чего́ не приго́дный** not suitable for anything; **ни с чем не согла́сен** I don't agree with anything; **ни о чём не прошу́** I

don't ask for anything; ~ **мне не интерéсно** nothing interests me; **~егó с ним не случи́тся** nothing will happen to him; **~егó подóбного не ви́дел** I've never seen anything like it; **~егó подóбного!** (*разг: совсем не так*) nothing like it!; **всегó ~егó** (*разг*) next to nothing; **ни за что!** (*ни в коем случае*) no way!; **ни за что не соглашáйся** whatever you do, don't agree; **ни за что ни про что** for nothing; **я здесь ни при чём** it has nothing to do with me; **~егó не поде́лаешь** there's nothing to be done.
ничтóжен *прил см* **ничтóжный.**
ничтóжеств|о (-а) *ср* nonentity.
ничтóж|ный (-ен, -на, -но) *прил* paltry.
ничу́ть *местоимённое нареч* (*нисколько*) not at all; (*не лучше, не больше*) no; (*не испугался, не огорчился*) at all; ~ **не бывáло** not at all.
ничь|я́ (-е́й) *ж* (*СПОРТ*) draw; **сыгрáть** *(perf)* **в ~ю́** to draw (*BRIT*), tie (*US*).
ни́ш|а (-и) *ж* niche.
нищá|ть (-ю; *perf* **обнищáть**) *несов неперех* to become impoverished.
ни́щая (-ей; *decl like adj*) *ж* beggar.
ни́щен|ка (-ки; *gen pl* **-ок**) *ж* = **ни́щая.**
ни́щенск|ий (-ая, -ое, -ие) *прил* (*ничтожный*) beggarly; **~ая жизнь** life of begging.
нищет|á (-ы́) *ж* poverty.
ни́щ|ий (-ая, -ее, -ие) *прил* poverty-stricken ◆ (-его; *decl like adj*) *м* beggar.
НЛО *м сокр* (= *неопóзнанный летáющий объéкт*) UFO (= *unidentified flying object*).
но *союз* but ◆ *ср нескл* (*препятствие*) setback ◆ *межд* gee up; **я предложи́л ему́ пóмощь,** ~ **он отказáлся** I offered to help him, but he refused; ~ **вдруг** then suddenly; ~ **тóлько** only; **~-но, осторóжнее!** now then, be more careful!
новáтор (-а) *м* innovator.
новáторств|о (-а) *ср* innovation.
новáци|я (-и) *ж* innovation.
новéлл|а (-ы) *ж* novella.
новелли́ст (-а) *м* writer of novellas.
новелли́ст|ка (-ки; *gen pl* **-ок**) *ж см* **новелли́ст.**
нóвеньк|ая (-ой; *decl like adj*) *ж* newcomer; (*в классе*) new pupil.
нóвеньк|ий (-ая, -ое, -ие) *прил* (*разг*) new ◆ (-ого; *decl like adj*) *м* newcomer; (*в классе*) new pupil; **что ~ого?** what's new?
новизн|á (-ы́) *ж* (*идей, подхода*) novelty.
нови́н|ка (-ки; *gen pl* **-ок**) *ж* new product; ~ **мóды** new fashion item; **кни́жная** ~ new book; **мне э́то в ~ку** it's new to me.
нович|óк (-кá) *м* newcomer; (*в классе*) new pupil; **я** ~ **в** *+prp* I am a newcomer to.
нóво *как сказ*: **здесь мне всё** ~ it's all new to me here.
новобрáн|ец (-ца) *м* new recruit.
новобрáчн|ая (-ой; *decl like adj*) *ж см* **новобрáчный.**
новобрáчн|ый (-ого; *decl like adj*) *м* newlywed.
нововведéни|е (-я) *ср* innovation.
новогóдн|ий (-яя, -ее, -ие) *прил* New Year *опред*; **новогóдняя ёлка** ≈ Christmas tree.
новозелáндск|ий (-ая, -ое, -ие) *прил* New Zealand *опред*.
новоиспечённый *прил* (*разг*) new.
новокаи́н (-а) *м* (*МЕД*) Novocaine ®.
новолу́ни|е (-я) *ср* new moon.
новорождённ|ая (-ой; *decl like adj*) *ж* newborn girl.
новорождённ|ый *прил* newborn ◆ (-ого; *decl like adj*) *м* newborn boy.
новосёл (-а) *м* (*дома*) new owner.
новосéл|ье (-ья; *gen pl* **-ий**) *ср* house-warming.
Новосиби́рск (-а) *м* Novosibirsk.
новострó|йка (-йки; *gen pl* **-ек**) *ж* (*строительство*) construction of new buildings; (*новое здание*) new building; **больни́ца-~** newly-built hospital.
нóвост|ь (-и; *gen pl* **-éй**) *ж* (*известие*) news; (*медицины, техники*) innovation.
новоя́вленный *прил* new.
нóвшеств|о (-а) *ср* (*в жизни, в обществе*) novelty; (*техническое*) innovation.
нóв|ый (-, -á, -о) *прил* new; **нóвая истóрия** modern history; **Нóвый Завéт** the New Testament; **Нóвая Зелáндия** New Zealand; **Нóвая Земля́** Novaya Zemlya.
нов|ь (-и) *ж* new era.
ног|á (-и́; *acc sg* **-у**, *nom pl* **-и**, *gen pl* **-**, *dat pl* **-áм**) *ж* (*ступня*) foot; (*выше ступни*) leg; **переступáть** *(impf)* *или* **перемина́ться** *(impf)* **с ~и́ нá ~у** to shift from one foot to the other; **идти́** *(impf)* **в нóгу со врéменем** (*перен*) to move with the times; **он бежáл со всех ног** he ran as fast as his legs would carry him; **сби́ться** *(perf)* **с ног** to be run off one's feet; **постáвить** *(perf)* **когó-н нá ~и** (*перен: больного*) to get sb back on his *umn* feet; (*детей*) to make sb stand on his *umn* own two feet; **с ног нá голову перевопрáчивать (перевернýть** *perf*) *или* **стáвить (постáвить** *perf*) **что-н** to turn *или* put sth on its head; **éле нóги унести́** *(perf)* to escape by the skin of one's teeth; **~и́ моéй там не бýдет** (*разг*) I won't step foot there again; **в ~х** (*постели*) at the foot of the bed; **вверх ~ми** upside down; **в дóме все вверх ~ми** the house is completely topsy turvy; **жить** *(impf)* **на ширóкую нóгу** to live lavishly; **на корóткой** *или* **дрýжеской ~é с** *+instr* on friendly terms with.
ноготк|и́ (-óв) *мн* marigold.
нóг|оть (-тя; *gen pl* **-тéй**) *м* nail; **до кóнчиков ногтéй** (*перен: совершенно*) from top to toe.
нож (-á) *м* knife; **быть** *(impf)* **с кем-н на ~áх** (*враждовать*) to be at daggers drawn with sb; **твой постýпки мне – ~ óстрый** (*перен: разг*) your behaviour gives me a lot of grief.
ножевóй *прил* (*рана*) knife *опред*.
нóжек *сущ см* **нóжка.**
нóжен *сущ см* **нóжны.**
нóжик (-а) *м*: **перочи́нный** ~ penknife; **складнóй** ~ flick knife (*BRIT*), switchblade (*US*).

но́ж|ка (**-ки**; *gen pl* **-ек**) *ж уменьш от* **нога́**; (*стула, стола итп*) leg; (*циркуля*) arm; **подставля́ть (подста́вить** *perf*) **~ку кому́-н** (*также перен*) to trip sb up.
но́жниц|ы (-) *мн* (*инструмент*) scissors *мн*, pair *ед* of scissors (*мн* pairs of scissors); (*расхождение*) disproportion.
ножно́й *прил* foot *опред*.
но́ж|ны (**-ен**) *мн* (*для кинжала*) sheath *ед*; (*для шпаги, сабли итп*) scabbard *ед*.
ножо́в|ка (**-ки**; *gen pl* **-ок**) *ж* hacksaw.
ноздрева́т|ый (**-, -а, -о**) *прил* (*сыр*) holey.
ноздр|я́ (**-и́**; *nom pl* **-и**, *gen pl* **-е́й**) *ж* (*обычно мн*) nostril.
нока́ут (**-а**) *м* knockout.
нокаути́р|овать (**-ую**) *(не)сов перех* to knock out.
нокда́ун (**-а**) *м* knockdown.
нол|ь (**-я́**) *м* (*МАТ*) zero, nought; (*при исчислении температуры*) zero; (*перен*: *человек*) nothing; **~ це́лых пять деся́тых, 0.5** zero *или* nought point five, 0.5; **встре́титься** (*perf*) **в де́сять ~-ноль** to meet at exactly ten o'clock.
номенклату́р|а (**-ы**) *ж* (*товаров, услуг*) list ◆ *собир* (*номенклатурные работники*) nomenklatura.
номенклату́рный *прил* (*единица*) listed; **номенклату́рный рабо́тник** nomenklatura.
но́мер (**-а**; *nom pl* **-а́**) *м* number; (*журнала, газеты*) issue; (*перчаток*) size; (*в гостинице*) room; (*концерта*) number, turn; **но́мер маши́ны** registration (number).
номерка́ *сущ см* **номеро́к**.
номерно́й *прил* (*завод*) *identified only by a number*; **номерно́й знак (автомоби́ля)** (car) number (*BRIT*) *или* license (*US*) plate; **номерно́й счёт (в ба́нке)** numbered account.
номер|о́к (**-ка́**) *ж* (*для пальто*) ≈ ticket.
номина́л (**-а**) *м* (*КОММ*) face value.
номина́л|ьный (**-ен, -ьна, -ьно**) *прил* (*зарплата*) nominal; **~ьная цена́** face value.
но́нсенс (**-а**) *м* nonsense.
нор|а́ (**-ы́**; *nom pl* **-ы**) *ж* (*зайца*) burrow; (*лисы*) den; (*барсука*) set; (*перен*) hole.
Норве́ги|я (**-и**) *ж* Norway.
норве́ж|ец (**-ца**) *м* Norwegian.
норве́ж|ка (**-ки**; *gen pl* **-ек**) *ж см* **норве́жец**.
норве́жск|ий (**-ая, -ое, -ие**) *прил* Norwegian; **~ язы́к** Norwegian.
норве́жца *итп сущ см* **норве́жец**.
но́р|ка (**-ки**; *gen pl* **-ок**) *ж* mink.
но́рковый *прил* mink *опред*.
но́рм|а (**-ы**) *ж* standard; (*выработки, прибыли*) rate; **~ поведе́ния** behavioural norm; **войти́** (*perf*) *или* **прийти́** (*perf*) **в ~у** (*в обычное состояние*) to return to normal; **он сего́дня в ~е** (*разг*) he's fine today.
норма́лен *прил см* **норма́льный**.
нормализа́ци|я (**-и**) *ж* normalization.
нормализ|ова́ть (**-у́ю**) *(не)сов перех* (*обстановку, отношения*) to normalize
▸ **нормализова́ться** *(не)сов возв* to stabilize.
норма́льно *нареч* normally ◆ *как сказ*: **э́то вполне́ ~** this is quite normal; **как дела́? – ~** how are things? – not bad; **у нас всё ~** everything's fine with us.
норма́льност|ь (**-и**) *ж* normality.
норма́л|ьный (**-ен, -ьна, -ьно**) *прил* normal; (*психически*) of sound mind.
Норма́нди|я (**-и**) *ж* Normandy.
нормати́в (**-а**) *м* norm.
нормати́вный *прил* normative.
норми́ровани|е (**-я**) *ср* (*цен*) standardization; (*мяса*) rationing.
норми́р|овать (**-ую**) *(не)сов перех* to standardize.
норов|и́ть (**-лю́, -и́шь**) *несов неперех* (*разг*): **~** *+infin* to take pains to do.
но́рок *сущ см* **но́рка**.
нос (**-а**; *part gen* **-у**, *loc sg* **-у́**, *nom pl* **-ы́**) *м* nose; (*корабля*) bow; (*птицы*) beak, bill; (*ботинка*) toe; **из-под но́са у** *+gen* from under the nose of; **отъе́зд/экза́мен на ~у́** (*разг*) the departure/exam is imminent; **под но́сом** (*разг*: *близко*) under one's (very) nose; **с но́сом оста́ться** (*perf*) (*разг*) to be left with nothing; **води́ть** (*impf*) **кого́-н за́ ~** to lead sb by the nose; **он не ви́дит да́льше со́бственного но́са** (*разг*) he can't see further than his own nose; **сова́ть** (*impf*) **~ в** *+acc* (*разг*) to poke *или* stick one's nose into.
носа́т|ый (**-, -а, -о**) *прил* with a big nose.
но́сик (**-а**) *м* (*человека*) small nose; (*чайника*) spout.
носи́л|ки (**-ок**) *мн* (*для раненых*) stretcher.
носи́льщик (**-а**) *м* porter.
носи́тел|ь (**-я**) *м* (*идей, прогресса*) bearer; (*инфекции*) carrier; (*данных, информации*) transmitter; **носи́тель языка́** native speaker.
носи́тельниц|а (**-ы**) *ж* (*идей, прогресса*) bearer.
но|си́ть (**-шу́, -сишь**) *несов перех* (*вещи, камни*) to carry; (*платье, очки*) to wear; (*усы, бороду, прическу*) to sport; (*фамилию мужа*) to use; (*отличаться*: *подлеж*: *предложение, спор,*) to be characterized by; **на́ши отноше́ния но́сят делово́й хара́ктер** our relations are of a business nature; **~** (*impf*) **на рука́х** to carry; (*перен*: *любить*) to adore
▸ **носи́ться** *несов возв* (*человек*) to rush; (*слухи*) to spread; (*одежда*) to wear; (*разг*: *увлекаться*): **~ся с** *+instr* (*с идеей*) to be preoccupied with; (*с человеком*) to make a fuss of; **~ся** (*impf*) **в во́здухе** (*настроения*) to be in the air; (*идея*) to be widespread.
но́ск|а (**-и**) *ж* (*одежды, обуви*) wearing; **удо́бный в ~е** comfortable (to wear).

носка́ *итп сущ см* **носо́к.**
но́с|кий (**-кая, -кое, -кие; -ок, -ка́, -ко**) *прил* (*туфли, ткань*) hard-wearing.
носов|о́й *прил* (*звук*) nasal; **~а́я часть** bow; **носово́й плато́к** handkerchief.
но́сок *прил см* **но́ский.**
нос|о́к (**-ка́**; *gen pl* **-о́к**) *м* (*обычно мн*: *чулок*) sock; (*gen pl* **-ко́в**; *ботинка, чулка, ноги*) toe; **встава́ть** (**встать** *perf*) **на ~ки́** to stand on tiptoe.
носоро́г (**-а**) *м* rhinoceros, rhino (*inf*).
ностальги́ческ|ий (**-ая, -ое, -ие**) *прил* nostalgic.
ностальги́|я (**-и**) *ж* (*по дому*) homesickness, nostalgia; (*по утраченному*) nostalgia.
но́т|а (**-ы**) *ж* note; *см также* **но́ты.**
нотариа́льный *прил* (*услуги*) notarial; **нотариа́льная householdконто́ра** notarial office.
нота́риус (**-а**) *м* notary (public).
нота́ци|я (**-и**) *ж* (*выговор*) lecture.
но́тн|ый *прил*: **~ое письмо́** musical notation.
но́т|ы (-) *мн* (*муз*) sheet music; **как по ~ам** (*перен*) smoothly.
но́у-ха́у *ср нескл* know-how.
ноч|ева́ть (**-у́ю**; *perf* **переночева́ть**) *несов неперех* to spend the night.
ночёв|ка (**-ки**; *gen pl* **-ок**) *ж*: **останови́ться на ~ку** to spend the night; **они́ прие́хали с ~кой** they came and stayed the night.
ночле́г (**-а**) *м* (*место*) somewhere to spend the night; **останови́ться** (*perf*) **на ~** to spend the night.
ночле́жный *прил*: **~ дом** hostel.
ночни́к (**-а́**) *м* night-light.
ночно́й *прил* (*час, холод*) night *опред*; **ночна́я руба́шка** nightshirt; **ночна́я сме́на** night shift.
ноч|ь (**-и**; *loc sg* **-и́**, *nom pl* **-и**, *gen pl* **-е́й**) *ж* night; **с утра́ до́ ~и** from dawn to dusk; **на́ ~** before bed; **споко́йной но́чи!** good night!
но́чью *нареч* at night; **и днём и ~** day and night.
но́ш|а (**-и**) *ж* burden.
ноше́ни|е (**-я**) *ср* (*действие*) wearing; **~ ору́жия** (*ЮР*) carrying of offensive weapons.
но́шеный *прил* (*одежда, туфли*) second-hand.
ношу́(сь) *несов см* **носи́ть(ся).**
но́ю *итп несов см* **ныть.**
ноя́бр|ь (**-я́**) *м* November; *см также* **октя́брь.**
ноя́брьск|ий (**-ая, -ое, -ие**) *прил* November *опред.*
нрав (**-а**) *м* (*человека*) temperament; **э́то мне по нра́ву** this is to my liking; *см также* **нра́вы.**
нра́в|иться (**-люсь, -ишься**; *perf* **понра́виться**) *несов возв* (*+dat*): **мне ~ится э́тот фильм** I like this film; **мне ~ится чита́ть/гуля́ть** I like to read/go for a walk.
нравоуче́ни|е (**-я**) *ср* lecture on morals; (*в басне*) moral; **чита́ть** (*impf*) **кому́-н ~я** to give sb a lecture on morals.
нравоучи́тел|ьный (**-ен, -ьна, -ьно**) *прил* (*рассказ, история*) with a moral; (*тон*) moralizing.
нра́вственност|ь (**-и**) *ж* morals *мн.*
нра́вствен|ный (**-, -на, -но**) *прил* moral.
нра́в|ы (**-ов**) *мн* (*обычаи*) customs *мн.*
н.с. *сокр* (= *но́вого сти́ля*) NS (New Style).
НТР *ж сокр* = *нау́чно-техни́ческая револю́ция.*

KEYWORD

ну *межд* **1** (*выражает побуждение*) come on; **ну, начина́й!** come on, get started!
2 (*выражает восхищение*) what; **ну и си́ла!** what strength!
3 (*выражает иронию*) well (well); **ну и у́мник же ты!** well (well), what a clever fellow you are!
◆ *част* **1** (*неужели*): **(да) ну?!** not really?!; **я женю́сь – да ну?!** I'm getting married – not really?!
2 (*усиливает выразительность*): **ну коне́чно!** why of course!; **ну, я тебе́ покажу́!** why, I'll show you!
3 (*допустим*): **ты говори́шь по-англи́йски? – ну, говорю́** do you speak English? – what if I do
4 (*во фразах*); **ну и ну!** (*разг*) well well!; **ну-ка!** (*разг*) come on!; **ну тебя́/его́!** (*разг*) to hell with you/him!

нувори́ш (**-а**) *м* nouveau riche.
нуг|а́ (**-и́**) *ж* nougat.
ну́ден *прил см* **ну́дный.**
нуди́ст (**-а**) *м* nudist.
нуди́стк|а (**-и**) *ж см* **нуди́ст.**
ну́дно *нареч* tediously.
ну́д|ный (**-ен, -на́, -но**) *прил* tedious.
нужд|а́ (**-ы́**; *nom pl* **-ы**) *ж* (*no pl*; *бедность*) poverty; (*потребность*): **~ (в** *+prp*) need (for); **ну́жды населе́ния** the needs of the population; **в э́том нет ~ы́** there is no need for it.
нужд|а́ться (**-юсь**) *несов возв* (*бедствовать*) to be needy; **~** (*impf*) **в** *+prp* to need, be in need of.
ну́жен *прил см* **ну́жный.**
ну́жно *как сказ* (*необходимо*): **~ им помо́чь** *или* **~, что́бы им помогли́** it is necessary to help them; **~ хоро́шего специали́ста** a good specialist is needed; **мне ~ идти́** I have to go, I must go; **мне ~ 10 рубле́й** I need 10 roubles; **о́чень ~!** (*разг*) my foot!
ну́ж|ный (**-ен, -на́, -но, -ны́**) *прил* necessary.
нулев|о́й *прил*: **~а́я температу́ра** temperature of zero; **~а́я отме́тка** (mark of) zero; **~ результа́т** no result.
нул|ь (**-я́**) *м* (*МАТ*) zero, nought; (*при исчислении температуры*) zero; (*перен*: *человек*) nothing; **начина́ть** (**нача́ть** *perf*) **с ~я́** to start from scratch; **своди́ться** (**свести́сь** *perf*) **к ~ю́** to come to nothing.
нумера́ци|я (**-и**) *ж* numbering.
нумер|ова́ть (**-у́ю**; *perf* **пронумерова́ть**) *несов перех* to number.
нумизма́т (**-а**) *м* numismatist.
нумизма́тик|а (**-и**) *ж* numismatics.
ну́три|я (**-и**) *ж* (*зоол*) coypu.
нутр|о́ (**-а́**) *ср* (*разг*: *интуиция*) instincts *мн*; **э́то**

мне не по ~ý I'm not too keen on this.
НФ *м сокр* (= *национáльный фронт*) NF (= *National Front*;) (= *наýчная фантáстика*) sci-fi, SF (= *science fiction*).
НФС *сокр* (= *Национáльная федерáция спорт*) national federation of sport.
НХЛ *ж сокр* (= *Национáльная хоккéйная лúга*) NHL (= *National Hockey League*).
НЧ *сокр* (= *нúзкая частотá*) LF (= *low frequency*) ◆ *прил* (*низкочастóтный*) LF (= *low-frequency*).
нынe *нареч* today.
нынешн|ий (-яя, -ее, -ие) *прил* (*события, правительство*) the present; (*молодёжь*) today's; **~ее лéто** this summer.
нынче *нареч* (*разг*: *сегодня*) today; (: *теперь*) nowadays.
нырн|ýть (-ý, -ёшь) *сов неперех* (*также перен*) to dive.
ныря́льщик (-а) *м* diver.
ныря́льщиц|а (-ы) *ж см* **ныря́льщик**.
ныря́|ть (-ю) *несов неперех* (*также перен*) to dive.
ныть (нóю, нóешь) *несов неперех* (*рана, зуб*) to ache; (*жаловаться*) to moan.
Нью-Йóрк (-а) *м* New York.
н.э. *сокр* (= *нáшей э́ры*) AD (= *anno Domini*).
НЭП *м сокр* (*ист*: = *нóвая экономúческая полúтика*) NEP (= *New Economic Policy*).
нюáнс (-а) *м* nuance.
Ню́рнберг (-а) *м* Nuremberg.
нюх (-а) *м* (*собаки*) nose; (*перен*: *разг*): **~ на** *+acc* nose for.
ню́ха|ть (-ю; *perf* **поню́хать**) *несов перех* (*цветы, воздух*) to smell; (*спирт*) to sniff; ~ (*impf*) **табáк** to take snuff.
ня́нек *сущ см* **ня́нька**.
ня́неч|ка (-ки; *gen pl* **-ек**) *ж* (*разг*) = **ня́ня**.
ня́нч|ить (-у, -ишь) *несов перех* to mind
▸ **ня́нчиться** *несов возв*: **~ся с** *+instr* (*с младенцем*) to mind; (*разг*: *с лентяем, с мужем*) to fuss over.
ня́н|ька (-ьки; *gen pl* **-ек**) *ж* (*разг*: *ребёнка*) nanny.
ня́н|я (-и; *gen pl* **-ь**) *ж* nanny; (*работающая на дому*) child minder; (*в больнице*) auxiliary nurse; (*в детском саду*) cleaner; **приходя́щая** ~ babysitter.

~О,о~

О, о *сущ нескл (буква) the 15th letter of the Russian alphabet.*
о *предл* (*+prp*) about; (*+acc*; *опереться, удариться*) against; (*споткнуться*) over ◆ *межд* oh; **книга ~ России** a book on *или* about Russia; **мысли ~ доме** thoughts of home; **волны бьются ~ скалы** the waves are beating against the cliffs; **~ да/нет!** oh yes/no!; **~, если бы ты знал!** oh, if only you knew!
о. *сокр* (= **остров**) I (= *island*); (= *озеро*) L (= *lake*).
о- *префикс* (*in verbs*; *сделать каким-нибудь*) *indicating change of state eg.* *округлить*; (*снабдить чем-н*) *indicating suppy of sth eg.* *озаглавить*; (*распространить действие на всю поверхность*) *indicating covering of a surface with sth eg.* *охватить*; (*распространить действие на многих*) *indicating action involving many people eg.* *одарить*.
оазис (-а) *м* (*также перен*) oasis.
ОАЕ *ж сокр* (= *Организация африканского единства*) OAU (= *Organization of African Unity*).
ОАПЕК *ж сокр* (= *Организация арабских стран-экспортёров нефти*) OAPEC (= *Organization of Arab Petroleum-Exporting Countries*).
об *предл* = **о**.
об- *префикс см* **о-**.
об|а (-оих; *см* **Table 26**; *f* **обе**, *nt* **оба**) *м чис* both; **смотреть** (*impf*) **в ~** (*разг*: *быть осторожным*) to watch out; (: *быть внимательным*) to keep one's eyes peeled.
обалде|ть (-ю; *impf* **обалдевать**) *сов неперех* (*разг*) to go crazy.
обанкро|титься (-чусь, -тишься) *сов возв* to go bankrupt; (*перен*: *идея, политика*) to prove (to be) bankrupt.
обаяни|е (-я) *ср* charm.
обаятел|ьный (-ен, -ьна, -ьно) *прил* charming.
обвал (-а) *м* (*в шахте, в штольне*) rock fall; (*снежный*) avalanche; (*здания, этажа, рубля*) collapse.
обвалива|ть (-ю) *несов от* **обвалять**.
обвал|иться (*3sg* **-ится**, *3pl* **-ятся**, *impf* **обваливаться**) *сов возв* to collapse; (*потолок, крыша*) to cave in, collapse.
обваля|ть (-ю; *impf* **обваливать**) *сов перех*: **~ кого-н/что-н в** *+prp* to roll sb/sth in.
обв|арить (-арю, -аришь; *impf* **обваривать**) *сов перех* to pour boiling water over; (*КУЛИН*) to blanch; (*обжечь*) to scald
▸ **обвариться** (*impf* **обвариваться**) *сов возв* (*обжечься*) to scald o.s.
обведу *итп сов см* **обвести**.
обвенча|ть (-ю; *impf* **венчать**) *сов перех* to marry
▸ **обвенчаться** (*impf* **венчаться**) *сов возв* to get married, marry.
обв|ести (-еду, -едёшь; *pt* **-ёл, -ела, -ело**, *impf* **обводить**) *сов перех* (*букву, чертёж*) to go over (*drawing, outline etc*); (*окаймить*: *заголовок, рисунок*) to edge; (*футболиста*) to pass (*while keeping possession of the ball/puck etc*); **обводить (~** *perf*) **вокруг** *+gen* (*стола, дома*) to lead *или* take round; **обводить (~** *perf*) **что-н/кого-н глазами** to run one's eye over sth/sb; **~** (*perf*) **кого-н вокруг пальца** (*разг*) to twist sb round one's little finger.
обветренный *прил* weather-beaten.
обветр|иться (-юсь, -ишься; *impf* **обветриваться**) *сов возв* to become weather-beaten.
обветшалый *прил* dilapidated.
обвива|ть(ся) (-ю(сь)) *несов от* **обвить(ся)**.
обвинени|е (-я) *ср*: **~ (в** *+prp*) accusation (of); (*ЮР*) charge (of) ◆ *ссбир* (*обвиняющая сторона*) the prosecution; **свидетели ~я** witnesses for the prosecution.
обвинител|ь (-я) *м* accuser; (*ЮР*) prosecutor.
обвинительный *прил* (*речь, выступление*) accusatory; **~ приговор** (*ЮР*) verdict of guilty; **~ акт** (*ЮР*) indictment.
обвин|ить (-ю, -ишь; *impf* **обвинять**) *сов перех*: **~ кого-н (в** *+prp*) to accuse sb (of); (*ЮР*) to charge sb (with).
обвиняем|ая (-ой; *decl like adj*) *ж см* **обвиняемый**.
обвиняем|ый (-ого; *decl like adj*) *м* the accused *или* defendant.
обвиня|ть (-ю) *несов от* **обвинить** ◆ *перех* (*ЮР*) to prosecute.
обвиса|ть (*3sg* **-ет**, *3pl* **-ют**, *perf* **обвиснуть**) *несов неперех* to droop.
обвислый *прил* (*разг*: *кожа*) sagging; (: *усы*) drooping; (: *тело*) flabby.
обвис|нуть (*3sg* **-нет**, *3pl* **-нут**, *pt* **-, -ла, -ло**) *сов от* **обвисать**.

об|ви́ть (-овью́, -овьёшь; *impf* **обвива́ть**) *сов перех* (*подлеж*: *плющ, вьюн*) to twine around; **обвива́ть (~** *perf*) **кого́-н/что-н чем-н** to wind sth round sb/sth; **обвива́ть (~** *perf*) **чью-н ше́ю рука́ми** to wrap one's arms around sb's neck
▸ **обви́ться** (*impf* **обвива́ться**) *сов возв*: **~ся вокру́г** *+gen* to twine around.
обв|оди́ть (-ожу́, -о́дишь) *несов от* **обвести́**.
обводн|и́ть (-ю́, -и́шь; *impf* **обводня́ть**) *сов перех* to irrigate.
обво́дный *прил*: **~ кана́л** *canal encircling a town*.
обводня́|ть (-ю) *несов от* **обводни́ть**.
обвожу́ *несов см* **обводи́ть**.
оборо́жива|ть (-ю) *несов от* **обворожи́ть**.
обвор|ова́ть (-у́ю; *impf* **обворо́вывать**) *сов перех* (*разг*: *квартиру*) to do over; (: *соседа*) to rob.
обворожи́тел|ьный (-ен, -ьна, -ьно) *прил* captivating.
обворож|и́ть (-у́, -и́шь; *impf* **обвора́живать**) *сов перех* to captivate.
обв|яза́ть (-яжу́, -я́жешь; *impf* **обвя́зывать**) *сов перех*: **~ кого́-н/что-н чем-н** (*верёвкой, платком*) to tie sth round sb/sth; **~** (*perf*) **что-н спи́цами/крючко́м** to knit/crochet a border on sth
▸ **обвяза́ться** (*impf* **обвя́зываться**) *сов возв*: **~ся чем-н** to tie sth round o.s.
обгл|ода́ть (-ожу́, -о́жешь; *impf* **обгла́дывать**) *сов перех* to pick clean.
обговор|и́ть (-ю́, -и́шь; *impf* **обгова́ривать**) *сов перех* (*разг*) to discuss.
обго́н (-а) *м* overtaking.
обгоню́ *итп сов см* **обогна́ть**.
обгоня́|ть (-ю) *несов от* **обогна́ть**.
обгора́|ть (-ю) *несов от* **обгоре́ть**.
обгоре́лый *прил* (*дом, дерево*) burnt; (*разг*: *спина, плечи*) sunburnt.
обгор|е́ть (-ю́, -и́шь; *impf* **обгора́ть**) *сов неперех* (*дом*) to be burnt; (*разг*: *на пожаре*) to get burnt; (: *на солнце*) to get sunburnt.
обгры́з|ть (-у́, -ёшь; *impf* **обгрыза́ть**) *сов перех* (*яблоко, кость*) to gnaw; **обгрыза́ть (~** *perf*) **но́гти** to bite one's nails right down.
обд|ели́ть (-елю́, -е́лишь; *impf* **обделя́ть**) *сов перех*: **он ~ели́л её деньга́ми** he didn't give her the money; **приро́да ~ели́ла его́ умо́м/си́лой** he is not blessed with intelligence/strength; **всем да́ли пода́рки, а его́ ~ели́ли** everybody got a present but he was left out.
обдеру́ *итп сов см* **ободра́ть**.
обдира́|ть (-ю) *несов от* **ободра́ть**.
обду́ман|ный (-, -на, -но) *прил* considered.
обду́ма|ть (-ю; *impf* **обду́мывать**) *сов перех* to consider, think over.
обдур|и́ть (-ю́, -и́шь; *impf* **обдуря́ть**) *сов перех*: **~ кого́-н** (*разг*: *обмануть*) to pull the wool over sb's eyes; (: *смошенничать*) to rip sb off.
о́б|е (-е́их) *ж чис см* **о́ба**.
обе́га|ть (-ю; *impf* **обега́ть**) *сов перех* (*разг*) to rush round.
обега́|ть (-ю) *несов от* **обе́гать, обежа́ть**.
обегу́ *итп сов см* **обежа́ть**.
обе́д (-а) *м* lunch, dinner; (*время*) lunch *или* dinner time; (*разг*: *перерыв*) lunch break; **за ~ом** at lunch *или* dinner; **по́сле ~а** after lunch *или* dinner; (*после 12 часов дня*) in the afternoon; **закры́т на ~** closed for lunch.
обе́да|ть (-ю; *perf* **пообе́дать**) *несов неперех* to have lunch *или* dinner; (*разг*: *уходить на перерыв*) to take a lunch break.
обе́ден *сущ см* **обе́дня**.
обе́денный *прил* (*стол, сервиз*) dinner *опред*; (*часы, время*) lunch *опред*, dinner *опред*.
обедне́вш|ий (-ая, -ее, -ие) *прил* impoverished.
обедне́|ть (-ю) *сов от* **бедне́ть**.
обе́д|ня (-ни; *gen pl* **-ен**) *ж* (*РЕЛ*) Mass; **идти́ (пойти́** *perf*) **к ~не** to go to Mass; **служи́ть** (*impf*) **~ню** to hear Mass.
обежа́ть (*как* **бежа́ть**; *см* **Table 20**; *impf* **обега́ть**) *сов перех* (*разг*: *магазины*) to rush round ◆ *неперех*: **~ вокру́г** *+gen* to run round.
обезбо́ливани|е (-я) *ж* anaesthetization (*BRIT*), anesthetization (*US*).
обезбо́лива|ть (-ю) *несов от* **обезбо́лить**.
обезбо́ливающ|ее (-его; *decl like adj*) *ср* (*разг*) painkiller.
обезбо́ливающ|ий (-ая, -ее, -ие) *прил* anaesthetic *опред* (*BRIT*), anesthetic *опред* (*US*).
обезбо́л|ить (-ю, -ишь; *impf* **обезбо́ливать**) *сов перех* to anaesthetize (*BRIT*), anesthetize (*US*); **обезбо́ливать (~** *perf*) **кому́-н ро́ды** to give sb an anaesthetic (*BRIT*) *или* anesthetic (*US*) during childbirth.
обезво́|дить (-жу, -дишь; *impf* **обезво́живать**) *сов перех* (*землю*) to drain; (*организм*) to dehydrate.
обезво́жу *сов см* **обезво́дить**.
обезвре́|дить (-жу, -дишь; *impf* **обезвре́живать**) *сов перех* (*бомбу*) to defuse; (*воду*) to purify; (*преступника*) to make powerless.
обезгла́в|ить (-лю, -ишь; *impf* **обезгла́вливать**) *сов перех* to behead; (*перен*: *восстание*) to leave without a leader.
обездо́лен|ный (-, -на, -но) *прил* deprived.
обездо́л|ить (-ю, -ишь) *сов перех* to deprive.
обезжи́ренный *прил* fat-free.
обезжи́р|ить (-ю, -ишь; *impf* **обезжи́ривать**) *сов перех* (*молоко, творог*) to skim; (*шерсть*) to remove fat from.
обезли́ч|ить (-у, -ишь; *impf* **обезли́чивать**) *сов перех* to depersonalize; (*работу, руководство*) to remove individual responsibility from.
обезобра́|зить (-жу, -зишь; *impf*

обезобра́живать) *сов перех* to disfigure.

обезопа́|сить (-шу, -сишь) *сов перех* (*себя, друга*) to protect

▸ **обезопа́ситься** *сов возв* to protect o.s.

обезору́ж|ить (-у, -ишь; *impf* **обезору́живать)** *сов перех* (*также перен*) to disarm.

обезу́ме|ть (-ю) *сов неперех*: **~ от** *+gen* (*страха, горя итп*) to go out of one's mind with.

обезья́н|а (-ы) *ж* (*с хвостом*) monkey; (*без хвоста*) ape; (*перен*: *разг*) copycat.

обезья́н|ий (-ья, -ье, -ьи) *прил* (*хвост*) monkey's; (*повадки*) apelike.

обезья́ннича|ть (-ю; *impf* **собезья́нничать)** *несов неперех* (*разг*) to be a copycat.

обе́их *чис см* **о́бе**.

обе́й(те) *сов см* **оби́ть.**

обели́ск (-а) *м* obelisk.

обел|и́ть (-ю́, -и́шь; *impf* **обеля́ть)** *сов перех* to whitewash.

оберега́|ть (-ю) *несов перех* (*человека*) to protect; (*имущество*) to guard.

оберн|у́ть (-у́, -ёшь; *impf* **обёртывать** *или* **обора́чивать)** *сов перех* (*книгу, посылку*) to wrap (up); (*impf* **обора́чивать;** *капитал*) to turn over; **обёртывать** *или* **обора́чивать (~** *perf***) что-н вокру́г** *+gen* (*талии, головы*) to wrap sth round; **обора́чивать (~** *perf***) де́ло в свою́ по́льзу** (*перен*) to turn things to one's own advantage

▸ **оберну́ться** (*impf* **обора́чиваться**) *сов возв* (*повернуться назад*) to turn (round); (*капитал, деньги*) to be recovered; **обора́чиваться (~ся** *perf***)** *+instr* (*неприятностями, сюрпризом*) to turn out to be; (*лебедем, волком*) to turn into.

обёрт|ка (-ки; *gen pl* **-ок)** *ж* (*книжная, конфетная*) wrapper; (*на посылке*) wrapping.

обёрточн|ый *прил*: **~ая бума́га** wrapping paper.

обёртыва|ть (-ю) *несов от* **оберну́ть.**

оберу́(сь) *итп сов см* **обобра́ть(ся).**

обескро́в|ить (-лю, -ишь) *сов перех* (*перен*) to sap the strength of.

обескура́жен|ный (-, -на, -но) *прил* baffled.

обескура́ж|ить (-у, -ишь; *impf* **обескура́живать)** *сов перех* (*озадачить*) to baffle.

обеспе́чени|е (-я) *ср* (*мира, безопасности, договора*) guarantee; **~** *+instr* (*сырьём, продуктами*) provision of; **материа́льное ~** financial security.

обеспе́ченност|ь (-и) *ж* (material) comfort; (*школ, завода итп*) provision; **фина́нсовая ~** financial security.

обеспе́чен|ный (-, -на, -но) *прил* well-off, well-to-do.

обеспе́ч|ить (-у, -ишь; *impf* **обеспе́чивать)** *сов перех* (*семью*) to provide for; (*мир, успех*) to guarantee, ensure; **обеспе́чивать (~** *perf***) кого́-н/что-н чем-н** to provide *или* supply sb/sth with sth, provide *или* supply sth for sb/sth.

обеспоко́|ить (-ю, -ишь) *сов от* **беспоко́ить.**

обесси́ле|ть (-ю; *impf* **обесси́левать)** *сов неперех* to become *или* grow weak.

обесси́л|ить (-ю, -ишь; *impf* **обесси́ливать)** *сов перех* to weaken.

обессла́в|ить (-лю, -ишь) *сов перех* to besmirch.

обессме́р|тить (-чу, -тишь) *сов перех* to immortalize.

обесто́ч|ить (-у, -ишь; *impf* **обесто́чивать)** *сов перех* (*ТЕХ*) to cut off the power to.

обесцве́|тить (-чу, -тишь; *impf* **обесцве́чивать)** *несов перех* to bleach; (*перен*: *рассказ*) to tone down

▸ **обесцве́титься** (*impf* **обесцве́чиваться**) *сов возв* to be bleached; (*ткань*: *от времени*) to fade; (*перен*: *рассказ*) to become flat.

обесце́нивани|е (-я) *ср* (*валюты*) depreciation; (*: намеренное*) devaluation.

обесце́н|ить (-ю, -ишь; *impf* **обесце́нивать)** *сов перех* (*также перен*) to devalue

▸ **обесце́ниться** (*impf* **обесце́ниваться**) *сов возв* to be devalued; (*вещь*) to depreciate.

обесче́|стить (-щу, -стишь) *сов от* **бесче́стить.**

обе́т (-а) *м* vow.

обетова́нн|ый *прил*: **~ая земля́** the Promised Land.

обеща́ни|е (-я) *ср* promise.

обеща́|ть (-ю; *perf* **обеща́ть** *или* **пообеща́ть)** *несов (не)перех* to promise.

обжа́ловани|е (-я) *ср* appeal.

обжа́л|овать (-ую) *сов перех* to appeal against.

обжа́р|ить (-ю, -ишь; *impf* **обжа́ривать)** *сов перех* to brown.

об|же́чь (-ожгу́, -ожжёшь *итп*, **-ожгу́т;** *pt* **-жёг, -ожгла́, -ожгло́)** *сов от* **жечь ◆** (*impf* **обжига́ть**) *перех* to burn; (*кирпич итп*) to fire; (*дерево итп*) to scorch; (*подлеж*: *крапива*) to sting

▸ **обже́чься** *сов от* **же́чься ◆** (*impf* **обжига́ться**) *возв* to burn o.s.; (*перен*: *потерпеть неудачу*) to get one's fingers burnt.

обжира́|ться (-юсь) *несов от* **обожра́ться.**

обжито́й *прил* (*дом*) lived-in.

обжо́р|а (-ы) *м/ж* (*разг*) pig, greedy guts.

обжо́рств|о (-а) *ср* (*разг*) greediness.

обжу́л|ить (-ю, -ишь; *impf* **обжу́ливать)** *сов перех* (*разг*) to con.

обзаве|сти́сь (-ду́сь, -дёшься; *impf* **обзаводи́ться**) *сов возв* (*+instr*; *разг*) to get o.s.

обзвон|и́ть (-ю́, -и́шь; *impf* **обзва́нивать)** *сов перех* (*разг*) to phone round.

обзову́ *итп сов см* **обозва́ть.**

обзо́р (-а) *м* view; (*статьи, новостей*) review.

обзо́рн|ый *прил* general; **~ая статья́** review.

обзыва́|ть (-ю) *несов от* **обозва́ть**

▸ **обзыва́ться** *несов возв* (*разг*) to call people names.

обива́|ть (-ю) *несов от* **оби́ть.**

оби́вк|а (-и) *ж* upholstery.

оби́д|а (-ы) *ж* (*несправедливость*) insult;

(*горечь*) grievance; **какáя ~!** what a pity!; **наносúть (нанестú** *perf*) **~у комý-н** to hurt *или* offend sb; **не давáть (дать** *perf*) **когó-н в ~у** (*разг*) to stand *или* stick up for sb; **быть** (*impf*) **в ~е на когó-н** to be in a huff with sb.
обúден *прил см* **обúдный**.
обú|деть (-жу, -дишь; *impf* **обижáть**) *сов перех* to hurt, offend; **он ~жен умóм/красотóй** (*разг*) he's not too smart/good-looking
▸ **обúдеться** (*impf* **обижáться**) *сов возв*: **~ся (на** *+acc*) to be hurt *или* offended (by).
обúдно *как сказ* (*см прил*) it's offensive; it's annoying; **мне ~ слы́шать э́то** it hurts me to hear this; **~, что мы не встрéтились** it's annoying that we didn't meet.
обúд|ный (-ен, -на, -но) *прил* (*оскорбительный*) offensive; (*разг: досадный*) annoying.
обúдчив|ый (-, -а, -о) *прил* touchy.
обижá|ть(ся) (-ю(сь)) *несов от* **обúдеть(ся)**.
обúжен|ный (-, -на, -но) *прил* aggrieved.
обúжу(сь) *сов см* **обúдеть(ся)**.
обúлен *прил см* **обúльный**.
обúли|е (-я) *ср* abundance.
обúль|ный (-ен, -ьна, -ьно) *прил* abundant; (*+instr*; *рыбой, талантами*) rich in; **~ьная едá** food in abundance.
обиня́к (-á) *м*: **без обиняко́в** plainly.
обирá|ть (-ю) *несов от* **обобрáть**.
обитáем|ый (-, -а, -о) *прил* inhabited.
обитáтел|ь (-я) *м* inhabitant.
обитá|ть (-ю) *несов неперех* to live.
об|úть (-обью́, -обьёшь; *imper* **обéй(те)**, *impf* **обивáть**) *сов перех*: **~ (**+*instr*) to cover (with); **обивáть (~** *perf*) **порóги у когó-н** to camp on sb's doorstep.
обихóд (-а) *м*: **быть в ~е** to be in use; **входúть (войтú** *perf*) **в ~** to come into use; **выходúть (вы́йти** *perf*) **из ~а** to go out of use.
обихóд|ный (-ен, -на, -но) *прил* everyday.
обкатá|ть (-ю; *impf* **обкáтывать**) *сов перех* (*поверхность, дорогу*) to flatten (out); (*машину*) to run in; (*станок итп*) to test (out).
обкáтк|а (-и) *ж* (*дороги*) flattening; (*машины, станка*) testing.
обкáтыва|ть (-ю) *несов от* **обкатáть**.
обклáдыва|ть(ся) (-ю(сь)) *несов от* **обложúть(ся)**.
обклé|ить (-ю, -ишь; *impf* **обклéивать**) *сов перех* (*плакатами, бумагой*) to cover; (*обоями*) to (wall)paper.
обкóм (-а) *м сокр* = *областнóй комитéт*; (*профсоюза, партии*) ≈ regional committee.
обкрадý *итп сов см* **обокрáсть**.
обкрáдыва|ть (-ю) *несов от* **обокрáсть**.
обк|урúть (-урю́, -ýришь; *impf* **обкýривать**) *сов перех* (*разг: комнату*) to fill with smoke; **ты меня́ совсéм ~урúл** your smoke is suffocating me.
обкусá|ть (-ю; *impf* **обкýсывать**) *сов перех* to nibble; **обкýсывать (~** *perf*) **нóгти** to bite one's nails.
обл. *сокр* = **óбласть**.
облáв|а (-ы) *ж* (*на преступников*) roundup; **устрóить** (*perf*) **~у на** *+acc* (*на зверя*) to close in on.
облагá|ть (-ю) *несов от* **обложúть**.
облагодéтельств|овать (-ую) *сов перех*: **~ когó-н** to do sb a great favour (*BRIT*) *или* favor (*US*).
обладáтел|ь (-я) *м* possessor.
обладá|ть (-ю) *несов неперех* (*+instr*) to possess; (*женщиной*) to have; **~** (*impf*) **здорóвьем** to enjoy good health; **~** (*impf*) **красотóй** to be beautiful.
облá|зить (-жу, -зишь) *сов перех* (*разг*) to go round.
облáива|ть (-ю) *несов от* **облáять**.
óблак|о (-а; *nom pl* **-á**, *gen pl* **-óв)** *ср* (*также перен*) cloud; **витáть** (*impf*) **в облакáх** to have one's head in the clouds.
облáмыва|ть(ся) (-ю(сь)) *несов от* **обломáть(ся)**.
обласкá|ть (-ю) *сов перех* to be kind to.
областнóй *прил* (*центр, театр*) ≈ regional, oblast *опред*; (*выражение, слово*) regional.
óбласт|ь (-и; *gen pl* **-éй)** *ж* region; (*АДМИН*) ≈ region, oblast; (*науки, искусства*) field; **в ~и** *+gen* (*в сфере*) in the field of.
óблачен *прил см* **óблачный**.
óблачност|ь (-и) *ж* cloud.
óблач|ный (-ен, -на, -но) *прил* cloudy.
облá|ять (-ю; *impf* **облáивать**) *сов перех* to bark at; (*перен: разг*) to swear at.
облёг *итп сов см* **облéчь**.
облегá|ть (-ю) *несов от* **облéчь ♦** *перех* to fit.
облегáющ|ий (-ая, -ее, -ие) *прил* close-fitting.
облегчá|ть (-ю) *несов от* **облегчúть**.
облегчéни|е (-я) *ср* (*условий труда, жизни*) improvement; (*успокоение*) relief.
облегчённо *нареч* with relief.
облегчённый *прил* (*ткань, инструмент*) light; (*труд, экзамен*) easier; (*ответ, улыбка*) relieved.
облегч|úть (-ý, -úшь; *impf* **облегчáть**) *сов перех* (*вес*) to lighten; (*экзамен, жизнь*) to make easier; (*боль, страдание*) to relieve; **облегчáть (~** *perf*) **дýшу** to ease one's mind.
обледенéлый *прил* (*ступени, горка*) icy; (*борода*) frozen.
обледенé|ть (-ю) *сов неперех* (*см прил*) to become icy; to freeze.
облезá|ть (-ю) *несов от* **облéзть**.
облéзлый *прил* (*разг: собака, птица*) mangy; (*вид, внешность*) scruffy; (*стены*) peeling.
облéз|ть (-у, -ешь; *impf* **облезáть**) *сов неперех*

(*разг*) to grow mangy; (*краска, обои*) to peel (off); (*стены*) to peel.
облёк *итп сов см* **облéчь.**
облекá|ть (-ю) *несов от* **облéчь.**
облекý *сов см* **облéчь.**
обл|ени́ться (-еню́сь, -éнишься) *сов возв* to grow lazy.
обл|епи́ть (-еплю́, -éпишь; *impf* **облепля́ть**) *сов перех* (*подлеж: грязь, глина*) to stick to; (*перен: подлеж: люди, мухи*) to surround; (*разг: покрыть*): ~ **что-н чем-н** to plaster sth with sth.
обле|тéть (-чý, -ти́шь; *impf* **облетáть**) *сов перех* to fly round; (*новость*) to spread ◆ *неперех* (*листья*) to fall off.
обл|éчь (-екý, -ечёшь *итп*, -екýт; *pt* -ёк, -еклá, -ekлó, *impf* **облекáть**) *сов перех*: ~ **когó-н/что-н чем-н** (*властью, доверием*) to vest sb/sth with sth; (*тайной*) to shroud sb/sth in sth; (*impf* **облегáть**, *3sg* **-ля́жет**, *3pl* **-ля́гут**, *pt* **-ёг, -еглá, -еглó**) to envelop; **облекáть** (~ *perf*) **что-н в** +*acc* to express sth in.
обливá|ть (-ю) *несов от* **обли́ть**
▸ **обливáться** *несов от* **обли́ться** ◆ *возв*: ~**ся слезáми** to be in floods of tears; **у меня́ сéрдце крóвью ~ется** my heart bleeds.
облигáци|я (-и) *ж* (*комм*) debenture (bond); **премиáльные ~и** premium bond; **прави́тельственные ~и** government stock.
обл|изáть (-ижý, -и́жешь; *impf* **обли́зывать**) *сов перех* (*губы, ложку*) to lick; **пирóг – пáльчики ~и́жешь** (*разг*) the pie is scrumptious
▸ **облизáться** (*impf* **обли́зываться**) *сов возв* (*человек*) to lick one's lips; (*собака, кошка*) to lick itself.
óблик (-а) *м* (*внешний вид*) appearance; (*характер, также перен*) character.
облиня́|ть (-ю) *сов от* **линя́ть.**
обл|и́ть (-олью́, -ольёшь; *impf* **обливáть**) *сов перех*: ~ **когó-н/что-н чем-н** (*намеренно*) to pour sth over sb/sth; (*случайно*) to spill sth over sb/sth; **обливáть** (~ *perf*) **когó-н гря́зью** (*перен*) to throw mud at sb; **обливáть** (~ *perf*) **когó-н презрéнием** to pour scorn on sb; **обливáть** (~ *perf*) **что-н слезáми** to shed tears over sth
▸ **обли́ться** (*impf* **обливáться**) *сов возв*: ~**ся** +*instr* (*водой*) to sluice o.s. with; (*соком*) to spill over o.s.; **обливáться** (~**ся** *perf*) **пóтом** to be bathed in sweat.
облицевáть (-ýю; *impf* **облицóвывать**) *сов перех*: ~ **что-н чем-н** to face sth with sth.
облицóвк|а (-и) *ж* facing.
облицóвыва|ть (-ю) *несов от* **облицевáть.**
обличá|ть (-ю) *несов от* **обличи́ть.**
обличи́тел|ьный (-ен, -ьна, -ьно) *прил* damning.
обличи́|ть (-ý, -и́шь; *impf* **обличáть**) *сов перех* to expose.
облóжек *сущ см* **облóжка.**
обложéни|е (-я) *ср* (*действие: налогом итп*) imposition; (*сбор*) levy.
обл|ожи́ть (-ожý, -óжишь; *impf* **облагáть**) *сов перех*: ~**налóгом** to tax; (*impf* **обклáдывать**) to surround; (*печь*) to face; (*подлеж: тучи, облака*) to cover; (*разг: обругать*) to swear at; **гóрло ~ожи́ло** my throat is furred
▸ **обложи́ться** (*impf* **обклáдываться**) *сов возв*: ~**ся** +*instr* to surround o.s. with.
облóж|ка (-ки; *gen pl* -ек) *ж* (*книги, тетради*) cover; (*для паспорта итп*) holder.
облок|оти́ться (-очýсь, -óтишься; *impf* **облокáчиваться**) *сов возв*: ~ **на** +*acc* to lean on (*with elbows*).
обломá|ть (-ю; *impf* **обла́мывать**) *сов перех* (*ветки, ногти итп*) to break off; (*перен: разг*): ~ **когó-н** to talk sb round
▸ **обломáться** (*impf* **обла́мываться**) *сов возв* (*ветка, ногти итп*) to break off.
облóм|ок (-ка) *м* fragment.
обл|упи́ть (-уплю́, -ýпишь) *сов от* **лупи́ть** ◆ (*impf* **облýпливать**) *перех* to peel
▸ **облупи́ться** *сов от* **лупи́ться** ◆ (*impf* **облýпливаться**) *возв* (*разг*) to peel.
облýпленн|ый *прил* (*разг*) peeling; **знать** (*impf*) **когó-н как ~ого** (*разг*) to know sb inside out.
облýплива|ть(ся) (-ю(сь)) *несов от* **облупи́ть(ся).**
облуплю́(сь) *сов см* **облупи́ть(ся).**
облучá|ть(ся) (-ю(сь)) *несов от* **облучи́ть(ся).**
облучéни|е (-я) *ср* irradiation.
облучи́|ть (-ý, -и́шь; *impf* **облучáть**) *сов перех* to irradiate
▸ **облучи́ться** (*impf* **облучáться**) *сов возв* to be irradiated.
облущи́|ть (-ý, -и́шь) *сов от* **лущи́ть.**
облысé|ть (-ю) *сов от* **лысéть.**
облюб|овáть (-ýю; *impf* **облюбóвывать**) *сов перех* to choose.
обля́жет *итп сов см* **облéчь.**
обмá|зать (-жу, -жешь; *impf* **обмáзывать**) *сов перех*: ~ **когó-н/что-н чем-н** to coat sb/sth with sth; (*разг: испачкать*) to get sb/sth covered in sth.
обмакн|ýть (-ý, -ёшь; *impf* **обмáкивать**) *сов перех*: ~ **что-н в** +*acc* to dip sth into.
обмáн (-а) *м* deception; ~ **зрéния** optical illusion.
обмáнный *прил* fraudulent; **обмáнным путём** fraudulently.
обм|анýть (-анý, -áнешь; *impf* **обмáнывать**) *сов перех* to deceive; (*поступить нечестно*) to cheat; (*не выполнить обещание*) to fail
▸ **обманýться** (*impf* **обмáнываться**) *сов возв*: ~**ся в** +*prp* to be disappointed in.
обмáнчив|ый (-, -а, -о) *прил* deceptive.
обмáнщик (-а) *м* cheat.
обмáнщиц|а (-ы) *ж см* **обмáнщик.**
обмáныва|ть(ся) (-ю(сь)) *несов от* **обманýть(ся).**
обмáтыва|ть(ся) (-ю(сь)) *несов от* **обмотáть(ся).**

обмахн|ýть (**-ý, -ёшь**; *impf* **обмáхивать**) *сов перех* (*пыль*) to brush off; (*стол*) to wipe down; **обмáхивать (~** *perf*) **лицó вéером** to fan one's face *или* o.s.
▸ **обмахнýться** (*impf* **обмáхиваться**) *сов возв*: **~ся вéером** to fan o.s.
обмелé|ть (**-ю**) *сов от* **мелéть**.
обмéн (**-а**) *м* (*также ЭКОН*) exchange; (*документов*) renewal; (*также:* **~ вещéств**: *БИО*) metabolism; (*также:* **~ жилплóщадью**) exchange (*of flats etc*); **в ~ на** *+acc* in exchange for.
обменя́|ть (**-ю**; *impf* **обмéнивать**) *сов перех* (*вещи, билеты*) to change
▸ **обменя́ться** (*impf* **обмéниваться**) *сов возв*: **~ся** *+instr* to exchange.
обмéр|ить (**-ю, -ишь**; *impf* **обмéривать**) *сов перех* (*участок итп*) to measure.
обме|стú (**-тý, -тёшь**; *impf* **обметáть**) *сов перех* (*песок, паутину*) to brush away.
обм|етáть (**-ечý, -éтишь**; *impf* **обмётывать**) *сов перех* to oversew ◆ *безл* (*разг*): **гýбы ~етáло** my lips are chapped.
обметý *итп сов см* **обместú**.
обмётыва|ть (**-ю**) *несов от* **обметáть**.
обмечý *сов см* **обметáть**.
обмолáчива|ть (**-ю**) *несов от* **обмолотúть**.
обмóлв|иться (**-люсь, -ишься**) *сов возв* (*разг*: *сказать невзначай*) to slip in; (: *оговориться*) to slip up; **слóвом не ~** (*perf*) (*разг*) to keep mum.
обмолóт (**-а**) *м* (*действие*) threshing; (*количество*) yield (*from threshing*).
обмол|отúть (**-очý, -óтишь**; *impf* **обмолáчивать**) *сов перех* to thresh.
обморó|зить (**-жу, -зишь**; *impf* **обморáживать**) *сов перех*: **~ нóгу/рýку** to get frostbite in one's foot/hand
▸ **обморóзиться** (*impf* **обморáживаться**) *сов возв* to suffer from frostbite.
óбморок (**-а**) *м* faint; **пáдать (упáсть** *perf*) **в ~** to faint.
обмотá|ть (**-ю**; *impf* **обмáтывать**) *сов перех*: **~ когó-н/чтó-н чем-н** to wrap sth round sb/sth; (*обвить*): **~ чтó-н вокрýг** *+gen* (*пальца, столба*) to wind sth round
▸ **обмотáться** (*impf* **обмáтываться**) *сов возв*: **~ся вокрýг** *+gen* to be wound round; **обмáтываться (~ся** *perf*) *+instr* (*разг*: *шарфом, одеялом*) to wrap o.s. in.
обмóтк|а (**-и**) *ж* (*ЭЛЕК*) winding.
обмóю *итп сов см* **обмы́ть**.
обмундировáни|е (**-я**) *ср* (*ВОЕН*: *действие*) fitting out; (*комплект одежды*) uniform.
обмундир|овáть (**-ýю**; *impf* **обмундирóвывать**) *сов перех* to fit out.
обм|ы́ть (**-óю, -óешь**; *impf* **обмывáть**) *сов перех* (*рану*) to bathe; (*разг*: *событие, премию*) to celebrate (*by drinking*).
обнаглé|ть (**-ю**) *сов от* **наглéть**.
обнадёж|ить (**-у, -ишь**; *impf* **обнадёживать**) *сов перех* to reassure; (*обещать*) to assure.
обнажá|ть(ся) (**-ю(сь)**) *несов от* **обнажúть(ся)**.
обнажённый (**-ён, -енá, -енó**) *прил* bare; (*корни*) exposed.
обнаж|úть (**-ý, -úшь**; *impf* **обнажáть**) *сов перех* to expose; (*руки, ноги*) to bare; (*ветки*) to strip bare; (*шпагу, мечь*) to draw
▸ **обнажúться** (*impf* **обнажáться**) *сов возв* to be exposed; (*человек*) to strip; (*рука, нога итп*) to be bared; (*лес, дерево*) to become bare.
обнарóдовани|е (**-я**) *ср* (*см глаг*) publication; promulgation.
обнарóд|овать (**-ую**) *сов перех* (*факты, статью*) to make public; (*закон, указ*) to promulgate.
обнарýж|ить (**-у, -ишь**; *impf* **обнарýживать**) *сов перех* (*найти*) to find; (*проявить*) to show; (*раскрыть*) to reveal
▸ **обнарýжиться** (*impf* **обнарýживаться**) *сов возв* (*найтись*) to be found; (*проявиться*) to show; (*стать явным*) to become evident.
обнáшива|ться (**-юсь**) *несов от* **обносúться**.
обн|естú (**-есý, -есёшь**; *pt* **-ёс, -еслá, -еслó**, *impf* **обносúть**) *сов перех*: **~ чтó-н/когó-н вокрýг** *+gen* to carry sth/sb round; (*огородить*): **~ чтó-н чем-н** to surround sth with sth; **обносúть (~** *perf*) **когó-н чем-н** (*вином*) to serve sb with sth.
обнимá|ть(ся) (**-ю(сь)**) *несов от* **обня́ть(ся)**.
обнúмк|а *ж*: **в ~у** (*разг*) with their arms around each other.
обнимý(сь) *итп сов см* **обня́ть(ся)**.
обнищá|ть (**-ю**) *сов от* **нищáть**.
обнов|úть (**-лю́, -úшь**; *impf* **обновля́ть**) *сов перех* (*оборудование, гардероб*) to replenish; (*репертуар, знания*) to refresh; (*памятник, дом*) to renovate; (*жизнь, искусство*) to revitalize; (*разг*: *платье*) to christen
▸ **обновúться** (*impf* **обновля́ться**) *сов возв* (*оборудование, гардероб*) to be replenished; (*репертуар*) to be refreshed; (*организм, природа*) to be regenerated; (*жизнь, искусство*) to be revitalized.
обновлéни|е (**-я**) *ср* (*см возв*) replenishment; refreshment; regeneration; revitalization.
обновлю́(сь) *сов см* **обновúть(ся)**.
обновля́|ть(ся) (**-ю(сь)**) *несов от* **обновúть(ся)**.
обн|осúть (**-ошý, -óсишь**) *несов от* **обнестú**.
обн|осúться (**-ошýсь, -óсишься**; *impf* **обнáшиваться**) *сов возв* (*разг*: *старик, ребёнок*) to wear out one's clothes; (: *одежда*) to become worn to bits.
обнóск|и (**-ов**) *мн* old clothes *мн*.

обношу́(сь) *несов см* **обноси́ть(ся)**.
обню́ха|ть (**-ю**; *impf* **обню́хивать**) *сов перех* to sniff.
обн|я́ть (**-иму́, -и́мешь**; *pt* **-ял, -яла́, -яло**, *impf* **обнима́ть**) *сов перех* to embrace
▸ **обня́ться** (*impf* **обнима́ться**) *сов возв* to embrace (each other).
обо *предл см* **о**.
об|обра́ть (**-еру́, -ерёшь**; *impf* **обира́ть**) *сов перех* (*смородину, черешню*) to pick; (*разг*: *прохожего, клиента*) to fleece
▸ **обобра́ться** *сов возв*: **забо́т не ~ерёшься** (*разг*) no end of worries.
обобща́|ть (**-ю**) *несов от* **обобщи́ть**.
обобще́ни|е (**-я**) *ср* generalization.
обобщён|ный (**-, -на́, -но**) *прил* general.
обобществ|и́ть (**-лю́, -и́шь**; *impf* **обобществля́ть**) *сов перех* (*производство, хозяйство*) to socialize; (*землю, труд*) to collectivize.
обобществле́ни|е (**-я**) *ср* socialization.
обобществлю́ *сов см* **обобществи́ть**.
обобществля́|ть (**-ю**) *несов от* **обобществи́ть**.
обобщ|и́ть (**-у́, -и́шь**; *impf* **обобща́ть**) *сов перех* (*результаты, факты*) to generalize from; (*статью, выступление*) to summarize.
обобью́ *итп сов см* **оби́ть**.
обовью́(сь) *итп сов см* **обви́ть(ся)**.
обога|ти́ть (**-щу́, -ти́шь**; *impf* **обогаща́ть**) *сов перех* to enrich; (*руду*) to concentrate
▸ **обогати́ться** (*impf* **обогаща́ться**) *сов возв* (*человек, страна*) to be enriched; (*почва, руда*) to be concentrated.
об|огна́ть (**-гоню́, -го́нишь**; *impf* **обгоня́ть**) *сов перех* to overtake; (*перен*) to outstrip.
обогн|у́ть (**-у́, -ёшь**; *impf* **огиба́ть**) *сов перех* (*стол, дом*) to go round.
обогре́в (**-а**) *м* heating.
обогре́|ть (**-ю**; *impf* **обогрева́ть**) *сов перех* (*помещение*) to heat; (*замёрзших*) to warm; (*перен*: *приласкать*) to be kind to
▸ **обогре́ться** (*impf* **обогрева́ться**) *сов возв* (*согреться*: *человек*) to warm o.s.; (*помещение*) to heat up; (*душа*) to be warmed.
о́б|од (**-ода**; *nom pl* **-о́дья**, *gen pl* **-о́дьев**) *м* rim; (*ракетки*) frame.
обод|о́к (**-ка́**) *м уменьш от* **о́бод**; (*на рисунке, платье*) border.
обо́дран|ный (**-, -а, -о**) *прил* (*стена*) stripped; (*дом, одежда*) shabby; (*руки*) scratched; (*колени*) skinned.
об|одра́ть (**-деру́, -дерёшь**; *impf* **обдира́ть**) *сов перех* (*кору, шкуру*) to strip; (*руки*) to scratch; (*колени*) to skin; (*перен*: *разг*: *покупателя, клиента*) to fleece.
ободре́ни|е (**-я**) *ср* encouragement.
ободри́тель|ный (**-ен, -ьна, -ьно**) *прил* encouraging.
ободр|и́ть (**-ю́, -и́шь**; *impf* **ободря́ть**) *сов перех* to encourage.
обожа́|ть (**-ю**) *несов перех* to adore; ~ (*impf*) **что-н**/*+infin* (*разг*) to adore sth/doing.
обожгу́(сь) *итп сов см* **обже́чь(ся)**.
обожеств|и́ть (**-лю́, -и́шь**; *impf* **обожествля́ть**) *сов перех* to worship.
обожествле́ни|е (**-я**) *ср* worship.
обожествлю́ *сов см* **обожестви́ть**.
обожествля́|ть (**-ю**) *несов от* **обожестви́ть**.
обожжёшь(ся) *итп сов см* **обже́чь(ся)**.
обожр|а́ться (**-у́сь, -ёшься**; *pt* **-а́лся, -ала́сь, -ало́сь**, *impf* **обжира́ться**) *сов возв* (*разг*) to stuff o.s.
обо́з (**-а**) *м* convoy.
об|озва́ть (**-зову́, -зовёшь**; *impf* **обзыва́ть**) *сов перех*: ~ **кого́-н кем-н** (*разг*) to call sb sth.
обозл|и́ть(ся) (**-ю́(сь), -и́шь(ся)**) *сов от* **злить(ся)**.
обозна́|ться (**-юсь**) *сов возв* (*разг*) to be mistaken.
обознача́|ть (**-ю**) *несов от* **обозна́чить** ◆ *перех* (*о знаках*) to signify
▸ **обознача́ться** *несов от* **обозна́читься**.
обозначе́ни|е (**-я**) *ср* (*границы, направления*) marking; (*на карте, в тексте итп*) symbol.
обозна́ч|ить (**-у, -ишь**; *impf* **обознача́ть**) *сов перех* (*границу, направление*) to mark; (*no impf*): ~ **что-н** (*нос, черты лица*) to make sth stand out
▸ **обозна́читься** (*impf* **обознача́ться**) *сов возв* to appear; (*становиться ощутимым*) to become noticeable.
обозрева́тел|ь (**-я**) *м* (*событий*) observer; (*на радио и телевидении*) editor; **междунаро́дный/полити́ческий ~** international/political editor.
обозре́ни|е (**-я**) *ср* review; (*представление*) revue.
обозри́м|ый (**-, -а, -о**) *прил* (*пространство*) visible; (*события*) observable; **~ое бу́дущее** the foreseeable future.
обо́|и (**-ев**) *мн* wallpaper *ед*.
обо́их *чис см* **о́ба**.
обойду́(сь) *итп сов см* **обойти́(сь)**.
обо́йм|а (**-ы**) *ж* (*ВОЕН*) (cartridge) clip; (*ТЕХ*) ring, hoop; (*перен*: *вопросов, аргументов*) round.
обо|йти́ (*как* **идти́**; *см* **Table 18**; *impf* **обходи́ть**) *сов перех* to go round; (*пройти стороной*: *лужу, канаву*) to skirt, go round; (*перен*: *вопрос, тему*) to skirt; (: *закон, указ*) to get round; (*обогнать*) to pass; (*перен*: *обмануть*) to take in; **обходи́ть** (**~** *perf*) **что-н молча́нием** to ignore
▸ **обойти́сь** (*impf* **обходи́ться**) *сов возв* (*уладиться*) to turn out; (*стоить*): **~сь в** *+acc* to cost; **обходи́ться** (**~сь** *perf*) **с кем-н/чем-н** to treat sb/sth; **обходи́ться** (**~сь** *perf*) *+instr* (*разг*) to get by with; **обходи́ться** (**~сь** *perf*) **без** *+gen* (*разг*) to get by without; (*без скандала*) to be settled without.
об|окра́сть (**-краду́, -крадёшь**; *impf*

обкра́дывать) *сов перех* to rob.
обол|га́ть (**-гу́, -жёшь**; *pt* **-га́л, -гала́, -га́ло**) *сов перех* (*разг*: *человека*) to slander.
оболо́ч|ка (**-ки**; *gen pl* **-ек**) *ж* (*плода*) pericarp; (*зерна*) testa, (seed) coat; (*Земли*) crust; (*перен*: *человека*) shell; (: *вопроса*) surface; (*аэростата*) hull; **слизистая ~** mucous membrane.
обо́лтус (**-а**) *м* (*разг*) waster.
оболь|сти́ть (**-щу́, -сти́шь**; *impf* **обольща́ть**) *сов перех* (*соблазнить*) to seduce; (*увлечь*) to captivate.
обольща́|ться (**-юсь**) *несов возв* to be under a delusion.
обольщу́ *сов см* **обольсти́ть**.
оболью́(сь) *итп сов см* **обли́ть(ся)**.
обомле́|ть (**-ю**) *сов неперех* (*разг*) to freeze.
обоня́ни|е (**-я**) *ср* sense of smell.
обопру́сь *итп сов см* **опере́ться**.
обора́чиваемост|ь (**-и**) *ж* (*КОММ*) turnover.
обора́чива|ть(ся) (**-ю(сь)**) *несов от* **оберну́ть(ся)**.
оборва́н|ец (**-ца**) *м* (*разг*) scruff.
обо́рван|ный (**-, -а, -о**) *прил* (*разг*: *одежда*) tattered; (: *рассказ, мысли*) fragmented.
оборва́нца *итп сущ см* **оборва́нец**.
оборв|а́ть (**-у́, -ёшь**; *pt* **-а́л, -ала́, -а́ло**, *impf* **обрыва́ть**) *сов перех* (*верёвку, нитку*) to break, snap; (*ягоды, цветы*) to pick; (*перен*: *разговор, дружбу*) to break off; (: *разг*: *говорящего*) to cut short
▸ **оборва́ться** (*impf* **обрыва́ться**) *сов возв* (*верёвка, нитка*) to break, snap; (*со скалы*) to fall; (*перен*: *жизнь, разговор, дружба*) to be cut short suddenly.
обо́р|ка (**-ки**; *gen pl* **-ок**) *ж* frill.
оборо́н|а (**-ы**) *ж* defence (*BRIT*), defense (*US*); (*линия сооружений*) defences *мн* (*BRIT*), defenses *мн* (*US*); **занима́ть (заня́ть** *perf*) **~у** to take up a defensive position; **держа́ть** (*impf*) **~у** to hold the defence.
оборо́нный *прил* (*промышленность*) defence *опред* (*BRIT*), defense *опред* (*US*).
обороноспосо́бност|ь (**-и**) *ж* defence (*BRIT*) *или* defense (*US*) capacity.
обороня́|ть (**-ю**) *несов перех* to defend
▸ **обороня́ться** *несов возв* (*защищаться*) to defend o.s.
оборо́т (**-а**) *м* (*полный круг*) revolution; (*КОММ*) turnover; (*обратная сторона*) back; (*перен*: *поворот событий*) turn; (*судов, вагонов*) turnaround; (*словесное выражение*) turn of phrase; **в ~е** in use; **входи́ть (войти́** *perf*) **в ~** to come into use; **пуска́ть (пусти́ть** *perf*) **в ~** (*деньги*) to put into circulation; (*средства, сбережения*) to invest; **брать (взять** *perf*) **кого́-н в ~** (*разг*) to take sb in hand.
оборо́тлив|ый (**-, -а, -о**) *прил* resourceful.
оборо́тный *прил* (*КОММ*) working *опред*.
обору́довани|е (**-я**) *ср* (*действие*: *завода*) equipping; (*предметы*) equipment; (*КОМП*) hardware.
обору́д|овать (**-ую**) (*не*)*сов перех* to equip.
обоснова́ни|е (**-я**) *ср* (*действие*: *теории*) substantiation; (*довод*) basis.
обосно́ван|ный (**-, -на, -но**) *прил* substantiated; **~ изно́с** (*КОММ*) fair wear and tear.
обосн|ова́ть (**-у́ю**; *impf* **обосно́вывать**) *сов перех* (*теорию, вывод*) to substantiate
▸ **обоснова́ться** (*impf* **обосно́вываться**) *сов возв* (*расположиться*) to be (situated); (*разг*: *прочно устроиться*) to settle.
обосо́б|ить (**-лю, -ишь**; *impf* **обособля́ть**) *сов перех* to set apart; (*предложение*) to detach
▸ **обосо́биться** (*impf* **обособля́ться**) *сов возв* (*от коллектива, от семьи*) to alienate o.s.
обосо́блен|ный (**-, -на, -но**) *прил* (*дом, также ЛИНГ*) detached; (*комната*) separate; (*жизнь*) solitary.
обосо́блю(сь) *сов см* **обосо́бить(ся)**.
обособля́|ть(ся) (**-ю(сь)**) *несов от* **обосо́бить(ся)**.
обостре́ни|е (**-я**) *ср* (*см глаг*) sharpening; intensification; aggravation; straining.
обостр|и́ть (**-ю́, -и́шь**; *impf* **обостря́ть**) *сов перех* to sharpen; (*желания, конфликт*) to intensify; (*боль, какое-нибудь чувство*) to aggravate; (*отношения*) to strain
▸ **обостри́ться** (*impf* **обостря́ться**) *сов возв* to sharpen; (*желание, разногласия*) to intensify; (*боль, какое-нибудь чувство*) to become more acute; (*отношения*) to become strained.
оботру́(сь) *итп сов см* **обтере́ть(ся)**.
обо́чин|а (**-ы**) *ж* verge.
обошёл(ся) *итп сов см* **обойти́(сь)**.
обошью́ *итп сов см* **обши́ть**.
обою́дный (**-ен, -на, -но**) *прил* mutual.
обрабо́та|ть (**-ю**; *impf* **обраба́тывать**) *сов перех* (*камень*) to cut; (*кожу*) to cure; (*деталь*: *на станке*) to turn; (*статью, песню*) to polish up; (*землю, поле*) to till; (*перен*: *разг*: *человека*) to work on.
обрабо́т|ка (**-ки**; *gen pl* **-ок**) *ж* (*см глаг*) cutting; curing; turning; polishing up; tilling; (*перен*: *человека*) influencing; **~ да́нных** (*КОМП*) computing; **пла́та за ~ку** (*КОММ*) handling charge.
обра́д|овать(ся) (**-ую(сь)**) *сов от* **ра́довать(ся)**.
о́браз (**-а**) *м* image; (*человека, зверя*) appearance; (*ЛИТЕРАТУРА*) figure; (*жизни, мыслей*) way; (*икона*) icon; **каки́м ~ом?** in what way?; **таки́м ~ом** in this way; (*следовательно*) consequently; **гла́вным ~ом** mainly; **ра́вным ~ом** similarly; **не́которым ~ом** to some extent.

óбразен *прил см* **óбразный.**
образ|éц (-цá) *м* (*ткани, изделий, оружия*) sample; (*скромности, мужества, также ТЕХ*) model.
óбраз|ный (-ен, -на, -но) *прил* vivid; **óбразное выражéние** (*линг*) figure of speech.
образовáни|е (-я) *ср* formation; (*получение знаний*) education.
образóван|ный (-, -на, -но) *прил* educated.
образ|овáть (-ýю; *impf* **образовáть** *или* **образóвывать)** *сов перех* to form
▸ **образовáться** (*impf* **образовáться** *или* **образóвываться)** *сов возв* (*трещина, опухоль*) to form; (*группа, комиссия*) to be formed; (*разг*: *уладиться*) to turn out all right.
образýм|ить (-лю, -ишь) *сов перех*: **~ когó-н** to make sb see sense
▸ **образýмиться** *сов возв* (*стать благоразумным*) to come to one's senses.
образцá *итп сущ см* **образéц.**
образцóв|ый (-, -а, -о) *прил* exemplary.
обраст|ú (-ý, -ёшь; *pt* **обрóс, оброслá, оброслó,** *impf* **обрастáть)** *сов неперех*: **~** *+instr* (*травой, деревьями*) to become overgrown with; (*разг*: *волосами, грязью*) to be covered in; (: *хозяйством, барахлом*) to surround o.s. with.
обратúм|ый (-, -а, -о) *прил* reversible.
обра|тúть (-щý, -тúшь; *impf* **обращáть)** *сов перех* (*взгляд, мысли*) to turn; **обращáть (~** *perf***) когó-н/что-н в** *+acc* to turn sb/sth into; **обращáть (~** *perf***) внимáние на** *+acc* to pay attention to; **обращáть (~** *perf***) когó-н в бéгство** to force sb to take flight; **обращáть (~** *perf***) когó-н в свою вéру** to convert sb to one's own faith
▸ **обратúться** (*impf* **обращáться)** *сов возв* (*подлеж*: *взгляд*) to turn; (*с вопросом*) to inquire; (*превратиться*): **~ся в** *+acc* to turn into; **обращáться (~ся** *perf***) к** *+dat* (*к врачу итп*) to consult; (*к зрителям*) to address; **обращáться (~ся** *perf***) в суд** to go to court; **обращáться (~ся** *perf***) в бéгство** to take flight.
обрáтно *нареч* back; **тудá и ~** there and back; **билéт тудá и ~** return ticket (*BRIT*), round-trip ticket (*US*).
обрáтн|ое (-ого; *decl like adj*) *ср* the opposite; **убеждáть (убедúть** *perf***) когó-н в ~ом** to convince sb of the opposite.
обрáтн|ый *прил* (*порядок, движение, мысль*) reverse; (*дорога, путь*) return *опред*; **на ~ом путú** on the way back; **в ~ую стóрону** in the opposite direction; **в ~ом направлéнии** the other way; **обрáтная сторонá** reverse (side); **обрáтный áдрес** return address; **обрáтный билéт** return (*BRIT*) *или* round-trip (*US*) ticket.
обращá|ть (-ю) *несов от* **обратúть**
▸ **обращáться** *несов от* **обратúться** ◆ *возв* (*деньги, товар*) to circulate; **~ся** *(impf)* **с** *+instr* (*применять*) to use; (*уметь справляться*) to handle; (*с человеком*) to treat.
обращéни|е (-я) *ср* address; (*ЭКОН*) circulation; **~ к** *+dat* (*к народу итп*) address to; **~ с** *+instr* (*с прибором, с огнём*) handling of; (*с животными, с больным*) treatment of; **находúться** *(impf)* **в ~и** to be in circulation.
обращý(сь) *сов см* **обратúть(ся).**
обрéжу *итп сов см* **обрéзать.**
обрéз (-а) *м* (*книги, альбома*) edge; (*оружие*) sawn-off (*BRIT*) *или* sawed-off (*US*) shotgun; **врéмени/дéнег в ~** (*разг*) there's just enough time/money.
обрé|зать (-жу, -жешь; *impf* **обрезáть)** *сов перех* to trim; (*разг*: *прервать*) to cut short; (*РЕЛ*) to circumcise.
обрéз|ок (-ка) *м* scrap.
обрёк *итп сов см* **обрéчь.**
обрекá|ть (-ю) *несов от* **обрéчь.**
обрекý *итп сов см* **обрéчь.**
обременúтел|ьный (-ен, -ьна, -ьно) *прил* onerous.
обремен|úть (-ю, -úшь; *impf* **обременять)** *сов перех*: **~ когó-н чем-н** to load sb down with sth.
обр|естú (-етý, -етёшь; *pt* **-ёл, -елá, -елó,** *impf* **обретáть)** *сов перех* to find.
обречённый (-ён, -енá, -енó) *прил* doomed.
обр|éчь (-екý, -ечёшь *итп*, **-екýт;** *pt* **-ёк, -еклá, -еклó,** *impf* **обрекáть)** *сов перех*: **~ когó-н на что-н** to condemn sb to sth.
обрис|овáть (-ýю; *impf* **обрисóвывать)** *сов перех* (*перен*) to describe.
обр|онúть (-оню, -óнишь) *сов перех* to drop; (*замечание, фразу*) to let drop.
обрóс *итп сов см* **обрастú.**
обр|убúть (-ублю, -ýбишь; *impf* **обрубáть)** *сов перех* to lop off.
обрýб|ок (-ка) *м* (*пень, хвоста*) stump; (*дерева*) chunk.
обругá|ть (-ю) *сов перех* (*выбранить*) to curse; (*обозвать*) to swear at; (*разг*: *раскритиковать*) to pan, slate (*BRIT*).
óбруч (-а) *м* hoop; (*для волос*) (Alice) band.
обручáльн|ый *прил*: **~ое кольцó** wedding ring.
обручá|ть(ся) (-ю(сь)) *несов от* **обручúть(ся).**
обручéни|е (-я) *ср* betrothal.
обруч|úть (-ý, -úшь; *impf* **обручáть)** *сов перех* to betroth
▸ **обручúться** (*impf* **обручáться)** *сов возв* to get betrothed.
обрýш|ить (-у, -ишь; *impf* **обрýшивать)** *сов перех* (*стену, крышу*) to bring down; **обрýшивать (~** *perf***) что-н на** *+acc* to bring sth down onto; **~** *(perf)* **обвинéния/угрóзы на когó-н** to bombard sb with accusations/threats
▸ **обрýшиться** (*impf* **обрýшиваться)** *сов возв* (*крыша, здание*) to collapse; **обрýшиваться (~ся** *perf***) на** *+acc* (*на голову*) to crash down onto; (*на врага*) to fall upon; (*на человека*: *с упрёками*) to come down on; **на негó ~илась бедá** he was struck down by misfortune.
обры́в (-а) *м* (*ГЕО*) precipice; (*на линии*) break.
обрывá|ть(ся) (-ю(сь)) *несов от*

оборва́ть(ся).
обры́вист|ый (-, -а, -о) *прил* (*склон, берег*) steep; (*мысли, фразы*) fragmentary.
обры́в|ок (-ка) *м* (*верёвки*) piece; (*бумаги*) scrap; (*обычно мн*: *мыслей, воспоминаний*) fragment; (: *разговора*) snatch.
обры́воч|ный (-ен, -на, -но) *прил* fragmentary.
обры́зга|ть (-ю; *impf* **обры́згивать**) *сов перех*: ~ **кого́-н/что-н** +*instr* (*водой*) to splash sb/sth with; (*грязью, краской*) to splatter sb/sth with
▸ **обры́згаться** (*impf* **обры́згиваться**) *сов возв*: ~**ся** +*instr* (*см перех*) to get splashed with; to get splattered with.
обря́д (-а) *м* ritual.
обря́довый *прил* (*песни*) ceremonial; (*действия*) ritual.
обса́сыва|ть (-ю) *несов от* **обсоса́ть**.
обсервато́ри|я (-и) *ж* observatory.
обсле́довани|е (-я) *ср* (*см глаг*) inspection; examination.
обсле́д|овать (-ую) *(не)сов перех* to inspect; (*больного*) to examine.
обслу́живани|е (-я) *ср* service; **медици́нское** ~ health care; **сфе́ра** ~**я** service industry.
обслу́жива|ть (-ю) *несов от* **обслужи́ть** ◆ *перех* (*подлеж*: *магазин*) to supply; (: *поликлиника*) to see to.
обслу́живающ|ий (-ая, -ее, -ие) *прил*: ~ **персона́л** ancilliary staff.
обсл|ужи́ть (-ужу́, -у́жишь; *impf* **обслу́живать**) *сов перех* (*покупателей*) to serve; (*клиентов*) to attend to; (*подлеж*: *поликлиника, магазин*) to see to; (*станки*) to operate.
обсос|а́ть (-у́, -ёшь; *impf* **обса́сывать**) *сов перех* to suck.
обста́в|ить (-лю, -ишь; *impf* **обставля́ть**) *сов перех* (*квартиру, кабинет*) to furnish; **обставля́ть** (~ *perf*) **стол сту́льями** to put chairs around the table.
обстано́в|ка (-ки; *gen pl* -ок) *ж* (*квартиры, кабинета*) furnishings *мн*; (*в мире, в семье*) situation; **междунаро́дная** ~ the international situation.
обстоя́тельно *нареч* in detail.
обстоя́тел|ьный (-ен, -ьна, -ьно) *прил* detailed; (*разг*: *человек*) solid.
обстоя́тельств|о (-а) *ср* circumstance; (*линг*) adverbial modifier; **ни при каки́х** ~**ах** under no circumstances; **стече́ние обстоя́тельств** coincidence; **смотря́ по** ~**ам** depending on the circumstances; (*как ответ на вопрос*) it depends.
обсто|я́ть (*3sg* **-и́т**, *3pl* **-я́т**) *несов неперех* (*дела, работа, учёба*) to be; **как** ~**и́т дела́?** how are things going?; **всё** ~**и́т хорошо́** everything is going well.
обстра́гива|ть (-ю) *несов от* **обстрога́ть**.
обстре́л (-а) *м* fire; **артиллери́йский** ~ artillery fire.
обстреля́|ть (-ю; *impf* **обстре́ливать**) *сов перех* to fire at.
обстри́|чь (-гу́, -жёшь *итп*, -гу́т) *сов от* **стричь**.
обстрога́|ть (-ю; *impf* **обстра́гивать**) *сов перех* to plane.
обстру́кци|я (-и) *ж* obstruction.
обст|упи́ть (*3sg* **-у́пит**, *3pl* **-у́пят**, *impf* **обступа́ть**) *сов перех* to surround.
обс|уди́ть (-ужу́, -у́дишь; *impf* **обсужда́ть**) *сов перех* to discuss.
обсужде́ни|е (-я) *ср* discussion; **предложи́ть** (**предлага́ть** *impf*) **что-н на** ~ to bring sth up for discussion.
обсужу́ *сов см* **обсуди́ть**.
обсчита́|ть (-ю; *impf* **обсчи́тывать**) *сов перех* to overcharge; (*результат, параметры*) to calculate
▸ **обсчита́ться** (*impf* **обсчи́тываться**) *сов возв* (*разг*) to miscalculate.
обсы́п|ать (-лю, -лешь; *impf* **обсыпа́ть**) *сов перех*: ~ **что-н чем-н** to sprinkle sth with sth
▸ **обсы́паться** (*impf* **обсыпа́ться**) *сов возв*: ~**ся** +*instr* to get covered in.
обта́чива|ть (-ю) *несов от* **обточи́ть**.
обтека́ем|ый (-, -а, -о) *прил* (*поверхность, форма*) streamlined; (*разг*: *ответ, объяснение*) ambiguous.
об|тере́ть (-отру́, -отрёшь; *impf* **обтира́ть**) *сов перех* to wipe
▸ **обтере́ться** (*impf* **обтира́ться**) *сов возв* to sponge o.s. down.
обт|еса́ть (-ешу́, -е́шешь; *impf* **обтёсывать**) *сов перех* (*бревно*) to trim; (*разг*: *манеры, человека*) to bring up to scratch.
обтира́|ть(ся) (-ю(сь)) *несов от* **обтере́ть(ся)**.
обт|очи́ть (-очу́, -о́чишь; *impf* **обта́чивать**) *сов перех* (*на станке*) to turn; (*на точильном камне*) to sharpen.
обто́чк|а (-и) *ж* (*см глаг*) turning; sharpening.
обтрёпан|ный (-, -на, -но) *прил* shabby.
обтр|епа́ть (-еплю́, -е́плешь) *сов перех* to wear out
▸ **обтрепа́ться** *сов возв* (*износиться*) to wear out.
обтя́гива|ть (-ю) *несов от* **обтяну́ть**.
обтя́жк|а (-и) *ж*: **в** ~**у** skintight.
обт|яну́ть (-яну́, -я́нешь; *impf* **обтя́гивать**) *сов перех* (*кресло, диван*) to cover; (*фигуру*) to fit tightly.
обува́|ть(ся) (-ю(сь)) *несов от* **обу́ть(ся)**.
обувно́й *прил* shoe *опред*.
о́був|ь (-и) *ж* footwear.
обу́гл|иться (*3sg* **-ится**, *3pl* **-ятся**, *impf* **обу́гливаться**) *сов возв* to become charred.
обу́жива|ть (-ю) *несов от* **обу́зить**.
обу́жу *сов см* **обу́зить**.
обу́з|а (-ы) *ж* burden; **быть** (*impf*) ~**ой для**

кого́-н (*разг*) to be a burden to sb.

обу́|зить (**-жу, -зишь**; *impf* **обу́живать**) *сов перех* to make too tight.

обусло́в|ить (**-лю, -ишь**; *impf* **обусла́вливать**) *сов перех* (*явиться причиной*) to lead to; **обусла́вливать** (*~ perf*) **что-н чем-н** to make sth conditional on sth.

обу́т|ый (**-, -а, -о**) *прил*: **~ в ту́фли/сапоги́** wearing shoes/boots; (*no full form*; *обеспеченный обувью*) provided with shoes or boots.

обу|ть (**-ю**; *impf* **обува́ть**) *сов перех* (*туфли, сапоги*) to put on; (*разг*: *снабдить обувью*) *to provide with shoes or boots*; (*ребёнка*) to put shoes on

▸ **обу́ться** (*impf* **обува́ться**) *сов возв to put on one's shoes or boots*; (*разг*: *обеспечить себя обувью*) *to provide o.s. with shoes or boots.*

о́бух (**-а**) *м* (*топора*) blunt end; **как ~ом по голове́** like a bolt from the blue.

обуча́|ть(ся) (**-ю(сь)**) *несов от* **обучи́ть(ся)**.

обуче́ни|е (**-я**) *ср*: **~** *+dat* (*преподавание*) teaching of, instruction in; (*изучение*) education in.

об|учи́ть (**-учу́, -у́чишь**; *impf* **обуча́ть**) *сов перех*: **~ кого́-н чему́-н/***+infin* to teach sb sth/to do

▸ **обучи́ться** (*impf* **обуча́ться**) *сов возв*: **~ся чему́-н/***+infin* to learn sth/to do.

обуя́|ть (*3sg* **-ет**, *3pl* **-ют**) *сов перех* to overcome.

обхам|и́ть (**-лю́, -и́шь**) *сов перех* (*разг*) to be rude to.

обхва́т (**-а**) *м* circumference (*measured by putting arms around object*); **в ~е** in circumference.

обхв|ати́ть (**-ачу́, -а́тишь**; *impf* **обхва́тывать**) *сов перех*: **~ что-н (рука́ми)** to put one's arms round sth.

обхо́д (**-а**) *м* (*путь*) way round; (*в больнице, на предприятии*) round; (*ВОЕН*) turning movement; **в ~** *+gen* (*озера, закона*) bypassing; **идти́** (*impf*) **в ~ чего́-н** to go round sth; (*закона, правил*) to evade sth.

обходи́тел|ьный (**-ен, -ьна, -ьно**) *прил* courteous.

обх|оди́ть(ся) (**-ожу́(сь), -о́дишь(ся)**) *несов от* **обойти́(сь)**.

обходно́й *прил* (*путь*) detour *опред*; (*маневр, движение*) turning; **обходно́й лист** *a certificate which must be signed on leaving job to prove that all property has been returned.*

обхожде́ни|е (**-я**) *ср* manners *мн*.

обхожу́(сь) *несов см* **обходи́ть(ся)**.

обхох|ота́ться (**-очу́сь, -о́чешься**) *сов возв* (*разг*) to kill o.s. laughing.

обчи́|стить (**-щу, -стишь**) *сов от* **чи́стить**.

обша́р|ить (**-ю, -ишь**; *impf* **обша́ривать**) *сов перех* (*разг*) to ransack.

обшива́|ть (**-ю**) *несов от* **обши́ть**.

обши́в|ка (**-ки**; *gen pl* **-ок**) *ж* (*платья, пальто*) trim; (*корабля*) plating; (*дома*) cladding.

обши́р|ный (**-ен, -на, -но**) *прил* extensive; (*комната*) spacious.

обши́т|ый (**-, -а, -о**) *прил*: **~** *+instr* (*бахромой, мехом*) trimmed with; (*досками*) faced with; (*металлом*) plated with.

об|ши́ть (**-ошью́, -ошьёшь**; *impf* **обшива́ть**) *сов перех* (*разг*: *семью итп*) to make clothes for; **обшива́ть** (*~ perf*) (*+instr*) (*мехом, бахромой*) to trim (with); (*деревом*) to face (with); (*металлом*) to plate *или* cover (with).

обшл|а́г (**-ага́**; *nom pl* **-ага́**) *м* cuff.

обща́|ться (**-юсь**) *несов возв*: **~ с** *+instr* (*с друзьями, с родственниками*) to spend time with; (*с политиками, с преступниками итп*) to associate with; **я бо́льше с ним не ~юсь** I don't see him any more.

общевойсково́й *прил* military.

общегородско́й *прил* town *опред*, city *опред*.

общегосуда́рственный *прил* state *опред*.

общедосту́пный *прил* (*средства, способ*) available to everyone; (*цены*) affordable; (*изложение, лекция*) accessible.

о́бщ|ее (**-его**; *decl like adj*) *ср* similarity; **в ~ем** (*разг*) on the whole; **в ~ем и це́лом** by and large; **у них мно́го/нет ничего́ ~его** they have a lot/nothing in common.

общежи́ти|е (**-я**) *ср* (*рабочее*) hostel; (*студенческое*) hall of residence (*BRIT*), dormitory *или* hall (*US*); (*сосуществование*) communal living.

общеизве́ст|ный (**-ен, -на, -но**) *прил* well-known.

общенаро́дный *прил* national *опред*.

общенациона́льный *прил* national *опред*.

обще́ни|е (**-я**) *ср* (*деловые, дружеские*) relations *мн*; (*с природой, с друзьями*) communication.

общеобразова́тельный *прил* comprehensive.

общепи́т (**-а**) *м сокр* (= *обще́ственное пита́ние*) public catering.

общепри́знанный *прил* universally recognized.

общепри́нят|ый *прил* generally accepted; **в ~ом смы́сле сло́ва** in the accepted sense of the word.

общераспространённый *прил* widespread.

обще́ственност|ь (**-и**) *ж собир* community.

обще́ственный *прил* social; (*признание, собственность, жизнь*) public; (*организация*) civic; **обще́ственное мне́ние** public opinion; **обще́ственные нау́ки** social sciences.

о́бществ|о (**-а**) *ср* society; (*компания*) company; **в ~е** *+gen* in the company of.

обществове́дени|е (**-я**) *ср* social science.

общеупотреби́тел|ьный (**ен, -ьна, -ьно**) *прил* commonly-used.

общечелове́ческ|ий (**-ая, -ое, -ие**) *прил* universal.

о́бщ|ий (**-ая, -ее, -ие**) *прил* general; (*труд*) communal; (*дом, книги*) shared; (*друзья*) mutual; (*интересы, увлечения, ненависть*) common; (*стоимость, количество*) total; (**-, -а́,**

-ó; *картина, описание*) general; **~ими усилиями** together; **в ~ей сло́жности** altogether; **на ~их основа́ниях** on equal terms; **в ~их черта́х** in general terms; **находи́ть (найти́** *perf*) **~ язы́к** to find a common language; **~ие слова́** waffle; **о́бщее образова́ние** general education.
общи́н|а (**-ы**) *ж* community.
общипа́ть (**-иплю́, -и́плешь**; *impf* **общи́пывать**) *сов перех* to pluck.
общи́телен *прил см* **общи́тельный**.
общи́тельност|ь (**-и**) *ж* sociability.
общи́тел|ьный (**-ен, -ьна, -ьно**) *прил* sociable.
о́бщност|ь (**-и**) *ж* (*взглядов, целей*) similarity; (*историческая, социальная*: *community*).
объеда́|ть(ся) (**-ю(сь)**) *несов от* **объе́сть(ся)**.
объе́дешь *итп сов см* **объе́хать**.
объеди́м(ся) *сов см* **объе́сть(ся)**.
объедине́ни|е (**-я**) *ср* (*сил, усилий, талантов*) concentration; (*литераторов, производственное*) association; (*ВОЕН*) unit.
объединённ|ый *прил* (*заседание, собрание*) joint; (*усилия, ресурсы*) joint, united; **О~ые Ара́бские Эмира́ты** United Arab Emirates.
объедин|и́ть (**-ю́, -и́шь**; *impf* **объединя́ть**) *сов перех* to join, unite; (*ресурсы*) to pool; (*компании*) to amalgamate
▸ **объедини́ться** (*impf* **объединя́ться**) *сов возв* (*люди*) to unite; (*компании*) to amalgamate.
объеди́те(сь) *сов см* **объе́сть(ся)**.
объе́дк|и (**-ов**) *мн* (*разг*) leftovers *мн*.
объе́ду *итп сов см* **объе́хать**.
объедя́т(ся) *сов см* **объе́сть(ся)**.
объе́зд (**-а**) *м* detour; (*с целью осмотра*) tour; **е́хать (пое́хать** *perf*) **в ~** to make a detour.
объе́з|дить (**-жу, -дишь**; *impf* **объезжа́ть**) *сов перех* (*место*) to travel round; (*лошадь*) to break in; (*друзей*) to visit.
объезжа́|ть (**-ю**) *несов от* **объе́здить, объе́хать**.
объе́зжу *сов см* **объе́здить**.
объе́кт (**-а**) *м* (*изучения, наблюдения*) subject; (*СТРОИТ, ВОЕН*) site.
объекти́в (**-а**) *м* lens.
объекти́вен *прил см* **объекти́вный**.
объекти́вност|ь (**-и**) *ж* objectivity.
объекти́в|ный (**-ен, -на, -но**) *прил* objective.
объе́л(ся) *итп сов см* **объе́сть(ся)**.
объе́м(ся) *сов см* **объе́сть(ся)**.
объём (**-а**) *м* (*ГЕОМ*) volume; (*ведра, чашки*) capacity; (*работы, знаний*) amount.
объёмен *прил см* **объёмный**.
объёмист|ый (**-, -а, -о**) *прил* bulky.
объём|ный (**-ен, -на, -но**) *прил* (*ГЕОМ*) volumetric; (*изображение, кино*) three-dimensional; (*книга, папка*) bulky.
объе́сть (*как* **есть**; *см* **Table 15**; *impf* **объеда́ть**) *сов перех* (*кость, яблоко*) to nibble (at); ~ (*perf*) **кого́-н** (*разг*) to eat sb out of house and home
▸ **объе́сться** (*impf* **объеда́ться**) *сов возв* to overeat.
объе́хать (*как* **е́хать**; *см* **Table 19**; *impf* **объезжа́ть**) *сов перех* (*камень, яму*) to go *или* drive round; (*с велью осмотра*) to travel round; (*друзей, страны*) to visit.
объе́шь(ся) *сов см* **объе́сть(ся)**.
объ|яви́ть (**-явлю́, -я́вишь**; *impf* **объявля́ть**) *сов перех* to announce; (*войну*) to declare ◆ *неперех*: ~ **о** +*prp* (*о решении, о случившемся*) to announce; **объявля́ть (~** *perf*) **собра́ние закры́тым/кого́-н победи́телем** to declare the meeting closed/sb the winner
▸ **объяви́ться** (*impf* **объявля́ться**) *сов возв* (*разг*) to turn up.
объявле́ни|е (**-я**) *ср* announcement; (*войны*) declaration; (*рекламное сообщение*) advertisement; (*извещение*) notice.
объявлю́(сь) *сов см* **объяви́ть(ся)**.
объявля́|ть(ся) (**-ю(сь)**) *несов от* **объяви́ть(ся)**.
объясне́ни|е (**-я**) *ср* explanation; **~ в любви́** declaration of love.
объясни́м|ый (**-, -а, -о**) *прил* explicable.
объясн|и́ть (**-ю́, -и́шь**; *impf* **объясня́ть**) *сов перех* to explain
▸ **объясни́ться** (*impf* **объясня́ться**) *сов возв*: **~ся (с** +*instr*) to clear things up (with); **всё ~и́лось** everything became clear; **объясня́ться (~ся** *perf*) **(кому́-н) в любви́** to declare one's love (to sb).
объясня́|ться (**-юсь**) *несов от* **объясни́ться** ◆ *возв* (*жестами, на английском языке*) to communicate; ~ (*impf*) +*instr* (*трудностями, усталостью*) to be explained by.
объя́ти|е (**-я**) *ср* embrace; **встреча́ть (встре́тить** *perf*) **кого́-н с распростёртыми ~ями** to welcome sb with open arms.
обыва́тел|ь (**-я**) *м* (*пренебр*) philistine; (*ИСТ*) resident.
обыва́тельск|ий (**-ая, -ое, -ие**) *прил* philistine.
обыгра́|ть (**-ю**; *impf* **обы́грывать**) *сов перех* (*команду, соперника*) to beat; (*разг*: *ошибку, оговорку*) to turn to one's advantage.
обы́ден|ный (**-, -на, -но**) *прил* mundane.
обыкнове́ни|е (**-я**) *ср* habit; **име́ть** (*impf*) ~ +*infin* to be in the habit of doing; **по ~ю** as usual; **про́тив ~я** against the norm; **по своему́ ~ю** as is his *итп* wont.
обыкнове́нно *нареч* usually.
обыкнове́н|ный (**-ен, -на, -но**) *прил* (*заурядный*: *человек, явление*) ordinary; (*частый*) common.
о́быск (**-а**) *м* search; **производи́ть (произвести́** *perf*) **~** to carry out a search.
об|ыска́ть (**-ыщу́, -ы́щешь**; *impf* **обы́скивать**)

сов перех to search.
обы́ча|й (-я) *м* custom.
обы́чен *прил см* **обы́чный**.
обы́чно *нареч* usually.
обы́ч|ный (-ен, -на, -но) *прил* usual; (*заурядный*) ordinary.
обыщу́ *итп сов см* **обыска́ть**.
обяжу́(сь) *итп сов см* **обяза́ть(ся)**.
обя́занност|и (-ей) *мн* (*директора итп*) duties *мн*, responsibilities *мн*; **исполня́ть** *(impf)* ~ *+gen* to act as; **он исполня́ет ~ дире́ктора** he is the acting director.
обя́занност|ь (-и) *ж* duty; *см также* **обя́занности**.
обя́зан|ный (-, -а, -о) *прил*: ~ *+infin* (*помочь, сделать итп*) obliged to do; ~ *+dat* obliged *или* indebted to; **я Вам о́чень обя́зан** I am greatly obliged to you.
обяза́телен *прил см* **обяза́тельный**.
обяза́тельно *нареч* definitely, without fail; **не** ~ not necessarily.
обяза́тел|ьный (-ен, -ьна, -ьно) *прил* (*правило, условие*) binding; (*исполнение, обучение*) compulsory, obligatory; (*человек, работник*) reliable; **в ~ьном поря́дке** as a compulsory measure.
обяза́тельств|о (-а) *ср* commitment, obligation; (*обычно мн*: *КОММ*) liability; **долгово́е** ~ (*КОММ*) promissory note; **брать (взять** *perf*) **на себя́** ~ to take on some commitment.
об|яза́ть (-яжу́, -я́жешь; *impf* **обя́зывать)** *сов перех*: ~ **кого́-н** *+infin* to oblige sb to do; **Вы меня́ ~я́жите, е́сли сде́лаете э́то** I would be very much obliged if you would do this; **он ~яза́л меня́ свое́й доброто́й** I am obliged to him for his kindness
▸ **обяза́ться** (*impf* **обя́зываться**) *сов возв* to pledge.
обя́зыва|ть (-ю) *несов от* **обяза́ть** ◆ *перех* (*подлеж: правила, закон, факты*) to oblige; **положе́ние ~ет** his *итп* position demands it
▸ **обя́зываться** *несов от* **обяза́ться**.
ова́л (-а) *м* oval; **у неё краси́вый ~ лица́** her face is a lovely shape.
ова́л|ьный (-ен, -ьна, -ьно) *прил* oval.
ова́ци|я (-и) *ж* ovation.
ОВД *м сокр* = *отде́л вну́тренних дел*.
овдове́|ть (-ю) *сов неперех* (*женщина*) to become a widow, be widowed; (*мужчина*) to become a widower, be widowed.
Ов|е́н (-на́) *м* (*созвездие*) Aries.
ов|ёс (-са́) *м собир* oats *мн*.
ове́ц *сущ см* **овца́**.
ове́ч|ий (-ья, -ье, -ьи) *прил* (*шерсть, сыр*) sheep's; (*молоко*) ewe's.
ОВИР *м сокр* = *Отде́л виз и регистра́ции иностра́нных гра́ждан*.
овладе́|ть (-ю, -ешь; *impf* **овладева́ть)** *сов неперех*: ~ *+instr* (*городом, высотой*) to capture, seize; (*перен: разговором*) to take control of; (: *вниманием*) to capture; (: *языком, профессией*) to master; **им ~ла ра́дость** he was overcome with joy.
Овна́ *сущ см* **Ове́н**.
о́вод (-а) *м* gadfly.
о́вощ (-а) *м* vegetable; *см также* **о́вощи**.
о́вощ|и (-е́й) *мн* vegetables *мн*.
овощно́й *прил* (*суп, блюдо*) vegetable *опред*; **овощно́й магази́н** greengrocer's (*BRIT*), fruit and vegetable shop.
овра́г (-а) *м* ravine.
овса́ *итп сущ см* **овёс**.
овся́нк|а (-и) *ж собир* (*разг: крупа*) oats *мн*; (*каша*) porridge (*BRIT*), oatmeal (*US*).
овся́ный *прил* oat *опред*.
овуля́ци|я (-и) *ж* ovulation.
ов|ца́ (-цы́; *nom pl* **-цы**, *gen pl* **-е́ц)** *ж* sheep (*мн* sheep); (*самка*) ewe.
овцево́дств|о (-а) *ср* sheep-farming.
ОВЧ *сокр* (= *о́чень высо́кая частота́*) VHF (= *very high frequency*).
овча́р|ка (-ки; *gen pl* **-ок)** *ж* sheepdog.
овча́рн|я (-и) *ж* sheepfold.
овчи́н|а (-ы) *ж* sheepskin.
ога́р|ок (-ка) *м* candle end.
огиба́|ть (-ю) *несов от* **обогну́ть**.
оглавле́ни|е (-я) *ср* (table of) contents.
огла|си́ть (-шу́, -си́шь; *impf* **оглаша́ть)** *сов перех* (*решение, проект*) to announce; (*приказ, закон*) to proclaim; (*телеграмму*) to read out; ~ *(perf)* **что-н чем-н** to fill sth with sth
▸ **огласи́ться** (*impf* **оглаша́ться**) *сов возв*: **~ся** *+instr* to resound with.
огла́ск|а (-и) *ж* publicity; **предава́ть (преда́ть** *perf*) **что-н ~е** to make sth public.
оглаша́|ть(ся) (-ю(сь)) *несов от* **огласи́ть(ся)**.
оглашу́(сь) *сов см* **огласи́ть(ся)**.
огло́бл|я (-ли; *gen pl* **-ель)** *ж* shaft (*on cart*).
огло́хн|уть (-у, -ешь) *сов от* **гло́хнуть**.
оглуша́|ть (-ю) *несов от* **оглуши́ть**.
оглуши́тел|ьный (-ен, -ьна, -ьно) *прил* deafening.
огл|уши́ть (-ушу́, -у́шишь; *impf* **оглуша́ть)** *сов перех*: ~ **кого́-н чем-н** (*звуками, криками*) to deafen sb with sth; (*ударом*) to stun sb with sth.
огля|де́ть (-жу́, -ди́шь; *impf* **огля́дывать)** *сов перех* to look round
▸ **огляде́ться** (*impf* **огля́дываться**) *сов возв* to look around.
огля́дк|а (-и) *ж*: **с ~ой** with caution; **де́лать (сде́лать** *perf*) **что-н без ~и** to do sth resolutely; **он бежа́л без ~и** (*разг*) he ran as fast as his legs would carry him.
огля́дыва|ть (-ю) *несов от* **огляде́ть**
▸ **огля́дываться** *несов от* **огляде́ться**, **огляну́ться**.
огляжу́(сь) *сов см* **огляде́ть(ся)**.
огл|яну́ться (-яну́сь, -я́нешься; *impf* **огля́дываться)** *сов возв* to look back; **(я) не успе́л ~, как ...** before I knew it ....
огнево́й *прил* (*характер, взгляд*) fiery; **огнева́я**

завеса (*ВОЕН*) curtain of fire; **огневая позиция** firing position; **огневая точка** (*ВОЕН*) emplacement.
огнедыш|ащий (**-ая, -ее, -ие**) *прил* (*дракон*) fire-breathing; (*вулкан*) erupting.
огнемёт (**-а**) *м* flame-thrower.
огненный *прил* (*цвет, глаза, характер*) fiery; (*поцелуй*) passionate; ~ **столб** burst of flames.
огнеопас|ный (**-ен, -на, -но**) *прил* (in)flammable.
огнесто|йкий (**-йкая, -йкое, -йкие; -ек, -йка, -йко**) *прил* fireproof.
огнестрельн|ый *прил*: **~ое оружие** firearms *мн*; **огнестрельная рана** bullet wound.
огнетушител|ь (**-я**) *м* fire-extinguisher.
огнеупор|ный (**-ен, -на, -но**) *прил* (*материал*) fire-proof; **огнеупорная глина** fire clay; **огнеупорный кирпич** firebrick.
огня *итп сущ см* **огонь**.
ого *межд*: ~! well!; ~, **каким ты стал взрослым!** my, how you've grown!
оговор|ить (**-ю, -ишь**; *impf* **оговаривать**) *сов перех* to slander; (*условия, срок*) to agree (on); (*подлеж*: *правила*) to stipulate
▸ **оговориться** (*impf* **оговариваться**) *сов возв*: **я ~ился** it was a slip of the tongue.
оговор|ка (**-ки**; *gen pl* **-ок**) *ж* (*обмолвка*) slip of the tongue; (*условие*) proviso; **я могу сказать без ~ок, что** ... I can say without reservation that ....
оголённый (**-ён, -ена, -ено**) *прил* bare.
огол|ить (**-ю, -ишь**; *impf* **оголять**) *сов перех* to bare, expose; (*деревья, провод, землю*) to strip; (*меч, кинжал*) to draw; (*фронт, участок*) to expose
▸ **оголиться** (*impf* **оголяться**) *сов возв* (*шея, плечо итп*) to become uncovered; (*деревья, земля*) to become bare; (*провод*) to be exposed; (*фронт, участок*) to become exposed.
оголтел|ый (**-, -а, -о**) *прил* mad.
оголя|ть(ся) (**-ю(сь)**) *несов перех от* **оголить(ся)**.
огон|ёк (**-ька**) *м уменьш от* **огонь**; (*блеск глаз*) twinkle; **работать** (*impf*) **с ~ьком** to work enthusiastically *или* with enthusiasm; **заходить** (**зайти** *perf*) **на** ~ to drop in.
ог|онь (**-ня**) *м* fire; (*фонарей, в окне*) light; (*перен*: *любви, негодования*) flame; **разводить** (**развести** *perf*) ~ to light a fire; **зажигать** (**зажечь** *perf*) ~ to turn on the light; **открывать** (**открыть** *perf*) ~ to open fire; **в ~не сражения** in the heat of battle; **бояться** (*impf*) **чего-н/кого-н как ~ня** to be terrified by sb/sth; **играть** (*impf*) **с ~нём** (*перен*) to play with fire; **между двух ~ней** between two fires.
огонька *итп сущ см* **огонёк**.
огоражива|ть (**-ю**) *несов от* **огородить**.
огород (**-а**) *м* vegetable *или* kitchen garden.
огор|одить (**-ожу, -одишь**; *impf* **огораживать**) *сов перех*: ~ **что-н** (**чем-н**) to fence sth in (with sth).
огорош|ить (**-у, -ишь**; *impf* **огорошивать**) *сов перех* (*разг*) to astound.
огорча|ть(ся) (**-ю(сь)**) *несов от* **огорчить(ся)**.
огорчени|е (**-я**) *ср* distress; **к моему ~ю** to my dismay.
огорч|ённый (**-ён, -ена, -ено**) *прил* distressed; **у него был ~ вид** he looked upset.
огорчител|ьный (**-ен, -ьна, -ьно**) *прил* distressing.
огорч|ить (**-у, -ишь**; *impf* **огорчать**) *сов перех* to distress
▸ **огорчиться** (*impf* **огорчаться**) *сов возв* to be upset *или* distressed.
ограб|ить (**-лю, -ишь**) *сов от* **грабить**.
ограблени|е (**-я**) *ср* robbery.
ограблю *сов см* **ограбить**.
ограда|а (**-ы**) *ж* (*стена*) wall; (*забор*) fence; (*решётка*) railings *мн*.
огра|дить (**-жу, -дишь**; *impf* **ограждать**) *сов перех* (*перен*) to defend, protect.
ограждени|е (**-я**) *ср* barrier.
огражу *сов см* **оградить**.
огран|ить (**-ю, -ишь**; *impf* **огранивать**) *сов перех* to cut.
ограничени|е (**-я**) *ср* restriction, limitation; (*правило*) restriction.
ограничен|ный (**-, -на, -но**) *прил* limited; (*человек*) narrow-minded.
ограничива|ть(ся) (**-ю(сь)**) *несов от* **ограничить(ся)**.
ограничител|ьный (**-ен, -ьна, -ьно**) *прил*: **~ьные меры** restrictive measures *мн*.
огранич|ить (**-у, -ишь**; *impf* **ограничивать**) *сов перех* to limit, restrict
▸ **ограничиться** (*impf* **ограничиваться**) *сов возв*: **~ся** +*instr* (*удовлетвориться*) to content o.s with; (*свестись*) to become limited to.
огре|ть (**-ю**) *сов перех* (*разг*) to whack.
огром|ный (**-ен, -на, -но**) *прил* enormous.
огрубелый *прил* (*руки, кожа*) coarse; (*сердце, душа*) hardened.
огрубе|ть (**-ю**) *сов от* **грубеть**.
огрыза|ться (**-юсь**) *несов возв* to snap.
огрызнуться (**-усь, -ёшься**) *сов возв* to snap.
огрыз|ок (**-ка**) *м* (*огурца, яблока*) half-eaten bit; (*карандаша, ластика*) stub; (*бумажки*) scrap.
огул|ьный (**-ен, -ьна, -ьно**) *прил* unfounded.
огур|ец (**-ца**) *м* cucumber; (*маринованный*) gherkin.
од|а (**-ы**) *ж* ode.
одалжива|ть (**-ю**) *несов от* **одолжить**.
одарён|ный (**-, -на, -но**) *прил* gifted.
одар|ить (**-ю, -ишь**; *impf* **одаривать** *или* **одарять**) *сов перех*: ~ **кого-н чем-н** to give sb sth; **природа ~ила её красотой** she is blessed

with good looks.
одева́|ть (-ю) *несов от* **оде́ть**
▸ **одева́ться** *несов от* **оде́ться** ◆ *возв (носить одежду)* to dress.
оде́жд|а (-ы) *ж* clothes *мн*.
одеколо́н (-а) *м* eau de Cologne.
одел|и́ть (-ю́, -и́шь; *impf* **оделя́ть)** *сов перех*: ~ **кого́-н чем-н** to give sth out to sb.
оде́ну(сь) *итп сов см* **оде́ть(ся)**.
одёргива|ть (-ю) *несов от* **одёрнуть**.
одеревене́лый *прил (руки, пальцы)* numb; *(человек)* paralysed (*BRIT*), paralyzed (*US*).
одеревене́|ть (-ю) *сов от* **деревене́ть**.
од|ержа́ть (-ержу́, -е́ржишь; *impf* **оде́рживать)** *сов перех*: ~ **побе́ду** to be victorious; **оде́рживать** (~ *perf*) **верх на соревнова́нии/в спо́ре** to win a competition/argument.
одержи́м|ый (-, -а, -о) *прил*: ~ *+instr (эмоциями)* possessed by; *(мыслью)* obsessed by.
одёрн|уть (-у, -ешь; *impf* **одёргивать)** *сов перех (одежду)* to straighten; *(разг: человека)* to check.
Оде́сс|а (-ы) *ж* Odessa.
оде́т|ый (-, -а, -о) *прил* dressed; *(разг: обеспеченный одеждой)* clothed; *(покрытый)*: ~ *+instr (снегом итп)* covered with.
оде́|ть (-ну, -нешь; *impf* **одева́ть)** *сов перех* to dress; *(разг: снабдить одеждой)* to clothe; *(перен: снегом)* to cover
▸ **оде́ться** (*impf* **одева́ться**) *сов возв* to get dressed; *(также разг: тепло, легко, приобретать одежду)* to dress; *(покрываться)*: **~ся** *+instr* to be covered with.
одея́л|о (-а) *ср (шерстяное)* blanket; *(стёганое)* quilt; *(пуховое)* eiderdown.

KEYWORD

од|и́н (-ного́; *см* **Table 22;** *f* **одна́**, *nt* **одно́**, *pl* **одни́)** *м чис* one; **одна́ кни́га** one book; **одни́ брю́ки** one pair of trousers; **ей оди́н год** she is one (year old); **они́ живу́т в до́ме но́мер оди́н** they live at number one; **кни́га сто́ит оди́н рубль** the book costs one rouble; **я́блоки продаю́тся по одно́й шту́ке** the apples are sold singly
◆ *прил* alone; *(единственный, единый)* one; *(одинаковый, тот же самый)* the same; **он идёт в кино́ оди́н** he goes to the cinema alone; **есть то́лько оди́н вы́ход** there is only one way out; **у них одни́ взгля́ды** they hold similar views; **я оди́н** *(без супруги)* I am single
◆ *мест* ***1*** *(какой-то)*: **оди́н мой знако́мый** a friend; **одни́ неприя́тности** nothing but problems
2 *(во фразах)*: **оди́н из** *+gen pl* one of; **оди́н и то́т же** the same; **одно́ и то́ же** the same thing; **оди́н раз** once; **оди́н на оди́н** one to one; **все до одного́** all to a man; **ни оди́н** not one; **оди́н за други́м** one after the other; **по одному́** one by one; **одно́ к одному́** *(разг)* one thing after another; **оди́н к одному́** one as good as another; **одно́ из двух** one of two things; **одно́ вре́мя** for some time; **в оди́н го́лос** with one voice; **оди́н-еди́нственный** only one; **оди́н-одинёшенек** *(разг)* all alone.

одина́ково *нареч* in the same way.
одина́ков|ый (-, -а, -о) *прил* similar.
одина́рный *прил* single.
одиннадцатичасово́й *прил* eleven-hour; *(отправление)* eleven-o'clock.
оди́ннадцат|ый (-ая, -ое, -ые) *чис* eleventh; *см также* **пя́тый**.
оди́ннадцат|ь (-и; *как* **пять**; *см* **Table 27)** *чис* eleven; *см также* **пять**.
одино́к|ий (-ая, -ое, -ие; -, -а, -о) *прил (дом, дерево)* solitary; *(жизнь, человек)* lonely; *(без семьи: женщина, мужчина)* single.
одино́чек *сущ см* **одино́чка**.
одино́честв|о (-а) *ср* loneliness.
одино́ч|ка (-ки; *gen pl* **-ек)** *ж (человек)*: **жить ~кой** to live alone; **байда́рка-~** one-man canoe; **в ~ку** on one's own; **сиде́ть** *(impf)* **в ~ке** *(разг)* to be in solitary confinement.
одино́чн|ый *прил (стук, выстрел)* single, lone; *(прохожие, дома)* solitary; ~ **полёт** solo flight; **~ое заключе́ние** solitary confinement; **одино́чное ката́ние (на конька́х)** (*СПОРТ*) singles figure skating.
одио́з|ный (-ен, -на, -но) *прил* odious.
одича́лый *прил* wild.
одича́|ть (-ю) *сов от* **дича́ть**.
одн|а́ (-о́й) *ж чис см* **оди́н**.
одна́жды *нареч* once.
одна́ко *союз, вводн сл* however; **его́ повы́сили – ~!** he's been promoted – no, really!; ~ **же** even so.
одни́ (-х) *мн чис см* **оди́н**.
одн|о́ (-ого́) *ср чис см* **оди́н**.
одноа́ктный *прил* one-act, in one act.
однобо́ртный *прил* single-breasted.
одновре́ме́нно *нареч*: ~ **(с** *+instr*) at the same time (as).
одновре́ме́нный *прил* simultaneous.
одного́ *итп чис см* **оди́н, одно́**.
однoго́д|ок (-ка) *м (разг)*: **он мой ~** he was born in the same year as me.
одноднéвн|ый *прил (зарплата, работа)* one day's; **~ая пое́здка** day trip.
однозву́ч|ный (-ен, -на, -но) *прил* monotonous.
однозна́ч|ный (-ен, -на, -но) *прил (тождественный)* synonymous; *(с одним значением: слово)* monosemantic; (: *выражение, ответ)* unambiguous; (*МАТ*) single-figure; **однозна́чное число́** single-digit number.
одноимённый *прил* of the same name.
однокла́ссник (-а) *м* classmate.
однокла́ссниц|а (-ы) *ж см* **однокла́ссник**.
одноклéточный *прил* single-cell.
одноколе́йный *прил* single-lane.
однокра́тный *прил* single.
однолéтн|ий (-яя, -ее, -ие) *прил* annual.

одноме́стный *прил* (*купе, номер*) single; (*каюта*) single-berth.
однообра́зи|е (**-я**) *ср* monotony.
однообра́зный *прил* monotonous.
однопо́лый *прил* unisexual.
одноразо́вый *прил* disposable; **~ про́пуск** temporary pass (*valid only once*).
одноро́д|ный (**-ен, -на, -но**) *прил* (*явления, понятия*) similar; (*жидкость, масса*) homogenous.
однослож|ный (**-ен, -на, -но**) *прил* (*также перен*) monosyllabic.
односторо́н|ний (**-няя, -нее, -ние**) *прил* (*ткань*) one-sided; (*разоружение*) unilateral; (*движение, связь*) one-way; (**-ен, -ня, -не;** *перен*: *воспитание, развитие*) narrow; (: *мышление*) parochial; **у него́ ~ парали́ч** he is paralysed (*BRIT*) *или* paralyzed (*US*) down one side.
одноти́п|ный (**-ен, -на, -но**) *прил* of the same type *или* kind.
одното́мный *прил* one-volume.
однофами́л|ец (**-ьца**) *м* namesake (*with same surname*).
однофами́лица (**-ы**) *ж см* **однофами́лец**.
однофами́льца *итп сущ см* **однофами́лец**.
одноцве́т|ный (**-ен, -на, -но**) *прил* plain.
одночле́н (**-а**) *м* monomial.
одноэта́жный *прил* single-storey (*BRIT*), single-story (*US*), one-storey (*BRIT*), one-story (*US*).
одобре́ни|е (**-я**) *ср* approval.
одобри́телен *прил см* **одобри́тельный**.
одобри́тельно *нареч* favourably.
одобри́тел|ьный (**-ен, -ьна, -ьно**) *прил* (*отзыв, реакция*) favourable (*BRIT*), favorable (*US*); (*восклицание, взгляд*) of approval; (*статья*) positive.
одо́бр|ить (**-ю, -ишь;** *impf* **одобря́ть**) *сов перех* to approve.
одоле́|ть (**-ю;** *impf* **одолева́ть**) *сов перех* (*врага*) to overpower; (*смущение, неприязнь*) to overcome; (*разг*: *книгу, задачу*) to get through; (: *подлеж*: *жара, комары*) to bug; (*науку*) to master; **его́ ~ла грусть/лень** he was overwhelmed by sadness/a feeling of laziness.
одолже́ни|е (**-я**) *ср* favour (*BRIT*), favor (*US*); **сде́лайте ~** would you do me a favour?; (*ответ*) be my guest.
одолж|и́ть (**-у́, -и́шь;** *impf* **ода́лживать**) *сов перех*: **~ что-н кому́-н** to lend sth to sb; **ода́лживать (~** *perf*) **что-н у кого́-н** (*разг*) to borrow sth from sb.
одряхле́|ть (**-ю**) *сов от* **дряхле́ть**.
одува́нчик (**-а**) *м* dandelion.
оду́ма|ться (**-юсь;** *impf* **оду́мываться**) *сов возв* to think again.
одура́ч|ить (**-у, -ишь**) *сов от* **дура́чить**.
одуре́лый *прил* (*разг*) befuddled.
одуре́|ть (**-ю**) *сов от* **дуре́ть**.
одурма́н|ить (**-ю, -ишь**) *сов от* **дурма́нить**.
о́дур|ь (**-и**) *ж*: **напи́ться до ~и** (*разг*) to drink o.s. silly; **набе́гаться** (*perf*) **до ~и** (*разг*) to run until one is ready to drop; **я насмотре́лся детекти́вов до ~и** (*разг*) I've watched thrillers until I'm sick of them.
одутлова́т|ый (**-, -а, -о**) *прил* puffed up, puffy.
одухотворё|нный (**-, -на, -но**) *прил* (*вид, лицо*) spiritual; (*речь*) inspired.
одухотвор|и́ть (**-ю́, -и́шь;** *impf* **одухотворя́ть**) *сов перех* to inspire.
оды́шк|а (**-и**) *ж*: **у него́ ~** he is short of breath; **страда́ть** (*impf*) **~ой** to be short-winded.
ОЕЭС *ж сокр* (= *Организа́ция европе́йского экономи́ческого сотру́дничества*) OEEC (= *Organization for European Economic Cooperation*).
ожереб|и́ться (*3sg* **-и́тся**, *3pl* **-я́тся**) *сов от* **жереби́ться**.
ожере́ль|е (**-я**) *ср* necklace.
ожесточа́|ть(ся) (**-ю(сь)**) *несов от* **ожесточи́ть(ся)**.
ожесточе́ни|е (**-я**) *ср* bitterness; **с ~м** furiously.
ожесточё|нный (**-, -на, -но**) *прил* (*человек*) hardened, embittered; (*спор, сражение*) fierce.
ожесточ|и́ть (**-у́, -и́шь;** *impf* **ожесточа́ть**) *сов перех* (*человека*) to harden, embitter
▸ **ожесточи́ться** (*impf* **ожесточа́ться**) *сов возв* to become hardened *или* embittered.
ожива́|ть (**-ю**) *несов от* **ожи́ть**.
ожив|и́ть (**-лю́, -и́шь;** *impf* **оживля́ть**) *сов перех* to revive; (*глаза, лицо*) to light up; (*улицу, долину*) to bring to life; (*торговлю, работу*) to revitalize
▸ **оживи́ться** (*impf* **оживля́ться**) *сов возв* to liven up; (*лицо*) to brighten; (*улица, школа*) to come to life.
оживле́ни|е (**-я**) *ср* (*на улице, в доме*) bustle; (*организма, растения*) revival.
оживлё|нный (**-, -на, -но**) *прил* (*беседа, спор*) animated; (*улица, место, деятельность*) lively; (*торговля*) brisk; (**-, -а́, -о́;** *человек*) lively.
оживлю́(сь) *сов см* **оживи́ть(ся)**.
оживля́|ть(ся) (**-ю(сь)**) *несов от* **оживи́ть(ся)**.
оживу́ *итп сов см* **ожи́ть**.
ожида́ни|е (**-я**) *ср* anticipation; (*обычно мн*: *надежды*) expectation; **в ~и чего́-н** in anticipation of sth; **обма́нывать (обману́ть** *perf*) **чьи-н ~я** to fail to come up to sb's expectations.
ожида́|ть (**-ю**) *несов перех* (*ждать*) to expect; (*+gen*; *надеяться*) to expect; **его́ ~ет блестя́щая карье́ра** he has a brilliant career ahead of him; **э́того мо́жно бы́ло ~** that was to be expected
▸ **ожида́ться** *несов возв* to be expected.

ожирéни|е (-я) *ср* obesity.
ожирé|ть (-ю) *сов от* **жирéть.**
ож|и́ть (**-иву́, -ивёшь**; *impf* **оживáть**) *сов неперех* to come to life; (*перен*: *чувства, человек*) to revive.
ожóг (-а) *м* burn.
озабóт|ить (**-чу, -тишь**) *сов перех* to worry, trouble.
озабóчен|ный (-, -на, -но) *прил* worried.
озабóчу *сов см* **озабóтить.**
озаглáв|ить (**-лю, -ишь**; *impf* **озаглáвливать**) *сов перех* to entitle.
озадáчен|ный (-, -на, -но) *прил* puzzled.
озадáч|ить (**-у, -ишь**; *impf* **озадáчивать**) *сов перех* to puzzle, perplex.
озар|и́ть (**-ю́, -и́шь**; *impf* **озаря́ть**) *сов перех* (*подлеж*: *солнце, улыбка*) to light up; (: *идея, догадка*) to dawn on
▸ **озари́ться** (*impf* **озаря́ться**) *сов возв*: **~ся** *+instr* (*также перен*) to be lit up by.
озверé|ть (-ю) *сов от* **зверéть** ◆ *неперех* to become violent.
озву́ч|ить (**-у, -ишь**; *impf* **озву́чивать**) *сов перех*: **~ фильм** to record the soundtrack for a film.
оздоровúтельн|ый *прил*: **~ые мероприя́тия** health-improving measures; **оздоровúтельный кóмплекс** ≈ health farm.
оздоров|и́ть (**-лю́, -и́шь**; *impf* **оздоровля́ть**) *сов перех* (*перен*: *коллектив, обстановку*) to clean up; **оздоровля́ть** (**~** *perf*) **органи́зм** to improve one's health; **~** (*perf*) **мéстность** to improve the ecology of an area.
озелен|и́ть (**-ю́, -и́шь**; *impf* **озеленя́ть**) *несов перех* to green.
óз|еро (**-ера**; *nom pl* **-ёра**) *ср* lake.
ози́м|ые (**-ых**; *decl like adj*) *мн* winter crops *мн*.
ози́м|ый *прил*: **~ая пшени́ца/рожь** winter wheat/rye; *см также* **ози́мые.**
озирá|ться (**-юсь**) *несов возв*: **~ (по сторонáм)** to glance about *или* around.
озлóб|ить (**-лю, -ишь**; *impf* **озлобля́ть**) *сов перех* to anger
▸ **озлóбиться** (*impf* **озлобля́ться**) *сов возв* to become angry.
озлоблéни|е (-я) *ср* anger.
озлóблен|ный (-, -на, -но) *прил* angry.
озлóблю(сь) *сов см* **озлóбить(ся).**
озлобля́|ть(ся) (**-ю(сь)**) *несов от* **озлóбить(ся).**
ознакóм|ить (**-лю, -ишь**) *сов от* **знакóмить** ◆ (*impf* **ознакомля́ть**) *перех*: **~ когó-н с** *+instr* to familiarize sb with
▸ **ознакóмиться** *сов от* **знакóмиться** ◆ (*impf* **ознакомля́ться**) *возв*: **~ся с** *+instr* to familiarize o.s. with.
ознаменовáни|е (-я) *ср*: **в ~** *+gen* (*в память*) in commemoration of.
ознамен|овáть (**-у́ю**; *impf* **ознаменóвывать**) *сов перех* to commemorate, mark; **егó побéда ~овáла э́тот год** his victory made this a memorable year
▸ **ознаменовáться** (*impf* **ознаменóвываться**) *сов возв* (*+instr*) to be remembered for.
означá|ть (-ю) *несов перех* to mean.
ознóб (-а) *м* shivering.
ОЗО *ср сокр* (= *отделéние заóчного обучéния*) *extra-mural department*.
озóн (-а) *м* ozone.
озóновый *прил*: **~ слой** ozone layer; **озóновая дырá** hole in the ozone layer.
озорни́к (**-á**) *м* (*разг*) scallywag.
озорнóй *прил* mischievous.
озорств|ó (**-á**) *ср* mischief.
озя́бн|уть (**-у, -ешь**) *сов от* **зя́бнуть.**
ой *межд*: **~!** (*выражает испуг*) argh!; (*выражает удивление, восхищение*) oh!; (*выражает боль*) ouch!, ow!; **им жилóсь ~ как тру́дно** their life was ever so difficult.
ОК *м сокр* (= *отдéл кáдров*) personnel department.
ок|азáть (**-ажу́, -áжешь**; *impf* **окáзывать**) *сов перех*: **~ пóмощь/содéйствие комý-н** to provide help/assistance for sb; **окáзывать (~** *perf*) **влия́ние на** *+acc* to exercise influence over *или* on; **окáзывать (~** *perf*) **давлéние на** *+acc* to put pressure on *или* upon; **окáзывать (~** *perf*) **внимáние комý-н** to pay attention to sb; **окáзывать (~** *perf*) **предпочтéние комý-н** to give preference to sb; **окáзывать (~** *perf*) **сопротивлéние (комý-н)** to offer resistance (to sb); **окáзывать (~** *perf*) **услу́гу комý-н** to do sb a service
▸ **оказáться** (*impf* **окáзываться**) *сов возв* (*найтись*: *на столе итп*) to appear; (*очутиться*: *на острове итп*) to find o.s.; **окáзываться (~ся** *perf*) *+instr* (*вором, шпионом*) to turn out to be; **~áзывается, онá былá правá** it turns out that she was right; **у негó не ~азáлось дéнег** it turned out that he didn't have any money.
окáзи|я (**-и**) *ж* opportunity; **посылáть (послáть** *perf*) **что-н с ~ей** to send sth with somebody.
окáзыва|ть(ся) (**-ю(сь)**) *несов от* **оказáть(ся).**
окайм|и́ть (**-лю́, -и́шь**; *impf* **окаймля́ть**) *сов перех* (*рисунок*) to frame; (*платок*) to border.
окаменивá|ть (-ю) *сов от* **каменéть.**
окаменéлый *прил* (*дерево, растение*) fossilized; (*хлеб, сыр*) rock-hard; (*перен*: *человек, взгляд, лицо*) motionless.
окаменé|ть (**-ю**; *impf* **окаменевáть** *или* **каменéть**) *сов неперех* (*дерево, растение*) to fossilize; (*хлеб, сыр*) to go stale; (*перен*: *лицо, взгляд*) to freeze; (: *душа, сердце*) to turn to stone; **~** (*perf*) **от стрáха** to turn rigid with fear; **~** (*perf*) **от гóря** to be numb with grief.
окант|овáть (**-у́ю**; *impf* **окантóвывать**) *сов перех* (*картину, фотографию*) to frame; (*воротник, платок*) to border.
окáнчива|ть (-ю) *несов от* **окóнчить**
▸ **окáнчиваться** *несов от* **окóнчиться** ◆ *возв*: **~ся на глáсную/соглáсную** to end in a vowel/

consonant; **э́та у́лица ~ется тупико́м** this (street) is a dead end.
ока́пыва|ть(ся) (**-ю(сь)**) *несов от* **окопа́ть(ся)**.
ок|ати́ть (**-ачу́, -а́тишь**; *impf* **ока́чивать**) *сов перех*: ~ **кого́-н/что-н чем-н** to pour sth over sb/sth.
океа́н (**-а**) *м* (*также перен*) ocean.
Океа́ни|я (**-и**) *ж* Oceania.
океаноло́ги|я (**-и**) *ж* oceanography.
оки́н|уть (**-у, -ешь**; *impf* **оки́дывать**) *сов перех*: ~ **кого́-н/что-н взгля́дом** to glance over at sb/sth.
о́кис|ел (**-ла**) *м* oxide.
окисле́ни|е (**-я**) *ср* oxidation.
окисл|и́ть (*3sg* **-и́т**, *3pl* **-я́т**, *impf* **окисля́ть**) *сов перех* to oxidize
▸ **окисли́ться** (*impf* **окисля́ться**) *сов возв* to oxidize.
о́кис|ь (**-и**) *ж* oxide.
оккупа́нт (**-а**) *м* (*захватчик*) occupier.
оккупацио́нный *прил* occupation *опред*.
оккупа́ци|я (**-и**) *ж* occupation.
оккупи́р|овать (**-ую**) *(не)сов перех* to occupy.
окла́д (**-а**) *м* (*зарплата*) salary; (*на иконе*) overlay.
оклев|ета́ть (**-ещу́, -е́щешь**) *сов перех* to slander.
окле́|ить (**-ю, -ишь**; *impf* **окле́ивать**) *сов перех*: ~ **что-н чем-н** to cover sth with sth; **окле́ивать** (~ *perf*) **сте́ны обо́ями** to paper the walls.
окли́кн|уть (**-у, -ешь**; *impf* **оклика́ть**) *сов перех* to call out to.
ок|но́ (**-на́**; *nom pl* **-на**, *gen pl* **-он**) *ср* window; (*подоконник*) windowsill; (*разг: между уроками*) gap.
око́в|ы (**-**) *мн* (*также перен*) fetters *мн*.
окола́чива|ться (**-юсь**) *несов возв* (*разг*) to hang about.
околд|ова́ть (**-у́ю**; *impf* **околдо́вывать**) *сов перех* (*также перен*) to bewitch.
околева́|ть (**-ю**) *несов от* **околе́ть**.
околе́сиц|а (**-ы**) *ж* (*разг*) claptrap, tripe; **нести́** (*impf*) ~**у** to talk tripe.
околе́|ть (**-ю**; *impf* **околева́ть**) *сов неперех* (*животное*) to die.
о́коло *нареч* nearby ◆ *предл* (*+gen*; *рядом с*) near; (*приблизительно*) about.
околозе́мн|ый *прил* around the earth; ~**ая орби́та** the earth's orbit.
око́льн|ый *прил* roundabout *опред*; (*перен: метод*) devious; **мы пошли́ ~ым путём** we took a roundabout route.
окольцева́ть (**-у́ю**) *сов от* **кольцева́ть**.
о́кон *сущ см* **окно́**.
оконе́чност|ь (**-и**) *ж* tip.
око́нн|ый *прил*: ~**ая ра́ма** window frame; ~**ое стекло́** windowpane.
оконча́ни|е (**-я**) *ср* end; (*линг*) ending.
оконча́телен *прил см* **оконча́тельный**.
оконча́тельно *нареч* (*решить, ответить*) definitely; (*разбить, победить, влюбиться*) completely; (*отредактировать, проверить*) finally.
оконча́тел|ьный (**-ен, -ьна, -ьно**) *прил* (*вывод, редакция, ответ*) final; (*победа, свержение*) complete.
око́нч|ить (**-у, -ишь**; *impf* **ока́нчивать**) *сов перех* to finish; (*вуз*) to graduate from
▸ **око́нчиться** (*impf* **ока́нчиваться**) *сов возв* to finish; ~**ся** (*perf*) *+instr* (*скандалом, свадьбой*) to result in.
око́п (**-а**) *м* trench.
окопа́|ть (**-ю**; *impf* **ока́пывать**) *сов перех*: ~ **расте́ние** to loosen the soil around a plant
▸ **окопа́ться** (*impf* **ока́пываться**) *сов возв* (*ВОЕН*) to dig (o.s.) in; (*разг: в библиотеке, в кабинете*) to bury o.s.
о́корок (**-а**; *nom pl* **-а́**) *м* gammon.
окосе́|ть (**-ю**) *сов неперех* (*разг: косить*) to squint; (: *ослепнуть*) to lose an eye; (: *опьянеть*) to get drunk.
окостенева́|ть (**-ю**) *несов от* **окостене́ть**.
окостене́лый *прил* ossified; (*руки, ноги*) stiff; (*ум, жизнь*) fossilized.
окостене́|ть (**-ю**; *impf* **окостенева́ть**) *сов неперех* to ossify; (*руки, ноги*) to stiffen; (*ум*) to fossilize.
око́т (**-а**) *м* (*кошки*) birth of kittens; (*овцы*) lambing.
окот|и́ться (*3sg* **-и́тся**, *3pl* **-я́тся**) *сов от* **коти́ться**.
окочене́лый *прил* stiff with cold.
окочене́|ть (**-ю**) *сов от* **кочене́ть**.
окра́ин|а (**-ы**) *ж* (*поля, леса*) edge; (*города*) outskirts *мн*; (*страны*) remote parts *мн*.
окра́|сить (**-шу, -сишь**; *impf* **окра́шивать**) *сов перех* (*ткань, волосы*) to dye; (*рассказ, жизнь*) to colour (*BRIT*), color (*US*)
▸ **окра́ситься** (*impf* **окра́шиваться**) *сов возв*: ~**ся в чёрный/кра́сный цвет** to come out black/red; **облака́ ~сились в ро́зовый цвет** the clouds were tinged with pink.
окра́с|ка (**-ки**; *gen pl* **-ок**) *ж* (*ткани, волос*) dyeing; (*животного, выражения*) colouring (*BRIT*), coloring (*US*); **принима́ть** (**приня́ть** *perf*) **совсе́м другу́ю ~ку** (*перен*) to take on a different complexion.
окра́шива|ть(ся) (**-ю(сь)**) *несов от* **окра́сить(ся)**.
окра́шу(сь) *сов см* **окра́сить(ся)**.
окре́пн|уть (**-у, -ешь**) *сов от* **кре́пнуть**.
окр|ести́ть (**-ещу́, -е́стишь**) *сов от* **крести́ть** ◆ *сов перех*: ~ **кого́-н/что-н чем-н** (*разг*) to nickname sb/sth sth
▸ **окрести́ться** *сов от* **крести́ться**.
окре́стност|ь (**-и**) *ж* (*города, деревни*) environs

мн; **в ~и** *+gen* in the vicinity of.
окре́стн|ый *прил* (*города́, деревни*) neighbouring (*BRIT*), neighboring (*US*); **~ое населе́ние** the population of the surrounding area.
окрещу́(сь) *сов см* **окрести́ть(ся)**.
окриве́|ть (-ю) *сов от* **криве́ть**.
о́крик (-а) *м* shout.
окри́кн|уть (-у, -ешь; *impf* **окри́кивать**) *сов перех*: ~ **кого́-н** to shout to sb.
окрова́влен|ный (-, -а, -о) *прил* bloodstained.
окроп|и́ть (-лю́, -и́шь) *сов от* **кропи́ть**.
окро́шк|а (-и) *ж* okroshka (*cold kvass soup with vegetables and cooked meat*).
о́круг (-а) *м* (*администрати́вный, вое́нный*) district; (*избира́тельный*) ward; (*национа́льный*) territory; (*города*) area.
окру́г|а (-и) *ж* (*разг*) neighbourhood (*BRIT*), neighborhood (*US*).
округле́|ть (-ю) *сов от* **кругле́ть**.
округл|и́ть (-ю́, -и́шь; *impf* **округля́ть**) *сов перех* (*форму, заготовку*) to round off; (*цифру, результат*) to round up *или* down; (*разг*: *сумму, капитал*) to increase; **округля́ть** (~ *perf*) **глаза́** (*от удивления, от страха*) to open one's eyes wide
▸ **округли́ться** (*impf* **округля́ться**) *сов возв* (*фигура, лицо*) to fill out; (*перен*: *разг*: *капитал, сумма*) to increase; **у неё ~и́лись глаза́** her eyes widened.
окру́глый *прил* rounded; (*лицо*) round.
округля́|ть(ся) (-ю(сь)) *несов от* **округли́ть(ся)**.
окружа́|ть (-ю) *несов от* **окружи́ть** ♦ *перех* to surround.
окружа́ющ|ее (-его; *decl like adj*) *ср* environment.
окружа́ющ|ие (-их; *decl like adj*) *мн* (*также*: ~ **лю́ди**) *the people around one*; **ничего́ нельзя́ скрыть от ~их** you can't hide anything from (other) people.
окружа́ющ|ий (-ая, -ее, -ие) *прил* surrounding; **окружа́ющая среда́** environment.
окруже́ни|е (-я) *ср* (*среда*) environment; (*компания*) company; (*ВОЕН*) encirclement; **в ~и** *+gen* (*в сопровождение*) in the company of; (*среди*) surrounded by.
окруж|и́ть (-у́, -и́шь; *impf* **окружа́ть**) *сов перех* to surround; **окружа́ть** (~ *perf*) **что-н** *+instr* to surround sth by; **окружа́ть** (~ *perf*) **кого́-н** *+instr* to surround sb with.
окружно́й *прил* (*центр, конференция*) regional; **окружна́я доро́га** bypass; **окружна́я избира́тельная комиссия** constituency electoral committee.
окру́жност|ь (-и) *ж* circle; **на три киломе́тра в ~и** three kilometres (*BRIT*) *или* kilometers (*US*) in circumference.
О́ксфорд (-а) *м* Oxford.
окта́в|а (-ы) *ж* octave.
октя́бр|ь (-я́) *м* October; **прие́ду пе́рвого октября́** I shall arrive on the first of October; **в про́шлом/бу́дущем октябре́** last/next October; **в конце́/нача́ле/середи́не октября́** at the end of/beginning of/in the middle of October.
октя́брьск|ий (-ая, -ое, -ие) *прил* October *опред*.
окули́ст (-а) *м* ophthalmologist.
окун|у́ть (-у́, -ёшь; *impf* **окуна́ть**) *сов перех* to dip
▸ **окуну́ться** (*impf* **окуна́ться**) *сов возв* to plunge.
о́кун|ь (-я) *м* (*ЗООЛ*) perch.
окупа́емост|ь (-и) *ж* viability.
окупи́ть (-уплю́, -у́пишь; *impf* **окупа́ть**) *сов перех* (*расходы*) to cover; (*поездку, проект*) to cover the cost of
▸ **окупи́ться** (*impf* **окупа́ться**) *сов возв* to pay for itself; (*перен*: *усилия, работа*) to be rewarded.
оку́р|ок (-ка; *nom pl* -ки) *м* stub, butt.
оку́та|ть (-ю; *impf* **оку́тывать**) *сов перех* (*подлеж*: *туман, дым*) to envelop; **оку́тывать** (~ *perf*) **что-н/кого́-н чем-н** to wrap sth/sb (up) in sth
▸ **оку́таться** (*impf* **оку́тываться**) *сов возв*: **~ся** *+instr* to wrap up in; (*перен*: *земля итп*) to be enveloped in.
оку́ч|ить (-у, -ишь; *impf* **оку́чивать**) *сов перех* to earth up.
ола́д|ья (-ьи; *gen pl* -ий) *ж* ≈ drop scone, ≈ (Scotch) pancake.
оледене́ни|е (-я) *ср* freezing.
оледене́|ть (-ю) *сов от* **ледене́ть**.
оленёнок (-ёнка; *nom pl* -я́та, *gen pl* -я́т) *м* fawn.
оле́н|ий (-ья, -ье, -ьи) *прил* deer's; **~ьи рога́** antlers.
олени́н|а (-ы) *ж* venison.
оле́н|ь (-я) *м* deer (*мн* deer).
оленя́та *итп сущ см* **оленёнок**.
оли́вк|а (-и) *ж* olive.
оли́вковый *прил* olive *опред*; (*цвет*) olive-green.
олимпиа́д|а (-ы) *ж* (*СПОРТ*) the Olympics *мн*; (*по физике итп*) Olympiad; **Бе́лая/Ле́тняя О~** the Winter/Summer Olympics.
олимпи́йск|ий (-ая, -ое, -ие) *прил* Olympic *опред*; **~ое споко́йствие** superhuman calm; **олимпи́йские и́гры** the Olympic Games.
оли́ф|а (-ы) *ж* drying oil.
олицетвор|и́ть (-ю́, -и́шь; *impf* **олицетворя́ть**) *сов перех* to personify.
о́лов|о (-а) *ср* (*ХИМ*) tin.
оловя́нный *прил* tin.
о́лух (-а) *м* (*разг*) oaf.
О́льстер (-а) *м* Ulster.
ольх|а́ (-и́) *ж* alder.
ом (-а) *м* ohm.
Ома́н (-а) *м* Oman.
ома́р (-а) *м* lobster.
оме́г|а (-и) *ж* omega.
омерзе́ни|е (-я) *ср* disgust.

омерзи́тел|ьный (-ен, -ьна, -ьно) *прил* disgusting.
омертве́лый *прил* dead.
омертве́|ть (-ю) *сов от* **мертве́ть**.
омле́т (-а) *м* omelette.
омоло|ди́ть (-жу́, -ди́шь; *impf* **омола́живать)** *сов перех* to rejuvenate
▸ **омолоди́ться** (*impf* **омола́живаться**) *сов возв* to be rejuvenated.
ОМОН *м сокр* (= *отря́д мили́ции осо́бого назначе́ния*) *special police force*.
омо́ним (-а) *м* homonym.
омоно́в|ец (-ца) *м member of ОМОН*.
омо́ю *итп сов см* **омы́ть**.
омрач|и́ть (-у́, -и́шь; *impf* **омрача́ть)** *сов перех* (*настроение, радость, лицо*) to cloud; (*праздник, встречу*) to cast a cloud over
▸ **омрачи́ться** (*impf* **омрача́ться**) *сов возв* (*взгляд, лицо, настроение*) to darken.
о́мут (-а) *м* (*водоворот*) whirlpool.
омыва́|ть (-ю) *несов от* **омы́ть** ◆ *перех* (*подлеж: море, океан*) to wash.
ом|ы́ть (-о́ю, -о́ешь; *impf* **омыва́ть)** *сов перех* to wash.
он (его́; *см* **Table 5a)** *мест* (*человек*) he; (*животное, предмет*) it.
она́ (её; *см* **Table 5a)** *мест* (*человек*) she; (*животное, предмет*) it.
онани́зм (-а) *м* masturbation.
онда́тр|а (-ы) *ж* musquash, muskrat.
онеме́лый *прил* numb.
онеме́|ть (-ю) *сов от* **неме́ть**.
они́ (их; *см* **Table 5b)** *мест* they.
онко́лог (-а) *м* oncologist.
онкологи́ческ|ий (-ая, -ое, -ие) *прил* oncological; **~ая кли́ника** cancer clinic.
онла́йновый *прил* on-line.
оно́ (его́; *см* **Table 5a)** *мест* it; **~ и ви́дно!** (*разг*) sure! (*used ironically*); **я хоте́л помо́чь Вам – ~ и ви́дно** I was only trying to help you – sure you were; **вот ~ что** *или* **как!** (*разг*) so that's what it is!
ОНЧ *сокр* (= *о́чень ни́зкая частота́*) VLF (= *very low frequency*).
ООН *ж сокр* (= *Организа́ция Объединённых На́ций*) UNO (= *United Nations Organization*).
ООП *ж сокр* (= *Организа́ция освобожде́ния Палести́ны*) PLO (= *Palestine Liberation Organization*).
опада́|ть (*3sg* **-ет**, *3pl* **-ют**) *несов от* **опа́сть**.
опаду́т *итп сов см* **опа́сть**.
опа́здыва|ть (-ю) *несов от* **опозда́ть**.
опа́л (-а) *м* opal.
опа́л|а (-ы) *ж* (*перен*) disfavour (*BRIT*), disfavor (*US*); **быть** *(impf)* **в ~е (у** *+gen*) to be out of favour (with).
опал|и́ть (-ю́, -и́шь; *impf* **опа́ливать** *или* **опаля́ть)** *сов перех* (*волосы, крылья, дерево итп*) to singe; (*кожу, лицо*) to burn; (*impf* **опа́ливать**; *курицу, утку*) to singe.
опа́р|а (-ы) *ж* leaven.
опаса́|ться (-юсь) *несов возв*: ~ *+gen* (*неприятеля, рецензента*) to be afraid of; (*сквозняка, простуды*) to avoid; ~ *(impf)* **за** *+acc* to be worried about.
опа́сен *прил см* **опа́сный**.
опасе́ни|е (-я) *ср* apprehension.
опа́ск|а (-и) *ж*: **с ~ой** cautiously; **без ~и** fearlessly.
опа́сно *нареч* dangerously ◆ *как сказ* it's dangerous; **э́то ~ для жи́зни** it's life-threatening.
опа́сност|ь (-и) *ж* danger; **в ~и** in danger; **с ~ю для жи́зни** endangering one's life.
опа́с|ный (-ен, -на, -но) *прил* dangerous.
опа́|сть (*3sg* **-дёт**, *3pl* **-ду́т**, *impf* **опада́ть**) *сов неперех* (*цветы, листья*) to fall; (*опухоль, шишка*) to go down; (*разг: щёки, бока*) to get thinner.
ОПЕК *м/ж сокр* (= *Организа́ция стран-экспортёров не́фти*) OPEC (= *Organization of Petroleum-Exporting Countries*).
опе́к|а (-и) *ж* (*попечительство: государства*) guardianship; (: *матери, отца*) custody; (*забота*) care ◆ *собир* guardians *мн*; **брать (взять** *perf*) **кого́-н под ~у** to take sb into one's care; **она́ рабо́тает под мое́й ~ой** she works under my supervision.
опека́|ть (-ю) *несов перех* to take care of; (*сироту*) to be guardian to.
опеку́н (-а́) *м* (*сироты*) guardian; (*наследника, наследства*) trustee.
опеку́нш|а (-и) *ж* (*сироты*) guardian.
оп|ёнок (-ёнка; *nom pl* **-я́та**, *gen pl* **-я́т)** *м* (*БОТ*) honey agaric.
о́пера (-ы) *ж* opera.
операти́вен *прил см* **операти́вный**.
операти́вност|ь (-и) *ж* efficiency.
операти́в|ный (-ен, -на, -но) *прил* (*работа, группа, штаб*) executive *опред*; (*меры, действия, руководство*) efficient; (*хирургический*) surgical; **операти́вное вмеша́тельство** surgical intervention.
опера́тор (-а) *м* operator.
операцио́нн|ая (-ой; *decl like adj*) *ж* (*МЕД*) operating theatre (*BRIT*) *или* room (*US*).
операцио́нный *прил* (*инструменты, отделение*) surgical; **операцио́нный стол** operating table.
опера́ци|я (-и) *ж* operation.
опере|ди́ть (-жу́, -ди́шь; *impf* **опережа́ть)** *сов перех* (*в беге, в учёбе, в развитии*) to outstrip; ~ *(perf)* **кого́-н** (*в разговоре*) to beat sb to it.
опере́ни|е (-я) *ср* (*ЗООЛ*) plumage; (*АВИА*): **хвостово́е ~** tail.
опере́тт|а (-ы) *ж* operetta.

опере́ться (**обопру́сь, обопрёшься**; *pt* **опёрся, оперла́сь, оперло́сь**, *impf* **опира́ться**) *сов неперех*: ~ **на** *+acc* (*дерево, трость*) to lean on; (*перен*: *на товарища, на коллектив*) to rely on; (*перен*: *на факты, на теорию*) to be supported *или* backed up by.
опери́р|овать (-**ую**; *perf* **опери́ровать** *или* **прооперúровать**) *несов перех* (*больного*) to operate on ◆ *неперех* (*no perf*; *ВОЕН*) to operate; ~ *(impf) +instr* (*акциями, ценными бумагами*) to deal in; (*перен*: *цифрами, фактами*) to use.
опер|и́ться (*3sg* **-и́тся**, *3pl* **-я́тся**, *impf* **оперя́ться**) *сов возв* to become fully fledged.
о́перный *прил* (*ария, партитура*) operatic; (*певец*) opera *опред*; ~ **теа́тр** opera house.
оперя́|ться (*3sg* **-ется**, *3pl* **-ются**) *несов от* **опери́ться**.
опеча́л|иться (-**юсь**) *сов от* **печа́литься**.
опеча́та|ть (-**ю**; *impf* **опеча́тывать**) *сов перех* to seal.
опеча́т|ка (-**ки**; *gen pl* **-ок**) *ж* misprint; **список** ~**ок** errata.
опеча́тыва|ть (-**ю**) *несов от* **опеча́тать**.
опе́ш|ить (-**у, -ишь**) *сов неперех* (*разг*) to be taken aback.
опи́л|ки (-**ок**) *мн* (*древесные*) sawdust *ед*; (*металлические*) filings *мн*.
опира́|ться (-**юсь**) *несов от* **опере́ться**.
описа́ни|е (-**я**) *ср* description.
описа́тел|ьный (-**ен, -ьна, -ьно**) *прил* descriptive.
оп|иса́ть (-**ишу́, -и́шешь**; *impf* **опи́сывать**) *сов перех* to describe; (*составить перечень*) to make a list *или* an inventory of; (*наложить арест*) to distrain.
опи́са|ться (-**юсь**) *сов возв* (*разг*) to wet o.s.
опи́сыва|ть (-**ю**) *несов от* **описа́ть**.
о́пис|ь (-**и**) *ж* (*список*) list, inventory; (*арест*) distraint.
о́пиум (-**а**) *м* opium.
опишу́ *итп сов см* **описа́ть**.
опла́|кать (-**чу, -чешь**; *impf* **опла́кивать**) *сов перех* to mourn.
опла́т|а (-**ы**) *ж* payment.
опл|ати́ть (-**ачу́, -а́тишь**; *impf* **опла́чивать**) *сов перех* (*работу, труд*) to pay for; (*счёт*) to pay.
опла́чу *итп сов см* **опла́кать**.
оплачу́ *сов см* **оплати́ть**.
оплеу́х|а (-**и**) *ж* (*разг*) clout; (*перен*: *оскорбление*) slap in the face.
оплодотворе́ни|е (-**я**) *ср* fertilization.
оплодотвор|и́ть (-**ю́, -и́шь**; *impf* **оплодотворя́ть**) *сов перех* to fertilize.
опломбир|ова́ть (-**у́ю**) *сов от* **пломбирова́ть**.
опло́т (-**а**) *м* stronghold, bastion.
оплоша́|ть (-**ю**) *сов неперех* (*разг*) to boob.
оплóшност|ь (-**и**) *ж* mistake; **допуска́ть** (**допусти́ть** *perf*) ~ to make a mistake.
опове|сти́ть (-**щу́, -сти́шь**; *impf* **оповеща́ть**) *сов перех* to notify.
оповеще́ни|е (-**я**) *ср* notification.
оповещу́ *сов см* **оповести́ть**.
опога́н|ить (-**ю**) *сов от* **пога́нить**.
опозда́вш|ий (-**его**; *decl like adj*) *м* latecomer.
опозда́ни|е (-**я**) *ср* lateness; (*поезда, самолёта*) late arrival; **приходи́ть** (**прийти́** *perf*) **с** ~**м/без опозда́ния** to arrive late/on time.
опозда́|ть (-**ю**; *impf* **опа́здывать**) *сов неперех*: **опа́здывать** (**в/на** *+acc*) (*в школу, на работу итп*) to be late (for); **опа́здывать** (~ *perf*) **с чем-н** to be late with sth; ~ *(perf)* **на по́езд/самолёт** to miss the train/plane.
опознава́тельный *прил* (*знак*) identifying; (*огни*) distinguishing.
опозна|ва́ть (-**ю́**) *несов от* **опозна́ть**.
опозна́ни|е (-**я**) *ср* identification.
опозна́|ть (-**ю**; *impf* **опознава́ть**) *сов перех* to identify.
опозо́р|ить(ся) (-**ю(сь)**) *сов от* **позо́рить(ся)**.
ополо́скива|ть (-**ю**) *несов от* **ополосну́ть**.
о́ползень (-**ня**) *м* landslide.
ополосн|у́ть (-**у́, -ёшь**; *impf* **ополо́скивать**) *сов перех* (*посуду*) to rinse; (*лицо, руки*) to wash.
ополоу́ме|ть (-**ю**) *сов неперех* (*разг*) to go wild.
ополча́|ться (-**юсь**) *несов от* **ополчи́ться**.
ополче́н|ец (-**ца**) *м* member of the home guard.
ополче́ни|е (-**я**) *ср* home guard.
ополче́нца *итп сущ см* **ополче́нец**.
ополч|и́ться (-**у́сь, -и́шься**; *impf* **ополча́ться**) *сов возв*: ~ **на** *+acc или* **про́тив** *+gen* (*человека*) to turn against; (*теорию, недостатки*) to attack.
опо́мн|иться (-**юсь, -ишься**) *сов возв* (*прийти в сознание*) to come round; (*одуматься*) to come to one's senses; ~**ись, что ты де́лаешь!** think what you're doing!
опо́р (-**а**) *м*: **во весь** ~ at top speed.
опо́р|а (-**ы**) *ж* (*также перен*) support; (*СТРОИТ*) pile; **то́чка** ~**ы** fulcrum; **опо́ра электропереда́ч** (*обычно мн*) electricity pylon.
опо́рный *прил* supporting *опред*; **опо́рный прыжо́к** vault; **опо́рный пункт** base; (*ВОЕН*) strongpoint.
опорожн|и́ть (-**ю́, -и́шь**; *impf* **опорожня́ть**) *сов перех* to drain, empty.
опоро́с (-**а**) *м* farrowing.
опоро́ч|ить (-**у, -ишь**) *сов от* **поро́чить**.
опохмел|и́ться (-**ю́сь, -и́шься**; *impf* **опохмеля́ться**) *сов возв* (*разг*) to take the hair of the dog (*to cure a hangover*).
опо́шл|ить (-**ю, -ишь**; *impf* **опошля́ть**) *сов перех* (*мысль, человека, имя*) to debase, demean; (*слово, песню*) to vulgarize.
опоэтизи́р|овать (-**ую**) *сов от* **поэтизи́ровать**.
оппозицио́н|ный (-**ен, -на, -но**) *прил* (*партия, блок*) opposition; ~**ные настрое́ния** mood of opposition.
оппози́ци|я (-**и**) *ж* opposition; **быть** *(impf)* **в** ~**и** (*ПОЛИТ*) to be in opposition; **быть** *(impf)* **в** ~**и к** *+dat* to oppose.

оппоне́нт (-а) *м* external examiner (*for doctoral thesis*); (*в споре*) opponent.
опра́в|а (-ы) *ж* frame.
оправда́ни|е (-я) *ср* justification; (*ЮР*) acquittal; (*извинение*) excuse; **говори́ть (сказа́ть** *perf*) **что-н в своё** ~ to say sth in one's defence (*BRIT*) *или* defense (*US*).
опра́вдан|ный (-, -на, -но) *прил* justified.
оправда́|ть (-ю; *impf* **опра́вдывать**) *сов перех* to justify; (*ЮР*) to acquit, find not guilty
▸ **оправда́ться** (*impf* **опра́вдываться**) *сов возв* to justify o.s.; (*надежды, опасения, расходы*) to be justified.
опра́в|ить (-лю, -ишь; *impf* **оправля́ть**) *сов перех* (*платье, постель*) to straighten; (*драгоценный камень, зеркало*) to mount; (*линзы*) to frame
▸ **опра́виться** (*impf* **оправля́ться**) *сов возв*: **~ся от** *+gen* to recover from.
опра́шива|ть (-ю) *несов от* **опроси́ть**.
определе́ни|е (-я) *ср* determination; (*понятия, значения*) definition; (*ЛИНГ*) attribute; (*ЮР*) ruling.
определён|ный (-ен, -на, -но) *прил* (*установленный*) definite; (*некоторый*) certain; (*явный*: *успех, способности*) unqualified; **при ~ных обстоя́тельствах** under certain circumstances.
определ|и́ть (-ю́, -и́шь; *impf* **определя́ть**) *сов перех* to determine; (*явление, понятие*) to define
▸ **определи́ться** (*impf* **определя́ться**) *сов возв* (*болезнь*) to be diagnosed; (*задачи*) to become clear; (*разг*: *характер*) to take shape; (*пилот*) to get one's bearings.
опре́лост|ь (-и) *ж* rash; (*у младенца*) nappy (*BRIT*) *или* diaper (*US*) rash.
опресн|и́ть (-ю́, -и́шь; *impf* **опресня́ть**) *сов перех* to desalinate.
оприхо́д|овать (-ую) *сов от* **прихо́довать**.
опро́б|овать (-ую) *(не)сов перех* to test.
опрове́ргн|уть (-у, -ешь; *impf* **опроверга́ть**) *сов перех* to refute.
опроверже́ни|е (-я) *ср* refutation.
опроки́н|уть (-у, -ешь; *impf* **опроки́дывать**) *сов перех* (*стакан, стул*) to knock over; (*лодку*) to capsize, overturn; (*прохожего, ребёнка*) to knock down *или* over; (*перен*: *войска, наступление*) to repel; (: *взгляды, представления*) to demolish
▸ **опроки́нуться** (*impf* **опроки́дываться**) *сов возв* (*стакан, стул, человек*) to fall over; (*лодка*) to capsize.
опроме́тчив|ый (-, -а, -о) *прил* precipitate, hasty.
о́прометью *нареч* headlong.
опро́с (-а) *м* (*свидетелей*) questioning; (*населения*) survey; **опро́с обще́ственного мне́ния** opinion poll.
опр|оси́ть (-ошу́, -о́сишь; *impf* **опра́шивать**) *сов перех* (*свидетелей*) to question; (*население*) to survey.
опро́сный *прил*: ~ **лист** questionnaire.
опротест|ова́ть (-у́ю; *impf* **опротесто́вывать**) *сов перех* (*ЮР*) to appeal against; (*вексель*) to protest.
опроти́ве|ть (-ю) *сов неперех*: **мне э́то ~ло** I am sick of it.
опрошу́ *сов см* **опроси́ть**.
опры́ска|ть (-ю; *impf* **опры́скивать**) *сов перех* to spray.
опры́скивател|ь (-я) *м* sprayer; (*садовый*) sprinkler.
опры́скива|ть (-ю) *несов от* **опры́скать**.
опря́т|ный (-ен, -на, -но) *прил* neat, tidy.
о́птик|а (-и) *ж* (*раздел физики*) optics ◆ *собир* optical instruments *мн*.
оптима́л|ьный (-ен, -ьна, -ьно) *прил* optimum.
оптими́зм (-а) *м* optimism.
оптими́ст (-а) *м* optimist.
оптимисти́ч|ный (-ен, -на, -но) *прил* optimistic.
опти́ческ|ий (-ая, -ое, -ие) *прил* optical.
оптови́к (-а́) *м* wholesaler.
опто́в|ый *прил* wholesale; **~ые заку́пки** (*КОММ*) bulk buying.
о́птом *нареч*: **купи́ть/прода́ть** ~ to buy/sell wholesale.
опубликова́ни|е (-я) *ср* (*статьи, книги*) publication; (*закона*) promulgation.
опублик|ова́ть (-у́ю; *impf* **опублико́вывать** *или* **публикова́ть**) *сов перех* (*статью, книгу*) to publish; (*закон*) to promulgate.
опуска́|ть(ся) (-ю(сь)) *несов от* **опусти́ть(ся)**.
опусте́лый *прил* (*дом, сад*) empty; (*улица*) deserted.
опусте́|ть (*3sg* -ет, *3pl* -ют) *сов от* **пусте́ть**.
оп|усти́ть (-ущу́, -у́стишь; *impf* **опуска́ть**) *сов перех* to lower; (*голову*) to bow; (*воротник*) to turn down; (*слово, параграф*) to miss out; **опуска́ть** (~ *perf*) **в** *+acc* (*в стакан, в ящик*) to drop *или* put in(to); (*человека*: *в яму*) to lower into; **опуска́ть** (~ *perf*) **ру́ки** (*перен*) to give up
▸ **опусти́ться** (*impf* **опуска́ться**) *сов возв* (*человек*: *на диван, на землю*) to sit (down); (*солнце*) to sink; (*мост, шлагбаум*) to be lowered; (*перен*: *человек*) to let o.s. go.
опустоша́|ть (-ю) *несов от* **опустоши́ть**.
опустошён|ный (-, -а, -о) *прил* (*человек, душа*) empty.
опустоши́тел|ьный (-ен, -ьна, -ьно) *прил* devastating.
опустош|и́ть (-у́, -и́шь; *impf* **опустоша́ть**) *сов перех* (*страну, поле*) to devastate; (*разг*: *бутылку, ящик*) to empty; (*перен*: *жизнь, человека*) to ruin.

опу́та|ть (-ю; *impf* **опу́тывать**) *сов перех* (*подлеж: ветки, плющ*) to entangle; **опу́тывать** (*~ perf*) **чем-н** (*верёвками, интригами*) to enmesh in sth.
опу́хн|уть (-у, -ешь) *сов от* **пу́хнуть** ◆ (*impf* **опуха́ть**) *неперех* to swell (up).
о́пухол|ь (-и) *ж* (*на руке, на ноге*) swelling; (*внутренняя*) tumour (*BRIT*), tumor (*US*).
опу́хш|ий (-ая, -ее, -ие) *прил* swollen.
опу́шк|а (-и) *ж* (*леса*) edge; (*шапки, воротника*) trim(ming).
опуще́ни|е (-я) *ср* (*деталей, слов*) omission; (*желудка, матки*) prolapse.
опущу́(сь) *сов см* **опусти́ть(ся)**.
опыле́ни|е (-я) *ср* pollination.
опыл|и́ть (-ю́, -и́шь; *impf* **опыля́ть**) *сов перех* to pollinate; (*от вредителей*) to spray (*with insecticide*).
о́пыт (-а) *м* (*знания*) experience; (*эксперимент*) experiment; (*попытка*) attempt; **на со́бственном ~е** from (one's own) experience.
о́пыт|ный (-ен, -на, -но) *прил* (*врач, рабочий*) experienced; (*лаборатория, отдел*) experimental; (*экземпляр*) sample *опред*; (*полёт*) test *опред*; **~ экземпля́р** (test) sample; **дока́зывать** (**доказа́ть** *perf*) **что-н ~ным путём** to prove sth by experiment; **~ный образе́ц** sample.
опьяне́ни|е (-я) *ср* intoxication.
опьяне́|ть (-ю) *сов от* **пьяне́ть**.
опьян|и́ть (-ю́, -и́шь; *impf* **опьяня́ть** *или* **пьяни́ть**) *сов перех* (*также перен*) to intoxicate.
опя́та *итп сущ см* **опёнок**.
опя́ть *нареч* again; **~ же** (*разг*) yet again; **~ два́дцать пять!** (*разг*) not again!
ора́в|а (-ы) *ж* (*разг*) gang.
орангута́н(г) (-а) *м* orang-utan.
ора́нжевый *прил* orange.
оранжере́йный *прил* hothouse *опред*.
оранжере́|я (-и) *ж* hothouse.
ора́тор (-а) *м* orator; (*выступающий*) speaker.
орато́ри|я (-и) *ж* oratorio.
ора́торск|ий (-ая, -ое, -ие) *прил* oratorical.
ор|а́ть (-у́, -ёшь) *несов неперех* (*разг*) to yell; (: *ребёнок*) to bawl, howl; **~** (*impf*) **во всё го́рло** (*разг*) to yell at the top of one's voice.
орби́т|а (-ы) *ж* orbit.
орбита́льный *прил* orbital.
о́рган (-а) *м* (*также АНАТ*) organ; (*здравоохранения*) body; (*орудие*): **~** *+gen* (*пропаганды*) vehicle for; **ме́стные ~ы вла́сти** local authorities (*BRIT*) *или* government (*US*); **половы́е ~ы** genitals; *см также* **о́рганы**.
орга́н (-а) *м* (*МУЗ*) organ.
организа́тор (-а) *м* organizer.
организа́торск|ий (-ая, -ое, -ие) *прил* organizational.
организацио́нный *прил* organizational.
организа́ци|я (-и) *ж* organization; (*устройство*) system; **Организа́ция Объединённых На́ций** United Nations Organization.
органи́зм (-а) *м* organism.
организо́ван|ный (-, -на, -но) *прил* organized; **организо́ванная престу́пность** organized crime.
организ|ова́ть (-у́ю) (*не*)*сов перех* (*создать*) to organize
▸ **организова́ться** (*не*)*сов возв* to be organized; (*в отряд, в ансамбль*) to organize o.s.; (*разг: жизнь*) to sort o.s. out.
органи́ст (-а) *м* organist.
органи́ческ|ий (-ая, -ое, -ие) *прил* organic; (*перен: неприязнь, отвращение*) natural; **~ поро́к се́рдца** heart defect.
о́рган|ы (-ов) *мн* (*разг*) *the Ministry of Internal Affairs and the KGB*.
о́рги|я (-и) *ж* orgy.
оргкомите́т (-а) *м сокр* (= *организацио́нный комите́т*) organizational committee.
оргрàбо́т|а (-ы) *ж сокр* (= *организацио́нная рабо́та*) organizational work.
оргте́хник|а (-и) *ж* office automation equipment.
орд|а́ (-ы́; *nom pl* **о́рды**) *ж* horde.
о́рден (-а; *nom pl* -а́) *м* order; (*nom pl* -ы; *рыцарский, масонский*) order.
орденоно́сный *прил* (*батальон, театр*) order-bearing.
орденоно́сца *итп сущ см* **орденоно́сец**.
о́рдер (-а) *м* (*на арест, на обыск*) warrant; (*на квартиру*) authorization.
ордина́р|ный (-ен, -на, -но) *прил* ordinary.
ордина́тор (-а) *м* (*МЕД*) ≈ registrar (*BRIT*), ≈ resident (*US*).
ордина́ту́р|а (-ы) *ж* *two-year period in which junior doctor specializes in particular field*.
орёл (**орла́**; *nom pl* **орлы́**) *м* eagle; (*перен: человек*) hero; **~ или ре́шка?** (*разг*) heads or tails?
Оренбу́рг (-а) *м* Orenburg.
орео́л (-а) *м* halo; (*перен: славы, таинственности*) aura.
оре́х (-а) *м* nut; (*древесина*) walnut; **мне доста́лось на ~и** (*разг*) I got it in the neck.
оре́ховый *прил* nut; (*мебель*) walnut.
оре́шник (-а) *м* (*кустарник*) hazel; (*собир: заросль*) hazel grove.
ОРЗ *ср сокр* (= *о́строе респирато́рное заболева́ние*) ARD (= *acute respiratory disease*).
оригина́л (-а) *м* original; (*разг: чудак*) eccentric.
оригина́л|ьный (-ен, -ьна, -ьно) *прил* original.
ориента́ци|я (-и) *ж* orientation; **име́ть** (*impf*) **хоро́шую ~ю в чём-н** to have a good grasp of sth.
ориенти́р (-а) *м* landmark.
ориенти́р|овать (-ую) (*не*)*сов перех* to orient, orientate; (*перен*): **~ кого́-н на** *+acc* to orient *или* orientate sb towards
▸ **ориенти́роваться** (*perf* **ориенти́роваться**

или **сориенти́роваться**) *несов возв* to find *или* get one's bearings; (*перен: в ситуации*) to find one's feet; (*разбираться*) to be versed; **~ся** *(impf/perf)* **на** *+acc* (*перен*) to be oriented *или* orientated towards; (*на маяк, на солнце*) to find one's bearings by.

ориентиро́воч|ный (-ен, -на, -но) *прил* provisional; ~ **пункт** landmark.

орке́стр (-а) *м* orchestra.

оркестра́нт (-а) *м* member of an orchestra.

оркестро́вк|а (-ки; *gen pl* **-ок)** *ж* orchestration.

оркне́йск|ий (-ая, -ое, -ие) *прил*: **О~ие острова́** Orkney Islands, Orkneys.

орла́ *итп сущ см* **орёл**.

орли́ный *прил* (*клюв, гнездо*) eagle's; ~ **взгляд** proud look.

орна́мент (-а) *м* (decorative) pattern.

орнито́лог (-а) *м* ornithologist.

орнитоло́ги|я (-и) *ж* ornithology.

оробе́|ть (-ю) *сов от* **робе́ть**.

ороси́тельный *прил* irrigation *опред*.

оро|си́ть (-шу́, -си́шь; *impf* **ороша́ть)** *сов перех* to irrigate; (*подлеж: дождь*) to water.

ороше́ни|е (-я) *ср* irrigation.

орошу́ *сов см* **ороси́ть**.

ортодокса́л|ьный (-ен, -ьна, -ьно) *прил* orthodox.

ортопе́д (-а) *м* orthopaedic (*BRIT*) *или* orthopedic (*US*) surgeon.

ортопеди́ческ|ий (-ая, -ое, -ие) *прил* orthopaedic (*BRIT*), orthopedic (*US*).

ору́ди|е (-я) *ср* (*также перен*) tool; (*ВОЕН*) gun (*used of artillery*).

ору́д|овать (-ую) *несов неперех* (*+instr; разг: вёслами, лопатой*) to work away with; (*: вор, браконьер*) to be at work.

оруже́йный *прил*: ~ **заво́д** arsenal; ~ **ма́стер** armourer (*BRIT*), armorer (*US*); **Оруже́йная пала́та** The Armoury Palace.

ору́жи|е (-я) *ж* (*также перен*) weapon; (*собир*) arms *мн*.

орфографи́ческ|ий (-ая, -ое, -ие) *прил* orthographical.

орфогра́фи|я (-и) *ж* (*правописание*) spelling; (*правила*) orthography.

орхиде́|я (-и) *ж* orchid.

ос|а́ (-ы́; *nom pl* **о́сы)** *ж* wasp.

оса́д|а (-ы) *ж* siege; **снима́ть (снять** *perf*) **~у** to lift a siege.

оса|ди́ть (-жу́, -ди́шь; *impf* **осажда́ть)** *сов перех* to besiege; (*ХИМ*) to precipitate; (*impf* **оса́живать;** *коня, лошадь*) to rein in; **осажда́ть** (~ *perf*) **кого́-н чем-н** (*перен*) to besiege sb with sth; ~ *(perf)* **кого́-н** (*разг*) to put sb in his *итп* place.

оса́дка *сущ см* **оса́док**.

оса́дк|и (-ов) *мн* precipitation *ед*.

оса́дн|ый *прил*: **~ое положе́ние** state of siege.

оса́д|ок (-ка) *м* sediment; **у меня́ оста́лся неприя́тный ~ от э́той встре́чи** the meeting left me with an unpleasant aftertaste.

оса́дочный *прил* sedimentary.

осажда́|ть (-ю) *несов от* **осади́ть**

▸ **осажда́ться** *несов возв* to precipitate.

оса́жива|ть (-ю) *несов от* **осади́ть**.

осажу́ *сов см* **осади́ть**.

оса́нист|ый (-, -а, -о) *прил* imposing.

оса́нк|а (-и) *ж* posture.

осатанева́|ть (-ю) *несов от* **осатане́ть**.

осатане́лый *прил* (*разг*) frenzied; (*: человек*) furious.

осатане́|ть (-ю; *impf* **осатанева́ть)** *сов неперех* (*разг*) to go wild; (*: надоедать*): ~ **кому́-н** to drive sb mad.

ОСВ *сокр = ограниче́ние стратеги́ческих наступа́тельных вооруже́ний*: **перегово́ры/догово́р** ~ SALT (= *Strategic Arms Limitation Talks/Treaty*).

осва́ива|ть(ся) (-ю(сь)) *несов от* **осво́ить(ся)**.

осведоми́тел|ь (-я) *м* informer.

осведоми́тельниц|а (-ы) *ж см* **осведоми́тель**.

осве́дом|ить (-лю́, -ишь; *impf* **осведомля́ть)** *сов перех* to inform

▸ **осве́домиться** (*impf* **осведомля́ться**) *сов возв*: **~ся о** *+prp* to inquire about; **осведомля́ться (~ся** *perf*) **о чьём-н здоро́вье** to inquire after sb's health.

осведомлён|ный (-, -на, -но) *прил* knowledgeable.

осведомлю́(сь) *сов см* **осве́домить(ся)**.

осведомля́|ть(ся) (-ю(сь)) *несов от* **осве́домить(ся)**.

освеж|и́ть (-у́, -и́шь; *impf* **освежа́ть)** *сов перех* (*воздух*) to freshen; (*комнату, платье*) to freshen up; (*краски*) to liven up; (*воспоминания, знания*) to refresh; **о́тдых ~и́л меня́** I feel refreshed after my rest

▸ **освежи́ться** (*impf* **освежа́ться**) *сов возв* (*воздух*) to freshen; (*человек: под душем итп*) to freshen up; (*краски*) to brighten up; (*воспоминания, знания*) to be refreshed.

освети́тел|ь (-я) *м* (*ТЕАТР*) lighting technician.

освети́тельный *прил*: ~ **прибо́р** light; **освети́тельная раке́та** flare.

осве|ти́ть (-щу́, -ти́шь; *impf* **освеща́ть)** *сов перех* (*также перен*) to light up; (*вопрос, проблему, дело*) to highlight

▸ **освети́ться** (*impf* **освеща́ться**) *сов возв* (*также перен*) to be lit up; (*лицо*) to light up.

освеще́ни|е (-я) *ср* lighting; (*вопроса, проблемы, дела*) coverage.

освещу́(сь) *сов см* **освети́ть(ся)**.

осв|иста́ть (-ищу́, -и́щешь; *impf* **осви́стывать)** *сов перех* to boo.

освободи́тел|ь (-я) *м* liberator.

освободи́тельниц|а (-ы) *ж см* **освободи́тель.**
освободи́тельн|ый *прил* liberation *опред*; **~ая война́** war of liberation.
освобо|ди́ть (-жу́, -ди́шь; *impf* **освобожда́ть)** *сов перех* to release; (*из капкана*) to free; (*город, деревню*) to liberate; (*полку, комнату*) to clear; (*дом, квартиру*) to vacate; (*время, день*) to leave free; **~** *(perf)* **кого́-н от хлопо́т/наказа́ния** to spare sb the trouble/from punishment; **~** *(perf)* **кого́-н от эксплуата́ции** to liberate sb from exploitation; **~** *(perf)* **кого́-н от до́лжности** to dismiss sb
▸ **освободи́ться** (*impf* **освобожда́ться**) *сов возв* (*из тюрьмы*) to be released; (*из капкана*: *зверь*) to free itself; (: *человек*) to free o.s.; (*квартира, дом*) to be vacated; (*место, полка*) to be cleared; **~ся** *(perf)* **от наказа́ния** to escape punishment; **~ся** *(perf)* **от рабо́ты** to finish work.
освобожде́ни|е (-я) *ср* release, freeing; (*города, деревни*) liberation; **~ от до́лжности** dismissal; **~ от нало́гов** tax exemption.
освобожу́(сь) *сов см* **освободи́ть(ся).**
ОСВОД *м сокр = Всероссийское общество спасения на водах.*
освое́ни|е (-я) *ср* (*см глаг*) mastering; cultivation.
осво́|ить (-ю, -ишь; *impf* **осва́ивать)** *сов перех* (*технику, язык*) to master; (*земли, пустыню*) to cultivate
▸ **осво́иться** (*impf* **осва́иваться**) *сов возв* (*на новой работе*) to find one's feet.
освя|ти́ть (-щу́, -ти́шь; *impf* **освяща́ть** *или* **святи́ть)** *сов перех* (*РЕЛ*) to bless.
оседа́|ть (-ю) *несов от* **осе́сть.**
оседла́|ть (-ю) *сов от* **седла́ть** ◆ (*impf* **осёдлывать**) *несов перех* (*разг*: *стул, бревно*) to straddle; (: *родственников, знакомых*) to take advantage of.
осе́длый *прил* settled.
осека́|ться (-юсь) *несов от* **осе́чься.**
осёкся *итп сов см* **осе́чься.**
осеку́сь *итп сов см* **осе́чься.**
ос|ёл (-ла́) *м* donkey; (*перен*: *разг*) ass.
осен|и́ть (*3sg* **-и́т**, *3pl* **-я́т**, *impf* **осеня́ть**) *сов перех* (*подлеж*: *мысль*) to strike; **меня́ ~и́ло, что ...** it struck me that ...; **осеня́ть (~** *perf*) **кресто́м** to bless.
осе́нн|ий (-яя, -ее, -ие) *прил* autumn *опред*, fall *опред* (*US*); (*похожий на осень*: *погода, день*) autumnal, fall.
о́сен|ь (-и) *ж* autumn, fall (*US*).
о́сенью *нареч* in autumn, in the fall (*US*).
осеня́|ть (-ю) *несов от* **осени́ть.**
ос|е́сть (-я́ду, -я́дешь; *impf* **оседа́ть)** *сов неперех* (*пол, дом*) to subside; (*пыль, осадок*) to settle; **они́ ~е́ли в го́роде** they settled in the city.
осети́н (-а; *gen pl* **-)** *м* Ossetian.
осети́н|ка (-ки; *gen pl* **-ок)** *ж см* **осети́н.**
Осе́ти|я (-и) *ж*: **Се́верная/Ю́жная ~** North/South Ossetia.
ос|ётр (-етра́) *м* sturgeon (*ZOOL*).
осетри́н|а (-ы) *ж* sturgeon (*CULIN*).
осе́ч|ка (-ки; *gen pl* **-ек)** *ж* (*перен*: *разг*) cockup (*BRIT*), mess (*US*); **дава́ть (дать** *perf*) **~ку** to misfire.
ос|е́чься (-еку́сь, -ечёшься *итп*, **-еку́тся;** *pt* **ёкся, -е́клась, -е́клось,** *impf* **осека́ться)** *сов неперех* to stop short.
оси́л|ить (-ю, -ишь; *impf* **оси́ливать)** *сов перех* (*противника*) to overpower; (*разг*: *книгу*) to get through; (: *физику, упражнение*) to get to grips with.
оси́н|а (-ы) *ж* aspen.
оси́новый *прил* aspen *опред.*
оси́н|ый *прил*: **~ое гнездо́** wasp's nest; (*перен*) hornet's nest.
оси́пн|уть (-у, -ешь) *сов от* **си́пнуть.**
осироте́вш|ий (-ая, -ее, -ие) *прил* (*ребёнок*) orphaned; (*перен*: *дом, сад*) abandoned.
осироте́лый *прил* **= осироте́вший.**
осироте́|ть (-ю) *сов от* **сироте́ть.**
оска́л|ить (-ю, -ишь; *impf* **оска́ливать** *или* **ска́лить)** *сов перех*: **~ зу́бы** (*также перен*) to bare one's teeth
▸ **оска́литься** (*impf* **оска́ливаться** *или* **ска́литься**) *сов возв* (*также перен*) to bare one's teeth; (*разг*: *осклабиться*) to smirk.
осканда́л|иться (-юсь, -ишься) *сов возв* (*разг*) to show o.s. up.
оскверн|и́ть (-ю́, -и́шь; *impf* **оскверня́ть)** *сов перех* to defile; (*чувства, идеи*) to debase.
оскла́б|иться (-люсь, -ишся) *сов неперех* to grin.
оско́л|ок (-ка) *м* (*стекла, чашки*) piece; (: *мелкий*) sliver; (*бомбы, снаряда*) shrapnel *только ед*; (*перен*: *прошлого*) fragment.
оско́лочный *прил* (*рана, бомба*) shrapnel *опред.*
оско́мин|а (-ы) *ж* acidic taste; **наби́ть** *(perf)* **кому́-н ~у** (*перен*) to bore sb stupid.
оскоп|и́ть (-лю́, -и́шь; *impf* **оскопля́ть)** *сов перех* to castrate.
оскорби́тел|ьный (-ен, -ьна, -ьно) *прил* offensive.
оскорб|и́ть (-лю́, -и́шь; *impf* **оскорбля́ть)** *сов перех* to insult, offend; **оскорбля́ть (~** *perf*) **кого́-н в лу́чших чу́вствах** to offend sb's finer feelings; **оскорбля́ть (~** *perf*) **слух** to offend the ear
▸ **оскорби́ться** (*impf* **оскорбля́ться**) *сов возв* to be offended, take offence *или* offense (*US*).
оскорбле́ни|е (-я) *ср* insult.
оскорблю́(сь) *сов см* **оскорби́ть(ся).**
оскорбля́|ть(ся) (-ю(сь)) *несов от* **оскорби́ть(ся).**
оскуде́|ть (-ю; *impf* **оскудева́ть** *или* **скуде́ть)** *сов неперех* (*страна*) to become impoverished; (*запасы итп*) to become depleted.
осла́ *итп сущ см* **осёл.**

ослабе́|ть (**-ю**; *impf* **ослабева́ть** *или* **слабе́ть**) *сов неперех* to weaken; (*давление, ветер*) to drop; (*внимание*) to wander; (*дождь*) to slacken *или* ease off; (*шум*) to die down; (*ремень*) to loosen; (*дисциплина*) to slacken.

осла́б|ить (**-лю, -ишь**; *impf* **ослабля́ть**) *сов перех* to weaken; (*внимание*) to let wander; (*ремень*) to loosen; (*дисциплина*) to relax.

ослабле́ни|е (**-я**) *ср* weakening; (*давления, шума*) reduction; (*внимания*) slackening; (*дисциплины*) decline; **за́втра ожида́ется ~ ве́тра/дождя́** the wind/rain should ease off by tomorrow.

осла́блю *сов см* **осла́бить**.

ослабля́|ть (**-ю**) *несов от* **осла́бить**.

осла́бн|уть (**-у, -ешь**) *сов от* **сла́бнуть**.

осла́в|ить (**-лю, -ишь**) *сов перех* (*разг*) to smear

▸ **осла́виться** *сов возв* (*разг*) to get o.s. a bad name.

осл|ёнок (**-ёнка**; *nom pl* **-я́та**, *gen pl* **-я́т**) *м* foal (*of donkey*).

ослепи́тел|ьный (**-ен, -ьна, -ьно**) *прил* dazzling.

ослеп|и́ть (**-лю́, -и́шь**; *impf* **ослепля́ть**) *сов перех* (*также перен*) to blind; (*подлеж: солнце, красота*) to dazzle.

ослепле́ни|е (**-я**) *ср* (*перен*) blindness.

ослеплю́ *сов см* **ослепи́ть**.

ослепля́|ть (**-ю**) *несов от* **ослепи́ть**.

осле́п|нуть (**-ну, -нешь**; *pt* **-, -ла, -ло**) *сов от* **сле́пнуть** ◆ *неперех* (*перен*): **~ от не́нависти/любви́** to be blinded by hatred/love.

осли́н|ый *прил* donkey's; **~ое упря́мство** pig-headedness.

осли́ц|а (**-ы**) *ж* female donkey.

О́сло *м нескл* Oslo.

осложне́ни|е (**-я**) *ср* complication.

осложн|и́ть (**-ю́, -и́шь**; *impf* **осложня́ть**) *сов перех* to complicate

▸ **осложни́ться** (*impf* **осложня́ться**) *сов возв* to become complicated; (*болезнь*) to develop complications.

ослы́ш|аться (**-усь, -ишься**) *сов возв* to mishear.

осля́та *итп сущ см* **ослёнок**.

осма́трива|ть(ся) (**-ю(сь)**) *несов от* **осмотре́ть(ся)**.

осме́ива|ть (**-ю**) *несов от* **осмея́ть**.

осмеле́|ть (**-ю**) *несов от* **смеле́ть**.

осме́л|иться (**-юсь, -ишься**) *сов возв* to dare.

осме|я́ть (**-ю́**; *impf* **осме́ивать**) *сов перех* (*поведение, человека*) to mock; (*теорию*) to ridicule.

осмо́тр (**-а**) *м* inspection; (*больного*) examination; (*выставки, музея*) visit.

осм|отре́ть (**-отрю́, -о́тришь**; *impf* **осма́тривать**) *сов перех* (*см сущ*) to inspect; to examine; to visit

▸ **осмотре́ться** (*impf* **осма́триваться**) *сов возв* (*по сторонам*) to look around; (*перен: на новом месте*) to settle in.

осмотри́тельност|ь (**-и**) *ж* circumspection.

осмотри́тельный *прил* prudent, cautious.

осмысле́ни|е (**-я**) *ср* comprehension.

осмы́слен|ный (**-, -на, -но**) *прил* (*взгляд*) intelligent; (*поступок, поведение*) premeditated.

осмы́сл|ить (**-ю, -ишь**; *impf* **осмы́сливать** *или* **осмысля́ть**) *сов перех* to comprehend.

осна|сти́ть (**-щу́, -сти́шь**; *impf* **оснаща́ть**) *сов перех* (*предприятие, лабораторию*) to equip; (*судно*) to rig.

оснаще́ни|е (**-я**) *ср* (*предприятия, лаборатории, армии*) equipment; (*судна*) rigging.

оснащённост|ь (**-и**) *ж* equipping.

оснащу́ *сов см* **оснасти́ть**.

осно́в|а (**-ы**) *ж* (*сооружения*) foundation; (*общества, развития*) basis; (*ткани, материи*) warp; (*линг*) stem; **на ~е** *+gen* on the basis of; **класть (положи́ть** *perf*) **в ~у чего́-н** to use as a basis for sth; **быть** (*impf*) *или* **лежа́ть** (*impf*) **в ~е чего́-н** to be the basis of sth; *см также* **осно́вы**.

основа́ни|е (**-я**) *ср* (*также МАТ, ХИМ*) base; (*города, общества*) founding; (*теории, науки*) basis; (*опоздания, поступка*) grounds *мн*; (*здания*) foundation; **без вся́ких ~й** without any reason; **до ~я** completely; **на ~и** *+gen* on the grounds of; **на како́м ~и?** on what grounds?; **на о́бщем ~и** on an equal basis; **с по́лным ~м** with good reason.

основа́телен *прил см* **основа́тельный**.

основа́тел|ь (**-я**) *м* founder.

основа́тельниц|а (**-ы**) *ж см* **основа́тель**.

основа́тел|ьный (**-ен, -ьна, -ьно**) *прил* (*причины, довод*) good; (*сооружение, человек*) solid; (*разг: вес, сумма*) fair; (*проверка, осмотр*) thorough.

основа́|ть (*pt* **-л, -ла, -ло**, *impf* **осно́вывать**) *сов перех* to found; **осно́вывать** (**~** *perf*) **что-н на** *+prp* to base sth on *или* upon

▸ **основа́ться** (*impf* **осно́вываться**) *сов возв* (*общество, компания*) to be founded; (*разг: в Москве, на новом месте*) to settle down.

основн|о́й *прил* (*цель, задача*) main; (*закон, принцип*) fundamental, basic; **в ~о́м** on the whole.

основополо́жник (**-а**) *м* founder.

осно́выва|ть (**-ю**) *несов от* **основа́ть**

▸ **осно́вываться** *несов от* **основа́ться** ◆ *возв*: **~ся на** *+prp* to be based on.

осно́в|ы (**-**) *мн* (*физики итп*) basics *мн*, rudiments *мн*.

осо́б|а (**-ы**) *ж* individual.

осо́бенен *прил см* **осо́бенный**.

осóбенно *нареч* particularly; (*смотреть, вести себя*) in an unusual way; (*приятно, хорошо*) especially, particularly; **не ~** (*разг*) not particularly.
осóбенност|ь (-и) *ж* (*не обыкновенность*) uniqueness; (*свойство*) peculiarity; **в ~и** in particular.
осóбен|ный (-ен, -на, -но) *прил* special; **ничегó ~ного** (*разг*) nothing special.
особня́к (-á) *м* mansion.
особнякóм *нареч* by oneself.
осóб|ый *прил* (*вид, случай*) special, particular; (*вход, помещение*) separate; **у негó ~ое мнéние на э́тот счёт** he has his own opinion about this.
óсоб|ь (-и) *ж* individual.
осовремéн|ить (-ю, -ишь; *impf* **осовремéнивать**) *сов перех* to update.
осозна|вáть (-ю́, -ёшь) *несов от* **осознáть**.
осóзнанный *прил* (*риск, поступок*) calculated; (*необходимость*) acknowledged.
осознá|ть (-ю; *impf* **осознавáть**) *сов перех* to realize.
осóк|а (-и) *ж* sedge.
осоловé|ть (-ю) *сов от* **соловéть**.
óсп|а (-ы) *ж* smallpox; (*разг: шрам*) pockmarks *мн*.
оспáрива|ть (-ю) *несов от* **оспóрить** ◆ *перех* (*первенство*) to contend *или* compete for.
óспин|а (-ы) *ж* pockmark.
оспóр|ить (-ю, -ишь; *impf* **оспáривать**) *сов перех* (*мнение, решение*) to question.
осрам|ить(ся) (-лю́(сь), -и́шь(ся)) *сов от* **срамить(ся)**.
оста|вáться (-ю́сь, -ёшься) *несов от* **остáться** ◆ *возв*: **счастли́во ~!** good luck!, all the best!
остáв|ить (-лю, -ишь; *impf* **оставля́ть**) *сов перех* to leave; (*сохранить*) to keep; (*задержать: после уроков*) to keep in; (*работу, занятие, разговор*) to stop; (*перен: мысли, мечты, надежды*) to give up; **~ь!** stop it!; **оставля́ть (~ *perf*) когó-н позади́** (*перен*) to leave sb standing; **оставля́ть (~ *perf*) когó-н/что-н в покóе** to leave sb/sth in peace *или* alone; **оставля́ть (~ *perf*) когó-н на вторóй год** (*ПРОСВЕЩ*) to make sb repeat a year; **оставля́ть (~ *perf*) когó-н в дуракáх** to make a fool of sb; **мы ~или гостéй ночевáть** we asked our guests to stay overnight; **сознáние ~ило егó** he lost consciousness.
остальн|óе (-óго; *decl like adj*) *ср* the rest; **в ~óм** in other respects.
остальн|óй *прил* (*часть*) the remaining; **~ые дéньги/дéти** the rest of the money/children; **~óе врéмя** the rest of the time.
остальн|ые (-ы́х; *decl like adj*) *мн* the others; **все ~** all the others; (*вещи*) all the rest.
останáвлива|ть(ся) (-ю(сь)) *несов от* **останови́ть(ся)**.
остáнк|и (-ов) *мн* remains *мн*.
остан|ови́ть (-овлю́, -óвишь; *impf* **останáвливать**) *сов перех* to stop; **останáвливать (~ *perf*) взгляд/внимáние на чём-н** to let one's gaze/attention rest on sth; **останáвливать (~ *perf*) свой вы́бор на** *+acc* to choose
▸ **останови́ться** (*impf* **останáвливаться**) *сов возв* to stop; (*в гостинице, у друзей*) to stay; **~ся** (*perf*) **на** *+prp* (*на вопросе, на описании*) to dwell on; (*на решении, на заключении*) to come to; (*взгляд*) to rest on; **не останáвливаться (~ся *perf*) ни перед чем** to stop at nothing.
остановк|а (-и) *ж* (*мотора, часов, эксперимента*) stopping; (*в речи, в работе*) pause; (*автобусная, поезда, в пути*) stop; **за кем/чем ~?** (*разг*) who/what is holding us up?
остановлю́(сь) *сов см* **останови́ть(ся)**.
остáнусь *итп сов см* **остáться**.
остáт|ок (-ка) *м* (*пищи, дня*) the remainder, the rest; (*материи*) remnant; (*МАТ*) remainder; **~ки** (*дома, стены*) remains *мн*; (*еды*) leftovers *мн*; (*красоты, чувства*) traces *мн*; **всё без ~ка** absolutely everything.
остá|ться (-нусь, -нешься; *impf* **оставáться**) *сов неперех* to stay; (*сохраниться: дом, чувство*) to remain; (*оказаться*) to be left; (*разг: проиграть*) to lose; **оставáться (~ *perf*) сидéть/стоя́ть** to remain sitting/standing; **мне ~лось дочитáть 2 страни́цы** I have 2 pages left to read; **оставáться (~ *perf*) на вторóй год** (*ПРОСВЕЩ*) to repeat a year; **оставáться (~ *perf*) при своём мнéнии** to stick to one's opinion; **оставáться (~ *perf*) ни с чем** to end up with nothing; **оставáться (~ *perf*) ни при чём** to be left out; **оставáться (~ *perf*) в живы́х** to survive; **не остаётся ничегó другóго как ...** there is nothing for it but ....
остекленé|ть (-ю) *сов от* **стекленéть**.
остепен|и́ться (-ю́сь, -и́шься; *impf* **остепеня́ться**) *сов неперех* to settle down.
остервенéлый *прил* frenzied, furious.
остервенé|ть (-ю) *сов от* **стервенéть**.
остерегá|ть (-ю; *perf* **остерéчь**) *несов перех* to warn
▸ **остерегáться** (*perf* **остерéчься**) *несов возв*: **~ся** *+gen* to be wary of; **~йтесь просту́ды!** mind you don't catch cold!
óстов (-а) *м* (*здания, корабля*) frame; (*зверя*) skeleton; (*словаря, романа*) framework.
остолбенé|ть (-ю) *сов от* **столбенéть**.
остолóп (-а) *м* (*разг*) dimwit.
осторóжен *прил см* **осторóжный**.
осторóжно *нареч* (*взять, поднять*) carefully; (*ходить, выступать, говорить*) cautiously; **~!** look out!
осторóжност|ь (-и) *ж* (*обращения, ухода*) care; (*поступка, поведения*) caution; **забывáть (забы́ть *perf*) о вся́кой ~и** to throw caution to the winds.
осторóж|ный (-ен, -на, -но) *прил* careful; (*осмотрительный*) cautious.
осточертé|ть (-ю; *impf* **осточертевáть**) *сов*

неперех (*+dat*; *разг*) to bore rigid.
остёр *прил см* **óстрый.**
остригу́(сь) *сов см* **остри́чь(ся).**
остри|ё (**-я́**) *ср* (*пера, иглы, шпиля*) point; (*ножа, меча, бритвы*) edge; (*критики, сатиры*) cutting edge.
остр|и́ть (**-ю́, -и́шь**) *несов перех* (*нож, меч*) to sharpen ◆ (*perf* **състри́ть**) *неперех* (*шутить*) to make witty remarks.
остр|и́чь(ся) (**-игу́(сь), -ижёшь(ся)** *umn*, **-игу́т(ся)**) *сов от* **стри́чь(ся).**
óстров (**-а**; *nom pl* **-á**) *м* (*также перен*) island.
острово́к (**-ка́**) *м* island; **острово́к безопа́сности** traffic island.
остроконе́ч|ный (**-ен, -на, -но**) *прил* pointed.
острно́с|ый (**-, -а, -о**) *прил* (*человек*) sharp-nosed; (*туфли*) pointed.
острсло́в|ить (**-лю, -ишь**) *несов неперех* to be witty.
остросовреме́н|ный (**-ен, -на, -но**) *прил* (*пьеса*) extremely topical.
остросюже́т|ный (**-ен, -на, -но**) *прил* (*фильм, пьеса*) gripping; **~ фильм, ~ рома́н** thriller.
остро́т|а (**-ы**) *ж* witticism.
острот|а́ (**-ы́**) *ж* (*ножа*) sharpness; (*зрения, слуха*) sharpness, keenness; (*шутки, слова*) wit; (*запаха, вкуса*) pungency; (*пищи*) spiciness; (*желания, радости*) poignancy; (*положения, ситуации*) acuteness; (*игры*) tension.
остроуго́л|ьный (**-ен, -ьна, -ьно**) *прил* acute-angled.
остроу́мен *прил см* **остроу́мный.**
остроу́ми|е (**-я**) *ср* wit; (*рассказа*) wittiness.
остроу́м|ный (**-ен, -на, -но**) *прил* witty.
óст|рый (**-р** *или* **-ёр, -pá, -pó** *или* **-po**) *прил* (*нож, память, вкус*) sharp; (*борода, нос, носок*) pointed; (*зрение, слух*) keen; (*шутка, слово*) witty; (*запах*) pungent; (*блюдо, еда*) spicy; (*сыр*) strong; (*желание*) burning; (*боль*) acute; (*ситуация*) critical; (*игра*) tense; (*no short form*; *аппендицит, воспаление лёгких*) acute; **óстрый у́гол** acute angle; **óстрый язы́к** sharp tongue.
остря́к (**-á**) *м* (*разг*) wit.
остря́ч|ка (**-ки**; *gen pl* **-ек**) *ж* (*разг*) *см* **остря́к.**
ост|уди́ть (**-ужу́, -у́дишь**; *impf* **остужа́ть** *или* **студи́ть**) *сов перех* (*молоко, чай, суп*) to cool; (*перен: желания*) to curb; (*: чувства*) to restrain.
ост|упи́ться (**-уплю́сь, -у́пишься**; *impf* **оступа́ться**) *сов возв* to trip, stumble; (*разг: совершить ошибку*) to trip up.
осты́|ть (**-ну, -нешь**; *impf* **остыва́ть**) *сов неперех* (*также перен*) to cool down; (*чувства, желание*) to cool; (*суп*) to get cold; **остыва́ть** (*~ perf*) **к** *+dat* (*перен*) to lose interest in.
ос|уди́ть (**-ужу́, -у́дишь**; *impf* **осужда́ть**) *сов перех* to condemn; (*приговорить*) to convict.
осужде́ни|е (**-я**) *ср* (*см глаг*) condemnation; conviction.
осуждённ|ая (**-ой**; *decl like adj*) *ж см* **осуждённый.**
осуждённ|ый (**-ого**; *decl like adj*) *м* convict.
осужу́ *сов см* **осуди́ть.**
осу́н|уться (**-усь, -ешься**) *сов возв* to look drawn.
осуша́|ть (**-ю**) *несов от* **осуши́ть.**
осуше́ни|е (**-я**) *ср* drainage.
осуши́тельный *прил* drainage *опред.*
ос|уши́ть (**-ушу́, -у́шишь**; *impf* **осуша́ть**) *сов перех* to drain.
осуществи́м|ый (**-, -а, -о**) *прил* (*мечты, желания*) realizable.
осуществле́ни|е (**-я**) *ср* (*мечты, идеи, намерения*) realization; (*плана, реорганизации*) implementation.
осуществ|и́ть (**-лю́, -и́шь**; *impf* **осуществля́ть**) *сов перех* (*мечту, намерение*) to realize; (*идею*) to put into practice; (*план, реорганизацию*) to implement
▸ **осуществи́ться** (*impf* **осуществля́ться**) *сов возв* (*мечты*) to come true; (*идея*) to materialize; (*надежды*) to be fulfilled.
осчастли́в|ить (**-лю, -ишь**) *сов перех* to make happy.
осы́п|ать (**-лю, -лешь**; *impf* **осыпа́ть**) *сов перех* (*кучу песка, землю*) to knock down; **осыпа́ть** (*~ perf*) **кого́-н/что-н чем-н** to scatter sth over sb/sth; (*перен: подарками, поцелуями*) to shower sb/sth with sth; (*оскорблениями*) to heap sth on sb/sth
▸ **осы́паться** (*impf* **осыпа́ться**) *сов возв* (*земля, насыпь, песок*) to subside; (*штукатурка, потолок*) to crumble; (*листья, цветы*) to fall.
ос|ь (**-и**; *loc sg* **-и́**) *ж* (*колеса, механизма*) axle; (*ГЕОМ*) axis (*мн* axes); (*перен: событий, происходящего*) centre (*BRIT*), center (*US*), hub.
осьмино́г (**-а**) *м* octopus (*мн* octopuses).
ося́ду *umn сов см* **осе́сть.**
осяза́ем|ый (**-, -а, -о**) *прил* (*перен: результат*) tangible.
осяза́ни|е (**-я**) *ср* touch.
осяза́тельный *прил* (*нервные окончания, органы*) tactile; (*перен: результат, разница, успех*) tangible.

KEYWORD

от *предл* (*+gen*) ***1*** from; **он отошёл от стола́** he moved away from the table; **недалеко́ от меня́** not far from me; **он узна́л об э́том от дру́га** he found out about it from a friend; **у него́ есть сын от пе́рвого бра́ка** he has a son from his first marriage; **от ча́са до двух** from one (o'clock) to two (o'clock); **он ушёл от семьи́** he left his family
2 (*указывает на причину*): **бума́га размо́кла**

от дождя́ the paper got wet with rain; **от злости** with anger; **от рáдости** for *или* in joy; **от удивлéния** in surprise; **от разочаровáния/стрáха** out of disappointment/fear
3 (*о подлежащем устранению*): **отмóй лицó от грязи** wash the dirt off your face
4 (*указывает на что-н, против чего направлено действие*) for; **лекáрство от кáшля** medicine for a cough, cough medicine
5 (*о части целого*): **рýчка/ключ от двéри** door handle/key; **я потеря́л пýговицу от пальтó** I lost the button off my coat
6 (*при противопоставлении*) from; **они́ не мóгут отличи́ть добрó от зла** they can't tell right from wrong
7 (*в датах*): **письмó от пéрвого февраля́** a letter of *или* dated the first of February
8 (*о временной последовательности*): **год от гóда** from year to year; **врéмя от врéмени** from time to time.

от- *префикс* (*in verbs*; *прекращение действия*) *indicating cessation of action eg. отзвучáть*; (*удаление от чего-н*) *indictaing removal from sth eg. отклéить*; (*об уклонении от чего-н*) *indicating avoidance of sth eg. отшути́ться*.
отáпливa|ть (**-ю**) *несов перех* to heat
▸ **отáпливаться** *несов возв* to be heated.
отáр|а (**-ы**) *ж* flock (*of sheep*).
отбáв|ить (**-лю, -ишь**; *impf* **отбавля́ть**) *сов перех* (*сахар, порцию*) to take away; (*молоко, воду*) to pour off; **хоть отбавля́й** (*разг*) more than enough.
отбарабáн|ить (**-ю, -ишь**; *impf* **отбарабáнивать**) *сов перех* (*мелодию*) to tap out; (*разг*: *ответ, вопрос*) to rattle off.
отбежáть (*как* **бежáть**; *см* **Table 20**; *impf* **отбегáть**) *сов неперех* to run off.
отбéливател|ь (**-я**) *м* bleach.
отб|ели́ть (**-елю́, -éлишь**; *impf* **отбéливать**) *сов перех* to bleach.
отберý *итп сов см* **отобрáть**.
отбивá|ть(ся) (**-ю**) *несов от* **отби́ть(ся)**.
отбивн|áя (**-óй**; *decl like adj*) *ж* tenderized steak; (*также:* ~ **котлéта**) chop.
отбирá|ть (**-ю**) *несов от* **отобрáть**.
от|би́ть (**-обью́, -обьёшь**; *impf* **отбивáть**) *сов перех* (*отколоть*) to break off; (*мяч, удар*) to parry; (*атаку, нападение*) to repulse; (*город, пленных*) to recapture; (*разг*: *жениха, невесту*) to pinch; (*такт, мелодию*) to beat out; (*мясо*) to tenderize; **зáпах ~би́л у меня́ желáние есть** the smell put me off my food; **я ~би́л себé нóги** my feet are sore
▸ **отби́ться** (*impf* **отбивáться**) *сов возв* (*отколоться*) to break off; **~ся** *(perf)* (**от** *+gen*) (*от нападающих, от собак*) to defend o.s. (against); (*от компании, от стада*) to fall behind; **~ся** *(perf)* **от рук** to get out of hand.
отблагодар|и́ть (**-ю́, -и́шь**) *сов перех* to show one's gratitude to.
óтблеск (**-а**) *м* reflection.
отбó|й (**-я**) *м* (*ВОЕН*: *ко сну*) the last post; (: *после воздушной тревоги*) all-clear (signal); (: *к отступлению*) retreat; **у неё ~ю нет от поклóнников** (*разг*) she has an endless stream of admirers.
отбóйный *прил*: ~ **молотóк** pickaxe (*BRIT*), pickax (*US*).
отбóр (**-а**) *м* selection.
отбóрн|ый *прил* (*картофель, семена*) selected; (*ругань, выражения*) well-chosen; **~ые войскá** crack troops.
отбóрочн|ый *прил* (*СПОРТ*) qualifying; **~ая комиссия** selection committee.
отбрó|сить (**-шу, -сишь**; *impf* **отбрáсывать**) *сов перех* to throw aside; (*противника, войска*) to repel; (*перен*: *сомнения, тревоги umn*) to cast aside; (*тень, свет*) to cast.
отбрóс|ы (**-ов**) *мн* (*производства*) waste *ед*; (*пищевые*) scraps *мн*.
отбрóшу *сов см* **отбрóсить**.
отб|ы́ть (*как* **быть**; *см* **Table 21**; *impf* **отбывáть**) *сов неперех*: ~ (**из** *+gen*/**в** *+acc*) to depart (from/for) ◆ (*pt* **-ы́л,-ылá,-ы́ло**) *перех*: ~ **наказáние** to serve a sentence.
отвáг|а (**-и**) *ж* bravery.
отвá|дить (**-жу, -дишь**; *impf* **отвáживать**) *сов перех* (*разг*): ~ **когó-н от чегó-н** (*от вредных привычек*) to wean sb off sth; (*от дома*) to drive sb away from sth.
отвáжен *прил см* **отвáжный**.
отвáживa|ть (**-ю**) *несов от* **отвáдить**.
отвáж|иться (**-усь, -ишься**; *impf* **отвáживаться**) *сов возв*: ~ *+infin* (*пойти, сказать umn*) to find the courage to do; ~ *(perf)* **на** *+acc* to venture on.
отвáж|ный (**-ен, -на, -но**) *прил* brave.
отвáжу *сов см* **отвáдить**.
отвáжусь *сов см* **отвáжиться**.
отвáл (**-а**) *м* (*породы, земли*) heap; **наéсться** *(perf)* **до ~а** (*разг*) to eat one's fill; **накорми́ть** *(perf)* **когó-н до ~а** to stuff sb with food.
отв|али́ть (**-алю́, -áлишь**; *impf* **отвáливать**) *сов перех* (*камень, бревно*) to push aside; (*разг*: *кучу денег*) to fork out
▸ **отвали́ться** (*impf* **отвáливаться**) *сов возв* (*обои, штукатурка*) to fall off; (*разг*: *откинуться назад*) to slump.
отвáр (**-а**; *part gen* **-у**) *м* (*из трав*) decoction; **мяснóй** ~ meat broth.
отв|ари́ть (**-арю́, -áришь**; *impf* **отвáривать**) *сов перех* to boil
▸ **отвари́ться** (*impf* **отвáриваться**) *сов возв* to boil.
отварнóй *прил* boiled.
отведý *итп сов см* **отвести́**.
отв|езти́ (**-езý, -езёшь**; *pt* **-ёз, -езлá, -езлó**, *impf* **отвози́ть**) *сов перех* (*увезти*) to take away; **отвози́ть** (~ *perf*) **когó-н/что-н в гóрод/на дáчу** to take sb/sth off to town/the dacha.
отвéргн|уть (**-у, -ешь**; *impf* **отвергáть**) *сов*

перех (*решение, помощь*) to reject; (*жениха*) to spurn.
отверде́|ть (*3sg* **-ет**, *3pl* **-ют**, *impf* **отвердева́ть**) *сов неперех* to harden.
отве́рженн|ая (**-ой**; *decl like adj*) *ж см* **отве́рженный.**
отве́рженн|ый *прил* outcast *опред* ◆ (**-ого**; *decl like adj*) *м* outcast.
отверн|у́ть (**-у́, -ёшь**; *impf* **отвёртывать**) *сов перех* (*гайку, пробку*) to unscrew; (*кран*) to be turned on; (*пола, рукав*) to turn back; (*impf* **отвора́чивать**; *лицо, голову*) to turn aside; (*разг: отломать: ручку*) to twist off
▸ **отверну́ться** (*impf* **отвёртываться**) *сов возв* (*гайка, пробка*) to come unscrewed; (*кран*) to be turned on; (*поля, рукав*) to be turned back; (*impf* **отвора́чиваться**; *человек*) to turn away; **~ся** (*perf*) **от кого́-н** to ostracize sb.
отве́рсти|е (**-я**) *ср* opening.
отвёрт|ка (**-ки**; *gen pl* **-ок**) *ж* screwdriver.
отвёртывать(ся) (**-ю(сь)**) *несов от* **отверну́ть(ся).**
отве́с (**-а**) *м* (*груз*) plumb; **~ скалы́** cliff face.
отве́сен *прил см* **отве́сный.**
отве́|сить (**-шу, -сишь**; *impf* **отве́шивать**) *сов перех* to weigh out; **~** (*perf*) **кому́-н пощёчину** (*разг*) to give sb a slap in the face.
отве́с|ный (**-ен, -на, -но**) *прил* (*склон, берег, стена*) vertical.
отв|ести́ (**-еду́, -едёшь**; *pt* **-ёл, -ела́, -ело́**, *impf* **отводи́ть**) *сов перех* (*человека: домой, к врачу*) to take (off); (*: от окна*) to lead away; (*войска, полк*) to relocate, move; (*воду, реку*) to divert; (*ветки*) to push aside; (*глаза, взгляд*) to avert, turn away; (*перен: беду, удар*) to avert; (*заявление, кандидатуру*) to reject; (*участок, сад*) to allot; (*средства*) to allocate; **отводи́ть** (**~** *perf*) **кого́-н в сто́рону** to take *или* lead sb aside; **отводи́ть** (**~** *perf*) **вре́мя на что-н** (*себе*) to set aside time for sth; (*другим*) to allocate time for sth; **отводи́ть** (**~** *perf*) **ду́шу** to unburden one's soul.
отве́т (**-а**) *м* (*на вопрос*) answer; (*реакция*) response; (*на письмо, на приглашение*) reply; **в ~** (**на** *+acc*) in response (to); **быть** (*impf*) **в ~е за** *+acc* to be answerable for; **призыва́ть** (**призва́ть** *perf*) **к ~у** to call to account.
ответв|и́ться (*3sg* **-и́тся**, *3pl* **-я́тся**, *impf* **ответвля́ться**) *сов возв* to branch.
ответвле́ни|е (**-я**) *ср* (*дерева, дороги*) branch; (*перен: движения, религии*) branch, offshoot.
ответвля́|ться (*3sg* **-ется**, *3pl* **-ются**) *несов от* **ответви́ться.**
отве́|тить (**-чу, -тишь**; *impf* **отвеча́ть**) *сов неперех*: **~** (**на** *+acc*) to answer, reply (to); (*на увольнение, на грубость*) to retaliate (against); **~** (*perf*) **за** *+acc* (*за преступление, за поступок*) to answer for; **отвеча́ть** (**~** *perf*) **любо́вью на** (**чью-н**) **любо́вь** to return sb's love.
отве́тственност|ь (**-и**) *ж* (*задания, заказа*) importance; (*за поступки, за действия*) responsibility; **нести́** (**понести́** *perf*) **~ за** *+acc* to be responsible for; **привлека́ть** (**привле́чь** *perf*) **кого́-н к ~и** to call sb to account.
отве́тствен|ный (**-, -на, -но**) *прил* responsible; (*работа, поручение, момент*) important; **отве́тственный квартиросъёмщик** responsible tenant; **отве́тственный рабо́тник** executive.
отве́тчик (**-а**) *м* (*ЮР*) defendant.
отве́тчиц|а (**-ы**) *ж см* **отве́тчик.**
отвеча́|ть (**-ю**) *несов от* **отве́тить** ◆ *неперех*: **~** *+dat* (*требованиям*) to meet; (*описанию*) to answer; (*интересам итп*) to suit; **~** (*impf*) **за кого́-н/что-н** to be responsible for sb/sth.
отве́чу *сов см* **отве́тить.**
отве́шива|ть (**-ю**) *несов от* **отве́сить.**
отве́шу *сов см* **отве́сить.**
отви́лива|ть (**-ю**; *perf* **отвильну́ть**) *несов неперех*: **~ от** *+gen* (*разг: от работы итп*) to dodge.
отвин|ти́ть (**-чу́, -ти́шь**; *impf* **отви́нчивать**) *сов перех* to unscrew
▸ **отвинти́ться** (*impf* **отви́нчиваться**) *сов возв* to come unscrewed.
отвиса́|ть (*3sg* **-ет**, *3pl* **-ют**) *несов от* **отви́снуть.**
отви́слый *прил* (*щёки*) sagging; (*уши*) droopy.
отви́сн|уть (*3sg* **-ет**, *3pl* **-ут**, *impf* **отвиса́ть**) *сов неперех* to sag.
отвлёк(ся) *сов см* **отвле́чь(ся).**
отвлека́|ть(ся) (**-ю(сь)**) *несов от* **отвле́чь(ся).**
отвлеку́(сь) *итп сов см* **отвле́чь(ся).**
отвлече́ни|е (**-я**) *ср* (*внимания, интереса*) distraction; (*абстракция*) abstraction.
отвлечён|ный (**-, -на, -но**) *прил* abstract.
отвл|е́чь (**-еку́, -ечёшь** *итп*, **-еку́т**; *pt* **-ёк, -екла́, -екло́**, *impf* **отвлека́ть**) *сов перех*: **~** (**от** *+gen*) (*противника*) to divert (from); (*от дел*) to distract (from); **отвлека́ть** (**~** *perf*) **чьё-н внима́ние** to distract sb's attention
▸ **отвле́чься** (*impf* **отвлека́ться**) *сов возв*: **~ся** (**от** *+gen*) to be distracted (from); (*от темы*) to digress (from); (*абстрагироваться*) to abstract o.s. (from).
отво́д (**-а**) *м* (*воды, газа*) diversion; (*войск*) relocation; (*кандидатуры, судьи*) rejection; **для ~а глаз** (*разг*) as a distraction.
отв|оди́ть (**-ожу́, -о́дишь**) *несов от* **отвести́.**
отводно́й *прил* drainage *опред.*
отво|ева́ть (**-ю́ю**; *impf* **отвоёвывать**) *сов перех* (*также перен*) to win back ◆ *неперех* (*разг: кончить воевать*) to finish fighting
▸ **отвоева́ться** *сов возв* (*разг: солдат, полк*) to finish fighting.
отвожу́ *несов см* **отводи́ть.**

отв|ози́ть (**-ожу́, -о́зишь**) *несов от* **отвезти́**.
отвора́чива|ть(ся) (**-ю(сь)**) *несов от* **отверну́ть(ся)**.
отвор|и́ть (**-ю́, -и́шь;** *impf* **отворя́ть**) *сов перех* to open.
отвра́тен *прил см* **отвра́тный**.
отврати́телен *прил см* **орврати́тельный**.
отврати́тельно *нареч* (*пахнуть*) disgusting; (*поступить*) abominably ◆ *как сказ* it's disgusting.
отврати́тел|ьный (**-ен, -ьна, -ьно**) *прил* disgusting.
отвра|ти́ть (**-щу́, -ти́шь;** *impf* **отвраща́ть**) *сов перех* to avert.
отвра́т|ный (**-ен, -на, -но**) *прил* (*разг*) revolting.
отвраща́|ть (**-ю**) *несов от* **отврати́ть**.
отвраще́ни|е (**-я**) *ср* disgust, repulsion.
отвращу́ *сов см* **отврати́ть**.
отвы́к|нуть (**-ну, -нешь;** *pt* **-, -ла, -ло,** *impf* **отвыка́ть**) *сов неперех*: **~ от** *+gen* (*от наркотиков*) to give up; (*от людей, от дома, от работы*) to become unaccustomed to; **отвыка́ть** (**~** *perf*) **от куре́ния** to give up smoking; **он отвы́к от до́ма/рабо́ты** he is not used to living at home/working any more.
отв|яза́ть (**-яжу́, -я́жешь;** *impf* **отвя́зывать**) *сов перех* (*верёвку*) to untie; (*собаку, коня*) to untie, untether
▸ **отвяза́ться** (*impf* **отвя́зываться**) *сов возв* (*верёвка*) to come undone; (*собака, конь*) to break loose; (*разг*): **~ся от** *+gen* (*от человека*) to leave in peace; (*отделаться*) to get rid of; **~яжи́сь (от меня́)!** (*разг*) get lost!
отгада́|ть (**-ю;** *impf* **отга́дывать**) *сов перех* to guess.
отга́д|ка (**-ки;** *gen pl* **-ок**) *ж* answer (*to riddle*).
отга́дыва|ть (**-ю**) *несов от* **отгада́ть**.
отгиба́|ть(ся) (**-ю(сь)**) *несов от* **отогну́ть(ся)**.
отглаго́льный *прил* verbal.
отгла́|дить (**-жу, -дишь;** *impf* **отгла́живать**) *сов перех* to iron
▸ **отгла́диться** (*impf* **отгла́живаться**) *сов возв* to be ironed.
отговор|и́ть (**-ю́, -и́шь;** *impf* **отгова́ривать**) *сов перех*: **~ кого́-н от чего́-н/**+*infin* to dissuade sb from sth/from doing
▸ **отговори́ться** (*impf* **отгова́риваться**) *сов возв* (+*instr*; *разг*: *незнанием, болезнью*) to plead; **~** (*perf*) **незна́нием** to plead ignorance; **он ~и́лся боле́знью** he gave the excuse that he was ill.
отгово́р|ка (**-ки;** *gen pl* **-ок**) *ж* excuse.
отголо́с|ок (**-ка;** *nom pl* **-ки**) *м* (*также перен*) echo.
отгоню́ *umn сов см* **отогна́ть**.
отгоня́|ть (**-ю**) *несов от* **отогна́ть**.
отгор|оди́ть (**-ожу́, -о́дишь;** *impf* **отгора́живать**) *сов перех* (*дом, участок*) to fence off; (*часть комнаты*) to partition off; (*от жизни*) to isolate; (*от забот*) to shelter
▸ **отгороди́ться** (*impf* **отгора́живаться**) *сов возв* (*забором*) to fence o.s. off; (*ширмой*) to screen o.s. off; (*от жизни, от забот*) to cut o.s. off.
отгрёб *umn сов см* **отгрести́**.
отгреба́|ть (**-ю**) *несов от* **отгрести́**.
отгребу́ *umn сов см* **отгрести́**.
отгрем|е́ть (*3sg* **-и́т**, *3pl* **-я́т**) *сов неперех* (*гром, аплодисменты*) to stop; **его́ сла́ва ~е́ла** he is no longer famous; **бой ~е́л** the battle is over.
отгр|ести́ (**-ебу́, -ебёшь;** *pt* **-ёб, -ебла́, -ебло́,** *impf* **отгреба́ть**) *сов перех* (*листья, снег*) to rake away ◆ *неперех* (*от берега*) to row away.
отгр|узи́ть (**-ужу́, -у́зишь;** *impf* **отгружа́ть**) *сов перех* (*отправить*) to ship.
отгру́зк|а (**-и**) *ж* shipment.
отгры́з|ть (**-у́, -ёшь;** *pt* **-, -ла, -ло,** *impf* **отгрыза́ть**) *сов перех* to bite off.
отгу́л (**-а**) *м* day off.
отгуля́|ть (**-ю;** *impf* **отгу́ливать**) *сов перех* (*разг*: *отпуск, праздники*) to finish (*one's holidays etc*); (: *за дежурство, за сверхурочные*) to have time off; **мы ~ли о́тпуск** our holidays are over.
отда|ва́ть (**-ю́, -ёшь**) *несов от* **отда́ть** ◆ *неперех*: **~** +*instr* (*разг*: *пахнуть*) to reek of
▸ **отдава́ться** *несов от* **отда́ться**.
отд|ави́ть (**-авлю́, -а́вишь;** *impf* **отда́вливать**) *сов перех* to crush.
отдади́м(ся) *umn сов см* **отда́ть(ся)**.
отда́й(ся) *сов см* **отда́ть(ся)**.
отда́йте(сь) *сов см* **отда́ть(ся)**.
отдале́ни|е (**-и**) *ср*: **в ~и, на ~и** in the distance; **в ~и от** +*gen* some way away from.
отдалён|ный (**-, -на, -но**) *прил* distant; (*место, сходство*) remote.
отдал|и́ть (**-ю́, -и́шь;** *impf* **отдаля́ть**) *сов перех* (*смерть, разлуку*) to postpone; (*сына, друзей*) to alienate
▸ **отдали́ться** (*impf* **отдаля́ться**) *сов возв*: **~ся от** +*gen* (*от берега, от города*) to move away from; (*от темы, от дел*) to digress from; (*от друзей, от семьи*) to become alienated from.
отда́|ть (*как* **дать**; *см* **Table 14**; *impf* **отдава́ть**) *сов перех* (*возвратить*) to return; (*дать*) to give; (*сдать*: *город, крепость*) to surrender; (*ребёнка*: *в школу, в детский сад*) to send; (*разг*: *заплатить*) to pay; (*подлеж*: *ружьё*) to kick; (: *боль*) to spread; **он ~л жизнь нау́ке** he devoted his life to science; **отдава́ть (~** *perf*) **ту́фли в ремо́нт** to put one's shoes in for repair; **отдава́ть (~** *perf*) **что-н за бесце́нок** to give sth away; **отдава́ть (~** *perf*) **дочь за́муж** to give one's daughter away (*in marriage*); **отдава́ть (~** *perf*) **(кому́-н) распоряже́ние/прика́з** to give (sb) instructions/an order; **отдава́ть (~** *perf*) **кому́-н/чему́-н предпочте́ние** to give preference to sb/sth; **отдава́ть (~** *perf*) **кого́-н под суд** to prosecute sb; **отдава́ть (~** *perf*) **кому́-н честь** to salute sb; **отдава́ть (~** *perf*) **себе́ отчёт** to realize; **отдава́ть (~** *perf*) **до́лжное** *или* **справедли́вость кому́-н** to give

sb his *umn* due; **отдавáть (~ *perf*) комý-н послéдний долг** to pay one's last respects to sb; **отдавáть (~ *perf*) концы́** (*разг*: *умереть*) to kick the bucket
▸ **отдáться** (*impf* **отдавáться**) *сов возв* (*голос, эхо*) to resound, reverberate; **отдавáться (~ся *perf*) +*dat*** to give o.s. up *или* surrender to; (*воспоминаниям*) to lose o.s. in; (*искусству*) to devote o.s. to; (*любовнику*) to give o.s. to; **боль отдавáлась в спинé** the pain spread to his back.
отдáч|а (-и) *ж* (*при выстреле*) recoil; (*СПОРТ*) return; **рабóтать** (*impf*) **с пóлной ~ей** to put a lot into one's work.
отдáшь(ся) *сов см* **отдáть(ся)**.
отдéл (-а) *м* (*учреждения, универмага*) department; (*книги, газеты*) section; (*истории, науки*) branch; **отдéл здравоохранéния** health department; **отдéл кáдров** personnel department; **отдéл отпрáвки** dispatch department.
отдéла|ть (-ю; *impf* **отдéлывать**) *сов перех* (*квартиру*) to do up; (*разг*: *поколотить*) to do over; **отдéлывать (~ *perf*) что-н чем-н** (*пальто*: *мехом*) to trim sth with sth; (*комнату*: *деревом*) to do sth out with sth
▸ **отдéлаться** (*impf* **отдéлываться**) *сов возв*: **~ся от +*gen*** (*разг*: *от работы, от дел*) to get away from; (: *от человека*) to get rid of; **~ся** (*perf*) **+*instr*** (*разг*: *лёгким ушибом*) to get away with; **легкó ~ся** (*perf*) to get off lightly; **он ~лся обещáниями** he did no more than make a few promises; **он ~лся испýгом** more than anything he got a fright.
отделéни|е (-я) *ср* (*действие*: *от семьи итп*) separation; (*пенала, стола*) section; (*сумки*) compartment; (*учебного заведения, больницы*) department; (*банка*) branch; (*концерта*) part; (*ВОЕН*) section; **отделéние свя́зи** post office; **отделéние милиции** police station.
отд|ели́ть (-елю́, -éлишь; *impf* **отделя́ть**) *сов перех*: **~ (от +*gen*)** to separate (from); (*участок, часть комнаты*) to separate *или* divide off (from)
▸ **отдели́ться** (*impf* **отделя́ться**) *сов возв*: **~ся (от +*gen*)** to separate (from); **~ся** (*perf*) **от родителей** to alienate o.s. from one's parents.
отдéл|ка (-ки; *gen pl* -ок) *ж* decoration; (*в квартире*) decor; (*на платье*) trimmings *мн*.
отдéлочный *прил* (*материалы, тесьма, пуговицы*) decorative; **отдéлочные рабóты** decorating.
отдéлыва|ть(ся) (-ю(сь)) *несов от* **отдéлать(ся)**.
отдéльно *нареч* separately.
отдéльност|ь (-и) *ж*: **в ~и** separately.
отдéльный *прил* separate; (*единичный*: *примеры, возражения*) isolated.
отделя́|ть(ся) (-ю(сь)) *несов от* **отдели́ть(ся)**.

отдёрн|уть (-у, -ешь; *impf* **отдёргивать**) *сов перех* to pull back.
отдерý(сь) *итп сов см* **отодрáть(ся)**.
отдирá|ть (-ю) *несов от* **отодрáть**.
отдохн|ýть (-ý, -ёшь; *impf* **отдыхáть**) *сов неперех* to (have a) rest; (*на море*) to have a holiday; **я хорошó ~ýл** I had a good rest.
отдувá|ться (-юсь) *несов неперех* (*разг*) to pant; (: *за ошибки, за других*) to carry the can.
отдýшин|а (-ы) *ж* vent; (*перен*) escape.
óтдых (-а) *м* rest; (*отпуск*) holiday; **на ~е** (*в отпуске*) on holiday; **он на заслýженном ~е** (*на пенсии*) he is having a well-earned rest; **дом ~а** holiday centre; **без ~а** without a moment's rest.
отдыхá|ть (-ю) *несов от* **отдохнýть**.
отдыхáющ|ая (-ей; *decl like adj*) *ж см* **отдыхáющий**.
отдыхáющ|ий (-его; *decl like adj*) *м* holidaymaker (*BRIT*).
отд|ышáться (-ышýсь, -ы́шишься) *сов возв* to get one's breath back.
отёк (-а) *м* swelling; **отёк лёгких** (*МЕД*) emphysema.
отёк *итп сов см* **отéчь**.
откá|ть (-ю) *несов от* **отéчь**.
отекý *итп сов см* **отéчь**.
отёл (-а) *м* calving.
от|ели́ться (*3sg* -éлится, *3pl* -éлятся) *сов от* **тели́ться**.
отéл|ь (-я) *м* hotel.
от|éц (-цá) *м* (*также РЕЛ, перен*) father.
отéческ|ий (-ая, -ое, -ие) *прил* fatherly, paternal.
отéчественн|ый *прил* (*не иностранный*: *промышленность*) domestic; **товáр ~ого произвóдства** home-produced goods; **Вели́кая О~ая Войнá** Great Patriotic War (*World War II*); **Отéчественная Войнá** patriotic war (*fought in defence of one's country*).
отéчеств|о (-а) *ср* fatherland.
отёчный *прил* swollen.
от|éчь (-екý, -ечёшь *итп*, -екýт; *pt* **отёк, -еклá, -еклó**, *impf* **отекáть**) *сов неперех* to swell up.
от|жáть (-ожмý, -ожмёшь; *impf* **отжимáть**) *сов перех* (*руками*) to wring out; (*в стиральной машине*) to spin dry.
отзвен|éть (*3sg* -и́т, *3pl* -я́т) *сов неперех* to stop ringing.
отзвон|и́ть (-ю́, -и́шь) *сов перех* (*подлеж*: *колокол*) to ring out; **часы́ ~и́ли пóлночь** the clock struck midnight.
óтзвук (-а) *м* (*также перен*) echo.
отзвуч|áть (*3sg* -и́т, *3pl* -áт) *сов неперех* to come to an end (*of music, speeches etc*).
отзовý(сь) *итп сов см* **отозвáть(ся)**.
óтзыв (-а) *м* (*мнение*) impression; (*рецензия*) review; (*перен*: *в душе*) echo; (*ВОЕН*) reply (*to a password*).

отзы́в (-а) *м* (*представителя, посла*) recall.
отзыва́|ть(ся) (-ю(сь)) *несов от* **отозва́ть(ся)**.
отзы́вчив|ый (-, -а, -о) *прил* ready to help.
оти́т (-а) *м* (*МЕД*) otitis (*ear infection*).
ОТК *м сокр* = *отде́л техни́ческого контро́ля*.
откажу́(сь) *итп сов см* **отказа́ть(ся)**.
отка́з (-а) *м* refusal; (*на заявление, от решения*) rejection; (*механизма*) failure; **закру́чивать (закрути́ть** *perf*) **до ~а** to turn full on; **рабо́тать** (*impf*) **без ~а** to operate smoothly; **набива́ть (наби́ть** *perf*) **до ~а** to cram.
отк|аза́ть (**-ажу́, -а́жешь**; *impf* **отка́зывать**) *сов неперех*: **~ кому́-н в чём-н** to refuse sb sth; (*лишить кого-н чего-н*) to deny sb sth; (*мотор, нервы*) to fail; **ему́ не ~а́жешь в тала́нте** you can't deny that he's talented
▸ **отказа́ться** (*impf* **отка́зываться**) *сов возв*: **~ся (от** *+gen*) to refuse; **отка́зываться (~ся** *perf*) **от свои́х слов** to retract one's words; **отка́зываться (~ся** *perf*) **от мы́сли** to give up on an idea; **не ~ажу́сь** I wouldn't say no.
отка́лыва|ть(ся) (-ю(сь)) *несов от* **отколо́ть(ся)**.
отка́пыва|ть (-ю) *несов от* **откопа́ть**.
отка́рмлива|ть (-ю) *несов от* **откорми́ть**.
отк|ати́ть (**-ачу́, -а́тишь**; *impf* **отка́тывать**) *сов перех* (*что-н круглое*) to roll away; (*что-н на колёсах*) to wheel away ◆ *неперех* (*разг*: *быстро отъехать*) to speed off
▸ **откати́ться** (*impf* **отка́тываться**) *сов возв* to roll away.
откача́|ть (-ю; *impf* **отка́чивать**) *сов перех* (*жидкость, газ*) to pump (out); (*привести в чувство*) to resuscitate.
откачу́(сь) *сов см* **откати́ть(ся)**.
отка́шлива|ться (-юсь) *несов от* **отка́шляться**.
отка́шлян|уть (-у, -ешь; *impf* **отка́шливать**) *сов перех* to cough up.
отка́шля|ться (-юсь; *impf* **отка́шливаться**) *сов возв* to clear one's throat.
откидно́й *прил* foldaway.
отки́н|уть (-у, -ешь; *impf* **отки́дывать**) *сов перех* to throw; (*перен*: *тревоги, сомнения*) to cast aside; (*верх, сидение*) to open; (*руку*) to throw back; (*волосы, голову*) to toss back; (*в дуршлаг*: *макароны, рис*) to tip out; (*разг*: *войска, противника*) to push back
▸ **отки́нуться** (*impf* **отки́дываться**) *сов возв*: **~ся на** *+acc* to lean back against; **отки́дываться (~ся** *perf*) **наза́д** to lean backwards.
откла́дыва|ть (-ю) *несов от* **отложи́ть**.
откле́|ить (-ю, -ишь; *impf* **откле́ивать**) *сов перех* to peel off
▸ **откле́иться** (*impf* **откле́иваться**) *сов возв* to come off.
о́тклик (-а) *м* response; (*перен*) echo; (*обычно мн*: *в печати*) comment.
откли́кн|уться (**-усь, -ешься**; *impf* **отклика́ться**) *сов возв*: **~ (на** *+acc*) to answer; (*на события, на просьбу*) to respond (to).
отклоне́ни|е (-я) *ср* deflection; (*перен*: *просьбы*) rejection; (*от курса*) deviation; (*МЕД*) abnormality; **~ от те́мы** digression.
откл|они́ть (**-оню́, -о́нишь**; *impf* **отклоня́ть**) *сов перех* (*стрелку*) to deflect; (*перен*: *предложение, просьбу*) to reject
▸ **отклони́ться** (*impf* **отклоня́ться**) *сов возв* (*стрелка*) to deflect; (*перен*: *в сторону, от удара*) to dodge; (*от курса, на север*) to be deflected; **отклоня́ться (~ся** *perf*) **от те́мы** to digress.
отключ|и́ть (-у́, -и́шь; *impf* **отключа́ть**) *сов перех* to switch off; (*телефон*) to cut off
▸ **отключи́ться** (*impf* **отключа́ться**) *сов возв* (*также перен*) to switch off.
отковыря́|ть (-ю; *impf* **отковы́ривать**) *сов перех* to pick off.
откозыря́|ть (-ю) *сов от* **козыря́ть**.
откол|оти́ть (**-очу́, -о́тишь**) *сов перех* (*разг*): **~ кого́-н** to give sb a thrashing.
отк|оло́ть (**-олю́, -о́лешь**; *impf* **отка́лывать**) *сов перех* (*кусок*) to break off; (*бант, булавку*) to unpin; **~** (*perf*) **но́мер** (*разг*) to pull a fast one
▸ **отколо́ться** (*impf* **отка́лываться**) *сов возв* (*также перен*) to break off; (*бант, булавка*) to come unpinned.
отколочу́ *сов см* **отколоти́ть**.
откомандир|ова́ть (-у́ю; *impf* **откомандиро́вывать**) *сов перех* to post, second.
откопа́|ть (-ю; *impf* **отка́пывать**) *сов перех* to dig up; (*перен*: *книгу, сведения*) to unearth.
отк|орми́ть (**-ормлю́, -о́рмишь**; *impf* **отка́рмливать**) *сов перех* to fatten (up).
откоррект|и́р|овать (-ую) *сов от* **корректи́ровать**.
отко́с (-а) *м* (*горы, берега*) slope; (*железной дороги*) embankment; **пуска́ть (пусти́ть** *perf*) **по́езд под ~** to derail a train.
откреп|и́ть (-лю́, -и́шь; *impf* **открепля́ть**) *сов перех* (*значок, вывеску*) to unfasten; (*снять с учёта*) to take off the register
▸ **открепи́ться** (*impf* **открепля́ться**) *сов возв* (*вывеска*) to come unfastened; (*сняться с учёта*) to sign o.s. off the register.
открове́нен *прил см* **открове́нный**.
открове́ни|е (-я) *ср* revelation.
открове́нничa|ть (-ю) *несов неперех*: **~ (с** *+instr*) to bare one's soul (to).
открове́нно *нареч* frankly; **~ говоря́** frankly speaking.
открове́нност|ь (-и) *ж* frankness.
открове́н|ный (**-ен, -на, -но**) *прил* frank; (*хамство, обман*) blatant; (*разг*: *платье, туалет*) revealing.
откро́ю(сь) *итп сов см* **откры́ть(ся)**.
откр|ути́ть (**-учу́, -у́тишь**; *impf* **откру́чивать**) *сов перех* to unscrew.
открыва́л|ка (**-ки**; *gen pl* **-ок**) *ж* (*для консервов*) tin-opener; (*для бутылок*) bottle-opener.

открыва́|ть(ся) **(-ю(сь))** *несов от* **откры́ть(ся).**

откры́ти|е **(-я)** *ср* (*также перен*) discovery; (*сезона, выставки, клуба*) opening.

откры́т|ка **(-ки;** *gen pl* **-ок)** *ж* postcard.

откры́т|ый **(-, -а, -о)** *прил* open; (*голова, шея*) bare; (*лицо, взгляд, человек*) frank; **в ~ую** openly; **на ~ом во́здухе** outside, outdoors; **музей под ~ым не́бом** open-air museum; **~ая маши́на** open-top car; **~ое пла́тье** low-cut dress; **откры́тая ра́на** open wound; **откры́тое голосова́ние/письмо́** open vote/letter; **откры́тый вопро́с** open question.

откр|ы́ть **(-о́ю, -о́ешь;** *impf* **открыва́ть)** *сов перех* to open; (*лицо итп*) to uncover; (*намерения, правду итп*) to reveal; (*воду, кран*) to turn on; (*возможность, путь, позицию*) to open up; (*явление, закон*) to discover; **открыва́ть (~** *perf***) торго́влю чем-н** to start selling sth; **открыва́ть (~** *perf***) Аме́рику** (*перен*) to reinvent the wheel; **открыва́ть (~** *perf***) счёт** (*КОММ*) to open an account; (*СПОРТ*) to open the scoring; **открыва́ть (~** *perf***) ого́нь** to open fire

▸ **откры́ться** (*impf* **открыва́ться**) *сов возв* to open; (*возможность, путь, позиция*) to open up; (*тайна*) to be revealed; (*пейзаж, река*) to open out; **~** *(perf)* **кому́-н** to open up to sb; **у него́ глаза́ ~ы́лись** (*перен*) he has begun to see things clearly.

отку́да *нареч* where from ◆ *союз* whence, from where; **Вы ~ ?** where are you from?; **~ Вы прие́хали?** where have you come from?; **~ ты э́то зна́ешь?** how do you know about that?; **он не мог поня́ть, ~ слы́шался звук** he couldn't work out where the sound was coming from; **~ сле́дует...** hence ...; **~ ни возьми́сь** out of nowhere; **~ я зна́ю?** (*разг*) how do I know?

отку́да-нибудь *нареч* from somewhere (or other).

отку́да-то *нареч* from somewhere.

откуп|и́ться **(-лю́сь, -ишься;** *impf* **откупа́ться)** *сов возв*: **~ от** *+gen* to buy one's way out of.

отку́пор|ить **(-ю, -ишь;** *impf* **отку́поривать)** *сов перех* to unseal.

отк|уси́ть **(-ушу́, -у́сишь;** *impf* **отку́сывать)** *сов перех* (*зубами*) to bite off; (*кусачками*) to snip off.

отл. *сокр* (*= отлично*) ≈ O (*US*) (*= outstanding*), ≈ A (*BRIT*).

отлага́тельств|о **(-а)** *ср* delay.

отла́дк|а **(-и)** *ж* (*КОМП*) debugging.

отлакир|ова́ть **(-у́ю)** *сов от* **лакирова́ть.**

отла́мыва|ть(ся) **(-ю)** *несов от* **отлома́ть(ся), отломи́ть(ся).**

отлеж|а́ть **(-у́, -и́шь)** *сов перех*: **я ~а́л но́гу/ру́ку** my leg/arm has gone dead

▸ **отлежа́ться** (*impf* **отлёживаться**) *сов возв* (*разг*) to rest up.

отл|епи́ть **(-еплю́, -е́пишь;** *impf* **отлепля́ть)** *сов перех* to peel off

▸ **отлепи́ться** (*impf* **отлепля́ться**) *сов возв* to peel off.

отлёт **(-а)** *м* (*птиц*) flight; (*самолёта*) departure; **на ~е** (*жить*) on the outskirts; (*держать*) in one's outstretched hand.

отле|те́ть **(-чу́, -ти́шь;** *impf* **отлета́ть)** *сов неперех* to fly off; (*мяч*) to fly back; (*человек: от удара*) to be sent flying back.

отл|е́чь (*3sg* **-я́жет,** *3pl* **-я́гут,** *pt* **-ёг, -егла́, -егло́)** *сов безл*: **у меня́ ~егло́ от се́рдца** a weight has been lifted from my mind.

отли́в **(-а)** *м* (*в море*) ebb; (*оттенок*) sheen.

отлива́|ть **(-ю)** *несов от* **отли́ть** ◆ *неперех* (*+instr*; *серебром, лиловым*) to be tinted with.

отли́вк|а **(-и)** *ж* (*деталей, форм*) casting.

от|ли́ть **(-олью́, -ольёшь;** *pt* **-ли́л, -лила́, -ли́ло,** *impf* **отлива́ть)** *сов перех* (*воду, вино*) to pour off; (*ТЕХ: деталь, форму*) to cast; **у него́ кровь ~лила́ от лица́** the blood drained from his face.

отлича́|ть **(-ю)** *несов от* **отличи́ть** ◆ *перех* (*подлеж: красота, новизна*) to be a feature of

▸ **отлича́ться** *несов от* **отличи́ться** ◆ *возв* (*не походить*): **~ся (от** *+gen***)** to be different (from); **~ся** *(impf) +instr* (*оригинальностью, красотой итп*) to be distinguished by; **она́ ~ется умо́м** she has a distinguished mind.

отли́чен *прил см* **отли́чный.**

отли́чи|е **(-я)** *ср* distinction; **знаки ~я** decorations; **дипло́м с ~м** ≈ first-class degree with distinction; **в ~ от** *+gen* unlike.

отличи́тельный *прил* distinguishing.

отлич|и́ть **(-у́, -и́шь;** *impf* **отлича́ть)** *сов перех*: **~ кого́-н/что-н от** *+gen* to tell sb/sth from; (*наградить*) to honour (*BRIT*), honor (*US*); **отлича́ть (~** *perf***) плохо́е от хоро́шего** to tell the difference between good and bad; **я не могу́ ~ их (друг от дру́га)** I can't tell them apart

▸ **отличи́ться** (*impf* **отлича́ться**) *сов возв* to distinguish o.s.; (*разг: сделать что-н необычное*) to outdo o.s.

отли́чник **(-а)** *м* 'A' grade pupil.

отли́чниц|а **(-ы)** *ж см* **отли́чник.**

отли́чно *нареч* extremely well ◆ *как сказ* it's great ◆ *ср нескл* (*ПРОСВЕЩ*) ≈ excellent *или* outstanding (*school mark*); **он ~ зна́ет, что он винова́т** he knows perfectly well that he's wrong; **здесь ~** it's great here; **учи́ться** *(impf)* **на ~** to get top marks; **~!** (that's) excellent!

отли́ч|ный **(-ен, -на, -но)** *прил* excellent; (*иной*): **~ от** *+gen* distinct from.

отло́г|ий **(-ая, -ое, -ие; -, -а, -о)** *прил* sloping.

отложе́ни|е **(-я)** *ср* (*ГЕО, МЕД*) deposit.

отл|ожи́ть **(-ожу́, -о́жишь;** *impf* **откла́дывать)** *сов перех* to put aside; (*отсрочить*) to postpone; (*яйцо*) to lay.

отложно́й *прил* (*воротник, манжеты*) turndown.
отлома́|ть (-ю; *impf* **отла́мывать**) *сов перех* to break off
▸ **отлома́ться** (*impf* **отла́мываться**) *сов возв* to break off.
отл|оми́ть (-омлю́, -о́мишь; *impf* **отла́мывать**) *сов перех* to break off
▸ **отломи́ться** (*impf* **отла́мываться**) *сов возв* to break off.
отл|упи́ть (-уплю́, -у́пишь) *сов от* **лупи́ть**.
отлуч|и́ть (-у́, -и́шь; *impf* **отлуча́ть**) *сов перех*: ~ **кого́-н от** +*gen* (*от дома, от семьи*) to take sb from; **отлуча́ть** (~ *perf*) **кого́-н от це́ркви** to excommunicate sb
▸ **отлучи́ться** (*impf* **отлуча́ться**) *сов возв*; **я до́лжен ~ся на полчаса́** I'll have to go out for half an hour.
отлы́нива|ть (-ю) *несов неперех*: ~ **от** +*gen* to try to get out of.
отма́лчива|ться (-юсь) *несов от* **отмолча́ться**.
отма́тыва|ть (-ю) *несов от* **отмота́ть**.
отмахн|у́ться (-у́сь, -ёшься; *impf* **отма́хиваться**) *сов возв*: ~ **от** +*gen* (*от мухи*) to brush away; (*от человека, от предложения*) to brush *или* wave aside.
отма́чива|ть (-ю) *несов от* **отмочи́ть**.
отмеж|ева́ться (-у́юсь; *impf* **отмежёвываться**) *сов возв*: ~ **от** +*gen* (*перен*) to distance o.s. from.
о́тмел|ь (-и) *ж*: **песча́ная** ~ sandbank.
отме́н|а (-ы) *ж* (*см глаг*) repeal; reversal; abolition; cancellation.
отм|ени́ть (-еню́, -е́нишь; *impf* **отменя́ть**) *сов перех* (*закон*) to repeal; (*решение, приговор*) to reverse; (*налог*) to abolish; (*лекцию*) to cancel.
от|мере́ть (*3sg* **-омрёт**, *3pl* **-омру́т**, *pt* **-мер, -мерла́, -мерло**, *impf* **отмира́ть**) *сов неперех* (*ткань, ветка*) to die; (*перен*: *обычаи, привычки*) to die (out).
отмёрз|нуть (*3sg* **-нет**, *3pl* **-нут**, *pt* **-, -ла, -ло**, *impf* **отмерза́ть**) *сов неперех* (*ветки, побеги*) to freeze; (*разг*: *руки, ноги*) to be frozen.
отме́р|ить (-ю, -ишь; *impf* **отмеря́ть**) *сов перех* to measure out.
отм|ести́ (-ету́, -етёшь; *pt* **-ёл, -ела́, -ело́**, *impf* **отмета́ть**) *сов перех* (*мусор, снег*) to sweep away; (*перен*: *доводы, возражения*) to sweep aside.
отме́стк|а (-и) *ж*: **в ~у за** +*acc* in revenge for.
отмета́|ть (-ю) *несов от* **отмести́**.
отме́тин|а (-ы) *ж* mark.
отме́|тить (-чу, -тишь; *impf* **отмеча́ть**) *сов перех* (*на карте, в книге*) to mark; (*затраты, расходы*) to record; (*присутствующих, отсутствующих*) to take a note of; (*достоинства, недостатки, успехи*) to recognise; (*юбилей, день рождения*) to celebrate; **ну́жно ~, что** ... it should be noted that ...
▸ **отме́титься** (*impf* **отмеча́ться**) *сов возв* to register.
отме́т|ка (-ки; *gen pl* **-ок**) *ж* mark; (*в документе, в паспорте*) note.
отмету́ *итп сов см* **отмести́**.
отмеча́|ть (-ю) *несов от* **отме́тить**
▸ **отмеча́ться** *несов от* **отме́титься** ◆ *возв* (*успехи, талант*) to be apparent.
отме́чу(сь) *сов см* **отме́тить(ся)**.
отмира́|ть (*3sg* **-ет**, *3pl* **-ют**) *несов от* **отмере́ть**.
отмо́к|нуть (*3sg* **-нет**, *3pl* **-нут**, *pt* **-, -ла, -ло**, *impf* **отмока́ть**) *сов неперех* to get damp; (*бельё*) to soak; (*отклеиться*) to come off (*as a result of soaking*).
отмолч|а́ться (-у́сь, -и́шься; *impf* **отма́лчиваться**) *сов неперех* to keep silent.
отморо́|зить (-жу, -зишь; *impf* **отмора́живать**) *сов перех*: ~ **ру́ки/но́ги** to get frostbite in one's hands/feet.
отмота́|ть (-ю; *impf* **отма́тывать**) *сов перех* to unwind.
отм|очи́ть (-очу́, -о́чишь; *impf* **отма́чивать**) *сов перех* (*наклейку, бинт*) to soak off; (*разг*: *глупость*) to come out with.
отмо́ю(сь) *итп сов см* **отмы́ть(ся)**.
отму́ч|иться (-усь, -ишься) *сов возв*: **он наконе́ц ~ился** his suffering has finally come to an end.
отм|ы́ть (-о́ю, -о́ешь; *impf* **отмыва́ть**) *сов перех*: ~ **что-н** to get sth clean; (*грязь, пятно*) to wash out
▸ **отмы́ться** (*impf* **отмыва́ться**) *сов возв* (*см перех*) to wash; to wash out; **у меня́ ру́ки не ~ыва́ются** I can't get my hands clean.
отмы́чк|а (-и) *ж* skeleton key.
отне́кива|ться (-юсь) *несов неперех* (*разг*: *отказываться*) to keep saying no; (*не признаваться*) to refuse to own up.
отн|ести́ (-есу́, -есёшь; *pt* **-ёс, -есла́, -есло́**, *impf* **относи́ть**) *сов перех* to take (off); (*подлеж*: *течение, ветер*) to carry off; (*причислить к*): ~ **что-н к** +*dat* (*к периоду, к году*) to date sth back to; (*к разряду, к категории*) to classify sth as; **относи́ть** (~ *perf*) **что-н за** *или* **на счёт** +*gen* to put sth down to, attribute sth to
▸ **отнести́сь** (*impf* **относи́ться**) *сов возв*: **~сь к** +*dat* (*к человеку*) to treat; (*к предложению, к событию*) to take; **как он ~ёсся к Ва́шему предложе́нию?** what did he think of your suggestion?
отникелир|ова́ть (-у́ю) *сов от* **никелирова́ть**.
отнима́|ть(ся) (-ю(сь)) *несов от* **отня́ть(ся)**.
отниму́(сь) *итп сов см* **отня́ть(ся)**.
относи́телен *прил см* **относи́тельный**.
относи́тельно *нареч* relatively ◆ *предл* (+*gen*; *в отношении*) regarding, with regard to.
относи́тел|ьный (-ен, -ьна, -ьно) *прил* relative; **относи́тельное местоиме́ние/прилага́тельное** (*линг*) relative pronoun/adjective.
отн|оси́ть (-ошу́, -о́сишь) *несов от* **отнести́**

▸ **относи́ться** *несов от* **отнести́сь** ◆ *возв*: **~ся к** *+dat* to relate to; (*к классу, к категории*) to belong to; (*к году, к эпохе*) to date from; **он к ней хорошо́ ~о́сится** he likes her; **как ты ~о́сишься к нему́?** what do you think about him?; **э́то к нам не ~о́сится** it has nothing to do with us.

отноше́ни|е (**-я**) *ср*: **~ к** *+dat* attitude (to); (*связь*) relation (to); (*МАТ*) ratio; (*документ*) letter; **в ~и** *+gen* with regard to; **по ~ю к** *+dat* towards; **в э́том ~и** in this respect *или* regard; **в не́котором ~и** in certain respects *или* regards; **во всех ~ях** in all respects *или* regards; **име́ть** *(impf)* **~ к** *+dat* to be connected with; **не име́ть** *(impf)* **~я к** *+dat* to have nothing to do with; *см также* **отноше́ния**.

отноше́ни|я (**-й**) *мн* (*политические, семейные итп*) relations *мн*.

отношу́(сь) *сов см* **относи́ть(ся)**.

отны́не *нареч* henceforth.

отню́дь *нареч*: **~ не** by no means, far from; **~ нет** absolutely not.

отн|я́ть (**-иму́, -и́мешь**; *pt* **-я́л, -яла́, -я́ло**, *impf* **отнима́ть**) *сов перех* to take away; (*силы, время*) to take up; (*ногу, руку*) to take off; **отнима́ть** (**~** *perf*) **от груди́** to wean; **э́того у него́ не ~и́мешь** (*перен*) you can't take that away from him

▸ **отня́ться** (*impf* **отнима́ться**) *сов возв*: **у него́ ~яли́сь но́ги/ру́ки** he has lost the use of his legs/arms; **у меня́ язы́к ~я́лся** (*перен: разг*) I was left speechless.

ото *предл см* **от**.

отобража́|ть (**-ю**) *несов от* **отобрази́ть**.

отображе́ни|е (**-я**) *ср* representation.

отобра|зи́ть (**-жу́, -зи́шь**; *impf* **отобража́ть**) *сов перех* to represent.

от|обра́ть (**-беру́, -берёшь**; *pt* **-обра́л, -обрала́, -обра́ло**, *impf* **отбира́ть**) *сов перех* (*отнять*) to take away; (*выбрать*) to select.

отобью́(сь) *итп сов см* **отби́ть(ся)**.

отовсю́ду *нареч* from all around.

от|огна́ть (**-гоню́, -го́нишь**; *impf* **отгоня́ть**) *сов перех* to chase away; (*перен: мысли, сомнения*) to drive out.

отогн|у́ть (**-у́, -ёшь**; *impf* **отгиба́ть**) *сов перех* (*металл*) to bend back; (*скатерть, страницу*) to fold back

▸ **отогну́ться** (*impf* **отгиба́ться**) *сов возв* to bend back.

отогре́|ть (**-ю**; *impf* **отогрева́ть**) *сов перех* to warm

▸ **отогре́ться** (*impf* **отогрева́ться**) *сов возв* to get warm.

отодви́н|уть (**-у, -ешь**; *impf* **отодвига́ть**) *сов перех* (*шкаф*) to move; (*щеколду, засов*) to slide back; (*срок, экзамен*) to put back

▸ **отодви́нуться** (*impf* **отодвига́ться**) *сов возв* (*человек*) to move; (*срок, экзамен*) to be put back.

от|одра́ть (**-деру́, -дерёшь**; *impf* **отдира́ть**) *сов перех* (*разг: оторвать*) to rip off; (*: высечь*) to thrash

▸ **отодра́ться** *сов возв* (*разг*) to come off.

отождеств|и́ть (**-лю́, -и́шь**; *impf* **отождествля́ть**) *сов перех* to equate.

отождествле́ни|е (**-я**) *ср* equating.

отождествлю́ *сов см* **отождестви́ть**.

отождествля́|ть (**-ю**) *несов от* **отождестви́ть**.

отожму́ *итп сов см* **отжа́ть**.

от|озва́ть (**-зову́, -зовёшь**; *impf* **отзыва́ть**) *сов перех* to call back; (*посла, представителя, документы*) to recall; **отзыва́ть** (**~** *perf*) **кого́-н в сто́рону** to take sb aside; **отзыва́ть** (**~** *perf*) **иск** (*ЮР*) to drop a case

▸ **отозва́ться** (*impf* **отзыва́ться**) *сов возв*: **~ся** (**на** *+acc*) to respond (to); **хорошо́/пло́хо ~ся** *(perf)* **о** *+prp* to speak well/badly of; **~ся** *(perf)* **о** *+prp* (*о книге*) to voice one's opinion about.

ото|йти́ (*как* **идти́**; *см* **Table 18**; *impf* **отходи́ть**) *сов неперех*: **~ от** *+gen* to move away from; (*перен: от друзей, от взглядов*) to distance o.s. from; (*от темы, от оригинала*) to depart from; (*поезд, автобус*) to leave; (*войска, полк*) to withdraw; (*обои, краска*) to come off; (*пятно, грязь*) to come out; (*отлучиться*) to go off; (*оттаять*) to thaw; (*перестать сердиться*) to calm down; **я ~йду́ на 5 мину́т** I'll be back in 5 minutes.

отолью́ *итп сов см* **отли́ть**.

отоларинго́лог (**-а**) *м* ear, nose and throat specialist.

отомрёт *итп сов см* **отмере́ть**.

отом|сти́ть (**-щу́, -сти́шь**) *сов от* **мстить**.

отопи́тельный *прил* (*прибор*) heating *опред*; **~ сезо́н** the cold season.

отопле́ни|е (**-я**) *ср* heating.

отопру́(сь) *итп сов см* **отпере́ть(ся)**.

отопью́ *итп сов см* **отпи́ть**.

ото́рван|ный (**-, -а, -о**) *прил*: **~ от** *+gen* (*от жизни, от друзей*) cut off from; (*воротник, пуговица*) torn-off.

оторв|а́ть (**-у́, -ёшь**; *impf* **отрыва́ть**) *сов перех*: **~** (**от** *+gen*) to tear away (from); (*воротник, пуговицу*) to tear off; **ему́ ~а́ло но́гу** his leg was blown off; **отрыва́ть** (**~** *perf*) **что-н от себя́** to sacrifice sth

▸ **оторва́ться** (*impf* **отрыва́ться**) *сов возв*: **~ся** (**от** *+gen*) (*от работы*) to tear o.s. away (from); (*от отряда, от бегунов, от преследователей*) to break away (from); (*от семьи, от друзей, от жизни*) to lose touch (with); (*воротник, штанина*) to tear; (*пуговица*) to come off; **отрыва́ться** (**~ся** *perf*) **от земли́** to take off.

оторопе́лый *прил* (*разг*) dumbstruck.

отороп\é|ть (**-ю**) *сов неперех* (*разг*) to be dumbstruck.
ото|сл\á|ть (**-шлю́, -шлёшь**; *impf* **отсыла́ть**) *сов перех*: ~ **кого́-н к** *+dat* to refer sb to; (*письмо, посылку*) to send (off); (*человека, машину*) to send back.
отосп|а́ться (**-лю́сь, -и́шься**; *impf* **отсыпа́ться**) *сов перех* (*разг*) to have a good sleep.
ототру́ *итп сов см* **оттере́ть**.
от|очи́ть (**-очу́, -о́чишь**) *сов перех* to sharpen.
отошёл *итп сов см* **отойти́**.
отошлю́ *итп сов см* **отосла́ть**.
отоща́|ть (**-ю**) *сов от* **тоща́ть**.
отпада́ет *итп сов см* **отпа́сть**.
отпада́|ть (**-ю**) *несов от* **отпа́сть**.
отпа́ива|ть (**-ю**) *несов от* **отпая́ть, отпои́ть**.
отпа́рива|ть (**-ю**) *несов от* **отпа́рить**.
отпари́р|овать (**-ую**) *сов от* **пари́ровать**.
отпа́р|ить (**-ю, -ишь**; *impf* **отпа́ривать**) *сов перех* (*брюки, юбку*) to steam press.
отпа́рыва|ть(ся) (**-ю(сь)**) *несов от* **отпоро́ть(ся)**.
отпа́|сть (*3sg* **-дёт**, *3pl* **-ду́т**, *impf* **отпада́ть**) *сов неперех* (*обои, штукатурка*) to come off; (*желание, необходимость*) to pass; **у меня́ ~ла охо́та идти́ туда́** I don't feel like going there any more.
отпая́|ть (**-ю**; *impf* **отпа́ивать**) *сов перех* to melt off.
отпева́ни|е (**-я**) *ср* funeral service.
отпева́|ть (**-ю**) *несов от* **отпе́ть**.
от|пере́ть (**-опру́, -опрёшь**; *pt* **-пер, -перла́, -перло**, *impf* **отпира́ть**) *сов перех* to unlock
▸ **отпере́ться** (*impf* **отпира́ться**) *сов возв* (*дверь, ворота, шкаф*) to open.
отпе́тый *прил* (*разг*) out-and-out.
отп|е́ть (**-ою́, -оёшь**; *impf* **отпева́ть**) *сов перех* (*РЕЛ*) to read a service for.
отпеча́та|ть (**-ю**; *impf* **отпеча́тывать**) *сов перех* (*также ФОТО*) to print; (*на компьютере*) to finish typing; (*следы*) to leave; (*помещение*) to open up
▸ **отпеча́таться** (*impf* **отпеча́тываться**) *сов возв* (*на земле, на песке*) to leave a print; (*перен: в памяти, в сознании*) to imprint itself.
отпеча́т|ок (**-ка**) *м* (*также перен*) imprint; **отпеча́тки па́льцев** fingerprints.
отпеча́тыва|ть(ся) (**-ю(сь)**) *несов от* **отпеча́тать(ся)**.
отпива́|ть (**-ю**) *несов от* **отпи́ть**.
отп|или́ть (**-илю́, -и́лишь**; *impf* **отпи́ливать**) *сов перех* to saw off.
отпира́тельств|о (**-а**) *ср* denial.
отпира́|ть (**-ю**) *несов от* **отпере́ть**
▸ **отпира́ться** *несов от* **отпере́ться** ◆ *возв*: **~ся** (**от** *+gen*) (*от слов итп*) to deny.
отп|иса́ться (**-ишу́сь, -и́шешься**; *impf* **отпи́сываться**) *сов неперех* (*разг*) to send a formal reply.
отпи́с|ка (**-ки**; *gen pl* **-ок**) *ж* formal reply.
отпи́сыва|ться (**-юсь**) *несов от* **отписа́ться**.
от|пи́ть (**-опью́, -опьёшь**; *impf* **отпива́ть**) *сов перех* (*полстакана итп*) to drink; ~ (*perf*) **глото́к** to take a sip.
отпихн|у́ть (**-у́, -ёшь**; *impf* **отпи́хивать**) *сов перех* (*разг*) to shove
▸ **отпихну́ться** (*impf* **отпи́хиваться**) *сов возв* (*разг*): **~ся** (**от** *+gen*) (*от берега*) to push off (from).
отпишу́сь *итп сов см* **отписа́ться**.
отпла́т|а (**-ы**) *ж* repayment (*fig*); **в ~у за** *+acc* in repayment *или* as a reward for.
отпл|ати́ть (**-ачу́, -а́тишь**; *impf* **отпла́чивать**) *сов неперех* (*+dat*; *наградить*) to repay; (*отомстить*) to pay back.
отплыва́|ть (**-ю**) *несов от* **отплы́ть**.
отплыву́ *итп сов см* **отплы́ть**.
отплы́ти|е (**-я**) *ср* (*отправление*) departure.
отплы́|ть (**-ву́, -вёшь**; *impf* **отплыва́ть**) *сов неперех* (*человек*) to swim off; (*корабль*) to set sail.
о́тповед|ь (**-и**) *ж* rebuke.
отпо|и́ть (**-ю́, -и́шь**; *impf* **отпа́ивать**) *сов перех*: ~ **кого́-н чем-н** (*разг*) to give sb sth (to drink).
отполз|ти́ (**-у́, -ёшь**; *impf* **отполза́ть**) *сов неперех* to crawl away.
отполир|ова́ть (**-у́ю**) *сов от* **полирова́ть**.
отпо́р (**-а**) *м*: **дать** ~ *+dat* (*врагу*) to repel, repulse; (*идее*) to rebuff; **получа́ть** (**получи́ть** *perf*) **реши́тельный** ~ to be rebuffed.
отп|оро́ть (**-орю́, -о́решь**; *impf* **отпа́рывать**) *сов перех* (*рукав, пуговицу*) to unstitch
▸ **отпоро́ться** (*impf* **отпа́рываться**) *сов возв* (*рукав*) to come unstitched; (*пуговица*) to come off.
отпою́ *итп сов см* **отпои́ть**.
отправи́тел|ь (**-я**) *м* sender.
отпра́в|ить (**-лю, -ишь**; *impf* **отправля́ть**) *сов перех* to send; **отправля́ть** (~ *perf*) **кого́-н на тот свет** to do away with sb
▸ **отпра́виться** (*impf* **отправля́ться**) *сов возв* (*человек*) to set off; (*поезд, теплоход*) to depart.
отпра́в|ка (**-ки**; *gen pl* **-ок**) *ж* (*письма, посылки*) posting; (*груза*) dispatch; (*поезда, теплохода*) departure.
отправле́ни|е (**-я**) *ср* (*письма, посылки*) dispatch; (*поезда, теплохода*) departure; (*обязанностей, правосудия*) administration; (*заказное, почтовое*) item; **отправле́ния органи́зма** bodily function.
отпра́влю(сь) *сов см* **отпра́вить(ся)**.
отправля́|ть (**-ю**) *несов от* **отпра́вить** ◆ *перех* (*обязанности*) to exercise; (*правосудие*) to adminster
▸ **отправля́ться** *несов от* **отпра́виться**.
отправн|о́й *прил*: ~ **пункт** point of departure; **~а́я цена́** (*КОММ*) reserve price (*BRIT*), upset price (*US*); **отправна́я то́чка** (*перен*) starting point.
отпра́здн|овать (**-ую**) *сов от* **пра́здновать**.
отпра́шива|ться (**-юсь**) *несов от* **отпроси́ться**.

отпресс|ова́ть (-у́ю) *сов от* **прессова́ть**.
отпр|оси́ться (-ошу́сь, -о́сишься; *impf* **отпра́шиваться**) *сов возв* to ask to be let off; **он ~оси́лся домо́й** he asked to be allowed to go home.
отпры́гн|уть (-у, -ешь; *impf* **отпры́гивать**) *сов неперех* to jump.
о́тпрыск (-а) *м* shoot; (*перен*) offspring.
отпря́г *итп сов см* **отпря́чь**.
отпряга́|ть (-ю) *несов от* **отпря́чь**.
отпрягу́ *итп сов см* **отпря́чь**.
отпря́н|уть (-у, -ешь) *сов неперех* to recoil.
отпря́|чь (-гу́, -жёшь *итп*, -гу́т; *pt* -г, -гла́, -гло́, *impf* **отпряга́ть**) *сов перех* to unharness.
отпугн|у́ть (-у́, -ёшь; *impf* **отпу́гивать**) *сов перех* to scare off.
о́тпуск (-а) *м* leave, holiday (*BRIT*), vacation (*US*); (*ВОЕН*) leave; (*товаров*) sale; **ежего́дный ~** annual leave; **быть** (*impf*) **в ~е** to be on holiday; **идти́ (пойти́** *perf*) **в ~** to go on holiday; **брать (взять** *perf*) **~** to take leave.
отпуска́|ть (-ю) *несов от* **отпусти́ть**.
отпускни́к (-а́) *м* holiday-maker; (*ВОЕН*) soldier on leave.
отпускни́ц|а (-ы) *ж* (*разг*) *см* **отпускни́к**.
отпускны́|е (-х; *decl like adj*) *мн* (*также:* **~ де́ньги**) holiday pay *ед*.
отп|усти́ть (-ущу́, -у́стишь; *impf* **отпуска́ть**) *сов перех* to let out; (*из рук*) to let go of; (*товар, продукты*) to sell; (*деньги, средства*) to release; (*бороду, волосы*) to grow ◆ *безл* (*разг: боль*) to ease off; **отпуска́ть** (~ *perf*) **кому́-н грехи́** (*РЕЛ*) to absolve sb of his sins; **отпуска́ть** (~ *perf*) **комплиме́нт** (*разг*) to compliment sb; **отпуска́ть** (~ *perf*) **шу́тку** (*разг*) to crack a joke.
отраба́тыва|ть (-ю) *несов от* **отрабо́тать**.
отрабо́танный *прил* (*порода*) worked out; (*газ*) waste *опред*.
отрабо́та|ть (-ю; *impf* **отраба́тывать**) *сов перех* (*долги*) to work off; (*какое-то время*) to work; (*освоить*) to work on, polish ◆ *неперех* (*кончить работать*) to finish work.
отра́в|а (-ы) *ж* poison.
отрави́тел|ь (-я) *м* poisoner.
отрави́тельниц|а (-ы) *ж см* **отрави́тель**.
отр|ави́ть (-авлю́, -а́вишь; *impf* **отравля́ть**) *сов перех* to poison; (*перен: удовольствие, праздник итп*) to spoil
▸ **отрави́ться** *сов от* **трави́ться** ◆ (*impf* **отравля́ться**) *возв* to poison o.s.; (*едой*) to get food-poisoning; (*газом итп*) to be poisoned.
отравле́ни|е (-я) *ср* poisoning.
отравлю́(сь) *сов см* **отрави́ть(ся)**.
отравля́|ть(ся) (-ю(сь)) *несов от* **отрави́ть(ся)**.
отравля́ющ|ий (-ая, -ее, -ие) *прил* poisonous, toxic.
отра́д|а (-ы) *ж* joy.
отра́д|ный (-ен, -на, -но) *прил* satisfying.
отража́тел|ь (-я) *м* reflector.
отража́|ть(ся) (-ю(сь)) *несов от* **отрази́ть(ся)**.
отраже́ни|е (-я) *ср* (*см глаг*) reflection; deflection.
отра|зи́ть (-жу́, -зи́шь; *impf* **отража́ть**) *сов перех* (*также перен*) to reflect; (*нападение, удар*) to deflect
▸ **отрази́ться** (*impf* **отража́ться**) *сов возв* (*также перен*) to be reflected; **отража́ться** (**~ся** *perf*) **на** +*prp* (*на здоровье, на успехах итп*) to have an effect on.
отрапорт|ова́ть (-у́ю) *сов от* **рапортова́ть**.
отраслево́й *прил related to a particular branch of industry*.
о́трасл|ь (-и) *ж* branch (*of research, industry*).
отр|асти́ (*3sg* -астёт, *3pl* -асту́т, *pt* -о́с, -осла́, -осло́, *impf* **отраста́ть**) *сов неперех* to grow.
отра|сти́ть (-щу́, -сти́шь; *impf* **отра́щивать**) *сов перех* to grow.
отреаги́р|овать (-ую) *сов от* **реаги́ровать**.
отре́бь|е (-я) *ср собир* (*пренебр*) scum.
отрегули́р|овать (-ую) *сов от* **регули́ровать**.
отредакти́р|овать (-ую) *сов от* **редакти́ровать**.
отре́жу *итп сов см* **отре́зать**.
отре́з (-а) *м* piece of fabric; **ли́ния ~а** dotted line.
отре́|зать (-жу, -жешь; *impf* **отреза́ть**) *сов перех* to cut off ◆ *несов перех* (*разг: резко ответить*) to cut short.
отрезве́|ть (-ю) *сов от* **трезве́ть**.
отрезв|и́ть (-лю́, -и́шь; *impf* **отрезвля́ть**) *сов перех* (*также перен*) to sober up.
отре́зка *итп сущ см* **отре́зок**.
отрезно́й *прил* (*талон*) tear-off; (*рукав*) detachable.
отре́з|ок (-ка) *м* (*ткани*) piece; (*пути*) section; (*времени*) period; (*ГЕОМ*) segment.
отрека́|ться (-юсь) *несов от* **отре́чься**.
отрекоменд|ова́ть (-у́ю) *сов от* **рекомендова́ть**.
отрёкся *итп сов см* **отре́чься**.
отреку́сь *итп сов от* **отре́чься**.
отремонти́р|овать (-ую) *сов от* **ремонти́ровать**.
отрепети́р|овать (-ую) *сов от* **репети́ровать**.
отреставри́р|овать (-ую) *сов от* **реставри́ровать**.
отрецензи́р|овать (-ую) *сов от* **рецензи́ровать**.
отрече́ни|е (-я) *ср*: **~ от** +*gen* renunciation of; **отрече́ние от престо́ла** abdication.
отр|е́чься (-еку́сь, -ечёшься *итп*, -еку́тся; *pt* -ёкся, -екла́сь, -екло́сь, *impf* **отрека́ться**) *сов возв*: **~ от** +*gen* to renounce; **отрека́ться** (~ *perf*) **от престо́ла** to abdicate.
отреша́|ться (-юсь) *несов от* **отреши́ться**.

отрешён|ный (-, -а, -о) *прил* resolute.
отреш|и́ться (-у́сь, -и́шься; *impf* **отреша́ться**) *сов возв*: ~ **от** +*gen* to reject.
отрица́ни|е (-я) *ср* denial; (*линг*) negation.
отрица́тел|ьный (-ен, -ьна, -ьно) *прил* (*также мат, элек*) negative.
отрица́|ть (-ю) *несов перех* to deny; (*литературу, моду итп*) to reject.
отро́г (-а) *м* (*гео*) spur.
о́троду *нареч*: ~ **не** +*pt* (*разг*) never; **я ~ тако́го не ви́дел** I've never ever seen anything like it.
отро́дь|е (-я) *ср* (*разг*: *пренебр*) scum.
отро́с *итп сов см* **отрасти́**.
отро́ст|ок (-ка) *м* (*побег*) shoot; (*ответвление*) branch; ~ **слепо́й кишки́** appendix.
о́трочеств|о (-а) *ср* adolescence.
отро́ю *итп сов см* **отры́ть**.
отруба́|ть (-ю) *несов от* **отруби́ть**.
о́труб|и (-е́й) *мн* bran *ед*.
отр|уби́ть (-ублю́, -у́бишь; *impf* **отруба́ть**) *сов перех* (*ветку, голову*) to chop off ◆ *неперех* (*разг*: *резко ответить*) to cut short.
отруга́|ть (-ю) *сов от* **руга́ть**.
отры́в (-а) *м*: ~ **от** +*gen* (*отряда, семьи*) separation from; **ли́ния ~а** perforated line; **учи́ться** (*impf*) **без ~а от произво́дства** *to study without giving up work*; **быть** (*impf*) **в ~е от** +*gen* to be cut off from.
отрыва́|ть (-ю) *несов от* **оторва́ть, отры́ть**
▸ **отрыва́ться** *несов от* **оторва́ться**.
отры́вист|ый (-, -а, -о) *прил* (*смех*) spasmodic; (*сигнал*) interrupted; (*речь, замечания*) disjointed.
отры́вка *итп сущ см* **отры́вок**.
отрывно́й *прил* (*блокнот, талоны*) tear-off.
отры́в|ок (-ка) *м* excerpt.
отры́воч|ный (-ен, -на, -но) *прил* fragmented, disjointed.
отрыгн|у́ть (-у́, -ёшь; *impf* **отры́гивать**) *сов* (*не*)*перех* to burp (*inf*).
отры́жк|а (-и) *ж* burp (*inf*).
отр|ы́ть (-о́ю, -о́ешь; *impf* **отрыва́ть**) *сов перех* (*также перен*) to dig up.
отря́д (-а) *м* party, group; (*воен*) detachment; (*зоол*) order; **поиско́вый** ~ search party.
отряхн|у́ть (-у́, -ёшь; *impf* **отря́хивать**) *сов перех* (*снег, пыль*) to shake off; (*пальто, сапоги*) to shake down
▸ **отряхну́ться** (*impf* **отря́хиваться**) *сов возв* to shake o.s. down.
отса|ди́ть (-жу́, -а́дишь; *impf* **отса́живать**) *сов перех* (*ученика, болтуна*) to move; (*растение, цветок*) to add new soil to.
отса́жива|ться (-юсь) *несов от* **отсе́сть**.
отсажу́ *сов см* **отсади́ть**.
отсалют|ова́ть (-у́ю) *сов от* **салютова́ть**.
отса́сыва|ть (-ю) *несов от* **отсоса́ть**.
о́тсвет (-а) *м* reflection.
отсве́чива|ть (*3sg* **-ет**, *3pl* **-ют**) *несов неперех* to reflect the light.
отсебя́тин|а (-ы) *ж* (*разг*: *пренебр*): **нести́ ~у** to say whatever comes into one's head; **занима́ться** (*impf*) **~ой** to do whatever comes into one's head.
отсе́в (-а) *м* (*действие*: *шелухи*) separation; (*то, что отсеяно*) siftings *мн*; (*кандидатов*) elimination; (*студентов*) expulsion.
отсе́ива|ть(ся) (-ю(сь)) *несов от* **отсе́ять(ся)**.
отсе́к (-а) *м* (*судна, помещения*) compartment; (*ракеты*) module.
отсёк *итп сов см* **отсе́чь**.
отсека́|ть (-ю) *несов от* **отсе́чь**.
отсеку́ *итп сов см* **отсе́чь**.
отс|е́сть (-я́ду, -я́дешь; *impf* **отса́живаться**) *сов неперех*: ~ (**от** +*gen*) to move away (from); ~ (*impf*) **пода́льше** to sit further away.
отс|е́чь (-еку́, -ечёшь *итп*, -ку́т; *pt* -ёк, -екла́, -екло́, *impf* **отсека́ть**) *сов перех* to cut off.
отсе́|ять (-ю; *impf* **отсе́ивать**) *сов перех* (*семена, шелуху*) to sift out; (*перен*: *кандидатов*) to eliminate; (: *учеников*) to expel
▸ **отсе́яться** (*impf* **отсе́иваться**) *сов возв* (*см перех*) to be separated; to be eliminated; to drop out.
отси|де́ть (-жу́, -ди́шь; *impf* **отси́живать**) *сов неперех* (*просидеть*) to wait; (*лекцию*) to sit through; (*разг*: *в тюрьме*) to do time ◆ *перех*: **я ~де́л но́гу** my leg has gone dead; **я ~де́л там два часа́** I sat (and waited) there for two hours
▸ **отсиде́ться** (*impf* **отси́живаться**) *сов возв* (*разг*) to sit tight.
отска́блива|ть (-ю) *несов от* **отскобли́ть**.
отска́кива|ть (-ю) *несов от* **отскочи́ть**.
отскобл|и́ть (-ю, -и́шь; *impf* **отска́бливать**) *сов перех* to scrub off.
отск|очи́ть (-очу́, -о́чишь; *impf* **отска́кивать**) *сов неперех*: ~ **от** +*gen* (*мяч*) to bounce off; (*человек*) to jump off; (*в сторону, назад*) to jump; (*разг*: *пуговица, кнопка*) to come off; **отска́кивать** (~ *perf*) **в сто́рону/наза́д** to jump to the side/back.
отскре|сти́ (-бу́, -бёшь; *impf* **отскреба́ть**) *сов перех* to scratch off.
отсло|и́ть (-ю́, -и́шь; *impf* **отсла́ивать**) *сов перех* to strip away.
отсл|ужи́ть (-ужу́, -у́жишь) *сов неперех* (*какое-то время*) to serve ◆ *перех* (*военную службу*) to serve out; (*панихиду, молебен*) to conduct.
отсн|я́ть (-иму́, -и́мешь) *сов перех* (*плёнку*) to finish off, use up; (*фильм, серию*) to finish shooting.
отсове́т|овать (-ую) *сов неперех*: ~ **кому́-н** +*infin* (*делать, ездить итп*) to advise sb not to do *или* against doing.
отсоедин|и́ть (-ю́, -и́шь; *impf* **отсоединя́ть**) *сов перех* to disconnect.
отсо́с (-а) *м* (*действие*) suction; (*устройство*) suction pump.
отсос|а́ть (-у́, -ёшь; *impf* **отса́сывать**) *сов перех* to draw off.
отсо́хн|уть (-у, -ешь; *impf* **отсыха́ть**) *сов*

неперех to wither.
отсрóч|ить (-у, -ишь; *impf* **отсрóчивать**) *сов перех* to defer.
отсрóчк|а (-и) *ж* deferral.
отставáни|е (-я) *ср* (*в работе, в учёбе*) falling behind; (*в развитии*) retardation.
отста|вáть (-ю́, -ёшь) *несов от* **отстáть**.
отстáв|ить (-лю, -ишь; *impf* **отставля́ть**) *сов перех* to move aside; ~! (*ВОЕН*) as you were!
отстáв|ка (-ки; *gen pl* -ок) *ж* (*ВОЕН*) retirement; (*с государственной службы*) resignation; **подавáть (подáть** *perf*) **в ~ку** to offer one's resignation; **уходи́ть (уйти́** *perf*) **в ~ку** to resign one's commission; **офицéр в ~ке** retired officer; ~ **прави́тельства/кабинéта** resignation of the government/cabinet.
отстáвлю *сов см* **отстáвить**.
отставля́|ть (-ю) *несов от* **отстáвить**.
отстáвок *сущ см* **отстáвка**.
отстáива|ть(ся) (-ю) *несов от* **отстоя́ть(ся)**.
отстáлост|ь (-и) *ж* backwardness.
отстáлый *прил* backward.
отстá|ть (-ну, -нешь; *impf* **отставáть**) *сов неперех*: ~ **(от** *+gen*) (*от группы, от друзей*) to fall behind; (*от поезда, от автобуса*) to be left behind; (*перен: в учёбе, в работе, в развитии*) to fall behind; (*обои, пластырь*) to come off; (*часы*) to be slow; **~нь от меня́!** stop pestering me!; **часы́ отстаю́т на 5 мину́т** the clock is 5 minutes slow; **отставáть (~** *perf*) **от врéмени** (*перен*) to be behind the times; **отставáть (~** *perf*) **от жи́зни** to be out of touch.
отстегá|ть (-ю) *сов от* **стегáть**.
отстегн|у́ть (-у́, -ёшь; *impf* **отстёгивать**) *сов перех* (*крючок*) to unfasten; (*капюшон, рукава*) to detach
▸ **отстегну́ться** (*impf* **отстёгиваться**) *сов возв* (*крючок*) to come unfastened.
отстирá|ть (-ю; *impf* **отсти́рывать**) *сов перех* (*пятно, грязь*) to wash out; (*рубашку, юбку*) to wash clean
▸ **отстирáться** (*impf* **отсти́рываться**) *сов возв* (*см перех*) to wash out; to wash clean.
отстó|й (-я) *м* sediment.
отстóйник (-а) *м* (*ТЕХ*) settling tank.
отсто|я́ть (-ю́, -и́шь; *impf* **отстáивать**) *сов перех* (*город, своё мнение*) to defend; (*воду, раствор*) to allow to stand; (*службу, концерт*) to stand through; (*два часа итп*) to wait; **мы ~я́ли всю слу́жбу** we stood through the whole service; **я ~я́л два часá в óчереди** I stood (and waited) for two hours in the queue ◆ *несов неперех* (*no perf*): ~ **от** *+gen* to be situated away from; **их дом ~и́т на 3 киломéтра от гóрода** their house is situated 3 kilometres from the town
▸ **отстоя́ться** (*impf* **отстáиваться**) *сов возв* to settle.
отстрáива|ть (-ю) *несов от* **отстрóить**.
отстран|и́ть (-ю́, -и́шь; *impf* **отстраня́ть**) *сов перех* (*уволить*): ~ **от** *+gen* (*от должности*) to relieve of; (*отодвинуть*) to push away
▸ **отстрани́ться** (*impf* **отстраня́ться**) *сов возв*: **~ся от** *+gen* (*от должности*) to relinquish; (*отодвинуться*) to draw back.
отстреля́|ться (-юсь; *impf* **отстрéливаться**) *сов возв*: ~ **от** *+gen* to drive back (*with gunfire*); (*разг: кончить дела*) to do one's bit.
отстр|и́чь (-игу́, -ижёшь *итп*, -игу́т; *impf* **отстригáть**) *сов перех* to cut off.
отстрó|ить (-ю, -ишь; *impf* **отстрáивать**) *сов перех* to finish building.
óтступ (-а) *м* (*в начале строки*) indentation.
отст|упи́ть (-уплю́, -у́пишь; *impf* **отступáть**) *сов неперех* to step back; (*ВОЕН*) to retreat; (*перен: перед трудностями, перед опасностью*) to give up; (*морозы, холода*) to abate; **отступáть (~** *perf*) **назáд** to step back; **он ~упи́л на 2 шагá** he took 2 steps back; **отступáть (~** *perf*) **от свои́х взгля́дов** to retreat from one's beliefs; **отступáть (~** *perf*) **от тéмы** to digress
▸ **отступи́ться** (*impf* **отступáться**) *сов возв*: **~ся от** *+gen* (*от взглядов, от требований итп*) to abandon.
отступлéни|е (-я) *ср* (*также ВОЕН*) retreat; (*от темы*) digression.
отступлю́(сь) *сов см* **отступи́ть(ся)**.
отсту́пник (-а) *м* apostate.
отсту́пниц|а (-ы) *ж см* **отсту́пник**.
отсту́пничеств|о (-а) *ср* apostasy.
отступя́ *нареч* away, off; **немнóго от** *+gen* away from.
отсу́тстви|е (-я) *ср* (*человека*) absence; (*денег, вкуса*) lack; **в ~** *+gen* in the absence of.
отсу́тств|овать (-ую) *несов неперех* (*в классе итп*) to be absent; (*желание, аппетит*) to be lacking.
отсу́тствующ|ий (-ая, -ее, -ие) *прил* (*взгляд, вид*) absent ◆ (-его: *decl like adj*) *м* absentee.
отсчёт (-а) *м* (*шагов, минут*) calculation; ~ **врéмени** time-keeping.
отсчитá|ть (-ю; *impf* **отсчи́тывать**) *сов перех* (*шаги, минуты*) to count; (*деньги*) to count out.
отсылá|ть (-ю) *несов от* **отослáть**.
отсы́лк|а (-и) *ж* cross-reference.
отсы́п|ать (-лю, -лешь; *impf* **отсыпáть**) *сов перех* (*+gen*) to pour off; **отсыпáть (~** *perf*) **комý-н чегó-н** to give sb sth.
отсыпá|ться (-юсь) *несов от* **отоспáться**.
отсы́плю *сов см* **отсы́пать**.
отсырé|ть (-ю; *impf* **отсыревáть**) *сов неперех* to get damp.
отсыхá|ть (*3sg* -ет, *3pl* -ют) *несов от* **отсóхнуть**.
отсю́да *нареч* from here; ~ **мóжно заключи́ть, что** ... from this we can conclude that ....

отсю́ду *итп сов см* **отсе́сть.**
Отта́в|а (-ы) *ж* Ottawa.
отта́ива|ть (-ю) *несов от* **оттая́ть.**
отта́лкива|ть(ся) (-ю(сь)) *несов от* **оттолкну́ть(ся).**
отта́лкивающ|ий (-ая, -ее, -ие) *прил* repellent.
отт|ащи́ть (-ащу́, -а́щишь; *impf* **отта́скивать**) *сов перех*: ~ **(от** *+gen***)** (*от огня, от окна*) to drag away (from); (*в сторону, назад*) to drag.
отта́|ять (-ю; *impf* **отта́ивать**) *сов неперех* (*земля*) to thaw; (*мясо, рыба*) to thaw out; (*перен*: *человек*) to soften ◆ *перех* (*разморозить*) to defrost.
оттен|и́ть (-ю́, -и́шь; *impf* **оттеня́ть**) *сов перех* (*рисунок, контур*) to shade in; (*перен*: *главное, подробности*) to highlight.
отте́н|ок (-ка) *м* (*также перен*) shade.
оттеня́|ть (-ю) *несов от* **оттени́ть.**
о́ттепел|ь (-и) *ж* thaw; (*полит*) the Thaw (*the period of political liberalization*).
от|тере́ть (-отру́, -отрёшь; *pt* **-тёр, -тёрла, -тёрло**, *impf* **оттира́ть**) *сов перех* (*грязь, пятно*) to rub out; (*щёки, руки*) to rub.
оттесн|и́ть (-ю́, -и́шь; *impf* **оттесня́ть**) *сов перех* to drive back.
оттира́|ть (-ю) *несов от* **оттере́ть.**
о́ттиск (-а) *м* (*ступни, ладони*) impression; (*рисунка, гравюры*) print; (*также*: **корректу́рный** ~) proof; (*статьи*) offprint.
оттого́ *нареч* that is why; ~ **что** because.
оттолкн|у́ть (-у́, -ёшь; *impf* **отта́лкивать**) *сов перех* to push away; (*перен*: *друзей*) to shun
▸ **оттолкну́ться** (*impf* **отта́лкиваться**) *сов возв*: ~**ся от** *+gen* (*от берега*) to push o.s. away *или* back from; (*перен*: *от какого-н положения, от данных*) to take as one's starting point.
оттопы́ренный *прил* (*карманы*) bulging; (*губа*) pouting; (*уши*) protruding.
оттопы́р|иться (*3sg* **-ится**, *3pl* **-ятся**, *impf* **оттопы́риваться**) *сов возв* to stick out; (*карман*) to bulge.
отто́ргн|уть (-у, -ешь; *impf* **отторга́ть**) *сов перех* (*МЕД*: *орган, ткань*) to reject; (*земли, имущество*) to seize.
отторже́ни|е (-я) *ср* (*см глаг*) rejection; seizure.
отту́да *нареч* from there.
оття́гива|ть (-ю) *несов от* **оттяну́ть.**
оття́ж|ка (-ки; *gen pl* **-ок**) *ж* delay.
отт|яну́ть (-яну́, -я́нешь; *impf* **оття́гивать**) *сов перех* to pull back; (*разг*: *человека*) to pull away; (*карман*) to stretch; (*разг*: *выполнение, решение*) to delay; **оття́гивать (**~ *impf***) вре́мя** to play for time.
отупе́лый *прил* glazed, dazed.
отупе́ни|е (-я) *ср* stupor.
отупе́|ть (-ю) *сов от* **тупе́ть.**
отутю́ж|ить (-у, -ишь) *сов от* **утю́жить.**
от|учи́ть (-учу́, -у́чишь; *impf* **отуча́ть**) *сов перех*: ~ **от** *+gen* (*от курения, от бутылки*) to wean sb off; (*+infin*; *воровать, врать*) to teach sb not to do
▸ **отучи́ться** (*impf* **отуча́ться**) *сов возв* (*+infin*) to get out of the habit of doing; **отуча́ться (**~**ся** *perf***) от плохи́х привы́чек** to get out of bad habits.
отфильтр|ова́ть (-у́ю; *impf* **отфильтро́вывать**) *сов перех* to filter off.
отфутбо́л|ить (-ю, -ишь; *impf* **отфутбо́ливать**) *сов перех* (*разг*): ~ **кого́-н** to send sb packing.
отха́ркивающ|ий (-ая, -ее, -ие) *прил* (*МЕД*): ~**ее сре́дство** expectorant.
отхв|ати́ть (-ачу́, -а́тишь; *impf* **охва́тывать**) *сов перех* (*разг*: *отрубить*) to cut off; (: *достать*) to get.
отхлебн|у́ть (-у́, -ёшь; *impf* **отхлёбывать**) *сов перех* (*разг*) to take a swig of.
отхлеста́|ть (-ю; *impf* **отхлёстывать**) *сов перех* (*разг*): ~ **кого́-н** to give sb a hiding.
отхлы́н|уть (*3sg* **-ет**, *3pl* **-ут**) *сов неперех* (*волны*) to roll back; (*кровь от лица*) to drain; (*перен*: *толпа*) to draw back.
отхо́д (-а) *м* departure; (*ВОЕН*) withdrawal; ~ **от тради́ций/действи́тельности** departure from tradition/reality; *см также* **отхо́ды.**
отх|оди́ть (-ожу́, -о́дишь) *несов от* **отойти́.**
отхо́дн|ая (-ой; *decl like adj*) *ж* (*РЕЛ*) prayer for the dying.
отхо́дчив|ый (-, -а, -о) *прил*: **он** ~ he doesn't stay angry for long.
отхо́д|ы (-ов) *мн* (*промышленности итп*) waste *мн*.
отхожу́ *несов см* **отходи́ть.**
отца́ *итп сущ см* **оте́ц.**
отцве|сти́ (-ту́, -тёшь; *impf* **отцвета́ть**) *сов неперех* to finish blossoming.
отце|ди́ть (-жу́, -дишь; *impf* **отце́живать**) *сов перех* to strain off.
отц|епи́ть (-еплю́, -е́пишь; *impf* **отцепля́ть**) *сов перех* (*вагон, паровоз*) to uncouple; (*колючку*) to unsnag
▸ **отцепи́ться** (*impf* **отцепля́ться**) *сов возв* (*вагон, паровоз*) to come uncoupled; ~**епи́сь от меня́!** (*разг*) leave me alone!
отцо́вск|ий (-ая, -ое, -ие) *прил* father's; (*перен*) paternal, fatherly.
отцо́вств|о (-а) *ср* fatherhood.
отча́ива|ться (-юсь) *несов от* **отча́яться.**
отча́л|ить (-ю, -ишь; *impf* **отча́ливать**) *сов неперех* to set sail.
отча́сти *нареч* partially.
отча́яни|е (-я) *ср* despair.
отча́янно *нареч* (*пытаться*) desperately; (*кричать*) in despair; (*спорить*) terribly.
отча́ян|ный (-, -на, -но) *прил* desperate; (*смелый*) daring; (*разг*: *врун, болтун итп*) terrible.
отча́|яться (-юсь; *impf* **отча́иваться**) *сов возв*: ~ (*+infin*) to despair (of doing).
отчего́ *нареч* (*почему*) why ◆ *союз* (*вследствие чего*) which is why; ~ **же?** (*разг*) what for?
отчего́-либо *нареч* = **отчего́-нибудь.**
отчего́-нибудь *нареч* for any reason.

отчего́-то *нареч* for some reason.
отчека́н|ить (-ю, -ишь; *impf* **отчека́нивать)** *сов перех* (*монету*) to mint; (*изделие*) to emboss; (*перен*: *слово*) to pronounce distinctly; **отчека́нивать (~** *perf***) отве́т** to answer distinctly.
о́тчеств|о (-а) *ср* patronymic.
отчёт (-а) *м* account; **фина́нсовый ~** financial report; **годово́й ~** annual report; **отдава́ть (отда́ть** *perf***) себе́ ~ в чём-н** to realize sth.
отчётлив|ый (-, -а, -о) *прил* (*звук, отпечаток*) distinct; (*объяснение, повествование*) clear.
отчётност|ь (-и) *ж* accountability ♦ *собир* (*финансовая, административная*) records *мн*.
отчётный *прил* (*собрание*) review *опред*; (*год*) current; **~ докла́д** report; **отчётный пери́од** accounting period.
отчи́зн|а (-ы) *ж* mother country.
о́тч|ий (-ая, -ее, -ие) *прил* (*ласка, совет*) fatherly; **~ дом** one's father's house.
о́тчим (-а) *м* stepfather.
отчисле́ни|е (-я) *ср* (*работника*) dismissal; (*студента*) expulsion; (*обычно мн*: *на строительство*) allocation *ед*; (: *денежные*: *удержание*) deduction; (: *выделение*) assignment.
отчи́сл|ить (-ю, -ишь; *impf* **отчисля́ть)** *сов перех* (*работника*) to dismiss; (*студента*) to expel; (*деньги*: *удержать*) to deduct; (: *выделить*) to assign
▸ **отчи́слиться** (*impf* **отчисля́ться)** *сов возв*: **~ся (из** *+gen*) to leave.
отчи́|стить (-щу, -стишь; *impf* **отчища́ть)** *сов перех* (*грязь*) to clean off; (*пятно*) to remove; (*пальто, туфли*) to clean
▸ **отчи́ститься** (*impf* **отчища́ться)** *сов возв* (*грязь*) to come off; (*пятно*) to come out; (*пальто, туфли*) to come clean.
отчита́|ть (-ю; *impf* **отчи́тывать)** *сов перех* (*ребёнка*) to tell off
▸ **отчита́ться** (*impf* **отчи́тываться)** *сов возв* to report; **отчи́тываться (~ся** *perf***) пе́ред** *+instr* **/ о** *+prp* to report to/on.
отчища́|ть(ся) (-ю(сь)) *несов от* **отчи́стить(ся)**.
отчи́щу(сь) *сов см* **отчи́стить(ся)**.
отчуд|и́ть (-и́шь) *сов перех* (*разг*): **он сего́дня тако́е ~и́л!** he did something really weird today!
отчужда́|ть (-ю) *несов перех* (*также ЮР*) to alienate.
отчужде́ни|е (-я) *ср* (*прекращение отношений*) estrangement; (*ЮР*) alienation.
отчуждённост|ь (-и) *ж* alienation.
отчуждён|ный (-, -на, -но) *прил* (*взгляд, вид*) indifferent.
отшатн|у́ться (-у́сь, -ёшься; *impf* **отша́тываться)** *сов возв* (*от удара*) to recoil; (*назад, в сторону*) to move; **отша́тываться (~** *perf***) от** *+gen* (*разг*: *от друзей итп*) to ditch.
отшвырн|у́ть (-у́, -ёшь; *impf* **отшвы́ривать)** *сов перех* (*разг*: *предмет*) to toss away; (: *человека*) to shove aside.
отше́льник (-а) *м* (*также перен*) hermit.
отше́льниц|а (-ы) *ж см* **отше́льник**.
отши́б (-а) *м*: **на ~е** (*разг*: *жить*) alone, on one's tod (*BRIT*); (*стоять*: *дом итп*) on its own.
отшиб|и́ть (-у́, -ёшь; *impf* **отшиба́ть)** *сов перех* (*разг*: *руку, ногу*) to hurt; **у меня́ па́мять отши́бло** (*разг*) my memory's gone.
отшлёпа|ть (-ю; *impf* **отшлёпывать)** *сов перех* (*разг*): **~ кого́-н** (*ребёнка*) to give sb a walloping.
отшлиф|ова́ть (-у́ю; *impf* **отшлифо́вывать)** *сов перех* (*деталь, поверхность*) to grind; (*рассказ, пьесу*) to put the finishing touches to.
отштамп|ова́ть (-у́ю) *сов от* **штампова́ть**.
отштукату́р|ить (-ю, -ишь) *сов от* **штукату́рить**.
отш|ути́ться (-учу́сь, -у́тишься; *impf* **отшу́чиваться)** *сов возв* to reply with a joke.
отщеп|и́ть (-лю́, -и́шь; *impf* **отщепля́ть)** *сов перех* (*кусочек дерева итп*) to chip off
▸ **отщепи́ться** (*impf* **отщепля́ться)** *сов возв* (*кусочек дерева итп*) to split off.
отъеда́|ться (-юсь) *несов от* **отъе́сться**.
отъе́дешь *итп сов см* **отъе́хать**.
отъеди́мся *итп сов см* **отъе́сться**.
отъе́ду *итп сов см* **отъе́хать**.
отъедя́тся *сов см* **отъе́сться**.
отъе́зд (-а) *м* departure; **быть** (*impf*) **в ~е** to be away.
отъезжа́|ть (-ю) *несов от* **отъе́хать**.
отъе́сться (*как* **есть**; *см* **Table 15**; *impf* **отъеда́ться)** *сов возв* (*после голода*) to eat one's fill; (*потолстеть*) to grow fat.
отъе́хать (*как* **е́хать**; *см* **Table 19**; *impf* **отъезжа́ть)** *сов неперех* to travel; **отъезжа́ть (~** *perf***) от** *+gen* to move away from.
отъе́шься *сов см* **отъе́сться**.
отъя́вленный *прил* (*мошенник итп*) absolute.
отыгра́|ть (-ю; *impf* **оты́грывать)** *сов перех* to win back
▸ **отыгра́ться** (*impf* **оты́грываться)** *сов возв* (*в карты, в шахматы*) to win again; (*перен*) to get one's own back.
от|ыска́ть (-ыщу́, -ы́щешь; *impf* **оты́скивать)** *сов перех* to hunt out; (*КОМП*) to retrieve
▸ **отыска́ться** (*impf* **оты́скиваться)** *сов возв* to turn up.
отяго|ти́ть (-щу́, -ти́шь; *impf* **отягоща́ть)** *сов перех*: **~ кого́-н чем-н** to burden sb with sth.
отягча́ющ|ий (-ая, -ее, -ие) *прил*: **~ие обстоя́тельства** (*ЮР*) aggravating circumstances.
отягч|и́ть (-у́, -и́шь; *impf* **отягча́ть)** *сов перех*

(*вину, положение*) to aggravate.

отяжелé|ть (**-ю**) *сов от* **тяжелéть**.

óфис (**-а**) *м* office.

офицéр (**-а**) *м* (*ВОЕН*) officer; (*разг*: *ШАХМАТЫ*) bishop.

офицéрск|ий (**-ая, -ое, -ие**) *прил* (*звание, форма*) officer's; (*комната, столовая*) officers'.

офицéрств|о (**-а**) *ср собир* officers *мн*.

официáл|ьный (**-ен, -ьна, -ьно**) *прил* official; **официáльное лицó** official.

официáнт (**-а**) *м* waiter.

официáнт|ка (**-ки**; *gen pl* **-ок**) *ж* waitress.

официóз|ный (**-ен, -на, -но**) *прил*: **~ная газéта** *newspaper which supports the government*.

оформúтел|ь (**-я**) *м*: **~ интерьéра/спектáкля** interior/set designer; **~ витрúны** window-dresser.

оформúтельниц|а (**-ы**) *ж см* **оформúтель**.

офóрм|ить (**-лю, -ишь**; *impf* **оформля́ть**) *сов перех* (*книгу*) to design the layout of; (*витрину*) to dress; (*спектакль*) to design the sets for; (*документы, договор*) to draw up; **оформля́ть** (**~** *perf*) **когó-н на рабóту** (**+***instr*) to take sb on (as)

▸ **офóрмиться** (*impf* **оформля́ться**) *сов возв* (*мнение, взгляды*) to form; **оформля́ться** (**~ся** *perf*) **на рабóту** (**+***instr*) to be taken on (as).

оформлéни|е (**-я**) *ср* design; (*документов, договора*) drawing up; (*на работу*) taking on; **музыкáльное ~** music.

офóрмлю(сь) *сов см* **офóрмить(ся)**.

оформля́|ть(ся) (**-ю(сь)**) *несов от* **офóрмить(ся)**.

офóрт (**-а**) *м* etching.

офсéт (**-а**) *м* offset (process).

офтальмóлог (**-а**) *м* ophthalmologist.

ох *межд* oh.

охáива|ть (**-ю**) *несов от* **охáять**.

охамé|ть (**-ю**) *сов от* **хамéть**.

охáп|ка (**-ки**; *gen pl* **-ок**) *ж* armful; **схватúть** (*perf*) **что-н в ~ку** to grab sth in one's arms.

охарактериз|овáть (**-ýю**) *сов от* **характеризовáть**.

óха|ть (**-ю**) *несов неперех* (*от боли*) to groan; (*от сожаления, печали*) to sigh.

охá|ять (**-ю**; *impf* **охáивать**) *сов перех* (*разг*) to slate (*BRIT*), to slag (off).

охв|атúть (**-ачý, -áтишь**; *impf* **охвáтывать**) *сов перех* (*подлеж: пламя, чувства, темнота*) to engulf; (*подписчиков, население*) to cover; (*ВОЕН*) to envelop; **охвáтывать** (**~** *perf*) **что-н чем-н** (*руками, лентой*) to put sth round sth; **охвáтывать** (**~** *perf*) **взгля́дом** to take in; **охвáтывать** (**~** *perf*) **умóм** to grasp.

охладé|ть (**-ю**; *impf* **охладевáть**) *сов неперех* (*отношения*) to cool; **охладевáть** (**~** *perf*) **к** *+dat* (*к мужу, к невесте*) to grow cool towards; (*к футболу, к сладкому*) to go off.

охла|дúть (**-жý, -дúшь**; *impf* **охлаждáть**) *сов перех* (*воду, чувства*) to cool; (*забияку*) to cool down

▸ **охладúться** (*impf* **охлаждáться**) *сов возв* (*печка, вода*) to cool down; (*человек: водой*) to cool off.

охлаждéни|е (**-я**) *ср* (*также перен*) cooling.

охлажý(сь) *сов см* **охладúть(ся)**.

охламóн (**-а**) *м* (*разг: пренебр*) loafer.

охмур|úть (**-ю, -úшь**; *impf* **охмуря́ть**) *сов перех* (*разг*) to lead on.

óхн|уть (**-у, -ешь**) *сов неперех* to gasp.

охóт|а (**-ы**) *ж* hunt; (*желание*): **~ к чемý-н/**+*infin* desire for sth/to do; **~ на лис** fox hunting (*to kill*); **~ за лисóй** fox hunting (*to catch*); **ходúть/идтú (пойтú** *perf*) **на ~у** to go hunting; **~ за престýпником/убúйцей** the hunt for a criminal/murderer; **мне ~ посмотрéть э́ту передáчу** (*разг*) I fancy watching that programme; **что Вам за ~ спóрить с ней?** (*разг*) what do you get out of arguing with her?; **~ тебé спóрить!** (*разг*) do you really have to argue?

охó|титься (**-чусь, -тишься**) *несов возв*: **~ на** *+acc* to hunt (*to kill*); **~** (*impf*) **за** *+instr* to hunt (*to catch*); (*перен: разг*) to hunt for.

охóтник (**-а**) *м* hunter; **~** *+infin* volunteer to do; **быть** (*impf*) **большúм ~ом до** *+gen* (*разг: до женщин, сладкого*) to be crazy about.

охóтнич|ий (**-ья, -ье, -ьи**) *прил* hunting *опред*.

охóтно *нареч* gladly.

охóчусь *несов см* **охóтиться**.

óхр|а (**-ы**) *ж* ochre, ocher (*US*).

охрáн|а (**-ы**) *ж* (*защита: помещения, президента*) security; (*группа людей: президента*) bodyguard; (*: помещения*) guard; (*здоровья, растений, животных*) protection; **под ~ой закóна** protected by law; **охрáна поря́дка** maintenance of law and order; **охрáна прирóды** nature conservation; **охрáна трудá** health and safety regulations *мн*.

охранéни|е (**-я**) *ср* (*также ВОЕН*) protection.

охрáнник (**-а**) *м* guard.

охрáнниц|а (**-ы**) *ж см* **охрáнник**.

охрáнн|ый *прил* (*зона, территория*) guarded; **~ая рóта** security company.

охраня́|ть (**-ю**) *несов перех* (*помещение, президента*) to guard; (*здоровье*) to look after; (*природу*) to protect.

охрúплый *прил* (*разг: голос, крик*) hoarse.

охрúпн|уть (**-у, -ешь**) *сов от* **хрúпнуть**.

охрúпш|ий (**-ая, -ее, -ие**) *прил* hoarse.

охромé|ть (**-ю**) *сов неперех* to go lame.

оцарáпа|ть(ся) (**-ю(сь)**) *сов от* **царáпать(ся)**.

оц|енúть (**-еню́, -éнишь**; *impf* **оцéнивать**) *сов перех* (*определить цену*) to value; (*определить уровень*) to assess; (*признать достоинства*) to appreciate; **оцéнивать** (**~** *perf*) **что-н по достóинству** to appreciate the true value of sth.

оцéн|ка (**-ки**; *gen pl* **-ок**) *ж* (*вещи*) valuation; (*работника, поступка*) assessment; (*отметка*) mark.

оце́нщик (**-а**) *м* valuer.
оцепене́лый *прил* (*взгляд, человек*) stunned; **оцепене́лое состоя́ние** stupor.
оцепене́ни|е (**-я**) *ср* numbness; (*БИО*) dormancy.
оцепене́|ть (**-ю**) *сов от* **цепене́ть**.
оц|епи́ть (**-еплю́, -е́пишь**; *impf* **оцепля́ть**) *сов перех* to cordon off.
оцепле́ни|е (**-я**) *ср* (*действие*) cordoning off; (*группа*) cordon.
оцеплю́ *сов см* **оцепи́ть**.
оцепля́|ть (**-ю**) *несов от* **оцепи́ть**.
оцинк|ова́ть (**-у́ю**; *impf* **оцинко́вывать**) *сов перех* (*ТЕХ*) to galvanize.
оча́г (**-а́**) *м* hearth; (*перен*: *заболевания*) source; (: *культуры*) heart; **~ войны́** flash point; **дома́шний ~** hearth and home.
очарова́ни|е (**-я**) *ср* charm.
очарова́тел|ьный (**-ен, -ьна, -ьно**) *прил* charming.
очар|ова́ть (**-у́ю**; *impf* **очаро́вывать**) *сов перех* to charm.
очеви́ден *прил см* **очеви́дный**.
очеви́д|ец (**-ца**) *м* eyewitness.
очеви́дно *нареч, част* obviously ◆ *как сказ*: **~, что он винова́т** it's obvious that he is guilty ◆ *вводн сл*: **~, он не придёт** apparently he's not coming; **э́то соверше́нно ~!** it is perfectly obvious!; **он винова́т? – ~!** is he guilty? – obviously!
очеви́д|ный (**-ен, -но, -на**) *прил* (*факт, истина*) plain; (*желание, намерение*) obvious.
очеви́дца *итп сущ см* **очеви́дец**.
о́чень *нареч* (*+adv, +adj*) very; (*+vb*) very much; **~ удо́бный/удо́бно** very comfortable/comfortably; **мы ~ хоти́м, что́бы она́ пришла́** we would very much like her to come.
очередно́й *прил* next; (*ближайший*: *задача*) immediate; (: *номер газеты*) latest; (*следующий по порядку*: *собрание, отпуск*) regular; (*повторяющийся*: *ссора, глупость*) usual.
о́черед|ь (**-и**) *ж* (*порядок*) order; (*место в порядке*) turn; (*группа людей*) queue (*BRIT*), line (*US*); (*тоннеля, завода итп*) section; **в пе́рвую ~** in the first instance; **в поря́дке ~и** when one's turn comes; **в свою́ ~** in turn; **~ за ни́ми** it is their turn; **по ~и** in turn; **стоя́ть** *(impf)* **на ~и на** *+acc* (*на квартиру итп*) to be on the waiting list for; **пулемётная ~** (*ВОЕН*) burst of automatic rifle fire; **на ~и стои́т вопро́с/зада́ча** this is the next question/task.
о́черк (**-а**) *м* (*литературный*) essay; (*газетный*) sketch.
очерн|и́ть (**-ю́, -и́шь**) *сов от* **черни́ть**.
очерстве́|ть (**-ю**) *сов от* **черстве́ть**.
очерта́ни|е (**-я**) *ср* (*обычно мн*) outline *ед*.
оч|ерти́ть (**-ерчу́, -е́ртишь**; *impf* **оче́рчивать**) *сов перех* to outline.
оче́чник (**-а**) *м* spectacle case.
оч|ини́ть (**-иню́, -и́нишь**; *impf* **очиня́ть**) *сов перех* to sharpen.
очисти́тельный *прил* purifying, purification *опред*.
очи́|стить (**-щу, -стишь**; *impf* **очища́ть**) *сов перех* to clean; (*газ, воду*) to purify; (*совесть, город, квартиру*) to clear; (*душу*) to cleanse; (*разг*: *обокрасть*: *дом итп*) to clean out; (*impf* **очища́ть** *или* **чи́стить**; *яблоко, картошку*) to peel; (*рыбу*) to clean
▸ **очи́ститься** (*impf* **очища́ться**) *сов возв* (*газ, вода*) to be purified; (*перен*: *совесть*) to be cleared; (: *душа*) to be cleansed; **не́бо ~стилось от туч** the sky cleared.
очи́стк|а (**-и**) *ж* purification; **для ~и со́вести** to ease one's conscience; *см также* **очи́стки**.
очи́стк|и (**-ов**) *мн* peelings *мн*.
очистн|о́й *прил*: **~ы́е сооруже́ния** purification plant *ед*.
очища́|ть(ся) (**-ю(сь)**) *несов от* **очи́стить(ся)**.
очи́щенный *прил* (*ХИМ*) purified; (*яблоко, картошка*) peeled; (*рыба*) cleaned.
очи́щу(сь) *сов см* **очи́стить(ся)**.
очк|и́ (**-о́в**) *мн* (*для чтения*) glasses *мн*, spectacles *мн*; (*для плавания*) goggles *мн*; **со́лнечные ~** sunglasses; **защи́тные ~** safety specs.
очк|о́ (**-а**) *ср* (*СПОРТ*) point; (*КАРТЫ*) pip; **дать** *(perf)* **сто ~в вперёд** to be miles better.
очковтира́тел|ь (**-я**) *м* deceiver.
очковтира́тельств|о (**-а**) *ср* deception.
очко́в|ый *прил*: **~ая змея́** cobra.
очн|у́ться (**-у́сь, -ёшься**) *сов возв* (*после сна*) to wake up; (*после обморока*) to come to; (*после испуга*) to steady o.s.
о́чный *прил* (*обучение, институт итп*) *with direct contact between students and teachers*; **о́чная ста́вка** (*ЮР*) confrontation.
очуме́|ть (**-ю**) *сов неперех* (*разг*) to go off one's head.
оч|ути́ться (*2sg* **-у́тишься**, *3sg* **-у́тится**) *сов возв* to find o.s.
ошара́ш|ить (**-у, -ишь**; *impf* **ошара́шивать**) *сов перех* (*разг*: *вопросом, поведением*) to dumbfound.
оше́йник (**-а**) *м* collar.
ошеломи́тел|ьный (**-ен, -ьна, -ьно**) *прил* stunning.
ошелом|и́ть (**-лю́, -и́шь**; *impf* **ошеломля́ть**) *сов перех* to stun.
ошеломля́ющ|ий (**-ая, -ее, -ие**; **-, -а, -е**) *прил* = **ошеломи́тельный**.
ош|иби́ться (**-ибу́сь, -ибёшься**; *pt* **-и́бся, -и́блась, -и́блось**, *impf* **ошиба́ться**) *сов возв* to make a mistake; **ошиба́ться** (**~** *perf*) **в ком-н** to misjudge sb.
оши́б|ка (**-ки**; *gen pl* **-ок**) *ж* mistake, error; (*КОМП*)

bug; **по ~ке** by mistake.
ошибоч|ный (-ен, -на, -но) *прил* (*мнение, представление*) mistaken, erroneous; (*суждение, вывод*) wrong.
ошива́|ться (-юсь) *несов возв* (*разг*: *пренебр*) to hang about.
ошпа́р|ить (-ю, -ишь; *impf* **ошпа́ривать)** *сов перех* (*разг*: *ногу, палец, помидор*) to scald
▸ **ошпа́риться** (*impf* **ошпа́риваться**) *сов возв* (*разг*) to scald o.s.
оштраф|ова́ть (-у́ю) *сов от* **штрафова́ть.**
оштукату́р|ить (-ю, -ишь) *сов от* **штукату́рить.**
ощен|и́ться (*3sg* **-и́тся**, *3pl* **-я́тся**) *сов от* **щени́ться.**
ощети́нива|ться (*3sg* **-ется**, *3pl* **-ются**) *несов* = **щети́ниться.**
ощети́н|иться (*3sg* **-ится**, *3pl* **-ятся**) *сов от* **щети́ниться.**
ощ|ипа́ть (-иплю́, -и́плешь) *сов от* **щипа́ть.**
щи́пыва|ть (-ю) *несов перех* = **щипа́ть.**
ощу́па|ть (-ю; *impf* **ощу́пывать)** *сов перех* (*стол*) to feel for; (*лицо*) to feel.
о́щуп|ь (-и) *ж*: **на ~** by touch; **пробира́ться** (*impf*) **на ~** to grope one's way through.
о́щупью *нареч* by touch; (*перен*) blindly; **пробира́ться** (*impf*) **~** to grope one's way through.
ощути́м|ый (-, -а, -о) *прил* (*потепление, запах*) noticeable; (*успех, расходы*) appreciable.
ощути́тел|ьный (-ен, -ьна, -ьно) *прил* = **ощути́мый.**
ощу|ти́ть (-щу́, -ти́шь; *impf* **ощуща́ть)** *сов перех* (*запах*) to notice; (*радость, желание, боль*) to feel.
ощуща́|ть (-ю) *несов от* **ощути́ть.**
ощуще́ни|е (-я) *ср* (*прикосновения, запаха*) sense; (*радости, боли*) feeling.
ощущу́ *сов см* **ощути́ть.**
ОЭСР *ж сокр* (= *Организа́ция экономи́ческого сотру́дничества и разви́тия*) OECD (= *Organization for Economic Cooperation and Development*).
оягн|и́ться (*3sg* **-и́тся**, *3pl* **-я́тся**) *сов от* **ягни́ться.**

~ П, п ~

П, п *сущ нескл* (*буква*) *the 16th letter of the Russian alphabet.*
п. *сокр* (= **пара́граф**) par. (= *paragraph*); = **посёлок.**
па *ср нескл* (dance) step.
п.а. *сокр* (= *почто́вый а́дрес*) postal address.
павиа́н (**-а**) *м* baboon.
павильо́н (**-а**) *м* pavilion; (*КИНО*) studio.
павли́н (**-а**) *м* peacock.
па́вод|ок (**-ка**) *м* flood.
па́губ|ный (**-ен, -на, -но**) *прил* (*последствия*) ruinous; (*влияние, привычка*) pernicious.
па́дал|ь (**-и**) *ж собир* carrion.
па́да|ть (**-ю**; *perf* **упа́сть** *или* **пасть**) *несов неперех* to fall; (*настроение*) to sink; (*дисциплина, нравы*) to decline; (*умирать: животное*) to die; (*no perf; снег*) to fall; ~ (**упа́сть** *perf*) **на** *+acc* (*ложиться: тень*) to fall on; ~ (**пасть** *perf*) **на** *+acc* (*подозрение*) to fall on; (*ответственность*) to fall to *или* on; ~ (**упа́сть** *perf*) **ду́хом** to lose heart; **у неё упа́ло настрое́ние** her spirits sank; ~ (**упа́сть** *perf*) **в чьих-н глаза́х** to fall in sb's estimation; ~ (**упа́сть** *perf*) **в о́бморок** to faint.
паде́ж (**-а́**) *м* (*линг*) case.
паде́жный *прил* (*линг*) case *опред.*
Па-де-Кале́ *м нескл* Pas de Calais.
паде́ни|е (**-я**) *ср* (*также перен*) fall; (*нравов, дисциплины*) decline.
па́д|кий (**-кая, -кое, -кие; -ок, -ка, -ко**) *прил*: ~ **на** *+acc* greedy for.
паду́ *итп сов см* **пасть.**
па́дчериц|а (**-ы**) *ж* stepdaughter.
па́дш|ий (**-ая, -ее, -ие**) *прил* fallen.
паев|о́й *прил* (*ЭКОН*) share *опред*; **на ~ы́х нача́лах** on a shareholder basis.
па|ёк (**-йка́**) *м* ration; **сухо́й** ~ dry ration.
паж (**-а́**) *м* page(boy).
ПАЗ *м сокр* = *Па́вловский авто́бусный заво́д*; (*авто́бус*) *vehicle manufactured at the Pavlovsk car factory.*
паз (**-а**; *loc sg* **-у́**, *nom pl* **-ы**) *м* (*ТЕХ*) groove.
па́зух|а (**-и**) *ж* bosom; **держа́ть** *(impf)* **ка́мень за ~ой на кого́-н** to bear a grudge against sb, bear sb a grudge; **жить** *(impf)* **как у Христа́ за ~ой** (*разг*) to be without a care in the world.

па|й (**-я**; *nom pl* **-и́**) *м* (*ЭКОН*) share; **на ~я́х** jointly.
пайка́ *итп сущ см* **паёк.**
па́йщик (**-а**) *м* shareholder.
пакга́уз (**-а**) *м* warehouse.
паке́т (**-а**) *м* (*бумажный свёрток, КОМП*) package; (*мешок*) (paper *или* plastic) bag; (*конверт*) official envelope (*containing important or secret documents*); (*КОММ*): (**контро́льный**) ~ **а́кций** (controlling) shareholding; ~ **програ́мм** (*КОМП*) software package; ~ **прикладны́х програ́мм** (*КОМП*) applications package.
паке́т|ный *прил*: **~ая обрабо́тка** (*КОМП*) batch processing.
Пакиста́н (**-а**) *м* Pakistan.
пакиста́н|ец (**-ца**) *м* Pakistani.
пакиста́н|ка (**-ки**; *gen pl* **-ок**) *ж см* **пакиста́нец.**
пакиста́нск|ий (**-ая, -ое, -ие**) *прил* Pakistani.
пакиста́нца *сущ см* **пакиста́нец.**
пак|ова́ть (**-у́ю**; *perf* **запакова́ть** *или* **упакова́ть**) *несов перех* to pack.
па́костен *прил см* **па́костный.**
па́ко|стить (**-щу, -стишь**; *perf* **запа́костить**) *несов перех* (*разг*) to soil, dirty ◆ (*perf* **напа́костить**) *неперех*: ~ (**кому́-н**) to play a dirty trick (on sb).
па́кост|ный (**-ен, -на, -но**) *прил* (*разг*) vile, nasty.
па́кощу *несов см* **па́костить.**
пакт (**-а**) *м* pact.
ПАЛ *сокр* PAL (= *phase alternation line*).
пала́с (**-а**) *м double-sided woven rug.*
пала́т|а (**-ы**) *ж* (*в больнице*) ward; (*полит*) chamber, house; **ве́рхняя/ни́жняя** ~ (*полит*) Upper/Lower Chamber; ~ **о́бщин/ло́рдов** House of Commons/Lords; **Кни́жная** ~ Book Chamber (*Bibliographical centre in Moscow*); **Торго́вая** ~ Chamber of Commerce.
пала́т|ка (**-ки**; *gen pl* **-ок**) *ж* (*туристическая*) tent; (*ларёк*) stall.
пала́ч (**-а́**) *м* executioner.
Палести́н|а (**-ы**) *ж* Palestine.
палести́нск|ий (**-ая, -ое, -ие**) *прил* Palestinian.
па́л|ец (**-ьца**) *м* (*руки*) finger; (*ноги*) toe; **безымя́нный** ~ fourth *или* ring finger; **большо́й** ~ (*руки*) thumb; (*ноги*) big toe;

сре́дний ~ middle finger; **указа́тельный** ~ index finger; **знать** *(impf)* **что-н как свой пять ~ьцев** to know sth like the back of one's hand; **он ~ о ~ не уда́рил, он па́льцем не шевельну́л** he didn't lift a finger; **смотре́ть** *(impf)* **сквозь ~ьцы на что-н** to shut one's eyes to sth.
палиса́дник (-а) *м* (small) front garden (*BRIT*) *или* yard (*US*).
пали́тр|а (-ы) *ж* (*также перен*) palette.
пал|и́ть (-ю́, -и́шь; *perf* **опали́ть**) *несов перех* (*волосы*) to singe; (*perf* **спали́ть**; *подлеж*: *солнце*) to scorch; (*perf* **вы́палить**; *разг*: *стрелять*) to fire.
па́л|ка (-ки; *gen pl* **-ок**) *ж* stick; **лы́жные ~ки** ski poles; **де́лать (сде́лать** *perf*) **что-н из-под ~ки** (*разг*) to be bludgeoned into doing sth; **э́то ~ о двух конца́х** it cuts both ways; **~ки в колёса вставля́ть** *(impf)* **кому́-н** to put a spoke in sb's wheel.
пало́мник (-а) *м* pilgrim.
пало́мничеств|о (-а) *ср* pilgrimage.
па́лоч|ка (-ки; *gen pl* **-ек**) *ж уменьш от* **па́лка**; (*МЕД*) bacillus (*мн* bacilli); **дирижёрская** ~ (conductor's) baton; **волше́бная** ~ magic wand.
па́лочн|ый *прил*: **~ая дисципли́на** (*перен*) heavy-handed discipline.
па́луб|а (-ы) *ж* (*МОР*) deck.
па́льм|а (-ы) *ж* palm (tree).
пальто́ *ср нескл* overcoat.
па́льца *итп сущ см* **па́лец**.
памфле́т (-а) *м* lampoon.
па́мятен *прил см* **па́мятный**.
па́мят|ка (-ки; *gen pl* **-ок**) *ж* (*туриста, отдыхающих*) guidelines *мн*; (*на работе*) memorandum (*мн* memoranda).
па́мятник (-а) *м* monument; (*на могиле*) tombstone; (*археологический*) relic; **~и старины́** ancient monuments; **па́мятники пи́сьменности** ancient manuscripts.
па́мят|ный (-ен, -на, -но) *прил* (*незабываемый*) memorable; (*no short form*; *сделанный в память*) commemorative.
па́мяток *сущ см* **па́мятка**.
па́мят|ь (-и) *ж* (*также КОМП*) memory; (*воспоминание*) memories *мн*; **в чью-н ~, в ~ о ком-н** in memory of sb; **на ~** (*читать стихи*) from memory; (*подарить, взять*) as a memento; **быть** *(impf)* **без ~и** to be unconscious; **он лю́бит её без ~и** (*разг*) he is crazy about her; **она́ без ~и от э́того актёра** (*разг*) she's mad about that actor.
Пана́м|а (-ы) *ж* Panama.
пана́м|а (-ы) *ж* Panama (hat).
пана́мск|ий (-ая, -ое, -ие) *прил*: **П~ кана́л** Panamanian Canal.
панаце́|я (-и) *ж* panacea.
па́нд|а (-ы) *ж* panda.
пандеми́|я (-и) *ж* pandemia.
пане́л|ь (-и) *ж* (*тротуар*) pavement (*BRIT*), sidewalk (*US*); (*СТРОИТ*) panel; (*ТЕХ*) control panel.
панибра́тств|о (-а) *ср* familiarity.
па́ник|а (-и) *ж* panic.
паник|ова́ть (-у́ю) *несов неперех* (*разг*) to panic.
панихи́д|а (-ы) *ж* (*РЕЛ*) funeral service; **гражда́нская** ~ civil funeral.
пани́ческ|ий (-ая, -ое, -ие) *прил* (*состояние, бегство итп*) panic-stricken; (*слухи*) alarming.
панно́ *ср нескл* decorative panel.
панора́м|а (-ы) *ж* panorama.
пансио́н (-а) *м* (*школа*) boarding school; (*полное содержание*) (full) board and lodging.
пансиона́т (-а) *м* boarding house.
пантео́н (-а) *м* pantheon.
панте́р|а (-ы) *ж* panther.
пантоми́м|а (-ы) *ж* mime.
па́нцир|ь (-я) *м* (*черепахи*) shell; (*рыцаря*) coat of armour (*BRIT*) *или* armor (*US*).
па́п|а (-ы) *м* dad; (*также*: **Ри́мский** ~) the Pope.
папа́х|а (-и) *ж* papakha (*tall fur cap*).
папа́ш|а (-и) *м* (*разг*: *папа*) old man; (: *как обращение*) grandad.
па́перт|ь (-и) *ж* church porch.
папиро́с|а (-ы) *ж* *type of cheap Russian cigarette with cardboard filter*.
папиро́сн|ый *прил*: **~ая бума́га** (*для курения*) cigarette paper; (*тонкая бумага*) tissue paper.
папи́рус (-а) *м* papyrus.
па́п|ка (-ки; *gen pl* **-ок**) *ж* folder (*BRIT*), file (*US*).
па́поротник (-а) *м* fern.
папье́-маше́ *ср нескл* papier-mâché.
пар (-а; *loc sg* **-у́**, *nom pl* **-ы́**) *м* steam; (*С-Х*) fallow land; **на всех ~а́х** (*перен*) full steam ahead; *см также* **пары́**.
па́р|а (-ы) *ж* (*туфель итп*) pair; (*супружеская*) couple; (*ПРОСВЕЩ*) ≈ poor (*school mark*); **~ слов/мину́т** (*разг*) a couple of words/minutes; **рабо́тать** *(impf)***/игра́ть** *(impf)* **в ~е с кем-н** to work/play with sb; **э́то ~ пустяко́в** (*разг*) it's child's play; **они́ два сапога́ ~** (*разг*) they are as bad as each other.
Парагва́|й (-я) *м* Paraguay.
пара́граф (-а) *м* paragraph.
пара́д (-а) *м* parade; **в по́лном** *или* **при всём ~е** (*разг*) dressed up to the nines.
пара́дн|ая (-ой; *decl like adj*) *ж* = **пара́дное**.
пара́дн|ое (-ого; *decl like adj*) *ср* entrance.
пара́дн|ый *прил* (*обед*) formal; (*стол*) festive; (*вид*) smart (*BRIT*), stylish (*US*); (*вход, лестница*) front *опред*, main; **пара́дный костю́м, пара́дная фо́рма** full dress.
парадо́кс (-а) *м* paradox.
парадокса́л|ьный (-ен, -ьна, -ьно) *прил* paradoxical.
парази́т (-а) *м* parasite.
парализ|ова́ть (-у́ю) *(не)сов перех* (*также перен*) to paralyze; **у́жас ~ова́л его́** he was paralyzed with fear.
парали́ч (-а́) *м* paralysis.
паралле́лен *прил см* **паралле́льный**.

паралле́л|ь (**-и**) *ж* (*также перен*) parallel.
паралле́л|ьный (**-ен, -ьна, -ьно**) *прил* parallel.
параме́дик (**-а**) *м* paramedic.
пара́метр (**-а**) *м* (*также перен*) parameter; (*КОМП*) default option.
паранджа́ (**-и́**) *ж* yashmak.
парано́й|я (**-и**) *ж* paranoia.
парапе́т (**-а**) *м* parapet.
парапсихоло́ги|я (**-и**) *ж* parapsychology.
парафи́н (**-а**) *м* paraffin (wax).
парафи́новый *прил* paraffin *опред*.
парашю́т (**-а**) *м* parachute.
парашюти́ст (**-а**) *м* parachutist.
парашюти́ст|ка (**-ки**; *gen pl* **-ок**) *ж см* **парашюти́ст**.
па́р|ень (**-ня**; *gen pl* **-не́й**) *м* (*разг*: *юноша*) lad, boy; (: *мужчина*) chap *или* fellow (*BRIT*), guy (*US*); **он сво́й ~** (*разг*) he's an easy-going guy.
пари́ *ср нескл* bet; **держа́ть** (*impf*) **~, что ...** to bet that ...; **заключа́ть (заключи́ть** *perf*) **~ с кем-н (на что-н)** to make a bet with sb (about sth).
Пари́ж (**-а**) *м* Paris.
парижа́н|ин (**-ина**; *nom pl* **-е**, *gen pl* **-**) *м* Parisian.
парижа́н|ка (**-ки**; *gen pl* **-ок**) *ж* Parisienne.
пари́жск|ий (**-ая, -ое, -ие**) *прил* Parisian.
пари́к (**-а́**) *м* wig.
парикма́хер (**-а**) *м* hairdresser.
парикма́херск|ая (**-ой**; *decl like adj*) *ж* hairdresser's (*BRIT*), beauty salon (*US*).
пари́л|ка (**-ки**; *gen pl* **-ок**) *ж* steam room (*in sauna*).
пари́р|овать (**-ую**; *perf* **пари́ровать** *или* **отпари́ровать**) *несов перех* (*также перен*) to parry.
парите́т (**-а**) *м* parity.
па́р|ить (**-ю, -ишь**) *несов перех* (*овощи*) to steam
▸ **па́риться** *несов возв* (*овощи*) to be steamed; (*в бане*) to have a sauna; (*разг*: *в тёплой одежде*) to sweat.
пар|и́ть (**-ю́, -и́шь**) *несов неперех* to glide; **~** (*impf*) **в облака́х** (*перен*) to have one's head in the clouds.
парк (**-а**) *м* park; (*трамвайный*) depot; **ваго́нный ~** rolling stock; **автомоби́льный ~** fleet of cars.
парке́т (**-а**) *м* parquet.
парк|ова́ть (**-у́ю**) *несов перех* to park.
парла́мент (**-а**) *м* parliament.
парламента́ри|й (**-я**) *м* parliamentarian.
парла́ментск|ий (**-ая, -ое, -ие**) *прил* parliamentary.
парни́к (**-а́**) *м* (*из стекла*) greenhouse; (*из полиэтилена*) (poly)tunnel.
парнико́в|ый *прил* (*растение*) hothouse *опред*; **~ое хозя́йство** glasshouse nursery; **парнико́вый эффе́кт** greenhouse effect.
парно́й *прил* fresh.
па́рн|ый *прил*: **~ боти́нок/носо́к** one of a pair of boots/socks; **~ое ка́танье (на конька́х)** pairs' ice-skating; **где ~ боти́нок?** where is the other boot?
па́рня *итп сущ см* **па́рень**.
парово́з (**-а**) *м* steam engine *или* locomotive.
парово́й *прил* steam *опред*.
пароди́р|овать (**-ую**) (*не*)*сов перех* to parody.
паро́ди|я (**-и**) *ж* (*также перен*): **~ (на** +*acc*) parody (of).
паро́л|ь (**-я**) *м* password.
паро́м (**-а**) *м* ferry.
парохо́д (**-а**) *м* steamer, steamship.
парохо́дств|о (**-а**) *ср* shipping; (*учреждения*) ≈ port and navigation authority; (*фирма*) shipping company.
па́рт|а (**-ы**) *ж* desk.
партбиле́т (**-а**) *м сокр* (= *парти́йный биле́т*) (Party) membership card (*of the Communist Party*).
парте́р (**-а**) *м* the stalls *мн*.
партиза́н (**-а**; *gen pl* **-**) *м* partisan, guerrilla.
парти́йн|ый *прил* (*съезд*) party *опред* ◆ (**-ого**; *decl like adj*) *м* Party member.
партиту́р|а (**-ы**) *ж* score.
па́рти|я (**-и**) *ж* (*полит*) party; (: *в СССР*) the (Communist) Party; (*муз*) part; (*груза*) consignment; (*изделий*: *в производстве*) batch, lot; (*группа*): **по́исковая ~** search party; (*СПОРТ*): **~ в ша́хматы/волейбо́л** a game of chess/volleyball.
партко́м (**-а**) *м сокр* (= *парти́йный комите́т*) (Communist) Party committee.
партнёр (**-а**) *м* partner.
партнёрств|о (**-а**) *ср* (*ЭКОН*) partnership.
парторганиза́ци|я (**-и**) *ж сокр* (= *парти́йная организа́ция*) (Communist) Party organization.
па́рус (**-а**; *nom pl* **-а́**) *м* sail; **на всех паруса́х** (*перен*) at full speed.
паруси́н|а (**-ы**) *ж* canvas.
паруси́новый *прил* canvas *опред*.
па́русник (**-а**) *м* sailing vessel.
парфюме́ри|я (**-и**) *ж собир perfume and cosmetic goods*.
парч|а́ (**-и́**) *ж* brocade.
парши́в|ый (**-, -а, -о**) *прил* (*разг*) lousy, rotten.
пар|ы́ (**-о́в**) *мн* vapour *ед* (*BRIT*), vapor *ед* (*US*).
пас (**-а**) *м* (*СПОРТ*) pass.
пас(ся) *итп несов см* **пасти́(сь)**.
па́сек|а (**-и**) *ж* apiary.
па́сечник (**-а**) *м* bee keeper.
па́сквил|ь (**-я**) *м* send-up (*inf*).
паску́д|ный (**-ен, -на, -но**) *прил* (*разг*) nasty.
па́смурен *прил см* **па́смурный**.
па́смурно *как сказ*: **сего́дня ~** it is overcast today.
па́смур|ный (**-ен, -на, -но**) *прил* overcast, dull; (*перен*) gloomy.
пас|ова́ть (**-у́ю**) *несов перех* (*мяч*) to pass ◆

(*perf* **спасова́ть**) *неперех*: ~ **пе́ред** *+instr* to give in to.
па́спорт (-а; *nom pl* **-а́**) *м* passport; (*автомобиля, станка*) registration document; **заграни́чный ~** passport (*for foreign travel*).
пасса́ж (-а) *м* arcade; (*МУЗ*) passage.
пассажи́р (-а) *м* passenger.
пассажи́р|ка (**-ки**; *gen pl* **-ок**) *ж см* **пассажи́р.**
пассажи́рск|ий (**-ая, -ое, -ие**) *прил* passenger *опред.*
пасси́в (-а) *м* (*КОММ*) liabilities *мн*; (*ЛИНГ*) passive (voice).
пасси́в|ный (**-ен, -на, -но**) *прил* (*также ЛИНГ*) passive; (*no short form*; *КОММ*): ~ **бала́нс** unfavourable (*BRIT*) *или* unfavorable (*US*) balance; ~ **партнёр** (*КОММ*) silent partner.
па́ст|а (**-ы**) *ж* (*томатная*) purée; (*в ручке*) ink; **зубна́я ~** toothpaste.
па́стбищ|е (-а) *ср* pasture.
пасте́л|ь (**-и**) *ж* pastel.
пасте́льный *прил* pastel *опред.*
пастеризо́ванный *прил* pasteurized.
пастериз|ова́ть (**-у́ю**) *(не)сов перех* to pasteurize.
пастерна́к (-а) *м* parsnip.
пас|ти́ (**-у́, -ёшь**; *pt* **-, ла́, -ло́**) *несов перех* (*скот*) to graze
▸ **пасти́сь** *несов возв* to graze.
паст|ила́ (**-илы́**; *nom pl* **-и́лы**) *ж* ≈ marshmallow.
па́стор (-а) *м* minister, pastor.
пасту́х (**-а́**) *м* (*коров*) herdsman (*мн* herdsmen); (*овец*) shepherd.
па́стыр|ь (**-я**) *м* pastor.
па|сть (**-ду́, -дёшь**; *pt* **-л, -ла, -ло**) *сов от* **па́дать** ◆ *неперех* (*no impf*; *крепость, правительство*) to fall ◆ (**-сти**) *ж* (*зверя*) mouth.
па́сх|а (**-и**) *ж* (*в иудаизме*) Passover; (*в христианстве*) ≈ Easter; (*кушанье*) paskha (*sweet dish made with cream cheese at Easter*).
па́сын|ок (**-ка**) *м* stepson.
пат (-а) *м* (*в шахматах*) stalemate.
пате́нт (-а) *м* (*на изобретение*) patent; (*торговый*) licence (*BRIT*), license (*US*).
пате́нтный *прил* patent *опред*; **пате́нтное бюро́/пра́во** patent office/rights.
патент|ова́ть (**-у́ю**; *perf* **запатентова́ть**) *несов перех* to patent.
патети́ческ|ий (**-ая, -ое, -ие**) *прил* (*страстный*) passionate, emotional.
па́ток|а (**-и**) *ж* treacle.
патологи́ческ|ий (**-ая, -ое, -ие**) *прил* (*также перен*) pathological.
патоло́ги|я (**-и**) *ж* pathology.
патриа́рх (-а) *м* patriarch.
патриарха́льный *прил* patriarchal.
патриа́рхи|я (**-и**) *ж* patriarchate.
патрио́т (-а) *м* patriot.
патриоти́зм (-а) *м* patriotism.
патрио́т|ка (**-ки**; *gen pl* **-ок**) *ж см* **патрио́т.**
патро́н (-а) *м* (*ВОЕН*) cartridge; (*дрели*) chuck; (*лампы*) socket; (*покровитель*) patron.
патрона́ж (-а) *м* (*МЕД*) *home visiting by a district nurse for newborn babies or the chronically ill.*
патрона́жн|ый *прил*: **~ая сестра́** (*МЕД*) ≈ district (*BRIT*) *или* visiting (*US*) nurse.
па́трубо|к (**-ка**) *м* branch pipe.
патрули́р|овать (**-ую**) *несов (не)перех* to patrol.
патру́л|ь (**-я́**) *м* patrol.
па́уз|а (**-ы**) *ж* (*также МУЗ*) pause.
пау́к (**-а́**) *м* spider.
паути́н|а (**-ы**) *ж* spider's web, spiderweb (*US*); (*в помещении*) cobweb; (*перен*) web.
па́фос (-а) *м* zeal, fervour (*BRIT*), fervor (*US*).
пах (-а; *loc sg* **-у́**) *м* groin.
пах *итп несов см* **па́хнуть.**
па́хар|ь (**-я**) *м* ploughman (*BRIT*), plowman (*US*) (*мн* ploughmen *или* plowmen).
па|ха́ть (**-шу́, -шешь**; *perf* **вспаха́ть**) *несов перех* to plough (*BRIT*), plow (*US*).
па́х|нуть (**-ну, -нешь**; *pt* **-, -ла, -ло**) *несов неперех*: ~ (*+instr*) to smell (of); (*разг*): ~ *+instr* (*скандалом*) to smack of; **от неё ~нет ду́хами** she smells of perfume.
пахн|у́ть (*3sg* **-ёт**, *3pl* **-у́т**) *сов неперех* (*+instr*): **~у́ло ро́зами** the scent of roses wafted by.
па́хот|а (**-ы**) *ж* ploughing (*BRIT*), plowing (*US*).
паху́ч|ий (**-ая, -ее, -ие**; **-, -а, -е**) *прил* strong-smelling.
паца́н (**-а́**) *м* (*разг*) boy, lad.
пацие́нт (-а) *м* patient.
пацие́нт|ка (**-ки**; *gen pl* **-ок**) *ж см* **пацие́нт.**
пацифи́ст (-а) *м* pacifist.
па́ч|ка (**-ки**; *gen pl* **-ек**) *ж* (*бумаг, денег итп*) bundle; (*чая, сигарет итп*) packet; (*балерины*) tutu.
па́чка|ть (**-ю**; *perf* **запа́чкать** *или* **испа́чкать**) *несов перех*: ~ **что-н** to get sth dirty; (*perf* **запа́чкать**; *перен*: *репутацию*) to sully, tarnish
▸ **па́чкаться** (*perf* **запа́чкаться** *или* **испа́чкаться**) *несов возв* to get dirty.
па́ш|ня (**-ни**; *gen pl* **-ен**) *ж* ploughed (*BRIT*) *или* plowed (*US*) field.
паште́т (-а) *м* pâté.
пашу́ *итп несов см* **паха́ть.**
па́юсн|ый *прил*: **~ая икра́** pressed caviar(e).
пая́льник (-а) *м* soldering iron.
пая́снича|ть (**-ю**) *несов неперех* (*разг*) to play the fool.
пая́|ть (**-ю**) *несов перех* to solder.
пая́ц (-а) *м* clown.
ПВО *ж сокр* (= *противовозду́шная оборо́на*) anti-aircraft defence (*BRIT*) *или* defense (*US*) system.
ПДВ *м сокр* (= *преде́льно допусти́мый вы́брос*) maximum permitted discharge.
пев|е́ц (**-ца́**) *м* singer.
певи́ц|а (**-ы**) *ж см* **пев́ец.**
певца́ *итп сущ см* **пев́ец.**
пе́вч|ий (**-ая, -ее, -ие**) *прил*: **~ая пти́ца** songbird ◆ (**-его**; *decl like adj*) *м* chorister.
пе́г|ий (**-ая, -ое, -ие**) *прил* piebald *опред.*

педагóг (-а) *м* (*учитель*) teacher.
педагóгик|а (-и) *ж* education science.
педагоги́ческ|ий (-ая, -ое, -ие) *прил* (*коллектив*) teaching *опред*; ~ **институ́т** teacher-training (*BRIT*) *или* teachers' (*US*) college; **у неё ~ тала́нт** she has a talent for teaching; **у него́ ~ое образова́ние** he trained as a teacher.
педа́л|ь (-и) *ж* pedal.
педа́нт (-а) *м* pedant.
педиа́тр (-а) *м* paediatrician (*BRIT*), pediatrician (*US*).
педиатри́|я (-и) *ж* paediatrics (*BRIT*), pediatrics (*US*).
педикю́р (-а) *м* pedicure.
udинститу́т (-а) *м сокр* (= *педагоги́ческий институ́т*) teacher-training college.
педсове́т (-а) *м сокр* (= *педагоги́ческий сове́т*) staff meeting.
педучи́лищ|е (-а) *ср сокр* (= *педагоги́ческое учи́лище*) teacher-training college (*for nursery and primary level*).
пей *несов см* **пить**.
пейза́ж (-а) *м* (*также* *ИСКУССТВО*) landscape; **морско́й** ~ (*ИСКУССТВО*) seascape.
пейзажи́ст (-а) *м* landscape painter.
пе́йте *несов см* **пить**.
пёк(ся) *итп несов см* **печь(ся)**.
пека́р|ня (-ни; *gen pl* -ен) *ж* bakery.
пе́кар|ь (-я) *м* baker.
Пеки́н (-а) *м* Beijing, Peking.
пе́кл|о (-а) *ср* (*зной*) scorching heat; (*перен*: *ад*) hell.
пеку́(сь) *итп несов см* **печь(ся)**.
пелен|а́ (-ы́) *ж* (*тумана, облаков*) veil, shroud; **у него́ сло́вно ~ с глаз упа́ла** the scales fell from his eyes.
пелена́|ть (-ю; *perf* **запелена́ть**) *несов перех* to swaddle.
пеленг|ова́ть (-у́ю; *perf* **запеленгова́ть**) *несов перех* (*TEX*) to take the bearings of.
пелён|ка (-ки; *gen pl* -ок) *ж* swaddling clothes *мн*; **с ~ок** (*перен*) from a very early age.
пелика́н (-а) *м* pelican.
пельме́н|ь (-я; *nom pl* -и) *м* (*обычно мн*) ≈ ravioli *только ед*.
пе́мз|а (-ы) *ж* pumice (stone).
пе́н|а (-ы) *ж* (*мыльная*) suds *мн*; (*морская*) foam; (*бульонная*) froth; **говори́ть** (*impf*) **с ~ой у рта́** to foam at the mouth.
пена́л (-а) *м* pencil case.
пена́льти *ср нескл* penalty.
Пенджа́б (-а) *м* Punjab.
пенджа́бск|ий (-ая, -ое, -ие) *прил* Punjabi.
пе́ней *сущ см* **пе́ня**.
пе́н|и (-ей) *мн* = **пе́ня**.
пе́ни|е (-я) *ср* singing.
пе́нистый *прил* frothy.
пе́н|иться (*3sg* -ится, *3pl* -ятся, *perf* **вспе́ниться**) *несов возв* to foam, froth.
пеницилли́н (-а) *м* penicillin.
пе́нк|а (-и) *ж* (*на молоке*) skin; **снима́ть** (*impf*) **~и** (*перен*) to cream off the best for o.s.
пе́нни *ср нескл* penny.
пенопла́ст (-а) *м* foam plastic.
пенс (-а) *м* pence *мн*.
пенсионе́р (-а) *м* pensioner.
пенсионе́р|ка (-ки; *gen pl* -ок) *ж см* **пенсионе́р**.
пенсио́нный *прил* (*фонд*) pension *опред*; **пенсио́нный во́зраст** pension age.
пе́нси|я (-и) *ж* pension; ~ **по инвали́дности** ≈ invalidity benefit; **выходи́ть (вы́йти** *perf*) **на ~ю** to retire.
пенсне́ *ср нескл* pince-nez.
пень (**пня**) *м* (tree) stump; (*разг*: *пренебр*: *о человеке*) dolt, blockhead.
пеньк|а́ (-и́) *ж* hemp (*fibre*).
пеньюа́р (-а) *м* negligee.
пе́н|я (-и; *gen pl* -ей) *ж* fine.
пеня́|ть (-ю) *несов неперех*: ~ **на себя́** (*разг*) to blame *или* reproach o.s.; **пусть он ~ет на себя́** he has only himself to blame.
пе́п|ел (-ла) *м* ash; (*хлопья*) ashes *мн*.
пепели́щ|е (-а) *ср* site of a fire.
пе́пельниц|а (-ы) *ж* ashtray.
пе́пла *итп сущ см* **пе́пел**.
пер. *сокр* = **переу́лок**.
пёр *итп несов см* **пере́ть**.
перве́йш|ий (-ая, -ее, -ие) *прил* primary.
пе́рвен|ец (-ца) *м* first-born.
пе́рвенств|о (-а) *ср* (*положение*) first place; (*соревнование*) championship.
пе́рвенств|овать (-ую) *несов неперех* to take first place, come first.
пе́рвенца *итп сущ см* **пе́рвенец**.
перви́чный *прил* (*самый ранний*) initial *опред*, primary; (*низовой*) grass root.
первобы́т|ный *прил* primeval; (-ен, -на, -но; *перен*: *методы*) primitive.
пе́рв|ое (-ого; *decl like adj*) *ср* first course.
первозда́нный *прил* primordial.
первоисто́чник (-а) *м* primary source.
первокла́ссник (-а) *м* *pupil in first year at school (usually seven years old)*.
первокла́ссниц|а (-ы) *ж см* **первокла́ссник**.
первокла́ссн|ый *прил*: **~ые инвести́ции** (*КОММ*) blue-chip investment.
пе́рво-на́перво *нареч* (*разг*) first of all.
первонача́л|ьный (-ен, -ьна, -ьно) *прил* (*исходный*) original, initial *опред*.
первоо́браз (-а) *м* prototype.
первооткрыва́тел|ь (-я) *м* discoverer.
первоочередно́й *прил* (*неотложный*) immediate.
первоочерёдный *прил* = **первоочередно́й**.
первопрохо́д|ец (-ца) *м* (*поселенец*) pioneer; (*исследователь*) explorer.

перворазря́дный *прил* first-class, top-class.
первосо́рт|ный (**-ен, -на, -но**) *прил* top-quality, top-grade, first-rate.
первостепе́н|ный (**-ен, -на, -но**) *прил* (*задача, значение*) paramount.
первоцве́т (**-а**) *м* primrose.
пе́рв|ый (**-ая, -ое, -ые**) *чис* first; (*по времени*) first, earliest; ~ **эта́ж** ground (*BRIT*) *или* first (*US*) floor; **~ое вре́мя** at first; **в ~ую о́чередь** in the first place *или* instance; ~ **час дня/но́чи** after midday/midnight; **из ~ых рук** first-hand; **он ~ учени́к** he is top of the class; **~ым де́лом** *или* **до́лгом** first of all; **това́р ~ого со́рта** top grade product (*on a scale of 1-3*); **пе́рвая по́мощь** first aid; *см также* **пя́тый**.
перга́мент (**-а**) *м* parchment.
пере- *префикс* (*in verbs*; *о направлении действия через что-н*) *indicating movement over or across sth eg. переходи́ть*; (*о направлении действия из одного места в другое*) *indicating movement from one place to another eg. передви́нуть*; (*разделение что-н на две части*) *indicating division of sth into two parts eg. перепили́ть*; (*изменение направленности действия*) *indicating redirection of sth eg. передове́рить*; (*повторение действия*) *indicating repetition of sth eg. переде́лать*; (*обозначает превосходство в чём-н*) *indicating superiority in sth eg. переспо́рить*; (*чрезмерность действия*) *indicating excessive action eg. перепи́ть*; (*прекращение действия после длительного проявления*) *indicating cessation of action after certain length of time eg. переволнова́ться*; (*распространение действия на много лиц или предметов*) *indicating action involving of many people or objects eg. перечита́ть*; (*обозначает взаимность действия*) *indicating reciprocal nature of action eg. перепи́сываться*; (*in nouns*; *обозначает промежуточность*) *indicating intermediate stage of sth eg. переми́рие*.
переадрес|ова́ть (**-у́ю**; *impf* **переадресо́вывать**) *сов перех* to readdress.
перебази́р|овать (**-ую**) *сов перех* to relocate.
переба́рщива|ть (**-ю**) *несов от* **переборщи́ть**.
перебежа́ть (*как* **бежа́ть**; *см* **Table 20**; *impf* **перебега́ть**) *сов неперех*: ~ (**че́рез** *+acc*) to run across; **перебега́ть** (~ *perf*) **к** *+dat* (*разг*: *к противнику итп*) to go over to.
перебе́й(те) *сов см* **переби́ть**.
переберу́(сь) *итп сов см* **перебра́ть(ся)**.
переб|еси́ться (**-ешу́сь, -е́сишься**) *сов возв* to run riot; (*разг*) to sow one's wild oats.
перебива́|ть(ся) (**-ю(сь)**) *несов от* **переби́ть(ся)**.
перебира́|ть (**-ю**) *несов от* **перебра́ть** ◆ *перех*: ~ **кла́виши** to run one's fingers over the keys
▸ **перебира́ться** *несов от* **перебра́ться**.
переб|и́ть (**-ью́, -ьёшь**; *impf* **перебива́ть**) *сов перех* to interrupt; (*убить*) to kill; (*разбить*) to break; (*обить*) to reupholster; **перебива́ть** (~ *perf*) **аппети́т** to spoil *или* ruin one's appetite; **перебива́ть** (~ *perf*) **мысль** to interrupt one's train of thought; **перебива́ть** (~ *perf*) **за́пах чего́-н** to conceal the smell of sth
▸ **переби́ться** (*impf* **перебива́ться**) *сов возв* to make ends meet, get by; (*no impf*; *обойтись*): **~ся** (**без** *+gen*) (*разг*) to do without; **они́ с трудо́м ~и́лись до зарпла́ты** they managed to get by till payday; **он ~ьётся!** he'll survive *или* manage!
перебо́|й (**-я**) *м* (*сердца*) irregularity; (*двигателя*) misfire; (*задержка*) interruption, break.
переболе́|ть (**-ю**) *сов неперех*: ~ *+instr* to recover from; (*дети, люди*: *корью, гриппом*) to come down with; **у него́ душа́ ~ла** he is over the heartache.
перебо́р (**-а**) *м* (*муз*) strumming; (*излишнее*): **э́то уже́** ~ that's too much.
переб|оро́ть (**-орю́, -о́решь**) *сов перех* to overcome.
переборщ|и́ть (**-у́, -и́шь**; *impf* **переба́рщивать**) *сов неперех*: ~ **в** *+prp* (*разг*) to go over the top with.
перебра́сыва|ть(ся) (**-ю(сь)**) *несов от* **перебро́сить(ся)**.
переб|ра́ть (**-еру́, -ерёшь**; *impf* **перебира́ть**) *сов перех* (*пересмотреть*: *бумаги*) to sort out; (: *крупу, ягоды*) to sort; (*мысленно воспроизвести*) to go over *или* through (in one's mind); (*взять слишком много*) to take too much; (*выпить лишнее*) to drink too much; (*струны*) to pluck (*BRIT*), pick (*US*)
▸ **перебра́ться** (*impf* **перебира́ться**) *сов возв* (*разг*: *через реку*) to manage to get across; (*на новую квартиру*) to move.
перебро́|сить (**-шу, -сишь**; *impf* **перебра́сывать**) *сов перех* (*мяч, мешок*) to throw over; (*войска*) to transfer, move
▸ **перебро́ситься** (*impf* **перебра́сываться**) *сов возв* (*войска*) to be transferred; **перебра́сываться** (**~ся** *perf*) *+instr* (*мячом*) to throw (to each other); (*словами*) to exchange (with one another).
перебыва́|ть (**-ю**) *сов неперех* (*у многих людей*) to call on; (*во многих местах*): **он везде́ ~л** he has been all over the world.
перебью́(сь) *итп сов см* **переби́ть(ся)**.
перева́л (**-а**) *м* (*в горах*) pass.
перев|али́ть (**-алю́, -а́лишь**; *impf* **перева́ливать**) *сов неперех*: ~ (**че́рез** *+acc*) to cross; **перева́ливать** (~ *perf*) **за** *+acc* (*разг*) to top.
перева́лочный *прил*: ~ **пункт/ла́герь** transit area/camp.
перев|ари́ть (**-арю́, -а́ришь**; *impf* **перева́ривать**) *сов перех* to overcook (*by boiling*); (*пищу, информацию*) to digest
▸ **перевари́ться** (*impf* **перева́риваться**) *сов*

возв to be overdone *или* overcooked; (*пища*) to be digested.
переведу́(сь) *итп сов см* **перевести́(сь)**.
перев|езти́ (**-езу́, -езёшь**; *pt* **-ёз, -езла́, -езло́**, *impf* **перевози́ть**) *сов перех* (*переместить*) to take *или* transport across; (*доставить*) to transport, take.
переверн|у́ть (**-у́, -ёшь**; *impf* **перевёртывать** *или* **перевора́чивать**) *сов перех* to turn over; (*изменить*) to change (completely); (*no impf*; *комнату*) to turn upside down
▸ **перевернýться** (*impf* **перевёртываться** *или* **перевора́чиваться**) *сов возв* (*человек*) to turn over; (*лодка, машина*) to overturn.
переве́с (**-а**) *м* (*преимущество*) advantage.
переве́|сить (**-шу, -сишь**; *impf* **переве́шивать**) *сов перех* (*товар*) to reweigh; (*подлеж*: *аргумент*) to outweigh.
перев|ести́ (**-еду́, -едёшь**; *pt* **-ёл, -ела́, -ело́**, *impf* **переводи́ть**) *сов перех* (*помочь перейти*) to take across; (*часы*) to reset; (*учреждение, сотрудника*) to transfer, move; (*текст*) to translate; (: *устно*) to interpret; (*переслать*: *деньги*) to send, transfer; (*доллары, метры итп*) to convert; (*разг*: *израсходовать*) to waste; **переводи́ть** (**~** *perf*) **разгово́р** to change the subject; **переводи́ть** (**~** *perf*) **текст с ру́сского языка́ на англи́йский** to translate a text from Russian into English; **переводи́ть** (**~** *perf*) **дух** *или* **дыха́ние** to take a (deep) breath
▸ **перевести́сь** (*impf* **переводи́ться**) *сов возв* to move; (*разг*: *исчезнуть*) to die out.
переве́шива|ть (**-ю**) *несов от* **переве́сить**.
переве́шу *сов см* **переве́сить**.
перевида́|ть (**-ю**) *сов перех* to see.
перевира́|ть (**-ю**) *несов от* **переврáть**.
перево́д (**-а**) *м* (*на другую должность*) transfer; (*стрелки часов*) resetting; (*текст*) translation; (*деньги*) remittance; **~ строки́** (*комп*) line feed; **креди́тный ~** (*комм*) credit transfer, bank giro.
перев|оди́ть(ся) (**-ожу́(сь), -о́дишь(ся)**) *несов от* **перевести́(сь)**.
перево́дный *прил* in translation.
перево́дчик (**-а**) *м* translator; (*устный*) interpreter.
перево́дчиц|а (**-ы**) *ж см* **перево́дчик**.
перевожу́ *несов см* **перевози́ть**.
перевожу́(сь) *несов см* **переводи́ть(ся)**.
перево́з (**-а**) *м* (*груза*) transportation.
перев|ози́ть (**-ожу́, -о́зишь**) *несов от* **перевезти́**.
перево́з|ка (**-ки**; *gen pl* **-ок**) *ж* transportation, conveyance.
переволн|ова́ться (**-у́юсь**) *сов возв* to be worried sick.
перевооруж|и́ть (**-у́, -и́шь**; *impf* **перевооружа́ть**) *сов перех* (*армию*) to rearm; (*промышленность*) to re-equip.
перевопло|ти́ться (**-щу́сь, -ти́шься**; *impf* **перевоплоща́ться**) *сов возв* (*актёр*) to be transformed.
перевора́чива|ть(ся) (**-ю(сь)**) *несов от* **переверну́ться(ся)**.
переворо́т (**-а**) *м* (*полит*) coup (d'état); (*в судьбе*) upheaval.
перевоспита́|ть (**-ю**; *impf* **перевоспи́тывать**) *сов перех* to re-educate.
перевр|а́ть (**-у́, -ёшь**; *impf* **перевира́ть**) *сов перех* (*разг*: *содержание*) to muddle.
перевы́бор|ы (**-ов**) *мн* election *ед* (*occurring at regular intervals*).
перевы́полн|ить (**-ю, -ишь**; *impf* **перевыполня́ть**) *сов перех* (*задание, план*) to overfulfil; (*норму*) to exceed.
перев|яза́ть (**-яжу́, -я́жешь**; *impf* **перевя́зывать**) *сов перех* (*руку, раненого*) to bandage; (*рану*) to dress, bandage; (*коробку*) to tie up; (*чулки, свитер*) to reknit.
перевя́з|ка (**-ки**; *gen pl* **-ок**) *ж* (*раны, раненых*) bandaging.
перевя́зочный *прил*: **~ материа́л** bandage.
перевя́зыва|ть (**-ю**) *несов от* **перевяза́ть**.
пе́ревяз|ь (**-и**) *ж* shoulder-belt; (*для руки*) sling.
перега́р (**-а**) *м* *smell or taste of (stale) alcohol*; **от него́ несёт ~ом** he reeks of alcohol.
переги́б (**-а**) *м* (*страницы, ткани*) fold; (*перен*: *крайность*) excesses *мн*.
перегиба́|ть (**-ю**) *несов от* **перегну́ть**.
перегл|яну́ться (**-яну́сь, -я́нешься**; *impf* **перегля́дываться**) *сов возв*: **~ (с** *+instr***)** to exchange glances (with).
перег|на́ть (**-оню́, -о́нишь**; *pt* **-на́л,-нала́,-на́ло**, *impf* **перегоня́ть**) *сов перех* (*переместить*: *скот, машину*) to drive; (*обогнать*: *бегуна, конкурента*) to overtake; (*нефть*) to refine; (*спирт*) to distil (*BRIT*), distill (*US*).
перегно́|й (**-я**) *м* humus.
перегн|у́ть (**-у́, -ёшь**; *impf* **перегиба́ть**) *сов перех* (*бумагу*) to fold (over) ◆ *неперех* (*с критикой*) to go too far; **перегиба́ть** (**~** *perf*) **па́лку** (*перен*) to go too far.
перегова́рива|ться (**-юсь**) *несов возв*: **~ (с** *+instr***)** to exchange remarks (with).
переговор|и́ть (**-ю́, -и́шь**) *сов неперех*: **~ с** *+instr* (*обсудить*) to have a talk with ◆ *перех* (*разг*) to outtalk.
перегово́рный *прил*: **~ пункт** telephone office (*for long-distance calls*).
перегово́р|ы (**-ов**) *мн* negotiations *мн*, talks *мн*; (*по телефону*) call *ед*; **зака́зывать** (**заказа́ть** *perf*) **~ с** *+instr* to book a call to.
перего́н (**-а**) *м* (*на железной дороге*) stage (*between two railway stations*).
перего́н|ка (**-ки**; *gen pl* **-ок**) *ж* (*нефти*) refining; (*спирта*) distillation.
перегоню́ *итп сов см* **перегна́ть**.

The spelling rules for Russian are shown on page xvii.

перегоня́|ть (-ю) *несов от* **перегна́ть.**
перегора́жива|ть (-ю) *несов от* **перегороди́ть.**
перегор|е́ть (*3sg* **-и́т**, *3pl* **-я́т**, *impf* **перегора́ть**) *сов неперех* (*лампочка*) to fuse; (*двигатель*) to burn out.
перегоро|ди́ть (-жу́, -ди́шь; *impf* **перегора́живать**) *сов перех* (*комнату*) to partition (off); (*дорогу*) to block.
перегоро́д|ка (-ки; *gen pl* **-ок)** *ж* partition.
перегорожу́ *сов см* **перегороди́ть.**
перегре́|ть (-ю; *impf* **перегрева́ть**) *сов перех* to overheat
▸ **перегре́ться** (*impf* **перегрева́ться**) *сов возв* to overheat; **он ~лся на со́лнце** he got a touch of sunstroke.
перегр|узи́ть (-ужу́, -у́зишь; *impf* **перегружа́ть**) *сов перех* to overload.
перегру́з|ка (-ки; *gen pl* **-ок)** *ж* overload; (*обычно мн*: *нервные*) strain.
перегры́з|ть (-у́, -ёшь; *impf* **перегрыза́ть**) *сов перех* to gnaw through
▸ **перегры́зться** (*impf* **перегрыза́ться**) *сов возв* to fight.

KEYWORD

пе́ред *предл* (*+instr*) ***1*** (*о положении, в присутствии*: *in front of*); **пе́ред до́мом/зе́ркалом** in front of the house/mirror; **он робе́л пе́ред де́вушками** he was shy in front of girls; **моли́ться** *(impf)* **пе́ред ико́ной** to pray before an icon
2 (*раньше чего-н*: *ужином, войной, концом итп*) before; **я говори́л с ним пе́ред уро́ком** I spoke to him before the lesson
3 (*об объекте воздействия*): **устоя́ть пе́ред тру́дностями** to stand one's ground in the face of difficulties; **извиня́ться (извини́ться** *perf*) **пе́ред кем-н** to apologize to sb; **я винова́т пе́ред тобо́й** I am guilty in your eyes; **отчи́тываться (отчита́ться** *perf*) **пе́ред** *+instr* to report to
4 (*по сравнению*) compared to; **пе́ред ним ты челове́к ничто́жный** compared to him, you are a nonentity
5 (*как союз*): **пе́ред тем как** before; **пе́ред тем как уйти́/зако́нчить** before leaving/finishing.

перёд (пе́реда) *м* front.
переда|ва́ть(ся) (-ю́(сь); *imper* **передава́й(те)**) *несов от* **переда́ть(ся).**
переда́м(ся) *итп сов см* **переда́ть(ся).**
переда́тчик (-а) *м* (*ТЕХ*) transmitter.
переда́|ть (*как* **дать**; *см* **Table 14**; *impf* **передава́ть**) *сов перех*: **~ что-н (кому́-н)** (*письмо, подарок*) to pass *или* hand sth (over) (to sb); (*известие, любовь, интерес*) to pass sth on (to sb); (*идеи, эмоции*) to convey sth *или* get sth across (to sb); **~йте ему́ (мой) приве́т** give him my regards; **~йте ей, что я не приду́** tell her I am not coming; **передава́ть (~** *perf*) **что-н по телеви́дению/ра́дио** to televise/broadcast sth; **передава́ть (~** *perf*) **де́ло в суд** to take a case to court
▸ **переда́ться** (*impf* **передава́ться**) *сов возв* (*+dat*; *эмоция*): **его́ страх ~лся други́м** his fear communicated itself to the others; **ему́ ~лся тала́нт отца́** he has inherited his father's talent.
переда́ч|а (-и) *ж* (*известия*) passing on; (*концерта, новостей*) transmission; (*ТЕЛ, РАДИО*: *интересная*) programme (*BRIT*), program (*US*); (*больному, заключённому*) parcel; **програ́мма переда́ч** television and radio guide.
переда́шь(ся) *сов см* **переда́ть(ся).**
передвига́|ть (-ю) *несов от* **передви́нуть**
▸ **передвига́ться** *несов от* **передви́нуться** ◆ *возв* (*на машине, на танке итп*) to move.
передвиже́ни|е (-я) *ср* (*предмета, войск*) movement; (*срока*) alteration, change; **сре́дства ~я** means of transport.
передвижно́й *прил* (*выставка, цирк*) travelling (*BRIT*), traveling (*US*); (*лаборатория, библиотека*) mobile.
передви́н|уть (-у, -ешь; *impf* **передвига́ть**) *сов перех* to move
▸ **передви́нуться** (*impf* **передвига́ться**) *сов возв* to move.
переде́ла|ть (-ю; *impf* **переде́лывать**) *сов перех* (*работу*) to redo; (*характер*) to change; (*рассказ*) to rewrite; **~** *(perf)* **все дела́** to get everything done.
переде́л|ка (-ки; *gen pl* **-ок)** *ж* (*одежды*) alteration; (*характера*) change; **попада́ть (попа́сть** *perf*) **в ~ку** (*разг*) to get into a fix; **побыва́ть** *(perf)* **в ~х** (*разг*) to be in a fix.
переде́лыва|ть (-ю) *несов от* **переде́лать.**
передёргива|ть (-ю) *несов от* **передёрнуть.**
перед|ержа́ть (-ержу́, -е́ржишь; *impf* **переде́рживать**) *сов перех*: **он ~ержа́л мя́со в духо́вке** he left the meat in the oven for too long.
передёрн|уть (-у, -ешь; *impf* **передёргивать**) *сов перех* (*разг*: *факты, цифры*) to massage ◆ *безл* (*+acc*): **его́ ~уло от хо́лода** he convulsed from the cold; **его́ ~уло от отвраще́ния** he shuddered in disgust.
пере́дн|ий (-яя, -ее, -ие) *прил* front; **П~яя А́зия** the Middle East; **~ план** (*КОМП*) foreground; **пере́дний край** (*ВОЕН, перен*) front line.
пере́дник (-а) *м* apron.
пере́дн|яя (-ей; *decl like adj*) *ж* (entrance) hall.
пе́редо *предл*: **~ мно́й** in front of me; **= пе́ред.**
передов|а́я (-о́й; *decl like adj*) *ж* (*также:* **~ статья́**) editorial; (*также:* **~ пози́ция**: *ВОЕН*) vanguard.
передово́й *прил* (*отряд*) advance, forward; (*машина*) front *опред*; (*технология*) advanced; (*писатель, взгляды*) progressive.
передохн|у́ть (-у́, -ёшь) *сов неперех* (*разг*) to take a breather (*BRIT*) *или* break (*US*).
передр|азни́ть (-азню́, -а́знишь; *impf* **передра́знивать**) *сов перех* to mimic.

передýма|ть (-ю; *impf* **передýмывать**) *сов неперех* to change one's mind.
передыш|ка (-ки; *gen pl* **-ек**) *ж* rest; (*перерыв*) (short) break.
переéду *итп сов см* **переéхать**.
переéзд (-а) *м* (*в новый дом*) move; (*на железной дороге*) level crossing.
переé|хать (*как* **éхать**; *см* **Table 19**; *impf* **переезжáть**) *сов неперех* (*переселиться*) to move; **переезжáть** (~ *perf*) (**чéрез** +*acc*) to cross.
пережгý *итп сов см* **пережéчь**.
пережд|áть (-ý, -ёшь; *impf* **пережидáть**) *сов перех*: ~ **дождь** to wait for the rain to pass.
переж|éчь (-гý, -жёшь *итп*, -гýт; *pt* **-ёг, -глá, -глó**, *impf* **пережигáть**) *сов перех* (*зерна кофе*) to burn; (*глину*) to overfire.
переживáни|е (-я) *ср* (*обычно мн*) feeling.
переживá|ть (-ю) *несов от* **пережить** ◆ *неперех*: ~ (**за** +*acc*) (*разг*) to worry (about).
переживý *итп сов см* **пережить**.
пережигá|ть (-ю) *несов от* **пережéчь**.
пережидá|ть (-ю) *несов от* **переждáть**.
пережит|ок (-ка) *м* relic.
пережи|ть (-вý, -вёшь; *impf* **переживáть**) *сов перех* (*прожить дольше*) to outlive; (*выжить*) to survive; (*испытать*) to experience; (*вытерпеть*) to suffer.
перезаря|дить (-жý, -дишь; *impf* **перезаряжáть**) *сов перех* (*аккумулятор*) to recharge; (*ружьё*) to reload.
перезвон|ить (-ю, -ишь; *impf* **перезвáнивать**) *сов неперех* to phone (*BRIT*) *или* call (*US*) back.
перезим|овáть (-ýю) *сов от* **зимовáть**.
перезрé|ть (-ю; *impf* **перезревáть**) *сов неперех* to become overripe.
переигрá|ть (-ю; *impf* **перейгрывать**) *сов перех* (*играть снова*) to replay ◆ *неперех* (*разг*) to overact; **это дéло нáдо** ~ (*разг*) this will have to be looked at again.
переизб|рáть (-ерý, -ерёшь; *pt* **-рáл, -ралá, -рáло**, *impf* **переизбирáть**) *сов перех* to re-elect.
переизда|вáть (-ю; *imper* **переиздáй(те)**) *несов от* **переиздáть**.
переиздáм *итп сов см* **переиздáть**.
переиздáни|е (-я) *ср* (*действие*) republication; (*исправленное, дополненное*) new edition.
переиздá|ть (*как* **дать**; *см* **Table 14**; *impf* **переиздавáть**) *сов перех* to republish.
переимен|овáть (-ýю; *impf* **переименóвывать**) *сов перех* to rename.
перейдý *итп сов см* **перейти**.
перейму *итп сов см* **перенять**.
пере|йти (*как* **идти**; *см* **Table 18**; *impf* **переходить**) *сов перех*: ~ (**чéрез** +*acc*) to cross ◆ *неперех*: ~ **в/на** +*acc* (*поменять место*) to go to; (*на другую работу*) to move to; **переходить** (~ *perf*) **к** +*dat* (*к сыну итп*) to pass to; (*к делу, к обсуждению*) to turn to; **переходить** (~ *perf*) **в атáку** to launch an attack; **переходить** (~ *perf*) **на** +*acc* to switch to; **переходить** (~ *perf*) **границу** to cross the frontier *или* border; (*перен*) to overstep the bounds *или* mark; **переходить** (~ *perf*) **из рук в рýки** to change hands; **переходить** (~ *perf*) **на грýбости** to resort to bad language; **дрýжба ~шлá в любóвь** friendship turned *или* developed into love.
перекáпыва|ть (-ю) *несов от* **перекопáть**.
перекáрмлива|ть (-ю) *несов от* **перекормить**.
перек|атить (-ачý, -áтишь; *impf* **перекáтывать**) *сов перех* (*что-н круглое*) to roll; (*что-н на колёсах*) to wheel.
перекáшива|ть(ся) (-ю(сь)) *несов от* **перекосить(ся)**.
переквалифицир|оваться (-уюсь) *сов возв* to retrain.
перекиднóй *прил*: ~ **мост** gangplank; ~ **календáрь** desk calendar.
перекин|уть (-у, -ешь; *impf* **перекидывать**) *сов перех* to throw over
▸ **перекинуться** (*impf* **перекидываться**) *сов возв*: ~+*instr* (*мячом*) to throw to each other.
переклáдин|а (-ы) *ж* crossbeam; (*СПОРТ*) (horizontal *или* high) bar.
переклaдн|ые (-ых; *decl like adj*) *мн* stagecoach *ед*.
переклáдыва|ть (-ю) *несов от* **переложить**.
перекликá|ться (-юсь) *несов возв* (*люди, животные*) to call to each other; ~ (*impf*) (**с** +*instr*) (*перен*: *образы, идеи*) to have something in common (with).
перекличк|а (-ки; *gen pl* **-ек**) *ж* roll call.
переключáтел|ь (-я) *м* switch.
переключá|ть(ся) (-ю(сь)) *несов от* **переключить(ся)**.
переключéни|е (-я) *ср* switching; (*скорости*) changing (*BRIT*), shifting (*US*).
переключ|ить (-ý, -ишь; *impf* **переключáть**) *сов перех* to switch; **переключáть** (~ *perf*) **скóрость** to change (*BRIT*) *или* shift (*US*) gear; **переключáть** (~ *perf*) **разговóр** to change the subject
▸ **переключиться** (*impf* **переключáться**) *сов возв*: **~ся** (**на** +*acc*) (*внимание*) to shift (to).
перек|овáть (-ую; *impf* **перекóвывать**) *сов перех* (*коня*) to reshoe; (*изделие, деталь*) to reforge.
перекопá|ть (-ю; *impf* **перекáпывать**) *сов перех* (*огород*) to dig up; (*разг*: *чемодан, шкаф*) to rummage through.
перекорм|ить (-лю, -ишь; *impf* **перекáрмливать**) *сов перех* to overfeed.
переко|сить (-шý, -сишь; *impf* **перекáшивать**)

сов перех (*рисуя*) to draw crooked; (*вырезая*) to cut crooked
▸ **перекоси́ться** (*impf* **перека́шиваться**) *сов возв* (*деталь, рисунок*) to come out crooked; (*лицо, тело*) to become distorted.
перекоч|ева́ть (**-у́ю**; *impf* **перекочёвывать**) *сов неперех* (*стадо, табор*) to move on.
перекошу́(сь) *сов см* **перекоси́ть(ся)**.
перекра́ива|ть (**-ю**) *несов от* **перекрои́ть**.
перекр|ести́ть (**-ещу́, -е́стишь**) *сов от* **крести́ть**
▸ **перекрести́ться** *сов от* **крести́ться** ◆ (*impf* **перекре́щиваться**) *возв* (*также перен*) to cross.
перекрёстка *сущ см* **перекрёсток**.
перекрёстный *прил* intersecting; **перекрёстный допро́с** cross-examination; **перекрёстный ого́нь** crossfire.
перекрёст|ок (**-ка**) *м* crossroads.
перекре́щива|ться (**-юсь**) *несов от* **перекрести́ться**.
перекрещу́(сь) *сов см* **перекрести́ть(ся)**.
перекрич|а́ть (**-у́, -и́шь**; *impf* **перекри́кивать**) *сов перех* (*в споре*) to shout down; (*шум, музыку*) to shout above.
перекро|и́ть (**-ю́, -и́шь**; *impf* **перекра́ивать**) *сов перех* (*платье*) to cut differently; (*карту*) to redraw.
перекро́ю *итп сов см* **перекры́ть**.
перекр|ути́ть (**-учу́, -у́тишь**; *impf* **перекру́чивать**) *сов перех* (*гайку, кран*) to overtighten
▸ **перекрути́ться** (*impf* **перекру́чиваться**) *сов возв* to get tangled up.
перекрыва́|ть (**-ю**) *несов от* **перекры́ть**.
перекры́ти|е (**-я**) *ср* ceiling; (*реки*) damming.
перекр|ы́ть (**-о́ю, -о́ешь**; *impf* **перекрыва́ть**) *сов перех* (*покрыть заново*) to re-cover; (*реку*) to dam; (*дорогу, улицу*) to close off; (*воду, газ*) to cut off; (*разг*: *план*) to exceed.
перек|упи́ть (**-уплю́, -у́пишь**; *impf* **перекупа́ть**) *сов перех* to buy.
переку́пщик (**-а**) *м* dealer.
переку́р (**-а**) *м* (*разг*: *перерыв*) cigarette break.
перек|ури́ть (**-урю́, -у́ришь**; *impf* **переку́ривать**) *сов перех* (*разг*) to break for a cigarette; (: *сделать перерыв*) to take a break.
перек|уси́ть (**-ушу́, -у́сишь**; *impf* **переку́сывать**) *сов перех* to bite through ◆ *неперех* (*разг*) to have a snack.
перела́влива|ть (**-ю**) *несов от* **перелови́ть**.
перелага́|ть (**-ю**) *несов от* **переложи́ть**.
перела́мыва|ть (**-ю**) *несов от* **переломи́ть**.
переле́з|ть (**-у, -ешь**; *pt* **-, -ла, -ло**, *impf* **перелеза́ть**) *сов (не)перех*: ~ (**че́рез** *+acc*) (*забор, канаву*) to climb (over); **перелеза́ть** (~ *perf*) **в/на** *+acc* to get *или* climb into.
переле́с|ок (**-ка**) *м* (*небольшой лес*) copse, coppice; (*редкий лес*) sparsely wooded area.
перелёт (**-а**) *м* flight; (*птиц*) migration.
переле|те́ть (**-чу́, -ти́шь**; *impf* **перелета́ть**) *сов (не)перех*: ~ (**че́рез** *+acc*) to fly over.
перелётный *прил* (*птицы*) migratory.
перелечу́ *сов см* **перелете́ть**.
перели́в (**-а**) *м* (*красок, звуков*) (subtle) gradation; (*голоса*) modulation.
переливá́ни|е (**-я**) *ср*: ~ **кро́ви** blood transfusion.
перелива́|ть (**-ю**) *несов от* **перели́ть** ◆ *неперех* (*блестеть*): ~ *+instr* to shimmer with; ~ (*impf*) **все́ми цвета́ми ра́дуги** to be iridescent.
перелиста́|ть (**-ю**; *impf* **перели́стывать**) *сов перех* (*просмотреть*) to leaf through; (*быстро перебрать*) to flick through.
перел|и́ть (**-ью́, -ьёшь**; *impf* **перелива́ть**) *сов перех* to pour (*from one container to another*); **перелива́ть** (~ *perf*) **кровь кому́-н** to give sb a blood transfusion.
перел|ови́ть (**-овлю́, -о́вишь**; *impf* **перела́вливать**) *сов перех* to catch.
переложе́ни|е (**-я**) *ср* (*пьесы, повести*) adaptation; (*музыкального произведения*) arrangement.
перел|ожи́ть (**-ожу́, -о́жишь**; *impf* **перекла́дывать**) *сов перех* to move, shift; (*impf* **перекла́дывать** *или* **перелага́ть**; *повесть, пьесу*) to adapt; **перекла́дывать** (~ *perf*) **что-н на кого́-н** (*ответственность, работу итп*) to pass sth onto sb; ~ (*perf*) **со́ли в суп** to put too much salt in the soup.
перело́м (**-а**) *м* (*МЕД*) fracture; (*перен*) turning point.
перелома́|ть (**-ю**) *сов перех* to break.
перел|оми́ть (**-омлю́, -о́мишь**; *impf* **перела́мывать**) *сов перех* (*палку*) to break in two; (*перен*: *ход событий*) to change dramatically.
перело́мный *прил* critical.
перелью́ *итп сов см* **перели́ть**.
перема́|зать (**-жу, -жешь**; *impf* **перема́зывать**) *сов перех* to cover.
перема́лыва|ть (**-ю**) *несов от* **перемоло́ть**.
перем|ани́ть (**-аню́, -а́нишь**; *impf* **перема́нивать**) *сов перех* (*разг*) to entice.
перема́тыва|ть (**-ю**) *несов от* **перемота́ть**.
перемежа́|ть (**-ю**) *несов перех*: ~ **что-н с чем-н** to alternate sth with sth
▸ **перемежа́ться** *несов возв*: ~**ся с** *+instr* to alternate with.
перемелю́ *итп сов см* **перемоло́ть**.
переме́н|а (**-ы**) *ж* change; (*в школе*) break (*BRIT*), recess (*US*).
перем|ени́ть (**-еню́, -е́нишь**) *сов перех* to change
▸ **перемени́ться** *сов возв* (*жизнь, погода*) to change; **он** ~**ени́лся в лице́** (*от волнения итп*) his expression changed.
переме́нный *прил* (*погода*) changeable; (*успех, ветер*) variable; **переме́нный ток** alternating current.
переме́р|ить (**-ю, -ишь**; *impf* **переме́ривать**)

сов перех (*измерить снова*) to remeasure; (*примерить*) to try on.

переме|сти́ть (**-щу́, -сти́шь**; *impf* **перемеща́ть**) *сов перех* (*предмет*) to move, shift; (*людей*) to transfer

▸ **перемести́ться** (*impf* **перемеща́ться**) *сов возв* to move.

переметну́ть (**-у́, -ёшь**) *сов (не)перех*: ~ (**че́рез** *+acc*) to throw over

▸ **переметну́ться** *сов возв* (*на сторону противника итп*) to go over; **~ся** (*perf*) **че́рез** *+acc* to leap over.

перемеша́|ть (**-ю**; *impf* **переме́шивать**) *сов перех* (*кашу*) to stir; (*угли, дрова*) to poke; (*вещи, бумаги*) to mix up

▸ **перемеша́ться** (*impf* **переме́шиваться**) *сов возв* to get mixed up.

перемеща́|ть(ся) (**-ю(сь)**) *несов от* **перемести́ть(ся)**.

перемеще́ни|е (**-я**) *ср* reshuffle (*in government, of jobs*); (*передвижение*) transfer.

перемещённ|ый *прил*: **~ое лицо́** (*обычно мн*) displaced person (*мн* people).

перемещу́(сь) *сов см* **перемести́ть(ся)**.

перемигну́ться (**-у́сь, -ёшься**; *impf* **перемигиваться**) *сов возв* (*разг*) to wink at each other; **он ~у́лся с де́вушкой** he winked at the girl and she winked back.

перемина́|ться (**-юсь**) *несов возв*: ~ **с ноги́ на́ ногу** to shift from one foot to the other.

переми́ри|е (**-я**) *ср* truce.

перемно́ж|ить (**-у, -ишь**; *impf* **перемножа́ть**) *сов перех* (*числа*) to multiply.

перемо́лв|иться (**-люсь, -ишься**) *сов возв*: ~ (**сло́вом**) **с кем-н** (*разг*) to pass the time of day with sb.

перем|оло́ть (**-елю́, -е́лешь**; *impf* **перема́лывать**) *сов перех* to grind.

перемота́|ть (**-ю**; *impf* **перема́тывать**) *сов перех* (*нитку, шерсть*) to wind; (*магнитофонную плёнку*) to rewind.

перем|ы́ть (**-о́ю, -о́ешь**; *impf* **перемыва́ть**) *сов перех* to wash; (*вымыть заново*) to wash again, rewash; **перемыва́ть** (~ *perf*) **ко́сточки кому́-н** (*разг*) to gossip about sb.

перемы́ч|ка (**-ки**; *gen pl* **-ек**) *ж* (*соединение*) crosspiece; (*перекрытие: окна, двери*) lintel.

перенапря́г *итп сов см* **перенапря́чь**.

перенапряга́|ть (**-ю**) *несов от* **перенапря́чь**.

перенапрягу́ *итп сов см* **перенапря́чь**.

перенапряже́ни|е (**-я**) *ср* (*физическое, умственное*) overexertion.

перенапря́|чь (**-гу́, -жёшь** *итп*, **-гу́т**; *pt* **-г, -гла́, -гло́**, *impf* **перенапряга́ть**) *сов перех* to overstrain, overexert.

перенаселённ|ый (**-, -á, -ó**) *прил* overpopulated.

перенасы́|тить (**-щу, -тишь**; *impf* **перенасыща́ть**) *сов перех* to oversaturate; **он ~тил свою́ речь цита́тами** his speech was riddled with quotations.

перен|ести́ (**-есу́, -есёшь**; *pt* **-ёс, -есла́, -есло́**, *impf* **переноси́ть**) *сов перех*: ~ **что-н че́рез** *+acc* to carry sth over *или* across; (*поменять место*) to move; (*встречу, заседание*) to reschedule; (*болезнь*) to suffer from; (*несчастье, голод, холод итп*) to endure; **переноси́ть** (~ *perf*) **сло́во на другу́ю строку́** to carry a word over to the next line

▸ **перенести́сь** (*impf* **переноси́ться**) *сов возв* (*также перен*) to be transported.

перенима́|ть (**-ю**) *несов от* **переня́ть**.

перено́с (**-а**) *м* (*вещей, предметов*) transfer; (*заседания*) rescheduling; (*лИНГ*) hyphen.

перен|оси́ть (**-ошу́, -о́сишь**) *несов от* **перенести́** ◆ *перех*: **не ~ антибио́тиков/самолёта** to react badly to antibiotics/flying; **он хорошо́ ~ёс доро́гу** he coped well with the journey; **она́ не ~о́сит его́** she can't stand him

▸ **переноси́ться** *несов от* **перенести́сь**.

перено́сиц|а (**-ы**) *ж* bridge of the nose.

перено́сно́й *прил* portable.

перено́сный *прил* (*значение*) figurative.

перено́счик (**-а**) *м* (*МЕД*) carrier.

переноч|ева́ть (**-у́ю**) *сов от* **ночева́ть**.

переношу́(сь) *несов см* **переноси́ть(ся)**.

пере|ня́ть (**-йму́, -ймёшь**; *pt* **-ня́л, -няла́, -ня́ло**, *impf* **перенима́ть**) *сов перех* (*опыт, идеи*) to assimilate; (*обычаи, привычки*) to adopt.

переоборуд|овать (**-ую**) *сов перех* to re-equip.

переобу́|ть (**-ю, -ешь**; *impf* **переобува́ть**) *сов перех* (*туфли*) to change (out of); **переобува́ть** (~ *perf*) **кого́-н** to change sb's shoes.

переоде́|ть (**-ну, -нешь**; *impf* **переодева́ть**) *сов перех* (*одежду*) to change (out of); **переодева́ть** (~ *perf*) **кого́-н** to change sb's clothes

▸ **переоде́ться** (*impf* **переодева́ться**) *сов возв* to change, get changed.

переосмы́сл|ить (**-ю, -ишь**; *impf* **переосмы́сливать**) *сов перех* (*осмыслить заново*) to reassess.

переоц|енить (**-еню́, -е́нишь**; *impf* **переоце́нивать**) *сов перех* (*дать новую цену*) to re-evaluate, revalue; (*оценить слишком высоко*) to overestimate.

переоце́н|ка (**-ки**; *gen pl* **-ок**) *ж* (*см глаг*) re-evaluation, revaluation; overestimation; ~ **це́нностей** (*перен*) reappraisal *или* reassessment of values.

перепа́д (**-а**) *м*: ~ *+gen* drop in.

перепада́|ть (*3sg* **-ет**, *3pl* **-ют**) *несов от* **перепа́сть**.

перепадёт *итп сов см* **перепа́сть**.

перепа́л|ка (**-ки**; *gen pl* **-ок**) *ж* (*разг*) row.

перепа́|сть (*3sg* **-дёт**, *3pl* **-ду́т**, *impf* **перепада́ть**) *сов неперех* (*+dat*; *достаться*) to come one's way; **мне ~ла ко́е-кака́я ме́бель** some furniture has come my way.

перепа́чка|ть (**-ю**) *сов перех* (*разг*) to get filthy.

перепева́|ть (**-ю**) *несов перех* (*перен*) to rehash.

пе́репел (**-а**; *nom pl* **-а́**) *м* quail.

перепёл|ка (**-ки**; *gen pl* **-ок**) *ж см* **пе́репел**.

перепеча́та|ть (**-ю**) *сов перех* (*статью*) to reprint; (*рукопись*) to type.

переп|или́ть (**-илю́, -и́лишь**; *impf* **перепи́ливать**) *сов перех* (*много дров*) to saw; (*доску*) to saw in two.

переп|иса́ть (**-ишу́, -и́шешь**; *impf* **перепи́сывать**) *сов перех* (*написать заново*) to rewrite; (*скопировать*) to copy; (*сделать список*) to list, make a list of; (*КОМП*) to overwrite.

перепи́с|ка (**-ки**; *gen pl* **-ок**) *ж* (*см глаг*) rewriting; copying; listing; (*деловая*) correspondence ◆ *собир* (*письма*) letters *мн*; **быть** (*impf*) **в ~ке с** *+instr* to be in correspondence with.

перепи́сыва|ть (**-ю**) *несов от* **переписа́ть**

▸ **перепи́сываться** *несов возв*: **~ся** (**с** *+instr*) to correspond (with).

пе́репис|ь (**-и**) *ж* (*населения*) census; (*имущества*) inventory.

перепишу́ *итп сов см* **переписа́ть**.

перепл|ати́ть (**-ачу́, -а́тишь**; *impf* **перепла́чивать**) *сов неперех* to pay too much.

перепл|ести́ (**-ету́, -етёшь**; *pt* **-ёл, -ела́, -ело́**, *impf* **переплета́ть**) *сов перех* (*книгу, диссертацию*) to bind; (*верёвки, пальцы*) to interlace

▸ **переплести́сь** (*impf* **переплета́ться**) *сов возв* to intertwine; (*перен*: *события*) to become interwoven.

переплёт (**-а**) *м* (*обложка*) binding; **попада́ть** (**попа́сть** *perf*) **в ~** (*перен*: *разг*) to get into a fix; **отдава́ть** (**отда́ть** *perf*) **книгу/диссерта́цию в ~** to have a book/thesis bound; **око́нный ~** window sash.

переплета́|ть(ся) (**-ю(сь)**) *несов от* **переплести́(сь)**.

переплётн|ая (**-ой**; *decl like adj*) *ж* (book) bindery.

переплету́(сь) *итп сов см* **переплести́(сь)**.

перепл|ы́ть (**-ву́, -вёшь**; *pt* **-л, -ла́, -ло**, *impf* **переплыва́ть**) *сов* (*не*)*перех*: **~** (**че́рез** *+acc*) (*вплавь*) to swim (across); (*на лодке, на корабле*) to sail (across).

переплю́н|уть (**-у, -ешь**) *сов перех* (*перен*: *разг*) to go one up on.

переподгото́в|ка (**-ки**; *gen pl* **-ок**) *ж* retraining.

перепол|зти́ (**-у́, -ёшь**; *pt* **-, -ла́, -ло́**, *impf* **переполза́ть**) *сов* (*не*)*перех* to crawl; **переполза́ть** (**~** *perf*) (**че́рез** *+acc*) (*дорогу, поле итп*) to crawl across.

перепо́лн|ить (**-ю, -ишь**; *impf* **переполня́ть**) *сов перех* (*сосуд, контейнер*) to overfill; (*вагон, автобус итп*) to overcrowd; **моё се́рдце ~ено любо́вью** my heart is overflowing with love

▸ **перепо́лниться** (*impf* **переполня́ться**) *сов возв* (*сосуд*) to be overfilled; (*душа, сердце*) to overflow.

переполо́х (**-а**) *м* hullabaloo.

переполоши́ть (**-у́, -и́шь**) *сов перех* (*разг*) to alarm

▸ **переполоши́ться** *сов возв* (*разг*) to become alarmed.

перепо́н|ка (**-ки**; *gen pl* **-ок**) *ж* membrane; **бараба́нная ~** eardrum.

перепра́в|а (**-ы**) *ж* crossing.

перепра́в|ить (**-лю, -ишь**; *impf* **переправля́ть**) *сов перех* (*через реку, границу*) to take across; (*посылку, письмо*) to forward; (*ошибку, фразу*) to correct

▸ **перепра́виться** (*impf* **переправля́ться**) *сов возв* (*через реку, горы итп*) to cross.

перепро́б|овать (**-ую**) *сов перех* (*еду*) to taste; (*способы*) to try (out).

перепрода|ва́ть (**-ю́**; *imper* **перепродава́й(те)**) *несов от* **перепрода́ть**.

перепрода́ть (*как* **дать**; *см* **Table 14**; *impf* **перепродава́ть**) *сов перех* to resell.

перепроизво́дств|о (**-а**) *ср* overproduction.

перепры́гн|уть (**-у, -ешь**; *impf* **перепры́гивать**) *сов* (*не*)*перех*: **~** (**че́рез** *+acc*) to jump (over).

перепу́г (**-а**) *м* (*разг*): **с ~у** in fright.

перепуга́|ть (**-ю**) *сов перех*: **~ кого́-н** to scare the life out of sb.

перепу́та|ть (**-ю**; *impf* **перепу́тывать** *или* **пу́тать**) *сов перех* (*нитки, провода*) to tangle (up); (*факты*) to confuse; (*имена, адреса*) to mix up

▸ **перепу́таться** (*impf* **перепу́тываться** *или* **пу́таться**) *сов возв* (*нитки, провода*) to get tangled up; (*перен*: *мысли, воспоминания*) to get confused.

перепу́ть|е (**-я**) *ср* crossroads; **на ~** (*перен*) at a crossroads.

перерабо́та|ть (**-ю**; *impf* **перераба́тывать**) *сов перех* (*сырьё, нефть*) to process; (*идеи, статью, теорию*) to rework ◆ *неперех* (*переутомиться*) to be overworked.

перераспредел|и́ть (**-ю́, -и́шь**; *impf* **перераспределя́ть**) *сов перех* to redistribute.

перер|асти́ (**-асту́, -астёшь**; *pt* **-о́с, -осла́, -осло́**, *impf* **перераста́ть**) *сов перех* (*также перен*) to outgrow; **перераста́ть** (**~** *perf*) **в** *+acc* (*превратиться*) to escalate into.

перерасхо́д (**-а**) *м* (*энергии, денег*) overexpenditure; (*КОММ*) overdraft.

перерасхо́д|овать (**-ую**) *сов перех*: **~ эне́ргию/де́ньги** to expend too much energy/money.

перерасчёт (**-а**) *м* (*счёт заново*) recalculation; (*КОММ*: *в другие единицы*) conversion.

переpе́|зать (**-жу, -жешь**; *impf* **перереза́ть**) *сов перех* (*провод*) to cut in two; (*перен*:

преградить) to cut off.
перерис|ова́ть (**-у́ю**; *impf* **перерисо́вывать**) *сов перех* to copy.
переро|ди́ться (**-жу́сь, -ди́шься**; *impf* **перерожда́ться**) *сов возв* (*природа, общество*) to be regenerated; (*человек*) to be transformed.
перерожде́ни|е (**-я**) *ср* (*см глаг*) regeneration; transformation.
перерожу́сь *сов см* **перероди́ться**.
перерóс *итп сов см* **перерасти́**.
перерóю *итп сов см* **перерыть**.
переруга́|ться (**-юсь**) *сов возв* to quarrel.
переры́в (**-а**) *м* break; **обе́денный ~** lunch break; **де́лать** (**сде́лать** *perf*) **~** to take a break.
перер|ы́ть (**-óю, -óешь**) *сов перех* (*перекопать*) to dig up; (*разг*: *вещи, книги*) to rummage through.
перес|ади́ть (**-ажу́, -а́дишь**; *impf* **переса́живать**) *сов перех* to move; (*на другой поезд, самолёт итп*) to transfer; (*дерево, цветок, сердце*) to transplant; (*кость, кожу*) to graft; **переса́живать** (**~** *perf*) **кого́-н на друго́е ме́сто** to move sb to another seat.
переса́д|ка (**-ки**; *gen pl* **-ок**) *ж* (*растения*) transplantation; (*на поезд итп*) change; (*МЕД*: *сердца*) transplant; (: *кожи*) graft; **де́лать** (**сде́лать** *perf*) **~ку в Москве́** to change in Moscow.
переса́жива|ть (**-ю**) *несов от* **пересади́ть**.
переса́жива|ться (**-юсь**) *несов от* **пересе́сть**.
пересажу́ *сов см* **пересади́ть**.
переса́лива|ть (**-ю**) *несов от* **пересоли́ть**.
переcда|ва́ть (**-ю́**; *imper* **передава́й(те)**) *несов перех* to resit.
пересда́ть (*как* **дать**; *см* **Table 14**) *сов перех* (*экзамен, зачёт*) to pass (*after resit*).
пересёк(ся) *итп сов см* **пересе́чь(ся)**.
пересека́|ть(ся) (**-ю(сь)**) *несов от* **пересе́чь(ся)**.
пересеку́(сь) *итп сов см* **пересе́чь(ся)**.
переселе́н|ец (**-ца**) *м* (*на новую территорию*) settler; (*временно переселяемый*) *person having to move to temporary accommodation.*
переселе́н|ка (**-ки**; *gen pl* **-ок**) *ж см* **переселе́нец**.
переселе́нца *итп сущ см* **переселе́нец**.
пересел|и́ть (**-ю́, -и́шь**; *impf* **переселя́ть**) *сов перех* (*на новые земли*) to settle; (*в новую квартиру*) to move
▸ **пересели́ться** (*impf* **переселя́ться**) *сов возв* (*в другую страну*) to emigrate; (*в новый дом*) to move.
перес|е́сть (**-я́ду, -я́дешь**; *impf* **переса́живаться**) *сов неперех* (*на другое место*) to move; **переса́живаться** (**~** *perf*) **на друго́е ме́сто** to move to another seat; **переса́живаться** (**~** *perf*) **на друго́й по́езд/самолёт** to change trains/planes.
пересече́ни|е (**-я**) *ср* (*действие*) crossing; (*место*) intersection.
пересечённый *прил* (*ГЕО*: *местность итп*) broken.
перес|е́чь (**-еку́, -ечёшь** *итп*, **-еку́т**; *pt* **-ёк, -екла́, -екло́**, *impf* **пересека́ть**) *сов перех* to cross
▸ **пересе́чься** (*impf* **пересека́ться**) *сов возв* to intersect; (*интересы*) to cross.
переси́л|ить (**-ю, -ишь**; *impf* **переси́ливать**) *сов перех* (*человека*) to overpower; (*чувство*) to overcome.
перескажу́ *итп сов см* **пересказа́ть**.
переска́з (**-а**) *м* (*содержания фильма*) retelling; (*изложение*) exposition.
переск|аза́ть (**-ажу́, -а́жешь**; *impf* **переска́зывать**) *сов перех* to tell.
перес|кочи́ть (**-очу́, -о́чишь**; *impf* **переска́кивать**) *сов (не)перех*: **~** (**че́рез** *+acc*) to jump (over); (*перен*): **~ на** *+acc* (*на другую тему*) to jump to.
пересла|сти́ть (**-щу́, -сти́шь**; *impf* **пересла́щивать**) *сов перех*: **~ что-н** to put too much sugar in sth.
пере|сла́ть (**-шлю́, -шлёшь**; *impf* **пересыла́ть**) *сов перех* (*отослать*) to send; (*по другому адресу*) to forward.
пересла́щива|ть (**-ю**) *несов от* **пересласти́ть**.
переслащу́ *сов см* **пересласти́ть**.
пересма́трива|ть (**-ю**) *несов от* **пересмотре́ть**.
пересме́ива|ться (**-юсь**) *несов возв* to smile at each other.
пересме́н|а (**-ы**) *ж* (*на заводе, на вахте*) change of shift.
пересме́шник (**-а**) *м* mockingbird.
пересм|отре́ть (**-отрю́, -о́тришь**; *impf* **пересма́тривать**) *сов перех* (*книги, вещи*) to look through; (*решение, вопрос, позицию*) to reconsider.
пересн|я́ть (**-иму́, -и́мешь**; *pt* **-я́л,-яла́,-я́ло**, *impf* **переснима́ть**) *сов перех* (*документ*) to make a copy of; (*сцену в фильме*) to reshoot; (*фотографию*) to take again.
перес|оли́ть (**-олю́, -о́лишь**; *impf* **переса́ливать**) *сов перех*: **~ что-н** to put too much salt in sth.
пересо́х|нуть (*3sg* **-нет**, *3pl* **-нут**, *pt* **-, -ла, -ло**, *impf* **пересыха́ть**) *сов неперех* (*почва, бельё*) to dry out; (*река, ручей*) to dry up.
пересп|а́ть (**-лю́, -и́шь**; *impf* **пересыпа́ть**) *сов неперех* (*спать слишком долго*) to oversleep; **~** (*perf*) **с кем-н** (*разг*) to sleep with sb.
переспе́лый *прил* overripe.
переспе́|ть (*3sg* **-ет**, *3pl* **-ют**) *сов неперех* to become overripe.
пересплю́ *сов см* **переспа́ть**.

переспо́р|ить (**-ю, -ишь**) *сов перех*: ~ **кого́-н** to defeat sb in an argument.
переспр|оси́ть (**-ошу́, -о́сишь**; *impf* **переспра́шивать**) *сов перех* to ask again.
перессо́р|иться (**-юсь, -ишься**) *сов возв*: ~ (**с** +*instr*) to quarrel *или* fall out (with).
переста|ва́ть (**-ю́**; *imper* **перестава́й(те)**) *несов от* **переста́ть**.
переста́в|ить (**-лю, -ишь**; *impf* **переставля́ть**) *сов перех* to move; (*изменить порядок*) to rearrange.
переста́ну *итп сов см* **переста́ть**.
перестара́|ться (**-юсь**) *сов возв* to overdo it.
переста́|ть (**-ну, -нешь**; *impf* **перестава́ть**) *сов неперех* to stop; **перестава́ть** (~ *perf*) +*infin* to stop doing; ~**ньте!** stop it!
перестира́|ть (**-ю**; *impf* **перести́рывать**) *сов перех* (*все вещи*) to wash; (*постирать заново*) to wash again, rewash.
престо|я́ть (*3sg* **-и́т**, *3pl* **-я́т**) *сов неперех* (*квас, суп*) to stand too long; (*молоко*) to go off.
перестрада́|ть (**-ю**) *сов (не)перех* to suffer.
перестра́ива|ть(ся) (**-ю(сь)**) *несов от* **перестро́ить(ся)**.
перестрах|ова́ться (**-у́юсь**; *impf* **перестрахо́вываться**) *сов возв* (*комм*) to reinsure; (*перен*) to play safe.
перестрахо́в|ка (**-ки**; *gen pl* **-ок**) *ж* (*см глаг*) reinsurance; playing safe.
перестрахо́выва|ться (**-юсь**) *несов от* **перестрахова́ться**.
перестре́л|ка (**-ка**; *gen pl* **-ок**) *ж* exchange of fire.
перестро́ек *сущ см* **перестро́йка**.
перестро́ечный *прил* (*процессы, явления*) perestroika *опред*.
перестро́|ить (**-ю, -ишь**; *impf* **перестра́ивать**) *сов перех* (*дом, мост*) to rebuild, reconstruct; (*програму, экономику*) to reorganize; (*ряды, колонны*) to re-form; (*музыкальный инструмент*) to retune
▸ **перестро́иться** (*impf* **перестра́иваться**) *сов возв* (*человек*) to reorganize o.s.; (*фабрика, коллектив*) to restructure; (*солдаты, шеренги*) to re-form.
пере́стро́|йка (**-йки**; *gen pl* **-ек**) *ж* (*дома*) rebuilding, reconstruction; (*расписания, экономики*) reorganization; (*муз*) retuning; (*ист*) perestroika.
перест|упи́ть (**-уплю́, -у́пишь**; *impf* **переступа́ть**) *сов (не)перех* (*перен*) to overstep; **переступа́ть** (~ *perf*) (**че́рез** +*acc*) (*порог, предмет*) to step over.
пересу́д|ы (**-ов**) *мн* (*разг*) gossip *ед*.
пересчёт (**-а**) *м* count; (*повторный*) re-count; **ско́лько э́то в** ~**е на рубли́?** how much is it when converted into roubles?
пересчита́|ть (**-ю**; *impf* **пересчи́тывать**) *сов перех* to count; (*повторно*) to re-count, count again; (*в других единицах*) to convert.
пересыла́|ть (**-ю**) *несов от* **пересла́ть**.
пересы́л|ка (**-ки**; *gen pl* **-ок**) *ж* sending; (*тюрьма*) transit prison (*where prisoners stay temporarily*).
пересы́п|ать (**-лю, -лешь**; *impf* **пересыпа́ть**) *сов перех* (*насыпать*) to pour; (*перен*: *речь, рассказ*) to intersperse.
пересыпа́|ть (**-ю**) *несов от* **переспа́ть**.
пересы́плю *итп сов см* **пересы́пать**.
пересыха́|ть (*3sg* **-ет**, *3pl* **-ют**) *несов от* **пересо́хнуть**.
переся́ду *итп сов см* **пересе́сть**.
перета́скива|ть (**-ю**) *несов от* **перетащи́ть**.
перетас|ова́ть (**-у́ю**; *impf* **перетасо́вывать**) *сов перех* (*карты*) to shuffle; (*перен*: *министров*) to reshuffle.
перет|ащи́ть (**-ащу́, -а́щишь**; *impf* **перета́скивать**) *сов перех* (*мешок*) to drag over.
перетр|уди́ться (**-ужу́сь, -у́дишься**; *impf* **перетружда́ться**) *сов возв* (*разг*) to be burnt out.
перетру́|сить (**-шу, -сишь**) *сов неперех* (*разг*) to be scared out of one's wits.
перетряс|ти́ (**-у́, -ёшь**; *pt* **-, -ла́, -ло́**) *сов перех* to shake out.
пере́ть (**пру, прёшь**; *pt* **пёр, пёрла, пёрло**) *несов неперех* (*разг*: *идти*) to trudge; (*ломиться*) to barge through; (*perf* **спере́ть**; *красть*) to pinch
▸ **пере́ться** *несов возв* (*разг*: *идти*) to trudge.
перет|януть (**-яну́, -я́нешь**; *impf* **перетя́гивать**) *сов перех* (*передвинуть*) to pull, tow; (*быть более тяжёлым*) to outweigh; (*стянуть*): ~ **что-н чем-н** to tie sth tightly round sth.
переубе|ди́ть (**-жу́, -ди́шь**; *impf* **переубежда́ть**) *сов перех*: ~ **кого́-н** to make sb change his mind.
переу́л|ок (**-ка**) *м* lane, alley.
переустро́йств|о (**-а**) *ср* reconstruction.
переутом|и́ться (**-лю́сь, -и́шься**; *impf* **переутомля́ться**) *сов возв* to tire o.s. out.
переутомле́ни|е (**-я**) *ср* exhaustion.
переутомлю́сь *сов см* **переутоми́ться**.
переутомля́|ться (**-юсь**) *несов от* **переутоми́ться**.
переучёт (**-а**) *м* stocktaking.
переуч|и́ть (**-учу́, -у́чишь**; *impf* **переу́чивать**) *сов перех* to retrain
▸ **переучи́ться** (*impf* **переу́чиваться**) *сов возв* to undergo retraining.
переформати́р|овать (**-ую**) *(не)сов перех* (*комп*) to reformat.
перефрази́р|овать (**-ую**) *(не)сов перех* to paraphrase.
перехв|ати́ть (**-ачу́, -а́тишь**; *impf* **перехва́тывать**) *сов перех* (*захватить на пути*) to intercept; (*разг*: *переборщить*) to go too far; (*обвязать*): ~ **что-н чем-н** to tie sth round sth; **у него́** ~**а́тило дыха́ние** he caught his breath; **перехва́тывать** (~ *perf*) **бутербро́д** (*разг*) to grab a sandwich; **перехва́тывать** (~ *perf*) **чей-н взгляд** (*перен*) to catch sb's eye.

перехитр|и́ть (-ю́, -и́шь) *сов перех* to outwit.
перехо́д (-а) *м* crossing; (*к другой системе*) transition; (*в здании, между зданиями*) passage.
перех|оди́ть (-ожу́, -о́дишь) *несов от* **перейти́.**
перехо́дный *прил* (*промежуточный*) transitional; **перехо́дный глаго́л** transitive verb.
переходя́щ|ий (-ая, -ее, -ие) *прил*: ~ **ку́бок** (*СПОРТ*) challenge cup.
перехожу́ *несов см* **переходи́ть.**
пе́р|ец (-ца) *м* pepper; (*зёрнышко*) peppercorn; **жгу́чий** ~ chilli pepper; **болга́рский** ~ capsicum.
пе́реч|ень (-ня) *м* list; ~ **служе́бных обя́занностей** job specification.
перечеркн|у́ть (-у́, -ёшь; *impf* **перечёркивать)** *сов перех* to cross out; (*перен*: *надежды*) to shatter.
переч|ерти́ть (-ерчу́, -е́ртишь; *impf* **перече́рчивать)** *сов перех* (*начертить снова*) to draw again; (*скопировать*) to copy.
переч|е́сть (-ту́, -тёшь; *pt* **-ёл, -ла́, -ло́)** *сов перех* (*пересчитать*) to re-count, count again; (*перечитать*) to reread, read again.
перечисле́ни|е (-я) *ср* transfer; **плати́ть (заплати́ть** *perf*) **по ~ю** to pay by transfer.
перечи́сл|ить (-ю, -ишь; *impf* **перечисля́ть)** *сов перех* (*упомянуть*) to list; (*КОММ*) to transfer.
перечита́|ть (-ю; *impf* **перечи́тывать)** *сов перех* to read; (*читать заново*) to reread, read again.
пе́речня *итп сущ см* **пе́речень.**
перечту́ *итп сов см* **перече́сть.**
перешагн|у́ть (-у́, -ёшь; *impf* **переша́гивать)** *сов (не)перех*: ~ **(че́рез** *+acc*) to step over.
переше́|ек (-йка) *м* isthmus.
перешёл *итп сов см* **перейти́.**
перешёптыва|ться (-юсь) *несов возв* to whisper to each other.
переш|и́ть (-ью́, -ьёшь; *impf* **перешива́ть)** *сов перех* (*платье, костюм*) to alter; (*пуговицу, крючок*) to move (*by sewing on somewhere else*).
перешлю́ *сов см* **пересла́ть.**
перещеголя́|ть (-ю) *сов перех* (*разг*) to outshine.
переэкзамено́в|ка (-ки; *gen pl* **-ок)** *ж* resit.
пери́л|а (-) *мн* railing *ед*; (*лестницы*) banisters *мн*.
пери́метр (-а) *м* perimeter.
пери́н|а (-ы) *ж* feather bed.
пери́од (-а) *м* period; **пе́рвый/второ́й ~ игры́** (*СПОРТ*) first/second half (of the game).
перио́дик|а (-и) *ж собир* periodicals *мн*.
периоди́чески *нареч* periodically.
периоди́ческ|ий (-ая, -ое, -ие) *прил* periodical *опред*; **периоди́ческая печа́ть** the periodical press.
периоди́чност|ь (-и) *ж* regularity.
перипети́|я (-и) *ж* (*обычно мн*) upheaval.
перитони́т (-а) *м* peritonitis.
периферийный *прил* peripheral.
перифери́|я (-и) *ж* the provinces *мн* ♦ *собир* (*КОМП*) peripherals *мн*, peripheral devices *мн*.
перифрази́р|овать (-ую) *(не)сов перех* to paraphrase.
перл (-а) *м* (*также перен*) pearl.
перламу́тр (-а) *м* mother-of-pearl.
перламу́тровый *прил* mother-of-pearl *опред*; (*цвет*) pearly.
перло́в|ка (-ки; *gen pl* **-ок)** *ж* (*разг*) pearl barley.
перло́в|ый *прил* (*суп, каша*) barley *опред*; **~ая крупа́** pearl barley.
перлюстри́р|овать (-ую) *сов перех* to censor.
пермане́нт (-а) *м* perm (= *permanent wave*).
пермане́нт|ный (-ен, -на, -но) *прил* permanent.
перна́т|ый (-ого; *decl like adj*) **м** (*обычно мн*) bird.
пёрн|уть (-у, -ешь) *сов неперех* (*груб!*) to fart (*!*)
пер|о́ (-а́; *nom pl* **-ья,** *gen pl* **-ьев)** *ср* (*птицы*) feather; (*для письма*: *гусиное*) quill; (: *стальное, золотое*) nib.
перочи́нный *прил*: ~ **нож** penknife (*мн* penknives).
перпендикуля́р|ный (-ен, -на, -но) *прил* perpendicular.
перро́н (-а) *м* platform (*RAIL*).
перс (-а) *м* Persian.
перси́дск|ий (-ая, -ое, -ие) *прил* Persian; **Перси́дский зали́в** Persian Gulf.
пе́рсик (-а) *м* (*дерево*) peach tree; (*плод*) peach.
Пе́рси|я (-и) *ж* Persia.
персия́н|ка (-ки; *gen pl* **-ок)** *ж см* **перс.**
персо́н|а (-ы) *ж* person; **со́бственной ~ой** in person.
персона́ж (-а) *м* character.
персона́л (-а) *м* (*АДМИН*) personnel, staff.
персона́льный *прил* personal; **персона́льная вы́ставка** one-man exhibition; **персона́льный компью́тер** PC (= *personal computer*).
перспекти́в|а (-ы) *ж* (*ГЕОМ*) perspective; (*вид*) view; **~ы** (*планы*) prospects *мн*; **в ~е** (*в будущем*) in store.
перспекти́вный *прил* (*изображение*) in perspective; (*планирование*) long-term; (*многообещающий*) promising; ~ **план** plan of future developments.
пе́рст|ень (-ня) *м* ring.
Перу́ *ж нескл* Peru.
перуа́нск|ий (-ая, -ое, -ие) *прил* Peruvian.
перфока́рт|а (-ы) *ж сокр* (= *перфорацио́нная ка́рта*) punched *или* punch (*BRIT*) card.
перфоле́нт|а (-ы) *ж сокр* (= *перфорацио́нная ле́нта*) punched tape.

пéрхот|ь (-и) *ж собир* dandruff.
пéрца *итп сущ см* **пéрец**.
перчáт|ка (-ки; *gen pl* **-ок)** *ж* glove; (*боксёра*) (boxing) glove; **пéрвая ~** (*СПОРТ*) champion boxer.
пéрч|ить (-у, -ишь; *perf* **наперчи́ть** *или* **поперчи́ть)** *сов перех* to pepper.
перш|и́ть (*3sg* **-и́т**) *несов безл* (*разг*): **у меня́ ~и́т в гóрле** I've got a frog in my throat.
пéрья *итп сущ см* **перó**.
пёс (пса) *м* dog.
пéсен *сущ см* **пéсня**.
пéсенник (-а) *м* songbook; (*композитор*) songwriter.
пес|éц (-цá) *м* arctic fox.
пескá *итп сущ см* **песóк**.
пескáр|ь (-я́) *м* gudgeon.
песк|и́ (-óв) *мн* sands *мн*.
песн|ь (-и; *gen pl* **-ей)** *ж* (*в поэме*) canto.
пéс|ня (-ни; *gen pl* **-ен)** *ж* song; **стáрая ~** (*разг*) the same old story.
пес|óк (-кá; *part gen* **-кý)** *м* sand; **сáхарный ~** granulated sugar; *см также* **пески́**.
песóчниц|а (-ы) *ж* sandpit (*BRIT*), sandbox (*US*).
песóчный *прил* (*цвет*) sandy; (*тесто, печенье*) short; **песóчные часы́** hourglass.
пессими́ст (-а) *м* pessimist.
пессимисти́ч|ный (-ен, -на, -но) *прил* pessimistic.
пестици́д (-а) *м* pesticide.
пéст|овать (-ую; *perf* **вы́пестовать)** *несов перех* (*перен*) to nurture.
пестр|éть (*3sg* **-ет**, *3pl* **-ют**) *несов неперех* (*виднеться*) to be colourful (*BRIT*) *или* colorful (*US*); (*3pl* **-я́т**; *мелькать*) to make a colo(u)rful display; **в садý/на лугý ~ют цветы́** the garden/meadow is bright with flowers.
пестр|и́ть (*3sg* **-и́т**, *3pl* **-я́т**) *несов неперех*: **~** *+instr* to be full of.
пёстр|ый (-, -á, -о) *прил* (*ткань, ковёр*) multi-coloured (*BRIT*), multi-colored (*US*); (*перен: разнородный*) mixed.
песцá *итп сущ см* **песéц**.
песчáник (-а) *м* sandstone.
песчáн|ый *прил* (*берег, дно реки*) sandy; **песчáная бýря** sandstorm.
пéтель *сущ см* **пéтля**.
Петербýрг *сущ* = **Санкт-Петербýрг**.
пети́ци|я (-и) *ж* petition.
петли́ц|а (-ы) *ж* (*петля*) buttonhole; (*нашивка*) tab (*on uniform*).
пé|тля (-ли; *gen pl* **-ель)** *ж* loop; (*в вязании*) stitch; (*двери, крышки*) hinge; (*в одежде: для пуговицы*) buttonhole; (*: для крючка*) eye.
петля́|ть (-ю) *несов неперех* to meander.
петрýшк|а (-и) *ж* parsley.
петýнь|я (-и) *ж* petunia.
петýх (-á) *м* cock, rooster (*US*).
петуши́ный *прил* (*пение*) cocks'; **~ бой** cock-fight; **~ гóлос** a squeaky voice.
пе|ть (пою́, поёшь; *pt* **-л, -ла, -лo**, *imper* **пóй(те)**, *perf* **спеть)** *несов перех* to sing.
пехóт|а (-ы) *ж* infantry.
пехоти́н|ец (-ца) *м* infantryman (*мн* infantrymen).
пехóтный *прил* infantry *опред*.
печáлен *прил см* **печáльный**.
печáл|иться (-юсь, -ишься; *perf* **опечáлиться)** *несов возв* to be sad.
печáл|ь (-и) *ж* (*грусть*) sadness, sorrow; **нé было ~и!** (*разг*) what a nuisance!
печáльно *нареч* (*петь, выглядеть*) sadly ◆ *как сказ* it's sad; **~, что мы не встрéтились** it's sad that we didn't meet; **~ извéстный** notorious.
печáл|ьный (-ен, -ьна, -ьно) *прил* sad; (*ошибка, судьба, память*) unhappy; **~ьная извéстность** *или* **слáва** ill repute.
печáта|ть (-ю; *perf* **напечáтать)** *несов перех* (*также ФОТО*) to print; (*публиковать*) to publish; (*на пишущей машинке*) to type
▸ **печáтаться** (*perf* **напечáтаться**) *несов возв* to have one's work published.
печáтающ|ий (-ая, -ее, -ие) *прил*: **~ая голóвка** (*КОМП*) printhead; **~ее колесó** (*КОМП*) printwheel.
печáт|ка (-ки; *gen pl* **-ок)** *ж* signet.
печáтник (-а) *м* (*работник*) printer.
печáтн|ый *прил* (*станок*) printing *опред*; (*цех*) print *опред*; (*интервью итп*) published; **писáть (написáть** *perf***) ~ыми бýквами** to print; **печáтные бýквы** block letters; **печáтный лист** (*единица измерения*) printer's sheet.
печáток *сущ см* **печáтка**.
печáт|ь (-и) *ж* stamp, seal; (*на дверях, на сейфе*) seal; (*издательское дело*) printing; (*след: страданий*) mark ◆ *собир* (*пресса*) press; **выходи́ть (вы́йти** *perf***) из ~и** to come out, be published.
пéчек *сущ см* **пéчка**.
печён|ка (-ки; *gen pl* **-ок)** *ж* liver; **в ~х сидéть** (*impf*) **у когó-н** (*разг*) to get on sb's nerves.
печёный *прил* baked.
пéчен|ь (-и) *ж* (*АНАТ*) liver.
печéнь|е (-я) *ср* biscuit (*BRIT*), cookie (*US*).
пéч|ка (-ки; *gen pl* **-ек)** *ж* stove.
пе|чь (-чи; *loc sg* **-чи́**, *gen pl* **-éй)** *ж* stove; (*ТЕХ*) furnace; (*: обжиговая*) kiln; ◆ **(-кý, -чёшь** *итп*, **-кýт**; *pt* **пёк, -клá, -клó**, *perf* **испéчь)** *несов перех* to bake; **микроволнóвая ~** microwave oven
▸ **пéчься** (*perf* **испéчься**) *несов возв* to bake; (*заботиться*): **пéчься о** *+prp* to look after (*BRIT*), take care of (*US*).
пéшек *сущ см* **пéшка**.
пешехóд (-а) *м* pedestrian.
пешехóдный *прил* pedestrian *опред*; (*совершаемый пешком*) on foot; **пешехóдный мост** footbridge.
пéш|ий (-ая, -ее, -ие) *прил* (*солдат*) foot *опред*; (*движение*) pedestrian *опред*; (*совершаемый пешком*) on foot; **~им хóдом** on foot.
пéш|ка (-ки; *gen pl* **-ек)** *ж* (*также перен*) pawn.
пешкóм *нареч* on foot.

пещéр|а (-ы) *ж* cave.
пещéрный *прил* (*живопись*) cave *опред*; **пещéрный человéк** caveman (*мн* cavemen).
ПЗУ *ср сокр* (= *постоя́нное запомина́ющее устрóйство*) ROM (= *read-only memory*).
пиал|á (-ы́) *ж* *handleless cup used in Central Asia*.
пиани́но *ср нескл* (upright) piano.
пиани́ст (-а) *м* pianist.
пиани́ст|ка (-ки; *gen pl* -ок) *ж см* **пиани́ст**.
пивн|áя (-óй; *decl like adj*) *ж* ≈ bar, ≈ pub (*BRIT*).
пивнóй *прил* (*бар, бочка*) beer *опред*; (*дрожжи*) brewer's.
пи́в|о (-а) *ср* beer.
пи́галиц|а (-ы) *ж* (*перен: пренебр*) pipsqueak.
пигмé|й (-я) *м* pygmy.
пигмéнт (-а) *м* pigment.
пигментáци|я (-и) *ж* pigmentation.
пиджáк (-á) *м* jacket.
пижáм|а (-ы) *ж* pyjamas *мн*.
пи́жм|а (-ы) *ж* (*трава*) feverfew; (*дерево*) wild rowan.
пижóн (-а) *м* (*разг: пренебр*) pose(u)r.
пик (-а) *м* (*также перен*) peak ◆ *прил неизм* (*часы, период, время*) peak *опред*; **часы́ ~** (*в работе транспорта*) rush hour; (*электростанции, телефона итп*) peak period.
пи́к|а (-и) *ж* (*рыцаря*) lance; (*солдата*) pike; **в ~у комý-н** to get at sb.
пикáнт|ный (-ен, -на, -но) *прил* (*вкус*) piquant; (*случай, слухи*) spicy; (*женщина, внешность*) alluring.
пикéт (-а) *м* picket.
пикети́р|овать (-ую) *несов перех* to picket.
пи́к|и (-) *мн* (*в картах*) spades *мн*.
пики́р|овать (-ую) *(не)сов неперех* (*АВИА*) to dive.
пикирóвщик (-а) *м* (*АВИА*) dive-bomber.
пикни́к (-á) *м* picnic.
пи́кн|уть (-у, -ешь) *сов неперех* (*разг: животное*) to let out a squeak; (*: птица*) to let out a squawk; **он при ней не смел и ~** he wouldn't dare speak out in her presence.
пи́ков|ый *прил* (*наивысший*) peak *опред*; (*в картах*) of spades; **~ое положéние** (*разг*) mess.
пи́ксел|ь (-я) *м* (*КОМП*) pixel.
пил *итп несов см* **пить**.
пил|á (-ы́; *nom pl* -ы) *ж* saw.
пилигри́м (-а) *м* pilgrim.
пили́ка|ть (-ю) *несов неперех* (*разг*): **~ на** *+prp* (*на скрипке*) to scrape away on.
пил|и́ть (-ю́, -ишь) *несов перех* to saw; (*перен: разг*) to nag.
пи́л|ка (-ки; *gen pl* -ок) *ж* nail file.
пиломатериáл|ы (-ов) *мн* sawn timber *ед*.
пилóт (-а) *м* pilot; (*СПОРТ*) driver.
пилоти́р|овать (-ую) *несов перех* to pilot.
пилóт|ка (-ки; *gen pl* -ок) *ж* *cloth cap worn as part of uniform*.
пилю́л|я (-и) *ж* pill; **проглоти́ть** *(perf)* **~ю** (*перен*) to swallow a bitter pill.
пиля́стр|а (-ы) *ж* pilaster.
пинá|ть (-ю) *несов перех* to kick.
пингви́н (-а) *м* penguin.
пинг-пóнг (-а) *м* table tennis, ping-pong.
пинéт|ка (-ки; *gen pl* -ок) *ж* (*обычно мн*) bootee.
пин|óк (-кá) *м* kick.
пинцéт (-а) *м* (*МЕД*) tweezers *мн*; (*ТЕХ*) pincers *мн*.
пиóн (-а) *м* peony.
пионéр (-а) *м* pioneer; (*в СССР*) *member of Communist Youth organisation*.
пипéт|ка (-ки; *gen pl* -ок) *ж* pipette.
пир (-а; *loc sg* -ý, *nom pl* -ы́) *м* feast.
пирами́д|а (-ы) *ж* pyramid.
пирáт (-а) *м* pirate.
пирáтский (-ая, -ое, -ие) *прил* pirate *опред*.
Пиренé|и (-ев) *мн* Pyrenees.
пир|овáть (-ýю) *несов неперех* to feast.
пирóг (-á) *м* pie.
пирожкá *итп сущ см* **пирожóк**.
пирожкóв|ая (-ой; *decl like adj*) *ж* (*тип закусочной*) snack-bar.
пирóжн|ое (-ого; *decl like adj*) *ср* cake, sweet pastry.
пирож|óк (-кá) *м* (*с мясом*) pasty, pie; (*с вареньем*) turnover, tart.
пирс (-а) *м* pier.
пируэ́т (-а) *м* pirouette.
пи́ршеств|о (-а) *ср* feast.
писáк|а (-и) *м/ж* (*разг: пренебр*) scribbler.
писáни|е (-я) *ср* (*действие*) writing; **Свящéнное П~** Holy Scripture.
писани́н|а (-ы) *ж* (*разг: пренебр*) scribblings *мн*.
пи́сан|ый *прил* (*разг*): **онá ~ая красáвица** she is a picture of beauty ◆ (-ого; *decl like adj*) *м*: **говори́ть как по ~ому** to speak fluently.
пи́сар|ь (-я) *м* clerk.
писáтел|ь (-я) *м* writer.
писáтельниц|а (-ы) *ж см* **писáтель**.
пи|сáть (-шý, -шешь; *perf* **написáть**) *несов перех* to write; (*картину, пейзаж*) to paint ◆ *неперех* (*no perf*, *ребёнок, ученик*) to be able to write; (*ручка*) to write; **он написáл, как доéхал/где устрóился** he wrote to say he had arrived safely/where he was staying; **~ши́ пропáло** (*разг*) it is as good as lost
▸ **писáться** *несов возв* (*слово*) to be spelt *или* spelled; **как пи́шется э́то слóво?** how do you spell this word?; **мне сегóдня не пи́шется** I don't feel like writing today.
пи́сем *сущ см* **письмó**.
пис|éц (-цá) *м* (*ИСТ*) scribe.
писк (-а) *м* (*ребёнка*) squeak; (*птицы*) cheep.
пискли́вый *прил* (*голос*) squeaky.
пискля́вый *прил* = **пискли́вый**.

пи́скн|уть (**-у, -ешь**) *сов неперех* (*ребёнок, животное*) to give a squeak; (*птица*) to give a cheep.

пистоле́т (**-а**) *м* pistol.

листо́н (**-а**) *м* (*в патроне*) percussion cap.

писца́ *итп сущ см* **писе́ц.**

писчебума́жный *прил*: ~ **магази́н** stationer's.

пи́сч|ий (**-ая, -ее, -ие**) *прил* writing *опред.*

пи́сьменно *нареч* in writing.

пи́сьменност|ь (**-и**) *ж* written language; (*памятники*) literary texts *мн.*

пи́сьменн|ый *прил* (*просьба, экзамен*) written; (*стол, прибор*) writing; **в ~ой фо́рме** in writing.

пис|ьмо́ (**-ьма́**; *nom pl* **-ьма**, *gen pl* **-ем**) *ср* letter; (*no pl*; *иероглифическое, алфавитное*) script; (*искусство*: *манера*) style.

пита́ни|е (**-я**) *ср* (*больного, ребёнка*) feeding; (*ТЕХ*) supply; (*вегетарианское, плохое*) diet; **обще́ственное** ~ public catering.

пита́тел|ьный *прил* (*соли, вещества*) nutritious; (*крем, лосьон итп*) nourishing; (*клапан, станция, насос*) supply *опред*; (**-ен, -ьна, -ьно**; *каша, бульон*) filling; **пита́тельная среда́** (*БИО*: *перен*) breeding ground.

пита́|ть (**-ю**) *несов перех* (*кормить*) to feed; (*снабжать*) to supply; (*перен*: *испытывать*) to feel

▸ **пита́ться** *несов возв*: **~ся** *+instr* (*человек, растение*) to live on; (*животное*) to feed on; (*ТЕХ*) to run on, use.

пито́м|ец (**-ца**) *м* (*воспитанник*) pupil.

пито́мник (**-а**) *м* (*БОТ*) nursery.

пито́н (**-а**) *м* python.

пи|ть (**пью, пьёшь**; *pt* **-л, -ла́, -ло**, *imper* **пе́й(те)**, *perf* **вы́пить**) *несов перех* to drink ◆ *неперех*: ~ **за кого́-н/что-н** to drink to sb/sth; **как ~ дать** (*разг*) for sure.

питьев|о́й *прил*: **~а́я вода́** drinking water.

пиха́|ть (**-ю**) *несов перех* (*разг*: *толкать*) to shove; (*разг*: *засовывать*) to cram

▸ **пиха́ться** *несов возв* to push and shove (each other).

пихн|у́ть (**-у́, -ёшь**) *сов перех* to give a shove; (*сунуть*) to push.

пи́хт|а (**-ы**) *ж* fir (tree).

пи́цц|а (**-ы**) *ж* pizza.

пиццери́|я (**-и**) *ж* pizzeria.

пи́чка|ть (**-ю**; *perf* **напи́чкать**) *несов перех* (*разг*): ~ **кого́-н чем-н** (*конфетами итп*) to stuff sb with sth; (*лекарствами*) to pour sth down sb's neck.

пишу́(сь) *итп несов см* **писа́ть(ся).**

пи́шущ|ий (**-ая, -ее, -ие**) *прил*: **~ая маши́нка** typewriter.

пи́щ|а (**-и**) *ж* food; ~ **для размышле́ний** *или* **ума́** food for thought; ~ **для воображе́ния** fuel to the imagination.

пищ|а́ть (**-у́, -и́шь**) *несов неперех* (*птицы*) to cheep; (*животные*) to squeak; (*ребёнок*) to cry.

пищебло́к (**-а**) *м* kitchen (*for catering*).

пищеваре́ни|е (**-я**) *ср* digestion.

пищево́й *прил* food *опред*; (*соль*) edible; **пищева́я со́да** baking soda.

пия́в|ка (**-ки**; *gen pl* **-ок**) *ж* leech.

ПК *м сокр* (= *персона́льный компью́тер*) PC (= *personal computer*).

пл. *сокр* (= *пло́щадь*) Sq. (= *Square*).

плав (**-а**) *м*: **на ~у́** afloat.

пла́вани|е (**-я**) *ср* swimming; (*на судне*) sailing; (*рейс*) voyage; **занима́ться** (*impf*) **~м** to train as a swimmer.

пла́вательный *прил* swimming *опред* **пла́вательный бассе́йн** swimming pool.

пла́ва|ть (**-ю**) *несов неперех* (*человек, животное*) to swim; (*корабль*) to sail; (*лист, облако*) to float; (*перен*: *на экзамене итп*) to be out of one's depth; (*служить на судне*): ~ *+instr* to work (at sea) as.

пла́вен *прил см* **пла́вный.**

пла́в|ить (**-лю, -ишь**; *perf* **распла́вить**) *несов перех* to smelt

▸ **пла́виться** (*perf* **распла́виться**) *несов возв* to smelt; (*стекло, пластмасса*) to melt.

пла́в|ка (**-ки**; *gen pl* **-ок**) *ж* (*действие*) smelting; (*продукт*) smelted metal.

пла́в|ки (**-ок**) *мн* swimming trunks *мн.*

плавле́ни|е (**-я**) *ср*: **температу́ра** *или* **то́чка ~я** melting point.

пла́вленый *прил*: ~ **сыр** processed cheese.

пла́влю(сь) *несов см* **пла́вить(ся).**

плавни́к (**-а́**) *м* (*у рыб*) fin; (*у водных животных*) flipper.

пла́в|ный (**-ен, -на, -но**) *прил* smooth.

пла́вок *сущ см* **пла́вка, пла́вки.**

плаву́ч|ий (**-ая, -ее, -ие**) *прил* floating; **плаву́чая ба́за** (*в рыболовстве*) *floating unit for storing and processing fish.*

плагиа́т (**-а**) *м* plagiarism.

плагиа́тор (**-а**) *м* plagiarist.

пла́зм|а (**-ы**) *ж* plasma.

плака́т (**-а**) *м* poster.

пла́|кать (**-чу, -чешь**) *несов неперех* to cry, weep; ~ (*impf*) **от** *+gen* (*от боли итп*) to cry from; (*от радости*) to cry with; (*от горя*) to cry in; **~кал мой выходно́й** (*разг*) so much for my day off; **~кали мои́ де́ньги** (*разг*) that's my money up the spout; **па́лка по нему́ ~чет** (*разг*) he's asking for a beating

▸ **пла́каться** *несов возв* (*разг*): **~ся** (**на** *+acc*) (*на судьбу, на участь*) to moan (about).

плакир|ова́ть (**-у́ю**) (*не*)*сов перех* (*ТЕХ*) to plate.

пла́кс|а (**-ы**) *м/ж* crybaby.

плаку́ч|ий (**-ая, -ее, -ие**) *прил*: **~ая и́ва** weeping willow.

пла́мени *итп сущ см* **пла́мя.**

пла́менный *прил* (*цвета пламени*) flame-coloured (*BRIT*), flame-colored (*US*); (*горячий*) burning; (*перен*: *страстный*) ardent.

пла́м|я (**-ени**; *как* **вре́мя**; *см* **Table 4**) *ср* flame.

план (**-а**) *м* plan; (*чертёж*) plan, map; **кру́пный**

~ (*КИНО, ФОТО*) close-up; **планы на будущее** future plans; **передний ~** foreground; **задний ~** background; **на первом плане у неё учёба** her priority is studying; **в теоретическом плане** in theory; **отходить (отойти** *perf*) *или* **отступать (отступить** *perf*) **на второй ~** to become less important.
планёр (**-а**) *м* glider.
планеризм (**-а**) *м* gliding.
планет|а (**-ы**) *ж* planet.
планетари|й (**-я**) *м* planetarium.
планировани|е (**-я**) *ср* planning; ~ **семьи** family planning.
планир|овать (**-ую**) *несов перех* to plan ◆ *неперех* (*perf* **запланировать**; *намереваться*) to plan; (*АВИА*) to glide.
планир|овать (**-ую**; *perf* **распланировать**) *несов перех* to lay out.
планировк|а (**-и**) *ж* (*участка, квартиры*) layout.
планировщик (**-а**) *м* planner.
план|ка (**-ки**; *gen pl* **-ок**) *ж* (*деревянная*) strip of wood; (*металлическая*) strip of metal.
планктон (**-а**) *м* plankton.
плановик (**-а**) *м* planner.
плановый *прил* (*задание, продукция*) planned; (*отдел, комиссия*) planning.
планок *сущ см* **планка**.
планомер|ный (**-ен, -на, -но**) *прил* systematic.
плантаци|я (**-и**) *ж* plantation.
планшет (**-а**) *м* mapcase.
пласт (**-а**) *м* (*также перен*) stratum (*мн* strata).
пластик (**-а**) *м* = **пластмасса**.
пластик|а (**-и**) *ж* (*скульптура*) the plastic arts *мн*; (*гармония*) grace; (*балетная*) eurhythmics; (*МЕД*) plastic surgery.
пластилин (**-а**) *м* plasticine.
пластин|а (**-ы**) *ж* (*ГЕО*) plate.
пластин|ка (**-ки**; *gen pl* **-ок**) *ж* (*уменьш от* **пластина**; (*МУЗ*) record; **долгоиграющая ~** album, L.P. (= *long-playing record*).
пластичен *прил см* **пластичный**.
пластическ|ий (**-ая, -ое, -ие**) *прил* plastic *опред*; **пластическая масса** plastic; **пластическая операция** (*МЕД*) plastic surgery.
пластич|ный (**-ен, -на, -но**) *прил* (*жесты, движения*) graceful; (*материалы, вещества*) plastic *опред*.
пластмасс|а (**-ы**) *ж сокр* (= *пластическая масса*) plastic.
пластунск|ий (**-ая, -ое, -ие**) *прил*: **ползти по-~и** to crawl on one's belly.
пластыр|ь (**-я**) *м* (*МЕД*) plaster.
плат|а (**-ы**) *ж* (*за труд, за услуги*) pay, salary; (*за квартиру*) payment; (*за проезд*) fee; (*перен: награда, кара*) reward; **заработная ~** wages *мн*.
платан (**-а**) *м* plane (tree).
плат|ёж (**-ежа**) *м* payment; **наложенным ~ежом** cash on delivery.
платёжеспособен *прил см* **платёжеспособный**.
платёжеспособност|ь (**-и**) *ж* solvency.
платёжеспособ|ный (**-ен, -на, -но**) *прил* (*КОММ*) solvent.
платёжн|ый *прил* (*КОММ*): ~ **бланк** payslip; **~ая ведомость** payroll; **~ое поручение** *или* **требование** payment order.
платин|а (**-ы**) *ж* platinum.
пла|тить (**-чу, -тишь**; *perf* **заплатить** *или* **уплатить**) *несов перех* to pay ◆ *неперех* (*перен*): ~ **чем-н за что-н** to repay sth with sth; ~ (**заплатить** *или* **уплатить** *perf*) **наличными/натурой** to pay in cash/in kind
▸ **платиться** (*perf* **поплатиться**) *несов возв*: **~ся чем-н за что-н** to pay for sth with sth.
платка *итп сущ см* **платок**.
платный *прил* (*вход, стоянка*) chargeable; (*школа*) fee-paying; (*больница*) private.
плато *ср нескл* plateau.
плат|ок (**-ка**) *м* (*головной*) headscarf (*мн* headscarves); (*наплечный*) shawl; (*также:* **носовой ~**) handkerchief.
платформ|а (**-ы**) *ж* platform; (*маленькая станция*) halt; (*открытый вагон*) open goods truck; (*основание*) foundation.
платьe|e (**-я**; *gen pl* **-ев**) *ср* dress ◆ *собир* (*одежда*) clothing, clothes *мн*.
плафон (**-а**) *м* decorated ceiling; (*абажур*) shade (*for ceiling light*).
плах|а (**-и**) *ж* (*ИСТ*) (executioner's) block.
плац (**-а**; *loc sg* **-у**) *м* (*ВОЕН*) parade ground.
плацдарм (**-а**) *м* (*ВОЕН*) bridgehead.
плацент|а (**-ы**) *ж* placenta.
плацкартный *прил*: ~ **вагон** *railway car with open berths instead of compartments*.
плач (**-а**) *м* crying.
плачев|ный (**-ен, -на, -но**) *прил* (*бедственный*) lamentable; (*жалкий*) pitiful.
плачу(сь) *итп несов см* **плакать(ся)**.
плачу(сь) *несов см* **платить(ся)**.
плашмя *нареч* flat.
плащ (**-а**) *м* cloak; (*пальто*) raincoat.
плащаниц|а (**-ы**) *ж* (*РЕЛ*) the shroud of Christ.
плащ-палат|ка (**-ки**; *gen pl* **-ок**) *ж* (*ВОЕН*) waterproof cape.
плебе|й (**-я**) *м* plebeian.
плебейск|ий (**-ая, -ое, -ие**) *прил* plebeian *опред*.
пл|евать (**-юю**) *несов неперех* to spit; (*perf* **наплевать**; *перен*): ~ **на** *+acc* (*разг: на правила, на мнение других*) to not give a damn about; ~ *(impf)* **в потолок** (*разг*) to loaf (about)
▸ **плеваться** *несов возв* to spit.
плев|ок (**-ка**) *м* spit, spittle.
плеврит (**-а**) *м* pleurisy.
плёв|ый *прил*: (**это**) **~ое дело** (*разг*) it's a piece

of cake.
плед (**-а**) *м* (tartan) rug.
плéйер (**-а**) *м* Walkman®.
плёл *итп несов см* **плести́**.
плéмени *итп сущ см* **плéмя**.
племенн|óй *прил* (*язык, территория*) tribal; (*с.-х.: скот*) purebred; (*хозяйство, животноводство*) (pure-strain) stockbreeding *опред*; **племеннóй бык** pedigree bull; **племеннáя лóшадь** thoroughbred (horse).
плéм|я (**-ени**; *как* **врéмя**; *см* **Table 4**) *ср* (*также перен*) tribe; **молодóе** ~ the younger generation.
племя́нник (**-а**) *м* nephew.
племя́нниц|а (**-ы**) *ж* niece.
плен (**-а**; *loc sg* **-ý**) *м* captivity; **брáть (взять** *perf*) **когó-н в** ~ to take sb prisoner; **попадáть (попáсть** *perf*) **в** ~ to be taken prisoner.
пленáрный *прил* plenary.
плени́тел|ьный (**-ен, -ьна, -ьно**) *прил* captivating, charming.
плен|и́ть (**-ю́, -и́шь**; *impf* **пленя́ть**) *сов перех* (*очаровывать*) to captivate, charm.
плён|ка (**-ки**; *gen pl* **-ок**) *ж* (*также ФОТО*) film; (*кожица*) film, membrane; (*магнитофонная*) tape; **записывать (записáть** *perf*) **что-н на ~ку** to record sth (on tape).
плéнн|ая (**-ой**; *decl like adj*) *ж см* **плéнный**.
плéнник (**-а**) *м* (*пленный*) prisoner, captive.
плéнниц|а (**-ы**) *ж см* **плéнник**.
плéнн|ый *прил* captive *опред* ◆ (**-ого**; *decl like adj*) *м* prisoner, captive.
плёнок *сущ см* **плёнка**.
плéнум (**-а**) *м* plenum.
пленя́|ть (**-ю**) *несов от* **плени́ть**.
плéсен|ь (**-и**) *ж* mould (*BRIT*), mold (*US*).
плеск (**-а**) *м* splash.
пле|скáть (**-щý, -щешь**) *несов неперех* to splash; (*слегка*) to lap
▸ **плескáться** *несов возв* to splash; (*волны: слегка*) to lap.
плéсневе|ть (*3sg* **-ет**, *3pl* **-ют**, *perf* **заплéсневеть**) *несов неперех* to go mouldy (*BRIT*) *или* moldy (*US*).
пл|ести́ (**-етý, -етёшь**; *pt* **-ёл, -елá, -елó**, *perf* **сплести́**) *несов перех* (*сети*) to weave; (*венок, волосы*) to plait; (*глупости*) to spout; ~ (*impf*) **интри́ги** *или* **кóзни** to weave a web of intrigue; ~ (*impf*) **небыли́цы** (*разг*) to spin yarns
▸ **плести́сь** *несов возв* (*разг: человек: медленно идти*) to trudge, plod.
плетёный *прил* (*корзина, мебель*) wicker; (*сандалии*) woven.
плет|éнь (**-ня́**) *м* wattle fence.
плёт|ка (**-ки**; *gen pl* **-ок**) *ж* whip.
плетня́ *итп сущ см* **плетéнь**.
плёток *сущ см* **плётка**.
плетý(сь) *итп несов см* **плести́(сь)**.
плет|ь (**-и**; *gen pl* **-éй**) *ж* whip.
плéчик|и (**-ов**) *мн* (*вешалка*) coat hangers *мн*; (*подкладки*) shoulder pads *мн*.
плечи́ст|ый (**-, -а, -о**) *прил* broad-shouldered.
плеч|ó (**-á**; *nom pl* **-и**) *ср* shoulder; **~м к ~ý** shoulder to shoulder; **э́то мне не по ~ý** I am not up to it; **за ~áми у негó 5 лет учёбы** he has 5 years of study behind him *или* under his belt; **с чужóго ~á** (*одежда*) second-hand; **выноси́ть (вы́нести** *perf*) **что-н на свои́х ~áх** to carry sth on one's shoulders.
плеши́в|ый (**-, -а, -о**) *прил* bald.
плеш|ь (**-и**) *ж* bald patch.
плéщет(ся) *итп несов см* **плескáть(ся)**.
плещýсь *итп несов см* **плескáться**.
плея́д|а (**-ы**) *ж* (*учёных, музыкантов итп*) galaxy.
Пли́мут (**-а**) *м* Plymouth.
пли́нтус (**-а**) *м* skirting board (*BRIT*), baseboard (*US*).
плиссé *ср нескл* pleats *мн* ◆ *прил неизм*: **юбка/плáтье** ~ pleated skirt/dress.
плит|á (**-ы́**; *nom pl* **-ы**) *ж* (*каменная*) slab; (*металлическая*) plate; (*печь*) cooker, stove.
пли́т|ка (**-ки**; *gen pl* **-ок**) *ж* (*керамическая, кафельная*) tile; (*шоколада*) bar; (*электрическая*) hot plate; (*газовая*) camping stove.
плов (**-а**) *м* pilaff.
плов|éц (**-цá**) *м* swimmer.
пловчи́х|а (**-и**) *ж см* **пловéц**.
плод (**-á**) *м* (*БОТ*) fruit; (*БИО*) foetus (*BRIT*), fetus (*US*); ~ *+gen* (*перен*) fruits of.
плод|и́ться (*3sg* **-и́тся**, *3pl* **-я́тся**, *perf* **расплоди́ться**) *несов возв* (*также перен*) to multiply.
плодови́т|ый (**-, -а, -о**) *прил* fertile; (*перен*) prolific.
плодовóдств|о (**-а**) *ср* fruit-growing.
плодорóд|ный (**-ен, -на, -но**) *прил* fertile.
плодотвóр|ный (**-ен, -на, -но**) *прил* fruitful.
плóмб|а (**-ы**) *ж* (*в зубе*) filling; (*на дверях, сейфе*) seal.
пломби́р (**-а**) *м* *rich creamy ice-cream*.
пломбир|овáть (**-ýю**; *perf* **запломбировáть**) *несов перех* (*зуб*) to fill; (*perf* **опломбировáть**; *дверь, сейф*) to seal.
плóс|кий (**-кая, -кое, -кие**; **-ок, -кá, -ко**) *прил* flat; (*перен: неоригинальный*) feeble.
плоскогýбц|ы (**-ев**) *мн* pliers *мн*.
плóскост|ь (**-и**; *gen pl* **-éй**) *ж* (*также перен*) plane.
плóсок *прил см* **плóский**.
плот (**-á**; *loc sg* **-ý**) *м* raft.
плóтен *прил см* **плóтный**.
плоти́н|а (**-ы**) *ж* dam.
плóтник (**-а**) *м* carpenter.
плóтно *нареч* (*закрыть дверь*) tightly; (*пообедать*) well.
плóтност|ь (**-и**) *ж* density.
плóт|ный (**-ен, -нá, -но**) *прил* (*дым, туман*) dense, thick; (*население, толпа, лес*) dense; (*бумага, кожа*) thick; (*тело, человек*) thick-set; (*завтрак, обед*) substantial.

плотоя́д|ный (**-ен, -на, -но**) *прил* carnivorous; (*перен*) lustful.
пло́тск|ий (**-ая, -ое, -ие**) *прил* (*желания*) carnal.
пло́ттер (**-а**) *м* (*КОМП*) plotter.
плот|ь (**-и**) *ж* flesh; **~ и кровь** flesh and blood; **а́нгел/дья́вол во ~и́** angel/devil incarnate.
пло́хо *нареч* (*учиться, работать*) badly ◆ *как сказ* it's bad ◆ *ср нескл* (*ПРОСВЕЩ*) ≈ poor (*school mark*); **без друзе́й ~** it's bad not to have friends; **мне ~** I feel bad; **в го́роде ~ с хле́бом** there's a shortage of bread in the town; **у меня́ ~ с деньга́ми** I am short of money.
плох|о́й (**-а́я, -о́е, -и́е; -, -а́, -о**) *прил* bad; **мать ста́ла ~а́** mother is in a bad way.
площа́д|ка (**-ки**; *gen pl* **-ок**) *ж* (*детская*) playground; (*спортивная*) ground; (*строительная*) site; (*часть вагона*) corridor; **ле́стничная ~** landing; **поса́дочная ~** landing pad.
пло́щад|ь (**-и**; *gen pl* **-е́й**) *ж* (*место*) square; (*пространство, также МАТ*) area; (*разг*: *также*: **жила́я ~**) living space.
пло́ще *сравн прил от* **пло́ский**.
плуг (**-а**; *nom pl* **-и́**) *м* plough (*BRIT*), plow (*US*).
плут (**-а́**) *м* (*мошенник*) cheat; (*хитрец*) rogue.
плута́|ть (**-ю**) *несов неперех* (*разг*) to wander.
плут|ова́ть (**-у́ю**; *perf* **сплутова́ть**) *несов неперех* to cheat.
Плуто́н (**-а**) *м* Pluto.
плуто́ни|й (**-я**) *м* plutonium.
плы|ть (**-ву́, -вёшь**; *pt* **-л, -ла́, -ло**) *несов неперех* (*человек, животное*) to swim; (*судно*) to sail; (*лист, облако*) to float.
плюга́в|ый (**-, -а, -о**) *прил* (*разг*: *пренебр*) wimpish.
плю́н|уть (**-у, -ешь**) *сов неперех* to spit; **~** *(perf)* **на что-н** (*разг*) to stop bothering about sth; **плюнь!** (*разг*) forget it!; **э́то мне раз ~** (*разг*) it's a doddle (for me).
плюрали́зм (**-а**) *м* pluralism.
плюралисти́ческ|ий (**-ая, -ое, -ие**) *прил* pluralist(ic).
плюс *м нескл, союз* plus ◆ (**-а**) *м* (*разг*: *преимущество*) plus (*мн* plusses); **два ~ два – четы́ре** two plus two is four; **~ми́нус 2см** plus or minus *или* give or take 2cm.
плю́хн|уться (**-усь, -ешься**; *impf* **плю́хаться**) *сов возв* (*человек*) to flop down.
плюш (**-а**) *м* plush.
плю́ш|ка (**-ки**; *gen pl* **-ек**) *ж* bun.
плющ (**-а́**) *м* ivy.
плю́щить (**-у, -ишь**; *perf* **сплю́щить**) *несов перех* to flatten.
пляж (**-а**) *м* beach.
пля|са́ть (**-шу́, -шешь**; *perf* **спляса́ть**) *несов перех* to dance.
пля́с|ка (**-ки**; *gen pl* **-ок**) *ж* dance.
пляшу́ *итп несов см* **пляса́ть**.

пневмати́ческ|ий (**-ая, -ое, -ие**) *прил* pneumatic.
пневмони́|я (**-и**) *ж* pneumonia.
Пномпе́н|ь (**-я**) *м* Pnomh Penh.
пн|уть (**-у, -ёшь**) *сов перех* (*разг*) to boot.
пня *итп сущ см* **пень**.
ПО *ср сокр* = *произво́дственное объедине́ние*.

KEYWORD

по *предл* (*+dat*) ***1*** (*о месте действия, вдоль*) along; **де́вочка идёт по у́лице** the little girl is walking along the street; **по берега́м расту́т кусты́** bushes grow along the banks; **ло́дка плывёт по реке́** the boat is sailing on the river; **спуска́ться (спусти́ться** *perf*) **по ле́стнице** to go down the stairs
2 (*при глаголах движения*) round; **ходи́ть** *(impf)* **по ко́мнате/са́ду** to walk round the room/garden; **путеше́ствовать** *(impf)* **по стране́** to travel round the country; **плыть** *(impf)* **по тече́нию** to go downstream; (*перен*) to swim with the tide; **идти́** *(impf)* **по ве́тру** to sail with the wind
3 (*об объекте воздействия*) on; **уда́рить** *(impf)* **кого́-н по плечу́/лицу́** to hit on the shoulder/face; **уда́рить** *(impf)* **по врагу́/по контрабанди́стам** to deal a blow to the enemy/to the smugglers
4 (*в соответствии с*): **де́йствовать по зако́ну/пра́вилам** to act in accordance with the law/the rules; **по расписа́нию/пла́ну** according to schedule/plan; **он ушёл по со́бственному жела́нию** he left voluntarily; **получа́ть (получи́ть** *perf*) **де́ньги по счёту** to receive payment of a bill
5 (*об основании*): **суди́ть по вне́шности** to judge by appearances; **жени́ться** *(impf/perf)* **по любви́** to marry for love
6 (*вследствие*) due to; **отсу́тствовать** *(impf)* **по боле́зни** to be absent due to illness; **по невнима́тельности** due to carelessness; **по необходи́мости** out of necessity
7 (*посредством*): **говори́ть по телефо́ну** to speak on the phone; **отправля́ть (отпра́вить** *perf*) **что-н по по́чте** to send sth by post; **передава́ть (переда́ть** *perf*) **что-н по ра́дио/по телеви́дению** to broadcast sth on radio/television
8 (*с целью, для*): **рабо́та по повыше́нию эффекти́вности** work towards increased efficiency; **о́рганы по борьбе́ с престу́пностью** organizations in the fight against crime; **опера́ция по захва́ту моста́** an operation to seize the bridge; **я позва́л тебя́ по де́лу** I called on you on business
9 (*о какой-н характеристике объекта*) in; **по интере́сам/до́лжности** in interests/position; **по профе́ссии** by profession; **дед по ма́тери** maternal grandfather; **това́рищ по шко́ле**

school friend
10 (*о сфере деятельности*) in; **заня́тия по литерату́ре** studies in literature; **иссле́дование по хи́мии** research in chemistry
11 (*о мере времени*): **по вечера́м/утра́м** in the evenings/mornings; **по воскресе́ньям/пя́тницам** on Sundays/Fridays; **я рабо́таю по це́лым дням** I work all day long; **рабо́та расчи́тана по мину́там** the work is planned by the minute
12 (*о единичности предметов*): **ма́ма дала́ всем по я́блоку** Mum gave them each an apple; **мы купи́ли по одно́й кни́ге** we bought a book each
◆ *предл* (*+acc*) **1** (*вплоть до*) up to; **стоя́ть** (*impf*) **по по́яс в воде́** to stand up to the waist in water; **по настоя́щее вре́мя** up to the present time; **с пе́рвой по пя́тую главу́** from the first to (*BRIT*) *или* through (*US*) the fifth chapter; **я за́нят по го́рло** (*разг*: *перен*) I am up to my eyes in work; **он по́ уши в неё влюблён** he is head over heels in love with her
2 (*при обозначении цены*): **по два/три рубля́ за шту́ку** two/three roubles each
3 (*при обозначении количества*): **по два/три челове́ка** in twos/threes
◆ *предл* (*+prp*; *после*) on; **по оконча́нии рабо́ты** on finishing work; **по прие́зде** on arrival.

по- *префикс* (*in verbs*; *о начале действия*) *indicating the beginning of an action eg.* *побежа́ть*; (*об ограниченном действии*) *indicating limitation of an action eg.* *поговори́ть*; (*о прерывистом действии*) *indicating action carried out at intervals eg.* *погля́дывать*; (*о действии, совершаем многими*) *indicating action undertaken by many people eg.* *повскака́ть*; (*in adjectives and adverbs*; *о неинтенсивном качестве*) *indicating non-intensive quality of sth eg.* *помя́гче*; (*подобно чем-н*) *indicating comparison with sth eg.* *по-но́вому*.
п/о *сокр* = *почто́вое отделе́ние*; *произво́дственное объедине́ние*.
по-англи́йски *нареч* in English; **как ~ э́то сло́во?** what is this word in English?
побагрове́|ть (**-ю**) *сов от* **багрове́ть**.
поба́ива|ться (**-юсь**) *несов возв*: ~ *+gen* to be a bit frightened of.
поба́лива|ть (*3sg* **-ет**, *3pl* **-ют**) *несов неперех* (*разг*: *иногда*) to ache now and again; (: *слегка*) to hurt a bit.
побе́г (**-а**) *м* (*из тюрьмы*) escape; (*БОТ*) shoot, sprout.
побегу́ *итп сов см* **побежа́ть**.
побегу́шк|и *мн* (*разг*): **быть на ~ах у кого́-н** to run errands for sb; (*перен*) to be at sb's beck and call.
побе́д|а (**-ы**) *ж* victory; **оде́рживать** (**одержа́ть** *perf*) **~у над кем-н/чем-н** to win a victory over sb/sth.
победи́тел|ь (**-я**) *м* (*в войне*) victor; (*в состязании*) winner.
победи́тельниц|а (**-ы**) *ж см* **победи́тель**.
побед|и́ть (*2sg* **-и́шь**, *3sg* **-и́т**, *impf* **побежда́ть**) *сов перех* to defeat ◆ *неперех* to win.
побе́дный *прил* victorious, triumphant; (*марш, салют*) victory *опред*.
победоно́с|ный (**-ен, -на, -но**) *прил* (*армия, атака*) victorious; (*перен*: *вид, слова*) triumphant.
побежа́ть (*как* **бежа́ть**; *см* **Table 20**) *сов неперех* (*человек, животное*) to start running; (*дни, годы*) to start to fly by; (*ручьи, слёзы*) to begin to flow.
побежда́|ть (**-ю**) *несов от* **победи́ть**.
побежи́шь *итп сов см* **побежа́ть**.
побеле́|ть (**-ю**) *сов от* **беле́ть**.
побел|и́ть (**-ю́, -ишь**) *сов от* **бели́ть**.
побе́лк|а (**-и**) *ж* whitewash; (*действие*) whitewashing.
поберёг(ся) *итп сов см* **побере́чь(ся)**.
поберегу́(сь) *итп сов см* **побере́чь(ся)**.
побере́жь|е (**-я**) *ср* coast.
побер|е́чь (**-егу́, -ежёшь** *итп*, **-егу́т**; *pt* **-ёг, -егла́, -егло́**) *сов перех* (*деньги, время*) to save; (*здоровье, мать*) to take care of, look after
▸ **побере́чься** *сов возв* to take care of o.s.
побесед|ова́ть (**-у́ю**) *сов неперех* to have a chat.
побеспоко́|ить (**-ю, -ишь**) *сов перех* to disturb, bother; **позво́льте Вас ~** may I trouble you?; ~ (*perf*) **кого́-н прие́здом** to inconvenience sb by one's arrival
▸ **побеспоко́иться** *сов возв* (*проявить заботу*) to concern o.s.
поб|и́ть (**-ью́, -ьёшь**) *сов от* **бить** ◆ *перех* (*повредить*) to destroy; (*перебить*) to kill; (*разбить*) to break; (*impf* **побива́ть**; *СПОРТ*) to beat; **побива́ть** (~ *perf*) **реко́рд** to break a record.
поблагодар|и́ть (**-ю́, -и́шь**) *сов от* **благодари́ть**.
побла́жк|а (**-ки**; *gen pl* **-ек**) *ж* (*разг*) indulgence.
побледне́|ть (**-ю**) *сов от* **бледне́ть**.
поблёк|нуть (**-ну, -нешь**; *pt* **-, -ла, -ло**) *сов от* **блёкнуть**.
побли́зости *нареч* nearby ◆ *предл*: ~ **от** *+gen* near (to), close to.
побо́|и (**-ев**) *мн* beating *ед*.
побо́рник (**-а**) *м* champion (*of cause*).
побо́рниц|а (**-ы**) *ж см* **побо́рник**.
поб|оро́ть (**-орю́, -о́решь**) *сов перех* (*также перен*) to overcome.
побо́р|ы (**-ов**) *мн* (*ИСТ*) taxes *мн*, levies *мн*.
побо́ч|ный (**-ен, -на, -но**) *прил* (*продукт, реакция*) secondary; ~ **эффе́кт** side effect.
побо|я́ться (**-ю́сь, -и́шься**) *сов от* **боя́ться** ◆ *возв*: **побо́йся Бо́га!** (*разг*) have a heart!
побрати́м (**-а**) *м*: **города́-~ы** twin towns *или* cities.

побреду́ *итп сов см* **побрести́**.
побре́згa|ть (-ю) *сов от* **бре́згать**.
побре́зг|овать (-ую) *сов от* **бре́зговать**.
побр|ести́ (-еду́, -едёшь; *pt* **-ёл, -ела́, -ело́)** *сов неперех* to trudge.
побр|и́ть(ся) (-е́ю(сь), -е́ешь(ся)) *сов от* **бри́ть(ся)**.
поброса́|ть (-ю) *сов перех* (*вещи*) to throw about.
побряку́ш|ка (-ки; *gen pl* **-ек)** *ж* (*обычно мн*) trinket.
поб|уди́ть (-ужу́, -у́дишь; *impf* **побужда́ть)** *сов перех*: ~ **кого́-н к чему́-н/**+*infin* to prompt sb (in)to sth/to do.
побу́ду *итп сов см* **побы́ть**.
побужда́|ть (-ю) *несов от* **побуди́ть**.
побужде́ни|е (-я) *ср* (*действие*) prompting; (*стремление*) motive.
побужу́ *сов см* **побуди́ть**.
побыва́|ть (-ю) *сов неперех*: ~ **в А́фрике/у роди́телей** to visit Africa/one's parents.
поб|ы́ть (*как* **быть**; *см* **Table 21**) *сов неперех* to stay.
побью́ *итп сов см* **поби́ть**.
пова́|диться (-жусь, -дишься) *сов неперех*: ~ +*infin* to get into the way of doing.
пова́д|ка (-ки; *gen pl* **-ок)** *ж* (*разг*) way.
пова́жусь *сов см* **пова́диться**.
пова́лен *прил см* **пова́льный**.
пов|али́ть (-алю́, -а́лишь) *сов от* **вали́ть** ◆ *неперех* (*снег, град*) to begin to fall; (*толпа*) to come pouring in
▸ **повали́ться** *сов от* **вали́ться**.
пова́л|ьный (-ен, -ьна, -ьно) *прил* mass.
по́вар (-а; *nom pl* **-а́)** *м* cook.
пова́ренн|ый *прил*: **~ая кни́га** cookery (*BRIT*) *или* cook (*US*) book; **~ая соль** table salt.
повари́х|а (-и) *ж см* **по́вар**.
пове́дат|ь (-ю) *сов (не)перех*: ~ **что-н** *или* **о чём-н кому́-н** to tell sb sth.
поведе́ни|е (-я) *ср* behaviour (*BRIT*), behavior (*US*).
поведу́(сь) *итп сов см* **повести́(сь)**.
повез|ти́ (-у́, -ёшь; *pt* **-ёз, -езла́, -езло́)** *сов от* **везти́** ◆ *перех* to take.
повели́тел|ьный (-ен, -ьна, -ьно) *прил* imperious; **повели́тельное наклоне́ние** (*линг*) imperative mood.
повенча́|ть (-ю) *сов от* **венча́ть**.
пове́ргн|уть (-у, -ешь; *impf* **поверга́ть)** *сов перех* (*перен*: *врага*) to conquer; **поверга́ть (~** *perf*) **кого́-н в** +*acc* (*в отчаяние, в уныние итп*) to plunge sb into.
пове́ренн|ый (-ого; *decl like adj*) *м*: ~ **в дела́х** chargé d'affaires; **прися́жный** ~ (*ИСТ*) barrister (*in tsarist Russia*).
пове́р|ить (-ю, -ишь) *сов от* **ве́рить** ◆ (*impf* **поверя́ть**) *перех*: ~ **что-н кому́-н** to confide sth to sb
▸ **пове́риться** *сов от* **ве́риться**.
пове́рк|а (-и) *ж* (*перекличка*) rollcall; **на ~у** in fact.
поверн|у́ть (-у́, -ёшь; *impf* **повора́чивать)** *сов (не)перех* to turn
▸ **поверну́ться** (*impf* **повора́чиваться**) *сов возв* to turn; **де́ло ~у́лось к лу́чшему/ху́дшему** things took a turn for the better/worse; **у меня́ язы́к не ~ётся сказа́ть э́то** (*разг*) I wouldn't have the guts to say that; **~ся не́где** there isn't even room to turn round.
пове́рх *предл* (+*gen*) over.
пове́рхност|ный *прил* surface *опред*; **(-ен, -на, -но;** *перен*) superficial.
пове́рхност|ь (-и) *ж* surface; **лежа́ть** (*impf*) **на ~и** to be perfectly obvious.
пове́р|ье (-ья; *gen pl* **-ий)** *ср* (popular) belief.
поверя́|ть (-ю) *несов от* **пове́рить**.
повеселе́|ть (-ю) *сов от* **веселе́ть**.
пове́|сить(ся) (-шу(сь), -сишь(ся)) *сов от* **ве́шать(ся)**.
повествова́ни|е (-я) *ср* narrative.
повеств|ова́ть (-у́ю) *несов неперех*: ~ **о** +*prp* (*роман итп*) to tell (the story) of.
пов|ести́ (-еду́, -едёшь; *pt* **-ёл, -ла́, -ло́)** *сов перех* (*начать вести*: *человека*) to take; (: *войска*) to lead; (*машину, поезд*) to drive; (*войну, следствие итп*) to begin ◆ (*impf* **поводи́ть**) *неперех*: ~ +*instr* (*бровью*) to raise; (*плечом*) to shrug; ~ (*perf*) **себя́ наха́льно** to start to behave impudently; **он и бро́вью не ~ёл** (*разг*) he didn't bat an eyelid
▸ **повести́сь** *сов возв* (*войти в обыкновение*) to become the custom; **~сь** (*perf*) **с кем-н** to become friends with sb.
пове́ст|ка (-ки; *gen pl* **-ок)** *ж* summons (*мн* summonses); (*также*: ~ **дня**) agenda.
по́вест|ь (-и) *ж* story.
пове́три|е (-я) *ср* tendency.
пове́шени|е (-я) *ср* hanging; **сме́ртная казнь че́рез** ~ sentence of death by hanging.
пове́шу(сь) *сов см* **пове́сить(ся)**.
пове́|ять (*3sg* **-ет**, *3pl* **-ют**) *сов безл* (+*instr*): **~яло прохла́дой/све́жестью** there was a breath of cool/fresh air; **~яло свобо́дой/сча́стьем** there was a feeling of freedom/happiness in the air.
повздо́р|ить (-ю, -ишь) *сов от* **вздо́рить**.
повзросле́|ть (-ю) *сов от* **взросле́ть**.
повида́|ть(ся) (-ю(сь)) *сов от* **вида́ть(ся)**.
по-ви́димому *вводн сл* apparently.
пови́дл|о (-а) *ср* jam (*BRIT*), jelly (*US*).
пови́нн|ая (-ой; *decl like adj*) *ж* confession; **яви́ться** (*perf*) *или* **прийти́** (*perf*) **с ~ой** to give o.s. up.
пови́нност|ь (-и) *ж* duty; **во́инская** ~ conscription.

пови́н|ный (**-ен, -на, -но**) *прил* guilty.
повин|ова́ться (**-у́юсь**) *сов возв* (*+dat*) to obey.
повинове́ни|е (**-я**) *ср* obedience.
пови́с|нуть (**-ну, -нешь**; *pt* **-, -ла, -ло**, *impf* **повиса́ть**) *сов неперех* to hang; (*тучи*) to hang motionless; (*птица, вертолёт*) to hover.
повл|е́чь (**-еку́, -ечёшь** *итп*, **-еку́т**; *pt* **-ёк, -екла́, -екло́**) *сов от* **влечь**.
по́в|од (**-ода**; *loc sg* **-оду́**, *nom pl* **-о́дья**, *gen pl* **-ьев**) *м* (*лошади*) rein; (*nom pl* **-оды**; *причина*) reason ◆ *предл*: **по ~у** *+gen* regarding, concerning; **дава́ть (дать** *perf*) **кому́-н ~ для чего́-н** to give sb cause for sth; **идти́** (*impf*) *или* **быть** (*impf*) **на поводу́ у кого́-н** to be under sb's thumb.
пов|оди́ть (**-ожу́, -о́дишь**) *несов от* **повести́** ◆ *перех* (*водить недолго*) to walk.
повод|о́к (**-ка́**) *м* lead, leash.
пово́дья *итп сущ см* **по́вод**.
повожу́ *сов см* **поводи́ть**.
пово́з|ка (**-ки**; *gen pl* **-ок**) *ж* cart.
поволо́к|а (**-и**) *ж* shroud, haze.
повора́чива|ть (**-ю**) *несов от* **поверну́ть**
▸ **повора́чиваться** *несов от* **поверну́ться** ◆ *возв* (*разг*: *быстро действовать*) to get a move on.
поворо́т (**-а**) *м* (*действие*) turning; (*место*) bend, turn; (*перен*) turning point.
поворо́тлив|ый (**-, -а, -о**) *прил* (*человек*) agile, nimble.
поворо́тный *прил* (*ТЕХ*) revolving; **~ пункт** *или* **моме́нт** (*перен*) turning point; **~ день** crucial day; **поворо́тный круг** turntable.
повре|ди́ть (**-жу́, -ди́шь**) *сов от* **вреди́ть** ◆ (*impf* **поврежда́ть**) *перех* (*поранить*) to injure; (*поломать*) to damage.
поврежде́ни|е (**-я**) *ср* (*см глаг*) injury; damage.
поврежу́ *сов см* **повреди́ть**.
повремен|и́ть (**-ю́, -и́шь**) *сов неперех*: **~ с чем-н** to delay sth a little; **~** (*perf*) **с отве́том** to wait a little before answering.
повреме́нный *прил*: **повреме́нная опла́та** payment by the hour.
повседне́вен *прил см* **повседне́вный**.
повседне́вност|ь (**-и**) *ж* everyday routine.
повседне́в|ный (**-ен, -на, -но**) *прил* everyday; (*занятия, встречи*) daily.
повсеме́ст|ный (**-ен, -на, -но**) *прил* widespread.
повск|ака́ть (*3sg* **-а́чет**, *3pl* **-а́чут**) *сов неперех* (*разг*) to jump up.
повстреча́|ть (**-ю**) *сов перех* (*разг*) to bump into
▸ **повстреча́ться** *сов возв* (*разг*): **~ся с кем-н** to bump into sb.
повсю́ду *нареч* everywhere.
по-вся́кому *нареч* in different ways.
повто́рен *прил см* **повто́рный**.
повторе́ни|е (**-я**) *ср* repetition.
повтор|и́ть (**-ю́, -и́шь**; *impf* **повторя́ть**) *сов перех* to repeat
▸ **повтори́ться** (*impf* **повторя́ться**) *сов возв* (*ситуация*) to repeat itself; (*болезнь*) to recur.
повто́р|ный (**-ен, -на, -но**) *прил* repeated.
повторя́|ть(ся) (**-ю(сь)**) *несов от* **повтори́ть(ся)**.
повы́|сить (**-шу, -сишь**; *impf* **повыша́ть**) *сов перех* to increase; (*интерес*) to heighten; (*качество, культуру*) to improve; (*работника*) to promote; **повыша́ть (~** *perf*) **кого́-н в обще́ственном мне́нии** to raise sb in the opinion of the public; **повыша́ть (~** *perf*) **го́лос** to raise one's voice
▸ **повы́ситься** (*impf* **повыша́ться**) *сов возв* to increase; (*интерес*) to heighten; (*качество, культура*) to improve.
повы́шенный *прил* (*спрос*) increased; (*интерес, чувствительность*) heightened; (*качество*) improved; **повы́шенное давле́ние** high blood pressure.
повы́шу(сь) *сов см* **повы́сить(ся)**.
пов|яза́ть (**-яжу́, -я́жешь**; *impf* **повя́зывать**) *сов перех* to tie.
повя́з|ка (**-ки**; *gen pl* **-ок**) *ж* bandage; (*стерильная*) dressing; **ги́псовая ~** plaster.
повя́зыва|ть (**-ю**) *несов от* **повяза́ть**.
погада́|ть (**-ю**) *сов от* **гада́ть**.
пога́н|ить (**-ю, -ишь**; *perf* **опога́нить**) *несов перех* (*разг*) to mess up.
пога́н|ка (**-ки**; *gen pl* **-ок**) *ж* toadstool.
пога́ный *прил* (*разг*: *отвратительный*) lousy; **~ гриб** toadstool.
пога́с *итп сов см* **пога́снуть**.
пог|аси́ть (**-ашу́, -а́сишь**) *сов от* **гаси́ть** ◆ (*impf* **погаша́ть**) *перех* (*задолженность, вексель,*) to pay (off).
пога́с|нуть (**-ну, -нешь**; *pt* **-, -ла, -ло**) *сов от* **га́снуть**.
погаша́|ть (**-ю**) *несов от* **погаси́ть**.
погаше́ни|е (**-я**) *ср*: **срок ~я** (*КОММ*) maturity date.
погашу́ *сов см* **погаси́ть**.
поги́б *итп сов см* **поги́бнуть**.
погиба́|ть (**-ю**) *несов от* **поги́бнуть**.
поги́бел|ь (**-и**) *ж*: **согну́ться в три ~и** (*разг*) to bend double.
поги́б|нуть (**-ну, -нешь**; *pt* **-, -ла, -ло**) *сов от* **ги́бнуть**.
поги́бш|ий (**-его**; *decl like adj*) *м* dead person; **~ие** the dead.
погла́|дить (**-жу, -дишь**) *сов от* **гла́дить**.
погл|оти́ть (**-ощу́, -о́тишь**; *impf* **поглоща́ть**) *сов перех* to absorb; (*средства, время*) to take up; (: *усилия*) to demand.
поглоще́ни|е (**-я**) *ср*: **попы́тка ~я** (*КОММ*) takeover bid.
поглощу́ *сов см* **поглоти́ть**.
поглупе́|ть (**-ю**) *сов от* **глупе́ть**.
погля|де́ть (**-жу́, -ди́шь**) *сов от* **гляде́ть**.
погля́дыва|ть (**-ю**) *несов неперех* (*разг*) to have *или* take a squint.
погляжу́ *сов см* **погляде́ть**.

пог|нáть (-оню́, -óнишь) *сов перех* (*стадо, лошадь*) to drive; (*машину, поезд*) to drive fast
▸ **погнáться** *сов возв*: **~ся за кем-н/чем-н** (*также перен*) to set off in pursuit of sb/sth.
погнушá|ться (-юсь) *несов от* **гнушáться**.
поговáрива|ть (-ю) *несов неперех*: **~ о** +*prp* to talk about; **~ют, что** ... they say that ....
поговóр|ка (-ки; *gen pl* -ок) *ж* saying.
погóд|а (-ы) *ж* weather; **э́то не дéлает ~у** it doesn't make a lot of difference.
пого|ди́ть (-жу́, -ди́шь) *сов неперех*: **~ с** +*instr* (*разг*: *подождать*) to take one's time with; **немнóго ~дя́** after a while; **~ди́!** (*угроза*) just you wait!
погóдный *прил* weather *опред*.
погóж|ий (-ая, -ее, -ие; -, -а, -е) *прил* fine.
погожу́ *сов см* **погоди́ть**.
поголóвный *прил* (*всеобщий*) general.
поголóвь|е (-я) *ср* (*скота, лошадей*) total number.
поголубé|ть (-ю) *сов от* **голубéть**.
погóн (-а) *м* (*обычно мн*) (shoulder) stripe.
погóнщик (-а) *м* (cattle) driver.
погоню́(сь) *итп сов см* **погнáть(ся)**.
погóн|я (-и) *ж*: **~ за** +*instr* (*также перен*) pursuit of ◆ *собир* (*преследователи*) pursuers *мн*; **в ~е за** +*instr* in pursuit of.
погоня́|ть (-ю) *несов перех* (*лощадь, скот*) to drive; (*перен*: *разг*): **~ когó-н** to hurry sb up.
погор|éть (-ю́, -и́шь; *impf* **погорáть**) *сов неперех* to lose everything (*in a fire*); **погорáть** (**~** *perf*) **на взя́тках/крáже** (*разг*) to be caught taking bribes/stealing.
погоряч|и́ться (-у́сь, -и́шься) *сов возв* to get worked up.
погранзастáв|а (-ы) *ж сокр* (= *пограни́чная застáва*) frontier post.
пограни́чник (-а) *м* frontier *или* border guard.
пограни́чный *прил* (*город, район*) frontier *опред*, border *опред*; (*конфликт, знак*) border *опред*.
пóгреб (-а; *nom pl* -á) *м* cellar; **ви́нный ~** wine cellar.
погребáльный *прил* funeral *опред*.
погребéни|е (-я) *ср* (*похороны*) burial, interment; (*могила*) grave.
погремýш|ка (-ки; *gen pl* -ек) *ж* rattle.
погрé|ть (-ю; *impf* **погревáть**) *сов перех* to warm up
▸ **погрéться** *сов возв* to warm up.
погреш|и́ть (-у́, -и́шь) *сов от* **греши́ть**.
погрéшност|ь (-и) *ж* error, mistake.
погро|зи́ть (-жу́, -зи́шь) *сов от* **грози́ть**.
погрóм (-а) *м* pogrom; (*разг*: *беспорядок*) chaos.
погрубé|ть (-ю) *сов от* **грубéть**.
погр|узи́ть (-ужу́, -у́зишь) *сов перех от* **грузи́ть** ◆ *перех*: (-ужу́, -узи́шь; *impf* **погружáть**; **~ что-н в** +*acc*) to immerse sth in
▸ **погрузи́ться** *сов от* **грузи́ться** ◆ (*impf* **погружáться**) *возв* (*человек*) to immerse o.s.; (*предмет*) to sink; **погружáться** (**~ся** *perf*) **в** +*acc* (*в сон, в апатию*) to sink into; **погружáться** (**~ся** *perf*) **в размышлéния** to be deep in thought.
погру́з|ка (-ки; *gen pl* -ок) *ж* loading.
погру́зочн|ый *прил* (*машина*) loading *опред*; **~ые рабóты** loading.
погры́з|ться (-у́сь, -ёшься) *несов от* **гры́зться**.
погря́зн|уть (-у, -ешь; *impf* **погрязáть**) *сов неперех*: **~ в** +*prp* (*в грязи*) to get stuck in; (*в долгах, во лжи*) to sink into; (*в разврате*) to wallow in.
по|губи́ть (-ублю́, -у́бишь) *сов от* **губи́ть**.
погуля́|ть (-ю) *сов от* **гуля́ть**.
погустé|ть (-ю) *сов от* **густéть**.

KEYWORD

под *предл* (+*acc*) ***1*** (*в направлении ниже*) under; **я положи́л су́мку под стол** I put the bag under the table; **идти́** (*impf*) **пóд гору** to go downhill
2 (*поддерживая снизу*) by; **брать** (**взять** *perf*) **когó-н пóд руку** to take sb by the arm
3 (*указывает на положение, состояние*) under; **под контрóль/наблюдéние** under control/observation; **отдавáть** (**отдáть** *perf*) **когó-н под суд** to prosecute sb; **попадáть** (**попáсть** *perf*) **под дождь** to be caught in the rain
4 (*близко к*): **под у́тро/вéчер** towards morning/evening; **под прáздники** coming up to the holidays; **под стáрость** approaching old age
5 (*указывает на функцию*) as; **мы приспосóбили помещéние под магази́н** we fitted out the premises as a shop
6 (*в виде чего-н*): **вáза под хрустáль** an imitation crystal vase; **стéны под мрáмор** marble-effect walls
7 (*в обмен на*) on; **брать** (**взять** *perf*) **что-н под залóг/чéстное слóво** to take sth on security/trust
8 (*в сопровождении*): **под роя́ль/скри́пку** to the piano/violin; **мне э́то не под си́лу** that is beyond my powers
◆ *предл* (+*instr*) ***1*** (*ниже чего-н*: *о расположении*) under; **чемодáн под столóм** the suitcase is under the table
2 (*около*) near; **под Петербу́ргом** near St. Petersburg; **под бóком у когó-н** very near to sb; **под нóсом у когó-н** under sb's nose; **под рукóй** to hand, at hand
3 (*об условиях существования объекта*) under; **быть** (*impf*) **под наблюдéнием/арéстом** to be under observation/arrest; **под назвáнием, под и́менем** under the name of
4 (*вследствие*) under; **под влия́нием/тя́жестью чегó-н** under the influence/weight of

sth; **понимать** *(impf)*/**подразумевать** *(impf)* **под чем-н** to understand/imply by sth.

под- *префикс (in verbs; о движении снизу вверх) indicating movement upwards eg. подбросить; (о действиии, содершающемся внизу) indicating movement below sth eg. подбить; (приближение) indicating movement towards eg. подбежать; (добавление) indicating addition to sth eg. подлить; (ослабленная степень действия) indicating non-intensive quality of sth eg. подкрасить; (тайное действие) indicating unaercover nature oj sth eg. подслушать; (in adjectives; расположенный ниже какой-нибудь поверхности)* under-; *(находящийся в ведении) indicating supervision of sth eg. поднадзорный; (in nouns; часть чего-н)* sub-; *(ниже по званию) indicating lower position or rank eg. подмастерье.*

пода|вать(ся) (**-ю(сь)**) *несов от* **подать(ся)**.

пода|вить (**-влю, -вишь**; *impf* **подавлять**) *сов перех* to suppress; **подавлять** (~ *perf*) **кого-н чем-н** to intimidate sb with sth

▸ **подавиться** *сов от* **давиться**.

подавлени|е (**-я**) *ср (восстания)* suppression.

подавленност|ь (**-и**) *ж* depression.

подавленный *прил (настроение, состояние, человек)* depressed; *(смех, стон)* suppressed.

подавлю(сь) *сов см* **подавить(ся)**.

подавля|ть (**-ю**) *несов от* **подавить**.

подавляющ|ий (**-ая, -ее, -ие**) *прил* overwhelming.

подавно *нареч*: **он богат, а она и** ~ *(разг)* he is rich and she is even more so; **если я не могу это сделать, то ты и** ~ *(разг)* if I can't do this, then you certainly can't.

подам(ся) *umn сов см* **подать(ся)**.

подарить (**-арю, -аришь**) *сов от* **дарить**.

подар|ок (**-ка**) *м* gift, present.

подарочный *прил (магазин umn)* gift *опред*.

подаст(ся) *сов см* **подать(ся)**.

податлив|ый (**-, -а, -о**) *прил* pliable; *(тело)* supple.

подат|ь (**-и**) *ж (ИСТ)* tax.

пода|ть (*как* **дать**; *см* **Table 14**; *impf* **подавать**) *сов перех* to give; *(еду)* to serve up; *(поезд, такси umn)* to bring; *(заявление, жалобу umn)* to submit; *(СПОРТ: в теннисе)* to serve; *(: в футболе)* to pass; **подавать** (~ *perf*) **что-н кому-н** to give sth to sb, give sb sth; *(еду)* to serve sb up with sth; **подавать** (~ *perf*) **голос за** *+acc* to cast a vote for; **подавать** (~ *perf*) **идею** to put forward an idea; **подавать** (~ *perf*) **реплику** to make a comment; **подавать** (~ *perf*) **в отставку** to hand in *или* submit one's resignation; **подавать** (~ *perf*) **на кого-н в суд** to take sb to court; **подавать** (~ *perf*) **кому-н руку** *(при встрече)* to give sb one's hand; *(в трудной ситуации)* to give sb a hand; **подавать** (~ *perf*) **кому-н пальто** to help sb into their coat

▸ **податься** (*impf* **подаваться**) *сов возв (сдвинуться)* to give way; *(разг: уехать)* to make tracks.

подач|а (**-и**) *ж (действие: заявления, прошения)* submission; *(: обеда)* serving up; *(СПОРТ: в теннисе)* serve; *(: в футболе)* pass.

подач|ка (**-ки**; *gen pl* **-ек**) *ж (собаке)* scraps *мн*; *(человеку)* hand-out.

подашь(ся) *сов см* **подать(ся)**.

подаяни|е (**-я**) *ср* alms *мн*.

подбав|ить (**-лю, -ишь**; *impf* **подбавлять**) *сов перех* to add.

подбадрива|ть (**-ю**) *несов от* **подбодрить**.

подбежать (*как* **бежать**; *см* **Table 20**; *impf* **подбегать**) *сов неперех* to run up.

подберёзовик (**-а**) *м (БОТ)* shaggy boletus.

подберу(сь) *umn сов см* **подобрать(ся)**.

подбива|ть (**-ю**) *несов от* **подбить**.

подбира|ть(ся) (**-ю(сь)**) *несов от* **подобрать(ся)**.

под|бить (**-обью, -обьёшь**; *impf* **подбивать**) *сов перех (птицу, самолёт)* to shoot down; *(глаз, крыло)* to injure; **подбивать** (~ *perf*) **каблуки на** *+prp* to reheel.

подбодр|ить (**-ю, -ишь**; *impf* **подбадривать**) *сов перех* to cheer up.

подбор (**-а**) *м* selection; *(собрание)* collection; **как на** ~ *all alike and all the very best.*

подборк|а (**-и**) *ж (журнальная) collection of articles on one general theme.*

подбород|ок (**-ка**) *м* chin.

подбро|сить (**-шу, -сишь**; *impf* **подбрасывать**) *сов перех (мяч, шар, камень umn)* to toss; *(+acc или +gen; добавить)* to put; *(тайно подложить: анонимку)* to leave; *(: ворованный товар, наркотик)* to plant; *(разг: подвезти)* to give a lift.

подвал (**-а**) *м* cellar; *(для жилья)* basement.

подвальный *прил (помещение)* basement *опред*; **подвальный этаж** basement.

подведени|е (**-я**) *ср (линии электропередачи)* connecting; **подведение итогов** summing-up.

подведу *umn сов см* **подвести**.

подв|езти (**-езу, -езёшь**; *pt* **-ёз, -езла, -езло**, *impf* **подвозить**) *сов перех (машину, товар)* to take up; *(человека)* to give a lift.

подверг|нуть (**-ну, -нешь**; *pt* **-, -ла, -ло**, *impf* **подвергать**) *сов перех*: ~ **кого-н/что-н чему-н** to subject sb/sth to sth; **подвергать** (~ *perf*) **кого-н риску/опасности** to put sb at risk/in danger

▸ **подвергнуться** (*impf* **подвергаться**) *сов возв*: **~ся** *+dat* to be subjected to.

подвержен|ный (**-, -а, -о**) *прил*: ~ *+dat (дурному влиянию)* subject to; *(простуде)* susceptible to.

подверн|уть (**-у, -ёшь**; *impf* **подворачивать**) *сов перех (сделать короче)* to turn up; **подворачивать** (~ *perf*) **ногу** to turn *или* twist one's ankle

▸ **подверну́ться** (*impf* **подвора́чиваться**) *сов возв* (*разг*: *попасться*) to turn up; **мне ~у́лась по́д руку интере́сная кни́га** I came across an interesting book; **у меня́ нога́ ~у́лась** I've twisted my ankle.
подве́|сить (**-шу, -сишь**; *impf* **подве́шивать**) *сов перех* to hang up.
подве́с|ка (**-ки**; *gen pl* **-ок**) *ж* pendant.
подвесно́й *прил* (*в висячем положении*) hanging *опред*; **подвесно́й мост** suspension bridge.
подве́сок *сущ см* **подве́ска**.
подве|сти́ (**-еду́, -едёшь**; *pt* **-ёл, -ела́, -ело́**, *impf* **подводи́ть**) *сов перех*: **~ к** *+dat* (*человека*) to bring up to; (*машину*) to drive up to; (*поезд*) to bring into; (*корабль*) to sail up to; (*электричество*) to bring to; (*дорогу*) to link to; (*разочаровать*) to let down; **подводи́ть** (**~** *perf*) **глаза́/гу́бы** to put eyeliner/lipstick on; **подводи́ть** (**~** *perf*) **ито́ги** to sum up.
подве́шива|ть (**-ю**) *несов от* **подве́сить**.
подве́шу *сов см* **подве́сить**.
по́двиг (**-а**) *м* exploit.
подвига́|ть(ся) (**-ю(сь)**) *несов от* **подви́нуть(ся)**.
подви́жен *прил см* **подви́жный**.
подви́жник (**-а**) *м* devotee.
подвижно́й *прил*: **~ соста́в** (*на железной дороге*) rolling stock.
подви́ж|ный (**-ен, -на, -но**) *прил* (*человек, животное*) agile; (*no short form*; *войска, контакт*) mobile.
подви́н|уть (**-у, -ешь**; *impf* **подвига́ть**) *сов перех* (*передвинуть*: *человека, предмет*) to move; (*перен*: *работу, дело*) to push ahead with
▸ **подви́нуться** (*impf* **подвига́ться**) *сов возв* (*человек*) to move.
подвла́ст|ный (**-ен, -на, -но**) *прил*: **~** *+dat* (*закону*) subject to; (*президенту*) under the control of.
подво́д|а (**-ы**) *ж* cart.
подв|оди́ть (**-ожу́, -о́дишь**) *несов от* **подвести́**.
подво́дник (**-а**) *м* (*моряк*) submariner; (*водолаз*) diver.
подво́дный *прил* (*растение, работы*) underwater *опред*; **подво́дная ло́дка** submarine; **подво́дное тече́ние** undercurrent.
подвожу́ *сов см* **подводи́ть**.
подв|ози́ть (**-ожу́, -о́зишь**) *несов от* **подвезти́**.
подвора́чива|ть (**-ю**) *несов от* **подверну́ть**.
подворо́т|ня (**-ни**; *gen pl* **-ен**) *ж* passage(way).
подво́х (**-а**) *м* (*разг*: *ловушка*) catch.
подв|яза́ть (**-яжу́, -я́жешь**; *impf* **подвя́зывать**) *сов перех* to tie.
подгиба́|ть(ся) (**-ю(сь)**) *несов от* **подогну́ть(ся)**.
подгля|де́ть (**-жу́, -ди́шь**; *impf* **подгля́дывать**) *сов перех* to peep through.
подговор|и́ть (**-ю́, -и́шь**; *impf* **подгова́ривать**) *сов перех*: **~ кого́-н на что-н/** *+infin* to put sb up to sth/to doing.
подгоню́ *итп сов см* **подогна́ть**.
подгоня́|ть (**-ю**) *несов от* **подогна́ть**.
подгор|е́ть (*3sg* **-и́т**, *3pl* **-я́т**, *impf* **подгора́ть**) *сов неперех* (*мясо, пирог*) to burn slightly.
подгота́влива|ть(ся) (**-ю(сь)**) *несов от* **подгото́вить(ся)**.
подготови́тельный *прил* (*предварительный*) preparatory; **подготови́тельный класс** (*в начальной школе*) reception.
подгото́в|ить (**-лю, -ишь**; *impf* **подгота́вливать**) *сов перех* to prepare
▸ **подгото́виться** (*impf* **подгота́вливаться**) *сов возв* to prepare (o.s.).
подгото́вк|а (**-и**) *ж* (*к экзамену, к отъезду*) preparation; (*запас знаний, умений*) training.
подгото́влю(сь) *сов см* **подгото́вить(ся)**.
подгу́зник (**-а**) *м* nappy (*BRIT*), diaper (*US*).
подда|ва́ться (**-ю́сь**) *несов от* **подда́ться** ◆ *возв*: **не ~ сравне́нию/описа́нию** to be beyond comparison/words.
поддади́мся *итп сов см* **подда́ться**.
подда́кива|ть (**-ю**) *несов неперех*: **~** *+dat* (*разг*) to agree with.
подда́мся *сов см* **подда́ться**.
по́дданн|ая (**-ой**; *decl like adj*) *ж см* **по́дданный**.
по́дданн|ый (**-ого**; *decl like adj*) *м* subject, citizen.
по́дданств|о (**-а**) *ср* nationality, citizenship.
подда́ться (*как* **дать**; *см* **Table 14**; *impf* **поддава́ться**) *сов возв* (*дверь итп*) to give way; **поддава́ться** (**~** *perf*) *+dat* (*панике*) to give way to; (*влиянию, соблазну*) to give in to; **поддава́ться** (**~** *perf*) *+dat или* **на** *+acc* (*на просьбы*) to give in to.
поддева́|ть (**-ю**) *несов от* **подде́ть**.
подде́ла|ть (**-ю**; *impf* **подде́лывать**) *сов перех* to forge
▸ **подде́латься** (*impf* **подде́лываться**) *сов возв*: **~ся под** *+acc* to imitate.
подде́л|ка (**-ки**; *gen pl* **-ок**) *ж* forgery.
подде́лыва|ть(ся) (**-ю(сь)**) *несов от* **подде́лать(ся)**.
подде́льный *прил* (*документ*) forged; (*радость, гостеприимство*) feigned.
подде́ну *итп сов см* **подде́ть**.
подд|ержа́ть (**-ержу́, -е́ржишь**; *impf* **подде́рживать**) *сов перех* to support; (*падающего*) to hold on to; (*выступление, предложение итп*) to second; (*беседу*) to keep up.
подде́ржива|ть (**-ю**) *несов от* **поддержа́ть** ◆ *перех* to support; (*переписку*) to keep up; (*порядок, отношения*) to maintain.
подде́ржк|а (**-и**) *ж* support.

поддé|ть (**-ну, -нешь**; *impf* **поддевáть**) *сов перех* (*приподнять*) to prise (*BRIT*) *или* prize (*US*) off; (*перен*: *разг*) to gibe at; **поддевáть** (**~** *perf*) **свúтер под кýртку** to put on a sweater under(neath) one's jacket; **поддевáть** (**~** *perf*) **крючкóм** to hook.

поддóн (**-а**) *м* (*для грузов*) pallet; (*для жидкости*) tray.

поддувáл|о (**-а**) *ср* damper.

подевá|ть(ся) (**-ю(сь)**) *сов от* **девáть(ся)**.

подéйств|овать (**-ую**) *сов от* **дéйствовать**.

подéла|ть (**-ю**) *сов перех* (*разг*) to do; **ничегó не ~ешь, ничегó нельзя́ ~** (*разг*) it can't be helped.

под|елúть(ся) (**-елю́(сь), -éлишь(ся)**) *сов от* **делúть(ся)**.

подéл|ка (**-ки**; *gen pl* **-ок**) *ж any kind of handmade craft*.

поделóм *нареч*: **~ емý** it serves him right.

подёргива|ться (**-юсь**) *несов от* **подёрнуться** ♦ *возв* (*лицо*) to twitch.

подéржанный *прил* (*одежда, мебель итп*) second-hand.

подёрн|уться (*3sg* **-ется**, *3pl* **-утся**, *impf* **подёргиваться**) *сов возв*: **~** *+instr* (*покрыться*) to be covered with; **у негó вóлосы ~улись сединóй** he had a lot of grey hair.

подерýсь *итп сов см* **подрáться**.

подешевé|ть (**-ю**) *сов от* **дешевéть**.

поджáрист|ый (**-, -а, -о**) *прил* (*мясо*) well-done; (*картошка, пирожок*) crisp.

поджáр|ый (**-, -а, -о**) *прил* lean.

поджáть (**-ожмý, -ожмёшь**; *impf* **поджимáть**) *сов перех* (*губы*) to purse; (*живот*) to pull in; **поджимáть** (**~** *perf*) **нóги под себя́** to tuck one's legs under o.s.; **поджимáть** (**~** *perf*) **колéни** to pull one's knees up.

поджелýдочн|ый *прил*: **~ая железá** pancreas.

поджéчь (**-ожгý, -ожжёшь** *итп*, **-ожгýт**; *impf* **поджигáть**) *сов перех* to set fire to.

поджигáтел|ь (**-я**) *м* arsonist.

поджигá|ть (**-ю**) *несов от* **поджéчь**.

поджидá|ть (**-ю**) *несов перех* to wait for.

поджимá|ть (**-ю**) *несов от* **поджáть** ♦ *перех* (*разг*): **нас ~ют срóки** we are working to a tight deadline.

поджóг (**-а**) *м* arson.

подзаголóв|ок (**-ка**) *м* subheading.

подзатыльник (**-а**) *м* (*разг*) clip round the ear.

подзащúтн|ая (**-ой**; *decl like adj*) *ж* (*ЮР*) *см* **подзащúтный**.

подзащúтн|ый (**-ого**; *decl like adj*) *м* (*ЮР*) client.

подземéл|ье (**-ья**; *gen pl* **-ий**) *ср* (*комната*) vault; (*проход*) underground passage; (*ряд помещений*) catacombs *мн*.

подзéмный *прил* underground.

подзовý *итп сов см* **подозвáть**.

подзóрн|ый *прил*: **~ая трубá** telescope.

подзывá|ть (**-ю**) *несов от* **подозвáть**.

подú *сов* (*разг*) go ♦ *вводн сл* (*наверное*) probably.

подирá|ть (*3sg* **-ет**) *несов безл*: **у меня́ морóз по кóже ~ет от э́того** (*разг*) it makes my skin crawl *или* my flesh creep.

подкáлыва|ть (**-ю**) *несов от* **подколóть**.

подкáпыва|ться (**-юсь**) *несов от* **подкопáться**.

подкараýл|ить (**-ю, -ишь**; *impf* **подкараýливать**) *сов перех* (*разг*) to lie in wait for.

подкáрмлива|ть (**-ю**) *несов от* **подкормúть**.

подк|атúть (**-ачý, -áтишь**; *impf* **подкáтывать**) *сов перех* (*что-н круглое*) to roll; (*что-н на колёсах*) to wheel ♦ *неперех* (*машина, экипаж*) to race up.

подкачá|ть (**-ю**) *сов* (*не*)*перех* (*разг*) to fail.

подкачý *сов см* **подкатúть**.

подкáшива|ть(ся) (**-ю(сь)**) *несов от* **подкосúть(ся)**.

подкúдыва|ть (**-ю**) *несов от* **подкúнуть**.

подкúдыш (**-а**) *м* abandoned baby.

подкúн|уть (**-у, -ешь**; *impf* **подкúдывать**) *сов перех* (*кинуть вверх*) to toss; (*+acc или +gen*; *добавить*) to put; (*тайно подложить*: *анонимку*) to leave; (: *ворованный товар, наркотик*) to plant; **подкúдывать** (**~** *perf*) **комý-н дéнег** (*разг*) to give sb a sub; **подкúдывать** (**~** *perf*) **когó-н** (*разг*) to give sb a lift.

подклáд|ка (**-ки**; *gen pl* **-ок**) *ж* lining.

подклáдыва|ть (**-ю**) *несов от* **подложúть**.

подклé|ить (**-ю, -ишь**; *impf* **подклéивать**) *сов перех* to stick on.

подключ|úть (**-ý, -úшь**; *impf* **подключáть**) *сов перех* (*телефон*) to connect; (*лампу*) to plug in; (*специалистов*) to involve; **подключáть** (**~** *perf*) **к систéме/центрáльной сетú** (*КОМП*) to network, hook up to the main network

▸ **подключúться** (*impf* **подключáться**) *сов возв* to get involved.

подкóв|а (**-ы**) *ж* (*лошади итп*) shoe.

подк|овáть (**-ую́**) *сов от* **ковáть** ♦ (*impf* **подкóвывать**) *перех* (*лошадь итп*) to shoe.

подк|олóть (**-олю́, -óлешь**; *impf* **подкáлывать**) *сов перех* (*скрепить*) to pin up; (*разг*: *уязвить*) to taunt; **подкáлывать** (**~** *perf*) **докумéнт к дéлу** to file a document.

подкóп (**-а**) *м* (*ход*) secret underground passage.

подкопá|ться (**-юсь**; *impf* **подкáпываться**) *сов возв*: **~ под** *+acc* (*под здание*) to tunnel under; (*разг*: *под начальника итп*) to undermine.

подк|ормúть (**-ормлю́, -óрмишь**; *impf* **подкáрмливать**) *сов перех* (*животных*) to fatten up; (*ребёнка, больного*) to feed up.

подк|осúть (**-ошý, -óсишь**; *impf* **подкáшивать**) *сов перех* (*подлеж*: *удар, пуля*) to fell; (*несчастье*) to devastate; (*усталость*) to overcome

▸ **подкосúться** (*impf* **подкáшиваться**) *сов возв*: **у негó нóги/колéни ~осúлись** his legs/knees gave way.

подкрá|сться (**-дýсь, -дёшься**; *impf*

подкра́дываться) *сов возв* to sneak *или* steal up.
подкреп|и́ть (-лю́, -и́шь; *impf* **подкрепля́ть)** *сов перех* (*стену, крышу*) to support; (*мысли, утверждение*) to support, back up
▸ **подкрепи́ться** (*impf* **подкрепля́ться**) *несов возв* to fortify o.s.
подкрепле́ни|е (-я) *ср* (*ВОЕН*) reinforcement.
подкреплю́(сь) *сов см* **подкрепи́ть(ся)**.
подкрепля́|ть(ся) (-ю(сь)) *несов от* **подкрепи́ть(ся)**.
по́дкуп (-а) *м* bribery.
подк|упи́ть (-уплю́, -у́пишь; *impf* **подкупа́ть)** *сов перех* to bribe; (*перен: добротой*) to win over.
подла́мыва|ться (*3sg* **-ется**, *3pl* **-ются)** *несов от* **подломи́ться**.
по́дле *нареч* (*рядом*) nearby ◆ *предл* (+*gen*) beside, next to.
подлеж|а́ть (*3sg* **-и́т**, *3pl* **-а́т)** *несов неперех*: ~ +*dat* (*проверке, обложению налогом*) to be subject to; **пригово́р не ~и́т обжа́лованию** (*ЮР*) the sentence is not open to appeal; **э́то не ~и́т сомне́нию** there can be no doubt about that.
подлежа́щ|ее (-его; *decl like adj*) *ср* (*ЛИНГ*) subject.
подле|те́ть (-чу́, -ти́шь; *impf* **подлета́ть)** *сов неперех* (*самолёт*) to fly in; (*птица*) to fly up; (*разг: человек*) to race up.
подле́ц (-а́) *м* scoundrel.
подл|ечи́ть (-ечу́, -е́чишь; *impf* **подле́чивать)** *сов перех* to treat
▸ **подлечи́ться** (*impf* **подле́чиваться**) *сов возв* to undergo a short course of treatment.
подлечу́ *сов см* **подлете́ть**.
подлива́|ть (-ю) *несов от* **подли́ть**.
подли́в|ка (-ки; *gen pl* **-ок)** *ж* (*КУЛИН*) sauce.
подли́з|а (-ы) *ж* crawler.
подли́зыва|ться (-юсь; *perf* **подлиза́ться)** *несов возв*: ~ **к** +*dat* (*разг*) to crawl to.
по́длинен *прил см* **по́длинный**.
по́длинник (-а) *м* original.
по́длин|ный (-ен, -на, -но) *прил* original; (*документ*) authentic; (*no short form; герой, друг*) true.
подл|и́ть (-олью́, -ольёшь; *pt* **-ли́л, -лила́, -ли́ло**, *impf* **подлива́ть)** *сов перех* to add; **подлива́ть (~** *perf*) **вина́ в стака́н** to top up a glass with wine; **подлива́ть (~** *perf*) **ма́сла в ого́нь** to add fuel to the fire *или* flames.
по́дло *нареч* (*поступить*) meanly ◆ *как сказ* it's mean.
подло́г (-а) *м* forgery.
подло́жен *прил см* **подло́жный**.
подл|ожи́ть (-ожу́, -о́жишь; *impf* **подкла́дывать)** *сов перех* (*анонимку*) to leave; (*ворованный товар*) to plant; (+*acc или* +*gen*; *добавить*) to put; (*дров, сахара*) to add; **подкла́дывать (~** *perf*) **что-н под что-н** to put sth under sth.
подло́ж|ный (-ен, -на, -но) *прил* forged.
подлоко́тник (-а) *м* arm(rest).
подл|оми́ться (*3sg* **-о́мится**, *3pl* **-о́мятся**, *impf* **подла́мываться**) *сов возв*: ~ **под тя́жестью чего́-н** to give way under the weight of sth.
по́длост|ь (-и) *ж* (*качество*) baseness; **кака́я ~!** what a base thing to do!
по́дл|ый (-, -а́, -о) *прил* base.
подмастéрь|е (-я) *м* apprentice.
подма́чива|ть (-ю) *несов от* **подмочи́ть**.
подм|ени́ть (-еню́, -е́нишь; *impf* **подме́нивать)** *сов перех* (*заменить*) to substitute; **подме́нивать (~** *perf*) **кого́-н** (*разг*) to stand in for sb.
подм|ести́ (-ету́, -етёшь; *pt* **-ёл, -ела́, -ело́)** *сов от* **мести́** ◆ (*impf* **подмета́ть**) *перех* (*пол*) to sweep; (*мусор*) to sweep up.
подме́|тить (-чу, -тишь; *impf* **подмеча́ть)** *сов перех* to notice.
подмётк|а (-и) *ж* (*подошва*) sole; **он в ~и ей не годи́тся** (*разг*) he's not worth her little finger.
подмету́ *итп сов см* **подмести́**.
подмеча́|ть (-ю) *несов от* **подме́тить**.
подме́чу *сов см* **подме́тить**.
подмигн|у́ть (-у́, -ёшь; *impf* **подми́гивать)** *сов неперех*: ~ **кому́-н** to wink at sb.
подмина́|ть (-ю) *несов от* **подмя́ть**.
подмо́г|а (-и) *ж* (*разг*) help.
подмо́стк|и (-ов) *мн* (*ТЕАТР*) stage *ед*.
подм|очи́ть (-очу́, -о́чишь; *impf* **подма́чивать)** *сов перех* to dampen, moisten; (*разг: репутацию*) to blacken.
подмо́ю *итп сов см* **подмы́ть**.
подмыва́|ть (-ю) *несов от* **подмы́ть** ◆ *безл* (*разг*): **его́ ~ло** +*infin* ... he felt an urge to ....
подм|ы́ть (-о́ю, -о́ешь; *impf* **подмыва́ть)** *сов перех* (*ребёнка, больного*) to wash; (*берег, мост*) to undermine.
подмы́ш|ка (-ки; *gen pl* **-ек)** *ж* armpit.
под|мя́ть (-омну́, -омнёшь; *impf* **подмина́ть)** *сов перех* to crush.
поднево́л|ьный (-ен, -ьна, -ьно) *прил* (*человек*) subordinate; (*труд*) forced.
поднес|ти́ (-у́, -ёшь; *impf* **подноси́ть)** *сов перех*: ~ **к** +*dat* to bring up to; (*подарить*): ~ **что-н кому́-н** to present sth to sb.
поднима́|ть(ся) (-ю(сь)) *несов от* **подня́ть(ся)**.
подниму́(сь) *итп сов см* **подня́ть(ся)**.
поднов|и́ть (-лю́, -и́шь; *impf* **подновля́ть)** *сов перех* (*здание*) to refurbish; (*краску*) to touch up.
подного́тн|ая (-ой; *decl like adj*) *ж*: **(вся) ~** the true nature.
подно́жек *сущ см* **подно́жка**.

поднóжи|е (**-я**) *ср* (*горы, памятника*) foot.
поднóж|ка (**-ки**; *gen pl* **-ек**) *ж* (*трамвая, автобуса итп*) step; **дать** *(perf) или* **постáвить** *(perf)* **~ку комý-н** to trip sb up.
поднóжн|ый *прил*: **быть на ~ом кормý** (*с.-х.*) to be out at pasture.
поднóс (**-а**) *м* tray.
подн|осить (**-ошý, -óсишь**) *несов от* **поднести́**.
подн|я́ть (**-имý, -и́мешь**; *impf* **поднимáть**) *сов перех* to raise; (*что-н лёгкое*) to pick up; (*что-н тяжёлое*) to lift (up); (*флаг*) to hoist; (*спящего человека*) to rouse; (*панику, восстание*) to start; (*экономику, дисциплину*) to improve; (*архивные материалы, документацию итп*) to unearth; **поднимáть (~** *perf)* **крик** *или* **шум** to make a fuss; **поднимáть (~** *perf)* **чьё-н настроéние** *или* **чей-н дух** to raise sb's spirits; **поднимáть (~** *perf)* **когó-н нá смех** to make a laughing stock of sb
▸ **подня́ться** (*impf* **поднимáться**) *сов возв* to rise; (*на другой этаж, на сцену*) to go up; (*с постели, со стула*) to get up; (*паника, метель, драка*) to break out; **поднимáться (~ся** *perf)* **нá гору** to climb a hill; **~я́лся крик** there was an uproar; **~я́лся вéтер** the wind got up.
подо *предл см* **под**.
подобá|ть (*3sg* **-ет**, *3pl* **-ют**) *несов неперех*: **~** *+dat* to befit; **Вам не ~ет откáзываться** it does not befit you to refuse.
подобáющ|ий (**-ая, -ее, -ие**) *прил* appropriate.
подóбен *прил см* **подóбный**.
подóбно *предл*: **~** *+dat* like, similar to ◆ *союз*: **~ томý как** in the same way as, just as.
подóб|ный (**-ен, -на, -но**) *прил*: **~** *+dat* (*сходный с*) like, similar to; **~ные лю́ди – рéдкость** there are very few people like this *или* of this type; **и томý ~ное** et cetera, and so on; **ничегó ~ного** (*разг*) nothing of the sort.
подобострáст|ный (**-ен, -на, -но**) *прил* obsequious, servile.
подо|брáть (**-берý, -берёшь**; *impf* **подбирáть**) *сов перех* to pick up; (*приподнять вверх*) to gather (up); (*выбрать подходящее*) to select, pick
▸ **подобрáться** (*impf* **подбирáться**) *сов возв* (*коллектив*) to get together; (*библиотека, коллекция*) to be built up; (*подкрасться*) to steal up.
подобрé|ть (**-ю**) *сов от* **добрéть**.
подобрý-поздорóву *нареч* (*разг*): **убирáйся ~!** get out while the going's good!
подобью *итп сов см* **подби́ть**.
под|огнáть (**-гоню́, -гóнишь**; *impf* **подгоня́ть**) *сов перех*: **~ к** *+dat* (*стадо, машину*) to drive up to; (*лодку*) to take in to; **подгоня́ть (~** *perf)* **под** *+acc* to fit.
подогн|ýть (**-ý, -ёшь**; *impf* **подгибáть**) *сов перех* (*рукава, штанину*) to turn up
▸ **подогнýться** (*impf* **подгибáться**) *сов возв* to curl under; **у негó нóги/колéни ~ýлись** his legs/knees gave way.
подогрé|ть (**-ю**; *impf* **подогревáть**) *сов перех* to warm up; (*перен: любопытство*) to heighten.
пододви́н|уть (**-у, -ешь**; *impf* **пододвигáть**) *сов перех* to move closer.
пододея́льник (**-а**) *м* ≈ duvet cover.
подожд|áть (**-ý, -ёшь**; *pt* **-áл, -алá, -áло**) *сов перех* to wait for; **~** *(perf)* **с чем-н** to put sth off; **~** *(perf) +infin* to put off doing; **~и́те!** wait a minute!; **~и́те, мóжет всё не так плóхо** wait a bit, maybe it won't be all that bad; **~и́те, я ведь знал Вáшего отцá** wait a minute, I think I knew your father.
подожгý *итп сов см* **поджéчь**.
подожмý *итп сов см* **поджáть**.
под|озвáть (**-зовý, -зовёшь**; *pt* **-озвáл, -озвалá, -озвáло**, *impf* **подзывáть**) *сов перех* to call over.
подозревá|ть (**-ю**) *несов перех* to suspect; **~** *(impf)* **когó-н в чём-н** to suspect sb of sth; **~** *(impf)* **(о чём-н)** to have an idea (about sth).
подозрéни|е (**-я**) *ср* suspicion; **~ на** *+acc* (*предположение*) suspicion of; **быть** *(impf)* **под ~м** *или* **на ~и** to be under suspicion; **он был задéржан/арестóван по ~ю в убийстве** he was held/arrested on suspicion of murder.
подозри́тел|ьный (**-ен, -ьна, -ьно**) *прил* suspicious.
подо|и́ть (**-ю́, -ишь**) *сов от* **дои́ть**.
подой|ти́ (*как* **идти́**; *см* **Table 18**; *impf* **подходи́ть**) *сов неперех*: **~ к** *+dat* (*также перен*) to approach; (*соответствовать*): **~ти́ к** *+dat* (*юбка*) to go (well) with; **подходи́ть (~** *perf)* **на дóлжность** to be suited to a position; **э́то мне подхóдит** this suits me; **подходи́ть (~** *perf)* **к концý** to come to an end.
подокóнник (**-а**) *м* windowsill.
подóл (**-а**) *м* hem.
подóлгу *нареч* for a long time.
подолью *итп сов см* **подли́ть**.
подомнý *итп сов см* **подмя́ть**.
подóн|ок (**-ка**) *м* scum.
подопéчн|ый (**-ого**; *decl like adj*) *м* ward ◆ *прил*: **~ ребёнок** ward; **подопéчная территóрия** (*под опекой ООН*) trust territory, trusteeship.
подоплёк|а (**-и**) *ж* underlying reason.
подопрý *итп сов см* **подперéть**.
подóпытн|ый *прил*: **~ое живóтное** animal used in experiments; **~ крóлик** (*перен*) guinea pig.
подорв|áть (**-ý, -ёшь**; *pt* **-áл, -алá, -áло**, *impf* **подрывáть**) *сов перех* to blow up; (*перен: авторитет, доверие*) to undermine; (*: здоровье*) to destroy
▸ **подорвáться** (*impf* **подрывáться**) *сов возв* to be blown up; (*перен: авторитет*) to be undermined; (*: здоровье*) to be destroyed.
подорожá|ть (**-ю**) *сов от* **дорожáть**.
подорóжник (**-а**) *м* plantain.
подо|слáть (**-шлю́, -шлёшь**; *impf* **подсылáть**) *сов перех* to send (*secretly*).

подоспе́|ть (**-ю**; *impf* **подоспева́ть**) *сов неперех* to arrive in time.
подотру́ *итп сов см* **подотере́ть**.
подотчёт|ный (**-ен, -на, -но**) *прил* (*организация, работник итп*) accountable; **счёт ~ных сумм** expense account; **подотчётные де́ньги** expenses.
подо́хн|уть (**-у, -ешь**) *сов от* **до́хнуть**.
подохо́дный *прил*: **~ нало́г** income tax.
подо́шв|а (**-ы**) *ж* (*обуви*) sole.
подошёл *итп сов см* **подойти́**.
подошлю́ *итп сов см* **подосла́ть**.
подошью́ *итп сов см* **подши́ть**.
подпа́|сть (**-ду́, -дёшь**) *сов неперех*: **~ под** *+acc* to fall under.
подпева́|ть (**-ю**; *perf* **подпе́ть**) *несов неперех* (*+dat*) to join in with; (*перен: разг: пренебр*) to echo.
под|пере́ть (**-опру́, -опрёшь**; *pt* **-пёр, -пёрла, -пёрло**, *impf* **подпира́ть**) *сов перех*: **~ что-н чем-н** to prop up; **подпира́ть** (**~** *perf*) **щёку кула́ком** to rest one's head in one's hands.
подп|е́ть (**-ою́, -оёшь**) *сов от* **подпева́ть**.
подпира́|ть (**-ю**) *несов от* **подпере́ть**.
подписа́ни|е (**-я**) *ср* signing.
подп|иса́ть (**-ишу́, -и́шешь**; *impf* **подпи́сывать**) *сов перех* to sign
▸ **подписа́ться** (*impf* **подпи́сываться**) *сов возв*: **~ся под** *+instr* to sign; **подпи́сываться** (**~ся** *perf*) **на** *+acc* (*на газету, на журнал*) to subscribe to.
подпи́с|ка (**-ки**; *gen pl* **-ок**) *ж* subscription; (*о невыезде, о неразглашении*) signed statement.
подписно́й *прил* subscription *опред*; **~ акционе́рный капита́л** (*комм*) subscribed capital; **подписно́й лист** list of subscribers.
подпи́сок *сущ см* **подпи́ска**.
подпи́счик (**-а**) *м* subscriber.
подпи́сыва|ть(ся) (**-ю(сь)**) *несов от* **подписа́ть(ся)**.
по́дпис|ь (**-и**) *ж* (*фамилия*) signature; (*под картиной*) title, caption; (*под стихами*) title.
подпишу́(сь) *итп сов см* **подписа́ть(ся)**.
подплы́|ть (**-ву́, -вёшь**; *pt* **-л, -ла́, -ло**, *impf* **подплыва́ть**) *сов неперех* (*лодка*) to sail (up); (*пловец, рыба*) to swim (up).
подполко́вник (**-а**) *м* lieutenant colonel.
подпо́ль|е (**-я**) *ср* (*подвал*) cellar; (*конспирация*) underground activities *мн*; **уходи́ть** (**уйти́** *perf*) **в ~** to go underground.
подпо́льный *прил* underground *опред*.
подпо́р|ка (**-ки**; *gen pl* **-ок**) *ж* prop, support.
подпою́ *итп сов см* **подпе́ть**.
подпоя́|сать (**-шу, -шешь**; *impf* **подпоя́сывать**) *сов перех* to belt.
подпра́в|ить (**-лю, -ишь**; *impf* **подправля́ть**) *сов перех* to make minor corrections to.
подпрогра́мм|а (**-ы**) *ж* (*комп*) subroutine.
подпру́г|а (**-и**) *ж* girth.
подпры́гн|уть (**-у, -ешь**; *impf* **подпры́гивать**) *сов неперех* to jump.
подпуска́|ть (**-ю**) *несов от* **подпусти́ть** ◆ *перех*: **~ к** *+dat* to allow access to.
подп|усти́ть (**-ущу́, -у́стишь**; *impf* **подпуска́ть**) *сов перех* (*человека, зверя*) to allow to approach.
подрабо́та|ть (**-ю**; *impf* **подраба́тывать**) *сов перех* (*статью*) to polish up ◆ *(не)перех* (*+acc или +gen*) to earn extra.
подра́внива|ть (**-ю**) *несов от* **подровня́ть**.
подра́гива|ть (**-ю**) *сов неперех* to tremble; (*ресницы*) to flutter.
подража́ни|е (**-я**) *ср* imitation.
подража́|ть (**-ю**) *несов неперех* (*+dat*) to imitate.
подразделе́ни|е (**-я**) *ср* (*воинское*) subunit; (*производственное*) subdivision.
подраздел|и́ть (**-ю́, -и́шь**; *impf* **подразделя́ть**) *сов перех* to subdivide.
подразделя́|ться (*3sg* **-ется**, *3pl* **-ются**) *несов возв* to be subdivided.
подразумева́|ть (**-ю**) *несов перех* to mean
▸ **подразумева́ться** *несов возв* to be implied.
подра́мник (**-а**) *м* stretcher.
подр|асти́ (**-асту́, -астёшь**; *pt* **-о́с, -осла́, -осло́**, *impf* **подраста́ть**) *сов неперех* to grow (a little).
под|ра́ться (**-еру́сь, -ерёшься**) *сов от* **дра́ться**.
подре́|зать (**-жу, -жешь**; *impf* **подреза́ть**) *сов перех* (*платье*) to shorten; (*волосы*) to cut; **~** (*perf*) **кры́лья кому́-н** (*перен*) to clip sb's wings.
подро́бен *прил см* **подро́бный**.
подро́бност|ь (**-и**) *ж* detail; **вдава́ться** (*impf*) **в ~и** to go into detail.
подро́б|ный (**-ен, -на, -но**) *прил* detailed.
подровня́|ть (**-ю**; *impf* **подра́внивать**) *сов перех* to trim.
подро́с *итп сов см* **подрасти́**.
подро́стка *сущ см* **подро́сток**.
подростко́вый *прил* (*одежда итп*) teenage *опред*; (*проблемы*) adolescent *опред*; **подростко́вый во́зраст** teens *мн*.
подро́ст|ок (**-ка**) *м* teenager, adolescent.
подру́г|а (**-и**) *ж* (girl)friend; **подру́га жи́зни** wife.
по-друго́му *нареч* (*иначе*) differently.
подр|ужи́ть (**-ужу́, -у́жишь**) *сов от* **дружи́ть**
▸ **подружи́ться** *сов от* **дружи́ться** ◆ *возв*: **~ся с** *+instr* to make friends with; **они́ бы́стро ~ужи́лись** they quickly became friends.
подрул|и́ть (**-ю́, -и́шь**; *impf* **подру́ливать**) *сов неперех* (*самолёт*) to taxi; (*автомобиль*) to drive (up).
подрумя́н|иться (**-юсь, -ишься**) *сов от* **румя́ниться** ◆ (*impf* **подрумя́ниваться**) *возв* (*женщина*) to put on blusher; (*пирожки,*

булочки) to brown.
подру́ч|ный *прил*: ~ **материа́л/инструме́нт** the material/instrument to hand ◆ (**-ого**; *decl like adj*) *м* assistant.
подрыва́|ть(ся) (**-ю(сь)**) *несов от* **подорва́ть(ся)**.
подрывно́й *прил* subversive.
подря́д *нареч* in succession ◆ (**-а**) *м* (*рабочий договор*) contract; **рабо́тали 5 дней** ~ they worked 5 days in a row *или* in succession; **все/всё** ~ everyone/everything without exception.
подря́дный *прил* contract *опред*.
подря́дчик (**-а**) *м* contractor.
подряхле́|ть (**-ю**) *сов от* **дряхле́ть**.
подс|ади́ть (**-ажу́, -а́дишь**; *impf* **подса́живать**) *сов перех* (*на коня*) to help to mount; (*на высокий стул*) to help up; (*посадить рядом*) to place nearby.
подса́жива|ться (**-юсь**) *несов от* **подсе́сть**.
подсажу́ *сов см* **подсади́ть**.
подсве́чник (**-а**) *м* candlestick.
подсе́к *umn сов см* **подсе́чь**.
подсека́|ть (**-ю**) *несов от* **подсе́чь**.
подсеку́ *umn сов см* **подсе́чь**.
подс|е́сть (**-я́ду, -я́дешь**; *impf* **подса́живаться**) *сов неперех*: ~ **к** *+dat* to sit down beside.
подс|е́чь (**-еку́, -ечёшь** *umn*, **-еку́т**; *pt* **-ёк, -екла́, -екло**, *impf* **подсека́ть**) *сов перех* to cut down; (*перен*: *подлеж*: *несчастье, болезнь*) to lay low.
подсин|и́ть (**-ю́, -и́шь**) *сов от* **сини́ть**.
подск|аза́ть (**-ажу́, -а́жешь**; *impf* **подска́зывать**) *сов перех* (*перен*: *идею, решение*) to suggest; (*разг*: *адрес, телефон*) to tell; **подска́зывать** (~ *perf*) **что-н кому́-н** to prompt sb with sth; **не ~а́жите, где у́лица Пу́шкина?** can you please tell me where Pushkin Street is?
подска́з|ка (**-ки**; *gen pl* **-ок**) *ж* prompt; **де́йствовать** (*impf*) **по чьей-н ~ке** (*перен*) to do as sb says.
подска́зыва|ть (**-ю**) *несов от* **подсказа́ть**.
подск|очи́ть (**-очу́, -о́чишь**; *impf* **подска́кивать**) *сов неперех* (*также перен*) to jump; (*подбежать*) to run up; **подска́кивать** (~ *perf*) **от испу́га/неожи́данности** to start (in fright/surprise).
подсла|сти́ть (**-щу́, -сти́шь**; *impf* **подсла́щивать**) *сов перех* to sweeten.
подсле́дственн|ая (**-ой**; *decl like adj*) *ж см* **подсле́дственный**.
подсле́дственн|ый (**-ого**; *decl like adj*) *м* the accused, the defendant; **~ые** the accused.
подслу́ша|ть (**-ю**; *impf* **подслу́шивать**) *сов перех* to eavesdrop on.
подсма́трива|ть (**-ю**) *несов от* **подсмотре́ть**.
подсме́ива|ться (**-юсь**) *сов возв*: ~ **над** *+instr* to poke gentle fun at.
подсм|отре́ть (**-отрю́, -о́тришь**; *impf* **подсма́тривать**) *сов перех* (*увидеть*) to spy on; ~ (*perf*), **что ...** to notice that ...; **я ~отре́л, как он брал конфе́ты** I saw him take the sweets.
подсне́жник (**-а**) *м* snowdrop.
подсо́бный *прил* (*помещение, хозяйство*) subsidiary; **подсо́бный рабо́чий** auxiliary.
подсо́выва|ть (**-ю**) *несов от* **подсу́нуть**.
подсозна́ни|е (**-я**) *ср* the subconscious.
подсозна́тел|ьный (**-ен, -ьна, -ьно**) *прил* subconscious.
подсо́лнечник (**-а**) *м* sunflower.
подсо́лнечн|ый *прил*: **~ое ма́сло** sunflower oil.
подсо́лнух (**-а**) *м* (*разг*) sunflower.
подсо́х|нуть (**-ну, -нешь**; *pt* **-, -ла, -ло**, *impf* **подсыха́ть**) *сов неперех* to dry out a little.
подспо́рь|е (**-я**) *ср* help.
подспу́д|ный (**-ен, -на, -но**) *прил* hidden.
подста́в|ить (**-лю, -ишь**; *impf* **подставля́ть**) *сов перех*: ~ **под** *+acc* to put under; **подставля́ть** (~ *perf*) **кого́-н под уда́р** (*перен*) to lay sb open to attack.
подста́в|ка (**-ки**; *gen pl* **-ок**) *ж* stand.
подста́влю *сов см* **подста́вить**.
подставля́|ть (**-ю**) *несов от* **подста́вить**.
подставно́й *прил* (*ложный*) false.
подста́вок *сущ см* **подста́вка**.
подстака́нник (**-а**) *м* glassholder.
подста́нци|я (**-и**) *ж* substation.
подстегн|у́ть (**-у́, -ёшь**; *impf* **подстёгивать**) *сов перех* to urge on; (*перен*: *разг*): ~ **кого́-н** to get sb moving.
подст|ели́ть (**-елю́, -е́лишь**; *impf* **подстила́ть**) *сов перех* (*плед, простыню*) to spread out.
подстерега́|ть (**-ю**) *несов от* **подстере́чь** ◆ *перех* (*ожидать*) to await.
подстере́|чь (**-гу́, -жёшь** *umn*, **-гу́т**; *impf* **подстерега́ть**) *сов перех* to lie in wait for.
подстила́|ть (**-ю**) *несов от* **подстели́ть**.
подсти́л|ка (**-ки**; *gen pl* **-ок**) *ж* covering.
подстра́ива|ть (**-ю**) *несов от* **подстро́ить**.
подстрах|ова́ть (**-у́ю**; *impf* **подстрахо́вывать**) *сов перех* (*гимнаста*) to be on hand for; (*в рискованном деле*) to insure.
подстрека́тел|ь (**-я**) *м* instigator.
подстрека́|ть (**-ю**) *несов перех*: ~ **кого́-н к** *+dat* to drive sb to.
подстр|ели́ть (**-елю́, -е́лишь**; *impf* **подстре́ливать**) *сов перех* to wing.
подстри́|чь (**-гу́, -жёшь** *umn*, **-гу́т**; *pt* **-г, -ла, -ло**, *impf* **подстрига́ть**) *сов перех* to trim; (*для укорачивания*) to cut
▸ **подстри́чься** (*impf* **подстрига́ться**) *сов возв* to have one's hair cut.
подстро́|ить (**-ю, -ишь**; *impf* **подстра́ивать**) *сов перех* to fix.
подстро́чн|ый *прил*: **~ое примеча́ние** footnote; ~ **перево́д** word-for-word translation.
по́дступ (**-а**) *м* (*обычно мн*) approach.
подст|упи́ть (**-уплю́, -у́пишь**; *impf* **подступа́ть**) *сов неперех* (*слёзы*) to well up; (*рыдания*) to

rise; **подступа́ть** (*~ perf*) **к** *+dat* to approach
▸ **подступи́ться** (*impf* **подступа́ться**) *сов возв*: **~ся к** *+dat* to approach.
подсу́ден *прил см* **подсу́дный**.
подсуди́м|ая (**-ой**; *decl like adj*) *ж см* **подсуди́мый**.
подсуди́м|ый (**-ого**; *decl like adj*) *м* (*ЮР*) the accused, the defendant; **~ые** the accused.
подсу́д|ный (**-ен, -на, -но**) *прил* (*ЮР*) sub judice; **~ное де́ло** (*подлежащий суду*) *case due to come before court*; (*преступление*) crime.
подсу́н|уть (**-у, -ешь**; *impf* **подсо́вывать**) *сов перех* to shove; (*разг*: *что-н ненужное, плохое*) to get rid of.
подс|уши́ть (**-ушу́, -у́шишь**; *impf* **подсу́шивать**) *сов перех* to dry slightly.
подсчёт (**-а**) *м* counting; (*обычно мн*: *итог*) calculation.
подсчита́|ть (**-ю**; *impf* **подсчи́тывать**) *сов перех* to count (up).
подсыла́|ть (**-ю**) *несов см* **подосла́ть**.
подсыха́|ть (**-ю**) *несов от* **подсо́хнуть**.
подся́ду *итп сов см* **подсе́сть**.
подта́лкива|ть (**-ю**) *несов от* **подтолкну́ть**.
подтас|ова́ть (**-у́ю**; *impf* **подтасо́вывать**) *сов перех* to juggle (with).
подта́чива|ть (**-ю**) *несов от* **подточи́ть**.
подтвер|ди́ть (**-жу́, -ди́шь**; *impf* **подтвержда́ть**) *сов перех* to confirm; (*фактами, цифрами*) to back up
▸ **подтверди́ться** (*impf* **подтвержда́ться**) *сов возв* to be confirmed.
подтвержде́ни|е (**-я**) *ср* confirmation.
подтвержу́(сь) *сов см* **подтверди́ть(ся)**.
подтёк (**-а**) *м* bruise.
подте́кст (**-а**) *м* hidden meaning.
под|тере́ть (**-отру́, -отрёшь**; *impf* **подтира́ть**) *сов перех* to mop up.
подтолкн|у́ть (**-у́, -ёшь**; *impf* **подта́лкивать**) *сов перех* to nudge; (*перен*) to urge on.
подт|очи́ть (**-очу́, -о́чишь**; *impf* **подта́чивать**) *сов перех* to sharpen (a little); (*перен*: *силы*) to weaken; (: *здоровье*) to destroy.
подтя́гива|ть(ся) (**-ю(сь)**) *несов от* **подтяну́ть(ся)**.
подтя́ж|ка (**-ки**; *gen pl* **-ек**) *ж* (*обычно мн*) braces *мн* (*BRIT*), suspenders *мн* (*US*).
подтя́нут|ый (**-, -а, -о**) *прил* smart.
подт|яну́ть (**-яну́, -я́нешь**; *impf* **подтя́гивать**) *сов перех* (*тяжёлый предмет*) to haul up; (*гайку, болт*) to tighten; (*войска*) to bring up
▸ **подтяну́ться** (*impf* **подтя́гиваться**) *сов возв* (*на брусьях, на перекладине*) to pull o.s. up; (*войска*) to move up; (*перен*) to get one's act together.
поду́ма|ть (**-ю**) *сов от* **ду́мать** ◆ *неперех*: **~** (**о** *+prp*) to think (about); **~** (*perf*) **над** *+instr* *или* **о** *+prp* to think about; **~, что...** to think that ...; **он и не ~л извини́ться** he didn't even think of apologizing *или* to apologize; **~ешь! купи́л но́вую маши́ну** so what if he's bought a new car!; **~ то́лько!** (*разг*) just think!; **кто бы мог ~!** who would have thought it!; **и не ~ю!** (*разг*) I won't hear of it!
▸ **поду́маться** *сов от* **ду́маться**.
поду́мыва|ть (**-ю**) *несов неперех* (*разг*): **~ о** *+prp*/*+infin* to think about/of doing.
подурне́|ть (**-ю**) *сов от* **дурне́ть**.
поду́|ть (**-ю**) *сов неперех* to blow; (*ветер*) to begin to blow.
подучи́ть (**-учу́, -у́чишь**; *impf* **поду́чивать**) *сов перех* (*разг*: *выучить*) to learn; (*научить*) to teach.
поду́шек *сущ см* **поду́шка**.
под|уши́ть (**-ушу́, -у́шишь**) *сов перех* to spray lightly with perfume.
поду́ш|ка (**-ки**; *gen pl* **-ек**) *ж* (*для сидения*) cushion; (*под голову*) pillow.
поду́шный *прил*: **~ нало́г** poll tax.
подхали́м (**-а**) *м* toady.
подхали́м|ка (**-ки**; *gen pl* **-ок**) *ж см* **подхали́м**.
подхва́т (**-а**) *м*: **быть на ~е** (*разг*) to be at hand.
подхв|ати́ть (**-ачу́, -а́тишь**; *impf* **подхва́тывать**) *сов перех* (*падающее*) to catch; (*подлеж*: *течение, толпа*) to carry away; (*слова, идею, болезнь*) to pick up; (*песню, мелодию*) to join in.
подхлестн|у́ть (**-у́, -ёшь**; *impf* **подхлёстывать**) *сов перех* to whip on.
подхо́д (**-а**) *м* approach; **экза́мены на ~е** the exams are approaching.
подх|оди́ть (**-ожу́, -о́дишь**) *несов от* **подойти́**.
подходя́щ|ий (**-ая, -ее, -ие**) *прил* (*дом*) suitable; (*момент, слова*) appropriate.
подхожу́ *несов см* **подходи́ть**.
подц|епи́ть (**-еплю́, -е́пишь**) *сов перех* to attach; (*разг*: *болезнь, девушку, жениха*) to pick up.
подча́с *нареч* at times.
подчеркн|у́ть (**-у́, -ёшь**; *impf* **подчёркивать**) *сов перех* (*в тексте*) to underline; (*в речи*) to emphasize.
подчине́ни|е (**-я**) *ср* obedience.
подчинённ|ый *прил* subordinate *опред* ◆ (**-ого**; *decl like adj*) *м* subordinate.
подчин|и́ть (**-ю́, -и́шь**; *impf* **подчиня́ть**) *сов перех* (*народ, страну*) to subjugate; **подчиня́ть** (*~ perf*) **что-н кому́-н** to place sth under the control of sb
▸ **подчини́ться** (*impf* **подчиня́ться**) *сов возв* (*+dat*) to obey.
подчи|сти́ть (**-щу, -сти́шь**; *impf* **подчища́ть**) *сов перех* (*пол итп*) to clean; (*написанное*) to erase.
подше́й(те) *сов см* **подши́ть**.
подше́фный *прил*: **~ де́тский дом** children's

home under patronage.
подшивá|ть (-ю) *несов от* **подши́ть.**
подши́в|ка (-ки; *gen pl* **-ок)** *ж (газет, документов)* bundle.
подши́пник (-а) *м (ТЕХ)* bearing.
под|ши́ть (-ошью́, -ошьёшь; *imper* **-ше́й(те),** *impf* **подшивáть)** *сов перех (рукав)* to hem; *(подол)* to take up; *(документ)* to file; *(пачку газет)* to bundle up.
подш|ути́ть (-учу́, -у́тишь; *impf* **подшу́чивать)** *сов неперех:* ~ **над** *+instr* to make fun of.
подъ- *преф см* **под-.**
подъе́ду *итп сов см* **подъе́хать.**
подъе́зд (-а) *м (к городу, к дому)* approach; *(в здании)* entrance.
подъезжа́й(те) *сов см* **подъе́хать.**
подъезжá|ть (-ю) *несов от* **подъе́хать.**
подъём (-а) *м (груза)* lifting; *(флага)* raising; *(на гору)* ascent; *(промышленный, культурный итп)* revival; *(в речи, в действиях)* enthusiasm; *(сигнал: к пробуждению)* reveille.
подъёмник (-а) *м* lift (*BRIT*), elevator (*US*).
подъёмн|ые (-ых; *decl like adj*) *мн (также:* ~ **де́ньги)** relocation costs *мн.*
подъёмный *прил* lifting *опред;* **подъёмный кран** crane.
подъе́хать (*как* **е́хать;** *см* **Table 19;** *impf* **подъезжáть)** *сов неперех (на автомобиле)* to drive up; *(на коне)* to ride up; *(разг)* to call in.
подыгрá|ть (-ю; *impf* **поды́грывать)** *сов неперех (+dat; разг)* to accompany.
поды|скáть (-щу́, -щешь; *impf* **поды́скивать)** *сов перех* to find.
подыто́ж|ить (-у, -ишь) *сов перех (расходы, доходы)* to add up; *(сделанное, сказанное)* to sum up.
подыхá|ть (-ю) *несов неперех (животные)* to be dying; *(разг):* ~ **от** *+gen (от голода, от скуки итп)* to be dying of.
под|ышáть (-ышу́, -ы́шешь) *сов неперех* to breathe.
подыщу́ *итп сов см* **подыскáть.**
поедá|ть (-ю) *несов от* **пое́сть.**
пое́дешь *итп сов см* **пое́хать.**
поеди́м *итп сов см* **пое́сть.**
поеди́н|ок (-ка) *м* duel.
поеди́те *сов см* **пое́сть.**
пое́ду *итп сов см* **пое́хать.**
поедя́т *сов см* **пое́сть.**
поёж|иться (-усь, -ишься; *impf* **поёживаться)** *сов возв* to shiver slightly.
по́езд (-а; *nom pl* **-á)** *м* train; **ско́рый** ~ express train; ~ **дáльнего сле́дования** long-distance train; **е́хать** *(impf)* **~ом** *или* **на ~е** to travel by train; **е́хать** *(impf)* **в ~е метро́** to travel by tube (*BRIT*) *или* subway (*US*).
пое́зд|ка (-ки; *gen pl* **-ок)** *ж* trip.
поезжа́й(те) *сов см* **пое́хать.**
пое́сть (*как* **есть;** *см* **Table 15)** *сов от* **есть ◆** *(impf* **поедáть)** *перех:* ~ **чего́-н** to eat a little bit of sth; *(съесть всё)* to eat sth up; *(подлеж: моль)* to eat sth away.
пое́хать (*как* **е́хать;** *см* **Table 19)** *сов неперех (автомобиль, поезд итп)* to set off.
пое́шь *сов см* **пое́сть.**
пожáднича|ть (-ю) *сов от* **жáдничать.**
пожале́|ть (-ю) *сов от* **жале́ть.**
пожáл|овать (-ую) *сов от* **жáловать ◆** *неперех:* ~ **к** *+dat (посетить)* to visit; **добро́** ~ welcome.
пожáлуй *вводн сл (возможно)* perhaps; *(выражает предпочтение)* likely; **он, ~, не придёт** he may not come; **я, ~, пойду́** I'd better go.
пожáлуйста *част* please; *(в ответ на благодарность)* don't mention it, you're welcome; **~, помоги́те мне** please help me; **скажи́те ~!** you don't say!; **зако́нчил шко́лу и, ~, жени́лся** he left school and then, would you believe it, he got married.
пожáр (-а) *м* fire; *(+gen; перен: войны, революции)* the inferno.
пожáрищ|е (-а) *ср* site of fire.
пожáрник (-а) *м (разг)* fireman (*мн* firemen).
пожáрн|ый (-ого; *decl like adj*) *м* fireman (*мн* firemen) **◆** *прил:* **~ая комáнда** fire brigade (*BRIT*) *или* department (*US*); **~ая маши́на** fire engine; **на вся́кий ~ (слу́чай)** *(разг)* in case of emergency.
пожáти|е (-я) *ср:* ~ **(руки́)** handshake.
пож|áть (-му́, -мёшь; *impf* **пожимáть)** *сов перех* to squeeze; **он ~áл мне ру́ку** he shook my hand; **пожимáть (~** *perf***) плечáми** to shrug one's shoulders.
пожелáни|е (-я) *ср* wish; **при́мите мой наилу́чшие ~я** please accept my best wishes.
пожелá|ть (-ю) *сов от* **желáть.**
пожелте́|ть (-ю) *сов от* **желте́ть.**
пож|ени́ть (-еню́, -е́нишь) *сов от* **жени́ть ◆** *перех (разг)* to marry
▸ пожени́ться *сов от* **жени́ться ◆** *возв* to marry, get married.
поже́ртвовани|е (-я) *ср* donation.
поже́ртв|овать (-ую) *несов от* **же́ртвовать.**
поживá|ть (-ю) *несов неперех (разг):* **как ты ~ешь?** how are you?
пожив|и́ться (-лю́сь, -и́шься) *сов возв (+instr; разг)* to live off.
поживу́ *итп сов см* **пожи́ть.**
пожи́зненный *прил* lifelong, life *опред;* **пожи́зненное заключе́ние** life imprisonment.
пожило́й *прил* elderly.
пожимá|ть (-ю) *несов от* **пожáть.**
пожирá|ть (-ю) *несов от* **пожрáть ◆** *перех (книги)* to devour; **любопы́тство/честолю́бие ~ло его́** he was devoured by curiosity/ambition; ~ *(impf)* **кого́-н глазáми** to devour sb with one's eyes.
пожи́тк|и (-ов) *мн (разг)* belongings *мн.*
пож|и́ть (-иву́, -ивёшь; *pt* **-и́л, -илá, -и́ло)** *сов неперех (пробыть где-нибудь)* to stay for a while; **~ивём – уви́дим** we shall see.

пожму́ *итп сов см* **пожа́ть.**
пожр|а́ть (**-у́, -ёшь**; *impf* **пожира́ть**) *сов перех* (*подлеж: животное*) to devour; (*no impf; разг: подлеж: человек*) to gobble up.
по́з|а (**-ы**) *ж* posture; (*перен: поведение*) pose.
позабо́|титься (**-чусь, -тишься**) *сов от* **забо́титься.**
позави́д|овать (**-ую**) *сов от* **зави́довать.**
поза́втрака|ть (**-ю**) *несов от* **за́втракать.**
позавчера́ *нареч* the day before yesterday.
позади́ *нареч* (*сзади*) behind; (*в прошлом*) in the past ♦ *предл* (*+gen*) behind.
позаимств|овать (**-ую**) *сов от* **заимствовать.**
позапро́шл|ый *прил* before last; **~ая неде́ля** the week before last.
позаре́з *нареч* (*разг*) terribly.
поз|ва́ть (**-ову́, -овёшь**) *сов от* **звать.**
позволе́ни|е (**-я**) *ср* permission; **с Ва́шего ~я** with your permission.
позво́л|ить (**-ю, -ишь**; *impf* **позволя́ть**) *сов непepex* (*погода, обстоятельства*) to permit ♦ *перех*: **~ что-н кому́-н** to allow sb sth; **позволя́ть** (**~** *perf*) **кому́-н** *+infin* to allow sb to do; **~ьте!** excuse me!; **~ьте мне предста́вить моего́ колле́гу** allow me to introduce my colleague; **~ьте пройти́** excuse me please; **позволя́ть** (*impf*) **себе́ что-н** to afford sth.
позвон|и́ть (**-ю́, -и́шь**) *сов от* **звони́ть.**
позвон|о́к (**-ка́**) *м* vertebra (*мн* vertebrae).
позвоно́чник (**-а**) *м* spine, spinal column.
поздне́е *сравн нареч от* **по́здно** ♦ *нареч* later ♦ *предл* (*+gen*) after; (**не**) **~** *+gen* (no) later than.
по́здн|ий (**-яя, -ее, -ие**) *прил* late; **са́мое ~ее** (*разг*) at the latest.
по́здно *нареч* late ♦ *как сказ* it's late.
поздоро́ва|ться (**-юсь**) *сов от* **здоро́ваться.**
поздоро́в|иться (*3sg* **-ится**) *сов безл*: **ему́ не ~ится** (*разг*) he's in trouble.
поздрави́тельный *прил* greetings *опред.*
поздра́в|ить (**-лю, -ишь**; *impf* **поздравля́ть**) *сов перех*: **~ кого́-н с** *+instr* to congratulate sb on; **поздравля́ть** (**~** *perf*) **кого́-н с днём рожде́ния** to wish sb a happy birthday.
поздравле́ни|е (**-я**) *ср* congratulation; (*с днём рождения*) greeting.
поздра́влю *сов см* **поздра́вить.**
поздравля́|ть (**-ю**) *несов от* **поздра́вить.**
позелене́|ть (**-ю**) *сов от* **зелене́ть.**
по́зже *нареч* = **поздне́е.**
пози́р|овать (**-ую**) *сов непереx* (*+dat*) to pose for.
пози́ти́в (**-а**) *м* (*ФОТО*) positive.
позити́вн|ый (**-ен, -на, -но**) *прил* positive.
пози́ци|я (**-и**) *ж* position; (*контракта, проекта*) item.
познава́тел|ьный (**-ен, -ьна, -ьно**) *прил* educational.
позна|ва́ть (**-ю́**) *несов от* **позна́ть**
▸ **познава́ться** *несов возв* to become known.
познако́м|ить(ся) (**-лю(сь), -ишь(ся)**) *сов от* **знако́мить(ся).**
позна́ни|е (**-я**) *ср* familiarization; (*приобретение знаний*) cognition; *см также* **позна́ния.**
позна́ни|я (**-й**) *мн* knowledge *ед.*
позна́|ть (**-ю**; *impf* **познава́ть**) *сов перех* (*любовь, бедность итп*) to experience.
позову́ *итп сов см* **позва́ть.**
позоло́т|а (**-ы**) *ж* gilding, gilt.
позоло|ти́ть (**-чу́, -ти́шь**) *сов от* **золоти́ть.**
позо́р (**-а**) *м* disgrace; **выставля́ть** (**вы́ставить** *perf*) **кого́-н на ~** to bring disgrace on sb.
позо́рен *прил см* **позо́рный.**
позо́р|ить (**-ю, -ишь**; *perf* **опозо́рить**) *несов перех* to disgrace
▸ **позо́риться** (*perf* **опозо́риться**) *несов возв* to disgrace o.s.
позо́р|ный (**-ен, -на, -но**) *прил* disgraceful.
позывн|ы́е (**-ы́х**; *decl like adj*) *мн* call sign *ед.*
поимённый *прил*: **~ спи́сок** list of names.
поймк|а (**-ки**; *gen pl* **-ок**) *ж* capture.
по-ино́му *нареч* differently.
поинтерес|ова́ться (**-у́юсь**) *сов возв* (*+instr*) to take an interest in.
по́иск (**-а**) *м* (*научный, творческий итп*) quest; (*КОМП*) search; **„~ и заме́на"** "search and replace"; *см также* **по́иски.**
по|иска́ть (**-ищу́, -и́щешь**) *сов перех* to have a look for.
по́иск|и (**-ов**) *мн*: **~** (*+gen*) search *ед* (for); **в ~ах** *+gen* in search of.
поисти́не *нареч* truly.
по|и́ть (**-ю́, -ишь**; *imper* **пои́(те)**, *perf* **напои́ть**) *несов перех*: **~ кого́-н чем-н** to give sb sth to drink; **его́ напои́ли во́дкой** he was plied with vodka.
поищу́ *итп сов см* **поиска́ть.**
пойду́ *итп сов см* **пойти́.**
по́йм|а (**-ы**) *ж* flood plain.
пойма́|ть (**-ю**) *сов перех* to catch.
пойму́ *итп сов см* **поня́ть.**
по́йнтер (**-а**) *м* pointer (*dog*).
по́й(те) *несов см* **петь.**
пойти́ (*как* **идти́**; *см* **Table 18**) *сов непереx* to set off; (*по пути рефирм*) to start off; (*о механизмах, к цели*) to start working; (*дождь, снег*) to begin to fall; (*дым, пар*) to begin to rise; (*кровь*) to start flowing; (*фильм итп*) to start showing; (*подойти*): **~** *+dat* *или* **к** *+dat* (*шляпа, поведение*) to suit; **~** (*perf*) **в кого́-н** (*в мать, в деда итп*) to look like sb; **е́сли на то пошло́** if it comes to that; **так не пойдёт** that won't work.

KEYWORD

пока́ *нареч* **1** (*некоторое время*) for a while; **я пока́ подожду́** I'll wait for a while
2 (*тем временем*) in the meantime; **я ушёл, а**

она́ пока́ остава́лась в до́ме I left, and in the meantime she stayed at home
◆ *союз* **1** (*в то время как*) while; **пока́ он чита́л, я вы́шел на балко́н** while he was reading, I went out onto the balcony
2 (*до того времени как*): **пока́ не** until; **ребёнок бу́дет крича́ть, пока́ не полу́чит конфе́ту** the child will go on shouting until he gets a sweet; **пока́!** so long!; **пока́ что** for the moment.

покажу́(сь) *итп сов см* **показа́ть(ся)**.
пока́з (-а) *м* (*фильма*) showing; (*опыта*) demonstration; (*изменений, тенденций итп*) portrayal, depiction.
показа́ни|е (-я) *ср* (*ЮР*: *обычно мн*) evidence *ед*; (*на счётчике итп*) reading.
показа́телен *прил см* **показа́тельный**.
показа́тел|ь (-я) *м* indicator; (*МАТ, ЭКОН*) index (*мн* indices).
показа́тел|ьный (-ен, -ьна, -ьно) *прил* (*явление, пример итп*) revealing; (*no short form*): **~ьное выступле́ние гимна́стов** gymnastics display; **~ о́пыт** demonstration (*of an experiment*).
пока|за́ть (-жу́, -жешь; *impf* **пока́зывать**) *сов перех* to show; (*подлеж*: *часы, счётчик итп*) to say; (*на суде*) to testify; **пока́зывать (~** *perf*) **что-н/кого́-н кому́-н** to show sth/sb to sb; **пока́зывать (~** *perf*) **на что-н/кого́-н** to point to sth/sb; **пока́зывать (~** *perf*) **приме́р** to set an example; **пока́зывать (~** *perf*) **себя́** to prove o.s.; **он ~за́л себя́ не в лу́чшем све́те** he didn't show himself in a very good light; **я тебе́ ~жу́!** (*разг*) I'll show you!
▸ **показа́ться** *сов от* **каза́ться** ◆ (*impf* **пока́зываться**) *возв* to appear; **~ся** (*perf*) **врачу́** to see a doctor.
показно́й *прил* (*энтузиазм, радость итп*) affected; (*роскошь*) ostentatious.
пока́зыва|ть(ся) (-ю(сь)) *несов от* **показа́ть(ся)**.
пока́ка|ть (-ю) *сов от* **ка́кать**.
покале́ч|ить (-у, -ишь) *сов от* **кале́чить**.
пока́лыва|ть (*3sg* -ет) *несов неперех*: **у меня́ ~ет се́рдце/желу́док** I keep getting stabbing pains in my chest/stomach.
пока́мест *нареч* (*разг*) in the meantime ◆ *союз* (*разг*) while.
покапри́знича|ть (-ю) *сов от* **капри́зничать**.
покара́|ть (-ю) *сов от* **кара́ть**.
поката́|ть (-ю) *сов перех*: **~ кого́-н на маши́не** to take sb for a drive; **~** (*perf*) **ребёнка на саня́х** to take a child sledging
▸ **поката́ться** *сов возв* to go for a ride.
по|кати́ть (-качу́, -ка́тишь) *сов перех* (*что-н круглое*) to roll; (*что-н на колёсах*) to wheel ◆ *неперех* (*машина*) to shoot off
▸ **покати́ться** *сов возв* to start rolling, start to roll; **~ся** (*perf*) **со́ сме́ху** (*разг*) to burst out laughing.
пока́тыва|ться (-юсь) *несов возв*: **~ со́ сме́ху** (*разг*) to roll about with laughter *или* laughing.
пока́т|ый (-, -а, -о) *прил* sloping.
покача́|ть (-ю) *сов перех* to rock; **~** (*perf*) **голово́й** to shake one's head
▸ **покача́ться** *сов возв* (*на качелях*) to swing.
пока́чива|ться (-юсь) *несов возв* to rock.
покачу́(сь) *сов см* **покати́ть(ся)**.
покая́ни|е (-я) *ср* repentance.
пока́|яться (-юсь) *несов от* **ка́яться**.
по́кер (-а) *м* poker (*CARDS*).
поки́н|уть (-у, -ешь; *impf* **покида́ть**) *сов перех* to abandon.
поклада́|ть (-ю) *несов перех*: **не ~я рук** tirelessly.
покла́дист|ый (-, -а, -о) *прил* flexible.
покло́н (-а) *м* (*жест*) bow; (*приветствие*) greeting; **посыла́ть (посла́ть** *perf*) *или* **передава́ть (переда́ть** *perf*) **кому́-н ~** to send sb one's regards.
покл|они́ться (-оню́сь, -о́нишься) *сов от* **кла́няться** ◆ (*impf* **поклоня́ться**) *возв*: **~ (**+*dat*) (*святым местам*) to pay homage (at).
покло́нник (-а) *м* admirer.
поклоня́|ться (-юсь) *несов от* **поклони́ться** ◆ *возв* (+*dat*) to worship.
покля́|сться (-ну́сь, -нёшься) *сов от* **кля́сться**.
поко́|иться (-юсь, -ишься) *несов возв* (*быть похороненным*) to be at rest; (*основываться*): **~ на** +*prp* to rest on.
поко́|й (-я) *м* peace; **оставля́ть (оста́вить** *perf*) **кого́-н в ~е** to leave sb in peace; **он не даёт мне ~я** he doesn't give me any peace.
поко́йн|ая (-ой; *decl like adj*) *ж см* **поко́йный**.
поко́йник (-а) *м* the deceased.
поко́йниц|а (-ы) *ж см* **поко́йник**.
поко́йн|ый *прил* the late ◆ (-ого; *decl like adj*) *м* the deceased.
поколеба́|ть (-ю) *сов от* **колеба́ть**
▸ **поколеба́ться** *сов от* **колеба́ться** ◆ *возв* to waver.
поколе́ни|е (-я) *ср* generation.
поко́нч|ить (-у, -ишь) *сов неперех*: **~ с** +*instr* (*с делами, с ремонтом итп*) to be finished with; (*с бедностью, с проблемой*) to put an end to; **~** (*perf*) **с собо́й** to kill o.s, commit suicide.
покорёж|ить (-у, -ишь) *несов от* **корёжить**.
поко́рен *прил см* **поко́рный**.
покори́тел|ь (-я) *м* conqueror.
покор|и́ть (-ю́, -и́шь; *impf* **покоря́ть**) *сов перех* (*страну, народ*) to conquer; (*подлеж*: *женщина, стихи*) to conquer the heart of; **~** (*perf*) **чьё-н се́рдце** to win sb's heart
▸ **покори́ться** (*impf* **покоря́ться**) *сов возв*: **~ся (**+*dat*) to submit (to).
по|корми́ть (-ормлю́, -о́рмишь) *сов от* **корми́ть**.
поко́р|ный (-ен, -на, -но) *прил* submissive.
покоро́б|ить(ся) (-лю(сь), -ишь(ся)) *сов от* **коро́бить(ся)**.

покоря́|ть(ся) (-ю(сь)) *несов от* **покори́ть(ся)**.
поко́с (-а) *м* (*трав*) mowing; (*время покоса*) haymaking.
поко|си́ть(ся) (-шу́(сь), -си́шь(ся)) *сов от* **коси́ть(ся)**.
покра́|сить(ся) (-шу(сь), -сишь(ся)) *сов от* **кра́сить(ся)**.
покрасне́|ть (-ю) *сов от* **красне́ть**.
покрас|ова́ться (-у́юсь) *сов от* **красова́ться**.
покра́шу(сь) *сов см* **покра́сить(ся)**.
покрив|и́ть(ся) (-лю́(сь), -и́шь(ся)) *несов от* **криви́ть(ся)**.
покри́кива|ть (-ю) *несов неперех* (*разг*): ~ (**на** *+acc*) to yell (at).
покро́в (-а) *м* (*верхний слой*) layer; (*РЕЛ*) shroud; **сне́жный** ~ a blanket of snow; **под ~ом но́чи** under cover of darkness.
покрови́тел|ь (-я) *м* protector.
покрови́тельниц|а (-ы) *ж см* **покрови́тель**.
покрови́тельствен|ный (-ен, -на, -но) *прил* patronizing.
покрови́тельств|о (-а) *ср* protection.
покро́|й (-я) *ср* cut (*of clothing*).
покро́ю(сь) *итп сов см* **покры́ть(ся)**.
покрупне́|ть (-ю) *сов от* **крупне́ть**.
покрыва́л|о (-а) *ср* bedspread.
покрыва́|ть(ся) (-ю(сь)) *несов от* **покры́ть(ся)**.
покры́ти|е (-я) *ср* covering; ~ **дивиде́нда** (*КОММ*) dividend cover.
покр|ы́ть (-о́ю, -о́ешь) *сов от* **крыть** ◆ (*impf* **покрыва́ть**) *перех* (*звуки, шум*) to cover up; (*расходы, убытки, расстояние*) to cover; **покрыва́ть** (~ *perf*) (**что-н/кого́-н чем-н**) to cover (sth/sb with sth)
▸ **покры́ться** (*impf* **покрыва́ться**) *сов возв* (*+instr*; *одеялом*) to cover o.s. with; (*румянцем, снегом итп*) to be covered in.
покры́шк|а (-ки; *gen pl* -ек) *ж* (*АВТ*) tyre (*BRIT*), tire (*US*).
покупа́тел|ь (-я) *м* (*в магазине*) customer; (*товара, дома итп*) buyer, purchaser.
покупа́тельниц|а (-ы) *ж см* **покупа́тель**.
покупа́тельн|ый *прил*: **~ая спосо́бность** purchasing power.
покупа́тельск|ий (-ая, -ое, -ие) *прил* (*спрос, интересы*) consumer *опред*.
покупа́|ть (-ю) *несов от* **купи́ть**.
поку́п|ка (-ки; *gen pl* -ок) *ж* purchase; **де́лать (сде́лать** *perf*) **~ки** to go shopping.
покупно́й *прил* (*торт*) bought.
поку́почн|ый *прил*: **~ая цена́** purchase price.
поку́ша|ть (-ю) *сов от* **ку́шать** ◆ (*не*)*перех*: ~ **чего́-н** to have sth to eat.
покуша́|ться (-юсь) *несов возв*: ~ **на** *+acc* to attempt to take.
покуше́ни|е (-я) *ср*: ~ (**на** *+acc*) (*на свободу, на права*) infringement (of); (*на жизнь*) attempt (on); **соверша́ть (соверши́ть** *perf*) ~ **на кого́-н** to make an attempt on sb's life.
пол (-а; *loc sg* -у́, *nom pl* -ы́) *м* floor; (*nom pl* -ы, *gen pl* -о́в, *dat pl* -а́м) sex, gender.
пол|а́ (-ы́; *nom pl* -ы) *ж* (*обычно мн*: *пальто, пиджака итп*) side; **продава́ть (прода́ть** *perf*) **из-под ~ы́** to sell under the counter.
полага́|ть (-ю) *несов неперех* (*думать*) to suppose; **на́до** ~ supposedly; ~ (*impf*) **нача́ло чему́-н** to make a start on sth; ~ (*impf*) **коне́ц чему́-н** to put an end to sth.
полага́|ться (-юсь) *несов от* **положи́ться** ◆ *возв* (*быть должным*) to be expected; **~ется приходи́ть во́ вре́мя** one is expected to be punctual.
пола́|дить (-жу, -дишь) *сов от* **ла́дить**.
пола́ком|иться (-люсь, -ишься) *сов от* **ла́комиться**.
полбеды́ *ж нескл*: **э́то ещё** ~ (*разг*) it could be worse.
пол|ве́ка (-уве́ка) *м* half a century.
пол|го́да (-уго́да) *м* half a year.
по́лдень (**полу́дня** *или* **по́лдня**) *м* midday, noon; **2 часа́ по́сле полу́дня** 2 p.m.
по́лдник (-а) *м* (afternoon) tea.
по́лдня *сущ см* **по́лдень**.
полдоро́г|и (-) *ж*: **на ~е** halfway; **остана́вливаться (останови́ться** *perf*) **на ~е** (*также перен*) to stop halfway.
по́л|е (-я; *nom pl* -я́, *gen pl* -е́й) *ср* field; ~ **де́ятельности** sphere of activity; ~ **зре́ния** field of vision; *см также* **поля́**.
полево́дств|о (-а) *ср* crop cultivation.
полев|о́й *прил* field *опред*; **~ы́е рабо́ты** work in the fields; **полево́й госпита́ль** field hospital.
полёг *итп сов см* **поле́чь**.
полежа́ть (-у́, -и́шь) *сов неперех* (*человек*) to have a lie down; (*книга на полке, продукты в ящике итп*) to lie.
поleза́й(те) *сов см* **лезть**.
поле́з|ный (-ен, -на, -но) *прил* useful; (*пища*) healthy; **чем могу́ быть ~ен?** how can I be of help?; **~ная нагру́зка** (*КОММ*) payload; **поле́зные ископа́емые** minerals; **поле́зная жила́я пло́щадь** living space.
поле́з|ть (-у, -ешь) *сов неперех* (*начать лезть*) to start climbing, start to climb; (*в драку, в спор*) to get involved.
поле́мик|а (-и) *ж* polemic.
полеми́ческ|ий (-ая, -ое, -ие) *прил* polemical.
пол|ени́ться (-еню́сь, -е́нишься) *сов от* **лени́ться**.
поле́н|о (-а; *nom pl* -ья, *gen pl* -ьев) *ср* log.
полёт (-а) *м* flight; ~ **фанта́зии** *или* **мы́сли** flight of fancy.
поле|те́ть (-чу́, -ти́шь) *сов от* **лете́ть** ◆ *неперех* (*птица, самолёт*) to fly off; (*годы, дни*) to start to fly by; (*слухи, новости*) to start to fly.

пол|éчь (**-я́гу, -я́жешь** *итп*, **-я́гут**; *pt* **-ёг, -еглá, -егло́**) *сов неперех* (*травы*) to be flattened; (*перен*: *погибнуть*) to fall, perish.
по́лза|ть (**-ю**) *несов неперех* to crawl; ~ (*impf*) **в ногáх у когó-н** to come crawling to sb.
ползко́м *нареч*: **продвигáться** ~ to crawl along on one's stomach.
полз|тú (**-у́, -ёшь**; *pt* **-, -лá, -ло́**) *несов неперех* to crawl; (*разг*: *медленно двигаться*) to crawl (along).
ползунк|ú (**-о́в**) *мн* (*одежда*) rompers *мн*.
ползу́ч|ий (**-ая, -ее, -ие**) *прил* (*животные*) crawling *опред*; (*растения*) creeping *опред*.
поливá|ть (**-ю**) *несов от* **полúть**.
поливитамúн|ы (**-ов**) *мн* multivitamins *мн*.
полигáми|я (**-и**) *ж* polygamy.
полиго́н (**-а**) *м* (*для учений*) shooting range; (*для испытания оружия*) test(ing) site.
полиграфúст (**-а**) *м* printer.
полигрáфи|я (**-и**) *ж* printing.
поликлúник|а (**-и**) *ж* clinic.
полиня́|ть (*3sg* **-ет**, *3pl* **-ют**) *сов от* **линя́ть**.
полиомиелúт (**-а**) *м* polio(myelitis).
полир|овáть (**-у́ю**; *perf* **отполировáть**) *несов перех* to polish.
по́лис (**-а**) *м*: **страховóй** ~ insurance policy.
полисемú|я (**-и**) *ж* polysemy.
политбюро́ *ср нескл* the Politburo.
политéхникум (**-а**) *м* technical college.
политехнúческ|ий (**-ая, -ое, -ие**) *прил*: ~ **институ́т** polytechnic.
полúтик (**-а**) *м* politician.
полúтик|а (**-и**) *ж* (*курс*) policy; (*события, наука*) politics.
политикáн (**-а**) *м* (*пренебр*) politico.
политúческ|ий (**-ая, -ое, -ие**) *прил* political; **политúческая эконо́мия** political economy; **политúческий обозревáтель** political observer.
политóлог (**-а**) *м* political scientist.
пол|úть (**-ью́, -ьёшь**; *pt* **-úл, -илá, -úло**, *impf* **поливáть**) *сов неперех* (*дождь*) to start pouring, start to pour ◆ *перех*: ~ **что-н чем-н** to pour sth on sth; **поливáть** (~ *perf*) **цветы́** to water the flowers
▸ **полúться** *сов возв* to pour out.
политэконо́ми|я (**-и**) *ж сокр* (= *политúческая эконо́мия*) Pol. Econ. (= *political economy*).
полицéйск|ий (**-ая, -ое, -ие**) *прил* police *опред* ◆ (**-ого**; *decl like adj*) *м* policeman (*мн* policemen); **полицéйский учáсток** police station.
полúци|я (**-и**) *ж* the police; **вызывáть** (**вы́звать** (*perf*)) ~**ю** to call the police.
полúчн|ое (**-ого**; *decl like adj*) *ср*: **поймáть когó-н с** ~**ым** to catch sb at the scene of a crime; (*перен*) to catch sb red-handed *или* in the act.
полиэтилéн (**-а**) *м* polythene.
полиэтилéновый *прил* polythene *опред*.
полк (**-á**; *loc sg* **-у́**) *м* regiment.
по́л|ка (**-ки**; *gen pl* **-ок**) *ж* shelf; (*в поезде*: *для багажа*) luggage rack; (: *для лежания*) berth.
полко́вник (**-а**) *м* colonel.
полково́д|ец (**-ца**) *м* commander.
пол-лúтра (**полулúтра**) *м* half a litre (*BRIT*) *или* liter (*US*).
полнé|ть (**-ю**; *perf* **пополнéть**) *несов неперех* to put on weight.
по́лно *как сказ* that's enough; ~ **сердúться/расстрáиваться** stop getting so angry/upset.
полно́ *как сказ* (*+gen*; *разг*): **в до́ме** ~ **книг** the house is stacked full of books; **наро́ду** ~ there are a lot of people.
полновéс|ный (**-ен, -на, -но**) *прил* (*аргумент, статья*) weighty; (*описание*) full-bodied.
полновлáст|ный (**-ен, -на, -но**) *прил* fully empowered.
полново́д|ный (**-ен, -на, -но**) *прил* deep.
полнокро́в|ный (**-ен, -на, -но**) *прил* (*жизнь*) full-blooded.
полнолу́ни|е (**-я**) *ср* full moon.
полнометрáжный *прил*: ~ **фильм** full-length film.
полномо́чен *прил см* **полномо́чный**.
полномо́чи|е (**-я**) *ср* authority; (*обычно мн*: *право*) power; **облекáть** (**облéчь** (*perf*)) **когó-н** ~**ями** *+infin* to authorize sb to do; **слагáть** (**сложúть** (*perf*)) **с себя́** ~**я** to relinquish one's authority; **э́то не вхо́дит в мои́** ~**я** it is not within my jurisdiction.
полномо́ч|ный (**-ен, -на, -но**) *прил* fully authorized.
полноправ|ный (**-ен, -на, -но**) *прил* (*гражданин*) fully-fledged; (*наследник*) rightful; **он** ~ **владéлец** he has full ownership rights.
по́лностью *нареч* fully, completely.
полнот|á (**-ы́**) *ж* (*целостность*) completeness; (*тучность*) stoutness; **обладáть** (*impf*) **всей** ~**о́й влáсти/прав** to enjoy full power/rights; **опúсывать** (**описáть** *perf*) **что-н во всей** ~**é** to describe sth in its entirety; **от** ~**ы́ чувств** *или* **душú** overcome by emotion.
полноцéн|ный (**-ен, -на, -но**) *прил* (*отдых, пища*) proper; (*работа, исследование*) valuable; (*деньги, валюта*) valued.
по́л|ночь (**-у́ночи**) *ж* midnight.
по́л|ный (**-он, -нá, -но́** *или* **-но**) *прил* full; (*no short form*; *победа, власть, счастье итп*) complete, total; (*толстый*) stout; ~ *+gen или +instr* full of; (*тревоги, любви итп*) filled with; **ведро́,** ~**ное воды́** a bucket, full of water; **ко́мната былá полнá людьмú** the room was full of people; **онá былá полнá тревогú** she was filled with anxiety; ~**ным хо́дом** at full speed; **в** ~**ную сúлу** at full strength; **полны́м-полно́** (*+gen*) (*разг*) loads and loads (of); **по́лное собрáние сочинéний** complete works.
по́ло *ср нескл*: (**во́дное**) ~ (water) polo.
половúк (**-á**) *м* mat.
половúн|а (**-ы**) *ж* half; **на** ~**е доро́ги** halfway; **сейчáс** ~ **пéрвого/второ́го** it's (now) half past

twelve/one; **приходите в ~е двенадцатого** come at half past eleven; **встреча назначена на ~у десятого** the meeting has been set for half past nine.

половинчат|ый (-, -а, -о) *прил (меры, решение)* half-baked.

половник (-а) *м* ladle.

половодь|е (-я) *ср* high water.

половой *прил (тряпка, мастика)* floor *опред*; (*БИО*) sexual; **половая жизнь** sex life; **половая зрелость** puberty; **половой орган** reproductive organ; **половые органы** genitals.

полог|ий (-ая, -ое, -ие; -, -а, -о) *прил (склон)* gentle; *(гора, берег)* gently sloping.

положени|е (-я) *ср* situation; *(географическое)* location, position; *(тела, головы итп)* position; *(социальное, семейное итп)* status; *(правила)* regulations *мн*; *(обычно мн: тезис)* point; **быть** *(impf)* **на высоте ~я** to be on top of the situation; **входить (войти** *perf*) **в чьё-н ~** to put o.s. in sb's position; **выходить (выйти** *perf*) **из трудного/неприятного ~я** to get o.s. out of a difficult/unpleasant situation; **она в ~и** *(разг)* she's expecting; **положение дел** the state of affairs.

положенный *прил* due.

положител|ьный (-ен, -ьна, -ьно) *прил* positive.

пол|ожить (-ожу, -ожишь) *сов от* **класть** ◆ *(не)перех*: **~ожим, ты прав/это так** let us assume that you're right/this is the case; **~ожа руку на сердце** *(перен)* with hand on heart

▸ **положиться** (*impf* **полагаться**) *сов возв*: **~ся на** *+acc* to count on.

пол|оз (-оза; *nom pl* **-озья)** *м (обычно мн)* runner (*on sledge*).

полок *сущ см* **полка**.

полома|ть(ся) (-ю(сь)) *сов от* **ломать(ся)**.

полом|ка (-ки; *gen pl* **-ок)** *ж (действие)* breakdown; *(поврежденное место)* damage.

полон *прил см* **полный**.

полос|а (-ы; *nom pl* **полосы**, *gen pl* **полос**, *dat pl* **полосам**) *ж (ткани, металла итп)* strip; *(на ткани, на рисунке итп)* stripe; *(тумана, леса итп)* belt; *(неудач, плохой погоды)* spell; *(в газете)* column.

полосат|ый (-, -а, -о) *прил* striped, stripy.

полос|ка (-ки; *gen pl* **-ок)** *ж (ткани, бумаги, металла)* (thin) strip; *(на одежде, на ткани)* (thin) stripe; **в ~ку** striped.

пол|оскать (-ощу, -ощешь; *perf* **прополоскать**) *несов перех (бельё, посуду)* to rinse; *(рот)* to rinse out; **~ (прополоскать** *perf*) **горло** to gargle.

полосок *сущ см* **полоска**.

полост|ь (-и; *gen pl* **-ей)** *ж (АНАТ)* cavity.

полотен *сущ см* **полотно**.

полотен|це (-ца; *gen pl* **-ец)** *ср* towel.

полотнищ|е (-а) *ср*: **~ флага** flag.

пол|отно (-отна; *nom pl* **-отна**, *gen pl* **-отен**) *ср (ткань)* sheet; *(картина)* canvas; **бледный как ~** white as a sheet.

пол|оть (-ю, -ешь; *perf* **прополоть**) *несов перех* to weed.

полоумный *прил (разг: идея, речь)* crackpot *опред*.

полощу *итп несов см* **полоскать**.

полпред (-а) *м (= полномочный представитель)* plenipotentiary.

полпути *м нескл* half (*of journey*); **на ~** halfway; *(перен: остановиться, бросить дело итп)* halfway through; **вернуться** *(perf)* **с ~** to turn back halfway.

полслова (- *или* **полуслова)** *ср* half of the word; **можно Вас на ~?** could I have a quick word?; **прерывать (прервать** *perf*) **кого-н на пол(у)слове** to cut sb short; **понимать (понять** *perf*) **с пол(у)слова** to understand in an instant.

полтинник (-а) *м (сумма)* 50 kopecks; *(монета)* 50-kopeck piece.

пол|тора (-утора; *f* **полторы**) *м/ср чис* one and a half; **ей ~ года** she is one and a half; **ей около ~утора лет** she is about one and a half; **книга стоит ~ рубля/полторы марки** the book costs one and a half roubles/one and a half marks.

пол|тораста (-утораста) *чис* one hundred and fifty.

полуботин|ок (-ка) *м (обычно мн)* ankle *или* desert boot.

полувека *сущ см* **полвека**.

полугода *сущ см* **полгода**.

полугоди|е (-я) *ср (ПРОСВЕЩ)* semester; *(ЭКОН)* half (*of the year*).

полугодичный *прил* six-month.

полугодовой *прил* six-monthly, half-yearly.

полудня *сущ см* **полдень**.

полузащит|а (-ы) *ж* midfield.

полузащитник (-а) *м* midfielder.

полукруг (-а) *м* semicircle.

полукруглый *прил* semicircular.

полумер|а (-ы) *ж* half-measure (*fig*).

полумесяц (-а) *м* half-moon.

полумрак (-а) *м* semidarkness.

полуночи *сущ см* **полночь**.

полуостров (-а) *м* peninsular.

полупальто *ср нескл* jacket, short coat.

полупроводник (-а) *м (ЭЛЕК)* semiconductor.

полусапож|ек (-ка; *gen pl* **-ек)** *м (обычно мн)* half-boot.

полуслова *сущ см* **полслова**.

полутон (-а) *м (МУЗ)* semitone, half step (*US*).

полутора *чис см* **полтора**.

полуфабрикат (-а) *м (КУЛИН) any products such as frozen foods and cake mixes which require partial preparation*; *(ТЕХ)* semifinished article.

полуфинáл (-а) *м* semifinal.
получáса *сущ см* **полчасá**.
получáтел|ь (-я) *м* recipient.
получá|ть(ся) (-ю(сь)) *несов от* **получúть(ся)**.
полýчек *сущ см* **полýчка**.
получéни|е (-я) *ср* receipt; (*урожая, результата*) obtaining.
пол|учúть (-учý, -ýчишь; *impf* **получáть**) *сов перех* to receive, get; (*урожай, результат, насморк, удовольствие*) to get; (*известность, распространение, применение итп*) to gain ◆ *неперех* (*разг*: *быть наказанным*) to get it in the neck
▸ **получúться** (*impf* **получáться**) *сов возв* to turn out; (*удасться*) to work; (*фотография*) to come out; **из негó ~ýчится хорóший учúтель** he'll make a good teacher; **пирóг хорошó ~учúлся** the pie turned out well; **у меня́ э́то не ~учáется** I can't do it; **из э́того ничегó не ~ýчится** it won't come to anything.
полý|ка (-ки; *gen pl* -ек) *ж* (*разг*) pay.
полушáри|е (-я) *ср* hemisphere.
полушýб|ок (-ка) *м* (*из овчины*) sheepskin jacket; (*из меха*) short fur coat.
полцены́ *ж нескл* (*разг*): **за** ~ for next to nothing.
пол|часá (-учáса) *м* half an hour; **кáждые** ~ every half hour; **прошлó** *или* **прошлú** ~ half an hour went by.
пóлчищ|е (-а) *ср* (*обычно мн*: *врагов*) horde; (: *насекомых, крыс*) swarm.
пóл|ый (-, -а, -о) *прил* hollow.
полы́н|ь (-и) *ж* wormwood.
полысé|ть (-ю) *сов от* **лысéть**.
полыхá|ть (-ю) *несов неперех* to blaze.
пóльз|а (-ы) *ж* benefit; **в ~у** *+gen* in favour (*BRIT*) *или* favor (*US*) of; **идтú (пойтú** *perf*) **на ~у комý-н** to be of benefit to sb.
пóльзовани|е (-я) *ср*: ~ (*+instr*) use (of).
пóльзовател|ь (-я) *м* (*также КОМП*) user.
пóльз|оваться (-уюсь; *perf* **воспóльзоваться**) *несов возв* (*+instr*) to use; (*no perf*; *авторитетом, успехом итп*) to enjoy.
пóл|ька (-ьки; *gen pl* -ек) *ж см* **поля́к**; (*танец*) polka.
пóльск|ий (-ая, -ое, -ие) *прил* Polish; ~ **язы́к** Polish.
поль|стúть (-щý, -стúшь) *сов от* **льстить**.
Пóльш|а (-и) *ж* Poland.
польщён|ный (-, -á, -ó) *прил*: ~ (*+instr*) flattered (by).
польщý *сов см* **польстúть**.
полью́(сь) *итп сов см* **полúть(ся)**.
пол|юбúть (-юблю́, -ю́бишь) *сов перех* (*человека*) to come to love; ~ (*perf*) **что-н**/*+infin* to develop a love for sth/doing.
полюб|овáться (-ýюсь) *сов от* **любовáться** ◆ *возв* (*разг*): **~ýйтесь на негó/э́то!** take a look at him/that!
пóлюс (-а; *nom pl* -á) *м* (*ГЕО, ЭЛЕК*) pole.
пол|я́ (-éй) *мн* (*шляпы*) brim *ед*; (*на странице*) margin *ед*.
поля́гу *итп сов см* **полéчь**.
поля́к (-а) *м* Pole.
поля́н|а (-ы) *ж* glade.
поля́рный *прил* (*ГЕО*) polar *опред*; (*интересы, точки зрения итп*) diametrically opposed; **поля́рная звездá** the Pole Star; **поля́рная ночь** Arctic night; **поля́рный день** Arctic day.
помáд|а (-ы) *ж* (*также*: **губнáя ~**) lipstick.
помá|зать (-жу, -жешь) *сов от* **мáзать**.
помалéньку *нареч* (*разг*) bit by bit; **живём ~** we're getting by.
помáлкива|ть (-ю) *несов неперех* (*разг*) to keep quiet.
пом|анúть (-аню́, -áнишь) *несов от* **манúть**.
помáр|ка (-ки; *gen pl* -ок) *ж* crossing out (*мн* crossings out).
помáсл|ить (-ю, -ишь) *сов от* **мáслить**.
пом|ахáть (-ашý, -áшешь) *сов неперех* (*+instr*) to wave.
помéдл|ить (-ю, -ишь) *сов неперех*: ~ **с** *+instr*/*+infin* to linger over sth/over doing.
помелю́ *итп сов см* **помолóть**.
поменя́|ть(ся) (-ю(сь)) *сов от* **меня́ть(ся)**.
померéщиться (*3sg* -ится, *3pl* -атся) *сов от* **мерéщиться**.
помéр|ить(ся) (-ю(сь), -ишь(ся)) *сов от* **мéрить(ся)**.
помéркн|уть (-у, -ешь) *сов от* **мéркнуть**.
помертвé|ть (-ю) *сов от* **мертвéть**.
пом|естúть (-ещý, -естúшь; *impf* **помещáть**) *сов перех* to put; (*поставить*) to place, put; (*поселить*) to put up; (*устроить*) to settle
▸ **поместúться** (*impf* **помещáться**) *сов возв* (*уместиться*) to fit.
помéст|ье (-ья; *gen pl* -ий) *ср* estate.
помёт (-а) *м* dung.
помéт|а (-ы) *ж* (*в словаре*) explanatory note.
помé|тить (-чу, -тишь) *сов от* **мéтить** ◆ (*impf* **помечáть**) *перех* to note.
помéт|ка (-ки; *gen pl* -ок) *ж* note.
помéх|а (-и) *ж* hindrance; (*СВЯЗЬ*: *обычно мн*) interference *ед*.
помечá|ть (-ю) *несов от* **помéтить**.
помéчу *сов см* **помéтить**.
помéшан|ный (-, -а, -о) *прил* mad; (*разг*): ~ **на** *+prp* (*перен*) crazy about.
помешáтельств|о (-а) *ср* madness.
помешá|ть (-ю) *сов от* **мешáть**
▸ **помешáться** *сов возв* to go mad; (*разг*): **~ся на** *+prp* to become crazy about.
помещá|ть (-ю) *несов от* **поместúть**
▸ **помещáться** *несов от* **поместúться** ◆ *возв* (*находиться*) to be situated.
помещéни|е (-я) *ср* room; (*под офис*) premises *мн*; **жилóе ~** living space.
помéщик (-а) *м* landowner.
помéщиц|а (-ы) *ж см* **помéщик**.
помещý(сь) *сов см* **поместúть(ся)**.
помидóр (-а) *м* tomato (*мн* tomatoes).
помúловани|е (-я) *ср* (*преступника*) pardon.

помил|овать (-ую) *сов от* **миловать** ◆ *неперех*: **~уйте!** (*разг*) you can't be serious!

помимо *предл* (*+gen*) besides; (*без участия*) bypassing; **~ денег нам нужна машина** besides money we need a car; **~ того/всего прочего** apart from that/everything else.

помин (-а) *м*: **этого и в ~е нет** it's nowhere to be found; **его у нас и в ~е не было** we haven't seen hide nor hair of him; **лёгок на ~е** (*разг*) speak of the devil.

поминальный *прил* (*РЕЛ*) funeral *опред*.

помина|ть (-ю) *несов от* **помянуть** ◆ *неперех*: **~й как звали** (*разг*) just like that.

помин|ки (-ок) *мн* wake *ед*; **справлять (справить** *perf*) **~ по кому-н** to give a wake for sb.

поминут|ный (-ен, -на, -но) *прил* at intervals of one minute; (*очень частый*) constant; (*оплата*) by the minute.

помир|ить(ся) (-ю(сь), -ишь(ся)) *сов от* **мирить(ся)**.

помн|ить (-ю, -ишь) *несов (не)перех*: **~ (о** *+prp***/ про** *+acc***)** to remember; **я ~ю Вашу просьбу** *или* **о Вашей просьбе** I remember your request; **я ~ю, что Вы просили об этом** I remember that you asked about that

▸ **помниться** *несов возв* to be remembered; **мне ~ится наша встреча** I remember our meeting; **~ится, мы об этом говорили** I remember that we spoke about that.

помножа|ть (-ю) *несов перех* = **множить**.

помнож|ить (-у, -ишь) *сов от* **множить**.

помню(сь) *итп сов см* **помять(ся)**.

помог *итп сов см* **помочь**.

помога|ть (-ю) *несов от* **помочь**.

помогу *итп сов см* **помочь**.

помоек *сущ см* **помойка**.

по-моему *нареч* my way ◆ *вводн сл* in my opinion.

поможешь *итп сов см* **помочь**.

помо|и (-ев) *мн* dishwater; (*отходы*) slops *мн*.

помо|йка (-йки; *gen pl* -ек) *ж* (*помойная яма*) cesspit; (*для мусора*) rubbish (*BRIT*) *или* garbage (*US*) heap.

помол (-а) *м*: **мука/кофе мелкого/крупного ~а** fine-/coarse-ground flour/coffee.

помолв|ить (-лю, -ишь) *сов перех*: **они ~лены** they are engaged; **она ~лена с ним** she is engaged to him.

пом|олиться (-олюсь, -олишься) *сов от* **молиться**.

помолоде|ть (-ю) *сов от* **молодеть**.

пом|олоть (-елю, -елешь) *несов от* **молоть**.

помолча|ть (-у, -ишь) *сов неперех* to pause.

помор|ить (-ю, -ишь) *сов от* **морить**.

поморщ|иться (-усь, -ишься) *сов возв* to screw up one's face.

помост (-а) *м* (*для обозрения*) platform; (*для выступлений*) rostrum; (*для казни*) scaffold.

помота|ть (-ю) *сов от* **мотать**.

пом|очиться (-очусь, -очишься) *сов от* **мочиться**.

пом|очь (-огу, -ожешь *итп*, -огут; *pt* -ог, -огла, -огло, *impf* **помогать**) *сов неперех* (*+dat*) to help; (*в работе*) to help, assist; (*другой стране*) to aid.

помощник (-а) *м* helper; (*должностное лицо*) assistant; **~ капитана** mate.

помощниц|а (-ы) *ж* helper.

помощ|ь (-и) *ж* help, assistance; **с ~ю, при помощи** with; **звать (позвать** *perf*) **на ~** to call for help; **оказывать (оказать** *perf*) **кому-н ~** to help *или* assist sb; **просить (попросить** *perf*) **о ~и** to ask for help.

помою(сь) *итп сов см* **помыть(ся)**.

помпон (-а) *м* pompom.

помрачне|ть (-ю) *сов от* **мрачнеть**.

помут|ить(ся) (*3sg* **-ит(ся)**, *3pl* **-ят(ся)**) *сов от* **мутить(ся)**.

помутне|ть (-ю) *сов от* **мутнеть**.

помуч|ить (-у, -ишь) *сов перех* to torment

▸ **помучиться** *сов возв* to suffer.

помыс|ел (-ла) *м* intention.

помысл|ить (-ю, -ишь; *impf* **помышлять**) *сов неперех*: **~ о чём-н** to have sth in mind.

пом|ыть(ся) (-ою(сь), -оешь(ся)) *сов от* **мыть(ся)**.

помышля|ть (-ю) *несов от* **помыслить**.

пом|януть (-яну, -янешь; *impf* **поминать**) *сов перех* (*упомянуть*) to mention; (*устроить поминки*) to give a wake for; **~яните моё слово** mark my words.

помят|ый (-, -а, -о) *прил* (*разг*: *одежда, внешность*) rumpled; (*бок машины*) dented.

пом|ять(ся) (-ну(сь), -нёшь(ся)) *сов от* **мять(ся)**.

понадеяться (-юсь) *сов от* **надеяться**.

понадоб|иться (-люсь, -ишься) *сов возв* to be needed *или* required.

понаслышке *нареч*: **знать ~ о ком-н/чём-н** to hear a rumour (*BRIT*) *или* rumor (*US*) about sb/sth.

по-настоящему *нареч* properly.

поначалу *нареч* (*разг*) at first.

по-нашему *нареч* our way ◆ *вводн сл* in our opinion.

поневоле *нареч* against one's will.

понедельник (-а) *м* Monday; *см также* **вторник**.

понемногу *нареч* a little; (*постепенно*) little by little; **как поживаете? – ~** how's life? – not too bad.

пон|ести (-есу, -есёшь; *pt* -ёс, -есла, -есло) *сов от* **нести** ◆ *перех* (*начать нести*) to take

▸ **понестись** *сов возв* (*человек*) to tear off; (*лошадь*) to charge off; (*машина*) to speed off.

пóни *м нескл* pony.
понижá|ть(ся) (-ю(сь)) *несов от* **понизить(ся)**.
понижéни|е (-я) *ср* reduction; (*в должности*) demotion.
пони́|зить (-жу, -зишь; *impf* **понижáть**) *сов перех* to reduce; (*в должности*) to demote; (*голос*) to lower
▸ **пони́зиться** (*impf* **понижáться**) *сов возв* to be reduced.
пóнизу *нареч* (*близко к земле*) low.
пони́кн|уть (-у, -ешь) *сов от* **ни́кнуть**.
пони́мáни|е (-я) *ср* (*способность ума*) understanding; (*толкование*) interpretation; **относи́ться (отнести́сь** *perf*) **к чему́-н с ~м** to be understanding about sth; **э́то вы́ше моего́ ~я** this is beyond me.
понимá|ть (-ю) *несов от* **поня́ть** ◆ *перех* to understand ◆ *неперех*: ~ **в** +*prp* to know about; **~ете** you see; **вот э́то я ~ю!** (*разг*) that's great!
пономáр|ь (-я́) *м* (*РЕЛ*) ≈ acolyte.
понóс (-а) *м* diarrhoea (*BRIT*), diarrhea (*US*).
пон|оси́ть (-ошу́, -óсишь) *сов перех* to carry for a while; (*одежду*) to wear ◆ *несов перех* (*ругать*) to curse.
понóшен|ный (-, -на, -но) *прил* (*одежда*) worn.
поношу́ *(не)сов см* **поноси́ть**.
понрáв|иться (-люсь, -ишься) *сов от* **нрáвиться**.
понт (-а) *м* (*разг*) pretence.
понтóн (-а) *м* pontoon bridge.
понукá|ть (-ю) *несов перех* to urge on.
пону́р|ить (-ю, -ишь) *сов перех*: ~ **гóлову** to hang one's head.
пону́рый *прил* downcast.
пóнчик (-а) *м* doughnut (*BRIT*), donut (*US*).
пону́не *нареч* to this day.
понюха|ть (-ю) *сов от* **ню́хать**.
поня́тен *прил см* **поня́тный**.
поня́ти|е (-я) *ср* (*времени, пространства итп*) conception; (*о политике, о литературе*) idea; **~я не имéю** (*разг*) I've no idea.
поня́тлив|ый (-, -а, -о) *прил* quick.
поня́тно *нареч* intelligibly ◆ *как сказ*: **мне** ~ I understand; ~! I see!
поня́т|ный (-ен, -на, -но) *прил* intelligible; (*ясный*) clear; (*оправданный*) understandable.
понят|óй (-óго; *decl like adj*) *м* (*ЮР*) witness (*during official search*).
по|ня́ть (-йму́, -ймёшь; *pt* -нял, -нялá, -няло, *impf* **понимáть**) *сов перех* to understand; **давáть (дать** *perf*) ~ **кому́-н** to give sb to understand.
пообéда|ть (-ю) *сов от* **обéдать**.
пообещá|ть (-ю) *сов от* **обещáть**.
поóдаль *нареч* a little way away ◆ *предл*: ~ **от** +*gen* a little way from.
поодинóчке *нареч* one at a time.
поочерёдный *прил* (*дежурство, обслуживание*) alternating.
поощрéни|е (-я) *ср* (*действие*) encouragement; (*то, чем поощряют*) incentive.
поощри́тельн|ый *прил*: **~ая плáта** (*КОММ*) incentive bonus.
поощр|и́ть (-ю́, -и́шь; *impf* **поощря́ть**) *сов перех* to encourage.
поп (-á) *м* (*разг*) priest.
пóп|а (-ы) *ж* (*разг*) bottom, bum.
попадáни|е (-я) *ср* hit.
попадá|ть(ся) (-ю(сь)) *несов от* **попáсть(ся)**.
попаду́(сь) *итп сов см* **попáсть(ся)**.
попáрно *нареч* in pairs.
попá|сть (-ду́, -дёшь; *impf* **попадáть**) *сов неперех*: ~ **в** +*acc* (*в цель*) to hit; (*в ворота*) to end up in; (*в чужой город*) to find o.s. in; (*в беду*) to land in; **мы́ло ~ло в глазá** the soap got in my eyes; **он ~л мячóм в корзи́ну** he put the ball in the basket; ~ (*perf*) **в университéт/на ку́рсы** to get into university/onto a course; **попадáть (~** *perf*) **в авáрию** to have an accident; ~ (*perf*) **в плен** to be taken prisoner; **попадáть (~** *perf*) **под дождь** to be caught in the rain; **ему́ ~ло** (*разг*) he got a hiding; **(Вы) не тудá ~ли** you've got the wrong number; **где ~ло** (*разг*) anywhere; **как ~ло** (*разг*) anyhow; **что ~ло** (*разг*) anything
▸ **попáсться** (*impf* **попадáться**) *сов возв* (*быть пойманным*) to be caught; **~ся** (*perf*) **на взя́тках/воровствé** to be caught taking bribes/ stealing; **мне ~лась интерéсная кни́га** I came across an interesting book; **попадáться (~ся** *perf*) **кому́-н на глазá** to catch sb's eye.
попéй(те) *сов см* **попи́ть**.
поперёк *нареч* crossways ◆ *предл* (+*gen*) across.
попеременно *нареч* in turns.
попере́чный *прил* horizontal.
поперхн|у́ться (-у́сь, -ёшься) *сов возв* to choke.
попéрч|ить (-у, -ишь) *сов от* **перчи́ть**.
попечéни|е (-я) *ср* (*о детях*) care; (*о делах, о доме*) charge; **оставля́ть (остáвить** *perf*) **когó-н/чтó-н на чьё-н** ~ to leave sb/sth in sb's care.
попечи́тел|ь (-я) *м* guardian; (*КОММ*) trustee.
попирá|ть (-ю) *несов от* **попрáть**.
поп|исáть (-ишу́, -и́шешь) *сов (не)перех* to write; **ничегó не ~и́шешь** (*разг*) there's nothing you can do.
поп|и́ть (-ью́, -ьёшь; *pt* -и́л, -илá, -и́ло, *imper* -е́й(те)) *сов перех* to have a drink of.
попишу́ *итп сов см* **пописáть**.
пóпкорн (-а) *м* popcorn.
поплав|óк (-кá) *м* (*на удочке*) float.
попл|ати́ться (-ачу́сь, -áтишься) *сов от* **плати́ться**.
попли́н (-а) *м* poplin.
поплы́|ть (-ву́, -вёшь; *pt* -л, -лá, -ло) *сов неперех* (*человек, животное*) to start swimming; (*судно*) to set sail.
пополáм *нареч* in half; ~ **с** +*instr* mixed with.
пополнéни|е (-я) *ср* (*запасов*) replenishment; (*коллекции*) expansion; (*то, чем пополняется*) reinforcement.

пополне́|ть (**-ю**) *сов от* **полне́ть**.
попо́лн|ить (**-ю, -ишь**; *impf* **пополня́ть**) *сов перех*: ~ **что-н** +*instr* (*запасы*) to replenish sth with; (*коллекцию*) to expand sth with; (*коллектив*) to reinforce sth with; (*образование*) to supplement sth with
▸ **попо́лниться** (*impf* **пополня́ться**) *сов возв* (*запасы*) to be replenished; (*коллекция*) to be expanded.
поправи́м|ый (**-, -а, -о**) *прил* (*дело, ошибка*) rectifiable.
попра́в|ить (**-лю, -ишь**; *impf* **поправля́ть**) *сов перех* to correct; (*галстук, платье итп*) to straighten; (*причёску*) to tidy; (*здоровье, дела*) to improve
▸ **попра́виться** (*impf* **поправля́ться**) *сов возв* to improve; (*пополнеть*) to put on weight.
попра́в|ка (**-ки**; *gen pl* **-ок**) *ж* (*в решение, в закон*) amendment; **вноси́ть** (**внести́** *perf*) **~ку в зако́н** to make an amendment to a law; **де́ло идёт на ~ку** things are looking up.
попра́влю(сь) *сов см* **попра́вить(ся)**.
поправля́|ть(ся) (**-ю(сь)**) *несов от* **попра́вить(ся)**.
попра́вок *сущ см* **попра́вка**.
попра́|ть (*pt* **-л, -ла, -ло**, *impf* **попира́ть**) *сов перех* (*права*) to disregard; (*гордость*) to offend; (*закон*) to flout.
по-пре́жнему *нареч* as before.
попрека́|ть (**-ю**) *несов перех* to reproach.
попрекн|у́ть (**-у́, -ёшь**) *сов перех* to reproach.
поприве́тств|овать (**-ую**) *сов от* **приве́тствовать**.
по́прищ|е (**-а**) *ср* (*науки итп*) field.
попро́б|овать (**-ую**) *сов от* **про́бовать** ◆ *неперех*: **~уйте!** (*разг*) just you try!
попр|оси́ть(ся) (**-ошу́(сь), -о́сишь(ся)**) *сов от* **проси́ть(ся)**.
по́просту *част* simply; **он ~ уста́л** he's just *или* simply tired.
попрошу́(сь) *сов см* **попроси́ть(ся)**.
попроща́|ться (**-юсь**) *сов возв*: ~ **с** +*instr* to say goodbye to.
попуга́|й (**-я**) *м* parrot.
популя́рен *прил см* **популя́рный**.
популяризи́р|овать (**-ую**) *(не)сов перех* to popularize.
популяриз|ова́ть (**-у́ю**) *(не)сов* = **популяризи́ровать**.
популя́рност|ь (**-и**) *ж* popularity.
популя́р|ный (**-ен, -на, -но**) *прил* popular; (*изложение*) accessible.
популя́ци|я (**-и**) *ж* population (*of plants or animals*).
попурри́ *ср нескл* (*МУЗ*) medley.
попусти́тельств|овать (**-ую**) *несов неперех* (+*dat*) to tolerate.
по́пусту *нареч* (*разг*) in vain.
попу́тн|ый *прил* (*замечание, исправление*) accompanying; (*машина*) passing; (*ветер*) favourable (*BRIT*), favorable (*US*); (: *МОР*) fair.
попу́тчик (**-а**) *м* travelling (*BRIT*) *или* traveling (*US*) companion.
попыта́|ть (**-ю**) *сов перех*: ~ **сча́стья** to try one's luck
▸ **попыта́ться** *сов от* **пыта́ться**.
попы́т|ка (**-ки**; *gen pl* **-ок**) *ж* attempt; ~ **к бе́гству** attempted escape; **со второ́й/с тре́тьей ~ки** on *или* at the second/third attempt.
попью́ *итп сов см* **попи́ть**.
попя́|титься (**-чусь, -тишься**) *сов возв* to take a few steps backward.
попя́тн|ый *прил*: **идти́** *или* **пойти́ на ~** *или* **на ~ую** to go back on one's word.
попя́чусь *сов см* **попя́титься**.
по́р|а (**-ы**) *ж* pore.
пор|а́ (**-ы́**; *acc sg* **-ру**, *dat sg* **-ре́**, *nom pl* **-ры**) *ж* time ◆ *как сказ* it's time; **до каки́х ~р?** until when?; **до ~ры́ до вре́мени** for the time being; **до сих пор** (*раньше*) up till now; (*всё ещё*) still; **до тех пор** until then; **до тех пор, пока́** until; **на пе́рвых ~х** at first; **с каки́х пор?** since when?; **(мне) ~** it's time (for me) to go; **(мне) ~ спать/рабо́тать** it's time (for me) to go to bed/to work.
порабо|ти́ть (**-щу́, -ти́шь**; *impf* **порабоща́ть**) *сов перех* to enslave.
порабоще́ни|е (**-я**) *ср* enslavement.
порабощу́ *сов см* **поработи́ть**.
поравня́|ться (**-юсь**) *сов возв*: ~ **с** +*instr* (*человек*) to draw level with; (*машина*) to come alongside.
пора́д|овать(ся) (**-ую(сь)**) *сов от* **ра́довать(ся)**.
поража́|ть(ся) (**-ю(сь)**) *несов от* **порази́ть(ся)**.
пораже́ни|е (**-я**) *ср* (*цели*) hitting; (*МЕД*: *лёгких*) damage; (*в войне, в состязании итп*) defeat; **наноси́ть** (**нанести́** *perf*) **кому́-н ~** to defeat sb; **терпе́ть** (**потерпе́ть** *perf*) **~** to be defeated.
поражу́(сь) *сов см* **порази́ть(ся)**.
порази́тел|ьный (**-ен, -ьна, -ьно**) *прил* (*красота, талант*) striking; (*жестокость*) astonishing.
пора|зи́ть (**-жу́, -зи́шь**; *impf* **поража́ть**) *сов перех* (*цель*) to hit; (*подлеж*: *болезнь*) to affect; (*изумить*) to astonish
▸ **порази́ться** (*impf* **поража́ться**) *сов возв* to be astonished.
пора́н|ить (**-ю, -ишь**) *сов перех* to hurt.
пор|асти́ (*3sg* **-астёт**, *3pl* **-асту́т**, *pt* **-о́с, -осла́, -осло́**, *impf* **порасти́ть**) *сов неперех*: ~ +*instr* to become overgrown with.
порв|а́ть (**-у́, -ёшь**) *сов от* **рвать** ◆ *перех* to tear ◆ (*impf* **порыва́ть**) *неперех*: ~ **с** +*instr* (*с женой, с друзьями*) to break up with; **порыва́ть** (~ *perf*) **что-н с кем-н** to break off sth with sb

▸ **порва́ться** *сов от* **рва́ться** ◆ *возв* (*нить*) to break; (*платье*) to tear.
поредé|ть (*3sg* **-ет**, *3pl* **-ют**) *несов от* **редéть**.
порéжу(сь) *итп сов см* **порéзать(ся)**.
порéз (-а) *м* cut.
порé|зать (**-жу, -жешь**) *сов перех* to cut
▸ **порéзаться** *сов возв* to cut o.s.
поpé|й (**-я**) *м* leek.
порекомендова́ть (**-у́ю**) *сов от* **рекомендова́ть**.
по́рист|ый (**-, -а, -о**) *прил* porous.
порица́ни|е (**-я**) *ср* reprimand.
порица́|ть (**-ю**) *несов перех* to reprimand.
порнографи́ческ|ий (**-ая, -ое, -ие**) *прил* pornographic.
порногра́фи|я (**-и**) *ж* pornography.
по́ровну *нареч* equally.
поро́г (-а) *м* (*также перен*) threshold; (*на реке*) rapids *мн*; **переступа́ть (переступи́ть** *perf*) **~** to cross the threshold; **я его́ на ~ не пущу́** he won't darken my door again.
поро́д|а (**-ы**) *ж* (*животных*) breed; (*древесная*) species; (*горная*) rock; (*перен*: *людей*) type.
поро́дист|ый (**-, -а, -о**) *прил* pedigree *опред*; (*лицо*) aristocratic.
поро|ди́ть (**-жу́, -ди́шь**; *impf* **порожда́ть**) *сов перех* (*стать причиной*) to give rise to.
породн|и́ться (**-ю́сь, -и́шься**) *сов от* **родни́ться**.
порожда́|ть (**-ю**) *несов от* **породи́ть**.
поро́жн|ий (**-яя, -ее, -ие**) *прил* empty; **перелива́ть** (*impf*) **из пусто́го в ~ее** to rabbit on.
порожня́к (**-а́**) *м* empty vehicle.
порожняко́м *нареч* without a load.
порожу́ *сов см* **породи́ть**.
по́рознь *нареч* apart.
порозовé|ть (**-ю**) *сов от* **розовéть**.
поро́й *нареч* from time to time.
поро́к (-а) *м* vice; **поро́к сéрдца** heart disease.
поролóн (**-а**) *м* foam rubber.
поро́с *итп сов см* **порасти́**.
поросёнок (**-ёнка**; *nom pl* **-я́та**, *gen pl* **-я́т**) *м* piglet.
по́росл|ь (**-и**) *ж* (*побеги*) shoots *мн*; (*перен*) generation.
порося́та *итп сущ см* **поросёнок**.
пор|о́ть (**-ю́, -ешь**; *perf* **распоро́ть**) *несов перех* (*швы*) to unpick; (*perf* **вы́пороть**; *бить*) to belt; **~ (напоро́ть** *perf*) **чушь** *или* **ерунду́** *или* **чепуху́** to talk nonsense; **~** (*impf*) **горя́чку** (*разг*) to get a move on.
по́рох (**-а**; *part gen* **-у**) *м* gunpowder.
поро́чен *прил см* **поро́чный**.
поро́ч|ить (**-у, -ишь**; *perf* **опоро́чить**) *несов перех* to bring shame on; (*чернить*: *человека*) to defame; (: *работу*) to bring into disrepute.
поро́ч|ный (**-ен, -на, -но**) *прил* (*безнравственный*) depraved; (*неправильный*) flawed.
порош|о́к (**-ка́**) *м* powder.
поро́ю *нареч* = **поро́й**.
порт (-а; *loc sg* **-у́**, *nom pl* **-ы**, *gen pl* **-о́в**) *м* port; **возду́шный ~** airport.
порта́л (**-а**) *м* (*АРХИТ*) portal.
портати́вный *прил* portable.
портвéйн (**-а**) *м* port (*wine*).
по́р|тить (**-чу, -тишь**; *perf* **испо́ртить**) *несов перех* (*механизм, здоровье, карьеру*) to damage; (*настроение, праздник, ребёнка*) to spoil; **~** (*impf*) **себé нéрвы** to worry
▸ **по́ртиться** (*perf* **испо́ртиться**) *сов возв* (*механизм*) to be damaged; (*здоровье, погода*) to deteriorate; (*настроение*) to be spoiled; (*молоко*) to go off; (*мясо, овощи*) to go bad.
портни́х|а (**-и**) *ж* dressmaker.
портн|о́й (**-о́го**; *decl like adj*) *м* tailor.
порто́вый *прил* port *опред*.
портрéт (**-а**) *м* portrait.
портсига́р (**-а**) *м* cigarette case.
Портсму́т (**-а**) *м* Portsmouth.
Португа́ли|я (**-и**) *ж* Portugal.
португа́льск|ий (**-ая, -ое, -ие**) *прил* Portuguese; **~ язы́к** Portuguese.
портфéл|ь (**-я**) *м* briefcase; (*ПОЛИТ, КОММ*) portfolio; **~ цéнных бума́г** (*КОММ*) investment portfolio.
портьé *м нескл* (*в гостинице*) porter.
портьéр|а (**-ы**) *ж* curtain.
портя́н|ка (**-ки**; *gen pl* **-ок**) *ж* (*обычно мн*) puttee.
поруга́ни|е (**-я**) *ср* desecration.
поруга́|ть (**-ю**) *сов перех* (*разг*) to scold
▸ **поруга́ться** *сов от* **руга́ться** ◆ *возв* (*разг*): **~ся (с** *+instr*) to fall out (with).
пору́к|а (**-и**) *ж*: **брать кого́-н на ~и** to take sb on probation; (*ЮР*) to stand bail for sb; **кругова́я ~** mutual dependence; (*у преступников*) mutual cover-up; **отпуска́ть (отпусти́ть** *perf*) **кого́-н на ~и** to release sb on bail.
по-ру́сски *нареч* (*разговаривать, написать*) in Russian; **говори́ть** (*impf*)**/понима́ть** (*impf*) **~** to speak/understand Russian; **как ~ «book»?** what is the Russian for "book"?
поруча́|ть (**-ю**) *несов от* **поручи́ть**.
поручéни|е (**-я**) *ср* (*задание*) errand; (: *важное*) mission; **по ~ю** *+gen* on behalf of.
по́ручен|ь (**-ня**) *м* handrail.
пору́чик (**-а**) *м* (*ИСТ*) first lieutenant.
поручи́тел|ь (**-я**) *м* (*КОММ*) guarantor.
поручи́тельств|о (**-а**) *ср* guarantee.
пор|учи́ть (**-учу́, -у́чишь**; *impf* **поруча́ть**) *сов неперех*: **~ кому́-н что-н** to entrust sb with sth; **поруча́ть** (**~** *perf*) **кому́-н** *+infin* to instruct sb to do; **поруча́ть** (**~** *perf*) **кому́-н кого́-н/что-н** (*отдать на попечение*) to leave sb/sth in sb's care.
пор|учи́ться (**-учу́сь, -у́чишься**) *сов от* **руча́ться**.
по́ручня *итп сущ см* **по́ручень**.
порха́|ть (**-ю**) *несов неперех* (*бабочка*) to flutter about; (*птица*) to flit about.
по́рци|я (**-и**) *ж* portion; **принеси́те нам две ~и**

жа́реной говя́дины bring us two steaks.
по́рч|а (**-и**) *ж* damage.
по́рчу(сь) *сов см* **по́ртить(ся)**.
по́рш|ень (**-ня**) *м* (*в двигателе*) piston; (*в насосе*) plunger.
поры́в (**-а**) *м* (*ветра*) gust; (*негодования, восторга итп*) surge.
порыва́|ть (**-ю**) *несов от* **порва́ть**
▸ **порыва́ться** *несов возв*: **~ся** *+infin* (*стремиться*) to strive to do.
поры́вист|ый (**-, -а, -о**) *прил* (*ветер*) gusty; (*движения*) jerky; (*характер, человек*) impetuous.
поря́дка *итп сущ см* **поря́док**.
поря́дковый *прил* (*номер*) ordinal; **поря́дковое числи́тельное** ordinal number.
поря́дком *нареч* (*разг*) pretty; **я ~ уста́л** I'm pretty tired.
поря́д|ок (**-ка**) *м* order; (*правила*) procedure; **в ~ке** *+gen* (*в качестве*) as; **~ка** *+gen* about; **в рабо́чем ~ке** in the course of the proceedings; **э́то в ~ке веще́й** (*это нормально*) that's nothing out of the ordinary; **в ~ке** in order; **всё в ~ке** everything's OK; **поря́док дня** agenda; **поря́док слов** (*линг*) word order.
поря́дочно *нареч* decently; (*устал*) pretty; (*хорошо*) quite well.
поря́доч|ный (**-ен, -на, -но**) *прил* (*честный*) decent; (*значительный*) fair.
пос. *сокр* = **посёлок**.
пос|ади́ть (**-ажу́, -а́дишь**) *сов от* **сажа́ть**.
поса́д|ка (**-ки**; *gen pl* **-ок**) *ж* (*овощей, деревьев*) planting; (*пассажиров*) boarding; (*самолёта итп*) landing; **произво́дится ~ на самолёт ...** the flight ... is boarding.
поса́дочный *прил* (*трап, талон*) boarding *опред*; (*площадка, огни*) landing *опред*.
посажу́ *сов см* **посади́ть**.
посва́та|ть(ся) (**-ю(сь)**) *сов от* **сва́таться**.
посвеже́|ть (**-ю**) *сов от* **свеже́ть**.
посве|ти́ть (**-чу́, -тишь**) *сов от* **свети́ть**.
посветле́|ть (**-ю**) *сов от* **светле́ть**.
посвечу́ *сов см* **посвети́ть**.
по-сво́ему *нареч* his *итп* way.
посвя|ти́ть (**-щу́, -ти́шь**; *impf* **посвяща́ть**) *сов перех*: **~ что-н** *+dat* to devote sth to; (*книгу, стихи*) to dedicate sth to; **посвяща́ть** (**~** *perf*) **кого́-н в** *+acc* (*в тайну*) to let sb into.
посвяща́|ть (**-ю**) *несов от* **посвяти́ть**.
посвяще́ни|е (**-я**) *ср* (*в книге*) dedication.
посвящу́ *сов см* **посвяти́ть**.
посе́в (**-а**) *м* sowing; *см также* **посе́вы**.
посевн|о́й *прил*: **~ы́е рабо́ты** sowing; **посевны́е пло́щади** (*с.-х.*) area sown with crops.
посе́в|ы (**-ов**) *мн* crops *мн*.
поседе́|ть (**-ю**) *сов от* **седе́ть**.
поселе́н|ец (**-ца**) *м* settler; (*высланный*) deportee.
поселе́ни|е (**-я**) *ср* (*селение*) settlement; (*как наказание*) deportation.
поселе́нца *итп сущ см* **поселе́нец**.
пос|ели́ть(ся) (**-елю́(сь), -е́лишь(ся)**) *сов от* **сели́ть(ся)**.
посёл|ок (**-ка**) *м* village; **да́чный ~** *village made up of dachas*.
поселя́|ть(ся) (**-ю(сь)**) *несов* = **сели́ть(ся)**.
посеребр|и́ть (**-ю́, -и́шь**) *сов от* **серебри́ть**.
посреди́не *нареч* in the middle ◆ *предл* (*+gen*) in the middle of.
посере́|ть (**-ю**) *сов от* **сере́ть**.
посети́тел|ь (**-я**) *м* visitor.
посети́тельница (**-ы**) *ж см* **посети́тель**.
посе|ти́ть (**-щу́, -ти́шь**; *impf* **посеща́ть**) *сов перех* to visit.
посе́т|овать (**-ую**) *сов от* **се́товать**.
посеща́емост|ь (**-и**) *ж* attendance.
посеща́|ть (**-ю**) *несов от* **посети́ть**.
посеще́ни|е (**-я**) *ср* visit.
посещу́ *сов см* **посети́ть**.
посе́|ять (**-ю**) *сов от* **се́ять** ◆ *перех* (*разг: потерять*) to lose.
поси|де́ть (**-жу́, -ди́шь**) *сов неперех* to sit for a while.
поси́л|ьный (**-ен, -ьна, -ьно**) *прил* feasible.
посине́|ть (**-ю**) *сов от* **сине́ть**.
посин|и́ть (**-ю́, -и́шь**) *сов от* **сини́ть**.
поска|ка́ть (**-чу́, -чешь**) *сов от* **скака́ть**.
поскanда́л|ить (**-ю, -ишь**) *сов от* **сканда́лить**.
поскачу́ *итп сов см* **поскака́ть**.
поскользн|у́ться (**-у́сь, -ёшься**) *сов возв* to slip.
поско́льку *союз* as.
поскуп|и́ться (**-лю́сь, -и́шься**) *сов от* **скупи́ться**.
посла́ *итп сущ см* **посо́л**.
послабле́ни|е (**-я**) *ср* leniency.
посла́н|ец (**-ца**) *м* envoy.
посла́ни|е (**-я**) *ср* (*официальное*) dispatch; (*дружеское, любовное*) message.
посла́нник (**-а**) *м* (*дипломатический*) diplomat.
посла́нца *итп сущ см* **посла́нец**.
по|сла́ть (**-шлю́, -шлёшь**; *impf* **посыла́ть**) *сов перех* to send; **посыла́ть** (**~** *perf*) **кого́-н к чёрту** (*разг*) to tell sb to go to hell.
по́сле *нареч* (*потом*) afterwards ◆ *предл* (*+gen*) after ◆ *союз*: **~ того́ как** after.
послевое́нный *прил* postwar.
после́д (**-а**) *м* placenta.
после́дн|ее (**-его**; *decl like adj*) *ср* the last; **до ~его** to the utmost.
после́дн|ий (**-яя, -ее, -ие**) *прил* last; (*новости, мода*) latest; (*разг*); **~ негодя́й** utter rascal; **за** *или* **в ~ее вре́мя** recently; **руга́ться** (*impf*) **~ими слова́ми** to use foul language.
после́дователь|ь (**-я**) *м* follower.

после́довательност|ь (-и) *ж* sequence; (*политики*) consistency.
после́довательный *прил* (*этапы, движения*) consecutive; (*вывод, ход мысли*) consistent.
после́д|овать (-ую) *сов от* **сле́довать**.
после́дстви|е (-я) *ср* consequence.
после́дующ|ий (-ая, -ее, -ие) *прил* subsequent.
послеза́втра *нареч* the day after tomorrow.
послеродово́й *прил* postnatal.
послесло́ви|е (-я) *ср* (*в книге*) epilogue.
посло́виц|а (-ы) *ж* proverb, saying; **войти** *(perf)* **в ~у** to become proverbial.
посл|ужи́ть (-ужу́, -у́жишь) *сов от* **служи́ть**.
послужно́й *прил*: **~ спи́сок** (*военного*) service record; (*работника*) work record.
послуша́ни|е (-я) *ср* (*покорность*) obedience.
послу́ша|ть (-ю) *сов от* **слу́шать** ◆ *перех*: **~ что-н** to listen to sth for a while; **~йте!** listen!
▸ **послу́шаться** *сов от* **слу́шаться**.
послу́шен *прил см* **послу́шный**.
послу́шник (-а) *м* (*РЕЛ*) novice.
послу́шниц|а (-ы) *ж см* **послу́шник**.
послу́ш|ный (-ен, -на, -но) *прил* (*ребёнок, ученик*) obedient; (*механизм*) user-friendly.
послы́ш|аться (*3sg* **-ется**, *3pl* **-атся**) *сов от* **слы́шаться**.
послюня́в|ить (-лю, -ишь) *сов от* **слюня́вить**.
посма́трива|ть (-ю) *несов неперех* to glance occasionally.
посме́ива|ться (-юсь) *несов возв* (*смеяться*) to chuckle; **~** *(impf)* **(над** *+instr*) (*насмехаться*) to laugh at.
посме́нный *прил* shift *опред*.
посме́ртный *прил* posthumous.
посме́|ть (-ю) *сов от* **сметь**.
посме́шищ|е (-а) *ср* laughing stock; **выставля́ть** *(impf)* **кого́-н на ~** to make a laughing stock of sb.
посме|я́ться (-ю́сь, -ёшься) *сов от* **сме́яться**.
посм|отре́ть (-отрю́, -о́тришь) *сов от* **смотре́ть** ◆ *неперех*: **~о́трим** (*разг*) we'll see; **там ~о́трим** (*разг*) we'll see later
▸ **посмотре́ться** *сов от* **смотре́ться**.
посо́би|е (-я) *ср* (*помощь*) benefit; (*ПРОСВЕЩ*: *учебное*) handout; (: *наглядное*) visual aids *мн*; **посо́бие по безрабо́тице** unemployment benefit; **посо́бие по инвали́дности** disability living allowance.
посо́бник (-а) *м* accomplice.
посове́т|овать(ся) (-ую(сь)) *сов от* **сове́товать(ся)**.
посоде́йств|овать (-ую) *сов от* **соде́йствовать**.
пос|о́л (-ла́) *м* ambassador; (**-о́ла**; *засол*) salting.
пос|оли́ть (-олю́, -о́лишь) *сов от* **соли́ть**.
посо́льств|о (-а) *ср* embassy.
поспе́|ть (-ю) *сов от* **спеть** ◆ (*impf* **поспева́ть**) *неперех* (*успеть*) to make it.
поспе́шен *прил см* **поспе́шный**.
поспеш|и́ть (-у́, -и́шь) *сов от* **спеши́ть**.
поспе́ш|ный (-ен, -на, -но) *прил* rushed.
поспо́р|ить (-ю, -ишь) *сов от* **спо́рить** ◆ *неперех* to argue.
поспосо́бств|овать (-ую) *сов от* **спосо́бствовать**.
посрам|и́ть (-лю́, -и́шь; *impf* **посрамля́ть**) *сов перех* to disgrace.
посреди́ *нареч* in the middle ◆ *предл* (*+gen*) in the middle of; **~ толпы́** in the midst of the crowd.
посреди́не *нареч* in the middle ◆ *предл* (*+gen*) in the middle of.
посре́дник (-а) *м* intermediary; (*при конфликте*) mediator; **торго́вый ~** middleman (*мн* middlemen).
посре́дническ|ий (-ая, -ое, -ие) *прил* (*КОММ*) intermediary *опред*.
посре́дничеств|о (-а) *ср* mediation.
посре́дственно *нареч* (*учиться, писать, сочинять*) averagely ◆ *ср нескл* (*ПРОСВЕЩ*) ≈ satisfactory (*school mark*).
посре́дствен|ный (-, -на, -но) *прил* mediocre.
посре́дств|о (-а) *ср*: **при ~е** *или* **че́рез ~** *+gen* by means of.
посре́дством *предл* (*+gen*) by means of.
поссо́р|ить(ся) (-ю(сь), -ишь(ся)) *сов от* **ссо́рить(ся)**.
пост (-а́; *loc sg* **-у́**) *м* (*люди*) guard; (*место*) lookout post; (*должность*) position, post; (*РЕЛ*) fast; **~ автоинспе́кции** (traffic) police checkpoint.
поста́в|ить (-лю, -ишь) *сов от* **ста́вить** ◆ (*impf* **поставля́ть**) *перех* (*товар*) to supply.
поста́в|ка (-ки; *gen pl* **-ок**) *ж* (*снабжение*) supply.
поста́влю *сов см* **поста́вить**.
поставля́|ть (-ю) *несов от* **поста́вить**.
поста́вок *сущ см* **поста́вка**.
поставщи́к (-а́) *м* supplier; **судово́й ~** ship chandler.
постаме́нт (-а) *м* pedestal.
постан|ови́ть (-овлю́, -о́вишь; *impf* **постановля́ть**) *сов неперех*: **~** *+infin* to resolve to do.
постано́в|ка (-ки; *gen pl* **-ок**) *ж* (*памятника*) erection; (*учебного процесса*) organization; (*ТЕАТР*) production; **у неё хоро́шая ~ головы́** she holds her head well; **~ вопро́са/пробле́мы** the formulation of the question/problem.
постановле́ни|е (-я) *ср* (*решение*) resolution; (*распоряжение*) decree.
постановлю́ *сов см* **постанови́ть**.
постановля́|ть (-ю) *несов от* **постанови́ть**.
постано́вок *сущ см* **постано́вка**.
постано́вщик (-а) *м* producer.
постара́|ться (-юсь) *сов от* **стара́ться**.
постаре́|ть (-ю) *сов от* **старе́ть**.
пост|ели́ть(ся) (-елю́(сь), -е́лишь(ся)) *сов от* **стели́ть(ся)**.
посте́л|ь (-и) *ж* bed.
посте́ль|ный *прил*: **~ое бельё** bedclothes *мн*; **он на ~ом режи́ме** he is confined to bed.
постелю́ *итп сов см* **постла́ть**.

постепе́нно *нареч* gradually.
постепе́н|ный (**-ен, -на, -но**) *прил* gradual.
постесня́|ться (**-юсь**) *сов от* **стесня́ться**.
пости́г *итп сов см* **пости́чь**.
постига́|ть (**-ю**) *несов от* **пости́чь**.
пости́гну *итп сов см* **пости́чь**.
пости́г|нуть (**-ну, -нешь**; *pt* **-, -ла, -ло**) *сов* = **пости́чь**.
постила́|ть (**-ю**) *несов* = **стели́ть**.
постира́|ть (**-ю**) *сов от* **стира́ть**.
по|сти́ться (**-щу́сь, -сти́шься**) *несов возв* (*РЕЛ*) to fast.
пости́|чь (**-гну, -гнешь**; *pt* **-г, -гла, -гло**, *impf* **постига́ть**) *сов перех* (*смысл, значение*) to grasp; (*подлеж*: *несчастье*) to befall; **я не могу́ ~, как он мог э́то сде́лать** I can't comprehend how he could do something like that; **его́ ~гло разочарова́ние** he was disappointed.
пост|ла́ть (**-елю́, -е́лешь**) *сов от* **стлать**.
по́стный *прил* (*суп, обед*) vegetarian; (*мясо*) lean; (*разг*: *хмурый*) cheesed off; **по́стное ма́сло** vegetable oil.
постов|о́й *прил* (*служба, будка*) sentry *опред* ◆ (**-о́го**; *decl like adj*) *м militiaman on duty*.
посто́льку *союз*: **~ ... поско́льку** in so far as ....
постор|они́ться (**-оню́сь, -о́нишься**) *сов от* **сторони́ться**.
посторо́нн|ий (**-яя, -ее, -ие**) *прил* (*чужой*) strange; (*помощь, влияние*) outside; (*вопрос*) irrelevant ◆ (**-его**; *decl like adj*) *м* stranger, outsider; **~им вход воспрещён** authorized entry only.
постоя́н|ный (**-ен, -на, -но**) *прил* (*работа, адрес*) permanent; (*шум, разговоры*) constant; (*вкус, взгляды*) consistent; **постоя́нная а́рмия** regular army; **постоя́нный ток** direct current.
посто|я́ть (**-ю́, -и́шь**) *сов от* **стоя́ть** ◆ *неперех* (*стоять недолго*) to stand for a while; **постойте!** (*подождите*) hang on!; **он за ценой не ~и́т** (*разг*) money is no object to him.
пострада́|ть (**-ю**) *сов от* **страда́ть**.
постри́г(ся) *итп сов см* **постри́чь(ся)**.
постригу́(сь) *итп сов см* **постри́чь(ся)**.
постриже́ни|е (**-я**) *ср* (*мужчины*) taking the habit; (*женщины*) taking the veil.
постри́|чь (**-гу́, -жёшь** *итп*, **-гу́т**; *pt* **-г, -гла, -гло**) *сов перех*: **~ кого́-н** to cut sb's hair; **~** (*perf*) **кого́-н в монасты́рь** to initiate sb into a monastery
▸ **постри́чься** *сов возв* to have a haircut; **~ся** (*perf*) **в монасты́рь** to be initiated into a monastery.
постро́ек *сущ см* **постро́йка**.
построе́ни|е (**-я**) *ср* (*предложения, фразы*) construction.
постро́|ить(ся) (**-ю(сь), -ишь(ся)**) *сов от* **стро́ить(ся)**.
постро́|йка (**-йки**; *gen pl* **-ек**) *ж* construction.
поступа́тельн|ый *прил* (*движение*) forward *опред*; **~ое разви́тие** progress.
пост|упи́ть (**-уплю́, -у́пишь**; *impf* **поступа́ть**) *сов неперех* (*благородно, разумно*) to act; (*товар, известия*) to come in; (*жалоба*: *в суд*) to be received; **поступа́ть** (**~** *perf*) **в** *+acc* (*в университет*) to enter; **поступа́ть** (**~** *perf*) **на** *+acc* (*на работу, на курсы*) to start
▸ **поступи́ться** (*impf* **поступа́ться**) *сов возв*: **~ся** *+instr* to give up.
посту́пка *сущ см* **посту́пок**.
поступле́ни|е (**-я**) *ср* (*действие*: *в университет*) entrance; (: *на работу*) starting; (: *жалобы*: *в суд*) receipt; (*то, что поступило*: *бюджетное*) revenue; (: *в библиотеке*) acquisition.
поступлю́(сь) *сов см* **поступи́ть(ся)**.
посту́п|ок (**-ка**) *м* (*благородный, подлый*) deed.
по́ступ|ь (**-и**) *ж* (*походка*) gait.
постуч|а́ть(ся) (**-у́(сь), -и́шь(ся)**) *сов от* **стуча́ть(ся)**.
посты́ден *прил см* **посты́дный**.
посты|ди́ться (**-жу́сь, -ди́шься**) *сов от* **стыди́ться**.
посты́д|ный (**-ен, -на, -но**) *прил* shameful.
постыжу́сь *сов см* **постыди́ться**.
посу́д|а (**-ы**) *ж собир* crockery; **ку́хонная ~** kitchenware; **стекля́нная ~** glassware; **мыть** (**помы́ть** *perf*) **~у** to wash *или* do (*BRIT*) the dishes.
посу|ди́ть (**-жу́, -дишь**) *сов*: **~ди́те са́ми** judge for yourself.
посул|и́ть (**-ю́, -и́шь**) *сов от* **сули́ть**.
посчастли́в|иться (*3sg* **-ится**) *сов безл*: **мне ~илось** *+infin* ... I was lucky enough to ....
посчита́|ть(ся) (**-ю(сь)**) *сов от* **счита́ть(ся)**.
посыла́|ть (**-ю**) *несов от* **посла́ть**.
посы́л|ка (**-ки**; *gen pl* **-ок**) *ж* (*действие*: *книг, денег*) sending; (*отправление*) parcel; (*основание*) premise.
посы́льн|ый (**-ого**; *decl like adj*) *м* messenger.
посы́п|ать (**-лю, -лешь**) *сов перех* to sprinkle.
посяга́тельств|о (**-а**) *ср*: **~ на что-н** infringement on *или* of sth; **~ на чью-н жизнь** an attempt on sb's life.
посягн|у́ть (**-у́, -ёшь**; *impf* **посяга́ть**) *сов неперех*: **~ на** *+acc* to infringe; **посяга́ть** (**~** *perf*) **на чью-н жизнь** to make an attempt on sb's life.
пот (**-а**; *part gen* **-у**, *loc sg* **-у́**, *nom pl* **-ы́**) *м* sweat; **в по́те лица́** hard; **по́том и кро́вью добыва́ть** (**добы́ть** *perf*) **что-н** to sweat blood to get sth; **рабо́тать** (*impf*) **в по́те лица́** to sweat blood.
потайно́й *прил* secret *опред*.
потака́|ть (**-ю**) *несов неперех*: **~** *+dat* (*агрессии*) to turn a blind eye to; (*агрессору*) to ignore.
потаску́х|а (**-и**) *ж* (*разг*: *пренебр*) hussy.
потасо́в|ка (**-ки**; *gen pl* **-ок**) *ж* (*разг*) punch-up.

по-твóему *нареч* your way ◆ *вводн сл* in your opinion.
потвóрств|овать (**-ую**) *несов неперех*: ~ *+dat* (*агрессии*) to turn a blind eye to; (*агрессору*) to ignore.
потёк *итп сов см* **потéчь**.
потекýт *сов см* **потéчь**.
потём|ки (**-ок**) *мн* darkness *ед*.
потемнé|ть (**-ю**) *сов от* **темнéть**.
потёмок *сущ см* **потёмки**.
потенциáл (**-а**) *м* potential.
потенциáл|ьный (**-ен, -ьна, -ьно**) *прил* potential.
потеплéни|е (**-я**) *ср* warmer spell.
потеплé|ть (*3sg* **-ет**, *3pl* **-ют**) *сов от* **теплéть**.
пот|ерéть (**-рý, -рёшь**; *pt* **-ёр, -ёрла, -ёрло**) *сов перех* (*ушиб*) to rub; (*морковь*) to grate
▸ **потерéться** *сов от* **терéться**.
потерпéвш|ая (**-ей**; *decl like adj*) *ж см* **потерпéвший**.
потерпéвш|ий (**-его**; *decl like adj*) *м* (*ЮР*) victim ◆ *прил*: (**-ая, -ее, -ие**) **~ая сторонá** injured party.
пот|ерпéть (**-ерплю, -éрпишь**) *сов от* **терпéть**.
потёртый *прил* (*одежда*) worn.
потéр|я (**-и**) *ж* loss; **нести** (**понести** *perf*) **~и** (*в войне*) to suffer losses.
потéрянно *нареч* (*смотреть*) lost.
потéрян|ный (**-, -на, -но**) *прил* (*растерянный*: *вид итп*) lost.
потерá|ть(ся) (**-ю(сь)**) *сов от* **терять(ся)**.
потесн|ить (**-ю, -ишь**) *сов от* **теснить** ◆ *перех*: ~ **когó-н** to make sb squeeze up
▸ **потесниться** *сов возв* to squeeze up.
потé|ть (**-ю**; *impf* **вспотéть**) *несов неперех* to sweat.
пот|éчь (*3sg* **-ечёт**, *3pl* **-екýт**, *pt* **-ёк, -еклá, -еклó**) *сов неперех* (*вода*) to start flowing; (*дни, жизнь*) to begin.
потéш|ить(ся) (**-ю(сь)**) *сов от* **тéшить(ся)**.
потихóньку *нареч* (*разг*: *медленно*) at a snail's pace; (: *тайно*) on the sly.
потницá|а (**-ы**) *ж* (*МЕД*) heat rash.
пóтный *прил* sweaty.
потогóнн|ый *прил* (*перен*): **~ая систéма** slave labour (*BRIT*) *или* labor (*US*).
потóк (**-а**) *м* (*также ПРОСВЕЩ*) stream; **положительный/отрицáтельный ~ налúчности** (*КОММ*) positive/negative cash flow.
потол|óк (**-кá**) *м* (*также перен*) ceiling; **брать** (**взять** *perf*) **что-н с ~кá** (*разг*) to pluck sth out of thin air.
потолстé|ть (**-ю**) *сов от* **толстéть**.
потóм *нареч* (*после*: *пойдем, закончим итп*) later ◆ *союз* (*после*) then; (*разг*: *кроме того*) anyhow; **на ~** (*разг*) for later.
потóмк|и (**-ов**) *мн* descendants *мн*.
потóмственный *прил* (*имение, деньги*) inherited; **он – ~ музыкáнт** he is descended from a family of musicians.
потóмств|о (**-а**) *ср собир* descendants *мн*; (*дети*) offspring *мн*.
потомý *нареч*: **~ (и)** that's why; **я не придý, ~ что устáл** I'm not coming because I'm tired; **потомý что** because.
пот|онýть (**-онý, -óнешь**) *сов от* **тонýть**.
потóп (**-а**) *м* flood.
пот|опúть (**-оплю, -óпишь**) *сов от* **топúть**.
потоп|тáть (**-чý, -чешь**) *сов от* **топтáть**.
торáпливa|ть (**-ю**) *несов перех*: **~ когó-н** to hurry sb up
▸ **поторáпливаться** *несов возв* to hurry.
потороп|úть(ся) (**-лю(сь), -ишь(ся)**) *сов от* **торопúть(ся)**.
потóчный *прил* (*производство*) mass *опред*; **потóчная лúния** production line.
потрав|úть (**-лю, -ишь**) *сов от* **травúть**.
потрá|тить(ся) (**-чу(сь), -тишь(ся)**) *сов от* **трáтить(ся)**.
потребúтел|ь (**-я**) *м* consumer.
потребúтельск|ий (**-ая, -ое, -ие**) *прил* (*спрос, товар*) consumer *опред*; **потребúтельская кооперáция** cooperative (society).
потреб|úть (**-лю, -úшь**) *сов от* **потреблять**.
потреблéни|е (**-я**) *ср* (*действие*) consumption; **товáры ширóкого ~я** consumer goods.
потреблю *сов см* **потребúть**.
потребля|ть (**-ю**; *perf* **потребúть**) *несов перех* to consume.
потрéбност|ь (**-и**) *ж* (*надобность*) requirement, demand; (*желание*) need.
потрéб|овать(ся) (**-ую(сь)**) *сов от* **трéбовать(ся)**.
Потребсоюз (**-а**) *м сокр* = *Союз потребúтельских кооперáций*.
потревóж|ить(ся) (**-у(сь), -ишь(ся)**) *сов от* **тревóжить(ся)**.
потрёпан|ный (**-, -на, -но**) *прил* (*книга, одежда*) tattered, tatty; (*вид, лицо*) worn.
потреп|áть(ся) (**-лю(сь), -лешь(ся)**) *сов от* **трепáть(ся)**.
потрéска|ться (*3sg* **-ется**, *3pl* **-ются**) *сов от* **трéскаться**.
потрох|á (**-óв**) *мн* (*птицы*) giblets *мн*.
потрош|úть (**-ý, -úшь**; *perf* **выпотрошить**) *несов перех* (*курицу, рыбу*) to gut.
потрý(сь) *итп сов см* **потерéть(ся)**.
потруд|úться (**-жýсь, -дишься**) *сов возв* to work; ~ (*perf*) *+infin* to take the trouble to do; **~úтесь передáть э́то письмó** if you could be so kind as to pass on this letter.
потрясá|ть (**-ю**) *несов от* **потрясти**.
потрясáющ|ий (**-ая, -ее, -ие**) *прил* (*музыка, стихи*) fantastic; (*красота*) stunning.
потрясéни|е (**-я**) *ср* breakdown.
потряс|тú (**-ý, -ёшь**; *pt* **-, -лá, -лó**) *сов перех* to shake; (*impf* **потрясáть**; *взволновать*) to stun ◆ *неперех*: **~** *+instr* to shake.
потýг|а (**-и**) *ж* (*обычно мн*) contraction; (*перен*: *пренебр*: *усилия*) pathetic attempt.
потýп|ить (**-лю, -ишь**; *impf* **потуплять**) *сов*

перех (*голову, глаза*) to lower
▸ **потупиться** *сов возв* to lower one's eyes.
потускне́|ть (-ю) *сов от* **тускне́ть.**
потусторо́нн|ий (-яя, -ее, -ие) *прил* (*РЕЛ*) on the other side.
поту́хн|уть (*3sg* **-ет**, *3pl* **-ут**, *impf* **потуха́ть**) *сов неперех* (*лампа, свет*) to go out; (*жизнь, веселье*) to end.
пот|уши́ть (-ушу́, -у́шишь) *сов от* **туши́ть.**
потяга́|ться (-юсь) *сов от* **тяга́ться.**
потя́гива|ть (-ю) *несов перех* (*верёвку*) to pull; (*вино, чай*) to sip
▸ **потя́гиваться** *несов от* **потяну́ться.**
потяжеле́|ть (-ю) *сов от* **тяжеле́ть.**
пот|яну́ть (-яну́, -я́нешь) *сов от* **тяну́ть**
▸ **потяну́ться** *сов возв* to start to drag; (*impf* **потя́гиваться**; *в постели, в кресле*) to stretch out.
поу́жина|ть (-ю) *сов от* **у́жинать.**
поумне́|ть (-ю) *сов от* **умне́ть.**
поуча́|ть (-ю) *несов перех* to teach.
поуче́ни|е (-я) *ср* preaching.
поучи́тел|ьный (-ен, -ьна, -ьно) *прил* (*пример, история*) instructive; (*тон, голос*) didactic; **его́ приме́р был для нас ~ен** we learnt from his example.
поха́б|ный (-ен, -на, -но) *прил* (*непристойный*) dirty.
поха́жива|ть (-ю) *несов неперех* (*в парке итп*) to stroll.
похвал|а́ (-ы́) *ж* praise; **отзыва́ться (отозва́ться** *perf*) **с ~о́й о ком-н** to praise sb.
похва́лен *прил см* **похва́льный.**
похв|али́ть(ся) (-алю́(сь), -а́лишь(ся)) *сов от* **хвали́ть(ся).**
похва́л|ьный (-ен, -ьна, -ьно) *прил* praiseworthy; (*отзыв*) complimentary; **~ьное сло́во** word of praise; **похва́льная гра́мота** certificate of merit.
похва́ста|ть(ся) (-ю(сь)) *сов от* **хва́стать(ся).**
похити́тел|ь (-я) *м* (*см глаг*) thief; abductor; kidnapper.
похити́тельниц|а (-ы) *ж см* **похити́тель.**
похи́|тить (-щу, -тишь; *impf* **похища́ть**) *сов перех* (*предмет*) to steal; (*человека*) to abduct; (: *для выкупа*) to kidnap.
похище́ни|е (-я) *ср* (*см глаг*) theft; abduction; kidnap(ping).
похи́щу *сов см* **похи́тить.**
похло́па|ть (-ю) *сов перех* to pat ◆ *неперех* (*человек: в ладоши*) to clap; (*птица*) to flap.
похлоп|ота́ть (-очу́, -о́чешь) *сов от* **хлопота́ть.**
похме́ль|е (-я) *ср* hangover.
похо́д (-а) *м* (*военный*) campaign; (*туристический*) hike (*walking and camping expedition*).
походата́йств|овать (-ую) *сов от* **хода́тайствовать.**
пох|оди́ть (-ожу́, -о́дишь) *несов неперех*: **~ на кого́-н/что-н** to resemble sb/sth ◆ *сов неперех* to walk.
похо́дк|а (-и) *ж* gait.
похожде́ни|е (-я) *ср* (*обычно мн*) adventure.
похо́ж|ий (-ая, -ее, -ие) *прил*: **~ (на** *+acc* *или* **с** *+instr*) similar (to); **он похо́ж на бра́та, они́ с бра́том ~и** he looks like his brother; **они́ ~и** they look alike; **~е на то, что ...** it looks as if ...; **э́то на него́ не ~е** it's not like him.
похожу́ *(не)сов см* **походи́ть.**
похолода́ни|е (-я) *ср* cold spell.
похолода́|ть (*3sg* **-ет**) *сов от* **холода́ть.**
похолоде́|ть (-ю) *сов от* **холоде́ть.**
похор|они́ть (-оню́, -о́нишь) *сов от* **хорони́ть.**
похоро́нный *прил* funeral *опред*; **похоро́нное бюро́** undertaker's.
по́хор|оны (-о́н; *dat pl* **-она́м**) *мн* funeral *ед*.
похороше́|ть (-ю) *сов от* **хороше́ть.**
по́хот|ь (-и) *ж* lust.
похуде́|ть (-ю) *сов от* **худе́ть.**
поцара́па|ть (-ю) *сов от* **цара́пать.**
поцел|ова́ть(ся) (-у́ю(сь)) *сов от* **целова́ть(ся).**
поцелу́|й (-я) *м* kiss.
поцеремо́н|иться (-юсь) *сов от* **церемо́ниться.**
почасови́к (-а́) *м* part-time worker (*paid by the hour*).
почасов|о́й *прил* (*оплата*) hourly; **~а́я рабо́та** hourly-paid work.
поча́т|ок (-ка) *м* (*кукурузы*) cob.
по́чв|а (-ы) *ж* soil; (*перен*) basis; **на ~е** *+gen* owing to; **он потеря́л ~у под нога́ми** he lost his confidence.
по́чек *сущ см* **по́чка.**
почём *нареч* (*разг*) how much; **~ я́блоки?** how much are the apples?
почему́ *нареч* why; **(и) вот ~** and that is why.
почему́-либо *нареч* for some reason.
почему́-нибудь *нареч* = **почему́-либо.**
почему́-то *нареч* for some reason.
по́черк (-а) *м* handwriting; (*перен: художника, грабителя*) hallmark.
почерне́|ть (-ю) *сов от* **черне́ть.**
почерпн|у́ть (-у́, -ёшь) *сов перех* (*сведения*) to obtain; (*идею*) to draw.
почерстве́|ть (-ю) *сов от* **черстве́ть.**
поче|са́ть(ся) (-шу́(сь), -шешь(ся)) *сов от* **чеса́ть(ся).**
по́чест|ь (-и) *ж* (*обычно мн*) homage *ед*; **воздава́ть (возда́ть** *perf*) **~и кому́-н** to pay homage to sb.
поч|е́сть (-ту́, -тёшь; *pt* **-ёл, -ла́, -ло́**, *impf* **почита́ть**) *сов неперех*: **~ за долг/честь** *+infin* to consider it one's duty/an honour (*BRIT*) *или* honor (*US*) to do.

почёт (-а) *м* honour (*BRIT*), honor (*US*).
почётный *прил* (*гость*) honoured (*BRIT*), honored (*US*); (*член академии*) honorary; (*обязанность*) honourable (*BRIT*), honorable (*US*); **почётный карау́л** guard of honour (*BRIT*) *или* honor (*US*).
по́чечный *прил* kidney *опред*, renal; (*камни*) kidney *опред*.
почешу́(сь) *итп сов см* **почеса́ть(ся)**.
почи́н (-а) *м* initiative.
поч|ини́ть (-иню́, -и́нишь) *сов от* **чини́ть**.
почи́н|ка (-ки; *gen pl* -ок) *ж* (*обуви, телевизора*) repair.
почи́|стить (-щу, -стишь) *сов от* **чи́стить**.
почита́тел|ь (-я) *м* admirer.
почита́тельниц|а (-ы) *ж см* **почита́тель**.
почита́|ть (-ю) *несов от* **поче́сть** ◆ *перех* (*поклоняться*) to admire ◆ *сов перех* to read.
почи́щу *сов см* **почи́стить**.
по́ч|ка (-ки; *gen pl* -ек) *ж* (*БОТ*) bud; (*АНАТ*) kidney; **~ки** (*КУЛИН*) kidneys.
по́чт|а (-ы) *ж* (*учреждение*) post office; (*корреспонденция*) mail, post; **отправля́ть (отпра́вить** *perf*) **что-н ~ой** *или* **по ~е** to send sth by post.
почтальо́н (-а) *м* postman (*BRIT*) (*мн* postmen), mailman (*US*) (*мн* mailmen).
почта́мт (-а) *м* main post office.
почте́ни|е (-я) *ср* esteem.
почте́нн|ый *прил* venerable; **~ые го́ды** advanced years.
почти́ *нареч* almost, nearly; **~ что** (*разг*) almost.
почти́тел|ьный (-ен, -ьна, -ьно) *прил* respectful; **на ~ьном расстоя́нии** at a respectful distance.
почт|и́ть (*как* **чтить**; *см* **Table 17**) (-у́, -и́шь) *сов перех* (*память*) to pay homage to; **~** (*perf*) **кого́-н свои́м прису́тствием** to honour (*BRIT*) *или* honor (*US*) sb with one's presence.
почто́вый *прил* (*служба, связь*) postal; (*марка*) postage *опред*; **почто́вая откры́тка** postcard; **почто́вая бума́га** writing paper; **почто́вый и́ндекс** postcode (*BRIT*), zip code (*US*); **почто́вый перево́д** (*деньги*) postal order; **почто́вый я́щик** postbox.
почту́ *итп сов см* **поче́сть**.
почу́вств|овать (-ую) *сов от* **чу́вствовать**.
почу́д|иться (*3sg* -ится, *3pl* -ятся) *сов от* **чу́диться**.
почу́|ять (-ю) *сов от* **чу́ять**.
пошатн|у́ть (-у́, -ёшь) *сов перех* (*веру*) to shake; (*здоровье*) to affect
▸ **пошатну́ться** *сов возв* to sway; (*авторитет*) to be undermined; (*здоровье*) to suffer.
поша́тыва|ться (-юсь) *несов возв* (*человек*) to sway slightly.
пошеве́лива|ться (-юсь) *несов возв* to stir; (*разг: поторапливаться*) to get a move on.
пошевел|и́ть(ся) (-ю́(сь), -и́шь(ся)) *сов от* **шевели́ть(ся)**.
пошевельн|у́ться (-у́сь, -ёшься) *сов возв* to stir.
пошёл *сов см* **пойти́**.
пошелохну́ться (-у́сь, -ёшься) *сов* = **шелохну́ться**.
поши́б (-а) *м* (*разг: пренебр*): **они́ лю́ди одного́ ~а** they are cut from the same cloth; **ни́зкий** *или* **невысо́кий ~** second-rate.
поши́в (-а) *м* (*действие*) sewing; **индивидуа́льный ~** tailoring.
пошла́ *итп сов см* **пойти́**.
по́шлин|а (-ы) *ж* duty; **суде́бная ~** legal costs *или* expenses; **облага́ть (обложи́ть** *perf*) **что-н ~ой** to impose a duty on sth.
по́шлинный *прил* customs *опред*.
пошло́ *сов см* **пойти́**.
по́шлост|ь (-и) *ж* vulgarity; **говори́ть** (*impf*) **~и** to make trite and vulgar comments.
по́шл|ый (-, -а́, -о) *прил* (*человек, поступок*) vulgar; (*анекдот*) corny; (*картинка*) kitsch; (*речи*) trite and vulgar.
пошлю́ *итп сов см* **посла́ть**.
пошля́к (-а́) *м* (*разг*) vulgar person.
пош|ути́ть (-учу́, -у́тишь) *сов от* **шути́ть**.
поща́д|а (-ы) *ж* mercy.
поща|ди́ть (-жу́, -ди́шь) *сов от* **щади́ть**.
пощек|ота́ть (-очу́, -о́чешь) *сов от* **щекота́ть**.
пощёчин|а (-ы) *ж* slap in the face.
пощу́па|ть (-ю) *сов от* **щу́пать**.
пощу́сь *несов см* **пости́ться**.
поэ́зи|я (-и) *ж* (*также перен*) poetry.
поэ́м|а (-ы) *ж* poem.
поэ́т (-а) *м* poet.
поэте́сс|а (-ы) *ж см* **поэ́т**.
поэтизи́р|овать (-ую; *perf* **опоэтизи́ровать**) *несов перех* to wax poetic about.
поэти́ческ|ий (-ая, -ое, -ие) *прил* poetic.
поэ́тому *нареч* therefore.
пою́ *итп несов см* **петь, пои́ть**.
по|яви́ться (-явлю́сь, -я́вишься; *impf* **появля́ться**) *сов возв* to appear; **у него́ ~яви́лись иде́и/сомне́ния** he has had an idea/begun to have doubts; **появля́ться (~** *perf*) **на свет** to come into the world.
появле́ни|е (-я) *ср* appearance.
появлю́сь *сов см* **появи́ться**.
появля́|ться (-юсь) *несов от* **появи́ться**.
по́яс (-а; *nom pl* -а́) *м* (*ремень*) belt; (*талия*) waist; (*ГЕО*) zone; **спаса́тельный ~** life belt; **тари́фный ~** (*ЭКОН*) tariff zone.
поясне́ни|е (-я) *ср* explanation.
поясн|и́ть (-ю́, -и́шь; *impf* **поясня́ть**) *сов перех* to explain.
поясни́ц|а (-ы) *ж* small of the back.
поясня́|ть (-ю) *несов от* **поясни́ть**.
ППГ *м сокр* (= *полево́й подви́жный го́спиталь*) field hospital, ≈ MASH (*US*) (= *mobile army surgical hospital*).
пр. *сокр* = **прое́зд, проспе́кт, про́чее, про́чие**.
праба́б|ка (-ки; *gen pl* -ок) *ж* great-grandmother.
праба́буш|ка (-ки; *gen pl* -ек) *ж* = **праба́бка**.

прав|а́ (-) *мн* (*также:* **води́тельские ~**) driving licence (*BRIT*), driver's license (*US*); **права́ челове́ка** human rights.
пра́вд|а (-ы) *ж* truth ◆ *нареч* really ◆ *вводн сл* true; **он ~ измени́лся** he really has changed; **он, ~, сам созна́лся** true, he did confess; **ты винова́т в э́том – ~** you are to blame, it's true; **~у** *или* **по ~е говоря́** *или* **сказа́ть** to tell the truth; **он уже́ уе́хал, не ~ ли?** he's already gone, hasn't he?; **хоро́шая пого́да, не ~ ли?** the weather's good, isn't it?
правди́в|ый (-, -а, -о) *прил* truthful.
правдоподо́б|ный (-ен, -на, -но) *прил* plausible.
пра́веден *прил см* **пра́ведный**.
пра́ведник (-а) *ж* (*РЕЛ*) righteous man (*мн* men).
пра́вед|ный (-ен, -на, -но) *прил* (*человек*) righteous; (*суд*) just.
пра́вилен *прил см* **пра́вильный**.
пра́вил|о (-а) *ср* rule; **э́то не в мои́х ~ах** that's not my way; **как ~** as a rule; **по всем ~ам** by the rules; **пра́вила доро́жного движе́ния** rules of the road, ≈ Highway Code.
пра́вильно *нареч* correctly ◆ *как сказ* that's correct.
пра́вил|ьный (-ен, -ьна, -ьно) *прил* (*написание, произношение*) correct; (*вывод, ответ*) right; (*совет, суждение*) sound.
прави́тел|ь (-я) *м* ruler.
прави́тельственный *прил* government *опред*.
прави́тельств|о (-а) *ср* government.
пра́в|ить (-лю, -ишь) *несов перех* (*исправлять*) to correct ◆ *неперех*: **~** *+instr* (*страной*) to rule, govern; (*машиной*) to drive.
пра́в|ка (-ки; *gen pl* -ок) *ж* proofreading.
правле́ни|е (-я) *ср* government; (*орган*) board.
пра́влю *несов см* **пра́вить**.
пра́внук (-а) *м* great-grandson.
пра́в|о (-а; *nom pl* -а́) *ср* (*нормы, наука*) law; (*свобода*) right ◆ *вводн сл* (*разг*) really; **име́ть** *(impf)* **~ на что-н/***+infin* to have the right *или* be entitled to sth/to do; **быть** *(impf)* **в ~е** *+infin* to be entitled *или* have the right to do; **на права́х** *+gen* as; **по ~у** (*законно*) by rights; (*с полным основанием*) rightly; **на ра́вных права́х с** *+instr* on equal terms with; *см также* **права́**.
правове́д (-а) *м* jurisprudent.
правове́дени|е (-я) *ср* jurisprudence.
правове́р|ный (-ен, -на, -но) *прил* orthodox.
правово́й *прил* (*нормы*) legal; **правово́е госуда́рство** lawful state.
правозащи́тник (-а) *м* human rights activist.
правозащи́тниц|а (-ы) *ж см* **правозащи́тник**.
пра́вок *сущ см* **пра́вка**.
правоме́р|ный (-ен, -на, -но) *прил* (*вопрос*) valid; (*сомнения*) justifiable; (*действие, поступок*) lawful.
правомо́ч|ный (-ен, -на, -но) *прил* (*орган*) competent; (*лицо*) authorized.
правонаруше́ни|е (-я) *ср* offence.
правонаруши́тел|ь (-я) *м* offender.
правоохрани́тельный *прил* (*орган*) law-enforcement.
правописа́ни|е (-я) *ср* spelling.
правопоря́д|ок (-ка) *м* law and order.
правосла́ви|е (-я) *ср* orthodoxy.
правосла́вн|ая (-ой; *decl like adj*) *ж см* **правосла́вный**.
правосла́вн|ый *прил* (*церковь, обряд*) orthodox ◆ (-ого; *decl like adj*) *м member of the Orthodox Church*.
правоспосо́б|ный (-ен, -на, -но) *прил* (*ЮР*) capable.
правосу́ди|е (-я) *ср* justice.
правот|а́ (-ы) *ж* correctness; **я не сомнева́юсь в Ва́шей ~е́** I don't doubt that you are right.
пра́в|ый *прил* right; (*ПОЛИТ*) right-wing; (-, -а́, -о; *справедливый*) just; (*невиновный*) innocent; (*no full form*): **он прав** he is right; **~ суд** fair trial.
пра́вящ|ий (-ая, -ее, -ие) *прил* ruling *опред*.
Пра́г|а (-и) *ж* Prague.
прагмати́зм (-а) *м* pragmatism.
прагма́тик (-а) *м* pragmatist.
пра́дед (-а) *м* great-grandfather.
праде́душ|ка (-ки; *gen pl* -ек) *м* = **пра́дед**.
пра́зднеств|о (-а) *ср* festival.
пра́здник (-а) *м* (*по случаю какого-н события*) public holiday; (*религиозный*) festival; (*нерабочий день*) holiday; (*радость, торжество*) celebration; **с ~ом!** best wishes!
пра́здни́ч|ный (-ен, -на, -но) *прил* (*салют, обед*) celebratory; (*одежда, настроение*) festive; **~ день, пра́здничная да́та** holiday.
пра́здн|овать (-ую) *несов перех* to celebrate.
пра́зд|ный (-ен, -на, -но) *прил* idle; **~ная жизнь** life of idleness.
пра́ктик (-а) *м* (*о каком-н специалисте*) expert; (*практичный человек*) practical person (*мн* people); **он хоро́ший ~, но плохо́й теоре́тик** he's technically very good, but not so good at the theory.
пра́ктик|а (-и) *ж* practice; (*часть учёбы*) practical experience *или* work; **на ~е** in practice.
практика́нт (-а) *м* trainee (*on a placement*).
практика́нт|ка (-ки; *gen pl* -ок) *ж см* **практика́нт**.
практик|ова́ть (-у́ю) *несов перех* to practise (*BRIT*), practice (*US*)
▸ **практикова́ться** *несов возв* (*методы, приёмы*) to be used; (*обучаться*): **~ся в чем-н** to practise sth.
практи́чен *прил см* **практи́чный**.
практи́чески *нареч* (*на практике*) in practice; (*по сути дела*) practically.
практи́ческ|ий (-ая, -ое, -ие) *прил* practical.
практи́ч|ный (-ен, -на, -но) *прил* practical.
пра́порщик (-а) *м* (*ВОЕН*) ≈ warrant officer.

прах (-а) *м* (*умершего*) ashes *мн*; **пойти́** *(perf)* **пра́хом** (*усилия, работа*) to be wasted.
пра́чек *сущ см* **пра́чка**.
пра́чечн|ая (-ой; *decl like adj*) *ж* laundry.
пра́ч|ка (-ки; *gen pl* -ек) *ж* laundress.
преа́мбул|а (-ы) *ж* preamble.
пребыва́ни|е (-я) *ср* (*в каком-н месте*) stay; ~ **у вла́сти** term of office.
пребыва́|ть (-ю) *несов неперех* (*находиться*) to be.
превали́р|овать (-ую) *несов неперех*: ~ **(над** *+instr*) to prevail (over).
превенти́вный *прил* preventive; ~ **уда́р** pre-emptive strike.
превзойти́ (*как* **идти́**: *см* **Table 18**; *impf* **превосходи́ть**) *сов перех* (*соперника, врага*) to beat; (*прежние результаты, ожидания*) to surpass; (*доходы, скорость*) to exceed; ~ *(perf)* **самого́ себя́** to surpass o.s.
превозм|о́чь (-огу́, -о́жешь *итп*, -о́гут; *pt* -о́г, -огла́, -огло́, *impf* **превозмога́ть**) *сов перех* to overcome.
превозн|ести́ (-есу́, -есёшь; *pt* -ёс, -есла́, -есло́) *сов перех* to extol.
превосхо́ден *прил см* **превосхо́дный**.
превосхо|ди́ть (-жу́, -дишь) *несов от* **превзойти́**.
превосхо́дно *нареч* excellently ◆ *как сказ* it's excellent.
превосхо́д|ный (-ен, -на, -но) *прил* superb; **превосхо́дная сте́пень** superlative degree.
превосхо́дств|о (-а) *ср* superiority.
превосхожу́ *несов см* **превосходи́ть**.
превра́тен *прил см* **превра́тный**.
превра|ти́ть (-щу́, -ти́шь; *impf* **превраща́ть**) *сов перех*: ~ **что-н в** *+acc* to turn sth into; **превраща́ть** (~ *perf*) **кого́-н в** *+acc* to turn *или* transform sb into
▸ **преврати́ться** (*impf* **превраща́ться**) *сов возв* to turn.
превра́т|ный (-ен, -на, -но) *прил* wrong.
превраща́|ть(ся) (-ю(сь)) *несов от* **преврати́ть(ся)**.
превраще́ни|е (-я) *ср* transformation.
превращу́(сь) *сов см* **преврати́ть(ся)**.
превы́|сить (-шу́, -сишь; *impf* **превыша́ть**) *сов перех* to exceed; (*рекорд*) to break.
прегра́д|а (-ы) *ж* barrier.
прегра|ди́ть (-жу́, -ди́шь; *impf* **прегражда́ть**) *сов перех*: ~ **кому́-н доро́гу/вход** to block *или* bar sb's way/entrance.
преда|ва́ть(ся) (-ю́(сь)) *несов от* **преда́ть(ся)**.
преда́м(ся) *итп сов см* **преда́ть(ся)**.
преда́ни|е (-я) *ср* legend.
пре́дан|ный (-, -на, -но) *прил* devoted; **он пре́дан де́лу/жене́** he is devoted to the cause/his wife.
преда́ст(ся) *сов см* **преда́ть(ся)**.
преда́тел|ь (-я) *м* traitor.
преда́тельниц|а (-ы) *ж см* **преда́тель**.
преда́тельск|ий (-ая, -ое, -ие) *прил* treacherous.
преда́тельств|о (-а) *ср* treachery.
преда́ть (*как* **дать**; *см* **Table 14**; *impf* **предава́ть**) *сов перех* to betray; **предава́ть** (~ *perf*) **что-н гла́сности** to make sth public; **предава́ть** (~ *perf*) **кого́-н су́ду** to prosecute sb; **предава́ть** (~ *perf*) **забве́нию** to consign to oblivion
▸ **преда́ться** (*impf* **предава́ться**) *сов возв*: ~**ся** *+dat* (*мечтам итп*) to give o.s. up to.
предвари́тел|ьный (-ен, -ьна, -ьно) *прил* preliminary; (*продажа билетов*) advance *опред*; ~ **счёт-факту́ра** (*КОММ*) pro-forma invoice; **предвари́тельное заключе́ние** (*ЮР*) remand.
предвар|и́ть (-ю́, -и́шь; *impf* **предваря́ть**) *сов перех* (*события*) to anticipate.
предве́сти|е (-я) *ср* indication.
предвеща́|ть (-ю) *несов перех* (*будущее, успех*) to foretell; (*изменения, кризис*) to portend; (*плохую погоду*) to herald.
предвзя́т|ый (-, -а, -о) *прил* prejudiced.
предви́дени|е (-я) *ср* foresight; (*предположение*) prediction.
предви́|деть (-жу, -дишь) *сов перех* to foresee, predict
▸ **предви́деться** *сов неперех* to be expected.
предвкуша́|ть (-ю) *несов перех* to look forward to, anticipate.
предвкуше́ни|е (-я) *ср* anticipation.
предводи́тел|ь (-я) *м* leader.
предвосхи́|тить (-щу́, -ти́шь; *impf* **предвосхища́ть**) *сов перех* to anticipate.
предвы́борн|ый *прил* (*собрание*) pre-election *опред*; ~**ая кампа́ния** election campaign.
предго́рный *прил*: ~ **райо́н** foothills *мн*.
преддве́ри|е (-я) *ср*: **в** ~**и чего́-н** on the threshold of sth.
преде́л (-а) *м* (*обычно мн*: *города, страны*) boundary; (*перен*: *приличия*) bound; (: *терпения*) limit; (*изнеможения*) peak; (*совершенства, подлости*) height; (*мечтаний, желаний*) pinnacle; **на** ~**е** at breaking point; **дойти́** *(perf)* **до** ~**а** to reach the limit; **в** ~**ах** *+gen* (*закона, года*) within; (*приличия*) within the bounds of; **за** ~**ами** *+gen* (*страны, города*) outside.
преде́л|ьный (-ен, -ьна, -ьно) *прил* maximum; (*восторг, важность*) utmost; **преде́льный срок** deadline.
предзнаменова́ни|е (-я) *ср* omen.
предика́т (-а) *м* (*лииг*) predicate.
предисло́ви|е (-я) *ср* foreword, preface.
пре́дка *сущ см* **пре́док**.
пре́дк|и (-ов) *мн* ancestors *мн*.
предлага́|ть (-ю) *несов от* **предложи́ть**.
предло́г (-а) *м* pretext; (*лииг*) preposition; **под** ~**ом** *+gen* on the pretext of; **под** ~**ом того́ что, под тем** ~**ом что** on the pretext that.
предложе́ни|е (-я) *ср* (*конкретное, умное*) proposal, suggestion; (*замужества*) proposal;

(*КОММ*) offer; (*ЭКОН*) supply; (*ЛИНГ*) sentence; **де́лать (сде́лать** *perf*) **~ кому́-н** (*девушке*) to propose to sb; (*КОММ*) to make sb an offer; **вноси́ть (внести́** *perf*) **~** (*на собрании, на съезде*) to propose a motion.

предл|ожи́ть (**-ожу́, -о́жишь**; *impf* **предлага́ть**) *сов перех* to offer; (*план, кандидатуру*) to propose ◆ *неперех* to suggest, propose; (*попросить*) to ask, invite; (*потребовать*) to ask; **предлага́ть (~** *perf*) **что-н кому́-н** to offer sth to sb, offer sb sth; **он ~ожи́л нам пойти́ туда́** he suggested that we went there.

предло́жный *прил* (*ЛИНГ*) prepositional; **предло́жный паде́ж** prepositional case.

предме́сть|е (**-я**) *ср* suburb.

предме́т (**-а**) *м* object; (*обсуждения, изучения*) subject; **на ~** *+gen* concerning; **предме́ты дома́шнего обихо́да** household goods; **предме́ты пе́рвой необходи́мости** necessities.

предназнача́|ть (**-ю**) *несов от* **предназна́чить**

▸ **предназнача́ться** *несов возв* (*+dat*) to be destined for.

предназначе́ни|е (**-я**) *ср* role.

предназна́ч|ить (**-у, -ишь**; *impf* **предназнача́ть**) *сов перех*: **~ что-н/кого́-н** *+dat* to intend sth/sb for.

преднаме́рен|ный (**-, -на, -но**) *прил* (*преступление*) premeditated; (*обман итп*) deliberate.

пре́д|ок (**-ка**) *м* ancestor; *см также* **пре́дки**.

предопредел|и́ть (**-ю́, -и́шь**; *impf* **предопределя́ть**) *сов перех* (*определить*) to predetermine; (*обусловить*) to bring about.

предоста́в|ить (**-лю, -ишь**) *сов перех*: **~ что-н кому́-н** to give sb sth ◆ *неперех*: **~ кому́-н** *+infin* (*выбирать, решать*) to let sb do; **предоставля́ть (~** *perf*) **кого́-н самому́ себе́** to leave sb to his own devices; **предоставля́ть (~** *perf*) **кому́-н сло́во** to call upon sb to speak.

предостерёг *итп сов см* **предостере́чь**.

предостерега́|ть (**-ю**) *несов от* **предостере́чь**.

предостерегу́ *итп сов см* **предостере́чь**.

предостереже́ни|е (**-я**) *ср* warning.

предостер|е́чь (**-егу́, -ежёшь** *итп*, **-егу́т**; *pt* **-ёг, -егла́, -егло́**, *impf* **предостерега́ть**) *сов перех*: **~ кого́-н (от** *+gen*) to warn sb (about).

предосторо́жност|ь (**-и**) *ж* caution; **ме́ры ~и** precautionary measures, precautions.

предосуди́тел|ьный (**-ен, -ьна, -ьно**) *прил* reprehensible.

предотвра|ти́ть (**-щу́, -ти́шь**; *impf* **предотвраща́ть**) *сов перех* (*войну, кризис*) to avert; (*болезнь, аварии*) to prevent.

предотвраще́ни|е (**-я**) *ср* (*см глаг*) averting; prevention.

предотвращу́ *сов см* **предотврати́ть**.

предохрани́тел|ь (**-я**) *м* safety device; (*электрический*) fuse (*BRIT*), fuze (*US*); (*ружейный*) safety catch; (*замка*) snib.

предохрани́тельный *прил* (*TEX*) safety *опред*.

предохран|и́ть (**-ю́, -и́шь**; *impf* **предохраня́ть**) *сов перех* to protect.

предписа́ни|е (**-я**) *ср* (*распоряжение*) instruction; (: *президента, полиции*) order; (: *врача*) prescription.

предп|иса́ть (**-ишу́, -и́шешь**; *impf* **предпи́сывать**) *сов перех*: **~ что-н кому́-н** (*назначить*) to prescribe sth for sb ◆ *неперех*: **~ кому́-н** *+infin* to order sb to do.

предполага́|ть (**-ю**) *несов от* **предположи́ть** ◆ *перех* to demand ◆ *неперех*: **~** *+infin* (*намереваться*) to intend to do

▸ **предполага́ться** *несов неперех* (*намечаться*) to be planned.

предположе́ни|е (**-я**) *ср* (*догадка*) supposition; (*намерение*) intention.

предположи́тел|ьный (**-ен, -ьна, -ьно**) *прил* (*результат, вопрос*) hypothetical; (*срок, доход*) anticipated.

предпол|ожи́ть (**-ожу́, -о́жишь**; *impf* **предполага́ть**) *сов перех* (*допустить возможность*) to allow for; **~о́жим** (*возможно*) suppose; **~о́жим, он опозда́ет** suppose he is late.

предпо|сла́ть (**-шлю́, -шлёшь**; *impf* **предпосыла́ть**) *сов перех*: **~ что-н чему́-н** to preface sth with sth.

предпосле́дн|ий (**-яя, -ее, -ие**) *прил* (*номер журнала*) penultimate; (*в очереди*) last but one.

предпосыла́|ть (**-ю**) *несов от* **предпосла́ть**.

предпосы́л|ка (**-ки**; *gen pl* **-ок**) *ж* (*условие*) precondition, prerequisite; (*исходное положение*) premise.

предпоч|е́сть (**-ту́, -тёшь**; *pt* **-ёл, -ла́, -ло́**, *impf* **предпочита́ть**) *сов перех*: **~ что-н/кого́-н** *+dat* to prefer sth/sb to ◆ *неперех*: **~** *+infin* to prefer to do.

предпочте́ни|е (**-я**) *ср* preference; **ока́зывать (оказа́ть** *perf*) *или* **отдава́ть (отда́ть** *perf*) **~ кому́-н/чему́-н** to show a preference for sb/sth.

предпочти́тел|ьный (**-ен, -ьна, -ьно**) *прил* preferable.

предпочту́ *итп сов см* **предпоче́сть**.

предпошлю́ *итп сов см* **предпосла́ть**.

предприи́мчив|ый (**-, -а, -о**) *прил* enterprising.

предприму́ *итп сов см* **предприня́ть**.

предпринима́тел|ь (**-я**) *м* entrepreneur, businessman (*мн* businessmen).

предпринима́тельск|ий (**-ая, -ое, -ие**) *прил* enterprise *опред*, business *опред*.

предпринима́тельств|о (**-а**) *ср* enterprise.

предпр|иня́ть (**-иму́, -и́мешь**; *pt* **-и́нял,-иняла́,-и́няло**, *impf* **предпринима́ть**) *сов перех* to

undertake; (*атаку, наступление итп*) to launch; (*меры*) to take.
предприя́ти|е (**-я**) *ср* enterprise, business.
предрасположе́ни|е (**-я**) *ср* predisposition.
предрасполо́женност|ь (**-и**) *ж* = **предрасположе́ние.**
предрассу́д|ок (**-ка**) *м* prejudice.
предрека́|ть (**-ю**) *несов перех* (*успех*) to foretell; (*плохую погоду*) to herald.
предреш|и́ть (**-у́, -и́шь**; *impf* **предреша́ть**) *сов перех* to predetermine.
председа́тел|ь (**-я**) *м* chairman (*мн* chairmen).
председа́тельств|о (**-а**) *ср* chairmanship; **под ~м** *+gen* under the chairmanship of.
председа́тельств|овать (**-ую**) *несов неперех* (*на заседании*) to be in the chair; (*работать председателем*) to be chairman; ~ *(impf)* **на собра́нии** to chair a meeting.
предскажу́ *итп сов см* **предсказа́ть.**
предсказа́ни|е (**-я**) *ср* (*действие*) predicting; (*то, что предсказано*) prediction.
предск|аза́ть (**-ажу́, -а́жешь**; *impf* **предска́зывать**) *сов перех* to predict; (*чью-н судьбу*) to foretell.
предсме́ртный *прил* (*агония*) death *опред*; (*вздох*) dying; (*воля*) last.
предста|ва́ть (**-ю́**) *несов от* **предста́ть.**
представи́тел|ь (**-я**) *м* representative; (*разряда животных итп*) specimen.
представи́тельниц|а (**-ы**) *ж* representative.
представи́тельный *прил* representative; (*видный*) imposing.
представи́тельств|о (**-а**) *ср* (*учреждение*) representatives *мн*; (*наличие представителей*) representation; **торго́вое ~** trade mission; **дипломати́ческое ~** diplomatic corps.
предста́в|ить (**-лю, -ишь**; *impf* **представля́ть**) *сов перех* to present; **представля́ть (~** *perf***) кого́-н кому́-н** (*познакомить*) to introduce sb to sb; **представля́ть (предста́вить** *perf***) кого́-н к** *+dat* (*к награде, к премии итп*) to recommend sb for, put sb forward for; **представля́ть (~** *perf***) интере́с** to be of interest; **представля́ть (~** *perf***) себе́** to imagine; **~ьте (себе́)!** (just) imagine!
▸ **предста́виться** (*impf* **представля́ться**) *несов возв* (*при знакомстве*) to introduce o.s.; (*появиться: возможность*) to present itself; **представля́ться (~ся** *perf***) кому́-н** (*вид*) to appear before sb; (*интересная картина*) to meet sb's eyes; **ему́ ~илась бу́дущая встре́ча** he pictured the future meeting; **ей ~илась возмо́жность пое́хать в Ло́ндон** an opportunity arose for her to go to London; **представля́ться (~ся** *perf***) больны́м/спя́щим** to pretend to be ill/asleep.
представле́ни|е (**-я**) *ср* presentation; (*документ*) statement; (*ТЕАТР*) performance; (*знание*) idea; (*ПСИХОЛ*) representation; **не име́ть** *(impf)* **(никако́го) ~я о** *+prp* to have no idea about.
предста́влю(сь) *сов см* **предста́вить(ся).**
представля́|ть (**-ю**) *несов от* **предста́вить** ◆ *перех* (*действовать от имени*) to represent; ~ *(impf)* **собо́й** *или* **из себя́** (*являться*) to be; ~ *(impf)* **себе́ что-н** (*понимать*) to understand sth; (*осознавать*) to appreciate sth; **он ничего́ из себя́ не ~ет** he doesn't amount to much
▸ **представля́ться** *несов от* **предста́виться** ◆ *возв*: **мне ~ется, (что) он прав** I think he's right; **~ется, что ...** it appears that ....
предста́|ть (**-ну, -нешь**; *impf* **представа́ть**) *сов неперех*: **~ пе́ред** *+instr* (*появиться*) to appear before; (*проявиться: человек*) to show o.s.; (*: характер*) to show itself.
предсто|я́ть (*3sg* **-и́т**, *3pl* **-я́т**) *несов неперех* to lie ahead; **нам ~и́т мно́го рабо́ты** there is a lot of work ahead of us.
предстоя́щ|ий (**-ая, -ее, -ие**) *прил* (*сезон*) coming; (*трудности*) impending; (*работа, встреча*) forthcoming.
предубежде́ни|е (**-я**) *ср* prejudice.
предугада́|ть (**-ю**; *impf* **предуга́дывать**) *сов перех* to anticipate.
предупреди́тел|ьный (**-ен, -ьна, -ьно**) *прил* (*предохраняющий*) preventive; (*любезный*) solicitous, attentive.
предупре|ди́ть (**-жу́, -ди́шь**; *impf* **предупрежда́ть**) *сов перех* to warn; (*предотвратить*) to prevent; (*опередить*) to anticipate; **предупрежда́ть (~** *perf***) кого́-н о** *+prp* to warn sb about.
предупрежде́ни|е (**-я**) *ср* warning; (*аварии, заболевания*) prevention; (*извещение*) notice.
предупрежу́ *сов см* **предупреди́ть.**
предусм|отре́ть (**-отрю́, -о́тришь**; *impf* **предусма́тривать**) *сов перех* (*учесть*) to foresee; (*принять меры*) to make provision for; (*подлеж: программа, закон*) to provide for.
предусмотри́тел|ьный (**-ен, -ьна, -ьно**) *прил* prudent.
предчу́встви|е (**-я**) *ср* premonition.
предчу́вств|овать (**-ую**) *несов перех* to have a premonition of.
предше́ственник (**-а**) *м* predecessor.
предше́ствующ|ий (**-ая, -ее, -ие**) *прил* previous; (*событие*) foregoing.
предъяви́тел|ь (**-я**) *м* bearer.
предъяви́тельниц|а (**-ы**) *ж см* **предъяви́тель.**
предъ|яви́ть (**-явлю́, -я́вишь**; *impf* **предъявля́ть**) *сов перех* (*паспорт, билет итп*) to show; (*доказательства*) to produce; (*требования, претензии*) to make; (*иск*) to bring; **предъявля́ть (~** *perf***) права́ на что-н** to lay claim to sth.
предъявле́ни|е (**-я**) *ср* (*паспорта, билета итп*) showing; (*претензий*) making; (*иска*) bringing; **по ~ю** (*КОММ*) at sight.
предъявлю́ *сов см* **предъяви́ть.**
предъявля́|ть (**-ю**) *несов от* **предъяви́ть.**
предыду́щ|ий (**-ая, -ее, -ие**) *прил* previous.

предыстóри|я (-и) *ж* background.
преéмник (-а) *м* successor.
преéмница (-ы) *ж см* **преéмник**.
преéмственност|ь (-и) *ж* (*власти, традиций*) continuity.
преéмственный *прил* successive.
прéжде *нареч* (*в прошлом*) formerly; (*сначала*) first ◆ *предл* (+*gen*) before; ~ **всегó** first of all; ~ **чем** before; ~ **онá никогдá об э́том не дýмала** she never used to think about it.
преждеврéмен|ный (-ен, -на, -но) *прил* premature.
прéжн|ий (-яя, -ее, -ие) *прил* former.
презентáци|я (-и) *ж* presentation.
презервати́в (-а) *м* condom.
президéнт (-а) *м* president.
прези́диум (-а) *м* presidium.
презирá|ть (-ю) *несов перех* to hold in contempt.
презрéни|е (-я) *ср* (*ко лжи, к предателю*) contempt; (*к опасности*) disregard; (*к богатству итп*) scorn.
презри́тел|ьный (-ен, -ьна, -ьно) *прил* contemptuous.
преимýщественно *нареч* chiefly.
преимýществ|о (-а) *ср* advantage; (*юр*) privilege; **по** ~**у** (*главным образом*) chiefly; **имéть** (*impf*) ~ **пéред** +*instr* to have an advantage over.
преиспóлн|иться (-юсь; *impf* **преисполня́ться**) *сов возв*: ~ +*instr* to be filled with.
прейскурáнт (-а) *м* price list.
преклонéни|е (-я) *ср*: ~ (**пéред** +*instr*) admiration (for).
преклóнный *прил*: ~ **вóзраст** old age.
преклоня́|ться (-юсь) *несов возв*: ~ **пéред** +*instr* to admire.
прекрáсен *прил см* **прекрáсный**.
прекрáсн|ое (-ого; *decl like adj*) *ср* beauty.
прекрáс|ный (-ен, -на, -но) *прил* (*красивый: женщина, природа*) beautiful; (*: город, вид, день*) fine, beautiful; (*отличный*) excellent; **в оди́н** ~ **день** (*однажды*) one fine day.
прекра|ти́ть (-щý, -ти́шь; *impf* **прекращáть**) *сов перех* to stop; (*подачу энергии*) to cut off ◆ *неперех*: ~ +*infin* to stop doing; **прекращáть** (~ *perf*) **отношéния с кем-н** to break off relations with sb
▸ **прекрати́ться** (*impf* **прекращáться**) *сов возв* (*дождь, занятия*) to stop; (*отношения, знакомство*) to end.
прекращéни|е (-я) *ср* (*работы*) stopping; (*поставок*) cutting off; (*отношений*) breaking off.
прекращý(сь) *сов см* **прекрати́ть(ся)**.
прелéст|ный (-ен, -на, -но) *прил* charming.
прéлест|ь (-и) *ж* charm; **какáя** ~! how charming!
прел|оми́ться (*3sg* **-óмится**, *3pl* **-óмятся**, *impf* **преломля́ться**) *сов возв* (*физ*) to be refracted; (*перен*) to take on a different cast.
прéлый *прил* rotten.
прель|сти́ть (-щý, -сти́шь; *impf* **прельщáть**) *сов перех* to attract; (*увлечь*): ~ **когó-н чем-н** to entice sb with sth
▸ **прельсти́ться** (*impf* **прельщáться**) *сов возв*: ~**ся** +*instr* (*возможностями*) to be attracted by; (*богатством*) to be enticed by.
прелю́ди|я (-и) *ж* prelude.
премиáльн|ые (-ых; *decl like adj*) *мн* bonus *ед*.
премиáльный *прил* bonus *опред*; *см также* **премиáльные**.
премир|овáть (-ýю) *(не)сов перех* (*работника*) to give a bonus to; (*победителя*) to award a prize to.
прéми|я (-и) *ж* (*работнику*) bonus; (*победителю*) prize; (*комм*) premium.
премýдрост|ь (-и) *ж* (*разг: обычно мн*) ins *мн* and outs *мн*.
премьéр (-а) *м* (*также:* ~**-мини́стр**) prime minister, premier.
премьéр|а (-ы) *ж* première.
премьéр-мини́стр (-а) *м* prime minister, premier.
пренебрёг *итп сов см* **пренебрéчь**.
пренебрегá|ть (-ю) *несов от* **пренебрéчь**.
пренебрегý *итп сов см* **пренебрéчь**.
пренебрежéни|е (-я) *ср* (*законами итп*) disregard; (*: обязанностями*) neglect; (*высокомерие*) contempt.
пренебрежёшь *итп сов см* **пренебрéчь**.
пренебрежи́тел|ьный (-ен, -ьна, -ьно) *прил* contemptuous.
пренебр|éчь (-егý, -ежёшь *итп*, -гýт; *pt* -ёг, -еглá, -еглó, *impf* **пренебрегáть**) *сов неперех*: ~ +*instr* (*опасностью, последствиями*) to disregard; (*модной одеждой, правилами*) to scorn; (*советом, просьбой*) to ignore.
прéни|я (-й) *мн* debate *ед*.
преобладá|ть (*3sg* **-ет**, *3pl* **-ют**) *несов неперех*: ~ (**над** +*instr*) to predominate (over).
преобра|зи́ть (-жý, -зи́шь; *impf* **преображáть**) *сов перех* to transform
▸ **преобрази́ться** (*impf* **преображáться**) *сов возв* to be transformed.
преобразовáни|е (-я) *ср* (*общества, жизни*) transformation; (*тока, энергии*) conversion; (*революционное, социальное*) reform.
преобразовáтел|ь (-я) *м* (*тока, радиосигналов*) transformer; (*общества*) reformer.
преобраз|овáть (-ýю; *impf* **преобразóвывать**) *сов перех* to reorganize; **преобразóвывать** (~ *perf*) **что-н в** +*acc* (*превратить*) to convert sth into.

преодоле́|ть (-ю; *impf* **преодолева́ть**) *сов перех* to overcome; (*преграду*) to break down; (*трудный переход итп*) to get through.
препара́т (-а) *м* (*МЕД, ХИМ*) preparation.
препина́ни|е (-я) *ср*: **знаки ~я** punctuation marks *мн*.
препира́|ться (-юсь) *несов возв*: ~ (**с** +*instr*) to squabble *или* bicker (with).
преподава́ни|е (-я) *ср* teaching.
преподава́тел|ь (-я) *м* (*школы, курсов*) teacher; (*вуза*) lecturer.
преподава́тельниц|а (-ы) *ж см* **преподава́тель**.
препода|ва́ть (-ю́, -ёшь) *несов перех* to teach.
препода́ть (*как* **дать**; *см* **Table 14**) *сов перех* to teach; ~ (*perf*) **кому́-н уро́к терпе́ния** to teach sb patience.
препродн|ести́ (-есу́, -есёшь; *pt* -ёс, -есла́, -есло́, *impf* **преподноси́ть**) *сов перех*: ~ **что-н кому́-н** to present sb with sth; (*новость, сюрприз*) to give sb sth.
преподо́би|е (-я) *ср* (*РЕЛ*): **Ва́ше/Его́** ~ Your/His Eminence.
преподо́бный *прил* (*РЕЛ*) venerable.
препя́тстви|е (-я) *ср* obstacle.
препя́тств|овать (-ую; *perf* **воспрепя́тствовать**) *несов неперех* (+*dat*) to impede.
прерв|а́ть (-у́, -ёшь; *impf* **прерыва́ть**) *сов перех* (*разговор, работу итп*) to cut short; (*отношения, знакомство*) to break off; (*говорящего*) to interrupt; (*КОМП*) to abort
▸ **прерва́ться** (*impf* **прерыва́ться**) *сов возв* (*разговор, игра*) to be cut short; (*отношения, знакомство*) to be broken off.
пререка́|ться (-юсь) *несов возв* to squabble *или* bicker.
прерогати́в|а (-ы) *ж* prerogative.
прерыва́|ть(ся) (-ю(сь)) *несов от* **прерва́ть(ся)**.
преры́вист|ый (-, -а, -о) *прил* (*звонок*) intermittent; (*линия*) broken.
пресёк *итп сов см* **пресе́чь**.
пресека́|ть (-ю) *несов от* **пресе́чь**.
пресеку́ *итп сов см* **пресе́чь**.
пре́сен *прил см* **пре́сный**.
пресече́ни|е (-я) *ср* suppression; **ме́ра ~я** (*ЮР*) injunction.
прес|е́чь (-еку́, -ечёшь *итп*, -еку́т; *pt* -ёк, -екла́, -екло́, *impf* **пресека́ть**) *сов перех* to suppress.
пресле́довани|е (-я) *ср* pursuit; (*инакомыслия*) persecution.
пресле́д|овать (-ую) *несов перех* to pursue; (*перен: женщину*) to chase; (*подлеж: мысли, чувства*) to haunt; (*правозащитника*) to persecute.
преслову́тый *прил* notorious.
пресмыка́|ться (-юсь) *несов возв* (*пренебр*): ~ **пе́ред** +*instr* (*унижаться*) to crawl to.
пресмыка́ющееся (-егося; *nom pl* **-иеся**) *ср* reptile.
пресново́дный *прил* freshwater.
пре́с|ный (-ен, -на, -но) *прил* (*вода*) fresh; (*пища*) bland; (*перен: шутка*) feeble; (: *история, разговоры итп*) tedious.
пресс (-а) *м* (*ТЕХ*) press.
пре́сс|а (-ы) *ж собир* the press; **общенациона́льная** ~ national press.
пресс-конфере́нци|я (-и) *ж* press conference.
пресс|ова́ть (-у́ю; *perf* **спрессова́ть**) *несов перех* (*детали*) to press; (*порошок, газ*) to compress.
пресс-центр (-а) *м* press office.
престаре́л|ый *прил* aged; **дом (для) ~ых** old people's home.
прести́ж (-а) *м* prestige.
прести́ж|ный (-ен, -на, -но) *прил* prestigious.
престо́л (-а) *м* (*трон*) throne; **вступа́ть (вступи́ть** *perf*) *или* **восходи́ть (взойти́** *perf*) **на** ~ to ascend the throne; **сверга́ть (све́ргнуть** *perf*) **кого́-н с ~а** to dethrone sb.
преступен *прил см* **престу́пный**.
прест|упи́ть (-уплю́, -у́пишь; *impf* **преступа́ть**) *сов перех* to breach.
преступле́ни|е (-я) *ср* crime.
преступлю́ *сов см* **преступи́ть**.
престу́пник (-а) *м* criminal.
престу́пниц|а (-ы) *ж см* **престу́пник**.
престу́пност|ь (-и) *ж* criminal nature; (*количество*) crime; **организо́ванная** ~ organized crime.
престу́п|ный (-ен, -на, -но) *прил* criminal.
пресы́|титься (-щусь, -тишься; *impf* **пресыща́ться**) *сов возв* (+*instr*) to satiate o.s. with.
претвор|и́ть (-ю́, -и́шь; *impf* **претворя́ть**) *сов перех*: ~ **что-н в жизнь** *или* **в де́ло** *или* **в действи́тельность** (*планы, замыслы*) to put sth into practice; (*мечту*) to realize sth.
претенде́нт (-а) *м* (*на престол*) claimant; (*на должность*) candidate; (*на руку женщины*) suitor; (*СПОРТ*) contender; (*ШАХМАТЫ*) challenger.
претенд|ова́ть (-у́ю) *несов неперех*: ~ **на** +*acc* (*стремиться*) to aspire to; (*заявлять права*) to lay claim to.
прете́нзи|я (-и) *ж* (*обычно мн: на наследство, на престол*) claim *ед*; (: *на ум, на красоту итп*) pretension; (*жалоба*) complaint; **быть** (*impf*) **в ~и на** +*acc* to bear a grudge against.
претенцио́з|ный (-ен, -на, -но) *прил* pretentious.
прет|ерпе́ть (-ерплю́, , -е́рпишь; *impf* **претерпева́ть**) *сов перех* (*изменения*) to undergo; (*невзгоды*) to suffer.
прет|и́ть (*3sg* -и́т, *3pl* -я́т) *несов безл* (+*dat*): **ему́ ~и́т жа́дность** greed disgusts *или* sickens him.
преткнове́ни|е (-я) *ср*: **ка́мень ~я** stumbling block.
Прето́ри|я (-и) *ж* Pretoria.
пре|ть (-ю; *perf* **сопре́ть**) *несов неперех* (*листья*) to rot; (*пища*) to stew.

преувеличе́ни|е (-я) *ср* exaggeration.
преувели́ч|ить (-у, -ишь; *impf* **преувели́чивать**) *сов перех* to exaggerate.
преуме́ньш|ить (-у, -ишь; *impf* **преуменьша́ть**) *сов перех* (*недооценивать*) to underestimate; (*показать в меньших размерах*) to understate.
преуспева́|ть (-ю) *несов от* **преуспе́ть** ♦ *неперех* (*бизнесмен, писатель*) to be successful.
преуспе́|ть (-ю; *impf* **преуспева́ть**) *сов неперех* to be successful.
префе́кт (-а) *м* *head of administrative area of Moscow.*
преходя́щий (-ая, -ее, -ие; -, -а, -е, -и) *прил* (*временный*) transient.
прецеде́нт (-а) *м* precedent.

KEYWORD

при *предл* (*+prp*) **1** (*возле*) by, near; **при доро́ге/до́ме** by *или* near the road/house; **сраже́ние при Ватерло́о** the battle of Waterloo
2 (*указывает на прикреплённость*) at; **при институ́те есть столо́вая** there is a canteen at the institute; **я бу́ду при гостя́х** I will be with the guests
3 (*в присутствии*) in front of; **при мне он не хо́чет говори́ть** he doesn't want to speak in front of me; **при свиде́телях** in front of *или* in the presence of witnesses; **он всегда́ чита́ет при све́те ла́мпы** he always reads by the light of a lamp
4 (*о времени*) under; **при коммуни́стах/консерва́торах** under the communists/Conservatives; **при короле́ве Викто́рии** in the time of Queen Victoria
5 (*о наличии чего-н у кого-н*) on; **он всегда́ при деньга́х** he always has money on him; **я оста́влю э́то при себе́** I'll keep it on me; **при жела́нии мо́жно всё измени́ть** if you wish everything can be changed; **при слу́чае переда́й ему́ приве́т** if the occasion arises, give him my regards ; **он при́ сме́рти** he is close to death; **я здесь ни при чём** it has nothing to do with me.

при- *префикс* (*in verbs*; *о доведении движения до конечной цели*) *indicating achievement of final goal eg.* *прибежа́ть*; (*добавление*) *indicating addition eg.* *пристро́ить*; (*скрепление*) *indicating fastening onto sth eg.* *привинти́ть*; (*сближение*) *indicating approach of sth eg.* *придви́нуться*; (*о слабой мере действия*) *indicating slight action eg.* *приоткры́ть*; (*о сопутствующем действии*) *indicating accompanying action eg.* *припева́ть*; (*in nouns and adjectives*; *примыкающий*) *indicating adjoining position eg.* *примо́рский*.
приба́в|ить (-лю, -ишь; *impf* **прибавля́ть**) *сов перех* to add; (*увеличить*) to increase; **прибавля́ть** (~ *perf*) **в ве́се** to put on weight
▸ **приба́виться** (*impf* **прибавля́ться**) *сов возв* (*проблемы, работа итп*) to mount up ♦ *безл* (*воды в реке*) to rise; (*народу в толпе*) to grow.
прибавле́ни|е (-я) *ср* addition; (*к зарплате, воды в реке*) rise; ~ **семе́йства** new addition to the family.
приба́влю(сь) *сов см* **приба́вить(ся)**.
прибавля́|ть (-ю) *несов от* **приба́вить**.
прибау́т|ка (-ки; *gen pl* -ок) *ж* catch phrase.
прибега́|ть (-ю) *несов от* **прибе́гнуть, прибежа́ть**.
прибе́гн|уть (-у, -ешь; *impf* **прибега́ть**) *сов неперех*: ~ **к** *+dat* to resort to.
прибегу́ *итп сов см* **прибежа́ть**.
прибедня́|ться (-юсь) *несов возв* (*разг*) to pretend to be poor; (*преуменьшать свои возможности*) to show false modesty.
прибежа́ть (*как* **бежа́ть**; *см* **Table 20**) *сов неперех* to come running.
прибе́жищ|е (-а) *ср* refuge.
прибе́й(те) *сов см* **приби́ть**.
приберу́ *итп сов см* **прибра́ть**.
прибива́|ть(ся) (-ю(сь)) *несов от* **приби́ть(ся)**.
прибира́|ть (-ю) *несов от* **прибра́ть**.
приб|и́ть (-ью́, -ьёшь; *imper* -е́й(те), *impf* **прибива́ть**) *сов перех* (*прикрепить гвоздями*) to nail; (*подлеж*: *вода, волна итп*) to wash up
▸ **приби́ться** (*impf* **прибива́ться**) *сов возв* (*лодка к берегу*) to be washed up.
приближа́|ть(ся) (-ю(сь)) *несов от* **прибли́зить(ся)**.
приближе́ни|е (-я) *ср* (*дня, события*) approach.
прибли́жу(сь) *сов см* **прибли́зить(ся)**.
приблизи́тел|ьный (-ен, -ьна, -ьно) *прил* approximate.
прибли́|зить (-жу, -зишь; *impf* **приближа́ть**) *сов перех* (*придвинуть*) to move nearer; (*ускорить*) to bring nearer
▸ **прибли́зиться** (*impf* **приближа́ться**) *сов возв* (*человек к окну, машина к дому*) to approach; (*развязка, победа итп*) to draw near.
прибо́|й (-я) *м* breakers *мн*.
прибо́р (-а) *м* (*измерительный*) device; (*оптический*) instrument; (*нагревательный*) appliance; (*бритвенный, чернильный*) set.
приб|ра́ть (-еру́, -ерёшь; *impf* **прибира́ть**) *сов перех* to clear up; **прибира́ть** (~ *perf*) **что-н к рука́м** to lay one's hands on sth; **прибира́ть** (~ *perf*) **кого́-н к рука́м** to take sb in hand.
прибре́жный *прил* (*у берега моря*) coastal; (*у берега реки*) riverside *опред*.
прибу́ду *итп сов см* **прибы́ть**.
прибыва́|ть (-ю) *несов от* **прибы́ть**.
при́был|ь (-и) *ж* profit; **нереализо́ванная** ~ (*КОММ*) paper profit.

при́был|ьный (**-ен, -ьна, -ьно**) *прил* profitable.
прибы́ти|е (**-я**) *ср* arrival.
приб|ы́ть (*как* **быть**; *см* **Table 21**; *impf* **прибыва́ть**) *сов неперех* to arrive; (*вода в реке*) to rise.
прибью́(сь) *итп сов см* **приби́ть(ся)**.
прива́л (**-а**) *м* (*в пути*) stop; (*место остановки*) stopping place.
прив|али́ть (**-алю́, -а́лишь**; *impf* **прива́ливать**) *сов перех* (*придвинуть что-н тяжёлое*) to heave ◆ *неперех* (*перен*: *разг*) to turn up.
приватиза́ци|я (**-и**) *ж* (*ЭКОН*) privatization.
приватизи́р|овать (**-ую**) *(не)сов перех* to privatize.
приведе́ни|е (**-я**) *ср* (*чего-н в порядок*) bringing; (*примеров*) introduction; ~ **к прися́ге** swearing in; ~ **пригово́ра в исполне́ние** (*ЮР*) carrying out of a sentence; ~ **в движе́ние** setting in motion.
приведу́ *итп сов см* **привести́**.
прив|езти́ (**-езу́, -езёшь**; *pt* **-ёз, -езла́, -езло́**, *impf* **привози́ть**) *сов перех* to bring.
привере́длив|ый (**-, -а, -о**) *прил* fussy.
приве́ржен|ец (**-ца**) *м* (*идеи, традиции*) adherent.
приве́ржен|ный (**-, -а, -о**) *прил*: ~ (**к** *+dat*) dedicated (to).
приве́рженца *итп сущ см* **приве́рженец**.
прив|ести́ (**-еду́, -едёшь**; *pt* **-ёл,-ела́,-ело́**, *impf* **приводи́ть**) *сов перех* (*ребёнка*: *домой*) to bring; (*подлеж*: *дорога*: *к дому*) to take; (*пример*) to give; (*чьи-н слова*) to quote; ~ *(perf)* **в у́жас** to horrify; ~ *(perf)* **в отча́яние** to bring to the point of despair; ~ *(perf)* **в восто́рг** to delight; ~ *(perf)* **в изумле́ние** to astonish; ~ *(perf)* **в исполне́ние** to put into effect; ~ *(perf)* **в гото́вность** to make ready; ~ *(perf)* **в поря́док** to put in order; ~ *(perf)* **в движе́ние** to set in motion.
приве́т (**-а**) *м* greetings *мн*, regards *мн*; (*разг*: *при встрече*) hi; (: *при расставании*) bye; **посыла́ть (посла́ть** *perf*) *или* **передава́ть (переда́ть** *perf*) **кому́-н** ~ to send one's regards to sb; ~**! рад тебя́ ви́деть** hi! it's nice to see you.
приве́тлив|ый (**-, -а, -о**) *прил* friendly.
приве́тстви|е (**-я**) *ср* (*при встрече*) greeting; (*съезду, делегации*) welcome.
приве́тств|овать (**-ую**; *perf* **поприве́тствовать**) *несов перех* (*также перен*) to welcome.
привива́|ть(ся) (**-ю(сь)**) *несов от* **приви́ть(ся)**.
приви́в|ка (**-ки**; *gen pl* **-ок**) *ж* (*МЕД*) vaccination.
привиде́ни|е (**-я**) *ср* ghost.
приви́д|еться (*3sg* **-ится**, *3pl* **-ятся**, *impf* **ви́деться**) *сов безл* (*+dat*) to appear to; **мне ~елся стра́шный сон** I had a terrifying dream.
привилегиро́ванный *прил* privileged.
привиле́ги|я (**-и**) *ж* privilege.
привин|ти́ть (**-чу́, -ти́шь**; *impf* **приви́нчивать**) *сов перех* to screw on.
прив|и́ть (**-ью́, -ьёшь**; *impf* **привива́ть**) *сов перех* (*растение*) to graft; (*МЕД*): ~ **кому́-н что-н** to inoculate *или* vaccinate sb against sth; (*перен*) to cultivate sth in sb
▸ **приви́ться** (*impf* **привива́ться**) *сов возв* (*прививка, черенок*) to take; (*новшество*) to catch on.
при́вкус (**-а**) *м* flavour (*BRIT*), flavor (*US*).
привлёк *итп сов см* **привле́чь**.
привлека́тел|ьный (**-ен, -ьна, -ьно**) *прил* attractive.
привлека́|ть (**-ю**) *несов от* **привле́чь**.
привлеку́ *итп сов см* **привле́чь**.
привлече́ни|е (**-я**) *ср* (*покупателей, внимания*) attraction; (*ресурсов*) use; ~ **к суду́** taking to court; ~ **к отве́тственности** calling to account.
привл|е́чь (**-еку́, -ечёшь** *итп*, **-еку́т**; *pt* **-ёк, -екла́, -екло́**, *impf* **привлека́ть**) *сов перех* to attract; **привлека́ть (**~ *perf*) **кого́-н к** *+dat* (*к работе, к участию*) to coax sb into; (*к суду*) to take sb to; **привлека́ть (**~ *perf*) **кого́-н к разгово́ру** to draw sb into a conversation; **привлека́ть (**~ *perf*) **кого́-н к отве́тственности** to call sb to account.
привн|ести́ (**-есу́, -есёшь**; *pt* **-ёс, -есла́, -есло́**, *impf* **привноси́ть**) *сов перех*: ~ **что-н в** *+acc* to inject sth into.
привн|оси́ть (**-ошу́, -о́сишь**) *несов от* **привнести́**.
при́вод (**-а**) *м* (*электрический*) drive; (*ручной*) gear.
приво́д (**-а**) *м* (*ЮР*) arrest.
прив|оди́ть (**-ожу́, -о́дишь**) *несов от* **привести́**.
привожу́ *несов см* **привози́ть**.
приво́з (**-а**) *м* (*товаров, сырья*) supply.
прив|ози́ть (**-ожу́, -о́зишь**) *несов от* **привезти́**.
привозно́й *прил* imported.
приво́лен *прил см* **приво́льный**.
приво́ль|е (**-я**) *ср* (*степное, полевое*) expanse.
приво́л|ьный (**-ен, -ьна, -ьно**) *прил* (*луга, поля итп*) expansive; (*жизнь*) free and easy.
привра́тник (**-а**) *м* doorman (*мн* doormen).
привста|ва́ть (**-ю́**) *несов от* **привста́ть**.
привста́|ть (**-ну, -нешь**; *impf* **привстава́ть**) *сов неперех* to half rise.
привы́к|нуть (**-ну, -нешь**; *pt* **-, -ла, -ло**, *impf* **привыка́ть**) *сов неперех*: ~ *+infin* (*гулять, тратить деньги*) to get into the habit of doing; **привыка́ть (**~ *perf*) **к** *+dat* (*к новым друзьям, к школе*) to get used to; **он ~, что́бы ему́ все помога́ли** he is used to everyone helping him.
привы́чек *сущ см* **привы́чка**.
привы́чен *прил см* **привы́чный**.
привы́ч|ка (**-ки**; *gen pl* **-ек**) *ж* habit; **по ~ке** out of habit.
привы́ч|ный (**-ен, -на, -но**) *прил* (*работа, звуки*) familiar.
привью́(сь) *итп сов см* **приви́ть(ся)**.
привяжу́(сь) *итп сов см* **привяза́ть(ся)**.

привязанност|ь (**-и**) *ж* attachment.
прив|язать (**-яжу, -яжешь**; *impf* **привязывать**) *сов перех*: ~ **что-н/кого-н к** *+dat* to tie sth/sb to; **привязывать** (~ *perf*) **к себе** *+acc* (*вызвать любовь*) to endear o.s. to
▸ **привязаться** (*impf* **привязываться**) *сов возв*: ~**ся к** *+dat* (*ремнём к сиденью*) to fasten o.s. to; (*полюбить*) to become attached to; (*разг: надоедать*) to pester.
привяз|ь (**-и**) *ж* tie.
пригиба|ть(ся) (**-ю(сь)**) *несов от* **пригнуть(ся)**.
пригладить (**-жу, -дишь**; *impf* **приглаживать**) *сов перех* (*складки на платье*) to smooth out; (*волосы*) to smooth back.
пригласительный *прил*: ~ **билет** invitation.
пригла|сить (**-шу, -сишь**; *impf* **приглашать**) *сов перех* to invite; (*врача*) to call; **приглашать** (~ *perf*) **кого-н в гости** to invite sb; **приглашать** (~ *perf*) **кого-н на танец** to ask sb to dance.
приглашени|е (**-я**) *ср* invitation; (*комп*) prompt.
приглашу *сов см* **пригласить**.
приглуш|ить (**-у, -ишь**; *impf* **приглушать**) *сов перех* (*звуки*) to deaden; (*радио*) to turn down; (*краски*) to tone down; (*тона*) to soften; (*перен: боль, тоску*) to lessen.
пригля|деть (**-жу, -дишь**; *impf* **приглядывать**) *сов неперех*: ~ **за** *+instr* to look after ◆ *перех* to search out, find
▸ **приглядеться** (*impf* **приглядываться**) *сов возв*: ~**ся** (**к** *+dat*) (*к картине, к незнакомцу*) to look closely (at).
пригл|януться (**-янусь, -янешься**) *сов возв*: ~ **кому-н** to attract sb.
приг|нать (**-оню, -онишь**; *impf* **пригонять**) *сов перех* to drive; (*костюм*) to adjust, alter.
пригн|уть (**-у, -ёшь**; *impf* **пригибать**) *сов перех* (*ветку, кусты*) to bend
▸ **пригнуться** (*impf* **пригибаться**) *сов возв* (*нагнуться: человек*) to bend down; (*ветки, кусты*) to bend.
приговарива|ть (**-ю**) *несов от* **приговорить** ◆ *неперех* (*сопровождать словами*) to talk at the same time (*as doing sth*).
приговор (**-а**) *м* (*юр*) sentence; (*перен*) condemnation; **выносить** (**вынести** *perf*) ~ to pass sentence.
приговор|ить (**-ю, -ишь**; *impf* **приговаривать**) *сов перех*: ~ **кого-н к** *+dat* to sentence sb to.
пригоден *прил см* **пригодный**.
приго|диться (**-жусь, -дишься**; *impf* **пригождаться**) *сов возв* (*+dat*) to be useful to.
пригод|ный (**-ен, -на, -но**) *прил* suitable.
пригожда|ться (**-юсь**) *несов от* **пригодиться**.
пригожусь *сов см* **пригодиться**.
пригоню *итп сов см* **пригнать**.
пригоня|ть (**-ю**) *несов от* **пригнать**.
пригора|ть (*3sg* **-ет**, *3pl* **-ют**) *несов от* **пригореть**.
пригорелый *прил* burnt.
пригор|еть (*3sg* **-ит**, *3pl* **-ят**, *impf* **пригорать**) *сов неперех* to burn.
пригорка *сущ см* **пригорок**.
пригород (**-а**) *м* suburb.
пригородный *прил* (*посёлок, житель*) suburban; (*поезд, автобус*) local.
пригор|ок (**-ка**) *м* hillock.
пригорш|ня (**-ни**; *gen pl* **-ен**) *ж* handful.
приготов|ить (**-лю, -ишь**) *сов от* **готовить** ◆ (*impf* **приготавливать** *или* **приготовлять**) *перех* to prepare; (*постель*) to make; (*ванну*) to run
▸ **приготовиться** *сов от* **готовиться** ◆ *возв*: ~**ся** (**к** *+dat*) (*к путешествию*) to get ready (for); (*к уроку*) to prepare (o.s.) (for).
приготовлени|е (**-я**) *ср* preparation.
приготовлю(сь) *сов см* **приготовить(ся)**.
приготовля|ть (**-ю**) *несов от* **приготовить**.
пригрева|ть (**-ю**) *несов от* **пригреть**.
пригре|зиться (**-жусь, -зишься**) *сов от* **грезиться**.
пригре|ть (**-ю**; *impf* **пригревать**) *сов перех* (*подлеж: солнце: землю*) to warm; (*перен: сироту*) to take in.
пригро|зить(ся) (**-жу(сь), -зишь(ся)**) *сов от* **грозить(ся)**.
пригуб|ить (**-лю, -ишь**; *impf* **пригубливать**) *сов перех* to take a sip of.
прида|вать (**-ю, -ёшь**) *несов от* **придать**.
прид|авить (**-авлю, -авишь**; *impf* **придавливать**) *сов перех* to press, to squash.
придам *итп сов см* **придать**.
придан|ое (**-ого**; *decl like adj*) *ср* (*невесты*) dowry; (*новорождённого*) layette.
придаст *сов см* **придать**.
придат|ок (**-ка**) *м* (*также перен*) appendage.
придаточный *прил*: **придаточное предложение** (*линг*) subordinate clause.
придать (*как* **дать**; *см* **Table 14**; *impf* **придавать**) *сов неперех*: ~ **чего-н кому-н** (*уверенности*) to instil sth in sb; **придавать** (~ *perf*) **что-н чему-н** (*вид, форму*) to give sth to sth; (*важность*) to attach sth to sth; **придавать** (~ *perf*) **бодрости кому-н** to hearten sb; **придавать** (~ *perf*) **сил кому-н** to strengthen sb.
придач|а (**-и**) *ж*: **в** ~**у** in addition.
придашь *сов см* **придать**.
придвин|уть (**-у, -ешь**; *impf* **придвигать**) *сов перех*: ~ (**к** *+dat*) to move over *или* up (to).
придворн|ый *прил* court *опред* ◆ (**-ого**; *decl like adj*) *м* courtier.
придела|ть (**-ю**; *impf* **приделывать**) *сов перех*: ~ **что-н к** *+dat* to attach *или* fix sth to.
прид|ержать (**-ержу, -ержишь**; *impf* **придерживать**) *сов перех* (*дверь*) to hold

(steady); (*лошадь*) to restrain.
приде́ржива|ться (**-юсь**) *несов возв* (*+gen*: *каких-н взглядов*) to hold; (*за перила*): **~ за** *+acc* to hold onto.
придеру́сь *итп сов см* **придра́ться**
придира́|ться (**-ю**) *несов от* **придра́ться**.
приди́р|ка (**-ки**; *gen pl* **-ок**) *ж* quibble.
приди́рчив|ый (**-, -а, -о**) *прил* (*человек*) fussy; (*замечание, взгляд*) critical.
прид|ра́ться (**-еру́сь, -ерёшься**; *impf* **придира́ться**) *сов возв*: **~ к** *+dat* to find fault with.
приду́(сь) *итп сов см* **прийти́(сь)**.
приду́ма|ть (**-ю**; *impf* **приду́мывать**) *сов перех* (*отговорку, причину*) to think of *или* up; (*новый прибор*) to devise; (*песню, стихотворение*) to make up; **он ~л, как спасти́ положе́ние** he thought of how to save the situation.
приду́рива|ться (**-юсь**) *несов возв* (*разг*) to pretend to be ignorant.
приду́сь *итп сов см* **прийти́сь**.
придыха́ни|е (**-я**) *ср* (*ЛИНГ*) aspiration.
приеда́|ться (**-юсь**) *несов от* **прие́сться**.
приеди́мся *итп сов см* **прие́сться**.
прие́ду *итп сов см* **прие́хать**.
приедя́тся *сов см* **прие́сться**.
прие́зд (**-а**) *м* arrival.
приезжа́|ть (**-ю**) *несов от* **прие́хать**
прие́зж|ий (**-ая, -ее, -ие**) *прил* visiting
приём (**-а**) *м* reception; (*у врача*) surgery (*BRIT*), office (*US*); (*борьбы, гимнастический*) technique; (*наказания, воздействия*) means; **за оди́н ~** in one go; **в два/в три ~а** in two/three attempts; **устра́ивать (устро́ить** *perf*) **~** to organize a reception; **запи́сываться (записа́ться** *perf*) **на ~ к** *+dat* to make an appointment to see.
приёмк|а (**-и**) *ж* (*товаров*) receipt.
приёмн|ая (**-ой**; *decl like adj*) *ж* (*также*: **~ ко́мната**) reception.
приёмник (**-а**) *м* (*радиоприёмник*) radio; (*связь*) receiver.
приёмный *прил* (*часы*) reception *опред*; (*день*) visiting *опред*; (*экзамены*) entrance *опред*; (*комиссия*) selection *опред*; (*родители, дети*) adoptive; **приёмный поко́й** *room where newly-arrived patients register and are given inital checkup before going to the ward*.
приёмся *сов см* **прие́сться**.
при|е́сться (*как* **есть**; *см* **Table 15**; *impf* **приеда́ться**) *сов возв*: **~ кому́-н** (*разг*) to bore sb stiff.
прие́|хать (*как* **е́хать**; *см* **Table 19**; *impf* **приезжа́ть**) *сов неперех* to arrive *или* come (*by transport*).
приёшься *сов см* **прие́сться**.
приж|а́ть (**-му́, -мёшь**; *impf* **прижима́ть**) *сов перех* (*разг*: *притеснить*) to put the screws on; **прижима́ть (~** *perf*) **что-н/кого́-н к** *+dat* to press sth/sb to *или* against
▸ **прижа́ться** (*impf* **прижима́ться**) *сов возв*: **~ся к** *+dat* to press o.s. against; (*ребёнок к груди*) to snuggle up to.
приж|е́чь (**-гу́, -жёшь** *итп*, **-гу́т**; *impf* **прижига́ть**) *сов перех* to cauterize.
прижива́|ться (**-юсь**) *несов от* **прижи́ться**
приживу́сь *итп сов см* **прижи́ться**
прижига́|ть (**-ю**) *несов от* **приже́чь**.
прижи́зненн|ый *прил*: **~ая сла́ва** fame during one's lifetime; **он ви́дел мно́го ~ых изда́ний свои́х поэ́м** many books of his poems were published during his lifetime.
прижима́|ть(ся) (**-ю(сь)**) *несов от* **прижа́ть(ся)**.
прижи́мист|ый (**-, -а, -о**) *прил* (*разг*) tightfisted.
прижи́|ться (**-ву́сь, -вёшься**; *pt* **-лся, -ла́сь, -ло́сь**, *impf* **прижива́ться**) *сов возв* (*человек*) to settle in, get o.s. settled; (*животные*) to adapt, become acclimatized (*BRIT*) *или* acclimated (*US*); (*растения*) to take rest.
прижму́(сь) *сов см* **прижа́ть(ся)**.
приз (**-а**; *nom pl* **-ы́**) *м* prize.
призаду́ма|ться (**-юсь**; *impf* **призаду́мываться**) *сов возв*: **~ над** *+instr* *или* **о** *+prp* to reflect upon.
призва́ни|е (**-я**) *ср* (*к искусству, к науке итп*) vocation; (*предназначение*) calling; **~ теа́тра – воспи́тывать** the purpose of the theatre is to educate.
приз|ва́ть (**-ову́, -овёшь**; *pt* **-ва́л, -вала́, -ва́ло**, *impf* **призыва́ть**) *сов перех* (*на борьбу, к защите страны*) to call, summon; **призыва́ть (~** *perf*) **к ми́ру/разоруже́нию** to call for peace/disarmament; **призыва́ть (~** *perf*) **кого́-н к споко́йствию/повинове́нию** to appeal to sb to be calm/obedient; **призыва́ть (~** *perf*) **кого́-н к поря́дку** to call sb to order; **призыва́ть (~** *perf*) **в а́рмию** to call up (to join the army).
призе́мист|ый (**-, -а, -о**) *прил* (*человек*) squat.
приземл|и́ть (**-ю́, -и́шь**; *impf* **приземля́ть**) *сов перех* to land
▸ **приземли́ться** (*impf* **приземля́ться**) *сов возв* to land
призёр (**-а**) *м* prizewinner.
при́зм|а (**-ы**) *ж* prism; **сквозь** *или* **че́рез ~у** *+gen* (*перен*) in the light of.
призна|ва́ть(ся) (**-ю́(сь), -ёшь(ся)**) *несов от* **призна́ть(ся)**.
при́знак (**-а**) *м* (*кризиса, успеха*) sign; (*отравления*) symptom; **без ~ов жи́зни** not showing any sign of life.
призна́ни|е (**-я**) *ср* (*государства, писателя*) recognition; (*своего бессилия, чьих-н достижений*) acknowledgment, recognition; (*в любви*) declaration; (*в преступлении*) confession.
при́знан|ный (**-, -а, -о**) *прил* recognized.
призна́телен *прил см* **призна́тельный**.
призна́тельност|ь (**-и**) *ж* gratitude.
призна́тел|ьный (**-ен, -ьна, -ьно**) *прил* grateful.
призна́|ть (**-ю**; *impf* **признава́ть**) *сов перех*

(*правительство, чьи-н права*) to recognize; (*положительно оценить: книгу, фильм*) to acclaim; (*счесть*): **~ что-н/кого-н** *+instr* to recognize sth/sb as

▸ **призна́|ться** (*impf* **признава́ться**) *сов возв*: **~ся кому́-н в чём-н** (*в преступлении*) to confess sth to sb; **признава́ться (~ся** *perf***) кому́-н в любви́** to make a declaration of love to sb; **~ся** *или* **призна́юсь, я Вас не понима́ю** I have to admit that I don't understand you.

призов|о́й *прил* (*деньги*) prize *опред*; **~а́я меда́ль** prizewinner's medal; **~о́е ме́сто** medal position.

призову́ *итп сов см* **призва́ть.**

призо́р (-а) *м*: **без ~а** (*разг*) unattended.

при́зрак (-а) *м* ghost.

при́зрач|ный (-ен, -на, -но) *прил* (*успех, надежды*) illusory; (*опасность*) imagined.

призы́в (-а) *м* (*к восстанию, к защите*) call; (*: в армию*) conscription; (*лозунг*) slogan ◆ *собир* call-up.

призыва́|ть (-ю) *несов от* **призва́ть.**

призывни́к (-а́) *м* conscript.

призывно́й *прил* (*возраст*) call-up *опред*; (*пункт*) recruiting *опред*.

призы́вный *прил* summoning *опред*.

при́иск (-а) *м* mine.

прийти́ (*как* **идти́**; *см* **Table 18**; *impf* **приходи́ть**) *сов неперех* (*идя, достичь*) to come (*on foot*); (*письмо, телеграмма*) to arrive; (*весна, час свободы*) to come; (*достигнуть*): **~ к** *+dat* (*к власти, к выводу*) to come to; (*к демократии*) to achieve; **приходи́ть (~** *perf***) в у́жас/недоуме́ние** to be horrified/bewildered; **приходи́ть (~** *perf***) в восто́рг** to go into raptures; **приходи́ть (~** *perf***) в него́дность** to become worthless; **приходи́ть (~** *perf***) в упа́док** to go into decline; **приходи́ть (~** *perf***) в запу́щенность** to fall into neglect; **приходи́ть (~** *perf***) кому́-н в го́лову** *или* **на ум** to occur to sb; **приходи́ть (~** *perf***) в себя́** (*после обморока*) to come to *или* round; (*успокоиться*) to come to one's senses

▸ **прийти́сь** (*impf* **приходи́ться**) *сов возв*: **~сь на** *+acc* to fall on; (*попасть*): **~сь по** *+dat* to land on; (*подойти*): **~сь по** *+dat*/**к** *+dat* (*одежда, ключ*) to fit; (*вещь: по вкусу*) to suit ◆ *безл* (*+infin; уступить, пойти на компромисс итп*) to have to do; **(нам) придётся согласи́ться** we'll have to agree; **нам пришло́сь тяжело́** we had a hard time; **как придётся** anyhow; **где придётся** anywhere; **что придётся** anything.

прикажу́ *итп сов см* **приказа́ть.**

прика́з (-а) *м* order; **отдава́ть (отда́ть** *perf***) ~** to give an order.

приказа́ни|е (-я) *ср* = **прика́з.**

прик|аза́ть (-ажу́, -а́жешь; *impf* **прика́зывать**) *сов неперех*: **~ кому́-н** *+infin* to order sb to do; **как ~а́жете** as you like.

приказно́й *прил* (*тон, жест*) commanding; **в приказно́м поря́дке** in the form of an order.

прика́зчик (-а) *м* (*в магазине*) sales assistant (*BRIT*) *или* clerk (*US*); (*в помещичьем хозяйстве*) *manager of estate or farm.*

прика́зыва|ть (-ю) *несов от* **приказа́ть.**

прика́лыва|ть (-ю) *несов от* **приколо́ть.**

прика́нчива|ть (-ю) *несов от* **прико́нчить.**

прикарма́н|ить (-ю, -ишь; *impf* **прикарма́нивать**) *сов перех* (*разг*) to pocket.

прика́рмлива|ть (-ю) *несов перех* (*младенца*) to supplement the diet of.

прикаса́ни|е (-я) *ср* (*рук*) touch.

прикаса́|ться (-юсь) *несов от* **прикосну́ться.**

прик|ати́ть (-ачу́, -а́тишь; *impf* **прика́тывать**) *сов перех* to roll up ◆ *неперех* (*разг: приехать*) to show up.

прики́н|уть (-у, -ешь; *impf* **прики́дывать**) *сов неперех* (*разг: посчитать*) to work out (roughly)

▸ **прики́нуться** (*impf* **прики́дываться**) *сов возв* (*+instr; разг*) to pretend to be.

прикла́д (-а) *м* (*ружья, автомата*) butt (*of gun etc*).

прикладно́й *прил* applied; **прикладна́я програ́мма** (*КОМП*) application program; **прикладно́е иску́сство** applied art.

прикла́дыва|ть(ся) (-ю(сь)) *несов от* **приложи́ть(ся).**

прикле́|ить (-ю, -ишь; *impf* **прикле́ивать**) *сов перех* to glue, stick

▸ **прикле́иться** (*impf* **прикле́иваться**) *сов возв* to stick.

приключа́|ться (*3sg* **-ется**, *3pl* **-ются**) *несов от* **приключи́ться.**

приключе́ни|е (-я) *ср* adventure.

приключе́ническ|ий (-ая, -ое, -ие) *прил* adventure *опред*.

приключ|и́ться (*3sg* **-и́тся**, *3pl* **-а́тся**, *impf* **приключа́ться**) *сов возв* (*разг: произойти*) to happen.

прик|ова́ть (-ую́; *impf* **прико́вывать**) *сов перех* (*перен: внимание, взгляд*) to fix; **прико́вывать (~** *perf***) кого́-н к** *+dat* to chain sb to; (*перен*) to confine sb to.

прико́л (-а) *м*: **стоя́ть на ~е** to be moored.

прик|оло́ть (-олю́, -о́лешь; *impf* **прика́лывать**) *сов перех* to fasten, fix.

прикомандир|ова́ть (-у́ю; *impf* **прикомандиро́вывать**) *сов перех* to second.

прико́нч|ить (-у, -ишь; *impf* **прика́нчивать**) *сов перех* (*умертвить*) to finish off.

прикорн|у́ть (-у́, -ёшь) *сов неперех* (*разг*) to curl up.

прикосн|у́ться (-у́сь, -ёшься; *impf* **прикаса́ться**) *сов возв*: **~ к** *+dat* to touch lightly.

прикреп|и́ть (-лю́, -и́шь; *impf* **прикрепля́ть)** *сов перех*: ~ **что-н к** *+dat* (*деталь, бант*) to fix sth to; **прикрепля́ть (~** *perf***) кого́-н/что-н к** *+dat* (*советника к предприятию, институт к заводу*) to attach sb/sth to.
прикри́кн|уть (-у, -ешь; *impf* **прикри́кивать)** *сов неперех*: ~ **на** *+acc* to shout *или* yell at.
прикро́ю(сь) *итп сов см* **прикры́ть(ся)**.
прикрыва́|ть(ся) (-ю) *несов от* **прикры́ть(ся)**.
прикры́ти|е (-я) *ср* (*махинаций*) cover-up; (*тыла, ВОЕН*) cover; **под ~м** *+gen* under the guise of.
прикр|ы́ть (-о́ю, -о́ешь; *impf* **прикрыва́ть)** *сов перех* to cover; (*закрыть*) to close (over); (*разг: ликвидировать*) to wind up; (*скрывать*) to cover up
▸ **прикры́ться** (*impf* **прикрыва́ться)** *сов возв* (*+instr; одеялом, плащом*) to cover o.s. with; (*отговорками, риторикой*) to hide behind; (*разг: ликвидироваться*) to close down.
прик|ури́ть (-урю́, -у́ришь; *impf* **прику́ривать)** *сов неперех* to get a light (*from lit cigarette*).
прик|уси́ть (-ушу́, -у́сишь; *impf* **прику́сывать)** *сов перех* (*губу, язык*) to bite.
прила́в|ок (-ка) *м* (*в магазине*) counter; (*на рынке*) stall.
прилага́тельн|ое (-ого; *decl like adj*) *ср* (*ЛИНГ: также:* **имя** ~) adjective.
прилага́|ть (-ю) *несов от* **приложи́ть**.
прила́|дить (-жу, -дишь; *impf* **прила́живать)** *сов перех*: ~ **что-н к** *+dat* to fit sth on to.
приласка́|ть(ся) (-ю(сь)) *сов от* **ласка́ть(ся)**.
прилёг *итп сов см* **приле́чь**.
прилега́|ть (*3sg* **-ет**, *3pl* **-ют)** *несов неперех*: ~ **к** *+dat* (*касаться*) to fit tightly; (*находиться рядом*) to adjoin.
прилежа́ни|е (-я) *ср* diligence.
приле́ж|ный (-ен, -на, -но) *прил* diligent.
прил|епи́ть (-еплю́, -е́пишь; *impf* **прилепля́ть)** *сов перех* to stick.
приле|те́ть (-чу́, -ти́шь; *impf* **прилета́ть)** *сов неперех* to arrive (*by air*), fly in.
прил|е́чь (-я́гу, -я́жешь *итп*, **-я́гут;** *pt* **-ёг, -егла́, -егло́)** *сов неперех* to lie down for a while.
прили́в (-а) *м* (*в море, в океане*) tide; (*денег, туристов*) flood; (*негодования, энергии*) surge.
прилива́|ть (-ю) *несов от* **прили́ть**.
прилижу́ *итп сов см* **прилиза́ть**.
прили́занный *прил* (*разг: волосы*) slicked-down; (*вид*) fastidious; (*человек*) pernickety (*BRIT*), persnickety (*US*).
прил|иза́ть (-ижу́, -и́жешь; *impf* **прили́зывать)** *сов перех* (*разг: волосы*) to slick down.
прили́п|нуть (-ну, -нешь; *pt* **-, -ла, -ло**, *impf* **прилипа́ть** *или* **ли́пнуть)** *сов неперех*: ~ **к** *+dat* to stick to; (*разг: к девушке, к незнакомцу*) to cling to.
прил|и́ть (*3sg* **-ьёт**, *3pl* **-ью́т**, *pt* **-и́л, -ила́, -и́ло**, *impf* **прилива́ть)** *сов неперех* (*вода в море*) to flow; (*кровь*) to rush.
прили́чен *прил см* **прили́чный**.
прили́чи|е (-я) *ср* decency; (*обычно мн*) manners *мн*.
прили́ч|ный (-ен, -на, -но) *прил* (*пристойный: человек*) decent; (*: манеры*) proper; (*достаточно хороший, большой*) fair, decent.
приложе́ни|е (-я) *ср* (*силы, энергии*) application; (*к журналу*) supplement; (*к документации*) addendum (*мн* addenda).
прил|ожи́ть (-ожу́, -о́жишь; *impf* **прилага́ть)** *сов перех* (*присоединить*) to affix; (*силу, знания итп*) to apply; (*impf* **прикла́дывать)**: ~ **что-н к** *+dat* (*руку ко лбу*) to put sth to; (*трубку к уху*) to hold sth to; **прилага́ть (~** *perf***) ру́ку к** *+dat* to put one's hand to; **ума́ не ~ожу́** (*разг*) I don't have a clue
▸ **приложи́ться** (*impf* **прикла́дываться)** *сов возв*: **~ся у́хом/губа́ми к** *+dat* to press one's ear/lips against; **остально́е ~о́жится** the rest is a matter of course.
прильёт *итп сов см* **прили́ть**.
прильн|у́ть (-у́, -ёшь) *сов от* **льнуть ♦** *неперех* (*приникнуть*): ~ **к** *+dat* (*к чьей-н груди*) to cling to; (*к двери, к окну*) to press o.s. against.
приля́гу *итп сов см* **приле́чь**.
при́м|а (-ы) *ж* (*МУЗ: ведущий голос*) lead; (*разг: о балерине*) prima ballerina.
при́м|а-балери́н|а (-ы, -ы) *ж* prima ballerina.
прим|ани́ть (-аню́, -а́нишь) *сов перех* (*разг*) to lure.
прима́н|ка (-ки; *gen pl* **-ок)** *ж* bait.
примелька́|ться (-юсь) *сов возв* to become familiar.
примене́ни|е (-я) *ср* (*оружия*) use; (*машин, лекарств*) application; (*мер, метода*) adoption; **в ~и к** *+dat* in application to.
примени́м|ый (-, -а, -о) *прил* applicable.
примени́тельно *предл*: ~ **к** *+dat* in conformity with.
прим|ени́ть (-еню́, -е́нишь; *impf* **применя́ть)** *сов перех* (*меры*) to implement; (*силу*) to use; **применя́ть (~** *perf***) что-н (к** *+dat***)** (*метод, теорию*) to apply sth (to); **применя́ть (~** *perf***) са́нкции к** *+dat* to impose sanctions on.
применя́|ться (*3sg* **-ется**, *3pl* **-ются)** *несов неперех* (*использоваться*) to be used.
приме́р (-а) *м* example; **к ~у** for example; **не в ~** *+dat* unlike; **по ~у** *+gen* (*сходно с*) after the example of; **ста́вить (поста́вить** *perf***) кого́-н/что-н в** ~ to hold sb/sth up as an example; **брать (взять** *perf***) ~ с** *+gen* to follow the example of.
приме́рен *прил см* **приме́рный**.
примёрз|нуть (-ну, -нешь; *pt* **-, -ла, -ло**, *impf* **примерза́ть)** *сов неперех*: ~ **(к** *+dat***)** to freeze (to).
приме́р|ить (-ю, -ишь; *impf* **примеря́ть)** *сов перех* to try on.
приме́р|ка (-ки; *gen pl* **-ок)** *ж* trying on.
приме́рно *нареч* (*образцово*) in an exemplary fashion; (*приблизительно*) approximately.

приме́р|ный (-ен, -на, -но) *прил* (*образцовый*) exemplary; (*приблизительный*) approximate.
приме́рок *сущ см* **приме́рка.**
примеря́|ть (-ю) *несов от* **приме́рить.**
при́мес|ь (-и) *ж* dash.
приме́т|а (-ы) *ж* (*признак*) sign; (*суеверная*) omen; **она́ у него́ на ~е** he has his eye on her.
примета́|ть (-ю; *impf* **примётывать)** *сов перех* to stitch on, tack on (*BRIT*).
приме́тен *прил см* **приме́тный.**
приме́|тить (-чу, -тишь; *impf* **примеча́ть)** *сов перех* (*разг*) to notice.
приме́т|ный (-ен, -на, -но) *прил* (*заметный: человек*) conspicuous; (: *событие*) prominent.
примётыва|ть (-ю) *несов от* **примета́ть.**
примеча́ни|е (-я) *ср* note, comment.
примеча́тел|ьный (-ен, -ьна, -ьно) *прил* (*событие, внешность*) remarkable; (*изменение*) notable.
примеча́|ть (-ю) *несов от* **приме́тить.**
примечу́ *сов см* **приме́тить.**
примеша́|ть (-ю; *impf* **приме́шивать)** *сов перех* (*перен*) to bring; **приме́шивать (~** *perf*) **(в** *+acc*) to add (to), mix in(to).
примина́|ть (-ю) *несов от* **примя́ть.**
примире́ни|е (-я) *ср* reconciliation.
примир|и́ть (-ю́, -и́шь; *impf* **примиря́ть** *или* **мири́ть)** *сов перех*: **~ кого́-н с кем-н** to reconcile sb with sb; **примиря́ть (~** *perf*) **кого́-н с чем-н** to help sb come to terms with sth
▸ **примири́ться** (*impf* **примиря́ться**) *сов возв*: **~ся с** *+instr* (*с врагом, с мужем*) to be reconciled with; (*с действительностью*) to reconcile o.s. to.
примити́в|ный (-ен, -на, -но) *прил* primitive.
примкн|у́ть (-у́, -ёшь; *impf* **примыка́ть)** *сов неперех*: **~ к** *+dat* (*к партии*) to join; (*к большинству*) to side with.
примну́ *итп сов см* **примя́ть.**
примо́лкн|уть (-у, -ешь) *сов неперех* (*разг: умолкнуть*) to shush.
примо́рск|ий (-ая, -ое, -ие) *прил* seaside *опред.*
примо́рь|е (-я) *ср* seaside.
примо|сти́ться (-щу́сь, -сти́шься) *сов возв* (*разг*) to perch o.s.
примо́ч|ка (-ки; *gen pl* **-ек)** *ж* (*процедура*) bathing; (*лекарство*) lotion.
примощу́сь *сов см* **примости́ться.**
приму́(сь) *итп сов см* **приня́ть(ся).**
при́мул|а (-ы) *ж* (*БОТ*) primrose.
при́мус (-а) *м* Primus (stove) ®.
примч|а́ться (-у́сь, -и́шься) *несов возв* to come tearing up.
примыка́|ть (-ю) *несов от* **примкну́ть ◆** *неперех* (*прилегать*): **~ к** *+dat* to adjoin.
примя́|ть (-ну́, -нёшь; *impf* **примина́ть)** *сов перех* (*траву*) to trample on.
принадлеж|а́ть (-у́, -и́шь) *несов неперех*: **~** *+dat* to belong to; (*заслуга*) to go to; (*роль*) to be played by; **~** (*impf*) **к** *+dat* (*входить в состав*) to belong to, be a member of.
принадле́жност|ь (-и) *ж* characteristic; (*обычно мн: охотничьи, рыболовные*) tackle; (*письменные*) accessories *мн*; (*вхождение в состав*): **~ к** *+dat* membership of.
принево́л|ить (-ю, -ишь) *сов от* **нево́лить.**
прин|ести́ (-есу́, -есёшь; *pt* **-ёс, -есла́, -есло́,** *impf* **приноси́ть)** *сов перех* (*стул, ребёнка, удачу итп*) to bring; (*подлеж: животные*) to bear; (: *растения*) to yield; (*доход, прибыль итп*) to bring in; (*извинения, благодарность*) to express; (*присягу*) to take; **приноси́ть (~** *perf*) **по́льзу** to be of use; **приноси́ть (~** *perf*) **вред** to harm; **приноси́ть (~** *perf*) **что-н в же́ртву** to sacrifice sth.
прини́|зить (-жу, -зишь; *impf* **принижа́ть)** *сов перех* (*унизить*) to humiliate; (*умалить*) to belittle.
прини́к|нуть (-ну, -нешь; *pt* **-, -ла, -ло,** *impf* **приника́ть)** *сов неперех*: **~ к** *+dat* (*к земле*) to press o.s. to; (*к подушке итп*) to nestle up against; (*к другу*) to snuggle up to; (*к двери, к окну*) to press o.s. against.
принима́|ть(ся) (-ю(сь)) *несов от* **приня́ть(ся).**
принорови́|ться (-лю́сь, -и́шься; *impf* **принора́вливаться)** *сов возв*: **~ к** *+dat* (*к обстоятельствам*) to adapt o.s. to; (*к машине*) to get used to; (*+infin*) to get used to doing.
прино|си́ть (-ошу́, -о́сишь) *несов от* **принести́.**
при́нтер (-а) *м* (*КОМП*) printer.
принуди́тел|ьный (-ен, -ьна, -ьно) *прил* (*труд, лечение итп*) forced; (*меры*) compulsory.
прину́|дить (-жу, -дишь; *impf* **принужда́ть)** *сов перех*: **~ кого́-н/что-н к** *+dat/+infin* to force sb/sth into/to do.
принужде́ни|е (-я) *ср* compulsion; **по ~ю** under compulsion.
принуждён|ный (-ён, -на, -но) *прил* forced.
прину́жу *сов см* **прину́дить.**
принц (-а) *м* prince.
принце́сс|а (-ы) *ж* princess.
при́нцип (-а) *м* principle; **в ~е** (*в основном*) in principle; **из ~а** on principle; **по ~у** *+gen* on the principle of.
принципиа́л|ьный (-ен, -ьна, -ьно) *прил* (*человек, политика*) of principle; (*согласие, договорённость*) in principle.
при́нят|ый (-, -а, -о) *прил* accepted.
при|ня́ть (-му́, -мешь; *pt* **-ня́л, -няла́, -няло́,** *impf* **принима́ть)** *сов перех* to take; (*подарок, критику, условия*) to accept; (*какой-н пост*) to take up; (*гостей, делегацию, телеграмму*) to receive; (*закон, резолюцию, поправку*) to pass;

(*отношение, вид*) to take on; (*христианство итп*) to adopt; **принима́ть (~ *perf*) в/на** *+acc* (*в университет, на работу*) to accept for; **принима́ть (~ *perf*) что-н/кого-н за** *+acc* to mistake sth/sb for; (*счесть*) to take sth/sb as; **принима́ть (~ *perf*) ро́ды** to deliver a baby
▸ **приня́ться** (*impf* **принима́ться**) *сов возв* (*растение*) to take root; (*+infin; приступить*) to get down to doing; **принима́ться (~ся *perf*) за** *+acc* (*приступить*) to get down to; (*за лентяев, за преступников*) to take in hand; (*за десерт, за вино*) to start *или* get started on.
приободр|и́ть (-ю́, -и́шь; *impf* **приободря́ть)** *сов перех* to cheer up
▸ **приободри́ться** (*impf* **приободря́ться**) *несов возв* to cheer up.
приобр|ести́ (-ету́, -етёшь; *pt* **-ёл, -ела́, -ело́,** *impf* **приобрета́ть)** *сов перех* to acquire; (*друзей, врагов*) to make; (*опыт*) to gain.
приобрете́ни|е (-я) *ср* acquisition; (*КОММ*) procurement.
приобрету́ *итп сов см* **приобрести́.**
приобщ|и́ть (-у́, -и́шь; *impf* **приобща́ть)** *сов перех* (*приложить*) to attach; (*познакомить*): ~ **кого́-н/что-н к** *+dat* to introduce sb/sth to; **приобща́ть (~ *perf*) к де́лу** to file
▸ **приобщи́ться** (*impf* **приобща́ться**) *сов возв*: ~ **к** *+dat* to become involved in.
приоде́|ть (-ну, -нешь) *сов перех* (*разг*) to dress up.
приорите́т (-а) *м* priority.
приорите́т|ный (-ен, -на, -но) *прил* main.
приостан|ови́ть (-овлю́, -о́вишь; *impf* **приостана́вливать)** *сов перех* to suspend.
приоткр|ы́ть (-о́ю, -о́ешь; *impf* **приоткрыва́ть)** *сов перех* (*дверь*) to open slightly; (*глаза*) to half open.
припада́|ть (-ю) *несов от* **припа́сть.**
припа́д|ок (-ка) *м* (*сердечный*) attack; (*гнева*) fit; (*веселья*) outburst; **истери́ческий** ~ fit of hysterics.
припаду́ *итп сов см* **припа́сть.**
припа́ива|ть (-ю) *несов от* **припая́ть.**
припа́р|ка (-ки; *gen pl* **-ок)** *ж* (*МЕД*) poultice.
прип|асти́ (-асу́, -асёшь; *pt* **-а́с, -асла́, -асло́,** *impf* **припаса́ть)** *сов перех* (*еду*) to store up; (*деньги*) to save up.
припа́|сть (-ду́, -дёшь; *impf* **припада́ть)** *сов неперех*: ~ **к** *+dat* to throw o.s. at.
припасу́ *итп сов см* **припасти́.**
припа́с|ы (-ов) *мн* (*еды, денежные*) supplies; (*ВОЕН: боевые, ружейные*) ammunition.
припая́|ть (-ю; *impf* **припа́ивать)** *сов перех* (*приделать паянием*) to solder on.
припе́в (-а) *м* (*песни*) chorus, refrain.
припева́ючи *нареч* (*разг*): **жить** ~ to live the life of Riley.
припека́|ть (*3sg* **-ет**) *несов неперех* (*солнце*) to be burning hot.
прип|ере́ть (-ру́, -рёшь; *pt* **-ёр, -ёрла, -ёрло,** *impf* **припира́ть)** *сов перех* (*разг*): ~ **к** *+dat* (*прижать*) to shove against; **припира́ть (~ *perf*) к сте́нке** (*перен: разг*) to put in a tight spot.
прип|иса́ть (-ишу́, -и́шешь; *impf* **припи́сывать)** *сов перех* (*написать в дополнение*) to add; (*прикрепить*): ~ **кого́-н/что-н к** *+dat* to attach sb/sth to; (*счесть следствием*): ~ **что-н чему́-н** to put sth down to sth; (*счесть принадлежащим*): ~ **что-н кому́-н** to attribute sth to sb.
припи́с|ка (-ки; *gen pl* **-ок)** *ж* (*в письме*) postscript; (: *в документе*) addition; (*обычно мн: ложные данные: в отчёте, в докладе*) tampering with facts and figures.
припи́сыва|ть (-ю) *несов от* **приписа́ть.**
припишу́ *итп сов см* **приписа́ть.**
припл|ести́ (-ету́, -етёшь; *pt* **-ёл, -ела́, -ело́,** *impf* **приплета́ть)** *сов перех* (*вплетая, присоединить*) to plait in; (*перен: разг: имя*) to drag in; (: *событие, факт*) to drag up
▸ **приплести́сь** *сов возв* (*разг*) to drag o.s. along.
приплю́снут|ый (-, -а, -о) *прил* (*нос*) flat.
припля́сыва|ть (-ю) *несов неперех* to skip.
приподнима́|ть(ся) (-ю(сь)) *несов от* **приподня́ть(ся).**
приподниму́(сь) *итп сов см* **приподня́ть(ся).**
припо́днят|ый (-, -а, -о) *прил* (*оживлённый*) cheerful; (*торжественный*) elevated.
приподн|я́ть (-иму́, -и́мешь; *impf* **приподнима́ть)** *сов перех* (*чемодан*) to lift slightly; (*занавес*) to raise slightly
▸ **приподня́ться** (*impf* **приподнима́ться**) *сов возв* to raise o.s. a little.
припо́мн|ить (-ю, -ишь; *impf* **припомина́ть)** *сов перех* to remember; **припомина́ть (~ *perf*) что-н кому́-н** to make sb remember sth.
припра́в|а (-ы) *ж* seasoning.
припру́ *итп сов см* **приперéть.**
припря́|тать (-чу, -чешь; *impf* **припря́тывать)** *сов перех* (*разг*) to stash (away).
припугн|у́ть (-у́, -ёшь; *impf* **припу́гивать)** *сов перех* (*разг*) to put the wind up.
при́пуск (-а) *м* allowance.
прип|усти́ть (-ущу́, -у́стишь; *impf* **припуска́ть)** *сов неперех* (*разг: побежать*) to speed up.
припу́хлый *прил* slightly swollen.
припущу́ *сов см* **припусти́ть.**
приравня́|ть (-ю; *impf* **прира́внивать)** *сов перех*: ~ **кого́-н/что-н к** *+dat* to equate sb/sth with.
прир|асти́ (-асту́, -астёшь; *pt* **-о́с, -осла́, -осло́,** *impf* **прираста́ть)** *сов неперех* (*прижиться*) to take; (*увеличиться*) to increase; (*перен*): ~ **к** *+dat* to become rooted to.
приро́д|а (-ы) *ж* nature; (*места вне города*) countryside; **от ~ы, по ~е** by nature; **жива́я** ~ natural world.
приро́дный *прил* natural; (*врождённый*) innate; **приро́дные бога́тства** natural resources; **приро́дный газ** natural gas.
природове́дени|е (-я) *ср* natural history.

природоохра́н|а (-ы) *ж* nature conservation.
природоохра́нный *прил* conservation *опред.*
прирождённый *прил* (*чувство, грация*) inborn; (*учитель, художник*) born.
прирóс *итп сов см* **прирасти́.**
прирóст (-а) *м* (*населения*) growth; (*доходов, урожая*) increase.
приручи́ть (-у́, -и́шь; *impf* **прируча́ть)** *сов перех* (*животное*) to tame; (*перен: человека*) to bring to heel.
приса́жива|ться (-юсь) *несов от* **присе́сть.**
приса́сыва|ться (-юсь) *несов от* **присоса́ться.**
присво́|ить (-ю, -ишь; *impf* **присва́ивать)** *сов перех* to appropriate; (*дать*): **~ что-н кому́-н** to confer sth on sb.
приседа́ни|е (-я) *ср* squatting (*physical exercise*).
приседа́|ть (-ю) *несов от* **присе́сть.**
присе́ст (-а) *м* (*разг*): **в** *или* **за оди́н ~** at one sitting *или* a single sitting.
прис|е́сть (-я́ду, -я́дешь; *impf* **приседа́ть)** *сов неперех* to squat; (*impf* **приса́живаться**) to sit down (*for a short while*).
приск|ака́ть (-ачу́, -а́чешь; *impf* **приска́кивать)** *сов неперех* (*лошадь, всадник*) to gallop up, come galloping up; (*разг: быстро прийти/приехать*) to come tearing up.
прискóрбен *прил см* **прискóрбный.**
прискóрби|е (-я) *ср*: **к мóему глубóкому ~ю** to my deepest regret; **с глубóким ~м** with deepest regret.
прискóрб|ный (-ен, -на, -но) *прил* regrettable.
при|сла́ть (-шлю́, -шлёшь; *impf* **присыла́ть)** *сов перех* to send.
прислон|и́ть (-ю́, -и́шь; *impf* **прислоня́ть)** *сов перех*: **~ что-н к** *+dat* to lean sth against
▸ **прислони́ться** (*impf* **прислоня́ться**) *сов возв*: **~ся к** *+ dat* to lean against.
прислу́г|а (-и) *ж собир* servants *мн.*
прислу́жива|ть (-ю) *несов неперех* (*+dat; официант*) to wait on
▸ **прислу́живаться** *несов возв* to ingratiate o.s., grovel.
прислу́ша|ться (-юсь; *impf* **прислу́шиваться)** *сов возв*: **~ к** *+dat* (*к звуку*) to listen to; (*к совету*) to take heed of.
присма́трива|ть (-ю) *несов от* **присмотре́ть** ◆ *перех* to look for
▸ **присма́триваться** *несов от* **присмотре́ться.**
присмире́|ть (-ю) *сов неперех* to quieten (*BRIT*) *или* quiet (*US*) down, calm down.
присмир|и́ть (-ю́, -и́шь; *impf* **присмиря́ть)** *сов перех* to quieten (*BRIT*), quiet (*US*).
присмóтр (-а) *м* care.
присм|отре́ть (-отрю́, -óтришь) *сов перех* (*разг*) to find ◆ (*impf* **присма́тривать**) *неперех*: **~ за** *+instr* to look after
▸ **присмотре́ться** (*impf* **присма́триваться**) *сов возв*: **~ся (к** *+dat*) to take a good look (at).
присн|и́ться (*3sg* **-и́тся**, *3pl* **-я́тся**) *сов от* **сни́ться.**
присовокуп|и́ть (-лю́, -и́шь; *impf* **присовокупля́ть)** *сов перех* (*к делу*) to file; (*к сказанному*) to add.
присоедине́ни|е (-я) *ср* (*см глаг*) attachment; connection; annexation; (*к протесту итп*) joining; (*к чьему-н мнению*) supporting.
присоедин|и́ть (-ю́, -и́шь; *impf* **присоединя́ть)** *сов перех*: **~ что-н к** *+dat* to attach sth to; (*провод*) to connect sth to; (*территорию*) to annex sth to
▸ **присоедини́ться** (*impf* **присоединя́ться**) *сов возв*: **~ся к** *+dat* (*к экскурсии, к протесту итп*) to join; (*к чьему-н мнению*) to support.
присос|а́ться (-у́сь, -ёшься; *impf* **приса́сываться)** *сов возв* to attach itself by suction.
приспе́шник (-а) *м* (*пренебр*) accomplice.
приспосо́б|ить (-лю, -ишь; *impf* **приспоса́бливать** *или* **приспособля́ть)** *сов перех* to adapt
▸ **приспосо́биться** (*impf* **приспоса́бливаться** *или* **приспособля́ться**) *сов возв* (*к условиям, к климату*) to adapt (o.s.); (*делать что-н*) to get used to.
приспосо́блен *прил см* **приспосо́бленный.**
приспособле́ни|е (-я) *ср* (*к условиям итп*) adaptation; (*устройство, механизм итп*) appliance.
приспосо́блен|ный (-, -а, -о) *прил*: **~ к** *+dat* (*пригодный*) fit for, well-suited to.
приспосо́блю(сь) *сов см* **приспосо́бить(ся).**
приспособля́|ть(ся) (-ю(сь)) *несов от* **приспосо́бить(ся).**
пристава́ни|е (-я) *ср* pestering.
приста|ва́ть (-ю́, -ёшь) *несов от* **приста́ть.**
приста́в|ить (-лю, -ишь; *impf* **приставля́ть)** *сов перех*: **~ что-н к** *+dat* to put sth against; (*пистолет: к груди*) to put sth to; **приставля́ть** (**~** *perf*) **когó-н к** *+dat* to assign sb to look after.
приста́в|ка (-ки; *gen pl* **-ок)** *ж* fitting; (*линг*) prefix.
приста́влю *сов см* **приста́вить.**
приставля́|ть (-ю) *несов от* **приста́вить.**
приста́вок *сущ см* **приста́вка.**
при́стал|ьный (-ен, -ьна, -ьно) *прил* (*взгляд, внимание*) fixed; (*интерес, наблюдение*) determined, resolute.
приста́нищ|е (-а) *ср* refuge.
приста́ну *итп сов см* **приста́ть.**
при́стан|ь (-и) *ж* pier.
приста́|ть (-ну, -нешь; *impf* **пристава́ть)** *сов неперех*: **~ к** *+dat* (*прилипнуть*) to stick to; (*присоединиться*) to join; (*разг: с вопросами*) to pester; (*причалить*) to put into; **ему́ не ~ло**

так поступа́ть (*разг*) he shouldn't behave like that.
пристегн|у́ть (**-у́, -ёшь**; *impf* **пристёгивать**) *сов перех* to fasten
▸ **пристегну́ться** (*impf* **пристёгиваться**) *сов возв* (*в самолёте, в автомобиле*) to fasten one's seat belt.
присто́|йный (**-ен, -йна, -йно**) *прил* (*приличный*) decent.
пристра́ива|ть(ся) (**-ю(сь)**) *несов от* **пристро́ить(ся)**.
пристра́стен *прил см* **пристра́стный**.
пристра́сти|е (**-я**) *ср* (*склонность*) passion; (*предубеждение*) bias.
пристра|сти́ться (**-щу́сь, -сти́шься**) *сов возв*: ~ **к** +*dat* to develop a liking for.
пристра́ст|ный (**-ен, -на, -но**) *прил* bias(s)ed.
пристращу́сь *сов см* **пристрасти́ться**.
пристр|ели́ть (**-елю́, -е́лишь**; *impf* **пристре́ливать**) *сов перех* (*животное*) to put down; (*разг*: *человека*) to shoot.
пристро́ек *сущ см* **пристро́йка**.
пристро́|ить (**-ю, -ишь**; *impf* **пристра́ивать**) *сов перех* (*комнату*) to build onto; (*разг*: *устроить*) to fix up
▸ **пристро́иться** (*impf* **пристра́иваться**) *сов возв* (*на диване, в углу*) to settle o.s.; (*разг*: *на работу, на службу*) to get fixed up.
пристро́|йка (**-йки**; *gen pl* **-ек**) *ж* extension.
при́ступ (**-а**) *м* (*атака*) attack; (*смеха, гнева*) fit; (*кашля*) bout; (*припадок*): **серде́чный** ~ heart attack; ~ **уду́шья** asthma attack.
прист|упи́ть (**-уплю́, -у́пишь**; *impf* **приступа́ть**) *сов неперех*: ~ **к** +*dat* (*начать*) to get down to.
присты|ди́ть (**-жу́, -ди́шь**) *сов от* **стыди́ть**.
прис|уди́ть (**-ужу́, -у́дишь**; *impf* **присужда́ть**) *сов перех*: ~ **что-н кому́-н** (*приз, алименты итп*) to award sth to sb; (*учёную степень*) to confer sth on sb; (*приговорить*): ~ **кого́-н к** +*dat* to sentence sb to.
прису́тственный *прил* (*день, часы*) working *опред*.
прису́тстви|е (**-я**) *ср* presence; **в ~и** +*gen* in the presence of; ~ **ду́ха** presence of mind.
прису́тств|овать (**-ую**) *несов неперех* to be present.
прису́тствующ|ие (**-их**; *decl like adj*) *мн* those present.
прису́щ|ий (**-ая, -ее, -ие; -, -а, -о**) *прил*: ~ +*dat* characteristic of.
присыла́|ть (**-ю**) *несов от* **присла́ть**.
присы́л|ка (**-ки**; *gen pl* **-ок**) *ж* (*письма*) sending.
присы́п|ка (**-ки**; *gen pl* **-ок**) *ж* powder.
прися́г|а (**-и**) *ж* oath; **под ~ой** under oath.
присяга́|ть (**-ю**; *perf* **присягну́ть**) *несов неперех* (+*dat*) to swear an oath to.
прися́ду *итп сов см* **присе́сть**.
прися́жн|ый (**-ого**; *decl like adj*) *м* (*ЮР*: *также:* ~ **заседа́тель**) juror; **суд ~ых** jury.
прита|и́ться (**-ю́сь, -и́шься**; *impf* **прита́иваться**) *сов возв* to hide.
прит|ащи́ть (**-ащу́, -а́щишь**; *impf* **прита́скивать**) *сов перех* (*что-н тяжёлое или громоздкое*) to drag; (*заставить пойти*) to drag along.
притво́рен *прил см* **притво́рный**.
притв|ори́ть (**-орю́, -о́ришь**; *impf* **притворя́ть**) *сов перех* to shut (*not fully*).
притвор|и́ться (**-ю́сь, -и́шься**; *impf* **притворя́ться**) *сов возв* (+*instr*) to pretend to be.
притво́р|ный (**-ен, -на, -но**) *прил* feigned.
притво́рств|о (**-а**) *ср* pretence.
притворю́(сь) *сов см* **притвори́ть(ся)**.
притворя́|ть(ся) (**-ю(сь)**) *несов от* **притвори́ть(ся)**.
притесне́ни|е (**-я**) *ср* (*людей*) oppression; (*обычно мн*: *гонения*) persecution.
притесни́тел|ь (**-я**) *м* oppressor.
притесн|и́ть (**-ю́, -и́шь**; *impf* **притесня́ть**) *сов перех* to oppress.
прити́х|нуть (**-ну, -нешь**; *pt* **-, -ла, -ло**, *impf* **притиха́ть**) *сов неперех* to grow quiet.
приткн|у́ть (**-у́, -ёшь**; *impf* **притыка́ть**) *сов перех* to stick.
прито́к (**-а**) *м* (*река*) tributary; ~ +*gen* (*сил, энергии, средств*) supply of; (*населения*) influx of.
прито́м *союз* and what's more.
прито́н (**-а**) *м* den.
при́тор|ный (**-ен, -на, -но**) *прил* (*вкус, торт итп*) sickly sweet; (*перен*: *улыбка, выражение лица*) unctuous.
притро́н|уться (**-усь, -ешься**; *impf* **притра́гиваться**) *сов возв*: ~ **к** +*dat* to touch.
прит|упи́ться (*3sg* **-у́пится**, *3pl* **-у́пятся**, *impf* **притупля́ться**) *сов возв* (*нож, бритва, топор*) to go blunt; (*перен*: *внимание итп*) to diminish; (: *чувства*) to fade; (: *слух*) to fail.
при́тч|а (**-и**) *ж* parable.
притыка́|ть (**-ю**) *несов от* **приткну́ть**.
притяга́тел|ьный (**-ен, -ьна, -ьно**) *прил* attractive.
притя́гива|ть (**-ю**) *несов от* **притяну́ть**.
притяжа́тельный *прил* (*ЛИНГ*) possessive.
притяза́ни|е (**-я**) *ср*: ~ **на** +*acc* (*на наследство, на территорию*) claim to; (*на остроумие, на красоту итп*) pretensions *мн* of.
прит|яну́ть (**-яну́, -я́нешь**; *impf* **притя́гивать**) *сов перех* (*подтащить*) to drag up; (*привлечь*) to attract; **притя́гивать (**~ *perf***) факт за́ уши** to come up with a far-fetched fact.
приукра́|сить (**-шу, -сишь**; *impf* **приукра́шивать**) *сов перех* (*события, чьи-н достоинства*) to exaggerate.
приумно́ж|ить (**-у, -ишь**; *impf* **приумножа́ть**) *сов перех* to increase.
приун|ы́ть (**-о́ю, -о́ешь**; *impf* **приунывать**) *сов неперех* to get depressed.
приуро́ч|ить (**-у, -ишь**; *impf* **приуро́чивать**) *сов перех*: ~ **что-н к** +*dat* to time sth to coincide with.

приуса́дебный *прил*: ~ **уча́сток** allotment.
при|учи́ть (-учу́, -у́чишь; *impf* **приу́чивать)** *сов перех*: ~ **кого́-н к** *+dat/+infin* to train sb for/to do
▸ **приучи́ться** (*impf* **приу́чиваться**) *сов возв*: ~**ся к** *+dat/+infin* to train for/to do.
прифронтово́й *прил* front(line) *опред*.
прихвастн|у́ть (-у́, -ёшь) *сов неперех* (*разг*) to blow one's own trumpet a bit.
прихв|ати́ть (-ачу́, -а́тишь; *impf* **прихва́тывать)** *сов перех* (*разг*: *схватить*) to grab; (: *взять с собой*) to take ◆ *безл* (*о боли*) to grip.
прихлеба́тел|ь (-я) *м* (*разг*: *пренебр*) sponger.
прихло́пн|уть (-у, -ешь; *impf* **прихло́пывать)** *сов перех* (*крышку*) to slam shut; (*разг*: *насекомое*) to swat.
прихлы́н|уть (*3sg* **-ет**, *3pl* **-ут**) *сов перех* (*волна, толпа*) to surge; (*перен*: *воспоминания*) to come flooding back.
прихо́д (-а) *м* (*поезда, гостя, весны*) arrival; (*КОММ*) receipts *мн*; (*РЕЛ*) parish; ~ **и расхо́д** (*КОММ*) credit and debit.
прих|оди́ть (-ожу́, -о́дишь) *несов от* **прийти́**
▸ **приходи́ться** *несов от* **прийти́сь** ◆ *возв*: ~**ся кому́-н дя́дей/ро́дственником** to be sb's uncle/relative; **раз на раз не ~о́дится** no two times are ever the same.
прихо́дн|ый *прил* (*КОММ*): ~**ая кни́га** receipt book.
прихо́д|овать (-ую; *perf* **оприхо́довать)** *несов перех* (*КОММ*: *сумму*) to enter (*in receipt book*).
прихо́дск|ий (-ая, -ое, ие) *прил* (*РЕЛ*) parish *опред*.
приходя́щ|ий (-ая, -ее, -ие) *прил* nonresident; (*медсестра*) visiting *опред*; ~**ая ня́ня** babysitter; ~ **больно́й** outpatient.
прихожа́н|ин (-ина; *nom pl* **-е)** *м* (*РЕЛ*) parishioner.
прихожа́н|ка (-ки; *gen pl* **-ок)** *ж* (*РЕЛ*) *см* **прихожа́нин**.
прихо́ж|ая (-ей; *decl like adj*) *ж* entrance hall.
прихожу́(сь) *несов см* **приходи́ть(ся)**.
прихора́шива|ться (-юсь) *несов возв* (*разг*) to smarten o.s. up.
прихотли́в|ый (-, -а, -о) *прил* (*человек*) capricious, whimsical; (*вкус*) quirky; (*узор*) intricate.
при́хот|ь (-и) *ж* whim.
прихра́мыва|ть (-ю) *сов неперех* to limp slightly.
прице́л (-а) *м* (*ружья, пушки*) sight(s); (*прицеливание*) aiming; **брать (взять** *perf*) **кого́-н/что-н на** ~ to aim at sb/sth; (*перен*) to keep a close watch on sb/sth.
прице́л|иться (-юсь, -ишься; *impf* **прице́ливаться)** *сов возв* to take aim.
прицен|и́ться (-еню́сь, -е́нишься; *impf* **прице́ниваться)** *сов возв*: ~ **к** *+dat* to enquire about the price of.

прице́п (-а) *м* trailer.
прицеп|и́ть (-еплю́, -е́пишь; *impf* **прицепля́ть)** *сов перех* (*вагон*) to couple
▸ **прицепи́ться** (*impf* **прицепля́ться**) *сов возв* (*перен*: *разг*: *пристать*) to be a pain in the neck; **прицепля́ться (~ся** *perf*) **к** *+dat* to stick to; (*перен*: *разг*: *к человеку*) to nag; (: *к словам*) to find fault with.
прича́л (-а) *м* mooring; (*пассажирский*) quay; (*грузовой, ремонтный*) dock.
прича́л|ить (-ю, -ишь; *impf* **прича́ливать)** *сов* (*не*)*перех* to moor.
прича́стен *прил см* **прича́стный**.
прича́сти|е (-я) *ср* (*ЛИНГ*) participle; (*РЕЛ*) communion.
прича|сти́ть (-щу́, -сти́шь; *impf* **причаща́ть)** *сов перех* (*РЕЛ*) to give communion to
▸ **причасти́ться** (*impf* **причаща́ться**) *сов возв* (*РЕЛ*) to receive communion.
прича́ст|ный *прил* (*ЛИНГ*) participial; (**-ен, -на, -но**; *связанный*): ~ **к** *+dat* connected with.
причаща́|ть(ся) (-ю(сь)) *несов от* **причасти́ть(ся)**.
причаще́ни|е (-я) *ср* (*РЕЛ*) Eucharist.
причащу́(сь) *сов см* **причасти́ть(ся)**.
причём *союз* moreover.
приче|са́ть (-ешу́, -е́шешь; *impf* **причёсывать)** *сов перех* (*волосы*) to comb, brush; **причёсывать (~** *perf*) **кого́-н** to comb *или* brush sb's hair; **причёсывать (~** *perf*) **го́лову** to do one's hair
▸ **причеса́ться** (*impf* **причёсываться**) *сов возв* to comb *или* brush one's hair.
причё́с|ка (-ки; *gen pl* **-ок)** *ж* hairstyle.
причёсыва|ть(ся) (-ь(сь)) *несов от* **причеса́ть(ся)**.
причешу́(сь) *итп сов см* **причеса́ть(ся)**.
причи́н|а (-ы) *ж* cause, reason; **по ~е** *+gen* on account of.
причин|и́ть (-ю, -и́шь; *impf* **причиня́ть)** *сов перех* to cause.
причисл|ить (-ю, -ишь; *impf* **причисля́ть)** *сов перех*: ~ **кого́-н/что-н к** *+dat* (*отнести к*) to number sb/sth among.
причита́ни|е (-я) *ср* lamentation; (*похоронные*) keening; **сва́дебные ~я** *old Russian wedding ritual where women wail and lament the bride*.
причита́|ть (-ю) *несов неперех* (*на похоронах*) to wail
▸ **причита́ться** *несов возв*: **мне ~ется 10 рубле́й** I am owed 10 roubles; **с Вас ~ется 10 рубле́й** you owe 10 roubles.
причу́д|а (-ы) *ж* whim.
причу́длив|ый (-, -а, -о) *прил* (*узор*) intricate.
пришварт|ова́ть (-ую) *сов от* **швартова́ть**.
037пришей(те) *сов см* **приши́ть**.
пришёл(ся) *сов см* **прийти́(сь)**.
прише́л|ец (-ьца) *м* stranger.

пришéстви|е (**-я**) *ср* (*РЕЛ*) advent.
пришиб́ленный *прил* crestfallen.
приш·|ить (**-ью́, -ьёшь**; *imper* **-éй(те)**, *impf* **пришивáть**) *сов перех* to sew on; (*перен*: *разг*): ~ **комý-н что-н** to pin sth on sb.
пришлá *umn сов см* **прийти́**.
при́шлый *прил* (*человек*) strange; (*кошка*) stray.
пришлю́ *umn сов см* **прислáть**.
пришпóр|ить (**-ю, -ишь**; *impf* **пришпóривать**) *сов перех* to spur.
пришью́ *umn сов см* **приши́ть**.
прищеми́|ть (**-лю́, -и́шь**; *impf* **прищемля́ть**) *сов перех* to catch.
прищéп|ка (**-ки**; *gen pl* **-ок**) *ж* clothes peg (*BRIT*), clothespin (*US*).
прищýр|ить (**-ю, -ишь**; *impf* **прищýривать**) *сов перех* (*глаза*) to screw up
▸ **прищýриться** (*impf* **прищýриваться**) *сов возв* to screw up one's eyes.
приют (**-а**) *м* shelter; (*для сирот*) orphanage.
приюти́ть (**-чý, -ти́шь**) *сов перех* to shelter
▸ **приюти́ться** *сов возв* to take shelter.
прия́тел|ь (**-я**) *м* friend.
прия́тельниц|а (**-ы**) *ж см* **прия́тель**.
прия́тен *прил см* **прия́тный**.
прия́тно *нареч* (*удивлён, поражён*) pleasantly ◆ *как сказ* it is nice *или* pleasant; **мне ~ э́то слы́шать** I'm glad to hear that; **о́чень ~** (*при знакомстве*) pleased to meet you.
прия́т|ный (**-ен, -на, -но**) *прил* (*встреча, поездка*) pleasant, enjoyable; (*разговор, вкус*) pleasant; (*человек, лицо, улыбка*) nice, pleasant.
ПРО *ж сокр* (= *противоракéтная оборóна*) antimissile defence (*BRIT*) *или* defense (*US*) system.
про *предл* (+*acc*) about.
про- *префикс* (*in verbs*; *о действии, направленном сквозь что-н*) *indicating action through sth eg*. *прострели́ть*; (*о действии, распространяющемся на весь предмет*) *indicating action involving whole object eg*. *прогрéть*; (*о движении мимо чего-н*) *indicating movement past sth eg*. *проéхать*; (*об исчерпанности действия*) *indicating completion of action eg*. *пронумеровáть*; (*о звучании, осуществляемом в один приём*) *indicating single occurence of sound eg*. *протруби́ть*; (*о длительном действии*) *indicating prolonged action eg*. *прорабóтать*; (*in nouns and adjectives*; *сторонник чего-н*) pro-.
проанализи́р|овать (**-ую**) *сов от* **анализи́ровать**.
проаннотиŕ|овать (**-ую**) *сов от* **аннотиŕовать**.
прóб|а (**-ы**) *ж* (*испытание*) test; (*образец*) sample; (*драгоценного металла*) standard (*of precious metals*); (*клеймо*) hallmark.
пробéг (**-а**) *м* (*СПОРТ*: *автомобильный, марафонский*) race; (: *лыжный*) run; (*АВТ*) mileage.
пробéга|ть (**-ю**) *сов неперех* to run around.
пробеж|áть (*как* **бежáть**; *см* **Table 20**; *impf* **пробегáть**) *сов перех* (*бегло прочитать*) to skim; (*5 километров*) to cover ◆ *неперех* (*время, годы*) to pass; (*миновать бегом*): ~ **ми́мо** +*gen* to run past; (*появиться и исчезнуть*): ~ **по** +*dat* (*шум, дрожь*) to run through; (*по земле*) to run along; **пробегáть** (~ *perf*) **чéрез** +*acc* to run through
▸ **пробежáться** *сов возв* to run.
пробéж|ка (**-ки**; *gen pl* **-ек**) *ж* run.
пробéл (**-а**) *м* (*также перен*) gap.
проберý(сь) *umn сов см* **пробрáть(ся)**.
пробивá|ть(ся) (**-ю(сь)**) *несов от* **проби́ть(ся)**.
пробивнóй *прил* (*сила снаряда*) penetrating; (*перен*: *разг*: *человек*) pushy.
пробирá|ть(ся) (**-ю(сь)**) *несов от* **пробрáть(ся)**.
проби́р|ка (**-ки**; *gen pl* **-ок**) *ж* test-tube.
проб|и́ть (**-ью́, -ьёшь**) *сов от* **бить** ◆ (*impf* **пробивáть**) *перех* (*дыру, отверстие*) to knock; (*крышу, стену*) to make a hole in; (*разг*: *с трудом добиться*) to force through; **пробивáть** (~ *perf*) **себé дорóгу** (*перен*) to carve one's way
▸ **проби́ться** (*impf* **пробивáться**) *сов возв* (*прорваться*) to fight one's way through; (*растения, ростки*) to push through *или* up; (*разг*: *прожить с трудом*) to struggle through.
прóб|ка (**-ки**; *gen pl* **-ок**) *ж* (*no pl*; *древесной коры*) cork; (*для закупоривания*) cork, stopper; (*перен*: *транспортная*) jam; (*ЭЛЕК*) fuse.
проблéм|а (**-ы**) *ж* problem.
проблемáтик|а (**-и**) *ж собир* problems *мн*.
проблемати́чен *прил см* **проблемати́чный**.
проблемати́ческ|ий (**-ая, -ое, -ие**) *прил* problematic(al).
проблемати́ч|ный (**-ен, -на, -но**) *прил* = **проблемати́ческий**.
прóблеск (**-а**) *м* (*блеск*) ray; (*таланта, понимания*) hint; ~ **надéжды** ray of hope.
прóбный *прил* (*образец, экземпляр*) trial *опред*; (*полёт*) test *опред*; ~ **кáмень** (*перен*) touchstone.
прóб|овать (**-ую**; *perf* **попрóбовать**) *несов перех* (*мотор*) to test; (*пирог, вино*) to taste; (+*infin*; *пытаться*) to try to do.
прободéни|е (**-я**) *ср* (*МЕД*) perforation.
пробóин|а (**-ы**) *ж* hole.
прóбок *сущ см* **прóбка**.
проболтá|ться (**-юсь**) *сов возв* (*разг*: *проговориться*) to blab; (: *пробездельничать*) to loaf about.
пробóр (**-а**) *м* parting (*of hair*).
проб|рáть (**-ерý, -ерёшь**; *impf* **пробирáть**) *сов перех* (*разг*: *страх*) to strike; (*дрожь*) to come over; (*мороз*) to chill
▸ **пробрáться** (*impf* **пробирáться**) *сов возв* (*с трудом пройти*) to fight one's way through;

(*тихо пройти*) to steal past *или* through.
пробу́дешь *итп сов см* **пробы́ть**.
пробу|ди́ть (-ужу́, -у́дишь; *impf* **пробужда́ть** *или* **буди́ть)** *сов перех* (*массы, людей*) to rouse, stir; (*перен*: *желания, чувства*) to arouse
▸ **пробуди́ться** (*impf* **пробужда́ться**) *сов возв* (*проснуться*) to awake, wake up; (*перен*: *появиться*) to appear.
пробу́ду *итп сов см* **пробы́ть**.
пробу́дь(те) *сов см* **пробы́ть**.
пробужда́|ть(ся) (-ю(сь)) *несов от* **пробуди́ть(ся)**.
пробужде́ни|е (-я) *ср* (*ото сна*) waking up; (*сознания, чувств*) awakening.
пробужу́(сь) *сов см* **пробуди́ть(ся)**.
пробура́в|ить (-лю, -ишь) *сов от* **бура́вить**.
пробур|и́ть (-ю́, -и́шь) *сов от* **бури́ть**.
пробурч|а́ть (-у́, -и́шь) *сов от* **бурча́ть**.
пробы́ть (*как* **быть**; *см* **Table 21**) *сов неперех* (*прожить*) to stay, remain; (*провести*) to go; **он пробы́л 10 лет учи́телем** he was a teacher for 10 years.
пробью́(сь) *итп сов см* **проби́ть(ся)**.
прова́л (-а) *м* (*в почве, в стене*) hole; (*перен*: *неудача*) flop; (: *памяти*) failure.
пров|али́ть (-алю́, -а́лишь; *impf* **прова́ливать)** *сов перех* (*крышу, пол*) to cause to collapse; (*разг*: *перен*: *дело, затею*) to make a mess of; (: *студента*) to fail
▸ **провали́ться** (*impf* **прова́ливаться**) *сов возв* (*упасть*) to fall; (*рухнуть*) to collapse; (*разг*: *перен*: *студент, попытка*) to fail; (: *исчезнуть*) to vanish; **как сквозь зе́млю ~али́лся** he disappeared into thin air.
пров|ари́ть (-арю́, -а́ришь; *impf* **прова́ривать)** *сов перех* to boil (*for a long time*).
прове́да|ть (-ю; *impf* **прове́дывать)** *сов перех* (*навестить*) to call on; (*разг*: *узнать*) to find out.
проведе́ни|е (-я) *ср* (*урока*) taking; (*репетиции, конкурса*) holding; (*границы*) drawing; (*линии передачи*) installation; (*машины*) driving; (*судна*) piloting.
проведу́ *итп сов см* **провести́**.
прове́дыва|ть (-ю) *несов от* **прове́дать**.
пров|езти́ (-езу́, -езёшь; *pt* **-ёз, -езла́, -езло́,** *impf* **провози́ть)** *сов перех* (*везя, доставить*): **~ по** *+dat*/**ми́мо** *+gen*/**че́рез** *+acc* to take along/past/across; (*контрабанду, наркотики*) to smuggle.
провентили́р|овать (-ую) *сов от* **вентили́ровать**.
прове́р|ить (-ю, -ишь; *impf* **проверя́ть)** *сов перех* to check; (*выполнение правил*) to monitor; (*знание ученика, двигатель*) to test
▸ **прове́риться** (*impf* **проверя́ться**) *сов возв* (*у врача*) to get a check-up.
прове́р|ка (-ки; *gen pl* **-ок)** *ж* (*см глаг*) check; monitoring; test.
проверн|у́ть (-у́, -ёшь; *impf* **провора́чивать)** *сов перех* (*кран, винт*) to crank; (*перен*: *разг*: *дело, обмен квартиры*) to rush through.
прове́рок *прил см* **прове́рка**.
проверя́ющ|ий (-его; *decl like adj*) *м* examiner.
проверя́|ть(ся) (-ю(сь)) *несов от* **прове́рить(ся)**.
пров|ести́ (-еду́, -едёшь; *pt* **-ёл, -ела́, -ело́,** *impf* **проводи́ть)** *сов перех* (*черту, границу*) to draw; (*дорогу, ход итп*) to build; (*линию передачи*) to install; (*план, реформу*) to implement; (*урок, репетицию*) to hold; (*операцию*) to carry out; (*детство, день*) to spend; (*обмануть*) to trick; **проводи́ть (~** *perf*) **ми́мо** *+gen*/**че́рез** *+acc* (*людей, экскурсантов*) to take past/across; **проводи́ть (~** *perf*) **что-н в жизнь** to put sth into effect.
прове́тр|ить (-ю, -ишь; *impf* **прове́тривать)** *сов перех* to air
▸ **прове́триться** (*impf* **прове́триваться**) *сов возв* (*комната, одежда*) to have an airing; (*человек*: *на свежем воздухе*) to take a breath of fresh air; (*перен*: *разг*) to have a change of scene.
прове́|ять (-ю) *сов от* **ве́ять**.
провиа́нт (-а) *м* provisions *мн*.
прови́дени|е (-я) *ср* foresight.
провиде́ни|е (-я) *ср* (*РЕЛ*) Providence.
провин|и́ться (-ю́сь, -и́шься) *сов возв*: **~ (в** *+prp*) to be guilty (of).
прови́нност|ь (-и) *ж* fault.
провинциа́л (-а) *м* provincial.
провинциа́л|ка (-ки; *gen pl* **-ок)** *ж см* **провинциа́л**.
провинциа́льный *прил* provincial.
прови́нци|я (-и) *ж* province; (*отдалённая местность*) provinces *мн*.
про́вод (-а; *nom pl* **-а́)** *м* cable.
проводи́мост|ь (-и) *ж* conductivity.
пров|оди́ть (-ожу́, -о́дишь) *несов от* **провести́** ◆ (*impf* **провожа́ть**) *сов перех* to see off; (*сына*: *в армию*) to send off; **провожа́ть (~** *perf*) **глаза́ми/взгля́дом кого́-н** to follow sb with one's eyes/gaze.
прово́д|ка (-ки; *gen pl* **-ок)** *ж* (*ЭЛЕК*) wiring.
проводни́к (-а́) *м* (*в горах*) guide; (*в поезде*) steward (*BRIT*) *или* porter (*US*); (*ЭЛЕК*) conductor; (*перен*: *идей, политики итп*) vehicle.
проводни́ц|а (-ы) *ж* (*в поезде*) stewardess (*BRIT*) *или* porter (*US*).
прово́док *сущ см* **прово́дка**.
про́вод|ы (-ов) *мн* (*прощание*) send-off *ед*.
провожа́т|ый (-ого; *decl like adj*) *м* escort.
провожа́|ть (-ю) *несов от* **проводи́ть**.
провожу́ (*не*)*сов см* **проводи́ть**.
провожу́(сь) *несов см* **провози́ть(ся)**.

прово́з (-а) *м* (*багажа*) transport; (*незаконный*) smuggling.
провозгла|си́ть (-шу́, -си́шь; *impf* **провозглаша́ть**) *сов перех* to proclaim; **провозглаша́ть** (~ *perf*) **кого́-н/что-н** *+instr* to hail sb/sth as.
провозглаше́ни|е (-я) *ср* proclamation.
провозглашу́ *сов см* **провозгласи́ть.**
прово|зи́ть (-жу́, -зишь) *несов от* **провезти́**
▸ **провози́ться** *сов возв* (*разг*) to muck around *или* about; **~ся** (*perf*) **с кем-н/чем-н** to spend time with sb/on sth.
провока́тор (-а) *м* agent provocateur.
провокацио́нный *прил* provocative.
провока́ци|я (-и) *ж* provocation; **поддава́ться** (**подда́ться** *perf*) **на ~ю** to give in to provocation.
про́волок|а (-и) *ж* wire.
проволо́ч|ка (-ки; *gen pl* **-ек**) *ж* (*разг*) hold-up.
провора́чива|ть (-ю) *несов от* **провернуть.**
прово́р|ный (-ен, -на, -но) *прил* agile.
проворо|ва́ться (-у́юсь; *impf* **проворо́вываться**) *сов возв* (*разг*) to be caught stealing.
проворо́н|ить (-ю, -ишь) *сов от* **воро́нить.**
проворч|а́ть (-у́, -и́шь) *сов неперех* (*человек*) to grumble ◆ *перех* to mutter.
провоци́р|овать (-ую; *perf* **спровоци́ровать**) *несов перех* to provoke; ~ (**спровоци́ровать** *perf*) **кого́-н/что-н на что-н** to provoke sb/sth into sth.
провя́л|ить (-ю, -ишь) *сов от* **вя́лить.**
прогада́|ть (-ю; *impf* **прога́дывать**) *сов неперех* (*разг*) to miscalculate.
проги́б (-а) *м* (*пола, балки*) sagging; (*место*) sag.
прогиба́|ть(ся) (-ю(сь)) *несов от* **прогну́ть(ся).**
прогл|оти́ть (-очу́, -о́тишь; *impf* **прогла́тывать** *или* **глота́ть**) *сов перех* (*также перен*) to swallow; (*перен: разг: книгу*) to devour; **язы́к ~о́тишь, так вку́сно** (*разг*) it's so tasty it makes your mouth water.
прогля|де́ть (-жу́, -ди́шь) *сов перех* (*ошибку, изменения*) to overlook.
прогл|яну́ть (*3sg* **-я́нет**, *3pl* **-я́нут**) *сов неперех* (*солнце*) to peek out; **на его́ лице́ ~яну́ла улы́бка** there was a hint of a smile on his face.
прог|на́ть (-оню́, -о́нишь; *pt* **-на́л, -нала́, -на́ло**, *impf* **прогоня́ть**) *сов перех* (*заставить двигаться*) to drive; (*заставить уйти*) to turn out; (*уволить*) to dismiss; (*избавиться*) to drive away.
прогнев|и́ть (-лю́, -и́шь) *сов от* **гневи́ть.**
прогни́|ть (*3sg* **-ёт**, *3pl* **-ю́т**, *impf* **прогнива́ть**) *сов неперех* to rot through.
прогно́з (-а) *м* forecast.
прогнози́р|овать (-ую) (*не*)*сов перех* to forecast.
прогн|у́ть (-у́, -ёшь; *impf* **прогиба́ть**) *сов перех*: **~ что-н** to cause sth to sag
▸ **прогну́ться** (*impf* **прогиба́ться**) *сов возв* to sag.
проговор|и́ть (-ю́, -и́шь; *impf* **прогова́ривать**) *сов перех* (*произнести*) to utter ◆ *неперех* (*no impf; разговаривать*) to chat
▸ **проговори́ться** (*impf* **прогова́риваться**) *сов возв* to let out a secret; **~ся** (*perf*) **о чём-н** to reveal sth.
прогого|та́ть (-чу́, -чешь) *сов от* **гогота́ть.**
проголос|ова́ть (-у́ю) *сов от* **голосова́ть.**
прогоню́ *итп сов см* **прогна́ть.**
прогоня́|ть (-ю) *несов от* **прогна́ть.**
прогор|е́ть (-ю́, -и́шь; *impf* **прогора́ть**) *сов неперех* (*дрова*) to burn through; (*перен: разг: дело*) to go bust.
прого́рклый *прил* (*масло*) rancid.
прого́ркн|уть (*3sg* **-ет**, *3pl* **-ут**) *сов от* **го́ркнуть.**
програ́мм|а (-ы) *ж* programme (*BRIT*), program (*US*); (*ПОЛИТ*) manifesto; (*также:* **веща́тельная** ~) channel; (*ПРОСВЕЩ*) curriculum; (*КОМП*) program.
программи́ровани|е (-я) *ср* (*КОМП*) programming.
программи́р|овать (-ую; *perf* **запрограмми́ровать**) *несов перех* (*КОМП*) to program.
программи́ст (-а) *м* (*КОМП*) programmer.
програ́мм|ка (-ки; *gen pl* **-ок**) *ж* (*разг: в театре*) programme (*BRIT*), program (*US*).
програ́ммный *прил* programmed (*BRIT*), programed (*US*); (*экзамен, зачёт*) set; (*КОМП*) programming (*BRIT*), programing (*US*); **програ́ммное обеспе́чение** (*КОМП*) software; **програ́ммное управле́ние** (*КОМП*) programmed (*BRIT*) *или* programed (*US*) control.
прогрева́|ть(ся) (-ю(сь)) *сов от* **прогре́ть(ся).**
прогрем|е́ть (-лю́, -и́шь) *сов от* **греме́ть.**
прогре́сс (-а) *м* progress.
прогресси́вный *прил* (*писатель, идеи*) progressive.
прогресси́р|овать (-ую) *несов неперех* to progress.
прогре́|ть (-ю; *impf* **прогрева́ть**) *сов перех* to warm up
▸ **прогре́ться** (*impf* **прогрева́ться**) *сов возв* to warm up.
прогромыха́|ть (-ю) *сов от* **громыха́ть.**
прогрохо|та́ть (-чу́, -чешь) *сов от* **грохота́ть.**
прогры́з|ть (-у́, -ёшь; *pt* -, **-ла, -ло**, *impf* **прогрыза́ть**) *сов перех* to gnaw through.
прогу|де́ть (-жу́, -ди́шь) *сов от* **гуде́ть.**
прогу́л (-а) *м* (*на работе*) absence; (*в школе*) truancy.
прогу́лива|ть (-ю) *несов от* **прогуля́ть** ◆ *перех* (*разг: собаку*) to take
▸ **прогу́ливаться** *несов от* **прогуля́ться.**
прогу́л|ка (-ки; *gen pl* **-ок**) *ж* walk; (*недалекая поездка*) trip.
прогу́льщик (-а) *м* (*работник*) absentee; (*ученик*) truant.
прогу́льщиц|а (-ы) *ж см* **прогу́льщик.**

прогуля|ть (**-ю**; *impf* **прогу́ливать**) *сов перех* (*работу*) to be absent from; (*уроки*) to miss ◆ *неперех* (*no impf*) to walk
▸ **прогуля́ться** (*impf* **прогу́ливаться**) *сов возв* to go for a walk.
продава́|ть(ся) (**-ю(сь)**) *несов от* **прода́ть(ся)**.
продав|е́ц (**-ца́**) *м* seller; (*в магазине*) (shop-) assistant.
прод|ави́ть (**-авлю́, -а́вишь**; *impf* **прода́вливать**) *сов перех* (*стекло*) to go through; **прода́вливать** (**~** *perf*) **сиде́нье сту́ла** to make the seat of a chair sag.
продавца́ *итп сущ см* **продаве́ц**.
продавщи́ц|а (**-ы**) *ж см* **продаве́ц**.
продади́м(ся) *итп сов см* **прода́ть(ся)**.
прода́ж|а (**-и**) *ж* (*дома, товара*) sale; (*торговля*) trade; **быть** (*impf*) **в ~е, поступа́ть** (**поступи́ть** *perf*) **в ~у** to be on sale.
прода́ж|ный *прил* (*цена*) sale *опред*; (*вещь*) for sale; (**-ен, -на, -но**; *человек, пресса*) corrupt.
прода́лблива|ть (**-ю**) *несов от* **продолби́ть**.
прода́ть (*как* **дать**; *см* **Table 14**; *impf* **продава́ть**) *сов перех* to sell; (*перен*: *друга*) to betray
▸ **прода́ться** (*impf* **продава́ться**) *сов возв* (*врагам*) to sell out.
продвига́|ть(ся) (**-ю(сь)**) *несов от* **продви́нуть(ся)**.
продвиже́ни|е (**-я**) *ср* (*по территории*) advance; (*по службе*) promotion.
продви́н|уть (**-у, -ешь**; *impf* **продвига́ть**) *сов перех* to move; (*перен*: *работника*) to promote
▸ **продви́нуться** (*impf* **продвига́ться**) *сов возв* to move; (*войска*) to advance; (*перен*: *работник*) to be promoted; (: *работа, строительство*) to progress.
продева́|ть (**-ю**) *несов от* **проде́ть**.
продезинфици́р|овать (**-ую**) *сов от* **дезинфици́ровать**.
продеклами́р|овать (**-ую**) *сов от* **деклами́ровать**.
проде́ла|ть (**-ю**; *impf* **проде́лывать**) *сов перех* (*отверстие*) to make; (*работу*) to do.
проде́л|ка (**-ки**; *gen pl* **-ок**) *ж* trick.
проде́лыва|ть (**-ю**) *несов от* **проде́лать**.
продемонстри́р|овать (**-ую**) *сов от* **демонстри́ровать**.
проде́ну *итп сов см* **проде́ть**.
прод|ержа́ть (**-ержу́, -е́ржишь**) *сов перех* (*держать*) to hold; (: *библиотечную книгу, человека*) to keep
▸ **продержа́ться** *сов возв* (*держаться*) to hold out.
продеру́сь *итп сов см* **продра́ться**.
проде́|ть (**-ну, -нешь**; *impf* **продева́ть**) *сов перех* to thread; **продева́ть** (**~** *perf*) **ни́тку в иго́лку** to thread a needle.
продикт|ова́ть (**-у́ю**) *сов от* **диктова́ть**.
продира́|ться (**-юсь**) *несов от* **продра́ться**.
продлева́|ть (**-ю**) *несов от* **продли́ть**.
продле́ни|е (**-я**) *ср* (*см глаг*) extension; prolongation.
продлённый *прил*: **~ день** (ПРОСВЕЩ) extended school day (*for children whose parents work late*).
продл|и́ть (**-ю́, -и́шь**; *impf* **продлева́ть**) *сов перех* (*командировку, отпуск*) to extend; (*жизнь*) to prolong.
продл|и́ться (*3sg* **-и́тся**, *3pl* **-я́тся**) *сов от* **дли́ться**.
продма́г (**-а**) *м* (= *продово́льственный магази́н*) grocer's (shop) (BRIT), grocery (US).
продово́льственный *прил* food *опред*; **продово́льственный магази́н** grocer's (shop) (BRIT), grocery (US).
продово́льстви|е (**-я**) *ср* provisions *мн*.
продолб|и́ть (**-лю́, -и́шь**) *сов от* **долби́ть**.
продолгова́т|ый (**-, -а, -о**) *прил* elongated.
продолжа́тел|ь (**-я**) *м* successor.
продолжа́|ть (**-ю**; *perf* **продо́лжить**) *несов перех* to continue, carry on; **~** (**продо́лжить** *perf*) *+impf infin* to continue *или* carry on doing
▸ **продолжа́ться** (*perf* **продо́лжиться**) *несов возв* to continue, carry on.
продолже́ни|е (**-я**) *ср* (*борьбы, лекции*) continuation; (*романа, рассказа*) sequel; **в ~** *+gen* for the duration of.
продолжи́телен *прил см* **продолжи́тельный**.
продолжи́тельност|ь (**-и**) *ж* duration; **сре́дняя ~ жи́зни** life expectancy; **продолжи́тельность жи́зни** lifespan.
продолжи́тел|ьный (**-ен, -ьна, -ьно**) *прил* (*болезнь, разговор*) prolonged; (*урок*) extended.
продо́лж|ить(ся) (**-у(сь), -ишь(ся)**) *сов от* **продолжа́ть(ся)**.
продо́льный *прил* longitudinal.
продр|а́ться (**-еру́сь, -ерёшься**; *impf* **продира́ться**) *сов возв*: **~ сквозь** *+acc* to fight one's way through.
продро́г|нуть (**-у, -ешь**) *сов неперех* to be frozen to the bone.
продува́|ть (**-ю**) *несов от* **проду́ть** ◆ *перех*: **сквозня́к ~л ко́мнату** the draught blew through the room.
проду́кт (**-а**) *м* product; *см также* **проду́кты**.
продукти́вен *прил см* **продукти́вный**.
продукти́вност|ь (**-и**) *ж* productivity; (КОМП) throughput.
продукти́в|ный (**-ен, -на, -но**) *прил* productive.
продукто́вый *прил* food *опред*.
проду́кт|ы (**-ов**) *мн* (*также*: **~ пита́ния**) foodstuffs *мн*.
проду́кци|я (**-и**) *ж* produce.
проду́ман|ный (**-, -на, -но**) *прил* well thought-out.
проду́ма|ть (**-ю**; *impf* **проду́мывать**) *сов перех*

(*действия, выступление*) to think out; (*ответ*) to consider ◆ *неперех* to think.
продý|ть (-ю, -ешь; *impf* **продува́ть)** *сов перех* (*трубу*) to blow through; (*разг: проиграть*) to lose ◆ *безл* (*+acc*): **меня́ ~ло** I've caught a chill.
продыря́в|ить (-лю, -ишь) *сов перех* to make a hole in.
продю́сер (-а) *м* producer.
проеда́|ть (-ю) *несов от* **прое́сть.**
прое́дешь *итп сов см* **прое́хать.**
проеди́м *итп сов см* **прое́сть.**
прое́ду(сь) *итп сов см* **прое́хать(ся).**
проедя́т *сов см* **прое́сть.**
прое́зд (-а) *м* (*в транспорте*) journey; (*место*) passage.
проездно́й *прил* (*документ*) travel *опред*; **проездно́й биле́т** travel card.
прое́здом *нареч* en route.
проезжа́й(те) *сов см* **прое́хать.**
проезжа́|ть (-ю) *несов от* **прое́хать.**
прое́зж|ий (-ая, -ее, -ие) *прил* (*человек*) passing ◆ **(-его;** *decl like adj*) *м* traveller (*BRIT*), traveler (*US*); **~ая часть (у́лицы)** road.
прое́кт (-а) *м* (*дома, памятника итп*) design; (*закона, договора*) draft; (*замысел*) project.
проекти́р|овать (-ую; *perf* **спроекти́ровать)** *несов перех* (*дом*) to design; (*perf* **запроекти́ровать**; *наметить*) to plan.
проектиро́вщик (-а) *м* designer.
прое́ктор (-а) *м* (*ОПТИКА*) projector.
прое́кци|я (-и) *ж* (*также ГЕОМ*) projection.
проём (-а) *м* (*дверной, оконный*) aperture.
прое́сть (*как* **есть**; *см* **Table 15**; *impf* **проеда́ть)** *сов перех* to eat through; (*разг: деньги*) to blow on food.
прое́хать (*как* **е́хать**; *см* **Table 19**) *сов перех* (*миновать*) to pass; (*остановку, поворот итп*) to miss ◆ (*impf* **проезжа́ть**) *неперех*: **~ ми́мо** *+gen*/**по** *+dat*/**че́рез** *+acc итп* to drive past/along/across *итп*
▸ **прое́хаться** *сов возв* (*на велосипеде, на санках*) to go for a ride; (*на машине*) to go for a drive.
прое́шь *сов см* **прое́сть.**
прожа́р|ить (-ю, -ишь; *impf* **прожа́ривать)** *сов перех* to fry
▸ **прожа́риться** (*impf* **прожа́риваться**) *сов возв* to be well-fried.
прожгý *итп сов см* **проже́чь.**
прожд|а́ть (-ý, -ёшь) *сов перех* to wait a long time for.
прожёг *итп сов см* **проже́чь.**
проже́ктор (-а) *м* floodlight.
прож|е́чь (-гý, -жёшь *итп*, **-гýт**; *pt* **-ёг, -гла́, -гло́,** *impf* **прожига́ть)** *сов перех* (*огнём, кислотой*) to burn a hole in.
прожива́ни|е (-я) *ср* (*в гостинице*) stay.
прожива́|ть (-ю) *несов от* **прожи́ть** ◆ *неперех* to live.
проживý *итп сов см* **прожи́ть.**
прожига́|ть (-ю) *несов от* **проже́чь** ◆ *перех*: **~ жизнь** (*перен*) to live life in the fast lane.
прожи́л|ка (-ки; *gen pl* **-ок)** *ж* vein; (*дерева*) grain.
прожи́ти|е (-я) *ср*: **на ~** to live on.
прожи́точный *прил*: **~ ми́нимум** minimum living wage.
прожи́|ть (-вý, -вёшь) *сов неперех* (*пробыть живым*) to live; (*жить*) to spend ◆ *перех* (*деньги, состояние*) to squander.
прожо́рлив|ый (-, -а, -о) *прил* voracious.
про́з|а (-ы) *ж* prose; (*повседневность*) routine.
проза́ик (-а) *м* prosaist.
прозаи́ческ|ий (-ая, -ое, -ие) *прил* (*произведение*) prose *опред*; (*жизнь*) prosaic.
прозва́ни|е (-я) *ср* nickname.
проз|ва́ть (-овý, -овёшь; *impf* **прозыва́ть)** *сов перех* to nickname.
прозвен|е́ть (*3sg* **-и́т**, *3pl* **-я́т**) *сов от* **звене́ть.**
про́звищ|е (-а) *ср* nickname.
прозвуч|а́ть (*3sg* **-и́т**, *3pl* **-а́т**) *сов неперех* (*стать слышным*) to resound; (*проявиться*) to come through.
прозева́|ть (-ю) *сов от* **зева́ть.**
прозим|ова́ть (-ýю) *сов от* **зимова́ть.**
прозовý *итп сов см* **прозва́ть.**
прозонди́р|овать (-ую) *сов от* **зонди́ровать.**
прозорли́в|ый (-, -а, -о) *прил* (*человек, ум*) perceptive; (*политика*) farsighted.
прозра́ч|ный (-ен, -на, -но) *прил* (*стекло, намерение*) transparent; (*воздух, вода*) clear; (*ткань, одежда*) see-through.
прозре́|ть (-ю; *impf* **прозрева́ть)** *сов неперех* to gain one's sight; (*перен*) to see the light.
прозыва́|ть (-ю) *несов от* **прозва́ть.**
прозяба́|ть (-ю) *несов неперех* (*человек*) to vegetate.
проигнори́р|овать (-ую) *сов от* **игнори́ровать.**
проигра́|ть (-ю; *impf* **прои́грывать)** *сов перех* to lose; (*играть*) to play ◆ *неперех* (*по impf*; *играть*) to play.
прои́грывател|ь (-я) *м* record player.
прои́грыва|ть (-ю) *несов от* **проигра́ть.**
про́игрыш (-а) *м* loss.
произведе́ни|е (-я) *ср* (*литературы, искусства*) work; (*МАТ*) product.
произв|ести́ (-едý, -едёшь; *pt* **-ёл, -ела́, -ело́,** *impf* **производи́ть)** *сов перех* (*обыск, операцию*) to carry out; (*впечатление, суматоху*) to create; **производи́ть (~** *perf*) **поса́дку** to land; **производи́ть (~** *perf*) **кого́-н в офице́ры/в генера́лы** to confer the rank of an officer/a general on sb.
производи́телен *прил см* **производи́тельный.**
производи́тел|ь (-я) *м* producer.
производи́тельност|ь (-и) *ж* productivity.
производи́тел|ьный (-ен, -ьна, -ьно) *прил* (*продуктивный*) productive; **производи́тельные си́лы** (*ЭКОН*) labour (*BRIT*) *или* labor (*US*) force.

произв|оди́ть (**-ожу́, -о́дишь**) *несов от* **произвести́** ◆ *перех* (*изготовлять*) to produce.
произво́дный *прил* derivative *опред*; **произво́дное сло́во** derivative.
произво́дственный *прил* (*процесс, план*) production *опред*; ~ **спрос** (*КОММ*) derived demand; ~ **несча́стный слу́чай** occupational accident; **произво́дственные отноше́ния** industrial relations.
произво́дств|о (**-а**) *ср* (*товаров*) production, manufacture; (*отрасль*) industry; (*завод, фабрика*) factory; (*опыта*) carrying out; **сельскохозя́йственное** ~ agricultural yield; (*отрасль*) agriculture; **промы́шленное** ~ industrial output; (*отрасль*) industry.
производу́ *несов см* **производи́ть**.
произво́л (**-а**) *м* (*самовластие*) arbitrary rule; **оставля́ть (оста́вить** *perf*) *или* **броса́ть (бро́сить** *perf*) **кого́-н на** ~ **судьбы́** to leave sb in the hands of fate.
произво́л|ьный (**-ен, -ьна, -ьно**) *прил* (*свободный*) free; (*no short form*; *СПОРТ*) freestyle *опред*; (*неосновательный*) arbitrary.
произн|ести́ (**-есу́, -есёшь**; *pt* **-ёс, -есла́, -есло́**, *impf* **произноси́ть**) *сов перех* (*выговорить*) to pronounce; (*сказать*) to say; **произноси́ть** (~ *perf*) **речь/тост** to make a speech/toast.
произн|оси́ть (**-ошу́, -о́сишь**) *несов от* **произнести́**.
произноше́ни|е (**-я**) *ср* pronunciation.
произношу́ *несов см* **произноси́ть**.
произойти́ (*как* **идти́**; *см* **Table 18**; *impf* **происходи́ть**) *сов неперех* (*случиться*) to occur; **происходи́ть** (~ *perf*) **из** +*gen* to come from.
проиллюстри́р|овать (**-ую**) *сов от* **иллюстри́ровать**.
проинспекти́р|овать (**-ую**) *сов от* **инспекти́ровать**.
проинструкти́р|овать (**-ую**) *сов от* **инструкти́ровать**.
проинтервьюи́р|овать (**-ую**) *сов от* **интервьюи́ровать**.
проинформи́р|овать (**-ую**) *сов от* **информи́ровать**.
про́иск|и (**-ов**) *мн* machinations *мн*.
проистека́|ть (*3sg* **-ет**, *3pl* **-ют**) *несов неперех*: ~ **из/от** +*gen* to result from.
происх|оди́ть (**-ожу́, -о́дишь**) *несов от* **произойти́** ◆ *неперех*: ~ **от/из** +*gen* to come from.
происхожде́ни|е (**-я**) *ср* origin; **по ~ю** by birth.
происхожу́ *несов см* **происходи́ть**.
происше́стви|е (**-я**) *ср* event; **доро́жное** ~ road accident.
пройдёш|ь(ся) *итп сов см* **пройти́(сь)**.
пройдо́х|а (**-и**) *м/ж* (*разг*) cad.
пройду́(сь) *итп сов см* **пройти́(сь)**.
пройму́ *итп сов см* **проня́ть**.
пройти́ (*как* **идти́**; *см* **Table 18**; *impf* **проходи́ть**) *сов неперех* to pass; (*расстояние*) to cover; (*слух, весть итп*) to spread; (*дорога, канал итп*) to stretch; (*дождь, снег*) to fall; (*состояться: операция, переговоры итп*) to go ◆ *перех* (*завершить: практику, службу итп*) to complete; (*изучить: тему итп*) to do; **проходи́ть** (~ *perf*) **в** +*acc* (*в институт итп*) to get into
▸ **пройти́сь** (*impf* **проха́живаться**) *сов возв* (*по комнате*) to pace; (*по парку*) to stroll; **~сь** (*perf*) **на чей-н счёт** *или* **по чьему́-н а́дресу** (*разг*) to give sb a bad write-up.
прок (**-а**; *gen part* **-у**) *м* (*разг*) use.
прока́з|а (**-ы**) *ж* mischief; (*МЕД*) leprosy.
прока́зник (**-а**) *м* mischief-maker.
прока́знича|ть (**-ю**; *perf* **напрока́зничать**) *несов неперех* to get up to mischief.
прока́лыва|ть (**-ю**) *несов от* **проколо́ть**.
прока́пчива|ть (**-ю**) *несов от* **прокопти́ть**.
прока́пыва|ть (**-ю**) *несов от* **прокопа́ть**.
прока́т (**-а**) *м* (*телевизора, палатки итп*) hire; (*металл*) rolled iron; **брать (взять** *perf*) **что-н на** ~ to hire sth; **выпуска́ть (вы́пустить** *perf*) **фильм в** ~ to release a film.
прок|ати́ть (**-ачу́, -а́тишь**; *impf* **прока́тывать**) *сов перех* (*разг: раскритиковать*) to pick holes in; (*: обмануть*) to cheat ◆ *неперех* (*разг*) to whizz past; **прока́тывать** (~ *perf*) **кого́-н** (*на машине итп*) to take sb for a ride
▸ **прокати́ться** (*impf* **прока́тываться**) *сов возв* (*также перен: гром*) to roll; (*на машине*) to go for a spin; (*перен: выстрел*) to ring out.
прока́тк|а (**-и**) *ж* (*ТЕХ*) rolling.
прока́тный *прил* (*производство, цех*) rolling; (*пункт, плата*) hire.
прока́тчик (**-а**) *м* (*в цеху*) worker (*in steel rolling mill*).
прока́тыва|ть(ся) (**-ю(сь)**) *несов от* **прокати́ть(ся)**.
прокачу́(сь) *сов см* **прокати́ть(ся)**.
прокипя|ти́ть (**-чу́, -ти́шь**) *сов перех* to boil.
прокис|нуть (*3sg* **-нет**, *3pl* **-нут**, *pt* **-, -ла, -ло**) *сов от* **киснуть** ◆ (*impf* **прокиса́ть**) *неперех* to go off.
прокла́д|ка (**-ки**; *gen pl* **-ок**) *ж* (*действие: труб*) laying out; (*: линий передачи*) laying; (*защитная*) padding.
прокла́дыва|ть (**-ю**) *несов от* **проложи́ть**.
проклина́|ть (**-ю**) *несов от* **прокля́сть** ◆ *перех* to curse.
прокл|я́сть (**-яну́, -янёшь**; *pt* **-ял, -яла́, -яло**, *impf* **проклина́ть**) *сов перех* to curse.
прокля́ти|е (**-я**) *ср* curse.
прокля́тый *прил* damned; **рабо́тать** (*impf*) **как про́клятый** (*разг*) to work like a dog.

прокóл (-а) *м* (*действие: шины*) puncturing; (: *нарыва*) lancing; (: *ушей*) piercing; (*отверстие: в шине*) puncture; (*в ушах*) hole; (*разг: неудача*) flop.
проко|лóть (-олю́, -óлешь; *impf* **прокáлывать**) *сов перех* (*шину*) to puncture; (*уши*) to pierce; (*нарыв*) to lance.
прокомментиŕр|овать (-ую) *сов от* **комментиŕровать**.
прокомпостиŕр|овать (-ую) *сов от* **компостиŕровать**.
проконсультиŕр|овать(ся) (-ую(сь)) *сов от* **консультиŕровать(ся)**.
прокопá|ть (-ю; *impf* **прокáпывать**) *сов перех* (*канаву, ход*) to dig out.
прокоп|тить (-чу́, -ти́шь) *сов от* **коптить** ◆ (*impf* **прокáпчивать**) *перех* (*копотью*) to cover with soot; (*дымом*) to fill with smoke.
прокóрм (-а) *м* feeding.
про|корми́ть(ся) (-ормлю́(сь), -óрмишь(ся)) *сов от* **корми́ть(ся)**.
прокр|áсться (-аду́сь, -адёшься; *impf* **прокрáдываться**) *сов возв*: ~ **в** *+acc*/**ми́мо** *+gen*/**чéрез** *+acc* *итп* to creep (*BRIT*) *или* sneak (*US*) in(to)/past/through *итп*.
прокрич|áть (-у́, -и́шь) *сов перех* (*выкрикнуть*) to shout out ◆ *неперех* (*ребёнок*) to cry.
прокр|ути́ть (-учу́, -у́тишь; *impf* **прокру́чивать**) *сов перех* (*провернуть*) to turn; (*мясо*) to mince; (*комп*) to scroll; (*разг: фильм*) to roll; (: *пластинку, видеоплёнку*) to play; (: *деньги*) to invest illegally.
прокру́чивани|е (-я) *ср* (*см глаг*) turning; mincing; rolling; playing.
прокру́чива|ть (-ю) *несов от* **прокрути́ть**.
прокручу́ *сов см* **прокрути́ть**.
прокурату́р|а (-ы) *ж* (*юр*) public prosecution office ◆ *собир* procurators *мн*.
проку|ри́ть (-урю́, -у́ришь; *impf* **проку́ривать**) *сов перех* to fill with smoke.
прокурóр (-а) *м* (*района, города*) procurator; (*на суде*) counsel for the prosecution; **Генерáльный** ~ (*юр*) general procurator, attorney general (*US*).
прокурóрск|ий (-ая, -ое, -ие) *прил*: ~ **надзóр** (*юр*) procurator's powers *мн*.
проку|си́ть (-ушу́, -у́сишь; *impf* **проку́сывать**) *сов перех* to bite through.
пролагá|ть (-ю) *несов от* **проложи́ть**.
пролáмыва|ть (-ю) *несов от* **проломи́ть**.
пролá|ять (-ю) *сов от* **лáять**.
пролегá|ть (*3sg* -ет, *3pl* -ют) *несов от* **пролéчь**.
пролеж|áть (-у́, -и́шь) *сов неперех* to lie.
пролé|зть (-у, -ешь; *impf* **пролезáть**) *сов неперех* to get through; (*перен: разг: в руководство*) to worm one's way in.
пролёт (-а) *м* span; ~ **лéстницы** a flight of stairs.
пролетариáт (-а) *м* proletariat.
пролетáрск|ий (-ая, -ое, -ие) *прил* proletarian.
проле|тéть (-чу́, -ти́шь; *impf* **пролетáть**) *сов неперех* to fly; (*человек, поезд*) to fly past; (*лето, отпуск*) to fly by.
прол|éчь (*3sg* -я́жет, *3pl* -я́гут, *impf* **пролегáть**) *сов неперех* (*дорога, тропинка*) to stretch.
проли́в (-а) *м* strait(s) (*мн*).
проливá|ть(ся) (-ю(сь)) *несов от* **проли́ть(ся)**.
проливнóй *прил*: ~ **дождь** pouring rain.
прол|и́ть (-ью́, -ьёшь; *pt* -и́л, -илá, -и́ло, *impf* **проливáть**) *сов перех* to spill; **проливáть** (~ *perf*) **чью-н кровь** to spill sb's blood
▸ **проли́ться** (*impf* **проливáться**) *сов возв* to spill.
пролóг (-а) *м* prologue (*BRIT*), prolog (*US*).
прол|ожи́ть (-ожу́, -óжишь; *impf* **проклáдывать**) *сов перех* (*протянуть*) to lay; **проклáдывать** (~ *perf*) **что-н чем-н** to interlay sth with sth; ~ (*perf*) **дорóгу** *или* **путь комý-н/чемý-н** to pave the way for sb/sth.
пролóм (-а) *м* (*льда*) cracking; (*место*) crack.
проломá|ть (-ю; *impf* **пролáмывать**) *сов перех* to break through.
прол|оми́ть (-омлю́, -óмишь; *impf* **пролáмывать**) *сов перех* (*лёд*) to break; (*череп*) to fracture; **пролáмывать** (~ *perf*) **дыру́ в чём-н** to make a hole in sth.
пролью́(сь) *итп сов см* **проли́ть(ся)**.
проля́жет *итп сов см* **пролéчь**.
промá|зать (-жу, -жешь) *сов от* **мáзать**.
промарширов|áть (-у́ю) *сов неперех* to march past.
промáсл|ить (-ю, -ишь; *impf* **промáсливать**) *сов перех* (*растительным маслом*) to oil; (*сливочным маслом*) to grease.
промáтыва|ть (-ю) *несов от* **промотáть**.
прóмах (-а) *м* miss; (*перен*) blunder; **давáть** (**дать** *perf*) ~ to miss the target; (*перен*) to make a blunder.
промахн|у́ться (-у́сь, -ёшься; *impf* **промáхиватся**) *сов возв* to miss; (*перен: разг*) to blunder.
промáчива|ть (-ю) *несов от* **промочи́ть**.
промáш|ка (-ки; *gen pl* -ек) *ж* stroke of bad luck; (*упущение*) blunder.
промедлéни|е (-я) *ср* delay.
промéдл|ить (-ю, -ишь) *сов неперех*: ~ **с** *+instr* to delay.
промежу́т|ок (-ка) *м* (*пространство*) gap; (*перерыв*) break.
промежу́точный *прил* (*участок, период*) intervening; (*стадия, положение*) intermediate.
промелькн|у́ть (-у́, -ёшь) *сов неперех* to flash past; ~ (*perf*) **в** *+prp* (*в голове, в памяти*) to flash through.
променя́|ть (-ю; *impf* **промéнивать**) *сов перех*: ~ **когó-н/что-н на** *+acc* to prefer sb/sth to.
промёрзн|уть (-у, -ешь; *impf* **промерзáть**) *сов неперех* (*комната, дом*) to be chilled through; (*человек*) to freeze.
прометá|ть (-ю) *сов от* **метáть**.

промо́зглый *прил* cold and wet.
промока́тельн|ый *прил*: **~ая бума́га** blotting paper.
промока́|ть (**-ю**) *несов от* **промо́кнуть** ◆ *неперех* to let water through.
промока́шк|а (**-ки**; *gen pl* **-ек**) *ж* (*разг*) blotting paper.
промо́кн|уть (**-у, -ешь**; *impf* **промока́ть**) *сов неперех* (*одежда, ноги*) to get soaked.
промокн|у́ть (**-у́, -ёшь**; *impf* **промока́ть**) *сов перех* to blot.
промо́лв|ить (**-лю, -ишь**) *сов перех* to utter.
промолч|а́ть (**-у́, -и́шь**) *сов неперех* to say nothing.
промота́|ть (**-ю**; *impf* **прома́тывать**) *сов перех* (*разг*) to blow.
пром|очи́ть (**-очу́, -о́чишь**; *impf* **прома́чивать**) *сов перех* to get wet.
промо́ю *итп сов см* **промы́ть**.
промтова́рный *прил*: **~ магази́н** *shop selling manufactured goods*.
промтова́р|ы (**-ов**) *мн* (= *промышленные това́ры*) manufactured goods *мн*.
промурлы́ка|ть (**-ю**) *сов от* **мурлы́кать**.
промч|а́ться (**-у́сь, -и́шься**) *сов возв* (*год, лето, жизнь*) to fly by; **~** *(perf)* **ми́мо** *+gen*/ **че́рез** *+acc* (*поезд, человек*) to fly past/through.
промыва́ни|е (**-я**) *ср* (*желудка*) pumping; (*глаза, раны*) bathing.
промыва́|ть (**-ю**) *несов от* **промы́ть**.
про́мыс|ел (**-ла**) *м* (*ремесло*) trade; **охо́тничий ~** hunting; **пушно́й ~** trapping; **ры́бный ~** fishing; *см также* **про́мыслы**.
промысло́вый *прил* trading; (*рыба, зверь*) marketable.
про́мысл|ы (**-ов**) *мн* (*нефтяные*) fields *мн*; (*горные, соляные*) mines *мн*.
пром|ы́ть (**-о́ю, -о́ешь**; *impf* **промыва́ть**) *сов перех* (*желудок*) to pump; (*рану, глаз*) to bathe; (*золотой песок*) to pan out.
промыч|а́ть (**-у́, -и́шь**) *сов от* **мыча́ть**.
промы́шленник (**-а**) *м* industrialist.
промы́шленност|ь (**-и**) *ж* industry; **лёгкая/тяжёлая ~** light/heavy industry.
промы́шленный *прил* industrial.
промышля́|ть (**-ю**) *несов неперех*: **~ охо́той** to hunt; **~** *(impf)* **ры́бой** to fish; **~** *(impf)* **перево́дами** (*разг*) to earn a living from translation.
промя́мл|ить (**-ю, -ишь**) *сов от* **мя́млить**.
промяу́ка|ть (**-ю**) *сов от* **мяу́кать**.
пронаблюда́|ть (**-ю**) *сов от* **наблюда́ть**.
прон|ести́ (**-есу́, -есёшь**; *pt* **-ёс, -есла́, -есло́**, *impf* **проноси́ть**) *сов перех* to carry; (*тайком*) to sneak in; (*сохранить*) to preserve ◆ *безл* (*перен*) to blow over
▸ **пронести́сь** (*impf* **проноси́ться**) *сов возв* (*машина, пуля, бегун*) to shoot by; (*лето, годы итп*) to fly by; (*буря, тайфун итп*) to whirl past.
пронжу́ *сов см* **пронзи́ть**.
пронза́|ть (**-ю**) *несов от* **пронзи́ть**.
пронзи́тел|ьный (**-ен, -ьна, -ьно**) *прил* piercing; (*свет, цвет*) glaring.
прон|зи́ть (**-жу́, -зи́шь**; *impf* **пронза́ть**) *сов перех* (*также перен*) to pierce.
прон|иза́ть (**-ижу́, -и́жешь**; *impf* **прони́зывать**) *сов перех* to penetrate (into).
прони́к(ся) *итп сов см* **прони́кнуть(ся)**.
проника́|ть(ся) (**-ю(сь)**) *несов от* **прони́кнуть(ся)**.
проникнове́н|ный (**-ен, -на, -но**) *прил* (*слова*) heartfelt; (*голос*) emotional.
прони́кнут|ый (**-, -а, -о**) *прил* (*+instr*) full of.
прони́к|нуть (**-ну, -нешь**; *pt* **-, -ла, -ло**, *impf* **проника́ть**) *сов перех*: **~ в** *+acc* to penetrate (into); (*залезть*) to break into; (*распространиться*) to spread into; (*понять*) to understand
▸ **прони́кнуться** (*impf* **проника́ться**) *сов возв* (*+instr*) to be filled with.
понима́|ть (**-ю**) *несов от* **проня́ть**.
проница́тел|ьный (**-ен, -ьна, -ьно**) *прил* (*человек, ум*) shrewd; (*взгляд*) penetrating.
проница́|ть (**-ю**) *несов неперех*: **~ в** *+acc* (*свет*) to penetrate (into).
прон|оси́ть(ся) (**-ошу́(сь), -о́сишь(ся)**) *несов от* **пронести́(сь)**.
пронумер|ова́ть (**-у́ю**) *сов от* **нумерова́ть**.
проны́р|а (**-ы**) *ж* (*разг*) dodgy character.
проны́рлив|ый (**-, -а, -о**) *прил* (*разг*) dodgy.
про|ня́ть (**-йму́, -ймёшь**; *impf* **пронима́ть**) *сов перех* (*разг*: *подлеж*: *холод*) to seize; (: *музыка*) to move.
прообраз (**-а**) *м* (*образец*) model; (*прототип*) prototype.
прооперир|ова́ть (**-ую**) *сов от* **опери́ровать**.
пропага́нд|а (**-ы**) *ж* propaganda; (*спорта*) promotion.
пропаганди́р|овать (**-ую**) *несов перех* (*политическое учение*) to spread propaganda about; (*знаний, спорт*) to promote.
пропаганди́ст (**-а**) *м* propagandist.
пропаганди́стск|ий (**-ая, -ое, -ие**) *прил* (*шумиха, кампания*) propagandist *опред*.
пропада́|ть (**-ю**) *несов от* **пропа́сть** ◆ *неперех* (*разг*) to stay for a long time; **он вечера́ми ~ет на рабо́те** he spends all his evenings at work.
про́падом *нареч*: **пропади́ ~** (*разг*) to hell with it.
пропаду́ *итп сов см* **пропа́сть**.
пропа́ж|а (**-и**) *ж* (*денег, документов*) loss; (*то, что пропало*) lost object.
пропа́лыва|ть (**-ю**) *несов от* **пропо́лоть**.
про́паст|ь (**-и**) *ж* precipice; (*перен*: *во взглядах*) abyss; (*no pl*; *разг*) masses *мн*.

проп|а́сть (**-аду́, -адёшь**; *impf* **пропада́ть**) *сов неперех* to disappear; (*деньги, письмо*) to go missing; (*аппетит, голос, слух*) to go; (*усилия, билет в театр*) to be wasted; (*погибнуть*) to die; **пропада́ть** (~ *perf*) **бе́з вести** (*человек*) to go missing.

проп|аха́ть (**-ашу́, -а́шешь**; *impf* **пропа́хивать**) *сов перех* to plough (*BRIT*), plow (*US*).

пропа́х|нуть (**-ну, -нешь**; *pt* **-, -ла, -ло**) *сов неперех* (+*instr*) to become filled with the smell of.

пропашу́ *итп сов см* **пропаха́ть**.

пропа́щ|ий (**-ая, -ее, -ие**) *прил* (*разг*: *безнадёжный*) hopeless; (*долго не приходивший*) long-lost; **э́ти де́ньги – ~ие** (*разг*) that money is lost for good.

пропе́й(те) *сов см* **пропи́ть**.

пропёк(ся) *итп сов см* **пропе́чь(ся)**.

пропека́|ть(ся) (**-ю(сь)**) *несов от* **пропе́чь(ся)**.

пропеку́(сь) *сов см* **пропе́чь(ся)**.

пропе́ллер (**-а**) *м* (*АВИА*) propeller.

проп|е́ть (**-ою́, -оёшь**) *сов от* **петь** ♦ *перех* (*петь*) to sing.

проп|е́чь (**-еку́, -ечёшь** *итп*, **-еку́т**; *pt* **-ёк, -екла́, -екло́**, *impf* **пропека́ть**) *сов перех* to bake

▸ **пропе́чься** (*impf* **пропека́ться**) *сов возв* to be well-baked.

пропива́|ть (**-ю**) *несов от* **пропи́ть**.

проп|или́ть (**-илю́, -и́лишь**; *impf* **пропи́ливать**) *сов перех* to saw through.

проп|иса́ть (**-ишу́, -и́шешь**; *impf* **пропи́сывать**) *сов перех* (*человека*) to register; (*лекарство*) to prescribe; (*статью, письмо*) to write

▸ **прописа́ться** *сов возв* to register.

пропи́с|ка (**-ки**) *ж* (*в городе, в доме*) registration.

прописн|о́й *прил* (*общеизвестный*) commonplace; **~а́я и́стина** truism; **прописна́я бу́ква** capital letter.

пропи́сыва|ть (**-ю**) *несов от* **прописа́ть**.

про́пис|ь (**-и**) *ж* (*ПРОСВЕЩ*) writing samples *мн*.

про́писью *нареч* in full; **писа́ть (написа́ть** *perf*) **су́мму ~** to write out a sum *или* amount in words.

пропита́ни|е (**-я**) *ср* food.

пропита́|ть (**-ю**; *impf* **пропи́тывать**) *сов перех* (*смочить*) to soak; (*насытить*: *бумагу*) to saturate; (: *комнату, воздух*) to fill

▸ **пропита́ться** (*impf* **пропи́тываться**) *сов возв*: **~ся чем-н** (*водой*) to be soaked in sth; (*запахом*: *воздух*) to be filled with sth; (: *одежда*) to be saturated with sth.

пропи́т|ка (**-ки**; *gen pl* **-ок**) *ж* (*ткани, дерева*) soaking; (*водонепроницаемая*) impregnation; (*ромовая*) flavouring.

пропи́тыва|ть(ся) (**-ю(сь)**) *несов от* **пропита́ть(ся)**.

проп|и́ть (**-ью́, -ьёшь**; *pt* **-и́л, -ила́, -и́ло**, *imper* **пропе́й(те)**, *impf* **пропива́ть**) *сов перех* (*деньги, состояние*) to squander on drink; (*талант, карьеру*) to ruin (*through drinking*); (*no impf*; *пить*) to drink.

пропихну́ть (**-у́, -ёшь**) *сов перех* (*разг*: *в дверь итп*) to shove; (: *в университет итп*) to push.

пропишу́(сь) *итп сов см* **прописа́ть(ся)**.

пропла́ва|ть (**-ю**) *сов неперех* (*человек*) to swim; (*судно*) to sail.

пропла́|кать (**-чу, -чешь**) *сов неперех* to cry; ~ (*perf*) **все глаза́** to cry one's eyes out.

проплута́|ть (**-ю**) *сов неперех* to wander.

пропл|ы́ть (**-ыву́, -ывёшь**; *impf* **проплыва́ть**) *сов неперех* (*человек*) to swim; (: *миновать*) to swim past; (*судно*) to sail; (: *миновать*) to sail past; (*перен*: *птица, облака*) to sail by *или* past; (: *воспоминания, мысли итп*) to flash past.

пропове́дник (**-а**) *м* (*РЕЛ*) preacher; (*перен*: *убеждений, теории*) advocate.

пропове́дниц|а (**-ы**) *ж см* **пропове́дник**.

пропове́д|овать (**-ую**) *несов перех* (*РЕЛ*) to preach; (*идею*) to advocate.

про́поведь (**-и**) *ж* (*РЕЛ*) preaching; (*идей*) endorsement; (*речь*) sermon.

пропо́йц|а (**-ы**) *м* (*разг*) soak.

пропола́скива|ть (**-ю**) *несов от* **прополоска́ть**.

пропол|з|ти́ (**-у́, -ёшь**; *pt* **-, -ла́, -ло́**) *сов неперех*: **~ по** +*dat*/**в** +*acc итп* (*насекомое, человек*) to crawl along/in(to) *итп*; (*змея*) to slither along/in (to) *итп*.

пропо́лис (**-а**) *м* propolis.

пропо́л|ка (**-ки**; *gen pl* **-ок**) *ж* weeding.

прополоска́|ть (**-ю**; *impf* **пропола́скивать** *или* **полоска́ть**) *сов перех* to rinse (out); **пропола́скивать** *или* **полоска́ть** (~ *perf*) **го́рло** to gargle.

проп|оло́ть (**-олю́, -о́лешь**; *impf* **пропа́лывать** *или* **поло́ть**) *сов перех* (*грядку итп*) to weed.

пропорциона́лен *прил см* **пропорциона́льный**.

пропорциона́льност|ь (**-и**) *ж* proportion.

пропорциона́л|ьный (**-ен, -ьна, -ьно**) *прил* (*фигура, тело*) well-proportioned; (*развитие, распределение*) proportional; **пропорциона́льное представи́тельство** proportional representation.

пропо́рци|я (**-и**) *ж* proportion.

пропоте́|ть (**-ю**; *impf* **пропотева́ть**) *сов неперех* to sweat profusely; (*пропитаться потом*) to be soaked with sweat.

пропою́ *итп сов см* **пропе́ть**.

про́пуск (**-а**) *м* (*действие*: *в зал, через границу итп*) admission; (: *в школе*) non-attendance; (*в тексте, в изложении*) gap; (*неявка*: *на работу, в школу*) absence; (*nom pl* **-а́**; *документ*) pass.

пропуска́|ть (**-ю**) *несов от* **пропусти́ть** ♦ *перех* (*чернила, свет итп*) to let through; (*воду, холод*) to let in.

проп|усти́ть (**-ущу́, -у́стишь**; *impf* **пропуска́ть**) *сов перех* to miss; (*дать дорогу, обслужить*) to admit; (*разрешить*) to allow; (*заставить пройти*) to put through; (*выпустить*) to miss out; **пропуска́ть** (~ *perf*) **кого́-н че́рез грани́цу** to let sb across the border; **пропуска́ть** (~ *perf*)

кого́-н вперёд to let sb go ahead.
пропылесо́с|ить (**-ю, -ишь**) *сов от* **пылесо́сить**.
пропыл|и́ться (**-ю́сь, -и́шься**) *сов возв* to be full of dust.
пропью́ *итп сов см* **пропи́ть**.
прора́б (**-а**) *м* (= *производи́тель рабо́т*) foreman (*мн* foremen).
прорабо́та|ть (**-ю**; *impf* **прораба́тывать**) *сов неперех* to work ◆ *перех* (*учебник, статью, урок*) to study in detail; (*разг*: *критиковать*) to rip into.
прор|асти́ (*3sg* **-астёт**, *3pl* **-асту́т**, *pt* **-о́с, -осла́, -осло́**, *impf* **прораста́ть**) *сов неперех* (*семена*) to germinate; (*трава*) to sprout.
про́рв|а (**-ы**) *ж* (*разг*: *очень много*) heaps *мн*, masses *мн*; (: *о человеке*) pig.
прорв|а́ть (**-у́, -ёшь**; *pt* **-а́л, -ала́, -а́ло**, *impf* **прорыва́ть**) *сов перех* (*одежду, сумку*) to tear; (*плотину*) to burst; (*оборону, фронт*) to break through ◆ *безл* (*+acc*; *перен*) to explode; **наконе́ц его́ ~а́ло** (*перен*) he finally exploded
▸ **прорва́ться** (*impf* **прорыва́ться**) *сов возв* (*карман, сумка*) to tear; (*плотина, шарик*) to burst; (*гнев, раздражение*) to erupt; (*горе*) to break out; **прорыва́ться** (**~ся** *perf*) **в** *+acc* to burst in(to).
прореаги́р|овать (**-ую**) *сов от* **реаги́ровать**.
проре|ди́ть (**-жу́, -ди́шь**; *impf* **проре́живать**) *сов* (*грядки, всходы*) to thin out.
проре́|зать (**-жу, -жешь**) *сов от* **ре́зать** ◆ (*impf* **проре́зывать**) *перех* to cut through; (*резать*: *мясо, рыбу итп*) to cut; (: *овощи, фрукты итп*) to chop
▸ **проре́заться** *сов от* **ре́заться** ◆ (*impf* **проре́зываться**) *возв* (*появиться*: *зубы*) to come through; (: *листья*) to come out.
прорези́н|ить (**-ю, -ишь**; *impf* **прорези́нивать**) *сов перех* to cover with rubber.
прорезн|о́й *прил*: **~ карма́н** slit pocket; **~а́я пе́тля** buttonhole.
проре́зыва|ть(ся) (**-ю(сь)**) *несов от* **проре́зать(ся)**.
про́резь (**-и**) *ж* (*на ткани*) slit; (*на прицеле орудия*) aperture.
проре́ктор (**-а**) *м* vice-principal.
прорепети́р|овать (**-ую**) *сов от* **репети́ровать**.
прореферир|овать (**-ую**) *сов от* **реферирова́ть**.
проре́х|а (**-и**) *ж* (*дыра*) tear; (*разг*: *недостаток*) shortcoming.
прорецензи́р|овать (**-ую**) *сов от* **рецензи́ровать**.
проржа́ве|ть (*3sg* **-ет**, *3pl* **-ют**) *сов неперех* to rust through.
прорица́ни|е (**-я**) *ср* prophecy.
прорица́тел|ь (**-я**) *м* prophet.
прорица́тельниц|а (**-ы**) *ж см* **прорица́тель**.
прорица́|ть (**-ю**) *несов перех* to prophesy.
проро́к (**-а**) *м* (*РЕЛ, перен*) prophet.
прор|они́ть (**-оню́, -о́нишь**) *сов перех* (*сказать*) to utter.
проро́с *итп сов см* **прорасти́**.
проро́ческ|ий (**-ая, -ое, -ие**) *прил* (*сон, слова, дар*) prophetic.
проро́честв|о (**-а**) *ср* prophecy.
проро́ч|ить (**-у, -ишь**; *perf* **напроро́чить**) *несов перех* to predict.
пророю́ *итп сов см* **проры́ть**.
прор|уби́ть (**-ублю́, -у́бишь**; *impf* **прoруба́ть**) *сов перех* (*стену, лёд, гору*) to make a hole in; **проруба́ть** (**~** *perf*) **про́секу в лесу́** to make a clearing in a forest.
про́рубь (**-и**) *ж* ice-hole.
проры́в (**-а**) *м* (*фронта*) break-through; (*плотины*) bursting; (*прорванное место*) breach.
прорыва́|ть(ся) (**-ю(сь)**) *несов от* **прорва́ть(ся)**.
прор|ы́ть (**-о́ю, -о́ешь**; *impf* **прорыва́ть**) *сов перех* (*прокопать*) to dig.
прос|ади́ть (**-ажу́, -а́дишь**; *impf* **проса́живать**) *сов перех* (*разг*: *истратить*) to blow.
проса́лива|ть (**-ю**) *несов от* **просоли́ть**.
проса́чива|ться (*3sg* **-ется**, *3pl* **-ются**) *несов от* **просочи́ться**.
просверл|и́ть (**-ю́, -и́шь**; *impf* **просве́рливать** *или* **сверли́ть**) *сов перех* to bore, drill.
просве́т (**-а**) *м* (*в тучах, в облаках*) break; (*в заборе, в занавесе*) crack; (*перен*: *в тяжёлой ситуации*) light at the end of the tunnel.
просвети́тел|ь (**-я**) *м* *person who enlightens others about progressive ideas*.
просвети́тельниц|а (**-ы**) *ж см* **просвети́тель**.
просвети́тельный *прил* enlightening.
просв|ети́ть (**-ещу́, -ети́шь**; *impf* **просвеща́ть**) *сов перех* to enlighten; (**-ечу́, -е́тишь**; *impf* **просве́чивать**; *лёгкие*) to x-ray
▸ **просве|ти́ться** ◆ (**-щу́сь, -ти́шься**; *impf* **просвеща́ться**) *сов возв* to enlighten o.s.
просветле́ни|е (**-я**) *ср* (*ясность*) lucidity.
просветлённый *прил* lucid.
просветле́|ть (**-ю**) *сов от* **светле́ть**.
просве́чива|ть (**-ю**) *несов от* **просвети́ть** ◆ *неперех* (*солнце*) to shine through; (*небо*) to be visible through; (*ткань*) to let light through.
просвечу́ *сов см* **просвети́ть**.
просвеща́|ть(ся) (**-ю(сь)**) *несов от* **просвети́ть(ся)**.
просвеще́ни|е (**-я**) *ср* education; **Министе́рство ~я** ≈ Department of Education.
просвещён|ный (**-, -на, -но**) *прил* educated.
просвещу́(сь) *сов см* **просвети́ть(ся)**.
просвир|а́ (**-ы́**) *ж* (*РЕЛ*) communion bread, Host.
просви|сте́ть (**-щу́, -сти́шь**) *сов от* **свисте́ть** ◆

(*impf* **просви́стывать**) *перех* (*мотив, песню*) to whistle (through) ◆ *неперех* (*пуля, снаряд*) to whistle past.

про́сед|ь (**-и**) *ж* grey (*BRIT*) *или* gray (*US*) streak.

просе́ивани|е (**-я**) *ср* (*муки, песка*) sifting.

просе́ива|ть (**-ю**) *несов от* **просе́ять.**

про́сек|а (**-и**) *ж* (*в лесу*) clearing.

просёл|ок (**-ка**) *м* dirt-track.

просёлочн|ый *прил*: **~ая доро́га** dirt-track.

просе́|ять (**-ю**; *impf* **просе́ивать**) *сов перех* (*муку, песок*) to sift.

просигнализи́р|овать (**-ую**) *сов от* **сигнализи́ровать.**

просигна́л|ить (**-ю, -ишь**) *сов от* **сигна́лить.**

проси|де́ть (**-жу́, -ди́шь**; *impf* **просиживать**) *сов неперех* (*сидеть*) to sit; (*пробыть*) to stay.

проси́тельный *прил* pleading.

про|си́ть (**-шу́, -сишь**; *perf* **попроси́ть**) *несов перех* to ask; (*приглашать*) to invite; **~шу́ Вас!** if you please!; ~ **(попроси́ть** *perf*) **кого́-н о чём-н**/+*infin* to ask sb for sth/to do; ~ **(попроси́ть** *perf*) **кого́-н за кого́-н** to ask sb a favour (*BRIT*) *или* favor (*US*) on behalf of sb

▸ **проси́ться** (*perf* **попроси́ться**) *несов возв* (*просить разрешения*) to ask permission; **сло́во так и ~ся** (*impf*) **с языка́** to have a word on the tip of one's tongue; **её лицо́ про́сится на карти́ну** her face was crying out to be painted.

прося́|ть (**-ю**) *сов неперех* (*солнце*) to begin to shine; (*радуга*) to appear; (*перен*: *человек*) to beam; (: *лицо*) to light up.

проск|ака́ть (**-ачу́, -а́чешь**) *сов неперех* (*человек*) to hop; ~ (*perf*) **че́рез/сквозь** +*acc* (*лошадь*) to gallop across/through; (*олень, заяц*) to bound across *или* by/through.

проска́кива|ть (**-ю**) *несов от* **проскочи́ть.**

проска́льзыва|ть (**-ю**) *несов от* **проскользну́ть.**

проскачу́ *итп сов см* **проскака́ть.**

просквоз|и́ть (*3sg* **-и́т**, *3pl* **-я́т**) *сов безл* (+*acc*): **меня́ ~и́ло** I caught a chill.

просклоня́|ть (**-ю**) *сов от* **склоня́ть.**

проскользн|у́ть (**-у́, -ёшь**; *impf* **проска́льзывать**) *сов неперех* (*монета*) to slide in; (*человек*) to slip in; (*перен*: *сомнение, страх*) to creep in.

проск|очи́ть (**-очу́, -о́чишь**; *impf* **проска́кивать**) *сов неперех* (*проскользнуть*) to slide in; (*пройти, проехать*): ~ **в** +*acc*/**ми́мо** +*gen итп* to race in(to)/past *итп*; (*проникнуть*): ~ **в/че́рез** +*acc* to break in(to)/through.

проскуча́|ть (**-ю**) *сов неперех* to be bored.

просла́б|ить (*3sg* **-ит**, *3pl* **-ят**) *сов от* **сла́бить.**

просла́в|ить (**-лю, -ишь**; *impf* **прославля́ть**) *сов перех* (*сделать известным*) to make famous; (*impf* **прославля́ть** *или* **сла́вить**; *восхвалить*) to glorify

▸ **просла́виться** (*impf* **прославля́ться**) *сов возв* (*актёр, писатель*) to become famous; (*перен*: *разг*: *преступник*) to become notorious.

просла́вленный *прил* renowned.

просла́влю(сь) *сов см* **просла́вить(ся).**

прославля́|ть(ся) (**-ю(сь)**) *несов от* **просла́вить(ся).**

просле|ди́ть (**-жу́, -ди́шь**; *impf* **просле́живать**) *сов перех* (*следить глазами*) to follow; (*исследовать*) to trace ◆ *неперех*: ~ **за** +*instr* to follow; (*за выполнением приказа, за чьим-н поведением*) to monitor.

просле́д|овать (**-ую**) *сов неперех*: ~ **(ми́мо** +*gen*/**сквозь** +*acc*) to pass slowly (by/through).

просле́жива|ть (**-ю**) *несов от* **проследи́ть.**

прослежу́ *сов см* **проследи́ть.**

просле|зи́ться (**-жу́сь, -зи́шься**) *сов возв* to cry.

просло́|йка (**-йки**; *gen pl* **-ек**) *ж* (*слой*) layer; (*в горной породе*) stratum (*мн* strata).

прослу|жи́ть (**-ужу́, -у́жишь**) *сов неперех* to serve; (*туфли, пальто итп*) to last.

прослу́ша|ть (**-ю**; *impf* **прослу́шивать**) *сов перех* to listen to; (*курс, лекции*) to attend; (*ответ, объяснение итп*) to miss; (*no impf*; *радио, музыку*) to listen to.

прослу́шива|ть (**-ю**) *несов от* **прослу́шать** ◆ *перех*: **их кварти́ру ~ют** their flat (*BRIT*) *или* apartment (*US*) is bugged.

просл|ы́ть (**-ыву́, -ывёшь**) *сов неперех* (+*instr*) to acquire a reputation as.

прослы́шать (**-у, -ишь**) *сов неперех* (*разг*): ~ **о** +*prp* to hear about.

просма́лива|ть (**-ю**) *несов от* **просмоли́ть.**

просма́трива|ть (**-ю**) *несов от* **просмотре́ть**

▸ **просма́триваться** *несов возв* to be visible.

просмол|и́ть (**-ю́, -и́шь**; *impf* **просма́ливать**) *сов перех* to coat with tar.

просмо́тр (**-а**) *м* (*фильма, спектакля*) viewing; (*документов*) inspection; (*ошибка*) blunder.

просм|отре́ть (**-отрю́, -о́тришь**; *impf* **просма́тривать**) *сов перех* (*ознакомиться*: *читая*) to look through; (: *смотря*) to view; (*пропустить*) to overlook.

просну́ться (**-у́сь, -ёшься**; *impf* **просыпа́ться**) *сов возв* to wake up; (*перен*: *любовь, страх итп*) to be awakened.

про́с|о (**-а**) *ср* millet.

просо́выва|ть(ся) (**-ю(сь)**) *несов от* **просу́нуть(ся).**

просо́ди|я (**-и**) *ж* prosody.

просо|ли́ть (**-олю́, -о́лишь**; *impf* **проса́ливать**) *сов перех* to salt.

просо́х|нуть (**-ну, -нешь**; *pt* **-, -ла, -ло**, *impf* **просыха́ть**) *сов неперех* to dry out.

просоч|и́ться (*3sg* **-и́тся**, *3pl* **-а́тся**, *impf* **проса́чиваться**) *сов возв* (*также перен*) to filter through.

просп|а́ть (**-лю́, -и́шь**; *pt* **-а́л, -ала́, -а́ло**) *сов неперех* (*спать*) to sleep; (*impf* **просыпа́ть**; *встать поздно*) to oversleep ◆ *перех* (*разг*: *остановку*) to sleep through.

проспе́кт (**-а**) *м* avenue; (*план*) draft; (*издание*) brochure.

просплю́ *сов см* **проспа́ть.**

проспо́р|ить (**-ю, -ишь**; *impf* **проспо́ривать**) *сов перех* to lose in a bet ◆ *неперех* (*no impf*, *спорить*) to argue.
проспряга́|ть (**-ю**) *сов от* **спряга́ть.**
просро́чек *сущ см* **просро́чка.**
просро́ч|ить (**-у, -ишь**; *impf* **просро́чивать**) *сов перех* (*платёж*) to be late with; (*паспорт, билет*) to let expire.
просро́ч|ка (**-ки**; *gen pl* **-ек**) *ж* (*платежа*) expiry of time limit; (*паспорта, билета*) expiry.
проста́в|ить (**-лю, -ишь**; *impf* **проставля́ть**) *сов перех* to fill in.
проста́ива|ть (**-ю**) *несов от* **простоя́ть.**
проста́к (**-а́**) *м* simpleton.
простега́|ть (**-ю**) *сов от* **стега́ть.**
просте́н|ок (**-ка**) *м section of wall between windows or doors.*
прост|ере́ть(ся) (*pt* **-ёр(ся), -ёрла(сь), -ёрло(сь)**) *сов от* **простира́ть(ся).**
просте́цк|ий (**-ая, -ое, -ие**) *прил* (*разг*) informal.
простира́|ть (**-ю**; *perf* **простере́ть**) *несов перех* (*планы, замыслы*) to raise; (*протягивать*): ~ **ру́ки** to hold out one's hands ◆ (*impf* **прости́рывать**) *сов перех* (*стирать тщательно*) to wash thoroughly ◆ *неперех* (*стирать*) to wash
▸ **простира́ться** (*perf* **простере́ться**) *несов возв* to extend.
простирн|у́ть (**-у́, -ёшь**) *сов перех* (*разг*): ~ **что-н** to give sth a quick wash.
прости́рыва|ть (**-ю**) *несов от* **простира́ть.**
прости́тел|ьный (**-ен, -ьна, -ьно**) *прил* excusable, forgivable.
проститу́т|ка (**-ки**; *gen pl* **-ок**) *ж* prostitute.
проститу́ци|я (**-и**) *ж* prostitution.
прости́ть (**прощу́, прости́шь**; *impf* **проща́ть**) *сов перех* (*врага, ошибку итп*) to forgive; **проща́ть** (~ *perf*) **что-н кому́-н** to excuse *или* forgive sb (for) sth; **проща́ть** (~ *perf*) **долг кому́-н** to cancel sb's debt; **прости́те меня́, я был о́чень груб** forgive me, I was very rude; **прости́те, как пройти́ на ста́нцию?** excuse me, how do I get to the station?; **нет (уж) прости́те, я не согла́сен** I'm sorry, but I cannot agree
▸ **прости́ться** (*impf* **проща́ться**) *сов возв*: ~**ся с** *+instr* to say goodbye to; (*покинуть*) to leave.
про́сто *нареч* (*делать*) easily; (*интерпретировать*) simply ◆ *част* just; **я зашёл ~ повида́ться** I just popped in to see you; **всё э́то ~ недоразуме́ние** all this is simply a misunderstanding; ~ **(так)** for no particular reason; **~-на́просто** (*разг*) just.
простова́т|ый (**-, -а, -о**) *прил* simple-minded.
простоволо́сый *прил* (*разг*) bareheaded.
простоду́шен *прил см* **простоду́шный.**
простоду́ши|е (**-я**) *ср* ingenuousness.
простоду́ш|ный (**-ен, -на, -но**) *прил* ingenuous.
прост|о́й (**-, -а́, -о**) *прил* simple; (*незамысловатый, грубый*) plain; (*не трудный*) easy, simple; (*прямой и нецеремонный*) unaffected; (*no short form*; *обыкновенный*) ordinary ◆ (**-о́я**) *м* downtime, idle time; (*рабочих*) stoppage; **маши́на на ~о́е** the machine is standing idle; **пла́та за ~ су́дна** demurrage; **~ы́м глазо́м** with the naked eye; **про́ще ~о́го** (*разг*) as easy as pie; **просто́е письмо́** ordinary letter; **просто́й каранда́ш** lead pencil; **просты́е чулки́** cotton stockings.
простоква́ш|а (**-и**) *ж* soured milk (*type of yoghurt*).
простонаро́дный *прил* of the common people.
прост|она́ть (**-ону́, -о́нешь**) *сов (не)перех* to groan.
просто́р (**-а**) *м* expanse; (*свобода*) scope.
просто́рен *прил см* **просто́рный.**
простoréчи|е (**-я**) *ср* common speech; **э́то ~** it's a colloquial expression.
простоpе́чный *прил* common.
просто́р|ный (**-ен, -на, -но**) *прил* roomy.
простосерде́ч|ный (**-ен, -на, -но**) *прил* open-hearted.
простот|а́ (**-ы́**) *ж* simplicity; (*задачи*) easiness, simplicity; (*одежды, рисунка*) plainness; (*характера*) unaffectedness; **по ~е́ душе́вной** *или* **серде́чной** in all innocence.
простофи́л|я (**-и**) *м/ж* dimwit.
просто|я́ть (**-ю́, -и́шь**; *impf* **проста́ивать**) *сов неперех* to stand; (*бездействуя*) to stand idle; (*no impf*; *просуществовать*) to stand.
простра́н|ный (**-ен, -на, -но**) *прил* (*подробный*) verbose.
простра́нственный *прил* spatial.
простра́нств|о (**-а**) *ср* (*также АСТРОНОМИЯ*) space; (*территория*) expanse.
простре́л (**-а**) *м* backache.
простре́лива|ть (**-ю**) *несов от* **прострели́ть** ◆ *перех* (*обстреливать*) to cover (*with artillery fire*).
простр|ели́ть (**-елю́, -е́лишь**; *impf* **простре́ливать**) *сов перех* to shoot through.
простр|очи́ть (**-очу́, -о́чишь**) *сов от* **строчи́ть.**
просту́д|а (**-ы**) *ж* (*МЕД*) cold.
прост|уди́ть (**-ужу́, -у́дишь**; *impf* **простужа́ть**) *сов перех*: ~ **кого́-н** to give a cold to sb; **простужа́ть** (~ *perf*) **у́ши/го́рло** to get a cold in one's ears/throat
▸ **простуди́ться** (*impf* **простужа́ться**) *сов возв* to catch a cold.
просту́дный *прил* cold-related.
простужа́|ть(ся) (**-ю(сь)**) *несов от* **простуди́ть(ся).**
просту́жен|ный (**-, -а, -о**) *прил*: **ребёнок просту́жен** the child has got a cold; **у Вас ~ го́лос** you sound as if you've got a cold.
простужу́(сь) *сов см* **простуди́ть(ся).**
прост|упи́ть (*3sg* **-у́пит**, *3pl* **-у́пят**, *impf*

проступáть) *сов неперех* (*пот, пятна*) to come through; (*очертания*) to appear.
простýп|ок (-ка) *м* misconduct; (*ЮР*) misdemeanour (*BRIT*), misdemeanor (*US*).
простывá|ть (-ю) *несов от* **простыть.**
простыну *итп сов см* **простыть.**
простын|я́ (-и́; *nom pl* **прóстыни**, *gen pl* **просты́нь**, *dat pl* **-я́м)** *ж* sheet.
просты́|ть (-ну, -нешь; *impf* **простывáть)** *сов неперех* (*разг*) to catch a cold; **егó и след ~л** (*разг*) he disappeared without a trace.
просýн|уть (-у, -ешь; *impf* **просóвывать)** *сов перех*: **~ сквозь/в** *+acc итп* to push through/in (to) *итп*
▸ **просýнуться** (*impf* **просóвываться**) *сов возв* (*разг*): **в дверь/в окнó ~улась головá** a head came round the door/appeared at the window.
прос|ушить (-ушý, -ýшишь; *impf* **просýшивать**) *сов перех* to dry.
просуществ|овáть (-ýю) *сов неперех* to exist.
просфор|á (-ы) *ж* (*РЕЛ*) communion bread, Host.
просчёт (-а) *м* (*счёт*) counting; (*ошибка*: *в подсчёте*) error; (: *в действиях*) miscalculation.
просчитá|ть (-ю; *impf* **просчитывать**) *сов перех* (*считать*) to count; (*ошибиться*) to miscount
▸ **просчитáться** (*impf* **просчитываться**) *сов возв* (*при счёте*) to miscount; (*в планах, в предположениях*) to miscalculate; **мы ~лись на сто рублéй** we are out by one hundred roubles.
просы́п|ать (-лю, -лешь; *impf* **просыпáть**) *сов перех* to spill
▸ **просы́паться** (*impf* **просыпáться**) *сов возв* to spill.
просыпá|ть (-ю) *несов от* **проспáть. просыпать**
▸ **просыпáться** *несов от* **проснýться, просыпаться.**
просыплю(сь) *итп сов см* **просыпать(ся).**
просыхá|ть (-ю) *сов от* **просóхнуть.**
прóсьб|а (-ы) *ж* request; **выполнять (выполнить** *perf*) **~у** to fulfil a request; **обращáться (обратиться** *perf*) **к комý-н с ~ой** to make a request to sb.
протáлин|а (-ы) *ж* bare patch (*where snow has melted*).
протáлкива|ть(ся) (-ю(сь)) *несов от* **протолкнýть(ся).**
протáплива|ть (ю) *несов от* **протопить.**
протáптыва|ть (-ю) *несов от* **протоптáть.**
протарáн|ить (-ю, -ишь) *сов от* **тарáнить.**
протаскá|ть (-ю) *сов перех* (*разг*: *сумку*) to carry round; (: *платье*) to wear.
протáскива|ть (-ю) *несов от* **протащить.**
протáчива|ть (ю) *несов от* **проточить.**
прот|ащить (-ащý, -áщишь; *impf* **протáскивать**) *сов перех* (*разг*: *перен*: *силой устроить*) to wangle; (: *критиковать*) to pan; **протáскивать (~** *perf*) **что-н по** *+dat***/сквозь** *+acc* to drag sth along/through.

протежé *м/ж нескл* protégé(e).
протéз (-а) *м* artificial *или* prosthetic limb; **зубнóй ~** denture.
протеи́н (-а) *м* protein.
протеи́новый *прил* protein *опред.*
протёк *сов см* **протéчь.**
протекáни|е (-я) *ср* (*болезни, явлений*) progression; (*в крыше*) leakage.
протекá|ть (*3sg* **-ет**, *3pl* **-ют**) *несов от* **протéчь** ◆ *неперех* (*вода*) to flow, run; (*болезнь, явление*) to progress.
протекýт *итп сов см* **протéчь.**
протекционизм (-а) *м* (*ЭКОН*) protectionism.
протéкци|я (-и) *ж* patronage; **окáзывать (оказáть** *perf*) **~ю комý-н** to use one's influence on behalf of sb.
протелеграфи́р|овать (-ую) *сов от* **телеграфировать.**
прот|ерéть (-рý, -рёшь; *pt* **-ёр, -ёрла, -ёрло,** *impf* **протирáть**) *сов перех* (*сделать дыру*) to wear a hole in; (*очистить*) to wipe; **протирáть (~** *perf*) **что-н чéрез сито** to rub sth through a sieve; **~** (*perf*) **глазá** to rub one's eyes
▸ **протерéться** (*impf* **протирáться**) *сов возв* (*одежда итп*) to wear through.
протёртый *прил* mashed.
протéст (-а) *м* protest; (*ЮР*) objection.
протестáнт (-а) *м* Protestant.
протестáнтск|ий (-ая, -ое, -ие) *прил* Protestant *опред.*
протест|овáть (-ýю) *несов неперех*: **~ (прóтив** *+gen*) to protest (against) ◆ (*perf* **опротестовáть**) *перех* (*вексель, решение суда*) to object to.
протестýющ|ий (-его; *decl like adj*) *м* (*обычно мн*) protestor.
протéчек *сущ см* **протéчка.**
протечёт *итп сов см* **протéчь.**
протéч|ка (-ки; *gen pl* **-ек)** *ж* leak.
прот|éчь (*3sg* **-ечёт**, *3pl* **-екýт**, *pt* **-ёк, -еклá, -еклó**, *impf* **протекáть**) *сов неперех* (*вода*) to seep; (*крыша*) to leak; (*время, юность итп*) to pass by.
прóтив *предл* (*+gen*) against; (*прямо перед*) opposite ◆ *как сказ*: **я ~ дáнного предложéния** I am against the motion; **кто ~?** who is against?; **~ дóма магазин** opposite the house (there) is a shop; **~ имени/наименовáния** against a name/designation; **~ вéтра/течéния/сóлнца** against the wind/current/sun; **~ прáвил/вóли родителей** against the rules/one's parents wishes; **~ ожидáния** contrary to expectation; **~ конкурéнтов/врагá** against the competition/enemy; **лекáрство ~ кáшля/головнóй бóли** medicine for a cough/headache.
проти́вен *прил см* **проти́вный.**
прóтив|ень (-ня) *м* baking tray.
проти́в|иться (-люсь, -ишься; *perf* **воспроти́виться**) *несов возв* (*+dat*) to oppose.
проти́вник (-а) *м* opponent ◆ *собир* (*ВОЕН*) the enemy.

проти́вниц|а (**-ы**) *ж* opponent.
проти́вно *нареч* offensively ◆ *как сказ безл* it's disgusting; **мне ~ ви́деть э́то** it disgusts me to see this.
проти́вн|ое (**-ого**; *decl like adj*) *ср* the opposite.
проти́в|ный *прил* (*точка зрения, мнение*) opposite *опред*, contrary *опред*; (**-ен, -на, -но;** *человек, работа*) disgusting, revolting; **~** *+dat* (*закону, разуму*) contrary to; **в ~ном слу́чае** otherwise; **проти́вная сторона́** the opposing side.
про́тивня *итп сущ см* **про́тивень.**
противоа́томн|ый *прил* (*защита*) anti-nuclear; **~ое укры́тие** nuclear shelter.
противобо́рств|о (**-а**) *ср* struggle.
противобо́рств|овать (**-ую**) *несов неперех* (*+dat*) to fight.
противове́с (**-а**) *м* (*ТЕХ, перен*) counterbalance; **в ~ обще́ственному мне́нию** contrary to public opinion.
противовозду́шный *прил* anti-aircraft.
противога́з (**-а**) *м* gas mask.
противоде́йстви|е (**-я**) *ср* opposition; **встреча́ть (встре́тить** *perf*) **~ чему́-н** to meet with opposition over sth.
противоде́йств|овать (**-ую**) *несов неперех* (*+dat*) to oppose.
противоесте́ствен|ный (**-, -на, -но**) *прил* unnatural.
противозако́н|ный (**-ен, -на, -но**) *прил* unlawful.
противозача́точный *прил* contraceptive *опред*; **противозача́точное сре́дство** contraceptive.
противопожа́рный *прил* (*меры*) fire-prevention; (*техника*) fire-fighting.
противопоказа́ни|е (**-я**) *ср* contraindication.
противопока́зан|ный (**-, -а, -о**) *прил*: **ему́ ~о есть жи́рное** he's been advised not to eat fatty things.
противополо́жен *прил см* **противополо́жный.**
противополо́жност|ь (**-и**) *ж* (*мнений, политики*) contrast; (*противоположное явление*) opposite; **в ~** *+dat* in contrast to.
противополо́ж|ный (**-ен, -на, -но**) *прил* (*берег, сторона итп*) opposite; (*мнение, политика итп*) opposing.
противопоста́в|ить (**-лю, -ишь**; *impf* **противопоставля́ть**) *сов перех*: **~ кого́-н/что-н** *+dat* to contrast sb/sth with; (*направить против*) to oppose sb/sth with.
противопоставле́ни|е (**-я**) *ср* (*мнений, взглядов*) contrasting; (*силы*) opposing.
противопоста́влю *сов см* **противопоста́вить.**
противопоставля́|ть (**-ю**) *несов от* **противопоста́вить.**

противоречи́вост|ь (**-и**) *ж* paradox.
противоречи́в|ый (**-, -а, -о**) *прил* paradoxical.
противоре́чи|е (**-я**) *ср* contradiction; (*классовое, политические*) conflict; (*возражение*): **~** (*+dat*) (*закону, старшим*) defiance (of); **быть** (*impf*) **в ~и с** *+instr* to be in conflict with.
противоре́ч|ить (**-у, -ишь**) *несов неперех*: **~** *+dat* (*человеку*) to contradict; (*логике, закону итп*) to defy; **их показа́ния ~ат друг дру́гу** their evidence is contradictory.
противосто|я́ть (**-ю́, -и́шь**) *несов неперех*: **~** *+dat* (*ветру, буре*) to withstand; (*уговорам, давлению*) to resist; **~** (*impf*) **друг дру́гу** to confront each other.
противоя́ди|е (**-я**) *ср* (*также перен*) antidote.
протира́|ть(ся) (**-ю(сь)**) *несов от* **протере́ть(ся).**
проти́сн|уть (**-у, -ешь**; *impf* **проти́скивать**) *сов перех* to squeeze through
▸ **проти́снуться** (*impf* **проти́скиваться**) *сов возв*: **~ся в** *+acc*/**сквозь** *+acc* to squeeze in(to)/through; **~ся** (*impf*) **вперёд** to push forward.
проткн|у́ть (**-у́, -ёшь**; *impf* **протыка́ть**) *сов перех* to pierce.
протодья́кон (**-а**) *м* archdeacon.
протоиере́|й (**-я**) *м* high priest.
прото́к (**-а**) *м* (*рукав реки*) tributary; (*соединяющая река*) channel; (*МЕД*) duct.
протоко́л (**-а**) *м* (*собрания*) minutes *мн*; (*допроса*) transcript; (*соглашение*) protocol; **Дипломати́ческий ~** Diplomatic Protocol; **вести́** (*impf*) **~ собра́ния** to take the minutes of a meeting; **составля́ть (соста́вить** *perf*) **~ о́быска** to record the details of a search; **журна́л ~ов** minute book.
протоколи́р|овать (**-ую**; *perf* **запротоколи́ровать**) *несов перех* (*собрание, заседание*) to minute; (*осмотр, обыск*) to record.
протоко́льный *прил* (*стиль*) condensed; **протоко́льная за́пись** record of proceedings; **~ журна́л** minutes book.
протолкн|у́ть (**-у́, -ёшь**; *impf* **прота́лкивать**) *сов перех* (*также перен*) to push through
▸ **протолкну́ться** (*impf* **прота́лкиваться**) *сов возв* to push one's way through.
прот|опи́ть (**-оплю́, -о́пишь**; *impf* **прота́пливать**) *сов перех* (*комнату, дом*) to warm through; (*печь*) to stoke up.
прот|опта́ть (**-опчу́, -о́пчешь**; *impf* **прота́птывать**) *сов перех* (*тропинку, дорожку*) to beat.
проторг|ова́ть (**-у́ю**; *impf* **проторго́вывать**) *сов перех* (*потерять*) to make a loss of; (*no impf*; *торговать*: *товары*) to sell; (*жизнь*) to fritter away.
проторённ|ый *прил* (*дорога, путь*) well-

trodden.
протор|úть (-ю, -úшь; *impf* **проторять**) *сов перех* to beat.
прототúп (-а) *м person upon which a character of a novel, play etc is based.*
прото|чúть (-очý, -óчишь; *impf* **протáчивать**) *сов перех* (*прогрызть отверстие*) to nibble through; (*ТЕХ*) to bore.
протóчн|ый *прил* (*вода*) running; **~ое óзеро** *lake with rivers flowing out of it*; **~ая трубá** pipe.
протрáл|ить (-ю, -ишь) *сов от* **трáлить**.
протрезвé|ть (-ю) *сов неперех* = **протрезвúться**.
протрезв|úть (-лю́, -úшь; *impf* **протрезвлять**) *сов перех*: **~ когó-н** to sober sb up
▸ **протрезвúться** (*impf* **протрезвляться**) *сов возв* to sober up.
протрý(сь) *итп сов см* **протерéть(ся)**.
протрубúть (-лю́, -úшь) *сов от* **трубúть**.
протýхн|уть (*3sg* **-ет**, *3pl* **-ут**, *impf* **протухáть** *или* **тýхнуть**) *сов неперех* to go bad *или* off.
протыкá|ть (-ю) *несов от* **проткнýть**.
протя́гива|ть(ся) (-ю(сь)) *несов от* **протянýть(ся)**.
протя́жен *прил см* **протя́жный**.
протяжéни|е (-я) *ср*: **на ~и двух недéль/мéсяцев** over a period of two weeks/months; **на всём ~и путú** the whole way; **на ~и всегó нáшего визúта** for the whole duration of our visit.
протяжённост|ь (-и) *ж* length.
протяжён|ный (-, -на, -но) *прил* prolonged.
протя́жный (-ен, -на, -но) *прил* (*песня, крик итп*) long drawn-out.
прот|янýть (-янý, -я́нешь; *impf* **протя́гивать**) *сов перех* (*верёвку*) to stretch; (*линию передачи*) to extend; (*руки, ноги*) to stretch (out); (*предмет*) to hold out; (*слово, ответ итп*) to say slowly; (*разг*: *критиковать*) to pan ◆ *неперех* (*разг*: *прожить*) to last; **~** (*perf*) **нóги** (*разг*) to turn up one's toes; **протя́гивать** (**~** *perf*) **рýку пóмощи** to lend a (helping) hand
▸ **протянýться** (*impf* **протя́гиваться**) *сов возв* (*дорога*) to stretch; (*линия передачи*) to extend; (*рука*) to stretch out.
проýл|ок (-ка) *м* (*разг*) lane.
про|учúть (-учý, -ýчишь; *impf* **проýчивать**) *сов перех* (*разг*: *наказать*) to teach a lesson; (*no impf*; *учить*) to study
▸ **проучúться** *сов возв* to study.
проф. *сокр* (= **профéссор**) Prof. (= *Professor*).
профáн (-а) *м* ignoramus.
профанáци|я (-и) *ж* (*непочтительное отношение*) profanity; (*обман*) sham.
профашúст (-а) *м* fascist sympathizer.
профашúстск|ий (-ая, -ое, -ие) *прил* fascist *опред*.
профбюрó *ср нескл сокр* (= *профсоюзное бюрó*) trade-union office.
профессионáл (-а) *м* professional.
профессионалúзм (-а) *м* professionalism.
профессионáльный *прил* professional *опред*; (*болезнь, привычка, обучение*) occupational; **профессионáльный союз** trade (*BRIT*) *или* labor (*US*) union.
профéсси|я (-и) *ж* profession; **по ~и он инженéр** he is an engineer by profession; **получáть** (**получúть** *perf*) *или* **приобретáть** (**приобрестú** *perf*) **~ю** to get professional qualifications.
профéссор (-а; *nom pl* **-á**) *м* professor.
профессýр|а (-ы) *ж* professorship ◆ *собир* professors *мн*.
профилáктик|а (-и) *ж* prevention.
профилактúческ|ий (-ая, -ое, -ие) *прил* (*меры*) prevent(at)ive; (*прививка*) prophylactic *опред*; **~ое срéдство** prophylactic.
прóфил|ь (-я) *м* profile; (*предмета, дороги*) cross section; (*учебного заведения*) type; (*работника*) field.
профильтр|овáть (-ýю) *сов от* **фильтровáть**.
профкóм (-а) *м сокр* (= *профсоюзный комитéт*) trade-union committee.
профóрг (-а) *м сокр* (= *профсоюзный организáтор*) trade-union boss.
профóрм|а (-ы) *ж* formality.
профсоюз (-а) *м сокр* (= *профессионáльный союз*) trade (*BRIT*) *или* labor (*US*) union.
профсоюзный *прил* trade-union.
прохáжива|ться (-юсь) *несов от* **пройтúсь**.
прохв|атúть (*3sg* **-áтит**, *3pl* **-áтят**, *impf* **прохвáтывать**) *сов перех* (*подлеж*: *холод, мороз итп*) to chill to the bone.
прохвóст (-а) *м* (*разг*) crook.
прохлáд|а (-ы) *ж* cool.
прохладúтельный *прил*: **~ напúток** cool soft drink.
прохлáдно *нареч* (*встретить*) coolly ◆ *как сказ* it's cool.
прохлáдный *прил* (*также перен*) cool.
прохлáдц|а (-ы) *ж*: **с ~ей** coolly.
прохлаждá|ться (-юсь) *несов возв* (*разг*: *бездельничать*) to doss about.
прохлóпа|ть (-ю; *impf* **прохлóпывать**) *сов перех* (*разг*) to miss.
прохóд (-а) *м* passage; **зáдний ~** (*AHAT*) back passage, anus; **~а нет от когó-н/чегó-н** you can't get away from sb/sth; **не давáть** (*impf*) **~а комý-н** to pester sb.
проходúм|ец (-ца) *м* swindler.
проходúмост|ь (-и) *ж* (*местности*) passability; (*ABT*) off-road capability; (*МЕД*) permeability.
проходúм|ый (-, -а, -о) *прил* passable.
прох|одúть (-ожý, -óдишь) *несов от* **пройтú** ◆ *сов неперех* (*ходить*) to walk.
прохóд|ка (-ки; *gen pl* **-ок**) *ж* sinking of shafts.
проходн|áя (-óй; *decl like adj*) *ж* checkpoint (*at entrance to factory etc*).
проходн|óй *прил*: **~áя кóмната** hall;

проходнóй балл pass mark.
прохóдок *сущ см* **прохóдка**.
прохóдчик (-а) *м person who sinks shafts*.
прохóж|ая (-ей; *decl like adj) ж см* **прохóжий**.
прохождéни|е (-я) *ср* (*по дороге*) passage; (*испытаний*) passing; (*службы*) term.
прохóж|ий (-его; *decl like adj*) *м* passer-by.
прохожý *(не)сов см* **проходи́ть**.
прохуди́|ться (*3sg* **-и́тся**, *3pl* **-я́тся**) *сов неперех* (*разг*) to wear thin.
процветá|ть (-ю) *несов неперех* (*фирма, бизнесмен*) to prosper; (*театр, наука*) to flourish; (*разг: человек, семья*) to thrive.
процеди́ть (-ежý, -éдишь; *impf* **процéживать**) *сов перех* (*бульон, сок*) to strain; (*no impf; произнести*): **~ (сквозь зýбы)** to say through one's teeth.
процедýр|а (-ы) *ж* procedure; (*МЕД: обычно мн*) course of treatment.
процедýрн|ый *прил* procedural; (*МЕД*): **~ая сестрá** nurse; **~ кабинéт** treatment room.
процéжива|ть (-ю) *несов от* **процеди́ть**.
процежý *сов см* **процеди́ть**.
процéнт (-а) *м* percentage; **в размéре 5 ~ов годовы́х** at a yearly rate of 5 percent; **на все сто ~ов** (*доверять, поддерживать*) one hundred percent; *см также* **процéнты**.
процéнтный *прил* (*выраженный в процентах*) percentage *опред*; **процéнтная стáвка** interest rate.
процéнт|ы (-ов) *мн* (*КОММ*) interest *ед*; (*: вознаграждение*) commission; **простые/слóжные/нарóсшие ~** simple/compound/accrued interest.
процéсс (-а) *м* process; (*ЮР: порядок разбирательства*) proceedings *мн*; (*: также: судéбный ~*) trial; **воспали́тельный ~** inflammation; **в ~е** *+gen* in the course of; **возбуждáть (возбуди́ть** *perf*) **~** to institute proceedings.
процéсси|я (-и) *ж* procession.
процéссор (-а) *м* word processor.
процессуáльный *прил* (*ЮР*) procedural; **процессуáльный кóдекс** procedural code.
процити́р|овать (-ую) *сов от* **цити́ровать**.
прочёл *сов см* **прочéсть**.
прóчен *прил см* **прóчный**.
прóчерк (-а) *м* line.
прочерти́ть (-ерчý, -éртишь; *impf* **прочéрчивать**) *сов перех*: **~ ли́нию** to draw a line.
проч|есáть (-ешý, -éшешь; *impf* **прочёсывать**) *сов перех* (*также перен*) to comb.
проч|éсть (-тý, -тёшь; *pt* **-ёл, -лá, -лó**) *сов от* **читáть**.
прочёсыва|ть (-ю) *несов от* **прочесáть**.
прочешý *итп сов см* **прочесáть**.
прóч|ий (-ая, -ее, -ие) *прил* other; **поми́мо всегó ~его** on top of everything else; **и прóчее** and so on.
прочи́|стить (-щу, -стишь; *impf* **прочищáть**) *сов перех* to clean out; (*нос*) to clear.
прочитá|ть (-ю) *сов от* **читáть**.
прóч|ить (-у, -ишь) *несов перех*: **~ что-н комý-н** to predict sth for sb; **егó роди́тели ~или егó во врачи́** his parents intended him to be a doctor.
прочищá|ть (-ю) *несов от* **прочи́стить**.
прочи́щу *сов см* **прочи́стить**.
прочлá *итп сов см* **прочéсть**.
прóчно *нареч* (*закрепить*) firmly; (*заучить*) well.
прóчност|ь (-и) *ж* (*материала итп*) durability; (*отношений, семьи*) stability; **запáс ~и** reliability.
прóч|ный (-ен, -нá, -но) *прил* (*материал итп*) durable; (*постройка*) solid, stable; (*знания*) sound; (*отношение, семья*) stable; (*мир, счастье*) lasting.
прочтéни|е (-я) *ср* reading.
прочтý *итп сов см* **прочéсть**.
прочýвствованный *прил* heartfelt.
прочýвств|овать (-ую) *сов перех* to feel deeply; **~** (*perf*) **роль** to get inside a role.
прочь *нареч* (*в сторону*) away; **рýки ~!** hands off!; **~ с дорóги!** get out of the way!; **он не ~ вы́пить** he won't say no to a drink.
прошвырн|ýться (-ýсь, -ёшься) *сов возв* (*разг*) to stretch one's legs.
прошéдш|ий (-ая, -ее, -ие) *прил* (*прошлый*) past; **прошéдшее врéмя** past tense.
прошéй(те) *сов см* **проши́ть**.
прошёл(ся) *сов см* **пройти́(сь)**.
прошéни|е (-я) *ср* plea; (*письменное ходатайство*) petition; **подавáть (подáть** *perf*) **~ в** *+acc* to present a petition to.
прош|ептáть (-епчý, -éпчешь) *сов перех* to whisper.
прошéстви|е (-я) *ср*: **по ~и гóда/мéсяца** after a year's/month's lapse.
прошиб|и́ть (-ý, -ёшь; *pt* **-, -ла, -ло**, *impf* **прошибáть**) *сов перех* (*разг: дверь, окно итп*) to smash through; **пот прошиб егó** he broke out in a sweat; **дрожь ~ла её** a shiver went down her spine.
прош|и́ть (-ью, -ьёшь; *imper* **-éй(те)**, *impf* **прошивáть**) *сов перех* (*пришить*) to sew a seam on; (*перен: пулями стены*) to pepper.
прошлá *итп сов см* **пройти́**.
прошлогóдн|ий (-яя, -ее, -ие) *прил* last year's; **~ие собы́тия** the events of last year.
прóшло|е (-го; *decl like adj*) *ср* the past; **отходи́ть (отойти́** *perf*) **в ~** to become a thing of the past.
прóшл|ый *прил* last; (*прежний*) past; **в ~ раз** last time; **на ~ой недéле** last week; **в ~ом годý/мéсяце** last year/month; **дéло ~ое** it's in

the past.

прошмыгн|у́ть (-у́, -ёшь; *impf* **прошмы́гивать**) *сов неперех*: ~ **ми́мо** *+gen*/**сквозь** *+acc итп* (*разг*) to dart past/through *итп*.

проштамп|ова́ть (-у́ю) *сов от* **штампова́ть**.

проштра́ф|иться (-люсь, -ишься) *сов возв* (*разг*) to lapse.

проштуди́р|овать (-ую) *сов от* **штуди́ровать**.

прошу́(сь) *несов см* **проси́ть(ся)**.

прошью́ *итп сов см* **прошить**.

проща́йте *част* goodbye, farewell.

проща́льный *прил* parting *опред*; (*вечер, визит*) farewell *опред*.

проща́ни|е (-я) *ср* (*действие*) parting; **на** ~ on parting.

проща́|ть(ся) (-ю(сь)) *несов от* **прости́ть(ся)**.

про́ще *сравн нареч от* **про́сто** ◆ *сравн прил от* **просто́й**.

проще́ни|е (-я) *ср* (*ребёнка, друга итп*) forgiveness; (*преступника*) pardon; **проси́ть** (**попроси́ть** *perf*) ~**я** to say sorry; **прошу́ ~я!** (I'm) sorry!

прощу́(сь) *сов см* **прости́ть(ся)**.

прощу́па|ть (-ю; *impf* **прощу́пывать**) *сов перех* to feel for; (*перен*) to check out; **прощу́пывать** (~ *perf*) **по́чву** to see how the land lies.

проэкзамен|ова́ть (-у́ю) *сов от* **экзаменова́ть**.

проявите́л|ь (-я) *м* (*ФОТО*) developer.

про|яви́ть (-явлю́, -я́вишь; *impf* **проявля́ть**) *сов перех* to display; (*ФОТО*) to develop; **проявля́ть** (~ *perf*) **себя́ пло́хо/хорошо́** to show o.s. in a bad/good light

► **прояви́ться** (*impf* **проявля́ться**) *сов возв* (*талант, потенциал итп*) to reveal itself; (*решительность, смелость итп*) to show itself; (*ФОТО*) to be developed.

проявле́ни|е (-я) *ср* display; (*обычно мн: жизни*) manifestation.

проявлю́(сь) *сов см* **прояви́ть(ся)**.

проявля́|ть(ся) (-ю(сь)) *несов от* **прояви́ть(ся)**.

проясне́ни|е (-я) *ср* (*погоды*) brightening *или* clearing up; (*ситуации*) clarification; **у меня́ наступи́ло ~ созна́ния** *или* **ума́** my mind cleared.

проясн|и́ть (-ю́, -и́шь; *impf* **проясня́ть**) *сов перех* (*обстановку*) to clarify; (*мысли*) to sort out; **проясня́ть** (~ *perf*) **чьё-н созна́ние** to bring sb round

► **проясни́ться** (*impf* **проясня́ться**) *сов возв* (*погода, небо*) to brighten *или* clear up; (*обстановка*) to be clarified; (*мысли*) to be sorted out; **у него́ ~и́лось созна́ние** his mind cleared.

пру(сь) *итп несов см* **пере́ть(ся)**.

пруд (-а́; *loc sg* -у́) *м* (*естественный*) pool, pond; (*искусственный*) pond.

пр|уди́ть (-ужу́, -у́дишь; *perf* **запруди́ть**) *несов перех* to dam; **де́нег у него́ хоть ~уд пруди́** (*разг*) he is rolling in cash.

пружи́н|а (-ы) *ж* (*ТЕХ*) spring; (*перен: движущая сила*) mainspring.

пружи́нист|ый (-, -а, -о) *прил* springy; **у него́ ~ шаг** he has a spring in his step.

пружу́ *сов см* **пруди́ть**.

прут (-а́; *nom pl* -ья) *м* (*БОТ*) twig; (*ТЕХ*) rod.

пры́гал|ка (-ки; *gen pl* -ок) *ж* skipping-rope (*BRIT*), skip rope (*US*).

пры́га|ть (-ю) *несов неперех* to jump; (*мяч*) to bounce.

пры́гн|уть (-у, -ешь) *сов неперех* to jump; (*мяч*) to bounce.

пры́гу́н (-а́) *м* (*СПОРТ*) jumper; ~ **в длину́** long jumper; ~ **в высоту́** high jumper.

прыгу́н|ья (-ьи; *gen pl* -ий) *ж см* **прыгу́н**.

пры|жо́к (-жка́) *м* (*через лужу, с парашютом*) jump; (*в воду*) dive; **~жки́ в высоту́/длину́** high/long jump; **~жки́ с шесто́м** pole vault; **опо́рный** ~ (*СПОРТ*) vault.

пры́сн|уть (-у, -ешь; *impf* **пры́скать**) *сов неперех* (*кровь*) to spurt; (*+instr*; *водой*) to sprinkle with; (*духами*) to spray with; **пры́скать** (~ *perf*) **со́ смеху** (*разг*) to go into a fit of giggles.

пры́т|кий (-кая, -кое, -кие; -ок, -ка́, -ко) *прил* (*разг: подвижный*) bouncy.

пры́т|ь (-и) *ж* (*разг: быстрота*) bounce; **во всю** ~ (*разг*) at full tilt.

прыщ (-а́) *м* spot.

прыща́в|ый (-, -а, -о) *прил* spotty.

пряди́льный *прил* spinning *опред*.

пряди́льщик (-а) *м* spinner.

пряди́льщиц|а (-ы) *ж см* **пряди́льщик**.

пряду́ *итп несов см* **прясть**.

пряд|ь (-и) *ж* lock (*of hair*).

пря́ж|а (-и) *ж* yarn.

пря́ж|ка (-ки; *gen pl* -ек) *ж* (*на ремне*) buckle; (*на юбке*) clasp.

пря́л|ка (-ки; *gen pl* -ок) *ж* spinning wheel.

прям|а́я (-о́й; *decl like adj*) *ж* straight line; **по ~о́й** in a straight line.

прямико́м *нареч*: **он прошёл ~ че́рез сад** (*разг*) he went straight across the garden.

пря́мо *нареч* (*в прямом направлении*) straight ahead; (*ровно*) upright; (*непосредственно*) straight; (*откровенно*) directly ◆ *част* (*действительно*) really; **приступа́ть** (**приступи́ть** *perf*) ~ **к де́лу** to get straight down to business; **у меня́ ~ сил нет!** I really haven't (got) the strength!; **помоги́те ему́ – (ну) ~!** (*разг*) help him? no way!

прямоду́ш|ный (-ен, -на, -но) *прил* (*человек*) forthright; (*ответ*) candid.

прям|о́й (-, -а́, -о) *прил* straight; (*путь, слова, человек*) direct; (*ответ, политика*) open; (*вызов, обман*) obvious; (*улики*) solid; (*no short form*; *сообщение, рейс, обязанность итп*) direct; (*выгода, смысл, польза итп*) real; (*значение слова*) literal; **~ы́е изде́ржки** direct cost; **пряма́я кишка́** rectum; **пряма́я**

трансля́ция live broadcast; **прямо́е дополне́ние** direct object; **прямо́е попада́ние** direct hit; **прямо́й до́ступ** (*КОМП*) direct access; **прямо́й репорта́ж** live coverage; **прямо́й у́гол** right angle; **прямы́е вы́боры/нало́ги** direct elections/taxes.
прямолине́|йный (-ен, -йна, -йно) *прил* (*движение*) along a straight line; (*перен*) blunt.
пря́мо-таки *нареч* (*разг*) really.
прямоуго́льник (-а) *м* rectangle.
прямоуго́льный *прил* rectangular.
пря́ник (-а) *м* ≈ gingerbread.
пря́ност|ь (-и) *ж* spice.
пря́н|ый (-, -а, -о) *прил* spicy.
пря|сть (-ду́, -дёшь; *perf* **спрясть)** *несов перех* to spin.
пря́|тать (-чу, -чешь; *perf* **спря́тать)** *несов перех* to hide; **он ~тал глаза́ от меня́** he didn't look me straight in the eye
▸ **пря́таться** (*perf* **спря́таться**) *несов возв* to hide; (*человек: от холода, ветра*) to shelter; (*солнце*) to hide; **~ся (спря́таться** *perf*) **за чужу́ю спи́ну** to redirect responsibility.
пря́т|ки (-ок; *dat pl* **-кам)** *мн* hide-and-seek *ед*; **игра́ть** (*impf*) **в ~ с кем-н** to play hide-and-seek with sb; (*перен*) to avoid sb.
пря́чу(сь) *итп несов см* **пря́тать(ся)**.
пса *итп сущ см* **пёс**.
псал|о́м (-ма́) *м* psalm.
псало́мщик (-а) *м* sexton.
псалты́р|ь (-и) *ж* Psalter.
пса́рн|я (-и) *ж* kennels *мн* (*for hunting dogs*).
псевдони́м (-а) *м* pseudonym.
псих (-а) *м* (*разг*) psycho.
психиа́тр (-а) *м* psychiatrist.
психиатри́ческ|ий (-ая, -ое, -ие) *прил* psychiatric.
психиатри́|я (-и) *ж* psychiatry.
пси́хик|а (-и) *ж* psyche.
психи́ческ|ий (-ая, -ое, -ие) *прил* (*заболевание, отклонение итп*) mental.
психоана́лиз (-а) *м* psychoanalysis.
псих|ова́ть (-у́ю) *несов неперех* (*разг*) to freak out.
психо́з (-а) *м* (*МЕД*) psychosis; (*странность в психике*) neurosis.
психо́лог (-а) *м* psychologist.
психологи́ческ|ий (-ая, -ое, -ие) *прил* psychological.
психоло́ги|я (-и) *ж* psychology.
психопа́т (-а) *м* psychopath.
психопа́ти|я (-и) *ж* psychopathy.
психотерапе́вт (-а) *м* psychotherapist.
психотерапи́|я (-и) *ж* psychotherapy.
ПСС *м сокр* = *по́лное собра́ние сочине́ний*.
пта́х|а (-и) *ж* (*разг*) bird.
пта́ш|ка (-ки; *gen pl* **-ек)** *ж* bird.
птен|е́ц (-ца́) *м* chick.
пти́ц|а (-ы) *ж* bird ◆ *собир*: **(дома́шняя) ~** poultry; **ва́жная ~** (*разг*) big shot.
птицево́д (-а) *м* poulterer, poultry farmer.
птицево́дств|о (-а) *ср* poultry farming.
птицево́дческ|ий (-ая, -ое, -ие) *прил*: **~ая фе́рма** poultry farm.
птицефа́брик|а (-и) *ж* poultry farm.
пти́чек *сущ см* **пти́чка**.
пти́ч|ий (-ья, -ье, -ьи) *прил* (*корм, клетка*) bird *опред*; **вид с высоты́ ~ьего полёта** bird's eye view; **я сам здесь на ~ьих права́х** I don't have any rights here myself; **пти́чий база́р** bird colony.
пти́ч|ка (-ки; *gen pl* **-ек)** *ж уменьш от* **пти́ца**; (*разг: в тексте*) tick (*BRIT*), check (*US*).
пти́чник (-а) *м* ≈ hen house.
ПТУ *ср сокр* (= *профессиона́льно-техни́ческое учи́лище*) ≈ tech (= *technical college*).
пуа́нт (-а) *м* (*БАЛЕТ*) ballet shoe.
пу́блик|а (-и) *ж собир* audience; **широ́кая ~** the public; **игра́ть** (*impf*) **на ~у** to show off; **на ~у** in company.
публика́ци|я (-и) *ж* publication.
публик|ова́ть (-у́ю; *perf* **опубликова́ть)** *несов перех* to publish.
публици́ст (-а) *м* *writer of sociopolitical literature*.
публици́стик|а (-и) *ж собир* sociopolitical journalism.
публицисти́ческ|ий (-ая, -ое, -ие) *прил* sociopolitical.
публи́ч|ный (-ен, -на, -но) *прил* public; **публи́чный дом** brothel; **публи́чные торги́, публи́чная прода́жа** (public) auction, public sale.
пу́гал|о (-а) *ср* scarecrow; (*перен: некрасивый человек*) fright.
пуга́|ть (-ю; *perf* **испуга́ть** *или* **напуга́ть)** *несов перех* to frighten, scare
▸ **пуга́ться** (*perf* **испуга́ться** *или* **напуга́ться**) *несов возв* to be frightened *или* scared.
пугли́в|ый (-, -а, -о) *прил* timid.
пу́говиц|а (-ы) *ж* button; **застёгивать (застегну́ть** *perf*) **~у** to fasten a button.
пуд (-а; *nom pl* **-ы́)** *м* pood (*Russian measure of weight equivalent to 16 kilogrammes*).
пу́дел|ь (-я) *м* poodle.
пу́динг (-а) *м* ≈ pudding.
пудо́в|ый *прил*: **~ая гиря** a pood weight.
пу́др|а (-ы) *ж* powder; **са́харная ~** icing sugar.
пу́дрениц|а (-ы) *ж* powder compact.
пу́др|ить (-ю, -ишь; *perf* **напу́дрить)** *несов перех* to powder; **~** (*impf*) **мозги́ кому́-н** (*разг*) to pull the wool over sb's eyes
▸ **пу́дриться** (*perf* **напу́дриться**) *несов возв* to powder one's face.
пуза́т|ый (-, -а, -о) *прил* (*разг: человек*) tubby; (*перен: чайник, комод*) rounded.

пу́з|о (-а) *ср* (*разг*: *живот*) belly; (*брюхо*) paunch.
пузырёк (-ька́) *м* (*уменьш от* **пузы́рь**; (*для лекарства, чернил*) vial.
пузыр|и́ться (*3sg* **-и́тся**, *3pl* **-я́тся**) *несов возв* (*жидкость*) to bubble; (*краска*) to blister; (*разг*: *одежда*) to blow up.
пузы́р|ь (-я́) *м* (*мыльный*) bubble; (*на коже*) blister; (*с водой*) water bottle; **жёлчный ~** gall bladder; **мочево́й ~** (urinary) bladder.
пузырька́ *итп сущ см* **пузырёк**.
пук (-а; *nom pl* **-и́**) *м* bundle.
пу́ка|ть (-ю; *perf* **пу́кнуть**) *несов неперех* to fart.
пулево́й *прил* bullet *опред*.
пулемёт (-а) *м* machine gun.
пулемётчик (-а) *м* machine gunner.
пуленепробива́емый *прил* bullet-proof.
пуло́вер (-а) *м* pullover.
пульвериза́тор (-а) *м* atomizer.
пульс (-а) *м* (*МЕД, перен*) pulse.
пульси́р|овать (*3sg* **-ует**, *3pl* **-уют**) *несов неперех* (*артерии*) to pulsate; (*кровь*) to pulse; (*нарыв*) to throb.
пульт (-а) *м* panel; (*музыканта*) stand; **пульт управле́ния** control panel.
пу́л|я (-и) *ж* bullet; **~ей вы́лететь** (*perf*) (**из** *+gen*) (*перен*: *разг*) to shoot out (from).
пу́м|а (-ы) *ж* puma.
пункт (-а) *м* point; (*документа*) clause; (*медицинский*) centre (*BRIT*), center (*US*); (*наблюдательный, командный*) post; **населённый ~** inhabited area.
пункти́р (-а) *м* dotted line.
пунктуа́л|ьный (**-ен, -ьна, -ьно**) *прил* (*человек*) punctual.
пунктуа́ци|я (-и) *ж* punctuation.
пу́нкци|я (-и) *ж* (*МЕД*) lumber puncture.
пунцо́вый *прил* scarlet *опред*.
пунш (-а) *м* (*КУЛИН*) punch.
пуп (-а́) *м* (*разг*) belly button; **~ земли́** (*разг*) the bee's knees.
пупка́ *сущ см* **пупо́к**.
пупови́н|а (-ы) *ж* umbilical cord.
пуп|о́к (-ка́) *м* (*АНАТ*) navel.
пупы́рыш|ек (-ка) *м* (*разг*: *на коже*) pimple.
пург|а́ (-и́) *ж* snowstorm.
пурге́н (-а) *м* phenol phthalene (*used as laxative*).
пурита́н|ин (**-ина**; *nom pl* **-е**, *gen pl* **-**) *м* puritan.
пурита́н|ка (**-ки**; *gen pl* **-ок**) *ж см* **пурита́нин**.
пурита́нск|ий (**-ая, -ое, -ие**) *прил* puritanical.
пу́рпур (-а) *м* wine, Burgundy.
пурпу́рный *прил* wine *опред*, Burgundy *опред*.
пуск (-а) *м* (*завода итп*) starting up; **~ в эксплуата́цию** commission.
пуска́й *част, союз* (*разг*) = **пусть**.
пуска́|ть(ся) (**-ю(сь)**) *несов от* **пусти́ть(ся)**.
пусково́й *прил* (*период*) initial *опред*; (*механизм, установка*) starting *опред*; (*платформа*) launching *опред*.
пусте́|ть (*3sg* **-ет**, *3pl* **-ют**, *perf* **опусте́ть**) *несов неперех* to become empty.
пу|сти́ть (**-щу́, -стишь**; *impf* **пуска́ть**) *сов перех* (*руку, человека*) to let go of; (*лошадь, санки итп*) to send off; (*завод, станок, электростанцию*) to start; (*в вагон, в зал*) to let in; (*пар, дым*) to give off; (*камень, снаряд*) to throw; (*сплетни*) to spread; (*корни*) to put out; **пуска́ть** (**~** *perf*) **что-н на** *+acc*/**под** *+acc* (*использовать*) to use sth as/for; **пуска́ть** (**~** *perf*) **кого́-н куда́-нибудь** to let sb go somewhere; **пуска́ть** (**~** *perf*) **това́р в прода́жу** to put goods onto the market; **пуска́ть** (**~** *perf*) **пузыри́** to blow bubbles; **пуска́ть** (**~** *perf*) **слю́ни** to dribble; **пуска́ть** (**~** *perf*) **во́ду/газ** to turn on the water/gas
▶ **пусти́ться** (*impf* **пуска́ться**) *сов возв*: **~ся в** *+acc* (*в объяснения*) to go into; **пуска́ться** (**~ся** *perf*) **в подро́бности** to go into detail; **пуска́ться** (**~ся** *perf*) **в пляс** *или* **пляса́ть** to start dancing; **пуска́ться** (**~ся** *perf*) **в путь** to set off.
пу́сто *нареч* empty ◆ *как сказ* (*ничего нет*) there's nothing there; (*никого нет*) there's no-one there; **в го́роде/холоди́льнике ~** the town/fridge is empty.
пуст|ова́ть (*3sg* **-у́ет**, *3pl* **-у́ют**) *несов неперех* to be empty.
пуст|о́й (**-, -а́, -о, -ы**) *прил* empty; (*взгляд*) vacant; (*предлог, причина, затея*) trifling; **он – ~о́е ме́сто** he's a real nobody; **с ~ы́ми рука́ми** empty-handed.
пустосло́ви|е (-я) *ср* idle talk.
пуст|ота́ (**-оты́**; *nom pl* **-о́ты**) *ж* emptiness; (*полое место*) cavity.
пу́стош|ь (-и) *ж* wasteland.
пусты́н|ный *прил* desert *опред*; (**-ен, -на, -но**; *безлюдный*) deserted.
пусты́н|я (**-и**; *gen pl* **-ь**) *ж* desert; (*безлюдное место*) wilderness.
пусты́рник (-а) *м* motherwort.
пусты́р|ь (-я́) *м* wasteland.
пусты́ш|ка (**-ки**; *gen pl* **-ек**) *ж* (*разг*: *соска*) dummy (*BRIT*), pacifier (*US*); (*перен*: *о человеке*) airhead.

KEYWORD

пусть *част* (*+3sg/pl*) ***1*** (*выражает приказ, угрозу*): **пусть он придёт у́тром** let him come in the morning; **пусть она́ то́лько попро́бует отказа́ться** let her just try to refuse
2 (*выражает согласие*): **пусть бу́дет так** so be it; **пусть бу́дет по-тво́ему** have it your way
3 (*всё равно*) OK, all right; **она́ вини́т меня́, пусть!** OK *или* all right, so she blames me!
◆ *союз* (*допустим*) even if; **пусть он плохо́й дире́ктор, зато́ хоро́ший челове́к** even if he is a bad director, he is a good person; **на́до оправда́ть все, пусть да́же небольши́е, затра́ты** all expenses, even small ones, must be justified.

пустя́к (-а́) *м* trifle; (*неценный предмет*) trinket

◆ *как сказ*: **э́то** ~ it's nothing; **говори́ть** *(impf)* **пустяки́** to talk nonsense; **Вы огорчены́? – пустяки́!** are you upset? – it's nothing!

пустяко́вый *прил* (*разг*: *повод, жалоба*) trivial; **э́то пустяко́вая рабо́та** it's a piece of cake.

пустя́чный *прил* = **пустяко́вый.**

путáн|а **(-ы)** *ж prostitute working for hard currency.*

пу́таница **(-ы)** *ж* (*в мыслях, в делах*) muddle; (*дорог, дверей*) maze.

пу́тан|ый **(-, -а, -о)** *прил* (*объяснение, рассказ*) muddled.

пу́та|ть **(-ю;** *perf* **запу́тать** *или* **спу́тать)** *несов перех* (*нитки, волосы*) to tangle (up); (*разг*: *сбить с толку*) to bamboozle; (*perf* **спу́тать** *или* **перепу́тать**; *бумаги, факты итп*) to mix up; (*perf* **впу́тать**; *разг*): ~ **кого́-н в** *+acc* to get sb mixed up in; **я его́ с кем-то ~ю** I'm confusing him with somebody else; **он всегда́ ~л на́ши имена́** he always got our names mixed up

▸ **пу́таться** **(***perf* **запу́таться** *или* **спу́таться)** *несов возв* to get tangled (up); (*в рассказе, в объяснении*) to get mixed up; (*perf* **спу́таться**; *общаться*): **~ся с** *+instr* (*с мошенниками, с хулиганами итп*) to get mixed up with.

путёв|ка **(-ки;** *gen pl* **-ок)** *ж* holiday voucher (*given by employer*); (*водителя*) manifest (*of cargo drivers*).

путеводи́тел|ь **(-я)** *м* guidebook.

путево́дн|ый *прил* (*перен*: *идея, теория*) guiding; **~ая нить** guiding light.

путево́й *прил* (*пост, сигнал*) railway *опред*; (*записки, дневник*) travel *опред*; **путево́й лист** (*водителя*) = **путёвка.**

путёвок *сущ см* **путёвка.**

путёвый *прил* (*разг*) = **пу́тный.**

путе́й *сущ см* **пути́.**

путём *сущ см* **путь** ◆ *предл* (*+gen*) by means of.

путеше́ственник **(-а)** *м* traveller (*BRIT*), traveler (*US*).

путеше́стви|е **(-я)** *ср* journey, trip; (*морской*) voyage.

путеше́ствовать **(-ую)** *несов неперех* to travel.

пут|и́ *сущ см* **путь** ◆ **(-е́й)** *мн*: **дыха́тельные** ~ respiratory tract.

пу́тник **(-а)** *м* traveller (*BRIT*), traveler (*US*).

пу́тный *прил* (*человек*) decent; (*план, предложение*) practical.

путч **(-а)** *м* (*полит*) putsch.

пу́т|ы **(-)** *мн* (*также перен*) fetters *мн.*

пут|ь **(-и́;** *см* **Table 3)** *м* (*также перен*) way; (*платформа*) platform; (*рельсы*) track; (*путешествие*) journey; **запасно́й** ~ siding; **во́дные ~и́** waterways; **возду́шные ~и́** air lanes; **нам с Ва́ми не по ~и́** we're not going the same way; (*перен*) we don't see eye to eye; **счастли́вого ~и́!** have a good trip!; **быть** *(impf)* **на ~и́ к** *+dat* to be on the road *или* way to; **провожа́ть (проводи́ть** *perf*) **кого́-н в после́дний** ~ to lay sb to rest; **пути́ сообще́ния** transport network *ед*; *см также* **пути́.**

пуф **(-а)** *м* pouffe.

пух **(-а;** *loc sg* **-у́)** *м* (*у животных*) fluff; (*у птиц, у человека*) down; **в ~ и прах** (*разг*) totally and utterly; **ни пу́ха ни пера́!** good luck!

пух *итп несов см* **пу́хнуть.**

пу́хл|ый **(-, -а́, -о)** *прил* (*щёки, человек*) chubby; (*губы*) full; (*портфель, папка*) bulging.

пу́х|нуть **(-ну, -нешь;** *pt* **-, -ла, -ло,** *perf* **вспу́хнуть** *или* **опу́хнуть)** *несов неперех* to swell (up); **у меня́ голова́ ~нет** (*разг*) my head's buzzing.

пухо́в|ый *прил* (*подушка*) feather *опред*; (*платок*) angora *опред*; **~ая ку́ртка** padded jacket.

пучегла́зый *прил* (*разг*) goggle-eyed, pop-eyed.

пучи́н|а **(-ы)** *ж* the deep.

пу́ч|ить **(-у, -ишь;** *perf* **вы́пучить)** *несов перех*: ~ **глаза́** to goggle; **он вы́пучил глаза́** his eyes popped out of his head; **меня́ ~ит** I have flatulence

▸ **пу́читься** **(***perf* **вспу́читься)** *несов возв* to swell (up).

пуч|о́к **(-ка́)** *м* bunch; (*света*) beam.

пу́шек *сущ см* **пу́шка.**

пуши́н|ка **(-ки;** *gen pl* **-ок)** *ж* piece of fluff; (*снега*) flake.

пуши́ст|ый **(-, -а, -о)** *прил* (*мех, ковёр итп*) fluffy; (*волосы*) fuzzy; (*ткань*) fleecy; (*кот*) furry; (*цыплёнок*) downy.

пу́ш|ка **(-ки;** *gen pl* **-ек)** *ж* (*на танке*) artillery gun; (*ист*) cannon.

пушни́н|а **(-ы)** *ж собир* furs *мн.*

пушно́й *прил* furry; ~ **това́р** furs *мн.*

пуш|о́к **(-ка́)** *м уменьш от* **пух**; (*над губой*) fluff.

пу́щ|а **(-и)** *ж* dense forest.

пу́щий **(-ая, -ее, -ие)** *прил*: **для ~ей ва́жности** (*разг*) for more impact.

пущу́(сь) *сов см* **пусти́ть(ся).**

пфе́нинг **(-а)** *м* pfennig.

Пхенья́н **(-а)** *м* Pyongyang.

пчел|а́ **(-ы́;** *nom pl* **пчёлы)** *ж* bee.

пчели́ный *прил* (*мёд*) bee's; ~ **воск** beeswax; ~ **рой** swarm of bees.

пчелово́д **(-а)** *м* bee-keeper.

пчелово́дств|о **(-а)** *ср* bee-keeping.

пшени́ц|а **(-ы)** *ж* wheat.

пшени́чный *прил* wheat *опред.*

пшён|ка **(-ки)** *ж* (*разг*) millet porridge.

пшённ|ый *прил*: **~ая ка́ша** millet porridge.

пшен|о́ **(-а́)** *ср* millet.

пы́ж|иться **(-усь, -ишься;** *perf* **напы́житься)** *несов возв* (*разг*: *напрягаться*) to puff and pant; (*держаться важно*) to puff up.

пыл (**-а**; *loc sg* **-ý**) *м* (*перен*) ardour (*BRIT*), ardor (*US*); **в ~ý спóра/сражéния** in the heat of the argument/battle.
пылá|ть (**-ю**) *несов неперех* (*костёр*) to blaze; (*перен*: *лицо*) to burn; (*+instr*; *перен*: *любовью, гневом итп*) to burn with.
пы́лен *прил см* **пы́льный**.
пылесóс (**-а**) *м* vacuum cleaner, Hoover®.
пылесóс|ить (**-ишь**; *perf* **пропылесóсить**) *сов перех* to vacuum, hoover®.
пыли́н|ка (**-ки**; *gen pl* **-ок**) *ж* speck of dust.
пыл|и́ть (**-ю́, -и́шь**; *perf* **напыли́ть**) *несов неперех* to raise dust
▸ **пыли́ться** (*perf* **запыли́ться**) *несов возв* to get dusty.
пы́л|кий (**-кая, -кое, -кие**; **-ок, -кá, -ко**) *прил* passionate.
пыл|ь (**-и**; *loc sg* **-и́**) *ж* dust; **вытирáть** (**вы́тереть** *perf*) **~** to dust; **пускáть** (**пусти́ть** *perf*) **~ в глазá комý-н** to give sb the wrong idea.
пы́л|ьный (**-ен, -ьна, -ьно**) *прил* dusty.
пыльц|á (**-ы́**) *ж* pollen.
пырн|ýть (**-ý, -ёшь**) *сов перех* (*разг*) to stab; ~ (*perf*) **ножóм** to knife.
пытá|ть (**-ю**) *несов перех* to torture; ~ (*impf*) **когó-н о чём-н** to grill sb about sth
▸ **пытáться** (*perf* **попытáться**) *несов возв*: **~ся** *+infin* to try to do.
пы́т|ка (**-ки**; *gen pl* **-ок**) *ж* torment.
пытли́в|ый (**-, -а, -о**) *прил* inquisitive.
пы́ток *сущ см* **пы́тка**.
пы́|хать (**-шу, -шешь**) *несов неперех*: ~ *+instr* to give off; ~ (*impf*) **злóбой/зáвистью** to burn with anger/envy; **онá ~шет здорóвьем** she's bursting with health.
пых|тéть (**-чý, -ти́шь**) *несов неперех* (*тяжело дышать*) to pant; (*самовар*) to steam; (*паровоз*) to chug; ~ (*impf*) **над чем-н** (*разг*) to sweat over sth.
пы́шек *сущ см* **пы́шка**.
пы́шен *прил см* **пы́шный**.
пы́ш|ка (**-ки**; *gen pl* **-ек**) *ж* doughnut (*BRIT*), donut (*US*).
пышноволóс|ый (**-, -а, -о**) *прил* fuzzy-haired.
пышногрýд|ый (**-, -а, -о**) *прил* busty.
пы́шност|ь (**-и**) *ж* (*волос*) luxuriance; (*хвоста итп*) bushiness; (*обстановки, приёма итп*) splendour (*BRIT*), splendor (*US*); **придавáть** (**придáть** *perf*) **~ волосáм** to give body to one's hair.
пы́ш|ный (**-ен, -нá, -но**) *прил* (*волосы, хвост, усы итп*) bushy; (*полный*) voluptuous; (*роскошный*) splendid.
пышý *итп несов см* **пы́хать**.
пьедестáл (**-а**) *м* (*основание*) pedestal; (*для победителей*) winners' rostrum.
пьéс|а (**-ы**) *ж* (*ЛИТЕРАТУРА*) play; (*МУЗ*) piece.
пью *итп несов см* **пить**.
пью́щий (**-его**; *decl like adj*) *м* heavy drinker.
пьянé|ть (**-ю**; *perf* **опьянéть**) *несов неперех* to get drunk; (*перен*) to become intoxicated.
пьян|и́ть (**-ю́, -и́шь**; *perf* **опьяни́ть**) *несов перех* to get drunk; (*перен*: *подлеж*: *воздух, счастье итп*) to intoxicate.
пья́ниц|а (**-ы**) *м/ж* drunkard.
пья́н|ка (**-ки**; *gen pl* **-ок**) *ж* (*разг*) booze-up.
пья́нств|о (**-а**) *ср* heavy drinking; **борьбá с ~м** anti-drinking campaign.
пья́нств|овать (**-ую**) *несов неперех* to drink heavily.
пьянчýг|а (**-и**) *м/ж* (*разг*) (old) soak.
пья́н|ый (**-, -á, -о**) *прил* (*человек*) drunk; (*крики, песни итп*) drunken ◆ (**-ого**; *decl like adj*) *м* drunk; **под ~ую рýку** (*разг*) in a drunken rage.
пэр (**-а**) *м* peer.
пюпи́тр (**-а**) *м* lectern.
пюрé *ср нескл* (*фруктовое*) purée; **картóфельное ~** mashed potato.
п/я *сокр* (= **почтóвый я́щик**) POB (= *Post Office Box*).
пяд|ь (**-и**) *ж* (*мера*) span; (*небольшое пространство*) stretch; **семи́ пя́дей вó лбу** extraordinarily intelligent.
пя́лец *сущ см* **пя́льцы**.
пя́л|иться (**-юсь, -ишься**) *несов возв* (*разг*) to gawk.
пя́л|ьцы (**-ец**; *dat pl* **-ьцам**) *мн* tambour *ед*.
пят|á (**-ы́**) *ж*: **до пят** (*очень длинный*) to the ground; **с головы́ до пят** from head to toe; **ходи́ть** (*impf*) *или* **гнáться** (*impf*) **за кем-н по ~м** to follow hot on sb's heels.
пятáк (**-á**) *м* (*разг*) five-kopeck piece.
пятач|óк (**-кá**) *м* five-kopeck piece; (*небольшая площадка*) spot; (*небольшое пространство*) stretch; (*свиньи*) snout.
пя́т|ая (**-ой**; *decl like adj*) *ж*: **однá ~** one fifth.
пя́тен *сущ см* **пятнó**.
пятёр|ка (**-ки**; *gen pl* **-ок**) *ж* (*цифра, карта*) five; (*разг*: *денежный знак*) fiver; (*ПРОСВЕЩ*) ≈ A (*school mark*); (*группа из пяти*) group of five; (*разг*: *автобус, трамвай итп*) (number) five (*bus, tram etc*).
пятерн|я́ (**-и́**) *ж* (*разг*) paw.
пя́тер|о (**-ы́х**; *как* **чéтверо**; *см* **Table 36b**) *чис* five; *см также* **двóе**.
пятёрок *сущ см* **пятёрка**.
пяти́ *чис см* **пять**.
пятибóрь|е (**-я**) *ср* pentathlon.
пяти́десяти *чис см* **пятьдеся́т**.
пятидесятилéти|е (**-я**) *ср* fifty years *мн*; (*годовщина*) fiftieth anniversary.
пятидесятилéтн|ий (**-яя, -ее, -ие**) *прил* (*период*) fifty-year; (*человек*) fifty-year-old.
пятидеся́т|ый (**-ая, -ое, -ые**) *чис* fiftieth; **я читáю ~ую страни́цу** I am on page fifty; **я живý в ~ой кварти́ре** I live in flat fifty; **я приéхал в Петербýрг в ~ом годý** I came to Petersburg in nineteen fifty; **~ые гóды** the Fifties; **в ~ых годáх** in the Fifties.
пятиднéв|ка (**-ки**; *gen pl* **-ок**) *ж* (*разг*) five-day week.
пятиднéвный *прил* five-day.

пятикла́ссник (-а) *м pupil in fifth year at school (usually eleven years old).*
пятикла́ссниц|а (-ы) *ж см* **пятикла́ссник.**
пятикопе́ечный *прил* five-kopeck.
пятикра́тн|ый *прил*: **~ чемпио́н** five-times champion; **в ~ом разме́ре** fivefold.
пятиле́ти|е (-я) *ср* (*срок*) five years; (*юбилей*) fifth anniversary.
пятиле́т|ка (-ки; *gen pl* **-ок)** *ж* (*ИСТ, ЭКОН*) five-year plan.
пятиле́тн|ий (-яя, -ее, -ие) *прил* (*промежуток*) five-year; (*ребёнок*) five-year-old.
пятиле́ток *сущ см* **пятиле́тка.**
пятиме́сячный *прил* five-month; (*ребёнок*) five-month-old.
пятимину́т|ка (-ки; *gen pl* **-ок)** *ж* (*разг*) short meeting (*at work*).
пятинеде́льный *прил* five-week; (*ребёнок*) five-week-old.
пятисо́т *чис см* **пятьсо́т.**
пятисотле́ти|е (-я) *ср* (*срок*) five hundred years; (*годовщина*) quincentenary.
пятисотле́тн|ий (-яя, -ее, -ие) *прил* (*период*) five-hundred-year; (*дерево*) five hundred-year-old.
пятисо́т|ый (-ая, -ое, -ые) *чис* five-hundredth.
пя́|титься (-чусь, -тишься; *perf* **попя́титься)** *несов возв* to move backwards; **он попя́тился от меня́** he backed away from me.
пятиуго́льник (-а) *м* pentagon.
пятичасово́й *прил* (*рабочий день*) five-hour; (*поезд*) five-o'clock.
пятиэта́ж|ка (-ки; *gen pl* **-ек)** *ж* (*разг*) five-storey block of flats (*BRIT*), five-story apartment block (*US*).
пятиэта́жный *прил* five-storey.
пя́т|ка (-ки; *gen pl* **-ок)** *ж* heel; **наступа́ть** *(impf)* **кому́-н на ~ки** (*перен*) to tread on sb's toes.
пятна́дцат|ый (-ая, -ое, -ые) *чис* fifteenth; *см также* **пя́тый.**
пятна́дцат|ь (-и; *как* **пять**; *см* **Table 27)** *чис* fifteen; *см также* **пять.**
пятна́|ть (-ю; *perf* **запятна́ть)** *несов перех* to tarnish.
пятни́ст|ый (-, -а, -о) *прил* spotted.
пя́тниц|а (-ы) *ж* Friday; **в ~у** on Friday; **по ~м** on Fridays; **в сле́дующую/про́шлую ~у** next/last Friday; **сего́дная ~, деся́тое ма́я** today is Friday (the) tenth (of) May.
пят|но́ (-на́; *nom pl* **пя́тна**, *gen pl* **-ен)** *ср* (*также перен*) stain; (*выделяющееся по цвету*) spot.
пя́ток *сущ см* **пя́тка.**
пят|о́к (-ка) *м* (*разг*) five (*when buying eggs etc*).
пя́т|ый (-ая, -ое, -ые) *чис* fifth; **сего́дня ~ое ию́ля** today is the fifth of July *или* July the fifth; **прие́ду ~ого ию́ля** I will arrive on the fifth of July; **встре́ча отло́жена до ~ого ию́ля** the meeting was postponed until the fifth of July; **сего́дня у́же ~ое (число́)** today is already the fifth; **сейча́с де́сять мину́т ~ого** it is ten minutes past four; **я прие́хал в Петербу́рг в ты́сяча девятьсо́т пятьдеся́т ~ом году́** I came to Petersburg in nineteen fifty five; **ле́кция бу́дет в ~ой аудито́рии** the lecture will take place in room five; **я зако́нчил ~ым** I finished fifth; **я был ~ым ребёнком в семье́** I was child number five in the family; **~ое – деся́тое** (*разг*) this and that; **переска́кивать** *(impf)* **с ~ого на деся́тое** (*разг*) to skip from one subject to another.
пят|ь (-и́; *см* **Table 27)** *чис* five; (*ПРОСВЕЩ*) ≈ A (*school mark*); **ей ~ лет** she is five years old; **они́ живу́т в до́ме но́мер ~** they live at number five; **о́коло ~и́** about five; **кни́га сто́ит ~ рубле́й** the book costs five roubles; **~ с полови́ной часо́в** five and a half hours; **сейча́с ~ часо́в** it is five o'clock; **я́блоки продаю́тся по ~ штук** the apples are sold in fives; **дели́ть (раздели́ть** *perf)* **что-н на ~** to divide sth into five.
пят|ьдеся́т (-и́десяти; *см* **Table 29)** *чис* fifty; **здесь о́коло ~и́десяти челове́к** there are about fifty people here; **на сле́дующей неде́ле ему́ испо́лнится ~ (лет)** he will be fifty next week; **ему́ о́коло ~и́десят (лет)** he is about fifty (years old); **маши́на е́дет со ско́ростью ~ киломе́тров в час** the car is going at fifty kilometres (*BRIT*) *или* kilometers (*US*) per hour.
пят|ьсо́т (-исо́т; *см* **Table 34)** *чис* five hundred; *см также* **сто.**
пя́тью *нареч* five times; **~ два – де́сять** five times two is ten.
пятью́ *чис см* **пять.**
пя́чусь *несов см* **пя́титься.**

~ Р, р ~

Р, р *сущ нескл* (*буква*) *the 17th letter of the Russian alphabet*.
р. *сокр* (= **река́**) R., r. (= *river*); (= *роди́лся*) b. (= *born*); (= **рубль**) R., r. (= *rouble*).
раб (-а́) *м* (*также перен*) slave; **~ любви́/мо́ды** *итп* a slave to love/fashion *итп*.
раб|а́ (-ы́; *no pl*) *ж см* **раб**.
рабовладе́л|ец (-ьца) *м* slave owner.
рабовладе́льческ|ий (-ая, -ое, -ие) *прил* slave-owning.
раболе́п|ный (-ен, -на, -но) *прил* servile.
раболе́пств|овать (-ую) *несов неперех*: **~ (пе́ред** *+instr*) to crawl (to).
рабо́т|а (-ы) *ж* (*труд, произведе́ние*) work; (*исто́чник за́работка*) work, job; (*функциони́рование*) working; **поступа́ть (поступи́ть** *perf*) **на ~у** to start a job; **постоя́нная/вре́менная/случа́йная ~** permanent/temporary/casual work *или* employment; **сде́льная ~** piecework; **сме́нная ~** shiftwork.
рабо́та|ть (-ю) *несов неперех* to work; (*магази́н, библиоте́ка итп*) to be open; **~** (*impf*) **на кого́-н/что-н** to work for sb/sth; **~** (*impf*) **над чем-н** to work on sth; **кем Вы ~ете?** what do you do for a living?; **я ~ю инжене́ром** I'm an engineer
▸ **рабо́таться** *несов безл* (*+dat*): **сего́дня мне не ~ется** I can't get down to work today; **в библиоте́ке хорошо́ ~ется** the library is a good place to work.
рабо́тник (-а) *м* worker; (*учрежде́ния*) employee; **руководя́щие ~и** management; **нау́чный ~** researcher.
рабо́тниц|а (-ы) *ж* (female) worker.
работода́тел|ь (-я) *м* employer.
работоспосо́бност|ь (-и) *ж* (*челове́ка*) ability to work hard; (*маши́ны*) efficiency.
работоспосо́бный *прил* (*челове́к*) able to work hard; (*населе́ние*) working *опред*.
работя́г|а (-и) *м/ж* (*разг*) workhorse (*fig*).
работя́щ|ий (-ая, -ее, -ие) *прил* (*разг*) hard-working.
рабо́ч|ая (-ей; *decl like adj*) *ж см* **рабо́чий**.
рабо́ч|ий (-ая, -ее, -ие) *прил* (*движе́ние, посёлок, столо́вая*) worker's *опред*; (*челове́к, оде́жда, часть механи́зма, чертёж*) working *опред* ◆ **(-его**; *decl like adj*) *м* worker; **в ~ее вре́мя** during working hours; **у нас нехва́тка ~их рук** we are undermanned; **в ~ем поря́дке** in the course of the proceedings; **рабо́чая ло́шадь** workhorse; **рабо́чая си́ла** workforce; **рабо́чая ста́нция** (*КОМП*) work station; **рабо́чее ме́сто** (*помеще́ние*) workplace; (*пост*) position; **рабо́чие ру́ки** workers; **рабо́чий визи́т** working visit; **рабо́чий день** working day (*BRIT*), workday (*US*); **рабо́чий класс** the working class.
ра́бск|ий (-ая, -ое, -ие) *прил* (*существова́ние, усло́вия*) slave-like; (*послуша́ние, подража́ние*) slavish; **~ труд** slave labour (*BRIT*) *или* labor (*US*).
ра́бств|о (-а) *ср* slavery.
рабфа́к (-а) *м* (*ИСТ*: = *рабо́чий факульте́т*) ≈ working man's college.
рабы́н|я (-и) *ж* slave.
равви́н (-а) *м* rabbi.
ра́вен *прил см* **ра́вный**.
ра́венств|о (-а) *ср* equality; (*чи́сел*) equal value; **знак ~а** (*МАТ*) equals sign; **ста́вить (поста́вить** *perf*) **знак ~а ме́жду чем-н и чем-н** to equate sth with sth.
равни́н|а (-ы) *ж* plain.
равно́ *нареч* equally ◆ *союз*: **~ (как) и** as well as ◆ *как сказ*: **э́то всё ~** it doesn't make any difference; **мне всё ~** it's all the same to me; **я всё ~ приду́** I'll come just the same; **два плюс пять ~ семи́** two plus five equals seven.
равнове́си|е (-я) *ср* (*также перен*) equilibrium; **теря́ть (потеря́ть** *perf*) **~** to lose one's balance; **~ сил** balance of power.
равноде́нстви|е (-я) *ср* equinox.
равноду́шен *прил см* **равноду́шный**.
равноду́ши|е (-я) *ср*: **~ (к** *+dat*) indifference (to).
равноду́шно *нареч* indifferently.
равноду́ш|ный (-ен, -на, -но) *прил*: **~ (к** *+dat*) indifferent (to).
равноме́р|ный (-ен, -на, -но) *прил* even.
равнопра́вен *прил см* **равнопра́вный**.
равнопра́ви|е (-я) *ср* equal rights *мн*.
равнопра́в|ный (-ен, -на, -но) *прил* equal.
равноси́л|ьный (-ен, -ьна, -ьно) *прил*: **~** *+dat* equivalent *или* equal to.
равноце́н|ный (-ен, -на, -но) *прил* of equal value *или* worth.
ра́в|ный (-ен, -на́, -но) *прил* equal; **~ным о́бразом** equally; **на ~ных** (*разг*) on an equal

footing.

равня́|ть (**-ю**; *perf* **сравня́ть**) *несов перех*: **~ (с** *+instr*) (*делать равным*) to make equal (with); (*одинаково оценивать*): **~ кого́-н/что-н с** *+instr* to treat sb/sth the same as

▸ **равня́ться** (*perf* **сравня́ться**) *несов возв*: **~ся по** *+dat* to draw level with; (*считать себя равным*): **~ся с** *+instr* to compare o.s. with; (*быть равносильным*): **~ся** *+dat* to be equal to; (*следовать примеру*): **~ся на** *+acc* to emulate; **два плюс два ~ется четырём** two plus two equals four.

рагу́ *ср нескл* ragout.

рад (**-а, -о, -ы**) *как сказ*: **~** (*+dat*) glad (of); **~** *+infin* glad *или* pleased to do; **~ познако́миться с Ва́ми** pleased to meet you; **я ~ за него́** I'm pleased *или* happy for him; **я всегда́ ~ помо́чь** I'm always glad to be of help; **я уже́ и не ра́да, что согласи́лась** I'm already regretting that I agreed.

ра́ди *предл*: **~** (*+gen*) for the sake of; **чего́ ~?** (*разг*) what for?; **шу́тки ~** (*разг*) for a joke; **~ Бо́га!** (*разг*) for God's sake!

радиа́льный *прил* radial.

радиа́тор (**-а**) *м* radiator.

радиа́ци|я (**-и**) *ж* radiation.

ра́ди|й (**-я**) *м* radium.

радика́л (**-а**) *м* (*ПОЛИТ, МАТ*) radical.

радика́л|ьный (**-ен, -ьна, -ьно**) *прил* radical.

радикули́т (**-а**) *м* lower back pain.

ра́дио *ср нескл* radio; **по ~** on the radio; **слу́шать** *(impf)* **~** to listen to the radio.

радиоакти́вност|ь (**-и**) *ж* radioactivity.

радиоакти́вный *прил* radioactive.

радиовеща́ни|е (**-я**) *ср* (radio) broadcasting.

радиолока́тор (**-а**) *м* radar (*device*).

радиолока́ци|я (**-и**) *ж* radar (*system*).

радиолюби́тел|ь (**-я**) *м* radio ham.

радиопереда́ч|а (**-и**) *ж* radio programme (*BRIT*) *или* program (*US*).

радиоприёмник (**-а**) *м* radio (set).

радиосвя́з|ь (**-и**) *ж* radiocommunication.

радиослу́шател|ь (**-я**) *м* (radio) listener.

радиослу́шательниц|а (**-ы**) *ж см* **радиослу́шатель**.

радиоста́нци|я (**-и**) *ж* radio station.

радиотелефо́н (**-а**) *м* radiotelephone.

радиоте́хник|а (**-и**) *ж* radio engineering.

радиоу́з|ел (**-ла́**) *м* public-address facilities *мн*.

радиоэлектро́ник|а (**-и**) *ж* radio electronics.

ради́ст (**-а**) *м* radio operator.

ради́ст|ка (**-ки**; *gen pl* **-ок**) *ж см* **ради́ст**.

ра́диус (**-а**) *м* radius; (*перен*: *влияния, действия*) range.

ра́д|овать (**-ую**; *perf* **обра́довать**) *несов перех*: **~ кого́-н** to make sb happy, please sb; **~** *(impf)* **глаз/слух** to be a joy to behold/hear

▸ **ра́доваться** *несов возв* (*перен*: *душа, сердце*) to rejoice; (*perf* **обра́доваться**; *+dat*; *солнцу, успехам*) to take pleasure in; **я обра́довалась ему́** *или* **встре́че с ним** I was overjoyed to see him.

ра́достен *прил см* **ра́достный**.

ра́достно *нареч* joyfully; **они́ меня́ ~ встре́тили** they gave me a very warm welcome.

ра́дост|ный (**-ен, -на, -но**) *прил* joyful; (*день, новость*) joyous.

ра́дос|ть (**-ти**) *ж* joy; **от ~ти** (*плакать, смеяться*) with joy; **пры́гать** *(impf)* **от ~ти** to jump for joy; **с ~ю** gladly; **на ~тях я его́ прости́л** (*разг*) I was so happy, I forgave him.

ра́дуг|а (**-и**) *ж* rainbow.

ра́дуж|ный (**-ен, -на, -но**) *прил* (*перен*: *настроение, надежды*) bright; **~ные цвета́** rainbow colours; **ра́дужная оболо́чка** (*АНАТ*) iris.

раду́шен *прил см* **раду́шный**.

раду́ши|е (**-я**) *ср* warmth.

раду́ш|ный (**-ен, -на, -но**) *прил* warm.

раз (**-а**; *nom pl* **-ы**, *gen pl* **-**) *м* time ◆ *нескл* (*один*) one ◆ *нареч* (*разг*: *однажды*) once ◆ *союз* (*разг*: *если*) if; **в два/три/четы́ре ра́за бо́льше/ ме́ньше** two/three/four times bigger/smaller; **в пять/шесть/семь** *итп* **~ бо́льше/ме́ньше** five/six/seven *итп* times bigger/smaller; **не ~** more than once; **в пе́рвый ~** (*впервые*) for the first time; (*в первом случае*) on the first occasion; **в тот/про́шлый/сле́дующий ~** that/ last/next time; **на э́тот ~** this time; **ещё ~** (once) again; **~ и навсегда́** once and for all; **ни ра́зу** not once; **(оди́н) ~ в день** once a day; **вот тебе́ и ~!** (*разг*) that's a turn up for the books!; **в са́мый ~** (*разг*: *о размере*) just right; (: *о времени*) at just the right time: **~... то ...** (*разг*) if ... then ...; **~ на ~ не прихо́дится** you can't win all the time; **~ пришёл – сади́сь** now that you're here, have a seat.

раз- *префикс* (*in verbs*; *о разделении на части*) *indicating division into parts eg.* *развяза́ть*; (*о распределении по местам, по поверхности*) *indicating positioning of sth somewhere eg.* *разложи́ть*; (*об интенсивном действии*) *indicating intensive action eg.* *разбушева́ться*; (*о направлении движения в разные стороны*) *indicating movement in different directions eg.* *разбежа́ться*; (*о прекращении действия*) *indicating cessation of action eg.* *разлюби́ть*; (*in adjectives*; *разг*: *о высшей степени качества*) *indicating a great degree of a certain quality eg.* *развесёлый*.

разба́в|ить (**-лю, -ишь**; *impf* **разбавля́ть**) *сов перех* to dilute.

разбаза́р|ить (**-ю, -ишь**; *impf* **разбаза́ривать**) *сов перех* to squander.

разба́лива|ться (**-юсь**) *несов от* **разболе́ться**.

разба́лтыва|ть(ся) (**-ю(сь)**) *несов от* **разболта́ть(ся)**.
разбе́г (**-а**) *м* (*машины*) acceleration; (*атлета*) run-up; **прыжо́к с ~а** *или* **~у** running jump.
разбежа́ться (*как* **бежа́ть**; *см* **Table 20**; *impf* **разбега́ться**) *сов возв* to run off, scatter; (*перед прыжком*) to take a run-up; (*перен*: *мысли*) to wander; **у меня́ глаза́ разбега́ются** (*разг*) I'm spoilt for choice.
разбе́й(те) *сов см* **разби́ть**.
разберу́(сь) *сов см* **разобра́ть(ся)**.
разбива́|ть(ся) (**-ю(сь)**) *несов от* **разби́ть(ся)**.
разби́в|ка (**-ки**; *gen pl* **-ок**) *ж* (*данных, людей*) arranging; (*сада, парка*) layout.
разбира́тельств|о (**-а**) *ср* (*ЮР*) examination.
разбира́|ть (**-ю**) *несов от* **разобра́ть** ◆ *перех* (*разг*: *сотрудника, нарушителя*) to take to task
▸ **разбира́ться** *несов от* **разобра́ться** ◆ *возв* (*разг*: *понимать*): **~ся в** *+prp* to understand.
разбитно́й *прил* carefree.
раз|би́ть (**-обью́, -обьёшь**; *imper* **-бе́й(те)**, *impf* **разбива́ть**) *сов перех* (*стекло, тарелку, голову*) to break; (*машину*) to smash up; (*врага, армию*) to crush; (*на участки, на части*) to break up; (*аллею, клумбу*) to lay; (*счастье, мечты*) to ruin; **разбива́ть** (**~** *perf*) **ла́герь** to set up camp
▸ **разби́ться** (*impf* **разбива́ться**) *сов возв* to break, smash; (*при падении, в аварии*) to be badly hurt; (*на группы, на участки*) to break up.
разбогате́|ть (**-ю**) *сов от* **богате́ть**.
разбо́|й (**-я**) *м* robbery.
разбо́йник (**-а**) *м* robber; (*разг*: *шалун*) troublemaker.
разбо́йниц|а (**-ы**) *ж см* **разбо́йник**.
разбо́йнича|ть (**-ю**) *несов неперех* to thieve; (*разг*: *шалить*) to get up to mischief.
разбо́йн|ый *прил*: **~ое нападе́ние** (*ЮР*) armed assault.
разболе́|ться (**-юсь**; *impf* **разба́ливаться**) *сов возв* (*разг*: *человек*) to be taken ill; (: *рука, живот итп*) to hurt badly; **у меня́ голова́ ~лась** I've got a splitting headache.
разбо́лтан|ный (**-, -на, -но**) *прил* (*разг*) slack; **~ная похо́дка** swagger.
разболта́|ть (**-ю**; *impf* **разба́лтывать**) *сов перех* (*порошок, смесь итп*) to mix in; (*замок, гайку*) to weaken; (*разг*: *секрет, новость*) to blab; **~** (*perf*) **дисципли́ну** (*разг*) to let discipline slip; **~** (*perf*) **ребёнка** (*разг*) to lose control over a child
▸ **разболта́ться** (*impf* **разба́лтываться**) *сов возв* (*порошок, мука*) to mix in; (*дверь, запор*) to come loose; (*дисциплина, поведение*) to slacken off; (*no impf*; *болтать*) to babble on.
разбомб|и́ть (**-лю́, -и́шь**) *сов перех* to bomb.
разбо́р (**-а**) *м* (*статьи, вопроса итп*) analysis; (*ЮР*) examination; (*ЛИНГ*) parsing; **без ~а** without exception.
разбо́рк|а (**-и**) *ж* (*обычно мн*) infighting.
разбо́рный *прил* collapsible.
разбо́рчивост|ь (**-и**) *ж* (*требовательность*) discernment; (*почерка*) legibility.
разбо́рчив|ый (**-, -а, -о**) *прил* (*человек, вкус*) discerning; (*почерк*) legible.
разбра́сыва|ть (**-ю**) *несов от* **разброса́ть**
▸ **разбра́сываться** *несов возв* (*разг*) to try to do too much (at once); (*+instr*; *друзьями, поклонниками итп*) to underrate.
разбр|ести́сь (**-еду́сь, -едёшься**; *pt* **-ёлся, -ела́сь, -ело́сь**, *impf* **разбреда́ться**) *сов возв* to wander off (*in different directions*).
разброса́|ть (**-ю**; *impf* **разбра́сывать**) *сов перех* to scatter.
разб|уди́ть (**-ужу́, -у́дишь**) *сов от* **буди́ть**.
разбу́х|нуть (**-ну, -нешь**; *pt* **-, -ла, -ло**, *impf* **разбуха́ть**) *сов неперех* to swell; (*папка, чемодан итп*) to bulge; (*лицо, рука итп*) to swell up.
разбуш|ева́ться (**-у́юсь**) *сов возв* (*море*) to rage; (*разг*) to rant.
разва́л (**-а**) *м* (*в квартире, в делах*) chaos; (*экономики*) ruin; (*системы*) break-up; **у нас до́ма по́лный ~** our home is in a state of chaos.
разва́лива|ть(ся) (**-ю(сь)**) *несов от* **развали́ть(ся)**.
разва́лин|а (**-ы**) *ж* (*обычно мн*) ruins *мн*; (*перен*: *человек*) wreck.
разв|али́ть (**-алю́, -а́лишь**; *impf* **разва́ливать**) *сов перех* (*стену, дом*) to knock down; (*дело, хозяйство*) to ruin
▸ **развали́ться** (*impf* **разва́ливаться**) *сов возв* to collapse; **он ~али́лся в кре́сле** he sat slumped in the armchair.
разв|ари́ться (*3sg* **-а́рится**, *3pl* **-а́рятся**, *impf* **разва́риваться**) *сов возв* to be overcooked; **бы́стро ~а́риваться** (*impf*) to cook quickly.
ра́зве *част* really; **~ он согласи́лся/не знал?** did he really agree/not know?; **~ то́лько** *или* **что** except that.
развева́|ться (*3sg* **-ется**, *3pl* **-ются**) *несов возв* (*флаг*) to flutter; (*волосы*) to flow.
разве́да|ть (**-ю**; *impf* **разве́дывать**) *сов перех* (*ГЕО*) to prospect; (*ВОЕН*) to reconnoitre (*BRIT*), reconnoiter (*US*); **~** (*perf*) (**о** *+prp*) to find out (about).
разведе́ни|е (**-я**) *ср* (*животных*) breeding; (*растений*) cultivation; (*костра*) building; (*клея, краски*) dilution; **~ пчёл** beekeeping.
разведён|ный (**-, -а́, -ы́**) *прил* (*в разводе*) divorced; (*no short form*; *раствор, водка*) diluted.
разве́д|ка (**-ки**; *gen pl* **-ок**) *ж* (*ГЕО*) prospecting; (*ПОЛИТ*) intelligence; (*ВОЕН*) reconnaissance.
разведу́(сь) *итп сов см* **развести́(сь)**.
разве́дчик (**-а**) *м* (*ГЕО*) prospector; (*ПОЛИТ*) intelligence agent; (*ВОЕН*) scout; (*самолёт*) reconnaissance plane.
разве́дчиц|а (**-ы**) *ж* (*ВОЕН*) scout.
разве́дыва|ть (**-ю**) *несов от* **разве́дать**.
разв|езти́ (**-езу́, -езёшь**; *pt* **-ёз, -езла́, -езло́**, *impf* **развози́ть**) *сов перех* to deliver ◆ *безл*: **меня́ ~езло́ от жары́/во́дки** the heat/vodka knocked me out; **доро́гу ~езло́** the road has become impassable.

развéива|ть(ся) (-ю(сь)) *несов от* **развéять(ся)**.
развéй(те) *сов см* **развить**.
развенчá|ть (-ю; *impf* **развéнчивать**) *сов перех* to discredit.
развёрнут|ый (-, -а, -о) *прил* detailed; (*строительство*) extensive.
разверн|ýть (-ý, -ёшь; *impf* **развёртывать** *или* **разворáчивать**) *сов перех* (*бумагу, карту*) to unfold; (*ковёр*) to unroll; (*парус, флаг*) to unfurl; (*проект, торговлю итп*) to launch; (*выставку, лагерь*) to set up; (*свои силы, талант*) to develop fully; (*корабль, машину, самолёт*) to turn around; (*батальон, полк итп*) to deploy; ~ (*perf*) **плéчи** to pull one's shoulders back
▸ **развернýться** (*impf* **развёртываться** *или* **разворáчиваться**) *сов возв* (*борьба, кампания, работа*) to get under way; (*талант, человек*) to develop fully; (*автомобиль, судно*) to turn around; (*батальон*) to be deployed; (*вид, зрелище*) to open up.
развесел|ить (-ю, -ишь) *сов от* **веселить**.
развéсист|ый (-, -а, -о) *прил* spreading *опред*.
развé|сить (-шу, -сишь; *impf* **развéшивать**) *сов перех* (*ветви*) to spread; (*картины, вещи*) to hang; (*бельё*) to hang up *или* out; ~ (*perf*) **ýши** (*разг*) to listen wide-eyed.
развеснóй *прил* sold by weight.
разв|ести (-едý, -едёшь; *pt* -ёл, -елá, -елó, *impf* **разводить**) *сов перех* to take; (*разъединить*) to divorce; (*порошок*) to dissolve; (*сок, краску*) to dilute; (*животных*) to breed; (*цветы, сад*) to grow; (*мост*) to raise; **разводить (~ *perf*) детéй по домáм** to take the children home; **разводить (~ *perf*) огóнь** to get a fire going; **разводить (~ *perf*) рукáми** ≈ to shrug one's shoulders; **разводить (~ *perf*) пустýю болтовню** (*разг*) to talk hot air
▸ **развестись** (*impf* **разводиться**) *сов возв* (*животные*) to breed; **разводиться (~сь *perf*) (с +*instr*)** to divorce, get divorced (from).
разветв|ить (-лю, -ишь; *impf* **разветвлять**) *сов перех* to expand
▸ **разветвиться** (*impf* **разветвляться**) *сов возв* (*дерево, река, дорога*) to branch; (*компания, учреждение*) to branch out.
разветвлéни|е (-я) *ср* (*действие: дорог, кроны деревьев*) branching; (: *компании*) expansion; (*место: железной дороги, канала*) fork.
разветвл|ённый (-ён, -енá, -енó) *прил* extensive.
разветвлю(сь) *сов см* **разветвить(ся)**.
разветвля|ть(ся) (-ю(сь)) *несов от* **разветвить(ся)**.
развéша|ть (-ю; *impf* **развéшивать**) *сов перех* (*картины, фотографии*) to hang; (*бельё*) to hang up *или* out.
развéшива|ть (-ю) *несов от* **развéсить, развéшать**.
развéшу *сов см* **развéсить**.
развé|ять (-ю; *impf* **развéивать**) *сов перех* (*облака, туман*) to disperse; (*подозрения, сомнения, грусть*) to dispel; **развéивать (~ *perf*) миф** to shatter a myth
▸ **развéяться** (*impf* **развéиваться**) *сов возв* (*облака*) to disperse; (*туман*) to lift; (*тоска, сомнения, мрачные мысли*) to be dispelled; (*человек*) to relax.
развивá|ть(ся) (-ю(сь)) *несов от* **развить(ся)**.
развивáющ|ийся (-аяся, -ееся, -иеся) *прил*: ~**аяся странá** developing country.
развил|ка (-ки; *gen pl* -ок) *ж* fork (*in road*).
развити|е (-я) *ср* development; **высóкое/ низкое** ~ a high/low level of development.
рáзвит|ой (-, -а, -о) *прил* developed; (*духовно зрелый*) mature.
раз|вить (-овью, -овьёшь; *pt* -вил, -вилá, -вило, *imper* -вéй(те), *impf* **развивáть**) *сов перех* to develop; (*наступление, деятельность*) to step up; (*верёвку, плётку*) to unwind; (*волосы*) to straighten; **развивáть (~ *perf*) скóрость** to gather speed; **развивáть (~ *perf*) ребёнка** to help a child to develop
▸ **развиться** (*impf* **развивáться**) *сов возв* to develop; (*скорость*) to build up; (*верёвка, коса, плётка*) to come unwound; (*волосы*) to become straighter.
развлёк(ся) *итп сов см* **развлéчь(ся)**.
развлекáтел|ьный (-ен, -ьна, -ьно) *прил* entertaining.
развлекá|ть(ся) (-ю(сь)) *несов от* **развлéчь(ся)**.
развлекý(сь) *итп сов см* **развлéчь(ся)**.
развлечéни|е (-я) *ср* (*гостей, публики*) entertaining; (*спектакль итп*) entertainment.
развл|éчь (-екý, -ечёшь *итп*, -екýт; *pt* -ёк, -еклá, -еклó, *impf* **развлекáть**) *сов перех* to entertain
▸ **развлéчься** (*impf* **развлекáться**) *сов возв* to have fun.
развóд (-а) *м* (*расторжение брака*) divorce; (*моста*) opening; **они в ~е** they are divorced; **подавáть (подáть *perf*) на ~** to apply for a divorce.
разв|одить(ся) (-ожý(сь), -óдишь(ся)) *несов от* **развести(сь)**.
разводнóй *прил*: ~ **ключ** monkey wrench; **разводнóй мост** drawbridge.
развóд|ы (-ов) *мн* (*узор*) design *ед*; (*подтёки, пятна*) stains *мн*.
развожý(сь) *несов см* **разводить(ся)**.
разв|озить (-ожý, -óзишь) *несов от* **развезти**.
разволн|овáть (-ýю) *сов перех* to alarm
▸ **разволновáться** *сов возв* to be alarmed.
разворáчива|ть(ся) (-ю(сь)) *несов от*

развернýть(ся).
развор|ова́ть (**-ýю**; *impf* **развoрóвывать**) *сов перех* to loot.
разворóт (**-а**) *м* (*машины*) U-turn; (*в книге*) double page.
разворо|ти́ть (**-чý, -ти́шь**) *сов перех* (*дорогу*) to dig up.
развра́т (**-а**) *м* promiscuity; (*духовный*) depravity.
развра́тен *прил см* **развра́тный.**
развра|ти́ть (**-щý, -ти́шь**; *impf* **развраща́ть**) *сов перех* to pervert; (*деньгами*) to corrupt
▸ **разврати́ться** (*impf* **развраща́ться**) *сов возв* (*см перех*) to become promiscuous; to become corrupted.
развра́тник (**-а**) *м* promiscuous man (*мн* men).
развра́тниц|а (**-ы**) *ж* promiscuous woman (*мн* women).
развра́тнича|ть (**-ю**) *несов неперех* to lead a life of promiscuity.
развра́т|ный (**-ен, -на, -но**) *прил* promiscuous.
развраща́|ть(ся) (**-ю(сь)**) *несов от* **разврати́ть(ся).**
развращý(сь) *несов см* **разврати́ть(ся).**
развя|за́ть (**-яжý, -я́жешь**; *impf* **развя́зывать**) *сов перех* (*узел, шнурки, мешок*) to untie; (*перен*: *инициативу*) to unshackle; (: *войну, реакцию*) to unleash; **развя́зывать** (**~** *perf*) **комý-н рýки** (*перен*) to free sb's hands; **развя́зывать** (**~** *perf*) **комý-н язы́к** to loosen sb's tongue
▸ **развяза́ться** (*impf* **развя́зываться**) *сов возв* (*шнурки, бант итп*) to come untied: **~ся с** *+instr* (*разг*: *с людьми, с экзаменами*) to be through with; (: *с долгами*) to get rid of.
развя́з|ка (**-ки**; *gen pl* **-ок**) *ж* (*конец*) ending; (*АВТ*) junction.
развя́з|ный (**-ен, -на, -но**) *прил* overly familiar.
развя́зок *сущ см* **развя́зка.**
развя́зыва|ть(ся) (**-ю(сь)**) *несов от* **развяза́ть(ся).**
разгада́|ть (**-ю**; *impf* **разга́дывать**) *сов перех* (*кроссворд, загадку*) to solve; (*замыслы, тайну*) to guess; (*сны*) to decipher; (*человека*) to fathom out.
разга́д|ка (**-ки**; *gen pl* **-ок**) *ж* (*снов, мыслей*) deciphering; (*тайны*) key; (*феномена*) explanation; (*решение загадки*) solution.
разга́дыва|ть (**-ю**) *несов от* **разгада́ть.**
разга́р (**-а**) *м*: **в ~е** *+gen* (*сезона*) at the height of; (*боя*) in the heart of; **кани́кулы в (пóлном) ~е** the holidays are in full swing.
разгиба́|ть(ся) (**-ю(сь)**) *несов от* **разогнýть(ся).**
разгильдя́|й (**-я**) *м* (*разг*) layabout.
разгла́|дить (**-жу, -дишь**; *impf* **разгла́живать**) *сов перех* to smooth out.
разгла|си́ть (**-шý, -си́шь**; *impf* **разглаша́ть**) *сов перех* to divulge, disclose.
разгля|де́ть (**-жý, -ди́шь**; *impf* **разгля́дывать**) *сов перех* (*рассмотреть*) to scrutinize; (*no impf*; *понять*) to discern.
разгне́ван|ный (**-, -а, -о**) *прил*: **~** (*+instr*) angry (with).
разгова́рива|ть (**-ю**) *несов неперех*: **~** (**с** *+instr*) to talk (to); **онá бóльше со мной не ~ет** she doesn't talk to me any more.
разговóр (**-а**) *м* conversation; **э́то другóй ~!** (*разг*) that's another matter!; **без ~ов** without a word; *см также* **разговóры.**
разговóрник (**-а**) *м* phrase book.
разговóрный *прил* colloquial.
разговóрчив|ый (**-, -а, -о**) *прил* talkative.
разговóр|ы (**-ов**) *мн* (*толки*) gossip *ед.*
разгóн (**-а**) *м* (*демонстрации*) breaking up; (*самолёта, автомобиля*) acceleration; **устра́ивать** (**устрóить** *perf*) **комý-н ~** (*разг*) to give sb a roasting.
разгоня́|ть(ся) (**-ю(сь)**) *несов от* **разогна́ть(ся).**
разгор|е́ться (*3sg* **-и́тся**, *3sg* **-я́тся**, *impf* **разгора́ться**) *сов возв* (*костёр, спор*) to flare up; (*закат*) to be ablaze; (*щёки, уши*) to burn; (*перен*: *страсти, любопытство*) to become inflamed.
разгорячён|ный (**-, -á, -ó**) *прил*: **~** (*+instr*) (*человек*) inflamed (by); (**-, -нá, -нó**; *лицо*) excited.
разгоряч|и́ться (**-ýсь, -и́шься**) *сов от* **горячи́ться** ◆ *возв* (*от волнения, от работы*) to get het up; (*от бега*) to be hot.
разграни́ч|ить (**-у, -ишь**; *impf* **разграни́чивать**) *сов перех* (*район, земли*) to demarcate; (*обязанности, понятия*) to delimit.
разграф|и́ть (**-лю́, -и́шь**) *сов от* **графи́ть.**
разгр|ести́ (**-ебý, -ебёшь**; *pt* **-ёб, -ебла́, -ебло́**, *impf* **разгреба́ть**) *сов перех* to sweep aside.
разгрóм (**-а**) *м* rout; (*разг*: *беспорядок*) mayhem, havoc; (*статьи*) savaging.
разгром|и́ть (**-лю́, -и́шь**) *сов перех* (*врага, сопротивление*) to crush; (*город, страну*) to destroy; (*политику, статью, соперника*) to savage.
разгрóмный *прил* (*речь, критика*) savage.
разгр|узи́ть (**-ужý, -ýзишь**; *impf* **разгружа́ть**) *сов перех* to unload; (*программу*) to ease; **разгружа́ть** (**~** *perf*) **когó-н** to lighten sb's load.
разгрýз|ка (**-ки**; *gen pl* **-ок**) *ж* (*вагонов, баржи*) unloading; (*перен*: *человека*) unburdening; (: *программы, плана*) easing up.
разгрýзочн|ый *прил*: **~ые рабóты** unloading; **разгрýзочный день** *day during dieting programme on which diet is relaxed.*
разгры́з|ть (**-у, -ёшь**) *сов от* **грызть** ◆ (*impf* **разгрыза́ть**) *перех* (*редиску, кость*) to gnaw at; (*орех*) to crack open.
разгýл (**-а**) *м* revelry; (*+gen*; *реакции, национализма итп*) outburst of.
разгýлива|ть (**-ю**) *несов неперех* to have a wander
▸ **разгýливаться** *несов от* **разгуля́ться.**
разгуля́|ться (**-юсь**; *impf* **разгýливаться**) *сов*

возв (*дать себе волю*) to let o.s. go; (*перен*: *ветер, море*) to get up; (: *погода, день*) to clear up.
раздаjвать(ся) (**-ю(сь), -ёшь(ся)**) *несов от* **раздать(ся)**.
раздавить (**-авлю, -авишь**) *сов от* **давить** ◆ (*impf* **раздавливать**) *перех* to squash.
раздам(ся) *итп сов см* **раздать(ся)**.
раздаточный *прил*: ~ **пункт** distribution centre (*BRIT*) *или* center (*US*).
раздать (*как* **дать**; *см* **Table 14**; *impf* **раздавать**) *сов перех* to give out, distribute
▸ **раздаться** (*impf* **раздаваться**) *сов возв* (*голос, шум итп*) to be heard; (*толпа*) to make way; (*обувь, сапоги*) to stretch; **раздаваться** (~**ся** *perf*) **в бёдрах** (*разг*) to put weight on around the hips.
раздача (**-и**) *ж* distribution.
раздашь(ся) *сов см* **раздать(ся)**.
раздваиваться (**-юсь**) *несов от* **раздвоиться**.
раздвигать(ся) (**-ю**) *несов от* **раздвинуть(ся)**.
раздвижной *прил*: ~ **занавес** curtain (*THEAT*); ~ **стол** extending table.
раздвинуть (**-у, -ешь**; *impf* **раздвигать**) *сов перех* to move apart; (*шторы*) to open; (*толпу*) to part; (*перен*: *рамки наблюдения, исследования*) to broaden
▸ **раздвинуться** (*impf* **раздвигаться**) *сов возв* (*шторы*) to open; (*толпа*) to part; (*перен*: *мир, возможности*) to open up.
раздвоение (**-я**) *ср*: ~ **личности** split personality.
раздвоиться (**-юсь, -ишься**; *impf* **раздваиваться**) *сов возв* (*дорога, река*) to divide into two; (*перен*: *мнение*) to be divided.
раздевалка (**-ки**; *gen pl* **-ок**) *ж* changing room.
раздевать(ся) (**-ю(сь)**) *несов от* **раздеть(ся)**.
раздел (**-а**) *м* (*действие*: *имущества*) division; (*часть, область*) section.
разделать (**-ю**; *impf* **разделывать**) *сов перех* (*мясо, рыбу*) to dress; (*грядки*) to prepare; (*мебель*): ~ **что-н под дуб/мрамор** to give sth an oak/a marble finish
▸ **разделаться** (*impf* **разделываться**) *сов возв* (*разг*): ~**ся с** +*instr* (*с делами, с долгами*) to settle; (*с соперником, с хулиганом*) to take care of.
разделение (**-я**) *ср* division; ~ **труда** division of labour (*BRIT*) *или* labor (*US*).
разделить (**-елю, -елишь**) *сов от* **делить** ◆ (*impf* **разделять**) *перех* (*мнение, взгляды, энтузиазм*) to share
▸ **разделиться** *сов от* **делиться** ◆ (*impf* **разделяться**) *возв* (*мнения, общество*) to become divided.
разделывать(ся) (**-ю(сь)**) *несов от* **разделать(ся)**.
разделять(ся) (**-ю(сь)**) *несов от* **разделить(ся)**.
раздеру *итп сов см* **разодрать**.
раздеть (**-ну, -нешь**; *impf* **раздевать**) *сов перех* to undress; (*разг*: *ограбить*): ~ **кого-н** to strip sb bare
▸ **раздеться** (*impf* **раздеваться**) *сов возв* to get undressed.
раздирать (**-ю**) *несов от* **разодрать** ◆ *перех* (*душу, человека, общество*) to tear apart.
раздобреть (**-ю**) *сов от* **добреть**.
раздобыть (*как* **быть**; *см* **Table 21**; *impf* **раздобывать**) *сов перех* (*разг*) to get hold of, lay one's hands on.
раздолен *прил см* **раздольный**.
раздолье (**-я**) *ср* expanse; (*перен*) freedom; **мне здесь** ~ I feel free here.
раздольный (**-ен, -ьна, -ьно**) *прил* vast; (*перен*) free.
раздор (**-а**) *м* (*обычно мн*) strife *ед*.
раздосадовать (**-ую**) *сов перех* to upset.
раздражать(ся) (**-ю(сь)**) *несов от* **раздражить(ся)**.
раздражение (**-я**) *ср* irritation.
раздражённо *нареч* (*сказать*) irritably.
раздражённый (**-ён, -ена, -ено**) *прил* (*человек, голос*) irritated; (**-ён, -енна, -енно**; *тон*) irritable; **у меня нервы ~ены до предела** my nerves are on edge.
раздражительный (**-ен, -ьна, -ьно**) *прил* irritable.
раздражить (**-у, -ишь**; *impf* **раздражать**) *сов перех* (*также МЕД*) to irritate; (*нервы*) to agitate; (*аппетит*) to stimulate
▸ **раздражиться** (*impf* **раздражаться**) *сов возв* (*кожа, глаза*) to become irritated; (*человек*): ~**ся** (+*instr*) to be irritated (by).
раздробить (**-лю, -ишь**) *сов от* **дробить** ◆ (*impf* **раздроблять**) *перех* to shatter.
раздробленный (**-, -а, -о**) *прил* fragmented.
раздроблю *сов см* **раздробить**.
раздроблять (**-ю**) *несов от* **раздробить**.
раздувать(ся) (**-ю(сь)**) *несов от* **раздуть(ся)**.
раздумать (**-ю**; *impf* **раздумывать**) *сов неперех*: ~ +*infin* (*пойти, жениться итп*) to decide not to do, decide against doing.
раздумывать (**-ю**) *несов от* **раздумать** ◆ *неперех*: ~ (**о** +*prp*) (*долго думать*) to contemplate.
раздумье (**-я**; *gen pl* **-ий**) *ср* contemplation; (*обычно мн*) thought; **впадать** (**впасть** *perf*) **в** ~ to sink deep into thought; **после долгих ~ий** on *или* after lengthy consideration.
раздуть (**-ую**; *impf* **раздувать**) *сов перех* (*огонь, костёр*) to fan; (*пузырь*) to blow; (*разг*: *дело, скандал*) to blow up; (: *штаты*) to overstaff; **раздувать** (~ *perf*) **ноздри** to flare

one's nostrils; **у неё ~уло щёку/нóгу** her cheek/leg has swollen up
▸ **раздýться** (*impf* **раздувáться**) *сов возв* (*парус*) to swell; (*щека, губа, также перен*) to swell up; (*карманы, портфель*) to bulge.
разевá|ть (-ю) *несов от* **разинуть.**
разжáлоб|ить (-лю, -ишь) *сов перех*: ~ **когó-н** to evoke sympathy in sb.
разжáл|овать (-ую) *сов перех* to demote; ~ (*perf*) **когó-н в рядовые** to reduce sb to the ranks.
раз|жáть (-ожмý, -ожмёшь; *impf* **разжимáть)** *сов перех* (*пальцы, губы*) to relax; (*пружину*) to uncoil
▸ **разжáться** (*impf* **разжимáться**) *сов возв* (*см перех*) to relax; to uncoil.
разж|евáть (-ую; *impf* **разжёвывать)** *сов перех* to chew; (*перен: разг: мысль*) to spell out in simple terms.
раз|жéчь (-ожгý, -ожжёшь *итп*, **-ожгýт;** *pt* **-жёг, -ожглá, -ожглó,** *impf* **разжигáть)** *сов перех* (*также перен*) to kindle; (*войну, ненависть*) to incite.
разживýсь *итп сов см* **разжиться.**
разжигá|ть (-ю) *несов от* **разжéчь.**
разжимá|ть(ся) (-ю(сь)) *несов от* **разжáть(ся).**
разжирé|ть (-ю) *сов от* **жирéть.**
разж|иться (-ивýсь, -ивёшься; *pt* **-йлся, -илáсь, -илóсь)** *сов возв* (*разг: жить в достатке*) to do well for o.s.; ~ (*perf*) +*instr* (*деньгами*) to rake in.
раззадóр|ить (-ю, -ишь; *impf* **раззадóривать)** *сов перех* to excite.
разин|уть (-у, -ешь; *impf* **разевáть)** *сов перех* (*разг*): ~ **рот** to gape; **слýшать** (*impf*) **~ув рот** to listen open-mouthed.
разин|я (-и) *м/ж* (*разг*) scatterbrain.
разитель|ный (-ен, -ьна, -ьно) *прил* striking.
ра|зить (-жý, -зишь) *сов перех* to strike; (*перен: пороки*) to strike out at ◆ *безл* (+*instr*; *разг*): **от неё ~зит духáми/чеснокóм** she reeks of perfume/garlic.
разлагá|ть(ся) (-ю(сь)) *несов от* **разложить(ся).**
разлáд (-а) *м* (*в делах, в работе*) disorder; (*с женой*) discord.
разлáмыва|ть (-ю) *несов от* **разломáть, разломить**
▸ **разлáмываться** *несов от* **разломáться, разломиться** ◆ *возв* (*разг*): **у меня ~ется спинá/головá** my back/head is killing me.
разлёгся *итп сов см* **разлéчься.**
разле|тéться (-чýсь, -тишься; *impf* **разлетáться)** *сов возв* (*птицы, перья*) to fly off (*in different directions*); (*перен: выросшие дети*) to fly the nest; (*разг: стекло, ваза итп*) to shatter; (: *новости*) to get around; (: *поезд*) to speed up.
разл|éчься (-ягусь, -яжешься *итп*, **-ягутся;** *pt* **-ёгся, -еглáсь, -еглóсь)** *сов возв* (*разг*) to stretch out.
разлив (-а) *м* flooding; (*место, залитое водой*) flood plain; (*вина, воды*) bottling; (*металла*) casting.
разливá|ть (-ю) *несов от* **разлить**
▸ **разливáться** *несов от* **разлиться** ◆ *возв* (*соловьи*) to sing; (*перен*): **~ся соловьём** to wax lyrical.
разливн|óй *прил*: **~óе пиво** beer on tap.
разлин|овáть (-ýю; *impf* **разлинóвывать)** *сов перех* to rule (*page*).
раз|лить (-олью, -ольёшь; *pt* **-лил, -лилá, -лило,** *impf* **разливáть)** *сов перех* to pour out; (*по бутылкам*) to bottle; (*пролить*) to spill; **их водóй не ~ольёшь** they are never apart
▸ **разлиться** (*impf* **разливáться**) *сов возв* (*пролиться*) to spill; (*река*) to overflow; **румянец ~лился по егó щекáм** the colour flooded into his cheeks; **по её лицý ~лилáсь улыбка** a smile spread across her face.
различá|ть (-ю) *несов от* **различить**
▸ **различáться** *несов возв*: **~ся по** +*dat* to differ in.
различен *прил см* **различный.**
различи|е (-я) *ср* difference; **без ~я** indiscriminately.
различ|ить (-ý, -ишь; *impf* **различáть)** *сов перех* (*увидеть, услышать*) to make out; (*отличить*): ~ (**по** +*dat*) to distinguish (by); **я их не ~áю** I can't tell them apart.
различ|ный (-ен, -на, -но) *прил* different.
разложéни|е (-я) *ср* (*ХИМ, БИО*) decomposition; (*общества, армии итп*) disintegration; (*МАТ*) expansion (*of equation*).
разл|ожить (-ожý, -óжишь; *impf* **раскладывать)** *сов перех* (*расположить*) to place, arrange; (*еду по тарелкам*) to dish out, serve; (*карту, диван, стол*) to open out; (*impf* **разлагáть**; *ХИМ, БИО*) to decompose; (*МАТ*) to expand; (*перен: армию*) to demoralize; **раскладывать** (~ *perf*) **костёр** to build a fire
▸ **разложиться** (*impf* **раскладываться**) *сов возв* (*разг: разместить свои вещи*) to spread; (*impf* **разлагáться**; *ХИМ, БИО*) to decompose; (*МАТ*) to expand; (*перен: армия, общество*) to fall apart.
разломá|ть (-ю) *сов от* **ломáть** ◆ (*impf* **разлáмывать**) *перех* to break up
▸ **разломáться** (*impf* **разлáмываться**) *сов возв* to break up; (*постройка*) to fall to pieces.
разл|омить (-омлю, -óмишь; *impf* **разлáмывать)** *сов перех* (*на части: хлеб итп*) to break up
▸ **разломиться** (*impf* **разлáмываться**) *сов возв* to break up.
разлýк|а (-и) *ж* separation; **жить** (*impf*) **в ~е с кем-н** to live apart from sb.
разлуч|ить (-ý, -ишь; *impf* **разлучáть)** *сов перех*: ~ **когó-н с** +*instr* to separate sb from
▸ **разлучиться** (*impf* **разлучáться**) *сов возв*: **~ся (с** +*instr*) to be separated (from).

разл|юби́ть (**-юблю́, -ю́бишь**) *сов перех*: ~ *+infin* (*читать, гулять итп*) to lose one's enthusiasm for doing; **он меня́ ~ю́бил** he doesn't love me any more.

разля́гусь *итп сов см* **разле́чься**.

разма́|зать (**-жу, -жешь**; *impf* **разма́зывать**) *сов перех* to smear

▸ **разма́заться** (*impf* **разма́зываться**) *сов возв* to be smeared.

размазн|я́ (**-и́**) *м/ж* ditherer.

разма́зыва|ть(ся) (**-ю**) *несов от* **разма́зать(ся)**.

разма́лыва|ть (**-ю**) *несов от* **размоло́ть**.

разма́рива|ть (*3sg* **-ет**, *3pl* **-ют**) *несов от* **разморить**

▸ **разма́риваться** *несов от* **разморя́ться**.

разма́тыва|ть (**-ю**) *несов от* **размота́ть**.

разма́х (**-а**) *м* (*рук, крыльев*) span; (*маятника, колокола*) swing; (*перен*: *деятельности*) scope; (: *проекта*) scale; **уда́рить** (*perf*) **кого́-н с ~у** to take a swing at sb; **он челове́к с ~ом** he thinks on a large scale.

разма́хива|ть (**-ю**) *несов от* **размахну́ть** ◆ *неперех*: ~ *+instr* (*руками, флажком*) to wave; (*шашкой*) to brandish

▸ **разма́хиваться** *несов от* **размахну́ться**.

размахн|у́ть (**-у́, -ёшь**; *impf* **разма́хивать**) *сов перех* (*руки, крылья*) to spread ◆ *неперех*: ~ *+instr* (*кнутом, топором*) to swing

▸ **размахну́ться** (*impf* **разма́хиваться**) *сов возв* to swing one's arm back; (*перен*: *разг*: *со свадьбой, в делах итп*) to go to town.

разма́шист|ый (**-, -а, -о**) *прил* sweeping.

размельч|и́ть (**-у́, -и́шь**) *сов от* **мельчи́ть**.

размелю́ *итп сов см* **размоло́ть**.

разме́н (**-а**) *м* (*денег, пленных*) exchange; ~ **кварти́ры** flat swap (*in which one large flat is exchanged for two smaller ones*).

разме́нива|ть(ся) (**-ю(сь)**) *несов от* **разменя́ть(ся)**.

разме́нн|ый *прил*: ~ **автома́т** change machine; **~ая моне́та** (small) change.

разменя́|ть (**-ю**; *impf* **разме́нивать**) *сов перех* (*деньги*) to change; (*квартиру*) to exchange; (*перен*: *талант*) to waste; ~ (*perf*) **со́весть** to sell out (*fig*)

▸ **разменя́ться** (*impf* **разме́ниваться**) *сов возв* (*перен*: *разг*: *обменять жилплощадь*) to do a flat swap (*of one large flat for two smaller ones*); **разме́ниваться** (*impf*) **по мелоча́м** *или* **пустяка́м** (*разг*) to waste o.s.

разме́р (**-а**) *м* size; (*обычно мн*: *строительства*: *масштабы*) dimension; (*ЛИНГ*) metre (*BRIT*), meter (*US*); **како́й у тебя́ ~?** what size do you take?

разме́рен|ный (**-, -на, -но**) *прил* (*звон, шаги*) measured; (*жизнь*) well-regulated.

разме|сти́ть (**-щу́, -сти́шь**; *impf* **размеща́ть**) *сов перех* (*найти место для*) to place; (*расположить*) to arrange

▸ **размести́ться** (*impf* **размеща́ться**) *сов возв* to accommodate o.s.; **го́сти ~сти́лись за столо́м** the guests took their seats at the table.

разм|ета́ть (**-ечу́, -е́чешь**) *сов перех* (*листву, пепел итп*) to scatter; (*руки*) to fling open

▸ **размета́ться** *сов возв* (*волосы*) to fly everywhere; (*человек*: *во сне*) to sprawl out.

разме́|тить (**-чу, -тишь**; *impf* **размеча́ть**) *сов перех* to mark out.

размечта́|ться (**-юсь**) *сов возв* to start dreaming.

разме́чу *сов см* **разме́тить**.

размечу́(сь) *итп сов см* **размета́ть(ся)**.

размеша́|ть (**-ю**; *impf* **разме́шивать**) *сов перех* to stir.

размеща́|ть(ся) (**-ю(сь)**) *несов от* **размести́ть(ся)**.

размеще́ни|е (**-я**) *ср* (*вещей*) placing; (*расположение*) arrangement; (*людей*: *по комнатам*) accommodation.

размещу́(сь) *сов см* **размести́ть(ся)**.

размина́|ть(ся) (**-ю(сь)**) *несов от* **размя́ть(ся)**.

размини́р|овать (**-ую**) (*не*)*сов перех*: ~ **по́ле** to clear a field of mines.

разми́н|ка (**-ки**; *gen pl* **-ок**) *ж* (*ног, мускулов*) loosening up; (*спортсменов*) warm-up.

размин|у́ться (**-у́сь, -ёшься**) *сов возв* (*не встретиться*) to miss each other; (*дать пройти*) to pass; **мы с ним ~у́лись (на 5 мину́т)** we missed each other (by 5 minutes).

размножа́|ть (**-ю**) *несов от* **размно́жить**

▸ **размножа́ться** *несов от* **размно́житься** ◆ *возв* (*БИО*) to reproduce.

размноже́ни|е (**-я**) *ср* (*также БИО*) reproduction.

размно́ж|ить (**-у, -ишь**; *impf* **размножа́ть**) *сов перех* to make (multiple) copies of

▸ **размно́житься** (*perf* **размножа́ться**) *сов возв* (*БИО*) to reproduce.

размо́ет *итп сов см* **размы́ть**.

размозж|и́ть (**-у́, -и́шь**) *сов перех* to smash.

размо́к|нуть (**-ну, -нешь**; *pt* **-, -ла, -ло**, *impf* **размока́ть**) *сов неперех* (*хлеб, картон*) to go soggy; (*почва*) to become sodden.

размо́лв|ка (**-ки**; *gen pl* **-ок**) *ж* squabble.

разм|оло́ть (**-елю́, -е́лешь**; *impf* **разма́лывать**) *сов перех* to grind.

размора́жив|ать(ся) (**-ю(сь)**) *несов от* **разморо́зить(ся)**.

размор|и́ть (*3sg* **-и́т**, *3pl* **-я́т**, *impf* **разма́ривать**) *сов перех* (*сон, усталость*) to come over; **меня́ ~и́ло от жары́/све́жего во́здуха** the heat/fresh air has made me drowsy

▸ **размори́ться** (*impf* **разма́риваться**) *сов возв* to become drowsy.

разморо́|зить (**-жу, -зишь**; *impf*

разморА́живать) *сов перех* to defrost
▸ **разморо́зиться** (*impf* **разморА́живаться**) *сов возв* to defrost.
размота́|ть (**-ю**; *impf* **разма́тывать**) *сов перех* to unwind.
размыва́|ть (*3sg* **-ет**, *3pl* **-ют**) *несов от* **размы́ть**.
размыка́|ть(ся) (**-ю**) *несов от* **разомкну́ть(ся)**.
размы́т|ый (**-, -а, -о**) *прил* blurred.
разм|ы́ть (*3sg* **-о́ет**, *3sg* **-о́ют**, *impf* **размыва́ть**) *сов перех* to wash away.
размышле́ни|е (**-я**) *ср* reflection.
размышля́|ть (**-ю**) *несов неперех*: ~ (**о** +*prp*) to think (about), reflect (on).
размягч|и́ть (**у́, -и́шь**; *impf* **размягча́ть**) *сов перех* (*воск, кожу, душу*) to soften; (*перен*: *человека*) to soften up.
размя́к|нуть (**-ну, -нешь**; *pt* **-, -ла, -ло**, *impf* **размяка́ть**) *сов неперех* (*глина, почва*) to soften; (*перен*: *от спиртного, от духоты*) to (become) mellow; (: *от похвалы*) to soften up.
раз|мя́ть (**-омну́, -омнёшь**) *сов от* **мять** ◆ (*impf* **размина́ть**) *перех* to loosen up
▸ **размя́ться** (*impf* **размина́ться**) *сов возв* to warm up.
разнаря́д|ка (**-ки**; *gen pl* **-ок**) *м* directive.
разна́шива|ть(ся) (**-ю**) *несов от* **разноси́ть(ся)**.
разн|ести́ (**-есу́, -есёшь**; *pt* **-ёс, -есла́, -есло́**, *impf* **разноси́ть**) *сов перех* (*письма, посылки*) to deliver; (*еду*) to serve (up); (*тарелки, чашки*) to put out; (*тучи, обрывки бумаги*) to disperse; (*заразу, слухи*) to spread; (*разг*: *разбить*) to smash up; (: *раскритиковать*) to slam, pan ◆ *безл* (*разг*: *опухнуть*) to puff up; (: *пополнеть*) to get fat; **разноси́ть** (~ *perf*) **что-н в клочья** to smash sth to pieces
▸ **разнести́сь** (*impf* **разноси́ться**) *сов возв* (*весть, слух, запах*) to spread; (*звон, гудок, крик*) to resound.
разнима́|ть (**-ю**) *несов от* **разня́ть**.
разниму́ *итп сов см* **разня́ть**.
ра́зниц|а (**-ы**) *ж* difference; **кака́я** ~**?** what difference does it make?; ~ **в ве́се/в во́зрасте** weight/age difference; **без** ~**ы** (*разг*) it makes no difference.
разнобо́|й (**-я**) *м* (*в работе, в действиях*) lack of coordination; (*в правилах*) contradictions *мн*.
разнове́с (**-а**) *м* weights *мн* (*for set of scales*).
разнови́дност|ь (**-и**) *ж* (*БИО*) variety; (*людей*) type, kind.
разногла́си|е (**-я**) *ср* disagreement.
разнообра́жу *сов см* **разнообра́зить**.
разнообра́зен *прил см* **разнообра́зный**.
разнообра́зи|е (**-я**) *ср* variety; **для** ~**я** for a change.
разнообра́|зить (**-жу, -зишь**) *несов перех* to vary.
разнообра́з|ный (**-ен, -на, -но**) *прил* (*вкусы, звуки, мнения*) various; ~**ные лю́ди** different sorts of people; ~**ная пу́блика** a diverse audience.
разнорабо́ч|ий (**-его**; *decl like adj*) *м* labourer (*BRIT*), laborer (*US*).
разноречи́в|ый (**-, -а, -о**) *прил* conflicting.
разноро́д|ный (**-ен, -на, -но**) *прил* (*состав*) heterogeneous; (*вещества, предметы*) of various sorts; (*впечатления*) varied.
разно́с (**-а**) *м* delivery; (*разг*: *выговор*) pounding.
разн|оси́ть (**-ошу́, -о́сишь**) *несов от* **разнести́** ◆ (*impf* **разна́шивать**) *сов перех* (*туфли, сапоги*) to break in
▸ **разноси́ться** *несов от* **разнести́сь** ◆ (*impf* **разна́шиваться**) *сов возв* to wear loose.
разносторо́н|ний (**-няя, -нее, -ние; -ен, -ня, -не**) *прил* (*деятельность*) wide-ranging; (*соглашение, договор*) multilateral; (*ум, личность*) multifaceted; **он** ~ **челове́к** he has a wide range of interests; ~**ее образова́ние** a broad education.
ра́зност|ь (**-и**) *ж* (*также МАТ*) difference.
разно́счик (**-а**) *м* (*товара*) delivery man (*мн* men); (*телеграмм*) bearer; (*инфекции*) carrier.
разноцве́тный *прил* multicoloured (*BRIT*), multicolored (*US*).
разночи́н|ец (**-ца**) *м* (*ИСТ*) raznochinets (*educated person of nonaristocratic descent in 19th century Russia*).
разношёрстный *прил* (*перен*) motley.
разношу́(сь) (*не*)*сов см* **разноси́ть(ся)**.
разноязы́чный *прил* speaking different languages.
разну́здан|ный (**-, -на, -но**) *прил* (*человек, поведение*) unruly.
ра́зный *прил* different.
разн|я́ть (**-иму́, -и́мешь**; *pt* **-я́л, -яла́, -я́ло**, *impf* **разнима́ть**) *сов перех* (*руки, зубы*) to unclench; (*драчунов, боксёров*) to separate, pull apart.
разоблач|и́ть (**-у́, -и́шь**; *impf* **разоблача́ть**) *сов перех* to expose.
раз|обра́ть (**-беру́, -берёшь**; *impf* **разбира́ть**) *сов перех* (*разг*: *раскупить, взять*) to snatch up; (*привести в порядок*) to sort out; (*подвергнуть анализу*) to analyse (*BRIT*), analyze (*US*); (*распознать*: *вкус, подпись итп*) to make out; **разбира́ть** (~ *perf*) (**на ча́сти**) (*часы, механизм итп*) to take apart; **его́** ~**бира́ет смех** (*разг*) he can hardly control his laughter
▸ **разобра́ться** (*impf* **разбира́ться**) *сов возв*: ~**ся в** +*prp* (*в вопросе, в деле*) to form an understanding of.
разобщён|ный (**-, -на, -но**) *прил* isolated.
ра́зовый *прил*: ~ **биле́т** single (*BRIT*) *или* one-way ticket.
разовью́(сь) *итп сов см* **разви́ть(ся)**.
раз|огна́ть (**-гоню́, -го́нишь**; *pt* **-огна́л, -огнала́, -огна́ло**, *impf* **разгоня́ть**) *сов перех* (*толпу, демонстрацию*) to break up; (*разг*: *организацию*) to purge; (: *бездельников, тунеядцев*) to come down on; (*тучи, туман*) to

disperse; (*перен*: *сон, тоску, мысли*) to drive away; (*машину, самолёт*) to increase the speed of
▸ **разогна́ться** (*impf* **разгоня́ться**) *сов возв* to build up speed.
разогн|у́ть (**-у́, -ёшь**; *impf* **разгиба́ть**) *сов перех* (*спину*) to straighten up; (*проволоку, скрепку*) to straighten out
▸ **разогну́ться** (*impf* **разгиба́ться**) *сов возв* to straighten up.
разогре́|ть (**-ю**; *impf* **разогрева́ть**) *сов перех* (*чайник, суп*) to heat
▸ **разогре́ться** (*impf* **разогрева́ться**) *сов возв* (*суп*) to heat up; (*человек, двигатель*) to warm up.
разоде́т|ый (**-, -а, -о**) *прил* overdressed.
разоде́|ться (**-нусь, -нешься**) *сов возв* (*разг*) to get dressed up.
раз|одра́ть (**-деру́, -дерёшь**; *impf* **раздира́ть**) *сов перех* to tear up.
разожгу́ *итп сов см* **разже́чь.**
разожму́(сь) *итп сов см* **разжа́ть(ся).**
разозл|и́ть (**-ю́, -и́шь**) *сов от* **злить** ◆ *перех* to anger
▸ **разозли́ться** *сов от* **зли́ться** ◆ *возв* to get angry.
разойти́сь (*как* **идти́**; *см* **Table 18**; *impf* **расходи́ться**) *сов возв* (*гости*) to leave; (*облака, туман, толпа*) to disperse; (*запасы, деньги*) to run out; (*тираж*) to sell out; (*не встретиться*) to miss each other; (*дать дорогу*) to pass each other; (*супруги*) to split up; (*прекратить дружбу*) to part company; (*шов, крепления*) to come apart; (*перен*: *мнения, взгляды*) to diverge; (: *разг*: *дать волю себе*) to get going; **на э́той доро́ге не** ~ the road is too narrow for passing.
разолью́(сь) *итп сов см* **разли́ть(ся).**
ра́зом *нареч* (*разг*: *все вместе*) all at once; (: *в один приём*) all in one go.
разомкн|у́ть (**-у́, -ёшь**; *impf* **размыка́ть**) *сов перех* (*цепь, крепление*) to unfasten; (*пальцы*) to uncurl; ~ *(perf)* **ру́ки** to let go (of each other's hands)
▸ **разомкну́ться** (*impf* **размыка́ться**) *сов возв* (*цепь, крепление*) to come unfastened; (*пальцы*) to open.
разомну́(сь) *итп сов см* **размя́ть(ся).**
разопью́ *итп сов см* **распи́ть.**
разорв|а́ть (**-у́, -ёшь**; *pt* **-а́л, -ала́, -а́ло**) *сов от* **рвать** ◆ (*impf* **разрыва́ть**) *перех* (*письмо, бумагу*) to tear *или* rip up; (*конверт, обёртку*) to tear *или* rip open; (*одежду*) to tear, rip; (*перен*: *знакомство, связь*) to break off; (: *договор, контракт*) to break ◆ *безл* (*ногу, руку*) to be blown off; (*танк, стену*) to be blown up
▸ **разорва́ться** *сов от* **рва́ться** ◆ (*impf* **разрыва́ться**) *возв* (*одежда*) to tear, rip; (*верёвка, цепь*) to break; (*связь, знакомство*) to be severed; (*снаряд, ракета*) to explode.
разоре́ни|е (**-я**) *ср* (*см глаг*) plundering; impoverishment; ruin.
разори́тел|ьный (**-ен, -ьна, -ьно**) *прил* ruinous.
разор|и́ть (**-ю́, -и́шь**; *impf* **разоря́ть**) *сов перех* (*деревню, гнездо*) to plunder; (*семью, население*) to impoverish; (: *компанию, страну*) to ruin
▸ **разори́ться** (*impf* **разоря́ться**) *сов возв* to go to rack and ruin; (*человек*) to become impoverished; (*разг*): **~ся на** *+acc* (*потратить деньги*) to splash out on.
разоружа́|ть(ся) (**-ю(сь)**) *несов от* **разоружи́ть(ся).**
разоруже́ни|е (**-я**) *ср* (*противника, пленных*) disarming; (*политический процесс*) disarmament.
разоруж|и́ть (**-у́, -и́шь**; *impf* **разоружа́ть**) *сов перех* (*также перен*) to disarm
▸ **разоружи́ться** (*impf* **разоружа́ться**) *сов возв* to disarm.
разоря́|ть(ся) (**-ю(сь)**) *несов от* **разори́ть(ся).**
разо|сла́ть (**-шлю́, -шлёшь**; *impf* **рассыла́ть**) *сов перех* to send out.
разостла́ть (**расстелю́, рассте́лешь**) *несов =* **расстели́ть.**
разотру́(сь) *итп сов см* **растере́ть(ся).**
разочарова́ни|е (**-я**) *ср* disappointment; (*потеря веры*): ~ **в** *+prp* (*в друге, в идеалах*) disenchantment with.
разочаро́ван|ный (**-, -на, -но**) *прил* disappointed; (**-, -а, -о**): ~ **в** *+prp* disenchanted with.
разочар|ова́ть (**-у́ю**; *impf* **разочаро́вывать**) *сов перех* to disappoint
▸ **разочарова́ться** (*impf* **разочаро́вываться**) *сов возв*: **~ся в** *+prp* to become disenchanted with.
разошёлся *итп сов см* **разойти́сь.**
разошлю́ *итп сов см* **разосла́ть.**
разошью́ *итп сов см* **расши́ть.**
разрабо́та|ть (**-ю**; *impf* **разраба́тывать**) *сов перех* (*план, технологию, теорию*) to develop; (*месторождение*) to exploit.
разрабо́т|ка (**-ки**) *ж* (*см глаг*) development; exploitation; (*gen pl* **-ок**; *обычно мн*: *научные*) groundwork *ед*; *см также* **разрабо́тки.**
разрабо́т|ки (**-ок**) *мн* (*ГЕО*): **га́зовые** ~ gas fields *мн*; **нефтяны́е** ~ oilfields *мн*; **методи́ческие** ~ guidelines *мн*.
разра́внива|ть (**-ю**) *несов от* **разровня́ть.**
разра|зи́ться (**-жу́сь, -зи́шься**; *impf* **разража́ться**) *сов возв* (*гроза, катастрофа*) to break out; ~ *(perf)* **аплодисме́нтами/сме́хом** to break into applause/laughter.
разр|асти́сь (*3sg* **-астётся**, *3pl* **-асту́тся**, *pt* **-о́сся, -осла́сь, -о́слось**, *impf* **разраста́ться**)

сов возв (*лес, растение*) to spread; (*город, движение*) to grow.

разреве́|ться (**-у́сь, -ёшься**) *сов возв* (*разг*) to start bawling.

разрежён|ный (**-, -а́, -о́**) *прил* rarified.

разре́жу *сов см* **разре́зать.**

разре́з (**-а**) *м* (*на юбке*) slit; (*ГЕОМ*) section; **в ~е** *+gen* in the context of; **~ глаз** the shape of one's eyes.

разре́|зать (**-жу, -жешь**) *сов от* **ре́зать.**

разреза́|ть (**-ю**) *несов перех* to cut up.

разреклами́р|овать (**-ую**) *сов перех* to publicize.

разреша́|ть (**-ю**) *несов от* **разреши́ть**

▸ **разреша́ться** *несов от* **разреши́ться** ◆ *неперех* (*допускаться*) to be allowed *или* permitted; **здесь не ~ется кури́ть** smoking is not permitted here.

разреше́ни|е (**-я**) *ср* (*действие*) authorization; (*позволение, право*) permission, authorization; (*документ*) permit; (*решение*) resolution; **с Ва́шего ~я** with your permission.

разреш|и́ть (**-у́, -и́шь**; *impf* **разреша́ть**) *сов перех* (*решить*) to resolve; (*позволить*): **~ кому́-н** *+infin* to allow *или* permit sb to do; **~и́те** *+infin* ... may I ...; **~?** may I come in?; **~и́те пройти́** let me through; **разреша́ть** (**~** *perf*) **фильм/кни́гу** to pass a film for screening/book for publication

▸ **разреши́ться** (*impf* **разреша́ться**) *сов возв* to be resolved.

разрис|ова́ть (**-у́ю**; *impf* **разрисо́вывать**) *сов перех* (*карандашом*) to draw all over; (*краской*) to paint all over.

разровня́|ть (**-ю**) *сов от* **ровня́ть** ◆ (*impf* **разра́внивать**) *перех* to level.

разро́знен|ный (**-, -на, -но**) *прил* (*действия, силы*) uncoordinated; (*коллекция, сервиз*) made up of odd parts; (*тома*) odd.

разро́сся *итп сов см* **разрасти́сь.**

разр|уби́ть (**-ублю́, -у́бишь**; *impf* **разруба́ть**) *сов перех* to chop in two; **разруба́ть** (**~** *perf*) **на куски́** to chop up.

разрумя́н|ить(ся) (**-ю(сь)**) *сов от* **румя́нить(ся).**

разру́х|а (**-и**) *ж* ruin; **в стране́ ~** the country is in ruins.

разруша́|ть(ся) (**-ю(сь)**) *несов от* **разру́шить(ся).**

разруши́тел|ьный (**-ен, -ьна, -ьно**) *прил* destructive.

разру́ш|ить (**-у, -ишь**; *impf* **разруша́ть**) *сов перех* to destroy; (*планы, жизнь*) to ruin

▸ **разру́шиться** (*impf* **разруша́ться**) *сов возв* (*см перех*) to be destroyed; to be ruined.

разры́в (**-а**) *м* (*дипломатических отношений, связей*) severance; (*провода, цепи*) breaking; (*разорванная часть*) tear; (*снаряда, гранаты*) explosion; (*несоответствие, промежуток времени*) gap; **с ~ом в 10 лет** with a gap of 10 years; **разры́в се́рдца** (*МЕД*) heart attack.

разрыва́|ть(ся) (**-ю(сь)**) *несов от* **разорва́ть(ся).**

разрыхл|и́ть (**-ю́, -и́шь**) *сов от* **рыхли́ть.**

разря́д (**-а**) *м* (*людей, растений*) class; (*спортивный*) grade; (*профессиональный*) status; (*ФИЗ*) discharge.

разря|ди́ть (**-жу́, -ди́шь**; *impf* **разряжа́ть**) *сов перех* (*ружьё, батарейку*) to discharge; **разряжа́ть** (**~** *perf*) **обстано́вку** to diffuse the situation

▸ **разряди́ться** (*impf* **разряжа́ться**) *сов возв* (*перен*) to become less tense.

разря́дк|а (**-и**; *gen pl* **-ок**) *ж* release, outlet; (*в тексте*) spacing; **~ (междунаро́дной напряжённости** détente.

разряжа́|ть(ся) (**-ю(сь)**) *несов от* **разряди́ть(ся).**

разряжу́(сь) *сов см* **разряди́ть(ся).**

разубе|ди́ть (**-жу́, -ди́шь**; *impf* **разубежда́ть**) *сов перех*: **~ кого́-н** (**в** *+prp*) to dissuade sb (from).

разува́|ть(ся) (**-ю(сь)**) *несов от* **разу́ть(ся).**

разуве́р|иться (**-юсь, -ишься**; *impf* **разуверя́ться**) *сов возв*: **~ в** *+prp* to lose faith in.

разузна́|ть (**-ю**; *impf* **разузнава́ть**) *сов перех* (*разг*) to find out.

разукра́|сить (**-шу, -сишь**; *impf* **разукра́шивать**) *сов перех* to decorate.

ра́зум (**-а**) *м* reason.

разу́мен *прил см* **разу́мный.**

разуме́|ться (*3sg* **-ется**) *сов возв*: **под э́тим ~ется, что** ... by this is meant that ...; **(само́ собо́й) ~ется** that goes without saying; **он, ~ется, не знал об э́том** it goes without saying that he knew nothing about it.

разу́м|ный (**-ен, -на, -но**) *прил* intelligent; (*поступок, решение, довод*) reasonable.

разу́т|ый (**-, -а, -о**) *прил* (*без обуви*) barefoot; (*разг: нуждающийся в обуви*) shoeless.

раз|у́ть (**-у́ю**; *impf* **разува́ть**) *сов перех*: **~ кого́-н** to take sb's shoes off

▸ **разу́ться** (*impf* **разува́ться**) *сов возв* to take one's shoes off.

раз|учи́ть (**-учу́, -у́чишь**; *impf* **разу́чивать**) *сов перех* to learn

▸ **разучи́ться** (*impf* **разу́чиваться**) *сов возв*: **~ся** *+infin* to forget how to do.

разъеда́|ть (*3sg* **-ет**, *3pl* **-ют**) *несов от* **разъе́сть** ◆ *перех* (*перен: душу*) to eat away at

▸ **разъеда́ться** *несов от* **разъе́сться.**

разъе́дешься *итп сов см* **разъе́хаться.**

разъеди́м(ся) *сов см* **разъе́сть(ся).**

разъедин|и́ть (**-ю́, -и́шь**; *impf* **разъединя́ть**) *сов перех* (*провода, телефон*) to disconnect; (*друзей, любимых*) to separate.

разъеди́те(сь) *сов см* **разъе́сть(ся).**

разъе́дусь *итп сов см* **разъе́хаться.**

разъедя́т(ся) *сов см* **разъе́сть(ся).**

разъе́зд (**-а**) *м* (*гостей*) departure; (*для поездов*) siding (*BRIT*), sidetrack (*US*); *см также*

разъе́зды.
разъе́зд|ы (**-ов**) *мн* (*поездки*) travel *ед*; **он всё вре́мя в ~ах** he does a lot of travelling.
разъезжа́|ть (**-ю**) *несов неперех* (*по делам, по городам*) to travel around; (*кататься: на тройке, на автомобиле*) to ride about; ~ *(impf)* **по гостя́м** to go around visiting friends
▸ **разъезжа́ться** *несов от* **разъе́хаться**.
разъе́сть (*как* **есть**; *см* **Table 15**; *impf* **разъеда́ть**) *сов перех* to corrode
▸ **разъе́сться** (*impf* **разъеда́ться**) *сов возв* (*разг*) to get fat.
разъе́|хаться (*как* **е́хать**; *см* **Table 19**; *impf* **разъезжа́ться**) *сов возв* to leave; (*разг: лыжи, ноги на льду*) to slide apart; **она́ ~халась с му́жем/ма́терью** she doesn't live with her husband/mother any more; **мы с ни́ми ~хались в темноте́** we missed each other in the darkness; **маши́ны не могли́** ~ the cars couldn't get past each other.
разъе́шь(ся) *сов см* **разъе́сть(ся)**.
разъярённый *прил* (*зверь, человек, лицо*) furious; (*перен: река, стихия*) raging.
разъяр|и́ть (**-ю́, -и́шь**; *impf* **разъяря́ть**) *сов перех* (*толпу, человека*) to infuriate, enrage; (*зверя*) to provoke
▸ **разъяри́ться** (*impf* **разъяря́ться**) *сов возв* to become infuriated.
разъясне́ни|е (**-я**) *ср* clarification.
разъясн|и́ть (**-ю́, -и́шь**; *impf* **разъясня́ть**) *сов перех* to clarify
▸ **разъясни́ться** (*impf* **разъясня́ться**) *сов возв* to be clarified.
разыгра́|ть (**-ю**; *impf* **разы́грывать**) *сов перех* (*МУЗ, СПОРТ*) to play; (*сцену*) to act out; (*в лотерею, по жребию*) to raffle; (*разг: подшутить*) to play a joke *или* trick on
▸ **разыгра́ться** (*impf* **разы́грываться**) *сов возв* (*увлечься игрой*) to get carried away with one's game; (*начать лучше играть*) to get going; (*перед концертом*) to warm up; (*перен: буря*) to rage; (: *драма, сражение*) to unfold; **у меня́ ~лась мигре́нь** I had a nasty migraine; **по́сле прогу́лки у него́ ~лся аппети́т** the walk gave him a big appetite.
раз|ыска́ть (**-ыщу́, -ы́щешь**; *impf* **разы́скивать**) *сов перех* to find
▸ **разыска́ться** (*impf* **разы́скиваться**) *сов возв* to turn up.
РАИС *ср сокр* (= *Российское аге́нтство интеллектуа́льной со́бственности*) copyright protection agency.
ра|й (**-я**; *loc sg* **-ю́**) *м* (*также перен*) paradise.
райко́м (**-а**) *м сокр* (*ИСТ: = райо́нный комите́т*) district committee (*of Communist Party or Komsomol*).
райо́н (**-а**) *м* region; (*ПОЛИТ*) district.
райо́нный *прил* district *опред*.
ра́йск|ий (**-ая, -ое, -ие**) *прил* (*также перен*) heavenly.
райце́нтр (**-а**) *м сокр* (= *райо́нный центр*) main town (*of district*).
рак (**-а**) *м* (*ЗООЛ: речной*) crayfish (*мн* crayfish); (: *морской*) crab; (*МЕД*) cancer; (*созвездие*): **Р~** Cancer.
раке́т|а (**-ы**) *ж* (*также КОСМОС*) rocket; (*ВОЕН*) missile; (*судно*) hydrofoil.
раке́т|ка (**-ки**; *gen pl* **-ок**) *ж* (*СПОРТ*) racket; **пе́рвая** ~ (*перен*) the top player.
раке́тный *прил* (*также КОСМОС*) rocket *опред*; (*ВОЕН*) missile *опред*; **раке́тное ору́жие** (*ВОЕН*) missiles *мн*.
раке́ток *сущ см* **раке́тка**.
ра́ковин|а (**-ы**) *ж* (*ЗООЛ*) shell; (*для умывания*) sink; **ушна́я** ~ aural cavity.
ра́ковый *прил* (*ЗООЛ, КУЛИН*) crab *опред*; (*МЕД*) cancer *опред*; **ра́ковая о́пухоль** malignant tumour.
ра́лли *ср нескл* (*СПОРТ*) rally.
ра́м|а (**-ы**) *ж* frame; (*АВТ*) chassis; **двойны́е ~ы** double glazing.
рамаза́н (**-а**) *м* Ramadan.
ра́м|ка (**-ки**; *gen pl* **-ок**) *ж* (*для фотографии, для картины*) frame; (*текста, рисунка*) border; *см также* **ра́мки**.
ра́м|ки (**-ок**) *мн*: ~ *+gen* (*рассказа, разговора, обязанностей*) framework *ед* of; (*закона, устава*) limits *мн* of; **в ~ках** *+gen* (*закона, приличия*) within the bounds of; (*дискуссии, переговоров*) within the framework of; **за ~ками** *+gen* beyond the bounds of; **держа́ть** *(impf)* **себя́ в ~ках** to control o.s.
ра́мп|а (**-ы**) *ж* (*ТЕАТР*): **огни́ ~ы** footlights *мн*.
РАН *м сокр* (= *Российская акаде́мия нау́к*) Russian Academy of Sciences.
ра́н|а (**-ы**) *ж* (*также перен*) wound.
Ранѓун (**-а**) *м* Rangoon.
ра́нен|ая (**-ой**; *decl like adj*) *ж см* **ра́неный**.
ране́ни|е (**-я**) *ср* injury.
ра́нен|ый *прил* injured; (*ВОЕН*) wounded ◆ (**-ого**; *decl like adj*) *м* injured person (*мн* people); (*ВОЕН*) wounded person (*мн* people).
ра́н|ец (**-ца**) *м* (*школьный*) satchel; (*солдатский, походный*) backpack.
рани́м|ый (**-, -а, -о**) *прил* vulnerable.
ра́н|ить (**-ю, -ишь**) *(не)сов перех* (*также перен*) to wound; ~ *(impf/perf)* **кого́-н в ру́ку/но́гу** to wound sb in the arm/leg; ~ *(impf/perf)* **кому́-н душу́** to wound sb (*fig*).
ра́нн|ий (**-яя, -ее, -ие**) *прил* early.
ра́но *нареч* early ◆ *как сказ* it's early; **ещё** ~ (*о раннем времени*) it's still early; ~ **де́лать** *(impf)* **вы́воды** it's too early to draw conclusions; **он жени́лся/у́мер** ~ he married/died young; ~ **и́ли по́здно** sooner or later.
ра́нца *итп сущ см* **ра́нец**.

ран|ь (-и) *ж* (*разг*) early morning.
раньше *сравн нареч от* **рано** ◆ *нареч* (*прежде*) before; (*сначала*) earlier ◆ *предл*: ~ +*gen* before; ~ **он жил в городе** he used to live in the city; ~ **подумай, потом отвечай** think before you answer; ~ **времени** (*радоваться итп*) too soon; ~ **вечера мы не закончим** we won't finish before the evening; **он закончил ~ всех** he finished before everybody else.
РАО *сокр* (= *Российское акционерное общество*) joint-stock company.
рапир|а (-ы) *ж* foil (*for fencing*).
рапорт (-а) *м* report; **подавать (подать** *perf*) ~ to submit a report.
рапорт|овать (-ую; *perf* **отрапортовать**) (*не*)*сов неперех*: ~ (**кому-н о** +*prp*) to report back (to sb on).
рас- *префикс см* **раз-**.
рас|а (-ы) *ж* race.
расизм (-а) *м* racism.
расист (-а) *м* racist.
расист|ка (-ки; *gen pl* -ок) *ж см* **расист**.
расистск|ий (-ая, -ое, -ие) *прил* racist *опред*.
раскаива|ться (-юсь) *несов от* **раскаяться**.
раскалённый *прил* burning hot.
раскал|ить (-ю, -ишь; *impf* **раскалять**) *сов перех* to bring to a high temperature
▸ **раскалиться** (*impf* **раскаляться**) *сов возв* to get very hot.
раскалыва|ть (-ю) *несов от* **расколоть**
▸ **раскалываться** *несов от* **расколоться** ◆ *возв*: **у меня ~ется голова** I have a splitting headache.
раскаля|ть(ся) (-ю(сь)) *несов от* **раскалить(ся)**.
раскапыва|ть (-ю) *несов от* **раскопать**.
раскармлива|ть (-ю) *несов от* **раскормить**.
раскат (-а) *м* (*обычно мн*: *грома, смеха*) peal.
раскат|ать (-ю; *impf* **раскатывать**) *сов перех* (*ковёр, рулон*) to unroll; (*тесто*) to roll out; (*дорогу, горку*) to flatten (out); (*брёвна, шары*) to send rolling (*in different directions*).
раскатист|ый (-, -а, -о) *прил* booming.
раскатыва|ть (-ю) *несов от* **раскатать**.
раскача|ть (-ю; *impf* **раскачивать**) *сов перех* to swing; (*качели, ребёнка*) to push
▸ **раскачаться** (*impf* **раскачиваться**) *сов возв* (*лодка*) to rock; (*качели*) to swing; (*разг*: *медлить*: *человек*) to dither.
раскаяни|е (-я) *ср* repentance.
раска|яться (-юсь; *impf* **раскаиваться**) *сов возв*: ~ (**в** +*prp*) to repent (of).
расквита|ться (-юсь) *сов возв* (*разг*): ~ **с** +*instr* (*с кредиторами*) to settle up with; (*перен*: *с врагом, с обидчиком*) to settle a score with.
раскида|ть (-ю; *impf* **раскидывать**) *сов перех* to throw around, scatter; **жизнь ~ла их по всему свету** life has scattered them across the globe.
раскидист|ый (-, -а, -о) *прил* spreading.
раскидыва|ть (-ю) *несов от* **раскидать**, **раскинуть**.
раскин|уть (-у, -ешь; *impf* **раскидывать**) *сов перех* (*руки*) to throw open; (*ковёр, сети*) to spread out; (*лагерь*) to set up; (*палатку, шатёр*) to pitch; ~ (*perf*) **что-н умом** *или* **мозгами** (*разг*) to think sth over
▸ **раскинуться** (*impf* **раскидываться**) *сов возв* to stretch out.
расклад|ка (-и) *ж* (*действие*) arranging; (*соотношение*: *сил, средств*) balance.
раскладной *прил* folding *опред*.
раскладу|шка (-ки; *gen pl* -ек) *ж* (*разг*) camp bed (*BRIT*), cot (*US*).
раскладыва|ть(ся) (-ю(сь)) *несов от* **разложить(ся)**.
раскланя|ться (-юсь; *impf* **раскланиваться**) *сов возв* (*актёр, выступающий*) to take a bow; (*при встрече, при расставании*) to bow.
раскле|ить (-ю, -ишь; *impf* **расклеивать**) *сов перех* (*конверт*) to unglue; (*плакаты, афиши, рекламы*) to paste up
▸ **расклеиться** (*impf* **расклеиваться**) *сов возв* to come unstuck; (*перен*: *разг*: *свадьба, дело*) to fall through; **я совсем ~ился** (*разг*) I feel (like) a complete wreck.
раскован|ный (-, -на, -но) *прил* relaxed.
раскол (-а) *м* (*организации, движения*) split; (*РЕЛ*) schism.
раск|олоть (-олю, -олешь; *impf* **раскалывать**) *сов перех* (*дрова, страну, движение*) to split; (*лёд, орех*) to crack
▸ **расколоться** (*impf* **раскалываться**) *сов возв* (*полено, орех*) to split open; (*перен*: *движение, организация*) to be split.
раскопа|ть (-ю; *impf* **раскапывать**) *сов перех* (*также перен*) to dig up.
раскоп|ка (-ки; *gen pl* -ок) *ж* (*действие*) excavation; *см также* **раскопки**.
раскоп|ки (-ок) *мн* (*работы*) excavations *мн*; (*место*) (archaeological) dig *ед*.
раск|ормить (-ормлю, -ормишь; *impf* **раскармливать**) *сов перех* to overfeed.
раскосый *прил* (*глаза*) slanting.
раскошел|иться (-юсь, -ишься; *impf* **раскошеливаться**) *сов возв* (*разг*): ~ (**на** +*acc*) to fork out (for).
раскраива|ть (-ю) *несов от* **раскроить**.
раскра|сить (-шу, -сишь; *impf* **раскрашивать**) *сов перех* (*рисунок, картинку*) to colour (*BRIT*), color (*US*); (*вазу, поделку*) to paint.
раскраск|а (-и) *ж* (*см глаг*) colouring (*BRIT*), coloring (*US*); painting; (*цветовая гамма*) colours *мн* (*BRIT*), colors *мн* (*US*).
раскрасне|ться (-юсь) *сов возв* to go red.
раскрашива|ть (-ю) *несов от* **раскрасить**.
раскрашу *сов см* **раскрасить**.
раскритик|овать (-ую) *сов перех* to criticize severely.
раскро|ить (-ю, -ишь; *impf* **раскраивать**) *сов перех* to cut.
раскр|утить (-учу, -утишь; *impf* **раскручивать**)

сов перех (*что-н сплетённое*) to untwist; (*что-н закрученное*) to unscrew; (*интригу, тайну*) to unravel; (*идею, политика*) to promote.
раскру́тк|а (-и) *ж* (*разг*) promotion.
раскр|ы́ть (-о́ю, -о́ешь; *impf* **раскрыва́ть**) *сов перех* to open; (*перен*) to discover; **раскрыва́ть** (~ *perf*) **свои́ ка́рты** (*перен*) to show one's hand
▸ **раскры́ться** (*impf* **раскрыва́ться**) *сов возв* to open; (*перен*: *характер, дарование*) to be revealed; **~ся** (*perf*) **пе́ред кем-н** to open up to sb.
раск|упи́ть (-уплю́, -у́пишь; *impf* **раскупа́ть**) *сов перех* to buy up.
раск|уси́ть (-ушу́, -у́сишь) *сов перех* (*разг*: *понять*) to suss out; (*impf* **раску́сывать**; *яблоко, конфету*) to bite into.
ра́совый *прил* racial.
распа́д (-а) *м* break-up, collapse; (*ХИМ*) decomposition.
распада́|ться (*3sg* **-ется**, *3pl* **-ются**) *несов от* **распа́сться** ◆ *возв* (*состоять из частей*): ~ **на** *+acc* to be divided into.
распадётся *итп сов см* **распа́сться**.
распа́рыва|ть (-ю; *perf* **распоро́ть**) *несов перех* = **поро́ть**.
распа́|сться (*3sg* **-дётся**, *3pl* **-ду́тся**, *impf* **распада́ться**) *сов возв* to break up; (*вещество, молекула*) to decompose; **распада́ться** (~ *perf*) **на ча́сти** to fall apart.
расп|аха́ть (-ашу́, -а́шешь; *impf* **распа́хивать**) *сов перех* to plough (*BRIT*) *или* plow (*US*) up.
распахн|у́ть (-у́, -ёшь; *impf* **распа́хивать**) *сов перех* to throw open; ~ (*perf*) **ду́шу** to bare one's soul
▸ **распахну́ться** (*impf* **распа́хиваться**) *сов возв* (*дверь, шуба*) to fly open; (*поля, равнина*) to open out.
распашо́н|ка (-ки; *gen pl* **-ок**) *ж* *cotton baby top*.
распашу́ *итп сов см* **распаха́ть**.
распева́|ть (-ю) *несов неперех* (*разг*) to sing loudly ◆ *перех* (*разг*): ~ **пе́сню** to sing away.
распеленá|ть (-ю; *impf* **распелёнывать**) *сов перех* to unwrap.
распеча́та|ть (-ю; *impf* **распеча́тывать**) *сов перех* (*письмо, пакет*) to open; (*помещение*) to unseal; (*размножить*) to print off; (*КОМП*) to print out.
распеча́т|ка (-ки; *gen pl* **-ок**) *ж* (*доклада*) print-out; (*КОМП*) hard copy.
распеча́тыва|ть (-ю) *несов от* **распеча́тать**.
распива́|ть (-ю) *несов от* **распи́ть**.
расп|или́ть (-илю́, -и́лишь; *impf* **распи́ливать**) *сов перех* to saw up.
распина́|ть (-ю) *несов от* **распя́ть**
▸ **распина́ться** *несов возв* (*разг*): **~ся пе́ред** *+instr* to go out of one's way for.
расписа́ни|е (-я) *ср* timetable.
расп|иса́ть (-ишу́, -и́шешь; *impf* **распи́сывать**) *сов перех* (*дела, мероприятия, расходы итп*) to arrange; (*день, месяц*) to fill up; (*стены, шкатулку, вазу*) to paint; (*перен*: *разг*: *будущее, приключения*) to paint a rosy picture of; (*разг*: *жениха и невесту*) to marry (*in registry office*)
▸ **расписа́ться** (*impf* **распи́сываться**) *сов возв* (*поставить подпись*) to sign one's name; (*перен*): **~ся в** *+prp* (*в невежестве, в бессилии*) to acknowledge; (*разг*): **~ся (с** *+instr*) (*зарегистрировать брак*) to get married (to) (*in registry office*); **распи́сываться (~ся** *perf*) **в получе́нии чего́-н** to sign for sth.
распи́с|ка (-ки; *gen pl* **-ок**) *ж* (*о получении денег*) receipt; (*гарантия*) warrant; **принима́ть (приня́ть** *perf*) **что-н под ~ку** to sign for sth.
расписно́й *прил* painted.
распи́сок *сущ см* **распи́ска**.
распи́сыва|ть(ся) (-ю(сь)) *несов от* **расписа́ть(ся)**.
расп|и́ть (разопью́, разопьёшь; *pt* **-и́л, -ила́, -и́ло**, *impf* **распива́ть**) *сов перех* (*разг*) to get through.
распиха́|ть (-ю; *impf* **распи́хивать**) *сов перех* (*разг*: *толпу, очередь*) to push through; (: *вещи, бумаги*): ~ **по** *+dat* to stuff into.
распишу́(сь) *итп сов см* **расписа́ть(ся)**.
распла́в|ить (-лю, -ишь) *сов от* **пла́вить** ◆ (*impf* **расплавля́ть**) *перех* to melt
▸ **распла́виться** *сов от* **пла́виться** ◆ (*impf* **расплавля́ться**) *возв* to melt.
распла́|каться (-чусь, -чешься) *сов возв* to burst into tears.
распласта́|ть (-ю; *impf* **распла́стывать**) *сов перех* (*крылья, руки*) to spread
▸ **распласта́ться** (*impf* **распла́стываться**) *сов возв* to sprawl out.
распла́т|а (-ы) *ж* payment; (*перен*) retribution; **час ~ы** (*перен*) the day of reckoning.
распл|ати́ться (-ачу́сь, -а́тишься; *impf* **распла́чиваться**) *сов возв*: ~ **(с** *+instr*) (*с продавцом, с кредитором*) to pay; (*перен*: *с предателем, с негодяем*) to get even (with); **распла́чиваться (~** *perf*) **за оши́бку/преступле́ние** to pay for a mistake/crime.
распла́чусь *итп сов см* **распла́каться**.
расплёл(ся) *итп сов см* **расплести́(сь)**.
распл|еска́ть (-ещу́, -е́щешь; *impf* **расплёскивать**) *сов перех* to spill
▸ **расплеска́ться** (*impf* **расплёскиваться**) *сов возв* to spill.
распл|ести́ (-ету́, -етёшь; *pt* **-ёл, -ела́, -ело́**, *impf* **расплета́ть**) *сов перех* (*плётку*) to untwist; (*косу*) to unplait
▸ **расплести́сь** (*impf* **расплета́ться**) *сов возв* to come untwisted; (*коса*) to come out.
расплещу́(сь) *сов см* **расплеска́ть(ся)**.

расплод|и́ться (*3sg* **-и́тся**, *3pl* **-я́тся**) *сов от* **плоди́ться**.
расплыва́|ться (**-юсь**) *несов от* **расплы́ться**.
расплыву́сь *итп сов см* **расплы́ться**.
расплы́вчат|ый (**-, -а, -о**) *прил* (*рисунок, очертания*) blurred; (*перен*: *мысли, ответ, намёк*) vague.
расплы́|ться (**-ву́сь, -вёшься**; *pt* **-лся, -ла́сь, -лось**, *impf* **расплыва́ться**) *сов возв* (*утки итп*) to swim off; (*чернила, краски*) to run; (*нефть, дым*) to diffuse; (*облака*) to disperse; (*перен*: *фигуры, силуэт*) to be blurred; (*разг*: *располнеть*) to spread; (: *широко улыбнуться*) to beam; **он ~лся** *или* **его́ лицо́ ~лось в улы́бке** a smile spread across his face.
расплю́щ|ить (**-у, -ишь**; *impf* **расплю́щивать**) *сов перех* to crush.
распну́ *итп сов см* **распя́ть**.
распого́д|иться (*3sg* **-ится**) *сов возв* to clear up (*weather*).
распозна́|ть (**-ю**; *impf* **распознава́ть**) *сов перех* to identify.
располага́|ть (**-ю**) *несов от* **расположи́ть** ♦ *неперех*: ~ *+instr* (*данными, временем итп*) to have at one's disposal, have available; **Вы мо́жете мной** ~ I am entirely at your disposal
располага́ться *несов от* **расположи́ться** ♦ *возв* (*находиться*) to be situated *или* located.
располага́ющий (**-ая, -ее, -ие**) *прил* welcoming.
располз|ти́сь (*3sg* **-ётся**, *3pl* **-у́тся**, *impf* **располза́ться**) *сов возв* to crawl off; (*туман, плющ*) to spread; (*пятно, строчки*) to smudge; (*разг*: *ткань, одежда*) to become threadbare.
расположе́ни|е (**-я**) *ср* (*действие*: *предметов*) arranging; (*место*: *отряда, лагеря*) location; (*комнат*) layout; (*мебели*) arrangement; (*симпатия*) disposition; ~ **ду́ха** mood; **я испы́тываю к нему́** ~ I am well-disposed towards him; **у меня́ нет сейча́с ~я е́хать туда́** I'm not in the mood for going there right now.
располо́жен|ный (**-, -а, -о**) *прил*: ~ **к** *+dat* (*к человеку*) well-disposed towards; (*к инфекции, к простуде*) susceptible to; ~ *+infin* (*читать, работать, играть*) in the mood for doing; **я не располо́жен э́то сейча́с обсужда́ть** I am not in the mood to discuss it right now.
распол|ожи́ть (**-ожу́, -о́жишь**; *impf* **располага́ть**) *сов перех* (*мебель, вещи итп*) to arrange; (*отряд*) to station; (*лагерь*) to set up; **располага́ть** (~ *perf*) **кого́-н к себе́** to win sb over
▸ **расположи́ться** (*impf* **располага́ться**) *сов возв* (*человек*: *в кресле, под деревом итп*) to settle down; (*отряд*) to position itself.
расп|оро́ть (**-орю́, -о́решь**) *сов от* **поро́ть**.
распоряди́тел|ь (**-я**) *м* (*КОММ*) manager; (*церемониала, вечера*) organizer.
распоряди́тельный *прил* (*хозяйка, начальник*) efficient; **распоряди́тельный дире́ктор** managing director; **распоряди́тельный комите́т** management committee.
распоря|ди́ться (**-жу́сь, -ди́шься**; *impf* **распоряжа́ться**) *сов возв* to give out instructions; (*+infin*; *сделать что-н*) to order to do; (*+instr*; *деньгами, ресурсами*) to manage; **он ~ди́лся, что́бы все яви́лись к шести́** he instructed everyone to be there by six (o'clock).
распоря́д|ок (**-ка**) *м* routine; **пра́вила вну́треннего ~ка** regulations *мн*.
распоряжа́|ться (**-юсь**) *несов от* **распоряди́ться** ♦ *возв*: ~ (*+instr*) to be in charge (of).
распоряже́ни|е (**-я**) *ср* (*управление*) management; (*приказ*) instructions *мн*; (*указ*) enactment; **ба́нковское** ~ banker's order; **в** ~ *+gen* at sb's/sth's disposal; **предоставля́ть** (**предоста́вить** *perf*) **что-н в чьё-н** ~ to place sth at sb's disposal; **я в Ва́шем ~и** I am at your disposal.
распоряжу́сь *сов см* **распоряди́ться**.
распоя́са|ться (**-юсь**; *impf* **распоя́сываться**) *сов возв* (*перен*: *разг*) to get cocky.
распра́в|а (**-ы**) *ж* reprisals *мн*.
распра́в|ить (**-лю, -ишь**; *impf* **расправля́ть**) *сов перех* (*складки, смятую бумагу*) to straighten out; (*грудь, плечи*) to straighten (up); (*крылья*) to spread
▸ **распра́виться** (*impf* **расправля́ться**) *сов возв* (*см перех*) to be straightened out; to straighten up; to spread; (*парус*) to unfurl; (*наказать*): **~ся с** *+instr* (*с демонстрантами, с забастовщиками*) to take reprisals against; (*перен*: *разг*: *с делами, с обедом итп*) to be finished with.
распределе́ни|е (**-я**) *ср* distribution; (*после института*) work placement.
распредел|и́ть (**-ю́, -и́шь**; *impf* **распределя́ть**) *сов перех* (*обязанности, доходы*) to distribute; (*книги по полкам*) to arrange; (*учеников по классам*) to divide up; (*разг*): ~ **кого́-н** (*выпускника*) to give sb a work placement
▸ **распредели́ться** (*impf* **распределя́ться**) *сов возв* (*разг*: *выпускники*) to get work placements; **распределя́ться** (**~ся** *perf*) (**по** *+dat*) (*по группам, по бригадам*) to divide up (into).
распрода|ва́ть (**-ю́, -ёшь**) *несов от* **распрода́ть**.
распродади́м *итп сов см* **распрода́ть**.
распрода́ж|а (**-и**) *ж* sale.
распрода́ть (*как* **дать**; *см* **Table 14**; *impf* **распродава́ть**) *сов перех* (*вещи, имущество, товар*) to sell off; (*билеты*) to sell out of.
распросте́ртый *прил* (*руки*) outstretched; (*тело*) prostrate; **встреча́ть** (**встре́тить** *perf*) **кого́-н с распросте́ртыми объя́тиями** to welcome sb with open arms.
распро|сти́ться (**-щу́сь, -сти́шься**) *сов возв*: ~ **с** *+instr* to say *или* bid farewell to.
распростране́ни|е (**-я**) *ср* (*информации,*

опыта, знаний) dissemination; (*инфекции*) spreading; (*ядерного оружия*) proliferation; (*приказа, правила*) extension.
распространён|ный (-, -на, -но) *прил* widespread.
распростран|и́ть (-ю́, -и́шь; *impf* **распространя́ть**) *сов перех* (*информацию, знания*) to disseminate; (*опыт*) to share; (*сплетни, инфекцию*) to spread; (*правило, приказ*) to apply; (*владения*) to widen; (*газеты*) to distribute; (*запах*) to emit
▸ **распространи́ться** (*impf* **распространя́ться**) *сов возв* to spread; (*разг: подробно говорить*) to go into detail; **~ся** (*perf*) **на** *+acc* to extend to; **э́тот прика́з ~я́ется на всех** this order applies to everybody.
распроща́|ться (-юсь) *сов возв* = **распрости́ться**.
распрощу́сь *сов см* **распрости́ться**.
ра́спр|я (-и; *gen pl* -ей) *ж* (*обычно мн*) feud.
распря́г *итп сов см* **распря́чь**.
распряга́|ть (-ю) *несов от* **распря́чь**.
распрягу́ *итп сов см* **распря́чь**.
распряжёшь *итп сов см* **распря́чь**.
распрям|и́ть (-лю́, -и́шь; *impf* **распрямля́ть**) *сов перех* (*проволоку, крючок*) to straighten (out); (*спину, грудь, плечи*) to straighten (up).
распря́|чь (-гу́, -жёшь *итп*, -гу́т; *pt* -г, -гла́, -гло́, *impf* **распряга́ть**) *сов перех* to unharness.
распуга́|ть (-ю; *impf* **распу́гивать**) *сов перех* to scare away *или* off.
расп|усти́ть (-ущу́, -у́стишь; *impf* **распуска́ть**) *сов перех* (*армию*) to disband; (*студентов, школьников*) to dismiss; (*шнурки, корсет, ремень*) to loosen; (*волосы, косу*) to let down; (*шов, вязанье*) to unpick; (*перен*): ~ **кого́-н** (*ребёнка итп*) to let sb run wild; **распуска́ть** (~ *perf*) **парла́мент** to dissolve parliament; **распуска́ть** (~ *perf*) **слу́хи** to spread rumours
▸ **распусти́ться** (*impf* **распуска́ться**) *сов возв* (*цветы, почки*) to open out; (*шнуровка, завязки*) to come undone; (*дети, люди*) to get out of hand.
распу́та|ть (-ю; *impf* **распу́тывать**) *сов перех* (*узел, нитки*) to untangle; (*перен: дело, преступление, загадку*) to unravel; (*лошадь*) to unfetter
▸ **распу́таться** (*impf* **распу́тываться**) *сов возв* (*см перех*) to come untangled; to unravel itself.
распу́тиц|а (-ы) *ж* *period during autumn and spring when the roads become impassable*.
распу́тник (-а) *м* libertine.
распу́тниц|а (-ы) *ж см* **распу́тник**.
распу́т|ный (-ен, -на, -но) *прил* depraved.
распу́тыва|ть(ся) (-ю(сь)) *несов от* **распу́тать(ся)**.
распу́т|ье (-ья; *nom pl* -ий) *ср* crossroads; **быть** (*impf*) **на** ~ (*перен*) to be at a crossroads.

распу́хн|уть (-у, -ешь; *impf* **распуха́ть**) *сов неперех* (*лицо, нога итп*) to swell up; (*бумажник, папка*) to bulge.
распу́щен|ный (-, -на, -но) *прил* unruly; (*безнравственный*) dissolute.
распущу́(сь) *сов см* **распусти́ть(ся)**.
распыли́тел|ь (-я) *м* spray.
распыл|и́ть (-ю́, -и́шь; *impf* **распыля́ть**) *сов перех* to spray.
распя́ти|е (-я) *ср* crucifixion.
расп|я́ть (-ну́, -нёшь; *impf* **распина́ть**) *сов перех* to crucify.
расса́д|а (-ы) *ж собир* (*БОТ*) seedlings *мн*.
расс|ади́ть (-ажу́, -а́дишь; *impf* **расса́живать**) *сов перех* (*гостей, публику*) to seat; (*болтунов*) to seat apart; (*цветы*) to thin out.
расса́дник (-а) *м* (*перен*) hotbed.
расса́жива|ть (-ю) *несов от* **рассади́ть**
▸ **расса́живаться** *несов от* **рассе́сться**.
рассажу́ *сов см* **рассади́ть**.
расса́сыва|ться (*3sg* -ется, *3pl* -ются) *несов от* **рассоса́ться**.
рассве|сти́ (*3sg* -тёт, *pt* -ло́, *impf* **рассвета́ть**) *сов безл*: **~та́ет** dawn is breaking; **уже́ ~ло́** it's already light.
рассве́т (-а) *м* daybreak.
рассвета́|ть (*3sg* -ет) *несов от* **рассвести́**.
рассветёт *сов см* **рассвести́**.
рассвирепе́|ть (-ю) *сов от* **свирепе́ть**.
расседла́|ть (-ю; *impf* **рассёдлывать**) *сов перех* to unsaddle.
рассе́ива|ть(ся) (-ю(сь)) *несов от* **рассе́ять(ся)**.
рассёк *итп сов см* **рассе́чь**.
рассека́|ть (-ю) *несов от* **рассе́чь**.
рассеку́ *итп сов см* **рассе́чь**.
рассе́лин|а (-ы) *ж* fissure.
расс|ели́ть (-елю́, -е́лишь; *impf* **расселя́ть**) *сов перех* (*по комнатам, по квартирам*) to accommodate, put up; **расселя́ть** (~ *perf*) **коммуна́льную кварти́ру** *to move the occupants of a communal flat into self-contained accommodation*.
рассе́лся *итп сов см* **рассе́сться**.
расселя́|ть (-ю) *несов от* **расселить**.
расс|ерди́ть(ся) (-ержу́(сь), -е́рдишь(ся)) *сов от* **серди́ть(ся)**.
расс|е́сться (-я́дусь, -я́дешься; *pt* -е́лся, -е́лась, -е́лось) *сов возв* (*по столам, в зале*) to take one's seat; (*разг: развалиться: на диване, в кресле*) to slump.
рассе́|чь (-еку́, -ечёшь *итп*, -еку́т; *pt* -ёк, -екла́, -екло́, *impf* **рассека́ть**) *сов перех* (*тушу, канат*) to cut in two; (*губу, лоб*) to cut; **рассека́ть** (~ *perf*) **во́лны** to cut through the water.
рассе́ян|ный (-, -на, -но) *прил* (*человек*) absent-minded; (*свет*) diffuse.

рассе́|ять (**-ю**; *impf* **рассе́ивать**) *сов перех* (*семена, людей*) to scatter; (*свет*) to diffuse; (*перен*: *сомнения, подозрения*) to dispel; (*горе, тоску*) to alleviate
▸ **рассе́яться** (*impf* **рассе́иваться**) *сов возв* (*люди, семена*) to be scattered; (*тучи, туман, дым*) to disperse; (*сомнения, печаль*) to be dispelled; (*развлечься*) to find a distraction.
расскажу́ *итп сов см* **рассказа́ть**.
расска́з (**-а**) *м* story; (*свидетеля*) account.
расск|аза́ть (**-ажу́, -а́жешь**; *impf* **расска́зывать**) *сов перех* to tell.
расска́зчик (**-а**) *м* storyteller; (*автор*) narrator.
расска́зчиц|а (**-ы**) *ж см* **расска́зчик**.
расска́зыва|ть (**-ю**) *несов от* **рассказа́ть**.
рассла́б|ить (**-лю, -ишь**; *impf* **расслабля́ть**) *сов перех* (*мышцы, ноги, руки*) to relax; (*ремень, галстук*) to loosen; (*подлеж*: *болезнь, работа*) to weaken
▸ **рассла́биться** (*impf* **расслабля́ться**) *сов возв* to relax.
рассла́блен|ный (**-, -на, -но**) *прил* relaxed.
рассла́блю(сь) *сов см* **рассла́бить(ся)**.
расслабля́|ть(ся) (**-ю(сь)**) *несов от* **рассла́бить(ся)**.
рассла́ива|ться (*3sg* **-ется**, *3pl* **-ются**) *несов от* **расслои́ться**.
рассле́довани|е (**-я**) *ср* investigation.
рассле́д|овать (**-ую**) *(не)сов перех* to investigate.
рассло|и́ться (*3sg* **-и́тся**, *3pl* **-я́тся**, *impf* **рассла́иваться**) *сов возв* (*горная порода, общество*) to stratify; (*пирог, фанера*) to split.
рассл́ыш|ать (**-у, -ишь**) *сов перех* to hear; **извини́те, я не ~ал** I'm sorry, I didn't catch what you said.
рассма́трива|ть (**-ю**) *несов от* **рассмотре́ть** ♦ *перех*: **~ что-н как** to regard sth as.
рассмеш|и́ть (**-у́, -и́шь**) *сов от* **смеши́ть**.
рассме|я́ться (**-ю́сь, -ёшься**) *сов возв* to start laughing.
рассмотре́ни|е (**-я**) *ср* examination.
рассм|отре́ть (**-отрю́, -о́тришь**; *impf* **рассма́тривать**) *сов перех* to examine; (*различить*: *в темноте, вдали*) to discern.
рассо|ва́ть (**-у́ю**; *impf* **рассо́вывать**) *сов перех* (*разг*): **~ что-н в** *+acc или* **по** *+dat* to stuff sth into.
рассо́л (**-а**; *part gen* **-у**) *м* brine.
рассо́льник (**-а**; *part gen* **-у**) *м soup made with meat and pickled cucumbers.*
рассос|а́ться (*3sg* **-ётся**, *3pl* **-у́тся**, *impf* **расса́сываться**) *сов возв* (*опухоль*) to go down; (*перен*: *очередь, пробка*) to ease off; (: *толпа*) to thin out.
расспра́шива|ть (**-ю**) *несов от* **расспроси́ть**.
расспро́с (**-а**) *м* (*действие*: *свидетелей*) questioning; (*обычно мн*: *вопросы*) question.
расспр|оси́ть (**-ошу́, -о́сишь**; *impf* **расспра́шивать**) *сов перех*: **~ (о** *+prp*) to question (about).
рассро́ч|ка (**-ки**; *gen pl* **-ек**) *ж* installment (*BRIT*), instalment (*US*); **в ~ку** (*купить, продать*) on hire purchase (*BRIT*), on the installment plan (*US*); **выпла́чивать (вы́платить** *perf*) **в ~ку** to pay in instal(l)ments.
расстава́ни|е (**-я**) *ср* parting.
расста|ва́ться (**-ю́сь, -ёшься**) *сов от* **расста́ться**.
расста́в|ить (**-лю, -ишь**; *impf* **расставля́ть**) *сов перех* (*книги, мебель итп*) to arrange; (*шахматы*) to set up *или* out; (*знаки препинания, ударения*) to add; (*ножки циркуля*) to open; (*пальцы*) to splay; (*разг*: *расширить*: *платье, воротник*) to let out; **расставля́ть (~** *perf*) **но́ги** to open one's legs.
расстано́в|ка (**-ки**; *gen pl* **-ок**) *ж* (*мебели, книг*) arrangement; **~ сил** distribution of power; **чита́ть** (*impf*)/**говори́ть** (*impf*) **с ~кой** to read/ speak slowly and clearly.
расста́|ться (**-нусь, -нешься**; *impf* **расстава́ться**) *сов возв*: **~ с** *+instr* to part with; (*с любимым делом*) to abandon; (*перен*: *с мечтой, с детством*) to say goodbye to.
расстегн|у́ть (**-у́, -ёшь**; *impf* **расстёгивать**) *сов перех* to undo
▸ **расстегну́ться** (*impf* **расстёгиваться**) *сов возв* (*человек*) to unbutton o.s.; (*рубашка, молния, пуговица*) to come undone.
расст|ели́ть (**-елю́, -е́лешь**; *impf* **расстила́ть**) *сов перех* to spread out.
расстила́|ться (*3sg* **-ется**, *3pl* **-ются**) *несов возв* (*равнина, степь*) to extend; (*туман*) to spread.
расстоя́ни|е (**-я**) *ср* distance; **держа́ть** (*impf*) **кого́-н на ~и** (*перен*) to keep sb at arm's length; **держа́ться** (*impf*) **на ~и** to keep one's distance.
расстра́ива|ть(ся) (**-ю(сь)**) *несов от* **расстро́ить(ся)**.
расстре́л (**-а**) *м*: **~** *+gen* shooting *или* firing at; (*казнь*) execution (*by firing squad*); **пригова́ривать (приговори́ть** *perf*) **кого́-н к ~у** to sentence sb to be shot.
расстреля́|ть (**-ю**; *impf* **расстре́ливать**) *сов перех* (*демонстрацию*) to open fire on; (*казнить*) to shoot; (*патроны, снаряды*) to use up.
расстро́ен|ный (**-, -а, -о**) *прил* (*здоровье, нервы*) weak; (*человек, вид*) upset; (*рояль, скрипка*) out of tune.
расстро́|ить (**-ю, -ишь**; *impf* **расстра́ивать**) *сов перех* (*планы, дела, свадьбу*) to disrupt; (*нервы*) to unsettle; (*человека, желудок*) to upset; (*здоровье*) to compromise; (*ряды противника*) to throw into confusion *или* disarray; (*муз*) to put out of tune
▸ **расстро́иться** (*impf* **расстра́иваться**) *сов возв* (*поездка, планы*) to fall through; (*дела, бизнес*) to fall apart; (*человек*) to get upset; (*колонна, ряды*) to fall into disarray; (*нервы*) to weaken; (*здоровье*) to become poorly; (*муз*) to go out of tune.
расстро́йств|о (**-а**) *ср* (*в делах, в хозяйстве*)

disorder; (*в рядах противника*) confusion, disarray; (*огорчение*) upset; (*речи, нервной системы*) dysfunction; ~ **желу́дка** stomach upset; **приходи́ть (прийти́** *perf*) **в** ~ (*дела, хозяйство*) to be thrown into confusion; (*человек*) to become upset.

расст|упи́ться (*3sg* **-у́пится**, *impf* **расступа́ться**) *сов возв* (*толпа*) to make way; (*перен*: *тайга, волны, земля*) to part.

расстык|ова́ться (**-у́юсь**; *impf* **расстыко́вываться**) *сов возв* (*КОСМОС*) to undock.

расстыко́в|ка (**-ки**) *ж* undocking.

расстыко́выва|ться (**-юсь**) *несов от* **расстыкова́ться**.

рассуди́тел|ьный (**-ен, -ьна, -ьно**) *прил* judicious.

расс|уди́ть (**-ужу́, -у́дишь**) *сов перех* (*спор*) to settle; (*людей*) to settle a dispute between ◆ *неперех*: **она́ ~уди́ла пра́вильно** she made the correct decision.

рассу́д|ок (**-ка**) *м* reason; **быть** (*impf*) **в своём ~ке** to be in possession of one's facilities.

рассужда́|ть (**-ю**) *несов неперех* to reason; ~ (*impf*) **о** +*prp* to debate.

рассужде́ни|е (**-я**) *ср* (*умозаключение*: *логическое итп*) judg(e)ment; (*обычно мн*: *о морали*) reasoning *ед*; **без ~й** without arguing.

рассужу́ *сов см* **рассуди́ть**.

рассчита́|ть (**-ю**; *impf* **рассчи́тывать**) *сов перех* (*стоимость, траекторию, политику*) to calculate; (*работника*) to lay off; **слова́рь рассчи́тан на студе́нтов** the dictionary is designed for students

▸ **рассчита́ться** (*impf* **рассчи́тываться**) *сов возв* (*уволиться*) to hand in one's notice; (*ВОЕН*: *в строю*) to call out one's number; **рассчи́тываться (~ся** *perf*) **(с** +*instr*) (*с продавцом, в гостинице*) to settle up (with); (*перен*: *с врагом итп*) to settle a score (with).

рассчи́тыва|ть (**-ю**) *несов от* **рассчита́ть** ◆ *неперех*: ~ **на** +*acc* (*надеяться*: *на удачу, на друга*) to count *или* rely on; ~ (*impf*) +*infin* to count on doing

▸ **рассчи́тываться** *несов от* **рассчита́ться**.

рассыла́|ть (**-ю**) *несов от* **разосла́ть**.

рассы́п|ать (**-лю, -лешь**; *impf* **рассыпа́ть**) *сов перех* to spill; (*распределить*): ~ **по** +*dat* to pour into

▸ **рассы́паться** (*impf* **рассыпа́ться**) *сов возв* (*сахар, песок, бусы*) to spill; (*стена, холм*) to crumble; (*волосы*) to fall loose; (*толпа, стая*) to scatter; **он ~ался в благода́рностях** he was effusive in his thanks.

рассыпно́й *прил* sold loose.

рассы́пчат|ый (**-, -а, -о**) *прил* (*каша, рис*) fluffy; (*печенье, пирог*) crumbly.

расся́дусь *итп сов см* **рассе́сться**.

раста́лкива|ть (**-ю**) *несов от* **растолка́ть**.

растамо́ж|ить (**-у, -ишь**) (*не*)*сов перех* to obtain customs clearance for.

раста́плива|ть (**-ю**) *несов от* **растопи́ть**.

раста́птыва|ть (**-ю**) *несов от* **растопта́ть**.

растаска́|ть (**-ю**; *impf* **раста́скивать**) *сов перех* (*разг*: *по комнатам*) to drag; (: *разворовать*) to filch.

раст|ащи́ть (**-ащу́, -а́щишь**) *сов* = **растаска́ть** ◆ *перех* (*разг*: *мальчишек*) to drag apart.

раста́|ять (**-ю**) *сов от* **та́ять**.

раство́р (**-а**) *м* (*ХИМ*) solution; (*циркуля*) span, spread; (*строительный*) mortar; **цеме́нтный** ~ cement.

раствори́м|ый (**-, -а, -о**) *прил* soluble; **раствори́мый ко́фе** instant coffee.

раствори́тел|ь (**-я**) *м* solvent.

раствор|и́ть (**-ю́, -и́шь**; *impf* **растворя́ть**) *сов перех* (*окно, дверь*) to open; (*порошок, сахар*) to dissolve

▸ **раствори́ться** (*impf* **растворя́ться**) *сов возв* (*см перех*) to open; to dissolve; (*перен*): ~ **в** +*prp* (*в темноте, в тумане*) to vanish into.

растека́|ться (*3sg* **-ется**, *3pl* **-ются**) *несов от* **растечься**.

растёкся *итп сов см* **расте́чься**.

растеку́тся *итп сов см* **расте́чься**.

расте́ни|е (**-я**) *ср* plant.

растениево́дств|о (**-а**) *ср* horticulture.

раст|ере́ть (**разотру́, разотрёшь**; *pt* **-ёр, -ёрла, -ёрло**, *impf* **растира́ть**) *сов перех* (*рану, тело*) to massage; **растира́ть (~** *perf*) **(в порошо́к)** to grind (into a powder); **растира́ть (~** *perf*) **кре́мом/ма́зью** to rub cream/ointment into; **растира́ть (~** *perf*) **но́гу** to get blisters

▸ **растере́ться** (*impf* **растира́ться**) *сов возв*: **~ся** (+*instr*) (*полотенцем, мочалкой*) to rub o.s. down (with).

растерза́|ть (**-ю**) *сов от* **терза́ть**.

расте́рянност|ь (**-и**) *ж* confusion; **она́ стоя́ла в ~и** she stood there looking confused.

расте́рян|ный (**-, -а, -о**) *прил* confused.

растеря́|ться (**-юсь**) *сов возв* (*человек*) to be confused; (*письма*) to go missing.

раст|е́чься (*3sg* **-ечётся**, *3pl* **-еку́тся**, *pt* **-ёкся, -екла́сь, -екло́сь**, *impf* **растека́ться**) *сов возв* (*ручьи, вода*) to spill; (*чернила, краска*) to run.

раст|и́ (**-у́, -ёшь**; *pt* **рос, росла́, росло́**, *perf* **вы́расти**) *несов неперех* to grow; (*проводить детство*) to grow up; **он вы́рос за грани́цей** he grew up abroad; ~ **(вы́расти** *perf*) **в чьих-н глаза́х** to grow in sb's estimation.

растира́|ть(ся) (**-ю(сь)**) *несов от* **растере́ть(ся)**.

расти́тельност|ь (**-и**) *ж собир* vegetation.

расти́тельн|ый *прил* (*БОТ*) plant *опред*; **расти́тельное ма́сло** vegetable oil; **расти́тельный мир** the plant kingdom;

растительный покров vegetation.
ра|сти́ть (-щу́, -сти́шь; *perf* **вы́растить)** *несов перех* (*детей*) to raise; (*цветы*) to grow; (*животных*) to rear; (*перен*: *кадры*) to nurture; (: *талант, дарование*) to cultivate.
растолка́|ть (-ю; *impf* **раста́лкивать)** *сов перех* (*толпу, людей*) to push away; (*разг*: *разбудить*) to shake.
растолк|ова́ть (-у́ю; *impf* **растолко́вывать)** *сов перех*: ~ **что-н (кому́-н)** to clarify sth (for sb).
растол|о́чь (-ку́, -чёшь *итп*, **-ку́т;** *pt* **-о́к, -кла́, -кло́)** *сов от* **толо́чь.**
растолсте́|ть (-ю) *сов неперех* to put on weight.
раст|опи́ть (-оплю́, -о́пишь; *impf* **раста́пливать)** *сов перех* (*печку*) to light; (*воск, жир, лёд*) to melt
▸ **растопи́ться** *сов от* **топи́ться.**
раст|опта́ть (-опчу́, -о́пчешь; *impf* **раста́птывать)** *сов перех* (*также перен*) to trample on.
растопы́р|ить (-ю, -ишь; *impf* **растопы́ривать)** *сов перех* to spread.
расто́рг|нуть (-ну, -нешь; *pt* **-, -ла, -ло,** *impf* **расторга́ть)** *сов перех* to annul.
растормош|и́ть (-у́, -и́шь) *сов перех* (*разг*) to shake.
расторо́п|ный (-ен, -на, -но) *прил* quick, efficient.
расточи́тел|ьный (-ен, -ьна, -ьно) *прил* extravagant.
расточи́тельств|о (-а) *ср* extravagance.
растр|ави́ть (-авлю́, -а́вишь; *impf* **растравля́ть)** *сов перех* (*перен*): ~ **кому́-н ду́шу** to torment sb.
растранжи́р|ить (-ю, -ишь) *сов от* **транжи́рить.**
растра́т|а (-ы) *ж* (*времени, сил, денег*) waste; (*хищение*) embezzlement; (*растраченная сумма*) loss.
растра́|тить (-чу, -тишь; *impf* **растра́чивать)** *сов перех* to waste; (*расхитить*) to embezzle.
растрево́ж|ить (-у, -ишь) *сов перех* to alarm; ~ (*perf*) **кому́-н ду́шу** to stir sb's emotions
▸ **растрево́житься** *сов возв* to become alarmed.
растрёпан|ный (-, -на, -но) *прил* (*вид, внешность*) bedraggled; (*волосы*) tousled; (*тетрадь, книга*) tatty; **быть** (*impf*) **в ~ных чу́вствах** (*разг*) to be all confused.
растр|епа́ть (-еплю́, -е́плешь) *сов перех* (*волосы*) to mess up; (*тетрадь, книгу*) to tatter; (*разг*: *разболтать*) to blab
▸ **растрепа́ться** *сов возв* (*разг*: *волосы*) to get messed up; (: *тетрадь, книга*) to become tattered.
растро́ган|ный (-, -на, -но) *прил* (*человек*) moved, touched; (*голос*) full of emotion.
растро́га|ть (-ю) *сов перех*: ~ **кого́-н (+***instr***)** (*письмом, вниманием*) to touch *или* move sb (by)
▸ **растро́гаться** *сов возв* to be touched *или* moved; **~ся** (*perf*) **до слёз** to be moved to tears.
раструб|и́ть (-лю́, -и́шь) *сов от* **труби́ть.**
растя́гива|ть(ся) (-ю(сь)) *несов от* **растяну́ть(ся).**
растяже́ни|е (-я) *ср* (*МЕД*) strain.
растяжи́м|ый (-, -а, -о) *прил*: **~ое поня́тие** a loose concept.
растя́нут|ый (-, -а, -о) *прил* lengthy.
раст|яну́ть (-яну́, -я́нешь; *impf* **растя́гивать)** *сов перех* to stretch; (*скатерть*) to spread out; (*связки, сухожилие*) to strain; (*ногу, руку*) to sprain; (*доклад, рассказ*) to drag out; (*удовольствие*) to prolong; (*средства*) to stretch out
▸ **растяну́ться** (*impf* **растя́гиваться)** *сов возв* to stretch; (*человек, обоз*) to stretch out; (*связки, сухожилие*) to be strained; (*собрание, работа*) to drag on.
растя́п|а (-ы) *м/ж* (*разг*) bungler.
расфас|ова́ть (-у́ю) *сов от* **фасова́ть.**
расформир|ова́ть (-у́ю; *impf* **расформиро́вывать)** *сов перех* to disband.
расха́жива|ть (-ю) *несов неперех* to saunter.
расхв|али́ть (-алю́, -а́лишь; *impf* **расхва́ливать)** *сов перех* to enthuse about.
расхвата́|ть (-ю; *impf* **расхва́тывать)** *сов перех* (*разг*) to snatch up.
расхити́тел|ь (-я) *м* embezzler.
расхи́|тить (-щу, -тишь; *impf* **расхища́ть)** *сов перех* to embezzle.
расхище́ни|е (-я) *ср* embezzlement.
расхля́бан|ный (-, -на, -но) *прил* (*жест, движение*) irreverent; (*человек, поведение*) lax.
расхо́д (-а) *м* (*энергии, воды*) consumption; (*обычно мн*: *затраты*) expense; (: *КОММ*: *в бухгалтерской книге*) expenditure; **~ы произво́дства** production costs; **вводи́ть (ввести́** *perf*) **кого́-н в ~** to leave sb out of pocket.
расх|оди́ться (-ожу́сь, -о́дишься) *несов от* **разойти́сь.**
расхо́дный *прил*: ~ **о́рдер** (*КОММ*) expenses form.
расхо́д|овать (-ую; *perf* **израсхо́довать)** *несов перех* (*деньги*) to spend; (*материалы, энергию*) to expend; (*потреблять*: *бензин*) to consume.
расхожде́ни|е (-я) *ср* (*между словом и делом*) discrepancy; (*во взглядах*) divergence.
расхо́ж|ий (-ая, -ее, -ие) *прил* (*мнение*) widely accepted.
расхожу́сь *несов см* **расходи́ться.**
расхоте́ть (*как* **хоте́ть;** *см* **Table 16)** *сов неперех*: ~ **+***infin* (*спать, гулять итп*) to no longer want to do; **я расхоте́л есть** I don't feel hungry any more
▸ **расхоте́ться** *сов безл*: **(мне) расхоте́лось спать** I don't feel sleepy any more.
расхох|ота́ться (-очу́сь, -о́чешься) *сов возв* to burst out laughing.

расхочу́(сь) *итп сов см* **расхоте́ть(ся).**
расцара́па|ть (-ю) *сов перех* to scratch.
расцв|ести́ (-ету́, -етёшь; *pt* -ёл, -ела́, -ело́, *impf* **расцвета́ть**) *сов неперех* (*также перен*) to blossom; (*от радости*) to light up.
расцве́т (-а) *м* (*перен: науки, таланта*) blossoming; **он в ~е сил** he is in the prime of life.
расцвета́|ть (-ю) *несов от* **расцвести́.**
расцве́т|ка (-ки; *gen pl* -ок) *ж* colour (*BRIT*) *или* color (*US*) scheme.
расцвету́ *итп сов см* **расцвести́.**
расцел|ова́ть (-у́ю) *сов перех* to kiss
▸ **расцелова́ться** *сов возв* to kiss each other.
расце́нива|ться (*3sg* -ется, *3pl* -ются) *несов возв*: **~ как** to be regarded as.
расц|ени́ть (-еню́, -е́нишь; *impf* **расце́нивать**) *сов перех* to judge; **расце́нивать** (~ *perf*) **что-н как** to regard sth as.
расце́н|ка (-ки; *gen pl* -ок) *ж* (*оплата работы*) rate; (*цена*) tariff.
расц|епи́ть (-еплю́, -е́пишь; *impf* **расцепля́ть**) *сов перех* (*состав*) to uncouple; (*дерущихся, пальцы*) to pull apart.
расч|ерти́ть (-ерчу́, -е́ртишь; *impf* **расче́рчивать**) *сов перех* to rule, line.
расч|еса́ть (-ешу́, -е́шешь; *impf* **расчёсывать**) *сов перех* (*волосы, гриву*) to comb; (*шерсть, лён*) to card; (*руку, царапину*) to scratch; **расчёсывать** (~ *perf*) **кого́-н** to comb sb's hair.
расчё́с|ка (-ки; *gen pl* -ок) *ж* comb.
расчёсыва|ть (-ю) *несов от* **расчеса́ть.**
расчёт (-а) *м* (*налога, стоимости итп*) calculation; (*оплата*) payment; (*предложение*) calculation; (*выгода*) advantage; (*бережливость*) economy; (*увольнение*) dismissal; (*ВОЕН, МОР*) crew; **из ~а** *+gen* on the basis of; **из ~а 5 проце́нтов годовы́х** at 5 percent per annum; **он ведёт дела́ с ~ом** he runs his business economically; **де́йствовать** (*impf*) **по ~у** to act in a calculated way; **исходи́ть** (*impf*) **из ~а, что ...** to act on the assumption that ...; **брать (взять** *perf*) *или* **принима́ть (приня́ть** *perf*) **что-н в ~** to take sth into account; **по мои́м ~ам мы зако́нчим к ве́черу** by my reckoning we will finish by evening; **я с Ва́ми в ~е** we are all even; **брать (взять** *perf*) **~** to hand in one's notice.
расчётлив|ый (-, -а, -о) *прил* (*экономный*) thrifty; (*руководитель, игрок*) calculating; (*движения*) deliberate.
расчётн|ый *прил* (*ТЕХ: скорость итп*) estimated; **расчётный день** payday; **расчётный счёт** debit account.
расчешу́ *итп сов см* **расчеса́ть.**
расчи́|стить (-щу, -стишь; *impf* **расчища́ть**) *сов перех* to clear
▸ **расчи́ститься** (*impf* **расчища́ться**) *сов возв* to clear.
расчлен|и́ть (-ю́, -и́шь) *сов от* **расчленя́ть, члени́ть.**
расчленя́|ть (-ю) *несов от* **расчлени́ть.**
расчу́вств|оваться (-уюсь) *сов возв* (*разг*) to be overcome with emotion.
расшата́|ть (-ю; *impf* **расша́тывать**) *сов перех* (*стол, стул*) to make wobbly; (*здоровье*) to damage; **он ~л себе́ не́рвы** he's become a nervous wreck
▸ **расшата́ться** (*impf* **расша́тываться**) *сов возв* (*забор, столб*) to become wobbly; (*перен: нервы*) to give out; (*здоровье*) to be damaged.
расшвыря́|ть (-ю) *сов перех* (*разг*) to hurl around; (*: перен: деньги*) to fritter away.
расшевел|и́ть (-ю́, -и́шь) *сов перех* (*разг*): **~ кого́-н** to give sb a shake; (*перен: слушателей*) to liven sb up
▸ **расшевели́ться** *сов возв* to stir; (*перен: начальство, игроки*) to get moving.
расшиб|и́ть (-у́, -ёшь; *impf* **расшиба́ть**) *сов перех* (*разг*) to smash
▸ **расшиби́ться** (*impf* **расшиба́ться**) *сов возв* (*о дверь, при падении*) to hurt o.s.; (*разг: для друга, для семьи*) to put o.s. out.
расшива́|ть (-ю) *несов от* **расши́ть.**
расшире́ни|е (-я) *ср* widening; (*связей, производства*) expansion; (*знаний*) broadening.
расши́рен|ный (-, -на, -но) *прил* (*проход*) widened; (*комитет, заседание*) expanded; (*зрачки, сосуды*) dilated.
расши́р|ить (-ю, -ишь; *impf* **расширя́ть**) *сов перех* to widen; (*производство*) to expand; **расширя́ть** (~ *perf*) **кругозо́р** to broaden one's horizons
▸ **расши́риться** (*impf* **расширя́ться**) *сов возв* to widen; (*завод, контакты, знания*) to expand; (*зрачки*) to dilate.
расши́тый *прил* embroidered.
ра|сши́ть (-зошью́, -зошьёшь; *impf* **расшива́ть**) *сов перех* (*вышить*) to embroider.
расшифр|ова́ть (-у́ю; *impf* **расшифро́вывать**) *сов перех* (*текст, шифровку*) to decode, decipher; (*перен: тайну, смысл слов*) to decipher.
расшнур|ова́ть (-у́ю; *impf* **расшнуро́вывать**) *сов перех* to unlace.
расшум|е́ться (-лю́сь, -и́шься) *сов возв* (*разг*) to make a racket; (*: начать спорить*) to kick up a fuss.
расще́др|иться (-юсь, -ишься; *impf* **расще́дриваться**) *сов возв* (*разг*) to become generous.
расще́лин|а (-ы) *ж* (*скалы, горы*) crevice; (*в дереве, в камне*) cleft.
расщеп|и́ть (-лю́, -и́шь; *impf* **расщепля́ть**) *сов перех* (*также ФИЗ*) to split; (*ХИМ*) to decompose
▸ **расщепи́ться** (*impf* **расщепля́ться**) *сов возв*

to splinter; (*физ*) to split; (*хим*) to decompose.
расщеплéни|е (-я) *ср* splintering; (*физ*) fission; (*хим*) decomposition.
расщеплю́(сь) *сов см* **расщепи́ть(ся)**.
расщепля́|ть(ся) (-ю) *несов от* **расщепи́ть(ся)**.
ратификáци|я (-и) *ж* ratification.
ратифици́р|овать (-ую) *(не)сов перех* to ratify.
рáунд (-а) *м* (*спорт*) round; (*полит*): ~ **переговóров** round of talks.
рáфик (-а) *м* (*разг*) minibus.
рафинáд (-а) *м* sugar cubes *мн*.
рафини́рованный *прил* refined.
рахи́т (-а) *м* (*мед*) rickets.
рациóн (-а) *м* ration.
рационáлен *прил см* **рационáльный**.
рационализáтор (-а) *м* innovator.
рационализáци|я (-и) *ж* rationalization.
рационализи́р|овать (-ую) *(не)сов перех* to rationalize.
рационали́ст (-а) *м* rationalist.
рационáл|ьный (-ен, -ьна, -ьно) *прил* (*поступок*) rational; (*использование ресурсов, организация*) effective; **~ьное питáние** well-balanced diet.
рáци|я (-и) *ж* walkie-talkie.
рацпредложéни|е (-я) *ср сокр* (= *рационализáторское предложéние*) innovation proposal.
рачи́тел|ьный (-ен, -ьна, -ьно) *прил* thrifty.
рвану́ть (-у, -ёшь) *сов перех* to pull at; (*разг*) to explode ◆ *неперех* (*разг: лошадь, бегун*) to shoot off; ~ *(perf)* **когó-н за пиджáк/зá руку** to tug at sb's jacket/arm; ~ *(perf)* **пéсню** (*разг*) to break into song
▸ **рвану́ться** *сов возв* to tear off.
рвáный *прил* torn; (*ботинки*) ripped; (*рана*) lacerated.
рв|ать (-у, -ёшь; *perf* **порвáть** *или* **разорвáть**) *несов перех* (*письмо, одежду, книгу*) to tear, rip; (*перен: отношения, дружбу*) to break off; (*perf* **вы́рвать**; *предмет из рук*) to snatch; (*no perf*; *подлеж: ветер: одежды, занавес*) to tear at; (*perf* **сорвáть**; *цветы, траву*) to pick; (*ветки*) to break off ◆ (*perf* **вы́рвать**) *безл*: **егó** *итп* **~áло всю ночь** he was vomiting *или* being sick all night; ~ **(разорвáть** *perf*) **когó-н/что-н на чáсти** to tear sb/sth to bits; **меня́ ~ут на чáсти** (*перен*) I'm in demand from all sides; ~ **(порвáть** *perf*) **с прóшлым** to break with the past; ~ **(вы́рвать** *perf*) **комý-н зуб** (*разг*) to pull sb's tooth out; ~ *(impf)* **и метáть** *(impf)* (*разг*) to rant and rave
▸ **рвáться** (*perf* **порвáться** *или* **разорвáться**) *несов возв* (*бумага, одежда*) to tear, rip; (*обувь*) to rip; (*перен: отношения, связи*) to be severed; (*perf* **разорвáться**; *снаряд*) to explode; **~áться** *(impf)* **к приключéниям/влáсти** to be hungry for adventure/power; **~áться** *(impf)* **в дрáку** to be spoiling for a fight; **у меня́ сéрдце** *или* **душá ~ётся на чáсти** my heart is being torn in two.
рвач (-á) *м* (*разг: пренебр*) taker.
рвéни|е (-я) *ср* (*в учёбе, в работе*) enthusiasm; (*патриотический, религиозный*) zeal; ~ *+infin* desire to do.
рвóт|а (-ы) *ж* vomiting.
рвóтн|ый *прил*: **~ое (срéдство)** emetic.
ре *ср нескл* (*муз*) re.
реабилитáци|я (-и) *ж* rehabilitation.
реабилити́р|овать (-ую) *(не)сов перех* to rehabilitate.
реаги́р|овать (-ую) *несов неперех*: ~ **(на** *+acc*) (*на свет, на раздражение*) to react (to); (*perf* **отреаги́ровать** *или* **прореаги́ровать**; *на критику, на слова*) to react *или* respond (to).
реакти́в (-а) *м* (*хим*) reagent.
реакти́вный *прил* (*хим*) reactive; (*тех*) jet-propelled; **реакти́вный дви́гатель** jet engine; **реакти́вный самолёт** jet (plane).
реáктор (-а) *м* reactor.
реакционéр (-а) *м* reactionary.
реакциóнный *прил* reactionary.
реáкци|я (-и) *ж* reaction.
реáлен *прил см* **реáльный**.
реализáци|я (-и) *ж* (*см глаг*) implementation; realization.
реали́зм (-а) *м* realism.
реализ|овáть (-ýю) *(не)сов перех* (*реформы, проект, предложение*) to implement; (*товар, ценные бумаги*) to realize.
реали́ст (-а) *м* realist.
реалисти́чен *прил см* **реалисти́чный**.
реалисти́ческ|ий (-ая, -ое, -ие) *прил* realistic; (*искусство*) realist *опред*.
реалисти́ч|ный (-ен, -на, -но) *прил* realistic.
реáльност|ь (-и) *ж* reality; (*политики, плана, задачи*) practicability, feasibility; **~и нáшего врéмени** modern-day realities.
реáл|ьный (-ен, -ьна, -ьно) *прил* (*не воображаемый*) real; (*осуществимый, практический*) realistic; **в ~ьном врéмени** (*комп*) real-time; **реáльная зáработная плáта** (*экон*) real wage.
реанимáци|я (-и) *ж* resuscitation; **отделéние ~и** intensive care unit.
ребён|ок (-ка; *nom pl* **дéти** *или* **ребя́та**) *м* child (*мн* children); (*грудной*) baby; **дом ~ка** children's home.
ребр|ó (-á; *nom pl* **рёбра**, *gen pl* **рёбер**) *ср* (*анат*) rib; (*монеты, стола, кубика итп*) edge; **стáвить (постáвить** *perf*) **вопрóс ~м** to put a question bluntly.
рéбус (-а) *м* rebus; (*перен*) riddle.
ребя́т|а (-) *мн от* **ребёнок**; (*разг: парни*) guys *мн*.
ребя́ческ|ий (-ая, -ое, -ие) *прил* (*душа, сознание*) child's *опред*; (*перен: поведение, суждение*) childish.
рёв (-а) *м* roar; (*разг: громкий плач*) howling.
ревальвáци|я (-и) *ж* (*экон*) revaluation.
ревáнш (-а) *м* revenge; (*игра*) revenge match; **взять** *(perf)* ~ to take revenge.

реваншизм (-а) *м* revanchism.
ревень (-я) *м* rhubarb.
ревјеть (-у, -ёшь) *несов неперех* to roar; (*разг: плакать*) to howl.
ревизионнјый *прил*: **~ая комиссия** audit commission.
ревизија (-и) *ж* (*комм*) audit; (*взглядов, учения*) revision.
ревизјовать (-ую) *(не)сов перех* (*предприятие*) to inspect; (*бухгалтерские книги*) to audit.
ревизор (-а) *м* (*комм*) auditor.
ревматизм (-а) *м* rheumatism.
ревматическјий (-ая, -ое, -ие) *прил* rheumatoid.
ревматолог (-а) *м* rheumatologist.
ревнивјый (-, -а, -о) *прил* jealous.
ревнјовать (-ую) *несов неперех*: **~ (кого-н)** to be jealous (of sb); **он ~ует меня к своему брату** he is jealous of my relationship with his brother.
ревностнјый (-ен, -на, -но) *прил* ardent, zealous.
ревностјь (-и) *ж* jealousy.
револьвер (-а) *м* revolver.
революционер (-а) *м* revolutionary.
революционерјка (-ки; *gen pl* -ок) *ж см* **революционер**.
революционный *прил* revolutionary.
революцијя (-и) *ж* revolution.
ревю *ср нескл* revue.
регалија (-и) *ж* (*обычно мн*) regalia *ед*.
регатја (-ы) *ж* regatta.
регби *ср нескл* rugby.
регбист (-а) *м* rugby player.
регион (-а) *м* region.
региональный *прил* regional.
регистр (-а) *м* (*муз, комп, мор*) register; (*на пишущей машинке*): **верхний/нижний ~** upper/lower case.
регистратор (-а) *м* (*в поликлинике*) receptionist; (*в загсе*) registrar.
регистратурја (-ы) *ж* (*в поликлинике*) reception; (*на предприятии*) records department.
регистрацијя (-и) *ж* registration.
регистрирјовать (-ую; *perf* **регистрировать** *или* **зарегистрировать**) *несов перех* to register
▸ **регистрироваться** *(не)сов возв* to register; (*оформлять брак*) to get married (*at a registry office*).
регламент (-а) *м* (*порядок заседаний*) order of business; (*время для выступления*) speaking time.
реглан *прил неизм* raglan ◆ (-а) *м*: **(пальто-)/(платье-)~** raglan coat/dress.
регулирјовать (-ую) *несов перех* to regulate; (*perf* **урегулировать**; *отношения*) to normalize; (*perf* **отрегулировать**; *мотор, громкость*) to adjust.
регулировщик (-а) *м* traffic policeman (*мн* policemen).
регулярен *прил см* **регулярный**.
регулярно *нареч* regularly.
регулярностјь (-и) *ж* regularity.
регулярнјый (-ен, -на, -но) *прил* regular; **регулярные войска** regular army *ед*.
редактирјовать (-ую; *perf* **отредактировать**) *несов перех* to edit.
редактор (-а) *м* (*также комп*) editor.
редакционнјый *прил* (*поправки*): **~ая коллегия** editorial board; **редакционная статья** editorial.
редакцијя (-и) *ж* (*действие: текста, статьи*) editing; (*вариант произведения*) edition; (*формулировка: статьи закона*) wording; (*учреждение*) editorial offices *мн*; (*на радио*) desk; (*на телевидении*) division; **под ~ей** *+gen* edited by.
редејть (*3sg* **-ет**, *3pl* **-ют**, *perf* **поредеть**) *несов неперех* to thin out.
редис (-а) *м* radish.
редискја (-и) *ж* (*разг*) (red) radish ◆ *собир* radishes *мн*.
редкий (-кая, -кое, -кие; -ок, -ка, -ко) *прил* rare; (*выстрелы, письма, гость*) occasional; (*волосы*) thin; (*зубы*) gappy; (*лес*) sparse; (*ткань, материал*) loose-weave.
редко *нареч* rarely, seldom; (*расти*) sparsely.
редколлегија (-и) *ж сокр* = **редакционная коллегия**.
редкостјь (-и) *ж* rarity; **на ~** unusually; **он на ~ добрый человек** he is a person of uncommon kindness; **такие примеры не ~** such examples are not uncommon.
редок *прил см* **редкий**.
редькја (-и) *ж* (white) radish ◆ *собир* radishes *мн*.
режим (-а) *ж* (*питания, также полит*) regime; (*больничный, тюремный итп*) routine; (*условия работы*) conditions *мн*; (*комп*) mode; **~ безопасности** security system; **рабочий ~ двигателя** the operating conditions of the engine.
режиссёр (-а) *м* director (*of film, play etc*); **режиссёр-постановщик** (stage) director.
режиссурја (-ы) *ж* (*профессия*) directing; (*фильма, спектакля*) direction.
резјать (-жу, -жешь; *perf* **разрезать**) *несов перех* (*хлеб*) to slice, cut up; (*металл, кожу*) to cut; (*разг: нарыв, живот*) to cut open; (*perf* **зарезать**; *разг: гуся, свинью*) to slaughter; (*перен: разг: диссертацию*) to flunk; (*perf* **срезать**; *студента*) to fail; (*no perf*; *ложки, фигурки итп*) to carve; (*причинять боль: подлеж: воротник*) to dig into; (*: дым, ветер*)

to sting; (*наносить изображения*): **~ по** *+dat* (*по дереву, по камню*) to carve; (*по стеклу*) to cut; (*по металлу*) to engrave; **реза́ть** *(impf)* **слух** *или* **у́хо** to grate

▸ **ре́заться** (*perf* **проре́заться**) *несов возв* (*зубы, рога*) to come through; (*no perf; разг*): **~ся в** *+acc* (*в карты итп*) to play.

резв|и́ться (**-лю́сь, -и́шься**) *несов возв* to frolic, frisk about.

ре́зво *нареч* (*бежать*) energetically.

ре́зв|ый (**-, -а́, -о**) *прил* (*ребёнок*) playful; (*быстрый в беге: конь, заяц*) frisky.

резе́рв (**-а**) *м* (*СПОРТ*) reserve team; (*обычно мн: материальные итп*) reserve; **ка́ссовый ~** (*КОММ*) cash reserves.

резе́рвн|ый *прил* reserve *опред*; (*КОМП*) backup *опред*; **~ые войска́** (army) reserves; **резе́рвная валю́та** reserve currency; **резе́рвный капита́л** capital reserve; **резе́рвный фонд** reserve fund.

резервуа́р (**-а**) *м* reservoir (*tank*).

рез|е́ц (**-ца́**) *м* (*инструмент*) cutting tool; (*АНАТ*) incisor.

резиде́нт (**-а**) *м* spy.

резиде́нци|я (**-и**) *ж* residence.

рези́н|а (**-ы**) *ж* rubber; **тяну́ть** *(impf)* **~у** (*разг*) to drag things out.

рези́н|ка (**-ки**; *gen pl* **-ок**) *ж* (*ластик*) rubber (*BRIT*), eraser (*esp US*); (*тесёмка*) elastic; (*жвачка*) chewing gum.

рези́новый *прил* rubber *опред*.

рези́нок *сущ см* **рези́нка**.

ре́з|кий (**-кая, -кое, -кие; -ок, -ка́, -ко**) *прил* sharp; (*свет, звук, голос*) harsh; (*запах*) pungent; (*стиль, манера*) abrupt.

ре́зко *нареч* sharply; (*встать, высказать*) abruptly.

ре́зкост|ь (**-и**) *ж* (*поведения, манеры*) abruptness; (*ФОТО*) focus; **говори́ть (сказа́ть** *perf*) **кому́-н ~и** to be rude to sb.

резно́й *прил* carved.

резн|я́ (**-и́**) *ж* slaughter.

ре́зок *прил см* **ре́зкий**.

резолю́ци|я (**-и**) *ж* (*съезда, заседания*) resolution; (*распоряжение*) directive.

резона́нс (**-а**) *м* (*ФИЗ*) resonance; (*перен*) response.

резо́н|ный (**-ен, -на, -но**) *прил* reasonable.

результа́т (**-а**) *м* result; **в ~е** as a result; (*в итоге*) in the end.

результати́в|ный (**-ен, -на, -но**) *прил* (*дело, встреча*) productive; (*спортсмен*) successful.

ре́зче *сравн прил от* **ре́зкий** ◆ *сравн нареч от* **ре́зко**.

ре́зус (**-а**) *м* (*также:* **~-фа́ктор**) rhesus factor.

резца́ *итп сущ см* **резе́ц**.

рез|ь (**-и**) *ж* sharp pain.

резьб|а́ (**-ы́**) *ж* carving; (*винта, шурупа*) thread; **~ по де́реву/ка́мню** carving in wood/stone.

резюме́ *ср нескл* resumé, summary.

резюми́р|овать (**-ую**) *(не)сов перех* to summarize.

рейд (**-а**) *м* raid; (*МОР*) anchorage.

ре́й|ка (**-йки**; *gen pl* **ек**) *ж* batten; (*измерительная*) measuring rod.

Ре́йкьявик (**-а**) *м* Reykjavik.

Рейн (**-а**) *м* (the) Rhine.

рейнве́йн (**-а**) *м* hock (*wine*).

рейс (**-а**) *м* (*самолёта*) flight; (*автобуса*) run; (*парахода*) sailing.

ре́йсовый *прил* regular.

ре́йтинг (**-а**) *м* popularity rating.

рейту́з|ы (**-**) *мн* thermal pants.

рек|а́ (**-и́**; *acc sg* **-у**, *dat sg* **-е́**, *nom pl* **-и**) *ж* (*также перен*) river.

ре́квием (**-а**) *м* requiem.

реквизи́р|овать (**-ую**) *(не)сов перех* to requisition.

реквизи́т (**-а**) *м* (*ТЕАТР, КИНО*) props *мн*; (*обычно мн: в документе*) stipulation.

рекла́м|а (**-ы**) *ж* (*действие: торговая*) advertising; (*средство*) advert (*BRIT*), advertisement; (*театральная*) publicity; **де́лать (сде́лать** *perf*) **себе́ ~у** to draw attention to o.s.

реклами́р|овать (**-ую**) *(не)сов перех* to advertise.

рекла́мный *прил* (*отдел, колонка*) advertising *опред*; (*статья, фильм, справочник*) publicity *опред*; **рекла́мный ро́лик** advertisement; (*фильма*) trailer.

рекоменда́тельн|ый *прил*: **~ое письмо́** letter of recommendation.

рекоменда́ци|я (**-и**) *ж* recommendation.

рекоменд|ова́ть (**-у́ю**; *perf* **рекомендова́ть** *или* **порекомендова́ть**) *несов перех* to recommend; **~ (порекомендова́ть** *perf*) **кого́-н кому́-н/на рабо́ту** to recommend sb to sb/for a job; **~ (порекомендова́ть** *perf*) **кому́-н** *+infin* to recommend sb to do.

реконструи́р|овать (**-ую**) *(не)сов перех* (*промышленность*) to rebuild; (*памятник, здание*) to reconstruct.

реконстру́кци|я (**-и**) *ж* reconstruction.

реко́рд (**-а**) *м* record; **устана́вливать (установи́ть** *perf*)/**поби́ть** *(perf)* **~** to set/break a record.

реко́рдный *прил* record(-breaking) *опред*.

рекордсме́н (**-а**) *м* recordholder.

рекордсме́н|ка (**-ки**; *gen pl* **-ок**) *ж см* **рекордсме́н**.

ре́ктор (**-а**) *м* ≈ principal.

ректора́т (**-а**) *м* principal's office.

религио́з|ный (**-ен, -на, -но**) *прил* religious.

рели́ги|я (**-и**) *ж* religion.

рели́кви|я (**-и**) *ж* relic; (*семейная*) heirloom.

релье́ф (**-а**) *м* (*ГЕО, ИСКУССТВО*) relief.

рельс (**-а**) *м* (*обычно мн*) rail; **на ре́льсы** *+gen* (*перен*) towards.

ре́льсовый *прил*: **~ путь** railway (*BRIT*) *или* railroad (*US*) track.

рема́рк|а (**-и**) *ж* (*ТЕАТР*) stage directions *мн*;

(*замечание*) remark.
рем|éнь (**-ня́**) *м* (*брюк, платья, также ТЕХ*) belt; (*сумки*) strap; **привязны́е ~ни́** seat belt; **приводно́й ~** drive-belt.
ремёсел *сущ см* **ремесло́**.
ремéсленник (**-а**) *м* artisan, craftsman (*мн* craftsmen).
ремéсленный *прил* (*труд, мастерская*) artisan's, craftsman's; (*изделие*) handcrafted; (*перен*: *не творческий*) mechanical.
ремесл|о́ (**-á**; *nom pl* **ремёсла**, *gen pl* **ремёсел**) *ср* trade; (*перен*: *нетворческая работа*) hack work.
ремеш|óк (**-кá**) *м* strap.
ремня́ *итп сущ см* **ремéнь**.
ремóнт (**-а**) *м* repair; (*здания*) refurbishment; (: *мелкий*) redecoration; **на ~е** under repair; **теку́щий ~** maintenance; **сдавáть (сдать** *perf***) что-н в ~** to put sth in for repair; **у нас дóма сейчáс идёт ~** our house is being redecorated.
ремонти́р|овать (**-ую**; *perf* **ремонти́ровать** *или* **отремонти́ровать**) *несов перех* to repair; (*квартиру, здание*) to do up.
ремóнтн|ый *прил*: **~ые рабóты** repairs *мн*; **~ая мастерскáя** repair workshop.
рéнт|а (**-ы**) *ж* rent; **земéльная ~** ground rent.
рентáбел|ьный (**-ен, -ьна, -ьно**) *прил* profitable.
рентгéн (**-а**) *м* (*МЕД*) X-ray; (*ФИЗ*) roentgen; **дéлать (сдéлать** *perf***) кому́-н ~** to X-ray sb.
рентгéновск|ий (**-ая, -ое, -ие**) *прил*: **~ кабинéт/аппарáт** X-ray room/machine; **~ сни́мок** X-ray; **~ие лучи́** X-rays.
рентгенóлог (**-а**) *м* radiologist.
реорганизáци|я (**-и**) *ж* reorganization.
реорганиз|овáть (**-у́ю**) (*не*)*сов перех* to reorganize.
рéп|а (**-ы**) *ж* (*no pl*) swede (*BRIT*), rutabaga (*US*).
репатриáнт (**-а**) *м* repatriate.
репатриáци|я (**-и**) *ж* repatriation.
репатрии́р|овать (**-ую**) (*не*)*сов перех* to repatriate.
реп|éй (**-ья́**) *м* (*разг*) = **репéйник**.
репéйник (**-а**) *м* (*БОТ*) burdock.
репертуáр (**-а**) *м* repertoire.
репети́р|овать (**-ую**; *perf* **отрепети́ровать** *или* **прорепети́ровать**) *несов* (*не*)*перех* (*диалог, спектакль*) to rehearse.
репети́тор (**-а**) *м* (*преподаватель*) coach, private tutor.
репети́ци|я (**-и**) *ж* rehearsal.
рéплик|а (**-и**) *ж* (*слушателей*) remark; (*ТЕАТР*) line; (*ЮР*) objection.
репортáж (**-а**) *м* (*статья, передача*) report.
репортёр (**-а**) *м* reporter.
репрéсси|я (**-и**) *ж* (*обычно мн*) repression.
репроду́ктор (**-а**) *м* loudspeaker.
репроду́кци|я (**-и**) *ж* reproduction (*of painting etc*).
репти́ли|я (**-и**) *ж* reptile.
репутáци|я (**-и**) *ж* reputation.
рéпчатый *прил*: **~ лук** onions *мн*.
репья́ *итп сущ см* **репéй**.
ресни́ц|а (**-ы**) *ж* (*обычно мн*) eyelash.
респектáбел|ьный (**-ен, ьна, ьно**) *прил* respectable.
респондéнт (**-а**) *м* respondent.
респу́блик|а (**-и**) *ж* republic.
республикáнск|ий (**-ая, -ое, -ие**) *прил* republican.
рессóр|а (**-ы**) *ж* spring.
реставрáтор (**-а**) *м* restorer.
реставрáци|я (**-и**) *ж* restoration.
реставри́р|овать (**-ую**; *perf* **реставри́ровать** *или* **отреставри́ровать**) *несов перех* to restore.
ресторáн (**-а**) *м* restaurant.
ресу́рс (**-а**) *м* (*обычно мн*) resource; **прирóдные ~ы** natural resources.
рéтро *прил неизм* (*мода, мебель*) retro.
ретрогрáд (**-а**) *м* reactionary.
ретроспекти́в|а (**-ы**) *ж* retrospective.
реферáт (**-а**) *м* synopsis (*мн* synopses).
рефере́ндум (**-а**) *м* referendum (*мн* referenda).
референт (**-а**) *м* (*директора, министра*) aide.
рефери́ *м нескл* referee.
рефери́р|овать (**-ую**; *perf* **рефери́ровать** *или* **прорефери́ровать**) (*не*)*сов перех* to summarize.
рефлéкс (**-а**) *м* reflex.
рефлéктор (**-а**) *м* reflector.
реформ|а (**-ы**) *ж* reform.
реформáтор (**-а**) *м* reformer.
рефрижерáтор (**-а**) *м* (*судно*) refrigerator ship; (*грузовик*) refrigerated lorry (*BRIT*) *или* truck (*US*).
рехну́ться (**-у́сь, -ёшься**) *сов возв* (*разг*) to crack (up), flip; **~** (*perf*) **на чём-н** to be nuts about sth.
рецензи́р|овать (**-ую**; *perf* **прорецензи́ровать**) *несов перех* to review.
рецéнзи|я (**-и**) *ж*: **~ (на** *+acc***)** review (of).
рецéпт (**-а**) *м* (*МЕД*) prescription; (*КУЛИН, перен*) recipe.
рециди́в (**-а**) *м* (*преступления*) repetition; (*болезни*) recurrence.
рецидиви́ст (**-а**) *м* recidivist, habitual offender.
речев|óй *прил* speech *опред*; **~ дефéкт** speech defect; **~ы́е нáвыки** speaking skills.
рéч|ка (**-ки**; *gen pl* **-ек**) *ж* stream; (*разг*) river.
речни́к (**-а**) *м* river-transport worker.
речн|óй *прил* river *опред*; **~áя ры́ба** freshwater fish; **речнóй трамвáй** river bus.
реч|ь (**-и**) *ж* speech; (*стиль*: *разговорная итп*) language; (*русская, французская*) spoken language; **ру́сская ~** spoken Russian; **часть рéчи** part of speech; **прямáя/кóсвенная ~**

direct/indirect speech; **устная/письменная ~** spoken/written language; **дар речи** the gift of speech; **терять (потерять** *perf*) **дар речи** to be left speechless; **произносить** (*impf*) **умные/пустые речи** to make clever/empty pronouncements; **~ идёт о** *+prp* ... we are talking about ...; **о чём идёт ~?** what are you talking about?; **~ идёт о том, как/где/кто** *итп* ... the matter in question is how/where/who *итп* ...; **заводить (завести** *perf*) **~ о** *+prp* to raise the matter of; **об этом не может быть и речи** there can be absolutely no question of this; **об этом речи не было** nothing was said about this; **о чём ~!** (*разг*) sure!, of course!

реша́|ть(ся) (**-ю(сь)**) *несов от* **решить(ся)**.

реша́ющ|ий (**-ая, -ее, -ие**) *прил* decisive; (*слово, матч*) deciding *опред*; **решающий голос** casting vote.

реше́ни|е (**-я**) *ср* (*суда, собрания итп*) decision; (*ответ к задаче*) solution; (*действие: вопроса, дела*) solution, solving; (: *судьбы*) deciding.

решё́т|ка (**-ки**; *gen pl* **-ок**) *ж* (*садовая*) trellis; (*оконная*) grille; (*в камине*) grate; (*в духовке*) oven rack; **за ~кой** (*разг*) behind bars.

решет|о́ (**-а́**) *ср* sieve.

решёток *сущ см* **решётка**.

решётчат|ый *прил* lattice *опред*, trellis *опред*; **~ое окно** lattice window.

реши́мост|ь (**-и**) *ж* resolve.

реши́телен *прил см* **решительный**.

реши́тельно *нареч* (*заявить, отказать*) resolutely; (*действовать*) with resolve, decisively; **я ~ не понимаю, о чём Вы говорите** I've got absolutely no idea what you are talking about.

реши́тел|ьный (**-ен, -ьна, -ьно**) *прил* (*человек, взгляд*) resolute; (*меры*) drastic; (*решающий*) decisive.

реш|и́ть (**-у́, -и́шь**; *impf* **решать**) *сов перех* to decide; (*задачу, вопрос*) to solve; **решать (~** *perf*) *+infin* to decide to do

▸ **реши́ться** (*impf* **решаться**) *сов возв* (*вопрос, судьба*) to be decided; **решаться (~ся** *perf*) **на** *+acc*/*+infin* to make up one's mind on/to do.

ре́шк|а (**-и**) *ж* (*на монете*) tails *мн*; **орёл или ~?** heads or tails?

реэ́кспорт (**-а**) *м* re-export.

реэкспорти́р|овать (**-ую**) (*не*)*сов перех* re-export.

ре́|ять (*3sg* **-ет**, *3sg* **-ют**) *сов неперех* (*птица*) to soar; (*флаг*) to fly.

ржа́ве|ть (*3sg* **-ет**, *3pl* **-ют**, *perf* **заржаветь**) *несов неперех* to rust, go rusty.

ржа́вчин|а (**-ы**) *ж* rust.

ржа́в|ый *прил* rusty; (*вода*) brown; (*листва*) rust-coloured (*BRIT*) *или* -colored (*US*); **~ое пятно** rust mark.

ржано́й *прил* rye *опред*.

рж|ать (**-у, -ёшь**) *несов неперех* to neigh; (*разг: смеяться*) to roar with laughter.

ржи *итп сущ см* **рожь**.

РЖУ *ср сокр* = *районное жилищное управление*.

РИА *ср сокр* (= *Российское информационное агентство*) Russian News Agency.

Ривье́р|а (**-ы**) *ж* the Riviera.

Ри́г|а (**-и**) *ж* Riga.

ри́з|а (**-ы**) *ж* (*одежда*) vestments *мн*; (*на иконе*) overlay.

рикоше́т (**-а**) *м* ricochet, rebound; **отскакивать (отскочить** *perf*) **~ом** to ricochet, rebound.

Рим (**-а**) *м* Rome.

ри́мск|ий (**-ая, -ое, -ие**) *прил* Roman; **Папа Р~** the Pope; **римские цифры** Roman numerals.

ри́мско-католи́ческ|ий (**-ая, -ое, -ие**) *прил* Roman Catholic.

ринг (**-а**) *м* (boxing) ring.

ри́н|уться (**-усь, -ешься**) *сов возв* to charge; **~** (*perf*) **в работу** to throw o.s. into one's work.

Рио-де-Жане́йро *м нескл* Rio de Janeiro.

рис. *сокр* (= **рисунок**) diag. (= *diagram*).

рис (**-а**) *м* rice.

риск (**-а**) *м* (*no pl*) risk; **на свой страх и ~** at one's own risk.

рискн|у́ть (**-у́, -ёшь**) *сов от* **рисковать**.

риско́ван|ный (**-, -на, -но**) *прил* risky; (*перен: разговор, шутка*) risqué.

риск|ова́ть (**-у́ю**; *perf* **рискнуть**) *несов неперех* to take risks; **~ (рискнуть** *perf*) *+instr* (**жизнью, здоровьем**) to risk; **~** (*impf*) *+infin* to risk doing; **Вы (сильно) ~уете** you are taking a (big) risk.

ри́слинг (**-а**) *м* Riesling.

рисова́ни|е (**-я**) *ср* (*карандашом*) drawing; (*красками*) painting.

рис|ова́ть (**-у́ю**; *perf* **нарисовать**) *несов перех* (*карандашом*) to draw; (*красками*) to paint; (*перен: описывать*) to depict, portray; (: *подлеж: воображение, сознание*) to evoke a picture of

▸ **рисова́ться** *несов возв* (*видneться*) to be seen; (*перен: в воображении*) to be conjured up; (*манерничать*) to show off.

ри́совый *прил* rice *опред*.

рису́н|ок (**-ка**) *м* drawing; (*на ткани, на обоях*) pattern; (*картины*) sketch; **акварельный ~** watercolour (*BRIT*), watercolor (*US*).

ритм (**-а**) *м* (*сердца, стиха*) rhythm; (*перен: жизни, работы*) pace.

ритми́чен *прил см* **ритмичный**.

ритми́ческ|ий (**-ая, -ое, -ие**) *прил* rhythmic(al); **ритмическая гимнастика** aerobics.

ритми́ч|ный (**-ен, -на, -но**) *прил* (*музыка, стук*) rhythmic(al); (*работа, процесс*) smooth-running.

рито́рик|а (**-и**) *ж* rhetoric.

ритуа́л (**-а**) *м* ritual.

риф (**-а**) *м* reef.

рифлёный *прил* (*подошва*) grooved; **рифлёное железо** corrugated iron.

ри́фм|а (**-ы**) *ж* rhyme.

рифм|ова́ть (**-у́ю**; *perf* **срифмовать**) *несов перех* (*строчки, слова*) to make rhyme

▸ **рифмова́ться** *несов возв* to rhyme.
РКП(б) *ж сокр* (*ист*) = *Росси́йская Коммунисти́ческая па́ртия (большевико́в)*.
р-н *сокр* = **райо́н**.
РНК *ж сокр* (= *рибонуклеи́новая кислота́*) RNA (= *ribonucleic acid*).
робе́|ть (**-ю**; *perf* **оробе́ть**) *несов неперех* to go shy.
ро́б|кий (**-кая, -кое, -кие**; **-ок, -ка́, -ко**) *прил* shy.
ро́бот (**-а**) *м* robot.
робототе́хник|а (**-и**) *ж* robotics.
р|ов (**-ва**; *loc sg* **-ву**) *м* ditch.
ро́вен *прил см* **ро́вный**.
рове́сник (**-а**) *м*: **он мой ~** he is the same age as me.
рове́сниц|а (**-ы**) *ж*: **она́ моя́ ~** she is the same age as me.
ро́вно *нареч* (*писать*) evenly; (*чертить*) straight; (*дышать*) regularly; (*через год*) exactly; **~ в два часа́** at two o'clock sharp; **я ~ ничего́ не по́нял** I didn't understand a thing.
ро́в|ный (**-ен, -на́, -но**) *прил* even; (*степь*) flat; (*пробор, линия*) straight; (*дыхание, пульс*) regular; (*перен*: *характер, человек*) stable; **~ счёт** round number; **~ным счётом ничего́** (*разг*) absolutely nothing.
ровня́|ть (**-ю**; *perf* **сровня́ть** *или* **вы́ровнять**) *несов перех* (*строй, шеренгу*) to straighten (up); (*perf* **разровня́ть** *или* **сровня́ть**; *дорожку, площадку*) to level; **сровня́ть** *(perf)* **с землёй** to raze to the ground.
рог (**-а**; *nom pl* **-а́**) *м* (*также муз*) horn; (*полумесяца*) cusp; **оле́ний ~** antler; **~ изоби́лия** horn of plenty; **у чёрта на ~а́х** (*разг*) in the middle of nowhere; **взять** *(perf)* **быка́ за ~а́** (*разг*) to take the bull by the horns.
рога́лик (**-а**) *м* *crescent-shaped roll*.
рога́т|ка (**-ки**; *gen pl* **-ок**) *ж* (*для метания камешков*) catapult; (*на дороге*) roadblock: **ста́вить** *(impf)* **~ки кому́-н** to create obstacles for sb.
рога́т|ый (**-, -а, -о**) *прил* horned; **кру́пный ~ скот** cattle.
рогови́ц|а (**-ы**) *ж* cornea.
рогово́й *прил* horn *опред*; **рогова́я оболо́чка** cornea.
рого́ж|а (**-и**) *ж* (*ткань*) sacking.
род (**-а**; *part gen* **-у**, *loc sg* **-у́**, *nom pl* **-ы́**) *м* clan; (*ряд поколений*) family; (*происхождение*) stock; (*растений, животных*) genus (*мн* genera); (*деятельности, войск*) type; (*линг*) gender; (*одно поколение*) generation; **он ро́дом из По́льши** he comes from Poland; **он ро́дом из дворя́н** he is of noble stock; **своего́ ро́да** a kind of; **в не́котором ро́де** to some extent; **что-то в э́том** *или* **тако́м ро́де** something like that; **вся́кого** *или* **ра́зного ро́да** all kinds of; **вести́** *perf* **свой ~ от кого́-н** to be descended from sb; **э́то у нас в ~у́** it runs in the family; **из ро́да в ~** from generation to generation; **ему́ два́дцать лет о́т ~у** (*разг*) he is twenty years old; **он о́т ~у ничего́ тако́го не слы́шал** he had never heard anything like this in his life.
род. *сокр* (= *роди́лся*) b. (= *born*).
роддо́м (**-а**) *м сокр* (= *роди́льный дом*) maternity hospital.
роди́льный *прил*: **~ дом** maternity hospital.
роди́мый *прил* (*разг*: *край, земля*) native; **~ дом** family home; **роди́мое пятно́** birthmark.
ро́дин|а (**-ы**) *ж* (*отечество*) homeland; (*место рождения, появления*) birthplace.
ро́дин|ка (**-ки**; *gen pl* **-ок**) *ж* birthmark.
роди́тел|и (**-ей**) *мн* parents *мн*.
роди́тельный *прил*: **~ паде́ж** genitive case.
роди́тельский (**-ая, -ое, -ие**) *прил* (*обязанности, права, дом*) parental; (*деньги*) parents'; **роди́тельское собра́ние** parents' meeting.
ро|ди́ть (**-жу́, -ди́шь**; *pt perf* **-ди́л, -дила́, -ди́ло**, *pt impf* **-ди́л, -ди́ла, -ди́ло**, *impf* **рожа́ть** *или* **рожда́ть**) *сов перех* to give birth to; (*подлеж*: *земля, яблоня*) to bear a crop of
▸ **роди́ться** (*impf* **рожда́ться**) *сов возв* to be born ◆ (*perf* **уроди́ться**) *несов* (*пшеница, яблоки*) to give a good yield; **у них ~дила́сь дочь** they had a daughter; **~ся** *(perf)* **в руба́шке** (*разг*) to always land on one's feet.
родни́к (**-а́**) *м* spring (*water*).
родн|и́ть (*3sg* **-и́т**, *3pl* **-я́т**) *несов перех*: **~ кого́-н** (**с** *+instr*) to bring sb closer (to)
▸ **родни́ться** ◆ (**-ю́сь, -и́шься**; *perf* **породни́ться**) *несов возв*: **~ся** (**с** *+instr*) to become related (to).
родно́й *прил* (*брат, мать итп*) natural *опред*; (*город, страна*) native; (*в обращении*) dear; **родно́й язы́к** mother tongue; *см также* **родны́е**.
родны́|е (**-х**; *decl like adj*) *мн* relations *мн*, relatives *мн*.
родн|я́ (**-и́**) *ж собир* (*родственники*) relations *мн*, relatives *мн* ◆ *ж/м* (*разг*: *родственник*) relative.
родови́т|ый (**-, -а, -о**) *прил* of noble birth.
родово́й *прил* (*ист*: *строй, быт*) tribal; (*понятие, признак*) generic; (*линг*) gender *опред*; (*имение*) family *опред*; (*мед*: *судороги, травма*) birth *опред*.
родовспоможе́ни|е (**-я**) *ср* midwifery.
родонача́льник (**-а**) *м* (*семьи, династии*) forefather; (*перен*: *учения*) founder; (: *теории*) originator.
родосло́ви|е (**-я**) *ср* genealogy.
родосло́вн|ая (**-ой**; *decl like adj*) *ж* (*семьи*) ancestry; (*собаки*) pedigree.
родосло́вн|ый *прил*: **~ое де́рево** family tree.
ро́дственник (**-а**) *м* relation, relative.
ро́дственниц|а (**-ы**) *ж см* **ро́дственник**.

ро́дствен|ный (-, -на, -но) *прил* family *опред*; (*языки, науки*) related; **ро́дственные свя́зи** family ties.

родств|о́ (-а́) *ср* relationship; (*душ, идей итп*) affinity.

ро́д|ы (-ов) *мн* labour *ед* (*BRIT*), labor *ед* (*US*); **умере́ть** *(perf)* **от ~ов** to die in childbirth; **принима́ть (приня́ть** *perf***) ~** to deliver a baby.

ро́ж|а (-и) *ж* (*разг: лицо*) face; (*неприятное лицо*) mug; (*МЕД*) erysipelas (*skin complaint*); **стро́ить** *(impf)* **~и** (*разг*) to make faces.

рожа́|ть (-ю) *несов от* **роди́ть**.

рожда́емост|ь (-и) *ж* birth rate.

рожда́|ть(ся) (-ю(сь)) *несов от* **роди́ть(ся)**.

рожде́ни|е (-я) *ср* birth; **день ~я** birthday.

рождественск|ий (-ая, -ое, -ие) *прил* Christmas *опред*.

Рождеств|о́ (-а́) *ср* (*РЕЛ*) Nativity; (*праздник*) Christmas; **с ~м!** Happy *или* Merry Christmas!

роже́ниц|а (-ы) *ж* (*рожающая женщина*) *woman in labour*; (*только что родившая*) *woman who has given birth*.

рожка́ *итп сущ см* **рожо́к**.

рожна́ *итп сущ см* **рожо́н**.

рож|о́к (-ка́) *м* (*МУЗ*) horn; (*рогалик*) *crescent-shaped roll*; (*для надевания обуви*) shoehorn; (*макароны*) macaroni.

рож|о́н (-на́) *м* (*разг*): **лезть на ~** to ask for trouble; **како́го ~на́ тебе́ на́до?** (*разг*) what the hell do you want?

рожу́(сь) (*не*)*сов см* **роди́ть(ся)**.

рожь (**ржи**) *ж* rye.

ро́з|а (-ы) *ж* (*растение*) rose(bush); (*цветок*) rose.

роза́ри|й (-я) *м* rose garden.

ро́з|га (-ги; *gen pl* -ог) *ж* birch (*for punishment*).

розе́т|ка (-ки; *gen pl* -ок) *ж* power point; (*блюдечко*) jam (*BRIT*) *или* jelly (*US*) dish; (*украшение*) rosette.

ро́зниц|а (-ы) *ж* retail goods *мн*; **продава́ть** *(impf)* **в ~у** to retail.

ро́зничный *прил* retail; **(рекомендо́ванная) ро́зничная цена́** (recommended) retail price.

розн|ь (-и) *ж*: **студе́нт студе́нту ~** there are students and students.

розове́|ть (-ю; *perf* **порозове́ть**) *несов неперех* to turn *или* go pink; **у него́ на лбу ~л шрам** he had a pink scar on his forehead.

ро́зовый *прил* rose *опред*; (*цвет*) pink; (*ребёнок, мечты*) rosy; **ви́деть** *(impf)* **кого́-н/что-н в ро́зовом све́те** to see sb/sth through rose-coloured spectacles (*BRIT*) *или* rose-colored glasses (*US*).

ро́зог *сущ см* **ро́зга**.

ро́зыгрыш (-а) *м* draw; (*шутка*) prank.

ро́зыск (-а) *м* search; **уголо́вный ~** Criminal Investigation Department (*BRIT*), Federal Bureau of Investigation (*US*).

ро|и́ться (*3sg* -и́тся, *3pl* -я́тся) *несов возв* to swarm; (*перен: мысли*) to flood.

ро|й (-я; *nom pl* -и́) *м* (*пчёл, комаров*) swarm; (*снежинок, искр*) flurry; (*пыли*) cloud; (*перен: воспоминаний*) flood.

рок (-а) *м* (*злая судьба*) fate; (*рок-музыка*) rock ♦ *прил неизм* (*танец, стиль*) rock *опред*.

ро́кер (-а) *м* (*разг*) rocker.

рок-му́зык|а (-и) *ж* rock music.

рок-н-ро́лл (-а) *м* rock and roll.

рокова́й *прил* fatal.

ро́кот (-а) *м* rumble.

рок|ота́ть (*3sg* -о́чет, *3pl* -о́чут) *несов неперех* to rumble.

рокфо́р (-а) *м* Roquefort.

ро́лик (-а) *м* (*вращающийся валик*) roller; (*на ножке*) caster; (*ЭЛЕК*) cleat; (*фотоплёнки, бумаги*) roll; (*обычно мн: разг: коньки на колесиках*) roller skate; **~ новосте́й** newsreel; **рекла́мный ~** advertisement; (*фильма*) trailer; *см также* **ро́лики**.

ро́лик|и (-ов) *мн* roller skates *мн*.

ро́ликов|ый *прил* (*ТЕХ*) roller *опред*; **~ые коньки́** roller skates.

рол|ь (-и; *gen pl* -е́й, *dat pl* -я́м) *ж* role; (*текст*) part; **в ро́ли** *+gen* as; **игра́ть** *(impf)* **~** to play a part; **входи́ть (войти́** *perf***) в ~** to get into the part.

ром (-а) *м* rum.

рома́н (-а) *м* (*исторический, биографический*) novel; (*любовная связь*) affair.

романи́ст (-а) *м* (*писатель*) novelist; (*учёный*) Romance language philologist.

рома́нс (-а) *м* (*МУЗ*) romance.

рома́нск|ий (-ая, -ое, -ие) *прил* Romance *опред*; (*архитектура*) Romanesque.

романти́зм (-а) *м* (*художественное течение*) Romanticism; (*умонастроение*) romantic mood.

рома́нтик (-а) *м* (*мечтатель*) romantic; (*писатель, композитор итп*) romanticist.

рома́нтик|а (-и) *ж* romance.

рома́ш|ка (-ки; *gen pl* -ек) *ж* camomile.

ромб (-а) *м* rhombus.

ро́мовый *прил* rum *опред*; **ро́мовая ба́ба** rum baba.

ромште́кс (-а) *м* rump steak.

РОНО *м сокр* (= *ра́йонный отде́л наро́дного образова́ния*) ≈ district education department.

роня́|ть (-ю; *perf* **урони́ть**) *несов перех* to drop; (*перен: честь, авторитет*) to lose; (*no perf*; *листву, перья*) to shed; **~** *(impf)* **слёзы** to shed tears; **~** *(impf)* **себя́ в чьих-н глаза́х** to lose face with sb; **~** *(impf)* **слова́** to make haughty remarks.

ро́пот (-а) *м* rumble.

рос *итп несов см* **расти́**.

рос|а́ (-ы́; *nom pl* -ы) *ж* dew.

роси́н|ка (-ки; *gen pl* -ок) *ж* dewdrop.

роско́ш|ный (-ен, -на, -но) *прил* (*наряд, дом*) luxurious; (*еда*) sumptuous; (*разг: волосы, растительность*) luxuriant; (*: день, погода*) splendid; **~ная жизнь** a life of luxury.

ро́скош|ь (-и) *ж* luxury; (*излишества*)

extravagance; (*природы*) luxuriance; **предме́ты ~и** luxury items; **жить** *(impf)* **в ~и** to live in luxury.
ро́слый *прил* tall.
ро́спис|ь (-и) *ж* (*действие*: *собора, купола*) painting; (*узор*: *на шкатулке*) design; (: *на стенах*) mural; (*расходов, имущества*) list; (*подпись*) signature.
ро́спуск (-а) *м* (*армии*) disbandment; (*парламента*) dissolution.
росси́йск|ий (-ая, -ое, -ие) *прил* Russian; **Росси́йская Федера́ция** the Russian Federation.
Росси́|я (-и) *ж* Russia.
россия́н|ин (-ина; *nom pl* **-е**, *gen pl* **-**) *м* Russian.
россия́н|ка (-ки; *gen pl* **-ок)** *ж см* **россия́нин**.
ро́ссказн|и (-ей) *мн* (*разг*) old wives' tale.
ро́ссып|и (-ей) *мн* (*алмазов, золотые итп*) deposit *ед*.
ро́ссып|ь (-и) *ж* (*грибов*) scattering; *см также* **ро́ссыпи**.
рост (-а) *м* growth; (*перен*: *мастерства, производительности*) increase; (*размер*: *человека*) height; (*nom pl* **-а́**; *длина*: *пальто, платья*) length; **встава́ть (встать** *perf*) **во весь ~** (*человек*) to stand up straight; (*проблема, задача*) to become fully apparent.
ро́стбиф (-а) *м* roast beef.
ростка́ *итп сущ см* **росто́к**.
ростовщи́к (-а́) *м* moneylender.
ростовщи́ц|а (-ы) *ж см* **ростовщи́к**.
рост|о́к (-ка́) *м* (*БОТ*) shoot; (*перен*): **~ки́** *+gen* (*демократии, нового*) beginnings *мн* of.
ро́счерк (-а) *м* stroke; **реша́ть (реши́ть** *perf*) **что-н одни́м ~ом пера́** to decide sth with one stroke of the pen.
рот (рта; *loc sg* **рту́)** *м* mouth; **говори́ть** *(impf)* **не закрыва́я рта́** (*разг*) to talk nonstop; **смотре́ть** *(impf)* **в ~ кому́-н** (*перен*) to hang on sb's every word; **она́ в ~ не берёт ры́бы** (*разг*) she doesn't touch fish.
ро́т|а (-ы) *ж* (*ВОЕН*) company.
ротапри́нт (-а) *м* offset duplicator.
ротозе́|й (-я) *м* (*разг*: *бездельник*) loafer; (*разиня*) scatterbrain.
ро́тор (-а) *м* rotor.
Ро́ттердам (-а) *м* Rotterdam.
ро́щ|а (-и) *ж* grove.
роя́л|ь (-я) *м* grand piano.
р-р *сокр* (= **раство́р**) sol. (= *solution*).
р/с *сокр* = **расчётный счёт**.
РСО *ж сокр* (= *раке́та сре́дней да́льности*) MRBM (= *medium-range ballistic missile*).
РСУ *ср сокр* = *ремо́нтно-строи́тельное управле́ние*.
РСФСР *ж сокр* (*ИСТ*: = *Росси́йская Сове́тская Федерати́вная Социалисти́ческая Респу́блика*) RSFSR (= *Russian Soviet Federal Socialist Republic*).
рта *итп сущ см* **рот**.
рту́тный *прил* mercury *опред*; **~ сто́лбик** mercury column.
рту́т|ь (-и) *ж* mercury.
руб. *сокр* (= **рубль**) R., r., rouble.
руба́н|ок (-ка) *м* plane (*tool*).
руба́х|а (-и) *ж* (*разг*) shirt; **~-па́рень** (*разг*) straightforward chap (*BRIT*) *или* guy (*US*).
руба́ш|ка (-ки; *gen pl* **-ек)** *ж* (*мужская*) shirt; (*игральной карты*) back; **ни́жняя ~** (*женская*) slip; **ночна́я ~** nightshirt; **смири́тельная ~** (*перен*) straitjacket.
рубе́ж (-а́) *м* (*государства*) border; (: *водный, лесной*) boundary; (*ВОЕН*) line; **он живёт за рубежо́м** he lives abroad; **он уе́хал за ~** he went abroad; **на рубеже́ эпо́х** between the two eras.
руб|е́ц (-ца́) *м* (*от ран, после операции*) scar; (*КУЛИН*) tripe.
руби́льник (-а) *м* knife switch.
руби́н (-а) *м* ruby.
руби́новый *прил* ruby *опред*.
руб|и́ть (-лю́, -ишь; *perf* **сруби́ть)** *сов перех* (*дерево*) to fell; (*ветку*) to chop off; (*no perf*; *мясо, капусту*) to chop (up); (*голову*) to hack off; (*дачу, избу*) to erect; **он ~ит сплеча́** (*перен*) he doesn't mince his words.
ру́бк|а (-и) *ж* (*действие*: *деревьев*) felling; (*избы*) erection; (*мяса*) chopping; (*на судне, на радиостанции*) cabin.
рублёвый *прил* (*монета, банкнота*) rouble *опред*; (*печенье, конфеты*) for one rouble; (*разг*: *товар, подарок*) cheap.
ру́блен|ый *прил* (*мясо, овощи*) chopped; (*амбар, изба*) made from logs; **~ые котле́ты** rissoles.
рубл|ь (-я́) *м* rouble; **переводно́й ~** convertible rouble.
рублю́ *сов см* **руби́ть**.
ру́брик|а (-и) *ж* (*раздел*) column; (*заголовок*) heading.
рубца́ *итп сущ см* **рубе́ц**.
рубцева́ться (*3sg* **-у́ется**, *3pl* **-у́ются**, *perf* **зарубцева́ться**) *несов возв* to form a scar.
ру́бчат|ый (-, -а, -о) *прил* ribbed.
ру́бчик (-а) *м* rib.
ру́ган|ь (-и) *ж* bad language.
руга́тельн|ый *прил*: **~ое сло́во** swearword; **пье́са получи́ла мно́го ~ых о́тзывов** the play got a lot of bad reviews.
руга́тельств|о (-а) *ср* swearword.
руга́|ть (-ю; *perf* **вы́ругать** *или* **отруга́ть)** *несов перех* (*мужа, ученика*) to scold; (*perf* **обруга́ть**; *пьесу, статью*) to take to pieces
▸ **руга́ться** *несов возв* (*бранить*): **~ся с** *+instr* to scold; (*perf* **вы́ругаться**) to swear; (*perf* **поруга́ться**): **~ся с** *+instr* (*с мужем, с родными*)

to fall out with.
ругн|у́ться (-у́сь, -ёшься) *сов возв* (*разг*) to swear (*once*).
руд|а́ (-ы́; *nom pl* -ы) *ж* ore.
рудни́к (-а́) *м* mine.
руднико́вый *прил* (*предприятие*) ore-mining.
рудни́чный *прил* = **рудни́ко́вый.**
руже́йный *прил* rifle *опред.*
руж|ьё (-ья́; *nom pl* -ья, *gen pl* -ей) *ср* rifle.
руи́н|а (-ы) *ж* (*обычно мн*) ruin.
рук|а́ (-и́; *acc sg* -у, *nom pl* -и, *gen pl* -, *dat pl* -а́м) *ж* hand; (*верхняя конечность*) arm; (*разг*: *в верхах, в руководстве*) contact; **из пе́рвых рук** first hand; **в э́том чу́вствуется ~ ма́стера** one can tell this is the work of clever hands; **у неё на ~х трое дете́й** she has three children on her hands; **под руко́й, под ~ми** to hand, handy; **она́ шла с ним под ~у** she walked arm in arm with him; **проси́ть** (*impf*) **чьей-н ~и́** to ask for sb's hand (in marriage); **подня́ть** (*perf*) **ру́ку на кого́-н** to raise one's hand to sb; **его́/э́то с ~ми оторву́т** (*разг*) he/it will be snapped up; **у меня́ всё ру́ки не дохо́дят до э́того** I haven't got round to (doing) it; **отсю́да до го́рода ~о́й пода́ть** it's a stone's throw from here to the town; **у меня́ ру́ки че́шутся** +*infin* ... (*разг*) I'm itching to ...; **э́то ему́ на́ ~у** that's what suits him; **брать (взять** *perf*) **себя́ в ру́ки** to get a grip of o.s.; **ему́ всё схо́дит с рук** (*разг*) he gets away with everything; **э́то де́ло рук ма́фии** this is the work of the Mafia; **у него́ золоты́е ру́ки** he's very good with his hands; **де́ла иду́т из рук вон пло́хо** things have hit rock bottom; **прибира́ть (прибра́ть** *perf*) **что-н к ~м** to get one's hands on sth.
рука́в (-а́) *м* (*одежды*) sleeve; (*реки*) branch; (*пожарный, напорный*) hose; (*зерновой*) chute.
рукави́ц|а (-ы) *ж* (*обычно мн*) mitten.
руководи́тел|ь (-я) *м* leader; (*кафедры, предприятия*) head.
руководи́тельниц|а (-ы) *ж см* **руководи́тель.**
руков|оди́ть (-ожу́, -оди́шь) *несов неперех*: ~ +*instr* (*наступлением, действиями*) to lead; (*учреждением, цехом, лабораторией*) to be in charge of; (*страной*) to govern; (*аспирантами*) to supervise; **им ~оди́ла жа́дность** he was governed by greed.
руково́дств|о (-а) *м* (*походом, мероприятием*) leadership; (*заводом, институтом*) management; (*лабораторией*) supervision; (*к действию, в поведении*) guidelines *мн*; (*по рукоделию, по фотографии*) handbook, manual; (*по эксплуатации, по уходу*) instructions *мн* ◆ *собир* (*партии, страны*) leadership (*leaders*); **под ~м** +*gen* under the leadership of.
руково́дств|оваться (-уюсь) *несов возв*: ~ +*instr* to follow; (*здравым смыслом*) to be guided by.
руководя́щ|ий (-ая, -ее, -ие) *прил* (*работник, кадры*) managerial; (*орган*) governing *опред*; **~ие указа́ния** instructions.
руковожу́ *несов см* **руководи́ть.**
рукоде́ли|е (-я) *ср* needlework.
рукоде́льниц|а (-ы) *ж* needlewoman.
рукомо́йник (-а) *м* washstand.
рукопа́шный *прил*: **они́ пошли́ в ~ бой** they went off to fight with their bare hands.
рукопи́сный *прил* (*текст*) handwritten; (*отдел библиотеки*) manuscript *опред.*
ру́копис|ь (-и) *ж* manuscript.
рукопл|еска́ть (-ещу́, -е́щешь) *несов неперех*: ~ +*dat* to applaud.
рукопожа́ти|е (-я) *ср* handshake.
рукоприкла́дств|о (-а) *ср* beating.
рукоя́т|ка (-ки; *gen pl* -ок) *ж* (*кинжала, молотка*) handle; (*пульта управления*) crank.
рулев|о́й (-о́го; *decl like adj*) *м* (*МОР*) helmsman (*мн* helmsmen); (*перен*: *ведущий вперёд*) leader ◆ *прил*: **~о́е колесо́** steering wheel; **~о́е управле́ние** steering.
руле́т (-а) *м* (*картофельный*) croquette; (*с маком, с джемом*) ≈ swiss roll; (*окорок без кости*) boned ham; **мясно́й ~** meat loaf.
руле́т|ка (-ки; *gen pl* -ок) *ж* (*для измерения*) tape measure; (*в игорных домах*) roulette.
рул|и́ть (-ю́, -и́шь) *несов перех* to steer.
руло́н (-а) *м* roll.
рул|ь (-я́) *м* steering wheel; **стоя́ть** (*impf*) **у ~я́** (*перен*) to be at the helm.
румы́н (-а) *м* Romanian.
Румы́ни|я (-и) *ж* Romania.
румы́н|ка (-ки; *gen pl* -ок) *ж см* **румы́н.**
румы́нск|ий (-ая, -ое, -ие) *прил* Romanian; **~ язы́к** Romanian.
румя́н|а (-) *мн* blusher *ед.*
румя́н|ец (-ца) *м* glow.
румя́н|ить (-ю, -ишь; *perf* **нарумя́нить**) *несов перех* (*щёки, лицо*) to put blusher on; (*perf* **разрумя́нить**): **моро́з ~ит ли́ца** the frost makes faces glow
▸ **румя́ниться** (*perf* **разрумя́ниться**) *несов возв* to flush; (*perf* **нарумя́ниться**; *женщина*) to put on blusher; (*perf* **подрумя́ниться**; *пирог*) to brown.
румя́нца *итп сущ см* **румя́нец.**
румя́н|ый (-, -а, -о) *прил* rosy; (*пирог*) browned.
РУОП *сокр* (= *Региона́льное управле́ние по борьбе́ с организо́ванной престу́пностью*) department fighting against organized crime.
ру́пор (-а) *м* loudspeaker; ~ +*gen* (*о газете, о журнале*) mouthpiece of.
руса́л|ка (-ки; *gen pl* -ок) *ж* mermaid.
руса́лоч|ий (-ья, -ье, -ьи) *прил* mermaid's.
ру́сел *сущ см* **ру́сло.**
руси́ст (-а) *м* Russianist.
руси́стик|а (-и) *ж* Russian studies.
руси́ст|ка (-ки; *gen pl* -ок) *ж см* **руси́ст.**
русифика́ци|я (-и) *ж* Russification.
русифици́р|овать (-ую) (*не*)*сов перех* to Russify
▸ **русифици́роваться** (*не*)*сов возв* to be

Russified.

ру́с|ло (-ла; *gen pl* **-ел**) *ср* bed (*of river, stream etc*); (*перен: путь развития чего-н*) course; **жизнь вошла́ в обы́чное ~** life has taken its usual course.

ру́сск|ая (-ой; *decl like adj*) *ж см* **ру́сский**.

ру́сск|ий (**-ая, -ое, -ие**) *прил* Russian ♦ (**-ого**; *decl like adj*) *м* Russian; **~ язы́к** Russian.

ру́с|ый *прил* (*волосы, борода*) light brown; (*человек*) with light brown hair.

Рус|ь (**-и́**) *ж* Russia.

рути́н|а (**-ы**) *ж* rut (*fig*).

рути́нный *прил* stale.

ру́хлядь (**-и**) *ж собир* (*разг*) junk.

ру́хн|уть (**-у, -ешь**) *сов* (*дерево, человек итп*) to crash down; (*дом, мост*) to collapse; (*перен: счастье, надежда*) to be shattered.

руча́тельств|о (**-а**) *ср* guarantee.

руча́|ться (**-юсь**; *perf* **поручи́ться**) *несов возв*: **~ за** +*acc* to guarantee; **я голово́й ~юсь, что мы успе́ем** (*разг*) I'll bet my life that we'll do it.

руч|е́й (**-ья́**) *м* stream; **~ слёз** floods of tears.

ру́ч|ка (**-ки**; *gen pl* **-ек**) *ж уменьш от* **рука́**; (*двери, чемодана итп*) handle; (*кресла, дивана*) arm; (*для письма*) pen; **ша́риковая ~** ballpoint (pen).

ручн|о́й *прил* hand *опред*; (*животное, человек*) tame; **~а́я прода́жа** sale without a prescription; **ручна́я кладь, ручно́й бага́ж** hand luggage; **ручны́е часы́** (wrist)watch.

ручья́ *сущ см* **руче́й**.

ру́ш|ить (**-у, -ишь**; *perf* **обру́шить**) *несов перех* (*дома, деревья*) to pull down; (*no perf*; *разг*: *счастье, семью*) to wreck

▸ **ру́шиться** *несов возв* (*дом, строение*) to collapse; (*перен: семья, планы*) to be wrecked.

РФ *ж сокр* (= *Росси́йская Федера́ция*) the Russian Federation.

ры́б|а (**-ы**) *м* fish; **ни ~ ни мя́со** neither here nor there; **чу́вствовать** (*impf*) **себя́ как ~ в воде́** to feel at home; *см также* **Ры́бы**.

рыба́к (**-а́**) *м* fisherman (*мн* fishermen).

рыба́л|ка (**-ки**; *gen pl* **-ок**) *ж* fishing.

рыба́цк|ий (**-ая, -ое, -ие**) *прил* fishing *опред*.

рыба́чек *сущ см* **рыба́чка**.

рыба́ч|ий (**-ья, -ье, -ьи**) *прил* = **рыба́цкий**.

рыба́ч|ить (**-у, -ишь**) *несов неперех* to fish.

рыба́ч|ка (**-ки**; *gen pl* **-ек**) *ж* fisherwoman (*мн* fisherwomen); (*разг: жена рыбака*) fisherman's wife (*мн* wives).

ры́б|ий (**-ья, -ье, -ьи**) *прил* (*чешуя, хвост, клей*) fish *опред*; (*плавник*) fish's; **ры́бий жир** cod-liver oil.

рыбнадзо́р (**-а**) *м* fishing patrol.

ры́бный *прил* (*магазин*) fish *опред*; (*промышленность, хозяйство*) fishing *опред*; (*река, озеро*) full of fish; **ры́бные консе́рвы** tinned (*BRIT*) *или* canned fish; **~ день** *day when only fish is served in a canteen or restaurant*.

рыболо́в (**-а**) *м* fisherman (*мн* fishermen), angler.

рыболо́вный *прил* fishing *опред*.

Ры́б|ы (-) *мн* (*созвездие*) Pisces.

рыв|о́к (**-ка́**) *м* (*человека, машины*) jerk; (*перен: в работе*) push; (: *бегуна*) dash.

рыга́|ть (**-ю**) *несов неперех* (*разг*) to belch, burp.

рыда́ни|е (**-я**) *ср* sobbing.

рыда́|ть (**-ю**) *несов неперех* to sob.

рыжеволо́с|ый (**-, -а, -о**) *прил* red-haired.

ры́ж|ий (**-ая, -ее, -ие; -, -а́, -е**) *прил* (*усы, волосы, животное*) red *опред*; (*человек*) red-haired.

ры́ка|ть (**-ю**) *несов неперех* to roar.

ры́лец *сущ см* **ры́льце**.

ры́л|о (**-а**) *ср* (*свиное*) snout; (*разг: лицо*) mug.

ры́л|ьце (**-ьца**; *gen pl* **-ец**) *ср* (*БОТ*) stigma (*мн* stigmata).

ры́н|ок (**-ка**) *м* market; **~ труда́** labour (*BRIT*) *или* labor (*US*) market; **~ки сбы́та** markets.

ры́ночный *прил* (*КОММ*) market *опред*; (*яйца, овощи*) from the market; **ры́ночная цена́** market price; **ры́ночная сто́имость** market value.

рыса́к (**-а́**) *м* trotter (*horse*).

ры́с|ий (**-ья, -ье, -ьи**) *прил* lynx *опред*.

ры́|скать (**-щу, -щешь**) *несов неперех* to roam, rove; **~** (*impf*) **глаза́ми** (*перен*) to let one's eyes roam.

рысц|а́ (**-ы́**) *ж* jog trot.

рыс|ь (**-и**) *ж* lynx; (*бег лошади*) trot.

ры́твин|а (**-ы**) *ж* pothole.

рыть (**ро́ю, ро́ешь**; *perf* **вы́рыть**) *несов перех* (*окопы, канал*) to dig; (*картошку итп*) to dig up

▸ **ры́ться** *несов возв* (*в земле, в песке*) to dig; (*в карманах, в шкафу*) to rummage; (*перен: в бумагах, в книгах*) to dig about; **ры́ться** (*impf*) **в па́мяти** to delve into one's memory.

рыхл|и́ть (**-ю, -и́шь**; *perf* **взрыхли́ть** *или* **разрыхли́ть**) *несов перех* to loosen.

ры́хл|ый (**-, -а, -о**) *прил* (*снег, земля*) loose; (*кирпич, камень*) crumbly; (*перен: статья, план*) rough; (: *разг: тело, человек*) podgy (*BRIT*), pudgy (*US*).

ры́царск|ий (**-ая, -ое, -ие**) *прил* (*доспехи, честь долг*) knight's; (*турнир*) jousting *опред*; (*поступок, поведение*) chivalrous, knightly; **ры́царский рома́н** tale of chivalry.

ры́цар|ь (**-я**) *м* knight; **он настоя́щий ~** he's very chivalrous.

рыча́г (**-а́**) *м* (*ТЕХ: управления, скорости*) lever; (*телефона*) cradle; (*перен: воздействия, реформ*) linchpin.

рыч|а́ть (**-у́, -и́шь**) *несов неперех* to growl; (*разг*): **~ на** +*acc* (*на подчинённых, на учеников итп*) to snarl at.

ры́щу *итп несов см* **ры́скать**.

рья́н|ый (**-, -а, -о**) *прил* zealous.

рэ́кет (**-а**) *м* racket.
рэкети́р (**-а**) *м* racketeer.
рюкза́к (**-а́**) *м* rucksack.
рю́м|ка (**-ки**; *gen pl* **-ок**) *ж* (*сосуд*) ≈ liqueur glass; (*водки, коньяка итп*) shot.
рю́мочн|ая (**-ой**; *decl like adj*) *ж small bar selling alcohol and sandwiches.*
рю́ш|ка (**-ки**; *gen pl* **-ек**) *ж* frill.
ряби́н|а (**-ы**) *ж* (*дерево*) rowan, mountain ash ◆ *собир* (*ягоды*) rowan berry; (*разг*: *на коже*) pockmark; (*тёмное пятно*) speck.
ряби́новый *прил* (*куст*) rowan *опред*, mountain ash *опред*; (*настойка, варенье*) rowan-berry.
ряб|и́ть (*3sg* **-и́т**) *несов перех* (*воду*) to ripple; **у меня́ ~и́т в глаза́х** I'm seeing stars.
ряб|о́й (**-, -а́, -о**) *прил* (*лицо, тело*) pockmarked; (*курица, скворец*) speckled; (*гладь озера*) rippling; **Ку́рочка-ря́ба** speckled hen (*in fairytales*).
ря́бчик (**-а**) *м* hazelhen.
ряб|ь (**-и**) *ж* (*на воде*) ripple; (*в глазах*) stars *мн*.
ря́вка|ть (**-ю**) *несов неперех* (*разг*): **~** (**на** *+acc*) to bark (at).
ряд (**-а**; *loc sg* **-у́**, *nom pl* **-ы́**) *м* row; (*бойцов*) line; (*явлений, событий*) sequence; (*обычно мн*: *торговые, овощной*) stalls *мн*; (*prp sg* **-е**): **~** *+gen* (*вопросов, причин*) a number of; **из ря́да вон выходя́щий** extraordinary; *см также* **ряды́**.
рядов|о́й *прил* (*случай, жизнь, работник итп*) ordinary; (*член партии, боец*) rank-and-file ◆ (**-о́го**; *decl like adj*) *м* (*ВОЕН*) private.
ря́дом *нареч* close (by), near(by); **они́ сиде́ли ~** they sat side by side; **~ с** *+instr* next to; **э́то совсе́м ~** it's really near.
ряд|ы́ (**-о́в**) *мн* (*состав*: *армии, партии*) ranks *мн*.
ря́женк|а (**-и**) *ж type of yoghurt*.
Ряза́н|ь (**-и**) *ж* Ryazan.
ря́с|а (**-ы**) *ж* cassock.

~ С, с ~

С, с *сущ нескл* (*буква*) *the 18th letter of the Russian alphabet.*

с *сокр* (= *сéвер*) N (= *North*;) (= **секýнда**) s (= *second*).

KEYWORD

с *предл* (+*gen*) **1** (*указывает на объект, от которого что-н отделяется*) off; **лист упáл с дéрева** a leaf fell off the tree; **мáльчик прыгнул с крыши** the boy jumped off the roof; **письмó с рóдины/Украины** a letter from home/the Ukraine; **с лéкции/рабóты/свидáния** from a lecture/work/a meeting
2 (*следуя чему-н*) from; **эскиз с натýры** a sketch from nature; **перевóд с рýсского** a translation from Russian; **кóпия с докумéнта** a copy of a document
3 (*об источнике*) from; **дéньги с закáзчика** money from a customer; **с ребёнка спрос мáленький** one can't demand much from a child; **с меня́/негó достáточно** I've/he's had enough
4 (*начиная с*) since; **жду тебя́ с утрá** I've been waiting for you since morning; **с января́ по май** from January to May; **с утрá до вéчера** from morning till evening
5 (*на основании чего-н*) with; **закóн введён с одобрéния парлáмента** the law was brought in with the approval of parliament
6 (*по причине*): **с гóлоду/хóлода/гóря** of hunger/cold/grief; **с испýга/досáды** with fright/anger; **со зла** out of spite; **я устáл с дорóги** I was tired from the journey
◆ *предл* (+*acc*; *приблизительно*) about; **с киломéтр/тóнну** about a kilometre (*BRIT*) *или* kilometer (*US*)/ton *или* tonne
◆ *предл* (+*instr*) **1** (*совместно*) with; **я идý гуля́ть с дрýгом** I am going for a walk with a friend; **он познакóмился с дéвушкой** he has met a girl; **мы с ним óчень рáзные** he and I are very different
2 (*о наличии чего-н в чём-н*): **пирóг с мя́сом** a meat pie; **хлеб с мáслом** bread and butter; **диктáнт с ошибками** a dictation containing mistakes; **человéк с ю́мором** a man with a sense of humour (*BRIT*) *или* humor (*US*)
3 (*при указании на образ действия*) with; **слýшать** (*impf*) **с удивлéнием** to listen with *или* in surprise; **ждать** (*impf*) **с нетерпéнием** to wait impatiently *или* with impatience; **ждём с нетерпéнием встрéчи с Вáми** we look forward to meeting you; **одевáться** (*impf*) **со вкýсом** to dress with (good) taste; **он ел с жáдностью** he ate greedily
4 (*при посредстве*): **с курьéром** by courier; **я уéхал с пéрвым пóездом** I left on the first train
5 (*при наступлении чего-н*): **с вóзрастом** with age; **мы вы́ехали с рассвéтом** we left at dawn; **с отъéздом гостéй нам стáло скýчно** when the guests left we got bored
6 (*об объекте воздействия*) with; **покóнчить** (*perf*) **с несправедли́востью** to do away with injustice; **поспеши́ть** (*perf*) **с вы́водами** to draw hasty conclusions; **случáться (случи́ться** *perf*) **с** +*instr* to happen to; **что с тобóй?** what's the matter with you?

с. *сокр* = **селó**; (= **страни́ца**) p. (= *page*).

СА *ж сокр* (*ИСТ*) = *Совéтская Áрмия.*

сáб|ля (**-ли**; *gen pl* **-ель**) *ж* sabre (*BRIT*), saber (*US*).

сабó *м/ср нескл* (*обычно мн*) clog.

саботáж (**-а**) *м* sabotage.

саботи́р|овать (**-ую**) (*не*)*сов перех* to sabotage.

сáван (**-а**) *м* shroud.

савáнн|а (**-ы**) *ж* savannah.

сáг|а (**-и**) *ж* saga.

сагити́р|овать (**-ую**) *сов от* **агити́ровать**.

сáго *ср нескл* sago.

сад (**-а**; *loc sg* **-ý**, *nom pl* **-ы́**) *м* garden; (*фруктовый*) orchard; (*также:* **дéтский ~**) nursery (school) (*BRIT*), kindergarten (*US*).

сади́зм (**-а**) *м* sadism.

сáдик (**-а**) *м уменьш от* **сад**; (*разг: детский сад*) nursery (*BRIT*), kindergarten (*US*).

сади́ст (**-а**) *м* sadist.

са|ди́ться (**-жýсь, -ди́шься**) *несов от* **сесть**.

садóвник (**-а**) *м* (professional) gardener.

садовóд (**-а**) *м* (*любитель*) gardener; (*специалист*) horticulturalist.

садовóдств|о (**-а**) *ср* (*хобби*) gardening; (*наука*) horticulture.

The spelling rules for Russian are shown on page xvii.

садóв|ый *прил* garden *опред*; **головá твоя́ ~ая** (*разг*) you've got a head like a sieve.
сáек *сущ см* **сáйка.**
сáж|а **(-и)** *ж* soot.
сажá|ть **(-ю;** *perf* **посади́ть)** *несов перех* (*человека: на стол, в кресло*) to seat; (: *в поезд, в автобус*) to put; (*растения, дерево*) to plant; (*разг: заключить*) to lock up; (*самолёт*) to land; ~ **(посади́ть** *perf***) когó-н в пóезд/на самолёт** to put sb on a train/plane; ~ **(посади́ть** *perf***) когó-н за рабóту** to sit sb down to work; ~ **(посади́ть** *perf***) когó-н в тюрьмý/под арéст** to put sb in prison/under arrest.
сáжен|ец **(-ца)** *м* (*дерева*) sapling; (*растения*) seedling.
сажýсь *несов см* **сади́ться.**
сазáн **(-а)** *м* carp.
сá|йка **(-йки;** *gen pl* **-ек)** *ж* (bread) roll.
сайт **(-а)** *м* (*КОМП*) web site.
саквоя́ж **(-а)** *м* travelling (*BRIT*) *или* traveling (*US*) bag.
сакраментáл|ьный **(-ен, -ьна, -ьно)** *прил* (*РЕЛ*) sacramental; (*перен*) sacred.
саксофóн **(-а)** *м* saxophone.
салáз|ки **(-ок)** *мн* (*сани*) toboggan *ед*.
салáк|а **(-и)** *ж* Baltic herring.
салáт **(-а)** *м* (*БОТ*) lettuce; (*КУЛИН*) salad.
салáтниц|а **(-ы)** *ж* salad bowl.
салáтный *прил* salad *опред*; (*цвет*) pale green.
сáл|о **(-а)** *ср* (*животного*) fat; (*КУЛИН*) lard.
салóн **(-а)** *м* salon; (*автобуса, самолёта итп*) passenger section; (*в гостинице*) lounge; (*на корабле*) saloon; **худóжественный** ~ art salon.
салфéт|ка **(-ки;** *gen pl* **-ок)** *ж* (*столовая*) napkin, serviette (*BRIT*); (*маленькая скатерть*) doily.
Сальвадóр **(-а)** *м* El Salvador.
сальди́р|овать **(-ую)** *несов перех* (*КОММ*) to balance.
сáльдо *ср нескл* (*КОММ*) balance; ~ **с перенóса** balance brought forward.
сáльный *прил* greasy; (*шутка, слова*) dirty.
сáльто *ср нескл* somersault.
салю́т **(-а)** *м* salute.
салют|овáть **(-ýю)** *(не)сов неперех* (+*dat*) to salute.
саля́ми *ж нескл* salami.
сам **(-огó;** *f* **самá,** *nt* **самó,** *pl* **сáми)** *мест* (*я*) myself; (*ты*) yourself; (*он*) himself; (*как таковой*) itself; **он ~ предложи́л э́то** he himself suggested it; **я ~ могý провéрить** I can check it myself; **ты (и) ~ знáешь** you know yourself; **~á егó принципиáльность важнá** his integrity itself is important; **~ по себé** (*в отдельности*) per se, by itself; **~ собóй** (*непроизвольно*) of its own accord, by itself; **фáкты говоря́т ~и за себя́** the facts speak for themselves.
сам|á **(-óй)** *мест* (*я*) myself; (*ты*) yourself; (*она*) herself; *см также* **сам.**
Самáр|а **(-ы)** *ж* Samara.
самби́ст **(-а)** *м* sambo wrestler.
сáмбо *ср нескл* sambo (wrestling).
сам|éц **(-цá)** *м* male (*ZOOL*).
сáм|и **(-и́х)** *мест* (*мы*) ourselves; (*они*) themselves; *см также* **сам.**
сáм|ка **(-ки;** *gen pl* **-ок)** *ж* female (*ZOOL*).
сáммит **(-а)** *м* (*ПОЛИТ*) summit.
сам|ó **(-огó)** *мест* itself; ~ **собóй (разумéется)** it goes without saying; *см также* **сам.**
самоанáлиз **(-а)** *м* self-analysis.
самобичевáни|е **(-я)** *ср* (*перен*) self-reproach.
самобы́тен *прил см* **самобы́тный.**
самобы́тност|ь **(-и)** *ж* originality.
самобы́т|ный **(-ен, -на, -но)** *прил* original.
самовáр **(-а)** *м* samovar.
самовлюблённый *прил* (*человек*) vain.
самовóли|е **(-я)** *ср* wilfulness (*BRIT*), willfulness (*US*).
самовóл|ьный **(-ен, -ьна, -ьно)** *прил* (*человек*) self-willed; (*уход*) unauthorized.
самогóн **(-а)** *м* home-made vodka.
самодéл|ка **(-ки;** *gen pl* **-ок)** *ж* home-made thing.
самодéльный *прил* home-made.
самодержáви|е **(-я)** *ср* autocracy.
самодержáвный *прил* autocratic.
самодéятельност|ь **(-и)** *ж* initiative, self-motivation; (*также:* **худóжественная ~**) amateur art and performance.
самодéятельный *прил* (*по личному почину*) self-motivated; (*не профессиональный*) amateur.
самодисципли́н|а **(-ы)** *ж* self-discipline.
самодовлéющ|ий **(-ая, -ее, -ие)** *прил* self-sufficient.
самодовóл|ьный **(-ен, -ьна, -ьно)** *прил* self-satisfied.
самодýр **(-а)** *м* tyrant (*fig*).
самозабвéнен *прил см* **самозабвéнный.**
самозабвéни|е **(-я)** *ср* selflessness.
самозабвéн|ный **(-ен, -на, -но)** *прил* selfless.
самозвáн|ец **(-ца)** *м* impostor.
самозвáн|ка **(-ки;** *gen pl* **-ок)** *ж см* **самозвáнец.**
самозвáнный *прил* self-appointed.
самозвáнок *сущ см* **самозвáнка.**
самозвáнца *итп сущ см* **самозвáнец.**
сáмок *сущ см* **сáмка.**
самокáт **(-а)** *м* scooter (*child's*).
самоконтрóл|ь **(-я)** *м* self-control.
самокри́тик|а **(-и)** *ж* self-criticism.
самокрити́ч|ный **(-ен, -на, -но)** *прил* self-critical.
самолёт **(-а)** *м* (aero)plane (*BRIT*), (air)plane (*US*).
самолётостроéни|е **(-я)** *ср* aircraft manufacturing.
самолюби́в|ый **(-, -а, -о)** *прил* self-enamoured.
самолю́би|е **(-я)** *ср* self-esteem.
самомнéни|е **(-я)** *ср* self-importance.
самонадéян|ный **(-, -на, -но)** *прил* self-important.
самообладáни|е **(-я)** *ср* self-possession.
самообмáн **(-а)** *м* self-deception.
самооборóн|а **(-ы)** *ж* self-defence (*BRIT*), self-

defense (*US*).
самообразова́ни|е (-я) *ср* self-education.
самообслу́живани|е (-я) *ср* self-service.
самоокупа́емост|ь (-и) *ж* (*экон*) self-sufficiency.
самоопределе́ни|е (-я) *ср* self-determination.
самоопредел|и́ться (-ю́сь, -и́шься; *impf* **самоопределя́ться**) *сов возв* (*человек*) to determine one's position; (*нация*) to make its position clear.
самоотве́ржен|ный (-, -на, -но) *прил* self-sacrificing.
самоотво́д (-а) *м* withdrawal.
самоотрече́ни|е (-я) *ср* self-denial.
самооце́н|ка (-ки; *gen pl* -ок) *ж* self-appraisal.
самоочеви́дный (-ен, -на, -но) *прил* self-evident.
самопа́л (-а) *м* (*разг*: *кустарная вещь*) cheap fake.
самопоже́ртвовани|е (-я) *ср* self-sacrifice.
самопрове́р|ка (-ки; *gen pl* -ок) *ж* (*КОМП*) self-test.
самопроизво́л|ьный (-ен, -ьна, -ьно) *прил* spontaneous.
самоpекла́м|а (-ы) *ж* self-advertisement.
самоpо́д|ок (-ка) *м* (*золотой*) nugget; (*перен*: *талант*) natural.
самосва́л (-а) *м* dump truck.
самосоверше́нствовани|е (-я) *ср* self-improvement.
самосозна́ни|е (-я) *ср* self-awareness.
самосохране́ни|е (-я) *ср* self-preservation.
самостоя́телен *прил см* **самостоя́тельный**.
самостоя́тельно *нареч* (*независимо*) independently; (*без помощи других*) on one's own.
самостоя́тел|ьный (-ен, -ьна, -ьно) *прил* independent.
самосу́д (-а) *м* mob law.
самотёк (-а) *м* (*перен*) chaos; **пуска́ть (пусти́ть** *perf*) **де́ло на** ~ to let things slide.
самоуби́йств|о (-а) *ср* suicide; **поко́нчить** (*perf*) **жизнь ~м** to commit suicide.
самоуби́йц|а (-ы) *м/ж* suicide (victim).
самоуваже́ни|е (-я) *ср* self-respect.
самоуве́рен|ный (-, -на, -но) *прил* self-confident, self-assured.
самоуниже́ни|е (-я) *ср* self-abasement, self-degradation.
самоуничиже́ни|е (-я) *ср* self-humiliation.
самоуправле́ни|е (-я) *ср* self-administration.
самоупра́вств|о (-а) *ср* (*произвол*) arbitrariness.
самоуспокое́ни|е (-я) *ср* complacency.
самоустран|и́ться (-ю́сь, -и́шься) *сов возв*: ~ **от** *+gen* to evade, dodge.
самоутвержде́ни|е (-я) *ср* self-assertion.
самоу́чек *сущ см* **самоу́чка**.
самоучи́тел|ь (-я) *м* teach-yourself book.
самоу́ч|ка (-ки; *gen pl* -ек) *м/ж*: **он/она́** ~ he/she is self-taught.
самофинанси́ровани|е (-я) *ср* self-financing.
самохо́дный *прил* self-propelled.
самоцве́т (-а) *м* gem.
самоцве́тный *прил*: ~ **ка́мень** gemstone.
самоце́л|ь (-и) *ж* an end in itself.
самочу́встви|е (-я) *ср*: **как Ва́ше ~?** how are you feeling?
самца́ *итп сущ см* **саме́ц**.
са́м|ый (-ая, -ое, -ые) *мест* (*+noun*) the very; (*+adj*; *вкусный, красивый итп*) the most; **на ~ верх** to the very top; **в ~ом низу́** at the very bottom; **в ~ом нача́ле/конце́** right at the beginning/end; ~ **большо́й/ма́ленький/лу́чший/ху́дший** the biggest/smallest/best/worst; **тот же** ~ the same; **э́то тот ~ челове́к, о кото́ром мы говори́ли** this is the (same) person that we were talking about; **~ое вре́мя** *или* **~ая пора́ уйти́/нача́ть** it is high time to go/start; **в ~ раз** (*разг*: *вовремя*) at just the right time; **э́ти ту́фли мне в ~ раз** (*разг*) these shoes are a perfect fit; **~ая ма́лость** the tiniest little bit; **в ~ом де́ле** really; **на ~ом де́ле** in actual fact.
сан (-а) *м* (*звание*) rank; **духо́вный** ~ holy orders *мн*.
санато́ри|й (-я) *м* sanatorium (*BRIT*), sanitarium (*US*) (*мн* sanatoriums *или* sanatoria).
санда́ли|я (-и) *ж* (*обычно мн*) sandal.
са́н|и (-е́й) *мн* sledge *ед* (*BRIT*), sled *ед* (*US*); (*спортивные*) toboggan *ед*.
санита́р (-а) *м* (*МЕД*) orderly.
санитари́|я (-и) *ж* sanitation.
санита́р|ка (-ки; *gen pl* -ок) *ж* auxiliary.
санита́рный *прил* sanitary; **санита́рная те́хника = санте́хника**;; **санита́рное состоя́ние** sanitation; **санита́рный день** cleaning day; **санита́рный инспе́ктор** environmental health officer.
санита́рок *сущ см* **санита́рка**.
са́н|ки (-ок) *мн* sledge *ед* (*BRIT*), sled *ед* (*US*).
Санкт-Петербу́рг (-а) *м* St. Petersburg.
санкт-петербу́ргск|ий (-ая, -ое, -ие) *прил* St. Petersburg *опред*.
санкциони́ровани|е (-я) *ср* sanctioning.
санкциони́р|овать (-ую) (*не*)*сов перех* to sanction.
са́нкци|я (-и) *ж* (*разрешение*) sanction; (*мера*): **экономи́ческие/полити́ческие ~и** economic/political sanctions; ~ **на о́быск** search warrant; **с ~и** *+gen* with the sanction of; **дава́ть (дать** *perf*) **~ю на** *+acc* to sanction.
са́нок *сущ см* **са́нки**.
са́ночник (-а) *м* (*СПОРТ*) tobogganist.
санте́хник (-а) *м сокр* (= *санита́рный те́хник*) plumber.
санте́хник|а (-и) *ж сокр* (= *санита́рная*

те́хника) collective term for plumbing equipment and bathroom accessories.

сантиме́тр (**-а**) *м* centimetre (*BRIT*), centimeter (*US*); (*линейка*) tape measure.

Сантья́го *м нескл* Santiago.

сану́з|ел (**-ла́**) *м сокр* (= *санита́рный у́зел*) bathroom facilities *мн*.

Сан-Франци́ско *м нескл* San Francisco.

санча́ст|ь (**-и**) *ж сокр* = *санита́рная часть*; (*ВОЕН*) medical unit.

сапёр (**-а**) *м* field engineer, sapper.

сапо́г (**-а́**; *nom pl* **-и́**, *gen pl* **-**) *м* boot.

сапо́жник (**-а**) *м* shoemaker; (*разг*: *пренебр*) bungler.

сапфи́р (**-а**) *м* sapphire.

сапфи́ровый *прил* sapphire *опред*.

Сара́ев|о (**-а**) *ср* Sarajevo.

сара́|й (**-я**) *м* (*для дров, скотины*) shed; (*для сена*) barn.

саранч|а́ (**-и́**) *ж собир* locusts *мн*.

сарафа́н (**-а**) *м* (*платье*) pinafore (dress) (*BRIT*), jumper (*US*).

сарде́л|ька (**-ьки́**; *gen pl* **-ек**) *ж* sausage.

сарди́н|а (**-ы**) *ж* sardine.

са́рж|а (**-и**) *ж* serge.

сарка́зм (**-а**) *м* sarcasm.

саркасти́ческ|ий (**-ая, -ое, -ие**) *прил* sarcastic.

саркофа́г (**-а**) *м* sarcophagus (*мн* sarcophaguses *или* sarcophagi).

сары́ч (**-а́**) *м* buzzard.

сатан|а́ (**-ы**) *м* Satan.

сателли́т (**-а**) *м* (*также полит*) satellite.

сати́н (**-а**) *м* sateen.

сати́новый *прил* sateen *опред*.

сати́р|а (**-ы**) *ж* satire.

сати́рик (**-а**) *м* satirist.

сатири́ческ|ий (**-ая, -ое, -ие**) *прил* satirical.

Сату́рн (**-а**) *м* Saturn.

сау́довск|ий (**-ая, -ое, -ие**) *прил*: **С~ая Ара́вия** Saudi Arabia.

са́ун|а (**-ы**) *ж* sauna.

Сахали́н (**-а**) *м* Sakhalin.

са́хар (**-а**; *part gen* **-у**) *м* sugar; **рабо́та у меня́ не** ~ (*разг*) my work is no picnic; **хара́ктер у неё не** ~ (*разг*) she's not all sweetness and light.

Саха́р|а (**-ы**) *ж* Sahara.

сахари́н (**-а**) *м* saccharin.

са́харниц|а (**-ы**) *ж* sugar bowl.

са́харный *прил* sugary; (*перен*: *белый*) white; (: *слащавый*) sugary; **са́харная ва́та** candy floss; **са́харная кость** marrowbone; **са́харная свёкла** sugar beet; **са́харный диабе́т** diabetes; **са́харный песо́к** granulated sugar; **са́харный тростни́к** sugar cane.

сахаро́з|а (**-ы**) *ж* sucrose.

сач|о́к (**-ка́**) *м* (*для ловли рыб*) landing net; (*для бабочек*) butterfly net.

СБ *ж сокр* (= *слу́жба бы́та*) service industries *мн*.

сб. *сокр* (= **сбо́рник**) coll. (= *collection*).

сба́в|ить (**-лю, -ишь**; *impf* **сбавля́ть**) *сов перех* to reduce.

сба́гр|ить (**-ю, -ишь**) *сов перех* (*разг*) to get rid *или* shot of.

сбаланси́рованный *прил* balanced.

сбаланси́р|овать (**-ую**) *сов от* **баланси́ровать**.

сба́лтыва|ть (**-ю**) *несов от* **сболта́ть**.

сбе́га|ть (**-ю**) *сов неперех* (*разг*): **~ в магази́н/за молоко́м** to run to the shop/for milk.

сбе|жа́ть (*как* **бежа́ть**; *см* **Table 20**; *impf* **сбега́ть**) *сов неперех* (*убежать*) to run away; **сбега́ть** (~ *perf*) **с** +*gen* (*с горы итп*) to run down; **сбега́ть** (~ *perf*) **с ле́стницы** to run downstairs; **сбега́ть** (~ *perf*) **из тюрьмы́** to escape from prison; **улы́бка ~жа́ла с его́ лица́** the smile vanished from his face

▸ **сбежа́ться** (*impf* **сбега́ться**) *сов возв* to come running.

сбе́й(те) *сов см* **сбить**.

сберёг *итп сов см* **сбере́чь**.

сберега́тельный *прил*: ~ **банк** savings bank; **сберега́тельная ка́сса** = **сберка́сса**;; **сберега́тельная кни́жка** = **сберкни́жка**.

сберега́|ть (**-ю**) *несов от* **сбере́чь**.

сберегу́ *итп сов см* **сбере́чь**.

сбереже́ни|е (**-я**) *ср* (*действие*) saving; **~я** savings *мн*.

сбер|е́чь (**-егу́, -ежёшь** *итп*, **-егу́т**; *pt* **-ёг, -егла́, -егло́**, *impf* **сберега́ть**) *сов перех* (*имущество*) to protect; (*здоровье, любовь, отношение*) to preserve; (*деньги*) to save (up).

сберка́сс|а (**-ы**) *ж ссокр* (= *сберега́тельная ка́сса*) savings bank.

сберкни́ж|ка (**-ки**; *gen pl* **-ек**) *ж сокр* (= *сберега́тельная кни́жка*) savings book.

сбива́|ть(ся) (**-ю(сь)**) *несов от* **сбить(ся)**.

сби́вчив|ый (**-, -а, -о**) *прил* confused.

сбить (**собью́, собьёшь**; *imper* **сбе́й(те)**, *impf* **сбива́ть**) *сов перех* to knock down; (*птицу, самолёт*) to shoot down; (*каблуки, туфли*) to wear down; (*цену, температуру*) to bring down; (*ящик из досок*) to knock together; (*сливки, яйца*) to beat; **сбива́ть** (~ *perf*) **кого́-н с пути́** (*перен*) to lead sb astray; **сбива́ть** (~ *perf*) **кого́-н с то́лку** to mislead sb

▸ **сби́ться** (*impf* **сбива́ться**) *сов возв* (*шапка, повязка итп*) to slip; (*каблуки, копыта*) to wear down; (*собраться вместе*) to flock together; (*сливки, крем, яйца*) to stiffen; **сбива́ться** (**сби́ться** *perf*) **с пути́** (*также перен*) to lose one's way; **сбива́ться** (**сби́ться** *perf*) **со счёта** to lose count; **сбива́ться** (**сби́ться** *perf*) **с ног** to be run off one's feet.

сближа́|ть(ся) (**-ю(сь)**) *несов от* **сбли́зить(ся)**.

сближе́ни|е (**-я**) *ср* (*между государствами*) rapprochement; (*между людьми*) closeness.

сбли́|зить (**-жу, -зишь**; *impf* **сближа́ть**) *сов перех* to bring closer together

▸ **сбли́зиться** (*impf* **сближа́ться**) *сов возв*: **~ся** (**друг с дру́гом**) to approach (one another); (*люди, государства*) to become closer.

СБО *м сокр* = *спра́вочно-библиографи́ческий отде́л.*

сбо|й (**-я**) *м* (*перебой*) failure; (*в работе людей*) disruption.

сбо́ку *нареч* at the side ◆ *предл*: ~ **от** *+gen* at the side of, beside.

сболта́|ть (**-ю**; *impf* **сба́лтывать**) *сов перех* to shake (up).

сболтн|у́ть (**-у́, -ёшь**) *сов перех* (*разг*): ~ **ли́шнее/глу́пость** to say too much/something stupid.

сбор (**-а**) *м* (*урожая, данных*) gathering; (*налогов, взносов*) collection; (*валовой, годовой*) yield; (*плата*: *страховой, аукционный итп*) fee; (*выручка*: *от концерта, спектакля*) takings *мн*, receipts *мн*; (*собрание*) assembly, gathering; (*обычно мн*: *армейского запаса, спортсменов*) training *ед*; ~ **фру́ктов** fruit-picking; **тамо́женный/ге́рбовый** ~ customs/stamp duty; ~ **информа́ции** (*комп*) data capture; **порто́вые сбо́ры** harbour dues; **все в сбо́ре** everyone is present; *см также* **сбо́ры.**

сбо́рищ|е (**-а**) *ср* (*разг*: *пренебр*) gang; (: *собрание*) mob.

сбо́р|ка (**-ки**; *gen pl* **-ок**) *ж* (*изделия*) assembly; (*обычно мн*: *на юбке*) gather.

сбо́рн|ая (**-ой**; *decl like adj*) *ж* (*также*: ~ **кома́нда**) national team.

сбо́рник (**-а**) *м* collection (*of stories, articles*).

сбо́рный *прил*: ~ **пункт** assembly point; **сбо́рная ме́бель** kit furniture; **сбо́рная моде́ль** model kit.

сбо́рок *сущ см* **сбо́рка.**

сбо́рочный *прил* assembly *опред*; ~ **конве́йер** assembly line.

сбо́рщик (**-а**) *м* (*данных, урожая*) gatherer; (*машин*) assembler; **сбо́рщик нало́гов** tax collector.

сбо́р|ы (**-ов**) *мн* (*приготовления*) preparations *мн*.

сбра́сыва|ть(ся) (**-ю(сь)**) *несов от* **сбро́сить(ся).**

сбр|ить (**-е́ю, -е́ешь**; *impf* **сбрива́ть**) *сов перех* to shave off.

сброд (**-а**) *м* (*разг*: *пренебр*) rabble.

сброс (**-а**) *м* (*отходов*) discharge; (*воды*) overflow.

сбро́|сить (**-шу, -сишь**; *impf* **сбра́сывать**) *сов перех* (*бросить вниз*) to throw down; (*спустить*) to let down; (*свергнуть*) to overthrow; (*пальто итп*) to throw off; (*скорость, давление*) to reduce; (*карту*) to throw away; (*комп*) to reset

▸ **сбро́ситься** (*impf* **сбра́сываться**) *сов возв* (*разг*: *сложиться*) to chip in; **сбра́сываться** (**~ся** *perf*) **с** *+gen* to throw o.s. from.

сбру|я́ (**-и́**) *ж* harness.

СБСЕ *ср сокр* (= *Совеща́ние по безопа́сности и сотру́дничеству в Евро́пе*) CSCE (= *Conference on Security and Cooperation in Europe*).

сбу́ду(сь) *итп сов см* **сбы́ть(ся).**

сбыва́|ть(ся) (**-ю(сь)**) *несов от* **сбы́ть(ся).**

сбыт (**-а**) *м* sale; **ры́нок сбы́та** market; **отде́л сбы́та** sales department.

сбытово́й *прил* retail *опред.*

сб|ыть (*как* **быть**; *см* **Table 21**; *impf* **сбыва́ть**) *сов перех* (*товар*) to sell; (*разг*: *избавиться*) to get rid of; ~ (*perf*) **кого́-н/что-н с рук** to get sb/sth off one's hands

▸ **сбы́ться** (*impf* **сбыва́ться**) *сов возв* (*надежды, предсказания*) to come true.

СВ *сокр* (= *сре́дние во́лны*) MW= *medium wave* *ед* ◆ *прил* (*средневолново́й*) MW (= *medium-wave*).

св. *сокр* (= **свято́й**) St (= *Saint*).

сва́деб *сущ см* **сва́дьба.**

сва́дебный *прил*: ~ **пода́рок** wedding present; **сва́дебное пла́тье** wedding dress.

сва́дьба (**-ьбы**; *gen pl* **-еб**) *ж* wedding; **игра́ть** (**сыгра́ть** *perf*) **~ьбу** to celebrate a wedding.

св|али́ть (**-алю́, -а́лишь**) *сов от* **вали́ть** ◆ (*impf* **сва́ливать**) *перех* to throw down; (*разг*: *свергнуть*) to topple; **меня́ ~али́ла уста́лость** (*разг*) I feel whacked; **её ~али́л грипп** (*разг*) she's come down with the flu

▸ **свали́ться** *сов от* **вали́ться** ◆ (*impf* **сва́ливаться**) *возв* (*разг*: *появиться*) to turn up; (: *заболеть и слечь*) to collapse; **вся рабо́та ~али́лась на него́** he was landed with all (of) the work.

сва́л|ка (**-ки**; *gen pl* **-ок**) *ж* (*действие*) dumping; (*место*) rubbish dump.

сваля́|ть (**-ю**) *сов от* **валя́ть**

▸ **сваля́ться** *сов возв* (*волосы, шерсть*) to become matted.

СВАПО *ж сокр* SWAPO (= *South-West Africa People's Organization*).

св|ари́ть (**-арю́, -а́ришь**) *сов от* **вари́ть** ◆ (*impf* **сва́ривать**) *перех* (*шов*) to weld

▸ **свари́ться** *сов от* **вари́ться.**

сва́рк|а (**-и**) *ж* welding.

сварли́в|ый (**-, -а, -о**) *прил* quarrelsome.

сва́рочный *прил* welding *опред.*

сва́рщик (**-а**) *м* welder.

сва́стик|а (**-и**) *ж* swastika.

сват (**-а**) *м* (*сватающий*) matchmaker; (*родственник*) *the father of one's son-in-law or daughter-in-law.*

сва́та|ть (**-ю**; *perf* **посва́тать** *или* **сосва́тать**) *несов перех*: ~ **кого́-н** (**за** *+acc*) (*предлагать в супруги*) to try to marry sb off (to); (*no perf*, *перен*): ~ **кого́-н** (**кому́-н**) to fix sb up (with sb)

▸ **сва́таться** (*perf* **посва́таться**) *несов возв*: **~ся к** *+dat* *или* **за** *+acc* to court.

сватья (-и) *ж mother of one's son-in-law or daughter-in-law.*
сваха (-и) *ж* matchmaker.
сваія (-и) *ж* (*СТРОИТ*) pile.
сведениіе (-я) *ср* (*обычно мн*: *известия, данные*) information *ед*; **доводить (довести** *perf*) **что-н до ~я кого-н** to bring sth to sb's attention; **принимать (принять** *perf*) **что-н к ~ю** to take sth into consideration; **к Вашему ~ю** for your information; *см также* **сведения.**
сведениіе (-я) *ср* (*пятен, грязи*) removal; (*в таблицу, в график итп*) arrangement; **~ к** *+dat* reduction to.
сведениія (-й) *мн* (*знания*) knowledge *ед*.
сведу(сь) *итп сов см* **свести(сь).**
сведущіий (-ая, -ее, -ие; -, -а, -е) *прил*: **~ (в** *+prp*) knowledgeable (about).
свежезамороженный *прил* fresh-frozen.
свежеиспечённый *прил* freshly-baked.
свежестіь (-и) *ж* (*продуктов итп*) freshness; (*воздуха, воды*) cleanliness; (*погоды*) briskness; **эти овощи не первой ~и** these vegetables aren't very fresh.
свежеіть (-ю; *perf* **посвежеть**) *несов неперех* (*ветер*) to turn brisk; (*воздух*) to clear; (*человек*) to look fresher.
свежіий (-ая, -ее, -ие; -, -а, -о, -и) *прил* fresh; (*воздух, вода*) clean; (*ветер*) brisk; (*журнал*) recent; **к вечеру стало свежо** it grew chilly towards evening; **обдумывать (обдумать** *perf*) **что-н на ~ую голову** to come back to sth with a clear head.
свіезти (-езу, -езёшь; *pt* **-ёз, -езла, -езло,** *impf* **свозить**) *сов перех*: **~ (с** *+gen*) (*спустить*) to drive down; (*собрать*) to bring; (*разг*: *отвезти*: *на дачу*) to take.
свёклІа (-ы) *ж* beetroot.
свекольный *прил* beetroot *опред*; (*цвет*) beetroot(-coloured (*BRIT*) *или* colored (*US*)).
свёкіор (-ра) *м* father-in-law, husband's father.
свекровіь (-и) *ж* mother-in-law, husband's mother.
свёл(ся) *итп сов см* **свести(сь).**
свергніуть (-у, -ешь; *impf* **свергать**) *сов перех* to overthrow.
свержениіе (-я) *ср* overthrow.
свеіріить (-ю, -ишь; *impf* **сверять**) *сов перех*: **~ (с** *+instr*) to check (against)
▸ **свериться** (*impf* **сверяться**) *сов возв*: **~ся с** *+instr* to check in.
сверкаіть (-ю) *несов неперех* (*звезда, глаза*) to twinkle; (*огни*) to flicker; **~** (*impf*) **умом/красотой** to sparkle with intelligence/beauty.
сверкніуть (-у, -ёшь) *сов неперех* to flash; **у меня ~ула мысль** a thought flashed through my mind.
сверлильніый *прил* (*ТЕХ*): **~ станок** drill; **~ая головка** drillstock.
сверліить (-ю, -ишь; *perf* **просверлить**) *несов перех* to drill, bore; (*no perf*; *подлеж*: *сомнения итп*) to gnaw away at.
свіерло (-ерла; *nom pl* **свёрла**) *ср* drill.
свернуіть (-у, -ёшь; *impf* **свёртывать** *или* **сворачивать**) *сов перех* (*скатать*: *карту, ковёр итп*) to roll up; (: *сигарету*) to roll; (*сократить*) to cut, reduce; (*временно прекратить*) to hold up ◆ (*impf* **сворачивать**) *неперех* (*повернуть*) to turn; **~** (*perf*) **себе шею** to break one's neck; **~** (*perf*) **кому-н шею** (*перен*) to wring sb's neck; **сворачивать (~** *perf*) **направо/налево** to turn right/left
▸ **свернуться** (*impf* **свёртываться** *или* **сворачиваться**) *сов возв* (*карта, ковёр итп*) to roll up; (*человек, животное*) to curl up; (*молоко*) to curdle; (*кровь*) to clot.
сверстаіть (-ю) *сов от* **верстать.**
сверстник (-а) *м* peer; **мы с ней ~и** she and I are the same age.
сверстницІа (-ы) *ж см* **сверстник.**
свёртіок (-ка) *м* package.
свёртываіть(ся) (-ю(сь)) *несов от* **свернуть(ся).**
сверх *предл* (*+gen*; *нормы*) over and above; **это ~ моих возможностей** it is out of my reach; **~ ожидания** beyond all expectation; **~ обыкновения** unusually; **~ того** moreover; **~ всего** on top of everything else.
сверхзвуковой *прил* supersonic.
сверхплановый *прил* over and above the plan.
сверхприбыліь (-и) *ж* surplus profit.
сверхсрочніый *прил*: **~ая военная служба** extended military service.
сверху *нареч* (*о направлении*) from the top; (*в верхней части*) on the surface; **приказы ~** orders from above; **смотреть** (*impf*) **~ вниз на кого-н** to look down on sb.
сверхурочно *нареч*: **работать ~** to work overtime.
сверхурочніые (-ых; *decl like adj*) *мн* (*плата*) overtime pay *ед*.
сверхурочніый *прил*: **~ая работа** overtime; **работать** (*impf*) **в ~ые часы** to work on after hours.
сверхчеловечесікий (-ая, -ое, -ие) *прил* superhuman.
сверхъестественный *прил* (*РЕЛ*) supernatural; (*перен*: *усилие, терпение итп*) superhuman.
сверчіок (-ка) *м* (*ЗООЛ*) cricket.
свершаіть(ся) (-ю(сь)) *несов от* **свершить(ся).**
свершениіе (-я) *ср* (*надежд*) fulfilment (*BRIT*), fulfillment (*US*); (*дел, подвига итп*) accomplishment; (*кары*) exacting.
сверші́ить (-у, -ишь; *impf* **свершать**) *сов перех* to accomplish
▸ **свершиться** (*impf* **свершаться**) *сов возв* (*событие*) to take place; (*надежды, замыслы*) to be fulfilled.
сверяіть(ся) (-ю(сь)) *несов от* **сверить(ся).**
свеісить (-шу, -сишь; *impf* **свешивать**) *сов*

перех to lower
▸ **све́ситься** (*impf* **све́шиваться**) *сов возв*: **~ся из** +*gen*/**че́рез** +*acc* to hang from/over; (*ветви, деревья*) to overhang.
св|ести́ (**-еду́, -едёшь**; *pt* **-ёл, -ела́, -ело́**, *impf* **своди́ть**) *сов перех*: ~ **с** +*gen* to lead down; (*направить в другую сторону*) to lead off; (*пятно, грязь*) to shift; (*познакомить*) to introduce; (*собрать*) to arrange; **своди́ть** (~ *perf*) **к ми́нимуму** to minimize; **своди́ть** (~ *perf*) **кого́-н с ума́** to drive sb mad; **у меня́ ~ело́ но́гу** I've got cramp in my leg; **своди́ть** (~ *perf*) **бро́ви** to knit one's brows; **своди́ть** (~ *perf*) **ру́ки** to clasp one's hands (together)
▸ **свести́сь** (*impf* **своди́ться**) *сов возв*: **~сь к** +*dat* to be reduced to; **своди́ться** (**~сь** *perf*) **к нулю́** to come to nothing.
свет (**-а**; *loc sg* **-у́**) *м* light; (*Земля*) the world; (*аристократия*) (high) society; **при све́те луны́/свечи́** by moonlight/candlelight; **в све́те** +*gen* (*новой политики, последних событий*) in the light of; **в мра́чном/оптимисти́ческом све́те** in a gloomy/optimistic light; **ни ~ ни заря́** at the crack of dawn; **чуть ~** at daybreak; **выводи́ть** (**вы́вести** *perf*) **в ~** (*книга*) to be published; **выпуска́ть** (**вы́пустить** *perf*) **в ~** (*книгу*) to publish; **включа́ть** (**включи́ть** *perf*)/**выключа́ть** (**вы́ключить** *perf*) to switch *или* turn the light on/off; **пролива́ть** (**проли́ть** *perf*) **~ на что-н** to shed *или* throw light on sth; **тот ~** (*РЕЛ*) the next world; **ни за что на све́те не сде́лал бы э́то** (*разг*) I wouldn't do it for the world; **руга́ть** (*impf*) *или* **брани́ть** (*impf*) **кого́-н на чём ~ стои́т** (*разг*) to give sb hell.
света́|ть (*3sg* **-ет**) *несов безл* to get *или* grow light; **ле́том ра́но ~ет** it gets light early in summer.
све́тел *прил см* **све́тлый**.
свети́л|о (**-а**) *ср*: **небе́сное ~** heavenly body; (*перен*: *науки итп*) leading light.
свети́льник (**-а**) *м* lamp.
св|ети́ть (**-ечу́, -е́тишь**) *несов неперех* to shine; (*perf* **посвети́ть**): **~ кому́-н** (*фонарем итп*) to light the way for sb
▸ **свети́ться** *несов возв* (*также перен*) to shine; **её глаза́ ~ети́лись любо́вью** her eyes shone with love; **он ~ети́лся от ра́дости** he was radiant with joy.
светле́|ть (**-ю**; *perf* **посветле́ть** *или* **просветле́ть**) *несов неперех* (*также перен*) to lighten; (*ткань, волосы*) to go lighter; (*no perf*; *виднеться*) to shine light; **за о́кнами ~ет** it's getting light outside.
светло́ *как сказ*: **на у́лице ~** it's light outside.
све́т|лый (**-ел, -ла́, -ло**) *прил* bright; (*комната*) light, bright; (*волосы, глаза, краски*) light; (*ум, мысли*) lucid; **~ло-кра́сный/-зелёный** light-red/-green; **у него́ ~лая голова́** he is very bright.
светово́й *прил* light *опред*; **светово́й день** *time of the day during which it's light.*
светопреставле́ни|е (**-я**) *ср* doomsday.
светофо́р (**-а**) *м* traffic light.
светочувстви́тельный *прил* light-sensitive.
све́тск|ий (**-ая, -ое, -ие**) *прил* (*круг, манеры*) refined; (*не духовный*) secular; **~ое о́бщество** high society; **~ челове́к** man of the world.
свеч|а́ (**-и́**; *nom pl* **-и**, *gen pl* **-е́й**) *ж* candle; (*МЕД*) suppository; (*ТЕХ*) spark(ing) plug; (*СПОРТ*) lob.
све́ч|ка (**-ки**; *gen pl* **-ек**) *ж* candle.
свечу́(сь) *сов см* **свети́ть(ся)**.
све́ша|ть (**-ю**) *сов от* **ве́шать**.
све́шива|ть(ся) (**-ю(сь)**) *несов от* **све́сить(ся)**.
све́шу(сь) *сов см* **све́сить(ся)**.
свива́|ть (**-ю**; *perf* **свить**) *несов перех* to weave
▸ **свива́ться** *несов от* **сви́ться**.
свида́ни|е (**-я**) *ср* rendezvous; (*деловое*) appointment; (*с заключённым, с больным*) visit; (*влюблённых*) date; **до ~я** goodbye; **до ско́рого ~я** see you soon; **назнача́ть** (**назна́чить** *perf*) **кому́-н ~** to arrange to meet sb; (*о влюблённых*) to make a date with sb.
свиде́тел|ь (**-я**) *м* witness.
свиде́тельниц|а (**-ы**) *ж см* **свиде́тель**.
свиде́тельск|ий (**-ая, -ое, -ие**) *прил* witness's.
свиде́тельств|о (**-а**) *ср* evidence; (*документ*) certificate; **свиде́тельство о рожде́нии/бра́ке** birth/marriage certificate.
свиде́тельств|овать (**-ую**) *несов неперех*: **~ о** +*prp* (*свидетель*) to give evidence about; (*цифры, события*) to testify to ♦ (*perf* **засвиде́тельствовать**) *перех* (*подпись*) to certify.
свина́рник (**-а**) *м* (*также перен*) pigsty.
свин|е́ц (**-ца́**) *м* lead (*metal*).
свини́н|а (**-ы**) *ж* pork.
сви́нк|а (**-и**) *ж* (*МЕД*) mumps; **морска́я ~** guinea pig.
свиново́дств|о (**-а**) *ср* pig farming.
свино́й *прил* (*сало, корм*) pig *опред*; (*из свинины*) pork *опред*; **свина́я ко́жа** pigskin.
сви́нск|ий (**-ая, -ое, -ие**) *прил* (*разг*) filthy.
сви́нств|о (**-а**) *ср* (*разг*) filth.
свин|ти́ть (**-чу́, -ти́шь**; *impf* **сви́нчивать**) *сов перех* (*соединить*) to screw together.
свинца́ *итп сущ см* **свине́ц**.
свинцо́вый *прил* lead *опред*; (*цвет*) leaden.
сви́нчива|ть (**-ю**) *несов от* **свинти́ть**.
свинчу́ *сов см* **свинти́ть**.
свин|ья́ (**-ьи́**; *nom pl* **-ьи**, *gen pl* **-е́й**) *ж* pig; (*разг*: *пренебр*) pig, swine; **подложи́ть** *perf* **~ью́ кому́-н** (*разг*) to do the dirty on sb.
свире́л|ь (**-и**) *ж* (*МУЗ*) reed pipe.
свирепе́|ть (**-ю**; *perf* **рассвирепе́ть**) *несов неперех* to turn savage.

свирéпств|овать (**-ую**) *несов неперех* to rage.
свирéп|ый (**-, -а, -о**) *прил* fierce, ferocious.
свисá|ть (*3sg* **-ет**, *3pl* **-ют**) *несов неперех* to hang.
свист (**-а**) *м* whistle; (*ветра*) whistling.
сви|стéть (**-щý, -стúшь**; *perf* **просвистéть**) *несов неперех* to whistle.
свисткá *сущ см* **свистóк.**
свúстн|уть (**-у, -ешь**) *сов неперех* to give a whistle ◆ *перех* (*разг*: *украсть*) to nick (*BRIT*), pinch.
свист|óк (**-кá**) *м* whistle.
свúт|а (**-ы**) *ж* retinue.
свúтер (**-а**) *м* sweater.
свить (**совью, совьёшь**) *сов от* **вить, свивáть**
▸ **свúться** (*impf* **свивáться**) *сов возв* (*растения*) to intertwine.
свихн|ýться (**-ýсь, -ёшься**) *сов возв* (*разг*: *помешаться*) to go round the bend *или* twist; ~ (*perf*) **на чём-н** (*на футболе, на кино*) to be mad *или* crazy about sth.
свищ (**-á**) *м* (*МЕД*) fistula.
свищý *несов от* **свистéть.**
свобóд|а (**-ы**) *ж* freedom; **лишéние ~ы** imprisonment; **лишáть** (**лишúть** *perf*) **когó-н ~ы** to imprison sb; **выпускáть** (**вы́пустить** *perf*) **когó-н на ~у** to set sb free; **свобóда лúчности/печáти** freedom of the individual/ press; **свобóда слóва** freedom of speech.
свобóден *прил см* **свобóдный.**
свобóдно *нареч* (*передвигаться*) freely; (*говорить*) fluently; (*облегать*) loosely ◆ *как сказ*: **мне здесь** ~ I feel free here; **в дóме** ~ there's a lot of room in the house; **здесь** ~? is this place free?; **он ~ говорúт по-рýсски** he speaks Russian fluently.
свобóд|ный (**-ен, -на, -но**) *прил* free; (*незанятый*: *место, номер*) vacant; (: *комната*) spare; (*одежда*) loose-fitting; (*помещение*) spacious; (*движение, речь*) fluent; (*дыхание*) unrestricted; ~ **от** *+gen* (*от недостатков итп*) free from *или* of; **вход** ~ free admission; **телефóн ~ен** the telephone is free; **Вы ~ны, мóжете идтú** you are free to go; **у меня сейчáс нет ~ных дéнег** I don't have any money to spare; **свобóдный перевóд** free translation; **свобóдный стиль** (*в плавании*) free style; **свобóдный удáр** (*в футболе*) free kick.
свободолюбúв|ый (**-, -а, -о**) *прил* freedom-loving.
свободомы́сли|е (**-я**) *ср* free thinking.
свод (**-а**) *м* (*пятен, грязи*) removal; (*частей в целое, данных в таблицу*) arrangement; (*правил итп*) set; (*летописей*) collection; (*здания, тоннеля*) vaulting; ~ **прáвил** (*профессиональный*) code of practice; **свод закóнов** legal code.
св|одúть (**-ожý, -óдишь**) *несов от* **свестú** ◆ *сов перех* (*отвести*) to take
▸ **сводúться** *несов от* **свестúсь.**
свóд|ка (**-ки**; *gen pl* **-ок**) *ж*: ~ **погóды/новостéй** weather/news summary; **оперативная** ~ (*ВОЕН*) situation report.
свóдный *прил* (*таблица, график*) summary *опред*; **свóдный брат** stepbrother; **свóдная сестрá** stepsister.
свóдок *прил см* **свóдка.**
свóдчатый *прил* vaulted.
сво|ё (**-егó**) *мест см* **свой.**
своевóл|ьный (**-ен, -ьна, -ьно**) *прил* self-willed.
своеврéмен|ный (**-ен, -на, -но**) *прил* timely.
своём *итп мест см* **свой, своё.**
своенрáв|ный (**-ен, -на, -но**) *прил* wilful (*BRIT*), willful (*US*).
своеобрáзен *прил см* **своеобрáзный.**
своеобрáзи|е (**-я**) *ср* distinctiveness.
своеобрáз|ный (**-ен, -на, -но**) *прил* (*оригинальный*) original; (*no short form*; *своего рода*) peculiar.
свожý(сь) (*не*)*сов см* **сводúть(ся).**
св|озúть (**-ожý, -óзишь**) *несов от* **свезтú** ◆ *сов перех* to take; **он ~озúл нас в кинó** he took us to the cinema.

KEYWORD

сво|й (**-егó**; *f* **своя́**, *nt* **своё**, *pl* **свои́**; *как* **мой**; *см* **Table 8**) *мест* ***1*** (*я*) my; (*ты*) your; (*он*) his; (*она*) her; (*оно*) its; (*мы*) our; (*вы*) your; (*они*) their; **я люблю́ свою́ рабóту** I love my work; **мы собрáли свои́ вéщи** we collected our things; **дéлать** (**сдéлать** *perf*) **что-н своúми рукáми** to make sth oneself; **жить** (*impf*) **своúм трудóм** to live by one's own hard work; **кричáть** (*impf*) **не своúм гóлосом** to shout wildly; **называ́ть** (*impf*) **вéщи своúми именáми** to call a spade a spade
2 (*собственный*) one's own; **у неё свой компью́тер** she has her own computer; **у меня́ своя́ машúна** I have my own car
3 (*своеобразный*) its; **э́тот план имéет свои́ недостáтки** this plan has its shortcomings
4 (*близкий*): **свой человéк** one of us; **он сам не свой пóсле случúвшегося** he is not himself after what happened

свóйск|ий (**-ая, -ое, -ие**) *прил* (*разг*) easy-going, laid-back.
свóйствен|ный (**-, -на, -но**) *прил* (*+dat*) characteristic of; **емý ~но сердúться** he has a tendency to get angry.
свóйств|о (**-а**) *ср* (*человека*) characteristic; (*предмета*) property.
свóлоч|ь (**-и**; *gen pl* **-éй**) *ж* (*груб!*) bastard (*!*)
свóр|а (**-ы**) *ж собир* (*волков*) pack; (*перен*: *хулиганов, мошенников*) pack, gang.
сворáчива|ть (**-ю**) *несов от* **свернýть, своротúть**
▸ **сворáчиваться** *несов от* **свернýться.**
свор|отúть (**-очý, -óтишь**; *impf* **сворáчивать**) *сов неперех* (*разг*: *сдвинуть*) to shift, budge; (: *свернуть*) to turn.
сво|я́ (**-éй**) *мест см* **свой.**

своя́к (-á) *м* brother-in-law (*wife's sister's husband*).
своя́чениц|а (-ы) *ж* sister-in-law (*wife's sister*).
СВЧ *сокр* (= *сверхвысо́кая частота́*) SHF, shf (= *superhigh frequency*) ◆ *прил сокр* (*сверхвысокочастотный*) SHF, shf (= *superhigh frequency*).
СВЧ-печ|ь (-и) *ж* microwave.
свы́кн|уться (**-усь, -ешься**; *impf* **свыка́ться**) *сов возв*: ~ **с** *+instr* to get *или* become used to.
свысока́ *нареч* condescendingly; **смотре́ть** (*impf*) **на кого́-н** ~ to look down on sb.
свы́ше *предл*: ~ *+gen* (*выше*) beyond; (*больше*) over, more than; **э́то** ~ **мои́х сил** it's beyond me.
свяжу́(сь) *итп сов см* **связа́ть(ся)**.
свя́зан|ный (**-, -а, -о**) *прил*: ~ (**с** *+instr*) connected (to *или* with); (*имеющий связи*): ~ **с** *+instr* (*с деловыми кругами, с художниками итп*) associated with; (**-, -на, -но**; *несвободный*: *движения, речь*) restricted; **э́то** ~**о со значи́тельными расхо́дами** it involves considerable expense; **он был не́сколько лет свя́зан с э́той фи́рмой** he was involved with the company for several years.
свя|за́ть (**-жу́, -жешь**) *сов от* **вяза́ть** ◆ (*impf* **свя́зывать**) *перех* (*веревку итп*) to tie; (*вещи, человека*) to tie up; (*перен*: *действия, инициативу*) to bind; (*установить сообщение, зависимость*): ~ **что-н с** *+instr* to connect *или* link sth to; **с чем Вы э́то свя́зываете?** to what do you attribute this?; **я могу́ Вас с ним** ~ I can put you in touch with him; **он** ~**за́л свою́ жизнь с нау́кой** he devoted his life to science; **он двух слов** ~ **не мо́жет** (*перен*) he can't string two words together; **свя́зывать** (~ *perf*) **кого́-н по рука́м и нога́м** (*перен*) to bind sb hand and foot
▸ **связа́ться** (*impf* **свя́зываться**) *сов возв*: ~**ся с** *+instr* to contact; (*разг*: *с ворами итп*) to get mixed up with; (: *с невыгодным делом*) to get o.s. caught up in; **свя́зываться** (~**ся** *perf*) **с кем-н по телефо́ну** to get in touch with sb by phone.
свя́з|и (**-ей**) *мн* (*знакомства*) connections *мн*; ~ **с обще́ственностью** public relations; **отде́л по** ~**ям с обще́ственностью** public relations department.
связи́ст (**-а**) *м* (*ВОЕН*) signalman (*мн* signalmen).
свя́з|ка (**-ки**; *gen pl* **-ок**) *ж* bunch; (*бумаг, дров*) bundle; (*АНАТ*) ligament; (*ЛИНГ*) copula.
связн|о́й (**-о́го**; *decl like adj*) *м* messenger.
свя́зный *прил* coherent.
свя́зок *сущ см* **свя́зка**.
связу́ющ|ий (**-ая, -ее, -ие**) *прил* connecting.
свя́зывани|е (**-я**) *ср* tying.
свя́зыва|ть(ся) (**-ю(сь)**) *несов от* **связа́ть(ся)**.
связ|ь (**-и**) *ж* tie; (*причинная*) connection, link; (*почтовая итп*) communications *мн*; (*также*: **любо́вная** ~) relationship; **в** ~**и́ с** *+instr* (*вследствие*) due to; (*по поводу*) in connection with; **в э́той** ~**и́** in this regard; **Министе́рство Свя́зи** Ministry of Communications; *см также* **свя́зи**.
свят|а́я (**-о́й**; *decl like adj*) *ж см* **свято́й**.
святи́лищ|е (**-а**) *ср* (*РЕЛ*) sanctuary.
свя|ти́ть (**-щу́, -ти́шь**; *perf* **освяти́ть**) *несов перех* (*РЕЛ*) to sanctify.
свя́т|ки (**-ок**) *мн* ≈ Christmas(tide) *ед*.
свят|о́й *прил* holy; (**-, -а, -о**; *дело, обязанность, истина*) sacred ◆ (**-о́го**; *decl like adj*) *м* (*РЕЛ*) saint; ~**а́я святы́х** the holy of holies; ~ **оте́ц** father (*used to address a priest*); **он/она́** ~ **челове́к** he/she is a real saint.
свя́ток *сущ см* **свя́тки**.
свя́тост|ь (**-и**) *ж* holiness; (*дела, чувства*) sanctity.
святота́тств|о (**-а**) *ср* sacrilege.
святы́н|я (**-и**) *ж* (*место*) sacred place; (*предмет*) sacred object.
свяще́нник (**-а**) *м* priest.
священноде́йстви|е (**-я**) *ср* religious ceremony.
священноде́йств|овать (**-ую**) *несов неперех* to conduct a religious ceremony.
священнослужи́тел|ь (**-я**) *м* clergyman (*мн* clergymen).
свяще́нный *прил* holy, sacred; (*долг, обязанность*) sacred; **Свяще́нное Писа́ние** Holy Scripture.
свяще́нств|о (**-а**) *ср собир* the priesthood.
свящу́ *несов см* **святи́ть**.
с.г. *сокр* = *сего́ го́да*.
сгиб (**-а**) *м* bend.
сгиба́|ть (**-ю**; *perf* **согну́ть**) *несов перех* to bend
▸ **сгиба́ться** (*perf* **согну́ться**) *несов возв* to bend down.
сги́н|уть (**-у, -ешь**) *сов неперех* (*разг*) to vanish.
сгла́|дить (**-жу, -дишь**; *impf* **сгла́живать**) *сов перех* to smooth out; (*перен*: *противоречия, остроту горя*) to smooth over; **сгла́живать** (~ *perf*) **углы́** (*перен*) to iron out difficulties
▸ **сгла́диться** (*impf* **сгла́живаться**) *сов возв* to be smoothed out.
сгла́|зить (**-жу, -зишь**) *сов перех* (*РЕЛ*) to put the evil eye on; (*разг*) to jinx.
сглуп|и́ть (**-лю́, -и́шь**) *сов от* **глупи́ть**.
сгнива́|ть (*3sg* **-ет**, *3pl* **-ют**) *несов неперех* to rot.
сгни|ть (**-ю, -ёшь**) *сов от* **гнить**.
сгно|и́ть (**-ю́, -и́шь**) *сов от* **гнои́ть**.
сгова́рива|ться (**-юсь**) *несов от* **сговори́ться**.
сго́вор (**-а**) *м* agreement.
сговор|и́ться (**-ю́сь, -и́шься**; *impf* **сгова́риваться**) *сов возв*: ~ **с** *+instr* (*о встрече, о сделке*) to come to an arrangement with; (*в дискуссии, в беседе*) to reach an agreement with.

сговорчив|ый (-, -а, -о) *прил* cooperative.
сгоню *итп сов см* **согнать**.
сгоня|ть (-ю) *несов от* **согнать** ◆ *сов неперех* (*разг*: *сбегать*) to run ◆ *перех* (*послать*) to send.
сгорани|е (-я) *ср* (*ТЕХ*) combustion.
сгора|ть (-ю) *несов от* **сгореть** ◆ *неперех*: ~ **от любопытства/нетерпения** to be burning with curiosity/impatience.
сгорб|ить(ся) (-лю(сь), -ишь(ся)) *сов от* **горбить(ся)**.
сгор|еть (-ю, -ишь; *impf* **сгорать** *или* **гореть**) *сов неперех* to burn; (*impf* **сгорать**; *ЭЛЕК*) to fuse; (*на солнце*) to get burnt; (*перен*: *на работе*) to burn o.s. out.
сгоряча *нареч* in the heat of the moment.
сготов|ить (-лю, -ишь) *сов от* **готовить**.
сгр|ести (-ебу, -ебёшь; *pt* -ёб, -ебла, -ебло, *impf* **сгребать**) *сов перех* (*собрать*) to rake up; (*скинуть*): ~ **с** +*gen* to shovel off.
сгрудиться (*3sg* -ится, *1pl* -имся) *сов неперех* (*разг*) to crowd together.
сгр|узить (-ужу, -узишь; *impf* **сгружать**) *сов перех*: ~ **(с** +*gen*) to unload (from).
сгруппир|овать(ся) (-ую(сь)) *сов от* **группировать(ся)**.
сг|убить (-ублю, -убишь) *сов от* **губить**.
сг|устить (-ущу, -устишь; *impf* **сгущать**) *сов перех* to thicken; **сгущать (~** *perf*) **краски** (*перен*) to paint an exaggerated picture
▸ **сгуститься** (*impf* **сгущаться**) *сов возв* to thicken.
сгуст|ок (-ка) *м* blob.
сгуща|ть(ся) (-ю(сь)) *несов от* **сгустить(ся)**.
сгущённ|ый *прил*: **~ое молоко** condensed milk.
сгущу(сь) *сов см* **сгустить(ся)**.
с.-д. *сокр* = *социал-демократический*.
сда|вать (-ю, -ёшь; *imper* -вай(те)) *несов от* **сдать** ◆ *перех*: ~ **экзамен** to sit an exam
▸ **сдаваться** *несов от* **сдаться** ◆ *возв* (*отдаваться внаём*) to be leased out ◆ *безл* (+*dat*; *разг*): **~ётся мне, что ...** I reckon that ...; **„~ётся внаём"** "to let".
сд|авить (-авлю, -авишь; *impf* **сдавливать**) *сов перех* to squeeze.
сдавлен|ный (-, -на, -но) *прил* (*голос, плач*) choked.
сдавлива|ть (-ю) *несов от* **сдавить**.
сдавлю *сов см* **сдавить**.
сдам(ся) *итп сов см* **сдать(ся)**.
сдатчик (-а) *м* supplier.
сдать (*как* **дать**; *см* **Table 14**; *impf* **сдавать**) *сов перех* (*пальто, багаж, работу*) to hand in; (*сырьё, продукцию*) to supply; (*дежурство, рабочее место итп*) to hand over; (*дом, комнату итп*) to rent out; (*город, позицию*) to surrender; (*сдачу*) to give (back); (*no impf*; *экзамен, зачёт итп*) to pass ◆ *неперех* (*ослабеть*) to give out; **сдать** (*perf*) **дела** to step down; **сдавать (сдать** *perf*) **оружие** to lay down one's arms; **он сдал мне 5 рублей** he gave me 5 roubles change
▸ **сдаться** (*impf* **сдаваться**) *сов возв* to give up; (*солдат, город*) to surrender; **сдаваться (~ся** *perf*) **на** +*acc* (*на уговоры итп*) to give in to; **на что мне сдались эти деньги?** (*разг*) what use is this money to me?; **сдаваться (~ся** *perf*) **в плен кому-н** to give o.s. up to sb.
сдач|а (-и) *ж* (*сырья*) supply; (*экзамена*) passing; (*дежурства*) handing over; (*дома*) letting; (*города врагу*) surrender; (*излишек денег*) change; (*КАРТЫ*) deal; **давать (дать** *perf*) **кому-н ~у** (*в магазине*) to give sb his *итп* change; **дать** (*perf*) **кому-н ~и** (*разг*) to match sb blow for blow; **~ с 10 рублей** change from 10 roubles.
сдашь(ся) *сов см* **сдать(ся)**.
сдвиг (-а) *м* (*в работе, в учёбе*) progress; (*в сознании*) change; **у него ~** (*разг*) he's not all there.
сдвин|уть (-у, -ешь; *impf* **сдвигать**) *сов перех* (*переместить*) to move; (*сблизить*) to move together; (*заставить тронуться*) to shift
▸ **сдвинуться** (*impf* **сдвигаться**) *сов возв*: **~ся (с места)** to move; (*сместиться*) to shift.
сдела|ть(ся) (-ю(сь)) *сов от* **делать(ся)**.
сдел|ка (-ки; *gen pl* -ок) *ж* deal; **заключать (заключить** *perf*) **~ку (с** +*instr*) to do a deal (with); **пойти** (*perf*) **на ~ку с совестью** to do a deal with the devil.
сдельн|ый *прил*: **~ая работа** piecework.
сдельщик (-а) *м* pieceworker.
сдельщиц|а (-ы) *ж см* **сдельщик**.
сдёргива|ть (-ю) *несов от* **сдёрнуть**.
сдержанно *нареч* (*сказать, плакать итп*) with restraint; (*отнестись, принять*) with reserve.
сдержан|ный (-, -на, -но) *прил* (*человек*) reserved; (*чувства*) contained.
сд|ержать (-ержу, -ержишь; *impf* **сдерживать**) *сов перех* to contain, hold back; **сдерживать (~** *perf*) **себя** to contain o.s.; **сдерживать (~** *perf*) **слово/обещание** to keep one's word/promise; **сдерживать (~** *perf*) **клятву** to honour an oath
▸ **сдержаться** (*impf* **сдерживаться**) *сов возв* to restrain o.s.
сдёрн|уть (-у, -ешь; *impf* **сдёргивать**) *сов перех* to pull off.
сдеру *итп сов см* **содрать**.
сдира|ть (-ю; *perf* **содрать**) *несов перех* (*кожуру, кору*) to peel off.
сдоб|а (-ы) *ж* (*добавки*) shortening ◆ *собир* (*булки*) buns *мн*.
сдобный *прил* rich.
сдохн|уть (-у, -ешь) *сов от* **дохнуть**.
сдр|ужить (-ужу, -ужишь) *сов перех* to bring together
▸ **сдружиться** *сов возв* to become friends.
сдублир|овать (-ую) *сов от* **дублировать**.
сдува|ть (-ю) *несов см* **сдуть**.
сдуру *нареч* (*разг*) stupidly.
сду|ть (-ю; *impf* **сдувать**) *сов перех* to blow away; (*разг*: *списать*) to copy.
сдыха|ть (-ю) *несов неперех* (*разг*: *человек*) to

snuff it.
сё (**сего́**) *мест* this; **то да** ~ (*разг*) this and that; **ни то ни** ~ (*разг*) neither one thing nor the other.
сеа́нс (**-а**) *м* (*кино*) show; (*психотерапии итп*) session.
СЕАТО *ср сокр* (= *Организа́ция догово́ра Юго-Восто́чной А́зии*) SEATO (= *Southeast Asia Treaty Organization*).
себе́ *мест см* **себя́** ◆ *част* (*разг*): **так** ~ so-so; **ничего́** ~! wow!; **иди́** ~, **не вме́шивайся!** just stay out of it!
себесто́имост|ь (**-и**) *ж* cost price.

KEYWORD

себя́ *мест* (*я*) myself; (*ты*) yourself; (*он*) himself; (*она*) herself; (*оно*) itself; (*мы*) ourselves; (*вы*) yourselves; (*они*) themselves; **он тре́бователен к себе́** he asks a lot of himself; **она́ вини́т себя́** she blames herself; **представля́ть** (**предста́вить** *perf*) **что-н себе́** to imagine sth; **испы́тывать** (**испыта́ть** *perf*) **что-н на себе́** (*лекарство*) to test sth on o.s.; (*трудности*) to experience sth; **к себе́** (*домой*) home; (*в свою комнату*) to one's room; **«к себе́»** (*на двери*) "pull"; **«от себя́»** (*на двери*) "push"; **по себе́** (*по своим вкусам*) to one's taste; **убира́ть** (**убра́ть** *perf*) **по́сле себя́** to tidy up after o.s.; **приходи́ть** (**прийти́** *perf*) **в себя́** to come to one's senses; **говори́ть** (*impf*)/**чита́ть** (*impf*) **про себя́** to talk/read to o.s.; **она́ себе́ на уме́** (*разг*) she is secretive; **он у себя́** (*в своём доме*) he is at home; (*в своём кабинете*) he is in the office.

себялюби́в|ый (**-, -а, -о**) *прил* egotistical.
себялю́би|е (**-я**) *ср* self-love.
сев (**-а**) *м* sowing.
Севасто́пол|ь (**-я**) *м* Sevastopol.
се́вер (**-а**) *м* north; **С**~ (*Арктика*) the Arctic North.
се́верн|ый *прил* north *опред*; (*ветер, направление*) northerly; (*климат, полушарие*) northern; **С**~ **Кавка́з** the Northern Caucasus; **С**~**ая Коре́я** North Korea; **С**~ **Ледови́тый океа́н** Arctic Ocean; **се́верное сия́ние** the northern lights *мн*; **Се́верный по́люс** the North Pole.
се́веро-восто́к (**-а**) *м* northeast.
се́веро-за́пад (**-а**) *м* northwest.
северя́н|ин (**-ина**; *nom pl* **-е**, *gen pl* **-**) *м* northerner.
северя́н|ка (**-ки**; *gen pl* **-ок**) *ж см* **северя́нин**.
севрю́г|а (**-и**) *ж* sturgeon.
сегме́нт (**-а**) *м* segment.
сего́ *мест см* **сей, сие́**.
сего́дня *нареч, сущ нескл* today; ~ **у́тром/днём/ве́чером** this morning/afternoon/evening; **встре́ча назна́чена на** ~ this meeting has been set for today; **на** ~ **у нас ма́ло ресу́рсов** we currently have very few resources; **не** ~**-за́втра** any day now.
сего́дняшн|ий (**-яя, -ее, -ие**) *прил* today's; ~ **день** today; **на** ~ **день** at present; **жить** (*impf*) ~**им днём** to live for the present.
сегрега́ци|я (**-и**) *ж* segregation.
сёдел *сущ см* **седло́**.
седе́|ть (**-ю**; *perf* **поседе́ть**) *несов неперех* to go grey (*BRIT*) *или* gray (*US*).
сед|ина́ (**-ины́**; *nom pl* **-и́ны**) *ж* grey (*BRIT*) *или* gray (*US*) hair.
седла́|ть (**-ю**; *perf* **оседла́ть**) *несов перех* to saddle.
седл|о́ (**-а́**; *nom pl* **сёдла**, *gen pl* **сёдел**) *ср* saddle; **вы́шибить** (*perf*) *или* **вы́бить** (*perf*) **кого́-н из** ~**а́** (*перен*) to knock sb out of his *umn* stride.
седовла́с|ый (**-, -а, -о**) *прил* grey-haired (*BRIT*), gray-haired (*US*).
седоволо́с|ый (**-, -а, -о**) *прил* = **седовла́сый**.
сед|о́й (**-, -а́, -о**) *прил* (*волосы*) grey (*BRIT*), gray (*US*); (*человек*) grey-haired (*BRIT*), gray-haired (*US*); ~**а́я старина́** ancient times.
седо́к (**-а́**) *м* (*всадник*) rider; (*пассажир*) passenger.
седьм|о́й (**-а́я, -о́е, -ы́е**) *чис* seventh; **сейча́с** ~ **час** it's after six; **быть** (*impf*) **на** ~**о́м не́бе** to be in seventh heaven; *см также* **пя́тый**.
сезо́н (**-а**) *м* season; ~ **дожде́й** the rainy season.
сезо́нник (**-а**) *м* seasonal worker.
сезо́нный *прил* seasonal; **сезо́нный биле́т** season ticket.
сей (**сего́**; *см* **Table 12**) *мест* this; **сию́ мину́ту** *или* **секу́нду!** this minute!; **на** ~ **раз** on this occasion; **по** ~ **день** to this day; **5-го ма́я сего́ го́да** on the 5th (of) May this year; **от сих до сих** (*разг*) from here to here.
сейсми́ческ|ий (**-ая, -ое, -ие**) *прил* (*колебания, волны*) seismic; (*станция, прибор*) seismological.
сейсмо́лог (**-а**) *м* seismologist.
сейф (**-а**) *м* (*ящик*) safe; (*помещение*) vault.
сейча́с *нареч* (*теперь*) now; (*скоро*) just now; (*разг*: *недавно*) (only) just; **он** ~ **рабо́тает** he's working just now; ~ **приду́** I'm just on my way; ~ **же!** right now!
сёк *итп сов см* **сечь**.
СЕКАМ *м сокр* (= *систе́ма цветно́го телеви́дения*) SECAM (= *séquentiel couleur à mémoire*).
сека́тор (**-а**) *м* secateurs *мн*.
секре́т (**-а**) *м* secret; **по** ~**у** in secret; **под** ~**ом** confidentially; **держа́ть** (*impf*) **что-н в** ~**е** to keep sth a secret.
секретариа́т (**-а**) *м* secretariat.
секрета́рш|а (**-и**) *ж* (*разг*) secretary (*female*).
секрета́р|ь (**-я́**) *м* secretary; **генера́льный** ~ secretary-general; **секрета́рь-машини́стка**

secretary.
секре́тен *прил см* **секре́тный.**
секрете́р (-а) *м* bureau (*BRIT*), secretaire.
секре́тнича|ть (-ю) *несов неперех* (*скрытничать*) to be secretive; (*разговаривать по секрету*) to talk secretively.
секре́т|ный (-ен, -на, -но) *прил* secret.
секс (-а) *м* sex.
сексопи́льност|ь (-и) *ж* sex appeal.
сексопи́льный *прил* sexy.
сексуа́л|ьный *прил* sexual; **(-ен, -ьна, -ьно;** *эротичный*) sexy; **сексуа́льная жизнь** sex life; **сексуа́льное образова́ние** sex education; **сексуа́льное домога́тельство** *или* **пресле́дование** sexual harassment.
се́кт|а (-ы) *ж* sect.
секта́нт (-а) *м* sect member.
секта́нт|ка (-ки; *gen pl* **-ок)** *ж см* **секта́нт.**
секта́нтск|ий (-ая, -ое, -ие) *прил* sectarian.
се́ктор (-а) *м* (*также ЭКОН, ГЕОМ*) sector; (*здания*) section; (*учреждения*) department.
се́кторный *прил*: **се́кторная диагра́мма** pie chart.
секу́ *итп сов см* **сечь.**
секу́нд|а (-ы) *ж* second; **(одну́) ~у!** just one *или* a second!
секунда́нт (-а) *м* second (*of boxer, duellist*).
секу́ндн|ый *прил* (*пауза, заминка*) second's; **~ая стре́лка** second hand (*on clock*).
секундоме́р (-а) *м* stopwatch.
секцио́нный *прил* divided into sections.
се́кци|я (-и) *ж* section.
сел *итп сов см* **сесть.**
селёд|ка (-ки; *gen pl* **-ок)** *ж* herring.
селезён|ка (-и) *ж* spleen.
се́лез|ень (-ня) *м* drake.
селе́ктор (-а) *м* (*ТЕЛ*) intercom.
селекционе́р (-а) *м* breeder.
селе́кци|я (-и) *ж* (*БИО*) selective breeding.
селе́ни|е (-я) *ср* village.
сел|и́ть (-ю́, -ишь; *perf* **посели́ть)** *несов перех* (*в местности*) to settle; (*в доме*) to house
▸ **сели́ться** (*perf* **посели́ться)** *несов возв* to settle.
сел|о́ (-а́; *nom pl* **сёла)** *ср* (*селение*) village; (*no pl*; *местность*) the country; **ни к ~у́ ни к го́роду** (*разг*) inappropriately.
сел|ь (-я) *м* mountain torrent.
сельдере́|й (-я) *м* celery.
сельд|ь (-и; *gen pl* **-е́й)** *ж* herring.
сельпо́ *ср нескл* (*= се́льское потреби́тельское о́бщество*) village shop.
се́льск|ий (-ая, -ое, -ие) *прил* (*см сущ*) village *опред*; country *опред*, rural; **се́льское хозя́йство** agriculture.
сельскохозя́йственный *прил* agricultural.
сельча́н|ин (-ина; *nom pl* **-е,** *gen pl* **-)** *м* villager.
сельча́н|ка (-ки; *gen pl* **-ок)** *ж см* **сельча́нин.**
сём *мест см* **сей, сиё.**
сема́нтик|а (-и) *ж* semantics.
семанти́ческ|ий (-ая, -ое, -ие) *прил* semantic.
семафо́р (-а) *м* semaphore.
сёмг|а (-и) *ж* salmon.
семе́йный *прил* family *опред*; **~ челове́к** family man.
семе́йственност|ь (-и) *ж* nepotism.
семе́йств|о (-а) *ср* family.
се́мени *итп сущ см* **се́мя.**
семен|и́ть (-ю́, -и́шь) *несов неперех* to mince.
семенно́й *прил* (*для посева*) seed; (*БИО*) sperm.
семёр|ка (-ки; *gen pl* **-ок)** *ж* (*цифра, карта*) seven; (*группа из семи*) group of seven; (*разг: автобус, трамвай итп*) (number) seven (*bus, tram etc*).
се́мер|о (-ы́х; *как* **че́тверо;** *см* **Table 36b)** *чис* seven; *см также* **дво́е.**
семёрок *сущ см* **семёрка.**
семе́стр (-а) *м* term (*BRIT*), semester (*US*).
се́меч|ки (-ек) *мн* (*БОТ*) sunflower seeds *мн*.
се́меч|ко (-ка; *gen pl* **-ек)** *ср* seed; *см также* **се́мечки.**
семи́ *чис см* **семь.**
семи́десяти *чис см* **се́мьдесят.**
семидесятиле́ти|е (-я) *ср* (*промежуток*) seventy years; (*годовщина*) seventieth anniversary.
семидесятиле́тн|ий (-яя, -ее, -ие) *прил* seventy-year; (*человек*) seventy-year-old.
семидеся́т|ый (-ая, -ое, -ые) *чис* seventieth; *см также* **пятидеся́тый.**
семидне́вный *прил* seven-day.
семикла́ссник (-а) *м* *pupil in seventh year at school (usually 13 years old).*
семикла́ссниц|а (-ы) *ж см* **семикла́ссник.**
семикра́тн|ый *прил*: **~ чемпио́н** seven-times champion; **в ~ом разме́ре** sevenfold.
семиле́ти|е (-я) *ср* (*срок*) seven years; (*годовщина*) seventh anniversary.
семиле́тн|ий (-яя, -ее, -ие) *прил* seven-year; (*ребёнок*) seven-year-old.
семиме́сячный *прил* seven-month; (*ребёнок*) seven-month-old.
семина́р (-а) *м* seminar.
семинари́ст (-а) *м* seminarist.
семина́ри|я (-и) *ж* seminary.
семинеде́льный *прил* seven-week; (*ребёнок*) seven-week-old.
семисо́т *чис см* **семьсо́т.**
семисотле́ти|е (-я) *ср* (*срок*) seven hundred years *мн*; (*годовщина*) seven hundredth anniversary.
семисотле́тн|ий (-яя, -ее, -ие) *прил* (*период*) seven-hundred-year; (*дерево*) seven-hundred-year-old.
семисо́т|ый (-ая, -ое, -ые) *чис* seven hundredth.
семиуго́льник (-а) *м* heptagon.
семичасово́й *прил* (*рабочий день*) seven-hour; (*поезд*) seven o'clock.
семна́дцати *чис см* **семна́дцать.**
семна́дцат|ый (-ая, -ое, -ые) *чис* seventeenth; *см также* **пя́тый.**
семна́дцат|ь (-и; *как* **пять;** *см* **Table 27)** *чис* seventeen; *см также* **пять.**

сему́ *мест см* **сей, сие́**.
сем|ь (**-и́**; *как* **пять**; *см* **Table 27**) *чис* seven; *см также* **пять**.
се́м|ьдесят (**-идесяти**; *как* **пятьдеся́т**; *см* **Table 29**) *чис* seventy; *см также* **пятьдеся́т**.
сем|ьсо́т (**-исо́т**; *как* **пятьсо́т**; *см* **Table 34**) *чис* seven hundred; *см также* **сто**.
се́мью *нареч*: **~ пять** *umn* seven times five *umn*.
семью́ *чис см* **семь**.
семь|я́ (**-и́**; *nom pl* **-и**) *ж* family.
семьяни́н (**-а**) *м* family man.
се́м|я (**-ени**; *как* **вре́мя**; *см* **Table 4**) *ср* (*БОТ*, *также перен*) seed; (*no pl*; *БИО*) semen.
Се́н|а (**-ы**) *ж* Seine.
сена́т (**-а**) *м* senate.
сена́тор (**-а**) *м* senator.
Сенега́л (**-а**) *м* Senegal.
се́н|и (**-ей**) *мн* hall *ед*.
сенн|о́й *прил*: **~а́я лихора́дка** hay fever.
се́н|о (**-а**) *м* hay.
сенова́л (**-а**) *м* hayloft.
сеноко́с (**-а**) *м* (*косьба*) haymaking; (*место*) hayfield.
сенсацио́нный *прил* sensational.
сенса́ци|я (**-и**) *ж* sensation.
сенте́нци|я (**-и**) *ж* maxim.
сентимента́л|ьный (**-ен, -ьна, -ьно**) *прил* sentimental.
сентя́бр|ь (**-я́**) *м* September; *см также* **октя́брь**.
сентя́брьск|ий (**-ая, -ое, -ие**) *прил* September *опред*.
сен|ь (**-и**; *prp sg* **-и́**) *ж* canopy; **под се́нью** *+gen* under the protection of.
сепарати́зм (**-а**) *м* separatism.
сепара́тный *прил* separate.
се́псис (**-а**) *м* septicaemia (*BRIT*), septicemia (*US*).
септи́ческ|ий (**-ая, -ое, -ие**) *прил* septic.
се́р|а (**-ы**) *ж* sulphur (*BRIT*), sulfur (*US*); (*в ушах*) earwax.
серб (**-а**) *м* Serb.
Се́рби|я (**-и**) *ж* Serbia.
се́рб|ка (**-ки**; *gen pl* **-ок**) *ж см* **серб**.
се́рбск|ий (**-ая, -ое, -ие**) *прил* Serbian.
серва́нт (**-а**) *м* buffet unit.
серви́з (**-а**) *м*: **столо́вый/ча́йный ~** dinner/tea service.
сервир|ова́ть (**-у́ю**) *(не)сов перех*: **~ стол** to set *или* lay the table.
се́рвис (**-а**) *м* service (*in shop, restaurant etc*).
серде́ц *umn сущ см* **се́рдце**.
серде́чен *прил см* **серде́чный**.
серде́чник (**-а**) *м* (*ТЕХ*) core; (*разг*): **он ~** he's got a bad heart.
серде́чниц|а (**-ы**) *ж* (*разг*) *см* **серде́чник**.
серде́ч|ный *прил* heart *опред*, cardiac; (*любовный*) loving; (*волнения, обида*) deep-felt; (**-ен, -на, -но**; *человек*) warm-hearted; (*приём, разговор*) cordial; **~ная тоска́** heartache; **серде́чная боле́знь** heart disease; **серде́чный при́ступ** acute angina.
серди́т|ый (**-, -а, -о**) *прил* angry.
серд|и́ть (**-жу́, -дишь**; *perf* **рассерди́ть**) *несов перех* to anger, make angry
▸ **серди́ться** (*perf* **рассерди́ться**) *несов возв*: **~ся (на кого́-н/что-н)** to be angry (with sb/about sth).
сердобо́л|ьный (**-ен, -ьна, -ьно**) *прил* soft-hearted.
сердоли́к (**-а**) *м* carnelian.
се́рд|це (**-ца**; *nom pl* **-ца́**, *gen pl* **-е́ц**, *dat pl* **-ца́м**) *ср* (*также перен*) heart; **в сердца́х** in a fit of temper; **в глубине́ ~ца** in one's heart of hearts; **от всего́ ~ца** from the bottom of one's heart; **принима́ть (приня́ть** *perf*) **что-н бли́зко к ~цу** to take sth to heart; **он мне по́ сердцу** he's a man after my own heart; **у него́ ~ не лежи́т к э́той рабо́те** his heart isn't in the work.
сердцебие́ни|е (**-я**) *ср* (*нормальное*) heartbeat; (*учащённое*) palpitations *мн*.
сердцеви́н|а (**-ы**) *ж* (*стебля, плода*) core; (*перен*: *событий*) heart.
серебри́ст|ый (**-, -а, -о**) *прил* silver(-coloured (*BRIT*) *или* -colored (*US*)); (*перен*: *голос, смех*) silvery.
серебр|и́ть (**-ю́, -и́шь**; *perf* **посеребри́ть**) *несов перех* (*покрыть серебром*) to silver-plate; (*перен*) to turn silver.
серебр|о́ (**-а́**) *ср, собир* silver.
сере́бряник (**-а**) *м* silversmith.
сере́бряный *прил* silver; **сере́бряная сва́дьба** silver wedding (anniversary).
серёг *сущ см* **серьга́**.
середи́н|а (**-ы**) *ж* middle; **в ~е** *+gen* in the middle of.
середи́нный *прил* middle-of-the-road.
серёдк|а (**-и**) *ж* (*разг*) middle.
серёж|ка (**-ки**; *gen pl* **-ек**) *ж уменьш от* **серьга́**; (*БОТ*) catkin.
серена́д|а (**-ы**) *ж* serenade.
сере́|ть (**-ю**; *perf* **посере́ть**) *несов неперех* to turn grey (*BRIT*) *или* gray (*US*); (*no perf*; *цветы*) to show grey.
сержа́нт (**-а**) *м* sergeant.
сержу́(сь) *несов см* **серди́ть(ся)**.
сери́йн|ый *прил*: **~ое произво́дство** serial production; **сери́йный но́мер** serial number.
се́ри|я (**-и**) *ж* series *ед*; (*кинофильма*) part.
се́рн|а (**-ы**) *ж* chamois.
се́рн|ый *прил*: **~ая кислота́** sulphuric (*BRIT*) *или* sulfuric (*US*) acid.
серп (**-а́**) *м* sickle; **лу́нный ~** crescent moon.
серпанти́н (**-а**) *м* (*бумажная лента*) streamer; (*дорога*) sharply winding road (*in the mountains*).
сертифика́т (**-а**) *м* certificate; (*товара*) guarantee (certificate).

се́р|ый *прил* grey (*BRIT*), gray (*US*); (**-, -а́, -о**; *перен*: *погода, жизнь*) grey, drab; (*разг*: *малообразованный*) dim; **се́рый хлеб** brown bread.
сер|ьга́ (**-ьги́**; *nom pl* **-ьги**, *gen pl* **-ёг**, *dat pl* **-ьга́м**) *ж* earring.
серьёзен *прил см* **серьёзный.**
серьёзно *нареч, вводн сл* seriously; **~, ты согла́сен?** do you really agree?
серьёзност|ь (**-и**) *ж* seriousness.
серьёз|ный (**-ен, -на, -но**) *прил* serious.
се́сси|я (**-и**) *ж* (*суда, парламента*) session; (*также:* **экзаменацио́нная ~**) examinations *мн*.
сестр|а́ (**-ы́**; *nom pl* **сёстры**, *gen pl* **сестёр**) *ж* sister; (*также:* **медици́нская ~**) nurse.
сесть (**ся́ду, ся́дешь**; *pt* **сел, се́ла, се́ло**, *impf* **сади́ться**) *сов неперех* to sit down; (*птица, самолёт*) to land; (*солнце, луна*) to go down; (*одежда*) to shrink; (*батарейка, аккумулятор*) to run down; **сади́ться (~ *perf*) в по́езд/на самолёт** to get on a train/plane; **сади́ться (~ *perf*) за руль** to get behind the wheel; **сади́ться (~ *perf*) за рабо́ту** to sit down to work; **сади́ться (~ *perf*) в тюрьму́** to go to prison; **сади́ться (~ *perf*) под аре́ст** to be placed under arrest; **сади́ться (~ *perf*) за стол** to sit down at the table.
сет (**-а**) *м* (*ТЕННИС итп*) set.
се́т|ка (**-ки**; *gen pl* **-ок**) *ж* net; (*разг*: *сумка*) string bag; **тари́фная ~** scale of charges.
се́товани|е (**-я**) *ср* (*обычно мн*) complaint.
се́т|овать (**-ую**; *perf* **посе́товать**) *несов неперех*: **~ на** *+acc* to complain about.
се́ток *сущ см* **се́тка.**
сет|ь (**-и**; *prp sg* **-и́**, *gen pl* **-е́й**) *ж* (*для ловли рыб итп*) net; (*система, также КОМП*) network; **расставля́ть (расста́вить *perf*) кому́-н се́ти** to set a trap for sb; **Сеть** the Net, Internet.
Сеу́л (**-а**) *м* Seoul.
сече́ни|е (**-я**) *ср* (*поперечное, продольное итп*) section; **ке́сарево ~** Caesarean (*BRIT*) *или* Cesarean (*US*) (section).
се́чк|а (**-и**) *ж* (*крупа*) chaff.
сечь (**секу́, сечёшь** *итп*, **секу́т**; *pt* **сёк, секла́, секло́**) *несов перех* (*рубить*) to cut up; (*perf* **вы́сечь**; *розгами итп*) to lash, flog.
се́ял|ка (**-ки**; *gen pl* **-ок**) *ж* seed drill.
се́|ять (**-ю**; *perf* **посе́ять**) *несов перех* (*также перен*) to sow ◆ *неперех* (*no perf*): **~ет дождь** it's drizzling; **~ (посе́ять *perf*) зна́ния/зло** to sow the seeds of knowledge/evil.
СЖ *м сокр* (= *Сою́з журнали́стов*) ≈ NUJ (= *National Union of Journalists*).
сжа́л|иться (**-юсь, ишься**) *сов возв*: **~ (над** *+instr*) to have *или* take pity (on).
сжа́ти|е (**-я**) *ср* (*воздуха, газа*) compression; (*в груди, в горле*) constriction; (*сердца*) contraction.
сжа́т|ый (**-, -а, -о**) *прил* (*воздух, газ*) compressed; (*краткий*) condensed; **в ~ые сро́ки** in a short space of time.
сжать (**сожну́, сожнёшь**) *сов от* **жать** ◆ (**сожму́, сожмёшь**; *impf* **сжима́ть**) *перех* to squeeze; (*воздух, газ*) to compress; (*текст, статью*) to condense; (*срок*) to reduce; **сжима́ть (~ *perf*) зу́бы** to grit one's teeth; **сжима́ть (~ *perf*) гу́бы** to purse one's lips
▸ **сжа́ться** (*impf* **сжима́ться**) *сов возв* (*пружина, губка, воздух*) to contract; (*человек*: *от боли, испуга*) to tense up; (*перен*: *сердце*) to seize up.
сжечь (**сожгу́, сожжёшь** *итп*, **сожгу́т**; *pt* **сжёг, сожгла́, сожгло́**, *impf* **сжига́ть** *или* **жечь**) *сов перех* to burn; (*impf* **сжига́ть**; *перен*: *подлеж*: *страсть, желание*) to consume; (: *солнце*) to scorch; **его́ сжига́ла за́висть** he was consumed with envy; **~ (*perf*) свой корабли́** *или* **за собо́й мосты́** to burn one's boats *или* bridges.
сжива́|ть(ся) (**-ю(сь)**) *несов от* **сжи́ть(ся).**
сживу́(сь) *итп сов см* **сжи́ть(ся).**
сжига́|ть (**-ю**) *несов от* **сжечь.**
сжима́|ть(ся) (**-ю(сь)**) *несов от* **сжа́ть(ся).**
сжи|ть (**-ву́, -вёшь**; *pt* **-л, -ла́, -ло**, *impf* **сжива́ть**) *сов перех*: **~ кого́-н со све́та** *или* **свету́** to drive sb to his *итп* grave.
сжи́|ться (**-ву́сь, -вёшься**; *pt* **-лся, -ла́сь, -лось**, *impf* **сжива́ться**) *сов возв*: **~ с** *+instr* to become close to; (*привыкнуть*) to grow used to; **~ (*perf*) с ро́лью** to get inside a role.
сжу́льнича|ть (**-ю**) *сов от* **жу́льничать.**
сза́ди *нареч* (*подойти*) from behind; (*находиться*) behind ◆ *предл* (*+gen*) behind.
сзыва́|ть (**-ю**) *несов от* **созва́ть.**
си *ср нескл* (*МУЗ*) te.
сиби́рск|ий (**-ая, -ое, -ие**) *прил* Siberian.
Сиби́р|ь (**-и**) *ж* Siberia.
сибиря́к (**-а́**) *м* Siberian.
сибиря́ч|ка (**-ки**; *gen pl* **-ек**) *ж см* **сибиря́к.**
си́вый *прил* (*масть лошади*) grey (*BRIT*), gray (*US*).
сига́р|а (**-ы**) *ж* cigar.
сигаре́т|а (**-ы**) *ж* cigarette.
сигна́л (**-а**) *м* signal; (*АВТ*) horn.
сигнализа́тор (**-а**) *м* signalling device.
сигнализа́ци|я (**-и**) *ж* (*действие*) signalling; (*система*) signalling system; (*в квартире*) burglar alarm; **пожа́рная/автомоби́льная ~** fire/car alarm.
сигнализи́р|овать (**-ую**; *perf* **сигнализи́ровать** *или* **просигнализи́ровать**) *несов неперех*: **~ (о** *+prp*) to signal.
сигна́л|ить (**-ю, -ишь**; *perf* **просигна́лить**) *несов неперех* (*флажками, фарами*) to signal; (*АВТ*) to honk.
сигна́льный *прил* signal *опред*; **сигна́льный экземпля́р** proof copy; **сигна́льная бу́дка** signal box; **сигна́льные огни́** (*АВТ*) indicators.
СИД *м сокр* (= *светоизлуча́ющий дио́д*) LED (= *light-emitting diode*).
сиде́л|ка (**-ки**; *gen pl* **-ок**) *ж* (sick) nurse.
сиде́ни|е (**-я**) *ср* sitting.
сиде́нь|е (**-я**) *ср* seat.
си|де́ть (**-жу́, -ди́шь**) *несов неперех* to sit; (*не*

работать, отдыхать) to sit around; (*одежда*) to fit; ~ *(impf)* **дома** to stay at home; ~ *(impf)* **в тюрьме** to be in prison; ~ *(impf)* **с ребёнком** to look after a child; ~ *(impf)* **без денег/дела** to have no money/nothing to do; **он ~дел за книгой/работой** he was sitting reading a book/ doing his work; ~ *(impf)* **на телефоне** (*разг*) to spend ages on the phone

▸ **сидеться** *безл*: **ему не ~дится на месте/дома** he can't keep still/bear sitting at home.

Сидне|й (-я) *м* Sydney.

сидя *нареч*: **работать/есть** ~ to work/eat sitting down.

сидяч|ий (-ая, -ее, -ие) *прил* (*положение*) sitting *опред*; (*образ жизни*) sedentary; **сидячая забастовка** sit-down strike; **сидячие места** (*разг*) seats *мн*.

сие *мест см* **сей**.

сижу *несов см* **сидеть**.

СИЗО *сокр* = *следственный изолятор*.

сиз|ый (-, -а, -о) *прил* blue-grey (*BRIT*), blue-gray (*US*).

сий *мест см* **сей**.

сил|а (-ы) *ж* strength; (*тока, ветра, закона*) force; (*воли, слова*) power; (*обычно мн*: *душевные, творческие*) energy; **в ~у того, что ...** owing to the fact that ...; **изо всей ~ы** *или* **всех сил** as hard as one can; **от ~ы** (*разг*) at (the) most; **это задание ему по ~м** *или* **под силу** he is capable of (doing) this task; **я не в ~х это сделать** I'm not able to do that; **он всё делает через ~у** it's an effort for him to do anything; **он ест через ~у** he's forcing himself to eat; **вступать (вступить** *perf*) *или* **входить (войти** *perf*) **в ~у** to come into *или* take effect; **терять (потерять** *perf*) *или* **утрачивать (утратить** *perf*) **~у** to cease to be effective; **всё остаётся в ~е** everything will stay as it is; **применять (применить** *perf*) **~у** to use force; *см также* **силы**.

силач (-а) *м* strong man (*мн* men).

силён *прил см* **сильный**.

сил|иться (-юсь, -ишься) *несов возв*: ~ *+infin* to make an effort to do.

силовой *прил* power *опред*; **силовая борьба** wrestling; **силовой приём** throw (*in martial arts*).

силой *нареч* by force.

силос (-а) *м* silage.

силуэт (-а) *м* (*контур*) silhouette; (*одежды*) outline.

сил|ы (-) *мн* forces *мн*; **~ами кого-н** with the help of; **своими ~ами** by o.s.; **производительные** ~ production force; **силы быстрого реагирования** quick-deployment forces.

сильно *нареч* strongly; (*ударить*) hard; (*хотеть, понравиться итп*) very much.

сильнодействующ|ий (-ая, -ее, -ие) *прил* (*лекарство, яд*) powerful.

сил|ьный (-ён, -ьна, -ьно) *прил* strong; (*мороз*) hard; (*впечатление, желание*) powerful; (*шум*) loud; (*дождь*) heavy.

сим *мест см* **сей, сие, сий**.

символ (-а) *м* symbol; (*КОМП*) character.

символизир|овать (-ую) *несов перех* to symbolize.

символизм (-а) *м* (*ИСКУССТВО*) symbolism.

символик|а (-и) *ж* (*символическое значение*) symbolism ◆ *собир* (*военная, морская итп*) symbols *мн*.

символическ|ий (-ая, -ое, -ие) *прил* symbolic.

сими *мест см* **сий**.

симметрическ|ий (-ая, -ое, -ие) *прил* symmetrical.

симметричный *прил* = **симметрический**.

симметри|я (-и) *ж* symmetry.

симпатизир|овать (-ую) *несов неперех*: ~ **кому-н** to like *или* be fond of sb.

симпатич|ный (-ен, -на, -но) *прил* nice, pleasant.

симпати|я (-и) *ж* liking, fondness.

симпозиум (-а) *м* symposium.

симптом (-а) *м* symptom.

симптоматич|ный (-ен, -на, -но) *прил* symptomatic.

симулир|овать (-ую) *(не)сов перех* (*нападение*) to simulate; (*болезнь*) to fake.

симфоническ|ий (-ая, -ое, -ие) *прил* symphonic; **симфонический оркестр** symphony orchestra.

симфони|я (-и) *ж* (*МУЗ*) symphony.

синагог|а (-и) *ж* synagogue.

Сингапур (-а) *м* Singapore.

синдикат (-а) *м* (*ЭКОН*) syndicate.

синдром (-а) *м* (*МЕД*) syndrome.

синев|а (-ы) *ж* (*синий цвет*) blue; (*моря, неба*) blueness.

сине|ть (-ю; *perf* **посинеть**) *несов неперех* to turn blue; (*no perf*; *видняться*) to show blue.

син|ий (-яя, -ее, -ие) *прил* blue; **синий чулок** bluestocking.

син|ить (-ю, -ишь; *perf* **посинить**) *несов перех* (*красить*) to paint blue.

синиц|а (-ы) *ж* tit.

синкретизм (-а) *м* syncretism.

синод (-а) *м* synod.

синоним (-а) *м* synonym.

синонимическ|ий (-ая, -ое, -ие) *прил* synonymous.

синонимi|я (-и) *ж* synonimity.

синоптик (-а) *м* weather forecaster.

синтаксис (-а) *м* syntax.

синтаксическ|ий (-ая, -ое, -ие) *прил* syntactic; **~ая ошибка** (*КОМП*) syntax error.

си́нтез (-а) *м* (*также хим*) synthesis (*мн* syntheses).
синтези́р|овать (-ую) *(не)сов перех* (*также хим*) to synthesize.
синте́тик|а (-и) *ж собир* (*материалы*) synthetic material; (*изделия*) synthetics *мн*.
синтети́ческ|ий (-ая, -ое, -ие) *прил* (*материал*) synthetic.
синхро́нн|ый *прил* (*движение*) synchronous; (*перевод*) simultaneous; **~ое пла́вание** synchronized swimming.
син|ь (-и) *ж* = **синева́**.
си́ньк|а (-и) *ж* blue.
синя́к (-а́) *м* bruise.
сиони́зм (-а) *м* Zionism.
сиони́ст (-а) *м* Zionist.
сип|е́ть (-лю́, -и́шь) *несов неперех* to croak.
си́пл|ый (-, -а́, -о) *прил* hoarse.
сиплю́ *несов см* **сипе́ть**.
си́пн|уть (-у, -ешь; *perf* **оси́пнуть**) *несов неперех* to grow hoarse.
сире́н|а (-ы) *ж* (*гудок*) siren.
сире́невый *прил* lilac.
сире́н|ь (-и) *ж* (*кустарник*) lilac bush ◆ *собир* (*цветы*) lilac.
сири́ек *сущ см* **сири́йка**.
сири́|ец (-йца) *м* Syrian.
сири́|йка (-йки; *gen pl* **-ек**) *ж см* **сири́ец**.
сири́йск|ий (-ая, -ое, -ие) *прил* Syrian.
сири́йца *итп сущ см* **сири́ец**.
Си́ри|я (-и) *ж* Syria.
сиро́п (-а) *м* syrup.
сир|ота́ (-оты́; *nom pl* **-о́ты**) *м/ж* orphan.
сироте́|ть (-ю; *perf* **осироте́ть**) *несов неперех* to be orphaned.
сиротли́в|ый (-, -а, -о) *прил* sad and lonely.
систе́м|а (-ы) *ж* system; (*конструкция*) make; **приводи́ть (привести́** *perf*) **в ~у** to put into order.
систематизи́р|овать (-ую) *(не)сов перех* to order.
системати́ческ|ий (-ая, -ое, -ие) *прил following a defined system*; (*регулярный*) regular.
системати́чный *прил* = **системати́ческий**.
систе́мный *прил relating to or based on a system*; **систе́мный ана́лиз** systems analysis; **систе́мный диск** (*КОМП*) system disk.
си́т|ец (-ца) *м* cotton.
си́теч|ко (-ка; *gen pl* **-ек**) *ср уменьш от* **си́то**; (*для чая*) (tea) strainer.
си́т|о (-а) *ср* sieve.
ситро́ *ср нескл* soft drink.
ситуа́ци|я (-и) *ж* situation.
си́тца *итп сущ см* **си́тец**.
си́тцевый *прил* (*ткань*) cotton.
СИФ *м сокр* c.i.f. (= *cost, insurance, freight*).
си́филис (-а) *м* syphilis.
сифо́н (-а) *м* siphon.
сих *мест см* **сий**.
сицилиа́нск|ий (-ая, -ое, -ие) *прил* Sicilian.
Сици́ли|я (-и) *ж* Sicily.
сию́ *мест см* **сия́**.
сиюмину́т|ный (-ен, -на, -но) *прил* immediate.
сия́ *мест см* **сей**.
сия́ни|е (-я) *ср* (*солнца, луны, глаз*) shining; (*лица*) radiance; (*славы, успеха*) dazzle; **се́верное ~** the Northern lights *мн*.
сия́|ть (-ю) *несов неперех* (*солнце, звезда*) to shine; (*огонь*) to glow; ~ (*impf*) **от сча́стья** to beam with happiness; **ко́мната ~ла чистото́й** the room was spotlessly clean; **же́нщина ~ла красото́й** the woman was dazzlingly beautiful.
сия́ющ|ий (-ая, -ее, -ие) *прил* (*глаза*) shining; (*лицо, улыбка*) beaming; (*человек*) radiant.
СК *м сокр* (= *Союз композиторов*) ≈ MU (= *Musicians' Union*).
скажу́(сь) *итп сов см* **сказа́ть(ся)**.
сказа́ни|е (-я) *ср* legend.
ск|аза́ть (-ажу́, -а́жешь) *сов от* **говори́ть** ◆ *перех*; **~а́жем** (*разг*) let's say; **~ажи́те!** (*разг*) I say!; **как ~** (*разг*) how shall I put it; **кста́ти ~** by the way; **не́чего ~** (*разг*: *действительно*) indeed; **~ажи́те пожа́луйста** could you please tell me; **~ажи́те пожа́луйста!** well I never!; **так ~** so to speak
▸ **сказа́ться** (*impf* **ска́зываться**) *сов возв* (*способности, опыт итп*) to show; (*отразиться*): **~ся на** *+prp* to take its toll on; **ска́зываться (~ся** *perf*) *+instr* (*родственником, журналистом*) to pose as; **ска́зываться (~ся** *perf*) **больны́м** to pretend to be ill (*BRIT*) *или* sick (*US*).
ска́з|ка (-ки; *gen pl* **-ок**) *ж* fairy tale *или* story.
ска́зочен *прил см* **ска́зочный**.
ска́зочник (-а) *м* story teller.
ска́зочниц|а (-ы) *ж см* **ска́зочник**.
ска́зоч|ный *прил* fairy-tale; (**-ен, -на, -но**; *перен*: *необычайный*) fantastic.
сказу́ем|ое (-ого; *decl like adj*) *ср* (*ЛИНГ*) predicate.
ска́зыва|ться (-юсь) *несов от* **сказа́ться**.
скак *м*: **на (всём) ~у́** at top speed.
скака́л|ка (-ки; *gen pl* **-ок**) *ж* skipping rope.
ск|ака́ть (-ачу́, -а́чешь) *несов неперех* (*человек*) to skip; (*животное*) to hop; (*мяч*) to bounce; (*разг*: *температура, цены итп*) to rise and fall; (*лошадь, всадник*) to gallop.
скакн|у́ть (-у́, -ёшь) *сов неперех* to leap.
скаков|о́й *прил*: **~а́я ло́шадь** racehorse; **скаковы́е соревнова́ния** race meeting.
скаку́н (-а́) *м* racehorse.
ск|ала́ (-алы́; *nom pl* **-а́лы**) *ж* cliff.
скаламбу́р|ить (-ю, -ишь) *сов от* **каламбу́рить**.
скали́ст|ый *прил* rocky; **С~ые го́ры** the Rocky Mountains *или* Rockies.
ска́л|ить (-ю, -ишь; *perf* **оска́лить**) *несов перех*: **~ зу́бы** to bare one's teeth
▸ **ска́литься** (*perf* **оска́литься**) *несов возв* to bare one's teeth.
ска́л|ка (-ки; *gen pl* **-ок**) *ж* (*КУЛИН*) rolling-pin.
скалола́з (-а) *м* rock-climber.

скалола́зани|е (-я) *ср* rock-climbing.
ска́лыва|ть (-ю) *несов от* **сколо́ть.**
скалькиро́|вать (-ую) *сов от* **калькирова́ть.**
ска́льпел|ь (-я) *м* scalpel.
скаме́|йка (-йки; *gen pl* -ек) *ж* bench.
скам|ья́ (-ьи́; *gen pl* -е́й) *ж* (*для сидения*) bench; ~ **подсуди́мых** (*ЮР*) the dock; **сесть** (*perf*) **на ~ью́ подсуди́мых** to stand trial; **со шко́льной/студе́нческой ~ьи́** from one's school/student days.
сканда́л (-а) *м* (*политический*) scandal; (*ссора*) quarrel.
сканда́лен *прил см* **сканда́льный.**
скандализи́р|овать (-ую) *(не)сов перех* to scandalize.
скандали́ст (-а) *м* troublemaker.
скандали́ст|ка (-ки; *gen pl* -ок) *ж см* **скандали́ст.**
сканда́л|ить (-ю, -ишь; *perf* **насканда́лить**) *несов неперех* to quarrel.
сканда́л|ьный (-ен, -ьна, -ьно) *прил* (*история, поступок*) scandalous; (*no short form*; *человек*) quarrelsome.
сканди́р|овать (-ую) *(не)сов перех* (*подлеж: толпа итп*) to chant.
ска́нер (-а) *м* scanner.
ска́плива|ть(ся) (-ю(сь)) *несов от* **скопи́ть(ся).**
скарб (-а) *м собир* (*разг*: *вещи*) stuff.
ска́ред|ный (-ен, -на, -но) *прил* (*разг*) mingy.
скарлати́н|а (-ы) *ж* scarlet fever.
ска́рмлива|ть (-ю) *несов от* **скорми́ть.**
скат (-а) *м* slope; (*АВТ*: *колесо*) wheel; (*ось*) axle.
ската́|ть (-ю) *сов от* **ката́ть** ◆ (*impf* **ска́тывать**) *перех* to roll up.
ска́терт|ь (-и; *gen pl* -е́й) *ж* tablecloth; **~ю доро́га** (*разг*) good riddance.
с|кати́ть (-ачу́, -а́тишь; *impf* **ска́тывать**) *сов перех* to roll down
▸ **скати́ться** (*impf* **ска́тываться**) *сов возв* (*слеза*) to roll down; (*перен*): **~ся к** *+dat*/**на** *+acc* to slide towards/into; **~ся** (*perf*) **на лы́жах/на са́нях** to ski/sledge down.
ска́тыва|ть (-ю) *несов от* **ската́ть, скати́ть**
▸ **ска́тываться** *несов от* **скати́ться.**
скафа́ндр (-а) *м* (*водолаза*) diving suit; (*космонавта*) spacesuit.
ска́чек *итп сущ см* **ска́чки.**
ска́чк|а (-и) *ж* galloping.
скачка́ *итп сущ см* **скачо́к.**
ска́ч|ки (-ек) *мн* the races *мн.*
скач|о́к (-ка́) *м* leap.
скачу́(сь) *сов см* **скати́ть(ся).**
скачу́ *итп несов см* **скака́ть.**
ска́шива|ть (-ю) *несов от* **скоси́ть.**
СКВ *ж сокр* (= *свобо́дно конверти́руемая валю́та*) convertible currency.
сква́жин|а (-ы) *ж* (*нефтяная, газовая*) well; **замо́чная** ~ keyhole; **бурова́я** ~ borehole.
сквер (-а) *м* *small public garden.*
скве́рен *прил см* **скве́рный.**
скверносло́ви|е (-я) *ср* foul language.
скверносло́в|ить (-лю, -ишь) *несов неперех* to use foul language.
скве́р|ный (-ен, -на́, -но) *прил* foul; (*история, поступок*) nasty.
сквита́|ться (-юсь) *сов возв*: **~ (с** *+instr*) (*отомстить*) to get even (with); (*рассчитаться*) to pay in full.
сквоз|и́ть (*3sg* -и́т, *3pl* -я́т) *несов неперех* (*чувство*) to show ◆ *безл*: **здесь ~и́т** it's draughty here.
сквозн|о́й *прил* (*поезд*) through *опред*; **он получи́л ~у́ю ра́ну** the bullet has gone right through him; ~ **ве́тер** crosswinds *мн.*
сквозня́к (-а́) *м* (*в комнате*) draught (*BRIT*), draft (*US*).
сквозь *предл* (*+acc*) through; **я слы́шал что́-то ~ сон** I heard something in my sleep.
сквор|е́ц (-ца́) *м* starling.
скворе́чник (-а) *м* nesting box.
скворца́ *итп сущ см* **скворе́ц.**
скеле́т (-а) *м* (*также перен*) skeleton.
ске́псис (-а) *м* scepticism.
ске́птик (-а) *м* sceptic.
скептици́зм (-а) *м* scepticism.
скепти́ческ|ий (-ая, -ое, -ие) *прил* sceptical.
ски́д|ка (-ки; *gen pl* -ок) *ж* (*с цены*) discount, reduction; **де́лать (сде́лать** *perf*) **~ку на что-н** to make an allowance for sth; **со ~кой на что-н** taking sth into account; **нало́говая** ~ tax allowance.
ски́н|уть (-у, -ешь; *impf* **ски́дывать**) *сов перех* (*сбросить*) to throw down; (: *одежду, одеяло*) to throw off; (*разг*: *с цены*) to knock off
▸ **ски́нуться** *сов возв* (*разг*) to have a whip-round.
ски́петр (-а) *м* sceptre (*BRIT*), scepter (*US*).
скирд|а́ (-ы́) *ж* stack.
ски́с|нуть (-ну, -нешь; *pt* -, -ла, -ло) *сов от* **ки́снуть** ◆ (*impf* **скиса́ть**) *неперех* to turn sour; (*перен*: *разг*) to lose interest.
скита́л|ец (-ьца) *м* wanderer.
скита́ни|е (-я) *ср* wandering.
скита́|ться (-юсь) *несов возв* to wander.
склад (-а) *м* (*помещение*: *товарный*) store; (*жизни*) way; (*оружия итп*) cache; **~ ума́** mentality; ~ **боеприпа́сов** ammunition dump.
скла́ден *прил см* **скла́дный.**
складир|овать (-ую) *(не)сов перех* to store.
скла́д|ка (-ки; *gen pl* -ок) *ж* (*на одежде*) pleat; (*на лице*) furrow; (*на ткани*) crease; **ю́бка в ~ку** *или* **со ~ми** pleated skirt.
складн|о́й *прил* folding.
скла́д|ный (-ен, -на, -но) *прил* (*статный*) well-built; (*связный*) coherent.

скла́док *сущ см* **скла́дка.**
складско́й *прил* storage *опред.*
скла́дчин|а (**-ы**) *ж* (*сбор*) pool; **купи́ть** *(perf)* **что-н в ~у** to pool together to buy sth.
скла́дывани|е (**-я**) *ср* (*действие: предметов*) stacking; (*чисел*) addition.
скла́дыва|ть(ся) (**-ю(сь)**) *несов от* **сложи́ть(ся).**
скле́|ить (**-ю, -ишь**) *сов от* **кле́ить** ♦ (*impf* **скле́ивать**) *перех* to glue together.
склеп (**-а**) *м* crypt.
склепа́|ть (**-ю**) *сов от* **клепа́ть.**
склеро́з (**-а**) *м* (*сосудов, лёгких*) sclerosis; **~ мо́зга** senility.
склеро́зный *прил* sclerotic.
склеро́тик (**-а**) *м* sclerotic.
склероти́ческ|ий (**-ая, -ое, -ие**) *прил* = **склеро́зный.**
скло́к|а (**-и**) *ж* squabble.
склон (**-а**) *м* slope; **на скло́не лет** *или* **жи́зни** *или* **дней** in one's later life.
скло́нен *прил см* **скло́нный.**
склоне́ни|е (**-я**) *ср* (*линг*) declension.
скл|они́ть (**-оню́, -о́нишь**; *impf* **склоня́ть**) *сов перех* (*опустить*) to lower; **склоня́ть** (**~** *perf*) **кого́-н к побе́гу/на преступле́ние** to talk sb into escaping/committing a crime; **я ~они́л её на свою́ сто́рону** I talked her over to my side
▸ **склони́ться** (*impf* **склоня́ться**) *сов возв* (*нагнуться*) to bend; (*перен*): **~ся к** *+dat* to come round to.
скло́нност|ь (**-и**) *ж*: **~ к** *+dat* (*к музыке, к математике*) aptitude for; (*к меланхолии, к полноте*) tendency to.
скло́н|ный (**-ен, -на́, -но**) *прил*: **~ к** *+dat* (*к простудам*) prone *или* susceptible to; **~** *+infin* (*согласиться, помириться*) inclined to do; **он ~ен к фи́зике** he has an aptitude for physics.
склоня́емый *прил* declinable.
склоня́|ть (**-ю**) *несов от* **склони́ть** ♦ (*perf* **просклоня́ть**) *перех* (*линг*) to decline; **~** *(impf)* **кого́-н** to talk about sb a lot
▸ **склоня́ться** *несов от* **склони́ться** ♦ *возв* (*линг*) to decline.
скло́чен *прил см* **скло́чный.**
скло́чник (**-а**) *м* (*разг*) quarrelsome man (*мн* men).
скло́чница (**-ы**) *ж* (*разг*) quarrelsome woman (*мн* women).
скло́ч|ный (**-ен, -на, -но**) *прил* quarrelsome.
скля́н|ка (**-ки**; *gen pl* **-ок**) *ж* (*разг: сосуд*) bottle.
ск|оба́ (**-обы́**; *nom pl* **-о́бы**) *ж* (*для опоры, для держания*) clamp; (*для крепления*) staple.
ско́б|ка (**-ки**; *gen pl* **-ок**) *ж уменьш от* **скоба́**; (*обычно мн: знак*) bracket, parentheses *мн*; **кру́глые/квадра́тные ~ки** round/square brackets; **брать** (**взять** *perf*) **сло́во в ~ки** to put a word in brackets *или* parentheses.
скобл|и́ть (**-ю́, -и́шь**) *несов перех* to scrape.
ско́бок *сущ см* **ско́бка.**
ско́ван|ный (**-, -на, -но**) *прил* (*человек, движения*) inhibited.
ск|ова́ть (**-ую́**) *сов от* **кова́ть** ♦ (*impf* **ско́вывать**) *перех* (*соединить*) to weld together; **страх ~ова́л его́** he was paralysed with fear; **лёд ~ова́л ре́ку** the river froze over.
сковород|а́ (**-ы́**; *nom pl* **ско́вороды**) *ж* frying-pan (*BRIT*), skillet (*US*).
сковоро́д|ка (**-ки**; *gen pl* **-ок**) *ж* = **сковорода́.**
ско́выва|ть (**-ю**) *несов от* **скова́ть.**
скол|оти́ть (**-очу́, -о́тишь**; *impf* **скола́чивать**) *сов перех* to hammer together; (*разг: банду, капитал*) to get together.
ск|оло́ть (**-олю́, -о́лешь**; *impf* **ска́лывать**) *сов перех* (*снять*) to chop off; (*соединить*) to pin together.
сколочу́ *сов см* **сколоти́ть.**
сколь *нареч* (*как*) how; (*возможно*) as much as; **~ ... сто́ль (же)** ... as much ... as ....
сколь|зи́ть (**-жу́, -зи́шь**) *несов неперех* to glide; (*теряя устойчивость*) to slide.
ско́льз|кий (**-кая, -кое, -кие; -ок, -ка, -ко**) *прил* slippery; (*ситуация, тема*) tricky; (*вопрос*) sensitive.
скользн|у́ть (**-у́, -ёшь**) *сов неперех* to glide; (*быстро пройти*) to slip.
ско́льзок *прил см* **ско́льзкий.**
скользя́щ|ий (**-ая, -ее, -ие**) *прил* (*шаг*) gliding; (*непостоянный*) flexible.

KEYWORD

ско́льк|о (**-их**) *местоимённое нареч* ***1*** (*+gen*; *книг, часов, дней итп*) how many; (*сахара, сил, работы итп*) how much; **ско́лько люде́й пришло́?** how many people came?; **ско́лько де́нег тебе́ на́до?** how much money do you need?; **ско́лько э́то сто́ит?** how much is it?; **ско́лько тебе́ лет?** how old are you?
2 (*относительное*) as much; **бери́, ско́лько хо́чешь** take as much as you want; **ско́лько уго́дно** as much as you like
♦ *нареч* ***1*** (*насколько*) as far as; **ско́лько по́мню, он всегда́ был агресси́вный** as far as I remember, he was always aggressive
2 (*много*): **ско́лько люде́й!** what a lot of people!; **ско́лько вре́мени он отня́л у нас!** what a long time he has kept us!; **не сто́лько ... ско́лько** ... not so much ... as ....

скома́нд|овать (**-ую**) *сов от* **кома́ндовать.**
скомбини́р|овать (**-ую**) *сов от* **комбини́ровать.**
ско́мка|ть (**-ю**) *сов от* **ко́мкать.**
скоморо́х (**-а**) *м* (*комедиант*) mummer; (*перен*) buffoon.
скомпили́р|овать (**-ую**) *сов от* **компили́ровать.**
скомплект|ова́ть (**-у́ю**) *сов от* **комплектова́ть.**
скомпон|ова́ть (**-у́ю**) *сов от* **компонова́ть.**
скомпромети́р|овать (**-ую**) *сов от* **компромети́ровать.**
сконструи́р|овать (**-ую**) *сов от*

конструи́ровать.
сконфу́|зить(ся) (**-жу(сь), -зишь(ся)**) *сов от* **конфу́зить(ся)**.
сконцентри́р|овать(ся) (**-ую(сь)**) *сов от* **концентри́ровать(ся)**.
сконча́ни|е (**-я**) *ср*: **до ~я ве́ка** to the end of time.
сконча́|ться (**-юсь**) *сов возв* to pass away.
скоордини́р|овать (**-ую**) *сов от* **координи́ровать**.
скопидо́м (**-а**) *м* miser.
скопи́р|овать (**-ую**) *сов от* **копи́ровать**.
скоп|и́ть(ся) (**-лю́(сь), -ишь(ся)**) *сов от* **копи́ть(ся)**.
ско́пищ|е (**-а**) *ср* horde.
скопле́ни|е (**-я**) *ср* (*людей, предметов*) mass.
скоплю́(сь) *сов см* **скопи́ть(ся)**.
ско́пом *нареч* (*разг*) in a crowd.
ско́р|ая (**-ой**; *decl like adj*) *ж* (*разг*: *также*: **~ по́мощь**) ambulance.
ско́рбен *прил см* **ско́рбный**.
скорб|е́ть (**-лю́, -и́шь**) *несов неперех*: **~ о** *+prp* to grieve for.
ско́рб|ный (**-ен, -на, -но**) *прил* sorrowful; **в ~ную мину́ту** at a time of sorrow.
скорб|ь (**-и**; *gen pl* **-е́й**) *ж* grief.
скоре́е *сравн прил от* **ско́рый** ◆ *сравн нареч от* **ско́ро** ◆ *част* rather; **~...чем** *или* **нежели** (*в большей степени*) more likely ... than; (*лучше, охотнее*) rather ... than; **~ всего́ они́ до́ма** it's most likely they'll be (at) home; **~ всего он сего́дня не придёт** he is most unlikely to come today; **~ бы он верну́лся** I wish he would come back soon.
скорл|упа́ (**-упы́**; *nom pl* **-у́пы**) *ж* shell; **яи́чная ~** eggshell; **оре́ховая ~** nutshell.
скорм|и́ть (**-лю́, -ишь**; *impf* **ска́рмливать**) *сов перех*: **~ что-н кому́-н** to feed sth to sb.
скорня́ж|ный *прил*: **~ая мастерская** furrier's workshop; **~ое де́ло** furriery.
скорня́к (**-а́**) *м* furrier.
ско́ро *нареч* soon ◆ *как сказ* it's soon; **~ зима́** it will soon be winter; **я ~ верну́сь** I will be back soon.
скорова́р|ка (**-ки**; *gen pl* **-ок**) *ж* pressure cooker.
скорогово́р|ка (**-ки**; *gen pl* **-ок**) *ж* tongue-twister; (*быстрая речь*) gabble.
скоро́мн|ый *прил*: **~ая пи́ща** *food forbidden on fasting days.*
скоропали́тел|ьный (**-ен, -ьна, -ьно**) *прил* hasty.
скоропо́ртящ|ийся (**-аяся, -ееся, -иеся**) *прил* (*кулин*) perishable.
скоропости́ж|ный (**-ен, -на, -но**) *прил*: **~ная смерть** sudden death.
скоропе́лый *прил* (*БОТ*) early.
скоростно́й *прил* (*поезд*) high-speed; (*строительство*) speedy.

ско́рост|ь (**-и**; *gen pl* **-е́й**) *ж* speed; (*физ*) velocity; **со ~ю 5 киломе́тров в час** at (a speed of) 5 kilometres (*BRIT*) *или* kilometers (*US*) per hour; **на (большо́й) ~и** at (great) speed; **~ переда́чи (в бо́дах)** (*КОМП*) baud rate.
скорошива́тел|ь (**-я**) *м* (loose-leaf) binder.
скорота́|ть (**-ю**) *сов от* **корота́ть**.
скороте́ч|ный (**ен, -на, -но**) *прил* short-lived.
скорпио́н (**-а**) *м* scorpion; (*созвездие*): **С~** Scorpio.
скорректи́р|овать (**-ую**) *сов от* **корректи́ровать**.
ско́рч|ить(ся) (**-у(сь), -ишь(ся)**) *сов от* **ко́рчить(ся)**.
ско́р|ый (**-, -а́, -о**) *прил* (*езда, движение*) fast; (*разлука, визит*) impending; **до ~ого свида́ния** see you soon; **в ~ом вре́мени** shortly; **пригото́вить** *(perf)* **что-н на ~ую ру́ку** to rustle sth up; **ско́рая по́мощь** (*учреждение*) ambulance service; (*автомашина*) ambulance; **ско́рый по́езд** express (train).
скос (**-а**) *м* (*скошенная сторона*) slant; (*склон*) slope.
ск|оси́ть (**-ошу́, -о́сишь**) *сов от* **коси́ть** ◆ (*impf* **ска́шивать**) *перех* (*траву*) to mow; (*пшеницу*) to reap; (*крышу*) to set on a slant; **ска́шивать** *или* **коси́ть** (**~** *perf*) **глаза́** to squint
▸ **скоси́ться** *сов от* **коси́ться**.
скот (**-а́**) *м собир* livestock; (*перен*: *разг*) animal; **моло́чный/мясно́й ~** dairy/beef cattle.
скоти́н|а (**-ы**) *ж собир* livestock ◆ *ж* (*разг*: *человек*) swine.
ско́тник (**-а**) *м* herdsman (*мн* herdsmen).
ско́тница (**-ы**) *ж* dairy maid.
ско́тный *прил*: **~ двор** cattle-yard.
скотово́дств|о (**-а**) *ср* livestock farming.
ско́тск|ий (**-ая, -ое, -ие**) *прил* (*подлый*) beastly; (*грязный*) bestial.
скошу́ *сов см* **скоси́ть**.
скра́дыва|ть (*3sg* **-ет**, *3pl* **-ют**) *несов перех* (*звуки*) to keep out; (*полноту, морщины*) to conceal.
скра́|сить (**-шу, -сишь**; *impf* **скра́шивать**) *сов перех* to ease.
скрёб(ся) *итп несов см* **скрести́(сь)**.
скреб|о́к (**-ка́**) *м* scraper.
скребу́(сь) *итп несов см* **скрести́(сь)**.
скре́жет (**-а**) *м* (*металла*) grating; (*колёс*) screech.
скреж|ета́ть (**-ещу́, -е́щешь**) *несов неперех* (*что-н металлическое*) to grate; **~** *(impf)* **зуба́ми** to grate one's teeth.
скреп|и́ть (**-лю́, -и́шь**; *impf* **скрепля́ть**) *сов перех* (*соединить*) to fasten together; (*перен*: *дружбу*) to strengthen; (*удостоверить*) to endorse; **~я се́рдце** reluctantly.
скре́п|ка (**-ки**; *gen pl* **-ок**) *ж* paperclip.
скреплю́ *сов см* **скрепи́ть**.

скрепля́|ть (-ю) *несов от* **скрепи́ть.**
скре́пок *сущ см* **скре́пка.**
скр|ести́ (**-ебу́, -ебёшь**; *pt* **-ёб, -ебла́, -ебло́**) *несов неперех* (*мышь, кошка*) to scratch ◆ *перех* (*сковородку*) to scour; (*дерево*) to sand; **~ебёт на душе́** *или* **на се́рдце** he *umn* has a nagging feeling inside
▸ **скрести́сь** *несов возв* (*мышь*) to scratch about; **соба́ка ~ебётся в дверь** the dog is scratching at the door.
скре|сти́ть (**-щу́, -сти́шь**; *impf* **скре́щивать**) *сов перех* to cross
▸ **скрести́ться** (*impf* **скре́щиваться**) *сов возв* to cross; (*перен*: *интересы, устремления*) to clash.
скреще́ни|е (**-я**) *ср* crossing; (*интересов*) clash; ~ **доро́г** crossroads.
скре́щивани|е (**-я**) *ср* cross-breeding.
скре́щива|ть(ся) (**-ю(сь)**) *несов от* **скрести́ть(ся).**
скрещу́(сь) *сов см* **скрести́ть(ся).**
скрив|и́ть(ся) (**-лю́(сь), -и́шь(ся)**) *сов от* **криви́ть(ся).**
скрип (**-а**) *м* (*двери, пола*) creak; (*металла*) grate; (*снега*) crunch; **со скри́пом** (*перен*: *разг*) with a struggle.
скрипа́ч (**-а́**) *м* violinist.
скрипа́ч|ка (**-ки**; *gen pl* **-ек**) *ж см* **скрипа́ч.**
скрип|е́ть (**-лю́, -и́шь**) *несов неперех* to creak; (*перен*: *разг*) to struggle along.
скри́п|ка (**-ки**; *gen pl* **-ок**) *ж* violin; (*в народной музыке*) fiddle; **пе́рвая** ~ (*в оркестре*) first violin; (*в деле*) first fiddle.
скриплю́ *несов см* **скрипе́ть.**
скри́пок *сущ см* **скри́пка.**
скрипу́ч|ий (**-ая, -ее, -ие**) *прил* (*дверь, пол*) creaky; (*голос*) croaky.
скро|и́ть (**-ю́, -и́шь**) *сов от* **кро́ить.**
скро́мен *прил см* **скро́мный.**
скро́мник (**-а**) *м* (*разг*) modest lad (*BRIT*) *или* guy (*US*).
скро́мниц|а (**-ы**) *ж* (*разг*) modest girl.
скро́мност|ь (**-и**) *ж* modesty; (*одежды umn*) plainness.
скро́м|ный (**-ен, -на́, -но**) *прил* modest; (*служащий, должность*) humble.
скро́ю(сь) *umn сов см* **скры́ть(ся).**
скрупулёз|ный (**-ен, -на, -но**) *прил* scrupulous.
скр|ути́ть (**-учу́, -у́тишь**) *сов от* **крути́ть** ◆ (*impf* **скру́чивать**) *перех* (*провода, волосы*) to twist together; (*разг*: *арестованного*) to tie up; (: *подлеж*: *болезнь, горе*) to take a grip
▸ **скрути́ться** *сов возв* to twist together.
скрыва́|ть (**-ю**) *несов от* **скрыть**
▸ **скрыва́ться** *несов от* **скры́ться** ◆ *возв* (*от полиции, от властей*) to hide; (*раздражение в голосе*) to lurk; **~ся** (*impf*) **под чужи́м и́менем** to hide behind another name.
скры́т|ный (**-ен, -на, -но**) *прил* secretive; (*возможности*) potent.
скры́тый *прил* (*смысл, возможности umn*) hidden; (*ненависть, оппозиция*) secret; **скры́тая ка́мера** *или* **съёмка** hidden camera.
скр|ыть (**-о́ю, -о́ешь**; *impf* **скрыва́ть**) *сов перех* (*спрятать*) to hide; (*факты*) to conceal
▸ **скры́ться** (*impf* **скрыва́ться**) *сов возв* (*от дождя, от погони*) to take cover; (*солнце, луна*) to disappear; **от него́ ничего́ не ~о́ется** nothing escapes him.
скрю́ч|ить (**-у, -ишь**) *сов от* **крю́чить** ◆ (*impf* **скрю́чивать**) *перех* to bend
▸ **скрю́читься** *сов от* **крю́читься** ◆ (*impf* **скрю́чиваться**) *возв* to be stooped.
скря́г|а (**-и**) *м/ж* (*разг*) skinflint.
ску́ден *прил см* **ску́дный.**
скуде́|ть (**-ю**; *perf* **оскуде́ть**) *несов неперех* to run thin.
ску́д|ный (**-ен, -на́, -но**) *прил* (*запасы, средства*) meagre (*BRIT*), meager (*US*); (*язык, сведения*) limited; (*растительность*) sparse; ~ *+instr* (*событиями, витаминами*) lacking in.
ску́к|а (**-и**) *ж* boredom; **там ужа́сная** ~ it's dreadfully boring there.
ск|ула́ (**-улы́**; *nom pl* **-у́лы**) *ж* (*обычно мн*) cheekbone.
скула́ст|ый (**-, -а, -о**) *прил*: **~ое лицо́** a face with prominent cheekbones.
скул|и́ть (**-ю́, -и́шь**) *несов неперех* to whine.
ску́льптор (**-а**) *м* sculptor.
скульпту́р|а (**-ы**) *ж* sculpture.
ску́мбри|я (**-и**) *ж* mackerel.
скупа́|ть (**-ю**) *несов от* **скупи́ть** ◆ *перех* (*для перепродажи*) to buy up; (*краденное*) to buy.
ск|упи́ть (**-уплю́, -у́пишь**; *impf* **скупа́ть**) *сов перех* to buy up.
скуп|и́ться (**-лю́сь, -и́шься**; *perf* **поскупи́ться**) *несов возв*: ~ **на** *+acc* to skimp on; **он не ~и́тся на обеща́ния/комплиме́нты** he's generous with his promises/compliments.
ску́пк|а (**-и**) *ж* (*действие*) buying up; (*магазин*) second-hand shop.
скуплю́ *сов см* **скупи́ть.**
скуп|о́й (**-, -á, -о**) *прил* mean; (*свет*) dim; (*речь*) terse; (*растительность*) sparse; **он скуп на де́ньги/похвалу́** he's sparing with money/ praise.
ску́почный *прил*: ~ **магази́н** second-hand shop; ~ **пункт** collection point.
ску́пщик (**-а**) *м* buyer.
скуфь|я́ (**-и́**; *gen pl* **-е́й**) *ж tall hat worn by Orthodox priests.*
скуча́|ть (**-ю**) *несов неперех* to be bored; (*тосковать*): ~ **по** *+dat или* **о** *+prp* to miss.
ску́чен *прил см* **ску́чный.**
ску́чно *нареч* (*жить, рассказывать umn*) boringly ◆ *как сказ*: **здесь** ~ it's boring here; **мы о́чень ~ живём** we lead a boring life; **как** ~! oh, how boring!; **на уро́ке бы́ло** ~ the lesson was boring; **мне** ~ I'm bored.
ску́ч|ный (**-ен, -на́, -но**) *прил* (*человек, жизнь umn*) boring, dreary; (*испытывающий скуку*: *человек, голос umn*) bored.

ску́ша|ть (-ю) *сов от* **ку́шать.**
слабе́|ть (-ю; *perf* **ослабе́ть)** *несов неперех* (*человек*) to grow weak; (*здоровье, интерес итп*) to weaken; (*мороз*) to ease off; (*ветер*) to drop; (*дисциплина*) to slacken.
слаби́тельн|ое (-ого; *decl like adj*) *ср* laxative.
слаби́тельный *прил* laxative.
сла́б|ить (*3sg* **-ит**) *несов перех*: **~ кого́-н** to give sb diarrhoea (*BRIT*) *или* diarrhea (*US*); **его́ ~ит** he has diarrhoea.
сла́б|нуть (-ну, -нешь; *perf* **осла́бнуть)** *несов* = **слабе́ть.**
сла́бо *нареч* (*вскрикнуть*) weakly; (*нажать*) lightly; (*знать*) badly.
слабово́л|ьный (-ен, -ьна, -ьно) *прил* weak-willed.
сла́бост|ь (-и) *ж* weakness; (*голоса*) feebleness; (*дисциплины*) slackness; (*пристрастие*): **~ к** *+dat* weakness for.
слабоу́мный *прил* feeble-minded.
слабохара́ктер|ный (-ен, -на, -но) *прил* weak.
сла́б|ый (-, -а́, -о) *прил* weak; (*ветер*) light; (*голос*) feeble; (*знания, доказательство итп*) poor; (*резинка, дисциплина итп*) slack; **сла́бая сторона́, сла́бое ме́сто** weak spot.
сла́в|а (-ы) *ж* (*героя*) glory; (*писателя, актёра итп*) fame; (*дурная, хорошая*) repute; (*разг*: *слухи*) rumour (*BRIT*), rumor (*US*); **во ~у** *+gen* to the greater glory of; **на ~у** splendidly; **~ Бо́гу!** thank God!
сла́вен *прил см* **сла́вный.**
слави́р|овать (-ую) *сов от* **лави́ровать.**
сла́в|ить (-лю, -ишь) *несов от* **просла́вить ♦** *перех* (*героев*) to glorify
▸ **сла́виться** *несов возв*: **~ся** *+instr* to be renowned for.
сла́в|ный (-ен, -на́, -но) *прил* (*человек, отдых*) pleasant; (*подвиг, имя*) famous.
славосло́в|ить (-лю, -ишь) *несов перех* to extol.
слав|яни́н (-яни́на; *nom pl* **-я́не,** *gen pl* **-я́н)** *м* Slav.
славя́н|ка (-ки; *gen pl* **-ок)** *ж см* **славяни́н.**
славя́нск|ий (-ая, -ое, -ие) *прил* Slavonic.
слага́ем|ое (-ого; *decl like adj*) *ср* (*MAT*) item; (*успеха*) component.
слага́|ть (-ю) *несов от* **сложи́ть.**
сла́|дить (-жу, -дишь; *impf* **сла́живать)** *сов неперех*: **~ с** *+instr* (*с машиной, с лошадью*) to handle; (*с ребёнком*) to cope with.
сла́д|кий (-кая, -кое, -кие; -ок, -ка́, -ко) *прил* sweet; (*жизнь*) pleasant.
сла́дко *нареч* (*пахнуть*) sweet; (*спать*) deeply; (*улыбаться*) sweetly; **♦** *как сказ безл*: **во рту ~** I am left with a sweet taste in my mouth; **мне здесь не ~** (*разг*) I can't stand it here.
сла́дк|ое (-ого; *decl like adj*) *ср* sweet things *мн*; (*разг*: *десерт*) afters (*BRIT*), dessert (*US*); **что сего́дня на ~?** what's for afters today?
сладкое́ж|ка (-ки; *gen pl* **-ек)** *м/ж* (*разг*) = **сластёна.**
сла́док *прил см* **сла́дкий.**
сла́достен *прил см* **сла́достный.**
сла́дост|и (-ей) *мн* sweet things *мн*.
сла́дост|ный (-ен, -на, -но) *прил* sweet.
сладостра́ст|ный (-ен, -на, -но) *прил* sensual.
сла́дост|ь (-и) *ж* (*см прил*) sweetness; pleasantness; *см также* **сла́дости.**
сла́жен|ный (-, -на, -но) *прил* orderly.
сла́жива|ть (-ю) *несов от* **сла́дить.**
сла́жу *сов от* **сла́дить.**
сла́|зить (-жу, -зишь) *сов неперех* to climb.
слайд (-а) *м* (*ФОТО*) slide.
сла́лом (-а) *м* slalom; **гига́нтский ~** giant slalom.
слаломи́ст (-а) *м* slalom skier.
сластён|а (-ы) *м/ж*: **он/она́ ~** he/she has a sweet tooth.
сла|сти́ть (-щу́, -сти́шь) *несов перех* to sweeten.
слать (шлю́, шлёшь) *несов перех* to send.
слаща́в|ый (-, -а, -о) *прил* sugary.
сла́ще *сравн прил от* **сла́дкий ♦** *сравн нареч от* **сла́дко.**
слащу́ *сов см* **сласти́ть.**
сле́ва *нареч* on the left.
слёг *итп сов см* **слечь.**
слегка́ *нареч* slightly.
след (-а; *nom pl* **-ы́)** *м* trace; (*колес*) track; (*перен*) sign; (*ноги*) footprint; **пре́жней уста́лости и ~а́ нет** all traces of my earlier tiredness have gone; **напада́ть (напа́сть** *perf*) **на чей-н ~** (*также перен*) to get on sb's trail.
сле|ди́ть (-жу́, -ди́шь) *несов неперех*: **~ за** *+instr* to follow; (*заботиться*) to take care of; (*за шпионом*) to watch; (*perf* **наследи́ть;** *грязными ногами*) to leave a trail; **~** (*impf*) **за собо́й** to take care of o.s..
сле́довани|е (-я) *ср* (*моде, советам итп*) following; **по́езд/авто́бус да́льнего ~я** long-distance train/bus.
сле́дователь (-я) *м* detective.
сле́довательно *вводн сл* consequently **♦** *союз* therefore.
сле́д|овать (-ую; *perf* **после́довать)** *несов неперех* (*вывод, неприятность*) to follow **♦** *безл*: **Вам ~ует поду́мать** you should think about it; **его́ ~ует за э́то наказа́ть** he should be punished for this; **~ (после́довать** *perf*) **за кем-н/чем-н** to follow sb/sth; **~ (после́довать** *perf*) **чему́-н** (*правилам, советам*) to follow sth; **как ~ует** properly.
сле́дом *нареч*: **ходи́ть ~ за кем-н** to follow sb **♦** *предл*: **~ за** *+instr* following.
сле́дственный *прил* investigative, investigatory.
сле́дстви|е (-я) *ср* (*последствие*) consequence;

(*юр*: *после преступления*) investigation.
сле́дующ|ий (-ая, -ее, -ие) *прил* next ◆ *мест* following; **на ~ день** the next day; **кто ~?** who is next?
слеже́ни|е (**-я**) *ср* observation.
сле́ж|ка (**-ки**; *gen pl* **-ек**) *ж* shadowing.
слежу́ *сов см* **следи́ть**.
слез *итп сов см* **слезть**.
сл|еза́ (**-езы́**; *nom pl* **-ёзы**, *dat pl* **-еза́м**) *ж* tear; **доводи́ть (довести́** *perf*) **кого́-н до ~ёз** to reduce sb to tears; **мне оби́дно до ~ёз** I'm so hurt I could cry.
слеза́|ть (**-ю**) *несов от* **слезть**.
слез|и́ться (*3sg* **-и́тся**, *3pl* **-я́тся**) *несов возв* (*глаза*) to water.
слезли́в|ый (**-, -а, -о**) *прил* (*человек*) weepy; (*перен*: *тон, голос*) tearful.
слёзный *прил* lacrimal; (*жалобный*) pitiful.
слезоточи́вый *прил*: **~ газ** tear gas.
слез|ть (**-у, -ешь**; *pt* **-, ла, -ло**, *impf* **слеза́ть**) *сов неперех*: **~ (с** *+gen*) (*с дерева*) to climb down; (*с лошади, с велосипеда*) to climb off; (*разг*: *с автобуса, с поезда итп*) to get off; (: *очки, платок*) to slip off; (*кожа, краска*) to peel off.
сле́й(те) *сов см* **слить**.
сленг (**-а**) *м* slang.
слеп|е́нь (**-ня́**) *м* horsefly (*мн* horseflies), cleg.
слеп|и́ть (*3sg* **-и́т**, *3pl* **-я́т**) *сов перех*: **~ глаза́ кому́-н** to blind sb.
сл|епи́ть (**-еплю́, -е́пишь**) *сов от* **лепи́ть** ◆ (*impf* **слепля́ть**) *перех* to stick together
▸ **слепи́ться** (*impf* **слепля́ться**) *сов возв* to stick together.
сле́пка *итп сущ см* **сле́пок**.
слеплю́(сь) *сов см* **слепя́ть(ся)**.
слепля́|ть(ся) (**-ю(сь)**) *несов от* **слепи́ть(ся)**.
сле́пн|уть (**-у, -ешь**; *perf* **осле́пнуть**) *несов неперех* to go blind.
слепня́ *итп сущ см* **слепе́нь**.
слеп|о́й (**-, -а́, -о**) *прил* (*также перен*) blind ◆ (**-о́го**; *decl like adj*) *м* blind person (*мн* people); **слепа́я кишка́** appendix (*мн* appendices); **слепо́й ме́тод печа́тания** touch-typing.
сле́п|ок (**-ка**) *м* cast.
слепот|а́ (**-ы́**) *ж* (*также перен*) blindness.
слеса́рн|ый *прил*: **~ая мастерска́я** metal workshop; **~ стано́к** lathe.
сле́сар|ь (**-я**; *nom pl* **-я́**, *gen pl* **-е́й**) *м* maintenance man (*мн* men).
слёт (**-а**) *м* (*пионеров*) rally.
слета́|ть (**-ю**) *несов от* **слете́ть** ◆ *неперех* (*на юг, на море*) to fly; (*разг*: *сбегать*) to nip
▸ **слета́ться** *несов от* **слете́ться**.
сле|те́ть (**-чу́, -ти́шь**; *impf* **слета́ть**) *сов неперех*: **~ (с** *+gen*) (*птица*) to fly down (from); (*разг*: *спесь*) to vanish (from); (: *шляпа, ребёнок*) to fall off; **вопро́с ~те́л с губ** *или* **с языка́** the question slipped out
▸ **слете́ться** (*impf* **слета́ться**) *сов возв* (*птицы*) to flock; (*мухи*) to swarm.
сл|ечь (**-я́гу, -я́жешь** *итп*, **-я́гут**; *pt* **-ёг, -егла́, -егло́**) *сов неперех* to take to one's bed.
слив (**-а**) *м* (*действие*) discharge; (*устройство*) drain.
сли́в|а (**-ы**) *ж* (*дерево*) plum (tree); (*плод*) plum.
слива́|ть(ся) (**-ю(сь)**) *несов от* **сли́ть(ся)**.
сли́в|ки (**-ок**) *мн* (*также перен*) cream *ед*.
сли́вовый *прил* plum *опред*.
сли́вок *сущ см* **сли́вки**.
сли́вочный *прил* *made with cream*; **сли́вочное ма́сло** butter.
сл|иза́ть (**-ижу́, -и́жешь**; *impf* **сли́зывать**) *сов перех* (*языком*) to lick off.
сли́зистый *прил* mucous *опред*; **сли́зистая оболо́чка** mucous membrane.
сли́зыва|ть (**-ю**) *несов от* **слиза́ть**.
слиз|ь (**-и**) *ж* mucus; (*от сырости, от грязи*) slime.
слипа́|ться (*3sg* **-ется**, *3pl* **-ются**) *несов от* **сли́пнуться** ◆ *возв* (*перен*): **у меня́ глаза́ ~ются** I can't keep my eyes open.
сли́п|нуться (*3sg* **-нется**, *3pl* **-нутся**, *pt* **-ся, -лась, -лось**, *impf* **слипа́ться**) *сов возв* to stick together.
сли́тка *итп сущ см* **сли́ток**.
сли́тн|ый *прил* (*звучание*) unified; **~ое написа́ние** spelt as one word.
сли́т|ок (**-ка**) *м* (*металлический*) bar; (*золота, серебра*) ingot.
сли|ть (**солью́, сольёшь**; *pt* **-л, -ла́, -ло**, *imper* **сле́й(те)**, *impf* **слива́ть**) *сов перех* to pour; (*вылить*) to pour out; (*перен*: *соединить*) to merge
▸ **сли́ться** (*impf* **слива́ться**) *сов возв* (*реки*) to flow together; (*голоса, судьбы, компании*) to merge.
слич|и́ть (**-у́, -и́шь**; *impf* **слича́ть**) *сов перех*: **~ что-н с чем-н** to check sth against sth.
сли́шком *нареч* too; **э́то уже́ ~** (*разг*) that's just too much.
слов|а́ (**-**) *мн*: **~ пе́сни** lyrics *мн*.
слова́к (**-а**) *м* Slovak.
Слова́ки|я (**-и**) *ж* Slovakia.
слова́рный *прил* (*работа, статья*) dictionary *опред*, lexicographic(al); (*фонд, состав языка*) lexical; **слова́рный запа́с** vocabulary.
слова́р|ь (**-я́**) *м* (*книга*) dictionary; (*запас слов*) vocabulary.
слова́цк|ий (**-ая, -ое, -ие**) *прил* Slovak, Slovakian.
слова́ч|ка (**-ки**; *gen pl* **-ек**) *ж см* **слова́к**.
слове́н|ец (**-ца**) *м* Slovene.
Слове́ни|я (**-и**) *ж* Slovenia.
слове́н|ка (**-ки**; *gen pl* **-ок**) *ж см* **слове́нец**.
слове́нск|ий (**-ая, -ое, -ие**) *прил* Slovene, Slovenian.
слове́нца *итп сущ см* **слове́нец**.
слове́сност|ь (**-и**) *ж* literature.
слове́сный *прил* oral; (*заявление, протест*) verbal; **слове́сный портре́т** description.
сло́вно *союз* (*как*) like; (*как будто*) as if.
сло́в|о (**-а**; *nom pl* **-а́**) *ср* word; **~ в ~** word for

word; **он двух слов связáть не мóжет** (*разг*) he can't string two words together; **на словáх** (*передать, согласиться*) verbally; **онá сочýвствует тóлько на словáх** her sympathy is just empty words; **со слов свидéтелей/егó друзéй** according to witnesses/his friends; **просúть (попросúть** *perf*) **~а** (*на собрании*) to ask to speak; **предоставля́ть (предостáвить** *perf*) **комý-н ~** to allow sb to speak; **лаборатóрия оборýдована по послéднему ~у наýки** the laboratory is equipped with the latest technology; **к ~у пришлóсь** it sprang to mind; **(однúм) ~м** in a word; **слов нет, ты прав** what can I say, you're right; *см также* **словá**.

словоизменéни|е (**-я**) *ср* inflection.

слóвом *вводн сл* in a word.

словообразовáни|е (**-я**) *ср* word formation.

словоохóтлив|ый (**-, -а, -о**) *прил* loquacious.

словосочетáни|е (**-я**) *ср* word combination.

словоупотреблéни|е (**-я**) *ср* word usage.

словц|ó (**-á**) *ср* witticism; **для крáсного ~á** for effect.

слог (**-а**; *nom pl* **-и**, *gen pl* **-óв**) *м* syllable; (*стиль*) style.

слóек *сущ см* **слóйка.**

слоён|ый *прил*: **~ое тéсто** puff pastry.

слóжен *прил см* **слóжный.**

сложéни|е (**-я**) *ср* (*в математике*) addition; (*телосложение*) build; (*полномочий, обязанностей*) relinquishing; (*чисел*) adding.

сложён|ный (**-, -á, -о**) *прил*: **он хорошó сложён** he is well-built.

сл|ожúть (**-ожý, -óжишь**; *impf* **склáдывать**) *сов перех* (*вещи*) to put; (*книги*) to stack; (*чемодан, сумку итп*) to pack; (*бумагу, рубашку итп*) to fold (up); (*impf* **склáдывать** *или* **слагáть**; *числа*) to add (up); (*картинку*) to make; (*песню, стихи*) to make up; **~** (*perf*) **гóлову/орýжие** to lay down one's life/weapons; **~** (*perf*) **рýки** to fold one's arms; **слагáть (~** *perf*) **с себя́ полномóчия/отвéтственность** to relinquish one's authority/responsibility; **сидéть** (*impf*) **~ожá рýки** to sit back and do nothing

▸ **сложúться** (*impf* **склáдываться**) *сов возв* (*коллектив*) to come together; (*ситуация, обстоятельства*) to turn out; (*характер*) to form; (*собрать деньги*) to have a collection; (*зонт, палатка*) to fold up; (*впечатление*) to form; **у нас ~ожúлось хорóшее впечатлéние о нём** we formed a good impression of him.

слóжно *нареч* (*делать*) in a complicated way; (*сложиться*) in a difficult way ◆ *как сказ* it's difficult; **мне ~ поня́ть егó** I find it difficult to understand him.

сложносокращённ|ый *прил*: **~ое слóво** compound.

слóжност|ь (**-и**) *ж* (*многообразие*) complexity; (*затейливость*) intricacy; (*обычно мн*: *трудность*) difficulty; **в óбщей ~и** all in all.

слóж|ный (**-ен, -нá, -но**) *прил* (*дело, предложение, человек*) complex; (*узор*) intricate; (*вопрос, работа*) difficult.

слоúст|ый (**-, -а, -о**) *прил* stratified.

сло|й (**-я**; *nom pl* **-ú**) *м* layer.

слó|йка (**-йки**; *gen pl* **-ек**) *ж* sweet pastry.

слом (**-а**) *м*: **на ~** for demolition; **дом идёт на ~** this house is due for demolition.

сломá|ть (**-ю**) *сов от* **ломáть**

▸ **сломáться** *сов от* **ломáться** ◆ *возв* (*перен*: *разг*: *человек*) to break.

слом|úть (**-лю́, -ишь**) *сов перех* (*сопротивление, волю итп*) to break; (*подлеж*: *болезнь, усталость*) to knock out; **~я́ гóлову** (*разг*) at breakneck speed

▸ **сломúться** *сов возв* (*перен*: *человек*) to break.

слон (**-á**) *м* elephant; (*ШАХМАТЫ*) bishop.

слон|ёнок (**-ёнка**; *nom pl* **-я́та**, *gen pl* **-я́т**) *м* elephant calf (*мн* calves).

слонúх|а (**-и**) *ж* cow (*elephant*).

слонóвый *прил* elephant *опред*; **слонóвая кость** ivory.

слоня́та *итп сущ см* **слонёнок.**

слоня́|ться (**-юсь**) *несов возв* (*разг*) to loaf around.

слóпа|ть (**-ю**) *сов от* **лóпать.**

слуг|á (**-ú**; *nom pl* **-и**) *м* servant.

служáк|а (**-и**) *м* (*разг*) trouper.

служáн|ка (**-ки**; *gen pl* **-ок**) *ж* maid.

слýжащ|ий (**-его**; *decl like adj*) *м* white collar worker; **госудáрственный ~** civil servant; **контóрский ~** clerk.

слýжб|а (**-ы**) *ж* service; (*работа*) work; **срок ~ы** durability; **Слýжба бы́та** consumer services; **Слýжба зáнятости** ≈ Employment Service.

служéбн|ый *прил* (*дела, обязанности итп*) official; (*роль, помещение итп*) auxiliary; **~ое положéние** rank; **служéбное слóво** connective word; **служéбная собáка** working dog.

служéни|е (**-я**) *ср* (*действие*: *родине*) serving; (*РЕЛ*) service.

служúтел|ь (**-я**) *м* (*в музее, в зоопарке*) keeper; (*на автозаправке*) attendant; (*науки, искусства*) servant; **служúтель цéркви** clergyman (*мн* clergymen).

служúтельниц|а (**-ы**) *ж* keeper.

сл|ужúть (**-ужý, -ýжишь**) *несов неперех* (*в банке, в конторе итп*) to work; (*в армии*) to serve ◆ *перех* (*РЕЛ*) to hear ◆ *неперех* (*собака*) to beg; (*perf* **послужúть**; *+instr*; *функционировать*) to serve as; **~** (*impf*) **рóдине/пáртии** to serve one's country/party; **чем могý ~?** what can I do for you?

слукáв|ить (**-лю, -ишь**) *сов от* **лукáвить.**

слух (**-а**) *м* hearing; (*музыкальный*) ear;

(*известие*) rumour (*BRIT*), rumor (*US*); **на ~** by hearing; **игрáть** *(impf)* **по слýху** to play by ear; **о нём ни слýху ни дýху** there's been no word of him; **по слýхам** from what people are saying.
слуховóй *прил* (*нерв, орган*) auditory; **слуховóй аппарáт** hearing aid.
случáен *прил см* **случáйный.**
слýча|й (-я) *м* occasion; (*подходящий момент*) chance, opportunity; (*случайность*) chance; **в ~е** *+gen* in the event of; **в ~е чегó** (*разг*) if there is anything; **во вся́ком ~е** in any case; **на ~** *+gen* in case of; **на вся́кий ~** just in case; **по ~ю** *+gen* (*годовщины*) on the occasion of; **при ~е** if the opportunity arises; **несчáстный ~** accident.
случáйно *нареч* accidentally, by chance ♦ *вводн сл* by any chance; **Вы, ~, не знáете, где здесь банк?** you don't by any chance know where there is a bank?; **не ~** not by chance.
случáйност|ь (-и) *ж* (*chance*); **по счастли́вой ~и** by sheer luck.
случá|йный (-ен, -йна, -йно) *прил* (*встреча*) accidental, chance *опред*; (*знакомство*) casual; (*КОМП*) random; **~ зáработок** casual earnings.
случá|ть (-ю) *несов от* **случи́ть**
▸ **случáться** *несов от* **случи́ться** ♦ *возв*: **он, ~ется, прихóдит серди́тый** occasionally he arrives in a temper.
случ|и́ть (-ý, -и́шь; *impf* **случáть)** *сов перех* to mate
▸ **случи́ться** (*impf* **случáться**) *сов возв* (*произойти*) to happen ♦ *безл*: **мне ~и́лось с ним познакóмиться** I happened to become acquainted with him.
слýшани|е (-я) *ср* (*ЮР*) hearing.
слýшател|ь (-я) *м* listener; (*ПРОСВЕЩ*) student.
слýшательниц|а (-ы) *ж см* **слýшатель.**
слýша|ть (-ю) *несов перех* (*музыку, речь*) to listen to; (*ЮР*) to hear; (*курс лекций*) to attend; (*perf* **послýшать**; *совет*) to listen to; (*perf* **вы́слушать**; *сердце, лёгкие*) to listen to; **~йте!** (*разг*) listen!
▸ **слýшаться** (*perf* **послýшаться**) *несов возв*: **~ся** *+gen* to obey; (*совета*) to follow; **~юсь!** yes, sir!
слы|ть (-вý, -вёшь; *pt* **-л, -лá, -ло)** *несов неперех*: **~** *+instr или* **за** *+acc* to be reputed to be.
слы́хан|ный *прил*: **где э́то ~о?** *(разг)* whoever heard of such a thing?
слыхá|ть (*pt* **-л, -ла, -ло**) *несов перех* to hear; **мне ничегó не ~** (*разг*) I can't hear a thing.
слы́ш|ать (-у, -ишь) *несов неперех* to hear ♦ (*perf* **услы́шать**) *перех* to hear; **~** *(impf)* **о** *+prp* to hear about: **и ~ об э́том не хочý** I won't hear of it; **он плóхо ~ит** he's hard of hearing
▸ **слы́шаться** *несов возв* to be heard.
слы́шен *прил см* **слы́шный.**
слы́шимост|ь (-и) *ж* (*в зале*) acoustics *мн*; (*радио, телевизора*) audibility.
слы́шно *как сказ* it can be heard; **мне ничегó не ~** I can't hear a thing; **о ней ничегó не ~** there's no news of her; **что у Вас ~?** how are things?
слы́ш|ный (-ен, -нá, -но) *прил* (*звук, пение*) audible ♦ *как сказ* (*no full form*): **в егó гóлосе слышнá тревóга** anxiety can be heard in his voice.
слюд|á (-ы́) *ж* mica.
слюн|á (-ы́) *ж* saliva.
слю́н|ки (-ок) *мн*: **у меня́ ~ текýт** my mouth's watering.
слюня́в|ить (-лю, -ишь) *несов перех* (*разг*) to lick.
сля́гу *итп сов см* **слечь.**
сля́кот|ь (-и) *ж* slush.
сля́па|ть (-ю) *сов от* **ля́пать.**
см *сокр* (= **сантимéтр**) cm(= *centimetre* (*BRIT*) *или centimeter* (*US*)).
см. *сокр* (= *смотри́*) v. (= *vide*,) qv (= *quod vide*).
с.м. *сокр* (= *сегó мéсяца*) inst. (= *instant*).
смá|зать (-жу, -жешь; *impf* **смáзывать)** *сов перех* (*маслом*) to lubricate; (*разг*: *испортить впечатление*) to slur; **смáзывать (~** *perf*) **что-н мáзью** to put ointment on sth.
смáзк|а (-и) *ж* (*действие*) lubrication; (*вещество*) lubricant.
смазли́в|ый (-, -а, -о) *прил* (*разг*) pretty.
смáзочный *прил* lubricating.
смáзыва|ть (-ю) *несов от* **смáзать.**
смак|овáть (-ýю) *несов перех* (*еду*) to savour (*BRIT*), savor (*US*); (*перен*: *новость, книгу итп*) to relish.
смалодýшнича|ть (-ю) *сов от* **малодýшничать.**
смáльт|а (-ы) *ж* smalto.
сманеври́р|овать (-ую) *сов от* **маневри́ровать.**
см|ани́ть (-аню́, -áнишь; *impf* **смáнивать)** *сов перех* (*переманить*) to lure, entice.
смастер|и́ть (-ю́, -и́шь) *сов от* **мастери́ть.**
смáтыва|ть(ся) (-ю(сь)) *несов от* **смотáть(ся).**
смáхива|ть (-ю) *несов от* **смахнýть** ♦ *неперех* (*разг*): **~ на** *+acc* (*походить*) to look a bit like.
смахн|ýть (-ý, -ёшь) *сов перех* to brush off.
смáчен *прил см* **смáчный.**
смáчива|ть (-ю) *несов от* **смочи́ть.**
смáч|ный (-ен, -нá, -но) *прил* (*разг*: *вкусный*) scrumptious; (*перен*: *слово*) juicy.
смéжен *прил см* **смéжный.**
смéжник (-а) *м* (*предприятие*) related company.
смéж|ный (-ен, -на, -но) *прил* (*с общей границей*) adjoining, adjacent; (*производство, предприятие*) affiliated; (*наука*) related.
смекáлист|ый (-, -а, -о) *прил* astute.
смекáлк|а (-и) *ж* astuteness.
смекá|ть (-ю; *perf* **смекнýть)** *несов перех* to catch onto.
смелé|ть (-ю; *perf* **осмелéть)** *несов неперех* to grow bolder.
смéло *нареч* boldly; (*без колебаний*) confidently.

сме́лост|ь (**-и**) *ж* (*храбрость*) bravery; (*поступка, поведения*) boldness, audacity; **брать (взять** *perf*) **на себя́** ~ *+infin* to have the audacity to do.
сме́л|ый (**-, -а́, -о**) *прил* (*человек, поступок*) brave; (*идея, проект*) ambitious; (*перен*: *нескрайный*) risqué.
смельча́к (**-а́**) *м* brave person (*мн* people).
смелю́ *итп сов см* **смоло́ть**.
сме́н|а (**-ы**) *ж* (*руководства*) change; (*караула, одежды*) changing; (*на производстве*) shift; (*молодое поколение*) successors *мн*; (*также:* ~ **белья́**) change of sheets (*BRIT*) *или* bed-linen (*US*); **приходи́ть (прийти́** *perf*) **на ~у кому́-н/чему́-н** to succeed sb/sth.
см|ени́ть (**-еню́, -е́нишь**; *impf* **сменя́ть**) *сов перех* to change; (*коллегу*) to relieve
▸ **смени́ться** (*impf* **сменя́ться**) *сов возв* (*руководство*) to change; (*радость, день*): **~ся** *+instr* to give way to; **сменя́ться (~ся** *perf*) **(с** *+gen*) (*с дежурства, с вахты*) to go off duty (from).
сме́нн|ый *прил* (*работа, задание*) shift *опред*; (*колесо*) spare; **~ое бельё** a change of sheets (*BRIT*) *или* bed-linen (*US*); (*нижнее*) a change of underwear.
сменя́|ть(ся) (**-ю(сь)**) *несов от* **смени́ть(ся)**.
смёрзн|уться (*3sg* **-ется**, *3pl* **-утся**) *сов возв* to freeze together.
сме́р|ить (**-ю, -ишь**) *сов от* **ме́рить**.
смерка́|ться (*3sg* **-ется**, *perf* **сме́ркнуться**) *несов безл* to start to get dark.
смерте́л|ьный (**-ен, -ьна, -ьно**) *прил* mortal; (*рана*) fatal; (*скука, усталость*) deadly; **смерте́льный исхо́д** fatal ending; **смерте́льный слу́чай** fatality.
сме́ртен *прил см* **сме́ртный**.
сме́ртник (**-а**) *м* (*приговорённый к казни*) prisoner on death row; (*террорист*) kamikaze.
сме́ртност|ь (**-и**) *ж* death-rate, mortality.
сме́рт|ный (**-ен, -на, -но**) *прил* mortal; (*разг*: *скука*) deadly; ~ **час** hour of death; ~ **бой** (*перен*) fight to the death; **просто́й** ~ ordinary mortal; **сме́ртный пригово́р** death sentence; **сме́ртная казнь** death penalty.
смертоно́сный *прил* lethal.
смерт|ь (**-и**) *ж* death; **быть** (*impf*) **при́ ~и** to be at death's door; **умира́ть (умере́ть** *perf*) **свое́й сме́ртью** to die a natural death; **я до́ ~и бою́сь** I'm scared to death.
смерч (**-а**) *м* tornado.
смеси́тел|ь (**-я**) *м* mixer.
сме|си́ть (**-шу́, -сишь**) *сов от* **меси́ть**.
см|ести́ (**-ету́, -етёшь**; *pt* **-ёл, -ела́, -ело́**, *impf* **смета́ть**) *сов перех* to sweep; (*подлеж*: *ураган, смерч*) to sweep away.
сме|сти́ть (**-щу́, -сти́шь**; *impf* **смеща́ть**) *сов перех* (*уволить*) to remove; (*сдвинуть*) to shift
▸ **смести́ться** (*impf* **смеща́ться**) *сов возв* to shift.
смес|ь (**-и**) *ж* mixture; **моло́чная** ~ powdered baby milk.
сме́т|а (**-ы**) *ж* (*экон*) estimate.
смета́н|а (**-ы**) *ж* sour cream.
смета́|ть (**-ю**) *несов от* **смести́** ◆ *сов от* **мета́ть**.
сметли́в|ый (**-, -а, -о**) *прил* quick.
сме́тный *прил* estimated; **сме́тная сто́имость** estimated cost.
сме|ть (**-ю**; *perf* **посме́ть**) *несов неперех*: ~ *+infin* to dare to do; **как Вы сме́ете!** how dare you!; **не сме́й!** don't you dare!
смету́ *итп сов см* **смести́**.
смех (**-а**; *part gen* **-у**) *м* laughter ◆ *как сказ* (*смешно*) it's ridiculous; **слу́шать э́то – ~** it makes me laugh to hear it; **поднима́ть (подня́ть** *perf*) **кого́-н на́ ~** to make a laughing stock of sb; **и ~ и грех** one can see the funny side of it.
смехотво́р|ный (**-ен, -на, -но**) *прил* (*смешной*) funny; (*жалкий*) ludicrous.
сме́шанный *прил* mixed.
смеша́|ть (**-ю**) *сов от* **меша́ть** ◆ (*impf* **сме́шивать**) *перех* (*спутать*) to mix up; ~ (*perf*) **чьи-н ка́рты** to spoil sb's plans
▸ **смеша́ться** *сов от* **меша́ться** ◆ *возв* (*смутиться*) to be taken aback; (*impf* **сме́шиваться**; *слиться*) to mingle; (*краски, цвета*) to blend; (*чувства*) to become confused.
смеше́ни|е (**-я**) *ср* (*стилей, чувств*) mixture.
сме́шивани|е (**-я**) *ср* mixing.
сме́шива|ть(ся) (**-ю(сь)**) *несов от* **смеша́ть(ся)**.
смеш|и́ть (**-у́, -и́шь**; *perf* **насмеши́ть** *или* **рассмеши́ть**) *несов перех*: ~ **кого́-н** to make sb laugh.
смешка́ *итп сущ см* **смешо́к**.
смешли́в|ый (**-, -а, -о**) *прил* (*человек*) jolly; (*настроение*) giggly.
смешно́ *нареч* (*смотреться*) funny ◆ *как сказ* it's funny; (*глупо*) it's ludicrous; **мне не** ~ I don't find it funny; ~ **наде́яться** it's ludicrous to hope; ~ **сказа́ть, но** ... it sounds funny, but ...; **э́то про́сто** ~ that's just ridiculous.
смеш|но́й (**-о́н, -на́, -но́**) *прил* funny; (*требования, претензии итп*) ludicrous; **до ~но́го** to the point of absurdity; **дохо́дит до ~но́го** it's a real joke.
смеш|о́к (**-ка́**) *м* giggle.
смешо́н *прил см* **смешно́й**.
смеща́|ть(ся) (**-ю(сь)**) *несов от* **смести́ть(ся)**.
смеще́ни|е (**-я**) *ср* (*руководства*) removal; (*понятий, критериев*) shift.
смещённый (**-ён, -ена́, -ено́**) *прил* upset; (*понятия*) disturbed.
смещу́(сь) *сов см* **смести́ть(ся)**.
сме|я́ться (**-ю́сь**) *несов возв* to laugh;

(*шутить*) to joke; (*perf* **посмеяться**; *насмехаться*): ~ **над** *+instr* to laugh at.
СМИ *сокр* (= *Сре́дства ма́ссовой информа́ции*) the media.
сми́лостив|иться (**-люсь, -ишься**) *сов возв*: ~ (**над** *+instr*) to take pity (on).
смина́|ть (**-ю**) *несов от* **смять**.
сми́рен *прил см* **сми́рный**.
смире́ни|е (**-я**) *ср* (*покорность*) humility.
смире́н|ный (**-, -на, -но**) *прил* humble.
смири́тельн|ый *прил*: ~**ая руба́шка** strait-jacket.
смир|и́ть (**-ю́, -и́шь**; *impf* **смиря́ть**) *сов перех* to subdue
▸ **смири́ться** (*impf* **смиря́ться**) *сов возв* (*покориться*) to submit; (*примириться*): ~**ся с** *+instr* to resign o.s. to.
сми́рно *нареч* (*сидеть, вести себя*) quietly; (*ВОЕН*: *команда*) attention; **стоя́ть** (*impf*) **по сто́йке** „~" to stand to attention.
сми́р|ный (**-ен, -на́, -но**) *прил* docile.
смиря́|ть(ся) (**-ю(сь)**) *несов от* **смири́ть(ся)**.
смог (**-а**) *м* smog.
смог *итп сов см* **смочь**.
смогу́ *итп сов см* **смочь**.
смоделйр|овать (**-ую**) *сов от* **моделйровать**.
смо́жешь *итп сов см* **смочь**.
смол|а́ (**-ы́**; *nom pl* **-ы**) *ж* (*дерева*) resin; (*дёготь*) tar.
смоли́ст|ый (**-, -а, -о**) *прил* (*дерево*) resinous.
смо́лк|нуть (**-ну, -нешь**; *pt* **-, -ла, -ло**, *impf* **смолка́ть**) *сов неперех* (*голоса*) to fall silent; (*звуки*) to fade away.
смо́лоду *нареч* from one's youth.
смол|оти́ть (**-очу́, -о́тишь**) *сов от* **молоти́ть**.
см|оло́ть (**-елю́, -е́лешь**) *сов от* **моло́ть**.
смолочу́ *сов см* **смолоти́ть**.
смолч|а́ть (**-у́, -и́шь**) *сов неперех* to keep quiet.
смол|ь (**-и**) *ж*: **чёрный как** ~ jet-black.
смонти́р|овать (**-ую**) *сов от* **монти́ровать**.
сморка́|ть (**-ю**; *perf* **вы́сморкать**) *несов перех*: ~ **нос** to blow one's nose
▸ **сморка́ться** (*perf* **вы́сморкаться**) *несов возв* to blow one's nose.
сморо́дин|а (**-ы**) *ж*: **кра́сная** ~ (*кустарник*) redcurrant bush; (*ягоды*) redcurrants *мн*; **чёрная** ~ (*кустарник*) blackcurrant bush; (*ягоды*) blackcurrants *мн*.
сморо́|зить (**-жу, -зишь**) *сов перех* to say.
смо́рщенный *прил* wrinkled.
смо́рщ|ить (**-у, -ишь**) *сов от* **мо́рщить**
▸ **смо́рщиться** *сов от* **мо́рщиться** ◆ *возв* to become wrinkled.
смота́|ть (**-ю**; *impf* **сма́тывать**) *сов перех* to wind
▸ **смота́ться** (*impf* **сма́тываться**) *сов возв* (*нитки*) to wind; (*разг*: *убежать*) to leg it; (: *быстро пойти*) to nip.
смотр (**-а**; *loc sg* **-у́**, *nom pl* **-ы́**) *м* presentation; (*ВОЕН*) inspection.
см|отре́ть (**-отрю́, -о́тришь**; *perf* **посмотре́ть**) *несов неперех* to look ◆ *перех* (*фильм, игру*) to watch; (*газеты, почту*) to look through; (*квартиру, картину*) to look at; (*музей, выставку*) to look round; (*пациента*) to examine; (*следить*): ~ **за** *+instr* to look after; ~ (*impf*) **в/на** *+acc* to look onto; ~ (**посмотре́ть** *perf*) **на** *+acc* (*относиться*) to look at; ~**отри́те, не упади́те** watch, don't fall; ~**отрю́, ты осво́ился здесь** (*разг*) I see you've settled down here; ~**отря́ по** *+dat* depending on; **Вы хоти́те пойти́ погуля́ть? – ~отря́ куда́** would you like to go for a walk? – it depends where to
▸ **смотре́ться** (*perf* **посмотре́ться**) *несов возв*: ~**ся в** *+acc* (*в зеркало, в воду*) to look at o.s. in; (*разг*: *хорошо выглядеть*) to look good; **э́та вы́ставка ~о́трится легко́** this exhibition is not too demanding.
смотри́тел|ь (**-я**) *м* (*в музее*) attendant.
смотри́тельниц|а (**-ы**) *ж см* **смотри́тель**.
смотров|о́й *прил* (*площадка*) viewing *опред*; ~**а́я ба́шня** watch tower; ~**о́е отве́рстие** peephole; **смотрово́й кабине́т** medical examination room.
см|очи́ть (**-очу́, -о́чишь**; *impf* **сма́чивать**) *сов перех* to dampen.
смо|чь (**-гу́, -жешь** *итп*, **-гут**; *pt* **-г, -гла́, -гло́**) *сов от* **мочь**.
смоше́нничa|ть (**-ю**) *сов от* **моше́нничать**.
смо́ю(ся) *итп сов от* **смы́ть(ся)**.
смрад (**-а**) *м* (*вонь*) stench.
смра́д|ный (**-ен, -на, -но**) *прил* stinking.
сму́гл|ый (**-, -а́, -о**) *прил* swarthy.
сму́т|а (**-ы**) *ж* (*социальная*) unrest; **у меня́ на душе́** ~ my soul is troubled.
сму́тен *прил см* **сму́тный**.
сму|ти́ть (**-щу́, -ти́шь**; *impf* **смуща́ть**) *сов перех* to embarrass
▸ **смути́ться** (*impf* **смуща́ться**) *сов возв* to get embarrassed.
сму́т|ный (**-ен, -на, -но**) *прил* (*очертания, воспоминания*) vague; (*настроение, время итп*) troubled.
смуща́|ть(ся) (**-ю(сь)**) *несов от* **смути́ть(ся)**.
смуще́ни|е (**-я**) *ср* embarrassment.
смущённый *прил* embarrassed.
смущу́(сь) *сов см* **смути́ть(ся)**.
смыва́|ть(ся) (**-ю(сь)**) *несов от* **смы́ть(ся)**.
смыка́|ть(ся) (**-ю(сь)**) *несов от* **сомкну́ть(ся)**.
смысл (**-а**) *м* (*книги, статьи*) point; (*слов*) meaning; (*ЛИНГ*) sense; **в смы́сле** *+gen* as regards; **здра́вый** ~ common sense; **прямо́й/перено́сный** ~ **сло́ва** the literal/figurative sense of a word; **како́й ~ на э́то соглаша́ться?** what is the point of agreeing to that?; **есть ~ е́хать сего́дня** it makes sense to go today.
смы́сл|ить (**-ю, -ишь**) *несов неперех* (*разг*: *разбираться*): ~ **в** *+prp* to have a knack for.
см|ыть (**-о́ю, -о́ешь**; *impf* **смыва́ть**) *сов перех* to wash off; (*подлеж*: *волна, течение*) to wash away
▸ **смы́ться** (*impf* **смыва́ться**) *сов возв* to wash

off; (*разг*: *незаметно уйти*) to do a bunk.
смыч|о́к (**-ка́**) *м* (*муз*) bow.
смышлён|ый (**-, -а, -о**) *прил* sharp.
смягча́|ть(ся) (**-ю(сь)**) *несов от* **смягчи́ть(ся)**.
смягча́ющ|ий (**-ая, -ее, -ие**) *прил*: **~ие обстоя́тельства** (*ЮР*) extenuating circumstances *мн*.
смягче́ни|е (**-я**) *ср* (*действие*) softening; (: *наказания*) mitigation.
смягч|и́ть (**-у́, -и́шь**; *impf* **смягча́ть**) *сов перех* (*кожу, ткань, удар*) to soften; (*боль*) to ease; (*наказание, приговор*) to mitigate; (*человека*) to appease
▸ **смягчи́ться** (*impf* **смягча́ться**) *сов возв* to soften.
смяте́ни|е (**-я**) *ср* turmoil.
смять (**сомну́, сомнёшь**) *сов от* **мять** ♦ (*impf* **смина́ть**) *перех* (*противника, оборону*) to crush
▸ **смя́ться** *сов от* **мя́ться**.
сна *итп сущ см* **сон**.
снабд|и́ть (**-жу́, -ди́шь**; *impf* **снабжа́ть**) *сов перех*: **~ кого́-н/что-н чем-н** to supply sb/sth with sth.
снабже́ни|е (**-я**) *ср* supply.
снабжу́ *сов см* **снабди́ть**.
сна́йпер (**-а**) *м* (*стрелок*) sniper.
снару́жи *нареч* (*покрасить, расположиться*) on the outside; (*закрыть*) from the outside.
снаря́д (**-а**) *м* (*ВОЕН*) shell; (*СПОРТ*) apparatus.
снаря|ди́ть (**-жу́, -ди́шь**; *impf* **снаряжа́ть**) *сов перех* to equip.
снаряже́ни|е (**-я**) *ср* (*действие*) equipping; (*лыжное, охотничье*) equipment; (*солдата*) kit.
снаряжу́ *сов см* **снаряди́ть**.
снаст|ь (**-и**) *ж* (*МОР*: *обычно мн*) rigging *только ед*; (*рыболовная*) tackle.
снача́ла *нареч* at first; (*ешё раз*) all over again.
сна́шива|ть (**-ю**) *несов от* **сноси́ть**.
СНГ *м сокр* (= *Содру́жество Незави́симых Госуда́рств*) CIS (= *Commonwealth of Independent States*).
снег (**-а**; *part gen* **-у**, *loc sg* **-у́**, *nom pl* **-а́**) *м* snow; **идёт ~** it's snowing; **вы́пал ~** it's been snowing; **как ~ на́ голову** like a bolt from the blue.
снеги́р|ь (**-я́**) *м* bullfinch.
снегови́к (**-а́**) *м* snowman (*мн* snowmen).
снегоочисти́тел|ь (**-я**) *м* snowplough (*BRIT*), snowplow (*US*).
снегопа́д (**-а**) *м* snowfall.
снегоубо́рочн|ый *прил*: **~ая маши́на** snowplough (*BRIT*), snowplow (*US*).
снегу́роч|ка (**-ки**; *gen pl* **-ек**) *ж* Snow Maiden.
снед|ь (**-и**) *ж собир* food.
снежи́н|ка (**-ки**; *gen pl* **-ок**) *ж* snowflake.
снежка́ *итп сущ см* **снежо́к**.
сне́жн|ый *прил* snow *опред*; **~ая зима́** snowy winter; **сне́жная ба́ба** snowman (*мн* snowmen).
снеж|о́к (**-ка́**) *м* (*комок*) snowball; **игра́ть** (*impf*) **в ~ки́** to have a snowball fight.
сн|ести́ (**-есу́, -есёшь**; *pt* **-ёс, -есла́, -есло́**) *сов от* **нести́** ♦ (*impf* **сноси́ть**) *перех* (*отнести*) to take; (*подлеж*: *буря*) to carry away; (*сверху вниз*) to take down; (*перен*: *вытерпеть*) to take; (*дом*) to demolish
▸ **снести́сь** *сов от* **нести́сь** ♦ *возв* (*связаться*): **~сь с** +*instr* to contact.
снижа́|ть(ся) (**-ю(сь)**) *несов от* **сни́зить(ся)**.
сниже́ни|е (**-я**) *ср* (*цен итп*) lowering; (*самолёта*) descent; (*производительности итп*) reduction.
сни́|зить (**-жу, -зишь**; *impf* **снижа́ть**) *сов перех* (*цены, давление итп*) to lower; (*самолёт*) to bring down ; (*скорость*) to reduce
▸ **сни́зиться** (*impf* **снижа́ться**) *сов возв* (*цены, производительность итп*) to fall; (*самолёт*) to descend.
снизойти́ (*как* **идти́**; *см* **Table 18**; *impf* **снисходи́ть**) *сов неперех*: **~ к кому́-н** *или* **до кого́-н** to condescend to sb; **он снизошёл к моей про́сьбе** *или* **до мое́й про́сьбы** he condescended to grant my request.
сни́зу *нареч* (*внизу*) at the bottom; (*по направлению вверх*) from the bottom; (*перен*: *со стороны народа*) from the masses; **~ до́верху** from top to bottom.
сни́к|нуть (**-ну, -нешь**; *pt* **-, -ла, -ло**) *сов от* **ни́кнуть** ♦ *неперех* to flag.
снима́|ть(ся) (**-ю(сь)**) *несов от* **снять(ся)**.
сни́м|ок (**-ка**) *м* (*ФОТО*) snap(shot).
сниму́(сь) *итп сов см* **снять(ся)**.
сни|ска́ть (**-щу́, -щешь**) *сов перех* to win; **э́тот посту́пок ~ска́л ему́ большу́ю сла́ву** this deed won him great fame.
снисходи́тел|ьный (**-ен, -ьна, -ьно**) *прил* (*не строгий*) lenient; (*с оттенком высокомерия*) condescending.
снисх|оди́ть (**-ожу́, -о́дишь**) *несов от* **снизойти́**.
снисхожде́ни|е (**-я**) *ср* leniency.
снисхожу́ *несов см* **снисходи́ть**.
сн|и́ться (**-юсь, -и́шься**; *perf* **присни́ться**) *несов безл*: **мне ~и́лся стра́шный сон** I was having a terrible dream; **мне ~и́лось, что я в гора́х** I dreamt I was in the mountains; **ты ча́сто ~и́шься мне** I often dream of you.
снищу́ *итп сов см* **сниска́ть**.
сноб (**-а**) *м* snob.
снобизм (**-а**) *м* snobbery.
сно́ва *нареч* again.
сн|ова́ть (**-ую́**) *несов неперех* (*люди*) to dash about; (*машины*) to zoom about.
сновиде́ни|е (**-я**) *ср* dream.
сногсшиба́тел|ьный (**-ен, -ьна, -ьно**) *прил*

(*разг*) stunning.
сноп (-á) *м* (*с-х*) sheaf; (*перен*) shaft.
сноро́вк|а (-и) *ж* knack.
снос (-а) *м* demolition; **дом идёт на ~** the house is due for demolition; **э́тим боти́нкам сно́су нет** these boots are hard-wearing.
сн|оси́ть (-ошу́, -о́сишь) *несов от* **снести́** ◆ (*impf* **сна́шивать**) *сов перех* (*износить*) to wear out.
сно́с|ка (-ки; *gen pl* **-ок)** *ж* footnote.
сно́с|ный (-ен, -на, -но) *прил* (*разг*) tolerable.
сно́сок *сущ см* **сно́ска.**
снотво́рн|ое (-ого; *decl like adj*) *ср* sleeping pill *или* tablet.
снотво́рн|ый *прил*: **~ое сре́дство** sedative.
снох|á (-и́) *ж* daughter-in-law (*of husband's father*).
сноше́ни|е (-я) *ср* relations *мн*; **входи́ть (войти́** *perf*) **в ~я с** *+instr* to enter into relations with.
сношу́ (*не*)*сов см* **сноси́ть.**
сня́ти|е (-я) *ср* removal.
сн|ять (-иму́, -и́мешь; *impf* **снима́ть**) *сов перех* to take down; (*плод*) to pick; (*одежду*) to take off; (*запрет, ответственность*) to remove; (*копию*) to make; (*дом, комнату итп*) to rent; (*уволить*) to dismiss; **снима́ть (~** *perf*) **фотогра́фию** to take a picture; **снима́ть (~** *perf*) **фильм** to shoot a film; **снима́ть (~** *perf*) **показа́ния** to take down evidence; **снима́ть (~** *perf*) **урожа́й** to gather the harvest
▸ **сня́ться** (*impf* **снима́ться**) *сов возв* (*сфотографироваться*) to have one's photograph taken; (*покинуть: со стоянки*) to move off; (*актёр*) to appear; (*корабль*): **~я́ться с я́коря** to up anchor.
со *предл* = **с.**
соа́втор (-а) *м* coauthor.
соа́вторств|о (-а) *ср* coauthorship; **в ~е с** *+instr* in coauthorship with.
соба́к|а (-и) *ж* dog; (*разг*) rat, dog; **он на э́том ~у съел** (*разг*) he knows it inside out; **вот где ~ зары́та!** so that's what it is!
собаково́д (-а) *м* dog-breeder.
собаково́дств|о (-а) *ср* dog-breeding.
соба́ч|ий (-ья, -ье, -ьи) *прил* (*лай, нюх*) dog's; **~ья жизнь** (*разг*) it's a dog's life; **на у́лице хо́лод ~** (*разг*) it's blooming cold outside.
соба́чник (-а) *м* (*ловящий собак*) dog-catcher; (*разг: любитель собак*) dog-lover.
собезья́ннича|ть (-ю) *сов от* **обезья́нничать.**
соберу́(сь) *итп сов см* **собра́ть(ся).**
собе́с (-а) *м сокр* (= *социа́льное обеспе́чение*) social security; (*учреждение*) ≈ social security department.
собесе́дник (-а) *м* interlocutor; **мой ~ замолча́л** the person I was talking to fell silent.
собесе́дниц|а (-ы) *ж см* **собесе́дник.**
собесе́довани|е (-я) *ср* interview.
собира́ни|е (-я) *ср* (*материала, данных итп*) collection, gathering; (*коллекционирование*) collecting; (*ягод, грибов*) picking; **~ ма́рок** *итп* stamp *итп* collecting.
собира́телен *прил см* **собира́тельный.**
собира́тел|ь (-я) *м* collector.
собира́тел|ьный (-ен, -ьна, -ьно) *прил* (*также линг*) collective.
собира́|ть (-ю) *несов от* **собра́ть**
▸ **собира́ться** *несов от* **собра́ться** ◆ *возв*: **я ~юсь пойти́ туда́** I'm going to go there.
собко́р (-а) *м сокр* = *со́бственный корреспонде́нт*: **э́то сообще́ние от на́шего ~а в Москве́** this report is from our own correspondent in Moscow.
собла́зн (-а) *м* temptation; **устоя́ть** (*perf*) **пе́ред ~ом** *или* **про́тив ~а** to resist temptation; **вводи́ть (ввести́** *perf*) **кого́-н в ~** to tempt sb.
соблазни́тел|ь (-я) *м* seducer.
соблазни́тел|ьный (-ен, -ьна, -ьно) *прил* tempting; (*женщина*) seductive.
соблазн|и́ть (-ю́, -и́шь; *impf* **соблазня́ть**) *сов перех* to seduce; (*прельстить*): **~ кого́-н чем-н** to tempt sb with sth
▸ **соблазни́ться** (*impf* **соблазня́ться**) *сов возв*: **~ся** *+instr/+infin* to be tempted by/to do.
соблюда́|ть (-ю) *несов от* **соблюсти́** ◆ *перех* (*дисциплину, порядок*) to maintain; **«~йте чистоту́»** "please keep this area tidy".
соблю|сти́ (-ду́, -дёшь) *сов от* **блюсти́** ◆ (*impf* **соблюда́ть**) *перех* (*закон, правила*) to observe.
соболе́зновани|е (-я) *ср* condolences *мн*; **выража́ть (вы́разить** *perf*) **кому́-н ~** to express one's condolences to sb.
соболе́зн|овать (-ую) *несов неперех*: **~ кому́-н** to condole with sb.
со́б|оль (-оля; *nom pl* **-оля́)** *м* sable.
собо́р (-а) *м* cathedral; (*съезд*) council (*of churches*).
собо́рн|ый *прил* (*здание, колокол*) cathedral *опред*; **~ое постановле́ние** decree of the church council.
СОБР *сокр* (= *Сво́дный отря́д бы́строго реаги́рования*) flying squad.
собра́ни|е (-я) *ср* (*партийное, профсоюзное*) meeting; (*представителей*) assembly; (*картин итп*) collection; **собра́ние сочине́ний** collected works *мн*.
со́бран|ный (-, -на, -но) *прил* self-disciplined.
соб|ра́ть (-еру́, -ерёшь; *pt* **-ра́л, -рала́, -ра́ло,** *impf* **собира́ть**) *сов перех* to gather (together); (*ягоды, грибы*) to pick; (*урожай*) to gather; (*станок, приёмник итп*) to assemble; (*марки, налоги, подписи*) to collect; (*перен: мужество*) to muster up; (*: силы*) to summon; (*приготовить*): **~ кого́-н в** *+acc* (*в школу итп*) to get sb ready for; **собира́ть (~** *perf*) **чемода́н/ве́щи** to pack one's suitcase/things
▸ **собра́ться** (*impf* **собира́ться**) *сов возв* (*гости, делегаты*) to assemble, gather; (*в экспедицию, на урок итп*) to get ready to go; (*приготовиться*): **~ся** *+infin* to get ready to do; **собира́ться (~ся** *perf*) **с** *+instr* (*с силами, с мыслями*) to gather; **собира́ться (~ся** *perf*) **с**

ду́хом to pluck up the courage; **ты куда́ ~ра́лся?** where were you going?; **то́лько ~ра́лся лечь спать, как зазвони́л телефо́н** I was about to go to bed when the telephone rang.
со́бственник (-а) *м* (*владелец*) owner.
со́бственниц|а (-ы) *ж см* **со́бственник**.
со́бственническ|ий (-ая, -ое, -ие) *прил* proprietorial.
со́бственно *част* actually ◆ *вводн сл*: ~ **(говоря́)** as a matter of fact.
собственнору́чный *прил* (*расписка*) own.
со́бственност|ь (-и) *ж* (*имущество*) property; (*владение*) ownership; ~ **на** *+acc* right of ownership of; **быть** *(impf) или* **находи́ться** *(impf)* **в чьей-н ~и** to be in sb's possession; **приобрета́ть (приобрести́** *perf*) **в ~ что-н** to become the owner of sth.
со́бственн|ый *прил* (one's) own; **по ~ому жела́нию** of one's own volition; **и́мя ~ое** proper name; **чу́вство ~ого досто́инства** self-respect; **со́бственный корреспонде́нт** *см* **собко́р**.
собуты́льник (-а) *м* (*разг*: *пренебр*) drinking mate (*BRIT*) *или* buddy (*US*).
собы́ти|е (-я) *ср* event.
собью́(сь) *итп сов см* **сбить(ся)**.
сов|а́ (-ы́; *nom pl* -ы) *ж* owl.
сова́ть (**сую́, суёшь**; *perf* **су́нуть**) *несов перех* to put in; ~ **(су́нуть** *perf*) **нос во что-н** to poke one's nose into sth
▸ **сова́ться** (*perf* **су́нуться**) *несов возв* (*разг*: *лезть*): **~ся вперёд** to push through; **~ся (су́нуться** *perf*) **не в своё де́ло** to poke one's nose into other people's business.
сов|ёнок (-ёнка; *nom pl* -я́та, *gen pl* -я́т) *м* owlet.
соверша́|ть(ся) (-ю(сь)) *несов от* **соверши́ть(ся)**.
соверше́нен *прил см* **соверше́нный**.
соверше́ни|е (-я) *ср* (*сделки*) conclusion; (*преступления*) committing.
соверше́нно *нареч* (*играть, исполнять*) perfectly; (*совсем*) absolutely, completely; **у меня́ ~ нет сил** I have absolutely no energy; **э́то ~ ве́рно** it's absolutely *или* completely true.
совершеннолети|е (-я) *ср*: **дости́гнуть ~я** to come of age.
совершенноле́тн|ий (-яя, -ее, -ие) *прил*: **стать ~им** to come of age.
соверше́н|ный (-ен, -на, -но) *прил* (*безукоризненный*) perfect; (*абсолютный*) absolute, complete; **соверше́нный вид** perfective aspect.
соверше́нств|о (-а) *ср* perfection; **доводи́ть (довести́** *perf*) **что-н до ~а** to do sth to perfection; **в ~е владе́ть** *(impf)* **чем-н** to have a perfect command of sth.
соверше́нств|овать (-ую; *perf* **усоверше́нствовать**) *несов перех* to improve
▸ **соверше́нствоваться** (*perf* **усоверше́нствоваться**) *несов возв*: **~ся в** *+prp* to improve.
соверш|и́ть (-у́, -и́шь; *impf* **соверша́ть**) *сов перех* to make; (*сделку*) to conclude; (*преступление, проступок итп*) to commit; (*богослужение, обряд, подвиг*) to perform
▸ **соверши́ться** (*impf* **соверша́ться**) *сов возв* to take place.
со́вестлив|ый (-, -а, -о) *прил* conscientious.
со́вестно *как сказ*: **мне ~** *+infin* ... I am ashamed to do; **как ему́ не ~!** he ought to be ashamed of himself!
со́вест|ь (-и) *ж* conscience; **на ~** (*сделанный*) very well; **по ~и говоря́** to be honest; **поступа́ть (поступи́ть** *perf*) **по ~и** to behave as one's conscience dictates; **со споко́йной ~ю** with a clear conscience.
сове́т (-а) *м* advice *только ед*; (*семейный*) discussion; (*военный*) council; (*ИСТ*) Soviet; **учёный ~** academic council; **С~ Безопа́сности ООН** United Nations Security Council; **дава́ть (дать** *perf*) **кому́-н ~** to give sb advice; **держа́ть** *(impf)* **~** to hold a council.
сове́тник (-а) *м* (*юстиции итп*) councillor; (*президента*) adviser.
сове́т|овать (-ую; *perf* **посове́товать**) *несов неперех*: **~ кому́-н** *+infin* to advise sb to do; ~ *(impf)* **кому́-н что-н** to recommend sth to sb
▸ **сове́товаться** (*perf* **посове́товаться**) *несов возв*: **~ся с кем-н** (*с другом*) to ask sb's advice; (*с врачом, с юристом*) to consult sb.
сове́тск|ий (-ая, -ое, -ие) *прил* Soviet.
сове́тчик (-а) *м* confidant(e); **в да́нном вопро́се я тебе́ не ~** I can't advise you on this subject.
совеща́ни|е (-я) *ср* (*собрание*) meeting; (*конференция*) conference.
совеща́тельный *прил* (*орган, голос*) consultative.
совеща́|ться (-юсь) *несов возв* to deliberate.
Совинформбюро́ *ср нескл сокр* (*ИСТ*) = *Сове́тское информацио́нное бюро́*.
совка́ *итп сущ см* **сово́к**.
сово́в|ый *прил*: **~ая лопа́та** shovel.
совлада́|ть (-ю) *сов неперех*: **~ с** *+instr* to control; ~ *(perf)* **с собо́й** to control o.s.
совладе́л|ец (-ьца) *м* joint owner.
совладе́ни|е (-я) *ср* joint ownership.
совме́стен *прил см* **совме́стный**.
совмести́мост|ь (-и) *ж* compatibility.
совмести́м|ый (-, -а, -о) *прил* compatible.
совмести́тельств|о (-а) *ср*: **я рабо́таю по ~у секретарём** my second job is as a secretary.
совме|сти́ть (-щу́, -сти́шь; *impf* **совмеща́ть**) *сов перех* to combine; **он ~ща́л в себе́ учёного и администра́тора** he was both a scholar and an administrator.

совме́стно *нареч* (*работать, решать итп*) jointly; ~ **с** *+instr* jointly with.
совме́ст|ный (**-ен, -на, -но**) *прил* (*общий*) joint; **совме́стное предприя́тие** joint venture.
совмеща́|ть (**-ю**) *несов от* **совмести́ть** ♦ *перех* (*две должности*) to combine.
совмеще́ни|е (**-я**) *ср* combining.
совмещу́ *сов см* **совмести́ть.**
сов|о́к (**-ка́**) *м* (*для мусора*) dustpan; (*для муки*) scoop; (*строительный*) shovel.
совоку́пен *прил см* **совоку́пный.**
совоку́пност|ь (**-и**) *ж* (*факторов, причин*) combination; **в ~и** in total.
совоку́п|ный (**-ен, -на, -но**) *прил* (*усилие*) combined, joint.
совпада́|ть (*3sg* **-ет**, *3pl* **-ют**) *несов от* **совпа́сть.**
совпаде́ни|е (**-я**) *ср* (*событий, обстоятельств*) coincidence; (*данных, цифр*) tallying; (*интересов, мнений*) meeting.
совпа́|сть (*3sg* **-дёт**, *3pl* **-ду́т**, *impf* **совпада́ть**) *сов неперех* (*события*) to coincide; (*данные, цифры итп*) to agree; (*интересы, мнения*) to meet.
соврати́тел|ь (**-я**) *м* seducer.
совра|ти́ть (**-щу́, -ти́шь**; *impf* **совраща́ть**) *сов перех* (*сбить с пути*) to lead astray; (*женщину*) to seduce.
совр|а́ть (**-у́, -ёшь**) *сов от* **врать.**
совраща́|ть (**-ю**) *несов от* **соврати́ть.**
совращу́ *сов см* **соврати́ть.**
совреме́нен *прил см* **совреме́нный.**
совреме́нник (**-а**) *м* contemporary.
совреме́нниц|а (**-ы**) *ж см* **совреме́нник.**
совреме́нно *нареч* (*одеваться*) fashionably; (*звучать*) modern.
совреме́нност|ь (**-и**) *ж* (*взглядов, идей*) progressiveness; (*современная эпоха*) the present day.
совреме́н|ный *прил* contemporary; (**-ен, -на, -но**; *техника*) up-to-date; (*человек, идеи*) modern.
совсе́м *нареч* (*новый, негодный итп*) completely; (*молодой*) very; (*нисколько: не пригодный, не нужный*) totally; **не** ~ (*не вполне*) not quite.
совхо́з (**-а**) *м сокр* (= *сове́тское хозя́йство*) Sovkhoz (*state farm in the Soviet Union*).
совью́(сь) *итп сов см* **свить(ся).**
совя́та *итп сущ см* **совёнок.**
согла́сен *прил см* **согла́сный.**
согла́си|е (**-я**) *ср* consent; (*в семье*) harmony, accord; **в ~и с** *+instr* (*с человеком*) in agreement with; **с чьего́-н ~я** with sb's consent; **дава́ть (дать** *perf*) ~ **на что-н** to give one's consent to sth; **приходи́ть (прийти́** *perf*) **к ~ю** to come to an agreement; **жить** (*impf*) **в ~и** to live in harmony.
согла|си́ться (**-шу́сь, -си́шься**; *impf* **соглаша́ться**) *сов возв*: ~ **на что-н/** *+infin* to agree to sth/to do; ~ (*perf*) **с** *+instr* (*с мнением, с высказыванием*) to agree with; ~ (*perf*) **на чём-н** (*разг*) to agree on sth.
согла́сно *нареч* (*жить, работать*) in harmony ♦ *предл*: ~ *+dat или* **с** *+instr* in accordance with.
согла́с|ный *прил*: ~ **звук** consonant ♦ (**-ного**; *decl like adj*) *м* consonant; (**-ен, -на, -но**; *дающий согласие*): ~ **на** *+acc* (*на условия, на ограничения*) agreeable to; **Вы ~ны (со мной)?** do you agree (with me)?; **все ~ны?** are we all agreed?; **я не ~ен** *+infin* ... I am not prepared to ....
согласова́ни|е (**-я**) *ср* (*действий, мер*) coordinating; (*обсуждение: плана*) coordination.
согласо́ван|ный (**-, -на, -но**) *прил* (*политика*) concerted; (*стратегия*) agreed.
соглас|ова́ть (**-у́ю**; *impf* **согласо́вывать**) *сов перех* (*усилия, действия*) to coordinate; (*обговорить*): ~ **что-н с** *+instr* (*план, цену*) to agree sth with; ~ (*perf*) **что-н с чем-н** (*спрос с предложением*) to make sth meet sth; (*прилагательное с существительным*) to make sth agree with sth
▸ **согласова́ться** (*не*)*сов возв*: **~ся с** *+instr* to correspond with.
соглаша́|ться (**-юсь**) *несов от* **согласи́ться.**
соглаше́ни|е (**-я**) *ср* agreement; **приходи́ть (прийти́** *perf*) **к ~ю** to come to an agreement; **заключа́ть (заключи́ть** *perf*) ~ to conclude an agreement.
соглашу́сь *сов см* **согласи́ться.**
согн|а́ть (**сгоню́, сго́нишь**; *pt* **-а́л, -ала́, -а́ло,** *impf* **сгоня́ть**) *сов перех* (*заставить удалиться*) to drive away; (*собрать*) to round up; **сгоня́ть** (~ *perf*) **улы́бку с лица́** to wipe a smile off somebody's face.
согн|у́ть (**-у́, -ёшь**) *сов от* **гнуть, сгиба́ть.**
согр|ажда́ни́н (**-ажданина**; *nom pl* **-а́ждане,** *gen pl* **-а́ждан**) *м* fellow citizen.
согрева́ни|е (**-я**) *ср* (*воды, пищи*) heating up; (*тела*) warming up.
согре́|ть (**-ю**; *impf* **согрева́ть**) *сов перех* (*воду*) to heat up; (*землю, ноги, руки*) to warm up; (*подлеж: мысль, ласка*) to warm
▸ **согре́ться** (*impf* **согрева́ться**) *сов возв* (*вода*) to heat up; (*человек, печка*) to warm up.
согреш|и́ть (**-у́, -и́шь**) *сов от* **греши́ть.**
со́д|а (**-ы**) *ж* soda; **питьева́я** ~ bicarbonate of soda.
соде́йстви|е (**-я**) *ср* assistance.
соде́йств|овать (**-ую**) (*не*)*сов неперех* (*+dat*) to assist.
содержа́ни|е (**-я**) *ср* (*семьи, детей*) upkeep; (*магазина, фермы*) keeping; (*книги, статьи*) contents *мн*; (*человека: под арестом*) holding; (*сахара, витаминов*) content; (*заработная плата*) allowance; (*оглавление*) contents *мн*; **о́тпуск без ~я** unpaid leave.
содержа́телен *прил см* **содержа́тельный.**
содержа́тел|ь (**-я**) *м* (*ресторана*) owner; (*магазина, пансиона*) keeper.

содержа́тел|ьный (-ен, -ьна, -ьно) *прил* (*статья, доклад*) informative.

соде́ржа́ть (-ержу́, -е́ржишь) *несов перех* (*детей, родителей, магазин*) to keep; (*ресторан*) to own; (*сахар, ошибки, информацию итп*) to contain; (*человека: под арестом*) to hold; ~ (*impf*) **что-н в чистоте́/в поря́дке** to keep sth clean/in order

▸ **содержа́ться** *несов возв* (*под арестом*) to be held; **в кни́ге ~е́ржится интере́сная информа́ция** the book contains interesting information; **~ся** (*impf*) **в чистоте́/в поря́дке** to be kept clean/in order.

содержи́м|ое (-ого; *decl like adj*) *ср* (*банки, сумки итп*) contents *мн*.

со́довый *прил* (*раствор*) soda *опред*.

содр|а́ть (сдеру́, сдерёшь; *pt* **-а́л, -ала́, -а́ло,** *impf* **сдира́ть)** *сов перех* (*слой, одежду*) to tear off; **сдира́ть (~** *perf*) **ко́жу с чего́-н** to skin sth; ~ (*perf*) **что-н с кого́-н** (*разг: дорого взять*) to sting sb for sth.

содрога́ни|е (-я) *ср* (*стен, стёкол*) shaking; (*от боли, от ужаса*) shuddering.

содрога́|ться (-юсь; *perf* **содрогну́ться)** *несов возв* (*стены, земля*) to shake; (*от боли, от страха итп*) to shudder.

содру́жеств|о (-а) *ср* (*дружба*) cooperation; (*союз*) commonwealth; **Содру́жество Незави́симых Госуда́рств** the Commonwealth of Independent States.

со́евый *прил* soya *опред*.

соедине́ни|е (-я) *ср* (*сил*) joining; (*проводов*) connection; (*учёбы с работой*) combination; (*место соединения*) contact; (*ВОЕН*) formation.

соедини́тел|ь (-я) *м* (*ЭЛЕК*) adaptor.

соедини́тельный *прил* (*провод, труба*) connecting.

соедин|и́ть (-ю́, -и́шь; *impf* **соединя́ть)** *сов перех* (*силы, усилия, детали*) to join; (*людей*) to unite; (*провода, трубы, по телефону*) to connect; (*установить сообщение*) to link; (*сочетать*): ~ **что-н с** +*instr* to combine sth with; **в ней ~ены́ ум и красота́** she is both clever and beautiful

▸ **соедини́ться** (*impf* **соединя́ться**) *сов возв* (*люди, отряды*) to join together; **~ся** (*perf*) **с кем** to make contact with sb.

сожале́ни|е (-я) *ср* (*сострадание*) pity; ~ **(о** +*prp*) (*о прошлом, о потере*) regret (about); **к ~ю** unfortunately; **к мо́ему (вели́кому** *или* **глубо́кому) ~ю** to my (great *или* deep) regret.

сожале́|ть (-ю) *несов неперех*: ~ **(о** +*prp*) (*об ошибке, о поступке*) to regret.

сожгу́ *итп сов см* **сжечь**.

сожже́ни|е (-я) *ср* (*еретика*) burning.

сожи́тел|ь (-я) *м* cohabiter.

сожи́тельниц|а (-ы) *ж см* **сожи́тель**.

сожму́(сь) *итп сов см* **сжа́ть(ся)**.

сожну́ *итп сов см* **сжать**.

сожр|а́ть (-у́, -ёшь) *сов от* **жрать**.

созва́нива|ться (-юсь) *несов см* **созвони́ться**.

соз|ва́ть (-ову́, -овёшь; *pt* **-ва́л, -вала́, -ва́ло,** *impf* **сзыва́ть)** *сов перех* (*пригласить*) to summon; (*impf* **созыва́ть**; *съезд, конференцию итп*) to convene.

созве́зди|е (-я) *ср* constellation.

созвон|и́ться (-ю́сь, -и́шься; *impf* **созва́ниваться)** *сов возв*: ~ **с** +*instr* to phone (*BRIT*) *или* call (*US*); (*договориться*): **нам на́до ~** we should fix something over the phone.

созву́чен *прил см* **созву́чный**.

созву́чи|е (-я) *ср* (*МУЗ*) sonority.

созву́ч|ный (-ен, -на, -но) *прил* harmonious; (*слова*) assonant; **~но** +*dat* (*соответствующий*) in keeping with; **~но с** +*instr* in keeping with.

созда|ва́ть(ся) (-ю́(сь), -ёшь(ся)) *несов от* **созда́ть(ся)**.

созда́м(ся) *итп сов см* **созда́ть(ся)**.

созда́ни|е (-я) *ср* creation; (*школы*) foundation; (*человек, животное*) creature.

созда́ст(ся) *сов см* **созда́ть(ся)**.

созда́тел|ь (-я) *м* creator; (*школы*) founder.

созда́тельниц|а (-ы) *ж см* **созда́тель**.

созда́ть (*как* **дать**; *см* **Table 14**; *impf* **создава́ть**) *сов перех* to create; (*школу*) to found

▸ **созда́ться** (*impf* **создава́ться**) *сов возв* (*обстановка*) to emerge; (*впечатление*) to be created.

созерца́ни|е (-я) *ср* (*рассматривание*) contemplation; (*душевное*) reflection.

созерца́|ть (-ю) *несов перех* (*рассматривать*) to contemplate.

созида́тел|ьный (-ен, -ьна, -ьно) *прил* creative.

созна|ва́ть (-ю́, -ёшь) *несов от* **созна́ть** ♦ *перех* to be aware of; ~ (*impf*), **что ...** to realize that ...

▸ **сознава́ться** *несов от* **созна́ться**.

созна́ни|е (-я) *ср* consciousness; (*вины, долга*) awareness; **приходи́ть (прийти́** *perf*) **в ~** to come round; **теря́ть (потеря́ть** *perf*) **~** to lose consciousness; **он рабо́тал до поте́ри ~я** he worked himself senseless.

созна́телен *прил см* **созна́тельный**.

созна́тельност|ь (-и) *ж* (*политическая, социальная*) awareness.

созна́тел|ьный (-ен, -ьна, -ьно) *прил* (*жизнь, возраст*) conscious; (*отношение, человек*) intelligent; (*обман, поступок*) deliberate, intentional.

созна́|ть (-ю; *impf* **сознава́ть)** *сов перех* (*вину, долг*) to realize

▸ **созна́ться** (*impf* **сознава́ться**) *сов возв*: **~ся (в** +*prp*) (*в ошибке, в каком-н намерении*) to admit (to); (*преступник*) to confess (to); **на́до ~ся** admittedly.

созову́ *итп сов см* **созва́ть**.

созрева́|ть (-ю) *несов неперех* = **зреть**.

созре́|ть (-ю) *сов от* **зреть**.

созы́в (-а) *м* (*съезда, собрания*) calling.

созыва́|ть (-ю) *несов от* **созва́ть**.

СОИ *ж сокр* (= *стратеги́ческая оборо́нная инициати́ва*) SDI (*US*) (= *Strategic Defense Initiative*).

соизмери́м|ый (-, -а, -о) *прил* (*величины*) proportional; (*понятия, ценности*) comparable.

соизме́р|ить (-ю, -ишь; *impf* **соизмеря́ть)** *сов перех* to compare.

соиска́ни|е (-я) *ср*: **на ~ чего́-н** pursuing sth.

соиска́тел|ь (-я) *м* (*приза, награды*) competitor; (*учёной степени*) candidate.

со|йти́ (*как* **идти́**; *см* **Table 18**; *impf* **сходи́ть)** *сов неперех* (*с горы, с лестницы*) to go down; (*с дороги*) to leave; (*подлеж*: *краска, загар итп*) to come off; (*разг*): **~ с** *+instr* (*с поезда, с автобуса*) to get off; **~** *(perf)* **за** *+acc* (*за актёра, за богача*) to pass as; **сходи́ть (~** *perf*) **с ума́** to go mad; **фильм ~шёл с экра́на** the film is not shown anymore; **с ума́ сойдёшь** *или* **~** (*разг*) the mind boggles; **всё ~шло́ благополу́чно** everything's turned out well; **~йдёт (и так)** (*разг*) it will do (as it is); **ему́ всё схо́дит с рук** he gets away with everything

▸ **сойти́сь** (*impf* **сходи́ться)** *сов возв* (*встретиться*) to meet; (*собраться*) to gather; (*цифры, показания*) to tally; (*перен*): **~сь с** *+instr* (*подружиться*) to become friendly with; **~шли́сь на том, что ...** it was agreed that ...; **~сь** *(perf)* **во взгля́дах/во вку́сах** (*перен*) to have similar views/tastes; **сходи́ться (~сь** *perf*) **на цене́/усло́виях** to agree on a price/ conditions; **~сь** *(perf)* **хара́ктерами** to get on.

сок (-а; *part gen* **-у,** *loc sg* **-у́)** *м* juice; (*также:* **фрукто́вый ~**) (fruit) juice.

соковыжима́л|ка (-ки; *gen pl* **-ок)** *ж* juice extractor.

со́кол (-а) *м* falcon.

соко л|ёнок (-ёнка; *nom pl* **-я́та,** *gen pl* **-я́т)** *ж* falcon chick.

соколи́н|ый *прил* (*гнездо*) falcon's *опред*; **~ая охо́та** falconry.

соколя́та *итп сущ см* **соколёнок**.

сокра|ти́ть (-щу́, -ти́шь; *impf* **сокраща́ть)** *сов перех* (*путь, рабочий день, статью*) to shorten; (*расходы*) to cut down, reduce

▸ **сократи́ться** (*impf* **сокраща́ться**) *сов возв* (*расстояние, сроки*) to be shortened; (*расходы, снабжение*) to be reduced.

сокраще́ни|е (-я) *ср* (*см глаг*) shortening; cutting down, reduction; (*сокращённое название*) abbreviation; (*также:* **~ шта́тов**) staff reduction; **попада́ть (попа́сть** *perf*) **под ~ (шта́тов)** to be made redundant.

сокращённый *прил* (*вариант текста*) abridged; (*рабочий день*) shortened; (*слово*) abbreviated.

сокращу́(сь) *сов см* **сократи́ть(ся)**.

сокрове́н|ный (-ен, -на, -но) *прил* (*мысли итп*) innermost; (*смысль, мечта*) intimate.

сокро́вищ|е (-а) *ср* (*обычно мн*: *также перен*) treasure.

сокро́вищниц|а (-ы) *ж* (*место*) treasury; (*совокупность*): **~** *+gen* wealth.

сокруша́|ть (-ю) *несов от* **сокруши́ть**

▸ **сокруша́ться** *несов возв* (*огорчаться*) to be distressed.

сокруше́ни|е (-я) *ср* (*противника*) destruction; (*огорчение*) distress.

сокруши́тел|ьный (-ен, -ьна, -ьно) *прил* devastating.

сокруш|и́ть (-у́, -и́шь; *impf* **сокруша́ть)** *сов перех* (*армию*) to crush; (*режим*) to overthrow.

соку́рсник (-а) *м*: **он мой ~** he is in my year.

соку́рсниц|а (-ы) *ж*: **она́ моя́ ~** she is in my year.

сол|га́ть (-гу́, -жёшь *итп,* **-гу́т)** *сов от* **лгать**.

солда́т (-а) *м* soldier.

солда́тик (-а) *м уменьш от* **солда́т**; (*игрушка*) toy soldier.

солда́т|ка (-ки; *gen pl* **-ок)** *ж* soldier's wife (*мн* wives).

солда́тск|ий (-ая, -ое, -ие) *прил* soldier's.

солдафо́н (-а) *м* (*разг*: *пренебр*) squaddie.

соле́ни|е (-я) *ср* (*огурцов*) pickling; (*рыбы*) salting.

солён|ое (-ого; *decl like adj*) *ср* salty food.

сол|ёный *прил* (*ветер*) salty; (*овощи*) pickled in brine; (*вода*) salt *опред*; (*рыба*) salted; (**-он, -она́, -оно**; *пища*) salty.

соле́нь|е (-я) *ср* (*обычно мн*) ≈ pickle.

солжёшь *итп сов см* **солга́ть**.

солида́рен *прил см* **солида́рный**.

солида́рност|ь (-и) *ж* solidarity.

солида́р|ный (-ен, -на, -но) *прил*: **я с ним ~ен** I am on his side.

соли́д|ный (-ен, -на, -но) *прил* (*постройка*) solid; (*знания, работа*) sound; (*фирма, специалист*) established; (*человек, манеры*) respectable; (*мебель, одежда*) quality; **~ во́зраст** respectable age.

соли́р|овать (-ую) *несов* to play a solo part.

соли́ст (-а) *м* soloist.

солист|ка (-ки; *gen pl* **-ок)** *ж см* **соли́ст**.

сол|и́ть (-ю́, -ишь; *perf* **посоли́ть)** *несов перех* (*суп, рагу*) to salt; (*засаливать*) to preserve in brine.

со́лнеч|ный *прил* (*энергия, лучи итп*) solar; (**-ен, -на, -но**; *день, погода*) sunny; **со́лнечное сплете́ние** solar plexus; **со́лнечный уда́р** sunstroke; **со́лнечные очки** sunglasses.

со́лнц|е (-а) *ср* sun.

солнцезащи́тный *прил*: **~ крем** suncream.

солнцепёк (-а) *м*: **на ~е** in a sunny spot.

солнцестоя́ни|е (-я) *ср* solstice.

со́ло *ср нескл нареч* solo.

солов|е́й (-ья́) *м* nightingale.

соловé|ть (-ю; *perf* **осоловéть)** *несов неперех* (*разг*) to become dazed.
соловьи́ный *прил* nightingale *опред*.
соловья́ *итп сущ см* **соловéй.**
сóлод (-а) *м* malt.
солóм|а (-ы) *ж* straw.
солóменный *прил* (*шляпа*) straw *опред*; (*крыша*) thatched; (*цвет*) straw-coloured (*BRIT*), straw-colored (*US*).
соломи́н|а (-ы) *ж* straw.
солóмин|ка (-ки; *gen pl* **-ок)** *ж уменьш от* **соломи́на**; (*перен*): **хватáться за ~ку** to clutch at straws.
солóм|ка (-ки; *gen pl* **-ок)** *ж уменьш от* **солóма**; (*печенье*) *long thin biscuit or bread stick.*
сóлон *итп прил см* **солёный.**
солóн|ка (-ки; *gen pl* **-ок)** *ж* saltcellar.
солончáк (-á) *м* saltmarsh.
сол|ь (-и) *ж* salt; (*gen pl* **-éй**; *ХИМ*) salt; (*перен*): ~ *+gen* (*вопроса, рассказа*) point of ◆ *ср нескл* (*МУЗ*) soh; **столóвая ~** table salt.
сóльный *прил* solo *опред*.
солью́(сь) *сов см* **сли́ть(ся).**
соля́н|ка (-ки; *gen pl* **-ок)** *ж spicy meat and vegetable soup*; (*рагу*) ragout.
солянóй *прил* (*раствор*) saline; (*промысел, залежи*) salt *опред*.
соля́нок *сущ см* **соля́нка.**
сом (-á) *м* catfish.
Сомали́ *ср нескл* Somalia.
сомкн|у́ть (-у́, -ёшь; *impf* **смыкáть)** *сов перех* to close; **я глаз не ~у́л всю ночь** I didn't sleep a wink all night
▸ **сомкну́ться** (*impf* **смыкáться**) *сов возв* to close.
сомневá|ться (-юсь) *несов возв*: **~ (в** *+prp*) to doubt; **~юсь, что э́то прáвда** I doubt that is true; **не ~йся приду́** don't worry, I'll come.
сомнéни|е (-я) *ср* (*неуверенность*) doubt; **вне** *или* **без (вся́кого) ~я** without a doubt; **брать (взять** *perf*) **что-н под ~** to doubt sth.
сомни́телен *прил см* **сомни́тельный.**
сомни́тельно *как сказ* it's doubtful; **~, чтóбы он согласи́лся** it's doubtful he'll agree; **он придёт?- ~** he's coming? – it's unlikely *или* not likely.
сомни́тел|ьный (-ен, -ьна, -ьно) *прил* (*дело, личность*) shady; (*предложение, знакомство*) dubious; (*комплимент, речи*) ambiguous; (*победа*) questionable.
сомну́(сь) *итп сов см* **смя́ть(ся).**
сон (сна) *м* sleep; (*сновидение*) dream; **ви́деть (уви́деть** *perf*) **что-н во сне** to have a dream about sth; **ви́деть** (*impf*) **~** to have a dream; **сквозь ~ слы́шать (услы́шать** *perf*) to hear in one's sleep; **со сна** half-awake.
сонáт|а (-ы) *ж* sonata.
сонéт (-а) *м* sonnet.

сонли́вый *прил* sleepy.
сóнн|ый *прил* (*заспанный*) sleepy, somnolent; (*вялый*) drowsy; **~ые видéния** dreams.
сóн|я (-и) *ж* (*животное*) dormouse (*мн* dormice) ◆ *м/ж* (*разг*) sleepyhead.
соображá|ть (-ю) *несов от* **сообрази́ть** ◆ *неперех* (*разг*: *быть сообразительным*) to be quick; (*смыслить*): **~ в** *+prp* to be good at; **я сегóдня плóхо ~ю** I'm slow on the uptake today.
соображéни|е (-я) *ср* (*суждение*) reasoning; (*обычно мн*: *мотивы*) reason; **из финáнсовых/педагоги́ческих ~й** for financial/educational reasons.
соображу́ *сов см* **сообрази́ть.**
сообрази́тел|ьный (-ен, -ьна, -ьно) *прил* bright.
сообра|зи́ть (-жу́, -зи́шь; *impf* **соображáть)** *сов неперех* to work out; **нам нáдо ~, что дéлать дáльше** we've got to work out what to do next.
сообрáзно *предл*: **~** *+dat или* **с** *+instr* in accordance with.
сообрáзный *прил*: **~ с** *+instr* in agreement with.
сообщá *нареч* together.
сообщá|ть (-ю) *несов от* **сообщи́ть**
▸ **сообщáться** *несов от* **сообщи́ться** ◆ *возв*: **~ся с** *+instr* (*связываться*) to communicate with.
сообщéни|е (-я) *ср* (*действие*: *новостей, результатов*) reporting; (*по радио*) report; (*правительственное*) announcement; (*срочное*) communication; (*автобусное, почтовое*) communications *мн*; **~ об оши́бке** (*КОМП*) error message.
соóбществ|о (-а) *ср* association; **в ~е с** *+instr* in association with; **мировóе** *или* **междунарóдное ~** international community.
сообщ|и́ть (-у́, -и́шь; *impf* **сообщáть)** *сов неперех*: **~ кому́-н о** *+prp* to inform sb of ◆ *перех* (*новости, тайну*) to tell
▸ **сообщи́ться** (*impf* **сообщáться**) *сов возв* (*+dat*) to be communicated to.
соóбщник (-а) *м* accomplice.
соóбщниц|а (-ы) *ж см* **соóбщник.**
соору|ди́ть (-жу́, -ди́шь; *impf* **сооружáть)** *сов перех* (*построить*) to erect; (*разг*: *смастерить*) to put together; (: *ужин, выпить*) to knock up.
сооружá|ть (-ю) *несов от* **соорди́ть.**
сооружéни|е (-я) *ср* (*действие*: *здания*) erection; (*крупная постройка*) structure.
сооружу́ *сов см* **соорди́ть.**
соотвéтственно *нареч* (*как следует*) accordingly ◆ *предл*: **~** *+dat* (*обстановке*) according to; **~ с** *+instr* in accordance with.
соотвéтствен|ный (-, -на, -но) *прил* (*оплата*) appropriate; (*результаты*) fitting.
соотвéтстви|е (-я) *ср* (*интересов, стилей*

итп) conformity; **в ~и с** *+instr* in accordance with.
соотве́тств|овать (-ую) *несов неперех*: ~ *+dat* (*интересам, должности итп*) to correspond with; (*требованиям*) to meet; **э́то не ~ует действи́тельности** it does not correspond with reality.
соотве́тствующ|ий (-ая, -ее, -ие) *прил* appropriate; **~им о́бразом** accordingly.
соотéчественник (-а) *м* compatriot.
соотéчественниц|а (-ы) *ж см* **соотéчественник.**
соотн|ести́ (-есу́, -есёшь; *pt* -ёс, -есла́, -есло́, *impf* **соотноси́ть**) *сов перех*: ~ **что-н с чем-н** to correlate sth with sth.
соотноси́тел|ьный (-ен, -ьна, -ьно) *прил* correlating.
соотн|оси́ть (-ошу́, -о́сишь) *несов от* **соотнести́**
▸ **соотноси́ться** *несов возв* to correlate.
соотноше́ни|е (-я) *ср* correlation.
соотношу́(сь) *несов см* **соотноси́ть(ся).**
со́пел *сущ см* **со́пло.**
сопережива́|ть (-ю) *несов неперех* to empathize.
сопе́рник (-а) *м* rival; (*в спорте*) competitor.
сопе́рниц|а (-ы) *ж см* **сопе́рник.**
сопе́рнича|ть (-ю) *несов неперех*: ~ **с кем-н в чём-н** to rival sb in sth.
соп|е́ть (-лю́, -и́шь) *несов неперех* to snort.
со́п|ка (-ки; *gen pl* -ок) *ж* (*холм*) hill; (*вулкан*) volcano.
со́пл|и (-е́й) *мн* (*разг*) snot *ед*.
сопли́вый *прил* (*разг*: *ребёнок*) snotty; **он ещё ~ мальчи́шка!** (*разг*) he's still just a young whippersnapper!
со́п|ло (-ла́; *nom pl* -ла, *gen pl* -ел) *ср* nozzle.
соплю́ *несов см* **сопе́ть.**
со́пок *сущ см* **со́пка.**
сопостави́м|ый (-, -а, -о) *прил* comparable.
сопоста́в|ить (-лю, -ишь; *impf* **сопоставля́ть**) *сов перех*: ~ **что-н** (**с** *+instr*) to collate sth (with).
сопра́но *ср нескл* soprano.
сопреде́л|ьный (-ен, -ьна, -ьно) *прил* (*область, страна итп*) neighbouring *опред* (*BRIT*), neighboring *опред* (*US*); (*наука, понятие*) related.
сопре́|ть (*3sg* -ет, *3pl* -ют) *сов от* **преть.**
соприкаса́|ться (-юсь; *perf* **соприкосну́ться**) *несов возв* (*предметы, участки*) to adjoin; (*интересы*) to cross over; ~ (**соприкосну́ться** *perf*) **с кем-н** to come into contact with sb.
сопроводи́тел|ь (-я) *м* escort.
сопроводи́тельный *прил* (*документ*) accompanying *опред*; **сопроводи́тельное письмо́** covering letter.
сопрово|ди́ть (-жу́, -ди́шь; *impf* **сопровожда́ть**) *сов перех* to accompany; (*no impf*; *дополнить*): ~ **что-н чем-н** to attach sth to sth.
сопровожда́|ть (-ю) *несов от* **сопроводи́ть** ◆ *перех* (*рассказ, пение*) to accompany
▸ **сопровожда́ться** *несов возв*: **~ся** *+instr* to be accompanied by.
сопровожде́ни|е (-я) *ср* (*действие*) escorting; (*аккомпанемент*) accompaniment; **в ~и** *+gen* accompanied by.
сопровожу́ *сов см* **сопроводи́ть.**
сопротивле́ни|е (-я) *ср* resistance; (*ИСТ*) the Resistance; **ока́зывать (оказа́ть** *perf*) ~ **кому́-н** to put up resistance to sb.
сопротивля́емост|ь (-и) *ж* resistance.
сопротивля́|ться (-юсь) *несов возв* (*+dat*) to resist.
сопру́ *итп сов см* **спере́ть.**
сопряжён|ный (-, -а́, -о) *прил*: ~ **с** *+instr* (*с опасностями итп*) involving.
сопу́тств|овать (*3sg* -ует, *3pl* -уют) *несов неперех* (*+dat*) to accompany.
сопью́сь *итп сов см* **спи́ться.**
сор (-а; *part gen* -у) *м* rubbish; **выноси́ть** (*impf*) ~ **из избы́** (*перен*) to wash one's dirty linen in public.
соразме́рен *прил см* **соразме́рный.**
соразме́р|ить (-ю, -ишь; *impf* **соразмеря́ть**) *сов перех*: ~ **что-н с чем-н** to measure sth against sth.
соразме́р|ный (-ен, -на, -но) *прил*: ~ *+dat* proportionate to; **~но** *+dat или* **с** *+instr* according to.
соразмеря́|ть (-ю) *несов от* **соразме́рить.**
сора́тник (-а) *м* comrade in arms.
сора́тниц|а (-ы) *ж см* **сора́тник.**
сорван|е́ц (-ца́) *м* (*разг*) scamp.
сорв|а́ть (-у́, -ёшь; *pt* -а́л, -ала́, -а́ло, *impf* **срыва́ть**) *сов перех* (*цветок, яблоко*) to pick; (*дверь, крышу, одежду итп*) to tear off; (*лекцию, переговоры*) to sabotage; (*планы*) to frustrate; (*разг*: *аплодисменты*) to get; (: *перен*): ~ **что-н на ком-н** (*гнев, злобу*) to take sth out on sb; ~ (*perf*) **го́лос** to lose one's voice
▸ **сорва́ться** (*impf* **срыва́ться**) *сов возв*: **~ся с** *+gen* (*с петель*) to come away from; (*с лестницы*) to fall off; (*перен*: *потерять самообладание*) to lose one's temper; (*планы*) to be frustrated; (*лекция*) to have to be cancelled; **~ся** (*perf*) **с ме́ста** to dash off; **у него́ срыва́лся го́лос** his voice was faltering; **он как с цепи́ ~а́лся** (*пренебр*) he's gone completely berserk.
сорганиз|ова́ться (-у́юсь) *сов от* **организова́ться.**
соревнова́ни|е (-я) *ср* competition; **кома́ндные ~я** team event; **отбо́рочные ~я** elimination contests.
соревн|ова́ться (-у́юсь) *несов возв* to compete.
сориенти́р|оваться (-уюсь) *сов от* **ориенти́роваться.**
сори́н|ка (-ки; *gen pl* -ок) *ж* speck.
сор|и́ть (-ю́, -и́шь; *perf* **насори́ть**) *несов неперех* to make a mess; ~ (*impf*) **деньга́ми** to throw

one's money about *или* around.
со́рн|ый *прил* refuse *опред*; **~ая трава́** weeds.
сорня́к (-а́) *м* weed.
со́рок (-а́; *см* **Table 28**) *чис* forty; **ему́ за ~** he's over forty; *см также* **пятьдеся́т**.
соро́к|а (-и) *ж* magpie; (*о болтливом человеке*) chatterbox.
сорокале́ти|е (-я) *ср* (*срок*) forty years; (*годовщина события*) fortieth anniversary.
сорокале́тн|ий (-яя, -ее, -ие) *прил* (*период*) forty-year; (*человек*) forty-year-old.
сороков|о́й (-а́я, -о́е, -ы́е) *чис* fortieth; *см также* **пятидеся́тый**.
сороконо́жка (-ки; *gen pl* **-ек)** *ж* centipede.
соро́ч|ка (-ки; *gen pl* **-ек)** *ж* (*мужская*) shirt; **ночна́я ~** nightgown; **ни́жняя ~** undergarment.
сорт (-а; *nom pl* **-а́)** *м* (*товара, продукта*) sort; (*пшеницы*) grade; **пе́рвый ~** Grade 1; (*перен*) first rate; **това́р пе́рвого со́рта** a Grade 1 product.
сорта́мент (-а) *м* assortment.
сортирова́льный *прил* sorting *опред*.
сортир|ова́ть (-у́ю) *несов перех* (*также комп*) to sort; (*по сортам, качеству*) to grade.
сортиро́в|ка (-ки; *gen pl* **-ок)** *ж* (*см глаг*) sorting; grading.
со́ртный *прил* ≈ Grade A *или* 1 *опред*.
сортово́й *прил* = **со́ртный**.
сос|а́ть (-у́, -ёшь) *несов перех* to suck; (*младенец, детёныш*) to suckle; **у меня́ ~ёт под ло́жечкой** (*разг*) I've got a sore stomach.
сосва́та|ть (-ю) *сов от* **сва́тать**.
сосе́д (-а; *nom pl* **-и**, *gen pl* **-ей)** *м* neighbour (*BRIT*), neighbor (*US*).
сосе́дн|ий (-яя, -ее, -ие) *прил* neighbouring (*BRIT*), neighboring (*US*).
сосе́дств|о (-а) *ср*: **жить по ~у** to live nearby; **в ~е с** *+instr* near.
со́сен *сущ см* **сосна́**.
соси́с|ка (-ки; *gen pl* **-ок)** *ж* sausage.
со́с|ка (-ки; *gen pl* **-ок)** *ж* (*на бутылке*) teat; (*пустышка*) dummy.
соска́ *итп сущ см* **сосо́к**.
соска́блива|ть (-ю) *несов от* **соскобли́ть**.
соска́кива|ть (-ю) *несов от* **соскочи́ть**.
соска́льзыва|ть (-ю) *несов от* **соскользну́ть**.
соскобл|и́ть (-ю́, -и́шь; *impf* **соска́бливать)** *сов перех* to scrape off.
соскользн|у́ть (-у́, -ёшь; *impf* **соска́льзывать)** *сов неперех* (*с горы*) to slide down; (*платок*) to slip off.
соск|очи́ть (-очу́, -о́чишь; *impf* **соска́кивать)** *сов неперех* (*с лошади, с поезда итп*) to jump off; (*с головы, с ноги*) to slip off.
соскреба́|ть (-ю) *несов от* **соскрести́**.
соскр|ести́ (-ебу́, -ебёшь; *pt* **-ёб, -ебла́, -ебло́**, *impf* **соскреба́ть)** *сов перех* to scrape away *или* off.
соску́ч|иться (-усь, -ишься) *сов возв* (*в чужом городе*) to be bored; (*затосковать*): **~ по** *+dat* to miss.
сослага́тельн|ый *прил*: **~ое наклоне́ние** subjunctive mood.
со|сла́ть (-шлю́, -шлёшь; *impf* **ссыла́ть)** *сов перех* to exile
▸ **сосла́ться** (*impf* **ссыла́ться)** *сов возв*: **~ся на** *+acc* to refer to.
со́слепу *нареч* (*разг*) being unable to see properly.
сосло́ви|е (-я) *ср* social class.
сосло́вный *прил* class *опред*.
сослужи́в|ец (-ца) *м* colleague.
сослужи́виц|а (-ы) *ж см* **сослужи́вец**.
сослужи́вца *итп сущ см* **сослужи́вец**.
сосл|ужи́ть (-ужу́, -у́жишь) *сов перех*: **~ слу́жбу кому́-н** (*человек*) to do sb a good turn; (*вещь*) to serve sb well.
сос|на́ (-ны́; *nom pl* **-ны**, *gen pl* **-ен)** *ж* pine (tree); **заблуди́ться** (*perf*) **в трёх со́снах** (*перен*: *разг*) to fail to solve a simple problem; **сиби́рская ~** cedar.
сосно́вый *прил* pine *опред*.
сосн|у́ть (-у́, -ёшь) *сов неперех* to take a nap.
со́сок *сущ см* **со́ска**.
сос|о́к (-ка́) *м* nipple.
сосредота́чива|ть(ся) (-ю(сь)) *несов от* **сосредото́чить(ся)**.
сосредото́чен|ный (-, -на, -но) *прил* (*атака, взгляд*) concentrated; (*ученик, работник*) attentive.
сосредото́ч|ить (-у, -ишь; *impf* **сосредота́чивать)** *сов перех* (*войска*) to concentrate; (*мысли, внимание*) to concentrate, focus
▸ **сосредото́читься** (*impf* **сосредота́чиваться)** *сов возв* (*войска*) to be concentrated; (*внимание*) to concentrate, focus.
соста́в (-а) *м* (*товарный, пассажирский*) train; (*классовый*) structure; **~** *+gen* (*комитета, комиссии*) members *мн* of; (*вещества*) composition of; **руководя́щий ~** management (staff); **преподава́тельский ~** teaching staff; **в ~е** *+gen* among(st); **входи́ть** (*impf*) **в ~** *+gen* to be a member of; **войти́** (*perf*) **в ~** *+gen* to become a member of; **гру́ппа верну́лась в по́лном ~е** all members of the group returned; **в ~ делага́ции вошли́ ...** the delegation was made up of ...; **коми́ссия в ~е 10 челове́к** a commission consisting of 10 members; **соста́в преступле́ния** (*ЮР*) constitution of a crime.
составите́л|ь (-я) *м* (*словаря*) compiler; (*сборника*) editor.
соста́в|ить (-лю, -ишь; *impf* **составля́ть)** *сов перех* (*фразу*) to make; (*словарь, список*) to compile; (*план*) to draw up; (*коллекцию, мнение, впечатление*) to form; (*какую-нибудь*

сумму) to constitute; (*мебель*) to put together; ~ *(perf)* **себе имя** to make a name for o.s.; **составлять (~** *perf)* **кому-н компанию** to join sb; **составлять (~** *perf)* **себе представление о чём-н** to form an impression about sth; **это не ~ит большого труда** it won't take a lot of effort

▸ **составиться** (*impf* **составляться**) *сов возв* (*коллекция, хор, коллектив*) to be formed; (*мнение, впечатление*) to form; **у нас ~илось благоприятное мнение о нём** we formed a good impression of him.

составлени|е (**-я**) *ср* (*словаря*) compilation; (*плана*) drawing up; (*коллекции*) forming; (*фразы*) making.

составлю(сь) *сов см* **составить(ся).**

составля|ть(ся) (**-ю(сь)**) *несов от* **составить(ся).**

составн|ой *прил*: **~ая мебель** kit furniture; **~ая часть, ~ элемент** component.

состар|ить (**-ю, -ишь**) *сов от* **старить**

▸ **состариться** *сов возв* (*человек*) to grow old.

состояни|е (**-я**) *ср* (*экономическое, эмоциональное*) state; (*больного*) condition; (*собственность*) capital; **быть** *(impf)* **в ~и** *+infin* to be able to do.

состоятел|ьный (**-ен, -ьна, -ьно**) *прил* (*идея, вывод итп*) sound; (*богатый*) well-off.

состо|ять (**-ю, -ишь**) *несов неперех*: **~ из** *+gen* (*книга*) to consist of; (*квартира*) to comprise; (*заключаться*): **~ в** *+prp* to be; (*в партии*) to be a member of; ~ *(impf)* *+instr* (*директором итп*) to be; **проблема ~ит в том, что ...** the problem is that ...

▸ **состояться** *несов возв* (*собрание, концерт*) to take place; **как учёный, он не ~ялся** he didn't make it as a scholar.

сострадани|е (**-я**) *ср* compassion.

состриг *итп сов см* **сострячь.**

сострига|ть (**-ю**) *несов от* **состричь.**

состригу *итп сов см* **состричь.**

состр|ить (**-ю, -ишь**) *сов от* **острить.**

стри|чь (**-гу, -жёшь** *итп*, **-гут**; *pt* **-г, -гла, -гло,** *impf* **состригать**) *сов перех* (*волосы*) to cut off; (*шерсть*) to shear off.

состро|ить (**-ю, -ишь**) *сов от* **строить.**

состряпа|ть (**-ю**) *несов от* **стряпать** ◆ *сов перех* (*перен: сделать плохо*) to concoct.

состык|овать(ся) (**-ую(сь)**) *сов от* **стыковать(ся).**

состязани|е (**-я**) *ср* contest.

состяза|ться (**-юсь**) *несов возв* to compete; ~ *(impf)* **в беге, ~** *(impf)* **в плавании** to race; **они ~лись в щедрости** they were competing to show who was the most generous.

сосуд (**-а**) *м* vessel.

сосудистый *прил* vascular.

сосул|ька (**-ьки**; *gen pl* **-ек**) *ж* icicle.

сосуществовани|е (**-я**) *ср* coexistence.

сосуществ|овать (**-ую**) *несов неперех* to coexist.

сосчита|ть (**-ю**) *сов от* **считать.**

сот *чис см* **сто.**

сот|ая (**-ой**; *decl like adj*) *ж*: **одна ~** one hundredth.

сотворени|е (**-я**) *ср*: **~ мира** Creation.

сотвор|ить (**-ю, -ишь**) *сов от* **творить** ◆ *перех* to create.

сотен *сущ см* **сотня.**

сот|ка (**-ки**; *gen pl* **-ок**) *ж one tenth of a hectare.*

сотк|ать (**-у, -ёшь**) *сов от* **ткать.**

сотник (**-а**) *м* sotnik (*lieutenant of Cossack troops*).

сот|ня (**-ни**; *gen pl* **-ен**) *ж* (*сто*) a hundred; (*деньги*) one hundred roubles; (*войска*) *Cossack squadron*; **~ни людей/вопросов/писем** hundreds of people/questions/letters.

соток *сущ см* **сотка.**

сотру(сь) *итп сов см* **стереть(ся).**

сотрудник (**-а**) *м* (*служащий*) employee; (*коллега*) colleague; **научный ~** research worker.

сотрудниц|а (**-ы**) *ж см* **сотрудник.**

сотруднича|ть (**-ю**) *несов неперех* (*в газете, в учреждении*) to work; ~ *(impf)* **с** *+instr* (*с фирмой*) to work with; (*с секретными службами*) to collaborate with.

сотрудничеств|о (**-а**) *ср* (*культурное, экономическое*) cooperation; (*в газете, в журнале*) work.

сотряса|ть(ся) (**-ю(сь)**) *несов от* **сотрясти(сь).**

сотрясени|е (**-я**) *ср* (*от взрыва, от удара*) shaking; (*также:* **~ мозга**) concussion.

сотряс|ти (**-у, -ёшь**; *impf* **сотрясать**) *сов перех* (*стены, землю*) to shake

▸ **сотрястись** (*impf* **сотрясаться**) *сов возв* (*стены, земля*) to shake.

сот|ы (**-ов**) *мн*: **(пчелиные) ~** honeycomb *ед.*

сот|ый (**-ая, -ое, -ые**) *чис* hundredth.

соус (**-а**) *м* sauce.

соусник (**-а**) *м* ≈ gravy boat.

соучасти|е (**-я**) *ср* complicity.

соучастник (**-а**) *м* accomplice.

соучастниц|а (**-ы**) *ж см* **соучастник.**

соф|а (**-ы**; *nom pl* **-ы**) *ж* sofa.

Софи|я (**-и**) *ж* Sofia.

сох|а (**-и**; *nom pl* **-и**) *ж* wooden plough (*BRIT*) *или* plow (*US*).

сох|нуть (**-ну, -нешь**; *pt* **-, -ла, -ло,** *perf* **высохнуть**) *несов неперех* (*мокрое бельё, кожа*) to dry; (*perf* **высохнуть** *или* **засохнуть**; *растения, дерево*) to wither; (*от болезни, от переживаний*) to go thin; (*краска, клей*) to dry; (*чернила*) to dry up.

сохран|ить (**-ю, -ишь**; *impf* **сохранять**) *сов перех* to preserve; (*КОМП*) to save

▸ **сохраниться** (*impf* **сохраняться**) *сов возв* to survive, be preserved; **она хорошо ~илась** (*разг*) she's well-preserved.

сохранност|ь (**-и**) *ж* (*груза*) good condition; (*вкладов, документов*) security; **в (полной) ~и**

(fully) intact.
сохраня́|ть(ся) (**-ю(сь)**) *несов от* **сохрани́ть(ся)**.
соцве́ти|е (**-я**) *ср* inflorescence.
социа́л-демокра́т (**-а**) *м* social democrat.
социа́л-демократи́ческ|ий (**-ая, -ое, -ие**) *прил* social democrat *опред*.
социали́зм (**-а**) *м* socialism.
социали́ст (**-а**) *м* socialist.
социалисти́ческ|ий (**-ая, -ое, -ие**) *прил* socialist.
социа́льный *прил* social; **социа́льная защищённость** social security.
социо́лог (**-а**) *м* sociologist.
социоло́ги|я (**-и**) *ж* sociology.
соче́льник (**-а**) *м* (*рождественский*) Christmas Eve; (*крещенский*) Twelfth Night.
со́чен *прил см* **со́чный**.
сочета́ни|е (**-я**) *ср* (*учёбы и работы*) combining; (*единство*: *красок, звуков*) combination.
сочета́|ть (**-ю**) *(не)сов перех* to combine
▸ **сочета́ться** *(не)сов возв* (*соединиться*) to combine; (*гармонировать*) to match, go with; **в ней ~ются ум и доброта́** she is both kind and intelligent.
сочине́ни|е (**-я**) *ср* (*музыки*) composing; (*стихов*) writing; (*литературное*) work; (*музыкальное*) composition; (*ПРОСВЕЩ*) essay.
сочин|и́ть (**-ю́, -и́шь**; *impf* **сочиня́ть**) *сов перех* (*музыку*) to compose; (*стихи, песню*) to write; (*разг*: *письмо*) to concoct; (: *солгать*) to make up.
соч|и́ться (*3sg* **-и́тся**, *3pl* **-а́тся**) *несов возв* to ooze; ~ *(impf)* **чем-н** to ooze with sth.
со́ч|ный (**-ен, -на́, -но**) *прил* (*плод*) juicy; (*трава*) lush; (*краски*) vibrant; (*язык*) expressive.
сочту́ *итп сов см* **счесть**.
сочу́вствен|ный (**-ен, -на, -но**) *прил* sympathetic.
сочу́встви|е (**-я**) *ср* sympathy; **встреча́ть** (**встре́тить** *perf*) **что-н с ~м** to be sympathetic to sth.
сочу́вств|овать (**-ую**) *несов неперех*: ~ *+dat* to sympathize with.
сочу́вствующ|ий (**-его**; *decl like adj*) *м* sympathizer.
сошёл(ся) *итп сов см* **сойти́(сь)**.
сошлю́(сь) *итп сов см* **сосла́ть(ся)**.
сошью́ *итп сов см* **сшить**.
сощу́р|ить(ся) (**-ю(сь), -ишь(ся)**) *сов от* **щу́рить(ся)**.
сою́з (**-а**) *м* alliance; (*республик, профессиональный*) union; (*ЛИНГ*) conjunction.
сою́зник (**-а**) *м* ally.
сою́зническ|ий (**-ая, -ое, -ие**) *прил* ally's.
сою́зный *прил* (*государство, армия*) allied; (*слово, связь*) conjunctive.
со́|я (**-и**) *ж собир* soya beans *мн*.
СП *м сокр* = *Сою́з писа́телей* ◆ *ср сокр* = *совме́стное предприя́тие*.
спаге́тти *мн нескл* spaghetti *ед*.
спад (**-а**) *м* (*температуры, давления*) drop; **экономи́ческий ~** recession; **идти́** (**пойти́** *perf*) **на ~** (*температура, давление*) to go down; (*экономика, производство*) to go into recession.
спада́|ть (*3sg* **-ет**, *3pl* **-ют**) *несов от* **спасть** ◆ *неперех* (*волосы, складки*) to fall.
спадёт *итп сов см* **спасть**.
спа́ек *сущ см* **спа́йка**.
спазм (**-а**) *м* spasm.
спа́ива|ть (**-ю**) *несов от* **спои́ть, спая́ть**.
спа́|йка (**-йки**; *gen pl* **-ек**) *ж* (*действие*) soldering; (*место*) join (*from soldering*).
спа́лен *прил см* **спа́льня**.
спал|и́ть (**-ю́, -и́шь**) *сов от* **пали́ть**.
спа́льник (**-а**) *м* (*разг*) sleeping bag.
спа́льный *прил* (*место*) sleeping *опред*; **спа́льный ваго́н** sleeping car; **спа́льный мешо́к** sleeping bag.
спа́л|ьня (**-ьни**; *gen pl* **-ен**) *ж* (*комната*) bedroom; (*мебель*) bedroom suite.
спа́рж|а (**-и**) *ж* asparagus.
спа́р|ить (**-ю, -ишь**; *impf* **спа́ривать**) *сов перех* (*телефон*) to connect (*to a shared line*); (*вагоны, трубы*) to couple; (*собак, кошек*) to mate.
спа́рыва|ть (**-ю**) *несов от* **споро́ть**.
Спас (**-а**) *м* (*РЕЛ*) the Day of the Saviour (*in the Orthodox Church*); (: *икона*) the Saviour.
спас(ся) *итп сов см* **спасти́(сь)**.
спаса́ни|е (**-я**) *ср* rescue.
спаса́тел|ь (**-я**) *м* rescuer; (*судно*) lifeboat.
спаса́тельный *прил* (*станция*) rescue *опред*; **спаса́тельная ло́дка** lifeboat; **спаса́тельный жиле́т** lifejacket; **спаса́тельный по́яс** lifebelt.
спаса́|ть(ся) (**-ю(сь)**) *несов от* **спасти́(сь)**.
спасе́ни|е (**-я**) *ср* rescue; (*РЕЛ*) Salvation.
спаси́бо *част*: ~ (**Вам**) thank you; **большо́е ~!** thank you very much!; **~ за по́мощь/сове́т** thanks for the help/advice; **~, что мили́ция во́время пришла́** (*разг*) thank God the police got here on time.
спаси́телен *прил см* **спаси́тельный**.
спаси́тел|ь (**-я**) *м* saviour; (*РЕЛ*) the Saviour.
спаси́тельниц|а (**-ы**) *ж* saviour.
спаси́тел|ьный (**-ен, -ьна, -ьно**) *прил* lifesaving.
спас|ова́ть (**-у́ю**) *сов от* **пасова́ть**.
спас|ти́ (**-у́, -ёшь**; *pt* **-, -ла́, -ло́**, *impf* **спаса́ть**) *сов перех* (*также РЕЛ*) to save; **спаса́ть** (~ *perf*) **кому́-н жизнь** to save sb's life; ~ *(perf)* **положе́ние** to rescue the situation
▸ **спасти́сь** (*impf* **спаса́ться**) *сов возв*: **~сь** (**от** *+gen*) to escape; (*РЕЛ*) to be saved (from).

спа|сть (*3sg* **-дёт**, *3pl* **-ду́т**, *impf* **спада́ть**) *сов неперех* (*вода*) to drop; (*упасть вниз*): ~ **с** *+gen* (*одежда, покрывало*) to fall off; **жара́ к ве́черу спа́ла** the heat lessened towards evening.

сп|ать (**-лю, -ишь**; *pt* **-ал, -ала́, -а́ло**) *несов неперех* to sleep; (*перен*: *разг*: *быть невнимательным*) to daydream; **ложи́ться** (**лечь** *perf*) ~ to go to bed; **пора́** ~ it's time for bed; ~ *(impf)* **кре́пким сном** to sleep like a log; **по́сле рабо́ты хорошо́ ~и́тся** one sleeps well after working

▸ **спа́ться** *несов безл*: **мне не ~и́тся** I can't (get to) sleep.

спа́ян|ный (**-, -на, -но**) *прил* (*перен*: *коллектив*) unified.

спая́|ть (**-ю**; *impf* **спа́ивать**) *сов перех* (*трубы*) to weld; (*перен*: *сплотить*) to unite.

СПБ *сокр* (= *Санкт-Петербу́рг*) St Petersburg.

СПб *сокр* = **СПБ**.

Спб *сокр* = **СПБ**.

спекта́кл|ь (**-я**) *м* performance.

спектр (**-а**) *м* (*также перен*) spectrum.

спекули́р|овать (**-ую**) *несов неперех* (*дефицитом*) to profiteer; (*КОММ*): ~ *+instr* (*на бирже*: *ценными бумагами*) to speculate in; (*с дурными целями*): ~ **на** *+prp* (*на трудностях, на слабостях*) to exploit.

спекуля́нт (**-а**) *м* (*КОММ*: *биржевой*) speculator; (*дефицитом*) profiteer.

спекуляти́в|ный (**-ен, -на, -но**) *прил* speculative.

спекуля́ци|я (**-и**) *ж* (*КОММ*) speculation; (*дефицитом*) profiteering.

спеку́тся *итп сов см* **спе́чься**.

спелена́|ть (**-ю**) *сов от* **пелена́ть**.

спе́л|ый (**-, -а́, -о**) *прил* ripe.

сперва́ *нареч* (*разг*: *вначале*) (at) first.

спе́реди *нареч* in front ◆ *предл* (*+gen*) in front of.

сп|ере́ть (**сопру́, сопрёшь**; *pt* **-ёр, -ёрла, -ёрло**) *сов от* **пере́ть**.

спе́рм|а (**-ы**) *ж* sperm.

спёрт|ый (**-, -а, -о**) *прил* (*разг*: *воздух*) stuffy.

спеси́в|ый (**-, -а, -о**) *прил* (*человек, тон*) haughty, arrogant.

спес|ь (**-и**) *ж* haughtiness, arrogance.

сп|еть (*3sg* **-е́ет**, *3pl* **-е́ют**, *perf* **поспе́ть**) *несов неперех* (*фрукты, овощи*) to ripen; ◆ (**-ою́, -оёшь**) *сов от* **петь**

▸ **спе́ться** *сов возв* (*хор, ансамбль*) to achieve a good sound; (*разг*: *пренебр*): **~е́ться с** *+instr* (*с ворами, со спекулянтами*) to get in with.

спех (**-а**) *м*: **мне не к спе́ху** (*разг*) I'm in no hurry.

спец (**-а́**) *м сокр* = **специали́ст**.

спец (**-а́**) *м* (*разг*: *мастер, знаток*) buff.

специализа́ци|я (**-и**) *ж* (*производства*) specialization; (*научная*) specialism.

специализи́рованный *прил* specialized.

специализи́р|оваться (**-уюсь**) *(не)сов возв*: ~ **в** *+prp* или **по** *+dat* to specialize in.

специали́ст (**-а**) *м*: ~ (**по** *+dat*) specialist (in).

специали́ст|ка (**-ки**; *gen pl* **-ок**) *ж см* **специали́ст**.

специа́льно *нареч* specially; (*намеренно*) on purpose.

специа́льност|ь (**-и**) *ж* (*профессия*) profession; (*ПРОСВЕЩ*) main subject.

специа́льный *прил* (*помещение, одежда итп*) special; (*образование*) specialist; **~ те́рмин** technical term; **специа́льный корреспонде́нт** special correspondent.

специ́фик|а (**-и**) *ж* specific nature.

спецификá́ци|я (**-и**) *ж* specification.

специфици́р|овать (**-ую**) *(не)сов перех* to specify.

специфи́чен *прил см* **специфи́чный**.

специфи́ческ|ий (**-ая, -ое, -ие**) *прил* specific.

специфи́ч|ный (**-ен, -на, -но**) *прил* = **специфи́ческий**.

спе́ци|я (**-и**) *ж* spice.

спецко́р (**-а**) *м сокр* = **специа́льный корреспонде́нт**.

спецку́рс (**-а**) *м сокр* = *специа́льный курс*; (*в вузе*) *course of lectures in a specialist field*.

спецо́вк|а (**-и**) *ж* (*разг*) workman's jacket.

спецоде́жд|а (**-ы**) *ж сокр* (= *специа́льная оде́жда*) work clothes *мн*.

спе́|чься (*3sg* **-чётся**, *3pl* **-ку́тся**) *сов* = **запе́чься**.

спе́шен *прил см* **спе́шный**.

спеш|и́ть (**-у́, -и́шь**; *perf* **поспеши́ть**) *несов неперех* (*часы*) to be fast; (*прийти закончить*): ~ *+infin*/**с** *+instr* to be in a hurry to do/with; ~ *(impf)* **на по́езд/в шко́лу** to rush for the train/to school; **я ~у́ (домо́й/на рабо́ту)** I am in a hurry (to get home/to work); **поспеши́!** hurry up; **он поспеши́л с отве́том** he gave a rash answer; **~у́ сообщи́ть, что ...** I hasten to inform you that ...; **рабо́тать** *(impf)* **не ~а́** to work at a relaxed pace.

спе́шк|а (**-и**) *ж* (*разг*) hurry, rush; **в ~е я забы́л ша́пку** in the rush I forgot my hat; **нет никако́й ~и** there's no hurry.

спе́шно *нареч* (*уйти, закончить*) hurriedly.

спе́ш|ный (**-ен, -на, -но**) *прил* (*дело, задание*) urgent.

спива́|ться (**-юсь**) *несов от* **спи́ться**.

СПИД (**-а**) *м сокр* (= *синдро́м приобретённого иммунодефици́та*) AIDS (= *acquired immune deficiency syndrome*).

спидо́метр (**-а**) *м* speedometer.

спи́кер (**-а**) *м* speaker.

спики́р|овать (**-ую**) *сов от* **пики́ровать**.

спил|и́ть (**-ю́, -ишь**; *impf* **спи́ливать**) *сов перех* to saw down.

спин|а́ (**-ы́**; *acc sg* **-у**, *dat sg* **-е́**, *nom pl* **-ы**) *ж* (*человека, животного*) back; **за ~о́й у него́ бога́тая жизнь** he has lead a full life.

спи́н|ка (**-ки**; *gen pl* **-ок**) *ж уменьш от* **спина́**; (*дивана, стула итп*) back; (*кровати*) bedstead.

спи́ннинг (**-а**) *м* spinner.

спинно́й *прил* (*позвонок*) spinal; **спинно́й мозг**

spinal cord.
спи́нок *сущ см* **спи́нка**.
спира́л|ь (-и) *ж* (*линия*) spiral; (*также:* **внутрима́точная ~**) coil (*contraceptive*).
спира́льный *прил* spiral.
спирт (-а; *loc sg* **-у)** *м* (*технический, медицинский*) spirit.
спиртн|о́е (-о́го; *decl like adj*) *ср* alcohol.
спиртно́й *прил* (*запах, раствор*) of alcohol; **спиртно́й напи́ток** alcoholic drink.
списа́ни|е (-я) *ср* (*КОММ*) writing off; (*МОР*) discharge.
сп|иса́ть (-ишу́, -и́шешь; *impf* **спи́сывать)** *сов перех* to copy; (*КОММ*) to write off; (*МОР*) to discharge; **спи́сывать (~** *perf*) **что-н с** *+gen* to copy sth from
▸ **списа́ться** (*impf* **спи́сываться)** *сов возв* (*моряк*) to leave ship; **спи́сываться (~ся** *perf*) **с** *+instr* (*со старым другом*) to write to.
спи́с|ок (-ка) *м* (*делегатов, присутствующих*) list; (*документов, романа*) manuscript copy; **кни́га разошла́сь в ~ках** the book was distributed in handwritten copies.
спи́сыва|ть(ся) (-ю(сь)) *несов от* **списа́ть(ся)**.
спи́ться (сопью́сь, сопьёшься; *impf* **спива́ться)** *сов возв* to take to drink.
спихн|у́ть (-у́, -ёшь; *impf* **спи́хивать)** *сов перех* to push aside *или* down; (*разг*: *конкурента, начальника*) to oust; **спи́хивать (~** *perf*) **что-н на кого́-н** (*разг*: *плохой товар, ответственность*) to push sth onto sb.
спи́ц|а (-ы) *ж* (*для вязания*) knitting needle; (*колеса*) spoke.
спи́чек *сущ см* **спи́чка**.
спи́чечн|ый *прил*: **~ая коро́бка** matchbox; **~ая голо́вка** matchhead.
спи́ч|ка (-ки; *gen pl* **-ек)** *ж* match; (*разг*: *худой человек*) beanpole.
спишу́(сь) *итп сов см* **списа́ть(ся)**.
сплав (-а) *м* (*(не)металический*) alloy; (*леса*) floating.
спла́в|ить (-лю, -ишь; *impf* **сплавля́ть)** *сов перех* (*металлы*) to alloy; (*лес*) to float; (*перен*: *разг*: *избавиться*) to get rid of.
сплани́р|овать (-ую) *сов от* **плани́ровать**.
спланир|ова́ть (-у́ю) *сов от* **планирова́ть**.
спла́чива|ть(ся) (-ю(сь)) *несов от* **сплоти́ть(ся)**.
сплёвыва|ть (-ю) *несов от* **сплю́нуть**.
спл|ести́ (-ету́, -етёшь; *pt* **-ёл, -ела́, -ело́)** *сов от* **плести́** ◆ (*impf* **сплета́ть**) *перех* to plait; (*пальцы, ноги, руки*) to intertwine
▸ **сплести́сь** (*impf* **сплета́ться**) *сов возв* (*водоросли*) to be interwoven; (*руки, тела*) to be intertwined.
сплётен *сущ см* **сплётня**.
сплете́ни|е (-я) *ср* (*лент, верёвок*) interlacing; (*то, что сплетено*) tissue; (*перен*: *причин, обстоятельств*) combination.
сплётник (-а) *м* gossip.
сплётниц|а (-ы) *ж см* **сплётник**.
сплётнича|ть (-ю) *несов неперех* to gossip.
сплёт|ня (-ни; *gen pl* **-ен)** *ж* gossip; **распуска́ть** (*impf*) **~ни** to spread gossip; **пуска́ть (пусти́ть** *perf*) **~ню** to start gossip.
сплету́(сь) *итп сов см* **сплести́(сь)**.
сплеча́ *нареч* (*ударить*) straight from the shoulder; (*разг*: *решать*) impulsively.
спло|ти́ть (-чу́, -ти́шь; *impf* **спла́чивать)** *сов перех* to unite
▸ **сплоти́ться** (*impf* **спла́чиваться**) *сов возв* to unite.
сплох|ова́ть (-у́ю) *сов неперех* (*разг*) to slip up.
сплочённый *прил* united.
сплочу́(сь) *сов см* **сплоти́ть(ся)**.
сплошно́й *прил* (*стена, поток итп*) continuous; (*грамотность, перепись*) universal; (*разг*: *мучение, неудачи*) utter; (: *восторг, маразм*) complete and utter.
сплошь *нареч* (*по всей поверхности*) all over; (*без исключения*) completely; **~ и ря́дом** (*разг*) more often than not.
сплут|ова́ть (-у́ю) *сов от* **плутова́ть**.
сплы|ть (*3sg* **-вёт**, *3pl* **-ву́т**, *impf* **сплыва́ть)** *сов неперех* (*уплыть*) to be carried away; **был да ~л** (*разг*) it's gone forever
▸ **сплы́ться** (*impf* **сплыва́ться**) *сов возв* (*буквы, краски итп*) to run together, merge.
сплю *несов см* **спать**.
сплю́н|уть (-у, -ешь; *impf* **сплёвывать)** *сов перех* to spit; (*шелуху*) to spit out.
сплю́щ|ить (-у, -ишь) *сов от* **плю́щить** ◆ (*impf* **сплю́щивать**) *перех* to flatten
▸ **сплю́щиться** (*impf* **сплю́щиваться**) *сов возв* to become flattened.
спл|яса́ть (-яшу́, -я́шешь) *сов от* **пляса́ть**.
сподви́жник (-а) *м* loyal supporter.
сподо́б|иться (-люсь, -ишься) *сов возв*: **~** *+infin* (*разг*) to be honoured (*BRIT*) *или* honored (*US*) to do.
спозара́нку *нареч* (*разг*) very early (*in the morning*).
спо|и́ть (-ю́, -и́шь; *imper* **-и́(те)**, *impf* **спа́ивать)** *сов перех*: **~ кого́-н** to get sb drunk; (*приучить пьянствовать*) to make a drunkard of sb.
споко́ен *прил см* **споко́йный**.
споко́йно *нареч* (*жить, говорить*) quietly; (*спать*) peacefully ◆ *как сказ безл* it's quiet; **у меня́ на душе́ ~** I feel calm.
споко́|йный (-ен, -йна, -йно) *прил* (*море*) calm; (*улица, жизнь*) quiet; (*человек, тон, беседа*) serene; (*характер*) placid; (*цвет*) gentle, restful; **~йная со́весть** clear conscience.
споко́йстви|е (-я) *ср* (*в городе, в лесу*) calm, tranquillity; (*на душе*) calm; **сохраня́ть** (*impf*) **~**

to keep calm.

споласкива|ть (-ю) *несов от* **сполоснуть.**

сполз|ти (-у, -ёшь; *pt* **-, -ла, -ло,** *impf* **сползать)** *сов неперех* to climb down; (*шапка, платок, чулки*) to slip down; (*перен: к национализму*) to slide

▸ **сползтись** (*impf* **сползаться)** *сов возв* to congregate.

сполна *нареч* in full.

сполосн|уть (-у, -ёшь; *impf* **споласкивать)** *сов перех* to rinse.

спонсор (-а) *м* sponsor.

спонсорск|ий (-ая, -ое, -ие) *прил* sponsoring *опред.*

спор (-а) *м* debate; (*имущественный*) dispute; (*спортивный*) competition; **вести** (*impf*) **~** to have an argument; **спору нет** there is no doubt; **на ~** (*разг*) as a bet.

спор|а (-ы) *ж* (*БОТ*) spore.

спорадическ|ий (-ая, -ое, -ие) *прил* sporadic.

спорен *прил см* **спорный.**

спор|ить (-ю, -ишь; *perf* **поспорить)** *несов неперех* (*вести спор*) to argue, debate; (*держать пари*) to bet; **~** (*impf*) **с кем-н о чем-н** *или* **за что-н** (*о наследстве*) to dispute sth with sb; **~им, ты не посмеешь ему возразить** I bet you wouldn't dare to contradict him

▸ **спориться** *несов возв* (*работа, дело*) to go well.

спор|ный (-ен, -на, -но) *прил* (*дело*) disputed; (*победа, преимущество*) doubtful; **~ вопрос** moot point.

сп|ороть (-орю, -орешь; *impf* **спарывать)** *сов перех* to nip off.

спорт (-а) *м* sport.

спортзал (-а) *м* sports hall, gymnasium.

спортивный *прил* (*площадка, комментатор*) sports *опред*; (*фигура, человек*) sporty; **спортивный костюм** tracksuit.

спортлото *ср нескл* sports lottery.

спортсмен (-а) *м* sportsman (*мн* sportsmen).

спортсмен|ка (-ки; *gen pl* **-ок)** *ж* sportswoman (*мн* sportswomen).

спорттовар|ы (-ов) *мн* sports goods *мн.*

спорхн|уть (-у, -ёшь) *сов неперех* to flutter off.

спорщик (-а) *м* debater.

спорщиц|а (-ы) *ж см* **спорщик.**

спорый *прил* efficient.

способ (-а) *м* way.

способен *прил см* **способный.**

способност|ь (-и) *ж* ability; (*обычно мн: талант*) aptitude *ед*; **математические ~и** aptitude for mathematics; **пропускная ~** (*дороги, метро*) capacity; **покупательная ~ населения** purchasing power (of the population).

способ|ный (-ен, -на, -но) *прил* capable; (*талантливый*) able; **~** *+infin* capable of doing; **он ~ен к математике** he has a gift for mathematics; **она ~на на всё** she is capable of anything.

способств|овать (-ую) *сов неперех*: **~** *+dat* (*успеху, развитию*) to promote.

споткн|уться (-усь, -ёшься; *impf* **спотыкаться)** *сов возв* (*при ходьбе, при беге*) to trip; (*при чтении*) to get stuck; (*перен: совершить проступок*) to slip up.

спохв|атиться (-ачусь, -атишься; *impf* **спохватываться)** *сов возв* (*вспомнить*) to remember suddenly; (*понять ошибку*) to realize.

спою *итп несов см* **спеть.**

справа *нареч* to the right; **~ от чего-н** to the right of sth.

справедливо *нареч* fairly, justly ◆ *как сказ*: **это ~** that's fair *или* just.

справедливост|ь (-и) *ж* justice; **отдать** (*perf*) **кому-н ~** (*оценить по заслугам*) to do justice to sb; **~и ради ...** to be fair ....

справедлив|ый (-, -а, -о) *прил* just; (*утверждение*) correct; (*подозрение*) justified.

справ|ить (-лю, -ишь; *impf* **справлять)** *сов перех* (*разг: день рождения*) to celebrate; (*шубу, туфли*) to get

▸ **справиться** (*impf* **справляться)** *сов возв*: **~ся с** *+instr* (*с работой, с заданием*) to manage; (*с противником*) to deal with; (*с волнением, с детьми*) to cope with; (*узнавать*): **~ся о** *+prp* to enquire *или* ask about.

справ|ка (-ки; *gen pl* **-ок)** *ж* (*сведения*) information; (*документ*) certificate; **обращаться (обратиться** *perf*) **за ~кой** to apply for information; **наводить (навести** *perf*) **~ки** to make enquiries.

справлю(сь) *сов см* **справить(ся).**

справля|ть(ся) (-ю(сь)) *несов от* **справить(ся).**

справок *сущ см* **справка.**

справочник (-а) *м* (*телефонный*) directory; (*грамматический*) reference book.

справочный *прил* (*литература, пособие*) reference *опред*; **справочное бюро** information office *или* bureau.

спрашива|ть (-ю) *несов от* **спросить**

▸ **спрашиваться** *несов от* **спроситься** ◆ *возв*: **~ется, где ты был в это время** the question is, where were you at that time?

спресс|овать (-ую) *сов от* **прессовать.**

спринт (-а) *м* sprint.

спринтер (-а) *м* sprinter.

спровад|ить (-жу, -дишь; *impf* **спроваживать)** *сов перех* (*разг*) to send off.

спровоцир|овать (-ую) *сов от* **провоцировать.**

спроектир|овать (-ую) *сов от* **проектировать.**

спрос (-а) *м*: **~ на** *+acc* (*на товары, на специалистов*) demand for; (*требование*): **~ с** *+gen* (*с родителей, с начальника*) demands *мн* on; **без спроса** *или* **спросу** without permission; **с тебя ~ особый** there are special demands on you; ~ **и предложение** (*ЭКОН*) supply and demand.

спр|осить (**-ошу, -осишь**; *impf* **спрашивать**) *сов перех* (*дорогу, время*) to ask; (*совета, денег*) to ask for; (*взыскать*): ~ **что-н с** *+gen* to call sb to account for; (*осведомиться*): ~ **кого-н о чём-н** to ask sb about sth; **спрашивать** (~ *perf*) **ученика** to question *или* test a pupil; **я ~осил, который час/когда поезд** I asked what the time was/when the train would be

▸ **спроситься** (*impf* **спрашиваться**) *сов возв*: ~**ся** *+gen или* **у** *+gen* (*у родителей, у учителя итп*) to ask permission of; **с нас ~осится за это** we will be answerable for that.

спросонок *нареч* (*разг*) half asleep.

спрошу(сь) *сов см* **спросить(ся)**.

спрут (**-а**) *м* octopus.

спрыг|нуть (**-ну, -нешь**; *impf* **спрыгивать**) *сов неперех*: ~ **с** *+gen* to jump off.

спряга|ть (**-ю**; *perf* **проспрягать**) *несов перех* (*ЛИНГ*) to conjugate.

спряду *итп сов см* **спрясть**.

спряжени|е (**-я**) *ср* (*ЛИНГ*) conjugation.

спря|сть (**-ду, -дёшь**) *сов от* **прясть**.

спря|тать(ся) (**-чу(сь), -чешь(ся)**) *сов от* **прятать(ся)**.

спуг|нуть (**-ну, -нёшь**; *impf* **спугивать**) *сов перех* to frighten off.

спуд (**-а**) *м*: **держать что-н под спудом** (*идею, план*) to keep sth back; **извлекать** (**извлечь** *perf*) **что-н из-под спуда** to bring sth into the light of day.

спуск (**-а**) *м* (*действие*: *флага*) lowering; (: *корабля*) launch; (: *воды, газа*) draining; (*место*: *к реке, с горы*) descent; (*в оружии*) trigger; **нажимать** (**нажать** *perf*) (**на**) ~ to pull the trigger; **я не дал ему спуску** (*разг*) I didn't let him off.

спускаемый *прил*: ~ **аппарат** (*КОСМОС*) landing gear.

спуска|ть (**-ю**) *несов от* **спустить** ◆ *перех*: **я не ~л глаз с неё** I didn't take my eyes off her

▸ **спускаться** *несов от* **спуститься** ◆ *возв* (*дорога, берег*) to descend, go down; (*волосы, фалды*) to hang down.

спусковой *прил* (*трап*) exit *опред*; (*механизм*) trigger *опред*.

спу|стить (**-щу, -стишь**; *impf* **спускать**) *сов перех* to lower; (*директиву, план*) to send out; (*собаку*) to let loose; (*газ, воду*) to drain; (*разг*: *зарплату, наследство*) to squander; (*простить*): ~ **что-н кому-н** to let sb off with sth, forgive sb for sth; **~стя рукава** (*разг*: *небрежно*) carelessly; **спускать** (~ *perf*) **корабль** (**на воду**) to launch a ship; **спускать** (~ *perf*) **курок** to pull the trigger; **спускать** (~ *perf*) **кого-н с лестницы** to kick sb downstairs; (*выгнать*) to kick sb out; **у моей машины ~стила шина** my car has a flat tyre (*BRIT*) *или* tire (*US*)

▸ **спуститься** (*impf* **спускаться**) *сов возв* to go down; (*чулки, юбка итп*) to slip down; (*туман, мгла, ночь итп*) to descend.

спустя *нареч*: ~ **три дня/год** three days/a year later.

спутанный *прил* (*волосы, верёвки*) tangled; (*речь*) muddled.

спута|ть(ся) (**-ю(сь)**) *сов от* **путать(ся)**.

спутник (**-а**) *м* (*в пути*) travelling (*BRIT*) *или* traveling (*US*) companion; (*городок*) satellite town; (*АСТРОНОМИЯ*) satellite; (*КОСМОС*: *также*: **искусственный** ~) sputnik, satellite; (*перен*): ~ *+gen* (*бедности, прогресса итп*) concomitant of; ~ **жизни** (*муж*) life's companion.

спутниковый *прил* (*связь*) satellite *опред*; **спутниковое телевидение** satellite TV.

спутниц|а (**-ы**) *ж* (*в пути*) travelling (*BRIT*) *или* traveling (*US*) companion; ~ **жизни** (*жена*) life's companion.

спутыва|ть (**-ю**; *perf* **спутать**) *несов перех* = **путать**.

спущу(сь) *сов см* **спустить(ся)**.

спя|тить (**-чу, -тишь**) *сов неперех* (*разг*) to go daft.

спячк|а (**-и**) *ж* (*животных*) hibernation; (*перен*: *бездеятельность*) lethargy.

спячу *сов см* **спятить**.

ср. *сокр* (= *сравни*) cp. (= *compare*).

срабатыва|ть (*3sg* **-ет**, *3pl* **-ют**) *несов от* **сработать**.

сработанност|ь (**-и**) *ж* harmony.

сработа|ть (*3sg* **-ет**, *3pl* **-ют**, *impf* **срабатывать**) *сов неперех* to operate.

сравнени|е (**-я**) *ср* comparison; **в ~и** *или* **по ~ю с** *+instr* compared with; **не может быть никакого ~я с** *+instr* there can be no comparison with; **не поддаваться** (*impf*) **никакому ~ю** to be unspeakable.

сравнива|ть (**-ю**) *несов от* **сравнить, сравнять**.

сравним|ый (**-, -а, -о**) *прил* comparable.

сравнителен *прил см* **сравнительный**.

сравнительно *нареч* comparatively; ~ **с** *+instr* compared to *или* with.

сравнител|ьный (**-ен, -ьна, -ьно**) *прил* comparative; **сравнительная степень** (*ЛИНГ*) comparative degree.

сравн|ить (**-ю, -ишь**; *impf* **сравнивать**) *сов перех*: ~ **что-н/кого-н** (**с** *+instr*) to compare sth/sb (with); (*уподобить*): ~ **что-н/кого-н с** *+instr* to compare sth/sb to

▸ **сравниться** *сов возв*: **~ся с** *+instr* to compare with.

сравня|ть (**-ю**; *impf* **сравнивать**) *сов перех* (*расход с доходом*) to balance; **сравнивать** (~ *perf*) **счёт** to equalize

► **сравня́ться** *сов возв*: **~ся с** *+instr* to become the equal of.
сража́ть(ся) (**-ю(сь)**) *несов от* **срази́ть(ся)**.
сраже́ни|е (**-я**) *ср* (*битва*) battle.
сра|зи́ть (**-жу́, -зи́шь**; *impf* **сража́ть**) *сов перех* (*пулей, ударом*) to slay; (*подлеж: горе, тяжёлая весть*) to crush
► **срази́ться** (*impf* **сража́ться**) *сов возв* to join battle.
сра́зу *нареч* (*немедленно*) straight away; (*в один приём*) (all) at once; (*рядом*) right.
срам (**-а**) *м* (*разг*) shame; **~ ви́деть тако́е** it's a disgrace *или* shame.
срам|и́ть (**-лю́, -и́шь**; *perf* **осрами́ть**) *несов перех* (*позорить*) to shame; (*бранить*) to put to shame
► **срами́ться** (*perf* **осрами́ться**) *несов возв* to bring shame on o.s.
сраста́ни|е (**-я**) *ср* (*костей*) knitting.
сраст|и́сь (*3sg* **-ётся**, *3pl* **-у́тся**, *impf* **сраста́ться**) *сов возв* (*кости*) to knit (together); (*стволы*) to grow together; (*перен: компании*) to merge.
сраще́ни|е (**-я**) *ср* (*костей*) knitting.
среаги́р|овать (**-ую**) *сов от* **реаги́ровать**.
сред|а́ (**-ы́**; *nom pl* **-ы**) *ж* medium; (*no pl*; *природная, социальная*) environment; (*артистическая, литературная*) milieu; (*acc sg* **-у**; *день недели*) Wednesday; *см также* **пя́тница**; **окружа́ющая ~** environment; **охра́на окружа́ющей ~ы́** conservation.
среди́ *предл* (*+gen*) in the middle of; (*в пределах*) in the middle of, amidst; (*в окружении*) amidst; (*в среде, в числе*) among.
средизе́мн|ый *прил*: **С~ое мо́ре** the Mediterranean (Sea).
среди́н|а (**-ы**) *ж* = **середи́на**.
среди́нный *прил* = **середи́нный**.
среднеазиа́тск|ий (**-ая, -ое, -ие**) *прил* Central Asian.
средневеко́вый *прил* medieval.
средневеко́вь|е (**-я**) *ср* the Middle Ages *мн*.
среднево́лновый *прил* medium-wave.
среднегодово́й *прил* average annual.
среднеме́сячный *прил* average monthly.
среднесу́точный *прил* average daily.
сре́дн|ий (**-яя, -ее, -ие**) *прил* medium; (*комната, окно итп*) middle; (*посредственный*) average; **в ~ем** on average; **вы́ше/ни́же ~его** above/below average; **он ~их лет** he is middle-aged; **сре́днее образова́ние** secondary education; **сре́дние века́** the Middle Ages *мн*; **сре́дний па́лец** middle finger; **сре́дняя шко́ла** secondary school.
средото́чи|е (**-я**) *ср* focus, centre (*BRIT*), center (*US*).
сре́дств|а (**-**) *мн* means *мн*; (*деньги*) means *мн*, funds *мн*; **отпуска́ть (отпусти́ть** *perf*) *или* **выделя́ть (вы́делить** *perf*) **~ на что-н** to allocate funds to sth; **остава́ться (оста́ться** *perf*) **без средств** to be without means; **сре́дства произво́дства** (*ЭКОН*) means of production; **сре́дства существова́ния** livelihood.
сре́дств|о (**-а**) *ср* means *мн*; (*лекарство*) remedy, medicine; **добива́ться** (*impf*) **чего́-н всéми ~ами** to use all means to get sth; **сре́дство передвиже́ния** means of conveyance; *см также* **сре́дства**.
сре́жу(сь) *итп сов см* **сре́зать(ся)**.
срез (**-а**) *м* (*место*) cut; (*тонкий слой*) section.
сре́|зать (**-жу, -жешь**; *impf* **среза́ть**) *сов перех* (*траву, цветок*) to cut; (*разг: дотации, кредиты*) to cut off; (*: студента*) to flunk
► **сре́заться** (*impf* **среза́ться**) *сов возв* (*разг: студент*) to flunk.
Сре́тени|е (**-я**) *ср* (*РЕЛ*) Candlemas, Feast of the Purification.
срис|ова́ть (**-у́ю**; *impf* **срисо́вывать**) *сов перех* to copy.
срифм|ова́ть (**-у́ю**) *сов от* **рифмова́ть**.
сровня́|ть (**-ю**) *сов от* **ровня́ть**.
сродни́ *предл* (*+dat*) akin to.
срод|ни́ть (**-ню́, -ни́шь**) *сов перех*: **~ кого́-н с** *+instr* to bring sb close to
► **сродни́ться** *сов возв*: **~ся с** *+instr* to become close to.
сродств|о́ (**-а́**) *ср* affinity.
сро́ду *нареч*: **~ не ви́дел/не слы́шал ...** never in my life have I seen/heard ....
сро|и́ться (*3sg* **-и́тся**, *3pl* **-я́тся**) *сов от* **рои́ться**.
срок (**-а**; *part gen* **-у**) *м* (*длительность*) time, period; (*дата*) date; (*разг: тюремный*) term; **в ~** (*во время*) in time; **после́дний** *или* **преде́льный ~** deadline; **сро́ком на** *+acc* for a term of; **испыта́тельный ~** trial period; **~ произво́дства платежа́** due date; **срок го́дности** (*товара*) sell-by date; **срок де́йствия** period of validity.
сро́чен *прил см* **сро́чный**.
сро́чно *нареч* quickly, urgently.
сро́чност|ь (**-и**) *ж* urgency; **нет никако́й ~и** there's no hurry.
сро́ч|ный (**-ен, -на, -но**) *прил* (*дело, заказ*) urgent; (*ссуда, вклад*) fixed-term; **сро́чная телегра́мма** express telegram.
сро́ю *итп сов см* **срыть**.
сруб (**-а**) *м* (*место сруба*) cut; (*постройка*) log shell (*of building, well etc*).
сруба́|ть (**-ю**; *perf* **сруби́ть**) *несов перех* = **руби́ть**.
ср|уби́ть (**-ублю́, -у́бишь**) *сов от* **руби́ть**.
срыв (**-а**) *м* (*плана итп*) disruption; (*с горы, с крыши итп*) fall; (*на экзамене итп*) failure; (*обрыв*) precipice.
срыва́ни|е (**-я**) *ср* picking.
срыва́|ть (**-ю**) *несов от* **сорва́ть, срыть**
► **срыва́ться** *несов от* **сорва́ться**.
срыва́ющ|ийся (**-аяся, -ееся, -иеся**) *прил* (*голос*) breaking.
ср|ыть (**-о́ю, -о́ешь**; *impf* **срыва́ть**) *сов перех*

(*насыпь, холм*) to level.
СС *м сокр* SS.
ссадин|а (-ы) *ж* scratch.
ссад|ить (-ажу́, -дишь; *impf* **ссаживать**) *сов перех* (*со стула, с колен*) to help down; (*безбилетника*) to put off.
ссо́р|а (-ы) *ж* quarrel.
ссо́р|ить (-ю, -ишь; *perf* **поссо́рить**) *несов перех* (*друзей, родственников*) to cause to quarrel; ~ (**поссо́рить** *perf*) **кого́-н с** *+instr* to make sb quarrel with
▸ **ссо́риться** (*perf* **поссо́риться**) *несов возв* to quarrel.
СССР *м сокр* (*ист*: = *Союз Советских Социалистических Республик*) USSR (= *Union of Soviet Socialist Republics*).
ссу́д|а (-ы) *ж* loan; **брать** (**взять** *perf*) **~у** to take out a loan; ~ **под проце́нты** interest-bearing loan; ~ **под зало́г** loan on collateral.
ссу|ди́ть (-жу́, -дишь; *impf* **ссужа́ть**) *сов перех* (*деньги*) to lend.
ссу́дный *прил* (*операция, ведомость*) loan *опред*; **ссу́дный банк** lending bank; **ссу́дный капита́л** (*комм*) loan capital.
ссужа́|ть (-ю) *несов от* **ссуди́ть**.
ссужу́ *сов см* **ссуди́ть**.
ссуту́л|ить(ся) (-ю(сь), -ишь(ся)) *сов от* **суту́лить(ся)**.
ссыла́|ть(ся) (-ю(сь)) *несов от* **сосла́ть(ся)** ◆ *возв*: **~ясь на** *+acc* with reference to.
ссы́л|ка (-ки; *gen pl* -ок) *ж* exile; (*на автора, на источник*) reference; (*цитата*) quotation.
ссы́льн|ая (-ой; *decl like adj*) *ж см* **ссы́льный**.
ссы́льн|ый (-ого; *decl like adj*) *м* exile.
ссы́п|ать (-лю, -лешь; *impf* **ссыпа́ть**) *сов перех* (*насыпать*) to pour.
ст. *сокр* (= **ста́нция**) sta. (= *station*); (= **ста́рший**) Sen. (= *senior*); = **ста́рый**.
ста *чис см* **сто**.
стаби́лен *прил см* **стаби́льный**.
стабилиза́тор (-а) *м* (*тех*) stabilizer.
стабилиза́ци|я (-и) *ж* stabilization.
стабилизи́р|овать (-ую) (*не*)*сов перех* to stabilize
▸ **стабилизи́роваться** (*не*)*сов возв* to stabilize.
стаби́л|ьный (-ен, -ьна, -ьно) *прил* stable; **стаби́льный уче́бник** standard textbook.
ста́в|ень (-ня) *м* (*обычно мн*) shutter.
ста́в|ить (-лю, -ишь; *perf* **поста́вить**) *несов перех* to put; (*назначать: министром, дежурным*) to appoint; (*памятник*) to erect; (*телефон*) to install; (*парус, сроки*) to set; (*пятно, оценку*) to make; (*точку, запятую итп*) to put in; (*оперу, фильм итп*) to stage; (*выдвигать: задачу, цель*) to present; (: *вопрос*) to raise; ~ (**поста́вить** *perf*) **де́ньги на что-н** to put money on sth; ~ (**поста́вить** *perf*) **печа́ть на что-н** to stamp sth; ~ (**поста́вить** *perf*) **часы́** to set a clock; ~ (**поста́вить** *perf*) **диа́гноз** to make a diagnosis; ~ (**поста́вить** *perf*) **что-н на голосова́ние** to put sth to the vote; ~ (**поста́вить** *perf*) **что-н кому́-н в вину́** to lay the blame for sth on sb; ~ (**поста́вить** *perf*) **что-н кому́-н в заслу́гу** to put sth at sb's service; ~ (**поста́вить** *perf*) **что-н кому́-н в досто́инство** to give sb credit for sth; ~ (**поста́вить** *perf*) **себе́ за пра́вило** to make it a rule; ~ (**поста́вить** *perf*) **кого́-н в изве́стность** to fill sb in; ~ (**поста́вить** *perf*) **что-н под контро́ль** to bring sth under control; **его́ здесь ни во что не ~ят** he counts for nothing here.
ста́в|ка (-ки; *gen pl* -ок) *ж* (*также комм*) rate; (*воен*) headquarters *мн*; (*в азартных играх*) stake; (*перен*): ~ **на** *+acc* (*расчёт*) counting on; **проце́нтные ~ки** (*комм*) interest rates; **ба́зовая ссу́дная** ~ base rate; **минима́льная ссу́дная** ~ minimum lending rate; **учётная** ~ (*банка*) discount rate.
ста́вленник (-а) *м* protégé.
ста́вленниц|а (-ы) *ж* protégée.
ста́влю *сов см* **ста́вить**.
ста́вня *итп сущ см* **ста́вень**.
ста́вок *сущ см* **ста́вка**.
ставри́д|а (-ы) *ж* (*зоол*) horse mackerel, scad.
стагна́ци|я (-и) *ж* stagnation.
стадио́н (-а) *м* stadium (*мн* stadia).
ста́ди|я (-и) *ж* stage.
ста́дный *прил* (*животное*) herd *опред*; (*перен: чувство*) gregarious.
ста́д|о (-а; *nom pl* -а́) *ср* (*коров*) herd; (*овец*) flock.
стаж (-а) *м* (*рабочий*) length of service; **испыта́тельный** ~ probation.
стажёр (-а) *м* probationer.
стажир|ова́ться (-у́юсь) *несов возв* to work on probation.
стажиро́в|ка (-ки; *gen pl* -ок) *ж* probationary period.
ста́ива|ть (-ю) *несов от* **стая́ть**.
ста́йер (-а) *м* long-distance runner.
ста́йерск|ий (-ая, -ое, -ие) *прил*: **~ая диста́нция** long distance.
стака́н (-а) *м* glass; **бума́жный** ~ paper cup.
стака́нчик (-а) *м* glass; **моро́женое в ~ах** ice cream in tubs.
стакка́то *нареч* staccato.
сталагми́т (-а) *м* stalagmite.
сталакти́т (-а) *м* stalactite.
стале́ва́р (-а) *м* steel founder.
сталелите́йный *прил* steel-founding.
сталеплави́льный *прил* steel-smelting.
сталепрока́тный *прил* steel-rolling.
сталийн|ый *прил*: **~ое вре́мя** (*комм*) lay days *мн*.
сталини́зм (-а) *м* Stalinism.

ста́лкива|ть(ся) (**-ю(сь)**) *несов от* **столкну́ть(ся)**.
стал|ь (**-и**) *ж* steel.
стально́й *прил* (*кабель, рельсы, решимость*) steel *опред*; (*мускулы, нервы*) of steel; (*воля*) iron *опред*; (*цвет: глаза*) steel-blue; (*: море*) steel-grey (*BRIT*), steel-gray (*US*).
стам *итп чис см* **сто**.
Стамбу́л (**-а**) *м* Istanbul.
стаме́с|ка (**-ки**; *gen pl* **-ок**) *ж* chisel.
стан (**-а**) *м* (*человека*) torso; (*стоянка*) camp; (*ТЕХ*) mill.
станда́рт (**-а**) *м* (*также перен*) standard; **по ~у** (*изготовить*) in line with the standard; (*перен: действовать*) conventionally.
станда́ртен *прил см* **станда́ртный**.
стандартиза́ци|я (**-и**) *ж* standardization; (*личности, отношений*) stereotyping.
стандартизи́р|овать (**-ую**) *(не)сов перех* to standardize.
станда́рт|ный (**-ен, -на, -но**) *прил* (*детали, машина*) standard; (*вопросы, тема*) stock.
стани́н|а (**-ы**) *ж* (*ТЕХ*) bed.
стани́ц|а (**-ы**) *ж* stanitsa (*large Cossack village*).
станка́ *итп сущ см* **стано́к**.
станко́вый *прил* (*живопись*) easel *опред*.
станкострое́ни|е (**-я**) *ср* machine-tool construction.
станкострои́тельный *прил* (*завод, промышленность*) machine-tool.
стан|ови́ться (**-овлю́сь, -о́вишься**) *несов от* **стать**.
становле́ни|е (**-я**) *ср* formation.
становлю́сь *несов см* **станови́ться**.
стан|о́к (**-ка́**) *м* (*слесарный итп*) machine (tool); (*ИСКУССТВО*) frame; (*балетный*) barre; **тока́рный ~** lathe.
ста́ну(сь) *итп сов см* **стать(ся)**.
станцио́нный *прил* station *опред*.
ста́нци|я (**-и**) *ж* station; **запра́вочная ~** filling station; **телефо́нная ~** telephone exchange.
ста́пел|ь (**-я**; *nom pl* **-я́**) *м* (*МОР*) building berth (*BRIT*), slip (*US*).
ста́плива|ть (**-ю**) *несов от* **стопи́ть**.
ста́птыва|ть(ся) (**-ю(сь)**) *несов от* **стопта́ть(ся)**.
стара́ни|е (**-я**) *ср* effort; **при всём ~и не смогу́ тебе́ помо́чь** no matter how much I try, I can't help you.
стара́телен *прил см* **стара́тельный**.
стара́тел|ь (**-я**) *м* (gold) prospector.
стара́тельност|ь (**-и**) *ж* (*см прил*) diligence; painstakingness.
стара́тел|ьный (**-ен, -ьна, -ьно**) *прил* (*работник, ученик*) diligent; (*работа, подсчёт*) painstaking.
стара́|ться (**-юсь**; *perf* **постара́ться**) *несов возв*: **~** *+infin* to try to do.
старе́йш|ий (**-ая, -ее, -ие**) *превос прил от* **ста́рый**.
старе́йшин|а (**-ы**) *ж* elder.
старе́ни|е (**-я**) *ср* ageing.
старе́|ть (**-ю**; *perf* **постаре́ть**) *несов неперех* (*человек*) to grow old(er), age; (*perf* **устаре́ть**; *оборудование*) to become out of date.
ста́р|ец (**-ца**) *м* elder; (*РЕЛ*) elderly monk.
стари́к (**-а́**) *м* old man (*мн* men); **старики́** old people.
старико́вск|ий (**-ая, -ое, -ие**) *прил* (*привычки*) old people's.
старин|а́ (**-ы́**) *ж* (*прошлое*) the olden days *мн* ◆ *м* (*обращение*) old man *или* chap (*BRIT*).
стари́нк|а (**-и**) *ж*: **по ~е** in the old way.
стари́нный *прил* ancient; (*давний: друг*) old.
ста́р|ить (**-ю, -ишь**; *perf* **соста́рить**) *несов перех* to age.
ста́рк|а (**-и**) *ж* (*сорт водки*) starka (*type of vodka*).
старо́ *как сказ*: **э́то всё ~** it's all outdated; (*не ново*) there's nothing new in it; **~ как мир** it's as old as the hills.
старове́р (**-а**) *м* (*РЕЛ*) Old Believer.
старове́р|ка (**-ки**; *gen pl* **-ок**) *ж см* **старове́р**.
старожи́л (**-а**) *м* old resident.
старомо́д|ный (**-ен, -на, -но**) *прил* old-fashioned.
старообря́д|ец (**-ца**) *м* (*РЕЛ*) Old Believer.
старообря́д|ка (**-ки**; *gen pl* **-ок**) *ж см* **старообря́дец**.
старообря́дца *итп сущ см* **старообря́дец**.
старообря́дчеств|о (**-а**) *ср* Old Belief.
старославя́нск|ий (**-ая, -ое, -ие**) *прил*: **старословя́нский язы́к** Old Church Slavonic.
ста́рост|а (**-ы**) *м* (*курса*) senior student; (*класса: мальчик*) head boy; (*: девушка*) head girl; (*клуба*) head, president; (*артели*) foreman (*мн* foremen).
ста́рост|ь (**-и**) *ж* (*человека*) old age; **на ~и лет** in one's old age.
старпо́м (**-а**) *м* = *ста́рший помо́щник*; (*МОР*) first mate.
старт (**-а**) *м* (*СПОРТ*) start; (*ракеты*) takeoff point; **дава́ть** (**дать** *perf*) **~** to start; **брать** (**взять** *perf*) **~** to start; (*перен*) to take off.
ста́ртер (**-а**) *м* (*АВТ*) starter.
стартёр (**-а**) *м* (*СПОРТ*) starter.
старт|ова́ть (**-у́ю**) *(не)сов неперех* (*спортсмен*) to start; (*ракета*) to take off.
ста́ртовый *прил* starting *опред*.
стару́х|а (**-и**) *ж* old woman (*мн* women).
стару́шек *сущ см* **стару́шка**.
стару́шеч|ий (**-ья, -ье, -ьи**) *прил* old woman's.
стару́ш|ка (**-ки**; *gen pl* **-ек**) *ж* = **стару́ха**.
ста́рца *итп сущ см* **ста́рец**.
ста́рческ|ий (**-ая, -ое, -ие**) *прил* old person's *или* people's; **ста́рческий во́зраст** old age; **ста́рческий мара́зм** (*МЕД*) senility.
ста́рше *сравн прил от* **ста́рый** ◆ *как сказ*: **я ~ сестры́ на́ год** I am a year older than my sister; **я ~ его́ по зва́нию** I am senior to him.
старшекла́ссник (**-а**) *м* senior pupil.
старшекла́ссница (**-ы**) *ж см*

старшекла́ссник.
старшеку́рсник (-а) *м* senior student.
старшеку́рсница (-ы) *ж см* **старшеку́рсник.**
ста́рш|ий (-ая, -ее, -ие) *прил* senior *опред*; (*сестра, брат*) elder *опред* ◆ **(-его;** *decl like adj*) *м* (*группы, отделения*) senior; **~ие** (*взрослые люди*) grown-ups *мн*, adults *мн*.
старшин|а́ (-ы́; *nom pl* **-ы)** *м* (*ВОЕН*) sergeant major; (*милиции*) sergeant.
старшинств|о́ (-а́) *ср* seniority; **по ~у́** by seniority.
ста́р|ый (-, -а́, -о́, -ы) *прил* old; **и стар и млад** old and young; **ста́рый стиль** (*летосчисления*) Old Style.
старь|ё (-я́) *ср собир* old things *мн*.
старьёвщик (-а) *м* junk dealer.
ста́скива|ть (-ю) *несов от* **стащи́ть.**
стас|ова́ть (-у́ю) *сов от* **тасова́ть.**
ста́тен *прил см* **ста́тный.**
ста́тик|а (-и) *ж* (*наука*) statics; (*неподвижность*) stasis.
стати́ст (-а) *м* (*ТЕАТР*) extra.
стати́стик (-а) *м* statistician.
стати́стик|а (-и) *ж* statistics.
статисти́ческ|ий (-ая, -ое, -ие) *прил* statistical; **Центра́льное ~ое управле́ние** *central statistics office.*
стати́чен *прил см* **стати́чный.**
стати́ческ|ий (-ая, -ое, -ие) *прил* static.
стати́ч|ный (-ен, -на, -но) *прил* static.
ста́т|ный (-ен, -на, -но) *прил* stately.
ста́тус (-а) *м* status.
ста́тус-кво *м нескл* status quo.
стату́т (-а) *м* (*правила*) statute.
статуэ́т|ка (-ки; *gen pl* **-ок)** *ж* statuette.
ста́ту|я (-и) *ж* statue.
ста|ть (-ти) *ж* (*осанка*) bearing; ◆ **(-ну, -нешь;** *impf* **станови́ться)** *сов неперех* to stand; (*к станку, за прилавок*) to take up position; (*no impf; часы, завод, движение*) to stop; (*начать*): ~ *+infin* to begin *или* start doing; (*обойтись*): ~ **в** *+acc* to cost ◆ *безл* (*наличествовать*): **нас ста́ло бо́льше/тро́е** there are more/three of us; **под ~ кому́-н/чему́-н** (*подобно*) like sb/sth; **с како́й ста́ти?** (*разг*) why?; **станови́ться (~** *perf*) *+instr* (*учителем*) to become; **его́ не ста́ло** he passed away; **не ста́ло де́нег/сил** I have no more money/energy; **с него́ ста́нет** (*разг*) that's all you can expect from him; **ста́ло быть** (*значит*) so; **во что бы то ни ста́ло** no matter what; **что с ним ста́ло?** what has become of him?; **станови́ться (~** *perf*) **у вла́сти** to come to power; **станови́ться (~** *perf*) **на путь чего́-н** to set out on the path of sth
▸ **ста́ться** *сов безл* (*случиться*) to happen; **мо́жет ста́ться** it is possible.
стать|я́ (-ьи́; *gen pl* **-е́й)** *ж* (*в газете, в сборнике*) article; (*в словаре*) entry; (*в законе, в договоре*) paragraph, clause; (*экспорта, импорта*) type; (*КОММ: расхода, дохода*) item; **по всем ~м** (*разг*) in all respects.
стафилоко́кк (-а) *м* (*МЕД*) staphylococcus.
стациона́р (-а) *м* (*МЕД*) hospital.
ста́чек *сущ см* **ста́чка.**
ста́чечник (-а) *м* striker.
ста́чечниц|а (-ы) *ж см* **ста́чечник.**
ста́чива|ть (-ю) *несов от* **сточи́ть.**
ста́ч|ка (-ки; *gen pl* **-ек)** *ж* (*ЭКОН*) strike.
стащ|и́ть (-у́, -ишь) *сов от* **тащи́ть** ◆ (*impf* **ста́скивать**) *перех* (*что-н сверху*) to pull down; (*что-н в подвал*) to drag down; (*сапоги, чулки*) to pull off; (*no impf; разг: украсть*) to nick.
ста́|я (-и) *ж* (*птиц*) flock; (*волков*) pack; (*рыб*) shoal.
ста́|ять (*3sg* **-ет,** *3pl* **-ют,** *impf* **ста́ивать)** *сов неперех* to melt.
ствол (-а́) *м* (*дерева*) trunk; (*ружья, пушки*) barrel.
ство́р|ка (-ки; *gen pl* **-ок)** *ж* door; (*ставней*) shutter; (*зеркала*) leaf.
ство́рчатый *прил* (*окно, шкаф*) double (*opening in the middle*).
сте́б|ель (-ля) *м* (*цветка*) stem.
стёган|ка (-ки; *gen pl* **-ок)** *ж* quilted jacket.
стёганый *прил* quilted; **стёганое одея́ло** quilt.
стега́|ть (-ю; *perf* **простега́ть)** *несов перех* (*одеяло*) to quilt; (*no perf; хлыстом*) to lash.
стегн|у́ть (-у́, -ёшь) *сов перех* to lash.
стёж|ка (-ки; *gen pl* **-ек)** *ж* stitch.
стеж|о́к (-ка́) *м* stitch.
стез|я́ (-и́) *ж* path (*fig*).
стёк(ся) *итп сов см* **сте́чь(ся).**
стека́|ть(ся) (*3sg* **-ет(ся),** *3pl* **-ют(ся))** *несов от* **сте́чь(ся).**
стеклене́|ть (*3sg* **-ет,** *3pl* **-ют,** *perf* **остеклене́ть)** *несов неперех* to become glassy.
стекл|и́ть (-ю́, -и́шь; *perf* **остекли́ть)** *несов перех* (*окно*) to glaze.
стекл|о́ (-а́; *nom pl* **стёкла,** *gen pl* **стёкол)** *ср* glass; (*также:* **око́нное ~**) (window) pane; (*для очков*) lenses *мн* ◆ *собир* (*изделия*) glassware.
стёклыш|ко (-ка; *gen pl* **-ек)** *ср уменьш от* **стекло́**; (*осколок*) piece of glass.
стекля́нный *прил* glass; (*перен: взгляд, глаза*) glassy.
стекля́рус (-а) *м собир* glass beads *мн*.
стекля́ш|ка (-ки; *gen pl* **-ек)** *ж* (*осколок*) piece of glass; (*пренебр: изделие*) bauble.
стёкол *сущ см* **стекло́.**
стеко́льный *прил* (*завод*) glass.
стеко́льщик (-а) *м* glazier.
стеку́т(ся) *итп сов см* **сте́чь(ся).**
сте́лек *сущ см* **сте́лька.**
стел|и́ть (-ю́, -ишь; *perf* **постели́ть)** *несов перех* (*скатерть, подстилку*) to spread out; (*perf*

настели́ть; *пол, паркет*) to lay; ~ **(постели́ть** *perf*) **посте́ль** to make up a bed
▸ **стели́ться** *несов возв* (*туман*) to spread; (*perf* **постели́ться**; *разг*: *приготовить постель*) to get ready for bed.
стелла́ж (-á) *м* shelf (*мн* shelves).
сте́ль|ка (-ьки; *gen pl* -ек) *ж* (*в обуви*) insole.
стелю́(сь) *итп несов см* **стла́ть(ся)**.
стемне́|ть (*3sg* -ет) *сов от* **темне́ть**.
стен|á (-ы́; *acc sg* -у, *dat sg* -é, *nom pl* -ы, *dat pl* -áм) *ж* (*также перен*) wall; **в ~х** +*gen* (*школы, учреждения*) within the confines of; **сиде́ть** (*impf*) **в четырёх ~х** to be cooped up indoors.
стена́ни|е (-я) *ср* groan.
стена́|ть (-ю) *несов неперех* to groan.
стенгазе́т|а (-ы) *ж* (= *стенна́я газе́та*) *newsletter displayed on wall in school or place of work.*
стенд (-а) *м* (*выставочный*) display stand; (*испытательный*) test-bed; (*для стрельбы*) rifle range.
сте́ндовый *прил*: **сте́ндовая стрельба́** target practice.
сте́н|ка (-ки; *gen pl* -ок) *ж уменьш от* **стена́**; (*комнаты, желудка, также* ФУТБОЛ) wall; (*разг*: *мебель*) wall unit; (*ящика*) side; **прижима́ть (прижа́ть** *perf*) **кого́-н к ~ке** (*разг*) to push sb to the wall.
стенно́й *прил* wall *опред*; **стенна́я ро́спись** mural.
стеногра́мм|а (-ы) *ж* shorthand record.
стенографи́р|овать (-ую; *perf* **стенографи́ровать** *или* **застенографи́ровать**) *несов перех* to take down in shorthand.
стенографи́ст (-а) *м* shorthand typist (BRIT), stenographer (US).
стенографи́ст|ка (-ки; *gen pl* -ок) *ж см* **стенографи́ст**.
стеногра́фи|я (-и) *ж* shorthand (BRIT), stenography (US).
сте́нок *сущ см* **сте́нка**.
стенокарди́|я (-и) *ж* angina.
сте́нопис|ь (-и) *ж* mural painting.
сте́ньг|а (-и) *ж* (МОР) topmast.
степе́н|ный (-ен, -на, -но) *прил* sedate.
сте́пен|ь (-и; *gen pl* -е́й) *ж* (*также* ПРОСВЕЩ) degree; (МАТ) power; **в вы́сшей ~и** in the extreme; **до изве́стной** *или* **не́которой ~и** to some *или* a certain extent; **ожо́г пе́рвой** *итп* **~и** first *итп* degree burn.
степно́й *прил* steppe *опред*.
степ|ь (-и; *loc sg* -и́, *gen pl* -е́й) *ж* the steppe.
сте́рв|а (-ы) *ж* (*груб!*) bastard (*!*); (: *женщина*) bitch (*!*)
стервене́|ть (-ю; *perf* **остервене́ть**) *несов неперех* (*разг*) to get mad.
стервя́тник (-а) *м* carrion crow.
стерёг *итп несов см* **стере́чь**.
стерегу́ *итп несов см* **стере́чь**.
стереоза́пис|ь (-и) *ж* stereo recording.
стереозвуча́ни|е (-я) *ср* stereo (*sound*).
стереомагнитофо́н (-а) *м* stereo tape recorder.
стереопро́игрыватель (-я) *м* stereo record player.
стереосисте́м|а (-ы) *ж* stereo.
стереоти́п (-а) *м* (ТИПОГ, *перен*) stereotype.
стереоти́п|ный *прил* (-ен, -на, -но; *ответ, мышление итп*) stereotyped.
стере́ть (сотру́, сотрёшь; *pt* **стёр, стёрла, стёрло**, *impf* **стира́ть**) *сов перех* (*грязь, пыль, грим*) to wipe off; (*надпись, память, различия*) to erase; **стира́ть (~** *perf*) **что-н/кого́-н в порошо́к** (*также перен*) to pulverize sth/sb; **стира́ть (~** *perf*) **с лица́ земли́** to wipe off the face of the earth
▸ **стере́ться** (*impf* **стира́ться**) *сов возв* (*надпись, краска*) to be worn away; (*подошвы*) to wear down; (*перен*: *различия, границы*) to be erased; **стира́ться (~ся** *perf*) **в па́мяти** to become blurred.
стер|е́чь (-егу́, -ежёшь *итп*, -егу́т; *pt* -ёг, -егла́, -егло́) *несов перех* to watch over; (*подстерегать*) to lie in wait for.
сте́рж|ень (-ня) *м* rod; (*винта*) stem; (*ось*) pivot; (*шариковой ручки*) (ink) cartridge; (*перен*: *политики, романа*) backbone.
стержнево́й *прил* (*осевой*) pivoted; (*перен*: *вопрос, проблема*) crucial.
сте́ржня *итп сущ см* **сте́ржень**.
стери́лен *прил см* **стери́льный**.
стерилиза́тор (-а) *м* sterilizer.
стерилиза́ци|я (-и) *ж* sterilization.
стерилиз|ова́ть (-у́ю) *(не)сов перех* to sterilize.
стери́л|ьный (-ен, -ьна, -ьно) *прил* sterile, sterilized.
сте́рлинг (-а) *м* (ЭКОН) sterling; **10 фу́нтов ~ов** 10 pounds sterling.
сте́рляд|ь (-и; *gen pl* -е́й) *ж* sterlet.
стерп|е́ть (-лю́, -ишь) *сов перех* to endure
▸ **стерпе́ться** *сов возв*: **~ся с** +*instr* to learn to endure.
стёрт|ый (-, -а, -о) *прил* (*надпись*) worn; (*монета*) effaced; (*перен*: *фразы*) hackneyed.
сте|са́ть (-шу́, -шешь; *impf* **стёсывать**) *сов перех* (*кору*) to strip off.
стесне́ни|е (-я) *ср* constraints *мн*; (*в груди*) constriction; (*смущение*) shyness.
стеснённ|ый *прил* (*дыхание*) constricted; **в ~ых обстоя́тельствах** in financial straits.
стесни́телен *прил см* **стесни́тельный**.
стесни́тельност|ь (-и) *ж* shyness.
стесни́тел|ьный (-ен, -ьна, -ьно) *прил* shy.
стесн|и́ть (-ю́, -и́шь) *сов от* **тесни́ть** ♦ (*impf* **стесня́ть**) *перех* (*хозяев*) to inconvenience; (*дыхание*) to constrict; **стесня́ть (~** *perf*) **кого́-н в расхо́дах** to restrict sb's spending.
стесня́|ться (-юсь; *perf* **постесня́ться**) *несов возв*: **~** (+*gen*) (*женщин, незнакомых*) to be shy (of); (+*infin*; *сказать, просить итп*) to be too

shy to do; ~ *(impf)* **пéред кем-н** to feel shy in sb's presence; **онá не ~ется в срéдствах** she won't stop at anything; **он не ~ется в выражéниях** he doesn't mince his words.
стёсыва|ть (-ю) *несов от* **стесáть.**
стетоскóп (-а) *м* stethoscope.
стечéни|е (-я) *ср* (*нарóда*) gathering; (*случáйностей*) combination; ~ **обстоя́тельств** coincidence; **при большóм ~и нарóда** in front of a large number of people.
ст|ечь (*3sg* **-ечёт**, *3pl* **-екýт**, *pt* **-ёк, -еклá, -еклó**, *impf* **стекáть**) *сов неперех*: ~ **(с** *+gen***)** to run down (from)
▸ **стéчься** (*impf* **стекáться**) *сов возв* (*ручьи, реки*) to flow; (*люди*) to congregate.
стешý *итп сов см* **стесáть.**
сти́лен *прил см* **сти́льный.**
стилизáци|я (-и) *ж* (*подражание*) imitation; (*о произведении*) stylized work.
стилизóван|ный (-, -на, -но) *прил* stylized.
стилиз|овáть (-ýю) *(не)сов перех* to stylize.
стилисти́ческ|ий (-ая, -ое, -ие) *прил* (*приём*) stylistic.
стил|ь (-я) *м* style; (*летосчисления*) calendar; **он в своём сти́ле** he's being his usual self; **6 ию́ня по стáрому/нóвому сти́лю** 6th June Old Style/New Style.
сти́л|ьный (-ен, -ьна, -ьно) *прил* stylish; (*разг: причёска, одежда*) snazzy.
стиля́г|а (-и) *м/ж* (*разг: пренебр*) fashion victim.
сти́мул (-а) *м* incentive, stimulus (*мн* stimuli).
стимули́ровани|е (-я) *ср* stimulation; **материáльное** ~ financial incentive.
стимули́р|овать (-ую) *(не)сов перех* to stimulate; (*работу, прогресс*) to encourage; ~ *(impf/perf)* **рост экономики** to encourage economic growth.
стимуля́ци|я (-и) *ж* stimulation; (*родов*) induction.
стипендиáльный *прил*: ~ **фонд** scholarship fund; **стипендиáльная коми́ссия** grants committee.
стипéнди|я (-и) *ж* (*государственная*) grant; (*за особые достижения*) scholarship.
сти́пль-чéз (-а) *м* (*СПОРТ*) steeplechase.
стирáльный *прил*: ~ **порошóк** washing powder; **стирáльная маши́на** washing machine.
стирáни|е (-я) *ср* (*надписи*) erasure; (*различий*) erosion.
сти́раный *прил* washed.
стирá|ть (-ю) *несов от* **стерéть** ◆ (*perf* **вы́стирать** *или* **постирáть)** *перех* to wash
▸ **стирáться** *несов от* **стерéться.**
сти́р|ка (-ки; *gen pl* **-ок)** *ж* washing; **отдавáть (отдáть** *perf***) что-н в ~ку** to put sth in for a service wash.
сти́сн|уть (-у, -ешь; *impf* **сти́скивать)** *сов перех* (*в руке, в зубах*) to clench; (*подлеж: толпа*) to squeeze; **сти́скивать (~** *perf***) когó-н в объя́тиях** to clutch sb in one's arms; ~ *(perf)* **зýбы** (*перен*) to grit one's teeth.
стих (-á) *м* verse.
стихá|ть (-ю) *несов от* **сти́хнуть.**
стих|и́ (-ов) *мн* (*поэзия*) poetry *ед*; **ромáн в ~áх** novel in verse.
стихи́|йный (-ен, -йна, -йно) *прил* (*сила*) elemental; (*развитие, становление*) uncontrolled; (*протест, демонстрации*) spontaneous; **стихи́йное бéдствие** natural disaster.
стихи́|я (-и) *ж* (*вода, огонь итп*) element; (*рынка, инфляции*) natural force; **борóться** *(impf)* **со ~ей** to do battle with the elements; **быть** *(impf)* **в своéй ~и** to be in one's element; **би́знес – егó** ~ business is his forte.
сти́х|нуть (-ну, -нешь; *pt* **-, -ла, -ло**, *impf* **стихáть)** *сов неперех* to die down.
стихосложéни|е (-я) *ср* versification.
стихотворéни|е (-я) *ср* poem.
стихотвóрный *прил* (*произведение*) poetic; (*пародия*) in verse; **стихотвóрный размéр** metre (*in poetry*).
стлать (стелю́, стéлешь; *perf* **постлáть)** *несов перех* = **стели́ть**
▸ **стлáться** *несов возв* = **стели́ться.**
сто (ста; *см* **Table 30)** *чис* one hundred; (*разг: много*): ~ *+gen* hundreds of; ~ **книг/столóв** a hundred books/tables; **óколо ста** about a hundred; ~ **пéрвый** hundred and first; **я увéрен на ~ процéнтов** I am one hundred percent sure; **мнóго сот** many hundreds; **нéсколько сот** several hundred.
стог (-а; *loc sg* **-ý**, *nom pl* **-á)** *м*: ~ **сéна** haystack.
стограммóвый *прил* (*гиря*) one-hundred-gram; ~ **стакáн** ≈ shot glass.
стóек *сущ см* **стóйка** ◆ *прил см* **стóйкий.**
стóимостн|ый *прил* (*ЭКОН*): **~ые показáтели/отношéния** cost indices/relations.
стóимост|ь (-и) *ж* cost; (*ценность*) value; ~ **по торгóвым кни́гам** (*КОММ*) book value; ~ **и фрахт** cost and freight.
стó|ить (-ю, -ишь) *несов (не)перех* (*+acc или +gen; денег*) to cost; (*усилий, труда итп*) to take ◆ *неперех*: ~ *+gen* (*внимания, любви*) to be worth ◆ *безл*: **~ить** *+infin* to be worth doing; **кни́га ~ит 10 рублéй** the book costs 10 roubles; **дом ~ит бóльшие дéньги** *или* **бóльших дéнег** the house costs a lot of money; **на э́ту вы́ставку ~ит пойти́** it is worth going to see this exhibition; **мне ничегó не ~ит сдéлать э́то** it's no trouble for me to do it; **спаси́бо! – не ~ит** thank you! – don't mention it; **чегó ~ят твои́ обещáния!** what are your promises worth?; **~ит (тóлько) захотéть/постарáться** (*об условии*) you only have to wish/try; **~ит мне (тóлько)**

войти́ в дом, как сра́зу начина́ет звони́ть телефо́н the minute I come through the door the phone starts ringing.
сто́йчески *нареч* stoically.
стои́ческ|ий (**-ая, -ое, -ие**) *прил* stoical.
стой(те) *несов см* **стоя́ть.**
сто́йбищ|е (**-а**) *ср* (*кочевников*) nomad camp.
сто́|йка (**-йки**; *gen pl* **-ек**) *ж* (*положение тела*) stance; (*собаки*) pose; (*подпорка*) prop; (*прилавок*) counter; (*воротник*) stand-up collar; **стоя́ть** *(impf)* **по ~йке сми́рно/во́льно** to stand to attention/at ease; **сто́йка на рука́х** handstand; **сто́йка на голове́** headstand.
сто́|йкий (**-йкая, -йкое, -йкие**; **-ек, -йка, -йко**) *прил* (*человек, характер*) steadfast, resilient; (*краска, материал*) durable, hard-wearing; (*запах*) stubborn.
сто́йко *нареч* steadfastly.
сто́йкост|ь (**-и**) *ж* (*см прил*) resilience; durability; stubborness.
сто́йл|о (**-а**) *ср* stall (*in a stable*).
стоймя́ *нареч* upright.
сто́йче *сравн прил от* **сто́йкий** ◆ *сравн нареч от* **сто́йко.**
сток (**-а**) *м* (*действие*) drainage; (*приспособление*) drain.
Стокго́льм (**-а**) *м* Stockholm.
стокра́тный *прил* hundredfold.
стол (**-а́**) *м* table; (*письменный*) desk; (*еда*) food; **а́дресный ~** *residents' registration office*; **кру́глый ~** round table (*fig*); **сади́ться (сесть** *perf*) **за ~** to sit down at the table; **за ~о́м** at table; **убира́ть (убра́ть** *perf*) **со ~а́** to clear the table; **встава́ть (встать** *perf*) **из-за ~а́** to get up from the table; **стол нахо́док** lost property (office); **стол перегово́ров** negotiating table.
столб (**-а́**) *м* (*пограничный, указательный*) post; (*телеграфный*) pole; (*перен*: *пыли, дыма*) cloud.
столбене́|ть (**-ю**; *perf* **остолбене́ть**) *несов неперех* to be rooted to the spot.
столб|е́ц (**-ца́**) *м* column (*on page*).
сто́лбик (**-а**) *м уменьш от* **столб**; (*бумаг*) ream; (*цифр*) column; **рту́тный ~** mercury column; **~ом** in a column.
столбня́к (**-а́**) *м* tetanus.
столбово́й *прил*: **~ дворяни́н** (*ИСТ*) *a member of the old Russian nobility*; **столбова́я доро́га** (*ИСТ*) highway.
столбца́ *итп сущ см* **столбе́ц.**
столе́ти|е (**-я**) *ср* (*срок*) century; (*годовщина*): **~** *+gen* centenary of.
столе́тн|ий (**-яя, -ее, -ие**) *прил* (*период*) hundred-year; (*старик, дерево*) hundred-year-old.
столе́тник (**-а**) *м* (*БОТ*) aloe.
сто́лечко *нареч* (*разг*) = **сто́лько.**
сто́лик (**-а**) *м уменьш от* **стол**; (*в ресторане, в кафе*) table; **туале́тный ~** dressing table.
столи́ц|а (**-ы**) *ж* capital (city).
столи́чный *прил* (*газеты, жители, театры*) of the capital; **столи́чный го́род** capital city.
столкнове́ни|е (**-я**) *ср* clash; (*машин, судов*) collision; **вооружённое ~** armed clash.
столкн|у́ть (**-у́, -ёшь**; *impf* **ста́лкивать**) *сов перех*: **~ (с** *+gen*) to push off; (*сблизить толчком*) to push together; (*подлеж*: *случей, судьба*) to bring together; **~** *(perf)* **кого́-н в во́ду** to push sb into the water
▸ **столкну́ться** (*impf* **ста́лкиваться**) *сов возв* (*машины, поезда*) to collide; (*интересы, характеры*) to clash; (*встретиться*): **~ся с** *+instr* (*встречаться*) to come into contact with; (*случайно*) to bump *или* run into; (*с трудностями, с непониманием*) to encounter; **я ста́лкивался с ним по рабо́те** I have come into contact with him through work.
столк|ова́ться (**-у́юсь**; *impf* **столко́вываться**) *сов возв*: **~ (с** *+instr*) to come to an agreement (with).
столо́в|ая (**-ой**; *decl like adj*) *ж* (*заведение*) canteen; (*команта*) dining room.
столо́в|ка (**-ки**; *gen pl* **-ок**) *ж* (*разг*) canteen.
столо́вый *прил* (*мебель, часы*) dining room *опред*; **столо́вая ло́жка** (*для супа*) tablespoon; **столо́вая соль** table salt; **столо́вое вино́** table wine; **столо́вый серви́з** dinner service.
столп (**-а́**) *м* (*обычно мн*: *перен*) pillar.
столп|и́ться (*3sg* **-и́тся**, *3pl* **-я́тся**) *сов возв* to crowd.
столпотворе́ни|е (**-я**) *ср* chaos.
столь *нареч* so; **~ же ... ско́лько ...** as ... as ....
сто́льк|о *нареч* (*об исчисляемом количестве*) so many; (*о неисчисляемом количестве*) so much ◆ (**-их**) *мест* (*см нареч*) this many; this much; **я не хочу́ дава́ть ему́ ~ де́нег** I don't want to give him that much money; **она́ ~ пережила́!** she has been through so much!; **где ты был ~ вре́мени?** where have you been all this time?; **у меня́ ~ (же) де́нег/пробле́м, ско́лько (и) у тебя́** I've got as much money/as many problems as you; **он не ~ глуп, ско́лько лени́в** he is not so much stupid as lazy.
сто́лько-то *нареч* (*об исчисляемом количестве*) X number of; (*об неисчисляемом количестве*) X amount of; **~ сде́лано, ~ оста́лось** this much has been done and this much is left.
столя́р (**-а́**) *м* joiner.
столя́рнича|ть (**-ю**) *несов неперех* (*разг*) to do carpentry.
столя́рн|ый *прил*: **~ая мастерка́я** joiner's; **столя́рное де́ло** joinery; **столя́рные инструме́нты** carpentry tools; **столя́рный клей** wood glue.
стомати́т (**-а**) *м* mouth ulcer.
стомато́лог (**-а**) *м* dental surgeon.
стоматологи́ческ|ий (**-ая, -ое, -ие**) *прил* dental; **стоматологи́ческий кабине́т/поликли́ника** dental surgery/hospital.
стоматоло́ги|я (**-и**) *ж* dentistry.
стометро́в|ка (**-ки**; *gen pl* **-ок**) *ж* (*разг*: *СПОРТ*)

the hundred metres (*BRIT*) *или* meters (*US*).
стометро́в|ый *прил*: **~ая диста́нция** one hundred metres (*BRIT*) *или* meters (*US*).
стон (-а) *м* (*см глаг*) groan; moan.
стон|а́ть (-у́, -ешь) *несов неперех* to groan; (*перен*: *жаловаться*) to moan.
стоп *межд* stop.
стоп|а́ (-ы́; *nom pl* -ы) *ж* (*в стихах*) foot; (*nom pl* -ы́; *АНАТ*) sole; **идти́ (пойти́ *perf*) по чьим-н ~м** to follow in sb's footsteps.
стоп|и́ть (-лю́, -ишь; *impf* **ста́пливать**) *сов перех* (*дрова*) to burn up.
сто́п|ка (-ки; *gen pl* -ок) *ж* (*бумаг, писем*) pile; (*стаканчик*) glass (*for vodka etc*).
стоп-кра́н (-а) *м* emergency handle (*on train*).
стоплю́ *сов см* **стопи́ть**.
сто́пок *сущ см* **сто́пка**.
сто́пор (-а) *м* (*ТЕХ*) lock.
сто́пор|ить (-ю, -ишь; *perf* **засто́порить**) *несов перех* (*машину*) to stop; (*дело, работу*) to hold up; (*фиксировать*) to lock.
стопроце́нтный *прил* one-hundred percent; (*разг*: *негодяй, лгун итп*) absolute.
стоп|та́ть (-чу́, -чешь; *impf* **ста́птывать**) *сов перех* to wear out
▸ **стопта́ться** (*impf* **ста́птываться**) *сов возв* to wear out.
сторг|ова́ть(ся) (-у́ю(сь)) *сов от* **торгова́ть(ся)**.
стори́цей *нареч*: **возда́ть ~ кому́-н** to reward sb in full.
сто́рож (-а; *nom pl* -а́, *gen pl* -е́й) *м* watchman (*мн* watchmen).
сторожево́й *прил*: **~ пост** lookout post; **сторожева́я вы́шка** watchtower; **сторожево́й ка́тер** patrol boat.
сторо́жек *сущ см* **сторо́жка**.
сторож|и́ть (-у́, -и́шь) *несов перех* (*дом, сад*) to guard; (*зверя, вора*) to lie in wait for.
сторо́ж|ка (-ки; *gen pl* -ек) *ж* hut.
стор|она́ (-оны́; *acc sg* -ону, *dat sg* -оне́, *nom pl* -оны, *gen pl* -о́н, *dat pl* -она́м) *ж* side; (*направление*: *левая, правая*) direction; (*страна*) land; **стоя́ть** (*impf*) **в ~оне́ от** +*gen* to stand apart from; **в ~оне́** a little way off; **держа́ться** (*impf*) **в ~оне́** to keep one's distance; **в сто́рону** +*gen* towards; **смотре́ть (посмотре́ть *perf*) в сто́рону** to look away; **на́ ~ону** (*разг*: *продавать*) on the side; **подраба́тывать** (*impf*) **на ~оне́** (*разг*) to work on the side; **брать (взять *perf*) кого́-н со ~оны́** to bring sb in from outside (*fig*); **со ~оны́** +*gen* from; **со ~оны́ ма́тери/отца́** on one's mother's/father's side; **э́то о́чень любе́зно с Ва́шей ~оны́** that is very good of you; **с одно́й ~оны́ ... с друго́й ~оны́** ... on the one hand ... on the other hand ...; **принима́ть (приня́ть *perf*) чью-н сто́рону** to take sb's side; **встава́ть (встать *perf*) на чью-н сто́рону** to come out in sb's defence (*BRIT*) *или* defense (*US*); **быть** (*impf*) **на чьей-н ~оне́** to be on sb's side; **смотре́ть** (*impf*) **по ~м** to look around; (*отвлекаться*) to let one's attention wander.
стор|они́ться (-оню́сь, -о́нишься; *perf* **посторони́ться**) *несов возв* (*дать дорогу*) to make way; (*избегать*): **~** +*gen* to avoid.
сторо́нн|ий (-яя, -ее, -ие) *прил* outside *опред*.
сторо́нник (-а) *м* supporter, advocate.
сторо́нниц|а (-ы) *ж см* **сторо́нник**.
сторублёвый *прил* (*ассигнация*) one-hundred-rouble; (*о стоимости*) worth one hundred roubles.
стоск|ова́ться (-у́юсь) *сов возв*: **~ по** +*dat* to miss.
сточ|и́ть (-у́, -ишь; *impf* **ста́чивать**) *сов перех* to smooth down.
сто́чн|ый *прил*: **~ая кана́ва** gutter (*in street*); **сто́чная труба́** drainpipe; **сто́чные во́ды** effluent; **сто́чный жёлоб** gutter (*on roof*).
стошн|и́ть (-и́т) *сов от* **тошни́ть**.
сто́я *нареч* standing up.
стоя́ни|е (-я) *ср* standing.
стоя́н|ка (-ки; *gen pl* -ок) *ж* (*поезда, судна*) stop; (*автомобилей*) car park (*BRIT*), parking lot (*US*); (*геологов, путешественников*) camp; (*первобытного человека*) site; **стоя́нка такси́** taxi rank.
сто|я́ть (-ю́, -и́шь; *imper* **сто́й(те)**) *несов неперех* to stand; (*находиться*) to be; (*полк*) to be stationed; (*бездействовать*) to stand idle; (*сохраняться*: *цветы*) to last; (: *продукты*) to keep; (*perf* **постоя́ть**; *защищать*): **~ за** +*acc* (*за друга, за идею*) to stand up for; **пе́ред на́ми ~и́т тру́дная зада́ча/интере́сная пробле́ма** we are faced with a difficult task/interesting problem; **на бла́нке ~и́т по́дпись дире́ктора** the document bears the director's signature; **по́езд ~и́т здесь 15 мину́т** the train stops here for 15 minutes; **ча́йник ~и́т на плите́** the kettle is on the stove; **цветы́ ~я́т в ва́зе** the flowers are in the vase; **посу́да ~и́т в шкафу́** the crockery is in the cupboard; **~я́ла весна́/о́сень** it was spring/autumn (*BRIT*) *или* fall (*US*); **всё ле́то ~я́ла жара́** it was hot all through the summer; **в до́ме ~я́л шум/смех** the house was full of noise/laughter; **~** (*impf*) **у вла́сти** to be in power; **~** (*impf*) **на свои́х пози́циях** to stand one's ground; **он ~и́т на своём** he refuses to budge.
стоя́ч|ий (-ая, -ее, -ие) *прил* (*предложение*) standing *опред*; (*воротник*) stand-up; (*вода*) stagnant.
сто́ящ|ий (-ая, -ее, -ие) *прил* (*дело, предложение*) worthwhile; (*человек*) worthy; (*вещь*) useful.
стр. *сокр* (= **страни́ца**) pg. (= *page*).

страв|ить (-лю, -ишь) *сов от* **травить** ◆ (*impf* **стравливать**) *перех* to set on; **он их ~ил** he set them on each other.
страд|а (-ы) *ж* harvesting.
страдал|ец (-ьца) *м* martyr.
страдалиц|а (-ы) *ж см* **страдалец.**
страдальца *итп сущ см* **страдалец.**
страдальческ|ий (-ая, -ое, -ие) *прил* martyred.
страдани|е (-я) *ср* suffering.
страдательный *прил*: **~ залог** passive voice.
страда|ть (-ю) *несов неперех* to suffer; (*дисциплина, грамотность итп*) to be poor; (*сочувствовать*): **~ за** *+acc* to suffer for; (*потерпеть ущерб*): **~ от** *+gen* (*от засухи, от инфляции итп*) to suffer as a result of; (*perf* **пострадать**; *поплатиться*) to suffer; **~** *(impf)* **(от** *+gen***)** (*от боли, от голода*) to suffer; **~** *(impf) +instr* (*болезнью, самомнением*) to suffer from; **~** *(impf)* **от любви** to be lovesick.
страж (-а) *м* guardian.
страж|а (-и) *ж собир* guard; **быть** *(impf) или* **стоять** *(impf)* **на ~е** *+gen* to guard; **под ~ей** in custody; **брать (взять** *perf***) кого-н под ~у** to take sb into custody; **содержать** *(impf)* **кого-н под ~ей** to remand sb in custody.
стран|а (-ы; *nom pl* **-ы)** *ж* country; **страны света** cardinal points (*on compass*).
странен *прил см* **странный.**
страниц|а (-ы) *ж* (*также перен*) page; (*перен: истории, жизни*) chapter; **на ~х газет** in the papers.
странник (-а) *м* wanderer; (*РЕЛ*) pilgrim.
странниц|а (-ы) *ж см* **странник.**
странно *нареч* strangely ◆ *как сказ* that is strange *или* odd; **он ~ выглядит** he looks strange; **~, что её ещё нет** it is strange *или* odd that she isn't here yet; **мне ~, что ...** I find it strange that ....
странност|ь (-и) *ж* strangeness; (*обычно мн: человека, поведения*) oddity.
стран|ный (-ен, -на, -но) *прил* strange; **~ное дело** that's strange *или* odd.
страноведени|е (-я) *ср* national studies *мн.*
странстви|е (-я) *ср* wandering.
странств|овать (-ую) *несов неперех* to wander.
Страсбург (-а) *м* Strasbourg.
страстен *прил см* **страстный.**
страстн|ой *прил*: **~ая неделя** Holy Week.
страстност|ь (-и) *ж* passion.
страст|ный (-ен, -на, -но) *прил* passionate; (*коллекционер итп*) ardent.
страст|ь (-и) *ж* passion; (*разг: ужас*) horror; **страсти разгорелись** passions were running high; **~ к музыке/книгам** a passion for music/books.
стратег (-а) *м* strategist.
стратегическ|ий (-ая, -ое, -ие) *прил* strategic.
стратеги|я (-и) *ж* strategy.
стратосфер|а (-ы) *ж* stratosphere.
страус (-а) *м* ostrich.
страусовый *прил* ostrich *опред.*
страх (-а) *м* fear; (*разг: обычно мн: страшное событие*) horror; **~ за детей/за близких** fear for one's children/loved ones; **~ смерти/разоблачения** fear of death/exposure; **~ перед неизвестным** fear of the unknown; **со страху** in fright; **начальник держал их в страхе** they lived in fear of their boss; **под страхом смерти** on pain of death; **на свой ~ (и риск)** at one's own risk.
страховани|е (-я) *ср* insurance; **~ от** *+gen* insurance against; **государственное ~** national insurance (*BRIT*); **страхование жизни** life insurance; **страхование имущества** property insurance.
страховател|ь (-я) *м person taking out insurance.*
страх|овать (-ую) *несов перех* (*гимнаста*) to stand by (*to prevent sb from falling*); (*perf* **застраховать**): **~ (от** *+gen***)** (*имущество, автомобиль*) to insure (against); (*от неожиданностей*) to protect (against)
▸ **страховаться** (*perf* **застраховаться**) *несов возв*: **~ся (от** *+gen***)** to insure o.s. (against); (*от неожиданностей*) to protect o.s (from).
страхов|ка (-ки; *gen pl* **-ок)** *ж* insurance; **для ~ки** to be on the safe side.
страховой *прил* (*фирма, агент*) insurance *опред*; **~ брокер** insurance broker; **страховой взнос** *или* **страховая премия** insurance premium; **страховой полис** insurance policy.
страховок *сущ см* **страховка.**
страховщик (-а) *м* insurer.
страшен *прил см* **страшный.**
страшил|а (-ы) *м/ж* = **страшилище.**
страшилищ|е (-а; *gen pl* -) *ср* (*разг*) fright.
страш|ить (-у, -ишь) *несов перех* to frighten, scare
▸ **страшиться** *несов возв*: **~ся** *+gen* to be frightened *или* scared of.
страшно *нареч* (*кричать*) in a frightening way; (*разг: усталый, довольный*) terribly ◆ *как сказ* it's frightening; **мне ~** I'm frightened *или* scared; **~ подумать** it's frightening to think; **он ~ доволен собой** (*разг*) he's awfully *или* terribly pleased with himself; **она ~ устала** (*разг*) she's awfully *или* terribly tired; **она ~ любит болтать** (*разг*) she really likes to chat.
страш|ный (-ен, -на, -но) *прил* terrible, awful; (*фильм, сон, путь*) terrifying; **ничего ~ного** it doesn't matter.
стрежень (-ня) *м* deep part (*of river*).
стрек|оза (-озы; *nom pl* **-озы)** *ж* dragonfly (*мн* dragonflies); (*ребёнок*) fidget.
стрек|отать (-очу, -очешь) *несов неперех* to chirp.
стрел|а (-ы; *nom pl* **-ы)** *ж* (*для стрельбы*) arrow; (*крана*) arm; (*поезд*) express (train).
стрел|ец (-ьца) *м* Strelets (*regular soldier of special regiment in 16th-17th century*); (*созвездие*): **С~** Sagittarius.

стрéл|ка (**-ки**; *gen pl* **-ок**) *ж уменьш от* **стрелá**; (*часов*) hand; (*компаса, барометра*) needle; (*знак*) arrow; (*железнодорожная*) switch; (*ГЕО*) spit; (*лука*) shoot.
стрелкá *итп сущ см* **стрелóк**.
стрелкóвый *прил*: ~ **полк** infantry regiment; **стрелкóвый спорт** shooting.
стрéлок *сущ см* **стрéлка**.
стрел|óк (**-кá**) *м* (*ВОЕН*) rifleman (*мн* riflemen); **он хорóший** ~ he is a good shot.
стрéлочник (**-а**) *м* signalman (*мн* signalmen).
стрéлочниц|а (**-ы**) *ж см* **стрéлочник**.
стрельб|á (**-ы́**) *ж* shooting, firing.
стрéльбищ|е (**-а**) *ср* shooting range.
стрельцá *итп сущ см* **стрелéц**.
стрéльчатый *прил* (*окна, свод*) arched.
стрéляный *прил* (*дичь*) shot *опред*; ~ **патрóн** spent cartridge; ~ **солдáт** *soldier who has been under fire*; ~ **воробéй** (*разг*) old hand.
стреля́|ть (**-ю**) *несов неперех*: ~ (**в** *+acc*) (*в цель, во врага*) to shoot (at); (*мотор*) to backfire ◆ *перех* (*убивать*: *птиц*) to shoot; (*выпрашивать*) to cadge; ~ *(impf)* **из ружья́/пýшки** to fire a rifle/canon; **у меня́ ~ет в бокý** I have a shooting pain in my side
▸ **стреля́ться** *несов возв* (*самоубийца*) to shoot o.s.; (*на дуэли*): **~ся с** *+instr* to fight a duel with.
стремглáв *нареч* headlong.
стрéмени *итп сущ см* **стрéмя**.
стреми́тельно *нареч* (*мчаться*) headlong; (*меняться*) rapidly.
стреми́тельност|ь (**-и**) *ж* (*движений*) swiftness; (*изменений*) rapidity.
стреми́тельный *прил* (*движение, бег, атака*) swift; (*человек*) energetic; (*изменения*) rapid.
стрем|и́ться (**-лю́сь, -и́шься**) *несов возв*: ~ **в** *+acc* (*в университет, на родину*) to want to go to; (*добиваться*): ~ **к** *+dat* (*к славе, к добру, к правде*) to strive for.
стремлéни|е (**-я**) *ср*: ~ (**к** *+dat*) striving (for).
стремлю́сь *несов см* **стреми́ться**.
стремни́н|а (**-ы**) *ж* rapid (*in river*).
стрéм|я (**-ени**; *как* **врéмя**; *см* **Table 4**) *ср* stirrup.
стремя́н|ка (**-ки**; *gen pl* **-ок**) *ж* step-ladder.
стрептокóкк (**-а**) *м* streptococcus.
стресс (**-а**) *м* stress.
стрéссовый *прил* (*состояние*) stressed; (*ситуация, нагрузки*) stressful.
стри́г(ся) *итп несов см* **стри́чь(ся)**.
стригý(сь) *итп несов см* **стри́чь(ся)**.
стриж (**-á**) *м* swift.
стри́жек *сущ см* **стри́жка**.
стри́женый *прил* shorn; (*трава*) cut; (*мальчик*) short-haired.
стри́ж|ка (**-ки**; *gen pl* **-ек**) *ж* (*см глаг*) cutting; shearing; mowing; pruning; (*причёска*) haircut.
стрипти́з (**-а**) *м* striptease.
стрихни́н (**-а**) *м* strychnine.

стри|чь (**-гý, -жёшь** *итп*, **-гýт**; *pt* **-г, -гла, -гло**, *perf* **пострúчь** *или* **острúчь**) *несов перех* (*волосы, траву*) to cut; (*овцу*) to shear; (*газон*) to mow; (*кусты*) to prune; ~ (**постри́чь** *perf*) **когó-н** to cut sb's hair; ~ *(impf)* **всех под однý гребёнку** to tar everyone with the same brush
▸ **стри́чься** (*perf* **постри́чься** *или* **остри́чься**) *несов возв* (*остричь себе волосы*) to cut one's hair; (*в парикмахерской*) to have one's hair cut; (*no perf*; *носить короткую стрижку*) to wear one's hair short.
стрóганый *прил* planed.
строгá|ть (**-ю**; *perf* **вы́строгать**) *несов перех* to plane.
стрóг|ий (**-ая, -ое, -ие**; **-, -á, -о**) *прил* strict; (*красота, причёска, наказание, выговор*) severe; (*меры*) harsh; (*черты лица*) regular.
стрóго *нареч* (*воспитывать*) strictly; (*наказать, сказать*) severely; **~-нáстрого** (*разг*) very strictly; ~ **говоря́** strictly speaking.
стрóгост|ь (**-и**) *ж* (*см прил*) strictness; severity; harshness; regularity; (*обычно мн*: *строгие порядки*) harsh regulation.
строевóй *прил* (*ВОЕН*: *командир*) line *опред*; **строевáя подготóвка** drill; **строевáя часть** line unit; **строевóй лес** timber forest; **строевóй шаг** goose step.
стрóек *сущ см* **стрóйка**.
стрóен *прил см* **стрóйный**.
строéни|е (**-я**) *ср* (*здание*) building; (*организации, вещества*) structure.
стрóже *сравн прил от* **стрóгий** ◆ *сравн нареч от* **стрóго**.
строи́тел|ь (**-я**) *м* builder; (*+gen*; *нового общества*) creator of.
строи́тельный *прил* building *опред*, construction *опред*; **строи́тельный учáсток** building site; **строи́тельные материáлы** building materials.
строи́тельств|о (**-а**) *ср* (*зданий*) building, construction; (*нового общества*) building.
стрó|ить (**-ю, -ишь**; *perf* **вы́строить** *или* **пострóить**) *несов перех* (*дом, дорогу, мост*) to build, construct; (*perf* **пострóить**; *общество, быт, семью*) to create; (*фразу, мысль*) to compose; (*план, догадку*) to make; (*полк, отряд*) to draw up; ~ (**пострóить** *perf*) **ромáн на чём-н** to base a novel on sth; ~ (**сострóить** *perf*) (**из себя́**) **дуракá** to make o.s. out to be a fool; ~ (**сострóить** *perf*) **глáзки комý-н** to make eyes at sb; ~ (**сострóить** *perf*) **гримáсы** to make *или* pull faces
▸ **стрóиться** (*perf* **пострóиться**) *несов возв* to build o.s. a house; (*perf* **вы́строиться**; *солдаты, пленные*) to form up; (*no perf*): **~ся на** *+prp* (*сюжет, роман*) to be based on.
стро|й (**-я**) *м* (*социальный*) system; (*языка, предложения*) structure; (*loc sg* **-ю́**; *ВОЕН*:

шеренга) line; (: *походный, боевой*) formation; (: *действующие войска*) ranks *мн*; **входи́ть (войти́** *perf*) **в ~** (*завод*) to come into operation; **вводи́ть (ввести́** *perf*) **что-н в ~** (*завод*) to put sth into operation; **выводи́ть (вы́вести** *perf*) **что-н из стро́я** (*танк, машину*) to put sth out of commission; **выходи́ть (вы́йти** *perf*) **из стро́я** to fall out; (*перен*) to break down; **~ мышле́ния** way of thinking.

стро́|йка (-йки; *gen pl* **-ек**) *ж* (*здания*) building; (*место*) building *или* construction site.

стройматериа́л|ы (-ов) *мн сокр* (= *строительные материа́лы*) building materials *мн*.

стро́|йный (-ен, -йна́, -йно) *прил* (*фигура*) shapely; (*человек*) well-built; (*ряд, шеренга*) orderly; (*речь, фраза*) well-constructed; (*пение*) harmonious.

строк|а́ (-и́; *nom pl* **-и**, *dat pl* **-а́м**) *ж* (*в тексте*) line; **кра́сная ~** new paragraph; **чита́ть** (*impf*) **ме́жду строк** to read between the lines.

стро́н|уться (-усь, -ешься) *сов возв* to start moving.

строп (-а) *м* sling.

стропи́л|о (-а) *ср* beam, rafter.

стропти́в|ый (-, -а, -о) *прил* headstrong.

строф|а́ (-ы́; *nom pl* **-ы**, *dat pl* **-а́м**) *ж* stanza.

стро́чек *сущ см* **стро́чка**.

строч|и́ть (-у́, -и́шь; *perf* **прострочи́ть**) *несов перех* (*рукав, подол*) to stitch; (*perf* **настрочи́ть**; *сочинение, статью*) to scribble; (*no perf*; *перен*: *из автомата*) to fire away.

стро́ч|ка (-ки; *gen pl* **-ек**) *ж уменьш от* **строка́**; (*шов*) stitch.

строчн|о́й *прил*: **~а́я бу́ква** small *или* lower case letter.

струга́|ть (-ю; *perf* **вы́стругать**) *несов перех* = **строга́ть**.

стру́ек *сущ см* **стру́йка**.

стру́ж|ка (-ки; *gen pl* **-ек**) *ж* shaving (*of wood, metal etc*).

стру|и́ться (*3sg* **-и́тся**, *3pl* **-я́тся**) *несов возв* (*вода, ручей*) to stream; (*пот, дым*) to pour.

стру́|йка (-йки; *gen pl* **-ек**) *ж* trickle.

стру́йный *прил*: **~ при́нтер** inkjet printer.

структу́р|а (-ы) *ж* structure.

структурали́зм (-а) *м* structuralism.

структу́рный *прил* structural.

струн|а́ (-ы́; *nom pl* **-ы**) *ж* (*скрипки, ракетки*) string; (*перен*: *поэтическая*) streak.

стру́н|ка (-ки; *gen pl* **-ок**) *ж* string; **стать** (*perf*) *или* **вытя́гиваться (вы́тянуться** (*perf*) **в ~ку** to stand to attention; **ходи́ть** (*impf*) **по ~ке у кого́-н** *или* **пе́ред кем-н** to be under sb's thumb.

стру́нный *прил* (*инструмент*) stringed; **стру́нный кварте́т** string quartet.

стру́нок *сущ см* **стру́нка**.

струп (-а; *nom pl* **-ья**, *gen pl* **-ьев**) *м* scab.

стру́|сить (-шу, -сишь) *сов от* **тру́сить**.

струхн|у́ть (-у́, -ёшь) *сов неперех* (*разг*) to get a fright.

стручка́ *итп сущ см* **стручо́к**.

стручко́вый *прил*: **~ пе́рец** chilli; **стручко́вая фасо́ль** runner beans *мн*; **стручко́вый горо́х** peas *мн* in the pod.

стручо́|к (-ка́) *м* pod.

стру́шу *сов см* **стру́сить**.

стру|я́ (-и́; *nom pl* **-и**) *ж* (*воды, воздуха*) stream; (*перен*: *сатирическая, бодрая*) streak; **попа́сть** (*perf*) **в ~ю́** (*перен*) to fit in.

стря́па|ть (-ю; *perf* **состря́пать**) *несов перех* (*разг*: *еду*) to cook; (: *рассказ, стихи*) to cobble together.

стряпн|я́ (-и́) *ж* (*разг*) cooking; (*перен*) rubbish.

стряс|ти́ (-у́, -ёшь; *pt* **-, -ла́, -ло́**, *impf* **стряса́ть**) *сов перех* to shake off

► **стрясти́сь** *сов возв* (*разг*) to happen; **с ним ~ла́сь беда́** he's in trouble; **что там ~ло́сь?** what happened here?

стряхн|у́ть (-у́, -ёшь; *impf* **стря́хивать**) *сов перех* (*также перен*) to shake off.

ст.с *сокр* (= *ста́рого сти́ля*) OS (= *Old Style*).

ст.ст. *сокр* = **ст.с**.

студене́|ть (*3sg* **-ет**, *3pl* **-ют**) *несов неперех* (*заливное*) to gel.

студени́ст|ый (-, -а, -о) *прил* gelatinous.

студе́нт (-а) *м* student.

студе́нт|ка (-ки; *gen pl* **-ок**) *ж см* **студе́нт**.

студе́нческ|ий (-ая, -ое, -ие) *прил* student *опред*; **студе́нческий биле́т** student card.

студе́нчеств|о (-а) *ср* student days *мн* ◆ *собир* (*студенты*) students *мн*.

студёный (-, -а, -о) *прил* icy cold.

сту́д|ень (-ня) *м* jellied meat.

студи́ек *сущ см* **студи́йка**.

студи́|ец (-йца) *м* student (*at art or drama school*).

студи́|йка (-йки; *gen pl* **-ек**) *ж см* **студи́ец**.

студи́йца *итп сущ см* **студи́ец**.

сту|ди́ть (-жу́, -дишь; *perf* **остуди́ть**) *несов перех* to cool.

сту́ди|я (-и) *ж* studio; (*школа*) school (*for actors, dancers, artists etc*); (*мастерская*) workshop.

сту́дня *итп сущ см* **сту́день**.

сту́ж|а (-и) *ж* severe cold.

стужу́ *несов см* **студи́ть**.

стук (-а) *м* (*в дверь*) knock; (*машин, падающего предмета*) thud; (*сердца*) thump; **входи́ть (войти́** *perf*) **без сту́ка** to enter without knocking.

сту́ка|ть(ся) (-ю(сь)) *несов от* **сту́кнуть(ся)**.

стука́ч (-а́) *м* (*разг пренебр*) grass (*informer*).

сту́кн|уть (-у, -ешь) *сов неперех* (*в дверь, в окно*) to knock; (*по столу*) to bang; (*impf* **сту́кать**; *разг*: *ударить*) to knock ◆ *безл* (*no impf*): **мне ~уло 60** I've hit 60

► **сту́кнуться** (*impf* **сту́каться**) *сов возв* to bang o.s.

стул (-а; *nom pl* **-ья**, *gen pl* **-ьев**) *м* chair; (*no pl*; *ФИЗИОЛОГИЯ*) stools *мн*.

сту́п|а (-ы) *ж* mortar.

ступа́|ть (-ю) *несов от* **ступи́ть** ◆ *неперех*

(*осторожно, медленно*) to tread; **~йте!** off you go!

ступе́нек *сущ см* **ступе́нька**.

ступе́нчат|ый (**-, -а, -о**) *прил* (*спуск, водопад*) terraced; (*процесс*) in stages.

ступе́н|ь (**-и**) *ж* step; (*gen pl* **-е́й**, *dat pl* **-я́м**; *процесса*) stage; (*муз*) degree.

ступе́н|ька (**-ьки**; *gen pl* **-ек**) *ж* step.

ступ|и́ть (**-лю́, -ишь**; *impf* **ступа́ть**) *сов неперех* to step, tread.

ступи́ц|а (**-ы**) *ж* (*ТЕХ*) hub.

сту́п|ка (**-ки**; *gen pl* **-ок**) *ж* mortar.

ступлю́ *сов см* **ступи́ть**.

ступн|я́ (**-и́**) *ж* (*стопа*) foot (*мн* feet); (*подошва*) sole.

сту́пок *сущ см* **сту́пка**.

сту́пор (**-а**) *м* stupor.

стуч|а́ть (**-у́, -и́шь**; *perf* **постуча́ть**) *несов неперех* (*в дверь, в окно*) to knock; (*по столу, по доске*) to bang; (*колёса*) to rattle; (*сердце*) to thump; (*зубы*) to chatter; (*perf* **настуча́ть**; *разг*: *доносить*) to grass; **(у меня́) ~и́т в виска́х** my temples are throbbing; **~ (постуча́ть** *perf***) в окно́/в дверь** to bang on the window/door

▸ **стуча́ться** (*perf* **постуча́ться**) *несов возв*: **~ся (в** *+acc*) to knock (at); **~ся (постуча́ться** *perf***) к кому́-н** to knock at sb's door.

стуш|ева́ться (**-у́юсь**; *impf* **тушева́ться**) *сов возв* to go shy.

стыд (**-а́**) *м* shame; **к ~у́ своему́** to one's shame; **сгора́ть (сгоре́ть** *perf***) от ~а́** to burn with shame; **у тебя́ нет ни ~а́, ни со́вести** (*разг*) you've no shame.

сты|ди́ть (**-жу́, -ди́шь**; *perf* **пристыди́ть**) *несов перех* to (put to) shame

▸ **стыди́ться** (*perf* **постыди́ться**) *несов возв*: **~ся** *+gen/+infin* to be ashamed of/to do; **~ся (постыди́ться** *perf***) кого́-н/чего́-н пе́ред кем-н** to be ashamed of sb/sth in front of sb.

стыдли́в|ый (**-, -а, -о**) *прил* bashful.

сты́дно *как сказ* it's a shame; **мне ~** I am ashamed; **мне ~ друзе́й** *или* **пе́ред друзья́ми** I'm ashamed in front of my friends; **как тебе́ не ~!** you ought to be ashamed of yourself!

стыжу́(сь) *несов см* **стыди́ть(ся)**.

стык (**-а**) *м* (*труб, рельсов*) join; (*улиц*) junction; (*перен: двух наук, двух эпох*) meeting point.

стык|ова́ть (**-у́ю**; *perf* **состыкова́ть**) *несов перех* (*рельсы, трубы*) to join; (*КОСМОС*) to dock

▸ **стыкова́ться** (*perf* **состыкова́ться**) *несов возв* (*КОСМОС*) to dock.

стыко́в|ка (**-ки**; *gen pl* **-ок**) *ж* docking.

сты́н|уть (**-у, -ешь**; *perf* **осты́нуть**) *несов неперех* = **стыть**.

сты|ть (**-ну, -нешь**; *perf* **осты́ть**) *несов неперех* to go cold; (*perf* **просты́ть**; *мёрзнуть*) to freeze; **кровь сты́нет (в жи́лах)** the blood runs cold.

сты́ч|ка (**-ки**; *gen pl* **-ек**) *ж* (*военная*) clash; (*разг*: *с начальником, с милицией*) run-in.

стюа́рд (**-а**) *м* steward.

стюарде́сс|а (**-ы**) *ж* air hostess.

стяг (**-а**; *nom pl* **-и**) *м* banner.

стя́гива|ть(ся) (**-ю(сь)**) *несов от* **стяну́ть(ся)**.

стяжа́тел|ь (**-я**) *м* taker.

стяжа́тельниц|а (**-ы**) *ж см* **стяжа́тель**.

стяжа́тельск|ий (**-ая, -ое, -ие**) *прил* grasping.

стян|у́ть (**-у́, -ешь**; *impf* **стя́гивать**) *сов перех* (*пояс, шнуровку*) to tighten; (*войска*) to round up; (*no impf*; *разг*: *украсть*) to nick, pinch; (*перевязать*): **~ что-н чем-н** (*талию поясом*) to pull sth in with sth; (*чемодан ремнём*) to strap sth up with sth; (*обувь, перчатку*) to pull off

▸ **стяну́ться** (*impf* **стя́гиваться**) *сов возв* (*узел*) to tighten; (*войска*) to gather; (*разг*: *поясом*) to pull o.s. in.

СУ *ср сокр* (= *статисти́ческое управле́ние*) *statistics office*.

субаре́нд|а (**-ы**) *ж* sub-lease, sub-let.

суббо́т|а (**-ы**) *ж* Saturday; *см также* **пя́тница**.

суббо́тн|ий (**-яя, -ее, -ие**) *прил* (*вечер, работа*) Saturday *опред*; (*события*) Saturday's.

сублима́ци|я (**-и**) *ж* sublimation.

субордина́ци|я (**-и**) *ж* subordination.

субподря́д (**-а**) *м* subcontract; **заключа́ть (заключи́ть** *perf***) ~** to subcontract.

субподря́дчик (**-а**) *м* subcontractor.

субсиди́р|овать (**-ую**) (*не*)*сов перех* to subsidize.

субси́ди|я (**-и**) *ж* subsidy; **инвестицио́нные ~и** (*КОММ*) investment grant *ед*.

субстантиви́рованн|ый *прил*: **~ое прилага́тельное** substantivized adjective.

субста́нци|я (**-и**) *ж* substance.

субти́тр (**-а**) *м* subtitle.

субтро́пик|и (**-ов**) *мн* subtropics *мн*.

субъе́кт (**-а**) *м* (*индивид, также ЮР*) individual; (*разг*: *о мужчине*) character.

субъекти́вност|ь (**-и**) *ж* subjectivity.

субъекти́вный *прил* subjective.

сувени́р (**-а**) *м* souvenir.

сувере́нен *прил см* **суверéнный**.

суверените́т (**-а**) *м* sovereignty.

суверéн|ный (**-ен, -на, -но**) *прил* sovereign.

сугли́н|ок (**-ка**) *м* loam.

сугро́б (**-а**) *м* snowdrift.

сугу́бо *нареч* highly.

сугу́бый *прил* particular.

суд (**-а́**) *м* court session; (*орган*) court; (*процесс*) trial; (*мнение*) judgement, verdict ◆ *собир* the judges *мн*; **отдава́ть (отда́ть** *perf***) кого́-н под ~** to prosecute sb; **подава́ть (пода́ть** *perf***) на кого́-н в ~** to take sb to court; **предава́ть (преда́ть** *perf***) кого́-н ~у́** (*преступника*) to prosecute sb; **попада́ть (попа́сть** *perf***) под ~** to

be taken to court; **встать, ~ идёт!** please stand for the court!; **на нет и ~á нет** oh well, that's that then.
судá *итп сущ см* **сýдно**.
судáк (-á) *м* pike-perch.
Судáн (-а) *м* (the) Sudan.
судáрын|я (-и; *gen pl* -ь) *ж* Madame.
сýдар|ь (-я) *м* Sir.
сýдеб *сущ см* **судьбá**.
судéбно-медицúнск|ий (-ая, -ое, -ие) *прил*: **судéбно-медицúнская экспертúза** forensics.
судéбн|ый *прил* (*заседание, органы*) court *опред*; (*издержки, практика*) legal; **~ая ошúбка** miscarriage of justice; **~ое решéние** adjudication; **судéбное дéло** court case; **судéбный исполнúтель** bailiff; **судéбный приговóр** sentence.
судéйск|ий (-ая, -ое, -ие) *прил* (*ЮР*) judge's; **судéйская коллéгия** (*ЮР*) the bench; (*СПОРТ*) panel of judges.
судéйств|о (-а) *ср* refereeing.
сýден *сущ см* **сýдно**.
судúмост|ь (-и) *ж* conviction.
су|дúть (-жý, -дишь) *несов перех* (*преступника*) to try; (*матч*) to referee; (*укорять*) to judge ◆ *неперех* (*на матче*) to referee; (*на соревнованиях*) to judge; ~ *(impf)* **о ком-н/чём-н** to judge sb/sth; **сýдя по** *+dat* judging by
▸ **судúться** *несов возв*: **~ся с кем-н** to take sb to court.
сýд|но (-на; *nom pl* -á, *gen pl* -óв) *ср* vessel; (*gen pl* -ен; *МЕД*) bedpan.
сýдный *прил*: **~ день** Judgement Day.
судовéрф|ь (-и) *ж сокр* (= *судостроúтельная верфь*) shipyard.
судовладéл|ец (-ьца) *м* shipowner.
судовождéни|е (-я) *ср* navigation.
судов|óй *прил*: **~áя комáнда** ship's crew; **судовóй журнáл** ship's log.
судопроизвóдств|о (-а) *ср* legal proceedings *мн*.
судоремóнтн|ый *прил*: **~ые мастерскúе** shipyards *мн*.
сýдорог|а (-и) *ж* (*от боли*) spasm; (*от холода, от отвращения итп*) shudder.
сýдорож|ный (-ен, -на, -но) *прил* (*движения, плач*) convulsive; (*перен*: *приготовления*) feverish.
судостроéни|е (-я) *ср* ship building.
судостроúтельный *прил* ship-building.
судохóдный *прил* navigable; **~ канáл** shipping canal.
судохóдств|о (-а) *ср* navigation.
суд|ьбá (-ьбы́; *nom pl* -ьбы, *gen pl* -еб) *ж* fate; (*будущее*) destiny; **~ э́той пьéсы óчень интерéсна** this play has had a very interesting fate; **какúми ~мú!** fancy seeing you here!; **(нам) не ~ встрéтиться** we are not fated to meet.
суд|ья́ (-ьú; *nom pl* -ьи, *gen pl* -éй) *ж* judge; (*СПОРТ*) referee; **я тебé не ~** who am I to judge you?
суевéрен *прил см* **суевéрный**.
суевéри|е (-я) *ср* superstition.
суевéр|ный (-ен, -на, -но) *прил* superstitious.
сует|á (-ы́) *ж* (*житейская, мелочная*) futility; (*хлопоты*) hustle and bustle.
сýетен *прил см* **сýетный**.
сует|úться (-чýсь, -тúшься) *несов возв* to fuss (about).
суетлúв|ый (-, -а, -о) *прил* fussy; (*жизнь, работа*) busy.
сýет|ный (-ен, -на, -но) *прил* (*интересы, желания, жизнь итп*) futile; (*человек*) superficial; (*день, жизнь*) busy.
суечýсь *несов см* **суетúться**.
сужá|ть (-ю) *несов от* **сýзить**.
суждéни|е (-я) *ср* (*мнение*) opinion; (*заключение*) judgement.
сужденó *как сказ*: **(нам) не ~ бы́ло встрéтиться** we weren't fated to meet.
сýжен|ая (-ой; *decl like adj*) *ж*: **егó ~** his intended.
сужéни|е (-я) *ср* (*см глаг*) narrowing; taking in.
сýжен|ый (-ого; *decl like adj*) *м*: **её ~** her intended.
сужý(сь) *несов см* **судúть(ся)**.
сý|зить (-жу, -зишь; *impf* **сужáть**) *сов перех* to narrow; (*платье*) to take in
▸ **сýзиться** *сов возв* to narrow.
су|к (-кá; *loc sg* -кý, *nom pl* -чья, *gen pl* -чьев) *м* (*дерева*) bough.
сýк|а (-и) *ж* bitch ◆ *м/ж* (*груб!*: *о женщине*) bitch (*!*); (*: о мужчине*) bastard (*!*); **~ин сын** (*разг*) son of a bitch (*!*)
сук|нó (-нá; *nom pl* -на, *gen pl* -он) *ср* (*шерстяное*) felt; (*хлопчатобумажное*) coarse cloth; **класть (положúть** *perf*) **что-н под ~** (*перен*) to shelve sth.
сукóнный *прил* (*см сущ*) felt *опред*; coarse cloth *опред*.
сул|úть (-ю́, -úшь; *perf* **посулúть**) *несов перех*: **~ что-н комý-н** (*обещать*) to promise sb sth, promise sth to sb; (*предвещать*) to bode for.
султáн (-а) *м* (*монарх*) sultan; (*украшение*) plume.
сульфáт (-а) *м* sulphate.
сум|á (-ы́) *ж* (*старушечья*) (tote) bag; (*охотничья*) pouch; **ходúть** *(impf)* **с ~óй** (*перен*) to go begging.
сумасбрóд (-а) *м* maverick.
сумасбрóден *прил см* **сумасбрóдный**.
сумасбрóд|ка (-ки; *gen pl* -ок) *ж см* **сумасбрóд**.
сумасбрóд|ный (-ен, -на, -но) *прил* (*человек, поведение*) maverick; (*идея*) madcap.
сумасбрóдок *сущ см* **сумасбрóдка**.
сумасбрóдств|о (-а) *ср* (*поведение*) maverick behaviour; (*поступок*) exploit.
сумасшéдш|ая (-ей; *decl like adj*) *ж* madwoman (*мн* madwomen).
сумасшéдш|ий (-ая, -ее, -ие) *прил* mad; (*разг*: *успех*) amazing; (*: скорость*) lunatic ◆ (-его; *decl like adj*) *м* madman (*мн* madmen); **~ие**

де́ньги ridiculous amounts of money; **сумасше́дший дом** asylum; (*разг*) madhouse.

сумасше́стви|е (**-я**) *ср* madness, lunacy; **до ~я** like mad.

сумато́х|а (**-и**) *ж* chaos.

сумато́ш|ный (**-ен, -на, -но**) *прил* (*разг*) chaotic.

сумбу́р (**-а**) *м* muddle.

сумбу́р|ный (**-ен, -на, -но**) *прил* muddled.

су́мерек *сущ см* **су́мерки.**

су́мереч|ный (**-ен, -на, -но**) *прил* twilight.

су́мер|ки (**-ек**) *мн* twilight *ед*, dusk *ед*.

суме́|ть (**-ю**) *сов неперех*: ~ *+infin* to manage to do.

су́м|ка (**-ки**; *gen pl* **-ок**) *ж* bag; (*кенгуру*) pouch.

су́мм|а (**-ы**) *ж* sum.

сумма́р|ный (**-ен, -на, -но**) *прил* (*количество, затраты*) total *опред*; (*оценка, обзор, описание*) overall.

сумми́р|овать (**-ую**) *(не)сов перех* (*затраты итп*) to add up; (*информацию, данные, сказанное*) to summarize.

су́мок *сущ см* **су́мка.**

су́моч|ка (**-ки**; *gen pl* **-ек**) *ж уменьш от* **су́мка**; (*дамская, вечерняя*) handbag.

су́мрак (**-а**) *м* gloom.

су́мрачен *прил см* **су́мрачный.**

су́мрачно *нареч* (*посмотреть*) gloomily; (*выглядеть*) gloomy ◆ *как сказ* (*на улице, в доме*) it's gloomy; **у меня́ на душе́** ~ I have a heavy heart.

су́мрач|ный (**-ен, -на, -но**) *прил* (*также перен*) gloomy.

су́мчатый *прил* (*ЗООЛ*) marsupial *опред*.

сумя́тиц|а (**-ы**) *ж* mishmash.

сунду́к (**-а́**) *м* trunk, chest.

су́н|уть(ся) (**-у(сь), -ешь(ся)**) *сов от* **сова́ть(ся).**

суп (**-а**; *part gen* **-у**, *nom pl* **-ы́**) *м* soup.

суперма́ркет (**-а**) *м* supermarket.

суперме́н (**-а**) *м* superman (*мн* supermen).

супермо́дный *прил* very trendy.

супероблóж|ка (**-ки**; *gen pl* **-ек**) *ж* dust jacket.

су́пниц|а (**-ы**) *ж* soup tureen.

супру́г (**-а**; *nom pl* **-и**) *м* spouse; **~и** husband and wife.

супру́г|а (**-и**) *ж* spouse.

супру́жеск|ий (**-ая, -ое, -ие**) *прил* marital; (*чета*) married.

супру́жеств|о (**-а**) *ср* matrimony.

сургу́ч (**-а́**) *м* sealing wax.

суро́вост|ь (**-и**) *ж* (*см прил*) bleakness; severity; hardship; harshness; sternness.

суро́в|ый (**-, -а, -о**) *прил* (*природа, зима*) bleak; (*приговор*) severe; (*жизнь*) tough; (*действительность*) harsh; (*человек, взгляд*) stern; (*no short form*; *ткань, нити*) coarse.

суррога́т (**-а**) *м* (*также перен*) substitute.

суррога́тный *прил* substitute *опред*.

суса́льн|ый *прил*: **~ое зо́лото** gold leaf.

су́слик (**-а**) *м* ground squirrel (*BRIT*), gopher (*US*).

суспе́нзи|я (**-и**) *ж* suspension.

суста́в (**-а**) *м* (*АНАТ*) joint.

суста́вный *прил*: ~ **ревмати́зм** rheumatism of the joints.

сутенёр (**-а**) *м* pimp.

су́т|ки (**-ок**) *мн* twenty four hours *мн*; **кру́глые ~** day and night.

су́толок|а (**-и**) *ж* hurly-burly.

су́точн|ые (**-ых**; *decl like adj*) *мн* subsistence allowance *ед*.

су́точный *прил* twenty-four-hour.

суту́л|ить (**-ю, -ишь**; *perf* **ссуту́лить**) *несов перех* to hunch

► **суту́литься** (*perf* **ссуту́литься**) *несов возв* to stoop.

суту́л|ый (**-, -а, -о**) *прил* stooped.

сут|ь (**-и**) *ж* essence; ~ **де́ла** the crux of the matter; **по су́ти (де́ла)** as a matter of fact ◆ *как сказ*: **э́то не ~ ва́жно** it's not all that important; **таки́е слу́чаи ~ гро́зное предупрежде́ние** such incidents serve as a severe warning.

суфле́ *ср нескл* soufflé.

суфлёр (**-а**) *м* prompter.

суфлёрск|ий (**-ая, -ое, -ие**) *прил*: **~ая бу́дка** prompt box.

су́ффикс (**-а**) *м* suffix.

суха́р|ь (**-я́**) *м* cracker; (*разг*: *о человеке*) cold fish.

су́хо *нареч* drily ◆ *как сказ* (*о сухой погоде*) it is dry; **на у́лице** ~ it's dry outside.

сухове́|й (**-я**) *м* hot dry wind.

сухогру́з (**-а**) *м* dry-cargo ship.

сухожи́ли|е (**-я**) *ср* tendon.

сух|о́й (**-, -а́, -о**) *прил* dry; (*ветка, листья*) dried; (*no short form*; *фрукты, овощи*) dried; **сухо́е вино́** dry wine; **сухо́е молоко́** dried milk; **сухо́й зако́н** dry law, prohibition; **сухо́й счёт** (*СПОРТ*) lockout.

сухопа́р|ый (**-, -а, -о**) *прил* bony.

сухопу́тный *прил* land *опред*; **сухопу́тные войска́** ground forces *мн*.

су́хост|ь (**-и**) *ж* dryness.

сухофру́кт|ы (**-ов**) *мн* dried fruit *ед*.

сухоща́в|ый (**-, -а, -о**) *прил* lean.

суч|о́к (**-ка́**) *м* twig.

су́чья *итп сущ см* **сук.**

су́ш|а (**-и**) *ж* (dry) land.

су́ше *сравн прил от* **сухо́й** ◆ *сравн нареч от* **су́хо.**

су́шек *сущ см* **су́шка.**

сушёный *прил* dried.

суши́л|ка (**-ки**; *gen pl* **-ок**) *ж* (*помещение*) drying room; (*приспособление*) dryer.

суш|и́ть (**-у́, -ишь**; *perf* **вы́сушить**) *несов перех* (*бельё, одежду, сено*) to dry; (*perf* **вы́сушить**

или **засушить**; *травы итп*) to dry
▸ **сушиться** (*perf* **высушиться**) *несов возв* to dry; (*человек*) to dry off.
сўш|ка (**-ки**; *gen pl* **-ек**) *ж* (*действие*) drying; (*бублик*) *small dry biscuit in the shape of a doughnut.*
суш|ь (**-и**) *ж* dry spell.
сущéственно *нареч* (*улучшить, изменить*) substantially.
сущéствен|ный (**-, -на, -но**) *прил* (*черта, качество*) essential; (*изменения*) substantial; (*замечания*) major; (*вопрос*) important.
существительн|ое (**-ого**; *decl like adj*) *ср* (*также:* **имя ~**) noun.
существ|ó (**-á**) *ср* (*вопроса, дела итп*) essence; (*nom pl* **-á**; *животное*) creature; (*человек*) being; **по ~ý** (*говорить*) to the point; (*вводн сл*) essentially; **всем своим ~м** with one's whole being.
существовáни|е (**-я**) *ср* existence; **прекращáть** (**прекратить** *perf*) **~** to cease to exist; **срéдства к ~ю** livelihood; **отравлять** (**отравить** *perf*) **комý-н ~** to make sb's life a misery.
существ|овáть (**-ýю**) *несов неперех* to exist; **~** (*impf*) *+instr* *или* **на** *+acc* to make one's living from.
сýщ|ий (**-ая, -ее, -ие**) *прил* (*правда*) honest; (*мучение, пустяки*) utter; **онá ~ ребёнок** she is a real baby.
сýщност|ь (**-и**) *ж* (*вопроса, проблемы*) essence; **в ~и** (**говорят**) in essence, essentially.
Суэ́ц (**-а**) *м* Suez.
суэ́цк|ий (**-ая, -ое, -ие**) *прил*: **С~ канáл** the Suez Canal.
СФ *м сокр* (= *Совéт Федерáций*) *upper chamber of the Russian parliament.*
сфабрик|овáть (**-ýю**) *сов от* **фабриковáть**.
сфальшив|ить (**-лю, -ишь**) *сов от* **фальшивить**.
сфантазир|овать (**-ую**) *сов от* **фантазировать**.
сфéр|а (**-ы**) *ж* sphere; (*производства, торговли, науки*) area; (*театральная, дипломатическая*) circles *мн*; **земнáя ~** the globe; **высшие ~ы** upper echelons; **в ~е** *+gen* in the field of; **сфéра обслýживания** *или* **услýг** service industry.
сферическ|ий (**-ая, -ое, -ие**) *прил* spherical.
сфинкс (**-а**) *м* sphinx.
сформир|овáть(ся) (**-ýю(сь)**) *сов от* **формировáть(ся)**.
сформулир|овать (**-ую**) *сов от* **формулировать**.
сфотографир|овать(ся) (**-ую(сь)**) *сов от* **фотографировать(ся)**.
схалтýр|ить (**-ю, -ишь**) *сов от* **халтýрить**.
схва|тить (**-чý, -тишь**) *сов от* **хватáть** ◆ (*impf* **схвáтывать**) *перех* (*скрепить*) to secure; (*разг: простуду*) to catch; (*мысль, смысл*) to grasp; **у меня ~тило живóт** I've got stomach cramps
▸ **схватиться** *сов от* **хватáться** ◆ (*impf* **схвáтываться**) *возв* (*борцы, оппоненты*) to lock together.
схвáт|ка (**-ки**; *gen pl* **-ок**) *ж* fight; *см также* **схвáтки**.
схвáт|ки (**-ок**) *мн* (*МЕД*) contractions *мн*.
схвáтыва|ть(ся) (**-ю(сь)**) *несов от* **схватить(ся)**.
схвачý(сь) *сов см* **схватить(ся)**.
схéм|а (**-ы**) *ж* (*метро, улиц*) plan; (*ЭЛЕК: радио итп*) circuit board; (*статьи итп*) outline.
схематизир|овать (**-ую**) (*не*)*сов перех* to schematize.
схематизм (**-а**) *м* schematism.
схемати́чен *прил см* **схемати́чный**.
схемати́ческ|ий (**-ая, -ое, -ие**) *прил* (*ТЕХ*) diagrammatic; (*изложение*) sketchy.
схемати́ч|ный (**-ен, -на, -но**) *прил* (*изложение*) sketchy.
схим|а (**-ы**) *ж* schema (*strict vow taken by orthodox monks*).
схимник (**-а**) *м monk who has taken strict vows.*
схитр|ить (**-ю, -ишь**) *сов от* **хитрить**.
схлестн|ýться (**-ýсь, -ёшься**; *impf* **схлёстываться**) *сов возв* (*разг*) to lock together.
схлоп|отáть (**-очý, -óчешь**) *сов перех* (*разг*): **~ вы́говор** to get a telling off; **ты у меня ~óчешь!** you're asking for it!
схлы́н|уть (*3sg* **-ет**, *3pl* **-ут**) *сов неперех* (*вода*) to subside; (*толпа*) to thin out.
сход (**-а**) *м* (*с горы, с трапа*) descent.
схóден *прил см* **схóдный**.
схо|дить (**-жý, -дишь**) *сов от* **ходить** ◆ *неперех* (*разг: в театр, на прогулку*) to go ◆ *несов от* **сойти**
▸ **сходиться** *несов от* **сойтись**.
схóд|ка (**-ки**; *gen pl* **-ок**) *ж* assembly.
схóдн|и (**-ей**) *мн* gangplank *ед*.
схóд|ный (**-ен, -на, -но**) *прил* similar.
схóдок *сущ см* **схóдка**.
схóдств|о (**-а**) *ср* similarity.
схóж|ий (**-ая, -ее, -ие**) *прил* (*разг*) = **схóдный**.
схожý(сь) (*не*)*сов см* **сходить(ся)**.
схолáстик|а (**-и**) *ж* (*философия*) scholasticism; (*отвлечённые знания*) speculation.
схоласти́ч|ный (**-ен, -на, -но**) *прил* scholastic.
схорон|ить (**-ю, -ишь**) *сов от* **хоронить**.
сцáпа|ть (**-ю**) *сов от* **цáпать**.
сце|дить (**-жу, -дишь**; *impf* **сцеживать**) *сов перех* (*жидкость, сок*) to strain off; (*грудное молоко*) to express.
сцементир|овать (**-ую**) *сов от* **цементировать**.
сцéн|а (**-ы**) *ж* (*подмостки*) stage; (*эпизод: в пьесе, на улице*) scene; **сходить** (**сойти** *perf*) **со ~ы** to leave the stage; (*политик*) to fade from the scene; **устрáивать** (**устрóить** *perf*) **~у** to make a scene.
сценáри|й (**-я**) *м* (*фильма*) script; (*вечера, праздника*) programme.
сценарист (**-а**) *м* scriptwriter.
сцени́чен *прил см* **сцени́чный**.

сцени́ческ|ий (-ая, -ое, -ие) *прил* stage *опред*; **~ое мастерство́** acting skills; **~ о́браз** dramatic character; **сцени́ческое иску́сство** dramatic art.
сцени́ч|ный (-ен, -на, -но) *прил*: **~ная пье́са** play well-suited for the theatre (*BRIT*) *или* theater (*US*).
сце́н|ка (-ки; *gen pl* **-ок)** *ж уменьш от* **сце́на**; (*зарисовка*) sketch.
сцеп|и́ть (-лю́, -ишь; *impf* **сцепля́ть)** *сов перех* (*вагоны, прицепы*) to couple; (*пальцы, руки*) to clasp
▸ **сцепи́ться** (*impf* **сцепля́ться)** *сов возв* (*ветви*) to be caught together; (*разг*: *схватиться*): **~ся (с** *+instr*) (*дети, спорщики*) to get into a fight (with).
сцепле́ни|е (-я) *ср* (*вагонов*) coupling; (*ТЕХ*: *механизм*) clutch.
сцеплю́(сь) *сов см* **сцепи́ть(ся)**.
сцепля́|ть(ся) (-ю(сь)) *несов от* **сцепи́ть(ся)**.
счастли́в|ец (-ца) *м* lucky man (*мн* men).
счастли́виц|а (-ы) *ж* lucky woman (*мн* women).
сча́стливо *нареч* (*жить, рассмеяться*) happily; **~ отде́латься** *(perf)* to have a lucky escape; **счастли́во!** all the best!; **счастли́во остава́ться!** good luck!
счастли́вца *итп сущ см* **счастли́вец**.
счастли́вчик (-а) *м* (*разг*) lucky devil.
счастл|и́вый (-ив, -ива, -иво) *прил* (*человек, жизнь, лицо*) happy; (*делец, игрок, случай*) lucky; **у него́ ~и́вая рука́** he's got a lucky touch; **~и́вого пути́!** have a good journey!
сча́сть|е (-я) *ср* (*личное, семейное*) happiness; (*удача*) luck; **к ~ю** luckily, fortunately; **на на́ше ~** luckily for us; **како́е ~, что ты пришёл** how nice that you've come; **возьми́ э́то на ~** take that for good luck; **твоё ~, что ...** you're lucky that ....
счесть (сочту́, сочтёшь; *pt* **счёл, сочла́, сочло́**) *сов от* **счита́ть** ◆ *неперех*: **пробле́м у меня́ не ~** I've got countless problems.
счёт (-а; *part gen* **-у**, *loc sg* **-у́**, *nom pl* **-а́)** *м* (*действие*) counting; (*КОММ*: *в банке*) account; (: *накладная*) invoice; (*ресторанный, телефонный*) bill; (*no pl*; *СПОРТ*) score; **в ~** *+gen* in lieu of; **за ~** *+gen* (*фирмы*) at the expense of; (*эффективности, внедрений итп*) due to; **на ~ кого́-н** at sb's expense; **на э́тот ~** in this respect; **быть** *(impf)* **на хоро́шем/плохо́м счету́ у** *+gen* to be in the good/bad books with; **у неё ка́ждая копе́йка на счету́** she counts every penny; **э́то не в ~** that doesn't count; **по большо́му ~у** having set a high standard; **име́ть** *(impf)* **что-н на счету́** (*победы*) to have sth to one's name; **предъявля́ть (предъяви́ть** *perf*) **~ кому́-н** to invoice sb; **принима́ть (приня́ть** *perf*) **что-н на свой ~** to take sth personally; **он не зна́ет ~а деньга́м** he's rolling in money; **лицево́й ~** (*КОММ*) personal account; **теку́щий ~** (*КОММ*) current (*BRIT*) *или* checking (*US*) account; **~ поступле́ний** (*КОММ*) revenue account; **ссу́дный ~** (*КОММ*) loan account; **~ ассигнова́ний** (*КОММ*) appropriation account; **счета́ креди́торов/дебито́ров** (*КОММ*) account payable/receivable; **открыва́ть (откры́ть** *perf*) **~ в ба́нке** to open a bank account.
счётн|ый *прил*: **~ая коми́ссия** vote counting committee; **счётная маши́на** calculator.
счётчик (-а) *м* (*человек*: *голосов*) counter; (*электричества, в такси*) meter.
счёт|ы (-ов) *мн* (*приспособление*) abacus; (*деловые*) dealings *мн*; **поко́нчить** *(perf)* **все ~ с кем-н** (*расчитаться*) to pay off one's debts to sb; (*прекратить связи*) to break off ties with sb; **сбра́сывать (сбро́сить** *perf*) **кого́-н/что-н со счето́в** to dismiss sb/sth; **своди́ть (свести́** *perf*) **~ с кем-н** to settle a score with sb; **у него́ с ни́ми свой ~** he's got his own scores to settle with them.
счи́|стить (-щу, -стишь; *impf* **счища́ть)** *сов перех* to clean off.
счита́л|ка (-ки; *gen pl* **-ок)** *ж* counting rhyme.
счи́танн|ый *прил*: **~ые дни/мину́ты** only a few days/minutes; **~ое коли́чество** very few.
счита́|ть (-ю) *несов неперех* to count ◆ (*perf* **посчита́ть** *или* **сосчита́ть**) *перех* (*деньги итп*) to count; (*perf* **посчита́ть** *или* **счесть**): **~ что-н/кого́-н** *+instr* to regard sth/sb as; **~ (посчита́ть** *или* **счесть** *perf*) **что-н необходи́мым** to consider sth (to be) necessary; **~я** *+gen* (*принимая в расчёт*) considering; **не ~я** *+gen* excluding; **~я от** *+gen или* **с** *+gen* starting with; **~ (счесть** *perf*) **что-н/кого́-н за** *+acc* to regard sb/sth as; **я ~ю, что ...** I believe *или* think that ...
▸ **счита́ться** *несов возв*: **~ся** *+instr* to be considered to be; (*уважать*): **~ся с** *+instr* (*с родителями, с другом итп*) to be considerate to.
счи́тыва|ть (-ю; *perf* **счита́ть)** *несов перех* to read (*meter etc*).
счища́|ть (-ю) *несов от* **счи́стить**.
счи́щу *сов см* **счи́стить**.
США *мн сокр* (= *Соединённые Шта́ты Аме́рики*) USA (= *United States of America*).
сшиб|и́ть (-у́, -ёшь; *pt* **-, -ла, -ло**, *impf* **сшиба́ть)** *сов перех* (*разг*: *подлеж*: *машина*) to hit
▸ **сшиби́ться** (*impf* **сшиба́ться**) *сов возв* (*разг*) to get into a fight.
сшива́|ть (-ю) *несов от* **сшить**.
сшить (сошью́, сошьёшь; *imper* **сше́й(те))** *сов от* **шить** ◆ (*impf* **сшива́ть**) *перех* (*соединить шитьём*) to sew together.
съеда́|ть (-ю) *несов от* **съесть**.
съе́дем(ся) *сов см* **съе́хать(ся)**.
съеде́ни|е (-я) *ср*: **отдава́ть кого́-н на ~**

кому́-н (*также перен*) to leave sb at the mercy of sb.
съе́дешь(ся) *итп сов см* **съе́хать(ся)**.
съеди́м *итп сов см* **съесть**.
съедо́б|ный (-ен, -на, -но) *прил* edible.
съе́ду(сь) *итп сов см* **съе́хать(ся)**.
съедя́т *сов см* **съесть**.
съёж|иться (-усь, -ишься) *сов от* **ёжиться** ◆ *возв* (*от холода, от страха*) to huddle; (*листья*) to shrivel up.
съезд (-а) *м* (*действие: гостей, делегатов*) gathering; (*к реке, в долину*) descent; (*партийный*) congress.
съе́з|дить (-жу, -дишь) *сов неперех* (*за покупками, к родителям*) to go; ~ *(perf) +dat* (*разг: ударить*) to whack.
съе́здовск|ий (-ая, -ое, -ие) *прил* (*документы, решения*) congress *опред*.
съезжа́|ть(ся) (-ю(сь)) *несов от* **съе́хать(ся)**.
съе́зжу *сов см* **съе́здить**.
съем *сов см* **съесть**.
съём|ка (-ки; *gen pl* **-ок)** *ж* (*копии*) making, taking; (*местности*) survey; (*обычно мн: фильма*) shooting; (*гипса*) removal.
съёмный *прил* detachable.
съёмок *сущ см* **съёмка**.
съёмочн|ый *прил*: **~ая площа́дка** film set; **съёмочная гру́ппа** film crew.
съёмщик (-а) *м* tennant.
съёмщиц|а (-ы) *ж см* **съёмщик**.
съестн|о́й *прил*: **~ые припа́сы** food supplies *мн*.
съе|сть (*как* **есть**; *см* **Table 15**; *impf* **есть** *или* **съеда́ть)** *сов перех* (*хлеб, кашу*) to eat; (*подлеж: моль, ржавчина*) to eat away at; (: *тоска, ревность*) to gnaw at; (*impf* **съеда́ть**; *разг: деньги, зарплату*) to eat up.
съе́хать (*как* **е́хать**; *см* **Table 19**; *impf* **съезжа́ть)** *сов неперех*: **~ (с** *+gen***)** (*спуститься: с горки*) to go down; (*платок*) to slip; (*шапка*) to tilt; **съезжа́ть (~** *perf***) (с кварти́ры)** to move out (of one's flat); ~ *(perf)* **с ле́стницы** (*упасть*) to tumble down the stairs
▸ **съе́хаться** (*impf* **съезжа́ться**) *сов возв* (*гости, делегаты*) to gather.
съехи́днича|ть (-ю) *сов от* **ехи́дничать**.
съешь *сов см* **съесть**.
съязв|и́ть (-лю́, -и́шь) *сов от* **язви́ть**.
сы́ворот|ка (-ки; *gen pl* **-ок)** *ж* (*молочная*) whey; (*МЕД*) serum.
сы́гранный *прил* well-coordinated.
сыгра́|ть (-ю) *сов от* **игра́ть**
▸ **сыгра́ться** (*impf* **сы́грываться**) *сов возв* (*музыканты*) to play well together; (*спортсмены*) to play well as a team.
сы́змала *нареч* from an early age.
сы́знова *нареч* (*разг*) anew.
сымити́р|овать (-ую) *сов от* **имити́ровать**.
сымпровизи́р|овать (-ую) *сов от* **импровизи́ровать**.
сын (-а; *nom pl* **-овья́**, *gen pl* **-ове́й**, *dat pl* **-овья́м)** *м* son; (*nom pl* **-ы́**, *gen pl* **-о́в**; *перен*): ~ *+gen* (*народа*) son of.
сынка́ *итп сущ см* **сыно́к**.
сыновья́ *итп сущ см* **сын**.
сыно́вн|ий (-яя, -ее, -ие) *прил* (*любовь, долг*) son's.
сын|о́к (-ка́) *м уменьш от* **сын**; (*как обращение*) son.
сы́п|ать (-лю, -лешь; *imper* **сы́пь(те))** *несов перех* to pour ◆ *неперех*: ~ *+instr* (*цитатами, остротами*) to pour forth with
▸ **сы́паться** *несов возв* (*мука, песок, яблоки итп*) to pour; (*вопросы, письма итп*) to pour forth; **на него́ посы́пались уда́ры со всех сторо́н** blows rained down on him from all sides.
сыпно́й *прил*: **~ тиф** typhus.
сыпу́ч|ий (-ая, -ее, -ие) *прил* (*вещество*) friable; (*грунт*) shifting.
сып|ь (-и) *ж* rash.
сыр (-а; *part gen* **-у**, *nom pl* **-ы́)** *м* cheese; **как ~ в ма́сле ката́ться** *(impf)* to live the life of Riley.
сыре́|ть (*3sg* **-ет**, *3pl* **-ют**) *несов неперех* to get damp.
сыр|е́ц (-ца́) *м*: **хло́пок-~** rough cotton; **шёлк-~** raw silk.
сырка́ *итп сущ см* **сыро́к**.
сырко́в|ый *прил*: **~ая ма́сса** cream cheese.
сы́рник (-а) *м small thick pancake made with cream cheese*.
сы́ро *как сказ*: **здесь ~** it's damp here.
сырое́жк|а (-и) *ж* russula.
сыр|о́й (-, -а́, -о) *прил* (*бельё, земля, воздух*) damp; (*статья, стихи*) rough; (*no short form; мясо, овощи*) raw, uncooked; **сыра́я вода́** tap water.
сыр|о́к (-ка́) *м*: **творо́жный ~** sweet curd cheese; **пла́вленный ~** processed cheese.
сы́рост|ь (-и) *ж* dampness.
сырца́ *итп сущ см* **сыре́ц**.
сырь|ё (-я́) *ср собир* raw material.
сырьево́й *прил* (*ресурсы, база*) raw material *опред*.
сыск (-а) *м* criminal detection.
сы|ска́ть (-щу́, -щешь) *сов перех* (*разг: отыскать*) to find
▸ **сыска́ться** *сов возв* (*разг: обнаружиться*) to turn up.
сы́т|ный (-ен, -на́, -но) *прил* filling.
сы́т|ый (-, -а́, -о) *прил* (*не голодный*) full, satisfied; (*откормленный*) well-fed; (*no short form; перен: вид, улыбка*) contented; (: *мещанство*) smug; **спаси́бо, я сыт** thank you, I'm full; **я сыт по го́рло** (*перен*) I'm fed up.
сыч (-а́) *м* little owl; (*о человеке*) loner.
сы́щик (-а) *м* detective.
сыщу́(сь) *итп сов см* **сыска́ть(ся)**.
СЭВ (-а) *м сокр* (*ИСТ: = Сове́т Экономи́ческой Взаимопо́мощи*) Comecon, CMEA (= *Council for Mutual Economic Assistance*).

СЭЗ *ж сокр = свобóдная экономúческая зóна.*
сэконóм|ить (-лю, -ишь) *сов от* **экономить.**
СЭС *м сокр = Совéтский Энциклопедúческий Словáрь.*
сюдá *нареч* here; **(и) тудá и ~** both here and there; **то тудá, то ~** sometimes here, sometimes there; **ни тудá ни ~** neither here nor there; **тудá-~** (*туда и обратно*) backwards and forwards; (*в разные стороны*) everywhere; **иди ~!** come here!; **э́то ещё тудá-~** that's bearable.
сюжéт (-а) *м* plot.
сюжéтн|ый *прил*: **~ая лúния** storyline; **сюжéтное развúтие** development of the plot.
сюúт|а (-ы) *ж* (*муз*) suite.
сюрпрúз (-а) *м* surprise.
сюрреалúзм (-а) *м* surrealism.
сюрреалúст (-а) *м* surrealist.
сюртýк (-á) *м* frock-coat.
сюсю́кани|е (-я) *ср* (*см глаг*) lisping; fussing.
сюсю́ка|ть (-ю) *несов неперех* (*в речи*) to lisp; (*потворствовать*): **~ с кем-н** to fuss over sb
▸ **сюсю́каться** *несов возв*: **~ся с кем-н** to fuss over sb.
ся́ду *итп сов см* **сесть.**
сяк *нареч*: **(и) так и ~** *или* **то так, то ~** (*разг*) by hook or by crook; **э́то ещё так-~** (*разг*) it's so-so.
сякóй *прил*: **ах ты такóй-~** (*разг*) you little so-and-so.
сям *нареч*: **(и) там и ~** (*разг*) here and there; **то там, то ~** now here, now there.

~T, т~

Т, т *сущ нескл* (*буква*) *the 19th letter of the Russian alphabet.*
т *сокр* (= **тонна**) t (= *tonne*).
т. *сокр* = **товарищ**; (= **том**) v., vol. (= *volume*); = **тысяча.**
та (**той**) *мест см* **тот**.
табак (**-а**; *part gen* **-у**) *м* tobacco.
табака *нескл*: **цыплёнок** ~ char-grilled chicken.
табакер|ка (**-ки**; *gen pl* **-ок**) *ж* snuffbox.
табаковод (**-а**) *м* tobacco grower.
табаководств|о (**-а**) *ср* tobacco-growing.
табачный *прил* tobacco *опред.*
табел|ь (**-я**) *м* (*ПРОСВЕЩ*) school report (*BRIT*), report card (*US, SCOTTISH*); (*на работе*) *board on which employees mark their time of arrival and departure*; (*график*) chart.
таблет|ка (**-ки**; *gen pl* **-ок**) *ж* tablet.
табли|ца (**-ы**) *ж* table; (*СПОРТ*) (league) table; **таблица умножения** multiplication table.
табличк|а (**-ки**; *gen pl* **-ек**) *ж* (*с названием улицы*) street sign; (*экспоната*) plate; (*на двери*) nameplate.
табло *ср нескл* (*на вокзале, в аэропорту*) (information) board; (*на стадионе*) scoreboard.
табор (**-а**) *м* camp.
табу *ср нескл* taboo; **налагать** (**наложить** *perf*) **на что-н** ~ to make a taboo of sth.
табун (**-а**) *м* herd.
табурет (**-а**) *м* = **табуретка**.
табурет|ка (**-ки**; *gen pl* **-ок**) *ж* stool.
тавтологи|я (**-и**) *ж* tautology.
таджик (**-а**) *м* Tajik.
Таджикистан (**-а**) *м* Tajikistan.
таджикск|ий (**-ая, -ое, -ие**) *прил* Tajiki.
таджич|ка (**-ки**; *gen pl* **-ек**) *ж см* **таджик**.
таёжный *прил* taiga *опред.*
таз (**-а**; *loc sg* **-у**, *nom pl* **-ы**) *м* (*сосуд*) basin; (*АНАТ*) pelvis.
тазобедренный *прил*: ~ **сустав** hip joint.
тазовый *прил* (*АНАТ*) pelvic.
Таиланд (**-а**) *м* Thailand.
таиланд|ец (**-ца**) *м* Thai.
таиланд|ка (**-ки**; *gen pl* **-ок**) *ж см* **таиландец**.
таиландца *итп сущ см* **таиландец**.
таинствен|ный (**-, -на, -но**) *прил* mysterious; (*цель, намерение*) secret.
таинств|о (**-а**) *ср* (*РЕЛ*) sacrament.
Таити *м нескл* Tahiti.
та|ить (**-ю, -ишь**) *несов перех* to conceal; (*перен*): ~ **в себе** (*возможности, угрозу итп*) to conceal; ~ (*impf*) **злобу на кого-н** to harbour (*BRIT*) *или* harbor (*US*) malice towards sb; **что греха** ~ (*разг*) there's no point in pretending otherwise
▸ **таиться** *несов возв* (*скрывать что-н*) to cover up; (*опасность, неожиданность*) to lurk; **в нём ~ится надежда/злоба** he harbo(u)rs a secret hope/feeling of malice.
таитянск|ий (**-ая, -ое, -ие**) *прил* Tahitian.
Тайван|ь (**-я**) *м* Taiwan.
тайг|а (**-и**) *ж* the taiga.
тайком *нареч* in secret, secretly.
тайм (**-а**) *м* (*СПОРТ*) period; **первый/второй** ~ (*ФУТБОЛ*) the first/second half.
тайм-аут (**-а**) *м* (*СПОРТ*) time-out.
тайн|а (**-ы**) *ж* (*секрет*) secret; (*загадка*) mystery; **держать** (*impf*) **что-н в ~е** to keep sth secret; **хранить** (*impf*) **~у** to keep a secret.
тайник (**-а**) *м* hiding place.
тайный *прил* secret.
тайфун (**-а**) *м* typhoon.

KEYWORD

так *нареч* **1** (*указательное*: *таким образом*) like this, this way; **делайте так** do it like this *или* this way; **пусть будет так** so be it; **так не пойдёт** that won't do; **она всё делает не так** she does everything wrong
2 (*настолько*) so; **я так испугался, что начал кричать** I was so frightened I started to shout; **всё случилось так неожиданно!** it all happened so unexpectedly!
3 (*без последствий*) just like that; **так это не пройдёт** you won't get away with it
4 (*разг*: *без какого-н намерения*) for no (special) reason; **я сказал это просто так** I said it for no (special) reason; **почему ты плачешь? – да так** why are you crying? – for no reason
◆ *част* **1** (*разг*: *ничего*) nothing; **что с тобой? – так** what's wrong? – nothing
2 (*разг*: *усилительная*): **а она так жаловалась!** she didn't half complain!; **так я тебе и поверил!** I'm not falling for that!
3 (*разг*: *приблизительно*) about; **дня так через два** in about two days
4 (*например*) for example; **поведение у него плохое; так, вчера сломал окно** his behaviour is bad, for example, yesterday he broke a window

5 *(да)* OK; **так, всё хорошо́/пра́вильно** OK, that's fine/correct
◆ *союз* **1** *(в таком случае)* then; **пло́хо себя́ чу́вствуешь, так иди́ спать** if you feel ill, (then) go and have a sleep; **е́хать, так е́хать** if we are going, (then) let's go
2 *(таким образом)* so; **так ты пое́дешь?** so, you are going?
3 *(но)* but; **я пыта́лся его́ убеди́ть, так он не слу́шает** I tried to convince him but he wouldn't listen
4 *(в разделительных вопросах)*: **э́то поле́зная кни́га, не так ли?** it's a useful book, isn't it?; **он хоро́ший челове́к, не так ли?** he's a good person, isn't he?; **у них есть соба́ка, не так ли?** they have a dog, don't they?
5 *(во фразах)*: **и так** *(и без того уже)* anyway; **е́сли** *или* **раз так** in that case; **так и быть!** so be it!; **так и есть** *(разг)* sure enough; **так ему́!** serves him right!; **та́к себе** *(разг)* so-so; **так как** since; **так что** so; **так что́бы** so that.

такела́ж (-а) *м* rigging.
та́кже *союз, нареч* also; **я ~ подде́рживаю Ва́ше предложе́ние** I also *или* too am in favour (*BRIT*) *или* favor (*US*) of your suggestion; **мне нра́вится ~ и Ва́ше предложе́ние** I like your suggestion too *или* as well; **с Но́вым Го́дом! – и Вас ~** Happy New Year! – the same to you; **а ~** and also.
-таки *част (разг: всё же) emphatic particle*; **ты~ отказа́лся** so you decided to refuse then; **он~ пришёл** so he did come then; **она́ пря́мо~ исхо́дит от гне́ва** she is really furious; **опя́ть~** but having said that; **та́к~** *(разг)* so that's the way it is.
тако́в (-á, -ó, -ы́) *как сказ* such; **~ тебе́ мой сове́т** that is my advice to you; **ситуа́ция такова́, что** ... the situation is such that ...; **и был ~** *(разг)* and we never saw him again.
таково́й *мест*: **как ~** as such.
так|о́е (-о́го) *ср (о чём-н интересном, важном итп)* something; **я ~ слы́шала!** I've heard something; **~ происхо́дит!** something is going on!; **что тут ~о́го?** what is so special about that?
так|о́й *мест* such; **~ие лю́ди встреча́ются ре́дко** you rarely meet such people; **до ~ сте́пени** to such an extent; **~а́я жара́!** such heat!; **кто ~?** who is it?; **он сего́дня како́й-то не ~** he is not quite himself today; **что ~о́е?** what is it?; **~-то** *(о лице)* so-and-so; *(о предмете)* such-and-such.
тако́й-сяко́й *мест (разг)*: **ах ты ~** you little so-and-so.
та́кс|а (-ы) *ж (ЗООЛ)* dachshund; *(КОММ)* (fixed) rate; **пла́та по ~е** fixed-rate payment.
такса́ци|я (-и) *ж* rating.
такси́ *ср нескл* taxi.
такси́р|овать (-ую) *(не)сов перех (услуги итп)* to set a rate for.
такси́ст (-а) *м* taxi driver.
таксомото́р (-а) *м* taxicab.
таксопа́рк (-а) *м сокр (= таксомото́рный парк)* taxi depot.
таксофо́н (-а) *м* payphone.
такт (-а) *м (тактичность)* tact; *(МУЗ)* bar (*BRIT*), measure (*US*); *(ритм)* beat; **в ~ му́зыке** in time with the music.
та́ктик (-а) *м* tactician.
та́ктик|а (-и) *ж* tactic; *(ВОЕН)* tactics *мн*.
такти́чен *прил см* **такти́чный**.
такти́ческ|ий (-ая, -ое, -ие) *прил* tactical.
такти́ч|ный (-ен, -на, -но) *прил* tactful.
тала́нт (-а) *м* talent.
тала́нтлив|ый (-, -а, -о) *прил* talented.
талисма́н (-а) *м* charm, talisman.
та́ли|я (-и) *ж* waist; **пла́тье в ~ю** dress fitted at the waist.
Та́ллин (-а) *м* Tallin(n).
талму́д (-а) *м* the Talmud.
тало́н (-а) *м* ticket; *(на бензин, на продукты итп)* coupon.
та́лый *прил (снег, лёд)* melted.
тальк (-а) *м* talcum powder, talc.
там *нареч* there; **бу́ду ~ ско́ро** I'll be there soon; **~ посмо́трим** *(разг)* we'll see; **каки́е ~ сомне́ния** *(разг)* what's there to be unsure about?; **како́е ~!** *(разг)* not a chance!; **я ду́мал, что он догада́ется – куда́ уж ~!** *(разг)* I thought he'd guess, but not a bit of it!; **что ~ ни говори́, а мы оши́блись** whatever you say, we still made a mistake; **и ~ и сям** *(разг)* here, there and everywhere.
тамад|а́ (-ы́) *ж (мужчина)* toastmaster; *(женщина)* toastmistress.
та́мбур (-а) *м section at door of train carriage.*
тамбури́н (-а) *м (барабан)* tambourin (*small drum*); *(бубен)* tambourine.
тамо́жен *сущ см* **тамо́жня**.
тамо́женник (-а) *м* customs officer.
тамо́женный *прил (досмотр)* customs *опред*; **тамо́женная по́шлина** customs (duty).
тамо́ж|ня (-ни; *gen pl* -ен) *ж* customs.
та́мпекс (-а) *м* Tampax ®.
тампо́н (-а) *м* tampon.
та́нгенс (-а) *м (МАТ)* tangent.
та́нго *ср нескл* tango.
та́н|ец (-ца) *м* dance; *см также* **та́нцы**.
танзани́йск|ий (-ая, -ое, -ие) *прил* Tanzanian.
Танзани́|я (-и) *ж* Tanzania.
тани́н (-а) *м* tannin.
танк (-а) *м (ВОЕН, ТЕХ)* tank.
та́нкер (-а) *м* tanker (*ship*).
танке́т|ка (-ки; *gen pl* -ок) *ж (обычно мн: обувь)* wedge heel.
танки́ст (-а) *м* tank crew member.

та́нца *итп сущ см* **та́нец**.
танцева́льный *прил* dance *опред*; ~ **зал** dance hall.
танц|ева́ть (-у́ю) *несов (не)перех* to dance.
танцо́вщик (-а) *м* dancer.
танцо́вщиц|а (-ы) *ж см* **танцо́вщик**.
танцплоща́д|ка (-ки; *gen pl* -ок) *ж сокр* (= *танцева́льная площа́дка*) dance floor.
танцо́р (-а) *м* dancer.
та́нц|ы (-ев) *мн* (*вечер*) dance *ед*; **идти́ (пойти́** *perf*) **на** ~ to go dancing.
та́поч|ка (-ки; *gen pl* -ек) *ж* (*обычно мн*: *домашняя*) slipper; (: *спортивная*) plimsoll (*BRIT*), sneaker (*US*).
та́р|а (-ы) *ж собир* containers *мн*.
тараба́н|ить (-ю, -ишь) *несов неперех* (*разг*) to rap.
тараба́рщин|а (-ы) *ж* (*разг*) gobbledegook.
тарака́н (-а) *м* cockroach.
тара́н (-а) *м* (*ВОЕН*) ram.
тара́н|ить (-ю, -ишь; *perf* **протара́нить**) *несов перех* to ram.
таранта́с (-а) *м* tarantass (*large springless carriage*).
тара́нтул (-а) *м* tarantula.
тарара́м (-а) *м* (*разг*) hullaballoo.
тарато́р|ить (-ю, -ишь) *несов неперех* (*разг*) to gabble on.
тарах|те́ть (-чу́, -ти́шь) *несов неперех* (*колёса, мотор*) to rattle; (*человек*) to rattle on.
тара́щ|ить (-у, -ишь; *perf* **вы́таращить**) *несов перех*: ~ **глаза́ (на** *+acc*) to stare (at)
▸ **тара́щиться** (*perf* **вы́таращиться**) *несов возв* (*разг*): ~**ся (на** *+acc*) to gawp *или* gawk (at).
таре́л|ка (-ки; *gen pl* -ок) *ж* plate; **глубо́кая** ~ soup plate; **лета́ющая** ~ flying saucer; **я здесь не в свое́й** ~**ке** (*разг*) I feel out of place here; *см также* **таре́лки**.
таре́л|ки (-ок) *мн* (*МУЗ*) cymbals *мн*.
тари́ф (-а) *м* tariff.
тарифика́ци|я (-и) *ж* tariffing.
тарифици́р|овать (-ую) *(не)сов перех* (*перевозки, услуги*) to tariff; ~ *(impf/perf)* **окла́ды/нало́ги** to set the salary/tax scale.
тари́фн|ый *прил*: ~**ая табли́ца/се́тка** list/scale of charges.
таска́|ть (-ю) *несов перех* to lug; (*разг*: *воровать*) to pinch; (: *одевать*) to wear; ~ *(impf)* **с собо́й** to carry around; ~ *(impf)* **кого́-н за́ волосы** to pull sb's hair
▸ **таска́ться** *несов возв* (*по магазинам итп*) to traipse around; ~**ся** *(impf)* **за кем-н** to trail around after sb.
Тасма́ни|я (-и) *ж* Tasmania.
тас|ова́ть (-у́ю; *perf* **стасова́ть**) *несов перех* to shuffle.
ТАСС *м сокр* (= *Телегра́фное аге́нтство Сове́тского Сою́за*) Tass (*main news agency of the Soviet Union*).
тата́рин (-а; *nom pl* **тата́ры**) *м* Tatar.
тата́р|ка (-ки; *gen pl* -ок) *ж см* **тата́рин**.
тата́ры *итп сущ см* **тата́рин**.
татуиро́в|ка (-ки; *gen pl* -ок) *ж* tattoo.
тахт|а́ (-ы́) *ж* divan (*BRIT*), ottoman (*US*).
та́ч|ка (-ки; *gen pl* -ек) *ж* wheelbarrow.
Ташке́нт (-а) *м* Tashkent.
тащ|и́ть (-у́, -ишь) *несов перех* (*тянуть*) to pull; (*волочить, также перен*) to drag; (*нести*) to haul; (*perf* **вы́тащить**; *перен*: *в театр, на прогулку*) to drag out; (*perf* **стащи́ть**; *разг*: *красть*) to nick; **он та́щит всю рабо́ту на себе́** he is lumbered with (*BRIT*) *или* has got landed with all the work
▸ **тащи́ться** *несов возв* (*медленно ехать*) to trundle along; (*идти неохотно*) to drag o.s. along; (*волочиться*: *подол*) to drag; **не хо́чется** ~**ся в таку́ю даль** I don't feel like traipsing all that way.
та́|ять (-ю; *perf* **раста́ять**) *несов неперех* to melt; (*перен*: *силы, деньги*) to dwindle; (: *от любви, от похвал*) to melt; (: *от болезни*) to waste away; ~ *(impf)* **во рту** (*перен*) to melt in the mouth.
Тбили́си *м нескл* Tbilisi.
ТВ *м сокр* (= **телеви́дение**) TV (= *television*).
твар|ь (-и) *ж* creature; (*разг*: *пренебр*) swine.
тверде́|ть (*3sg* -ет, *3pl* -ют, *perf* **затверде́ть**) *несов неперех* (*также перен*) to harden.
твер|ди́ть (-жу́, -ди́шь; *perf* **затверди́ть**) *несов перех* (*стихотворение, урок итп*) to learn by rote; ~ *(impf)* **о** *+prp* (*говорить*) to go on about.
твёрдо *нареч* (*верить, сказать*) firmly; (*заучить, запомнить*) properly; **я** ~ **зна́ю, что** ... I know for sure that ....
твердоло́б|ый (-, -а, -о) *прил* hard-headed.
твёрдост|ь (-и) *ж* firmness; (*цен*) stability; (*воли, характера*) toughness.
твёрд|ый *прил* (*физ*) solid; (-, -а́, -о; *земля, предмет*) hard; (*решение, сторонник, тон итп*) firm; (*цены, ставки*) stable; (*порядок*) set; (*знания*) solid; (*воля, характер*) tough; (*ЛИНГ*: *звук*) hard, nonpalatalized; **здесь нужна́** ~**ая рука́** a firm hand is needed; **твёрдый знак** (*ЛИНГ*) hard sign.
тверды́н|я (-и) *ж* (*перен*) stronghold.
твёрже *сравн прил от* **твёрдый** ◆ *сравн нареч от* **твёрдо**.
твержу́ *несов см* **тверди́ть**.
твид (-а) *м* tweed.
твист (-а) *м* the twist.
тво|й (-его́; *f* -я́, *nt* -ё, *pl* -и́; *как* **мой**; *см* **Table 8**) *притяж мест* your; **вот** ~ **чай** here is your tea; **мой оте́ц врач – а** ~? my father is a doctor – what does yours do?; **э́то всё** ~**ё** this is all yours; **приве́т (всем) ~и́м** say hello to your folks; **по-~ему́ мне́нию** in your opinion; **как по-тво́ему?** what is your opinion?; **дава́й сде́лаем по-тво́ему** let's do it your way.
творе́ни|е (-я) *ср* creation.
твор|е́ц (-ца́) *м* creator; **Т**~ (*РЕЛ*) the Creator.
твори́тельный *прил*: ~ **паде́ж** (*ЛИНГ*) the instrumental (case).

твор|и́ть (-ю́, -и́шь) *несов неперех* to create ◆ (*perf* **сотвори́ть**) *перех* (*шедевр, симфонию итп*) to create; (*perf* **натвори́ть**; *разг*) to get up to; ~ **(сотвори́ть** *perf*) **чудеса́** to work miracles; ~ **(сотвори́ть** *perf*) **добро́** to do good; ~ (*impf*) **беззако́ния** to commit unjust acts
▸ **твори́ться** *несов возв*: **что тут ~и́тся?** what's going on here?; **с ним ~и́тся что́-то стра́нное** something strange has come over him.
творо́г (-а́; *part gen* **-у́)** *м* ≈ curd cheese.
творо́жник (-а) *м* curd pancake.
творо́жный *прил* curd-cheese.
творца́ *итп сущ см* **творе́ц.**
тво́рческ|ий (-ая, -ое, -ие) *прил* creative; **тво́рческий о́тпуск** sabbatical.
тво́рчеств|о (-а) *ср* creative work; (*писателя, композитора*) work; **худо́жественное ~** artistic creativity; **наро́дное ~** folk art.
тво|я́ (-е́й) *притяж мест см* **твой.**
ТВЧ *сокр* (= *то́ки высо́кой частоты́*) high frequency currents *мн.*
т.д. *сокр* (= **так да́лее**) etc. (= *et cetera*).
те (тех) *мест см* **тот.**
т.е. *сокр* (= **то есть**) i.e. (= *id est*).
теа́тр (-а) *м* theatre (*BRIT*), theater (*US*); ~ **Го́голя/Шекспи́ра** Gogol's/Shakespeare's theatrical works; ~ **вое́нных де́йствий** the theatre of operations.
театра́л (-а) *м* theatregoer (*BRIT*), theatergoer (*US*).
театрализ|ова́ть (-у́ю) *(не)сов перех* to dramatize.
театра́л|ка (-ки; *gen pl* **-ок)** *ж см* **театра́л.**
театра́льный *прил* (*афиша, сезон*) theatre *опред* (*BRIT*), theater *опред* (*US*); (*деятельность, жест*) theatrical; **театра́льная ка́сса** theatre box office; **театра́льная сту́дия** theatre studio; **театра́льный зал** theatre; **театра́льный институ́т** drama school.
театрове́д (-а) *м* theatre (*BRIT*) *или* theater (*US*) specialist.
тебе́ *мест см* **ты** ◆ *как част* (*разг*): **здесь ~ и по́мощь и понима́ние** you can get help and understanding here; **я ~ поспо́рю!** don't you dare to argue!; **я ~ дам** *или* **покажу́!** I'll show you!
тебя́ *мест см* **ты.**
Тегера́н (-а) *м* Teheran.
теза́урус (-а) *м* thesaurus.
те́зис (-а) *м* (*идея*) thesis (*мн* theses); (: *в логике*) proposition; (*обычно мн*: *доклада*) abstract.
тёз|ка (-ки; *gen pl* **-ок)** *м/ж* namesake.
тёк *итп несов см* **течь.**
текст (-а) *м* text; (*песни*) words *мн*, lyrics *мн.*
тексти́л|ь (-я) *м собир* textiles *мн.*
тексти́льн|ый *прил*: **~ые изде́лия** textiles; **~ая промы́шленность** textile industry.
теку́т *итп несов см* **течь.**

теку́чест|ь (-и) *ж* fluidity; ~ **ка́дров** high staff turnover.
теку́ч|ий (-ая, -ее, -ие; -, -а, -е) *прил* fluid; **~ие ка́дры** fluctuating workforce.
теку́чк|а (-и) *ж* (*разг*) daily routine.
теку́щ|ий (-ая, -ее, -ие) *прил* (*год*) current; (*повседневный*: *дела*) routine; **~ие обяза́тельства** (*КОММ*) current liabilities *мн*; **теку́щие собы́тия** current affairs; **теку́щий ремо́нт** running repairs, maintenance; **теку́щий счёт** (*КОММ*) current (*BRIT*) *или* checking (*US*) account.
тел. *сокр* (= **телефо́н**) tel. (= *telephone*).
телевеща́ни|е (-я) *ср* television broadcasting.
телеви́дени|е (-я) *ср* television; **по ~ю** on television.
телевизио́нный *прил* television *опред.*
телевизио́нщик (-а) *м* broadcaster.
телеви́зор (-а) *м* television (set); **смотре́ть** (*impf*) ~ to watch television; **по ~у** on television.
теле́г|а (-и) *ж* cart.
телегра́мм|а (-ы) *ж* telegram.
телегра́ф (-а) *м* (*способ связи*) telegraph; (*учреждение*) telegraph office.
телеграфи́р|овать (-ую) *(не)сов перех* to wire.
телеграфи́ст (-а) *м* telegraphist.
телеграфи́ст|ка (-ки; *gen pl* **-ок)** *ж см* **телеграфи́ст.**
телегра́фный *прил* (*также перен*) telegraphic; **телегра́фное аге́нтство** news agency; **телегра́фный де́нежный перево́д** telegraphic transfer; **телегра́фный столб** telegraph pole.
теле́ж|ка (-ки; *gen pl* **-ек)** *ж уменьш от* **теле́га;** (*для багажа, в супермаркете*) trolley.
телезри́тел|ь (-я) *м* viewer.
телека́мер|а (-ы) *ж* television camera.
те́лекс (-а) *м* telex.
тел|ёнок (-ёнка; *nom pl* **-я́та**, *gen pl* **-я́т)** *м* calf (*мн* calves).
телепа́ти|я (-и) *ж* telepathy.
телепереда́ч|а (-и) *ж* TV programme (*BRIT*) *или* program (*US*).
теле́сен *прил см* **теле́сный.**
телеско́п (-а) *м* telescope.
телескопи́ческ|ий (-ая, -ое, -ие) *прил* (*антенна, очки*) telescopic; (*наблюдения*) long-distance.
теле́с|ный (-ен, -на, -но) *прил* bodily; **~ого цве́та** flesh-coloured; **теле́сное наказа́ние** corporal punishment.
телеста́нци|я (-и) *ж* television station.
телесту́ди|я (-и) *ж* television studio.
телета́йп (-а) *м* teleprinter (*BRIT*), teletypewriter (*US*), Teletype ®.
телефо́н (-а) *м* telephone; (*разг*: *номер*) (phone) number.
телефони́ст (-а) *м* telephonist.
телефони́ст|ка (-ки; *gen pl* **-ок)** *ж см*

телефонист.
телефóнный *прил* telephone *опред*; **телефóнная стáнция** telephone exchange; **телефóнная кни́га** telephone book *или* directory.
телéц *сущ см* **тéльце.**
Тел|éц (-ьцá) *м* (*созвездие*) Taurus.
телецéнтр (-а) *м* television centre (*BRIT*) *или* center (*US*).
тел|и́ться (*3sg* **-ится**, *3pl* **-ятся**, *perf* **отели́ться**) *несов возв* to calve.
тёл|ка (-ки; *gen pl* **-ок)** *ж* heifer.
тéл|о (-а; *nom pl* **-á)** *ср* body; **небéсные телá** heavenly bodies; **дрожáть** *(impf)* **всем ~м** to tremble all over; **держáть** *(impf)* **когó-н в чёрном ~е** to treat sb badly.
телогрé|йка (-йки; *gen pl* **-ек)** *ж* body warmer.
телодвижéни|е (-я) *ср* movement.
тёлок *сущ см* **тёлка.**
телосложéни|е (-я) *ср* physique.
телохрани́тел|ь (-я) *м* bodyguard.
Тель-Ави́в (-а) *м* Tel Aviv.
тельня́ш|ка (-ки; *gen pl* **-ек)** *ж* sailor top.
Тельцá *итп сущ см* **Телéц.**
тéль|це (-ьца; *nom pl* **-ьцá**, *gen pl* **-éц)** *ср уменьш от* **тéло**; (*ребёнка*) body; (*обычно мн*: *кровяные*) corpuscle.
теля́та *итп сущ см* **телёнок.**
теля́тин|а (-ы) *ж* veal.
теля́тник (-а) *м* (*помещение*) calf shed.
теля́ч|ий (-ья, -ье, -ьи) *прил*: **~ья кóжа** calfskin *опред*; (*КУЛИН*) veal *опред*; **~ьи нéжности** (*разг*) lovey-dovey behaviour; **~ востóрг** (*разг*) wide-eyed enthusiasm.
тем *мест см* **тот, то** ◆ *союз* (*+comparative*): **чем бóльше, ~ лýчше** the more the better; **~ бóлее!** all the more so!; **~ бóлее что ...** especially as ...; **э́то трýдно, ~ бóлее для меня́** it's difficult, especially for me; **~ лýчше/хýже** that's even better/worse; **~ лýчше для меня́** all the better for me; **не хóчет слýшать? ~ хýже для негó** if he doesn't want to listen then it's his loss; **~ не мéнее** nevertheless; **~ сáмым** thus.
тéм|а (-ы) *ж* subject, topic; (*МУЗ, ЛИТЕРАТУРА*) theme.
темáтик|а (-и) *ж* theme.
темати́чес|кий (-ая, -ое, -ие) *прил* (*выставка, показ фильмов итп*) theme-based.
тембр (-а) *м* timbre.
тёмен *прил см* **тёмный.**
тéмени *итп сущ см* **тéмя.**
Тéмз|а (-ы) *ж* the Thames.
тéми *мест см* **тот, то.**
темнé|ть (*3sg* **-ет**, *3pl* **-ют**, *perf* **потемнéть**) *несов неперех* (*небо, краска*) to darken ◆ (*perf* **стемнéть**) *безл* to get dark; (*no perf*; *видняться*) to loom dark; **зимóй рáно ~ет** it gets dark early in winter.
темн|и́ть (-ю́, -и́шь) *несов неперех* (*разг*) to confuse the issue.
темни́ц|а (-ы) *ж* dungeon.
темнó *как сказ*: **на ýлице/в кóмнате ~** it's dark outside/inside; **на душé у неё былó ~** she felt gloomy.
темнот|á (-ы́) *ж* darkness; (*перен*: *невежество*) ignorance.
тём|ный (-ен, -нá, -нó) *прил* dark; (*смысл, теория*) obscure; (*прошлое, дела*) shady; (*невежественный*: *человек*) ignorant; **~ное пятнó** (*перен*) blemish; **~ные временá** dark times.
темп (-а) *м* speed; (*МУЗ*) tempo; **в тéмпе** (*разг*) quickly; **ускоря́ть (ускóрить** *perf*) **~** *+gen* to speed up.
тéмпер|а (-ы) *ж* tempera.
темперáмент (-а) *м* temperament, disposition; **он человéк с ~ом** he is a temperamental character.
темперáмент|ный (-ен, -на, -но) *прил* (*речь, исполнение, человек*) spirited.
температýр|а (-ы) *ж* temperature; **у меня́ ~** I've got a temperature; **ходи́ть** *(impf)* **с ~ой** (*разг*) to go about with a temperature.
температýр|ить (-ю, -ишь) *несов неперех* (*разг*) to be running a temperature.
тéм|я (-ени; *как* **врéмя**; *см* **Table 4**) *ср* crown (*of the head*).
тéнг|е (-а) *м* tenga (*currency unit of Kazakhstan*).
тенденциóзност|ь (-и) *ж* bias.
тенденциóзный *прил* bias(s)ed.
тендéнци|я (-и) *ж*: **~ (к** *+dat*) tendency (towards); (*предвзятость*) bias.
теневóй *прил* shady; (*перен*: *стороны жизни*) shadowy; **теневáя экинóмика** shadow economy; **теневóй кабинéт** (*ПОЛИТ*) shadow cabinet.
тенелюби́в|ый (-, -а, -о) *прил* (*БОТ*) shade-loving.
тéн|и (-éй) *мн* (*также*: **~ для век**) eye shadow *ед*.
тени́ст|ый (-, -а, -о) *прил* shady.
тéннис (-а) *м* tennis.
теннисúст (-а) *м* tennis player.
теннисúст|ка (-ки; *gen pl* **-ок)** *ж см* **теннисúст.**
тéннис|ка (-ки; *gen pl* **-ок)** *ж* polo shirt.
тéннисн|ый *прил*: **~ая ракéтка** tennis racket; **тéннисный корт/мяч** tennis court/ball.
тéннисок *сущ см* **тéнниска.**
тéнор (-а; *nom pl* **-á)** *м* (*МУЗ*) tenor.
тент (-а) *м* awning.
тен|ь (-и; *prp sg* **-и́**, *gen pl* **-éй)** *ж* (*тенистое место*) shade; (*предмета, человека*) shadow; (*+gen*; *перен*: *волнения, печали итп*) flicker of; **отбрáсывать (отбрóсить** *perf*) **~** to cast a shadow; **держáться** *(impf)* **в ~и́** (*перен*) to remain in the background; **бросáть (брóсить** *perf*) **~ на** *+acc* (*перен*) to cast a slur on; **без тéни сомнéния** without a shadow of a doubt; **нет ни тéни сомнéния, что ...** there is not the slightest doubt that ...; *см также* **тéни.**
теологи́чес|кий (-ая, -ое, -ие) *прил* theological.
теолóги|я (-и) *ж* theology.

теоре́м|а (**-ы**) *ж* theorem.
теоре́тик (**-а**) *м* theoretician.
теорети́ческ|ий (**-ая, -ое, -ие**) *прил* theoretical.
тео́ри|я (**-и**) *ж* theory.
тепе́решн|ий (**-яя, -ее, -ие**) *прил* (*разг*) present.
тепе́рь *нареч* (*сейчас*) now; (*в наше время*) nowadays ◆ *союз*: ~ **обсу́дим сле́дующий вопро́с** let us now move on to the next question.
тепле́|ть (*3sg* **-ет**, *3pl* **-ют**, *perf* **потепле́ть**) *несов неперех* to get warmer; (*отношения*) to become warmer.
те́пл|иться (*3sg* **-ится**, *3pl* **-ятся**) *несов возв* to flicker; **в нём ещё ~ится наде́жда** he still holds out a faint hope.
тепли́ц|а (**-ы**) *ж* hothouse.
тепли́чный *прил* (*растение*) hothouse *опред*; (*перен*: *условия*) sheltered.
тепл|о́ *нареч* warmly ◆ (**-а́**) *ср* (*также перен*) warmth ◆ *как сказ* it's warm; **на у́лице/в ко́мнате ~** it's warm outside/inside; **нас ~ встре́тили** we were given a warm welcome; **10 гра́дусов ~а́** 10 degrees (centigrade); **мне ~** I'm warm.
теплово́з (**-а**) *м* locomotive.
теплово́й *прил* (*лучи, энергия*) thermal; **теплово́й дви́гатель** heat engine; **теплово́й уда́р** (*МЕД*) heatstroke.
теплолюби́в|ый (**-, -а, -о**) *прил* (*БОТ*) heat-loving.
теплообме́н (**-а**) *м* (*ФИЗ*) heat exchange.
теплот|а́ (**-ы́**) *ж* heat; (*перен*: *чувств, отношений, красок*) warmth.
теплохо́д (**-а**) *м* motor ship *или* vessel.
теплоцентра́л|ь (**-и**) *ж* generator plant (*supplying central heating systems*).
тёп|лый (**-ел, -ла́, -ло́**) *прил* warm; **~лое месте́чко** (*разг*) cushy job; **сказа́ть** (*perf*) **кому́-н па́ру ~лых слов** (*разг*) to give sb a piece of one's mind.
тера́кт (**-а**) *м* (*= террористи́ческий акт*) act of terrorism.
терапе́вт (**-а**) *м* ≈ general practitioner.
терапи́|я (**-и**) *ж* (*МЕД*: *наука*) internal medicine; (*лечение*) therapy; **интенси́вная ~** intensive care.
тереб|и́ть (**-лю́, -и́шь**) *несов перех* (*волосы, бороду*) to twiddle; (*разг*: *надоедать*) to pester.
тере́ть (**тру, трёшь**; *pt* **тёр, тёрла, тёрло**) *несов перех* to rub; (*чистить*) to scrub; (*овощи*) to grate ◆ *неперех* (*обувь, воротник*) to rub
▸ **тере́ться** *несов возв* (*человек*): **~ся о** *+acc* to rub o.s. up against; (*перен*: *разг*): **~ся о́коло** *или* **во́зле** *+gen* to hang around.
терза́ни|е (**-я**) *ср* (*обычно мн*: *душевные*) torment.
терза́|ть (**-ю**; *perf* **растерза́ть**) *несов перех* (*добычу*) to savage; (*perf* **истерза́ть**; *перен*: *упрёками, ревностью*) to torment
▸ **терза́ться** *несов возв* (*+instr*; *сомнениями, раскаянием*) to be racked by.
тёр|ка (**-ки**; *gen pl* **-ок**) *ж* grater.
те́рмин (**-а**) *м* term.
термина́л (**-а**) *м* terminal.
терминологи́ческ|ий (**-ая, -ое, -ие**) *прил*: **~ слова́рь** specialized dictionary.
терминоло́ги|я (**-и**) *ж* terminology.
терми́ческ|ий (**-ая, -ое, -ие**) *прил* thermal.
термо́метр (**-а**) *м* thermometer.
те́рмос (**-а**) *м* Thermos®.
термоста́т (**-а**) *м* thermostat.
термосто́йк|ий (**-ая, -ое, -ие**) *прил* heat-resistant.
термоя́дерный *прил* thermonuclear; **термоя́дерное ору́жие** thermonuclear weapon.
терни́ст|ый (**-, -а, -о**) *прил*: **~ путь** (*перен*) difficult path.
терно́вник (**-а**) *м* blackthorn.
тёрок *сущ см* **тёрка**.
терпели́в|ый (**-, -а, -о**) *прил* patient.
терпе́ни|е (**-я**) *ср* patience; **выводи́ть** (**вы́вести** *perf*) **кого́-н из ~я** to exhaust sb's patience; **~ у меня́ ло́пнуло** I lost my patience; **запаса́ться** (**запасти́сь** *perf*) **~м** to call on one's reserve of patience.
терп|е́ть (**-лю́, -ишь**) *несов перех* (*боль, холод итп*) to suffer, endure; (*perf* **потерпе́ть**; *неудачу*) to suffer; (*мириться*: *грубость, наглеца итп*) to tolerate; **~** (**потерпе́ть** *perf*) **неуда́чу/пораже́ние** to suffer failure/a defeat; **~** (**потерпе́ть** *perf*) **круше́ние** (*корабль*) to be wrecked; (*поезд*) to crash; **вре́мя не те́рпит** time waits for no man; **де́ло не те́рпит отлага́тельств** this matter won't wait; **~ не могу́ таки́х люде́й** (*разг*) I can't stand people like that; **~ не могу́ спо́рить** I hate arguing
▸ **терпе́ться** *несов безл*: (**мне**) **не те́рпится** *+infin* I can't wait to do.
терпи́мост|ь (**-и**) *ж*: **~** (**к** *+dat*) tolerance (of).
терпи́м|ый (**-, -а, -о**) *прил* tolerable; (*человек, отношение*): **~** (**к** *+dat*) tolerant (towards).
те́рп|кий (**-кая, -кое, -кие**; **-ок, -ка, -ко**) *прил* tart.
терплю́(сь) *несов см* **терпе́ть(ся)**.
те́рпок *прил см* **те́рпкий**.
террако́т|а (**-ы**) *ж* terracotta.
террако́товый *прил* terracotta.
терра́с|а (**-ы**) *ж* (*также ГЕО*) terrace.
территориа́льный *прил* territorial.
террито́ри|я (**-и**) *ж* (*страны*) territory; (*школы, усадьбы*) grounds *мн*; **о́бщая ~ заво́да – 100 кв миль** the plant occupies an area of 100 sq miles.
терро́р (**-а**) *м* terror.
терроризи́р|овать (**-ую**) (*не*)*сов перех* to terrorize.
террори́зм (**-а**) *м* terrorism.
террори́ст (**-а**) *м* terrorist.
террористи́ческ|ий (**-ая, -ое, -ие**) *прил*

terrorist *опред*.
террори́ст|ка (**-ки**; *gen pl* **-ок**) *ж см* **террори́ст**.
тёртый *прил* (*сыр, овощи*) grated; **челове́к он** ~ (*разг*) he's been around.
терье́р (**-а**) *м* terrier.
теря́|ть (**-ю**; *perf* **потеря́ть**) *несов перех* to lose; ~ **(потеря́ть** *perf*) **го́лову** to lose one's head; ~ **(потеря́ть** *perf*) **из ви́ду** (*перестать видеть*) to lose sight of; (*не иметь сведений о*) to lose touch with; ~ **(потеря́ть** *perf*) **по́чву под нога́ми** (*перен*) to lose one's way
▸ **теря́ться** (*perf* **потеря́ться**) *несов возв* to get lost; (*робеть*) to lose one's nerve; (*утрачиваться: память, уверенность*) to disappear; **~ся** *(impf)* **в дога́дках** to get caught up in conjecture.
тёс (**-а**) *м собир* planks *мн*.
тёсаный *прил* hewn.
те|са́ть (**-шу́, -шешь**) *несов перех* to hew (out).
тесём|ка (**-ки**; *gen pl* **-ок**) *ж* = **тесьма́**; (*завязка*) drawstring.
те́сен *прил см* **те́сный**.
тесн|и́ть (**-ю́, -и́шь**; *perf* **потесни́ть**) *несов перех* (*друг друга в толпе*) to squeeze; (*кого-н к стене*) to press; (*противника*) to press back; (*perf* **стесни́ть**; *перен*): **~и́т в груди́** he *итп* has got a tight feeling in his chest
▸ **тесни́ться** *несов возв* (*люди: в толпе, в тесной комнате*) to be squashed together; (*мысли*) to crowd; **семья́ ~и́тся в одно́й ко́мнате** the whole family lives crammed together in one room; **в голове́ ~я́тся воспомина́ния** his *итп* mind is crowded with memories.
те́сно *нареч* (*стоять, расположить итп*) close together; (*сотрудничать*) closely ◆ *как сказ*: **в кварти́ре о́чень** ~ the flat is very cramped; **мы с ним ~ знако́мы** he and I know each other very well.
теснот|а́ (**-ы**) *ж* (*помещения*) cramped conditions *мн*; (*скопление людей*) crowd; (*в груди*) tightness; **в ~е́, да не в оби́де** ≈ the more the merrier.
те́с|ный (**-ен, -на́, -но**) *прил* (*проход*) narrow; (*помещение*) cramped; (*одежда*) tight; (*дружба, ряды*) close; **мир ~ен** it's a small world.
тест (**-а**) *м* test.
те́ст|о (**-а**) *ср* (*дрожжевое*) dough; (*слоёное, песочное*) pastry (*BRIT*), paste (*US*); (*для блинов*) batter; (*для кекса*) mixture; (*бетонное*) mix.
тест|ь (**-я**) *м* father-in-law, wife's father.
тесьм|а́ (**-ы́**) *ж* tape; (*для украшения*) trimming.
те́терев (**-а**) *м* black grouse.
тетёр|я (**-и**) *ж* (*разг*) clot; **глуха́я** ~ cloth-ears; **со́нная** ~ sleepyhead.
тетив|а́ (**-ы́**) *ж* (*лука*) bowstring.
тёт|ка (**-ки**; *gen pl* **-ок**) *ж* auntie; (*разг: пренебр: женщина*) old dear.
тетра́д|ка (**-ки**; *gen pl* **-ок**) *ж* exercise book.
тетра́д|ь (**-и**) *ж* exercise book; **но́тная** ~ manuscript book.
тёт|я (**-и**; *gen pl* **-ь**) *ж* aunt; (*разг: женщина*) lady.
те́фтел|и (**-ей**) *мн* meatballs *мн*.
тех *мест см* **те**.
Теха́с (**-а**) *м* Texas.
те́хник (**-а**) *м* technician.
те́хник|а (**-и**) *ж* technology; (*приёмы: музыкальная, плавания итп*) technique ◆ *собир* (*машины*) machinery; (*разг: муз*) hi-fi; **вычисли́тельная** ~ (*комп*) computers *мн*; **те́хника безопа́сности** industrial safety.
те́хникум (**-а**) *м* technical college.
техни́чек *сущ см* **техни́чка**.
техни́чен *прил см* **техни́чный**.
техни́ческ|ий (**-ая, -ое, -ие**) *прил* technical; (*масло, волокно*) industrial; **техни́ческие нау́ки** engineering sciences; **техни́ческие сре́дства обуче́ния** educational technology; **техни́ческий осмо́тр** (*АВТ*) ≈ MOT (*BRIT*) (*annual roadworthiness check*); **техни́ческий реда́ктор** copy editor; **техни́ческое обслу́живание** maintenance, servicing.
техни́ч|ка (**-ки**; *gen pl* **-ек**) *ж* (*автомобиль*) emergency vehicle; (*уборщица*) cleaner.
техни́ч|ный (**-ен, -на, -но**) *прил* (*спортсмен, музыкант*) technically good.
технокра́т (**-а**) *м* technocrat.
техно́лог (**-а**) *м* technologist; (*производственного процесса*) process engineer.
технологи́ческ|ий (**-ая, -ое, -ие**) *прил* technological; (*не строительный*) engineering *опред*; (*не вспомогательный*) basic, major; **технологи́ческий институ́т** institute of technology.
техноло́ги|я (**-и**) *ж* technology.
тече́ни|е (**-я**) *ср* (*воды, жизни*) flow; (*поток: морское, атмосферное*) current; (*в политике, в искусстве*) trend, current; **в** ~ *+gen* during; **с ~м вре́мени** in the course of time; **по ~ю** with the current; **плыть** *(impf)* **по ~ю** (*перен*) to go with the flow; **про́тив ~я** against the current.
те́чк|а (**-и**) *ж* (*зоол*) heat; **у на́шей соба́ки** ~ our dog is on *или* in heat.
те|чь (*3sg* **-чёт**, *3pl* **-ку́т**, *pt* **тёк, текла́, текло́**) *несов неперех* (*вода, кровь итп*) to flow; (*крыша, лодка итп*) to leak; (*перен: жизнь, время*) to go by ◆ (**-чи**) *ж* leak; **дава́ть (дать** *perf*) ~ to spring a leak.
те́ш|ить (**-у, -ишь**; *perf* **поте́шить**) *несов перех* to amuse; (*самолюбие*) to indulge
▸ **те́шиться** (*perf* **поте́шиться**) *несов возв*: **~ся** *+instr* (*игрушкой*) to amuse o.s. with; (*мыслью*) to console o.s. with; (*издеваться*): **~ся над** *+instr* to make fun of.
тёщ|а (**-и**) *ж* mother-in-law, wife's mother.
тешу́ *итп несов см* **теса́ть**.
Тибе́т (**-а**) *м* Tibet.
тибе́тск|ий (**-ая, -ое, -ие**) *прил* Tibetan.
Тибр (**-а**) *м* Tiber (*river*).
Тигр (**-а**) *м* Tigris (*river*).

тигр (-а) *м* tiger.
тигр|ёнок (-ёнка; *nom pl* **-ята**, *gen pl* **-ят**) *м* tiger cub.
тигри́ц|а (-ы) *ж* tigress.
тигро́вый *прил* tiger *опред*; **тигро́вый глаз** (*камень*) tiger's-eye.
тигря́та *итп сущ см* **тигрёнок**.
тик (-а) *м* (*нервный*) tic; (*ткань*) ticking.
ти́кани|е (-я) *ср* ticking.
ти́ка|ть (*3sg* **-ет**, *3pl* **-ют**) *несов неперех* to tick.
ти́н|а (-ы) *ж* slime; (*перен*: *обывательщины итп*) mire.
тип (-а) *м* type; (*разг*: *о мужчине*) character; **ти́па** *+gen* (*разг*) sort of.
типа́ж (-а́) *м* character type.
типи́чен *прил см* **типи́чный**.
типи́ческ|ий (-ая, -ое, -ие) *прил* typical.
типи́ч|ный (-ен, -на, -но) *прил*: ~ (**для** *+gen*) typical (of).
типово́й *прил* standard-type.
типогра́фи|я (-и) *ж* press, printing house.
типогра́фск|ий (-ая, -ое, -ие) *прил* typographical; **типогра́фская кра́ска** printing ink; **типогра́фский стано́к** printing press.
типу́н (-а) *м*: ~ **тебе́ на язы́к!** (*разг*) don't say that!
тир (-а) *м* shooting gallery.
тира́д|а (-ы) *ж* tirade.
тира́ж (-а́) *м* (*газеты*) circulation; (*книги*) printing; (*лотереи, облигаций*) drawing; **кни́га вы́шла тиражо́м в ты́сячу экземпля́ров** one thousand copies of the book were printed; **выходи́ть (вы́йти** *perf*) **в** ~ (*заём, облигации*) to be issued; (*книга*) to be printed; (*перен*) to fade from the scene.
тира́н (-а) *м* tyrant.
Тира́н|а (-ы) *ж* Tirana.
тира́н|ить (-ю, -ишь) *несов перех* to tyrannize.
тирани́ческ|ий (-ая, -ое, -ие) *прил* tyrannical.
тирани́|я (-и) *ж* tyranny.
тире́ *ср нескл* dash.
тис (-а) *м* yew (tree).
ти́ска|ть (-ю) *несов перех* to squeeze.
тиск|и́ (-о́в) *мн* (*ТЕХ*) vice *ед* (*BRIT*), vise *ед* (*US*); **в ~а́х** *+gen* (*перен*) in the grip of.
тисне́ни|е (-я) *ср* (*по коже*) stamping.
тиснёный *прил* (*переплёт*) impressed.
тита́н (-а) *м* (*в мифологии*) titan; (*перен*: *науки, мысли итп*) giant; (*ХИМ*) titanium; (*для нагрева воды*) boiler, urn.
титани́ческ|ий (-ая, -ое, -ие) *прил* titanic.
титр (-а) *м* (*обычно мн*) credit (*of a film*).
ти́тул (-а) *м* (*также КОММ*) title; ~ **на иму́щество** (*ЮР*) title (*to property*).
ти́тульный *прил*: ~ **лист** title page.
тиф (-а) *м* typhus; **брюшно́й** ~ typhoid fever.
тифо́зн|ый *прил*: **~ая лихора́дка** typhoid fever ◆ (**-ого**; *decl like adj*) *м* typhus patient.
ти́х|ий (-ая, -ое, -ие; -, -а́, -о) *прил* quiet; (*течение, ход*) gentle; **Ти́хий океа́н** the Pacific (Ocean).
ти́х|нуть (*3sg* **-нет**, *3pl* **-нут**, *pt* **-**, **-ла**, **-ло**) *несов неперех* to go quiet.
ти́хо *нареч* (*говорить, жить итп*) quietly; (*идти*) slowly ◆ *как сказ*: **в до́ме** ~ the house is quiet; **~!** (be) quiet!
тихо́н|я (-и) *м/ж* (*разг*) quiet operator.
ти́ше *сравн прил от* **ти́хий** ◆ *сравн нареч от* **ти́хо**; **~!** quiet!, hush!
тишин|а́ (-ы́) *ж* quiet.
тиш|ь (-и) *ж* = **тишина́**.
т.к. *сокр* = **так как**.
тка́ный *прил* woven.
ткан|ь (-и) *ж* fabric, material; (*АНАТ*) tissue; (*перен*: *рассказа*) fabric.
тк|ать (-у, -ёшь; *perf* **соткать**) *несов перех* to weave; (*паутину*) to spin.
тка́цк|ий (-ая, -ое, -ие) *прил*: **~ое произво́дство** weaving; **тка́цкая фа́брика** mill (*for fabric production*); **тка́цкий стано́к** loom.
ткач (-а́) *м* weaver.
ткачи́х|а (-и) *ж см* **ткач**.
ткн|у́ть(ся) (-у(сь), -ёшь(ся)) *сов от* **ты́кать(ся)**.
тлен (-а) *м* decay.
тлетво́р|ный (-ен, -на, -но) *прил* pernicious.
тле|ть (*3sg* **-ет**, *3pl* **-ют**) *несов неперех* (*навоз, мусор*) to decay; (*дрова, угли*) to smoulder (*BRIT*), smolder (*US*); (*пламя*) to die out; (*перен*: *надежда*) to flicker
➢ **тле́ться** *несов возв* (*костёр, угли*) to smo(u)lder; (*надежда*) to flicker.
тл|я (-и) *ж* aphid.
тмин (-а) *м* (*БОТ*) tumin.
т.н. *сокр* = **так называ́емый**.
ТНК *ж сокр* = *транснациона́льная корпора́ция*.
то *союз* (*условный*): **е́сли** ... ~ ... if ... then ...; (*разделительный*): ~ ... ~ ... sometimes ... sometimes ...; **е́сли его́ не бу́дет там, ~ я не пойду́** if he isn't going to be there, (then) I'm not going; **и** ~ even; **он и ~ зна́ет об э́том** even he knows about it; ~ **есть** that is; ~ **и де́ло** time and again.
то (**того́**) *мест см* **тот**.
т.о. *сокр* = **таки́м о́бразом**.
-то *част* (*для выделения*): **письмо́-то ты получи́л?** did you (at least) receive the letter?; **где-то она́ сейча́с** if only I knew where she is now; **когда́-то мы встре́тимся?** when on earth shall we meet?; **э́тот-то всё съел** this one here has eaten everything.
тобо́й *мест см* **ты**.
тобо́ю *мест* = **тобо́й**.
тов. *сокр* = **това́рищ**.
това́р (-а; *part gen* **-у**) *м* product; (*ЭКОН*) commodity ◆ *собир* goods *мн*.
това́рищ (-а) *м* (*приятель*) friend; (*по партии*)

comrade; ~ **по шкóле/рабóте** school-/ workmate.

товáрищеск|ий (-ая, -ое, -ие) *прил* comradely; **товáрищеский матч** (*СПОРТ*) friendly (match).

товáриществ|о (-а) *ср* camaraderie; (*КОММ*) partnership.

товáрный *прил* (*производство*) goods *опред*; (*рынок*) commodity *опред*; **товáрная бíржа** commodity exchange; **товáрный вагóн** goods wagon (*BRIT*), freight car (*US*); **товáрный знак** trademark; **товáрный пóезд** goods (*BRIT*) *или* freight (*US*) train; **товáрный склад** warehouse.

товаровéд (-а) *м* merchandiser.

товарообмéн (-а) *м* barter.

товарооборóт (-а) *м* turnover.

товаропроизводíтел|ь (-я) *м* (goods) manufacturer.

тогдá *нареч* then; ~ **как** (*хотя*) while; (*при противопоставлении*) whereas; **не хóчешь, ~ не нáдо** if you don't want to, then don't.

тогдáшн|ий (-яя, -ее, -ие) *прил* (*разг*): **в ~ие временá** in those days.

тогó *мест см* **тот, то.**

тождéствен|ный (-, -на, -но) *прил* identical.

тóждеств|о (-а) *ср* (*также МАТ*) identity.

тóже *нареч* (*также*) too, as well, also ◆ *част* as if; **я ~ пойдý** I'm going too *или* as well, I'm also going; ~ **мне поэ́т нашёлся!** as if he's a poet!; **я ~ люблю́ я́блоки** I too like apples; **я идý купáться – я ~!** I'm going swimming – me too!

той *мест см* **та.**

ток (-а) *м* (*ЭЛЕК*) current; (*для зерна*) threshing floor.

токáрный *прил*: ~ **станóк** lathe.

тóкар|ь (-я; *nom pl* -я́) *м* turner.

Тóкио *м нескл* Tokyo.

токсикóз (-а) *м* toxicosis; (*беременной*) hyperemesis.

токсíчен *прил см* **токсíчный.**

токсíческ|ий (-ая, -ое, -ие) *прил* toxic.

токсíч|ный (-ен, -на, -но) *прил* = **токсíческий.**

толк (-а; *part gen* -у) *м* (*в рассуждениях*) sense; (*разг*: *польза*) use; **рассуждáть** *(impf) или* **говорíть** *(impf)* **с тóлком** to talk sense; **от негó нет тóлку** (*разг*) he's no use; **всё без ~у** it's all for nothing; **взять** *(perf)* **что-н себé в ~** (*разг*) to get sth; **знать** *(impf) или* **понимáть** *(impf)* **~ в чём-н** to have a good understanding of sth; **сбивáть (сбить** *perf*) **когó-н с тóлку** to confuse sb.

толкáтел|ь (-я) *м*: ~ **ядрá** shot-putter.

толкá|ть (-ю; *perf* **толкнýть**) *несов перех* to push; (*перен*): ~ **когó-н на** *+acc* (*подлеж*: *голод*) to force sb into; (: *человек*) to put sb up to; ~ *(impf)* **лóктем** to nudge; ~ *(impf)* **ядрó** to put the shot; ~ *(impf)* **штáнгу** to lift weights; ~ **(толкнýть** *perf*) **речь** (*разг*) to have one's say

▸ **толкáться** *несов возв* (*в толпе*) to push (one's way); (*разг*: *без дела*) to hang about *или* around; **~ся (толкнýться** *perf*) **в** *+acc* (*разг*: *в дверь*) to push; (*перен*: *в учреждения*) to approach.

тóлк|и (-ов) *мн* (*разг*) gossip *ед.*

толкн|ýть(ся) (-ý(сь), -ёшь(ся)) *сов от* **толкáть(ся).**

толковáни|е (-я) *ср* interpretation; (*слова*) definition.

толк|овáть (-ýю) *несов перех* (*явления, события итп*) to interpret; (*разг*): ~ **что-н** *+dat* to spell sth out to; ~ *(impf)* **с кем-н о чём-н** (*разг*) to have a chat with sb about sth.

толкóв|ый (-, -а, -о) *прил* (*ученик, работник*) intelligent; (*объяснение*) clear; **толкóвый словáрь** dictionary with definitions.

тóлком *нареч* (*разг*) properly; **я ~ ничегó не узнáл** I didn't manage to find anything out.

толкотн|я́ (-и́) *ж* (*разг*: *в толпе, в очереди*) crush.

толкý(сь) *итп несов см* **толóчь(ся).**

толкýч|ка (-ки; *gen pl* -ек) *ж* (*разг*: *рынок*) flea market; (*место скопления людей*) crush.

толóк(ся) *итп несов см* **толóчь(ся).**

толокн|ó (-á) *ср* oatmeal.

тол|óчь (-кý, -чёшь *итп*, -кýт; *pt* -óк, -клá, -клó, *perf* **истолóчь** *или* **растолóчь**) *несов перех* (*зерна, сухари*) to pound; ~ *(impf)* **вóду в стýпе** (*разг*) to pound the air

▸ **толóчься** *несов возв* (*разг*) to crowd about *или* around.

толп|á (-ы́; *nom pl* -ы) *ж* (*народа*) crowd; (*перен*: *в противопоставление личности*) the crowd.

толп|íться (*3sg* -íтся, *3pl* -я́тся) *несов возв* to crowd around.

толстé|ть (-ю; *perf* **потолстéть**) *несов неперех* to get fatter.

толст|íть (*3sg* -íт, *3pl* -я́т) *несов перех* (*разг*): **Вас ~íт э́то плáтье** that dress makes you look fat.

толстокóж|ий (-ая, -ее, -ие; -, -а, -о) *прил* (*также перен*) thick-skinned.

толстýх|а (-и) *ж* (*разг*) = **толстýшка.**

толстýш|ка (-ки; *gen pl* -ек) *ж* (*разг*) fatty.

тóлст|ый (-, -á, -о) *прил* thick; (*человек, ноги итп*) fat; **тóлстая кишкá** large intestine.

толстя́к (-á) *м* (*разг*) fatso.

толчёный *прил* crushed.

толче|я́ (-и́) *ж* (*разг*) crush.

толч|óк (-кá) *м* (*в спину, в грудь*) shove; (*при торможении, при встряхивании*) jolt; (*при землетрясении*) tremor; (*перен*: *к работе, к началу*) push; (*СПОРТ*: *штанги*) thrust; (: *ядра*) put; (*разг*: *рынок*) flea market.

тóлщ|а (-и) *ж* (*льда, облаков*) mass.

тóлще *сравн прил от* **тóлстый.**

толщин|á (-ы́) *ж* (*тела, фигуры*) corpulence; (*слоя, бревна*) thickness.

тол|ь (-я) *м* roofing felt.

KEYWORD

тóлько *част* ***1*** only; **тóлько 5 книг** only 5 books; **он читáет тóлько газéты** he only reads newspapers

2 (*+pron/+adv*; *усиливает выразительность*):

зачём только я согласился! why on earth did I agree!; **где только он не побывал** where has he NOT been!; **попробуй только отказаться!** just try to refuse!; **подумать только!** imagine that!
◆ *союз* **1** (*сразу после*) as soon as; **только напишешь, я приеду** as soon as you write, I'll come
2 (*однако, но*) only; **позвони, только разговаривай недолго** phone (*BRIT*) *или* call (*US*), only don't talk for long
◆ *нареч* **1** (*недавно*) (only) just; **ты давно здесь?- нет, только вошла** have you been here long? – no, I've (only) just come in
2 (*во фразах*): **только лишь** (*разг*) only; **только и всего** (*разг*) that's all; **как** *или* **лишь** *или* **едва только** (*сразу после того, как*) as soon as; **не только ..., но и ...** not only ... but also ...; **только бы** if only; **только бы знать, где он!** if only I knew where he was!; **только что** only just.

том *мест см* **тот, то.**
том (**-а**; *nom pl* **-а**) *м* volume.
томат (**-а**) *м* (*помидор*) tomato (*мн* tomatoes); (*соус*) tomato purée.
томатный *прил*: ~ **сок/суп** tomato juice/soup.
томен *прил см* **томный**.
томител|ьный (**-ен, -ьна, -ьно**) *прил* tormenting.
том|ить (**-лю, -ишь**; *perf* **истомить**) *несов перех* (*расспросами, ожиданием*) to torment
▸ **томиться** (*perf* **истомиться**) *несов возв* (*ожиданием, жаждой*) to be tormented.
томлени|е (**-я**) *ср* languor.
томлю(сь) *несов см* **томить(ся)**.
том|ный (**-ен, -на, -но**) *прил* languid.
тому *мест см* **тот, то.**
тон (**-а**) *м* (*также МУЗ, МЕД*) tone.
тональност|ь (**-и**) *ж* (*МУЗ*) key; (*картины*) tones *мн*; (*перен*: *стихотворения*) tone.
тонзиллит (**-а**) *м* tonsillitis.
тонизирующ|ий (**-ая, -ее, -ие**) *прил* (*прогулка, напиток*) refreshing; **~ее средство** tonic.
тон|кий (**-кая, -кое, -кие; -ок, -ка, -ко**) *прил* thin; (*фигура, пальцы*) slender; (*черты лица, работа, ум*) fine; (*запах, вкус*) delicate; (*обращение, различия, намёк*) subtle; (*слух*) sharp; **тонкая кишка** small intestine.
тонко *нареч* (*резать*) thinly; (*пахнуть*) delicately; (*намекать, чувствовать*) subtly; **она ~ чувствует музыку/поэзию** she has a fine appreciation of music/poetry.
тонкокож|ий (**-ая, -ее, -ие; -, -а, -о**) *прил* thin-skinned.
тонкост|ь (**-и**) *ж* (*см прил*) thinness; slenderness; fineness; delicacy; subtlety; sharpness; (*частность*) detail; **до ~ей** down to the last detail; **вдаваться** *(impf)* **в ~и** to go into detail.

тонн|а (**-ы**) *ж* tonne.
тоннаж (**-а**) *м* (*судна*) tonnage; (*вагона*) capacity.
тоннел|ь (**-я**) *м* tunnel.
тонок *прил см* **тонкий**.
тонус (**-а**) *м* (*сердца, тканей*) tone; **жизненный** ~ vitality.
тон|уть (**-у, -ешь**; *perf* **утонуть** *или* **потонуть**) *несов неперех* (*человек*) to drown; (*perf* **утонуть**; *дерево, камень*) to sink; (*perf* **затонуть**; *корабль*) to sink; (*увязать*): **~ в** *+prp* (*в снегу, в грязи*) to get stuck in; (*перен*: *в делах*) to be up to one's eyes in; (*no perf*; *перен*: *в зелени*) to get lost; (*в шуме*) to drown.
тоньше *сравн прил от* **тонкий** ◆ *сравн нареч от* **тонко**.
топаз (**-а**) *м* topaz.
топа|ть (**-ю**) *несов неперех* (*разг*: *идти*) to go; ~ *(impf)* **ногами** to stamp one's feet; **~й отсюда!** (*разг*) scram!
топ|ить (**-лю, -ишь**) *несов перех* (*печь*) to stoke (up); (*дом*) to warm (up); (*плавить*: *масло, воск*) to melt; (*perf* **утопить** *или* **потопить**; *корабль*) to sink; (*человека*) to drown; (*perf* **потопить**; *перен*: *дело*) to ruin; **~ (потопить** *perf*) **горе** to drown one's sorrows
▸ **топиться** *несов возв* (*печь*) to burn; (*помещение*) to be heated; (*perf* **растопиться**; *воск*) to melt; (*perf* **утопиться**; *лишить себя жизни*) to drown o.s.
топк|а (**-и**) *ж* (*действие*: *печи*) stoking; (*часть печи*) furnace.
топ|кий (**-кая, -кое, -кие; -ок, -ка, -ко**) *прил* (*дорога, почва*) muddy.
топлён|ый *прил* (*КУЛИН*: *масло, жир*) melted; **~ое молоко** boiled milk.
топлив|о (**-а**) *ср* fuel; **жидкое/твёрдое** ~ liquid/solid fuel.
топлю(сь) *несов см* **топить(ся)**.
топографи|я (**-и**) *ж* topography.
топок *прил см* **топкий**.
тополь|ь (**-я**) *м* poplar.
топонимик|а (**-и**) *ж* toponymy.
топор (**-а**) *м* axe (*BRIT*), ax (*US*).
топорен *прил см* **топорный**.
топорищ|е (**-а**) *ср* axe (*BRIT*) *или* ax (*US*) handle.
топор|ный (**-ен, -на, -но**) *прил* (*перен*: *работа, стиль*) crude.
топорщ|ить (**-у, -ишь**; *perf* **встопорщить**) *несов перех* (*разг*: *перья, шерсть*) to fluff up
▸ **топорщиться** (*perf* **встопорщиться**) *несов возв* (*разг*: *усы, хвост*) to bristle; (*платье, складки*) to puff up.
топот (**-а**) *м* clatter.
топ|тать (**-чу, -чешь**; *perf* **потоптать**) *несов перех* (*траву*) to trample; (*пол*) to dirty
▸ **топтаться** *несов возв* (*разг*) to shift from one foot to the other; **~ся** *(impf)* **на месте** (*перен*) to

go round in circles.
топ-топ *звукоподражание* pitter-patter.
топча́н (**-а**) *м* trestle bed.
топчу́(сь) *итп несов см* **топта́ть(ся)**.
топ|ь (**-и**) *ж* marsh.
торг (**-а**) *м* trading.
торга́ш (**-а́**) *м* (*разг*: *пренебр*) money-grubber.
торг|и́ (**-о́в**) *мн* (*аукцион*) auction *ед*; (*состязание*) tender *ед*.
торг|ова́ть (**-у́ю**) *несов неперех* (*перен*: *совестью, убеждениями*) to forfeit; (*магазин*) to trade; ~ *(impf)* *+instr* (*мясом, мебелью*) to trade in; ~ *(impf)* **с** *+instr* to (do) trade with
▸ **торгова́ться** (*perf* **сторгова́ться**) *несов возв* (*разг*: *спорить о цене*) to haggle; (*перен*: *спорить*) to bicker.
торго́в|ец (**-ца**) *м* merchant; (*мелкий, уличный*) trader.
торго́в|ка (**-ки**; *gen pl* **-ок**) *ж* (*уличная, базарная*) trader.
торго́вл|я (**-и**) *ж* trade.
торго́вок *сущ см* **торго́вка**.
торго́вца *итп сущ см* **торго́вец**.
торго́вый *прил* (*договор, прибыль, барьеры*) trade *опред*; (*судно, флот*) merchant *опред*; **торго́вая сеть** retail network; **торго́вая то́чка** retail outlet; **торго́вое представи́тельство** trade mission; **торго́вый рабо́тник** retail industry worker; **торго́вый центр** shopping centre (*BRIT*), mall (*US*).
торгпре́д (**-а**) *м сокр* (= *торго́вый представи́тель*) head of the trade mission.
торгпре́дств|о (**-а**) *ср сокр* (= *торго́вое представи́тельство*) trade mission.
тореадо́р (**-а**) *м* toreador.
тор|е́ц (**-ца́**) *м* (*доски, книги*) butt; (*здания*) gable end.
торже́ственен *прил см* **торже́ственный**.
торже́ственно *нареч* (*обещать*) solemnly; (*праздновать*) fully.
торже́ствен|ный *прил* (*день, случай*) special; (*собрание*) celebratory; (**-ен, -на, -но**; *вид, обстановка*) festive; (*no short form*; *обещание, клятва*) solemn.
торжеств|о́ (**-а́**) *ср* (*семейное, национальное*) celebration; (*в голосе, в словах*) triumph; ~ *+gen* (*справедливости итп*) the triumph of.
торжеств|ова́ть (**-у́ю**; *perf* **восторжествова́ть**) *несов неперех*: ~ (**над** *+instr*) to triumph (over); (*no perf*; *внутренно, открыто*) to rejoice.
торма́ш|ки (**-ек**) *мн* (*разг*): **вверх ~ками** upside down.
торможе́ни|е (**-я**) *ср* (*машины*) braking; (*рефлексов*) inhibition.
торможу́(сь) *несов см* **тормози́ть(ся)**.
то́рмоз (**-а**; *nom pl* **-а́**) *м* brake; (*nom pl* **-ы**; *перен*: *в работе*) hindrance, obstacle.
тормо|зи́ть (**-жу́, -зи́шь**; *perf* **затормози́ть**) *несов перех* (*машину, поезд*) to slow down; (*перен*: *движение, работу*) to hamper, impede ◆ *неперех* (*машина, поезд*) to brake
▸ **тормози́ться** (*perf* **затормози́ться**) *несов возв* (*дело, работа итп*) to be hindered *или* impeded.
тормозн|о́й *прил* (*механизм, педаль*) brake *опред*; (*БИО*: *рефлекс*) inhibitory; **~а́я жи́дкость** brake fluid.
тормош|и́ть (**-у́, -и́шь**) *несов перех* to shake; ~ *(impf)* **кого́-н за рука́в** to tug at sb's sleeve; ~ *(impf)* **кого́-н** (*вопросами*) to pester sb.
тор|опи́ть (**-оплю́, -о́пишь**; *perf* **поторопи́ть**) *несов перех* (*коня*) to urge on; (*ребёнка, события*) to hurry; ~ (**поторопи́ть** *perf*) **кого́-н с чем-н** to hurry sb with sth
▸ **торопи́ться** (*perf* **поторопи́ться**) *несов возв* (*на поезд, в школу итп*) to hurry; (*с работой, с выполнением*): **~ся с** *+instr* to hurry with.
торопли́в|ый (**-, -а, -о**) *прил* (*человек*) hasty; (*шаг*) hurried; (*суждение, вывод*) hasty, hurried.
тороплю́(сь) *несов см* **торопи́ть(ся)**.
торпе́д|а (**-ы**) *ж* torpedo (*мн* torpedoes).
торпеди́р|овать (**-ую**) *(не)сов перех* (*также перен*) to torpedo.
торс (**-а**) *м* torso.
торт (**-а**) *м* cake.
торф (**-а**) *м* peat.
торца́ *итп сущ см* **торе́ц**.
торч|а́ть (**-у́, -и́шь**) *несов неперех* (*вверх*) to stick up; (*в стороны*) to stick out; (*разг*: *на улице, в ресторане*) to hang around.
торчко́м *нареч* (*разг*) on end.
торше́р (**-а**) *м* standard lamp.
тоск|а́ (**-и́**) *ж* (*на сердце, во взгляде*) melancholy; (*скука*) boredom; ~ **по ро́дине** homesickness.
тоскли́в|ый (**-, -а, -о**) *прил* (*настроение, музыка итп*) melancholy; (*погода, разговор итп*) dreary.
тоск|ова́ть (**-у́ю**) *несов неперех* to pine away; ~ *(impf)* **по** *+dat* *или* *+prp* to miss.
тост (**-а**) *м* toast; ~ **за** *+acc* toast to.

KEYWORD

то|т (**-го́**; *f* **та**, *nt* **то**, *pl* **те**; *см* **Table 11**) *мест* ***1*** that; **тот дом** that house; **та ру́чка** that pen; **те кни́ги** those books; **по ту сто́рону** on that side
2 (*указывает на ранее упомянутое*) that; **в тот раз/день** that time/day
3 (*разг*: *о прошлом*) last; (: *о будущем*) next; **я ви́дел его́ на той неде́ле** I saw him last week; **уви́димся на той неде́ле** we'll meet next week
4 (*в главных предложениях*): **э́то тот челове́к, кото́рый приходи́л вчера́** it's the man who came yesterday; **мы обра́довались тому́, что он ушёл** we were pleased that he had gone
5 (*о последнем из названных лиц*): **я посмотре́л на дру́га, тот стоя́л мо́лча** I looked at my friend, he stood silently
6 (*обычно с отрицанием*): **зашёл не в тот дом** I called at the wrong house; **э́то всё не то** it's not that
7 (*об одном из перечисляемых предметов*): **ни тот, ни друго́й** neither one nor the other; **тем или ины́м спо́собом** by some means or other;

тот же the same; **та же маши́на, что и в про́шлый раз** the same car as last time; **он сказа́л то же са́мое** he said the same thing *8 (во фразах)*: **до того́** so; **он до того́ испуга́лся, что не мог усну́ть** he was so frightened he couldn't sleep; **мне не до того́** I have no time for that; **не то что́(бы) ... , а ...** not so much that ... but ...; **она́ не то что́(бы) глупа́, а засте́нчива** she's not so much stupid, as just shy; **к тому́ же** moreover; **с тем, что́бы** in order to; **ни с того́ ни с сего́** *(разг)* out of the blue; **тому́ наза́д** ago; **и тому́ подо́бное** et cetera, and so on.

тота́лен *прил см* **тота́льный**.
тотализа́тор (-а) *м* totalizer.
тоталитари́зм (-а) *м* totalitarianism.
тоталита́рный *прил* totalitarian.
тота́л|ьный (-ен, -ьна, -ьно) *прил* total.
то-то *част (разг: вот именно)* exactly, that's just it; *(вот почему)* that's why; *(выражает удовлетворение)*: ~ **же** pleased to hear it; **он не сдал экза́мен – ~ он тако́й гру́стный** he didn't pass the exam – that's why he's so sad; ~ **он удиви́тся!** he WILL be surprised!
то́тчас *нареч* immediately.
то́чек *сущ см* **то́чка**.
то́чен *прил см* **то́чный**.
точёный *прил (острый: нож)* sharpened; *(деталь, грань итп)* turned; *(перен: фигура)* shapely; (: *черты лица*) fine.
то́чечн|ый *прил (линия)* dotted; ~ **масса́ж** shiatsu, acupressure; **~ая электросва́рка** spot-welding.
точи́л|ка (-ки; *gen pl* -ок) *ж* pencil sharpener.
точ|и́ть (-у́, -ишь; *perf* **наточи́ть**) *несов перех (нож, карандаш)* to sharpen; *(perf* **вы́точить**; *деталь)* to turn; *(no perf; подлеж: червь, ржавчина)* to eat away at; *(перен: подлеж: болезнь, тоска итп)* to drain.
то́ч|ка (-ки; *gen pl* -ек) *ж* point; *(пятнышко)* dot; *(линг)* full stop *(BRIT)*, period *(esp US)*; *(действие: детали, карандаша)* sharpening; ~ **зре́ния** point of view; **попада́ть (попа́сть** *perf*) **в (са́мую) ~ку** to hit the bull's-eye; **дойти́** *(perf)* **до ~ки** *(разг)* to reach one's limit; **то́чка с запято́й** semicolon.
точне́е *вводн сл* to be exact *или* precise; **приходи́ ве́чером, ~, в 5 часо́в** come in the evening, at 5 o'clock to be exact *или* precise.
то́чно *нареч* exactly; *(объяснить)* exactly, precisely; *(подсчитать, перевести)* accurately ♦ *част (разг: действительно)* precisely ♦ *союз (как будто)* as if *или* though; ~ **тако́й дом** exactly the same house; **он ~ та́к и сде́лал/сказа́л** that's exactly what he did/said; ~, **он уе́хал** that's right, he's gone; **так ~!** yes, sir!; **распла́кался, ~ ребёнок** he burst into tears, just like a child; **он говори́л со мной, ~ я ребёнок** he talked to me as if *или* though I were a child.
то́чност|ь (-и) *ж (часов, попадания)* accuracy; *(работы)* precision; **я подсчита́л затра́ты с ~ю до рубля́** I counted the expenditure right down to the last rouble; **в ~и** *(разг)* exactly.
то́ч|ный (-ен, -на́, -но) *прил (часы, перевод, попадание)* accurate; *(описание, приказ)* precise; *(адрес, копия)* exact; **то́чное вре́мя** exact time; **то́чные нау́ки** exact sciences.
точь-в-точь *нареч (разг)* just like.
тошн|и́ть (*3sg* -и́т, *perf* **стошни́ть**) *несов безл*: **меня́ ~и́т** I feel sick; *(перен)* it makes me sick; **меня́ ~и́т от твоего́ лицеме́рия** your hypocrisy makes me sick.
то́шно *как сказ (перен: разг)* it's nauseating *или* sickening.
тошнот|а́ (-ы́) *ж (чувство)* nausea; **мне э́то до ~ы́ надое́ло** I'm sick to death of it.
тошнотво́р|ный (-ен, -на, -но) *прил (также перен)* nauseating, sickening.
то́щ|ий (-ая, -ее, -ие; -, -а́, -е) *прил (человек)* gaunt; *(кошелёк)* empty; *(почва)* poor; *(растительность)* sparse.
т.п. *сокр* (= **тому́ подо́бное**) etc. (= *et cetera*).
ТПП *м сокр* (= *Торго́во-промы́шленная пала́та*) ≈ Chamber of Commerce.
тпру *межд (лошадям)* whoa.
т-р *сокр* = **теа́тр**.
трав|а́ (-ы́; *nom pl* -ы) *ж* grass; *(лекарственная)* herb; **со́рная ~** weed; **хоть ~ не расти́** *(разг)* he *итп* couldn't care less.
трави́н|ка (-ки; *gen pl* -ок) *ж* blade of grass.
трав|и́ть (-лю́, -ишь) *несов перех (также перен)* to poison; *(perf* **потрави́ть**; *посевы)* to damage; *(perf* **затрави́ть**; *дичь)* to hunt; *(перен: разг: притеснять)* to harass, hound; *(perf* **вы́травить**; *узор)* to etch
▸ **трави́ться** *(perf* **отрави́ться**) *несов возв* to poison o.s.
травле́ни|е (-я) *ср* etching.
травлю́(сь) *несов см* **трави́ть(ся)**.
тра́вл|я (-и) *ж* hunting; *(демократов, радикалов)* hounding.
тра́вм|а (-ы) *ж (физическая)* injury; *(психическая)* trauma.
травмато́лог (-а) *м* specialist in traumatology.
травматологи́ческ|ий (-ая, -ое, -ие) *прил*: ~ **отде́л** casualty; ~ **пункт** first-aid room.
травматоло́ги|я (-и) *ж* traumatology.
травми́р|овать (-ую) *(не)сов перех (голову)* to injure; *(перен: грубостью)* to traumatize.
травоя́д|ный (-ен, -на, -но) *прил* herbivorous.
травяни́ст|ый *прил* herbaceous; (-, -а, -о; *луг*) grassy.
травяно́й *прил (настойка)* herbal; ~ **покро́в** grass.

трагéди|я (**-и**) *ж* tragedy.
трагúзм (**-а**) *м* tragedy.
трагикомéди|я (**-и**) *ж* tragicomedy.
трагикомúческ|ий (**-ая, -ое, -ие**) *прил* tragicomic.
трагúческ|ий (**-ая, -ое, -ие**) *прил* tragic; ~ **актёр** (*трагик*) tragedy actor.
трагúч|ный (**-ен, -на, -но**) *прил* tragic.
традициóн|ный (**-ен, -на, -но**) *прил* traditional.
традúци|я (**-и**) *ж* tradition; **входúть (войтú** *perf*) **в ~ю** to become a tradition.
траектóри|я (**-и**) *ж* trajectory.
тракт (**-а**) *м* (*ИСТ*) highway; (*АНАТ*): **пищеварúтельный** ~ alimentary canal.
трактáт (**-а**) *м* treatise.
трактúр (**-а**) *м* inn.
трактúрщик (**-а**) *м* innkeeper.
трактúрщиц|а (**-ы**) *ж см* **трактúрщик**.
тракт|овáть (**-ýю**) *несов перех* to interpret.
трактóв|ка (**-ки**; *gen pl* **-ок**) *ж* interpretation.
трáктор (**-а**) *м* tractor.
тракторúст (**-а**) *м* tractor driver.
тракторúст|ка (**-ки**; *gen pl* **-ок**) *ж см* **трактoрúст**.
трал (**-а**) *м* (*сеть*) trawl; **мúнный** ~ minesweeping operation.
трáл|ить (**-ю, -ишь**; *perf* **протрáлить**) *несов перех* to trawl; ~ **(протрáлить** *perf*) **мúны** to sweep for mines.
трамб|овáть (**-ýю**; *perf* **утрамбовáть**) *несов перех* to tamp.
трамвá|й (**-я**) *м* tram (*BRIT*), streetcar (*US*); **éздить/éхать** (*impf*) **на ~е** to go by tram.
трамвáйн|ый *прил* tram *опред* (*BRIT*), streetcar *опред* (*US*); **~ые пути** tramlines; **трамвáйный парк** tram *или* streetcar depot.
трамплúн (**-а**) *м* (*также перен*) springboard; **лыжный** ~ ski jump.
транжúр (**-а**) *м* spendthrift.
транжúр|ить (**-ю, -ишь**; *perf* **растранжúрить**) *несов перех* (*разг*: *деньги*) to blow.
транжúр|ка (**-ки**; *gen pl* **-ок**) *ж см* **транжúр**.
транзúстор (**-а**) *м* (*усилитель*) transistor; (*радиоприёмник*) transistor (radio).
транзúт (**-а**) *м* transit; (*о грузе*) transit goods.
транзúтный *прил* transit *опред*.
транквилизáтор (**-а**) *м* tranquillizer (*BRIT*), tranquilizer (*US*).
транс (**-а**) *м* (*ПСИХОЛ*) trance; (*КОММ*: *документ*) transport document; **нóмер трáнса** trans number.
трансгéнный *прил* genetically modified.
трансконтинентáльный *прил* transcontinental.
транскрúпци|я (**-и**) *ж* transcription.
транслúр|овать (**-ую**) (*не*)*сов перех* to broadcast.
транслятор (**-а**) *м* (*ТЕХ*) translator.
трансляци|я (**-и**) *ж* (*передачи*) transmission, broadcasting; (*передача*) broadcast; **прямáя** ~ live broadcast.
транспарáнт (**-а**) *м* banner.
трансплантáци|я (**-и**) *ж* transplant.
трáнспорт (**-а**) *м* transport.
транспортёр (**-а**) *м* (*конвейер*) conveyor belt; (*ВОЕН*) troop carrier.
транспортúр|овать (**-ую**) (*не*)*сов перех* to transport.
транспортирóвк|а (**-и**) *ж* transportation.
трáнспортный *прил* transport *опред*.
транссексуáл (**-а**) *м* transsexual.
трансформáтор (**-а**) *м* transformer.
трансформáци|я (**-и**) *ж* transformation.
трансформúр|овать (**-ую**) (*не*)*сов перех* to transform.
траншé|я (**-и**) *ж* trench.
трап (**-а**) *м* gangway; **подавáть (подáть** *perf*) ~ to put down the gangway.
трáпез|а (**-ы**) *ж communal meal in monastery*.
трáпезн|ая (**-ой**; *decl like adj*) *ж* refectory.
трапéци|я (**-и**) *ж* (*ГЕОМ*) trapezium; (*цирковая, гимнастическая*) trapeze.
трáсс|а (**-ы**) *ж* (*лыжная*) run; (*трубопровода, канала*) route; **автомобúльная** ~ motorway (*BRIT*), expressway (*US*); **воздýшная** ~ airway.
трассáт (**-а**) *м* (*КОММ*) drawee.
трáт|а (**-ы**) *ж* spending; **пустáя ~ врéмени/дéнег** a waste of time/money.
трá|тить (**-чу, -тишь**; *perf* **истрáтить** *или* **потрáтить**) *несов перех* to spend
▸ **трáтиться** (*perf* **истрáтиться** *или* **потрáтиться**) *несов возв*: **~ся на** +*acc* to spend a lot of money on.
трáулер (**-а**) *м* trawler.
трáур (**-а**) *м* mourning; ~ **по** +*prp* mourning for; **носúть** (*impf*) ~ to wear mourning.
трáур|ный *прил* (*процессия, платье*) mourning *опред*; (**-ен, -на, -но**; *перен*: *обстановка, тон*) mournful.
трафарéт (**-а**) *м* stencil; **мыслить** (*impf*) **по ~у** (*перен*) to think in clichés.
трафарéт|ный (**-ен, -на, -но**) *прил* (*рисунок, черчение*) stencilled; (*перен*: *фразы*) trite.
трах *межд* bang; **а он ~ по столý** and he banged against the table.
трáха|ть(ся) (**-ю(сь)**) *несов от* **трáхнуть(ся)**.
трахé|я (**-и**) *ж* trachea.
трáхн|уть (**-у, -ешь**; *impf* **трáхать**) *сов неперех* (*разг*: *выстрел*) to ring out ♦ *перех* (*ударить*) to thump; (*переспать*: *женщину*) to lay
▸ **трáхнуться** (*impf* **трáхаться**) *сов возв* (*разг*: *удариться*) to bang o.s.; (: *мужчина и женщина*) to have it off; **трáхаться (~ся** *perf*) **головóй о стéнку** to bang one's head against the wall.
трáчу(сь) *несов см* **трáтить(ся)**.
трéбовани|е (**-я**) *ср* (*объяснений, денег*) request; (*решительное, категорическое*) demand; (*устава, экзаменационные*) requirement; (*документ*: *на книгу*) order; **~я** (*моральные, эстетические*) needs *мн*.
трéбовател|ьный (**-ен, -ьна, -ьно**) *прил* demanding; (*тон, голос*) peremptory.
трéб|овать (**-ую**; *perf* **потрéбовать**) *несов перех* (*квитанцию*) to ask for; (*в суд, к*

начальнику) to summon; ~ **(потре́бовать** *perf*) **что-н/***+infin* to demand sth/to do; ~ **(потре́бовать** *perf*) *+gen* (*сочувствия, правдивости*) to expect; (*помощи, переделки*) to need, require
▸ **тре́боваться** (*perf* **потре́боваться**) *несов возв* to be needed *или* required.
требух|а́ (-и́) *ж* entrails *мн.*
трево́г|а (-и) *ж* (*волнение*) anxiety; (*на улице, в доме*) alarm; **возду́шная** ~ air-raid warning; **поднима́ть (подня́ть** *perf*) *или* **бить** (*impf*) **~у** (*перен*) to raise the alarm.
трево́жен *прил см* **трево́жный.**
трево́ж|ить (-у, -ишь; *perf* **встрево́жить)** *несов перех* (*родителей, правительство*) to alarm; (*perf* **потрево́жить**; *подлеж*: *шум, посетители*) to disturb; (*перен*: *рану*) to reopen
▸ **трево́житься** (*perf* **встрево́житься**) *несов возв* (*за детей*) to be concerned; (*perf* **потрево́житься**; *затруднять себя*) to trouble o.s.
трево́жно *нареч* (*посмотреть*) anxiously ◆ *как сказ*: **на се́рдце** ~ I feel anxious; **в го́роде** ~ there is a sense of alarm in the city.
трево́ж|ный (-ен, -на, -но) *прил* (*голос, взгляд*) anxious; (*сведения*) alarming; **~ное вре́мя** time of unrest; **трево́жный сигна́л** alarm.
тре́звенник (-а) *м* teetotaller.
трезве́|ть (-ю; *perf* **отрезве́ть)** *несов неперех* to sober up.
трезво́н (-а) *м* (*колокольный*) peal; (*разг*: *толки*) gossip.
трезво́н|ить (-ю, -ишь) *несов неперех* (*колокола*) to peal; (*телефон, звонок*) to ring; (*разг*: *сплетничать*) to spread gossip.
тре́звост|ь (-и) *ж* (*неупотребление алкоголя*) sobriety; (*перен*: *взгляда, суждений*) soberness.
тре́зв|ый (-, -а́, -о) *прил* (*состояние, человек*) sober; (*перен*: *рассуждение, решение*) sensible.
трек (-а) *м* track.
трел|ь (-и) *ж* warble.
трелья́ж (-а) *м* (*зеркало*) triple mirror.
трём *итп чис см* **три.**
трёмста́м *итп чис см* **триста.**
тренажёр (-а) *м equipment used for physical training.*
тре́нер (-а) *м* coach; **гла́вный** ~ manager (*of sports team*).
тре́ни|е (-я) *ср* friction; (*обычно мн*: *перен*) friction *ед.*
трениров|а́ть (-у́ю; *perf* **натренирова́ть)** *несов перех* to train; (*спортсменов*) to coach.
▸ **тренирова́ться** (*perf* **натренирова́ться**) *несов возв* (*спортсмен*) to train; (*ученик, работник*) to train o.s.
трениро́в|ка (-ки; *gen pl* **-ок)** *ж* (*памяти, лошади итп*) training; (*отдельное занятие*) training (session).
трениро́вочный *прил* training *опред*; **трениро́вочный костю́м** tracksuit.
трено́жник (-а) *м* tripod.
трёп (-а; *part gen* **-у)** *м* (*разг*) blethering, blathering.
трепана́ци|я (-и) *ж* (*МЕД*) trepanation.
трёпаный *прил* (*разг*) tattered.
треп|а́ть (-лю́, -лешь; *perf* **потрепа́ть)** *несов перех* (*подлеж*: *ветер*) to blow about; (*по плечу*) to pat; (*перен*: *корабль*) to toss; (*perf* **истрепа́ть** *или* **потрепа́ть**; *разг*: *обувь, книги*) to wear out; ~ **(потрепа́ть** *perf*) **кого́-н за во́лосы/за у́ши** to pull sb's hair/ears; ~ **(потрепа́ть** *perf*) **не́рвы кому́-н** to wear sb's nerves down; ~ (*impf*) **языко́м** (*разг ЦМИ*) to chatter
▸ **трепа́ться** *несов возв* (*no perf*; *флаги, волосы*) to be blown about; (*perf* **истрепа́ться** *или* **потрепа́ться**; *разг*: *одежда, обувь*) to wear out; (*perf* **потрепа́ться**; *разг*: *о пустяках*) to chatter.
трепа́ч (-а́) *м* (*разг*) chatterbox.
тре́пет (-а) *м* (*листьев*) quivering; (*волнение*) tremor; (*страх*) trepidation.
треп|ета́ть (-ещу́, -е́щешь) *несов неперех* (*листья, флаги*) to quiver; (*от ужаса*) to quake, tremble.
тре́пет|ный (-ен, -на, -но) *прил* tremulous.
трепещу́ *итп несов см* **трепета́ть.**
треплю́(сь) *итп несов см* **трепа́ть(ся).**
трепыха́|ться (-юсь) *несов возв* (*разг*: *животное, рыба*) to wriggle; (*флаг, парус*) to flutter; (*перен*: *волноваться*) to be in a flutter.
треск (-а) *м* (*ломающихся сучьев*) snapping; (*выстрелов*) crackling; **с тре́ском прова́ливаться (провали́ться** *perf*) (*разг*: *пьеса*) to be a flop; (: *студент*) to come a cropper.
треск|а́ (-и́) *ж* cod.
тре́ска|ться (*3sg* **-ется**, *3pl* **-ются**, *perf* **потре́скаться)** *несов возв* (*земля, стекло*) to crack.
трескотн|я́ (-и́) *ж* (*разг*: *кузнечиков*) chirp; (*перен*: *болтовня*) chitchat.
треску́ч|ий (-ая, -ее, -ие; -, -а, -е) *прил* (*перен*: *речи, слова*) bombastic; ~ **моро́з** hard frost.
тре́сн|уть (*3sg* **-ет**, *3pl* **-ут**) *сов неперех* (*ветка*) to snap; (*стакан, кожа*) to crack; (*разг*): ~ **чем-н по чему́-н** (*кулаком*: *по столу*) to bang sth on sth ◆ *перех* (*разг*): ~ **кого́-н по** *+dat* (*по шее, по руке*) to thump sb on
▸ **тре́снуться** *сов возв* (*разг*): **~ся чем-н о** *+acc* to bang sth on.
трест (-а) *м* (*ЭКОН*) trust.
тре́т|ий (-ья, -ье, -ьи) *чис* third; **фильм/врач ~ьего со́рта** a third-rate film/doctor; **~ьего дня** the day before yesterday; **Т~ мир** the Third World; **тре́тий сорт** (*товара*) Grade 3 (*denoting product of inferior quality*); **тре́тье**

лицо (*линг*) the third person; **третья сторона, третьи лица** third party; *см также* **пятый.**
третир|овать (**-ую**) *сов перех* to patronize.
третичный *прил* tertiary.
трет|ь (**-и**; *nom pl* **-и**, *gen pl* **-ей**) *ж* third.
треть|е (**-его**; *decl like adj*) *ср* (*кулин*) sweet (*BRIT*), dessert.
третьеклассник (**-а**) *м pupil in third year at school (usually nine years old).*
третьеклассниц|а (**-ы**) *ж см* **третьеклассник.**
третьесорт|ный (**-ен, -на, -но**) *прил* third-rate.
треть|я (**-ей**; *decl like adj*) *ж*: **одна** ~ one third.
треугольник (**-а**) *м* triangle.
треугольный *прил* triangular.
треф|ы (**-**) *мн* (*карты*) clubs *мн*.
трёх *чис см* **три.**
трёхгодичный *прил* three-year.
трёхгодовалый *прил* three-year-old.
трёхдневный *прил* three-day.
трёхкратн|ый *прил*: ~ **чемпион** three-times champion; **в ~ом размере** threefold.
трёхлети|е (**-я**) *ср* (*срок*) three years; (*годовщина*) third anniversary.
трёхлетн|ий (**-яя, -ее, -ие**) *прил* (*период*) three-year; (*ребёнок*) three-year-old.
трёхмерный *прил* 3-D, three-dimensional.
трёхмесячный *прил* three-month; (*ребёнок*) three-month-old.
трёхнедельный *прил* three-week; (*ребёнок*) three-week-old.
трёхсот *чис см* **триста.**
трёхсотлети|е (**-я**) *ср* (*срок*) three hundred years; (*годовщина*) tercentenary.
трёхсотлетн|ий (**-яя, -ее, -ие**) *прил* (*период*) three hundred-year; (*дерево*) three hundred-year-old.
трёхсот|ый (**-ая, -ое, -ые**) *чис* three hundredth.
трёхстах *чис см* **триста.**
трёхсторонн|ий (**-яя, -ее, -ие**) *прил* (*соглашение, союз*) trilateral.
трёхчасовой *прил* (*операция*) three-hour; (*поезд*) three o'clock.
трёш|ка (**-ки**; *gen pl* **-ек**) *ж* (*разг*) three-rouble note.
трещ|ать (**-у, -ишь**) *несов неперех* (*лёд, доски итп*) to crack; (*кузнечики*) to chip; (*пулемёты*) to crackle; (*разг*: *тараторить*) to jabber (on); **у меня ~ит голова** I've got a splitting headache; ~ *(impf)* **по швам** (*также перен*) to be falling apart at the seams.
трещин|а (**-ы**) *ж* (*также перен*) crack; **давать** (**дать** *perf*) **~у** to crack.
трещот|ка (**-ки**; *gen pl* **-ок**) *ж* rattle ◆ *м/ж* (*перен*: *болтун*) chatterbox.
тр|и (**-ёх**; *см* **Table 24**) *чис* three ◆ *нескл* (*ПРОСВЕЩ*) ≈ C (*school mark*); **ей ~ года** she is three (years old); **они живут в доме номер** ~ they live at number three; **около ~ёх** about three; **книга стоит ~ рубля** the book costs three roubles; ~ **с половиной часа** three and a half hours; **сейчас ~ часа** it is three o'clock; **яблоки продаются по ~ штуки** the apples are sold in threes; **делить** (**разделить** *perf*) **что-н на** ~ to divide sth into three.
трибун|а (**-ы**) *ж* platform; (*стадиона*) stand.
трибунал (**-а**) *м* tribunal; **военный** ~ military court.
тривиал|ьный (**-ен, -ьна, -ьно**) *прил* trivial.
тригонометри|я (**-и**) *ж* trigonometry.
тридевять: **за ~ земель** (*ФОЛЬКЛОР*) in far off lands.
тридесят|ый *прил* (*ФОЛЬКЛОР*): **в ~ом государстве** in a far off country.
тридцати *чис см* **тридцать.**
тридцатилети|е (**-я**) *ср* (*срок*) thirty years; (*годовщина события*) thirtieth anniversary.
тридцатилетн|ий (**-яя, -ее, -ие**) *прил* (*период*) thirty-year; (*человек*) thirty-year-old.
тридцат|ый (**-ая, -ое, -ые**) *чис* thirtieth; *см также* **пятидесятый.**
тридцат|ь (**-и**; *как* **пять**; *см* **Table 27**) *чис* thirty; *см также* **пятьдесят.**
трижды *нареч* three times; ~ **два – шесть** three times two is six; **он ~ прав** he's absolutely right.
трико *ср нескл* leotard.
трикотаж (**-а**) *м* (*ткань*) knitted fabric ◆ *собир* (*одежда*) knitwear.
трикотажный *прил* knitted; ~ **магазин** knitwear shop.
трилер (**-а**) *м* thriller.
трилистник (**-а**) *м* trefoil.
триллион (**-а**) *м* trillion.
трилоги|я (**-и**) *ж* trilogy.
тринадцати *чис см* **тринадцать.**
тринадцат|ый (**-ая, -ое, -ые**) *чис* thirteenth; *см также* **пятый.**
тринадцат|ь (**-и**; *как* **пять**; *см* **Table 27**) *чис* thirteen; *см также* **пять.**
трио *ср нескл* trio.
Триполи *м нескл* Tripoli.
триптих (**-а**) *м* triptych.
триста (**трёхсот**; *как* **сто**; *см* **Table 32**) *чис* three hundred; *см также* **сто.**
тритон (**-а**) *м* newt.
триумф (**-а**) *м* triumph.
триумфальный *прил* triumphant; **триумфальная арка** triumphal arch.
трогател|ьный (**-ен, -ьна, -ьно**) *прил* touching.
трога|ть (**-ю**; *perf* **тронуть**) *несов перех* (*также перен*) to touch; (*разг*: *беспокоить*: *вопросами*) to pester; (*подлеж*: *рассказ, событие*) to move ◆ *неперех* (*лошадь, повозка*) to start moving; **улыбка тронула её губы** a smile flickered across her lips; **седина тронула его волосы** his hair was touched with grey
▸ **трогаться** (*perf* **тронуться**) *несов возв* (*поезд*) to move off; (*лёд*) to (begin to) break; **~ся** (**тронуться** *perf*) **в путь** to set off.
тр|ое (**-оих**; *см* **Table 35a**) *чис* three: *см также* **двое.**
троеборь|е (**-я**) *ср* triathlon.
троек *сущ см* **тройка.**

тро́ен *сущ см* **тро́йня.**
троих *чис см* **тро́е.**
тро́иц|а (-ы) *ж* (*также:* **свята́я ~**) the Holy Trinity; (*праздник: также:* **Т~ын день**) ≈ Trinity Sunday; (*разг: о друзьях*) threesome.
тро́|йка (-йки; *gen pl* -ек) *ж* (*цифра, карта*) three; (*ПРОСВЕЩ*) ≈ C (*school mark*); (*лошадей*) troika; (*группа людей*) threesome; (*разг: автобус, трамвай итп*) (number) three (*bus, tram etc*); (*костюм*) three-piece suit.
тройни́к (-а́) *м* (*ЭЛЕК*) (three-way) adaptor.
тройн|о́й *прил* triple; **в ~о́м разме́ре** triple the size; **тройно́й прыжо́к** (*СПОРТ*) triple jump.
тро́|йня (-йни; *gen pl* -ен) *ж* triplets *мн.*
тро́йствен|ный (-ен, -на, -но) *прил* (*связь*) threefold; (*no short form; ПОЛИТ: союз, соглашение*) tripartite.
тройча́тк|а (-и) *ж* (*разг*) *mild painkiller taken for headaches etc.*
тролле́йбус (-а) *м* trolleybus.
тромб (-а) *м* blood clot.
тромбо́з (-а) *м* thrombosis.
тромбо́н (-а) *м* trombone.
трон (-а) *м* throne.
тро́нн|ый *прил*: **~ зал** throne room; **~ая речь** royal address.
тро́н|уть (-у, -ешь) *сов от* **тро́гать**
▸ **тро́нуться** *сов от* **тро́гаться** ◆ *возв*: **~ся (умо́м)** (*разг*) to be (a bit) touched.
троп|а́ (-ы́; *nom pl* -ы) *ж* pathway.
тро́пик (-а) *м*: **се́верный/ю́жный ~** the tropic of Cancer/Capricorn; *см также* **тро́пики.**
тро́пик|и (-ов) the tropics *мн.*
тропи́н|ка (-ки; *gen pl* -ок) *ж* footpath.
тропи́ческ|ий (-ая, -ое, -ие) *прил* tropical.
трос (-а) *м* cable.
тростин|ка (-ки; *gen pl* -ок) *ж* (*камыша*) cane; (*травинка*) stem.
тростни́к (-а́) *м* reed; **са́харный ~** sugar cane.
трост|ь (-и; *gen pl* -е́й) *ж* walking stick.
тротуа́р (-а) *м* pavement (*BRIT*), sidewalk (*US*).
трофе́|й (-я) *м* trophy.
трою́родный *прил*: **~ брат** second cousin (*male*); **трою́родная сестра́** second cousin (*female*).
троя́к|ий (-ая, -ое, -ие; -, -а, -о) *прил* triple.
тру(сь) *итп несов см* **тере́ть(ся).**
труб|а́ (-ы́; *nom pl* -ы) *ж* (*газовая, водосточная итп*) pipe; (*дымовая*) chimney; (*МУЗ*) trumpet; (*АНАТ*): **фалло́пиева ~** Fallopian tube; **в ~у́ вылета́ть (вы́лететь** *perf*) (*разг*) to go to the wall.
труба́ч (-а́) *м* trumpeter.
труб|и́ть (-лю́, -и́шь; *perf* **протруби́ть**) *несов неперех*: **~ в** +*acc* (*МУЗ*) to blow; (*подлеж: труба*) to sound; (*перен: разг*): **~ о** +*prp* to trumpet ◆ *перех* (*сбор, отбой*) to sound.
тру́б|ка (-ки; *gen pl* -ок) *ж* tube; (*курительная*) pipe; (*телефона*) receiver; (*МЕД*) stethoscope; **брать (взять** *perf*) *или* **поднима́ть (подня́ть** *perf*) **~ку** (*ТЕЛ*) to pick up the receiver; **свора́чивать (сверну́ть** *perf*) **что-н в ~ку** to roll sth into a tube.
трублю́ *несов см* **труби́ть.**
тру́бок *сущ см* **тру́бка.**
трубопрово́д (-а) *м* pipeline.
тру́бочек *сущ см* **тру́бочка.**
трубочи́ст (-а) *м* chimney sweep.
тру́боч|ка (-ки; *gen pl* -ек) *ж уменьш от* **тру́бка**; (*КУЛИН*) cream horn.
труд (-а́) *м* work; (*ЭКОН*) labour (*BRIT*), labor (*US*); (*ПРОСВЕЩ*) *home economics and design*; **бескоры́стный ~** labo(u)r of love; **брать (взять** *perf*) **на себя́ ~** +*infin* to take the trouble to do; **без ~а́** without any difficulty; **с (больши́м) ~о́м** with (great) difficulty.
тру́ден *прил см* **тру́дный.**
тру|ди́ться (-жу́сь, -дишься) *несов возв* to work hard; **~** (*impf*) **над** +*instr* to labour (*BRIT*) *или* labor (*US*) over; **не ~ди́тесь писа́ть мне** don't bother to write.
тру́дно *как сказ* it's hard *или* difficult; **у меня́ ~ с деньга́ми** I've got money problems; **мне ~ поня́ть э́то/найти́ вре́мя** I find it hard to understand/to find the time; **(мне) ~ бе́гать/стоя́ть** I have trouble running/standing up; **~ сказа́ть** it's hard to say.
трудновоспиту́ем|ый (-, -а, -о) *прил*: **~ ребёнок** problem child (*мн* children).
труднодосту́п|ный (-ен, -на, -но) *прил* (*горы, место*) hard to get to.
труднопроходи́м|ый (-, -а, -о) *прил* (*дорога*) almost impassable.
тру́дност|ь (-и) *ж* difficulty.
тру́д|ный (-ен, -на́, -но) *прил* difficult.
трудов|о́й *прил* working; **~о́е законода́тельство** employment legislation; **~ы́е дохо́ды** earned income; **~ стаж** working life; **~а́я дисципли́на** discipline in the workplace; **трудова́я кни́жка** employment record book; **трудово́е соглаше́ние** contract (of employment).
трудоём|кий (-кая, -кое, -кие; -ок, -ка, -ко) *прил* labour-intensive (*BRIT*), labor-intensive (*US*).
трудолюби́в|ый (-, -а, -о) *прил* hard-working, industrious.
трудоспосо́бност|ь (-и) *ж* fitness to work; **утра́та ~и** disablement.
трудоспосо́бный *прил* fit to work.
трудотерапи́|я (-и) *ж* occupational therapy.
трудоустро́|ить (-ю, -ишь; *impf* **трудоустра́ивать**) *сов перех* to find work for.
трудоустро́йств|о (-а) *ср* placement.
трудя́щ|ийся (-аяся, -ееся, -иеся) *прил* working ◆ (-егося; *decl like adj*) *м* worker.
тру́женик (-а) *м* worker.

тру́жениц|а (-ы) *ж см* **тру́женик.**
тружу́сь *несов см* **труди́ться.**
труп (-а) *м* corpse; **то́лько че́рез мой ~!** over my dead body!
тру́пп|а (-ы) *ж* (*ТЕАТР*) company.
трус (-а) *м* coward.
тру́сик|и (-ов) *мн* (*женские, детские*) knickers *мн* (*BRIT*), panties *мн* (*US*).
тру́|сить (-шу, -сишь; *perf* **стру́сить**) *несов неперех* to get scared; ~ *(impf)* **перед кем-н** to cower before sb.
тру|си́ть (-шу́, -си́шь) *несов неперех* to trot along ◆ *перех* (*содержимое мешка*) to shake out; (*плоды: с дерева*) to shake.
трусли́в|ый (-, -а, -о) *прил* cowardly.
тру́сост|ь (-и) *ж* cowardice.
трусц|а́ (-ы́) *ж* trot; **бег ~о́й** jogging; **бе́гать** *(impf)* **~о́й** to jog.
трус|ы́ (-о́в) *мн* (*бельё: обычно мужские*) underpants *мн*; (*спортивные*) shorts *мн*.
тру́т|ень (-ня) *м* (*ЗООЛ*) drone; (*перен: человек*) parasite.
трух|а́ (-и́) *ж* dust.
трухля́в|ый (-, -а, -о) *прил* crumbly.
тру́шу *несов см* **тру́сить.**
трушу́ *несов см* **труси́ть.**
трущо́б|а (-ы) *ж* (*бедный район*) slum; (*лесная*) jungle (*fig*).
трюк (-а) *м* trick; (*акробатический*) stunt.
трюка́ч (-а́) *м* (*в цирке*) acrobat; (*мошенник*) fraudster.
трюм (-а) *м* hold (*of ship*).
трюмо́ *ср нескл* dresser (*piece of furniture*).
трю́фел|ь (-я; *nom pl* -я́) *м* (*также конфета*) truffle.
тряпи́чн|ый *прил*: **~ая ку́кла** rag doll.
тря́п|ка (-ки; *gen pl* -ок) *ж* (*половая, для пыли*) cloth; (*лоскут*) rag; (*перен: разг: о человеке*) drip; **~ки** (*разг: пренебр*) rags.
тряпь|ё (-я́) *ср собир* rags *мн*.
тряси́н|а (-ы) *ж* quagmire; (*перен*) mire.
тря́с|кий (-кая, -кое, -кие; -ок, -ка, -ко) *прил* (*вагон, машина*) rickety; (*дорога*) bumpy.
трясогу́з|ка (-ки; *gen pl* -ок) *ж* wagtail.
тря́сок *прил см* **тря́ский.**
тряс|ти́ (-у́, -ёшь) *несов перех* to shake; (*perf* **вы́трясти**; *ковёр, мешок*) to shake down; ~ *(impf)* +*instr* (*головой, кулаком*) to shake; (*гривой*) to toss; **в маши́не ~ёт** the car is jolting; **его́ ~ёт от стра́ха** he's shaking with fear
▸ **трясти́сь** *несов возв* (*машина*) to jolt; (*разг: в машине, в поезде итп*) to rattle along; **~сь** *(impf)* **пе́ред** +*instr* (*перед начальством*) to tremble before; **~сь** *(impf)* **над** +*instr* (*разг: над ребёнком, над деньгами*) to fret over *или* about; **~сь** *(impf)* **от сме́ха/стра́ха/хо́лода** to shake with laughter/fear/cold.
тряхн|у́ть (-у́, -ёшь) *сов перех* to shake; ~ *(perf)* **старино́й** (*разг*) to turn the clock back.
т/с *сокр* (= **теку́щий счёт**) C/A (= *current account*).
т/счёт *сокр* = **т/с.**
тт *сокр* = *тома́*.
т.т. *сокр* = *това́рищи*.
ТУ *м сокр* = *самолёт констру́кции А.Н.Ту́полева.*
Ту *м сокр* = **ТУ**
туале́т (-а) *м* toilet; (*гардероб*) outfit.
туале́тн|ый *прил*: **~ая бума́га** toilet paper; **туале́тное мы́ло** toilet soap; **туале́тные принадле́жности** toiletries; **туале́тный сто́лик** dressing table.
туберкулёз (-а) *м* TB, tubercolosis.
туберкулёзный *прил* TB, tubercolosis *опред*.
ту́го *нареч* tightly; (*набить*) tight ◆ *как сказ* (*разг*): **(у нас) ~ с деньга́ми** money is tight (for us); **(у нас) ~ со вре́менем** we're hard-pressed for time; **дела́ иду́т** ~ (*разг*) things aren't going too well.
тугоду́м (-а) *м* dimwit.
туг|о́й (-, -а́, -о) *прил* (*струна, пружина*) taut; (*узел, одежда*) tight; (*чемодан*) tightly-packed; (*кошелёк*) bulging; **он туг на́ ухо** (*разг*) he's a bit hard of hearing.
туда́ *нареч* there; **~ и обра́тно** there and back; **биле́т ~ и обра́тно** return (*BRIT*) *или* round-trip (*US*) ticket; **ни ~ ни сюда́!** (*разг*) it won't budge!; **~ ему́ и доро́га** (*разг*) that's the best place for him; **он тако́й молодо́й, а ~ же, командуе́т** (*разг*) he is so young, and look at him ordering everyone around.
туда́-сюда́ *нареч* all over the place; (*раскачиваться*) backwards and forwards ◆ *как сказ* (*разг*) it's so-so.
ту́же *сравн прил от* **туго́й** ◆ *сравн нареч от* **ту́го.**
туж|и́ть (-у́, -ишь) *несов неперех*: ~ **(о** +*prp*) to pine (for).
туз (-а́) *м* (*финансовый, городской*) bigwig.
тузе́м|ец (-ца) *м* native.
тузе́м|ка (-ки; *gen pl* -ок) *ж см* **тузе́мец.**
тузе́мный *прил* (*население, обычай*) native *опред*.
тузе́мок *сущ см* **тузе́мка.**
тузе́мца *итп сущ см* **тузе́мец.**
тук *межд* knock.
ту́ловищ|е (-а) *ср* torso.
тулу́п (-а) *м* (*овчинный*) sheepskin coat.
тума́к (-а́) *м* (*разг*) thump, whack.
тума́н (-а; *part gen* -у) *м* mist; (*перен: в голове*) haze.
тума́нен *прил см* **тума́нный.**
тума́н|ить (*3sg* -ит, *3pl* -ят *perf* **затума́нить**); *несов перех* (*подлеж: дым, дождь*) to obscure; **слёзы затума́нили ей глаза́** her eyes were misty with tears; **вино́ затума́нило мне го́лову** the wine has addled my brain
▸ **тума́ниться** (*perf* **затума́ниться**) *несов возв* to become shrouded in mist; (*перен: глаза*) to mist over; (*: лицо*) to cloud.
тума́нност|ь (-и) *ж* (*АСТРОНОМИЯ*) nebula; (*перен: в мыслях, в изложении*) cloudiness.

тума́н|ный (**-ен, -на, -но**) *прил* (*воздух, утро*) misty; (*перен*: *взгляд*) dull; (: *смысл, объяснение*) nebulous.
ту́мб|а (**-ы**) *ж* (*причальная, уличная*) bollard; (*для цветов*) stand; (*для скульптуры, стола*) pedestal; **афи́шная ~** *cylindrical advertising hoarding*.
ту́мблер (**-а**) *м* (*КОМП*) toggle switch.
ту́мбоч|ка (**-ки**; *gen pl* **-ек**) *ж уменьш от* **ту́мба**; (*мебель*) bedside cabinet.
ту́ндр|а (**-ы**) *ж* tundra.
ту́ндровый *прил* tundra *опред*.
тун|е́ц (**-ца́**) *м* tuna (fish).
тунея́д|ец (**-ца**) *м* parasite (*fig*).
тунея́дств|о (**-а**) *ср* parasitism.
тунея́дца *итп сущ см* **тунея́дец**.
Туни́с (**-а**) *м* (*город*) Tunis; (*страна*) Tunisia.
туни́сск|ий (**-ая, -ое, -ие**) *прил* Tunisian.
тунне́л|ь (**-я**) *м* = **тонне́ль**.
тунца́ *итп сущ см* **туне́ц**.
тупе́|ть (**-ю**) *несов неперех* (*боль*) to become less acute; (*perf* **отупе́ть**; *разг*: *человек*) to become stupid; (*чувства*) to dull.
тупи́к (**-а́**) *м* (*улица*) dead end, cul-de-sac; (*для поездов*) siding; (*перен*: *в переговорах итп*) deadlock; **ста́вить (поста́вить** *perf*) **кого́-н в ~** to stump sb; **стать** (*perf*) **в ~** to be stumped; **заходи́ть (зайти́** *perf*) **в ~** (*переговоры*) to reach a deadlock.
тупико́вый *прил* (*ситуация*) dead-end; (*станция*) at the end of the line.
туп|и́ть (**-лю́, -ишь**; *perf* **затупи́ть**) *несов перех* to blunt
▸ **тупи́ться** (*perf* **затупи́ться**) *несов возв* to become blunt.
тупи́ц|а (**-ы**) *м/ж* (*разг*) dunce.
туплю́(сь) *несов см* **тупи́ть(ся)**.
туп|о́й (**-, -а́, -о**) *прил* (*нож, карандаш*) blunt; (*человек*) stupid; (*боль, ум*) dull; (*покорность, страх*) blind; **тупо́й у́гол** obtuse angle.
ту́пост|ь (**-и**) *ж* (*человека, поведения*) stupidity; (*ума*) dullness.
тур (**-а**) *м* (*конкурса, переговров, выборов*) round; (*в танце*) turn; (*ЗООЛ*) mountain goat.
тур|а́ (**-ы́**) *ж* (*разг*: *в шахматах*) castle.
турби́н|а (**-ы**) *ж* turbine.
туре́цк|ий (**-ая, -ое, -ие**) *прил* Turkish; **~ язы́к** Turkish.
тури́зм (**-а**) *м* tourism.
тури́ст (**-а**) *м* tourist; (*в походе*) hiker.
туристи́ческ|ий (**-ая, -ое, -ие**) *прил* tourist *опред*.
тури́стск|ий (**-ая, -ое, -ие**) *прил* tourist's; **~ маршру́т** trail; **~ое снаряже́ние** *camping and walking equipment*.
ту́рка *итп сущ см* **ту́рок**.
туркме́н (**-а**) *м* Turkmen.
Туркме́ни|я (**-и**) *ж* Turkmenia.
туркме́н|ка (**-ки**; *gen pl* **-ок**) *ж см* **туркме́н**.
туркме́нск|ий (**-ая, -ое, -ие**) *прил* Turkmenian.
турне́ *ср нескл* (*ТЕАТР, СПОРТ*) tour.
турне́пс (**-а**) *м* turnip.
турни́к (**-а́**) *м* horizontal bar.
турнике́т (**-а**) *м* turnstile.
турни́р (**-а**) *м* tournament.
ту́р|ок (**-ка**) *м* Turk.
Ту́рци|я (**-и**) *ж* Turkey.
турча́н|ка (**-ки**; *gen pl* **-ок**) *ж см* **ту́рок**.
ту́скл|ый (**-, -а́, -о**) *прил* (*стекло*) opaque; (*лак, краска, позолота*) matt; (*свет, стиль, взгляд*) dull.
тускне́|ть (*3sg* **-ет**, *3pl* **-ют**, *perf* **потускне́ть**) *несов неперех* (*краска, талант*) to fade; (*серебро, позолота, краски*) to tarnish.
тут *нареч* here; **что ~ говори́ть!** (*разг*) what is there to say?; **я ~ ни при чём** it has nothing to do with me; **и всё ~** (*разг*) and that's that; **он уже́ ~ как ~** (*разг*) right at that moment he appeared; **не ~-то бы́ло** (*разг*) it wasn't to be.
ту́тов|ый *прил*: **~ое де́рево** mulberry tree; **ту́товый шелкопря́д** silkworm.
ту́фл|я (**-ли**; *nom pl* **-ли**, *gen pl* **-ель**) *ж* (*обычно мн*) shoe.
ту́хл|ый (**-, -а́, -о**) *прил* (*еда*) rotten; (*запах*) putrid.
ту́х|нуть (*3sg* **-нет**, *3pl* **-нут**, *pt* **-, -ла, -ло**, *perf* **поту́хнуть**) *несов неперех* (*костёр, свет, свеча*) to go out; (*perf* **проту́хнуть**; *мясо, рыба*) to go off.
ту́ч|а (**-и**) *ж* rain cloud; (*перен*: *мух, стрел*) cloud; **он сего́дня, как ~** he's been in a black mood all day.
ту́ч|ный (**-ен, -на́, -но**) *прил* (*человек*) stout; (*почва*) fertile; (*трава, луга*) lush.
туш (**-а**) *м* (*МУЗ*) flourish.
ту́ш|а (**-и**) *ж* carcass; (*разг*: *о тучном человеке*) hulk.
туш|ева́ть (**-у́ю**; *perf* **затушева́ть**) *несов перех* (*рисунок, фотографию*) to shade in; (*перен*: *разницу, противоречия*) to gloss over.
туш|ева́ться (**-у́юсь**) *несов от* **стушева́ться**.
тушён|ка (**-ки**; *gen pl* **-ок**) *ж* (*разг*) tinned (*BRIT*) *или* canned meat.
тушёный *прил* (*кулин*) braised.
туш|и́ть (**-у́, -ишь**; *perf* **затуши́ть** *или* **потуши́ть**) *несов перех* (*свечу, костёр, пожар*) to put out; (*perf* **потуши́ть**; *свет*) to put out; (*КУЛИН*) to braise.
тушка́нчик (**-а**) *м* jerboa.
туш|ь (**-и**) *ж* (*для рисования*) Indian ink; (*для ресниц*) mascara.
ту́|я (**-и**) *ж* red cedar.
т/х *сокр* = **теплохо́д**.
тчк *сокр* = **то́чка**.
тща́тел|ьный (**-ен, -ьна, -ьно**) *прил* thorough.
тщеду́ш|ный (**-ен, -на, -но**) *прил* feeble.

тщесла́вен *прил см* **тщесла́вный.**
тщесла́ви|е (**-я**) *ср* vanity.
тщесла́в|ный (**-ен, -на, -но**) *прил* vain.
тщётен *прил см* **тщётный.**
тщётност|ь (**-и**) *ж* futility.
тщёт|ный (**-ен, -на, -но**) *прил* futile.
ты (**тебя́**; *см* **Table 5a**) *мест* you; (*разг*: *для усиления*): **ах ~, кака́я жа́лость!** oh, what a pity!; **быть** *(impf)* **с кем-н на ~** to be on familiar terms with sb; **вот тебе́ раз!** good grief!
ты́|кать (**-чу, -чешь**; *perf* **ткнуть**) *несов перех* (*разг*: *ударять*): **тыка́ть что-н/кого́-н чем-н** to poke sth/sb with sth; (: *вонзать*): **тыка́ть что-н в** *+acc* to stick sth into; (: *обращаться на „ты"*) *to address somebody using the informal form of "you"*; **~** *(impf)* **кого́-н но́сом во что-н** (*разг*) to rub sb's face in sth; **~** (**ткнуть** *perf*) **па́льцем на** *+acc* (*разг*) to point at
▸ **ты́каться** (*perf* **ткну́ться**) *несов возв* (*разг*: *суетливо двигаться*) to rush about; **~ся** (**ткну́ться** *perf*) **в** *+acc* (*в стену, в дверь итп*) to bang into; (*соваться*) to nuzzle.
тыкв|а (**-ы**) *ж* pumpkin.
тыл (**-а**; *loc sg* **-у́**, *nom pl* **-ы́**) *м* (*ВОЕН*: *сторона, территория*) the rear; (: *вся страна*) the home front; (: *воинские организации*) rear units.
тылово́й *прил* (*ВОЕН*) rear.
ты́льн|ый *прил* back; **~ая часть руки́** the back of one's hand.
тыс. *сокр* = **ты́сяча.**
ты́сяч|а (**-и**; *см* **Table 35**) *ж чис* thousand.
тысячеле́ти|е (**-я**) *ср* millenium; (*годовщина*) thousandth anniversary.
тысячеле́тн|ий (**-яя, -ее, -ие**) *прил* (*период*) thousand-year; (*дерево*) thousand-year-old.
ты́сячи *чис см* **ты́сяча.**
ты́сячн|ая (**-ой**; *decl like adj*) *ж*: **одна́ ~** one thousandth.
ты́сячн|ый (**-ая, -ое, -ие**) *чис* thousandth; (*толпа, армия*) of many thousands.
ты́сячу *чис см* **ты́сяча.**
тычи́нк|а (**-ки**; *gen pl* **-ок**) *ж* stamen.
ты́чу(сь) *итп несов см* **ты́кать(ся).**
тьм|а (**-ы**) *ж* (*мрак*) darkness, gloom; (*множество*) swarm.
тьфу *межд* yuk.
ТЭС *ж сокр* = *теплоэлектроста́нция.*
ТЭЦ *ж сокр* = *теплоэлектроцентра́ль.*
тюбете́|йка (**-йки**; *gen pl* **-ек**) *ж* skullcap (*worn in Central Asia*).
тю́бик (**-а**) *м* tube.
ТЮЗ (**-а**) *м сокр* (= *теа́тр ю́ного зри́теля*) youth theatre (*BRIT*) *или* theater (*US*).
тюз (**-а**) *м сокр* = **ТЮЗ.**
тюк (**-а́**) *м* bale.
тю́левый *прил* tulle.
тюле́н|ь (**-я**) *м* (*ЗООЛ*) seal.
тюл|ь (**-я**) *м* tulle.
тюльпа́н (**-а**) *м* tulip.
тюрба́н (**-а**) *м* turban.
тюре́мный *прил* prison *опред*; **тюре́мное заключе́ние** imprisonment.
тюрьм|а́ (**-ы́**) *ж* prison; **сажа́ть** (**посади́ть** *perf*) **кого́-н в ~у́** to put sb in prison.
тюфя́к (**-а́**) *м* straw mattress; (*разг*: *о человеке*) wimp.
тя́вка|ть (**-ю**) *несов неперех* to yap.
тя́вкн|уть (**-у, -ешь**) *сов неперех* to yap.
тя́г|а (**-и**) *ж* (*в печи*) draught (*BRIT*), draft (*US*); (*насоса, пылесоса*) suction; (*ТЕХ*) traction; (*реактивная*) thrust; **~ к** *+dat* (*перен*) attraction to; **на электри́ческой ~е** powered by electricity; **на ко́нной ~е** horse-drawn.
тяга́|ться (**-юсь**; *perf* **потяга́ться**) *несов возв* (*разг*): **~ с кем-н** (**в** *+prp*) to compete with sb (in); **~** (**потяга́ться** *perf*) **с кем-н умо́м** to pit one's wits against sb.
тяга́ч (**-а́**) *м* tractor.
тя́гост|ный (**-ен, -на, -но**) *прил* burdensome; (*впечатления*) depressing.
тя́гост|ь (**-и**) *ж* (*ожидания, зависимости*) burden; (*обычно мн*: *войны, бедности*) hardship; (*на сердце, на душе*) heavy feeling; **быть** *(impf)* **в ~ кому́-н** to be a burden to sb.
тяготе́ни|е (**-я**) *ср* (*ФИЗ*) gravity; (*перен*): **~ к** *+dat* attraction to.
тяготе́|ть (**-ю**) *несов неперех*: **~ к** *+dat* (*к культуре, к прогрессу, к общению*) to gravitate *или* be drawn towards; (*к мнению*) to tend towards; (*перен*): **~ над** *+instr* (*обвинение, подозрение*) to hang over; (*чья-н власть, воля*) to oppress.
тяго|ти́ть (**-щу́, -ти́шь**) *несов перех* to weigh (heavy) on
▸ **тяготи́ться** *несов возв* (*+instr*) to be weighed down by.
тя́гот|ы (**-**) *мн* hardships *мн.*
тягощу́(сь) *несов см* **тяготи́ть(ся).**
тягу́ч|ий (**-ая, -ее, -ие; -, -а, -е**) *прил* (*клей, краска итп*) viscous; (*резинка, ткань*) stretchy; (*перен*: *речь, голос*) droning.
тя́жб|а (**-ы**) *ж* dispute.
тя́жек *прил см* **тя́жкий.**
тяжеле́|ть (**-ю**; *perf* **отяжеле́ть** *или* **потяжеле́ть**) *несов неперех* to get heavier; (*голова, ноги*: *от усталости*) to grow heavy.
тяжело́ *нареч* heavily; (*больной, раненый*) seriously ♦ *как сказ* (*нести*) it's heavy; (*понять, согласиться*) it's hard; **мне ~ здесь** I find it hard here; **больно́му ~** the patient is suffering.
тяжелоатле́т (**-а**) *м* weightlifter.
тяжелоатлети́ческ|ий (**-ая, -ое, -ие**) *прил*: **~ие соревнова́ния** weightlifting competiton.
тяжелове́с (**-а**) *м* (*СПОРТ*) heavyweight.
тяжелове́с|ный *прил* (**-ен, -на, -но**; *перен*: *речь, шутка, стиль*) laboured (*BRIT*), labored (*US*); (*архитектура*) heavy; **~ по́езд** freight train.
тяж|ёлый (**-ёл, -ела́, -ело́**) *прил* heavy; (*трудный*: *труд, обязанность, дорога итп*) hard, tough; (*сон*) restless; (*запах*) thick;

(*воздух*) close; (*преступление, болезнь, рана*) serious; (*горестный*: *зрелище, день трудный*) grim; (*мрачный*: *мысли, настроение*) sombre (*BRIT*), somber (*US*); (*no short form*; *трудный*: *человек, характер*) difficult; **с ~ёлым сердцем** with a heavy heart; **тяжёлая атлетика** weightlifting; **тяжёлая промышленность** heavy industry.

тяжест|ь (**-и**) *ж* heaviness, weight; (*работы, задачи*) difficulty; (*болезни, раны, преступления*) seriousness, severity; (*обычно мн*: *тяжёлый предмет*) weight; **сила ~и** (*физ*) gravitational pull; **центр ~и** (*физ*) centre of gravity.

тяж|кий (**-кая, -кое, -кие; -ек, -ка́, -ко**) *прил* (*труд*) arduous; (*характер*) oppressive; (*зрелище*) grim; (*сомнения, подозрение, преступление*) grave.

тян|у́ть (**-у́, -ешь**) *несов перех* (*канат, сеть итп*) to pull; (*вытягивать*: *шею, руку*) to stretch out; (*дело, разговор, заседание*) to drag out; (*напиток*) to sip (at); (*perf* **протяну́ть**; *трубопровод, кабель*) to lay; (*perf* **вытянуть**; *жребий, номер*) to draw ◆ *неперех*: **~ с** *+instr* (*с ответом, с решением*) to delay; (*разг*): **~ на** *+acc* (*на килограмм итп*) to weigh; **~ (потяну́ть** *perf*) **кого́-н за́ руку** to pull at sb's arm; **~** (*impf*) **кого́-н в кино́** to tempt sb out to the cinema; **меня́ тя́нет в Петербу́рг** I want to go to Petersburg; **меня́ тя́нет ко сну** I'm feeling drowsy; **он не тя́нет на ли́дера** he is not leadership material

▸ **тяну́ться** *несов возв* to stretch; (*заседание, дни, зима итп*) to drag on; (*дым, запах*) to waft; **~ся** (*impf*) **к** *+dat* to be attracted *или* drawn to; **он тя́нется к зна́ниям** he has a thirst for knowledge; **~ся** (*impf*) **за кем-н** to try to keep up with sb.

тяну́ч|ка (**-ки**; *gen pl* **-ек**) *ж* toffee.

тя́п|ка (**-ки**; *gen pl* **-ок**) *ж* hoe.

тяп-ля́п *нареч* (*разг*: *пренебр*): **де́лать что-н ~** to do sth in a slapdash way.

тя́пн|уть (**-у, -ешь**) *сов неперех* (*разг*: *укусить*) to nip.

тя́пок *сущ см* **тя́пка**.

~ У, у ~

У, у *сущ нескл* (*буква*) *the 20th letter of the Russian alphabet.*

KEYWORD

у *предл* (*+gen*) **1** (*около*) by; **у окна́/стены́** by the window/wall; **у мо́ря/реки́** by the sea/river; **у вхо́да** at the entrance
2 (*обозначает орудие, место работы*) at; **сиде́ть** (*impf*) **у руля́** to sit at the helm; **стоя́ть** (*impf*) **у станка́** to stand at the workbench
3 (*обозначает обладателя чего-н*): **у меня́ есть дом/де́ти** I have a house/children; **у таких люде́й быва́ют интере́сные иде́и** people like that have interesting ideas; **голова́ у меня́ совсе́м разболе́лась** I have a terrible headache
4 (*обозначает объект, с которым соотносится действие*): **я живу́ у друзе́й** I live with friends; **я учи́лся у него́** I was taught by him
5 (*указывает на источник получения чего-н*) from; **я взял/попроси́л у дру́га де́нег** I got/asked for money from a friend; **мы получи́ли разреше́ние у нача́льства** we got permission from the authorities
◆ *межд* (*выражает угрозу*) hey; (*выражает испуг, восторг*) oh; **у, негодя́й!** hey, you rascal!; **у, как высоко́!** oh, how high it is!; **у, кака́я красота́!** oh, how beautiful!

УАЗ *м сокр = Улья́новский автомоби́льный заво́д*; (*автомобиль*) *vehicle produced at the Ul'ianovskiy car factory.*
уба́в|ить (**-лю, -ишь**; *impf* **убавля́ть**) *сов перех* (*цену, размеры*) to reduce; (*рукава*) to shorten
▸ **уба́виться** (*impf* **убавля́ться**) *сов возв* (*расходы*) to decrease; (*срок*) to be reduced; (*дни*) to get shorter.
убаю́ка|ть (**-ю**) *сов от* **баю́кать**.
убега́|ть (**-ю**) *несов от* **убежа́ть**.
убегу́ *итп сов см* **убежа́ть**.
убеди́тел|ьный (**-ен, -ьна, -ьно**) *прил* (*пример, доказательство*) convincing; (*просьба*) urgent.
убед|и́ть (**-и́шь, -и́т**; *impf* **убежда́ть**) *сов перех*: ~ **кого́-н** *+infin* to persuade sb to do; **убежда́ть** (~ *perf*) **кого́-н в чём-н** to convince sb of sth
▸ **убеди́ться** (*impf* **убежда́ться**) *сов возв*: ~**ся в чём-н** to be convinced of sth.
убежа́|ть (*как* **бежа́ть**; *см* **Table 20**; *impf* **убега́ть**) *сов неперех* to run away; **молоко́ ~ло** (*разг*) the milk has boiled over.
убежда́|ть(ся) (**-ю(сь)**) *несов от* **убеди́ть(ся)**.
убежде́ни|е (**-я**) *ср* (*внушение*) assurance; (*взгляд*) conviction; **поддава́ться (подда́ться** *perf*) **~ям** to give in to persuasion.
убеждённост|ь (**-и**) *ж* (*уверенность*) assurance, conviction.
убеждённый (**-ён, -ена́, -ено́**) *прил*: ~ **в** *+prp* convinced of; (**-ён, -ённа, -ённо**; *тон*) assured; (*no short form*; *католик*) convinced.
убежи́шь *итп сов см* **убежа́ть**.
убе́жищ|е (**-а**) *ср* (*от дождя, от бомб*) shelter; **полити́ческое** ~ political asylum.
убелённый *прил*: ~ **седи́нами** silver-haired.
убер|е́чь (**-егу́, -ежёшь** *итп*, **-егу́т**; *pt* **-ёг, -егла́, -егло́**, *impf* **уберега́ть**) *сов перех* to protect
▸ **убере́чься** (*impf* **уберега́ться**) *сов возв* (*от опасности итп*) to protect o.s.; **~ся** (*perf*) **от просту́ды** to avoid catching cold.
уберу́(сь) *итп сов см* **убра́ть(ся)**.
убива́|ть (**-ю**) *несов от* **уби́ть**
▸ **убива́ться** *несов возв* (*разг: страдать*) to grieve; (*: на работе*) to break one's back.
уби́йственный *прил* (*оружие*) deadly; (*новость, результат*) devastating; (*разг: жара, климат*) unbearable.
уби́йств|о (**-а**) *ср* murder.
уби́йц|а (**-ы**) *м/ж* murderer.
убира́|ть(ся) (**-ю(сь)**) *несов от* **убра́ть(ся)**.
уби́т|ая (**-ой**; *decl like adj*) *ж* dead woman (*мн* women).
уби́т|ый *прил* (*перен: лицо*) crushed ◆ (**-ого**; *decl like adj*) *м* dead man (*мн* men); **спит как** ~ (*перен*) he is sleeping like a log.
уб|и́ть (**-ью́, -ьёшь**; *impf* **убива́ть**) *сов перех* to kill; (*совершить преступление*) to murder; (*перен: надежды, инициативу*) to destroy; ~ (*perf*) **вре́мя** (*перен*) to kill time.
ублаж|и́ть (**-у́, -и́шь**; *impf* **ублажа́ть**) *сов перех* (*разг*) to please.
убо́г|ий (**-ая, -ое, -ие**) *прил* (*дом, человек*) wretched; (*перен: идеи, фильм*) mediocre.
убо́жеств|о (**-а**) *ср* (*мыслей, идей*) mediocrity; (*обстановки*) wretchedness.
убо́|й (**-я**) *м* slaughter.
убо́р (**-а**) *м*: **головно́й** ~ hat.
убо́рист|ый (**-, -а, -о**) *прил* (*почерк, печать*) close, dense.
убо́рк|а (**-и**) *ж* (*помещения*) cleaning;

занимáться (заня́ться *perf*) **~** to do the cleaning; **~ урожáя** harvest.
убóрн|ая (-ой; *decl like adj*) *ж* (*артистическая*) dressing-room; (*туалет*) toilet, lavatory.
убóрочн|ый *прил* harvesting *опред*; **~ая машúна** harvester.
убóрщик (-а) *м* cleaner.
убóрщиц|а (-и) *ж см* **убóрщик**.
убр|áть (уберý, уберёшь; *pt* **-áл, -алá, -áло,** *impf* **убирáть)** *сов перех* (*унести: вещи*) to take away, remove; (*поместить*) to put away; (*паруса, якорь*) to stow; (*шасси*) to retract, draw in; (*комнату*) to tidy; (*разг: параграф: из текста*) to remove; (*урожай*) to gather in; **убирáть (~** *perf*) **со столá** to clear the table
▸ **убрáться** (*impf* **убирáться)** *сов возв* (*разг: удалиться*) to get out; (*сделать уборку*) to clear *или* tidy up; **убирáйся отсю́да!** get lost!
убу́ду *итп сов см* **убы́ть**.
убывá|ть (-ю) *несов от* **убы́ть**.
у́был|ь (-и) *ж* (*рабочей силы*) decrease; **идтú (пойтú** *perf*) **на ~** (*дни*) to get shorter; (*болезнь, эпидемия*) to run its course.
убы́т|ок (-ка) *м* loss; **терпéть** (*impf*) *или* **нестú** (*impf*) **~ки** to incur losses.
убы́точ|ный (-ен, -на, -но) *прил* unprofitable.
убы́ть (*как* **быть**; *см* **Table 21**; *impf* **убывáть)** *сов неперех* to decrease; **егó от э́того не убу́дет** he won't be any worse off for it.
убью́ *итп сов см* **убúть**.
уважáем|ый *прил* respected, esteemed; **У~ые дáмы и господá!** Ladies and Gentlemen!
уважá|ть (-ю) *несов перех* to respect.
уважéни|е (-я) *ср* respect.
уважúтел|ьный (-ен, -ьна, -ьно) *прил* (*отношение*) respectful; (*довод, причина*) respectable.
увáж|ить (-у, -ишь) *сов перех* (*угодить*) to humour (BRIT), humor (US); **~** (*perf*) **чью-н прóсьбу** to grant sb's request.
у́вал|ень (-ьня) *м* lumbering oaf.
ув|арúться (*3sg* **-áрится,** *3pl* **-áрятся,** *impf* **увáриваться)** *сов возв* (*сироп, щи*) to boil down, reduce.
УВД *ср сокр* (= *Управлéние вну́тренних дел*) *administration of internal affairs within a town or region.*
увéдом|ить (-лю, -ишь; *impf* **уведомля́ть)** *сов перех* to inform.
уведомлéни|е (-я) *ср* (*документ*) notification.
увéдомлю *сов см* **увéдомить**.
уведомля́|ть (-ю) *несов от* **увéдомить**.
уведу́ *итп сов см* **увестú**.
увез|тú (-у́, -ёшь; *pt* **увёз, увезлá, увезлó,** *impf* **увозúть)** *сов перех* to take away.
увековéч|ить (-у, -ишь) *сов перех* (*героя*) to immortalize.
увеличéни|е (-я) *ср* increase.
увелúчива|ть(ся) (-ю(сь)) *несов от* **увелúчить(ся)**.
увеличúтельн|ый *прил*: **~ое стеклó** magnifying glass.
увелúч|ить (-у, -ишь; *impf* **увелúчивать)** *сов перех* to increase; (*фотографию*) to enlarge
▸ **увелúчиться** (*impf* **увелúчиваться)** *сов возв* to increase, be increased.
увенчá|ться (-юсь) *сов возв*: **~ успéхом** to result in success.
увéренност|ь (-и) *ж* confidence; **~ в себé** self-confidence; **поколебáть** (*perf*) **чью-н ~ в чём-н/в том, что ...** to shake sb's conviction in sth/that ...; **я был в пóлной ~и, что ...** I was absolutely sure that ....
увéрен|ный (-, -на, -но, -ы) *прил* (*шаг, ответ, голос*) confident; (*рука*) sure; **~ в** *+prp* sure of; **~ в себé** self-confident, sure of o.s.
увéр|ить (-ю, -ишь) *сов от* **уверя́ть**.
уверн|у́ться (-у́сь, -ёшься; *impf* **увёртываться)** *сов возв* to swerve; **увёртываться (~** *perf*) **от удáра** to dodge a blow; **увёртываться (~** *perf*) **от пря́мого отвéта** to avoid giving a straight answer.
увéр|овать (-ую) *сов неперех*: **~ в** *+acc* to (come to) believe in.
увёртлив|ый (-, -а, -о) *прил* (*подвижный*) nimble; (*перен: хитрый*) evasive.
увёртыва|ться (-юсь) *несов от* **увернýться**.
увертю́р|а (-ы) *ж* overture.
уверя́|ть (-ю; *perf* **увéрить)** *несов перех*: **~ когó-н/что-н (в чем-н)** to assure sb/sth (of sth); **~ю Вас, что я был прóтив э́того** I assure you that I was against it.
увеселúтельн|ый *прил* (*зрелище*) entertaining; **~ая прогу́лка** jaunt.
увéсист|ый (-, -а, -о) *прил* heavy.
уве|стú (-ду́, -дёшь; *pt* **-ёл, -елá, -елó,** *impf* **уводúть)** *сов перех* to lead off *или* away; (*разг: похитить*) to nick.
увéчь|е (-я) *ср* injury; **наносúть (нанестú** *perf*) **комý-н ~** to maim sb; **получáть (получúть** *perf*) **~** to be maimed.
увéша|ть (-ю; *impf* **увéшивать)** *сов перех*: **~ когó-н/что-н чем-н** to cover sb/sth with sth.
увещевá|ть (-ю) *несов перех* to exhort.
увивá|ться (-юсь) *несов возв* (*ухаживать*): **~ (за кем-н)** (*за женщиной*) to hang around (sb).
увú|деть (-жу, -дишь) *сов от* **вúдеть** ◆ *перех* to catch sight of
▸ **увúдеться** *сов от* **вúдеться**.
увильн|у́ть (-у́, -ёшь) *сов неперех*: **~ от** *+gen* (*разг*) to dodge; (*от ответственности*) to get *или* wriggle out of.
увлажн|úть (-ю́, -úшь; *impf* **увлажня́ть)** *сов перех* to moisten
▸ **увлажнúться** (*impf* **увлажня́ться)** *сов возв* to become moist.

увлёк(ся) *итп сов см* **увле́чь(ся)**.
увлека́тел|ьный *прил* (*захватывающий*) absorbing; (**-ен, -ьна, -ьно**; *занимательный*) entertaining.
увлека́|ть(ся) (**-ю(сь)**) *несов от* **увле́чь(ся)**.
увлека́ющ|ийся (**-аяся, -ееся, -иеся**) *прил* easily carried away.
увлеку́(сь) *итп сов см* **увле́чь(ся)**.
увлече́ни|е (**-я**) *ср* (*влюблённость*) infatuation; ~ (*+instr*) (*работой, балетом*) enthusiasm *или* passion (for).
увл|е́чь (**-еку́, -ечёшь** *итп*, **-еку́т**; *pt* **-ёк, -екла́, -екло́**, *impf* **увлека́ть**) *сов перех* to lead away; (*перен*) to captivate
▸ **увле́чься** (*impf* **увлека́ться**) *сов возв*: **~ся** *+instr* to get carried away with; (*влюбиться*) to fall for; (*шахматами итп*) to become keen on.
ув|оди́ть (**-ожу́, -о́дишь**) *несов от* **увести́**.
ув|ози́ть (**-ожу́, -о́зишь**) *несов от* **увезти́**.
увола́кива|ть (**-ю**) *несов от* **уволо́чь**.
уво́л|ить (**-ю, -ишь**; *impf* **увольня́ть**) *сов перех* (*с работы*) to dismiss, sack; **увольня́ть** (**~** *perf*) **в запа́с** to transfer to the reserve
▸ **уво́литься** (*impf* **увольня́ться**) *сов возв*: **~ся с рабо́ты** to leave one's job.
уволо́|чь (**-ку́, -чёшь** *итп*, **-ку́т**; *pt* **-к, -кла́, -кло́**, *impf* **увола́кивать**) *сов перех* to drag away *или* off; (*разг*: *украсть*) to nick.
увольне́ни|е (**-я**) *ср* (*со службы*) dismissal; (*ВОЕН*) leave.
увольни́тельн|ая (**-ой**; *decl like adj*) *ж* (*ВОЕН*) leave-pass.
увольня́|ть(ся) (**-ю(сь)**) *несов от* **уво́лить(ся)**.
УВЧ *сокр* (= *ультравысо́кая частота́*) UHF (= *ultrahigh frequency*) ◆ *прил сокр* (*ультравысокочасто́тный*) UHF (= *ultrahigh-frequency*).
увы́ *межд* alas.
увяда́ни|е (**-я**) *ср* (*цветов*) withering; (*красоты*) fading.
увя́дш|ий (**-ая, -ее, -ие**) *прил* (*цветок*) withered; (*красота*) faded.
ув|яза́ть (**-яжу́, -я́жешь**; *impf* **увя́зывать**) *сов перех* (*вещи*) to tie up; (*перен*: *согласовать*) to tie in
▸ **увяза́ться** *сов возв* (*разг*): **~ся** (**за** *+instr*) to tag along (behind).
увя́зн|уть (**-у, -ешь**) *сов от* **вя́знуть**.
увя́зыва|ть (**-ю**) *несов от* **увяза́ть**.
увя́н|уть (**-у, -ешь**) *сов от* **вя́нуть**.
угада́|ть (**-ю**; *impf* **уга́дывать**) *сов перех* to guess.
Уга́нд|а (**-ы**) *ж* Uganda.
уга́р (**-а**) *м* (*воздух*) fume-filled air; (*отравление*) carbon-monoxide poisoning; **пья́ный** ~ drunken haze.
уга́рный *прил*: ~ **дым** poisonous smoke; **уга́рный газ** carbon monoxide.
угаса́|ть (**-ю**; *perf* **уга́снуть**) *несов неперех* (*костёр, закат*) to die down.
уга́сн|уть (**-у, -ешь**) *сов от* **га́снуть**.
угла́ *итп сущ см* **у́гол**.
углево́д (**-а**) *м* carbohydrate.
углеводоро́д (**-а**) *м* hydrocarbon.
углекислот|а́ (**-ы́**) *ж* carbon dioxide.
углеки́слый *прил*: ~ **газ** carbon dioxide.
углепромы́шленност|ь (**-и**) *ж* coal industry.
углеро́д (**-а**) *м* (*ХИМ*) carbon.
углова́тост|ь (**-и**) *ж* (*лица*) angularity; (*человека, движений*) awkwardnes.
углова́тый *прил* (*лицо*) angular; (*человек, движения*) awkward.
углово́й *прил* corner *опред*; (*также*: ~ **уда́р**: *СПОРТ*) corner.
углуб|и́ть (**-лю́, -и́шь**; *impf* **углубля́ть**) *сов перех* to deepen
▸ **углуби́ться** (*impf* **углубля́ться**) *сов возв* (*также перен*) to deepen; **углубля́ться** (**~ся** *perf*) **в** *+acc* (*в книгу, в чтение*) to become absorbed in; **~ся** (*perf*) **в воспомина́ния/мы́сли** to become lost in memories/thought; **~ся** (*perf*) **в лес** to go deep into the forest.
углубле́ни|е (**-я**) *ср* (*кризиса*) deepening; (*впадина*) depression.
углубл|ённый (**-ён, -ена́, -ено́**) *прил* profound.
углублю́(сь) *сов см* **углуби́ть(ся)**.
углубля́|ть(ся) (**-ю(сь)**) *несов от* **углуби́ть(ся)**.
угля́ *итп сущ см* **у́голь**.
угля|де́ть (**-жу́, -ди́шь**) *сов перех* (*разг*: *увидеть*) to spot.
угн|а́ть (**угоню́, уго́нишь**; *pt* **-а́л, -ала́, -а́ло**, *impf* **угоня́ть**) *сов перех* to drive off; (*разг*: *украсть*) to steal; (*самолёт*) to hijack
▸ **угна́ться** *сов возв*: **~ся за** *+instr* (*также перен*) to catch up with.
угнета́тел|ь (**-я**) *м* oppressor.
угнета́|ть (**-ю**) *несов перех* (*притеснять*) to oppress; (*тяготить*) to depress.
угнете́ни|е (**-я**) *ср* (*народа*) oppression.
угнетённост|ь (**-и**) *ж* depression.
угнетённый *прил* (*народ*) oppressed; (*МЕД*) depressed.
угова́рива|ть (**-ю**) *несов от* **уговори́ть** ◆ *перех* to try to persuade.
угово́р (**-а**) *м* (*обычно мн*: *наставление*) persuasion; (*соглашение*) agreement, arrangement; **поддава́ться** (**подда́ться** *perf*) **на ~ы** to give in to persuasion.
уговор|и́ть (**-ю́, -и́шь**; *impf* **угова́ривать**) *сов перех* to persuade.
уго́д|а (**-ы**) *ж*: **в ~у кому́-н** to please sb.
уго́ден *прил см* **уго́дный**.
уго|ди́ть (**-жу́, -ди́шь**; *impf* **угожда́ть**) *сов неперех*: ~ *+dat*/**на** *+acc* to please; (*попасть*) to end up; ~ (*perf*) **под маши́ну** to get run over; ~ (*perf*) **ного́й в я́му** to put one's foot in a hole.
уго́длив|ый (**-, -а, -о**) *прил* obsequious.
уго́дник (**-а**) *м* (*РЕЛ*) saint; **да́мский** ~ ladies' man.
уго́днича|ть (**-ю**) *несов неперех*: ~ (**пе́ред**

+*instr*) to fawn (on).

угóдно *част*: **что ~** whatever you like ♦ *как сказ*: **что Вам ~?** what can I do for you?; **кто ~** anyone; **когдá/какóй ~** whenever/whichever you like; **скóлько ~** any amount; **комý ~ начáть?** who would like to start?; **возьмите всё, что Вам ~** take whatever you like; **от них мóжно ожидáть чегó ~** they might do anything.

угóд|ный (-ен, -на, -но) *прил* (+*dat*; *родителям, властям*) pleasing to.

угóд|ья (-ий) *мн*: **земéльные ~** arable and pasture land; **лéсные ~** forestry; **вóдные ~** fisheries and waterways.

угождá|ть (-ю) *несов от* **угодить.**

угожý *сов см* **угодить.**

ýг|ол (-лá; *loc sg* **-лý)** *м* (*ГЕОМ*) angle; (*стола, дома, комнаты*) corner; **заворáчивать (завернýть** *perf*) **зá угол** to turn the corner; **за углóм** round the corner; **из-за углá** from around the corner; **~ зрéния** perspective, standpoint; **он снимáет ~** he's renting a tiny little place.

уголкá *сущ см* **уголóк.**

уголóвник (-а) *м* criminal.

уголóвный *прил* criminal *опред*; **уголóвный кóдекс** criminal code; **уголóвный престýпник** criminal; **уголóвный рóзыск** Criminal Investigation Department.

уголóвщин|а (-ы) *ж* (*разг*) crime.

угол|óк (-кá) *м уменьш от* **ýгол**; (*место*) corner; **тúхий ~** secluded spot.

ýг|оль (-ля́; *nom pl* **-ли,** *gen pl* **-лей)** *м* coal.

угóльник (-а) *м* (*чертёжный*) set square.

ýгольный *прил* coal.

угомон|и́ться (-ю́сь, -и́шься) *сов возв* (*разг*) to quieten down.

угóн (-а) *м* (*самолёта*) hijacking; (*машины, коня*) theft.

угóнщик (-а) *м* (*самолёта*) hijacker.

угоню́(сь) *итп сов см* **угнáть(ся).**

угоня́|ть (-ю) *несов от* **угнáть.**

угорáзд|ить (3*sg* **-ит)** *сов безл*: **~ило тебя́ сказáть э́то!** what on earth made you say that?; **как э́то тебя́ ~ило** how on earth did you manage that?

угорéлый *прил*: **бегáть как ~** to run around like a mad thing.

угор|éть (-ю́, -и́шь) *сов неперех* to get gas-poisoning.

ýг|орь (-ря́; *nom pl* **-ри́)** *м* (*ЗООЛ*) eel; (*на лице*) blackhead.

уго|сти́ть (-щý, -сти́шь; *impf* **угощáть)** *сов перех*: **~ когó-н чем-н** (*дома*) to offer sb sth; (*в ресторане*) to treat sb to sth.

угощá|ться (-юсь) *несов возв*: **~йтесь!** help yourself!

угощéни|е (-я) *ср* (*гостей*) entertaining; (*вкусное, изысканное*) food.

угощý *сов см* **угости́ть.**

угрóб|ить (-лю, -ишь) *сов от* **грóбить.**

угрожá|ть (-ю) *несов неперех*: **~ комý-н (чем-н)** to threaten sb (with sth); **емý ~ет банкрóтство** he is threatened with bankruptcy.

угрожáющ|ий (-ая, -ее, -ие) *прил* threatening; (*вид*) menacing.

угрóз|а (-ы) *ж* (*обычно мн*) threat.

угрóха|ть (-ю) *сов перех* (*разг*: *деньги*) to blow; (*продукты*) to use (up).

угрызéни|е (-я) *ср*: **~я сóвести** pangs *мн* of conscience.

угрю́м|ый (-, -а, -о) *прил* gloomy.

угря́ *итп сущ см* **ýгорь.**

удáбрива|ть (-ю) *несов от* **удóбрить.**

удáв (-а) *м* boa constrictor.

уда|вáться (3*sg* **-ётся,** 3*pl* **-ю́тся)** *несов от* **удáться.**

удади́мся *итп сов см* **удáться.**

удал|éц (-ьцá) *м* (*разг*) hero.

удал|и́ть (-ю́, -и́шь; *impf* **удаля́ть)** *сов перех* (*детей, посторонних*) to send away, remove; (*игрока*: *с поля*) to send off; (*пятно, занозу, орган*) to remove; (*зуб*) to extract; (*КОМП*) to delete

▸ **удали́ться** (*impf* **удаля́ться**) *сов возв* to move away; (*перен*: *от темы*) to digress; (*в свою комнату*) to withdraw.

удалóй *прил* daring.

ýдал|ь (-и) *ж* daring.

удальцá *итп сущ см* **удалéц.**

удаля́|ть(ся) (-ю(сь)) *несов от* **удали́ть(ся).**

удáр (-а) *м* blow; (*ногой*) kick; (*звук, инсульт*) stroke; (*пульса, сердца*) beat; **~ грóма** clap of thunder; **быть** (*impf*) **в ~е** (*разг*) to be on the ball; **стáвить (постáвить** *perf*) **когó-н под ~** to put sb in a vulnerable position; **наноси́ть (нанести́** *perf*) **~ комý-н** to deal a blow to sb.

ударéни|е (-я) *ср* (*также ЛИНГ*) stress.

удáр|ить (-ю, -ишь; *impf* **ударя́ть)** *сов перех* to hit; (*подлеж*: *часы*) to strike; (: *морозы*) to set in; **ударя́ть (~** *perf*) **когó-н по головé/спинé** to hit sb on the head/back; **ударя́ть (~** *perf*) **в барабáн** to beat a drum; **~** (*perf*) **по спекуля́нтам** to crack down on profiteers; **винó ~ило емý в гóлову** the wine has gone to his head; **~ил гром** there was a clap of thunder; **он не ~ил лицóм в грязь** he didn't disgrace himself

▸ **удáриться** (*impf* **ударя́ться**) *сов возв* (*натолкнуться на что-н*): **~ся о** +*acc* (*о дверь, о стену итп*) to bang (o.s.) against; **~ся** (*perf*) **в пáнику** to fly into a panic; **~ся** (*perf*) **в спорт/в наýку/в поли́тику** to become obsessed with sport/science/politics; **он ~ился головóй о шкаф** he hit his head on *или* against the cupboard.

удáрник (-а) *м* (*музыкант*) percussionist; (*ружья, пистолета*) striker, firing pin.

уда́рный *прил* (*инструмент*) percussion *опред*; (*войска, труд*) shock *опред*; (*слог*) stressed; **уда́рная волна́** shock wave.
ударя́|ть(ся) (**-ю(сь)**) *несов от* **уда́рить(ся)**.
уда́ться (*как* **дать**; *см* **Table 14**; *impf* **удава́ться**) *сов возв* (*получиться*: *опыт, испытание*) to be successful, work; (*пирог*) to turn out well; **нам удало́сь/не удало́сь поговори́ть/зако́нчить рабо́ту** we managed/didn't manage to talk to one another/finish the work.
уда́ч|а (**-и**) *ж* (good) luck; **нам вы́пала больша́я** ~ we had a great stroke of luck; **жела́ю ~и!** good luck!
уда́чен *прил см* **уда́чный**.
уда́члив|ый (**-, -а, -о**) *прил* lucky.
уда́ч|ный (**-ен, -на, -но**) *прил* successful; (*хороший*: *выбор, выражение*) good.
удва́ива|ть(ся) (**-ю(сь)**) *несов от* **удво́ить(ся)**.
удвое́ни|е (**-я**) *ср* doubling.
удво́енный *прил* (*зарплата*) doubled; (*энергия, сила итп*) redoubled.
удво́|ить (**-ю, -ишь**; *impf* **удва́ивать**) *сов перех* to double; (*внимание, усилия*) to redouble
▸ **удво́иться** (*impf* **удва́иваться**) *сов возв* to double; (*усилия итп*) to be redoubled.
уде́л (**-а**) *м* (*судьба*) lot, fate.
удел|и́ть (**-ю́, -и́шь**; *impf* **уделя́ть**) *сов перех*: ~ **что-н кому́-н/чему́-н** to devote sth to sb/sth.
уде́льный *прил*: ~ **вес** (*физ*) specific gravity.
уделя́|ть (**-ю**) *несов от* **удели́ть**.
у́держ (**-у**) *м*: **без ~у** uncontrollably; **он не зна́ет ~у в тра́тах** he doesn't know when to stop spending.
уд|ержа́ть (**-ержу́, -е́ржишь**; *impf* **уде́рживать**) *сов перех* to restrain; (*часть зарплаты*) to deduct; (*первенство, позиции*): ~ **(за собо́й)** to retain; ~ *(perf)* **что-н в рука́х** to hold onto sth, not let go of sth; **уде́рживать (~** *perf*) **кого́-н от пое́здки** to keep sb from going on a journey; **уде́рживать (~** *perf*) **кого́-н до́ма** to keep sb at home
▸ **удержа́ться** (*impf* **уде́рживаться**) *сов возв* (*остановить себя*) to stop *или* restrain o.s.; (*устоять*: *на краю обрыва*) to hang on; **~ся** *(perf)* **на нога́х** to stay on one's feet; **~ся** *(perf)* **на свои́х пози́циях** to hold one's ground; **~ся** *(perf)* **от сме́ха** to stop *или* keep o.s. from laughing; **~ся** *(perf)* **от слёз** to hold back the tears.
удеру́ *итп сов см* **удра́ть**.
удесятер|и́ть (**-ю́, -и́шь**) *сов перех* to increase tenfold; (*усилия*) to triple.
удешев|и́ть (**-лю́, -и́шь**; *impf* **удешевля́ть**) *сов перех* to make cheaper
▸ **удешеви́ться** (*impf* **удешевля́ться**) *сов возв* to get cheaper.
удешевле́ни|е (**-я**) *ср*: ~ **цен (на** *+acc*) reduction in the price (of).
удешевлю́(сь) *сов см* **удешеви́ть(ся)**.
удешевля́|ть(ся) (**-ю(сь)**) *несов от* **удешеви́ть(ся)**.
удиви́телен *прил см* **удиви́тельный**.
удиви́тельно *нареч* (*красивый, вкусный*) amazingly ◆ *как сказ* it's amazing; **мне ~, что ты э́того не понима́ешь** I'm amazed that you don't understand this; **~, как ты не простуди́лся** it's amazing that you didn't catch (a) cold; **и не** ~ and no wonder.
удиви́тел|ьный (**-ен, -ьна, -ьно**) *прил* amazing.
удив|и́ть (**-лю́, -и́шь**; *impf* **удивля́ть**) *сов перех* to surprise
▸ **удиви́ться** (*impf* **удивля́ться**) *сов возв*: **~ся** *+dat* (*известию, приезду итп*) to be surprised at *или* by; **я ~и́лся, что он не позвони́л** I was surprised that he didn't phone.
удивле́ни|е (**-я**) *ср* surprise; **к на́шему ~ю, она́ ушла́** to our surprise she left; **с ~м** with surprise; **от ~я** in surprise; **краси́вый/у́мный на** ~ amazingly beautiful/clever.
удивлённый *прил* surprised.
удивлю́(сь) *сов см* **удиви́ть(ся)**.
удивля́|ть(ся) (**-ю(сь)**) *несов от* **удиви́ть(ся)**.
удила́ (**уди́л**) *мн* bit *ед* (*of bridle*).
уди́лищ|е (**-а**) *ср* (*часть удочки*) (fishing-)rod.
удира́|ть (**-ю**) *несов от* **удра́ть**.
уди́ть (**ужу́, у́дишь**) *несов неперех* to angle.
удлине́ни|е (**-я**) *ср* (*рукава*) lengthening; (*срока*) extension.
удлинённый *прил* (*пальто*) long; (*лицо*) elongated.
удлин|и́ть (**-ю́, -и́шь**; *impf* **удлиня́ть**) *сов перех* (*рукав, пальто*) to lengthen; (*рабочий день, срок*) to extend
▸ **удлини́ться** (*impf* **удлиня́ться**) *сов возв* to grow longer.
удо́бен *прил см* **удо́бный**.
удо́бно *нареч* (*усесться, лечь*) comfortably ◆ *как сказ*: **мне здесь** ~ I'm comfortable here; **мне ~ прийти́ ве́чером** it's convenient for me to come in the evening.
удо́б|ный (**-ен, -на, -но**) *прил* (*мебель*) comfortable; (*время, формат, место*) convenient; **дожида́ться (дожда́ться** *perf*) **~ного слу́чая** to wait for the right opportunity.
удобре́ни|е (**-я**) *ср* (*действие*) fertilizing; (*минералное, химическое*) fertilizer.
удо́бр|ить (**-ю, -ишь**; *impf* **удобря́ть (или** **уда́бривать**) *сов перех* to fertilize.
удо́бств|о (**-а**) *ср* comfort; **кварти́ра со все́ми ~ами** a flat with all (modern) conveniences.
удовлетворе́ни|е (**-я**) *ср* satisfaction; (*требований*) fulfilment.
удовлетворённый *прил* satisfied.
удовлетвори́телен *прил см* **удовлетвори́тельный**.
удовлетвори́тельно *нареч* satisfactorily; (*ПРОСВЕЩ*) ≈ satisfactory (*school mark*).
удовлетвори́тел|ьный (**-ен, -ьна, -ьно**) *прил* satisfactory.
удовлетвор|и́ть (**-ю́, -и́шь**; *impf* **удовлетворя́ть**) *сов перех* to satisfy;

(*потребности, спрос, просьбу*) to meet; (*жалобу*) to respond to; **удовлетворя́ть** (~ *perf*) +*dat* (*требованиям, вкусам, правилам*) to satisfy
▸ **удовлетвори́ться** (*impf* **удовлетворя́ться**) *сов возв*: **~ся** +*instr* to be satisfied with.
удово́льстви|е (**-я**) *ср* pleasure; **получа́ть** (**получи́ть** *perf*) **~ от чего́-н** to enjoy sth; **доставля́ть** (**доста́вить** *perf*) **кому́-н ~** to make sb happy; **с ~м** with pleasure; **я бы с ~м пошёл с Ва́ми** I would love to go with you.
удово́льств|оваться (**-уюсь**) *сов от* **дово́льствоваться**.
удо́д (**-а**) *м* (*зоол*) hoopoe.
удо́|й (**-я**) *м* yield (*of milk*).
удо́йлив|ый (**-, -а, -о**) *прил*: **~ая коро́ва** good milking cow.
удорожа́ни|е (**-я**) *ср*: **~ проду́ктов пита́ния** rise in food prices.
удоста́ива|ть(ся) (**-ю(сь)**) *несов от* **удосто́ить(ся)**.
удостовере́ни|е (**-я**) *ср* (*подписи*) verification; (*документ*) identification (card); **удостовере́ние ли́чности** identity card.
удостове́р|ить (**-ю, -ишь**; *impf* **удостоверя́ть**) *сов перех* (*факт*) to verify
▸ **удостове́риться** (*impf* **удостоверя́ться**) *сов возв*: **~ся в** +*prp* (*в чьей-н невиновности, в верности сообщения*) to assure o.s. of; **он ~ился, что она́ до́ма** he made sure that she was at home.
удосто́|ить (**-ю, -ишь**; *impf* **удоста́ивать**) *сов перех*: **~ кого́-н чего́-н** to bestow sth on sb; **удоста́ивать** (~ *perf*) **кого́-н свои́м визи́том** to honour (*BRIT*) *или* honor (*US*) sb with a visit; ~ (*perf*) **кого́-н улы́бки** to bestow a smile on sb
▸ **удосто́иться** (*impf* **удоста́иваться**) *сов возв*: **~ся** +*gen* (*награды*) to be honoured (*BRIT*) *или* honored (*US*) with.
удосу́ж|иться (**-усь, -ишься**; *impf* **удосу́живаться**) *сов возв*: ~ +*infin* to find time to do.
у́дочек *сущ см* **у́дочка**.
удочере́ни|е (**-я**) *ср* adoption (*of daughter*).
удочер|и́ть (**-ю́, -и́шь**; *impf* **удочеря́ть**) *сов перех* to adopt (*daughter*).
у́доч|ка (**-ки**; *gen pl* **-ек**) *ж* (fishing-)rod; **он попа́лся на ~ку** (*перен*) he fell for it; **заки́дывать** (**заки́нуть** *perf*) **~ку** (*рыболов*) to cast; (*перен*) to put out feelers.
удр|а́ть (**удеру́, удерёшь**; *pt* **-а́л, -ала́, -а́ло**, *impf* **удира́ть**) *сов неперех* (*разг*) to make off.
удруж|и́ть (**-у́, -и́шь**) *сов неперех*: **~ кому́-н** to do sb a favour (*BRIT*) *или* favor (*US*).
удручённый *прил* (*взгляд, лицо, вид*) dejected; (**-ён, -ена́, -ено́**; *человек*) dejected, depressed.
уд|уши́ть (**-ушу́, -у́шишь**) *сов от* **души́ть** ◆ (*impf* **удуша́ть**) *перех* (*человека*) to strangle; (*свободу*) to stifle.
уду́шливый *прил* (*газ, вещество*) suffocating; (*жара*) stifling.
уду́шь|е (**-я**) *ср* (*no pl*) suffocation.
ужу́ *несов см* **уди́ть**.
уе́дешь *итп сов см* **уе́хать**.
уедине́ни|е (**-я**) *ср* solitude.
уединён|ный (**-, -на, -но**) *прил* (*место, остров*) solitary.
уедин|и́ться (**-ю́сь, -и́шься**; *impf* **уединя́ться**) *сов возв* to go off, withdraw.
уе́ду *итп сов см* **уе́хать**.
уе́зд (**-а**) *м* (*ист*) uezd (*administrative division in pre-Revolutionary Russia*).
уезжа́й(те) *сов см* **уе́хать**.
уезжа́|ть (**-ю**) *несов от* **уе́хать**.
УЕФА́ *м сокр* (= *Европе́йский сою́з футбо́льных ассоциа́ций*) UEFA (= *Union of European Football Associations*).
уе́ха|ть (*как* **е́хать**; *см* **Table 19**; *impf* **уезжа́ть**) *сов неперех* to leave, go away; **он ~л в о́тпуск/в Москву́** he has gone on holiday/to Moscow; **мы ско́ро уезжа́ем** we are leaving soon.
уж (**-а́**) *м* (*зоол*) grass snake ◆ *нареч* (*уже*) already ◆ *част* (*выражает усиление*): **здесь не так ~ пло́хо** it's not as bad as all that here; **э́то ~ о́чень до́рого** it really is too expensive.
ужа́л|ить (**-ю, -ишь**) *сов от* **жа́лить**.
у́жас (**-а**) *м* horror; (*страх*) terror ◆ *как сказ* (*разг*): (**э́то**) **~!** it's awful *или* terrible! ◆ *нареч*: **он ~ како́й бога́тый** (*разг*) he's incredibly rich; **~ы войны́** horrors of war; **прийти́** (*perf*) **в ~ от чего́-н** to be horrified by sth; **к моему́ ~у** to my horror; **он дрожа́л от ~а** he was shaking in terror; **~ как бы́стро вре́мя идёт** it's awful *или* terrible how time flies; **ти́хий ~!** (*разг*) horror of horrors!; **до ~а** (*разг*) terribly.
ужасн|у́ть (**-у́, -ёшь**; *impf* **ужаса́ть**) *сов перех* to horrify
▸ **ужасну́ться** (*impf* **ужаса́ться**) *сов возв* to be horrified.
ужаса́ющ|ий (**-ая, -ее, -ие**) *прил* (*крик, зрелище*) horrific; (*запах, холод*) terrible.
ужа́сен *прил см* **ужа́сный**.
ужа́сно *нареч* (*разг*: *умный, красивый итп*) terribly ◆ *как сказ*: **здесь сейча́с ~** it's terrible here now; **он чу́вствует себя́ ~** he feels terrible.
ужа́с|ный (**-ен, -на, -но**) *прил* terrible, horrible, awful.
у́же *сравн прил от* **у́зкий**.
уже́ *нареч, част* already; **мы не ви́делись ~ 3 го́да** it's now 3 years since we've seen each other; **ты же ~ не ма́ленький** you're not a child any more; **~ по э́тому мо́жно суди́ть, что ...** one can judge from this alone that ....
ужива́|ться (**-юсь**) *несов от* **ужи́ться**.

уживу́сь *итп сов см* **ужи́ться.**
ужи́вчив|ый (-, -а, -о) *прил* (*человек*) easy to get along with.
ужи́м|ка (-ки; *gen pl* -ок) *ж* (*обычно мн*) grimace.
у́жин (-а) *м* supper.
у́жина|ть (-ю; *perf* **поу́жинать**) *несов неперех* to have supper.
ужи́|ться (-ву́сь, -вёшься; *pt* -лся, -ла́сь, -ло́сь, *impf* **ужива́ться**) *сов возв*: ~ **с кем-н** to get on with sb.
узако́ненный *прил* (*порядок, ритуал*) established.
узако́н|ить (-ю, -ишь; *impf* **узако́нивать**) *сов перех* (*отношения, порядок*) to legalize.
узбе́к (-а) *м* Uzbek.
Узбекиста́н (-а) *м* Uzbekistan.
узбе́кск|ий (-ая, -ое, -ие) *прил* Uzbek; ~ **язы́к** Uzbek.
узбе́ч|ка (-ки; *gen pl* -ек) *ж см* **узбе́к.**
узд|а́ (-ы́; *nom pl* -ы) *ж* bridle; **держа́ть** *(impf)* **кого́-н в ~е́** to keep sb in check.
узде́чк|а (-и) *ж* = **узда́.**
уздцы́: **под** ~ by the bridle.
у́з|ел (-ла́) *м* knot; (*мешок*) bundle; **телефо́нный** ~ telephone exchange; **железнодоро́жный** ~ railway junction; **санита́рный** ~ bathroom and toilet; **морско́й** ~ hitch; **не́рвный** ~ ganglion; ~ **противоре́чий** a mass of contradictions.
у́з|кий (-кая, -кое, -кие; -ок, -ка́, -ко) *прил* narrow; (*тесный*) tight; (*перен: человек, взгляд*) narrow-minded; **~кая специа́льность** narrow specialism; ~ **круг друзе́й** small circle of friends.
узкоколе́йн|ый *прил*: **~ая желе́зная доро́га** narrow-gauge railway.
узколо́бый *прил* (*перен*) narrow-minded.
узла́ *итп сущ см* **у́зел.**
узлова́т|ый (-, -а, -о) *прил* knotty.
узлов|о́й *прил* (*перен: вопрос, задачи*) key; **~а́я ста́нция** junction.
узна́|ть (-ю; *impf* **узнава́ть**) *сов перех* (*знакомого, свою вещь итп*) to recognize; (*новости*) to find out, learn; (*познать: нужду, любовь*) to know; **я ~л, что ты прие́хал** I heard that you had come; **он ~л о состоя́нии дел** he found out how things stood.
у́зник (-а) *м* captive.
у́зок *прил см* **у́зкий.**
узо́р (-а) *м* pattern.
узо́рный *прил* = **узо́рчатый.**
узо́рчатый *прил* patterned.
у́зост|ь (-и) *ж* (*улиц, взглядов*) narrowness; (*платья*) tightness; (*человека*) narrow-mindedness.
узурпа́тор (-а) *м* usurper.
узурпи́р|овать (-ую) *(не)сов перех* to usurp.
у́з|ы (-) *мн* (*перен*) bonds *мн.*
уйду́ *итп сов см* **уйти́.**
у́йм|а (-ы) *ж* (*разг*): ~ **де́нег/вре́мени** heaps *или* loads of money/time.
уйму(сь) *итп сов см* **уня́ть(ся).**
уйти́ (*как* **идти́**; *см* **Table 18**; *impf* **уходи́ть**) *сов неперех* (*человек*) to go away, leave; (*пароход, поезд*) to go, leave; (*молодость*) to go; (*время, годы*) to pass; (*отдаться*): ~ **в** *+acc* (*в бизнес*) to go into; (*избежать*): ~ **от** *+gen* (*от опасности итп*) to get away from; (*потребоваться*): ~ **на** *+acc* (*деньги, время*) to be spent on; **уходи́ть (~ *perf*) из до́ма** to leave the house; **уходи́ть (~ *perf*) со слу́жбы/со сце́ны** to leave one's job/the stage; **уходи́ть (~ *perf*) от му́жа** to leave one's husband; **уходи́ть (~ *perf*) из жи́зни** to pass away; **уходи́ть (~ *perf*) на пе́нсию** to retire; **у нас ушло́ мно́го де́нег на поку́пки** we spent a lot of money on shopping.
укажу́ *итп сов см* **указа́ть.**
ука́з (-а) *м* (*президента*) decree; **он мне не ~** (*разг*) I don't take orders from him.
указа́ни|е (-я) *ср* pointing out, indication; (*разъяснение*) instruction; (: *начальства*) directive; **~я врача́** doctor's orders.
указа́тел|ь (-я) *м* (*дорожный*) sign; (*книга*) guide; (*список в книге*) index; (*прибор*) indicator.
указа́тельный *прил* (*жест*) pointing; **указа́тельное местоиме́ние** demonstrative pronoun; **указа́тельный па́лец** index finger.
ук|аза́ть (-ажу́, -а́жешь; *impf* **ука́зывать**) *сов перех* to point out; (*дорогу*) to show; (*свой адрес, интересы, срок*) to indicate; (*движением, жестом*): ~ **на** *+acc* (*на дверь, на картину итп*) to point to; (*на ошибки, на недостатки*) to point out; ~ *(perf)* **кому́-н на дверь** (*перен*) to show sb the door.
ука́з|ка (-ки; *gen pl* -ок) *ж* pointer; **де́лать (сде́лать *perf*) что́-нибудь по чужо́й ~ке** to blindly follow somebody else's directions.
ука́зыва|ть (-ю) *несов от* **указа́ть** ♦ *неперех* (*свидетельствовать*): ~ **на** *+acc* (*факты, цифры*) to indicate, point to.
ука́лыва|ть (-ю) *несов от* **уколо́ть.**
уката́|ть (-ю; *impf* **ука́тывать**) *сов перех* (*дорогу*) to roll, flatten.
ук|ати́ть (-ачу́, -а́тишь) *сов перех* (*мяч*) to roll away; (*тачку*) to wheel away ♦ *неперех* (*разг: уехать*) to go off.
ука́тыва|ть (-ю) *несов от* **уката́ть.**
укача́|ть (-ю; *impf* **despite** **ука́чивать**) *сов перех* (*усыпить: ребёнка*) to rock to sleep; (*довести до тошноты*): **его́ ~ло (в маши́не/на парохо́де)** he got (car-/sea-)sick.
укачу́ *сов см* **укати́ть.**
укла́д (-а) *м* (*экон: капиталистический, феодальный*) order; ~ **жи́зни** way of life.
укла́дк|а (-и) *ж* (*действие: дров, рельс*) laying; (*причёска*) set.
укла́дчик (-а) *м* (*путей, паркета*) layer.
укла́дывани|е (-я) *ср* (*вещей, чемодана*) packing; (*ребёнка*) putting to bed.
укла́дыва|ть (-ю) *несов от* **уложи́ть**
▸ **укла́дываться** *несов от* **уложи́ться,**

улéчься ◆ *возв*: **э́то не ~ется в обы́чные рáмки** this is out of the ordinary; **э́то не ~ется в головé** *или* **в сознáнии** it's beyond me.

уклóн (-а) *м (также перен)* slant; **пóезд/дорóга идёт под ~** the train/road is going downhill.

уклонéни|е (-я) *ср (дороги в сторону)* bending; *(от ответа, от обязанностей)* evasion.

укл|они́ться (-оню́сь, -óнишься; *impf* **уклоня́ться)** *сов возв (отстраниться: в сторону)* to swerve; *(отойти от главного)*: **~ от** *+gen* to dodge; *(от темы, от предмета)* to digress from; *(от поручения)* to evade; **уклоня́ться (~** *perf***) от отвéта** to avoid giving an answer.

уклóнчив|ый (-, -а, -о) *прил (ответ)* evasive.

уклоня́|ться (-юсь) *несов от* **уклони́ться**.

уклю́чин|а (-ы) *ж* rowlock.

укóл (-а) *м (иголкой)* prick; *(перен: замечание)* dig; *(МЕД)* injection; **дéлать (сдéлать** *perf***) комý-н ~** to give sb an injection; **~ самолю́бию** blow to one's ego.

ук|олóть (-олю́, -óлешь) *сов от* **колóть** ◆ *(impf* **укáлывать)** *перех (иглой, шипом)* to prick; *(перен: самолюбие)* to wound

▸ **уколóться** *сов от* **колóться**.

укомплектóванный *прил* complete.

укомплект|овáть (-ýю) *сов от* **комплектовáть**.

укóр (-а) *м (упрёк)* reproach; **~ы сóвести** the pangs of conscience; **живóй ~ комý-н** living indictment of sb; **стáвить (постáвить** *perf***) комý-н что-н в ~** to reproach sb with sth.

укорáчива|ть(ся) (-ю(сь)) *несов от* **укороти́ть(ся)**.

укоренéни|е (-я) *ср* taking root, establishment.

укорен|и́ть (-ю́, -и́шь; *impf* **укореня́ть)** *сов перех (рассаду)* to allow to take root.

укорен|и́ться *(3sg* **-и́тся**, *3pl* **-я́тся**, *impf* **укореня́ться)** *сов возв (также перен)* to take root.

укори́зн|а (-ы) *ж (укор)* reproach.

укори́зненно *нареч* reproachfully.

укори́знен|ный (-, -на, -но) *прил* reproachful.

укор|и́ть (-ю́, -и́шь; *impf* **укоря́ть)** *сов перех* to reproach.

укоро|ти́ть (-чý, -ти́шь; *impf* **укорáчивать)** *сов перех (платье, палку, путь)* to shorten; *(жизнь, сроки)* to reduce; **~** *(perf)* **рýки комý-н** *(перен)* to take sb down a peg

▸ **укороти́ться** *(impf* **укорáчиваться)** *сов возв (юбка итп)* to be shortened; *(сроки)* to be reduced.

укорóченный *прил (пальто, юбка)* short; *(рабочий день)* reduced.

укорчý(сь) *сов см* **укороти́ть(ся)**.

укоря́|ть (-ю) *несов от* **укори́ть**.

укоря́ющ|ий (-ая, -ее, -ие) *прил (взгляд)* reproachful.

укрáдкой *нареч* secretly.

украдý *итп сов см* **укрáсть**.

Украи́н|а (-ы) *ж* (the) Ukraine.

украи́н|ец (-ца) *м* Ukrainian.

украи́н|ка (-ки; *gen pl* **-ок)** *ж см* **украи́нец**.

украи́нск|ий (-ая, -ое, -ие) *прил* Ukrainian; **~ язы́к** Ukrainian.

украи́нца *итп сущ см* **украи́нец**.

укрá|сить (-шу, -сишь; *impf* **украшáть)** *сов перех (комнату)* to decorate; *(ёлку)* to decorate *(BRIT)*, trim *(US)*; *(речь)* to embellish; *(существование, жизнь итп)* to brighten

▸ **укрáситься** *(impf* **украшáться)** *сов возв*: **~ся** *+instr (деревья, поля)* to be decorated with *(fig)*; *(жизнь, существование)* to be brightened up by.

укрá|сть (-дý, -дёшь) *сов от* **красть**.

украшá|ть (-ю) *несов от* **укрáсить** ◆ *перех*: **такóе поведéние тебя́ не ~ет** that kind of behaviour doesn't suit you

▸ **украшáться** *несов от* **укрáситься**.

украшéни|е (-я) *ср* decoration; *(коллектива)* pride; *(коллекции)* jewel; *(также:* **ювели́рное ~**) jewellery *(BRIT)*, jewelry *(US)*.

укрáшу(сь) *сов см* **укрáсить(ся)**.

укреп|и́ть (-лю́, -и́шь; *impf* **укрепля́ть)** *сов перех (мир, семью, организм)* to strengthen; *(стену, строение)* to reinforce; *(город, перевал)* to fortify; **укрепля́ть (~** *perf***) здорóвье** to get fit(ter)

▸ **укрепи́ться** *(impf* **укрепля́ться)** *сов возв (нервы, организм)* to become stronger; *(хозяйство, авторитет)* to become established; *(здоровье)* to improve; *(дисциплина)* to be tightened up; **~ся** *(perf)* **в свои́х убеждéниях** to become surer of one's convictions; **за ним ~и́лась дурнáя репутáция** he has earned a bad reputation.

укреплéни|е (-я) *ср (здоровья)* improving; *(авторитета)* reinforcement; *(ВОЕН: обычно мн)* fortification.

укреплю́(сь) *сов см* **укрепи́ть(ся)**.

укрепля́|ть(ся) (-ю(сь)) *несов от* **укрепи́ть(ся)**.

укрепля́ющ|ий (-ая, -ее, -ие) *прил* fortifying.

укрóмный *прил (уголок)* secluded.

укрóп (-а) *м, собир* dill.

укрóпный *прил* dill; **укрóпная водá** *(МЕД)* gripe water.

укроти́тел|ь (-я) *м* tamer; **~ львов** lion-tamer.

укроти́тельница (-ы) *ж см* **укроти́тель**.

укро|ти́ть (-щý, -ти́шь; *impf* **укрощáть)** *сов перех (животного, гнев, страсти)* to tame; *(человека)* to bring to heel.

укрощéни|е (-я) *ср (действие)* taming.

укрощý *сов см* **укроти́ть**.

укрóю(сь) *итп сов см* **укры́ть(ся)**.

укрупнéни|е (-я) *ср* enlargement.

укрупн|и́ть (-ю́, -и́шь; *impf* **укрупня́ть)** *сов*

перех to enlarge
▸ **укрупни́ться** (*impf* **укрупня́ться**) *сов возв* (*завод, производство*) to get larger; (*черты лица*) to grow more pronounced.
укрыва́тельств|о (**-а**) *ср* (*преступника итп*) harbouring.
укрыва́|ть(ся) (**-ю(сь)**) *несов от* **укры́ть(ся)**.
укры́ти|е (**-я**) *ср* (*место: подземное, от бомб*) shelter.
укр|ы́ть (**-о́ю, -о́ешь**; *impf* **укрыва́ть**) *сов перех* (*закрыть: платком, снегом*) to cover; (*спрятать: преступника*) to harbour; (: *беженца*) to shelter
▸ **укры́ться** (*impf* **укрыва́ться**) *сов возв* (*одеялом, платком*) to cover o.s.; (*от обстрела, от дождя*) to take cover; (*от погони*) to hide; **от моего́ взгля́да не ~ы́лось, что** ... it has not escaped my notice that ....
у́ксус (**-а**) *м* vinegar.
у́ксусный *прил* (*запах, эссенция*) vinegar *опред*; **у́ксусная кислота́** acetic acid.
уку́с (**-а**) *м* bite.
ук|уси́ть (**-ушу́, -у́сишь**) *сов перех* to bite.
уку́та|ть (**-ю**; *impf* **уку́тывать**) *сов перех* (*больного, шею итп*) to wrap up
▸ **уку́таться** (*impf* **уку́тываться**) *сов возв* to wrap o.s. up.
укушу́ *сов см* **укуси́ть**.
ул. *сокр* (= *у́лица*) St (= *street*).
ула́влива|ть (**-ю**) *несов от* **улови́ть**.
ула́|дить (**-жу, -дишь**; *impf* **ула́живать**) *сов перех* to settle
▸ **ула́диться** (*impf* **ула́живаться**) *сов возв* to sort o.s. out.
ула́живани|е (**-я**) *ср* (*ссоры, конфликта*) settling.
ула́жива|ть(ся) (**-ю(сь)**) *несов от* **ула́дить(ся)**.
ула́жу(сь) *сов см* **ула́дить(ся)**.
ула́мыва|ть (**-ю**) *несов от* **улома́ть**.
ула́н (**-а**) *м* (*ист*) uhlan (*lancer*).
Ула́н-Ба́тор (**-а**) *м* Ulan Bator.
улёгся *итп сов см* **уле́чься**.
у́л|ей (**-ья**) *м* (bee-)hive.
уле|те́ть (**-чу́, -ти́шь**; *impf* **улета́ть**) *сов неперех* (*птица*) to fly away; (*самолёт*) to leave; (*перен: стремительно уйти*) to fly off.
улету́ч|иться (**-усь, -ишься**; *impf* **улету́чиваться**) *сов возв* (*также перен*) to evaporate; (*перен: разг*) to vanish.
улечу́ *сов см* **улете́ть**.
ул|е́чься (**-я́гусь, -я́жешься** *итп*, **-я́гутся**; *pt* **-ёгся, -егла́сь, -егло́сь**, *impf* **укла́дываться**) *сов возв* to lie down; (*no impf*; *пыль*) to settle; (*перен: буря, страсти, гнев*) to subside.
улизн|у́ть (**-у́, -ёшь**) *сов неперех* (*разг*) to slip away.
ули́к|а (**-и**) *ж* (piece) of evidence (*мн* evidence); **ко́свенная/пряма́я** ~ circumstantial/hard evidence.
ули́т|ка (**-ки**; *gen pl* **-ок**) *ж* snail.
у́лиц|а (**-ы**) *ж* (*в городе, в селе*) street; (*перен: некультурная среда*) the gutter; **на ~е** outside; **остава́ться (оста́ться** *perf*) **на ~е** to be out on the street; **выбра́сывать (вы́бросить** *perf*) **на ~у** (*выселить*) to throw sb out onto the streets.
улич|и́ть (**-у́, -и́шь**; *impf* **улича́ть**) *сов перех*: ~ **кого́-н в чём-н** to face sb with sth.
у́личный *прил* street *опред*; **у́личное движе́ние** traffic.
уло́в (**-а**) *м* catch (*of fish*).
улови́м|ый (**-, -а, -о**) *прил*: **едва́** *или* **чуть** *или* **е́ле** ~ barely perceptible.
ул|ови́ть (**-овлю́, -о́вишь**; *impf* **ула́вливать**) *сов перех* (*звуки, шум, запах*) to catch, detect; (*перен: мысль, связь*) to catch, grasp; **ула́вливать (~** *perf*) **(подходя́щий) моме́нт** to find the right moment.
уло́в|ка (**-ки**; *gen pl* **-ок**) *ж* ruse.
уловлю́ *сов см* **улови́ть**.
уло́вок *сущ см* **уло́вка**.
ул|ожи́ть (**-ожу́, -о́жишь**; *impf* **укла́дывать**) *сов перех* (*ребёнка*) to put to bed; (*вещи, чемодан*) to pack; (*волосы*) to set; (*шпалы, рельсы*) to lay; (*бельё*) to fold away; (*no impf*, *разг*): ~ **кого́-н на ме́сте** to kill sb; **хозя́йка ~ожи́ла нас в гости́ной** our hostess put us (up) in the living room
▸ **уложи́ться** (*impf* **укла́дываться**) *сов возв* (*сложить вещи*) to pack; **укла́дываться (~ся** *perf*) **в сро́ки** to keep to the deadline; **~ся** (*perf*) **в полчаса́** to keep it down to half an hour.
улома́|ть (**-ю**; *impf* **ула́мывать**) *сов перех* (*разг*): ~ **кого́-н** to talk sb round; **ула́мывать (~** *perf*) **кого́-н** +*infin* to talk sb into doing.
у́лоч|ка (**-ки**; *gen pl* **-ек**) *ж* lane.
улуч|и́ть (**-у́, -и́шь**; *impf* **улуча́ть**) *сов перех* (*момент, полчаса*) to find.
улучша́|ть (**-ю**) *несов от* **улу́чшить**.
улучше́ни|е (**-я**) *ср* improvement.
улу́чш|ить (**-у, -ишь**; *impf* **улучша́ть**) *сов перех* to improve.
улыба́|ться (**-юсь**; *perf* **улыбну́ться**) *несов возв*: ~ +*dat* to smile at; (*перен: счастье, жизнь*) to smile on; **мне не ~ется э́та рабо́та/пое́здка** this work/trip doesn't appeal to me.
улы́б|ка (**-ки**; *gen pl* **-ок**) *ж* smile.
улыбн|у́ться (**-у́сь, -ёшься**) *сов от* **улыба́ться**.
улы́бок *сущ см* **улы́бка**.
улы́бчив|ый (**-, -а, -о**) *прил* smiley.
ультима́тум (**-а**) *м* ultimatum; **предъявля́ть (предъяви́ть** *perf*) **кому́-н** ~ to give sb an ultimatum.
ультразву́к (**-а**) *м* ultrasound.
ультразвуково́й *прил* ultrasonic.
ультрамари́н (**-а**) *м* ultramarine.
ультрафиоле́тов|ый *прил*: **~ые лучи́** ultraviolet rays *мн*.
у́лья *итп сущ см* **у́лей**.
улюлю́ка|ть (**-ю**) *несов неперех* to halloo;

(*перен*) to hoot (*in derision*).
улягусь *итп сов см* **улечься**.
ум (**-á**) *м* mind; **быть** *(impf)* **без ~á от кого-н/чего-н** to be wild about sb/sth; **в ~é** (*считать, держать*) in one's head; **в своём ~é** in one's right mind; **браться (взяться** *perf*) **за ~** to see sense; **сходить (сойти** *perf*) **с ~á** to go mad; **сводить (свести** *perf*) **кого-н с ~á** to drive sb mad; (*перен*: *увлечь*) to drive sb wild; **природный ~** native wit; **~á не приложу, куда/сколько/кто ...** I can't think where/how much/who ...; **с ~óм** (*рассудительно*) sensibly; **приходить (прийти** *perf*) **на ~ кому-н** to come into sb's head.
умал|ить (**-ю, -ишь**; *impf* **умалять**) *сов перех* (*значение, роль*) to diminish, belittle.
умалишённый *прил* insane.
умалчива|ть (**-ю**) *несов от* **умолчать**.
умаля|ть (**-ю**) *несов от* **умалить**.
умá|яться (**-юсь**) *сов от* **маяться**.
умéл|ец (**-ьца**) *м* skilled artisan.
умéло *нареч* skilfully (*BRIT*), skillfully (*US*).
умéл|ый (**-, -а, -о**) *прил* (*рука, ремесленник, политик*) skilful (*BRIT*), skillful (*US*); (*работник*) able.
умéльца *итп сущ см* **умéлец**.
умён *прил см* **умный**.
умéни|е (**-я**) *ср* ability, skill; **с ~м** (*делать что-н*) with skill.
уменьшá|ть(ся) (**-ю(сь)**) *несов от* **умéньшить(ся)**.
уменьшéни|е (**-я**) *ср* reduction.
уменьшительный *прил* (*суффикс*) diminutive.
умéньш|ить (**-у, -ишь**; *impf* **уменьшать**) *сов перех* to reduce; **~** *(perf)* **шаг** to slow down
▸ **умéньшиться** (*impf* **уменьшаться**) *сов возв* (*объём, опасность*) to diminish, decrease.
умéренност|ь (**-и**) *ж* moderateness; (*климата*) temperate nature.
умéрен|ный (**-, -на, -но**) *прил* (*аппетит, скорость, политика*) moderate; (*no short form*; *климат, характер*) temperate.
ум|ерéть (**-рý, -рёшь**; *pt* **-ер, -ерлá, -ерло**, *impf* **умирать**) *сов неперех* to die; (*традиция*) to die out; **хоть ~рú, но сдéлай** (*разг*) do it, even if it kills you; **~** *(perf)* **от голода/рака** to die of hunger/cancer; **со смеху ~ мóжно** (*разг*) I could die laughing.
умéр|ить (**-ю, -ишь**; *impf* **умерять**) *сов перех* (*требования, желания*) to moderate; (*гнев*) to restrain.
умер|твить (**-щвлю, -твишь**; *impf* **умерщвлять**) *сов перех* (*также перен*) to kill.
умерщвлéни|е (**-я**) *ср* killing.
умерщвлю *сов см* **умертвить**.
умерщвля|ть (**-ю**) *несов от* **умертвить**.
умеря|ть (**-ю**) *несов от* **умéрить**.

уме|стить (**-щý, -стишь**; *impf* **умещать**) *сов перех* to fit, find room for
▸ **уместиться** (*impf* **умещаться**) *сов возв* to fit; **мы все умéстимся в машину** there's room for all of us in the car; **мой вéщи не ~щаются в чемодан** my things won't fit in my suitcase.
умé|ть (**-ю**) *несов неперех* can, to be able to; (*иметь способность*) to know how to; **он ~ет плáвать/читать** he can swim/read; **Мария ~ет хорошó одеваться** Maria knows how to dress well.
умещá|ть(ся) (**-ю(сь)**) *несов от* **уместить(ся)**.
умещý(сь) *сов см* **уместить(ся)**.
умéючи *нареч* (*разг*): **это нáдо дéлать ~** you need to have the knack (to do this).
умилéни|е (**-я**) *ср* tenderness; **слёзы ~я** fond tears.
умилитель|ный (**-ен, -ьна, -ьно**) *прил* touching.
умил|ить (**-ю, -ишь**; *impf* **умилять**) *сов перех* to touch
▸ **умилиться** (*impf* **умиляться**) *сов возв* to be touched.
умильный *прил* (*нежный*) touching; (*льстивый*) smarmy.
умиля|ть(ся) (**-ю(сь)**) *несов от* **умилить(ся)**.
уминá|ть (**-ю**) *несов от* **умять**.
умирáни|е (**-я**) *ср* dying.
умирá|ть (**-ю**) *несов от* **умерéть** ◆ *неперех* (*перен*): **~ю, как хочý есть/спать** I'm dying for something to eat/to go to sleep; **я ~ю от скýки** I'm bored to death.
умиротворéни|е (**-я**) *ср* (*сердца, души*) bringing of peace; (*агрессора*) appeasement.
умиротворённый *прил* serene, tranquil.
умиротвор|ить (**-ю, -ишь**; *impf* **умиротворять**) *сов перех* (*душу*) to bring peace to; (*враждующих*) to pacify; (*агрессора*) to appease
▸ **умиротвориться** (*impf* **умиротворяться**) *сов возв* (*враждующие, спорщики итп*) to be pacified.
умнé|ть (**-ю**; *perf* **поумнéть**) *несов неперех* (*человек*) to grow wiser; (*ребёнок*) to become more intelligent; **это помóжет тебé поумнéть** (*перен*) that'll teach you a lesson.
ýмник (**-а**) *м* clever boy; (*пренебр*: *умничающий*) clever dick, knowall.
ýмница (**-ы**) *ж* clever girl ◆ *м/ж* (*разг*): **вот ~!** good for you!, well done!; **он ~** he's a clever one.
ýмнича|ть (**-ю**) *несов неперех* (*разг*: *пренебр*) to show off how clever one is, be clever; (*своевольничать*) to try to be clever.
ýмно *нареч* (*вести себя*) sensibly; (*говорить*) intelligently.
умножá|ть (**-ю**) *несов от* **умнóжить**.
умножéни|е (**-я**) *ср* (*см глаг*) multiplication; increase; **таблица ~я** (*МАТ*) multiplication table.

умнóж|ить (-у, -ишь; *impf* **мнóжить** *или* **умножáть**) *сов перех* (*МАТ*) to multiply; (*доходы, опыт, славу итп*) to increase; **умножáть** (~ *perf*) **пять нá два** to multiply five by two
▸ **умнóжиться** *сов от* **мнóжиться**.
умнý *итп сов см* **умя́ть**.
ýм|ный (-ён, -нá, -нó *или* -но) *прил* (*человек*) clever, intelligent; (*лицо*) intelligent; (*собака, машина, прибор*) clever; (*речи, совет, политика*) sensible.
умозаключéни|е (-я) *ср* (*вывод*) deduction.
умозрúтел|ьный (-ен, -ьна, -ьно) *прил* (*построение, рассуждения*) speculative.
умол|úть (-ю́, -и́шь; *impf* **умоля́ть**) *сов перех*: ~ **когó-н** (+*infin*) to prevail upon sb (to do) (*by pleading*).
ýмолк *м*: **без ~у** incessantly.
умóлкн|уть (-у, -ешь; *impf* **умолкáть**) *сов неперех* (*голос, скрипка*) to fall silent; (*смех, звон*) to stop.
умолчáни|е (-я) *ср* (*фактов*) supression, hushing up.
умолч|áть (-ý, -и́шь; *impf* **умáлчивать**) *сов неперех*: ~ **о чём-н** (*о преступлении, о недостатках итп*) to keep quiet about sth.
умоля́|ть (-ю) *несов от* **умолúть** ◆ *перех* to implore.
умоля́ющ|ий (-ая, -ее, -ие) *прил* (*взгляд, голос*) pleading.
умонастроéни|е (-я) *ср* frame of mind.
умопомешáтельств|о (-а) *ср* insanity.
умопомрачéни|е (-я) *ср* temporary loss of one's senses; **до ~я** (*устать*) terribly; (*любить, влюбиться*) madly; **рабóтать** *(impf)*/**танцевáть** *(impf)* **до ~я** to work/dance until one is ready to drop.
умопомрачи́тел|ьный (-ен, -ьна, -ьно) *прил* (*разг: красота, богатство*) staggering.
умóра *ж нескл*: **э́то прóсто** ~ (*разг*) it's hilarious.
уморúтел|ьный (-ен, -ьна, -ьно) *прил* (*разг*) hilarious.
умор|úть (-ю́, -и́шь) *сов от* **морúть**.
умотá|ть (-ю) *сов от* **мотáть**.
умрý *итп сов см* **умерéть**.
умóю(сь) *сов см* **умы́ть(ся)**.
ýмственно *нареч*: ~ **отстáлый** mentally retarded.
ýмственный *прил* (*способности*) mental; ~ **труд** brainwork.
умудр|ённый (-ён, -енá, -енó) *прил*: ~ **óпытом/годáми** wise from experience/with age.
умудр|úться (-ю́сь, -и́шься; *impf* **умудря́ться**) *сов возв* (*разг*) to manage; **я ~и́лся простудúться/опоздáть на пóезд** I managed to catch a cold/miss the train.
умч|áть (-ý, -и́шь) *сов перех* to whisk off *или* away
▸ **умчáться** *сов возв* (*кони, всадники, дети*) to dash off; (*годы, детство*) to fly by.
умывáльник (-а) *м* washstand.
умывáльн|ый *прил*: **~ые принадлéжности** washing things *мн*.
умывáни|е (-я) *ср* washing.
умывá|ть(ся) (-ю(сь)) *несов от* **умы́ть(ся)**.
умы́кн|уть (-ý, -ёшь; *impf* **умыкáть**) *сов перех* (*разг: украсть*) to nick; (*невесту*) to abduct (*as part of wedding ritual*).
ýмыс|ел (-ла) *м* intent; **дéлать (сдéлать** *perf*) **что-н без ~ла/с ýмыслом** to do sth without/with intent.
умы́ть (умóю, умóешь; *impf* **умывáть**) *сов перех* to wash
▸ **умы́ться** (*impf* **умывáться**) *сов возв* to wash.
умы́шленно *нареч* deliberately, intentionally.
умы́шленност|ь (-и) *ж* (*поступка*) deliberateness; (*преступления*) premeditated nature.
умы́шлен|ный (-, -на, -но) *прил* (*поступок*) deliberate, intentional; (*преступление, убийство*) premeditated.
ум|я́ть (-нý, -нёшь; *impf* **уминáть**) *сов перех* (*снег, землю*) to flatten; (*разг: съесть много*) to stuff down.
унавó|зить (-жу, -зишь) *сов от* **навóзить**.
унаслéдовать (-ую) *сов от* **наслéдовать**.
ун|ести́ (-есý, -есёшь; *pt* -ёс, -еслá, -еслó, *impf* **уноси́ть**) *сов перех* to take away; (*разг: украсть*) to carry off; (*подлеж: война, эпидемия*) to claim; **лóдку ~еслó течéнием** the boat drifted away; **бумáги ~еслó вéтром** the papers blew away
▸ **унести́сь** (*impf* **уноси́ться**) *сов возв* (*тучи, кони, поезд*) to speed off; **мои́ мы́сли ~ели́сь в прóшлое** his thoughts flashed back to the past; **он ~ёсся в мир фантáзий** he was carried into the world of fantasy.
универмáг (-а) *м* (= *универсáльный магази́н*) department store.
универсáл (-а) *м* all-rounder.
универсáльност|ь (-и) *ж* (*знаний*) breadth; (*средств*) universality.
универсáльн|ый *прил* (*проблема*) universal; (*образование*) all-round; (*человек*) versatile, multitalented; (*знания*) encyclopaedic (*BRIT*), encyclopedic (*US*); (*машина, инструмент*) versatile, multipurpose; **~ое срéдство** cure-all; **~ая вычисли́тельная маши́на** (*КОМП*) mainframe; ~ **си́мвол** (*КОМП*) wildcard; **универсáльный магази́н** department store.
универсáм (-а) *м* supermarket.
университéт (-а) *м* university.
университéтск|ий (-ая, -ое, -ие) *прил* university *опред*.
унижá|ть(ся) (-ю(сь)) *несов от* **уни́зить(ся)**.
унижéни|е (-я) *ср* humiliation; **идти́ (пойти́** *perf*) **на** ~ to humble o.s.
уни́жен|ный (-, -на, -но) *прил* (*человек*) humbled; (*взгляд, просьба*) humble.
уни́жу(сь) *сов см* **уни́зить(ся)**.

ун|изáть (**-ижу́, -и́жешь**; *impf* **уни́зывать**) *сов перех* to string; (*пояс*: *жемчугом*) to stud.
унизи́телен *прил см* **унизи́тельный**.
унизи́тельност|ь (**-и**) *ж* humiliation.
унизи́тел|ьный (**-ен, -ьна, -ьно**) *прил* humiliating, degrading.
уни́|зить (**-жу, -зишь**; *impf* **унижáть**) *сов перех* to humiliate; **унижáть** (**~** *perf*) **себя́** to abase o.s.
▸ **уни́зиться** (*impf* **унижáться**) *сов возв*: **~ся** (**пéред** *+instr*) to abase o.s. (before).
уни́зыва|ть (**-ю**) *несов от* **унизáть**.
уникáл|ьный (**-ен, -ьна, -ьно**) *прил* unique.
у́никум (**-а**) *м*: **он настоя́щий ~** he's one of a kind.
унимá|ть(ся) (**-ю(сь)**) *несов от* **уня́ть(ся)**.
унисо́н (**-а**) *м* unison; **в ~** (**с** *+instr*) (*также перен*) in unison (with).
унитáз (**-а**) *м* toilet.
унификáци|я (**-и**) *ж* standardization.
унифици́р|овать (**-ую**) (*не*)*сов перех* to standardize.
унифо́рм|а (**-ы**) *ж* (*одежда*) uniform.
уничижá|ть (**-ю**) *несов перех* to disparage.
уничижи́тел|ьный (**-ен, -ьна, -ьно**) *прил* disparaging.
уничтожá|ть (**-ю**) *несов от* **уничто́жить**.
уничтожáющ|ий (**-ая, -ее, -ие**) *прил* (*огонь, удар, критика*) devastating; (*взгляд*) scathing, withering.
уничто́ж|ить (**-у, -ишь**; *impf* **уничтожáть**) *сов перех* to destroy; (*насекомых, вредителей*) to exterminate; (*память о чём-н, следы*) to wipe out; (*безработицу, преступность итп*) to do away with; (*перен*: *унизить*) to crush.
ун|оси́ть(ся) (**-ошу́(сь), -о́сишь(ся)**) *несов от* **унести́(сь)**.
у́нтер-офицéр (**-а**) *м* non-commissioned officer.
у́нци|я (**-и**) *ж* ounce.
унывá|ть (**-ю**) *несов неперех* (*человек*) to be downcast *или* despondent; (*впадать в уныние*) to lose heart.
уны́ло *нареч* despondently.
уны́лый *прил* (*человек*) despondent; (*мысли*) depressing; (*природа*) cheerless, dreary.
уны́ни|е (**-я**) *ср* despondency.
уня́|ть (**уйму́, уймёшь**; *pt* **-л, -лá, -ло**, *impf* **унимáть**) *сов перех* (*ребёнка, хулигана*) to restrain; (*слёзы, волнение*) to suppress
▸ **уня́ться** (*impf* **унимáться**) *сов возв* (*ребёнок, шалун итп*) to calm down; (*буря, боль*) to die down.
упáвш|ий (**-ая, -ее, -ие**) *прил* (*голос*) fallen.
упáд (**-у**) *м*: **мы танцевáли до ~у** (*разг*) we danced till we were ready to drop; **я смея́лся до ~у** (*разг*) I laughed my head off.
упáд|ок (**-ка**) *м* decline; **~ сил** exhaustion; **~ ду́ха** despondency.

упáдочническ|ий (**-ая, -ое, -ие**) *прил* decadent.
упаду́ *итп сов см* **упáсть**.
упак|овáть (**-у́ю**) *сов от* **паковáть**.
упако́вк|а (**-и**) *ж* packing; (*паковочный материал*) packaging.
упако́вочный *прил* packaging *опред*.
упако́выва|ть (**-ю**; *perf* **упаковáть**) *несов* = **паковáть** ◆ *перех* (*КОМП*) to pack.
упако́вщик (**-а**) *м* packer.
упако́вщиц|а (**-ы**) *ж см* **упако́вщик**.
упасти́ *сов перех*: **упаси́ Бог** *или* **Бо́же** *или* **Го́споди!** God forbid!
упá|сть (**-ду́, -дёшь**) *сов от* **пáдать** ◆ *неперех*: **~ в но́ги кому́-н** to go down on one's knees to sb.
упекá|ть (**-ю**) *несов от* **упéчь**.
упеку́ *итп сов см* **упéчь**.
уперéть (**упру́, упрёшь**; *pt* **упёр, упёрла, упёрло**, *impf* **упирáть**) *сов перех* (*разг*: *украсть*) to nick, pinch; **упирáть** (**~** *perf*) **что-н в** *+acc* (*в стену итп*) to prop sth against
▸ **уперéться** (*impf* **упирáться**) *сов возв*: **~ся чем-н в** *+acc* (*в землю*) to dig sth into; (*в плот*) to stick sth into; (*натолкнуться на преграду*): **~ся в** *+acc* (*в ограду, в забор итп*) to come up against; (*перен*: *взглядом, глазами*) to stare; **упирáться** (**~ся** *perf*) (**на** *+prp*) (*перен*: *разг*: *настоять*) to dig one's heels in (on).
упé|чь (**-ку́, -чёшь** *итп*, **-ку́т**; *impf* **упекáть**) *сов перех* (*разг*: *в тюрьму*) to fling.
упивá|ться (**-юсь**) *несов от* **упи́ться**.
упирá|ть (**-ю**) *несов от* **уперéть**
▸ **упирáться** *несов от* **уперéться** ◆ *возв* (*иметь причиной*): **~ся в** *+prp* to arise from.
упи́тан|ный (**-, на, -но**) *прил* plump.
уп|и́ться (**-ью́сь, -ьёшься**; *impf* **упивáться**) *сов возв* (*разг*: *напиться допьяна*) to get very drunk; (*перен*): **~** *+instr* (*счастьем, свободой итп*) to be intoxicated by; (*: чьим-н несчастьем*) to revel in.
УПК *м сокр* (= *Уголо́вно-процессуа́льный ко́декс*) *criminal code*.
уплáт|а (**-ы**) *ж* payment.
упл|ати́ть (**-ачу́, -áтишь**) *сов от* **плати́ть**.
уплáчива|ть (**-ю**; *perf* **уплати́ть**) *несов перех* = **плати́ть**.
уплачу́ *сов см* **уплати́ть**.
упл|ести́ (**-ету́, -етёшь**) *сов от* **уплетáть**.
уплетá|ть (**-ю**) *несов перех* (*разг*) to tuck *или* get stuck into.
уплотнéни|е (**-я**) *ср* (*почвы, снега*) compression; (*под кожей*) lump (*ANAT*).
уплотн|и́ть (**-ю́, -и́шь**; *impf* **уплотня́ть**) *сов перех* (*также перен*) to compress
▸ **уплотни́ться** (*impf* **уплотня́ться**) *сов возв* (*песок, грунт*) to become firmer; (*рабочий день, график*) to become busier.
уплы́|ть (**-ву́, -вёшь**; *pt* **-л, -лá, -ло**, *impf*

уплыва́ть) *сов неперех* (*человек, рыба итп*) to swim away *или* off; (*пароход*) to sail away *или* off; (*плавно уйти*) to float away *или* off; (*перен*: *пройти*) to pass; (: *разг*: *деньги, наследство итп*) to vanish.
упова́ни|е (**-я**) *ср* hope; **возлага́ть** *(impf)* **~я на** *+acc* to set one's hopes on.
упова́|ть (**-ю**) *несов неперех*: **~ на** *+acc* to count on.
уподо́б|ить (**-лю, -ишь**; *impf* **уподобля́ть**) *сов перех*: **~ что-н/кого́-н** *+dat* to compare sth/sb to
▸ **уподо́биться** (*impf* **уподобля́ться**) *сов возв*: **~ся** *+dat* to become like.
упое́ни|е (**-я**) *ср* elation; **с ~м** with relish.
упо|ённый (**-ён, -ена́, -ено́**) *прил*: **~** *+instr* (*успехом итп*) elated by; (*счастьем*) intoxicated with.
упои́тел|ьный (**-ен, -ьна, -ьно**) *прил* (*воздух*) intoxicating; (*поцелуй*) rapturous.
упоко́|й (**-я**) *м*: **моли́тва за ~ (душ́и) кого́-н** prayer for sb's eternal rest.
упол3|ти́ (**-у́, -ёшь**; *pt* **-, -ла́, -ло́**) *сов неперех* (*змея*) to slither away; (*червь*) to wriggle away; (*ребёнок*) to crawl away.
уполномо́ченн|ая (**-ой**; *decl like adj*) *ж см* **уполномо́ченный**.
уполномо́ченн|ый (**-ого**; *decl like adj*) *м* authorized person (*мн* people).
уполномо́ч|ить (**-у, -ишь**; *impf* **уполномо́чивать**) *сов перех*: **~ кого́-н** *+infin* to authorize sb to do.
упомина́ни|е (**-я**) *ср* (*см глаг*) mention; reference.
упомина́|ть (**-ю**) *несов от* **упомяну́ть**
▸ **упомина́ться** *несов неперех* (*имя, событие*) to be mentioned.
упом|яну́ть (**-яну́, -я́нешь**; *impf* **упомина́ть**) *сов* (*не*)*перех* (*назвать*): **~** *+acc* *или* **о** *+prp* to mention; (*коснуться*) to refer to.
упо́р (**-а**) *м* (*для ног, для рук*) rest; **в ~** (*стрелять*) point-blank; (*смотреть*) intently; **де́лать (сде́лать** *perf*) **~ на** *+prp* to put emphasis on.
упо́рно *нареч* persistently.
упо́р|ный (**-ен, -на, -но**) *прил* persistent; (*сопротивление*) unrelenting.
упо́рств|о (**-а**) *ср* persistence.
упо́рств|овать (**-ую**) *несов неперех* to persist *или* be persistent.
упорхн|у́ть (**-у́, -ёшь**) *сов неперех* (*также перен*) to flit away.
упоря́дочени|е (**-я**) *ср* (*корреспонденции, информации*) sorting; (*торговли, процедуры*) regulation.
упоря́доченный *прил* ordered.
упоря́доч|ить (**-у, -ишь**; *impf* **упоря́дочивать**) *сов перех* to put in order; (*цены, процедуру*) to regulate
▸ **упоря́дочиться** (*impf* **упоря́дочиваться**) *сов возв* (*дела*) to be put in order; (*процедура*) to be regulated.
употреби́телен *прил см* **употреби́тельный**.
употреби́тельност|ь (**-и**) *ж* frequency (*of use*).
употреби́тел|ьный (**-ен, -ьна, -ьно**) *прил* frequently used.
употреб|и́ть (**-лю́, -и́шь**; *impf* **употребля́ть**) *сов перех* to use; **употребля́ть** (**~** *perf*) **что-н в пи́щу** to eat sth.
употребле́ни|е (**-я**) *ср* (*лекарства, наркотиков*) taking; (*алкоголя*) consumption; (*слова, термина*) usage; **находи́ться** *(impf)* **в ~и** to be in use; **выходи́ть (вы́йти** *perf*) **из ~я** (*слово*) to go out of usage; **вводи́ть (ввести́** *perf*) **в ~** (*слово*) to introduce; (*одежду, предмет быта*) to bring into use.
употреблю́ *сов см* **употреби́ть**.
употребля́|ть (**-ю**) *несов от* **употреби́ть**
▸ **употребля́ться** *несов возв* to be used.
упр. *сокр* (**= управле́ние**) admin (= *administration*).
упра́в|а (**-ы**) *ж* (*ист*) office; (*разг*: *мера пресечения*): **иска́ть ~у** to seek justice; **найти́** *(perf)* **~у на кого́-н** to make sure that sb is punished; **на него́ нет ~ы** there's no control over him.
упра́в|иться (**-люсь, -ишься**; *impf* **управля́ться**) *сов возв*: **~ с** *+instr* (*разг*: *с делами, с уборкой*) to manage; (*с шалуном, с плохим учеником*) to deal with.
управле́ни|е (**-я**) *ср* (*судном, самолётом*) navigation; (*делами, финансами*) administration; (*оркестром, хором*) conducting; (*учреждение*) office; (*система приборов*) controls *мн*; **симфо́ния испо́лнена под ~м а́втора** the symphony was conducted by the composer; **теря́ть (потеря́ть** *perf*) **~** to lose control.
управле́нческ|ий (**-ая, -ое, -ие**) *прил*: **~ аппара́т** ruling body.
упра́влюсь *сов см* **упра́виться**.
управля́ем|ый (**-, -а, -о**) *прил*: **~ая раке́та** guided missile; **~ (с по́мощью) меню́** (*комп*) menu-driven.
управля́|ть (**-ю**) *несов неперех*: **~** *+instr* (*автомобилем*) to drive; (*судном*) to navigate; (*конём*) to ride; (*государством*) to govern; (*учреждением, фирмой итп*) to manage; (*оркестром, хором*) to conduct
▸ **управля́ться** *несов от* **упра́виться**.
управля́ющ|ий (**-его**; *decl like adj*) *м* (*хозяйством*) manager; (*имением, поместьем*) bailiff.
упражне́ни|е (**-я**) *ср* (*мускулов, памяти*) exercising; (*грамматические, гимнастические*) exercise.
упражня́|ть (**-ю**) *несов перех* to exercise
▸ **упражня́ться** *несов возв* to practise.
упраздн|и́ть (**-ю, -и́шь**; *impf* **упраздня́ть**) *сов перех* to abolish.
упра́шива|ть (**-ю**) *несов от* **упроси́ть**.
упрёк (**-а**) *м* reproach; **броса́ть (бро́сить** *perf*) **~ кому́-н** to reproach sb; **ста́вить (поста́вить**

perf) **что-н в ~ кому-н** to hold sth against sb.
упрека|ть (-ю; *perf* **упрекнуть**) *несов перех*: ~ **кого-н (в** *+prp*) to reproach sb (for).
упр|осить (-ошу, -осишь; *impf* **упрашивать**) *сов перех*: ~ **кого-н** *+infin* to persuade sb to do.
упро|стить (-щу, -стишь; *impf* **упрощать**) *сов перех* to simplify; (*сделать слишком простым*) to oversimplify
▸ **упроститься** (*impf* **упрощаться**) *сов возв* to become simpler.
упрочени|е (-я) *ср* consolidation.
упроч|ить (-у, -ишь; *impf* **упрочивать**) *сов перех* to consolidate
▸ **упрочиться** (*impf* **упрочиваться**) *сов возв* (*работник*) to establish o.s.; (*положение, позиции*) to be consolidated; (*перен*): **за ним ~илась репутация хорошего редактора** his reputation as a good editor was established.
упрошу *сов см* **упросить**.
упроща|ть(ся) (-ю(сь)) *несов от* **упростить(ся)**.
упрощени|е (-я) *ср* simplification.
упрощённый *прил* (*простой*) simplified; (*излишне простой*) oversimplified.
упрощу(сь) *сов см* **упростить(ся)**.
упру(сь) *итп сов см* **упереть(ся)**.
упруг|ий (-ая, -ое, -ие; -, -а, -о) *прил* (*пружина, тело*) elastic; (*походка, движения*) bouncy, springy.
упругост|ь (-и) *ж* (*пружины, мышц*) elasticity; (*походки*) springiness.
упряж|ка (-ки; *gen pl* -ек) *ж* team (*of horses, dogs etc*); (*упряжь*) harness.
упряж|ь (-и) *ж* (*no pl*) harness.
упрям|ец (-ца) *м* stubborn person (*мн* people).
упрям|иться (-люсь, -ишься) *несов возв* to be obstinate *или* stubborn.
упрямица (-ы) *ж см* **упрямец**.
упрямо *нареч* (*сказать*) obstinately, stubbornly; (*искать*) persistently.
упрямств|о (-а) *ср* obstinacy, stubbornness.
упрямца *итп сущ см* **упрямец**.
упрям|ый (-, -а, -о) *прил* obstinate, stubborn; (*поиски, стремление*) persistent.
упря|тать (-чу, -чешь) *сов перех* (*разг*) to put away.
упуска|ть (-ю; *perf* **упустить**) *несов перех* (*мяч*) to let go of; (*момент, случай*) to miss; ~ **(упустить** *perf*) **из виду** to overlook.
уп|устить (-ущу, -устишь) *сов от* **упускать**.
упущени|е (-я) *ср* omission.
упыр|ь (-я) *м* vampire.
упьюсь *итп сов см* **упиться**.
ура *межд* hooray, hurrah; **на ~** (*с энтузиазмом*) enthusiastically; (*без подготовки*) just like that.
уравнени|е (-я) *ср* (*сил*) equalization; (*МАТ*) equation.
уравнива|ть (-ю) *несов от* **уравнять**, **уровнять**.
уравниловк|а (-и) *ж* (*разг: пренебр*) *equal rewarding regardless of contribution*.
уравнове|сить (-шу, -сишь; *impf* **уравновешивать**) *сов перех* to balance
▸ **уравновеситься** (*impf* **уравновешиваться**) *сов возв* (*чаши весов*) to balance; (*силы*) to be counterbalanced.
уравновешенност|ь (-и) *ж* composure.
уравновешен|ный (-, -на, -но) *прил* balanced, steady.
уравновешива|ть(ся) (-ю(сь)) *несов от* **уравновесить(ся)**.
уравновешу(сь) *сов см* **уравновесить(ся)**.
уравня|ть (-ю; *impf* **уравнивать**) *сов перех* (*размеры, доли итп*) to make equal; **уравнивать (~** *perf*) **кого-н в правах с кем-н** to give sb the same rights as sb.
ураган (-а) *м* hurricane; (*перен: страстей*) storm.
ураганный *прил*: ~ **ветер** gale.
Уралмаш (-а) *м сокр* = *Уральский машиностроительный завод*.
уран (-а) *м* uranium; (*планета*): **У~** Uranus.
урановый *прил* uranium.
ура-патриот (-а) *м* (*пренебр*) jingoist.
ура-патриотизм (-а) *м* jingoism.
урбанизаци|я (-и) *ж* urbanization.
урв|ать (-у, -ёшь; *impf* **урывать**) *сов перех* (*разг: материальные блага*) to grab; (*: время*) to snatch.
урегулировани|е (-я) *ср* settlement.
урегулир|овать (-ую) *сов от* **регулировать** ♦ *перех* (*отношения*) to put to rights; (*конфликт*) to settle.
урежу *итп сов см* **урезать**.
урезанный *прил* (*демократия, свобода*) limited.
уре|зать (-жу, -жешь; *impf* **урезать**) *сов перех* (*расходы, штаты*) to cut down.
урезон|ить (-ю, -ишь; *impf* **урезонивать**) *сов перех*: ~ **кого-н** (*разг*) to make sb see reason.
уреми|я (-и) *ж* uraemia (*BRIT*), uremia (*US*).
уретр|а (-ы) *ж* urethra.
урн|а (-ы) *ж* (*погребальная*) urn; (*для мусора, для окурков*) bin; **избирательная ~** ballot box.
уров|ень (-ня) *м* level; (*техники*) standard; (*зарплаты, доходов*) rate; **в ~ с** *+instr* on a level with; **на ~не земли** at ground level; **встреча на высшем ~не** summit meeting; **выше/ниже ~ня моря** above/below sea level; **моя работа была на ~не** my work was up to standard; **уровень жизни** living standard.
уровня|ть (-ю; *impf* **уравнивать**) *сов перех* (*дорогу, землю*) to level.
урод (-а) *м person with a deformity*; (*нравственный*) monster.
уродин|а (-ы) *м/ж* ugly person (*мн* people).

уро|ди́ться (**-жу́сь, -ди́шься**) *сов возв* (*пшеница*) to give a good yield; ~ *(perf)* **в кого́-н** (*в деда, в отца итп*) to take after sb.
уро́д|ка (**-ки**; *gen pl* **-ок**) *ж см* **уро́д**.
уро́дливост|ь (**-и**) *ж* (*см прил*) deformity; distortion; ugliness.
уро́длив|ый (**-, -а, -о**) *прил* (*с уродством*) deformed; (*представление*) distorted; (*безобразный*) ugly.
уро́д|овать (**-ую**; *perf* **изуро́довать**) *несов перех* (*калечить*) to deform; (*делать некрасивым*) to make ugly; (*сознание*) to distort; (*душу, молодёжь*) to corrupt.
уро́дств|о (**-а**) *ср* (*физический недостаток*) deformity; (*некрасивая внешность*) ugliness.
урожа́|й (**-я**) *м* (*зерна, картофеля итп*) harvest; (*большое количество*) abundance; **снима́ть (снять** *perf***)** *или* **собира́ть (собра́ть** *perf***)** ~ to gather the harvest; **убира́ть (убра́ть** *perf***)** ~ to take in the harvest.
урожа́йност|ь (**-и**) *ж* yield.
урожа́йный *прил* (*год*) productive.
урождённая *прил* née.
урожéн|ец (**-ца**) *м* native.
урожу́сь *сов см* **уроди́ться**.
уро́к (**-а**) *м* lesson; (*задание*) task; (*обычно мн*: *домашняя работа*) homework *ед*; **де́лать (сде́лать** *perf***)** **~и** to do one's homework; **э́то послу́жит тебе́ хоро́шим ~ом** let it be a (good) lesson to you; **брать** *(impf)* **~и чего́-н у кого́-н** to take lessons in sth from sb; **дава́ть** *(impf)* ~ to give a lesson; **дава́ть** *(impf)* **~и где́-нибудь/кому́-н** to teach somewhere/sb.
уро́лог (**-а**) *м* urologist.
урологи́ческ|ий (**-ая, -ое, -ие**) *прил* urological.
уроло́ги|я (**-и**) *ж* urology.
уро́н (**-а**) *м* (*потери*) losses *мн*; **нести́ (понести́** *perf***)** ~ to suffer losses; **наноси́ть (нанести́** *perf***)** **кому́-н** ~ to inflict loss on sb.
ур|они́ть (**-оню́, -о́нишь**) *сов от* **роня́ть**.
уро́чищ|е (**-а**) *ср* natural boundary.
Уругва́|й (**-я**) *м* Uruguay.
уругва́йск|ий (**-ая, -ое, -ие**) *прил* Uruguayan.
урча́ни|е (**-я**) *ср* (*воды*) gurgling; (*собаки*) growling; (*кошки*) purring.
урч|а́ть (**-у́, -и́шь**) *несов неперех* (*вода*) to gurgle; (*тигр*) to growl; (*кошка*) to purr; **у меня́ ~и́т в желу́дке** my tummy's rumbling.
урыва́|ть (**-ю**) *несов от* **урва́ть**.
уры́вками *нареч* at odd times.
урю́к (**-а**) *м собир* dried apricots *мн*.
ус (**-а**) *м* whisker; *см также* **усы́**.
ус|ади́ть (**-ажу́, -а́дишь**; *impf* **уса́живать**) *сов перех*: ~ **госте́й** to show the guests to their seats; (*заставить делать*): ~ **кого́-н за что-н/**+*infin* to sit sb down to sth/to do; **уса́живать (~** *perf***)** **сад цвета́ми** to plant the garden with lots of flowers.
уса́дьб|а (**-ы**) *ж* (*помещичья*) country estate; (*крестьянская*) farmstead.
уса́жива|ть (**-ю**) *несов от* **усади́ть**
▸ **уса́живаться** *несов от* **усе́сться**.
усажу́ *сов см* **усади́ть**.
уса́т|ый (**-, -а, -о**) *прил*: ~ **мужчи́на** man with a moustache; ~ **кот** cat with whiskers.
усва́ива|ть (**-ю**) *несов от* **усво́ить**.
усвое́ни|е (**-я**) *ср* (*урока, науки*) mastering; (*пищи*) assimilation.
усво́|ить (**-ю, -ишь**; *impf* **усва́ивать**) *сов перех* (*привычку*) to acquire; (*урок*) to master; (*пищу, лекарство*) to assimilate.
усвоя́емост|ь (**-и**) *ж* assimilability.
усёк *итп сов см* **усе́чь**.
усека́|ть (**-ю**) *несов от* **усе́чь**.
усеку́ *итп сов см* **усе́чь**.
усе́рден *прил см* **усе́рдный**.
усе́рди|е (**-я**) *ср* diligence.
усе́рд|ный (**-ен, -на, -но**) *прил* diligent.
усе́рдств|овать (**-ую**) *несов неперех* to make an effort.
ус|е́сться (**-я́дусь, -я́дешься**; *pt* **-е́лся, -е́лась, -е́лось**, *impf* **уса́живаться**) *сов возв* to settle down; (*заняться чем-н*): ~ **за** +*acc* (*за работу, за письмо*) to sit down to.
ус|е́чь (**-еку́, -ечёшь** *итп*, **-еку́т**; *pt* **-ёк, -екла́, -екло́**, *impf* **усека́ть**) *сов перех* (*укоротить*) to truncate; (*разг*: *понять*) to catch on to.
усе́|ять (**-ю**) *сов перех* (*поле, небо*) to cover
▸ **усе́яться** *сов возв*: **~ся** +*instr* to be dotted *или* strewn with; (*цветами*) to be full of.
уси|де́ть (**-жу́, -ди́шь**) *сов неперех* (*остаться сидеть*) to stay sitting; (*не упасть*) to stay in one's seat; **он е́ле ~де́л на ме́сте** he could hardly sit still; **он не мог ~ до́ма** he couldn't just sit at home.
усе́дчивост|ь (**-и**) *ж* assiduity.
усе́дчив|ый (**-, -а, -о**) *прил* assiduous.
усижу́ *сов см* **усиде́ть**.
у́сик|и (**-ов**; *nom sg* **-**) *мн* (*маленькие усы*) small moustache *ед*; (*у растений*) tendril *ед*; (*у членистоногих*) feelers *мн*.
уси́ленн|ый *прил* (*охрана*) reinforced; (*просьбы, напоминания*) persistent; (*внимание*) increased; **~ое пита́ние** high calorie diet.
уси́лива|ть(ся) (**-ю(сь)**) *несов от* **уси́лить(ся)**.
уси́ли|е (**-я**) *ср* effort; (*физическое*) exertion; **де́лать (сде́лать** *perf***)** ~ **над собо́й** to force o.s.
усили́тел|ь (**-я**) *м* amplifier.
усили́тельный *прил* amplifying.
уси́л|ить (**-ю, -ишь**; *impf* **уси́ливать**) *сов перех* to intensify; (*охрану*) to reinforce; (*внимание*) to increase; (*звук*) to amplify
▸ **уси́литься** (*impf* **уси́ливаться**) *сов возв* (*ветер*) to get stronger; (*сопротивление*) to intensify; (*волнение*) to increase.
уск|ака́ть (**-ачу́, -а́чешь**) *сов неперех* (*кони*) to gallop away *или* off; (*перен*: *разг*: *человек*) to whizz off.
ускользну́ть (**-у́, -ёшь**; *impf* **ускольза́ть**) *сов неперех* (*рыба, змея итп*) to slip off; (*перен*): ~ **из** +*gen***/от** +*gen* to slip out of/away from; **ускольза́ть (~** *perf***)** **от чьего́-н внима́ния** to

escape sb's attention.
ускоре́ни|е (-я) *ср* acceleration; (*шага*) quickening.
уско́ренный *прил* (*шаг*) quickened; (*дыхание, пульс, темпы*) accelerated; ~ **курс** crash course.
ускори́тел|ь (-я) *м* accelerator; **раке́тный** ~ rocket booster.
уско́р|ить (-ю, -ишь; *impf* **ускоря́ть**) *сов перех* (*шаги*) to quicken; (*ход механизма, прогресс*) to accelerate; (*выздоровление, отъезд*) to be speeded up
▸ **уско́риться** (*impf* **ускоря́ться**) *сов возв* (*ход поезда*) to accelerate; (*шаги*) to quicken; (*отъезд, решение вопроса*) to speed up.
усла́влива|ться (-юсь) *несов от* **усло́виться**.
усла́д|а (-ы) *ж* delight, joy.
усла|ди́ть (-жу́, -ди́шь; *impf* **услажда́ть**) *сов перех* (*слух, зрение*) to delight
▸ **услади́ться** (*impf* **услажда́ться**) *сов возв*: ~**ся** *+instr* (*зрелищем, ароматом*) to delight in.
усл|а́ть (**ушлю́, ушлёшь**; *impf* **усыла́ть**) *сов перех* (*курьера, слуг*) to dispatch; (*на каторгу*) to send away.
усле|ди́ть (-жу́, -ди́шь) *сов неперех*: ~ **за** *+instr* (*за ребёнком*) to keep an eye on; (*за ходом разговора*) to follow.
усло́вен *прил см* **усло́вный**.
усло́ви|е (-я) *ср* condition; (*договора, платежа*) term; (*соглашение*) agreement; (*обычно мн*: *поступления в институт, приёма на работу*) requirement; **ста́вить** (**поста́вить** *perf*) **что-н** ~**м** to make sth a condition; **при** ~**и хоро́шей пого́ды** on the condition that the weather is good; **при** ~**и, что он согласи́тся** on the condition *или* provided that he agrees; *см также* **усло́вия**.
усло́в|иться (-люсь, -ишься; *impf* **усла́вливаться**) *сов возв*: ~ **о** *+prp* (*договориться*) to agree on.
усло́ви|я (-й) *мн* (*природные*) conditions *мн*; (*задачи, теоремы*) factors *мн*; (*пользования чем-н, какого-н режима*) terms *мн*; **жили́щные** ~ housing; ~ **труда́** working conditions; **в** ~**х** *+gen* in an atmosphere of; **по** ~**м догово́ра** on the terms of the agreement; **на льго́тных** ~**х** on special terms; **на сле́дующих** ~**х** on the following conditions; **для рабо́ты здесь – все** ~ (*разг*) everything you need for working here is laid on.
усло́вленный *прил* agreed.
усло́влюсь *сов см* **усло́виться**.
усло́вност|ь (-и) *ж* conditional nature; (*обычай*) convention.
усло́в|ный (-ен, -на, -но) *прил* (*срок, согласие итп*) conditional; (*знак, сигнал*) code *опред*; . (*линия*) imaginary; (*no short form*; *линг*) conditional; **усло́вный рефле́кс** conditional reflex; **усло́вный срок** suspended sentence.
усложн|и́ть (-ю́, -и́шь; *impf* **усложня́ть**) *сов перех* to complicate
▸ **усложни́ться** (*impf* **усложня́ться**) *сов возв* to get more complicated.
услу́г|а (-и) *ж* (*одолжение*) favour (*BRIT*), favor (*US*); (*обычно мн*: *облуживание*) service; **коммуна́льные** ~**и** public utilities; **бюро́ (до́брых) услу́г** domestic services agency; **к Ва́шим** ~**м!** at your service!; **ока́зывать (оказа́ть** *perf*) **кому́-н** ~**у** to do sb a good turn.
услуже́ни|е (-я) *ср*: **быть в** ~**и (у** *+gen*) to be in service (with).
усл|ужи́ть (-ужу́, -у́жишь) *сов неперех*: ~ **кому́-н** to do sb a good turn.
услу́жлив|ый (-, -а, -о) *прил* obliging.
услы́ш|ать (-у, -ишь) *сов от* **слы́шать**.
усма́трива|ть (-ю) *несов от* **усмотре́ть**.
усмехн|у́ться (-у́сь, -ёшься; *impf* **усмеха́ться**) *сов возв* to smile slightly.
усме́шк|а (-и) *ж* slight smile; **зла́я** ~ sneer.
усмире́ни|е (-я) *ср* (*тигра*) taming; (*страстей, мятежа*) suppression.
усмир|и́ть (-ю́, -и́шь; *impf* **усмиря́ть**) *сов перех* (*льва*) to tame; (*детей*) to discipline; (*страсти, мятеж, восстание*) to suppress
▸ **усмири́ться** (*impf* **усмиря́ться**) *сов возв* (*лев*) to become tame; (*дети*) to calm down.
усмотре́ни|е (-я) *ср* discretion; **предоставля́ть (предоста́вить** *perf*) **на** ~ **нача́льства** to be left to the management's discretion; **де́йствовать** (*impf*) **по своему́** ~**ю** to use one's own discretion *или* judgement; **на Ва́ше** ~ at your discretion.
усм|отре́ть (-отрю́, -о́тришь; *impf* **усма́тривать**) *сов перех* (*разг*) to spot; (*счесть*): ~ **что-н в** *+prp* to see sth in ◆ *неперех* (*разг*: *уследить*): ~ **за** *+instr* to keep an eye on.
усна|сти́ть (-ащу́, -сти́шь; *impf* **уснаща́ть**) *сов перех*: ~ **что-н чем-н** to pepper sth with sth.
усн|у́ть (-у́, -ёшь) *сов неперех* (*заснуть*) to fall asleep, go to sleep; ~ (*perf*) **наве́ки** *или* **ве́чным сном** to go to one's eternal rest.
усоверше́нствовани|е (-я) *ср* improvement, refinement.
усоверше́нств|овать(ся) (-ую(сь)) *сов от* **соверше́нствовать(ся)**.
усо́ве|стить (-щу, -стишь; *impf* **усо́вещивать**) *сов перех*: ~ **кого́-н** to make sb (feel) ashamed.
усомн|и́ться (-ю́сь, -и́шься) *сов возв*: ~ **в** *+prp* to doubt.
усо́пш|ая (-ей; *decl like adj*) *ж см* **усо́пший**.
усо́пш|ий (-его; *decl like adj*) *м* deceased.
усо́хн|уть (-у, -ешь; *impf* **усыха́ть**) *сов неперех* (*также перен*) to shrivel (up); (*шерсть*) to shrink.
успева́емост|ь (-и) *ж* performance (*in studies*).
успева́|ть (-ю) *несов от* **успе́ть** ◆ *неперех* to make progress (*in one's studies*).
успе́ется *сов безл* there's no hurry *или* rush.

Успéни|е (-я) *ср* the Assumption.
успé|ть (-ю; *impf* **успевáть**) *сов неперех* (*сделать что-н в срок*) to manage; (*прийти вовремя*) to be *или* make it in time; **я не ~л это сдéлать, как ...** I'd hardly done it when ...; **не ~л оглянýться, как он ужé ушёл** I hardly had time to blink before he'd already gone.
успéх (-а) *м* success; (*обычно мн*: *в спорте, в учёбе*) achievement; **как Вáши ~и?** how are you doing?; **с ~ом** (*успешно*) successfully; (*без затруднений*) easily; **добивáться (добиться** *perf*) **~а** to achieve success; **с тем же ~ом** just as well.
успéшно *нареч* successfully.
успéш|ный (-ен, -на, -но) *прил* successful.
успокáива|ть(ся) (-ю(сь)) *несов от* **успокóить(ся)**.
успокоéни|е (-я) *ср* (*боли, совести*) easing; (*плачущего*) pacifying; **эти мысли принеслú ей ~** these thoughts brought her peace of mind.
успокóенност|ь (-и) *ж* complacency.
успокоительн|ое (-ого; *decl like adj*) *ср* sedative.
успокоительный *прил* (*известие, ответ*) calming, soothing; (*лекарство*) sedative *опред.*
успокó|ить (-ю, -ишь; *impf* **успокáивать**) *сов перех* to calm (down); (*совесть*) to ease; (*боль*) to soothe
▸ **успокóиться** (*impf* **успокáиваться**) *сов возв* (*человек*) to calm down; (*море*) to calm; (*боль, совесть, волнения*) to be eased; (*ветер*) to drop; **успокáиваться (~ся** *perf*) **на достúгнутом** to be content with one's achievements; **он не ~ился, покá не раскрыли всё дéло** he couldn't rest until they'd uncovered the whole business.
уст|á (-) *мн* lips *мн*; **в егó ~х это звучит стрáнно** it sounds strange coming from him; **из уст в ~** by word of mouth; **из пéрвых уст** from the horse's mouth; **это у всех на ~х** it's on everyone's lips.
устáв (-а) *м* (*партийный*) rules *мн*; (*воинский*) regulations *мн*; (*корпорации*) statute; **~ акционéрной компáнии** (*комм*) articles of association.
уста|вáть (-ю, -ёшь) *несов от* **устáть**.
устáв|ить (-лю, -ишь; *impf* **уставлять**) *сов перех* (*разместить*) to place, put; (*занять*): **~ что-н чем-н** (*стол*) to cover sth with; (*полку*) to fill sth with; (*разг*: *устремить*): **~ что-н в** *+acc* to fix sth on
▸ **устáвиться** (*impf* **уставляться**) *сов возв* (*разг*): **~ся на/в** *+acc* (*на собеседника, в стену*) to gaze at.
устáвный *прил* statutory; **устáвный капитáл** (*комм*) authorized capital.
устáло *нареч* wearily.
устáлост|ь (-и) *ж* tiredness, fatigue.
устáлый *прил* tired, weary.
ýстал|ь (-и) *ж*: **без** *или* **не знáя ~и** tirelessly, indefatigably.
устан|овúть (-овлю, -óвишь; *impf* **устанáвливать**) *сов перех* to establish; (*размер оплаты, сроки*) to set; (*прибор, машину*) to install; **устанáвливать (~** *perf*) **рекóрд** to set a record
▸ **установúться** (*impf* **устанáвливаться**) *сов возв* to be established; (*погода*) to become settled; (*характер*) to be formed.
установк|а (-и) *ж* installation; (*директива*) directive; (*цель*) objective.
установлю(сь) *сов см* **установúть(ся)**.
устáну *итп сов см* **устáть**.
устарé|ть (-ю) *сов от* **старéть** ◆ (*impf* **устаревáть**) *неперех* (*оборудование*) to become obsolete.
устá|ть (-ну, -нешь; *impf* **уставáть**) *сов неперех* to get tired.
уст|лáть (-елю, -éлешь; *impf* **устилáть**) *сов перех*: **~ что-н (чем-н)** to cover sth (with sth).
ýстный *прил* (*экзамен*) oral; (*обещание, приказ*) verbal; **ýстная речь** spoken language.
устó|й (-я) *м* (*опора*) support; **~и** (*основы*) foundations.
устóйчивост|ь (-и) *ж* stability.
устóйчив|ый (-, -а, -о) *прил* (*также перен*) stable; (*лестница*) steady; **устóйчивое (слово)сочетáние** set phrase.
усто|ять (-ю, -úшь) *сов неперех* (*не упасть*) to remain standing; (*в споре, в борьбе итп*) to stand one's ground; (*не поддаться*) to resist; **~** (*perf*) **на ногáх** to keep one's balance
▸ **устояться** *сов возв* (*характер*) to be formed; (*жидкость*) to settle; (*взгляды*) to become fixed.
устрáива|ть(ся) (-ю(сь)) *несов от* **устрóить(ся)**.
устран|úть (-ю, -úшь; *impf* **устранять**) *сов перех* (*препятствие*) to remove; (*недостатки, соперника*) to eliminate; (*работника*) to dismiss
▸ **устранúться** (*impf* **устраняться**) *сов возв* to resign.
устрашá|ть(ся) (-ю(сь)) *несов от* **устрашúть(ся)**.
устрашáющ|ий (-ая, -ее, -ие) *прил* frightening.
устраш|úть (-ý, -úшь; *impf* **устрашáть**) *сов перех* to frighten
▸ **устрашúться** (*impf* **устрашáться**) *сов возв*: **~ся** *+gen* to be frightened of.
устрем|úть (-лю, -úшь; *impf* **устремлять**) *сов перех* (*удар, глаза итп*) to direct; (*внимание, помыслы*) to focus
▸ **устремúться** (*impf* **устремляться**) *сов возв*: **~ся на** *+acc* (*конница, толпа*) to charge at; (*перен*: *внимание, мысли*) to be focused on; (*взгляд, глаза*) to be fixed on.
устремлéни|е (-я) *ср* aspiration.
устремлённост|ь (-и) *ж* tendency.
устремлю(сь) *сов см* **устремúть(ся)**.
устремля|ть(ся) (-ю(сь)) *несов от* **устремúть(ся)**.
ýстриц|а (-ы) *ж* oyster.
ýстричный *прил* oyster.

устро́ен|ный (-, -а, -о) *прил* (*жизнь*) ordered; (*квартира*) habitable.
устрои́тел|ь (-я) *м* organizer.
устро́|ить (-ю, -ишь; *impf* **устра́ивать**) *сов перех* (*жизнь, дела*) to organize; (*спектакль, выставку*) to arrange; (*подлеж: предложение, цена*) to suit; **устра́ивать (~ *perf*) кого́-н на рабо́ту/кварти́ру** to help sb find work/a flat; **устра́ивать (~ *perf*) сканда́л** to make a scene; **э́то меня́ ~ит** that suits me
▸ **устро́иться** (*impf* **устра́иваться**) *сов возв* (*расположиться*) to settle down; (*прийти в порядок*) to work out; **устра́иваться (~ся *perf*) на рабо́ту** to get a job; **он ~ился на заво́д** he got a job in a factory.
устро́йств|о (-а) *ср* (*действие: выставки*) organization; (*: на работу*) finding; (*дома, прибора*) construction; (*государственное, общественное*) structure; (*техническое*) device, mechanism; **~ опти́ческого счи́тывания си́мволов** (*КОМП*) optical character reader.
усту́п (-а) *м* ledge.
уст|упи́ть (-уплю́, -у́пишь; *impf* **уступа́ть**) *сов перех*; **~ что-н кому́-н** to give sth up for sb ◆ *неперех*: **~ кому́-н/чему́-н** (*сильному, силе, желанию итп*) to give in to sb/sth; **уступа́ть (~ *perf*) в** *+prp* (*в силе, в уме*) to be inferior in; **уступа́ть (~ *perf*) доро́гу кому́-н** to make way for sb; **он ~упи́л мне кни́гу за 10 рубле́й** he let me have the book for 10 roubles.
усту́п|ка (-ки; *gen pl* **-ок**) *ж* (*компромисс*) compromise; (*силе, врагу*) surrender; (*скидка*) discount; **пойти́** (*perf*) **на ~ку** to compromise.
уступлю́ *сов см* **уступи́ть**.
усту́пок *сущ см* **усту́пка**.
усту́пчив|ый (-, -а, -о) *прил* compliant.
усты|ди́ть (-жу́, -ди́шь) *сов перех* to shame
▸ **устыди́ться** *сов возв*: **~ся** *+gen* to be ashamed of.
у́сть|е (-я) *ср* (*реки*) mouth; (*шахты*) entrance.
усугу́б|ить (-лю, -ишь; *impf* **усугубля́ть**) *сов перех* (*вину, опасность*) to increase; (*болезнь, положение*) to aggravate
▸ **усугу́биться** (*impf* **усугубля́ться**) *сов возв* (*вина*) to increase; (*страдания, болезнь*) to be aggravated.
усу́шк|а (-и) *ж* (*зерна*) loss of weight (*through drying*).
ус|ы́ (-о́в) *мн* (*у человека*) moustache *ед*; (*у животных*) whiskers *мн*; **он (и) в ус (себе́) не ду́ет** (*разг*) he's completely unruffled; **на ус мота́ть (намота́ть *perf*) что-н** (*разг*) to take good note of sth; **са́ми с ~а́ми** (*разг*) we weren't born yesterday.
усыла́|ть (-ю) *несов от* **усла́ть**.
усынов|и́ть (-лю́, -и́шь; *impf* **усыновля́ть**) *сов перех* to adopt (*son*).
усыновле́ни|е (-я) *ср* adoption (*son*).
усыновлю́ *сов см* **усынови́ть**.
усыновля́|ть (-ю) *несов от* **усынови́ть**.
усыпа́льниц|а (-ы) *ж* burial chamber.
усы́п|ать (-лю, -лешь; *impf* **усыпа́ть**) *сов перех*: **~ что-н чем-н** (*путь, дорогу*) to scatter sth with sth.
усып|и́ть (-лю́, -и́шь; *impf* **усыпля́ть**) *сов перех* (*больного*) to anaesthetize (*BRIT*), anesthetize (*US*); (*ребёнка*) to lull to sleep; (*перен: внимание, бдительность*) to weaken; (*больную собаку итп*) to put to sleep; **он ~и́л меня́ свои́ми ску́чными разгово́рами** his boring conversation sent me to sleep.
усы́плю *итп сов см* **усы́пать**.
усыплю́ *сов см* **усыпи́ть**.
усыпля́|ть (-ю) *несов от* **усыпи́ть**.
усыха́|ть (-ю) *несов от* **усо́хнуть**.
уся́дусь *итп сов см* **усе́сться**.
ута|и́ть (-ю́, -и́шь; *impf* **ута́ивать**) *сов перех* (*правду*) to keep secret; (*деньги, документы*) to appropriate.
ута́йк|а (-и) *ж*: **без ~и** (*разг*) openly.
ута́птыва|ть (-ю) *несов от* **утопта́ть**.
ут|ащи́ть (-ащу́, -а́щешь; *impf* **ута́скивать**) *сов перех* (*унести*) to drag away *или* off; (*разг: украсть*) to make off with.
у́твар|ь (-и) *ж собир* utensils *мн*.
утверди́тел|ьный (-ен, -ьна, -ьно) *прил* (*также линг*) affirmative.
утвер|ди́ть (-жу́, -ди́шь; *impf* **утвержда́ть**) *сов перех* (*проект, график*) to approve; (*господство, демократию итп*) to establish; **~ (*perf*) кого́-н в подозре́ниях** to confirm sb's suspicions; **~ (*perf*) кого́-н в до́лжности** to approve sb's appointment to office; **~ (*perf*) кого́-н в мне́нии/наме́рении** to strengthen sb's conviction/intention
▸ **утверди́ться** (*impf* **утвержда́ться**) *сов возв* to be established; (*увериться*): **~ся в** *+prp* (*в намерении*) to become convinced of.
утвержда́|ть (-ю) *несов от* **утверди́ть** ◆ *перех* (*правильность, достоверность*) to maintain; **он ~л, что ничего́ не зна́ет** he maintained that he didn't know anything
▸ **утвержда́ться** *несов от* **утверди́ться**.
утвержде́ни|е (-я) *ср* (*см глаг*) approval; establishment; (*правильное, интересное*) statement.
утвержу́(сь) *сов см* **утверди́ть(ся)**.
утёк *итп сов см* **уте́чь**.
утека́|ть (*3sg* **-ет**, *3pl* **-ют**) *несов от* **уте́чь**.
утеку́т *итп сов см* **уте́чь**.
ут|ёнок (-ёнка; *nom pl* **-я́та**, *gen pl* **-я́т**) *м* duckling.
утеплённый *прил* (*гараж*) insulated; (*обувь*) lined.
утепл|и́ть (-ю́, -и́шь; *impf* **утепля́ть**) *сов перех* to insulate.

ут|ере́ть (**-ру́, -рёшь**; *pt* **-ёр, -ёрла, -ёрло**, *impf* **утира́ть**) *сов перех* (*пот*) to wipe off; (*слёзы*) to wipe away; (*лицо, нос*) to wipe; ~ *(perf)* **нос кому́-н** (*перен: разг*) to show sb what's what

▸ **утере́ться** (*impf* **утира́ться**) *сов возв* to wipe one's face; (*нос*) to wipe one's nose.

уте́р|я (**-и**) *ж* loss.

утеря́|ть (**-ю**) *сов от* **теря́ть**.

утёс (**-а**) *м* cliff.

уте́чк|а (**-и**) *ж* (*также перен*) leak; (*кадров*) turnover; **уте́чка мозго́в** brain drain.

ут|е́чь (*3sg* **-ечёт**, *3pl* **-еку́т**, *pt* **-ёк, -екла́, -екло́**, *impf* **утека́ть**) *сов неперех* (*вода, газ*) to leak; (*годы*) to go by, pass; (*информация*) to be leaked.

утеша́|ть(ся) (**-ю(сь)**) *несов от* **уте́шить(ся)**.

утеше́ни|е (**-я**) *ср* (*плачущего*) comforting; (*о чём-н утешающем*) consolation.

уте́ш|ить (**-у, -ишь**; *impf* **утеша́ть**) *сов перех* (*плачущего, несчастного*) to comfort, console; (*подлеж: мысль, успехи детей*) to comfort

▸ **уте́шиться** (*impf* **утеша́ться**) *сов возв* to cheer up.

утилиза́ци|я (**-и**) *ж* recycling.

утилизи́р|овать (**-ую**) *(не)сов перех* to recycle.

утилита́р|ный (**-ен, -на, -но**) *прил* (*взгляды*) utilitarian; (*знания*) practical.

ути́л|ь (**-я**) *м собир* recyclable waste.

ути́ный *прил* (*гнездо*) duck's; (*яйцо, охота*) duck *опред*.

утира́|ть(ся) (**-ю(сь)**) *несов от* **утере́ть(ся)**.

ути́хн|уть (**-у, -ешь**; *impf* **утиха́ть**) *сов неперех* (*спор*) to calm down; (*гром, звон*) to die away; (*ветер*) to drop; (*вьюга*) to die down.

утихоми́р|ить (**-ю, -ишь**; *impf* **утихоми́ривать**) *сов перех* to pacify

▸ **утихоми́риться** (*impf* **утихоми́риваться**) *сов возв* to calm down.

у́т|ка (**-ки**; *gen pl* **-ок**) *ж* duck; (*ложный слух*) canard; (*сосуд*) bedpan; **пуска́ть** (**пусти́ть** *perf*) **~ку** to spread a false rumour (*BRIT*) *или* rumor (*US*).

уткн|у́ть (**-у́, -ёшь**) *сов перех* (*разг: подбородок*) to bury; ~ *(perf)* **нос в** *+acc* to bury one's nose in; ~ *(perf)* **глаза́ в зе́млю** to fix one's eyes on the ground

▸ **уткну́ться** *сов возв* (*разг*): **~ся в** *+acc* (*в книгу, в газету*) to bury one's nose in; **она́ ~у́лась голово́й в поду́шку** she buried her face in the pillow.

утконо́с (**-а**) *м* duck-billed platypus (*мн* platypus).

у́тлый *прил* (*лодка*) decrepit.

у́ток *сущ см* **у́тка**.

утол|и́ть (**-ю́, -и́шь**; *impf* **утоля́ть**) *сов перех* (*жажду*) to quench; (*голод, любопытство*) to satisfy; (*боль*) to ease.

утол|сти́ть (**-щу́, -сти́шь**; *impf* **утолща́ть**) *сов перех* to thicken.

утолще́ни|е (**-я**) *ср* widening.

утолщу́ *сов см* **утолсти́ть**.

утоля́|ть (**-ю**) *несов от* **утоли́ть**.

утоми́тел|ьный (**-ен, -ьна, -ьно**) *прил* tedious, tiresome; (*ребёнок*) tiring.

утом|и́ть (**-лю́, -и́шь**; *impf* **утомля́ть**) *сов перех* to tire

▸ **утоми́ться** (*impf* **утомля́ться**) *сов возв* to get tired.

утомле́ни|е (**-я**) *ср* tiredness, fatigue.

утомлю́(сь) *сов см* **утоми́ть(ся)**.

утомля́емост|ь (**-и**) *ж* (*также ТЕХ*) fatigue.

утомля́|ть(ся) (**-ю(сь)**) *несов от* **утоми́ть(ся)**.

ут|ону́ть (**-ону́, -о́нешь**) *сов от* **тону́ть**.

утончённост|ь (**-и**) *ж* refinement.

утончён|ный (**-, -на, -но**) *прил* refined.

утонч|и́ть (**-у́, -и́шь**) *сов перех* (*нитку*) to make thinner

▸ **утончи́ться** *сов возв* (*вкусы, восприятие*) to become refined.

утопа́|ть (**-ю**) *несов неперех* (*тонуть*) to drown; (*перен*): **~ в** *+prp* (*в кружевах, в цветах*) to be smothered in; (*в роскоши, в разврате*) to wallow in.

утопи́ст (**-а**) *м* utopian.

ут|опи́ть(ся) (**-оплю́(сь), -о́пишь(ся)**) *сов от* **топи́ть(ся)**.

утопи́чен *прил см* **утопи́чный**.

утопи́ческ|ий (**-ая, -ое, -ие**) *прил* utopian.

утопи́ч|ный (**-ен, -на, -но**) *прил* utopian.

уто́пи|я (**-и**) *ж* utopia.

уто́пленник (**-а**) *м* drowned man (*мн* men).

уто́пленница (**-ы**) *ж* drowned woman (*мн* women).

утоплю́(сь) *сов см* **утопи́ть(ся)**.

ут|опта́ть (**-опчу́, -о́пчешь**; *impf* **уtáптывать**) *сов перех* to stamp down.

уточне́ни|е (**-я**) *ср* elaboration; **вноси́ть** (**внести́** *perf*) **~я в** *+acc* to elaborate on.

уточн|и́ть (**-ю́, -и́шь**; *impf* **уточня́ть**) *сов перех* (*пункт договора, выводы*) to elaborate on; (*сведения, факты*) to clarify.

утрамб|ова́ть (**-у́ю**) *сов от* **трамбова́ть**.

утра́т|а (**-ы**) *ж* loss; **~ трудоспосо́бности** disablement; **понести́** *(perf)* **~у** to suffer a loss.

утра́|тить (**-чу, -тишь**; *impf* **утра́чивать**) *сов перех* (*потерять*) to lose; ~ *(perf)* **си́лу** (*документ итп*) to become invalid.

у́тренн|ий (**-яя, -ее, -ие**) *прил* morning *опред*; (*событие, известие*) this morning's.

у́тренник (**-а**) *м* matinée; (*с участием детей*) children's party.

утри́рованный *прил* exaggerated.

утри́р|овать (**-ую**) *(не)сов перех* to exaggerate.

у́тр|о (**-а́**; *nom pl* **-а**, *gen pl* **-**, *dat pl* **-ам**) *ср* morning; **до утра́** till morning; **с утра́** since this morning; **дава́й встре́тимся с утра́** let's meet in the morning; **с утра́ до́ ночи** from morn till night; **до́брое ~!, с до́брым ~м!** good morning!; **на ~** next morning; **по утра́м** in the mornings; **под ~, к утру́** in the early hours of the morning.

утро́б|а (**-ы**) *ж* (*материнская*) womb; (*брюхо*) belly.

утро́бный *прил* (*БИО*) f(o)etal; (*истошный*) hollow.
утро́|ить (**-ю, -ишь**) *сов перех* to treble, triple
▸ **утро́иться** *сов возв* to treble, triple.
у́тром *нареч* in the morning; **ра́но ~** early in the morning.
утру́(сь) *итп сов см* **утере́ть(ся)**.
утружда́|ть (**-ю**) *несов перех*: **~ кого́-н чем-н** to trouble sb with sth; **не ~йте себя́** don't trouble yourself
▸ **утружда́ться** *несов возв* to trouble o.s.
утру́ск|а (**-и**) *ж* spillage.
утр|ясти́ (**-ясу́, -ясёшь**; *impf* **утряса́ть**) *сов перех* (*перен*: *разг*: *вопрос, проблему*) to settle; (*муку*) to shake down
▸ **утрясти́сь** *сов возв* (*разг*) to settle.
уты́|кать (**-чу, -чешь**; *impf* **утыка́ть**) *сов перех*: **~ что-н чем-н** to stick sth into sth.
утю́г (**-а́**) *м* iron (*appliance*).
утю́ж|ить (**-у, -ишь**; *perf* **выутюжить** *или* **отутю́жить**) *несов перех* to iron.
утяжел|и́ть (**-ю́, -и́шь**; *impf* **утяжеля́ть**) *сов перех* to make heavier, increase the weight of.
утя́та *итп сущ см* **утёнок**.
утя́тин|а (**-ы**) *ж* (*мясо*) duck.
уф *межд*: **~!** phew!
ух *межд*: **~!** ooh!
ух|а́ (**-и́**) *ж* fish broth.
уха́б (**-а**) *м* pothole.
уха́бист|ый (**-, -а, -о**) *прил*: **~ая доро́га** road full of potholes.
ухажёр (**-а**) *м* (*разг*) admirer.
уха́живани|е (**-я**) *ср* courting.
уха́жива|ть (**-ю**) *несов неперех*: **~ за** *+instr* (*за больным, за ранеными*) to nurse; (*за цветами, за садом*) to tend; (*за женщиной*) to court.
у́хань|е (**-я**) *ср* (*no pl*) hooting.
у́ха|ть (**-ю**) *несов от* **у́хнуть**.
ухва́т (**-а**) *м* oven fork.
ухв|ати́ть (**-ачу́, -а́тишь**; *impf* **ухва́тывать**) *сов перех* (*человека*: *за руку, за рукав*) to get hold of; (*перен*: *идею, смысл*) to grasp
▸ **ухвати́ться** (*impf* **ухва́тываться**) *сов возв*: **~ся за** *+acc* (*за перила, за руку*) to grab hold of; (*за дело, за мысль*) to latch onto; (*за предложение*) to jump at.
ухва́т|ки (**-ок**) *мн* manners *мн*.
ухва́тыва|ть(ся) (**-ю(сь)**) *несов от* **ухвати́ть(ся)**.
ухвачу́(сь) *сов см* **ухвати́ть(ся)**.
ухитр|и́ться (**-ю́сь, -и́шься**; *impf* **ухитря́ться**) *сов возв* = **умудри́ться**.
ухищре́ни|е (**-я**) *ср* (*уловка*) trick; **прибега́ть (прибе́гнуть** *perf*) **к ра́зным ~ям** to resort to various tricks.
ухищрённый *прил* crafty.
ухищря́|ться (**-юсь**) *несов возв* to contrive.
ухло́па|ть (**-ю**; *impf* **ухло́пывать**) *сов перех* (*разг*: *истратить*) to blow.
ухмы́лк|а (**-и**) *ж* (*разг*) smirk.
ухмыля́|ться (**-юсь**; *perf* **ухмыльну́ться**) *несов возв* (*разг*) to smirk.
у́хн|уть (**-у, -ешь**; *impf* **у́хать**) *сов неперех* (*снаряд*) to thud; (*гром*) to rumble; (*филин, сова*) to hoot; (*разг*: *упасть*) to come a cropper ♦ *перех* (*разг*: *все деньги*) to blow; (*: камень*) to hurl; **~** (*perf*) **кулако́м по столу́** to bang one's fist down on the table.
у́х|о (**-а**; *nom pl* **у́ши**, *gen pl* **уше́й**) *ср* ear; (*у шапки*) flap; **говори́ть (сказа́ть** *perf*) **что-н кому́-н на́ ухо** to whisper sth in sb's ear; **не вида́ть тебе́ де́нег как свои́х уше́й** (*разг*) you've got no chance of getting the money; **слу́шать** (*impf*) **во все у́ши** to be all ears; **слы́шать (услы́шать** *perf*) **что-н кра́ем ~а** *или* **одни́м ~м** to listen to sth with half an ear; **по́ уши влюби́ться** (*perf*) **в кого́-н** (*разг*) to fall head over heels in love with sb; **уши́ вя́нут от твои́х шу́ток** your jokes make me sick.
ухо́д (**-а**) *м* (*со службы, из семьи*) leaving; (*от погони, от реальности*) escape; (*в монастырь*) retreat; (*с собрания, со сцены*) exit; (*за больным, за ребёнком*) care; **~ в отста́вку** resignation; **~ на пе́нсию** retirement.
ух|оди́ть (**-ожу́, -о́дишь**) *несов от* **уйти́** ♦ *неперех* (*простираться*) to extend.
ухо́женный *прил* (*лицо, руки*) well-looked-after; (*сад*) well-kept; (*лошадь, человек*) well-groomed.
ухожу́ *несов см* **уходи́ть**.
ухудша́|ть(ся) (**-ю(сь)**) *несов от* **уху́дшить(ся)**.
ухудше́ни|е (**-я**) *ср* deterioration, worsening.
уху́дш|ить (**-у, -ишь**; *impf* **ухудша́ть**) *сов перех* to make worse
▸ **уху́дшиться** (*impf* **ухудша́ться**) *сов возв* to get worse, deteriorate.
уцеле́|ть (**-ю**) *сов неперех* to survive.
уценённый *прил* reduced.
уц|ени́ть (**-еню́, -е́нишь**; *impf* **уце́нивать**) *сов перех* to reduce (the price of).
уце́н|ка (**-ки**; *gen pl* **-ок**) *ж* reduction.
уц|епи́ть (**-еплю́, -е́пишь**) *сов перех* to hook
▸ **уцепи́ться** *сов возв* (*ухватиться*): **~ся за** *+acc* (*за руку*) to get hold of; (*за предложение, за возможность*) to jump at.
уча́ств|овать (**-ую**) *сов неперех*: **~ в** *+prp* (*в собрании, в спектакле*) to take part in; (*в предприятии, в прибылях*) to have a share in.
уча́сти|е (**-я**) *ср* (*в собрании, в спектакле итп*) participation; (*в предприятии, в прибылях*) share; (*родственное, дружеское*) concern; **принима́ть (приня́ть** *perf*) **~ в** *+prp* to take part in; **принима́ть (приня́ть** *perf*) **~ в ком-н** to show concern for sb.
уча|сти́ть (**-щу́, -сти́шь**; *impf* **учаща́ть**) *сов*

перех (*шаг*) to quicken; (*контакты, встречи*) to make more frequent
▸ **участиться** (*impf* **учащаться**) *сов возв* (*пульс, дыхание*) to quicken; (*столкновения, контакты*) to become more frequent.
участка *сущ см* **участок.**
участков|ый *прил* local ◆ **(-ого**; *decl like adj*) *м* (*разг*) local policeman (*мн* policemen); (*также:* **~ врач**) local GP *или* doctor; (*также:* **~ инспектор**) local policeman (*мн* policemen).
участливо *нареч* sympathetically.
участливый *прил* sympathetic.
участник (-а) *м* (*кружка, экспедиции*) member; (*восстания, репетиции, переговоров*) participant; **~ соревнования** competitor, contestant; **~ выставки** exhibitor; **~ войны** (war) veteran.
участниц|а (-ы) *ж см* **участник.**
участ|ок (-ка) *м* (*земли, кожи итп*) area; (*дороги, реки, фронта*) stretch; (*врачебный*) catchment area; (*приусадебный, земельный*) plot; (*строительный*) site; (*работы, деятельности*) field; **избирательный ~** polling station; **садовый ~** allotment.
участ|ь (-и) *ж* lot; **его постигла страшная ~** fate dealt him a terrible blow.
учаща|ть(ся) (-ю(сь)) *несов от* **участить(ся).**
учащ|аяся (-ейся; *decl like adj*) *ж см* **учащийся.**
учащ|ийся (-егося; *decl like adj*) *м* (*школы*) pupil; (*училища*) student.
учащу(сь) *сов см* **участить(ся).**
учёб|а (-ы) *ж* studies *мн.*
учебник (-а) *м* textbook; **~ истории** *или* **по истории** history textbook.
учебный *прил* (*работа*) academic; (*процесс, фильм*) educational; (*стрельба*) practice; (*бой*) mock; (*мастерская, судно*) training *опред*; (*методы*) teaching *опред*; **учебная программа** curriculum; **учебное заведение** educational establishment; **учебный год** academic year; **учебный план** course outline; **учебный отпуск** block release.
учёл *итп сов см* **учесть.**
учён|ая (-ой; *decl like adj*) *ж см* **учёный.**
учени|е (-я) *ср* (*в школе, в вузе*) study; (*теория*) teachings *мн*; *см также* **учения.**
ученик (-а) *м* (*школы*) pupil; (*училища*) student; (*мастера*) apprentice; (*последователь*) follower.
учениц|а (-ы) *ж см* **ученик.**
ученическ|ий (-ая, -ое, -ие) *прил* (*дневник, тетради*) school *опред*; (*перен: рассуждение, работа*) primitive.
ученичеств|о (-а) *ср* (*у мастера*) apprenticeship; **годы ~а** schooldays *мн.*
учени|я (-й) *мн* exercises *мн.*
учёност|ь (-и) *ж* learning.
учён|ый *прил* (*спор, круги*) academic; (*разг: опытом, каким-н событием*) educated; (*труды*) scholarly; (*кот, собака*) trained; **(-, -а, -о**; *человек*) learned, scholarly ◆ **(-ого**; *decl like adj*) *м* (*научный работник*) academic, scholar; (: *в области точных и естественных наук*) scientist; **учёное звание** academic title; **учёный совет** academic council.
уч|есть (-ту, -тёшь; *pt* **-ёл, -ла, -ло**, *impf* **учитывать**) *сов перех* (*обстоятельства, сложности*) to take into account; (*материал, имущество*) to make an inventory of; (*присутствующих*) to make a list of; **~тите, что** ... bear in mind that ...; **~** (*perf*) **вексель** to discount a bill.
учёт (-а) *м* (*потребностей, обстоятельств*) consideration; (*товара*) stock-taking; (*военный, медицинский*) registration; (*векселей*) discount; (*затрат, поступлений*) record; **бухгалтерский ~** (*учебный предмет*) accountancy; (*практическая деятельность*) bookkeeping; **брать (взять** *perf*) **на ~** to register; **вести** (*impf*) **~** to keep a record; **с ~ом всех обстоятельств** bearing in mind all the circumstances; **с ~ом сезонных колебаний** allowing for seasonal fluctuations.
учётн|ый *прил*: **~ая карточка** registration form; **~ая книга** record book; **~ процент** (*КОММ*) rate of discount; **~ дом** (*КОММ*) discount house.
училищ|е (-а) *ср* college; **профессионально-техническое ~** technical college.
учин|ить (-ю, -ишь; *impf* **учинять**) *сов перех* (*драку*) to start; **учинять** (~ *perf*) **скандал** to make a scene.
учител|ь (-я; *nom pl* **-я**) *м* (*школьный*) teacher; (*nom pl* **-и**; *мудрости*) master.
учительниц|а (-ы) *ж* teacher.
учительск|ая (-ой; *decl like adj*) *ж* staffroom.
учительств|о (-а) *ср* (*профессия*) teaching ◆ *собир* (*учителя*) teachers *мн.*
учительств|овать (-ую) *несов неперех* to teach, work as a teacher.
учитыва|ть (-ю) *несов от* **учесть.**
уч|ить (-у, -ишь; *perf* **выучить**) *несов перех* (*урок, роль*) to learn; (*perf* **выучить** *или* **научить** *или* **обучить**): **~ кого-н чему-н/**+*infin* to teach sb sth/to do; **история/эта теория учит, что** ... history/this theory teaches that ...
▸ **учиться** *несов возв* (*в школе, училище*) to study; (*perf* **выучиться** *или* **научиться**; *получить навыки*): **~ся чему-н/**+*infin* to learn sth/to do.
учредител|ь (-я) *м* founder.
учредительниц|а (-ы) *ж см* **учредитель.**
учредительн|ый *прил*: **~ое собрание** inaugural meeting.
учре|дить (-жу, -дишь; *impf* **учреждать**) *сов перех* (*фонд, банк*) to set up; (*контроль, порядок*) to introduce.
учреждени|е (-я) *ср* (*фонда, организации итп*) setting up; (*контроля*) introduction; (*научное, исследовательское*) establishment; (*финансовое, общественное*) institution; (*страховое*) agency.
учрежу *сов см* **учредить.**

учти́вост|ь (**-и**) *ж* courtesy.
учти́в|ый (**-, -а, -о**) *прил* courteous, civil.
учту́ *итп сов см* **уче́сть**.
учу́|ять (**-ю, -ешь**) *сов перех* (*разг*: *собака*) to sniff; (: *перен*: *человек*) to sense.
уша́н|ка (**-ки**; *gen pl* **-ок**) *ж cap with ear-flaps*.
уша́ст|ый (**-, -а, -о**) *прил*: ~ **ма́льчик** boy with big ears.
уша́т (**-а**) *м* tub.
у́шек *сущ см* **у́шко**.
ушёл *сов см* **уйти́**.
у́ши *итп сущ см* **у́хо**.
уши́б (**-а**) *м* bruise.
ушиб|и́ть (**-у́, -ёшь**; *pt* **-, -ла, -ло**, *impf* **ушиба́ть**) *сов перех* to bang
► **ушиби́ться** *сов возв* to bang o.s.
уш|и́ть (**-ью́, -ьёшь**; *impf* **ушива́ть**) *сов перех* (*сделать уже*) to take in; (*сделать короче*) to shorten, take up.
у́ш|ко (**-ка**; *nom pl* **-ки**, *gen pl* **-ек**) *ср уменьш от* **у́хо**; (*медали*) eyelet; (*иголки*) eye.
ушла́ *итп сов см* **уйти́**.
у́шлый *прил* smart.
ушлю́ *итп сов см* **усла́ть**.
ушни́к (**-а́**) *м* (*разг*) ear specialist.
ушн|о́й *прил* ear *опред*; **~а́я боль** earache; **~а́я ра́ковина** (*АНАТ*) auricle.
ушью́ *итп сов см* **уши́ть**.
уще́л|ье (**-ья**; *gen pl* **-ий**) *ср* gorge, ravine.
ущем|и́ть (**-лю́, -и́шь**; *impf* **ущемля́ть**) *сов перех* (*права, возможности*) to limit; (*палец*) to trap; **ущемля́ть** (~ *perf*) **чьё-н самолю́бие** to hurt *или* wound sb's pride.
ущемле́ни|е (**-я**) *ср* (*прав, возможностей*) limitation; ~ **чьего́-н самолю́бия** wound to sb's pride.
ущемлённый *прил* (*самолюбие, гордость*) wounded; (*права*) limited.
ущемлю́ *сов см* **ущеми́ть**.
ущемля́|ть (**-ю**) *несов от* **ущеми́ть**.
уще́рб (**-а**) *м* (*материальный*) loss; (*здоровью*) detriment; **в** ~ *+dat* to the detriment of; **на ~е** on the wane; **наноси́ть (нанести́** *perf*) *или* **причиня́ть (причини́ть** *perf*) ~ **кому́-н/чему́-н** to inflict loss on sb/sth.
уще́рбен *прил см* **уще́рбный**.
уще́рбност|ь (**-и**) *ж* (*см прил*) waning; abnormality.
уще́рб|ный *прил* (*луна*) waning; (**-ен, -на, -но**; *характер, психика*) abnormal.
ущипн|у́ть (**-у́, -ёшь**) *сов перех* to nip, pinch.
Уэ́льс (**-а**) *м* Wales.
уэ́льск|ий (**-ая, -ое, -ие**) *прил* Welsh; ~ **язы́к** Welsh.
ую́т (**-а**) *м* comfort, cosiness.
ую́тен *прил см* **ую́тный**.
ую́тно *нареч* (*расположиться*) comfortably ◆ *как сказ*: **здесь** ~ it's cosy here; **мне здесь** ~ I feel comfortable here.
ую́т|ный (**-ен, -на, -но**) *прил* cosy.
уязви́мост|ь (**-и**) *ж* vulnerability.
уязви́м|ый (**-, -а, -о**) *прил* vulnerable; **~ое ме́сто** weak spot.
уязв|и́ть (**-лю́, -и́шь**) *сов перех* to wound, hurt.
уясне́ни|е (**-я**) *ср* clarification.
уясн|и́ть (**-ю́, -и́шь**; *impf* **уясня́ть**) *сов перех* (*смысл, значение*) to comprehend; **уясня́ть** (~ *perf*) **(себе́)** to clarify for o.s.

~Ф, ф~

Ф, ф *сущ нескл* (*буква*) *the 21st letter of the Russian alphabet*.
фа *ср нескл* (*муз*) fa.
фа́брик|а (**-и**) *ж* factory; (*ткацкая, бумажная*) mill.
фабрик|ова́ть (**-у́ю**; *perf* **сфабрикова́ть**) *несов перех* (*перен*) to fabricate.
фабри́чный *прил* factory *опред*; **фабри́чная ма́рка** trademark.
фа́була|а (**-ы**) *ж* plot.
фавори́т (**-а**) *м* (*также спорт*) the favourite (*BRIT*) *или* favorite (*US*).
фавори́т|ка (**-ки**; *gen pl* **-ок**) *ж см* **фавори́т**.
фаго́т (**-а**) *м* bassoon.
фа́з|а (**-ы**) *ж* phase; (*работы, строительства*) stage.
фаза́н (**-а**) *м* pheasant.
файл (**-а**) *м* (*комп*) file.
фак. *сокр* (= **факульте́т**) Fac. (= *Faculty*).
фа́кел (**-а**) *м* torch; (*дыма, выбросов*) column.
факс (**-а**) *м* fax; **посыла́ть** (**посла́ть** *perf*) ~ to send a fax.
факси́миле *ср нескл* facsimile.
факси́мильный *прил* facsimile *опред*.
факт (**-а**) *м* fact; **ста́вить** (**поста́вить** *perf*) **кого́-н пе́ред фа́ктом** to present sb with a fait accompli; **го́лые фа́кты** the bare facts; ~ **тот, что ...** (*разг*) the fact of the matter is that ....
факти́чески *нареч* actually, in fact.
факти́ческ|ий (**-ая, -ое, -ие**) *прил* (*материал, данные*) factual; (*руководитель, положение дел*) real, actual.
фа́ктор (**-а**) *м* factor.
факту́р|а (**-ы**) *ж* texture; (*комм*) invoice.
факультати́в (**-а**) *м* optional *или* elective course.
факультати́в|ный (**-ен, -на, -но**) *прил* optional, elective.
факульте́т (**-а**) *м* faculty.
фала́нг|а (**-и**) *ж* (*анат, воен*) phalanx.
фа́лд|а (**-ы**) *ж* tail (*of coat*); (*складка*) crease.
фальсифика́тор (**-а**) *м* falsifier.
фальсифика́ци|я (**-и**) *ж* falsification.
фальсифици́р|овать (**-ую**) (*не*)*сов перех* to falsify.
фальста́рт (**-а**) *м* (*спорт*) false start.
фальце́т (**-а**) *м* falsetto.
фальши́в|ить (**-лю, -ишь**; *perf* **сфальши́вить**) *несов неперех* (*петь*) to sing out of tune; (*играть*) to play out of tune; (*лицемерить*) to pretend, put on an act.
фальши́в|ка (**-ки**; *gen pl* **-ок**) *ж* (*разг*) forgery.
фальши́влю *несов см* **фальши́вить**.
фальши́вок *сущ см* **фальши́вка**.
фальшивомоне́тчик (**-а**) *м* counterfeiter.
фальшивомоне́тчиц|а (**-ы**) *ж см* **фальшивомоне́тчик**.
фальши́в|ый *прил* (*документ, паспорт*) false, forged; (*монета, банкнот*) counterfeit; (*пение, инструмент*) out of tune; (*борода, улыбка, нота*) false; (**-, -а, -о**; *игра актёра*) unnatural, artificial; (*человек, поведение*) insincere.
фальш|ь (**-и**) *ж* insincerity.
фами́ли|я (**-и**) *ж* surname; (*королевская, старинная*) family; **де́вичья** ~ maiden name; **как Ва́ша ~?** what is your surname?; **моя́ ~ Серо́в** my surname is Serov.
фами́льный *прил* family *опред*.
фамилья́рен *прил см* **фамилья́рный**.
фамилья́рнича|ть (**-ю**) *несов неперех*: ~ (**с** +*instr*) to be too familiar (with).
фамилья́р|ный (**-ен, -на, -но**) *прил* over(ly)-familiar.
фанати́зм (**-а**) *м* fanaticism.
фана́тик (**-а**) *м* (*также перен*) fanatic.
фанати́ч|ный (**-ен, -на, -но**) *прил* fanatical.
фане́р|а (**-ы**) *ж* (*для облицовки*) veneer; (*древесный материал*) plywood.
фане́рный *прил* plywood *опред*.
фант (**-а**) *м* forfeit.
фантазёр (**-а**) *м* dreamer.
фантазёр|ка (**-ки**; *gen pl* **-ок**) *ж см* **фантазёр**.
фантази́р|овать (**-ую**) *несов неперех* (*мечтать*) to dream; (*выдумывать*) to make up stories.
фанта́зи|я (**-и**) *ж* (*художника, писателя*) imagination; (*мечта*) fantasy; (*выдумка*) fib; (*муз*) fantasia.
фанта́ст (**-а**) *м* writer of fantasy; (*научный*) science-fiction writer.
фанта́стик|а (**-и**) *ж* (*сказок, преданий*) fantastic element ◆ *собир* (*литература*) fantasy; **нау́чная** ~ science fiction; **э́то ~!** (*разг*) it's incredible!
фантасти́ческ|ий (**-ая, -ое, -ие**) *прил* fantastic; (*причудливый*) fantastical; (*проект*) fantastic, far-fetched.
фа́нтик (**-а**) *м* wrapper.
фанфа́р|а (**-ы**) *ж* (*инструмент*) bugle; (*обычно*

мн: сигнал) fanfare.
ФАО *сокр* FAO (= *Food and Agriculture Organization*).
фа́р|а (-ы) *ж* (*АВТ, АВИА*) light; **пере́дние ~ы** headlights, headlamps; **за́дние ~ы** rear lights (*BRIT*), taillights *или* taillamps (*US*).
фарао́н (-а) *м* pharaoh.
фарва́тер (-а) *м* (*МОР*) fairway, channel.
Фаренге́йт (-а) *м* Fahrenheit; **70 гра́дусов по ~у** 70 degrees Fahrenheit.
фаре́рск|ий (-ая, -ое, -ие) *прил*: **Ф~ие острова́** the Faroe Islands, the Faroes.
фаринги́т (-а) *м* pharyngitis.
фарисе́|й (-я) *м* Pharisee.
фарисе́йств|о (-а) *ср* hypocrisy.
фармаколо́ги|я (-и) *ж* pharmacology.
фармаце́вт (-а) *м* chemist, pharmacist.
фарс (-а) *м* farce.
фа́ртук (-а) *м* apron.
фарфо́р (-а) *м, собир* porcelain, china.
фарфо́ровый *прил* porcelain, china.
фарцо́вщик (-а) *м* (*разг*) *illegal trader who sells imported goods to Russians*.
фарцо́вщиц|а (-ы) *ж см* **фарцо́вщик**.
фарш (-а) *м* stuffing, forcemeat; (*мясной*) mince, minced *или* ground (*US*) meat.
фарширо́ванный *прил* (*кулин*) stuffed.
фарширова́ть (-у́ю; *perf* **зафаршировать**) *несов перех* to stuff.
ФАС *сокр* f.a.s. (= *free alongside ship*).
фас (-а) *м* (*ФОТО*) front.
фаса́д (-а) *м* (*лицевая сторона*) facade, front; **за́дний ~** back; **боково́й ~** side.
фас|ова́ть (-у́ю; *perf* **расфасова́ть**) *несов перех* to prepack.
фасо́вк|а (-и) *ж* packing.
фасо́вочн|ый *прил* (*цех, машина*) packing *опред*; **~ая бума́га** wrapping paper.
фасо́л|ь (-и) *ж* (*растение*) bean plant ◆ *собир* (*БОТ; семена*) beans *мн*; **кра́сная ~** kidney beans *мн*.
фасо́н (-а) *м* style.
фат|а́ (-ы́) *ж* veil.
фата́л|ьный (-ен, -ьна, -ьно) *прил* fatal, fateful.
фа́ун|а (-ы) *ж* fauna.
фаши́зм (-а) *м* fascism.
фаши́ст (-а) *м* fascist.
фаши́стск|ий (-ая, -ое, -ие) *прил* fascist.
фая́нс (-а) *м* (*материал*) faïence ◆ *собир* (*изделия*) faïence, glazed earthenware.
фая́нсовый *прил* (*посуда, изделия*) glazed earthenware *опред*.
ФБР *ср сокр* (= *Федера́льное бюро́ рассле́дований (США)*) FBI (= *Federal Bureau of Investigation*).
февра́л|ь (-я́) *м* February; *см также* **октя́брь**.
февра́льск|ий (-ая, -ое, -ие) *прил* February *опред*.
федера́льный *прил* federal; **Федера́льное бюро́ рассле́дований** Federal Bureau of Investigation; **Федера́льное собра́ние** (*ПОЛИТ*) the Federal Assembly (*upper house of the Russian parliament*).
федерати́вный *прил* federal.
федера́ци|я (-и) *ж* federation; **Росси́йская Ф~** the Russian Federation; **Сове́т Ф~й** *upper chamber of the Russian parliament*.
фее́ри|я (-и) *ж* magic show.
фейерве́рк (-а) *м* firework.
фе́льдшер (-а) *м* medical assistant.
фельето́н (-а) *м* satirical article.
фемини́ст|ка (-ки; *gen pl* -ок) *ж* feminist.
фен (-а) *м* hairdryer.
фено́мен (-а) *м* phenomenon (*мн* phenomena).
феномена́л|ьный (-ен, -ьна, -ьно) *прил* phenomenal.
феода́л (-а) *м* feudal lord.
феодали́зм (-а) *м* feudalism.
феода́льный *прил* feudal.
ферз|ь (-я́) *м* (*ШАХМАТЫ*) queen.
фе́рм|а (-ы) *ж* farm.
ферме́нт (-а) *м* ferment, enzyme.
фе́рмер (-а) *м* farmer.
фе́рмерск|ий (-ая, -ое, -ие) *прил*: **~ое хозя́йство** farm.
фестива́л|ь (-я) *м* festival.
фетр (-а) *м* felt.
фе́тровый *прил* felt.
фехтова́льщик (-а) *м* fencer.
фехтова́льщиц|а (-ы) *ж см* **фехтова́льщик**.
фехтова́ни|е (-я) *ср* (*СПОРТ*) fencing.
фешене́бел|ьный (-ен, -ьна, -ьно) *прил* fashionable.
фе́|я (-и) *ж* fairy.
фи *межд*: **~!** ugh!
фиа́л|ка (-ки; *gen pl* -ок) *ж* violet.
фиа́ско *ср нескл* fiasco; **терпе́ть (потерпе́ть** *perf*) **~** to suffer an embarrassment.
фи́г|а (-и) *ж* (*БОТ*) fig; (*разг*) fig (*gesture of refusal*); **ни фига́ не полу́чишь (от них)** (*разг*) you won't get a thing out of them; **иди́ на́ фиг** (*разг*) get lost, clear off.
фи́говый *прил* fig *опред*.
фиго́вый *прил* (*разг*) lousy, rotten.
фигу́р|а (-ы) *ж* (*ГЕОМ, перен*) figure; (*ШАХМАТЫ*) (chess)piece; **фигу́ра вы́сшего пилота́жа** aerobatic figure.
фигура́л|ьный (-ен, -ьна, -ьно) *прил* figurative.
фигури́р|овать (-ую) *несов неперех* (*присутствовать*) to be present; (*имя, тема*) to figure; **~** *(impf)* **на суде́ в ка́честве свиде́теля** to appear as a witness.
фигури́ст (-а) *м* figure skater.
фигури́ст|ка (-ки; *gen pl* -ок) *ж см* **фигури́ст**.
фигу́р|ка (-ки; *gen pl* -ок) *ж* (*скульптура*) figurine, statuette; (*обычно мн: игральная*) piece.

фигу́рный *прил* (*резьба*) figured; (*СПОРТ*) figure *опред*; **фигу́рное ката́ние** figure skating; **фигу́рные ско́бки** curly *или* brace brackets.
фигу́рок *сущ см* **фигу́рка.**
Фи́джи *ср нескл* Fiji.
фи́зик (-а) *м* physicist.
фи́зик|а (-и) *ж* physics.
физио́лог (-а) *м* physiologist.
физиологи́ческ|ий (**-ая, -ое, -ие**) *прил* physiological.
физиоло́ги|я (-и) *ж* physiology.
физионо́ми|я (-и) *ж* (*разг*) face.
физиотерапе́вт (-а) *м* physiotherapist.
физиотерапевти́ческ|ий (**-ая, -ое, -ие**) *прил* physiotherapy *опред*.
физиотерапи́|я (-и) *ж* physiotherapy.
физи́ческ|ий (**-ая, -ое, -ие**) *прил* (*также СПОРТ, ФИЗ*) physical; (*труд*) manual; **физи́ческая культу́ра** physical education; **физи́ческие упражне́ния** physical exercise *ед*; **физи́ческое лицо́** (*ЮР*) individual; **физи́ческое наси́лие** physical violence.
физкульту́р|а (-ы) *ж сокр* (= *физи́ческая культу́ра*) PE (= *physical education*).
физма́т (-а) *м сокр* = *фи́зико-математи́ческий факульте́т*.
фикс *м*: **иде́я** ~ idée fixe.
фикса́ж (-а) *м* (*ФОТО*) fixer.
фикса́ци|я (-и) *ж* (*ТЕХ*) clamping; (*ФОТО*) fixing.
фикси́р|овать (-ую; *perf* **зафикси́ровать**) *несов перех* (*события, факты, показания*) to record, chronicle; (*срок, дату, цены*) to fix, set; (*внимание, взгляд*) to fix; (*груз, тормоз*) to clamp, fix.
фикти́в|ный (**-ен, -на, -но**) *прил* fictitious; **фикти́вный брак** (*ЮР*) marriage of convenience.
фи́кус (-а) *м* ficus; (*каучуконосный*) rubber plant.
фи́кци|я (-и) *ж* fiction.
филармо́ни|я (-и) *ж* (*зал*) concert hall; (*организация*) philharmonic society.
филатели́ст (-а) *м* philatelist.
филе́ *ср нескл* (*сорт мяса*) fillet.
филиа́л (-а) *м* branch.
филигра́н|ный (**-ен, -на, -но**) *прил* (*изделия, орнамент*) filigree; (*перен: работа*) intricate.
фи́лин (-а) *м* eagle owl.
филиппи́н|ец (**-ца**) *м* Filipino.
филиппи́н|ка (**-ки**; *gen pl* **-ок**) *ж см* **филиппи́нец.**
филиппи́нск|ий (**-ая, -ое, -ие**) *прил* Filipino, Philippine.
филиппи́нца *итп сущ см* **филиппи́нец.**
Филиппи́н|ы (-) *мн* the Philippines *мн.*
фило́лог (-а) *м* philologist (*specialist in languages and literature*).
филологи́ческ|ий (**-ая, -ое, -ие**) *прил* philological; **филологи́ческий факульте́т** faculty of philology.
филоло́ги|я (-и) *ж* philology (*study of language and literature*).
фило́н|ить (**-ю, -ишь**) *несов неперех* (*разг*) to skive.
фило́соф (-а) *м* philosopher.
филосо́фи|я (-и) *ж* philosophy.
филфа́к (-а) *м сокр* = *филологи́ческий факульте́т*.
фильм (-а) *м* film; **сего́дня идёт хоро́ший** ~ there's a good film on today.
фильмоско́п (-а) *м* slide projector.
фильтр (-а) *м* filter.
фильтр|ова́ть (**-у́ю**; *perf* **профильтрова́ть**) *несов перех* to filter.
фин. *сокр* (= **фина́нсовый**) fin. (= *financial*).
фина́л (-а) *м* (*спектакля, концерта*) finale; (*СПОРТ*) final; **выходи́ть** (**вы́йти** *perf*) **в** ~ to reach the final.
фина́льный *прил* (*также СПОРТ, КОММ*) final *опред*.
финанси́ровани|е (-я) *ср* financing.
финанси́р|овать (-ую) *несов перех* to finance.
финанси́ст (-а) *м* (*предприниматель*) financier; (*специалист*) *specialist in financial matters*.
фина́нсовый *прил* financial; (*год*) fiscal; (*отдел, инспектор, комиссия*) finance *опред*; ~ **институ́т** institute of finance; ~ **отчёт** financial statement.
фина́нс|ы (**-ов**) *мн* finances *мн*; (*деньги*) cash *ед*; **Министе́рство ~ов** ≈ the Treasury (*BRIT*), ≈ the Treasury Department *или* Department of the Treasury (*US*).
фи́ник (-а) *м* (*плод*) date; (*дерево*) date palm.
фини́фт|ь (-и) *ж, собир decorated Russian enamel.*
фи́ниш (-а) *м* (*СПОРТ*) finish; **приходи́ть** (**прийти́** *perf*) **к ~у** to reach the finish.
финиши́р|овать (**-ую**) (*не*)*сов неперех* to finish, come in.
фи́нишн|ый *прил* finishing *опред*; **выходи́ть** (**вы́йти** *perf*) **на ~ую пряму́ю** to reach the final straight; (*перен*) to be on the home straight; **~ая черта́/ле́нточка** finishing line/tape.
фи́н|ка (**-ки**; *gen pl* **-ок**) *ж см* **финн**; (*разг: нож*) Finnish knife.
Финля́нди|я (-и) *ж* Finland.
финн (-а) *м* Finn.
фи́нок *сущ см* **фи́нка.**
фи́нск|ий (**-ая, -ое, -ие**) *прил* Finnish; ~ **язы́к** Finnish; **Фи́нский зали́в** Gulf of Finland.
финт (**-а́**) *м* (*СПОРТ*) feint; (*разг: уловка*) trick.
фин|ти́ть (**-чу́, -ти́шь**) *несов неперех* (*разг*) to be tricky.
Ф.И.О. *сокр* (= *фами́лия, и́мя, о́тчество*) *surname, first name, patronymic*.
ф.и.о. *сокр* = **Ф.И.О.**.
фиоле́товый *прил* purple.
фи́рм|а (**-ы**) *ж* firm; (*разг: модная вещь*) quality; **секре́т ~ы** (*разг*) trade secret.
фи́рменный *прил* (*марка, ресторан*) firm's, company *опред*; (*магазин*) chain *опред*; (*разг:*

джинсы, юбка, костюм итп) quality *опред* (*usually of imported brand names*); **фи́рменный знак** brand name.
фиста́шк|а (-и) *ж* pistachio.
фити́л|ь (-я́) *м* wick; (*взрывных устройств*) fuse.
ФИФА́ *ж сокр* (= *Междунаро́дная федера́ция футбо́ла*) FIFA (= *Fédération Internationale de Football Association*).
фи́ф|а (-ы) *ж* (*разг*) bimbo, dolly bird.
фи́ш|ка (-ки; *gen pl* **-ек)** *ж* counter, chip.
флаг (-а) *м* flag.
фла́гман (-а) *м* (*командующий*) flag officer; (*корабль*) flagship.
флагшто́к (-а) *м* flagpole.
флаж|о́к (-ка́) *ж* flag.
флако́н (-а) *м* bottle.
флама́нд|ец (-ца) *м* Fleming.
флама́нд|ка (-ки; *gen pl* **-ок)** *ж см* **флама́ндец**.
флама́ндск|ий (-ая, -ое, -ие) *прил* Flemish; **~ язы́к** Flemish.
флама́ндца *итп сущ см* **флама́ндец**.
флами́нго *м нескл* flamingo.
фланг (-а) *м* flank.
Фла́ндри|я (-и) *ж* Flanders.
флане́левый *прил* flannel.
флане́л|ь (-и) *ж* flannel.
флегма́тик (-а) *м*: **он ~** he is phlegmatic.
флегмати́ч|ный (-ен, -на, -но) *прил* phlegmatic.
фле́йт|а (-ы) *ж* flute.
флейти́ст (-а) *м* flautist.
фле́кси|я (-и) *ж* inflection.
флекти́вный *прил* inflected.
фли́гел|ь (-я) *м* (*АРХИТ*) wing.
флирт (-а) *м* flirtation.
флирт|ова́ть (-у́ю) *несов неперех*: **~ (с** *+instr*) to flirt (with).
флокс (-а) *м* phlox.
флома́стер (-а) *м* felt-tip (pen).
фло́р|а (-ы) *ж* flora.
флоренти́йск|ий (-ая, -ое, -ие) *прил* Florentine.
Флоре́нци|я (-и) *ж* Florence.
флот (-а) *м* (*ВОЕН*) navy; (*МОР*) fleet.
флоти́ли|я (-и) *ж* flotilla.
флю́гер (-а) *м* wind gauge; (*на башне*) weather vane.
флюи́д|ы (-ов) *мн* (*разг*) vibes *мн*.
флюорогра́фи|я (-и) *ж* fluorography.
флюс (-а) *м* (dental) abscess, gumboil.
фля́г|а (-и) *ж* (*для воды, спирта*) flask; (*для молока, для сметаны*) churn.
ФНО *м сокр* (= *Фронт национа́льного освобожде́ния*) NLF (= *National Liberation Front*).
ФОБ *сокр* (= *фра́нко-борт*) f.o.b. (= *free on board*).
фойе́ *ср нескл* foyer.
фокстерье́р (-а) *м* fox terrier.
фокстро́т (-а) *м* foxtrot.
фо́кус (-а) *м* trick; (*ТЕХ, перен*) focus; **выки́дывать (вы́кинуть** *perf*) **~** (*перен*: *разг*) to start some nonsense.
фо́кусник (-а) *м* conjurer.
фолкле́ндск|ий (-ая, -ое, -ие) *прил*: **Ф~ие острова́** the Falkland Islands, the Falklands.
фольг|а́ (-и́) *ж* foil.
фолькло́р (-а) *м* folklore.
фолькло́рный *прил* (*фестиваль, ансамбль*) folk *опред*.
фон (-а) *м* background; **на фо́не чего́-н** against a background of sth; **на фо́не кого́-н** next to sb, compared to sb.
фона́р|ь (-я́) *м* (*уличный*) lamp; (*карманный*) torch; (*разг*: *синяк*) black eye, shiner; **ему́ всё до фонаря́** (*разг*) he doesn't give a toss about anything.
фонд (-а) *м* (*организация*) fund, foundation; (*денежные средства, запас*) fund; (*жилищный, семенной, земельный*) resources *мн*; **фо́нды** (*ценные бумаги*) stocks; **уставно́й ~** (*КОММ*) authorized capital.
фо́ндов|ый *прил*: **~ая би́ржа** stock exchange.
фоне́тик|а (-и) *ж* phonetics.
фоногра́мм|а (-ы) *ж* recording; **петь (спеть** *perf*) **под ~у** to mime to a recording.
фоноло́ги|я (-и) *ж* phonology.
фоноте́к|а (-и) *ж* record and tape collection.
фонта́н (-а) *м* fountain; (*нефти*) gusher.
фо́р|а (-ы) *ж*: **дать кому́-н ~у** (*разг*) to give sb a start *или* an advantage; (*перен*: *разг*) to be miles better than sb.
фо́рвард (-а) *м* forward.
форе́л|ь (-и) *ж* trout.
фо́рм|а (-ы) *ж* (*также ЛИНГ*) form; (*одежда*) uniform; (*ТЕХ*) mould; (*КУЛИН*) (cake) tin (*BRIT*) *или* pan (*US*); **быть** (*impf*) **в ~е** to be in good form; *см также* **фо́рмы**.
форма́лен *прил см* **форма́льный**.
формали́зм (-а) *м* (*в искусстве, в науке*) formalism; **~ в рабо́те** bureaucratic attitude to work.
формали́ст (-а) *м* (*бюрократ*) bureaucrat.
формали́стик|а (-и) *ж* bureaucracy.
форма́льно *нареч* (*относиться*) formally; **~ он прав** factually he's right.
форма́льност|ь (-и) *ж* formality.
форма́л|ьный (-ен, -ьна, -ьно) *прил* (*отношение, подход*) bureaucratic; (*ответ*) nominal; (*no short form*; *согласие, метод, логика*) formal.
форма́т (-а) *м* format.
формати́р|овать (-ую) *(не)сов перех* (*КОМП*) to format.
форма́ци|я (-и) *ж* (*общественная*) structure; **челове́к но́вой ~и** forward-thinking person.

фóрменн|ый *прил* (*безобразие, негодяй*) absolute; ~ **бланк** official form; **фóрменная одéжда** uniform.
формировáни|е (-я) *ср* formation; **воéнное** ~ military unit.
формир|овáть (-ýю; *perf* **сформировáть**) *несов перех* to form
▸ **формировáться** (*perf* **сформировáться**) *несов возв* to form.
фóрмул|а (-ы) *ж* formula.
формулúр|овать (-ую; *perf* **сформулúровать**) *несов перех* to formulate.
формулирóв|ка (-ки; *gen pl* -ок) *ж* (*мысли, предложения*) formulation; (*определение*) definition.
формулúр (-а) *м* library ticket *или* card.
фóрм|ы (-) *мн* (*разг*) curves *мн*.
форпóст (-а) *м* (*ВОЕН*) outpost; (*перен*: *демократии, науки*) stronghold.
форс (-а) *м* (*разг*) swank.
форсúр|овать (-ую) *(не)сов перех* to force.
фор|сúть (-шý, -сúшь) *несов неперех* (*разг*) to show off.
форсýн|ка (-ки; *gen pl* -ок) *ж* (*двигателя*) fuel injector.
форт (-а; *loc sg* -ý, *nom pl* -ы́) *м* fort.
фортепьáнный *прил* piano *опред*.
фортепьáно *ср нескл* piano.
фóрточ|ка (-ки; *gen pl* -ек) *ж hinged, upper pane for ventilation.*
фортýн|а (-ы) *ж* fortune.
фóрум (-а) *м* forum.
форшý *несов см* **форсúть**.
фосфáт (-а) *м* (*обычно мн*) phosphate.
фóсфор (-а) *м* phosphorous.
фóто *ср нескл* (*разг*) photo.
фотоаппарáт (-а) *м* camera.
фотоателье́ *ср нескл* photographic *или* photographer's studio.
фотобумáг|а (-и) *ж* photographic paper.
фотогенúч|ный (-ен, -на, -но) *прил* photogenic.
фотóграф (-а) *м* photographer.
фотографúр|овать (-ую; *perf* **сфотографúровать**) *несов перех* to photograph
▸ **фотографúроваться** (*perf* **сфотографúроваться**) *несов возв* to have one's photo(graph) taken.
фотогрáфи|я (-и) *ж* (*занятие*) photography; (*снимок*) photograph; (*учреждение*) photographer's studio.
фотокáрточ|ка (-ки; *gen pl* -ек) *ж* photo.
фоторóбот (-а) *м* Photofit®.
фотосúнтез (-а) *м* photosynthesis.
фототелегрáмм|а (-ы) *ж* phototelegram.
фотоэлемéнт (-а) *м* photocell.
фрагмéнт (-а) *м* (*фильма, спектакля*) excerpt; (*древних сосудов итп*) fragment.
фрагментáр|ный (-ен, -на, -но) *прил* fragmentary.
фрáз|а (-ы) *ж* phrase.
фразеолóги|я (-и) *ж* (*ЛИНГ*) phraseology; (*пустословие*) rhetoric.
фрак (-а) *м* tail coat, tails *мн*.
фракциóнный *прил* factional.
фрáкци|я (-и) *ж* faction.
франк (-а) *м* franc.
фрáнко *прил неизм* (*КОММ*): ~ **вдоль бóрта сýдна** free alongside ship; ~-**железнодорóжный вагóн** free on rail.
Фрáнкфурт (-а) *м* Frankfurt.
франт (-а) *м* dandy.
Фрáнци|я (-и) *ж* France.
францýжен|ка (-ки; *gen pl* -ок) *ж* Frenchwoman (*мн* Frenchwomen).
францýз (-а) *м* Frenchman (*мн* Frenchmen).
францýзск|ий (-ая, -ое, -ие) *прил* French; ~ **язы́к** French.
франшúз|а (-ы) *ж* (*КОММ*) franchise; **держáтель/предоставúтель ~ы** franchisee/ franchiser.
фрахт (-а) *м* freight; ~, **уплáчиваемый по прибы́тие** (*КОММ*) freight inward; ~, **уплáчиваемый в портý вы́грузки** (*КОММ*) freight forward.
фрахт|овáть (-ýю; *perf* **зафрахтовáть**) *несов перех* to charter.
ФРГ *ж сокр* (*ИСТ*: = *Федератúвная Респýблика Гермáнии*) FRG (= *Federal Republic of Germany*).
фрегáт (-а) *м* frigate.
фрéйлин|а (-ы) *ж* lady-in-waiting (*мн* ladies-in-waiting).
фрéс|ка (-ки; *gen pl* -ок) *ж* fresco.
фривóльност|ь (-и) *ж* frivolity.
фривóл|ьный (-ен, -ьна, -ьно) *прил* frivolous.
фриз (-а) *м* frieze.
фрикадéл|ька (-ьки; *gen pl* -ек) *ж* meatball.
фронт (-а; *nom pl* -ы́) *м* front; **рабóтать** *(impf)* **на два фрóнта** (*перен*) to do two things at the same time.
фронтáл|ьный (-ен, -ьна, -ьно) *прил* (*ВОЕН*) frontal; (*перен*) полный, general.
фронтиспúс (-а) *м* frontispiece.
фронтовúк (-á) *м* front line soldier; (*ветеран*) war veteran.
фронтóн (-а) *м* (*АРХИТ*) pediment.
фрукт (-а) *м* (*БОТ*) fruit; (*разг· пренебр*: *человек*) suspicious character.
фруктóвый *прил* fruit *опред*.
фруктóз|а (-ы) *ж* fructose.
ФСК *ж сокр* (= *Федерáльная слýжба контрразвéдки*) *Russian counterespionage intelligence service*.
фтор (-а) *м* fluorin(e).
фу *межд*: ~! ugh!
фýг|а (-и) *ж* fugue.
фýкси|я (-и) *ж* fuchsia.
фужéр (-а) *м* wineglass; (*для шампанского*) flute.
фундáмент (-а) *м* (*СТРОИТ*) foundation, base; (*перен*: *семьи, науки*) foundation, basis.

фундаментáл|ьный (-ен, -ьна, -ьно) *прил* (*здание, мост*) sound, solid; (*перен*: *знания, труд*) profound; **~ьные наýки** basic science.
фундýк (-á) *м* (*кустарник*) hazel; (*плод*) hazelnut.
фуникулёр (-а) *м* funicular railway.
функционáл|ьный (-ен, -ьна, -ьно) *прил* functional; **функционáльная клáвиша** (*КОМП*) function key.
функционéр (-а) *м* official, functionary.
функционúр|овать (-ую) *несов неперех* to function.
фýнкци|я (-и) *ж* function; (*круг обязанностей*) function, duties *мн*.
фунт (-а) *м* pound.
фурáж (-á) *м* fodder.
фурáж|ка (-ки; *gen pl* **-ек)** *ж* cap; (*ВОЕН*) forage cap.
фургóн (-а) *м* (*АВТ*) van; (*конная повозка*) (covered) wagon.
фýри|я (-и) *ж* (*разг*) virago.
фурóр (-а) *м* furore; **производúть (произвестú** *perf*) ~ to create a furore.
фурýнкул (-а) *м* boil.
фут (-а) *м* foot.
футбóл (-а) *м* football (*BRIT*), soccer; **америкáнский** ~ (American) football.
футболúст (-а) *м* footballer (*BRIT*), soccer player.
футбóл|ка (-ки; *gen pl* **-ок)** *ж* T-shirt, tee shirt.
футбóльный *прил* football *опред*, soccer *опред*; **футбóльный мяч** football.
футля́р (-а) *м* case.
фуфá|йка (-йки; *gen pl* **-ек)** *ж* (*ватник*) padded jacket; (*вязаная рубашка*) jersey.
фы́рка|ть (-ю) *несов неперех* (*животное*) to snort; (*разг*: *смеяться*) to snort with laughter; (: *брюзжать*) to complain.
фы́ркн|уть (-у, -ешь) *сов неперех* (*животное*) to give a snort; (*разг*: *издать смешок*) to snort with laughter.
фырч|áть (-ý, -úшь) *несов неперех* (*разг*) to snort; (*брюзжать*) to whinge.
фьючерс|ы (-ов) *мн* (*КОММ*) futures *мн*.

~ Х, х ~

Х, **х** *сущ нескл* (*буква*) *the 22nd letter of the Russian alphabet.*
ха́кер (**-а**) *м* hacker.
ха́ки *прил неизм, ср нескл* khaki.
хала́т (**-а**) *м* (*домашний*) dressing gown; **ба́нный** ~ bathrobe.
хала́тен *прил см* **хала́тный**.
хала́тност|ь (**-и**) *ж* negligence.
хала́т|ный (**-ен, -на, -но**) *прил* negligent.
халв|а́ (**-ы́**) *ж* halva.
халту́р|а (**-ы**) *ж* (*разг: плохая работа*) shoddy work; (: *работа на стороне*) moonlighting.
халту́р|ить (**-ю, -ишь**; *perf* **схалту́рить**) *несов неперех* (*разг*) to cut corners; (*no perf*; *разг: работать на стороне*) to moonlight.
хам (**-а**) *м* (*разг*) brute, lout.
хамелео́н (**-а**) *м* (*также перен*) chameleon.
хаме́|ть (**-ю**; *perf* **охаме́ть**) *несов неперех* to become impudent.
хам|и́ть (**-лю́, -и́шь**; *perf* **нахами́ть**) *несов неперех*: ~ (**+*dat***) (*разг*) to be cheeky (*BRIT*) *или* rude (*US*) (to).
ха́м|ка (**-ки**; *gen pl* **-ок**) *ж* (*разг*) hussy.
хамлю́ *сов см* **хами́ть**.
ха́мок *сущ см* **ха́мка**.
ха́мск|ий (**-ая, -ое, -ие**) *прил* (*разг*) brutish, loutish.
ха́мств|о (**-а**) *ср* rudeness.
хан (**-а**) *м* khan.
хандр|а́ (**-ы́**) *ж* depression.
хандр|и́ть (**-ю́, -и́шь**) *несов неперех* to feel down.
ханж|а́ (**-и́**; *gen pl* **-е́й**) *м/ж* prude, prig.
ха́нжеств|о (**-а**) *ср* prudishness, priggishness.
Хано́|й (**-я**) *м* Hanoi.
ха́ос (**-а**) *м* chaos.
хаоти́чен *прил см* **хаоти́чный**.
хаоти́ческ|ий (**-ая, -ое, -ие**) *прил* chaotic.
хаоти́ч|ный (**-ен, -на, -но**) *прил* = **хаоти́ческий**.
ха́па|ть (**-ю, -ешь**) *несов перех* (*разг: хватать*) to grab at; (: *присваивать*) to swipe.
хара́ктер (**-а**) *м* nature; (*человека*) personality; **он челове́к с ~ом** he has a lot of character; **выде́рживать (вы́держать *perf*) ~** to hold firm.
характе́рен *прил см* **характе́рный**.
характериз|ова́ть (**-у́ю**) *несов перех* to be typical of; (*perf* **охарактеризова́ть**; *персонаж, эпоху итп*) to characterize; **его́ ~у́ет доброта́** he is a kind person
▸ **характеризова́ться** *несов возв* (*+instr*) to be characterized by.
характери́стик|а (**-и**) *ж* (*документ*) (character) reference; (*описание*) description.
характе́р|ный (**-ен, -на, -но**) *прил* (*внешность, поведение*) distinctive; (*свойственный*): ~ (**для** ***+gen***) characteristic (of); (*no short form*; *обычаи, танцы итп*) typical; **для него́ ~ пери́оды депре́ссии** he tends to go through bouts of depression.
ха́рка|ть (**-ю**) *несов неперех* (*+instr*; *кровью, слизью*) to cough up.
ха́рти|я (**-и**) *ж* (*документ*) charter.
харч (**-а**; *nom pl* **-и́**, *gen pl* **-е́й**) *м* (*обычно мн*: *разг*) grub *ед*, chow *ед*.
харчо́ *ср нескл spicy Georgian meat and vegetable soup.*
ха́р|я (**-и**) *ж* (*разг*) mug (*face*).
ха́т|а (**-ы**) *ж* cottage (*in Southern Russia and Ukraine*); **моя́ ~ с кра́ю** (*разг*) it's nothing to do with me.
ха-ха *межд* ha-ha.
хачапу́ри *ср нескл flat Georgian cheese pie.*
ха́|ять (**-ю**) *несов перех* (*разг*) to slag off.
х/б *сокр* = **хлопчатобума́жный**.
хвал|а́ (**-ы́**) *ж* praise.
хвале́бный *прил* complimentary.
хвалёный *прил* celebrated.
хвал|и́ть (**-ю́, -ишь**; *perf* **похвали́ть**) *несов перех* to praise
▸ **хвали́ться** (*perf* **похвали́ться**) *несов возв*: **~ся** (***+instr***) (*разг*) to show off (about).
хва́ста|ться (**-юсь**; *perf* **похва́статься**) *несов возв*: ~ (***+instr***) to boast (about).
хвастли́в|ый (**-, -а, -о**) *прил* boastful.
хвастовств|о́ (**-а́**) *ср* boasting.
хвасту́н (**-а́**) *м* (*разг*) show-off.
хвасту́н|ья (**-ьи**; *gen pl* **-ий**) *ж см* **хвасту́н**.
хвата́|ть (**-ю**; *perf* **схвати́ть**) *несов перех* to grab (hold of); (*преступника*) to arrest; (*разг: простуду, насморк*) to catch; (: *плохую отметку, оплеуху*) to get ◆ (*perf* **хвати́ть**) *безл* (*+gen*; *денег, времени итп*) to have enough; **мне ~ет де́нег на еду́** I've got enough to buy food; **его́ не хвати́ло на э́то** he wasn't up to it; **он ~л всё подря́д** (*разг*) he grabbed whatever he could; ~ (*impf*) **за́ душу** to tug at one's heartstrings; ~ (**схвати́ть *perf***) **что-н на лету́** to grasp sth in an instant; **э́того ещё не ~ло!**

(*разг*) as if that wasn't enough!; **не ~ет то́лько, что́бы он отказа́лся** (*разг*) now all we need is for him to refuse

▸ **хвата́ться** (*perf* **схвати́ться**) *несов возв*: **~ся за** *+acc* (*за сердце*) to clutch at; (*за дверь, за оружие*) to grab; **~ся** (*impf*) **за всё сра́зу** (*разг*) to try to do everything at once; **~ся (схвати́ться** *perf*) **за соло́минку** to clutch at straws; **~ся (схвати́ться** *perf*) **за́ голову** (*перен*) to panic.

хва|ти́ть (-чу́, -тишь) *сов от* **хвата́ть** ◆ *перех* (*разг*): **~ по рю́мочке/чайку́** to have a quick drink/cuppa; (*+gen*; *беды, горя*) to suffer; (*разг: ударить*) to whack, thump ◆ *безл* (*разг*): **хва́тит!** that's enough!; **его́ ~ти́л парали́ч** he was paralysed; **её ~ти́л уда́р** she had a stroke; **он ~ти́л меня́ по голове́** he thumped me on the head; **он ~ти́л кулако́м по столу́** he banged on the table with his fist; **хва́тит спо́ров** *или* **спо́рить!** (*разг*) that's enough of this arguing!; ~ (*perf*) **че́рез край** to go too far; **с меня́ хва́тит!** I've had enough!

▸ **хвати́ться** *сов возв* (*разг*): **~ся чего́-н/кого́-н** to notice that sth/sb is gone.

хва́т|ка (-ки; *gen pl* **-ок**) *ж* grip; (*перен: ловкость*) skill; **делова́я ~** business acumen; **вцепля́ться (вцепи́ться** *perf*) **в что-н/кого́-н мёртвой ~кой** (*также перен*) to cling onto sth/sb for dear life.

хвать *как сказ* (*разг*): **он меня́ ~ по голове́** he whacked me right in the head; **я поверну́лся, и ~ – нет кошелька́** I turned round and my purse (*BRIT*) *или* wallet (*US*) had vanished.

хвачу́(сь) *сов см* **хвати́ть(ся)**.

х-во *сокр* = **хозя́йство**.

хво́йный *прил* coniferous; **хво́йное де́рево** conifer.

хвора́|ть (-ю) *несов неперех* to feel poorly (*BRIT*), to feel sick (*US*).

хво́рост (-а; *part gen* **-у**) *м собир* firewood; (*КУЛИН*) *sugar-coated strips of dough fried in oil*.

хворости́н|а (-ы) *ж* switch.

хво́рый *прил* (*разг*) ill.

хвор|ь (-и) *ж* ailment.

хвост (-а́) *м* tail; (*поезда*) tail end; (*перен: пыли, зевак итп*) trail; (*разг: очередь*) queue (*BRIT*), line (*US*); (*: по математике итп*) *an exam which has to be taken again*.

хво́стик (-а) *м* (*мыши, редиски*) tail; **ему́ 50 с ~ом** (*разг*) he's just over 50.

хвостов|о́й *прил* tail *опред*; **~а́я часть** (*самолёта, поезда*) the tail end.

хвощ (-а́) *м* (*БОТ*) horsetail.

хво́|я (-и) *ж собир* needles *мн* (*of a conifer*).

ХДС *м сокр* (= *Христиа́нско-демократи́ческий союз*) CDU (= *Christian Democratic Union*).

хек (-а) *м* whiting.

хе́кер (-а) *м* (*КОМП*) hacker.

Хе́льсинки *м нескл* Helsinki.

хе́рес (-а; *part gen* **-у**) *м* sherry.

хи́жин|а (-ы) *ж* hut.

хи́л|ый (-, -а́, -о) *прил* (*мужчина, рука*) puny; (*растение, ребёнок*) sickly; (*дом, постройка*) rickety.

хи́мик (-а) *м* chemist.

химика́т (-а) *м* chemical.

химиотерапи́|я (-и) *ж* chemotherapy.

хими́ческ|ий (-ая, -ое, -ие) *прил* chemical *опред*; (*факультет, кабинет*) chemistry *опред*; **хими́ческий каранда́ш** *graphite pencil which writes in purple when moistened*.

хи́ми|я (-и) *ж* chemistry; **бытова́я ~** household chemicals *мн*.

химчи́ст|ка (-ки; *gen pl* **-ок**) *ж сокр* = *хими́ческая чи́стка*; (*процесс*) dry-cleaning; (*пункт приёма*) dry-cleaner('s).

хини́н (-а) *м* quinine.

хи́ппи *м нескл* hippie.

хире́|ть (-ю; *perf* **захире́ть**) *несов неперех* (*человек*) to waste away; (*растение*) to wither; (*перен: творчество, талант*) to dry up.

хирома́нти|я (-и) *ж* palmistry.

Хироси́м|а (-ы) *ж* Hiroshima.

хиру́рг (-а) *м* surgeon.

хирурги́ческ|ий (-ая, -ое, -ие) *прил* surgical; (*больной, клиника*) surgery *опред*.

хирурги́|я (-и) *ж* surgery.

хит (-а) *м* (*МУЗ*) hit.

хитёр *прил см* **хи́трый**.

хитре́ц (-а́) *м* cunning devil.

хитр|и́ть (-ю́, -и́шь; *perf* **схитри́ть**) *несов неперех* to act slyly.

хи́тро *нареч* cunningly; (*сделанный*) intricately.

хи́трост|ь (-и) *ж* slyness; (*уловка*) cunning.

хитроу́ми|е (-я) *ср* ingenuity.

хитроу́м|ный (-ен, -на, -но) *прил* ingenious.

хи́т|рый (-ёр, -ра́, -ро) *прил* sly, cunning; (*изобретательный*) cunning; (*замысловатый*) intricate.

хихи́ка|ть (-ю) *несов неперех* (*разг*) to giggle; (*: смеяться исподтишка*) to snigger.

хи́щен *прил см* **хи́щный**.

хище́ни|е (-я) *ср* misappropriation.

хи́щник (-а) *м* (*также перен*) predator.

хи́щниц|а (-ы) *ж* (*перен*) predator.

хи́щническ|ий (-ая, -ое, -ие) *прил* (*политика, инстинкт*) predatory; (*истребление леса, охота*) ruthless; (*использование ресурсов*) rapacious.

хи́щ|ный (-ен, -на, -но) *прил* (*также перен*) predatory; (*делец, торгаш*) cutthroat; **~ная пти́ца** bird of prey.

хладнокро́вен *прил см* **хладнокро́вный**.

хладнокро́ви|е (-я) *ср* composure.

хладнокро́в|ный (-ен, -на, -но) *прил* composed; (*убийство итп*) cold-blooded.

хлам (-а) *м собир* (*также перен*) junk.

хлеб (-а) *м* bread; (*зерно*) grain; (*nom pl* **-ы**;

формовой, круглый) loaf (*мн* loaves); (*nom pl* **-á**; *озимые, яровые*) cereal; **зараба́тывать** *(impf)* **на ~** to earn a crust; **~ насу́щный** bread and butter (*fig*); **~-соль** bread and salt (*traditionally offered to guests as a symbol of hospitality*).

хлеба́|ть (-ю) *несов перех* (*разг*) to slurp.

хлеб|е́ц (-ца́) *м* loaf; **хрустя́щие ~цы́** ≈ crispbreads.

хле́бница (-ы) *ж* bread basket; (*для хранения*) bread bin.

хлебн|у́ть (-у́, -ёшь) *сов перех* (*разг*: *чай итп*) to take a gulp of; **~** *(perf)* **го́ря** to see a lot of sorrow.

хле́бн|ый *прил* bread *опред*; (*злак, растение*) corn *опред*; (*край, поле*) fertile; (*разг*: *местечко*) well-paid; **э́то год был ~** we had a good harvest this year; **~ые дро́жжи** baker's yeast.

хлебобу́лочн|ый *прил*: **~ые изде́лия** bread products *мн*.

хлебозаво́д (-а) *м* bakery.

хлеборе́зк|а (-ки; *gen pl* **-ок)** *ж* bread slicer.

хлебoро́б (-а) *м* harvester.

хлеборо́дный *прил* (*край, земля*) fertile; **э́тот год был ~** we had a good harvest this year.

хлебосо́льный *прил* hospitable.

хлебца́ *итп сущ см* **хлебе́ц**.

хлев (-а; *loc sg* **-у́**, *nom pl* **-а́)** *м* cowshed; (*перен*: *разг*) pigsty.

хл|еста́ть (-ещу́, -е́щешь) *несов перех* (*ремнём, кнутом*) to whip; (*по лицу, по щекам*) to slap; (*разг*: *водку, пиво*) to knock back ◆ *неперех* (*дождь*) to lash down; (*вода, кровь*) to gush; (*пули*) to rain down; **во́лны ~еста́ли о борт ло́дки** the waves lashed against the side of the boat.

хлёст|кий (-кая, -кое, -кие; -ок, -ка́, -ко) *прил* (*перен*) scathing.

хлестн|у́ть (-у́, -ёшь) *сов перех* to whip; (*по щеке*) to slap.

хлёсток *прил см* **хлёсткий**.

хлещу́ *итп несов см* **хлеста́ть**.

хли́пк|ий (-ая, -ое, -ие) *прил* (*разг*: *здоровье*) poor; (: *человек, земля*) weedy; (: *стол, строение*) wobbly.

хлоп *как сказ* (*разг*): **он меня́ ~ по спине́** he whacked me right in the back; **он ~ на крова́ть** he flopped onto the bed.

хло́па|ть (-ю) *несов перех* (*ладонью*) to slap; (*кнутом*) to lash ◆ *неперех* (*+instr*; *дверью, крышкой*) to slam; (*+dat*; *артисту, певцу*) to clap; (*хлопушка, выстрел*) to go bang; **~** *(impf)* **уша́ми/глаза́ми** (*разг*) to look stupid/baffled.

хло́пка *сущ см* **хло́пок**.

хлопка́ *сущ см* **хлопо́к**.

хлопково́дств|о (-а) *ср* cotton growing.

хло́пковый *прил* cotton.

хло́пн|уть (-у, -ешь) *сов перех* (*по спине*) to slap ◆ *неперех* (*в ладони*) to clap; (*дверь*) to slam shut; (*хлопушка, выстрел*) to go bang; (*+instr*; *дверью*) to slam; (*кнутом*) to crack.

хло́п|ок (-ка) *м* cotton.

хлоп|о́к (-ка́) *м* (*удар в ладоши*) clap; (*выстрела, кнута*) crack; (*по спине, по затылку*) slap.

хлоп|ота́ть (-очу́, -о́чешь) *несов неперех* (*по дому, по хозяйству*) to busy o.s.; (*добиваться*): **~ о** *+prp* (*о разрешении, о пособии итп*) to be busy trying to get; **~** *(impf)* **о ком-н** *или* **за кого́-н** to trouble o.s. on sb's behalf.

хлопотли́в|ый (-, -а, -о) *прил* (*человек*) busy; (*дело, обязанности*) troublesome.

хло́потный *прил* (*разг*) troublesome.

хло́п|оты (-о́т; *dat pl* **-отам)** *мн* (*по хозяйству, по дому итп*) things *мн* to do; (*о ком-н*) effort *ед*, trouble *ед*; **все мои́ ~ бы́ли напра́сны** all of my efforts were in vain; **хлопо́т по́лон рот** he *итп* has troubles galore.

хлопочу́ *итп несов см* **хлопота́ть**.

хлопу́ш|ка (-ки; *gen pl* **-ек)** *ж* (*для мух*) fly swatter; (*игрушка*) (Christmas) cracker.

хлопча́тник (-а) *м* (*БОТ*: *растение*) cotton.

хлопчатобума́жный *прил* cotton.

хло́пь|я (-ев) *мн* (*снега, мыла*) flakes *мн*; (*ваты, овчины*) clumps *мн*; **кукуру́зные ~** cornflakes.

хлор (-а) *м* chlorine.

хло́рк|а (-и) *ж* (*разг*) bleaching powder.

хло́рн|ый *прил*: **~ая и́звесть** bleaching powder; **хло́рная кислота́** hydrochloric acid.

хлы́н|уть (*3sg* **-ет**, *3pl* **-ут**) *сов неперех* to flood; (*перен*: *мысли, воспоминания*) to flood back.

хлыст (-а́) *м* whip.

хлыщ (-а́) *м* playboy.

хлю́па|ть (-ю) *несов неперех* (*разг*) to squelch; **~** *(impf)* **но́сом** to sniff.

хля́стик (-а) *м* half-belt.

хмеле́|ть (-ю) *несов неперех* to be drunk; **~** *(impf)* **от сча́стья/свобо́ды** to be drunk with happiness/freedom.

хмел|ь (-я) *м* (*БОТ*) hops *мн*; (*опьянение*) drunkenness; **во ~ю́** drunk.

хмельно́й *прил* drunken; (*напиток*) alcoholic; (*воздух, запах*) intoxicating.

хму́р|ить (-ю, -ишь; *perf* **нахму́рить)** *несов перех* (*лоб, брови*) to furrow

▸ **хму́риться** *несов возв* to frown; (*небо*) to become overcast; (*погода, день*) to turn gloomy.

хму́ро *нареч* gloomily ◆ *как сказ*: **сего́дня на у́лице ~** it's very gloomy outside; **у него́ на душе́ ~** he's feeling very gloomy.

хму́рый *прил* gloomy.

хмы́ка|ть (-ю) *несов неперех* (*разг*) *to say "hmm" as a sign of surprise, annoyance etc.*

хмы́кн|уть (-у, -ешь) *сов неперех to say "hmm" as a sign of surprise, annoyance etc.*

хн|а (-ы) *ж* henna.

хны́ка|ть (-ю) *несов неперех* (*разг*: *плакать*) to whimper; (*перен*: *жаловаться*) to whine.

хо́бби *ср нескл* hobby.

хо́бот (-а) *м* (*слона*) trunk.

хобот|о́к (-ка́) *м* (*насекомого*) proboscis.

ход (-а; *part gen* **-у**, *loc sg* **-у́)** *м* (*поезда, машины,* *руля, поршня*) movement; (*событий, дела итп*) course; (*часов, двигателя*) working; (*КАРТЫ*) go; (*маневр, также ШАХМАТЫ*) move; (*возможность*) chance; (*вход*) entrance; (*тоннель*) passage; **в хо́де** *+gen* in the course of; **~ мы́слей** train of thought; **идти́ (пойти́** *perf*) **в ~** to come into use; **пуска́ть (пусти́ть** *perf*) **что-н в ~** (*механизм*) to bring into use; (*слово, тип одежды*) to popularize; **быть** *(impf)* **в (большо́м) ~у́** to be (very) popular; **на ~у́** (*есть, разговаривать*) on the move; (*делать замечания, шутить*) in passing; **с хо́ду** straight off; **он с хо́ду взбежа́л на ле́стницу** he ran straight upstairs; **до до́ма три часа́ ~у́** it's three hours' walk to the house; **дава́ть (дать** *perf*) **~ де́лу** to set things in motion; **дава́ть (дать** *perf*) **~ но́вым лю́дям/ме́тодам** to give new people/methods a chance; **дава́ть (дать** *perf*) **за́дний ~** (*АВТ*) to reverse; (*человек*) to retreat; **знать** *(impf)* **все ~ы и вы́ходы** to know all the ins and outs; **де́ло идёт свои́м хо́дом** events are taking their natural course; **по хо́ду де́ла** during the course of events; **чей ~?** (*в игре*) whose go is it?

хода́тайств|о (-а) *ср* petition; **подава́ть (пода́ть** *perf*) **~** to submit a petition.

хода́тайств|овать (-ую; *perf* **походатайствовать**) *несов неперех*: **~ о чём-н/за кого́-н** to petition for sth/on sb's behalf.

хо́дики (-ов) *мн* wall clock *ед*.

хо|ди́ть (-жу́, -дишь) *несов неперех* to walk; (*по магазинам, в гости, в кино итп*) to go (*on foot*); (*поезд, автобус итп*) to go; (*слухи, грипп*) to go round; (*часы*) to work; (*+instr: тузом итп*) to play; (*конём, пешкой итп*) to move; (*носить*): **~ в** *+prp* (*в пальто, в сапогах итп*) to wear; (*ухаживать*): **~ за кем-н** to look after sb.

хо́д|кий (-кая, -кое, -кие; -ок, -ка́, -ко) *прил* (*разг: машина*) speedy; (*: товар*) popular.

ходово́й *прил* popular.

хо́док *прил см* **хо́дкий**.

ходо́к (-а́) *м*: **он хоро́ший ~** he's a good walker; **туда́ я бо́льше не ~** (*разг*) I'm not going there again.

ходу́л|я (-и; *gen pl* -ей) *ж* (*обычно мн*) stilt.

ходуно́м *нареч*: **ходи́ть ~** (*разг*) to shake.

ходьб|а́ (-ы́) *ж* walking; **полчаса́ ~ы́** half an hour's walk.

ходя́ч|ий (-ая, -ее, -ие) *прил* trendy; (*избитый*) hackneyed; (*больной*) able to walk; **он – ~ая доброде́тель** he is a paragon of virtue.

хожде́ни|е (-я) *ср* walking; (*слухов*) circulation; **име́ть** *(impf)* **~** (*валюта*) to be in circulation; (*выражение, товар*) to be popular.

хожу́ *несов см* **ходи́ть**.

хозрасчёт (-а) *м* (= *хозяйственный расчёт*) *system of management based on self-financing and self- governing principles.*

хозрасчётн|ый *прил*: **~ое предприя́тие** self-financing, self-governing enterprise.

хозя́ева *итп сущ см* **хозя́ин**.

хозя́ек *сущ см* **хозя́йка**.

хозя́|ин (-ина; *nom pl* -ева, *gen pl* -ев) *м* (*владелец*) owner; (*сдающий жильё*) landlord; (*пользующийся наёмным трудом*) employer; (*принимающий гостей*) host; (*ведущий хозяйство*) manager; (*перен: положения, своей судьбы*) master.

хозя́|йка (-йки; *gen pl* -ек) *ж* (*владелица*) owner; (*сдающая жильё*) landlady; (*принимающая гостей*) hostess; (*разг: жена*) missus, old lady; **дома́шняя ~** housewife.

хозя́йнича|ть (-ю) *несов неперех* (*в доме, на кухне*) to be in charge; (*командовать*) to be bossy.

хозя́йск|ий (-ая, -ое, -ие) *прил*: **(это) де́ло ~ое** (*разг*) have it your own way.

хозя́йственник (-а) *м* manager.

хозя́йственный *прил* (*деятельность, управление*) economic *опред*; (*постройка, инвентарь*) domestic *опред*; (*человек*) thrifty; **хозя́йственные това́ры** hardware; **хозя́йственный магази́н** hardware shop.

хозя́йств|о (-а) *ср* (*ЭКОН*) economy; (*производственная единица*) enterprise; (*оборудование*) equipment; (*предметы быта*) household goods *мн*; **городско́е/наро́дное ~** urban/national economy; **дома́шнее ~** housekeeping; **вести́** *(impf)* **~** to run the house.

хозя́йств|овать (-ую) *несов неперех*: **~ на предприя́тии/фи́рме** to manage an enterprise/firm; **он уме́ло ~ует** he is a good manager.

хокке́ист (-а) *м* hockey player.

хокке́|й (-я) *м* hockey; **~ с ша́йбой/на траве́** ice/field hockey.

хокке́йный *прил* hockey *опред*.

хо́лдинг (-а) *м* (*КОММ*) holding.

хо́лдингов|ый *прил*: **~ая компа́ния** holding company.

хо́леный *прил* (*человек, лошадь*) well-groomed; (*лицо, руки*) elegant.

холёный *прил* = **хо́леный**.

холе́р|а (-ы) *ж* (*МЕД*) cholera.

холестери́н (-а) *м* cholesterol.

холл (-а) *м* (*театра, гостиницы*) foyer, lobby; (*в квартире, в доме*) hall.

холм (-а́) *м* hill.

хо́лмик (-а) *м* hillock.

холми́стый (-, -а, -о) *прил* hilly.

хо́лод (-а; *nom pl* -а́) *м* cold; (*осенний, зимний*) cold weather; (*перен: равнодушие*) coldness; (*озноб*) cold shiver.

холода́|ть (*3sg* -ет, *perf* **похолода́ть**) *несов безл* to turn cold.

хо́лоден *прил см* **холо́дный**.

холоде́|ть (-ю; *perf* **похолоде́ть**) *несов неперех*

(*руки, ноги*) to get cold; (*от страха, при смерти*) to go cold.
холод|éц (**-цá**) *м* meat in aspic.
холоди́льник (**-а**) *м* (*домашний*) fridge, refrigerator; (*промышленный*) refrigerator; **двухкáмерный** ~ fridge-freezer.
хóлодно *нареч* coldly ◆ *как сказ* it's cold; (+*dat*): **мне** *итп* ~ I'm *итп* cold; **на ýлице сегóдня** ~ it's cold outside today.
хол|óдный (**-оден, -однá, -одно**) *прил* cold; **эта кýртка ~óдная** this jacket isn't very warm; **холóдная войнá** cold war; **холóдное орýжие** side arms *мн*.
холодцá *итп сущ см* **холодéц**.
холост|óй (**хóлост**) *прил* (*мужчина*) unmarried, single; (*no short form*; *выстрел, патрон*) blank; **рабóтать** (*impf*) **на ~óм ходý** (*АВТ, ТЕХ*) to idle, tick over; ~ **прогóн** dry run.
холостя́к (**-á**) *м* bachelor.
холý|й (**-я**) *м* sycophant.
холст (**-á**) *м* canvas.
хомýт (**-á**) *м* (*коня*) harness collar; (*ТЕХ*) clamp; (*перен*) bind; **повéсить** (*perf*) *или* **надéть** (*perf*) **себé ~ на шéю** to weigh o.s. down.
хомя́к (**-á**) *м* hamster.
хор (**-а**) *м* choir; (*перен*) chorus.
хорвáт (**-а**) *м* Croatian.
Хорвáти|я (**-и**) *ж* Croatia.
хорвáт|ка (**-ки**; *gen pl* **-ок**) *ж см* **хорвáт**.
хорвáтск|ий (**-ая, -ое, -ие**) *прил* Croatian.
хор|ёк (**-ькá**) *м* ferret.
хореóграф (**-а**) *м* choreographer.
хореогрáфи|я (**-и**) *ж* choreography.
хори́ст (**-а**) *м* chorister.
хори́ст|ка (**-ки**; *gen pl* **-ок**) *ж см* **хори́ст**.
хормéйстер (**-а**) *м* choirmaster.
хоровóд (**-а**) *м* round dance.
хоровóй *прил* choral.
хóром *нареч* in unison.
хорóм|ы (**-**) *мн* mansion *ед*.
хор|они́ть (**-oню́, -óнишь**; *perf* **похорони́ть**) *несов перех* to bury.
хорохóр|иться (**-юсь, -ишься**) *несов возв* (*разг*) to brag.
хорóшеньк|ий (**-ая, -ое, -ие**) *прил* (*симпатичный*) pretty; (*разг: плохой*) fine, nice.
хорошéнько *нареч* (*разг*) properly.
хорошé|ть (**-ю**; *perf* **похорошéть**) *несов неперех* to become more attractive.
хорóш|ий (**-ая, -ее, -ие; -, -á, -ó**) *прил* good; **он хорóш (собóю)** he's good-looking; **хорóш друг!** (*разг*) a fine friend!; **всегó ~его!** all the best!
хорошó *нареч* well ◆ *как сказ* it's good; (+*dat*): **мне** ~ I feel good ◆ *част, вводн сл* okay, all right ◆ *ср нескл* (*ПРОСВЕЩ*) ≈ good (*school mark*); ~ **отдыхáть (отдохнýть** *perf*) to have a good rest; **на мóре** ~ it's nice by the sea; **мне здесь** ~ I like it here; **~, я соглáсен** okay, I agree; **ну, ~!** (*разг: выражение угрозы*) right then!; ~ **бы поéсть/поспáть** (*разг*) I wouldn't mind a bite to eat/getting some sleep.
хóр|ы (**-ов**) *мн* (*в церкви, в большом зале*) gallery *ед*.
хорькá *итп сущ см* **хорёк**.
хот-дог (**-а**) *м* hot dog.
хо|тéть (*см* **Table 16**) *несов перех*: ~ +*infin* to want to do; **как ~ти́те** (*как вам угодно*) as you wish; (*а всё-таки*) no matter what you say; **хóчешь не хóчешь** whether you like it or not; ~ (*impf*) **есть/пить** to be hungry/thirsty
▸ **хотéться** *несов безл* (+*infin*): **мне** *итп* **хóчется плáкать/есть** I *итп* feel like crying/something to eat; **мне хóчется чáю** I feel like some tea.

KEYWORD

хоть *союз* **1** (*несмотря на то, что*) (al)though; **хоть я и оби́жен, я помогý тебé** although I am hurt, I will help you
2 (*до такой степени, что*) even if; **не соглашáется, хоть до утрá проси́** he won't agree, even if you ask all night; **хоть умри́, а дéнег достáнь** get hold of some money, even if it kills you; **хоть убéй, не могý пойти́ на э́то** I couldn't do that to save my life; **хоть..., хоть** either ..., or; **езжáй хоть сегóдня, хоть чéрез мéсяц** go either today, or in a month's time
◆ *част* **1** (*служит для усиления*) at least; **подвези́ егó хоть до стáнции** take him to the station at least; **поймú хоть ты** you of all people should understand
2 (*разг: например*) for example; **взять хоть Мари́ю: онá же всё врéмя рабóтает** take Maria for example, she works all the time
3 (*во фразах*): **хоть бы** at least; **хоть бы ты емý позвони́л!** you could at least phone him!; **хоть бы закóнчить сегóдня!** if only we could get finished today!; **хоть кто** anyone; **хоть какóй** any; **емý хоть бы что** it doesn't bother him; **хоть кудá!** (*разг*) excellent!; **хоть бы и так!** so what!

хотя́ *союз* although; ~ **и** even though; ~ **бы** at least; **он срáзу всё пóнял, ~ и не знал подрóбностей** even without knowing the details, he was able to understand at once; **возьми́те ~ бы примéр Áнглии** take England for example.
хотя́т(ся) *несов см* **хотéть(ся)**.
хохлá *итп сущ см* **хохóл**.
хохлом|á (**-ы́**) *ж* khokhloma (*traditional wooden articles decorated in red, gold and black*).
хóхм|а (**-ы**) *ж* (*разг*) joke; (*что-н смешное*) laugh.
хох|óл (**-лá**) *м* (*клок волос*) tuft of hair; (*разг: пренебр*) Ukrainian.
хóхот (**-а**) *м* guffaw; (*шакала*) laugh.
хох|отáть (**-очý, -óчешь**) *несов неперех* to laugh (loudly); (*филин, шакал*) to laugh; ~ (*impf*) **над** +*instr* to laugh at; **я ~отáл до слёз** I laughed till the tears ran down my face.
хочý(сь) *итп несов см* **хотéть(ся)**.

храбре́ц (-а́) *м* brave person (*мн* people).
храб|и́ться (**-ю́сь, -и́шься**) *несов возв* (*разг*) to try to appear brave.
хра́бро *нареч* bravely.
хра́брост|ь (**-и**) *ж* bravery, courage.
хра́бр|ый (**-, -а́, -о**) *прил* brave, courageous.
храм (**-а**) *м* (*РЕЛ*) temple.
хране́ни|е (**-я**) *ср* (*денег*) keeping; ~ **ору́жия** possession of firearms; **ка́мера для ~я багажа́** left-luggage office (*BRIT*), checkroom (*US*); **сдава́ть (сдать** *perf*) **ве́щи на** ~ to put things in for safekeeping.
храни́лищ|е (**-а**) *ср* store.
храни́тел|ь (**-я**) *м* curator, keeper.
хран|и́ть (**-ю́, -и́шь**) *несов перех* to keep; (*границы, достоинство*) to protect; (*традиции*) to preserve; ~ (*impf*) **что-н в та́йне** to keep sth secret
▸ **храни́ться** *несов возв* to be kept.
храп (**-а**) *м* (*во сне*) snoring.
храп|е́ть (**-лю́, -и́шь**) *несов неперех* (*человек*) to snore; (*лошадь*) to snort.
хреб|е́т (**-та́**) *м* (*АНАТ*) spine; (*разг*: *спина*) back; (*ГЕО*) ridge.
хребто́вый *прил* (*позвонки*) spinal; (*перевал, гряда*) mountain *опред*.
хрен (**-а**) *м* (*БОТ, КУЛИН*) horseradish; (*груб!*) willy (*!*); ~ **его́ зна́ет** (*разг*) who the hell knows; **ста́рый** ~ (*разг*) old fool.
хрено́вый *прил* (*БОТ, КУЛИН*) horseradish *опред*; (*груб!*) crappy (*!*) (*BRIT*), lousy (*US*).
хрестомати́йный *прил* (*идея, образ*) basic.
хрестома́ти|я (**-и**) *ж* study aid, reader.
хризанте́м|а (**-ы**) *ж* chrysanthemum.
хрип (**-а**) *м* wheezing; **предсме́ртный** ~ dying gasp.
хрип|е́ть (**-лю́, -и́шь**) *несов неперех* (*лошадь, больной*) to wheeze; (*пластинка*) to crackle.
хри́пл|ый (**-, -а́, -о**) *прил* (*голос*) hoarse; (*гармонь, звук*) wheezing.
хриплю́ *несов см* **хрипе́ть**.
хри́пн|уть (**-у, -ешь**; *perf* **охри́пнуть**) *несов неперех* to become *или* grow hoarse.
хрипот|а́ (**-ы́**) *ж* hoarseness.
христи|ани́н (**-ани́на**; *nom pl* **-а́не**, *gen pl* **-а́н**) *м* Christian.
христиа́н|ка (**-ки**; *gen pl* **-ок**) *ж см* **христиани́н**.
христиа́нск|ий (**-ая, -ое, -ие**) *прил* Christian.
христиа́нств|о (**-а**) *ср* Christianity.
Христ|о́с (**-а́**) *м* Christ; **~а́ ра́ди** (*разг*) for Christ's sake.
хром (**-а**) *м* (*ХИМ*) chrome; (*краска*) chrome yellow; (*кожа*) box calf.
хрома́|ть (**-ю**) *несов неперех* to limp; (*перен*: *разг*: *знания, дисциплина*) to be weak; **моя́ матема́тика ~ет** (*разг*) my maths is pretty shaky.
хро́мовый *прил* (*ХИМ*) chrome; (*кожа, сапоги итп*) box-calf.
хром|о́й (**-, -а́, -о**) *прил* lame; (*перен*: *разг*: *стол итп*) wobbly.
хромосо́м|а (**-ы**) *ж* chromosome.
хромот|а́ (**-ы́**) *ж* limp.
хро́ник (**-а**) *м* (*разг*) bad case.
хро́ник|а (**-и**) *ж* chronicle; (*КИНО*) film chronicle.
хроника́льный *прил* chronicle *опред*.
хроникёр (**-а**) *м* (*журналист*) reporter.
хрони́ческ|ий (**-ая, -ое, -ие**) *прил* chronic.
хронологи́ческ|ий (**-ая, -ое, -ие**) *прил* chronological; **в ~ой после́довательности** in chronological order.
хроноло́ги|я (**-и**) *ж* chronology.
хронометра́ж (**-а**) *м* time-keeping.
хру́п|кий (**-кая, -кое, -кие**; **-ок, -ка́, -ко**) *прил* (*лёд, стекло итп*) fragile; (*печенье, кости*) brittle; (*перен*: *фигура, девушка*) delicate; (: *здоровье, организм*) frail.
хру́пкост|ь (**-и**) *ж* (*см прил*) fragility; brittleness; delicacy; frailty.
хру́пок *прил см* **хру́пкий**.
хруст (**-а**) *м* crunch.
хруста́лик (**-а**) *м* (*АНАТ*) lens.
хруста́л|ь (**-я́**) *м, собир* crystal; **го́рный** ~ rock crystal.
хруста́льный *прил* crystal *опред*; (*перен*: *лёд, звон*) crystal clear.
хру|сте́ть (**-щу́, -сти́шь**) *несов неперех* to crunch; (*+instr*; *редиской, сахаром итп*) to crunch.
хрустя́щ|ий (**-ая, -ее, -ие**) *прил* crunchy; (*скатерть, бельё*) crisp; **хрустя́щий карто́фель** potato crisps (*BRIT*) *или* chips (*US*) *мн*.
хрущу́ *несов см* **хрусте́ть**.
хрю́ка|ть (**-ю**) *несов неперех* to grunt.
хрящ (**-а́**) *м* (*АНАТ*) cartilage.
ХСС *м сокр* (= *Христиа́нско-социалисти́ческий союз*) CSU (= *Christian Socialist Union*).
худе́|ть (**-ю**) *несов неперех* to grow thin; (*быть на диете*) to slim.
худо́жественный *прил* artistic; (*школа, выставка*) art *опред*; **худо́жественная литерату́ра** fiction; **худо́жественная самоде́ятельность** *amateur art and performance*; **худо́жественный сало́н** (*выставка*) art exhibition; (*магазин*) ≈ craft shop; **худо́жественный фильм** feature film.
худо́жеств|о (**-а**) *ср*: **акаде́мия худо́жеств** art school.
худо́жник (**-а**) *м* artist.
худо́жниц|а (**-ы**) *ж см* **худо́жник**.
худ|о́й (**-, -а́, -о**) *прил* thin; (*разг*: *плохой*) bad; (: *дырявый*) full of holes; **на ~ коне́ц** if the worst comes to the worst (*BRIT*), in the worst case scenario (*US*).
худоща́в|ый (**-, -а, -о**) *прил* thin.

ху́дш|ее (**-его**; *decl like adj*) *ср* the worst.
ху́дш|ий (**-ая, -ее, -ие**) *превос прил* the worst *опред*.
ху́же *сравн прил, нареч* worse.
ху|й (**-я**) *м* (*груб!*) cock (*!*), prick (*!*)
хулига́н (**-а**) *м* hooligan.
хулига́н|ить (**-ю, -ишь**; *perf* **нахулига́нить**) *несов неперех* to act like a hooligan.
хулига́н|ка (**-ки**; *gen pl* **-ок**) *ж см* **хулига́н**.
хулига́нск|ий (**-ая, -ое, -ие**) *прил*: **~ посту́пок** act of hooliganism; **~ое поведе́ние** hooliganism.
хулига́нств|о (**-а**) *ср* hooliganism.
хулиганьј|ё (**-я́**) *ср собир* hooligans *мн*, yobs *мн* (*BRIT*).
хул|и́ть (**-ю́, -и́шь**) *несов перех* (*порочить*) to abuse.
ху́нт|а (**-ы**) *ж* (*полит*) junta.
хурм|а́ (**-ы́**) *ж* (*дерево*) persimmon tree; (*плод*) persimmon, sharon fruit.
ху́тор (**-а**) *м* (*ферма*) farmstead; (*селение*) village (*in Southern Russia and the Ukraine*).
хуторя́н|ин (**-ина**; *nom pl* **-е**, *gen pl* **-**) *м* (*владелец хутора*) farmer; (*житель хутора*) villager.
хуторя́н|ка (**-ки**; *gen pl* **-ок**) *ж см* **хуторя́нин**.

Ц, ц

Ц, ц *сущ нескл* (*буква*) *the 23rd letter of the Russian alphabet*.
ц. *сокр* (= **центр**) ctr. (= *centre*); = **цена́**.
ца́па|ть (**-ю**) *несов перех* (*когтями, зубами*) to seize; (*perf* **сца́пать**; *разг*) to snatch, grab.
ца́п|ля (**-ли**; *gen pl* **-ель**) *ж* heron.
ца́пн|уть (**-у, -ешь**) *сов перех* to seize; (*разг*) to snatch, grab.
цара́пань|е (**-я**) *ср* scratching.
цара́па|ть (**-ю**; *perf* **оцара́пать**) *несов перех* (*раздирать*) to scratch; (*perf* **нацара́пать**; *разг*: *писать*) to scribble
▸ **цара́паться** (*perf* **оцара́паться**) *несов возв* to scratch; (*no perf*; *друг друга*) to scratch one another.
цара́пин|а (**-ы**) *ж* scratch.
царе́вен *сущ см* **царе́вна**.
царе́вич (**-а**) *м* tsarevich (*son of the tsar*).
царе́в|на (**-ны**; *gen pl* **-ен**) *ж* tsarevna (*daughter of the tsar*).
цари́зм (**-а**) *м* tsarism.
цар|и́ть (**-ю́, -и́шь**) *несов неперех* (*также перен*) to reign.
цари́ц|а (**-ы**) *ж* tsarina (*wife of the tsar*), empress; (*перен*: *бала, моды*) queen.
ца́рск|ий (**-ая, -ое, -ие**) *прил* (*двор, указ, семья*) tsar's, royal; (*режим, правительство*) tsarist; (*перен*: *роскошь, прием*) regal.
ца́рствен|ный (**-, -на, -но**) *прил* regal.
ца́рств|о (**-а**) *ср* (*государство*) tsardom; (*царствование*) reign; (*перен*: *любви, природы*) realm; **живо́тное/расти́тельное ~** the animal/plant kingdom.
ца́рствовани|е (**-я**) *ср* reign.
ца́рств|овать (**-ую**) *несов неперех* (*также перен*) to reign.
цар|ь (**-я́**) *м* tsar; (*перен*) king; **без ~я́ в голове́** (*разг*) completely daft.
ЦБ *м сокр* = *центра́льный банк*.
ЦБНТИ *ср сокр* = *Центра́льное бюро́ нау́чно-техни́ческой информа́ции*.
цве|сти́ (**-ту́, -тёшь**) *несов неперех* (*БОТ*) to blossom, flower; (*перен*: *страна, человек*) to flourish; ~ (*impf*) **здоро́вьем/от ра́дости** to be bursting with health/joy.
цвет (**-а**; *nom pl* **-а́**) *м* (*окраска*) colour (*BRIT*), color (*US*); (*part gen* **-у**, *loc sg* **-у́**; *БОТ*) blossom; **~ о́бщества** the cream of society; **во цве́те лет** in the prime of life.
цвета́ст|ый (**-, -а, -о**) *прил* colourful (*BRIT*), colorful (*US*).
цвете́ни|е (**-я**) *ср* blossoming.
цвети́ст|ый (**-, -а, -о**) *прил* (*узор*) floral; (*луг, поле*) flower-covered; (*речь, стиль*) flowery.
цветка́ *итп сущ см* **цвето́к**.
цветни́к (**-а́**) *м* flowerbed.
цветн|о́й *прил* (*карандаш*) coloured (*BRIT*), colored (*US*); (*одежда*) colourful (*BRIT*), colorful (*US*); (*фотография, фильм*) colour (*BRIT*), color (*US*) ◆ (**-о́го**; *decl like adj*) *м* (*человек*) colo(u)red; **цветна́я капу́ста** cauliflower; **цветно́й телеви́зор** colo(u)r television; **цветны́е мета́ллы** non-ferrous metals.
цвет|о́к (**-ка́**; *nom pl* **-ки́**) *м* flower (*reproductive part of a plant*); (*nom pl* **-ы**) flower (*bloom*); (*комнатный*) plant.
цветому́зык|а (**-и**) *ж* son et lumière, sound-and-light show (*US*).
цвето́чник (**-а**) *м* florist.
цвето́чниц|а (**-ы**) *ж см* **цвето́чник**.
цвето́чный *прил* flower *опред*; (*духи*) flower-scented; **цвето́чный горшо́к** flowerpot; **цвето́чный магази́н** florist's.
цвету́ *итп несов см* **цвести́**.
цвету́щ|ий (**-ая, -ее, -ие**) *прил* (*вид, женщина*) blossoming; (*область, экономика*) flourishing.
ЦГАЛИ *м сокр* = *Центра́льный госуда́рственный архи́в литерату́ры и иску́сства*.
ЦГИА *м сокр* = *Центра́льный госуда́рственный истори́ческий архи́в*.
це|ди́ть (**-жу́, -дишь**; *perf* **процеди́ть**) *несов перех* (*молоко, отвар*) to strain; (*no perf*; *заливить*: *в бутылку*) to siphon; (*perf* **процеди́ть**; *перен*: *слова*) to force out.
це́др|а (**-ы**) *ж* (dried) peel.
цежу́ *несов см* **цеди́ть**.
Цейло́н (**-а**) *м* Ceylon.
цейло́нск|ий (**-ая, -ое, -ие**) *прил* Ceylonese.
цейтно́т (**-а**) *м*: **быть в ~е** (*ШАХМАТЫ*) to be in time-trouble; (*перен*: *разг*) to be pushed for time.

The spelling rules for Russian are shown on page xvii.

целе́бен *прил см* **целе́бный**.
целе́бност|ь (-и) *ж* healing *или* medicinal properties *мн*.
целе́б|ный (-ен, -на, -но) *прил* medicinal; (*воздух*) healthy.
целево́й *прил* (*задание, установка*) special; (*финансирование, ссуды*) for a specified purpose; ~ **ры́нок** (*КОММ*) target market.
це́лен *прил см* **це́льный**.
целенапра́вленност|ь (-и) *ж* single-mindedness.
целенапра́вленный *прил* single-minded.
целесообра́зен *прил см* **целесообра́зный**.
целесообра́зно *нареч* expediently ♦ *как сказ* it makes sense; ~ **заверши́ть рабо́ту сейча́с** it makes sense to finish the work now.
целесообра́зност|ь (-и) *ж* expediency.
целесообра́з|ный (-ен, -на, -но) *прил* expedient.
целеустремлён|ный (-, -на, -но) *прил* purposeful.
целико́м *нареч*: **проглоти́ть/съесть что-н** ~ to swallow/eat sth whole; (*перен*: *без ограничений*) wholly, entirely.
целин|а́ (-ы́) *ж* (*также перен*) virgin territory; **сне́жная** ~ virgin snow.
цели́нный *прил* (*земля*) virgin *опред*.
цели́тель|ный (-ен, -ьна, -ьно) *прил* (*бальзам*) medicinal; (*действие, свойство*) healing *опред*; (*воздух*) healthy.
це́л|ить (-ю, -ишь; *perf* **наце́лить**) *несов неперех*: ~ **в** *+acc* to aim at; (*перен*: *в начальники*) to have one's sights set on
▸ **це́литься** (*perf* **наце́литься**) *несов возв*: ~**ся в** *+acc* to (take) aim at; ~**ся** (**наце́литься** *perf*) *+infin* (*разг*) to aim to do.
целлофа́н (-а) *м* cellophane®.
целлофа́новый *прил* cellophane® *опред*.
целлуло́ид (-а) *м* celluloid.
целлюло́з|а (-ы) *ж* cellulose.
цел|ова́ть (-у́ю; *perf* **поцелова́ть**) *несов перех* to kiss
▸ **целова́ться** (*perf* **поцелова́ться**) *несов возв* to kiss (each other).
це́л|ое (-ого; *decl like adj*) *ср* whole; (*МАТ*) integer; **еди́ное** ~ unified whole.
целому́дрен|ный (-, -на, -но) *прил* chaste.
целому́дри|е (-я) *ср* (*девственность*) chastity; (*нравственность*) chasteness.
це́лостен *прил см* **це́лостный**.
це́лостност|ь (-и) *ж* integrity.
це́лост|ный (-ен, -на, -но) *прил* integrated.
це́лост|ь (-и) *ж* (*машины, предмета*) safety; (*денег, инвестиций*) security, safety; **в** ~**и и сохра́нности** in one piece; **сохраня́ть** (**сохрани́ть** *perf*) **что-н в** ~**и** to keep sth safe.
це́л|ый *прил* whole, entire; (-, -а́, -о; *неповреждённый*: *машина, оборудование итп*) intact, undamaged; (: *одежда*) undamaged; **в** ~**ом** (*целиком*) as a whole; (*в общем*) on the whole; ~ **и невреди́мый** safe and sound; ~ **ряд** *+gen pl* a whole range of; **це́лое число́** (*МАТ*) whole number.
цел|ь (-и) *ж* (*при стрельбе*) target; (*перен*) aim, goal; **с це́лью** *+infin* with the object *или* aim of doing; **с це́лью** *+gen* for; **в це́лях** *+gen* for the purpose of; **в воспита́тельных/рекла́мных це́лях** for education/publicity purposes.
це́льност|ь (-и) *ж* integrity, completeness.
це́л|ьный *прил* (*кусок, камень*) solid; (-ен, -ьна, -ьно; *характер, произведение*) complete; (*теория*) integrated; ~**ьное молоко́** full-cream milk.
цеме́нт (-а) *м* cement.
цементи́р|овать (-ую; *perf* **зацементи́ровать**) *несов перех* to cement; (*perf* **сцементи́ровать**; *перен*) to cement.
цеме́нтный *прил* cement *опред*.
цен|а́ (-ы́; *acc sg* -у, *dat sg* -е́, *nom pl* -ы) *ж* price; (*перен*: *суждения, человека*) value; ~**о́ю** *+gen* at the expense of; **таки́е лю́ди/кни́ги в** ~**е́** such people/books are highly prized; **ему́** ~**ы́ нет** he is invaluable; ~ **продавца́** (*КОММ*) offer price; **торго́вая** ~ (*КОММ*) trade price.
це́нен *прил см* **це́нный**.
ценз (-а) *м* requirement.
це́нзор (-а) *м* censor.
цензу́р|а (-ы) *ж* censorship.
цензу́р|ный *прил* censorship *опред*; (-ен, -на, -но; *пристойный*) acceptable.
цени́тел|ь (-я) *м* judge (*of art, character etc*).
цени́тельница (-ы) *ж см* **цени́тель**.
цен|и́ть (-ю́, -ишь) *несов перех* (*дорожить*) to value; (*помощь, совет*) to appreciate; (*разг*: *назначать цену*) to name a price for
▸ **цени́ться** *несов неперех* to be (highly) valued.
це́нник (-а) *м* (*бирка*) price tag; (*список*) price list.
це́нност|ь (-и) *ж* value; (*обычно мн*: *духовные, культурные*) treasure; ~**и** valuables; **материа́льные** ~**и** commodities.
це́н|ный (-ен, -на, -но) *прил* valuable; (*no short form*; *посылка, письмо*) registered; **це́нные бума́ги** (*КОММ*) securities *мн*.
ценообразова́ни|е (-я) *ср* price formation.
цент (-а) *м* cent.
це́нтнер (-а) *м* centner (*100kg*).
центр (-а) *м* centre (*BRIT*), center (*US*); **в це́нтре внима́ния** in the limelight; **торго́вый центр** shopping centre (*BRIT*) *или* mall (*US*).
централи́зм (-а) *м* centralism.
централиз|ова́ть (-у́ю) (*не*)*сов перех* to centralize.
центра́льный *прил* central; ~ **проце́ссор** (*КОМП*) central processing unit; **центра́льная пре́сса** the national press; **центра́льное отопле́ние** central heating.
центров|о́й *прил*: ~ **напада́ющий/круг** centre forward/circle ♦ (-о́го; *decl like adj*) *м* (*в баскетболе*) centre (*BRIT*), center (*US*); (*в футболе*) midfielder.
цепене́|ть (-ю; *perf* **оцепене́ть**) *несов неперех*

(*от ужаса, от страха*) to freeze; ~ **(оцепене́ть** *perf***) от хо́лода** to be frozen stiff.
це́п|кий (-кая, -кое, -кие; -ок, -ка́, -ко) *прил* tenacious.
цепля́|ться (**-юсь**) *несов возв*: ~ **за** *+acc* (*также перен*) to cling *или* hang on to; ~ *(impf)* **рукаво́м/ного́й за что-н** to catch one's sleeve/leg on sth; ~ *(impf)* **к чему́-н** (*перен*: *разг*) to pick up on sth.
цепно́й *прил* chain *опред*; **цепна́я реа́кция** chain reaction; **цепна́я соба́ка** guard dog; **цепно́й мост** drawbridge.
це́пок *прил см* **це́пкий**.
цепо́ч|ка (-ки; *gen pl* **-ек)** *ж* (*тонкая цепь*) chain; (*машин, людей*) line; (*предложений*) string; **идти́** *(impf)* **~кой** to walk in single file.
цеп|ь (-и; *loc sg* **-и́)** *ж* (*также перен*) chain; (*ЭЛЕК*) circuit; **го́рная ~** mountain range; **сажа́ть (посади́ть** *perf***) кого́-н на ~** to chain sb up; **зако́вывать (закова́ть** *perf***) кого́-н в це́пи** to put sb in chains.
церемо́нен *прил см* **церемо́нный**.
церемо́н|иться (-юсь, -ишься) *несов возв* (*стесняться*) to stand on ceremony; (*быть снисходительным*): ~ **с кем-н** to be too soft on sb.
церемо́ни|я (-и) *ж* ceremony; **без ~й** without ceremony.
церемо́н|ный (-ен, -на, -но) *прил* ceremonious.
це́ркви *итп сущ см* **це́рковь**.
церко́вник (-а) *м* clergyman (*мн* clergymen).
церковнослужи́тел|ь (-я) *м* junior churchman (*мн* churchmen).
церко́вный *прил* church *опред*.
це́рк|овь (-ви; *instr sg* **-овью,** *nom pl* **-ви,** *gen pl* **-ве́й)** *ж* church.
цех (-а; *loc sg* **-у́,** *nom pl* **-а́)** *м* (work)shop (*in factory*).
цивилиза́ци|я (-и) *ж* civilization.
цивилизо́ванно *нареч* in a civilized manner.
цивилизо́ван|ный (-, -на, -но) *прил* civilized.
цивилиз|ова́ть (-у́ю) *(не)сов перех* to civilize.
циге́йк|а (-и) *ж* beaver lamb.
циге́йковый *прил* beaver-lamb.
цикл (-а) *м* cycle; (*лекций, концертов итп*) series.
цикламе́н (-а) *м* cyclamen.
цикли́чен *прил см* **цикли́чный**.
цикли́ческ|ий (-ая, -ое, -ие) *прил* cyclical.
цикли́ч|ный (-ен, -на, -но) *прил* = **цикли́ческий**.
цикло́н (-а) *м* cyclone.
цико́ри|й (-я) *м* chicory.
цили́ндр (-а) *м* cylinder; (*шляпа*) top hat.
цилиндри́ческ|ий (-ая, -ое, -ие) *прил* cylindrical.
цинг|а́ (-и́) *ж* scurvy.
цини́зм (-а) *м* cynicism.
ци́ник (-а) *м* cynic.
цини́чен *прил см* **цини́чный**.
цини́чност|ь (-и) *ж* cynicism.
цини́ч|ный (-ен, -на, -но) *прил* cynical.
цинк (-а) *м* zinc.
ци́нковый *прил* zinc.
цирк (-а) *м* circus; (*разг*: *смешное событие*) farce.
цирка́ч (-а́) *м* (*разг*) circus performer.
цирково́й *прил* circus *опред*.
циркули́р|овать (*3sg* **-ует**, *3pl* **-уют**) *несов неперех* to circulate.
ци́ркул|ь (-я) *м* (a pair of) compasses.
циркуля́р (-а) *м* circular.
циркуля́ци|я (-и) *ж* circulation.
цирро́з (-а) *м* cirrhosis.
цисте́рн|а (-ы) *ж* (*разервуар*) cistern; (*автомобиль*) tanker; (*вагон*) tank wagon (*BRIT*) *или* car (*US*).
цитаде́л|ь (-и) *ж* (*также перен*) citadel.
цита́т|а (-ы) *ж* quote, quotation.
цити́р|овать (-ую; *perf* **процити́ровать)** *несов перех* to quote.
ци́трус (-а) *м* (*обычно мн*) citrus fruit.
ци́трусовый *прил* citrus *опред*.
цифербла́т (-а) *м* dial; (*на часах*) face.
ци́фр|а (-ы) *ж* number; (*арабские, римские*) numeral; (*обычно мн*: *расчет*) figure.
цифрово́й *прил* numerical.
ЦК *м сокр* = *Центра́льный Комите́т*.
цо́ка|ть (-ю) *несов неперех* (*языком*) to tut; (*каблуки, копыта*) to clatter.
ЦП *сокр* (= *центра́льный проце́ссор*) CPU (= *central processing unit*).
ЦПКиО *м сокр* (= *Центра́льный парк культу́ры и о́тдыха*) *park used for recreational purposes*.
ЦПКО *м сокр* = **ЦПКиО**.
ЦРУ *ср сокр* (= *Центра́льное разве́дывательное управле́ние (США)*) CIA (= *Central Intelligence Agency*).
ЦСДФ *ж сокр* = *Центра́льная сту́дия документа́льных фи́льмов*.
ЦСКА *м сокр* = *Центра́льный спорти́вный клуб а́рмии*.
ЦСУ *ср сокр* = *Центра́льное статисти́ческое управле́ние*.
ЦТ *ср сокр* = *Центра́льное телеви́дение*.
цука́т (-а) *м* candied fruit.
ЦУМ (-а) *м сокр* = *центра́льный универса́льный магази́н*.
цум (-а) *м сокр* = **ЦУМ**.
цуна́ми *ср нескл* tidal wave.
цыга́н (-а; *nom pl* **-е)** *м* gypsy.
цыга́н|ка (-ки; *gen pl* **-ок)** *ж см* **цыга́н**.
цыга́нск|ий (-ая, -ое, -ие) *прил* gypsy *опред*.
цы́ка|ть (-ю) *несов неперех* (*разг*): ~ **на** *+acc* to snap at.
цыплёнок (-ёнка; *nom pl* **-я́та,** *gen pl* **-я́т)** *м* chick.
цыпля́ч|ий (-ья, -ье, -ьи) *прил* chicken *опред*; (*перен*: *шея, руки*) scrawny.
цы́почк|и (-ек) *мн*: **на ~ках** on tiptoe; **встава́ть (встать** *perf***) на ~** to stand on tiptoe.
Цю́рих (-а) *м* Zürich.

~Ч, ч~

Ч, ч *сущ нескл* (*буква*) *the 24th letter of the Russian alphabet*.
ча́вка|ть (-ю) *несов неперех* to chomp; (*перен*: *по грязи*) to squelch.
чад (-а; *loc sg* **-у́)** *м* fumes *мн*.
ча|ди́ть (-жу́, -ди́шь; *perf* **начади́ть)** *несов неперех* to give off fumes.
ча́д|о (-а) *ср* offspring (*мн* offspring).
чадр|а́ (-ы́) *ж* yashmak.
чаев|ы́е (-ы́х; *decl like adj*) *мн* tip *ед*; **дава́ть (дать** *perf*) **кому́-н** ~ to tip sb.
чаево́д (-а) *м* tea-grower.
чаево́дств|о (-а) *ср* tea-growing.
ча́ек *сущ см* **ча́йка**.
чаепити|е (-я) *ср* (*занятие*) tea-drinking; (*событие*) tea-party.
чажу́ *несов см* **чади́ть**.
чаи́н|ка (-ки; *gen pl* **-ок)** *ж* tea leaf.
ча|й (-я; *part gen* **-ю**, *nom pl* **-и́)** *м* tea; **зава́ривать (завари́ть** *perf*) ~ to make tea; **за ча́ем** over a cup of tea; **ча́шка ча́я** a cup of tea; **дава́ть (дать** *perf*) **кому́-н на** ~ to give sb a tip.
ча́|йка (-йки; *gen pl* **-ек)** *ж* (sea)gull.
ча́йн|ая (-ой; *decl like adj*) *ж* tearoom, teashop.
ча́йник (-а) *м* kettle; (*для заварки*) teapot.
ча́йн|ый *прил* (*плантация*) tea *опред*; **ча́йная ло́жка** teaspoon; **ча́йный серви́з** tea service *или* set.
чалм|а́ (-ы́) *ж* turban.
чан (-а) *м* (*деревянный*) vat; (*металлический*) tank.
ча́р|ка (-ки; *gen pl* **-ок)** *ж* chalice.
чар|ова́ть (-у́ю) *несов перех* (*красотой*) to charm; (*умом*) to captivate.
чароде́ек *сущ см* **чароде́йка**.
чароде́|й (-я) *м* sorcerer.
чароде́|йка (-йки; *gen pl* **-ек)** *ж* sorceress.
ча́рок *сущ см* **ча́рка**.
ча́ртер (-а) *м* (*КОММ*) charter.
ча́ртерный *прил* charter *опред*.
ча́р|ы (-) *мн* (*обаяние*) charms *мн*; (*волшебство*) magic *ед*.
час (-а́; *nom pl* **-ы́)** *м* hour; **академи́ческий** ~ (*ПРОСВЕЩ*) ≈ period; **кото́рый** ~? what time is it?; **сейча́с 3 ~а́ но́чи/дня** it's 3 o'clock in the morning/afternoon; **в 9 ~о́в утра́/ве́чера** at 9 o'clock in the morning/evening; **стоя́ть** (*impf*) **на ~а́х** to stand guard; **по ~а́м** by the clock; **~ от ~у не ле́гче** it gets worse by the hour; **в до́брый ~!** Godspeed!; **с ча́су на** ~ any moment; **он помо́г мне в тру́дный** ~ he helped me in my hour of need; *см также* **часы́**.
часо́в|ня (-ни; *gen pl* **-ен)** *ж* chapel.
часов|о́й *прил* (*лекция, перерыв итп*) one-hour; (*поезд*) one o'clock; (*механизм*: *ручных часов*) watch *опред*; (: *стенных часов*) clock *опред* ♦ **(-о́го**; *decl like adj*) *м* sentry; **~а́я стре́лка** the small hand; **~а́я опла́та** payment by the hour; **часово́й по́яс** time zone.
часовщи́к (-а́) *м* watchmaker.
ча́сом *нареч* (*разг*: *иногда*) the odd time ♦ *вводн сл* (*разг*: *случайно*) by any chance.
часосло́в (-а) *м* (*РЕЛ*) Book of Hours.
часте́нько *нареч* (*разг*) many's the time.
части́ц|а (-ы) *ж* (*маленькая часть*) fragment; (*ФИЗ, ЛИНГ*) particle; (*перен*: *правды*) grain.
части́чен *прил см* **части́чный**.
части́чно *нареч* partly.
части́ч|ный (-ен, -на, -но) *прил* partial.
ча́стник (-а) *м* (*разг*: *предприниматель*) entrepreneur; (*собственник*) proprietor.
частновладе́льческий (-ая, -ое, -ие) *прил* privately owned.
ча́стн|ое (-ого; *decl like adj*) *ср* quotient.
ча́стност|ь (-и) *ж* (*деталь*) detail; **в ~и** in particular.
ча́стн|ый *прил* private; (*нехарактерный*) certain; **в ~ых рука́х** in private hands; **~ слу́чай** isolated case; **ча́стная со́бственность** private property; **ча́стное лицо́** individual; **ча́стный капита́л** (*ЭКОН*) private capital; **ча́стный со́бственник** private owner; **ча́стная акционе́рная компа́ния** private limited company.
ча́сто *нареч* (*много раз*) often; (*тесно*) close together.
частоко́л (-а) *м* palings *мн*.
част|ота́ (-оты́) *ж* (*повторяемость*) frequency; (*nom pl* **-о́ты**; *ТЕХ*) frequency.
часто́тност|ь (-и) *ж* frequency.
частý́ш|ка (-ки; *gen pl* **-ек)** *ж* *traditional humorous folk song*.
ча́стый *прил* frequent; (*сито*) fine; (*лес, ряд предметов*) dense.
част|ь (-и; *gen pl* **-е́й**, *dat pl* **-я́м)** *ж* part; (*симфонии*) movement; (*отдел*) department; (*ВОЕН*) unit; **хозя́йственная** ~ supply department; **уче́бная** ~ academic studies office;

по ча́сти *+gen* when it comes to; **э́то не по мое́й ча́сти** this is not my department; **разрыва́ться** *(impf)* **на ча́сти** to have lots on the go at once; **её рвут на ча́сти** she is in constant demand; **часть ре́чи** part of speech; **часть све́та** continent.
ча́стью *нареч* partly.
час|ы́ (-о́в) *мн* (*карманные*) watch *ед*; (*стенные*) clock *ед*.
ча́хл|ый (-, -а, -о) *прил* (*цветок*) withered; (*человек*) sickly.
ча́х|нуть (-ну, -нешь; *pt* **-, -ла, -ло,** *perf* **зача́хнуть)** *несов неперех* (*растения*) to wither; (*человек, животное*) to fade away.
чахо́тк|а (-и) *ж* consumption.
ча́ш|а (-и) *ж* bowl; (*весов*) pan; **у них дом – по́лная ~** they've got everything imaginable in their house; **~ терпе́ния перепо́лнилась** this is the last straw.
ча́шек *сущ см* **ча́шка**.
ча́шеч|ка (-ки; *gen pl* **-ек)** *ж уменьш от* **ча́шка**; (*БОТ*) calyx; **коле́нная ~** kneecap.
ча́ш|ка (-ки; *gen pl* **-ек)** *ж* cup; (*весов*) pan.
ча́щ|а (-и) *ж* (*лес*) thick forest.
ча́ще *сравн прил от* **ча́стый** ♦ *сравн нареч от* **ча́сто**.
ча́яни|е (-я) *ср* (*обычно мн*) aspiration.
ча́|ять (-ю) *несов перех*: **он в ней души́ не ~ет** he dotes on her.
чванли́в|ый (-, -а, -о) *прил* conceited.
чва́нств|о (-а) *ср* conceit.
чебуре́к (-а) *м* ≈ meat pasty.
чего́ *мест см* **что**.
чей (чьего́; *см* **Table 7;** *f* **чья,** *nt* **чьё,** *pl* **чьи)** *мест* whose; **~ э́то ребёнок?** whose child is this?; **~ бы то ни́ был** no matter whose it is.
че́й-либо (чьего́-либо; *как* **чей;** *см* **Table 7;** *f* **чья́-либо,** *nt* **чьё-либо,** *pl* **чьи́-либо)** *мест* = **че́й-нибудь**.
че́й-нибудь (чьего́-нибудь; *как* **чей;** *см* **Table 7;** *f* **чья́-нибудь,** *nt* **чьё-нибудь,** *pl* **чьи́-нибудь)** *мест* anyone's.
че́й-то (чьего́-то; *как* **чей;** *см* **Table 7;** *f* **чья́-то,** *nt* **чьё-то,** *pl* **чьи́-то)** *мест* someone's, somebody's.
чек (-а) *м* (*банковский*) cheque (*BRIT*), check (*US*); (*товарный, кассовый*) receipt; **выбива́ть (вы́бить** *perf***) ~** to issue a receipt (*to be presented as proof of payment in Russian shops*).
Чека́ *ж сокр* (*ИСТ*: = *Чрезвыча́йная коми́ссия по борьбе́ с контрреволю́цией и сабота́жем*) Cheka (*state security police in Soviet Russia from 1918-1922*).
чека́н|ить (-ю, -ишь; *perf* **отчека́нить)** *несов перех* (*монеты*) to mint; (*узор*) to enchase; **~ (отчека́нить** *perf***) слова́** to enunciate one's words.
чека́нк|а (-и) *ж* (*монет*) minting; (*изделие*) enchased object.
чеки́ст (-а) *м* (*ИСТ*) Cheka officer.
че́ковый *прил* cheque *опред* (*BRIT*), check *опред* (*US*); **че́ковая кни́жка** cheque book.
чёл|ка (-ки; *gen pl* **-ок)** *ж* (*человека*) fringe (*BRIT*), bangs *мн* (*US*); (*лошади*) forelock.
челно́к (-а́) *м* (*лодка*) dugout; (*швейный*) shuttle.
челно́чный *прил* shuttle *опред*.
челове́к (-а; *nom pl* **лю́ди,** *gen pl* **люде́й)** *м* human (being); (*некто, личность*) person (*мн* people); **два/три/четы́ре ~а** two/three/four people; **пять/шесть** *umn* **~** five/six *umn* people; **будь ~ом, помоги́ нам!** (*разг*) be a sport and give us a hand!; **вот ~!** (*разг*) what a character!
челове́ко-день (-ня; *gen pl* **-ней)** *м* man-day.
человеколю́би|е (-я) *ср* philanthropy.
человеконенави́стник (-а) *м* misanthrope.
человеконенави́стническ|ий (-ая, -ое, -ие) *прил* misanthropic.
челове́ко-час (-а) *м* man-hour.
челове́чен *прил см* **челове́чный**.
челове́ческ|ий (-ая, -ое, -ие) *прил* human *опред*; (*человечный*) humane; **по-~и** in a humane way.
челове́честв|о (-а) *ср* humanity, mankind.
челове́чн|ый (-ен, -на, -но) *прил* humane.
чёлок *сущ см* **чёлка**.
че́люст|ь (-и) *ж* (*АНАТ*) jaw.
Челя́бинск (-а) *м* Chelyabinsk.
чем *мест см* **что** ♦ *союз* than; (*разг*: *вместо того чтобы*) instead of; **бо́льше, ~ де́сять челове́к** more than ten people; **~ спо́рить, дава́й спро́сим кого́-нибудь** instead of arguing, let's ask someone; **~ бо́льше/ра́ньше** *umn*, **тем лу́чше** the bigger/earlier *umn*, the better.
чемода́н (-а) *м* suitcase; **сиде́ть** *(impf)* **на ~ах** (*перен*: *разг*) to have one's bags packed.
чемпио́н (-а) *м* champion; **~ по те́ннису** tennis champion.
чемпиона́т (-а) *м* championship; **~ страны́ по хокке́ю** national hockey championships.
чемпио́н|ка (-ки; *gen pl* **-ок)** *ж см* **чемпио́н**.
чему́ *мест см* **что**.
чепе́ *ср нескл* (*разг*) crisis.
чепух|а́ (-и́) *ж* (*разг*) rubbish (*BRIT*), garbage (*US*).
че́пчик (-а) *м* bonnet (*hat*).
че́рв|и (-е́й) *мн* (*КАРТЫ*) hearts *мн*.
черви́в|ый (-, -а, -о) *прил* maggoty.
черво́н|ец (-ца) *м* (*разг*: *10 рублей*) ten roubles.
черво́нн|ый *прил* (*КАРТЫ*): **~ая да́ма/деся́тка** the queen/ten of hearts.
черво́нца *umn сущ см* **черво́нец**.
черв|ь (-я́; *gen pl* **-е́й)** *м* worm; (*личинка*) maggot.
червя́к (-а́) *м* worm.
червя́чный *прил* (*ТЕХ*) worm *опред*.
черда́к (-а́) *м* attic, loft.
черда́чный *прил* attic *опред*.
черёд *м* (*разг*) turn; **всё идёт свои́м чередо́м**

everything is going as normal.
чередá (**-ы**) *ж* (*людей*) stream; (*событий*) sequence.
черед|овáть (**-ýю**) *несов перех*: **~ что-н с** *+instr* to alternate sth with
▸ **чередовáться** *несов возв* to alternate; **~ся** *(impf)* **с** *+instr* to take turns with.

KEYWORD

чéрез *предл* (*+acc*) **1** (*поперёк*) across, over; **мост чéрез канáл/рéку** the bridge across *или* over the canal/river; **переходить (перейти** *perf***) чéрез дорóгу** to cross the road
2 (*сквозь*) through; **он влез чéрез окнó** he climbed through the window; **чéрез лýпу** through a magnifying glass
3 (*поверх*) over; **он перелéз чéрез забóр** he climbed over the fence; **дéти прыгают чéрез верёвку** the children are jumping over a rope
4 (*спустя*) in; **чéрез час** in an hour('s time); **чéрез мéсяц/год** in a month('s)/year('s) (time)
5 (*минуя какое-н пространство*): **чéрез три квартáла – стáнция** the station is three blocks away
6 (*при помощи*) via; **он передáл письмó чéрез знакóмого** he sent the letter via a friend
7 (*при повторении действия*) every; **принимáйте таблéтки чéрез кáждый час** take the tablets every hour.

черёмух|а (**-и**) *ж* bird cherry.
чёрен *прил см* **чёрный**.
черен|óк (**-кá**) *м* (*рукоятка*) handle; (*БОТ*) cutting.
чéреп (**-а**) *м* skull.
черепáх|а (**-и**) *ж* tortoise; (*морская*) turtle.
черепáховый *прил* (*суп*) turtle; (*гребень*) tortoiseshell.
черепáш|ий (**-ья, -ье, -ьи**) *прил* tortoise's; (*морской*) turtle's; **идти** *(impf)* **~ьим шáгом** to go at a snail's pace.
черепúц|а (**-ы**) *ж* tile ◆ *собир* tiles *мн*.
черепúчный *прил* tiled.
черепкá *сущ см* **черепóк**.
черепнóй *прил* skull *опред*; **черепнáя корóбка** cranium.
череп|óк (**-кá**) *м* pottery fragment.
чересчýр *нареч* far too; **это уж ~!** that's just too much!
черéш|ня (**-ни**; *gen pl* **-ен**) *ж* (*дерево*) cherry (tree); (*плод*) cherry.
черкá|ть (**-ю**; *perf* **начеркáть**) *несов перех* (*разг*) to draw lines on; (*зачёркивать*) to cross out.
черкн|ýть (**-ý, -ёшь**) *сов перех* (*разг*: *написать*) to scribble.
чернé|ть (**-ю**; *perf* **почернéть**) *несов неперех* (*становиться чёрным*) to turn black; (*no perf*; *виднеться*) to show black.
черникá|а (**-и**) *ж* (*кустарник*) bilberry (bush) ◆ *собир* bilberries *мн*.
чернúл|а (**-**) *мн* ink *ед*.
чернúльниц|а (**-ы**) *ж* inkwell.
чернúльный *прил* ink *опред*; **чернúльный карандáш** *graphite pencil which writes in purple when moistened.*
черн|úть (**-ю, -úшь**; *perf* **начернúть**) *несов перех* (*брови*) to tint; (*perf* **очернúть**; *имя, репутацию*) to tarnish; (*no perf*; *сталь, серебро*) to tarnish.
чёрно-бéлый *прил* black-and-white.
чернобýрк|а (**-и**) *ж* (*разг*: *мех*) silver fox.
черно-бýр|ый *прил*: **~ая лисá** silver fox.
черновúк (**-á**) *м* draft.
чернов|óй *прил* draft; **~áя рабóта** rough work.
черноволóс|ый (**-, -а, -о**) *прил* black-haired.
черногóр|ец (**-ца**) *м* Montenegrin.
Черногóри|я (**-и**) *ж* Montenegro.
черногóр|ка (**-ки**; *gen pl* **-ок**) *ж см* **черногóрец**.
черногóрск|ий (**-ая, -ое, -ие**) *прил* Montenegrin.
черногóрца *итп сущ см* **черногóрец**.
чернозём (**-а**) *м* black earth.
чернокóж|ий (**-ая, -ее, -ие**) *прил* black (*person*) ◆ (**-его**; *decl like adj*) *м* black (person) (*мн* people).
чернорабóч|ий (**-его**; *decl like adj*) *м* unskilled worker.
чернослúв (**-а**) *м собир* prunes *мн*.
чернот|á (**-ы́**) *ж* blackness.
чёр|ный (**-ен, -нá, -нó**) *прил* black; (*мрачный*) gloomy; (*no short form*; *преступный*) wicked; (*задний*) back *опред*; **держáть** *(impf)* **когó-н в ~ном тéле** to treat sb badly; **~ным по бéлому** in black and white; **~ная рабóта** dirty work; **чёрные метáллы** ferrous metals; **чёрный кóфе** black coffee; **чёрный ры́нок** black market; **чёрный нал** profits from the shadow economy.
чéрпа|ть (**-ю**) *несов перех* (*жидкость*) to ladle; (*песок*) to scoop (up); (*перен*: *знания, силы*) to derive.
черпн|ýть (**-ý, -ёшь**) *сов перех* (*жидкость*) to ladle; (*песок*) to scoop (up).
черствé|ть (**-ю**; *perf* **зачерствéть**) *несов неперех* (*хлеб*) to go stale; (*perf* **очерствéть**; *человек, душа*) to harden.
чёрств|ый (**-, -á, -о**) *прил* (*хлеб*) stale; (*человек, душа*) hard.
чёрт (**-а**; *nom pl* **чéрти**, *gen pl* **чертéй**) *м* (*дьявол*) devil; **у негó дéнег до ~а** (*разг*) he's rolling in money; **идú к ~у!** (*разг*) go to hell!; **к ~у!** *reply to a wish of good luck*; **ни чертá** not a thing; **~ меня́ дёрнул** I don't know what got into me; **чем ~ не шýтит** you never know; **~ возьмú** *или* **поберú** *или* **подерú!** (*разг*) damn it!; **~ егó знáет!** (*разг*) God knows!; **~ знáет что!** (*разг*) it's outrageous!; **он мóжет ~ знáет, что надéлать** it's frightening to think what he might do; **~ с ним!** (*разг*) to hell with him!; **он дал тебé дéнег? – ~а с два!** (*разг*) did he give you any money? – like hell he did!
черт|á (**-ы́**) *ж* (*линия*) line; (*граница*) limit; (*признак*) trait; **в óбщих ~х** in general terms; *см также* **черты́**.

чертёж (-á) *м* draft.
чертёжник (-а) *м* draughtsman (*BRIT*) (*мн* draughtsmen), draftsman (*US*) (*мн* draftsmen).
чертёжный *прил* drawing *опред*.
чер|ти́ть (-чу́, -тишь; *perf* **начерти́ть**) *несов перех* (*линию*) to draw; (*план, график*) to draw up.
чёртов (-а, -о, -ы) *прил* (*разг*: *холод, работа итп*) damn(ed); **чёртова дю́жина** baker's dozen.
чертóвски *нареч* (*разг*) dreadfully: **я ~ гóлоден** I'm ravenous.
чертóвск|ий (-ая, -ое, -ие) *прил* (*разг*) damn (ed).
чертополóх (-а) *м* thistle.
чёрточ|ка (-ки; *gen pl* -ек) *ж уменьш от* **чертá**; (*дефис*) hyphen; **э́то слóво пи́шется чéрез ~ку** this word is written with a hyphen.
черт|ы (-) *мн* (*также*: **~ лицá**) features *мн*.
черчéни|е (-я) *ср* (*действие*) drawing; (*ПРОСВЕЩ*) technical drawing.
черчу́ *несов см* **черти́ть**.
че|сáть (-шу́, -шешь; *perf* **почесáть**) *несов перех* (*спину*) to scratch; (*no perf*; *разг*: *гребнем*) to comb; (: *щёткой*) to brush; **~** *(impf)* **язы́к** *или* **языкóм** to natter
▸ **чесáться** (*perf* **почесáться**) *несов возв* to scratch o.s.; (*no perf*; *зудеть*) to itch; **он и не чéшется** (*разг*) he doesn't lift a finger; **у меня́ ру́ки ~шу́тся** *+infin* (*разг*) I'm itching to do.
чеснóк (-á) *м* garlic.
чесóтк|а (-и) *ж* (*МЕД*) scabies.
чéствовани|е (-я) *ср* (*действие*) honouring (*BRIT*), honoring (*US*).
чéств|овать (-ую) *несов перех* to honour (*BRIT*), honor (*US*).
чéстен *прил см* **чéстный**.
чéстно *нареч* honestly ♦ *как сказ*: **так бу́дет ~** that'll be fair.
чéстност|ь (-и) *ж* honesty.
чéст|ный (-ен, -нá, -но) *прил* honest; (*безупречный*) upright; **~ное и́мя** good name; **~ное слóво** honest to God; **держáться** *(impf)* **на ~ном слóве** (*разг*) to hang by a thread.
честолю́б|ец (-ца) *м* ambitious person (*мн* people).
честолюби́в|ый (-, -а, -о) *прил* (*человек, план*) ambitious.
честолю́би|е (-я) *ср* ambition.
честолю́бца *итп сущ см* **честолю́бец**.
чест|ь (-и) *ж* honour (*BRIT*), honor (*US*); (*loc sg* **-и́**; *почёт*) glory; **в ~** *+gen* in hono(u)r of; **к чéсти когó-н** to sb's credit; **дéлать** *(impf)* **~ кому́-н** to do sb credit; (*оказывать уважение*) to do sb an hono(u)r; **отдавáть (отдáть** *perf*) **кому́-н ~** to salute sb; **выходи́ть (вы́йти** *perf*) **с чéстью из чегó-н** to come out of sth with one's hono(u)r intact; **порá и ~ знать** (*разг*) it is time to wind up.
чет|á (-ы́) *ж* couple; **он мне не ~** he is no match for me.
четвéрг (-á) *м* Thursday; *см также* **втóрник**.
четверéн|ьки (-ек) *мн*: **вставáть (встать** *perf*) **на ~** to go down on all fours; **ходи́ть** *(impf)* **на ~ьках** to move on all fours.
четвёр|ка (-ки; *gen pl* -ок) *ж* (*цифра, карта*) four; (*ПРОСВЕЩ*) ≈ B (*school mark*); (*группа людей*) foursome; (*разг*: *автобус, трамвай итп*) (number) four (*bus, tram etc*).
четверн|я́ (-и́; *gen pl* -éй) *ж* quadruplets *мн*.
чéтвер|о (*см* **Table 36a**: **-ы́х**) *чис* four; *см также* **двóе**.
четвёрок *сущ см* **четвёрка**.
четвероклáссник (-а) *м pupil in fourth year at school (usually ten years old)*.
четвероклáссниц|а (-ы) *ж см* **четвероклáссник**.
четвероно́г|ий (-ая, -ое, -ие) *прил* four-legged.
четверости́ши|е (-я) *ср* quatrain.
четвёрт|ая (-ой; *decl like adj*) *ж*: **однá ~** one quarter.
четверт|овáть (-у́ю) *несов перех* to quarter (*at execution*).
четвёрт|ый (-ая, -ое, -ые) *чис* fourth; **сейчáс ~ час** it's after three; *см также* **пя́тый**.
чéтверт|ь (-и) *ж* quarter; (*МУЗ*) crotchet (*BRIT*), quarter note (*US*); (*ПРОСВЕЩ*) term.
четвертьфинáл (-а) *м* (*СПОРТ*) quarter final.
четверы́м *итп чис см* **чéтверо**.
чёт|кий (-кая, -кое, -кие; -ок, -кá, -ко) *прил* clear; (*движения, шаг*) precise.
чёткост|ь (-и) *ж* (*см прил*) clarity; precision.
чётный *прил* (*число*) even.
чёток *сущ см* **чёткий**.
четы́р|е (-ёх; *instr sg* **-ьмя́**; *см* **Table 25**) *чис* (*цифра, число*) four; (*ПРОСВЕЩ*) ≈ B (*school mark*); **ей ~ гóда** she is four (years old); **они́ живу́т в дóме нóмер ~** they live at number four; **óколо четырёх** about four; **кни́га стóит ~ рубля́** the book costs four roubles; **~ с полови́ной часá** four and a half hours; **сейчáс ~ часá** it is four o'clock; **я́блоки продаю́тся по ~ шту́ки** the apples are sold in fours; **дели́ть (раздели́ть** *perf*) **что-н на ~** to divide sth into four.
четы́р|еста (-ёхсóт; *см* **Table 33**) *чис* four hundred; *см также* **сто**.
четырёх *чис см* **четы́ре**.
четырёхднéвный *прил* four-day.
четырёхкрáтн|ый *прил*: **~ чемпиóн** four-times champion; **в ~ом размéре** fourfold.
четырёхлéти|е (-я) *ср* (*срок*) four years; (*годовщина*) fourth anniversary.
четырёхлéтн|ий (-яя, -ее, -ие) *прил* (*период*) four-year; (*ребёнок*) four-year-old.
четырёхмéсячный *прил* four-month;

(*ребёнок*) four-month-old.
четырёхнеде́льный *прил* four-week; (*ребёнок*) four-week-old.
четырёхсо́т *чис см* **четы́реста**.
четырёхсотле́ти|е **(-я)** *ср* (*срок*) four hundred years; (*годовщина*) quatercentenary.
четырёхсотле́тн|ий (-яя, -ее, -ие) *прил* (*период*) four-hundred-year; (*дерево*) four-hundred-year-old.
четырёхсо́т|ый (-ая, -ое, -ые) *чис* four-hundredth.
четырёхста́х *чис см* **четы́реста**.
четырёхуго́льник (-а) *м* quadrangle.
четырёхуго́льный *прил* quadrangular.
четырёхчасово́й *прил* (*рабочий день*) four-hour; (*поезд*) four o'clock.
четы́рнадцат|ый (-ая, -ое, -ые) *чис* fourteenth; *см также* **пя́тый**.
четы́рнадцат|ь (-и; *как* **пять;** *см* **Table 27)** *чис* fourteen; *см также* **пять**.
четырьмя́ *чис см* **четы́ре**.
четырьмяста́ми *чис см* **четы́реста**.
чех (-а) *м* Czech.
чехарда́ (-ы) *ж* (*разг: игра*) leapfrog; (*перен: путаница*) muddle.
Чехи|я (-и) *ж* the Czech Republic.
чех|о́л (-ла́) *м* (*для мебели*) cover; (*для гитары, для оружия*) case.
Чехослова́ки|я (-и) *ж* (*ИСТ*) Czechoslovakia.
чечеви́ца (-ы) *ж* lentil ◆ *собир* lentils *мн*.
чече́н|ец (-ца) *м* Chechen.
чече́н|ка (-ки; *gen pl* **-ок)** *ж см* **чече́нец**.
чече́нца *итп сущ см* **чече́нец**.
чечётк|а (-и) *ж* tap dance.
Чечн|я́ (-и́) *ж* Chechenia, Chechnya.
че́ш|ка (-ки; *gen pl* **-ек)** *ж см* **чех**.
че́шск|ий (-ая, -ое, -ие) *прил* Czech; ~ **язы́к** Czech.
чешу́(сь) *итп несов см* **чеса́ть(ся)**.
чешу́йк|а (-и) *ж* scale.
чешу́йчатый *прил* scaly.
чешу|я́ (-и́) *ж собир* scales *мн*.
чи́бис (-а) *м* lapwing.
чиж (-а́) *м* siskin.
чи́збургер (-а) *м* cheeseburger.
Чика́го *м нескл* Chicago.
Чи́ли *ср нескл* Chile.
чили́йск|ий (-ая, -ое, -ие) *прил* Chilean.
чин (-а; *nom pl* **-ы́)** *м* rank; **повыша́ть (повы́сить** *perf*) **кого́-н в чи́не** to promote sb to a higher rank.
чин|и́ть (-ю́, -ишь; *perf* **почини́ть)** *несов перех* to mend, repair; (*perf* **очини́ть;** *карандаш*) to sharpen; **(-ю́, -и́шь;** *perf* **учини́ть;** *насилие, произвол*) to commit; (*no perf; препятствия*) to create.
чино́вник (-а) *м* (*служащий*) official; (*бюрократ*) bureaucrat.
чино́вническ|ий (-ая, -ое, -ие) *прил* (*должность*) official; (*аппарат*) bureaucratic.
чи́пс|ы (-ов) *мн* crisps *мн*.
чири́ка|ть (-ю) *несов неперех* to twitter.
чи́рка|ть (-ю) *несов неперех*: ~ **спи́чкой** to strike a match.
чи́ркн|уть (-у, -ешь) *сов неперех* to strike.
чи́сел *сущ см* **число́**.
чи́сленност|ь (-и) *ж* (*армии*) numbers *мн*; (*учащихся*) number; ~ **населе́ния** population.
чи́сленный *прил* (*количественный*) numerical; **чи́сленное превосхо́дство** numerical advantage; **чи́сленный соста́в** (*армии*) total numbers *мн*.
числи́тел|ь (-я) *м* numerator.
числи́тельн|ое (-ого; *decl like adj*) *ср* numeral.
чи́сл|иться (-юсь, -ишься) *несов возв* (*в организации*) to be registered; ~ (*impf*) *+instr* (*больным, должником итп*) to be registered as; **он ~ится дире́ктором фи́рмы** he's officially the director of the firm; **за ним ~ится долг** he owes some money; **в спи́ске его́ фами́лия не ~ится** his name is not on the list.
чис|ло́ (-ла́; *nom pl* **-ла,** *gen pl* **-ел)** *ср* number; (*день месяца*) date; **еди́нственное** ~ singular; **мно́жественное** ~ plural; **быть** (*impf*) **в ~ле́** *+gen* to be among(st); **како́е сего́дня ~?** what is the date today?; **прие́ду в пе́рвых чи́слах ма́рта** I am coming at the beginning of March; **отмеча́ть (отме́тить** *perf*) **что-н за́дним ~м** to backdate sth; **узнава́ть (узна́ть** *perf*) **за́дним ~м** (*разг*) to find out later; **в том ~ле́** including; **оши́бкам нет ~ла́** there are countless mistakes.
числов|о́й *прил*: **~о́е програ́ммное управле́ние** (*КОМП*) numerically programmed (*BRIT*) *или* programed (*US*) control.
чисти́лищ|е (-а) *ср* purgatory.
чи́|стить (-щу, -стишь; *perf* **вы́чистить** *или* **почи́стить)** *несов перех* to clean; (*зубы*) to brush, clean; (*perf* **почи́стить;** *яблоко, картошку*) to peel; (*рыбу*) to scale; (*perf* **очи́стить;** *дно реки*) to dredge; (*сад*) to clean up; (*perf* **обчи́стить;** *разг: кассу, человека*) to clean out.
чи́ст|ка (-ки; *gen pl* **-ок)** *ж* (*действие*) cleaning; (: *овощей*) peeling; (*в партии*) purge.
чи́сто *нареч* (*только*) purely; (*убранный, сделанный*) neatly ◆ *как сказ*: **в до́ме** ~ the house is clean.
чистови́к (-а́) *м* fair copy.
чистово́й *прил* fair.
чи́сток *сущ см* **чи́стка**.
чистокро́вн|ый *прил* pure-breed; **~ая ло́шадь** thoroughbred.
чистопло́тен *прил см* **чистопло́тный**.
чистопло́тность (-и) *ж* cleanliness.
чистопло́т|ный (-ен, -на, -но) *прил* clean; (*перен: порядочный*) decent.
чистопро́бный *прил* (*золото*) pure.
чистосерде́чный (-ен, -на, -но) *прил* sincere.
чистот|а́ (-ы́) *ж* (*воздуха, спирта, раствора*) purity; **у него́ в до́ме всегда́** ~ his house is always extremely clean.
чи́ст|ый (-, -а́, -о) *прил* (*одежда, комната*) clean; (*любовь, сердце, человек*) pure and innocent;

(*совесть, небо, произношение*) clear; (*золото, спирт*) pure; (*язык*) proper; (*no short form*; *прибыль, вес*) net; (*совпадение, случайность*) pure; **выводи́ть (вы́вести** *perf*) **кого́-н на ~ую во́ду** (*разоблачить*) to expose sb.
чита́льный *прил*: **~ зал** reading room.
чита́тел|ь (-я) *м* reader.
чита́тельница (-ы) *ж см* **чита́тель.**
чита́|ть (-ю; *perf* **прочёсть** *или* **прочита́ть**) *несов перех* to read; (*декламировать*) to recite; (*курс*) to teach; (*лекцию*) to give.
чиха́|ть (-ю; *perf* **чихну́ть**) *несов неперех* to sneeze; (*разг*: *мотор*) to splutter: **ему́ ~ на пра́вила/свои́х роди́телей** he doesn't give a damn about the rules/his parents.
чи́ще *сравн прил от* **чи́стый** ◆ *сравн нареч от* **чи́сто.**
чи́щу *несов см* **чи́стить.**
ЧК *ж сокр* = **Чека́.**
член (-а) *м* member; (*обычно мн*: *конечности*) limb; **полово́й ~** penis; **~ предложе́ния** part of a sentence.
член|и́ть (-ю́, -и́шь; *perf* **расчлени́ть**) *несов перех* to break up.
членко́р (-а) *м сокр* = *член-корреспонде́нт.*
член-корреспонде́нт (-а, -а) *м* (*звание*) *academic title junior to academician.*
членоразде́л|ьный (-ен, -ьна, -ьно) *прил* intelligible.
чле́нск|ий (-ая, -ое, -ие) *прил* membership.
чле́нств|о (-а) *ср* membership.
ЧМ *сокр* (= *часто́тная модуля́ция*) FM (= *frequency modulation*).
чо́ка|ться (-юсь; *perf* **чо́кнуться**) *несов возв* to clink glasses (*during a toast*).
чо́кнут|ый (-, -а, -о) *прил* (*разг*: *человек*) barmy, crazy.
чо́кн|уться (-усь, -ешься) *сов от* **чо́каться.**
чо́пор|ный (-ен, -на, -но) *прил* prim.
ЧП *ср сокр* = **чрезвыча́йное происше́ствие.**
ЧПУ *ср сокр* = **числово́е програ́ммное управле́ние.**
чрезвыча́ен *прил см* **чрезвыча́йный.**
чрезвыча́йно *нареч* extremely.
чрезвыча́|йный (-ен, -йна, -йно) *прил* (*исключительный*) extraordinary; (*no short form*; *экстренный*) emergency *опред*; **чрезвыча́йный и полномо́чный посо́л** ambassador extraordinary and plenipotentiary; **чрезвыча́йное положе́ние** state of emergency; **чрезвыча́йное происше́ствие** crisis.
чрезме́р|ный (-ен, -на, -но) *прил* excessive.
чте́ни|е (-я) *ср* reading; *см также* **чте́ния.**
чте́ни|я (-й) *мн* course *ед* of lectures.
чтец (-а́) *м* reader.
чт|ить (*см* **Table 17**) *несов перех* to honour (*BRIT*), honor (*US*).

KEYWORD

что (чего́; (*см* **Table 6**) *мест* **1** (*вопросительное*) what; **что ты сказа́л?** what did you say?; **что с тобо́й?** what's the matter (with you)?; **что Вы говори́те?** you don't say!; **к чему́** *или* **на что тебе́ э́то?** what do you need it for?
2 (*относительное*) which; **она́ не поздоро́валась, что бы́ло мне неприя́тно** she did not say hello, which was unpleasant for me; **что ни говори́ ...** whatever you say ...
3 (*столько сколько*)**: она́ закрича́ла что бы́ло сил** she shouted with her all might
4 (*который*) that; **де́рево, что растёт у до́ма** the tree that grows by the house
5 (*разг*: *что-нибудь*) anything; **е́сли что слу́чится** if anything happens, should anything happen; **в слу́чае чего́** if anything crops up; **чуть что – сра́зу скажи́ мне** get in touch at the slightest thing
◆ *нареч* (*почему*) why; **что ты грусти́шь?** why are you sad?; **мне не хо́чется идти́ – что так?** I don't feel like going – why's that?
◆ *союз* **1** (*при сообщении, высказывании*): **я зна́ю, что на́до де́лать** I know what must be done; **я зна́ю, что он прие́дет** I know that he will come; **стра́нно то, что он молчи́т** it is strange that he remains silent; **что ни день, то но́вые пробле́мы** there isn't a day without new problems
2 (*во фразах*): **а что?** (*разг*) why (do you ask)?; **к чему́** (*зачем*) why; **не́ за что!** not at all! (*BRIT*), you're welcome! (*US*); **ни за что!** (*разг*) no way!; **ни за что ни про что** (*разг*) for no (good) reason; **что ты!** (*при возражении*) what!; **я здесь ни при чём** it has nothing to do with me; **э́то тут ни при чём** that's beside the point; **чего́ там!** forget it!; **что ж** (*да*) oh well; **что за чепуха́?** what kind of nonsense is this!; **са́мый что ни на есть лу́чший/о́пытный** best/most experienced there is; **что к чему́** (*разг*) what's what; **пое́хали, что ли?** (*разг*) shall we go or not?

чтоб *союз* = **что́бы.**

KEYWORD

что́бы *союз*: **что́бы** *+infin* (*выражает цель*) in order *или* so as to do; **я бу́ду рабо́тать но́чью, что́бы сдать сочине́ние за́втра** I will work at night in order *или* so as to hand in the composition tomorrow
◆ *союз* (*+pt*) **1** (*выражает цель*) so that; **учи́тель говори́т ме́дленно, что́бы мы всё понима́ли** the teacher speaks slowly so that we understand everything
2 (*выражает желательность*): **я хочу́, что́бы она́ пришла́** I want her to come
3 (*выражает возможность*): **не мо́жет быть,**

что́бы он так поступи́л it can't be possible that he should acted like that
◆ *част* **1** (*выражает пожелание*): **что́бы она́ заболе́ла!** I hope she gets ill!
2 (*выражает требование*): **что́бы я его́ здесь бо́льше не ви́дел!** I hope (that) I never see him here again!

что́-либо (**чего́-либо**; *как* **что**; *см* **Table 6**) *мест* = **что́-нибудь**.
что́-нибудь (**чего́-нибудь**; *как* **что**; *см* **Table 6**) *мест* (*в утвердительных предложениях*) something; (*в вопросительных предложениях*) anything; **скажи́ ~** say something; **есть ~ интере́сное?** is there anything interesting?
что́-то (**чего́-то**; *как* **что**; *см* **Table 6**) *мест* something; (*приблизительно*) something like ◆ *нареч* (*разг*: *почему-то*) somehow; **он получи́л ~ о́коло ста пи́сем** he got something like a hundred letters; **~ не по́мню тако́го** somehow I don't remember that.
чуб (**-а**) *м* forelock.
чува́ш (**-а**) *м* Chuvash.
чува́шек *сущ см* **чува́шка**.
Чува́ши|я (**-и**) *ж* Chuvashia.
чува́ш|ка (**-ки**; *gen pl* **-ек**) *ж см* **чува́ш**.
чу́вствен|ный (**-, -на, -но**) *прил* (*удовольствие, любовь итп*) sensual; (*no short form*; *восприятия*) sensory.
чувстви́телен *прил см* **чувстви́тельный**.
чувстви́тельност|ь (**-и**) *ж* sensitivity; (*стихов, музыки*) sentimentality.
чувстви́тел|ьный (**-ен, -ьна, -ьно**) *прил* sensitive; (*стихи, музыка*) sentimental; (*удар*) heavy; (*оскорбление*) deep; (*потери*) considerable.
чу́вств|о (**-а**) *ср* (*эмоция, ощущение*) feeling; (*+gen*; *юмора, долга, ответственности*) sense of; **лиша́ться** (**лиши́ться** *perf*) **чувств** to faint, lose consciousness; **приводи́ть** (**привести́** *perf*) **кого́-н в ~** to bring sb round.
чу́вств|овать (**-ую**; *perf* **почу́вствовать**) *несов перех* to feel; (*присутствие, опасность*) to sense; **~** (*impf*) **себя́ хорошо́/пло́хо/нело́вко** to feel good/bad/awkward
▸ **чу́вствоваться** *несов возв* (*жара, усталость*) to be felt; **~ется, что он волну́ется** you can tell he's worried.
чугу́н (**-а́**) *м* cast iron.
чугу́нный *прил* cast-iron.
чуда́к (**-а́**) *м* eccentric.
чу́ден *прил см* **чу́дный**.
чудён *прил см* **чудно́й**.
чудеса́ *итп сущ от* **чу́до**.
чуде́сен *прил см* **чуде́сный**.
чуде́сно *нареч* wonderfully ◆ *как сказ* it's wonderful.
чуде́с|ный (**-ен, -на, -но**) *прил* (*необычный*) miraculous; (*очень хороший*) marvellous (*BRIT*), marvelous (*US*), wonderful.
чуд|и́ть (*2sg* **-и́шь**, *3sg* **-и́т**) *несов неперех* to behave oddly.
чу́д|иться (*3sg* **-ится**, *3pl* **-ятся**, *perf* **почу́диться**) *несов возв* (*+dat*) to appear.
чу́дищ|е (**-а**) *ср* monster.
чуд|но́й (**-ён, -на́, -но́**) *прил* (*разг*) odd.
чу́д|ный (**-ен, -на, -но**) *прил* (*великолепный*) marvellous (*BRIT*), marvelous (*US*).
чу́д|о (**-а**; *nom pl* **-еса́**) *ср* miracle.
чудо́вищ|е (**-а**) *ср* monster.
чудо́вищ|ный (**-ен, -на, -но**) *прил* (*преступление, факт*) monstrous; (*перен*: *ураган, мороз*) terrible.
чудоде́йствен|ный (**-ен, -на, -но**) *прил* (*средство*) miraculous.
чу́дом *нареч* (*спастись*) by a miracle.
чужа́к (**-а́**) *м* stranger.
чужби́н|а (**-ы**) *ж* foreign country.
чужда́|ться (**-юсь**) *несов возв*: **~** *+gen* (*также перен*) to shun.
чу́жд|ый (**-, -а́, -о**) *прил* (*взгляды, ценности*) alien; **~** *+gen* devoid of; **ему́ чужда́ за́висть** he is devoid of envy.
чужезе́м|ец (**-ца**) *м* stranger.
чужезе́мный *прил* from foreign parts.
чужезе́мца *итп сущ см* **чужезе́мец**.
чужеро́дный *прил* (*элемент*) alien.
чуж|о́й *прил* (*принадлежащий другому*) someone *или* somebody else's; (*речь, обычай*) foreign; (*человек*) strange ◆ (**-о́го**; *decl like adj*) *м* stranger; **под ~и́м и́менем** under an assumed name.
чу́кч|а (**-и**) *м/ж нескл* Chukchi.
чула́н (**-а**) *м* storeroom.
чул|о́к (**-ка́**; *gen pl* **-о́к**, *dat pl* **-ка́м**) *м* (*обычно мн*) stocking.
чум|а́ (**-ы́**) *ж* plague.
чума́з|ый (**-, -а, -о**) *прил* (*разг*) mucky.
чур *межд* (*разг*): **~ я пе́рвый!** mind out, I'm first!; **~ меня́!** get away from me! (*to keep evil at bay*).
чурба́н (**-а**) *м* (*деревянный*) block; (*разг*: *пренебр*: *человек*) blockhead.
чу́т|кий (**-кая, -кое, -кие**; **-ок, -ка́, -ко**) *прил* sensitive; (*натура*) sympathetic; **~ сон** light sleep.
чу́ткост|ь (**-и**) *ж* (*см прил*) sensitivity; sympathy.
чу́ток *прил см* **чу́ткий**.
чу́точк|а (**-и**) *ж* (*разг*): **~у** a bit; **ни ~и** not a bit.
чуть *нареч* (*разг*: *едва*) hardly; (*немного*) a little ◆ *союз* (*как только*) as soon as; **~** (**бы́ло**) **не** almost, nearly; **~ ли не** almost certainly; **~ что** (*разг*) at the slightest thing.
чуть|ё (**-я́**) *ср* (*у животных*) scent; (*у людей*) intuition.
чу́чел|о (**-а**) *ср* (*также перен*) scarecrow; **~ живо́тного/пти́цы** stuffed animal/bird.
чушь (**-и**) *ж* (*разг*) rubbish (*BRIT*), garbage (*US*).
чу́|ять (**-ю**) *несов перех* (*также перен*) to scent; **я ног под собо́й не ~ю** I'm walking on air; (*от усталости*) my legs are giving way beneath me.
чьё (**чьего́**) *мест см* **чей**.
чьи (**чьих**) *мест см* **чей**.
чья (**чьей**) *мест см* **чей**.

~Ш, ш~

Ш, ш *сущ нескл* (*буква*) *the 25th letter of the Russian alphabet*.
ш *сокр* (= **широта́**) w. (= *width*).
ш. *сокр* (= **шту́ка**) ea. (= *each*).
ша́баш **(-а)** *м* Sabbath.
шаба́ш *част* (*кончено*) that's enough.
шабло́н **(-а)** *м* (*ТЕХ*) pattern, gauge; (*перен*: *в речи, в письме*) cliché.
шабло́н|ный *прил* (*об инструменте, о чертеже*) pattern *опред*; **(-ен, -на, -но**; *перен*: *фраза, ответ*) trite.
шаг **(-а**; *part gen* **-у**, *loc sg* **-у́**, *nom pl* **-и́)** *м* (*также перен*) step; **на ка́ждом ~у́** (*перен*) continually; **~ за ша́гом** step by step; **ша́гу не даю́т ступи́ть** (*перен*) one has no freedom of action; **прибавля́ть (приба́вить** *perf*) **ша́гу** to quicken one's pace; **предпринима́ть (предприня́ть** *perf*) **но́вые ~и́** to take a new initiative; **я услы́шал ~и́** I heard footsteps.
шага́|ть **(-ю)** *несов неперех* to march; (*делать шаг*) to step; **~й отсю́да!** (*разг*) get lost!
шагн|у́ть **(-у́, -ёшь)** *сов неперех* to step, take a step; **~** (*perf*) **вперёд** (*также перен*) to take a step forward.
ша́гом *нареч* (*идти*) at a walk, at walking pace; **~ марш!** (*ВОЕН*) quick march!
ша́ек *сущ см* **ша́йка**.
ша́йб|а **(-ы)** *ж* (*ТЕХ*: *прокладка*) spacer; (: *болта*) washer; (*СПОРТ*) puck.
ша́|йка **(-йки**; *gen pl* **-ек)** *ж* (*бандитская*) gang.
шака́л **(-а)** *м* jackal.
шала́нд|а **(-ы)** *ж* scow, barge.
шала́ш **(-а́)** *м* hut (*made of branches*).
ша́левый *прил*: **~ плато́к** shawl; **ша́левый воротни́к** shawl collar.
шале́|ть **(-ю**; *perf* **ошале́ть)** *несов неперех* (*разг*) to go crazy; **~ (ошале́ть** *perf*) **от ра́дости** to go mad with joy.
шал|и́ть **(-ю́, -и́шь)** *несов неперех* (*дети*) to be mischevious; (*разг*: *мотор, сердце*) to play up.
шаловли́в|ый **(-, -а, -о)** *прил* (*ребёнок*) mischevious; (*тон, глаза*) playful.
шалопа́|й **(-я)** *м* (*разг*) loafer, skiver.
ша́лост|ь **(-и)** *ж* (*проказа*) mischief.
шалу́н **(-а́)** *м* mischevious boy.
шалу́н|ья **(-ьи**; *gen pl* **-ий)** *ж* mischevious girl.
шалфе́|й **(-я)** *м* (*БОТ*) sage.
шал|ь **(-и)** *ж* shawl.
шально́й *прил* (*разг*) wild; (*пуля*) stray; (*деньги*) easy.
шаля́й-валя́й *нареч* (*разг*: *небрежно*) any(old) how.
шама́н **(-а)** *м* (*колдун*) shaman.
шама́н|ка **(-ки**; *gen pl* **-ок)** *ж см* **шама́н**.
ша́мка|ть **(-ю)** *несов неперех* to mumble.
шампа́нск|ое **(-ого**; *decl like adj*) *ср* champagne.
шампиньо́н **(-а)** *м* (*БОТ*) (field) mushroom.
шампу́н|ь **(-я)** *м* shampoo.
шампу́р **(-а)** *м* skewer.
шанс **(-а)** *м* chance; **~ на что-н** chance of sth.
шансоне́т|ка **(-ки**; *gen pl* **-ок)** *ж см* **шансонье́**.
шансонье́ *м нескл* singer.
шанта́ж **(-а́)** *м* blackmail.
шантажи́р|овать **(-ую)** *несов перех* to blackmail.
шантажи́ст **(-а)** *м* blackmailer.
шантажи́ст|ка **(-ки**; *gen pl* **-ок)** *ж см* **шантажи́ст**.
шантрап|а́ **(-ы́)** *м/ж собир* (*разг*) yobs *мн*.
Шанха́|й **(-я)** *м* Shanghai.
ша́п|ка **(-ки**; *gen pl* **-ок)** *ж* hat; (*перен*: *снежная*) cap; (*заголовок*) headline; **по ~ке дава́ть (дать** *perf*) *+dat* (*перен*: *разг*) to punish; **по ~ке получа́ть (получи́ть** *perf*) (*разг*) to be punished; **на воре́ ~ гори́т** he's given the game away.
ша́почн|ый *прил* of a hat; **~ое знако́мство** nodding acquaintance; **приходи́ть (прийти́** *perf*) **к ~ому разбо́ру** (*перен*) to miss the bus.
шар **(-а**; *nom pl* **-ы́)** *м* (*ГЕОМ*) sphere; (*кегли, бильярдный итп*) ball; **возду́шный ~** balloon; **земно́й ~** the Earth; **в до́ме хоть ~о́м покати́** the house is completely empty.
шара́д|а **(-ы)** *ж* charade.
шара́хн|уть **(-у, -ешь**; *impf* **шара́хать)** *сов* (*не*)*перех* (*разг*): **~** *+acc или +instr* (*ударять*) to thump
► **шара́хнуться** (*impf* **шара́хаться)** *сов возв* (*разг*: *отпрянуть*) to leap back; (: *удариться*): **~ся о** *+acc* to bang into.
шара́шкин *прил*: **~а кoнтóра** dodgy enterprise; (*несолидное учреждение*) pathetic place.
шарж **(-а)** *м* caricature.
шаржи́р|овать **(-ую)** *несов перех* to caricature.

The spelling rules for Russian are shown on page xvii.

ша́рик (**-а**) *м уменьш от* **шар**; (*АНАТ*): **кровяно́й ~** blood corpuscule.
ша́риков|ый *прил* (*подшипник*) ball *опред*; **~ая ру́чка** ballpoint pen.
шарикоподши́пник (**-а**) *м* (*ТЕХ*) ball bearing.
ша́р|ить (**-ю, -ишь**) *несов неперех* (*разг*) to grope; ~ *(impf)* **глаза́ми** to sweep; ~ *(impf)* **по (чужи́м) карма́нам** (*разг*) to pick pockets.
ша́рканьe (**-я**) *ср* shuffling.
ша́рка|ть (**-ю**) *несов неперех*: ~ *+instr* to shuffle.
ша́ркн|уть (**-у, -ешь**) *сов неперех*: ~ **ного́й** to click one's heels.
шарлата́н (**-а**) *м* charlatan.
шарлата́н|ка (**-ки**; *gen pl* **-ок**) *ж см* **шарлата́н**.
шарлата́нств|о (**-а**) *ср* charlatanism.
шарло́т|ка (**-ки**; *gen pl* **-ок**) *ж* (*КУЛИН*) charlotte.
шарм (**-а**) *м* (*обаяние*) charm.
шарма́н|ка (**-ки**; *gen pl* **-ок**) *ж* (*МУЗ*) barrel organ.
шарни́р (**-а**) *м* (*ТЕХ*) hinge; (*АВТ*) (suspension) joint.
шарова́р|ы (**-**) *мн* baggy trousers *мн*.
шарови́д|ный (**-ен, -на, -но**) *прил* spherical.
шарово́й *прил* (*ГЕОМ*) spherical; **~ кла́пан** ball valve; **шарова́я мо́лния** (*ГЕО*) fireball, globe lightning.
шарообра́з|ный (**-ен, -на, -но**) *прил* = **шарови́дный**.
шарф (**-а**) *м* scarf.
шасси́ *ср нескл* (*самолёта*) landing gear; (*автомобиля*) chassis.
ша́ста|ть (**-ю**) *несов неперех* (*разг*) to mooch about.
шата́ни|е (**-я**) *ср* (*хождение*) mooching about; (*раскачивание*) swaying; (*перен*: *идейные*) vacillation.
шата́|ть (**-ю**) *несов перех* (*раскачивать*) to rock; **меня́ ~ет от уста́лости** I am reeling with tiredness
▸ **шата́ться** *несов возв* (*зуб*) to be loose *или* wobbly; (*столб*) to shake; (*от усталости*) to reel, stagger; (*разг*: *по городу, по улицам итп*) to mooch about.
шате́н (**-а**) *м man with auburn hair*.
шат|ёр (**-ра́**) *м* tent.
ша́т|кий (**-кая, -кое, -кие**; **-ок, -ка, -ко**) *прил* (*стул*) wobbly, rickety; (*перен*: *положение*) precarious; (: *доводы*) shaky.
ша́ткост|ь (**-и**) *ж* (*см прил*) wobbliness; precariousness; shakiness.
шатн|у́ть (**-у́, -ёшь**) *сов перех* (*столб*) to shake
▸ **шатну́ться** *сов возв* (*столб*) to be unsteady; (*от усталости*) to reel.
ша́ток *прил см* **ша́ткий**.
шатра́ *итп сущ см* **шатёр**.
шатро́вый *прил* (*крыша, купол*) hipped; **шатро́вая архитекту́ра** hipped architecture.
шату́н (**-а́**) *м* (*ТЕХ*) connecting rod.
ша́фер (**-а**) *м* best man (*мн* men).
шафра́н (**-а**) *м* (*БОТ*) saffron.
шах (**-а**) *м* (*монарх*) shah; (*в шахматах*) check.
шахмати́ст (**-а**) *м* chess player.
шахмати́ст|ка (**-ки**; *gen pl* **-ок**) *ж см* **шахмати́ст**.
ша́хматный *прил* (*кружок, чемпионат*) chess *опред*; (*порядок, рисунок*) staggered; **ша́хматная доска́** chessboard.
ша́хмат|ы (**-**) *мн* (*игра*) chess *ед*; (*фигуры*) chessmen *мн*.
ша́хт|а (**-ы**) *ж* (*выработка*) mine, pit; (*предприятие*) mine; (*лифта*) shaft.
шахтёр (**-а**) *м* miner.
ша́шек *сущ см* **ша́шки**.
шаши́ст (**-а**) *м* draughts (*BRIT*) *или* checkers (*US*) player.
шаши́ст|ка (**-ки**; *gen pl* **-ок**) *ж см* **шаши́ст**.
ша́шк|а (**-и**) *ж* (*игральная*) draught (*BRIT*), checker (*US*); (*взрывчатка*) blasting cartridge; (*оружие*) sabre (*BRIT*), saber (*US*); *см также* **ша́шки**.
ша́ш|ки (**-ек**) *мн* (*игра*) draughts *мн* (*BRIT*), checkers *мн* (*US*).
шашлы́к (**-а́**) *м* shashlik, kebab.
шашлы́чн|ая (**-ой**; *decl like adj*) *ж* kebab-house.
ша́шн|и (**-ей**) *мн* (*разг*) affair *ед*.
шва *итп сущ см* **шов**.
шва́бр|а (**-ы**) *ж* mop.
шва́ркн|уть (**-у, -ешь**; *impf* **шва́ркать**) *сов перех* (*разг*) to hurl.
шварто́в (**-а**) *м* (*МОР*) mooring line; **отдава́ть (отда́ть** *perf*) **~ы** to cast off.
швартов|а́ть (**-у́ю**; *perf* **пришвартова́ть** *или* **ошвартова́ть**) *несов перех* (*МОР*) to moor.
швед (**-а**) *м* Swede.
шве́д|ка (**-ки**; *gen pl* **-ок**) *ж см* **швед**.
шве́дск|ий (**-ая, -ое, -ие**) *прил* Swedish; **~ язы́к** Swedish.
шве́йный *прил* (*машина, нитки*) sewing *опред*; (*фабрика*) clothing *опред*.
швейца́р (**-а**) *м* doorman (*мн* doormen).
швейца́р|ец (**-ца**) *м* Swiss.
Швейца́ри|я (**-и**) *ж* Switzerland.
швейца́р|ка (**-ки**; *gen pl* **-ок**) *ж см* **швейца́рец**.
швейца́рск|ий (**-ая, -ое, -ие**) *прил* Swiss.
швейца́рца *итп сущ см* **швейца́рец**.
Шве́ци|я (**-и**) *ж* Sweden.
шве|я́ (**-и́**) *ж* seamstress.
швырн|у́ть (**-у́, -ёшь**) *сов (не)перех*: ~ *+acc или +instr* to hurl.
швыря́|ть (**-ю**) *несов перех* to hurl, fling; ~ *(impf)* **де́ньги** *или* **деньга́ми** (*разг*) to throw one's money about
▸ **швыря́ться** *несов возв* (*разг*) to throw at each other; (*перен*): **~ся** *+instr* (*людьми*) to treat lightly; **~ся** *(impf)* **деньга́ми** (*разг*) to throw one's money about.
шевел|и́ть (**-ю́, -и́шь**; *perf* **пошевели́ть**) *несов перех* (*сено*) to turn over; (*подлеж*: *ветер*) to stir ♦ *неперех*: ~ *+instr* (*пальцами, губами*) to move; ~ (**пошевели́ть** *perf*) **мозга́ми** (*перен*: *разг*) to use one's head
▸ **шевели́ться** (*perf* **пошевели́ться**) *несов возв* to stir; **~и́сь!** (*разг*) get a move on!
шевельн|у́ть (**-у́, -ёшь**) *сов неперех*: ~ *+instr*

(*пальцами, плечом*) to move
▸ **шевельнуться** *сов возв* to stir.
шевелюр|а (-ы) *ж* (head of) hair.
шеврон (-а) *м* (*нашивка*) chevron, long-service stripe.
шедевр (-а) *м* masterpiece.
шеек *сущ см* **шейка.**
шезлонг (-а) *м* deckchair.
ше|йка (-йки; *gen pl* -ек) *ж уменьш от* **шея**; (*рельса*) web; (*гильзы*) neck; **шейка матки** (*АНАТ*) cervix.
шейный *прил* (*мышца*) neck *опред*; (*позвонок*) cervical; ~ **платок** neckerchief.
шейх (-а) *м* sheikh.
шёл *несов см* **идти.**
шелест (-а) *м* rustle.
шелест|еть (-ишь) *несов неперех* to rustle.
шёлк (-а; *nom pl* -а) *м* silk.
шелковист|ый (-, -а, -о) *прил* (*гладкий*) silky.
шелковичный *прил*: ~ **червь** silkworm.
шелководств|о (-а) *ср* sericulture, silkworm breeding.
шёлковый *прил* (*нить, одежда*) silk; (*перен*: *разг*: *человек*) meek.
шелкопряд (-а) *м* silkworm.
шелкопрядильный *прил* silk-spinning.
шелкоткацк|ий (-ая, -ое, -ие) *прил* silk-weaving.
шелохн|уть (-у, -ёшь) *сов перех* to stir, agitate
▸ **шелохнуться** *сов возв* to stir, move.
шелух|а (-и) *ж* (*картофельная*) skin, peel; (*гороховая*) pod; (*семечек*) chaff; (*перен*) dross.
шелушени|е (-я) *ср* (*зерна*) shelling; (*кожи*) peeling.
шелуш|ить (-у, -ишь) *несов перех* to shell
▸ **шелушиться** *несов возв* to peel.
шельм|а (-ы) *м/ж* (*разг*) rascal.
шельф (-а) *м* (*ГЕО*) shelf.
шепеляв|ить (-лю, -ишь) *несов неперех* to lisp.
шепеляв|ый (-, -а, -о) *прил* (*человек, речь*) lisping.
шепн|уть (-у, -ёшь) *сов перех* to whisper.
шёпот (-а) *м* whisper; (*перен*: *ручья, листьев*) murmuring.
шёпотом *нареч* (*сказать, подсказать*) in a whisper.
шептани|е (-я) *ср* (*см глаг*) whispering; murmuring.
шеп|тать (-чу, -чешь) *несов перех* to whisper ◆ *неперех* (*перен*: *ручей, листья*) to murmur
▸ **шептаться** *несов возв* to whisper to each other.
шербет (-а) *м* sherbet.
шеренг|а (-и) *ж* (*солдат*) rank; (*машин*) line.
шериф (-а) *м* sheriff.
шероховатост|ь (-и) *ж* (*см прил*) roughness; uneveness; (*шероховатое место*) rough area.
шероховат|ый (-, -а, -о) *прил* (*доска, кожа*) rough; (*перен*: *изложение*) uneven.
шерстин|ка (-ки; *gen pl* -ок) *ж* strand of wool.
шерстопрядильный *прил* wool-spinning.
шерст|ь (-и) *ж* (*животного*) hair; (*пряжа, ткань*) wool.
шерстяной *прил* (*пряжа, ткань*) woollen (*BRIT*), woolen (*US*).
шершав|ый (-, -а, -о) *прил* (*руки, ткань*) rough.
шест (-а) *м* pole; **прыжок с ~ом** pole vault.
шест|ая (-ой; *decl like adj*) *ж*: **одна ~** one sixth.
шестви|е (-я) *ср* procession.
шеств|овать (-ую) *несов неперех* to walk in procession.
шестерён|ка (-ки; *gen pl* -ок) *ж* (*ТЕХ*) gear (wheel).
шестёрк|а (-и) *ж* (*цифра, карта*) six; (*шлюпка*) six-oar boat; (*группа из шести*) group of six; (*разг*: *автобус, трамвай итп*) (number) six (*bus, tram etc*).
шестер|о (-ых; *см* **Table 36b**) *чис* six; *см также* **двое.**
шести *чис см* **шесть.**
шестидесяти *чис см* **шестьдесят.**
шестидесятилети|е (-я) *ср* (*срок*) sixty years *мн*; (*годовщина события*) sixtieth anniversary.
шестидесятилетн|ий (-яя, -ее, -ие) *прил* (*период*) sixty-year; (*юбилей*) sixtieth; (*человек*) sixty-year-old.
шестидесят|ый (-ая, -ое, -ые) *чис* sixtieth; *см также* **пятидесятый.**
шестидневный *прил* six-day.
шестиклассник (-а) *м pupil in sixth year at school (usually twelve years old).*
шестиклассниц|а (-ы) *ж см* **шестиклассник.**
шестикратн|ый *прил*: ~ **чемпион** six-times champion; **в ~ом размере** sixfold.
шестилети|е (-я) *ср* (*срок*) six years; (*годовщина*) sixth anniversary.
шестилетн|ий (-яя, -ее, -ие) *прил* (*отсутствие*) six-year; (*ребёнок*) six-year-old.
шестимесячный *прил* six-month; (*ребёнок*) six-month-old.
шестинедельный *прил* six-week; (*ребёнок*) six-week-old.
шестисот *чис см* **шестьсот.**
шестисотлети|е (-я) *ср* (*срок*) six hundred years *мн*; (*годовщина*) six hundredth anniversary, sexcentenary.
шестисотлетн|ий (-яя, -ее, -ие) *прил* (*период*) six hundred-year; (*дерево*) six hundred-year-old.
шестисот|ый (-ая, -ое, -ые) *чис* six-hundredth.
шестиугольник (-а) *м* hexagon.
шестичасовой *прил* (*рабочий день*) six-hour; (*поезд*) six-o'clock.
шестнадцати *чис см* **шестнадцать.**
шестнадцат|ый (-ая, -ое, -ые) *чис* sixteenth; *см*

также **пя́тый**.
шестна́дцат|ь (**-и**; *как* **пять**; *см* **Table 27**) *чис* sixteen; *см также* **пять**.
шест|о́й (**-а́я, -о́е, -ы́е**) *чис* sixth; *см также* **пя́тый**.
шест|ь (**-и́**; *как* **пять**; *см* **Table 27**) *чис* six; *см также* **пять**.
шест|ьдеся́т (**-и́десяти**; *как* **пятьдеся́т**; *см* **Table 29**) *чис* sixty; *см также* **пятьдеся́т**.
шест|ьсо́т (**-исо́т**; *как* **пятьсо́т**; *см* **Table 34**) *чис* six hundred; *см также* **сто**.
ше́стью *нареч* six times.
шестью́ *чис см* **шесть**.
шестьюста́ми *чис см* **шестьсо́т**.
шетла́ндск|ий (**-ая, -ое, -ие**) *прил*: **Ш~ие острова́** Shetland Islands.
шеф (**-а**) *м* (*полиции*) chief; (*разг*: *начальник*) boss; (*обычно мн*: *детского дома*) patron.
ше́фск|ий (**-ая, -ое, -ие**) *прил* (*помощь*) patronal.
ше́фств|о (**-а**) *ср*: **~ над** *+instr* patronage of.
ше́фств|овать (**-ую**) *несов неперех*: **~ над** *+instr* to be patron of.
ше́|я (**-и**) *ж* (*АНАТ*) neck; **на свою́ ~ю** (*разг*) to our loss; **сиде́ть** *(impf) или* **висе́ть** *(impf)* **у кого́-н на ~е** to live off sb; **гнать** *(impf)* **кого́-н в ~ю** (*разг*) to throw sb out on his *umn* ear.
ши́бко *нареч* terribly.
ши́ворот (**-а**) *м* (*разг*): **за ~** by the collar; **~-навы́ворот** back to front.
шизофре́ник (**-а**) *м* schizophrenic.
шизофрени́|я (**-и**) *ж* schizophrenia.
шик (**-а**; *part gen* **-у**) *м* chic, stylishness.
шика́рен *прил см* **шика́рный**.
шика́рно *нареч* (*разг*: *жить*) in style; (*обставленный*) stylishly ◆ *как сказ*: **в гости́нице ~** the hotel is stylish.
шика́р|ный (**-ен, -на, -но**) *прил* (*разг*) smart, stylish.
ши́ка|ть (**-ю**) *несов неперех* (*разг*): **~ на кого́-н** to hush sb.
ши́кн|уть (**-у, -ешь**) *сов неперех*: **~ на кого́-н** to hush sb.
шик|ова́ть (**-у́ю**) *несов неперех* (*разг*) to show off.
ши́ллинг (**-а**) *м* (*денежная единица*) shilling.
ши́л|о (**-а**; *nom pl* **-ья**, *gen pl* **-ьев**) *ср* awl.
шимпанзе́ *м нескл* chimpanzee.
ши́н|а (**-ы**) *ж* (*АВТ*) tyre (*BRIT*), tire (*US*); (*МЕД*) splint.
шине́л|ь (**-и**) *ж* (*солдатская*) greatcoat, overcoat.
шинкова́ни|е (**-я**) *ср* shredding.
шинк|ова́ть (**-у́ю**; *perf* **нашинкова́ть**) *несов перех* (*овощи*) to shred.
шиньо́н (**-а**) *м* chignon.
шип (**-а́**) *м* (*растения*) thorn; (*соединительный*) tenon, tongue; (*на колесе*) stud; (*на ботинке*) spike.
шипе́ни|е (**-я**) *ср* hissing.
шип|е́ть (**-лю́, -и́шь**) *несов неперех* (*также разг*) to hiss; (*шампанское, газировка*) to fizz.
шипо́в|ки (**-ок**) *мн* (*СПОРТ*) spikes *мн*.
шипо́вник (**-а**) *м* (*куст*) wild rose; (*плод*) (rose)hip; (*настой*) rosehip drink.
шипо́вок *сущ см* **шипо́вки**.
шипу́ч|ий (**-ая, -ее, -ие**; **-, -а, -е**) *прил* fizzy; (*вино*) sparkling.
шипя́щ|ий (**-ая, -ее, -ие**) *прил* (*ЛИНГ*) sibilant *опред*.
ши́ре *сравн прил от* **широ́кий** ◆ *сравн нареч от* **широко́**.
ширин|а́ (**-ы́**) *ж* width; **доро́жка метр ~о́й** *или* **в ~у́** a path a metre (*BRIT*) *или* meter (*US*) wide.
шири́н|ка (**-ки**; *gen pl* **-ок**) *ж* (*брюк*) fly.
ши́р|иться (*3sg* **-ится**, *3pl* **-ятся**) *несов возв* (*дела*) to expand; (*движение*) to grow.
ши́рм|а (**-ы**) *ж* (*также перен*) screen.
широ́к|ий (**-ая, -ое, -ие**; **-, -а́, -о́**) *прил* wide; (*степи, фронт, планы*) extensive; (*перен*: *общественность, публика*) general; (: *смысл, интерпретация*) broad; (: *масштабы*) large; (: *натура, жест*) generous; (: *образ жизни*) grand; **това́ры ~ого потребле́ния** (*ЭКОН*) consumer goods; **жить** *(impf)* **на ~ую но́гу** to live in grand style; **широ́кий экра́н** (*КИНО*) wide screen.
широко́ *нареч* (*раскинуться*) widely; (*улыбаться, интерпретировать*) broadly; (*жить*) in grand style; **~ раскрыва́ть** (**раскры́ть** *perf*) **глаза́** to open one's eyes wide; (*перен*) to be amazed.
широковеща́тел|ьный (**-ен, -ьна, -ьно**) *прил* broadcasting *опред*; **широковеща́тельная сеть** (*КОМП*) broadcast network.
широкопле́ч|ий (**-ая, -ее, -ие**; **-, -а, -е**) *прил* (*человек*) broad-shouldered.
широкопо́лый *прил* (*шляпа*) wide-brimmed; (*пальто*) with a full skirt.
широкоформа́тный *прил* (*экран*) wide-format.
широкофюзеля́жный *прил* (*самолёт*) wide-bodied.
широкоэкра́нный *прил* (*фильм*) wide-screen.
шир|ота́ (**-оты́**) *ж* breadth; (*nom pl* **-о́ты**; *ГЕО*) latitude.
ширпотре́б (**-а**) *м сокр* = *широ́кое потребле́ние*; (*разг*: *о товарах*) consumer goods *мн*; (: *о плохом товаре*) low-quality goods *мн*.
шир|ь (**-и**) *ж* expanse; **развора́чиваться** (**разверну́ться** *perf*) **во всю ~** (*перен*) to develop to one's full potential.
ши́то-кры́то *нареч* (*разг*): **всё ~** it's all being kept under wraps.
ши́тый *прил* embroidered.
шить (**шью, шьёшь**; *perf* **сшить**) *несов перех* (*платье umn*) to sew ◆ *неперех*: **~** *+instr* (*шёлком umn*) to embroider.
шить|ё (**-я́**) *ср* (*см глаг*) sewing; embroidery.
ши́фер (**-а**) *м* (*натуральный*) slate; (*СТРОИТ*) corrugated asbestos board.
шифо́н (**-а**) *м* chiffon.
шифонье́р (**-а**) *м* wardrobe.

шифр (**-а**) *м* (*для секретного письма*) code, cipher; (*книги, документа*) pressmark.
шифровáльщик (**-а**) *м* cipher-clerk; (*расшифровывающий*) code cracker.
шифр|овáть (**-ýю**; *perf* **зашифровáть**) *несов перех* (*донесение*) to encode, encipher.
шифрóв|ка (**-ки**; *gen pl* **-ок**) *ж* (*см глаг*) encoding, enciphering; (*сообщение*) coded message.
шиш (**-á**) *м* (*разг*: *кукиш*) fig (*rude gesture*); **ни ~á** (*разг*) damn all; **~ ты от меня полýчишь** (*разг*) you'll get damn all from me; **на какúе ~й?** (*разг*) who's paying?
шúш|ка (**-ки**; *gen pl* **-ек**) *ж* (*БОТ*) cone; (*на лбу*) bump, lump; (*разг*: *важный человек*) bigwig.
шишковáт|ый (**-, -а, -о**) *прил* (*руки*) knobbly; (*лоб*) lumpy; (*доска*) rough.
шкал|á (**-ы́**; *nom pl* **-ы**) *ж* scale; (*приёмника*) dial.
шкатýл|ка (**-ки**; *gen pl* **-ок**) *ж* casket; **музыкáльная ~** musical box.
шкаф (**-а**; *loc sg* **-ý**, *nom pl* **-ы́**) *м* (*для одежды*) wardrobe; (*для посуды*) cupboard; (*ТЕХ*: *сушильный итп*) oven; **духовóй ~** airing cupboard; **кни́жный ~** bookcase.
шквал (**-а**) *м* (*ветер*) squall; **~** *+gen* (*оваций, огня*) burst of.
шквáльный *прил* (*ветер*) squally; (*огонь*) heavy.
шкив (**-а**) *м* (*ТЕХ*) pulley.
шкúпер (**-а**) *м* (*МОР*) skipper.
шкúр|а (**-и**) *ж*: **брать когó-н за ~у** (*разг*) to take sb by the scruff of the neck; (*перен*) to twist sb's arm.
шкóл|а (**-ы**) *ж* school; (*милиции*) college, academy; (*выучка*) education, training; (*СПОРТ*) training; **вы́сшая ~** higher education; **начáльная ~** primary (*BRIT*) *или* elementary (*US*) school; **срéдняя ~** secondary (*BRIT*) *или* high (*US*) school.
шкóл|а-интернáт (**-ы, -а**) *м* boarding school.
шкóльник (**-а**) *м* schoolboy.
шкóльниц|а (**-ы**) *ж* schoolgirl.
шкóльный *прил* (*здание*) school *опред*; **шкóльные гóды** schooldays; **шкóльный вóзраст** school age; **шкóльный учéбник** school book; **шкóльный учúтель** school teacher.
шкýр|а (**-ы**) *ж* (*животного*) fur; (*убитого животного*) skin; (: *обработанная*) hide ◆ *м/ж* (*разг*: *продажный человек*) self-seeker; **быть** (*impf*) **в чьей-н ~е** to be in sb's shoes (*fig*); **спасáть** (*impf*) **свою́ ~у** (*разг*) to save one's (own) skin; **на своéй ~е узнáть** (*perf*) (*разг*) to experience first-hand.
шкýр|ить (**-ю, -ишь**) *сов перех* (*шлифовать*) to sand(paper).
шкýр|ка (**-и**) *ж уменьш от* **шкýра**; (*разг*: *плода*) rind, peel; (*абразив*) sandpaper.
шкýрник (**-а**) *м* (*разг*: *пренебр*) self-seeker.
шкýрный *прил* (*интересы*) selfish.
шла *несов см* **идтú**.
шлагбáум (**-а**) *м* barrier.
шлак (**-а**) *м* (*ТЕХ*) slag.
шлакобетóнный *прил* (*панель, кирпич*) slag-concrete.
шланг (**-а**) *м* hose.
шлейф (**-а**) *м* (*платья*) train; (*дыма*) trail.
шлем (**-а**) *м* helmet.
шлёпан|ец (**-ца**) *м* (*разг*: *обычно мн*) bedroom slipper.
шлёпа|ть (**-ю**) *несов перех* (*бить*) to slap ◆ *неперех*: **~ по** *+acc* (*по полу*) to shuffle; (*по воде*) to splash
▸ **шлёпаться** (*perf* **шлёпнуться**) *несов возв* (*разг*) to plop.
шли *несов см* **идтú**.
шлифовáльный *прил* (*ТЕХ*) grinding *опред*.
шлиф|овáть (**-ýю**; *perf* **отшлифовáть**) *несов перех* (*ТЕХ*) to grind; (*перен*: *стиль*) to polish.
шлифóвк|а (**-и**) *ж* (*детали*) grinding.
шлúц|а (**-ы**) *ж* (*ТЕХ*) spline; (*юбки*) slit.
шло *несов см* **идтú**.
шлю *итп несов см* **слать**.
шлюз (**-а**) *м* (*на канале*) lock; (*на реке*) sluice.
шлю́п|ка (**-ки**; *gen pl* **-ок**) *ж* (*МОР*) dinghy; **спасáтельная ~** lifeboat.
шлю́х|а (**-и**) *ж* (*разг*) tart.
шля́гер (**-а**) *м* (*МУЗ*) hit.
шля́п|а (**-ы**) *ж* hat ◆ *м/ж* (*перен*: *разг*: *человек*) wimp; **дéло в ~е** (*разг*) it's in the bag.
шля́п|ка (**-ки**; *gen pl* **-ок**) *ж* hat; (*гвоздя*) head; (*гриба*) cap.
шля́пник (**-а**) *м* (*мужской*) hatter; (*женский*) milliner.
шля́пный *прил* hat *опред*.
шля́пок *сущ см* **шля́пка**.
шля́|ться (**-юсь**) *несов возв* (*разг*) to mooch about.
шмел|ь (**-я́**) *м* bumblebee.
шмóт|ки (**-ок**) *мн* (*разг*) clobber *ед*.
шмы́га|ть (**-ю**) *несов неперех* (*разг*: *шнырять*) to rush; (*исчезнуть*) to slip, dart; **~** (*impf*) **нóсом** to sniff.
шмыгн|ýть (**-ý, -ёшь**) *сов неперех* (*быстро пройти*) to dart, nip; (*исчезнуть*) to slip, dart.
шмя́кн|уть (**-у, -ешь**; *impf* **шмя́кать**) *сов перех* (*разг*: *бросить*) to thump down
▸ **шмя́кнуться** (*impf* **шмя́каться**) *сов возв* (*разг*: *упасть*) to topple over.
шнúцел|ь (**-я**) *м* (*КУЛИН*) schnitzel.
шнур (**-á**) *м* (*верёвка*) cord; (*телефонный, лампы*) flex.
шнуркá *итп сущ см* **шнурóк**.
шнур|овáть (**-ýю**; *perf* **зашнуровáть**) *несов перех* (*ботинки*) to lace (up); (*perf* **прошнуровáть**; *прошивать шнуром*) to tie, bind.

шнуро́вк|а (-и) *ж* (*см глаг*) lacing up; tying, binding; (*на одежде, на обуви*) lacing.
шнур|о́к (-ка́) *м* (*ботинка*) lace.
шныря́|ть (-ю) *несов неперех* (*разг*: *в толпе, по улицам*) to dash about; **он ~л глаза́ми** (*перен*: *разг*) his eyes darted about.
шов (**шва**) *м* (*швейный*) seam; (*хирургический*) stitch, suture; (*намёточный, тамбурный итп*) stitch; (*кровельный*) joint, seam; **сварно́й ~** joint weld, weld seam; **накла́дывать (наложи́ть** *perf*) **/снима́ть (снять** *perf*) **швы** (*МЕД*) to put in/take out stitches; **треща́ть** *(impf)* **по всем швам** (*перен*: *разг*) to fall apart at the seams; **ру́ки по швам** stand at attention.
шовини́зм (-а) *м* chauvinism.
шовини́ст (-а) *м* chauvinist.
шовинисти́ческ|ий (-ая, -ое, -ие) *прил* chauvinist.
шок (-а) *м* (*МЕД, перен*) shock.
шоки́р|овать (-ую) *(не)сов перех* to shock.
шо́ков|ый *прил*: **~ое состоя́ние** state of shock; **шо́ковая терапи́я** (*МЕД, перен*) shock therapy.
шокола́д (-а) *м* chocolate; (*напиток*) (hot) chocolate.
шокола́д|ка (-ки; *gen pl* -ок) *ж* (*разг*) bar of chocolate.
шокола́дн|ый *прил* (*конфета*) chocolate; (*цвет*) chocolate-brown; **~ая пли́тка** bar of chocolate.
шокола́док *сущ см* **шокола́дка**.
шо́мпол (-а) *м* (*ВОЕН*) cleaning rod.
шо́рох (-а) *м* rustle.
шорт-лист (-а) *м* short list.
шо́рт|ы (-) *мн* shorts *мн*.
шоссе́ *ср нескл* highway.
шоссе́йн|ый *прил*: **~ая доро́га** highway.
шотла́нд|ец (-ца) *м* Scotsman (*мн* Scotsmen).
Шотла́нди|я (-и) *ж* Scotland.
шотла́нд|ка (-ки; *gen pl* -ок) *ж* Scotswoman (*мн* Scotswomen); (*ткань*) tartan (*BRIT*), plaid (*US*).
шотла́ндск|ий (-ая, -ое, -ие) *прил* Scottish, Scots.
шотла́ндца *итп сущ см* **шотла́ндец**.
шо́у *ср нескл* (*также перен*) show.
шофёр (-а) *м* driver.
шпа́г|а (-и) *ж* sword.
шпага́т (-а) *м* (*бечёвка*) string, twine; (*СПОРТ*) the splits.
шпажи́ст (-а) *м* (*СПОРТ*) fencer.
шпажи́ст|ка (-ки; *gen pl* -ок) *ж см* **шпажи́ст**.
шпакл|ева́ть (-ю́ю; *perf* **зашпаклева́ть**) *несов перех* (*трещины, дыры*) to fill.
шпаклёвк|а (-и) *ж* (*действие*) filling; (*замазка*) filler.
шпа́л|а (-ы) *ж* sleeper (*RAIL*).
шпале́р|а (-ы) *ж* (*обои*) handpainted wallpaper; (*для растений*) trellis.
шпан|а́ (-ы́) *ж собир* (*разг*) rabble.
шпарга́л|ка (-ки; *gen pl* -ок) *ж* (*разг*: *для экзаменов*) crib.
шпа́р|ить (-ю, -ишь) *несов неперех* (*разг*): **~ на гита́ре** to play away on the guitar; **~** *(impf)* **по-англи́йски** (*разг*) to speak fluent English; **~** *(impf)* **по у́лице** (*разг*) to rush along the street.
шпа́тел|ь (-я) *м* (*для шпаклёвки, для краски*) palette knife (*мн* knives); (*МЕД*) spatula.
шпиг|ова́ть (-у́ю; *perf* **нашпигова́ть**) *несов перех* (*КУЛИН, перен*) to lard.
шпик (-а; *part gen* -у) *м* (*сало*) lard; (*разг*: *сыщик*) detective.
шпи́лек *сущ см* **шпи́лька**.
шпил|ь (-я) *м* spire.
шпи́л|ька (-ьки; *gen pl* -ек) *ж* (*для волос*) hairpin; (*для шляпы*) hatpin; (*каблук*) stiletto (heel); (*перен*: *разг*: *замечание*) dig; **ту́фли на ~ьке** stilettos.
шпина́т (-а) *м* spinach.
шпингале́т (-а) *м* (*на окне*) catch; (*разг*: *о мальчишке*) little boy.
шпио́н (-а) *м* spy.
шпиона́ж (-а) *м* espionage.
шпио́н|ить (-ю, -ишь) *несов неперех* (*разг*) to spy; **~** *(impf)* **за** *+instr* (*за женой*) to spy on.
Шпицбе́рген (-а) *м* Spitzbergen.
шпо́р|а (-ы) *ж* spur.
шприц (-а) *м* syringe.
шпро́т|ы (-ов) *мн* sprats *мн*.
шпу́льк|а (-и) *ж* spool, bobbin.
шрам (-а) *м* (*на теле*) scar.
шрапне́л|ь (-и) *ж* (*ВОЕН*) shrapnel *только ед*.
Шри-Ла́нк|а (-и) *ж* Sri Lanka.
шрифт (-а; *nom pl* -ы́) *м* type, print; **жи́рный/курси́вный ~** bold/italic type; **набо́рный ~** (*ТИПОГ*) printing type.
шт. *сокр* = **ш**.
штаб (-а; *nom pl* -ы́) *м* headquarters *мн*; (*люди*) staff.
шта́бел|ь (-я; *nom pl* -я́) *м* (*дров*) stack.
штаб-кварти́р|а (-ы) *ж* (*ВОЕН*) headquarters *мн*.
штабно́й *прил* (*разведка, офицер*) staff *опред*.
штаке́тник (-а) *м* (*ограда*) palings *мн*.
штамп (-а) *м* (*печать*) stamp; (*перен*: *в речи*) cliché; (*ТЕХ*) die, stamp.
штамп|ова́ть (-у́ю; *perf* **проштампова́ть**) *несов перех* (*справки, документы*) to stamp; (*perf* **отштампова́ть**; *детали*) to punch, press; (*no perf*; *решения, ответы*) to rubber-stamp.
штампо́вочный *прил* (*ТЕХ*) punching *опред*, pressing *опред*.
шта́нг|а (-и) *ж* (*СПОРТ*: *в тяжёлой атлетике*) weight; (: *ворот*) post.
штангенци́ркул|ь (-я) *м* (*ТЕХ*) sliding calipers *мн*, slide gauge.
штанги́ст (-а) *м* (*СПОРТ*) weightlifter.
штанда́рт (-а) *м* (*ВОЕН*) standard.
штани́н|а (-ы) *ж* (*разг*) trouser leg.
штан|ы́ (-о́в) *мн* trousers *мн*.
шта́пел|ь (-я) *м* (*ткань*) *viscose manufactured to resemble cotton*.
шта́пельный *прил* (*ткань, платье*) *made with viscose manufactured to resemble cotton*.
штат (-а) *м* (*государства*) state; (*работники*)

staff; (*положение*) staff regulations *мн*; **эта дóлжность полагáется по штáту** this job is stipulated by the regulations; **зачислять (зачúслить** *perf*) **когó-н в ~** to take sb onto the staff.
штатúв (-а) *м* (*ФОТО*) tripod; (*микроскопа*) stand.
штáтный *прил* (*сотрудник*) permanent; **штáтная дóлжность** (*АДМИН*) established post; **штáтное расписáние** (*АДМИН*) staff register.
штáтск|ий (-ая, -ое, -ие) *прил* (*одежда*) civilian *опред* ◆ **(-ого**; *decl like adj*) *м* civilian.
штáтск|ое (-ого; *decl like adj*) *ср* civilian clothes *мн*, civvies *мн* (*inf*).
штéмпел|ь (-я) *м*: **почтóвый ~** postmark.
штéпсел|ь (-я) *м* (*ЭЛЕК*) plug.
штéпсельн|ый *прил*: **~ая розéтка** electric socket.
штиблéт|ы (-) *мн* lace-up boots *мн*.
штилевóй *прил* (*погода*) calm.
штил|ь (-я) *м* (*МОР*) calm.
штифт (-á) *м* (*ТЕХ*) pin.
штóл|ьня (-ьни; *gen pl* **-ен)** *ж* (*ГЕО*) gallery.
штóпаный *прил* darned.
штóпа|ть (-ю; *perf* **заштóпать)** *несов перех* to darn.
штóпк|а (-и) *ж* (*действие*) darning; (*нитки*) darning thread; (*разг*: *заштопанное место*) darn.
штóпор (-а) *м* corkscrew.
штóр|а (-ы) *ж* drapery; (*поднимающаяся*) blind.
шторм (-а) *м* gale.
штормúть (*3sg* **-úт)** *несов неперех* (*море*) to be rough; **сегóдня ~úт** it is rough today.
штормóв|ка (-ки; *gen pl* **-ок)** *ж* oilskin coat.
штормов|óй *прил* (*погода*) stormy; (*ветер*) gale-force; **штормовóе предупреждéние** (*МОР*) gale warning.
штормóвок *сущ см* **штормóвка**.
штраф (-а) *м* (*денежный*) fine; (*СПОРТ*) punishment; **наклáдывать (наложúть** *perf*) **~ на** *+acc* to impose a fine on.
штрафнúк (-á) *м* (*СПОРТ*) *player who has been sent off*; **скамéйка штрафникóв** penalty box (*in ice-hockey*).
штрафн|óй *прил* penal ◆ **(-óго**; *decl like adj*) *м* (*СПОРТ*: *также*: **~ удáр**) penalty (kick); **штрафнóе очкó** (*СПОРТ*) penalty point.
штраф|овáть (-ýю; *perf* **оштрафовáть)** *несов перех* to fine; (*СПОРТ*) to penalize.
штрейкбрéхер (-а) *м* strikebreaker, blackleg.
штрек (-а) *м* (*ГЕО*) drift.
штрих (-á) *м* (*черта*) stroke; (*частность*) feature.
штрих|овáть (-ýю; *perf* **заштриховáть)** *несов перех* (*рисунок*) to shade.
штудúр|овать (-ую; *perf* **проштудúровать)** *несов перех* to study.
штýк|а (-и) *ж* (*отдельный предмет*) item; (*разг*: *трудная, забавная*) thing; (: *проделка*) trick; **вот так ~!** (*разг*) what do you know!
штукатýр (-а) *м* plasterer.
штукатýр|ить (-ю, -ишь; *perf* **отштукатýрить** *или* **оштукатýрить)** *несов перех* to plaster.
штукатýрк|а (-и) *ж* (*действие*) plastering; (*раствор*) plaster; (*на стене*) plaster, stucco.
штукатýрный *прил* (*работы*) plaster *опред*.
штукóвин|а (-ы) *ж* (*разг*) thing.
штурвáл (-а) *м* (*судна, комбайна*) wheel; (*самолёта*) controls *мн*.
штурвáльный *прил* steering *опред*.
штурм (-а) *м* (*ВОЕН*) storm; (*перен*: *горной вершины*) conquest; **брать (взять** *perf*) **что-н штýрмом** to take sth by storm.
штýрман (-а) *м* (*МОР, АВИА*) navigator.
штýрманск|ий (-ая, -ое, -ие) *прил* navigator's.
штурм|овáть (-ýю) *несов перех* (*ВОЕН*) to storm; (*перен*) to conquer.
штýчный *прил* (*товар, изделие*) sold by the piece; (*работа, оплата*) piece *опред*.
штык (-á) *м* (*ВОЕН*) bayonet; **принимáть (принять** *perf*) *или* **встречáть (встрéтить** *perf*) **что-н/когó-н в ~ú** (*перен*) to give sth/sb a hostile reception; **как ~** (*разг*) on the dot.
штыковóй *прил* (*атака*) bayonet *опред*; **штыковáя лопáта** sharp-bladed spade.
штыр|ь (-я́) *м* (*ТЕХ*) pin, pintle.
шýб|а (-ы) *ж* (*меховая*) fur coat; (*разг*: *животного*) coat; **селёдка под ~ой** (*КУЛИН*) *herring served with an elaborate topping*.
шýлер (-а) *м* cardsharper.
шум (-а; *part gen* **-у)** *м* (*звук*) noise; (*перен*: *ажиотаж*) stir, sensation; (*МЕД*) murmur; (*разг*: *ссора*) row, racket; (*суета*) bustle, fuss; **вызывáть (вы́звать** *perf*) *или* **надéлать** (*perf*) **~** to cause a sensation.
шýмен *прил см* **шýмный**.
шум|éть (-лю́, -úшь) *несов неперех* to make a noise; (*разглашать*) to create a scene; (*ссориться*) to kick up a row; **у меня́ ~úт в головé/в ушáх** I have a buzzing in my head/ears.
шумúх|а (-и) *ж* (*разг*: *пренебр*: *толки*) sensation, stir; **поднимáть (подня́ть** *perf*) **~у вокрýг чегó-н** to create a sensation around sth; **газéтная ~** *sensation created by the press*.
шумлúвый (-, -а, -о) *прил* noisy.
шумлю́ *несов см* **шумéть**.
шýмно *нареч* noisily ◆ *как сказ* it is noisy.
шýм|ный (-ен, -нá, -но) *прил* noisy; (*разговор, компания*) loud; (*оживлённый*: *улица, залы итп*) bustling; (*перен*: *успех*) sensational.
шумóв|ка (-ки; *gen pl* **-ок)** *ж* perforated spoon.
шумовóй *прил* (*оформление*) sound *опред*.
шумóвок *сущ см* **шумóвка**.
шумóк *м* (*разг*): **под ~** (*разг*) on the quiet.

шу́рин (-а) *м* brother-in-law, wife's brother.
шуру́п (-а) *м* (*ТЕХ*) screw.
шурш|а́ть (-у́, -и́шь) *несов неперех* to rustle.
шу́ры-му́ры *мн нескл* (*разг*) love affairs *мн*.
шу́стр|ый (-, -а́, -о) *прил* (*разг*) nimble.
шут (-а́) *м* (*придворный*) jester; (*разг*: *человек*) fool, clown; ~ **горо́ховый** (*разг*) buffoon; ~ **с ним** (*разг*) forget it.
шу|ти́ть (-чу́, -тишь; *perf* **пошути́ть**) *несов неперех* to joke; (*смеяться*): ~ **над** +*instr* to make fun of; (*no perf*; *пренебрегать*): ~ +*instr* (*здоровьем*) to disregard; ~ *(impf)* **с огнём** (*перен*) to play with fire; **чем чёрт не шу́тит!** (*разг*) anything might happen!
шу́т|ка (-ки; *gen pl* -ок) *ж* joke; **без ~ок** joking apart, seriously; **кро́ме ~ок, ты пра́вда согла́сен?** joking apart *или* seriously, do you really agree?; **не на ~ку** (*рассердился, испугался итп*) in earnest; **сказа́ть** *(perf)* **что-н в ~ку** to say sth as a joke; **~ки пло́хи с кем-н/чем-н** sb/sth is not to be trifled with.
шутли́в|ый (-, -а, -о) *прил* (*человек, тон, замечание*) humourous (*BRIT*), humorous (*US*); (*настроение*) light-hearted.
шутни́к (-а́) *м* joker.
шутовск|о́й *прил*: **~и́е вы́ходки** buffoonery; ~ **колпа́к** jester's cap.
шутовств|о́ (-а́) *ср* buffoonery.
шу́ток *сущ см* **шу́тка**.
шу́точ|ный (-ен, -на, -но) *прил* (*рассказ*) comic, funny; **э́то де́ло не ~ное** it's no laughing matter.
шутя́ *нареч* (*разг*: *без труда*) easily.
шучу́ *несв см* **шути́ть**.
шу́шер|а (-ы) *ж собир* (*разг*) riffraff.
шушу́ка|ться (-юсь) *несов возв*: ~ (**с** +*instr*) to whisper (to).
шху́н|а (-ы) *ж* (*МОР*) schooner.
ш-ш *межд* sh.
шью *итп несов см* **шить**.

~ Щ, щ ~

Щ, щ *сущ нескл* (*буква*) *the 26th letter of the Russian alphabet.*
щаве́л|ь (-я́) *м* sorrel.
ща|ди́ть (-жу́, -ди́шь; *perf* **пощади́ть)** *несов перех* to spare; **он на ~дя́щем режи́ме** (*МЕД*) he's not allowed to exert himself.
щам *итп сущ см* **щи.**
щебёнк|а (-и) *ж* = **ще́бень.**
ще́б|ень (-ня) *м* (*СТРОИТ*) ballast.
ще́бет (-а) *м* twitter.
щеб|ета́ть (-ечу́, -е́чешь) *несов неперех* (*также перен*) to twitter.
ще́бня *итп сущ см* **ще́бень.**
щег|о́л (-ла́) *м* goldfinch.
щеголева́т|ый (-, -а, -о) *прил* (*одежда*) fancy; (*мужчина*) stylish.
щёгол|ь (-я) *м* dandy.
щегольн|у́ть (-у́, -ёшь) *сов неперех*: ~ *+instr* to show off.
щегольско́й *прил* stylish.
щегольств|о́ (-а́) *ср* dandyism.
щеголя́|ть (-ю) *несов неперех* to dress up; ~ *(impf) +instr* to show off; ~ *(impf)* **в** *+prp* to rig o.s. out in.
ще́дрост|ь (-и) *ж* generosity.
ще́др|ый (-, -а́, -о) *прил* generous; (*природа*) lush; (*климат*) fertile; ~ **на** *+acc* generous with.
щей *сущ см* **щи.**
щека́ (щеки́; *nom pl* **щёки**, *gen pl* **щёк**, *dat pl* **щека́м)** *ж* cheek; **за о́бе щеки́ есть** *(impf) или* **упи́сывать** *(impf)* (*разг*) to gobble one's food up *или* down.
щеко́лд|а (-ы) *ж* latch.
щек|ота́ть (-очу́, -о́чешь; *perf* **пощекота́ть)** *несов неперех* (*пятки итп*) to tickle; ~ *(impf)* **кому́-н не́рвы** to excite sb; **у меня́ ~о́чет в го́рле/носу́** I've got a tickle in my throat/nose.
щеко́тк|а (-и) *ж* tickling.
щекотли́в|ый (-, -а, -о) *прил* (*вопрос итп*) delicate.
щеко́тно *как сказ*: **мне** ~ it's tickling me; **здесь ~ ходи́ть босико́м** it's ticklish going barefoot here.
щекочу́ *итп несов см* **щекота́ть.**
щёлк|а (-и) *ж* small hole.
щёлка|ть (-ю) *несов перех* (*человека*) to flick; (*орехи, семечки*) to crack (open) ◆ *неперех*: ~ *+instr* (*языком*) to click; (*кнутом*) to crack.
щёлкн|уть (-у, -ешь) *сов неперех* to click; (*хлыстом*) to crack.
щелочно́й *прил* alkaline.
щёлоч|ь (-и) *ж* alkali.
щелч|о́к (-ка́) *м* flick; (*звук*) click; (*перен: оскорбление*) jibe.
щел|ь (-и; *loc sg* **-и́**, *gen pl* **-е́й)** *ж* (*отверстие*) crack; (*ТЕХ*) slit; **смотрова́я ~** vision slit.
щем|и́ть (*3sg* **-и́т**, *3pl* **-я́т)** *несов перех* (*перен: тревожить*) to trouble ◆ *безл* (*ныть*): **~и́т в боку́** his *итп* side is aching; **~и́т в груди́** his *итп* heart is heavy.
щемя́щ|ий (-ая, -ее, -ие) *прил* aching.
щен|и́ться (*3sg* **-и́тся**, *3pl* **-я́тся**, *perf* **ощени́ться)** *несов возв* (*собака*) to have pups; (*волчица, лиса*) to have cubs.
щен|о́к (-ка́; *nom pl* **-я́та**, *gen pl* **-я́т)** *м* (*собаки*) pup; (*лисы, волчицы*) cub; (*перен: разг*) whippersnapper.
щепети́лен *прил см* **щепети́льный.**
щепети́льност|ь (-и) *ж* (*в отношениях, денежных делах*) scrupulousness.
щепети́л|ьный (-ен, -ьна, -ьно) *прил* scrupulous.
ще́п|ка (-ки; *gen pl* **-ок)** *ж* splinter; (*для растопки*): **~ки** chippings *мн*; **худо́й как ~** thin as a rake.
щепо́т|ка (-ки; *gen pl* **-ок)** *ж* (*соли, табака*) pinch.
щерба́т|ый (-, -а, -о) *прил* (*рот*) gap-toothed; (*лицо*) pock-marked.
щерби́н|а (-ы) *ж* (*на лице, на коже*) pock-mark; (*во рту*) gap (between teeth); (*на посуде*) chink.
щети́н|а (-ы) *ж* (*животных, щётки*) bristle; (*у мужчины*) stubble.
щети́нист|ый (-, -а, -о) *прил* (*жёсткий*) bristly; (*небритый*) stubbly.
щети́н|иться (*3sg* **-ится**, *3pl* **-ятся**, *perf* **ощети́ниться)** *несов возв* (*также перен*) to bristle.
щёт|ка (-ки; *gen pl* **-ок)** *ж* brush; **зубна́я ~** toothbrush; **~ для воло́с** hairbrush.
щи (щей; *dat pl* **щам)** *мн* cabbage soup *ед*; **ки́слые ~** sour cabbage soup; **зелёные ~** sorrel soup.

The spelling rules for Russian are shown on page xvii.

щиколот|ка (**-ки**; *gen pl* **-ок**) *ж* ankle.

щип|áть (**-лю́, -лешь**) *несов перех* (*защемлять до боли*) to nip, pinch; (*no perf*; *подлеж*: *мороз*) to bite; (: *специя*, *кислое*) to sting; (*perf* **ощипáть**; *волосы*, *курицу*) to pluck

▸ **щипáться** *несов возв* (*разг*) to nip, pinch.

щипкá *итп сущ см* **щипóк**.

щипкóвый *прил* (*муз*): ~ **инструмéнт** plucked (*BRIT*) *или* picked (*US*) instrument.

щиплю́(сь) *итп несов см* **щипáть(ся)**.

щипн|у́ть (**-у́, -ёшь**) *сов перех* to nip, pinch.

щип|óк (**-кá**) *м* nip, pinch.

щипц|ы́ (**-óв**) *мн*: **ками́нные** ~ tongs *мн*; **кузнéчные** ~ pliers *мн*; **хирурги́ческие** ~ forceps *мн*; ~ **для сáхара** sugar-tongs *мн*.

щи́пчик|и (**-ов**) *мн уменьш от* **щипцы́**; (*для ногтей*, *бровей*) tweezers *мн*.

щит (**-á**) *м* shield; (*фанерный*, *металлический итп*) barrier; (*рекламный*, *баскетбольный*) board; (*ТЕХ*) panel; ~ **управлéния** control panel.

щитови́дн|ый *прил*: ~**ая железá** thyroid gland.

щу́к|а (**-и**) *ж* pike (*мн* pike).

щуп (**-а**) *м* (*ТЕХ*) probe.

щу́паль|це (**-ца**; *nom pl* **-ьца**, *gen pl* **-ец**) *ср* (*осьминога*) tentacle; (*насекомых*) feeler.

щу́па|ть (**-ю**; *perf* **пощу́пать**) *несов перех* (*опухоль*, *пульс*) to feel for; (*карманы*) to grope in.

щу́пл|ый (**-, -á, -о**) *прил* (*разг*) puny.

щу́р|ить (**-ю, -ишь**; *perf* **сощу́рить**) *несов перех*: ~ **глазá** to screw up one's eyes

▸ **щу́риться** (*perf* **сощу́риться**) *несов возв* (*от солнца*) to squint.

щу́ч|ий (**-ья, -ье, -ьи**) *прил*: **по ~ьему велéнью** (as if) by magic.

~ Э, э ~

Э, э *сущ нескл (буква) the 30th letter of the Russian alphabet.*

э *межд (выражает недоумение)* er ..., um ...; *(выражает решимость)* oh; **э, нет, я не пойду!** oh, no, I'm not going!

эбони́т (-а) *м* vulcanite, ebonite.

эвакуацио́нный *прил (пункт)* evacuation *опред*; *(госпиталь)* evacuee *опред*.

эвакуа́ци|я (-и) *ж* evacuation.

эвакуи́р|овать (-ую) *(не)сов перех* to evacuate

▸ **эвакуи́роваться** *(не)сов возв* to be evacuated.

Эвере́ст (-а) *м* Mount Everest.

эвкали́пт (-а) *м* eucalyptus.

эвкали́птов|ый *прил*: **~ое ма́сло** eucalyptus oil.

ЭВМ *ж сокр (= электро́нная вычисли́тельная маши́на)* computer.

эволюциони́р|овать (-ую) *(не)сов неперех* to evolve.

эволюцио́нный *прил* evolutionary.

эволю́ци|я (-и) *ж* evolution.

эвфеми́зм (-а) *м* euphemism.

эвфемисти́ческ|ий (-ая, -ое, -ие) *прил* euphemistic.

эги́д|а (-ы) *ж*: **под ~ой** *+gen* under the aegis of.

эгои́зм (-а) *м* egoism.

эгои́ст (-а) *м* egoist.

эгоисти́чен *прил см* **эгоисти́чный**.

эгоисти́ческ|ий (-ая, -ое, -ие) *прил* egotistic(al).

эгоисти́ч|ный (-ен, -на, -но) *прил* = **эгоисти́ческий**.

эгои́ст|ка (-ки; *gen pl* **-ок)** *ж см* **эгои́ст**.

эгоцентри́ст (-а) *м*: **он настоя́щий ~** he is very egocentric.

эдельве́йс (-а) *м* edelweiss.

Эдинбу́рг (-а) *м* Edinburgh.

эй *межд (разг)* hey; **~, кто идёт?** hey, who's there?

Эй-би-си *м сокр (= Америка́нская радиовеща́тельная компа́ния)* ABC (= *American Broadcasting Company*).

Эквадо́р (-а) *м* Ecuador.

эквадо́рск|ий (-ая, -ое, -ие) *прил* Ecuadorian.

эква́тор (-а) *м* equator.

экваториа́льный *прил* equatorial.

эквивале́нт (-а) *м* equivalent.

эквивале́нт|ный (-ен, -на, -но) *прил* equivalent.

эквилибри́стик|а (-и) *ж* tightrope walking.

ЭКГ *ж сокр* (**= электрокардиогра́мма)** ECG (= *electrocardiogram*).

экзальта́ци|я (-и) *ж* exhilaration.

экзальти́рован|ный (-, -на, -но) *прил* exhilarated.

экза́мен (-а) *м*: **~ (по** *+dat*) *(по истории, по языку)* exam(ination) (in); *(для получения звания, должности)*: **~ на перево́дчика** translator's test; *(перен)*: **~ (на** *+acc*) test (of); **выпускны́е ~ы** Finals *мн*; **сдава́ть** *(impf)* ~ to sit *(BRIT) или* take an exam(ination); **сдать** *(perf) или* **выде́рживать (вы́держать** *perf*) ~ to pass an exam(ination); **прова́ливать (провали́ть** *perf*) ~ to fail an exam(ination); **принима́ть (приня́ть** *perf*) ~ to hold an exam(ination).

экзамена́тор (-а) *м* examiner.

экзаменацио́нный *прил (комиссия, сессия)* examination *опред*; **экзаменацио́нный биле́т** exam(ination) paper.

экзамен|ова́ть (-у́ю; *perf* **проэкзаменова́ть)** *несов перех* to examine.

экзе́м|а (-ы) *ж* eczema.

экземпля́р (-а) *м (рукописи, документа)* copy; *(животного, растения)* specimen; **в двух/трёх ~ах** in duplicate/triplicate.

экзистенциали́зм (-а) *м* existentialism.

экзо́тик|а (-и) *ж* exotica *мн*.

экзоти́чен *прил см* **экзоти́чный**.

экзоти́ческ|ий (-ая, -ое, -ие) *прил (растение, страна)* exotic.

экзоти́ч|ный (-ен, -на, -но) *прил (наряд, декорации)* exotic.

э́к|ий (-ая, -ое, -ие; -а, -о, -и) *мест*: **~ая незада́ча!** what a nuisance!; **~ ты стра́нный** what a strange one you are!

экипа́ж (-а) *м (коляска)* carriage; *(команда)* crew.

экипир|ова́ть (-у́ю) *(не)сов перех (бойцов, экспедицию)* to equip.

экипиро́вк|а (-и) *ж (действие)* equipping; *(снаряжение)* equipment.

The spelling rules for Russian are shown on page xvii.

экологи́ческ|ий (**-ая, -ое, -ие**) *прил* ecological.
эколо́ги|я (**-и**) *ж* ecology.
эконо́мен *прил см* **эконо́мный.**
эконо́мик|а (**-и**) *ж* (*страны, региона*) economy; (*наука*) economics.
экономи́ст (**-а**) *м* economist.
эконо́м|ить (**-лю, -ишь**; *perf* **сэконо́мить**) *несов перех* (*энергию, деньги*) to save; (*выгадывать*): ~ **на** *+prp* to economize *или* save on.
экономи́чен *прил см* **экономи́чный.**
экономи́ческ|ий (**-ая, -ое, -ие**) *прил* economic.
экономи́ч|ный (**-ен, -на, -но**) *прил* economical.
эконо́ми|я (**-и**) *ж* (*в работе, в использовании чего-н*) economy; (*выгода*): ~ **в** *+prp* (*в топливе, в ресурсах*) economizing in; **соблюда́ть** *(impf)* **~ю** to economize; **полити́ческая** ~ political economy.
эконо́м|ка (**-ки**; *gen pl* **-ок**) *ж* housekeeper.
эконо́млю *несов см* **эконо́мить.**
эконо́м|ный (**-ен, -на, -но**) *прил* (*хозяин*) thrifty; (*метод*) economical.
эконо́мок *сущ см* **эконо́мка.**
экосисте́м|а (**-ы**) *ж* ecosystem.
экра́н (**-а**) *м* screen.
экраниза́ци|я (**-и**) *ж* screen adaptation.
экранизи́р|овать (**-ую**) *(не)сов перех* to screen.
экра́нн|ый *прил*: **~ая па́мять** (*КОМП*) screen memory; **~ое редакти́рование** (*КОМП*) screen editing.
экс- *префикс* ex-; **~чемпио́н** ex-champion.
экскава́тор (**-а**) *м* excavator, digger.
экскава́торщик (**-а**) *м* excavator operator.
эксклюзи́вный *прил* exclusive.
э́кскурс (**-а**) *м* excursus, digression.
экскурса́нт (**-а**) *м* tour group member.
экскурсио́нный *прил* excursion *опред.*
экску́рси|я (**-и**) *ж* (*посещение*) excursion; (*группа*) party.
экскурсово́д (**-а**) *м* guide.
экспанси́в|ный (**-ен, -на, -но**) *прил* enthusiastic.
экспа́нси|я (**-и**) *ж* (*ПОЛИТ*) expansion.
экспеди́тор (**-а**) *м* shipping agent.
экспеди́ци|я (**-и**) *ж* (*научная, студенческая*) field work; (*группа людей*) expedition; (*газетная*) dispatch.
экспериме́нт (**-а**) *м* experiment.
эксперимента́льный *прил* experimental.
экспериментир|овать (**-ую**) *несов неперех*: ~ (**над** *или* **с** *+instr*) to experiment (on *или* with).
экспе́рт (**-а**) *м* expert.
эксперти́з|а (**-ы**) *ж* (*медицинская*) medical assessment; (*судебная*) legal evaluation.
экспе́ртный *прил* expert *опред.*
эксплуата́тор (**-а**) *м* exploiter.
эксплуата́ци|я (**-и**) *ж* (*человека, ресурсов*) exploitation; (*машин, месторождений*) utilization; **сдава́ть (сдать** *perf*) **что-н в ~ю** to put sth into commission.
эксплуати́р|овать (**-ую**) *несов перех* to exploit; (*машины, дороги*) to use.
экспози́ци|я (**-и**) *ж* (*музейная*) exhibition; (*ФОТО*) exposure.
экспона́т (**-а**) *м* exhibit.
экспони́р|овать (**-ую**) *(не)сов перех* to exhibit.
э́кспорт (**-а**) *м* export; **на** ~ for export.
экспортёр (**-а**) *м* exporter.
экспорти́р|овать (**-ую**) *несов перех* to export.
э́кспортный *прил* (*товар*) exported; (*правила*) export *опред.*
экспре́сс (**-а**) *м* (*транспорт*) express.
экспресси́в|ный (**-ен, -на, -но**) *прил* expressive.
экспре́сси|я (**-и**) *ж* expression.
экспро́мт (**-а**) *м* impromptu.
экспро́мтом *нареч* spontaneously.
экста́з (**-а**) *м* ecstasy.
экстенси́в|ный (**-ен, -на, -но**) *прил* extensive.
экстравага́нт|ный (**-ен, -на, -но**) *прил* extravagant.
экстра́кт (**-а**) *м* extract.
экстраордина́р|ный (**-ен, -на, -но**) *прил* extraordinary.
экстрасе́нс (**-а**) *м* psychic.
экстрема́л|ьный (**-ен, -ьна, -ьно**) *прил* extreme.
экстреми́зм (**-а**) *м* extremism.
экстреми́ст (**-а**) *м* extremist.
экстреми́стск|ий (**-ая, -ое, -ие**) *прил* extremist.
э́кстрен|ный (**-ен, -на, -но**) *прил* (*отъезд, вызов*) urgent; (*расходы, заседание*) emergency *опред.*
эксце́нтрик (**-а**) *м* eccentric.
эксцентри́чен *прил см* **эксцентри́чный.**
эксцентри́ческ|ий (**-ая, -ое, -ие**) *прил* eccentric.
эксцентри́ч|ный (**-ен, -на, -но**) *прил* eccentric.
эксце́сс (**-а**) *м* excess.
ЭКЮ́ *сокр* ECU (= *European Currency Unit*).
эла́стик (**-а**) *м* stretchy material.
эласти́ч|ный (**-ен, -на, -но**) *прил* (*материал*) stretchy; (*походка*) springy.
элева́тор (**-а**) *м* (*С.-Х.*) grain store *или* elevator (*US*); (*ТЕХ*) elevator.
элега́нт|ный (**-ен, -на, -но**) *прил* elegant.
эле́ги|я (**-и**) *ж* elegy.
электриз|ова́ть (**-у́ю**; *perf* **наэлектризова́ть**) *несов перех* (*ФИЗ*) to electrify; (*перен*: *человека, атмосферу*) to stir up.
эле́ктрик (**-а**) *м* electrician.
электрифика́ци|я (**-и**) *ж* electrification.
электрифици́р|овать (**-ую**) *(не)сов перех* to connect an electricity supply to.
электри́чек *сущ см* **электри́чка.**
электри́ческ|ий (**-ая, -ое, -ие**) *прил* electric.
электри́честв|о (**-а**) *ср* (*энергия*) electricity; (*освещение*) light; **зажига́ть (заже́чь** *perf*) ~ to turn on the light.
электри́ч|ка (**-ки**; *gen pl* **-ек**) *ж* electric train.
электробытов|о́й *прил*: **~ы́е прибо́ры** electrical appliances.
электрово́з (**-а**) *м* electric locomotive.
эле́ктрогита́р|а (**-ы**) *ж* electric guitar.

электрóд (-а) *м* electrode.
электрокардиогрáмм|а (-ы) *ж* electrocardiogram.
электромонтёр (-а) *м* electrician.
электромотóр (-а) *м* electric motor.
электрóн (-а) *м* electron.
электрóник|а (-и) *ж* electronics *мн*.
электрóнн|ый *прил*: **~ микроскóп** electron microscope; **~ая доскá объявлéний** (*КОМП*) bulletin board; **~ая пóчта** (*КОМП*) electronic mail; **~ая таблúца** (*КОМП*) spreadsheet; **электрóнная вычислúтельная машúна** computer.
электропередáч|а (-и) *ж* power transmission; **лúния ~и** power line.
электропóезд (-а) *м* electric train.
электроприбóр (-а) *м* electrical device.
электропровóдк|а (-и) *ж* (electrical) wiring.
электропровóдност|ь (-и) *ж* conductivity.
электросвáрк|а (-и) *ж* (electric) welding.
электростáнци|я (-и) *ж* (electric) power station.
электротéхник (-а) *м* electrical engineer.
электротéхник|а (-и) *ж* electrical engineering.
электроэнéрги|я (-и) *ж* electric power.
элемéнт (-а) *м* (*также ХИМ. ЭЛЕК*) element; **преступные ~ы** criminal element; **прогрессúвные ~ы óбщества** progressive elements in society.
элементáр|ный *прил* (*также ФИЗ*) elementary; (**-ен, -на, -но**; *правила, условия*) basic.
эликсúр (-а) *м* elixir.
элúт|а (-ы) *ж собир* elite.
элитáрный *прил* elite.
э́ллипс (-а) *м* ellipse.
эл|ь (-я) *м* ale.
Э́льб|а (-ы) *ж* (*остров*) Elba; (*река*) Elbe.
Эльзáс (-а) *м* Alsace.
эльзáсск|ий (-ая, -ое, -ие) *прил* Alsatian.
эльф (-а) *м* elf.
эмáлевый *прил* enamel.
эмалирóванный *прил* enamelled.
эмалир|овáть (-ýю) *несов перех* to enamel.
эмáл|ь (-и) *ж* enamel.
эмансипáци|я (-и) *ж* emancipation.
эмансипúрованный *прил* emancipated.
эмбáрго *ср нескл* embargo; **налагáть (наложúть** *perf*) **~ на** *+acc* to place an embargo on.
эмблéм|а (-ы) *ж* emblem.
эмбриолóги|я (-и) *ж* embryology.
эмбриóн (-а) *м* embryo.
эмигрáнт (-а) *м* emigrant.
эмигрáнтск|ий (-ая, -ое, -ие) *прил* (*поселение*) emigrant *опред*; (*литература*) emigré *опред*.
эмиграциóнный *прил* emigration *опред*.
эмигрáци|я (-и) *ж* emigration ◆ *собир* emigrants *мн*.
эмигрúр|овать (-ую) *(не)сов неперех* to emigrate.
эмоционáл|ьный (-ен, -ьна, -ьно) *прил* emotional.
эмóци|я (-и) *ж* emotion.
эмýльси|я (-и) *ж* emulsion.
эмфатúческ|ий (-ая, -ое, -ие) *прил* emphatic.
эндокрúнн|ый *прил* (*ФИЗИОЛОГИЯ*) endocrine; **~ые жéлезы** endocrine glands.
эндокринолóги|я (-и) *ж* endocrinology.
энергéтик|а (-и) *ж* (*отдел физики*) energetics; (*промышленность*) power industry; (*наука*) power engineering.
энергетúческ|ий (-ая, -ое, -ие) *прил* (*проблемы, ресурсы*) energy *опред*; **энергетúческий крúзис** energy crisis.
энергúч|ный (-ен, -на, -но) *прил* (*человек, движения*) energetic; (*меры*) effective.
энéрги|я (-и) *ж* energy.
энергонезавúсим|ый *прил*: **~ая пáмять** (*КОМП*) nonvolatile memory.
э́нн|ый *прил*: **~ое числó/колúчество врéмени** X number/amount of time; **в ~ раз** yet again; **в ~ой стéпени** to the nth degree.
энтузиáзм (-а) *м* enthusiasm.
энтузиáст (-а) *м* enthusiast.
энциклопедúческ|ий (-ая, -ое, -ие) *прил* (*ум*) encyclopaedic (*BRIT*), encyclopedic (*US*); **энциклопедúческий словáрь** encyclopaedia (*BRIT*), encyclopedia (*US*).
энциклопéди|я (-и) *ж* encyclopaedia (*BRIT*), encyclopedia (*US*).
эпигрáмм|а (-ы) *ж* epigram.
эпúграф (-а) *м* epigraph.
эпидéми|я (-и) *ж* epidemic.
эпизóд (-а) *м* episode.
эпизодúческ|ий (-ая, -ое, -ие) *прил* (*случай, факт*) random.
эпизодúчный *прил* = **эпизодúческий**.
эпилéпси|я (-и) *ж* epilepsy.
эпилéптик (-а) *м* epileptic.
эпилóг (-а) *м* epilogue (*BRIT*), epilog (*US*).
эпистолярный *прил* epistolary.
эпúтет (-а) *м* epithet.
эпицéнтр (-а) *м* epicentre (*BRIT*), epicenter (*US*).
эпúческ|ий (-ая, -ое, -ие) *прил* epic.
эполéт|а (-ы) *ж* (*обычно мн*) epaulette.
эпопé|я (-и) *ж* epic.
э́пос (-а) *м* epic literature.
эпóх|а (-и) *ж* epoch.
эпохáл|ьный (-ен, -на, -но) *прил* epoch-making.
э́р|а (-ы) *ж* era; **1-ый век нáшей ~ы/до нáшей ~ы** the first century AD/BC.
эрéкци|я (-и) *ж* (*АНАТ*) erection.
эрзáц (-а) *м* substitute.
Эритрé|я (-и) *ж* Eritrea.
эритроцúт (-а) *м* erythrocyte, red blood cell.
эрóзи|я (-и) *ж* erosion.
эрóтик|а (-и) *ж* erotica *мн*.

эроти́ческ|ий (-ая, -ое, -ие) *прил* erotic.
Эр-Рия́д (-а) *м* Riyadh.
эруди́рован|ный (-, -на, -но) *прил* erudite.
эруди́т (-а) *м*: **он настоя́щий ~** he knows an enormous amount.
эруди́ци|я (-и) *ж* erudition.
эска́др|а (-ы) *ж* squadron (*navy*).
эскадри́ль|я (-и) *ж* squadron (*air force*).
эскадро́н (-а) *м* squadron (*army*).
эскала́тор (-а) *м* escalator.
эскала́ци|я (-и) *ж* escalation.
эскало́п (-а) *м* escalope.
эски́з (-а) *м* (*к картине*) sketch; (*к проекту*) draft.
эскимо́ *ср нескл* choc-ice, Eskimo (*US*).
эскимо́с (-а) *м* Eskimo.
эскимо́с|ка (-ки; *gen pl* **-ок)** *ж см* **эскимо́с**.
эско́рт (-а) *м* escort.
эсми́н|ец (-ца) *м* (= *эска́дренный миноно́сец*) destroyer.
эссе́ *ср нескл* essay.
эссе́нци|я (-и) *ж* essence.
эстака́д|а (-ы) *ж* (*на автомагистрали*) flyover (*BRIT*), overpass; (*на железной дороге*) viaduct; (*на пристани*) pier.
эста́мп (-а) *м* (*ИСКУССТВО*) print.
эстафе́т|а (-ы) *ж* (*СПОРТ*) relay (race); (: *палочка*) baton.
эсте́тик|а (-и) *ж* aesthetics.
эстети́чен *прил см* **эстети́чный**.
эстети́ческ|ий (-ая, -ое, -ие) *прил* aesthetic.
эстети́ч|ный (-ен, -на, -но) *прил* aesthetic.
эсто́н|ец (-ца) *м* Estonian.
Эсто́ни|я (-и) *ж* Estonia.
эсто́н|ка (-ки; *gen pl* **-ок)** *ж см* **эсто́нец**.
эсто́нск|ий (-ая, -ое, -ие) *прил* Estonian; **~ язы́к** Estonian.
эсто́нца *итп сущ см* **эсто́нец**.
эстра́д|а (-ы) *ж* (*для оркестра*) platform; (*вид искусства*) variety.
эстра́дный *прил*: **~ конце́рт** variety show; **~ арти́ст** variety performer.
э́т|а (-ой) *мест см* **э́тот**.
эта́ж (-а́) *м* floor, storey (*BRIT*), story (*US*); **пе́рвый/второ́й/тре́тий ~** ground/first/second floor (*BRIT*), first/second/third floor (*US*).
этаже́р|ка (-ки; *gen pl* **-ок)** *ж* (stack of) shelves.
э́так *нареч* (*разг*: *таким образом*) in such a way ◆ *вводн сл* (*приблизительно*): **~ 25 лет** 25 years or so; **~ у нас ничего́ не полу́чится** we won't get anywhere this way; **и так и ~** (*разг*) this way and that (way).
э́так|ий (-ая, -ое, -ие) *мест* (*разг*) such.
этало́н (-а) *м* (*веса, меры*) standard; (*перен*: *красоты, благородства итп*) model; **брать (взять** *perf*) **что-н за ~** to use sth as a standard.
эта́п (-а) *м* (*развития, работы*) stage; (*гонки*) lap; **ссы́льный ~** stopping point (*for deported convicts*); **отправля́ть** (*impf*) **~ом** *или* **по ~у** to deport (*under convoy*).
эта́пн|ый *прил* (*работа, произведение*) prominent; **~ое собы́тие** an event of great significance.
э́т|и (-их) *мест см* **э́тот**.
э́тик|а (-и) *ж* ethics.
этике́т (-а) *м* etiquette.
этике́т|ка (-ки; *gen pl* **-ок)** *ж* label.
эти́л (-а) *м* ethyl.
эти́ловый *прил* ethyl *опред*.
э́тим *мест см* **э́тот, э́то, э́ти**.
э́тими *мест см* **э́ти**.
этимоло́ги|я (-и) *ж* etymology.
эти́ч|ный (-ен, -на, -но) *прил* ethical.
этни́ческ|ий (-ая, -ое, -ие) *прил* ethnic.
этнографи́ческ|ий (-ая, -ое, -ие) *прил* ethnographic.
этногра́фи|я (-и) *ж* ethnography.

KEYWORD

э́т|о (-ого; *см* **Table 10)** *мест* **1** (*указательное*) this; **на́до успе́ть к ве́черу; э́то бу́дет тру́дно** we need to finish by this evening, this will be difficult; **он на всё соглаша́ется; э́то о́чень стра́нно** he is agreeing to everything, this is most strange
2 (*связка в сказуемом*): **любо́вь – э́то проще́ние** love is forgiveness
3 (*как подлежащее*): **с кем ты разгова́ривал? – э́то была́ моя́ сестра́** who were you talking to? – that was my sister; **как э́то произошло́?** how did it happen?
4 (*для усиления*): **э́то он во всём винова́т** he is the one who is to blame for everything; **э́то они́ нас подвели́** they are the ones who let us down
◆ *част* **1** (*служит для усиления*): **кто э́то звони́л?** who was it who phoned (*BRIT*) *или* called (*US*)?; **о чём э́то ты так беспоко́ишься?** what is it that you are so worried about?
2 (*указательная*): **э́то ты так крича́л?** was it you who called out?

KEYWORD

э́т|от (-ого; *f* **э́та**, *nt* **э́то**, *pl* **э́ти**; *см* **Table 10)** *мест* **1** (*указательное*: *о близком предмете*) this; (: *о близких предметах*) these; **э́тот дом** this house; **э́ти кни́ги** these books
2 (*о данном времени*) this; **э́тот год осо́бенно тру́дный** this year is particularly hard; **в э́ти дни я при́нял реше́ние** in the last few days I have come to a decision; **э́тот са́мый** that very
3 (*о чём-то только что упомянутом*) this; **он ложи́лся в 10 часо́в ве́чера; э́та привы́чка меня́ всегда́ удивля́ла** he used to go to bed at 10 pm, this habit always amazed me
◆ *ср* (*как сущ*: *об одном предмете*) this one; (: *о многих предметах*) these ones; **дай мне вот э́ти** give me these ones; **э́тот не всё спосо́бен** this one is capable of anything; **при э́том** in addition.

этю́д (-а) *м* (*ИСКУССТВО*) sketch; (*ЛИТЕРАТУРА*) study; (*МУЗ*) étude; (*шахматный*) problem.
эфеме́р|ный (-ен, -на, -но) *прил* ephemeral.
эфе́с (-а) *м* (*шпаги, сабли*) hilt.

эфиóп (**-а**) *м* Ethiopian.
Эфиóпи|я (**-и**) *ж* Ethiopia.
эфиóп|ка (**-ки**; *gen pl* **-ок**) *ж см* **эфиóп**.
эфиóпск|ий (**-ая, -ое, -ие**) *прил* Ethiopian.
эфи́р (**-а**) *м* (*хим*) ether; (*воздушное пространство*) air; **выходи́ть (вы́йти** *perf*) **в** ~ to go on the air; **прямóй** ~ live broadcast.
эфи́рн|ый *прил*: **~ое мáсло** essential oil; **~ое врéмя** airtime.
эффéкт (**-а**) *м* effect; (*обычно мн*: *шумовые, световые*) effects *мн*; **экономи́ческий** ~ economic result; **производи́ть (произвести́** *perf*) ~ **на** *+acc* to have an effect on; **давáть (дать** *perf*) **желáемый** ~ to have the desired effect.
эффéктен *прил см* **эффéктный**.
эффекти́вен *прил см* **эффекти́вный**.
эффекти́вност|ь (**-и**) *ж* effectiveness.
эффекти́в|ный (**-ен, -на, -но**) *прил* effective.
эффéкт|ный (**-ен, -на, -но**) *прил* (*одежда*) striking; (*речь*) impressive.
эх *межд* (*разг*) oh; ~ **ты, лентя́й !** oh, you're such a lazybones!
э́х|о (**-а**) *ср* echo (*мн* echoes).
эшафóт (**-а**) *м* scaffold; **всходи́ть (взойти́** *perf*) **на** ~ to mount the scaffold.
эшелóн (**-а**) *м* echelon; (*поезд*) special train; **~ы влáсти** echelons of power.

~Ю, ю~

Ю, ю *сущ нескл (буква) the 31st letter of the Russian alphabet.*
ю. *сокр* (**= юг**) S (= *South*); (**= ю́жный**) S (= *South*).
юа́н|ь (**-я**) *м* yuan (*мн* yuan).
ЮАР *ж сокр (= Южно-Африка́нская Респу́блика)* RSA (= *Republic of South Africa*).
юбиле́|й (**-я**) *м* (*годовщина*) anniversary; (*празднование*) jubilee.
юбиле́йный *прил* (*торжество*) anniversary *опред*; (*монета, значок итп*) jubilee *опред*.
юбиля́р (**-а**) *м*: **учёный-/заво́д-~** *scientist/factory whose anniversary is being celebrated.*
ю́б|ка (**-ки**; *gen pl* **-ок**) *ж* skirt; **держа́ться** *(impf)* **за чью-н ~ку** (*разг*) to be tied to sb's apron strings.
ювели́р (**-а**) *м* jeweller (*BRIT*), jeweler (*US*).
ювели́рн|ый *прил* jewellery *опред* (*BRIT*), jewelery *опред* (*US*); (*перен: работа, точность*) painstaking; **~ые изде́лия** jewel(l)ery; **~ магази́н** jeweller's (*BRIT*) *или* jeweler's (*US*) (shop).
юг (**-а**) *м* south; **на ю́ге страны́** in the south of the country; **к ю́гу от го́рода** to the south of the town.
ю́го-восто́к (**-а**) *м* south-east.
ю́го-за́пад (**-а**) *м* south-west.
Югосла́ви|я (**-и**) *ж* (*ИСТ*) Yugoslavia.
южа́н|ин (**-ина**; *nom pl* **-е**, *gen pl* **-**) *м* southerner.
южа́н|ка (**-ки**; *gen pl* **-ок**) *ж см* **южа́нин**.
ю́жный *прил* southern; **Ю́жная Коре́я** South Korea; **Ю́жный по́люс** the South Pole.
юл|а́ (**-ы́**) *ж* (*игрушка*) (spinning) top ◆ *м/ж* (*перен: разг*) fidget.
юл|и́ть (**-ю́, -и́шь**) *несов неперех* (*разг: суетиться*) to fidget; (*: хитрить*) to be shifty; ~ *(impf)* **пе́ред** *+instr* (*заискивать*) to play up to.
ю́мор (**-а**) *м* humour (*BRIT*), humor (*US*).
юморе́с|ка (**-ки**; *gen pl* **-ок**) *ж* (*МУЗ*) humoresque; (*ЛИТЕРАТУРА*) short comedy.
юмори́ст (**-а**) *м* (*автор*) humorist; (*шутливый человек*) comedian.
юмори́стик|а (**-и**) *ж* (*ЛИТЕРАТУРА*) humour (*BRIT*), humor (*US*).
юмористи́ческ|ий (**-ая, -ое, -ие**) *прил* humorous; **~ журна́л** satirical magazine.
юмори́ст|ка (**-ки**; *gen pl* **-ок**) *ж* comedienne.
ю́нг|а (**-и**) *м* cabin boy; (*младший матрос*) trainee sailor.
ЮНЕСКО *ср сокр* UNESCO (= *United Nations Educational Scientific and Cultural Organization*).
юн|е́ц (**-ца́**) *м* (*разг: юноша*) youth.
юнио́р (**-а**) *м* junior.
ЮНИСЕФ *м сокр* UNICEF (= *United Nations (International) Children's (Emergency) Fund*).
ю́нкер (**-а**; *nom pl* **-а́**) *м* (*ИСТ*) cadet.
ю́нкерск|ий (**-ая, -ое, -ие**) *прил* cadet *опред*; **~ое учи́лище** military school.
ю́ност|ь (**-и**) *ж* youth ◆ *собир* (*юношество*) young people *мн*; **в ~и он был любозна́телен** in his youth he was greedy for knowledge.
ю́нош|а (**-и**; *nom pl* **-и**, *gen pl* **-ей**) *м* young man (*мн* men).
ю́ношеск|ий (**-ая, -ое, -ие**) *прил* youthful; (*журнал*) young person's; (*организация, клуб*) youth; **~ие го́ды** youth.
ю́ношеств|о (**-а**) *ср собир* young people *мн*; (*юность*) youth.
юнца́ *итп сущ см* **юне́ц**.
ю́н|ый (**-, -а́, -о**) *прил* (*молодой*) young; (*силы, задор*) youthful; **теа́тр ~ого зри́теля** children's theatre (*BRIT*) *или* theater (*US*).
ЮПИ *м сокр* UPI (= *United Press International*).
юпи́тер (**-а**) *м* (*прибор*) floodlight; **Ю~** Jupiter.
юриди́чески *нареч*: **~ обяза́тельный** legally binding.
юриди́ческ|ий (**-ая, -ое, -ие**) *прил* (*сила*) juridical; (*образование*) legal; **~ факульте́т** law faculty; **юриди́ческая консульта́ция** ≈ legal advice office; **юриди́ческое лицо́** body corporate.
юрисди́кци|я (**-и**) *ж* (*ЮР*) jurisdiction; **подлежа́ть** *(impf)* **чье́й-н ~и** to come under sb's jurisdiction.
юриско́нсульт (**-а**) *м* legal adviser.
юриспруде́нци|я (**-и**) *ж* (*правоведение*) jurisprudence; (*практика юриста*) law.
юри́ст (**-а**) *м* lawyer.
ю́рк|ий (**-кая, -кое, -кие**; **-ок, -ка́, -ко**) *прил* nimble.
ю́ркн|уть (**-у, -ешь**) *сов неперех* to scurry away.
юро́див|ый *прил* (*разг*) crazy ◆ (**-ого**; *decl like adj*) *м* (*РЕЛ*) *holy fool*.
юро́дств|овать (**-ую**) *несов неперех* (*перен*) to behave like a lunatic.
ю́рок *прил см* **ю́ркий**.
ю́рск|ий (**-ая, -ое, -ие**) *прил* (*ГЕО*) Jurassic.
ю́рт|а (**-ы**) *ж* yurt (*skin tent used by nomads in*

Central Asia and Siberia).

ЮСИА *м сокр* USIA (= *United States Information Agency*).

юсти́ция (-и) *ж* (*правовые учреждения*) the judiciary; **Министе́рство ~и** the Ministry of Justice.

ю|ти́ться (-чу́сь, -ти́шься) *несов неперех* (*располагаться*) to huddle together; (*иметь приют*) to live in cramped conditions.

~ Я, я ~

Я, я *сущ нескл* (*буква*) *the 32nd letter of the Russian alphabet*.
я (**меня́**; *см* **Table 5a**) *мест* I ◆ *сущ нескл* (*личность*) the self, the ego; ~ **тебя́** *или* **тебе́!** (*разг*: *угроза*) I'll teach you!; **не ~ бу́ду, е́сли не ...** (*разг*) I'll be damned if I don't ...; **второ́е „я"** alter ego.
я́беда (**-ы**) *м/ж* sneak.
я́бедник (**-а**) *м* = **я́беда**.
я́беднича|ть (**-ю**; *perf* **ная́бедничать**) *несов неперех*: ~ **на** *+acc* (*разг*) to tell tales about.
я́блок|о (**-а**; *nom pl* **-и**) *ср* apple; **глазно́е ~** eyeball; **в ~ах** (*о масти лошадей*) dappled; **~у не́где упа́сть** (*перен*) there's not enough room to swing a cat.
я́блонев|ый *прил* (*цвет*) apple-green; **~ая ве́тка** branch of an apple tree.
я́блон|я (**-и**) *ж* apple tree.
я́блочк|о (**-а**) *ср уменьш от* **я́блоко**; (*на мишени*) bull's-eye.
я́блочный *прил* apple *опред*.
я́вен *прил см* **я́вный**.
яв|и́ться (**-лю́сь, -ишься**; *impf* **явля́ться**) *сов возв* (*в суд*) to appear; (*на службу*) to report; (*домой, в гости*) to arrive; (*мысль, образ*) to arise; **явля́ться** (~ *perf*) *+instr* (*причиной, следствием*) to turn out to be.
я́в|ка (**-ки**; *gen pl* **-ок**) *ж* (*действие*: *в суд, на допрос*) appearance; (: *на интервью итп*) attendance; (*место*: *конспираторов*) secret meeting place.
явле́ни|е (**-я**) *ср* phenomenon (*мн* phenomena); (*событие*) occurrence; (*ТЕАТР*) scene; (*РЕЛ*) manifestation.
явлю́сь *сов см* **яви́ться**.
явля́|ться (**-юсь**) *несов от* **яви́ться** ◆ *возв*: ~ *+instr* to be.
я́вно *нареч* (*очевидно*) obviously.
я́в|ный (**-ен, -на, -но**) *прил* (*вражда, благосклонность*) overt; (*ложь, лесть итп*) obvious.
я́вок *сущ см* **я́вка**.
я́вочн|ый *прил*; **~ая кварти́ра** secret meeting place; ~ **пункт** (*ВОЕН*) reporting point; **~ым поря́дком** without permission; **я́вочный лист** attendance sheet.
я́ствен|ный (**-, -на, -но**) *прил* (*звук*) distinct; (*сознание, понимание итп*) clear.
я́ств|овать (*3sg* **-ует**) *несов неперех* to be obvious; **из показа́ний ~ует, что он невино́вен** from the evidence it is obvious that he is innocent.
яв|ь (**-и**) *ж* reality.
яг|а́ (**-и́**) *ж* Baba-Yaga (*witch in Russian folk tales*).
я́гел|ь (**-я**) *м* Iceland moss.
ягн|ёнок (**-ёнка**; *nom pl* **-я́та**, *gen pl* **-я́т**) *м* lamb.
ягн|и́ться (*3sg* **-и́тся**, *3pl* **-я́тся**, *perf* **оягни́ться**) *несов возв* to lamb.
ягня́та *итп сущ см* **ягнёнок**.
я́год|а (**-ы**) *ж* berry; **одного́ по́ля ~** kindred spirit.
ягоди́ц|а (**-ы**) *ж* buttock.
я́годник (**-а**) *м* (*место*) berry patch; (*кустарник*) berry bush; (*разг*: *сборщик*) berry picker.
я́годный *прил* berry *опред*.
ягуа́р (**-а**) *м* jaguar.
яд (**-а**; *part gen* **-у**) *м* poison.
я́дер *сущ см* **ядро́**.
я́дерный *прил* nuclear.
я́дерщик (**-а**) *м* (*разг*) nuclear physicist.
ядови́т|ый (**-, -а, -о**) *прил* poisonous; (*перен*: *человек, слова*) venomous.
ядохимика́т (**-а**) *м* (*обычно мн*) chemical (*used as weedkiller or pesticide*).
ядрён|ый (**-, -а, -о**) *прил* (*яблоко*) juicy; (*перен*: *воздух*) fresh; (: *мороз*) hard.
яд|ро́ (**-ра́**; *nom pl* **-ра**, *gen pl* **-ер**) *ср* nucleus; (*ореха*) kernel; (*Земли, древесины*) core; (*ВОЕН*) projectile; (*СПОРТ*) shot; **толка́ние ~ра́** (*СПОРТ*) shot put.
яз. *сокр* (= **язы́к**) lang. (= *language*).
я́зв|а (**-ы**) *ж* (*МЕД*) ulcer; (*перен*: *общества*) evil ◆ *м/ж* (*перен*: *разг*) sarcastic person (*мн* people); **я́зва желу́дка** stomach ulcer.
я́звенн|ый *прил*: **~ая боле́знь** stomach ulcer.
язви́тел|ьный (**-ен, -ьна, -ьно**) *прил* scathing.
язв|и́ть (**-лю́, -и́шь**; *perf* **съязви́ть**) *несов неперех* (*+dat*) to speak sharply to; ~ (**съязви́ть** *perf*) **на чей-н счёт** to be scathing at sb's expense.
язы́к (**-а́**) *м* tongue; (*русский, разговорный итп*) language; (*ВОЕН*: *разг*) *prisoner captured for information*; **держа́ть** (*impf*) ~ **за зу́бами** (*разг*) to hold one's tongue; **вопро́с (был) у него́ на ~е** (*разг*) the question was on the tip of his tongue; **прикуси́ть** (*perf*) ~ (*разг*) to bite one's

tongue; **тяну́ть** *(perf)* **кого́-н за** ~ *(разг)* to make sb talk; ~ **не повернётся сказа́ть/попроси́ть** *(разг)* I could not bring myself to say/ask; **владе́ть** *(impf)* **языко́м** to speak a language; **находи́ть (найти́** *perf)* **общий** ~ to find a common language; ~ **программи́рования высо́кого/ни́зкого у́ровня** *(КОМП)* high-level/low-level language; ~ **ассе́мблера** *(КОМП)* assembly language.

языка́ст|ый (-, -а, -о) *прил (человек)* sharp-tongued.

языкове́д (-а) *м* linguist.

языкове́дени|е (-я) *ср* linguistics.

языков|о́й *прил (факультет, система)* language *опред*; **~о́е пра́вило** rule of a language.

языкозна́ни|е (-я) *ср* linguistics.

язы́ческ|ий (-ая, -ое, -ие) *прил* pagan *опред*.

язы́честв|о (-а) *ср* paganism.

язычка́ *итп сущ см* **язычо́к**.

язы́чник (-а) *м* pagan.

язы́чниц|а (-ы) *ж см* **язы́чник**.

язычо́|к (-ка́) *м уменьш от* **язы́к**; *(АНАТ)* uvula; *(ботинка)* tongue; *(замка)* catch.

яйц *сущ см* **яйцо́**.

яи́ч|ко (-ка; *gen pl* **-ек)** *ср уменьш от* **яйцо́**; *(АНАТ)* testicle.

яи́чник (-а) *м* ovary.

яи́чниц|а (-ы) *ж* fried eggs *мн*.

яи́чн|ый *прил*: ~ **бело́к** egg white; **~ая скорлупа́** eggshell.

яйцеви́д|ный (-ен, -на, -но) *прил* egg-shaped.

яйцево́д (-а) *м* oviduct.

яйцекле́т|ка (-ки; *gen pl* **-ок)** *ж* ovule.

яйцо́ (яйца́; *nom pl* **я́йца**, *gen pl* **яи́ц**, *dat pl* **я́йцам)** *ср* egg; *(АНАТ)* ovum; ~ **всмя́тку/вкруту́ю** soft-boiled/hard-boiled egg.

ЯК (-а) *м сокр = самолёт констру́кции А С. Я́ковлева*.

Як (-а) *м сокр =* **ЯК**.

як (-а) *м* yak.

я́кобы *союз (будто бы)* that ◆ *част* supposedly; **он утвержда́ет,** ~ **ничего́ не зна́ет** he claims that he doesn't know anything; **он предлага́ет** ~ **вы́годную сде́лку** he is supposedly proposing a good deal.

я́корный *прил* anchor *опред*.

я́кор|ь (-я; *nom pl* **-я́)** *м (МОР)* anchor; **броса́ть (бро́сить** *perf)* ~ to cast anchor; **стоя́ть** *(impf)* **на ~е** to ride at anchor; **снима́ться (сня́ться** *perf)* **с ~я** to weigh anchor.

яку́т (-а) *м* Yakut.

Яку́ти|я (-и) *ж* Yakutia.

яку́т|ка (-ки; *gen pl* **-ок)** *ж см* **яку́т**.

якша́|ться (-юсь) *несов возв*: ~ **с** *+instr* to consort with.

Я́лт|а (-ы) *ж* Yalta.

я́м|а (-ы) *ж (в земле)* pit; *(разг: впадина)* hollow; **рыть** *(impf)* **~у кому́-н** to lay a trap for sb; **возду́шная** ~ air pocket; **оркестро́вая** ~ orchestra pit.

Яма́йк|а (-и) *ж* Jamaica.

яма́йск|ий (-ая, -ое, -ие) *прил* Jamaican.

я́моч|ка (-ки; *gen pl* **-ек)** *ж* dimple.

ямщи́к (-а́) *м* coachman *(мн* coachmen).

янва́р|ь (-я́) *м* January; *см также* **октя́брь**.

янта́рный *прил* amber *опред*.

янта́р|ь (-я́) *м* amber.

япо́н|ец (-ца) *м* Japanese.

Япо́ни|я (-и) *ж* Japan.

япо́н|ка (-ки; *gen pl* **-ок)** *ж см* **япо́нец**.

япо́нск|ий (-ая, -ое, -ие) *прил* Japanese; ~ **язы́к** Japanese.

япо́нца *итп сущ см* **япо́нец**.

ярд (-а) *м* yard.

я́р|кий (-кая, -кое, -кие; -ок, -ка́, -ко) *прил* bright; *(перен: человек, речь)* brilliant; (: *талант)* outstanding.

я́ркост|ь (-и) *ж (цвета, краски)* brightness; *(человека, речи)* brilliance.

ярлы́к (-а́) *м* label; **ему́ накле́или** ~ **реакционе́ра** he was labelled as a reactionary.

я́рмар|ка (-ки; *gen pl* **-ок)** *ж* fair; **междунаро́дная** ~ international trade fair.

ярм|о́ (-а́) *ср (также перен)* yoke.

ярово|о́й *прил (злаки)* spring *опред*; **~о́е по́ле** field sown with spring crops.

я́рок *прил см* **я́ркий**.

я́рост|ный (-ен, -на, -но) *прил (взгляд, слова)* furious; *(перен: атака, критика)* fierce.

я́рост|ь (-и) *ж* fury; **приходи́ть (прийти́** *perf)* **в** ~ to fly into a rage.

я́рус (-а) *м (в зрительном зале)* circle; *(ряд)* tier; *(ГЕО)* layer.

я́рый *прил (преданный)* ardent.

я́сен *прил см* **я́сный**.

я́сен|ь (-я) *м* ash (tree).

я́сл|и (-ей) *мн (для скота)* trough *ед*; *(также:* **де́тские** ~) crèche, day nursery *(ВНIТ)*.

ясне́|ть *(3sg* **-ет**, *3pl* **-ют)** *несов неперех* to clear, become clear.

я́сно *нареч* clearly ◆ *как сказ (о погоде)* it's fine; *(понятно)* it's clear; **я** ~ **выража́юсь?** do I make myself clear?; **на у́лице сего́дня** ~ it's fine outside today; **тепе́рь мне всё** ~ it's all clear to me now; **~, что он недово́лен** it's clear that he's not happy; **с ним всё** ~ nothing more needs to be said about him.

ясновиде́ни|е (-я) *ср* clairvoyance.

ясновид|ец (-ца) *м* clairvoyant.

ясновидящ|ий (-ая, -ее, -ие) *прил (человек)* clairvoyant *опред* ◆ **(-его;** *decl like adj)* *м* clairvoyant.

я́сност|ь (-и) *ж* clarity; **вноси́ть (внести́** *perf)* ~ **в что-н** to clarify sth.

я́с|ный (-ен, -на́, -но) *прил* clear.

я́стреб (-а) *м* (*ЗООЛ*) hawk.
ястреби́н|ый *прил* (*клюв*) hawk's; **~ая охо́та** falconry; ~ **нос** (*перен*) hooked nose.
я́хонт (-а) *м* (*рубин*) ruby; (*сапфир*) sapphire.
я́хт|а (-ы) *ж* yacht.
яхт-клу́б (-а) *м* yacht club.
яхтсме́н (-а) *м* yachtsman (*мн* yachtsmen).
яче́|йка (-йки; *gen pl* **-ек)** *ж* (*сотовая, партийная*) cell; (*профсоюзная*) branch; (*для почты*) pigeonhole; **яче́йка па́мяти** (*КОМП*) memory cell.
ячме́нный *прил* barley *опред.*
ячме́н|ь (-я́) *м* (*С-Х*) barley; (*МЕД*) sty(e).
я́чневый *прил* crushed-barley.
я́шм|а (-ы) *ж* jasper.
я́щериц|а (-ы) *ж* lizard.
я́щик (-а) *м* (*вместилище*: *большой*) chest; (: *маленький*) box; (*в письменном столе итп*) drawer; (*также*: **мусо́рный** ~) dustbin (*BRIT*), garbage can (*US*); **почто́вый** ~ (*домашний*) letter box (*BRIT*), mailbox (*US*); (*уличный*: *как адрес*) post office box; (*разг*: *об учреждении*) *secret plant, institution etc*; (: *ТЕЛ*) the box; **откла́дывать (отложи́ть** *perf*) **что-н в до́лгий** ~ (*перен*) to shelve sth.
я́щур (-а) *м* (*болезнь*) foot-and-mouth disease.

GUIDE TO RUSSIAN GRAMMAR

It is not the purpose of this grammar section to attempt to give an exhaustive treatment of Russian grammar. Instead it is intended to outline the basic grammatical principles and to draw the user's attention to the most commonly encountered irregular forms.

NOUNS

1 Gender

A Russian noun has either masculine, feminine or neuter gender. In most cases it is grammatically determinable by its ending:

дом *m*
карти́на *f*
кре́сло *nt*

Gender of nouns is significant since, for example, it determines the ending of a qualifying adjective:

большо́й дом
больша́я карти́на
большо́е кре́сло

1.1 Masculine noun categories

I) All nouns ending in a hard consonant eg. кот, собо́р, а́дрес or in -й eg. кремато́рий, музе́й.
II) Some nouns ending in -а/-я which are natural masculine nouns eg.мужчи́на, дя́дя and masculine first names eg. Са́ша.
III) Numerous nouns ending in a soft sign, including:
  i) natural masculines eg. па́рень, коро́ль.
  ii) months of the year eg. ию́ль.

1.2 Feminine noun categories

I) The majority of nouns ending in -а/-я, eg. доро́га, ко́мната, тётя.
II) The majority of nouns ending in a soft sign, including:
  i) natural feminines eg. мать
  ii) all nouns ending in -жь,-чь,-шь,-щь,-знь,-мь,-пь,-фь.
  iii) most nouns ending in -сть,-бь,-вь,-дь,-зь,-сь,-ть.

1.3 Neuter noun categories

a) Almost all nouns ending in -о eg. окно́
b) Almost all nouns ending in -е eg. со́лнце
c) Nouns ending in -ё eg. копьё.
d) Nouns ending in -мя eg. вре́мя, пле́мя.
e) Most indeclinable loan words eg. ви́ски, ра́дио (a notable exception being ко́фе, which is masculine).

2 Declension

There are three declension patterns for nouns. The first covers most masculine and neut nouns, the second most feminine nouns and the third is specific to feminine nouns ending i a soft sign. For the first declension pattern hard-ending masculine and neuter nouns (eg мост, óзеро) have the genitive singular ending -а, whereas soft-ending masculine an neuter nouns (eg. крематóрий, гость, гóре) have the genitive ending -я. Similarly, th second declension pattern has a split between hard-ending feminine nouns (eg. лáмпа which have the genitive singular ending -ы, and soft-ending feminine nouns (eg. бáшня which have the genitive ending -и. All nouns in the third declension pattern, as they ar soft-ending, have the genitive ending -и.

The genitive singular declension generally sets the pattern for the other oblique cases of noun, ie. whether these will be hard- or soft-ending. The general pattern followed in all thre declensions is illustrated by the following table, using specific noun examples:

[NB. The table does not, of course, cover all the variations in declension or stress that exis

	Singular					*Plural*					
Nom	*Acc*	*Gen*	*Dat*	*Instr*	*Prp*	*Nom*	*Acc*	*Gen*	*Dat*	*Instr*	*Prp*
Masculine											
завóд	~	~а	~у	~ом	~е	~ы	~ы	~ов	~ам	~ами	~ах
музéй	~й	~я	~ю	~ем	~е	~и	~и	~ев	~ям	~ями	~ях
гость	~я	~я	~ю	~ем	~е	~и	~éй	~éй	~ям́	~ями́	~ях́
писáтель	~я	~я	~ю	~ем	~е	~и	~ей	~ей	~ям	~ями	~ях
двúгатель	~ь	~я	~ю	~ем	~е	~и	~и	~ей	~ям	~ями	~ях
Neuter											
мéсто	~о	~а	~у	~ом	~е	~á	~á	~	~áм	~áми	~áх
пóле	~е	~я	~ю	~ем	~е	~я́	~я́	~éй	~я́м	~я́ми	~я́х
здáние	~е	~я	~ю	~ем	~и	~я	~я	~й	~ям	~ями	~ях
Feminine											
лáмпа	~у	~ы	~е	~ой	~е	~ы	~ы	~	~ам	~ами	~ах
бáшня	~ню	~ни	~не	~ней	~не	~ни	~ни	~ен	~нят	~нями	~ня
пóвесть	~ь	~и	~и	~ью	~и	~и	~и	~ей	~ям	~ями	~ях
стáнция	~ю	~и	~и	~ей	~и	~и	~и	~й	~ям	~ями	~ях

One particularly important rule to bear in mind is that the accusative case of anima masculine singular nouns and of all animate plural nouns is identical with the genitive.

3 Stress patterns

Stress varies a great deal from one Russian noun to the next, and even oblique cases of particular noun frequently differ from each other in this respect.

Nouns ending in unstressed -а/-я and in -ия/-ие do not undergo any stress changes.

Fixed stem-stress is found in first declension masculine nouns such as стул, музé локомотúв, in nouns with medial stress, in nouns of three or more syllables, and in nour with unstressed prefixes or suffixes.

Fixed end-stress is found in many hard-ending and soft-ending first declension masculine nouns such as стол, дождь, словáрь, as well as in almost all nouns with the stressed suffixes -áк/-ѧ́к,-áч,-éж, -ёж,-ѝк,-ѝч,-ýн,-ýх.

A shift of stress from the stem in the singular to the end in the plural is found in first declension masculine nouns such as мост and сад, as well as in many nouns with nominative plural endings -ья́,-á/-я́. A similar stress shift occurs in neuter nouns such as дéло and мéсто. The reverse happens (ie. a shift of stress from the end in the singular to the stem in the plural) in other neuter nouns eg. письмó, винó, окнó. This is also true for many second declension feminine nouns eg. войнá, игрá, странá and others which undergo a vowel mutation in the stress change eg. женá » жёны, сестрá » сёстры.

Irregularity of stress pattern is greatest in end-stressed second declension feminine nouns, where the following patterns are possible: the accusative singular and nominative/accusative plural have stem stress eg. рукá, ногá, сторонá, or only the nominative/accusative plural have stem stress eg. губá, волнá. Alternatively, stem stress may be confined to: the singular accusative and all plural forms, as in the case of водá, ценá, стенá; all plural forms with the exception of the genitive and animate accusative, as in the case of семья́, судья́; the accusative singular and all plural forms excepting the genitive, as in the case of земля́.

2 ADJECTIVES

Russian adjectives generally have a long (attributive) form eg. вéжливый, вéжливая, вéжливое, вéжливые and a short (predicative) form eg. вéжлив, вéжлива, вéжливо, вéжливы.

1 Long form

Russian long adjectives are mostly used attributively and the majority have hard endings, the first vowel of the ending being -ы,-а or -о. The declension of such adjectives is seen as the regular one for the purposes of this dictionary. Thus, adjectives such as стáрый decline as follows:

	m	*f*	*nt*	*pl*
Nom	стáр|ый	стáр|ая	стáр|ое	стáр|ые
Acc	~ый/~ого	~ую	~ое	~ые/~ых
Gen	~ого	~ой	~ого	~ых
Dat	~ому	~ой	~ому	~ым
Instr	~ым	~ой	~ым	~ыми
Prp	о ~ом	о ~ой	о ~ом	о ~ых

(NB. The alternative forms of the accusative are animate and identical with the genitive. The feminine instrumental ending -ою also exists)

End-stressed adjectives with hard endings, eg. живóй, decline similarly, with the only difference being the masculine nominative singular and inanimate accusative singular, where the ending -óй replaces -ый. Alternative endings are determined by Russian spelling rules, according to which и replaces ы after г,к,х,ж,ч,ш,щ, and е replaces an unstressed о after ж,ч,ш,щ and ц. Thus, a stem-stressed adjective such as глáдкий declines as follows:

	m	*f*	*nt*	*pl*
Nom	гла́дк|ий	гла́дк|ая	гла́дк|ое	гла́дк|ие
Acc	~ий/~ого	~ую	~ое	~ие/~их
Gen	~ого	~ой	~ого	~их
Dat	~ому	~ой	~ому	~им
Instr	~им	~ой	~им	~ими
Prp	о ~ом	о ~ой	о ~ом	о ~их

(NB. The alternative forms of the accusative are animate and identical with the genitive. Th feminine instrumental ending -ою also exists)

End-stressed adjectives such as большо́й decline similarly, with only the masculin nominative and inanimate accusative singular differing in that they have the ending -о́ instead of -ий. In stem-stressed adjectives such as хоро́ший, however, the declensions ar as follows:

	m	*f*	*nt*	*pl*
Nom	хоро́ш|ий	хоро́ш|ая	хоро́ш|ее	хоро́ш|ие
Acc	~ий/~его	~ую	~ее	~ие/~их
Gen	~его	~ей	~его	~их
Dat	~ему	~ей	~ему	~им
Instr	~им	~ей	~им	~ими
Prp	о ~ем	о ~ей	о ~ем	о ~их

(NB. The alternative forms of the accusative are animate and identical with the genitive. Th feminine instrumental ending -ею also exists)

Soft-ending adjectives, ie. those ending in -ний, decline differently again. Thus, adjective such as осе́нний or сосе́дний decline as follows:

	m	*f*	*nt*	*pl*
Nom	осе́нн|ий	осе́нн|яя	осе́нн|ее	осе́нн|ие
Acc	~ий/~его	~юю	~ее	~ие/~их
Gen	~его	~ей	~его	~их
Dat	~ему	~ей	~ему	~им
Instr	~им	~ей	~им	~ими
Prp	о ~ем	о ~ей	о ~ем	о ~их

(NB. The alternative forms of the accusative are animate and, therefore, identical with th genitive. The feminine instrumental ending -ею also exists)

1.1 Possessive adjectives

These follow one of two declension patterns. Possessive adjectives like соба́чий an де́вичий decline as follows:

	m	*f*	*nt*	*pl*
Nom	соба́ч|ий	соба́ч|ья	соба́ч|ье	соба́ч|ьи
Acc	~ий/~ьего	~ью	~ье	~ьи/~ьих
Gen	~ьего	~ьей	~ьего	~ьих
Dat	~ьему	~ьей	~ьему	~ьим
Instr	~ьим	~ьей	~ьим	~ьими
Prp	о ~ьем	о ~ьей	о ~ьем	о ~ьих

(NB. The alternative forms of the accusative are animate and identical with the genitive. Th feminine instrumental ending -ьею also exists. The ordinal numeral трéтий declines according to the above table)

In addition, there are those possessive adjectives formed by adding the suffixes -ин,-нин or -ов to the stems of nouns. This form is mainly used with reference to particular family members, eg. мáмин, мýжнин, дéдов, but can also be derived from the familiar forms of first names, eg. Лéнин, Сáшин. These decline as follows:

	m	*f*	*nt*	*pl*
Nom	Сáшин	Сáшин|а	Сáшин|о	Сáшин|ы
Acc	~/~ого	~у	~о	~ы/~ых
Gen	~ого	~ой	~ого	~ых
Dat	~у	~ой	~у	~ым
Instr	~ым	~ой	~ым	~ыми
Prp	о ~ом	о ~ой	о ~ом	о ~ых

(NB. The alternative forms of the accusative are animate and identical with the genitive. The feminine instrumental ending -ою also exists)

Note that the animate accusative/genitive rule which affects nouns also applies to long adjectives.

1.2 Usage

Long adjectives are typically used attributively, for example:

на ýлице стои́т **бéлая** маши́на "a white car is parked on the street"

or showing the use of the accusative case:

он вóдит **бéлую** маши́ну "he drives a white car"

Long adjectives may be used predicatively when they denote characteristics inherent to the nouns they refer to.

э́та ýлица – **дли́нная** "this street is long"
э́тот груз – **тяжёлый** "this load is heavy"

2 Short adjectives

Short adjectives can be derived from most long adjectives. They are formed by replacing the long-form endings with contracted ones eg. **вéжливый**. This declines as follows:

	Long Form	*Short Form*
m	вéжлив|ый	вéжлив
f	~ая	~а
nt	~ое	~о
pl	~ые	~ы

The masculine short form of many adjectives requires a buffer vowel (е,о or ё) to be inserted between the last two consonants or to replace a soft sign. Thus, вáжный has masculine short form вáжен, ви́дный has ви́ден, лёгкий лёгок, ýмный умён etc. Masculine short forms of adjectives ending in -енный (ie. unstressed) generally have -ен endings, whereas those in -éнный (ie. stressed) are replaced by the short form -éнен.

Short-form adjectives have either fixed stem stress, eg. вéжлив, вéжлива, вéжливо, вéжливы, end stress in feminine, neuter and plural, eg. хорóш, хорошá, хорошó, хороши́, end stress in the feminine, eg. жив, жива́, жи́во, жи́вы, or end stress in the feminine and plural, eg. ви́ден, видна́, ви́дно, видны́.

2.1 Usage

In contrast to the predicative use of long adjectives, the short form on the whole is used when talking about a temporary state. For example, он **плох** "he is poorly" contrasts with он плохо́й "he is bad".

3 VERBS

1 Conjugation

Russian verbs can be divided into two groups, according to their endings when conjugated. The two groups are often referred to as "first-conjugation" and "second-conjugation" verbs and the following examples – one from either group – show the pattern of ending encountered in the present-tense conjugations of verbs from each group:

	1st Conjugation	*2nd Conjugation*
	рабо́тать	говори́ть
я	рабо́таю	говорю́
ты	рабо́таешь	говори́шь
он/она́	рабо́тает	говори́т
мы	рабо́таем	говори́м
вы	рабо́таете	говори́те
они́	рабо́тают	говоря́т

1.1 First-conjugation verbs

These include verbs with infinitive endings in -ать (eg. рабо́тать: see above), in -ять (eg. стреля́ть: стреля́ю,стреля́ешь etc), in -овать/-евать (eg. интересова́ть: интересу́ю,интересу́ешь etc), in -уть (eg. махну́ть: махну́,махнёшь etc), in -авать (eg. узнава́ть: узнаю́,узнаёшь etc), in -ыть (eg. мыть: мо́ю,мо́ешь etc), and in -зть,-оть,-сть and -ти, as well as monosyllabic verbs in -ить (eg. шить: шью,шьёшь etc). Note how under stress е is replaced by ё.

Many first-conjugation verbs – generally those with end-stressed infinitives – undergo consonant mutation in conjugation, which is frequently accompanied by a stress shift from the end to the stem after the first person singular; this is the general pattern for stress changes within the conjugation of first-conjugation verbs. For example:

	писа́ть	иска́ть
я	пишу́	ищу́
ты	пи́шешь	и́щешь
он/она́	пи́шет	и́щет
мы	пи́шем	и́щем
вы	пи́шете	и́щете
они́	пи́шут	и́щут

Stress change does not occur in first-conjugation verbs where the stress falls on the stem of the infinitive, eg. пла́кать: пла́чу, пла́чешь etc, and дви́гать: дви́жу,дви́жешь etc.

1.2 Second-conjugation verbs

These include most verbs with infinitive endings in -ить (the main exception being the monosyllabic ones), many verbs in -еть, some in -ать and two in -ять (боя́ться and стоя́ть).

Note that у replaces ю and а replaces я after ж,ч,ш, or щ. Thus, смотре́ть conjugates: смотрю́,смо́тришь,...смо́трят, whereas слы́шать conjugates: слы́шу,слы́шишь,...слы́шат.

As with first-conjugation verbs, stress change in second-conjugation verbs that are end-stressed in the infinitive is often accompanied by a consonant change in conjunction, eg. плати́ть: плачу́,пла́тишь,...пла́тят and суди́ть: сужу́,су́дишь,...су́дят. However, this mutation applies consistently only to the first person singular of second-conjugation verbs in -ить and -еть. Furthermore, the addition of л in the first person singular of verbs with the stem ending in п, б, в, ф and м is a salient feature of the second conjugation, eg. люби́ть: люблю́,лю́бишь,...лю́бят and корми́ть: кормлю́, ко́рмишь,...ко́рмят. In fact, a consonant change of one form or other, in the first person singular, is found in all second conjugation verbs in -ить whose stems end in -б,-в,-д,-з,-с,-т and -ф, and those in -еть and -ить whose stems end in -м,-п, and -ст.

2 Past Tense

The past tense for most Russian verbs, including all those with infinitive endings in -сть and -ть, is formed by replacing the infinitive ending by -л,-ла,-ло,-ли, giving the masculine, feminine, neuter and plural forms respectively.

For example:

infinitive	*past tense*
молча́ть	он молча́л
	она́ молча́ла
	оно́ молча́ло
	они́ молча́ли
укра́сть	он укра́л
	она́ укра́ла
	оно́ укра́ло
	они́ укра́ли
звони́ть	он звони́л
	она́ звони́ла
	оно́ звони́ло
	они́ звони́ли

The singular past tense always reflects the gender of the subject, so that even after the personal pronouns я and ты the gender is always marked, eg. я сказа́л (masculine subject)
я сказа́ла (feminine subject)

Verbs with infinitives ending in -ереть,-зть,-чь, and many in -ти have no -л in the masculine past tense, eg. умере́ть (у́мер,умерла́), лезть (лез,ле́зла), мочь (мог,могла́), нести́ (нёс,несла́). This is also the case with some verbs in -нуть, привы́кнуть (привы́к, привы́кла).

The verb быть, while not used in the present tense, is encountered frequently in the past tense:

был, была́, бы́ло, бы́ли

Note the stress changes when used in the negative, ie. preceded by **не**:

не́ был, не была́, не́ было, не́ были

3 Imperative Mood

The imperative mood has two forms – the familiar and the formal - which are used in accordance with the mode of address (ie. the familiar **ты** or the formal **Вы**) appropriate in any given situation. The formal imperative is obtained by simply adding **-те** to the end of the familiar form. The familiar imperative is formed by replacing the third person plural ending of a verb by **-й** where it is directly preceded by a vowel, eg.:

де́лать (*infin*) » **де́лают** (*3rd person pl*) » **де́лай(те)** (*imperative*)

similarly:

чита́ть » чита́ют » чита́й(те)

Alternatively, **-и(те)** replaces the third person plural ending where this is directly preceded by a consonant and the verb has mobile or end stress in conjunction, eg.:

подчеркну́ть » подчеркну́т » подчеркни́(те)
держа́ть » де́ржат » держи́(те)

The imperative ending **-ь(те)** replaces the third person plural ending where this is directly preceded by no more than one consonant and the verb has fixed stem stress in conjugation. eg.:

поста́вить » поста́вят » поста́вь(те)
оде́ть » оде́нут » оде́нь(те)

Note: stress in imperative forms is identical to that of the first person singular.

- **дава́|ть** and its compounds have imperative **-й(те)**.
- **пить** has imperative **пей(те)** (compare **петь** which has imperative **по́й(те)**). **бить**, **вить**, **лить** and **шить** also form the imperative like **пить**.
- the imperative of **быть** is **бу́дь(те)**.

4 Aspect

The majority of Russian verbs have two verb aspects, the **imperfective** for conveying the **frequency** of an action or describing a **process**, and the **perfective** for emphasis on a **single action** or a **result**. It follows that the perfective can only be used in the past and future, while the imperfective can also be used in the present tense.

Aspectual pairs can be differentiated either by the presence of a prefix in the perfective aspect, eg. **сде́лать** (cf imperfective **де́лать**), by the presence of a suffix in the imperfective aspect, eg. **пока́зывать** (cf perfective **показа́ть**), or by a change in conjugation, eg. perfective **ко́нчить** (2nd conjugation) and its imperfective counterpart **конча́ть** (1st conjugation).

It should be noted, though, that some aspectual pairs do not follow this pattern, for instance those that derive from different roots, eg. **говори́ть** (*impf*)/**сказа́ть** (*perf*), **брать** (*impf*)/**взять** (*perf*). Then there are a minority of verbs which exist in one aspect only, eg. **сто́ить** (*impf*), while some verbs incorporate the two aspects in one form, eg. **иссле́довать** (*impf/perf*).

Aspect also has a bearing on the use of the imperative mood, where, generally speaking, the perfective aspect is used in positive commands (ie. telling someone to do something), while the imperfective is used in negative commands (ie. telling someone not to do something), in other words where the imperative form is preceded by "не".

~ A, a ~

A, a [eɪ] *n* (*letter*) *1-ая бу́ква англи́йского алфави́та*; (*SCOL*: *mark*) ≈ отли́чно; **~ road** (*BRIT*: *AUT*) шоссе́ *nt ind* (пе́рвой катего́рии); **~ shares** (*BRIT*: *STOCK EXCHANGE*) а́кции *fpl* с ограни́ченным пра́вом го́лоса; **from ~ to Z** от "а" до "я".

A [eɪ] *n* (*MUS*) ля *nt ind*.

KEYWORD

a [eɪ] (*before vowel or silent h* **an**) *indef art*: **1**: **a book** кни́га; **an apple** я́блоко; **she's a student** она́ студе́нтка

2 (*instead of the number "one"*): **a week ago** неде́лю наза́д; **a hundred/thousand** *etc* **pounds** сто/ты́сяча *etc* фу́нтов

3 (*in expressing time*) в *+acc*; **3 a day/week** 3 в день/неде́лю; **10 km an hour** 10 км в час

4 (*in expressing prices*): **30p a kilo** 30 пе́нсов килогра́мм; **£5 a person** с ка́ждого 5 фу́нтов.

a. *abbr* = **acre**.

AA *n abbr* (*BRIT*: = *Automobile Association*) Автомоби́льная ассоциа́ция; (*US*: = *Associate in/of Arts*) член ассоциа́ции рабо́тников иску́сства; (= *Alcoholics Anonymous*) *о́бщество анони́много излече́ния от алкоголи́зма*; (= *anti-aircraft*) противовозду́шный.

AAA *n abbr* (= *American Automobile Association*) Америка́нская автомоби́льная ассоциа́ция; (*BRIT*: = *Amateur Athletics Association*) Люби́тельская ассоциа́ция лёгкой атле́тики.

A & R *n abbr* (*MUS*: = *artists and repertoire*) исполни́тели и репертуа́р.

AAUP *n abbr* = *American Association of University Professors.*

AB *abbr* (*BRIT*) = **able-bodied seaman**; (*CANADA*) = *Alberta.*

abaci ['æbəsaɪ] *npl of* **abacus**.

aback [ə'bæk] *adv*: **I was taken ~** я был поражён.

abacus ['æbəkəs] (*pl* **abaci**) *n* счёты *pl.*

abandon [ə'bændən] *vt* (*person*) покида́ть (поки́нуть *perf*); (*car*) броса́ть (бро́сить* *perf*); (*search, research*) прекраща́ть (прекрати́ть* *perf*); (*idea, hope*) отка́зываться (отказа́ться* *perf*) от *+gen* ◆ *n* (*wild behaviour*): **with ~** самозабве́нно; **to ~ ship** покида́ть (поки́нуть *perf*) кора́бль.

abandoned [ə'bændənd] *adj* поки́нутый; (*unrestrained*) безу́держный.

abase [ə'beɪs] *vt*: **to ~ o.s. (before)** унижа́ться (уни́зиться* *perf*) (пе́ред *+instr*).

abashed [ə'bæʃt] *adj* смущённый* (смущён).

abate [ə'beɪt] *vi* (*storm*) утиха́ть (ути́хнуть* *perf*); (*anger, terror*) ослабева́ть (ослабе́ть *perf*).

abatement [ə'beɪtmənt] *n*: **noise ~** сниже́ние у́ровня шу́ма.

abattoir ['æbətwɑ:'] *n* (*BRIT*) скотобо́йня.

abbey ['æbɪ] *n* абба́тство.

abbot ['æbət] *n* абба́т.

abbreviate [ə'bri:vɪeɪt] *vt* (*essay, word*) сокраща́ть (сократи́ть* *perf*).

abbreviation [əbri:vɪ'eɪʃən] *n* сокраще́ние.

ABC *n abbr* = *American Broadcasting Company.*

abdicate ['æbdɪkeɪt] *vt* (*responsibility, right*) слага́ть (сложи́ть *perf*) с себя́ ◆ *vi* (*monarch*) отрека́ться (отре́чься* *perf*) от престо́ла.

abdication [æbdɪ'keɪʃən] *n* (*see vb*) скла́дывание; отрече́ние от престо́ла.

abdomen ['æbdəmɛn] *n* брюшна́я по́лость *f*, живо́т.

abdominal [æb'dɔmɪnl] *adj* брюшно́й; **~ pain** бо́ли *fpl* в брюшно́й по́лости *or* в животе́.

abduct [æb'dʌkt] *vt* похища́ть (похи́тить* *perf*).

abduction [æb'dʌkʃən] *n* похище́ние.

Aberdeen [æbə'di:n] *n* Аберди́н.

Aberdonian [æbə'dəunɪən] *adj* аберди́нский ◆ *n* аберди́нец(-нка).

aberration [æbə'reɪʃən] *n* аберра́ция, отклоне́ние (от но́рмы); **in a moment of mental ~** в мину́ту помраче́ния рассу́дка.

abet [ə'bɛt] *vt see* **aid**.

abeyance [ə'beɪəns] *n*: **in ~** приостано́вленный (приостано́влен).

abhor [əb'hɔ:'] *vt* испы́тывать (*impf*) отвраще́ние к *+dat*.

abhorrent [əb'hɔrənt] *adj* отврати́тельный* (отврати́телен).

abide [ə'baɪd] *vt*: **I can't ~ it/him** я э́того/его́ не выношу́

* marks translations which have irregular inflections. The Russian-English side of the dictionary gives inflectional information.

▸ **abide by** *vt fus* (*law, decision*) соблюда́ть (соблюсти́* *perf*).
abiding [ə'baɪdɪŋ] *adj* неослабева́ющий.
ability [ə'bɪlɪtɪ] *n* (*capacity*) спосо́бность *f*; (*talent, skill*) спосо́бности *fpl*; **to the best of my ~** в ме́ру мои́х спосо́бностей.
abject ['æbdʒɛkt] *adj* (*poverty, coward*) жа́лкий*; (*apology*) уни́женный*.
ablaze [ə'bleɪz] *adj* (*building etc*) в огне́; **the city was ~ with light** го́род был за́лит огня́ми.
able ['eɪbl] *adj* (*capable*) спосо́бный* (спосо́бен); (*skilled*) уме́лый (уме́л); **he is/was ~ to ...** он спосо́бен/был спосо́бен *+infin* ....
able-bodied ['eɪbl'bɔdɪd] *adj* (*person*) кре́пкий*; **~ seaman** (*BRIT*) матро́с пе́рвого кла́сса.
ablutions [ə'blu:ʃənz] *npl* омове́ние *ntsg*.
ably ['eɪblɪ] *adv* (*skilfully*) уме́ло.
ABM *n abbr* (= *anti-ballistic missile*) ≈ ЗУРС= *зени́тный управля́емый реакти́вный снаря́д.*
abnormal [æb'nɔ:ml] *adj* ненорма́льный* (ненорма́лен).
abnormality [æbnɔ:'mælɪtɪ] *n* ненорма́льность *f*, анома́лия.
aboard [ə'bɔ:d] *prep* (*position*: *NAUT, AVIAT*) на борту́ *+gen*; (: *train, bus*) в *+prp*; (*motion*: *NAUT, AVIAT*) на борт *+gen*; (: *train, bus*) в *+acc* ◆ *adv*: **to climb ~** (*ship*) сади́ться (сесть* *perf*) на кора́бль; (*train*) сади́ться (сесть* *perf*) в/на по́езд.
abode [ə'bəud] *n* (*LAW*): **of no fixed ~** без постоя́нного местожи́тельства.
abolish [ə'bɔlɪʃ] *vt* отменя́ть (отмени́ть* *perf*).
abolition [æbə'lɪʃən] *n* отме́на.
abominable [ə'bɔmɪnəbl] *adj* отврати́тельный* (отврати́телен).
abominably [ə'bɔmɪnəblɪ] *adv* отврати́тельно.
aborigine [æbə'rɪdʒɪnɪ] *n* абориге́н(ка).
abort [ə'bɔ:t] *vt* (*plan, activity*) прекраща́ть (прекрати́ть* *perf*); (*COMPUT*) прерыва́ть (прерва́ть* *perf*); (*MED*): **to ~ a baby** де́лать (сде́лать *perf*) або́рт.
abortion [ə'bɔ:ʃən] *n* (*MED*) або́рт; **to have an ~** де́лать (сде́лать *perf*) або́рт.
abortionist [ə'bɔ:ʃənɪst] *n* *челове́к, де́лающий подпо́льные або́рты.*
abortive [ə'bɔ:tɪv] *adj* неуда́чный* (неуда́чен).
abound [ə'baund] *vi* быть* (*impf*) в изоби́лии; **to ~ in** *or* **with** изоби́ловать (*impf*) *+instr*.

KEYWORD

about [ə'baut] *adv* **1** (*approximately*: *referring to time, price etc*) приблизи́тельно *+acc*, приме́рно *+acc*, о́коло *+gen*; **it will take me about 3 hours** э́то займёт у меня́ приме́рно *or* приблизи́тельно 3 часа́; **at about 2 (o'clock)** приблизи́тельно *or* приме́рно в 2 (часа́), часа́ в 2, о́коло двух (часо́в); **I've just about finished** я почти́ зако́нчил
2 (*approximately*: *referring to height, size etc*) приме́рно *+nom*, приблизи́тельно *+nom*; **the room is about 10 metres wide** ко́мната приме́рно *or* приблизи́тельно 10 ме́тров в ширину́; **she is about your height/age** она́ приме́рно *or* приблизи́тельно Ва́шего ро́ста/во́зраста
3 (*referring to place*) повсю́ду; **to leave things lying about** разбра́сывать (разброса́ть *perf*) ве́щи повсю́ду; **to run/walk** *etc* **about** бе́гать (*impf*)/ходи́ть* (*impf*) *etc*
4: **to be about to do** собира́ться (собра́ться* *perf*) *+infin*; **he was about to go to bed** он собра́лся лечь спать
◆ *prep* **1** (*relating to*) о(б) *+prp*; **a book about London** кни́га о Ло́ндоне; **what is it about?** о чём э́то?; **we talked about it** мы говори́ли *or* разгова́ривали об э́том; **what** *or* **how about doing this?** как насчёт того́, что́бы *+infin*?
2 (*referring to place*) по *+dat*; **to walk about the town** ходи́ть* (*impf*) по го́роду; **her clothes were scattered about the room** её оде́жда была́ разбро́сана по ко́мнате.

about-face [ə'baut'feɪs] *n* (*MIL*) поворо́т круго́м; (*fig*) поворо́т на 180 гра́дусов.
about-turn [ə'baut'tə:n] *n* = **about-face**.
above [ə'bʌv] *adv* (*higher up*) наверху́; (*greater, more*) вы́ше, свы́ше ◆ *prep* (*higher than*) над *+instr*; (: *in rank etc*) вы́ше *+gen*; (: *in number*) свы́ше *+gen*, бо́лее *+gen*; **from ~** све́рху; **costing ~ £10** сто́ящий свы́ше £10; **~ the knees** вы́ше коле́н; **mentioned ~** вышеупомя́нутый; **he's not ~ a bit of blackmail** он не погнуша́ется шантажо́м; **~ suspicion/criticism** вне подозре́ния/кри́тики; **~ all** пре́жде всего́.
above board *adj* че́стный* (че́стен), откры́тый (откры́т).
abrasion [ə'breɪʒən] *n* тре́ние; (*on skin*) ссади́на.
abrasive [ə'breɪzɪv] *adj* (*substance*) абрази́вный; (*manner*) жёсткий* (жёсток).
abreast [ə'brɛst] *adv* (*people, vehicles*) в ряд; **three ~** по́ трое в ряд; **to keep ~ of** (*fig*) быть* (*impf*) в ку́рсе *+gen*.
abridge [ə'brɪdʒ] *vt* (*novel, play*) сокраща́ть (сократи́ть* *perf*).
abroad [ə'brɔ:d] *adv* (*to be*) за грани́цей *or* рубежо́м; (*to go*) за грани́цу *or* рубе́ж; (*from abroad*) из-за грани́цы *or* рубежа́; **there is a rumour ~ that ...** (*fig*) хо́дит слух, что ....
abrupt [ə'brʌpt] *adj* (*action, ending etc*) внеза́пный* (внеза́пен); (*person, manner*) ре́зкий* (ре́зок).
abruptly [ə'brʌptlɪ] *adv* (*leave, end*) внеза́пно; (*speak*) ре́зко.
abscess ['æbsɪs] *n* абсце́сс.
abscond [əb'skɔnd] *vi* (*thief*): **to ~ with** скрыва́ться (скры́ться* *perf*) с *+instr*; (*prisoner*): **to ~ (from)** сбега́ть (сбежа́ть* *perf*) (из *+gen*).
abseil ['æbseɪl] *vi* спуска́ться (спусти́ться* *perf*) при по́мощи кана́та.
absence ['æbsəns] *n* (*of person, thing*)

отсу́тствие; **in the ~ of** (*person*) в отсу́тствие *+gen*; (*thing*) при отсу́тствии *+gen*; **~ without leave** (*MIL*) самово́льная отлу́чка.

absent [*adj* 'æbsənt, *vb* æb'sɛnt] *adj* отсу́тствующий* ◆ *vt*: **to ~ o.s.** отлуча́ться (отлучи́ться *perf*).

absentee [æbsən'ti:] *n* отсу́тствующий*(-ая) *m(f) adj*.

absenteeism [æbsən'ti:ɪzəm] *n* прогу́лы *mpl*.

absent-minded ['æbsənt'maɪndɪd] *adj* рассе́янный* (рассе́ян).

absent-mindedly ['æbsənt'maɪndɪdlɪ] *adv* рассе́янно.

absent-mindedness ['æbsənt'maɪndɪdnɪs] *n* рассе́янность *f*.

absolute ['æbsəlu:t] *adj* абсолю́тный*.

absolutely [æbsə'lu:tlɪ] *adv* (*totally*) абсолю́тно, соверше́нно; (*certainly*) безусло́вно.

absolute monopoly *n* абсолю́тная монопо́лия.

absolution [æbsə'lu:ʃən] *n* (*REL*) отпуще́ние грехо́в.

absolve [əb'zɔlv] *vt*: **to ~ sb (from sth)** отпуска́ть (отпусти́ть* *perf*) кому́-н (что-н).

absorb [əb'zɔ:b] *vt* (*liquid, information*) впи́тывать (впита́ть *perf*); (*light, business*) поглоща́ть (поглоти́ть* *perf*); (*changes, effects*) воспринима́ть (восприня́ть* *perf*); **he is ~ed in a book** он поглощён кни́гой.

absorbent [əb'zɔ:bənt] *adj* гигроскопи́чный.

absorbent cotton *n* (*US*) гигроскопи́ческая ва́та.

absorbing [əb'zɔ:bɪŋ] *adj* (*book, film etc*) увлека́тельный* (увлека́телен).

absorption [əb'sɔ:pʃən] *n* (*see vt*) впи́тывание; поглоще́ние; восприя́тие; (*interest*) увлечённость *f*.

abstain [əb'steɪn] *vi*: **to ~ (from)** возде́рживаться (воздержа́ться* *perf*) (от *+gen*).

abstemious [əb'sti:mɪəs] *adj* (*person*) возде́ржанный* (возде́ржан).

abstention [əb'stɛnʃən] *n* (*refusal to vote*) неуча́стие в голосова́нии.

abstinence ['æbstɪnəns] *n* воздержа́ние.

abstract [*adj, n* 'æbstrækt, *vb* æb'strækt] *adj* абстра́ктный*; (*idea, quality*) отвлечённый ◆ *n* (*summary*) аннота́ция; (*of dissertation*) рефера́т ◆ *vt* (*remove*) извлека́ть (извле́чь* *perf*); (*summarize*) анноти́ровать (проанноти́ровать *perf*).

abstruse [æb'stru:s] *adj* замыслова́тый.

absurd [əb'sə:d] *adj* абсу́рдный* (абсу́рден), неле́пый (неле́п).

absurdity [əb'sə:dɪtɪ] *n* абсу́рдность *f*, неле́пость *f*.

ABTA ['æbtə] *n abbr* = *Association of British Travel Agents.*

Abu Dhabi ['æbu:'dɑ:bɪ] *n* Абу́-Да́би.

abundance [ə'bʌndəns] *n* изоби́лие; **in ~** в изоби́лии.

abundant [ə'bʌndənt] *adj* изоби́льный* (изоби́лен).

abundantly [ə'bʌndəntlɪ] *adv* в изоби́лии; **~ clear/obvious** соверше́нно я́сно/очеви́дно.

abuse [*n* ə'bju:s, *vb* ə'bju:z] *n* (*insults*) брань *f*; (*ill-treatment*) жесто́кое обраще́ние; (*misuse: of power, drugs etc*) злоупотребле́ние ◆ *vt* (*insult*) оскорбля́ть (оскорби́ть* *perf*); (*ill-treat*) жесто́ко обраща́ться (*impf*) с *+instr*; (*misuse*) злоупотребля́ть (злоупотреби́ть* *perf*) *+instr*; **this system is open to ~** э́той систе́мой легко́ злоупотребля́ть.

abuser [ə'bju:zəʳ] *n*: **drug ~** наркома́н; **child ~** *челове́к, подверга́ющий дете́й физи́ческому и́ли сексуа́льному наси́лию.*

abusive [ə'bju:sɪv] *adj* (*person*) гру́бый (груб); **~ language** брань *f*.

abysmal [ə'bɪzməl] *adj* (*performance, failure*) плаче́вный* (плаче́вен); (*ignorance etc*) вопию́щий* (вопию́щ).

abysmally [ə'bɪzməlɪ] *adv* (*see adj*) плаче́вно; вопию́ще.

abyss [ə'bɪs] *n* про́пасть *f*.

AC *abbr* = **alternating current**; (*US*: = *athletic club*) легкоатлети́ческий клуб.

a/c *abbr* (*COMM*) = **account**; (= *account current*) теку́щий* счёт*.

academic [ækə'dɛmɪk] *adj* (*system, standards*) академи́ческий*; (*qualifications*) учёный; (*work, books*) нау́чный*; (*person, child*) интеллектуа́льный*; (*pej: issue*) академи́чный (академи́чен) ◆ *n* учёный(-ая) *m(f) adj*.

academic year *n* (*in school*) уче́бный год*; (*in higher education*) академи́ческий* год*.

academy [ə'kædəmɪ] *n* (*learned body*) акаде́мия; (*school*) учи́лище; (: *in Scotland*) сре́дняя шко́ла; **~ of music** консервато́рия; **military/naval ~** вое́нная/вое́нно-морска́я акаде́мия.

ACAS ['eɪkæs] *n abbr* (*BRIT*: = *Advisory, Conciliation and Arbitration Service*) *слу́жба юриди́ческих консульта́ций и арбитра́жа.*

accede [æk'si:d] *vi*: **to ~ to** (*request*) удовлетворя́ть (удовлетвори́ть *perf*); (*opinion, contention*) соглаша́ться (согласи́ться* *perf*) с *+instr*.

accelerate [æk'sɛləreɪt] *vt* (*process*) ускоря́ть (уско́рить *perf*) ◆ *vi* (*AUT*) разгоня́ться (разогна́ться *perf*).

acceleration [æksɛlə'reɪʃən] *n* (*see vb*) ускоре́ние; разго́н.

accelerator [æk'sɛləreɪtəʳ] *n* акселера́тор.

accent ['æksɛnt] *n* акце́нт; (*stress mark*) знак

* marks translations which have irregular inflections. The Russian-English side of the dictionary gives inflectional information.

ударе́ния; **to speak with an Irish ~** говори́ть *(impf)* с ирла́ндским акце́нтом; **to have a strong ~** име́ть *(impf)* си́льный акце́нт.
accented [æk'sɛntɪd] *adj* с акце́нтом; **heavily ~** с си́льным акце́нтом.
accentuate [æk'sɛntjueɪt] *vt* (*syllable*) акценти́ровать *(impf/perf)*, проставля́ть (проста́вить *perf*) ударе́ние на *+acc*; (*need, difference*) подчёркивать (подчеркну́ть *perf*).
accept [ək'sɛpt] *vt* (*gift, proposal etc*) принима́ть (приня́ть* *perf*); (*fact, situation, risk*) мири́ться (примири́ться *perf*) с *+instr*; (*responsibility, blame*) принима́ть (приня́ть* *perf*) на себя́.
acceptable [ək'sɛptəbl] *adj* прие́млемый (прие́млем).
acceptance [ək'sɛptəns] *n* (*of gift, offer etc*) приня́тие; (*of fact, situation*) прия́тие; **to meet with general ~** находи́ть* (найти́* *perf*) всео́бщее одобре́ние.
access ['æksɛs] *n* до́ступ ◆ *vt* (*COMPUT*) испо́льзовать *(impf/perf)* до́ступ к *+dat*; (*: data*) обраща́ться (обрати́ться* *perf*) к *+dat*; **to have ~ to** (*child*) име́ть *(impf)* возмо́жность обще́ния с *+instr*; **the burglars gained ~ through a window** взло́мщики прони́кли че́рез окно́.
accessible [æk'sɛsəbl] *adj* досту́пный* (досту́пен).
accession [æk'sɛʃən] *n* прихо́д к вла́сти; (*of king*) вступле́ние на престо́л; (*to library*) поступле́ние.
accessory [æk'sɛsərɪ] *n* (*COMM, TECH, AUT*) принадле́жность *f*; (*LAW*): **~ to** соуча́стник(-ица) *+gen*; **accessories** *npl* (*DRESS*) аксессуа́ры *mpl*; **toilet accessories** (*BRIT*) туале́тные принадле́жности *fpl*.
access road *n* подъездно́й путь* *m*.
access time *n* (*COMPUT*) вре́мя* *nt* до́ступа.
accident ['æksɪdənt] *n* (*chance event*) случа́йность *f*; (*mishap, disaster*) несча́стный слу́чай, ава́рия; **to meet with** *or* **to have an ~** попада́ть (попа́сть *perf*) в ава́рию *or* катастро́фу; **he had an ~** с ним произошёл несча́стный слу́чай; **by ~** (*unintentionally*) неча́янно; (*by chance*) случа́йно.
accidental [æksɪ'dɛntl] *adj* случа́йный* (случа́ен).
accidentally [æksɪ'dɛntəlɪ] *adv* случа́йно, неча́янно.
accident insurance *n* страхова́ние от несча́стных слу́чаев.
accident-prone ['æksɪdənt'prəun] *adj* невезу́чий; **he is ~** его́ пресле́дуют несча́стья.
acclaim [ə'kleɪm] *n* призна́ние ◆ *vt*: **he was ~ed for his achievements** он получи́л призна́ние за свои́ достиже́ния.
acclamation [æklə'meɪʃən] *n* (*approval*) бу́рное *or* шу́мное одобре́ние; (*applause*) бу́рные аплодисме́нты *mpl*.
acclimate [ə'klaɪmət] *vt* (*US*) = **acclimatize**.
acclimatize [ə'klaɪmətaɪz] (*US* **acclimate**) *vt*: **to become ~d (to)** (*surroundings*) акклиматизи́роваться *(impf/perf)* (в *+prp*), осва́иваться (осво́иться *perf*) (в *+prp*); (*heat, cold*) привыка́ть (привы́кнуть* *perf*) (к *+dat*).
accolade ['ækəleɪd] *n* по́честь *f*.
accommodate [ə'kɔmədeɪt] *vt* (*subj: person*) предоставля́ть (предоста́вить* *perf*) жильё *+dat*; (*: car, hotel etc*) вмеща́ть (вмести́ть* *perf*); (*oblige, help*) ока́зывать (оказа́ть* *perf*) услу́гу *+dat*; **to ~ one's plans to** приспоса́бливать (приспосо́бить* *perf*) свои́ пла́ны к *+dat*.
accommodating [ə'kɔmədeɪtɪŋ] *adj* услу́жливый (услу́жлив).
accommodation [əkɔmə'deɪʃən] *n* (*to live in*) жильё; (*to work in*) помеще́ние; **~s** *npl* (*US: lodgings*) жильё *ntsg*; **"accommodation to let"** (*living*) "сдаётся жильё"; (*office*) "сдаётся помеще́ние"; **they have ~ for 500** они́ мо́гут размести́ть 500 челове́к; **the hall has seating ~ for 600** (*BRIT*) зал расчи́тан на 600 мест; **do you have any ~?** (*for yourself*) Вам есть где жить?; (*for me*) Вы предоставля́ете жильё?
accompaniment [ə'kʌmpənɪmənt] *n* сопровожде́ние; (*MUS*) аккомпанеме́нт.
accompanist [ə'kʌmpənɪst] *n* аккомпаниа́тор.
accompany [ə'kʌmpənɪ] *vt* (*escort, go along with*) сопровожда́ть (сопроводи́ть* *perf*); (*MUS*) аккомпани́ровать *(impf)* *+dat*.
accomplice [ə'kʌmplɪs] *n* соуча́стник(-ица), со́общник(-ица).
accomplish [ə'kʌmplɪʃ] *vt* (*task*) заверша́ть (заверши́ть *perf*); (*goal*) достига́ть (дости́гнуть* *or* дости́чь* *perf*) *+gen*.
accomplished [ə'kʌmplɪʃt] *adj* (*person*) тала́нтливый (тала́нтлив); (*performance*) соверше́нный* (соверше́нен).
accomplishment [ə'kʌmplɪʃmənt] *n* (*completion, bringing about*) заверше́ние; (*achievement*) достиже́ние; (*skill: usu pl*) уме́ние.
accord [ə'kɔ:d] *n* соглаше́ние ◆ *vt* ока́зывать (оказа́ть* *perf*); **of his own ~** по со́бственному жела́нию; **of its own ~** сам по себе́; **with one ~** единоду́шно; (*movement*) как по кома́нде; **he and I are in ~ on this issue** мы с ним в согла́сии на э́тот счёт *or* по э́тому по́воду.
accordance [ə'kɔ:dəns] *n*: **in ~ with** в согла́сии *or* соотве́тствии с *+instr*.
according [ə'kɔ:dɪŋ] *prep*: **~ to** согла́сно *+dat*; **~ to plan** по пла́ну.
accordingly [ə'kɔ:dɪŋlɪ] *adv* (*appropriately*) соотве́тствующим о́бразом; (*as a result*) соотве́тственно.
accordion [ə'kɔ:dɪən] *n* аккордео́н.
accost [ə'kɔst] *vt* пристава́ть* (приста́ть* *perf*) к *+dat*.
account [ə'kaunt] *n* (*bill*) счёт*; (*monthly*

account) ежемéсячныи счёт; (*in bank*) (расчётный) счёт; (*report*) отчёт; **~s** *npl* (*COMM*) счетá* *mpl*; (*books*) бухгáлтерские книги *fpl*; **"account payee only"** (*BRIT*) "подлежит уплáте тóлько на счёт получáтеля"; **to keep an ~ of** вести* *(impf)* счёт* *+gen or +dat*; **to bring sb to ~ for sth** призывáть (призвáть* *perf*) когó-н к отвéту за что-н; **by all ~s** по всем свéдениям; **of no ~** не вáжно; **on ~** в кредит; **to pay £5 on ~** платить* (заплатить* *perf*) £5 в задáток; **to buy sth on ~** покупáть (купить* *perf*) что-н в кредит; **on no ~** ни в кóем слýчае; **on ~ of** по причине *+gen*; **to take into ~, take ~ of** принимáть (принять* *perf*) в расчёт

▸ **account for** *vt fus* (*money spent, expenses*) отчитываться (отчитáться *perf*) за *+acc*; (*absence, failure*) объяснять (объяснить *perf*); (*represent*) составлять (состáвить* *perf*); **all the children were ~ed for** все дéти бы́ли на мéсте; **four people are still not ~ed for** не досчитáлись четырёх человéк.

accountability [ə'kauntə'bɪlɪtɪ] *n* отчётность *f*.

accountable [ə'kauntəbl] *adj* подотчётный* (подотчётен); **to be ~ to sb for sth** отвечáть *(impf)* за что-н пéред кем-н.

accountancy [ə'kauntənsɪ] *n* бухгалтéрия.

accountant [ə'kauntənt] *n* бухгáлтер.

account executive *n* делопроизводитель *m*.

accounting [ə'kauntɪŋ] *n* бухгáлтерское дéло*.

accounting period *n* отчётный периóд.

account number *n* (*at bank etc*) нóмер* счёта.

account payable *n* счёт кредитóров (*в балáнсе*).

account receivable *n* счёт дебитóров (*в балáнсе*).

accredited [ə'krɛdɪtɪd] *adj* (*agent etc*) аккредитóванный.

accretion [ə'kri:ʃən] *n* (*process*) нарастáние; (*layer*) нарóст.

accrue [ə'kru:] *vi* (*mount up*) нарастáть (нарасти* *perf*); **to ~ to** доставáться* (достáться* *perf*) *+dat*.

accrued charges *npl* нарóсшие процéнты *mpl*.

accrued interest *n* нарóсшие процéнты *mpl*.

accumulate [ə'kju:mjuleɪt] *vt* накáпливать (накопить* *perf*) ◆ *vi* накáпливаться (накопиться* *perf*).

accumulation [əkju:mju'leɪʃən] *n* накоплéние.

accuracy ['ækjurəsɪ] *n* тóчность *f*.

accurate ['ækjurɪt] *adj* тóчный* (тóчен); (*person, device*) аккурáтный* (аккурáтен); (*shot*) мéткий*.

accurately ['ækjurɪtlɪ] *adv* тóчно; (*shoot*) мéтко.

accusation [ækju'zeɪʃən] *n* обвинéние.

accusative [ə'kju:zətɪv] *n* (*LING*) винительный падéж*.

accuse [ə'kju:z] *vt*: **to ~ sb (of sth)** обвинять (обвинить *perf*) когó-н (в чём-н).

accused [ə'kju:zd] *n* (*LAW*): **the ~** обвиняемый(-ая) *m(f) adj*.

accuser [ə'kju:zə'] *n* обвинитель *m*.

accusing [ə'kju:zɪŋ] *adj* обвиняющий.

accustom [ə'kʌstəm] *vt* приучáть (приучить* *perf*); **to ~ o.s. to sth** приучáться (приучиться *perf*) *or* привыкáть (привы́кнуть* *perf*) к чемý-н.

accustomed [ə'kʌstəmd] *adj* (*usual*) привы́чный*; **I'm ~ to working late/to the heat** я привы́к рабóтать пóздно/к жарé.

AC/DC *abbr* (= *alternating current/direct current*) перемéнный ток/постоянный ток.

ACE [eɪs] *n abbr* = *American Council on Education*.

ace [eɪs] *n* (*CARDS*) туз; (*TENNIS*) вы́игрыш с подáчи.

acerbic [ə'sə:bɪk] *adj* (*remark*) éдкий* (éдок).

acetate ['æsɪteɪt] *n* ацетáт.

ache [eɪk] *n* боль *f* ◆ *vi* (*be painful*) болéть *(impf)*; (*yearn*): **to ~ to do** томиться* *(impf)* желáнием *+infin*; **I've got stomach ~** *or* **a stomach ~** у меня болит живóт; **I'm aching all over** у меня всё тéло нóет; **my head ~s** у меня болит головá.

achieve [ə'tʃi:v] *vt* (*aim, result*) достигáть (дости́гнуть* *or* дости́чь* *perf*) *+gen*; (*success, victory*) добивáться (добиться* *perf*) *+gen*.

achievement [ə'tʃi:vmənt] *n* достижéние.

Achilles heel [ə'kɪli:z-] *n* Ахиллéсова пятá.

acid ['æsɪd] *adj* (*CHEM*: *soil etc*) кислóтный*; (*taste*) ки́слый* ◆ *n* (*CHEM*) кислотá*; (*inf*: *DRUGS*) ЛСД (*наркóтик*).

acid house *adj* áсид хáус (*стиль поп-мýзыки*).

acidic [ə'sɪdɪk] *adj* ки́слый* (кисел).

acidity [ə'sɪdɪtɪ] *n* кислóтность *f*.

acid rain *n* кислóтный* дождь* *m*.

acid test *n* прóбный кáмень* *m*.

acknowledge [ək'nɔlɪdʒ] *vt* (*letter etc*: *also*: **~ receipt of**) подтверждáть (подтвердить* *perf*) получéние *+gen*; (*fact, situation*) признавáть* (признáть *perf*).

acknowledgement [ək'nɔlɪdʒmənt] *n* (*of letter etc*) подтверждéние получéния; **~s** *npl* (*in book*) выражéние *ntsg* благодáрности (*в предислóвии книги*).

ACLU *n abbr* = *American Civil Liberties Union*.

acme ['ækmɪ] *n* верх*, вершина.

acne ['æknɪ] *n* угри́* *mpl*, прыщи́ *mpl*.

acorn ['eɪkɔ:n] *n* жёлудь *m*.

acoustic [ə'ku:stɪk] *adj* (*guitar etc*) акустический*.

acoustic coupler *n* (*COMPUT*) акустический* соединитель *m*.

acoustics [ə'ku:stɪks] *n* (*science*) акýстика ◆ *npl* (*of hall, room*) акýстика *fsg*.

* marks translations which have irregular inflections. The Russian-English side of the dictionary gives inflectional information.

acquaint [ə'kweɪnt] *vt*: **to ~ sb with sth** (*inform*) ознакóмить* *(perf)* когó-н с чем-н; **I am/was ~ed with** (*person, fact*) я знакóм/был знакóм с *+instr*.

acquaintance [ə'kweɪntəns] *n* (*person*) знакóмый(-ая) *m(f) adj*; (*with person, subject*) знакóмство; **to make sb's ~** познакóмиться* *(perf)* с кем-н.

acquiesce [ækwɪ'ɛs] *vi*: **to ~ to** соглашáться (согласи́ться* *perf*) на *+acc*.

acquire [ə'kwaɪə'] *vt* приобретáть (приобрести́* *perf*).

acquired [ə'kwaɪəd] *adj* приобретённый; **it's an ~ taste** к э́тому нáдо привы́кнуть.

acquisition [ækwɪ'zɪʃən] *n* приобретéние.

acquisitive [ə'kwɪzɪtɪv] *adj* (*greedy*) приобретáтельский.

acquit [ə'kwɪt] *vt* (*LAW*) опрáвдывать (оправдáть *perf*); **to ~ o.s. well** хорошó проявля́ть (прояви́ть* *perf*) себя́.

acquittal [ə'kwɪtl] *n* оправдáние.

acre ['eɪkə'] *n* акр.

acreage ['eɪkərɪdʒ] *n* плóщадь* *f* в áкрах.

acrid ['ækrɪd] *adj* éдкий* (éдок).

acrimonious [ækrɪ'məunɪəs] *adj* язви́тельный* (язви́телен).

acrimony ['ækrɪmənɪ] *n* язви́тельность *f*.

acrobat ['ækrəbæt] *n* акробáт.

acrobatic [ækrə'bætɪk] *adj* (*movement, display*) акробати́ческий; (*person*) ги́бкий* (ги́бок) и лóвкий* (лóвок).

acrobatics [ækrə'bætɪks] *npl* акробáтика *fsg*.

acronym ['ækrənɪm] *n* бу́квенная аббревиату́ра.

Acropolis [ə'krɔpəlɪs] *n*: **the ~** (*GEO*) Акрóполь *m*.

across [ə'krɔs] *prep* (*from one side to the other of*) чéрез *+acc*; (*on the other side of*) на другóй сторонé *+gen*; (*crosswise over*) поперёк *+gen* ◆ *adv* на ту́ *or* другу́ю стóрону; (*measurement: width*) ширинóй; **to walk ~ the road** переходи́ть* (перейти́* *perf*) дорóгу; **to take sb ~ the road** переводи́ть* (перевести́* *perf*) когó-н чéрез дорóгу; **a road ~ the wood** дорóга чéрез лес; **the lake is 12 km ~** ширинá óзера – 12 км; **~ from** напрóтив *+gen*; **to get sth ~ (to sb)** втолкóвывать (втолковáть *perf*) что-н (комý-н).

acrylic [ə'krɪlɪk] *adj* акри́ловый ◆ *n* акри́л; **~s** *npl* (*ART*) акри́ловые крáски *fpl*.

ACT *n abbr = American College Test.*

act [ækt] *n* (*action, also LAW*) акт; (*deed*) постýпок*; (*of play*) дéйствие, акт; (*in music-hall etc*) нóмер* ◆ *vi* (*do sth, take action*) дéйствовать* *(impf)*; (*behave*) вести́* *(impf)* себя́; (*have effect*) дéйствовать (подéйствовать *perf*); (*THEAT*) игрáть (сыгрáть *perf*); (*pretend*) разы́грывать (разыгрáть *perf*) ◆ *vt* (*part*) игрáть (сыгрáть *perf*); **it's only an ~** э́то всегó лишь игрá; **~ of God** (*LAW*) стихи́йное бéдствие; **in the ~ of** в процéссе *+gen*; **to catch sb in the ~** поймáть *(perf)* когó-н на мéсте преступлéния; **to ~ as** дéйствовать* *(impf)* в кáчестве *+gen*; **it ~s as a deterrent** э́то дéйствует в кáчестве сдéрживающей си́лы; **~ing in my capacity as chairman, I ...** выступáя в кáчестве председáтеля, я ...; **to ~ the fool** (*BRIT*) валя́ть (сваля́ть *perf*) дуракá

▸ **act on** *vt*: **to ~ on sth** дéйствовать (подéйствовать *perf*) на что-н

▸ **act out** *vt* (*event*) разы́грывать (разыгрáть *perf*); (*fantasies*) выплёскивать (вы́плеснуть *perf*).

acting ['æktɪŋ] *adj*: **~ manager/director** исполня́ющий обя́занности управля́ющего/ди́ректора ◆ *n* (*activity, profession*) актёрская профéссия.

action ['ækʃən] *n* (*deed*) дéйствие; (*motion*) движéние; (*MIL*) воéнные дéйствия *ntpl*; (*LAW*) иск; **to bring an ~ against sb** (*LAW*) предъявля́ть (предъяви́ть* *perf*) иск комý-н; **he was killed in ~** (*MIL*) он был уби́т в бою́; **she/the machine was out of ~ for a week** онá/маши́на вы́шла из стрóя на недéлю; **to take ~** принимáть (приня́ть* *perf*) мéры; **to put a plan into ~** реализóвывать (реализовáть *perf*) план.

action replay *n* (*TV*) повторéние кáдра (*чáсто замéдленное*).

activate ['æktɪveɪt] *vt* (*mechanism*) приводи́ть* (привести́* *perf*) в дéйствие; (*CHEM*) активи́ровать *(impf/perf)*; (*PHYS*) дéлать (сдéлать *perf*) радиоакти́вным.

active ['æktɪv] *adj* (*person, life*) акти́вный* (акти́вен); (*volcano*) дéйствующий*; **to play an ~ part in** игрáть (сыгрáть *perf*) акти́вную роль в *+prp*.

active duty *n* (*US: MIL*) дéйствующая áрмия.

actively ['æktɪvlɪ] *adv* (*participate*) акти́вно; (*discourage, dislike*) си́льно.

active partner *n* (*COMM*) *глáвный партнёр с ограни́ченной (имýщественной) отвéтственностью.*

active service *n* (*BRIT: MIL*) дéйствующая áрмия.

active suspension *n автомати́ческая систéма амортизáции гóночного автомоби́ля, реаги́рующая на кáчество повéрхности.*

activist ['æktɪvɪst] *n* активи́ст(ка).

activity [æk'tɪvɪtɪ] *n* (*being active*) акти́вность *f*; (*action*) дéятельность *f*; (*pastime, pursuit*) заня́тие.

actor ['æktə'] *n* актёр.

actress ['æktrɪs] *n* актри́са.

actual ['æktjuəl] *adj* (*real*) действи́тельный* (действи́телен); (*emphatic use*): **the ~ work hasn't begun yet** самá рабóта ещё не начала́сь.

actually ['æktjuəlɪ] *adv* (*really*) действи́тельно; (*in fact*) факти́чески, на сáмом дéле; (*even*) да́же.

actuary [ˈæktjuərɪ] *n* (*COMM*) актуа́рий.

actuate [ˈæktjueɪt] *vt* приводи́ть* (привести́* *perf*) в де́йствие.

acuity [əˈkju:ɪtɪ] *n* острота́.

acumen [ˈækjumən] *n* сообрази́тельность *f*; **business** ~ делова́я хва́тка*.

acupuncture [ˈækjupʌŋktʃəʳ] *n* иглоука́лывание, акупункту́ра.

acute [əˈkju:t] *adj* (*illness, mind, angle*) о́стрый* (остр); (*anxiety*) си́льный*; (*person, observer*) проница́тельный* (проница́телен); (*LING*): ~ **accent** аку́т.

AD *adv abbr* (= *Anno Domini*) н.э.= *на́шей э́ры* ◆ *n abbr* (*US*: *MIL*) = **active duty**.

ad [æd] *n abbr* (*inf*) = **advertisement**.

adage [ˈædɪdʒ] *n* погово́рка*.

adamant [ˈædəmənt] *adj* непрекло́нный* (непрекло́нен).

Adam's apple [ˈædəmz-] *n* ада́мово я́блоко*, кады́к*.

adapt [əˈdæpt] *vt* (*alter, change*) приспоса́бливать (or) приспосабля́ть (приспосо́бить* *perf*) ◆ *vi*: **to ~ (to)** приспоса́бливаться *or* приспосабля́ться (приспосо́биться* *perf*) *or* адапти́роваться (*impf/perf*) (к +*dat*).

adaptability [ədæptəˈbɪlɪtɪ] *n* приспособля́емость *f*.

adaptable [əˈdæptəbl] *adj* (*device*) приспособля́емый; (*person*) легко́ приспоса́бливающийся.

adaptation [ædæpˈteɪʃən] *n* (*of story, novel etc*) переложе́ние; (*of machine, equipment etc*) приспособле́ние.

adapter [əˈdæptəʳ] *n* (*ELEC*) ада́птер, переходни́к.

adaptor [əˈdæptəʳ] *n* = **adapter**.

ADC *n abbr* (*MIL*) = *aide-de-camp*; (*US*: = *Aid to Dependent Children*) по́мощь нужда́ющимся де́тям.

add [æd] *vt* (*to a collection etc*) прибавля́ть (приба́вить* *perf*); (*comment etc*) добавля́ть (доба́вить* *perf*); (*figures*: *also*: ~ **up**) скла́дывать (сложи́ть* *perf*), сумми́ровать (*impf/perf*) ◆ *vi*: **to ~ to** (*increase*) увели́чивать (увели́чить *perf*)

▸ **add on** *vt*: ~ **on (to)** прибавля́ть (приба́вить* *perf*) (к +*dat*)

▸ **add up** *vt* скла́дывать (сложи́ть *perf*) в +*acc* ◆ *vi* (*fig*): **it doesn't ~ up** концы́ не схо́дятся; **it doesn't ~ up to much** (*fig*) э́то не впечатля́ет.

addenda [əˈdɛndə] *npl of* **addendum**.

addendum [əˈdɛndəm] (*pl* **addenda**) *n* приложе́ние.

adder [ˈædəʳ] *n* гадю́ка.

addict [ˈædɪkt] *n* (*also*: **drug ~**) наркома́н; (*enthusiast*) фана́тик.

addicted [əˈdɪktɪd] *adj*: **to be ~ to** (*drugs, drink etc*) пристрасти́ться* (*perf*) к +*dat*; (*fig*): **he's ~ to football/golf** он зая́длый люби́тель футбо́ла/го́льфа.

addiction [əˈdɪkʃən] *n* пристра́стие; **drug ~** наркома́ния.

addictive [əˈdɪktɪv] *adj* (*drug*) вызыва́ющий* привыка́ние; (*activity*) захва́тывающий*.

adding machine [ˈædɪŋ-] *n* счётная маши́на.

Addis Ababa [ˈædɪsˈæbəbə] *n* (*GEO*) Адди́с-Абе́ба *f*.

addition [əˈdɪʃən] *n* (*MATH*) сложе́ние; (*thing added*) добавле́ние; (*to collection*) пополне́ние; **in ~** вдоба́вок; **in ~ to** в дополне́ние к +*dat*.

additional [əˈdɪʃənl] *adj* дополни́тельный*.

additive [ˈædɪtɪv] *n* доба́вка*.

addled [ˈædld] *adj* (*BRIT*: *egg*) ту́хлый*; **his brain is ~** он сбит с то́лку.

address [əˈdrɛs] *n* а́дрес*; (*speech*) речь* *f* ◆ *vt* (*letter, parcel*) адресова́ть (*impf/perf*); (*person, problem*) обраща́ться (обрати́ться* *perf*) к +*dat*; **form of ~** фо́рма обраще́ния; **absolute/relative ~** (*COMPUT*) абсолю́тный/относи́тельный а́дрес; **to ~ o.s. to** обраща́ться (обрати́ться* *perf*) к +*dat*.

address book *n* записна́я кни́жка.

addressee [ædrɛˈsi:] *n* адреса́т.

Aden [ˈeɪdən] *n*: **Gulf of ~** А́денский зали́в.

adenoids [ˈædɪnɔɪdz] *npl* адено́иды *mpl*.

adept [ˈædɛpt] *adj*: **~ at** иску́сный* (иску́сен) в +*prp*.

adequacy [ˈædɪkwəsɪ] *n* (*in quantity*) доста́точность *f*; (*in quality*) адеква́тность *f*.

adequate [ˈædɪkwɪt] *adj* (*sufficient*) доста́точный (доста́точен); (*satisfactory*) удовлетвори́тельный* (удовлетвори́телен), адеква́тный* (адеква́тен).

adequately [ˈædɪkwɪtlɪ] *adv* адеква́тно.

adhere [ədˈhɪəʳ] *vi*: **to ~ to** прилипа́ть (прили́пнуть* *perf*) к +*dat*; (*fig*) приде́рживаться (*impf*) +*gen*.

adhesion [ədˈhi:ʒən] *n* прилипа́ние; (*fig*) приве́рженность *f*.

adhesive [ədˈhi:zɪv] *adj* кле́йкий* ◆ *n* клей*.

adhesive tape *n* (*BRIT*) кле́йкая ле́нта; (*US*: *MED*) лейкопла́стырь *m*.

ad hoc [ædˈhɔk] *adj* (*decision*) момента́льный; (*committee*) со́зданный на ме́сте ◆ *adv* (*decide, appoint*) тут же.

ad infinitum [ˈædɪnfɪˈnaɪtəm] *adv* до бесконе́чности.

adjacent [əˈdʒeɪsənt] *adj*: **~ (to)** сме́жный* (сме́жен) (с +*instr*).

adjective [ˈædʒɛktɪv] *n* прилага́тельное *nt adj*.

adjoining [əˈdʒɔɪnɪŋ] *adj* (*room*) сме́жный.

adjourn [əˈdʒə:n] *vt* откла́дывать (отложи́ть*

* marks translations which have irregular inflections The Russian-English side of the dictionary gives inflectional information

perf) ◆ *vi*: **the meeting ~ed** собрáние бы́ло отлóжено; **to ~ a meeting till the following week** отложи́ть* *(perf)* заседáние до слéдующей недéли; **they ~ed to the restaurant** (*BRIT*: *inf*) они́ перебрáлись в ресторáн.
adjournment [ə'dʒə:nmənt] *n* (*period*) перерь́ів.
Adjt. *abbr* (*MIL*) = **adjutant**.
adjudicate [ə'dʒu:dɪkeɪt] *vt* (*claim*) рассмáтривать (рассмотрéть* *perf*); (*competition*) суди́ть* *(impf)* ◆ *vi* суди́ть* *(impf)*.
adjudication [ədʒu:dɪ'keɪʃən] *n* (*LAW*) решéние судá.
adjudicator [ə'dju:dɪkeɪtə'] *n* судья́* *m/f*.
adjust [ə'dʒʌst] *vt* (*plans, views*) приспосáбливать (приспосóбить *perf*); (*clothing*) поправля́ть (попрáвить* *perf*); (*mechanism*) регули́ровать (отрегули́ровать *perf*) ◆ *vi*: **to ~ (to)** приспосáбливаться (приспосóбиться* *perf*) (к +*dat*).
adjustable [ə'dʒʌstəbl] *adj* регули́руемый.
adjuster [ə'dʒʌstə'] *n see* **loss**.
adjustment [ə'dʒʌstmənt] *n* (*to surroundings*) адаптáция; (*of prices, wages*) регули́рование; **to make ~s to** вноси́ть* (внести́* *perf*) изменéния в +*acc*.
adjutant ['ædʒətənt] *n* адъютáнт.
ad-lib [æd'lɪb] *vti* импровизи́ровать (сымпровизи́ровать *perf*) ◆ *adv*: **ad lib** (*speak*) экспрóмтом.
adman ['ædmæn] *irreg n* (*inf*) реклами́ст.
admin ['ædmɪn] *n abbr* (*inf*) = **administration**.
administer [əd'mɪnɪstə'] *vt* (*country, department*) управля́ть *(impf)* +*instr*, руководи́ть* *(impf)* +*instr*; (*justice*) отправля́ть *(impf)*; (*test*) проводи́ть* (провести́* *perf*); (*drug*) вводи́ть* (ввести́* *perf*).
administration [ədmɪnɪs'treɪʃən] *n* (*management*) администрáция; **the A~** (*US*) прави́тельство; **the Clinton A~** администрáция Кли́нтона.
administrative [əd'mɪnɪstrətɪv] *adj* административный.
administrator [əd'mɪnɪstreɪtə'] *n* администрáтор.
admirable ['ædmərəbl] *adj* (*quality*) восхити́тельный* (восхити́телен); (*action*) замечáтельный* (замечáтелен).
admiral ['ædmərəl] *n* адмирáл.
Admiralty ['ædmərəltɪ] *n* (*BRIT*): **the ~** (*also:* **the ~ Board**) ≈ адмиралтéйство (*воéнно-морскóе вéдомство*).
admiration [ædmə'reɪʃən] *n* восхищéние; **I have great ~ for her** онá вызывáет у меня́ большóе восхищéние.
admire [əd'maɪə'] *vt* (*respect, appreciate*) восхищáться (восхити́ться *perf*) +*instr*; (*gaze at*) любовáться *(impf)* +*instr*.
admirer [əd'maɪərə'] *n* поклóнник(-ица).
admiring [əd'maɪərɪŋ] *adj* восхищённый (восхищён), востóрженный* (востóржен).
admissible [əd'mɪsəbl] *adj* приéмлемый (приéмлем), допусти́мый* (допусти́м); **it is ~ evidence** э́то мóжет быть* при́нято в кáчестве доказáтельства.
admission [əd'mɪʃən] *n* (*admittance*) дóпуск; (*entry fee*) входнáя плáта; (*confession*) признáние; **to gain ~ to** (*official permission*) получáть (получи́ть* *perf*) дóпуск в/на +*acc*; **"admission free"**, **"free ~"** "вход свобóдный"; **by his own ~** по егó сóбственному признáнию.
admit [əd'mɪt] *vt* (*confess, accept*) признавáть* (признáть* *perf*); (*permit to enter*) впускáть (впусти́ть* *perf*); (*to club, organization*) принимáть (приня́ть* *perf*); (*to hospital*) госпитализи́ровать *(impf/perf)*; **"children not ~ted"** "дéтям вход воспрещён"; **this ticket ~s two** э́тот билéт нá два лицá
▸ **admit of** *vt fus* (*allow*) допускáть *(impf)*
▸ **admit to** *vt fus* (*murder etc*) сознавáться* (сознáться *perf*) в +*prp*.
admittance [əd'mɪtəns] *n* дóпуск; **no ~** вход воспрещён.
admittedly [əd'mɪtɪdlɪ] *adv*: **~ it is not easy** признáться, э́то не легкó.
admonish [əd'mɒnɪʃ] *vt* дéлать (сдéлать *perf*) внушéние +*dat*; (*LAW*) дéлать (сдéлать *perf*) предупреждéние +*dat*.
ad nauseam [æd'nɔ:sɪæm] *adv* бесконéчно.
ado [ə'du:] *n*: **without (any) more ~** без дальнéйших церемóний.
adolescence [ædəu'lɛsns] *n* подрóстковый вóзраст.
adolescent [ædəu'lɛsnt] *adj* подрóстковый ◆ *n* подрóсток*.
adopt [ə'dɒpt] *vt* (*son*) усыновля́ть (усынови́ть* *perf*); (*daughter*) удочеря́ть (удочери́ть *perf*); (*policy*) придéрживаться *(impf)* +*gen*; **to ~ sb as a candidate** выдвигáть (вы́двинуть *perf*) когó-н в кандидáты.
adopted [ə'dɒptɪd] *adj* (*child*) приёмный.
adoption [ə'dɒpʃən] *n* (*see vb*) усыновлéние; удочерéние; приня́тие.
adoptive [ə'dɒptɪv] *adj* (*parent*) приёмный.
adorable [ə'dɔ:rəbl] *adj* прелéстный* (прелéстен).
adoration [ædə'reɪʃən] *n* (*of person*) обожáние.
adore [ə'dɔ:'] *vt* обожáть *(impf)*.
adoring [ə'dɔ:rɪŋ] *adj* обожáющий.
adoringly [ə'dɔ:rɪŋlɪ] *adv* с обожáнием.
adorn [ə'dɔ:n] *vt* украшáть (укрáсить* *perf*).
adornment [ə'dɔ:nmənt] *n* украшéние.
ADP *n abbr* = **automatic data processing**.
adrenalin [ə'drɛnəlɪn] *n* адренали́н; **to get the ~ going** давáть* (дать* *perf*) заря́д энéргии.
Adriatic [eɪdrɪ'ætɪk] *n*: **the ~** Адриáтика.
adrift [ə'drɪft] *adv* (*NAUT*): **to be ~** дрейфовáть *(impf)*; (*fig*) плыть* *(impf)* по течéнию; **to go ~**

(*plans etc*) расстра́иваться (расстро́иться *perf*); **to come ~** (*boat*) лечь* *(perf)* в дрейф; (*fastening*) расслабля́ться (рассла́биться *perf*).

adroit [ə'drɔɪt] *adj* ло́вкий* (ло́вок).

adroitly [ə'drɔɪtlɪ] *adv* ло́вко.

ADT *abbr* (*US*) = *Atlantic Daylight Time*.

adulation [ædju'leɪʃən] *n* обожа́ние.

adult ['ædʌlt] *n* взро́слый(-ая) *m adj* ◆ *adj* (*grown-up*) взро́слый; (*for adults*) для взро́слых.

adult education *n* образова́ние для взро́слых.

adulterate [ə'dʌltəreɪt] *vt* (*food, drink: with additives*) по́ртить* (испо́ртить* *perf*) (*доба́вками*); (*: with water*) разбавля́ть (разба́вить* *perf*).

adulterer [ə'dʌltərəʳ] *n* неве́рный муж.

adulteress [ə'dʌltərɪs] *n* неве́рная жена́.

adultery [ə'dʌltərɪ] *n* супру́жеская неве́рность *f*.

adulthood ['ædʌlthud] *n* зре́лый во́зраст.

advance [əd'vɑ:ns] *n* (*progress*) успе́х; (*MIL*) наступле́ние; (*movement*) продвиже́ние; (*money*) ава́нс ◆ *adj* (*booking*) предвари́тельный ◆ *vt* (*theory, idea*) выдвига́ть (вы́двинуть *perf*) ◆ *vi* (*move forward: also fig*) продвига́ться (продви́нуться *perf*) вперёд; (*MIL*) наступа́ть *(impf)*; **in ~** предвари́тельно, зара́нее; **to make ~s (to sb)** заи́грывать *(impf)* (с кем-н); **to give sb ~ notice** *or* **~ warning (of sth)** предупрежда́ть (предупреди́ть* *perf*) кого́-н зара́нее (о чём-н); **to ~ sb money** плати́ть* (заплати́ть* *perf*) кому́-н ава́нсом; **we ~d 20 km** мы продви́нулись на 20 кило ме́тров.

advanced [əd'vɑ:nst] *adj* (*studies, course*) для продви́нутого у́ровня; (*child, country*) развито́й* (ра́звит); (*ideas, views*) прогресси́вный* (прогресси́вен); **~ maths** вы́сшая матема́тика; **a man of ~ years** *or* **~ in years** челове́к прекло́нного во́зраста.

advancement [əd'vɑ:nsmənt] *n* (*of science*) прогре́сс; (*in job, rank*) продвиже́ние (по слу́жбе).

advancing [əd'vɑ:nsɪŋ] *adj* надвига́ющийся.

advantage [əd'vɑ:ntɪdʒ] *n* преиму́щество; (*TENNIS*) "бо́льше"; **to take ~ of** (*person*) испо́льзовать *(perf)*; (*sb's hospitality*) злоупотребля́ть (злоупотреби́ть* *perf*) *+instr*; (*opportunity*) воспо́льзоваться *(perf) +instr*; **to our/his ~** в на́ших/его́ интере́сах; **to turn sth to one's ~** обраща́ть (обрати́ть* *perf*) что-н в свою́ по́льзу.

advantageous [ædvən'teɪdʒəs] *adj* (*position, situation*) вы́годный* (вы́годен); **it's ~ to us** нам э́то вы́годно.

advent ['ædvənt] *n* появле́ние; (*REL*): **A~** *ме́сяц до Рождества́*.

Advent calendar *n календа́рь с две́рцами на ка́ждый день ме́сяца до Рождества́*.

adventure [əd'vɛntʃəʳ] *n* (*exciting event*) приключе́ние; **to look for ~** иска́ть* *(impf)* приключе́ний.

adventure playground *n* де́тский городо́к.

adventurous [əd'vɛntʃərəs] *adj* (*action*) риско́ванный (риско́ван); (*person*) сме́лый (смел); **an ~ life** жизнь по́лная приключе́ний.

adverb ['ædvə:b] *n* наре́чие.

adversarial [ædvə'sɛərɪəl] *adj* противо-бо́рствующий, вражде́бный.

adversary ['ædvəsərɪ] *n* проти́вник(-ница).

adverse ['ædvə:s] *adj* неблагоприя́тный; **in ~ circumstances** при неблагоприя́тных обстоя́тельствах.

adversity [əd'və:sɪtɪ] *n* бе́дствие, невзго́да.

advert ['ædvə:t] *n abbr* (*BRIT*) = **advertisement**.

advertise ['ædvətaɪz] *vti* реклами́ровать *(impf)*; **to ~ on television/in a newspaper** дава́ть* (дать* *perf*) объявле́ние по телеви́дению/в газе́ту; **to ~ a job** объявля́ть (объяви́ть* *perf*) ко́нкурс на ме́сто; **to ~ for staff/ accommodation** дава́ть* (дать* *perf*) объявле́ние, что тре́буются рабо́тники/ тре́буется жильё.

advertisement [əd'və:tɪsmənt] *n* рекла́ма; (*in classified ads*) объявле́ние.

advertiser ['ædvətaɪzəʳ] *n* (*professional*) реклами́ст(ка); (*in newspaper, on television etc*) рекламода́тель *m*.

advertising ['ædvətaɪzɪŋ] *n* рекла́ма.

advertising agency *n* рекла́мное аге́нтство.

advertising campaign *n* рекла́мная кампа́ния.

advice [əd'vaɪs] *n* сове́т; (*notification*) уведомле́ние, извеще́ние; **a piece of ~** сове́т; **to ask sb for ~** (*friend*) сове́товаться (посове́товаться *perf*) с кем-н; (*professional*) обраща́ться (обрати́ться* *perf*) (за сове́том) к кому́-н; **to take legal ~** обраща́ться (обрати́ться* *perf*) (за сове́том) к юри́сту.

advice note *n* (*BRIT*) извеще́ние.

advisable [əd'vaɪzəbl] *adj* целесообра́зный* (целесообра́зен).

advise [əd'vaɪz] *vt* сове́товать (посове́товать *perf*) *+dat*; (*professionally*) консульти́ровать (проконсульти́ровать *perf*) *+gen*; (*inform*): **to ~ sb of sth** извеща́ть (извести́ть* *perf*) кого́-н о чём-н; **to ~ (sb) against doing** отсове́товать *(perf)* (кому́-н) *+impf infin*; **you would be well-/ill-~d to go** Вам бы сле́довало пойти́/ не сле́довало ходи́ть ....

advisedly [əd'vaɪzɪdlɪ] *adv* наме́ренно.

adviser [əd'vaɪzəʳ] *n* сове́тник, консульта́нт;

* marks translations which have irregular inflections. The Russian-English side of the dictionary gives inflectional information.

legal ~ юриско́нсульт.
advisor [əd'vaɪzə^r] *n* = **adviser**.
advisory [əd'vaɪzərɪ] *adj* (*body, role*) консультати́вный; **in an ~ capacity** в ка́честве сове́тника *or* консульта́нта.
advocate [*vb* 'ædvəkeɪt, *n* 'ædvəkɪt] *vt* выступа́ть *(impf)* за *+acc* ◆ *n* (*LAW*) защи́тник, адвока́т; (*supporter*): **~ of** сторо́нник(-ица) *+gen*.
advt. *abbr* = **advertisement.**
AEA *n abbr* (*BRIT*: = *Atomic Energy Authority*) Управле́ние а́томной эне́ргии.
AEC *n abbr* (*US*: = *Atomic Energy Commission*) Коми́ссия по а́томной эне́ргии.
AEEU *n abbr* (*BRIT*) = *Amalgamated Engineering and Electrical Union*.
Aegean [i:'dʒi:ən] *n*: **the ~** Эге́йское мо́ре.
aegis ['i:dʒɪs] *n*: **under the ~ of** под эги́дой *+gen*.
aeon ['i:ən] *n*: **for ~s** це́лую ве́чность.
aerial ['ɛərɪəl] *n* анте́нна ◆ *adj* возду́шный*; **~ photography** аэрофотосъёмка.
aerobatics ['ɛərəu'bætɪks] *npl* вы́сший* пилота́ж *msg*.
aerobics [ɛə'rəubɪks] *n* аэро́бика.
aerodrome ['ɛərədrəum] *n* (*BRIT*) аэродро́м.
aerodynamic ['ɛərəudaɪ'næmɪk] *adj* аэродинами́ческий*.
aeronautics [ɛərə'nɔ:tɪks] *n* аэрона́втика.
aeroplane ['ɛərəpleɪn] *n* (*BRIT*) самолёт.
aerosol ['ɛərəsɔl] *n* аэрозо́ль *m*.
aerospace industry ['ɛərəuspeɪs-] *n* аэро-косми́ческая промы́шленность *f*.
aesthetic [i:s'θɛtɪk] *adj* эстети́ческий*.
aesthetically [i:s'θɛtɪklɪ] *adv* эстети́чески.
afar [ə'fɑ:^r] *adv*: **from ~** издалека́.
AFB *n abbr* (*US*) = *Air Force Base*.
AFDC *n abbr* (*US*) = *Aid to Families with Dependent Children*.
affable ['æfəbl] *adj* (*person*) доброду́шный* (доброду́шен); (*behaviour*) доброжела́тельный* (доброжела́телен).
affair [ə'fɛə^r] *n* (*matter*) де́ло*; (*also*: **love ~**) рома́н; **~s** *npl* (*business*) дела́* *ntpl*.
affect [ə'fɛkt] *vt* (*influence*) де́йствовать (поде́йствовать *perf*) на *+acc*, влия́ть (повлия́ть *perf*) на *+acc*; (*afflict*) поража́ть (порази́ть* *perf*); (*move deeply*) тро́гать (тро́нуть *perf*); (*feign*) подде́лывать (подде́лать *perf*); **to ~ an American accent** говори́ть *(impf)* с де́ланным америка́нским акце́нтом.
affectation [æfɛk'teɪʃən] *n* (*in manner, speech*) наи́гранность *f*.
affected [ə'fɛktɪd] *adj* (*person*) претенцио́зный* (претенцио́зен); (*manner*) де́ланный.
affection [ə'fɛkʃən] *n* привя́занность *f*.
affectionate [ə'fɛkʃənɪt] *adj* не́жный*.
affectionately [ə'fɛkʃənɪtlɪ] *adv* не́жно.
affidavit [æfɪ'deɪvɪt] *n* (*LAW*) пи́сьменное свиде́тельство, афида́вит.
affiliated [ə'fɪlɪeɪtɪd] *adj* (*company*) доче́рний*; **to be ~ to** (*body*) явля́ться *(impf)* филиа́лом *+gen*.
affinity [ə'fɪnɪtɪ] *n*: **to have an ~ with** (*bond*) ощуща́ть (ощути́ть* *perf*) бли́зость с *+instr*; (*resemblance*) обнару́живать (обнару́жить *perf*) родство́ с *+instr*.
affirm [ə'fə:m] *vt* утвержда́ть (утверди́ть* *perf*).
affirmation [æfə'meɪʃən] *n* (*of facts*) подтвержде́ние; (*of ideas*) утвержде́ние.
affirmative [ə'fə:mətɪv] *adj* утверди́тельный* ◆ *n*: **in the ~** утверди́тельно.
affix [ə'fɪks] *vt* прикрепля́ть (прикрепи́ть* *perf*).
afflict [ə'flɪkt] *vt* постига́ть (пости́чь* *perf*); **to be ~ed by** (*illness*) страда́ть *(impf)* от *+gen*.
affliction [ə'flɪkʃən] *n* несча́стье.
affluence ['æfluəns] *n* благосостоя́ние.
affluent ['æfluənt] *adj* благополу́чный* (благополу́чен); **the ~ society** о́бщество благосостоя́ния.
afford [ə'fɔ:d] *vt* позво́лить *(perf)* себе́; (*provide*) предоставля́ть (предоста́вить* *perf*); **I can't ~ it** мне э́то не по карма́ну; **can we ~ a car?** мы мо́жем себе́ позво́лить купи́ть маши́ну?; **I can't ~ the time** мне вре́мя не позволя́ет.
affordable [ə'fɔ:dəbl] *adj* досту́пный по цене́.
affray [ə'freɪ] *n* (*BRIT*: *LAW*) дра́ка в обще́ственном ме́сте.
affront [ə'frʌnt] *n* оскорбле́ние.
affronted [ə'frʌntɪd] *adj* оскорблённый (оскорблён).
Afghan ['æfgæn] *adj* афга́нский ◆ *n* афга́нец*(-нка).
Afghanistan [æf'gænɪstæn] *n* Афганиста́н.
afield [ə'fi:ld] *adv*: **far ~** вдалеке́, вдали́; **from far ~** издалека́.
AFL-CIO *n abbr* = *American Federation of Labor and Congress of Industrial Organizations*.
afloat [ə'fləut] *adv* (*floating*) на плаву́; **to stay ~** (*fig*) держа́ться *(impf)* на пове́рхности; **to keep a business ~** не дава́ть* (дать* *perf*) потону́ть предприя́тию.
afoot [ə'fut] *adv*: **there is something ~** что́-то затева́ется.
aforementioned [ə'fɔ:mɛnʃənd] *adj* вышеупомя́нутый.
aforesaid [ə'fɔ:sɛd] *adj* вышеупомя́нутый.
afraid [ə'freɪd] *adj* (*frightened*) испу́ганный (испу́ган); **to be ~ of sth/sb/of doing** боя́ться* *(impf)* чего́-н/кого́-н/*+infin*; **to be ~ to** боя́ться (побоя́ться *perf*) *+infin*; **I am ~ that** (*apology*) бою́сь, что; **I am ~ that I'll be late** бою́сь, что я опозда́ю; **I am ~ so/not** бою́сь, что да/нет.
afresh [ə'frɛʃ] *adv* за́ново.
Africa ['æfrɪkə] *n* А́фрика.
African ['æfrɪkən] *adj* африка́нский* ◆ *n* африка́нец*(-нка).
Afrikaans [æfrɪ'kɑ:ns] *n* (язы́к*) африкаа́нс.
Afrikaner [æfrɪ'kɑ:nə^r] *n* африка́нер (*уроже́нец Ю́жной А́фрики голла́ндского происхожде́ния*).

Afro-American ['æfrəuə'mɛrɪkən] *adj* афро-американский*.

Afro-Caribbean ['æfrəkærɪ'bi:ən] *adj* афро-карибский.

AFT *n abbr* (*US*) = *American Federation of Teachers.*

after ['ɑ:ftə'] *prep* (*time*) после *+gen*, спустя *+acc*; (*place, order*) за *+instr*; (*style, technique*) в стиле *+gen* ◆ *adv* потом, после ◆ *conj* после того как; **~ dinner** после обеда; **the day ~ tomorrow** послезавтра; **~ three years they divorced** спустя три года они развелись; **what/who are you ~?** что/кто Вам нужно/нужен?; **the police are ~ him** его разыскивает полиция; **to name sb ~ sb** называть (назвать* *perf*) кого-н в честь кого-н; **it's twenty ~ eight** (*US*) сейчас двадцать минут девятого; **to ask ~ sb** справляться (справиться* *perf*) о ком-н; **~ all** в конце концов; **~ you!** после Вас!; **~ he left** после того, как он ушёл; **~ having done this** сделав это.

afterbirth ['ɑ:ftəbə:θ] *n* послед.

aftercare ['ɑ:ftəkɛə'] *n* (*BRIT: MED*) уход за выздоравливающим.

after-effects ['ɑ:ftərɪfɛkts] *npl* последствия *ntpl*.

afterlife ['ɑ:ftəlaɪf] *n* загробная жизнь *f*.

aftermath ['ɑ:ftəmɑ:θ] *n* последствия *ntpl*; **in the ~ of** после *+gen*.

afternoon ['ɑ:ftə'nu:n] *n* вторая половина дня; **in the ~** днём; **good ~!** (*goodbye*) до свидания!; (*hello*) добрый день!

afters ['ɑ:ftəz] *n* (*inf: dessert*): **for ~** на третье *or* десерт.

after-sales service [ɑ:ftə'seɪlz-] *n* (*BRIT*) гарантированное техобслуживание.

after-shave (lotion) ['ɑ:ftəʃeɪv-] *n* одеколон после бритья.

aftershock ['ɑ:ftəʃɔk] *n* толчок* (*после основного землетрясения*).

aftertaste ['ɑ:ftəteɪst] *n* привкус.

afterthought ['ɑ:ftəθɔ:t] *n*: **as an ~** машинально.

afterward ['ɑ:ftəwəd] *adv* (*US*) = **afterwards**.

afterwards ['ɑ:ftəwədz] (*US* **afterward**) *adv* позже, потом.

again [ə'gɛn] *adv* (*once more*) ещё раз, снова; (*repeatedly*) опять; **I won't see him/go there ~** я больше не увижу его/пойду туда; **to do sth ~** делать (сделать *perf*) что-н ещё раз *or* снова; **to begin ~** начать* (*perf*) сначала; **to see ~** смотреть* (посмотреть* *perf*) *or* видеть* (увидеть* *perf*) ещё раз; **he opened the door ~** он опять *or* снова открыл дверь; **~ and ~** снова и снова; **now and ~** время от времени.

against [ə'gɛnst] *prep* (*lean*) к *+dat*; (*hit, rub*) о *+acc*; (*standing*) у *+gen*; (*in opposition to*) против *+gen*; (*at odds with*) вопреки *+dat*; (*compared to*) по сравнению с *+instr*; **~ a blue background** на синем фоне; **(as) ~** в сравнении с *+instr*.

age [eɪdʒ] *n* (*of person*) возраст; (*period in history*) век* ◆ *vi* (*person*) стареть (постареть *perf*) ◆ *vt* (*subj: hairstyle, dress*) старить (*impf*); **what ~ is he?** сколько ему лет?; **he is 20 years of ~** ему двадцать лет; **under ~** несовершеннолетний*; **to come of ~** достигать (достичь* *perf*) совершеннолетия; **it's been ~s since I saw you** я не видел Вас целую вечность.

aged[1] ['eɪdʒd] *adj*: **a boy ~ ten** мальчик десяти лет.

aged[2] ['eɪdʒɪd] *npl*: **the ~** престарелые *pl adj*.

age group *n* возрастная группа; **the forty to fifty ~ ~** люди возрастом от сорока до пятидесяти лет.

ageing ['eɪdʒɪŋ] *adj* стареющий ◆ *n* старение.

ageless ['eɪdʒlɪs] *adj* (*building, ritual*) вечный* (вечен).

age limit *n* возрастной предел.

agency ['eɪdʒənsɪ] *n* (*COMM*) агентство, бюро *nt ind*; (*government body*) управление; **through** *or* **by the ~ of** при посредстве *+gen*.

agenda [ə'dʒɛndə] *n* (*of meeting*) повестка* (дня); **on the ~** на повестке (дня).

agent ['eɪdʒənt] *n* (*representative, spy*) агент; (*COMM*) посредник; (*CHEM*) реактив; (*fig*) фактор.

aggravate ['ægrəveɪt] *vt* (*situation*) усугублять (усугубить* *perf*); (*person*) раздражать (раздражить *perf*).

aggravating ['ægrəveɪtɪŋ] *adj*: **his behaviour is ~** его поведение раздражает меня.

aggravation [ægrə'veɪʃən] *n* (*see vt*) усугубление; раздражение.

aggregate ['ægrɪgɪt] *n* (*total*) совокупность *f* ◆ *vt* группировать (сгруппировать *perf*) в *+acc*.

aggression [ə'grɛʃən] *n* агрессия.

aggressive [ə'grɛsɪv] *adj* (*belligerent*) агрессивный* (агрессивен); (*assertive*) напористый (напорист).

aggressiveness [ə'grɛsɪvnɪs] *n* агрессивность *f*.

aggressor [ə'grɛsə'] *n* агрессор.

aggrieved [ə'gri:vd] *adj* огорчённый* (огорчён).

aggro ['ægrəu] *n* (*inf: aggressive behaviour*) напряжёнка; (*difficulties*) возня.

aghast [ə'gɑ:st] *adj*: **to be ~ at** быть* (*impf*) в ужасе от *+gen*.

agile ['ædʒaɪl] *adj* (*person*) проворный* (проворен); (*mind*) живой*.

agility [ə'dʒɪlɪtɪ] *n* подвижность *f*; **mental ~** живость *f* ума.

agitate ['ædʒɪteɪt] *vt* (*person*) возбуждать

* marks translations which have irregular inflections. The Russian-English side of the dictionary gives inflectional information.

(возбудить* *perf*); (*liquid*) взбалтывать (взболтать *perf*) ◆ *vi*: **to ~ for/against** агитировать (сагитировать *perf*) за +*acc*/ против +*gen*.

agitated ['ædʒɪteɪtɪd] *adj* возбуждённый* (возбуждён), взволнованный (взволнован).

agitator ['ædʒɪteɪtə'] *n* агитатор.

AGM *n abbr* (= *annual general meeting*) ежегодное общее собрание.

agnostic [æg'nɔstɪk] *n* агностик.

ago [ə'gəu] *adv*: **two days ~** два дня назад; **not long ~** недавно; **as long ~ as 1960** ещё в 1960 году; **how long ~?** как давно?

agog [ə'gɔg] *adj* (*excited*) взволнованный (взволнован); **to be (all) ~** (*with anticipation*) сгорать *(impf)* от нетерпения.

agonize ['ægənaɪz] *vi*: **he ~d over the problem** он мучился над проблемой.

agonizing ['ægənaɪzɪŋ] *adj* мучительный* (мучителен).

agony ['ægənɪ] *n* (*pain*) мучительная боль *f*; (*torment*) мука, мучение; **to be in ~** мучиться *(impf)* от боли.

agony aunt *n психолог "почты доверия", отвечающий на вопросы читателей.*

agony column *n рубрика "почта доверия".*

agree [ə'gri:] *vt* согласовывать (согласовать *perf*) ◆ *vi*: **to ~ with** (*have same opinion*) соглашаться (согласиться *perf*) с +*instr*; (*correspond*) согласоваться *(impf/perf)* с +*instr*; **to ~ that** согласиться* *(perf)*, что; **it was ~d that ...** было решено, что ...; **the price is still to be ~d** цену всё ещё надо согласовать; **I ~ (with you)** я согласен (с Вами); **to ~ (with)** (*LING*) согласовывать (согласовать* *perf*) (с +*instr*); **garlic doesn't ~ with me** я не переношу чеснока; **to ~ on sth** договариваться (договориться *perf*) о чём-н; **they ~d on this** они сошлись на этом; **they ~d on going/on a price** они договорились пойти/о цене; **to ~ to sth/to do** соглашаться (согласиться* *perf*) на что-н/+*infin*.

agreeable [ə'gri:əbl] *adj* (*pleasant*) приятный* (приятен); (*willing*) согласен; **are you ~ to this?** Вы согласны на это?

agreed [ə'gri:d] *adj* условленный (условлен).

agreement [ə'gri:mənt] *n* (*consent*) согласие; (*arrangement*) соглашение, договор; **in ~ with** в согласии с +*instr*; **we are in complete ~** между нами полное согласие; **by mutual ~** по взаимному соглашению.

agricultural [ægrɪ'kʌltʃərəl] *adj* сельскохозяйственный; **~ land** земельные угодья *ntpl*.

agriculture ['ægrɪkʌltʃə'] *n* сельское хозяйство.

aground [ə'graund] *adv*: **to run ~** садиться* (сесть* *perf*) на мель.

ahead [ə'hɛd] *adv* впереди; (*direction*) вперёд; **~ of** (*more advanced than*) впереди +*gen*; (*earlier than*) раньше +*gen*; **~ of time** *or* **schedule** досрочно; **go right** *or* **straight ~** идите вперёд *or* прямо; **go ~!** (*permission*) давайте!; **they were (right) ~ of us** они были (прямо) перед нами.

AI *n abbr* (= *Amnesty International*) Международная амнистия; (*COMPUT*) = **artificial intelligence.**

AIB *n abbr* (*BRIT*) = *Accident Investigation Bureau.*

AID *n abbr* (= *artificial insemination by donor*) искусственное оплодотворение семенем донора; (*US*) = *Agency for International Development.*

aid [eɪd] *n* (*assistance*) помощь *f*; (*device*) приспособление ◆ *vt* помогать (помочь* *perf*) +*dat*; **with the ~ of** при помощи +*gen*; **in ~ of** в помощь +*dat*; **to ~ and abet** (*LAW*) подстрекать *(impf)*; *see also* **hearing.**

aide [eɪd] *n* помощник.

aide-de-camp ['eɪddə'kɔŋ] *n* адъютант.

AIDS [eɪdz] *n abbr* (= *acquired immune deficiency syndrome*) СПИД= *синдром приобретённого иммунодефицита.*

AIH *n abbr* (= *artificial insemination by husband*) искусственное оплодотворение семенем мужа.

ailing ['eɪlɪŋ] *adj* больной* (болен); **an ~ economy** экономика пришедшая в упадок.

ailment ['eɪlmənt] *n* недуг.

aim [eɪm] *n* (*objective*) цель *f* ◆ *vi* (*also:* **take ~**) целиться (нацелиться *perf*) ◆ *vt*: **to ~ (at)** (*gun, camera*) наводить* (навести* *perf*) (на +*acc*); (*missile, blow*) целить *(impf) or* нацеливать (нацелить *perf*) (на +*acc*); (*remark*) направлять (направить* *perf*) (на +*acc*); **to ~ at** целиться *(impf)* в +*acc*, прицеливаться (прицелиться *perf*) в +*acc*; (*fig*) стремиться* *(impf)* к +*dat*; **to ~ to do** ставить* (поставить* *perf*) своей целью +*infin*; **he has a good ~** он меткий стрелок.

aimless ['eɪmlɪs] *adj* бесцельный* (бесцелен).

aimlessly ['eɪmlɪslɪ] *adv* бесцельно.

ain't [eɪnt] (*inf*) = **am not, aren't, isn't**; *see* **be.**

air [ɛə'] *n* воздух; (*tune*) мотив; (*appearance*) вид* ◆ *vt* (*room, bedclothes*) проветривать (проветрить *perf*); (*views*) обнародовать *(perf)* ◆ *cpd* (*currents, attack etc*) воздушный; **to throw sth into the ~** подбрасывать (подбросить* *perf*) что-н в воздух; **by ~** самолётом; **everything's still very much in the ~** всё до сих пор висит в воздухе; **on the ~** в эфире; **to go on the ~** выходить* (выйти* *perf*) в эфир.

airbag ['ɛəbæg] *n воздушная подушка, надувающаяся автоматически между рулём и шофёром, в случае аварии.*

air base *n* авиабаза.

airbed ['ɛəbɛd] *n* (*BRIT*) надувной матрас.

airborne ['ɛəbɔ:n] *adj* воздушный* (воздушен); (*troops*) воздушно-десантный; (*particles*) летучий*; **as soon as the plane was**

~ как только самолёт поднялся в воздух.
air cargo *n* воздушный груз.
air-conditioned ['ɛəkən'dɪʃənd] *adj* кондиционированный.
air conditioning *n* кондиционирование.
air-cooled ['ɛəku:ld] *adj* охлаждаемый воздухом.
aircraft ['ɛəkrɑ:ft] *n inv* самолёт.
aircraft carrier *n* авианосец*.
air cushion *n* воздушная подушка*.
airfield ['ɛəfi:ld] *n* аэродром.
Air Force *n* Военно-Воздушные Силы *fpl*.
air freight *n* авиагруз.
air freshener *n* освежитель *m* воздуха.
air gun *n* духовое ружьё*.
air hostess *n* (*BRIT*) бортпроводница, стюардесса.
airily ['ɛərɪlɪ] *adv* с лёгкостью, небрежно.
airing ['ɛərɪŋ] *n*: **to give an ~ to** (*ideas, views etc*) обнародовать *(perf)*.
air letter *n* (*BRIT*) письмо* авиа.
airlift ['ɛəlɪft] *n* воздушная переброска ◆ *vt* перебрасывать (перебросить* *perf*) по воздуху.
airline ['ɛəlaɪn] *n* авиакомпания.
airliner ['ɛəlaɪnəʳ] *n* пассажирский* (авиа)лайнер.
airlock ['ɛəlɔk] *n* воздушная пробка.
air mail *n*: **by ~ ~** авиапочтой.
air mattress *n* надувной матрас.
airplane ['ɛəpleɪn] *n* (*US*) самолёт.
air pocket *n* воздушная яма.
airport ['ɛəpɔ:t] *n* аэропорт.
air rage *n* агрессивное поведение на борт самолёта.
air raid *n* воздушный налёт.
air rifle *n* пневматическая винтовка.
airsick ['ɛəsɪk] *adj*: **to be ~** страдать *(impf)* воздушной болезнью.
airspace ['ɛəspeɪs] *n* воздушное пространство.
airspeed ['ɛəspi:d] *n* воздушная скорость *f*, скорость *f* в воздухе.
airstrip ['ɛəstrɪp] *n* взлётно-посадочная полоса*.
air terminal *n* аэровокзал.
airtight ['ɛətaɪt] *adj* герметический.
air time *n* время* *nt* в эфире.
air-traffic control ['ɛətræfɪk-] *n* воздушно-диспетчерская служба.
air-traffic controller *n* воздушный диспетчер.
airway ['ɛəweɪ] *n* воздушная трасса.
air waybill *n* транспортная накладная для авиагруза.
airy ['ɛərɪ] *adj* просторный* (просторен); (*manner*) беспечный* (беспечен).
aisle [aɪl] *n* проход.
ajar [ə'dʒɑ:ʳ] *adj* приоткрытый (приоткрыт).
AK *abbr* (*US*: *POST*) = *Alaska*.
aka *abbr* (= *also known as*) известный также под именем.
akin [ə'kɪn] *adj*: **~ to** сродни *+dat*.
AL (*US*: *POST*) *abbr* = *Alabama*.
ALA *n abbr* = *American Library Association*.
alabaster ['æləbɑ:stəʳ] *n* алебастр.
à la carte [ɑ:lɑ:'kɑ:t] *adv*: **dinner ~ ~ ~** *обед с заказом блюд по меню*.
alacrity [ə'lækrɪtɪ] *n* готовность *f*; **with ~** с готовностью.
alarm [ə'lɑ:m] *n* (*anxiety*) тревога; (*device*) сигнализация ◆ *vt* (*person*) тревожить (встревожить *perf*); (*car, house*) устанавливать (установить* *perf*) сигнализацию в *+prp*.
alarm call *n*: **I would like an ~ ~ for 6 a.m.** позвоните, пожалуйста, в 6 часов и разбудите меня.
alarm clock *n* будильник.
alarmed [ə'lɑ:md] *adj* встревоженный* (встревожен); **his car is ~** у него в машине сигнализация.
alarming [ə'lɑ:mɪŋ] *adj* тревожный* (тревожен).
alarmist [ə'lɑ:mɪst] *n* паникёр(ша).
alas [ə'læs] *excl* увы.
Alaska [ə'læskə] *n* Аляска.
Albania [æl'beɪnɪə] *n* Албания.
Albanian [æl'beɪnɪən] *adj* албанский* ◆ *n* албанец*(-нка); (*LING*) албанский* язык*.
albatross ['ælbətrɔs] *n* (*ZOOL*) альбатрос.
albeit [ɔ:l'bi:ɪt] *conj* хотя и.
album ['ælbəm] *n* альбом.
albumen ['ælbjumɪn] *n* белок*.
alchemy ['ælkɪmɪ] *n* алхимия.
alcohol ['ælkəhɔl] *n* алкоголь *m*.
alcohol-free ['ælkəhɔl'fri:] *adj* безалкогольный.
alcoholic [ælkə'hɔlɪk] *adj* алкогольный ◆ *n* алкоголик(-ичка).
alcoholism ['ælkəhɔlɪzəm] *n* алкоголизм.
alcove ['ælkəuv] *n* альков.
alderman ['ɔ:ldəmən] *irreg n* глава муниципалитета.
ale [eɪl] *n* пиво (*приготовленное без хмеля*).
alert [ə'lə:t] *adj* (*attentive*) внимательный* (внимателен); (*to danger*) бдительный* (бдителен) ◆ *n* (*alarm*) тревога ◆ *vt* (*police etc*) предупреждать (предупредить* *perf*); **to be on the ~** (*also MIL*) быть* *(impf)* начеку; **to ~ sb to sth** предупреждать (предупредить *perf*) кого-н о чём-н; **to ~ sb to the dangers of sth** предостерегать (предостеречь* *perf*) кого-н от опасности чего-н.
Aleutian Islands [ə'lu:ʃən-] *npl* Алеутские острова *mpl*.
Alexandria [ælɪg'zɑ:ndrɪə] *n* Александрия.
alfresco [æl'frɛskəu] *adj, adv* под открытым

* marks translations which have irregular inflections. The Russian-English side of the dictionary gives inflectional information.

небом.
algebra [ˈældʒɪbrə] *n* áлгебра.
Algeria [ælˈdʒɪərɪə] *n* Алжи́р.
Algerian [ælˈdʒɪərɪən] *adj* алжи́рский* ◆ *n* алжи́рец*(-рка).
Algiers [ælˈdʒɪəz] *n* Алжи́р (*го́род*).
algorithm [ˈælgərɪðəm] *n* алгори́тм.
alias [ˈeɪlɪəs] *n* (*of criminal*) вы́мышленное и́мя* *nt*; (*of writer*) псевдони́м ◆ *adv*: ~ **John Green** он же Джон Грин.
alibi [ˈælɪbaɪ] *n* а́либи *nt ind*.
alien [ˈeɪlɪən] *n* (*foreigner*) иностра́нец*(-нка); (*extraterrestrial*) инопланетя́нин*(-я́нка) ◆ *adj*: ~ **(to)** чу́ждый* (чужд) (+*dat*); **pity was ~ to his nature** чу́вство жа́лости ему́ бы́ло чу́ждо.
alienate [ˈeɪlɪəneɪt] *vt* (*person*) отчужда́ть *(impf)*, отта́лкивать (оттолкну́ть *perf*).
alienation [eɪlɪəˈneɪʃən] *n* отчужде́ние.
alight [əˈlaɪt] *adj*: **to be ~** горе́ть *(impf)*; (*eyes, face*) сия́ть *(impf)* ◆ *adv*: **to set ~** поджига́ть (подже́чь* *perf*) ◆ *vi*: **to ~ on** опуска́ться (опусти́ться* *perf*) на +*acc*; **to ~ from** (*boat*) сходи́ть* (сойти́* *perf*) с +*gen*; (*bus, train*) выходи́ть* (вы́йти* *perf*) из +*gen*.
align [əˈlaɪn] *vt* (*objects*) выра́внивать (вы́ровнять *perf*); **to ~ o.s. with** присоединя́ться (присоедини́ться *perf*) к +*dat*.
alignment [əˈlaɪnmənt] *n* сою́з; (*POL*) алья́нс; **out of ~** неро́вно.
alike [əˈlaɪk] *adj* одина́ковый (одина́ков) ◆ *adv* одина́ково; **they look ~** они́ похо́жи друг на дру́га; **winter and summer ~** и зимо́й и ле́том.
alimony [ˈælɪmənɪ] *n* алиме́нты* *pl*.
alive [əˈlaɪv] *adj* жив; (*place*) оживлённый*; (*active: person*) живо́й; ~ **with** по́лон +*gen*; **to be ~ to sth** осознава́ть (осозна́ть *perf*) что-н.
alkali [ˈælkəlaɪ] *n* щёлочь* *f*.
alkaline [ˈælkəlaɪn] *adj* щелочно́й.

KEYWORD

all [ɔ:l] *adj* весь* (*f* вся, *nt* всё, *pl* все); **all day** весь день* *m*; **all night** всю ночь* *f*; **all men are equal** все лю́ди равны́; **all five stayed** все пя́теро оста́лись; **all the books** все кни́ги; **all the time** всё вре́мя; **all his life** всю свою́ жизнь

◆ *pron* **1** всё; **I ate it all, I ate all of it** я всё съел; **all of us stayed** мы все оста́лись; **we all sat down** мы все се́ли; **is that all?** э́то всё?; (*in shop*) всё?

2 (*in phrases*): **above all** пре́жде всего́; **after all** в конце́ концо́в; **all in all** в це́лом *or* о́бщем; **not at all** (*in answer to question*) совсе́м нет, ничу́ть нет; (*in answer to thanks*) не́ за что; **I'm not at all tired** я совсе́м не уста́л

◆ *adv* совсе́м; **I am all alone** я совсе́м оди́н; **I did it all by myself** я всё сде́лал сам; **it's not as hard as all that** э́то совсе́м не так уж тру́дно; **all the more/the better** тем бо́лее/лу́чше; **I have all but finished** я почти́ что зако́нчил; **the score is two all** счёт-два два.

allay [əˈleɪ] *vt* (*fears etc*) разве́ивать (разве́ять *perf*).
all clear *n* отбо́й.
allegation [ælɪˈgeɪʃən] *n* обвине́ние; **according to his ~s** согла́сно его́ утвержде́ниям.
allege [əˈlɛdʒ] *vt* (*claim*) утвержда́ть *(impf)*; **he is ~d to have said that ...** утвержда́ют, что он сказа́л что ....
alleged [əˈlɛdʒd] *adj* подозрева́емый.
allegedly [əˈlɛdʒɪdlɪ] *adv* я́кобы.
allegiance [əˈli:dʒəns] *n* (*to people*) ве́рность *f*; (*to ideas*) приве́рженность *f*.
allegory [ˈælɪgərɪ] *n* аллего́рия.
all-embracing [ˈɔ:lɪmˈbreɪsɪŋ] *adj* всеобъе́млющий* (всеобъе́млющ).
allergic [əˈlə:dʒɪk] *adj* аллерги́ческий*; **he is ~ to** у него́ аллерги́я на +*acc*; (*fig*) он не выно́сит +*gen*.
allergy [ˈælədʒɪ] *n* (*MED*) аллерги́я.
alleviate [əˈli:vɪeɪt] *vt* облегча́ть (облегчи́ть *perf*).
alley [ˈælɪ] *n* (*street*) переу́лок*.
alleyway [ˈælɪweɪ] *n* проу́лок*.
alliance [əˈlaɪəns] *n* сою́з; (*POL*) алья́нс.
allied [ˈælaɪd] *adj* (*POL, MIL*) сою́зный; (*industries*) сме́жный*.
alligator [ˈælɪgeɪtə*] *n* аллига́тор.
all-important [ˈɔ:lɪmˈpɔ:tnt] *adj* суще́ственный.
all-in [ˈɔ:lɪn] *adj* (*BRIT: cost*) о́бщий*; **it cost me £100 ~** в о́бщей сло́жности мне э́то сто́ило £100.
all-in wrestling *n* во́льная борьба́.
alliteration [əlɪtəˈreɪʃən] *n* аллитера́ция.
all-night [ˈɔ:lˈnaɪt] *adj* (*café, cinema*) ночно́й.
allocate [ˈæləkeɪt] *vt* (*money, time, room*) выделя́ть (вы́делить *perf*); (*tasks*) поруча́ть (поручи́ть* *perf*).
allocation [æləuˈkeɪʃən] *n* (*of responsibilty*) распределе́ние; (*of resources*) выделе́ние; (*of money*) ассигнова́ние.
allot [əˈlɔt] *vt*: **to ~ (to)** отводи́ть* (отвести́* *perf*) (+*dat*); **in the ~ted time** в отведённое вре́мя.
allotment [əˈlɔtmənt] *n* (*share*) до́ля*; (*garden*) (земе́льный) уча́сток*.
all-out [ˈɔ:laut] *adj* (*effort*) максима́льный; (*attack*) масси́рованный; (*strike*) всео́бщий* ◆ *adv* по́лностью; **to go all out (for)** по́лностью выкла́дываться (вы́ложиться *perf*) (для +*gen*).
allow [əˈlau] *vt* (*permit*) разреша́ть (разреши́ть *perf*); (: *claim, goal*) признава́ть* (призна́ть *perf*) действи́тельным; (*set aside: sum*) выделя́ть (вы́делить *perf*); (*concede*): **to ~ that** допуска́ть (допусти́ть* *perf*), что; **to ~ sb to do** разреша́ть (разреши́ть *perf*) *or* позволя́ть (позво́лить *perf*) кому́-н +*infin*; **he was ~ed to ...** ему́ бы́ло разрешено́ +*infin* ...; **smoking is not ~ed** кури́ть воспреща́ется *or*

запреща́ется; **we must ~ 3 days for the journey** мы должны́ оста́вить три дня на доро́гу

▸ **allow for** *vt fus* учи́тывать (уче́сть* *perf*), принима́ть (приня́ть* *perf*) в расчёт.

allowance [ə'lauəns] *n* (*company expenses*) де́ньги* *pl* на расхо́ды; (*pocket money*) карма́нные де́ньги; (*welfare payment*) посо́бие; (*tax allowance*) нало́говая ски́дка*; **to make ~s for sb/sth** де́лать (сде́лать *perf*) ски́дку для кого́-н/на что-н.

alloy ['ælɔɪ] *n* сплав.

all right *adv* хорошо́, норма́льно; (*as answer: in agreement*) хорошо́, ла́дно ◆ *adj* неплохо́й*, норма́льный; **is everything ~~?** всё норма́льно *or* в поря́дке?; **are you ~~?** как Вы (себя́ чу́вствуете)?; **do you like him? – he's ~~** он Вам нра́вится? – ничего́.

all-rounder [ɔ:l'raundə^r] *n* универса́л.

allspice ['ɔ:lspaɪs] *n* души́стый пе́рец*.

all-time ['ɔ:l'taɪm] *adj* (*record*) непревзойдённый; **inflation is at an ~ low** инфля́ция на небыва́ло ни́зком у́ровне.

allude [ə'lu:d] *vi*: **to ~ to** намека́ть (намекну́ть *perf*) на *+acc*.

alluring [ə'ljuərɪŋ] *adj* соблазни́тельный* (соблазни́телен).

allusion [ə'lu:ʒən] *n*: **~ (to)** намёк (на *+acc*); (*LITERATURE*) аллю́зия (на *+acc*).

alluvium [ə'lu:vɪəm] *n* аллю́вий.

ally [*n* 'ælaɪ, *vb* ə'laɪ] *n* сою́зник ◆ *vt*: **to ~ o.s. with** объединя́ться (объедини́ться *perf*) с *+instr*.

Alma-Ata [ælmɑ:ə'tɑ:] *n* А́лма-Ата́ *f ind*.

almighty [ɔ:l'maɪtɪ] *adj* (*omnipotent*) всемогу́щий* (всемогу́щ); (*tremendous*) колосса́льный.

almond ['ɑ:mənd] *n* минда́ль* *m*.

almost ['ɔ:lməust] *adv* почти́; (*all but*) чуть *or* едва́ не; **he ~ fell** он чуть не упа́л.

alms [ɑ:mz] *npl* ми́лостыня *fsg*, подая́ние *ntsg*.

aloft [ə'lɔft] *adv* (*hold, carry*) над голово́й.

alone [ə'ləun] *adj, adv* оди́н (одна́); **to leave sb/sth ~** оставля́ть (оста́вить* *perf*) кого́-н/что-н в поко́е; **let ~ ...** не говоря́ уже́ о *+prp* ....

along [ə'lɔŋ] *prep* (*motion*) по *+dat*, вдоль *+gen*; (*position*) вдоль *+gen* ◆ *adv*: **is he coming ~ (with us)?** он идёт с на́ми?; **he was limping ~** он шёл хрома́я; **~ with** вме́сте с *+instr*; **all ~** с са́мого нача́ла.

alongside [ə'lɔŋ'saɪd] *prep* (*position*) ря́дом с *+instr*, вдоль *+gen*; (*motion*) к *+dat* ◆ *adv* ря́дом; **we brought our boat ~** мы прича́лили ло́дку.

aloof [ə'lu:f] *adj* отрешённый (отрешён) ◆ *adv*: **to stand ~** держа́ться (*impf*) в стороне́.

aloofness [ə'lu:fnɪs] *n* отрешённость *f*.

aloud [ə'laud] *adv* (*read, speak*) вслух.

alphabet ['ælfəbɛt] *n* алфави́т.

alphabetical [ælfə'bɛtɪkl] *adj* алфави́тный; **in ~ order** в алфави́тном поря́дке.

alphanumeric ['ælfənju:'mɛrɪk] *adj* алфави́тно-цифрово́й.

alpine ['ælpaɪn] *adj* высокого́рный, альпи́йский*.

Alps [ælps] *npl*: **the ~** А́льпы* *pl*.

already [ɔ:l'rɛdɪ] *adv* уже́.

alright ['ɔ:l'raɪt] *adv* (*BRIT*) **= all right**.

Alsace ['ælsæs] *n* Эльза́с.

Alsatian [æl'seɪʃən] *n* (*BRIT: dog*) неме́цкая овча́рка*; (*person*) эльза́сец(-ска).

also ['ɔ:lsəu] *adv* (*referring to subject*) та́кже, то́же; (*referring to object*) та́кже; (*moreover*) кро́ме того́, к тому́ же; **he ~ likes apples** он та́кже *or* то́же лю́бит я́блоки; **he likes apples ~** он лю́бит та́кже я́блоки.

altar ['ɔltə^r] *n* алта́рь* *m*.

alter ['ɔltə^r] *vt* изменя́ть (измени́ть* *perf*) ◆ *vi* изменя́ться (измени́ться* *perf*).

alteration [ɔltə'reɪʃən] *n* измене́ние; **~s** *npl* (*SEWING*) переде́лки *fpl*; **to make ~s to a building** перестра́ивать (перестро́ить *perf*) зда́ние.

altercation [ɔltə'keɪʃən] *n* препира́тельство.

alternate [*adj* ɔl'tə:nɪt, *vb* 'ɔltə:neɪt] *adj* череду́ющийся; (*US: alternative*) альтернати́вный ◆ *vi*: **to ~ (with)** чередова́ться (*impf*) (с *+instr*); **on ~ days** че́рез день.

alternately [ɔl'tə:nɪtlɪ] *adv* попереме́нно.

alternating current ['ɔltə:neɪtɪŋ-] *n* переме́нный ток*.

alternative [ɔl'tə:nətɪv] *adj* альтернати́вный ◆ *n* альтернати́ва.

alternatively [ɔl'tə:nətɪvlɪ] *adv*: **~ one could ...** кро́ме того́ мо́жно ....

alternative medicine *n* альтернати́вная *or* нетрадицио́нная медици́на.

alternator ['ɔltə:neɪtə^r] *n* (*AUT*) генера́тор переме́нного то́ка.

although [ɔ:l'ðəu] *conj* хотя́.

altitude ['æltɪtju:d] *n* (*of plane*) высота́*; (*of place*) высота́ над у́ровнем мо́ря.

alto ['æltəu] *n* (*female*) контра́льто *nt ind*; (*male*) альт*.

altogether [ɔ:ltə'gɛðə^r] *adv* (*completely*) соверше́нно; (*in all*) в о́бщем, в о́бщей сло́жности; **how much is that ~?** ско́лько бу́дет в о́бщей сло́жности?

altruism ['æltruɪzəm] *n* альтруи́зм.

altruistic [æltru'ɪstɪk] *adj* (*action*) альтруисти́ческий; (*person*) альтруисти́чный (альтруисти́чен).

aluminium [ælju'mɪnɪəm] *n* (*BRIT*) алюми́ний.

* marks translations which have irregular inflections. The Russian-English side of the dictionary gives inflectional information.

aluminum [ə'lu:mɪnəm] *n* (*US*) = **aluminium.**
always ['ɔ:lweɪz] *adv* всегда́.
Alzheimer's disease ['æltshaɪməz-] *n* боле́знь *f* Алцхе́ймера.
AM *abbr* (= *amplitude modulation*) амплиту́дная модуля́ция; (= *Assembly Member*) член ассамбле́и.
am [æm] *vb see* **be**.
a.m. *adv abbr* (= *ante meridiem*) до полу́дня.
AMA *n abbr* = *American Medical Association.*
amalgam [ə'mælgəm] *n* амальга́ма.
amalgamate [ə'mælgəmeɪt] *vi* слива́ться (сли́ться *perf*) ◆ *vt* слива́ть (слить *perf*).
amalgamation [əmælgə'meɪʃən] *n* (*of companies*) слия́ние.
amass [ə'mæs] *vt* нака́пливать (накопи́ть* *perf*).
amateur ['æmətə^r] *n* люби́тель *m*; ~ **sport/ dramatics** люби́тельский* спорт/теа́тр; ~ **photographer** фото́граф-люби́тель *m*.
amateurish ['æmətərɪʃ] *adj* (*work, efforts*) непрофессиона́льный (непрофессиона́лен).
amaze [ə'meɪz] *vt* поража́ть (порази́ть* *perf*), изумля́ть (изуми́ть* *perf*); **I was ~d (at)** я был поражён (*+instr*).
amazement [ə'meɪzmənt] *n* изумле́ние.
amazing [ə'meɪzɪŋ] *adj* (*surprising*) порази́тельный* (порази́телен); (*fantastic*) изуми́тельный* (изуми́телен), замеча́тельный* (замеча́телен).
amazingly [ə'meɪzɪŋlɪ] *adv* порази́тельно.
Amazon ['æməzən] *n* (*river*) Амазо́нка; (*woman*) амазо́нка*; **the ~ basin** бассе́йн реки́ Амазо́нки; **the ~ jungle** джу́нгли *pl* Амазо́нки.
Amazonian [æmə'zəunɪən] *adj* амазо́нский.
ambassador [æm'bæsədə^r] *n* посо́л*.
amber ['æmbə^r] *n* янта́рь* *m*; **the lights were at** ~ на светофо́ре был жёлтый свет.
ambidextrous [æmbɪ'dɛkstrəs] *adj одина́ково владе́ющий пра́вой и ле́вой руко́й.*
ambience ['æmbɪəns] *n* атмосфе́ра.
ambiguity [æmbɪ'gjuɪtɪ] *n* двусмы́сленность *f*, нея́сность *f*.
ambiguous [æm'bɪgjuəs] *adj* двусмы́сленный, нея́сный*.
ambition [æm'bɪʃən] *n* (*quality: positive*) честолю́бие; (: *negative*) амби́ция; (*aim*) цель *f*; **to achieve one's ~** достига́ть (дости́чь* *perf*) свое́й це́ли.
ambitious [æm'bɪʃəs] *adj* честолюби́вый (честолюби́в); амбицио́зный* (амбицио́зен).
ambivalence [æm'bɪvələns] *n* (*indecision*) дво́йственное отноше́ние; (*ambiguity*) несоотве́тствия *ntpl*.
ambivalent [æm'bɪvələnt] *adj* (*attitude*) дво́йственный (дво́йствен); (*person*) противоречи́вый (противоречи́в).
amble ['æmbl] *vi* прогу́ливаться (прогуля́ться *perf*).
ambulance ['æmbjuləns] *n* ско́рая по́мощь *f*.
ambulanceman ['æmbjulənsmən] *irreg n* фе́льдшер ско́рой по́мощи.
ambush ['æmbuʃ] *n* заса́да ◆ *vt* устра́ивать (устро́ить* *perf*) заса́ду *+dat*.
ameba [ə'mi:bə] *n* (*US*) = **amoeba**.
ameliorate [ə'mi:lɪəreɪt] *vt* (*situation*) улучша́ть (улу́чшить *perf*).
amen ['ɑ:'mɛn] *excl* ами́нь.
amenable [ə'mi:nəbl] *adj*: ~ **to** пода́тливый (пода́тлив) на *+acc*; **he's ~ to advice** он прислу́шивается к сове́там; ~ **to the law** отве́тственный (отве́тствен) пе́ред зако́ном.
amend [ə'mɛnd] *vt* пересма́тривать (пересмотре́ть *perf*); (*habits*) исправля́ть (испра́вить* *perf*) ◆ *vi* исправля́ться (испра́виться* *perf*) ◆ *n*: **to make ~s** загла́живать (загла́дить* *perf*) вину́.
amendment [ə'mɛndmənt] *n* попра́вка*.
amenities [ə'mi:nɪtɪz] *npl* удо́бства *ntpl*.
amenity [ə'mi:nɪtɪ] *n* удо́бство.
America [ə'mɛrɪkə] *n* Аме́рика.
American [ə'mɛrɪkən] *adj* америка́нский* ◆ *n* америка́нец*(-нка).
americanize [ə'mɛrɪkənaɪz] *vt* американизи́ровать *(impf/perf)*.
amethyst ['æmɪθɪst] *n* амети́ст.
Amex ['æmɛks] *n abbr* = *American Stock Exchange*.
amiable ['eɪmɪəbl] *adj* дружелю́бный* (дружелю́бен).
amiably ['eɪmɪəblɪ] *adv* дружелю́бно.
amicable ['æmɪkəbl] *adj* (*relationship*) дру́жеский*; (*divorce*) ми́рный* (ми́рен).
amicably ['æmɪkəblɪ] *adv* по-дру́жески, ми́рно
amid(st) [ə'mɪd(st)] *prep* посреди́ *+gen*.
amiss [ə'mɪs] *adj, adv*: **to take sth ~** оши́бочно истолко́вывать (истолкова́ть* *perf*) что-н; **there's something ~** что́-то нела́дно
ammeter ['æmɪtə^r] *n* амперме́тр.
ammo ['æməu] *n abbr* (*inf*) = **ammunition**.
ammonia [ə'məunɪə] *n* (*gas*) аммиа́к; (*liquid*) нашаты́рный спирт*.
ammunition [æmju'nɪʃən] *n* (*MIL*) боеприпа́сы *pl*; (*for gun*) патро́ны *mpl*; (*fig*) ору́жие.
ammunition dump *n* склад боеприпа́сов.
amnesia [æm'ni:zɪə] *n* амнези́я, утра́та па́мяти.
amnesty ['æmnɪstɪ] *n* амни́стия; **to grant an ~ to** объявля́ть (объяви́ть* *perf*) амни́стию *+dat*.
amoeba [ə'mi:bə] (*US* **ameba**) *n* амёба.
amok [ə'mɔk] *adv*: **to run ~** (*people*) бесноваться *(impf)*; (*animals*) беси́ться* (взбеси́ться *perf*).
among(st) [ə'mʌŋ(st)] *prep* среди́ *+gen*; (*between*) ме́жду *+instr*.
amoral [æ'mɔrəl] *adj* безнра́вственный* (безнра́вственен), амора́льный* (амора́лен).
amorous ['æmərəs] *adj* любо́вный.

amorphous [ə'mɔ:fəs] *adj* амо́рфный* (амо́рфен).
amortization [əmɔ:taɪ'zeɪʃən] *n* (*COMM*) амортиза́ция.
amount [ə'maunt] *n* коли́чество; (*sum of money*) су́мма ◆ *vi*: **to ~ to** (*total*) составля́ть (соста́вить* *perf*); **this ~s to a refusal** э́то равноси́льно отка́зу; **the total ~** (*of money*) о́бщая су́мма.
amp(ère) ['æmp(ɛə')] *n* ампе́р*; **a 13 amp plug** ви́лка в 13 ампе́р.
ampersand ['æmpəsænd] *n* знак "&" (*обознача́ющий "и"*).
amphetamine [æm'fɛtəmi:n] *n* амфетами́н.
amphibian [æm'fɪbɪən] *n* амфи́бия, земново́дное живо́тное *nt adj*.
amphibious [æm'fɪbɪəs] *adj* (*animal*) земново́дный; (*vehicle*) амфи́бийный; **~ tank** танк-амфи́бия.
amphitheatre ['æmfɪθɪətə'] (*US* **amphitheater**) *n* амфитеа́тр.
ample ['æmpl] *adj* (*large*) большо́й; (*abundant*) оби́льный* (оби́лен); (*enough*) доста́точный (доста́точен); **to have ~ time/room** име́ть (*impf*) доста́точно вре́мени/ме́ста; **this is ~** э́того вполне́ доста́точно.
amplifier ['æmplɪfaɪə'] *n* усили́тель *m*.
amplify ['æmplɪfaɪ] *vt* уси́ливать (уси́лить *perf*).
amply ['æmplɪ] *adv* вполне́.
ampoule ['æmpu:l] (*US* **ampule**) *n* а́мпула.
amputate ['æmpjuteɪt] *vt* ампути́ровать (*impf/perf*).
amputation [æmpju'teɪʃən] *n* ампута́ция.
amputee [æmpju'ti:] *n* инвали́д.
Amsterdam ['æmstədæm] *n* Амстерда́м.
amt *abbr* (= **amount**) кол-во= *коли́чество*.
amuck [ə'mʌk] *adv* = **amok**.
amuse [ə'mju:z] *vt* развлека́ть (развле́чь* *perf*); **to ~ o.s. with sth** заня́ться (*perf*) *or* развлека́ться (развле́чься* *perf*) чем-н; **he was ~d at this** его́ э́то позаба́вило; **he was not ~d** ему́ бы́ло не до сме́ха.
amusement [ə'mju:zmənt] *n* (*mirth*) удово́льствие; (*pastime*) развлече́ние; **much to my ~** к моему́ осо́бенному удово́льствию.
amusement arcade *n* павильо́н с игровы́ми аппара́тами.
amusement park *n* луна-парк.
amusing [ə'mju:zɪŋ] *adj* заба́вный* (заба́вен), занима́тельный* (занима́телен).
an [æn] *indef art see* **a**.
ANA *n abbr* = *American Newspaper Association*; *American Nurses Association*.
anachronism [ə'nækrənɪzəm] *n* анахрони́зм.
anaemia [ə'ni:mɪə] (*US* **anemia**) *n* анеми́я, малокро́вие.
anaemic [ə'ni:mɪk] (*US* **anemic**) *adj* (*MED, fig*) анеми́чный* (анеми́чен).
anaesthetic [ænɪs'θɛtɪk] (*US* **anesthetic**) *n* нарко́з; **under the ~** под нарко́зом; **local/general ~** ме́стный/о́бщий* нарко́з.
anaesthetist [æ'ni:sθɪtɪst] (*US* **anesthetist**) *n* анестезио́лог.
anagram ['ænəgræm] *n* анагра́мма.
anal ['eɪnl] *adj* ана́льный, заднепрохо́дный.
analgesic [ænæl'dʒi:sɪk] *adj* обезбо́ливающий* ◆ *n* обезбо́ливающее сре́дство.
analog ['ænəlɔg] *adj* = **analogue**.
analogous [ə'næləgəs] *adj* аналоги́чный* (аналоги́чен).
analogue ['ænəlɔg] *adj* (*computer*) ана́логовый.
analogy [ə'nælədʒɪ] *n* анало́гия; **to draw an ~ between** проводи́ть* (провести́* *perf*) анало́гию ме́жду *+instr*; **by ~** по анало́гии.
analyse ['ænəlaɪz] (*US* **analyze**) *vt* анализи́ровать (проанализи́ровать *perf*); (*PSYCH*): **to ~ sb** подверга́ть (подве́ргнуть* *perf*) кого́-н психоана́лизу.
analyses [ə'næləsi:z] *npl of* **analysis**.
analysis [ə'næləsɪs] (*pl* **analyses**) *n* ана́лиз; (*PSYCH*) психоана́лиз; **in the last ~** в коне́чном ито́ге.
analyst ['ænəlɪst] *n* (*political*) коммента́тор; (*financial, economic*) экспе́рт; (*US*: *psychiatrist*) психиа́тр.
analytic(al) [ænə'lɪtɪk(l)] *adj* аналити́ческий.
analyze ['ænəlaɪz] *vt* (*US*) = **analyse**.
anarchic [æ'na:kɪk] *adj* анархи́ческий.
anarchist ['ænəkɪst] *adj* анархи́ческий ◆ *n* анархи́ст.
anarchy ['ænəkɪ] *n* ана́рхия.
anathema [ə'næθɪmə] *n*: **that is ~ to him** для него́ э́то ана́фема.
anatomical [ænə'tɔmɪkl] *adj* анатоми́ческий.
anatomy [ə'nætəmɪ] *n* анато́мия; (*body*) органи́зм.
ANC *n abbr* (= *African National Congress*) АНК= *Африка́нский* национа́льный конгре́сс*.
ancestor ['ænsɪstə'] *n* пре́док*.
ancestral [æn'sɛstrəl] *adj* родово́й; **~ home** родово́е поме́стье.
ancestry ['ænsɪstrɪ] *n* происхожде́ние.
anchor ['æŋkə'] *n* я́корь* *m* ◆ *vi* (*also:* **to drop ~**) броса́ть (бро́сить* *perf*) я́корь; **to weigh ~** поднима́ть (подня́ть* *perf*) я́корь.
anchorage ['æŋkərɪdʒ] *n* я́корная стоя́нка*.
anchor man *n* веду́щий* *m adj* (програ́ммы).
anchovy ['æntʃəvɪ] *n* анчо́ус.
ancient ['eɪnʃənt] *adj* (*civilization, person*) дре́вний*; (*monument*) стари́нный.
ancient monument *n* па́мятник старины́.
ancillary [æn'sɪlərɪ] *adj* подсо́бный.

and [ænd] *conj* и; (*with pronouns*) с *+instr*; **you ~ I** мы с Вáми; **my father ~ I** мы с отцóм; **bread ~ butter** хлеб с мáслом; **~ so on** и так дáлее; **try ~ come** постарáйтесь прийти́; **he talked ~ talked** он всё говори́л и говори́л.
Andes ['ændi:z] *npl*: **the ~** Áнды* *pl*.
Andorra [æn'dɔ:rə] *n* Андóрра.
anecdote ['ænɪkdəut] *n* забáвная истóрия.
anemia *etc n* (*US*) = **anaemia** *etc*.
anemone [ə'nɛmənɪ] *n* вéтреница, анемóна.
anesthetic *etc* (*US*) = **anaesthetic** *etc*.
anew [ə'nju:] *adv* зáново.
angel ['eɪndʒəl] *n* áнгел.
angel dust *n* (*drug*) „áнгельская пыль" *f*.
angelic [æn'dʒɛlɪk] *adj* áнгельский*.
anger ['æŋgə^r] *n* гнев, возмущéние ◆ *vt* серди́ть* (рассерди́ть* *perf*), возмущáть (возмути́ть* *perf*).
angina [æn'dʒaɪnə] *n* грудная жáба.
angle ['æŋgl] *n* (*corner*) ýгол*; (*viewpoint*): **from their ~** с их тóчки зрéния ◆ *vi*: **to ~ for** (*invitation*) напрáшиваться (напроси́ться* *perf*) на *+acc* ◆ *vt*: **the idea is/was ~d towards** *or* **to** идéя рассчи́тана/былá рассчи́тана на *+acc*.
angler ['æŋglə^r] *n* рыболóв.
Anglican ['æŋglɪkən] *adj* англикáнский* ◆ *n* англикáнец(-áнка).
anglicize ['æŋglɪsaɪz] *vt* англизи́ровать *(impf)*.
angling ['æŋglɪŋ] *n* ры́бная лóвля.
Anglo- ['æŋgləu] *prefix* áнгло-.
Anglo-Saxon ['æŋgləu'sæksən] *adj* англосаксóнский; (*LING*) древнеангли́йский ◆ *n* англосáкс; (*LING*) древнеангли́йский язы́к*.
Angola [æŋ'gəulə] *n* Ангóла.
Angolan [æŋ'gəulən] *adj* ангóльский* ◆ *n* ангóлец*(-лка*).
angrily ['æŋgrɪlɪ] *adv* серди́то, гнéвно.
angry ['æŋgrɪ] *adj* серди́тый (серди́т), гнéвный* (гнéвен); (*wound*) воспалённый (воспалён); **to be ~ with sb/at sth** серди́ться* *(impf) or* зли́ться *(impf)* на когó-н/чтó-н; **to get ~** серди́ться* (рассерди́ться* *perf*), зли́ться (разозли́ться *perf*); **he gets ~ easily** егó легкó рассерди́ть; **to make sb ~** серди́ть* (рассерди́ть* *perf*) *or* злить (разозли́ть *perf*) когó-н.
anguish ['æŋgwɪʃ] *n* мýка.
anguished ['æŋgwɪʃt] *adj* страдáльческий*.
angular ['æŋgjulə^r] *adj* (*person, features*) углова́тый (углова́т).
animal ['ænɪməl] *n* живóтное *nt adj*; (*wild animal*) зверь* *m*; (*pej*: *person*) зверь, живóтное ◆ *adj* живóтный.
animal rights [-raɪts] *npl* правá *ntpl* живóтных; **the ~ ~ movement** движéние за правá живóтных.
animate [*vb* 'ænɪmeɪt, *adj* 'ænɪmɪt] *vt* оживля́ть (оживи́ть* *perf*) ◆ *adj* живóй*; (*LING*) одушевлённый.
animated ['ænɪmeɪtɪd] *adj* оживлённый* (оживлён), живóй*; (*film*) мультипликациóнный.
animation [ænɪ'meɪʃən] *n* (*CINEMA*) мультипликáция; (*enthusiasm*) оживлéние.
animosity [ænɪ'mɔsɪtɪ] *n* враждéбность *f*.
aniseed ['ænɪsi:d] *n* ани́с ◆ *adj* ани́совый.
Ankara ['æŋkərə] *n* Анкарá.
ankle ['æŋkl] *n* лоды́жка*.
ankle sock *n* носóк*.
annex ['ænɛks] *n* (*also*: **~e**: *BRIT*) пристрóйка; (: *separate building*) отдéльный кóрпус ◆ *vt* аннекси́ровать *(impf/perf)*.
annexation [ænɛk'seɪʃən] *n* аннéксия.
annihilate [ə'naɪəleɪt] *vt* уничтожáть (уничтóжить *perf*).
annihilation [ənaɪə'leɪʃən] *n* уничтожéние.
anniversary [ænɪ'və:sərɪ] *n* годовщи́на.
Anno Domini ['ænəu'dɔmɪnaɪ] *adv* нáшей э́ры.
annotate ['ænəuteɪt] *vt* составля́ть (состáвить *perf*) комментáрий на *+acc*.
announce [ə'nauns] *vt* (*decision, engagement*) объявля́ть (объяви́ть* *perf*) (о *+prp*); (*birth, death etc*) извещáть (извести́ть* *perf*) о *+prp*; **he ~d that he wasn't going** он заяви́л, что не пойдёт.
announcement [ə'naunsmənt] *n* объявлéние; (*in newspaper etc*) сообщéние; (*in letter etc*) извещéние; **I'd like to make an ~** я бы хотéл сдéлать заявлéние.
announcer [ə'naunsə^r] *n* (*RADIO, TV*) ди́ктор.
annoy [ə'nɔɪ] *vt* раздражáть (раздражи́ть *perf*); **I am ~ed with him** он меня́ раздражáет; **don't get ~ed!** не раздражáйтесь *or* серди́тесь!
annoyance [ə'nɔɪəns] *n* (*feeling*) раздражéние, досáда.
annoyed [ə'nɔɪd] *adj* раздражённый* (раздражён).
annoying [ə'nɔɪɪŋ] *adj* (*noise*) раздражáющий; (*mistake, event*) досáдный* (досáден); **he is ~** он меня́ раздражáет.
annual ['ænjuəl] *adj* (*meeting*) ежегóдный; (*income*) годовóй ◆ *n* (*BOT*) однолéтнее растéние; (*book*) ежегóдник.
annual general meeting *n* (*BRIT*) ежегóдное óбщее собрáние.
annually ['ænjuəlɪ] *adv* ежегóдно.
annual report *n* годовóй отчёт.
annuity [ə'nju:ɪtɪ] *n* рéнта; **life ~** пожи́зненная рéнта.
annul [ə'nʌl] *vt* (*contract*) аннули́ровать *(impf/perf)*; (*marriage*) расторгáть (растóргнуть* *perf*); (*law*) отменя́ть (отмени́ть* *perf*).
annulment [ə'nʌlmənt] *n* (*see vt*) аннули́рование; расторжéние; отмéна.
annum ['ænəm] *n see* **per**.
Annunciation [ənʌnsɪ'eɪʃən] *n* Благовéщение.
anode ['ænəud] *n* анóд.
anodyne ['ænədaɪn] *n* успокáивающее срéдство ◆ *adj* нейтрáльный* (нейтрáлен).
anoint [ə'nɔɪnt] *vt* помáзывать (помáзать*

perf).
anomalous [ə'nɔməlәs] *adj* анома́льный* (анома́лен).
anomaly [ə'nɔməlɪ] *n* анома́лия.
anon. [ə'nɔn] *abbr* = **anonymous.**
anonymity [ænə'nɪmɪtɪ] *n* анони́мность *f.*
anonymous [ə'nɔnɪməs] *adj* анони́мный* (анони́мен); (*place*) безли́кий* (безли́к); **to remain ~** сохраня́ть (сохрани́ть *perf*) анони́мность.
anorak ['ænəræk] *n* ку́ртка* с капюшо́ном.
anorexia [ænə'rɛksɪə] *n* аноре́ксия.
anorexic [ænə'rɛksɪk] *adj*: **she is ~** она́ страда́ет аноре́ксией.
another [ə'nʌðə^r] *pron* друго́й ◆ *adj*: **~ book** (*additional*) ещё одна́ кни́га; (*different*) друга́я кни́га; **I waited ~ week** я подожда́л ещё одну́ неде́лю; **~ drink?** Вам ещё нали́ть?; **in ~ 5 years** ещё че́рез 5 лет; *see also* **one.**
ANSI *n abbr* (= *American National Standards Institute*) Институ́т америка́нских национа́льных станда́ртов.
answer ['ɑ:nsə^r] *n* отве́т; (*to problem*) реше́ние ◆ *vi* отвеча́ть (отве́тить* *perf*) ◆ *vt* (*letter, question*) отвеча́ть (отве́тить* *perf*) на *+acc*; (*person*) отвеча́ть (отве́тить* *perf*) *+dat*; **in ~ to your letter** в отве́т на Ва́ше письмо́; **to ~ the phone** подходи́ть* (подойти́* *perf*) к телефо́ну; **to ~ the bell** *or* **the door** открыва́ть (откры́ть* *perf*) дверь; **our prayers were ~ed** на́ши моли́твы бы́ли услы́шаны
▸ **answer back** *vi* огрыза́ться *(impf)*
▸ **answer for** *vt fus* отвеча́ть (отве́тить* *perf*) за *+acc*
▸ **answer to** *vt fus* (*description*) соотве́тствовать *(impf) +dat.*
answerable ['ɑ:nsərəbl] *adj*: **~ to sb for sth** отве́тственный пе́ред кем-н за что-н; **I am ~ to no-one** я не отвеча́ю ни пе́ред кем.
answering machine ['ɑ:nsərɪŋ-] *n* автоотве́тчик.
ant [ænt] *n* мураве́й*.
ANTA *n abbr* = *American National Theater and Academy.*
antagonism [æn'tægənɪzəm] *n* антагони́зм.
antagonist [æn'tægənɪst] *n* проти́вник.
antagonistic [æntægə'nɪstɪk] *adj* (*feelings*) вражде́бный* (вражде́бен); **he is ~ to the government** он вражде́бен по отноше́нию к прави́тельству.
antagonize [æn'tægənaɪz] *vt*: **to ~ sb** вызыва́ть (вы́звать* *perf*) чьё-н вражде́бное отноше́ние.
Antarctic [ænt'ɑ:ktɪk] *n*: **the ~** Анта́рктика.
Antarctica [ænt'ɑ:ktɪkə] *n* Антаркти́да.
Antarctic Circle *n*: **the ~ ~** Ю́жный поля́рный круг.
Antarctic Ocean *n*: **the ~ ~** Антаркти́ческий* океа́н.
ante ['æntɪ] *n*: **to up the ~** повыша́ть (повы́сить* *perf*) ста́вку.
ante... ['æntɪ] *prefix* до..., пред....
anteater ['ænti:tə^r] *n* муравье́д.
antecedent [æntɪ'si:dənt] *n* предше́ственник; (*ancestor*) пре́док*.
antechamber ['æntɪtʃeɪmbə^r] *n* пере́дняя *f adj*, прихо́жая *f adj*.
antelope ['æntɪləup] *n* антило́па.
antenatal ['æntɪ'neɪtl] *adj* дородово́й.
antenatal clinic *n* ≈ же́нская консульта́ция.
antenna [æn'tɛnə] (*pl* **~e**) *n* у́сик; (*TV*) анте́нна.
antennae [æn'tɛni:] *npl of* **antenna.**
anteroom ['æntɪrum] *n* приёмная *f adj*.
anthem ['ænθəm] *n*: **national ~** госуда́рственный гимн.
ant hill *n* мураве́йник.
anthology [æn'θɔlədʒɪ] *n* антоло́гия.
anthropologist [ænθrə'pɔlədʒɪst] *n* антропо́лог.
anthropology [ænθrə'pɔlədʒɪ] *n* антрополо́гия.
anti... ['æntɪ] *prefix* а́нти..., про́тиво....
anti-aircraft ['æntɪ'ɛəkrɑ:ft] *adj* (*missile*) противовозду́шный.
anti-aircraft defence *n* противовозду́шная оборо́на.
antiballistic ['æntɪbə'lɪstɪk] *adj* (*missile*) антибаллисти́ческий.
antibiotic ['æntɪbaɪ'ɔtɪk] *n* (*MED*) антибио́тик.
antibody ['æntɪbɔdɪ] *n* антите́ло*.
anticipate [æn'tɪsɪpeɪt] *vt* (*expect*) ожида́ть *(impf) +gen*; (*foresee*) предви́деть* *(impf/perf)*; (*look forward to*) предвкуша́ть *(impf)*; (*forestall*) предвосхища́ть (предвосхи́тить* *perf*); **this is worse than I ~d** э́то ху́же, чем я ожида́л; **as ~d** как предполага́лось.
anticipation [æntɪsɪ'peɪʃən] *n* (*expectation*) ожида́ние; (*eagerness*) предвкуше́ние; **thanking you in ~** зара́нее благодарю́ Вас.
anticlimax ['æntɪ'klaɪmæks] *n* разочарова́ние.
anticlockwise ['æntɪ'klɔkwaɪz] *adv* (*BRIT*) про́тив часово́й стре́лки.
antics ['æntɪks] *npl* (*of animal, child*) ша́лости *fpl*; (*of politicians etc*) вы́ходки *pl.*
anticyclone ['æntɪ'saɪkləun] *n* антицикло́н.
antidepressant ['æntɪdɪ'presənt] *n* антидепресса́нт.
antidote ['æntɪdəut] *n* (*also fig*) противоя́дие.
antifreeze ['æntɪfri:z] *n* антифри́з.
antihistamine ['æntɪ'hɪstəmɪn] *n* антигистами́н.
Antilles [æn'tɪli:z] *npl*: **the ~** Анти́льские острова́ *mpl*.
antipathy [æn'tɪpəθɪ] *n* антипа́тия.
antiperspirant ['æntɪ'pə:spɪrənt] *n* дезодора́нт.
Antipodean [æntɪpə'di:ən] *adj* антипо́дный

* marks translations which have irregular inflections. The Russian-English side of the dictionary gives inflectional information.

(*обычно о жителях Австралии и Новой Зеландии*).

Antipodes [æn'tɪpədi:z] *npl*: **the ~** *Австралия и Новая Зеландия*.

antiquarian [æntɪ'kwɛərɪən] *n* антиквар ◆ *adj*: **~ bookshop** букинистический* магазин.

antiquated ['æntɪkweɪtɪd] *adj* устарелый.

antique [æn'ti:k] *n* предмет старины ◆ *adj* (*furniture etc*) антикварный*; (*pre-medieval*) античный.

antique dealer *n* антиквар.

antique shop *n* антикварный магазин.

antiquity [æn'tɪkwɪtɪ] *n* античность *f*.

anti-Semitic ['æntɪsɪ'mɪtɪk] *adj* антисемитский*.

anti-Semitism ['æntɪ'sɛmɪtɪzəm] *n* антисемитизм.

antiseptic [æntɪ'sɛptɪk] *n* антисептик ◆ *adj* антисептический*.

antisocial ['æntɪ'səuʃəl] *adj* (*behaviour*) антиобщественный; (*person*) необщительный* (необщителен).

antitank ['æntɪ'tæŋk] *adj* противотанковый.

antitheses [æn'tɪθɪsi:z] *npl of* **antithesis**.

antithesis [æn'tɪθɪsɪs] (*pl* **antitheses**) *n* антитеза.

antitrust ['æntɪ'trʌst] *adj*: **~ legislation** антимонопольное законодательство.

antlers ['æntləz] *npl* (оленьи) рога* *mpl*.

Antwerp ['æntwə:p] *n* Антверпен.

anus ['eɪnəs] *n* задний* проход.

anvil ['ænvɪl] *n* наковальня*.

anxiety [æŋ'zaɪətɪ] *n* (*also MED*) тревога; **~ to do** стремление *+infin*.

anxious ['æŋkʃəs] *adj* (*person*) беспокойный* (беспокоен); (*expression*) озабоченный* (озабочен); (*worrying*) тревожный* (тревожен); (*keen*): **she is ~ to do** она очень хочет *+infin*; **to be ~ about** беспокоиться (*impf*) о *+prp*; **I'm very ~ about you** я очень беспокоюсь за Вас.

anxiously ['æŋkʃəslɪ] *adv* беспокойно, тревожно.

KEYWORD

any ['ɛnɪ] *adj* **1** (*in questions etc*): **have you any butter/children?** у Вас есть масло/дети?; **do you have any questions/doubts?** у Вас есть какие-нибудь вопросы/сомнения?; **if there are any tickets left** если ещё остались билеты
2 (*with negative*): **I haven't any bread/books** у меня нет хлеба/книг; **I didn't buy/read any newspapers** я не купил/не читал газеты
3 (*no matter which*) любой; **any colour will do** любой цвет пойдёт; **choose any book you like** выбирайте любую книгу, какая Вам понравится
4 (*in phrases*): **in any case** в любом случае; **any day now** сейчас в любой день; **at any moment** в любой момент; **at any rate** во всяком случае; (*anyhow*) так или иначе; **any time** (*at any moment*) в любой момент; (*whenever*) в любое время; (*in answer to thanks*) не за что; **I need some black leather boots – have you any?** мне нужны чёрные кожаные сапоги – у Вас такие есть?; **I have run out of sugar, you don't have any?** у меня кончился сахар, у Вас не найдётся немного?
◆ *pron* **1** (*in questions etc*): **I need some money, have you got any?** мне нужны деньги, у Вас они есть?; **can any of you sing?** кто-нибудь из Вас умеет петь?
2 (*with negative*) ни один (*f* одна, *nt* одно, *pl* одни); **I haven't any (of those)** у меня таких нет
3 (*no matter which one(s)*) любой; **take any you like** возьмите то, что Вам нравится
◆ *adv* **1** (*in questions etc*): **do you want any more soup/sandwiches?** хотите ещё супа/бутерброды?; **are you feeling any better?** Вам хоть сколько-нибудь лучше?
2 (*with negative*): **I can't hear him any more** я больше его не слышу; **don't wait any longer** не ждите больше; **he isn't any better** ему нисколько *or* ничуть не лучше.

anybody ['ɛnɪbɔdɪ] *pron* = **anyone**.

anyhow ['ɛnɪhau] *adv* (*at any rate*) так или иначе; (*haphazardly*): **the work is done ~** работа сделана кое-как *or* как попало; **I shall go ~** я так или иначе пойду; **she leaves things just ~** она разбрасывает вещи как попало.

anyone ['ɛnɪwʌn] *pron* (*in questions etc*) кто-нибудь; (*with negative*) никто; (*no matter who*) кто угодно, любой, всякий*; **can you see ~?** Вы видите кого-нибудь?; **I can't see ~** я никого не вижу; **~ could do it** кто угодно *or* любой *or* всякий* может это сделать; **you can invite ~** Вы можете пригласить кого угодно.

anyplace ['ɛnɪpleɪs] *adv* (*US*) = **anywhere**.

KEYWORD

anything ['ɛnɪθɪŋ] *pron* **1** (*in questions etc*) что-нибудь; **can you see anything?** Вы видите что-нибудь?
2 (*with negative*) ничего; **I can't see anything** я ничего не вижу
3 (*no matter what*) (всё,) что угодно; **anything (at all) will do** всё, (что угодно) подойдёт; **he'll eat anything** он ест всё, что ему ни дай.

anyway ['ɛnɪweɪ] *adv* (*at any rate*) всё равно; (*besides*) всё равно, в любом случае; **I will be there ~** я всё равно там буду; **~, I couldn't stay even if I wanted to** всё равно *or* в любом случае, я не мог бы остаться, даже если бы я захотел; **why are you phoning, ~?** а что Вы звоните?

KEYWORD

anywhere ['ɛnɪwɛə^r] *adv* **1** (*in questions etc*: *position*) где-нибудь; (: *motion*) куда-

нибудь; **can you see him anywhere?** Вы его где-нибудь ви́дите?; **did you walk anywhere yesterday?** Вы вчера́ куда́-нибудь ходи́ли?
2 (*with negative*: *position*) нигде́; (: *motion*) никуда́; **I can't see him anywhere** я нигде́ его́ не ви́жу; **I'm not walking anywhere today** сего́дня я никуда́ не иду́
3 (*no matter where*: *position*) где уго́дно; (: *motion*) куда́ уго́дно; **anywhere in the world** где уго́дно в ми́ре; **put the books down anywhere** положи́те кни́ги куда́ уго́дно.

Anzac ['ænzæk] *n abbr* = *Australia-New Zealand Army Corps*.
apace [ə'peɪs] *adv* стреми́тельно.
apart [ə'pɑːt] *adv* (*position*) в стороне́; (*motion*) в сто́рону; (*separately*) разде́льно, врозь; **they are ten miles/a long way ~** они́ нахо́дятся на расстоя́нии десяти́ миль/на большо́м расстоя́нии друг от дру́га; **they are living ~** они́ живу́т врозь; **they jumped ~** они́ отпры́гнули в сто́роны; **with one's legs ~** с расста́вленными нога́ми; **to take ~** разбира́ть (разобра́ть* *perf*) (на ча́сти); **~ from** кро́ме *+gen*.
apartheid [ə'pɑːteɪt] *n* апартеи́д.
apartment [ə'pɑːtmənt] *n* (*US*) кварти́ра; (*room*) ко́мната.
apartment building *n* (*US*) многокварти́рный дом*.
apathetic [æpə'θɛtɪk] *adj* апати́чный* (апати́чен).
apathy ['æpəθɪ] *n* апа́тия.
APB *n abbr* (*US*: = *all points bulletin*) ≈ сигна́л всем поста́м.
ape [eɪp] *n* (*ZOOL*) человекообра́зная обезья́на ♦ *vt* копи́ровать (скопи́ровать *perf*).
Apennines ['æpənaɪnz] *npl*: **the ~** Апенни́ны *pl*.
aperitif [ə'pɛrɪtiːf] *n* аперити́в.
aperture ['æpətʃjuə'] *n* отве́рстие; (*PHOT*) диафра́гма.
apex ['eɪpɛks] *n* (*also fig*) верши́на.
aphid ['æfɪd] *n* тля*.
aphorism ['æfərɪzəm] *n* афори́зм.
aphrodisiac [æfrəu'dɪzɪæk] *n сре́дство, возбужда́ющее полово́е влече́ние* ♦ *adj* возбужда́ющий* полово́е влече́ние.
API *n abbr* = *American Press Institute*.
apiece [ə'piːs] *adv* (*each person*) на ка́ждого; (*each thing*) за шту́ку.
aplomb [ə'plɔm] *n* апло́мб.
APO *n abbr* (*US*) = *Army Post Office*.
apocalypse [ə'pɔkəlɪps] *n* (*end of world*) коне́ц* све́та; (*destruction*) катастро́фа.
apolitical [eɪpə'lɪtɪkl] *adj* аполити́чный* (аполити́чен).
apologetic [əpɔlə'dʒɛtɪk] *adj* (*tone*) извиня́ющийся*; (*person, expression*) винова́тый; **an ~ letter** письмо́* с извине́ниями; **he's very ~ about ...** он прино́сит свои́ извине́ния за *+acc* ....
apologize [ə'pɔlədʒaɪz] *vi*: **to ~ (for sth to sb)** извиня́ться (извини́ться *perf*) (за что-н пе́ред кем-н).
apology [ə'pɔlədʒɪ] *n* извине́ние; **to send one's apologies** извиня́ться (извини́ться* *perf*) за своё отсу́тствие; **please accept my apologies** пожа́луйста, приими́те мои́ извине́ния.
apoplectic [æpə'plɛktɪk] *adj* (*MED*) апоплекси́ческий; (*fig*): **~ with rage** разъярённый (разъярён).
apoplexy ['æpəplɛksɪ] *n* апопле́ксия.
apostle [ə'pɔsl] *n* апо́стол.
apostrophe [ə'pɔstrəfɪ] *n* апостро́ф.
apotheosis [əpɔθɪ'əusɪs] *n* (*deification*) обожествле́ние; (*fig*) апофео́з.
appal [ə'pɔːl] *vt* ужаса́ть (ужасну́ть *perf*); **to be ~led by** ужаса́ться (ужасну́ться *perf*) *+dat*.
Appalachian Mountains [æpə'leɪʃən-] *npl*: **the ~ ~** Аппала́чи *pl*.
appalling [ə'pɔːlɪŋ] *adj* (*awful*) ужа́сный* (ужа́сен); (*shocking*) ужаса́ющий*; **she's an ~ cook** она́ ужа́сно гото́вит.
apparatus [æpə'reɪtəs] *n* аппарату́ра; (*in gymnasium*) (гимнасти́ческий) снаря́д; (*of organization*) аппара́т.
apparel [ə'pærl] *n* (*esp US*) одея́ние.
apparent [ə'pærənt] *adj* (*seeming*) ви́димый; (*obvious*) очеви́дный* (очеви́ден); **it is ~ that ...** очеви́дно, что ....
apparently [ə'pærəntlɪ] *adv* по всей ви́димости.
apparition [æpə'rɪʃən] *n* виде́ние, при́зрак.
appeal [ə'piːl] *vi* (*LAW*) апелли́ровать *(impf/perf)*, подава́ть* (пода́ть* *perf*) апелля́цию ♦ *n* (*attraction*) привлека́тельность *f*; (*plea*) призы́в; (*LAW*) апелля́ция, обжа́лование; **to ~ (to sb) for** (*help, funds*) обраща́ться (обрати́ться* *perf*) (к кому́-н) за *+instr*; (*calm, order*) призыва́ть (призва́ть* *perf*) (кого́-н) к *+dat*; **to ~ to** (*be attractive to*) привлека́ть (привле́чь* *perf*), нра́виться (понра́виться *perf*) *+dat*; **to ~ to sb for mercy** взыва́ть (воззва́ть* *perf*) к кому́-н о милосе́рдии; **the idea doesn't ~ to me** э́та иде́я не привлека́ет меня́; **right of ~** пра́во на апелля́цию *or* на обжа́лование; **on ~** (*LAW*) на апелля́ции.
appealing [ə'piːlɪŋ] *adj* (*attractive*) привлека́тельный* (привлека́телен); (*touching*) тро́гательный* (тро́гателен); (*pleading*) умоля́ющий*.
appear [ə'pɪə'] *vi* (*come into view, develop*) появля́ться (появи́ться* *perf*); (*seem*) каза́ться* (показа́ться* *perf*); (*be published*) выходи́ть* (вы́йти* *perf*); **to ~ in court** представа́ть* (предста́ть* *perf*) пе́ред судо́м; **to ~ on TV** выступа́ть (вы́ступить* *perf*) по

* marks translations which have irregular inflections. The Russian-English side of the dictionary gives inflectional information.

телеви́дению; **to ~ in "Hamlet"** игра́ть (сыгра́ть *perf*) в "Га́млете"; **it would ~ that ...** похо́же (на то), что ....

appearance [ə'pɪərəns] *n* (*arrival*) появле́ние; (*look, aspect*) вне́шность *f*; (*in public, on TV*) выступле́ние; **to put in** *or* **make an ~** появля́ться (появи́ться* *perf*); **cast in** *or* **by order of ~** (*THEAT*) соста́в исполни́телей в поря́дке появле́ния; **to keep up ~s** соблюда́ть (соблюсти́* *perf*) прили́чия; **to** *or* **by all ~s** су́дя по всему́.

appease [ə'pi:z] *vt* (*person, country*) умиротворя́ть (умиротвори́ть *perf*).

appeasement [ə'pi:zmənt] *n* (*POL*) умиротворе́ние.

append [ə'pɛnd] *vt* (*COMPUT*) добавля́ть (доба́вить* *perf*) (в коне́ц), присоединя́ть (присоедини́ть *perf*).

appendage [ə'pɛndɪdʒ] *n* прида́ток*.

appendices [ə'pɛndɪsi:z] *npl of* **appendix**.

appendicitis [əpɛndɪ'saɪtɪs] *n* аппендици́т.

appendix [ə'pɛndɪks] (*pl* **appendices**) *n* приложе́ние; (*ANAT*) аппе́ндикс; **he had his ~ out** ему́ вы́резали аппендици́т.

appetite ['æpɪtaɪt] *n* аппети́т; (*fig*) страсть* *f*; **that walk has given me an ~** по́сле прогу́лки у меня́ разыгра́лся аппети́т.

appetizer ['æpɪtaɪzə'] *n* (*food*) заку́ска*; (*drink*) аперити́в.

appetizing ['æpɪtaɪzɪŋ] *adj* (*smell*) аппети́тный.

applaud [ə'plɔ:d] *vi* (*clap*) аплоди́ровать *(impf)*, рукоплеска́ть* *(impf)* ◆ *vt* аплоди́ровать *(impf)* *+dat*, рукоплеска́ть* *(impf)* *+dat*; (*praise*) одобря́ть (одо́брить *perf*).

applause [ə'plɔ:z] *n* (*clapping*) аплодисме́нты *pl*.

apple ['æpl] *n* я́блоко*; **he's the ~ of her eye** она́ в нём души́ не ча́ет.

apple tree *n* я́блоня.

apple turnover *n* шарло́тка.

appliance [ə'plaɪəns] *n* (*electrical, domestic*) прибо́р.

applicable [ə'plɪkəbl] *adj*: **~ (to)** примени́мый (примени́м) (к *+dat*); **the law is ~ from January** зако́н вступа́ет в си́лу с января́.

applicant ['æplɪkənt] *n* (*for job, scholarship*) кандида́т; (*for college*) абитурие́нт.

application [æplɪ'keɪʃən] *n* (*for a job, a grant etc*) заявле́ние; (*hard work*) стара́ние; (*of cream, paint*) нанесе́ние; **on ~** (*of rule, knowledge*) по зая́вке; (*of methods*) примене́ние.

application form *n* заявле́ние-анке́та.

application program *n* (*COMPUT*) прикладна́я програ́мма.

applications package *n* (*COMPUT*) паке́т прикладны́х програ́мм.

applied [ə'plaɪd] *adj* (*science, art*) прикладно́й.

apply [ə'plaɪ] *vt* (*paint, makeup*) наноси́ть* (нанести́* *perf*); (*bandage*) накла́дывать (наложи́ть *perf*); (*theory, law*) применя́ть (примени́ть* *perf*) ◆ *vi*: **to ~ to** (*be applicable*) применя́ться *(impf)* к *+dat*; (*ask*) обраща́ться (обрати́ться* *perf*) (с про́сьбой) к *+dat*; **to ~ the brakes** нажима́ть (нажа́ть* *perf*) на тормоза́; **to ~ o.s. to** сосредота́чиваться (сосредото́читься *perf*) на *+prp*; **to ~ for a grant/job** подава́ть* (пода́ть* *perf*) заявле́ние на стипе́ндию/о приёме на рабо́ту.

appoint [ə'pɔɪnt] *vt* назнача́ть (назна́чить *perf*).

appointed [ə'pɔɪntɪd] *adj*: **at the ~ time** в назна́ченное вре́мя*.

appointee [əpɔɪn'ti:] *n* получи́вший(-ая) *m(f)* *adj* назначе́ние.

appointment [ə'pɔɪntmənt] *n* (*of person*) назначе́ние; (*post*) до́лжность* *f*; (*arranged meeting*) приём; **to make an ~ (with sb)** назнача́ть (назна́чить *perf*) (кому́-н) встре́чу *or* свида́ние; **I have an ~ with the director/the doctor** я запи́сан на приём к мини́стру/к врачу́; **to make an ~ with the hairdresser/doctor** записа́ться* *(perf)* в парикма́херскую/на приём к врачу́; **by ~** по за́писи.

apportion [ə'pɔ:ʃən] *vt* распределя́ть (распредели́ть *perf*); **to ~ sth to sb** наделя́ть (надели́ть *perf*) кого́-н чем-н; **to ~ blame to sb** возлага́ть (возложи́ть *perf*) вину́ на кого́-н.

apposition [æpə'zɪʃən] *n* приложе́ние.

appraisal [ə'preɪzl] *n* оце́нка*.

appraise [ə'preɪz] *vt* оце́нивать (оцени́ть* *perf*).

appreciable [ə'pri:ʃəbl] *adj* значи́тельный.

appreciably [ə'pri:ʃəblɪ] *adv* заме́тно, ощути́мо.

appreciate [ə'pri:ʃɪeɪt] *vt* (*value*) цени́ть* *(impf)*; (*understand*) понима́ть (поня́ть* *perf*) ◆ *vi* (*COMM*) повыша́ться (повы́ситься* *perf*) в цене́; **I ~ your help** я благода́рен Вам за по́мощь; **he ~s good cooking/opera** он цени́тель хоро́шей ку́хни/о́перы.

appreciation [əpri:ʃɪ'eɪʃən] *n* (*understanding*) понима́ние; (*gratitude*) призна́тельность *f*; (*COMM*) повыше́ние сто́имости.

appreciative [ə'pri:ʃɪətɪv] *adj* (*person, audience*) призна́тельный* (призна́телен); (*comment*) одобри́тельный* (одобри́телен).

apprehend [æprɪ'hɛnd] *vt* (*arrest*) заде́рживать (задержа́ть* *perf*); (*understand*) понима́ть (поня́ть* *perf*).

apprehension [æprɪ'hɛnʃən] *n* опасе́ние; (*of criminal*) задержа́ние.

apprehensive [æprɪ'hɛnsɪv] *adj* (*glance etc*) опа́сливый; **to be ~ about sth** опаса́ться *(impf)* за что-н.

apprentice [ə'prɛntɪs] *n* подмастéрье*, учени́к* ◆ *vt*: **to be ~d to sb** быть *(impf)* в уче́нии у кого́-н.

apprenticeship [ə'prɛntɪsʃɪp] *n* (*also fig*) учени́чество; **to serve one's ~** проходи́ть* (пройти́* *perf*) обуче́ние.

appro. ['æprəu] *abbr* (*BRIT*: *inf*: *COMM*:) = *approval*): **on ~** на про́бу.

approach [ə'prəutʃ] *vi* приближа́ться (прибли́зиться* *perf*) ◆ *vt* (*ask, apply to*) обраща́ться (обрати́ться* *perf*) к +*dat*; (*come to*) приближа́ться (прибли́зиться* *perf*) к +*dat*; (*consider*) подходи́ть* (подойти́* *perf*) к +*dat* ◆ *n* (*advance*: *also fig*) приближе́ние; (*access*: *on foot*) подхо́д; (: *by transport*) подъе́зд; (*to problem, situation*) подхо́д; **to ~ sb about sth** обраща́ться (обрати́ться* *perf*) к кому́-н с предложе́нием о чём-н.
approachable [ə'prəutʃəbl] *adj* (*person, place*) досту́пный* (досту́пен).
approach road *n* подъездно́й путь* *m*.
approbation [æprə'beɪʃən] *n* одобре́ние.
appropriate [*adj* ə'prəuprɪɪt, *vb* ə'prəuprɪeɪt] *adj* (*behaviour*) подоба́ющий*; (*remarks*) уме́стный; (*tools*) подходя́щий* ◆ *vt* присва́ивать (присво́ить *perf*); **it would not be ~ for me to comment** бы́ло бы неуме́стно с мое́й стороны́ комменти́ровать; **it is not ~ for you to behave like that** Вам не подоба́ет вести́ себя́ так.
appropriately [ə'prəuprɪɪtlɪ] *adv* подоба́ющим *or* соотве́тствующим о́бразом.
appropriation [əprəuprɪ'eɪʃən] *n* присвое́ние.
appropriation account *n* счёт ассигнова́ний.
approval [ə'pru:vəl] *n* одобре́ние; (*permission*) согла́сие; **to meet with sb's ~** получа́ть (получи́ть* *perf*) чьё-н одобре́ние; **on ~** (*COMM*) на про́бу.
approve [ə'pru:v] *vt* (*motion, decision*) одобря́ть (одо́брить *perf*); (*publication, product*) утвержда́ть (утверди́ть* *perf*)
▸ **approve of** *vt fus* одобря́ть (одо́брить *perf*).
approved school [ə'pru:vd-] *n* (*BRIT*: *formerly*) исправи́тельная шко́ла.
approvingly [ə'pru:vɪŋlɪ] *adv* одобри́тельно.
approx. *abbr* = **approximately**.
approximate [*adj* ə'prɔksɪmɪt, *vb* ə'prɔksɪmeɪt] *adj* приблизи́тельный* (приблизи́телен) ◆ *vi*: **to ~ to** приближа́ться (прибли́зиться* *perf*) к +*dat*.
approximately [ə'prɔksɪmɪtlɪ] *adv* приблизи́тельно.
approximation [ə'prɔksɪ'meɪʃən] *n* приближе́ние.
APR *n abbr* (= *annual percentage rate*) годова́я проце́нтная ста́вка.
Apr. *abbr* = **April**.
apricot ['eɪprɪkɔt] *n* абрико́с.
April ['eɪprəl] *n* апре́ль *m*; **~ fool!** пе́рвое Апре́ля – никому́ не ве́рю!; *see also* **July**.
April Fool's Day *n* день *m* дурако́в.
apron ['eɪprən] *n* пере́дник, фа́ртук; (*AVIAT*) *площа́дка пе́ред анга́ром*.
apse [æps] *n* апси́да.
APT *n abbr* (*BRIT*: = *advanced passenger train*) пассажи́рский* суперэкспре́сс.
apt [æpt] *adj* (*suitable*: *comment, description etc*) уда́чный* (уда́чен), уме́стный (уме́стен); **~ to do** скло́нный +*infin*.
Apt. *abbr* (= **apartment**) кв.= *кварти́ра*.
aptitude ['æptɪtju:d] *n* скло́нность *f*.
aptitude test *n* тест на выявле́ние скло́нностей.
aptly ['æptlɪ] *adv* уме́стно; (*accurately*) то́чно.
aqualung ['ækwəlʌŋ] *n* аквала́нг.
aquarium [ə'kwɛərɪəm] *n* аква́риум.
Aquarius [ə'kwɛərɪəs] *n* Водоле́й; **he is ~** он – Водоле́й.
aquatic [ə'kwætɪk] *adj* во́дный.
aqueduct ['ækwɪdʌkt] *n* акведу́к.
AR *abbr* (*US*: *POST*) = *Arkansas*.
ARA *n abbr* (*BRIT*) = *Associate of the Royal Academy*.
Arab ['ærəb] *adj* ара́бский* ◆ *n* ара́б(ка).
Arabia [ə'reɪbɪə] *n* Ара́вия.
Arabian [ə'reɪbɪən] *adj* ара́бский*.
Arabian Desert *n*: **the ~ ~** Арави́йская пусты́ня.
Arabian Sea *n*: **the ~ ~** Арави́йское мо́ре*.
Arabic ['ærəbɪk] *adj* ара́бский* ◆ *n* ара́бский* язы́к*.
arable ['ærəbl] *adj* (*land*) па́хотный; (*farm*) полево́дческий.
Aral Sea ['ærəl-] *n* Ара́льское мо́ре.
ARAM *n abbr* (*BRIT*) = *Associate of the Royal Academy of Music*.
arbiter ['ɑ:bɪtə^r] *n* арби́тр (*в спо́ре*).
arbitrary ['ɑ:bɪtrərɪ] *adj* произво́льный* (произво́лен).
arbitrate ['ɑ:bɪtreɪt] *vi* выноси́ть* (вы́нести* *perf*) трете́йское реше́ние.
arbitration [ɑ:bɪ'treɪʃən] *n* (*of quarrel*) трете́йский суд*; (*INDUSTRY*) арбитра́ж; **the dispute went to ~** спо́р пе́редан в арбитра́ж.
arbitrator ['ɑ:bɪtreɪtə^r] *n* трете́йский судья́*, арби́тр.
ARC *n abbr* = *American Red Cross*.
arc [ɑ:k] *n* (*also MATH*) дуга́*.
arcade [ɑ:'keɪd] *n* (*round a square*) арка́да; (*shopping mall*) пасса́ж.
arch [ɑ:tʃ] *n* а́рка*, свод; (*of foot*) свод ◆ *vt* (*back*) выгиба́ть (вы́гнуть *perf*) ◆ *adj* (*playful*) игри́вый; (*knowing*) многозначи́тельный ◆ *prefix* а́рхи-.
archaeological [ɑ:kɪə'lɔdʒɪkl] (*US* **archeological**) *adj* археологи́ческий*.
archaeologist [ɑ:kɪ'ɔlədʒɪst] (*US* **archeologist**) *n* архео́лог.
archaeology [ɑ:kɪ'ɔlədʒɪ] (*US* **archeology**) *n* археоло́гия.
archaic [ɑ:'keɪɪk] *adj* архаи́ческий.
Archangel ['ɑ:keɪndʒəl] *n* Арха́нгельск.
archangel ['ɑ:keɪndʒəl] *n* арха́нгел.
archbishop [ɑ:tʃ'bɪʃəp] *n* архиепи́скоп.

* marks translations which have irregular inflections. The Russian-English side of the dictionary gives inflectional information.

arch-enemy [ˈɑːtʃˈɛnəmɪ] *n* заклятый враг*.
archeology *etc* [ɑːkɪˈɔlədʒɪ] (*US*) = **archaeology** *etc.*
archery [ˈɑːtʃərɪ] *n* стрельба* из лука.
archetypal [ˈɑːkɪtaɪpəl] *adj* типичный*.
archetype [ˈɑːkɪtaɪp] *n* образец.
archipelago [ɑːkɪˈpɛlɪgəu] *n* архипелаг.
architect [ˈɑːkɪtɛkt] *n* (*of building*) архитектор.
architectural [ɑːkɪˈtɛktʃərəl] *adj* архитектурный.
architecture [ˈɑːkɪtɛktʃəʳ] *n* архитектура.
archive [ˈɑːkaɪvz] *n* архив.
archive file *n* (*COMPUT*) архивный файл.
archives [ˈɑːkaɪvz] *npl* архив *msg*.
archivist [ˈɑːkɪvɪst] *n* архивариус.
archway [ˈɑːtʃweɪ] *n* арочный проход.
ARCM *n abbr* (*BRIT*) = ***Associate of the Royal College of Music.***
Arctic [ˈɑːktɪk] *adj* арктический* ◆ *n*: **the ~** Арктика.
Arctic Circle *n*: **the ~ ~** Северный Полярный круг.
Arctic Ocean *n*: **the ~ ~** Северный Ледовитый океан.
ARD *n abbr* (*US*: *MED*: = *acute respiratory disease*) ОРЗ= *острое респираторное заболевание*.
ardent [ˈɑːdənt] *adj* пылкий* (пылок).
ardour [ˈɑːdəʳ] (*US* **ardor**) *n* пыл*.
arduous [ˈɑːdjuəs] *adj* тяжёлый* (тяжёл).
are [ɑːʳ] *vb see* **be**.
area [ˈɛərɪə] *n* (*of country, knowledge*) область *f*; (*part*: *of place*) участок*; (: *of room*) часть *f*; (*GEOM etc*) площадь* *f*; **in the London ~** в районе Лондона.
area code *n* код зоны.
arena [əˈriːnə] *n* (*also fig*) арена.
aren't [ɑːnt] = **are not**; *see* **be**.
Argentina [ɑːdʒənˈtiːnə] *n* Аргентина.
Argentinian [ɑːdʒənˈtɪnɪən] *adj* аргентинский* ◆ *n* аргентинец*(-инка*).
arguable [ˈɑːgjuəbl] *adj* спорный* (спорен); **it is ~ whether this is necessary** нужно ли это – вопрос спорный; **it is ~ that ...** можно утверждать, что ....
arguably [ˈɑːgjuəblɪ] *adv* возможно; **he is ~ the best in his profession** можно утверждать, что он лучший специалист в своей области.
argue [ˈɑːgjuː] *vi* (*quarrel*) ссориться (поссориться *perf*); (*reason*) доказывать (доказать* *perf*) ◆ *vt* обсуждать (обсудить* *perf*); **to ~ that ...** доказывать (доказать* *perf*), что ...; **to ~ about sth** спорить (поспорить *perf*) о чём-н; **to ~ for/against sth** приводить* (привести* *perf*) доводы в пользу/против чего-н.
argument [ˈɑːgjumənt] *n* (*quarrel*) ссора; (*reasons*) аргумент, довод; (*debate*) обсуждение, спор*; **~ for/against** аргумент *or* довод в пользу/против *+gen*.
argumentative [ɑːgjuˈmɛntətɪv] *adj* (*person*) конфликтный; (*voice*) вызывающий*.
aria [ˈɑːrɪə] *n* ария.
ARIBA *n abbr* (*BRIT*) = ***Associate of the Royal Institute of British Architects.***
arid [ˈærɪd] *adj* безводный* (безводен); (*fig*) сухой.
aridity [əˈrɪdɪtɪ] *n* сухость *f*.
Aries [ˈɛərɪz] *n* Овен*; **he is ~** он – Овен.
arise [əˈraɪz] (*pt* **arose**, *pp* **arisen**) *vi* (*occur*) возникать (возникнуть* *perf*); **to ~ from** возникать (возникнуть* *perf*) вследствие *+gen*; **should the need ~** если возникнет необходимость.
arisen [əˈrɪzn] *pp of* **arise**.
aristocracy [ærɪsˈtɔkrəsɪ] *n* аристократия.
aristocrat [ˈærɪstəkræt] *n* аристократ(ка*).
aristocratic [ærɪstəˈkrætɪk] *adj* (*family*) аристократический*; (*features*) аристократичный.
arithmetic [əˈrɪθmətɪk] *n* (*MATH*) арифметика; (*calculation*) подсчёт.
arithmetical [ærɪθˈmɛtɪkl] *adj* арифметический*.
ark [ɑːk] *n*: **Noah's A~** Ноев ковчег.
arm [ɑːm] *n* рука*; (*of chair*) ручка*; (*of clothing*) рукав*; (*of organization*) подразделение ◆ *vt* вооружать (вооружить *perf*); **~s** *npl* (*MIL*) вооружение *ntsg*; (*HERALDRY*) герб; **~ in ~** под руку.
armaments [ˈɑːməmənts] *npl* вооружение *sg*.
armband [ˈɑːmbænd] *n* нарукавная повязка.
armchair [ˈɑːmtʃɛəʳ] *n* кресло*.
armed [ɑːmd] *adj* вооружённый (вооружён); **the ~ forces** вооружённые силы.
armed robbery *n* вооружённый грабёж*.
Armenia [ɑːˈmiːnɪə] *n* Армения.
Armenian [ɑːˈmiːnɪən] *adj* армянский* ◆ *n* армянин(-нка); (*LING*) армянский* язык*.
armful [ˈɑːmful] *n* охапка.
armistice [ˈɑːmɪstɪs] *n* перемирие.
armor *etc* (*US*) = **armour** *etc*.
armour [ˈɑːməʳ] (*US* **armor**) *n* (*also:* **suit of ~**) доспехи *mpl*; (*also:* **~-plating**) броня; (*tanks*) бронесилы *fpl*.
armoured car [ˈɑːməd-] *n* бронемашина.
armoury [ˈɑːmərɪ] *n* (*also fig*) арсенал.
armpit [ˈɑːmpɪt] *n* подмышка*.
armrest [ˈɑːmrɛst] *n* подлокотник.
arms control [ɑːmz-] *n* контроль *m* вооружений.
arms race *n*: **the ~ ~** гонка вооружений.
army [ˈɑːmɪ] *n* (*also fig*) армия.
aroma [əˈrəumə] *n* аромат.
aromatherapy [ərəuməˈθɛrəpɪ] *n* аромотерапия.
aromatic [ærəˈmætɪk] *adj* ароматный* (ароматен).
arose [əˈrəuz] *pt of* **arise**.
around [əˈraund] *adv* вокруг ◆ *prep* (*encircling*) вокруг *+gen*; (*near, about*) около *+gen*; **is he ~?** он здесь?; **~ £5/3 o'clock** около £5/3 часов; **~ here** здесь поблизости.

arousal [ə'rauzəl] *n* возбужде́ние.
arouse [ə'rauz] *vt* (*sleeping person*) буди́ть* (разбуди́ть* *perf*); (*interest, passions*) возбужда́ть (возбуди́ть* *perf*).
arpeggio [ɑ:'pɛdʒɪəu] *n* арпе́джио *nt ind*.
arrange [ə'reɪndʒ] *vt* (*organize*) устра́ивать (устро́ить *perf*); (*put in order*) расставля́ть (расста́вить *perf*); (*MUS*) аранжи́ровать (*impf/perf*) ◆ *vi*: **we have ~d for a car to pick you up** мы договори́лись, что́бы маши́на зае́хала за Ва́ми; **it was ~d that ...** бы́ло усло́влено, что ...; **to ~ to do** усла́вливаться (усло́виться* *perf*) +*infin*, догова́риваться (договори́ться *perf*) +*infin*.
arrangement [ə'reɪndʒmənt] *n* (*agreement*) договорённость *f*; (*MUS*) аранжиро́вка*; (*order, layout*) расположе́ние; **~s** *npl* (*preparations, plans*) приготовле́ния *ntpl*; **to come to an ~ with sb** приходи́ть* (прийти́* *perf*) к соглаше́нию с кем-н; **home deliveries by ~** доста́вка на́ дом по договорённости; **I'll make ~s for you to be met** я договорю́сь, что́бы Вас встре́тили.
arrant ['ærənt] *adj* отъя́вленный.
array [ə'reɪ] *n* (*MATH, COMPUT*) масси́в; **~ of** ма́сса +*gen*, мно́жество +*gen*.
arrears [ə'rɪəz] *npl* задо́лженность *fsg*; **to be in ~ with one's rent** име́ть (*impf*) задо́лженность по квартпла́те.
arrest [ə'rɛst] *vt* (*criminal*) аресто́вывать (арестова́ть *perf*); (*sb's attention*) прико́вывать (прикова́ть *perf*) ◆ *n* аре́ст, задержа́ние; **under ~** под аре́стом.
arresting [ə'rɛstɪŋ] *adj* порази́тельный.
arrival [ə'raɪvl] *n* прибы́тие; (*COMM*) приво́з; **new ~** (*person*) новичо́к*; (*baby*) новорождённый(-ая) *m(f) adj*.
arrive [ə'raɪv] *vi* (*traveller*) прибыва́ть (прибы́ть* *perf*); (*letter, news*) приходи́ть* (прийти́* *perf*); (*baby*) рожда́ться (роди́ться* *perf*)
▸ **arrive at** *vt fus* (*fig*) приходи́ть* (прийти́* *perf*) к +*dat*.
arrogance ['ærəgəns] *n* высокоме́рие.
arrogant ['ærəgənt] *adj* высокоме́рный* (высокоме́рен).
arrow ['ærəu] *n* (*weapon*) стрела́*; (*sign*) стре́лка*.
arse [ɑ:s] *n* (*BRIT: inf!*) жо́па (*!*)
arsenal ['ɑ:sɪnl] *n* арсена́л.
arsenic ['ɑ:snɪk] *n* мышья́к*.
arson ['ɑ:sn] *n* поджо́г.
art [ɑ:t] *n* (*also fig*) иску́сство; (*also:* **Fine A~**) изобрази́тельное иску́сство; **A~s** *npl* гуманита́рные нау́ки *fpl*; **work of ~** произведе́ние иску́сства.
artefact ['ɑ:tɪfækt] *n* худо́жественное изде́лие, поде́лка.
arterial [ɑ:'tɪərɪəl] *adj* (*ANAT*) артериа́льный; **~ road** магистра́ль *f*.
artery ['ɑ:tərɪ] *n* (*also fig*) арте́рия.
artful ['ɑ:tful] *adj* ло́вкий*.
art gallery *n* (*national*) карти́нная галере́я; (*private*) галере́я.
arthritic [ɑ:'θrɪtɪk] *adj* артрити́ческий*.
arthritis [ɑ:'θraɪtɪs] *n* артри́т.
artichoke ['ɑ:tɪtʃəuk] *n* (*also:* **globe ~**) артишо́к; (*also:* **Jerusalem ~**) земляна́я гру́ша.
article ['ɑ:tɪkl] *n* (*object, item*) предме́т; (*LING*) арти́кль *m*; (*in newspaper*) статья́*; (*in document*) пункт; **~s** *npl* (*BRIT: LAW*) *курс профессиона́льной подгото́вки адвока́тов*; **~ of clothing** предме́т оде́жды.
articles of association *npl* (*COMM*) уста́в акционе́рной компа́нии.
articulate [*adj* ɑ:'tɪkjulɪt, *vb* ɑ:'tɪkjuleɪt] *adj* (*speech, writing*) вразуми́тельный* (вразуми́телен) ◆ *vt* (*fears, ideas*) выража́ть (вы́разить* *perf*) ◆ *vi*: **to ~ well/badly** чётко/нечётко выгова́ривать (вы́говорить *perf*); **she is very ~** она́ чётко *or* я́сно выража́ет свои́ мы́сли.
articulated lorry *n* (*BRIT*) грузови́к* с прице́пом.
artifice ['ɑ:tɪfɪs] *n* (*trick*) приём; (*skill*) иску́сность *f*.
artificial [ɑ:tɪ'fɪʃəl] *adj* иску́сственный*; (*affected*) неесте́ственный* (неесте́ствен).
artificial insemination [-ɪnsɛmɪ'neɪʃən] *n* иску́сственное оплодотворе́ние.
artificial intelligence *n* иску́сственный интелле́кт.
artificial respiration *n* иску́сственное дыха́ние.
artillery [ɑ:'tɪlərɪ] *n* (*MIL: corps*) артилле́рия.
artisan ['ɑ:tɪzæn] *n* реме́сленник(-ица).
artist ['ɑ:tɪst] *n* худо́жник(-ица); (*performer*) арти́ст(ка).
artistic [ɑ:'tɪstɪk] *adj* худо́жественный; **an ~ person** худо́жественная ли́чность *f*.
artistry ['ɑ:tɪstrɪ] *n* мастерство́.
artless ['ɑ:tlɪs] *adj* безыску́сный (безыску́сен).
art school *n* худо́жественное учи́лище.
artwork ['ɑ:twə:k] *n* оформле́ние.
ARV *n abbr* (*BIBLE: = American Revised Version*) *америка́нский* вариа́нт Би́блии*.
AS *n abbr* (*US: = Associate in/of Science*) член ассоциа́ции нау́чных рабо́тников ◆ *abbr* (*POST*) = *American Samoa*.

KEYWORD

as [æz] *conj* **1** (*referring to time*) когда́; **as the years went by** с года́ми; **he came in as I was leaving** он вошёл, когда́ я уходи́л; **as from tomorrow** с за́втрашнего дня
2 (*in comparisons*): **as big as** тако́й же

* marks translations which have irregular inflections. The Russian-English side of the dictionary gives inflectional information.

большо́й, как; **twice as big as** в два ра́за бо́льше, чем; **as white as snow** бе́лый как снег; **as much money/many books as** сто́лько же де́нег/книг, ско́лько; **as soon as** как то́лько; **as soon as possible** как мо́жно скоре́е
3 (*since, because*) поско́льку, так как
4 (*referring to manner, way*) как; **do as you wish** де́лайте, как хоти́те; **as she said** как она́ сказа́ла
5 (*concerning*) **as for** *or* **to** что каса́ется *+gen*:
***6*: as if** *or* **though** так, как бу́дто бы; **he looked as if he had been ill** он вы́глядел так, как бу́дто бы он был бо́лен
◆ *prep* (*in the capacity of*): **he works as a driver/ waiter** он рабо́тает шофёром/официа́нтом; **as chairman of the company, he ...** как глава́ компа́нии, он ...; *see also* **long, same, such, well**.

ASA *n abbr* (= *American Standards Association*) Америка́нская ассоциа́ция станда́ртов.
a.s.a.p. *adv abbr* (= *as soon as possible*) как мо́жно скоре́е.
asbestos [æz'bɛstəs] *n* асбе́ст.
ascend [ə'sɛnd] *vt* (*hill*) всходи́ть* (взойти́* *perf*) на *+acc*; (*stairs*) всходи́ть* (взойти́* *perf*) по *+dat*; (*throne*) взойти́* (*perf*) на *+acc*.
ascendancy [ə'sɛndənsɪ] *n* госпо́дство; **~ over sb** госпо́дство над кем-н.
ascendant [ə'sɛndənt] *n*: **to be in the ~** госпо́дствовать *(impf)*.
ascension [ə'sɛnʃən] *n*: **the A~** (*REL*) Вознесе́ние.
Ascension Island *n* О́стров Вознесе́ния.
ascent [ə'sɛnt] *n* (*slope*) подъём; (*climb*) восхожде́ние.
ascertain [æsə'teɪn] *vt* устана́вливать (установи́ть* *perf*).
ascetic [ə'sɛtɪk] *adj* аскети́ческий*.
asceticism [ə'sɛtɪsɪzəm] *n* аскети́зм.
ASCII ['æski:] *n abbr* (*COMPUT*: = *American Standard Code for Information Interchange*) *америка́нский станда́ртный код для обме́на информа́цией*.
ascribe [ə'skraɪb] *vt*: **to ~ sth to** припи́сывать (приписа́ть* *perf*) что-н *+dat*.
ASCU *n abbr* (*US*) = *Association of State Colleges and Universities*.
ASEAN ['æsɪæn] *n abbr* (= *Association of South-East Asian Nations*) АСЕАН.
ASH [æʃ] *n abbr* (*BRIT*: = *Action on Smoking and Health*) О́бщество борьбы́ с куре́нием.
ash [æʃ] *n* (*of fire*) зола́, пе́пел*; (*of cigarette*) пе́пел; (*wood, tree*) я́сень *m*.
ashamed [ə'ʃeɪmd] *adj*: **to be ~ (of)** стыди́ться *(impf)* (*+gen*); **I'm ~ of ...** мне сты́дно *+gen ...*; **I'm ~ of myself for having done that** мне сты́дно, что я сде́лал э́то.
ashen ['æʃən] *adj* (*face*) мёртвенно-бле́дный*.
Ashkhabad [aʃxa'bat] *n* Ашхаба́д.
ashore [ə'ʃɔ:'] *adv* (*be*) на берегу́; (*swim, go*) на бе́рег.
ashtray ['æʃtreɪ] *n* пе́пельница.
Ash Wednesday *n* пе́рвый день* *m* Вели́кого Поста́.
Asia ['eɪʃə] *n* А́зия.
Asia Minor *n* Ма́лая А́зия.
Asian ['eɪʃən] *adj* азиа́тский* ◆ *n* азиа́т(ка*).
Asiatic [eɪsɪ'ætɪk] *adj* азиа́тский*.
aside [ə'saɪd] *adv* в сто́рону ◆ *n* ре́плика ◆ *prep*: **~ from** поми́мо *+gen*; **to brush objections ~** отмета́ть (отмести́* *perf*) возраже́ния в сто́рону.
ask [ɑ:sk] *vt* (*inquire*) спра́шивать (спроси́ть* *perf*); (*invite*) звать* (позва́ть* *perf*); **to ~ sb for sth/sb to do** проси́ть* (попроси́ть* *perf*) что-н у кого́-н/кого́-н *+infin*; **to ~ sb the time** спра́шивать (спроси́ть* *perf*) кого́-н, кото́рый час; **to ~ sb about sth** спра́шивать (спроси́ть* *perf*) кого́-н о чём-н; **to ~ about the price** спра́шивать (спроси́ть* *perf*) о цене́; **to ~ (sb) a question** задава́ть* (зада́ть* *perf*) (кому́-н) вопро́с; **to ~ sb out to dinner** приглаша́ть (пригласи́ть* *perf*) кого́-н в рестора́н
▸ **ask after** *vt fus* (*person*) справля́ться (спра́виться* *perf*) о *+prp*
▸ **ask for** *vt fus* (*request*) проси́ть* (попроси́ть* *perf*); (*look for*: *trouble*) напра́шиваться (напроси́ться* *perf*) на *+acc*; **he's just ~ing for trouble** *or* **for it** он про́сто напра́шивается на неприя́тности.
askance [ə'skɑ:ns] *adv*: **to look ~ at sb/sth** смотре́ть* (посмотре́ть* *perf*) на кого́-н/что-н ко́со.
askew [ə'skju:] *adv* (*clothes*) кри́во, ко́со.
asking price ['ɑ:skɪŋ-] *n*: **the ~ ~** запра́шиваемая цена́*.
asleep [ə'sli:p] *adj* спя́щий; **to be ~** спать* *(impf)*; **to fall ~** засыпа́ть (засну́ть *perf*).
ASLEF ['æzlɛf] *n abbr* (*BRIT*) = *Associated Society of Locomotive Engineers and Firemen*.
asp [æsp] *n* а́спид.
asparagus [əs'pærəgəs] *n* спа́ржа.
asparagus tips *npl* спа́ржевые голо́вки* *fpl*.
ASPCA *n abbr* (= *American Society for the Prevention of Cruelty to Animals*) Америка́нское о́бщество защи́ты живо́тных.
aspect ['æspɛkt] *n* (*element*) аспе́кт, сторона́*; (*quality, air*) вид*; **a room with a southern ~** ко́мната с ви́дом на юг.
aspersions [əs'pə:ʃənz] *npl*: **to cast ~ on** (*integrity, ability*) ста́вить* (поста́вить* *perf*) под сомне́ние; (*person*) очерня́ть (очерни́ть *perf*).
asphalt ['æsfælt] *n* асфа́льт.
asphyxiate [æs'fɪksɪeɪt] *vt* души́ть* (задуши́ть* *perf*).
asphyxiation [æsfɪksɪ'eɪʃən] *n* уду́шье.
aspirate [*vt* 'æspəreɪt, *adj* 'æspərɪt] *vt*

произноси́ть* (произнести́* *perf*) с придыха́нием ◆ *adj* придыха́тельный.
aspirations [æspəˈreɪʃənz] *npl* устремле́ния *ntpl*.
aspire [əsˈpaɪəʳ] *vi*: **to ~ to** стреми́ться* *(impf)* к *+dat*.
aspirin [ˈæsprɪn] *n* аспири́н.
aspiring [əsˈpaɪərɪŋ] *adj* начина́ющий*.
ass [æs] *n* (*also fig*) осёл*; (*US*: *inf!*) жо́па (*!*)
assail [əˈseɪl] *vt* (*person*) напада́ть (напа́сть* *perf*) на *+acc*; (*fig*): **he was ~ed by doubts** его́ одоле́ли сомне́ния.
assailant [əˈseɪlənt] *n*: **his/her ~** напа́вший(-ая) *m(f) adj* на него́/неё.
assassin [əˈsæsɪn] *n* полити́ческий* уби́йца *m/f*.
assassinate [əˈsæsɪneɪt] *vt* соверша́ть (соверши́ть *perf*) покуше́ние на *+acc*.
assassination [əsæsɪˈneɪʃən] *n* полити́ческое уби́йство.
assault [əˈsɔ:lt] *n* нападе́ние; (*MIL, fig*) ата́ка ◆ *vt* напада́ть (напа́сть* *perf*) на *+acc*; (*MIL*) атакова́ть *(impf/perf)*; (*sexually*) соверша́ть (соверши́ть *perf*) сексуа́льное посяга́тельство на *+acc*; **~ and battery** оскорбле́ние де́йствием.
assemble [əˈsɛmbl] *vt* собира́ть (собра́ть* *perf*) ◆ *vi* собира́ться (собра́ться* *perf*).
assembly [əˈsɛmblɪ] *n* (*meeting*) собра́ние; (*institution*) ассамбле́я, законода́тельное собра́ние; (*construction*) сбо́рка; **General A~ of the UN** Генера́льная Ассамбле́я ООН.
assembly language *n* (*COMPUT*) язы́к* ассе́мблера.
assembly line *n* сбо́рочный конве́йер.
assent [əˈsɛnt] *n* согла́сие ◆ *vi*: **to ~ (to)** соглаша́ться (согласи́ться* *perf*) (на *+acc*).
assert [əˈsə:t] *vt* (*opinion, authority*) утвержда́ть (утверди́ть* *perf*); (*rights, innocence*) отста́ивать (отстоя́ть *perf*); **to ~ o.s.** самоутвержда́ться (самоутверди́ться* *perf*).
assertion [əˈsə:ʃən] *n* (*claim*) утвержде́ние.
assertive [əˈsə:tɪv] *adj* самоуве́ренный (самоуве́рен).
assess [əˈsɛs] *vt* оце́нивать (оцени́ть* *perf*); **to ~ for tax** оцени́ть *(perf)* сто́имость для це́лей налогообложе́ния.
assessment [əˈsɛsmənt] *n*: **~ (of)** оце́нка* (*+gen*); **tax ~** оце́нка сто́имости в це́лях налогообложе́ния.
assessor [əˈsɛsəʳ] *n* (*LAW*) экспе́рт-(-консульта́нт).
asset [ˈæsɛt] *n* (*useful quality*) досто́инство; **~s** *npl* (*property, funds*) акти́вы *mpl*; (*COMM*) акти́в *msg* бала́нса; **he's an ~ to the company** он представля́ет собо́й большу́ю це́нность для компа́нии.
asset-stripping [ˈæsɛtˈstrɪpɪŋ] *n* (*COMM*) распрода́жа непри́быльных акти́вов (*при поглоще́нии одно́й компа́нии друго́й*).
assiduous [əˈsɪdjuəs] *adj* (*care, work*) усе́рдный* (усе́рден).
assign [əˈsaɪn] *vt* (*task*) поруча́ть (поручи́ть* *perf*), предпи́сывать (предписа́ть* *perf*); (*significance*) придава́ть* (прида́ть* *perf*); (*resources, role*) предназнача́ть (предназна́чить *perf*); **to ~ a date for a meeting** назнача́ть (назна́чить *perf*) да́ту заседа́ния.
assignment [əˈsaɪnmənt] *n* (*task*) предписа́ние; (*SCOL*) зада́ние.
assimilate [əˈsɪmɪleɪt] *vt* (*ideas*) усва́ивать (усво́ить *perf*); (*immigrants*): **to be ~d** ассимили́роваться *(impf/perf)*.
assimilation [əsɪmɪˈleɪʃən] *n* усвое́ние; (*of immigrants etc*) ассимиля́ция.
assist [əˈsɪst] *vt* помога́ть (помо́чь* *perf*) *+dat*; (*financially*) соде́йствовать *(impf/perf) +dat*.
assistance [əˈsɪstəns] *n* по́мощь *f*; (*financial*) соде́йствие.
assistant [əˈsɪstənt] *n* помо́щник(-ица); (*in office etc*) ассисте́нт(ка); (*BRIT*: *also*: **shop ~**) продаве́ц*(-вщи́ца); **laboratory ~** лабора́нт(ка).
assistant manager *n* замести́тель *m* заве́дующего.
assizes [əˈsaɪzɪz] *npl* (*BRIT*: *LAW*) выездна́я се́ссия суда́ прися́жных.
associate [*n, adj* əˈsəuʃɪɪt, *vb* əˈsəuʃɪeɪt] *n* (*colleague*) колле́га *m/f*, партнёр ◆ *adj* (*member, director, professor*) ассоции́рованный ◆ *vt* (*mentally*) ассоции́ровать *(impf/perf)*; **to ~ with sb** обща́ться *(impf)* с кем-н.
associated company [əˈsəuʃɪeɪtɪd-] *n* дочéрнее предприя́тие.
association [əsəusɪˈeɪʃən] *n* (*group, PSYCH*) ассоциа́ция; (*involvement*) связь* *f*; **in ~ with** в сотру́дничестве с *+instr*.
association football *n* футбо́л.
assorted [əˈsɔ:tɪd] *adj* разнообра́зный*; **hats in ~ sizes** шля́пы ра́зных разме́ров.
assortment [əˈsɔ:tmənt] *n* (*of clothes, colours*) ассортиме́нт; (*of books, people*) подбо́р.
Asst. *abbr* (= **assistant**) ассисте́нт.
assuage [əˈsweɪdʒ] *vt* (*grief, pain*) смягча́ть (смягчи́ть *perf*); (*thirst, hunger*) утоля́ть (утоли́ть *perf*).
assume [əˈsju:m] *vt* (*suppose*) предполага́ть (предположи́ть* *perf*), допуска́ть (допусти́ть* *perf*); (*responsibilities*) брать* (взять* *perf*) на себя́; (*command, appearance, air*) принима́ть (приня́ть* *perf*); (*power*) брать* (взять* *perf*).
assumed name [əˈsju:md-] *n* вы́мышленное и́мя* *nt*.
assumption [əˈsʌmpʃən] *n* (*supposition*) предположе́ние; (*of control, responsibility*)

* marks translations which have irregular inflections. The Russian-English side of the dictionary gives inflectional information.

принятие на себя́; **~ of power** прихо́д к вла́сти; **on the ~ that** ... предполага́я, что ....

assurance [ə'ʃuərəns] *n* (*promise*) завере́ние; (*confidence*) уве́ренность *f*; (*insurance*) страхова́ние; **I can give you no ~s** я не могу́ дать Вам никаки́х гара́нтий.

assure [ə'ʃuə^r] *vt* (*reassure*) уверя́ть (уве́рить *perf*), заверя́ть (заве́рить *perf*); (*guarantee*) обеспе́чивать (обеспе́чить *perf*).

assured [ə'ʃuəd] *adj* (*voice*) уве́ренный* (уве́рен); (*success*) несомне́нный* (несомне́нен).

AST *abbr* (*US*) = *Atlantic Standard Time*.

asterisk ['æstərɪsk] *n* звёздочка* (*знак* "*").

astern [ə'stə:n] *adv* (*NAUT*: *on ship*: *position*) на корме́; (: *motion*) на корму́; (*behind ship*) за кормо́й; **to move ~** идти́* (*impf*) за́дним хо́дом.

asteroid ['æstərɔɪd] *n* астеро́ид.

asthma ['æsmə] *n* а́стма.

asthmatic [æs'mætɪk] *adj* (*breathing*) астмати́ческий* ◆ *n* астма́тик; **~ attack** при́ступ а́стмы.

astigmatism [ə'stɪgmətɪzəm] *n* астигмати́зм.

astir [ə'stə:ʳ] *adv* на нога́х.

astonish [ə'stɔnɪʃ] *vt* изумля́ть (изуми́ть* *perf*), поража́ть (порази́ть* *perf*).

astonishing [ə'stɔnɪʃɪŋ] *adj* порази́тельный* (порази́телен); **I find it ~ that** ... меня́ поража́ет, что ....

astonishingly [ə'stɔnɪʃɪŋlɪ] *adv* порази́тельно; **the play, ~, was successful** порази́тельным о́бразом пье́са была́ уда́чной.

astonishment [ə'stɔnɪʃmənt] *n* удивле́ние, изумле́ние; **to my ~** к моему́ изумле́нию.

astound [ə'staund] *vt* поража́ть (порази́ть* *perf*), изумля́ть (изуми́ть* *perf*).

astounded [ə'staundɪd] *adj* поражённый (поражён), изумлённый (изумлён).

astounding [ə'staundɪŋ] *adj* порази́тельный* (порази́телен), изуми́тельный* (изуми́телен).

astray [ə'streɪ] *adv*: **to go ~** (*letter*) затеря́ться (*perf*); (*fig*) сбива́ться (сби́ться* *perf*) с пути́; **to lead ~** (*fig*) сбива́ть (сбить* *perf*) с пути́; **to go ~ in one's calculations** сбива́ться (сби́ться* *perf*) со счёта.

astride [ə'straɪd] *prep* верхо́м на *+prp* ◆ *adv* верхо́м.

astringent [əs'trɪndʒənt] *adj* вя́жущий* ◆ *n* вя́жущее вещество́.

astrologer [əs'trɔlədʒəʳ] *n* астро́лог.

astrology [əs'trɔlədʒɪ] *n* астроло́гия.

astronaut ['æstrənɔ:t] *n* астрона́вт, космона́вт.

astronomer [əs'trɔnəməʳ] *n* астроно́м.

astronomical [æstrə'nɔmɪkl] *adj* (*also fig*) астрономи́ческий*.

astronomy [əs'trɔnəmɪ] *n* астроно́мия.

astrophysics ['æstrəu'fɪzɪks] *n* астрофи́зика.

astute [əs'tju:t] *adj* (*person*) проница́тельный* (проница́телен); (*decision*) дальнови́дный* (дальнови́ден).

asunder [ə'sʌndəʳ] *adv*: **to tear ~** разрыва́ть (разорва́ть* *perf*) на куски́.

ASV *n abbr* (*BIBLE*: = *American Standard Version*) *америка́нский* станда́ртный вариа́нт Би́блии*.

asylum [ə'saɪləm] *n* (*refuge*) убе́жище; (*mental hospital*) сумасше́дший* дом*; **to seek political ~** иска́ть* (*perf*) полити́ческого убе́жища.

asymmetrical [eɪsɪ'mɛtrɪkl] *adj* ассиметри́чный* (ассиметри́чен).

KEYWORD

at [æt] *prep* **1** (*referring to position*) в/на *+prp*; **at the top** наверху́; **at home** до́ма; **at school** в шко́ле; **at the theatre** в теа́тре; **at the baker's** в бу́лочной; **at a concert** на конце́рте; **at the station** на ста́нции; **they are sitting at the table** они́ сидя́т за столо́м; **at my friend's (house)** у моего́ дру́га; **at the doctor's** у врача́
2 (*referring to direction*) в/на *+acc*; **to look at sb/sth** смотре́ть (посмотре́ть *perf*) на кого́-н/что-н; **to throw sth at sb** (*several objects*) броса́ться (*impf*) чем-н в кого́-н; (*one object*) броса́ть (бро́сить* *perf*) что-н в кого́-н
3 (*referring to time*): **at four o'clock** в четы́ре часа́; **at half past two** в полови́не тре́тьего; **at a quarter to two** без че́тверти два; **at a quarter past two** в че́тверть тре́тьего; **at dawn** на заре́; **at night** но́чью; **at Christmas** на Рождество́; **at lunch** за обе́дом; **at times** времена́ми
4 (*referring to rates*): **at £1 a kilo** по фу́нту за килогра́мм; **two at a time** по два за раз; **at fifty km/h** со ско́ростью пятьдеся́т км/ч; **at full speed** на по́лной ско́рости
5 (*referring to manner*): **at a stroke** одни́м ма́хом; **at peace** в ми́ре
6 (*referring to activity*): **to be at home/work** быть (*impf*) до́ма/на рабо́те; **to play at cowboys** игра́ть (*impf*) в ковбо́и; **to be good at doing sth** хорошо́ уме́ть (*impf*) что-н де́лать (*impf*)
7 (*referring to cause*): **shocked/surprised/annoyed at sth** шоки́рован/удивлён*/раздражён* чем-н; **I am surprised at you** Вы меня́ удивля́ете; **I stayed at his suggestion** я оста́лся по его́ предложе́нию.

ate [eɪt] *pt of* **eat**.

atheism ['eɪθɪɪzəm] *n* атеи́зм.

atheist ['eɪθɪɪst] *n* атеи́ст(ка*).

Athenian [ə'θi:nɪən] *adj* афи́нский ◆ *n* афиня́нин(-нка).

Athens ['æθɪnz] *n* Афи́ны* *pl*.

athlete ['æθli:t] *n* спортсме́н(ка*).

athletic [æθ'lɛtɪk] *adj* спорти́вный; (*physique*) атлети́ческий*.

athletics [æθ'lɛtɪks] *n* лёгкая атле́тика.

Atlantic [ət'læntɪk] *adj* атланти́ческий* ◆ *n*: **the ~ (Ocean)** Атланти́ческий* океа́н.
atlas ['ætləs] *n* а́тлас.
Atlas Mountains *npl*: **the ~ ~** Атла́сские го́ры* *fpl*.
ATM *abbr* (= *Automated Telling Machine*) банкома́т.
atmosphere ['ætməsfɪəʳ] *n* атмосфе́ра; (*air*) во́здух.
atmospheric [ætməs'fɛrɪk] *adj* атмосфе́рный.
atmospherics [ætməs'fɛrɪks] *npl* (*RADIO*) атмосфе́рные поме́хи *fpl*.
atoll ['ætɔl] *n* ато́лл.
atom ['ætəm] *n* а́том.
atomic [ə'tɔmɪk] *adj* а́томный.
atom(ic) bomb *n* а́томная бо́мба.
atomizer ['ætəmaɪzəʳ] *n* (*for perfume*) пульвериза́тор.
atone [ə'təun] *vi*: **to ~ for** искупа́ть (искупи́ть* *perf*).
atonement [ə'təunmənt] *n* искупле́ние.
ATP *n abbr* = *Association of Tennis Professionals*.
atrocious [ə'trəuʃəs] *adj* ужа́сный* (ужа́сен).
atrocity [ə'trɔsɪtɪ] *n* (*act*) зве́рство.
atrophy ['ætrəfɪ] *n* атрофи́я ◆ *vt* атрофи́ровать (*impf/perf*) ◆ *vi* атрофи́роваться (*impf/perf*).
attach [ə'tætʃ] *vt* прикрепля́ть (прикрепи́ть* *perf*); (*document, letter*) прилага́ть (приложи́ть* *perf*); **he is/was ~ed to** (*fond of*) он привя́зан/был привя́зан к *+dat*; (*connected with*) он свя́зан/был свя́зан с *+instr*; **to ~ importance to** придава́ть (прида́ть* *perf*) значе́ние *+dat*; **the ~ed letter** прилага́емое письмо́.
attaché [ə'tæʃeɪ] *n* атташе́ *m ind*.
attaché case *n* диплома́т (*портфе́ль*).
attachment [ə'tætʃmənt] *n* (*fastening*) крепле́ние; (*device*) приспособле́ние, наса́дка; (*love*): **~ (to sb)** привя́занность *f* (к кому́-н).
attack [ə'tæk] *vt* (*MIL, fig*) атакова́ть (*impf/perf*); (*assault*) напада́ть (напа́сть* *perf*) на *+acc*; (*tackle*: *problem*) бра́ться* (взя́ться* *perf*) энерги́чно за *+acc* ◆ *n* (*criticism, MIL*) ата́ка; (*assault*) нападе́ние; (*of illness*) при́ступ*; **heart ~** серде́чный при́ступ.
attacker [ə'tækəʳ] *n*: **his/her ~** напа́вший(-ая) *m(f) adj* на него́/неё.
attain [ə'teɪn] *vt* (*happiness, success*) достига́ть (дости́гнуть* *or* дости́чь* *perf*) *+gen*, добива́ться (доби́ться* *perf*) *+gen*; (*knowledge*) приобрета́ть (приобрести́* *perf*)
attainments [ə'teɪnmənts] *npl* достиже́ния *ntpl*
attempt [ə'tɛmpt] *n* (*try*) попы́тка* ◆ *vt* (*try*) пыта́ться (попыта́ться *perf*) *+infin*; **to make an ~ on sb's life** соверша́ть (соверши́ть *perf*) покуше́ние на чью-н жизнь; **he made no ~ to help** он соверше́нно не попыта́лся помо́чь.
attempted [ə'tɛmptɪd] *adj*: **~ murder** покуше́ние на жизнь; **~ suicide** попы́тка* самоуби́йства; **~ burglary** попы́тка* ограбле́ния.
attend [ə'tɛnd] *vt* (*school, church, lectures*) посеща́ть (*impf*); (*patient*) уха́живать (*impf*) за *+instr*; (*course*) слу́шать (прослу́шать *perf*); (*meeting, talk*) прису́тствовать (*impf*) на *+prp*
▸ **attend to** *vt fus* (*needs, patient*) занима́ться (заня́ться* *perf*) *+instr*; (*customer*) обслу́живать (обслужи́ть *perf*).
attendance [ə'tɛndəns] *n* прису́тствие; (*in school*) посеща́емость *f*; (*SPORT*: *gate*) коли́чество боле́льщиков на ма́тче.
attendant [ə'tɛndənt] *n* сопровожда́ющий(-ая) *m(f) adj*; (*in garage etc*) служи́тель(ница) *m(f)* ◆ *adj* (*dangers, risks*) сопу́тствующий.
attention [ə'tɛnʃən] *n* (*concentration*) внима́ние; (*care*) ухо́д ◆ *excl* (*MIL*) сми́рно; **~s** *npl* (*acts of courtesy*) зна́ки *mpl* внима́ния; **for the ~ of ...** (*ADMIN*) к све́дению *+gen*; **it has come to my ~ that ...** мне ста́ло изве́стно, что ...; **to stand to/at ~** (*MIL*) стоя́ть (*impf*) по сто́йке "сми́рно".
attentive [ə'tɛntɪv] *adj* (*audience*) внима́тельный* (внима́телен); (*polite*) предупреди́тельный* (предупреди́телен); (*kind*) забо́тливый (забо́тлив).
attentively [ə'tɛntɪvlɪ] *adv* внима́тельно, забо́тливо.
attenuate [ə'tɛnjueɪt] *vt* ослабля́ть (осла́бить* *perf*) ◆ *vi* ослабля́ться (осла́биться* *perf*).
attest [ə'tɛst] *vi*: **to ~ to** (*demonstrate*) свиде́тельствовать (*impf*) о *+prp*; (*LAW*) свиде́тельствовать (засвиде́тельствовать *perf*).
attic ['ætɪk] *n* (*living space*) манса́рда; (*storage space*) черда́к*.
attire [ə'taɪəʳ] *n* одея́ние.
attitude ['ætɪtju:d] *n* (*view, behaviour*): **~ (to** *or* **towards)** отноше́ние (к *+dat*); (*posture*) по́за.
attorney [ə'tə:nɪ] *n* (*US*: *lawyer*) юри́ст; (*having proxy*) пове́ренный(-ая) *m(f) adj*; **power of ~** дове́ренность *f*.
Attorney General *n* (*BRIT*) мини́стр юсти́ции; (*US*) Генера́льный прокуро́р.
attract [ə'trækt] *vt* привлека́ть (привле́чь* *perf*)
attraction [ə'trækʃən] *n* (*charm, appeal*) привлека́тельность *f*; (*usu pl*: *amusements*) аттракцио́ны *mpl*; (*PHYS*) притяже́ние; (*fig*: *towards sb, sth*) влече́ние.
attractive [ə'træktɪv] *adj* привлека́тельный* (привлека́телен).
attribute [*n* 'ætrɪbju:t, *vb* ə'trɪbju:t] *n* при́знак, атрибу́т ◆ *vt*: **to ~ sth to** (*cause*) относи́ть* (отнести́* *perf*) что-н за счёт *+gen*; (*painting, quality*) припи́сывать (приписа́ть* *perf*) что-н *+dat*.
attribution [ætrɪ'bju:ʃən] *n* припи́сывание.

* marks translations which have irregular inflections. The Russian-English side of the dictionary gives inflectional information.

attrition [əˈtrɪʃən] *n*: **war of ~** войнá* на изнурéние.
Atty. Gen. *abbr* = **Attorney General.**
ATV *n abbr* (= *all terrain vehicle*) вездехóд.
atypical [eiˈtɪpɪkl] *adj* нетипи́чный (нетипи́чен).
aubergine [ˈəubəʒi:n] *n* (*vegetable*) баклажáн; (*colour*) тёмно-лилóвый.
auburn [ˈɔ:bən] *adj* (*hair*) тёмно-ры́жий*.
auction [ˈɔ:kʃən] *n* (*also:* **sale by ~**) аукциóн ◆ *vt* продавáть (продáть* *perf*) с аукциóна.
auctioneer [ɔ:kʃəˈnɪə^r] *n* аукциони́ст.
auction room *n* аукциóнный зал.
audacious [ɔ:ˈdeɪʃəs] *adj* (*behaviour*) дéрзкий* (дéрзок).
audacity [ɔ:ˈdæsɪtɪ] *n* дéрзость *f*.
audible [ˈɔ:dɪbl] *adj* слы́шный* (слы́шен).
audience [ˈɔ:dɪəns] *n* аудитóрия, пу́блика; (*with queen etc*) аудиéнция.
audio typist [ˈɔ:dɪəu-] *n* фономашини́стка.
audiovisual [ˈɔ:dɪəuˈvɪzjuəl] *adj* (*materials, equipment*) áудио-визуáльный*.
audiovisual aids [ˈɔ:dɪəuˈvɪzjuəl-] *npl* техни́ческие срéдства *ntpl* обучéния.
audit [ˈɔ:dɪt] *vt* (*COMM*) проводи́ть* (провести́* *perf*) реви́зию *+gen* ◆ *n* реви́зия, аудúт.
audition [ɔ:ˈdɪʃən] *n* (*CINEMA, THEAT etc*) прослу́шивание ◆ *vi*: **to ~ (for)** проходи́ть* (пройти́* *perf*) прослу́шивание (на *+acc*).
auditor [ˈɔ:dɪtə^r] *n* реви́зия, ауди́тор.
auditorium [ɔ:dɪˈtɔ:rɪəm] *n* зал.
Aug. *abbr* = **August.**
augment [ɔ:gˈmɛnt] *vt* (*income etc*) увели́чивать (увели́чить *perf*).
augur [ˈɔ:gə^r] *vi*: **it ~s well** э́то хорóшее предзнаменовáние.
August [ˈɔ:gəst] *n* áвгуст; *see also* **July.**
august [ɔ:ˈgʌst] *adj* (*figure, building*) вели́чественный.
aunt [ɑ:nt] *n* тётя*.
auntie [ˈɑ:ntɪ] *n dimin of* **aunt.**
aunty [ˈɑ:ntɪ] *n dimin of* **aunt.**
au pair [ˈəuˈpɛə^r] *n* (*also:* **~ ~ girl**) *молодáя ня́ня-инострáнка, живу́щая в семьé.*
aura [ˈɔ:rə] *n* (*fig: air*) орeóл.
auspices [ˈɔ:spɪsɪz] *npl*: **under the ~ of** под эги́дой *+gen.*
auspicious [ɔ:sˈpɪʃəs] *adj* благоприя́тный.
austere [ɔsˈtɪə^r] *adj* (*room etc*) стрóгий*; (*person, manner*) сурóвый (сурóв).
austerity [ɔsˈtɛrɪtɪ] *n* (*simplicity*) стрóгость *f*; (*ECON: hardship*) лишéния *ntpl.*
Australasia [ɔ:strəˈleɪzɪə] *n* Австрáлия и Нóвая Зелáндия.
Australasian [ɔ:strəˈleɪzɪən] *adj* австрáло-азиáтский*.
Australia [ɔsˈtreɪlɪə] *n* Австрáлия.
Australian [ɔsˈtreɪlɪən] *adj* австрали́йский* ◆ *n* австрали́ец*(-и́йка).
Austria [ˈɔstrɪə] *n* Áвстрия.
Austrian [ˈɔstrɪən] *adj* австри́йский* ◆ *n* австри́ец*(-и́йка).
AUT *n abbr* (*BRIT*) = *Association of University Teachers.*
authentic [ɔ:ˈθɛntɪk] *adj* пóдлинный*.
authenticate [ɔ:ˈθɛntɪkeɪt] *vt* удостоверя́ть (удостовéрить *perf*) пóдлинность *+gen.*
authenticity [ɔ:θɛnˈtɪsɪtɪ] *n* пóдлинность *f*.
author [ˈɔ:θə^r] *n* (*of text, plan*) áвтор; (*profession*) писáтель*(ница).
authoritarian [ɔ:θɔrɪˈtɛərɪən] *adj* (*attitudes, conduct*) авторитáрный* (авторитáрен).
authoritative [ɔ:ˈθɔrɪtətɪv] *adj* авторитéтный* (авторитéтен).
authority [ɔ:ˈθɔrɪtɪ] *n* (*power*) власть *f*; (*government body*) управлéние; (*expert*) авторитéт; (*official permission*) полномóчие; **the authorities** *npl* (*ruling body*) влáсти* *fpl*; **to have the ~ to do** имéть *(impf)* полномóчия *+infin.*
authorization [ɔ:θəraɪˈzeɪʃən] *n*: **~ (for)** сáнкция (на *+acc*).
authorize [ˈɔ:θəraɪz] *vt* санкциони́ровать *(impf/perf)*; **to ~ sb to do** уполномáчивать (уполномóчить *perf*) когó-н *+infin.*
authorized capital [ˈɔ:θəraɪzd-] *n* (*COMM*) устáвный капитáл.
authorship [ˈɔ:θəʃɪp] *n* áвторство.
autistic [ɔ:ˈtɪstɪk] *adj* (*person*) страдáющий ауги́змом.
auto [ˈɔ:təu] *n* (*US: inf*) автó *nt ind.*
autobiographical [ˈɔ:təbaɪəˈgræfɪkl] *adj* автобиографи́ческий*.
autobiography [ɔ:təbaɪˈɔgrəfɪ] *n* автобиográфия.
autocracy [ɔ:ˈtɔkrəsɪ] *n* автокрáтия.
autocratic [ɔ:təˈkrætɪk] *adj* автократи́ческий.
Autocue® [ˈɔ:təukju:] *n* телесуфлёр.
autograph [ˈɔ:təgrɑ:f] *n* автóграф ◆ *vt* надпи́сывать (надписáть* *perf*).
auto-immune [ɔ:təuɪˈmju:n] *adj* аутоиммýнный.
automat [ˈɔ:təmæt] *n* (*vending machine*) автомáт; (*US: place*) кафé-автомáт.
automata [ɔ:ˈtɔmətə] *npl of* **automaton.**
automate [ˈɔ:təmeɪt] *vt* автоматизи́ровать *(impf/perf).*
automated [ˈɔ:təmeɪtɪd] *adj* автоматизи́рованный.
automatic [ɔ:təˈmætɪk] *adj* автомати́ческий* ◆ *n* (*US: gun*) (самозаря́дный) пистолéт; (*car*) автомоби́ль *m* с автомати́ческим переключéнием скоростéй; (*washing machine*) стирáльная маши́на-автомáт.
automatically [ɔ:təˈmætɪklɪ] *adv* автомати́чески.
automatic data processing *n* автомати́ческая обрабóтка дáнных.
automation [ɔ:təˈmeɪʃən] *n* автоматизáция.
automaton [ɔ:ˈtɔmətən] (*pl* **automata**) *n* автомáт.
automobile [ˈɔ:təməbi:l] *n* (*US*) автомоби́ль *m.*

autonomous [ɔː'tɔnəməs] *adj* (*region*) автоно́мный* (автоно́мен); (*person, organization*) самостоя́тельный* (самостоя́телен).
autonomy [ɔː'tɔnəmɪ] *n* (*of organization, country etc*) автоно́мия, самостоя́тельность *f*.
autopsy ['ɔːtɔpsɪ] *n* вскры́тие (*тру́па*).
autumn ['ɔːtəm] *n* о́сень *f*; **in ~** о́сенью.
autumnal [ɔː'tʌmnəl] *adj* осе́нний*.
auxiliary [ɔːg'zɪlɪərɪ] *adj* вспомога́тельный ◆ *n* помо́щник.
AV *n abbr* (*BIBLE*: = *Authorized Version*) *перево́д Би́блии, при́нятый в англика́нской це́ркви* ◆ *abbr* = **audiovisual**.
Av. *abbr* = **avenue**.
avail [ə'veɪl] *vt*: **to ~ o.s. of** воспо́льзоваться (*perf*) +*instr* ◆ *n*: **to no ~** напра́сно.
availability [əveɪlə'bɪlɪtɪ] *n* (*supply*) нали́чие.
available [ə'veɪləbl] *adj* (*article, service*) име́ющийся в нали́чии, досту́пный* (досту́пен); (*person, time*) свобо́дный* (свобо́ден); **every ~ means** все досту́пные сре́дства; **is the manager ~?** заве́дующий *m adj* свобо́ден?; **to make sth ~ to sb** предоставля́ть (предоста́вить* *perf*) что-н кому́-н.
avalanche ['ævəlɑːnʃ] *n* (*also fig*) лави́на.
avant-garde ['ævɑ̃ŋ'gɑːd] *adj* авангарди́стский*.
avarice ['ævərɪs] *n* а́лчность *f*.
avaricious [ævə'rɪʃəs] *adj* а́лчный* (а́лчен).
avdp. *abbr* (= *avoirdupois*) *систе́ма едини́ц ве́са, испо́льзуемая в англоязы́чных стра́нах*.
Ave. *abbr* = **avenue**.
avenge [ə'vɛndʒ] *vt* мстить* (отомсти́ть* *perf*) за +*acc*.
avenue ['ævənjuː] *n* (*street*) у́лица; (*drive*) алле́я; (*means, solution*) путь* *m*.
average ['ævərɪdʒ] *n* сре́днее *nt adj* ◆ *adj* сре́дний* ◆ *vt* достига́ть (дости́чь* *perf*) в сре́днем +*gen*, составля́ть (соста́вить* *perf*) в сре́днем; **on ~** в сре́днем; **above/below (the) ~** вы́ше/ни́же сре́днего у́ровня
▸ **average out** *vi*: **to ~ out at** равня́ться (*impf*) в сре́днем +*dat*.
averse [ə'vəːs] *adj*: **to be ~ to sth/doing** быть* (*impf*) про́тив чего́-н/того́, что́бы +*infin*; **I wouldn't be ~ to a drink** я непро́чь что́-нибудь вы́пить.
aversion [ə'vəːʃən] *n* неприя́знь *f*; **to have an ~ to sb/sth** испы́тывать (*impf*) неприя́знь к кому́-н/чему́-н.
avert [ə'vəːt] *vt* (*accident, war*) предотвраща́ть (предотврати́ть* *perf*); (*blow, eyes*) отводи́ть* (отвести́* *perf*).
aviary ['eɪvɪərɪ] *n* пти́чий* волье́р.
aviation [eɪvɪ'eɪʃən] *n* авиа́ция.
avid ['ævɪd] *adj* (*supporter, viewer*) стра́стный.
avidly ['ævɪdlɪ] *adv* стра́стно.
avocado [ævə'kɑːdəu] *n* (*also*: **~ pear**: *BRIT*) авока́до *nt ind*.
avoid [ə'vɔɪd] *vt* избега́ть* (избежа́ть* *perf*).
avoidable [ə'vɔɪdəbl] *adj* (*death, accident*) предотврати́мый.
avoidance [ə'vɔɪdəns] *n*: **~ (of)** (*of tax, issue*) уклоне́ние (от +*gen*).
avowed [ə'vaud] *adj* откры́тый.
AVP *n abbr* (*US*: = *assistant vice-president*) помо́щник ви́це-президе́нта.
avuncular [ə'vʌŋkjulə'] *adj* (*expression, tone*) оте́ческий*; (*person*) забо́тливый.
AWACS ['eɪwæks] *n abbr* (= *airborne warning and control system*) АВАКС (*авиацио́нная систе́ма да́льнего радиолокацио́нного обнаруже́ния и управле́ния*).
await [ə'weɪt] *vt* ожида́ть (*impf*) +*gen*; **~ing delivery** (*COMM*) отпра́вка предстои́т; **long ~ed** долгожда́нный.
awake [ə'weɪk] (*pt* **awoke**, *pp* **awoken** *or* **awaked**) *vt* буди́ть* (разбуди́ть* *perf*) ◆ *vi* просыпа́ться (просну́ться *perf*) ◆ *adj*: **he is ~** он просну́лся; **to be ~ to** (*dangers, possibilities*) сознава́ть* (*impf*); **he was still ~** он ещё не спал.
awakening [ə'weɪknɪŋ] *n* (*also fig*) пробужде́ние.
award [ə'wɔːd] *n* награ́да; (*LAW*) возмеще́ние ◆ *vt* награжда́ть (награди́ть* *perf*); (*LAW*) присужда́ть (присуди́ть* *perf*).
aware [ə'wɛə'] *adj*: **to be ~ (of)** (*realize*) сознава́ть (*impf*) (+*acc*); **to become ~ of/that** осознава́ть* (осозна́ть *perf*) +*acc*/, что; **politically/socially ~** полити́чески/социа́льно созна́тельный; **I am fully ~ that** я по́лностью созна́ю, что.
awareness [ə'wɛənɪs] *n* осозна́ние; **to develop people's ~ of** развива́ть (разви́ть* *perf*) обще́ственное осозна́ние +*gen*.
awash [ə'wɔʃ] *adj* зато́пленный; (*fig*): **~ with** наводнённый (наводнён) +*instr*.
away [ə'weɪ] *adv* (*movement*) в сто́рону; (*position*) в стороне́, по́одаль; (*far away*) далеко́; (*in time*): **the holidays are two weeks ~** до кани́кул (оста́лось) две неде́ли; **~ from** (*movement*) от +*gen*; (*position*) по́одаль от +*gen*; **two kilometres ~ from the town** в двух киломе́трах от го́рода; **two hours ~ by car** в двух часа́х езды́ на маши́не; **he's ~ for a week** он в отъе́зде на неде́лю; **he's ~ in Milan** он в отъе́зде в Мила́н; **to take ~ (from)** (*remove*) забира́ть (забра́ть* *perf*) (у +*gen*); (*subtract*) отнима́ть (отня́ть* *perf*) (от +*gen*); **he is working ~** он продолжа́ет рабо́тать ; **to fade ~** (*colour*) выцвета́ть (вы́цвести* *perf*); (*enthusiasm, light*) угаса́ть (уга́снуть *perf*).

* marks translations which have irregular inflections. The Russian-English side of the dictionary gives inflectional information.

away game *n* (*SPORT*) игрá на вы́езде.
awe [ɔ:] *n* благоговéние.
awe-inspiring ['ɔ:mspaiərıŋ] *adj* (*person, thing*) внушáющий благоговéние.
awesome ['ɔ:səm] *adj* = **awe-inspiring**.
awestruck ['ɔ:strʌk] *adj* охвáченный (охвáчен) благоговéнием.
awful ['ɔ:fəl] *adj* ужáсный* (ужáсен); **an ~ lot (of)** ужáсно мнóго (*+gen*).
awfully ['ɔ:fəlı] *adv* ужáсно.
awhile [ə'waıl] *adv* недóлго, какóе-то врéмя; **wait ~** подождúте немнóго.
awkward ['ɔ:kwəd] *adj* (*clumsy*) неуклю́жий* (неуклю́ж); (*inconvenient*) неудóбный* (неудóбен); (*embarrassing*) нелóвкий*.
awkwardness ['ɔ:kwədnıs] *n* (*see adj*) неуклю́жесть *f*; неудóбство; нелóвкость *f*.
awl [ɔ:l] *n* шилó*.
awning ['ɔ:nıŋ] *n* (*of tent*) навéс; (*of shop, hotel*) тент.
awoke [ə'wəuk] *pt of* **awake**.
awoken [ə'wəukən] *pp of* **awake**.
AWOL ['eıwɔl] *abbr* (*MIL*: = *absent without leave*) (находя́щийся) в самовóльной отлу́чке.
awry [ə'raı] *adv* (*crooked*) крúво, кóсо; **to go ~** (*plan*) спу́тываться (спу́таться *perf*).
axe [æks] (*US* **ax**) *n* топóр* ◆ *vt* (*employee*) увольня́ть (увóлить *perf*); (*project etc*) урéзывать (урéзать* *perf*); (*jobs*) сокращáть (сократúть* *perf*); **to have an ~ to grind** (*fig*) имéть (*impf*) коры́стные побуждéния.
axes[1] ['æksız] *npl of* **ax(e)**.
axes[2] ['æksi:z] *npl of* **axis**.
axiom ['æksıəm] *n* аксиóма.
axiomatic [æksıəu'mætık] *adj* аксиоматúчный (аксиоматúчен).
axis ['æksıs] (*pl* **axes**) *n* ось* *f*.
axle ['æksl] *n* (*also:* **~-tree**: *AUT*) ось* *f*.
aye [aı] *excl* да; **the ~s** *npl* голосу́ющие "за".
AYH *n abbr* = *American Youth Hostels*.
AZ *abbr* (*US*: *POST*) = *Arizona*.
azalea [ə'zeılıə] *n* азáлия.
Azerbaijan [[ae]zəbaı'dʒɑ:n] *n* Азербайджáн.
Azerbaijani [[ae]zəbaı'dʒɑ:nı] *n* (*person*) азербайджáнец*(-áнка*); (*LING*) азербайджáнский* язы́к* ◆ *adj* азербайджáнский*.
Azores [ə'zɔ:z] *npl*: **the ~** Азóрские островá *mpl*.
Azov ['ɑ:zɔv] *n*: **Sea of ~** Азóвское мóре.
AZT *n abbr* (= *azidothymidine*) аздотимидúн.
Aztec ['æztɛk] *n* ацтéк ◆ *adj*: **~ civilization/art** цивилизáция/иску́сство ацтéков.
azure ['eıʒə'] *adj* лазу́рный.

~ B, b ~

B, b [bi:] *n* (*letter*) *2-ая бу́ква англи́йского алфави́та*; (*SCOL*: *mark*) ≈ хорошо́; **~ road** (*BRIT*: *AUT*) шоссе́ *nt ind* (второ́й катего́рии).

B [bi:] *n* (*MUS*) си *nt ind*.

b. *abbr* (= **born**) род.= *роди́лся*.

BA *n abbr* (= *Bachelor of Arts*) бакала́вр гуманита́рных нау́к; (= *British Academy*) Брита́нская акаде́мия (*гуманита́рных нау́к*).

babble ['bæbl] *vi* лепета́ть* (залепета́ть* *perf*) ◆ *n*: **a ~ of voices** го́мон голосо́в.

babe [beɪb] *n* (*inf*) де́тка*, кро́шка*.

baboon [bə'bu:n] *n* бабуи́н.

baby ['beɪbɪ] *n* ребёнок*; (*US*: *inf*) де́тка*.

baby carriage *n* (*US*) коля́ска*.

baby grand *n* (*also:* **~ ~ piano**) кабине́тный роя́ль *m*.

babyhood ['beɪbɪhud] *n* младе́нчество.

babyish ['beɪbɪɪʃ] *adj* де́тский*.

baby-minder ['beɪbɪ'maɪndə^r] *n* (*BRIT*) ня́ня* (*присма́тривающая за детьми́ у себя́ до́ма*).

baby-sit ['beɪbɪsɪt] *vi* смотре́ть (*impf*) за детьми́.

baby-sitter ['beɪbɪsɪtə^r] *n* приходя́щая ня́ня*.

bachelor ['bætʃələ^r] *n* холостя́к*; **B~ of Arts/Science** ≈ бакала́вр гуманита́рных/ есте́ственных наук; **B~ of Arts/Science degree** ≈ сте́пень* *f* бакала́вра гуманита́рных/есте́ственных нау́к.

bachelorhood ['bætʃələhud] *n* холостя́цкая жизнь *f*.

bachelor party *n* (*US*) мальчи́шник.

KEYWORD

back [bæk] *n* **1** (*of person, animal*) спина́; **the back of the hand** ты́льная сторона́ ладо́ни; **he has his back to the wall** (*fig*) он прижа́т к сте́нке

2 (*of house, car etc*) за́дняя часть *f*; (*of chair*) спи́нка*; (*of page*) обра́тная сторона́, оборо́т; (*back cover*: *of book*) оборо́т; **back to front** за́дом напере́д; **to break the back of a job** (*BRIT*) выполня́ть (вы́полнить *perf*) гла́вную часть рабо́ты; **at the back** (*of crowd*) в за́дних ряда́х; (*of book*) в конце́

3 (*FOOTBALL*) защи́тник

◆ *vt* **1** (*candidate*: *also:* **back up**) подде́рживать (поддержа́ть *perf*)

2 (*financially*: *person*) финанси́ровать (*impf*), ока́зывать (оказа́ть *perf*) фина́нсовую подде́ржку; (: *horse*) ста́вить* (поста́вить* *perf*) на +*acc*

3 (*car*): **he backed the car into the garage** он дал за́дний ход и поста́вил маши́ну в гара́ж

◆ *vi* (*car etc*: *also:* **back up**) дава́ть* (дать* *perf*) за́дний* ход

◆ *adv* **1** (*not forward*) обра́тно, наза́д; **he ran back** он побежа́л обра́тно *or* наза́д

2 (*returned*): **he's back** он верну́лся; **when will you be back?** когда́ Вы вернётесь?

3 (*restitution*): **to throw the ball back** кида́ть (ки́нуть *perf*) мяч обра́тно; **can I have the pen back?** верни́те мне ру́чку, пожа́луйста

4 (*again*): **to call back** (*TEL*) перезва́нивать (перезвони́ть *perf*); (*visit again*) заходи́ть (зайти́ *perf*) ещё раз

◆ *cpd* **1** (*payment*) за́дним число́м

2 (*AUT*: *seat, wheels*) за́дний*; (*room, garden*) вну́тренний*; **to take a back seat** (*fig*) станови́ться* (стать* *perf*) пасси́вным наблюда́телем

▸ **back down** *vi* отступа́ть (отступи́ть* *perf*)

▸ **back on to** *vt fus*: **the house backs on to a park** дом выхо́дит за́дним фаса́дом в парк

▸ **back out** *vi* (*of promise*) отступа́ться (отступи́ться* *perf*)

▸ **back up** *vt* (*person, theory etc*) подде́рживать (поддержа́ть* *perf*); (*COMPUT*) резерви́ровать (*impf/perf*).

backache ['bækeɪk] *n* простре́лы *mpl*, боль *f* в поясни́це.

backbencher ['bæk'bɛntʃə^r] *n* (*BRIT*) "заднескаме́ечник".

backbiting ['bækbaɪtɪŋ] *n* злосло́вие.

backbone ['bækbəun] *n* позвоно́чник; **he's the ~ of the organization** на нём де́ржится вся организа́ция.

backchat ['bæktʃæt] *n* (*BRIT*: *inf*) препира́тельство.

backcloth ['bækklɔθ] *n* (*BRIT*: *THEAT*) за́дник.

backcomb ['bækkəum] *vt* (*BRIT*) начёсывать (начеса́ть* *perf*).

* marks translations which have irregular inflections. The Russian-English side of the dictionary gives inflectional information.

backdate [bæk'deɪt] *vt* (*pay rise*) проводи́ть* (провести́* *perf*) за́дним число́м; (*letter*) помеча́ть (поме́тить* *perf*) за́дним число́м; **~d pay rise (of 20%)** повыше́ние зарпла́ты за́дним число́м (на 20%).
backdrop ['bækdrɔp] *n* = **backcloth**.
backer ['bækəʳ] *n* (*COMM*) финанси́рующая сторона́*.
backfire [bæk'faɪəʳ] *vi* (*AUT*) дава́ть* (дать* *perf*) обра́тную вспы́шку; **his plan ~d** его́ план оберну́лся про́тив него́.
backgammon ['bækgæmən] *n* триктра́к.
background ['bækgraund] *n* (*of picture*) за́дний* план; (*of events*) предысто́рия; (*COMPUT*) фон; (*experience*) о́пыт ◆ *cpd* (*noise, music*) посторо́нний*; **he's from a working class ~** он из рабо́чей семьи́; **against a ~ of ...** на фо́не *+gen* ...; **~ reading (on)** дополни́тельное чте́ние (по *+dat*).
backhand ['bækhænd] *n* (*TENNIS*) уда́р сле́ва.
backhanded ['bæk'hændɪd] *adj* (*fig*) двусмы́сленный (двусмы́слен).
backhander ['bæk'hændəʳ] *n* (*BRIT: inf*) взя́тка*.
backing ['bækɪŋ] *n* (*support*) подде́ржка*; (*COMM*) финанси́рование; (*MUS*) сопровожде́ние.
back issue *n* ста́рый но́мер*.
backlash ['bæklæʃ] *n* (*fig*) обра́тная реа́кция.
backlog ['bæklɔg] *n*: **~ of work** невы́полненная рабо́та.
back number *n* = **back issue**.
backpack ['bækpæk] *n* рюкза́к*.
backpacker ['bækpækəʳ] *n молодо́й челове́к, путеше́ствующий с рюкзако́м*.
back pay *n* пла́та за́дним число́м.
backpedal ['bækpɛdl] *vi* (*fig*) идти́* (пойти́* *perf*) на попя́тный.
backseat driver ['bæksi:t-] *n пассажи́р, даю́щий сове́ты шофёру*.
backside ['bæksaɪd] *n* (*inf*) зад*.
backslash ['bækslæʃ] *n* коса́я черта́ вле́во.
backslide ['bækslaɪd] *vi* принима́ться (приня́ться *perf*) за ста́рое.
backspace ['bækspeɪs] *vi* реверси́ровать *(impf/ perf)*.
backstage [bæk'steɪdʒ] *adv* за кули́сами.
backstreet ['bækstri:t] *n* окра́ина ◆ *cpd*: **~ abortionist** *челове́к, де́лающий подпо́льные або́рты*.
backstroke ['bækstrəuk] *n* пла́вание на спине́; **to do the ~** пла́вать *(impf)* на спине́.
backtrack ['bæktræk] *vi* (*fig*) идти́* (пойти́* *perf*) на попя́тный.
backup ['bækʌp] *adj* (*train, plane*) дополни́тельный*; (*COMPUT*) резе́рвный ◆ *n* (*support*) подде́ржка*; (*also:* **~ disk**) дублика́т ги́бкого ди́ска.
backward ['bækwəd] *adj* (*movement*) обра́тный; (*person, country*) отста́лый.
backwards ['bækwədz] *adv* наза́д; (*in reverse order*) наоборо́т; (*fall*) на́взничь; **to know sth ~** *or (US)* **~ and forwards** знать *(impf)* что-н вдоль и поперёк; **to walk ~** пя́титься* (попя́титься* *perf*).
backwater ['bækwɔ:təʳ] *n* (*fig*) боло́то.
backyard [bæk'jɑ:d] *n* (*of house*) за́дний* двор*.
bacon ['beɪkən] *n* бeко́н.
bacteria [bæk'tɪərɪə] *npl* бакте́рии *fpl*.
bacteriology [bæktɪərɪ'ɔlədʒɪ] *n* бактериоло́гия.
bad [bæd] *adj* плохо́й*; (*mistake*) серьёзный; (*injury, crash*) тяжёлый* (тяжёл); (*food*) ту́хлый*; **his ~ leg** его́ больна́я нога́; **to go ~** (*food*) ту́хнуть (протýхнуть *perf*), по́ртиться* (испо́ртиться* *perf*); (*milk*) скиса́ть (ски́снуть *perf*); **she's having a ~ time of it** у неё тяжёлый пери́од; **I feel ~ about it** я чу́вствую себя́ винова́тым; **in ~ faith** нейскренне.
bad debt *n* спи́санный долг (по несостоя́тельности должника́).
baddy ['bædɪ] *n* (*inf*) плохо́й* *m adj* (*в кни́ге, фи́льме*).
bade [bæd] *pt of* **bid**.
badge [bædʒ] *n* значо́к*; (*of policeman*) бля́ха; (*sew-on*) наши́вка; (*fig*) си́мвол.
badger ['bædʒəʳ] *n* барсу́к ◆ *vt* пристава́ть* (приста́ть* *perf*) к *+dat*.
badly ['bædlɪ] *adv* пло́хо; **~ wounded** тяжело́ ра́неный; **he needs it ~** он си́льно в э́том нужда́ется; **to be ~ off (for money)** нужда́ться *(impf)* (в деньга́х).
bad-mannered ['bæd'mænəd] *adj* невоспи́танный.
badminton ['bædmɪntən] *n* бадминто́н.
bad-tempered ['bæd'tɛmpəd] *adj* (*by nature*) вспы́льчивый (вспы́льчив), раздражи́тельный (раздражи́телен); (*on one occasion*) раздражённый (раздражён).
baffle ['bæfl] *vt* озада́чивать (озада́чить *perf*).
baffling ['bæflɪŋ] *adj*: **I find his behaviour ~** его́ поведе́ние меня́ озада́чивает.
bag [bæg] *n* су́мка; (*paper, plastic*) паке́т; (*handbag*) су́мочка*; (*satchel*) ра́нец*; (*case*) портфе́ль *m*; (*of hunter*) ягдта́ш; (*pej: woman*) карга́; **~s of** (*inf*) у́йма *+gen*; **to pack one's ~s** собира́ть (собра́ть* *perf*) чемода́ны; **~s under the eyes** мешки́ под глаза́ми.
bagful ['bægful] *n* (*of flour etc*) (по́лный) паке́т; (*of shopping*) (по́лная) су́мка*.
baggage ['bægɪdʒ] *n* (*US*) бага́ж*.
baggage car *n* (*US*) бага́жный ваго́н.
baggage claim *n* (*US*) вы́дача багажа́.
baggy ['bægɪ] *adj* мешкова́тый.
Baghdad [bæg'dæd] *n* Багда́д.
bag lady *n* (*esp US*) городска́я бродя́жка.
bagpipes ['bægpaɪps] *npl* волы́нка* *fsg*.
bag-snatcher ['bægsnætʃəʳ] *n* (*BRIT*) вор*, выхва́тывающий су́мки.
Bahamas [bə'hɑ:məz] *npl*: **the ~** Бага́мские острова́ *mpl*.
Bahrain [bɑ:'reɪn] *n* Бахре́йн.

Baikal [baɪ'kɑ:l] *n*: **Lake ~** Байкáл.
bail [beɪl] *n* (*payment*) залóг ◆ *vt* (*also:* **to grant ~ to**) выпускáть (вы́пустить* *perf*) под залóг; **he was released on ~** он был вы́пущен на порýки
▸ **bail out** *vt* (*LAW*) платúть* (заплатúть* *perf*) залóговую сýмму за *+acc*; (*boat*) вычéрпывать (вы́черпать *perf*) вóду из *+gen*; (*firm, friend*) вырулáть (вы́ручить *perf*) ◆ *vi* выбрáсываться (вы́броситься* *perf*) с парашю́том.
bailiff ['beɪlɪf] *n* (*LAW*: *BRIT*) судéбный исполнúтель *m*; (: *US*) помóщник шерифа; (*BRIT*: *of estate*) управля́ющий(-ая) *m(f) adj* имéнием.
bait [beɪt] *n* (*for fish*) нажúвка*; (*for animal, criminal*) примáнка* ◆ *vt* (*hook, trap*) наживля́ть (наживúть* *perf*); (*person*) дразнúть* (*impf*).
baize [beɪz] *n* (зелёное) сукнó.
bake [beɪk] *vt* печь* (испéчь* *perf*); (*clay etc*) обжигáть (обжéчь* *perf*) ◆ *vi* (*bread etc*) пéчься* (испéчься* *perf*); (*make cakes etc*) печь* (испéчь* *perf*) пирогú.
baked beans [beɪkt-] *npl* консервúрованная фасóль *fsg*.
baker ['beɪkə^r] *n* пéкарь* *m*; (*also:* **the ~'s**) бýлочная *f adj*.
baker's dozen *n* чёртова дю́жина.
bakery ['beɪkərɪ] *n* (*factory*) пекáрня*; (*shop*) бýлочная *f adj*.
baking ['beɪkɪŋ] *n* вы́печка ◆ *adj* (*inf*): **it's ~ hot today** сегóдня печёт; **she does her ~ once a week** онá печёт раз в недéлю.
baking powder *n* разрыхлúтель *m*.
baking tin *n* (*for cake, meat*) фóрма.
baking tray *n* прóтивень* *m*.
Baku [ba'ku] *n* Бакý *m ind*.
balaclava [bælə'klɑ:və] *n* (*also:* **~ helmet**) вя́заный шлем.
balance ['bæləns] *n* (*equilibrium*) равновéсие; (*COMM*: *in account*) балáнс; (: *remainder*) остáток*; (*scales*) весы́ *pl* ◆ *vt* (*budget, account*) балансúровать (сбалансúровать *perf*); (*make equal*) уравновéшивать (уравновéсить* *perf*); **on ~** по зрéлом размышлéнии; **~ of trade/payments** тóрговый/платёжный балáнс; **~ carried forward** балáнс к перенóсу; **~ brought forward** балáнс с перенóса; **to ~ the books** балансúровать (сбалансúровать *perf*) кнúги; **to ~ the pros and cons** взвéшивать (взвéсить* *perf*) все за и прóтив.
balanced ['bælənst] *adj* (*report*) взвéшенный (взвéшен); (*diet*) сбалансúрованный (сбалансúрован); (*personality*) уравновéшенный.
balance sheet *n* свóдный балáнс.
balcony ['bælkənɪ] *n* балкóн.
bald [bɔ:ld] *adj* (*head*) лы́сый*; (*tyre*) стёртый; (*statement*) прямóй*.
baldness ['bɔ:ldnɪs] *n* лы́сина.
bale [beɪl] *n* (*of hay etc*) тюк*; (*of papers etc*) кúпа
▸ **bale out** *vti see* **bail out**.
Balearic Islands [bælɪ'ærɪk-] *npl*: **the ~ ~** Балéрские островá *mpl*.
baleful ['beɪlful] *adj* (*glance*) зловéщий* (зловéщ).
balk [bɔ:k] *vi*: **he ~ed at the idea** емý претúла э́та идéя; (*subj*: *horse*): **to ~ (at)** заартáчиться (*perf*) (пéред *+instr*).
Balkan ['bɔ:lkən] *adj* балкáнский; **the ~s** *npl* Балкáны *pl*.
ball [bɔ:l] *n* (*for football*) мяч*; (*for tennis, golf*) мя́чик; (*of wool, string*) клубóк*; (*dance*) бал*; **to set the ~ rolling** (*fig*) пускáть (пустúть* *perf*) дéло в ход; **to play ~ (with sb)** (*fig*) подыгрывать (подыгрáть *perf*) (комý-н); **to be on the ~** (*fig*) быть* (*impf*) на конé; **the ~ is in their court** (*fig*) óчередь за нúми.
ballad ['bæləd] *n* баллáда.
ballast ['bæləst] *n* баллáст.
ball bearing *n* шáрик подшúпника.
ballcock ['bɔ:lkɔk] *n* шаровóй клáпан.
ballerina [bælə'ri:nə] *n* балерúна.
ballet ['bæleɪ] *n* балéт.
ballet dancer *n* артúст(ка) балéта.
ballistic [bə'lɪstɪk] *adj* баллистúческий*.
ballistic missile *n* баллистúческий* снаря́д.
ballistics [bə'lɪstɪks] *n* баллúстика.
balloon [bə'lu:n] *n* воздýшный шар; (*also:* **hot air ~**) аэростáт; (*in comic strip*) *кóнтур, в котóрый вписываются рéплики герóев кóмиксов*.
balloonist [bə'lu:nɪst] *n* воздухоплáватель *m*.
ballot ['bælət] *n* голосовáние, баллотирóвка*.
ballot box *n* избирáтельная ýрна.
ballot paper *n* избирáтельный бюллетéнь *m*.
ballpark ['bɔ:lpɑ:k] *n* (*US*) бейсбóльное пóле.
ballpark figure *n* (*inf*) приблизúтельный подсчёт.
ballpoint (pen) ['bɔ:lpɔɪnt(-)] *n* шáриковая рýчка*.
ballroom ['bɔ:lrum] *n* бáльный зал.
balls [bɔ:lz] *npl* (*inf!*) я́йца* *ntpl* (*!*); (: *nonsense*) фигня́ *fsg* (*!*)
balm [bɑ:m] *n* бальзáм.
balmy ['bɑ:mɪ] *adj* (*breeze*) ласкáющий (ласкáющ); (*day*) прия́тный* (прия́тен); (*BRIT*: *inf*) = **barmy**.
BALPA ['bælpə] *n abbr* = *British Airline Pilots' Association*.
balsam ['bɔ:lsəm] *n* бальзáм.
balsa (wood) ['bɔ:lsə-] *n* бáльзовое дéрево*.

* marks translations which have irregular inflections. The Russian-English side of the dictionary gives inflectional information.

Baltic [bɔ:ltɪk] *n*: **the ~** Балти́йское Мо́ре ◆ *adj*: **the ~ States** прибалти́йские госуда́рства *ntpl*.
balustrade [bæləs'treɪd] *n* балюстра́да.
bamboo [bæm'bu:] *n* бамбу́к.
bamboozle [bæm'bu:zl] *vt* (*inf*) одура́чивать (одура́чить *perf*).
ban [bæn] *vt* (*prohibit*) запреща́ть (запрети́ть* *perf*); (*suspend, exclude*) отстраня́ть (отстрани́ть *perf*) ◆ *n* (*prohibition*) запре́т; (*suspension*): **~ from** отстране́ние от *+gen*; **he was ~ned from driving** (*BRIT*) у него́ отобра́ли води́тельские права́.
banal [bə'nɑ:l] *adj* (*remark, idea etc*) бана́льный* (бана́лен).
banana [bə'nɑ:nə] *n* бана́н.
band [bænd] *n* (*group*: *of people, rock musicians*) гру́ппа; (: *of jazz, military musicians*) орке́стр; (*strip*: *of light, colour*) полоса́*; (: *of cloth*) ле́нта; (*range*) диапазо́н
▸ **band together** *vi* объединя́ться (объедини́ться *perf*).
bandage ['bændɪdʒ] *n* повя́зка* ◆ *vt* (*wound, leg*) бинтова́ть (забинтова́ть *perf*); (*person*) перевя́зывать (перевяза́ть* *perf*).
Bandaid® ['bændeɪd] *n* (*US*) пла́стырь *m*.
bandit ['bændɪt] *n* банди́т.
bandstand ['bændstænd] *n* эстра́да.
bandwagon ['bændwægən] *n*: **to jump on the ~** примкну́ть (*perf*) к си́льной стороне́ *or* мо́дному тече́нию.
bandy ['bændɪ] *vt* (*jokes, ideas*) перебра́сываться (перебро́ситься* *perf*) *+instr*
▸ **bandy about** *vt* бесконе́чно упомина́ть (*impf*).
bandy-legged ['bændɪ'lɛgɪd] *adj* (*person*) кривоно́гий*.
bane [beɪn] *n*: **it/he is the ~ of my life** э́то/он несча́стье мое́й жи́зни.
bang [bæŋ] *n* стук; (*explosion*) вы́стрел; (*blow*) уда́р ◆ *excl* бах ◆ *vt* (*door*) хло́пать (хло́пнуть *perf*) *+instr*; (*one's head etc*) ударя́ть (уда́рить *perf*) ◆ *vi* (*door*) захло́пываться (захло́пнуться *perf*); (*fireworks*) хло́пать (*impf*) ◆ *adv*: **~ on time** (*BRIT*: *inf*) как раз во́ вре́мя; **to ~ at the door** колоти́ть* (*impf*) в дверь; **to ~ into sth** ста́лкиваться (столкну́ться *perf*) с че́м-н.
banger ['bæŋə'] *n* (*BRIT*: *inf*: *also:* **old ~**) драндуле́т; (: *sausage*) сарде́лька*; (: *firework*) хлопу́шка.
Bangkok [bæŋ'kɔk] *n* Бангко́к.
Bangladesh [bæŋglə'dɛʃ] *n* Бангладе́ш.
Bangladeshi [bæŋglə'dɛʃɪ] *n* (*person*) бангладе́шец*(-е́шка*) ◆ *adj* бангладе́шский.
bangle ['bæŋgl] *n* брасле́т.
bangs [bæŋz] *npl* (*US*) чёлка* *fsg*.
banish ['bænɪʃ] *vt* высыла́ть (вы́слать* *perf*).
banister ['bænɪstə'] *n* (*usu pl*) пери́ла *pl*.
banjo ['bændʒəu] (*pl* **~es** *or* **~s**) *n* ба́нджо *nt ind*.
bank [bæŋk] *n* банк; (*of river, lake*) бе́рег*; (*of earth*) на́сыпь *f*; (*of switches*) пане́ль *f* ◆ *vi* (*AVIAT*) крени́ться (накрени́ться *perf*); (*COMM*): **they ~ with Pitt's** они́ де́ржат де́ньги в ба́нке Питт
▸ **bank on** *vt fus* полага́ться (положи́ться* *perf*) на *+acc*.
bank account *n* ба́нковский* счёт.
bank balance *n* коли́чество де́нег на ба́нковском счету́.
bank card *n* ба́нковская ка́рточка*.
bank charges *npl* (*BRIT*) *пла́та, взима́емая ба́нком за услу́ги*.
bank draft *n* ба́нковская тра́тта.
banker ['bæŋkə'] *n* банки́р.
banker's card *n* (*BRIT*) = **bank card**.
banker's order *n* (*BRIT*) ба́нковское поруче́ние.
Bank Giro *n* Жи́ро *nt ind* банк.
bank holiday *n* (*BRIT*) нерабо́чий* день *m* (*обы́чно понеде́льник*).
banking ['bæŋkɪŋ] *n* ба́нковское де́ло*.
banking hours *npl* часы́ *mpl* рабо́ты ба́нка.
bank loan *n* ба́нковский* заём*.
bank manager *n* управля́ющий(-ая) *m(f) adj* ба́нком.
banknote ['bæŋknəut] *n* банкно́т.
bank rate *n* учётная ста́вка* ба́нка.
bankroll ['bæŋkrəul] *vt* обеспе́чивать (обеспе́чить *perf*) деньга́ми ◆ *n* (*esp US*) фина́нсовые ресу́рсы *pl*.
bankrupt ['bæŋkrʌpt] *adj* обанкро́тившийся ◆ *n* банкро́т; **to go ~** обанкро́титься* (*perf*); **I am ~** я – банкро́т.
bankruptcy ['bæŋkrʌptsɪ] *n* (*COMM, fig*) банкро́тство, несостоя́тельность *f*.
bank statement *n* вы́писка* с ба́нковского счёта.
banner ['bænə'] *n* транспара́нт.
banner headline *n* (газе́тная) ша́пка*.
bannister ['bænɪstə'] *n* = **banister**.
banns [bænz] *npl огла́шение в це́ркви имён вступа́ющих в бра́к*.
banquet ['bæŋkwɪt] *n* банке́т.
bantamweight ['bæntəmweɪt] *n* (*BOXING*) боксёр лёгкого ве́са.
banter ['bæntə'] *n* подшу́чивание.
BAOR *n abbr* = *British Army of the Rhine*.
baptism ['bæptɪzəm] *n* креще́ние.
Baptist ['bæptɪst] *n* бапти́ст(ка).
baptize [bæp'taɪz] *vt* крести́ть* (окрести́ть* *perf*).
bar [bɑ:'] *n* (*pub*) бар; (*counter*) сто́йка; (*rod*) прут; (*cake*: *of soap*) бруsóк*; (: *of chocolate*) пли́тка*; (*obstacle*) прегра́да; (*prohibition*) запре́т; (*MUS*) такт ◆ *vt* (*door, way*) загора́живать (загороди́ть* *perf*); (*road*) прегражда́ть (прегради́ть *perf*); (*person*) не допуска́ть (допусти́ть* *perf*); (*activity*) запреща́ть (запрети́ть* *perf*); **~s** *npl* (*on window etc*) решётка *fsg*; **behind ~s** за решёткой; **the B~** адвокату́ра; **~ none** без

исключе́ния.
Barbados [bɑ:'beɪdɔs] *n* Барба́дос.
barbaric [bɑ:'bærɪk] *adj* ва́рварский*.
barbarous ['bɑ:bərəs] *adj* ва́рварский*.
barbecue ['bɑ:bɪkju:] *n* барбекю́ *nt ind*.
barbed wire ['bɑ:bd-] *n* колю́чая про́волока.
barber ['bɑ:bəʳ] *n* парикма́хер.
barbiturate [bɑ:'bɪtjurɪt] *n* барбитура́т.
Barcelona [bɑ:sə'ləunə] *n* Барсело́на.
bar chart *n* гистогра́мма.
bar code *n* штрихово́й код.
bare [bɛəʳ] *adj* (*body*) го́лый*, обнажённый (обнажён); (*trees*) оголённый (оголён) ◆ *vt* (*one's body*) обнажа́ть (обнажи́ть *perf*); (*teeth*) ска́лить (оска́лить *perf*); **in** *or* **with ~ feet** босико́м; **the ~ essentials** предме́ты *mpl* пе́рвой необходи́мости; **~ minimum** то́лько ми́нимум; **to ~ one's soul** раскрыва́ть (раскры́ть* *perf*) свою́ ду́шу.
bareback ['bɛəbæk] *adv* без седла́.
barefaced ['bɛəfeɪst] *adj* бессты́дный*.
barefoot ['bɛəfut] *adj* босо́й* (бос) ◆ *adv* босико́м.
bareheaded [bɛə'hɛdɪd] *adj, adv* с непокры́той голово́й.
barely ['bɛəlɪ] *adv* едва́.
Barents Sea ['bærənts-] *n*: **the ~ ~** Ба́ренцево мо́ре.
bargain ['bɑ:gɪn] *n* сде́лка*; (*good buy*) вы́годная поку́пка* ◆ *vi*: **to ~ (with sb)** торгова́ться (сторгова́ться *perf*) (с кем-н); **into the ~** в прида́чу
▸ **bargain for** *vt fus*: **he got more than he ~ed for** он получи́л бо́льше, чем ожида́л.
bargaining ['bɑ:gənɪŋ] *n* торг.
bargaining position *n позиция, с кото́рой предъявля́ются тре́бования и усло́вия сде́лки и́ли догово́ра.*
barge [bɑ:dʒ] *n* ба́ржа
▸ **barge in** *vi* (*enter*) вва́ливаться (ввали́ться* *perf*); (*interrupt*) влеза́ть (влезть* *perf*)
▸ **barge into** *vt fus* (*person*) ната́лкиваться (натолкну́ться *perf*) на *+acc*.
bargepole ['bɑ:dʒpəul] *n*: **I wouldn't touch him with a ~** я к э́тому на пу́шечный вы́стрел не подойду́.
baritone ['bærɪtəun] *n* барито́н.
barium meal ['bɛərɪəm-] *n* ба́риевая миксту́ра.
bark [bɑ:k] *n* (*of tree*) кора́; (*of dog*) лай ◆ *vi* (*dog*) ла́ять *(impf)*; **she's ~ing up the wrong tree** она́ обраща́ется не по а́дресу.
barley ['bɑ:lɪ] *n* ячме́нь* *m*.
barley sugar *n* ≈ леденéц*.
barmaid ['bɑ:meɪd] *n* буфе́тчица.
barman ['bɑ:mən] *irreg n* ба́рмен.
barmy ['bɑ:mɪ] *adj* (*BRIT*: *inf*: *person*) чо́кнутый; (: *idea*) неле́пый.
barn [bɑ:n] *n* амба́р.
barn owl *n* сипу́ха.
barnacle ['bɑ:nəkl] *n* моллю́ск.
barometer [bə'rɔmɪtəʳ] *n* баро́метр.
baron ['bærən] *n* баро́н; (*of press, industry*) магна́т.
baroness ['bærənɪs] *n* барон́есса.
baronet ['bærənɪt] *n* барон́ет.
barracking ['bærəkɪŋ] *n* вы́крики *mpl*, неодобри́тельные во́згласы *mpl*.
barracks ['bærəks] *npl* (*MIL*) каза́рма *fsg*.
barrage ['bærɑ:ʒ] *n* (*MIL*) загради́тельный ого́нь *m*; (*dam*) да́мба; (*fig*) лави́на.
barrel ['bærəl] *n* (*of wine, beer*) бо́чка*; (*of oil*) барре́ль *m*; (*of gun*) ствол*.
barrel organ *n* шарма́нка*.
barren ['bærən] *adj* (*land*) беспло́дный* (беспло́ден).
barricade [bærɪ'keɪd] *n* баррика́да ◆ *vt* баррикади́ровать (забаррикади́ровать *perf*); **to ~ o.s. in** баррикади́роваться (забаррикади́роваться *perf*).
barrier ['bærɪəʳ] *n* (*at entrance*) барье́р; (*at frontier*) шлагба́ум; (*BRIT*: *also:* **crash ~**) *предохрани́тельный барье́р на шоссе́ и доро́гах*; (*fig*: *to progress etc*) препя́тствие; (: *to communication*) поме́ха.
barrier cream *n* (*BRIT*) защи́тный крем.
barring ['bɑ:rɪŋ] *prep* за исключе́нием *+gen*.
barrister ['bærɪstəʳ] *n* (*BRIT*) адвока́т.
barrow ['bærəu] *n* (*also:* **wheelbarrow**) та́чка*; (*cart*) двухколёсная теле́жка*.
bar stool *n высо́кое сиде́нье во́зле сто́йки ба́ра.*
Bart. *abbr* (*BRIT*: = *baronet*) барон́ет.
bartender ['bɑ:tɛndəʳ] *n* (*US*) ба́рмен.
barter ['bɑ:təʳ] *vi* производи́ть* (произвести́* *perf*) ба́ртерный обме́н ◆ *n* ба́ртер.
base [beɪs] *n* основа́ние; (*of monument etc*) постаме́нт; (*of make up*) осно́ва; (*MIL*) ба́за; (*for organization*) местонахожде́ние ◆ *adj* ни́зкий* (ни́зок) ◆ *vt*: **to ~ sth on** (*opinion, belief*) осно́вывать *(impf)* что-н на *+prp*; **to be ~d at** бази́роваться *(impf)* в/на *+prp*; **the film is ~d on the book** фильм осно́ван на кни́ге; **I'm ~d in London for now** сейча́с я бази́руюсь в Ло́ндоне (*inf*); **a Paris-~d firm** фи́рма бази́рующаяся в Пари́же; **computer-~d teaching** обуче́ние при по́мощи компью́теров.
baseball ['beɪsbɔ:l] *n* бейсбо́л.
baseboard ['beɪsbɔ:d] *n* (*US*) пли́нтус.
base camp *n* ба́зовый ла́герь* *m*.
Basel [bɑ:l] *n* = **Basle**.
baseline ['beɪslaɪn] *n* (*SPORT*) ли́ния пода́чи; (*starting point*) исхо́дная черта́.
basement ['beɪsmənt] *n* подва́л.
base rate *n* тари́фная ста́вка.

* marks translations which have irregular inflections. The Russian-English side of the dictionary gives inflectional information.

bases[1] ['beɪsɪz] *npl of* **base**.
bases[2] ['beɪsi:z] *npl of* **basis**.
bash [bæʃ] *(inf) vt* колоти́ть* (поколоти́ть* *perf*) ◆ *n*: **I'll have a ~ (at it)** *(BRIT)* я попыта́юсь
▸ **bash up** *vt (car)* разбива́ть (разби́ть* *perf*); *(BRIT: person)* избива́ть (изби́ть* *perf*).
bashful ['bæʃful] *adj* засте́нчивый (засте́нчив).
bashing ['bæʃɪŋ] *n (inf)*: **union-~** я́ростные напа́дки на профсою́зы.
BASIC ['beɪsɪk] *n (COMPUT)* Бэ́йсик.
basic ['beɪsɪk] *adj (fundamental)* фундамента́льный; *(elementary)* нача́льный; *(primitive)* элемента́рный (элемента́рен).
basically ['beɪsɪklɪ] *adv* по существу́; *(on the whole)* в основно́м.
basic rate *n* ба́зисная ста́вка.
basics ['beɪsɪks] *npl*: **the ~** осно́вы *fpl*.
basil ['bæzl] *n* базили́к.
basin ['beɪsn] *n (also: washbasin)* ра́ковина; *(BRIT: for food)* ми́ска*; *(GEO)* бассе́йн.
basis ['beɪsɪs] *(pl* **bases***) n* основа́ние; **on a part-time ~** на непо́лной ста́вке; **on a trial ~** на испыта́тельный срок; **on the ~ of what you've said** на осно́ве ска́занного Ва́ми.
bask [bɑ:sk] *vi*: **to ~ in the sun** гре́ться *(impf)* на со́лнце.
basket ['bɑ:skɪt] *n* корзи́на.
basketball ['bɑ:skɪtbɔ:l] *n* баскетбо́л.
basketball player *n* баскетболи́ст(ка).
Basle [bɑ:l] *n* Ба́зель *m*.
Basque [bæsk] *adj* ба́скский ◆ *n* баск.
bass [beɪs] *n* бас* ◆ *adj* бассо́вый.
bass clef *n* басо́вый ключ*.
bassoon [bə'su:n] *n* фаго́т.
bastard ['bɑ:stəd] *n* внебра́чный ребёнок*; *(inf!)* ублю́док* *(!)*
baste [beɪst] *vt (CULIN)* полива́ть (поли́ть* *perf*) жи́ром и со́ком; *(SEWING)* смётывать (смета́ть* *perf*).
bastion ['bæstɪən] *n (fig)* опло́т.
bat [bæt] *n (ZOOL)* лету́чая мышь *f*; *(SPORT)* бита́; *(BRIT: TABLE TENNIS)* раке́тка* ◆ *vt*: **he didn't ~ an eyelid** он и гла́зом не моргну́л; **off one's own ~** по со́бственному почи́ну.
batch [bætʃ] *n (of bread)* вы́печка*; *(of papers etc)* па́чка*; *(of applicants, goods)* па́ртия.
batch processing *n (COMPUT)* паке́тная обрабо́тка *(да́нных)*.
bated ['beɪtɪd] *adj*: **with ~ breath** затаи́в дыха́ние.
bath [bɑ:θ] *n* ва́нна ◆ *vt* купа́ть (вы́купать *perf*); **to have a ~** принима́ть (приня́ть* *perf*) ва́нну; *see also* **baths**.
bathe [beɪð] *vi (swim)* купа́ться *(impf)*; *(US: have a bath)* принима́ть (приня́ть* *perf*) ва́нну ◆ *vt (wound)* промыва́ть (промы́ть* *perf*).
bather ['beɪðə'] *n* купа́льщик(-ица).
bathing ['beɪðɪŋ] *n* купа́ние.
bathing cap *n* купа́льная ша́почка*.
bathing costume *(US* **bathing suit***) n* купа́льный костю́м.
bath mat *n* ко́врик для ва́нной.
bathrobe ['bɑ:θrəub] *n* купа́льный хала́т.
bathroom ['bɑ:θrum] *n* ва́нная *f adj*.
baths [bɑ:ðz] *npl (also: swimming ~)* пла́вательный бассе́йн *msg*.
bath towel *n* ба́нное полоте́нце.
bathtub ['bɑ:θtʌb] *n* ва́нна.
batman ['bætmən] *irreg n (BRIT)* денщи́к.
baton ['bætən] *n (MUS)* дирижёрская па́лочка*; *(ATHLETICS)* эстафе́тная па́лочка*; *(POLICE)* дуби́нка*.
battalion [bə'tælɪən] *n* батальо́н.
batten ['bætn] *n (CARPENTRY)* ре́йка; *(NAUT)* ре́я
▸ **batten down** *vt (NAUT)*: **to ~ down the hatches** задра́ивать (задра́ить *perf*) лю́ки.
batter ['bætə'] *vt (child, wife)* бить (изби́ть* *perf*); *(subj: wind, rain)* бить* (поби́ть* *perf*) ◆ *n (CULIN)* жи́дкое те́сто.
battered ['bætəd] *adj (hat)* потрёпанный (потрёпан); *(pan)* покорёженный (покорёжен); **~ wife** подверга́емая побо́ям жена́*.
battering ram ['bætərɪŋ-] *n* тара́н.
battery ['bætərɪ] *n (of torch etc)* батаре́йка*; *(AUT)* аккумуля́тор; *(of tests, reporters)* ряд*.
battery charger *n* заря́дное устро́йство (батаре́и).
battery farm *n* птицефа́брика.
battery hens *npl* инкуба́торные ку́ры *mpl*.
battle ['bætl] *n* би́тва, бой* ◆ *vi* боро́ться* *(impf)*, сража́ться *(impf)*; **that's half the ~** э́то уже́ пол де́ла; **it's a** *or* **we're fighting a losing ~** *(fig)* э́то безнадёжная борьба́, мы ведём безнадёжную борьбу́.
battle dress *n* похо́дная фо́рма.
battlefield ['bætlfi:ld] *n* по́ле* би́твы *or* бо́я.
battlements ['bætlmənts] *npl* сте́ны* *fpl* с бойни́цами.
battleship ['bætlʃɪp] *n* вое́нный кора́бль* *m*.
batty ['bætɪ] *adj (inf)* чо́кнутый (чо́кнут).
bauble ['bɔ:bl] *n* безделу́шка*.
baud [bɔ:d] *n (COMPUT)* бод.
baud rate *n (COMPUT)* ско́рость *f* переда́чи (в бо́дах).
baulk [bɔ:lk] *vi* = **balk**.
bauxite ['bɔ:ksaɪt] *n* бокси́т.
Bavaria [bə'vɛərɪə] *n* Бава́рия.
Bavarian [bə'vɛərɪən] *adj* бава́рский* ◆ *n* бава́рец(-рка).
bawdy ['bɔ:dɪ] *adj (joke, song)* скабрёзный* (скабрёзен).
bawl [bɔ:l] *vi* ора́ть* (заора́ть* *perf*).
bay [beɪ] *n* зали́в; *(smaller)* бу́хта; *(horse)* гнеда́я ло́шадь *f*; **parking ~** *(BRIT)* ме́сто* парко́вки; **loading ~** погру́зочная площа́дка*; **to hold sb at ~** держа́ть *(impf)* кого́-н на расстоя́нии.
bay leaf *n* лавро́вый лист*.
bayonet ['beɪənɪt] *n* штык*.
bay tree *n* ла́вровое де́рево*.
bay window *n* э́ркер.

bazaar [bə'zɑ:ʳ] *n* (*market*) база́р, ры́нок*; (*fete*) благотвори́тельный база́р.
bazooka [bə'zu:kə] *n* базу́ка, гранатомёт.
BB *n abbr* (*BRIT*: = *Boys' Brigade*) ≈ отря́д бойска́утов.
B & B *n abbr* = **bed and breakfast**.
b & b *n abbr* = **B & B**.
BBC *n abbr* (= *British Broadcasting Corporation*) Би-Би-Си *nt ind*.
BC *adv abbr* (= *before Christ*) до рождества́ Христо́ва ◆ *abbr* (*CANADA*) = *British Columbia*.
BCG *n abbr* (= *Bacillus Calmette-Guérin*) БЦЖ.
BD *n abbr* (= *Bachelor of Divinity*) бакала́вр богосло́вия.
B/D *abbr* = **bank draft**.
BDS *n abbr* (= *Bachelor of Dental Surgery*) бакала́вр стоматоло́гии.

KEYWORD

be [bi:] (*pt* **was, were**, *pp* **been**) *aux vb* ***1*** (*with present participle*: *forming continuous tenses*): **what are you doing?** что Вы де́лаете?; **it is raining** идёт дождь; **they're working tomorrow** они́ рабо́тают за́втра; **the house is being built** дом стро́ится/стро́ят; **I've been waiting for you for ages** я жду Вас уже́ це́лую ве́чность
2 (*with pp*: *forming passives*): **he was killed** он был уби́т; **the box had been opened** я́щик открыва́ли; **the thief was nowhere to be seen** во́ра нигде́ не́ было ви́дно
3 (*in tag questions*) пра́вда, да; **she's back again, is she?** она́ верну́лась, да?; **she is pretty, isn't she?** она́ хоро́шенькая, пра́вда?
4 (*to +infin*): **the house is to be sold** дом бу́дет про́дан; **you're to be congratulated for all your work** Вы бу́дете отме́чены за всю ва́шу рабо́ту; **he's not to open it** он не до́лжен открыва́ть э́то
◆ *vb* ***1*** (*+ complement*: *in present tense*): **he is English** он англича́нин; (*in past/future tense*) быть (*impf*) +*instr or* +nom; **he was a doctor** он был врачо́м; **she is going to be very tall** она́ бу́дет о́чень высо́кая *or* высо́кой; **he is going to be an actor** он бу́дет актёром; **I'm tired** я уста́л; **I was hot/cold** мне бы́ло жа́рко/хо́лодно; **two and two are four** два́жды два – четы́ре; **she's tall/pretty** она́ высо́кая/симпати́чная; **be careful!** бу́дьте осторо́жны!; **be quiet!** ти́ше!
2 (*of health*): **how are you feeling?** как Вы себя́ чу́вствуете?; **he's very ill** он о́чень бо́лен; **I'm better now** мне сейча́с лу́чше
3 (*of age*): **how old are you?** ско́лько Вам лет?; **I'm sixteen (years old)** мне шестна́дцать (лет); **I was only 5 (years old) then** мне тогда́ бы́ло всего́ 5 (лет)
4 (*cost*): **how much is/was the wine?** ско́лько сто́ит/сто́ило вино́?; **that'll be £5.75, please** с Вас £5.75, пожа́луйста
◆ *vi* ***1*** (*exist*) быть (*impf*); **there are people who...** есть лю́ди, кото́рые...; **there is one drug that...** есть одно́ лека́рство, кото́рое...; **is there a God?** Бог есть на све́те?
2 (*occur*) быва́ть (*impf*); **there are frequent accidents on this road** на э́той доро́ге ча́сто быва́ют ава́рии; **be that as it may** как бы то ни́ было; **so be it** так и бы́ть, быть по сему́
3 (*referring to place*): **I won't be here tomorrow** меня́ здесь за́втра не бу́дет; **Edinburgh is in Scotland** Эдинбу́рг нахо́дится в Шотла́ндии; **the book is on the table** кни́га на столе́; **there are pictures on the wall** на стене́ карти́ны; **there is someone in the house** в до́ме кто-то есть; **we've been here for ages** мы здесь уже́ о́чень давно́
4 (*referring to movement*) быть (*impf*); **where have you been?** где Вы бы́ли?; **I've been to the post office** я был на по́чте
◆ *impers vb* ***1*** (*referring to time*): **it's five o'clock (now)** сейча́с пять часо́в; **it's the 28th of April (today)** сего́дня 28-ое апре́ля
2 (*referring to distance, weather*: *in present tense*): **it's 10 km to the village** до дере́вни 10 км; (: *in past/future tense*) быть (*impf*); **it's too hot/cold (today)** сего́дня сли́шком жа́рко/хо́лодно; **it was very windy yesterday** вчера́ бы́ло о́чень ве́трено; **it will be sunny tomorrow** за́втра бу́дет со́лнечно
3 (*emphatic*): **it's (only) me/the postman** э́то я/почтальо́н; **it was Maria who paid the bill** счёт оплати́ла Мари́я.

B/E *abbr* = **bill of exchange**.
beach [bi:tʃ] *n* (*stony*) бе́рег* мо́ря; (*sandy*) пляж ◆ *vt* (*boat*) выта́скивать (вы́тащить *perf*) на бе́рег.
beach buggy *n* пля́жный вездехо́д.
beachcomber ['bi:tʃkəuməʳ] *n* бич*.
beachwear ['bi:tʃwɛəʳ] *n* пля́жная оде́жда.
beacon ['bi:kən] *n* (*lighthouse*) мая́к*; (*marker*) сигна́льный ого́нь* *m*; (*also*: **radio ~**) радиомая́к*.
bead [bi:d] *n* бу́сина; (*of sweat*) ка́пля*; **~s** *npl* (*necklace*) бу́сы *pl*.
beady ['bi:dɪ] *adj*: **~ eyes** глаза́-бу́синки *mpl*.
beagle ['bi:gl] *n* го́нчая *f adj* (соба́ка).
beak [bi:k] *n* клюв.
beaker ['bi:kəʳ] *n* (*cup*) пластма́ссовый стака́н.
beam [bi:m] *n* (*ARCHIT*) ба́лка*; (*of light*) луч*; (*RADIO*) радиосигна́л ◆ *vi* (*smile*) сия́ть (*impf*) ◆ *vt* (*signal*) передава́ть* (переда́ть* *perf*); **to drive on full** *or* **main** *or* (*US*) **high ~** е́хать* (*impf*) с включёнными да́льними фа́рами.
beaming ['bi:mɪŋ] *adj* сия́ющий*.

* marks translations which have irregular inflections. The Russian-English side of the dictionary gives inflectional information.

bean [bi:n] *n* боб*; **French ~** фасо́ль *f no pl*; **runner ~** фасо́ль о́гненная; **coffee ~** кофе́йное зерно́.

beanpole ['bi:npəul] *n* (*inf*) каланча́* (*высо́кий челове́к*).

beansprouts ['bi:nsprauts] *npl* побе́ги *mpl* бобо́в.

bear [bɛə'] (*pt* **bore**, *pp* **borne**) *n* медве́дь(-дица) *m(f)*; (*STOCK EXCHANGE*) "медве́дь" (*спекуля́нт, игра́ющий на пониже́ние ку́рса*) ◆ *vt* (*responsibility, cost*) нести́* (понести́* *perf*); (*weight*) нести́* (*impf*); (*examination, scrutiny*) выде́рживать (вы́держать* *perf*); (*situation, person*) выноси́ть* (вы́нести* *perf*); (*traces, signs*) нести́* (*impf*) на себе́; (*children*) рожда́ть (роди́ть* *perf*); (*fruit*) приноси́ть* (принести́* *perf*); (*COMM*): **to ~ interest** приноси́ть* (принести́* *perf*) проце́нты ◆ *vi*: **to ~ right/left** (*AUT*) держа́ться (*impf*) пра́вого/ле́вого поворо́та; **to ~ the responsibility of** нести́* (понести́* *perf*) отве́тственность за *+acc*; **to ~ comparison with** выде́рживать (вы́держать *perf*) сравне́ние с *+instr*; **I can't ~ him** я его́ не выношу́; **the road ~s to the right/left** доро́га идёт впра́во/вле́во; **to bring pressure to ~ on sb** ока́зывать (оказа́ть* *perf*) давле́ние на кого́-н

▸ **bear out** *vt* подде́рживать (поддержа́ть *perf*)

▸ **bear up** *vi* держа́ться (*impf*); **he bore up well** он держа́лся молодцо́м

▸ **bear with** *vt fus* терпе́ть (*impf*) с *+instr*; **~ with me a minute** потерпи́те мину́ту.

bearable ['bɛərəbl] *adj* терпи́мый (терпи́м).

beard [bɪəd] *n* борода́*.

bearded ['bɪədɪd] *adj* борода́тый.

bearer ['bɛərə'] *n* (*of letter*) пода́тель(ница) *m(f)*; (*of news*) ве́стник; (*of cheque, passport etc*) владе́лец*, предъяви́тель *m*; (*of title*) носи́тель(ница) *m(f)*.

bearing ['bɛərɪŋ] *n* (*manner*) мане́ра держа́ть себя́; (*connection*) отноше́ние; (*TECH*) подши́пник; **~s** *npl* (*also:* **ball ~s**) ша́рики *mpl* подши́пника; **to take a ~** ориенти́роваться (*impf/perf*); **to get one's ~s** ориенти́роваться (сориенти́роваться *perf*).

beast [bi:st] *n* (*also inf*) зверь* *m*.

beastly ['bi:stlɪ] *adj* ужа́сный (ужа́сен), жу́ткий* (жу́ток).

beat [bi:t] (*pt* **beat**, *pp* **beaten**) *n* (*of heart*) бие́ние; (*MUS: rhythm*) ритм; (*: in bar*) такт; (*POLICE*) уча́сток* ◆ *vt* (*wife, child*) бить* (поби́ть* *perf*); (*eggs etc*) взбива́ть (взби́ть* *perf*); (*opponent, record*) побива́ть (поби́ть* *perf*); (*drum*) бить* (*impf*) в *+acc* ◆ *vi* (*heart*) би́ться* (*impf*); (*rain, wind*) стуча́ть (*impf*); **to ~ time** отбива́ть (*impf*) такт; **~ it!** (*inf*) кати́сь!; **that ~s everything** э́то превосхо́дит всё; **to ~ about the bush** ходи́ть* (*impf*) вокру́г да о́коло; **off the ~en track** по непротоpённому пути́

▸ **beat down** *vt* (*door*) выла́мывать (вы́ломать *perf*); (*price*) сбива́ть (сбить* *perf*); (*seller*) добива́ться (доби́ться* *perf*) ски́дки у *+gen* ◆ *vi* (*rain*) хлеста́ть* (*impf*); (*sun*) пали́ть (*impf*)

▸ **beat off** *vt* отбива́ть (отби́ть* *perf*)

▸ **beat up** *vt* (*person*) избива́ть (изби́ть* *perf*); (*eggs etc*) взбива́ть (взби́ть* *perf*).

beaten ['bi:tn] *pp of* **beat**.

beater ['bi:tə'] *n* ве́нчик.

beating ['bi:tɪŋ] *n* (*thrashing*) по́рка*; **to take a ~** (*fig*) терпе́ть* (потерпе́ть* *perf*) пораже́ние.

beat-up ['bi:t'ʌp] *adj* (*inf*) искоре́женный (искоре́жен).

beautician [bju:'tɪʃən] *n* космети́чка*.

beautiful ['bju:tɪful] *adj* (*woman, place*) краси́вый (краси́в); (*day, experience*) прекра́сный* (прекра́сен).

beautifully ['bju:tɪflɪ] *adv* (*play, sing etc*) краси́во, прекра́сно; (*quiet, empty etc*) замеча́тельно.

beautify ['bju:tɪfaɪ] *vt* украша́ть (укра́сить* *perf*).

beauty ['bju:tɪ] *n* красота́*; (*woman*) краса́вица; **the ~ of it is that ...** (*fig*) пре́лесть *f* э́того в том, что ....

beauty contest *n* ко́нкурс красоты́.

beauty queen *n* короле́ва красоты́.

beauty salon *n* сало́н красоты́.

beauty sleep *n сон до полу́ночи, по пове́рию де́лающий челове́ка молоды́м и здоро́вым.*

beauty spot *n* (*BRIT: TOURISM*) живопи́сная ме́стность *f*.

beaver ['bi:və'] *n* (*ZOOL*) бобр*.

becalmed [bɪ'kɑ:md] *adj* заштиле́вший.

became [bɪ'keɪm] *pt of* **become**.

because [bɪ'kɔz] *conj* потому́ что; (*since, as*) так как; **~ of** (*illness etc*) из-за *+gen*.

beck [bɛk] *n*: **to be at sb's ~ and call** быть* (*impf*) у кого́-н на побегу́шках.

beckon ['bɛkən] *vt* (*also:* **~ to**) мани́ть* (помани́ть* *perf*) ◆ *vi* (*fame, glory*) мани́ть* (*impf*).

become [bɪ'kʌm] (*irreg: like* **come**) *vi* станови́ться* (стать* *perf*) *+instr*; **to ~ fat** толсте́ть (потолсте́ть *perf*); **to ~ thin** худе́ть (похуде́ть *perf*); **to ~ angry** серди́ться* (рассерди́ться* *perf*); **it became known that** ста́ло изве́стно, что; **what has ~ of him?** что с ним ста́лось?

becoming [bɪ'kʌmɪŋ] *adj* (*behaviour*) прили́чествующий; (*clothes*): **your dress is ~** э́то пла́тье Вам к лицу́.

BECTU *n abbr* (*BRIT*) = *Broadcasting Entertainment Cinematographic and Theatre Union*.

BEd *n abbr* (= *Bachelor of Education*) бакала́вр педаго́гики.

bed [bɛd] *n* крова́ть *f*; (*of coal, clay*) пласт*; (*of river, sea*) дно*; (*of flowers*) клу́мба; **to go to ~** ложи́ться (лечь* *perf*) спать

▸ **bed down** *vi* располагáться (расположи́ться* *perf*) на ночлéг.
bed and breakfast *n ма́ленькая ча́стная гости́ница с за́втраком*; (*terms*) ночлéг и за́втрак.
bedbug [ˈbɛdbʌg] *n* клоп*.
bedclothes [ˈbɛdkləuðz] *npl* постéльное бельё *ntsg*.
bedding [ˈbɛdɪŋ] *n* постéльные принадлéжности *fpl*.
bedevil [bɪˈdɛvl] *vt* (*person*) опу́тывать (опу́тать *perf*); (*plans*) спу́тывать (спу́тать *perf*); **to be ~led by** вя́знуть (увя́знуть *perf*) в *+prp*.
bedfellow [ˈbɛdfɛləu] *n*: **they are strange ~s** (*fig*) они́ стра́нная па́ра.
bedlam [ˈbɛdləm] *n* бедла́м.
bedpan [ˈbɛdpæn] *n* (подкладно́е) су́дно*.
bedpost [ˈbɛdpəust] *n* сто́лбик крова́тного по́лога.
bedraggled [bɪˈdrægld] *adj* (*person, clothes*) потрёпанный (потрёпан); (*hair*) всклоко́ченный (всклоко́чен).
bedridden [ˈbɛdrɪdn] *adj* прико́ванный (прико́ван) к постéли.
bedrock [ˈbɛdrɔk] *n* (*fig*) краеуго́льный ка́мень* *m*; (*GEO*) материко́вая поро́да.
bedroom [ˈbɛdrum] *n* спа́льня*.
Beds *abbr* (*BRIT: POST*) = *Bedfordshire*.
bed settee *n* дива́н-крова́ть *f*.
bedside [ˈbɛdsaɪd] *n*: **at sb's ~** у постéли кого́-н ◆ *cpd* (*lamp, cabinet*) прикрова́тный.
bedsit(ter) [ˈbɛdsɪt(əʳ)] *n* (*BRIT*) *ко́мната, соединя́ющая в себé спа́льню, гости́ную и иногда́ ку́хню*.
bedspread [ˈbɛdsprɛd] *n* покрыва́ло.
bedtime [ˈbɛdtaɪm] *n* врéмя* *nt* ложи́ться спать; **it's ~** пора́ (ложи́ться) спать.
bee [bi:] *n* пчела́*; **to have a ~ in one's bonnet about sth** помеша́ться (*impf*) на чём-н.
beech [bi:tʃ] *n* бук.
beef [bi:f] *n* говя́дина; **roast ~** ро́стбиф
▸ **beef up** *vt* (*inf: support*) придава́ть (прида́ть* *perf*) си́лы *+dat*; (: *essay*) напо́лнить (*perf*) *+instr*.
beefburger [ˈbi:fbə:gəʳ] *n* говя́жья котлéта, га́мбургер.
Beefeater [ˈbi:fi:təʳ] *n лейб-гвардéец охра́ны Та́уэра в Ло́ндоне*.
beehive [ˈbi:haɪv] *n* у́лей*.
beekeeping [ˈbi:ki:pɪŋ] *n* пчеловóдство.
beeline [ˈbi:laɪn] *n*: **to make a ~ for** мча́ться (помча́ться *perf*) пря́мо в *+acc*.
been [bi:n] *pp of* **be**.
beep [bi:p] *n* гудо́к* ◆ *vi* сигна́лить (просигна́лить *perf*).
beer [bɪəʳ] *n* пи́во.
beer belly *n* (*inf*) брю́хо.
beer can *n* ба́нка из-под пи́ва.
beet [bi:t] *n* (*vegetable*) кормова́я свёкла; (*US: also:* **red ~**) свёкла.
beetle [ˈbi:tl] *n* жук*.
beetroot [ˈbi:tru:t] *n* (*BRIT*) свёкла *no pl*.
befall [bɪˈfɔ:l] (*irreg: like* **fall**) *vt* выпада́ть (вы́пасть* *perf*) *+dat*.
befit [bɪˈfɪt] *vt* прили́чествовать (*impf*) *+dat*.
before [bɪˈfɔ:ʳ] *prep* пéред *+instr*, до *+gen* ◆ *conj* до того́ *or* пéред тéм, как ◆ *adv* (*time*) ра́ньше, прéжде; (*space*) впереди́; **the day ~ yesterday** позавчера́; **do this ~ you forget** сдéлайте э́то пока́ Вы не забы́ли; **~ going** пéред ухо́дом; **~ she goes** до того́ *or* пéред тем, как она уйдёт; **the week ~** недéлю наза́д, на про́шлой недéле; **I've never seen it ~** я никогда́ э́того ра́ньше не ви́дел.
beforehand [bɪˈfɔ:hænd] *adv* зара́нее.
befriend [bɪˈfrɛnd] *vt* подружи́ться (*perf*) с *+instr*.
befuddled [bɪˈfʌdld] *adj* одурма́ненный (одурма́нен).
beg [bɛg] *vi* ни́щенствовать (*impf*) ◆ *vt* (*also:* **~ for**: *food, money*) проси́ть* (*impf*); (: *forgiveness, mercy etc*) умоля́ть (умоли́ть *perf*) о *+prp*; **to ~ sb to do** умоля́ть (умоли́ть *perf*) кого́-н *+infin*; **I ~ your pardon** (*apologizing*) прошу́ прощéния; (*not hearing*) прости́те, не расслы́шал; **to ~ the question** счита́ть (счесть* *perf*) спо́рный вопро́с решённым; **to ~ a favour of sb** проси́ть* (попроси́ть* *perf*) об одолжéнии у кого́-н.
began [bɪˈgæn] *pt of* **begin**.
beggar [ˈbɛgəʳ] *n* ни́щий*(-ая) *m(f) adj*.
begin [bɪˈgɪn] (*pt* **began**, *pp* **begun**) *vt* начина́ть (нача́ть* *perf*) ◆ *vi* начина́ться (нача́ться* *perf*); **to ~ doing** *or* **to do** начина́ть (нача́ть* *perf*) *+impf infin*; **~ning (from) Monday** начина́я с понедéльника; **I can't ~ to thank you** не зна́ю, как Вас благодари́ть; **we'll have soup to ~ with** мы начнём с су́па; **to ~ with, I'd like to know ...** для нача́ла, я бы хотéл знать ....
beginner [bɪˈgɪnəʳ] *n* начина́ющий*(-ая) *m(f) adj*.
beginning [bɪˈgɪnɪŋ] *n* нача́ло; **right from the ~** с са́мого нача́ла.
begrudge [bɪˈgrʌdʒ] *vt*: **he ~s me my success** он зави́дует моему́ успéху.
beguile [bɪˈgaɪl] *vt* соблазня́ть (соблазни́ть *perf*).
beguiling [bɪˈgaɪlɪŋ] *adj* соблазни́тельный, зама́нчивый.
begun [bɪˈgʌn] *pp of* **begin**.
behalf [bɪˈhɑ:f] *n*: **on** *or* (*US*) **in ~ of** от и́мени *+gen*; (*for benefit of*) ра́ди *+gen*, в интерéсах *+gen*; **on my/his ~** от моего́/его́ и́мени.
behave [bɪˈheɪv] *vi* вести́* (*impf*) себя́; (*well: also:* **~ o.s.**) вести́* (*impf*) себя́ хорошо́.

* marks translations which have irregular inflections. The Russian-English side of the dictionary gives inflectional information.

behaviour [bɪ'heɪvjə'] (*US* **behavior**) *n* поведе́ние.
behead [bɪ'hɛd] *vt* обезгла́вливать (обезгла́вить* *perf*).
beheld [bɪ'hɛld] *pt, pp of* **behold**.
behind [bɪ'haɪnd] *prep* (*at the back of*) за +*instr*, позади́ +*gen*; (*supporting*) за +*instr*; (*lower in rank etc*) ни́же +*gen* ◆ *adv* сза́ди, позади́ ◆ *n* (*buttocks*) зад*; **~ the scenes** за кули́сами; **we're ~ them in technology** мы отста́ли от них в техноло́гии; **to be ~ schedule** отстава́ть* (отста́ть* *perf*) от гра́фика; **to leave sth ~** (*forget*) оставля́ть (оста́вить* *perf*) что-н.
behold [bɪ'həuld] (*irreg*: *like* **hold**) *vt* узре́ть (*perf*).
beige [beɪʒ] *adj* бе́жевый.
Beijing ['beɪ'dʒɪŋ] *n* Пеки́н.
being ['bi:ɪŋ] *n* (*creature*) существо́*; (*existence*) существова́ние; **to come into ~** возника́ть (возни́кнуть* *perf*).
Beirut [beɪ'ru:t] *n* Бейру́т.
Belarus [bɛlə'rus] *n* Белару́сь *f*.
belated [bɪ'leɪtɪd] *adj* запозда́лый.
belch [bɛltʃ] *vi* отры́гивать (отрыгну́ть *perf*) ◆ *vt* (*also*: **~ out**) изверга́ть (изве́ргнуть* *perf*).
beleaguered [bɪ'li:gɪd] *adj* (*also fig*) осаждённый (осаждён); (*army*) окружённый*.
Belfast ['bɛlfɑ:st] *n* Бе́лфаст.
belfry ['bɛlfrɪ] *n* колоко́льня*.
Belgian ['bɛldʒən] *adj* бельги́йский* ◆ *n* бельги́ец*(-и́йка).
Belgium ['bɛldʒəm] *n* Бе́льгия.
Belgrade [bɛl greɪd] *n* Белгра́д.
belie [bɪ'laɪ] *vt* (*give false impression of*) дава́ть* (дать* *perf*) неве́рное представле́ние о +*prp*; (*disprove*) опроверга́ть (опрове́ргнуть *perf*).
belief [bɪ'li:f] *n* (*conviction*) убежде́ние; (*trust, faith*) ве́ра; **it's beyond ~** это невероя́тно; **in the ~ that** полагая, что.
believable [bɪ'li:vəbl] *adj* правдоподо́бный* (правдоподо́бен).
believe [bɪ'li:v] *vt* ве́рить (пове́рить *perf*) +*dat* *or* в(о) +*acc* ◆ *vi* верить (*impf*); **to ~ in** ве́рить (пове́рить *perf*) в +*acc*; **I don't ~ in corporal punishment** я не ве́рю в теле́сные наказания; **he is ~d to be abroad** полага́ют, что он за грани́цей.
believer [bɪ'li:və'] *n* сторо́нник(-ица); (*REL*) верующий*(-ая) *m(f) adj*; **she's a great ~ in healthy eating** она – сторонница здорового питания.
belittle [bɪ'lɪtl] *vt* преуменьша́ть (преуме́ньшить *perf*), уничижа́ть (*impf*).
Belize [bɛ'li:z] *n* Белиз.
bell [bɛl] *n* ко́локол*; (*small*) колоко́льчик; (*on door*) звоно́к*; **that rings a ~** я что́-то припомина́ю.
bell-bottoms ['bɛlbɔtəmz] *npl* брю́ки клёш *pl*.
bellboy ['bɛlbɔɪ] *n* (*BRIT*) коридо́рный *m adj*.
bellhop ['bɛlhɔp] *n* (*US*) = **bellboy**.
belligerence [bɪ'lɪdʒərəns] *n* войнственность *f*.
belligerent [bɪ'lɪdʒərənt] *adj* (*person, attitude*) во́инственный (во́инственен).
bellow ['bɛləu] *vi* реве́ть* (*impf*) ◆ *vt* (*orders*) прореве́ть* (*perf*).
bellows ['bɛləuz] *npl* (*for fire*) меха́ *mpl*.
bell push *n* (*BRIT*) звоно́к*.
belly ['bɛlɪ] *n* брю́хо.
bellyache ['bɛlɪeɪk] (*inf*) *n* бо́ли *fpl* в животе́ ◆ *vi* ныть* (*impf*).
bellybutton ['bɛlɪbʌtn] *n* пупо́к*.
bellyful ['bɛlɪful] *n*: **I've had a ~ of it** я сыт по го́рло э́тим.
belong [bɪ'lɔŋ] *vi*: **to ~ to** принадлежа́ть (*impf*) +*dat*; (*club etc*) состоя́ть (*impf*) в +*prp*; **this book ~s here** ме́сто э́той книги здесь.
belongings [bɪ'lɔŋɪŋz] *npl* ве́щи* *fpl*; **personal ~** ли́чные принадле́жности *fpl*.
Belorussia [bɛleu'rʌʃə] *n* Белору́ссия.
Belorussian [bɛleu'rʌʃən] *n* (*person*) белору́с(ска*); (*LING*) белору́сский* язы́к* ◆ *adj* белору́сский*.
beloved [bɪ'lʌvɪd] *adj* люби́мый ◆ *n* возлю́бленный(-ая) *m(f) adj*.
below [bɪ'ləu] *prep* (*position*) под(о) +*instr*; (*motion*) под(о) +*acc*; (*less than*) ни́же +*gen* ◆ *adv* (*position*) внизу́; (*motion*) вни́з; **temperatures ~ normal** температу́ры ни́же норма́льных; **see ~** смотрите ни́же.
belt [bɛlt] *n* (*leather etc*) реме́нь* *m*; (*cloth*) по́яс*; (*of land*) по́яс*, зо́на; (*TECH*) приводно́й реме́нь* ◆ *vt* (*thrash*) поро́ть* (вы́пороть *perf*) ◆ *vi* (*BRIT*: *inf*): **to ~ along** *or* **down the road** жа́рить (*impf*) по доро́ге; **industrial ~** индустриальная зона
▸ **belt out** *vt* горла́нить (*impf*)
▸ **belt up** *vi* (*inf*: *BRIT*) заткну́ться (*perf*); (: *AUT*) застёгиваться (застегну́ться *perf*).
beltway ['bɛltweɪ] *n* (*US*: *AUT*) кольцева́я доро́га; (*motorway*) кольцевая скоростна́я автомагистра́ль *f*.
bemoan [bɪ'məun] *vt* опла́кивать (опла́кать* *perf*).
bemused [bɪ'mju:zd] *adj* озадаченный.
bench [bɛntʃ] *n* скамья́*; (*in workshop*) верста́к*; (*in laboratory*) лаборато́рный стол*; (*BRIT*: *POL*) места́ па́ртий в Парла́менте; **the B~** (*LAW*) суде́йская колле́гия.
benchmark ['bɛntʃmɑ:k] *n* крите́рий.
bend [bɛnd] (*pt, pp* **bent**) *vt* (*pipe, leg etc*) гнуть (согну́ть *perf*), сгиба́ть (*impf*) ◆ *vi* (*person*) гну́ться (согну́ться *perf*) ◆ *n* (*BRIT*: *in road*) поворо́т; (*in pipe*) изги́б; (*in river*) излучина; **~s** *npl* (*MED*): **the ~s** кессонная боле́знь *fsg*
▸ **bend down** *vi* наклоня́ться (наклони́ться *perf*), нагиба́ться (нагну́ться *perf*)
▸ **bend over** *vt fus* (*book, child*) склоня́ться (склони́ться* *perf*) над +*instr*; (*fence*) перегиба́ться (перегну́ться *perf*) че́рез +*acc*.

beneath [bɪ'ni:θ] *prep* (*position*) под +*instr*; (*motion*) под(о) +*acc*; (*unworthy of*) ни́же +*gen* ◆ *adv* внизу́.
benefactor ['bɛnɪfæktə'] *n* (*to person*) благоде́тель *m*; (*to institution*) благотвори́тель *m*.
benefactress ['bɛnɪfæktrɪs] *n* благоде́тельница; благотвори́тельница.
beneficial [bɛnɪ'fɪʃəl] *adj*: **~ (to)** благотво́рный* (благотво́рен) (для +*gen*).
beneficiary [bɛnɪ'fɪʃərɪ] *n* (LAW) бенефициа́рий.
benefit ['bɛnɪfɪt] *n* (*advantage*) вы́года; (*money*) посо́бие; (*also:* **~ concert**) благотвори́тельный конце́рт; (*also:* **~ match**) благотвори́тельный матч ◆ *vt* приноси́ть* (принести́* *perf*) по́льзу +*dat* ◆ *vi*: **he'll ~ from it** он полу́чит от э́того вы́году.
Benelux ['bɛnɪlʌks] *n* Бенилю́кс.
benevolent [bɪ'nɛvələnt] *adj* (*person*) доброжела́тельный* (доброжела́телен); (*organization*) благотвори́тельный* (благотвори́телен).
BEng *n abbr* (= *Bachelor of Engineering*) ≈ бакала́вр инжене́рного де́ла.
Bengal [bɛn'gɔ:l] *n*: **Bay of ~** Бенга́льский зали́в.
Bengali [bɛn'gɔ:lɪ] *n* (*person*) бенга́лец*(-а́лка*); (LING) бенга́льский язы́к* ◆ *adj* бенга́льский.
benign [bɪ'naɪn] *adj* добросерде́чный* (добросерде́чен); (MED) доброка́чественный.
bent [bɛnt] *pt, pp of* **bend** ◆ *adj* (*wire, pipe*) по́гнутый; (*inf: dishonest*) жуликова́тый (жуликова́т); (: *pej: homosexual*): **he is ~** он – голубо́й ◆ *n*: **a ~ for** скло́нность *f* к +*dat*; **he is ~ on doing** он реши́тельно настро́ен +*infin*.
bequeath [bɪ'kwi:ð] *vt* завеща́ть (*impf/perf*).
bequest [bɪ'kwɛst] *n* насле́дство.
bereaved [bɪ'ri:vd] *adj* понёсший тяжёлую утра́ту ◆ *n*: **the ~** друзья́ *mpl* и ро́дственники *mpl* поко́йного.
bereavement [bɪ'ri:vmənt] *n* тяжёлая утра́та.
bereft [bɪ'rɛft] *adj*: **~ of** лишённый (лишён) +*gen*.
beret ['bɛreɪ] *n* бере́т.
Bering Sea ['beɪrɪŋ-] *n*: **the ~ ~** Бе́рингово мо́ре.
berk [bə:k] *n* (*inf: pej*) крети́н, деби́л.
Berks *abbr* (BRIT: POST) = *Berkshire*.
Berlin [bə:'lɪn] *n* Берли́н; **East/West ~** (*formerly*) Восто́чный/За́падный Берли́н.
Bermuda [bə:'mju:də] *n* Берму́дские острова́ *mpl*.
Bermuda shorts *npl* берму́ды *pl*.
Bern [bə:n] *n* Берн.
berry ['bɛrɪ] *n* я́года.
berserk [bə'sə:k] *adj*: **to go ~** разъяря́ться (разъяри́ться *perf*).
berth [bə:θ] *n* (*bed: in caravan*) ко́йка*; (: *on ship*) каю́та; (: *on train*) по́лка*; (*mooring*) прича́л ◆ *vi* прича́ливать (прича́лить *perf*); **to give sb/sth a wide ~** обходи́ть* (обойти́* *perf*) кого́-н/что-н за версту́.
beseech [bɪ'si:tʃ] (*pt, pp* **besought**) *vt* моли́ть* (*impf*).
beset [bɪ'sɛt] (*pt, pp* **beset**) *vt*: **we have been ~ with problems** нас одолева́ли пробле́мы.
beside [bɪ'saɪd] *prep* ря́дом с +*instr*, о́коло +*gen*, у +*gen*; (*compared with*) ря́дом с +*instr*; **to be ~ o.s. (with)** быть* (*impf*) вне себя́ (от +*gen*); **that's ~ the point** э́то к де́лу не отно́сится.
besides [bɪ'saɪdz] *adv* кро́ме того́ ◆ *prep* кро́ме +*gen*, поми́мо +*gen*.
besiege [bɪ'si:dʒ] *vt* (*also fig*) осажда́ть (осади́ть* *perf*).
besmirch [bɪ'smə:tʃ] *vt* очерня́ть (очерни́ть *perf*).
besotted [bɪ'sɔtɪd] *adj* (BRIT): **~ with** опьянённый (опьянён) +*instr*.
besought [bɪ'sɔ:t] *pt, pp of* **beseech**.
bespectacled [bɪ'spɛktɪkld] *adj* в очка́х.
bespoke [bɪ'spəuk] *adj* (BRIT) поши́тый (поши́т); **~ tailor** портно́й, рабо́тающий на зака́з.
best [bɛst] *adj* лу́чший* ◆ *adv* лу́чше всего́; **the ~ thing to do is ...** лу́чше всего́ +*infin* ...; **the ~ part of** (*quantity*) бо́льшая часть +*gen*; **at ~** в лу́чшем слу́чае; **to make the ~ of sth** испо́льзовать (*impf*) что-н наилу́чшим о́бразом; **to do one's ~** де́лать (сде́лать *perf*) всё возмо́жное; **to the ~ of my knowledge** наско́лько мне изве́стно; **to the ~ of my ability** в ме́ру мои́х спосо́бностей; **he's not exactly patient at the ~ of times** он не отлича́ется осо́бым терпе́нием.
bestial ['bɛstɪəl] *adj* ско́тский*.
best man *n* ша́фер*.
bestow [bɪ'stəu] *vt*: **to ~ sth on sb** (*title*) дарова́ть (*impf/perf*) что-н кому́-н; (*affection*) ода́ривать (одари́ть *perf*) кого́-н чем-н.
bestseller ['bɛst'sɛlə'] *n* бестсе́ллер.
bet [bɛt] (*pt, pp* **bet** *or* **betted**) *n* (*wager*) пари́ *nt ind*; (*in gambling*) ста́вка ◆ *vi* (*wager*) держа́ть (*impf*) пари́; (*expect, guess*) би́ться* (*impf*) об закла́д ◆ *vt*: **to ~ sb sth** би́ться* (поби́ться* *perf*) об закла́д с кем-н о чём-н, спо́рить (поспо́рить *perf*) с кем-н на что-н; **it's a safe ~** (*fig*) э́то ве́рное де́ло; **to ~ money on sth** ста́вить* (поста́вить* *perf*) де́ньги на что-н.
Bethlehem ['bɛθlɪhɛm] *n* Вифлее́м.
betray [bɪ'treɪ] *vt* (*friends*) предава́ть* (преда́ть* *perf*); (*trust*) обма́нывать (обману́ть* *perf*); (*emotion*) выдава́ть* (вы́дать* *perf*).

betrayal [bɪ'treɪəl] *n* предательство.
better ['bɛtəʳ] *adj* лучший* ◆ *adv* лучше ◆ *vt* (*score*) улучшать (улучшить *perf*) ◆ *n*: **to get the ~ of** брать* (взять* *perf*) верх над *+instr*; **I feel ~** я чувствую себя лучше; **to get ~** (*MED*) поправляться (поправиться* *perf*); **that's ~!** вот так(-то) лучше!; **I had ~ go** мне лучше уйти; **he thought ~ of it** он передумал; **a change for the ~** изменение к лучшему.
better off *adj* (*wealthier*) более состоятельный* (состоятелен); (*more comfortable etc*) лучше; (*fig*): **you'd be ~ ~ this way** так Вам будет лучше.
betting ['bɛtɪŋ] *n* пари *nt ind.*
betting shop *n* (*BRIT*) *место, где делают ставки.*
between [bɪ'twi:n] *prep* между *+instr* ◆ *adv*: **in ~** между тем; **the road ~ here and London** дорога отсюда до Лондона; **we only had £5 ~ us** у нас на двоих было всего £5.
bevel ['bɛvəl] *n* (*also:* **~ edge**) скос.
bevelled ['bɛvəld] *adj*: **a ~ edge** скошенный край*.
beverage ['bɛvərɪdʒ] *n* напиток*.
bevy ['bɛvɪ] *n*: **a ~ of** (*people*) группа *+gen*; (*things*) ряд *+gen.*
bewail [bɪ'weɪl] *vt* скорбеть *(impf)* о *+prp.*
beware [bɪ'wɛəʳ] *vi*: **to ~ (of)** остерегаться (остеречься* *perf*) (*+gen*); **"beware of the dog"** "осторожно, (злая) собака".
bewildered [bɪ'wɪldəd] *adj* изумлённый (изумлён).
bewildering [bɪ'wɪldrɪŋ] *adj* изумительный* (изумителен).
bewitching [bɪ'wɪtʃɪŋ] *adj* (*smile, person*) чарующий.
beyond [bɪ'jɔnd] *prep* (*position*) за *+instr*; (*motion*) за *+acc*; (*understanding*) выше *+gen*; (*expectations*) сверх *+gen*; (*age*) больше *+gen*; (*date*) после *+gen* ◆ *adv* (*position*) вдали; (*motion*) вдаль; **~ doubt** вне сомнения; **it's ~ repair** это невозможно починить; **it's ~ me** это выше моего понимания.
b/f *abbr* (*COMM*: = *brought forward*) перенесённый на следующую страницу.
BFPO *n abbr* = *British Forces Post Office.*
bhp *n abbr* (*AUT*: = *brake horsepower*) *эффективная мощность двигателя внутреннего сгорания в лошадиных силах.*
bi... [baɪ] *prefix* би..., дву(х)....
biannual [baɪ'ænjuəl] *adj* выходящий два раза в год.
bias ['baɪəs] *n* (*against*) предубеждение; (*towards*) пристрастие.
bias(s)ed ['baɪəst] *adj* (*jury*) пристрастный* (пристрастен); (*judgement*) предвзятый (предвзят); **he is/was ~ against** он предубеждён/был предубеждён против *+gen.*
bib [bɪb] *n* (*child's*) нагрудник.
Bible ['baɪbl] *n* Библия.
biblical ['bɪblɪkl] *adj* библейский*.
bibliography [bɪblɪ'ɔgrəfɪ] *n* библиография.
bicarbonate of soda [baɪ'kɑ:bənɪt-] *n* питьевая *or* пищевая сода.
bicentenary [baɪsɛn'ti:nərɪ] *n* двухсотлетие.
bicentennial [baɪsɛn'tɛnɪəl] *n* (*US*) = **bicentenary.**
biceps ['baɪsɛps] *n* бицепс.
bicker ['bɪkəʳ] *vi* препираться *(impf).*
bickering ['bɪkərɪŋ] *n* препирательство.
bicycle ['baɪsɪkl] *n* велосипед.
bicycle path *n* велосипедная дорожка.
bicycle pump *n* велосипедный насос.
bicycle track *n* велотрек.
bid [bɪd] (*pt* **bade** *or* **bid**, *pp* **bid(den)**) *n* (*at auction*) предложение цены; (*in tender*) заявка*; (*attempt*) попытка* ◆ *vt* (*offer*) предлагать (предложить* *perf*) ◆ *vi*: **to ~ for** (*at auction*) предлагать (предложить* *perf*) цену за *+acc*; (*CARDS*) объявлять (объявить* *perf*) (*масть или количество взяток*); **to ~ sb good day** здороваться (поздороваться *perf*) с кем-н.
bidden ['bɪdn] *pp of* **bid.**
bidder ['bɪdəʳ] *n*: **the highest ~** лицо, предлагающее наивысшую цену.
bidding ['bɪdɪŋ] *n* (*at auction*) предложение цены, торги *pl*; (*command*): **to do sb's ~** исполнять (исполнить *perf*) чьи-н приказания.
bide [baɪd] *vt*: **to ~ one's time** дожидаться (дождаться *perf*) своего часа.
bidet ['bi:deɪ] *n* биде *nt ind.*
bidirectional ['baɪdɪ'rɛkʃənl] *adj* (*COMPUT*: *printing*) двунаправленный; (: *drive*) реверсивный.
biennial [baɪ'ɛnɪəl] *adj* происходящий раз в два года ◆ *n* двухлетник.
bier [bɪəʳ] *n* катафалк.
bifocals [baɪ'fəuklz] *npl* бифокальные очки *pl.*
big [bɪg] *adj* большой; (*important*) важный* (важен); (*bulky*) крупный*; (*older*: *brother, sister*) старший*; **to do things in a ~ way** делать (сделать *perf*) что-н с широким размахом.
bigamist ['bɪgəmɪst] *n* (*man*) двоеженец*.
bigamous ['bɪgəməs] *adj* бигамный.
bigamy ['bɪgəmɪ] *n* бигамия.
big dipper [-'dɪpəʳ] *n* аттракцион "американские горы".
big end *n* большая головка (шатуна).
biggish ['bɪgɪʃ] *adj* довольно большой *or* крупный.
bigheaded ['bɪg'hɛdɪd] *adj* заносчивый (заносчив).
big-hearted ['bɪg'hɑ:tɪd] *adj* великодушный* (великодушен).
bigot ['bɪgət] *n* фанатик.
bigoted ['bɪgətɪd] *adj* фанатичный* (фанатичен).
bigotry ['bɪgətrɪ] *n* фанатизм.

big toe *n* большо́й па́лец* ноги́.
big top *n* ку́пол* ци́рка.
big wheel *n* колесо́* обозре́ния.
bigwig ['bɪgwɪg] *n* (*inf*) (ва́жная) ши́шка*.
bike [baɪk] *n* (*bicycle*) ве́лик; (*motorcycle*) мотоци́кл.
bikini [bɪ'ki:nɪ] *n* бики́ни *nt ind*.
bilateral [baɪ'lætərl] *adj* двусторо́нний*.
bile [baɪl] *n* жёлчь *f*; (*fig*) жёлчность *f*.
bilingual [baɪ'lɪŋgwəl] *adj* двуязы́чный*.
bilious ['bɪlɪəs] *adj* (*also fig*) тошнотво́рный (тошнотво́рен).
bill [bɪl] *n* (*invoice*) счёт*; (*POL*) законопрое́кт; (*US*: *banknote*) банкно́та; (*beak*) клюв ◆ *vt* (*item*) реклами́ровать *(impf/perf)*; (*customer*) присыла́ть (присла́ть* *perf*) счёт *+dat*; **"post no ~s"** "помеща́ть афи́ши воспреща́ется"; **to fit** *or* **fill the** ~ (*fig*) отвеча́ть *(impf)* всем тре́бованиям; **on the** ~ (*THEAT*) в афи́шах *or* програ́мме; **~ of exchange** ве́ксель* *m*; **~ of fare** меню́ *nt ind*; **~ of lading** коносаме́нт, (тра́нспортная) накладна́я *f adj*; **~ of sale** ку́пчая *f adj*.
billboard ['bɪlbɔ:d] *n* доска́ объявле́ний.
billet ['bɪlɪt] *n* (*MIL*) кварти́ры *fpl* ◆ *vt* расквартиро́вывать (расквартирова́ть *perf*).
billfold ['bɪlfəuld] *n* (*US*) бума́жник.
billiards ['bɪljədz] *n* билья́рд.
billion ['bɪljən] *n* (*BRIT*) биллио́н; (*US*) миллиа́рд.
billow ['bɪləu] *n* (*of smoke, steam*) клуб ◆ *vi* (*smoke*) клуби́ться *(impf)*; (*sail*) надува́ться (наду́ться* *perf*).
billy goat ['bɪlɪ-] *n* козёл*.
bimbo ['bɪmbəu] *n* (*inf*) ку́кла (*хоро́шенькая, но не у́мная же́нщина*).
bin [bɪn] *n* (*BRIT*: *also:* **rubbish** ~) му́сорное ведро́*; (*container*) я́щик.
binary ['baɪnərɪ] *adj* (*MATH, COMPUT*) двои́чный, бина́рный.
bind [baɪnd] (*pt, pp* **bound**) *vt* (*tie*) привя́зывать (привяза́ть* *perf*); (*tie together*: *hands and feet*) свя́зывать (связа́ть* *perf*); (*oblige*) обя́зывать (обяза́ть* *perf*); (*book*) переплета́ть (переплести́* *perf*) ◆ *n* (*inf*) обу́за
▸ **bind over** *vt* (*LAW*) обя́зывать (обяза́ть* *perf*)
▸ **bind up** *vt* (*wound*) перевя́зывать (перевяза́ть* *perf*); **he is/was bound up in** (*work etc*) он вовлечён/был вовлечён в *+acc*; **he is/was bound up with** (*person*) он свя́зан/был свя́зан с *+instr*.
binder ['baɪndə^r] *n* (*file*) скоросшива́тель *m*.
binding ['baɪndɪŋ] *adj* обя́зывающий ◆ *n* (*of book*) переплёт.
binge [bɪndʒ] *n* (*inf*): **to go on a** ~ (*drink a lot*) пья́нствовать *(impf)*.
bingo ['bɪŋgəu] *n* лото́ *nt ind*.
bin-liner ['bɪnlaɪnə^r] *n* мешо́к* для му́сора.
binoculars [bɪ'nɔkjuləz] *npl* бино́кль *msg*.
bio... [baɪəu] *prefix* био...; **~chemistry** биохи́мия.
biodegradable ['baɪəudɪ'greɪdəbl] *adj* биологи́чески разложи́мый (разложи́м).
biodiversity ['baɪəudaɪ'və:sɪtɪ] *n* биологи́ческое разнообра́зие.
biographer [baɪ'ɔgrəfə^r] *n* био́граф.
biographic(al) [baɪə'græfɪk(l)] *adj* биографи́ческий.
biography [baɪ'ɔgrəfɪ] *n* биогра́фия.
biological [baɪə'lɔdʒɪkl] *adj* (*science*) биологи́ческий*; (*warfare*) бактериологи́ческий*; (*washing powder*) содержа́щий* биопрепара́ты.
biological clock *n* биологи́ческие часы́ *pl*; **to upset sb's ~ ~** наруша́ть (нару́шить *perf*) чей-н режи́м.
biologist [baɪ'ɔlədʒɪst] *n* био́лог.
biology [baɪ'ɔlədʒɪ] *n* биоло́гия.
biophysics ['baɪəu'fɪzɪks] *n* биофи́зика.
biopic ['baɪəupɪk] *n* (*inf*) биографи́ческий фильм.
biopsy ['baɪɔpsɪ] *n* биопси́я.
biosphere ['baɪəsfɪə^r] *n* биосфе́ра.
biotechnology ['baɪəutɛk'nɔlədʒɪ] *n* биотехноло́гия.
biped ['baɪpɛd] *n* двуно́гое *nt adj*.
birch [bə:tʃ] *n* берёза.
bird [bə:d] *n* пти́ца; (*BRIT*: *inf*: *girl*) деви́ца.
bird of prey *n* хи́щная пти́ца.
bird's-eye view ['bə:dzaɪ-] *n* (*aerial view*) вид* с высоты́ пти́чьего полёта; (*overview*) о́бщая карти́на.
bird-watcher ['bə:dwɔtʃə^r] *n* орнито́лог-люби́тель *m*.
Birmingham ['bə:mɪŋəm] *n* Бирминге́м.
Biro® ['baɪərəu] *n* ша́риковая ру́чка*.
birth [bə:θ] *n* рожде́ние; **to give ~ to** рожа́ть (роди́ть* *perf*).
birth certificate *n* свиде́тельство о рожде́нии.
birth control *n* (*policy*) контро́ль *m* рожда́емости; (*methods*) противоза́чаточные ме́ры *fpl*.
birthday ['bə:θdeɪ] *n* день* *m* рожде́ния ◆ *cpd* ко дню рожде́ния; *see also* **happy**.
birthmark ['bə:θmɑ:k] *n* (*large*) роди́мое пятно́; (*small*) ро́динка*.
birthplace ['bə:θpleɪs] *n* (*also fig*) ро́дина.
birth rate *n* рожда́емость *f*.
Biscay ['bɪskeɪ] *n*: **the Bay of ~** Биска́йский зали́в.
biscuit ['bɪskɪt] *n* (*BRIT*) пече́нье; (*US*) ≈ кекс.
bisect [baɪ'sɛkt] *vt* (*MATH*) дели́ть* (раздели́ть* *perf*).
bisexual ['baɪ'sɛksjuəl] *adj* бисексуа́льный* (бисексуа́лен).
bishop ['bɪʃəp] *n* (*REL*) епи́скоп; (*CHESS*) слон*.

* marks translations which have irregular inflections. The Russian-English side of the dictionary gives inflectional information.

bistro ['bi:strəu] *n* бистро́ *nt ind.*
bit [bɪt] *pt of* **bite** ◆ *n* (*piece*) кусо́к*, кусо́чек*; (*of tool*) сверло́*; (*COMPUT*) бит; (*of horse*) удила́* *pl*; (*US*: *coin*) (ме́лкая) моне́та; **a ~ of** немно́го *+gen*; **a ~ dangerous** слегка́ опа́сный; **~ by ~** ма́ло-пома́лу; **to come to ~s** разла́мываться (разлома́ться* *perf*); **bring all your ~s and pieces** принеси́те все Ва́ши пожи́тки; **to do one's ~** вноси́ть* (внести́* *perf*) свой вклад.
bitch [bɪtʃ] *n* (*also inf!*) су́ка (*also !*)
bitching ['bɪtʃɪŋ] *n* хула́.
bite [baɪt] (*pt* **bit**, *pp* **bitten**) *vt* куса́ть (укуси́ть* *perf*) ◆ *vi* куса́ться (*impf*) ◆ *n* (*insect bite*) уку́с; **to ~ one's nails** куса́ть (*impf*) но́гти; **let's have a ~ (to eat)** (*inf*) дава́йте переку́сим; **he had a ~ of cake** он откуси́л кусо́к пирога́.
biting ['baɪtɪŋ] *adj* (*wind*) прони́зывающий; (*wit*) язви́тельный* (язви́телен).
bit part *n* проходна́я роль* *f*.
bitten ['bɪtn] *pp of* **bite**.
bitter ['bɪtəʳ] *adj* го́рький*; (*wind*) прони́зывающий; (*struggle*) ожесточённый ◆ *n* (*BRIT*) *пи́во с горькова́тым при́вкусом*; **to the ~ end** до са́мого конца́.
bitterly ['bɪtəlɪ] *adv* го́рько; (*oppose, criticize*) ожесточённо; (*jealous*) ужа́сно; **it's ~ cold today** сего́дня прони́зывающий хо́лод.
bitterness ['bɪtənɪs] *n* (*anger*) го́речь *f*, ожесточённость *f*; (*taste*) го́речь.
bittersweet ['bɪtəswi:t] *adj* горькова́то-сла́дкий*.
bitty ['bɪtɪ] *adj* (*BRIT*: *inf*) неро́вный* (неро́вен).
bitumen ['bɪtjumɪn] *n* би́тум.
bivouac ['bɪvuæk] *n* бива́к.
bizarre [bɪ'zɑ:ʳ] *adj* стра́нный, причу́дливый.
bk *abbr* = **bank, book**.
BL *n abbr* (= *Bachelor of Law*) ≈ бакала́вр правове́дения; (= *Bachelor of Letters*) ≈ бакала́вр литературове́дения; (*US*: = *Bachelor of Literature*) ≈ бакала́вр литературове́дения.
bl *abbr* (= *bill of lading*) ≈ тра́нспортная накладна́я *f adj*.
blab [blæb] *vi* (*inf*) проба́лтываться (проболта́ться *perf*).
black [blæk] *adj* чёрный*; (*tea, coffee*) без молока́; (*person*) чернoко́жий* ◆ *n* (*colour*) чёрный цвет, чёрное *nt adj*; (*person*): **B~** негр(итя́нка) ◆ *vt* (*BRIT*: *INDUSTRY*) бойкоти́ровать (*impf/perf*); **to give sb a ~ eye** подбива́ть (подби́ть* *perf*) кому́-н глаз; **~ and blue** в синяка́х; **there it is in ~ and white** (*fig*) вот оно́, чёрным по бе́лому напи́сано **to be in the ~** име́ть (*impf*) де́ньги в ба́нке
▸ **black out** *vi* па́дать (упа́сть* *perf*) в о́бморок.
black belt *n* (*JUDO*) чёрный по́яс*; (*US*: *area*) *ю́жные райо́ны США, в кото́рых преоблада́ет негритя́нское населе́ние*.
blackberry ['blækbərɪ] *n* ежеви́ка *no pl*.
blackbird ['blækbə:d] *n* (чёрный) дрозд*.
blackboard ['blækbɔ:d] *n* кла́ссная доска́*.
black box *n* (*AVIAT*) чёрный я́щик.
black coffee *n* чёрный ко́фе *m ind*.
Black Country *n* (*BRIT*): **the ~ ~** *индустриа́льные райо́ны Се́веро-За́падной А́нглии*.
blackcurrant ['blæk'kʌrənt] *n* чёрная сморо́дина.
black economy *n*: **the ~ ~** тенева́я эконо́мика.
blacken ['blækn] *vt* (*fig*) черни́ть (очерни́ть *perf*).
black eye *n* синя́к* *or* фона́рь* *m* под гла́зом.
Black Forest *n*: **the ~ ~** Шварцва́льд.
blackhead ['blækhɛd] *n* у́горь* *m*.
black hole *n* чёрная дыра́*.
black ice *n* гололе́дица.
blackjack ['blækdʒæk] *n* (*CARDS*) блэкдже́к; (*US*: *truncheon*) дуби́нка.
blackleg ['blæklɛg] *n* (*BRIT*: *INDUSTRY*) штрейкбре́хер.
blacklist ['blæklɪst] *n* чёрный спи́сок* ◆ *vt* (*person*) заноси́ть* (занести́* *perf*) в чёрный спи́сок.
blackmail ['blækmeɪl] *n* шанта́ж ◆ *vt* шантажи́ровать (*impf*).
blackmailer ['blækmeɪləʳ] *n* шантажи́ст.
black market *n* чёрный ры́нок*.
blackout ['blækaut] *n* (*in wartime*) затемне́ние; (*ELEC*) обесто́чка*; (*TV, RADIO*) приостановле́ние переда́ч; (*MED*) о́бморок.
black pepper *n* чёрный пе́рец*.
Black Sea *n*: **the ~ ~** Чёрное мо́ре.
black sheep *n* (*fig*) парши́вая овца́.
blacksmith ['blæksmɪθ] *n* кузне́ц*.
black spot *n* (*AUT*) ги́блое ме́сто*; (*ECON*) мёртвая зо́на.
bladder ['blædəʳ] *n* (*ANAT*) мочево́й пузы́рь* *m*.
blade [bleɪd] *n* ле́звие; (*of oar, propeller*) ло́пасть* *f*; **a ~ of grass** трави́нка*.
blame [bleɪm] *n* вина́* ◆ *vt*: **to ~ sb for sth** вини́ть (*impf*) кого́-н в чём-н; **he is/was to ~ (for sth)** он винова́т *or* вино́вен/был винова́т *or* вино́вен (в чём-н); **who's to ~?** кого́ сле́дует в э́том вини́ть?; **I'm not to ~** э́то не моя́ вина́.
blameless ['bleɪmlɪs] *adj* (*person*) невино́вный, безупре́чный.
blanch [blɑ:ntʃ] *vi* беле́ть (побеле́ть *perf*) ◆ *vt* (*CULIN*) обва́ривать (обвари́ть* *perf*) кипятко́м.
blancmange [blə'mɔnʒ] *n* бланманже́ *nt ind*.
bland [blænd] *adj* (*taste, food*) пре́сный (пре́сен).
blank [blæŋk] *adj* (*paper*) чи́стый* (чист); (*look*) безуча́стный* (безуча́стен) ◆ *n* (*of memory*) пробе́л; (*on form*) про́пуск; (*for gun*) холосто́й патро́н; **we drew a ~** (*fig*) мы оста́лись ни с чем.
blank cheque *n* незапо́лненный чек; **to give sb a ~ ~** (*fig*) предоставля́ть (предоста́вить*

perf) кому́-н карт-бла́нш.
blanket [ˈblæŋkɪt] *n* одея́ло; (*of snow*) покро́в; (*of fog*) пелена́ ◆ *adj* всеобъе́млющий*.
blanket cover *n* (*INSURANCE*) бла́нковый *or* блок по́лис.
blare [blɛəʳ] *vi* реве́ть *(impf)*
▸ **blare out** *vi* прореве́ть *(perf)*.
blarney [ˈblɑːnɪ] *n* лесть *f*.
blasé [ˈblɑːzeɪ] *adj* валья́жный.
blaspheme [blæsˈfiːm] *vi* богоху́льствовать *(impf)*, святота́тствовать *(impf)*.
blasphemous [ˈblæsfɪməs] *adj* (*words*) богоху́льный; **a ~ person** богоху́льник.
blasphemy [ˈblæsfɪmɪ] *n* богоху́льство, святота́тство.
blast [blɑːst] *n* (*of wind*) поры́в; (*of air, steam*) волна́*; (*of whistle*) пронзи́тельный свист; (*explosion*) взрыв ◆ *vt* (*blow up*) взрыва́ть (взорва́ть* *perf*) ◆ *excl* (*BRIT*: *inf*) пропади́ (всё) про́падом; **at full ~** (*play music etc*) на по́лную мо́щность
▸ **blast off** *vi* взлета́ть (взлете́ть* *perf*), взмыва́ть (взмыть* *perf*).
blast furnace *n* до́менная печь* *f*.
blast-off [ˈblɑːstɔf] *n* старт.
blatant [ˈbleɪtənt] *adj* я́вный (я́вен), неприкры́тый.
blatantly [ˈbleɪtəntlɪ] *adv* я́вно, неприкры́то; **it's ~ obvious** э́то абсолю́тно я́сно.
blaze [bleɪz] *n* (*fire*) пла́мя* *nt*; (*of colour*) полыха́ние; (*of glory*) сия́ние ◆ *vi* (*fire*) пыла́ть *(impf)*; (*guns*) пали́ть *(impf)*; (*fig*: *eyes*) сверка́ть *(impf)* ◆ *vt*: **to ~ a trail** пролага́ть (проложи́ть* *perf*) путь; **in a ~ of publicity** в газе́тной шуми́хе.
blazer [ˈbleɪzəʳ] *n* фо́рменная ку́ртка.
bleach [bliːtʃ] *n* (*also*: **household ~**) отбе́ливатель *m* ◆ *vt* (*fabric*) отбе́ливать (отбели́ть *perf*); (*hair*) обесцве́чивать (обесцве́тить* *perf*).
bleached [bliːtʃt] *adj* (*hair*) обесцве́ченный (обесцве́чен).
bleachers [ˈbliːtʃəz] *npl* (*US*: *SPORT*) откры́тая трибу́на *fsg*.
bleak [bliːk] *adj* (*weather, expression*) уны́лый (уны́л); (*prospect*) безра́достный* (безра́достен).
bleary-eyed [ˈblɪərɪˈaɪd] *adj* с воспалёнными глаза́ми.
bleat [bliːt] *vi* (*animal*) бле́ять (забле́ять *perf*) ◆ *n* (*of animal*) бле́яние.
bled [blɛd] *pt, pp of* **bleed**.
bleed [bliːd] (*pt, pp* **bled**) *vi* кровото́чить *(impf)*; (*colour*) течь* (поте́чь* *perf*) ◆ *vt* (*brakes, radiator*) опоро́жни́ть (опорожня́ть *perf*); **my nose is ~ing** у меня́ идёт кровь из но́са.
bleep [bliːp] *n* сигна́л; (*TEL*) гудо́к* ◆ *vi* сигна́лить (просигна́лить *perf*) ◆ *vt* (*doctor*) вызыва́ть (вы́звать* *perf*).
bleeper [ˈbliːpəʳ] *n* переносна́я ра́ция.
blemish [ˈblɛmɪʃ] *n* пятно́*.
blend [blɛnd] *n* (*of tea, whisky*) буке́т ◆ *vt* (*CULIN*) сме́шивать (смеша́ть *perf*); (*colours, styles etc*) сочета́ть *(impf)* ◆ *vi* (*also*: **~ in**) сочета́ться *(impf)*, слива́ться (сли́ться* *perf*).
blender [ˈblɛndəʳ] *n* смеси́тель *m*, ми́ксер.
bless [blɛs] (*pt, pp* **blessed** *or* **blest**) *vt* (*REL*) благословля́ть (благослови́ть* *perf*); **he is ~ed with** Бог награди́л его́ *+instr*; **~ you!** бу́дьте здоро́вы!
blessed [ˈblɛsɪd] *adj* блаже́нный; **it rains every ~ day** (*inf*) дождь идёт ка́ждый Бо́жий день.
blessing [ˈblɛsɪŋ] *n* благослове́ние; (*godsend*) бо́жий дар, благода́ть *f*; **to count one's ~s** не гневи́ть* *(impf)* Бо́га, не ропта́ть* *(impf)* по́пусту на судьбу́; **it was a ~ in disguise** ≈ не было бы сча́стья, да несча́стье помогло́.
blest [blɛst] *pt, pp of* **bless**.
blew [bluː] *pt of* **blow**.
blight [blaɪt] *vt* губи́ть* (погуби́ть* *perf*) ◆ *n* (*of plants*) головня́*.
blimey [ˈblaɪmɪ] *excl* (*BRIT*: *inf*) чтоб мне провали́ться.
blind [blaɪnd] *adj* слепо́й* ◆ *n* што́ра; (*also*: **Venetian ~**) жалюзи́ *pl ind* ◆ *vt* ослепля́ть (ослепи́ть* *perf*); **the ~** *npl* (*blind people*) слепы́е *pl adj*; **to be ~ (to)** (*fig*) не ви́деть* *(impf)* (*+acc*); **to turn a ~ eye (on** *or* **to)** закрыва́ть (закры́ть* *perf*) глаза́ (на *+acc*).
blind alley *n* (*fig*) тупи́к.
blind corner *n* (*BRIT*) непросма́тривающийся поворо́т.
blind date *n* *свида́ние с незнако́мцем*.
blinders [ˈblaɪndəz] *npl* (*US*) = **blinkers**.
blindfold [ˈblaɪndfəuld] *n* повя́зка ◆ *adv* вслепу́ю ◆ *vt* завя́зывать (завяза́ть* *perf*) глаза́ *+dat*.
blinding [ˈblaɪndɪŋ] *adj* ослепля́ющий (ослепля́ющ), слепя́щий; (*fig*) ослепи́тельный (ослепи́телен).
blindly [ˈblaɪndlɪ] *adv* (*without seeing*) вслепу́ю. (*without thinking*) сле́по.
blindness [ˈblaɪndnɪs] *n* слепота́; (*fig*) ослепле́ние.
blind spot *n* (*AUT*) опа́сное ме́сто*; (*fig*) сла́бое ме́сто*.
blink [blɪŋk] *vi* (*person, animal*) морга́ть *(impf)*; (*light*) мига́ть *(impf)* ◆ *n*: **the TV's on the ~** (*inf*) телеви́зор барахли́т.
blinkers [ˈblɪŋkəz] *npl* шо́ры *fpl*.
blinking [ˈblɪŋkɪŋ] *adj* (*BRIT*: *inf*): **this ~ weather** прокля́тая пого́да.
blip [blɪp] *n* вспы́шка* (*на экра́не*); (*scientific*) отражённый и́мпульс.
bliss [blɪs] *n* блаже́нство.
blissful [ˈblɪsful] *adj* блаже́нный (блаже́н);

(*event*) счастли́вый (сча́стлив); **in ~ ignorance** в счастли́вом неве́дении.
blissfully ['blɪsfəlɪ] *adv* блаже́нно; **~ happy** бесконе́чно счастли́вый; **~ unaware of ...** в счастли́вом неве́дении о *+prp* ....
blister ['blɪstə'] *n* (*on skin*) волды́рь* *m*; (*in paint, rubber*) пузы́рь* *m* ◆ *vi* (*paint*) пузы́риться *(impf)*.
blithely ['blaɪðlɪ] *adv* беспе́чно.
blithering ['blɪðərɪŋ] *adj* (*inf*): **this ~ idiot** э́тот зако́нченный дура́к.
BLit(t) *n abbr* = *Bachelor of Literature, Bachelor of Letters.*
blitz [blɪts] *n* (*MIL*) бомбёжка*; **to have a ~ on sth** (*fig*) нава́ливаться (навали́ться* *perf*) на что-н.
blizzard ['blɪzəd] *n* вью́га.
BLM *n abbr* (*US*) = *Bureau of Land Management.*
bloated ['bləutɪd] *adj* (*face, stomach*) взду́тый (вздут); **I feel ~** я весь разду́лся.
blob [blɔb] *n* (*of glue, paint*) сгу́сток*; (*indistinct shape*) сму́тное очерта́ние.
bloc [blɔk] *n* блок; **the Eastern ~** (*formerly*) стра́ны Восто́чного бло́ка.
block [blɔk] *n* (*of buildings*) кварта́л; (*of stone etc*) плита́*; (*in pipe etc*) про́бка; (*toy*) ку́бик ◆ *vt* (*entrance, road*) загора́живать (загороди́ть* *perf*); (*progress*) препя́тствовать *(impf)*; (*COMPUT*) блоки́ровать *(impf/perf)*; **~ of flats** (*BRIT*) многокварти́рный дом*; **three ~s from here** че́рез три у́лицы; **mental ~** прова́л па́мяти; **~ and tackle** лебёдка*; **to ~ sb's way** прегражда́ть (прегради́ть* *perf*) кому́-н доро́гу
▸ **block up** *vt* затыка́ть (заткну́ть *perf*) ◆ *vi* засоря́ться (засори́ться *perf*); **my nose is ~ed up** у меня́ нос заложи́ло.
blockade [blɔ'keɪd] *n* блока́да ◆ *vt* блоки́ровать (заблоки́ровать *perf*).
blockage ['blɔkɪdʒ] *n* блоки́рование.
block booking *n* группова́я бронь *f*.
blockbuster ['blɔkbʌstə'] *n* боеви́к*.
block capitals *npl* печа́тные бу́квы *fpl*.
blockhead ['blɔkhɛd] *n* (*inf*) болва́н.
block letters *npl* печа́тные бу́квы *fpl*.
block release *n* (*BRIT*) уче́бный о́тпуск.
block vote *n* (*BRIT*) представи́тельное голосова́ние.
bloke [bləuk] *n* (*BRIT*: *inf*) па́рень* *m*.
blond(e) [blɔnd] *adj* белоку́рый (белоку́р) ◆ *n*: **blonde** (*woman*) блонди́нка*.
blood [blʌd] *n* кровь* *f*; **new ~** (*fig*) све́жие си́лы *fpl*.
blood bank *n* храни́лище кро́ви.
bloodbath ['blʌdbɑ:θ] *n* бо́йня.
blood count *n* о́бщий* ана́лиз кро́ви.
bloodcurdling ['blʌdkə:dlɪŋ] *adj* леденя́щий* кровь.
blood donor *n* до́нор.
blood group *n* гру́ппа кро́ви.
bloodhound ['blʌdhaund] *n* ище́йка*.
bloodless ['blʌdlɪs] *adj* бескро́вный* (бескро́вен).
bloodletting ['blʌdlɛtɪŋ] *n* кровопуска́ние; (*fig*) кровопроли́тие.
blood poisoning *n* зараже́ние кро́ви.
blood pressure *n* кровяно́е давле́ние; **he has high/low ~ ~** у него́ высо́кое/ни́зкое давле́ние.
bloodshed ['blʌdʃɛd] *n* кровопроли́тие.
bloodshot ['blʌdʃɔt] *adj* (*eyes*) нали́тый кро́вью.
blood sport *n* охо́та (*как вид спо́рта*).
bloodstained ['blʌdsteɪnd] *adj* запя́тнанный кро́вью.
bloodstream ['blʌdstri:m] *n* кровообраще́ние.
blood test *n* ана́лиз кро́ви.
bloodthirsty ['blʌdθə:stɪ] *adj* кровожа́дный* (кровожа́ден).
blood transfusion *n* перелива́ние кро́ви.
blood type *n* гру́ппа кро́ви.
blood vessel *n* кровено́сный сосу́д.
bloody ['blʌdɪ] *adj* (*battle*) крова́вый; (*nose*) окрова́вленный (окрова́влен); (*BRIT*: *inf!*): **this ~ weather** э́та прокля́тая пого́да (*!*); **~ strong/good** (*inf!*) ужа́сно си́льный/ хоро́ший*.
bloody-minded ['blʌdɪ'maɪndɪd] *adj* (*BRIT*: *inf*) по́длый (подл).
bloom [blu:m] *n* (*BOT*) цвето́к ◆ *vi* (*BOT*) цвести́* *(impf)*; (*talent, person*) расцвета́ть (расцвести́* *perf*); **to be in ~** быть* *(impf)* в цвету́, цвести́* *(impf)*.
blooming ['blu:mɪŋ] *adj* (*BRIT*: *inf*): **this ~ weather** э́та чёртова пого́да.
blossom ['blɔsəm] *n* цвет ◆ *vi* цвести́* *(impf)*; (*fig*): **to ~ into** расцвести́* *(perf)* в *+acc*.
blot [blɔt] *n* (*on text*) кля́кса; (*on name etc*) пятно́* ◆ *vt* (*with ink etc*) ста́вить* (поста́вить* *perf*) кля́ксу на *+acc*; **to be a ~ on the landscape** по́ртить* *(impf)* вид; **to ~ one's copy book** (*fig*) мара́ть (замара́ть *perf*) свою́ репута́цию
▸ **blot out** *vt* (*view*) заслоня́ть (заслони́ть *perf*); (*memory*) уничтожа́ть (уничто́жить *perf*).
blotchy ['blɔtʃɪ] *adj* (*complexion*) пятни́стый (пятни́ст).
blotter ['blɔtə'] *n* бюва́р.
blotting paper ['blɔtɪŋ-] *n* промока́тельная бума́га.
blotto ['blɔtəu] *adj* (*inf*) пья́ный (пьян) в сте́льку.
blouse [blauz] *n* блу́за, блу́зка*.
blow [bləu] (*pt* **blew**, *pp* **blown**) *n* (*also fig*) уда́р ◆ *vi* (*wind, person*) дуть (поду́ть *perf*); (*fuse*) перегора́ть (перегоре́ть *perf*) ◆ *vt* (*subj*: *wind*) гнать* *(impf)*; (*instrument*) дуть *(impf)* в *+acc*; **to ~ one's nose** сморка́ться (вы́сморкаться *perf*); **to ~ a whistle** свисте́ть (просвисте́ть *perf*) в свисто́к; **to come to ~s** доходи́ть* (дойти́* *perf*) до дра́ки

▸**blow away** *vt* сдува́ть (сдуть *perf*) ◆ *vi* уноси́ться* (унести́сь* *perf*)
▸**blow down** *vt* вали́ть* (повали́ть* *perf*)
▸**blow off** *vt* сдува́ть (сдуть *perf*) ◆ *vi* слета́ть (слете́ть* *perf*); (*NAUT*): **the ship was ~n off course** кора́бль снесло́ с ку́рса
▸**blow out** *vi* га́снуть* (пога́снуть *perf*)
▸**blow over** *vi* (*storm, crisis*) проходи́ть* (пройти́* *perf*)
▸**blow up** *vi* (*storm, crisis*) разража́ться (разрази́ться* *perf*) ◆ *vt* (*bridge*) взрыва́ть (взорва́ть* *perf*); (*tyre*) надува́ть (наду́ть *perf*); (*PHOT*) увели́чивать (увели́чить *perf*).
blow-dry ['bləudraɪ] *n укла́дка воло́с фе́ном* ◆ *vt* укла́дывать (уложи́ть* *perf*) воло́сы фе́ном.
blowlamp ['bləulæmp] *n* (*BRIT*) пая́льная ла́мпа.
blown [bləun] *pp of* **blow**.
blow-out ['bləuaut] *n* (*of tyre*) разры́в; (*of oil well*) проры́в; (*inf: big meal*) кутёж*.
blowtorch ['bləutɔ:tʃ] *n* = **blowlamp**.
blow-up ['bləuʌp] *n* увели́ченный сни́мок*.
blowzy ['blauzɪ] *adj* (*BRIT*) обрю́зглый.
BLS *n abbr* (*US*) = *Bureau of Labor Statistics*.
blubber ['blʌbəʳ] *n* вы́топленный жир ◆ *vi* (*pej*) реве́ть* (зареве́ть* *perf*).
bludgeon ['blʌdʒən] *vt* бить* (изби́ть* *perf*) дуби́нкой; (*fig*): **to ~ sb into doing** заставля́ть (заста́вить* *perf*) кого́-н из-под па́лки *+infin*.
blue [blu:] *adj* (*colour: light*) голубо́й; (*: dark*) си́ний*; (*depressed*) гру́стный, пода́вленный; **~s** *npl* (*MUS*): **the ~s** блюз *msg*; **~ film** поха́бный фильм; **(only) once in a ~ moon** раз в сто лет; **out of the ~** (*fig*) как с не́ба свали́ться.
blue baby *n* синю́шный младе́нец*.
bluebell ['blu:bɛl] *n* колоко́льчик.
bluebottle ['blu:bɔtl] *n* наво́зная му́ха.
blue cheese *n* сыр* ти́па рокфо́р.
blue-chip ['blu:tʃɪp] *adj*: **~ investment/shares** вложе́ния/а́кции с высо́кими дивиде́ндами.
blue-collar worker ['blu:kɔləʳ-] *n* заводско́й рабо́чий*(-ая) *m(f) adj*.
blue jeans *npl* джи́нсы *pl*.
blueprint ['blu:prɪnt] *n* (*fig*): **a ~ (for)** прое́кт (*+gen*).
bluff [blʌf] *vi* (*pretend, threaten*) блефова́ть (*impf*) ◆ *n* блеф; (*GEO*) утёс; **to call sb's ~** заставля́ть (заста́вить* *perf*) кого́-н раскры́ть ка́рты.
blunder ['blʌndəʳ] *n* про́мах ◆ *vi* (*make mistake*) допуска́ть (допусти́ть* *perf*) про́мах; **to ~ into sb/sth** натыка́ться (наткну́ться *perf*) на кого́-н/что-н.
blunt [blʌnt] *adj* тупо́й* (туп); (*person*) прямолине́йный* (прямолине́ен); (*talk*) открове́нный* (открове́нен) ◆ *vt* (*chisel etc*) затупля́ть (затупи́ть* *perf*); (*feelings*) тупи́ть (притупи́ть* *perf*); **~ instrument** (*LAW*) тупо́е ору́дие.
bluntly ['blʌntlɪ] *adv* пря́мо.
bluntness ['blʌntnɪs] *n* прямолине́йность *f*.
blur [bləːʳ] *n* сму́тное очерта́ние; (*memory*) сму́тное воспомина́ние ◆ *vt* (*vision*) затума́нивать (затума́нить *perf*); (*distinction*) стере́ть* (стира́ть *perf*).
blurb [blə:b] *n* (*about book etc*) рекла́ма.
blurred [blə:d] *adj* стёртый, сму́тный.
blurt out [blə:t-] *vt* выпа́ливать (вы́палить *perf*).
blush [blʌʃ] *vi* красне́ть (покрасне́ть *perf*) ◆ *n* румя́нец*.
blusher ['blʌʃəʳ] *n* румя́на *pl*.
bluster ['blʌstəʳ] *n* взрыв гне́ва ◆ *vi* разбушева́ться* (*perf*).
blustering ['blʌstərɪŋ] *adj* (*person*) бу́йный* (бу́ен); (*tone etc*) громогла́сный* (громогла́сен).
blustery ['blʌstərɪ] *adj* ве́треный.
Blvd *abbr* = *boulevard*.
BM *n abbr* = *British Museum*; (= *Bachelor of Medicine*) ≈ бакала́вр медици́ны.
BMA *n abbr* = *British Medical Association*.
BMJ *n abbr* = *British Medical Journal*.
BMus *n abbr* (= *Bachelor of Music*) ≈ бакала́вр музыкове́дения.
BMX *n abbr* (= *bicycle motorcross*) велосипе́дные го́нки *pl*; **~ bike** *ма́рка велосипе́да*.
BNP *n abbr* (= *British National Party*) Брита́нская национа́льная па́ртия.
BO *n abbr* (*inf* = *body odour*): **he has ~** от него́ па́хнет по́том; (*US*) = **box office**.
boar [bɔːʳ] *n* бо́ров; (*wild pig*) каба́н*.
board [bɔ:d] *n* доска́*; (*cardboard*) карто́н; (*committee*) комите́т; (*in firm*) правле́ние ◆ *vt* (*ship*) сади́ться* (сесть* *perf*) на *+acc*; (*train*) сади́ться* (сесть* *perf*) в/на *+acc*; **on ~** (*NAUT, AVIAT*) на борту́; **full ~** (*BRIT*) по́лный пансио́н; **half ~** (*BRIT*) пансио́н с за́втраком и у́жином; **~ and lodging** прожива́ние и пита́ние; **the plan went by the ~** (*fig*) план был вы́брошен за́ борт; **above ~** (*fig*) зако́нным о́бразом; **across the ~** (*fig*) по всем катего́риям
▸**board up** *vt* забива́ть (заби́ть* *perf*), закола́чивать (заколоти́ть* *perf*).
boarder ['bɔ:dəʳ] *n* (*SCOL*) учени́к*(-и́ца) шко́лы-интерна́та.
board game *n* насто́льная игра́*.
boarding card ['bɔ:dɪŋ-] *n* (*AVIAT, NAUT*) = **boarding pass**.
boarding house *n* пансио́н.

boarding party *n спецгру́ппа тамо́женников и́ли полице́йских, проводя́щая инспе́кцию судо́в, подозрева́емых в прово́зе контраба́нды и нарко́тиков.*
boarding pass *n* поса́дочный тало́н.
boarding school *n* шко́ла-интерна́т.
board meeting *n* совеща́ние правле́ния.
board room *n* зал заседа́ний.
boardwalk ['bɔ:dwɔ:k] *n* (*US*) доща́тый насти́л.
boast [bəust] *vt* горди́ться *(impf)* +*instr* ◆ *vi*: **to ~ (about** *or* **of)** хва́статься (похва́статься *perf*) (+*instr*).
boastful ['bəustful] *adj* хвастли́вый (хвастли́в).
boastfulness ['bəustfulnɪs] *n* хвастовство́.
boat [bəut] *n* (*small*) ло́дка*; (*large*) кора́бль* *m*; **to go by ~** плыть* (поплы́ть* *perf*); **to be in the same ~** (*fig*) быть* *(impf)* това́рищами по несча́стью.
boater ['bəutə'] *n* соло́менная шля́па.
boating ['bəutɪŋ] *n* ката́ние на ло́дке.
boatswain ['bəusn] *n* бо́цман.
bob [bɔb] *vi* (*boat*: *also*: **~ up and down**) пока́чиваться *(impf)* ◆ *n* (*BRIT*: *inf*) = **shilling**
▸ **bob up** *vi* выска́кивать (вы́скочить *perf*).
bobbin ['bɔbɪn] *n* шпу́лька.
bobby ['bɔbɪ] *n* (*BRIT*: *inf*) мент.
bobsleigh ['bɔbsleɪ] *n* бо́бслей.
bode [bəud] *vi*: **to ~ well/ill** предвеща́ть *(impf)* *or* сули́ть *(impf)* хоро́шее/недо́брое.
bodice ['bɔdɪs] *n* корса́ж.
bodily ['bɔdɪlɪ] *adj* физи́ческий* ◆ *adv* целико́м.
body ['bɔdɪ] *n* те́ло*; (*torso*) ту́ловище; (*of speech, document*) основна́я часть* *f*; (*of car*) ко́рпус; (*of plane*) фюзеля́ж; (*fig*: *group*) гру́ппа; (: *organization*) о́рган, организа́ция; (*of information*) ма́сса; (*of wine*) консисте́нция; (*also*: **~stocking**) сви́тер-гольф (*по ти́пу закры́того купа́льника*), трико́ *nt ind*; **ruling ~** о́рган правле́ния; **in a ~** в по́лном соста́ве.
body blow *n* сокруши́тельный уда́р.
body-building ['bɔdɪ'bɪldɪŋ] *n* бо́ди-би́лдинг, атлети́зм.
body-double ['bɔdɪdʌbl] *n актёр, снима́ющийся в обнажённом ви́де вме́сто веду́щего актёра.*
bodyguard ['bɔdɪgɑ:d] *n* телохрани́тель *m*.
body language *n* язы́к* же́стов.
body repairs *npl* ремо́нт ко́рпуса.
body search *n* ли́чный досмо́тр.
bodywork ['bɔdɪwə:k] *n* ко́рпус.
boffin ['bɔfɪn] *n* (*BRIT*: *inf*) спец.
bog [bɔg] *n* (*GEO*) боло́то, тряси́на ◆ *vt*: **to get ~ged down in** (*fig*) вя́знуть (увя́знуть *perf*) в +*prp*.
bogey ['bəugɪ] *n* (*worry*) пу́гало; (*also*: **~man**) бу́ка *m/f*.
boggle ['bɔgl] *vi*: **the mind ~s** уму́ непостижи́мо.
bogie ['bəugɪ] *n* (*RAIL*) двухо́сная теле́жка*.
Bogotá [bəugə'tɑ:] *n* Богота́.
bogus ['bəugəs] *adj* (*claim*) фикти́вный* (фикти́вен); (*person*) сомни́тельный (сомни́телен).
Bohemia [bəu'hi:mɪə] *n* Боге́мия.
Bohemian [bəu'hi:mɪən] *adj* (*GEO*) боге́мский ◆ *n* боге́мец(ка); (*non-conformist*: *also*: **b~**) представи́тель(ница) *m(f)* боге́мы.
boil [bɔɪl] *vt* (*water*) кипяти́ть* (вскипяти́ть* *perf*); (*eggs, potatoes etc*) вари́ть (свари́ть *perf*), отва́ривать (отвари́ть *perf*) ◆ *vi* (*also fig*) кипе́ть* (вскипе́ть* *perf*) ◆ *n* фуру́нкул; **to come to the** (*BRIT*) **or a** (*US*) **~** вскипе́ть* *(perf)*
▸ **boil down to** *vt fus* (*fig*) своди́ться (свести́сь* *perf*) к +*dat*
▸ **boil over** *vi* (*milk*) убега́ть (убежа́ть* *perf*); (*potatoes*) выкипа́ть *(impf)*.
boiled egg [bɔɪld-] *n* варёное яйцо́*.
boiled potatoes *npl* варёная карто́шка *fsg*.
boiler ['bɔɪlə'] *n* (*device*) парово́й котёл*, бо́йлер.
boiler suit *n* (*BRIT*) комбинезо́н.
boiling ['bɔɪlɪŋ] *adj*: **I'm ~ (hot)** (*inf*) я запа́рился; **it's ~!** (*of weather*) жара́!, жари́ща!
boiling point *n* (*of liquid*) то́чка кипе́ния.
boisterous ['bɔɪstərəs] *adj* разбитно́й.
bold [bəuld] *adj* (*brave*) сме́лый* (смел); (*pej*: *cheeky*) на́глый (нагл); (*pattern, colours*) бро́ский* (бро́сок).
boldly ['bəuldlɪ] *adv* (*bravely*) сме́ло; (*impudently*) на́гло.
boldness ['bəuldnɪs] *n* (*see adv*) сме́лость *f*, на́глость *f*.
bold type *n* жи́рный шрифт.
Bolivia [bə'lɪvɪə] *n* Боли́вия.
Bolivian [bə'lɪvɪən] *adj* боливи́йский ◆ *n* боливи́ец(-и́йка).
bollard ['bɔləd] *n* (*BRIT*: *AUT*) ту́мба; (: *NAUT*) шварто́вая ту́мба.
bolshy ['bɔlʃɪ] *adj* (*BRIT*: *inf*) агресси́вный* (агресси́вен), во́инственный.
bolster ['bəulstə'] *n* ва́лик
▸ **bolster up** *vt* подкрепля́ть (подкрепи́ть* *perf*).
bolt [bəult] *n* (*lock*) засо́в; (*with nut*) болт* ◆ *vt* (*lock*) запира́ть (запере́ть* *perf*) на засо́в; (*also*: **~ together**) скрепля́ть (скрепи́ть* *perf*) болта́ми; (*devour*) загла́тывать (заглотну́ть* *perf*) ◆ *vi* (*run away*) понести́сь* *(perf)* ◆ *adv*: **~ upright** вы́тянувшись в стру́нку; **a ~ of lightning** разря́д мо́лнии; **a ~ from the blue** (*fig*) гром среди́ я́сного не́ба.
bomb [bɔm] *n* бо́мба ◆ *vt* бомби́ть* *(impf)*.
bombard [bɔm'bɑ:d] *vt* (*MIL, fig*) бомбардирова́ть *(impf)*.
bombardment [bɔm'bɑ:dmənt] *n* бомбардиро́вка.
bombastic [bɔm'bæstɪk] *adj* претенцио́зный* (претенцио́зен).

bomb disposal *n*: **~ ~ unit** отря́д сапёров; **~ ~ expert** сапёр.
bomber ['bɔmə^r] *n* (*AVIAT*) бомбардиро́вщик; (*person*) террори́ст.
bombing ['bɔmɪŋ] *n* бомбардиро́вка, бомбёжка.
bombshell ['bɔmʃɛl] *n* (*fig*): **my sacking was a real ~** изве́стие о моём увольне́нии произвело́ эффе́кт разорва́вшейся бо́мбы.
bomb site *n* разбомблённый уча́сток*.
bona fide ['bəunə'faɪdɪ] *adj* (*traveller etc*) по́длинный*; (*offer*) настоя́щий*.
bonanza [bə'nænzə] *n* золото́е дно.
bond [bɔnd] *n* у́зы *pl*; (*binding promise*) обяза́тельство; (*FINANCE*) облига́ция; (*COMM*): **goods in ~** това́ры, неопла́ченные по́шлиной.
bondage ['bɔndɪdʒ] *n* (*slavery*) нево́ля.
bonded goods ['bɔndɪd-] *npl* храня́щиеся това́ры *mpl* на тамо́женных скла́дах.
bonded warehouse *n* тамо́женный склад (*для това́ров неопла́ченных по́шлиной*).
bone [bəun] *n* кость* *f* ◆ *vt* отделя́ть (отдели́ть* *perf*) от косте́й; **I've got a ~ to pick with you** у меня́ к тебе́ претéнзия.
bone china *n* костяно́й фарфо́р.
bone-dry ['bəun'draɪ] *adj* соверше́нно сухо́й*.
bone idle *adj* пра́здный* (пра́зден); **he is ~ ~** он безде́льник.
bone marrow *n* ко́стный мозг.
boner ['bəunə^r] *n* (*US*) про́мах*.
bonfire ['bɔnfaɪə^r] *n* костёр*.
bonk [bɔŋk] (*inf*) *vt* тра́хать (тра́хнуть *perf*) ◆ *vi* тра́хаться (тра́хнуться *perf*).
bonkers ['bɔŋkəz] *adj* (*inf*) чо́кнутый.
Bonn [bɔn] *n* Бонн.
bonnet ['bɔnɪt] *n* (*hat*) ка́пор; (*BRIT*: *of car*) капо́т.
bonny ['bɔnɪ] *adj* (*esp SCOTTISH*) краси́вый (краси́в).
bonus ['bəunəs] *n* (*payment*) пре́мия; (*on wages*) премиа́льные *pl adj*; (*fig*) дополни́тельное преиму́щество.
bony ['bəunɪ] *adj* (*person, fingers*) костля́вый (костля́в); (*meat, fish*) кости́стый.
boo [bu:] *excl* фу ◆ *vt* осви́стывать (освиста́ть* *perf*).
boob [bu:b] *n* (*inf*: *breast*) грудь *f*; (*BRIT*: *mistake*) глу́пость *f*.
booby prize ['bu:bɪ-] *n* приз* проигра́вшему игроку́.
booby trap *n* (*MIL*) ми́на-лову́шка*; (*fig*) лову́шка*.
booby-trapped ['bu:bɪtræpt] *adj*: **a ~ car** маши́на с подло́женной ми́ной.
book [buk] *n* кни́га; (*of stamps, tickets*) кни́жечка* ◆ *vt* (*ticket, table*) зака́зывать (заказа́ть* *perf*); (*seat, room*) брони́ровать (заброни́ровать *perf*); (*subj*: *policeman, referee*) штрафова́ть (оштрафова́ть *perf*); **~s** *npl* (*COMM*: *accounts*) бухга́лтерские кни́ги *fpl*; **to keep the ~s** вести́* (*impf*) бухга́лтерские кни́ги; **by the ~** согла́сно инстру́кции; **to throw the ~ at sb** обвиня́ть (обвини́ть *perf*) кого́-н во всех сме́ртных греха́х
▸ **book in** *vi* (*BRIT*: *at hotel*) регистри́роваться (зарегистри́роваться *perf*)
▸ **book up** *vt*: **all seats are ~ed up** все биле́ты про́даны; **the hotel is ~ed up** в гости́нице нет мест; **I'm ~ed up that week** у меня́ э́та неде́ля по́лностью за́нята.
bookable ['bukəbl] *adj*: **all seats are ~** все биле́ты по предвари́тельным зака́зам.
bookcase ['bukkeɪs] *n* кни́жный шкаф*.
book end *n* книгодержа́тель *m*.
booking ['bukɪŋ] *n* (*BRIT*) зака́з.
booking office *n* (*BRIT*) биле́тная ка́сса.
book-keeping ['buk'ki:pɪŋ] *n* бухгалте́рия, счетово́дство.
booklet ['buklɪt] *n* брошю́ра.
bookmaker ['bukmeɪkə^r] *n* букме́кер.
bookseller ['buksɛlə^r] *n* книготорго́вец*.
bookshelf ['bukʃɛlf] *n* кни́жная по́лка.
bookshop ['bukʃɔp] *n* кни́жный магази́н.
bookstall ['bukstɔ:l] *n* кни́жный кио́ск.
book store *n* = **bookshop**.
book token *n* *пода́рочный тало́н на поку́пку кни́ги*.
book value *n* сто́имость *f* по торго́вым кни́гам.
bookworm ['bukwə:m] *n* кни́жный червь *m*.
boom [bu:m] *n* (*noise*) ро́кот; (*growth*: *in population etc*) бы́стрый рост; (*ECON*) бум ◆ *vi* (*guns, thunder*) грохота́ть* (прогрохота́ть* *perf*); (*voice*) рокота́ть* (пророкота́ть* *perf*); (*business*) процвета́ть (*impf*).
boomerang ['bu:məræŋ] *n* бумера́нг ◆ *vi*: **to ~ on sb** верну́ться (*perf*) к кому́-н бумера́нгом.
boom town *n* *го́род, процвета́ющий во вре́мя экономи́ческого подъёма*.
boon [bu:n] *n* бла́го.
boorish ['buərɪʃ] *adj* неотёсанный (неотёсан).
boost [bu:st] *n* (*to confidence etc*) толчо́к*, сти́мул ◆ *vt* стимули́ровать (*impf*), дава́ть* (дать* *perf*) толчо́к *+dat*; **to give a ~ to sb's spirits** *or* **to sb** окрыля́ть (окрыли́ть *perf*) кого́-н.
booster ['bu:stə^r] *n* (*MED*) повто́рная приви́вка*; (*TV, ELEC*) усили́тель *m*; (*also*: **~ rocket**) раке́та-носи́тель *m*.
booster cushion *n* *сиде́нье для дете́й в маши́не*.
boot [bu:t] *n* (*for winter*) сапо́г*; (*for football*) бу́тса; (*for walking*) боти́нок*; (*BRIT*: *of car*) бага́жник ◆ *vt* (*COMPUT*) загружа́ть (загрузи́ть* *perf*); **... to ~** (*in addition*) ... в

* marks translations which have irregular inflections. The Russian-English side of the dictionary gives inflectional information.

придáчу; **to give sb the ~** (*inf*) вы́турить *(perf)* кого́-н.
booth [bu:ð] *n* (*at fair*) ларёк*; (*TEL, for voting*) бу́дка*.
bootleg ['bu:tlɛg] *adj* контрабáндный.
bootlegger ['bu:tlɛgəʳ] *n* контрабандúст.
booty ['bu:tɪ] *n* трофéи *mpl*.
booze [bu:z] (*inf*) *n* вы́пивка ◆ *vi* выпивáть *(impf)*.
boozer ['bu:zəʳ] *n* (*BRIT*: *inf*: *pub*) пивнýшка*; **he's a real ~** (*inf*) он настоя́щий* пьянчýга.
border ['bɔ:dəʳ] *n* (*of a country*) грани́ца; (*for flowers*) бордю́р; (*on cloth etc*) каймá* ◆ *vt* (*road, river etc*) окаймля́ть (окайми́ть* *perf*); (*another country*: *also*: **~ on**) грани́чить *(impf)* с *+instr*; **B~s** *n*: **the B~s** *райóн на грани́це мéжду Áнглией и Шотлáндией*
▸ **border on** *vt fus* (*fig*) грани́чить *(impf)* с *+instr*.
borderline ['bɔ:dəlaɪn] *n*: **on the ~** на грáни.
borderline case *n* промежýточный слу́чай.
bore [bɔ:ʳ] *pt of* **bear** ◆ *vt* (*hole*) сверли́ть (просверли́ть *perf*); (*well, tunnel*) бури́ть (пробури́ть *perf*); (*person*) наскýчить *(perf)* *+dat* ◆ *n* (*person*) занýда *m/f*; (*of gun*) канáл стволá, кали́бр; **to be ~d** скучáть *(impf)*; **he's ~d to tears** *or* **~d to death** *or* **~d stiff** емý смертéльно скýчно.
boredom ['bɔ:dəm] *n* (*condition*) скýка; (*boring quality*) занýдство.
boring ['bɔ:rɪŋ] *adj* скýчный*.
born [bɔ:n] *adj* рождённый; **to be ~** рождáться (роди́ться* *perf*); **I was ~ in 1960** я роди́лся в 1960 годý; **~ blind** слепорождённый; **a ~ comedian** прирождённый кóмик.
born-again [bɔ:nə'gɛn] *adj*: **~ Christian** новообращённый(-ая) христиáнин*(-áнка).
borne [bɔ:n] *pp of* **bear**.
Borneo ['bɔ:nɪəu] *n* Борнéо *m ind*.
borough ['bʌrə] *n* администрати́вный óкруг*.
borrow ['bɔrəu] *vt*: **to ~ sth from sb** занимáть (заня́ть* *perf*) что-н у когó-н; **to ~ books from the library** брать* (взять* *perf*) кни́ги в библиотéке; **may I ~ your car?** мóжно взять на врéмя Вáшу маши́ну?
borrower ['bɔrəuəʳ] *n* заёмщик.
borrowing ['bɔrəuɪŋ] *n* (*word, custom*) заи́мствование; (*of money*) заём*.
borstal ['bɔ:stl] *n* (*BRIT*) *исправи́тельная колóния для несовершеннолéтних престýпников*.
Bosnia ['bɔznɪə] *n* Бóсния; **~-Herzegovina** Бóсния-Герцегови́на.
Bosnian ['bɔznɪən] *n* босни́ец(-и́йка).
bosom ['buzəm] *n* грудь* *f*; (*fig*: *of family*) лóно.
bosom friend *n* закады́чный друг*.
Bosphorus ['bɔsfərəs] *n*: **the ~** Босфóр.
boss [bɔs] *n* (*employer*) хозя́ин*(-я́йка*), босс; (*leader*) ли́дер, вожáк ◆ *vt* (*also*: **~ around, ~ about**) распоряжáться *(impf)*, комáндовать *(impf)* *+instr*; **stop ~ing everyone about!** перестáнь всéми комáндовать!
bossy ['bɔsɪ] *adj* влáстный (влáстен).
bosun ['bəusn] *n* бóцман.
botanical [bə'tænɪkl] *adj* ботани́ческий.
botanist ['bɔtənɪst] *n* ботáник.
botany ['bɔtənɪ] *n* ботáника.
botch [bɔtʃ] *vt* (*also*: **~ up**) состря́пать *(perf)*.
both [bəuθ] *adj, pron* óба* (*f* óбе*) ◆ *adv*: **~ A and B** и А, и Б; **~ (of them)** óба (они́); **~ of us went, we ~ went** мы óба пошли́; **they sell ~ meat and poultry** они́ торгýют и мя́сом, и пти́цей.
bother ['bɔðəʳ] *vt* (*worry*) беспокóить (обеспокóить *perf*); (*disturb*) беспокóить (побеспокóить *perf*) ◆ *vi* (*also*: **~ o.s.**) беспокóиться *(impf)* ◆ *n* (*trouble*) беспокóйство; (*nuisance*) хлóпоты* *pl* ◆ *excl*: **~!** чёрт возьми́!; **to ~ doing** брать* (взять* *perf*) на себя́ труд *+infin*; **I'm sorry to ~ you** извини́те за беспокóйство; **please don't ~** пожáлуйста, не беспокóйтесь; **don't ~!** не нáдо!; **it is a ~ to have to do** э́то так хлóпотно *+infin*; **it's no ~** э́то меня́ не затрудни́т; **I can't be ~ed** мне лень.
Botswana [bɔt'swɑ:nə] *n* Ботсвáна.
bottle ['bɔtl] *n* буты́лка*; (*for baby*) рожóк*; (*BRIT*: *inf*: *courage*) смéлость *f* ◆ *vt* (*beer, wine*) разливáть (разли́ть* *perf*) по буты́лкам; (*fruit*) консерви́ровать (законсерви́ровать *perf*); **~ of wine/milk** буты́лка* винá/молокá; **wine/milk ~** буты́лка* из-под винá/молокá
▸ **bottle up** *vt* скрывáть (скрыть* *perf*).
bottle bank *n контéйнер для стекля́нной тáры*.
bottle-fed ['bɔtlfɛd] *adj*: **~ baby** искýсственник.
bottleneck ['bɔtlnɛk] *n* (*AUT*) ýзкий* езд; (*fig*) затóр.
bottle-opener ['bɔtləupnəʳ] *n* штóпор.
bottom ['bɔtəm] *n* (*of container, sea etc*) дно*; (*ANAT*) зад*; (*of page, list*) низ*; (*of class*) неуспевáющий*(-ая) *m(f) adj*; (*of mountain etc*) поднóжие ◆ *adj* (*lowest*) ни́жний*; (*last*) послéдний*; **at the ~ of** на днé *+gen*; **to get to the ~ of sth** (*fig*) добирáться (добрáться* *perf*) до сýти чегó-н.
bottomless ['bɔtəmlɪs] *adj* (*funds, store*) бездóнный* (бездóнен).
bottom line *n* суть *f* дéла.
botulism ['bɔtjulɪzəm] *n* ботули́зм.
bough [bau] *n* сук*.
bought [bɔ:t] *pt, pp of* **buy**.
boulder ['bəuldəʳ] *n* валýн*.
boulevard ['bu:ləvɑ:d] *n* бульвáр.
bounce [bauns] *vi* (*ball*) отскáкивать (отскочи́ть *perf*); (*cheque*) вернýться *(perf)* (*о чéке, ввидý отсýтствия дéнег на счетý*) ◆ *vt* (*ball*) ударя́ть (удáрить *perf*); (*signal*) отражáть (отрази́ть* *perf*) ◆ *n* (*of ball*) отскóк; **he's got plenty of ~** (*fig*) он óчень живóй.

bouncer ['baunsə'] *n* (*inf*) вышибáла *m*.
bouncy castle ['baunsı-] *n* надувнóй воздýшный зáмок.
bound [baund] *pt, pp of* **bind** ◆ *n* (*leap*) прыжóк*, скачóк* ◆ *vi* (*leap*) прыгать (прыгнуть *perf*) ◆ *vt* (*border*) служить (*impf*) границей *+gen* ◆ *adj*: **he is ~ by law to ...** егó обязывает закóн *+infin...*; **~s** *npl* (*limits*) предéлы *mpl*; **he is/was ~ to do** он обязан/был обязан *+infin*; **he's ~ to come** он обязáтельно *or* непремéнно придёт; **~ for** направляющийся* в/на *+acc*; **this area is out of ~s** (*fig*: *place*) это мéсто является запрéтным.
boundary ['baundrı] *n* граница.
boundless ['baundlıs] *adj* безграничный* (безграничен).
bountiful ['bauntıful] *adj* (*person*) щéдрый* (щедр); (*supply*) обильный* (обилен).
bounty ['bauntı] *n* (*generosity*) щéдрость *f*; (*reward*) вознаграждéние.
bounty hunter *n охóтник за наградóй.*
bouquet ['bukeı] *n* букéт.
bourbon ['buəbən] *n* (*US*: *also*: **~ whiskey**) кукурýзное виски *nt ind*, бурбóн.
bourgeois ['buəʒwɑ:] *adj* буржуáзный* ◆ *n* буржуá *m ind*.
bout [baut] *n* (*of illness*) приступ; (*of activity*) всплéск; (*BOXING etc*) схвáтка*.
boutique [bu:'ti:k] *n* бутик.
bow[1] [bəu] *n* (*knot*) бант; (*weapon*) лук; (*MUS*) смычóк.
bow[2] [bau] *n* (*of the head, body*) поклóн; (*NAUT*: *also*: **~s**) нос ◆ *vi* (*with head, body*) клáняться (поклониться* *perf*); (*yield*): **to ~ to** *or* **before** поддавáться* (поддáться* *perf*) *+dat or* на *+acc*; **to ~ to the inevitable** покоряться (покориться *perf*) неизбéжному.
bowels ['bauəlz] *npl* кишéчник *msg*; (*of the earth etc*) нéдра *pl*.
bowl [bəul] *n* миска*, чáша; (*for washing*) таз*; (*ball*) шар*; (*of pipe*) голóвка*; (*US*: *stadium*) арéна ◆ *vi* подавáть* (подáть* *perf*) мяч
▸ **bowl over** *vt* (*fig*) сбивáть (сбить* *perf*).
bow-legged ['bəu'lɛgıd] *adj* кривонóгий*.
bowler ['bəulə'] *n* бóулер, подающий мяч; (*BRIT*: *also*: **~ hat**) котелóк*.
bowling ['bəulıŋ] *n* (*game*) кегельбáн.
bowling alley *n* кегельбан.
bowling green *n* площадка* для игры в шары.
bowls [bəulz] *n* игрá* в шары.
bow tie [bəu-] *n* бáбочка*.
box [bɔks] *n* ящик, корóбка*; (*also*: **cardboard ~**) картóнная корóбка*; (*THEAT*) ложа; (*BRIT AUT*) разграничительная линия; (*ADMIN*: *on form*) графá* ◆ *vt* (*put in a box*) упакóвывать (упаковáть *perf*) в корóбку; (*SPORT*) ударять (удáрить *perf*) ◆ *vi* (*SPORT*) боксировать (*impf*); **what's on the ~?** (*inf*: *TV*) что сегóдня по ящику?; **to ~ sb's ears** надирáть (надрáть* *perf*) комý-н ýши
▸ **box in** *vt* окружáть (окружить *perf*)
▸ **box off** *vt* отгорáживать (отгородить* *perf*).
boxer ['bɔksə'] *n* боксёр.
box file *n* ящик для хранéния докумéнтов.
boxing ['bɔksıŋ] *n* бокс.
Boxing Day *n* (*BRIT*) *день пóсле Рождествá.*
boxing gloves *npl* боксёрские перчáтки* *fpl*.
boxing ring *n* ринг.
box number *n* нóмер* абонéнтского ящика.
box office *n* театрáльная кáсса.
boxroom ['bɔksrum] *n* чулáн.
boy [bɔı] *n* мáльчик; (*son*) сынóк*.
boycott ['bɔıkɔt] *n* бойкóт ◆ *vt* бойкотировать (*impf/perf*).
boyfriend ['bɔıfrɛnd] *n* друг*.
boyish ['bɔııʃ] *adj* мальчишеский*.
boy scout *n* бойскáут.
Bp *abbr* = **bishop**.
BR *abbr* = **British Rail**.
bra [brɑ:] *n* лифчик.
brace [breıs] *n* (*on leg*) шина; (*on teeth*) пластинки *pl*; (*tool*) коловорóт; (*also*: **~ bracket**) скóбка* ◆ *vt* (*knees, shoulders*) напрягáть (напрячь* *perf*); **~s** *npl* (*BRIT*: *for trousers*) подтяжки* *pl*; **to ~ o.s.** (*for shock*) собирáться (собрáться* *perf*) с дýхом.
bracelet ['breıslıt] *n* браслéт.
bracing ['breısıŋ] *adj* бодрящий.
bracken ['brækən] *n* орляк.
bracket ['brækıt] *n* (*TECH*) кронштéйн; (*group, range*) категóрия; (*also*: **brace ~**) скóбка*; (*also*: **round ~**) крýглая скóбка*; (*also*: **square ~**) квадрáтная скóбка* ◆ *vt* (*fig*: *also*: **~ together**) группировáть (сгруппировáть *perf*); (*word, phrase*) заключáть (заключить *perf*) в скóбки; **income ~** ýровень *m* дохóда; **in ~s** в скóбках.
brackish ['brækıʃ] *adj* солоновáтый (солоновáт).
brag [bræg] *vi* хвáстаться (похвáстаться *perf*).
braid [breıd] *n* (*for clothes etc*) тесьмá; (*of hair*) косá*.
Braille [breıl] *n* шрифт Брáйля.
brain [breın] *n* (*ANAT, fig*) мозг*; **~s** *npl* (*CULIN*) мозги *mpl*; (*intelligence*) мозги *mpl*, сообразительность *f*; **he's got ~s** он пáрень с головóй.
brainchild ['breıntʃaıld] *n* детище.
braindead ['breındɛd] *adj*: **the patient was ~** у пациéнта наступила биологическая смерть
brain drain *n*: **the ~ ~** утéчка мозгóв.
brainless ['breınlıs] *adj* безмóзглый.
brainstorm ['breınstɔ:m] *n* (*fig*) умопомрачéние; (*US*: *brainwave*) озарéние

brainwash ['breɪnwɔʃ] *vt* промыва́ть (промы́ть* *perf*) мозги́ +*dat*.
brainwave ['breɪnweɪv] *n* озаре́ние; **he had a ~** на него́ нашло́ озаре́ние.
brainy ['breɪnɪ] *adj* мозгови́тый.
braise [breɪz] *vt* туши́ть* (потуши́ть* *perf*).
brake [breɪk] *n* (*also fig*) то́рмоз* ◆ *vi* тормози́ть* (затормози́ть* *perf*).
brake fluid *n* тормозна́я жи́дкость *f*.
brake light *n* тормозно́й сигна́л.
brake pedal *n* педа́ль *f* то́рмоза, тормоза́* *mpl*.
bramble ['bræmbl] *n* ежеви́ка.
bran [bræn] *n* о́труби *pl*.
branch [brɑːntʃ] *n* (*of tree*) ве́тка*, ветвь* *f*; (*fig*: *of family, organization*) ветвь*; (*COMM*: *of bank, company etc*) филиа́л ◆ *vi* разветвля́ться (разветви́ться* *perf*)
▸ **branch out** *vi* (*fig*) разветвля́ться (разветви́ться *perf*).
branch line *n* (железнодоро́жная) ве́тка*.
branch manager *n* дире́ктор* филиа́ла.
brand [brænd] *n* (*also*: **~ name**) фи́рменная ма́рка*; (*fig*: *type*) сорт ◆ *vt* (*cattle*) клейми́ть* (заклейми́ть* *perf*); (*fig*: *pej*): **to ~ sb a communist** *etc* клейми́ть* (заклейми́ть* *perf*) кого́-н коммуни́стом *etc*.
brandish ['brændɪʃ] *vt* разма́хивать *(impf)* +*instr*; (*weapon*) потряса́ть *(impf)* +*instr*.
brand name *n* фи́рменная ма́рка.
brand-new ['brænd'njuː] *adj* соверше́нно но́вый*.
brandy ['brændɪ] *n* бре́нди *nt ind*, конья́к*.
brash [bræʃ] *adj* наха́льный* (наха́лен).
Brasilia [brə'zɪlɪə] *n* Брази́лия.
brass [brɑːs] *n* (*metal*) лату́нь *f*; **the ~** (*MUS*) духовы́е инструме́нты *mpl*.
brass band *n* духово́й орке́стр.
brassiere ['bræsɪəʳ] *n* бюстга́льтер.
brass tacks *npl*: **to get down to ~ ~** доходи́ть* (дойти́* *perf*) до су́ти.
brassy ['brɑːsɪ] *adj* (*colour*) ме́дный; (*sound*) ре́зкий*; (*behaviour*) вызыва́ющий*.
brat [bræt] *n* (*pej*) отро́дье*.
Bratislava [brætɪ'slɑːvə] *n* Братисла́ва.
bravado [brə'vɑːdəu] *n* брава́да.
brave [breɪv] *adj* сме́лый (смел), хра́брый (храбр) ◆ *n* инде́йский во́ин ◆ *vt* сме́ло *or* хра́бро встреча́ть (встре́тить* *perf*).
bravely ['breɪvlɪ] *adv* сме́ло, хра́бро.
bravery ['breɪvərɪ] *n* сме́лость *f*, хра́брость *f*.
bravo [brɑː'vəu] *excl* бра́во.
brawl [brɔːl] *n* дра́ка ◆ *vi* дра́ться* (подра́ться* *perf*).
brawn [brɔːn] *n* (*strength*) му́скулы *mpl*; (*meat*) зельц, сту́день *m*.
brawny ['brɔːnɪ] *adj* мускули́стый (мускули́ст).
bray [breɪ] *vi* (*donkey*) реве́ть* *(impf)* ◆ *n* рёв осла́.
brazen ['breɪzn] *adj* (*woman*) бессты́жий (бессты́ж); (*lie, accusation*) на́глый (нагл) ◆ *vt*: **to ~ it out** выкру́чиваться (вы́крутиться* *perf*).
brazier ['breɪzɪəʳ] *n* жаро́вня*.
Brazil [brə'zɪl] *n* Брази́лия.
Brazilian [brə'zɪljən] *adj* брази́льский* ◆ *n* брази́лец*(-лья́нка*).
Brazil nut *n* америка́нский* оре́х.
breach [briːtʃ] *vt* (*defence, wall*) пробива́ть (проби́ть* *perf*) брешь в +*acc* ◆ *n* (*gap*) брешь *f*; (*estrangement*) разры́в; **~ of contract** наруше́ние догово́ра; **~ of the peace** наруше́ние обще́ственного поря́дка; **~ of trust** злоупотребле́ние дове́рием.
bread [brɛd] *n* хлеб; (*inf*: *money*) ба́бки *fpl*; **to earn one's daily ~** зараба́тывать (зарабо́тать *perf*) на хлеб *or* на жизнь; **to know which side one's ~ is buttered (on)** знать *(impf)* свою́ вы́году.
bread and butter *n* хлеб с ма́слом; (*fig*) хлеб насу́щный, жи́зненная осно́ва.
breadbin ['brɛdbɪn] *n* (*BRIT*) хле́бница.
breadboard ['brɛdbɔːd] *n* хле́бная доска́*; (*COMPUT*) маке́т, маке́тная пла́та.
breadbox ['brɛdbɔks] *n* (*US*) хле́бница.
breadcrumbs ['brɛdkrʌmz] *npl* кро́шки* *fpl*; (*CULIN*) панириро́вочные сухари́ *mpl*.
breadline ['brɛdlaɪn] *n*: **on the ~** за черто́й бе́дности.
breadth [brɛtθ] *n* (*of cloth etc*) ширина́; (*fig*: *of knowledge, subject*) широта́.
breadwinner ['brɛdwɪnəʳ] *n* корми́лец*(-лица).
break [breɪk] (*pt* **broke**, *pp* **broken**) *vt* (*cup, glass*) разбива́ть (разби́ть* *perf*); (*leg, arm*) лома́ть (слома́ть *perf*); (*promise, law*) наруша́ть (нару́шить *perf*); (*record*) побива́ть (поби́ть* *perf*) ◆ *vi* (*crockery*) разбива́ться (разби́ться *perf*); (*storm*) разрази́ться *(perf)*; (*weather*) по́ртиться (испо́ртиться *perf*); (*dawn*) бре́зжить (забре́зжить *perf*); (*story, news*) сообща́ть (сообщи́ть *perf*) ◆ *n* (*gap*) пробе́л; (*fracture*) перело́м; (*rest*) переды́шка*; (*interval*) переры́в; (*playtime*) переме́на; (*chance*) шанс; (*holiday*) о́тпуск*, о́тдых; **to ~ the news to sb** сообща́ть (сообщи́ть *perf*) кому́-н но́вость; **to ~ even** (*COMM*) зако́нчить *(perf)* без убы́тка; **to ~ with sb** порыва́ть (порва́ть* *perf*) с кем-н; **to ~ free** *or* **loose** вы́рваться* *(perf)* на свобо́ду; **to take a ~** (*few minutes*) де́лать (сде́лать *perf*) небольшо́й переры́в; (*holiday*) брать* (взять* *perf*) о́тпуск; **without a ~** без переры́ва; **a lucky ~** счастли́вый слу́чай
▸ **break down** *vt* (*figures etc*) разбива́ть (разби́ть* *perf*) по статья́м; (*door etc*) взла́мывать (взлома́ть *perf*) ◆ *vi* (*machine, car*) лома́ться (слома́ться *perf*); (*resistance*) быть* *(impf)* сло́мленным(-ой); (*person*) сломи́ться *(perf)*; (*talks*) срыва́ться (сорва́ться* *perf*)
▸ **break in** *vt* (*horse*) объу́здывать (обузда́ть

perf) ◆ *vi* (*burglar*) вла́мываться (вломи́ться *perf*); (*interrupt*) вме́шиваться (вмеша́ться *perf*)
▸ **break into** *vt fus* (*house*) вла́мываться (вломи́ться* *perf*) в +*acc*
▸ **break off** *vi* (*branch*) отла́мываться (отломи́ться* *perf*); (*speaker*) прерыва́ться (прерва́ться* *perf*) ◆ *vt* (*talks*) прерыва́ть (прерва́ть* *perf*); (*engagement*) расторга́ть (расто́ргнуть *perf*)
▸ **break open** *vt* взла́мывать (взлома́ть *perf*)
▸ **break out** *vi* (*begin*) разража́ться (разрази́ться* *perf*); (*escape*) сбега́ть (сбежа́ть* *perf*); **to ~ out in spots/a rash** покрыва́ться (покры́ться* *perf*) прыща́ми/сы́пью
▸ **break through** *vt fus* прорыва́ться (прорва́ться* *perf*) сквозь +*acc* ◆ *vi*: **the sun broke through** со́лнце проби́лось сквозь ту́чи
▸ **break up** *vi* (*ship*) разбива́ться (разби́ться* *perf*); (*crowd, meeting*) расходи́ться* (разойти́сь* *perf*); (*marriage, partnership*) распада́ться (распа́сться *perf*); (*SCOL*) закрыва́ться (закры́ться* *perf*) на кани́кулы ◆ *vt* (*rocks etc*) разла́мывать (разломи́ть* *perf*); (*journey*) прерыва́ть (прерва́ть* *perf*); (*fight etc*) прекраща́ть (прекрати́ть* *perf*); (*meeting*) распуска́ть (распусти́ть* *perf*); (*marriage*) разбива́ть (разби́ть* *perf*).
breakable ['breɪkəbl] *adj* хру́пкий* (хру́пок), ло́мкий* (ло́мок) ◆ *n*: **~s** хру́пкие предме́ты *mpl*.
breakage ['breɪkɪdʒ] *n* (*act of breaking*) поло́мка*; (*object*) бой; **to pay for ~s** плати́ть* (заплати́ть* *perf*) за бой.
breakaway ['breɪkəweɪ] *adj* (*group etc*) отдели́вшийся, отколо́вшийся.
break-dancing ['breɪkdɑ:nsɪŋ] *n* бре́йк.
breakdown ['breɪkdaun] *n* (*AUT*) небольша́я ава́рия; (*in communications*) наруше́ние; (*of marriage*) распа́д; (*of statistics*) разби́вка*; (*also:* **nervous ~**) не́рвный срыв.
breakdown service *n* (*BRIT*) авари́йная слу́жба.
breakdown van *n* (*BRIT*) фурго́н авари́йной слу́жбы.
breaker ['breɪkəʳ] *n* вал*.
breakeven ['breɪk'i:vn] *cpd*: **~ chart** гра́фик рента́бельности; **~ point** то́чка* безубы́точности.
breakfast ['brɛkfəst] *n* за́втрак ◆ *vi* за́втракать (поза́втракать *perf*).
breakfast cereal *n* крупа́ для за́втрака.
break-in ['breɪkɪn] *n* взлом.
breaking and entering ['breɪkɪŋən'ɛntrɪŋ] *n* (*LAW*) вторже́ние со взло́мом.
breaking point *n* преде́л.
breakthrough ['breɪkθru:] *n* (*fig: in technology*) перело́мное откры́тие.
break-up ['breɪkʌp] *n* (*of partnership, marriage*) распа́д.
break-up value *n* (*COMM*) ликвидацио́нная сто́имость *f*.
breakwater ['breɪkwɔ:təʳ] *n* волноре́з, мол*.
breast [brɛst] *n* грудь* *f*; (*of meat*) груди́нка; (*of poultry*) бе́лое мя́со.
breast-feed ['brɛstfi:d] (*irreg: like* **feed**) *vt* корми́ть* (покорми́ть* *perf*) гру́дью ◆ *vi* корми́ть (*impf*) (гру́дью).
breast pocket *n* (*of jacket etc*) нагру́дный карма́н.
breast-stroke ['brɛststrəuk] *n* брасс.
breath [brɛθ] *n* вдох; (*breathing*) дыха́ние; **to go out for a ~ of air** выходи́ть* (вы́йти* *perf*) подыша́ть *or* на све́жий во́здух; **to be out of ~** запы́хиваться (запыха́ться *perf*); **to get one's ~ back** отдыша́ться (*perf*).
breathalyse ['brɛθəlaɪz] *vt* проверя́ть (прове́рить *perf*) дыха́ние на алкого́ль.
Breathalyser® ['brɛθəlaɪzəʳ] *n* спирто́метр.
breathe [bri:ð] *vt* вдыха́ть (вдохну́ть *perf*) ◆ *vi* дыша́ть* (*impf*); **I won't ~ a word about it** я сло́вом не обмо́лвлюсь об э́том
▸ **breathe in** *vt* вдыха́ть (вдохну́ть *perf*) ◆ *vi* де́лать (сде́лать *perf*) вдох
▸ **breathe out** *vt* выдыха́ть (вы́дохнуть *perf*) ◆ *vi* де́лать (сде́лать *perf*) вы́дох.
breather ['bri:ðəʳ] *n* передышка*.
breathing ['bri:ðɪŋ] *n* дыхание.
breathing space *n* (*fig*) переды́шка*.
breathless ['brɛθlɪs] *adj* (*from exertion*) запыха́вшийся; (*after illness*) с затруднённым дыха́нием; **he was ~ with excitement** у него́ перехвати́ло дыха́ние от волне́ния.
breathtaking ['brɛθteɪkɪŋ] *adj* захва́тывающий* дух.
breath test *n* дыха́тельная про́ба.
bred [brɛd] *pt, pp of* **breed**.
-bred [brɛd] *suffix*: **well/ill-~** хорошо́/пло́хо воспи́танный* (воспи́тан).
breed [bri:d] (*pt, pp* **bred**) *vt* (*animals, plants*) разводи́ть* (развести́* *perf*); (*fig: give rise to*) порожда́ть (породи́ть* *perf*) ◆ *vi* размножа́ться (*impf*) ◆ *n* (*ZOOL*) поро́да; (*type, class*) сорт*, род*.
breeder ['bri:dəʳ] *n* (*person*) селекционе́р; (*PHYS: also:* **~ reactor**) реа́ктор-размножи́тель *m*; **cattle ~** скотово́д.
breeding ['bri:dɪŋ] *n* воспита́ние.
breeding ground *n* ме́сто* размноже́ния; (*fig*) расса́дник.
breeze [bri:z] *n* бриз.
breeze block ['bri:zblɔk] *n* (*BRIT*) шлакобето́нный кирпи́ч.
breezy ['bri:zɪ] *adj* (*manner, tone*) оживлённый

* marks translations which have irregular inflections. The Russian-English side of the dictionary gives inflectional information.

(оживлён); (*weather*) прохла́дный* (прохла́ден).
Bremen ['breımən] *n* Бре́мен.
Breton ['brɛtən] *adj* брето́нский ◆ *n* брето́нец*(-нка*).
brevity ['brɛvıtı] *n* кра́ткость *f*.
brew [bru:] *vt* (*tea*) зава́ривать (завари́ть* *perf*); (*beer*) вари́ть* (свари́ть* *perf*) ◆ *vi* (*tea*) зава́риваться (завари́ться *perf*); (*beer*) броди́ть* (вы́бродить* *perf*); (*storm*) надвига́ться (надви́нуться *perf*); (*fig*: *trouble*) назрева́ть (назре́ть *perf*).
brewer ['bru:əʳ] *n* пивова́р.
brewery ['bru:ərı] *n* пивова́ренный заво́д.
briar ['braıəʳ] *n* (*thorny bush*) колю́чий* куста́рник; (*wild rose*) шипо́вник.
bribe [braıb] *n* взя́тка*, по́дкуп ◆ *vt* (*person*) подкупа́ть (подкупи́ть* *perf*), дава́ть* (дать* *perf*) взя́тку; **to ~ sb to do** подкупа́ть (подкупи́ть* *perf*) кого́-н +*infin*.
bribery ['braıbərı] *n* по́дкуп.
bric-a-brac ['brıkəbræk] *n* безделу́шки* *fpl*.
brick [brık] *n* кирпи́ч*; (*of ice cream*) брике́т.
bricklayer ['brıkleıəʳ] *n* ка́менщик.
brickwork ['brıkwə:k] *n* (кирпи́чная) кла́дка.
bridal ['braıdl] *adj* подвене́чный, сва́дебный.
bride [braıd] *n* неве́ста.
bridegroom ['braıdgru:m] *n* жени́х*.
bridesmaid ['braıdzmeıd] *n* подру́жка* неве́сты.
bridge [brıdʒ] *n* (*TECH, ARCHIT, DENTISTRY*) мост*; (*NAUT*) капита́нский* мо́стик; (*CARDS*) бридж; (*of nose*) перено́сица ◆ *vt* (*fig*: *gap, gulf*) преодолева́ть (преодоле́ть *perf*); **to ~ a river** стро́ить (постро́ить *perf*) мост че́рез ре́ку.
bridging loan ['brıdʒıŋ-] *n* (*BRIT*: *COMM*) промежу́точный заём.
bridle ['braıdl] *n* узде́чка*, узда́ ◆ *vt* (*horse*) взну́здывать (взнузда́ть *perf*) ◆ *vi*: **to ~ at** взвива́ться (взви́ться* *perf*) на дыбы́, возмуща́ться (возмути́ться* *perf*).
bridle path *n* верхова́я тропа́*.
brief [bri:f] *adj* (*period of time*) коро́ткий* (ко́роток); (*description*) кра́ткий* (кра́ток) ◆ *n* (*LAW*) изложе́ние де́ла; (*task*) зада́ние ◆ *vt* (*inform*) знако́мить* (ознако́мить* *perf*) с +*instr*; (*MIL etc*): **to ~ sb (about)** инструкти́ровать (проинструкти́ровать *perf*) кого́-н (о +*prp*); **~s** *npl* (*for men*) трусы́ *pl*; (*for women*) тру́сики *pl*; **in ~ ...** вкра́тце ....
briefcase ['bri:fkeıs] *n* портфе́ль *m*.
briefing ['bri:fıŋ] *n* инструкта́ж; (*PRESS*) бри́финг.
briefly ['bri:flı] *adv* (*glance, smile*) бе́гло; (*visit*) на коро́ткое вре́мя; (*explain*) вкра́тце; **to glimpse ~** бро́сать (бро́сить* *perf*) бе́глый взгляд.
Brig. *abbr* = **brigadier**.
brigade [brı'geıd] *n* (*MIL*) брига́да.
brigadier [brıgə'dıəʳ] *n* бригади́р.
bright [braıt] *adj* (*light, colour*) я́ркий* (я́рок); (*room, future*) све́тлый* (све́тел); (*clever*: *person, idea*) блестя́щий*; (*lively*: *person*) живо́й*, весёлый*; **to look on the ~ side** ви́деть* (*impf*) све́тлую сто́рону.
brighten ['braıtn] *vt* (*also*: **~ up**: *room, event*) оживля́ть (оживи́ть* *perf*); (: *person*) ра́довать (обра́довать *perf*) ◆ *vi* (*weather*) проясня́ться (проясни́ться *perf*); (*person*) оживля́ться (оживи́ться* *perf*); (*face*) светле́ть (просветле́ть *perf*); (*prospects*) улучша́ться (улу́чшиться *perf*).
brightly ['braıtlı] *adv* (*shine*) я́рко; (*smile, talk*) ра́достно.
brill [brıl] (*inf*) *adj* здо́рово.
brilliance ['brıljəns] *n* блеск, я́ркость *f*; (*fig*: *of person*) гениа́льность *f*.
brilliant ['brıljənt] *adj* блестя́щий* (блестя́щ); (*sunshine, light*) я́ркий* (я́рок); (*inf*: *holiday etc*) великоле́пный* (великоле́пен).
brilliantly ['brıljəntlı] *adv* (*see adj*) блестя́ще; я́рко.
brim [brım] *n* (*of cup*) край; (*of hat*) поля́ *ntpl*.
brimful ['brım'ful] *adj*: **~ (of)** по́лный (по́лон) до краёв (+*gen*); (*fig*) перепо́лненный (перепо́лнен) (+*instr*).
brine [braın] *n* (*CULIN*) рассо́л.
bring [brıŋ] (*pt, pp* **brought**) *vt* (*thing*) приноси́ть* (принести́* *perf*); (*person*: *on foot*) приводи́ть* (привести́* *perf*); (: *by transport*) привози́ть* (привезти́* *perf*); (*fig*: *satisfaction, trouble*) доставля́ть (доста́вить* *perf*); **to ~ sth to an end** поко́нчить (*perf*) с чем-н; **I can't ~ myself to tell him** я не могу́ заста́вить себя́ сообщи́ть ему́
▸ **bring about** *vt* (*cause*: *unintentionally*) вызыва́ть (вы́звать* *perf*), порожда́ть (породи́ть *perf*); (: *intentionally*) осуществля́ть (осуществи́ть* *perf*)
▸ **bring back** *vt* (*restore*) возрожда́ть (возроди́ть* *perf*); (*return*) возвраща́ть (возврати́ть* *perf*), верну́ть (*perf*)
▸ **bring down** *vt* (*government*) сверга́ть (све́ргнуть* *perf*); (*plane*) сбива́ть (сбить* *perf*); (*price*) снижа́ть (сни́зить* *perf*)
▸ **bring forward** *vt* (*meeting*) переноси́ть* (перенести́* *perf*) на бо́лее ра́нний срок; (*proposal*) выдвига́ть (вы́двинуть *perf*); (*BOOKKEEPING*) переноси́ть* (перенести́* *perf*) на сле́дующую страни́цу
▸ **bring in** *vt* (*money*) приноси́ть* (принести́* *perf*); (*person, legislation*) вводи́ть* (ввести́* *perf*); (*verdict*) выноси́ть* (вы́нести* *perf*)
▸ **bring off** *vt* (*task, plan*) исполня́ть (испо́лнить *perf*); (*deal*) заключа́ть (заключи́ть *perf*)
▸ **bring out** *vt* вынима́ть (вы́нуть *perf*); (*meaning*) выявля́ть (вы́явить* *perf*); (*publish*) выпуска́ть (вы́пустить* *perf*)
▸ **bring round** *vt* (*MED*) приводи́ть* (привести́* *perf*) в чу́вство

▸ **bring up** *vt* (*carry up*) приносить* (принести* *perf*) наверх; (*educate*) воспитывать (воспитать *perf*); (*question*) поднимать (поднять* *perf*); (*vomit*): **he brought up his food** его стошнило.
bring and buy sale *n благотворительная перепродажа вещей между её организаторами.*
brink [brɪŋk] *n* (*of disaster, war etc*) грань *f*; **on the ~ of doing** чуть не *+infin*; **she was on the ~ of tears** она еле сдерживала слёзы.
brisk [brɪsk] *adj* (*tone*) отрывистый (отрывист); (*person, trade*) оживлённый* (оживлён); **business is ~** дела идут полным ходом.
bristle ['brɪsl] *n* щетина ◆ *vi* (*in anger*) щетиниться (ощетиниться *perf*); **bristling with** полный (полон) *+instr or +gen.*
bristly ['brɪslɪ] *adj* щетинистый; **your chin's all ~** у тебя подбородок щетинистый.
Brit [brɪt] *n abbr* (*inf*: = *British person*) британец*(-нка*).
Britain ['brɪtən] *n* (*also*: **Great ~**) Британия; **in ~** в Британии.
British ['brɪtɪʃ] *adj* британский*; **the ~** *npl* британцы* *mpl.*
British Isles *npl*: **the ~ ~** Британские острова* *mpl.*
British Rail *n* Британская железная дорога.
British Summer Time *n* Британское летнее время* *nt.*
Briton ['brɪtən] *n* британец*(-нка*).
Brittany ['brɪtənɪ] *n* Бретань *f.*
brittle ['brɪtl] *adj* хрупкий* (хрупок), ломкий* (ломок).
Bro. *abbr* (REL) = **brother.**
broach [brəutʃ] *vt* (*subject*) поднимать (поднять *perf*) вопрос о *+prp.*
broad [brɔ:d] *adj* (*wide*) широкий* (широк); (*general*) общий*; (*strong*) сильный* ◆ *n* (*US*: *inf*) баба; **in ~ daylight** средь бела дня; **~ hint** прозрачный намёк.
broad bean *n* фасоль *f no pl.*
broadcast ['brɔ:dkɑ:st] (*pt, pp* **broadcast**) *n* (RADIO) (радио)передача; (TV) (теле)передача ◆ *vt* (RADIO) передавать* (передать* *perf*) по радио, транслировать *(impf)*; (TV) передавать* (передать* *perf*) по телевидению, транслировать *(impf)* ◆ *vi* транслироваться *(impf).*
broadcaster ['brɔ:dkɑ:stə'] *n* (RADIO) радио-журналист; (TV) теле-журналист.
broadcasting ['brɔ:dkɑ:stɪŋ] *n* (RADIO) радиовещание; (TV) телевещание.
broadcasting station *n* (RADIO) радиостанция; (TV) телестанция.
broaden ['brɔ:dn] *vt* расширять (расширить *perf*) ◆ *vi* расширяться (расшириться *perf*); **to ~ one's horizons** расширять (расширить *perf*) свой кругозор.
broadly ['brɔ:dlɪ] *adv* вообще.
broad-minded ['brɔ:d'maɪndɪd] *adj* с широкими взглядами.
broadsheet ['brɔ:dʃi:t] *n* (*advertisement*) рекламный плакат *or* рекламная афиша; (*newspaper*) *газета, отпечатанная на одном развёрнутом листе бумаги.*
broccoli ['brɔkəlɪ] *n* брокколи *nt ind.*
brochure ['brəuʃjuə'] *n* брошюра.
brogue [brəug] *n* (*accent*) провинциальный акцент (*особенно ирландский или шотландский*); (*shoe*) башмак.
broil [brɔɪl] *vt* жарить (зажарить *perf*).
broiler ['brɔɪlə'] *n* бройлер.
broke [brəuk] *pt of* **break** ◆ *adj* (*inf*) прогоревший; **to go ~** прогорать (прогореть *perf*).
broken ['brəukn] *pp of* **break** ◆ *adj* (*window, cup etc*) разбитый (разбит); (*machine*) сломанный (сломан); (*promise, vow*) нарушенный (нарушен); **a ~ leg** сломанная нога*; **a ~ marriage** распавшийся брак; **a ~ home** неблагополучная семья; **in ~ English/Russian** на ломаном английском/русском.
broken-down ['brəukn'daun] *adj* (*car*) сломанный (сломан); (*house*) полуразрушенный.
broken-hearted ['brəukn'hɑ:tɪd] *adj* убитый горем, с разбитым сердцем.
broker ['brəukə'] *n* (COMM: *in shares*) брокер; (: *in insurance*) страховой агент.
brokerage ['brəukrɪdʒ] *n* (COMM: *commission*) брокераж; (: *business*) брокерское агентство.
brolly ['brɔlɪ] *n* (BRIT: *inf*) зонт.
bronchitis [brɔŋ'kaɪtɪs] *n* бронхит.
bronze [brɔnz] *n* (*metal*) бронза; (*sculpture*) бронзовая скульптура.
bronzed [brɔnzd] *adj* (*person, body*) загорелый, бронзовый.
brooch [brəutʃ] *n* брошь *f.*
brood [bru:d] *n* выводок* ◆ *vi* (*hen*) сидеть* (*impf*) на яйцах; (*person*) размышлять *(impf)*
▸ **brood on** *or* **over** *vt fus* грустить* *(impf) or* размышлять *(impf)* о *+prp.*
broody ['bru:dɪ] *adj* (*thoughtful, moody*) угрюмый (угрюм); **~ hen** наседка*.
brook [bruk] *n* ручей*.
broom [brum] *n* метла*; (BOT) ракитник.
broomstick ['brumstɪk] *n* (*broom handle*) ручка метлы.
Bros. *abbr* (COMM: = *brothers*) братья* *mpl.*
broth [brɔθ] *n* похлёбка*.
brothel ['brɔθl] *n* публичный дом*, бордель *m.*
brother ['brʌðə'] *n* (*also* REL) брат*; (*in association*) собрат*.

* marks translations which have irregular inflections. The Russian-English side of the dictionary gives inflectional information.

brotherhood ['brʌðəhud] *n* брáтство.
brother-in-law ['brʌðərɪn'lɔ:] *n* (*sister's husband*) зять* *m*; (*wife's brother*) шýрин*; (*husband's brother*) дéверь* *m*.
brotherly ['brʌðəlɪ] *adj* брáтский*.
brought [brɔ:t] *pt, pp of* **bring**.
brought forward *adj* перенесённый на слéдующую страни́цу.
brow [brau] *n* (*forehead*) лоб*, челó*; (*also:* **eyebrow**) бровь *f*; (*of hill*) гребень *m*.
browbeat ['braubi:t] *vt*: **to ~ sb (into doing)** запýгивать (запугáть *perf*) когó-н (для тогó, чтóбы *+infin*).
brown [braun] *adj* кори́чневый; (*hair*) каштáновый; (*eyes*) кáрий*; (*tanned*) загорéлый ◆ *n* (*colour*) кори́чневый цвет ◆ *vt* (*CULIN*) подрумя́нивать (подрумя́нить *perf*); **to go ~** (*person*) загорáть (загорéть *perf*); (*leaves*) желтéть (пожелтéть *perf*).
brown bread *n* чёрный хлеб.
Brownie ['braunɪ] *n* (*also:* **~ Guide**) *млáдшая дéвочка-скáут*.
brownie ['braunɪ] *n* (*US*: *cake*) *шоколáдное пирóжное с орéхами*.
brown paper *n* обёрточная бумáга.
brown rice *n* неочи́щенный рис.
brown sugar *n* неочи́щенный сáхар.
browse [brauz] *vi* (*in shop*) рассмáтривать (*impf*), разгля́дывать (*impf*); (*animal*) питáться (*impf*) поднóжным кóрмом ◆ *n*: **to have a ~ (around)** рассмáтривать (*impf*) *or* разгля́дывать (*impf*); **to ~ through a book** проли́стывать (пролистáть *perf*) кни́гу.
browser ['brauzəʳ] *n* (*COMPUT*) брáузер.
bruise [bru:z] *n* (*on face etc*) синя́к*; (*on fruit*) вмя́тина ◆ *vt* ушибáть (ушиби́ть* *perf*); (*fruit*) помя́ть* (*perf*) ◆ *vi* (*fruit*) помя́ться* (*perf*).
bruising ['bru:zɪŋ] *n* синяки́* *mpl*.
Brummie ['brʌmɪ] *n* (*inf*) бирмингéмец(-емка).
brunch [brʌntʃ] *n* пóздний* зáвтрак.
brunette [bru:'nɛt] *n* брюнéтка*.
brunt [brʌnt] *n*: **to bear the ~ of** принимáть (приня́ть* *perf*) на себя́ основнóй удáр *+gen*.
brush [brʌʃ] *n* (*for cleaning*) щётка*; (*for painting*) кисть* *f*; (*for shaving*) помазóк*; (*quarrel*) столкновéние ◆ *vt* (*sweep*) подметáть (подмести́* *perf*); (*groom*) чи́стить* (почи́стить* *perf*) щёткой; (*also:* **~ against**) слегкá задевáть (задéть* *perf*); **to have a ~ with sb** (*verbally*) вздóрить (повздóрить *perf*) с кéм-н; (*physically*) дрáться* (подрáться* *perf*) с кéм-н; **to have a ~ with the police** имéть (*impf*) столкновéние с поли́цией
▸ **brush aside** *vt* (*criticism, emotion*) отметáть (отмести́ *perf*)
▸ **brush past** *vt* проноси́ться* (пронести́сь* *perf*) ми́мо *+gen*
▸ **brush up** *vt* (*subject, language*) шлифовáть (отшлифовáть *perf*); (*knowledge*) освежáть (освежи́ть *perf*).
brushed [brʌʃt] *adj* (*steel, chrome etc*) мáтовый; (*nylon, denim etc*) ворси́стый.
brush-off ['brʌʃɔf] *n* (*inf*): **to give sb the ~** отбривáть (отбри́ть* *perf*) когó-н.
brushwood ['brʌʃwud] *n* хвóрост.
brusque [bru:sk] *adj* бесцеремóнный*.
Brussels ['brʌslz] *n* Брюссéль *m*.
Brussels sprout *n* брюссéльская капýста.
brutal ['bru:tl] *adj* (*person*) жестóкий*; (*actions*) звéрский*; (*honesty, frankness*) жёсткий*.
brutality [bru:'tælɪtɪ] *n* (*see adj*) жестóкость *f*; звéрство.
brutalize ['bru:təlaɪz] *vt* ожесточáть (ожесточи́ть *perf*).
brute [bru:t] *n* зверь* *m* ◆ *adj*: **by ~ force** грýбой си́лой.
brutish ['bru:tɪʃ] *adj* звéрский*, скóтский*.
BS *n abbr* (*US*: = *Bachelor of Science*) ≈ бакалáвр естéственных наýк.
bs *abbr* = **bill of sale**.
BSA *n abbr* (= *Boy Scouts of America*) Сою́з америкáнских бойскáутов.
BSE *n abbr* (= *bovine spongiform encephalopathy*) энцефалопáтия крýпного рогáтого скотá.
BSc *abbr* (= *Bachelor of Science*) ≈ бакалáвр естéственных наýк.
BSI *n abbr* (= *British Standards Institution*) Бритáнский* институ́т стандáртов.
BST *abbr* = *British Summer Time*.
Bt. *abbr* (*BRIT*) = **Bart**.
btu *n abbr* (= *British thermal unit*) бритáнская теплова́я едини́ца.
bubble ['bʌbl] *n* пузы́рь* *m* ◆ *vi* (*liquid*) пéниться (вспéниться *perf*); (*fig*): **to ~ with laughter** заливáться (*impf*) смéхом.
bubble bath *n* пéнистая вáнна.
bubble gum *n* жевáтельная рези́нка (*образýющая пузыри́*).
bubblejet printer ['bʌbldʒɛt-] *n тип компью́терного при́нтера*.
bubble pack *n* бли́стерная упакóвка*.
bubbly ['bʌblɪ] *adj* (*inf*: *girl*) живóй; (*mineral water*) шипу́чий*, газирóванный ◆ *n* (*inf*) шипу́чка*.
Bucharest [bu:kə'rɛst] *n* Бухарéст.
buck [bʌk] *n* (*rabbit*) крóлик; (*deer*) самéц* оленя́; (*US*: *inf*) бакс ◆ *vi* (*horse*) брыкáться (*impf*); **to pass the ~ (to sb)** переклáдывать (переложи́ть *perf*) отвéтственность (на когó-н)
▸ **buck up** *vi* (*cheer up*) встряхнýться (*perf*); (*hurry up*) пошевéливаться (*impf*) ◆ *vt*: **to ~ one's ideas up** исправля́ться (испрáвиться* *perf*).
bucket ['bʌkɪt] *n* ведрó* ◆ *vi* (*BRIT*: *inf*): **the rain is ~ing (down)** дождь льёт как из ведрá.
buckle ['bʌkl] *n* пря́жка* ◆ *vt* (*shoe, belt*) застёгивать (застегнýть *perf*); (*wheel*) деформи́ровать (*impf/perf*) ◆ *vi* (*wheel*) деформи́роваться (*impf/perf*); (*bridge,

support) прогибáться (прогнýться *perf*) (*knees, legs*) подгибáться (подогнýться *perf*)
▸ **buckle down** *vi*: **to ~ down (to sth)** засéсть* *(perf)* (за что-н).
Bucks [bʌks] *abbr* (*BRIT*: *POST*) = *Buckinghamshire*.
bud [bʌd] *n* (*of tree*) пóчка*; (*of flower*) бутóн ◆ *vi* (*flower*) распускáться (распусти́ться* *perf*); **the trees are ~ding** на дерéвьях распускáются пóчки; **to nip in the ~** пресекáть (пресéчь* *perf*) в кóрне.
Budapest [bju:də'pɛst] *n* Будапéшт.
Buddha ['budə] *n* Бýдда *m*.
Buddhism ['budɪzəm] *n* будди́зм.
Buddhist ['budɪst] *adj* будди́йский ◆ *n* будди́ст.
budding ['bʌdɪŋ] *adj* подаю́щий надéжды.
buddy ['bʌdɪ] *n* (*US*) приятель *m*.
budge [bʌdʒ] *vt* (*object*) сдвигáть (сдви́нуть *perf*) (с мéста); (*fig*: *person*) заставля́ть (застáвить* *perf*) уступи́ть* ◆ *vi* сдви́нуться *(perf)* (с мéста).
budgerigar ['bʌdʒərɪgɑ:'] *n* волни́стый попугáйчик.
budget ['bʌdʒɪt] *n* бюджéт ◆ *vi*: **to ~ for sth** ассигновáть *(impf/perf) or* отклáдывать (отложи́ть *perf*) дéньги на что-н; **I'm on a tight ~** у меня́ тýго с финáнсами; **she works out her ~ every month** онá рассчи́тывает свой бюджéт кáждый мéсяц.
budgie ['bʌdʒɪ] *n* = **budgerigar**.
Buenos Aires ['bweɪnəs'aɪrɪz] *n* Буэ́нос-А́йрес.
buff [bʌf] *adj* кори́чневый ◆ *n* (*inf*: *enthusiast*) знатóк*.
buffalo ['bʌfələu] (*pl* ~ *or* ~**es**) *n* (*BRIT*) бýйвол; (*US*: *bison*) бизóн.
buffer ['bʌfə'] *n* бýфер*.
buffering ['bʌfərɪŋ] *n* (*COMPUT*) буферизáция, испóльзование бýфера.
buffer state *n* бýферное госудáрство.
buffer zone *n* бýферная зóна.
buffet[1] ['bufeɪ] *n* (*BRIT*: *in station*) буфéт; (*food*) швéдский* стол*.
buffet[2] ['bʌfɪt] *vt* (*subj*: *wind, sea*) трепáть* *(perf)*, швыря́ть *(impf)*.
buffet car *n* (*BRIT*: *RAIL*) вагóн-ресторáн.
buffet lunch *n* швéдский* стол*.
buffoon [bə'fu:n] *n* фигля́р.
bug [bʌg] *n* (*esp US*: *insect*) насекóмое *nt adj*; (*COMPUT*: *of program*) оши́бка*; (*fig*: *germ*) ви́рус, зарáза; (*hidden microphone*) микрофóн, подслýшивающее устрóйство ◆ *vt* (*inf*: *annoy*) раздражáть (раздражи́ть *perf*); (: *bother*) надоедáть (надоéсть* *perf*) +*dat*; (*room etc*) прослýшивать *(impf)*; **I've got the travel ~** (*fig*) я помéшан на путешéствиях.
bugbear ['bʌgbɛə'] *n* проблéма.
bugger ['bʌgə'] (*inf!*) *n* свóлочь *m/f* (*!*) ◆ *vb*: **~ off!** кати́сь отсю́да! (*!*); **~ (it)!** твою́ мать! (*!*)
buggy ['bʌgɪ] *n* (*also:* **baby ~**) складнáя дéтская коля́ска*.
bugle ['bju:gl] *n* горн.
build [bɪld] (*pt, pp* **built**) *n* (*of person*) телосложéние ◆ *vt* стрóить (пострóить *perf*)
▸ **build on** *vt fus* (*fig*) пóльзоваться (воспóльзоваться *perf*) +*instr*
▸ **build up** *vt* (*forces, production*) наращивать *(impf)*; (*morale*) укрепля́ть (укрепи́ть* *perf*); (*stocks*) накáпливать (накопи́ть* *perf*); (*business*) создавáть* (создáть* *perf*); **don't ~ your hopes up too soon** не рáдуйтесь рáньше врéмени.
builder ['bɪldə'] *n* строи́тель *m*.
building ['bɪldɪŋ] *n* (*industry, construction*) строи́тельство; (*structure*) строéние; (: *residential, offices*) здáние.
building contractor *n* строи́тельный подря́дчик.
building industry *n* строи́тельная промы́шленность *f*.
building site *n* строи́тельный учáсток*.
building society *n* (*BRIT*) ≈ строи́тельно-сберегáтельная кáсса.
building trade *n* = **building industry**.
build-up ['bɪldʌp] *n* (*of gas etc*) скоплéние; (*publicity*): **to give sb/sth a good ~** обеспéчивать (обеспéчить *perf*) комý-н/ чемý-н хорóшую реклáму.
built [bɪlt] *pt, pp of* **build** ◆ *adj*: **~-in** встрóенный; **well-~ person** хорошó сложённый* человéк.
built-in obsolescence ['bɪltɪn-] *n* заплани́рованное устаревáние.
built-up area ['bɪltʌp-] *n* застрóенный райóн.
bulb [bʌlb] *n* (*BOT*) лýковица; (*ELEC*) лáмпа, лáмпочка*.
bulbous ['bʌlbəs] *adj* пузáтый (пузáт); (*nose*) тóлстый (толст).
Bulgaria [bʌl'gɛərɪə] *n* Болгáрия.
Bulgarian [bʌl'gɛərɪən] *adj* болгáрский* ◆ *n* болгáрин*(-рка*); (*LING*) болгáрский* язы́к*.
bulge [bʌldʒ] *n* (*bump*) вы́пуклость *f*; (*in birth rate*) врéменное увеличéние ◆ *vi* (*stomach*) выпя́чиваться (вы́пятиться* *perf*); (*pocket, file*) трещáть *(impf)* по швам; **her purse is bulging with money** её кошелёк наби́т деньгáми.
bulimia [bə'lɪmɪə] *n* булими́я.
bulimic [bə'li:mɪk] *adj*: **she is ~** онá страдáет булими́ей.
bulk [bʌlk] *n* громáда; **in ~** óптом; **the ~ of** бóльшая часть +*gen*.
bulk buying [-'baɪɪŋ] *n* оптóвая закýпка*.
bulk carrier *n* грузовóе сýдно, сухогрýз.
bulkhead ['bʌlkhɛd] *n* перегорóдка.
bulky ['bʌlkɪ] *adj* громóздкий* (громóздок).

* marks translations which have irregular inflections. The Russian-English side of the dictionary gives inflectional information.

bull [bul] *n* (*ZOOL*) бык*; (*male: whale*) саме́ц* кита́; (: *elephant*) слон; (*STOCK EXCHANGE*) *спекуля́нт, игра́ющий* на повыше́ние на би́рже*; (*REL*) бу́лла.
bulldog ['buldɔg] *n* бульдо́г.
bulldoze ['buldəuz] *vt* (*flatten*) расчища́ть (расчи́стить* *perf*) бульдо́зером; (*knock down*) лома́ть (слома́ть *perf*) бульдо́зером; **I was ~d into it** (*fig: inf*) меня́ заста́вили сде́лать э́то.
bulldozer ['buldəuzə'] *n* бульдо́зер.
bullet ['bulɪt] *n* пу́ля.
bulletin ['bulɪtɪn] *n*: **news ~** сво́дка* новосте́й; (*journal*) бюллете́нь *m*.
bulletin board *n* (*COMPUT*) электро́нная доска́ объявле́ний.
bulletproof ['bulɪtpru:f] *adj* пулене-пробива́емый.
bullfight ['bulfaɪt] *n* бой* быко́в.
bullfighter ['bulfaɪtə'] *n* тореадо́р.
bullfighting ['bulfaɪtɪŋ] *n* бой быко́в.
bullion ['buljən] *n* сли́ток*.
bullock ['bulək] *n* вол*.
bullring ['bulrɪŋ] *n* аре́на (*на кото́рой происхо́дит бой быко́в*)
bull's-eye ['bulzaɪ] *n* (*on a target*) я́блоко* мише́ни.
bullshit ['bulʃɪt] (*inf!*) *n* бред (соба́чий) (*!*) ◆ *vt* нести́* (*impf*) бред (*!*)
bully ['bulɪ] *n* зади́ра *m/f* ◆ *vt* трави́ть* (затрави́ть* *perf*); (*frighten*) запу́гивать (запуга́ть *perf*).
bullying ['bulɪɪŋ] *n* тра́вля, запу́гивание.
bum [bʌm] *n* (*inf: backside*) за́дница; (*esp US: tramp*) бродя́га *m/f*; (: *good-for-nothing*) безде́льник
▸ **bum around** *vi* (*inf*) шата́ться (*impf*).
bumblebee ['bʌmblbi:] *n* шмель* *m*.
bumf [bʌmf] *n* (*inf*) бума́жки* *fpl*.
bump [bʌmp] *n* (*minor accident*) столкнове́ние; (*jolt*) толчо́к; (*swelling*) ши́шка; (*on road*) уха́б ◆ *vt* (*strike*) ударя́ть (уда́рить *perf*); (*dent*) помя́ть* (*perf*); **he ~ed his head on the door** он уда́рился *or* сту́кнулся голово́й о дверь
▸ **bump along** *vi* трясти́сь* (*impf*) по *+dat*
▸ **bump into** *vt fus* ната́лкиваться (натолкну́ться *perf*) на *+acc*.
bumper ['bʌmpə'] *n* (*AUT*) ба́мпер ◆ *adj*: **~ crop** *or* **harvest** небыва́лый урожа́й.
bumper cars *npl* (*US*) аттракцио́нный электромоби́ль *m*.
bumper sticker *n* накле́йка на ба́мпер.
bumph [bʌmf] *n* = **bumf**.
bumptious ['bʌmpʃəs] *adj* самоуве́ренный (самоуве́рен).
bumpy ['bʌmpɪ] *adj* уха́бистый; **it was a ~ flight** нас всю доро́гу трясло́.
bun [bʌn] *n* (*CULIN*) сдо́бная бу́лка*; (*of hair*) у́зел*.
bunch [bʌntʃ] *n* (*of flowers*) буке́т; (*of keys*) свя́зка*; (*of bananas*) гроздь *f*; (*of people*) компа́ния; **~es** *npl* (*in hair*) хво́стики *mpl*; **~ of grapes** гроздь *or* кисть* *f* виногра́да.
bundle ['bʌndl] *n* (*of clothes*) у́зел*; (*of sticks*) вяза́нка*; (*of papers*) па́чка* ◆ *vt* (*also*: **~ up**) свя́зывать (связа́ть* *perf*) в у́зел; (*put*): **to ~ sth/sb into** зата́лкивать (затолкну́ть *perf*) что-н/кого́-н в *+acc*
▸ **bundle off** *vt* отсыла́ть (отосла́ть* *perf*)
▸ **bundle out** *vt* бы́стро уходи́ть* (уйти́* *perf*).
bun fight *n* (*BRIT: inf: official function*) банке́т; (: *tea party*) чаепи́тие.
bung [bʌŋ] *n* про́бка* ◆ *vt* (*BRIT: throw*) запи́хивать (запиха́ть *perf*); (*also*: **~ up**: *pipe, hole*) затыка́ть (заткну́ть *perf*); **my nose is ~ed up** у меня́ зало́жен нос.
bungalow ['bʌŋgələu] *n* бунга́ло *nt ind*.
bungee jumping ['bʌndʒi:'dʒʌmpɪŋ] *n* *прыжки́ с высоты́ вниз голово́й, в кото́рых челове́к привя́зан за но́ги к эласти́чному кана́ту*.
bungle ['bʌŋgl] *vt* зава́ливать (завали́ть *perf*).
bunion ['bʌnjən] *n* нато́птыш.
bunk [bʌŋk] *n* (*bed*) ко́йка.
bunk beds *npl* двухъя́русная крова́ть *fsg*.
bunker ['bʌŋkə'] *n* бу́нкер*; (*GOLF*) я́ма с песко́м (*на по́ле для го́льфа*).
bunny ['bʌnɪ] *n* (*also*: **~ rabbit**) за́йчик.
bunny girl *n* (*BRIT*) *официа́нтка ночно́го клу́ба, в облега́ющем костю́ме с кро́личьим хвосто́м и уша́ми*.
bunny hill *n* (*US: SKIING*) лягуша́тник.
bunting ['bʌntɪŋ] *n* флажки́ *mpl*.
buoy [bɔɪ] *n* буй*, ба́кен
▸ **buoy up** *vt* (*fig*) подба́дривать (подбодри́ть *perf*).
buoyancy ['bɔɪənsɪ] *n* плаву́честь *f*.
buoyant ['bɔɪənt] *adj* (*ship*) плаву́чий*; (*economy, market*) оживлённый* (оживлён); (*prices, currency*) твёрдый; (*fig: person*) жизнера́достный* (жизнера́достен).
burden ['bə:dn] *n* (*responsibility*) бре́мя* *nt*; (*load*) но́ша ◆ *vt* (*trouble*): **to ~ sb with** обременя́ть (обремени́ть *perf*) кого́-н *+instr*; **to be a ~ to sb** быть* (*impf*) в тя́гость кому́-н.
bureau ['bjuərəu] (*pl* **~x**) *n* (*BRIT*) бюро́ *nt ind*; (*US*) комо́д.
bureaucracy [bjuə'rɔkrəsɪ] *n* (*POL, COMM*) бюрокра́тия; (*system*) бюрократи́зм.
bureaucrat ['bjuərəkræt] *n* бюрокра́т.
bureaucratic [bjuərə'krætɪk] *adj* бюрократи́ческий*.
bureaux ['bjuərəuz] *npl of* **bureau**.
burgeon ['bə:dʒən] *vi* (*fig*) расцвета́ть (расцвести́* *perf*).
burger ['bə:gə'] *n* бу́ргер.
burglar ['bə:glə'] *n* взло́мщик.
burglar alarm *n* сигнализа́ция.
burglarize ['bə:gləraɪz] *vt* (*US*) соверша́ть (соверши́ть *perf*) кра́жу со взло́мом.
burglary ['bə:glərɪ] *n* (*crime*) кра́жа со взло́мом; (*act*) взлом.

burgle ['bə:gl] *vt* совершáть (совершúть *perf*) крáжу со взлóмом.
Burgundy ['bə:gəndɪ] *n* (*GEO*) Бургýндия.
burial ['bɛrɪəl] *n* погребéние, пóхороны *pl*.
burial ground *n* мéсто* погребéния.
burlesque [bə:'lɛsk] *n* парóдия.
burly ['bə:lɪ] *adj* дю́жий.
Burma ['bə:mə] *n* Бúрма.
Burmese [bə:'mi:z] *adj* бирмáнский ◆ *n inv* бирмáнец*(-нка*); (*LING*) бирмáнский язы́к*.
burn [bə:n] (*pt, pp* **burned** *or* **burnt**) *vt* жечь* (сжечь* *perf*), сжигáть (сжечь* *perf*); (*arson*) поджигáть (поджéчь* *perf*) ◆ *vi* (*house, wood*) горéть (сгорéть *perf*), сгорáть (сгорéть *perf*); (*cakes*) подгорáть (подгорéть *perf*) ◆ *n* ожóг; **the cigarette ~t a hole in her dress** сигарéта прожглá ды́рку в её плáтье; **she always ~s the meat** у неё всегдá подгорáет мя́со; **I've ~t myself!** я обжёгся!
▸ **burn down** *vt* сжигáть (сжéчь* *perf*) дотлá
▸ **burn out** *vt*: **to ~ o.s. out** вымáтываться (вы́мотаться *perf*); **the fire ~t itself out** огóнь догорéл.
burner ['bə:nə^r] *n* горéлка*.
burning ['bə:nɪŋ] *adj* (*building, forest*) горя́щий; (*sand, desert*) раскалённый; (*issue, ambition*) жгýчий*.
burnish ['bə:nɪʃ] *vt* полировáть (отполировáть *perf*).
burnt [bə:nt] *pt, pp of* **burn**.
burnt sugar *n* (*BRIT*) жжёный сáхар.
burp [bə:p] *n* отры́жка* ◆ *vt*: **to ~ a baby** вызывáть (вы́звать* *perf*) отры́жку у ребёнка ◆ *vi* отры́гивать (отрыгнýть *perf*).
burrow ['bʌrəu] *n* норá* ◆ *vi* (*dig*) рыть* (вы́рыть* *perf*) норý; (*rummage*) ры́ться* (*impf*).
bursar ['bə:sə^r] *n* казначéй.
bursary ['bə:sərɪ] *n* (*BRIT*) стипéндия.
burst [bə:st] (*pt, pp* **burst**) *vt* (*bag etc*) разрывáть (разорвáть* *perf*) ◆ *vi* (*pipe*) прорывáться (прорвáться* *perf*); (*tyre, balloon*) лóпаться (лóпнуть *perf*) ◆ *n* (*of gunfire*) залп; (*of shelling*) разры́в; (*also:* **~ pipe**) проры́в; **the river has ~ its banks** рекá вы́шла из берегóв; **to ~ into flames** вспы́хивать (вспы́хнуть *perf*); **to ~ into tears** распла́каться* (*perf*); **to ~ out laughing** расхохотáться* (*perf*); **to ~ into a room** врывáться (ворвáться* *perf*) в кóмнату; **~ blood vessel** разóрванный кровенóсный сосýд; **the room is/was ~ing with people** кóмната наби́та/бы́ла наби́та до откáза людьми́; **to be ~ing with** (*pride, anger*) раздувáться (раздýться *perf*) от +*gen*; **a ~ of energy/enthusiasm** прили́в энéргии/энтузиáзма; **~ of laughter/applause** взрыв смéха/рукоплескáний; **~ of machine gun fire** пулемётная óчередь *f*
▸ **burst into** *vt fus* (*room*) врывáться (ворвáться* *perf*)
▸ **burst open** *vi* (*door etc*) распáхиваться (распахнýться *perf*).
bury ['bɛrɪ] *vt* (*object*) зарывáть (зары́ть* *perf*), закáпывать (закопáть *perf*); (*person*) хорони́ть* (похорони́ть* *perf*); **many people were buried in the rubble** мнóго людéй бы́ло зары́то под облóмками; **to ~ one's face in one's hands** пря́тать* (спря́тать* *perf*) лицó в ладóни; **to ~ one's head in the sand** (*fig*) зарывáть (зары́ть* *perf*) гóлову в песóк; **to ~ the hatchet** (*fig*) забывáть (забы́ть* *perf*) раздóры, мири́ться (помири́ться *perf*).
bus [bʌs] *n* автóбус; (*double decker*) (двухэтáжный) автóбус.
bus boy *n* (*US*) *помóщник официáнта, убирáющий гря́зную посýду со столá.*
bush [buʃ] *n* куст*; (*scrubland*) *прострáнства, покры́тые кустáрниками (в Австрáлии и т.п.)*; **to beat about the ~** ходи́ть* (*impf*) вокрýг да óколо.
bushed [buʃt] *adj* (*inf*) вы́мотанный (вы́мотан).
bushel ['buʃl] *n* бýшель *m*.
bush fire *n* леснóй пожáр.
bushy ['buʃɪ] *adj* (*tail*) пуши́стый (пуши́ст); (*hair, eyebrows*) густóй* (густ); (*plant*) кусти́стый.
busily ['bɪzɪlɪ] *adv* (*actively*) делови́то, энерги́чно; **to be ~ doing sth** энерги́чно занимáться (*impf*) чем-н.
business ['bɪznɪs] *n* (*matter*) дéло*; (*trading*) би́знес; (*firm*) предпри́ятие, фи́рма; (*occupation*) заня́тие; **to be away on ~** быть (*impf*) в командирóвке; **I'm here on ~** я здесь по дéлу; **he's in the insurance/transport ~** он рабóтает в страховóм/трáнспортном би́знесе; **to do ~ with sb** имéть (*impf*) делá с кем-н; **it's my ~ to ...** э́то моя́ обя́занность +*infin* ...; **it's none of my ~** э́то не моё дéло; **he means ~** он серьёзно настрóен.
business address *n* áдрес* фи́рмы.
business card *n* визи́тная кáрточка*.
businesslike ['bɪznɪslaɪk] *adj* делови́тый (делови́т).
businessman ['bɪznɪsmən] *irreg n* бизнесмéн.
business trip *n* командирóвка*.
businesswoman ['bɪznɪswumən] *irreg n* жéнщина-бизнесмéн, деловáя жéнщина.
busker ['bʌskə^r] *n* (*BRIT*) ýличный музыкáнт.
bus lane *n* (*BRIT*) *часть дорóги, отведённая для движéния автóбусов.*
bus shelter *n* автóбусная останóвка (*с навéсом*).
bus station *n* автóбусная стáнция, автовокзáл.
bus-stop ['bʌsstɔp] *n* автóбусная останóвка*.

* marks translations which have irregular inflections. The Russian-English side of the dictionary gives inflectional information.

bust [bʌst] *n* (*ANAT*) бюст, грудь* *f*; (*measurement*) объём груди́; (*sculpture*) бюст ◆ *adj* (*inf*: *broken*) сло́манный (сло́ман) ◆ *vt* (*inf*: *arrest*) накрыва́ть (накры́ть* *perf*); **to go ~** (*company etc*) прогора́ть (прогоре́ть *perf*), вылета́ть (вы́лететь* *perf*) в трубу́.
bustle ['bʌsl] *n* (*activity*) сумато́ха, суета́ ◆ *vi* (*person*) суети́ться* (*impf*).
bustling ['bʌslɪŋ] *adj* (*place*) оживлённый, шу́мный*.
bust-up ['bʌstʌp] *n* (*BRIT*: *inf*) сканда́л, ссо́ра.
BUSWE *n abbr* (*BRIT*) = *British Union of Social Work Employees.*
busty ['bʌstɪ] *adj* (*inf*) груда́стый (груда́ст).
busy ['bɪzɪ] *adj* (*person*) занято́й; (*street*) оживлённый (оживлён), шу́мный* (шу́мен); (*TEL*): **the line is ~** ли́ния занята́ ◆ *vt*: **to ~ o.s. with** занима́ть (заня́ть* *perf*) себя́ *+instr*, занима́ться (заня́ться* *perf*) *+instr*; **he's a ~ man** (*normally*) он занято́й челове́к; **he's ~** (*temporarily*) он за́нят; **it's usually a very ~ shop** в э́том магази́не обы́чно мно́го наро́ду.
busybody ['bɪzɪbɔdɪ] *n*: **he is a ~** он суёт нос в чужи́е дела́.
busy signal *n* (*US*: *TEL*) коро́ткие гудки́ *mpl*.

KEYWORD

but [bʌt] *conj* ***1*** (*yet*) но; (: *in contrast*) а; **he's not very bright, but he's hard-working** он не о́чень умён, но усе́рден; **I'm tired but Paul isn't** я уста́л, а Па́вел не уста́л
2 (*however*) но; **I'd love to come, but I'm busy** я бы с удово́льствием пришёл, но я за́нят
3 (*showing disagreement, surprise etc*) но; **but that's fantastic!** но э́то же потряса́юще!
◆ *prep* (*apart from, except*): **no-one but him can do it** никто́, кро́ме него́, не мо́жет э́то сде́лать; **nothing but trouble/bad luck** сплошны́е неприя́тности/неуда́чи; **but for you/your help** е́сли бы не Вы/ва́ша по́мощь; **I'll do anything but that** я сде́лаю всё, что уго́дно, но то́лько не э́то
◆ *adv* (*just, only*): **she's but a child** она́ всего́ лишь ребёнок; **had I but known** е́сли бы то́лько я знал; **I can but try** ну я, коне́чно, могу́ попро́бовать; **the work is all but finished** рабо́та почти́ зако́нчена.

butane ['bju:teɪn] *n* (*also:* **~ gas**) бута́н.
butch [butʃ] *adj* (*pej*: *woman*) мужеподо́бный* (мужеподо́бен); **he's very ~** он (настоя́щий) мужи́к.
butcher ['butʃə'] *n* мясни́к*; (*pej*: *murderer*) пала́ч* ◆ *vt* (*cattle*) бить* (заби́ть* *perf*), ре́зать* (заре́зать* *perf*); (*prisoners*) выреза́ть* (вы́резать* *perf*).
butcher's (shop) ['butʃəz-] *n* мясно́й магази́н.
butler ['bʌtlə'] *n* дворе́цкий *m adj*.
butt [bʌt] *n* (*large barrel*) бо́чка*; (*thick end*) утолщённый коне́ц*; (*of rifle*) прикла́д; (*of pistol*) рукоя́тка; (*of cigarette*) оку́рок*; (*BRIT*: *of teasing*) посме́шище; (: *of criticism*) предме́т; (*US*: *inf!*) за́дница (*!*) ◆ *vt* (*subj*: *goat*) бода́ть (*impf*)
▸ **butt in** *vi* встрева́ть (встрять* *perf*).
butter ['bʌtə'] *n* (сли́вочное) ма́сло* ◆ *vt* (*bread*) нама́зывать (нама́зать* *perf*) (сли́вочным) ма́слом.
buttercup ['bʌtəkʌp] *n* лю́тик.
butter dish *n* маслёнка*.
butterfingers ['bʌtəfɪŋgəz] *n* (*inf*) растя́па *m/f*.
butterfly ['bʌtəflaɪ] *n* ба́бочка*; (*also:* **~ stroke**) баттерфля́й.
buttocks ['bʌtəks] *npl* я́годицы *fpl*.
button ['bʌtn] *n* (*on clothes*) пу́говица; (*on machine*) кно́пка*; (*US*: *badge*) значо́к* ◆ *vt* (*also:* **~ up**) застёгивать (застегну́ть *perf*).
buttonhole ['bʌtnhəul] *n* петля́*, петли́ца ◆ *vt*: **to ~ sb** пристава́ть* (приста́ть* *perf*) к кому́-н с разгово́рами.
buttress ['bʌtrɪs] *n* контрфо́рс.
buxom ['bʌksəm] *adj* (*woman*) полногру́дый (полногру́д).
buy [baɪ] (*pt, pp* **bought**) *vt* покупа́ть (купи́ть* *perf*); (*COMM*) приобрета́ть (приобрести́* *perf*) ◆ *n* поку́пка*; **to ~ sb sth/sth from sb** покупа́ть (купи́ть* *perf*) кому́-н что-н/что-н у кого́-н; **to ~ sb a drink** покупа́ть (купи́ть* *perf*) кому́-н вы́пить что́-нибудь; **that was a good/bad ~** э́то была́ уда́чная/неуда́чная поку́пка
▸ **buy back** *vt* выкупа́ть (вы́купить* *perf*)
▸ **buy in** *vt* (*BRIT*) закупа́ть (закупи́ть* *perf*)
▸ **buy into** *vt fus* (*BRIT*) покупа́ть (купи́ть* *perf*) часть *+gen*, входи́ть* (войти́* *perf*) в до́лю с *+instr*
▸ **buy off** *vt* подкупа́ть (подкупи́ть* *perf*)
▸ **buy out** *vt* выкупа́ть (вы́купить* *perf*)
▸ **buy up** *vt* скупа́ть (скупи́ть* *perf*).
buyer ['baɪə'] *n* покупа́тель(ница) *m(f)*; (*COMM*) заку́пщик(-ица).
buyer's market ['baɪəz-] *n рынок, выгодный для покупа́теля.*
buy-out ['baɪaut] *n*: **management ~** *вы́куп ча́стной фи́рмы у её владе́льца чле́нами администра́ции, рабо́тающими на фи́рме.*
buzz [bʌz] *n* жужжа́ние ◆ *vi* (*insect, saw*) жужжа́ть* (прожужжа́ть* *perf*); (*inf*: *place*) гуде́ть* (*impf*) ◆ *vt* (*call on intercom*) звони́ть (позвони́ть *perf*) по вну́треннему телефо́ну; (*with buzzer*) звони́ть (позвони́ть *perf*); (*AVIAT*) соверша́ть (соверши́ть *perf*) бре́ющий полёт над *+instr*; **to give sb a ~** (*inf*: *TEL*) звя́кнуть (*perf*) кому́-н; **my head is ~ing** у меня́ голова́ гуди́т
▸ **buzz off** *vi* (*inf*) отва́ливать (отвали́ть* *perf*).
buzzard ['bʌzəd] *n* каню́к*, сары́ч*.
buzzer ['bʌzə'] *n* зу́ммер, звоно́к.
buzz word *n* (*inf*) мо́дное слове́чко*.

KEYWORD

by [baɪ] *prep* ***1*** (*referring to cause, agent*): **he was killed by lightning** он был уби́т мо́лнией; **a**

painting by Van Gogh картúна Ван Гóга; **it's by Shakespeare** э́то Шекспúр
2 (*referring to manner, means*): **by bus/train** на автóбусе/пóезде, автóбусом/пóездом; **by car** на машúне; **by phone** по телефóну; **to pay by cheque** платúть* (заплатúть* *perf*) чéком; **by moonlight** при свéте луны́; **by candlelight** при свечáх; **by working constantly, he...** благодаря́ томý, что он рабóтал без остановки, он...
3 (*via, through*) чéрез *+acc*; **by land/sea** по сýше/мóрю; **by the back door** чéрез зáднюю дверь
4 (*close to*) óколо *+gen*, у *+gen*; **the house is by the river** дом* нахóдится óколо *or* у реки́; **a holiday by the sea** óтпуск на мóре
5 (*past*) ми́мо *+gen*; **she rushed by me** онá пронеслáсь ми́мо меня́
6 (*not later than*) к *+dat*; **by four o'clock** к четырём часáм; **by the time I got here it was too late** к томý врéмени, когдá я добрáлся сюдá, бы́ло сли́шком пóздно
7 (*during*): **by day** днём; **by night** нóчью
8 (*amount*): **to sell by the kilo/metre** продавáть* (*impf*) в килогрáммах/мéтрах; **she is paid by the hour** у неё почасовáя оплáта
9 (*MATH, measure*) на *+acc*; **to divide/multiply by three** дели́ть* (раздели́ть* *perf*)/умножáть (умнóжить *perf*) на три; **a room three metres by four** кóмната размéром три мéтра на четы́ре
10 (*according to*) по *+dat*; **to play by the rules** игрáть (*impf*) по прáвилам; **it's all right by me** я не возражáю; **by law** по закóнам
11: **(all) by oneself** (*alone*) (совершéнно) оди́н (*f* однá, *nt* однó, *pl* одни́); (*unaided*) сам (*f* самá, *nt* самó, *pl* сами́); **I did it all by myself** я сдéлал всё сам; **he was standing by himself in the corner** он стоя́л в углý оди́н/сам по себé
12: **by the way** кстáти, мéжду прóчим; **this wasn't my idea by the way** кстáти *or* мéжду прóчим, э́то былá не моя́ идéя
◆ *adv* *1* *see* **go, pass** *etc*
2: **by and by** вскóре; **by and large** в цéлом.

bye(-bye) ['baɪ('baɪ)] *excl* покá, всегó.
by(e)-law ['baɪlɔː] *n* постановлéние мéстной влáсти.
by-election ['baɪɪlɛkʃən] *n* (*BRIT*) дополни́тельные вы́боры *mpl*.
Byelorussia [bjɛləu'rʌʃə] *n* Белорýссия.
bygone ['baɪgɔn] *adj* минýвший* ◆ *n*: **let ~s be ~s** что бы́ло, то прошлó.
bypass ['baɪpɑːs] *n* (*AUT*) объéзд; (*MED*) обходнóе шунти́рование (*обы́чно в кардиохирурги́и*) ◆ *vt* (*town*) объезжáть (объéхать* *perf*); (*fig*) обходи́ть* (обойти́* *perf*).
by-product ['baɪprɔdʌkt] *n* (*of industrial process*) побóчный продýкт; (*of situation*) побóчный результáт.
byre ['baɪə^r] *n* (*BRIT*) корóвник.
bystander ['baɪstændə^r] *n* свидéтель(ница) *m(f)*, прохóжий(-ая) *m(f) adj*.
byte [baɪt] *n* (*COMPUT*) байт.
byway ['baɪweɪ] *n* (*in country*) просёлочная дорóга; (*in city*) ýлочка.
byword ['baɪwəːd] *n*: **to be a ~ for** быть* (*impf*) олицетворéнием *or* си́мволом *+gen*.
by-your-leave ['baɪjɔː'liːv] *n*: **without so much as a ~** без вся́кого разрешéния.

* marks translations which have irregular inflections. The Russian-English side of the dictionary gives inflectional information.

~ C, c ~

C, c [si:] *n* (*letter*) *3-ья бу́ква англи́йского алфави́та*; (*SCOL*: *mark*) ≈ удовлетвори́тельный.
C [si:] *n* (*MUS*) до *nt ind*.
C. *abbr* = **Celsius, centigrade**.
c *abbr* (= **century**) в.= *век*; (= *circa*) о́коло *+gen*; (*US etc*: = *cents*) це́нты *mpl*.
CA *n abbr* (*BRIT*) = **chartered accountant** ◆ *abbr* = **Central America**; (*US*: *POST*) = *California*.
ca. *abbr* (= *circa*) о́коло *+gen*.
c/a *abbr* (*COMM*) = **capital account, credit account, current account**.
CAA *n abbr* (*BRIT*: = *Civil Aviation Authority*) Управле́ние гражда́нской авиа́ции; (*US*) = *Civil Aeronautics Authority*.
CAB *n abbr* (*BRIT*: = *Citizens' Advice Bureau*) *бюро́, даю́щее беспла́тные сове́ты по широ́кому спе́ктру пробле́м*.
cab [kæb] *n* такси́ *nt ind*; (*of truck etc*) каби́на; (*horse-drawn*) экипа́ж, кэб.
cabaret ['kæbəreɪ] *n* кабаре́ *nt ind*.
cabbage ['kæbɪdʒ] *n* капу́ста.
cabbie ['kæbɪ] *n* такси́ст.
cab driver *n* шофёр такси́.
cabin ['kæbɪn] *n* (*on ship*) каю́та; (*on plane*) каби́на; (*house*) хи́жина.
cabin cruiser *n* пассажи́рский* ка́тер*.
cabinet ['kæbɪnɪt] *n* шкаф*; (*also*: **display ~**) го́рка; (*POL*) кабине́т (мини́стров).
cabinet-maker ['kæbɪnɪt'meɪkəʳ] *n* красноде́ревщик.
cabinet minister *n* член кабине́та мини́стров.
cable ['keɪbl] *n* (*strong rope*) кана́т; (*metal*) трос; (*ELEC, TEL, TV*) ка́бель *m*; (*also*: **~gram**) каблогра́мма, телегра́мма ◆ *vt* (*message*) телеграфи́ровать (*impf/perf*); (*money*) посыла́ть (посла́ть* *perf*) телегра́фом.
cable car *n* кана́тная доро́га.
cable railway *n* фуникулёр.
cable television *n* ка́бельное телеви́дение.
cache [kæʃ] *n* та́йный склад; **a ~ of food** запа́с продово́льствия.
cackle ['kækl] *vi* (*person*) хихи́кать (*impf*); (*hen*) кудáхтать* (*impf*).
cacti ['kæktaɪ] *npl of* **cactus**.
cactus ['kæktəs] (*pl* **cacti**) *n* ка́ктус.
CAD *n abbr* (= *computer-aided design*) автоматизи́рованное проекти́рование.
caddie ['kædɪ] *n* (*GOLF*) подру́чный *m adj* игрока́ в гольф.
caddy ['kædɪ] *n* = **caddie**.
cadence ['keɪdəns] *n* (*of voice*) интона́ция.
cadet [kə'dɛt] *n* курса́нт; **police ~** курса́нт полице́йской шко́лы.
cadge [kædʒ] *vt* (*inf*): **to ~ (from** *or* **off)** выкля́нчивать (вы́клянчить *perf*) (у *+gen*).
cadger ['kædʒəʳ] *n* (*BRIT*: *inf*) попроша́йка *m/f*.
cadre ['kædrɪ] *n* ка́дры *mpl*.
Caesarean [si:'zɛərɪən] *n* (*also*: **~ section**) ке́сарево сече́ние.
CAF *abbr* (*BRIT*: = *cost and freight*) КАФ (*сто́имость и фрахт*).
café ['kæfeɪ] *n* кафе́ *nt ind*.
cafeteria [kæfɪ'tɪərɪə] *n* кафете́рий.
caffein(e) ['kæfi:n] *n* кофеи́н.
cage [keɪdʒ] *n* (*of animal*) кле́тка; (*of lift*) каби́на ◆ *vt* сажа́ть (посади́ть* *perf*) в кле́тку.
cagey ['keɪdʒɪ] *adj* (*inf*: *person*) скры́тный* (скры́тен); (: *answer*) укло́нчивый (укло́нчив).
cagoule [kə'gu:l] *n* дождеви́к.
cahoots [kə'hu:ts] *npl*: **to be in ~ with sb** быть* (*impf*) в сго́воре с кем-н.
CAI *n abbr* (= *computer-aided instruction*) автоматизи́рованное обуче́ние.
Cairo ['kaɪərəu] *n* Каи́р.
cajole [kə'dʒəul] *vt*: **to ~ sb** склоня́ть (склони́ть *perf*) ле́стью кого́-н.
cake [keɪk] *n* (*large*) торт; (*small*) пиро́жное *nt adj*; (*of soap*) брусо́к*; **it's a piece of ~** (*inf*) э́то пустяко́вое де́ло*; **his books sell like hot ~s** его́ кни́ги иду́т на расхва́т.
caked [keɪkt] *adj*: **~ with** облеплённый *+instr*.
cake shop *n* бу́лочная-конди́терская *f adj*.
calamine lotion ['kæləmaɪn-] *n* калами́нный лосьо́н.
calamitous [kə'læmɪtəs] *adj* бе́дственный.
calamity [kə'læmɪtɪ] *n* бе́дствие.
calcium ['kælsɪəm] *n* ка́льций.
calculate ['kælkjuleɪt] *vt* (*work out*: *numbers, cost*) подсчи́тывать (подсчита́ть *perf*); (: *distance*) вычисля́ть (вы́числить *perf*); (*estimate*) рассчи́тывать (рассчита́ть *perf*)
▸ **calculate on** *vt fus*: **to ~ on sth** рассчи́тывать (*impf*) на что-н.
calculated ['kælkjuleɪtɪd] *adj* наме́ренный (наме́рен); **a ~ risk** созна́тельный риск.

calculating ['kælkjuleɪtɪŋ] *adj* расчётливый (расчётлив).
calculation [kælkju'leɪʃən] *n* (*see vb*) подсчёт; вычисле́ние; расчёт.
calculator ['kælkjuleɪtəʳ] *n* калькуля́тор.
calculus ['kælkjuləs] *n* исчисле́ние; **integral/ differential ~** интегра́льное/ дифференциа́льное исчисле́ние.
Calcutta [kæl'kʌtə] *n* Кальку́тта.
calendar ['kæləndəʳ] *n* календа́рь* *m* ◆ *cpd*: **~ month/year** календа́рный ме́сяц*/год*.
calf [kɑ:f] (*pl* **calves**) *n* (*of cow*) телёнок*; (*of elephant, seal*) детёныш; (*also*: **~skin**) теля́чья ко́жа; (*ANAT*) икра́*.
caliber ['kælɪbəʳ] (*US*) *n* = **calibre**.
calibrate ['kælɪbreɪt] *vt* калиброва́ть *(impf)*.
calibre ['kælɪbəʳ] (*US* **caliber**) *n* кали́бр.
calico ['kælɪkəu] *n* (*BRIT*) митка́ль* *m*; (*US*) си́тец*.
California [kælɪ'fɔ:nɪə] *n* Калифо́рния.
calipers ['kælɪpəz] (*US*) *npl* = **callipers**.
call [kɔ:l] *vt* (*name, label*) называ́ть (назва́ть* *perf*); (*TEL*) звони́ть (позвони́ть *perf*) +*dat*; (*summon*) вызыва́ть (вы́звать* *perf*); (*arrange*) созыва́ть (созва́ть* *perf*); (*announce*) объявля́ть (объяви́ть* *perf*) ◆ *vi* (*shout*) крича́ть (кри́кнуть *perf*); (*telephone*) звони́ть (позвони́ть *perf*); (*visit*: *also*: **~ in, ~ round**) заходи́ть* (зайти́* *perf*) ◆ *n* (*shout, cry*) крик; (*TEL*) звоно́к*; (*visit*) посеще́ние; (*demand*) призы́в; (*summons*: *for flight*) объявле́ние; (*fig*: *lure*) зов*; **she is ~ed Suzanne** её зову́т Сюза́нна; **the mountain is ~ed Ben Nevis** э́та гора́ называ́ется Бен Не́вис; **to ~ sb as a witness** призыва́ть (призва́ть* *perf*) кого́-н в свиде́тели; **who is ~ing?** (*TEL*) кто звони́т?; **London ~ing** (*RADIO*) говори́т Ло́ндон; **please give me a ~ at 7** позвони́те мне, пожа́луйста, в 7 часо́в; **to make a ~** звони́ть (позвони́ть *perf*); **to pay a ~ on sb** навеща́ть (навести́ть* *perf*) кого́-н; **there's not much ~ for these items** на э́ти предме́ты нет большо́го спро́са; **to be on ~** (*nurse, doctor*) дежу́рить *(impf)*; (*army, fire brigade*) быть* *(impf)* наготове
▸ **call at** *vt fus* (*subj*: *ship*) заходи́ть* (зайти́* *perf*) в +*prp*; (: *train*) остана́вливаться (останови́ться* *perf*) в +*prp*
▸ **call back** *vi* (*return*) заходи́ть* (зайти́* *perf*) опя́ть; (*TEL*) перезва́нивать (перезвони́ть *perf*) ◆ *vt* (*TEL*) перезва́нивать (перезвони́ть *perf*) +*dat*
▸ **call for** *vt fus* (*demand*) призыва́ть (призва́ть* *perf*) к +*dat*; (*fetch*) заходи́ть* (зайти́* *perf*) за +*instr*
▸ **call in** *vt* (*doctor*) вызыва́ть (вы́звать* *perf*) ◆ *vi* (*visit*) заходи́ть* (зайти́* *perf*); **to ~ sth in** (*books, stock*) отзыва́ть (отозва́ть* *perf*)
▸ **call off** *vt* отменя́ть (отмени́ть* *perf*); **the strike was ~ed off** забасто́вка была́ отменена́
▸ **call on** *vt fus* (*visit*) заходи́ть* (зайти́* *perf*) к +*dat*; (*appeal to*) призыва́ть (призва́ть* *perf*) к +*dat*; (*request*): **to ~ on sb to do** призыва́ть (призва́ть* *perf*) кого́-н +*infin*
▸ **call out** *vi* крича́ть (кри́кнуть *perf*) ◆ *vt* (*doctor, police*) вызыва́ть (вы́звать* *perf*)
▸ **call up** *vt* (*MIL*) призыва́ть (призва́ть* *perf*) (в а́рмию); (*TEL*) звони́ть (позвони́ть *perf*) +*dat*.
Callanetics® [kælə'nɛtɪks] *n* калланe´тика (*вид оздорови́тельной гимна́стики*).
call box *n* (*BRIT*) телефо́нная бу́дка.
call centre *n центр приёма комме́рческих итп звонко́в в большо́м объёме.*
caller ['kɔ:ləʳ] *n* (*visitor*) посети́тель(ница) *m(f)*; (*TEL*) звоня́щий(-ая) *m(f) adj*; **hold the line, ~!** не клади́те тру́бку!
call girl *n* проститу́тка* (*кото́рую вызыва́ют по телефо́ну*).
call-in ['kɔ:lɪn] *n* (*US*) програ́мма „Звони́те-отвеча́ем" .
calling ['kɔ:lɪŋ] *n* призва́ние.
calling card *n* (*US*) визи́тная ка́рточка*.
callipers ['kælɪpəz] (*US* **calipers**) *npl* (*MATH*) штангенци́ркуль *msg*.
callous ['kæləs] *adj* (*heartless*) безду́шный (безду́шен), жесто́кий.
callousness ['kæləsnɪs] *n* безду́шие.
callow ['kæləu] *adj*: **~ youth** птене́ц*.
calm [kɑ:m] *adj* споко́йный* (споко́ен); (*place*) ти́хий*; (*weather*) безве́тренный ◆ *n* тишина́, поко́й; (*at sea*) штиль *m* ◆ *vt* успока́ивать (успоко́ить *perf*)
▸ **calm down** *vt* (*person, animal*) успока́ивать (успоко́ить *perf*) ◆ *vi* (*person*) успока́иваться (успоко́иться *perf*).
calmly ['kɑ:mlɪ] *adv* споко́йно.
calmness ['kɑ:mnɪs] *n* споко́йствие.
Calor gas® ['kæləʳ-] *n фи́рменная ма́рка балло́нного га́за.*
calorie ['kælərɪ] *n* кало́рия; **low-~ product** низкокалори́йный проду́кт.
calve [kɑ:v] *vi* (*cow*) тели́ться* (отели́ться* *perf*); (*elephant, seal*) рожда́ть (роди́ть* *perf*) детёныша.
calves [kɑ:vz] *npl of* **calf**.
CAM *n abbr* (= *computer-aided manufacturing*) автоматизи́рованное произво́дство.
camber ['kæmbəʳ] *n* попере́чный укло́н.
Cambodia [kæm'bəudɪə] *n* Камбо́джа.
Cambodian [kæm'bəudɪən] *adj* камбоджи́йский* ◆ *n* камбоджи́ец(-и́йка).
Cambridge ['keɪmbrɪdʒ] *n* Ке́мбридж.
Cambs *abbr* (*BRIT*: *POST*) = *Cambridgeshire*.
camcorder ['kæmkɔ:dəʳ] *n* видеока́мера.
came [keɪm] *pt of* **come**.

camel ['kæməl] *n* верблю́д.
cameo ['kæmɪəu] *n* (*jewellery*) камéя; (*THEAT, LITERATURE*) миниатю́ра.
camera ['kæmərə] *n* (*PHOT*) фотоаппара́т; (*also:* **cine ~, movie ~**) кинока́мера; (*TV*) телека́мера; **35 mm ~** кинока́мера для 35-мм плёнки; **in ~** (*LAW*) при закры́тых дверя́х.
cameraman ['kæmərəmæn] *irreg n* (*CINEMA*) (кино)опера́тор; (*TV*) (теле)опера́тор.
Cameroon [kæmə'ru:n] *n* Камеру́н.
Cameroun [kæmə'ru:n] *n* = **Cameroon**.
camomile ['kæməumaɪl] *n* рома́шка; **~ tea** рома́шковый чай*.
camouflage ['kæməflɑ:ʒ] *n* (*MIL*) камуфля́ж, маскиро́вка; (*ZOOL*) защи́тная окра́ска ◆ *vt* (*also MIL*) маскирова́ть (замаскирова́ть *perf*).
camp [kæmp] *n* ла́герь* *m*; (*MIL*) вое́нный городо́к* ◆ *vi* (*set up camp*) разбива́ть (разби́ть* *perf*) ла́герь; (*go camping*) жить* (*impf*) в пала́тках ◆ *adj* (*effeminate*) женоподо́бный.
campaign [kæm'peɪn] *n* кампа́ния ◆ *vi*: **to ~ (for/against)** вести́* (*impf*) кампа́нию (за *+acc*/про́тив *+gen*).
campaigner [kæm'peɪnə^r] *n*: **~ (for/against)** боре́ц* (за *+acc*/про́тив *+gen*).
camp bed *n* (*BRIT*) раскладу́шка*.
camper ['kæmpə^r] *n* (*person*) тури́ст(ка) (*живу́щий* в пала́тке*); (*vehicle*) фурго́н (*обору́дованный для походно́й жи́зни*).
camping ['kæmpɪŋ] *n* ке́мпинг; **to go ~** отправля́ться (отпра́виться* *perf*) в похо́д.
camping site *n* = **camp site**.
camp site *n* ке́мпинг.
campus ['kæmpəs] *n* университе́тский* *or* студе́нческий* городо́к*.
camshaft ['kæmʃɑ:ft] *n* кулачко́вый вал*.
can[1] [kæn] *n* (*for foodstuffs*) консе́рвная ба́нка; (*for oil, beer*) ба́нка ◆ *vt* консерви́ровать (законсерви́ровать *perf*); **a ~ of beer** ба́нка пи́ва; **he had to carry the ~** (*BRIT: inf*) ему́ пришло́сь за всё отдува́ться.

KEYWORD

can[2] (*negative* **cannot, can't,** *conditional, pt* **could**) *aux vb* **1** (*be able to*) мочь* (смочь* *perf*); **you can do it (if you try)** Вы смо́жете э́то сде́лать(, е́сли Вы постара́етесь); **I'll help you all I can** я помогу́ Вам всем, чем могу́; **I can't go on any longer** я бо́льше не могу́; **I can't see/hear you** я не ви́жу/слы́шу Вас; **she couldn't sleep that night** в ту ночь она́ не могла́ усну́ть
2 (*know how to*) уме́ть (*impf*); **I can swim** я уме́ю пла́вать; **can you speak Russian?** Вы говори́те *or* уме́ете говори́ть по-ру́сски?
3 (*may*) мо́жно; **can I use your phone?** мо́жно от Вас позвони́ть?; **could I have a word with you?** мо́жно с Ва́ми поговори́ть?; **you can smoke if you like** Вы мо́жете кури́ть, е́сли хоти́те; **can I help you with that?** могу́ я Вам в э́том помо́чь?
4 (*expressing disbelief, puzzlement*): **it can't be true!** не мо́жет быть!; **what CAN he want?** что ему́ ну́жно?
5 (*expressing possibility, suggestion etc*): **he could be in the library** он мо́жет быть в библиоте́ке, возмо́жно, он в библиоте́ке; **she could have been delayed** возмо́жно, её что́-то задержа́ло.

Canada ['kænədə] *n* Кана́да.
Canadian [kə'neɪdɪən] *adj* кана́дский* ◆ *n* кана́дец*(-дка*).
canal [kə'næl] *n* кана́л.
Canaries [kə'nɛərɪz] *npl* = **Canary Islands**.
canary [kə'nɛərɪ] *n* канаре́йка*.
Canary Islands *npl*: **the ~ ~** Кана́рские острова́ *mpl*.
Canberra ['kænbərə] *n* Канбе́рра.
cancel ['kænsəl] *vt* отменя́ть (отмени́ть* *perf*); (*contract, cheque, visa*) аннули́ровать (*impf/perf*); (*words, figures*) вычёркивать (вы́черкнуть *perf*); (*stamp*) погаша́ть (погаси́ть* *perf*)
▸ **cancel out** *vt* нейтрализова́ть (*impf/perf*); **they ~ each other out** они нейтрализу́ют друг дру́га.
cancellation [kænsə'leɪʃən] *n* отме́на, аннули́рование.
cancer ['kænsə^r] *n* (*MED*) рак; (*fig*) бич; **C~** (*ASTROLOGY*) Рак; **he is C~** он – Рак.
cancerous ['kænsrəs] *adj* ра́ковый.
cancer patient *n* ра́ковый(-ая) больно́й(-а́я) *m(f) adj*.
cancer research *n* онкологи́ческие иссле́дования *ntpl*.
C and F *abbr* (*BRIT: COMM*) = **CAF**.
candid ['kændɪd] *adj* и́скренний* (и́скренен), чистосерде́чный* (чистосерде́чен).
candidacy ['kændɪdəsɪ] *n* кандидату́ра.
candidate ['kændɪdeɪt] *n* (*for job*) претенде́нт; (*in exam*) экзамену́емый(-ая) *m(f) adj*; (*POL*) кандида́т.
candidature ['kændɪdətʃə^r] (*BRIT*) *n* = **candidacy**.
candied ['kændɪd] *adj*: **~ fruit** цука́ты *mpl*; **~ apple** (*US*) я́блочный цука́т.
candle ['kændl] *n* свеча́*; (*smaller*) све́чка*.
candleholder ['kændlhəuldə^r] *n* = **candlestick**.
candlelight ['kændllaɪt] *n*: **by ~** при свеча́х.
candlestick ['kændlstɪk] *n* подсве́чник.
candour ['kændə^r] (*US* **candor**) *n* и́скренность *f*.
candy ['kændɪ] *n* (*also:* **sugar-~**) караме́ль *f*, ледене́ц*; (*US*) конфе́та.
candyfloss ['kændɪflɔs] *n* (*BRIT*) са́харная ва́та.
candy store *n* (*US*) конди́терская *f adj*.
cane [keɪn] *n* (*BOT*) тростни́к*; (*stick*) ро́зга*; (*for walking*) трость* *f* ◆ *vt* (*BRIT*) нака́зывать (наказа́ть* *perf*) ро́згами.
canine ['keɪnaɪn] *adj* соба́чий*.
canister ['kænɪstə^r] *n* (*for tea etc*) жестяна́я ба́нка*; (*pressurized container*) балло́н; (*of chemicals etc*) кани́стра.

cannabis ['kænəbɪs] *n* гашиш; (*also:* ~ **plant**) конопля.
canned [kænd] *adj* (*fruit, vegetables etc*) консервированный; (*inf: music*) в записи; (*BRIT: inf: drink*) баночный; (: *drunk*) наклюкавшийся.
cannibal ['kænɪbəl] *n* (*animal*) каннибал; (*person*) каннибал, людоед.
cannibalism ['kænɪbəlɪzəm] *n* каннибализм, людоедство.
cannon ['kænən] (*pl* ~ *or* ~**s**) *n* (*gun*) пушка*.
cannonball ['kænənbɔ:l] *n* пушечное ядро*.
cannon fodder *n* пушечное мясо.
cannot ['kænɔt] = **can not**; *see* **can²**.
canny ['kænɪ] *adj* смекалистый (смекалист).
canoe [kə'nu:] *n* (*boat*) челнок*; (*for competition*) каноэ *nt ind*.
canoeing [kə'nu:ɪŋ] *n* гребля на каноэ.
canon ['kænən] *n* (*clergyman*) каноник; (*rule*) канон; (*standard*) критерий.
canonize ['kænənaɪz] *vt* канонизировать *(impf/perf)*.
can-opener ['kænəupnə^r] *n* консервный нож* *or* ключ*.
canopy ['kænəpɪ] *n* (*above bed etc*) балдахин, полог; (*of leaves etc*) свод.
cant [kænt] *n* ханжество.
can't [kænt] = **can not**; *see* **can²**.
Cantab. *abbr* (*BRIT: in degree titles*) = *Cantabrigiensis*.
cantankerous [kæn'tæŋkərəs] *adj* сварливый (сварлив), придирчивый (придирчив).
canteen [kæn'ti:n] *n* столовая *f adj*; (*mobile*) походная кухня*; (*BRIT*): ~ **of cutlery** *походный ящик со столовыми принадлежностями*.
canter ['kæntə^r] *vi* ездить*/ехать* *(impf)* лёгким галопом ◆ *n* лёгкий* галоп.
cantilever ['kæntɪli:və^r] *n* консоль *f*, кронштейн; ~ **bridge** консольный мост*.
canvas ['kænvəs] *n* (*fabric, also ART*) холст*; (*for tents*) брезент; (*NAUT*) парусина ◆ *adj* (*shoes, bag*) парусиновый; **under** ~ (*camping*) в палатках.
canvass ['kænvəs] *vi*: **to** ~ **for** агитировать *(impf/perf)* за *+acc* ◆ *vt* (*opinions*) собирать *(impf)*.
canvasser ['kænvəsə^r] *n* агитатор.
canvassing ['kænvəsɪŋ] *n* предвыборная агитация.
canyon ['kænjən] *n* каньон.
CAP *n abbr* (= *Common Agricultural Policy*) общая сельскохозяйственная политика (*в странах Общего рынка*).
cap [kæp] *n* (*hat*) кепка*; (*of uniform*) фуражка*; (*of pen*) колпачок*; (*of bottle*) крышка*; (*also:* **Dutch** ~: *contraceptive*) колпачок*; (*for toy gun*) пистон; (*FOOTBALL*) *футбольный игрок, который получает кепку как знак отличия* ◆ *vt* (*outdo*) превосходить* (превзойти* *perf*); (*SPORT*): **he was ~ped ten times** он играл в сборной команде страны десять раз; **swimming** ~ купальная шапочка; **to be ~ped with** увенчиваться (увенчаться *perf*) *+instr*; **and to ~ it all, he ...** в довершение ко всему, он ....
capability [keɪpə'bɪlɪtɪ] *n* (*competence*) способность *f*; (*MIL*) потенциал.
capable ['keɪpəbl] *adj* (*person*) способный* (способен); ~ **of sth/doing** (*person, object*) способен к чему-н/*+infin*.
capacious [kə'peɪʃəs] *adj* вместительный* (вместителен).
capacity [kə'pæsɪtɪ] *n* (*of container*) ёмкость *f*; (*of ship, theatre etc*) вместительность *f*; (*of lift*) подъёмная способность *f*; (*of person: capability*) способность; (: *role*) роль* *f*; (*of factory*) производственная мощность *f*; **filled to** ~ заполнен до предела; **in his** ~ **as** в роли *+gen*; **in an advisory** ~ в роли советника; **this work is beyond my** ~ эта работа вне моей компетенции; **to work at full** ~ работать *(impf)* на полную мощность.
cape [keɪp] *n* (*GEO*) мыс*; (*cloak*) плащ.
Cape of Good Hope *n*: **the** ~ ~ ~ ~ Мыс Доброй Надежды.
caper ['keɪpə^r] *n* (*CULIN: usu pl*) каперсы *mpl*; (*prank*) розыгрыш.
Cape Town *n* Кейптаун.
capita ['kæpɪtə] *see* **per capita**.
capital ['kæpɪtl] *n* (*also:* ~ **city**) столица; (*money*) капитал; (*also:* ~ **letter**) заглавная буква.
capital account *n* баланс движения капитала.
capital allowance *n налоговая скидка, связанная с инвестициями в основной капитал*.
capital assets *npl* основной капитал *msg*, основные фонды *mpl*.
capital employed *n* применяемый капитал.
capital expenditure *n* капиталовложение.
capital gains tax *n* налог на реализованный прирост капитала.
capital goods *npl* капитальные товары *mpl*, средства *ntpl* производства.
capital-intensive ['kæpɪtlɪn'tɛnsɪv] *adj* капиталоёмкий.
capital investment *n* капиталовложение.
capitalism ['kæpɪtəlɪzəm] *n* капитализм.
capitalist ['kæpɪtəlɪst] *adj* капиталистический* ◆ *n* капиталист.
capitalize ['kæpɪtəlaɪz] *vt* (*COMM*) капитализировать *(impf/perf)* ◆ *vi*: **to** ~ **on** извлекать (извлечь* *perf*) выгоду из *+gen*.
capital punishment *n* смертная казнь *f*.

capital transfer tax *n* (*BRIT*) нало́г на перево́д капита́ла.
Capitol ['kæpɪtl] *n*: **the ~** Капито́лий.
capitulate [kə'pɪtjuleɪt] *vi*: **to ~ (to)** капитули́ровать *(impf/perf)* (пе́ред *+instr*).
capitulation [kəpɪtju'leɪʃən] *n* капитуля́ция.
capricious [kə'prɪʃəs] *adj* (*person*) капри́зный* (капри́зен), прихотли́вый (прихотли́в).
Capricorn ['kæprɪkɔ:n] *n* (*ASTROLOGY*) Козеро́г; **he is ~** он – Козеро́г.
caps [kæps] *abbr* = **capital letters**.
capsize [kæp'saɪz] *vt* опроки́дывать (опроки́нуть *perf*) ◆ *vi* опроки́дываться (опроки́нуться *perf*).
capstan ['kæpstən] *n* (*NAUT*) кабеста́н.
capsule ['kæpsju:l] *n* ка́псула.
Capt. *abbr* (*MIL*) = **captain**.
captain ['kæptɪn] *n* (*of ship, plane*) команди́р; (*of team, army*) капита́н ◆ *vt* (*ship*) кома́ндовать *(impf) +instr*; (*team*) явля́ться *(impf)* капита́ном *+gen*.
caption ['kæpʃən] *n* по́дпись *f*.
captivate ['kæptɪveɪt] *vt* пленя́ть (плени́ть *perf*).
captive ['kæptɪv] *adj* пле́нный ◆ *n* пле́нник(-ица).
captivity [kæp'tɪvɪtɪ] *n* плен*; **in ~** (*animal*) в нево́ле; (*person*) в плену́.
captor ['kæptə^r] *n* (*unlawful*) похити́тель(ница) *m(f)*; (*lawful*) взя́вший(-ая) *m(f) adj* в плен; **his ~s** взя́вшие его́ в плен.
capture ['kæptʃə^r] *vt* (*animal*) лови́ть* (пойма́ть *perf*); (*person, city, also COMM*) захва́тывать (захвати́ть* *perf*); (*attention*) прико́вывать (прикова́ть *perf*) ◆ *n* (*of person, town etc*) захва́т; (*of animal*) по́ймка*; (*COMPUT*): **data ~** сбор информа́ции; **to ~ the screen** (*COMPUT*) фикси́ровать (зафикси́ровать *perf*) изображе́ние с экра́на.
car [kɑ:^r] *n* автомоби́ль *m*, маши́на; (*RAIL*) ваго́н; **by ~** на автомоби́ле *or* маши́не; **dining ~** (*BRIT*) ваго́н-рестора́н.
Caracas [kə'rækəs] *n* Карака́с.
carafe [kə'ræf] *n* графи́н.
caramel ['kærəməl] *n* (*sweet*) караме́ль *f*; (*burnt sugar*) жжёный са́хар*.
carat ['kærət] *n* (*of diamond, gold*) кара́т; **24 ~ gold** чи́стое зо́лото.
caravan ['kærəvæn] *n* (*BRIT*) жило́й-автоприце́п; (*in desert*) карава́н.
caravan site *n* (*BRIT*) *площа́дка для стоя́нки жилы́х-автоприце́пов*.
caraway ['kærəweɪ] *n*: **~ seeds** тмин *msg*.
carbohydrate [kɑ:bəu'haɪdreɪt] *n* углево́д.
carbolic acid [kɑ:'bɔlɪk-] *n* карбо́ловая кислота́.
car bomb *n* бо́мба, подло́женная в *or* под маши́ну.
carbon ['kɑ:bən] *n* углеро́д.
carbonated ['kɑ:bəneɪtɪd] *adj* (*drink*) газиро́ванный.
carbon copy *n* ко́пия (*сде́ланная под копи́рку*).
carbon dioxide *n* двуо́кись *f* углеро́да.
carbon monoxide [mɔ'nɔksaɪd] *n* моноксӣд углеро́да.
carbon paper *n* копирова́льная бума́га, копи́рка.
carbon ribbon *n* ле́нта (*для пи́шущей маши́нки или при́нтера*).
car boot sale *n барахо́лка, на кото́рой това́р продаётся с маши́н*.
carburettor [kɑ:bju'rɛtə^r] (*US* **carburetor**) *n* карбюра́тор.
carcass ['kɑ:kəs] *n* ту́ша.
carcinogenic [kɑ:sɪnə'dʒɛnɪk] *adj* канцероге́нный.
card [kɑ:d] *n* (*material*) карто́н; (*also:* **record ~**) ка́рточка*; (*also:* **membership ~**) чле́нский* биле́т; (*also:* **playing ~**) (игра́льная) ка́рта; (*also:* **greetings ~**) откры́тка; (*also:* **visiting ~, business ~**) визи́тная ка́рточка*; **to play ~s** игра́ть *(impf)* в ка́рты.
cardamom ['kɑ:dəməm] *n* кардамо́н.
cardboard ['kɑ:dbɔ:d] *n* карто́н.
cardboard box *n* карто́нная коро́бка*.
cardboard city (*inf*) *n райо́н го́рода, за́нятый бездо́мными, живу́щими в карто́нных я́щиках*.
card-carrying ['kɑ:d'kærɪɪŋ] *adj*: **~ member** *полнопра́вный член полити́ческой организа́ции*.
card game *n* игра́* в ка́рты.
cardiac ['kɑ:dɪæk] *adj* серде́чный; (*unit*) кардиологи́ческий*.
Cardiff ['kɑ:dɪf] *n* Ка́рдифф.
cardigan ['kɑ:dɪgən] *n* жаке́т (*вя́заный*).
cardinal ['kɑ:dɪnl] *adj* (*also:* **~ number**) коли́чественное числи́тельное *nt adj*; (*sin*) сме́ртный; (*principle, importance*) кардина́льный ◆ *n* кардина́л.
card index *n* картоте́ка.
cardsharp ['kɑ:dʃɑ:p] *n* шу́лер*.
card vote *n* (*BRIT*) манда́тное голосова́ние.
CARE [kɛə^r] *n abbr* = *Cooperative for American Relief Everywhere*.
care [kɛə^r] *n* (*worry*) забо́та; (*of the ill*) ухо́д; (*attention*) внима́ние ◆ *vi*: **to ~ about** (*person, animal*) забо́титься* (позабо́титься* *perf*) о *+prp*; **in sb's ~** на чьём-н попече́нии; **the child has been taken into ~** ребёнок был взят в де́тский дом; **"handle with ~"** "не кантова́ть"; **to take ~ (to do)** позабо́титься *(perf)* (*+infin*); **to take ~ of** (*patient, child etc*) забо́титься* (позабо́титься* *perf*) о *+prp*; (*problem, situation*) занима́ться (заня́ться* *perf*) *+instr*; **~ of** для переда́чи *+dat*; **he ~s about environmental issues** его́ волну́ют пробле́мы защи́ты окружа́ющей среды́; **would you ~ to/for ...?** не хоти́те ли *+infin/+acc*; **I wouldn't ~ to repeat the experience** мне бы не хоте́лось испыта́ть э́то сно́ва; **I**

don't ~ мне всё равно́; **I couldn't ~ less** мне наплева́ть
► **care for** *vt fus* (*look after*) забо́титься* (позабо́титься* *perf*) о +*prp*; (*like*): **he ~s for her** он неравноду́шен к ней.
career [kə'rɪə^r] *n* карье́ра ◆ *vi* мча́ться* (помча́ться* *perf*); **my school ~** (*life*) мои́ шко́льные го́ды.
career girl *n* = **career woman**.
careers officer [kə'rɪəz-] *n консульта́нт по профессиона́льной ориента́ции*.
career woman *irreg n* делова́я же́нщина.
carefree ['kɛəfri:] *adj* беззабо́тный* (беззабо́тен).
careful ['kɛəful] *adj* (*cautious*) осторо́жный* (осторо́жен); (*thorough*) тща́тельный* (тща́телен); **(be) ~!** осторо́жно!, береги́сь!; **he is/was ~ with his money** он эконо́мен/был эконо́мен.
carefully ['kɛəfəlɪ] *adv* (*see adj*) осторо́жно; тща́тельно.
careless ['kɛəlɪs] *adj* (*negligent*) невнима́тельный* (невнима́телен); (*casual*: *remark*) небре́жный* (небре́жен); (*untroubled*) беззабо́тный* (беззабо́тен).
carelessly ['kɛəlɪslɪ] *adv* (*see adj*) невнима́тельно; небре́жно; беззабо́тно.
carelessness ['kɛəlɪsnɪs] *n* (*negligence*) невнима́тельность *f*; (*casualness*) небре́жность *f*; (*lack of concern*) беззабо́тность *f*.
carer ['kɛərə^r] *n челове́к, уха́живающий за больны́ми, престаре́лыми и т.п.*
caress [kə'rɛs] *n* ла́ска* ◆ *vt* ласка́ть *(impf)*.
caretaker ['kɛəteɪkə^r] *n* (*of building*) завхо́з.
caretaker government *n* (BRIT) вре́менное прави́тельство.
car ferry *n* автомоби́льный паро́м.
cargo ['kɑ:gəu] (*pl* **~es**) *n* груз.
cargo boat *n* грузово́е су́дно*.
cargo plane *n* грузово́й самолёт.
car hire *n* (BRIT) прока́т автомоби́лей.
Caribbean [kærɪ'bi:ən] *adj* кари́бский ◆ *n*: **the ~ (Sea)** Кари́бское мо́ре*.
caricature ['kærɪkətjuə^r] *n* карикату́ра; **~ of the truth** карикату́ра на пра́вду.
caring ['kɛərɪŋ] *adj* забо́тливый (забо́тлив).
carjack ['kɑ:dʒæk] *n* домкра́т.
carnage ['kɑ:nɪdʒ] *n* резня́.
carnal ['kɑ:nl] *adj* пло́тский*.
carnation [kɑ:'neɪʃən] *n* гвозди́ка.
carnival ['kɑ:nɪvl] *n* карнава́л; (*US*: *funfair*) аттракцио́нный городо́к*.
carnivorous [kɑ:'nɪvərəs] *adj* (*animal*) плотоя́дный*; (*plant*) насекомоя́дный.
carol ['kærəl] *n* (*also*: **Christmas ~**) Рожде́ственский* гимн.
carouse [kə'rauz] *vi* бра́жничать *(impf)*.
carousel [kærə'sɛl] *n* (*US*) карусе́ль *f*.
carp [kɑ:p] *n* карп
► **carp at** *vt fus* придира́ться (придра́ться* *perf*) к +*dat*.
car park *n* (BRIT) автостоя́нка*.
Carpathian Mountains [kɑ:'peɪθɪən-] *npl* Карпа́ты *pl*.
carpenter ['kɑ:pɪntə^r] *n* пло́тник.
carpentry ['kɑ:pɪntrɪ] *n* пло́тницкое де́ло.
carpet ['kɑ:pɪt] *n* (*also fig*) ковёр*; (*of snow*) покро́в ◆ *vt* (*room*) устила́ть (устла́ть* *perf*) ковра́ми; **fitted ~** (BRIT) ковро́вое покры́тие.
carpet bombing *n* ковро́вое бомбомета́ние.
carpet slippers *npl* шлёпанцы *mpl*.
carpet sweeper [-'swi:pə^r] *n* щётка для ковра́.
car phone *n* ра́дио-телефо́н (*в маши́не*).
carport ['kɑ:pɔ:t] *n* наве́с для маши́ны.
car rental *n* прока́т автомоби́лей.
carriage ['kærɪdʒ] *n* (*BRIT*: RAIL) (пассажи́рский*) ваго́н; (*horse-drawn*) экипа́ж; (*of goods*) перево́зка; (*of typewriter*) каре́тка*; (*transport costs*) сто́имость *f* перево́зки; **~ forward** *сто́имость перево́зки подлежи́т опла́те получа́телем*; **~ free** перево́зка осуществля́ется беспла́тно; **~ inwards** *су́мма, опла́чиваемая покупа́телем за доста́вку полу́ченного гру́за*; **~ outwards** *су́мма, предста́вленная продавцо́м к опла́те на покры́тие расхо́дов по доста́вке*; **~ paid** за перево́зку упла́чено.
carriage return *n* перево́д каре́тки.
carriageway ['kærɪdʒweɪ] *n* (BRIT) прое́зжая часть* *f* доро́ги.
carrier ['kærɪə^r] *n* (*transporter*) транспорти́ровщик; (MED) носи́тель *m*.
carrier bag *n* (BRIT) паке́тик (*для поку́пок*).
carrier pigeon *n* почто́вый го́лубь* *m*.
carrion ['kærɪən] *n* па́даль *f*.
carrot ['kærət] *n* морко́вь *f*; (*fig*): **~ and stick policy** поли́тика кнута́ и пря́ника.
carry ['kærɪ] *vt* (*take*) носи́ть*/нести́* *(impf)*; (*transport*) вози́ть*/везти́* *(impf)*; (*a motion, bill*) проводи́ть* (провести́* *perf*); (*involve*) влечь* (повле́чь* *perf*); (MED) переноси́ть* *(impf)*; (*have*: *picture, slogan*) содержа́ть* *(impf)* ◆ *vi* (*sound*) передава́ться* *(impf)*; **he carries the virus** он носи́тель ви́руса; **this loan carries 10% interest per annum** э́тот заём предоставля́ется под 10% годовы́х; **to get carried away (by)** (*fig*) увлека́ться (увле́чься* *perf*) (+*instr*)
► **carry forward** *vt* (*also* COMM) переноси́ть* (перенести́* *perf*) на другу́ю страни́цу
► **carry on** *vi* продолжа́ться (продо́лжиться *perf*); (*inf*: *make a fuss*) заводи́ться* (завести́сь* *perf*) ◆ *vt* продолжа́ть (продо́лжить *perf*); **to ~ on with sth/doing** продолжа́ть (продо́лжить *perf*) что-н/+*impf*

infin
▸ **carry out** *vt* (*orders*) выполня́ть (вы́полнить *perf*), исполня́ть (испо́лнить *perf*); (*investigation*) проводи́ть* (провести́* *perf*); (*threat*) осуществля́ть (осуществи́ть* *perf*).
carrycot ['kærɪkɔt] *n* (*BRIT*) переносна́я колыбе́ль *f*.
carry-on ['kærɪ'ɔn] *n* (*inf: fuss*) сумато́ха, суета́; (: *annoying behaviour*) капри́зы *mpl*; **I've had enough of your ~!** надое́ли мне твои́ капри́зы!; **what a ~!** кака́я сумато́ха *or* суета́!
cart [kɑ:t] *n* теле́га, пово́зка; (*handcart*) теле́жка* ◆ *vt* (*inf: people, objects*) таска́ть/тащи́ть* *(impf)*.
carte blanche ['kɑ:t'blɔŋʃ] *n*: **to give sb ~ ~** предоставля́ть (предоста́вить* *perf*) кому́-н по́лную свобо́ду де́йствий.
cartel [kɑ:'tɛl] *n* карте́ль *m*.
cartilage ['kɑ:tɪlɪdʒ] *n* хрящ*.
cartographer [kɑ:'tɔgrəfəʳ] *n* карто́граф.
cartography [kɑ:'tɔgrəfɪ] *n* картогра́фия.
carton ['kɑ:tən] *n* (*large box*) карто́нная коро́бка*; (*container*) паке́т.
cartoon [kɑ:'tu:n] *n* (*drawing*) карикату́ра; (*BRIT: comic strip*) ко́микс; (*TV*) мультфи́льм= *мультипликацио́нный фи́льм*.
cartoonist [kɑ:'tu:nɪst] *n* карикатури́ст(ка).
cartridge ['kɑ:trɪdʒ] *n* (*for gun*) ги́льза; (*for camera*) кассе́та с фотоплёнкой; (*music tape*) кассе́та; (*of record-player*) голо́вка*; (*of pen*) (черни́льный) балло́нчик; (*of printer*) ка́ртридж.
cartwheel ['kɑ:twi:l] *n* колесо́* теле́ги; **to turn a ~** де́лать (сде́лать *perf*) колесо́.
carve [kɑ:v] *vt* (*meat*) нареза́ть (наре́зать* *perf*); (*initials, design*) выреза́ть (вы́резать* *perf*); (*wood, stone*) выреза́ть *(impf)*
▸ **carve up** *vt* (*land, property*) раздробля́ть (раздроби́ть* *perf*); (*meat*) разреза́ть (разре́зать* *perf*).
carving ['kɑ:vɪŋ] *n* (*object*) резно́е изде́лие; (*design*) резьба́; (*art*) иску́сство резьбы́.
carving knife *n* разде́лочный нож*.
car wash *n* мо́йка автомоби́лей.
Casablanca [kæsə'blæŋkə] *n* Касабла́нка.
cascade [kæs'keɪd] *n* (*waterfall*) каска́д ◆ *vi* (*water*) низверга́ться *(impf)*; (*hair*) ниспада́ть *(impf)*.
case [keɪs] *n* (*instance, problem*) слу́чай; (*MED: patient*) больно́й(-а́я) *m(f) adj*; (*LAW*) (суде́бное) де́ло*; (*criminal investigation*) рассле́дование; (*for spectacles etc*) футля́р; (*BRIT: also:* **suitcase**) чемода́н; (*of wine etc*) я́щик (*содержа́щий** 12 *буты́лок*); (*TYP*): **lower/upper ~** ни́жный/ве́рхний* регистр; **to have a good ~** име́ть *(impf)* убеди́тельные до́воды; **there's a strong ~ for reform** есть все основа́ния для проведе́ния рефо́рмы; **in ~ (of)** (*fire, emergency*) в слу́чае (*+gen*); **in ~ he comes** в слу́чае, е́сли он придёт; **in any ~** во вся́ком слу́чае; **just in ~** на вся́кий* слу́чай.
case history *n* (*MED*) исто́рия боле́зни.
case study *n* изуче́ние конкре́тного слу́чая.
cash [kæʃ] *n* нали́чные *pl adj* (де́ньги) ◆ *vt*: **to ~ a cheque** обме́нивать (обменя́ть *perf*) чек на де́ньги; **to pay (in) ~** плати́ть* (заплати́ть* *perf*) нали́чными; **~ on delivery** нало́женный платёж; **~ with order** опла́та при соверше́нии зака́за
▸ **cash in** *vt* получа́ть (получи́ть* *perf*) де́ньги по *+dat*
▸ **cash in on** *vt fus* испо́льзовать *(impf)* в свои́х интере́сах.
cash account *n* нали́чный счёт*.
cash-and-carry [kæʃən'kærɪ] *n* мелкоопто́вый магази́н.
cash-book ['kæʃbuk] *n* ка́ссовая кни́га.
cash box *n* коро́бка для хране́ния ка́ссы.
cash card *n* (*BRIT*) *ка́рточка для получе́ния нали́чных из автома́та*.
cash cow *n* (*enterprise*) хле́бное де́ло*; (*product*) золото́е дно*.
cash crop *n* това́рная культу́ра.
cash desk *n* (*BRIT*) ка́сса.
cash discount *n ски́дка с цены́ това́ра в слу́чае упла́ты нали́чными*.
cash dispenser *n* (*BRIT*) банкома́т.
cashew [kæ'ʃu:] *n* (*also:* **~ nut**) оре́х ке́шью *m ind*.
cash flow *n* движе́ние де́нежной нали́чности.
cashier [kæ'ʃɪəʳ] *n* касси́р.
cashmere ['kæʃmɪəʳ] *n* (*wool, jersey*) кашеми́р.
cash point *n* банкома́т.
cash price *n цена́ това́ра при прода́же за нали́чные*.
cash register *n* ка́ссовый аппара́т.
cash reserves *npl* ка́ссовый резе́рв *msg*.
cash sale *n* прода́жа за нали́чные *pl adj*.
casing ['keɪsɪŋ] *n* оболо́чка*, футля́р.
casino [kə'si:nəu] *n* казино́ *nt ind*.
cask [kɑ:sk] *n* бочо́нок*.
casket ['kɑ:skɪt] *n* шкату́лка; (*US: coffin*) гроб*.
Caspian Sea ['kæspɪən-] *n* (*GEO*): **the ~ ~** Каспи́йское мо́ре*.
casserole ['kæsərəul] *n* рагу́ *nt ind*; (*also:* **~ dish**) ла́тка*.
cassette [kæ'sɛt] *n* кассе́та.
cassette deck *n* кассе́тный магнитофо́н (*стациона́рный*).
cassette player *n* кассе́тный пле́йер.
cassette recorder *n* кассе́тный магнитофо́н (*портати́вный*).
cast [kɑ:st] (*pt, pp* **cast**) *vt* (*light, shadow, glance*) броса́ть (бро́сить* *perf*); (*net, fishing line*) забра́сывать (забро́сить* *perf*); (*doubts*) се́ять (посе́ять *perf*); (*spell*) околдо́вывать (околдова́ть *perf*); (*skin*) сбра́сывать (сбро́сить* *perf*); (*statue*) отлива́ть (отли́ть*

perf) ♦ *vi* (*FISHING*) забрáсывать (забрóсить* *perf*) сéти ♦ *n* (*THEAT*) состáв (исполнúтелей); (*mould*) фóрма (*для отлúвки*); (*also:* **plaster ~**) гúпсовый слéпок*; **to ~ one's vote (for sb)** отдавáть* (отдáть* *perf*) свой гóлос (за когó-н); **to ~ sb as Hamlet** (*THEAT*) назначáть (назнáчить *perf*) когó-н на роль Гáмлета; **the ~ was full of celebrities** в спектáкле игрáло мнóго знаменúтостей
▸ **cast aside** *vt* отвергáть (отвéргнуть *perf*)
▸ **cast off** *vi* (*NAUT*) отчáливать (отчáлить *perf*); (*KNITTING*) сбрáсывать (сбрóсить* *perf*) пéтлю ♦ *vt* (*KNITTING*) сбрáсывать (сбрóсить* *perf*) (*пéтлю*)
▸ **cast on** *vi* (*KNITTING*) набирáть (набрáть* *perf*) пéтли ♦ *vt* набирáть (набрáть* *perf*) (*пéтли*).
castaway ['kɑ:stəweɪ] *n попáвший пóсле кораблекрушéния на необитáемый óстров*.
caste [kɑ:st] *n* кáста; **the ~ system** кáстовая систéма.
caster sugar ['kɑ:stə-] *n* (*BRIT*) сáхарная пýдра.
casting vote ['kɑ:stɪŋ-] *n* (*BRIT*) решáющий* гóлос (*при рáвном числé голосóв "за" и "прóтив"*).
cast iron *n* чугýн* ♦ *adj*: **~~~** (*fig*) желéзный.
castle ['kɑ:sl] *n* зáмок*; (*fortified*) крéпость *f*; (*CHESS*) ладья́*, турá.
cast-offs ['kɑ:stɔfs] *npl* обнóски *mpl*.
castor ['kɑ:stə^r] *n* (*wheel*) рóлик.
castor oil *n* кастóровое мáсло.
castrate [kæs'treɪt] *vt* кастрúровать (*impf/perf*).
casual ['kæʒjul] *adj* (*meeting*) случáйный* (случáен); (*attitude*) небрéжный* (небрéжен); (*clothes*) повседнéвный; **to do ~ work** дéлать (*impf*) случáйную рабóту; **~ wear** повседнéвная одéжда.
casual labour *n* врéменные рабóтники *mpl*.
casually ['kæʒjulɪ] *adv* (*behave*) небрéжно; (*dress*) повседнéвно; (*by chance*) случáйно; **he was ~ dressed** он был одéт в повсе-днéвную одéжду.
casualty ['kæʒjultɪ] *n* (*sb injured*) пострадáвший(-ая) *m(f) adj*; (*sb killed, victim*) жéртва; (*MED*: *department*) травматолóгия; **heavy casualties** тяжёлые потéри *fpl*.
casualty ward *n* (*BRIT*) травматологúческое отделéние.
cat [kæt] *n* (*pet*) кóшка*; (*tomcat*) кот; **big ~s** кошáчьи *pl adj*.
catacombs ['kætəku:mz] *npl* катакóмбы *fpl*.
catalogue ['kætəlɔg] (*US* **catalog**) *n* каталóг; (*of events, faults*) пéречень *m* ♦ *vt* (*books, collection*) каталогизúровать (*impf/perf*); (*events*) перечисля́ть (перечúслить *perf*).
catalyst ['kætəlɪst] *n* (*CHEM, fig*) катализáтор.
catalytic converter [kætə'lɪtɪk kən'və:tə^r] *n* (*AUT*) каталитúческий нейтрализáтор.
catapult ['kætəpʌlt] *n* (*BRIT*) рогáтка*; (*MIL*) катапýльта ♦ *vi* катапультúроваться (*impf/perf*) ♦ *vt* катапультúровать (*impf/perf*).
cataract ['kætərækt] *n* катарáкта.
catarrh [kə'tɑ:^r] *n* катáр.
catastrophe [kə'tæstrəfɪ] *n* катастрóфа.
catastrophic [kætə'strɔfɪk] *adj* катастрофúческий*.
catcall ['kætkɔ:l] *n* освúстывание.
catch [kætʃ] (*pt, pp* **caught**) *vt* ловúть* (поймáть *perf*); (*bus etc*) садúться (сесть* *perf*) на *+acc*; (*breath*) затáивать (затаúть *perf*); (*attention*) привлекáть (привлéчь* *perf*); (*hit*) ударя́ть (удáрить *perf*); (*hear*) улáвливать (уловúть* *perf*); (*illness*) подхвáтывать (подхватúть* *perf*); (*person*) заставáть* (застáть* *perf*) ♦ *vi* (*become trapped*) застревáть (застря́ть *perf*) ♦ *n* (*of fish*) улóв; (*criminal caught*) задéржанный(-ая) *m(f) adj*; (*of ball*) захвáт; (*hidden problem*) подвóх; (*of lock*) защёлка; (*game*) пятнáшки *pl*; **to ~ sb's attention** *or* **eye** привлекáть (привлéчь* *perf*) чьё-н внимáние; **to ~ sight of** увúдеть* (*perf*); **to ~ fire** загорéться (*perf*)
▸ **catch on** *vi* (*grow popular*) приживáться (прижúться* *perf*); (*understand*): **to ~ on (to sth)** понимáть (поня́ть* *perf*) (что-н)
▸ **catch out** *vt* (*BRIT*: *fig*) ловúть* (поймáть *perf*)
▸ **catch up** *vi* (*fig*) нагоня́ть (нагнáть* *perf*) ♦ *vt* (*also:* **~ up with**) догоня́ть (догнáть* *perf*).
catching ['kætʃɪŋ] *adj* (*fig*) заразúтельный*; (*MED*) зарáзный*.
catchment area ['kætʃmənt-] *n* (*BRIT*: *of school etc*) микрорайóн; (*GEO*) бассéйн.
catch phrase *n* мóдное выражéние.
catch-22 ['kætʃtwentɪ'tu:] *n*: **it's a ~ situation** это безвыходная ситуáция.
catchy ['kætʃɪ] *adj* легкó запоминáющийся.
catechism ['kætɪkɪzəm] *n* катехúзис.
categoric(al) [kætɪ'gɔrɪk(l)] *adj* категорúческий*.
categorize ['kætɪgəraɪz] *vt* (*classify*) классифицúровать (*impf/perf*).
category ['kætɪgərɪ] *n* категóрия.
cater ['keɪtə^r] *vi* (*provide food*): **to ~ (for)** организóвывать (организовáть *perf*) питáние (для *+gen*)
▸ **cater for** *vt fus* (*BRIT*: *needs, tastes*) удовлетворя́ть (удовлетворúть *perf*); (: *readers, consumers*) обслýживать (обслужúть* *perf*).
caterer ['keɪtərə^r] *n* организáтор питáния.
catering ['keɪtərɪŋ] *n* (*trade, business*) общéственное питáние.
caterpillar ['kætəpɪlə^r] *n* гýсеница ♦ *cpd* (*vehicle*) гýсеничный.
caterpillar track *n* гýсеница (*TEX*)
cat flap *n* кошáчий* лаз* (*в дверú*), кошáчья

двéрца.
cathedral [kəˈθiːdrəl] *n* собóр.
cathode [ˈkæθəud] *n* катóд.
cathode-ray tube [kæθəudˈreɪ-] *n* электроннолучевáя трýбка*.
Catholic [ˈkæθəlɪk] *adj* католи́ческий* ◆ *n* катóлик(-и́чка).
catholic *adj* (*tastes, interests*) разносторóнний*.
CAT scanner *n abbr* (MED: = *computerized axial tomography scanner*) аксиáльный компьютерный томóграф.
Catseye® [ˈkætsˈaɪ] *n* (BRIT: AUT) "кошáчий глаз" (*вмонти́рованный в дорóгу отражáтель свéта фар*).
catsup [ˈkætsəp] *n* (US) кéтчуп.
cattle [ˈkætl] *npl* скот* *msg*.
catty [ˈkætɪ] *adj* ехи́дный*.
catwalk [ˈkætwɔːk] *n* помóст *or* эстрáда (*для демонстрáции модéлей одéжды*).
Caucasian [kɔːˈkeɪzɪən] *adj* кавкáзский ◆ *n* кавкáзец*(-зка).
Caucasus [ˈkɔːkəsəs] *n* Кавкáз.
caucus [ˈkɔːkəs] *n* (POL: *group*) *влия́тельная группирóвка внутри́ пáртии*; (: US) *предвы́борный ми́тинг сторóнников пáртии*.
caught [kɔːt] *pt, pp of* **catch**.
cauliflower [ˈkɔlɪflauəʳ] *n* цветнáя капýста.
cause [kɔːz] *n* (*reason*) причи́на; (*aim*) дéло* ◆ *vt* явля́ться (яви́ться* *perf*) причи́ной *+gen*; **there is no ~ for concern** нет причи́н для беспокóйства; **to ~ sb trouble/harm** причиня́ть (причини́ть *perf*) комý-н неприя́тности/вред; **to ~ sb to do** (*force*) заставля́ть (застáвить* *perf*) когó-н *+infin*.
causeway [ˈkɔːzweɪ] *n* дорóга (*проложéнная чéрез тóнкое мéсто*).
caustic [ˈkɔːstɪk] *adj* каусти́ческий*; (*fig*) éдкий*.
cauterize [ˈkɔːtəraɪz] *vt* прижигáть (прижéчь* *perf*).
caution [ˈkɔːʃən] *n* осторóжность *f*; (*warning*) предупреждéние, предостережéние ◆ *vt* предупреждáть (предупреди́ть *perf*).
cautious [ˈkɔːʃəs] *adj* осторóжный* (осторóжен).
cautiously [ˈkɔːʃəslɪ] *adv* осторóжно.
cautiousness [ˈkɔːʃəsnɪs] *n* осторóжность *f*.
cavalier [kævəˈlɪəʳ] *adj* надмéнный*, пренебрежи́тельный.
cavalry [ˈkævəlrɪ] *n* кавалéрия; (*mechanized*) мотопехóта.
cave [keɪv] *n* пещéра ◆ *vi*: **to go caving** занимáться *(impf)* спелеолóгией
▸ **cave in** *vi* (*roof etc*) обвáливаться (обвали́ться *perf*); (*inf: give in*) сдавáться* (сдáться* *perf*).
caveman [ˈkeɪvmæn] *irreg n* пещéрный человéк*.
cavern [ˈkævən] *n* пещéра.
caviar(e) [ˈkævɪɑːʳ] *n* икрá*.
cavity [ˈkævɪtɪ] *n* пóлость* *f*; (*in tooth*) дуплó*.
cavity wall insulation *n* двойнáя стенá с изоля́цией.
cavort [kəˈvɔːt] *vi* скакáть* *(impf)*.
cayenne [keɪˈɛn] *n* (*also:* **~ pepper**) крáсный стручкóвый пéрец.
CB *n abbr* (= *Citizens' Band (Radio)*) *диапазóн частóт люби́тельской радиосвя́зи*; (BRIT: = *Companion of (the Order of) the Bath*) кавалéр óрдена Бáни.
CBC *n abbr* = *Canadian Broadcasting Corporation*.
CBE *n abbr* (BRIT: = *Companion of (the Order of) the British Empire*) кавалéр óрдена Бритáнской Импéрии.
CBI *n abbr* (= *Confederation of British Industries*) Конфедерáция бритáнской промы́шленности.
CBS *n abbr* (US) = *Columbia Broadcasting System*.
CC *abbr* (BRIT: = *county council*) ≈ совéт грáфства.
cc *abbr* (= *cubic centimetre*) куби́ческий* сантимéтр; = **carbon copy**.
CCA *n abbr* (US: = *Circuit Court of Appeals*) Окружнóй апелляциóнный суд.
CCTV *n abbr* = **closed-circuit television**.
CCU *n abbr* (US: = *coronary care unit*) *отделéние интенси́вной терапи́и для больны́х с óстрой сердéчной недостáточностью*.
CD *abbr* (BRIT: = *Corps Diplomatique*) ≈ дипкóрпус= *дипломати́ческий кóрпус* ◆ *n abbr* (MIL: BRIT: = *Civil Defence (Corps)*) граждáнская оборóна; (: US: = *Civil Defense*) граждáнская оборóна; = **compact disc**; **~ player** проигрыватель *m* для компáкт-ди́сков.
CDC *n abbr* (US) = *Center for Disease Control*.
CD-I *n abbr* (= *compact disc interactive*) компáктный диск-интеракти́вный (*устрóйство, позволя́ющее передавáть содержáние компáктного ди́ска на телеэкрáн*).
Cdr. *abbr* (MIL) = **commander**.
CD-ROM *abbr* (= *compact disc read-only memory*) пáмять, считывающая информáцию с компáкт-ди́ска.
CDT *abbr* (US) = *Central Daylight Time*.
cease [siːs] *vt* прекращáть (прекрати́ть* *perf*) ◆ *vi* прекращáться (прекрати́ться* *perf*).
cease-fire [ˈsiːsfaɪəʳ] *n* прекращéние огня́.
ceaseless [ˈsiːslɪs] *adj* непреры́вный*.
CED *n abbr* (US) = *Committee for Economic Development*.
cedar [ˈsiːdəʳ] *n* кедр.
cede [siːd] *vt* уступáть (уступи́ть* *perf*).
cedilla [sɪˈdɪlə] *n* седи́ль *m* (*орфографи́ческий знак*).
CEEB *n abbr* (US) = *College Entry Examination Board*.
Ceefax [ˈsiːfæks] *n информациóнная слýжба*

БиБиСи, осуществляемая путём вывода на экран телевизора информации, классифицированной по различным направлениям.
ceilidh ['keılı] *n* вечер народной музыки.
ceiling ['si:lıŋ] *n* (*also fig*) потолок*.
celebrate ['sɛlıbreıt] *vt* праздновать (отпраздновать *perf*) ◆ *vi* веселиться (повеселиться *perf*); **to ~ mass** отправлять *(impf)* церковную службу.
celebrated ['sɛlıbreıtıd] *adj* знаменитый (знаменит).
celebration [sɛlı'breıʃən] *n* (*event*) праздник; (*of anniversary etc*) празднование.
celebrity [sı'lɛbrıtı] *n* знаменитость *f*.
celeriac [sə'lɛrıæk] *n* корнеплод сельдерея.
celery ['sɛlərı] *n* сельдерей.
celestial [sı'lɛstıəl] *adj* небесный.
celibacy ['sɛlıbəsı] *n* сексуальное воздержание; (*unmarried state*) безбрачие.
cell [sɛl] *n* (*in prison*) камера; (*in monastery*) келья*; (*of revolutionaries etc*) ячейка*; (*BIO*) клетка*; (*ELEC*) элемент.
cellar ['sɛlə^r] *n* подвал; (*also:* **wine ~**) винный погреб*.
cellist ['tʃɛlıst] *n* виолончелист(ка).
cello ['tʃɛləu] *n* виолончель *f*.
cellophane ['sɛləfeın] *n* целлофан.
cellphone ['sɛlfəun] *n* портативный телефон.
cellular ['sɛljulə^r] *adj* (*BIO*) клеточный; (*fabrics*) сетчатый.
celluloid ['sɛljulɔıd] *n* целлулоид.
cellulose ['sɛljuləus] *n* клетчатка, целлюлоза.
Celsius ['sɛlsıəs] *adj*: **30 degrees ~** 30 градусов по Цельсию.
Celt [kɛlt] *n* кельт.
Celtic ['kɛltık] *adj* кельтский* ◆ *n* (*LING*) кельтский* язык*.
cement [sə'mɛnt] *n* цемент; (*glue*) клей* ◆ *vt* (*also fig*) цементировать *(impf/perf)*; (*stick, glue*): **to ~ to** приклеивать (приклеить *perf*) *or* прикреплять (прикрепить* *perf*) к *+dat*.
cement mixer *n* бетономешалка*.
cemetery ['sɛmıtrı] *n* кладбище.
cenotaph ['sɛnətɑ:f] *n памятник погибшим солдатам.*
censor ['sɛnsə^r] *n* цензор ◆ *vt* подвергать (подвергнуть* *perf*) цензуре.
censorship ['sɛnsəʃıp] *n* цензура.
censure ['sɛnʃə^r] *vt* осуждать (осудить* *perf*), порицать *(impf)* ◆ *n* осуждение, порицание.
census ['sɛnsəs] *n* (*of population*) перепись *f*.
cent [sɛnt] *n* (*US etc: coin*) цент; *see also* **per**.
centenary [sɛn'ti:nərı] *n* столетие.
centennial [sɛn'tɛnıəl] *n* (*US*) столетие.
center *etc n* (*US*) = **centre** *etc*.
centigrade ['sɛntıgreıd] *adj*: **30 degrees ~** 30 градусов по Цельсию.
centilitre ['sɛntıli:tə^r] (*US* **centiliter**) *n* центилитр.
centimetre ['sɛntımi:tə^r] (*US* **centimeter**) *n* сантиметр.
centipede ['sɛntıpi:d] *n* многоножка*.
central ['sɛntrəl] *adj* центральный*; **this flat is very ~** эта квартира расположена близко к центру города.
Central African Republic *n* Центрально-Африканская республика.
Central America *n* Центральная Америка.
central heating *n* центральное отопление.
centralize ['sɛntrəlaız] *vt* централизовать *(impf/perf)*.
central processing unit *n* центральный процессор.
central reservation *n* (*BRIT: AUT*) разделительная полоса.
centre ['sɛntə^r] (*US* **center**) *n* центр ◆ *vt* (*PHOT, TYP*) центрировать *(impf/perf)*; (*SPORT: ball*) подавать* (подать* *perf*) в центр поля; (*concentrate on*): **to ~ (on)** сосредоточиваться (сосредоточиться *perf*) (на *+prp*); **to ~ sth on** сосредоточивать (сосредоточить *perf*) что-н на *+acc*.
centrefold ['sɛntəfəuld] (*US* **centerfold**) *n* центральная вкладка*.
centre forward *n* (*SPORT*) центральный нападающий* *m adj*, центр-форвард.
centre half *n* (*SPORT*) центральный полузащитник.
centrepiece ['sɛntəpi:s] (*US* **centerpiece**) *n декоративный предмет, выставленный посередине стола, полки итд*; (*fig*) главное украшение.
centre spread *n* (*BRIT: PRESS*) разворот.
centre-stage [sɛntə'steıdʒ] *n* центр сцены.
centrifugal [sɛn'trıfjugl] *adj* (*PHYS*) центробежный.
centrifuge ['sɛntrıfju:ʒ] *n* центрифуга.
century ['sɛntjurı] *n* век*; (*CRICKET*) сто очков; **twentieth ~** двадцатый век; **in the twentieth ~** в двадцатом веке.
CEO *n abbr* (*US:* = *chief executive officer*) главный администратор.
ceramic [sı'ræmık] *adj* керамический*.
ceramics [sı'ræmıks] *npl* керамика *fsg*.
cereal ['si:rıəl] *n* (*plant, crop*): **~s** зерновые *pl adj*; (*also:* **breakfast ~**) хлопья *pl* к завтраку.
cerebral ['sɛrıbrəl] *adj* (*MED*) мозговой, церебральный; (*intellectual*) умозрительный* (умозрителен); **~ palsy** церебральный паралич.
ceremonial [sɛrı'məunıəl] *n* церемониал ◆ *adj* обрядовый.
ceremony ['sɛrımənı] *n* церемония; (*behaviour*) церемонии *fpl*; **with ~** со всеми

* marks translations which have irregular inflections. The Russian-English side of the dictionary gives inflectional information.

формáльностями; **to stand on ~** настáивать (настоя́ть* *perf*) на соблюдéнии формáльностей.
cert [sə:t] *n* (*BRIT*: *inf*): **it's a dead ~** э́то дéло вéрное.
certain ['sə:tən] *adj* (*sure*): **I'm ~ (that)** я увéрен (что); (*particular*): **~ days** определённые дни; (*some*): **a ~ pleasure** нéкоторое удовóльствие; **it's ~ (that)** несомнéнно (что); **in ~ circumstances** при определённых обстоя́тельствах; **a ~ Mr Smith** нéкий Ми́стер Смит; **to make ~ of/that** удостоверя́ться (удостовéриться *perf*) в +*prp*/что; **for ~** наверняќа.
certainly ['sə:tənlı] *adv* (*undoubtedly*) несомнéнно; (*of course*) конéчно.
certainty ['sə:təntı] *n* (*assurance*) увéренность *f*; (*inevitability*) несомнéнность *f*.
certificate [sə'tıfıkıt] *n* (*doctor's etc*) спрáвка; (*diploma*) диплóм; **birth ~** свидéтельство рождéнии; **marriage ~** свидéтельство о заключéнии брáка.
certified letter ['sə:tıfaıd-] *n* (*US*) гаранти́рованное письмó.
certified mail *n* (*US*) гаранти́рованная пóчта.
certified public accountant *n* (*US*) *бухгáлтер вы́сшей квалификáции.*
certify ['sə:tıfaı] *vt* (*fact*) удостоверя́ть (удостовéрить *perf*); (*after studies*) выдавáть* (вы́дать* *perf*) диплóм +*dat*; (*also:* **~ insane**) признавáть* (признáть* *perf*) душевнобольны́м(-ой); **he is a certified lawyer** он дипломи́рованный юри́ст.
cervical ['sə:vıkl] *adj*: **~ cancer** рак шéйки мáтки; **~ smear** мазóк* с шéйки мáтки.
cervix ['sə:vıks] *n* шéйка мáтки.
Cesarean [si:'zεərıən] *adj, n* (*US*) = **Caesarean**.
cessation [sə'seıʃən] *n* прекращéние.
cesspit ['sεspıt] *n* выгребнáя я́ма.
CET *abbr* (= *Central European Time*) центральноевропéйское врéмя* *nt*.
Ceylon [sı'lɔn] *n* Цейлóн.
cf. *abbr* = **compare**.
c/f *abbr* (*COMM*: = *carried forward*) перенесенó на слéдующую страни́цу.
CFC *n abbr* (= *chlorofluorocarbon*) хлорфтороуглерóд.
CG *n abbr* (*US*) = **coastguard**.
cg *abbr* (= *centigram*) сантигрáмм.
CH *n abbr* (*BRIT*: = *Companion of Honour*) *кавалéр óрдена.*
ch. *abbr* (= **chapter**) гл.= *главá.*
c.h. *abbr* (*BRIT*) = **central heating**.
Chad [tʃæd] *n* Чад.
chafe [tʃeıf] *vt* (*rub*) натирáть (натерéть *perf*) ◆ *vi* (*fig*): **to ~ at/under** раздражáться *(impf)* из-за +*gen*.
chaffinch ['tʃæfıntʃ] *n* зя́блик.
chagrin ['ʃægrın] *n* (*annoyance*) досáда; (*disappointment*) огорчéние.
chain [tʃeın] *n* (*also fig*) цепь* *f*; (*decorative, on bicycle*) цепóчка*; (*of shops, hotels*) сеть* *f*; (*of events, ideas*) верени́ца ◆ *vt* (*also:* **~ up**: *person*) прикóвывать (приковáть *perf*); (*dog*) сажáть (посади́ть* *perf*) на цепь; **a ~ of mountains** гóрная цепь.
chain reaction *n* цепнáя реáкция.
chain-smoke ['tʃeınsməuk] *vi* кури́ть* *(impf)* однý сигарéту за другóй.
chain store *n* филиáл (*магази́на*).
chair [tʃεə^r] *n* стул*; (*also:* **armchair**) крéсло*; (*of university*) кáфедра; (*of meeting*: *also:* **~person**) председáтель *m* ◆ *vt* председáтельствовать *(impf)* на +*prp*; **the ~** (*US*: *also:* **the electric ~**) электри́ческий* стул*; **to take the ~** председáтельствовать *(impf)*.
chair lift *n* канáтный подъёмник.
chairman ['tʃεəmən] *irreg n* председáтель *m*; (*BRIT*: *of company*) президéнт.
chairperson ['tʃεəpə:sn] *n* председáтель *m*.
chairwoman ['tʃεəwumən] *irreg n* председáтель *m*.
chalet ['ʃæleı] *n* ≈ коттéдж.
chalice ['tʃælıs] *n* (*REL*) поти́р.
chalk [tʃɔ:k] *n* мéл*
▸ **chalk up** *vt* (*fig*: *success etc*) заноси́ть* (занести́* *perf*) в спи́сок свои́х достижéний.
challenge ['tʃælındʒ] *n* вы́зов; (*challenging task*) испытáние ◆ *vt* (*rival*: *also SPORT*) бросáть (брóсить* *perf*) вы́зов +*dat*; (*authority, right etc*) оспáривать (оспóрить *perf*); **to ~ sb to sth** вызывáть (вы́звать* *perf*) когó-н на что-н.
challenger ['tʃælındʒə^r] *n* (*in sport*) претендéнт(ка).
challenging ['tʃælındʒıŋ] *adj* (*task*) трýдный* (трýден); (*tone, look*) вызывáющий*; **this work is very ~** э́та рабóта трéбует большóй отдáчи.
chamber ['tʃeımbə^r] *n* (*room*) кáмера; (*POL*) палáта; (*BRIT*: *LAW*: *usu pl*) адвокáтская контóра; **~ of commerce** Торгóвая Палáта.
chambermaid ['tʃeımbəmeıd] *n* гóрничная *f adj*.
chamber music *n* кáмерная мýзыка.
chamber pot *n* ночнóй горшóк*.
chameleon [kə'mi:lıən] *n* хамелеóн.
chamois ['ʃæmwɑ:] *n* (*ZOOL*) сéрна; (*also:* **~ leather**) зáмша.
champagne [ʃæm'peın] *n* шампáнское *nt adj*.
champers ['ʃæmpəz] *n* (*inf*) шампáнское *nt adj*.
champion ['tʃæmpıən] *n* (*SPORT*) чемпиóн; (*of cause*) побóрник(-ица); (*of person*) защи́тник(-ица) ◆ *vt* защищáть (защити́ть* *perf*).
championship ['tʃæmpıənʃıp] *n* (*contest*) чемпионáт; (*title*) звáние чемпиóна.
chance [tʃɑ:ns] *n* (*hope, possibility*) шанс; (*opportunity*) возмóжность *f*; (*risk*) риск ◆ *vt* (*risk*) рисковáть *(impf)* +*instr* ◆ *adj* случáйный; **the ~s are that** ... все шáнсы за то, что ...;

there is little ~ of his coming маловероя́тно, что он придёт; **to take a ~** рискну́ть *(perf)*; **by ~** случа́йно; **to leave to ~** оставля́ть (оста́вить* *perf*) на во́лю слу́чая; **it's the ~ of a lifetime** така́я возмо́жность представля́ется раз в жи́зни; **to ~ it** рискну́ть *(perf)*; **to ~ to overhear/see** (*happen*) случа́йно подслу́шать *(perf)*/уви́деть *(perf)*

▸ **chance (up)on** *vt fus* случа́йно наткну́ться *(perf)* на *+acc*.

chancel ['tʃɑːnsəl] *n* алта́рная часть *f*.

chancellor ['tʃɑːnsələʳ] *n* (*POL*) ка́нцлер; (*BRIT: of university*) почётный ре́ктор (*номина́льный пост*).

Chancellor of the Exchequer *n* (*BRIT*) ка́нцлер казначе́йства (*мини́стр фина́нсов*).

chancy ['tʃɑːnsɪ] *adj* риско́ванный (риско́ван).

chandelier [ʃændə'lɪəʳ] *n* лю́стра.

change [tʃeɪndʒ] *vt* меня́ть (поменя́ть *perf*); (*wheel, bulb etc*) заменя́ть (замени́ть* *perf*); (*job, address*) сменя́ть (смени́ть* *perf*); (*money: to different currency*) обме́нивать (обменя́ть *perf*); (: *for smaller notes or coins*) разме́нивать (разменя́ть *perf*) ◆ *vi* (*alter*) меня́ться *(impf)*, изменя́ться (измени́ться* *perf*); (*one's clothes*) переодева́ться (переоде́ться* *perf*); (*change trains, buses*) де́лать (сде́лать *perf*) переса́дку ◆ *n* (*alteration*) измене́ние; (*difference*) переме́на; (*replacement*) сме́на; (*coins: also:* **small** *or* **loose ~**) ме́лочь *f*; (*money returned*) сда́ча; **to ~ sb into** превраща́ть (преврати́ть* *perf*) кого́-н в *+acc*; **to ~ one's mind** переду́мывать (переду́мать *perf*); **to ~ gear** (*AUT*) переключа́ть (переключи́ть *perf*) ско́рость; **to ~ a baby's nappy** перепелёнывать (перепелена́ть *perf*) ребёнка; **to ~ into** (*be transformed*) превраща́ться (преврати́ться* *perf*) в *+acc*; **a ~ of clothes** сме́на оде́жды; **to give sb ~ for** *or* **of ten pounds** дава́ть* (дать* *perf*) кому́-н сда́чу с десяти́ фу́нтов; **keep the ~** сда́чи не на́до; **for a ~** для разнообра́зия.

changeable ['tʃeɪndʒəbl] *adj* (*weather, mood*) изме́нчивый (изме́нчив); (*person*) непостоя́нный* (непостоя́нен).

change machine *n* разме́нный автома́т.

changeover ['tʃeɪndʒəuvəʳ] *n*: **~ (to)** (*to new system*) перехо́д (к *+dat*).

changing ['tʃeɪndʒɪŋ] *adj* (*world*) изменя́ющийся; (*colours*) меня́ющийся.

changing room *n* (*BRIT: in shop*) приме́рочная *f adj*; (: *SPORT*) раздева́лка*.

channel ['tʃænl] *n* кана́л; (*for shipping*) тра́сса; (*groove*) жёлоб* ◆ *vt*: **to ~ into** (*money, interest*) направля́ть (напра́вить* *perf*) на *+acc*; **through the usual ~s** че́рез обы́чные кана́лы; **~s of communication** кана́лы свя́зи; **green/red ~** зелёный/кра́сный кана́л (*при тамо́женном контро́ле*); **the (English) C~** Ла-Ма́нш; **the C~ Islands** Норма́ндские острова́ *mpl*.

Channel Tunnel *n* тунне́ль *m* под Ла-Ма́ншем.

chant [tʃɑːnt] *n* (*of crowd, fans etc*) сканди́рование; (*REL: song*) пе́ние ◆ *vti* (*shout*) сканди́ровать *(impf)*; **the demonstrators ~ed their disapproval** демонстра́нты хо́ром выража́ли неодобре́ние.

chaos ['keɪɔs] *n* ха́ос.

chaos theory *n*: **the ~ ~** тео́рия ха́оса.

chaotic [keɪ'ɔtɪk] *adj* (*mess, situation*) хаоти́чный* (хаоти́чен).

chap [tʃæp] *n* (*BRIT: inf*) па́рень* *m*; (*term of address*): **old ~** старина́ *m*, стари́к.

chapel ['tʃæpl] *n* (*in church*)ириде́л; (*in hospital, prison, school etc*) часо́вня; (*BRIT: also:* **non-conformist ~**) протеста́нтская нон-конформи́стская це́рковь*; (: *of trade union*) *отделе́ние профсою́за полиграфи́стов*.

chaperone ['ʃæpərəun] *n* (*for woman*) компаньо́нка ◆ *vt* сопровожда́ть (сопроводи́ть* *perf*).

chaplain ['tʃæplɪn] *n* капелла́н.

chapped [tʃæpt] *adj* (*skin, lips etc*) потре́скавшийся.

chapter ['tʃæptəʳ] *n* (*of book*) глава́*; (*of life, history*) страни́ца; **a ~ of accidents** череда́ неуда́ч.

char [tʃɑːʳ] *vt* (*burn*) обу́гливать (обу́глить *perf*) ◆ *vi* (*BRIT*) рабо́тать *(impf)* убо́рщицей ◆ *n* (*BRIT*) = **charlady**.

character ['kærɪktəʳ] *n* (*personality*) ли́чность *f*; (*nature, strength of character*) хара́ктер; (*in novel, film*) персона́ж; (*eccentric*) оригина́л; (*letter, symbol*) знак; (: *COMPUT*) си́мвол; **a person of good ~** досто́йный челове́к.

character code *n* (*COMPUT*) код си́мвола.

characteristic ['kærɪktə'rɪstɪk] *n* характе́рная черта́ ◆ *adj*: **~ (of)** характе́рный* (характе́рен) (для *+gen*); **it is ~ of him** э́то характе́рно для него́.

characterize ['kærɪktəraɪz] *vt* (*typify*) характеризова́ть *(impf/perf)*; (*describe*): **to ~ (as)** характеризова́ть* *(impf/perf)* (как); **to be ~d by** характеризова́ться *(impf) +instr*.

charade [ʃə'rɑːd] *n* шара́да; (*fig*) коме́дия.

charcoal ['tʃɑːkəul] *n* (*fuel*) древе́сный у́голь* *m*; (*for drawing*) у́голь.

charge [tʃɑːdʒ] *n* (*fee*) пла́та; (*LAW: accusation*) обвине́ние; (*responsibility*) отве́тственность *f*; (*of gun, battery*) заря́д; (*MIL: attack*) ата́ка ◆ *vi* (*also MIL*) атакова́ть *(impf/perf)*; (*rush*) кида́ться (ки́нуться *perf*), броса́ться (бро́ситься *perf*) ◆ *vt* (*battery, gun*) заряжа́ть

* marks translations which have irregular inflections. The Russian-English side of the dictionary gives inflectional information.

(зарядить* *perf*); (*LAW*: *accuse*): **to ~ sb with** обвинять (обвинить *perf*) кого-н в *+prp*; (*entrust*) поручать (поручить* *perf*) кому-н *+acc*; **~s** *npl* (*bank charges*) денежный сбор *msg*; (*telephone charges*) телефонный тариф *msg*; **labour ~s** стоимость *fsg* рабочей силы; **to reverse the ~s** (*TEL*) звонить *(impf)* по коллекту; **is there a ~?** за это нужно платить?; **at no extra ~** без дополнительной оплаты; **free of ~** бесплатно; **to take ~ of** (*child*) брать* (взять* *perf*) на попечение; (*company*) брать* (взять* *perf*) на себя руководство *+instr*; **to be in ~ of** отвечать *(impf)* за *+acc*; **who's in ~ here?** кто здесь главный?; **to ~ (sb) (for)** (*demand fee*) просить* (попросить* *perf*) (у кого-н) плату (за *+acc*); **they ~d us £10 for the meal** с нас взяли £10 за еду; **how much do you ~ for?** сколько Вы просите за *+acc*?; **to ~ an expense (up) to sb's account** переводить* (перевести* *perf*) расходы на чей-н счёт.

charge account *n* кредит по открытому счёту.

charge card *n* кредитная карточка* (*определённого магазина*).

chargé d'affaires ['ʃɑ:ʒeɪ dæ'fɛə] *n* поверенный* *m adj* в делах.

charge hand *n* (*BRIT*) мастер* (*на производстве*).

charger ['tʃɑ:dʒəʳ] *n* (*also:* **battery ~**) зарядное устройство; (*warhorse*) боевой конь *m*.

chariot ['tʃærɪət] *n* колесница.

charisma [kæ'rɪsmə] *n* обаяние.

charitable ['tʃærɪtəbl] *adj* (*organization*) благотворительный; (*person*) милосердный* (милосерден).

charity ['tʃærɪtɪ] *n* (*organization*) благотворительная организация; (*kindness*) милосердие; (*money, gifts*) милостыня.

charlady ['tʃɑ:leɪdɪ] *n* (*BRIT*) уборщица.

charlatan ['ʃɑ:lətən] *n* шарлатан.

charm [tʃɑ:m] *n* (*attractiveness*) обаяние, очарование; (*spell*) заклинание; (*talisman*) амулет; (*on bracelet etc*) брелок ◆ *vt* (*please, delight*) очаровывать (очаровать *perf*).

charm bracelet *n* браслет с брелками.

charming ['tʃɑ:mɪŋ] *adj* очаровательный* (очарователен).

chart [tʃɑ:t] *n* (*graph, diagram*) график; (*NAUT*) навигационная карта; (*ASTRONOMY*) карта звёздного неба; (*weather chart*) синоптическая карта ◆ *vt* (*put on map*) наносить* (нанести* *perf*) на карту; (*keep track of*) фиксировать *(impf)*; **~s** *npl* (*hit parade*) хит-парад *msg*; **to be in the ~s** (*record*) *быть в списке наиболее популярных дисков*.

charter ['tʃɑ:təʳ] *vt* (*plane, ship etc*) фрахтовать (зафрахтовать *perf*) ◆ *n* (*of company*) устав; (*document, constitution*) хартия; **on ~** (*plane, train etc*) по чартеру.

chartered accountant ['tʃɑ:təd-] *n* (*BRIT*) *бухгалтер высшей квалификации*.

charter flight *n* чартерный рейс.

charwoman ['tʃɑ:wumən] *irreg n* = **charlady**.

chary ['tʃɛərɪ] *adj*: **to be ~ of** остерегаться *(impf)* *+gen*.

chase [tʃeɪs] *vt* (*pursue*: *also fig*) гнаться*/гоняться *(impf)* за *+instr* ◆ *n* погоня; **to ~ away** *or* **off** прогонять (прогнать* *perf*)

▸ **chase down** *vt* (*US*) = **chase up**

▸ **chase up** *vt* (*BRIT*: *information*) разыскивать (разыскать* *perf*); (: *person*: *remind*) напоминать (напомнить *perf*) *+dat*.

chasm ['kæzəm] *n* (*GEO*) ущелье; (*between people*) пропасть* *f*.

chassis ['ʃæsɪ] *n* шасси *nt ind*.

chaste [tʃeɪst] *adj* (*person, relationship etc*) целомудренный*.

chastened ['tʃeɪsnd] *adj* пристыженный (пристыжен).

chastening ['tʃeɪsnɪŋ] *adj* (*sobering*) отрезвляющий.

chastise [tʃæs'taɪz] *vt* отчитывать (отчитать *perf*).

chastity ['tʃæstɪtɪ] *n* целомудрие.

chat [tʃæt] *vi* болтать (поболтать *perf*) ◆ *n* беседа; **idle ~** болтовня

▸ **chat up** *vt* (*BRIT*: *inf*) заигрывать *(impf)* с *+instr*.

chatline ['tʃætlaɪn] *n телефонная служба, предоставляющая собеседника*.

chat show *n* (*BRIT*) ≈ шоу с участием знаменитостей.

chattel ['tʃætl] *n see* **goods**.

chatter ['tʃætəʳ] *vi* (*person, monkey, parrot*) трещать *(impf)*; (*magpie*) стрекотать* *(impf)*; (*teeth*) стучать *(impf)* ◆ *n* (*of people*) болтовня; (*of birds, animals*) трескотня; **my teeth are ~ing** я стучу зубами.

chatterbox ['tʃætəbɔks] *n* (*inf*) трещотка.

chattering classes ['tʃætərɪŋ 'klɑ:sɪz] *npl*: **the ~** ~ *псевдоинтеллигенция, любящая обсуждать современные политические и общественные проблемы*.

chatty ['tʃætɪ] *adj* (*letter*) живой; (*person*) говорливый (говорлив).

chauffeur ['ʃəufəʳ] *n* (персональный) шофёр.

chauvinism ['ʃəuvɪnɪzəm] *n* (*also:* **male ~**) мужской шовинизм; (*nationalism*) шовинизм.

chauvinist ['ʃəuvɪnɪst] *n* (*also:* **male ~**) шовинист.

chauvinistic [ʃəuvɪ'nɪstɪk] *adj* (*ideas, views*) шовинистический*.

ChE *abbr* = *chemical engineer*.

cheap [tʃi:p] *adj* (*also fig*) дешёвый*; (*reduced*) со скидкой ◆ *adv*: **to buy/sell sth ~** дёшево покупать (купить* *perf*)/продавать* (продать* *perf*) что-н.

cheapen ['tʃi:pn] *vt* (*person*) унижать

(униз́ить* *perf*).
cheaper ['tʃi:pə^r] *adj* дешёвле.
cheaply ['tʃi:plɪ] *adv* дёшево.
cheap money *n*: ~~ **policy** *ситуáция, когдá влáсти стремя́тся стимули́ровать экономи́ческий рост с пóмощью ни́зких процéнтных стáвок,* „дешёвые дéньги".
cheat [tʃi:t] *vi* (*at cards*) жу́льничать *(impf)*; (*in exam*) спи́сывать (списáть* *perf*) ◆ *n* (*person*) жу́лик ◆ *vt*: **to ~ sb (out of £10)** наду́ть *(perf)* когó-н (на £10); **to ~ on sb** (*inf*: *husband, wife etc*) изменя́ть (измени́ть* *perf*) комý-н.
cheating ['tʃi:tɪŋ] *n* жу́льничество, надувáтельство.
check [tʃɛk] *vt* проверя́ть (провéрить *perf*); (*halt*) приостанáвливать (приостанови́ть* *perf*); (*restrain*) сдéрживать (сдержáть* *perf*); (*US*: *items on list*) отмечáть (отмéтить* *perf*) ◆ *vi* проверя́ть (провéрить *perf*) ◆ *n* (*inspection*) провéрка*; (*US*: *bill*) счёт*; (: *COMM*) = **cheque**; (*pattern*: *usu pl*) клéтка* ◆ *adj* (*cloth, skirt*) клéтчатый; **to ~ with sb** посовéтоваться *(perf)* с кем-н; **to keep a ~ on sb/sth** контроли́ровать *(impf)* когó-н/что-н; **to act as a ~ on** (*curb*) явля́ться (яви́ться* *perf*) мéрой контрóля *+gen*
▸ **check in** *vi* (*at hotel, airport*) регистри́роваться (зарегистри́роваться *perf*) ◆ *vt* (*luggage*) сдавáть* (сдать* *perf*)
▸ **check off** *vt* (*items on list etc*) отмечáть (отмéтить* *perf*)
▸ **check out** *vi* (*of hotel*) выпи́сываться (вы́писаться* *perf*) ◆ *vt* (*investigate*: *story*) проверя́ть (провéрить *perf*); (: *building*) прочёсывать (прочесáть *perf*)
▸ **check up** *vi*: **to ~ up on sb/sth** наводи́ть (навести́* *perf*) спрáвки о ком-н/чём-н.
checkered ['tʃɛkəd] *adj* (*US*) = **chequered**.
checkers ['tʃɛkəz] *npl* (*US*: *draughts*) шáшки *pl*.
check guarantee card *n* (*US*) = **cheque card**.
check-in (desk) ['tʃɛkɪn-] *n* (*at airport*) стóйка регистрáции.
checking account ['tʃɛkɪŋ-] *n* (*US*: *current account*) текýщий* счёт*.
check list *n* контрóльный спи́сок*.
checkmate ['tʃɛkmeɪt] *n* (*CHESS*) мат.
checkout ['tʃɛkaut] *n* (*in shop*) контрóль *m*, кáсса.
checkpoint ['tʃɛkpɔɪnt] *n* (*on border*) контрóльно-пропускнóй пункт.
checkroom ['tʃɛkrum] *n* (*US*) кáмера хранéния.
checkup ['tʃɛkʌp] *n* (*MED*) осмóтр.
cheek [tʃi:k] *n* (*ANAT*) щекá*; (*impudence*) нáглость *f*; (*nerve*) дéрзость *f*.
cheekbone ['tʃi:kbəun] *n* скулá*.
cheeky ['tʃi:kɪ] *adj* нахáльный* (нахáлен), нáглый (нагл).
cheep [tʃi:p] *vi* пищáть* *(impf)* ◆ *n* писк.
cheer [tʃɪə^r] *vt* (*encourage*) привéтствовать (поприве́тствовать *perf*); (*gladden*) ободря́ть (ободри́ть *perf*) ◆ *vi* одобри́тельно восклицáть *(impf)*; **~s** *npl* (*of crowd*: *of welcome*) привéтственные вóзгласы *mpl*; (: *of approval*) одобри́тельные вóзгласы *mpl*; **~s!** (*toast*) (за) Вáше здорóвье!
▸ **cheer on** *vt* ободря́ть (ободри́ть *perf*)
▸ **cheer up** *vi* развесели́ться *(perf)*, повеселéть *(perf)* ◆ *vt* (*person*) развесели́ть *(perf)*; **~ up!** не грусти́(те)!
cheerful ['tʃɪəful] *adj* весёлый* (вéсел).
cheerfulness ['tʃɪəfulnɪs] *n* весёлость *f*.
cheerio [tʃɪərɪ'əu] *excl* (*BRIT*) покá!
cheerleader ['tʃɪəli:də^r] *n* заводи́ла (*дéвушка, подстрекáющая болéльщиков на спорти́вных состязáниях*).
cheerless ['tʃɪəlɪs] *adj* уны́лый* (уны́л).
cheese [tʃi:z] *n* сыр*.
cheeseboard ['tʃi:zbɔ:d] *n* доскá* для сы́ра; (*with cheese on it*) доскá* с сы́ром.
cheeseburger ['tʃi:zbə:gə^r] *n* чи́збургер.
cheesecake ['tʃi:zkeɪk] *n* ≈ творóжный кекс.
cheetah ['tʃi:tə] *n* гепáрд.
chef [ʃɛf] *n* шеф-пóвар*.
chemical ['kɛmɪkl] *adj* хими́ческий* ◆ *n* химикáт; (*in laboratory*) реакти́в.
chemical engineering *n* хими́ческая технолóгия.
chemist ['kɛmɪst] *n* (*BRIT*: *pharmacist*) фармацéвт; (*scientist*) хи́мик.
chemistry ['kɛmɪstrɪ] *n* хи́мия.
chemist's (shop) ['kɛmɪsts-] *n* (*BRIT*) аптéка.
chemotherapy [ki:məu'θɛrəpɪ] *n* химотерапи́я.
cheque [tʃɛk] *n* (*BRIT*) чек; **to pay by ~** плати́ть* (заплати́ть* *perf*) чéком.
chequebook ['tʃɛkbuk] *n* (*BRIT*) чéковая кни́жка*.
cheque card *n* (*BRIT*) *кáрточка, подтверждáющая платёжеспосóбность владéльца*.
chequered ['tʃɛkəd] (*US* **checkered**) *adj* (*fig*: *career*) пёстрый.
cherish ['tʃɛrɪʃ] *vt* лелéять (взлелéять *perf*).
cheroot [ʃə'ru:t] *n* сигáра (*с уплощёнными концáми*).
cherry ['tʃɛrɪ] *n* (*fruit, tree*) черéшня*; (: *sour variety*) ви́шня.
chervil ['tʃə:vɪl] *n* купы́рь *m*.
Ches *abbr* (*BRIT*: *POST*) = *Cheshire*.
chess [tʃɛs] *n* шáхматы *pl*.
chessboard ['tʃɛsbɔ:d] *n* шáхматная доскá*.
chessman ['tʃɛsmən] *irreg n* шáхматная фигýра.
chess player *n* шахмати́ст.
chest [tʃɛst] *n* (*ANAT*) грудь* *f*; (*box*) сундýк*;

I'm glad I got it off my ~ (*inf*) я рад, что облегчи́л ду́шу.
chest measurement *n* окру́жность *f* груди́.
chestnut ['tʃɛsnʌt] *n* кашта́н ◆ *adj* (*hair*) кашта́новый; (*horse*) гнедо́й.
chest of drawers *n* комо́д.
chesty ['tʃæstɪ] *adj* грудно́й.
chew [tʃu:] *vt* (*food*) жева́ть (*impf*); (*nails*) грызть* (*impf*); (*a hole*) прогрыза́ть (прогры́зть* *perf*).
chewing gum ['tʃu:ɪŋ-] *n* жева́тельная рези́нка.
chic [ʃi:k] *adj* шика́рный*, элега́нтный* (элега́нтен).
Chicago [ʃɪ'kɑ:geu] *n* Чика́го *m ind.*
chick [tʃɪk] *n* (*of hen*) цыплёнок; (*of wild bird*) птене́ц*; (*inf: girl*) пта́шка.
chicken ['tʃɪkɪn] *n* (*bird, meat*) ку́рица; (*inf: coward*) труси́шка *m/f*
▸ **chicken out** *vi* (*inf*) тру́сить (стру́сить* *perf*); **he ~ed out of going** он стру́сил и не пошёл.
chicken feed *n* (*fig*) гроши́ *mpl.*
chickenpox ['tʃɪkɪnpɔks] *n* ветря́нка.
chickpeas ['tʃɪkpi:z] *npl* туре́цкий горо́х* *msg.*
chicory ['tʃɪkərɪ] *n* цико́рий.
chide [tʃaɪd] *vt* (*person*): **to ~ sb (for)** брани́ть (вы́бранить *perf*) кого́-н (за *+acc*).
chief [tʃi:f] *n* (*of tribe*) вождь* *m*; (*of organization, department*) нача́льник ◆ *adj* гла́вный, основно́й.
chief constable *n* (*BRIT*) нача́льник поли́ции.
chief executive (*US* **chief executive officer**) *n* гла́вный исполни́тельный дире́ктор.
chiefly ['tʃi:flɪ] *adv* гла́вным о́бразом.
Chief of Staff *n* (*MIL*) нача́льник шта́ба.
chiffon ['ʃɪfɔn] *n* шифо́н.
chilblain ['tʃɪlbleɪn] *n* обморо́женное ме́сто* (*на па́льцах*).
child [tʃaɪld] (*pl* **~ren**) *n* ребёнок*; (*fig*): **~ (of)** дитя́ (*+gen*); **do you have any ~ren?** у Вас есть де́ти?
child benefit *n* (*BRIT*) *де́нежное посо́бие на ребёнка.*
childbirth ['tʃaɪldbə:θ] *n* ро́ды *pl.*
childhood ['tʃaɪldhud] *n* де́тство.
childish ['tʃaɪldɪʃ] *adj* (*games, attitude*) ребя́ческий*; (*person*) ребя́чливый (ребя́лчив).
childless ['tʃaɪldlɪs] *adj* безде́тный* (безде́тен).
childlike ['tʃaɪldlaɪk] *adj* (*smile, figure*) де́тский*.
child minder *n* (*BRIT*) ня́ня.
child prodigy *n* вундерки́нд.
children ['tʃɪldrən] *npl of* **child.**
children's home ['tʃɪldrənz-] *n* де́тский* дом*.
child's play ['tʃaɪldz-] *n*: **it was ~ ~** (*fig*) э́то бы́ло пустяко́вое де́ло.
Chile ['tʃɪlɪ] *n* Чи́ли *nt ind.*
Chilean ['tʃɪlɪən] *adj* чили́йский* ◆ *n* чили́ец(-и́йка).
chili ['tʃɪlɪ] *n* (*US*) = **chilli.**
chill [tʃɪl] *n* (*coldness*) прохла́да; (*MED*) просту́да ◆ *adj* холо́дный* ◆ *vt* (*food, drinks*) охлажда́ть (охлади́ть* *perf*); **to catch a ~** простужа́ться (простуди́ться* *perf*); **his words sent a ~ down my spine** от его́ слов у меня́ пробежа́л холодо́к по спине́; **a ~ reminder** (*fig*) злове́щее предзнаменова́ние; **I'm ~ed to the bone** я промёрз до косте́й; **"serve ~ed"** "подава́ть в охлаждённом ви́де"
▸ **chill out** *vi* (*inf*) кайфова́ть (*impf*).
chilli ['tʃɪlɪ] (*US* **chili**) *n* (*CULIN*) кра́сный стручко́вый пе́рец*.
chilling ['tʃɪlɪŋ] *adj* (*wind*) прохла́дный* (прохла́ден), холо́дный* (хо́лоден); (*tale*) ужаса́ющий*.
chilly ['tʃɪlɪ] *adj* (*weather*) холо́дный, промо́зглый; (*response, person*) холо́дный* (хо́лоден); **to feel ~** зя́бнуть* (*impf*).
chime [tʃaɪm] *n* (*of bell*) звон; (*of clock*) бой* ◆ *vi* (*bell*) звони́ть (*impf*); (*clock*) бить* (проби́ть* *perf*).
chimney ['tʃɪmnɪ] *n* (дымова́я) труба́.
chimney sweep *n* трубочи́ст.
chimpanzee [tʃɪmpæn'zi:] *n* шимпанзе́ *m ind.*
chin [tʃɪn] *n* подборо́док*.
China ['tʃaɪnə] *n* Кита́й.
china ['tʃaɪnə] *n* фарфо́р.
Chinese [tʃaɪ'ni:z] *adj* кита́йский* ◆ *n inv* (*person*) кита́ец(-а́янка); (*LING*) кита́йский* язы́к*.
chink [tʃɪŋk] *n* (*crack*) щель* *f*; (*clink*) звя́канье.
chintz [tʃɪnts] *n* набивно́й си́тец.
chinwag ['tʃɪnwæg] *n* (*inf*) дру́жеская болтовня́; **we had a good ~** мы хорошо́ поболта́ли.
chip [tʃɪp] *n* (*of wood*) ще́пка*; (*of glass, stone*) оско́лок*; (*in glass, cup etc*) щерби́нка; (*in gambling*) фи́шка*; (*COMPUT: also:* **microchip**) микросхе́ма ◆ *vt* (*cup, plate*) обива́ть (оби́ть* *perf*); **~s** *npl* (*BRIT: CULIN*) карто́фель *msg*-фри; (*US: also:* **potato ~s**) чи́псы *mpl*; **when the ~s are down** (*fig*) когда́ уда́ча отвернётся
▸ **chip in** *vi* (*inf: contribute*) сбра́сываться (сбро́ситься* *perf*); (*: interrupt*) встрева́ть (встрять *perf*).
chipboard ['tʃɪpbɔ:d] *n* древесно-стру́жечная плита́.
chipmunk ['tʃɪpmʌŋk] *n* бурунду́к.
chippings ['tʃɪpɪŋz] *npl*: **loose ~** ще́пки* *fpl.*
chiropodist [kɪ'rɔpədɪst] *n* (*BRIT*) мозо́льный опера́тор *m/f.*
chiropody [kɪ'rɔpədɪ] *n* (*BRIT*) *ухо́д за нога́ми.*
chirp [tʃə:p] *vi* (*bird*) чири́кать (*impf*); (*cricket, grasshopper*) стрекота́ть* (*impf*).
chirpy ['tʃə:pɪ] *adj* (*inf*) жизнера́достный* (жизнера́достен).
chisel ['tʃɪzl] *n* (*for wood*) долото́; (*for stone*) зуби́ло; (*of sculptor*) резе́ц*.
chit [tʃɪt] *n* (*note*) запи́ска*; (*receipt*) распи́ска.
chitchat ['tʃɪttʃæt] *n* болтовня́.

chivalrous ['ʃɪvəlrəs] *adj* гала́нтный* (гала́нтен).
chivalry ['ʃɪvəlrɪ] *n* гала́нтность *f.*
chives [tʃaɪvz] *npl* лук-ре́занец *msg.*
chloride ['klɔ:raɪd] *n* хлори́д.
chlorinate ['klɔrɪneɪt] *vt* хлори́ровать *(impf).*
chlorine ['klɔ:ri:n] *n* хлор.
chock [tʃɔk] *n* (*AUT, AVIAT*) тормозна́я коло́дка*.
chock-a-block ['tʃɔkə'blɔk] *adj* битко́м наби́тый (наби́т).
chock-full [tʃɔk'ful] *adj* = **chock-a-block.**
chocolate ['tʃɔklɪt] *n* шокола́д; (*sweet*) шокола́дная конфе́та ◆ *cpd* шокола́дный.
choice [tʃɔɪs] *n* (*selection*) вы́бор ◆ *adj* (*cut of meat, fruit etc*) отбо́рный; **this is a possible ~** э́то возмо́жный вариа́нт; **by** *or* **from ~** доброво́льно; **a wide ~** большо́й вы́бор; **to have first ~** выбира́ть (вы́брать* *perf*) пе́рвым; **I have no ~, but/but to** у меня́ нет друго́го вы́хода кро́ме *+gen*/кро́ме как *+infin.*
choir ['kwaɪə^r] *n* хор*; (*area of church*) хо́ры *pl.*
choirboy ['kwaɪə'bɔɪ] *n* пе́вчий* *m adj.*
choke [tʃəuk] *vi* (*on food, drink*) дави́ться* (подави́ться* *perf*); (*with smoke, anger*) задыха́ться (задохну́ться *perf*) ◆ *vt* (*strangle*) души́ть* (задуши́ть* *or* удуши́ть* *perf*) ◆ *n* (*AUT*) возду́шная засло́нка; **~d (with)** (*blocked*) засорённый (засорён) (*+instr*).
cholera ['kɔlərə] *n* холе́ра.
cholesterol [kə'lɛstərɔl] *n* холестери́н; **high/low ~** с высо́ким/ни́зким содержа́нием холестери́на.
choose [tʃu:z] (*pt* **chose**, *pp* **chosen**) *vt* выбира́ть (вы́брать *perf*); (*elect*) избира́ть (избра́ть* *perf*) ◆ *vi*: **to ~ between/from** выбира́ть (вы́брать* *perf*) ме́жду *+instr*/из *+gen*; **to ~ to do** реша́ть (реши́ть *perf*) *+infin.*
choosy ['tʃu:zɪ] *adj* привере́дливый (привере́длив); **he is ~ about his food** он привере́длив в еде́.
chop [tʃɔp] *vt* (*wood*) руби́ть* (наруби́ть* *perf*); (*also:* **~ up**: *vegetables, meat*) ре́зать* (наре́зать* *or* поре́зать* *perf*) ◆ *n* (*CULIN*) ≈ отбивна́я (котле́та); **~s** *npl* (*inf*: *jaws*): **to lick one's ~s** облизываться (облиза́ться* *perf*); **he got the ~** (*BRIT*: *inf*) его́ вы́гнали с рабо́ты
▸ **chop down** *vt* (*tree*) руби́ть* (сруби́ть* *perf*).
chopper ['tʃɔpə^r] *n* (*helicopter*) вертолёт.
choppy ['tʃɔpɪ] *adj* (*sea*) неспоко́йный* (неспоко́ен).
chopsticks ['tʃɔpstɪks] *npl* па́лочки* *fpl* для еды́.
choral ['kɔ:rəl] *adj* хорово́й; (*in church*) хора́льный.
chord [kɔ:d] *n* (*MUS*) акко́рд; (*MATH*) хо́рда.
chore [tʃɔ:^r] *n* (*domestic task*) рабо́та по до́му; (*routine task*) повседне́вная обя́занность *f*; **household ~s** дома́шние хло́поты.
choreographer [kɔrɪ'ɔgrəfə^r] *n* хорео́граф; (*of ballet*) балетме́йстер*.
choreography [kɔrɪ'ɔgrəfɪ] *n* хореогра́фия.
chorister ['kɔrɪstə^r] *n* пе́вчий* *m adj*, хори́ст.
chortle ['tʃɔ:tl] *vi* хохота́ть* *(impf).*
chorus ['kɔ:rəs] *n* (*choir, song, also fig*) хор*; (*church song*) хора́л; (*refrain*) припе́в; **in ~** хо́ром.
chose [tʃəuz] *pt of* **choose.**
chosen ['tʃəuzn] *pp of* **choose.**
chow [tʃau] *n* (*dog*) ча́у-ча́у *m/f ind.*
chowder ['tʃaudə^r] *n* ≈ похлёбка.
Christ [kraɪst] *n* Христо́с.
christen ['krɪsn] *vt* крести́ть* (окрести́ть* *perf*); (*with nickname*) окрести́ть* (*perf*) *+instr.*
christening ['krɪsnɪŋ] *n* креще́ние.
Christian ['krɪstɪən] *adj* христиа́нский* ◆ *n* христиани́н*(-а́нка).
Christianity [krɪstɪ'ænɪtɪ] *n* христиа́нство.
Christian name *n* и́мя* *nt.*
Christmas ['krɪsməs] *n* Рождество́; **Happy** *or* **Merry ~!** Счастли́вого Рождества́!
Christmas card *n* рожде́ственская откры́тка*.
Christmas Day *n* день *m* Рождества́.
Christmas Eve *n* соче́льник.
Christmas Island *n* о́стров* Рождества́.
Christmas tree *n* рожде́ственская ёлка*.
chrome [krəum] *n* = **chromium.**
chromium ['krəumɪəm] *n* хром; (*also:* **~ plating**) хроми́рование.
chromosome ['krəuməsəum] *n* хромосо́ма.
chronic ['krɔnɪk] *adj* хрони́ческий*.
chronicle ['krɔnɪkl] *n* (*of events*) хро́ника.
chronological [krɔnə'lɔdʒɪkl] *adj* (*order*) хронологи́ческий*.
chrysanthemum [krɪ'sænθəməm] *n* хризанте́ма.
chubby ['tʃʌbɪ] *adj* пу́хлый*.
chuck [tʃʌk] (*inf*) *vt* швыря́ть (швырну́ть *perf*); (*BRIT*: *also:* **~ up, ~ in**: *job, girlfriend*) броса́ть (бро́сить* *perf*)
▸ **chuck out** *vt* (*person, rubbish*) вышвы́ривать (вы́швырнуть *perf*).
chuckle ['tʃʌkl] *vi* посме́иваться *(impf)*; **"Yes", he ~d** Да, – сказа́л он, посме́иваясь.
chuffed [tʃʌft] *adj* (*inf*) дово́льный* (дово́лен).
chug [tʃʌg] *vi* пыхте́ть* *(impf)*; (*also:* **~ along**) пыхте́ть* (пропыхте́ть* *perf*).
chum [tʃʌm] *n* (*inf*: *friend*) закады́чный друг*.
chump [tʃʌmp] *n* (*inf*) болва́н.
chunk [tʃʌŋk] *n* (*of meat*) кусо́к*; (*of bread*) ло́моть* *m.*
chunky ['tʃʌŋkɪ] *adj* (*furniture etc*) громо́здкий* (громо́здок); (*person*) корена́стый (корена́ст); (*knitwear*) то́лстый.
church [tʃə:tʃ] *n* це́рковь* *f*; **the C~ of England**

* marks translations which have irregular inflections. The Russian-English side of the dictionary gives inflectional information.

Англика́нская Це́рковь*.
churchyard ['tʃə:tʃjɑ:d] *n* пого́ст.
churlish ['tʃə:lɪʃ] *adj* гру́бый (груб).
churn [tʃə:n] *n* (*machine*) маслобо́йка; (*also:* **milk ~**) бидо́н
▸ **churn out** *vt* производи́ть* (произвести́* *perf*) в большо́м коли́честве.
chute [ʃu:t] *n* (*also:* **rubbish ~**) мусоропрово́д; (*for parcels etc*) жёлоб*; (*BRIT: slide*) го́рка*.
chutney ['tʃʌtnɪ] *n* ча́тни *nt ind* (*инди́йская припра́ва*).
CIA *n abbr* (*US: = Central Intelligence Agency*) ЦРУ.
cicada [sɪ'kɑ:də] *n* цика́да.
CID *n abbr* (*BRIT: = Criminal Investigation Department*) Уголо́вный ро́зыск.
cider ['saɪdə^r] *n* сидр.
c.i.f. *abbr* (*COMM: = cost, insurance and freight*) СИФ (*сто́имость, страхова́ние, фрахт*).
cigar [sɪ'gɑ:^r] *n* сига́ра.
cigarette [sɪgə'rɛt] *n* сигаре́та.
cigarette case *n* портсига́р.
cigarette end *n* оку́рок*.
cigarette holder *n* мундшту́к*.
C-in-C *abbr* (*MIL: = commander in chief*) главнокома́ндующий*.
cinch [sɪntʃ] *n* (*inf*): **it's a ~** э́то пустя́к.
Cinderella [sɪndə'rɛlə] *n* Зо́лушка.
cinders ['sɪndəz] *npl* зола́ *fsg*.
cine camera ['sɪnɪ-] *n* (*BRIT*) кинока́мера.
cine film *n* (*BRIT*) киноплёнка*.
cinema ['sɪnəmə] *n* кинотеа́тр; (*film-making*) кинематогра́фия.
cine projector *n* (*BRIT*) кинопрое́ктор.
cinnamon ['sɪnəmən] *n* кори́ца.
cipher ['saɪfə^r] *n* шифр; (*fig*) пе́шка*; **a letter in ~** зашифро́ванное письмо́.
circa ['sə:kə] *prep* о́коло *+gen*.
circle ['sə:kl] *n* круг*; (*THEAT*) балко́н; (*of trees*) кольцо́ ◆ *vi* (*bird, plane*) кружи́ть* (*impf*) ◆ *vt* (*move round*) дви́гаться* (*impf*) вокру́г *+gen*; (*surround*) окружа́ть (окружи́ть *perf*); **to form a ~** встава́ть* (встать* *perf*) в круг.
circuit ['sə:kɪt] *n* (*ELEC*) цепь *f*; (*tour*) турне́ *nt ind*; (*track*) трек; (*lap*) зае́зд.
circuit board *n* монта́жная пла́та.
circuitous [sə:'kjuɪtəs] *adj* око́льный.
circular ['sə:kjulə^r] *adj* (*plate, pond etc*) кру́глый*; (*route*) окружно́й; (*argument*) несконча́емый ◆ *n* (*letter*) циркуля́р; (*advertisement*) проспе́кт.
circulate ['sə:kjuleɪt] *vi* (*blood, traffic*) циркули́ровать (*impf*); (*news, rumour etc*) передава́ться* (переда́ться* *perf*) ◆ *vt* передава́ть* (переда́ть* *perf*); **to ~ amongst the guests** переходи́ть (*impf*) от одного́ го́стя к друго́му.
circulating capital [sə:kju'leɪtɪŋ-] *n* оборо́тный капита́л.
circulation [sə:kju'leɪʃən] *n* (*of newspaper*) тира́ж*; (*MED*) кровообраще́ние; (*of money*) обраще́ние; (*of air, traffic*) циркуля́ция.
circumcise ['sə:kəmsaɪz] *vt* обреза́ть (обре́зать* *perf*) (*РЕЛ*).
circumference [sə'kʌmfərəns] *n* окру́жность *f*.
circumflex ['sə:kəmflɛks] *n* (*also:* **~ accent**) циркумфле́кс.
circumscribe ['sə:kəmskraɪb] *vt* (*GEOM*) впи́сывать (вписа́ть* *perf*) в окру́жность; (*fig*) ограни́чивать (ограни́чить *perf*).
circumspect ['sə:kəmspɛkt] *adj* осмотри́тельный* (осмотри́телен).
circumstances ['sə:kəmstənsɪz] *npl* обстоя́тельства *ntpl*; **in** *or* **under the ~** в да́нных обстоя́тельствах; **under no ~** ни в ко́ем слу́чае.
circumstantial [sə:kəm'stænʃl] *adj* обстоя́тельный* (обстоя́телен); **~ evidence** ко́свенные ули́ки *fpl*.
circumvent [sə:kəm'vɛnt] *vt* обходи́ть* (обойти́* *perf*).
circus ['sə:kəs] *n* цирк; (*also:* **C~**: *in place names*) ≈ пло́щадь *f*.
cirrhosis [sɪ'rəusɪs] *n* цирро́з.
CIS *n abbr* (*= Commonwealth of Independent States*) СНГ= *Содру́жество Незави́симых Госуда́рств*.
cissy ['sɪsɪ] *n* (*boy*) девчо́нка*; (*girl*) не́женка*.
cistern ['sɪstən] *n* (*water tank*) цисте́рна; (*of toilet*) бак.
citation [saɪ'teɪʃən] *n* (*from book etc*) цита́та; (*for bravery etc*) благода́рность *f*; (*US: LAW*) пове́стка (*в суд*).
cite [saɪt] *vt* (*quote*) цити́ровать (процити́ровать *perf*); (*LAW*) вызыва́ть (вы́звать* *perf*) в суд.
citizen ['sɪtɪzn] *n* (*of a country*) граждани́н*(-а́нка); (*of town*) жи́тель(ница) *m(f)*.
Citizens' Advice Bureau ['sɪtɪznz-] *n бюро́, даю́щее беспла́тные сове́ты по широ́кому кру́гу вопро́сов*.
citizenship ['sɪtɪznʃɪp] *n* (*of a country*) гражда́нство.
citric acid ['sɪtrɪk-] *n* лимо́нная кислота́*.
citrus fruit ['sɪtrəs-] *n* ци́трус.
city ['sɪtɪ] *n* го́род*; **the C~** Си́ти *nt ind*.
city centre *n* центр (го́рода).
City Hall *n* ра́туша.
civic ['sɪvɪk] *adj* муниципа́льный; (*duties, pride*) гражда́нский*.
civic centre *n* (*BRIT*) ≈ Дом* Культу́ры.
civil ['sɪvɪl] *adj* гражда́нский*; (*authorities*) госуда́рственный; (*polite*) учти́вый (учти́в).
Civil Aviation Authority *n* (*BRIT*) Управле́ние гражда́нской авиа́ции.
civil defence *n* гражда́нская оборо́на.
civil disobedience *n* гражда́нское неповинове́ние.
civil engineer *n* инжене́р-строи́тель *m*.
civil engineering *n* гражда́нское строи́тельство.

civilian [sɪ'vɪlɪən] *adj* (*life*) общéственный ◆ *n* мúрный(-ая) жúтель(ница) *m(f)*; **~ casualties** жéртвы средú мúрного населéния.
civilization [sɪvɪlaɪ'zeɪʃən] *n* цивилизáция.
civilized ['sɪvɪlaɪzd] *adj* (*society*) цивилизóванный; (*person*) культýрный; (*place*) комфортáбельный.
civil law *n* Граждáнское прáво.
civil liberties *npl* граждáнские свобóды *fpl*.
civil rights *npl* граждáнские правá *ntpl*.
civil servant *n* государственный слýжащий* *m adj*.
Civil Service *n* государственная слýжба.
civil war *n* граждáнская войнá*.
civvies ['sɪvɪz] *npl* (*inf*) цивúльная одéжда *fsg*.
cl *abbr* = **centilitre**.
clad [klæd] *adj*: **~ (in)** облачённый (облачён) (в *+acc*).
claim [kleɪm] *vt* (*responsibility, credit*) припúсывать (приписáть* *perf*) себé; (*rights, inheritance*) претендовáть (*impf*) *or* притязáть (*impf*) на *+acc*; (*compensation, damages*) трéбовать (потрéбовать *perf*) ◆ *vi* (*for insurance*) дéлать (сдéлать *perf*) страховýю заявку ◆ *n* (*assertion*) утверждéние; (*for compensation, pension*) требовáние; (*right*) прáво; (*to inheritance, land*) претéнзия, притязáние; (*for expenses*) заявка; **to ~ (that)** *or* **to be** (*assert*) утверждáть (*impf*), что; **(insurance) ~** страховáя заявка; **to put in a ~ for** (*expenses*) подавáть* (подáть* *perf*) заявку на *+acc*.
claimant ['kleɪmənt] *n* (*LAW*) претендéнт; (*ADMIN*) подáтель(ница) *m(f)* заявлéния.
claim form *n* бланк заявлéния.
clairvoyant [klɛə'vɔɪənt] *n* ясновúдец*(-дица).
clam [klæm] *n* двухствóрчатый моллюск
▸ **clam up** *vi* (*inf*) уходúть* (уйтú* *perf*) в себя.
clamber ['klæmbə'] *vi* карáбкаться (вскарáбкаться *perf*).
clammy ['klæmɪ] *adj* (*hands*) лúпкий*; (*weather*) дýшный*.
clamour ['klæmə'] (*US* **clamor**) *n* (*noise*) гул; (*protest*) рóпот ◆ *vi*: **to ~ for** шýмно трéбовать (*impf*) *+gen*.
clamp [klæmp] *n* зажúм ◆ *vt* зажимáть (зажáть* *perf*)
▸ **clamp down on** *vt fus* повестú* (*perf*) наступлéние прóтив *+gen*.
clampdown ['klæmpdaun] *n*: **~ (on)** стрóгие мéры *fpl* (прóтив *+gen*); **there was a ~ on drug dealing in the area** в райóне прикрыли торгóвлю наркóтиками.
clan [klæn] *n* клан.
clandestine [klæn'dɛstɪn] *adj* подпóльный.
clang [klæŋ] *vi* (*bell*) звенéть (*impf*); (*metal object*) лязгать (*impf*) ◆ *n* (*see vi*) звон; лязг.
clanger ['klæŋə'] *n* (*inf*) ляпсус.
clansman ['klænzmən] *irreg n* член клáна.
clap [klæp] *vi* хлóпать (*impf*) ◆ *vt*: **to ~ one's hands** хлóпать (*impf*) в ладóши; **a ~ of thunder** удáр грóма.
clapping ['klæpɪŋ] *n* хлопкú *mpl*, аплодисмéнты *fpl*.
claptrap ['klæptræp] *n* (*inf*) белибердá.
claret ['klærət] *n* бордó *nt ind*.
clarification [klærɪfɪ'keɪʃən] *n* (*fig*) разъяснéние.
clarify ['klærɪfaɪ] *vt* (*fig*) разъяснять (разъяснúть *perf*).
clarinet [klærɪ'nɛt] *n* кларнéт.
clarity ['klærɪtɪ] *n* (*of explanation, thought*) ясность *f*.
clash [klæʃ] *n* столкновéние; (*of events etc*) совпадéние; (*of metal objects*) звяканье ◆ *vi* (*gangs*) имéть (*impf*) столкновéние; (*political opponents*) вступáть (вступúть* *perf*) в столкновéние; (*beliefs*) стáлкиваться (столкнýться *perf*); (*colours*) не совмещáться (*impf*); (*events etc*) совпадáть (совпáсть* *perf*) (по врéмени); (*metal objects*) звякать (*impf*).
clasp [klɑːsp] *n* (*hold*) хвáтка*; (*of necklace, bag*) застёжка* ◆ *vt* сжимáть (сжать* *perf*).
class [klɑːs] *n* (*in school, society*) класс; (*lesson*) урóк; (*of goods: type*) разряд; (*: quality*) сорт ◆ *adj* клáссовый ◆ *vt* классифицúровать (*impf/perf*).
class-conscious ['klɑːs'kɔnʃəs] *adj* (*person*) осознаю́щий клáссовое разлúчие.
class-consciousness ['klɑːs'kɔnʃəsnɪs] *n* клáссовое сознáние.
classic ['klæsɪk] *adj* классúческий* ◆ *n* (*film, novel etc*) классúческое произведéние; (*author*) клáссик; **C~s** *npl* (*SCOL*) классúческая филолóгия *fsg*.
classical ['klæsɪkl] *adj* классúческий*.
classification [klæsɪfɪ'keɪʃən] *n* классификáция; (*category*) разряд.
classified ['klæsɪfaɪd] *adj* засекрéченный.
classified advertisement *n объявлéния под рýбрикой*.
classify ['klæsɪfaɪ] *vt* классифицúровать (*impf/perf*).
classless ['klaːslɪs] *adj* бесклáссовый.
classmate ['klɑːsmeɪt] *n* одноклáссник(-ица).
classroom ['klɑːsrum] *n* класс.
classy ['klɑːsɪ] *adj* (*inf: car, flat*) клáссный.
clatter ['klætə'] *n* (*of dishes etc*) звяканье; (*of hooves*) цóканье ◆ *vi* (*see n*) звякать (*impf*); цóкать (*impf*).
clause [klɔːz] *n* (*LAW*) пункт; (*LING*): **principal/subordinate ~** глáвное/придáточное предложéние.
claustrophobia [klɔːstrə'fəubɪə] *n* клаустрофóбия.
claustrophobic [klɔːstrə'fəubɪk] *adj*: **she is ~**

* marks translations which have irregular inflections. The Russian-English side of the dictionary gives inflectional information.

она́ страда́ет клаустрофо́бией, у неё клаустрофо́бия.
claw [klɔ:] *n* (*of animal, bird*) ко́готь* *m*; (*of lobster*) клешня́*
▸ **claw at** *vt fus* цепля́ться (*impf*) за *+acc*.
clay [kleɪ] *n* гли́на.
clean [kli:n] *adj* чи́стый*; (*fight*) че́стный*; (*reputation*) незапя́тнанный (незапя́тан); (*joke*) прили́чный* (прили́чен); (*edge, fracture*) ро́вный* (ро́вен) ◆ *vt* (*hands, face*) мыть (вы́мыть* *perf*); (*car, cooker*) чи́стить* (почи́стить* *perf*) ◆ *adv*: **he ~ forgot** он на́чисто забы́л; **~ driving licence** *or* (*US*) **record** чи́стые води́тельские права́ *ntpl*; **to ~ one's teeth** (*BRIT*) чи́стить* (почи́стить *perf*) зу́бы; **the thief got ~ away** во́ра и след просты́л; **to come ~** (*inf*) выкла́дывать (вы́ложить *perf*) всё начисту́ю
▸ **clean off** *vt* (*wash*) смыва́ть (смы́ть* *perf*); (*brush, dust etc*) счища́ть (счи́стить* *perf*)
▸ **clean out** *vt* (*cupboard etc*) вычища́ть (вы́чистить* *perf*); (*inf*: *person*) обчища́ть (обчи́стить* *perf*)
▸ **clean up** *vt* (*room*) убира́ть (убра́ть* *perf*); (*child*) мыть* (помы́ть* *perf*); (*fig*) проводи́ть* (провести́* *perf*) чи́стку в *+prp* ◆ *vi* убира́ться (убра́ться* *perf*); (*fig*) загреба́ть (загрести́* *perf*) больши́е де́ньги; **to ~ up after sb/sth** убира́ть (убра́ть* *perf*) за кем-н/чем-н.
clean-cut ['kli:n'kʌt] *adj* (*person*) опря́тный* (опря́тен); (*situation*) я́сный* (я́сен).
cleaner ['kli:nəʳ] *n* (*person*) убо́рщик(-ица); (*substance*) мо́ющее сре́дство.
cleaner's ['kli:nəz] *n* (*also*: **dry ~**) химчи́стка*.
cleaning ['kli:nɪŋ] *n* убо́рка*.
cleaning lady *n* убо́рщица.
cleanliness ['klɛnlɪnɪs] *n* чистопло́тность *f*.
cleanly ['kli:nlɪ] *adv* чи́сто.
cleanse [klɛnz] *vt* (*purify*) очища́ть (очи́стить* *perf*); (*face*) мыть* (вы́мыть* *perf*); (*cut*) промыва́ть (промы́ть* *perf*).
cleanser ['klɛnzəʳ] *n* (*for face*) очища́ющий лосьо́н.
clean-shaven ['kli:n'ʃeɪvn] *adj* чи́сто вы́бритый.
cleansing department ['klɛnzɪŋ-] *n* (*BRIT*) санита́рное управле́ние.
clean sweep *n*: **to make a ~ ~** (*in tournaments*) забира́ть (забра́ть* *perf*) все призы́.
cleanup ['kli:nʌp] *n* (*of house, room*) убо́рка*; (*of river, air*) очи́стка.
clear [klɪəʳ] *adj* я́сный* (я́сен); (*report, argument*) я́сный* (я́сен), поня́тный*; (*footprint*) чёткий*; (*writing*) разбо́рчивый (разбо́рчив); (*majority*) подавля́ющий*; (*glass, water*) прозра́чный* (прозра́чен); (*road*) свобо́дный* (свобо́ден); (*conscience, profit*) чи́стый* ◆ *vt* (*space, room*) освобожда́ть (освободи́ть* *perf*); (*ground*) расчища́ть (расчи́стить* *perf*); (*weeds, slums*) убира́ть (убра́ть* *perf*); (*suspect*) опра́вдывать (оправда́ть *perf*); (*fence etc*) брать* (взять* *perf*); (*goods*) распродава́ть* (распрода́ть* *perf*) ◆ *vi* (*sky*) проясня́ться (проясни́ться *perf*); (*fog, smoke*) рассе́иваться (рассе́яться *perf*); (*room etc*) обезлю́деть (*perf*) ◆ *adv*: **~ of** (*trouble, ground*) пода́льше от *+gen* ◆ *n*: **he is/was in the ~** (*out of debt*) он свобо́ден/был свобо́ден от долго́в; **to be in the ~** (*free of suspicion*) быть* (*impf*) вне подозре́ния; (*out of danger*) быть* (*impf*) вне опа́сности; **have I made myself ~?** я я́сно вы́разился?; **to make it ~ to sb that ...** дава́ть* (дать* *perf*) кому́-н поня́ть, что ...; **I have a ~ day tomorrow** (*BRIT*) у меня́ за́втра свобо́дный день; **to ~ the table** убира́ть (убра́ть* *perf*) со стола́; **to ~ one's throat** прочища́ть (прочи́стить* *perf*) го́рло; **to ~ a cheque** выпла́чивать (вы́платить* *perf*) де́ньги по че́ку; **to ~ a profit** получа́ть (получи́ть* *perf*) чи́стую при́быль; **to keep ~ of sb/sth** держа́ться* (*impf*) пода́льше от кого́-н/чего́-н
▸ **clear off** *vi* (*inf*: *leave*) убира́ться (убра́ться* *perf*)
▸ **clear up** *vt* (*room*) убира́ть (убра́ть* *perf*); (*mystery, problem*) разреша́ть (разреши́ть *perf*) ◆ *vi* убира́ться (убра́ться* *perf*); (*illness*) проходи́ть* (пройти́* *perf*); (*weather*) проясня́ться (проясни́ться *perf*).
clearance ['klɪərəns] *n* (*removal*) расчи́стка*; (*permission*) разреше́ние; (*above vehicle*) габари́тная высота́*.
clearance sale *n* распрода́жа.
clear-cut ['klɪə'kʌt] *adj* (*decision, issue*) я́сный* (я́сен); (*division*) чёткий*.
clearing ['klɪərɪŋ] *n* поля́на; (*BRIT*: *COMM*) кли́ринг.
clearing bank *n* (*BRIT*) кли́ринговый банк.
clearing house *n* кли́ринговая пала́та.
clearly ['klɪəlɪ] *adv* (*distinctly*) я́сно, отчётливо; (*obviously*) я́вно, очеви́дно; (*coherently*) я́сно, поня́тно.
clearway ['klɪəweɪ] *n* (*BRIT*) *автодоро́га, где остано́вка тра́нспорта запрещена́.*
cleavage ['kli:vɪdʒ] *n* я́мка*.
cleaver ['kli:vəʳ] *n* (*for meat*) топо́рик.
clef [klɛf] *n* (*MUS*) ключ*.
cleft [klɛft] *n* рассе́лина.
cleft palate *n* за́ячья губа́.
clemency ['klɛmənsɪ] *n* милосе́рдие.
clement ['klɛmənt] *adj* мя́гкий*.
clench [klɛntʃ] *vt* сжима́ть (сжать* *perf*).
clergy ['klə:dʒɪ] *n* духове́нство.
clergyman ['klə:dʒɪmən] *irreg n* свяще́нник, священнослужи́тель *m*.
clerical ['klɛrɪkl] *adj* (*job, error*) канцеля́рский*; (*skills*) секрета́рский; (*REL*) церко́вный.
clerk [klɑ:k, (*US*) klə:rk] *n* (*BRIT*: *office worker*) клерк, делопроизводи́тель*(ница) *m(f)*; (*US*: *sales person*) продаве́ц*(-вщи́ца).
Clerk of Court *n* секрета́рь* *m* суда́.

clever ['klɛvəʳ] *adj* (*intelligent*) у́мный* (умён); (*deft, crafty*) ло́вкий* (ло́вок).
cleverly ['klɛvəlɪ] *adv* ло́вко.
clew [klu:] *n* (*US*) = **clue**.
cliché ['kli:ʃeɪ] *n* клишé *nt ind*, штамп.
click [klɪk] *vt* (*tongue, heels*) щёлкать (щёлкнуть *perf*) *+instr* ◆ *vi* (*device, switch etc*) щёлкать (щёлкнуть *perf*); (*COMPUT*): **to ~ on the mouse** нажима́ть (нажа́ть* *perf*) на мышь.
client ['klaɪənt] *n* клие́нт.
clientele [kli:ɑ̃:n'tɛl] *n* клиенту́ра.
cliff [klɪf] *n* скала́*, утёс.
cliffhanger ['klɪfhæŋəʳ] *n* (*TV, also fig*) напряжённый моме́нт.
climactic [klaɪ'mæktɪk] *adj* кульминацио́нный.
climate ['klaɪmɪt] *n* (*weather, fig*) кли́мат; **~ of opinion** состоя́ние обще́ственного мне́ния.
climax ['klaɪmæks] *n* кульмина́ция, апофео́з; (*during sex*) орга́зм.
climb [klaɪm] *vi* (*sun*) поднима́ться (подня́ться* *perf*); (*plant*) ви́ться *(impf)*; (*plane*) набира́ть (набра́ть* *perf*) высоту́; (*prices, shares*) поднима́ться (подня́ться* *perf*) ◆ *vt* (*stairs, ladder*) взбира́ться (взобра́ться* *perf*) по *+prp*; (*tree, hill*) взбира́ться (взобра́ться* *perf*) *or* поднима́ться (подня́ться* *perf*) на *+acc* ◆ *n* подъём; **to ~ over a wall** переleза́ть (переле́зть* *perf*) че́рез сте́ну
▸ **climb down** *vi* (*fig*) уступа́ть (уступи́ть *perf*).
climb-down ['klaɪmdaun] *n* (*BRIT*) усту́пка*.
climber ['klaɪməʳ] *n* (*mountaineer*) альпини́ст(ка*); (*plant*) вью́щееся расте́ние.
climbing ['klaɪmɪŋ] *n* альпини́зм.
clinch [klɪntʃ] *vt* (*deal*) заключа́ть (заключи́ть *perf*); (*argument*) разреша́ть (разреши́ть *perf*).
clincher ['klɪntʃəʳ] *n* реша́ющий* до́вод.
cling [klɪŋ] (*pt, pp* **clung**) *vi* (*clothes, dress*) облега́ть *(impf)*; **to ~ to** (*mother, support*) вцепля́ться (вцепи́ться* *perf*) в *+acc*; (*idea, belief*) цепля́ться *(impf)* за *+acc*.
clingfilm ['klɪŋfɪlm] *n обёрточная плёнка для проду́ктов*.
clinic ['klɪnɪk] *n* (*medical centre*) кли́ника; (*session*) консульта́ция.
clinical ['klɪnɪkl] *adj* (*MED*) клини́ческий*; (*fig: attitude*) бесстра́стный (бесстра́стен); (*: room*) стери́льный.
clink [klɪŋk] *vi* звене́ть *(impf)* ◆ *vt* (*glasses*) чо́каться (чо́кнуться *perf*) *+instr*.
clip [klɪp] *n* (*also:* **paper ~**) скре́пка*; (*BRIT: also:* **bulldog ~**) зажи́м; (*for hair*) зако́лка*; (*TV, CINEMA*) клип ◆ *vt* (*fasten*) прикрепля́ть (прикрепи́ть* *perf*); (*also:* **~ together**: *papers*) скрепля́ть (скрепи́ть* *perf*); (*cut*) подстрига́ть (подстри́чь* *perf*).
clippers ['klɪpəz] *npl* (*for gardening*) сека́тор *msg*; (*also:* **nail ~**) щи́пчики *pl*.
clipping ['klɪpɪŋ] *n* (*PRESS*) вы́резка*.
clique [kli:k] *n* кли́ка.
clitoris ['klɪtərɪs] *n* кли́тор.
cloak [kləuk] *n* (*cape*) плащ* ◆ *vt* (*fig: in mist*) оку́тывать (оку́тать *perf*); **~ed in** оку́танный (оку́тан) *+instr*.
cloakroom ['kləukrum] *n* (*for coats*) гардеро́б; (*BRIT: toilet*) убо́рная *f adj*.
clobber ['klɔbəʳ] (*inf*) *n* мона́тки *pl* ◆ *vt* (*hit*) колошма́тить* (исколошма́тить* *perf*); (*defeat*) бить* (поби́ть* *perf*).
clock [klɔk] *n* часы́ *pl*; (*of taxi*) счётчик; **to sleep/work round the ~** спать* *(impf)*/ рабо́тать *(impf)* кру́глые су́тки; **this car has 30,000 miles on the ~** (*BRIT*) э́та маши́на нае́здила 30,000 миль; **to work against the ~** рабо́тать *(impf)* наперегонки́ со вре́менем
▸ **clock in** *vi* (*BRIT: for work*) отмеча́ться (отме́титься* *perf*) (*приходя́ на рабо́ту*)
▸ **clock off** *vi* (*BRIT: from work*) отмеча́ться (отме́титься* *perf*) (*уходя́ с рабо́ты*)
▸ **clock on** *vi* (*BRIT*) = **clock in**
▸ **clock out** *vi* (*BRIT*) = **clock off**
▸ **clock up** *vt* (*debts*) нака́пливать (накопи́ть* *perf*); (*miles*) накру́чивать (накрути́ть* *perf*); (*hours*) набира́ть (набра́ть* *perf*).
clockwise ['klɔkwaɪz] *adv* по часово́й стре́лке.
clockwork ['klɔkwə:k] *n* заво́д ◆ *adj* (*toy*) заводно́й.
clog [klɔg] *n* сабо́* *nt ind* ◆ *vt* (*drain*) засоря́ть (засори́ть *perf*) ◆ *vi* (*also:* **~ up**: *sink*) засоря́ться (засори́ться *perf*); **my nose is ~ged (up)** у меня́ зало́жен нос.
cloister ['klɔɪstəʳ] *n* перисти́ль *m*.
clone [kləun] *n* (*BIO*) клон.
close[1] [kləus] *adj* (*near*) бли́зкий* (бли́зок); (*writing*) убо́ристый (убо́рист); (*contact, ties*) те́сный* (те́сен); (*watch, attention*) при́стальный* (при́стален); (*weather, room*) ду́шный* (ду́шен) ◆ *adv* бли́зко; **~ to** (*near*) бли́зкий* (бли́зок) к *+dat*; **~ to** *or* **on** (*almost*) бли́зко к *+dat*; **~ by** *or* **at hand** ря́дом; **how ~ is Edinburgh to Glasgow?** как бли́зко от Эдинбу́рга нахо́дится Гла́зго?; **a ~ friend** бли́зкий* друг*; **a ~ contest** борьба́ на ра́вных; **I had a ~ shave** (*fig*) я был на волосо́к от э́того; **to keep a ~ eye on sb/sth** внима́тельно следи́ть *(impf)* за *+instr*; **at ~ quarters** на бли́зком расстоя́нии.
close[2] [kləuz] *vt* (*shut*) закрыва́ть (закры́ть* *perf*); (*finalize*) заключа́ть (заключи́ть *perf*); (*end*) заверша́ть (заверши́ть *perf*) ◆ *vi* (*shut*) закрыва́ться (закры́ться* *perf*); (*end*) заверша́ться(заверши́ться *perf*) ◆ *n* коне́ц*; **to bring sth to a ~** заверша́ть (заверши́ть *perf*) что-н
▸ **close down** *vt* закрыва́ть (закры́ть* *perf*) ◆ *vi* закрыва́ться (закры́ться* *perf*)

* marks translations which have irregular inflections. The Russian-English side of the dictionary gives inflectional information.

▸ **close in** *vi* (*night, fog*) опуска́ться (опусти́ться* *perf*); (*hunters*): **to ~ in (on sb/sth)** окружа́ть (окружи́ть *perf*) (кого́-н/что-н); **the days are closing in** дни стано́вятся коро́че
▸ **close off** *vt* (*area*) огора́живать (огороди́ть* *perf*); (*road*) блоки́ровать *(impf/perf)*.
closed [kləuzd] *adj* закры́тый (закры́т).
closed-circuit ['kləuzd'sə:kɪt] *adj*: **~ television** за́мкнутая телевизио́нная систе́ма.
closed shop *n* (*union*) *предприя́тие, на кото́ром рабо́тают то́лько чле́ны определённого профсою́за.*
close-knit ['kləus'nɪt] *adj* сплочённый (сплочён).
closely ['kləuslɪ] *adv* (*watch, examine*) при́стально; (*connected, related*) те́сно; **he ~ resembles his father** он о́чень похо́ж на отца́; **we are ~ related** мы бли́зкие ро́дственники; **a ~ guarded secret** тща́тельно оберега́емый секре́т.
close season ['kləus-] *n* закры́тый сезо́н.
closet ['klɔzɪt] *n* (*cupboard*) шкаф*; (*room*) чула́н.
close-up ['kləusʌp] *n* (*PHOT*) кру́пный план.
closing ['kləuzɪŋ] *adj* (*stages, remarks*) заключи́тельный.
closing price *n* (*COMM*) после́дняя цена́ *or* ста́вка*.
closing time *n* вре́мя* *nt* закры́тия (*ба́ра*).
closure ['kləuʒə'] *n* (*of factory*) закры́тие; (*of road*) блоки́рование.
clot [klɔt] *n* (*of blood etc*) сгу́сток*; (*inf*) балда́ *m/f* ◆ *vi* (*blood*) свора́чиваться (сверну́ться *perf*).
cloth [klɔθ] *n* (*material*) ткань *f*; (*for cleaning etc*) тря́пка*; (*BRIT*: *also:* **teacloth**) ку́хонное полоте́нце*; (*also:* **tablecloth**) ска́терть* *f*.
clothe [kləuð] *vt* одева́ть (оде́ть* *perf*).
clothes [kləuðz] *npl* оде́жда *fsg*; **to put one's ~ on** одева́ться (оде́ться* *perf*); **to take one's ~ off** раздева́ться (разде́ться* *perf*); **to change one's ~** переодева́ться (переоде́ться* *perf*).
clothes brush *n* одёжная щётка*.
clothesline ['kləuðzlaɪn] *n* бельева́я верёвка*.
clothes peg (*US* **clothes pin**) *n* прище́пка*.
clothing ['kləuðɪŋ] *n* = **clothes.**
clotted cream ['klɔtɪd-] *n* (*BRIT*) густы́е сли́вки *pl*.
cloud [klaud] *n* о́блако* ◆ *vt* (*liquid*) мути́ть* (замути́ть* *perf*); **every ~ has a silver lining** нет ху́да без добра́; **to ~ the issue** запу́тывать (запу́тать *perf*) де́ло
▸ **cloud over** *vi* (*sky*) покрыва́ться (покры́ться* *perf*) облака́ми; (*face*) тума́ниться (затума́ниться *perf*).
cloudburst ['klaudbə:st] *n* ли́вень* *m*.
cloud-cuckoo-land [klaud'kuku:lænd] *n* (*BRIT*): **he is living in ~** он живёт в безо́блачном ца́рстве.
cloudy ['klaudɪ] *adj* (*sky*) о́блачный* (о́блачен); (*liquid*) му́тный* (му́тен).
clout [klaut] *vt* (*inf*) долбану́ть *(perf)* ◆ *n* (*fig*) влия́ние.
clove [kləuv] *n* гвозди́ка; **~ of garlic** до́лька чеснока́.
clover ['kləuvə'] *n* кле́вер.
cloverleaf ['kləuvəli:f] *n* лист* кле́вера; (*AUT*) кле́верный лист* (*о констру́кции пересече́ния автомоби́льных доро́г*).
clown [klaun] *n* кло́ун ◆ *vi* (*also:* **~ about, ~ around**) пая́сничать *(impf)*.
cloying ['klɔɪɪŋ] *adj* (*taste, smell*) при́торный* (при́торен).
club [klʌb] *n* (*society, place*) клуб; (*weapon*) дуби́нка; (*implement*: *also:* **golf ~**) клю́шка* ◆ *vt* (*hit*) избива́ть (изби́ть* *perf*) ◆ *vi*: **to ~ together** скла́дываться (сложи́ться* *perf*); **~s** *npl* (*CARDS*) тре́фы *fpl*; **king of ~s** трефо́вый коро́ль *m*.
club car *n* (*US*: *RAIL*) ваго́н-рестора́н.
club class *n* осо́бый класс (*в самолётах*).
clubhouse ['klʌbhaus] *n* спорти́вный клуб (*зда́ние*).
club soda *n* со́довая вода́.
cluck [klʌk] *vi* (*hen*) куда́хтать* *(impf)*.
clue [klu:] *n* ключ*; (*for police*) ули́ка; **I haven't a ~** я поня́тия не име́ю.
clued-up ['klu:dʌp] (*US* **clued in**) *adj* (*inf*): **to be ~** быть* *(impf)* в ку́рсе (дел).
clueless ['klu:lɪs] *adj* без поня́тия.
clump [klʌmp] *n* (*of trees, plants*) за́росли *fpl*; (*of buildings*) скопле́ние.
clumsy ['klʌmzɪ] *adj* (*person, movement*) неуклю́жий* (неуклю́ж); (*object*) неудо́бный (неудо́бен).
clung [klʌŋ] *pt, pp of* **cling.**
cluster ['klʌstə'] *n* (*of people, stars*) скопле́ние; (*of flowers*) пучо́к* ◆ *vi* (*people*) сгруди́ться *(perf)*; (*things*) ска́пливаться (скопи́ться* *perf*).
clutch [klʌtʃ] *n* (*grip*) хва́тка; (*AUT*) сцепле́ние ◆ *vt* сжима́ть (сжать* *perf*) ◆ *vi*: **to ~ at** цепля́ться *(impf)* за *+acc*; **he has me in his ~es** я у него́ в рука́х.
clutter ['klʌtə'] *vt* (*also:* **~ up**: *room, table*) захламля́ть (захлами́ть* *perf*) ◆ *n* хлам.
CM *abbr* (*US*: *POST*) = *North Mariana Islands.*
cm *abbr* (= **centimetre**) см= *сантиме́тр.*
CNAA *n abbr* (*BRIT*) = *Council for National Academic Awards.*
CND *n abbr* = *Campaign for Nuclear Disarmament.*
CO *n abbr* = **commanding officer**; (*BRIT*: = *Commonwealth Office*) *отде́л по дела́м на́ций брита́нского Содру́жества* ◆ *abbr* (*US*: *POST*) = *Colorado.*
Co. *abbr* = **company, county.**
c/o *abbr* (= *care of*) для переда́чи *+dat*.
coach [kəutʃ] *n* (*bus*) авто́бус; (*horse-drawn*) каре́та; (*of train*) ваго́н; (*SPORT*) тре́нер; (*SCOL*) репети́тор ◆ *vt* (*SPORT*) тренирова́ть

(натренировáть *perf*); (*SCOL*): **to ~ sb for sth** готóвить* (подготóвить* *perf*) когó-н к чемý-н.
coach trip *n* автóбусная экскýрсия.
coagulate [kəu'ægjuleɪt] *vi* (*blood*) сворáчиваться (свернýться *perf*); (*paint*) сгущáться (сгустíться* *perf*).
coal [kəul] *n* ýголь* *m*.
coalface ['kəulfeɪs] *n* забóй.
coalfield ['kəulfi:ld] *n* каменноýгольный бассéйн.
coalition [kəuə'lɪʃən] *n* (*also POL*) коалíция.
coalman ['kəulmən] *irreg n* ýгольщик.
coalmine ['kəulmaɪn] *n* ýгольная шáхта.
coal miner *n* шахтёр.
coal mining *n* добы́ча ýгля.
coarse [kɔ:s] *adj* грýбый*; (*hair*) жёсткий*; (*salt, sand etc*) крýпный*.
coast [kəust] *n* бéрег*; (*area*) поберéжье ◆ *vi* (*car etc*) катíться* (покатíться* *perf*) по инéрции.
coastal ['kəustl] *adj* прибрéжный; (*services*) береговóй.
coaster ['kəustə'] *n* (*NAUT*) каботáжное сýдно*; (*for glass*) подстáвка* для стакáна.
coastguard ['kəustgɑ:d] *n* (*officer*) офицéр береговóй слýжбы; **the ~ (service)** береговáя слýжба.
coastline ['kəustlaɪn] *n* береговáя лíния.
coat [kəut] *n* пальтó *nt ind*; (*on animal*: *fur*) мех*; (: *wool*) шерсть*; (*of paint*) слой* ◆ *vt* покрывáть (покры́ть* *perf*).
coat hanger *n* вéшалка*.
coating ['kəutɪŋ] *n* слой.
coat of arms *n* герб*.
coauthor ['kəu'ɔ:θə'] *n* соáвтор.
coax [kəuks] *vt* уговáривать (уговорíть *perf*) лáской.
cob [kɔb] *n see* **corn**.
cobbler ['kɔblə'] *n* сапóжник.
cobbles ['kɔblz] *npl* булы́жники *mpl*.
cobblestones ['kɔblstəunz] *npl* = **cobbles**.
COBOL ['kəubɔl] *n* КОБОЛ.
cobra ['kəubrə] *n* кóбра.
cobweb ['kɔbwɛb] *n* паутíна.
cocaine [kə'keɪn] *n* кокаíн.
cock [kɔk] *n* (*rooster*) петýх*; (*male bird*) самéц* ◆ *vt* (*gun*) взводíть* (взвестí* *perf*); **to ~ one's ears** (*fig*) навострíть (*perf*) ýши.
cock-a-hoop [kɔkə'hu:p] *adj*: **to be ~** балдéть (*impf*).
cockerel ['kɔkərl] *n* петýх*.
cockeyed ['kɔkaɪd] *adj* (*fig*) дурáцкий*.
cockle ['kɔkl] *n* моллю́ск.
cockney ['kɔknɪ] *n* (*person*) кóкни *m/f ind* (*урожéнец райóна Ист-Энд в Лóндоне*); (*LING*) кóкни *m ind* (*диалéкт урожéнцев Ист-Э́нда*).
cockpit ['kɔkpɪt] *n* кабíна.
cockroach ['kɔkrəutʃ] *n* таракáн.
cocktail ['kɔkteɪl] *n* (*drink*) коктéйль *m*; (*with fruit, prawns etc*) салáт, закýска.
cocktail cabinet *n* бар (*в сервáнте*).
cocktail party *n* приём.
cocktail shaker [-'ʃeɪkə'] *n* míксер.
cockup ['kɔkʌp] *n* (*inf!*) лáжа, прокóл.
cocky ['kɔkɪ] *adj* дéрзкий* (дéрзок), задíристый (задíрист).
cocoa ['kəukəu] *n* какáо *nt ind*.
coconut ['kəukənʌt] *n* (*fruit*) кокóсовый орéх; (*flesh*) кокóс.
cocoon [kə'ku:n] *n* (*of butterfly*) кóкон; (*fig*) оболóчка.
COD *abbr* (= *cash on delivery*) налóженный платёж; (*US*: = *collect on delivery*) налóженный платёж.
cod [kɔd] *n* трескá *f no pl*.
code [kəud] *n* (*of behaviour*) кóдекс; (*cipher TEL*) код; **post ~** почтóвый íндекс; **~ of practice** свод прáвил (*профессионáльной дéятельности*).
codeine ['kəudi:n] *n* кодеíн.
codger ['kɔdʒə'] *n* чудáк*.
codicil ['kɔdɪsɪl] *n* (*LAW*) дополнíтельный парáграф завещáния.
codify ['kəudɪfaɪ] *vt* кодифицíровать (*impf/perf*).
cod-liver oil ['kɔdlɪvə-] *n* ры́бий* жир*.
co-driver ['kəu'draɪvə'] *n* (*in race*) штýрман; (*of lorry*) смéнный водíтель.
co-ed ['kəu'ɛd] *adj abbr* (*SCOL*) = **coeducational** ◆ *n abbr* (*US*: *female student*) студéнтка (*в учéбных заведéниях смéшанного тíпа*); (*BRIT*: *school*) смéшанная шкóла.
coeducational ['kəuɛdju'keɪʃənl] *adj* (*school*) смéшанный.
coerce [kəu'ə:s] *vt* принуждáть (принýдить* *perf*).
coercion [kəu'ə:ʃən] *n* принуждéние.
coexistence ['kəuɪg'zɪstəns] *n* сосуществовáние.
C. of C. *n abbr* (= *chamber of commerce*) Торгóвая палáта.
C of E *abbr* = **Church of England**.
coffee ['kɔfɪ] *n* кóфе *m ind*; **black ~** чёрный кóфе; **white ~** кóфе с молокóм; **~ with cream** кóфе со слíвками.
coffee bar *n* (*BRIT*) кофéйня.
coffee beans *npl* кофéйные зёрна *ntpl*.
coffee break *n* переры́в на кóфе.
coffee cake *n* (*US*) торт к кóфе.
coffee cup *n* кофéйная чáшка*.
coffeepot ['kɔfɪpɔt] *n* кофéйник.
coffee table *n* кофéйный стóлик.
coffin ['kɔfɪn] *n* гроб*.
C of I *abbr* = *Church of Ireland*.
C of S *abbr* = *Church of Scotland*.

cog [kɔg] *n* (*wheel*) зубча́тое колесо́*; (*tooth*) зубе́ц*.
cogent ['kəudʒənt] *adj* внуши́тельный* (внуши́телен).
cognac ['kɔnjæk] *n* конья́к*.
cogwheel ['kɔgwi:l] *n* зу́бчатое колесо́*.
cohabit [kəu'hæbɪt] *vi*: **to ~ (with sb)** сожи́тельствовать *(impf)* (с кем-н).
coherent [kəu'hɪərənt] *adj* свя́зный; **she was very ~** её речь была́ о́чень свя́зной.
cohesion [kəu'hi:ʒən] *n* це́льность *f*.
cohesive [kə'hi:sɪv] *adj* (*fig*) це́льный* (це́лен).
COI *n abbr* (*BRIT*: = *Central Office of Information*) Центра́льное управле́ние информа́ции.
coil [kɔɪl] *n* (*of rope, wire*) мото́к*; (*one loop*) вито́к*; (*of smoke*) кольцо́*; (*AUT*) кату́шка*; (*contraceptive*) спира́ль *f* ◆ *vt* (*rope*) сма́тывать (смота́ть *perf*).
coin [kɔɪn] *n* моне́та ◆ *vt* (*phrase*) приду́мывать (приду́мать *perf*).
coinage ['kɔɪnɪdʒ] *n* (*money*) де́нежные зна́ки *mpl*; (*system*) де́нежная систе́ма; (*LING*) неологи́зм.
coin box *n* (*BRIT*) телефо́н-автома́т.
coincide [kəuɪn'saɪd] *vi* совпада́ть (совпа́сть* *perf*).
coincidence [kəu'ɪnsɪdəns] *n* совпаде́ние.
coin-operated ['kɔɪn'ɔpəreɪtɪd] *adj*: **~ machine** автома́т.
Coke® [kəuk] *n* (*drink*) ко́ка-ко́ла; **I would like a ~, please** да́йте пожа́луйста ко́ка-ко́лу.
coke [kəuk] *n* (*coal*) кокс.
Col. *abbr* = **colonel**.
COLA *n abbr* (*US*: = *cost-of-living adjustment*) индекса́ция за́работной пла́ты.
colander ['kɔləndə'] *n* (*CULIN*) дуршла́г.
cold [kəuld] *adj* холо́дный* ◆ *n* хо́лод; (*MED*) просту́да; **it's ~** хо́лодно; **I am** *or* **feel ~** мне хо́лодно; **the wall is ~** э́та стена́ холо́дная; **to catch ~** *or* **a ~** простужа́ться (простуди́ться* *perf*); **in ~ blood** хладнокро́вно; **to have ~ feet** (*fig*) тру́сить* (стру́сить* *perf*); **I gave her the ~ shoulder** я был неприве́тлив с ней.
cold-blooded ['kəuld'blʌdɪd] *adj* (*ZOOL*) холоднокро́вный (холоднокро́вен); (*callous*) хладнокро́вный* (хладнокро́вен).
cold cream *n* ко́льд крем.
coldly ['kəuldlɪ] *adv* хо́лодно.
cold-shoulder [kəuld'ʃəuldə'] *vt* относи́ться* (отнести́сь* *perf*) неприве́тливо к *+dat*.
cold sore *n* лихора́дка* (*на губе́ и́ли носу́*).
cold sweat *n* холо́дный пот.
cold turkey *n* (*inf*): **he is going through ~ ~** у него́ ло́мка.
cold war *n*: **the ~ ~** холо́дная война́.
coleslaw ['kəulslɔ:] *n капу́стный сала́т с майоне́зом*.
colic ['kɔlɪk] *n* ко́лики *pl*.
colicky ['kɔlɪkɪ] *adj* страда́ющий ко́ликами.
collaborate [kə'læbəreɪt] *vi* сотру́дничать (*impf*).
collaboration [kəlæbə'reɪʃən] *n* сотру́дничество.
collaborator [kə'læbəreɪtə'] *n* (*on book etc*) соа́втор; (*with enemy*) коллаборациони́ст.
collage [kɔ'lɑ:ʒ] *n* (*ART*) колла́ж.
collagen ['kɔlədʒən] *n* коллаге́н.
collapse [kə'læps] *vi* (*building, system, plans*) ру́шиться (ру́хнуть *perf*); (*table etc*) скла́дываться (сложи́ться *perf*); (*company*) разоря́ться (разори́ться *perf*); (*government*) разва́ливаться (развали́ться *perf*); (*resistance*) сломи́ться (*perf*); (*MED*: *person*) свали́ться (*perf*) ◆ *n* (*of building*) обва́л; (*of system, plans*) круше́ние; (*of company*) разоре́ние; (*of government*) паде́ние; (*MED*) упа́док сил, колла́пс; **a ~d lung** колла́пс лёгкого.
collapsible [kə'læpsəbl] *adj* складно́й.
collar ['kɔlə'] *n* (*of shirt etc*) воротни́к*; (*of dog etc*) оше́йник; (*TECH*) ше́йка* ◆ *vt* (*inf*: *physically*) хва́тывать (схвати́ть* *perf*); (*to speak to*) заде́рживать (задержа́ть* *perf*).
collarbone ['kɔləbəun] *n* ключи́ца.
collate [kɔ'leɪt] *vt* сопоставля́ть (сопоста́вить* *perf*).
collateral [kə'lætərl] *n* (*COMM*) обеспече́ние креди́та.
collateral damage *n* сопу́тствующее разруше́ние.
collation [kə'leɪʃən] *n* сопоставле́ние, сличе́ние; (*CULIN*): **a cold ~** холо́дный буфе́т.
colleague ['kɔli:g] *n* колле́га *m/f*.
collect [kə'lɛkt] *vt* (*gather*) собира́ть (собра́ть* *perf*); (*stamps etc*) коллекциони́ровать (*impf*); (*BRIT*: *on foot*) заходи́ть* (зайти́* *perf*) за *+instr*; (: *by vehicle*) заезжа́ть* (зае́хать* *perf*) за *+instr*; (*debts etc*) взы́скивать (взыска́ть* *perf*); (*mail*) забира́ть (забра́ть* *perf*) ◆ *vi* (*crowd*) собира́ться (собра́ться* *perf*); **to call ~** (*US*) звони́ть (*impf*) по колле́кту; **to ~ one's thoughts** собира́ться (собра́ться *perf*) с мы́слями; **~ on delivery** (*US*) нало́женный платёж.
collected [kə'lɛktɪd] *adj*: **~ works** собра́ние сочине́ний.
collection [kə'lɛkʃən] *n* (*of stamps etc*) колле́кция; (*of poems etc*) сбо́рник; (*for charity, also REL*) поже́ртвования *ntpl*; (*of mail*) вы́емка*.
collective [kə'lɛktɪv] *adj* коллекти́вный ◆ *n* коллекти́в.
collective bargaining *n переговóры мéжду предпринимáтелем и профсоюзами об оплáте трудá рабóчих*.
collector [kə'lɛktə'] *n* (*of stamps etc*) коллекционе́р; (*of taxes etc*) сбо́рщик(-ица); (*of cash*) инкасса́тор; **~'s item** *or* **piece** *вещь, представля́ющая интере́с для коллекционе́ра*.
college ['kɔlɪdʒ] *n* (*of university*) ко́лледж; (*of*

technology etc) институ́т; **to go to ~** поступа́ть (поступи́ть* *perf*) в институ́т; **~ of education** уче́бное заведе́ние.
collide [kə'laɪd] *vi* (*cars, people*) ста́лкиваться (столкну́ться *perf*); **to ~ with sth** ната́лкиваться (натолкну́ться *perf*) на что-н.
collie ['kɔlɪ] *n* ко́лли *m ind*.
colliery ['kɔlɪərɪ] *n* (*BRIT*) у́гольная ша́хта.
collision [kə'lɪʒən] *n* (*of vehicles*) столкнове́ние; **to be on a ~ course** находи́ться* *(impf)* на пути́, веду́щем к столкнове́нию; (*fig*) встава́ть* (встать* *perf*) на путь конфронта́ции.
collision damage waiver *n страхо́вка, освобожда́ющая от вы́платы компенса́ции за поврежде́ние взя́той напрока́т маши́ны.*
colloquial [kə'ləukwɪəl] *adj* разгово́рный.
collusion [kə'lu:ʒən] *n* (*collaboration*) сго́вор; **in ~ with** в сго́воре с *+instr*.
Cologne [kə'ləun] *n* Кёльн.
cologne [kə'ləun] *n* (*also:* **eau de ~**) одеколо́н.
Colombia [kə'lɔmbɪə] *n* Колу́мбия.
Colombian [kə'lɔmbɪən] *adj* колумби́йский* ◆ *n* колумби́ец(-и́йка).
colon ['kəulən] *n* (*LING*) двоето́чие; (*ANAT*) пряма́я кишка́.
colonel ['kə:nl] *n* полко́вник.
colonial [kə'ləunɪəl] *adj* колониа́льный.
colonize ['kɔlənaɪz] *vt* (*country etc*) колонизи́ровать *(impf/perf)*.
colony ['kɔlənɪ] *n* (*of people, animals*) коло́ния.
color *etc* (*US*) = **colour** *etc*.
Colorado beetle [kɔlə'rɑ:dəu-] *n* колора́дский жук*.
colossal [kə'lɔsl] *adj* колосса́льный* (колосса́лен).
colour ['kʌlə^r] (*US* **color**) *n* цвет*; (*of spectacle etc*) кра́сочность *f* ◆ *vt* (*paint*) раскра́шивать (раскра́сить* *perf*); (*dye*) кра́сить* (покра́сить* *perf*); (*fig: judgement etc*) окра́шивать (окра́сить* *perf*) ◆ *vi* (*blush*) красне́ть (покрасне́ть *perf*) ◆ *cpd* цветно́й; **~s** *npl* (*of club etc*) эмбле́ма *fsg*; (*MIL*) флаг *msg*; **skin ~** цвет ко́жи; **in ~** в цве́те; **with flying ~s** с триу́мфом
▸ **colour in** *vt* раскра́шивать (раскра́сить* *perf*).
colour bar *n* ра́совый барье́р.
colour-blind ['kʌləblaɪnd] *adj*: **he is ~** он дальто́ник.
coloured ['kʌləd] *adj* цветно́й.
colour film *n* цветна́я плёнка.
colourful ['kʌləful] *adj* (*cloth*) цвети́стый (цвети́ст); (*story*) кра́сочный* (кра́сочен); (*personality*) я́ркий*.
colouring ['kʌlərɪŋ] *n* (*complexion*) цвет лица́; (*in food*) краси́тель *m*.
colour scheme *n* цветова́я га́мма.
colour supplement *n* (*BRIT: PRESS*) иллюстри́рованное приложе́ние.
colour television *n* цветно́й телеви́зор.
colt [kəult] *n* жеребёнок*.
column ['kɔləm] *n* (*of people, also ARCHIT*) коло́нна; (*of smoke*) столб*; (*PRESS*) ру́брика; **the editorial ~** реда́кторская статья́*.
columnist ['kɔləmnɪst] *n* (*PRESS*) обозрева́тель *m*.
coma ['kəumə] *n* (*MED*): **to be in a ~** находи́ться* *(impf)* в ко́ме.
comb [kəum] *n* (*for hair*) расчёска; (*: ornamental*) гре́бень* *m* ◆ *vt* (*hair*) расчёсывать (расчеса́ть* *perf*); (*area*) прочёсывать (прочеса́ть* *perf*).
combat [*n* 'kɔmbæt, *vt* kəm'bæt] *n* (*fighting*) бой*; (*battle*) би́тва ◆ *vt* боро́ться* *(impf)* про́тив *+gen*.
combination [kɔmbɪ'neɪʃən] *n* (*mixture*) сочета́ние, комбина́ция; (*code*) код.
combination lock *n* замо́к* с ши́фром.
combine [*vb* kəm'baɪn, *n* 'kɔmbaɪn] *vt* комбини́ровать (скомбини́ровать *perf*) ◆ *vi* (*groups*) объединя́ться (объедини́ться *perf*); (*CHEM*) вступа́ть (вступи́ть* *perf*) в соедине́ние ◆ *n* (*ECON*) объедине́ние; (*also:* **~ harvester**) комба́йн; **to ~ sth with sth** (*qualities*) сочета́ть *perf* что-н с чем-н; (*activities*) совмеща́ть (совмести́ть* *perf*) что-н с чем-н; **a ~d effort** совме́стное уси́лие.
combo ['kɔmbəu] *n* (*JAZZ*) ко́мбо.
combustible [kəm'bʌstɪbl] *adj* горю́чий*.
combustion [kəm'bʌstʃən] *n* (*act*) сгора́ние; (*process*) горе́ние.

KEYWORD

come [kʌm] (*pt* **came**, *pp* **come**) *vi* ***1*** (*move towards: on foot*) подходи́ть* (подойти́* *perf*); (*: by transport*) подъезжа́ть (подъе́хать* *perf*); **they came to a river** (*on foot*) они́ подошли́ к реке́; (*by transport*) они́ подъе́хали к реке́; **he came running up to us** он подбежа́л к нам; **to come running** подбега́ть (подбежа́ть* *perf*)
2 (*arrive: on foot*) приходи́ть* (прийти́* *perf*); (*: by transport*) приезжа́ть (прие́хать* *perf*); **to come home** (*on foot*) приходи́ть* (прийти́* *perf*) домо́й; (*by transport*) приезжа́ть (прие́хать* *perf*) домо́й; **he came running to tell us** он прибежа́л сказа́ть нам; **are you coming to my party?** Вы придёте ко мне на вечери́нку?; **I've only come for an hour** я зашёл то́лько на час
3 (*reach: power, decision, conclusion*): **to come to** приходи́ть* (прийти́* *perf*) к *+dat*; **the bill came to £40** счёт был £40; **her hair came to her waist** у неё бы́ли во́лосы до по́яса
4 (*occur*): **an idea came to me** мне в го́лову

* marks translations which have irregular inflections. The Russian-English side of the dictionary gives inflectional information.

пришла́ иде́я
5 (*be, become*): **to come into being** возника́ть (возни́кнуть *perf*); **to come loose** отходи́ть* (отойти́* *perf*); **I've come to like him** он стал мне нра́виться
▸ **come about** *vi*: **how did it come about?** каки́м о́бразом э́то получи́лось?; **it came about through...** э́то получи́лось из-за *+gen*
▸ **come across** *vt fus* ната́лкиваться (натолкну́ться *perf*) на *+acc*
◆ *vi*: **to come across well/badly** производи́ть* (произвести́* *perf*) хоро́шее/плохо́е впечатле́ние
▸ **come along** *vi* (*pupil, work*) продвига́ться (продви́нуться *perf*); **come along!** идёмте!, пошли́!
▸ **come apart** *vi* (*break*) лома́ться (слома́ться *perf*); (*can be dismantled*) разбира́ться *(impf)*; (*tear*) рва́ться* (разорва́ться* *perf*)
▸ **come away** *vi* (*leave*) уходи́ть* (уйти́* *perf*); (*to become detached*) отходи́ть* (отойти́* *perf*)
▸ **come back** *vi* (*return*) возвраща́ться (верну́ться *perf*); (*inf*): **can I come back to you on that one?** я ещё обращу́сь к Вам по э́тому вопро́су, ла́дно?
▸ **come by** *vt fus* (*acquire*) достава́ть* (доста́ть* *perf*)
▸ **come down** *vi* (*price*) понижа́ться (пони́зиться* *perf*); **the tree came down in the storm** де́рево снесло́ бу́рей; **the building will have to come down soon** зда́ние должны́ ско́ро снести́
▸ **come forward** *vi* (*volunteer*) вызыва́ться (вы́зваться* *perf*)
▸ **come from** *vt fus* (*place, source etc*): **she comes from India** она́ из И́ндии
▸ **come in** *vi* (*person*) входи́ть* (войти́* *perf*); (*on deal etc*): **to come in on** вступа́ть (вступи́ть* *perf*) в *+acc*; **where does he come in?** в чём состои́т его́ роль?
▸ **come in for** *vt fus* подверга́ться (подве́ргнуться* *perf*) *+dat*
▸ **come into** *vt fus* (*fashion*) входи́ть* (войти́* *perf*) в *+acc*; (*be involved in*) игра́ть *(impf)* роль в *+prp*; **to come into money** получа́ть (получи́ть* *perf*) большу́ю су́мму де́нег
▸ **come off** *vi* (*button*) отрыва́ться (оторва́ться *perf*); (*handle*) отла́мываться (отлома́ться *perf*); (*can be taken off*) снима́ться *(impf)*; (*attempt*) удава́ться* (уда́ться* *perf*)
▸ **come on** *vi* (*pupil*) де́лать (сде́лать *perf*) успе́хи; (*work etc*) продвига́ться *(impf)*; (*lights etc*) включа́ться (включи́ться* *perf*); **come on!** (ну,) дава́йте!
▸ **come out** *vi* (*fact*) станови́ться (стать* *perf*) изве́стным(-ой); (*book, sun*) выходи́ть* (вы́йти* *perf*); (*stain*) сходи́ть* (сойти́* *perf*); (*person*) выходи́ть* (вы́йти* *perf*); (*workers*): **to come out on strike** выходи́ть* (вы́йти* *perf*) на забасто́вку
▸ **come over** *vt fus*: **I don't know what's come over him!** я не зна́ю, что с ним тако́е!
▸ **come round** *vi* (*MED*) очну́ться *(perf)*, приходи́ть* (прийти́* *perf*) в себя́
▸ **come through** *vt fus* (*survive*) пережи́ть* *(perf)*; (: *operation*) переноси́ть* (перенести́* *perf*)
◆ *vi*: **his visa came through yesterday** его́ ви́за пришла́ вчера́
▸ **come to** *vi* (*MED*) очну́ться *(perf)*, приходи́ть* (прийти́* *perf*) в себя́
◆ *vt fus*: **how much does it come to?** ско́лько э́то всё бу́дет?
▸ **come under** *vt fus*: **to come under (the heading)** идти́* *(impf)* под заголо́вком; **to come under criticism from ...** подверга́ться (подве́ргнуться *perf*) кри́тике со стороны́ *+gen ...*; **he has come under pressure from his boss** нача́льник ока́зывал на него́ давле́ние
▸ **come up** *vi* (*sun*) всходи́ть* (взойти́* *perf*); (*approach*: *event*) приближа́ться *(impf)*; (*arise*: *questions*) встава́ть (встать* *perf*); (*to be mentioned*) быть *(impf)* затро́нутым; **I can't come with you, something important has come up** я не смогу́ пойти́ с тобо́й, у меня́ возни́кло ва́жное де́ло
▸ **come up against** *vt fus* ната́лкиваться (натолкну́ться *perf*) на *+acc*
▸ **come up to** *vt fus*: **the film didn't come up to our expectations** фильм не оправда́л на́ши ожида́ния
▸ **come up with** *vt fus* (*idea, solution*) приду́мывать (приду́мать *perf*); (*money*) находи́ть (найти́* *perf*)
▸ **come upon** *vt fus* ната́лкиваться (натолкну́ться *perf*) на *+acc*.

comeback ['kʌmbæk] *n* (*reaction*) язви́тельный отве́т; (*response*) возраже́ние; **to make a ~** (*of actor etc*) обрета́ть (обрести́* *perf*) но́вую популя́рность.
Comecon ['kɔmɪkɔn] *n abbr* (= *Council for Mutual Economic Aid*) ≈ СЭВ= *Сове́т Экономи́ческой Взаимопо́мощи.*
comedian [kə'mi:dɪən] *n* ко́мик.
comedienne [kəmi:dɪ'ɛn] *n* коми́ческая актри́са.
comedown ['kʌmdaun] *n* (*inf*: *humiliation*) униже́ние; (: *demotion*) пониже́ние.
comedy ['kɔmɪdɪ] *n* (*play, film*) коме́дия; (*humour*) коми́зм.
comet ['kɔmɪt] *n* коме́та.
comeuppance [kʌm'ʌpəns] *n*: **to get one's ~** получа́ть (получи́ть* *perf*) по заслу́гам.
comfort ['kʌmfət] *n* (*well-being*) комфо́рт; (*solace*) утеше́ние; (*relief*) облегче́ние ◆ *vt* утеша́ть (уте́шить *perf*); **~s** *npl* (*luxuries*) удо́бства *ntpl*.
comfortable ['kʌmfətəbl] *adj* (*furniture, room*)

удо́бный* (удо́бен), комфорта́бельный* (комфорта́белен); (*walk etc*) лёгкий*; (*majority*) прили́чный* (прили́чен); **to be ~** (*person*: *physically*) чу́вствовать *(impf)* себя́ удо́бно; (: *financially*) жить *(impf)* в доста́тке; (*patient*) чу́вствовать *(impf)* себя́ норма́льно; **I don't feel very ~ about it** я чу́вствую себя́ нело́вко в да́нном слу́чае; **make yourself ~** располага́йтесь поудо́бнее.

comfortably ['kʌmfətəblɪ] *adv* удо́бно.

comforter ['kʌmfətə^r] *n* (*US*) со́ска-пусты́шка*.

comfort station *n* (*US*) обще́ственный туале́т.

comic ['kɔmɪk] *adj* коми́ческий*, смешно́й ◆ *n* (*comedian*) ко́мик; (*BRIT*: *magazine*) ко́микс.

comical ['kɔmɪkl] *adj* смешно́й* (смешо́н), коми́чный* (коми́чен).

comic strip *n* ко́микс (*се́рия рису́нков*).

coming ['kʌmɪŋ] *n* прибы́тие ◆ *adj* (*approaching*) приближа́ющийся; (*next*) сле́дующий*; (*future*) бу́дущий*; **in the ~ weeks** в тече́ние сле́дующих неде́ль.

coming(s) and going(s) *n(pl)* прихо́д *msg* и ухо́д *msg*.

Comintern ['kɔmɪntə:n] *n* (*POL*) Коминте́рн.

comma ['kɔmə] *n* (*LING*) запята́я *f adj*.

command [kə'mɑ:nd] *n* (*order*) кома́нда; (*control*) контро́ль *m*; (*MIL*) кома́ндование; (*mastery*) владе́ние; (*COMPUT*) кома́нда, директи́ва ◆ *vt* (*troops*) кома́ндовать *(impf)* +*instr*; (*be able to get*) располага́ть *(impf)* +*instr*; (*deserve*) заслу́живать *(impf)* +*gen*; **to be in ~ of** (*situation*) владе́ть (овладе́ть *perf*) +*instr*; **to take ~ of** (*MIL*) принима́ть (приня́ть* *perf*) кома́ндование +*instr*; **to have at one's ~** (*resources etc*) име́ть *(impf)* в своём распоряже́нии; **he has a good ~ of English** он хоро́шо владе́ет англи́йским языко́м; **to ~ sb to do** прика́зывать (приказа́ть* *perf*) кому́-н +*infin*.

commandant ['kɔməndænt] *n* коменда́нт.

command economy *n* кома́ндная эконо́мика.

commandeer [kɔmən'dɪə^r] *vt* (*requisition*) реквизи́ровать *(impf/perf)*; (*fig*) присва́ивать (присво́ить *perf*).

commander [kə'mɑ:ndə^r] *n* (*MIL*: *of troops*) кома́ндующий *m adj*; (: *of batallion*) команди́р.

commander in chief *n* главнокома́ндующий *m adj*.

commanding [kə'mɑ:ndɪŋ] *adj* (*appearance*) внуши́тельный*; (*voice etc*) вла́стный*; (*situation*) госпо́дствующий*.

commanding officer *n* команди́р.

commandment [kə'mɑ:ndmənt] *n* за́поведь *f*.

command module *n* (*SPACE*) кома́ндный отсе́к корабля́.

commando [kə'mɑ:ndəu] *n* (*group*) деса́нтные войска́ *ntpl*; (*soldier*) деса́нтник.

commemorate [kə'mɛməreɪt] *vt* (*with statue etc*) увекове́чивать (увекове́чить *perf*); (*with celebration etc*) отмеча́ть (отме́тить* *perf*).

commemoration [kəmɛmə'reɪʃən] *n* ознаменова́ние.

commemorative [kə'mɛmərətɪv] *adj* (*stamp*) юбиле́йный; (*plaque*) мемориа́льный.

commence [kə'mɛns] *vt* приступа́ть (приступи́ть* *perf*) к +*dat* ◆ *vi* начина́ться (нача́ться* *perf*).

commend [kə'mɛnd] *vt* хвали́ть* (похвали́ть* *perf*); (*recommend*): **to ~ sth to sb** рекомендова́ть (порекомендова́ть *perf*) что-н кому́-н.

commendable [kə'mɛndəbl] *adj* похва́льный* (похва́лен).

commendation [kɔmɛn'deɪʃən] *n* благода́рность *f*.

commensurate [kə'mɛnʃərɪt] *adj*: **~ with** соразме́рный* (соразме́рен) +*dat or* с +*instr*.

comment ['kɔmɛnt] *n* (*remark*) замеча́ние; (*on situation*) коммента́рий ◆ *vi*: **to ~ (on)** комменти́ровать (прокомменти́ровать *perf*) (+*acc*); **to ~ that** поясня́ть (поясни́ть *perf*), что; **"no ~"** "возде́рживаюсь от коммента́риев".

commentary ['kɔməntərɪ] *n* репорта́ж; (*book, article*) коммента́рий.

commentator ['kɔmənteɪtə^r] *n* (*TV, RADIO*) коммента́тор; **(sports) ~** спорти́вный коммента́тор.

commerce ['kɔmə:s] *n* комме́рция.

commercial [kə'mə:ʃəl] *adj* (*organization*) комме́рческий*; (*success, failure*) фина́нсовый ◆ *n* (*TV, RADIO*) рекла́ма.

commercial bank *n* комме́рческий* банк.

commercial break *n* рекла́мная па́уза.

commercial college *n* институ́т комме́рции.

commercialism [kə'mə:ʃəlɪzəm] *n* меркантили́зм.

commercialized [kə'mə:ʃəlaɪzd] *adj* (*pej*) поста́вленный на комме́рческую осно́ву.

commercial radio *n* комме́рческое ра́дио.

commercial television *n* комме́рческое телеви́дение.

commercial traveller *n* коммивояжёр.

commercial vehicle *n* комме́рческий тра́нспорт.

commiserate [kə'mɪzəreɪt] *vi*: **to ~ with** сочу́вствовать (посочу́вствовать *perf*) +*dat*.

commission [kə'mɪʃən] *n* (*order for work*) зака́з; (*COMM*) комиссио́нные *pl adj*, комиссио́нное вознагражде́ние; (*committee*) коми́ссия; (*MIL*) офице́рский* чин ◆ *vt* (*order*) зака́зывать (заказа́ть* *perf*); (*MIL*) присва́ивать (присво́ить *perf*) офице́рский* чин +*dat*; **out of ~** (*NAUT*) не приго́дный

* marks translations which have irregular inflections. The Russian-English side of the dictionary gives inflectional information.

(приго́ден) к пла́ванию; (*machine*) неиспра́вный* (неиспра́вен); **I get 10% ~** я получа́ю 10% комиссио́нных; **~ of inquiry** сле́дственная коми́ссия; **to ~ sb to do** поруча́ть (поручи́ть* *perf*) кому́-н *+infin*; **to ~ sth from sb** зака́зывать (заказа́ть* *perf*) что-н кому́-н.

commissionaire [kəmɪʃə'nɛə'] *n* (*BRIT*) швейца́р.

commissioner [kə'mɪʃənə'] *n*: **(police) ~** полице́йский* комисса́р.

commit [kə'mɪt] *vt* (*crime*) соверша́ть (соверши́ть *perf*); (*money*) выделя́ть (выдели́ть *perf*); (*entrust*) вверя́ть (вве́рить *perf*); **to ~ o.s.** принима́ть (приня́ть* *perf*) на себя́ обяза́тельства; **to ~ suicide** соверша́ть (соверши́ть *perf*) самоуби́йство; **to ~ to writing** запи́сывать (записа́ть* *perf*); **to ~ to memory** запомина́ть (запо́мнить *perf*); **to ~ sb for trial** отдава́ть* (отда́ть* *perf*) кого́-н под суд.

commitment [kə'mɪtmənt] *n* (*belief*) пре́данность *f*; (*obligation*) обяза́тельство.

committed [kə'mɪtɪd] *adj* (*supporter*) приве́рженный (приве́ржен).

committee [kə'mɪtɪ] *n* комите́т; **to be on a ~** входи́ть* *(impf)* в соста́в комите́та.

committee meeting *n* заседа́ние комите́та.

commodity [kə'mɔdɪtɪ] *n* (*saleable item*) това́р; (*food*) проду́кт.

commodity exchange *n* това́рная би́ржа.

common ['kɔmən] *adj* (*shared*) о́бщий*; (*usual, ordinary*) обы́чный; (*vulgar*) вульга́рный* (вульга́рен) ◆ *n* обще́ственный луг*; **the C~s** *npl* (*also:* **the House of C~s**: *BRIT*) Пала́та *fsg* О́бщин; **to have sth in ~ (with sb)** име́ть *(impf)* что-н о́бщее (с кем-н); **in ~ use** в широ́ком употребле́нии; **it's ~ knowledge that** общеизве́стно, что; **to** *or* **for the ~ good** для всео́бщего бла́га.

common cold *n* обыкнове́нная просту́да.

common denominator *n* (*MATH*) о́бщий* знамена́тель *m*; (*characteristic*) о́бщая черта́; (*attitude*) о́бщее* мне́ние.

commoner ['kɔmənə'] *n* простолюди́н.

common ground *n* (*fig*) то́чки *fpl* соприкоснове́ния.

common land *n* обще́ственная земля́*.

common law *n* обы́чное пра́во.

common-law ['kɔmənlɔ:] *adj* гражда́нский*.

commonly ['kɔmənlɪ] *adv* обы́чно.

Common Market *n*: **the ~ ~** О́бщий* ры́нок*.

commonplace ['kɔmənpleɪs] *adj* обы́чный, обы́денный.

common room *n* ко́мната о́тдыха (*для студе́нтов, учителе́й и т.д.*).

common sense *n* здра́вый смысл.

Commonwealth ['kɔmənwɛlθ] *n* (*BRIT*): **the ~** Содру́жество.

commotion [kə'məuʃən] *n* сумато́ха.

communal ['kɔmju:nl] *adj* (*shared*) о́бщий*; (*life*) обще́ственный; **a ~ flat** коммуна́льная кварти́ра.

commune [*n* 'kɔmju:n, *vi* kə'mju:n] *n* комму́на ◆ *vi*: **to ~ with** обща́ться *(impf)* с *+instr*.

communicate [kə'mju:nɪkeɪt] *vt* передава́ть* (переда́ть* *perf*) ◆ *vi*: **to ~ (with)** обща́ться *(impf)* (с *+instr*); **to ~ (by letter)** обраща́ться (обрати́ться* *perf*) пи́сьменно.

communication [kəmju:nɪ'keɪʃən] *n* (*process*) коммуника́ция; (*letter etc*) сообще́ние.

communication cord *n* (*BRIT*) авари́йный сигна́л "стоп".

communications network [kəmju:nɪ'keɪʃənz-] *n* систе́ма коммуника́ций.

communications satellite *n* спу́тник свя́зи.

communicative [kə'mju:nɪkətɪv] *adj* (*person*) общи́тельный* (общи́телен).

communion [kə'mju:nɪən] *n* (*also:* **Holy C~**) Свято́е Прича́стие.

communiqué [kə'mju:nɪkeɪ] *n* коммюнике́ *nt ind*.

communism ['kɔmjunɪzəm] *n* коммуни́зм.

communist ['kɔmjunɪst] *adj* коммунисти́ческий* ◆ *n* коммуни́ст(ка).

community [kə'mju:nɪtɪ] *n* (*public*) обще́ственность *f*; (*within larger group*) о́бщина; **the business ~** делов́ые круги́ *mpl*.

community centre *n* ≈ обще́ственный центр.

community charge *n* (*BRIT: formerly*) поду́шный нало́г.

community chest *n* (*US*) объединённый благотвори́тельный фонд.

community health centre *n* райо́нная поликли́ника.

community home *n* (*BRIT: for children*) де́тский* дом.

community service *n* трудова́я пови́нность *f* (*как фо́рма наказа́ния*).

community spirit *n* чу́вство о́бщности *or* това́рищества.

commutation ticket [kɔmju'teɪʃən-] *n* (*US*) сезо́нный биле́т.

commute [kə'mju:t] *vi* (*to work*) *е́здить на рабо́ту из при́города в го́род* ◆ *vt* (*LAW*) смягча́ть (смягчи́ть *perf*) наказа́ние.

commuter [kə'mju:tə'] *n* *челове́к, кото́рый е́здит на рабо́ту из при́города в го́род*; **~ train** при́городный по́езд.

compact [*adj* kəm'pækt, *n* 'kɔmpækt] *adj* компа́ктный* (компа́ктен) ◆ *n* (*also:* **powder ~**) пу́дреница.

compact disc *n* компа́кт-диск.

compact-disc player [kɔmpækt'dɪsk-] *n* прои́грыватель *m* для компа́кт-ди́сков.

companion [kəm'pænjən] *n* спу́тник(-ица).

companionship [kəm'pænjənʃɪp] *n* обще́ние.

companionway [kəm'pænjənweɪ] *n* (*NAUT*) трап.

company ['kʌmpənɪ] *n* (*COMM*) компа́ния; (*THEAT*) тру́ппа; (*MIL*) ро́та; (*companionship*) компа́ния, о́бщество; **he's good ~** его́

общество приятно; **we have ~** у нас гости; **to keep sb ~** составлять (составить* *perf*) кому-н компанию; **to part ~ with** расходиться* (разойтись* *perf*) с *+instr*; **Smith and C~** Смит и Компания.
company car *n* служебная машина.
company director *n* директор* компании.
company secretary *n* (*BRIT*) секретарь* *m(f)* фирмы.
comparable ['kɔmpərəbl] *adj* (*size*) сравнимый (сравним); (*style*) сопоставимый (сопоставим); (*car, property etc*) подобный* (подобен).
comparative [kəm'pærətɪv] *adj* (*also LING*) сравнительный; (*relative*) относительный (относителен).
comparatively [kəm'pærətɪvlɪ] *adv* (*relatively*) относительно.
compare [kəm'pɛə'] *vt*: **to ~ sb/sth with** *or* **to** (*liken*) сравнивать (сравнить *perf*) кого-н/что-н с *+instr*; (*set side by side*) сопоставлять (сопоставить* *perf*) кого-н/что-н с *+instr* ◆ *vi*: **to ~ (with)** соотноситься (*impf*) (с *+instr*); **how do the prices ~?** как соотносятся цены?; **~d with** *or* **to** по сравнению *or* в сравнении с *+instr*.
comparison [kəm'pærɪsn] *n* (*see vt*) сравнение; сопоставление; **in ~ (with)** по сравнению *or* в сравнении (с *+instr*).
compartment [kəm'pɑ:tmənt] *n* (*RAIL*) купе *nt ind*; (*section*) отделение.
compass ['kʌmpəs] *n* (*instrument*) компас; (*fig*) диапазон; **~es** *npl* (*also:* **pair of ~es**) циркуль *msg*; **beyond the ~ of** за пределами *+gen*; **within the ~ of** в пределах *+gen*.
compassion [kəm'pæʃən] *n* сострадание.
compassionate [kəm'pæʃənɪt] *adj* сострадательный* (сострадателен); **on ~ grounds** по состоянию здоровья; **~ leave** отпуск по семейным обстоятельствам.
compatibility [kəmpætɪ'bɪlɪtɪ] *n* совместимость *f*.
compatible [kəm'pætɪbl] *adj* (*also COMPUT*) совместимый (совместим).
compel [kəm'pɛl] *vt* вынуждать (вынудить* *perf*).
compelling [kəm'pɛlɪŋ] *adj* (*fig: argument*) убедительный* (убедителен); (: *reason*) настоятельный.
compendium [kəm'pɛndɪəm] *n* (*summary*) резюме *nt ind*.
compensate ['kɔmpənseɪt] *vt*: **to ~ sb for sth** компенсировать (*impf/perf*) кому-н что-н ◆ *vi*: **to ~ for** (*loss, distress etc*) компенсировать (*impf/perf*).
compensation [kɔmpən'seɪʃən] *n* компенсация; (*money*) денежная компенсация.
compère ['kɔmpɛə'] *n* (*TV, RADIO*) ведущий*(-ая) *m(f) adj*.
compete [kəm'pi:t] *vi* (*in contest etc*) соревноваться (*impf*); **to ~ (with)** (*companies*) конкурировать (*impf*) (с *+instr*); (*rivals*) соперничать (*impf*) (с *+instr*); **to ~ (with one another)** (*theories etc*) соперничать (*impf*) друг с другом.
competence ['kɔmpɪtəns] *n* компетенция.
competent ['kɔmpɪtənt] *adj* (*person*) компетентный* (компетентен); (*piece of work*) искусный.
competing [kəm'pi:tɪŋ] *adj* (*firms*) конкурирующий; (*claims, explanations*) разноречивый (разноречив).
competition [kɔmpɪ'tɪʃən] *n* (*contest*) соревнование; (*between firms*) конкуренция; (*between rivals*) соперничество; **to be in ~ with** конкурировать (*impf*) с *+instr*.
competitive [kəm'pɛtɪtɪv] *adj* (*industry*) основанный на конкуренции; (*person*) честолюбивый (честолюбив); (*price etc*) конкурентноспособный* (конкурентноспособен); (*sport*) состязательный.
competitive examination *n* конкурс.
competitor [kəm'pɛtɪtə'] *n* (*rival*) соперник, конкурент; (*in musical competition*) конкурсант; (*participant*) участник(-ица) соревнования.
compile [kəm'paɪl] *vt* составлять (составить* *perf*).
complacency [kəm'pleɪsnsɪ] *n* безмятежность *f*.
complacent [kəm'pleɪsnt] *adj* безмятежный (безмятежен).
complain [kəm'pleɪn] *vi*: **to ~ (about)** жаловаться (пожаловаться *perf*) (на *+acc*); **to ~ of a pain** жаловаться (пожаловаться *perf*) на боль.
complaint [kəm'pleɪnt] *n* жалоба; **to make a ~ against** подавать* (подать* *perf*) жалобу на *+acc*.
complement [*n* 'kɔmplɪmənt, *vb* 'kɔmplɪmɛnt] *n* (*supplement*) дополнение; (*ship's crew*) экипаж ◆ *vt* (*enhance*) дополнять (*impf*); **to have a full ~ of** иметь (*impf*) полный комплект *+gen*.
complementary [kɔmplɪ'mɛntərɪ] *adj*: **they are ~ (to one another)** они дополняют друг друга.
complete [kəm'pli:t] *adj* полный*; (*finished*) завершённый (завершён) ◆ *vt* (*building, task*) завершать (завершить *perf*); (*set etc*) комплектовать (укомплектовать *perf*); (*a form*) заполнять (заполнить *perf*); **it's a ~ disaster** это полный провал.
completely [kəm'pli:tlɪ] *adv* полностью,

* marks translations which have irregular inflections. The Russian-English side of the dictionary gives inflectional information.

совершённо.
completion [kəm'pli:ʃən] *n* (*of building*) завершéние; (*of contract*) совершéние; **to be nearing** ~ близиться *(impf)* к завершéнию; **on** ~ по завершéнии.
complex ['kɔmplɛks] *adj* слóжный*, кóмплексный ◆ *n* (*also PSYCH*) кóмплекс.
complexion [kəm'plɛkʃən] *n* (*of face*) цвет* лицá; (*nature*) харáктер.
complexity [kəm'plɛksɪtɪ] *n* слóжность *f*.
compliance [kəm'plaɪəns] *n* (*submission*) послушáние; (*agreement*) соглáсие; ~ **with** слéдование *+dat*; **in ~ with** в соотвéтствии с *+instr*.
compliant [kəm'plaɪənt] *adj* послýшный* (послýшен).
complicate ['kɔmplɪkeɪt] *vt* усложня́ть (усложни́ть *perf*).
complicated ['kɔmplɪkeɪtɪd] *adj* слóжный* (слóжен).
complication [kɔmplɪ'keɪʃən] *n* (*also MED*) осложнéние.
complicity [kəm'plɪsɪtɪ] *n* соучáстие.
compliment [*n* 'kɔmplɪmənt, *vb* 'kɔmplɪmɛnt] *n* комплимéнт, хвалá ◆ *vt* хвлайть (похвали́ть *perf*); **~s** *npl* (*regards*) привéты *mpl*; **to ~ sb, pay sb a** ~ дéлать (сдéлать *perf*) комý-н комплимéнт; **to ~ sb (on sth** *or* **on doing)** поздравля́ть (поздрáвить* *perf*) когó-н (с чем-н).
complimentary [kɔmplɪ'mɛntərɪ] *adj* (*remark*) лéстный* (лéстен); (*ticket etc*) дáрственный.
compliments slip *n фи́рменный бланк для неофициáльных запи́сок*.
comply [kəm'plaɪ] *vi*: **to ~ (with)** подчиня́ться (подчини́ться *perf*) (*+dat*).
component [kəm'pəunənt] *adj* составнóй ◆ *n* компонéнт.
compose [kəm'pəuz] *vt* (*write*) сочиня́ть (сочини́ть *perf*); (*form*): **to be ~d of** состоя́ть *(impf)* из *+gen*; **to ~ o.s.** успокáиваться (успокóиться *perf*).
composed [kəm'pəuzd] *adj* спокóйный* (спокóен).
composer [kəm'pəuzəʳ] *n* композитор.
composite ['kɔmpəzɪt] *adj* составнóй; (*BOT*) сложноцвéтный; (*MATH*) слóжный.
composition [kɔmpə'zɪʃən] *n* (*structure*) состáв; (*essay*) сочинéние; (*MUS*) компози́ция.
compositor [kəm'pɔzɪtəʳ] *n* набóрщик.
compos mentis ['kɔmpɔs 'mɛntɪs] *adj* вменя́емый (вменя́ем).
compost ['kɔmpɔst] *n* компóст; (*also:* **potting** ~) удóбренная земля́.
composure [kəm'pəuʒəʳ] *n* самообладáние.
compound [*n, adj* 'kɔmpaund, *vt* kəm'paund] *n* (*CHEM*) соединéние; (*enclosure*) укреплённый кóмплекс; (*LING*) слóжное слóво* ◆ *adj* слóжный ◆ *vt* (*problem etc*) осложня́ть (осложни́ть *perf*).
compound fracture *n* откры́тый перелóм.
compound interest *n* слóжные процéнты *pl*.
comprehend [kɔmprɪ'hɛnd] *vt* постигáть (пости́гнуть *or* пости́чь* *perf*).
comprehension [kɔmprɪ'hɛnʃən] *n* понимáние.
comprehensive [kɔmprɪ'hɛnsɪv] *adj* исчéрпывающий* (исчéрпывающ) ◆ *n* = **comprehensive school**; ~ **insurance** всеобъéмлющее страховáние.
comprehensive school *n* (*BRIT*) срéдняя шкóла.
compress [*vt* kəm'prɛs, *n* 'kɔmprɛs] *vt* (*air*) сжимáть (сжать* *perf*); (*cotton, paper*) прессовáть (спрессовáть *perf*); (*text etc*) сокращáть (сократи́ть* *perf*) ◆ *n* компрéсс.
compressed air [kəm'prɛst-] *n* сжáтый вóздух.
compression [kəm'prɛʃən] *n* (*of air*) сжáтие; (*of text*) сокращéние.
comprise [kəm'praɪz] *vt* (*also:* **be ~d of**) включáть *(impf)* в себя́, состоя́ть *(impf)* из *+gen*; (*constitute*) составля́ть (состáвить* *perf*).
compromise ['kɔmprəmaɪz] *n* компроми́сс ◆ *vt* компромети́ровать (скомпромети́ровать *perf*) ◆ *vi* (*make concessions*) идти́* (пойти́* *perf*) на компроми́сс ◆ *cpd* компроми́ссный.
compulsion [kəm'pʌlʃən] *n* (*desire*) влечéние; (*force*) принуждéние; **under** ~ по принуждéнию.
compulsive [kəm'pʌlsɪv] *adj* (*gambler etc*) безрассýдный; (*behaviour*) маниакáльный; (*reading etc*) захвáтывающий* (захвáтывающ); **he's a ~ liar** он неисправи́мый лгун.
compulsory [kəm'pʌlsərɪ] *adj* (*attendance*) обязáтельный* (обязáтелен); (*redundancy*) принуди́тельный* (принуди́телен).
compulsory purchase *n* обязáтельная покýпка*.
compunction [kəm'pʌŋkʃən] *n* раскáяние; **to have no ~ about doing** дéлать (сдéлать *perf*) что-н без вся́кого сожалéния.
computer [kəm'pju:təʳ] *n* компью́тер ◆ *cpd* компью́терный; **the process is done by** ~ процéсс выполня́ется при пóмощи компью́тера.
computer game *n* компью́терная игрá*.
computerization [kəmpju:təraɪ'zeɪʃən] *n* компьютеризáция.
computerize [kəm'pju:təraɪz] *vt* компьютеризовáть *(impf/perf)*; **to ~ information** обрабáтывать (обрабóтать *perf*) информáцию на компью́тере.
computer literate *adj*: **to be ~ ~** умéть *(impf)* пóльзоваться компью́тером.
computer peripheral *n* перифери́йное устрóйство (*компью́тера*).
computer programmer *n* программи́ст.
computer programming *n* программ-и́рование.
computer science *n* электрóнно-

вычисли́тельная нау́ка.
computer scientist *n* специали́ст в о́бласти ЭВМ.
computing [kəm'pju:tɪŋ] *n* (*activity*) рабо́та на компью́тере; (*science*) электро́нно-вычисли́тельная нау́ка; **I've never done any ~** я никогда́ не рабо́тал на компью́тере.
comrade ['kɔmrɪd] *n* (*POL, MIL*) сора́тник; (*friend*) това́рищ.
comradeship ['kɔmrɪdʃɪp] *n* това́рищество.
Comsat® ['kɔmsæt] *n abbr* = **communications satellite**.
con [kɔn] *vt* надува́ть (наду́ть *perf*) ◆ *n* (*trick*) обма́н; **to ~ sb into doing** обма́ном заставля́ть (заста́вить• *perf*) кого́-н *+infin*.
concave ['kɔnkeɪv] *adj* (*mirror etc*) во́гнутый; (*cheeks*) впа́лый.
conceal [kən'si:l] *vt* (*hide*) укрыва́ть (укры́ть• *perf*); (*keep back*) скрыва́ть (скрыть• *perf*).
concede [kən'si:d] *vt* признава́ть• (призна́ть *perf*) ◆ *vi* (*admit error*) признава́ться (призна́ться *perf*); (*admit defeat*) сдава́ться• (сда́ться• *perf*).
conceit [kən'si:t] *n* высокоме́рие.
conceited [kən'si:tɪd] *adj* высокоме́рный.
conceivable [kən'si:vəbl] *adj* мы́слимый (мы́слим); **it is ~ that ...** вполне́ допусти́мо, что ....
conceivably [kən'si:vəblɪ] *adv*: **he may ~ be right** возмо́жно, что он прав.
conceive [kən'si:v] *vt* (*child*) зача́ть• (*perf*); (*idea*) заду́мывать (заду́мать *perf*) ◆ *vi* (*BIO*) забере́менеть (*perf*); **to ~ of sth** представля́ть (предста́вить• *perf*) что-н.
concentrate ['kɔnsəntreɪt] *vi* сосредото́чиваться (сосредото́читься *perf*), концентри́роваться (сконцентри́роваться *perf*) ◆ *vt*: **to ~ (on)** (*energies etc*) сосредото́чивать (сосредото́чить *perf*) *or* концентри́ровать (сконцентри́ровать *perf*) (на *+prp*).
concentration [kɔnsən'treɪʃən] *n* сосредото́чение, концентра́ция; (*attention*) сосредото́ченность *f*; (*CHEM*) концентра́ция.
concentration camp *n* концентрацио́нный ла́герь• *m*.
concentric [kɔn'sɛntrɪk] *adj* концентри́ческий•.
concept ['kɔnsɛpt] *n* поня́тие.
conception [kən'sɛpʃən] *n* (*idea*) конце́пция; (*BIO*) зача́тие.
concern [kən'sə:n] *n* (*affair*) де́ло•; (*worry*) озабо́ченность *f*; (*COMM*) предприя́тие ◆ *vt* (*worry*) беспоко́ить (*impf*); (*involve*) вовлека́ть (вовле́чь• *perf*); (*relate to*) каса́ться (*impf*) *+gen*; **to be ~ed (about)** беспоко́иться (*impf*) (о *+prp*); **"to whom it may ~"** "надлежа́щему лицу́"; **as far as I am ~ed** что каса́ется меня́; **the department ~ed** (*relevant*) отде́л, о кото́ром идёт речь; (*involved*) отде́л, кото́рый э́тим занима́ется.
concerning [kən'sə:nɪŋ] *prep* относи́тельно *+gen*.
concert ['kɔnsət] *n* конце́рт; **to be in ~** (*MUS*) дава́ть• (*impf*) конце́рт; **in ~ with** (*activities etc*) совме́стно *or* во взаимоде́йствии с *+instr*.
concerted [kən'sə:tɪd] *adj* совме́стный.
concert hall *n* конце́ртный зал.
concertina [kɔnsə'ti:nə] *n* гармо́ника ◆ *vi* (*fig*) скла́дываться (сложи́ться• *perf*) гармо́никой.
concerto [kən'tʃə:təu] *n* (*MUS*) конце́рт; **piano/violin ~** конце́рт для фортепья́но/скри́пки с орке́стром.
concession [kən'sɛʃən] *n* (*compromise*) усту́пка•; (*right*) конце́ссия; (*for pensioners, the unemployed*) льго́та; **tax ~** нало́говая ски́дка•.
concessionaire [kənsɛʃə'nɛəʳ] *n* концессионе́р.
concessionary [kən'sɛʃənrɪ] *adj* льго́тный.
conciliation [kənsɪlɪ'eɪʃən] *n* примире́ние.
conciliatory [kən'sɪlɪətrɪ] *adj* примири́тельный• (примири́телен).
concise [kən'saɪs] *adj* кра́ткий•.
conclave ['kɔnkleɪv] *n* та́йное совеща́ние; (*REL*) конкла́в.
conclude [kən'klu:d] *vt* (*speech, chapter*) зака́нчивать (зако́нчить *perf*); (*treaty, deal etc*) заключа́ть (заключи́ть *perf*); (*decide*) приходи́ть• (прийти́• *perf*) к заключе́нию *or* вы́воду ◆ *vi* (*speaker*) заключа́ть (заключи́ть *perf*) речь; (*events*): **to ~ (with)** заверша́ться (заверши́ться *perf*) (*+instr*); **"that," he ~d, "is why we did it"** "вот почему́, – заключи́л он, – мы сде́лали э́то"; **I ~ that ...** я прихожу́ к заключе́нию, что ....
concluding [kən'klu:dɪŋ] *adj* заключи́тельный.
conclusion [kən'klu:ʒən] *n* заключе́ние; (*of speech*) оконча́ние; (*of events*) заверше́ние; **to come to the ~ that** приходи́ть• (прийти́• *perf*) к заключе́нию, что.
conclusive [kən'klu:sɪv] *adj* (*evidence*) неопровержи́мый (неопровержи́м); (*defeat*) оконча́тельный• (оконча́телен).
concoct [kən'kɔkt] *vt* (*excuse*) приду́мывать (приду́мать *perf*); (*meal*) гото́вить• (пригото́вить• *perf*).
concoction [kən'kɔkʃən] *n* смесь *f*.
concord ['kɔŋkɔ:d] *n* (*harmony*) согла́сие; (*treaty*) соглаше́ние.
concourse ['kɔŋkɔ:s] *n* (*hall*) вестибю́ль *m*; (*crowd*) стече́ние.
concrete ['kɔŋkri:t] *n* бето́н ◆ *adj* бето́нный; (*fig*) конкре́тный• (конкре́тен).
concrete mixer *n* бетономеша́лка.
concur [kən'kə:ʳ] *vi* (*events*) совпада́ть

• marks translations which have irregular inflections. The Russian-English side of the dictionary gives inflectional information.

(совпа́сть* *perf*); **to ~ (with)** соглаша́ться (согласи́ться* *perf*) (с *+instr*).
concurrently [kən'kʌrntlı] *adv* одновре́ме́нно.
concussion [kən'kʌʃən] *n* сотрясе́ние мо́зга.
condemn [kən'dɛm] *vt* осужда́ть (осуди́ть* *perf*); (*building*) бракова́ть (забракова́ть *perf*).
condemnation [kɔndɛm'neıʃən] *n* (*criticism*) осужде́ние.
condensation [kɔndɛn'seıʃən] *n* конденса́ция.
condense [kən'dɛns] *vi* конденси́роваться (*impf/perf*) ◆ *vt* сжима́ть (сжать* *perf*).
condensed milk [kən'dɛnst-] *n* сгущённое молоко́.
condescend [kɔndı'sɛnd] *vi* вести́ (*impf*) себя́ снисходи́тельно; **to ~ to do** соизволя́ть (соизво́лить *perf*) *+infin*.
condescending [kɔndı'sɛndıŋ] *adj* снисходи́тельный* (снисходи́телен).
condition [kən'dıʃən] *n* (*also MED*) состоя́ние; (*requirement*) усло́вие ◆ *vt* (*person*) формирова́ть (сформирова́ть *perf*); (*hair, skin*) обраба́тывать (обрабо́тать *perf*); **~s** *npl* (*circumstances*) обстоя́тельства *ntpl*; **in good/ poor ~** в хоро́шем/плохо́м состоя́нии; **a heart ~** боле́знь *f* се́рдца; **weather ~s** пого́дные усло́вия; **~s of sale** усло́вия прода́жи; **on ~ that** при усло́вии, что.
conditional [kən'dıʃənl] *adj* усло́вный; **to be ~ upon** зави́сеть* (*impf/perf*) от *+gen*.
conditioner [kən'dıʃənəʳ] *n* (*for hair*) бальза́м; (*for fabrics*) смягча́ющий* раство́р.
condo ['kɔndəu] *n abbr* (*US*: *inf*) = **condominium**.
condolences [kən'dəulənsız] *npl* соболе́знования *ntpl*.
condom ['kɔndəm] *n* презервати́в.
condominium [kɔndə'mınıəm] *n* (*US*: *building*) *кооперати́вный многокварти́рный дом*; (: *rooms*) кооперати́вная кварти́ра.
condone [kən'dəun] *vt* мири́ться (примири́ться *perf*) с *+instr*.
conducive [kən'dju:sıv] *adj*: **~ to** спосо́бствующий *+dat*.
conduct [*n* 'kɔndʌkt, *vt* kən'dʌkt] *n* (*of person*) поведе́ние ◆ *vt* (*survey etc*) проводи́ть* (провести́* *perf*); (*MUS*) дирижи́ровать (*impf*); (*PHYS*) проводи́ть* (*impf*); **to ~ o.s.** (*behave*) вести́* (повести́* *perf*) себя́.
conducted tour [kən'dʌktıd-] *n* (*of museum etc*) экску́рсия с ги́дом.
conductor [kən'dʌktəʳ] *n* (*MUS*) дирижёр; (*US RAIL*) контролёр; (*PHYS*) проводни́к*; (*on bus*) конду́ктор.
conductress [kən'dʌktrıs] *n* конду́ктор.
conduit ['kɔndjuıt] *n* (*ELEC*) труба́ для электропрово́дки; (*TECH*) трубопрово́д.
cone [kəun] *n* (*shape*) ко́нус; (*on road*) *конусообра́зное доро́жное огражде́ние*; (*BOT*) ши́шка*; (*CULIN*) ва́фельная тру́бочка* (*для моро́женого*).
confectioner [kən'fɛkʃənəʳ] *n* конди́тер.
confectioner's (shop) [kən'fɛkʃənəz-] *n* конди́терская *f adj*.
confectionery [kən'fɛkʃənrı] *n* конди́терские изде́лия *ntpl*.
confederate [kən'fɛdrıt] *adj* конфедерати́вный ◆ *n* (*pej*) соо́бщник; (*US*) конфедера́т.
confederation [kənfɛdə'reıʃən] *n* конфедера́ция.
confer [kən'fə:ʳ] *vi* совеща́ться (*impf*) ◆ *vt*: **to ~ sth (on sb)** (*honour*) ока́зывать (оказа́ть* *perf*) что-н (кому́-н); (*degree*) присужда́ть (присуди́ть* *perf*) что-н (кому́-н); (*advantage*) дава́ть* (дать* *perf*) что-н (кому́-н); **to ~ (with sb about sth)** совеща́ться (*impf*) (с кем-н о чём-н).
conference ['kɔnfərəns] *n* конфере́нция; **to be in ~** быть* (*impf*) на совеща́нии.
conference room *n* зал заседа́ний, конфере́нцзал.
confess [kən'fɛs] *vt* (*guilt, ignorance*) признава́ть* (призна́ть *perf*); (*sin*) испове́доваться (испове́даться *perf*) в *+prp*; (*crime*) сознава́ться* (созна́ться *perf*) в *+prp* ◆ *vi* (*admit to crime*) признава́ться* (призна́ться *perf*); **to ~ to sth** сознава́ться* (созна́ться *perf*) в чём-н; **I must ~ that I didn't enjoy it at all** до́лжен призна́ться, мне э́то соверше́нно не понра́вилось.
confession [kən'fɛʃən] *n* призна́ние; (*REL*) и́споведь *f*; **to make a ~** де́лать (сде́лать *perf*) призна́ние.
confessor [kən'fɛsəʳ] *n* испове́дник.
confetti [kən'fɛtı] *n* конфетти́ *nt ind*.
confide [kən'faıd] *vi*: **to ~ in** доверя́ться (дове́риться *perf*) *+dat*.
confidence ['kɔnfıdns] *n* (*faith*) уве́ренность *f*; (*self-assurance*) уве́ренность в себе́; (*secret*) секре́т; **I have ~ in him** я уве́рен в нём; **she has (every) ~ that** она по́лностью уве́рена в том, что; **motion of no ~** выраже́ние недове́рия; **in ~** конфиденциа́льно; **to tell sb sth in strict ~** рассказа́ть* (*perf*) кому́-н что-н стро́го конфиденциа́льно.
confidence trick *n* моше́нничество.
confident ['kɔnfıdənt] *adj* (*positive*) уве́ренный (уве́рен); (*self-assured*) уве́ренный (уве́рен) в себе́.
confidential [kɔnfı'dɛnʃəl] *adj* (*report etc*) конфиденциа́льный* (конфиденциа́лен); (*tone*) довери́тельный (довери́телен); (*secretary*) по́льзующийся дове́рием.
confidentiality [kɔnfıdɛnʃı'ælıtı] *n* конфиденциа́льность *f*.
configuration [kənfıgju'reıʃən] *n* (*also COMPUT*) конфигура́ция.
confine [kən'faın] *vt* (*lock up*) запира́ть (запере́ть* *perf*); (*limit*): **to ~ (to)** ограни́чивать (ограни́чить *perf*) (*+instr*); **to ~ o.s. to sth** ограни́чиваться (ограни́читься *perf*) чем-н.

confined [kən'faɪnd] *adj* закры́тый.
confinement [kən'faɪnmənt] *n* (тюре́мное) заключе́ние; (*MED*) ро́ды *pl*.
confines ['kɔnfaɪnz] *npl* (*also fig*) преде́лы *mpl*.
confirm [kən'fə:m] *vt* подтвержда́ть (подтверди́ть* *perf*); **to be ~ed** (*REL*) получа́ть (получи́ть* *perf*) конфирма́цию.
confirmation [kɔnfə'meɪʃən] *n* подтвержде́ние; (*REL*) конфирма́ция.
confirmed [kən'fə:md] *adj* убеждённый.
confiscate ['kɔnfɪskeɪt] *vt* конфиско́вывать (конфискова́ть *perf*).
confiscation [kɔnfɪs'keɪʃən] *n* конфиска́ция.
conflagration [kɔnflə'greɪʃən] *n* пожа́рище.
conflict [*n* 'kɔnflɪkt, *vi* kən'flɪkt] *n* конфли́кт; (*of interests*) столкнове́ние ◆ *vi* противоре́чить (*impf*) друг дру́гу; **to ~ with sth** противоре́чить (*impf*) чему́-н.
conflicting [kən'flɪktɪŋ] *adj* (*reports*) противоречи́вый (противоречи́в); (*interests*) противополо́жный* (противополо́жен).
conform [kən'fɔ:m] *vi*: **to ~ (to)** подчиня́ться (подчини́ться *perf*) (+*dat*).
conformist [kən'fɔ:mɪst] *n* конформи́ст.
confound [kən'faund] *vt* (*confuse*) озада́чивать (озада́чить *perf*); (*amaze*) поража́ть (порази́ть* *perf*).
confounded [kən'faundɪd] *adj* (*nuisance*) прокля́тый; (*idiot*) зако́нченный.
confront [kən'frʌnt] *vt* (*problems*) ста́лкиваться (столкну́ться *perf*) с +*instr*; (*enemy*) противостоя́ть (*impf*) +*dat*.
confrontation [kɔnfrən'teɪʃən] *n* конфронта́ция.
confuse [kən'fju:z] *vt* (*perplex, complicate*) запу́тывать (запу́тать *perf*); (*mix up*: *two things, people etc*) пу́тать (спу́тать *perf*).
confused [kən'fju:zd] *adj* (*person*) озада́ченный (озада́чен); (*situation*) запу́танный (запу́тан); **to get ~** запу́тываться (запу́таться *perf*).
confusing [kən'fju:zɪŋ] *adj* запу́танный.
confusion [kən'fju:ʒən] *n* (*mix-up*) пу́таница; (*perplexity*) замеша́тельство; (*disorder*) беспоря́док.
congeal [kən'dʒi:l] *vi* (*blood*) запека́ться (запе́чься* *perf*); (*sauce, fat*) застыва́ть (засты́ть* *perf*).
congenial [kən'dʒi:nɪəl] *adj* (*atmosphere*) благоприя́тный* (благоприя́тен); (*person*) ро́дственный; (*place, job etc*) подходя́щий*.
congenital [kən'dʒɛnɪtl] *adj* (*MED*) врождённый.
conger eel ['kɔŋgər-] *n* морско́й у́горь* *m*.
congested [kən'dʒɛstɪd] *adj* (*road*) перегру́женный (перегру́жен); (*area*) перенаселённый (перенаселён); (*MED*) засто́йный.
congestion [kən'dʒɛstʃən] *n* (*of road*) перегру́женность *f*; (*of area*) перенаселённость *f*; (*MED*) засто́й.
conglomerate [kən'glɔmərɪt] *n* (*COMM*) конгломера́т.
conglomeration [kənglɔmə'reɪʃən] *n* конгломера́ция.
Congo ['kɔŋgəu] *n* Ко́нго *ind*.
congratulate [kən'grætjuleɪt] *vt*: **to ~ sb (on)** поздравля́ть (поздра́вить* *perf*) кого́-н (с +*instr*).
congratulations [kəngrætju'leɪʃənz] *npl* поздравле́ния *ntpl*; **~ (on)** (*from one person*) поздравля́ю (с +*instr*); (*from several people*) поздравля́ем (с +*instr*).
congregate ['kɔŋgrɪgeɪt] *vi* собира́ться (собра́ться* *perf*).
congregation [kɔŋgrɪ'geɪʃən] *n* прихожа́не* *mpl*.
congress ['kɔŋgrɛs] *n* (*conference*) конгре́сс; (*US*): **C~** конгре́сс США.
congressman ['kɔŋgrɛsmən] *irreg n* (*US*) конгрессме́н.
congresswoman ['kɔŋgrɛswumən] *irreg n* (*US*) конгрессме́н.
conical ['kɔnɪkl] *adj* кони́ческий*.
conifer ['kɔnɪfə'] *n* хво́йное де́рево*.
coniferous [kə'nɪfərəs] *adj* хво́йный.
conjecture [kən'dʒɛktʃə'] *n* предположе́ние ◆ *vi* предполага́ть (предположи́ть *perf*).
conjugal ['kɔndʒugl] *adj* супру́жеский*.
conjugate ['kɔndʒugeɪt] *vt* (*LING*) спряга́ть (проспряга́ть *perf*).
conjugation [kɔndʒə'geɪʃən] *n* (*LING*) спряже́ние.
conjunction [kən'dʒʌŋkʃən] *n* (*LING*) сою́з; **in ~ with** совме́стно с +*instr*.
conjunctivitis [kəndʒʌŋktɪ'vaɪtɪs] *n* (*MED*) конъюнктиви́т.
conjure ['kʌndʒə'] *vt* (*fig*) создава́ть* (созда́ть* *perf*) из ничего́ ◆ *vi* (*magician*) пока́зывать (показа́ть* *perf*) фо́кусы
▸ **conjure up** *vt* (*ghost*) вызыва́ть* (вы́звать* *perf*); (*memories*) пробужда́ть (пробуди́ть* *perf*).
conjurer ['kʌndʒərə'] *n* фо́кусник.
conjuring trick ['kʌndʒərɪŋ-] *n* фо́кус.
conker ['kɔŋkə'] *n* (*BRIT*) ко́нский* кашта́н.
conk out [kɔŋk-] *vi* (*inf*) сдыха́ть (сдо́хнуть *perf*).
con man *irreg n* моше́нник.
connect [kə'nɛkt] *vt* (*ELEC*) подсоединя́ть (подсоедини́ть *perf*); (*TEL*: *subscriber*) подключа́ть (подключи́ть *perf*); (*fig*: *associate*) свя́зывать (связа́ть* *perf*) ◆ *vi*: **to ~ with** согласо́вываться (согласова́ться *perf*) по расписа́нию с +*instr*; **to ~ sb/sth (to)** (*also TEL*) соединя́ть (соедини́ть *perf*) кого́-н/что-н

(с *+instr*); **he is/was ~ed with** он свя́зан/был свя́зан с *+instr*; **I am trying to ~ you** (*TEL*) я пыта́юсь нала́дить связь.
connection [kəˈnɛkʃən] *n* (*also fig, ELEC*) связь* *f*; (*train etc*) переса́дка*; (*TEL: caller*) соедине́ние; (: *subscriber*) подключе́ние; **in ~ with** в связи́ с *+instr*; **what is the ~ between them?** кака́я связь ме́жду ни́ми?; **business ~s** деловы́е свя́зи; **to miss one's ~** опа́здывать (опозда́ть *perf*) на переса́дку; **to get one's ~** де́лать (сде́лать *perf*) переса́дку.
connexion [kəˈnɛkʃən] *n* (*BRIT*) = **connection**.
conning tower [ˈkɔnɪŋ-] *n* (*NAUT*) ру́бка*.
connive [kəˈnaɪv] *vi*: **to ~ at** потво́рствовать (*impf*) *+dat*.
connoisseur [kɔnɪˈsəː] *n* знато́к*.
connotation [kɔnəˈteɪʃən] *n* коннота́ция.
connubial [kəˈnjuːbɪəl] *adj* бра́чный.
conquer [ˈkɔŋkə] *vt* (*MIL*) завоёвывать (завоева́ть* *perf*); (*overcome*) поборо́ть* (*perf*).
conqueror [ˈkɔŋkərə] *n* завоева́тель *m*.
conquest [ˈkɔŋkwɛst] *n* (*MIL*) завоева́ние; (*prize*) побе́да; (*of space*) покоре́ние.
cons [kɔnz] *npl see* **convenience, pro**.
conscience [ˈkɔnʃəns] *n* со́весть *f*; **he has a guilty/clear ~** у него́ со́весть нечиста́/чиста́; **in all ~** по со́вести.
conscientious [kɔnʃɪˈɛnʃəs] *adj* добросо́вестный* (добросо́вестен).
conscientious objector *n отка́зывающийся от призы́ва в а́рмию по убежде́нию*.
conscious [ˈkɔnʃəs] *adj* (*deliberate*) созна́тельный (созна́телен); (*aware*): **to be ~ of sth/that** сознава́ть* (*impf*) что-н/, что; (*awake*): **the patient was ~** пацие́нт находи́лся в созна́нии; **to become ~ of sth/ that** осознава́ть (осозна́ть *perf*) что-н/, что.
consciousness [ˈkɔnʃəsnɪs] *n* (*also MED*) созна́ние; (*of society etc*) самосозна́ние; **to lose ~** теря́ть (потеря́ть *perf*) созна́ние; **to regain ~** приходи́ть* (прийти́* *perf*) в созна́ние.
conscript [ˈkɔnskrɪpt] *n* призывни́к*, новобра́нец*.
conscription [kənˈskrɪpʃən] *n* во́инская пови́нность *f*.
consecrate [ˈkɔnsɪkreɪt] *vt* (*building etc*) освяща́ть (освяти́ть* *perf*).
consecutive [kənˈsɛkjutɪv] *adj*: **on three ~ occasions** в трёх слу́чаях подря́д; **on three ~ days** три дня подря́д.
consensus [kənˈsɛnsəs] *n* (*medical, scientific*) еди́ное мне́ние; **~ (of opinion)** консе́нсус.
consent [kənˈsɛnt] *n* согла́сие ◆ *vi*: **to ~ to** соглаша́ться (согласи́ться* *perf*) на *+acc*; **age of ~** совершенноле́тие; **by common ~** с о́бщего согла́сия.
consenting [kənˈsɛntɪŋ] *adj*: **~ adult** совершенноле́тний*(-яя) *m(f) adj*.
consequence [ˈkɔnsɪkwəns] *n* (*result*) сле́дствие; (*significance*): **of ~** значи́тельный (значи́телен); **it's of little ~** э́то не име́ет большо́го значе́ния; **in ~** (*consequently*) всле́дствие.
consequently [ˈkɔnsɪkwəntlɪ] *adv* сле́довательно.
conservation [kɔnsəˈveɪʃən] *n* (*preservation*) сохране́ние; (*also:* **nature ~**) охра́на приро́ды, природоохра́на; **energy ~** эконо́мия эне́ргии.
conservationist [kɔnsəˈveɪʃnɪst] *n* эко́лог(ист).
conservative [kənˈsəːvətɪv] *adj* (*person*) консервати́вный*; (*estimate*) скро́мный*; (*BRIT*): **C~** консервати́вный ◆ *n* (*BRIT*): **C~** консерва́тор.
conservatory [kənˈsəːvətrɪ] *n* застеклённая вера́нда; (*MUS*) консервато́рия.
conserve [kənˈsəːv] *vt* (*preserve*) сохраня́ть (сохрани́ть *perf*); (*energy*) рациона́льно испо́льзовать (*impf*) ◆ *n* варе́нье*.
consider [kənˈsɪdə] *vt* (*believe*) счита́ть (посчита́ть *perf*); (*study*) рассма́тривать (рассмотре́ть* *perf*); (*take into account*) учи́тывать (уче́сть* *perf*); (*regard*): **to ~ that ...** полага́ть (*impf*), что ...; **to ~ sth** поду́мывать (*impf*) о чём-н; **they ~ themselves to be superior** они́ счита́ют себя́ вы́ше; **she ~ed it a disaster** она́ счита́ла, что э́то катастро́фа; **~ yourself lucky** счита́йте, что Вам повезло́; **all things ~ed** приня́в всё во внима́ние.
considerable [kənˈsɪdərəbl] *adj* значи́тельный* (значи́телен).
considerably [kənˈsɪdərəblɪ] *adv* (*improve, deteriorate etc*) значи́тельно; (*bigger, smaller etc*) гора́здо.
considerate [kənˈsɪdərɪt] *adj* (*person*) забо́тливый (забо́тлив); (*action*) внима́тельный (внима́телен).
consideration [kənsɪdəˈreɪʃən] *n* (*deliberation*) рассмотре́ние, обду́мывание; (*factor*) соображе́ние; (*thoughtfulness*) внима́ние; (*reward*) вознагражде́ние; **out of ~ for** из уваже́ния к *+dat*; **to take sth into ~** принима́ть (приня́ть *perf*) что-н во внима́ние; **under ~** на рассмотре́нии; **my first ~ is my family** я пре́жде всего́ забо́чусь о свое́й семье́.
considered [kənˈsɪdəd] *adj* (*approach, answer*) обду́манный; **it is my ~ opinion that ...** у меня́ сложи́лось мне́ние, что ....
considering [kənˈsɪdərɪŋ] *prep* учи́тывая *+acc*; **~ (that)** учи́тывая (, что).
consign [kənˈsaɪn] *vt* (*send: goods*) отправля́ть (отпра́вить* *perf*); **to ~ to** (*thing: to place*) забра́сывать (забро́сить* *perf*) в *+acc*; (*person: to sb's care*) поруча́ть (поручи́ть *perf*) *+dat*; (: *to poverty*) обрека́ть (обре́чь* *perf*) на *+acc*.
consignee [kɔnsaɪˈniː] *n* грузополуча́тель *m*.
consignment [kənˈsaɪnmənt] *n* (*COMM*) па́ртия.

consignment note *n* (*COMM*) тра́нспортная накладна́я *f adj*.
consignor [kən'saɪnəʳ] *n* грузоотправи́тель *m*.
consist [kən'sɪst] *vi*: **to ~ of** состоя́ть *(impf)* из *+gen*.
consistency [kən'sɪstənsɪ] *n* (*of actions etc*) после́довательность *f*; (*of yoghurt etc*) консисте́нция.
consistent [kən'sɪstənt] *adj* (*person, argument*) после́довательный* (после́дователен); **~ with** соотве́тствующий* *+dat*.
consolation [kɔnsə'leɪʃən] *n* утеше́ние.
console [*vt* kən'səul, *n* 'kɔnsəul] *vt* утеша́ть (уте́шить *perf*) ◆ *n* (*panel*) пане́ль *f*.
consolidate [kən'sɔlɪdeɪt] *vt* (*position, power*) укрепля́ть (укрепи́ть* *perf*).
consolidated balance sheet [kən'sɔlɪdeɪtɪd-] *n* сво́дный бала́нсовый отчёт.
consols ['kɔnsɔlz] *npl* (*BRIT*) консо́ли *fpl* (*правительственные облигации*).
consommé [kən'sɔmeɪ] *n* прозра́чный бульо́н*.
consonant ['kɔnsənənt] *n* согла́сный *m adj*.
consort [*n* 'kɔnsɔ:t, *vb* kən'sɔ:t] *n* супру́г(а) ◆ *vi*: **to ~ with sb** свя́зываться (связа́ться* *perf*) с кем-н; **prince ~** принц-консо́рт, супру́г ца́рствующей короле́вы.
consortium [kən'sɔ:tɪəm] *n* консо́рциум.
conspicuous [kən'spɪkjuəs] *adj* (*person, feature*) заме́тный* (заме́тен); **to make o.s. ~** обраща́ть (обрати́ть* *perf*) на себя́ внима́ние.
conspiracy [kən'spɪrəsɪ] *n* за́говор.
conspiratorial [kən'spɪrə'tɔ:rɪəl] *adj* загово́рщический.
conspire [kən'spaɪəʳ] *vi* (*people*) устра́ивать (устро́ить *perf*) за́говор; **circumstances ~d against us** обстоя́тельства скла́дывались про́тив нас.
constable ['kʌnstəbl] (*BRIT*) *n* полице́йский *m adj*; **chief ~** нача́льник поли́ции.
constabulary [kən'stæbjulərɪ] *n* (*BRIT*) поли́ция.
constant ['kɔnstənt] *adj* (*continuous*) постоя́нный*; (*fixed*) неизме́нный*.
constantly ['kɔnstəntlɪ] *adv* (*continually*) постоя́нно.
constellation [kɔnstə'leɪʃən] *n* (*ASTRONOMY*) созве́здие.
consternation [kɔnstə'neɪʃən] *n* смяте́ние.
constipated ['kɔnstɪpeɪtɪd] *adj*: **he/she is ~** у него́/неё запо́р.
constipation [kɔnstɪ'peɪʃən] *n* запо́р.
constituency [kən'stɪtjuənsɪ] *n* (*area*) избира́тельный о́круг*; (*electors*) избира́тели *mpl* о́круга.
constituency party *n* ме́стная парти́йная организа́ция.
constituent [kən'stɪtjuənt] *n* (*POL*) избира́тель(ница) *m(f)*; (*component*) компоне́нт.
constitute ['kɔnstɪtju:t] *vt* (*represent*) явля́ться (яви́ться* *perf*) *+instr*; (*make up*) составля́ть (соста́вить* *perf*).
constitution [kɔnstɪ'tju:ʃən] *n* (*of country*) конститу́ция; (*of organization*) уста́в; (*health*) органи́зм; (*of committee etc*) строе́ние.
constitutional [kɔnstɪ'tju:ʃənl] *adj* конституцио́нный; **~ monarchy** конституцио́нная мона́рхия.
constrain [kən'streɪn] *vt* (*force*) вынужда́ть (вы́нудить* *perf*); (*limit*) сде́рживать (сдержа́ть *perf*).
constrained [kən'streɪnd] *adj* принуждённый*.
constraint [kən'streɪnt] *n* (*restriction*) ограниче́ние; (*compulsion*) принужде́ние; (*embarrassment*) стесне́ние.
constrict [kən'strɪkt] *vt* (*squeeze*) сжима́ть (сжать* *perf*); (*limit*) стесня́ть (стесни́ть *perf*).
constriction [kən'strɪkʃən] *n* (*in throat*) стесне́ние; (*restriction*) ограниче́ние.
construct [kən'strʌkt] *vt* (*build*) сооружа́ть (сооруди́ть* *perf*); (*formulate*) стро́ить (постро́ить *perf*).
construction [kən'strʌkʃən] *n* (*of building etc*) сооруже́ние; (*structure*) констру́кция; (*fig*: *interpretation*) истолкова́ние; **the building is under ~** зда́ние стро́ится.
construction industry *n* стро́ительная промы́шленность *f*.
constructive [kən'strʌktɪv] *adj* конструкти́вный* (конструкти́вен).
construe [kən'stru:] *vt* истолко́вывать (истолкова́ть *perf*).
consul ['kɔnsl] *n* ко́нсул.
consulate ['kɔnsjulɪt] *n* ко́нсульство.
consult [kən'sʌlt] *vt* (*friend*) сове́товаться (посове́товаться *perf*) с *+instr*; (*book, map etc*) справля́ться (спра́виться* *perf*) с *+instr*; **to ~ sb (about sth)** (*doctor etc*) консульти́роваться (проконсульти́роваться *perf*) с кем-н (о чём-н).
consultancy [kən'sʌltənsɪ] *n* (*company*) консульти́рующая фи́рма; (*MED*) до́лжность *f* врача́-консульта́нта.
consultant [kən'sʌltənt] *n* (*MED*) врач-консульта́нт; (*other specialist*) консульта́нт ◆ *cpd*: **~ engineer/paediatrician** инжене́р-/педиа́тр-консульта́нт; **legal ~** юриско́нсульт; **management ~** консульта́нт по ме́неджменту.
consultation [kɔnsəl'teɪʃən] *n* (*MED*) консульта́ция; (*discussion*) совеща́ние; (*LAW*) юриди́ческая консульта́ция; **in ~ with** с по́мощью *+gen*.
consultative [kən'sʌltətɪv] *adj* консультати́вный.

* marks translations which have irregular inflections. The Russian-English side of the dictionary gives inflectional information.

consulting room [kən'sʌltɪŋ-] *n* (*BRIT*) врачебный кабинет.
consume [kən'sju:m] *vt* (*food, drink*) потреблять (потребить* *perf*); (*fuel, energy etc*) расходовать (израсходовать *perf*); (*subj: emotion, fire etc*) охватывать (охватить* *perf*).
consumer [kən'sju:mə'] *n* (*COMM, also of gas etc*) потребитель *m*.
consumer credit *n* потребительский* кредит.
consumer durables *npl* потребительские товары *mpl* длительного пользования.
consumer goods *npl* потребительские товары *mpl*.
consumerism [kən'sju:mərizəm] *n* защита прав потребителей.
consumer society *n* общество потребления.
consummate ['kɔnsʌmeɪt] *vt* (*marriage, ambition etc*) осуществлять (осуществить* *perf*).
consumption [kən'sʌmpʃən] *n* потребление; (*amount consumed*) расход; (*MED*) туберкулёз лёгких; **not fit for human ~** не годен к потреблению.
cont. *abbr* (= *continued*): **~ on** продолжение на *+prp*.
contact ['kɔntækt] *n* (*communication*) контакт; (*touch*) соприкосновение; (*person*) деловой(-ая) знакомый(-ая) *m(f) adj* ◆ *vt* связываться (связаться* *perf*) с *+instr*; **to lose/be in ~ with sb/sth** терять (потерять *perf*)/поддерживать *(impf)* контакт с кем-н/чем-н; **business ~s** деловые связи.
contact lenses *npl* контактные линзы *fpl*.
contagious [kən'teɪdʒəs] *adj* (*disease*) заразный* (заразен); (*fig*) заразительный* (заразителен).
contain [kən'teɪn] *vt* (*hold*) вмещать (вместить* *perf*); (*include*) содержать* *(impf)*; (*curb*) сдерживать (сдержать* *perf*); **to ~ o.s.** сдерживаться (сдержаться* *perf*).
container [kən'teɪnə'] *n* (*also COMM*) контейнер ◆ *cpd* (*ship, lorry etc*) контейнерный.
containerization [kənteɪnəraɪ'zeɪʃən] *n* упаковка* грузов в контейнеры.
containerize [kən'teɪnəraɪz] *vt* осуществлять (осуществить* *perf*) контейнерные перевозки.
contaminate [kən'tæmɪneɪt] *vt* загрязнять (загрязнить *perf*).
contamination [kəntæmɪ'neɪʃən] *n* загрязнение.
cont'd *abbr* (= *continued*): **~ on** продолжение на *+prp*; **to be ~** продолжение следует.
contemplate ['kɔntəmpleɪt] *vt* (*consider*) размышлять *(impf)* о *+prp*; (*look at*) созерцать *(impf)*.
contemplation [kɔntəm'pleɪʃən] *n* (*see vb*) размышление; созерцание.
contemporary [kən'tɛmpərərɪ] *adj* (*present-day*) современный*; (*belonging to same time*) относящийся к тому времени ◆ *n* современник(-ица); **Samuel Pepys and his contemporaries** Самюэль Пипс и его современники.
contempt [kən'tɛmpt] *n* презрение; **~ of court** оскорбление суда; **to have ~ for sb/sth, to hold sb/sth in ~** презирать *(impf)* кого-н/что-н.
contemptible [kən'tɛmptəbl] *adj* (*conduct*) презренный.
contemptuous [kən'tɛmptjuəs] *adj* презрительный* (презрителен).
contend [kən'tɛnd] *vt*: **to ~ that** утверждать *(impf)*, что ◆ *vi* (*struggle*): **to ~ with** (*problem etc*) бороться* *(impf)* с *+instr*; (*compete*): **to ~ for** (*power etc*) бороться* *(impf)* за *+acc*; **to have to ~ with** сталкиваться (столкнуться *perf*) с *+instr*; **he has a lot to ~ with** ему приходится справляться со многим.
contender [kən'tɛndə'] *n* претендент(ка).
content [*n* 'kɔntɛnt, *adj, vt* kən'tɛnt] *n* содержание ◆ *adj* довольный* (доволен) ◆ *vt* (*satisfy*) удовлетворять (удовлетворить *perf*); **~s** *npl* (*of bottle etc*) содержимое *ntsg adj*; (*of book*) содержание *ntsg*; **(table of) ~s** оглавление; **she is ~ with her life** она довольна жизнью; **to ~ o.s. with sth** довольствоваться *(impf)* чем-н.
contented [kən'tɛntɪd] *adj* довольный* (доволен).
contentedly [kən'tɛntɪdlɪ] *adv* довольно, удовлетворённо.
contention [kən'tɛnʃən] *n* (*assertion*) утверждение; (*argument*) разногласие; **bone of ~** яблоко* раздора.
contentious [kən'tɛnʃəs] *adj* спорный* (спорен).
contentment [kən'tɛntmənt] *n* удовлетворённость *f*.
contest [*n* 'kɔntɛst, *vt* kən'tɛst] *n* (*competition: sport*) соревнование; (*: beauty*) конкурс; (*for power etc*) борьба* ◆ *vt* (*statement, decision, LAW*) оспаривать (оспорить *perf*); (*compete for*) бороться* *(impf)* за *+acc*; (*election, competition*) бороться* *(impf)* на *+prp*.
contestant [kən'tɛstənt] *n* (*in competition*) участник(-ница); (*in fight*) противник(-ница).
context ['kɔntɛkst] *n* контекст; **in ~** в контексте; **out of ~** вне контекста.
continent ['kɔntɪnənt] *n* континент, материк; **the C~** (*BRIT*) Европа (*кроме Британских островов*); **on the C~** в Европе (*кроме британских островов*).
continental [kɔntɪ'nɛntl] (*BRIT*) *adj* европейский* ◆ *n* европеец*(-ейка).
continental breakfast *n* европейский* завтрак (*лёгкий завтрак из кофе и булочки*).
continental quilt *n* (*BRIT*) стёганое одеяло.
contingency [kən'tɪndʒənsɪ] *n* возможность *f*.
contingency plan *n план действий на случай*

непредвиденных обстоятельств.
contingent [kən'tɪndʒənt] *n* (*also MIL*) контингент ◆ *adj*: **to be ~ upon** зависеть* (*impf*) от +*gen*.
continual [kən'tɪnjuəl] *adj* непрерывный*.
continually [kən'tɪnjuəlɪ] *adv* непрерывно, постоянно.
continuation [kəntɪnju'eɪʃən] *n* продолжение.
continue [kən'tɪnju:] *vi* (*carry on*) продолжаться (*impf*); (*after interruption*: *talk*) продолжаться (продолжиться *perf*); (: *person*) продолжать (продолжить *perf*) ◆ *vt* продолжать (продолжить *perf*); **to ~ to do** продолжать (продолжить *perf*) +*impf infin*; **to be ~d** продолжение следует; **~d on page 10** продолжение на странице 10.
continuing education [kən'tɪnjuɪŋ-] *n* курсы *mpl* вечернего обучения.
continuity [kɔntɪ'nju:ɪtɪ] *n* (*in management*) преемственность *f*; (*TV, CINEMA*) непрерывность *f* (*телевизионных программ и фильмов*); **~ announcer** *диктор, заполняющий пробелы*; **~ department** *отдел, обеспечивающий непрерывность телевизионных программ*.
continuous [kən'tɪnjuəs] *adj* (*process, growth etc*) непрерывный*; (*line*) сплошной; (*LING*) длительный*; **~ performance** (*CINEMA*) *показ кинофильма без перерыва между сеансами*.
continuously [kən'tɪnjuəslɪ] *adv* (*repeatedly*) неоднократно, постоянно; (*uninterruptedly*) непрерывно.
continuous stationery *n* (*COMPUT*) рулонная бумага (*для печатающего устройства*).
contort [kən'tɔ:t] *vt* (*body*) искривлять (искривить* *perf*); (*face*) кривить* (скривить* *perf*).
contortion [kən'tɔ:ʃən] *n* искривление.
contortionist [kən'tɔ:ʃənɪst] *n* пластический*(-ая) акробат(ка).
contour ['kɔntuə'] *n* (*also*: **~ line**) контурная линия; (*outline*: *usu pl*) контур.
contraband ['kɔntrəbænd] *n* контрабанда ◆ *adj* контрабандный.
contraception [kɔntrə'sɛpʃən] *n* предупреждение беременности.
contraceptive [kɔntrə'sɛptɪv] *adj* противозачаточный ◆ *n* противозачаточное средство, контрацептив.
contract [*n, cpd* 'kɔntrækt, *vb* kən'trækt] *n* (*LAW, COMM*) договор, контракт ◆ *vi* (*become smaller*) сжиматься (сжаться* *perf*) ◆ *vt* (*illness*) заболевать (заболеть *perf*) +*instr* ◆ *cpd* (*price, date*) договорный; **~ of employment** служебный контракт; **~ of service** *договор между компанией и руководящим сотрудником*; **to ~ to do** (*COMM*) обязывать (обязать *perf*) +*infin*; **~ work** работа по контракту
▸ **contract in** *vi* (*BRIT*) официально заявлять (заявить* *perf*) о желании участвовать в +*prp*
▸ **contract out** *vi* (*BRIT*) официально отказываться (отказаться* *perf*) от участия в +*prp*.
contraction [kən'trækʃən] *n* (*of metal*) сжатие; (*LING*) сокращение; (*MED*) родовая потуга.
contractor [kən'træktə'] *n* подрядчик.
contractual [kən'træktʃuəl] *adj* (*agreement etc*) договорный.
contradict [kɔntrə'dɪkt] *vt* (*person*) возражать (возразить* *perf*) +*dat*; (*statement*) возражать (возразить* *perf*) на +*acc*; (*be contrary to*) противоречить (*impf*) +*dat*.
contradiction [kɔntrə'dɪkʃən] *n* противоречие; **to be in ~ with** находиться* (*impf*) в противоречии с +*instr*; **a ~ in terms** логическое противоречие.
contradictory [kɔntrə'dɪktərɪ] *adj* противоречивый (противоречив).
contralto [kən'træltəu] *n* (*MUS*) контральто *nt ind*.
contraption [kən'træpʃən] *n* дурацкая вещь *f*.
contrary[1] ['kɔntrərɪ] *adj* (*opposite, different*) противоположный*; (*unfavourable*) неблагоприятный ◆ *n* противоположность *f*; **~ to what we thought** в противоположность тому, что мы думали; **on the ~** напротив, наоборот; **unless you hear to the ~** если не будет других инструкций.
contrary[2] [kən'trɛərɪ] *adj* своенравный*.
contrast [*n* 'kɔntrɑ:st, *vt* kən'trɑ:st] *n* (*difference*) контраст ◆ *vt* сопоставлять (сопоставить* *perf*); **in ~ to** *or* **with** по контрасту с +*instr*.
contrasting [kən'trɑ:stɪŋ] *adj* (*colours*) контрастирующий; (*attitudes, views*) противоположный.
contravene [kɔntrə'vi:n] *vt* преступать (преступить* *perf*).
contravention [kɔntrə'vɛnʃən] *n*: **in ~ of** в нарушение +*gen*.
contribute [kən'trɪbju:t] *vi* (*give*) делать (сделать *perf*) вклад ◆ *vt* (*money, an article*) вносить* (внести* *perf*); **to ~ to** (*to charity*) жертвовать (пожертвовать *perf*) на +*acc or* для +*gen*; (*to newspaper*) писать* (написать* *perf*) для +*gen*; (*to discussion*) участвовать (*impf*) в +*prp*; (*to problem*) усугублять (усугубить* *perf*).
contribution [kɔntrɪ'bju:ʃən] *n* (*donation*) пожертвование; (*BRIT*: *for social security*) взнос; (*to debate, campaign*) вклад; (*to journal*) публикация.
contributor [kən'trɪbjutə'] *n* (*to appeal*) жертвователь *m*; (*to newspaper*) автор.
contributory [kən'trɪbjutərɪ] *adj* способствующий; **it was a ~ factor in ...** это

* marks translations which have irregular inflections. The Russian-English side of the dictionary gives inflectional information.

явилось одним из способствующих факторов в ....
contributory pension scheme *n* (*BRIT*) *пенсионный договор, по которому работник принимает частичное участие в формировании своей будущей пенсии.*
contrite ['kɔntraɪt] *adj* (*person*) виноватый; **she looked ~** у неё был виноватый вид.
contrivance [kən'traɪvəns] *n* (*scheme*) уловка; (*device*) приспособление.
contrive [kən'traɪv] *vt* (*meeting*) затевать (затеять *perf*) ◆ *vi*: **to ~ to do** ухитряться (ухитриться *perf*) *+infin*.
control [kən'trəul] *vt* контролировать *(impf)* ◆ *n* (*of country, organization*) контроль *m*; (*of oneself*) самообладание; (*also:* **~ group**) контрольная группа; **~s** *npl* (*of vehicle*) рычаги *mpl* управления; (*on radio etc*) ручки *fpl* настройки; **to ~ o.s.** сохранять (сохранить *perf*) самообладание; **to take ~ of** брать* (взять* *perf*) в свои руки управление *+instr*; (*COMM*) брать* (взять* *perf*) под контроль *+acc*; **to be in ~ of** контролировать *(impf)*; **under ~** спокойный; **everything is under ~** всё под контролем; **out of ~** неуправляемый; **the car went out of ~** машина потеряла управление; **circumstances beyond our ~** не зависящие от нас обстоятельства; **governmental ~s** государственный контроль *msg*.
control key *n* управляющая клавиша, клавиша управления.
controller [kən'trəulə^r] *n* (*head*) руководитель *m*.
controlling interest [kən'trəulɪŋ-] *n* (*COMM*) контрольный пакет акций.
control panel *n* пульт управления.
control point *n* контрольный пункт.
control room *n* (*NAUT, MIL*) пункт управления; (*RADIO, TV*) аппаратная *f adj*.
control tower *n* контрольно-диспетчерский* пункт.
control unit *n* (*COMPUT*) блок управления.
controversial [kɔntrə'və:ʃl] *adj* (*topic etc*) спорный* (спорен); (*person, writer*) неоднозначный* (неоднозначен).
controversy ['kɔntrəvə:sɪ] *n* дискуссия, спор.
conurbation [kɔnə'beɪʃən] *n* агломерация.
convalesce [kɔnvə'lɛs] *vi* выздоравливать (выздороветь *perf*).
convalescence [kɔnvə'lɛsns] *n* выздоровление.
convalescent [kɔnvə'lɛsnt] *n* выздоравливающий*(-ая)*m(f) adj* ◆ *adj*: **~ home** санаторий; **~ leave** отпуск* по выздоровлению.
convector [kən'vɛktə^r] *n* (*also:* **~ heater**) конвектор.
convene [kən'vi:n] *vt* (*meeting*) созывать (созвать* *perf*) ◆ *vi* (*parliament etc*) собираться (собраться* *perf*).
convener [kən'vi:nə^r] *n* (*ADMIN*) *человек, ответственный за подготовку и созыв собрания, заседания итп.*
convenience [kən'vi:nɪəns] *n* удобство; **at your ~** когда *or* как Вам будет удобно; **at your earliest ~** при первой возможности; **a flat with all modern ~s** *or (BRIT)* **all mod cons** квартира со всеми удобствами.
convenience foods *npl* пищевые полуфабрикаты.
convenient [kən'vi:nɪənt] *adj* удобный* (удобен); **if it is ~ to you** если Вам удобно.
conveniently [kən'vi:nɪəntlɪ] *adv* (*happen*) как раз; (*situated*) удобно.
convenor [kən'vi:nə^r] *n* = **convener**.
convent ['kɔnvənt] *n* (*REL*) (женский*) монастырь* *m*.
convention [kən'vɛnʃən] *n* (*custom*) условность *f*; (*conference*) конференция; (*agreement*) конвенция; (*in art, literature*) приём.
conventional [kən'vɛnʃənl] *adj* обычный.
convent school *n* монастырская школа.
converge [kən'və:dʒ] *vi* (*roads*) сходиться* (сойтись* *perf*); (*people*) съезжаться (съехаться* *perf*); (*ideas*) совпадать (совпасть* *perf*).
conversant [kən'və:snt] *adj*: **he is/was ~ with** он сведущ/был сведущ в *+prp*.
conversation [kɔnvə'seɪʃən] *n* беседа, разговор; **to have a ~ with sb** разговаривать *(impf) or* беседовать *(perf)* с кем-н.
conversational [kɔnvə'seɪʃənl] *adj* разговорный; (*COMPUT*) диалоговый.
conversationalist [kɔnvə'seɪʃnəlɪst] *n*: **a good ~** интересный(-ая) собеседник(-ница).
converse [*n* 'kɔnvə:s, *vb* kən'və:s] *n* (*of statement*) противоположность *f* ◆ *vi*: **to ~ (with sb) (about sth)** беседовать (побеседовать *perf*) (с кем-н) (о чём-н).
conversely [kɔn'və:slɪ] *adv* наоборот.
conversion [kən'və:ʃən] *n* (*of weights*) перевод; (*of substances*) превращение; (*of currency, REL*) обращение; (*BRIT: of house*) перестройка; (*RUGBY*) *один из приёмов получения очков.*
conversion table *n* таблица преобразования.
convert [*vt* kən'və:t, *n* 'kɔnvə:t] *vt* (*person: REL, POL*) обращать (обратить* *perf*); (*building, vehicle*) преобразовывать (преобразовать *perf*); (*COMM*) переводить* (перевести* *perf*) ◆ *n* (*REL, POL*) новообращённый(-ая)*m(f) adj*; **to ~ sth into** превращать (превратить* *perf*) что-н в *+acc*.
convertible [kən'və:təbl] *adj* (*currency*) конвертируемый ◆ *n* автомобиль *m* с откидным верхом; **~ loan stock** (*COMM*) конвертабельные акции.
convex ['kɔnvɛks] *adj* выпуклый.
convey [kən'veɪ] *vt* (*information, idea, thanks*) передавать* (передать* *perf*); (*cargo, person*)

перевози́ть* (перевезти́* *perf*).
conveyance [kən'veɪəns] *n* (*of goods*) перево́зка*; (*vehicle*) тра́нспортное сре́дство.
conveyancing [kən'veɪənsɪŋ] *n* (*LAW*) *составле́ние нотариа́льного а́кта о переда́че прав на недви́жимость.*
conveyor belt [kən'veɪə[r]-] *n* конве́йер.
convict [*vt* kən'vɪkt, *n* 'kɔnvɪkt] *vt* осужда́ть (осуди́ть* *perf*) ◆ *n* ка́торжник.
conviction [kən'vɪkʃən] *n* (*belief*) убежде́ние; (*certainty*) убеждённость *f*; (*LAW: decision*) осужде́ние; (*previous*) суди́мость *f*.
convince [kən'vɪns] *vt* (*assure*) уверя́ть (уве́рить *perf*); (*persuade*) убежда́ть (убеди́ть* *perf*); **to ~ sb (of sth/that)** убежда́ть (убеди́ть* *perf*) кого́-н (в чём-н/, что).
convinced [kən'vɪnst] *adj*: **~ of/that** убеждённый в +*prp*/, что.
convincing [kən'vɪnsɪŋ] *adj* убеди́тельный* (убеди́телен).
convincingly [kən'vɪnsɪŋlɪ] *adv* убеди́тельно.
convivial [kən'vɪvɪəl] *adj* (*atmosphere*) дру́жеский*; (*person*) дружелю́бный* (дружелю́бен).
convoluted ['kɔnvəlu:tɪd] *adj* замыслова́тый (замыслова́т).
convoy ['kɔnvɔɪ] *n* (*of trucks*) коло́нна; (*of ships*) конво́й.
convulse [kən'vʌls] *vt*: **to be ~d with laughter/pain** содрога́ться *(impf)* от сме́ха/бо́ли.
convulsion [kən'vʌlʃən] *n* су́дорога, конву́льсия.
coo [ku:] *vi* (*dove, person*) воркова́ть *(impf)*.
cook [kuk] *vt* (*food*) гото́вить* (пригото́вить* *perf*) ◆ *vi* (*person*) гото́вить* *(impf)*; (*food*) гото́виться* *(impf)* ◆ *n* по́вар*
▸ **cook up** *vt* (*inf*) стря́пать (состря́пать *perf*).
cookbook ['kukbuk] *n* пова́ренная *or* кулина́рная кни́га.
cook-chill ['kuktʃɪl] *adj*: **~ food** заморо́женные полуфабрика́ты *mpl*.
cooker ['kukə[r]] *n* (*stove*) плита́*.
cookery ['kukərɪ] *n* кулинари́я.
cookery book *n* (*BRIT*) = **cookbook**.
cookie ['kukɪ] *n* (*US*) пече́нье*.
cooking ['kukɪŋ] *n* гото́вка ◆ *cpd* (*apples, chocolate*) испо́льзуемый в кулинари́и; **her ~ is very good** она́ хорошо́ гото́вит; **Italian ~** италья́нская ку́хня; **~ utensils** ку́хонные принадле́жности.
cookout ['kukaut] *n* (*US*) *пригото́вление пи́щи на откры́том во́здухе.*
cool [ku:l] *adj* (*temperature, drink etc*) прохла́дный*; (*dress, clothes*) лёгкий* (лёгок); (*person: calm, unemotional*) невозмути́мый (невозмути́м); (*: unfriendly*) холо́дный* (хо́лоден) ◆ *vt* (*tea, room*) охлажда́ть (охлади́ть* *perf*) ◆ *vi* (*water, air*) остыва́ть (осты́ть* *perf*); **it's ~** прохла́дно; **to keep sth ~** *or* **in a ~ place** держа́ть* *(impf)* что-н в прохла́дном ме́сте; **to keep one's ~** сохраня́ть (сохрани́ть *perf*) хладнокро́вие; **to lose one's ~** теря́ть (потеря́ть *perf*) самооблада́ние
▸ **cool down** *vi* остыва́ть (осты́ть* *perf*); (*situation*) нормализова́ться *(impf/perf)*.
coolant ['ku:lənt] *n* хладоаге́нт.
cool box (*US* **cooler**) *n* холоди́льный я́щик.
cooler ['ku:lə[r]] *n* (*US*) = **cool box**.
cooling ['ku:lɪŋ] *n* охлажде́ние ◆ *adj* прохлади́тельный, освежа́ющий (освежа́ющ).
cooling tower *n* гради́рня*.
coolly ['ku:lɪ] *adv* (*calmly*) невозмути́мо; (*coldly*) хо́лодно.
coolness ['ku:lnɪs] *n* (*see adj*) прохла́да; лёгкость *f*; невозмути́мость *f*; хо́лодность *f*.
coop [ku:p] *n* кле́тка* ◆ *vt*: **to ~ up** (*fig*) запира́ть (запере́ть* *perf*).
co-op ['kəuɔp] *n abbr* (= *cooperative (society)*) кооперати́вное о́бщество.
cooperate [kəu'ɔpəreɪt] *vi* (*collaborate*) сотру́дничать *(impf)*; (*assist*) соде́йствовать *(impf)*; **to ~ with sb** сотру́дничать *(impf)* с кем-н.
cooperation [kəuɔpə'reɪʃən] *n* (*see vb*) коопера́ция, сотру́дничество; соде́йствие.
cooperative [kəu'ɔpərətɪv] *adj* кооперати́вный ◆ *n* кооперати́в; **he is very ~** он всегда́ гото́в оказа́ть по́мощь.
coopt [kəu'ɔpt] *vt*: **to ~ sb onto a committee** коопти́ровать *(impf/perf)* кого́-н в чле́ны комите́та.
coordinate [*vt* kəu'ɔ:dɪneɪt, *n* kəu'ɔdɪnət] *vt* (*activity, attack*) согласо́вывать (согласова́ть *perf*); (*movements*) координи́ровать *(impf/perf)* ◆ *n* (*MATH*) координа́та; **~s** *npl* (*clothes*) *предме́ты оде́жды, составля́ющие оди́н анса́мбль.*
coordination [kəuɔ:dɪ'neɪʃən] *n* координа́ция.
co-ownership ['kəu'əunəʃɪp] *n* совме́стное владе́ние.
cop [kɔp] *n* (*inf*) мент.
cope [kəup] *vi*: **to ~ with** справля́ться (спра́виться* *perf*) с +*instr*.
Copenhagen ['kəupn'heɪgən] *n* Копенга́ген.
copier ['kɔpɪə[r]] *n* (*also:* **photocopier**) (фото)копирова́льная маши́на.
co-pilot ['kəu'paɪlət] *n* второ́й пило́т.
copious ['kəupɪəs] *adj* оби́льный* (оби́лен).
copper ['kɔpə[r]] *n* (*metal*) медь *f*; (*BRIT: inf*) мент; **~s** *npl* (*small change*) медяки́* *mpl*.
coppice ['kɔpɪs] *n* ро́щица.
copse [kɔps] *n* = **coppice**.

* marks translations which have irregular inflections. The Russian-English side of the dictionary gives inflectional information.

copulate ['kɔpjuleɪt] *vi* совокупля́ться (совокупи́ться* *perf*).
copy ['kɔpɪ] *n* (*duplicate*) ко́пия; (*of book etc*) экземпля́р; (*material: for printing*) пи́сьменный экземпля́р, ру́копись *f* ◆ *vt* (*person, idea, text*) копи́ровать (скопи́ровать *perf*); **to make good** ~ (*PRESS*) составля́ть (соста́вить* *perf*) хоро́ший материа́л (для печа́ти)
▸ **copy out** (*text*) копи́ровать (скопи́ровать *perf*)
▸ **copy down** (*text*) копи́ровать (скопи́ровать *perf*).
copycat ['kɔpɪkæt] *n* (*inf*) обезья́на *m/f*.
copyright ['kɔpɪraɪt] *n* а́вторское пра́во*; ~ **reserved** а́вторское пра́во сохранено́.
copy typist *n* машини́стка*.
copywriter ['kɔpɪraɪtə^r] *n* реклами́ст.
coral ['kɔrəl] *n* кора́лл.
coral reef *n* кора́лловый риф.
Coral Sea *n*: **the** ~ ~ Кора́лловое мо́ре*.
cord [kɔ:d] *n* (*string*) верёвка*; (*ELEC*) шнур*; (*fabric*) вельве́т; ~**s** *npl* (*trousers*) вельве́товые брю́ки *pl*.
cordial ['kɔ:dɪəl] *adj* (*friendly*) серде́чный* ◆ *n* (*BRIT*) фрукто́вый напи́ток*.
cordless ['kɔ:dlɪs] *adj* переносно́й.
cordon ['kɔ:dn] *n* кордо́н, оцепле́ние
▸ **cordon off** *vt* оцепля́ть (оцепи́ть* *perf*).
cordon bleu ['kɔ:dɔn 'blə:] *adj* (*cookery, cook*) вы́сшего кла́сса (*о кулина́рном иску́сстве*).
corduroy ['kɔ:dərɔɪ] *n* вельве́т*.
CORE [kɔ:^r] *n abbr* (*US*) = *Congress of Racial Equality*.
core [kɔ:^r] *n* (*of fruit, organization*) сердцеви́на; (*of earth*) ядро́*; (*of nuclear reactor*) серде́чник; (*of problem*) суть *f* ◆ *vt* выреза́ть (вы́резать* *perf*) сердцеви́ну +*gen*; **rotten to the** ~ (*fig*) прогни́вший до основа́ния.
Corfu [kɔ:'fu:] *n* Ко́рфу *m ind*.
coriander [kɔrɪ'ændə^r] *n* (*spice*) ки́нза, кориа́ндр.
cork [kɔ:k] *n* про́бка*.
corkage ['kɔ:kɪdʒ] *n* *дополни́тельная опла́та в рестора́не за отку́поривание и пода́чу принесённого с собо́й вина́*.
corked [kɔ:kt] (*US* **corky**) *adj* пропа́хший про́бкой.
corkscrew ['kɔ:kskru:] *n* што́пор.
corky ['kɔ:kɪ] *adj* (*US*) = **corked**.
cormorant ['kɔ:mərnt] *n* бакла́н.
Corn *abbr* (*BRIT: POST*) = *Cornwall*.
corn [kɔ:n] *n* (*BRIT*) зерно́; (*US: maize*) кукуру́за; (*on foot*) мозо́ль *f*; ~ **on the cob** поча́ток* кукуру́зы.
cornea ['kɔ:nɪə] *n* рогова́я оболо́чка*.
corned beef ['kɔ:nd-] *n* консерви́рованная говя́дина.
corner ['kɔ:nə^r] *n* у́гол*; (*SPORT: also:* ~ **kick**) углово́й *m adj* (уда́р) ◆ *vt* (*trap*) загоня́ть (загна́ть* *perf*) в у́гол; (*COMM: market*) приобрета́ть (приобрести́* *perf*) контро́ль над +*instr* ◆ *vi* (*in car*) де́лать (сде́лать *perf*) поворо́т; **to cut** ~**s** (*fig*) среза́ть (*impf*) углы́.
corner flag *n* углово́й флажо́к*.
corner kick *n* углово́й уда́р.
cornerstone ['kɔ:nəstəun] *n* (*fig*) краеуго́льный ка́мень* *m*.
cornet ['kɔ:nɪt] *n* (*MUS*) корне́т; (*BRIT: of ice-cream*) *моро́женое в ва́фельной тру́бочке*.
cornflakes ['kɔ:nfleɪks] *npl* кукуру́зные хло́пья* *pl*.
cornflour ['kɔ:nflauə^r] *n* (*BRIT*) кукуру́зная мука́.
cornice ['kɔ:nɪs] *n* карни́з.
Cornish ['kɔ:nɪʃ] *adj* корну́эльский.
corn oil *n* кукуру́зное ма́сло*.
cornstarch ['kɔ:nstɑ:tʃ] *n* (*US*) = **cornflour**.
cornucopia [kɔ:nju'kəupɪə] *n* рог* изоби́лия.
Cornwall ['kɔ:nwəl] *n* Ко́рнуолл.
corny ['kɔ:nɪ] *adj* (*inf*) пло́ский* (пло́сок).
corollary [kə'rɔlərɪ] *n* сле́дствие.
coronary ['kɔrənərɪ] *n* (*also:* ~ **thrombosis**) корона́рный тромбо́з.
coronation [kɔrə'neɪʃən] *n* корона́ция.
coroner ['kɔrənə^r] *n* (*LAW*) ко́ронер (*судья́, рассле́дующий причи́ны сме́рти, происше́дшей при подозри́тельных обстоя́тельствах*).
coronet ['kɔrənɪt] *n* диаде́ма.
Corp. *abbr* = **corporation**; (*MIL*) = **corporal**.
corporal ['kɔ:pərl] *n* капра́л ◆ *adj*: ~ **punishment** теле́сное наказа́ние.
corporate ['kɔ:pərɪt] *adj* (*COMM*) корпорацио́нный; (*ownership, effort*) о́бщий*; (*identity*) корпорати́вный.
corporate hospitality *n* *спецобслу́живание и привиле́гии, ока́зываемые корпора́цией осо́бо ва́жным и́ли це́нным клие́нтам*.
corporation [kɔ:pə'reɪʃən] *n* (*COMM*) корпора́ция; (*of town*) муниципалите́т.
corporation tax *n* корпорацио́нный нало́г.
corps [kɔ:^r] (*pl* ~) *n* (*also MIL*) ко́рпус*; **the press** ~ корреспонде́нтский ко́рпус.
corpse [kɔ:ps] *n* труп.
corpuscle ['kɔ:pʌsl] *n* (*BIO*) те́льце* (*кровяны́е*).
corral [kə'rɑ:l] *n* заго́н.
correct [kə'rɛkt] *adj* (*accurate*) пра́вильный* (пра́вилен); (*proper*) соотве́тствующий* ◆ *vt* (*mistake, fault*) исправля́ть (испра́вить* *perf*); (*exam*) проверя́ть (прове́рить *perf*); **you are** ~ Вы пра́вы.
correction [kə'rɛkʃən] *n* (*act of correcting*) исправле́ние; (*mistake corrected*) popра́вка*; (*of proofs*) корректу́ра.
correctly [kə'rɛktlɪ] *adv* пра́вильно.
correlate ['kɔrɪleɪt] *vt* соотноси́ть* (соотнести́* *perf*) ◆ *vi*: **to** ~ **with** соотноси́ться* (*impf*) *or* коррели́ровать (*impf*) с +*instr*.
correlation [kɔrɪ'leɪʃən] *n* соотноше́ние, корреля́ция.
correspond [kɔrɪs'pɔnd] *vi*: **to** ~ **(with)** (*write*)

переписываться *(impf)* (с +*instr*); (*tally*) согласо́вываться *(impf)* (с +*instr*); (*equate*): **to ~ (to)** соотве́тствовать *(impf)* (+*dat*).
correspondence [kɔrɪs'pɔndəns] *n* (*letters*) корреспонде́нция, перепи́ска; (*relationship*) соотноше́ние.
correspondence course *n* заочный курс.
correspondent [kɔrɪs'pɔndənt] *n* (*PRESS*) корреспонде́нт(ка).
corresponding [kɔrɪs'pɔndɪŋ] *adj* соотве́тствующий*.
corridor ['kɔrɪdɔ:'] *n* (*in building etc*) коридо́р; (*in train*) прохо́д.
corroborate [kə'rɔbəreɪt] *vt* подтвержда́ть (подтверди́ть* *perf*).
corrode [kə'rəud] *vt* (*metal*) разъеда́ть (разъе́сть* *perf*) ◆ *vi* (*metal*) ржаве́ть (заржаве́ть *perf*).
corrosion [kə'rəuʒən] *n* (*damage*) ржа́вчина; (*process*) корро́зия.
corrosive [kə'rəuzɪv] *adj* коррози́йный.
corrugated ['kɔrəgeɪtɪd] *adj* рифлёный.
corrugated iron *n* рифлёное желе́зо.
corrupt [kə'rʌpt] *adj* (*person*) прода́жный* (прода́жен), коррумпи́рованный; (*COMPUT*) испо́рченный, искажённый ◆ *vt* развраща́ть (разврати́ть* *perf*); (*COMPUT*) искажа́ть (искази́ть* *perf*); **~ practices** бесче́стные приёмы.
corruption [kə'rʌpʃən] *n* (*see adj*) корру́пция, прода́жность *f*; искаже́ние.
corset ['kɔ:sɪt] *n* (*also MED*) корсе́т.
Corsica ['kɔ:sɪkə] *n* Ко́рсика.
Corsican ['kɔ:sɪkən] *adj* корсика́нский ◆ *n* корсика́нец*(-нка*).
cortège [kɔ:'teɪʒ] *n* (*also:* **funeral ~**) проце́ссия.
cortisone ['kɔ:tɪzəun] *n* кортизо́н.
coruscating ['kɔrəskeɪtɪŋ] *adj* сверка́ющий.
c.o.s. *abbr* (= *cash on shipment*) *опла́та нали́чными при отпра́вке*.
cosh [kɔʃ] *n* (*BRIT*) дуби́нка*.
cosignatory ['kəu'sɪgnətərɪ] *n* *одна́ из сторо́н, подпи́сывающих докуме́нт*.
cosiness ['kəuzɪnɪs] *n* ую́т.
cos lettuce ['kɔs-] *n* лату́к (*сала́т*).
cosmetic [kɔz'mɛtɪk] *n* (*usu pl*) косме́тика ◆ *adj* (*fig*) космети́ческий*; **~ surgery** космети́ческая хирурги́я.
cosmic ['kɔzmɪk] *adj* косми́ческий*.
cosmonaut ['kɔzmənɔ:t] *n* космона́вт.
cosmopolitan [kɔzmə'pɔlɪtn] *adj* (*place*) космополити́ческий.
cosmos ['kɔzmɔs] *n*: **the ~** ко́смос.
cosset ['kɔsɪt] *vt* балова́ть (избалова́ть *perf*).
cost [kɔst] (*pt, pp* **cost**) *n* сто́имость *f*; (*fig*) цена́* ◆ *vt* (*be priced at*) сто́ить *(impf)*; (*pt, pp* **costed**; *find out cost of*) оце́нивать (оцени́ть *perf*) сто́имость +*gen*; **~s** *npl* (*COMM*) расхо́ды *mpl*; (*LAW*) суде́бные изде́ржки* *fpl*; **how much does it ~?** ско́лько э́то сто́ит?; **it ~s £5/too much** э́то сто́ит £5/сли́шком до́рого; **what will it ~ to have it repaired?** ско́лько бу́дет сто́ить ремо́нт?; **to ~ sb time/effort** сто́ить *(impf)* кому́-н вре́мени/уси́лий; **it ~ him his life/job** э́то сто́ило ему́ жи́зни/рабо́ты; **the ~ of living** сто́имость жи́зни; **to sell/buy at ~** продава́ть* (прода́ть* *perf*)/покупа́ть (купи́ть* *perf*) по себесто́имости; **at all ~s** любо́й цено́й.
cost accountant *n* бухга́лтер (*веду́щий учёт затра́т*).
co-star ['kəusta:'] *n* партнёр (*гла́вной ро́ли*).
Costa Rica ['kɔstə'ri:kə] *n* Ко́ста-Ри́ка.
cost-benefit analysis ['kɔstbɛnɪfɪt-] *n* ана́лиз изде́ржек и при́были.
cost centre *n* *счёт, фикси́рующий произво́дственные изде́ржки*.
cost control *n* контро́ль *m* за у́ровнем изде́ржек.
cost-effective ['kɔstɪ'fɛktɪv] *adj* вы́годный* (вы́годен); (*COMM*) рента́бельный.
cost-effectiveness ['kɔstɪ'fɛktɪvnɪs] *n* (*see adj*) вы́годность *f*; рента́бельность *f*.
costing ['kɔstɪŋ] *n* (*COMM*) оце́нка сто́имости.
costly ['kɔstlɪ] *adj* (*expensive*) дорого́й* (до́рог); (*in time, effort*) дорогосто́ящий.
cost of living *n* сто́имость *f* жи́зни.
cost price *n* (*BRIT*) себесто́имость *f*; **to sell/buy at ~ ~** продава́ть* (прода́ть* *perf*)/покупа́ть (купи́ть* *perf*) по себесто́имости.
costume ['kɔstju:m] *n* костю́м; (*BRIT: also:* **swimming ~**) купа́льник, купа́льный костю́м.
costume jewellery *n* бижуте́рия.
cosy ['kəuzɪ] (*US* **cozy**) *adj* (*room, atmosphere*) ую́тный* (ую́тен); (*bed*) удо́бный* (удо́бен); (*scarf, gloves*) тёплый*; (*person*) забо́тливый; (*chat, evening*) прия́тный* (прия́тен).
cot [kɔt] *n* (*BRIT: for baby*) де́тская крова́тка*; (*US: camp bed*) ко́йка*.
cot death *n* *внеза́пная сме́рть здоро́вого грудно́го ребёнка во сне*.
Cotswolds ['kɔtswəuldz] *npl*: **the ~** Ко́тсвольд *msg*.
cottage ['kɔtɪdʒ] *n* котте́дж.
cottage cheese *n* тво́рог.
cottage industry *n* надо́мный труд*.
cottage pie *n* *запека́нка из мя́са и карто́феля*.
cotton ['kɔtn] *n* (*fabric*) хло́пок*, хлопчатобума́жная тка́нь *f*; (*plant*) хлопча́тник; (*thread*) (шве́йная) ни́тка*; **~ dress** *etc* хлопчатобума́жное пла́тье* *etc*
▸ **cotton on** *vi* (*inf*): **he has ~ed on to the fact that ...** до него́ дошло́, что ....

* marks translations which have irregular inflections. The Russian-English side of the dictionary gives inflectional information.

cotton candy *n* (*US*) сахарная вата.
cotton wool *n* (*BRIT*) вата.
couch [kautʃ] *n* тахта, диван; (*for patients*) кушетка* ◆ *vt* излагать (изложить* *perf*).
couchette [ku:'ʃɛt] *n* спальное место*, полка*.
couch potato *n* лежебока *m/f*.
cough [kɔf] *vi* (*person*) кашлять *(impf)*; (*engine*) тарахтеть *(impf)* ◆ *n* кашель *m*.
cough drop *n* таблетка* от кашля.
cough mixture *n* микстура от кашля.
cough syrup *n* = **cough mixture**.
could [kud] *pt of* **can²**.
couldn't ['kudnt] = **could not**; *see* **can²**.
council ['kaunsl] *n* совет; **city** *or* **town** ~ городской совет, муниципалитет; **C~ of Europe** Совет Европейского Сообщества.
council estate *n* (*BRIT*) *жилой массив, принадлежащий муниципалитету*.
council house *n* (*BRIT*) *дом, принадлежащий муниципалитету*.
council housing *n* (*BRIT*) *жильё, принадлежащее муниципалитету и сдаваемое в аренду*.
councillor ['kaunslə'] *n* ≈ член муниципалитета.
council tax *n* муниципальный налог.
counsel ['kaunsl] *n* (*advice*) совет; (*lawyer*) адвокат, юрисконсульт ◆ *vt*: **to ~ sth/sb to do** советовать (посоветовать *perf*) что-н/кому-н *+infin*; **~ for the defence** защитник; **~ for the prosecution** обвинитель *m*.
counsellor ['kaunslə'] *n* (*advisor*) советник; (*US*: *lawyer*) адвокат.
count [kaunt] *vt* (*add up*) считать (посчитать *perf*); (*include*) считать *(impf)* ◆ *vi* пересчитывать (пересчитать *perf*); (*qualify*) считаться *(impf)*; (*matter*) иметь *(impf)* значение ◆ *n* (*of things, people*) подсчёт; (*level*) уровень* *m*; (*nobleman*) граф; **to ~ (up) to 10** считать (посчитать *perf*) до 10; **not ~ing the children** не считая детей; **10 ~ing him** 10, считая его; **to ~ the cost of** оценивать (оценить *perf*) стоимость *+gen*; **it ~s for very little** это имеет очень маленькое значение; **~ yourself lucky** считайте, что Вам повезло; **to keep/lose ~ of sth** вести* *(impf)*/терять (потерять *perf*) счёт чего-н
▸ **count on** *vt fus* рассчитывать *(impf)* на *+acc*; **to ~ on doing** рассчитывать *(impf) +infin*
▸ **count up** *vt* подсчитывать (подсчитать *perf*).
countdown ['kauntdaun] *n счёт в обратном направлении*.
countenance ['kauntınəns] *n* лицо* ◆ *vt* одобрять (одобрить *perf*).
counter ['kauntə'] *n* (*in shop, café*) прилавок*; (*in bank, post office*) стойка*; (*in game*) фишка*; (*TECH*) счётчик ◆ *vt* (*oppose*) опровергать (опровергнуть *perf*); (*blow*) отражать (отразить *perf*) ◆ *adv*: **~ to** в противовес *+dat*; **to buy under the ~** (*fig*) покупать (купить* *perf*) из-под прилавка; **to ~ sth with sth** противостоять *(impf/perf)* чему-н чем-н.
counteract ['kauntər'ækt] *vt* (*effect etc*) противодействовать *(impf) +dat*; (*poison etc*) нейтрализовать *(impf/perf)*, обезвреживать (обезвредить* *perf*).
counterattack ['kauntərə'tæk] *n* контратака ◆ *vi* контратаковать *(impf/perf)*.
counterbalance ['kauntə'bæləns] *vt* уравновешивать (уравновесить* *perf*).
counterclockwise ['kauntə'klɔkwaız] *adv* против часовой стрелки.
counterespionage ['kauntər'ɛspıənɑ:ʒ] *n* контрразведка*.
counterfeit ['kauntəfıt] *n* подделка* ◆ *vt* подделывать (подделать *perf*) ◆ *adj* (*coin*) фальшивый.
counterfoil ['kauntəfɔıl] *n* (*of cheque, money order*) корешок*.
counterintelligence ['kauntərın'tɛlıdʒəns] *n* контрразведка*.
countermand ['kauntəmɑ:nd] *vt* (*order*) отменять (отменить* *perf*).
countermeasure ['kauntəmɛʒə'] *n* контрмера.
counteroffensive ['kauntərə'fɛnsıv] *n* контрнаступление.
counterpane ['kauntəpeın] *n* покрывало.
counterpart ['kauntəpɑ:t] *n* (*of person*) коллега *m/f*; (*of document etc*) копия.
counterproductive ['kauntəprə'dʌktıv] *adj* непродуктивный* (непродуктивен).
counterproposal ['kauntəprə'pəuzl] *n* встречное предложение.
countersign ['kauntəsaın] *vt* заверять (заверить *perf*), засвидетельствовать *(perf)*.
countersink ['kauntəsıŋk] *vt* зенковать *(impf)*.
countess ['kauntıs] *n* графиня.
countless ['kauntlıs] *adj* несчётный*, бесчисленный.
countrified ['kʌntrıfaıd] *adj* деревенский*.
country ['kʌntrı] *n* (*state, nation*) страна*; (*native land*) родина; (*rural area*) деревня*; (*region*) район; **in the ~** в деревне; **mountainous ~** гористая местность *f*.
country and western (music) *n* кантри *nt ind*.
country dancing *n* (*BRIT*) народные танцы *mpl*.
country house *n* загородный дом*, ≈ дача.
countryman ['kʌntrımən] *irreg n* (*compatriot*) земляк*, соотечественник; (*country dweller*) деревенский* *or* сельский* житель *m*.
countryside ['kʌntrısaıd] *n* сельская местность *f*.
countrywide ['kʌntrı'waıd] *adj* общенациональный ◆ *adv* по всей стране.
county ['kauntı] *n* графство.
county council *n* ≈ областной совет, совет графства.
county town *n* (*BRIT*) главный город* графства.
coup [ku:] (*pl* **~s**) *n* (*also:* **~ d'état**)

государственный переворот; (*fig*) переворот.

coupé [ku:'peɪ] *n* (*AUT*) *закрытый автомобиль с двумя дверями и наклонным кузовом.*

couple ['kʌpl] *n* (*married couple*) супруги *pl*; (*of people, things*) пара ◆ *vt* (*ideas, names*) связывать (связать* *perf*); (*machinery*) сцеплять (сцепить* *perf*); **a ~ of** (*two, a few*) пара *+gen*.

couplet ['kʌplɪt] *n* двустишие.

coupling ['kʌplɪŋ] *n* (*RAIL*) сцепление.

coupon ['ku:pɔn] *n* (*voucher*) купон; (*detachable form*) талон; (*COMM*) отрывной бланк.

courage ['kʌrɪdʒ] *n* смелость *f*, храбрость *f*, мужество.

courageous [kə'reɪdʒəs] *adj* смелый* (смел), храбрый (храбр), мужественный (мужественен).

courgette [kuə'ʒɛt] *n* (*BRIT*) молодой кабачок*.

courier ['kurɪə'] *n* (*messenger*) курьер; (*for tourists*) руководитель *m* группы.

course [kɔ:s] *n* (*SCOL, MED, NAUT*) курс; (*of events, time etc*) ход; (*of argument, action*) направление; (*of river*) течение; (*part of meal*): **first/next/last ~** первое/второе/сладкое блюдо; **~ of lectures/treatment** курс лекций/лечения; **in the ~ of the next few days** в течение следующих нескольких дней; **in due ~** в своё время; **~ (of action)** линия поведения; **the best ~ would be ...** лучшим выходом было бы ...; **we have no other ~ but to ...** у нас нет другого выхода, кроме как ...; **of ~** (*naturally*) конечно; (*certainly*) безусловно; **of ~!** конечно!; **(no) of ~ not!** (нет,) конечно, нет!; **golf ~** *поле для игры в гольф.*

court [kɔ:t] *n* (*LAW*) суд*; (*SPORT*) корт; (*royal*) двор* ◆ *vt* (*woman*) ухаживать (*impf*) за *+instr*; (*fig*: *favour*) добиваться (добиться* *perf*) *+gen*; (: *death, disaster*) заигрывать (*impf*) с *+instr*; **to settle out of ~** приходить* (прийти* *perf*) к соглашению без судебного разбирательства; **to take sb to ~** подавать* (подать* *perf*) на кого-н в суд.

courteous ['kə:tɪəs] *adj* вежливый (вежлив).

courtesan [kɔ:tɪ'zæn] *n* куртизанка*.

courtesy ['kə:təsɪ] *n* вежливость *f*; **(by) ~ of** благодаря любезности *+gen*.

courtesy light *n лампочка в салоне автомобиля.*

courthouse ['kɔ:thaus] *n* (*US*) здание суда.

courtier ['kɔ:tɪə'] *n* придворный *m adj*.

court martial (*pl* **~s ~**) *n* военный трибунал.

court of appeal (*pl* **~s ~ ~**) *n* апелляционный суд*.

court of inquiry (*pl* **~s ~ ~**) *n* следственная комиссия.

courtroom ['kɔ:trum] *n* зал суда.

court shoe *n* лодочки *pl*.

courtyard ['kɔ:tjɑ:d] *n* внутренний* двор*.

cousin ['kʌzn] *n* (*relative*: *male*) неродной брат*; (: *female*) неродная сестра*; **first ~** (*male*) двоюродный брат*; (*female*) двоюродная сестра*.

cove [kəuv] *n* (*bay*) бухточка*.

covenant ['kʌvənənt] *n* (*promise*) обязательство ◆ *vt*: **to ~ £200 per year to charity** обязываться (обязаться* *perf*) перечислять £200 в год в благотворительный фонд.

Coventry ['kɔvəntrɪ] *n*: **send sb to ~** (*fig*) бойкотировать (*impf/perf*) кого-н.

cover ['kʌvə'] *vt* (*protect, hide*) закрывать (закрыть* *perf*), укрывать (укрыть* *perf*); (*distance*) покрывать (покрыть* *perf*); (*MIL*) прикрывать (прикрыть* *perf*); (*INSURANCE*) предусматривать (предусмотреть* *perf*); (*topic*) рассматривать (рассмотреть* *perf*); (*include*) охватывать (охватить* *perf*); (*PRESS*) освещать (осветить* *perf*) ◆ *n* (*for furniture, machinery etc*) чехол*; (*of book, magazine*) обложка*; (*shelter*) укрытие; (*INSURANCE*) покрытие; (*MIL*) прикрытие; (*fig*) прикрытие; **~s** *npl* (*bedclothes*) постельные принадлежности *fpl*; **he was ~ed in** *or* **with** (*mud*) он был весь в *+prp*; **to take ~** укрываться (укрыться* *perf*); **under ~** в укрытии; **under ~ of darkness** под покровом темноты; **under separate ~** (*COMM*) в отдельном пакете; **£10 will ~ my expenses** £10 покроют мои расходы

▸ **cover up** *vt* (*protect, hide*) закрывать (закрыть* *perf*); (*fig*: *facts, feelings*) скрывать (скрыть* *perf*) ◆ *vi* (*fig*): **to ~ up for sb** покрывать (покрыть* *perf*) кого-н.

coverage ['kʌvərɪdʒ] *n* (*TV, PRESS*) освещение; **television ~ of the conference** освещение конференции по телевидению; **to give full ~ to** давать* (дать* *perf*) полное освещение *+gen*.

coveralls ['kʌvərɔ:lz] *npl* (*US*) рабочий* комбинезон *msg*.

cover charge *n* (*in restaurant*) наценка.

covering ['kʌvərɪŋ] *n* (*layer*) пласт*; (*of snow, dust etc*) слой*; (*on floor*) настил.

covering letter (*US* **cover letter**) *n* сопроводительное письмо*.

cover note *n документ, удостоверяющий факт страхования.*

cover price *n* цена, указанная на обложке.

covert ['kʌvət] *adj* (*threat*) скрытый; (*attack*) неожиданный*; **she gave me a ~ glance** она украдкой на меня посмотрела.

cover-up ['kʌvərʌp] *n* ширма, прикрытие.

covet ['kʌvɪt] *vt* жаждать (*impf*) *+gen*.

* marks translations which have irregular inflections. The Russian-English side of the dictionary gives inflectional information.

cow [kau] *n* (*also inf!*) коро́ва (*also !*) ◆ *vt* запу́гивать (запуга́ть *perf*).
coward ['kauəd] *n* трус(и́ха).
cowardice ['kauədɪs] *n* тру́сость *f*.
cowardly ['kauədlɪ] *adj* трусли́вый (трусли́в).
cowboy ['kaubɔɪ] *n* (*in US*) ковбо́й; (*pej: tradesman*) шаба́шник.
cow elephant *n* слони́ха.
cower ['kauəʳ] *vi* съёживаться (съёжиться *perf*).
cow shed *n* коро́вник.
cowslip ['kauslɪp] *n* первоцве́т (настоя́щий* *or* весе́нний*).
cox [kɔks] *n abbr* = **coxswain**.
coxswain ['kɔksn] *n* (*ROWING*) старшина́ (байда́рки).
coy [kɔɪ] *adj* (*shy*) засте́нчивый (засте́нчив).
coyote [kɔɪ'əutɪ] *n* койо́т.
cozy ['kəuzɪ] *adj* (*US*) = **cosy**.
CP *n abbr* = *Communist Party*.
cp. *abbr* (= **compare**) ср.= *сравни́*.
c/p *abbr* (*BRIT*: = *carriage paid*) с опла́ченной доста́вкой.
CPA *n abbr* (*US*) = **certified public accountant**.
CPI *n abbr* (= *Consumer Price Index*) и́ндекс потреби́тельских цен.
Cpl. *abbr* (*MIL*) = **corporal**.
CP/M *n abbr* (= *Central Program for Microprocessors*) CPM (*операцио́нная систе́ма для микроЭВМ*).
c.p.s. *abbr* (*COMPUT, TYP*: = *characters per second*) зна́ков в секу́нду.
CPSA *n abbr* (*BRIT*) = *Civil and Public Services Association*.
CPU *n abbr* (*COMPUT*) (= **central processing unit**) ЦП= *центра́льный проце́ссор*.
cr. *abbr* = **credit**, **creditor**.
crab [kræb] *n* краб.
crab apple *n* ди́кое я́блоко*.
crack [kræk] *n* (*noise*) треск; (*gap*) щель* *f*; (*in bone, dish, wall*) тре́щина; (*joke*) хо́хма; (*DRUGS*) крэк (*фо́рма кокаи́на*) ◆ *vt* (*whip, twig*) щёлкать (щёлкнуть *perf*) +*instr*; (*bone, dish etc*) раска́лывать (расколо́ть* *perf*); (*nut*) коло́ть* (расколо́ть* *perf*); (*problem*) реша́ть (реши́ть *perf*); (*code*) разга́дывать (разгада́ть *perf*); (*joke*) отпуска́ть (отпусти́ть* *perf*) ◆ *adj* первокла́ссный*; **at the ~ of dawn** на заре́; **to have a ~ (at sth)** (*inf*) пыта́ть (попыта́ть *perf*) свои́ си́лы (в чём-н); **to get ~ing** (*inf*) пошеве́ливаться (*impf*)
▸ **crack down on** *vt fus* расправля́ться (распра́виться* *perf*) с +*instr*
▸ **crack up** *vi* (*with laughter*) пры́скать (пры́снуть *perf*) со́ смеху; **she ~ed up** (*under strain*) у неё был не́рвный срыв.
crackdown ['krækdaun] *n*: **~ (on)** распра́ва (с +*instr*).
cracked [krækt] *adj* (*inf*) сло́манный (сло́ман).
cracker ['krækəʳ] *n* (*biscuit*) кре́кер; (*Christmas cracker*) хлопу́шка*; (*firework*) шути́ха; **a ~ of a goal** (*BRIT*: *inf*) сногсшиба́тельный гол; **she's a ~** (*BRIT*: *inf*) она́ сногсшиба́тельная же́нщина; **he's ~s** (*BRIT*: *inf*) он спя́тил.
crackle ['krækl] *vi* потре́скивать (*impf*).
crackling ['kræklɪŋ] *n* треск; (*of pork*) шква́рки* *fpl*.
crackpot ['krækpɔt] *n* (*inf*) полоу́мный(-ая) *m(f) adj* ◆ *adj* полоу́мный.
cradle ['kreɪdl] *n* (*for baby*) колыбе́ль *f* ◆ *vt* прижима́ть (*impf*) к груди́.
craft [krɑ:ft] *n* (*skill*) мастерство́; (*trade*) ремесло́*; (*boat*: *pl inv*) кора́бль* *f*.
craftsman ['krɑ:ftsmən] *irreg n* (*artisan*) реме́сленник.
craftsmanship ['krɑ:ftsmənʃɪp] *n* (*quality*) вы́делка; (*skill*) мастерство́.
crafty ['krɑ:ftɪ] *adj* лука́вый (лука́в).
crag [kræg] *n* утёс.
craggy ['krægɪ] *adj* (*mountain, cliff*) отве́сный*; (*face*) с ре́зкими черта́ми.
cram [kræm] *vi* (*for exams*) зубри́ть (вы́зубрить *perf*) ◆ *vt* (*fill*): **to ~ sth with** набива́ть (наби́ть* *perf*) что-н +*instr*; (*put*): **to ~ sth into** вти́скивать (вти́снуть *perf*) что-н в +*acc*.
cramming ['kræmɪŋ] *n* зубрёжка.
cramp [kræmp] *n* су́дорога ◆ *vt* стесня́ть (стесни́ть *perf*).
cramped [kræmpt] *adj* (*accommodation*) те́сный (те́сен).
crampon ['kræmpən] *n* (*CLIMBING*) клещи́ *pl*.
cranberry ['krænbərɪ] *n* клю́ква.
crane [kreɪn] *n* (*machine*) (подьёмный) кран; (*bird*) жура́вль* *m* ◆ *vt*: **to ~ one's neck** вытя́гивать (вы́тянуть *perf*) ше́ю ◆ *vi*: **to ~ forward** высо́вываться (вы́сунуться *perf*).
crania ['kreɪnɪə] *npl of* **cranium**.
cranium ['kreɪnɪəm] (*pl* **crania**) *n* че́реп*.
crank [kræŋk] *n* (*person*) чуда́к*; (*handle*) заводна́я руко́ятка.
crankshaft ['kræŋkʃɑ:ft] *n* коле́нчатый вал*.
cranky ['kræŋkɪ] *adj* чудакова́тый (чудакова́т).
cranny ['krænɪ] *n see* **nook**.
crap [kræp] (*inf!*) *n* дерьмо́ (*!*) ◆ *vi* срать* (*impf*) (*!*); **to have a ~** посра́ть* (*perf*) (*!*)
crappy ['kræpɪ] *adj* (*inf!*) дерьмо́вый (*!*)
crash [kræʃ] *n* (*noise*) гро́хот; (*of car*) ава́рия; (*of plane, train*) круше́ние; (*COMM*) крах ◆ *vt* (*car, plane*) разбива́ть (разби́ть* *perf*) ◆ *vi* (*car, plane*) разбива́ться (разби́ться* *perf*); (*two cars*) ста́лкиваться (столкну́ться *perf*); (*COMM*) потерпе́ть* (*perf*) крах; **to ~ into** вреза́ться (вре́заться* *perf*) в +*acc*; **he ~ed the car into a wall** он вре́зался на маши́не в сте́ну.
crash barrier *n* (*BRIT*) предохрани́тельный барье́р (на доро́ге).
crash course *n* интенси́вный курс.
crash helmet *n* защи́тный шлем.
crash landing *n* вы́нужденная поса́дка*.

crass [kræs] *adj* тупо́й (туп).
crate [kreɪt] *n* (*box*) деревя́нный я́щик; (*for bottles*) упако́вочный я́щик (*для буты́лок*); (*inf*: *car*) драндуле́т.
crater ['kreɪtə'] *n* (*of volcano*) кра́тер; (*of bomb blast*) воро́нка*.
cravat [krə'væt] *n* ше́йный плато́к*.
crave [kreɪv] *vti*: **to ~ sth** *or* **for sth** жа́ждать *(impf)* чего́-н.
craven ['kreɪvən] *adj* трусли́вый (трусли́в).
craving ['kreɪvɪŋ] *n*: **~ (for)** жа́жда (*+gen*).
crawl [krɔ:l] *vi* по́лзать/ползти́* *(impf)*; (*inf*: *grovel*) пресмыка́ться *(impf)* ◆ *n* (SWIMMING) кроль *f*; **to ~ to sb** (*inf*) пресмыка́ться *(impf)* пе́ред кем-н; **I was driving along at a ~** моя́ маши́на е́ле ползла́.
crayfish ['kreɪfɪʃ] *n inv* (*freshwater*) речно́й рак; (*saltwater*) лангу́ст.
crayon ['kreɪən] *n* цветно́й мело́к*.
craze [kreɪz] *n* пова́льное увлече́ние.
crazed [kreɪzd] *adj* (*look, person*) безу́мный*; (*pottery etc*) потре́скавшийся.
crazy ['kreɪzɪ] *adj* сумасше́дший*; (*inf*): **he's ~ about skiing** (*inf*) он поме́шан на лы́жах; **to go ~** помеша́ться *(perf)*.
crazy paving *n* (BRIT) *насти́л из ка́менных плит разли́чной фо́рмы*.
creak [kri:k] *vi* скрипе́ть* *(impf)*.
cream [kri:m] *n* (*of milk*) сли́вки* *pl*; (*made artificially*) (иску́сственные) сли́вки*; (*cosmetic*) крем ◆ *adj* (*colour*) кре́мовый; **whipped ~** взби́тые сли́вки*; **soured ~** смета́на; **the ~ of society** сли́вки* о́бщества
▸ **cream off** *vt* (*fig*: *best talents*) отбира́ть (отобра́ть* *perf*); (*part of profits*) снима́ть *(impf)* пе́нки.
cream cake *n* пиро́жное *nt adj* с кре́мом.
cream cheese *n* сли́вочный сыр*.
creamery ['kri:mərɪ] *n* (*shop*) моло́чный магази́н; (*factory*) маслобо́йный заво́д.
creamy ['kri:mɪ] *adj* (*colour*) кре́мовый; (*taste*) сли́вочный.
crease [kri:s] *n* (*fold*) скла́дка*; (: *in trousers*) стре́лка*; (*wrinkle*: *in dress, on brow*) морщи́на ◆ *vt* мять* (помя́ть* *perf*) ◆ *vi* мя́ться* (помя́ться* *perf*).
crease-resistant ['kri:srɪzɪstənt] *adj* немну́щийся*.
create [kri:'eɪt] *vt* (*cause to happen, exist*) твори́ть (сотвори́ть *perf*), порожда́ть (породи́ть* *perf*); (*produce*: *impression*) создава́ть* (созда́ть* *perf*).
creation [kri:'eɪʃən] *n* созда́ние; (REL) сотворе́ние.
creative [kri:'eɪtɪv] *adj* (*artistic*) тво́рческий*; (*inventive*) изобрета́тельный* (изобрета́телен).
creativity [kri:eɪ'tɪvɪtɪ] *n* тво́рчество.
creator [kri:'eɪtə'] *n* созда́тель *m*.
creature ['kri:tʃə'] *n* (*animal*) существо́; (*person*) созда́ние.
creature comforts [- 'kʌmfəts] *npl* удо́бства *ntpl*.
crèche [krɛʃ] *n* (де́тские) я́сли *pl*.
credence ['kri:dns] *n*: **to lend** *or* **give ~ to** придава́ть* (прида́ть* *perf*) правдоподо́бность *+dat*.
credentials [krɪ'dɛnʃlz] *npl* (*references*) квалифика́ция *fsg*, достиже́ния *ntpl*; (*identity papers*) рекоменда́ция, рекоменда́тельное письмо́.
credibility [krɛdɪ'bɪlɪtɪ] *n* (*of fact*) правдоподо́бность *f*; (*of person*) авторите́т.
credible ['krɛdɪbl] *adj* (*thing*) вероя́тный* (вероя́тен), правдоподо́бный* (правдоподо́бен); (*person*) авторите́тный* (авторите́тен).
credit ['krɛdɪt] *n* (COMM) креди́т; (*recognition*) до́лжное *nt adj*; (SCOL) *курс, необходи́мый для получе́ния дипло́ма* ◆ *adj* (COMM) прихо́дный ◆ *vt* (COMM) кредитова́ть *(impf/perf)*; (*believe*: *also*: **give ~ to**) ве́рить (пове́рить *perf*) *+dat*; **~s** *npl* (CINEMA, TV) (вступи́тельные) ти́тры *mpl*; **he is/was in ~** он платёжеспосо́бен/был платёжеспосо́бен; **on ~** в креди́т; **to sb's ~** к чьей-н че́сти; **to take the ~ for** припи́сывать (приписа́ть* *perf*) себе́ *+acc*; **it does him ~** э́то де́лает ему́ честь; **he's a ~ to his family** он де́лает честь свое́й семье́; **to ~ sb with sth** (*fig*) припи́сывать (приписа́ть* *perf*) кому́-н что-н; **to ~ £5 to sb** вноси́ть* (внести́* *perf*) £5 на чей-н счёт.
creditable ['krɛdɪtəbl] *adj* (*behaviour*) досто́йный; (*mark*) похва́льный* (похва́лен).
credit account *n* креди́тный счёт (*в отде́льном магази́не*).
credit agency *n* (BRIT) кредитно-информацио́нное бюро́.
credit balance *n* креди́тный оста́ток* на счёте.
credit bureau *n* (US) = **credit agency**.
credit card *n* креди́тная ка́рточка*.
credit control *n* (ECON) креди́тный контро́ль *m*.
credit facilities *npl* креди́тный лими́т (*креди́тной ка́рточки заёмщика*).
credit limit *n* креди́тный лими́т (*в примене́нию к индивидуа́льному заёмщику и́ли определя́емый креди́тной ли́нией ба́нка*).
credit note *n* (BRIT) *докуме́нт, позволя́ющий купи́ть това́р взаме́н неиспра́вного*.
creditor ['krɛdɪtə'] *n* кредито́р.
credit transfer *n* креди́тный перево́д, жи́ро.
creditworthy ['krɛdɪt'wə:ðɪ] *adj* кредитоспосо́бный*.

* marks translations which have irregular inflections. The Russian-English side of the dictionary gives inflectional information.

credulity [krɪ'dju:lɪtɪ] *n* довéрчивость *f*.
creed [kri:d] *n* (*REL*) вероучéние.
creek [kri:k] *n* ýзкий* залив; (*US*) ручéй*; **to be up the ~** (*inf*) влипнуть *(perf)* в истóрию.
creel [kri:l] *n* (*also:* **lobster ~**) *клéтка для лóвли лангýстов.*
creep [kri:p] (*pt, pp* **crept**) *vi* (*person, animal*) крáсться* *(impf)*; (*plant*) виться* *(impf)* ◆ *n* (*inf*) подхали́м(ка); **it gives me the ~s** от э́того у меня́ морóз по кóже подирáет; **to ~ up on sb** подкрáдываться (подкрáсться* *perf*) к кому́-н.
creeper ['kri:pə'] *n* ползучее растение.
creepers ['kri:pəz] *npl* (*US*) ползунки́ *pl*.
creepy ['kri:pɪ] *adj* жýткий*.
creepy-crawly ['kri:pɪ'krɔ:lɪ] *n* (*inf*) букáшка*.
cremate [krɪ'meɪt] *vt* кремировать *(impf/perf)*.
cremation [krɪ'meɪʃən] *n* кремáция.
crematoria [krɛmə'tɔ:rɪə] *npl of* **crematorium**.
crematorium [krɛmə'tɔ:rɪəm] (*pl* **crematoria**) *n* крематóрий.
creosote ['krɪəsəut] *n* креозóт.
crêpe [kreɪp] *n* (*fabric*) креп; (*rubber*) *сорт каучýка*.
crêpe bandage *n* (*BRIT*) эласти́чная повя́зка*.
crêpe paper *n* крепи́рованная бумáга.
crêpe sole *n* каучýковая подóшва.
crept [krɛpt] *pt, pp of* **creep**.
crescendo [krɪ'ʃɛndəu] *n* (*MUS*) крещéндо *nt ind*; **the noise reached a ~** шум нарастáл крещéндо.
crescent ['krɛsnt] *n* (*shape*) полумéсяц; (*street*) серпообрáзная ýлица.
cress [krɛs] *n* кресс-салáт.
crest [krɛst] *n* (*of hill*) грéбень* *m*; (*of bird*) хохолóк*, гребешóк; (*coat of arms*) герб.
crestfallen ['krɛstfɔ:lən] *adj* удручённый* (удручён); **he looked ~** у негó был удручённый вид.
Crete [kri:t] *n* Крит.
crevasse [krɪ'væs] *n* рассéлина *or* расщéлина (*в леднике́*).
crevice ['krɛvɪs] *n* щель *f*.
crew [kru:] *n* (*NAUT, AVIAT*) экипáж; (*TV, CINEMA*) съёмочная грýппа; (*gang*) компáния.
crew cut *n* ёжик; **to have a ~~** стри́чься (постри́чься* *perf*) под ёжик.
crew neck *n* вы́рез под гóрло.
crib [krɪb] *n* (*cot*) дéтская кровáтка*; (*REL*) я́сли *pl* ◆ *vt* (*inf*) сдувáть (сдуть* *perf*).
cribbage ['krɪbɪdʒ] *n* кри́ббидж.
crick [krɪk] *n* (*in back*) болéзненный спазм; **~ in the neck** вы́вих шéйного позвонкá.
cricket ['krɪkɪt] *n* (*game*) кри́кет; (*insect*) сверчóк*.
cricketer ['krɪkɪtə'] *n* игрóк* в кри́кет.
crime [kraɪm] *n* (*also fig*) преступлéние; (*illegal activity*) престýпность *f*; **petty ~** мéлкое хулигáнство.
Crimea [kraɪ'mɪə] *n*: **the ~** Крым.
crime wave *n* волнá* престýпности.
criminal ['krɪmɪnl] *n* престýпник*(-ица) ◆ *adj* (*illegal*) кримина́льный, уголóвный; (*morally wrong*) престýпный*; **~ law** уголóвное прáво; **C~ Investigation Department** Уголóвный ро́зыск.
criminal code *n* уголóвный кóдекс.
crimp [krɪmp] *vt* (*fabric*) гофрировáть *(impf/perf)*; (*pastry*) защи́пывать (защипнýть *perf*); (*hair*) завивáть (зави́ть* *perf*).
crimson ['krɪmzn] *adj* мали́новый, тёмно-крáсный*.
cringe [krɪndʒ] *vi* съёживаться (съёжиться *perf*).
crinkle ['krɪŋkl] *vt* мять* (измя́ть* *perf*).
cripple ['krɪpl] *n* калéка *m/f* ◆ *vt* (*person*) калéчить (искалéчить *perf*); (*ship, plane*) повреждáть (повреди́ть* *perf*); (*production, exports*) наноси́ть* (нанести́* *perf*) вред *+dat*; **~d with rheumatism** искалéченный ревмати́змом.
crippling ['krɪplɪŋ] *adj* (*disease*) ведýщий* к инвали́дности; (*taxation, debts*) разори́тельный (разори́телен).
crises ['kraɪsi:z] *npl of* **crisis**.
crisis ['kraɪsɪs] (*pl* **crises**) *n* кри́зис.
crisp [krɪsp] *adj* (*vegetables*) хрустя́щий*; (*weather*) свéжий* (свеж); (*reply*) чёткий* (чёток).
crisps [krɪsps] *npl* (*BRIT*) чи́псы *pl*.
crisscross ['krɪskrɔs] *adj* перекрёстный ◆ *vt* пересекáть (пересéчь* *perf*).
criteria [kraɪ'tɪərɪə] *npl of* **criterion**.
criterion [kraɪ'tɪərɪən] (*pl* **criteria**) *n* критéрий.
critic ['krɪtɪk] *n* кри́тик.
critical ['krɪtɪkl] *adj* (*time, situation, analysis*) крити́ческий*; (*person, opinion*) крити́чный* (крити́чен); **he is ~** (*MED*) он в крити́ческом состоя́нии; **she is ~ of him/the system** она крити́чна по отношéнию к немý/систéме.
critically ['krɪtɪklɪ] *adv* (*speak, look*) крити́чески; (*ill*) опáсно; (*examine*) крити́чно.
criticism ['krɪtɪsɪzəm] *n* кри́тика; (*of book, play*) крити́ческий* разбóр.
criticize ['krɪtɪsaɪz] *vt* (*find fault with*) критиковáть *(impf)*.
critique [krɪ'ti:k] *n* крити́ческий* анáлиз.
croak [krəuk] *vi* (*frog*) квáкать *(impf)*; (*bird*) кáркать *(impf)*; (*person*) хрипéть *(impf)* ◆ *n* (*see vi*) квáканье; кáрканье; хрип.
Croatia [krəu'eɪʃə] *n* Хорвáтия.
Croatian [krəu'eɪʃən] *n* (*person*) хорвáт(ка*) ◆ *adj* хорвáтский*.
crochet ['krəuʃeɪ] *n* вязáние крючкóм.
crock [krɔk] *n* гли́няный кувши́н; (*inf: also:* **old ~**) развáлина.
crockery ['krɔkərɪ] *n* гли́няная *or* фая́нсовая посýда.
crocodile ['krɔkədaɪl] *n* крокоди́л.
crocus ['krəukəs] *n* шафрáн.
croft [krɔft] *n* (*BRIT: small farm*) хýтор*.
crofter ['krɔftə'] *n* (*BRIT*) хуторя́нин(-нка*).

crone [krəun] *n* карга́.
crony ['krəunɪ] *n* (*inf*) дружо́к.
crook [kruk] *n* (*criminal*) жу́лик; (*of shepherd*) по́сох; **the ~ of the arm** вну́тренний* сгиб ло́ктя.
crooked ['krukɪd] *adj* криво́й* (крив); (*dishonest*) нече́стный*.
crop [krɔp] *n* (*produce grown*) (сельскохозя́йственная) культу́ра; (*amount produced*: *cereals etc*) урожа́й; (: *honey, herbs*) сбор; (*also:* **riding ~**) плеть *f*; (*of bird*) зоб* ◆ *vt* (*hair*) ко́ротко подстрига́ть (подстри́чь* *perf*); (*subj*: *animal*) щипа́ть* (*impf*)
▸ **crop up** *vi* неожи́данно возника́ть (возни́кнуть* *perf*).
crop circle *n круг непоня́тного происхожде́ния на зерново́м по́ле.*
cropper ['krɔpə^r] *n* (*inf*): **to come a ~** (*fail*) сади́ться* (сесть *perf*) в лу́жу *or* в кало́шу; (*fall*) шлёпаться (шлёпнуться *perf*).
crop spraying [-'spreɪɪŋ] *n* опры́скивание посе́вов.
croquet ['krəukeɪ] *n* (*BRIT*) кроке́т.
croquette [krə'kɛt] *n* (*CULIN*) кроке́ты *pl*.
cross [krɔs] *n* (*shape, also REL*) крест; (*mark*) кре́стик; (*BIO*) по́месь *f*; (*BOT*) гибри́д ◆ *vt* (*street, room etc*) пересека́ть (пересе́чь* *perf*), переходи́ть* (перейти́* *perf*); (*cheque*) кросси́ровать (*impf/perf*); (*BIO, BOT, also arms etc*) скре́щивать (скрести́ть* *perf*); (*thwart*: *person, plan*) препя́тствовать* (*impf*) +*dat* ◆ *adj* серди́тый ◆ *vi*: **the boat ~es from ... to ...** кора́бль плывёт из +*gen*... в +*acc*...; **to ~ o.s.** крести́ться* (перекрести́ться* *perf*); **we have a ~ed line** (*BRIT*: *TEL*) кто́-то подсоедини́лся к на́шей ли́нии; **they've got their lines** *or* **wires ~ed** (*fig*) они́ совсе́м запу́тались; **the thought did not ~ my mind** э́та мысль не приходи́ла мне в го́лову; **to be/get ~ with sb (about sth)** серди́ться (*impf*)/рассерди́ться* *perf* на кого́-н (из-за чего́-н)
▸ **cross out** *vt* вычёркивать (вы́черкнуть *perf*).
crossbar ['krɔsbɑː^r] *n* (*FOOTBALL*) перекла́дина; (*on bicycle*) попере́чная пла́нка.
crossbow ['krɔsbəu] *n* самостре́л, арбале́т.
crossbreed ['krɔsbriːd] *n* по́месь *f*.
cross-Channel ferry ['krɔs'tʃænl-] *n* паро́м че́рез Ла-Ма́нш.
crosscheck ['krɔstʃɛk] *n* перепрове́рка ◆ *vt* перепроверя́ть (перепрове́рить *perf*).
cross-country (race) ['krɔs'kʌntrɪ-] *n* бег по пересечённой ме́стности.
cross-dressing [krɔs'drɛsɪŋ] *n переодева́ние в оде́жду противополо́жного по́ла.*
cross-examination ['krɔsɪgzæmɪ'neɪʃən] *n* перекрёстный допро́с.
cross-examine ['krɔsɪg'zæmɪn] *vt* (*LAW*) подверга́ть (подве́ргнуть* *perf*) перекрёстному допро́су.
cross-eyed ['krɔsaɪd] *adj* косогла́зый.
crossfire ['krɔsfaɪə^r] *n* перекрёстный ого́нь* *m*; **to get caught in the ~** (*MIL*) оказа́ться (*perf*) под перекрёстным огнём; (*fig*) оказа́ться (*perf*) ме́жду двух огне́й.
crossing ['krɔsɪŋ] *n* (*sea passage*) перепра́ва; (*also:* **pedestrian ~**) перехо́д.
crossing guard *n* (*US*) *регулиро́вщик движе́ния, кото́рый обеспе́чивает безопа́сный перехо́д у́лицы шко́льниками.*
cross-purposes ['krɔs'pəːpəsɪz] *npl*: **to be at ~ with sb** не находи́ть* (*impf*) о́бщего языка́ с кем-н; **we're (talking) at ~** мы говори́м о ра́зных веща́х.
cross-question ['krɔs'kwɛstʃən] *vt* подверга́ть (подве́ргнуть *perf*) перекрёстному допро́су.
cross-reference ['krɔs'rɛfrəns] *n* перекрёстная ссы́лка*.
crossroads ['krɔsrəudz] *n* перекрёсток*.
cross section *n* (*of population*) про́филь *m*; (*of object*) попере́чное сече́ние; (*BIO*) попере́чный разре́з *or* срез.
crosswalk ['krɔswɔːk] *n* (*US*) перехо́д.
crosswind ['krɔswɪnd] *n* боково́й ве́тер*.
crosswise ['krɔswaɪz] *adv* кре́ст-на́крест.
crossword ['krɔswəːd] *n* кроссво́рд.
crotch [krɔtʃ] *n* (*ANAT*) проме́жность *f*; **the trousers are tight in the ~** брю́ки жмут в шагу́.
crotchet ['krɔtʃɪt] *n* четвертна́я но́та.
crotchety ['krɔtʃɪtɪ] *adj* раздражи́тельный* (раздражи́телен), брюзгли́вый (брюзгли́в).
crouch [krautʃ] *vi* (*person, animal*) приседа́ть (присе́сть* *perf*).
croup [kruːp] *n* круп.
croupier ['kruːpɪə^r] *n* крупье́ *m ind*.
crouton ['kruːtɔn] *n* грено́к*.
crow [krəu] *n* (*bird*) воро́на; (*of cock*) кукаре́канье ◆ *vi* (*cock*) кукаре́кать (*impf*); (*fig*: *boast*): **to ~ about** хва́статься (*impf*) +*instr*.
crowbar ['krəubɑː^r] *n* лом*.
crowd [kraud] *n* толпа́*; (*clique*) компа́ния ◆ *vt* (*fill*) заполня́ть (запо́лнить *perf*); (*cram*): **to ~ sb/sth into sth** набива́ть (наби́ть* *perf*) что-н кем-н/чем-н ◆ *vi* (*gather*): **to ~ round** толпи́ться (*impf*); (*cram*): **to ~ into sth** набива́ться (наби́ться* *perf*) в что-н; **~s of people** то́лпы люде́й.
crowded ['kraudɪd] *adj* (*overpopulated*) перенаселённый (перенаселён); (*full*): **the room was ~** ко́мната была́ полна́ наро́ду; **~ with** по́лный* +*gen*, напо́лненный +*instr*.

* marks translations which have irregular inflections. The Russian-English side of the dictionary gives inflectional information.

crowd scene *n* массóвка*, мáссовая сцéна.
crown [kraun] *n* (*of monarch*) корóна; (*of head*) макýшка; (*of hill*) вершѝна; (*of tooth*) корóнка*; (*of hat*) тулья́* ◆ *vt* (*monarch*) короновáть *(impf/perf)*; (*tooth*) стáвить* (постáвить* *perf*) корóнку на *+acc*; (*fig*) венчáть (увенчáть *perf*); **the C~** (*monarchy*) корóна; **and to ~ it all ...** (*fig*) и в довершéние всегó ....
crown court *n* (*BRIT*) корóнный суд (*в отлѝчие от магистратýр с постоя́нными судья́ми и прися́жными заседáтелями*).
crowning ['krauniŋ] *adj* блистáтельный*.
crown jewels *npl* королéвские регáлии *fpl*.
crown prince *n* кронпрѝнц.
crow's-feet ['krəuzfi:t] *npl* гусѝные лáпки* *fpl*, морщѝнки* *fpl* (*в уголкáх глаз*).
crow's-nest ['krəuznɛst] *n* (*NAUT*) ворóнье гнездó.
crucial ['kru:ʃl] *adj* (*event, moment*) решáющий*; (*work*) вáжный* (вáжен); **~ to** вáжный (вáжен) для *+gen*.
crucifix ['kru:sɪfɪks] *n* распя́тие.
crucifixion [kru:sɪ'fɪkʃən] *n* распя́тие на кресте́.
crucify ['kru:sɪfaɪ] *vt* (*also fig*) распинáть (распя́ть* *perf*).
crude [kru:d] *adj* (*materials*) сырóй; (*fig*: *basic*) примитѝвный* (примитѝвен); (: *vulgar*) грýбый* (груб).
crude (oil) *n* сырáя нефть *f*.
cruel ['kruəl] *adj* жестóкий* (жестóк).
cruelty ['kruəltɪ] *n* жестóкость *f*.
cruet ['kru:ɪt] *n* судóк*.
cruise [kru:z] *n* (*on ship*) круѝз ◆ *vi* (*ship, aircraft*) крейсѝровать *(impf)*.
cruise missile *n* управля́емый снаря́д с я́дерной боеголóвкой.
cruiser ['kru:zə'] *n* (*motorboat*) кáтер*; (*warship*) крéйсер*.
cruising speed ['kru:zɪŋ-] *n* срéдняя (экономѝческая) скóрость *f*.
crumb [krʌm] *n* (*of bread, cake*) крóшка*; (*fig*: *of information*) обры́вок; (: *of sympathy, hope*) крупѝца.
crumble ['krʌmbl] *vt* (*bread, biscuit etc*) крошѝть* (раскрошѝть* *perf*) ◆ *vi* осыпáться (осы́паться* *perf*); (*fig*) рýшиться *(impf)*, рýхнуть *(perf)*.
crumbly ['krʌmblɪ] *adj* рассы́пчатый.
crummy ['krʌmɪ] *adj* (*inf*) задрѝпанный.
crumpet ['krʌmpɪt] *n* ≈ блин.
crumple ['krʌmpl] *vt* мять* (измя́ть* *perf*).
crunch [krʌntʃ] *vt* (*food etc*) грызть* (сгрызть* *perf*) ◆ *vi* (*stones, glass etc*) скрипéть* *(impf)*, хрустéть* *(impf)* ◆ *n* (*fig*): **the ~** критѝческий* *or* решáющий* момéнт; **if it comes to the ~** éсли настýпит критѝческий момéнт; **when the ~ comes** когдá настýпит критѝческий момéнт.
crunchy ['krʌntʃɪ] *adj* хрустя́щий*.
crusade [kru:'seɪd] *n* (*campaign*) крестóвый похóд ◆ *vi* (*fig*): **to ~ for/against** борóться* *(impf)* за *+acc*/прóтив *+gen*.
crusader [kru:'seɪdə'] *n* крестонóсец*; (*fig*): **~ (for)** бoрéц* (за *+acc*).
crush [krʌʃ] *vt* (*squash*) выжимáть (вы́жать* *perf*); (: *grapes*) давѝть* *(impf)*; (*crumple*) мять* (смять* *perf*); (*grind*: *garlic, ice*) размельчáть (размельчѝть *perf*); (*defeat*) сокрушáть (сокрушѝть *perf*); (*devastate*) уничтожáть (уничтóжить *perf*) ◆ *n* (*crowd*) дáвка; (*infatuation*): **to have a ~ on sb** сходѝть* (сойтѝ* *perf*) с умá по комý-н; (*drink*): **lemon ~** лимóнный напѝток*.
crush barrier *n* (*BRIT*) ограждéние (*сдéрживающее толпý*).
crushing ['krʌʃɪŋ] *adj* сокрушѝтельный*.
crust [krʌst] *n* кóрка*; (*of earth*) корá.
crustacean [krʌs'teɪʃən] *n* ракообрáзное *nt adj* (живóтное).
crusty ['krʌstɪ] *adj* хрустя́щий*; (*fig*) раздражѝтельный* (раздражѝтелен); (*bread*) кóрочкой; (*old gentleman*) жёлчный.
crutch [krʌtʃ] *n* (*MED*) косты́ль* *m*; (*support, TECH*) опóра; (*ANAT, in garment*) *see* **crotch**.
crux [krʌks] *n* суть *f*.
cry [kraɪ] *vi* (*weep*) плáкать* *(impf)*; (*also*: **~ out**) кричáть* *(impf)* ◆ *n* крик; **what are you ~ing about?** почемý Вы плáчете?; **he began to ~** он заплáкал *or* нáчал плáкать; **to ~ for help** звать* (позвáть* *perf*) на пóмощь; **she cried out suddenly in pain** онá вскрѝкнула от бóли; **she had a good ~** онá вы́плакалась; **it's a far ~ from ...** (*fig*) э́то сѝльно отличáется от *+gen*
▸ **cry off** *vi* (*inf*) откáзываться (отказáться* *perf*).
crying ['kraɪɪŋ] *adj* (*fig*: *need*) óстрый*; **it's a ~ shame** э́то весьмá прискóрбно.
crypt [krɪpt] *n* склеп.
cryptic ['krɪptɪk] *adj* (*remark*) загáдочный* (загáдочен); (*clue*) зашифрóванный.
crystal ['krɪstl] *n* гóрный хрустáль* *m*; (*glass*) хрустáль*; (*CHEM*) кристáлл.
crystal clear *adj* (*water, air*) кристáльно чѝстый*; (*sound, idea*) совершéнно я́сный.
crystallize ['krɪstəlaɪz] *vt* (*opinion etc*) формировáть (сформировáть *perf*) ◆ *vi* (*sugar etc*) кристаллизовáться *(impf/perf)*; **~d fruits** (*BRIT*) засáхаренные фрýкты.
CSA *n abbr* = *Confederate States of America*.
CSC *n abbr* (= *Civil Service Commission*) Комѝссия граждáнской слýжбы.
CSE *n abbr* (*BRIT*: *formerly*: = *Certificate of Secondary Education*) аттестáт о срéднем образовáнии.
CS gas *n* (*BRIT*) слезоточѝвый газ*.
CST *abbr* (*US*) = *Central Standard Time*.
CT *abbr* (*US*: *POST*) = *Connecticut*.
ct *abbr* = **carat**.
CTC *n abbr* (*BRIT*: = *city technology college*)

те́хникум.
cu. *abbr* (= **cubic**) куб.= *куби́ческий**.
cub [kʌb] *n* детёныш; (*also:* ~ **scout**) *член мла́дшего отря́да бойска́утов*.
Cuba ['kju:bə] *n* Ку́ба.
Cuban ['kju:bən] *adj* куби́нский* ◆ *n* куби́нец*(-нка*).
cubbyhole ['kʌbɪhəul] *n* закуто́к*.
cube [kju:b] *n* (*also MATH*) куб* ◆ *vt* возводи́ть* (возвести́* *perf*) в куб; **the ~ of 4 is 64** 4 в ку́бе равня́ется 64.
cube root *n* куби́ческий* ко́рень* *m*.
cubic ['kju:bɪk] *adj* куби́ческий*; ~ **metre** *etc* куби́ческий* метр *etc*.
cubic capacity *n* куби́ческий* объём.
cubicle ['kju:bɪkl] *n* (*at pool*) каби́нка*; (*in hospital*) бокс.
cuckoo ['kuku:] *n* куку́шка*.
cuckoo clock *n* часы́ *pl* с куку́шкой.
cucumber ['kju:kʌmbə'] *n* огуре́ц*.
cud [kʌd] *n*: **to chew the** ~ жева́ть* (*impf*) жва́чку.
cuddle ['kʌdl] *vt* обнима́ть (обня́ть* *perf*) ◆ *vi* обнима́ться (обня́ться* *perf*) ◆ *n* ла́ска.
cuddly ['kʌdlɪ] *adj* ми́ленький*.
cudgel ['kʌdʒl] *n* дуби́на ◆ *vt*: **to ~ one's brains about sth** лома́ть (*impf*) го́лову над чем-н.
cue [kju:] *n* (*SNOOKER etc*) кий*; (*THEAT etc*) ре́плика.
cuff [kʌf] *n* (*of sleeve*) манже́та; (*US*: *of trousers*) отворо́т; (*blow*) шлепо́к* ◆ *vt* (*hit*) шлёпать (шлёпнуть *perf*); **off the** ~ экспро́мтом.
cuff links *npl* за́понки* *fpl*.
cu. in. *abbr* (= *cubic inches*) куби́ческие дю́ймы.
cuisine [kwɪ'zi:n] *n* ку́хня* (*ку́шанья*).
cul-de-sac ['kʌldəsæk] *n* (*road*) тупи́к*.
culinary ['kʌlɪnərɪ] *adj* кулина́рный.
cull [kʌl] *vt* (*story, idea*) отбира́ть (отобра́ть* *perf*); (*animals*) отбрако́вывать (отбракова́ть *perf*) ◆ *n* отбрако́вка*.
culminate ['kʌlmɪneɪt] *vi*: **to ~ in** заверша́ться (заверши́ться *perf*) +*instr*.
culmination [kʌlmɪ'neɪʃən] *n* кульмина́ция.
culottes [kju:'lɔts] *npl* ю́бка-брю́ки *pl*.
culpable ['kʌlpəbl] *adj*: ~ **(of)** вино́вный (вино́вен) (в +*prp*).
culprit ['kʌlprɪt] *n* (*of crime*) вино́вник(-вница).
cult [kʌlt] *n* (*also REL*) культ.
cult figure *n* куми́р.
cultivate ['kʌltɪveɪt] *vt* (*crop, feeling*) культиви́ровать (*impf*); (*land*) возде́лывать (*impf*); (*person*) обха́живать (*impf*).
cultivation [kʌltɪ'veɪʃən] *n* (*AGR*) культива́ция.
cultural ['kʌltʃərəl] *adj* культу́рный*.
culture ['kʌltʃə'] *n* (*also BIO*) культу́ра.
cultured ['kʌltʃəd] *adj* (*individual*) культу́рный; (*pearl*) культиви́рованный.
cumbersome ['kʌmbəsəm] *adj* (*object, process*) громо́здкий* (громо́здок).
cumin ['kʌmɪn] *n* (*spice*) тмин*.
cumulative ['kju:mjulətɪv] *adj* (*effect, result*) сумма́рный; (*process*) нараста́ющий.
cunning ['kʌnɪŋ] *n* хи́трость *f* ◆ *adj* (*crafty*) хи́трый* (хитёр).
cunt [kʌnt] *n* (*inf!*) пизда́ (*!*)
cup [kʌp] *n* ча́шка*; (*as prize*) ку́бок*; (*of bra*) ча́шечка*; **a ~ of tea** ча́шка* ча́я.
cupboard ['kʌbəd] *n* шкаф*; (*built-in*) стенно́й шкаф*.
cup final *n* (*BRIT*: *SPORT*) фина́л ро́зыгрыша ку́бка.
cupful ['kʌpful] *n* по́лная ча́шка*.
cupid ['kju:pɪd] *n* (*figurine*) пу́тти *pl ind*; **C~** Купидо́н, Аму́р.
cupidity [kju:'pɪdɪtɪ] *n* а́лчность *f*.
cupola ['kju:pələ] *n* ку́пол*.
cuppa ['kʌpə] (*inf*) *n* ча́шка ча́я.
cup tie *n* (*BRIT*: *SPORT*) ку́бковый матч.
curable ['kjuərəbl] *adj* излечи́мый (излечи́м).
curate ['kjuərɪt] *n* вика́рий.
curator [kjuə'reɪtə'] *n* (*in museum*) храни́тель *m*.
curb [kə:b] *vt* (*powers, expenditure*) обу́здывать (обузда́ть *perf*); (*person*) сде́рживать (сдержа́ть* *perf*) ◆ *n* ограниче́ние; (*US*) бордю́р (*тротуа́ра*).
curd cheese [kə:d-] *n* творо́г*.
curdle ['kə:dl] *vi* (*milk*) свёртываться (сверну́ться *perf*).
curds [kə:dz] *npl* простоква́ша *fsg*.
cure [kjuə'] *vt* (*illness, patient*) выле́чивать (вы́лечить *perf*); (*CULIN*) обраба́тывать (обрабо́тать *perf*); (*problem*) устраня́ть (устрани́ть *perf*) ◆ *n* (*MED*) лека́рство; (*solution*) сре́дство; **to be ~d of sth** вы́лечиться (*perf*) *or* излечи́ться* (*perf*) от чего́-н.
cure-all ['kjuərɔ:l] *n* (*also fig*) панаце́я.
curfew ['kə:fju:] *n* коменда́нтский* час*.
curio ['kjuərɪəu] *n* ре́дкая антиква́рная ве́щь* *f*.
curiosity [kjuərɪ'ɔsɪtɪ] *n* (*see adj*) любозна́тельность *f*, любопы́тство.
curious ['kjuərɪəs] *adj* (*interested*) любозна́тельный* (любозна́телен); (*nosy, strange*) любопы́тный* (любопы́тен); **I'm ~ about him** он меня́ интересу́ет.
curiously ['kjuərɪəslɪ] *adv* стра́нно; (*inquisitively*) с любопы́тством; ~ **enough, ...** как ни стра́нно, ...
curl [kə:l] *n* (*of hair*) ло́кон, зави́ток; (*of smoke etc*) кольцо́* ◆ *vt* (*hair*: *loosely*) завива́ть (зави́ть* *perf*); (: *tightly*) закру́чивать (закрути́ть* *perf*) ◆ *vi* (*hair*) ви́ться* (*impf*); (*smoke*) клуби́ться (*impf*)
▸ **curl up** *vi* свора́чиваться (сверну́ться *perf*); **to ~ up into a ball** свора́чиваться (сверну́ться *perf*) клубко́м.

* marks translations which have irregular inflections. The Russian-English side of the dictionary gives inflectional information.

curler ['kə:lə'] *n* бигуди́ *ntpl ind*; (*SPORT*) игро́к в ке́рлинг.
curlew ['kə:lu:] *n* большо́й кроншне́п.
curling ['kə:lɪŋ] *n* (*SPORT*) ке́рлинг (*игра́ на льду, в кото́рой игроки́ сбива́ют цель при по́мощи специа́льных камне́й*).
curling tongs (*US* **curling irons**) *npl* щипцы́ *pl* для зави́вки.
curly ['kə:lɪ] *adj* вью́щийся; (*tightly curled*) кудря́вый.
currant ['kʌrnt] *n* (*dried grape*) изю́минка; (*bush, fruit*) сморо́динка; **~s** (*dried grapes*) изю́м *msg*; (*fruit*) сморо́дина *fsg*.
currency ['kʌrnsɪ] *n* (*system*) де́ньги *pl* в обраще́нии; (*money*) валю́та; **to gain ~** (*fig*) получа́ть (получи́ть *perf*) распростране́ние.
current ['kʌrnt] *n* (*of air, water*) струя́*, пото́к; (*ELEC*) ток*; (*of opinion*) направле́ние ◆ *adj* (*present*) теку́щий*, совреме́нный; (*accepted*) общепри́нятый; **direct/alternating ~** постоя́нный/переме́нный ток*; **the ~ issue of a magazine** теку́щий* но́мер* журна́ла; **this word is in ~ use** э́то сло́во явля́ется общепри́нятым.
current account *n* (*BRIT*) теку́щий* счёт*.
current affairs *npl* теку́щие собы́тия *ntpl*.
current assets *npl* теку́щие оборо́тные акти́вы *mpl*.
current liabilities *npl* теку́щие обяза́тельства *ntpl*.
currently ['kʌrntlɪ] *adv* в да́нный *or* настоя́щий моме́нт.
curricula [kə'rɪkjulə] *npl of* **curriculum**.
curriculum [kə'rɪkjuləm] (*pl* **~s** *or* **curricula**) *n* (*SCOL*) уче́бный план.
curriculum vitae [-'vi:taɪ] *n* автобиогра́фия (*обы́чно пи́шущаяся при поступле́нии на учёбу и́ли рабо́ту* *).
curry ['kʌrɪ] *n блю́до, с ке́рри* ◆ *vt*: **to ~ favour with** зае́скивать (*impf*) пе́ред *+instr*.
curry powder *n* порошо́к* ке́рри *nt ind*.
curse [kə:s] *vi* (*swear*) руга́ться (*impf*) ◆ *vt* проклина́ть (прокля́сть* *perf*) ◆ *n* (*spell, problem*) прокля́тие; (*swearword*) руга́тельство.
cursor ['kə:sə'] *n* ку́рсор.
cursory ['kə:sərɪ] *adj* (*glance, examination*) бе́глый.
curt [kə:t] *adj* ре́зкий*.
curtail [kə:'teɪl] *vt* (*freedom, rights*) ограни́чивать (ограни́чить *perf*); (*expenses, visit*) сокраща́ть (сократи́ть* *perf*).
curtain ['kə:tn] *n* (*light*) занаве́ска*; (*heavy, also THEAT*) за́навес; **to draw the ~s** (*together*) задёргивать (задёрнуть *perf*) занаве́ски; (*apart*) отдёргивать (отдёрнуть *perf*) занаве́ски.
curtain call *n* (*THEAT*) покло́ны *mpl*; **they took four ~ ~s** их вызыва́ли четы́ре ра́за.
curts(e)y ['kə:tsɪ] *vi* де́лать (сде́лать *perf*)争 ревера́нс, приседа́ть (присе́сть* *perf*) в ревера́нсе ◆ *n* ревера́нс.
curvature ['kə:vətʃə'] *n* (*of the earth*) кривизна́; (*of curve*) изги́б; (*of spine*) искривле́ние.
curve [kə:v] *n* изги́б ◆ *vi* изгиба́ться (изогну́ться *perf*) ◆ *vt* сгиба́ть (согну́ть *perf*), изгиба́ть (изогну́ть *perf*).
curved [kə:vd] *adj* изо́гнутый, со́гнутый.
cushion ['kuʃən] *n* поду́шка* ◆ *vt* (*collision, effect*) смягча́ть (смягчи́ть *perf*); (*seat*) подкла́дывать (подложи́ть *perf*) поду́шку под *+acc*.
cushy ['kuʃɪ] *adj* (*inf*): **a ~ job** тёпленькое месте́чко*; **to have a ~ time** бить* (*impf*) баклу́ши.
cussed ['kʌsɪd] *adj* упря́мый (упря́м).
custard ['kʌstəd] *n* заварно́й крем.
custard powder *n* (*BRIT*) заварно́й крем (*порошо́к*).
custodial [kʌs'təudɪəl] *adj*: **~ care** опеку́нство; **he was given a ~ sentence** он был приговорён к тюре́мному заключе́нию.
custodian [kʌs'təudɪən] *n* попечи́тель *m*.
custody ['kʌstədɪ] *n* (*of child*) опе́ка; (*for offenders*) содержа́ние под стра́жей, заключе́ние; **to take into ~** (*suspect*) брать* (взять* *perf*) под стра́жу, аресто́вывать (арестова́ть *perf*); **he was remanded in ~** он был оста́влен под стра́жей; **in the ~ of** под опе́кой *+gen*; **the mother has ~ of the children** де́ти нахо́дятся под опе́кой ма́тери.
custom ['kʌstəm] *n* (*traditional*) тради́ция; (*convention*) обы́чай; (*habit*) привы́чка*; **we get a lot of ~ from the locals** бо́льшая часть на́ших покупа́телей *or* на́шей клиенту́ры – ме́стные жи́тели.
customary ['kʌstəmərɪ] *adj* обы́чный*, традицио́нный; **it is ~ to** при́нято *+infin*.
custom-built ['kʌstəm'bɪlt] *adj* изгото́вленный на зака́з.
customer ['kʌstəmə'] *n* (*of shop*) покупа́тель*(ница) *m(f)*; (*of small business*) клие́нт; (*of large company*) зака́зчик; **he's an awkward ~** (*inf*) он тру́дный тип.
customer profile *n* про́филь *m* покупа́теля.
customized ['kʌstəmaɪzd] *adj* изгото́вленный на зака́з.
custom-made ['kʌstəm'meɪd] *adj* изгото́вленный на зака́з.
customs ['kʌstəmz] *npl* тамо́жня *fsg*; **to go through (the) ~** проходи́ть* (пройти́* *perf*) тамо́женный досмо́тр.
Customs and Excise *n* (*BRIT*) тамо́женно-акци́зное управле́ние.
customs officer *n* тамо́женник.
cut [kʌt] (*pt, pp* **cut**) *vt* (*bread, meat*) ре́зать* (разре́зать* *perf*); (*hand, knee*) ре́зать* (поре́зать* *perf*); (*grass, hair*) стричь* (постри́чь* *perf*); (*text, spending, supply*) уре́зывать (уре́зать* *perf*); (*prices*) снижа́ть (сни́зить* *perf*); (*cloth*) крои́ть (раскрои́ть *perf*); (*inf: lecture, appointment*) прогу́ливать

(прогуля́ть *perf*) ♦ *vi* (*knife, scissors*) ре́зать* (*impf*); (*lines*) пересека́ться (пересе́чься* *perf*) ♦ *n* (*in skin*) поре́з; (*in salary, spending etc*) сниже́ние; (*of meat*) кусо́к*; (*of garment*) покро́й; (*of jewel*) отде́лка*; **she is ~ting a tooth** у неё прореза́ется зуб; **to ~ one's finger** ре́зать (поре́зать* *perf*) па́лец*; **to get one's hair ~** стри́чься* (постри́чься* *perf*); **to ~ sth short** прерыва́ть (прерва́ть* *perf*) что-н; **to ~ sb short** обрыва́ть (оборва́ть* *perf*) кого́-н; **to ~ sb dead** соверше́нно игнори́ровать (*impf/perf*) кого́-н; **cold ~s** (*US*) холо́дные мясны́е заку́ски*; **we had a power ~** у нас отключи́лось электри́чество

▸ **cut back** *vt* (*plants*) подреза́ть (подре́зать* *perf*); (*production, expenditure*) сокраща́ть (сократи́ть* *perf*)

▸ **cut down** *vt* (*tree*) сруба́ть (сруби́ть* *perf*); (*consumption*) сокраща́ть (сократи́ть* *perf*); **to ~ sb down to size** (*fig*) поста́вить* (*perf*) кого́-н на ме́сто

▸ **cut down on** *vt fus*: **to ~ down on smoking/drinking** ме́ньше кури́ть (*impf*)/пить (*impf*)

▸ **cut in** *vi* (*AUT*) пересека́ть (пересе́чь* *perf*) путь*; (*interrupt*): **to ~ in on** вме́шиваться (вмеша́ться *perf*) в *+acc*

▸ **cut off** *vt* (*also fig*) отреза́ть (отре́зать* *perf*); (*water, electricity*) отключа́ть (отключи́ть *perf*); (*food*) прекраща́ть (прекрати́ть* *perf*) снабже́ние *+gen*; (*TEL*) разъединя́ть (разъедини́ть *perf*); **we've been ~ off** (*TEL*) нас разъедини́ли

▸ **cut out** *vt* (*remove*) выреза́ть (вы́резать* *perf*); (*stop*) прекраща́ть (прекрати́ть* *perf*)

▸ **cut up** *vt* разреза́ть (разре́зать* *perf*); **it really ~ me up** (*inf*) э́то о́чень подкоси́ло меня́; **she still feels ~ up about her sister's death** (*inf*) она́ всё ещё не опра́вилась по́сле сме́рти свое́й сестры́.

cut-and-dried ['kʌtən'draɪd] *adj* (*answer, solution*) гото́вый.

cut-and-dry ['kʌtən'draɪ] *adj* = **cut-and-dried**.

cutaway ['kʌtəweɪ] *n* (*coat*) визи́тка*; (*of machine, engine etc*): **a ~ model** моде́ль *f* в разре́зе; (*CINEMA, TV*) вста́вка*.

cutback ['kʌtbæk] *n* сокраще́ние.

cute [kju:t] *adj* (*sweet*) ми́лый (мил), преле́стный* (преле́стен); (*clever*) у́мный (умён).

cut glass *n* гранёное стекло́*.

cuticle ['kju:tɪkl] *n* (*of nail*) ко́жица; **~ remover** *жи́дкость и́ли крем размягча́ющий и уничтожа́ющий ко́жицу вокру́г ногтево́й лу́нки*.

cutlery ['kʌtlərɪ] *n* столо́вый прибо́р.

cutlet ['kʌtlɪt] *n* котле́та.

cutoff ['kʌtɔf] *n* (*also:* **~ point**) преде́л ♦ *cpd*: **~ date** преде́льный срок.

cutoff switch *n* автомати́ческий* выключа́тель *m*.

cutout ['kʌtaut] *n* (*switch*) автомати́ческий* выключа́тель *m*; (*shape*) вы́резанная фигу́ра; (*paper figure*) апплика́ция.

cut-price ['kʌt'praɪs] (*US* **cut-rate**) *adj* по сни́женной цене́.

cut-rate ['kʌt'reɪt] *adj* (*US*) = **cut-price**.

cutthroat ['kʌtθrəut] *n* головоре́з* ♦ *adj* (*fig*) беспоща́дный; **~ competition** жёсткая конкуре́нция.

cutting ['kʌtɪŋ] *adj* (*edge*) о́стрый*; (*remark etc*) язви́тельный* ♦ *n* (*BRIT: PRESS*) вы́резка*; (*: RAIL*) вы́емка*; (*from plant*) черено́к*.

cutting edge *n* остриё.

cuttlefish ['kʌtlfɪʃ] *n* карака́тица.

CV *n abbr* = **curriculum vitae**.

C & W *n abbr* = **country and western (music)**.

c.w.o. *abbr* (*COMM: = cash with order*) вы́дача това́ра по нали́чному расчёту.

cwt. *abbr* = **hundredweight**.

cyanide ['saɪənaɪd] *n* циа́н, циа́нистый ка́лий.

cybernetics [saɪbə'nɛtɪks] *n* киберне́тика.

cyclamen ['sɪkləmən] *n* (*BOT*) цикламе́н.

cycle ['saɪkl] *n* (*bicycle*) велосипе́д; (*series, also TECH*) цикл ♦ *vi* е́здить* (*impf*) на велосипе́де.

cycle race *n* велого́нка*.

cycle rack *n* *металли́ческая ра́ма для стоя́нки велосипе́дов*.

cycling ['saɪklɪŋ] *n* езда́ на велосипе́де; (*in competition*) велоспо́рт; **to go on a ~ holiday** (*BRIT*) е́хать (пое́хать* *perf*) в о́тпуск на велосипе́де.

cyclist ['saɪklɪst] *n* велосипеди́ст.

cyclone ['saɪkləun] *n* цикло́н.

cygnet ['sɪgnɪt] *n* (*ZOOL*) лебедёнок*.

cylinder ['sɪlɪndə'] *n* (*also TECH*) цили́ндр; (*of gas*) балло́н; **a five ~ engine** пятицили́ндровый дви́гатель *m*.

cylinder head *n* кры́шка* цили́ндра.

cylinder-head gasket ['sɪlɪndəhɛd-] *n* прокла́дка* кры́шки цили́ндра.

cymbals ['sɪmblz] *npl* (*MUS*) таре́лки* *fpl*.

cynic ['sɪnɪk] *n* ци́ник.

cynical ['sɪnɪkl] *adj* цини́чный* (цини́чен).

cynicism ['sɪnɪsɪzəm] *n* цини́зм.

CYO *n abbr* (*US*) = *Catholic Youth Organization*.

cypress ['saɪprɪs] *n* (*tree*) кипари́с.

Cypriot ['sɪprɪət] *adj* ки́прский ♦ *n* киприо́т(ка*).

Cyprus ['saɪprəs] *n* Кипр.

cyst [sɪst] *n* киста́.

cystitis [sɪs'taɪtɪs] *n* цисти́т.

CZ *n abbr* (*US*) = *Canal Zone*.

czar [zɑ:'] *n* царь *m*.

Czech [tʃɛk] *adj* че́шский* ♦ *n* чех (че́шка*); (*LING*) че́шский* язы́к*.

Czech Republic *n* Че́шская Респу́блика.

* marks translations which have irregular inflections. The Russian-English side of the dictionary gives inflectional information.

~ D, d ~

D, d [di:] *n* (*letter*) *4-ая бу́ква англи́йского алфави́та*; (*SCOL*) ≈ неудовлетвори́тельно.
D [di:] *n* (*MUS*) ре.
D *abbr* (*US*: *POL*) = **democrat(ic)**.
d *abbr* (*BRIT*: *formerly*) = **penny**.
d. *abbr* = *died*.
DA *n abbr* (*US*) = **district attorney**.
dab [dæb] *vt* (*eyes, wound*) просу́шивать (просуши́ть *perf*); (*paint, cream*) наноси́ть* (нанести́* *perf*) ◆ *n* мазо́к*; **she's a ~ hand at sth/doing** она́ до́ка в чём-н/+*infin*
▸ **dab at** *vt fus* просу́шивать (просуши́ть *perf*).
dabble ['dæbl] *vi*: **to ~ in** (*politics, antiques etc*) балова́ться (*impf*) +*instr*.
dachshund ['dækshund] *n* та́кса.
dad [dæd] *n* (*inf*) па́па *m*, па́почка* *m*.
daddy ['dædɪ] *n* (*inf*) = **dad**.
daddy-longlegs [dædɪ'lɔŋlɛgz] *n* (*inf*) долгоно́жка*.
daffodil ['dæfədɪl] *n* нарци́сс.
daft [dɑ:ft] *adj* (*ideas*) дура́цкий*; (*person*) чо́кнутый, ненорма́льный; **to be ~ about sb/sth** рехну́ться (*perf*) на ком-н/чём-н.
dagger ['dægəʳ] *n* кинжа́л; **to be at ~s drawn with sb** быть* (*impf*) на ножа́х с кем-н; **to look ~s at sb** пронза́ть (пронзи́ть* *perf*) кого́-н зло́бным взгля́дом.
dahlia ['deɪljə] *n* георги́н.
daily ['deɪlɪ] *adj* (*dose*) су́точный; (*routine*) повседне́вный; (*wages*) дневно́й ◆ *n* (*also:* **~ paper**) ежедне́вная газе́та; (*BRIT*: *also:* **~ help**) приходя́щая домрабо́тница ◆ *adv* ежедне́вно; **twice ~** два ра́за *or* два́жды в день.
dainty ['deɪntɪ] *adj* изя́щный* (изя́щен).
dairy ['dɛərɪ] *n* (*BRIT*: *shop*) моло́чный магази́н; (*company*) ≈ моло́чная фи́рма; (*on farm*: *for making butter*) маслоде́льня*; (: *for making cheese*) сырова́рня* ◆ *cpd* моло́чный.
dairy farm *n* моло́чная фе́рма.
dairy products *npl* моло́чные проду́кты *mpl*.
dairy store *n* (*US*) моло́чный магази́н.
dais ['deɪɪs] *n* помо́ст.
daisy ['deɪzɪ] *n* маргари́тка*.
daisywheel ['deɪzɪwi:l] *n* лепестко́вый шрифтоноси́тель *m*.
daisywheel printer *n* (*COMPUT*) лепестко́вый при́нтер.
Dakar ['dækəʳ] *n* Дака́р.
dale [deɪl] *n* (*BRIT*) доли́на.
dally ['dælɪ] *vi* болта́ться (*impf*) без де́ла; **to ~ with** (*idea, plan*) носи́ться* (*impf*) с +*instr*.
dalmatian [dæl'meɪʃən] *n* далма́тский дог.
dam [dæm] *n* (*on river*) да́мба; (*reservoir*) водохрани́лище ◆ *vt* перекрыва́ть (перекры́ть* *perf*) да́мбой.
damage ['dæmɪdʒ] *n* (*harm*) уще́рб; (*dents etc*) поврежде́ние; (*fig*) вред* ◆ *vt* (*object*) поврежда́ть (повреди́ть *perf*); (*reputation, economy*) наноси́ть (нанести́ *perf*) уро́н +*dat*; **~s** *npl* (*LAW*) компенса́ция *fsg*; **~ to property** иму́щественный уще́рб; **to pay £5,000 in ~s** выпла́чивать (вы́платить* *perf*) компенса́цию в разме́ре £5.000.
damaging ['dæmɪdʒɪŋ] *adj*: **~ (to)** вре́дный* (для +*gen*).
Damascus [də'mɑ:skəs] *n* Дама́ск.
dame [deɪm] *n* (*US*: *inf*) ба́ба; (*THEAT*) коми́ческая стару́ха; (*title*): **D~** Ле́ди *f ind*.
damn [dæm] *vt* (*condemn*) осужда́ть (осуди́ть* *perf*); (*curse at*) проклина́ть (прокля́сть* *perf*) ◆ *adj* (*inf*: *also:* **~ed**) прокля́тый ◆ *n* (*inf*): **I don't give a ~** мне плева́ть; **~ (it)!** чёрт возьми́ *or* побери́!; **~ good** (*inf*) черто́вски хоро́ший.
damnable ['dæmnəbl] *adj* отвра́тный* (отвра́тен).
damnation [dæm'neɪʃən] *n, excl* (*REL*: *also inf*) прокля́тие.
damning ['dæmɪŋ] *adj* изобличи́тельный.
damp [dæmp] *adj* (*building, wall*) сыро́й*; (*cloth*) вла́жный* ◆ *n* сы́рость *f* ◆ *vt* (*also:* **~en**: *cloth etc*) сма́чивать (смочи́ть* *perf*); (: *enthusiasm etc*) охлажда́ть (охлади́ть* *perf*).
dampcourse ['dæmpkɔ:s] *n* гидроизоля́ция.
damper ['dæmpəʳ] *n* (*MUS*) де́мпфер; (*of fire*) засло́нка*; **to put a ~ on** (*fig*: *atmosphere*) по́ртить* (испо́ртить* *perf*); (*enthusiasm*) охлажда́ть (охлади́ть* *perf*).
dampness ['dæmpnɪs] *n* сы́рость *f*.
damson ['dæmzən] *n* (*fruit*) тернosли́ва.
dance [dɑ:ns] *n* та́нец*; (*social event*) та́нцы* *mpl* ◆ *vi* танцева́ть (*impf*); **to ~ about** скака́ть* (*impf*).
dance hall *n* танцева́льный зал.
dancer ['dɑ:nsəʳ] *n* (*for pleasure*) танцо́р(ка*); (*professional*) танцо́вщик(-ица).

dancing ['dɑ:nsɪŋ] *n* тáнец.
D and C *n abbr* (*MED*: = *dilation and curettage*) расширéние шéйки мáтки и выскáбливание.
dandelion ['dændɪlaɪən] *n* одувáнчик.
dandruff ['dændrəf] *n* пéрхоть *f*.
dandy ['dændɪ] *n* дéнди *m ind*, щёголь *m* ◆ *adj* (*US*: *inf*) клáссный.
Dane [deɪn] *n* датчáнин*(-áнка*).
danger ['deɪndʒə^r] *n* опáсность *f*; **there is a ~ of** ... есть *or* существýет опáсность *+gen* ...; **"danger!"** "опáсно!"; **in/out of ~** в/вне опáсности; **he is in ~ of losing his job** емý грози́т потéря рабóты.
danger list *n*: **on the ~ ~** (*MED*) в спи́ске *or* числé óсобо тяжёлых больны́х.
dangerous ['deɪndʒrəs] *adj* опáсный* (опáсен).
dangerously ['deɪndʒrəslɪ] *adv* с ри́ском; **~ close (to)** в опáсной бли́зости (к *+dat*); **he is ~ ill** он опáсно бóлен.
danger zone *n* опáсная зóна.
dangle ['dæŋgl] *vt* болтáть *(impf) +instr* ◆ *vi* болтáться *(impf)*.
Danish ['deɪnɪʃ] *adj* дáтский* ◆ *n* (*LING*) дáтский* язы́к*; **the ~** *npl* датчáне.
Danish pastry *n* пирóжное *nt adj* по-дáтски (*с откры́той начи́нкой из фрýктов и́ли орéхов*).
dank [dæŋk] *adj* сырóй*.
Danube ['dænju:b] *n*: **the ~** Дунáй.
dapper ['dæpə^r] *adj* щеголевáтый (щеголевáт).
Dardanelles [dɑ:də'nɛlz] *npl*: **the ~** Дарданéллы *pl*.
dare [dɛə^r] *vt*: **to ~ sb to do** вызывáть (вы́звать* *perf*) когó-н *+infin* ◆ *vi*: **to ~ (to) do** сметь (посмéть *perf*) *+infin*; **I ~n't tell him** (*BRIT*) я не могý осмéлиться сказáть емý; **how ~ you say that!** как Вы смéете так говори́ть!; **I ~ say** смéю замéтить.
daredevil ['dɛədɛvl] *n* сорвиголовá* *m/f*.
Dar es Salaam ['dɑ:rɛssə'lɑ:m] *n* Дáр-эс-Салáм.
daring ['dɛərɪŋ] *adj* (*audacious*) дéрзкий* (дéрзок); (*bold*) смéлый* (смел) ◆ *n* дéрзость *f*.
dark [dɑ:k] *adj* тёмный* (тёмен); (*complexion*) смýглый*; (*fig*: *deed*) чёрный ◆ *n*: **in the ~** в темнотé; **~ blue** *etc* тёмно-си́ний* *etc*; **it is getting ~** темнéет; **it is ~** темнó; **~ chocolate** чёрный шоколáд*; **to be in the ~ about** (*fig*) быть* *(impf)* в невéдении относи́тельно *+gen*; **after ~** пóсле наступлéния темноты́.
Dark Ages *npl*: **the ~ ~** рáннее средневекóвье *ntsg*.
darken [dɑ:kn] *vt* затемня́ть (затемни́ть *perf*) ◆ *vi* (*sky, room*) темнéть (потемнéть *perf*).
dark glasses *npl* тёмные очки́ *pl*.
dark horse *n* тёмная лошáдка*.
darkly ['dɑ:klɪ] *adv* мрáчно.
darkness ['dɑ:knɪs] *n* темнотá.
darkroom ['dɑ:krum] *n* тёмная кóмната, проя́ви́тельная лаборатóрия.
darling ['dɑ:lɪŋ] *adj* (*child, spouse*) люби́мый ◆ *n* дорогóй(-áя) *m(f) adj*; (*favourite*): **he is the ~ of** он люби́мец *+gen*; **she is a ~** онá прéлесть.
darn [dɑ:n] *vt* штóпать (заштóпать *perf*).
dart [dɑ:t] *n* (*in game*) стрéлка* (*для игры́ в дартс*); (*in sewing*) вы́тачка* ◆ *vi*: **to (make a) ~ towards** бросáться (брóситься* *perf*) навстрéчу *+dat*; **to ~ along** промчáться *(perf)*; **to ~ away** умчáться *(perf)*.
dartboard ['dɑ:tbɔ:d] *n* мишéнь *f* в дáрте.
darts [dɑ:ts] *n* дарт.
dash [dæʃ] *n* (*drop*) кáпелька*; (*pinch*) щепóтка*; (*sign*) тирé *nt ind*; (*rush*) рывóк* ◆ *vt* (*throw*) швыря́ть (швырнýть *perf*); (*shatter*: *hopes*) разрушáть (разрýшить *perf*), разбивáть (разби́ть* *perf*) ◆ *vi*: **to ~ towards** рванýться *(perf)* к *+dat*; **we'll have to make a ~ for the house** мы должны́ бежáть к дóму
▸ **dash away** *vi* умчáться *(perf)*
▸ **dash off** *vi* = **dash away**.
dashboard ['dæʃbɔ:d] *n* (*AUT*) прибóрная панéль *f*.
dashing ['dæʃɪŋ] *adj* шикáрный* (шикáрен).
dastardly ['dæstədlɪ] *adj* пóдлый*, мéрзкий*.
DAT *n abbr* (= *digital audio tape*) дискретизи́рованная аудиокассéта.
data ['deɪtə] *npl* дáнные *pl adj*.
database ['deɪtəbeɪs] *n* бáза дáнных.
data capture *n* сбор дáнных.
data processing *n* обрабóтка дáнных.
data transmission *n* передáча дáнных.
date [deɪt] *n* (*day*) числó*, дáта; (*with friend*) свидáние; (*fruit*) фи́ник ◆ *vt* дати́ровать *(impf/perf)*; (*person*) встречáться *(impf)* с *+instr*; **what's the ~ today?** какóе сегóдня числó?; **~ of birth** дáта рождéния; **the closing ~ for applications is** ... срок подáчи заявлéний истекáет *+gen* ...; **to ~** на сегóдняшний* день; **out of ~** (*old-fashioned*) устарéлый (устарéл); (*expired*) просрóченный (просрóчен); **up to ~** совремéнный; **to bring up to ~** (*method*) обновля́ть (обнови́ть* *perf*); (*correspondence, information*) пополня́ть (попóлнить *perf*); (*person*) вводи́ть* (ввести́* *perf*) в курс дéла; **letter ~d 5th July** *or* (*US*) **July 5th** письмó, дати́рованное 5-ым ию́ля.
dated ['deɪtɪd] *adj* устарéлый.
dateline ['deɪtlaɪn] *n* указáние мéста и дáты (*опи́сываемого собы́тия*).
date rape *n* *изнаси́лование во врéмя свидáния*.
date stamp *n* календáрный штéмпель* *m*.
dative ['deɪtɪv] *n* (*also*: **~ case**) дáтельный падéж*.
daub [dɔ:b] *vt* размáзывать (размáзать* *perf*);

* marks translations which have irregular inflections. The Russian-English side of the dictionary gives inflectional information.

(*wall, face*): **to ~ with** мáзать* (намáзать* *perf*) *+instr*.
daughter ['dɔ:tə'] *n* дочь* *f*.
daughter-in-law ['dɔ:tərınlɔ:] *n* невéстка*, снохá*.
daunt [dɔ:nt] *vt* страшúть *(impf)*.
daunting ['dɔ:ntıŋ] *adj* устрашáющий*.
dauntless ['dɔ:ntlıs] *adj* бесстрáшный* (бесстрáшен).
dawdle ['dɔ:dl] *vi* копáться *(impf)*, возúться* *(impf)*; **to ~ over one's work** возúться* *(impf)* с рабóтой.
dawn [dɔ:n] *n* (*of day*) рассвéт; (*of period, situation*) зарá ◆ *vi* рассветáть (рассвестú* *perf*), светáть *(impf)*; (*fig*): **it ~ed on him that ...** егó осенúло, что ...; **from ~ to dusk** с рассвéта до закáта, от зари́ до зари́.
dawn chorus *n* (BRIT) *пéние птиц на рассвéте*.
day [deı] *n* (*period*) сýтки *pl*, день* *m*; (*daylight*) день*; (*working day*) рабóчий* день*; (*heyday*) врéмя *nt*; **the ~ before** наканýне; **the ~ after** на слéдующий* день; **the ~ after tomorrow** послезáвтра; **the ~ before yesterday** позавчерá; **the following ~** на слéдующий* день; **the ~ that ...** в тот день, когдá ...; **~ by ~** кáждый день; **~ after ~** изо дня́ в день; **by ~** днём; **he is paid by the ~** емý плáтят подённо; **I have a ~ off tomorrow** зáвтра у меня́ отгýл; **to work an 8 hour ~** рабóтать *(impf)* 8 часóв в день; **these ~s, in the present ~** в нáши дни, в настоя́щее врéмя.
daybook ['deıbuk] *n* (BRIT: ADMIN) журнáл.
dayboy ['deıbɔı] *n* приходя́щий ученúк* (*в интернáте*).
daybreak ['deıbreık] *n* рассвéт.
day-care centre ['deıkɛə-] *n* (BRIT) *дневнóй цéнтр по ухóду за больны́ми и престарéлыми*.
daydream ['deıdri:m] *vi* предавáться *(impf)* мечтáниям, грéзить* *(impf)* ◆ *n* мечтáние, грёза.
daygirl ['deıgə:l] *n* приходя́щая ученúца (*в интернáте*).
daylight ['deılaıt] *n* дневнóй свет*.
daylight robbery *n* грабёж средь бéла дня.
Daylight Saving Time *n* (US) лéтнее врéмя* *nt*.
day release *n*: **to be on ~ ~** *находúться на дневны́х кýрсах по повышéнию квалификáции*.
day return *n* (BRIT) обрáтный билéт (*действúтельный в течéние одногó дня*).
day shift *n* дневнáя смéна.
daytime ['deıtaım] *n* день* *m*.
day-to-day ['deıtə'deı] *adj* (*life, organization*) повседнéвный*, ежеднéвный; **on a ~ basis** ежеднéвно.
day trip *n* одноднéвная экскýрсия.
day-tripper ['deı'trıpə'] *n* *человéк на однодневной экскýрсии*.
daze [deız] *vt* (*stun*) ошеломля́ть (ошеломúть* *perf*); (*subj*: *drug*) тумáнить (затумáнить *perf*) сознáние *+dat*; (: *blow*) ошеломля́ть (ошеломúть *perf*) ◆ *n*: **in a ~** как в тумáне.
dazed [deızd] *adj* ошеломлённый.
dazzle ['dæzl] *vt* (*bewitch*) заворáживать (заворожúть *perf*); (*blind*) ослепля́ть (ослепúть* *perf*).
dazzling ['dæzlıŋ] *adj* (*also fig*) ослепúтельный* (ослепúтелен).
DC *abbr* = **direct current**; (US: POST) = *District of Columbia*.
DD *n abbr* (= *Doctor of Divinity*) ≈ дóктор богословия.
dd. *abbr* (COMM) = *delivered*.
D/D *abbr* = **direct debit**.
D-day ['di:deı] *n пéрвый день генерáльного сражéния*.
DDS *n abbr* (US: = *Doctor of Dental Surgery*) дóктор стоматолóгии.
DDT *n abbr* (= *dichlorodiphenyltrichloroethane*) ДДТ= *дихлордифенúл трихлорэтáн*.
DE *abbr* (US: POST) = *Delaware*.
DEA *n abbr* (US: = *Drug Enforcement Administration*) Управлéние по соблюдéнию закóнов о наркóтиках.
deacon ['di:kən] *n* дья́кон*.
dead [dɛd] *adj* (*person, place, flowers*) мёртвый* (мёртв); (*silence*) мёртвый*; (*arm, leg*) онемéлый; (*centre*) сáмый ◆ *adv* (*completely*) внезáпно; (*inf*: *directly*) пря́мо ◆ *npl*: **the ~** мёртвые *pl adj*; (*in an accident, war*) погúбшие *pl adj*; **the battery is ~** батарéйка сéла; **the telephone is ~** телефóн отключúлся; **to shoot sb ~** застрелúть* *(perf)* когó-н; **~ on time** тóчно вóвремя; **to stop ~** (*person*) останáвливаться (остановúться* *perf*) как вкóпанный; **~ tired** смертéльно устáлый* (устáл); **the line has gone ~** телефóн замолчáл.
dead-beat ['dɛdbi:t] *adj* смертéльно устáвший, совершéнно вы́мотанный (вы́мотан).
deaden [dɛdn] *vt* (*pain, sound*) заглушáть (заглушúть *perf*).
dead end *n* тупúк*.
dead-end ['dɛdɛnd] *adj*: **a ~ job** бесперспектúвная рабóта.
dead heat *n*: **to finish in a ~ ~** приходúть* (прийтú* *perf*) к фúнишу одновремéнно.
dead-letter office [dɛd'lɛtə-] *n* *отдéл невостребованной úли недостáвленной корреспондéнции*.
deadline ['dɛdlaın] *n* послéдний* *or* предéльный срок; **to work to a ~** рабóтать *(impf)* в рáмках ограни́ченного срóка.
deadlock ['dɛdlɔk] *n* тупúк; **the meeting ended in ~** собрáние зашлó в тупúк.
dead loss *n* (*inf*): **she is a ~ ~** онá никчёмна.
deadly ['dɛdlı] *adj* (*poison, weapon*) смертонóсный* (смертонóсен); (*insult*) смертéльный* (смертéлен); (*accuracy*)

ги́бельный ◆ *adv* (*dull*) смерте́льно.
deadpan ['dɛdpæn] *adj* невозмути́мый (невозмути́м).
Dead Sea *n*: **the ~ ~** Мёртвое мо́ре.
dead season *n* мёртвый сезо́н.
deaf [dɛf] *adj* (*totally*) глухо́й* (глух); (*partially*) туго́ухий (туго́ух); **to turn a ~ ear to sth** игнори́ровать *(impf)* что-н.
deaf aid *n* (*BRIT*) слухово́й аппара́т.
deaf-and-dumb ['dɛfən'dʌm] *adj* глухонемо́й; **~ alphabet** алфави́т для глухонемы́х.
deafen [dɛfn] *vt* оглуша́ть (оглуши́ть *perf*).
deafening ['dɛfnɪŋ] *adj* оглуши́тельный* (оглуши́телен).
deaf-mute ['dɛfmju:t] *n* глухонемо́й(-а́я) *m(f) adj*.
deafness ['dɛfnɪs] *n* глухота́.
deal [di:l] (*pt, pp* **dealt**) *n* (*agreement*) сде́лка* ◆ *vt* (*blow*) наноси́ть* (нанести́* *perf*); (*cards*) сдава́ть* (сдать* *perf*); **to strike a ~ with sb** заключа́ть (заключи́ть *perf*) сде́лку с кем-н; **it's a ~!** (*inf*) по рука́м!; **he got a fair/bad ~ from them** с ним обошли́сь че́стно/ нече́стно; **a good ~ (of)** мно́го (*+gen*); **a great ~ (of)** о́чень мно́го (*+gen*)
▸ **deal in** *vt fus* (*COMM*) торгова́ть *(impf)* *+instr*; (*drugs*) занима́ться *(impf)* прода́жей *+gen*
▸ **deal with** *vt fus* (*person, company*) име́ть *(impf)* де́ло с *+instr*; (*problem*) реша́ть (реши́ть *perf*); (*subject*) занима́ться (заня́ться* *perf*) *+instr*.
dealer ['di:ləʳ] *n* (*COMM*) торго́вец*; (*also:* **art ~**) ди́лер; (*CARDS*) сдаю́щий(-ая) *m(f) adj* ка́рты, банкомёт; **drug ~** наркоделе́ц.
dealership ['di:ləʃɪp] *n* (*COMM*) аге́нтство (*по прода́же проду́кции определённой фи́рмы*).
dealings ['di:lɪŋz] *npl* (*transactions*) опера́ции *fpl*; (*in business*) дела́ *ntpl*.
dealt [dɛlt] *pt, pp of* **deal**.
dean [di:n] *n* (*REL*) настоя́тель *m*; (*SCOL*) дека́н.
dear [dɪəʳ] *adj* (*person*) дорого́й*, ми́лый*; (*expensive*) дорого́й* ◆ *n*: **(my) ~** (*to man, boy*) дорого́й (мой); (*to woman, girl*) дорога́я (моя́) ◆ *excl*: **~ me!** о, Го́споди!; **D~ Sir** уважа́емый господи́н; **D~ Madam** уважа́емая госпожа́; **D~ Mr Smith** дорого́й *or* уважа́емый ми́стер Смит; **D~ Mrs Smith** дорога́я *or* уважа́емая ми́ссис Смит.
dearly ['dɪəlɪ] *adv* (*love*) о́чень; (*pay*) до́рого.
dear money *n* (*COMM*) „дороги́е де́ньги" *pl*.
dearth [də:θ] *n*: **a ~ of** нехва́тка *+gen*, недоста́ток* *+gen*.
death [dɛθ] *n* смерть* *f*.
deathbed ['dɛθbɛd] *n*: **to be on one's ~** быть* *(impf)* на сме́ртном одре́.
death certificate *n* свиде́тельство о сме́рти.
deathly ['dɛθlɪ] *adj* (*colour*) смерте́льный*; (*silence*) мёртвый ◆ *adv* смерте́льно.
death penalty *n* сме́ртная казнь *f*.
death rate *n* сме́ртность *f*.
death row [-rəu] *n* ка́меры *fpl* сме́ртников; **prisoners on ~ ~** заключённые *pl adj*, ожида́ющие сме́ртной ка́зни.
death sentence *n* сме́ртный пригово́р.
death toll *n* число́* поги́бших.
deathtrap ['dɛθtræp] *n* ги́блое ме́сто*.
deb [dɛb] *n abbr* (*inf*) = **debutante**.
debacle [deɪ'bɑ:kl] *n* (*defeat*) разгро́м; (*failure*) фиа́ско *nt ind*.
debar [dɪ'bɑ:ʳ] *vt*: **to ~ sb from doing** лиша́ть (лиши́ть *perf*) кого́-н возмо́жности *+infin*; **to ~ sb from a club** изгоня́ть (изгна́ть* *perf*) кого́-н из клу́ба.
debase [dɪ'beɪs] *vt* (*value, quality*) снижа́ть (сни́зить* *perf*); (*person*) унижа́ть (уни́зить* *perf*); **to ~ o.s.** унижа́ться (уни́зиться* *perf*).
debatable [dɪ'beɪtəbl] *adj* спо́рный*; **it is ~ whether he can come** смо́жет ли он прийти́ – вопро́с спо́рный.
debate [dɪ'beɪt] *n* деба́ты *pl* ◆ *vt* (*topic*) обсужда́ть (обсуди́ть* *perf*); (*course of action*) обду́мывать (обду́мать *perf*); **he ~d whether to stay** он размышля́л, сле́дует ли оста́ться.
debauchery [dɪ'bɔ:tʃərɪ] *n* (*drunkenness etc*) распу́щенность *f*.
debenture [dɪ'bɛntʃəʳ] *n* (*bond*) це́нная бума́га; **~ capital** *ссу́да, обеспе́ченная фикси́рованными и́ли други́ми акти́вами компа́нии*.
debilitate [dɪ'bɪlɪteɪt] *vt* истоща́ть (истощи́ть *perf*).
debilitating [dɪ'bɪlɪteɪtɪŋ] *adj* изнури́тельный* (изнури́телен).
debit ['dɛbɪt] *n* де́бет ◆ *vt*: **to ~ a sum to sb** *or* **to sb's account** дебетова́ть *(impf/perf)* су́мму с кого́-н *or* с чего́-н счёта; *see also* **direct debit**.
debit balance *n* дебето́вый оста́ток*.
debit note *n* дебето́вое ави́зо.
debonnaire [dɛbə'nɛəʳ] *adj* гала́нтный.
debrief [di:'bri:f] *vt* опра́шивать (опроси́ть* *perf*).
debriefing [di:'bri:fɪŋ] *n* расспро́с.
debris ['dɛbri:] *n* (*rubble*) обло́мки *mpl*, разва́лины *fpl*.
debt [dɛt] *n* (*sum*) долг*; (*state of owing money*) задо́лженность *f*; **to be in ~** быть* *(impf)* в долгу́; **bad ~** безнадёжный долг*.
debt collector *n* *челове́к, взы́скивающий долги́*.
debtor ['dɛtəʳ] *n* должни́к*.
debug ['di:'bʌg] *vt* отла́живать (отла́дить* *perf*).
debunk [di:'bʌŋk] *vt* (*claim*) опроверга́ть (опрове́ргнуть *perf*); (*person, institution,*

* marks translations which have irregular inflections. The Russian-English side of the dictionary gives inflectional information.

myth) развéнчивать (развенчáть *perf*).
début ['deɪbju:] *n* дебю́т.
debutante ['dɛbjutænt] *n девушка, выходящая в (высший) свет.*
Dec. *abbr* = **December**.
decade ['dɛkeɪd] *n* десятилéтие.
decadence ['dɛkədəns] *n* упáдок*.
decadent ['dɛkədənt] *adj* (*sentiments*) упáдочнический*; (*class*) упáдочный.
de-caff ['di:kæf] (*inf*) *adj* без кофеи́на ◆ *n* кóфе без кофеи́на.
decaffeinated [dɪ'kæfɪneɪtɪd] *adj* без кофеи́на.
decamp [dɪ'kæmp] *vi* (*inf*) удирáть (удрáть* *perf*).
decant [dɪ'kænt] *vt* переливáть (перели́ть* *perf*).
decanter [dɪ'kæntə'] *n* графи́н.
decarbonize [di:'kɑ:bənaɪz] *vt* очищáть (очи́стить* *perf*) от нагáра.
decathlon [dɪ'kæθlən] *n* десятибóрье.
decay [dɪ'keɪ] *n* разрушéние; (*of society*) разложéние ◆ *vi* (*body, leaves, society etc*) разлагáться (разложи́ться* *perf*); (*teeth*) разрушáться (разрýшиться *perf*).
decease [dɪ'si:s] *n* (*LAW*): **upon your ~** по Вáшей кончи́не.
deceased [dɪ'si:st] *n*: **the ~** покóйный(-ая) *m(f) adj*.
deceit [dɪ'si:t] *n* обмáн.
deceitful [dɪ'si:tful] *adj* лжи́вый (лжив).
deceive [dɪ'si:v] *vt* обмáнывать (обманýть* *perf*); **to ~ o.s.** обмáнываться (обманýться* *perf*).
decelerate [di:'sɛləreɪt] *vi* замедля́ть (замéдлить *perf*) скóрость.
December [dɪ'sɛmbə'] *n* декáбрь* *m*; *see also* **July**.
decency ['di:sənsɪ] *n* (*propriety*) благопристóйность *f*; (*kindness*) поря́дочность *f*.
decent ['di:sənt] *adj* (*wages, meal, sleep*) прили́чный* (прили́чен); (*interval, behaviour, person*) поря́дочный* (поря́дочен); **we expect you to do the ~ thing** мы ожидáем, что Вы постýпите поря́дочно; **they were very ~ about it** они́ отреаги́ровали на э́то óчень благорóдно; **it was very ~ of him** э́то бы́ло óчень поря́дочно с егó стороны́; **are you ~?** Вы прили́чно одéты?
decently ['di:səntlɪ] *adv* (*respectably*) прили́чно; (*kindly*) поря́дочно.
decentralization ['di:sɛntrəlaɪ'zeɪʃən] *n* децентрализáция.
decentralize [di:'sɛntrəlaɪz] *vt* децентрализовáть *(impf/perf)*.
deception [dɪ'sɛpʃən] *n* обмáн.
deceptive [dɪ'sɛptɪv] *adj* обмáнчивый* (обмáнчив).
decibel ['dɛsɪbɛl] *n* децибéл.
decide [dɪ'saɪd] *vt* (*person*: *persuade*) убеждáть (убеди́ть *perf*); (*settle*) решáть (реши́ть *perf*) ◆ *vi*: **to ~ to do/that** решáть (реши́ть *perf*) *+infin/*, что; **to ~ on sth** останáвливаться (останови́ться* *perf*) на чём-н; **to ~ on doing/against doing** решáть (реши́ть *perf*) *+infin*/не *+infin*.
decided [dɪ'saɪdɪd] *adj* (*character*) реши́тельный* (реши́телен); (*views, opinions*) определённый; (*dangers, improvement*) несомнéнный* (несомнéнен).
decidedly [dɪ'saɪdɪdlɪ] *adv* (*distinctly*) несомнéнно; (*emphatically*) реши́тельно.
deciding [dɪ'saɪdɪŋ] *adj* решáющий*.
deciduous [dɪ'sɪdjuəs] *adj* листопáдный.
decimal ['dɛsɪməl] *adj* десяти́чный ◆ *n* десяти́чная дробь *f*; **to three ~ places** с тóчностью до трéтьего знáка.
decimalize ['dɛsɪməlaɪz] *vt* (*BRIT*) переводи́ть* (перевести́* *perf*) в метри́ческую систéму мер.
decimal point *n* тóчка* *or* запятáя *f adj* (*отделяющая целое от дроби*).
decimate ['dɛsɪmeɪt] *vt* истребля́ть (истреби́ть* *perf*).
decipher [dɪ'saɪfə'] *vt* (*message etc*: *enigmatic*) расшифрóвывать (расшифровáть *perf*); (: *illegible*) разбирáть (разобрáть* *perf*).
decision [dɪ'sɪʒən] *n* решéние; (*decisiveness*) реши́мость *f*; **to make a ~** принимáть (приня́ть* *perf*) решéние.
decisive [dɪ'saɪsɪv] *adj* реши́тельный* (реши́телен).
deck [dɛk] *n* (*NAUT*) пáлуба; (*of cards*) колóда; (*also: record ~*) прои́грыватель *m*; (*of bus*): **top ~** вéрхний* этáж*; **to go up on ~** поднимáться (подня́ться* *perf*) на пáлубу; **below ~** под пáлубой; **cassette ~** кассéтная дéка.
deck chair *n* шезлóнг.
deck hand *n* матрóс.
declaration [dɛklə'reɪʃən] *n* (*statement*) декларáция; (*public announcement*) заявлéние.
declare [dɪ'klɛə'] *vt* (*state*) объявля́ть (объяви́ть* *perf*); (*for tax*) деклари́ровать *(impf/perf)*.
declassify [di:'klæsɪfaɪ] *vt* рассекрéчивать (рассекрéтить* *perf*).
decline [dɪ'klaɪn] *n* (*drop*) падéние; (*lessening*) уменьшéние; (*decay*) упáдок* ◆ *vt* (*invitation*) отклоня́ть (отклони́ть* *perf*) ◆ *vi* (*strength*) пáдать *(impf)*; (*business*) приходи́ть* (прийти́* *perf*) в упáдок; **~ in living standards** снижéние ýровня жи́зни; **to be in** *or* **on the ~** быть* *(impf)* в упáдке.
declutch ['di:'klʌtʃ] *vi* выключáть (вы́ключить *perf*) сцеплéние.
decode ['di:'kəud] *vt* (*message*) декоди́ровать *(impf/perf)*, расшифрóвывать (расшифровáть *perf*).
decoder [di:'kəudə'] *n* (*person*) *человéк, обращáющийся к словарю́ с цéлью поня́ть*

смысл слóва в инострáнном языкé; (*machine*) декóдер.
decompose [di:kəm'pəuz] *vi* разлагáться (разложи́ться* *perf*).
decomposition [di:kɔmpə'zɪʃən] *n* разложéние.
decompression [di:kəm'prɛʃən] *n* декомпрéссия.
decompression chamber *n* декомпрессиóнная кáмера.
decongestant [di:kən'dʒɛstənt] *n* сосудосужáющее срéдство.
decontaminate [di:kən'tæmɪneɪt] *vt* обеззарáживать (обеззарáзить* *perf*).
decontrol [di:kən'trəul] *vt* освобождáть (освободи́ть* *perf*) от (госудáрственного) контрóля.
décor ['deɪkɔ:ʳ] *n* (*in house*) отдéлка*; (*THEAT*) декорáция.
decorate ['dɛkəreɪt] *vt* (*room etc*) отдéлывать (отдéлать *perf*); (*adorn*): **to ~ (with)** украшáть (укрáсить* *perf*) *+instr*.
decoration [dɛkə'reɪʃən] *n* (*on tree, dress etc*) украшéние; (*of room*) отдéлка*; (*medal*) наградá.
decorative ['dɛkərətɪv] *adj* декорати́вный*.
decorator ['dɛkəreɪtəʳ] *n* обóйщик; **painter and ~** маля́р и обóйщик, отдéлочник.
decorum [dɪ'kɔ:rəm] *n* благопристóйность *f*, декóрум.
decoy ['di:kɔɪ] *n* примáнка*.
decrease ['di:kri:s] *vt* уменьшáть (умéньшить *perf*) ◆ *vi* уменьшáться (умéньшиться *perf*) ◆ *n*: **~ (in)** уменьшéние (*+gen*); **to be on the ~** идти́* (пойти́* *perf*) на ýбыль.
decreasing [di:'kri:sɪŋ] *adj* уменьшáющийся.
decree [dɪ'kri:] *n* (*ADMIN, LAW*) постановлéние; (*POL, REL*) укáз ◆ *vt*: **to ~ (that)** (*ADMIN, LAW*) постановля́ть (постанови́ть* *perf*)(, что).
decree absolute *n* окончáтельное решéние о развóде.
decree nisi [-'naɪsaɪ] *n* услóвно-окончáтельное решéние судá о развóде.
decrepit [dɪ'krɛpɪt] *adj* дря́хлый* (дряхл).
decry [dɪ'kraɪ] *vt* порицáть *(impf)*.
dedicate ['dɛdɪkeɪt] *vt*: **to ~ to** посвящáть (посвяти́ть* *perf*) *+dat*.
dedicated ['dɛdɪkeɪtɪd] *adj* (*person*) прéданный* (прéдан); (*COMPUT*) вы́деленный, назнáченный: **~ word processor** специализи́рованный процéссор для обрабóтки тéкстов.
dedication [dɛdɪ'keɪʃən] *n* (*devotion*) прéданность *f*; (*in book etc*) посвящéние.
deduce [dɪ'dju:s] *vt*: **to ~ that** заключáть (заключи́ть *perf*), что.
deduct [dɪ'dʌkt] *vt* вычитáть (вы́честь* *perf*); **to ~ sth (from)** (*from wage etc*) вычитáть (вы́честь* *perf*) что-н (из *+gen*).
deduction [dɪ'dʌkʃən] *n* (*conclusion*) умозаключéние; (*subtraction*) вычитáние; (*amount*) вы́чет.
deed [di:d] *n* (*feat*) деяние, постýпок*; (*LAW*) акт; **~ of covenant** акт о передáче.
deem [di:m] *vt* (*formal*) полагáть *(impf)*; **to ~ it wise to do** полагáть *(impf)* целесообрáзным *+infin*.
deep [di:p] *adj* глубóкий* (глубóк); (*voice*) ни́зкий* (ни́зок) ◆ *adv*: **the spectators stood 20 ~** зри́тели стоя́ли в 20 рядóв; **the lake is 4 metres ~** глубинá óзера – 4 мéтра; **knee-~ in water** по колéно в водé; **he took a ~ breath** он сдéлал глубóкий вздóх; **~ blue** тёмно-си́ний*.
deepen [di:pn] *vt* (*hole etc*) углубля́ть (углуби́ть* *perf*) ◆ *vi* (*crisis, mystery*) углубля́ться (углуби́ться* *perf*).
deepfreeze ['di:p'fri:z] *n* морози́льная кáмера.
deep-fry ['di:p'fraɪ] *vt* жáрить (зажáрить *perf*) во фритю́ре.
deeply ['di:plɪ] *adv* глубокó.
deep-rooted ['di:p'ru:tɪd] *adj* (*prejudice*) глубокó укорени́вшийся; (*affection*) глубóкий* (глубóк); (*habit*) закоренéлый (закоренéл).
deep-sea ['di:p'si:] *cpd* (*fishing*) глубоковóдный*; **~ diver** водолáз.
deep-seated ['di:p'si:tɪd] *adj* укорени́вшийся.
deep-set ['di:psɛt] *adj* глубокó посáженный (посáжен).
deer [dɪəʳ] *n inv* олéнь *m*; **(red) ~** благорóдный олéнь; **(roe) ~** косýля; **(fallow) ~** лань *f*.
deerskin ['dɪəskɪn] *n* зáмша.
deerstalker ['dɪəstɔ:kəʳ] *n* (*hat*) треýх.
deface [dɪ'feɪs] *vt* обезобрáживать (обезобрáзить* *perf*).
defamation [dɛfə'meɪʃən] *n* клеветá, диффамáция.
defamatory [dɪ'fæmətrɪ] *adj* клеветни́ческий*.
default [dɪ'fɔ:lt] *n* (*COMPUT*: *also*: **~ value**) значéние по умолчáнию ◆ *vi*: **to ~ on a debt** не выплáчивать (вы́платить* *perf*) долг; **by ~** (*win*) за неявкой проти́вника.
defaulter [dɪ'fɔ:ltəʳ] *n* неплатéльщик.
default option *n* (*COMPUT*) парáметр *or* вариáнт, выбираемый по умолчáнию.
defeat [dɪ'fi:t] *n* поражéние ◆ *vt* наноси́ть* (нанести́* *perf*) поражéние *+dat*.
defeatism [dɪ'fi:tɪzəm] *n* поражéнчество.
defeatist [dɪ'fi:tɪst] *adj* поражéнческий ◆ *n* поражéнец*.
defecate ['dɛfəkeɪt] *vi* испражня́ться (испражни́ться *perf*).
defect ['di:fɛkt] *n* (*of product*) дефéкт; (*of plan, society*) недостáток* ◆ *vi*: **to ~ to the enemy**

перебегáть (перебежáть* *perf*) на стóрону врагá; **physical/mental ~** физический*/ ýмственный недостáток*.
defective [dɪ'fɛktɪv] *adj* (*goods*) дефéктный (дефéктен).
defector [dɪ'fɛktəʳ] *n* перебéжчик(-ица).
defence [dɪ'fɛns] (*US* **defense**) *n* (*protection, justification*) защи́та; (*MIL*) оборóна; **in ~ of** в защи́ту *+gen*; **witness for the ~** свидéтель *m* защи́ты; **the Ministry of D~** Министéрство оборóны; **the Department of Defense** (*US*) Департáмент по оборóне.
defenceless [dɪ'fɛnslɪs] *adj* беззащи́тный* (беззащи́тен).
defend [dɪ'fɛnd] *vt* (*also SPORT*) защищáть (защити́ть* *perf*); (*LAW*) защищáть *(impf)*.
defendant [dɪ'fɛndənt] *n* (*in criminal case*) подсуди́мый(-ая) *m(f) adj*, обвиня́емый(-ая) *m(f) adj*; (*in civil case*) отвéтчик(-ица).
defender [dɪ'fɛndəʳ] *n* (*also fig*) защи́тник(-ица); (*SPORT*) защи́тник.
defending champion [dɪ'fɛndɪŋ-] *n чемпиóн, защищáющий своё звáние.*
defending counsel *n* адвокáт отвéтчика.
defense *etc* (*US*) = **defence** *etc*.
defensive [dɪ'fɛnsɪv] *adj* (*weapons, measures*) оборони́тельный; (*behaviour, manner*) вызывáющий* ◆ *n*: **he was on the ~** он был готóв к оборóне.
defer [dɪ'fəːʳ] *vt* отсрóчивать (отсрóчить *perf*).
deference ['dɛfərəns] *n* почтéние; **out of** *or* **in ~ to** из почтéния к *+dat*.
deferential [dɛfə'rɛnʃəl] *adj* почти́тельный* (почти́телен).
deferred creditor [dɪ'fəːd-] *n* кредитóр, получи́вший отсрóчку.
defiance [dɪ'faɪəns] *n* вы́зов; **in ~ of** вопреки́ *+dat*.
defiant [dɪ'faɪənt] *adj* (*person, reply*) дéрзкий* (дéрзок); (*tone*) вызывáющий*.
defiantly [dɪ'faɪəntlɪ] *adv* дéрзко, вызывáюще.
deficiency [dɪ'fɪʃənsɪ] *n* (*lack*) нехвáтка*; (*inadequacy*) недостáток*; (*COMM*) дефици́т.
deficiency disease *n* авитаминóз.
deficient [dɪ'fɪʃənt] *adj* (*inadequate*) несовершéнный* (несовершéнен); (*lacking*): **to be ~ in** испы́тывать *(impf)* недостáток в *+prp*.
deficit ['dɛfɪsɪt] *n* (*COMM*) дефици́т.
defile [dɪ'faɪl] *vt* оскверня́ть (оскверни́ть *perf*) ◆ *n* ущéлье*.
define [dɪ'faɪn] *vt* (*limits etc*) определя́ть (определи́ть *perf*); (*word etc*) давáть* (дать* *perf*) определéние *+dat*.
definite ['dɛfɪnɪt] *adj* определённый* (определёнен); **he was ~ about it** егó мнéние на э́тот счёт бы́ло определённым.
definite article *n* определённый арти́кль *m*.
definitely ['dɛfɪnɪtlɪ] *adv* (*positively*) определённо; (*certainly*) несомнéнно.
definition [dɛfɪ'nɪʃən] *n* (*of word*) определéние; (*of photograph etc*) чёткость *f*.
definitive [dɪ'fɪnɪtɪv] *adj* окончáтельный* (окончáтелен).
deflate [diː'fleɪt] *vt* (*tyre, balloon*) спускáть (спусти́ть* *perf*); (*person*) сбивáть (сбить* *perf*) спесь с *+gen*; (*ECON*): **to ~ the money supply** осуществля́ть (осуществи́ть* *perf*) дефля́цию.
deflation [diː'fleɪʃən] *n* (*ECON*) дефля́ция.
deflationary [diː'fleɪʃənrɪ] *adj* дефляциóнный.
deflect [dɪ'flɛkt] *vt* (*criticism, shot*) отклоня́ть (отклони́ть* *perf*); (*attention*) отвлекáть (отвлéчь* *perf*).
defog ['diː'fɔg] *vt* (*US*) устраня́ть (устрани́ть *perf*) запотевáние *+gen*.
defogger ['diː'fɔgəʳ] *n* (*US*: *AUT*) *устрóйство, устраня́ющее запотевáние стеклá.*
deform [dɪ'fɔːm] *vt* (*damage*) деформи́ровать *(impf/perf)*; (*distort*) искажáть (искази́ть* *perf*).
deformed [dɪ'fɔːmd] *adj* (*see vt*) деформи́рованный (деформи́рован); искажённый (искажён).
deformity [dɪ'fɔːmɪtɪ] *n* (*distorted part*) физи́ческий* недостáток; (*condition*) деформáция.
defraud [dɪ'frɔːd] *vt*: **to ~ sb of sth** обмáном лишáть (лиши́ть *perf*) когó-н чегó-н.
defray [dɪ'freɪ] *vt*: **to ~ sb's expenses** возмещáть (возмести́ть* *perf*) чьи-н расхóды.
defrost [diː'frɔst] *vt* (*fridge, food*) разморáживать (разморóзить* *perf*); (*windscreen*) очищáть (очи́стить* *perf*) ото льдá.
defroster [diː'frɔstəʳ] *n* (*US*: *demister*) дефрóстер.
deft [dɛft] *adj* лóвкий* (лóвок).
defunct [dɪ'fʌŋkt] *adj* бездéйственный (бездéйствен).
defuse [diː'fjuːz] *vt* (*also fig*) разряжáть (разряди́ть* *perf*).
defy [dɪ'faɪ] *vt* (*resist*) оспáривать (оспóрить *perf*); (*fig*: *description, explanation*) не поддавáться* *(impf) +dat*; (*challenge*): **to ~ sb to do** призывáть (призвáть* *perf*) когó-н *+infin*.
degenerate [*vb* dɪ'dʒɛnəreɪt, *adj* dɪ'dʒɛnərɪt] *vi* ухудшáться (ухýдшиться *perf*), деградúровать *(impf/perf)* ◆ *adj* растлéнный.
degradation [dɛgrə'deɪʃən] *n* деградáция.
degrade [dɪ'greɪd] *vt* (*debase*: *person*) унижáть (уни́зить* *perf*); (*worsen*) ухудшáть (ухýдшить *perf*).
degrading [dɪ'greɪdɪŋ] *adj* унизи́тельный* (унизи́телен).
degree [dɪ'griː] *n* (*extent*) стéпень* *f*; (*unit of measurement*) грáдус; (*SCOL*) (учёная) стéпень*; **10 ~s below (zero)** 10 грáдусов ни́же нуля́; **a considerable ~ of risk** значи́тельная стéпень* ри́ска; **by ~s** постепéнно; **to some ~, to a certain ~**

до не́которой сте́пени.
dehydrated [di:haɪ'dreɪtɪd] *adj* (*MED*) обезво́женный (обезво́жен); (*milk, eggs*) порошко́вый.
dehydration [di:haɪ'dreɪʃən] *n* обезво́живание.
de-ice ['di:'aɪs] *vt* удаля́ть (удали́ть *perf*) обледене́ние *+gen*.
de-icer ['di:'aɪsə'] *n* антиобледени́тель *m*.
deign [deɪn] *vi*: **to ~ to do** соизволя́ть (соизво́лить *perf*) *+infin*.
deity ['di:ɪtɪ] *n* божество́*.
déjà vu [deɪʒɑ:'vu:] *n чу́вство узнава́ния в незнако́мом ме́сте*; **I had a sense of ~ ~** у меня́ бы́ло тако́е чу́вство, бу́дто э́то уже́ бы́ло.
dejected [dɪ'dʒɛktɪd] *adj* уны́лый.
dejection [dɪ'dʒɛkʃən] *n* уны́ние.
del. *abbr* = **delete**.
delay [dɪ'leɪ] *vt* (*decision, ceremony etc*) откла́дывать (отложи́ть* *perf*); (*person, plane etc*) заде́рживать (задержа́ть* *perf*) ◆ *vi* ме́длить *(impf)* ◆ *n* заде́ржка*; **to be ~ed** заде́рживаться *(impf)*; **without ~** без отлага́тельств.
delayed-action [dɪ'leɪd'ækʃən] *adj*: **~ device** приспособле́ние с регули́руемой заде́ржкой де́йствия.
delectable [dɪ'lɛktəbl] *adj* (*person*) притяга́тельный* (притяга́телен); (*food*) ла́комый (ла́ком).
delegate [*n* 'dɛlɪgɪt, *vt* 'dɛlɪgeɪt] *n* делега́т ◆ *vt* (*person*) делеги́ровать *(impf/perf)*; (*task*) поруча́ть (поручи́ть *perf*); **to ~ sth to sb/sb to do** поруча́ть (поручи́ть *perf*) что-н кому́-н/ кому́-н *+infin*.
delegation [dɛlɪ'geɪʃən] *n* (*group*) делега́ция; (*by manager, leader*) переда́ча.
delete [dɪ'li:t] *vt* вычёркивать (вы́черкнуть *perf*); (*COMPUT*) удаля́ть (удали́ть *perf*).
Delhi ['dɛlɪ] *n* Де́ли *m ind*.
deli ['dɛlɪ] (*inf*) *n* магази́н деликате́сов.
deliberate [*adj* dɪ'lɪbərɪt, *vi* dɪ'lɪbəreɪt] *adj* (*intentional*) наме́ренный* (наме́рен); (*slow*) неторопли́вый (неторопли́в) ◆ *vi* обду́мывать (обду́мать *perf*).
deliberately [dɪ'lɪbərɪtlɪ] *adv* (*see adj*) наме́ренно, наро́чно; неторопли́во.
deliberation [dɪlɪbə'reɪʃən] *n* (*consideration*) размышле́ние; (*usu pl*: *discussion*) обсужде́ние.
delicacy ['dɛlɪkəsɪ] *n* то́нкость *f*; (*food*) деликате́с.
delicate ['dɛlɪkɪt] *adj* то́нкий* (то́нок); (*colour*) не́жный (не́жен); (*approach, problem*) делика́тный* (делика́тен); (*health*) хру́пкий* (хру́пок).
delicately ['dɛlɪkɪtlɪ] *adv* то́нко.
delicatessen [dɛlɪkə'tɛsn] *n* магази́н деликате́сов.
delicious [dɪ'lɪʃəs] *adj* (*food*) о́чень вку́сный* (вку́сен); (*smell, feeling, person*) восхити́тельный* (восхити́телен).
delight [dɪ'laɪt] *n* (*feeling*) восто́рг; (*person, experience etc*) пре́лесть *f* ◆ *vt* ра́довать (пора́довать *perf*); **to take (a) ~ in** находи́ть* (найти́* *perf*) удово́льствие в *+prp*; **her son was her ~** она́ души́ не ча́яла в своём сы́не; **she was a ~ to interview** брать *(impf)* у неё интервью́ бы́ло и́стинным удово́льствием; **the ~s of country life** пре́лести дереве́нской жи́зни.
delighted [dɪ'laɪtɪd] *adj*: **(to be) ~ (at** *or* **with)** (быть *(impf)*) в восто́рге (от *+gen*); **he was ~ to see her** он был рад ви́деть её; **I'd be ~ to help** я с ра́достью помогу́; **I am ~ to meet you** о́чень прия́тно познако́миться.
delightful [dɪ'laɪtful] *adj* восхити́тельный* (восхити́телен).
delimit [di:'lɪmɪt] *vt* определя́ть (определи́ть *perf*) грани́цы *+gen*.
delineate [dɪ'lɪnɪeɪt] *vt* оче́рчивать (очерти́ть* *perf*).
delinquency [dɪ'lɪŋkwənsɪ] *n* правонаруше́ние.
delinquent [dɪ'lɪŋkwənt] *adj* престу́пный ◆ *n* несовершенноле́тний(-яя) правонаруши́тель(ница) *m(f)*.
delirious [dɪ'lɪrɪəs] *adj*: **to be ~** (*with fever*) быть* *(impf)* в бреду́; (*with excitement*) быть* *(impf)* в забытьи́.
delirium [dɪ'lɪrɪəm] *n* (*MED*) бреди́.
deliver [dɪ'lɪvə'] *vt* (*goods*) доставля́ть (доста́вить* *perf*); (*letter*) вруча́ть (вручи́ть *perf*); (*message*) передава́ть* (переда́ть* *perf*); (*speech*) произноси́ть* (произнести́* *perf*); (*blow*) наноси́ть* (нанести́* *perf*); (*baby*) принима́ть (приня́ть* *perf*); (*warning, ultimatum*) предъявля́ть (предъяви́ть* *perf*); (*person*): **to ~ (from)** избавля́ть (изба́вить* *perf*) (от *+gen*); **to ~ the goods** (*fig*) выполня́ть (вы́полнить *perf*) обе́щанное.
deliverance [dɪ'lɪvrəns] *n* избавле́ние.
delivery [dɪ'lɪvərɪ] *n* (*of goods*) доста́вка*; (*of speaker*) стиль *m* изложе́ния; (*MED*) ро́ды *pl*; **to take ~ of** получа́ть (получи́ть* *perf*).
delivery note *n* тра́нспортная накладна́я *f adj*.
delivery van (*US* **delivery truck**) *n автофурго́н для доста́вки това́ров*.
delouse ['di:'laus] *vt* избавля́ть (изба́вить* *perf*) от вшей.
delta ['dɛltə] *n* (*GEO*) де́льта.
delude [dɪ'lu:d] *vt* вводи́ть* (ввести́* *perf*) в заблужде́ние; **to ~ o.s.** заблужда́ться *(impf)*.
deluge ['dɛlju:dʒ] *n* ли́вень *m*; (*fig*) лави́на.
delusion [dɪ'lu:ʒən] *n* заблужде́ние; **he has ~s of grandeur** у него́ ма́ния величия.

de luxe [də'lʌks] *adj* роско́шный* (роско́шен); **a ~ ~ car/hotel** маши́на/гости́ница люкс.
delve [dɛlv] *vi*: **to ~ into** (*subject*) углубля́ться (углуби́ться* *perf*) в +*acc*; (*handbag etc*) ры́ться* (*impf*) в +*acc*.
Dem. *abbr* (*US*: *POL*) = **democrat(ic)**.
demagogue ['dɛməgɔg] *n* демаго́г.
demand [dɪ'mɑ:nd] *vt* тре́бовать (потре́бовать *perf*) +*gen* ◆ *n* (*request, claim*) тре́бование; (*ECON*): **~ (for)** спрос (на +*acc*); **to ~ sth (from** *or* **of sb)** тре́бовать (потре́бовать *perf*) чего́-н (от кого́-н); **to be in ~** (*commodity*) по́льзоваться (*impf*) спро́сом; **specialists are in great ~** на специали́стов большо́й спрос; **on ~** (*available, payable*) по тре́бованию.
demand draft *n* (*COMM*) *ве́ксель, опла́чиваемый при предъявле́нии.*
demanding [dɪ'mɑ:ndɪŋ] *adj* (*boss, parents*) тре́бовательный* (тре́бователен); (*child*) тру́дный; (*work*: *involving responsibility*) отве́тственный; (: *requiring effort*) тяжёлый.
demarcation [di:mɑ:'keɪʃən] *n* разграниче́ние.
demarcation dispute *n* (*INDUSTRY*) *разногла́сие по по́воду разделе́ния труда́.*
demean [dɪ'mi:n] *vt*: **to ~ o.s.** унижа́ться (уни́зиться *perf*).
demeanour [dɪ'mi:nə^r] (*US* **demeanor**) *n* мане́ра поведе́ния.
demented [dɪ'mɛntɪd] *adj* (*person*) поме́шанный* (поме́шан).
demilitarized zone [di:'mɪlɪtəraɪzd-] *n* (*MIL*) демилитаризо́ванная зо́на.
demise [dɪ'maɪz] *n* упа́док; (*death*) кончи́на.
demist [di:'mɪst] *vt* (*BRIT*: *AUT*): **to ~ the windscreen** *суши́ть обогрева́телем запоте́вшее лобово́е стекло́.*
demister [di:'mɪstə^r] *n* (*BRIT*: *AUT*) *обогрева́тель для су́шки запоте́вших стёкол.*
demiveg ['dɛmɪvɛdʒ] *n* полу-вегетариа́нец*(-нка*).
demo ['dɛməu] *n abbr* (*inf*) = **demonstration**.
demob [de:'mɔb] *vt* (*MIL*: *inf*) демобилизова́ть (*impf/perf*).
demobilize [di:'məubɪlaɪz] *vt* (*MIL*) демобилизова́ть (*impf/perf*).
democracy [dɪ'mɔkrəsɪ] *n* (*system*) демокра́тия; (*country*) демократи́ческая страна́*.
democrat ['dɛməkræt] *n* демокра́т; **D~** (*US*) член па́ртии демокра́тов.
democratic [dɛmə'krætɪk] *adj* демократи́ческий*; **D~ Party** (*US*) па́ртия демокра́тов.
demography [dɪ'mɔgrəfɪ] *n* демогра́фия.
demolish [dɪ'mɔlɪʃ] *vt* (*building*) сноси́ть* (снести́* *perf*); (*argument*) разгроми́ть* (*perf*).
demolition [dɛmə'lɪʃən] *n* (*of building*) снос; (*of argument*) разгро́м.
demon ['di:mən] *n* де́мон ◆ *adj* (*skilled*) гениа́льный* (гениа́лен).
demonstrate ['dɛmənstreɪt] *vt* демонстри́ровать (продемонстри́ровать *perf*) ◆ *vi* (*POL*): **to ~ (for/against)** демонстри́ровать (*impf*) (за +*acc*/про́тив +*gen*).
demonstration [dɛmən'streɪʃən] *n* демонстра́ция; **to hold a ~** (*POL*) проводи́ть* (провести́* *perf*) демонстра́цию.
demonstrative [dɪ'mɔnstrətɪv] *adj* (*LING*) указа́тельный; **she's very ~** она́ откры́то выража́ет свои́ чу́вства.
demonstrator ['dɛmənstreɪtə^r] *n* (*POL*) демонстра́нт; (*sales person*) демонстра́тор.
demoralize [dɪ'mɔrəlaɪz] *vt* деморализова́ть (*impf/perf*).
demote [dɪ'məut] *vt* понижа́ть (пони́зить* *perf*) в до́лжности.
demotion [dɪ'məuʃən] *n* пониже́ние в до́лжности.
demur [dɪ'mə:^r] *vi* (*formal*) возража́ть (возрази́ть* *perf*) ◆ *n*: **without ~** без возраже́ний; **they ~red at his suggestion** они возрази́ли на его́ предложе́ние.
demure [dɪ'mjuə^r] *adj* (*smile, person*) чи́нный; (*dress*) скро́мный* (скро́мен).
demurrage [dɪ'mʌrɪdʒ] *n* (*COMM*) *пла́та за просто́й су́дна.*
den [dɛn] *n* (*of animal, person*) ло́гово; (*of thieves*) прито́н.
denationalization ['di:næʃnəlaɪ'zeɪʃən] *n* денационализа́ция.
denationalize [di:'næʃnəlaɪz] *vt* денационализи́ровать (*impf/perf*).
denatured alcohol [di:'neɪtʃəd-] *n* (*US*) денатура́т.
denial [dɪ'naɪəl] *n* отрица́ние; (*refusal*) отка́з.
denier ['dɛnɪə^r] *n* (*of tights, stockings*) денье́ *nt ind*.
denigrate ['dɛnɪgreɪt] *vt* принижа́ть (прини́зить* *perf*).
denim ['dɛnɪm] *n* джи́нсовая ткань *f*; **~s** *npl* (*jeans*) джи́нсы *pl*.
denim jacket *n* джи́нсовая ку́ртка*.
denizen ['dɛnɪzn] *n* (*inhabitant*) обита́тель(ница) *m(f)*.
Denmark ['dɛnmɑ:k] *n* Да́ния.
denomination [dɪnɔmɪ'neɪʃən] *n* (*of money*) досто́инство; (*REL*) конфе́ссия.
denominator [dɪ'nɔmɪneɪtə^r] *n* (*MATH*) знамена́тель *m*.
denote [dɪ'nəut] *vt* (*indicate*) ука́зывать (указа́ть* *perf*) на +*acc*; (*represent*) обознача́ть (обозна́чить *perf*).
denounce [dɪ'nauns] *vt* (*condemn*) осужда́ть (осуди́ть* *perf*); (*give information against*) доноси́ть* (донести́* *perf*) на +*acc*.
dense [dɛns] *adj* (*crowd*) пло́тный*; (*smoke, foliage etc*) густо́й* (густ); (*inf*: *person*) тупо́й* (туп).
densely ['dɛnslɪ] *adv*: **~ populated** гу́сто населённый; **~ wooded** покры́тый (покры́т)

густы́м ле́сом.
density ['dɛnsɪtɪ] *n* (*of population*: *also PHYS*) пло́тность *f*; **single/double-~ disk** (*COMPUT*) диск с одина́рной/двойно́й пло́тностью.
dent [dɛnt] *n* (*in metal*) вмя́тина ◆ *vt* (*also:* **make a ~ in**: *car etc*) оставля́ть (оста́вить* *perf*) вмя́тину в *+acc*; (*ego*) уда́рить *(perf)* по *+dat*.
dental ['dɛntl] *adj* зубно́й.
dental floss [-flɔs] *n нить для чи́стки межзу́бных промежу́тков*.
dental surgeon *n* зубно́й врач*, стомато́лог.
dentifrice ['dɛntɪfrɪs] *n* (*MED*: *paste*) зубна́я па́ста; (: *powder*) зубно́й порошо́к*.
dentist ['dɛntɪst] *n* зубно́й врач*, стомато́лог; (*also:* **~'s surgery**) зубоврачéбный кабине́т, стоматологи́ческий* кабине́т.
dentistry ['dɛntɪstrɪ] *n* стоматоло́гия.
dentures ['dɛntʃəz] *npl* зубно́й проте́з *sg*.
denuded [di:'nju:dɪd] *adj* оголённый* (оголён); **~ of** (*fig*) лишённый (лишён) *+gen*.
denunciation [dɪnʌnsɪ'eɪʃən] *n* (*accusation*) обличе́ние; (*condemnation*) осужде́ние.
deny [dɪ'naɪ] *vt* (*refute*) отрица́ть *(impf)*; (*allegation*) отверга́ть (отве́ргнуть *perf*); (*disown*) отрека́ться (отре́чься* *perf*) от *+gen*; (*refuse*): **to ~ sb sth** отка́зывать (отказа́ть* *perf*) кому́-н в чём-н; **he denies having said it** он отрица́ет, что он э́то сказа́л.
deodorant [di:'əudərənt] *n* дезодора́нт.
depart [dɪ'pɑ:t] *vi* (*person*) отбыва́ть (отбы́ть* *perf*); (*bus, train*) отправля́ться (отпра́виться* *perf*); (*plane*) улета́ть (улете́ть* *perf*); **to ~ from** (*fig*) отклоня́ться (отклони́ться* *perf*) от *+gen*.
departed [dɪ'pɑ:tɪd] *adj* поко́йный ◆ *n* поко́йный(-ая) *m(f) adj*, у́мерший*(-ая) *m(f) adj*.
department [dɪ'pɑ:tmənt] *n* (*in shop*) отде́л; (*in university, school*) отделе́ние; (*POL*) ве́домство, департа́мент; **D~ of Trade and Industry** Министе́рство торго́вли и промы́шленности; **that's not my ~** (*fig*) я не специали́ст в э́том де́ле; **D~ of State** (*US*) Госуда́рственный департа́мент.
departmental [di:pɑ:t'mɛntl] *adj* (*COMM, ADMIN*): **~ meeting/activities** собра́ние/де́ятельность *f* отде́ла; **~ manager** заве́дующий*(-ая) *m(f) adj* отде́лом.
department store *n* универса́льный магази́н.
departure [dɪ'pɑ:tʃə'] *n* (*of visitor etc*) отъе́зд; (*of employee*) ухо́д; (*of bus, train*) отправле́ние; (*of plane*) отлёт; (*fig*): **~ from** отклоне́ние от *+gen*; **a new ~** но́вое направле́ние.
departure lounge *n* (*at airport*) зал отлёта.
depend [dɪ'pɛnd] *vi*: **to ~ on** зави́сеть* *(impf)* от *+gen*; (*trust*) полага́ться (положи́ться* *perf*) на *+acc*; **it ~s** смотря́ по обстоя́тельствам, как полу́чится; **~ing on the outcome ...** в зави́симости от исхо́да ....
dependable [dɪ'pɛndəbl] *adj* надёжный* (надёжен).
dependant [dɪ'pɛndənt] *n* иждиве́нец(-нка).
dependence [dɪ'pɛndəns] *n* зави́симость *f*.
dependent [dɪ'pɛndənt] *adj*: **~ (on)** зави́симый (зави́сим) (от *+gen*) ◆ *n* = **dependant**.
depict [dɪ'pɪkt] *vt* изобража́ть (изобрази́ть* *perf*).
depilatory [dɪ'pɪlətrɪ] *n* (*also:* **~ cream**) крем для удале́ния воло́с.
depleted [dɪ'pli:tɪd] *adj* истощённый* (истощён).
deplorable [dɪ'plɔ:rəbl] *adj* (*conditions*) плаче́вный* (плаче́вен); (*behaviour*) возмути́тельный* (возмути́телен).
deplore [dɪ'plɔ:'] *vt* (*condemn*) негодова́ть *(impf)* по по́воду *+gen*.
deploy [dɪ'plɔɪ] *vt* (*troops*) дислоци́ровать *(impf/perf)*.
depopulate [di:'pɔpjuleɪt] *vt* обезлю́дить *(perf)*.
depopulation ['di:pɔpju'leɪʃən] *n* опустоше́ние.
deport [dɪ'pɔ:t] *vt* депорти́ровать *(impf/perf)*, высыла́ть (вы́слать* *perf*).
deportation [di:pɔ:'teɪʃən] *n* депорта́ция, вы́сылка*.
deportation order *n* (*LAW*) прика́з о депорта́ции.
deportee [di:pɔ:'ti:] *n* депорти́рованный(-ая) *m(f) adj*.
deportment [dɪ'pɔ:tmənt] *n* оса́нка.
depose [dɪ'pəuz] *vt* (*remove*) смеща́ть (смести́ть* *perf*); (*overthrow*) низлага́ть (низложи́ть *perf*).
deposit [dɪ'pɔzɪt] *n* (*in account*) депози́т, вклад; (*down payment*) пе́рвый взнос, зада́ток*; (: *when hiring, renting*) зало́г; (*on bottle etc*) сто́имость *f* посу́ды; (*CHEM*) оса́док*; (*of ore, oil*) за́лежь *f* ◆ *vt* (*money*) помеща́ть (помести́ть* *perf*); (*subj: river: sand, silt etc*) намыва́ть (намы́ть* *perf*); (*case, bag*) сдава́ть* (сдать* *perf*); **to put down a ~ of £50** дава́ть* (дать* *perf*) зада́ток £50.
deposit account *n* депози́тный счёт*.
depositor [dɪ'pɔzɪtə'] *n* вкла́дчик* *m/f*.
depository [dɪ'pɔzɪtərɪ] *n* (*person*) дове́ренное лицо́*; (*place*) храни́лище.
depot ['dɛpəu] *n* (*storehouse*) склад; (*for buses*) парк; (*for trains*) депо́ *nt ind*; (*US*: *station*) ста́нция.
depraved [dɪ'preɪvd] *adj* развращённый (развращён).
depravity [dɪ'prævɪtɪ] *n* развращённость *f*.
deprecate ['dɛprɪkeɪt] *vt* порица́ть *(impf)*.
deprecating ['dɛprɪkeɪtɪŋ] *adj* неодобри́тельный* (неодобри́телен).

* marks translations which have irregular inflections. The Russian-English side of the dictionary gives inflectional information.

depreciate [dɪ'pri:ʃɪeɪt] *vi* обесцéниваться (обесцéниться *perf*).
depreciation [dɪpri:ʃɪ'eɪʃən] *n* обесцéнивание.
depress [dɪ'prɛs] *vt* (*PSYCH*) подавля́ть *(impf)*, угнетáть *(impf)*; (*prices, profits*) снижáть (сни́зить* *perf*); (*lever, pedal*) нажимáть (нажáть* *perf*) на +*acc*.
depressant [dɪ'prɛsnt] *n* (*MED*) депрессáнт, успокои́тельное срéдство.
depressed [dɪ'prɛst] *adj* (*person*) подáвленный* (подáвлен), угнетённый* (угнетён); (*prices*) сни́женный; (*industry*): **to be** ~ находи́ться* *(impf)* в состоя́нии спáда; **to get** ~ впадáть (впасть* *perf*) в депрéссию; ~ **area** райóн, находя́щийся в состоя́нии экономи́ческого упáдка.
depressing [dɪ'prɛsɪŋ] *adj* (*time*) тяжёлый; (*news, outlook*) удручáющий.
depression [dɪ'prɛʃən] *n* (*PSYCH, ECON*) депрéссия; (*METEOROLOGY*) óбласть *f* ни́зкого давлéния; (*hollow*) углублéние; (: *in landscape*) впáдина.
deprivation [dɛprɪ'veɪʃən] *n* (*poverty*) нуждá; (*depriving*) лишéние.
deprive [dɪ'praɪv] *vt*: **to** ~ **sb of** лишáть (лиши́ть* *perf*) когó-н +*gen*.
deprived [dɪ'praɪvd] *adj* (*area, family*) бéдный* (бéден), обездóленный; ~ **child** обездóленный ребёнок.
dept. *abbr* = **department**.
depth [dɛpθ] *n* глубинá*; **in the ~s of despair/a crisis** в глубóком отчáянии/кри́зисе; **in the ~s of winter** глубóкой зимóй; **at a ~ of three metres** на глубинé трёх мéтров; **to be out of one's** ~ (*in water*) не доставáть* *(impf)* до днá; **I'm out of my ~ with this job** мне э́та рабóта не по плечу́; **to study sth in** ~ изучáть (изучи́ть* *perf*) что-н углублённо.
depth charge *n* глуби́нная бóмба.
deputation [dɛpju'teɪʃən] *n* депутáция.
deputize ['dɛpjutaɪz] *vi*: **to ~ for sb** замещáть *(impf)* когó-н.
deputy ['dɛpjutɪ] *n* замести́тель *m*; (*POL*) депутáт; (*US*: *also*: ~ **sheriff**) исполня́ющий обя́занности шери́фа ◆ *cpd*: ~ **leader/chairman** замести́тель ли́дера/председáтеля; ~ **head** (*BRIT*: *SCOL*) замести́тель дирéктора.
derail [dɪ'reɪl] *vt*: **to be ~ed** сходи́ть* (сойти́* *perf*) с рéльсов.
derailment [dɪ'reɪlmənt] *n*: **the cause of the ~ is unknown** причи́на, по котóрой пóезд сошёл с рéльсов, неизвéстна.
deranged [dɪ'reɪndʒd] *adj* (*person*) психи́чески больнóй; **he is** ~ он психи́чески бóлен.
derby ['də:rbɪ] *n* (*US*: *bowler hat*) котелóк.
Derbys *abbr* (*BRIT*: *POST*) = *Derbyshire*.
deregulate [dɪ'rɛgjuleɪt] *vt* (*INDUSTRY*) ослабля́ть (ослáбить* *perf*) государственное регули́рование +*gen*.
deregulation [dɪ'rɛgju'leɪʃən] *n* ослаблéние государ́ственного контрóля.
derelict ['dɛrɪlɪkt] *adj* заброшенный* (забрóшен).
deride [dɪ'raɪd] *vt* насмехáться *(impf)* над +*instr*.
derision [dɪ'rɪʒən] *n* презрéние.
derisive [dɪ'raɪsɪv] *adj* презри́тельный* (презри́телен).
derisory [dɪ'raɪsərɪ] *adj* (*ridiculous*) смехотвóрный* (смехотвóрен); (*derisive*) презри́тельный* (презри́телен).
derivation [dɛrɪ'veɪʃən] *n* происхождéние.
derivative [dɪ'rɪvətɪv] *n* (*CHEM*) деривáт; (*LING*) производнóе слóво, деривáт ◆ *adj* (*word, form*) произвóдный; (*not original*) неоригинáльный* (неоригинáлен).
derive [dɪ'raɪv] *vt* (*get*): **to ~ (from)** (*pleasure*) получáть (получи́ть* *perf*) (от +*gen*); (*benefit*) извлекáть (извлéчь* *perf*) (из +*gen*) ◆ *vi* (*originate in*): **to ~ from** происходи́ть* *(impf)* от +*gen*.
derived demand [dɪ'raɪvd-] *n* кóсвенный *or* произвóдственный спрос.
dermatitis [də:mə'taɪtɪs] *n* дермати́т.
dermatology [də:mə'tɔlədʒɪ] *n* дерматолóгия.
derogatory [dɪ'rɔgətərɪ] *adj* пренебрежи́тельный* (пренебрежи́телен).
derrick ['dɛrɪk] *n* (*on ship*) дéррик; (*on well*) буровáя вы́шка*.
derv [də:v] *n* (*BRIT*: *AUT*) ди́зельное тóпливо.
DES *n abbr* (*BRIT*: *formerly*: = *Department of Education and Science*) Министéрство просвещéния и нáуки.
desalination [di:sælɪ'neɪʃən] *n* опреснéние.
descend [dɪ'sɛnd] *vt* (*stairs*) спускáться (спусти́ться* *perf*) по +*dat*; (*hill*) спускáться (спусти́ться* *perf*) с +*gen* ◆ *vi* (*go down*) спускáться (спусти́ться* *perf*); **to ~ from** (*family, person*) происходи́ть* *(impf)* из +*gen*; **to ~ to** (*lying, begging etc*) опускáться (опусти́ться* *perf*) до +*gen*; **in ~ing order of importance** в нисходя́щем поря́дке
▸ **descend on** *vi fus* (*subj*: *enemy, misfortune*) обру́шиваться (обру́шиться *perf*) на +*acc*; (: *gloom, darkness*) опускáться (опусти́ться* *perf*) на +*acc*; (: *silence*) воцаря́ться (воцари́ться *perf*) на +*acc*; **visitors ~ed (up)on us** к нам нагря́нули гóсти.
descendant [dɪ'sɛndənt] *n* потóмок*.
descent [dɪ'sɛnt] *n* спуск; (*AVIAT*) снижéние; (*origin*) происхождéние.
describe [dɪs'kraɪb] *vt* опи́сывать (описáть* *perf*).
description [dɪs'krɪpʃən] *n* описáние; (*sort*) род*; **of every** ~ всевозмóжного рóда.
descriptive [dɪs'krɪptɪv] *adj* описáтельный.
desecrate ['dɛsɪkreɪt] *vt* осквернять (оскверни́ть *perf*).
desegregate [di:'sɛgrɪgeɪt] *vt*: **to ~ a society/school** ликвиди́ровать *(impf/perf)* сегрегáцию в óбществе/шкóле.
desert [*n* 'dɛzət, *vb* dɪ'zə:t] *n* (*also fig*) пусты́ня ◆

vt покидáть (покинуть *perf*) ◆ *vi* (*MIL*) дезертировать *(impf/perf)*; *see also* **deserts**.
deserter [dɪ'zə:tə'] *n* (*MIL*) дезертир.
desertion [dɪ'zə:ʃən] *n* (*MIL*) дезертирство; (*LAW*) оставлéние.
desert island *n* необитáемый óстров*.
deserts [dɪ'zə:ts] *npl*: **to get one's just ~** получáть (получить* *perf*) по заслýгам.
deserve [dɪ'zə:v] *vt* заслýживать (заслужить* *perf*).
deservedly [dɪ'zə:vɪdlɪ] *adv* заслýженно.
deserving [dɪ'zə:vɪŋ] *adj* достóйный*.
desiccated ['dɛsɪkeɪtɪd] *adj* (*coconut*) сушёный.
design [dɪ'zaɪn] *n* дизáйн; (*process*: *of dress*) моделирование; (*sketch*: *of building*) проéкт; (*type*: *of appliance etc*) модéль *f*; (*pattern*) рисýнок*; (*intention*) зáмысел* ◆ *vt* (*house, kitchen*) проектировать (спроектировать *perf*); (*product, test*) разрабáтывать (разрабóтать *perf*); **to have ~s on** имéть *(impf)* виды на *+acc*; **by ~** с ýмыслом.
designate [*vt* 'dɛzɪgneɪt, *adj* 'dɛzɪgnɪt] *vt* (*nominate*) назначáть (назнáчить *perf*); (*indicate*) обозначáть (обознáчить *perf*) ◆ *adj*: **minister ~** назнáченный министр (*до вступлéния в дóлжность*).
designation [dɛzɪg'neɪʃən] *n* (*description, name*) обозначéние.
designer [dɪ'zaɪnə'] *n* (*ART*) дизáйнер; (*of program*) разрабóтчик; (*of building*) проектирóвщик; (*of machine*) конструктор; (*also:* **fashion ~**) модельéр ◆ *adj* (*clothes*) модéльный; **~ label** фирменный знак (модельéра).
desirability [dɪzaɪərə'bɪlɪtɪ] *n*: **the ~ of** желáтельность *f +gen*.
desirable [dɪ'zaɪərəbl] *adj* (*proper*) желáтельный* (желáтелен); (*attractive*) привлекáтельный* (привлекáтелен); **it is ~ that** желáтельно, чтóбы.
desire [dɪ'zaɪə'] *n* желáние ◆ *vt* (*want*) желáть *(impf)*; **to ~ to do/that** желáть *(impf) +infin/*, чтóбы.
desirous [dɪ'zaɪərəs] *adj*: **to be ~ of doing** желáть *(impf) +infin*.
desist [dɪ'zɪst] *vi*: **to ~ (from)** воздéрживаться (воздержáться *perf*) (от *+gen*)
desk [dɛsk] *n* (*in office, study*) (письменный) стол*; (*for pupil*) пáрта; (*in hotel, at airport*) стóйка*; (*BRIT: also:* **cash-~**) кáсса.
desk job *n* канцелярская рабóта.
desktop ['dɛsktɔp] *adj* настóльный.
desktop publishing *n* (*COMPUT*) настóльное издáтельство, настóльная типогрáфия.
desolate ['dɛsəlɪt] *adj* (*place*) заброшенный*; (*person*) покинутый.
desolation [dɛsə'leɪʃən] *n* (*action*) опустошéние; (*quality*) опустошённость *f*.
despair [dɪs'pɛə'] *n* отчáяние ◆ *vi*: **to ~ of sth/doing** отчáиваться (отчáяться *perf*) в *+prp/+infin*; **to be in ~** быть* *(impf)* в отчáянии.
despatch [dɪs'pætʃ] *n, vt* = **dispatch**.
desperate ['dɛspərɪt] *adj* (*action, situation*) отчáянный* (отчáян); (*criminal*) отъявленный; (*person*): **he/she is ~** он/онá в отчáянии; **to be ~ to do** жáждать *(impf) +infin*; **to be ~ for money** стрáшно нуждáться *(impf)* в деньгáх.
desperately ['dɛspərɪtlɪ] *adv* отчáянно; (*very*) чрезвычáйно.
desperation [dɛspə'reɪʃən] *n* отчáяние; **in (sheer) ~** в (пóлном) отчáянии.
despicable [dɪs'pɪkəbl] *adj* презрéнный* (презрéнен).
despise [dɪs'paɪz] *vt* презирáть *(impf)*.
despite [dɪs'paɪt] *prep* несмотря на *+acc*.
despondent [dɪs'pɔndənt] *adj* унылый (уныл).
despot ['dɛspɔt] *n* дéспот.
dessert [dɪ'zə:t] *n* десéрт.
dessertspoon [dɪ'zə:tspu:n] *n* десéртная лóжка*.
destabilize [di:'steɪbɪlaɪz] *vt* (*also fig*) дестабилизировать *(impf/perf)*.
destination [dɛstɪ'neɪʃən] *n* (*of traveller*) цель *f*; (*of mail*) мéсто* назначéния.
destined ['dɛstɪnd] *adj*: **he/she is ~ to do** емý/ей суждено́ *+infin*; **to be ~ for** предназначáться *(impf)* для *+gen*.
destiny ['dɛstɪnɪ] *n* судьбá*.
destitute ['dɛstɪtju:t] *adj* (*person*) обездóленный (обездóлен).
destroy [dɪs'trɔɪ] *vt* (*also fig*) уничтожáть (уничтóжить *perf*), разрушáть (разрýшить *perf*); (*kill: pet*) усыплять (усыпить* *perf*); (: *farm animal*) забивáть (забить* *perf*).
destroyer [dɪs'trɔɪə'] *n* (*NAUT*) минонóсец*.
destruction [dɪs'trʌkʃən] *n* уничтожéние, разрушéние; (*fig: of reputation etc*) гибель *f*.
destructive [dɪs'trʌktɪv] *adj* (*capacity, force*) разрушительный; (*criticism*) деструктивный; (*emotion*) губительный* (губителен); (*child*): **he's very ~** он всё ломáет.
desultory ['dɛsəltərɪ] *adj* (*attempt*) слáбый (слаб); (*reading, work*) беспорядочный (беспорядочен).
detach [dɪ'tætʃ] *vt* снимáть (снять* *perf*); (*unstick*) отделять (отделить *perf*).
detachable [dɪ'tætʃəbl] *adj* съёмный
detached [dɪ'tætʃt] *adj* (*objective*) беспристрáстный* (беспристрáстен); **~ house** особняк*.
detachment [dɪ'tætʃmənt] *n* (*aloofness*) отдалённость *f*; (*MIL*) отряд.
detail ['di:teɪl] *n* детáль *f*, подрóбность *f* ◆ *vt* (*list*) перечислять (перечислить *perf*); **in ~**

* marks translations which have irregular inflections. The Russian-English side of the dictionary gives inflectional information.

подро́бно, в дета́лях; **to go into ~s** вдава́ться* *(impf)* в дета́ли *or* подро́бности.
detailed [ˈdi:teɪld] *adj* дета́льный* (дета́лен), подро́бный* (подро́бен).
detain [dɪˈteɪn] *vt* (*delay, confine*) заде́рживать (задержа́ть* *perf*); **to ~ in hospital** оставля́ть (оста́вить* *perf*) в больни́це.
detainee [di:teɪˈni:] *n* (*POL*) у́зник(-ица).
detect [dɪˈtɛkt] *vt* (*sense*) чу́вствовать (почу́вствовать *perf*); (*discover*) обнару́живать (обнару́жить *perf*).
detection [dɪˈtɛkʃən] *n* (*discovery*) обнаруже́ние; **crime ~** раскры́тие преступле́ний; **the criminal escaped ~** престу́пник не обнару́жен; **the mistake escaped ~** оши́бка оста́лась незаме́ченной.
detective [dɪˈtɛktɪv] *n* (*POLICE*) сы́щик, детекти́в.
detective story *n* детекти́в.
detector [dɪˈtɛktəʳ] *n* (*TECH*) дете́ктор.
détente [deɪˈtɑ:nt] *n* (*POL*) разря́дка.
detention [dɪˈtɛnʃən] *n* (*arrest*) задержа́ние; (*imprisonment*) содержа́ние под стра́жей; (*SCOL*): **to give sb ~** оставля́ть (оста́вить* *perf*) кого́-н по́сле уро́ков.
deter [dɪˈtə:ʳ] *vt* сде́рживать (сдержа́ть *perf*).
detergent [dɪˈtə:dʒənt] *n* мо́ющее сре́дство.
deteriorate [dɪˈtɪərɪəreɪt] *vi* ухудша́ться (уху́дшиться *perf*).
deterioration [dɪtɪərɪəˈreɪʃən] *n* ухудше́ние.
determination [dɪtə:mɪˈneɪʃən] *n* (*resolve*) реши́мость *f*; (*establishment*) установле́ние.
determine [dɪˈtə:mɪn] *vt* (*find out*) устана́вливать (установи́ть* *perf*); (*establish, dictate*) определя́ть (определи́ть *perf*); **to ~ that** (*establish*) устана́вливать (установи́ть* *perf*), что; **to ~ to do** (*decide*) реша́ть (реши́ть *perf*) +*infin*.
determined [dɪˈtə:mɪnd] *adj* (*person, effort*) реши́тельный* (реши́телен); (*quantity*) определённый*; **~ to do** по́лный (по́лон*) реши́мости +*infin*.
deterrence [dɪˈtɛrəns] *n* сде́рживание.
deterrent [dɪˈtɛrənt] *n* сре́дство сде́рживания, сде́рживающее сре́дство; **nuclear ~** сре́дство я́дерного сде́рживания; **to act as a ~** явля́ться (яви́ться* *perf*) сре́дством сде́рживания.
detest [dɪˈtɛst] *vt* ненави́деть* *(impf)*.
detestable [dɪˈtɛstəbl] *adj* отврати́тельный* (отврати́телен).
detonate [ˈdɛtəneɪt] *vi* взрыва́ться (взорва́ться* *perf*) ◆ *vt* взрыва́ть (взорва́ть* *perf*).
detonator [ˈdɛtəneɪtəʳ] *n* детона́тор.
detour [ˈdi:tuəʳ] *n* (*in vehicle, also US*) объе́зд; (*on foot*) обхо́д; **to make a ~** (*in vehicle*) е́хать* (пое́хать* *perf*) в объе́зд; (*on foot*) идти́* (пойти́* *perf*) в обхо́д.
detract [dɪˈtrækt] *vi*: **to ~ from** умаля́ть (умали́ть *perf*).
detractor [dɪˈtræktəʳ] *n* недоброжела́тель *m*.
detriment [ˈdɛtrɪmənt] *n*: **to the ~ of** в уще́рб +*dat*; **without ~ to** без уще́рба для +*gen*.
detrimental [dɛtrɪˈmɛntl] *adj*: **~ to** вре́дный* (вре́ден) для +*gen*.
deuce [dju:s] *n* (*TENNIS*) „ро́вно".
devaluation [dɪvæljuˈeɪʃən] *n* (*ECON*) девальва́ция.
devalue [ˈdi:ˈvælju:] *vt* (*currency*) обесце́нивать (обесце́нить *perf*); (*person, work*) недооце́нивать (недооцени́ть *perf*).
devastate [ˈdɛvəsteɪt] *vt* опустоша́ть (опустоши́ть *perf*); (*fig*): **she is ~d by** она́ потрясена́ +*instr*.
devastating [ˈdɛvəsteɪtɪŋ] *adj* (*weapon, storm*) разруши́тельный* (разруши́телен); (*news, effect*) сокруши́тельный.
devastation [dɛvəsˈteɪʃən] *n* разруше́ние, опустоше́ние.
develop [dɪˈvɛləp] *vt* (*idea, industry*) развива́ть (разви́ть* *perf*); (*plan, resource*) разраба́тывать (разрабо́тать *perf*); (*land*) застра́ивать (застро́ить *perf*); (*PHOT*) проявля́ть (прояви́ть* *perf*); (*disease*) заболева́ть (заболе́ть *perf*) +*instr* ◆ *vi* (*evolve, advance*) развива́ться (разви́ться* *perf*); (*appear*) проявля́ться (прояви́ться* *perf*); **the machine ~ed a fault** в маши́не возни́кли непола́дки; **to ~ a taste for sth** пристрасти́ться* *(perf)* к чему́-н; **to ~ into** превраща́ться (преврати́ться* *perf*) в +*acc*.
developer [dɪˈvɛləpəʳ] *n* (*also:* **property ~**: *company*) строи́тельная фи́рма; (: *person*) разрабо́тчик.
developing country [dɪˈvɛləpɪŋ-] *n* развива́ющаяся страна́*.
development [dɪˈvɛləpmənt] *n* разви́тие; (*of resources*) разрабо́тка; (*of land*) застро́йка; **housing ~** жили́щный ко́мплекс.
development area *n территория, на разви́тие кото́рой напра́влены дополни́тельные прави́тельственные сре́дства.*
deviant [ˈdi:vɪənt] *adj* отклоня́ющийся от но́рмы.
deviate [ˈdi:vɪeɪt] *vi*: **to ~ (from)** отклоня́ться (отклони́ться *perf*) (от +*gen*).
deviation [di:vɪˈeɪʃən] *n*: **~ (from)** отклоне́ние (от +*gen*).
device [dɪˈvaɪs] *n* устро́йство, прибо́р; (*ploy, stratagem*) сре́дство; **explosive ~** взры́вчатое устро́йство.
devil [ˈdɛvl] *n* дья́вол, чёрт*; **go on, be a ~!** дава́й, позво́ль себе́!; **talk of the ~!** лёгок* на поми́не!
devilish [ˈdɛvlɪʃ] *adj* дья́вольский*.
devil's advocate [dɛvlz-] *n* провока́тор.
devious [ˈdi:vɪəs] *adj* лука́вый (лука́в); (*route, path*) изви́листый (изви́лист).
devise [dɪˈvaɪz] *vt* разраба́тывать (разрабо́тать *perf*).

devoid [dɪ'vɔɪd] *adj*: ~ **of** лишённый (лишён) +*gen*.
devolution [di:və'lu:ʃən] *n* (*POL*) переда́ча вла́сти (*ме́стным о́рганам*).
devolve [dɪ'vɔlv] *vt* (*power, duty etc*) передава́ть* (переда́ть* *perf*) ◆ *vi*: **to ~ (up)on** переходи́ть* (перейти́* *perf*) к +*dat*.
devote [dɪ'vəut] *vt*: **to ~ sth to** посвяща́ть (посвяти́ть* *perf*) что-н +*dat*.
devoted [dɪ'vəutɪd] *adj* (*admirer, partner*) пре́данный* (пре́дан); (*service, friendship*) ве́рный; **he is ~ to her** он пре́дан ей; **his book is ~ to the history of Scotland** его́ кни́га посвящена́ исто́рии Шотла́ндии.
devotee [dɛvəu'ti:] *n* (*fan*) приве́рженец*; (*REL*) правове́рный(-ая) *m(f) adj*.
devotion [dɪ'vəuʃən] *n* пре́данность *f*; (*REL*) поклоне́ние.
devour [dɪ'vauə'] *vt* (*also fig*) пожира́ть (пожра́ть* *perf*).
devout [dɪ'vaut] *adj* (*REL*) благочести́вый (благочести́в).
dew [dju:] *n* роса́*.
dexterity [dɛks'tɛrɪtɪ] *n* (*manual*) ло́вкость *f*; (*mental*) сообрази́тельность *f*.
dext(e)rous ['dɛkstrəs] *adj* (*see n*) ло́вкий* (ло́вок); сообрази́тельный* (сообрази́телен).
dg *abbr* (= *decigram*) дециграмм.
DH *n abbr* (*BRIT*: = *Department of Health*) Министе́рство здравоохране́ния.
Dhaka ['dækə] *n* Да́ка.
DHSS *n abbr* (*BRIT*: *formerly*: = *Department of Health and Social Security*) Министе́рство здравоохране́ния и социа́льного обеспе́чения.
diabetes [daɪə'bi:ti:z] *n* диабе́т.
diabetic [daɪə'bɛtɪk] *n* диабе́тик ◆ *adj* диабети́ческий.
diabolical [daɪə'bɔlɪkl] *adj* дья́вольский*; (*inf*: *dreadful*) жу́ткий*.
diaeresis [daɪ'ɛrɪsɪs] *n* диере́за.
diagnose [daɪəg'nəuz] *vt* (*illness*) диагности́ровать *(impf/perf)*; (*problem*) определя́ть (определи́ть *perf*).
diagnoses [daɪəg'nəusi:z] *npl of* **diagnosis**.
diagnosis [daɪəg'nəusɪs] (*pl* **diagnoses**) *n* диа́гноз.
diagonal [daɪ'ægənl] *adj* диагона́льный ◆ *n* (*MATH*) диагона́ль *f*.
diagram ['daɪəgræm] *n* схе́ма.
dial ['daɪəl] *n* (*of clock*) цифербла́т; (*of indicator*) шкала́; (*of phone*) диск; (*of radio*) регуля́тор настро́йки ◆ *vt* (*number*) набира́ть (набра́ть* *perf*); **to ~ a wrong number** не туда́ попада́ть (попа́сть* *perf*); **can I ~ London direct?** могу́ я набра́ть Ло́ндон по автома́ту?
dial. *abbr* = **dialect**.
dial code *n* (*US*) = **dialling code**.
dialect ['daɪəlɛkt] *n* диале́кт.
dialling code ['daɪəlɪŋ-] (*US* **dial code**) *n* код; **the ~ ~ for London** код Ло́ндона.
dialling tone (*US* **dial tone**) *n* непреры́вный гудо́к*.
dialogue ['daɪəlɔg] (*US* **dialog**) *n* диало́г.
dial tone *n* (*US*) = **dialling tone**.
dialysis [daɪ'ælɪsɪs] *n* (*MED*) диа́лиз.
diameter [daɪ'æmɪtə'] *n* диа́метр.
diametrically [daɪə'mɛtrɪklɪ] *adv*: ~ **opposed (to)** диаметра́льно противополо́жный* (противополо́жен) (+*dat*).
diamond ['daɪəmənd] *n* алма́з; (*cut diamond*) бриллиа́нт; (*shape*) ромб; **~s** *npl* (*CARDS*) бу́бны* *fpl*.
diamond ring *n* бриллиа́нтовое кольцо́*.
diaper ['daɪəpə'] *n* (*US*) подгу́зник.
diaphragm ['daɪəfræm] *n* диафра́гма.
diarrhoea [daɪə'ri:ə] (*US* **diarrhea**) *n* поно́с.
diary ['daɪərɪ] *n* (*journal*) дневни́к*; (*engagements book*) записна́я кни́жка*; **to keep a ~** вести́* *(impf)* дневни́к.
diatribe ['daɪətraɪb] *n* ре́зкая кри́тика.
dice [daɪs] *npl of* **die**; (*in game*) ку́бик; (*game*) ко́сти* *fpl* ◆ *vt* (*CULIN*) ре́зать (наре́зать* *perf*) ку́биками.
dicey ['daɪsɪ] *adj* (*inf*): **it's a bit ~** э́то немно́го риско́ванно.
dichotomy [daɪ'kɔtəmɪ] *n* дихотоми́я.
dickhead ['dɪkhɛd] *n* (*inf*) муда́к.
Dictaphone® ['dɪktəfəun] *n* диктофо́н.
dictate [dɪk'teɪt] *vt* диктова́ть (продиктова́ть *perf*) ◆ *n* веле́ние ◆ *vi*: **to ~ to** диктова́ть (продиктова́ть *perf*) +*dat*; **the ~s of** веле́ние +*gen*; **I won't be ~d to by him** я не позволю́, что́бы он мне диктова́л.
dictation [dɪk'teɪʃən] *n* (*of letter*) дикто́вка*; (*SCOL*) дикта́нт; **at ~ speed** со ско́ростью дикто́вки.
dictator [dɪk'teɪtə'] *n* дикта́тор.
dictatorship [dɪk'teɪtəʃɪp] *n* диктату́ра.
diction ['dɪkʃən] *n* ди́кция.
dictionary ['dɪkʃənrɪ] *n* слова́рь* *m*.
did [dɪd] *pt of* **do**.
didactic [daɪ'dæktɪk] *adj* дидакти́ческий*, поучи́тельный* (поучи́телен).
diddle ['dɪdl] *vt* (*inf*) надува́ть (наду́ть* *perf*).
didn't ['dɪdnt] = **did not**.
die [daɪ] *n* (*pl* **dice**; *in game*) игра́льная кость* *f*; (*pl* **~s**; *TECH*) ма́трица, штамп ◆ *vi* (*person, emotion*) умира́ть (умере́ть* *perf*); (*smile, light*) угаса́ть (уга́снуть* *perf*); **to ~ of** *or* **from** умира́ть (умере́ть* *perf*) от +*gen*; **to be dying** умира́ть *(impf)*; **to be dying for sth/to do** до́ смерти хоте́ть* *(impf)* чего́-н/+*infin*
▶ **die away** *vi* (*sound*) замира́ть (замере́ть*

* marks translations which have irregular inflections. The Russian-English side of the dictionary gives inflectional information.

perf); (*light*) угаса́ть (уга́снуть* *perf*)
▸ **die down** *vi* (*wind, noise*) утиха́ть (ути́хнуть* *perf*); (*fire*) потуха́ть (поту́хнуть* *perf*); (*excitement*) уле́чься* (*perf*)
▸ **die out** *vi* (*custom*) умира́ть (умере́ть* *perf*); (*species*) вымира́ть (вы́мереть* *perf*).
diehard ['daɪhɑːd] *n* ретрогра́д ◆ *adj* непреклóнный.
diesel ['diːzl] *n* ди́зель* *m*; (*also:* **~ oil**) ди́зельное то́пливо.
diesel engine *n* ди́зельный мото́р.
diet ['daɪət] *n* дие́та ◆ *vi* (*also:* **be on a ~**) быть* (*impf*) на дие́те; **to live on a ~ of** пита́ться (*impf*) одни́м(-о́й) +*instr*.
dietician [daɪə'tɪʃən] *n* дието́лог.
differ ['dɪfəʳ] *vi*: **to ~ (from)** отлича́ться (*impf*) (от +*gen*); (*disagree*): **to ~ about** расходи́ться* (разойти́сь* *perf*) в вопро́се +*gen*; **we agreed to ~** ка́ждый из нас оста́лся при своём мне́нии.
difference ['dɪfrəns] *n* (*dissimilarity*) разли́чие; (: *in size, age*) ра́зница; (*disagreement*) разногла́сие; **it makes no ~ to me** мне всё равно́; **a ~ of opinion** расхожде́ние во мне́ниях; **to settle one's ~s** ула́живать (ула́дить* *perf*) разногла́сия.
different ['dɪfrənt] *adj* (*other*) друго́й, ино́й; (*various*) разли́чный, ра́зный; **to be ~ from** отлича́ться (*impf*) от +*gen*.
differential [dɪfə'rɛnʃəl] *n* (*MATH*) дифференциа́л; (*BRIT*: *in wages*) ра́зница в тари́фах.
differentiate [dɪfə'rɛnʃɪeɪt] *vi*: **to ~ (between)** проводи́ть* (провести́* *perf*) разли́чие (ме́жду +*instr*) ◆ *vt*: **to ~ from** отлича́ть (отличи́ть *perf*) от +*gen*.
differently ['dɪfrəntlɪ] *adv* (*otherwise*) ина́че, по-друго́му; (*in different ways*) по-ра́зному.
difficult ['dɪfɪkəlt] *adj* тру́дный* (тру́ден); (*person*) тяжёлый; **~ to understand/see** тру́дно поня́ть/ви́деть.
difficulty ['dɪfɪkəltɪ] *n* тру́дность *f*, затрудне́ние; **to have difficulties** испы́тывать (испыта́ть *perf*) тру́дности; **to be in difficulties** находи́ться* (*impf*) в тру́дном положе́нии.
diffidence ['dɪfɪdəns] *n* засте́нчивость *f*.
diffident ['dɪfɪdənt] *adj* засте́нчивый (засте́нчив).
diffuse [*vt* dɪ'fjuːz, *adj* dɪ'fjuːs] *vt* (*information*) распространя́ть (распространи́ть *perf*) ◆ *adj* (*idea, sense*) расплы́вчатый (расплы́вчат); (*light*) рассе́янный*.
dig [dɪg] (*pt, pp* **dug**) *vt* (*hole*) копа́ть (вы́копать *perf*), рыть* (вы́рыть* *perf*); (*garden*) вска́пывать (вскопа́ть *perf*) ◆ *n* (*prod*) толчо́к*; (*archaeological excavation*) раско́пки* *fpl*; (*remark*): **to have a ~ at sb** подка́лывать (подколо́ть *perf*) кого́-н; **to ~ one's nails/claws into sth** впива́ться (впи́ться* *perf*) ногтя́ми/когтя́ми во что-н
▸ **dig in** *vi* (*inf*: *eat*): **to ~ in (to)** налега́ть (нале́чь* *perf*) (на +*acc*) ◆ *vt*: **to ~ in (to)** (*compost*) вка́пывать (вкопа́ть *perf*) (в +*acc*); (*knife*) вонза́ть (вонзи́ть* *perf*) (в +*acc*); **to ~ in one's heels** (*fig*) упира́ться (упере́ться* *perf*)
▸ **dig into** *vt fus* (*snow, soil*) зарыва́ть (зары́ть* *perf*), зака́пывать (закопа́ть* *perf*); **to ~ into one's savings** нача́ть (*perf*) тра́тить сбереже́ния; **to ~ into one's pockets (for sth)** запуска́ть (запусти́ть* *perf*) руку́ в карма́н (за чем-н)
▸ **dig out** *vt* (*from snow, earth*) отка́пывать (откопа́ть *perf*)
▸ **dig up** *vt* (*plant*) выка́пывать (вы́копать *perf*); (*information*) раска́пывать (раскопа́ть *perf*).
digest [*vt* daɪ'dʒɛst, *n* 'daɪdʒɛst] *vt* (*food*) перева́ривать (перевари́ть* *perf*); (*facts*) усва́ивать (усво́ить *perf*) ◆ *n* (*book*) сбо́рник, дайдже́ст.
digestible [dɪ'dʒɛstəbl] *adj* удобовари́мый (удобовари́м).
digestion [dɪ'dʒɛstʃən] *n* пищеваре́ние.
digestive [dɪ'dʒɛstɪv] *adj* пищевари́тельный ◆ *n* (*also:* **~ biscuit**) *печéнье из муки́ гру́бого помо́ла.*
digit ['dɪdʒɪt] *n* (*number*) ци́фра; (*finger*) па́лец*.
digital ['dɪdʒɪtl] *adj*: **~ watch** электро́нные часы́ *mpl*; **~ recording** электро́нная за́пись.
digital camera *n* цифрова́я ка́мера.
digital compact cassette *n* оцифро́ванная компа́ктная кассе́та.
digital computer *n* электро́нно-вычисли́тельная маши́на.
digital TV *n* цифрово́е телеви́дение.
dignified ['dɪgnɪfaɪd] *adj* по́лный* (по́лон) досто́инства.
dignitary ['dɪgnɪtərɪ] *n* высокопоста́вленное лицо́*.
dignity ['dɪgnɪtɪ] *n* досто́инство.
digress [daɪ'grɛs] *vi*: **to ~ (from)** отступа́ть (отступи́ть* *perf*) (от +*gen*).
digression [daɪ'grɛʃən] *n* отступле́ние.
digs [dɪgz] *npl* (*BRIT*: *inf*) жили́ще.
dike [daɪk] *n* = **dyke**.
dilapidated [dɪ'læpɪdeɪtɪd] *adj* ве́тхий*.
dilate [daɪ'leɪt] *vi* расширя́ться (расши́риться *perf*) ◆ *vt* расширя́ть (расши́рить *perf*).
dilatory ['dɪlətərɪ] *adj* (*influence*) замедля́ющий; (*person*) медли́тельный* (медли́телен).
dilemma [daɪ'lɛmə] *n* диле́мма; **to be in a ~** стоя́ть (*impf*) пе́ред диле́ммой.
diligence ['dɪlɪdʒəns] *n* усе́рдие, прилежа́ние.
diligent ['dɪlɪdʒənt] *adj* (*worker*) усе́рдный* (усе́рден), приле́жный* (приле́жен); (*work*) тща́тельный* (тща́телен).
dill [dɪl] *n* укро́п*; (*seed*) укро́пное се́мя*.
dilly-dally ['dɪlɪ'dælɪ] *vi* ме́шкать (*impf*).
dilute [daɪ'luːt] *vt* (*liquid*) разбавля́ть (разба́вить* *perf*); (*belief, principle*) ослабля́ть (осла́бить* *perf*) ◆ *adj*

разба́вленный (разба́влен).

dim [dɪm] *adj* (*outline, feeling, memory*) сму́тный* (сму́тен); (*light*) ту́склый* (тускл); (*room*) пло́хо освещённый (освещён); (*eyesight*) сла́бый* (слаб); (*future, prospects*) мра́чный* (мра́чен); (*inf: person*) тупо́й* (туп) ◆ *vt* (*also US: light*) приглуша́ть (приглуши́ть* *perf*); **to take a ~ view of sth** неодобри́тельно смотре́ть* *(impf)* на что-н.

dime [daɪm] *n* (*US*) десятице́нтовая моне́та.

dimension [daɪ'mɛnʃən] *n* (*measurement*) измере́ние; (*also pl: scale, size*) разме́ры *mpl*; (*aspect*) аспе́кт.

diminish [dɪ'mɪnɪʃ] *vi* уменьша́ться (уме́ньшиться *perf*) ◆ *vt* (*belittle*) принижа́ть (прини́зить* *perf*).

diminished [dɪ'mɪnɪʃt] *adj*: **~ responsibility** (*LAW*) ограни́ченная отве́тственность *f*.

diminutive [dɪ'mɪnjutɪv] *adj* кро́шечный ◆ *n* (*LING*) уменьши́тельно-ласка́тельное сло́во.

dimly ['dɪmlɪ] *adv* (*glow, illuminate*) ту́скло; (*see, remember*) сму́тно.

dimmer ['dɪmə^r] *n* (*also:* **~ switch**) регуля́тор освещённости.

dimmers ['dɪməz] *npl* (*US: dipped headlights*) бли́жний* свет *msg* фар; (*parking lights*) стоя́ночный свет *msg*.

dimple ['dɪmpl] *n* я́мочка*.

dim-witted ['dɪm'wɪtɪd] *adj* (*inf*) тупоу́мный* (тупоу́мен).

din [dɪn] *n* гро́хот ◆ *vt* (*inf*): **to ~ sth into sb** вда́лбливать (вдолби́ть* *perf*) что-н в кого́-н.

dine [daɪn] *vi* обе́дать (пообе́дать *perf*).

diner ['daɪnə^r] *n* (*person*) обе́дающий(-ая) *m(f) adj*; (*US*) дешёвый рестора́нчик.

dinghy ['dɪŋgɪ] *n* (*also:* **sailing ~**) шлю́пка*; (*also:* **rubber ~**) надувна́я ло́дка.

dingy ['dɪndʒɪ] *adj* (*streets, room*) мра́чный* (мра́чен); (*clothes, curtains etc*) ве́тхий, замы́зганный.

dining car ['daɪnɪŋ-] *n* (*BRIT*) ваго́н-рестора́н.

dining room *n* столо́вая *f adj*.

dinner ['dɪnə^r] *n* (*evening meal*) у́жин; (*lunch, banquet*) обе́д.

dinner jacket *n* смо́кинг.

dinner party *n* зва́ный обе́д.

dinner service *n* столо́вый серви́з.

dinner time *n* (*midday*) обе́денное вре́мя* *nt*; (*evening*) вре́мя* у́жина.

dinosaur ['daɪnəsɔː^r] *n* диноза́вр.

dint [dɪnt] *n*: **by ~ of** посре́дством *+gen*.

diocese ['daɪəsɪs] *n* епа́рхия.

dioxide [daɪ'ɔksaɪd] *n* двуо́кись *f*.

dip [dɪp] *n* (*slope*) укло́н; (*depression*) впа́дина; (*CULIN*) со́ус*; (*AGR: for sheep*) дезинфици́рующий раство́р ◆ *vt* (*immerse*) погружа́ть (погрузи́ть* *perf*), окуна́ть (окуну́ть *perf*); (*: in liquid*) обма́кивать (обмакну́ть *perf*); (*BRIT: AUT: lights*) приглуша́ть (приглуши́ть* *perf*) ◆ *vi* (*ground, road*) идти́* (пойти́* *perf*) под укло́н; **to go for a ~ in the sea** окуна́ться (окуну́ться *perf*) в мо́ре.

Dip. *abbr* (*BRIT*) = **diploma**.

diphtheria [dɪf'θɪərɪə] *n* дифтери́т.

diphthong ['dɪfθɔŋ] *n* дифто́нг.

diploma [dɪ'pləumə] *n* дипло́м.

diplomacy [dɪ'pləuməsɪ] *n* диплома́тия.

diplomat ['dɪpləmæt] *n* диплома́т.

diplomatic [dɪplə'mætɪk] *adj* (*POL*) дипломати́ческий*; (*tactful*) дипломати́чный* (дипломати́чен); **to break off ~ relations (with)** (*POL*) разрыва́ть (разорва́ть* *perf*) дипломати́ческие отноше́ния (с *+instr*).

diplomatic corps *n* дипломати́ческий* ко́рпус*.

diplomatic immunity *n* дипломати́ческая неприкоснове́нность *f*.

dip stick *n* (*BRIT: AUT*) *щуп для измере́ния у́ровня ма́сла*.

dip switch *n* (*BRIT: AUT*) переключа́тель *m* све́та фар.

dire [daɪə^r] *adj* (*consequences*) злове́щий*; (*poverty, situation*) жу́ткий*.

direct [daɪ'rɛkt] *adj* прямо́й ◆ *adv* пря́мо ◆ *vt* (*company, project etc*) руководи́ть* *(impf)* *+instr*; (*play, film, programme*) ста́вить* (поста́вить* *perf*); (*letter*): **to ~ to** направля́ть (напра́вить* *perf*) *+dat*; (*attention, remark*): **to ~ (towards** *or* **at)** направля́ть (напра́вить* *perf*) (на *+acc*); (*order*): **to ~ sb to do** веле́ть *(impf)* кому́-н *+infin*; **can you ~ me to ...?** Вы не ука́жете, где нахо́дится ...?

direct access *n* (*COMPUT*) прямо́й до́ступ.

direct cost *n* (*COMM*) прямы́е затра́ты *fpl*.

direct current *n* постоя́нный ток.

direct debit *n* (*BRIT: COMM*) прямо́е дебетова́ние.

direct dialling *n* автомати́ческая телефо́нная связь *f*.

direct hit *n* (*MIL*) прямо́е попада́ние.

direction [dɪ'rɛkʃən] *n* (*way*) направле́ние; (*TV, CINEMA*) постано́вка; **~s** *npl* (*instructions*) указа́ния *ntpl*; **to have a good sense of ~** хорошо́ ориенти́роваться *(impf/perf)*; **~s for use** инстру́кция (по эксплуата́ции); **to ask for ~s (to)** спра́шивать (спроси́ть* *perf*) доро́гу (к *+dat*); **in the ~ of** в направле́нии *+gen*.

directional [dɪ'rɛkʃənl] *adj* (*TECH*) напра́вленный.

directive [dɪ'rɛktɪv] *n* (*POL, ADMIN*) директи́ва, постановле́ние; **a government ~** прави́тельственное постановле́ние.

direct labour *n* (*BRIT*) постоя́нная рабо́чая си́ла.

* marks translations which have irregular inflections. The Russian-English side of the dictionary gives inflectional information.

directly [dɪ'rɛktlɪ] *adv* пря́мо; (*at once*) сейча́с же; (*as soon as*) как то́лько.
direct mail *n* прода́жа това́ров по по́чте.
direct-mail shot [dɪ'rɛkt'meɪl-] *n* (*BRIT*) почто́вая рекла́ма.
directness [daɪ'rɛktnɪs] *n* прямота́.
director [dɪ'rɛktəʳ] *n* (*COMM*) дире́ктор*; (*of project*) руководи́тель(ница) *m(f)*; (*TV, RADIO, CINEMA*) режиссёр.
Director of Public Prosecutions *n* (*BRIT*) Гла́вный прокуро́р.
directory [dɪ'rɛktərɪ] *n* (*also COMPUT*) спра́вочник; (*also:* **street ~**) указа́тель *m*.
directory enquiries (*US* **directory assistance**) *n* (телефо́нная) спра́вочная *f adj*.
dirt [də:t] *n* грязь* *f*; **to treat sb like ~** ни во что́ не ста́вить *(impf)* кого́-н.
dirt-cheap ['də:t'tʃi:p] *adv* по дешёвке.
dirt road *n* грунтова́я доро́га.
dirty ['də:tɪ] *adj* гря́зный* ◆ *vt* па́чкать (испа́чкать *perf*).
dirty trick *n* зла́я шу́тка*.
disability [dɪsə'bɪlɪtɪ] *n* (*physical*) инвали́дность *f no pl*; (*mental*) у́мственная неполноце́нность *f*; **physical disabilities** физи́ческие недоста́тки.
disability allowance *n* посо́бие по инвали́дности.
disable [dɪs'eɪbl] *vt* (*subj*: *illness, accident*) кале́чить (искале́чить *perf*); (*tank, gun*) выводи́ть* (вы́вести* *perf*) из стро́я.
disabled [dɪs'eɪbld] *adj* (*mentally*) у́мственно неполноце́нный; (*physically*): **~ person** инвали́д ◆ *npl*: **the ~** инвали́ды *mpl*.
disabuse [dɪsə'bju:z] *vt*: **to ~ sb (of)** разуверя́ть (разуве́рить *perf*) кого́-н (в *+prp*).
disadvantage [dɪsəd'vɑ:ntɪdʒ] *n* недоста́ток*; **to be at a ~** быть* *(impf)* в невы́годном положе́нии.
disadvantaged [dɪsəd'vɑ:ntɪdʒd] *adj* (*person, region*) обездо́ленный* (обездо́лен).
disadvantageous [dɪsædvɑ:n'teɪdʒəs] *adj* невы́годный* (невы́годен).
disaffected [dɪsə'fɛktɪd] *adj* разочаро́вавшийся.
disaffection [dɪsə'fɛkʃən] *n*: **~ (with)** потеря́ дове́рия (к *+dat*).
disagree [dɪsə'gri:] *vi* (*differ*) расходи́ться* (разойти́сь* *perf*); (*be against, think otherwise*): **to ~ (with)** не соглаша́ться (согласи́ться* *perf*) (с *+instr*); **I ~ with you** я с Ва́ми не согла́сен; **we ~ on many things** мы во мно́гом расхо́димся; **garlic ~s with me** я пло́хо переношу́ чесно́к.
disagreeable [dɪsə'gri:əbl] *adj* неприя́тный* (неприя́тен).
disagreement [dɪsə'gri:mənt] *n* (*lack of consensus, argument*) разногла́сие; (*opposition*): **~ with sb/sth** несогла́сие с кем-н/чем-н; **to have a ~ with sb** име́ть *(impf)* разногла́сие с кем-н.
disallow ['dɪsə'lau] *vt* (*appeal*) отклоня́ть (отклони́ть *perf*); (*goal*) не засчи́тывать (засчита́ть *perf*).
disappear [dɪsə'pɪəʳ] *vi* исчеза́ть (исче́знуть* *perf*).
disappearance [dɪsə'pɪərəns] *n* исчезнове́ние.
disappoint [dɪsə'pɔɪnt] *vt* разочаро́вывать (разочарова́ть *perf*).
disappointed [dɪsə'pɔɪntɪd] *adj* разочаро́ванный* (разочаро́ван).
disappointing [dɪsə'pɔɪntɪŋ] *adj*: **the film is rather ~** э́тот фильм разочаро́вывает; **the election results were ~ for the Democrats** демокра́ты бы́ли разочаро́ваны результа́тами вы́боров.
disappointment [dɪsə'pɔɪntmənt] *n* разочарова́ние.
disapproval [dɪsə'pru:vəl] *n* неодобре́ние.
disapprove [dɪsə'pru:v] *vi*: **to ~ (of)** не одобря́ть *(impf)* (*+acc*).
disapproving [dɪsə'pru:vɪŋ] *adj* неодобри́тельный* (неодобри́телен).
disarm [dɪs'ɑ:m] *vt* (*MIL*) разоружа́ть (разоружи́ть *perf*); (*fig*) обезору́живать (обезору́жить *perf*) ◆ *vi* разоружа́ться (разоружи́ться *perf*).
disarmament [dɪs'ɑ:məmənt] *n* разоруже́ние.
disarming [dɪs'ɑ:mɪŋ] *adj* обезору́живающий.
disarray [dɪsə'reɪ] *n*: **in ~** (*army, organization, thoughts*) в смяте́нии; (*hair, clothes*) в беспоря́дке; **to throw into ~** приводи́ть* (привести́* *perf*) в смяте́ние.
disaster [dɪ'zɑ:stəʳ] *n* (*natural*) бе́дствие; (*man-made, also fig*) катастро́фа.
disaster area *n* (*also fig*) зо́на бе́дствия.
disastrous [dɪ'zɑ:strəs] *adj* губи́тельный* (губи́телен).
disband [dɪs'bænd] *vt* распуска́ть (распусти́ть* *perf*) ◆ *vi* расформиро́вываться (расформирова́ться *perf*).
disbelief ['dɪsbə'li:f] *n* неве́рие; **in ~** в недоуме́нии.
disbelieve ['dɪsbə'li:v] *vt* (*person*) не ве́рить *(impf) +dat*; (*story*) не ве́рить *(impf) +dat or* в *+acc*; **I don't ~ you** я не могу́ сказа́ть, что не ве́рю Вам.
disc [dɪsk] *n* (*ANAT*) межпозвоно́чный хрящ*; (*record*) диск; (*COMPUT*) = **disk**.
disc. *abbr* (*COMM*) = **discount**.
discard [dɪs'kɑ:d] *vt* (*old things*) выбра́сывать (вы́бросить* *perf*); (*idea, plan*) отбра́сывать (отбро́сить* *perf*).
disc brake *n* ди́сковый то́рмоз*.
discern [dɪ'sə:n] *vt* (*see*) различа́ть (различи́ть *perf*); (*identify*) определя́ть (определи́ть *perf*).
discernible [dɪ'sə:nəbl] *adj* различи́мый.
discerning [dɪ'sə:nɪŋ] *adj* разбо́рчивый (разбо́рчив); **he has ~ tastes** у него́ то́нкий вкус.
discharge [*vt* dɪs'tʃɑ:dʒ, *n* 'dɪstʃɑ:dʒ] *vt* (*duties*) выполня́ть (вы́полнить *perf*); (*debt*)

распла́чиваться (расплати́ться* *perf*) с +*instr*; (**waste**) выбра́сывать (вы́бросить* *perf*); (ELEC) разряжа́ть (разряди́ть* *perf*); (**pus etc**) выделя́ть *(impf)*; (**patient**) выпи́сывать (вы́писать* *perf*); (**employee**) увольня́ть (уво́лить *perf*); (**soldier**) демобилизова́ть *(impf/perf)*; (**defendant**) опра́вдывать (оправда́ть *perf*) ◆ *n* (CHEM, MED) выделе́ние; (ELEC) разря́д; (**of patient**) вы́писка; (**of employee**) увольне́ние; (**of soldier**) демобилиза́ция; (**of defendant**) оправда́ние; **to ~ a gun** разряжа́ть (разряди́ть* *perf*) ружьё.
discharged bankrupt [dɪs'tʃɑ:dʒd-] *n лицо́, восстано́вленное в права́х по́сле банкро́тства.*
disciple [dɪ'saɪpl] *n* (REL) апо́стол; (**fig**) учени́к*(-и́ца).
disciplinary ['dɪsɪplɪnərɪ] *adj* (**code, measures**) дисциплина́рный; **~ problems** пробле́мы с дисципли́ной; **to take ~ action against sb** принима́ть (приня́ть* *perf*) дисциплина́рные ме́ры к кому́-н.
discipline ['dɪsɪplɪn] *n* дисципли́на ◆ *vt* (**train**) дисциплини́ровать *(impf/perf)*; (**punish**) налага́ть (наложи́ть* *perf*) дисциплина́рное взыска́ние на +*acc*; **to ~ o.s. to do** приуча́ться (приучи́ться* *perf*) +*impf infin*.
disc jockey *n* диск-жоке́й.
disclaim [dɪs'kleɪm] *vt* отрица́ть *(impf)*.
disclaimer [dɪs'kleɪmə^r] *n* отка́з от отве́тственности; **to issue a ~** обнаро́довать *(perf)* отка́з *or* отрече́ние от отве́тственности.
disclose [dɪs'kləuz] *vt* раскрыва́ть (раскры́ть* *perf*).
disclosure [dɪs'kləuʒə^r] *n* раскры́тие.
disco ['dɪskəu] *n abbr* = **discotheque**.
discolour [dɪs'kʌlə^r] (US **discolor**) *vt* обесцве́чивать (обесцве́тить* *perf*) ◆ *vi* обесцве́чиваться (обесцве́титься* *perf*).
discolouration [dɪskʌlə'reɪʃən] (US **discoloration**) *n* обесцве́чивание.
discoloured [dɪs'kʌləd] (US **discolored**) *adj* вы́цветший.
discomfort [dɪs'kʌmfət] *n* (**unease**) нело́вкость *f*; (**pain etc**) недомога́ние.
disconcert [dɪskən'sə:t] *vt* смуща́ть (смути́ть* *perf*).
disconcerting [dɪskən'sə:tɪŋ] *adj* вызыва́ющий* чу́вство нело́вкости.
disconnect [dɪskə'nɛkt] *vt* (**pipe, telephone**) разъединя́ть (разъедини́ть *perf*); (ELEC, RADIO) отключа́ть (отключи́ть *perf*).
disconnected [dɪskə'nɛktɪd] *adj* (**speech, thoughts**) бессвя́зный* (бессвя́зен).
disconsolate [dɪs'kɔnsəlɪt] *adj* неуте́шный* (неуте́шен), безуте́шный* (безуте́шен).
discontent [dɪskən'tɛnt] *n* недово́льство.
discontented [dɪskən'tɛntɪd] *adj*: **~ (with)** недово́льный* (недово́лен) (+*instr*).
discontinue [dɪskən'tɪnju:] *vt* прекраща́ть (прекрати́ть* *perf*); **"discontinued"** (COMM) "сня́то с произво́дства".
discord ['dɪskɔ:d] *n* разла́д; (MUS) диссона́нс.
discordant [dɪs'kɔ:dənt] *adj* (**fig: note**) несогласу́ющийся; (MUS) диссони́рующий.
discotheque ['dɪskəutɛk] *n* дискоте́ка.
discount [*n* 'dɪskaunt, *vt* dɪs'kaunt] *n* ски́дка* ◆ *vt* (COMM) снижа́ть (сни́зить* *perf*) це́ну на +*acc*; (**idea, fact**) не принима́ть (приня́ть* *perf*) в расчёт; **to give sb a ~ on sth** де́лать (сде́лать *perf*) кому́-н ски́дку на что-н; **~ for cash** ски́дка* при усло́вии опла́ты нали́чными; **at a ~** со ски́дкой.
discount house *n* (**esp** BRIT: FINANCE) учётный дом*; (**esp** US: **also: discount store**) *магази́н, торгу́ющий по сни́женным це́нам.*
discount rate *n* сни́женная цена́.
discourage [dɪs'kʌrɪdʒ] *vt* (**dishearten**) отбива́ть (отби́ть* *perf*) жела́ние у +*gen*; (**advise against**): **to ~ sb from doing** отгова́ривать (отговори́ть *perf*) кого́-н +*infin*.
discouragement [dɪs'kʌrɪdʒmənt] *n* (**feeling**) разочарова́ние; **to act as a ~ to sb** отбива́ть (отби́ть* *perf*) охо́ту у кого́-н *or* +*infin or* к +*dat*.
discouraging [dɪs'kʌrɪdʒɪŋ] *adj* удруча́ющий.
discourteous [dɪs'kə:tɪəs] *adj* нелюбе́зный* (нелюбе́зен).
discover [dɪs'kʌvə^r] *vt* обнару́живать (обнару́жить *perf*).
discovery [dɪs'kʌvərɪ] *n* (**of object etc**) откры́тие; (**object etc found**) обнаруже́ние.
discredit [dɪs'krɛdɪt] *vt* дискредити́ровать *(impf/perf)* ◆ *n*: **it is to his ~ that he ...** его́ дискредити́рует то, что он ....
discreet [dɪs'kri:t] *adj* (**tactful**) такти́чный* (такти́чен); (**careful**) осмотри́тельный* (осмотри́телен); (**barely noticeable**) неприме́тный* (неприме́тен).
discreetly [dɪs'kri:tlɪ] *adv* (**see adj**) такти́чно; осмотри́тельно; неприме́тно.
discrepancy [dɪs'krɛpənsɪ] *n* расхожде́ние.
discretion [dɪs'krɛʃən] *n* (**tact**) такти́чность *f*; **at the ~ of** на усмотре́ние +*gen*; **use your (own) ~** поступа́йте по своему́ усмотре́нию.
discretionary [dɪs'krɛʃənrɪ] *adj* (**powers etc**) дискрецио́нный.
discriminate [dɪs'krɪmɪneɪt] *vi*: **to ~ between** различа́ть (различи́ть *perf*); **to ~ against** дискримини́ровать *(impf/perf)*.
discriminating [dɪs'krɪmɪneɪtɪŋ] *adj* (**discerning**)

разбо́рчивый (разбо́рчив); (*tax etc*) дифференциа́льный.
discrimination [dıskrımı'neıʃən] *n* (*bias*) дискримина́ция; (*discernment*) разбо́рчивость *f*; **racial** ~ ра́совая дискримина́ция; **sexual** ~ дискримина́ция по полово́му при́знаку.
discus ['dıskəs] *n* (*object*) диск; (*event*) мета́ние ди́ска.
discuss [dıs'kʌs] *vt* обсужда́ть (обсуди́ть* *perf*).
discussion [dıs'kʌʃən] *n* (*talk*) обсужде́ние; (*debate*) диску́ссия; **the matter is under** ~ э́тот вопро́с обсужда́ется.
disdain [dıs'deın] *n* презре́ние ◆ *vt* презира́ть (*impf*) ◆ *vi*: **to** ~ **to do** счита́ть (посчита́ть *perf*) ни́же своего́ досто́инства *+infin*.
disease [dı'zi:z] *n* боле́знь *f*.
diseased [dı'zi:zd] *adj* (*also fig*) больно́й* (бо́лен).
disembark [dısım'bɑ:k] *vt* (*goods*) выгружа́ть (вы́грузить* *perf*); (*passengers*) выса́живать (вы́садить* *perf*) ◆ *vi* выса́живаться (вы́садиться* *perf*).
disembarkation [dısɛmbɑ:'keıʃən] *n* (*see vt*) вы́грузка*; вы́садка*.
disembodied ['dısım'bɔdıd] *adj* (*limb, head*) отчленённый; (*voice*) беспеле́сный.
disembowel ['dısım'bauəl] *vt* потроши́ть (вы́потрошить *perf*).
disenchanted ['dısın'tʃɑ:ntıd] *adj*: ~ **(with)** разочаро́ванный* (разочаро́ван) (*+instr*).
disenfranchise ['dısın'fræntʃaız] *vt* (*POL*) лиша́ть (лиши́ть *perf*) избира́тельных прав; (*COMM*) лиша́ть (лиши́ть *perf*) франши́зы.
disengage [dısın'geıdʒ] *vt* (*TECH*) расцепля́ть (расцепи́ть* *perf*); (*AUT*): **to** ~ **the clutch** выключа́ть (вы́ключить *perf*) сцепле́ние.
disengagement [dısın'geıdʒmənt] *n* освобожде́ние; **military** ~ вы́вод во́йск.
disentangle [dısın'tæŋgl] *vt* (*from wreckage*) высвобожда́ть (вы́свободить* *perf*); (*wool, wire*) распу́тывать (распу́тать *perf*); **to** ~ **o.s. (from)** выпу́тываться (вы́путаться *perf*) (из *+gen*).
disfavour [dıs'feıvə^r] (*US* **disfavor**) *n* неми́лость *f*.
disfigure [dıs'fıgə^r] *vt* уро́довать (изуро́довать *perf*).
disgorge [dıs'gɔ:dʒ] *vt* (*subj: river*) выбра́сывать (вы́бросить* *perf*); (: *building, vehicle*) изверга́ть (изве́ргнуть* *perf*).
disgrace [dıs'greıs] *n* позо́р ◆ *vt* позо́рить (опозо́рить *perf*).
disgraceful [dıs'greısful] *adj* позо́рный* (позо́рен).
disgruntled [dıs'grʌntld] *adj* недово́льный* (недово́лен).
disguise [dıs'gaız] *n* (*make-up, costume*) маскиро́вка*; (*art*) гримиро́вка, маскиро́вка ◆ *vt* (*object*) маскирова́ть (замаскирова́ть *perf*); (*feelings*) скрыва́ть (скрыть* *perf*); (*person*): **to** ~ **(as)** (*dress up*) переодева́ть (переоде́ть* *perf*) (*+instr*); (*make up*) гримирова́ть (загримирова́ть *perf*) (под *+acc*); **in** ~ (*person*) переоде́тый; **to** ~ **o.s. as** переодева́ться (переоде́ться* *perf*) *+instr*; **there's no disguising the fact that ...** нельзя́ скрыть того́, что ....
disgust [dıs'gʌst] *n* отвраще́ние ◆ *vt* внуша́ть (внуши́ть *perf*) отвраще́ние *+dat*; **she walked off in** ~ она́ ушла́ в знак проте́ста.
disgusting [dıs'gʌstıŋ] *adj* отврати́тельный* (отврати́телен).
dish [dıʃ] *n* (*plate, food*) блю́до; (*also:* **satellite** ~) параболи́ческая анте́нна; **to do** *or* **wash the** ~**es** мыть* (вы́мыть* *perf*) посу́ду
▸ **dish out** *vt* (*money, advice etc*) раздава́ть* (разда́ть* *perf*); (*food*) раскла́дывать (разложи́ть* *perf*) (по таре́лкам)
▸ **dish up** *vt* (*food*) подава́ть* (пода́ть* *perf*) к столу́; (*inf: facts*) преподноси́ть* (преподнести́* *perf*).
dishcloth ['dıʃklɔθ] *n* тря́пка* для мытья́ посу́ды.
dishearten [dıs'hɑ:tn] *vt* приводи́ть* (привести́* *perf*) в уны́ние.
dishevelled [dı'ʃɛvəld] (*US* **disheveled**) *adj* растрёпанный* (растрёпан).
dishonest [dıs'ɔnıst] *adj* нече́стный* (нече́стен).
dishonesty [dıs'ɔnıstı] *n* нече́стность *f*.
dishonour [dıs'ɔnə^r] (*US* **dishonor**) *n* бесче́стье.
dishonourable [dıs'ɔnərəbl] *adj* бесче́стный* (бесче́стен).
dish soap *n* (*US*) хозя́йственное мы́ло*.
dishtowel ['dıʃtauəl] *n* (*esp US*) ку́хонное *or* посу́дное полоте́нце*.
dishwasher ['dıʃwɔʃə^r] *n* (*machine*) посудомо́ечная маши́на.
dishy [dıʃı] *adj* (*inf*): ~ **bloke** клёвый па́рень *m*.
disillusion [dısı'lu:ʒən] *vt* разочаро́вывать (разочарова́ть *perf*) ◆ *n* разочарова́ние; **to become** ~**ed (with)** разочаро́вываться (разочарова́ться *perf*) (в *+prp*).
disillusionment [dısı'lu:ʒənmənt] *n* разочарова́ние.
disincentive [dısın'sɛntıv] *n* сде́рживающее обстоя́тельство; **to be a** ~ **to sb** явля́ться (*impf*) сде́рживающим обстоя́тельством для кого́-н.
disinclined [dısın'klaınd] *adj*: **I am** ~ **to do it** мне не хо́чется э́то де́лать.
disinfect [dısın'fɛkt] *vt* дезинфици́ровать (*impf/perf*).
disinfectant [dısın'fɛktənt] *n* дезинфици́рующее сре́дство.
disinflation [dısın'fleıʃən] *n* (*ECON*) дезинфля́ция.
disinformation [dısınfə'meıʃən] *n* дезинформа́ция.

disingenuous [dɪsɪn'dʒɛnjuəs] *adj* нейскренний* (нейскренен).
disinherit [dɪsɪn'hɛrɪt] *vt*: **to ~ sb** лиша́ть (лиши́ть *perf*) кого́-н насле́дства.
disintegrate [dɪs'ɪntɪgreɪt] *vi* (*break up*) распада́ться (распа́сться* *perf*) на ча́сти; (*decay*) разлага́ться (разложи́ться* *perf*).
disinterested [dɪs'ɪntrəstɪd] *adj* (*impartial*) бескоры́стный* (бескоры́стен).
disjointed [dɪs'dʒɔɪntɪd] *adj* бессвя́зный* (бессвя́зен).
disk [dɪsk] *n* (COMPUT) диск; **single-/double-sided ~** односторо́нний/двусторо́нний диск.
disk drive *n* дисково́д.
diskette [dɪs'kɛt] *n* (*US*) = **disk**.
disk operating system *n* ди́сковая операцио́нная систе́ма.
dislike [dɪs'laɪk] *n* (*feeling*) неприя́знь *f*; (*usu pl*: *object of dislike*) нелюби́мая вещь *f* ◆ *vt* не люби́ть* *(impf)* +*gen*; **to take a ~ to sb/sth** невзлюби́ть* *(perf)* кого́-н/что-н; **I ~ the idea** мне не нра́вится э́та иде́я; **he ~s cooking** он не лю́бит гото́вить.
dislocate ['dɪsləkeɪt] *vt* вы́вихнуть *(perf)*; **he has ~d his shoulder** он вы́вихнул плечо́.
dislodge [dɪs'lɔdʒ] *vt* смеща́ть (смести́ть* *perf*).
disloyal [dɪs'lɔɪəl] *adj*: **~ (to)** неве́рный* (неве́рен) (+*dat*).
dismal ['dɪzml] *adj* уны́лый (уны́л), мра́чный* (мра́чен); **a ~ failure** жа́лкий прова́л.
dismantle [dɪs'mæntl] *vt* разбира́ть (разобра́ть* *perf*).
dismast [dɪs'mɑ:st] *vt* (*NAUT*) снима́ть (снять* *perf*) ма́чты с +*gen*.
dismay [dɪs'meɪ] *n* смяте́ние ◆ *vt* приводи́ть* (привести́* *perf*) в смяте́ние; **much to my ~** к моему́ смяте́нию; **he gasped in ~** он а́хнул в смяте́нии.
dismiss [dɪs'mɪs] *vt* (*worker*) увольня́ть (уво́лить *perf*); (*pupils, soldiers*) распуска́ть (распусти́ть* *perf*); (*LAW*: *case*) прекраща́ть (прекрати́ть* *perf*); (*possibility, idea*) отбра́сывать (отбро́сить* *perf*).
dismissal [dɪs'mɪsl] *n* (*sacking*) увольне́ние.
dismount [dɪs'maunt] *vi* (*from horse*) спе́шиваться (спе́шиться *perf*); (*from bicycle*) слеза́ть (слезть *perf*).
disobedience [dɪsə'bi:dɪəns] *n* непослуша́ние.
disobedient [dɪsə'bi:dɪənt] *adj* непослу́шный* (непослу́шен).
disobey [dɪsə'beɪ] *vt* не слу́шаться (послу́шаться *perf*).
disorder [dɪs'ɔ:də'] *n* беспоря́док*; (*MED*) расстро́йство; **civil ~** социа́льные беспоря́дки.
disorderly [dɪs'ɔ:dəlɪ] *adj* (*room etc*) беспоря́дочный; (*meeting*) неорганизо́ванный* (неорганизо́ван); (*behaviour*) бесчи́нствующий.
disorderly conduct *n* наруше́ние обще́ственного поря́дка.
disorganize [dɪs'ɔ:gənaɪz] *vt* дезорганизова́ть *(impf/perf)*.
disorganized [dɪs'ɔ:gənaɪzd] *adj* неорганизо́ванный.
disorientated [dɪs'ɔ:rɪɛnteɪtɪd] *adj* лишённый (лищён) чу́вства ориента́ции.
disown [dɪs'əun] *vt* (*action*) отка́зываться (отказа́ться* *perf*) от +*gen*; (*person*) отрека́ться (отре́чься* *perf*) от +*gen*.
disparaging [dɪs'pærɪdʒɪŋ] *adj* пренебрежи́тельный* (пренебрежи́телен); **to be ~ about sb/sth** относи́ться* (отнести́сь* *perf*) пренебрежи́тельно к кому́-н/чему́-н.
disparate ['dɪspərɪt] *adj* несравни́мый.
disparity [dɪs'pærɪtɪ] *n* нера́венство.
dispassionate [dɪs'pæʃənət] *adj* бесстра́стный* (бесстра́стен).
dispatch [dɪs'pætʃ] *vt* (*send*) отправля́ть (отпра́вить* *perf*); (*deal with*) разде́лываться (разде́латься *perf*) с +*instr*; (*kill*) поко́нчить *(perf)* с +*instr* ◆ *n* (*sending*) отпра́вка; (*PRESS*) сообще́ние; (*MIL*) донесе́ние.
dispatch department *n* отде́л отпра́вки.
dispatch rider *n* (*MIL*) мотоцикли́ст свя́зи.
dispel [dɪs'pɛl] *vt* рассе́ивать (рассе́ять *perf*).
dispensary [dɪs'pɛnsərɪ] *n* апте́ка.
dispensation [dɪspən'seɪʃən] *n* (*of justice, treatment*) осуществле́ние; (*permission*): **(special) ~** осо́бое разреше́ние.
dispense [dɪs'pɛns] *vt* (*medicines*) приготовля́ть (пригото́вить* *perf*) и отпуска́ть (отпусти́ть* *perf*); (*charity, advice*) раздава́ть* (разда́ть* *perf*); **to ~ justice** отправля́ть *(impf)* правосу́дие
▸ **dispense with** *vt fus* (*do without*) обходи́ться* (обойти́сь* *perf*) без +*gen*; (*make unnecessary*) освобожда́ть (освободи́ть* *perf*) от необходи́мости +*gen*.
dispenser [dɪs'pɛnsə'] *n* (*machine*) торго́вый автома́т.
dispensing chemist [dɪs'pɛnsɪŋ-] *n* (*BRIT*: *shop*) апте́ка.
dispersal [dɪs'pə:sl] *n* рассе́ивание.
disperse [dɪs'pə:s] *vt* (*objects*) рассе́ивать (рассе́ять *perf*); (*crowd*) разгоня́ть (разогна́ть* *perf*); (*knowledge*) распространя́ть (распространи́ть *perf*) ◆ *vi* (*crowd, clouds*) рассе́иваться (рассе́яться *perf*).
dispirited [dɪs'pɪrɪtɪd] *adj* удручённый* (удручён).
displace [dɪs'pleɪs] *vt* замеща́ть (замести́ть* *perf*).
displaced person [dɪs'pleɪst-] *n* перемещённое лицо́*.

* marks translations which have irregular inflections. The Russian-English side of the dictionary gives inflectional information.

displacement [dɪs'pleɪsmənt] *n* замеще́ние; (*PHYS*) вытесне́ние.
display [dɪs'pleɪ] *n* демонстра́ция; (*exhibition*) вы́ставка*; (*pej: bad manners*) выставле́ние напока́з; (*COMPUT, TECH*) диспле́й ◆ *vt* (*emotion, quality*) выка́зывать (вы́казать* *perf*); (*goods, exhibits*) выставля́ть (вы́ставить* *perf*) (напока́з); (*results, departure times*) пока́зывать (показа́ть* *perf*); **on ~** (*exhibits*) на вы́ставке; (*goods in window*) на витри́не.
display advertising *n* витри́нно-вы́ставочная рекла́ма.
displease [dɪs'pli:z] *vt* раздража́ть (раздражи́ть *perf*).
displeased [dɪs'pli:zd] *adj*: **~ with** раздражённый* (раздражён) *+instr*.
displeasure [dɪs'plɛʒə^r] *n* неудово́льствие.
disposable [dɪs'pəuzəbl] *adj* (*lighter, bottle*) однора́зового употребле́ния; (*syringe*) однора́зовый; **~ income** *дохо́д, кото́рым населе́ние располага́ет по́сле упла́ты нало́гов*.
disposable nappy *n* (*BRIT*) однора́зовая пелёнка*.
disposal [dɪs'pəuzl] *n* (*of goods for sale*) реализа́ция; (*of property etc: by selling*) распрода́жа; (: *by giving away*) удале́ние; (*of rubbish*) удале́ние; **to have sth at one's ~** распола́гать *(impf)* чем-н; **to put sth at sb's ~** предоставля́ть (предоста́вить* *perf*) что-н в чьё-н распоряже́ние.
dispose [dɪs'pəuz] *vi*: **~ of** (*body, unwanted goods*) избавля́ться (изба́виться* *perf*) от *+gen*; (*problem, task*) управля́ться (упра́виться* *perf*) с *+instr*; (*COMM: stock*) реализо́вывать (реализова́ть *perf*).
disposed [dɪs'pəuzd] *adj*: **I am ~ to do** я настро́ен *+infin*; **to be well ~ towards sb** хорошо́ относи́ться* *(impf)* к кому́-н.
disposition [dɪspə'zɪʃən] *n* (*nature*) нрав; (*inclination*) скло́нность *f*.
dispossess ['dɪspə'zɛs] *vt*: **to ~ sb (of)** лиша́ть (лиши́ть *perf*) кого́-н (*+gen*).
disproportion [dɪsprə'pɔ:ʃən] *n* диспропо́рция.
disproportionate [dɪsprə'pɔ:ʃənət] *adj* (*excessive*) неопра́вданно большо́й; **our income is ~ to our expenditure** на́ши дохо́ды не соизмери́мы с на́шими расхо́дами.
disprove [dɪs'pru:v] *vt* опроверга́ть (опрове́ргнуть* *perf*).
dispute [dɪs'pju:t] *n* (*domestic*) ссо́ра; (*POL, MIL, INDUSTRY*) спор; (*LAW*) тя́жба ◆ *vt* оспа́ривать (оспо́рить *perf*); **to be in** *or* **under ~** (*matter*) опротесто́вываться *(impf)*; (*territory*) оспа́риваться *(impf)*.
disqualification [dɪskwɔlɪfɪ'keɪʃən] *n*: **~ from sth** лише́ние пра́ва на уча́стие в чём-н; **~ from driving** (*BRIT*) лише́ние води́тельских прав.
disqualify [dɪs'kwɔlɪfaɪ] *vt* (*SPORT*) дисквалифици́ровать *(impf/perf)*; **to ~ sb for sth/from doing** (*status, situation*) лиша́ть (лиши́ть *perf*) кого́-н пра́ва на уча́стие в чём-н/*+infin*; (*authority*) лиша́ть (лиши́ть *perf*) *+gen*; **to ~ sb from driving** (*BRIT*) лиша́ть (лиши́ть *perf*) кого́-н води́тельских прав.
disquiet [dɪs'kwaɪət] *n* беспоко́йство.
disquieting [dɪs'kwaɪətɪŋ] *adj* трево́жный* (трево́жен).
disregard [dɪsrɪ'gɑ:d] *vt* пренебрега́ть (пренебре́чь* *perf*) ◆ *n*: **~ (for)** пренебреже́ние (к *+dat*).
disrepair ['dɪsrɪ'pɛə^r] *n*: **to fall into ~** приходи́ть* (прийти́* *perf*) в него́дность.
disreputable [dɪs'rɛpjutəbl] *adj* (*person, behaviour*) недосто́йный.
disrepute ['dɪsrɪ'pju:t] *n* дурна́я сла́ва; **to fall into ~** приобрета́ть (приобрести́* *perf*) дурну́ю сла́ву; **to bring sb/sth into ~** навлека́ть (навле́чь* *perf*) на кого́-н/что-н дурну́ю сла́ву.
disrespectful [dɪsrɪ'spɛktful] *adj* непочти́тельный* (непочти́телен).
disrupt [dɪs'rʌpt] *vt* наруша́ть (нару́шить *perf*).
disruption [dɪs'rʌpʃən] *n* (*interruption*) наруше́ние; (*disturbance*) социа́льные беспоря́дки *mpl*.
disruptive [dɪs'rʌptɪv] *adj* (*influence*) подрывно́й; (*action*) разруши́тельный.
dissatisfaction [dɪssætɪs'fækʃən] *n* недово́льство, неудовлетворённость *f*.
dissatisfied [dɪs'sætɪsfaɪd] *adj*: **~ (with)** недово́льный* (недово́лен) (*+instr*).
dissect [dɪ'sɛkt] *vt* (*ANAT*) вскрыва́ть (вскрыть* *perf*); (*theory, article*) анализи́ровать (проанализи́ровать *perf*).
disseminate [dɪ'sɛmɪneɪt] *vt* распространя́ть (распространи́ть *perf*).
dissent [dɪ'sɛnt] *n* инакомы́слие; **~ from the party line** отхо́д от парти́йной ли́нии.
dissenter [dɪ'sɛntə^r] *n* (*REL, POL*) инакомы́слящий*(-ая) *m(f) adj*.
dissertation [dɪsə'teɪʃən] *n* диссерта́ция.
disservice [dɪs'sə:vɪs] *n*: **to do sb a ~** ока́зывать (оказа́ть* *perf*) кому́-н плоху́ю услу́гу.
dissident ['dɪsɪdnt] *adj* (*faction, voice*) диссиде́нтский ◆ *n* (*POL, REL*) диссиде́нт.
dissimilar [dɪ'sɪmɪlə^r] *adj*: **~ (to)** несхо́дный (с *+instr*); **this is not ~ to ...** э́то схо́дно с *+instr* ....
dissipate ['dɪsɪpeɪt] *vt* (*heat, clouds*) рассе́ивать (рассе́ять *perf*); (*money, effort*) растра́чивать (растра́тить* *perf*).
dissipated ['dɪsɪpeɪtɪd] *adj* (*debauched*) распу́щенный* (распу́щен).
dissociate [dɪ'səuʃɪeɪt] *vt*: **to ~ from** отделя́ть (отдели́ть* *perf*) от *+gen*; **to ~ o.s. from** отмежёвываться (отмежева́ться *perf*) от *+gen*.
dissolute ['dɪsəlu:t] *adj* развра́тный* (развра́тен).
dissolution [dɪsə'lu:ʃən] *n* (*of parliament,*

organization) ро́спуск; (*of marriage*) расторже́ние.

dissolve [dɪ'zɔlv] *vt* (*substance*) растворя́ть (раствори́ть *perf*); (*organization, parliament*) распуска́ть (распусти́ть* *perf*); (*marriage*) расторга́ть (расто́ргнуть* *perf*) ◆ *vi* растворя́ться (раствори́ться *perf*); **to ~ in(to) tears** залива́ться (зали́ться* *perf*) слеза́ми.

dissuade [dɪ'sweɪd] *vt*: **to ~ sb (from sth)** отгова́ривать (отговори́ть *perf*) кого́-н (от чего́-н).

distaff ['dɪstɑ:f] *n*: **on the ~ side** по же́нской ли́нии.

distance ['dɪstns] *n* (*in space*) расстоя́ние; (*in sport*) диста́нция; (*in time*) отдалённость *f*; (*reserve*) сде́ржанность *f* ◆ *vt*: **to ~ o.s. (from)** отдаля́ться (отдали́ться *perf*) (от *+gen*); **in the ~** вдалеке́, вдали́; **from a ~** издалека́, и́здали; **what's the ~ to London?** каково́ расстоя́ние до Ло́ндона; **into the ~** вдаль; **it's within walking ~** туда́ мо́жно дойти́ пешко́м; **the town is some ~ from the sea** го́род нахо́дится в не́котором отдале́нии от мо́ря; **at a ~ of two metres** на расстоя́нии двух ме́тров; **keep your ~!** соблюда́йте диста́нцию!; **to keep sb at a ~** держа́ть *(impf)* кого́-н на расстоя́нии.

distant ['dɪstnt] *adj* (*place, time*) далёкий*; (*relative*) да́льний*; (*manner*) сде́ржанный*; **in the ~ past/future** в далёком про́шлом/-бу́дущем.

distaste [dɪs'teɪst] *n* неприя́знь *f*.

distasteful [dɪs'teɪstful] *adj* неприя́тный* (неприя́тен).

Dist. Atty. *abbr* (*US*) = **district attorney**.

distemper [dɪs'tɛmpəʳ] *n* (*paint*) те́мпера; (*disease*: *of dogs*) (соба́чья) чума́.

distend [dɪs'tɛnd] *vt* расширя́ть (расши́рить *perf*), раздува́ть (разду́ть *perf*) ◆ *vi* раздува́ться (разду́ться *perf*).

distended [dɪs'tɛndɪd] *adj* (*stomach*) взду́тый.

distil [dɪs'tɪl] (*US* **distill**) *vt* (*water*) дистилли́ровать *(impf/perf)*; (*whisky*) перегоня́ть (перегна́ть* *perf*); (*information etc*) извлека́ть (извле́чь* *perf*).

distillery [dɪs'tɪlərɪ] *n* спи́рто-во́дочный заво́д.

distinct [dɪs'tɪŋkt] *adj* (*clear*) отчётливый (отчётлив); (*unmistakable*) определённый; (*different*): **~ (from)** отли́чный* (отли́чен) (от *+gen*); **as ~ from** в отли́чие от *+gen*.

distinction [dɪs'tɪŋkʃən] *n* (*difference*) отли́чие; (*honour*) честь *f*; (*in exam*) ≈ "отли́чно"; **to draw a ~ between** проводи́ть* (провести́* *perf*) разли́чие ме́жду *+instr*; **to pass an exam with ~** сдава́ть* (сдать* *perf*) экза́мен на отли́чно; **he is a writer of ~** он выдаю́щийся писа́тель.

distinctive [dɪs'tɪŋktɪv] *adj* (*voice, walk etc*) своеобра́зный* (своеобра́зен), характе́рный* (характе́рен); (*feature*) отличи́тельный.

distinctly [dɪs'tɪŋktlɪ] *adv* (*remember, specify*) отчётливо; (*unhappy, better*) определённо.

distinguish [dɪs'tɪŋgwɪʃ] *vt* различа́ть (различи́ть *perf*); **to ~ (between)** проводи́ть* (провести́* *perf*) разли́чие (ме́жду *+instr*); **to ~ o.s.** отлича́ться (отличи́ться *perf*).

distinguished [dɪs'tɪŋgwɪʃt] *adj* (*eminent*) выдаю́щийся*; (*in appearance*) благоро́дный* (благоро́ден).

distinguishing [dɪs'tɪŋgwɪʃɪŋ] *adj* (*feature*) отличи́тельный.

distort [dɪs'tɔ:t] *vt* искажа́ть (искази́ть* *perf*).

distortion [dɪs'tɔ:ʃən] *n* искаже́ние.

distract [dɪs'trækt] *vt* отвлека́ть (отвле́чь* *perf*).

distracted [dɪs'træktɪd] *adj* (*dreaming*) невнима́тельный* (невнима́телен); (*look*) отсу́тствующий*; (*anxious*) встрево́женный* (встрево́жен).

distraction [dɪs'trækʃən] *n* (*inattention*) отвлече́ние; (*confusion*) пу́таница; (*amusement*) развлече́ние; **to drive sb to ~** доводи́ть* (довести́* *perf*) кого́-н до безу́мия.

distraught [dɪs'trɔ:t] *adj*: **~ (with)** (*pain, worry*) обезу́мевший (от *+gen*).

distress [dɪs'trɛs] *n* (*extreme worry, hardship*) отча́яние; (*through pain*) страда́ние ◆ *vt* огорча́ть (огорчи́ть *perf*); **the ship is in ~** кора́бль те́рпит бе́дствие; **he is in ~** он в бе́дственном положе́нии; **~ed area** (*BRIT*) райо́н бе́дствия.

distressing [dɪs'trɛsɪŋ] *adj* огорчи́тельный* (огорчи́телен).

distress signal *n* сигна́л бе́дствия.

distribute [dɪs'trɪbju:t] *vt* (*leaflets, prizes etc*) раздава́ть* (разда́ть* *perf*); (*profits, weight*) распределя́ть (распредели́ть* *perf*).

distribution [dɪstrɪ'bju:ʃən] *n* (*of goods*) распростране́ние; (*of profits, weight*) распределе́ние.

distribution cost *n* изде́ржки* *fpl* обраще́ния.

distributor [dɪs'trɪbjutəʳ] *n* (*COMM*) дистрибью́тер; (*AUT, TECH*) распредели́тель *m* зажига́ния.

district ['dɪstrɪkt] *n* райо́н.

district attorney *n* (*US*) ≈ окружно́й прокуро́р.

district council *n* (*BRIT*) райо́нный сове́т.

district nurse *n* (*BRIT*) уча́стковая медсестра́*.

distrust [dɪs'trʌst] *n* недове́рие ◆ *vt* не доверя́ть *(impf)* *+dat*.

distrustful [dɪs'trʌstful] *adj*: **~ (of)** недове́рчивый (недове́рчив) (к *+dat*).

disturb [dɪs'tə:b] *vt* (*person*) беспоко́ить (побеспоко́ить *perf*); (*interrupt*: *thoughts,*

* marks translations which have irregular inflections. The Russian-English side of the dictionary gives inflectional information.

peace etc) мешáть (помешáть *perf*) *+dat*; (*disorganize*) нарушáть (нарýшить *perf*); **sorry to ~ you** извини́те за беспокóйство.
disturbance [dɪs'tə:bəns] *n* расстрóйство; (*political etc*) волнéния *ntpl*; (*violent event*) беспоря́дки *mpl*; (*of mind*) расстрóйство; (*by drunks etc*) нарушéние (общéственного поря́дка; **to cause a ~** (*in street etc*) вызывáть (вы́звать* *perf*) беспоря́дки; **~ of the peace** нарушéние общéственного поря́дка.
disturbed [dɪs'tə:bd] *adj* (*person*: *upset*) расстрóенный* (расстрóен); (*childhood*) неспокóйный; **mentally ~** душевнобольнóй; **emotionally ~** психи́чески неуравновéшенный.
disturbing [dɪs'tə:bɪŋ] *adj* тревóжный* (тревóжен).
disuse [dɪs'ju:s] *n*: **to fall into ~** выходи́ть* (вы́йти* *perf*) из употреблéния.
disused [dɪs'ju:zd] *adj* забрóшенный* (забрóшен).
ditch [dɪtʃ] *n* ров, канáва; (*for irrigation*) канáл ◆ *vt* (*inf*: *person, car*) бросáть (брóсить* *perf*); (: *plan*) забрáсывать (забрóсить* *perf*).
dither ['dɪðə'] *vi* колебáться* *(impf)*.
ditto ['dɪtəu] *adv* так же.
divan [dɪ'væn] *n* (*also*: **~ bed**) тахтá.
dive [daɪv] *n* (*from board*) прыжóк* (*в вóду*); (*underwater*) ныря́ние; (*of submarine*) погружéние; (*pej*: *place*) забегáловка ◆ *vi* ныря́ть *(impf)*; (*submarine*) погружáться (погрузи́ться* *perf*); **to ~ into** (*bag, drawer etc*) запускáть (запусти́ть* *perf*) рýку в *+acc*; (*shop, car etc*) ныря́ть (нырнýть *perf*) в *+acc*.
diver ['daɪvə'] *n* водолáз.
diverge [daɪ'və:dʒ] *vi* расходи́ться (разойти́сь* *perf*).
divergent [daɪ'və:dʒənt] *adj* расходя́щийся*.
diverse [daɪ'və:s] *adj* разнообрáзный* (разнообрáзен).
diversification [daɪvə:sɪfɪ'keɪʃən] *n* диверсификáция.
diversify [daɪ'və:sɪfaɪ] *vi* разнообрáзить* *(impf)*; (*COMM*) расширя́ть (расши́рить *perf*) вы́бор.
diversion [daɪ'və:ʃən] *n* (*BRIT*: *AUT*) объéзд; (*of attention, funds*) отвлечéние.
diversionary [daɪ'və:ʃənrɪ] *adj* диверсиóнный.
diversity [daɪ'və:sɪtɪ] *n* разнообрáзие, многообрáзие.
divert [daɪ'və:t] *vt* (*funds, attention*) отвлекáть (отвлéчь* *perf*); (*traffic*) отводи́ть* (отвести́* *perf*).
divest [daɪ'vɛst] *vt*: **to ~ sb of** лишáть (лиши́ть *perf*) когó-н *+gen*.
divide [dɪ'vaɪd] *vt* (*separate*) разделя́ть (раздели́ть* *perf*); (*MATH*) дели́ть* (раздели́ть* *perf*); (*share out*) дели́ть* (подели́ть* *perf*) ◆ *vi* (*cells etc*) дели́ться* (раздели́ться* *perf*); (*road*) разделя́ться (раздели́ться* *perf*); (*people, groups*) дели́ться* *or* разделя́ться (раздели́ться* *perf*) ◆ *n* расхождéние; **to ~ (between** *or* **among)** дели́ть* (подели́ть* *perf*) (мéжду *+instr*); **40 ~d by 5** 40 раздели́ть на 5
▸ **divide out** *vt*: **to ~ out (between** *or* **among)** разделя́ть (раздели́ть* *perf*) (мéжду *+instr*).
divided [dɪ'vaɪdɪd] *adj* (*fig*: *country, couple*) разделённый* (разделён); **opinions were ~** мнéния раздели́лись.
divided highway *n* (*US*) шоссé *nt ind*.
dividend ['dɪvɪdɛnd] *n* (*COMM*) дивидéнд; (*fig*): **to pay ~s** окупáться (окупи́ться *perf*).
dividend cover *n* (*COMM*) покры́тие дивидéнда.
dividers [dɪ'vaɪdəz] *npl* (*MATH, TECH*) раздели́тельный ци́ркуль *msg*.
divine [dɪ'vaɪn] *adj* (*also fig*) божéственный ◆ *vt* (*future, truth*) угáдывать (угадáть *perf*); (*water, metal*) искáть* *(impf)*.
diving ['daɪvɪŋ] *n* ныря́ние; (*SPORT*) прыжки́ *mpl* в вóду.
diving board *n* вы́шка* (*для прыжкóв в вóду*).
diving suit *n* гидрокостю́м.
divinity [dɪ'vɪnɪtɪ] *n* (*holiness*) божéственность *f*; (*god*) божествó*; (*SCOL*) богослóвие.
divisible [dɪ'vɪzəbl] *adj* (*MATH*): **~ (by)** дели́мый (на *+acc*); **to be ~ into** подразделя́ться *(impf)* на *+acc*.
division [dɪ'vɪʒən] *n* (*also MATH*) делéние; (*sharing out*) разделéние; (*disagreement*) разноглáсие; (*BRIT*: *POL*) *парлáментское голосовáние, совершáемое в рáзных кóмнатах*; (*COMM*) подразделéние, отделéние; (*MIL*) диви́зия; (*SPORT*) ли́га; **~ of labour** разделéние трудá.
divisive [dɪ'vaɪsɪv] *adj* (*tactics, system etc*) вызывáющий* разноглáсия.
divorce [dɪ'vɔ:s] *n* развóд ◆ *vt* (*spouse*) разводи́ться* (развести́сь* *perf*) с *+instr*; (*dissociate*) отделя́ть (отдели́ть* *perf*).
divorced [dɪ'vɔ:st] *adj* разведённый* (разведён).
divorcee [dɪvɔ:'si:] *n* разведённый(-ая) *m(f) adj*.
divot ['dɪvət] *n* вы́рванный кусóк* дёрна.
divulge [daɪ'vʌldʒ] *vt* разглашáть (разгласи́ть* *perf*).
DIY *n abbr* (*BRIT*) = **do-it-yourself**.
dizziness ['dɪzɪnɪs] *n* головокружéние.
dizzy ['dɪzɪ] *adj* (*height*) головокружи́тельный; **~ turn** *or* **spell** при́ступ головокружéния; **I feel ~** у меня́ крýжится головá; **to make sb ~** приводи́ть* (привести́* *perf*) когó-н в смятéние.
DJ *n abbr* = **disc jockey**.
d.j. *n abbr* = **dinner jacket**.
Djakarta [dʒə'kɑ:tə] *n* Джакáрта.
DJIA *n abbr* (*US*: = *Dow-Jones Industrial Average*) *и́ндекс Доу Джóнса*.
dl *abbr* (= *decilitre*) децили́тр.
DLit(t) *n abbr* (= *Doctor of Literature, Doctor of Letters*) дóктор филолóгии.
DLO *n abbr* (= *dead-letter office*) Отдéл

недоста́вленной корреспонде́нции.
dm *abbr* (= *decimetre*) дм= *дециме́тр.*
DMus *n abbr* (= *Doctor of Music*) до́ктор музыкове́дения.
DMZ *n abbr* (= *demilitarized zone*) демилитаризо́ванная зо́на.
DNA *n abbr* (= *deoxyribonucleic acid*) ДНК= *дезоксирибонуклеи́новая кислота́.*
Dnieper ['dni:pə^r] *n*: **the ~** Днепр.

KEYWORD

do [du:] (*pt* **did**, *pp* **done**) *aux vb* **1** (*in negative constructions and questions*); **I don't understand** я не понима́ю; **she doesn't want it** она́ не хо́чет э́то; **didn't you know?** ра́зве Вы не зна́ли?; **what do you think?** как Вы ду́маете?
2 (*for emphasis*) да; **she does look rather pale** да, она́ вы́глядит о́чень бле́дной; **oh do shut up!** да, замолчи́те же!
3 (*in polite expressions*) пожа́луйста; **do sit down/help yourself** пожа́луйста, сади́тесь/-угоща́йтесь; **do take care!** пожа́луйста, береги́те себя́!
4 (*used to avoid repeating vb*): **she swims better than I do** она́ пла́вает лу́чше меня́ *or* чем я; **do you read/buy newspapers? – yes, I do/no, I don't** Вы чита́ете/покупа́ете газе́ты? – да, (чита́ю/покупа́ю)/нет, (не чита́ю/-покупа́ю); **she lives in Glasgow – so do I** она́ живёт в Гла́зго – и, я то́же; **he didn't like it and neither did we** ни ему́, ни нам э́то не понра́вилось; **who made this mess? – I did** кто здесь насори́л? – я; **he asked me to help him and I did** он попроси́л меня́ помо́чь ему́, что я и сде́лал
5 (*in question tags*) ве́рно, ведь; **you like him, don't you?** он Вам нра́вится, ве́рно?, он ведь Вам нра́вится; **I don't know him, do I?** я ведь его́ не зна́ю
◆ *vt* **1** де́лать (сде́лать *perf*); **what are you doing tonight?** что Вы де́лаете сего́дня ве́чером?; **I've got nothing to do** мне не́чего де́лать; **what can I do for you?** чем я могу́ Вам помо́чь?; **we're doing "Othello" at school** (*studying*) мы прохо́дим "Оте́лло" в шко́ле; (*performing*) мы ста́вим "Оте́лло" в шко́ле; **to do one's teeth** чи́стить* (почи́стить* *perf*) зу́бы; **to do one's hair** причёсываться (причеса́ться *perf*); **to do the washing-up** мыть (помы́ть *perf*) посу́ду
2 (*AUT etc*): **the car was doing 100 (km/h)** маши́на шла со ско́ростью 100 км/ч; **we've done 200 km already** мы уже́ прое́хали 200 км; **he can do 100 mph in that car** на э́той маши́не он мо́жет е́хать со ско́ростью 100 миль в час
◆ *vi* **1** (*act, behave*) де́лать (сде́лать *perf*); **do as I do** де́лайте, как я; **you did well to react so quickly** Вы молоде́ц, что так бы́стро среаги́ровали
2 (*get on, fare*): **he's doing well/badly at school** он хорошо́/пло́хо у́чится; **the firm is doing well** дела́ в фи́рме иду́т успе́шно; **how do you do?** о́чень прия́тно
3 (*be suitable*) подходи́ть (подойти́ *perf*); **will it do?** э́то подойдёт?
4 (*be sufficient*) хвата́ть (хвати́ть *perf*) +*gen*; **will ten pounds do?** десяти́ фу́нтов хва́тит?; **that'll do** ла́дно, хорошо́; **that'll do!** (*in annoyance*) дово́льно!, хва́тит!; **to make do (with)** обходи́ться (обойти́сь *perf*) (+*instr*)
◆ *n* (*inf*): **we're having a bit of a do on Saturday** у нас бу́дет вечери́нка в суббо́ту; **it was a formal do** э́то был официа́льный приём
▸ **do away with** *vt fus* (*kill*) прико́нчить (*perf*); (*abolish*) поко́нчить (*perf*) с +*instr*
▸ **do for** *vt fus* (*BRIT: inf*) убира́ть (*impf*) у +*gen*
▸ **do up** *vt* (*laces*) завя́зывать (завяза́ть* *perf*); (*dress, buttons*) застёгивать (застегну́ть *perf*); (*room, house*) ремонти́ровать* (отремонти́ровать* *perf*)
▸ **do with** *vt fus*: **I could do with a drink** я бы вы́пил чего́-нибудь; **I could do with some help** по́мощь мне бы не помеша́ла; **what has it got to do with you?** како́е э́то к Вам име́ет отноше́ние?; **I won't have anything to do with it** я не жела́ю име́ть к э́тому никако́го отноше́ния; **it has to do with money** э́то каса́ется де́нег
▸ **do without** *vt fus* обходи́ться* (обойти́сь* *perf*) без +*gen*; **if you're late for tea then you'll do without** е́сли Вы опозда́ете, то оста́нетесь без ча́я.

do. *abbr* = **ditto.**
DOA *abbr* (= *dead on arrival*): **he was ~** по прибы́тии в больни́цу он был мёртв.
d.o.b. *abbr* = **date of birth.**
doc [dɔk] *n* (*inf*) до́ктор.
docile ['dəusaɪl] *adj* кро́ткий* (кро́ток).
dock [dɔk] *n* (*NAUT*) док; (*LAW*) скамья́ подсуди́мых; (*BOT*) щаве́ль* *m* ◆ *vi* (*NAUT*) прича́ливать (прича́лить *perf*); (*SPACE*) стыкова́ться (состыкова́ться *perf*) ◆ *vt*: **they ~ed a third of his wages** они́ удержа́ли треть его́ зарпла́ты; **~s** *npl* (*NAUT*) док, верфь *f*.
dock dues [-dju:z] *npl* (*COMM*) пла́та за по́льзование до́ком.
docker ['dɔkə^r] *n* до́кер.
docket ['dɔkɪt] *n* (*ADMIN, COMM*: *certificate*) квита́нция; (*on parcel*) о́пись *f*.
dockyard ['dɔkjɑ:d] *n* док, верфь *f*.
doctor ['dɔktə^r] *n* (*MED*) врач*; (*SCOL*) до́ктор* ◆ *vt*: **I ~ed his coffee with arsenic** я подмеша́л в его́ ко́фе мышья́к; **~'s office** (*US*) враче́бный

* marks translations which have irregular inflections. The Russian-English side of the dictionary gives inflectional information.

кабинéт.
doctorate [ˈdɔktərɪt] *n* (*thesis*) дóкторская рабóта; (*degree*) дóкторская стéпень* *f*.
Doctor of Philosophy *n* (*degree, person*) дóктор филосóфии *or* филосóфских наýк.
doctrine [ˈdɔktrɪn] *n* доктрúна.
docudrama [ˈdɔkjudrɑːmə] *n фильм úли прогрáмма, в оснóву котóрых вошлú реáльные событuя.*
document [*n* ˈdɔkjumənt, *vb* ˈdɔkjumɛnt] *n* докумéнт ◆ *vt* документúровать *(impf/perf)*.
documentary [dɔkjuˈmɛntərɪ] *adj* документáльный ◆ *n* (*TV, CINEMA*) документáльный фúльм.
documentation [dɔkjumənˈteɪʃən] *n* (*also COMPUT*) документáция.
DOD *n abbr* (*US*: = *Department of Defense*) Департáмент оборóны.
doddering [ˈdɔdərɪŋ] *adj* дряхлый* (дряхл).
doddery [ˈdɔdərɪ] *adj* = **doddering**.
doddle [ˈdɔdl] *n* (*inf*) пустяк, пáра пустякóв.
Dodecanese [dəudɪkəˈniːz] *n*: **the ~ (Islands)** Додеканéзские острова* *mpl*.
dodge [dɔdʒ] *n* (*trick*) увёртка*, улóвка ◆ *vt* увёртываться (увернýться *perf*) от *+gen* ◆ *vi* увёртываться (увернýться *perf*); (*SPORT*) дéлать (сдéлать *perf*) обмáнное движéние; **to ~ out of the way** отскáкивать (отскочúть* *perf*) в сторонý; **to ~ through the traffic** лавúровать *(impf)* в потóке машúн.
dodgems [ˈdɔdʒəmz] *npl* (*BRIT*) аттракциóнный электромобúль *msg*.
dodgy [ˈdɔdʒɪ] *adj* (*inf*: *plan*) рискóванный* (рискóван); (: *person*): **~ character** подозрúтельный тип.
DOE *n abbr* (*BRIT*: = *Department of the Environment*) Департáмент охрáны окружáющей среды́; (*US*: = *Department of Energy*) Департáмент энергéтики.
doe [dəu] *n* (*deer*) сáмка* олéня; (*rabbit*) сáмка* крóлика.
does [dʌz] *vb see* **do**.
doesn't [ˈdʌznt] = **does not**.
dog [dɔg] *n* собáка ◆ *vt* преслéдовать *(impf)*; **to go to the ~s** (*fig*) приходúть* (прийтú* *perf*) в упáдок.
dog biscuits *npl* галéты *fpl* для собáк.
dog collar *n* ошéйник; (*REL*) *высóкий жёсткий воротнúк у свящéнников.*
dog-eared [ˈdɔgɪəd] *adj* потрёпанный* (потрёпан).
dog food *n* корм* для собáк.
dogged [ˈdɔgɪd] *adj* упóрный.
doggy bag [ˈdɔgɪ-] *n пакéт, в котóром посетúтели ресторáна мóгут унестú объéдки.*
dogma [ˈdɔgmə] *n* дóгма.
dogmatic [dɔgˈmætɪk] *adj* догматúческий*.
do-gooder [duːˈgudəʳ] *n* (*pej*) благодéтель(ница) *m(f)*.
dogsbody [ˈdɔgzbɔdɪ] *n* (*BRIT*: *inf*) ишáк*.
doily [ˈdɔɪlɪ] *n* ажýрная *or* кружевнáя салфéточка.
doing [ˈduɪŋ] *n*: **this is your ~** э́то твоúх рук дéло.
doings [ˈduɪŋz] *npl* (*activities*) дéйствия *ntpl*.
do-it-yourself [ˈduːɪtjɔːˈsɛlf] *n* сдéлай сам.
doldrums [ˈdɔldrəmz] *npl*: **to be in the ~** (*person*) хандрúть *(impf)*; (*business*) находúться *(impf)* в упáдке.
dole [dəul] *n* (*BRIT*) посóбие по безрабóтице; **to be on the ~** получáть *(impf)* посóбие по безрабóтице
▸ **dole out** *vt* (*food, money*) раздавáть* (раздáть* *perf*).
doleful [ˈdəulful] *adj* скóрбный* (скóрбен).
doll [dɔl] *n* (*also US*: *inf*) кýкла*.
dolled up *adj* (*inf*) разряженный (разряжен).
dollar [ˈdɔləʳ] *n* дóллар.
dollar area *n* дóлларовая зóна.
dollop [ˈdɔləp] *n*: **a ~ (of)** лóжка (*+gen*).
dolly [ˈdɔlɪ] *n* кýкла.
Dolomites [ˈdɔləmaɪts] *npl*: **the ~** Доломúтовые Áльпы *fpl*.
dolphin [ˈdɔlfɪn] *n* дельфúн.
domain [dəˈmeɪn] *n* (*sphere*) сфéра; (*empire*) владéние.
dome [dəum] *n* кýпол*.
domestic [dəˈmɛstɪk] *adj* домáшний*; (*trade, politics*) внýтренний*; (*happiness*) семéйный.
domesticated [dəˈmɛstɪkeɪtɪd] *adj* (*animal*) одомáшненный; (*person*) домовúтый (домовúт); **he's very ~** он óчень домовúтый.
domesticity [dəumɛsˈtɪsɪtɪ] *n* домáшняя жизнь *f*.
domestic servant *n* прислýга.
domicile [ˈdɔmɪsaɪl] *n* (*LAW, ADMIN*) мéсто* жúтельства.
dominant [ˈdɔmɪnənt] *adj* (*share, role*) преобладáющий, доминúрующий; (*partner*) влáстный* (влáстен).
dominate [ˈdɔmɪneɪt] *vt* доминúровать *(impf)* над *+instr*.
domination [dɔmɪˈneɪʃən] *n* преобладáние, доминúрование.
domineering [dɔmɪˈnɪərɪŋ] *adj* влáстный* (влáстен).
Dominican Republic [dəˈmɪnɪkən-] *n*: **the ~ ~** Доминикáнская Респýблика.
dominion [dəˈmɪnɪən] *n* (*territory*) доминиóн; (*authority*): **to have ~ over** владычествовать *(impf)* над *+instr*.
domino [ˈdɔmɪnəu] (*pl* **~es**) *n* доминó *nt ind*.
domino effect *n* цепнáя реáкция.
dominoes [ˈdɔmɪnəuz] *n* (*game*) доминó *nt ind*.
don [dɔn] *n* (*BRIT*: *SCOL*) преподавáтель(ница) *m(f)* ◆ *vt* (*clothing*) надевáть (надéть* *perf*).
donate [dəˈneɪt] *vt*: **to ~ (to)** жéртвовать (пожéртвовать *perf*) (*+dat or* на *+acc*).
donation [dəˈneɪʃən] *n* пожéртвование.
done [dʌn] *pp of* **do**.
donkey [ˈdɔŋkɪ] *n* осёл*, ишáк.

donkey-work ['dɔŋkɪwə:k] *n* (*BRIT: inf*) ишáчья рабóта.
donor ['dəunə^r] *n* (*MED: of blood, heart etc*) дóнор; (*to charity*) жéртвователь(ница) *m(f)*.
donor card *n* дóнорская кáрточка.
don't [dəunt] = **do not**.
donut ['dəunʌt] *n* (*US*) = **doughnut**.
doodle ['du:dl] *vi* чи́ркать *(impf)* ◆ *n* карáкули* *fpl*.
doom [du:m] *n* рок ◆ *vt*: **the plan was ~ed to failure** план был обречён на провáл.
doomsday ['du:mzdeɪ] *n* стрáшный суд*.
door [dɔ:^r] *n* дверь* *f*; **to go from ~ to ~** ходи́ть* *(impf)* от дóма к дóму.
doorbell ['dɔ:bɛl] *n* (двернóй) звонóк*.
door handle *n* дверная рýчка*; (*of car*) рýчка* двéри.
doorman ['dɔ:mən] *irreg n* (*in hotel*) швейцáр; (*in block of flats*) приврáтник.
doormat ['dɔ:mæt] *n* (*mat*) полови́к*; (*inf: person*) тря́пка* *m/f*.
doorpost ['dɔ:pəust] *n* дверной кося́к*.
doorstep ['dɔ:stɛp] *n* порóг; **on the ~** на порóге.
door-to-door ['dɔ:tə'dɔ:^r] *adj*: **~ salesman** *агéнт, сбывáющий товáры и различные ви́ды услýг непосрéдственно в домáх потреби́телей*; **~ selling** продáжа вразнóс.
doorway ['dɔ:weɪ] *n* дверной проём; **in the ~** в дверя́х.
dope [dəup] *n* (*inf: drug*) наркóтик; (*: in sport*) дóпинг; (*: person*) придýрок*; (*: information*) секрéтная информáция ◆ *vt* (*horse, person*) вводи́ть* (ввести́* *perf*) наркóтик *+dat*.
dopey ['dəupɪ] *adj* (*inf: groggy*) одурмáненный; (*: stupid*) одурéлый.
dormant ['dɔ:mənt] *adj* (*plant*) покóящийся; (*volcano*) спя́щий; (*idea, report etc*): **to lie ~** бездéйствовать *(impf)*.
dormer ['dɔ:mə^r] *n* (*also:* **~ window**) мансáрдное окнó*.
dormice ['dɔ:maɪs] *npl of* **dormouse**.
dormitory ['dɔ:mɪtrɪ] *n* (*room*) óбщая спáльня*; (*US: building*) общежи́тие.
dormouse ['dɔ:maus] (*pl* **dormice**) *n* сóня.
Dors *abbr* (*BRIT: POST*) = *Dorset*.
DOS [dɔs] *n abbr* (*COMPUT: = disk operating system*) ДОС= *ди́сковая операциóнная систéма*.
dosage ['dəusɪdʒ] *n* дóза.
dose [dəus] *n* дóза; (*BRIT: bout*) при́ступ ◆ *vt*: **to ~ o.s. with** принимáть (приня́ть* *perf*); **I had a ~ of flu last week** на прóшлой недéле у меня́ был грипп.
dosh [dɔʃ] *n* (*inf*) бáбки *pl*.
dosser ['dɔsə^r] (*inf*) *n* (*tramp*) бомж; (*layabout*) разгильдя́й.
doss house ['dɔs-] *n* (*BRIT: inf*) ночлéжка*.
dossier ['dɔsɪeɪ] *n* досьé *nt ind*.
DOT *n abbr* (*US: = Department of Transportation*) департáмент путéй сообщéния.
dot [dɔt] *n* тóчка*; (*speck*) пя́тнышко* ◆ *vt*: **~ted with** усéянный (усéян) *+instr*; **on the ~** минýта в минýту.
dote [dəut]: **to ~ on** *vt fus* души́ не ча́ять *(impf)* в *+prp*.
dot-matrix printer [dɔt'meɪtrɪks-] *n* (*COMPUT*) мáтричный при́нтер.
dotted line ['dɔtɪd-] *n* пункти́рная ли́ния; **to sign on the ~ ~** (*fig*) окончáтельно соглашáться (согласи́ться *perf*).
dotty ['dɔtɪ] *adj* (*inf*) трóнутый.
double ['dʌbl] *adj* двойнóй ◆ *adv*: **to cost ~** стóить *(impf)* вдвóе дорóже ◆ *n* двойни́к* ◆ *vt* удвáивать (удвóить *perf*); (*fold in two*) склáдывать (сложи́ть* *perf*) вдвóе ◆ *vi* (*increase*) удвáиваться (удвóиться *perf*); **to ~ as** (*person*) совмещáть *(impf)* обя́занности *+gen*; (*object*) служи́ть* *(impf)* одноврéменно *+instr*; **he ~s as a servant in this play** он тáкже исполня́ет роль слуги́ в э́том спектáкле; **on the ~**, (*BRIT*) **at the ~** бегóм; **~ five two six (5526)** (*TEL*) пятьдеся́т пять двáдцать шесть; **it's spelt with a ~ "l"** пи́шется с двумя́ „л"
▸ **double back** *vi* разворáчиваться (разверну́ться *perf*) и идти́* (пойти́* *perf*) назáд
▸ **double up** *vi* (*bend over*) скóрчиваться (скóрчиться *perf*); (*share room*) дели́ть *(impf)*.
double bass *n* контрабáс.
double bed *n* двуспáльная кровáть *f*.
double bend *n* (*BRIT*) изви́листая дорóга.
double blind *n* эксперимéнт, в котóром исслéдуемый объéкт неизвéстен ни эксперимéнтáторам, ни эксперименти́руемым (*в мáркетинге*).
double-breasted ['dʌbl'brɛstɪd] *adj* двубóртный.
double-check ['dʌbl'tʃɛk] *vti* перепроверя́ть (перепровéрить *perf*).
double-click ['dʌbl'klɪk] *vt* (*COMPUT*) двáжды нажимáть (нажáть* *perf*) на*+acc*.
double cream (*BRIT*) *n* густы́е сли́вки* *pl*.
double-cross ['dʌbl'krɔs] *vt* надувáть (надýть *perf*).
double-decker ['dʌbl'dɛkə^r] *n* (*also:* **double-decker bus**) двухэтáжный автóбус.
double exposure *n* (*PHOT*) двойнáя экспози́ция.
double glazing [-'gleɪzɪŋ] *n* (*BRIT*) двойны́е рáмы *fpl*.
double indemnity *n* (*US*) *вы́плата страховóй сýммы в двойнóм размéре*.
double-page spread ['dʌblpeɪdʒ-] *n* двойнóй разворóт (*газéты, журнáла*).
double parking *n* паркóвка вторы́м ря́дом.

* marks translations which have irregular inflections. The Russian-English side of the dictionary gives inflectional information.

double room *n* (*in hotel*) двухмéстный нóмер*; (*in house*) большáя кóмната.
doubles ['dʌblz] *n* (TENNIS) пáры *fpl*.
double time *n* двойнáя оплáта.
double whammy [-'wæmɪ] *n* двойнóй удáр.
doubly ['dʌblɪ] *adv* вдвойнé.
doubt [daut] *n* сомнéние ◆ *vt* сомневáться *(impf)*; (*mistrust*) сомневáться *(impf)* в *+prp*, не доверя́ть *(impf) +dat*; **without (a) ~** без сомнéния; **I ~ it (very much)** я (óчень) сомневáюсь; **I ~ if** *or* **whether she'll come** я сомневáюсь, что онá придёт; **I don't ~ that ...** я не сомневáюсь, что ....
doubtful ['dautful] *adj* сомни́тельный; **to be ~ about sth** сомневáться *(impf)* насчёт чегó-н; **I'm a bit ~** я нéсколько сомневáюсь; **it's ~ whether ...** сомни́тельно, что ....
doubtless ['dautlɪs] *adv* несомнéнно.
dough [dəu] *n* тéсто; (*inf: money*) бáбки* *fpl*.
doughnut ['dəunʌt] (US **donut**) *n* пóнчик.
dour [duə'] *adj* сурóвый* (сурóв).
douse [dauz] *vt*: **to ~ (with)** обливáть (обли́ть* *perf*) (*+instr*) ◆ *vt* (*extinguish*) туши́ть (потуши́ть *perf*), гаси́ть (погаси́ть *perf*).
dove [dʌv] *n* гóлубь *m*.
Dover ['dəuvə'] *n* Дувр; **Straits of ~** Па-де-Калé *m ind*.
dovetail ['dʌvteɪl] *vi* (*fig*) совпадáть (совпáсть* *perf*); (*schedules*) дополня́ть (допóлнить *perf*) друг дрýга ◆ *n* (TECH): **~ joint** лáсточкин хвост*.
dowager ['dauədʒə'] *n* престарéлая свéтская дáма; **the ~ duchess** вдóвствующая герцоги́ня.
dowdy ['daudɪ] *adj* неказúстый* (неказúст).
Dow-Jones average ['dau'dʒəunz-] *n* (US) и́ндекс ведýщих монопóлий Дóу Джóнса.
down [daun] *n* пух*; (*hill*) холм* ◆ *adv* (*motion*) вниз; (*position*) внизý ◆ *prep* (*towards lower level*) (вниз) с *+gen or* по *+dat*; (*movement along*) (вдоль) по *+dat* ◆ *vt* (*inf: drink*) проглáтывать (проглоти́ть* *perf*); **~ there** вот там; **~ here** вот здесь; **the price of meat is ~** ценá на мя́со упáла; **I've got it ~ somewhere** у меня́ гдé-то это запи́сано; **to pay £2 ~** плати́ть* (заплати́ть* *perf*) пéрвый взнос £2; **England is two goals ~** А́нглия проигрывает на два очкá; **to ~ tools** (BRIT) прекращáть (прекрати́ть *perf*) рабóту; **~ with the government!** долóй прави́тельство!
down-and-out ['daunəndaut] *n* бродя́га, бездóмный(-ая) *m(f) adj*.
down-at-heel ['daunət'hi:l] *adj* (*shoes etc*) стóптанный (стóптан); (*appearance, person*) потрёпанный* (потрёпан).
downbeat ['daunbi:t] *n* (MUS) си́льная дóля ◆ *adj* небрéжный* (небрéжен).
downcast ['daunkɑ:st] *adj* (*person*) подáвленный* (подáвлен); (*eyes*) опýщенный (опýщен).
downer ['daunə'] *n* (*inf: drug*) успокои́тельное *nt adj*; **to be on a ~** (*depressed*) быть* *(impf)* в депрéссии.
downfall ['daunfɔ:l] *n* падéние; (*from drinking, gambling etc*) ги́бель *f*.
downgrade ['daungreɪd] *vt*: **he was ~d** егó пони́зили.
downhearted ['daun'hɑ:tɪd] *adj* упáвший* дýхом.
downhill ['daun'hɪl] *n* (*also:* **~ race**: SKIING) скоростнóй спуск ◆ *adv* (*face, look*) вниз; **to go ~** (*person*) идти́* (пойти́* *perf*) пóд гору; (*road*) идти́* (пойти́* *perf*) под уклóн; (*car*) éхать* (поéхать* *perf*) пóд гору; (*fig: person*) кати́ться (покати́ться *perf*) по наклóнной плóскости; (: *business*) идти́* (пойти́* *perf*) пóд гору *or* под уклóн.
Downing Street ['daunɪŋ-] *n* (BRIT: POL) Дáунинг Стрит.
download ['daunləud] *vt* (COMPUT) загружáть (загрузи́ть* *perf*) (*в пáмять*).
down-market ['daun'mɑ:kɪt] *adj* (*product*) дешёвый.
down payment *n* пéрвый взнос.
downplay ['daunpleɪ] *vt* (US) преуменьшáть (преумéньшить *perf*).
downpour ['daunpɔ:'] *n* ли́вень* *m*.
downright ['daunraɪt] *adj* я́вный; (*refusal*) пóлный ◆ *adv* совершéнно.
Downs [daunz] *npl* (BRIT: GEO): **the ~** Дáунз (*известкóвые холмы́ на ю́ге А́нглии*).
Down's syndrome [daunz-] *n* синдрóм Дáуна.
downstairs ['daun'stɛəz] *adv* (*position*) внизý; (*motion*) вниз.
downstream ['daunstri:m] *adv* вниз по течéнию.
downtime ['dauntaɪm] *n* простóй.
down-to-earth ['dauntu'ə:θ] *adj* (*person*) простóй; (*solution*) практи́чный* (практи́чен).
downtown ['daun'taun] *adv* (*position*) в цéнтре; (*motion*) в центр ◆ *adj* (US): **~ Chicago** центр Чикáго.
downtrodden ['dauntrɔdn] *adj* (*person*) заби́тый (заби́т).
down under *adv* (BRIT: *inf: Australia etc*) другóй конéц* свéта (*Австрáлия и Нóвая Зелáндия*); **he lives ~ ~** он живёт на другóм концé свéта.
downward ['daunwəd] *adj* напрáвленный вниз ◆ *adv* вниз; **a ~ trend** понижáтельная тендéнция.
downwards ['daunwədz] *adv* = **downward**.
dowry ['daurɪ] *n* придáное *nt adj*.
doz. *abbr* = **dozen**.
doze [dəuz] *vi* дремáть* *(impf)*
▸ **doze off** *vi* задремáть* *(perf)*.
dozen ['dʌzn] *n* дю́жина; **a ~ books** дю́жина книг; **80 pence a ~** 80 пéнсов за дю́жину; **~s of** деся́тки *+gen*.
DPh *n abbr* (*= Doctor of Philosophy*) дóктор

философии.
DPhil *n abbr* (= *Doctor of Philosophy*) доктор философии.
DPP *n abbr* (*BRIT*: = *Director of Public Prosecutions*) Генеральный прокурор.
DPT *n abbr* (= *diphtheria, pertussis, tetanus*) коклюшно-дифтерийно-столбнячная вакцина.
DPW *n abbr* (*US*: = *Department of Public Works*) Департамент общественного строительства.
Dr *abbr* = **doctor**.
Dr. *abbr* (*in street names*) = **Drive**.
dr *abbr* (*COMM*) = **debtor**.
drab [dræb] *adj* (*weather, building, clothes*) серый (сер), унылый (уныл).
draft [drɑ:ft] *n* (*first version*) черновик*, набросок*; (*POL*: *of bill*) проект; (*COMM*) тратта; (*US*: *MIL*) призыв ◆ *vt* (*plan*) составлять (составить* *perf*); (*write roughly*) писать* (написать* *perf*) начерно; *see also* **draught**.
draftsman ['drɑ:ftsmən] *irreg n* (*US*) = **draughtsman**.
draftsmanship ['drɑ:ftsmənʃɪp] *n* (*US*) = **draughtsmanship**.
drag [dræg] *vt* тащить* (*impf*); (*lake, pond*) прочёсывать (прочесать* *perf*) ◆ *vi* (*time, a concert etc*) тянуться* (*impf*) ◆ *n* (*inf*: *person*) обуза; (: *task*) бремя* *nt*; (*NAUT, AVIAT*) лобовое сопротивление; **in ~** в костюме женщины (*о мужчине*)
▸ **drag away** *vt*: **to ~ sb away (from)** оттаскивать (оттащить* *perf*) кого-н (от *+gen*)
▸ **drag on** *vi* тянуться* (*impf*).
dragnet ['drægnɛt] *n* невод*, бредень* *m*; (*fig*) облава.
dragon ['drægn] *n* дракон.
dragonfly ['drægənflaɪ] *n* стрекоза*.
dragoon [drə'gu:n] *n* драгун* ◆ *vt*: **to ~ sb into sth** (*BRIT*) втягивать (втянуть* *perf*) кого-н во что-н.
drain [dreɪn] *n* (*in street*) водосток, водоотвод; (*on resources, manpower*) утечка*; (*on health, energy*) расход ◆ *vt* (*land, glass etc*) осушать (осушить* *perf*); (*vegetables*) сливать (слить* *perf*) ◆ *vi* (*liquid*) стекать (стечь* *perf*); **I feel ~ed** я истощён; **I feel ~ed of emotion** у меня истощились эмоции.
drainage ['dreɪnɪdʒ] *n* (*system*) канализация; (*process*) дренаж, осушение.
drainboard ['dreɪnbɔ:d] *n* (*US*) = **draining board**.
draining board ['dreɪnɪŋ-] (*US* **drainboard**) *n* сушка*.
drainpipe ['dreɪnpaɪp] *n* водосточная труба*.
drake [dreɪk] *n* селезень* *m*.
dram [dræm] *n* (*SCOTTISH*: *drink*) глоток* (*о спиртном*).
drama ['drɑ:mə] *n* (*also fig*) драма.
dramatic [drə'mætɪk] *adj* драматический*; (*increase etc*) резкий*; (*change*) разительный.
dramatically [drə'mætɪklɪ] *adv* драматически; (*increase, change*) резко.
dramatist ['dræmətɪst] *n* драматург.
dramatize ['dræmətaɪz] *vt* (*exaggerate*) драматизировать (*impf/perf*); (*adapt*: *for TV, cinema*) инсценировать (*impf/perf*).
drank [dræŋk] *pt of* **drink**.
drape [dreɪp] *vt* драпировать (задрапировать *perf*).
drapes [dreɪps] *npl* (*US*: *curtains*) занавески* *fpl*.
drastic ['dræstɪk] *adj* (*measure*) решительный* (решителен); (*change*) коренной.
drastically ['dræstɪklɪ] *adv* (*change*) коренным образом; (*reduce*) резко.
draught [drɑ:ft] (*US* **draft**) *n* (*of air*) сквозняк*; (*NAUT*) осадка*; (*of chimney*) тяга; **on ~** (*beer*) из бочки.
draught beer *n* бочковое пиво.
draughtboard ['drɑ:ftbɔ:d] *n* (*BRIT*) шашечная доска*.
draughts [drɑ:fts] *n* (*BRIT*) шашки* *pl*.
draughtsman ['drɑ:ftsmən] *irreg* (*US* **draftsman**) *n* чертёжник(-ица).
draughtsmanship ['drɑ:ftsmənʃɪp] (*US* **draftsmanship**) *n* черчение; (*art*) искусство черчения.
draw [drɔ:] (*pt* **drew**, *pp* **drawn**) *vt* (*ART*) рисовать (*impf*); (*TECH*) чертить* (*impf*); (*pull*: *cart*) тащить* (*impf*); (: *curtains*) задёргивать (задёрнуть *perf*); (*gun, tooth*) вырывать (вырвать* *perf*); (*attention*) привлекать (привлечь* *perf*); (*crowd*) собирать (собрать* *perf*); (*money*) снимать (снять* *perf*); (*wages*) получать (получить* *perf*) ◆ *vi* (*SPORT*) играть (сыграть *perf*) в ничью ◆ *n* (*SPORT*) ничья*; (*lottery*) лотерея; (: *of teams*) жеребьёвка*; **to ~ near** приближаться (приблизиться* *perf*); **to ~ to a close** подходить* (подойти* *perf*) к концу; **to ~ a conclusion** делать (сделать *perf*) вывод; **to ~ a comparison between** проводить* (провести* *perf*) сравнение между *+instr*
▸ **draw back** *vi*: **to ~ back (from)** отпрянуть (*perf*) (от *+gen*)
▸ **draw in** *vi* (*BRIT*: *car*) останавливаться (остановиться* *perf*); (: *train*) подъезжать (подъехать* *perf*); (*nights*) становиться* (стать* *perf*) длиннее
▸ **draw on** *vt* использовать (*impf/perf*)
▸ **draw out** *vi* (*lengthen*) растягивать (растянуть* *perf*) ◆ *vt* (*money*) снимать (снять* *perf*)
▸ **draw up** *vi* (*train, bus etc*) подъезжать

* marks translations which have irregular inflections. The Russian-English side of the dictionary gives inflectional information.

(подъéхать* *perf*) ◆ *vt* (*chair etc*) придвигáть (придви́нуть *perf*); (*document*) составля́ть (состáвить* *perf*).
drawback ['drɔ:bæk] *n* недостáток*.
drawbridge ['drɔ:brɪdʒ] *n* подъёмный *or* разводнóй мост*.
drawee [drɔ:'i:] *n* трассáт.
drawer [drɔ:ʳ] *n* я́щик.
drawing ['drɔ:ɪŋ] *n* (*picture*) рисýнок*; (*act*) рисовáние.
drawing board *n* чертёжная доскá*; **to go back to the ~ ~** (*fig*) всё начинáть (начáть* *perf*) сначáла.
drawing pin *n* (*BRIT*) (канцеля́рская) кнóпка*.
drawing room *n* гости́ная *f adj*.
drawl [drɔ:l] *n* протя́жное произношéние ◆ *vi* протя́гивать (протянýть* *perf*).
drawn [drɔ:n] *pp of* **draw** ◆ *adj* измýченный* (измýчен).
drawstring ['drɔ:strɪŋ] *n* шнур* (*котóрый продёрнут во чтó-нибудь*).
dread [drɛd] *n* ýжас ◆ *vt* боя́ться *(impf)* +*gen*.
dreadful ['drɛdful] *adj* ужáсный*; **I feel ~!** я ужáсно себя́ чýвствую!
dream [dri:m] (*pt, pp* **dreamed** *or* **dreamt**) *n* сон*; (*ambition*) мечтá ◆ *vt*: **I must have ~t it** мне, навéрное, э́то присни́лось ◆ *vi* ви́деть *(impf)* сон*; (*wish*) мечтáть *(impf)*; **I had a ~ about you** ты мне присни́лся; **sweet ~s!** прия́тных сновидéний!
▸ **dream up** *vt* выдýмывать (вы́думать *perf*).
dreamer ['dri:məʳ] *n* (*fig*) мечтáтель*(ница) *m(f)*.
dreamt [drɛmt] *pt, pp of* **dream**.
dream world *n*: **to live in a ~ ~** жить* *(impf)* в придýманном ми́ре.
dreamy ['dri:mɪ] *adj* (*expression, person*) мечтáтельный* (мечтáтелен); (*music*) убаю́кивающий.
dreary ['drɪərɪ] *adj* тоскли́вый (тоскли́в).
dredge [drɛdʒ] *vt* драги́ровать *(impf/perf)*
▸ **dredge up** *vt* драги́ровать *(impf/perf)*; (*fig: facts*) вытáскивать (вы́тащить *perf*).
dredger ['drɛdʒəʳ] *n* (*ship*) землечерпáлка, дрáга; (*BRIT: also:* **sugar ~**) *сосýд с мáленькими ды́рочками в кры́шке для сáхара*.
dregs [drɛgz] *npl* муть* *fsg*; **~ of society** отбрóсы óбщества.
drench [drɛntʃ] *vt*: **to be ~ed** мóкнуть (промóкнуть* *perf*): **~ed to the skin** насквóзь промóкший.
Dresden ['drɛzdən] *n* Дрéзден.
dress [drɛs] *n* (*frock*) плáтье*; (*no pl: clothing*) одéжда ◆ *vt* одевáть (одéть* *perf*); (*wound*) перевя́зывать (перевязáть* *perf*) ◆ *vi* одевáться (одéться* *perf*); **she ~es very well** онá óчень хорошó одевáется; **to ~ a shop window** оформля́ть (офóрмить* *perf*) витри́ну; **to get ~ed** одевáться (одéться* *perf*)
▸ **dress up** *vi* наряжáться (наряди́ться* *perf*).
dress circle *n* (*BRIT*) бельэтáж.
dress designer *n* модельéр.
dresser ['drɛsəʳ] *n* (*BRIT*) кýхонный шкаф*; (*US: chest of drawers*) туалéтный стóлик; (*also:* **window ~**) оформи́тель(ница) *m(f)* витри́н.
dressing ['drɛsɪŋ] *n* (*MED*) повя́зка*; (: *process*) перевя́зка*; (*CULIN*) заправка*.
dressing gown *n* (*BRIT*) халáт.
dressing room *n* (*THEAT*) артисти́ческая убóрная *f adj*; (*SPORT*) раздевáлка*.
dressing table *n* туалéтный стóлик.
dressmaker ['drɛsmeɪkəʳ] *n* портни́ха.
dressmaking ['drɛsmeɪkɪŋ] *n* поши́в жéнского плáтья.
dress rehearsal *n* генерáльная репети́ция.
dressy ['drɛsɪ] *adj* (*inf*) наря́дный* (наря́ден).
drew [dru:] *pt of* **draw**.
dribble ['drɪbl] *vi* (*liquid*) кáпать* *(impf)*; (*baby*) пускáть (пусти́ть* *perf*) слю́ни; (*SPORT*) вести́* *(impf)* мяч ◆ *vt* (*ball*) вести́* *(impf)*.
dried [draɪd] *adj* (*fruit*) сушёный; (*milk*) сухóй.
drier ['draɪəʳ] *n* = **dryer**.
drift [drɪft] *n* (*of current etc*) скóрость* *f*; (*of snow*) занóс, сугрóб; (*meaning*) смысл ◆ *vi* (*boat*) дрейфовáть *(impf)*; **sand/snow had ~ed over the road** дорóгу занеслó пескóм/снéгом; **to let things ~** пускáть (пусти́ть* *perf*) всё на самотёк; **to ~ apart** расходи́ться* (разойти́сь* *perf*); **I get** *or* **catch your ~** я понимáю кудá Вы клóните.
drifter ['drɪftəʳ] *n* (*person*) бродя́га *m/f*.
driftwood ['drɪftwud] *n* плавни́к.
drill [drɪl] *n* (*drill bit*) сверлó*; (*machine*) дрель *f*; (: *for mining etc*) бурáв*; (*MIL*) учéние ◆ *vt* (*hole*) сверли́ть (просверли́ть* *perf*); (*troops*) муштровáть (вы́муштровать *perf*); (*pupils*) натáскивать (натаскáть *perf*) ◆ *vi* (*for oil*) бури́ть *(impf)*.
drilling ['drɪlɪŋ] *n* (*for oil*) бурéние.
drilling rig *n* буровáя установка*.
drily ['draɪlɪ] *adv* = **dryly**.
drink [drɪŋk] (*pt* **drank**, *pp* **drunk**) *n* напи́ток*; (*alcoholic drink*) (спиртнóй) напи́ток*; (*sip*) глотóк* ◆ *vt* пить* (вы́пить* *perf*) ◆ *vi* пить* *(impf)*; **to have a ~** попи́ть* *(perf)*; (*alcohol*) вы́пить* *(perf)*; **a ~ of water** глотóк* воды́; (*glassful*) стакáн воды́; **would you like something to ~?** хоти́те чегó-нибудь вы́пить?: **we had ~s before lunch** мы вы́пили пéред обéдом
▸ **drink in** *vt* упивáться *(impf)* +*instr*.
drinkable ['drɪŋkəbl] *adj* (*water*) питьевóй; (*palatable: wine etc*) неплохóй (неплóх), прия́тный* (прия́тен).
drink-driving ['drɪŋk'draɪvɪŋ] *n* вождéние в нетрéзвом состоя́нии ◆ *cpd*: **they are running a ~ campaign** они́ ведýт кампáнию прóтив води́телей, садя́щихся за руль в нетрéзвом состоя́нии
drinker ['drɪŋkəʳ] *n* (*of alcohol*) пью́щий*(-ая)

m(f) adj.

drinking ['drɪŋkɪŋ] *n* питьё*; **there was a lot of ~ at the party** на вечеринке много пили.

drinking fountain *n* питьевой фонтанчик.

drinking water *n* питьевая вода*.

drip [drɪp] *n* капанье; (*one drip*) капля*; (*MED*) капельница ◆ *vi* (*water, rain*) капать* *(impf)*; **the tap is ~ping** кран течёт; **the washing is ~ping** с белья капает.

drip-dry ['drɪp'draɪ] *adj*: **~ material** *ткань, которой дают стечь после стирки и которую не гладят.*

drip-feed ['drɪpfi:d] *vt* (*MED*) вливать (влить* *perf*) через капельницу ◆ *n*: **to be on a ~** быть* *(impf)* на капельнице.

dripping ['drɪpɪŋ] *n* (*CULIN*) (топлёный) жир ◆ *adj* (*very wet*) мокрый (мокр); **I'm ~** с меня течёт; **~ wet** совершенно мокрый (мокр).

drive [draɪv] (*pt* **drove**, *pp* **driven**) *n* (*journey*) поездка*; (*also:* **~way**) подъезд; (*energy*) напористость *f*; (*campaign*) кампания; (*FOOTBALL*) удар; (*TENNIS*) драйв; (*COMPUT*: *also:* **disk ~**) дисковод; (*in street names*): **Rose D~** Роуз Драйв ◆ *vt* (*vehicle*) водить*/вести* *(impf)*; (*TECH*: *machine, motor, wheel*) приводить* (привести* *perf*) в движение; (*animal*) гнать* *(impf)*; (*ball*) ударять (ударить *perf*) (плоско); (*nail, stake etc*): **to ~ sth into sth** вбивать (вбить* *perf*) что-н во что-н ◆ *vi* (*AUT*: *at controls*) водить*/вести* *(impf)* (машину); (*travel*) ездить*/ехать* *(impf)*; **to go for a ~** поехать *(perf)* покататься; **the town is three hours' ~ from London** город в трёх часах езды от Лондона; **right-/left-hand ~** (*AUT*) право-/левосторонее управление; **front-/rear-wheel ~** (*AUT*) привод на передние/задние колёса; **economy ~** борьба за экономию; **he ~s a taxi** он водит такси; **to ~ at 50 km an hour** ездить*/ехать* *(impf)* со скоростью 50 км в час; **to ~ sb home/to the airport** отвозить* (отвезти* *perf*) кого-н домой/в аэропорт; **to ~ sb mad** сводить* (свести* *perf*) кого-н с ума; **to ~ sb to sth** доводить* (довести* *perf*) кого-н до чего-н; **what are you driving at?** куда Вы клоните?

▸ **drive off** *vt* (*repel*) отбрасывать (отбросить* *perf*)

▸ **drive out** *vt* (*force to leave*) вытеснять (вытеснить *perf*); (*person, animal, evil*) выгонять (выгнать* *perf*).

drive-by shooting ['draɪvbaɪ-] *n* стрельба из движущегося автомобиля.

drive-in ['draɪvɪn] *n* (*esp US*: *restaurant*) *кафе, где можно купить еду не выходя из машины.*

drivel ['drɪvl] *n* (*inf*) чушь *f*.

driven ['drɪvn] *pp of* **drive**.

driver ['draɪvə^r] *n* водитель *m*; (*of train*) машинист.

driver's license ['draɪvəz-] *n* (*US*) водительские права *nt pl*.

driveway ['draɪvweɪ] *n* подъезд.

driving ['draɪvɪŋ] *n* вождение ◆ *adj*: **~ rain** проливной дождь* *m*; **~ snow** метель *f*.

driving belt *n* приводной ремень* *m*.

driving force *n* движущая сила.

driving instructor *n* инструктор* по вождению.

driving lesson *n* урок по вождению.

driving licence *n* (*BRIT*) водительские права *ntpl*.

driving mirror *n* зеркало заднего вида.

driving school *n* автошкола.

driving test *n* экзамен по вождению.

drizzle ['drɪzl] *n* моросящий дождь* *m* ◆ *vi* моросить *(impf)*.

droll [drəul] *adj* забавный.

dromedary ['drɔmədərɪ] *n* одногорбый верблюд, дромедар.

drone [drəun] *n* (*noise*) гудение; (*male bee*) трутень* *m* ◆ *vi* (*bee*) жужжать *(impf)*; (*engine etc*) гудеть *(impf)*; (*also:* **~ on**) бубнить *(impf)*.

drool [dru:l] *vi*: **he is ~ing** у него текут слюни; **to ~ over sth/sb** (*inf*) ронять *(impf)* слюни по поводу чего-н/кого-н.

droop [dru:p] *vi* (*flower, head*) поникать (поникнуть *perf*); (*shoulders*) ссутулиться *(perf)*.

drop [drɔp] *n* (*of water*) капля*; (*reduction*) падение; (*fall*: *distance*) расстояние (*сверху вниз*); (: *in salary*) снижение; (*also:* **parachute ~**) сбрасывание на парашюте (*продовольствия, боеприпасов*) ◆ *vt* (*allow to fall*: *object*) ронять (уронить* *perf*); (*eyes*) опускать (опустить* *perf*); (*voice, price*) понижать (понизить* *perf*); (*set down from car*) высаживать (высадить* *perf*); (*exclude*) исключать (исключить *perf*) ◆ *vi* падать (упасть* *perf*); (*wind*) стихать (стихнуть* *perf*); **~s** *npl* (*MED*) капли* *fpl*; **cough ~s** леденцы от кашля; **there is a 30 ft ~ from the window to the ground** высота от окна до земли 30 футов; **there's been a ~ of 10% in profits** прибыль упала на 10%; **to ~ anchor** бросать (бросить* *perf*) якорь; **to ~ sb a line** черкнуть* *(perf)* кому-н несколько строчек

▸ **drop in** *vi* (*inf*): **to ~ in on sb** заглядывать (заглянуть* *perf*) к кому-н

▸ **drop off** *vi* (*go to sleep*) засыпать (заснуть *perf*) ◆ *vt* (*passenger*) высаживать (высадить* *perf*)

▸ **drop out** *vi* (*of game, agreement*) выходить* (выйти* *perf*); **to ~ out of college** бросать (бросить* *perf*) колледж.

droplet ['drɔplɪt] *n* капелька*.

drop-out ['drɔpaut] *n* (*from society*)

* marks translations which have irregular inflections. The Russian-English side of the dictionary gives inflectional information.

отщепéнец*(-нка*); (*SCOL*) недоýчка* *m/f*.
dropper ['drɔpəʳ] *n* пипéтка*.
droppings ['drɔpɪŋz] *npl* помёт *msg*.
dross [drɔs] *n* шлак; (*rubbish*) мýсор.
drought [draut] *n* зáсуха.
drove [drəuv] *pt of* **drive** ◆ *n*: **~s of people** тóлпы *fpl* людéй.
drown [draun] *vt* топи́ть* (утопи́ть* *perf*); (*also:* **~ out**: *sound, voice*) заглушáть (заглуши́ть *perf*) ◆ *vi* тонýть* (утонýть* *perf*).
drowse [drauz] *vi* дремáть* *(impf)*.
drowsy ['drauzɪ] *adj* сóнный.
drudge [drʌdʒ] *n* (*person*) работя́га *m/f*.
drudgery ['drʌdʒərɪ] *n* тяжёлая, нýдная рабóта; **housework is sheer ~** рабóта по дóму – тяжёлый труд.
drug [drʌg] *n* (*MED*) лекáрство; (*narcotic*) наркóтик ◆ *vt* (*person, animal*) вводи́ть* (ввести́* *perf*) наркóтик *+dat*; **to be on ~s** быть* *(impf)* на наркóтиках; **hard/soft ~s** си́льные/слáбые наркóтики.
drug addict *n* наркомáн.
druggist ['drʌgɪst] *n* (*US*) аптéкарь *m*.
drug peddler *n* торгóвец* наркóтиками.
drugstore ['drʌgstɔːʳ] *n* (*US*) аптéка (*иногдá с небольши́м кафé*).
drum [drʌm] *n* барабáн; (*for oil*) бóчка* ◆ *vi* барабáнить *(impf)*; **~s** *npl* (*kit*) удáрные инструмéнты *mpl*
▸ **drum up** *vt* (*support*) призывáть (призвáть* *perf*).
drummer ['drʌməʳ] *n* (*with military band*) барабáнщик; (*in rock group*) удáрник.
drum roll *n* барабáнный бой*.
drumstick ['drʌmstɪk] *n* барабáнная пáлочка*; (*of chicken*) нóжка*.
drunk [drʌŋk] *pp of* **drink** ◆ *adj* пья́ный* ◆ *n* пья́ный*(-ая) *m(f) adj*; (*also:* **~ard**) пья́ница *m/f*; **to get ~** напивáться (напи́ться* *perf*); **~ driving** вождéние в нетрéзвом состоя́нии.
drunken ['drʌŋkən] *adj* пья́ный* (пьян); **~ driving** вождéние в нетрéзвом состоя́нии.
drunkenness ['drʌŋkənnɪs] *n* пья́нство.
dry [draɪ] *adj* (*also fig*) сухóй* (сух); (*lake, riverbed*) вы́сохший; (*humour*) сдéржанный* (сдéржан); (*lecture, subject*) скýчный* (скýчен) ◆ *vt* (*clothes, ground*) суши́ть* (вы́сушить *perf*); (*surface*) вытирáть (вы́тереть* *perf*) ◆ *vi* (*paint, washing*) сóхнуть (вы́сохнуть *perf*); **on ~ land** на сýше; **to ~ one's hands/eyes** вытирáть (вы́тереть* *perf*) рýки/глазá; **to ~ one's hair** (*with towel*) вытирáть (вы́тереть* *perf*) вóлосы; (*with hairdryer*) суши́ть* (вы́сушить *perf*) вóлосы; **to ~ the dishes** вытирáть (вы́тереть* *perf*) посýду
▸ **dry up** *vi* (*river, well*) высыхáть (вы́сохнуть* *perf*); (*resources, speaker*) иссякáть (иссякнуть* *perf*).
dry clean *vt* чи́стить* (почи́стить* *perf*) (*в химчи́стке*).
dry cleaner *n* рабóтник химчи́стки.
dry-cleaner's ['draɪ'kliːnəz] *n* химчи́стка*.
dry-cleaning ['draɪ'kliːnɪŋ] *n* хими́ческая чи́стка.
dry dock *n* (*NAUT*) сухóй док.
dryer ['draɪəʳ] *n* (*for clothes*) суши́лка*.
dry goods *npl* (*US*) галантерéя *fsg* и ткáни *fpl*.
dry ice *n* сухóй* лёд*.
dryly ['draɪlɪ] *adv* ирони́чно.
dryness ['draɪnɪs] *n* сýхость *f*.
dry rot *n* сухáя гниль *f* (*болéзнь древеси́ны*).
dry run *n* (*fig: inf*) холостóй прогóн.
dry ski slope *n* склон с искýсственным покры́тием.
DSc *n abbr* (= *Doctor of Science*) дóктор естествознáния.
DSS *n abbr* (*BRIT*: = *Department of Social Security*) Министéрство социáльного обеспéчения.
DST *abbr* (*US*: = *Daylight Saving Time*) лéтнее врéмя* *nt*.
DT *n abbr* (*COMPUT*: = *data transmission*) передáча дáнных.
DTI *n abbr* (*BRIT*: = *Department of Trade and Industry*) Министéрство промы́шленности и торгóвли.
DTP *n abbr* = **desktop publishing**.
DT's *npl abbr* (*inf*: = *delirium tremens*) бéлая горя́чка; **to have the ~** страдáть *(impf)* бéлой горя́чкой.
dual ['djuəl] *adj* двойнóй; (*function, number*) двóйственный.
dual carriageway *n* (*BRIT*) шоссé *nt ind*.
dual nationality *n* двойнóе граждáнство.
dual-purpose ['djuəl'pəːpəs] *adj* двойнóго назначéния.
dubbed [dʌbd] *adj* (*CINEMA*) дубли́рованный (дубли́рован); (*nicknamed*) прóзванный (прóзван).
dubious ['djuːbɪəs] *adj* сомни́тельный; **I'm very ~ about it** у меня́ серьёзные сомнéния на э́тот счёт.
Dublin ['dʌblɪn] *n* Дýблин.
Dubliner ['dʌblɪnəʳ] *n* дýблинец*(-нка*).
duchess ['dʌtʃɪs] *n* герцоги́ня.
duck [dʌk] *n* ýтка* ◆ *vi* (*also:* **~ down**) пригибáться (пригнýться *perf*) ◆ *vt* (*blow*) увёртываться (увернýться *perf*) от *+gen*; (*responsibility etc*) уви́ливать (увильнýть *perf*) от *+gen*.
duckling ['dʌklɪŋ] *n* утёнок*.
duct [dʌkt] *n* (*ELEC*) кáбельный канáл; (*TECH*) трубопровóд; (*ANAT*) протóк, канáл.
dud [dʌd] *adj* (*object, tool*) бесполéзный* (бесполéзен); (*grenade*) неразорвáвшийся; (*BRIT*: *cheque*) недействи́тельный ◆ *n* (*note, coin*) поддéлка*.
due [djuː] *adj* (*expected*) предполагáемый; (*attention, consideration*) дóлжный; (*owed*): **I am ~ £20** мне должны́ *or* причитáется £20 ◆ *n*: **to give sb his (*or* her) ~** отдавáть*

(отда́ть* *perf*) кому́-н до́лжное ◆ *adv*: **~ north** пря́мо на се́вер; **~s** *npl* (*for club, union*) взно́сы *mpl*; (*in harbour*) порто́вые сбо́ры *mpl*; **in ~ course** в своё вре́мя; **~ to** из-за *+gen*; **he is ~ to go** он до́лжен идти́; **the rent is ~ on the 30th** за кварти́ру должно́ быть* запла́чено 30-ого числа́; **the train is ~ at 8** по́езд до́лжен прийти́ в 8 часо́в; **she is ~ back tomorrow** она́ должна́ верну́ться за́втра; **I am ~ 6 days' leave** мне причита́ется 6 свобо́дных дней.
due date *n* срок произво́дства платежа́.
duel ['djuəl] *n* дуэ́ль *f*, (*fig*) поеди́нок.
duet [dju:'ɛt] *n* дуэ́т.
duff [dʌf] *adj* (*BRIT*: *inf*) дрянно́й*
▸ **duff up** *vt* (*inf*) колошма́тить* (исколошма́тить* *perf*).
duffel bag ['dʌfl-] *n* су́мка-мешо́к*.
duffel coat *n шерстяно́е пальто́ с капюшо́ном*.
duffer ['dʌfəʳ] *n* (*inf*) тупи́ца *m/f*.
dug [dʌg] *pt, pp of* **dig**.
dugout ['dʌgaut] *n* (*canoe*) челно́к; (*shelter*) земля́нка.
duke [dju:k] *n* ге́рцог.
dull [dʌl] *adj* (*light, colour*) ту́склый* (тускл); (*weather, day*) се́рый* (сер); (*sound*) глухо́й* (глух); (*pain, wit*) тупо́й* (туп); (*event*) ску́чный* (ску́чен) ◆ *vt* притупля́ть (притупи́ть* *perf*).
duly ['dju:lɪ] *adv* (*properly*) до́лжным о́бразом; (*on time*) своевре́менно.
dumb [dʌm] *adj* (*mute*) немо́й*; (*inf*: *pej*: *stupid*: *person*) тупо́й*; (: *idea*) дура́цкий*; **to be struck ~** онеме́ть (*perf*).
dumbbell ['dʌmbɛl] *n* (*SPORT*) ганте́ль *f*.
dumbfounded [dʌm'faundɪd] *adj* ошеломлённый (ошеломлён).
dummy ['dʌmɪ] *n* (*tailor's model*) манеке́н; (*TECH*) маке́т; (*COMM*) моде́ль *f*; (*SPORT*) обма́нный приём; (*BRIT*: *for baby*) со́ска*, пусты́шка* ◆ *adj* (*bullet*) холосто́й; (*firm*) фикти́вный.
dummy run *n* испыта́тельный прого́н.
dump [dʌmp] *n* (*also*: **rubbish ~**) сва́лка*; (*inf*: *pej*: *place*) дыра́*; (*MIL*) полево́й склад ◆ *vt* (*put down*) сва́ливать (свали́ть* *perf*), выбра́сывать (вы́бросить* *perf*); (*car*) броса́ть (бро́сить* *perf*); (*COMPUT*: *data*) выгружа́ть (вы́грузить* *perf*), сбра́сывать (сбро́сить* *perf*); **to be down in the ~s** (*inf*) хандри́ть (*impf*); **"no ~ing"** "сва́лка му́сора запрещена́".
dumpling ['dʌmplɪŋ] *n* (*CULIN*) клёцка*.
dumpy ['dʌmpɪ] *adj* кря́жистый* (кря́жист).
dunce [dʌns] *n* тупи́ца *m/f*.
Dundee [dʌn'di:] *n* Данди́ *m ind*.
Dundonian [dʌn'dəunɪən] *adj* го́рода Данди́ ◆ *n* жи́тель(ница) *m(f)* го́рода Данди́.
dune [dju:n] *n* дю́на.
dung [dʌŋ] *n* наво́з*.
dungarees [dʌŋgə'ri:z] *npl* комбинезо́н *msg*.
dungeon ['dʌndʒən] *n* темни́ца.
dunk [dʌŋk] *vt* мака́ть (макну́ть *perf*).
Dunkirk [dʌn'kə:k] *n* Данке́рк.
duo ['dju:əu] *n* дуэ́т.
duodenal [dju:əu'di:nl] *adj* дуодена́льный; **~ ulcer** я́зва двенадцатипе́рстной кишки́.
duodenum [dju:əu'di:nəm] *n* двенадцатипе́рстная кишка́.
dupe [dju:p] *n* проста́к*, простофи́ля* *m/f* ◆ *vt* надува́ть (надýть* *perf*).
duplex ['dju:plɛks] *n* (*US*: *also*: **~ house**) одна́ из часте́й двухкварти́рного до́ма; (*also*: **~ apartment**) двухэта́жная кварти́ра.
duplicate [*n, adj* 'dju:plɪkət, *vt* 'dju:plɪkeɪt] *n* (*of document, key etc*) дублика́т, ко́пия ◆ *adj* (*key, copy etc*) запасно́й ◆ *vt* копи́ровать (скопи́ровать *perf*); (*repeat*) дубли́ровать (продубли́ровать *perf*); **in ~** в двойно́м экземпля́ре.
duplicating machine ['dju:plɪkeɪtɪŋ-] *n* копирова́льная маши́на.
duplicator ['dju:plɪkeɪtəʳ] *n* копирова́льная маши́на.
duplicity [dju:'plɪsɪtɪ] *n* двули́чие.
Dur *abbr* (*BRIT*: *POST*) = *Durham*.
durability [djuərə'bɪlɪtɪ] *n* про́чность *f*.
durable ['djuərəbl] *adj* про́чный.
duration [djuə'reɪʃən] *n* продолжи́тельность *f*.
duress [djuə'rɛs] *n*: **under ~** под давле́нием.
Durex® ['djuərɛks] *n* (*BRIT*) ма́рка презервати́ва.
during ['djuərɪŋ] *prep* (*in the course of*) во вре́мя *+gen*, в тече́ние *+gen*; (*from beginning to end*) в тече́ние *+gen*.
Dushanbe [du:'ʃɑ:nbɪ] *n* Душанбе́ *m ind*.
dusk [dʌsk] *n* су́мерки* *pl*.
dusky ['dʌskɪ] *adj* (*light*) су́меречный*; (*room*) тёмный.
dust [dʌst] *n* пыль* *f* ◆ *vt* вытира́ть (вы́тереть* *perf*) пыль с *+gen*; (*cake etc*): **to ~ with** посыпа́ть (посы́пать* *perf*) *+instr*
▸ **dust off** *vt* (*also fig*) стря́хивать (стряхну́ть *perf*) пыль с *+gen*.
dustbin ['dʌstbɪn] *n* (*BRIT*) му́сорное ведро́*.
dustbin liner *n целофа́новая прокла́дка для му́сорного ведра́*.
duster ['dʌstəʳ] *n* (*cloth*) тря́пка* для пы́ли.
dust jacket *n* суперобло́жка*.
dustman ['dʌstmən] *irreg n* (*BRIT*) му́сорщик.
dustpan ['dʌstpæn] *n* сово́к* для му́сора.
dusty ['dʌstɪ] *adj* пы́льный*.
Dutch [dʌtʃ] *adj* голла́ндский* ◆ *n* (*LING*) голла́ндский* язы́к*; **the ~** *npl* (*people*) голла́ндцы* *mpl*; **they decided to go ~** (*inf*) они́ реши́ли, что ка́ждый пла́тит за себя́.

Dutch auction *n* "голла́ндский* аукцио́н" (*аукцио́н со сниже́нием цен, пока́ не найдётся покупа́тель*).
Dutchman ['dʌtʃmən] *irreg n* голла́ндец*.
Dutchwoman ['dʌtʃwumən] *irreg n* голла́ндка*.
dutiable ['dju:tɪəbl] *adj* (*COMM*: *goods*) облага́емый по́шлиной.
dutiful ['dju:tɪful] *adj* (*son, daughter*) послу́шный* (послу́шен); (*husband, wife*) поко́рный* (поко́рен); (*employee*) исполни́тельный* (исполни́телен).
duty ['dju:tɪ] *n* (*responsibility*) обя́занность *f*; (*obligation*) долг; (*tax*) по́шлина; **duties** *npl* (*functions*) обя́занности *fpl*; **to make it one's ~ to do** счита́ть (посчита́ть *perf*) свои́м до́лгом *+infin*; **to pay ~ on sth** плати́ть* (заплати́ть* *perf*) по́шлину за что-н; **on ~** на дежу́рстве; **off ~** вне слу́жбы.
duty-free ['dju:tɪ'fri:] *adj* беспо́шлинный; **~ shop** магази́н това́ров не облага́емых по́шлиной.
duty officer *n* (*MIL*) дежу́рный офице́р.
duvet ['du:veɪ] *n* (*BRIT*) пухо́вое одея́ло.
DV *abbr* (= *Deo volente*) Бог даст.
DVD *abbr* (= *digital video disc*) цифрово́й диск.
DVLA *n abbr* (*BRIT*) = *Driver and Vehicle Licensing Authority*.
DVLC *n abbr* (*BRIT*) = *Driver and Vehicle Licensing Centre*.
DVM *n abbr* (*US*: = *Doctor of Veterinary Medicine*) до́ктор ветерина́рных нау́к.
dwarf [dwɔ:f] (*pl* **dwarves**) *n* ка́рлик ◆ *vt* де́лать (сде́лать *perf*) кро́хотным.
dwarves [dwɔ:vz] *npl of* **dwarf**.
dwell [dwɛl] (*pt, pp* **dwelt**) *vi* прожива́ть (прожи́ть* *perf*)
▸ **dwell on** *vt fus* заде́рживаться (задержа́ться* *perf*) на *+prp*.
dweller ['dwɛləʳ] *n* жи́тель(ница) *m(f)*, обита́тель(ница) *m(f)*; **city ~** городско́й(-а́я) жи́тель(ница).
dwelling ['dwɛlɪŋ] *n* (*house*) жили́ще.
dwelt [dwɛlt] *pt, pp of* **dwell**.
dwindle ['dwɪndl] *vi* (*interest, attendance*) сокраща́ться (сократи́ться* *perf*).
dwindling ['dwɪndlɪŋ] *adj* (*strength, interest*) убыва́ющий; (*resources, supplies*) сокраща́ющийся.
dye [daɪ] *n* (*for hair, cloth*) краси́тель *m*, кра́ска* ◆ *vt* кра́сить* (покра́сить* *perf*).
dyestuffs ['daɪstʌfs] *npl* краси́тели *mpl*.
dying ['daɪɪŋ] *adj* умира́ющий; (*moments, words*) предсме́ртный.
dyke [daɪk] *n* (*BRIT*: *wall*) да́мба; (*channel*) кана́ва; (*causeway*) насы́пь *f*.
dynamic [daɪ'næmɪk] *adj* (*leader, force*) динами́чный.
dynamics [daɪ'næmɪks] *n or npl* (*TECH*) дина́мика *fsg*.
dynamite ['daɪnəmaɪt] *n* динами́т ◆ *vt* взрыва́ть (взорва́ть* *perf*) динами́том.
dynamo ['daɪnəməu] *n* (*ELEC*) дина́мо-маши́на.
dynasty ['dɪnəstɪ] *n* дина́стия.
dysentery ['dɪsntrɪ] *n* дизентери́я.
dyslexia [dɪs'lɛksɪə] *n* дисле́ксия.
dyslexic [dɪs'lɛksɪk] *adj* дислекти́ческий ◆ *n* дисле́ктик.
dyspepsia [dɪs'pɛpsɪə] *n* диспепси́я.

~ E, e ~

E, e [iː] *n* (*letter*) *5-ая бу́ква англи́йского алфави́та*; (*SCOL: mark*) ≈ о́чень пло́хо.

E [iː] *n* (*MUS*) ми *nt ind*.

E *abbr* (= **east**) В= *восто́к* ◆ *n abbr* (= *Ecstasy*) “Экста́з” (*нарко́тик*).

E111 *n abbr* (*also:* **form** ~) *спра́вка, обеспе́чивающая медици́нскую по́мощь за преде́лами Великобрита́нии*.

ea. *abbr* = **each**.

E.A. *n abbr* (*US*) = *educational age*.

each [iːtʃ] *adj* ка́ждый ◆ *pron* (*each one*) ка́ждый; ~ **other** дру́г дру́га; **they hate ~ other** они́ ненави́дят друг дру́га; **they don't talk to ~ other** они́ не разгова́ривают друг с дру́гом; **they think about ~ other** они́ ду́мают друг о дру́ге; **they are jealous of ~ other** они́ зави́дуют дру́г дру́гу; ~ **day** ка́ждый де́нь; **they have two books ~** у ка́ждого из них по две кни́ги; **they cost £5 ~** они́ сто́ят £5 шту́ка *or* за шту́ку; ~ **of us** ка́ждый из нас.

eager [ˈiːgəʳ] *adj* (*keen*) нетерпели́во ожида́ющий; **to be ~ for** жа́ждать *(impf)* +*gen*; **he is ~ to ...** он по́лон жела́ния +*infin* ....

eagerly [ˈiːgəlɪ] *adv* с воодушевле́нием; (*awaited*) с нетерпе́нием.

eagle [ˈiːgl] *n* орёл*.

ear [ɪəʳ] *n* (*ANAT*) у́хо*; (*of corn*) ко́лос*; **up to one's ~s in debt/work/paint** по́ уши в долга́х/в рабо́те/в кра́ске; **to give sb a thick ~** дать* *(perf)* кому́-н в у́хо; **we'll play it by ~** (*fig*) мы посмо́трим по ситуа́ции.

earache [ˈɪəreɪk] *n* боль *f* в у́хе; **I have ~** у меня́ боли́т у́хо.

eardrum [ˈɪədrʌm] *n* бараба́нная перепо́нка*.

earful [ˈɪəful] *n* (*inf*): **to give sb an ~** устра́ивать (устро́ить *perf*) разно́с кому́-н.

earl [əːl] *n* (*BRIT*) граф.

earlier [ˈəːlɪəʳ] *adj* бо́лее ра́нний* ◆ *adv* ра́ньше; **I can't come any ~** я не могу́ прийти́ ра́ньше.

early [ˈəːlɪ] *adv* ра́но ◆ *adj* ра́нний*; (*death, departure*) преждевре́менный*; (*quick: reply*) незамедли́тельный; (*Christians, settlers*) пе́рвый; ~ **in the morning** ра́но у́тром; **to have an ~ night** ра́но ложи́ться (лечь* *perf*) спать; **in the ~ spring, ~ in the spring** ра́нней весно́й; **in the ~ 19th century, ~ in the 19th century** в нача́ле 19-го ве́ка; **you need to take the ~ train** Вам на́до е́хать* ра́нним по́ездом; **you're ~!** Вы пришли́ ра́но!; **she's in her ~ forties** ей немно́го за со́рок; **at your earliest convenience** в ближа́йшее удо́бное для Вас вре́мя.

early retirement *n*: **to take ~ ~** ра́но уходи́ть* (уйти́* *perf*) на пе́нсию.

early warning system *n* (*MIL*) систе́ма ра́ннего предупрежде́ния.

earmark [ˈɪəmɑːk] *vt*: **to ~ for** (*funds*) предназнача́ть (предназна́чить *perf*) для +*gen*.

earn [əːn] *vt* (*salary*) зараба́тывать (зарабо́тать *perf*); (*interest*) приноси́ть* (принести́* *perf*); (*praise*) заслу́живать (заслужи́ть* *perf*); **to ~ one's living** зараба́тывать *(impf)* на жизнь; **this ~ed him much praise, he ~ed much praise for this** э́то принесло́ ему́ мно́го похва́л, он заслужи́л мно́го похва́л за э́то; **he's ~ed his rest/reward** он заслужи́л сво́й о́тдых/свою́ награ́ду.

earned income [əːnd-] *n* (*COMM*) трудово́й дохо́д.

earnest [ˈəːnɪst] *adj* (*person, manner*) серьёзный* (серьёзен); (*wish, desire*) и́скренний* ◆ *n* (*also:* ~ **money**) зада́ток*; **in ~** всерьёз; **work on the tunnel soon began in ~** рабо́та по прокла́дке тунне́ля вско́ре начала́сь всерьёз; **is he in ~ about these proposals?** всерьёз ли он говори́т об э́тих предложе́ниях?

earnings [ˈəːnɪŋz] *npl* (*personal*) за́работок* *msg*; (*of company etc*) при́быль *fsg*.

ear nose and throat specialist *n* (*MED*) отоларинго́лог, врач* у́хо-го́рло-но́с.

earphones [ˈɪəfəunz] *npl* нау́шники *mpl*.

earplugs [ˈɪəplʌgz] *npl* зату́чки* *fpl* для уше́й.

earring [ˈɪərɪŋ] *n* серьга́*.

earshot [ˈɪəʃɔt] *n*: **within/out of ~** в преде́лах/вне преде́лов слы́шимости.

earth [əːθ] *n* земля́*; (*BRIT: ELEC*) заземле́ние; (*of fox*) нора́* ◆ *vt* (*BRIT: ELEC*) заземля́ть (заземли́ть *perf*); **E~** (*planet*) Земля́*.

* marks translations which have irregular inflections. The Russian-English side of the dictionary gives inflectional information.

earthenware ['ə:θnwɛəʳ] *n* кера́мика, гонча́рные изде́лия *pl* ♦ *adj* гли́няный.
earthly ['ə:θlɪ] *adj* земно́й; ~ **paradise** земно́й рай*; **there is no ~ reason to think** ... нет ни мале́йшей причи́ны ду́мать ....
earthquake ['ə:θkweɪk] *n* землетрясе́ние.
earthshattering ['ə:θʃætərɪŋ] *adj* (*surprising*) потряса́ющий* (потряса́ющ).
earth tremor *n* подзе́мный толчо́к*.
earthworks ['ə:θwə:ks] *npl* земляны́е рабо́ты *fpl*.
earthworm ['ə:θwə:m] *n* земляно́й червь* *m*.
earthy ['ə:θɪ] *adj* (*humour*) грубова́тый (грубова́т).
earwig ['ɪəwɪg] *n* уховёртка*.
ease [i:z] *n* лёгкость *f*; (*comfort*) поко́й* ♦ *vt* (*pain*) облегча́ть (облегчи́ть *perf*); (*problem*) уменьша́ть (уме́ньшить *perf*; (*tension*) ослабля́ть (осла́бить* *perf*); (*loosen*: *grip, belt*) отпуска́ть (отпусти́ть* *perf*) ♦ *vi* (*situation*) упроща́ться (упрости́ться* *perf*); (*pain, grief, grip*) слабе́ть (ослабе́ть *perf*); (*rain, snow*) станови́ться* (стать* *perf*) ти́ше; **to ~ sth into sth** вставля́ть (вста́вить* *perf*) что-н в что-н; **to ~ sth out of sth** выдвига́ть (вы́двинуть *perf*) что-н из чего́-н; **to ~ o.s. into** опуска́ться (опусти́ться *perf*) в +*acc*; **at ~!** (*MIL*) во́льно!; **with ~** с лёгкостью; **life of ~** жизнь в поко́е и дово́льстве
▸ **ease off** *vi* станови́ться* (стать* *perf*) ти́ше; (*slow down*) замедля́ться (заме́длиться *perf*)
▸ **ease up** *vi* = **ease off**.
easel ['i:zl] *n* мольбе́рт.
easily ['i:zɪlɪ] *adv* легко́; (*in a relaxed manner*) непринуждённо; (*without doubt*) несомне́нно.
easiness ['i:zɪnɪs] *n* лёгкость *f*; (*of manner*) непринуждённость *f*.
east [i:st] *n* восто́к ♦ *adj* восто́чный ♦ *adv* на восто́к; **the E~** Восто́к.
Easter ['i:stəʳ] *n* па́сха ♦ *adj* пасха́льный.
Easter egg *n* (*painted*) пасха́льное яйцо́*; (*chocolate*) шокола́дное пасха́льное яйцо́*.
Easter Island *n* о́стров Па́схи.
easterly ['i:stəlɪ] *adj* восто́чный.
Easter Monday *n* ≈ Све́тлый понеде́льник.
eastern ['i:stən] *adj* восто́чный; (*POL*) восто́чно-европе́йский; **E~ Europe** Восто́чная Евро́па; **the E~ bloc** (*formerly*) Восто́чно-Европе́йский* блок.
Easter Sunday *n* ≈ Све́тлое *or* Христо́во воскресе́нье.
East Germany *n* (*formerly*) Восто́чная Герма́ния.
eastward(s) ['i:stwəd(z)] *adv* на восто́к.
easy ['i:zɪ] *adj* лёгкий*; (*manner*) непринуждённый* ♦ *adv*: **to take it** *or* **things ~** не напряга́ться *(impf)*; (*not worry*) не волнова́ться *(impf)*; **payment on ~ terms** (*COMM*) платёж* на лёгких усло́виях; **that's easier said than done** ле́гче сказа́ть, чем сде́лать; **I'm ~** (*inf*) мне всё равно́.
easy chair *n* удо́бное кре́сло*.
easy-going ['i:zɪ'gəuɪŋ] *adj* с лёгким хара́ктером.
easy touch *n* (*inf*): **she is an ~ ~** её легко́ убеди́ть.
eat [i:t] (*pt* **ate**, *pp* **eaten**) *vt* есть* (съесть* *perf*) ♦ *vi* есть* *(impf)*
▸ **eat away** *vt* (*rock, metal*) разъеда́ть (разъе́сть* *perf*); (*savings*) съеда́ть (съесть* *perf*)
▸ **eat away at** *vt fus* = **eat away**
▸ **eat into** *vt fus* = **eat away**
▸ **eat out** *vi* есть* *(impf)* в рестора́не
▸ **eat up** *vt* (*food*) доеда́ть (дое́сть* *perf*); **it ~s up electricity** э́то потребля́ет мно́го электроэне́ргии.
eatable ['i:təbl] *adj* съедо́бный*.
eaten ['i:tn] *pp of* **eat**.
eau de Cologne ['əudəkə'ləun] *n* одеколо́н*.
eaves [i:vz] *npl* (*of house*) карни́з *msg*.
eavesdrop ['i:vzdrɔp] *vi*: **to ~ (on)** подслу́шивать (подслу́шать *perf*).
ebb [ɛb] *n* отли́в ♦ *vi* (*tide, sea*) отлива́ть *(impf)*; (*fig*: *also*: **~ away**) угаса́ть (уга́снуть *perf*); **the ~ and flow** отли́в и прили́в; **to be at a low ~** (*fig*) находи́ться* *(impf)* в состоя́нии упа́дка.
ebb tide *n* отли́в.
ebony ['ɛbənɪ] *n* эбе́новое *or* чёрное де́рево.
ebullient [ɪ'bʌlɪənt] *adj* по́лный* (по́лон) энтузиа́зма.
EC *n abbr* (= *European Community*) ЕС = *Европе́йское соо́бщество или сою́з*.
ECB *n abbr* (= *European Central Bank*) Европе́йский центра́льный банк.
eccentric [ɪk'sɛntrɪk] *adj* (*choice, views*) эксцентри́чный* ♦ *n* эксцентри́чный челове́к.
ecclesiastic(al) [ɪkli:zɪ'æstɪk(l)] *adj* духо́вный.
ECG *n abbr* = **electrocardiogram**.
echo ['ɛkəu] (*pl* **~es**) *n* э́хо *no pl* ♦ *vt* (*repeat*) вто́рить *(impf)* +*dat* ♦ *vi* (*sound*) отдава́ться* *(impf)*; **the room ~ed with her laughter** в ко́мнате раздава́лся её смех.
éclair ['eɪklɛəʳ] *n* экле́р.
eclipse [ɪ'klɪps] *n* затме́ние ♦ *vt* (*also fig*) затмева́ть (затми́ть* *perf*).
ECM *n abbr* (*US*: = *European Common Market*) О́бщий* ры́нок*.
eco- ['i:kəu] *prefix* э́ко-.
eco-friendly ['i:kəu'frɛndlɪ] *adj* экологи́чески безопа́сный* (безопа́сен).
ecological [i:kə'lɔdʒɪkəl] *adj* экологи́ческий*.
ecologist [ɪ'kɔlədʒɪst] *n* эко́лог.
ecology [ɪ'kɔlədʒɪ] *n* (*SCOL*) эколо́гия; (*environment*) окружа́ющая среда́.
economic [i:kə'nɔmɪk] *adj* экономи́ческий*; (*profitable*) рента́бельный* (рента́белен).
economical [i:kə'nɔmɪkl] *adj* (*cheap to run*) экономи́чный* (экономи́чен); (*thrifty*) эконо́мный*.
economically [i:kə'nɔmɪklɪ] *adv* эконо́мно;

(*regarding economics*) экономи́чески.
economics [i:kə'nɔmɪks] *n* эконо́мика ◆ *npl* (*of project, situation*) экономи́ческий* расчёт *msg*.
economic warfare *n* экономи́ческая война́.
economist [ɪ'kɔnəmɪst] *n* экономи́ст.
economize [ɪ'kɔnəmaɪz] *vi* эконо́мить* (сэконо́мить* *perf*).
economy [ɪ'kɔnəmɪ] *n* эконо́мика, хозя́йство; (*financial prudence*) эконо́мия; **economies of scale** (*COMM*) экономи́чность за счёт кру́пных объёмов опера́ций.
economy class *n* (*AVIAT*) *наибо́лее дешёвые поса́дочные места́*.
economy size *n* (*COMM*) *больша́я упако́вка како́го-либо това́ра, сто́ящая деше́вле, чем ма́ленькая*.
ecosystem ['i:kəusɪstəm] *n* экосисте́ма.
ECSC *n abbr* (= *European Coal & Steel Community*) *европе́йское соо́бщество производи́телей угля́ и ста́ли*.
ecstasy ['ɛkstəsɪ] *n* экста́з; **to go into ecstasies over** впада́ть (впасть* *perf*) в экста́з от *+gen*; **in ecstasy** в экста́зе.
ecstatic [ɛks'tætɪk] *adj* восто́рженный*.
ECT *n abbr* = **electroconvulsive therapy**.
ECU *n abbr* (= *European Currency Unit*) экю́ *ind*.
Ecuador ['ɛkwədɔ:ʳ] *n* Эквадо́р.
ecumenical [i:kju'mɛnɪkl] *adj* вселе́нский.
eczema ['ɛksɪmə] *n* экзе́ма.
eddy ['ɛdɪ] *n* (*of water*) водоворо́т; (*of air*) вихрь *m*.
edge [ɛdʒ] *n* край*; (*of knife etc*) остриё* ◆ *vt* (*trim*) окаймля́ть (окайми́ть* *perf*) ◆ *vi*: **to ~ forward** ме́дленно продвига́ться (продви́нуться *perf*); **on ~** (*fig*) = **edgy**; **to have the ~ on** име́ть (*impf*) преиму́щество пе́ред *+instr*; **to ~ past** проти́снуться (*perf*); **to ~ away from** отходи́ть* (отойти́* *perf*) бочко́м от *+gen*; **to ~ up** (*COMM*) незначи́тельно изменя́ться.
edgeways ['ɛdʒweɪz] *adv*: **he couldn't get a word in ~** он не мог слове́чка верну́ть *or* сло́ва вста́вить.
edging ['ɛdʒɪŋ] *n* кайма́*.
edgy ['ɛdʒɪ] *adj* (*nervous, agitated*) раздражённый*.
edible ['ɛdɪbl] *adj* съедо́бный* (съедо́бен).
edict ['i:dɪkt] *n* ука́з.
edifice ['ɛdɪfɪs] *n* вели́чественное зда́ние.
edifying ['ɛdɪfaɪɪŋ] *adj* поучи́тельный* (поучи́телен).
Edinburgh ['ɛdɪnbərə] *n* Э́динбург.
edit ['ɛdɪt] *vt* (*text, newspaper, COMPUT*) редакти́ровать (отредакти́ровать *perf*); (*book*) гото́вить* (подгото́вить* *perf*) к печа́ти; (*film, broadcast*) монти́ровать (смонти́ровать *perf*).
edition [ɪ'dɪʃən] *n* (*of book*) изда́ние; (*of newspaper, TV programme*) вы́пуск.
editor ['ɛdɪtəʳ] *n* реда́ктор*; **foreign/political ~** (*PRESS*) реда́ктор* отде́ла зарубе́жных новосте́й/поли́тики.
editorial [ɛdɪ'tɔ:rɪəl] *adj* редакцио́нный ◆ *n* передови́ца, передова́я статья́*.
EDP *n abbr* (*COMPUT*) = **electronic data processing**.
EDT *abbr* (*US*) = *Eastern Daylight Time*.
educate ['ɛdjukeɪt] *vt* (*teach*) дава́ть* (дать* *perf*) образова́ние *+dat*; (*instruct*) просвеща́ть (просвети́ть* *perf*); **to be ~d at ...** получа́ть (получи́ть *perf*) образова́ние в *+prp*.
educated guess ['ɛdjukeɪtɪd-] *n* *дога́дка располага́ющего предвари́тельной информа́цией*.
education [ɛdju'keɪʃən] *n* (*schooling*) образова́ние; (*teaching*) обуче́ние; (*knowledge*) образо́ванность *f*; **primary or** (*US*) **elementary/secondary ~** нача́льное/ сре́днее образова́ние.
educational [ɛdju'keɪʃənl] *adj* (*institution*) уче́бный; (*staff*) преподава́тельский; (*policy, practice*) уче́бный, воспита́тельный; (*toy*) обуча́ющий; **~ system** систе́ма образова́ния; **~ technology** техни́ческие сре́дства обуче́ния.
Edwardian [ɛd'wɔ:dɪən] *adj* *эпо́хи англи́йского короля́ Эдуа́рда VII*.
EE *abbr* = **electrical engineer**.
EEC *n abbr* (= **European Economic Community**) ЕЭС= *Европе́йское экономи́ческое соо́бщество*.
EEG *n abbr* = **electroencephalogram**.
eel [i:l] *n* у́горь* *m*.
EENT *n abbr* (*US*: *MED*: = *eye, ear, nose and throat*) ≈ у́хо-го́рло-нос.
EEOC *n abbr* (*US*: = *Equal Employment Opportunity Commission*) *коми́ссия ра́вных возмо́жностей при на́йме на рабо́ту*.
eerie ['ɪərɪ] *adj* жу́ткий*.
EET *abbr* (= *Eastern European Time*) восточноевропе́йское вре́мя* *nt*.
efface [ɪ'feɪs] *vt* (*erase*) стира́ть (стере́ть* *perf*): **to ~ o.s.** держа́ться* (*impf*) в тени́.
effect [ɪ'fɛkt] *n* (*result*) эффе́кт, после́дствие; (*impression*) впечатле́ние, эффе́кт ◆ *vt* (*carry out*) производи́ть* (произвести* *perf*); **~s** *npl* (*property*) иму́щество *ntsg*; (*THEAT, CINEMA*) эффе́кты *mpl*; **to take ~** (*drug*) де́йствовать (поде́йствовать *perf*); (*law*) вступа́ть (вступи́ть* *perf*) в си́лу; **to put into ~** осуществля́ть (осуществи́ть* *perf*); **to have an ~ on sb/sth** де́йствовать (поде́йствовать *perf*) на кого́-н/что-н; **in ~** в су́щности; **his letter is to the ~ that** ... суть его́ письма́ заключа́ется в том, что ....

effective [ɪ'fɛktɪv] *adj* (*successful*) эффективный* (эффективен); (*actual*) действительный*; **to become ~** (*LAW*) входить* (войти* *perf*) в силу; **~ date** дата вступления в силу.
effectively [ɪ'fɛktɪvlɪ] *adv* (*successfully*) эффективно; (*in reality*) фактически.
effectiveness [ɪ'fɛktɪvnɪs] *n* (*success*) эффективность *f*.
effeminate [ɪ'fɛmɪnɪt] *adj* женоподобный* (женоподобен).
effervescent [ɛfə'vɛsnt] *adj* (*drink*) шипучий*.
efficacy ['ɛfɪkəsɪ] *n* эффективность *f*.
efficiency [ɪ'fɪʃənsɪ] *n* (*see adj*) эффективность *f*; деловитость *f*.
efficiency apartment *n* (*US*) *квартира, соединяющая в себе спальню, гостиную и иногда кухню.*
efficient [ɪ'fɪʃənt] *adj* (*organization, method, machine*) эффективный* (эффективен); (*person*) деловитый.
efficiently [ɪ'fɪʃəntlɪ] *adv* эффективно.
effigy ['ɛfɪdʒɪ] *n* (*dummy*) чучело; (*image*) изображение.
effluent ['ɛfluənt] *n* сток, жидкие отходы *mpl*.
effort ['ɛfət] *n* (*attempt*) попытка*; (*exertion, concerted attempt*) усилие; **to make an ~ to do** прикладывать (приложить *perf*) усилия, чтобы *+infin*.
effortless ['ɛfətlɪs] *adj* (*achievement*) не требующий усилий; (*style*) лёгкий*.
effrontery [ɪ'frʌntərɪ] *n* нахальство, наглость *f*; **to have the ~ to do** иметь *(impf)* нахальство *or* наглость, чтобы *+infin*.
effusive [ɪ'fju:sɪv] *adj* экспансивный*.
EFL *n abbr* (*SCOL*) = *English as a Foreign Language*.
EFTA ['ɛftə] *n abbr* (= *European Free Trade Association*) ЕАСТ= *Европейская ассоциация свободной торговли*.
e.g. *adv abbr* (*for example*: = *exempli gratia*) например.
egalitarian [ɪgælɪ'tɛərɪən] *adj* эгалитарный ◆ *n* (*person*) поборник(-ица) равноправия.
egg [ɛg] *n* яйцо; **hard-boiled/soft-boiled ~** яйцо вкрутую/всмятку
▸ **egg on** *vt* (*encourage*) подстрекать (подстрекнуть *perf*).
egg cup *n* рюмка* для яйца.
eggplant ['ɛgplɑ:nt] *n* (*esp US*) баклажан*.
eggshell ['ɛgʃɛl] *n* яичная скорлупа* ◆ *adj* (*paint*) матовый.
egg timer *n* таймер.
egg white *n* яичный белок*.
egg yolk *n* яичный желток*.
ego ['i:gəu] *n* (*self-esteem*) самолюбие.
egoism ['ɛgəuɪzəm] *n* эгоизм.
egoist ['ɛgəuɪst] *n* эгоист(ка*).
egotism ['ɛgəutɪzəm] *n* эготизм.
egotist ['ɛgəutɪst] *n* эготист(ка*).
ego trip *n* (*pej*) самоублажение.
Egypt ['i:dʒɪpt] *n* Египет*.
Egyptian [ɪ'dʒɪpʃən] *adj* египетский* ◆ *n* египтянин*(-янка*).
eiderdown ['aɪdədaun] *n* (*quilt*) ватное одеяло.
eight [eɪt] *n* восемь*; *see also* **five**.
eighteen [eɪ'ti:n] *n* восемнадцать*; *see also* **five**.
eighteenth [eɪ'ti:nθ] *adj* восемнадцатый; *see also* **fifth**.
eighth [eɪtθ] *adj* восьмой ◆ *n* (*fraction*) восьмая *f adj*; *see also* **fifth**.
eightieth ['eɪtɪəθ] *adj* восьмидесятый; *see also* **fifth**.
eighty ['eɪtɪ] *n* восемьдесят*; *see also* **fifty**.
Eire ['ɛərə] *n* Эйре *nt ind*.
EIS *n abbr* = *Educational Institute of Scotland*.
either ['aɪðə'] *adj* (*one or other*) любой (из двух); (*both, each*) каждый ◆ *adv* также ◆ *pron*: **~ (of them)** любой (из них) ◆ *conj*: **~ yes or no** либо "да", либо "нет"; **on ~ side** на обеих сторонах; **I don't smoke – I don't ~** я не курю – я тоже; **I don't like ~** мне не нравится ни то, ни другое; **there was no sound from ~ of the flats** не было звука ни из одной из квартир; **I haven't seen ~** я не видел ни того, ни другого.
ejaculation [ɪdʒækju'leɪʃən] *n* (*PHYSIOL*) эякуляция.
eject [ɪ'dʒɛkt] *vt* выбрасывать (выбросить* *perf*); (*tenant*) выселять (выселить *perf*); (*gate-crasher*) выгонять (выгнать* *perf*) ◆ *vi* (*pilot*) катапультироваться *(impf/perf)*.
ejector seat [ɪ'dʒɛktə-] *n* (*AVIAT*) катапультируемое кресло*.
Ekaterinburg [jɪkətɪrin'burk] *n* Екатеринбург.
eke [i:k] *vt*: **to ~ out** (*income*) растягивать (растянуть *perf*); **to ~ out a living from** существовать *(impf)* за счёт *+gen*.
EKG *n abbr* (*US*) = **electrocardiogram**.
el [ɛl] *n abbr* (*US*: *inf*: = *elevated railroad*) *надземная железная дорога.*
elaborate [*adj* ɪ'læbərɪt, *vb* ɪ'læbəreɪt] *adj* сложный* ◆ *vt* (*expand*) развивать (развить* *perf*); (*refine*) тщательно разрабатывать (разработать *perf*) ◆ *vi*: **to ~ on** (*idea, plan etc*) рассматривать (рассмотреть* *perf*) в деталях.
elapse [ɪ'læps] *vi* (*time*) проходить* (пройти* *perf*).
elastic [ɪ'læstɪk] *n* (*material*) резинка ◆ *adj* (*stretchy*) эластичный* (эластичен); (*adaptable*) гибкий* (гибок).
elastic band *n* (*BRIT*) резинка*.
elasticity [ɪlæs'tɪsɪtɪ] *n* эластичность *f*.
elated [ɪ'leɪtɪd] *adj*: **to be ~** быть* *(impf)* в приподнятом настроении.
elation [ɪ'leɪʃən] *n* приподнятое настроение.
elbow ['ɛlbəu] *n* локоть* *m* ◆ *vt*: **to ~ one's way through the crowd** проталкиваться *(impf)* в толпе.
elbow grease *n*: **a lot of ~ ~ is required** придётся хорошенько потрудиться.

elbowroom ['ɛlbəurum] *n* простóр.
elder ['ɛldə^r] *adj* (*brother, sister etc*) стáрший* ◆ *n* (*tree*) бузинá; (*older person*): **~s** стáршие *pl adj.*
elderly ['ɛldəlɪ] *adj* пожилóй; **the ~** *npl* стáрые лю́ди *pl*, престарéлые *pl adj.*
elder statesman *irreg n* заслу́женный полити́ческий* дéятель *m.*
eldest ['ɛldɪst] *adj* (*child*) (сáмый) стáрший* ◆ *n* стáрший*(-ая) *m(f) adj.*
elect [ɪ'lɛkt] *vt* избирáть (избрáть* *perf*) ◆ *adj*: **the president ~** и́збранный президéнт; **to ~ to do** (*choose*) предпочитáть (предпочéсть* *perf*) *+infin.*
election [ɪ'lɛkʃən] *n* (*voting*) вы́боры *pl*; (*installation*) избрáние; **to hold an ~** проводи́ть* (провести́* *perf*) вы́боры.
election campaign *n* избирáтельная кампáния.
electioneering [ɪlɛkʃə'nɪərɪŋ] *n* агитáция.
elector [ɪ'lɛktə^r] *n* избирáтель(ница) *m(f).*
electoral [ɪ'lɛktərəl] *adj* избирáтельный.
electoral college *n* коллéгия вы́борщиков.
electorate [ɪ'lɛktərɪt] *n*: **the ~** избирáтели *mpl.*
electric [ɪ'lɛktrɪk] *adj* электри́ческий*.
electrical [ɪ'lɛktrɪkl] *adj* электри́ческий*; **~ failure** отключéние тóка.
electrical engineer *n* инженéр-элéктрик.
electric blanket *n* одеялó-грéлка*.
electric chair *n* (*US*) электри́ческий* стул*.
electric cooker *n* электри́ческая плитá*.
electric current *n* электри́ческий* ток.
electric fire *n* (*BRIT*) электри́ческий*ками́н.
electrician [ɪlɛk'trɪʃən] *n* электромонтёр, элéктрик.
electricity [ɪlɛk'trɪsɪtɪ] *n* электри́чество ◆ *cpd* электри́ческий*; **to switch on/off the ~** подключáть (подключи́ть *perf*)/отключáть (отключи́ть *perf*) электри́чество; **~ bill** счёт* за электри́чество.
electricity board *n* (*BRIT*) управлéние по электрификáции.
electric light *n* электри́ческий* свет.
electric shock *n* удáр тóком.
electrify [ɪ'lɛktrɪfaɪ] *vt* (*fence, rail network*) электрифици́ровать (*impf/perf*); (*thrill*) электризовáть (наэлектризовáть *perf*).
electro... [ɪ'lɛktrəu] *prefix* элéктро....
electrocardiogram [ɪ'lɛktrə'kɑːdɪəgræm] *n* электрокардиогрáмма.
electroconvulsive therapy [ɪ'lɛktrəkən'vʌlsɪv-] *n* электротóковая терапи́я.
electrocute [ɪ'lɛktrəkjuːt] *vt* (*person: kill*) убивáть (уби́ть* *perf*) электри́ческим тóком; (*: injure*) ударя́ть (удáрить *perf*) электри́ческим тóком.
electrode [ɪ'lɛktrəud] *n* электрóд.
electroencephalogram [ɪ'lɛktrəuɛn'sɛfələgræm] *n* электроэнцефалогрáмма.
electrolysis [ɪlɛk'trɔlɪsɪs] *n* электрóлиз.
electromagnetic [ɪ'lɛktrəmæg'nɛtɪk] *adj* электромагни́тный.
electron [ɪ'lɛktrɔn] *n* электрóн.
electronic [ɪlɛk'trɔnɪk] *adj* электрóнный
electronic data processing *n* электрóнная обрабóтка информáции.
electronic mail *n* (*COMPUT*) электрóнная пóчта.
electronics [ɪlɛk'trɔnɪks] *n* электрóника.
electron microscope *n* электрóнный микроскóп.
electroplated [ɪ'lɛktrə'pleɪtɪd] *adj покры́тый метáллом с пóмощью электрóлиза.*
electrotherapy [ɪ'lɛktrə'θɛrəpɪ] *n* электротерапи́я.
elegance ['ɛlɪgəns] *n* элегáнтность *f.*
elegant ['ɛlɪgənt] *adj* элегáнтный* (элегáнтен).
element ['ɛlɪmənt] *n* (*also CHEM*) элемéнт; (*of heater, kettle etc*) электронагревáтельный элемéнт; **the ~s** *npl* стихи́я *fsg*; **you are in your ~** Вы в своéй стихи́и.
elementary [ɛlɪ'mɛntərɪ] *adj* элементáрный* (элементáрен); (*school, education*) начáльный.
elephant ['ɛlɪfənt] *n* слон*(и́ха).
elevate ['ɛlɪveɪt] *vt* (*in rank*) повышáть (повы́сить* *perf*); (*in importance*) возводи́ть* (возвести́* *perf*); (*physically*) поднимáть (подня́ть* *perf*).
elevated railroad ['ɛlɪveɪtɪd-] *n* (*US*) надзéмная желéзная дорóга.
elevation [ɛlɪ'veɪʃən] *n* (*see vb*) повышéние; возведéние; поднятие; (*height*) высотá*; (*ARCHIT*) фасáд.
elevator ['ɛlɪveɪtə^r] *n* (*US*) лифт; (*in warehouse etc*) грузоподъёмник.
eleven [ɪ'lɛvn] *n* оди́ннадцать*; *see also* **five.**
elevenses [ɪ'lɛvnzɪz] *npl* (*BRIT*) *лёгкий зáвтрак óколо оди́ннадцати часóв утрá.*
eleventh [ɪ'lɛvnθ] *adj* оди́ннадцатый; **at the ~ hour** в послéднюю минýту; *see also* **fifth.**
elf [ɛlf] (*pl* **elves**) *n* эльф.
elicit [ɪ'lɪsɪt] *vt*: **to ~ (from)** (*information*) извлекáть (извлéчь* *perf*) (из *+gen*); (*response, reaction*) вызывáть (вы́звать* *perf*) (от *+gen*); **to ~ a reply** добивáться (доби́ться* *perf*) отвéта; **to ~ applause from the audience** вызывáть (вы́звать* *perf*) аплодисмéнты аудитóрии.
eligible ['ɛlɪdʒəbl] *adj* (*for marriage*) подходя́щий*; **to be ~ for sth** (*qualified, suitable*) быть* (*impf*) подходя́щей кандидатýрой для чегó-н; **to be ~ for a pension** имéть (*impf*) прáво на пéнсию.

eliminate [ɪ'lɪmɪneɪt] *vt* ликвиди́ровать *(impf/perf)*, исключа́ть (исключи́ть *perf*); (*candidate, team, contestant*) отсе́ивать (отсе́ять *perf*); **they were ~d in the first round** они́ бы́ли отсе́яны на пе́рвом ту́ре.
elimination [ɪlɪmɪ'neɪʃən] *n* ликвида́ция, исключе́ние; (*of team, candidate*) устране́ние; **by process of ~** путём исключе́ния *or* ликвида́ции.
élite [eɪ'li:t] *n* эли́та.
élitist [eɪ'li:tɪst] *adj* (*pej*) элита́рный.
elixir [ɪ'lɪksəʳ] *n* элекси́р.
Elizabethan [ɪlɪzə'bi:θən] *adj* (*house, music, period*) эпо́хи короле́вы Елизаве́ты.
ellipse [ɪ'lɪps] *n* (*MATH*) э́ллипс.
elliptical [ɪ'lɪptɪkl] *adj* (*MATH*) эллипти́ческий.
elm [ɛlm] *n* вяз.
elocution [ɛlə'kju:ʃən] *n* ора́торское иску́сство.
elongated ['i:lɔŋgeɪtɪd] *adj* удлинённый* (удлинён).
elope [ɪ'ləup] *vi*: **to ~ (with)** та́йно сбежа́ть* *(perf)* (с *+instr*).
elopement [ɪ'ləupmənt] *n* та́йное бе́гство.
eloquence ['ɛləkwəns] *n* (*see adj*) красноре́чие; я́ркость *f*.
eloquent ['ɛləkwənt] *adj* (*description, person*) красноречи́вый; (*speech*) я́ркий*.
El Salvador [ɛl'sælvədɔ:ʳ] *n* Сальвадо́р.
else [ɛls] *adv* (*other*) ещё; **nothing ~** бо́льше ничего́; **somewhere ~** (*be*) где́-нибудь ещё; (*go*) куда́-нибудь ещё; (*come from*) отку́да-то ещё; **everywhere ~** везде́; **where ~?** (*position*) где ещё?; (*motion*) куда́ ещё?; **is there anything ~ I can do to help?** я могу́ че́м-нибудь ещё помо́чь?; **there was little ~ to do** почти́ не́чем бы́ло заня́ться; **everyone ~** все остальны́е; **nobody ~ spoke** бо́льше никто́ не выступа́л; **or ~** ... не то (бу́дет ху́же) ....
elsewhere [ɛls'wɛəʳ] *adv* (*be*) где́-нибудь ещё (*в друго́м ме́сте*); (*go*) куда́-нибудь ещё (*в друго́е ме́сто*).
ELT *n abbr* (*SCOL*) = *English Language Teaching*.
elucidate [ɪ'lu:sɪdeɪt] *vt* разъясня́ть (разъясни́ть *perf*).
elude [ɪ'lu:d] *vt* (*captor, capture*) ускольза́ть (ускользну́ть *perf*) от *+gen*; (*subj: fact, idea*): **to ~ sb** не приходи́ть *(impf)* кому́-н на у́м.
elusive [ɪ'lu:sɪv] *adj* (*person, animal*) неулови́мый; (*quality*) не поддаю́щийся описа́нию; **he's very ~** он о́чень за́мкнутый.
elves [ɛlvz] *npl of* **elf**.
emaciated [ɪ'meɪsɪeɪtɪd] *adj* (*person, animal*) истощённый*.
E-mail *n abbr* (= *electronic mail*) электро́нная по́чта.
emanate ['ɛməneɪt] *vi*: **to ~ from** исходи́ть *(impf)* от *+gen*.
emancipate [ɪ'mænsɪpeɪt] *vt* освобожда́ть (освободи́ть* *perf*), эмансипи́ровать *(impf/perf)*.
emancipation [ɪmænsɪ'peɪʃən] *n* освобожде́ние, эмансипа́ция.
emasculate [ɪ'mæskjuleɪt] *vt* (*weaken*) ослабля́ть (осла́бить* *perf*).
embalm [ɪm'bɑ:m] *vt* бальзами́ровать (забальзами́ровать *perf*).
embankment [ɪm'bæŋkmənt] *n* (*of road, railway*) на́сыпь *f*; (*of river*) на́бережная *f adj*.
embargo [ɪm'bɑ:gəu] (*pl* **~es**) *n* эмба́рго *nt ind* ◆ *vt* запреща́ть (запрети́ть* *perf*); **to put** *or* **impose** *or* **place an ~ on sth** накла́дывать (наложи́ть* *perf*) эмба́рго на что-н; **to lift an ~ from** снима́ть (снять* *perf*) эмба́рго с *+gen*.
embark [ɪm'bɑ:k] *vi*: **to ~ (on)** (*ship*) грузи́ться* (погрузи́ться* *perf*) (на *+acc*); **to ~ on** (*journey*) отправля́ться (отпра́виться* *perf*) в *+acc*; (*task, course of action*) предпринима́ть (предприня́ть* *perf*).
embarkation [ɛmbɑ:'keɪʃən] *n* (*of people*) поса́дка; (*of cargo*) погру́зка.
embarkation card *n* поса́дочный тало́н.
embarrass [ɪm'bærəs] *vt* смуща́ть (смути́ть* *perf*); (*politician, government*) затрудня́ть (затрудни́ть *perf*).
embarrassed [ɪm'bærəst] *adj* (*laugh, silence*) смущённый*; **to be ~** смуща́ться (смути́ться* *perf*).
embarrassing [ɪm'bærəsɪŋ] *adj* вызыва́ющий* смуще́ние, щекотли́вый.
embarrassment [ɪm'bærəsmənt] *n* (*feeling*) смуще́ние; (*problem*) стыд*.
embassy ['ɛmbəsɪ] *n* посо́льство; **the French E~** Францу́зское посо́льство, посо́льство Фра́нции.
embedded [ɪm'bɛdɪd] *adj* (*object*) заде́ланный; (*attitude, belief*) устоя́вшийся.
embellish [ɪm'bɛlɪʃ] *vt* (*story*) приукра́шивать (приукра́сить* *perf*); (*place, dress*): **~ed with** укра́шенный *+instr*.
embers ['ɛmbəz] *npl* тле́ющие уго́льки́ *mpl*.
embezzle [ɪm'bɛzl] *vt* присва́ивать (присво́ить *perf*).
embezzlement [ɪm'bɛzlmənt] *n* растра́та.
embezzler [ɪm'bɛzləʳ] *n* растра́тчик(-ица).
embitter [ɪm'bɪtəʳ] *vt* (*fig*) озлобля́ть (озло́бить* *perf*).
embittered [ɪm'bɪtəd] *adj* (*person*) озло́бленный*.
emblem ['ɛmbləm] *n* эмбле́ма.
embodiment [ɪm'bɔdɪmənt] *n*: **she is the ~ of** она́ – воплоще́ние *+gen*.
embody [ɪm'bɔdɪ] *vt* (*incarnate*) воплоща́ть (воплоти́ть* *perf*); (*include, contain*) содержа́ть *(impf)* (в себе́).
embolden [ɪm'bəuldn] *vt* ободря́ть (обо́дрить *perf*).
embolism ['ɛmbəlɪzəm] *n* эмболи́я.
embossed [ɪm'bɔst] *adj* (*design, word*) релье́фный*; **~ with his initials** с релье́фными инициа́лами.

embrace [ɪm'breɪs] *vt* обнимать (обнять* *perf*); (*include*) охватывать (охватить* *perf*) ◆ *vi* обниматься *(impf)* ◆ *n* объятие.
embroider [ɪm'brɔɪdəʳ] *vt* (*cloth*) вышивать (вышить* *perf*); (*fig*: *story*) приукрашивать (приукрасить* *perf*).
embroidery [ɪm'brɔɪdərɪ] *n* (*stitching*) вышивка; (*activity*) вышивание.
embroil [ɪm'brɔɪl] *vt*: **to become ~ed (in sth)** оказываться (оказаться* *perf*) вовлечённым(-ой) (во что-н).
embryo ['ɛmbrɪəu] *n* (*BIO*) эмбрион; (*fig*) зародыш.
emend [ɪ'mɛnd] *vt* (*text*) исправлять (исправить* *perf*).
emerald ['ɛmərəld] *n* изумруд.
emerge [ɪ'mə:dʒ] *vi* (*fact*) всплывать (всплыть* *perf*); (*new industry, society*) появляться (появиться* *perf*); **to ~ from** (*from room, imprisonment*) выходить* (выйти* *perf*) из *+gen*; (*from sleep*) пробуждаться (пробудиться* *perf*) от *+gen*; **it ~s that** (*BRIT*) выяснилось, что.
emergence [ɪ'mə:dʒəns] *n* (*of new idea etc*) появление.
emergency [ɪ'mə:dʒənsɪ] *n* (*crisis*) крайняя необходимость *f* ◆ *cpd*: **~ repair** срочный ремонт; **in an ~** в случае опасности; **state of ~** чрезвычайное положение; **~ talks** экстренные переговоры.
emergency cord *n* (*US*) ≈ стоп-кран.
emergency exit *n* запасный выход.
emergency landing *n* (*AVIAT*) вынужденная посадка.
emergency lane *n* (*US*: *AUT*) аварийная полоса*.
emergency road service *n* (*US*) аварийная дорожная служба.
emergency services *npl*: **the ~ ~** аварийная служба *fsg*.
emergency stop *n* (*BRIT*: *AUT*) внезапная остановка (*в критической ситуации*).
emergent [ɪ'mə:dʒənt] *adj* (*nation, group*) получивший независимость, образовавшийся; **an ~ industrial class** заявивший о себе промышленный класс.
emeritus [ɪ'mɛrɪtəs] *adj*: **professor ~** заслуженный профессор в отставке.
emery board ['ɛmərɪ-] *n* пилка для ногтей (*покрытая корундом*).
emery paper *n* наждачная бумага.
emetic [ɪ'mɛtɪk] *n* (*MED*) рвотное *nt adj*.
emigrant ['ɛmɪgrənt] *n* эмигрант(ка*).
emigrate ['ɛmɪgreɪt] *vi* эмигрировать *(impf/perf)*.
emigration [ɛmɪ'greɪʃən] *n* эмиграция.
émigré ['ɛmɪgreɪ] *n* политический* эмигрант(ка).
eminence ['ɛmɪnəns] *n* (*importance*) знаменитость *f*.
eminent ['ɛmɪnənt] *adj* (*scientist, writer*) знаменитый (знаменит).
eminently ['ɛmɪnəntlɪ] *adv* (*practical etc*) весьма.
emirate ['ɛmɪrɪt] *n* эмират.
emission [ɪ'mɪʃən] *n* (*of gas, heat*) выделение *nt no pl*; (*of light, radiation*) излучение.
emit [ɪ'mɪt] *vt* (*smoke, smell*) испускать (испустить *perf*); (*sound*) издавать* (издать* *perf*); (*light, heat*) излучать *(impf)*.
emolument [ɪ'mɔljumənt] *n* (*usu pl*) доход; (*fee*) вознаграждение; (*salary*) жалованье*.
emotion [ɪ'məuʃən] *n* чувство; (*as opposed to reason*) эмоция.
emotional [ɪ'məuʃənl] *adj* эмоциональный* (эмоционален); (*issue*) волнующий.
emotionally [ɪ'məuʃnəlɪ] *adv* (*behave, speak*) эмоционально; **~ disturbed** эмоционально неуравновешенный*.
emotive [ɪ'məutɪv] *adj* (*subject, language*) вызывающий эмоции, эмоционально волнующий; **~ power** эмоциональная сила.
empathy ['ɛmpəθɪ] *n* сочувствие; **to feel ~ with sb** сочувствовать *(impf)* кому-н.
emperor ['ɛmpərəʳ] *n* император.
emphases ['ɛmfəsi:z] *npl of* **emphasis**.
emphasis ['ɛmfəsɪs] (*pl* **emphases**) *n* значение; (*in speaking*) ударение, акцент; **to lay** *or* **place ~ on sth** (*fig*) подчёркивать (подчеркнуть *perf*) что-н; **the ~ is on reading** наибольшее значение придаётся чтению.
emphasize ['ɛmfəsaɪz] *vt* подчёркивать (подчеркнуть *perf*); **I must ~ that ...** я должен подчеркнуть, что ....
emphatic [ɛm'fætɪk] *adj* (*statement, denial*) убедительный* (убедителен); (*person, manner*) настойчивый; **to be ~ about sth** настойчиво убеждать *(impf)* в чем-н.
emphatically [ɛm'fætɪklɪ] *adv* настойчиво; (*certainly*) убедительно.
emphysema [ɛmfɪ'si:mə] *n* эмфизема.
empire ['ɛmpaɪəʳ] *n* (*also fig*) империя.
empirical [ɛm'pɪrɪkl] *adj* (*knowledge, study*) эмпирический.
employ [ɪm'plɔɪ] *vt* (*workforce, person*) нанимать (нанять* *perf*), трудоустраивать (трудоустроить *perf*), давать* (дать* *perf*) работу *+dat*; (*tool, weapon*) применять (применить* *perf*); **he's ~ed in a bank** он работает в банке.
employee [ɪmplɔɪ'i:] *n* работник.
employer [ɪm'plɔɪəʳ] *n* работодатель *m*.
employment [ɪm'plɔɪmənt] *n* работа; **to find ~** трудоустраиваться (трудоустроиться *perf*); **without ~** без работы; **place of ~** место

* marks translations which have irregular inflections. The Russian-English side of the dictionary gives inflectional information.

работы.

employment agency *n* бюро́ *nt ind* по трудоустро́йству.

employment exchange *n* (*BRIT: formerly*) би́ржа труда́.

empower [ɪm'pauəʳ] *vt*: **to ~ sb to do** уполномо́чивать (уполномо́чить *perf*) кого́-н *+infin*.

empress ['ɛmprɪs] *n* императри́ца.

empties ['ɛmptɪz] *npl* (*bottles*) та́ра *fsg*.

emptiness ['ɛmptɪnɪs] *n* пустота́.

empty ['ɛmptɪ] *adj* (*also fig*) пусто́й* ◆ *vt* (*container*) опорожня́ть (опорожни́ть *perf*); (*place, house etc*) опустоша́ть (опустоши́ть *perf*) ◆ *vi* (*house, container*) пусте́ть (опусте́ть *perf*); (*liquid*) вытека́ть (вы́течь* *perf*); **on an ~ stomach** на пусто́й желу́док; **to ~ into** (*river*) впада́ть (*impf*) в *+acc*.

empty-handed ['ɛmptɪ'hændɪd] *adj* с пусты́ми рука́ми; **he returned ~** он верну́лся с пусты́ми рука́ми.

empty-headed ['ɛmptɪ'hɛdɪd] *adj* (*person*) пустоголо́вый.

EMS *n abbr* (= *European Monetary System*) ЕВС= *Европе́йская валю́тная систе́ма*.

EMT *n abbr* = *emergency medical technician*.

EMU *n abbr* = *economic and monetary union*.

emu ['iːmjuː] *n* э́му *m ind*.

emulate ['ɛmjuleɪt] *vt* (*hero, idol*) подража́ть (*impf*) *+dat*.

emulsion [ɪ'mʌlʃən] *n* (*liquid*) эму́льсия; (*also:* **~ paint**) эму́льсия, эмульсио́нная кра́ска*.

enable [ɪ'neɪbl] *vt* (*make possible*) спосо́бствовать (*impf*) *+dat*; **to ~ sb to do** (*permit, allow*) дава́ть* (дать* *perf*) возмо́жность кому́-н *+infin*.

enact [ɪ'nækt] *vt* (*law*) вводи́ть* (ввести́* *perf*); (*play*) ста́вить* (поста́вить* *perf*); (*role*) игра́ть (сыгра́ть *perf*).

enamel [ɪ'næməl] *n* эма́ль *f*; (*also:* **~ paint**) эма́ль, эма́левая кра́ска*.

enamoured [ɪ'næməd] (*US* **enamored**) *adj*: **to be ~ of** (*pastime, idea, belief*) пита́ть (*impf*) сла́бость к *+dat*.

encampment [ɪn'kæmpmənt] *n* бивуа́к.

encased [ɪn'keɪst] *adj*: **~ in** (*in plaster, armour*) зако́ванный в *+acc*; (*in shell*) заключённый в *+acc*.

encash [ɪn'kæʃ] *vt* инкасси́ровать (*impf/perf*).

enchant [ɪn'tʃɑːnt] *vt* (*delight*) очаро́вывать (очарова́ть *perf*).

enchanted [ɪn'tʃɑːntɪd] *adj* (*under a spell*) заколдо́ванный, зачаро́ванный.

enchanting [ɪn'tʃɑːntɪŋ] *adj* обворож- и́тельный* (обворожи́телен).

encircle [ɪn'səːkl] *vt* (*place, prisoner*) окружа́ть (окружи́ть *perf*).

encl. *abbr* (*on letters etc:* = *enclosed, enclosure*) приложе́ние.

enclave ['ɛnkleɪv] *n*: **an ~ of** анкла́в *+gen*, о́стров *+gen*.

enclose [ɪn'kləuz] *vt* (*land, space*) огора́живать (огороди́ть* *perf*); (*object*) заключа́ть (заключи́ть *perf*); (*letter etc*): **to ~ (with)** прилага́ть (приложи́ть *perf*) (к *+dat*); **please find ~d a cheque for £100** здесь прилага́ется чек на £100.

enclosure [ɪn'kləuʒəʳ] *n* (*area of land*) огоро́женное ме́сто*; (*in letter etc*) приложе́ние.

encoder [ɪn'kəudəʳ] *n* (*COMPUT*) коди́рующее устро́йство, ко́дер.

encompass [ɪn'kʌmpəs] *vt* (*include*) охва́тывать (охвати́ть* *perf*).

encore [ɔŋ'kɔːʳ] *excl* бис ◆ *n*: **as an ~** на би́с.

encounter [ɪn'kauntəʳ] *n* встре́ча; (*problem*) столкнове́ние ◆ *vt* (*person*) встреча́ться (встре́титься *perf*) с *+instr*; (*new experience, problem*) ста́лкиваться (столкну́ться *perf*) с *+instr*.

encourage [ɪn'kʌrɪdʒ] *vt* поощря́ть (поощри́ть *perf*); (*growth*) спосо́бствовать (*impf*) *+dat*; **to ~ sb to do** убежда́ть (*impf*) кого́-н *+infin*.

encouragement [ɪn'kʌrɪdʒmənt] *n* (*see vt*) поощре́ние; подде́ржка.

encouraging [ɪn'kʌrɪdʒɪŋ] *adj* (*situation, meeting, news*) обнадёживающий.

encroach [ɪn'krəutʃ] *vi*: **to ~ (up)on** (*rights, property, time*) покуша́ться (покуси́ться* *perf*) *or* посяга́ть (посягну́ть *perf*) на *+acc*.

encrusted [ɪn'krʌstɪd] *adj*: **~ with** покры́тый *+instr*.

encumber [ɪn'kʌmbəʳ] *vt*: **~ed with** (*suitcase, baggage etc*) загромождённый (загромождён) *+instr*; (*debts*) обременённый (обременён) *+instr*.

encyclop(a)edia [ɛnsaɪkləu'piːdɪə] *n* энциклопе́дия.

end [ɛnd] *n* коне́ц*; (*of town*) часть *f*; (*aim*) цель *f* ◆ *vt* (*also:* **bring to an ~, put an ~ to**) зака́нчивать (зако́нчить *perf*), прекраща́ть (прекрати́ть* *perf*) ◆ *vi* (*situation, activity, period etc*) конча́ться (ко́нчиться *perf*); **from ~ to ~** с нача́ла до конца́; **to come to an ~** подходи́ть* (подойти́* *perf*) к концу́, конча́ться (ко́нчиться *perf*); **to be at an ~** зака́нчиваться (зако́нчиться *perf*); **in the ~** в конце́ концо́в; **on ~** (*object*) стоймя́; **to stand on ~** (*hair*) стоя́ть (стать* *perf*) ды́бом; **for hours on ~** часа́ми; **for 5 hours on ~** 5 часо́в подря́д; **at the ~ of the street** в конце́ у́лицы; **at the ~ of the day** (*BRIT: fig*) в конце́ концо́в; **to this ~, with this ~ in view** с э́той це́лью

▸ **end up** *vi*: **to ~ up in** (*place*) конча́ть (ко́нчить *perf*) в *+prp*; **we ~ed up taking a taxi** мы ко́нчили тем, что взя́ли такси́.

endanger [ɪn'deɪndʒəʳ] *vt* подверга́ть (подве́ргнуть* *perf*) опа́сности; **an ~ed species** вымира́ющий вид.

endear [ɪn'dɪəʳ] *vt*: **to ~ o.s. to sb** внуша́ть (внуши́ть *perf*) кому́-н симпа́тию к себе́.

endearing [ɪn'dɪərɪŋ] *adj* (*personality, conduct*)

покоря́ющий.
endearment [ɪn'dɪəmənt] *n*: **to whisper ~s** шепта́ть* *(impf)* ла́сковые слова́; **term of ~** ла́сковое сло́во.
endeavour [ɪn'dɛvəʳ] (*US* **endeavor**) *n* (*attempt*) попы́тка*; (*effort*) стара́ние ◆ *vi*: **to ~ to do** (*attempt*) стара́ться (постара́ться *perf*) +*infin*; (*strive*) стреми́ться* *(impf)* +*infin*.
endemic [ɛn'dɛmɪk] *adj* эндеми́ческий.
ending ['ɛndɪŋ] *n* (*of book, play etc*) коне́ц*; (*LING*) оконча́ние.
endive ['ɛndaɪv] *n* (*curly*) энди́вый сала́т; (*chicory*) цико́рный сала́т.
endless ['ɛndlɪs] *adj* бесконе́чный* (бесконе́чен); (*forest, beach*) беспра́йний; (*patience, resources*) беспреде́льный* (беспреде́лен); (*possibilities*) неограни́ченный* (неограни́чен).
endorse [ɪn'dɔːs] *vt* (*cheque, document*) распи́сываться (расписа́ться* *perf*) на +*prp*; (*approve*: *proposal, candidate*) подде́рживать (поддержа́ть* *perf*).
endorsee [ɪndɔː'siː] *n* индосса́т.
endorsement [ɪn'dɔːsmənt] *n* индоссаме́нт; (*BRIT*: *on driving licence*) отме́тка*; (*approval*) подде́ржка.
endorser [ɪn'dɔːsəʳ] *n* индосса́нт.
endow [ɪn'dau] *vt* (*provide with money*) обеспе́чивать (обеспе́чить *perf*); **~ed with** (*talent, quality*) наделённый (наделён) +*instr*.
endowment [ɪn'daumənt] *n* (*money*) поже́ртвование (*для обеспече́ния ежего́дным дохо́дом*); (*quality*) спосо́бности *fpl*.
endowment mortgage *n ипоте́чная ссу́да в сочета́нии со страхова́нием жи́зни.*
endowment policy *n по́лис, включа́ющий страхова́ние жи́зни.*
end product *n* (*INDUSTRY*) коне́чный проду́кт; (*fig*) результа́т.
end result *n* коне́чный результа́т.
endurable [ɪn'djuərəbl] *adj* терпи́мый.
endurance [ɪn'djuərəns] *n* выно́сливость *f*.
endurance test *n* испыта́ние на про́чность.
endure [ɪn'djuəʳ] *vt* (*bear*) переноси́ть* (перенести́* *perf*) ◆ *vi* (*last*) выде́рживать (вы́держать *perf*) (*испыта́ние вре́менем*).
enduring [ɪn'djuərɪŋ] *adj* (*lasting*) про́чный* (про́чен).
end user *n* (*COMPUT*) коне́чный по́льзователь *m*.
enema ['ɛnɪmə] *n* (*MED*) кли́зма.
enemy ['ɛnəmɪ] *adj* (*forces, strategy*) неприя́тельский, вра́жеский ◆ *n* враг*; (*opponent*) проти́вник; (*MIL*) враг*, неприя́тель *m*; **to make an ~ of sb** нажива́ть (нажи́ть* *perf*) врага́ в ком-н.
energetic [ɛnə'dʒɛtɪk] *adj* энерги́чный* (энерги́чен).
energy ['ɛnədʒɪ] *n* эне́ргия; **Department of E~** Управле́ние по энергоснабже́нию.
energy crisis *n* энергети́ческий* кри́зис.
energy-saving ['ɛnədʒɪ'seɪvɪŋ] *adj* (*device*) сокраща́ющий расхо́д эне́ргии; **~ policy** поли́тика эконо́мии эне́ргии.
enervating ['ɛnəveɪtɪŋ] *adj* обесси́ливающий, отнима́ющий си́лы.
enforce [ɪn'fɔːs] *vt* (*law*) следи́ть* *(impf)* за соблюде́нием +*gen*.
enforced [ɪn'fɔːst] *adj* (*inactivity, unemployment*) вы́нужденный.
enfranchise [ɪn'fræntʃaɪz] *vt* предоставля́ть (предоста́вить* *perf*) избира́тельные права́ +*dat*.
engage [ɪn'geɪdʒ] *vt* (*attention, interest*) привлека́ть (привле́чь* *perf*); (*employ*) нанима́ть (наня́ть* *perf*); (*AUT*: *clutch*) зацепля́ть (зацепи́ть* *perf*); (*MIL*: *enemy*) вступа́ть (вступи́ть* *perf*) в бой с +*instr* ◆ *vi* (*TECH*) входи́ть* (войти́* *perf*) в зацепле́ние; **to ~ in** занима́ться (заня́ться* *perf*) +*instr*; **to ~ sb in conversation** вовлека́ть (вовле́чь* *perf*) кого́-н в разгово́р.
engaged [ɪn'geɪdʒd] *adj* обручённый (обручён); (*BRIT*: *busy*) за́нят; **~ to** обручён с +*instr*; **to get ~** обручи́ться *(perf)*; **he is ~ in research** он занима́ется иссле́дованием.
engaged tone *n* (*BRIT*: *TEL*) гудки́ *pl* "за́нято".
engagement [ɪn'geɪdʒmənt] *n* (*appointment*) договорённость *f*; (*hiring*) контра́кт; (*to marry*) обруче́ние; (*MIL*) бой*; **I have a previous ~** у меня́ уже́ есть договорённость.
engagement ring *n* обруча́льное кольцо́*.
engaging [ɪn'geɪdʒɪŋ] *adj* привлека́тельный* (привлека́телен).
engender [ɪn'dʒɛndəʳ] *vt* порожда́ть (породи́ть* *perf*).
engine ['ɛndʒɪn] *n* (*AUT*) дви́гатель *m*, мото́р; (*RAIL*) локомоти́в.
engine driver *n* (*BRIT*) машини́ст.
engineer [ɛndʒɪ'nɪəʳ] *n* (*designer*) инжене́р; (*for repairs, also NAUT*) меха́ник; (*US*: *RAIL*) машини́ст; **civil ~** инжене́р-строи́тель *m*; **mechanical ~** инжене́р-меха́ник.
engineering [ɛndʒɪ'nɪərɪŋ] *n* (*science*) инжене́рное де́ло; (*design*) техни́ческий* диза́йн; (*construction*: *of roads, ships*) строи́тельство; (*of cars, machines*) произво́дство ◆ *cpd*: **~ works** *or* **factory** машинострои́тельный заво́д.
engine failure *n* отка́з дви́гателя.
engine trouble *n* неиспра́вность *f* дви́гателя.
England ['ɪŋglənd] *n* А́нглия.
English ['ɪŋglɪʃ] *adj* англи́йский* ◆ *n* (*LING*) англи́йский* язы́к*; **the ~** *npl* (*people*) англича́не* *mpl*; **an ~ speaker**

* marks translations which have irregular inflections. The Russian-English side of the dictionary gives inflectional information.

англоговоря́щий(-ая) *m(f) adj*.

English Channel *n*: **the ~ ~** Ла-Ма́нш.

Englishman [ˈɪŋglɪʃmən] *irreg n* англича́нин*.

English-speaking [ˈɪŋglɪʃˈspi:kɪŋ] *adj* англоговоря́щий.

Englishwoman [ˈɪŋglɪʃwumən] *irreg n* англича́нка*.

engrave [ɪnˈgreɪv] *vt* гравирова́ть (вы́гравировать *perf*).

engraving [ɪnˈgreɪvɪŋ] *n* гравю́ра.

engrossed [ɪnˈgrəust] *adj*: **~ in** поглощённый (поглощён) *+instr*.

engulf [ɪnˈgʌlf] *vt* (*subj*: *water*) поглоща́ть (поглоти́ть* *perf*); (: *panic, fear, fire*) охва́тывать (охвати́ть* *perf*).

enhance [ɪnˈhɑ:ns] *vt* (*enjoyment*) увели́чивать (увели́чить *perf*); (*beauty, reputation*) улучша́ть (улу́чшить *perf*).

enigma [ɪˈnɪgmə] *n* зага́дка.

enigmatic [ɛnɪgˈmætɪk] *adj* зага́дочный* (зага́дочен).

enjoy [ɪnˈdʒɔɪ] *vt* люби́ть (*impf*); (*have benefit of*) облада́ть (*impf*) *+instr*; **to ~ o.s.** хорошо́ проводи́ть* (провести́* *perf*) вре́мя; **I ~ dancing** я люблю́ танцева́ть.

enjoyable [ɪnˈdʒɔɪəbl] *adj* прия́тный* (прия́тен).

enjoyment [ɪnˈdʒɔɪmənt] *n* (*feeling of pleasure*) удово́льствие.

enlarge [ɪnˈlɑ:dʒ] *vt* увели́чивать (увели́чить *perf*) ◆ *vi*: **to ~ on** распространя́ться (*impf*) о *+prp*.

enlarged [ɪnˈlɑ:dʒd] *adj* (*edition*) допо́лненный; (*MED, PHOT*) увели́ченный (увели́чен).

enlargement [ɪnˈlɑ:dʒmənt] *n* (*PHOT*) увеличе́ние.

enlighten [ɪnˈlaɪtn] *vt* просвеща́ть (просвети́ть* *perf*).

enlightened [ɪnˈlaɪtnd] *adj* просвещённый.

enlightening [ɪnˈlaɪtnɪŋ] *adj* просвеща́ющий.

enlightenment [ɪnˈlaɪtnmənt] *n*: **the E~** Просвеще́ние.

enlist [ɪnˈlɪst] *vt* (*person*) вербова́ть (завербова́ть *perf*); (*support*) заруча́ться (заручи́ться *perf*) *+instr* ◆ *vi*: **to ~ in** (*army, navy etc*) идти́* (пойти́* *perf*) в *+acc*; **~ed man** (*US*: *MIL*) военнослу́жащий* *m adj* (*рядово́го и́ли сержа́нтского соста́ва*).

enliven [ɪnˈlaɪvn] *vt* (*events*) оживля́ть (оживи́ть* *perf*); (*people*) подбодря́ть (подбодри́ть *perf*).

enmity [ˈɛnmɪtɪ] *n* вражде́бность *f*.

ennoble [ɪˈnəubl] *vt* возводи́ть* (возвести́* *perf*) в ти́тул; (*fig*) облагора́живать (облагоро́дить* *perf*).

enormity [ɪˈnɔ:mɪtɪ] *n* (*of problem, danger*) величина́.

enormous [ɪˈnɔ:məs] *adj* грома́дный* (грома́ден).

enormously [ɪˈnɔ:məslɪ] *adv* чрезвыча́йно.

enough [ɪˈnʌf] *adj* (*time, books, people etc*) доста́точно *+gen* ◆ *pron* доста́точно ◆ *adv*: **big ~** доста́точно большо́й; **I've had ~!** с меня́ хва́тит!; **have you got ~ work to do?** у Вас доста́точно рабо́ты?; **have you had ~ to eat?** Вы нае́лись?; **that's ~, thanks** доста́точно, спаси́бо; **I've had ~ of him** он мне надое́л; **he has not worked ~** он недоста́точно рабо́тал; **will five pounds be ~?** пяти́ фунтов бу́дет доста́точно?; **I do not have ~ money to buy it** у меня́ не хвата́ет де́нег, что́бы купи́ть э́то; **it's hot ~ as it is** и та́к дово́льно жа́рко; **he was kind ~ to lend me the money** он был насто́лько добр, что́бы одолжи́ть мне де́ньги; **~!** дово́льно!; **strangely** *or* **oddly ~ ...** как э́то ни стра́нно ....

enquire [ɪnˈkwaɪəʳ] *vti* = **inquire**.

enrage [ɪnˈreɪdʒ] *vt* беси́ть* (взбеси́ть* *perf*).

enrich [ɪnˈrɪtʃ] *vt* обогаща́ть (обогати́ть *perf*).

enrol [ɪnˈrəul] (*US* **enroll**) *vt* (*subj*: *administrator*) зачисля́ть (зачи́слить *perf*); (: *parents etc*) запи́сывать (записа́ть* *perf*) ◆ *vi* (*see vt*) зачисля́ться (зачи́слиться *perf*); запи́сываться (записа́ться* *perf*).

enrolment [ɪnˈrəulmənt] (*US* **enrollment**) *n* (*registration*) зачисле́ние; (*for course, club*) за́пись *f*.

en route [ɔnˈru:t] *adv* по пути́; **~ ~ for** *or* **to/from** по пути́ в *+acc*/из *+gen*.

ensconce [ɪnˈskɔns] *vt*: **to ~ o.s. in** устра́иваться (устро́иться *perf*) в *+prp*.

ensemble [ɔnˈsɔmbl] *n* анса́мбль *m*.

enshrine [ɪnˈʃraɪn] *vt* (*belief, right*) храни́ть (*impf*); **to be ~d in** сохраня́ться (сохрани́ться *perf*) в *+prp*.

ensue [ɪnˈsju:] *vi* сле́довать (после́довать *perf*); **a terrible argument ~d** (за э́тим) после́довала ужа́сная ссо́ра.

ensuing [ɪnˈsju:ɪŋ] *adj* после́дующий*.

ensure [ɪnˈʃuəʳ] *vt* обеспе́чивать (обеспе́чить *perf*); **to ~ that** обеспе́чивать (обеспе́чить *perf*), что.

ENT *n abbr* (*MED*: = *Ear, Nose and Throat*) у́хо-го́рло-нос.

entail [ɪnˈteɪl] *vt* влечь* (повле́чь* *perf*) за собо́й.

entangled [ɪnˈtæŋgld] *adj*: **to become ~ (in)** (*in net, rope etc*) запу́тываться (запу́таться *perf*) (в *+prp*).

enter [ˈɛntəʳ] *vt* (*room, building*) входи́ть* (войти́* *perf*) в *+acc*; (*university, college*) поступа́ть (поступи́ть* *perf*) в *+acc*; (*club, profession, contest*) вступа́ть (вступи́ть* *perf*) в *+acc*; (*in book*) запи́сывать (записа́ть* *perf*); (*COMPUT*) вводи́ть* (ввести́* *perf*) ◆ *vi* входи́ть* (войти́* *perf*); **I ~ed my son in the marathon** я по́дал зая́вку на включе́ние моего́ сы́на в марафо́н

► **enter for** *vt fus* (*competition, examination*) подава́ть* (пода́ть* *perf*) зая́вку на уча́стие в *+prp*

▸ **enter into** *vt fus* (*discussion, correspondence, agreement*) вступáть (вступи́ть* *perf*) в *+acc*
▸ **enter (up)on** *vt fus* (*career, policy*) начинáть (начáть* *perf*).
enteritis [ɛntə'raɪtɪs] *n* энтери́т.
enterprise ['ɛntəpraɪz] *n* (*company, undertaking*) предприя́тие; (*initiative*) предприи́мчивость *f*; **free/private ~** свобóдное/чáстное предпринимáтельство.
enterprising ['ɛntəpraɪzɪŋ] *adj* (*person*) предприи́мчивый (предприи́мчив); (*scheme*) предпринимáтельский*.
entertain [ɛntə'teɪn] *vt* (*amuse*) развлекáть (развлéчь* *perf*); (*play host to*) принимáть (приня́ть* *perf*); (*idea*) раздýмывать *(impf)* над *+instr*.
entertainer [ɛntə'teɪnə'] *n* ведýщий*(-ая) *m(f) adj* развлекáтельной прогрáммы.
entertaining [ɛntə'teɪnɪŋ] *adj* занимáтельный* (занимáтелен), развлекáтельный ◆ *n*: **we do a lot of ~** мы чáсто приглашáем к себé гостéй.
entertainment [ɛntə'teɪnmənt] *n* (*amusement*) развлечéние; (*show*) представлéние.
entertainment allowance *n* срéдства на представи́тельские расхóды.
enthral [ɪn'θrɔ:l] (*US* **enthrall**) *vt* приводи́ть* (привести́* *perf*) в востóрг.
enthralled [ɪn'θrɔ:ld] *adj* увлечённый (увлечён); **he was ~ by** *or* **with the book** он был увлечён книгóй.
enthralling [ɪn'θrɔ:lɪŋ] *adj* увлекáтельный* (увлекáтелен).
enthuse [ɪn'θu:z] *vi*: **to ~ about** *or* **over** приходи́ть* (прийти́* *perf*) в востóрг от *+gen*.
enthusiasm [ɪn'θu:zɪæzəm] *n* энтузиáзм.
enthusiast [ɪn'θu:zɪæst] *n* энтузиáст; **a jazz** *etc* **~** энтузиáст джáза *etc*.
enthusiastic [ɪnθu:zɪ'æstɪk] *adj* пóлный* (пóлон) энтузиáзма; (*response, reception*) востóрженный; **he is ~ about** он пóлон энтузиáзма по пóводу *+gen*.
entice [ɪn'taɪs] *vt* (*lure*) замáнивать (замани́ть* *perf*); (*tempt*) соблазня́ть (соблазни́ть *perf*).
enticing [ɪn'taɪsɪŋ] *adj* (*offer, food*) соблазни́тельный.
entire [ɪn'taɪə'] *adj* весь*.
entirely [ɪn'taɪəlɪ] *adv* пóлностью; (*for emphasis*) совершéнно; **~ different** совершéнно различный.
entirety [ɪn'taɪərətɪ] *n*: **in its ~** весь целикóм.
entitle [ɪn'taɪtl] *vt*: **to ~ sb to sth/to do** давáть* (дать* *perf*) прáво комý-н на что-н/*+infin*.
entitled [ɪn'taɪtld] *adj* (*book, film etc*) озаглáвленный; **to be ~ to sth/to do** имéть *(impf)* прáво на что-н/на то, чтóбы *+infin*.
entity ['ɛntɪtɪ] *n* (еди́ная) сýщность *f*; **a separate ~** (*person*) отдéльная ли́чность.
entourage [ɔntu'rɑ:ʒ] *n* антурáж, окружéние.
entrails ['ɛntreɪlz] *npl* внýтренности *fpl*.
entrance [*n* 'ɛntrns, *vt* ɪn'trɑ:ns] *n* (*way in*) вход; (*arrival*) вступлéние, появлéние; (*THEAT*) вы́ход (на сцéну) ◆ *vt* (*enchant*) очарóвывать (очаровáть *perf*); **to gain ~ to** (*university*) поступáть (поступи́ть* *perf*) в *+acc*; (*profession*) получáть (получи́ть *perf*) дóступ к *+dat*; **to make an ~** появля́ться (появи́ться* *perf*).
entrance examination *n* вступи́тельный экзáмен.
entrance fee *n* (*for museum etc*) входнáя плáта.
entrance ramp *n* (*US*: *AUT*) въезд на автострáду.
entrancing [ɪn'trɑ:nsɪŋ] *adj* восхити́тельный* (восхити́телен).
entrant ['ɛntrnt] *n* учáстник(-ица).
entreat [ɛn'tri:t] *vt* (*implore*): **to ~ sb to do** умоля́ть (умоли́ть *perf*) когó-н *+infin*.
entreaty [ɛn'tri:tɪ] *n* мольбá.
entrée ['ɔntreɪ] *n* (*CULIN*: *main course*) глáвное блю́до.
entrenched [ɛn'trɛntʃt] *adj* (*ideas etc*) укорени́вшийся.
entrepreneur ['ɔntrəprə'nə:'] *n* пред-принимáтель(ница) *m(f)*.
entrepreneurial ['ɔntrəprə'nə:rɪəl] *adj* предпринимáтельский*.
entrust [ɪn'trʌst] *vt* (*possessions, task*): **to ~ sth to sb** доверя́ть (довéрить *perf*) что-н комý-н; **to ~ sb with sth** (*task*) возлагáть (возложи́ть* *perf*) на когó-н что-н.
entry ['ɛntrɪ] *n* (*way in*) вход; (*in register, account book*) зáпись *f*; (*in reference book*) статья́*; (*in competition*: *participants*) числó учáстников; (*arrival*: *in country*) въезд; (: *in room*) вход; **"no ~"** (*to room, building*) "нет вхóда"; (*AUT*) "нет въéзда"; **single/double ~ book-keeping** (*COMM*) простáя/двойнáя бухгалтéрия.
entry form *n* зая́вка* на учáстие.
entry phone *n* (*BRIT*) домофóн.
entwine [ɪn'twaɪn] *vt*: **to ~ (with)** переплетáть (переплести́* *perf*) (с *+instr*).
enumerate [ɪ'nju:məreɪt] *vt* перечисля́ть (перечи́слить *perf*).
enunciate [ɪ'nʌnsɪeɪt] *vt* (*word*) произноси́ть* (произнести́* *perf*); (*principle, plan etc*) излагáть (изложи́ть* *perf*).
envelop [ɪn'vɛləp] *vt* (*cover, enclose*) облегáть (облéчь* *perf*).
envelope ['ɛnvələup] *n* конвéрт.
enviable ['ɛnvɪəbl] *adj* зави́дный* (зави́ден).
envious ['ɛnvɪəs] *adj* зави́стливый (зави́стлив); **to be ~ of sth/sb** зави́довать

* marks translations which have irregular inflections. The Russian-English side of the dictionary gives inflectional information.

(impf) чемý-н/комý-н.
environment [ɪn'vaɪərnmənt] *n* средá; **the ~** окружáющая средá; **Department of the E~** (*BRIT*) отдéл охрáны окружáющей среды́.
environmental [ɪnvaɪərn'mɛntl] *adj* свя́занный с окружáющей средóй, экологи́ческий*; **children respond to ~ stimuli** дéти реаги́руют на сти́мулы предлагáемые средóй; **~ studies** эколóгия.
environmentalist [ɪnvaɪərn'mɛntlɪst] *n* сторóнник(-ица) защи́ты окружáющей среды́.
environmentally [ɪnvaɪərn'mɛntlɪ] *adv* экологи́чески.
Environmental Protection Agency *n* (*US*) *агéнтство по охранé окружáющей среды́.*
envisage [ɪn'vɪzɪdʒ] *vt* (*foresee*) предви́деть* *(impf)*; **I ~ that** ... я предви́жу, что ....
envision [ɪn'vɪʒən] *vt* (*US*) = **envisage.**
envoy ['ɛnvɔɪ] *n* послáнник.
envy ['ɛnvɪ] *n* зáвисть *f* ◆ *vt* зави́довать (позави́довать *perf*) *+dat*; **to ~ sb sth** зави́довать (позави́довать *perf*) комý-н из-за чегó-н.
enzyme ['ɛnzaɪm] *n* (*BIO, MED*) энзи́м.
EPA *n abbr* (*US*: = *Environmental Protection Agency*) *агéнтство по охрáне окружáющей среды́.*
ephemeral [ɪ'fɛmərl] *adj* эфемéрный* (эфемéрен).
epic ['ɛpɪk] *n* эпопéя; (*poem*) эпи́ческая поэ́ма ◆ *adj* (*journey*) эпохáльный* (эпохáлен).
epicentre ['ɛpɪsɛntəʳ] (*US* **epicenter**) *n* эпицéнтр.
epidemic [ɛpɪ'dɛmɪk] *n* эпидéмия.
epigram ['ɛpɪgræm] *n* эпигрáмма.
epilepsy ['ɛpɪlɛpsɪ] *n* эпилéпсия.
epileptic [ɛpɪ'lɛptɪk] *adj* эпилепти́ческий ◆ *n* эпилéптик.
epilogue ['ɛpɪlɔg] *n* эпилóг.
Epiphany [ɪ'pɪfənɪ] *n* Богоявлéние, Крещéние.
episcopal [ɪ'pɪskəpl] *adj* (*REL*) епи́скопский; **the E~ Church** Епископáльная Цéрковь*.
episode ['ɛpɪsəud] *n* эпизóд.
epistle [ɪ'pɪsl] *n* послáние.
epitaph ['ɛpɪtɑ:f] *n* эпитáфия.
epithet ['ɛpɪθɛt] *n* эпи́тет.
epitome [ɪ'pɪtəmɪ] *n* воплощéние.
epitomize [ɪ'pɪtəmaɪz] *vt* воплощáть (воплоти́ть* *perf*).
epoch ['ɪ:pɔk] *n* эпóха.
epoch-making ['i:pɔkmeɪkɪŋ] *adj* эпохáльный* (эпохáлен).
eponymous [ɪ'pɔnɪməs] *adj*: **~ hero** *герóй, и́менем котóрого нáзвано произведéние.*
EPOS *n abbr* (= *electronic point of sale*) *электрóнное счи́тывание информáции с товáрных этикéток.*
equable ['ɛkwəbl] *adj* рóвный* (рóвен).
equal ['i:kwl] *adj* рáвный* (рáвен); (*intensity, quality*) одинáковый ◆ *n* рáвный(-ая) *m(f) adj* ◆ *vt* (*number*) равня́ться *(impf) +dat*; (*quality*) не уступáть (уступи́ть* *perf*) *+dat or* по *+dat*; **they are roughly ~ in size** они́ примéрно равны́ по размéру; **the number of exports should be ~ to imports** коли́чество э́кспорта должнó быть* равнó коли́честву и́мпорта; **he is ~ to** (*task*) он мóжет спрáвиться с *+instr.*
Equal Employment Opportunity Commission *n* (*US*) = **Equal Opportunities Commission.**
equality [i:'kwɔlɪtɪ] *n* рáвенство, равноправие; **~ of opportunity** рáвенство возмóжностей.
equalize ['i:kwəlaɪz] *vt* урáвнивать (уравня́ть *perf*) ◆ *vi* (*SPORT*) срáвнивать (сравня́ть *perf*) счёт.
equally ['i:kwəlɪ] *adv* (*share etc*) равнó; (*good, bad*) одинáково; **they are ~ clever** они́ в рáвной стéпени умны́.
Equal Opportunities Commission (*US* **Equal Employment Opportunity Commission**) *n* *коми́ссия рáвных возмóжностей при нáйме на рабóту.*
equal(s) sign *n* знак рáвенства.
equanimity [ɛkwə'nɪmɪtɪ] *n* (*calm*) хладнокрóвие; **with ~** хладнокрóвно.
equate [ɪ'kweɪt] *vt*: **to ~ sth with sth, ~ sth to sth** прирáвнивать (приравня́ть *perf*) что-н к чемý-н.
equation [ɪ'kweɪʃən] *n* (*MATH*) уравнéние.
equator [ɪ'kweɪtəʳ] *n* эквáтор.
equatorial [ɛkwə'tɔ:rɪəl] *adj* экваториáльный.
Equatorial Guinea *n* Экваториáльная Гвинéя.
equestrian [ɪ'kwɛstrɪən] *adj* кóнный ◆ *n* всáдник(-ица).
equilibrium [i:kwɪ'lɪbrɪəm] *n* равновéсие.
equinox ['i:kwɪnɔks] *n* равнодéнствие; **the spring/autumn ~** весéннее/осéннее равнодéнствие.
equip [ɪ'kwɪp] *vt*: **to ~ (with)** (*person, army*) снаряжáть (снаряди́ть* *perf*) (*+instr*); (*room, car etc*) оборýдовать *(impf/perf)* (*+instr*); **to ~ sb for** (*prepare*) готóвить* (подготóвить* *perf*) когó-н к *+dat.*
equipment [ɪ'kwɪpmənt] *n* оборýдование.
equitable ['ɛkwɪtəbl] *adj* справедли́вый (справедли́в).
equities ['ɛkwɪtɪz] *npl* (*BRIT*) обыкновéнные áкции *fpl.*
equity ['ɛkwɪtɪ] *n* справедли́вость *f.*
equity capital *n* капитáл в фóрме áкций.
equivalent [ɪ'kwɪvələnt] *n* эквивалéнт ◆ *adj*: **~ (to)** эквивалéнтный* (эквивалéнтен) (*+dat*); **it is ~ to** э́то эквивалéнтно *+dat.*
equivocal [ɪ'kwɪvəkl] *adj* (*ambiguous*) двусмы́сленный* (двусмы́слен); (*open to suspicion*) сомни́тельный* (сомни́телен).
equivocate [ɪ'kwɪvəkeɪt] *vi* говори́ть *(impf)* двусмы́сленно.
equivocation [ɪkwɪvə'keɪʃən] *n* уклóнчивость *f.*

ER *abbr* (*BRIT*) = *Elizabeth Regina.*
ERA *n abbr* (*US*: *POL*: = *Equal Rights Amendment*) попра́вка о ра́вных права́х (*к конститу́ции США*).
era ['ɪərə] *n* э́ра.
eradicate [ɪ'rædɪkeɪt] *vt* искореня́ть (искорени́ть *perf*).
erase [ɪ'reɪz] *vt* стира́ть (стере́ть* *perf*).
eraser [ɪ'reɪzəʳ] *n* рези́нка*, ла́стик для стира́ния.
erect [ɪ'rɛkt] *adj* (*posture*) прямо́й* (прям), вертика́льный* (вертика́лен); (*tail, ears*) по́днятый (по́днят) ◆ *vt* (*build*) возводи́ть* (возвести́* *perf*); (*assemble*) ста́вить* (поста́вить* *perf*).
erection [ɪ'rɛkʃən] *n* возведе́ние; (*of tent, machinery*) устано́вка*; (*PHYSIOL*) эре́кция.
ergonomics [ə:gə'nɔmɪks] *n* эргоно́мика.
ERISA *n abbr* (*US*) = *Employee Retirement Income Security Act.*
ERM *n abbr* (= *Exchange Rate Mechanism*) МВК= *механи́зм валю́тных ку́рсов.*
ermine ['ə:mɪn] *n* горноста́й.
ERNIE ['ə:nɪ] *n abbr* (*BRIT*: = *Electronic Random Number Indicator Equipment*) *ЭВМ, определя́ющая вы́игрышные номера́ госуда́рственного вы́игрышного за́йма.*
erode [ɪ'rəud] *vt* (*soil, rock*: *subj*: *wind*) выве́тривать (вы́ветрить *perf*); (: *water*) размыва́ть (размы́ть* *perf*); (*metal*) разъеда́ть (разъе́сть* *perf*); (*confidence, power*) подрыва́ть (подорва́ть* *perf*).
erogenous [ɪ'rɔdʒənəs] *adj* эроге́нный.
erosion [ɪ'rəuʒən] *n* эро́зия.
erotic [ɪ'rɔtɪk] *adj* эроти́ческий*.
eroticism [ɪ'rɔtɪsɪzəm] *n* эроти́зм.
err [ə:ʳ] *vi* допуска́ть (допусти́ть* *perf*) оши́бку; **to ~ on the side of ...** склоня́ться *(impf)* к +*dat* ....
errand ['ɛrənd] *n* поруче́ние; **to run ~s** выполня́ть *(impf)* поруче́ния; **~ of mercy** пое́здка* с до́брой ми́ссией.
erratic [ɪ'rætɪk] *adj* (*attempts*) беспоря́дочный* (беспоря́дочен); (*behaviour*) сумасбро́дный* (сумасбро́ден).
erroneous [ɪ'rəunɪəs] *adj* оши́бочный* (оши́бочен).
error ['ɛrəʳ] *n* оши́бка*; **typing ~** опеча́тка*; **spelling ~** орфографи́ческая оши́бка*; **in ~** по оши́бке; **~s and omissions excepted** не счита́я оши́бок и про́пусков.
error message *n* (*COMPUT*) сообще́ние об оши́бке.
erstwhile ['ə:stwaɪl] *adj* бы́вший*.
erudite ['ɛrjudaɪt] *adj* (*person*) эруди́рованный* (эруди́рован).
erupt [ɪ'rʌpt] *vi* (*war, crisis*) разража́ться (разрази́ться* *perf*); **the volcano ~ed** произошло́ изверже́ние вулка́на.
eruption [ɪ'rʌpʃən] *n* (*of volcano*) изверже́ние; (*of fighting*) взрыв.
ESA *n abbr* (= *European Space Agency*) ЕКА= *Европе́йское косми́ческое аге́нтство.*
escalate ['ɛskəleɪt] *vi* обостря́ться (обостри́ться *perf*).
escalation [ɛskə'leɪʃən] *n* обостре́ние, эскала́ция.
escalation clause *n оговорка о скользя́щих це́нах и́ли скользя́щей зарпла́те.*
escalator ['ɛskəleɪtəʳ] *n* эскала́тор.
escapade [ɛskə'peɪd] *n* (*adventure*) эскапа́да, авантю́ра.
escape [ɪs'keɪp] *n* (*from prison*) побе́г; (*from person*) избега́ние; (*TECH*) вы́ход; (*of gas*) выделе́ние, вы́пуск ◆ *vi* (*get away*) убега́ть (убежа́ть* *perf*); (*from jail*) бежа́ть* *(impf/perf)*; (*leak*) утека́ть (уте́чь* *perf*), дава́ть* (дать* *perf*) уте́чку ◆ *vt* (*avoid*: *consequences etc*) избега́ть (избежа́ть* *perf*) +*gen*; (*elude*): **his name ~s me** его́ и́мя вы́пало у меня́ из па́мяти; **to ~ from** (*place*) сбега́ть (сбежа́ть* *perf*) *or* убега́ть (убежа́ть* *perf*) из/от +*gen*; (*person*) сбега́ть (сбежа́ть* *perf*) *or* убега́ть (убежа́ть* *perf*) от +*gen*; **he ~d with minor injuries** он отде́лался лёгкими тра́вмами; **to ~ to** (*another place*) сбега́ть (сбежа́ть* *perf*) *or* убега́ть (убежа́ть* *perf*) в/на +*prp*; **to ~ to safety** скрыва́ться (скры́ться* *perf*) в безопа́сном ме́сте; **to ~ notice** ускольза́ть (ускользну́ть *perf*) незаме́ченным.
escape artist *n* трюка́ч.
escape clause *n пункт догово́ра, иебавля́ющий сто́рону от отве́тственности.*
escapee [ɪskeɪ'pi:] *n* сбежа́вший(-ая) *m(f) adj.*
escape hatch *n* авари́йный люк.
escape key *n* (*COMPUT*) кла́виша вы́хода.
escape route *n* (*from fire*) запасно́й (пожа́рный) вы́ход; (*of prisoners etc*) маршру́т побе́га.
escapism [ɪs'keɪpɪzəm] *n* бе́гство от действи́тельности, эскапи́зм.
escapist [ɪs'keɪpɪst] *adj* (*literature*) уводя́щий от пробле́м жи́зни, эскапи́стский.
escapologist [ɛskə'pɔlədʒɪst] *n* (*BRIT*) = **escape artist.**
escarpment [ɪs'kɑ:pmənt] *n* отко́с.
eschew [ɪs'tʃu:] *vt* (*company, violence*) сторони́ться *(impf)* +*gen.*
escort [*n* 'ɛskɔ:t, *vt* ɪs'kɔ:t] *n* (*companion*: *male*) сопровожда́ющий *m adj*; (: *female*) сопровожда́ющая *f adj*; (*MIL, POLICE*) конво́й ◆ *vt* сопровожда́ть *(impf)*; **his/her ~** его́/её сопровожда́ющий(-ая).
escort agency *n* бюро́ *nt ind* по на́йму

* marks translations which have irregular inflections. The Russian-English side of the dictionary gives inflectional information.

сопровожда́ющих.
Eskimo ['ɛskɪməu] *n* эскимо́с(ка*).
ESL *n abbr (SCOL) = English as a Second Language.*
esophagus [i:'sɔfəgəs] *n (US)* = **oesophagus**.
esoteric [ɛsə'tɛrɪk] *adj* эзотери́ческий.
ESP *n abbr* = **extrasensory perception**; *(SCOL) = English for Special Purposes.*
esp. *abbr* = **especially**.
especially [ɪs'pɛʃlɪ] *adv* осо́бенно.
espionage ['ɛspɪənɑ:ʒ] *n* шпиона́ж.
esplanade [ɛsplə'neɪd] *n* эспла́нада.
espouse [ɪs'pauz] *vt (policy, idea)* (целико́м) отдава́ться* (отда́ться* *perf*) *+dat*, подде́рживать (поддержа́ть *perf*).
Esq. *abbr* = **Esquire**.
Esquire [ɪs'kwaɪə^r] *n*: **J. Brown, ~** Дж. Бра́ун, эсква́йр.
essay ['ɛseɪ] *n (SCOL)* сочине́ние; *(LITERATURE)* о́черк.
essence ['ɛsns] *n* су́щность *f*; *(CULIN)* эссе́нция; **in ~** в су́щности; **speed is of the ~** всё де́ло в ско́рости.
essential [ɪ'sɛnʃl] *adj (vital)* суще́ственно необходи́мый* (необходи́м); *(basic)* основно́й ◆ *n (see adj)* суще́ственно необходи́мая вещь *f*; основно́е *nt adj*; **it is ~ that** суще́ственно ва́жно, что́бы.
essentially [ɪ'sɛnʃəlɪ] *adv* в су́щности.
EST *abbr (US) = Eastern Standard Time.*
est. *abbr = established*; *estimate(d).*
establish [ɪs'tæblɪʃ] *vt (organization)* учрежда́ть (учреди́ть* *perf*); *(facts, contact)* устана́вливать (установи́ть* *perf*); *(reputation)* утвержда́ть (утверди́ть* *perf*) за собо́й.
established [ɪs'tæblɪʃt] *adj (business)* соли́дный; *(custom, practice)* при́знанный.
establishment [ɪs'tæblɪʃmənt] *n (see vb)* учрежде́ние; установле́ние; утвержде́ние; *(shop etc)* заведе́ние; **the E~** исте́блишмент
estate [ɪs'teɪt] *n (land)* поме́стье*; *(BRIT: also:* **housing ~**) жило́й ко́мплекс; *(LAW)* состоя́ние.
estate agency *n (BRIT)* аге́нтство по прода́же недви́жимости.
estate agent *n (BRIT)* аге́нт по прода́же недви́жимости.
estate car *n (BRIT)* автомоби́ль *m*-пика́п.
esteem [ɪs'ti:m] *n*: **to hold sb in high ~** относи́ться* (отнести́сь* *perf*) к кому́-н с больши́м почте́нием.
esthetic [ɪs'θɛtɪk] *adj (US)* = **aesthetic**.
estimate [*vb* 'ɛstɪmeɪt, *n* 'ɛstɪmət] *vt (reckon, calculate)* предвари́тельно подсчи́тывать (подсчита́ть *perf*); (: *chances*) оце́нивать (оцени́ть *perf*) ◆ *n (calculation)* подсчёт; *(assessment)* оце́нка*; *(builder's etc)* сме́та ◆ *vi (BRIT: COMM)*: **to ~ for** составля́ть (соста́вить* *perf*) сме́ту *+gen*; **I ~ that** я полага́ю, что; **to give sb an ~** дава́ть* (дать* *perf*) кому́-н оце́нку сто́имости; **at a rough ~** по гру́бым подсчётам.
estimation [ɛstɪ'meɪʃən] *n (opinion)* оце́нка*; *(calculation)* подсчёт; **in my ~** по мои́м подсчётам.
estimator ['ɛstɪmeɪtə^r] *n* оце́нщик.
Estonia [ɛs'təunɪə] *n* Эсто́ния.
Estonian [ɛs'təunɪən] *n (person)* эсто́нец*-(-о́нка*); *(LING)* эсто́нский* язы́к* ◆ *adj* эсто́нский*.
estranged [ɪs'treɪndʒd] *adj (from spouse, family)* отчуждённый* (отчуждён); **his ~ wife** уше́дшая от него́ жена́; **he is ~ from his wife** он разошёлся с жено́й.
estrangement [ɪs'treɪndʒmənt] *n* отчужде́ние.
estrogen ['i:strəudʒən] *n (US)* = **oestrogen**.
estuary ['ɛstjuərɪ] *n* у́стье*.
ET *n abbr (BRIT: = Employment Training)* профессиона́льная подгото́вка ◆ *abbr (US) = Eastern Time.*
ETA *n abbr (= estimated time of arrival)* ожида́емое вре́мя* *nt* прибы́тия.
et al. *abbr (and others: = et alii)* и други́е.
etc. *abbr (= et cetera)* и т.д.= *и так да́лее.*
etch [ɛtʃ] *vt (surface)* гравирова́ть (вы́гравировать *perf*); *(design)*: **to ~ (on)** трави́ть* (вы́травить* *perf*) (на *+prp*); **it will be ~ed on my memory** э́то запечатле́ется в мое́й па́мяти.
etching ['ɛtʃɪŋ] *n (craft)* гравиро́вка*; *(product)* гравю́ра, офо́рт.
ETD *n abbr (= estimated time of departure)* ожида́емое вре́мя* *nt* отправле́ния.
eternal [ɪ'tə:nl] *adj* ве́чный* (ве́чен).
eternity [ɪ'tə:nɪtɪ] *n* ве́чность *f*.
ether ['i:θə^r] *n* эфи́р*.
ethereal [ɪ'θɪərɪəl] *adj (delicate)* эфи́рный.
ethical ['ɛθɪkl] *adj (relating to ethics)* эти́ческий; *(morally right)* эти́чный* (эти́чен).
ethics ['ɛθɪks] *n, npl* э́тика *fsg.*
Ethiopia [i:θɪ'əupɪə] *n* Эфио́пия.
Ethiopian [i:θɪ'əupɪən] *adj* эфио́пский* ◆ *n* эфио́п(ка).
ethnic ['ɛθnɪk] *adj* этни́ческий*.
ethnic cleansing *n* этни́ческая чи́стка*.
ethnology [ɛθ'nɔlədʒɪ] *n* этноло́гия.
ethos ['i:θɔs] *n* э́тос.
etiquette ['ɛtɪkɛt] *n* этике́т.
ETV *n abbr (US) = Educational Television.*
etymology [ɛtɪ'mɔlədʒɪ] *n* этимоло́гия.
eucalyptus [ju:kə'lɪptəs] *n* эвкали́пт.
Eucharist ['ju:kərɪst] *n (REL)*: **the ~** евхари́стия. прича́стие.
eulogy ['ju:lədʒɪ] *n* восхвале́ние.
euphemism ['ju:fəmɪzəm] *n* эвфеми́зм.
euphemistic [ju:fə'mɪstɪk] *adj* эвфемисти́ческий*.
euphoria [ju:'fɔ:rɪə] *n* эйфори́я.
Eurasia [juə'reɪʃə] *n* Евра́зия.
Eurasian [juə'reɪʃən] *adj* евразийский ◆ *n* еврази́ец* (и́йка*).

Euratom [juə'ræṭəm] *n abbr* (= *European Atomic Energy Community*) Европе́йский* комите́т по а́томной эне́ргии.
euro ['juərəu] *n* е́вро *ind*.
Euro- ['juərəu] *prefix* е́вро-.
eurocheque ['juərəutʃɛk] *n* еврочéк.
Eurocrat ['juərəukræt] *n служащий в организа́ции Европе́йского Соо́бщества.*
Eurodollar ['juərəudɔlə^r] *n* евродо́ллар.
Euroland ['juərəulænd] *n* (*inf*) Евроле́нд.
Europe ['juərəp] *n* Евро́па.
European [juərə'pi:ən] *adj* европе́йский* ◆ *n* европе́ец(-е́йка).
European Community *n*: **the ~ ~** Европе́йское Соо́бщество.
European Court of Justice *n*: **the ~ ~ ~ ~** Европе́йский* Суд*.
European Economic Community *n*: **the ~ ~ ~** Европе́йское Экономи́ческое Соо́бщество.
Euro-sceptic ['juərəuskɛptɪk] *n* евроске́птик.
euthanasia [ju:θə'neɪzɪə] *n* эвтана́зия.
evacuate [ɪ'vækjueɪt] *vt* (*people*) эвакуи́ровать (*impf/perf*); (*place*) очища́ть (очи́стить* *perf*).
evacuation [ɪvækju'eɪʃən] *n* (*see vb*) эвакуа́ция; очи́стка*.
evacuee [ɪvækju'i:] *n* эвакуи́рованный(-ая) *m(f) adj*.
evade [ɪ'veɪd] *vt* (*duties, question*) уклоня́ться (уклони́ться* *perf*) от *+gen*; (*person*) избега́ть (*impf*) *+gen*.
evaluate [ɪ'væljueɪt] *vt* оце́нивать (оцени́ть* *perf*).
evangelical [i:væn'dʒɛlɪkl] *adj* евангели́ческий*.
evangelist [ɪ'vændʒəlɪst] *n* евангели́ст.
evangelize [ɪ'vændʒəlaɪz] *vi* пропове́довать (*impf*) евангели́зм.
evaporate [ɪ'væpəreɪt] *vi* испаря́ться (испари́ться *perf*); (*feeling, attitude*) пропада́ть (пропа́сть* *perf*).
evaporated milk [ɪ'væpəreɪtɪd-] *n* сгущённое молоко́ (*без са́хара*).
evaporation [ɪvæpə'reɪʃən] *n* испаре́ние.
evasion [ɪ'veɪʒən] *n* (*of responsibility, tax etc*) уклоне́ние.
evasive [ɪ'veɪsɪv] *adj* (*reply, action*) укло́нчивый (укло́нчив).
eve [i:v] *n*: **on the ~ of** накану́не *+gen*; **Christmas E~** кану́н Рождества́; **New Year's E~** кану́н Но́вого го́да.
even ['i:vn] *adj* (*level, smooth*) ро́вный* (ро́вен); (*equal*) ра́вный* (ра́вен); (*number*) чётный ◆ *adv* да́же; **~ if** да́же е́сли; **~ though** хотя́ и; **~ more** ещё бо́льше; **he loves her ~ more** он лю́бит её ещё бо́льше; **the work is going ~ better/faster** рабо́та идёт ещё лу́чше/быстре́е; **~ so** всё же; **not ~** да́же не; **~ he was there** да́же он там был; **~ on Sundays** да́же по воскресе́ньям; **I am ~ more likely to leave now** тепе́рь да́же ещё бо́лее вероя́тно, что я уе́ду; **to break ~** *рабо́тать на у́ровне самоокупа́емости (но без дохо́да)*; **to get ~ with sb** (*inf*) расквита́ться (*perf*) с кем-н
▸ **even out** *vt* выра́внивать (вы́ровнять *perf*) ◆ *vi* выра́вниваться (вы́ровняться *perf*).
even-handed ['i:vnhændɪd] *adj* беспристра́стный* (беспристра́стен).
evening ['i:vnɪŋ] *n* ве́чер*; **in the ~** ве́чером; **this ~** сего́дня ве́чером; **tomorrow/yesterday ~** за́втра/вчера́ ве́чером.
evening class *n* вече́рние ку́рсы *mpl*.
evening dress *n* (*no pl*: *formal clothes*) вече́рний туале́т; (*gown*) вече́рнее пла́тье*.
evenly ['i:vnlɪ] *adv* (*distribute*) равноме́рно; (*divide, breathe*) ро́вно.
evensong ['i:vnsɔŋ] *n* вече́рня*.
event [ɪ'vɛnt] *n* (*occurrence*) собы́тие; (*SPORT*: *competition*) соревнова́ние, вид; **in the normal course of ~s** при норма́льном тече́нии собы́тий; **in the ~ of** в слу́чае *+gen*; **in the ~** в коне́чном счёте; **at all ~s** (*BRIT*), **in any ~** во вся́ком *or* любо́м слу́чае.
eventful [ɪ'vɛntful] *adj* насы́щенный* (насы́щен) собы́тиями.
eventing [ɪ'vɛntɪŋ] *n* (*HORSE-RIDING*) *уча́стие в ря́де состяза́ний по верхово́й езде́.*
eventual [ɪ'vɛntʃuəl] *adj* (*outcome, goal*) коне́чный.
eventuality [ɪvɛntʃu'ælɪtɪ] *n* (*possibility*) возмо́жность *f*.
eventually [ɪ'vɛntʃuəlɪ] *adv* в конце́ концо́в.
ever ['ɛvə^r] *adv* (*always*) всегда́; (*at any time*) когда́-либо, когда́-нибудь; **why ~ not?** почему́ же нет?; **the best ~** са́мый лу́чший*; **have you ~ been to Russia?** Вы когда́-нибудь бы́ли в Росси́и?; **for ~** навсегда́; **hardly ~** почти́ никогда́; **I hardly ~ read** я почти́ никогда́ не чита́ю; **better than ~** лу́чше чем бы то ни́ было *or* чем когда́-либо; **~ since** с те́х пор, как; **~ since that day** с того́ дня; **~ so pretty** ужа́сно симпати́чная; **thank you ~ so much** я Вам так благода́рен; **yours ~** (*BRIT*: *in letters*) пре́данный Вам.
Everest ['ɛvərɪst] *n* (*GEO*: *also*: **Mount ~**) Эвере́ст.
evergreen ['ɛvəgri:n] *n* вечнозелёный.
everlasting [ɛvə'lɑ:stɪŋ] *adj* (*love, life etc*) ве́чный* (ве́чен).

KEYWORD

every ['ɛvrɪ] *adj* ***1*** (*each*) ка́ждый; **every child will receive a present** ка́ждый ребёнок полу́чит пода́рок; **every one of them** ка́ждый из них; **every shop in the town was closed** все

* marks translations which have irregular inflections. The Russian-English side of the dictionary gives inflectional information.

магази́ны в го́роде бы́ли закры́ты
2 (*all possible*): **I gave you every assistance** я помо́г Вам, всем чем то́лько мо́жно; **I tried every option** я испро́бовал все пути́; **I have every confidence in him** я в нём соверше́нно уве́рен; **we wish you every success** мы же́лаем Вам вся́ческого успе́ха; **he's every bit as clever/stupid as his brother** он столь же умён/глуп, как и его́ брат
3 (*showing recurrence*) ка́ждый; **every week** ка́ждую неде́лю; **every other car** ка́ждая втора́я маши́на; **she visits me every third/other day** она прихо́дит ко мне́ ка́ждые два дня́/че́рез день; **every now and then** вре́мя* от вре́мени.

everybody [ˈɛvrɪbɔdɪ] *pron* (*each*) ка́ждый; (*all*) все *pl*; ~ **knows about it** об э́том ка́ждый зна́ет; ~ **else** все остальны́е.
everyday [ˈɛvrɪdeɪ] *adj* (*daily*) ежедне́вный; (*common*) повседне́вный*.
everyone [ˈɛvrɪwʌn] *pron* = **everybody**.
everything [ˈɛvrɪθɪŋ] *pron* всё; ~ **is ready** всё гото́во; **he did ~ possible** он сде́лал всё возмо́жное; **you think of ~** Вы ду́маете обо всём; **I don't agree with ~ he says** я не согла́сен со всем, что он говори́т.
everywhere [ˈɛvrɪwɛəʳ] *adv* везде́, повсю́ду; **~ you go you meet ...** куда́ ни пойдёшь, везде́ *or* повсю́ду встреча́ешь ....
evict [ɪˈvɪkt] *vt* выселя́ть (вы́селить *perf*).
eviction [ɪˈvɪkʃən] *n* выселе́ние.
eviction notice *n* предупрежде́ние о выселе́нии.
eviction order *n* прика́з о выселе́нии.
evidence [ˈɛvɪdns] *n* (*proof*) доказа́тельство; (*testimony*) показа́ние; (*indication*) при́знаки *mpl*; **to give ~** дава́ть* (дать* *perf*) (свиде́тельские) показа́ния; **to show ~ of** проявля́ть (прояви́ть* *perf*) при́знаки *+gen*; **in ~** (*obvious*) заме́тен.
evident [ˈɛvɪdnt] *adj* заме́тный* (заме́тен).
evidently [ˈɛvɪdntlɪ] *adv* очеви́дно.
evil [ˈiːvl] *adj* (*person, spirit*) злой* (зол); (*system, influence*) дурно́й* ◆ *n* зло.
evocative [ɪˈvɔkətɪv] *adj* (*description, music*) *навева́ющий чу́вства и воспомина́ния*.
evoke [ɪˈvəuk] *vt* вызыва́ть (вы́звать* *perf*).
evolution [iːvəˈluːʃən] *n* эволю́ция.
evolve [ɪˈvɔlv] *vt* развива́ть (разви́ть* *perf*) ◆ *vi* (*animal, plant*) эволюциони́ровать *(impf/perf)*; (*plan, idea*) развива́ться (разви́ться* *perf*).
ewe [juː] *n* овца́*.
ewer [ˈjuːəʳ] *n* кувши́н*.
ex- [ɛks] *prefix* (*former*) экс-, бы́вший*; (*out of*): **the price ex works** цена́ с предприя́тия.
exacerbate [ɛksˈæsəbeɪt] *vt* (*situation, pain*) обостря́ть (обостри́ть *perf*).
exact [ɪgˈzækt] *adj* то́чный* (то́чен) ◆ *vt*: **to ~ sth from** (*obedience*) тре́бовать (потре́бовать *perf*) чего́-н от *+gen*; (*payment*) взы́скивать (взыска́ть* *perf*) что-н с *+gen*.
exacting [ɪgˈzæktɪŋ] *adj* (*task*) тру́дный*; (*person*) взыска́тельный* (взыска́телен).
exactly [ɪgˈzæktlɪ] *adv* то́чно; ~! вот и́менно!
exaggerate [ɪgˈzædʒəreɪt] *vti* преувели́чивать (преувели́чить *perf*).
exaggerated [ɪgˈzædʒəreɪtɪd] *adj* преувели́ченный (преувели́чен).
exaggeration [ɪgzædʒəˈreɪʃən] *n* преувеличе́ние.
exalt [ɪgˈzɔːlt] *vt* превозноси́ть* (превознести́* *perf*).
exalted [ɪgˈzɔːltɪd] *adj* (*prominent*) высо́кий* (высо́к); (*elated*) восто́рженный* (восто́ржен).
exam [ɪgˈzæm] *n abbr* = **examination**.
examination [ɪgzæmɪˈneɪʃən] *n* (*inspection*) изуче́ние; (*plan*) рассмотре́ние; (*SCOL*) экза́мен; (*LAW*) допро́с; (*MED*) осмо́тр; **to take** *or* (*BRIT*) **sit an ~** сдава́ть* (сдать* *perf*) экза́мен; **the matter is under ~** де́ло нахо́дится на рассмотре́нии.
examine [ɪgˈzæmɪn] *vt* (*scrutinize*) смотре́ть (посмотре́ть *perf*) на *+acc*; (*inspect*) осма́тривать (осмотре́ть *perf*); (*plan*) рассма́тривать (рассмотре́ть *perf*); (*SCOL*) экзаменова́ть (проэкзаменова́ть *perf*); (*LAW*) допра́шивать (допроси́ть* *perf*); (*MED*) осма́тривать (осмотре́ть* *perf*).
examiner [ɪgˈzæmɪnəʳ] *n* (*SCOL*) экзамена́тор.
example [ɪgˈzɑːmpl] *n* приме́р; **for ~** наприме́р; **to set a good/bad ~** подава́ть* (пода́ть* *perf*) хоро́ший*/плохо́й приме́р.
exasperate [ɪgˈzɑːspəreɪt] *vt* изма́тывать (измота́ть *perf*); **~d by** *or* **with** измо́танный *+instr*.
exasperating [ɪgˈzɑːspəreɪtɪŋ] *adj* раздража́ющий.
exasperation [ɪgzɑːspəˈreɪʃən] *n* раздраже́ние; **in ~** в раздраже́нии.
excavate [ˈɛkskəveɪt] *vt* (*site*) раска́пывать (раскопа́ть *perf*); (*hole*) выка́пывать (вы́копать *perf*) ◆ *vi* производи́ть* (произвести́* *perf*) раско́пки.
excavation [ɛkskəˈveɪʃən] *n* (*activity*) раска́пывание; (*archeological dig*): **~s** раско́пки *fpl*.
excavator [ˈɛkskəveɪtəʳ] *n* экскава́тор.
exceed [ɪkˈsiːd] *vt* превыша́ть (превы́сить* *perf*); (*hopes*) превосходи́ть* (превзойти́* *perf*).
exceedingly [ɪkˈsiːdɪŋlɪ] *adv* чрезвыча́йно.
excel [ɪkˈsɛl] *vt* превосходи́ть* (превзойти́* *perf*) ◆ *vi*: **to ~ (in** *or* **at)** отлича́ться (отличи́ться *perf*) (в *+prp*); **to ~ o.s.** (*BRIT*) превосходи́ть* (превзойти́* *perf*) само́го себя́.
excellence [ˈɛksələns] *n* (*in sport, business*) мастерство́; (*superiority*) превосхо́дство.
Excellency [ˈɛksələnsɪ] *n*: **His ~** его́ Превосходи́тельство.
excellent [ˈɛksələnt] *adj* отли́чный* (отли́чен),

превосхо́дный* (превосхо́ден) ◆ *excl*: ~! отли́чно!, превосхо́дно!
except [ɪk'sɛpt] *prep* (*also:* **~ for**) кро́ме *+gen* ◆ *vt*: **to ~ sb (from)** исключа́ть (исключи́ть *perf*) кого́-н (из *+gen*); **~ if/when** кро́ме *or* за исключе́нием тех слу́чаев е́сли/когда́; **~ that** кро́ме того́, что.
excepting [ɪk'sɛptɪŋ] *prep* за исключе́нием *+gen*.
exception [ɪk'sɛpʃən] *n* исключе́ние; **to take ~ to** обижа́ться (оби́деться* *perf*) на *+acc*; **with the ~ of** за исключе́нием *+gen*.
exceptional [ɪk'sɛpʃənl] *adj* исключи́тельный* (исключи́телен).
excerpt ['ɛksə:pt] *n* отры́вок*.
excess [ɪk'sɛs] *n* избы́ток*; (*INSURANCE*) превыше́ние; **~es** *npl* (*of cruelty etc*) эксце́ссы *mpl*, кра́йности *fpl*; **an ~ of £15, a £15 ~** изли́шек* в £15; **in ~ of** сверх *+gen*, свы́ше *+gen*; **to drink to ~** пить (*impf*) сверх ме́ры.
excess baggage *n* изли́шек* багажа́.
excess fare *n* (*BRIT*) допла́та (*за биле́т*).
excessive [ɪk'sɛsɪv] *adj* чрезме́рный* (чрезме́рен).
excess supply *n* избы́точное предложе́ние.
exchange [ɪks'tʃeɪndʒ] *n* (*conversation*) обме́н мне́ниями; (*argument*) перепа́лка*; (*also:* **telephone ~**) коммута́тор ◆ *vt*: **to ~ (for)** (*goods etc*) обме́нивать (обменя́ть *perf*) (на *+acc*); **~ (of)** обме́н (*+instr*); **in ~ for** в обме́н на *+acc*; **foreign ~** валю́тная би́ржа.
exchange control *n* валю́тный контро́ль *m*.
exchange market *n* валю́тный ры́нок*.
exchange rate *n* валю́тный *or* обме́нный курс.
Exchequer [ɪks'tʃɛkə^r] *n* (*BRIT*): **the ~** казначе́йство.
excisable [ɪk'saɪzəbl] *adj* (*goods*) облага́емый акци́зным сбо́ром.
excise [*n* 'ɛksaɪz, *vt* ɛk'saɪz] *n* акци́з, акци́зный сбор ◆ *vt* (*remove*) выреза́ть (вы́резать* *perf*).
excise duties *npl* акци́зный сбор *msg*.
excitable [ɪk'saɪtəbl] *adj* (легко́) возбуди́мый.
excite [ɪk'saɪt] *vt* возбужда́ть (возбуди́ть* *perf*); (*stimulate*) заинтересо́вывать (заинтересова́ть *perf*); **to get ~d** волнова́ться (взволнова́ться *perf*).
excitement [ɪk'saɪtmənt] *n* (*agitation*) возбужде́ние; (*exhilaration*) оживле́ние.
exciting [ɪk'saɪtɪŋ] *adj* восхити́тельный.
excl. *abbr* = **excluding, exclusive (of)**.
exclaim [ɪks'kleɪm] *vi* восклица́ть (воскли́кнуть *perf*).
exclamation [ɛksklə'meɪʃən] *n* восклица́ние.
exclamation mark *n* восклица́тельный знак.
exclude [ɪks'klu:d] *vt* исключа́ть (исключи́ть *perf*).
excluding [ɪks'klu:dɪŋ] *prep* исключа́я *+acc*.
exclusion [ɪks'klu:ʒən] *n* исключе́ние; **to the ~ of** исключа́я *+acc*.
exclusion clause *n* статья́* об исключе́ниях.
exclusion zone *n* запре́тная зо́на.
exclusive [ɪks'klu:sɪv] *adj* (*select*) недосту́пный* (недосту́пен), для и́збранных; (*use*) исключи́тельный* (исключи́телен); (*interview*) уника́льный* (уника́лен) ◆ *n* (*PRESS*) эксклюзи́вный материа́л (*напеча́танный то́лько в одно́й газе́те*) ◆ *adv*: **~ of** (*COMM*) не счита́я *+gen*; **mutually ~** взаимоисключа́ющие; **~ of postage** без сто́имости почто́вых расхо́дов; **from the 1st to the 15th March ~** с 1-ого до 15-ого ма́рта, включи́тельно; **~ of tax** не счита́я нало́га.
exclusively [ɪks'klu:sɪvlɪ] *adv* исключи́тельно.
exclusive rights *npl* исключи́тельные права́ *ntpl*.
excommunicate [ɛkskə'mju:nɪkeɪt] *vt* отлуча́ть (отлучи́ть *perf*) от це́ркви.
excrement ['ɛkskrəmənt] *n* экскреме́нты *mpl*.
excruciating [ɪks'kru:ʃɪeɪtɪŋ] *adj* мучи́тельный* (мучи́телен).
excursion [ɪks'kə:ʃən] *n* экску́рсия.
excursion ticket *n* *дешёвый биле́т на коро́ткую экску́рсию*.
excusable [ɪks'kju:zəbl] *adj* прости́тельный* (прости́телен).
excuse [*n* ɪks'kju:s, *vt* ɪks'kju:z] *n* оправда́ние ◆ *vt* (*justify*) опра́вдывать (оправда́ть *perf*); (*forgive*) проща́ть (прости́ть* *perf*); **to make ~s for sb** находи́ть* (найти́* *perf*) оправда́ние кому́-н; **that's no ~!** э́то не причи́на!; **to ~ sb from sth/doing** освобожда́ть (освободи́ть* *perf*) кого́-н от чего́-н/от того́, что́бы *+infin*; **~ me!** (*attracting attention*) извини́те!, прости́те!; (*as apology*) извини́те *or* прости́те (меня́)!; **if you will ~ me, I have to ...** Вы прости́те, мне на́до ...; **to ~ o.s. for sth/ for having done sth** извиня́ться (извини́ться *perf*) за что-н/за то, что сде́лал что-н.
ex-directory ['ɛksdɪ'rɛktərɪ] *adj* (*BRIT*: *number*) не включённый (включён) в телефо́нный спра́вочник; **she's ~** её но́мер не включён в телефо́нный спра́вочник.
execrable ['ɛksɪkrəbl] *adj* отврати́тельный* (отврати́телен).
execute ['ɛksɪkju:t] *vt* (*kill*) казни́ть (*impf/perf*); (*carry out, perform*) выполня́ть (вы́полнить *perf*).
execution [ɛksɪ'kju:ʃən] *n* (*see vb*) казнь *f*; выполне́ние.
executioner [ɛksɪ'kju:ʃnə^r] *n* пала́ч*.
executive [ɪg'zɛkjutɪv] *n* (*person*) руководи́тель *m*; (*committee*) исполни́тельный о́рган ◆ *adj* (*board, role*) руководя́щий*; (*secretary*) отве́тственный;

(*car, plane, chair, toys*) для руководя́щих рабо́тников.
executive director *n* дире́ктор*-распоряди́тель *m*.
executor [ɪg'zɛkjutəʳ] *n* (*LAW*) исполни́тель *m*.
exemplary [ɪg'zɛmplərɪ] *adj* приме́рный* (приме́рен).
exemplify [ɪg'zɛmplɪfaɪ] *vt* (*typify*) служи́ть* (послужи́ть *perf*) приме́ром +*gen*; (*illustrate*) поясня́ть (поясни́ть *perf*) приме́ром.
exempt [ɪg'zɛmpt] *adj*: **~ from** освобождённый (освобождён) от +*gen* ◆ *vt*: **to ~ sb from** освобожда́ть (освободи́ть* *perf*) кого́-н от +*gen*.
exemption [ɪg'zɛmpʃən] *n* освобожде́ние.
exercise ['ɛksəsaɪz] *n* (*no pl*) гимна́стика; (*keep-fit*) заря́дка*; (*SCOL, MUS*) упражне́ние; (*of authority etc*) проявле́ние ◆ *vt* (*patience, authority*) проявля́ть (прояви́ть* *perf*); (*right*) осуществля́ть (осуществи́ть* *perf*); (*dog*) выгу́ливать *(impf)*; (*mind*) занима́ть *(impf)* ◆ *vi* (*also:* **to take ~**) упражня́ться *(impf)*; **military ~s** вое́нные уче́ния; **you need more ~** Вам на́до бо́льше дви́гаться.
exercise bike *n* велосипе́д-тренажёр.
exercise book *n* тетра́дь *f*.
exert [ɪg'zə:t] *vt* (*influence, pressure*) ока́зывать (оказа́ть* *perf*); (*authority*) применя́ть (примени́ть* *perf*); **to ~ o.s.** напряга́ться (напря́чься* *perf*).
exertion [ɪg'zə:ʃən] *n* (*effort*) уси́лие; (*strain*) напряже́ние.
ex gratia ['ɛks'greɪʃə] *adj*: **~ ~ payment** де́нежное вознагражде́ние.
exhale [ɛks'heɪl] *vti* выдыха́ть (вы́дохнуть *perf*).
exhaust [ɪg'zɔ:st] *n* (*also:* **~ pipe**) выхлопна́я труба́; (*fumes*) выхлопны́е га́зы *mpl* ◆ *vt* (*person*) изнуря́ть (изнури́ть *perf*); (*money, resources etc*) истоща́ть (истощи́ть *perf*); (*topic*) исче́рпывать (исче́рпать *perf*); **to ~ o.s.** доводи́ть* (довести́* *perf*) себя́ до изнеможе́ния *or* изнуре́ния.
exhausted [ɪg'zɔ:stɪd] *adj* (*person*) изнурённый* (изнурён), изнеможённый* (изнеможён).
exhausting [ɪg'zɔ:stɪŋ] *adj* изнури́тельный* (изнури́телен).
exhaustion [ɪg'zɔ:stʃən] *n* (*tiredness*) изнеможе́ние; **nervous ~** не́рвное истоще́ние.
exhaustive [ɪg'zɔ:stɪv] *adj* исче́рпывающий*.
exhibit [ɪg'zɪbɪt] *n* экспона́т; (*LAW*) веще́ственное доказа́тельство ◆ *vt* (*paintings*) экспони́ровать *(impf/perf)*; (*quality, emotion*) проявля́ть (прояви́ть* *perf*).
exhibition [ɛksɪ'bɪʃən] *n* (*of paintings etc*) вы́ставка*; (*of ability, emotion*) проявле́ние; **to make an ~ of o.s.** выставля́ть (вы́ставить* *perf*) себя́ на посме́шище.
exhibitionist [ɛksɪ'bɪʃənɪst] *n* эксгибициони́ст; (*show-off*): **he's a real ~** он всё де́лает напока́з.
exhibitor [ɪg'zɪbɪtəʳ] *n* экспоне́нт.
exhilarating [ɪg'zɪləreɪtɪŋ] *adj* волну́ющий.
exhilaration [ɪgzɪlə'reɪʃən] *n* взволно́ванность *f*.
exhort [ɪg'zɔ:t] *vt*: **to ~ sb to do** увещева́ть *(impf)* кого́-н +*infin*.
exile ['ɛksaɪl] *n* (*banishment*) ссы́лка*, изгна́ние; (*person*) ссы́льный(-ая) *m(f) adj*, изгна́нник ◆ *vt* ссыла́ть (converted сосла́ть* *perf*); (*abroad*) высыла́ть (вы́слать* *perf*); **in ~** в ссы́лке *or* изгна́нии.
exist [ɪg'zɪst] *vi* существова́ть *(impf)*.
existence [ɪg'zɪstəns] *n* существова́ние; **to be in ~** существова́ть *(impf)*.
existentialism [ɛgzɪs'tɛnʃlɪzəm] *n* экзистенциали́зм.
existing [ɪg'zɪstɪŋ] *adj* существу́ющий.
exit ['ɛksɪt] *n* (*way out*) вы́ход; (*on motorway*) вы́езд; (*departure*) ухо́д ◆ *vi* (*THEAT*) уходи́ть* (уйти́* *perf*); (*COMPUT*) выходи́ть* (вы́йти* *perf*); (*leave*): **to ~ from** (*room*) выходи́ть* (вы́йти* *perf*) из +*gen*; (*motorway*) съезжа́ть (съе́хать* *perf*) с +*gen*.
exit poll *n* предвари́тельный подсчёт голосо́в.
exit ramp *n* (*US*: *AUT*) съезд с автостра́ды.
exit visa *n* выездна́я ви́за.
exodus ['ɛksədəs] *n* ма́ссовое бе́гство; **the ~ to the cities** ма́ссовое переселе́ние в города́.
ex officio ['ɛksə'fɪʃɪəu] *adv* по до́лжности.
exonerate [ɪg'zɔnəreɪt] *vt*: **to ~ sb from guilt/responsibility** снима́ть (снять* *perf*) с кого́-н обвине́ние/отве́тственность.
exorbitant [ɪg'zɔ:bɪtnt] *adj* непоме́рный* (непоме́рен).
exorcize ['ɛksɔ:saɪz] *vt* (*person, place*) изгоня́ть (изгна́ть* *perf*) дья́вола из +*gen*; (*spirit*) изгоня́ть (изгна́ть* *perf*).
exotic [ɪg'zɔtɪk] *adj* экзоти́ческий*.
expand [ɪks'pænd] *vt* (*area, business, influence*) расширя́ть (расши́рить *perf*); (*numbers*) увели́чивать (увели́чить *perf*) ◆ *vi* (*gas, metal, business*) расширя́ться (расши́риться *perf*); (*population*) увели́чиваться (увели́читься *perf*); **to ~ on** (*story, idea etc*) подро́бно разъясня́ть (разъясни́ть *perf*).
expanse [ɪks'pæns] *n*: **an ~ of sea/sky** морско́й/небе́сный просто́р.
expansion [ɪks'pænʃən] *n* расшире́ние; (*of population*) увеличе́ние; (*of economy*) рост.
expansionism [ɪks'pænʃənɪzəm] *n* (*ECON*) экспансиони́зм.
expansionist [ɪks'pænʃənɪst] *adj* (*policy*) экспансиони́стский.
expatriate [ɛks'pætrɪət] *n* эмигра́нт(ка*).
expect [ɪks'pɛkt] *vt* (*anticipate, hope for, await*) ожида́ть *(impf)*; (*baby*) ждать* *(impf)*; (*suppose*) полага́ть *(impf)* ◆ *vi*: **to be ~ing** (*be pregnant*) ждать* *(impf)* ребёнка; **he ~s me to**

finish by Tuesday он ожидáет, что я закóнчу ко втóрнику; **to ~ to do** рассчи́тывать *(impf)* *+infin*; **as ~ed** как и ожидáлось; **I ~ so** я полагáю.

expectancy [ɪks'pɛktənsɪ] *n* предвкушéние; **life ~** срéдняя продолжи́тельность *f* жи́зни.

expectant [ɪks'pɛktənt] *adj* (*silence, crowd*) выжидáющий.

expectantly [ɪks'pɛktəntlɪ] *adv* с надéждой.

expectant mother *n* берéменная жéнщина.

expectation [ɛkspɛk'teɪʃən] *n* (*hope*) ожидáние; **in ~ of** в ожидáнии *+gen*; **contrary to** *or* **against all ~(s)** вопреки́ всем ожидáниям; **to come** *or* **live up to sb's ~s** оправдывать (оправдáть *perf*) чьи-н ожидáния.

expedience [ɪks'pi:dɪəns] *n* = **expediency**.

expediency [ɪks'pi:dɪənsɪ] *n* вы́года; **for the sake of ~** рáди вы́годы.

expedient [ɪks'pi:dɪənt] *adj* целесообрáзный* (целесообрáзен) ◆ *n* улóвка.

expedite ['ɛkspədaɪt] *vt* ускоря́ть (ускóрить *perf*).

expedition [ɛkspə'dɪʃən] *n* экспеди́ция; (*for shopping etc*) похóд.

expeditionary force [ɛkspə'dɪʃənrɪ-] *n* экспедициóнные войскá* *pl*.

expeditious [ɛkspə'dɪʃəs] *adj* эффекти́вный* (эффекти́вен).

expel [ɪks'pɛl] *vt* (*person*: *from school, organization*) исключáть (исключи́ть *perf*); (: *from place*) изгоня́ть (изгнáть* *perf*); (*substance*: *from body etc*) выводи́ть* (вы́вести* *perf*).

expend [ɪks'pɛnd] *vt* расхóдовать (израсхóдовать *perf*), трáтить* (затрáтить* *perf*).

expendable [ɪks'pɛndəbl] *adj* (*resources*) подлежáщий списáнию; **he is entirely ~** егó мóжно сбрóсить со счётов.

expenditure [ɪks'pɛndɪtʃə'] *n* (*money spent*) затрáты *fpl*; (*of money*) расхóдование; (*of energy, time*) затрáта.

expense [ɪks'pɛns] *n* (*cost*) стóимость *f*; **~s** *npl* (*travelling expenses etc*) расхóды *mpl*; (*expenditure*) затрáты *fpl*; **at the ~ of** за счёт *+gen*; **to go to the ~ of doing** трáтиться* (потрáтиться* *perf*) *+infin*; **at great/little ~** с большúми/небольшúми затрáтами.

expense account *n* счёт подотчётных сумм.

expensive [ɪks'pɛnsɪv] *adj* дорогóй* (дóрог); **to be ~** дóрого стóить *(impf)*; **to have ~ tastes** имéть *(impf)* вкус к дороги́м вещáм.

experience [ɪks'pɪərɪəns] *n* (*in job, of situation*) óпыт; (*event, activity*) слу́чай; (: *difficult, painful*) испытáние; (*of emotion*) переживáние ◆ *vt* испы́тывать (испытáть *perf*), переживáть (пережи́ть* *perf*); **to know by** *or* **from ~** знать *(impf)* по óпыту; **to learn by ~** учи́ться *(impf)* на óпыте.

experienced [ɪks'pɪərɪənst] *adj* óпытный* (óпытен).

experiment [ɪks'pɛrɪmənt] *n* эксперимéнт, óпыт ◆ *vi*: **to ~ (with/on)** эксперименти́ровать *(impf)* (с *+instr*/на *+prp*); **to carry out** *or* **perform an ~** проводи́ть* (провести́* *perf*) эксперимéнт; **as an ~** в кáчестве эксперимéнта; **to ~ with a new vaccine** проводи́ть* (провести́* *perf*) óпыты с нóвой вакци́ной.

experimental [ɪkspɛrɪ'mɛntl] *adj* (*methods, ideas*) эксперментáльный; (*tests*) прóбный; **at the ~ stage** на стáдии эксперимéнта.

expert ['ɛkspə:t] *n* экспéрт, специали́ст ◆ *adj* (*person*) умéлый; **~ opinion/advice** мнéние/совéт экспéрта *or* специали́ста; **an ~ on sth** специали́ст по чемý-н; **she is ~ at resolving disputes** онá прекрáсно умéет разрешáть спóры; **~ witness** (*LAW*) судéбный экспéрт.

expertise [ɛkspə:'ti:z] *n* знáния *ntpl* и óпыт.

expire [ɪks'paɪə'] *vi* истекáть (истéчь* *perf*); **my passport ~s in January** срок дéйствия моегó пáспорта истекáет в январé.

expiry [ɪks'paɪərɪ] *n* истечéние срóка.

expiry date *n* дáта истечéния срóка.

explain [ɪks'pleɪn] *vt* объясня́ть (объясни́ть *perf*)

▸ **explain away** *vt* (*mistake, situation*) находи́ть* (найти́* *perf*) оправдáние *+gen*.

explanation [ɛksplə'neɪʃən] *n* объяснéние; **to find an ~ for sth** находи́ть* (найти́* *perf*) объяснéние чемý-н.

explanatory [ɪks'plænətrɪ] *adj* (*comment etc*) объясни́тельный; **~ notes** примечáния *ntpl*.

expletive [ɪks'pli:tɪv] *n* брáнное слóво*, ругáтельство.

explicable [ɪks'plɪkəbl] *adj* объясни́мый; **for no ~ reason** по необъясни́мой причи́не.

explicit [ɪks'plɪsɪt] *adj* я́вный* (я́вен); (*sex, violence*) откровéнный.

explode [ɪks'pləud] *vi* (*bomb, person*) взрывáться (взорвáться* *perf*); (*population*) рéзко возрастáть (возрасти́* *perf*) ◆ *vt* (*bomb*) взрывáть (взорвáть* *perf*); (*myth, theory*) опровергáть* (опровéргнуть* *perf*); **to ~ with laughter** разражáться (разрази́ться* *perf*) смéхом.

exploit [*vt* ɪks'plɔɪt, *n* 'ɛksplɔɪt] *vt* (*resources, also pej*: *person, idea*) эксплуати́ровать *(impf)*; (*opportunity*) испóльзовать *(impf/perf)* ◆ *n* пóдвиг.

exploitation [ɛksplɔɪ'teɪʃən] *n* (*see vb*) эксплуатáция; испóльзование.

exploration [ɛksplə'reɪʃən] *n* (*of place*) исслéдование; (*of idea*) изучéние.

exploratory [ɪks'plɔrətrɪ] *adj* (*expedition*)

* marks translations which have irregular inflections. The Russian-English side of the dictionary gives inflectional information.

исслéдовательский*; (*talks, operation*) предварúтельный.
explore [ɪks'plɔ:ʳ] *vt* (*place*) исслéдовать *(impf/perf)*; (*with hands etc*) ощýпывать (ощýпать *perf*); (*idea, suggestion*) изучáть (изучúть* *perf*).
explorer [ɪks'plɔ:rəʳ] *n* исслéдователь(ница) *m(f)*.
explosion [ɪks'pləuʒən] *n* взрыв; **population ~** демографúческий* взрыв.
explosive [ɪks'pləusɪv] *adj* (*device, effect*) взрывнóй; (*situation*) взрывоопáсный* (взрывоопáсен) ◆ *n* (*substance*) взрывчатое веществó*; (*device*) взрывнóе устрóйство; **he has an ~ temper** он óчень вспыльчивый.
exponent [ɪks'pəunənt] *n* (*of idea, theory*) сторóнник(-ица); (*of skill, activity*) мáстер; (*MATH*) показáтель *m* стéпени.
exponential [ɛkspəu'nɛnʃl] *adj* (*growth*) стремúтельный* (стремúтелен); (*MATH*) экспоненциáльный ◆ *n* (*MATH*) экспонéнта.
export [*n, cpd* 'ɛkspɔ:t, *vt* ɛks'pɔ:t] *n* (*process*) экспорт, вывоз; (*product*) предмéт экспорта ◆ *vt* экспортúровать *(impf/perf)*, вывозúть* (вывезти* *perf*) ◆ *cpd* (*duty, licence*) экспортный.
exportation [ɛkspɔ:'teɪʃən] *n* экспортúрование.
exporter [ɛks'pɔ:təʳ] *n* экспортёр.
expose [ɪks'pəuz] *vt* (*object*) обнажáть (обнажúть *perf*); (*truth, plot*) раскрывáть (раскрыть* *perf*); (*person*) разоблачáть (разоблачúть *perf*); (*PHOT*) экспонúровать *(impf/perf)*; **to ~ sb to sth** подвергáть (подвéргнуть* *perf*) когó-н чемý-н; **to ~ o.s.** (*LAW*) демонстрúровать *(impf)* половые óрганы.
exposé [ɛks'pəuzeɪ] *n* разоблачéние.
exposed [ɪks'pəuzd] *adj* (*wire*) оголённый; (*place*): **~ (to)** открытый (открыт) (*+dat*).
exposition [ɛkspə'zɪʃən] *n* (*explanation*) изложéние; (*exhibition*) экспозúция.
exposure [ɪks'pəuʒəʳ] *n* (*of culprit*) разоблачéние; (*PHOT*) экспозúция, выдержка; (: *shot*) кадр; **~ to radiation** пребывáние под воздéйствием радиáции; **to suffer/die from ~** (*MED*) страдáть (пострадáть *perf*)/умирáть (умерéть* *perf*) от переохлаждéния.
exposure meter *n* (*PHOT*) экспонóметр.
expound [ɪks'paund] *vt* излагáть (изложúть* *perf*).
express [ɪks'prɛs] *adj* (*clear*) чёткий*; (*BRIT*: *service*) срóчный ◆ *n* (*train, coach etc*) экспрéсс ◆ *adv* (*send*) экспрéссом ◆ *vt* выражáть (выразить* *perf*); **to ~ o.s.** выражáть (выразить* *perf*) себя.
expression [ɪks'prɛʃən] *n* выражéние; (*expressiveness*) выразúтельность *f*.
expressionism [ɪks'prɛʃənɪzəm] *n* экспрессионúзм.
expressive [ɪks'prɛsɪv] *adj* выразúтельный* (выразúтелен).
expressly [ɪks'prɛslɪ] *adv* (*clearly*) определённо; (*intentionally*) специáльно.
expressway [ɪks'prɛsweɪ] *n* (*esp US*) скоростнáя автострáда.
expropriate [ɛks'prəuprɪeɪt] *vt* (*money, property*) экспроприúровать *(impf/perf)*.
expulsion [ɪks'pʌlʃən] *n* (*from school*) исключéние; (*from country*) изгнáние; (*of substance*) вывод.
expurgate ['ɛkspə:geɪt] *vt*: **to ~ a text** вычёркивать (вычеркнуть *perf*) нежелáтельные местá из тéкста; **the ~d version** вариáнт с купюрами.
exquisite [ɛks'kwɪzɪt] *adj* (*face, lace, taste, workmanship*) изысканный* (изыскан); (*pain, pleasure*) óстрый.
exquisitely [ɛks'kwɪzɪtlɪ] *adv* (*dressed, polite, carved*) изысканно; (*sensitive*) обострённо.
ex-serviceman ['ɛks'sə:vɪsmən] *irreg n* бывший* военнослýжащий* *m adj*.
ext. *abbr* (*TEL*) = **extension**.
extemporize [ɪks'tɛmpəraɪz] *vi* импровизúровать *(impf)*.
extend [ɪks'tɛnd] *vt* (*visit, deadline*) продлевáть (продлúть *perf*); (*building*) расширять (расшúрить *perf*); (*arm, hand*) протягивать (протянýть* *perf*); (*offer*) окáзывать (оказáть* *perf*); (*credit, help*) предоставлять (предостáвить* *perf*) ◆ *vi* (*land, road*) простирáться *(impf)*; (*period*) продолжáться (продóлжиться *perf*); **to ~ an invitation to sb** приглашáть (пригласúть* *perf*) когó-н.
extension [ɪks'tɛnʃən] *n* (*of time*) продлéние; (*of campaign, rights*) расширéние; (*of building*) пристрóйка*; (*of road*) продолжéние; (*ELEC*) удлинúтель *m*; (*TEL*: *in house*) параллéльный телефóн; (: *in office*) добáвочный телефóн; **~ 3718** (*TEL*) добáвочный (нóмер) 3718.
extension cable *n* удлинúтель *m*.
extension lead *n* = **extension cable**.
extensive [ɪks'tɛnsɪv] *adj* обшúрный* (обшúрен); **~ damage** значúтельный ущéрб.
extensively [ɪks'tɛnsɪvlɪ] *adv*: **he has travelled ~** он мнóго путешéствовал.
extent [ɪks'tɛnt] *n* (*size*: *of area etc*) протяжённость *f*; (: *of problem etc*) масштáб; (*degree*: *of damage, loss*) размéр; **to some ~** до нéкоторой стéпени; **to a large ~** в значúтельной стéпени; **to go to the ~ of ...** доходúть* (дойтú* *perf*) до тогó, что ...; **to such an ~ that ...** до такóй стéпени, что ...; **to what ~?** до какóй стéпени?
extenuating [ɪks'tɛnjueɪtɪŋ] *adj*: **~ circumstances** смягчáющие обстоятельства *ntpl*.
exterior [ɛks'tɪərɪəʳ] *adj* (*drain, light, paint*) нарýжный; (*world*) внéшний* ◆ *n* (*outside*) внéшняя сторонá*; (*appearance*) внéшность *f*.

exterminate [ɪks'tə:mɪneɪt] *vt* истребля́ть (истреби́ть* *perf*).
extermination [ɪkstə:mɪ'neɪʃən] *n* истребле́ние.
external [ɛks'tə:nl] *adj* вне́шний*; **the ~s** *npl* вне́шняя сторона́* *sg*; **"for ~ use only"** "для нару́жного употребле́ния"; **~ affairs** (*POL*) вне́шняя поли́тика*; **~ evidence** свиде́тельство со стороны́.
externally [ɛks'tə:nəlɪ] *adv* вне́шне.
extinct [ɪks'tɪŋkt] *adj* (*animal*) вы́мерший; (*plant*) исче́знувший; (*volcano*) поту́хший; **to become ~** вымира́ть (вы́мереть* *perf*).
extinction [ɪks'tɪŋkʃən] *n* (*see adj*) вымира́ние; исчезнове́ние.
extinguish [ɪks'tɪŋgwɪʃ] *vt* (*fire*) туши́ть* (потуши́ть* *perf*); (*light*) гаси́ть* (погаси́ть* *perf*); (*memory, hope*) уничтожа́ть (уничто́жить *perf*).
extinguisher [ɪks'tɪŋgwɪʃəʳ] *n* (*also:* **fire ~**) огнетуши́тель *m*.
extol [ɪks'təul] (*US* **extoll**) *vt* превозноси́ть* (превознести́* *perf*).
extort [ɪks'tɔ:t] *vt*: **to ~ sth (from)** вымога́ть (*impf*) что-н (у +*gen*).
extortion [ɪks'tɔ:ʃən] *n* вымога́тельство.
extortionate [ɪks'tɔ:ʃnɪt] *adj* (*price*) граби́тельский*; (*demands*) вымога́тельский.
extra ['ɛkstrə] *adj* (*additional*) дополни́тельный; (*spare*) ли́шний ◆ *adv* (*in addition*) дополни́тельно; (*especially*) осо́бенно ◆ *n* (*luxury*) изли́шество; (*surcharge*) допла́та; (*CINEMA*) стати́ст(ка*); **wine will cost ~** за вино́ ну́жно бу́дет заплати́ть отде́льно; **the room charge does not include ~s** цена́ но́мера не включа́ет пла́ту за дополни́тельные услу́ги и удо́бства.
extra... ['ɛkstrə] *prefix* экстра..., особо..., сверх....
extract [*vt* ɪks'trækt, *n* 'ɛkstrækt] *vt* (*tooth*) удаля́ть (удали́ть *perf*); (*mineral*) добыва́ть (добы́ть* *perf*); (*money, promise*) вытя́гивать (вы́тянуть *perf*) ◆ *n* (*from novel, recording*) отры́вок*; (*CULIN*) экстра́кт; **to ~ sth (from)** извлека́ть (извле́чь* *perf*) что-н (из +*gen*).
extraction [ɪks'trækʃən] *n* (*of object*) извлече́ние; (*of tooth*) удале́ние; (*of minerals etc*) добы́ча; (*descent*): **of Scottish ~** шотла́ндец(-дка) по происхожде́нию.
extractor fan [ɪks'træktə-] *n* вытяжно́е устро́йство, вентиля́тор.
extracurricular ['ɛkstrəkə'rɪkjuləʳ] *adj* внекла́ссный, внеуче́бный.
extradite ['ɛkstrədaɪt] *vt*: **to ~ sb to/from** выдава́ть* (вы́дать* *perf*) кого́-н +*dat*/из +*gen*.
extradition [ɛkstrə'dɪʃən] *n* вы́дача (*преступника*) ◆ *cpd*: **~ order/treaty** про́сьба/соглаше́ние о вы́даче.
extramarital ['ɛkstrə'mærɪtl] *adj* внебра́чный.
extramural ['ɛkstrə'mjuərl] *adj* зао́чный.
extraneous [ɛks'treɪnɪəs] *adj* посторо́нний*.
extraordinary [ɪks'trɔ:dnrɪ] *adj* незауря́дный* (незауря́ден), необыча́йный* (необыча́ен); (*meeting*) чрезвыча́йный; **the ~ thing is that** ... са́мое удиви́тельное в том, что ....
extraordinary general meeting *n* чрезвыча́йное о́бщее собра́ние.
extrapolation [ɛkstræpə'leɪʃən] *n* экстраполя́ция.
extrasensory perception ['ɛkstrə'sɛnsərɪ-] *n* сверхчу́вственное *or* экстрасе́нсорное восприя́тие.
extra time *n* дополни́тельное вре́мя* *nt*.
extravagance [ɪks'trævəgəns] *n* (*of behaviour*) экстравага́нтность *f*; (*with money*) расточи́тельство.
extravagant [ɪks'trævəgənt] *adj* (*lavish*) экстравага́нтный* (экстравага́нтен); (*wasteful*: *person*) расточи́тельный* (расточи́телен); (: *machine*) неэконо́мный* (неэконо́мен); (*wild*: *ideas, claims*) сумасбро́дный* (сумасбро́ден).
extreme [ɪks'tri:m] *adj* кра́йний*; (*heat, cold*) сильне́йший ◆ *n* (*of behaviour*) кра́йность *f*; **the ~ right/left** (*POL*) кра́йне пра́вые *pl adj*/ ле́вые *pl adj*; **~s of temperature** перепа́ды температу́ры.
extremely [ɪks'tri:mlɪ] *adv* кра́йне.
extremist [ɪks'tri:mɪst] *n* экстреми́ст(ка*) ◆ *adj* экстреми́стский.
extremities [ɪks'trɛmɪtɪz] *npl* (*ANAT*) коне́чности *fpl*.
extremity [ɪks'trɛmɪtɪ] *n* коне́чность *f*; (*of situation*) кра́йность *f*.
extricate ['ɛkstrɪkeɪt] *vt*: **to ~ sb/sth (from)** высвобожда́ть (вы́свободить* *perf*) кого́-н/ что-н (из +*gen*); **to ~ o.s. (from)** выпу́тываться (вы́путаться *perf*) (из +*gen*).
extrovert ['ɛkstrəvə:t] *n* экстрове́рт.
exuberance [ɪg'zju:bərns] *n* экспанси́вность *f*.
exuberant [ɪg'zju:bərnt] *adj* (*person, behaviour*) экспанси́вный* (экспанси́вен); (*imagination*) бу́йный* (бу́ен).
exude [ɪg'zju:d] *vt* (*confidence, enthusiasm*) источа́ть (*impf*); (*liquid*) выделя́ть (вы́делить *perf*); (*smell*) издава́ть* (*impf*).
exult [ɪg'zʌlt] *vi* (*rejoice*): **to ~ (in)** ликова́ть* (*impf*) (по по́воду +*gen*).
exultant [ɪg'zʌltənt] *adj* лику́ющий, торжеству́ющий; **to be ~** ликова́ть (*impf*), торжествова́ть (*impf*).
exultation [ɛgzʌl'teɪʃən] *n* экзальта́ция, ликова́ние.
eye [aɪ] *n* (*ANAT*) глаз*; (*of needle*) у́шко* ◆ *vt* разгля́дывать (разгляде́ть* *perf*); **to keep an**

* marks translations which have irregular inflections. The Russian-English side of the dictionary gives inflectional information.

~ **on** (*person, object*) присмáтривать (присмотрéть* *perf*) за *+instr*; (*time*) следи́ть* (*impf*) за *+instr*; **in the public** ~ на виду́, в цéнтре внимáния; **to have an ~ for sth** знать (*impf*) толк в чём-н; **with an ~ to doing** (*BRIT*) с расчётом *+infin*; **as far as the ~ can see** наскóлько мóжно охвати́ть взгля́дом; **there's more to this than meets the** ~ э́то не так прóсто, как кáжется на пéрвый взгляд.
eyeball [ˈaɪbɔːl] *n* глазнóе я́блоко*.
eyebath [ˈaɪbɑːθ] *n* (*BRIT*) глазнáя вáнночка*.
eyebrow [ˈaɪbrau] *n* бровь* *f*.
eyebrow pencil *n* карандáш* для бровéй.
eye-catching [ˈaɪkætʃɪŋ] *adj* бросáющийся в глазá.
eyecup [ˈaɪkʌp] *n* (*US*) = **eyebath**.
eye drops *npl* глазны́е кáпли *fpl*.
eyeful [ˈaɪful] *n*: **an ~ of sand/dust** пóлные глазá пескá*/пы́ли; **to get an ~ of sb/sth** (*inf*) разглядéть* (*perf*) когó-н/что-н.
eyeglass [ˈaɪglɑːs] *n* монóкль *m*.
eyelash [ˈaɪlæʃ] *n* ресни́ца.
eyelet [ˈaɪlɪt] *n* фестóн.
eye level *n*: **at ~ ~** на у́ровне глаз.
eyelevel [ˈaɪlɛvl] *adj* (*grill*) располóженный на у́ровне глаз.
eyelid [ˈaɪlɪd] *n* вéко*.
eyeliner [ˈaɪlaɪnəʳ] *n* карандáш* для глаз.
eye-opener [ˈaɪəupnəʳ] *n* откровéние.
eye shadow *n* тéни* *fpl* (для век).
eyesight [ˈaɪsaɪt] *n* зрéние.
eyesore [ˈaɪsɔːʳ] *n*: **that building is a real** ~ э́то здáние как бельмó на глазу́.
eyestrain [ˈaɪstreɪn] *n* чрезмéрное напряжéние глаз.
eyeteeth [ˈaɪtiːθ] *npl of* **eyetooth**.
eyetooth [ˈaɪtuːθ] (*pl* **eyeteeth**) *n* глазнóй зуб; **to give one's eyeteeth for sth/to do** жéртвовать (пожéртвовать *perf*) всем за что-н/за то, чтóбы *+infin*.
eyewash [ˈaɪwɔʃ] *n* примóчка* для глаз; (*fig*: *inf*) очковтирáтельство.
eyewitness [ˈaiwɪtnɪs] *n* очеви́дец* ◆ *cpd*: **an ~ account** свидéтельство очеви́дца.
eyrie [ˈɪərɪ] *n* (*nest*) орли́ное гнездó*.

~ F, f ~

F, f [ɛf] *n* (*letter*) *6-ая бу́ква англи́йского алфави́та.*
F [ɛf] *n* (*MUS*) фа.
F *abbr* = **Fahrenheit.**
FA *n abbr* (*BRIT*: = *Football Association*) Футбо́льная ассоциа́ция.
FAA *n abbr* (*US*: = *Federal Aviation Administration*) Федера́льное управле́ние авиа́цией.
fable ['feɪbl] *n* ба́сня*.
fabric ['fæbrɪk] *n* (*cloth*) ткань *f*; (*of society*) структу́ра; (*of building*) констру́кция.
fabricate ['fæbrɪkeɪt] *vt* (*make up*) фабрикова́ть (сфабрикова́ть *perf*); (*make*) производи́ть* (произвести́* *perf*).
fabrication [fæbrɪ'keɪʃən] *n* (*lie*) фабрика́ция; (*making*) произво́дство.
fabric ribbon *n* (*for typewriter*) печа́тная ле́нта.
fabulous ['fæbjuləs] *adj* (*extraordinary*) невероя́тный* (невероя́тен); (*mythical*) ска́зочный*; (*inf*: *super*) ска́зочный* (ска́зочен).
façade [fə'sa:d] *n* фаса́д; (*fig*: *pretence*) ви́димость *f*; **a ~ of gaiety/indifference** фаса́д весе́лья/равноду́шия.
face [feɪs] *n* (*of person, organization*) лицо́*; (*grimace*) грима́са; (*of clock*) цифербла́т; (*of mountain, cliff*) склон; (*of building*) фаса́д; (*surface*: *of cube etc*) сторона́* ◆ *vt* (*fact*) признава́ть* (призна́ть* *perf*); **the house is facing the sea** дом обращён к мо́рю; **he was facing the door** он был обращён лицо́м к двери́; **we are facing difficulties** нам предстоя́т тру́дности; **~ down** лицо́м вниз; **to lose/save ~** теря́ть (потеря́ть *perf*)/спаса́ть (спасти́* *perf*) репута́цию; **to make** *or* **pull a ~** де́лать (сде́лать *perf*) грима́су; **in the ~ of** (*difficulties etc*) несмотря́ на *+acc*; **on the ~ of it** на пе́рвый взгляд; **~ to ~ (with)** (*with person, problem*) лицо́м к лицу́ (с *+instr*); **to ~ the fact that ...** признава́ть* (призна́ть* *perf*) тот факт, что ...
▸ **face up to** *vt fus* (*obligations, responsibility*) признава́ть* (призна́ть* *perf*); (*difficulties*) справля́ться (спра́виться* *perf*) с *+instr*.
face cloth *n* (*BRIT*) махро́вая салфе́тка (*для обтира́ния лица́*).
face cream *n* крем* для лица́.
faceless ['feɪslɪs] *adj* безли́кий*.
face-lift ['feɪslɪft] *n* подтя́жка* ко́жи на лице́; (*of building etc*) облицо́вка*.
face powder *n* пу́дра для лица́.
face-saving ['feɪs'seɪvɪŋ] *adj* для спасе́ния репута́ции.
facet ['fæsɪt] *n* (*also fig*) грань *f*.
facetious [fə'si:ʃəs] *adj* остроу́мный.
face to face *adv* лицо́м к лицу́.
face value *n* номина́льная сто́имость *f*; **to take sth at ~ ~** (*fig*) принима́ть (приня́ть* *perf*) что-н за чи́стую моне́ту.
facia ['feɪʃə] *n* = **fascia.**
facial ['feɪʃl] *n* космети́ческая обрабо́тка лица́ ◆ *adj*: **~ expression** выраже́ние лица́; **~ hair** во́лосы, расту́щие на лице́.
facile ['fæsaɪl] *adj* пове́рхностный*.
facilitate [fə'sɪlɪteɪt] *vt* спосо́бствовать (*impf/perf*) *+dat*.
facilities *npl* (*buildings*) помеще́ние *ntsg*; (*equipment*) обору́дование *ntsg*; **credit ~** креди́тный лими́т (*креди́тной ка́рточки заёмщика*); **cooking ~** усло́вия *ntpl* для приготовле́ния пи́щи.
facility [fə'sɪlɪtɪ] *n* (*feature*) приспособле́ние; (*service*) услу́га; (*aptitude*): **to have a ~ for** име́ть (*impf*) спосо́бности к *+dat*.
facing ['feɪsɪŋ] *prep* (*opposite*) напро́тив *+gen* ◆ *n* (*SEWING*) отде́лка*.
facsimile [fæk'sɪmɪlɪ] *n* факси́миле *nt ind*; (*machine, document*) факс.
fact [fækt] *n* факт; **in ~** факти́чески; **to know for a ~ that ...** зна́ть (*impf*) наверняка́, что ...; **the ~ (of the matter) is that ...** де́ло в том, что ...; **the ~s of life** (*sex*) полова́я сторона́ жи́зни; (*fig*) реа́льности *fpl* жи́зни.
fact-finding ['fæktfaɪndɪŋ] *adj* для рассле́дования фа́ктов.
faction ['fækʃən] *n* (*group*) фра́кция.
factor ['fæktə'] *n* фа́ктор; (*COMM*) комиссионе́р; (: *agent*) аге́нт; **safety ~** фа́ктор безопа́сности; **human ~** челове́ческий* фа́ктор.

* marks translations which have irregular inflections. The Russian-English side of the dictionary gives inflectional information.

factory ['fæktərɪ] *n* (*for textiles etc*) фа́брика; (*for machinery etc*) заво́д.
factory farming *n* (BRIT) веде́ние животново́дства промы́шленными ме́тодами.
factory floor *n* (*fig*: *workers*) рабо́чие *pl adj* у станка́.
factory ship *n* плаву́чая фа́брика.
factual ['fæktjuəl] *adj* факти́ческий*.
faculty ['fækəltɪ] *n* спосо́бность *f*; (*of university*) факульте́т; (US: *teaching staff*) профе́ссорско-преподава́тельский соста́в.
fad [fæd] *n* причу́да.
fade [feɪd] *vi* (*colour*) выцвета́ть (вы́цвести* *perf*); (*light*) угаса́ть (уга́снуть* *perf*); (*sound*) замира́ть (замере́ть* *perf*); (*flower*) вя́нуть* (завя́нуть* *perf*); (*hope, smile*) угаса́ть (уга́снуть* *perf*); (*memory*) сгла́живаться (сгла́диться* *perf*)
▸ **fade in** *vt*: **to ~ the picture/sound in** постепе́нно увели́чивать *(impf)* чёткость изображе́ния/си́лу зву́ка
▸ **fade out** *vt*: **to ~ the picture/sound out** постепе́нно уменьша́ть *(impf)* чёткость изображе́ния/си́лу зву́ка.
faeces ['fi:si:z] (US **feces**) *npl* фека́лии *fpl*.
fag [fæg] (*inf*) *n* (BRIT: *cigarette*) сигаре́та; (US: *pej*: *homosexual*) го́мик; (BRIT: *chore*): **what a ~!** ну и работёнка!
Fahrenheit ['færənhaɪt] *n* Фаренге́йт.
fail [feɪl] *vt* (*exam, candidate*) прова́ливать (провали́ть* *perf*); (*subj*: *person, memory*) изменя́ть (измени́ть *perf*) *+dat*, подводи́ть (подвести́ *perf*); (: *courage*) покида́ть (поки́нуть *perf*) ◆ *vi* (*candidate, attempt*) прова́ливаться (провали́ться* *perf*); (*brakes*) отка́зывать (отказа́ть* *perf*); **my eyesight/health is ~ing** у меня́ слабе́ет зре́ние/здоро́вье; **to ~ to do** не смочь* *(perf) +infin*; **without ~** обяза́тельно; **the light is ~ing** смерка́ется.
failing ['feɪlɪŋ] *n* недоста́ток* ◆ *prep* за неиме́нием *+gen*; **~ that** за неиме́нием э́того.
fail-safe ['feɪlseɪf] *adj* (*device*) предохрани́тельный.
failure ['feɪljə^r] *n* неуда́ча; (*mechanical*) поврежде́ние; (*of crops*) неурожа́й; (*in exam*) прова́л; (*person*) неуда́чник(-ица); **his ~ to complete the work** то, что он не смог вы́полнить рабо́ту; **the evening was a complete ~** ве́чер был по́лным прова́лом.
faint [feɪnt] *adj* сла́бый* (слаб); (*recollection*) сму́тный* (сму́тен); (*mark*) едва́ заме́тный* (заме́тен); (*breeze, trace*) лёгкий* ◆ *n* (MED) о́бморок ◆ *vi* (MED) па́дать (упа́сть* *perf*) в о́бморок; **to feel ~** чу́вствовать (почу́вствовать *perf*) сла́бость.
faintest ['feɪntɪst] *adj* мале́йший*; **I haven't the ~ idea** я не име́ю ни мале́йшего поня́тия.
faint-hearted ['feɪnt'hɑ:tɪd] *adj* малоду́шный* (малоду́шен).
faintly ['feɪntlɪ] *adv* (*a bit*) сла́бо; (*hardly*) едва́.
fair [fɛə^r] *adj* (*person, decision*) справедли́вый (справедли́в); (*size, number*) значи́тельный; (*chance, guess*) хоро́ший*; (*skin, hair*) све́тлый* (све́тел); (*weather*) хоро́ший*, я́сный* ◆ *n* (*also:* **trade ~**) я́рмарка*; (BRIT: *also:* **funfair**) аттракцио́ны *mpl* ◆ *adv*: **to play ~** вести́* *(impf)* дела́ разу́мно *or* че́стно; **it's not ~!** э́то нече́стно!; **a ~ amount of money** значи́тельная су́мма де́нег; **a ~ amount of success** значи́тельный успе́х; **I had a pretty ~ idea** у меня́ была́ дово́льно хоро́шая иде́я; **~ wear and tear** обосно́ванный изно́с.
fair copy *n* чистово́й экземпля́р.
fair game *n*: **he is ~ ~** он зако́нная добы́ча.
fairground ['fɛəgraund] *n* лу́на-парк.
fair-haired [fɛə'hɛəd] *adj* светловоло́сый (светловоло́с).
fairly ['fɛəlɪ] *adv* (*justly*) справедли́во; (*quite*) дово́льно; **I'm ~ sure** я почти́ уве́рен.
fairness ['fɛənɪs] *n* (*justice*) справедли́вость *f*; **in all ~** со все́й справедли́востью.
fair play *n* че́стная игра́.
fairway ['fɛəweɪ] *n* (GOLF): **the ~** *травяни́стая доро́жка ме́жду лу́нками в го́льфе.*
fairy ['fɛərɪ] *n* фе́я.
fairy godmother *n* до́брая волше́бница.
fairy lights *npl* (BRIT) электри́ческая гирля́нда *fsg*.
fairy tale *n* ска́зка*.
faith [feɪθ] *n* (*also* REL) ве́ра; **to have ~ in sb/sth** ве́рить *(impf)* в кого́-н/что-н.
faithful ['feɪθful] *adj*: **~ (to)** ве́рный* (ве́рен) (*+dat*).
faithfully ['feɪθfəlɪ] *adv* ве́рно.
faith healer *n* зна́харь(-рка*) *m(f)*.
fake [feɪk] *n* (*painting, document*) подде́лка*; (*person*) притво́рщик(-ица) ◆ *adj* фальши́вый, подде́льный ◆ *vt* (*painting, document*) подде́лывать (подде́лать *perf*); (*illness, emotion*) симули́ровать *(impf)*; **his illness is a ~** его́ боле́знь – симуля́ция.
falcon ['fɔ:lkən] *n* со́кол.
Falkland Islands ['fɔ:klənd-] *npl*: **the ~ ~** Фолкле́ндские острова́* *mpl*.
fall [fɔ:l] (*pt* **fell**, *pp* **fallen**) *n* паде́ние; (US: *autumn*) о́сень *f* ◆ *vi* па́дать (упа́сть* *perf*); (*government, country*) пасть* *(perf)*; (*rain, snow*) выпада́ть (вы́пасть* *perf*); (*silence, hush, night*) наступа́ть (наступи́ть* *perf*); (*sadness*) охва́тывать (охвати́ть *perf*); **~s** *npl* (*waterfall*) водопа́д; **a ~ of snow** снегопа́д; **a ~ of earth** обва́л; **to ~ flat** (*plan*) не удава́ться* (уда́ться* *perf*); (*joke*) не име́ть *(impf)* успе́ха; **to ~ flat (on one's face)** па́дать (упа́сть* *perf*) ничко́м; **to ~ in love (with sb/sth)** влюбля́ться (влюби́ться* *perf*) (в кого́-н/во что-н); **to ~ short of (sb's expectations)** не опра́вдывать (оправда́ть *perf*) (чьих-н ожида́ний); **a lot of rain/snow fell yesterday** вчера́ вы́пало мно́го сне́га/дождя́; **darkness/**

night fell наступи́ла темнота́/ночь
▸**fall apart** *vi* разва́ливаться (развали́ться* *perf*); (*inf: emotionally*) раскле́иваться (раскле́иться *perf*)
▸**fall back** *vt fus* (*MIL*) отступа́ть (отступи́ть* *perf*)
▸**fall back on** *vt fus* прибега́ть (прибе́гнуть* *perf*) к +*dat*; **to have sth to ~ back on** (*money, job etc*) име́ть (*impf*) что-н в запа́се
▸**fall behind** *vi* отстава́ть* (отста́ть* *perf*); **to ~ behind with the payments** просро́чивать (просрочить *perf*) платежи́
▸**fall down** *vi* (*person*) па́дать (упа́сть* *perf*); (*building*) ру́шиться (ру́хнуть *perf*)
▸**fall for** *vt fus* (*trick etc*) попада́ться (попа́сться* *perf*) на +*acc*; (*story*) ве́рить (пове́рить *perf*) +*dat*; (*person*) влюбля́ться (влюби́ться* *perf*) в +*acc*
▸**fall in** *vi* (*roof*) обва́ливаться (обвали́ться *perf*); (*MIL*) стро́иться (постро́иться *perf*)
▸**fall in with** *vt fus* (*sb's plans etc*) соглаша́ться (согласи́ться* *perf*) с +*instr*
▸**fall off** *vi* па́дать (упа́сть* *perf*)
▸**fall out** *vi* (*hair, teeth*) выпада́ть (вы́пасть* *perf*); (*friends etc*): **to ~ out with sb** ссо́риться (поссо́риться *perf*) с кем-н
▸**fall over** *vi* па́дать (упа́сть* *perf*) ◆ *vt*: **to ~ over o.s. to do** лезть* (вы́лезть* *perf*) из ко́жи вон, что́бы +*infin*
▸**fall through** *vi* (*plan*) прова́ливаться (провали́ться* *perf*).
fallacy ['fæləsɪ] *n* (*misconception*) заблужде́ние.
fall-back ['fɔ:lbæk] *adj*: **~ position** пози́ция для отступле́ния.
fallen ['fɔ:lən] *pp of* **fall**.
fallible ['fæləbl] *adj* спосо́бный* (спосо́бен) ошиба́ться (ошиби́ться *perf*).
falling ['fɔ:lɪŋ] *adj*: **~ market** (*COMM*) понижа́тельная ры́ночная конъюнкту́ра.
falling off *n* сниже́ние.
falling out *n* размо́лвка.
Fallopian tube [fə'ləupɪən-] *n* фалло́пиевы тру́бы *fpl*.
fallout ['fɔ:laut] *n* радиоакти́вные оса́дки *pl*.
fallout shelter *n* убе́жище от радиоакти́вных оса́дков.
fallow ['fæləu] *adj* (*land, field*) парово́й.
false [fɔ:ls] *adj* (*untrue, wrong*) ло́жный* (ло́жен); (*insincere, artificial*) фальши́вый (фальши́в); **~ imprisonment** незако́нное лише́ние свобо́ды.
false alarm *n* ло́жная трево́га.
falsehood ['fɔ:lshud] *n* ложь* *f*.
falsely ['fɔ:lslɪ] *adv* (*accuse*) ло́жно.
false pretences *npl*: **under ~ ~** под ло́жным предло́гом.
false teeth *npl* (*BRIT*) иску́сственные зу́бы* *mpl*.
falsify ['fɔ:lsɪfaɪ] *vt* фальсифици́ровать (*impf/perf*), подде́лывать (подде́лать *perf*).
falter ['fɔ:ltə^r] *vi* (*engine*) ка́шлять (*impf*); (*person: hesitate*) замя́ться* (*perf*); (*: in speech*) запина́ться (запну́ться *perf*); (*: while moving*) спотыка́ться (споткну́ться *perf*).
fame [feɪm] *n* сла́ва.
familiar [fə'mɪlɪə^r] *adj* (*well-known*) знако́мый (знако́м); (*intimate*) дру́жеский*; **he is/was ~ with** (*subject*) он знако́м/был знако́м с +*instr*; **to make o.s. ~ with sth** знако́миться* (ознако́миться* *perf*) с чем-н; **to be on ~ terms with sb** быть* (*impf*) в прия́тельских *or* дру́жеских отноше́ниях с кем-н.
familiarity [fəmɪlɪ'ærɪtɪ] *n* (*knowledge*) зна́ние; (*informality*) фамилья́рность *f*.
familiarize [fə'mɪlɪəraɪz] *vt*: **to ~ o.s. with sth** ознакомля́ться (ознако́миться* *perf*) с чем-н.
family ['fæmɪlɪ] *n* семья́*; (*children*) де́ти* *pl*.
family business *n* семе́йный би́знес.
family credit *n* *де́нежное посо́бие, выпла́чиваемое госуда́рством се́мьям с ни́зким у́ровнем дохо́дов*.
family doctor *n* семе́йный врач*.
family life *n* семе́йная жизнь *f*.
family man *n* семьяни́н*, семе́йный челове́к*.
family planning *n* плани́рование семьи́; **~ ~ clinic** ≈ же́нская консульта́ция.
family tree *n* родосло́вное де́рево*.
famine ['fæmɪn] *n* го́лод*.
famished ['fæmɪʃt] (*inf*) *adj* голо́дный; **I'm ~** я умира́ю с го́лоду.
famous ['feɪməs] *adj* знамени́тый (знамени́т).
famously ['feɪməslɪ] *adv* (*get on*) великоле́пно.
fan [fæn] *n* (*folding*) ве́ер*; (*ELEC*) вентиля́тор; (*of famous person*) покло́нник(-ица), фэн; (*of sports team*) боле́льщик(-ица) ◆ *vt* (*face*) обма́хивать (обмахну́ть *perf*); (*fire, quarrel*) раздува́ть (разду́ть *perf*)
▸**fan out** *vi* (*people*) развёртываться (разверну́ться *perf*) ве́ером; (*roads*) расходи́ться* (разойти́сь* *perf*) ве́ером.
fanatic [fə'nætɪk] *n* (*extremist*) фана́тик.
fanatical [fə'nætɪkl] *adj* (*support, dedication*) фанати́чный* (фанати́чен).
fan belt *n* (*AUT*) вентиля́торный реме́нь* *m*.
fanciful ['fænsɪful] *adj* причу́дливый (причу́длив).
fan club *n* клуб покло́нников, фэн-клуб.
fancy ['fænsɪ] *n* (*whim*) при́хоть *f*; (*imagination*) воображе́ние; (*fantasy*) фанта́зия ◆ *adj* изы́сканный ◆ *vt* (*feel like, want*) хоте́ть* (захоте́ть* *perf*); (*imagine*) вообража́ть (вообрази́ть* *perf*); (*think*) ду́мать (*impf*); **to take a ~ to** увлека́ться (увле́чься* *perf*) +*instr*; **when the ~ takes him** когда́ ему́ взду́мается; **the idea took** *or* **caught my ~** иде́я пришла́сь

* marks translations which have irregular inflections. The Russian-English side of the dictionary gives inflectional information.

мне по вкýсу; **to ~ that** дýмать *(impf)*, что; **he fancies her** (*inf*) онá емý нрáвится; **~ that!** представьте себé.
fancy dress *n* маскарáдный костюм.
fancy-dress ball ['fænsɪdrɛs-] *n* костюмированный бал*.
fancy goods *npl* украшéния *ntpl* (*обычно для дóма*).
fanfare ['fænfɛə'] *n* фанфáра.
fanfold paper ['fænfəuld-] *n* перфорировáнная *or* фальцóванная бумáга.
fang [fæŋ] *n* клык*; (*of snake*) ядовитый зуб*.
fan heater *n* (*BRIT*) электрообогревáтель *m* (*нагнетáющий тёплый вóздух при пóмощи вентилятора*).
fanlight ['fænlaɪt] *n веерообрáзное окнó над двéрью*.
fanny ['fænɪ] *n* (*inf*) зáдница.
fantasize ['fæntəsaɪz] *vi* фантазировать *(impf)*.
fantastic [fæn'tæstɪk] *adj* фантастический*; **that's ~!** это фантáстика!
fantasy ['fæntəsɪ] *n* фантáзия.
fanzine ['fænzi:n] *n журнáл или газéта, самодéятельно издавáемый поклóнниками попгрýппы, телепрогрáммы, спóрта итп.*
FAO *n abbr* (= *Food and Agriculture Organization*) ФАО (*продовóльственная и сельскохозяйственная организáция ООН*).
f.a.q. *abbr* (= *free alongside quay*) фрáнко нáбережная.
far [fɑ:'] *adj* (*distant*) дáльний* ◆ *adv* (*a long way*) далекó; (*much*) горáздо; **at the ~ end** в дáльнем концé; **at the ~ side** на другóй сторонé; **the ~ left/right** (*POL*) крáйне лéвый/прáвый; **~ away, ~ off** далекó; **~ better** горáздо лýчше; **he was ~ from poor** он был далекó *or* отнюдь не бéден; **by ~** намнóго; **is it ~ to London?** далекó ли до Лóндона?; **it's not ~ from here** это недалекó отсюда; **go as ~ as the post office** дойдите до пóчты; **as ~ back as the 13th century** ещё в 13-ом вéке; **as ~ as I know** наскóлько мне извéстно; **as ~ as possible** наскóлько возмóжно; **how ~?** (*distance*) как далекó?; (*to what extent*) наскóлько?; **how ~ have you got with your work?** наскóлько Вы продвинулись в своéй рабóте?
faraway ['fɑ:rəweɪ] *adj* (*place*) дáльний*, далёкий*; (*look*) отсýтствующий*.
farce [fɑ:s] *n* (*also fig*) фарс.
farcical ['fɑ:sɪkl] *adj* (*fig*) нелéпый.
fare [fɛə'] *n* (*on trains, buses*) плáта за проéзд; (*in taxi*) стóимость *f* проéзда; (: *passenger*) пассажир; (*food*) едá ◆ *vi*: **how did you ~?** как успéхи?; **half/full ~** полстóимости/пóлная стóимость проéзда; **bus/train ~** плáта за проéзд в автóбусе/на пóезде; **they ~ better than we do under the present system** с ними обращáются лýчше, чем с нáми при нынешней систéме; **they ~d well/badly in the recent elections** им повезлó/не повезлó на недáвних выборах.
Far East *n*: **the ~ ~** Дáльний* Востóк.
farewell [fɛə'wɛl] *excl* прощáйте ◆ *n* прощáние ◆ *cpd* (*party etc*) прощáльный.
far-fetched ['fɑ:'fɛtʃt] *adj* неправдоподóбный, невероятный.
farm [fɑ:m] *n* фéрма ◆ *vt* (*land*) обрабáтывать (обрабóтать *perf*)
▸ **farm out** *vt* отдавáть* (отдáть* *perf*).
farmer ['fɑ:mə'] *n* фéрмер.
farm hand *n* рабóтник(-ица) фéрмы.
farmhouse ['fɑ:mhaus] *n* фéрмерский дом*.
farming ['fɑ:mɪŋ] *n* (*agriculture*) сéльское хозяйство; (*of crops*) выращивание; (*of animals*) разведéние; **sheep ~** разведéние овéц, овцевóдство; **intensive ~** интенсивное ведéние сéльского хозяйства.
farm labourer *n* рабóтник на фéрме.
farmland ['fɑ:mlænd] *n* сельскохозяйственные угóдья* *ntpl*.
farm produce *n* продýкты *mpl* сéльского хозяйства.
farm worker *n* = **farm hand**.
farmyard ['fɑ:mjɑ:d] *n* фéрмерский двор*.
Faroe Islands ['fɛərəu-] *npl*: **the ~ ~** Фарéрские островá* *mpl*.
Faroes ['fɛərəuz] *npl* = **Faroe Islands**.
far-reaching ['fɑ:'ri:tʃɪŋ] *adj* (*reform*) далекó идýщий; (*effect*) глубóкий*.
far-sighted ['fɑ:'saɪtɪd] *adj* (*US*) дальнозóркий* (дальнозóрок); (*fig*) дальновидный* (дальновиден); **he is ~** (*US*) у негó дальнозóркость.
fart [fɑ:t] (*inf!*) *vi* пердéть* (пёрнуть *perf*) (*!*) ◆ *n* пердéние (*!*)
farther ['fɑ:ðə'] *adv* дáльше ◆ *adj* бóлее дáльний*, далёкий*.
farthest ['fɑ:ðɪst] *superl of* **far**.
f.a.s. *abbr* (*BRIT*: = *free alongside ship*) ФАС (*свобóдно вдоль бóрта сýдна*).
fascia ['feɪʃə] *n* (*AUT*) панéль *f*.
fascinate ['fæsɪneɪt] *vt* захвáтывать (захватить* *perf*); (*subj*: *person*) очарóвывать (очаровáть *perf*).
fascinating ['fæsɪneɪtɪŋ] *adj* (*story*) захвáтывающий*; (*person*) очаровáтельный* (очаровáтелен).
fascination [fæsɪ'neɪʃən] *n* очаровáние.
fascism ['fæʃɪzəm] *n* (*POL*) фашизм.
fascist ['fæʃɪst] *adj* фашистский* ◆ *n* фашист(ка).
fashion ['fæʃən] *n* (*trend*) мóда; (*fashion industry*) индýстрия мóды ◆ *vt* (*make*) мастерить (смастерить *perf*); **in/out of ~** в/не в мóде; **in an animated ~** оживлённо; **in a friendly ~** по-дрýжески; **he did it after a ~** он сдéлал это кóе-кáк; **in the Greek ~** в грéческом стиле.
fashionable ['fæʃnəbl] *adj* мóдный* (мóден).
fashion designer *n* модельéр.
fashion show *n* покáз *or* демонстрáция мод.

fast [fɑ:st] *adv* (*quickly*) бы́стро; (*firmly*: *stick*) про́чно; (: *hold*) кре́пко ◆ *n* (*REL*) пост* ◆ *vi* (*REL*) пости́ться* *(impf)* ◆ *adj* бы́стрый* (быстр); (*progress*) стреми́тельный*; (*car*) скоростно́й; (*dye, colour*) про́чный; (*clock*): **to be ~** спеши́ть *(impf)*; **he is ~ asleep** он кре́пко спит; **as ~ as possible** как мо́жно быстре́е; **to make a boat ~** (*BRIT*) кре́пко привяза́ть* *(perf)* ло́дку; **my watch is 5 minutes ~** мои́ часы́ спеша́т на 5 мину́т.
fasten ['fɑ:sn] *vt* закрепля́ть (закрепи́ть* *perf*); (*door*) запира́ть (запере́ть* *perf*); (*shoe*) завя́зывать (завяза́ть *perf*); (*coat, dress*) застёгивать (застегну́ть *perf*); (*seat belt*) пристёгивать (пристегну́ть *perf*) ◆ *vi* (*coat, belt*) застёгиваться (застегну́ться *perf*); (*door*) запира́ться (запере́ться* *perf*)
▸ **fasten (up)on** *vt fus* (*idea etc*) сосредото́чиваться (сосредото́читься *perf*) на *+acc*.
fastener ['fɑ:snəʳ] *n* (*for clothing*) застёжка*.
fastening ['fɑ:snɪŋ] *n* = **fastener**.
fast food *n* быстропригота́вливаемая еда́ ◆ *cpd*: **~~ restaurant** рестора́н быстропригота́вливаемой еды́.
fastidious [fæs'tɪdɪəs] *adj* (*fussy*) скрупулёзный* (скрупулёзен).
fast lane *n* (*BRIT*: *AUT*): **the ~ ~** скоростно́й ряд*.
fat [fæt] *adj* то́лстый* (толст); (*inf*: *profit*) соли́дный* ◆ *n* жир*; **that's a ~ lot of use to us** (*inf*) нам э́то нигде́ не на́до; **to live off the ~ of the land** как сыр в ма́сле ката́ться *(impf)*.
fatal ['feɪtl] *adj* (*mistake*) фата́льный* (фата́лен), роково́й; (*injury, illness*) смерте́льный* (смерте́лен).
fatalistic [feɪtə'lɪstɪk] *adj* (*attitude*) фаталисти́ческий.
fatality [fə'tælɪtɪ] *n* (*death*) смерте́льный слу́чай.
fatally ['feɪtəlɪ] *adv* (*injured*) смерте́льно; (*flawed*) фата́льно, роковы́м о́бразом.
fate [feɪt] *n* судьба́*, рок; **to meet one's ~** находи́ть* (найти́* *perf*) свой коне́ц.
fated ['feɪtɪd] *adj* обречённый* (обречён); **it seemed ~** каза́лось, э́тому бы́ло суждено́ случи́ться.
fateful ['feɪtful] *adj* роково́й.
fat-free ['fæt'fri:] *adj* обезжи́ренный.
father ['fɑ:ðəʳ] *n* оте́ц*.
Father Christmas *n* ≈ Дед Моро́з.
fatherhood ['fɑ:ðəhud] *n* отцо́вство.
father-in-law ['fɑ:ðərənlɔ:] *n* (*wife's father*) свёкор*; (*husband's father*) тесть *m*.
fatherland ['fɑ:ðəlænd] *n* оте́чество.
fatherly ['fɑ:ðəlɪ] *adj* оте́ческий*.
fathom ['fæðəm] *n* (*NAUT*) фа́том, морска́я са́жень *f* ◆ *vt* (*understand*: *also*: **~ out**) постига́ть (пости́чь* *perf*).
fatigue [fə'ti:g] *n* утомле́ние; **~s** *npl* (*MIL*) солда́тская рабо́чая оде́жда *fsg*; **metal ~** уста́лость *f* мета́лла.
fatness ['fætnɪs] *n* (*of person*) полнота́; (*of wallet*) толщина́.
fatten ['fætn] *vt* (*animal*) отка́рмливать (откорми́ть* *perf*) ◆ *vi* жире́ть (разжире́ть *perf*); **chocolate is ~ing** от шокола́да толсте́ют.
fatty ['fætɪ] *adj* (*food*) жи́рный* ◆ *n* (*inf*) толстя́к*.
fatuous ['fætjuəs] *adj* бессмы́сленный*.
faucet ['fɔ:sɪt] *n* (*US*) (водопрово́дный) кран.
fault [fɔ:lt] *n* (*blame*) вина́*; (*defect*: *in person*) недоста́ток*; (: *in machine*) дефе́кт; (*GEO*) разло́м; (*TENNIS*) оши́бка* при пода́че ◆ *vt* (*criticize*) придира́ться *(impf)* к *+dat*; **it's my ~** э́то моя́ вина́; **to find ~ with** придира́ться (придра́ться* *perf*) к *+dat*; **I am at ~** я винова́т; **if my memory is not at ~** е́сли мне не изменя́ет па́мять; **generous to a ~** чрезме́рно ще́дрый*.
faultless ['fɔ:ltlɪs] *adj* безупре́чный* (безупре́чен).
faulty ['fɔ:ltɪ] *adj* (*goods*) испо́рченный*; (*machine*) повреждённый.
fauna ['fɔ:nə] *n* фа́уна.
faux pas ['fəu'pɑ:] *n inv* неве́рный шаг*.
favour ['feɪvəʳ] (*US* **favor**) *n* (*approval*) расположе́ние; (*help*) одолже́ние ◆ *vt* (*prefer*: *solution*) ока́зывать (оказа́ть* *perf*) предпочте́ние *+dat*; (: *pupil etc*) выделя́ть (вы́делить *perf*); (*assist*) благоприя́тствовать *(impf)* *+dat*; **to ask a ~ of sb** проси́ть* (попроси́ть* *perf*) кого́-н об одолже́нии; **to do sb a ~** ока́зывать (оказа́ть* *perf*) кому́-н услу́гу; **in ~ of** в по́льзу *+gen*; **to be in ~ of sth/doing** быть* *(impf)* за что-н/за то́, что́бы *+infin*; **to find ~ with sb** (*subj*: *person*) завоёвывать (завоева́ть* *perf*) расположе́ние кого́-н; (: *suggestion*) находи́ть* (найти́* *perf*) подде́ржку у кого́-н.
favourable ['feɪvrəbl] (*US* **favorable**) *adj* благоприя́тный* (благоприя́тен).
favourably ['feɪvrəblɪ] (*US* **favorably**) *adv* (*react*) положи́тельно, благоприя́тно; **to compare ~ with** вы́игрывать *(impf)* в сравне́нии с *+instr*.
favourite ['feɪvrɪt] (*US* **favorite**) *adj* люби́мый ◆ *n* (*of teacher, parent*) люби́мец*; (*SPORT*) фавори́т.
favouritism ['feɪvrɪtɪzəm] (*US* **favoritism**) *n* фаворити́зм.
fawn [fɔ:n] *n* молодо́й оле́нь *m* ◆ *adj* (*also*: **~-coloured**) желтова́то-кори́чневый ◆ *vi*: **to ~ (up)on** заи́скивать *(impf)* пе́ред *+instr*.
fax [fæks] *n* факс ◆ *vt* (*letter, document*)

* marks translations which have irregular inflections. The Russian-English side of the dictionary gives inflectional information.

посыла́ть (посла́ть* *perf*) фа́ксом.

FBI *n abbr* (*US*: = *Federal Bureau of Investigation*) ФБР= *Федера́льное бюро́ рассле́дований.*

FCC *n abbr* (*US*: = *Federal Communications Commission*) Федера́льная коми́ссия свя́зи.

FCO *n abbr* (*BRIT*: = *Foreign and Commonwealth Office*) *Министе́рство иностра́нных дел и снoше́ний со стра́нами Брита́нского содру́жества.*

FD *n abbr* (*US*) = **fire department**.

FDA *n abbr* (*US*: = *Food and Drug Administration*) *управле́ние по контро́лю за проду́ктами и медикаме́нтами.*

FE *abbr* (= *Further Education*) ≈ профессиона́льно-техни́ческое образова́ние.

fear [fɪəʳ] *n* страх; (*less strong*) боя́знь *f*; (*worry*) опасе́ние ◆ *vt* боя́ться *(impf) +gen* ◆ *vi* боя́ться *(impf)*; **to ~ for** боя́ться *(impf)* за *+acc*; **to ~ that** боя́ться *(impf)*, что; **~ of heights** боя́знь высоты́; **for ~ of missing my flight** (*in case*) боя́сь опозда́ть на самолёт.

fearful [ˈfɪəful] *adj* (*person*) боязли́вый (боязли́в); (*sight*) ужаса́ющий*; (*risk, noise*) стра́шный* (стра́шен); **to be ~ of** страши́ться *(impf) +gen.*

fearfully [ˈfɪəfəlɪ] *adv* (*timidly*) боязли́во; (*inf: very*) ужа́сно.

fearless [ˈfɪəlɪs] *adj* бесстра́шный* (бесстра́шен).

fearsome [ˈfɪəsəm] *adj* (*opponent*) внуша́ющий страх; (*sight*) устраша́ющий.

feasibility [fiːzəˈbɪlɪtɪ] *n* (*of plan*) осуществи́мость *f*.

feasibility study *n* те́хнико-экономи́ческое обоснова́ние.

feasible [ˈfiːzəbl] *adj* осуществи́мый (осуществи́м).

feast [fiːst] *n* (*banquet*) пир*; (*REL*: *also*: **~ day**) пра́здник ◆ *vi* пирова́ть *(impf)*; **to ~ on** ла́комиться* *(impf) +instr*; **to ~ one's eyes on sth** любова́ться *(impf)* чем-н.

feat [fiːt] *n* по́двиг.

feather [ˈfɛðəʳ] *n* перо́* ◆ *cpd* перьево́й ◆ *vt*: **to ~ one's nest** набива́ть (наби́ть* *perf*) себе́ карма́н; **~ bed** пери́на.

featherweight [ˈfɛðəweɪt] *n* (*BOXING*) боксёр полулёгкого ве́са.

feature [ˈfiːtʃəʳ] *n* черта́, осо́бенность *f*; (*of landscape*) осо́бенность; (*PRESS*) о́черк; (*TV, RADIO*) переда́ча ◆ *vi*: **to ~ in** фигури́ровать *(impf)* в *+prp* ◆ *vt*: **the film ~s 2 famous actors** в фи́льме снима́ются 2 изве́стных актёра; **~s** *npl* (*of face*) черты́ *fpl*; **a film featuring ...** фильм с уча́стием *+gen...*; **his article ~d in all the newspapers** его́ статья́ фигури́ровала во всех газе́тах; **a special ~ on sth/sb** специа́льная переда́ча о чём-н/ком-н.

feature film *n* худо́жественный фильм.

featureless [ˈfiːtʃəlɪs] *adj* невырази́тельный* (невырази́телен).

Feb. *abbr* = **February**.

February [ˈfɛbruərɪ] *n* февра́ль* *m*; *see also* **July**.

feces [ˈfiːsiːz] *npl* (*US*) = **faeces**.

feckless [ˈfɛklɪs] *adj* безотве́тственный.

Fed *abbr* (*US*) = **federal, federation**.

fed [fɛd] *pt, pp of* **feed**.

Fed. *n abbr* (*US*: *inf*: = *Federal Reserve Board*) *сове́т, управля́ющий федера́льной резе́рвной систе́мой.*

federal [ˈfɛdərəl] *adj* федера́льный.

Federal Republic of Germany *n* Федерати́вная Респу́блика Герма́нии.

Federal Reserve Board *n* (*US*) Федера́льное резе́рвное правле́ние.

Federal Trade Commission *n* (*US*) Федера́льная торго́вая коми́ссия.

federation [fɛdəˈreɪʃən] *n* федера́ция.

fed up *adj*: **he is ~ ~** ему́ надое́ло.

fee [fiː] *n* пла́та; (*of doctor, lawyer*) пла́та, гонора́р; **school ~s** пла́та за обуче́ние; **entrance ~** входна́я пла́та; **membership ~** чле́нский* взнос; **for a small ~** за небольшо́е вознагражде́ние.

feeble [ˈfiːbl] *adj* хи́лый (хил); (*joke*) сла́бый.

feeble-minded [ˈfiːblˈmaɪndɪd] *adj* слабоу́мный.

feed [fiːd] (*pt, pp* **fed**) *n* (*feeding*) кормле́ние; (*fodder*) корм*; (*on printer*) загру́зка* ◆ *vt* корми́ть* (накорми́ть* *perf*); **to ~ sth into sth** (*data, information*) загружа́ть (загрузи́ть* *perf*) что-н во что-н; (*material*) подава́ть* (пода́ть* *perf*) что-н во что-н

▸ **feed back** *vt* (*results*) подава́ть* (пода́ть* *perf*) обра́тно

▸ **feed on** *vt fus* пита́ться *(impf) +instr*.

feedback [ˈfiːdbæk] *n* (*response*) обра́тная связь *f*; (*from person*) о́тзыв.

feeding bottle [ˈfiːdɪŋ-] *n* (*BRIT*) буты́лочка* (*для кормле́ния младе́нца*).

feel [fiːl] (*pt, pp* **felt**) *n* ощуще́ние ◆ *vt* (*touch*) тро́гать (потро́гать *perf*); (*experience*) чу́вствовать *(impf)*; (*think, believe*): **to ~ (that)** счита́ть *(impf)* (, что); **to get the ~ of sth** осва́иваться (осво́иться *perf*) с чем-н; **I ~ that you ought to do it** я счита́ю, что Вы должны́ э́то сде́лать; **he ~s hungry** он го́лоден; **she ~s cold** ей хо́лодно; **to ~ lonely/better** чу́вствовать *(impf)* себя́ одино́ким/лу́чше; **I don't ~ well** я пло́хо себя́ чу́вствую; **he ~s sorry for me** ему́ меня́ жа́лко *or* жаль; **the material ~s soft/like velvet** э́тот материа́л на о́щупь мя́гкий/как ба́рхат; **it ~s colder here** здесь холодне́е; **I ~ like ...** (*want*) мне хо́чется ...; **I'm still ~ing my way** я всё ещё осва́иваюсь *or* присма́триваюсь

▸ **feel about** *vi*: **to ~ about for sth** иска́ть *(impf)* что-н на о́щупь; **to ~ about** *or* **around in one's pocket for** ша́рить (поша́рить *perf*) в карма́не в по́исках *+gen*

▸ **feel around** *vi* = **feel about**.

feeler [ˈfiːləʳ] *n* (*of insect*) у́сик, щу́пальце*;

to put out a ~ *or* **~s** (*fig*) зонди́ровать (прозонди́ровать *perf*) по́чву.
feeling ['fi:lɪŋ] *n* (*emotion, impression*) чу́вство; (*physical sensation*) ощуще́ние; **~s ran high** стра́сти разгоре́лись; **what are your ~s about the matter?** каково́ Ва́ше отноше́ние к э́тому вопро́су?; **I have a ~ that ...** у меня́ тако́е ощуще́ние, что ...; **my ~ is that ...** по-моему́ мне́нию ...; **to hurt sb's ~s** задева́ть (заде́ть* *perf*) чьи-н чу́вства.
fee-paying ['fi:peɪɪŋ] *adj*: **~ school** пла́тная шко́ла; **~ student** студе́нт, пла́тящий за обуче́ние.
feet [fi:t] *npl of* **foot**.
feign [feɪn] *vt* (*injury, interest*) симули́ровать (*impf/perf*).
feigned [feɪnd] *adj* притво́рный* (притво́рен).
feint [feɪnt] *n* (*of paper*) лино́вка; **a pad of narrow ~** блокно́т в у́зкую лине́йку.
felicitous [fɪ'lɪsɪtəs] *adj* уда́чный* (уда́чен).
feline ['fi:laɪn] *adj* коша́чий*.
fell [fɛl] *pt of* **fall** ◆ *vt* вали́ть (свали́ть *perf*) ◆ *n* (*BRIT*) *гора́, холм и́ли боло́то в назва́ниях* ◆ *adj*: **in one ~ swoop** одни́м ма́хом; **the ~s** *npl* (*moorland*) боло́тистая ме́стность *fsg*.
fellow ['fɛləu] *n* (*man*) па́рень *m*; (*comrade*) това́рищ; (*of learned society*) действи́тельный член; (*of university*) член сове́та ◆ *cpd*: **their ~ prisoners/students** их сока́мерники/соку́рсники; **his ~ workers** его́ това́рищи по рабо́те.
fellow citizens *npl* согра́ждане* *mpl*.
fellow countryman *irreg n* соотече́ственник.
fellow men *npl* бли́жние *pl adj*.
fellowship ['fɛləuʃɪp] *n* (*comradeship*) содру́жество; (*society*) чле́нство; (*SCOL*) стипе́ндия аспира́нта (*зва́ние чле́на сове́та колле́джа и́ли нау́чного о́бщества*).
fell-walking ['fɛlwɔ:kɪŋ] *n* (*BRIT*) *хожде́ние по гора́м, бола́тистой ме́стности итп*.
felon ['fɛlən] *n* (*LAW*) уголо́вный престу́пник.
felony ['fɛlənɪ] *n* (*LAW*) уголо́вное преступле́ние.
felt [fɛlt] *pt, pp of* **feel** ◆ *n* (*fabric*) фетр.
felt-tip pen ['fɛlttɪp-] *n* флома́стер.
female ['fi:meɪl] *n* (*also pej*) са́мка ◆ *adj* (*sex, character, profession*) же́нский*; (*child*) же́нского по́ла; (*ELEC*) охва́тывающий; **~ suffrage** избира́тельное пра́во для же́нщин; **male and ~ students** студе́нты и студе́нтки.
female impersonator *n* (*THEAT*) *актёр, игра́ющий* же́нщин*.
Femidom® ['fɛmɪdɔm] *n* фемидо́м (*же́нский презервати́в*).
feminine ['fɛmɪnɪn] *adj* (*clothes, behaviour*) же́нственный* (же́нственен); (*LING*) же́нского ро́да ◆ *n* (*LING*) же́нский* род.
femininity [fɛmɪ'nɪnɪtɪ] *n* же́нственность *f*.
feminism ['fɛmɪnɪzəm] *n* фемини́зм.
feminist ['fɛmɪnɪst] *n* фемини́ст(ка).
fen [fɛn] (*BRIT*) *n* (*marsh*) боло́то; **the F~s** *ни́зкая боло́тистая ме́стность в Ке́ймбредшире и Ли́нкольншире*.
fence [fɛns] *n* (*barrier*) забо́р, и́згородь *f*; (*SPORT*) препя́тствие ◆ *vt* (*also*: **~ in**) огора́живать (огороди́ть* *perf*) ◆ *vi* (*SPORT*) фехтова́ть (*impf*); **to sit on the ~** (*fig*) занима́ть (*impf*) выжида́тельную пози́цию в спо́ре.
fencing ['fɛnsɪŋ] *n* (*SPORT*) фехтова́ние.
fend [fɛnd] *vi*: **to ~ for o.s.** забо́титься* (позабо́титься* *perf*) о себе́
▸ **fend off** *vt* отража́ть (отрази́ть* *perf*).
fender ['fɛndəʳ] *n* (*of fireplace*) ками́нная решётка*; (*on boat*) кра́нец*; (*US*: *of car*) крыло́*.
fennel ['fɛnl] *n* фе́нхель *m* обыкнове́нный, сла́дкий* укро́п*.
ferment [*n* 'fə:mɛnt, *vi* fə'mɛnt] *n* (*unrest*) броже́ние ◆ *vi* броди́ть* (*impf*).
fermentation [fə:mɛn'teɪʃən] *n* броже́ние.
fern [fə:n] *n* па́поротник.
ferocious [fə'rəuʃəs] *adj* (*animal*) свире́пый (свире́п); (*behaviour*) ди́кий* (дик); (*competition, opposition, criticism*) жесто́кий* (жесто́к); (*heat*) ужа́сный* (ужа́сен).
ferocity [fə'rɔsɪtɪ] *n* жесто́кость *f*; (*of opposition*) я́рость *f*; **the ~ of the sun** невыноси́мое пе́кло.
ferret ['fɛrɪt] *n* хорёк*
▸ **ferret about** *vi* ша́рить (*impf*)
▸ **ferret around** *vi* = **ferret about**
▸ **ferret out** *vt* выве́дывать (вы́ведать *perf*).
ferry ['fɛrɪ] *n* (*also*: **~boat**) паро́м ◆ *vt* перевози́ть* (перевезти́* *perf*); **to ~ sth/sb across** *or* **over** переправля́ть (перепра́вить *perf*) что-н/кого́-н.
ferryman ['fɛrɪmən] *irreg n* паро́мщик.
fertile ['fə:taɪl] *adj* (*land, soil*) плодоро́дный* (плодоро́ден); (*imagination*) бога́тый (бога́т); (*woman*) спосо́бная к зача́тию; **~ period** плодотво́рный пери́од.
fertility [fə'tɪlɪtɪ] *n* (*see adj*) плодоро́дие; бога́тство; спосо́бность *f* к зача́тию.
fertility drug *n* препара́т от беспло́дия.
fertilization [fə:tɪlaɪ'zeɪʃən] *n* (*of egg*) оплодотворе́ние.
fertilize ['fə:tɪlaɪz] *vt* (*land*) удобря́ть (удо́брить *perf*); (*egg*) оплодотворя́ть (оплодотвори́ть *perf*); (*plant*) опыля́ть (опыли́ть *perf*).
fertilizer ['fə:tɪlaɪzəʳ] *n* удобре́ние.
fervent ['fə:vənt] *adj* (*admirer, belief*) пы́лкий*.
fervour ['fə:vəʳ] (*US* **fervor**) *n* пыл*.
fester ['fɛstəʳ] *vi* (*wound*) гнои́ться (загнои́ться *perf*); (*insult, row*) разраста́ться

* marks translations which have irregular inflections. The Russian-English side of the dictionary gives inflectional information.

(разрости́сь* *perf*).
festival ['fɛstɪvəl] *n* (*REL*) пра́здник; (*ART, MUS*) фестива́ль *m*.
festive ['fɛstɪv] *adj* (*mood, atmosphere*) пра́здничный* (пра́здничен); **the ~ season** (*BRIT*) свя́тки* *pl*.
festivities [fɛs'tɪvɪtɪz] *npl* пра́зднества *ntpl*.
festoon [fɛs'tu:n] *vt*: **to ~ with** украша́ть (укра́сить* *perf*) *+instr*.
fetch [fɛtʃ] *vt* (*object*) приноси́ть* (принести́* *perf*); (*person*) приводи́ть* (привести́* *perf*); (*by transport*) привози́ть* (привезти́* *perf*); **would you ~ me a jug of water please?** принеси́те мне, пожа́луйста, кувши́н воды́; **how much did the book ~?** ско́лько Вы вы́ручили за кни́гу?; **his pictures ~ very high prices** его́ карти́ны продаю́тся по высо́ким це́нам
▸ **fetch up** *vi* (*BRIT*) оказа́ться* *(perf)*.
fetching ['fɛtʃɪŋ] *adj* преле́стный* (преле́стен).
fête [feɪt] *n* благотвори́тельный пра́здник-база́р.
fetid ['fɛtɪd] *adj* воню́чий*.
fetish ['fɛtɪʃ] *n* (*also fig*) фети́ш*.
fetter ['fɛtəʳ] *vt* (*person*) зако́вывать (закова́ть *perf*); (*horse*) спу́тывать (спу́тать *perf*); (*fig*) ско́вывать (скова́ть *perf*).
fetters ['fɛtəz] *npl* (*also fig*) око́вы *pl*.
fettle ['fɛtl] *n* (*BRIT*): **in fine ~** (*person*) в прекра́сной фо́рме.
fetus ['fi:təs] *n* (*US*) = **foetus**.
feud [fju:d] *n* вражда́ ◆ *vi* враждова́ть *(impf)*; **a family ~** фами́льная вражда́.
feudal ['fju:dl] *adj* феода́льный.
feudalism ['fju:dlɪzəm] *n* феодали́зм.
fever ['fi:vəʳ] *n* (*temperature*) жар; (*disease*) лихора́дка*; **he has a ~** у него́ жар.
feverish ['fi:vərɪʃ] *adj* (*also fig*) лихора́дочный* (лихора́дочен); (*person*: *with excitement*) возбуждённый* (возбуждён); **he is ~** у него́ жар, его́ лихора́дит.
few [fju:] *adj* (*not many*) немно́гие; (*several*): **a ~** (*number*) не́сколько *+gen*; (*some*) не́которые *pl adj* ◆ *pron*: **(a) ~** немно́гие *pl adj*; **a ~ more** ещё не́сколько; **for a ~ days** на не́сколько дней; **with a ~ of them** с не́которыми из них; **they were ~** их бы́ло ма́ло *or* немно́го; **~ succeed** немно́гим удаётся; **very ~ survive** о́чень немно́гие выжива́ют; **I know a ~** я зна́ю не́скольких; **a good ~** дово́льно мно́гие; **quite a ~** дово́льно мно́го; **in the next ~ days** в ближа́йшие не́сколько дней; **in the past ~ days** за после́дние не́сколько дней; **every ~ days/months** че́рез ка́ждые не́сколько дней/ме́сяцев.
fewer ['fju:əʳ] *adj* ме́ньше *+gen*; **they are ~** их ме́ньше; **there are ~ buses on Sundays** по воскресе́ньям хо́дит ме́ньше авто́бусов.
fewest ['fju:ɪst] *adj* ме́ньше всего́ *+gen*.
FFA *n abbr* = *Future Farmers of America*.
FH *n abbr* (*BRIT*) = **fire hydrant**.
FHA *n abbr* (*US*) = *Federal Housing Administration*.
fiancé [fɪ'ɑ̃:ŋseɪ] *n* жени́х*.
fiancée [fɪ'ɑ̃:ŋseɪ] *n* неве́ста.
fiasco [fɪ'æskəu] *n* фиа́ско *nt ind*.
fib [fɪb] *n* враньё *nt no pl*; **to tell ~s** привира́ть (приврáть* *perf*); **a few small ~s don't hurt** немно́жко приврáть не повреди́т.
fibre ['faɪbəʳ] (*US* **fiber**) *n* волокно́*; (*dietary*) клетча́тка.
fibreboard ['faɪbəbɔ:d] (*US* **fiberboard**) *n* фи́бровый карто́н*.
fibreglass ['faɪbəglɑ:s] (*US* **fiberglass**) *n* стекловолокно́.
fibrositis [faɪbrə'saɪtɪs] *n* фибро́з.
FICA *n abbr* (*US*) = *Federal Insurance Contributions Act*.
fickle ['fɪkl] *adj* непостоя́нный* (непостоя́нен).
fiction ['fɪkʃən] *n* (*LITERATURE*) худо́жественная литерату́ра; (*invention*) вы́мысел*; (*lie*) вы́думка*.
fictional ['fɪkʃənl] *adj* (*character, event*) вы́мышленный (вы́мышлен); (*relating to fiction*) беллетристи́ческий.
fictionalize ['fɪkʃnəlaɪz] *vt* беллетризи́ровать *(impf/perf)*.
fictitious [fɪk'tɪʃəs] *adj* (*false, invented*) фикти́вный* (фикти́вен); (*character, event*) вы́мышленный* (вы́мышлен).
fiddle ['fɪdl] *n* (*MUS*) скри́пка*; (*swindle*) обма́н ◆ *vt* (*BRIT*: *accounts*) подде́лывать (подде́лать *perf*); **tax ~** махина́ции с нало́гами; **to work a ~** моше́нничать (смоше́нничать *perf*)
▸ **fiddle with** *vt fus* верте́ть* *(impf)* в рука́х.
fiddler ['fɪdləʳ] *n* скрипа́ч*(ка*).
fiddly ['fɪdlɪ] *adj* (*task*) трудновыполни́мый; (*object*) неудо́бный в обраще́нии.
fidelity [fɪ'dɛlɪtɪ] *n* ве́рность *f*; (*accuracy*) то́чность *f*.
fidget ['fɪdʒɪt] *vi* ёрзать *(impf)*.
fidgety ['fɪdʒɪtɪ] *adj* беспоко́йный* (беспоко́ен).
fiduciary [fɪ'dju:ʃɪərɪ] *n* (*LAW*) дове́ренное лицо́*.
field [fi:ld] *n* (*also ELEC, COMPUT*) по́ле; (*SPORT*) по́ле, площа́дка*; (*fig*: *area of interest*) о́бласть* *f* ◆ *cpd* (*study, trip, scientist etc*) полево́й; **the ~** (*competitors, entrants*) уча́стники *mpl* состяза́ния; **they lead the ~** (*COMM*) они́ веду́щие в свое́й о́бласти.
field day *n*: **to have a ~ ~** (*fig*) пра́здновать *(impf)*, торжествова́ть *(impf)*.
field glasses *npl* полево́й бино́кль *msg*.
field hospital *n* полево́й го́спиталь *m*.
field marshal *n* фельдма́ршал.
field work *n* полевы́е иссле́дования *ntpl*; (*GEO*) рабо́та в по́ле.
fiend [fi:nd] *n* злоде́й.
fiendish ['fi:ndɪʃ] *adj* дья́вольский*.

fierce [fɪəs] *adj* (*animal, person, look*) свирéпый; (*fighting*) я́ростный; (*loyalty*) горя́чий* (горя́ч); (*enemy, cold, hatred*) лю́тый* (лют); (*wind, heat, storm*) стрáшный* (стрáшен).
fiery ['faɪərɪ] *adj* (*burning*) жгу́чий*; (*sunset*) óгненный; (*taste*) обжигáющий; (*temperament*) горя́чий* (горя́ч); ~ **red** óгненно-крáсный.
FIFA ['fi:fə] *n abbr* (= *Fédération Internationale de Football Association*) ФИФА.
fifteen [fɪf'ti:n] *n* пятнáдцать*; *see also* **five**.
fifteenth [fɪf'ti:nθ] *adj* пятнáдцатый; *see also* **fifth**.
fifth [fɪfθ] *adj* пя́тый ◆ *n* (*fraction*) пя́тая *f adj*; (*AUT: also:* ~ **gear**) пя́тая скóрость *f*; **he came ~ in the competition** он зáнял пя́тое мéсто в соревновáнии; ~ **form** (*BRIT: SCOL*) пя́тый класс; **I was (the) ~ to arrive** я пришёл пя́тым; **Henry the F~** Гéнрих Пя́тый; **the ~ of July, July the ~** пя́тое ию́ля; **I wrote to him on the ~** я написáл емý пя́того числá.
fifth column *n* пя́тая колóнна.
fiftieth ['fɪftɪɪθ] *adj* пятидеся́тый; *see also* **fifth**.
fifty ['fɪftɪ] *n* пятьдеся́т*; **there are about ~ people here** здесь óколо пяти́десяти человéк; **he'll be ~ (years old) next week** на слéдующей недéле емý бу́дет пятьдеся́т (лет); **he's about ~** емý óколо пяти́десяти; **the Fifties (1950s)** пятидеся́тые гóды; **he is in his fifties** емý за пятьдеся́т лет; **the temperature was in the fifties** температу́ра былá вы́ше пяти́десяти грáдусов; **to do ~ (miles per hour)** (*AUT*) éхать (*impf*) со скóростью пятьдеся́т миль в час.
fifty-fifty ['fɪftɪ'fɪftɪ] *adj* (*deal, split*) рáвный* ◆ *adv* пополáм, пóровну; **to share ~ with sb** дели́ть* (раздели́ть* *perf*) пополáм с кем-н; **to have a ~ chance (of success)** имéть (*impf*) рáвные шáнсы (на успéх).
fig [fɪg] *n* инжи́р*.
fight [faɪt] (*pt, pp* **fought**) *n* дрáка; (*MIL*) бой*; (*campaign, struggle*) борьбá ◆ *vt* (*person*) дрáться* (подрáться* *perf*) с +*instr*; (*MIL*) воевáть* (*impf*) с +*instr*; (*illness, problem, emotion*) борóться* (*impf*) с +*instr*; (*POL: election*) учáствовать (*impf*) в +*prp*; (*LAW: case*) защищáть (*impf*) ◆ *vi* (*people*) дрáться* (*impf*); (*MIL*) воевáть* (*impf*); **to put up a ~** упóрно сопротивля́ться (*impf*); **to ~ one's way through a crowd/the undergrowth** проклáдывать (*impf*) себé дорóгу чéрез толпу́/зáросли; **to ~ with sb** дрáться* (*impf*) с кем-н; **to ~ (for/against)** борóться* (*impf*) (за +*acc*/прóтив +*gen*)
▸ **fight back** *vi* защищáться (защити́ться *perf*); (*SPORT, after illness*) верну́ть (*perf*) себé спорти́вную фóрму ◆ *vt fus* (*tears, fear etc*) сдéрживать (сдержáть* *perf*)
▸ **fight down** *vt* (*urge, emotion*) подавля́ть (подави́ть* *perf*)
▸ **fight off** *vt* (*attacker*) отбивáть (отби́ть* *perf*); (*sleep*) отгоня́ть (отогнáть* *perf*)
▸ **fight out** *vt*: **to ~ it out** отстáивать (отстоя́ть *perf*) чтó-нибудь в борьбé.
fighter ['faɪtəʳ] *n* (*also fig*) борéц*; (*MIL: soldier*) боéц*; (: *plane*) истреби́тель *m*.
fighter pilot *n* лётчик-истреби́тель *m*.
fighting ['faɪtɪŋ] *n* (*battle*) бой*; (*brawl*) дрáка.
figment ['fɪgmənt] *n*: **a ~ of the imagination** плод* воображéния.
figurative ['fɪgjurətɪv] *adj* (*style*) óбразный*; (*sense*) перенóсный.
figure ['fɪgəʳ] *n* (*shape, body, also GEOM*) фигу́ра; (*number*) ци́фра; (*personality*) ли́чность *f* ◆ *vt* (*esp US: think*) считáть (*impf*) ◆ *vi* (*appear*) фигури́ровать (*impf*); **to put a ~ on** назначáть (назнáчить *perf*) цéну +*gen or* на +*acc*; **public ~** извéстная ли́чность
▸ **figure out** *vt* понимáть (поня́ть* *perf*); (*cost*) подсчи́тывать (подсчитáть *perf*).
figurehead ['fɪgəhɛd] *n* (*NAUT*) фигу́ра на носу́ корабля́; (*pej: leader*) номинáльный главá *m*.
figure of speech *n* фигу́ра рéчи.
figure skating *n* фигу́рное катáние.
Fiji (Islands) ['fi:dʒi:-] *n(pl)* Фи́джи *ntpl ind*.
filament ['fɪləmənt] *n* (*ELEC, TECH*) нить *f* накáла; (*BIO*) тычи́ночная нить.
filch [fɪltʃ] *vt* (*inf*) стяну́ть (*perf*).
file [faɪl] *n* (*dossier*) дéло*; (*in cabinet*) картотéка; (*folder*) скоросшивáтель *m*; (: *for loose leaf*) пáпка*; (*COMPUT*) файл; (*row*) колóнна; (*tool*) напи́льник ◆ *vt* (*papers, document*) подшивáть (подши́ть* *perf*); (*in card index*) вноси́ть* (внести́* *perf*); (*LAW: claim*) подавáть* (подáть* *perf*); (*wood, fingernails*) шлифовáть (отшлифовáть *perf*) ◆ *vi*: **to ~ in/out/past** входи́ть* (войти́* *perf*)/выходи́ть* (вы́йти* *perf*)/проходи́ть* (пройти́* *perf*) колóнной; **in single ~** в колóнну по одномý; **to ~ a suit against sb** подавáть* (подáть* *perf*) в суд на когó-н; **to ~ for divorce** подавáть* (подáть* *perf*) на развóд.
filename ['faɪlneɪm] *n* (*COMPUT*) и́мя* *nt* фáйла.
filibuster ['fɪlɪbʌstəʳ] (*esp US: POL*) *n* (*also:* ~**er**) обструкциони́ст ◆ *vi* тормози́ть (*impf*) приня́тие закóна путём обстру́кции.
filing ['faɪlɪŋ] *n* (*ADMIN*) систематизáция.
filing cabinet *n* картотéчный шкаф*, шкаф* с картотéкой.
filing clerk *n* дéлопроизводи́тель *m*.
Filipino [fɪlɪ'pi:nəu] *n* филиппи́нец*(-нка*); (*LING*) филиппи́нский* язы́к*.
fill [fɪl] *vi* (*room, hall*) наполня́ться

* marks translations which have irregular inflections. The Russian-English side of the dictionary gives inflectional information.

(напо́лниться *perf*) ◆ *vt* (*tooth*) пломбирова́ть (запломбирова́ть *perf*); (*vacancy*) заполня́ть (запо́лнить *perf*); (*need*) удовлетворя́ть (удовлетвори́ть *perf*) ◆ *n*: **to eat one's ~** наеда́ться (нае́сться* *perf*); **to ~ (with)** (*container*) наполня́ть (напо́лнить *perf*) (+*instr*); (*space, area*) заполня́ть (запо́лнить *perf*) (+*instr*)

▸ **fill in** *vt* (*cavity, form*) заполня́ть (запо́лнить *perf*); (*time*) корота́ть *(impf)* ◆ *vi*: **to ~ in for sb** замеща́ть *(impf)* кого́-н вре́менно; **to ~ sb in** (*inf*) вводи́ть* (ввести́* *perf*) кого́-н в курс де́ла

▸ **fill out** *vt* (*form, receipt*) заполня́ть (запо́лнить *perf*)

▸ **fill up** *vt* (*container*) наполня́ть (напо́лнить *perf*); (*space*) заполня́ть (запо́лнить *perf*) ◆ *vi* (*AUT*) заправля́ться (запра́виться* *perf*); **~ it up, please** (*AUT*) запра́вьте мне маши́ну, пожа́луйста.

fillet ['fɪlɪt] *n* филе́ *nt ind* ◆ *vt* отделя́ть (отдели́ть *perf*) от косте́й.

fillet steak *n* вы́резка.

filling ['fɪlɪŋ] *n* (*for tooth*) пло́мба; (*of pie*) начи́нка; (*of layer cake*) просло́йка.

filling station *n* запра́вочная ста́нция.

fillip ['fɪlɪp] *n* (*fig*) толчо́к.

filly ['fɪlɪ] *n* молода́я кобы́ла.

film [fɪlm] *n* (*CINEMA*) фи́льм; (*PHOT, COMM*) плёнка*; (*of powder, liquid etc*) то́нкий* слой ◆ *vti* снима́ть (снять *perf*).

film star *n* кинозвезда́* *m/f*.

film strip *n* диафи́льм.

film studio *n* киносту́дия.

Filofax® ['faileufæks] *n записна́я кни́жка и́ли дневни́к.*

filter ['fɪltəʳ] *n* фильтр ◆ *vt* (*liquid*) фильтрова́ть (профильтрова́ть *perf*)

▸ **filter in** *vi* (*news*) проса́чиваться (просочи́ться *perf*)

▸ **filter through** *vi* = **filter in.**

filter coffee *n ко́фе то́нкого помо́ла для кофева́рок с фи́льтром.*

filter lane *n* (*BRIT: AUT*) *полоса́, по кото́рой на́до е́хать, что́бы поверну́ть по указа́нию стре́лки светофо́ра.*

filter tip *n* фильтр (*сигаре́ты*).

filter-tipped ['fɪltə'tɪpt] *adj* с фи́льтром.

filth [fɪlθ] *n* грязь *f*; (*fig: on TV etc*) непристо́йность *f*.

filthy ['fɪlθɪ] *adj* гря́зный* (гря́зен); (*fig*) ме́рзкий* (ме́рзок).

fin [fɪn] *n* (*of fish*) плавни́к*; (*TECH: of rocket*) стабилиза́тор.

final ['faɪnl] *adj* (*last*) после́дний*; (*SPORT*) фина́льный; (*ultimate*) заключи́тельный; (*definitive*) оконча́тельный* ◆ *n* (*SPORT*) фина́л; **~s** *npl* (*SCOL*) выпускны́е экза́мены *mpl*.

final demand *n* (*for bill etc*) оконча́тельное тре́бование.

final dividend *n* оконча́тельный дивиде́нд.

finale [fɪ'nɑːlɪ] *n* фина́л.

finalist ['faɪnəlɪst] *n* финали́ст.

finality [faɪ'nælɪtɪ] *n* оконча́тельность *f*; **to speak with an air of ~** говори́ть *(impf)* то́ном, не допуска́ющим возраже́ния.

finalize ['faɪnəlaɪz] *vt* (*arrangements, plans*) оконча́тельно уточня́ть (уточни́ть *perf*).

finally ['faɪnəlɪ] *adv* (*eventually*) в конце́ концо́в; (*lastly*) наконе́ц; (*irrevocably*) оконча́тельно.

finance [faɪ'næns] *n* фина́нсы *pl* ◆ *vt* (*back, fund*) финанси́ровать *(impf/perf)*; **~s** *npl* (*personal finances*) фина́нсы *pl*.

financial [faɪ'nænʃəl] *adj* (*difficulties, venture*) фина́нсовый; **~ statement** фина́нсовый отчёт.

financially [faɪ'nænʃəlɪ] *adv* в фина́нсовом отноше́нии.

financial management *n* фина́нсовое руково́дство.

financial year *n* фина́нсовый год*.

financier [faɪ'nænsɪəʳ] *n* финанси́ст.

find [faɪnd] (*pt, pp* **found**) *vt* находи́ть* (найти́* *perf*); (*discover*) обнару́живать (обнару́жить *perf*) ◆ *n* нахо́дка*; **to ~ sb at home** застава́ть* (заста́ть* *perf*) кого́-н до́ма; **to ~ sb guilty** (*LAW*) признава́ть* (призна́ть* *perf*) кого́-н вино́вным(-ой)

▸ **find out** *vt* (*fact, truth*) узнава́ть* (узна́ть* *perf*); (*person*) разоблача́ть (разоблачи́ть *perf*) ◆ *vi*: **to ~ out about** узнава́ть* (узна́ть* *perf*) о +*prp*.

findings ['faɪndɪŋz] *npl* (*LAW*) заключе́ние *ntsg*; (*in research*) результа́ты *mpl*.

fine [faɪn] *adj* (*quality, performance etc*) прекра́сный* (прекра́сен); (*hair, features*) то́нкий*; (*sand, powder, detail*) ме́лкий*; (*adjustment*) то́чный* (то́чен) ◆ *adv* (*well*) прекра́сно; (*small*) ме́лко ◆ *n* штраф ◆ *vt* штрафова́ть (оштрафова́ть *perf*); **he's ~** (*not ill*) он чу́вствует себя́ хорошо́; (*without problems*) у него́ всё в поря́дке; **the weather is ~** пого́да хоро́шая; **to cut it ~** (*of time*) оставля́ть (оста́вить* *perf*) сли́шком ма́ло вре́мени; **you're doing ~** у Вас всё в поря́дке.

fine arts *npl* изя́щные иску́сства *nt pl*.

finely ['faɪnlɪ] *adv* (*splendidly*) превосхо́дно; (*chop*) ме́лко; (*adjust: instrument*) то́нко.

fine print *n* напи́санное *or* напеча́танное ме́лким шри́фтом.

finery ['faɪnərɪ] *n* (*dress*) наря́д; (*jewellery*) украше́ния *ntpl*.

finesse [fɪ'nɛs] *n* то́нкость *f*, изя́щество.

fine-tooth comb ['faɪntuːθ-] *n*: **to go through sth with a ~ ~** (*fig*) скрупулёзно изуча́ть (изучи́ть* *perf*) что-н.

finger ['fɪŋgəʳ] *n* па́лец* ◆ *vt* тро́гать (потро́гать *perf*); **little ~** мизи́не́ц*; **index ~** указа́тельный па́лец*.

fingernail ['fɪŋgəneɪl] *n* но́готь* *m* (*на руке́*).

fingerprint ['fɪŋgəprɪnt] *n* отпеча́ток* па́льца ◆ *vt* (*person*) брать* (взять* *perf*) отпеча́тки па́льцев у *+gen*.
fingerstall ['fɪŋgəstɔ:l] *n* напа́льчник.
fingertip ['fɪŋgətɪp] *n* ко́нчик па́льца; **to have sth at one's ~s** (*at one's disposal*) име́ть *(impf)* что-н под руко́й; (*know well*) знать* *(impf)* что-н как свой пять па́льцев.
finicky ['fɪnɪkɪ] *adj* привере́дливый (привере́длив).
finish ['fɪnɪʃ] *n* коне́ц*; (SPORT) фи́ниш; (*polish etc*) отде́лка* ◆ *vt* зака́нчивать (зако́нчить *perf*), конча́ть (ко́нчить *perf*) ◆ *vi* зака́нчиваться (зако́нчиться *perf*); (*person*) зака́нчивать (зако́нчить *perf*); **have you ~ed?** Вы уже́ зако́нчили?; **to ~ doing** конча́ть (ко́нчить *perf*) *+infin*; **he ~ed third** (*in race etc*) он зако́нчил тре́тьим; **to ~ with sth** поко́нчить *(perf)* с чем-н; **she's ~ed with him** у неё с ним всё ко́нчено
▸ **finish off** *vt* (*complete*) зака́нчивать (зако́нчить *perf*); (*kill*) прика́нчивать (прико́нчить *perf*)
▸ **finish up** *vt* (*food*) доеда́ть (дое́сть* *perf*); (*drink*) допива́ть (допи́ть* *perf*) ◆ *vi* (*end up*) конча́ть (ко́нчить *perf*).
finished ['fɪnɪʃt] *adj* (*product*) отде́ланный (отде́лан); (*performance*) отто́ченный (отто́чен); (*inf: tired*) измо́танный (измо́тан).
finishing line ['fɪnɪʃɪŋ-] *n* (SPORT) фи́нишная черта́.
finishing school *n частный же́нский пансио́н.*
finishing touches *npl* после́дние штрихи́* *mpl*.
finite ['faɪnaɪt] *adj* (*time, space*) ограни́ченный* (ограни́чен), коне́чный* (коне́чен); (*verb*) ли́чный.
Finland ['fɪnlənd] *n* Финля́ндия; **Gulf of ~** Фи́нский* зали́в.
Finn [fɪn] *n* финн (фи́нка).
Finnish ['fɪnɪʃ] *adj* фи́нский* ◆ *n* фи́нский* язы́к*.
fiord [fjɔ:d] *n* = **fjord**.
fir [fə:ʳ] *n* ель *f*.
fire ['faɪəʳ] *n* (*flames*) пла́мя* *nt*; (*in hearth*) ого́нь* *m*; (*accidental*) пожа́р; (*bonfire*) костёр* ◆ *vt* (*shoot: gun, cannon etc*) вы́стрелить *(perf)* из *+gen*; (*stimulate: imagination etc*) разжига́ть (разже́чь* *perf*); (*inf: dismiss*) увольня́ть (уво́лить *perf*) ◆ *vi* (*shoot*) вы́стрелить *(perf)*; **the house is on ~** дом* гори́т; **to set ~ to sth, set sth on ~** поджига́ть (подже́чь* *perf*) что-н; **the house is insured against ~** дом* застрахо́ван на слу́чай пожа́ра; **electric ~** электро-обогрева́тель *m*; **to come under ~ (from)** (*fig*) ока́зываться (оказа́ться* *perf*) под обстре́лом (со стороны́ *+gen*); **to be under ~** быть* *(impf)* под обстре́лом; **to ~ a gun** стреля́ть (вы́стрелить *perf*) из пу́шки.
fire alarm *n* пожа́рная сигнализа́ция.
firearm ['faɪərɑ:m] *n* огнестре́льное ору́жие *nt no pl*.
fire brigade *n* пожа́рная кома́нда.
fire chief *n* нача́льник пожа́рной кома́нды.
fire department *n* (US) = **fire brigade**.
fire door *n* пожа́рная дверь* *f*.
fire drill *n* пожа́рное уче́ние.
fire engine *n* пожа́рная маши́на.
fire escape *n* пожа́рная ле́стница.
fire-extinguisher ['faɪərɪk'stɪŋgwɪʃəʳ] *n* огнетуши́тель *m*.
fireguard ['faɪəgɑ:d] *n* (BRIT) ками́нная решётка*.
fire hazard *n*: **that's a ~ ~** э́то огнеопа́сно.
fire hydrant *n* пожа́рный насо́с.
fire insurance *n* страхова́ние на слу́чай пожа́ра.
fireman ['faɪəmən] *irreg n* пожа́рный *m adj*, пожа́рник.
fireplace ['faɪəpleɪs] *n* ками́н.
fireplug ['faɪəplʌg] *n* (US) = **fire hydrant**.
fire practice *n* = **fire drill**.
fireproof ['faɪəpru:f] *adj* (*objects*) несгора́емый; (*materials*) огнеупо́рный*.
fire regulations *npl* пра́вила *ntpl* пожа́рной безопа́сности.
fire screen *n* (*decorative*) ками́нный экра́н; (*for protection*) противопожа́рное огражде́ние.
fireside ['faɪəsaɪd] *n*: **by the ~** (*indoors*) у ками́на.
fire station *n* пожа́рное депо́ *nt ind*.
firewood ['faɪəwud] *n* дрова́ *pl*.
fireworks ['faɪəwə:ks] *npl* фейерве́рк *msg*; (*display*) фейерве́рк *msg*, салю́т *msg*.
firing line ['faɪərɪŋ-] *n* ли́ния огня́; **to be in the ~ ~** (*fig*) находи́ться* *(impf)* на ли́нии огня́.
firing squad *n* расстре́льная кома́нда.
firm [fə:m] *adj* (*ground, decision, faith*) твёрдый* (твёрд); (*mattress*) жёсткий*; (*grasp, body, muscles*) кре́пкий* (кре́пок); (*offer*) оконча́тельный* (оконча́телен) ◆ *n* фи́рма; **to be a ~ believer in sth** твёрдо ве́рить *(impf)* во что-н.
firmly ['fə:mlɪ] *adv* (*believe, stand*) твёрдо; (*grasp, shake hands*) кре́пко.
firmness ['fə:mnɪs] *n* (*of ground, decision, faith*) твёрдость *f*; (*of mattress*) жёсткость *f*; (*of grip, hold*) кре́пость *f*.
first [fə:st] *adj* пе́рвый ◆ *adv* (*before all others*) пе́рвый; (*before other things*) снача́ла; (*when listing reasons etc*) во-пе́рвых; (*for the first time*) впервы́е ◆ *n* (*person: in race*) пе́рвый(-ая) *m(f) adj*; (AUT: *also:* **~ gear**)

пéрвая скóрость *f*; (*BRIT*: *SCOL*: ***degree***) диплóм пéрвой стéпени; **the ~ of January** пéрвое январá; **at ~** сначáла; **~ of all** прéжде всегó; **in the ~ instance** в пéрвую óчередь; **I'll do it ~ thing (tomorrow)** я сдéлаю э́то зáвтра в пéрвую óчередь; **from the very ~** с сáмого начáла; *see also* **fifth**.
first aid *n* пéрвая пóмощь *f*.
first-aid kit [fə:st'eɪd-] *n* пакéт пéрвой пóмощи.
first-class ['fə:st'klɑ:s] *adj* пéрвого клáсса; (***excellent***) первоклáссный* ◆ *adv* пéрвым клáссом.
first-hand ['fə:st'hænd] *adj* (***experience, knowledge***) ли́чный; **a ~ account** расскáз очеви́дца.
first lady *n* (*US*) пéрвая лéди *f ind*; **the ~ ~ of jazz** королéва джáза.
firstly ['fə:stlɪ] *adv* во-пéрвых.
first name *n* и́мя* *nt*.
first night *n* (*THEAT*) премьéра.
first-rate ['fə:st'reɪt] *adj* первоклáссный*; (***liar***) отмéнный.
first-time buyer ['fə:sttaɪm-] *n человéк, впервы́е покупáющий дом и́ли квартúру*.
fir tree *n* ель *f*.
FIS *n abbr* (*BRIT*: = ***Family Income Supplement***) дополнéние к семéйному дохóду (*посóбие для малоимýщих*).
fiscal ['fɪskl] *adj* фискáльный; **~ year** фискáльный *or* финáнсовый год.
fish [fɪʃ] *n inv* ры́ба ◆ *vt* (***river, area***) лови́ть* (*impf*) ры́бу в *+prp* ◆ *vi* (***commercially***) занимáться (*impf*) рыболóвством; (***as sport, hobby***) занимáться (*impf*) ры́бной лóвлей; **to go ~ing** ходи́ть*/идти́* (пойти́* *perf*) на рыбáлку
▸ **fish out** *vt* (***from water***) вы́уживать (вы́удить* *perf*); (***from box etc***) вытáскивать (вы́тащить *perf*).
fishbone ['fɪʃbəun] *n* ры́бья кость* *f*.
fish cake *n* ры́бная котлéта.
fisherman ['fɪʃəmən] *irreg n* рыбáк*.
fishery ['fɪʃərɪ] *n* (***fishing ground***) ры́бные местá *ntpl*; (***fish farm***) рыбовóдческое хозя́йство.
fish factory *n* (*BRIT*) рыбозавóд.
fish farm *n* рыбовóдческая фéрма.
fish fingers *npl* (*BRIT*) ры́бные пáлочки* *fpl*.
fish hook *n* рыболóвный крючóк*.
fishing boat ['fɪʃɪŋ-] *n* рыболóвное сýдно*.
fishing line *n* (***on rod***) лéса*.
fishing net *n* рыболóвная сеть *f*.
fishing rod *n* ýдочка*.
fishing tackle *n* рыболóвная снáсть *f*.
fish market *n* ры́бный ры́нок*.
fishmonger ['fɪʃmʌŋgəʳ] *n* (***esp BRIT***) торгóвец* ры́бой.
fishmonger's (shop) ['fɪʃmʌŋgəz-] *n* (***esp BRIT***) ры́бный магази́н.
fish slice *n* (*BRIT*) *лопáточка для переворáчивания ры́бы на сковородé*.
fish sticks *npl* (*US*) = **fish fingers**.
fishy ['fɪʃɪ] *adj* (*inf*: ***tale, story etc***) сомни́тельный.
fission ['fɪʃən] *n* расщеплéние; **atomic** *or* **nuclear ~** áтомное *or* я́дерное расщеплéние.
fissure ['fɪʃəʳ] *n* (***in rock***) расщéлина; (***in ground***) щель* *f*, трéщина.
fist [fɪst] *n* кулáк*.
fistfight ['fɪstfaɪt] *n* дрáка, кулáчный бой*.
fit [fɪt] *adj* (***suitable***) пригóдный* (пригóден); (***healthy***) в хорóшей фóрме ◆ *vt* (***be the right size for***) быть* (*impf*) впóру *+dat*, подходи́ть* (подойти́* *perf*) по размéру *+dat*; (***adjust to the right size***) подгоня́ть (подогнáть* *perf*); (: ***clothes***) примеря́ть (примéрить *perf*); (***match***: ***facts, description***) соотвéтствовать (*impf*) *+dat*; (***put in***: ***kitchen etc***) устанáвливать (установи́ть* *perf*); (***equip***) оборýдовать (*impf*); (***suit***: ***person***) подходи́ть (подойти́* *perf*) *+dat* ◆ *vi* (***clothes***) подходи́ть* (подойти́* *perf*) по размéру, быть* (*impf*) впóру; (***parts***) подходи́ть* (подойти́* *perf*) ◆ *n* (*MED*) припáдок*; (***of coughing, giggles***) при́ступ; **~ to do** (***ready***) готóвый (готóв) *+infin*; **~ to keep** пригóдный (пригóден) для хранéния; **~ for** (***suitable for***) пригóдный (пригóден) для *+gen*; **to keep ~** сохраня́ть (*impf*) фóрму; **~ for work** гóдный (гóден) к рабóте; **she's not ~ to be a teacher** рабóта учи́теля ей не подхóдит; **do as you think** *or* **see ~** дéлайте так, как Вы считáете нýжным; **the suit ~s her** костю́м сиди́т на ней хорошó; **to ~ into** входи́ть* (войти́* *perf*) в *+acc*; **a ~ of anger** при́ступ гнéва; **a ~ of pride** поры́в гóрдости; **he had a ~** (*MED*) у негó был припáдок; **he nearly had a ~ when he learned about it** (*fig*: *inf*) егó чуть удáр не хвати́л когдá он об э́том узнáл; **this dress is a good ~** э́то плáтье хорошó сиди́т; **by ~s and starts** уры́вками
▸ **fit in** *vi* (***person, object***) впи́сываться (вписáться* *perf*) ◆ *vt* (***fig***: ***appointment, visitor***) находи́ть* (найти́* *perf*) врéмя для *+gen*; **to ~ in with sb's plans** совпадáть (совпáсть* *perf*) с чьи́ми-н плáнами.
fitful ['fɪtful] *adj* (***sleep***) преры́вистый (преры́вист).
fitment ['fɪtmənt] *n* (***in room, cabin***) предмéт обстанóвки, оборýдование.
fitness ['fɪtnɪs] *n* (*MED*) состоя́ние здорóвья.
fitted carpet ['fɪtɪd-] *n* ковровóе покры́тие.
fitted cupboards *npl* встрóенные шкáфы *mpl*.
fitted kitchen *n* (*BRIT*) пóлностью оборýдованная кýхня.
fitter ['fɪtəʳ] *n* (***of machinery***) механик; (***of equipment***) устанóвщик.
fitting ['fɪtɪŋ] *adj* (***thanks***) надлежáщий* ◆ *n* (***of dress***) примéрка*; (***of piece of equipment***) устанóвка; **~s** *npl* (***in building***) обстанóвка *fsg*.
fitting room *n* (***in shop***) примéрочная *f adj*.

five [faɪv] *n* пять*; **she is ~ (years) old** ей пять лет; **they live at number 5/at 5 Green Street** они́ живу́т в до́ме но́мер 5/в до́ме но́мер 5 по Зелёной у́лице; **there are ~ of us** нас пя́теро; **all ~ of them came** все пя́теро пришли́; **about ~** о́коло пяти́; **the book costs ~ pounds** кни́га сто́ит пять фу́нтов; **~ and a half/quarter** пять с полови́ной/и одна́ че́тверть; **it's ~ (o'clock)** сейча́с пять часо́в; **to divide sth into ~** дели́ть (раздели́ть *perf*) что-н на пять; **they are sold in ~s** они́ продаю́тся по пять.
five-day week ['faɪvdeɪ-] *n* пятидне́вная рабо́чая неде́ля.
fiver ['faɪvə'] *n* (*inf*: *money*: BRIT) пять фу́нтов; (: US) пять до́лларов.
fix [fɪks] *vt* (*sort out, arrange*: *amount*) устана́вливать (установи́ть* *perf*); (: *date*) назнача́ть (назна́чить *perf*); (*mend*) нала́живать (нала́дить* *perf*); (*inf*: *meal, drink*) организова́ть (*impf/perf*); (: *game etc*) подстра́ивать (подстро́ить *perf*) ◆ *n* (*inf*): **to be in a ~** быть* (*impf*) в тру́дном положе́нии; **to ~ sth to** (*attach*) прикрепля́ть (прикрепи́ть *perf*) что-н к +*dat*; **to ~ one's eyes on** остана́вливать (останови́ть* *perf*) глаза́ на +*prp*; **to ~ one's attention on** сосредото́чивать (сосредото́чить *perf*) внима́ние на +*prp*; **the fight was a ~** (*inf*) исхо́д поеди́нка был предрешён
▸ **fix up** *vt* (*meeting*) устра́ивать (устро́ить *perf*); **to ~ sb up with sth** устра́ивать (устро́ить *perf*) кому́-н что-н.
fixation [fɪk'seɪʃən] *n* помеша́тельство; (*fig*): **she has a ~ about cleanliness** чистота́ – её пу́нктик.
fixative ['fɪksətɪv] *n* фиксати́в.
fixed [fɪkst] *adj* (*price*) твёрдый*; (*amount*) устано́вленный; (*ideas*) навя́зчивый; (*smile*) засты́вший*; **there's a ~ charge** существу́ет устано́вленная пла́та; **how are you ~ for money?** как у тебя́ с деньга́ми?
fixed assets *npl* недви́жимое иму́щество *ntsg*.
fixed charge *n* (COMM) постоя́нные изде́ржки* *pl*.
fixed-price contract [['fikstprais-]] *n* контра́кт с фикси́рованной цено́й.
fixture ['fɪkstʃə'] *n* (*fitting*) обору́дование; (SPORT) назна́ченный матч.
fizz [fɪz] *vi* (*drink*) шипе́ть (*impf*).
fizzle out ['fɪzl-] *vi* (*event*) ока́нчиваться (око́нчиться *perf*) неуда́чей; (*interest*) угаса́ть (уга́снуть* *perf*); (*plan*) прова́ливаться (провали́ться *perf*).
fizzy ['fɪzɪ] *adj* (*drink*) шипу́чий*, газиро́ванный.
fjord [fjɔ:d] *n* фьорд, фио́рд.
FL *abbr* (US: POST) = *Florida*.
flabbergasted ['flæbəgɑ:stɪd] *adj* изумлённый (изумлён).
flabby ['flæbɪ] *adj* дря́блый*.
flag [flæg] *n* флаг; (*for signalling*) флажо́к*; (*also*: **~stone**) ка́менная плита́* ◆ *vi* (*person*) выдыха́ться (вы́дохнуться *perf*); (*spirits*) пропада́ть* (пропа́сть* *perf*); **~ of convenience** "удо́бный" флаг (*пла́вание под кото́рым явля́ется осо́бенно вы́годным*); **to ~ down** (*taxi, car etc*) остана́вливать (останови́ть* *perf*).
flagging ['flægɪŋ] *adj*: **~ spirits** упа́док ду́ха.
flagon ['flægən] *n* буты́ль *f*; (*for cider, wine*) кувши́н.
flagpole ['flægpəul] *n* флагшто́к.
flagrant ['fleɪgrənt] *adj* (*injustice*) вопию́щий*.
flagship ['flægʃɪp] *n* (*also fig*) фла́гман.
flagstone ['flægstəun] *n* ка́менная плита́.
flag stop *n* (US: *for bus*) остано́вка* по тре́бованию.
flair [flɛə'] *n* (*style*) стиль *m*; (*talent*): **a ~ for** скло́нность *f* к +*dat*; **political ~** полити́ческий* тала́нт.
flak [flæk] *n* (MIL) зени́тная артилле́рия; (*inf*: *criticism*) нахлобу́чка*.
flake [fleɪk] *n* (*of snow, soap powder, cereal*) хло́пья* *pl*; (*of rust, paint*) слой ◆ *vi* (*also*: **~ off**: *enamel*) лупи́ться (облупи́ться *perf*); (: *paint*) тре́скаться (потре́скаться *perf*); (*skin*) шелуши́ться (*impf*)
▸ **flake out** *vi* (*inf*: *person*) отключа́ться (отключи́ться *perf*).
flaky ['fleɪkɪ] *adj* (*paintwork*) облу́пленный; (*skin*) шелуша́щийся.
flaky pastry *n* слоёное те́сто.
flamboyant [flæm'bɔɪənt] *adj* (*dress, design*) бро́ский* (бро́сок); (*person*) колори́тный* (колори́тен).
flame [fleɪm] *n* (*of fire*) пла́мя* *nt*; **to burst into ~s** вспы́хнуть (*perf*); **to be in ~s** пыла́ть (*impf*); **an old ~** (*inf*) ста́рая страсть.
flaming ['fleɪmɪ[mg]] *adj* (*inf*) дья́вольский*.
flamingo [flə'mɪŋgəu] *n* флами́нго *m ind*.
flammable ['flæməbl] *adj* легко́ воспламеня́ющийся.
flan [flæn] *n* (BRIT) откры́тый кру́глый пиро́г*.
Flanders ['flɑ:ndəz] *n* Фла́ндрия.
flange [flændʒ] *n* кро́мка*.
flank [flæŋk] *n* (*of animal*) бок*; (*of army*) фланг ◆ *vt* окаймля́ть (*impf*); **~ed by** ме́жду +*instr*.
flannel ['flænl] *n* (*fabric*) флане́ль *f*; (BRIT: *also*: **face ~**) махро́вая салфе́тка для лица́; **~s** *npl* (*trousers*) флане́левые брю́ки; **to give sb some ~** (BRIT: *inf*) моро́чить (*impf*) кому́-н го́лову.
flannelette [flænə'lɛt] *n* ба́йка.
flap [flæp] *n* (*of envelope*) отворо́т; (*of pocket*) кла́пан; (*of jacket*) пола́* ◆ *vt* (*arms*) маха́ть*

* marks translations which have irregular inflections. The Russian-English side of the dictionary gives inflectional information

(impf) *+instr*; (**wings**) хлóпать *(impf)* *+instr* ◆ *vi* (*sail, flag*) колыхáться* *(impf)*; (*inf: also:* **be in a** ~) волновáться *(impf)*.
flapjack [ˈflæpdʒæk] *n* (*US: pancake*) олáдья*; (*BRIT: biscuit*) овсяное печéнье*.
flare [flɛəʳ] *n* (*signal*) сигнáльная ракéта; (*in skirt etc*) клёш
▸ **flare up** *vi* (*fire*) вспыхивать (вспыхнуть *perf*) ярким плáменем; (*fig: person, fighting, trouble*) вспыхивать (вспыхнуть *perf*).
flared [ˈflɛəd] *adj*: ~ **trousers** брюки-клёш; ~ **skirt** юбка-клёш.
flash [flæʃ] *n* (*of light, also PHOT*) вспышка*; (*also:* **news** ~) "мóлния"; (*US: torch*) фонáрик ◆ *vt* (*light*) (внезáпно) освещáть (осветить* *perf*); (*send: news, message*) посылáть (послáть* *perf*) мóлнией; (*look*) метáть* (метнýть *perf*) ◆ *vi* (*lightning, light, eyes*) сверкáть (сверкнýть *perf*); (*light on ambulance etc*) мигáть *(impf)*; **in a** ~ мгновéнно; **quick as a** ~ с быстротóй мóлнии; ~ **of inspiration** порыв вдохновéния; **to ~ one's headlights** сигнáлить (просигнáлить *perf*); **to ~ a smile at sb** улыбáться (улыбнýться *perf*) мимохóдом комý-н; **the thought ~ed through his mind** у негó промелькнýла мысль; **to ~ by** *or* **past** (*person*) мчáться (промчáться *perf*) мимо *+gen*.
flashback [ˈflæʃbæk] *n* (*CINEMA*) ретроспективный кадр.
flashbulb [ˈflæʃbʌlb] *n* фотовспышка*, лáмпа-вспышка*.
flash card *n* (*SCOL*) *кáрточка со слóвом или бýквой, испóльзуемая при обучéнии чтéнию.*
flashcube [ˈflæʃkjuːb] *n* фотовспышка.
flasher [ˈflæʃəʳ] *n* (*AUT*) указáтель *m* поворóта; (*inf: man*) эксгибиционист.
flashlight [ˈflæʃlaɪt] *n* фонáрь* *m*, прожéктор.
flash point *n* (*fig*): **to be at ~ ~** находиться* *(impf)* на грáни взрыва.
flashy [ˈflæʃɪ] *adj* (*pej*) кричáщий*.
flask [flɑːsk] *n* (*bottle*) фляжка*; (*CHEM*) кóлба; (*also:* **vacuum** ~) тéрмос.
flat [flæt] *adj* (*surface*) плóский*; (*tyre*) спýщенный; (*battery*) сéвший; (*beer*) выдохшийся; (*refusal, denial*) категорический*; (*MUS: note*) бемóльный; (*voice*) однотóнный; (*rate, fee*) единый (един) ◆ *n* (*BRIT: apartment*) квартира; (*AUT: also:* ~ **tyre**) спýщенная шина; (*MUS*) бемóль *m*; **to work ~ out** выклáдываться *(impf)* пóлностью, рабóтать *(impf)* на изнóс; ~ **rate of pay** единая стáвка.
flat-footed [ˈflætˈfutɪd] *adj*: **he is** ~ у негó плоскостóпие.
flatly [ˈflætlɪ] *adv* (*deny*) нáчисто; (*refuse*) наотрéз.
flatmate [ˈflætmeɪt] *n* (*BRIT*) сосéд*(ка*) по квартире.
flatness [ˈflætnɪs] *n* (*of land*) рóвность *f*.
flat-screen [ˈflætskriːn] *adj*: ~ **TV set** телевизор с плóским экрáном.
flatten [ˈflætn] *vt* (*also:* ~ **out**) вырáвнивать (выровнять *perf*); (*building*) сносить* (снести* *perf*); (*crop*) побивáть (побить* *perf*); (*city*) сравнять *(perf)* с землёй; (*fig: inf: person*) разбивáть (разбить* *perf*) в пух и прах; **to ~ o.s. against a wall/door** *etc* плóтно прижимáться (прижáться* *perf*) к стенé/двéри *etc*.
flatter [ˈflætəʳ] *vt* льстить* (польстить* *perf*) *+dat*.
flatterer [ˈflætərəʳ] *n* льстéц*.
flattering [ˈflætərɪŋ] *adj* (*comment*) лéстный* (лéстен); (*clothes*): **that dress is very** ~ это плáтье скрывáет все недостáтки.
flattery [ˈflætərɪ] *n* лесть *f*.
flatulence [ˈflætjuləns] *n* (*MED*) метеоризм.
flaunt [flɔːnt] *vt* щеголять *(impf)* *+instr*.
flavour [ˈfleɪvəʳ] (*US* **flavor**) *vt* (*soups etc*) приправлять (приправить* *perf*) ◆ *n* (*of food, drink*) вкус; (*of ice-cream etc*) сорт*; (*fig*): **music with an African** ~ мýзыка с африкáнскими мотивами *or* в африкáнском стиле; **strawberry-~ed** с клубничным привкусом; **to give** *or* **add ~ to** придавáть* (придáть* *perf*) вкус *+dat*.
flavouring [ˈfleɪvərɪŋ] *n* ароматическое веществó.
flaw [flɔː] *n* (*in argument, character*) недостáток*, изъян; (*in cloth, glass*) дефéкт.
flawless [ˈflɔːlɪs] *adj* безупрéчный*.
flax [flæks] *n* лён*.
flaxen [ˈflæksən] *adj* (*hair*) льнянóй.
flea [fliː] *n* блохá*.
flea market *n* барахóлка*.
fleck [flɛk] *n* (*mark*) крáпинка* ◆ *vt*: **to ~ (with)** забрызгивать *(perf)* (*+instr*); **brown ~ed with white** коричневый в бéлую крáпинку.
fled [flɛd] *pt, pp of* **flee**.
fledg(e)ling [ˈflɛdʒlɪŋ] *n* (оперившийся) птенéц*.
flee [fliː] (*pt, pp* **fled**) *vt* (*danger, famine*) бежáть* *(impf)* от *+gen*; (*country*) бежáть* *(impf/perf)* из *+gen* ◆ *vi* (*refugees, escapees*) спасáться *(impf)* бéгством.
fleece [fliːs] *n* (*sheep's coat*) рунó*; (*sheep's wool*) овéчья шерсть *f* ◆ *vt* (*inf: cheat*) обирáть (обобрáть* *perf*).
fleecy [ˈfliːsɪ] *adj* пушистый.
fleet [fliːt] *n* (*of ships*) флот*; (*of lorries, cars*) парк.
fleeting [ˈfliːtɪŋ] *adj* мимолётный*.
Flemish [ˈflɛmɪʃ] *adj* фламáндский* ◆ *n* (*LING*) фламáндский* язык*; **the** ~ *npl* (*GEO*) Фламáндцы* *mpl*.
flesh [flɛʃ] *n* (*ANAT*) плоть *f*; (*skin*) тéло; (*of fruit*) мякоть *f*
▸ **flesh out** *vt* излагáть (изложить* *perf*) во всех детáлях.
flesh wound [-wuːnd] *n* повéрхностная рáна.

flew [flu:] *pt of* **fly**.
flex [flɛks] *n* ги́бкий* шнур* ◆ *vt* (*leg, muscles*) размина́ть (размя́ть* *perf*).
flexibility [flɛksɪ'bɪlɪtɪ] *n* ги́бкость *f*.
flexible ['flɛksəbl] *adj* ги́бкий*.
flexitime ['flɛksɪtaɪm] *n* ги́бкий* гра́фик (*рабо́чего дня*).
flick [flɪk] *n* щелчо́к* ◆ *vt* (*with finger*) сма́хивать (смахну́ть *perf*); (*ash*) стря́хивать (стряхну́ть *perf*); (*towel, whip*) хлестну́ть (*perf*) *+instr*; (*switch*) щёлкнуть (*perf*) *+instr*; **~s** *npl* (*inf*) кино́шка *fsg*
▸ **flick through** *vt fus* просма́тривать (просмотре́ть *perf*).
flicker ['flɪkə^r] *vi* (*light, flame*) мерца́ть (*impf*); (*eyelids*) трепета́ть (*impf*) ◆ *n* (*of light*) мерца́ние; (*of pain, fear*) вспы́шка*; (*of suspicion, doubt*) тень *f*; (*of interest, hope*) про́блеск; (*of eyelid*) трепета́ние.
flick knife *n* (*BRIT*) кно́почный нож.
flier ['flaɪə^r] *n* (*pilot*) лётчик.
flight [flaɪt] *n* полёт; (*escape*) бе́гство; (*of steps*) пролёт (*ле́стницы*); **to take ~** обраща́ться (обрати́ться* *perf*) в бе́гство; **to put to ~** обраща́ть (обрати́ть* *perf*) в бе́гство.
flight attendant *n* (*US*) стюа́рд(е́сса).
flight crew *n* экипа́ж самолёта.
flight deck *n* (*AVIAT*) каби́на экипа́жа; (*NAUT*) *взлётно-поса́дочная полоса́ на па́лубе*.
flight path *n* (*of plane*) курс полёта; (*of rocket*) траекто́рия полёта.
flight recorder *n* "чёрный я́щик".
flimsy ['flɪmzɪ] *adj* (*shoes, clothes*) лёгкий*; (*building, structure*) непро́чный*; (*excuse, evidence*) сла́бый*.
flinch [flɪntʃ] *vi* (*in pain, shock*) вздра́гивать (вздро́гнуть *perf*); **to ~ from** (*unpleasant duty*) уклоня́ться (уклони́ться* *perf*) от *+gen*.
fling [flɪŋ] (*pt, pp* **flung**) *vt* (*throw*) швыря́ть (швырну́ть *perf*) ◆ *n* (*love affair*) рома́н; **to ~ one's arms around sb's neck** обнима́ть (обня́ть* *perf*) кого́-н за ше́ю; **to ~ o.s.** (*move quickly*) кида́ться (ки́нуться *perf*), броса́ться (бро́ситься* *perf*).
flint [flɪnt] *n* креме́нь* *m*.
flip [flɪp] *vt* (*switch*) щёлкать (щёлкнуть *perf*) *+instr*; (*coin*) подбра́сывать (подбро́сить* *perf*) щелчко́м; (*US*: *pancake*) подбра́сывать (подбро́сить* *perf*) ◆ *vi*: **to ~ for sth** (*US*) броса́ть (бро́сить* *perf*) моне́ту
▸ **flip through** *vt fus* просма́тривать (просмотре́ть *perf*).
flippant ['flɪpənt] *adj* несерьёзный*.
flipper ['flɪpə^r] *n* (*of seal etc*) плавни́к*; (*for swimming*) ласт*.
flip side *n* оборо́т.
flirt [flə:t] *vi* (*with person*) флиртова́ть (*impf*), заи́грывать (*impf*); (*with idea*) заи́грывать (*impf*) ◆ *n* коке́тка*, люби́тель(ница) *m(f)* пофлиртова́ть.
flirtation [flə:'teɪʃən] *n* флирт.
flit [flɪt] *vi* (*birds*) перелета́ть (перелете́ть* *perf*); (*butterfly*) порха́ть (*impf*); (*expression, smile*) мелька́ть (*impf*).
float [fləut] *n* (*for fishing*) поплаво́к*; (*for swimming*) *пенопла́стовая доска́ для обуча́ющихся пла́вать*; (*lorry*) *укра́шенная платфо́рма на колёсах в пра́здничной проце́ссии*; (*money*) разме́нные де́ньги *pl* ◆ *vi* (*object*: *on water*) пла́вать (*impf*), держа́ться (*impf*) на пове́рхности; (*swimmer*) плы́ть* (*impf*); (*sound, smell, cloud*) плыть* (*impf*); (*paper*) лета́ть (*impf*); (*COMM*: *currency*) свобо́дно колеба́ться* (*impf*) ◆ *vt* (*idea, plan*) пуска́ть (пусти́ть* *perf*) в ход; **to ~ currency** вводи́ть* (ввести́* *perf*) пла́вающий валю́тный курс; **to ~ a company** выпуска́ть (вы́пустить* *perf*) а́кции компа́нии че́рез би́ржу
▸ **float around** *vi* (*idea, rumour*) носи́ться* (*impf*) в во́здухе; (*person, object*) пла́вать (*impf*).
flock [flɔk] *n* (*of sheep*) ста́до; (*of birds*) ста́я; (*REL*) па́ства ◆ *vi*: **to ~ to** (*place, event*) стека́ться (стёчься *perf*) в *+prp*.
floe [fləu] *n* (*also: ice ~*) плаву́чая льди́на.
flog [flɔg] *vt* (*whip*) сечь* (вы́сечь* *perf*); (*inf*: *sell*) сплавля́ть (спла́вить* *perf*).
flood [flʌd] *n* (*of water*) наводне́ние; (*of letters, imports etc*) пото́к ◆ *vt* (*subj*: *water*) залива́ть (зали́ть* *perf*); (: *people*) наводня́ть (наводни́ть *perf*); (*AUT*: *carburettor*) наполня́ть (напо́лнить *perf*) ◆ *vi* (*place*) наполня́ться (напо́лниться *perf*) водо́й; (*people, goods*): **to ~ into** хлы́нуть (*perf*) в/на *+acc*; **the river is in ~** река́ вы́шла из берего́в; **to ~ the market with** (*COMM*) наводня́ть (наводни́ть *perf*) ры́нок *+instr*.
flooding ['flʌdɪŋ] *n* наводне́ние.
floodlight ['flʌdlaɪt] *n* проже́ктор* ◆ *vt* (*area*) освеща́ть (освети́ть* *perf*) проже́ктором.
floodlit ['flʌdlɪt] *pt, pp of* **floodlight** ◆ *adj* освещённый проже́ктором.
flood tide *n* прили́в.
flood water *n* па́водковые во́ды *fpl*.
floor [flɔ:^r] *n* (*of room*) пол*; (*storey*) эта́ж*; (*of sea, valley*) дно* ◆ *vt* (*subj*: *blow*) вали́ть* (повали́ть* *perf*) на́ пол, сбива́ть (сбить* *perf*) с ног; (: *question, remark*) сража́ть (срази́ть* *perf*); **on the ~** на полу́; **ground** *or* *(US)* **first ~** пе́рвый эта́ж*; **first** *or* *(US)* **second ~** второ́й эта́ж*; **top ~** после́дний* эта́ж*; **to take the ~** (*fig*) брать* (взять* *perf*) сло́во; **to have the ~** (*speaker*) получа́ть (получи́ть *perf*) сло́во.

* marks translations which have irregular inflections. The Russian-English side of the dictionary gives inflectional information.

floorboard ['flɔ:bɔ:d] *n* полови́ца.
flooring ['flɔ:rɪŋ] *n* (*floor*) пол*; (*material to make floor*) насти́л; (*covering*) насти́лка поло́в.
floor lamp *n* (*US*) торше́р.
floor show *n* (*in nightclub*) развлека́тельная програ́мма.
floorwalker ['flɔ:wɔ:kəʳ] *n* (*esp US*) дежу́рный администра́тор магази́на.
floozy ['flu:zɪ] *n* (*inf*) шлю́ха.
flop [flɔp] *n* (*failure*) прова́л ◆ *vi* (*fail*) прова́ливаться (провали́ться* *perf*); (*fall*: *into chair, onto floor etc*) шлёпаться (шлёпнуться *perf*).
floppy ['flɔpɪ] *adj* свиса́ющий, отви́слый ◆ *n* (*also:* ~ **disk**) ги́бкий* диск, диске́та, фло́ппи-диск; ~ **hat** шля́па с отви́слыми поля́ми.
flora ['flɔ:rə] *n* фло́ра.
floral ['flɔ:rl] *adj* (*pattern*) цвети́стый.
Florence ['flɔrəns] *n* Флоре́нция.
Florentine ['flɔrəntaɪn] *adj* флоренти́йский*.
florid ['flɔrɪd] *adj* (*style*) цвети́стый; (*complexion*) кра́сный*.
florist ['flɔrɪst] *n* торго́вец* цвета́ми; (*female*) цвето́чница.
florist's (shop) ['flɔrɪsts-] *n* цвето́чный магази́н.
flotation [fləu'teɪʃən] *n* (*of shares*) свобо́дная прода́жа; (*of company*) распрода́жа а́кций компа́нии.
flotsam ['flɔtsəm] *n* (*also:* ~ **and jetsam**: *rubbish*) му́сор; (: *people*) бродя́ги *pl*.
flounce [flauns] *n* (*frill*) обо́рка*
▸ **flounce out** *vi*: **she ~d out of the room** она́ бро́силась вон из ко́мнаты.
flounder ['flaundəʳ] *vi* (*in water*) бара́хтаться (*impf*); (*fig*) спотыка́ться (*impf*), пу́таться (*impf*) ◆ *n* (*ZOOL*) ка́мбала.
flour ['flauəʳ] *n* мука́.
flourish ['flʌrɪʃ] *vi* (*business*) процвета́ть (*impf*); (*plant*) пы́шно расти́* (*impf*) ◆ *vt* (*document, handkerchief*) разма́хивать (*impf*) +*instr* ◆ *n* (*in writing*) завиту́шка; (*bold gesture*): **with a** ~ демонстрати́вно.
flourishing ['flʌrɪʃɪŋ] *adj* (*company, trade*) процвета́ющий.
flout [flaut] *vt* (*law, rules*) пренебрега́ть (пренебре́чь* *perf*).
flow [fləu] *n* (*of blood, river*) тече́ние; (*ELEC*) пото́к; (*of traffic, orders, information*) пото́к; (*of tide*) прили́в ◆ *vi* течь* (*impf*); (*clothes, hair*) ниспада́ть (*impf*), па́дать (*impf*).
flow chart *n* блок-схе́ма.
flow diagram *n* = **flow chart**.
flower ['flauəʳ] *n* цвето́к* ◆ *vi* (*plant, tree*) цвести́* (*impf*); **~s** цветы́; **in** ~ в цвету́.
flowerbed ['flauəbed] *n* клу́мба.
flowerpot ['flauəpɔt] *n* цвето́чный горшо́к*.
flowery ['flauərɪ] *adj* (*perfume*) цвето́чный (*pattern, speech*) цвети́стый.
flown [fləun] *pp of* **fly**.
flu [flu:] *n* (*MED*) грипп*.
fluctuate ['flʌktjueɪt] *vi* (*price, rate, temperature*) колеба́ться* (*impf*); (*opinions, attitudes*) меня́ться (*impf*).
fluctuation [flʌktju'eɪʃən] *n*: ~ **(in)** колеба́ние (в +*prp*).
flue [flu:] *n* дымохо́д.
fluency ['flu:ənsɪ] *n* бе́глость *f*; **his ~ in Russian** его́ бе́глость в ру́сском языке́.
fluent ['flu:ənt] *adj* (*linguist*) бе́гло говоря́щий; (*speech, writing etc*) бе́глый, пла́вный*; **he's a ~ speaker** он о́чень красноречи́в; **he's a ~ reader** он бы́стро чита́ет; **he speaks ~ Russian, he's ~ in Russian** он свобо́дно *or* бе́гло говори́т по-ру́сски.
fluently ['flu:əntlɪ] *adv* (*speak*) бе́гло; (*read, write*) свобо́дно.
fluff [flʌf] *n* (*on jacket, carpet*) ворс; (*fur, down*) пух* ◆ *vt* (*inf*: *do badly*: *lines*) спу́тывать (спу́тать *perf*; (: *exam*) зава́ливать (завали́ть* *perf*); (*also:* ~ **out**: *hair*) взбива́ть (взби́ть* *perf*); (: *feathers*) распуша́ть (распуши́ть *perf*).
fluffy ['flʌfɪ] *adj* пуши́стый; ~ **toy** мя́гкая игру́шка*.
fluid ['flu:ɪd] *adj* (*movement*) теку́чий*; (*situation, arrangement*) переме́нчивый (переме́нчив); (*opinion*) неусто́йчивый (неусто́йчив) ◆ *n* жи́дкость *f*.
fluid ounce *n* (*BRIT*: = *0.028l; 0.05 pints*) жи́дкая у́нция.
fluke [flu:k] *n* (*inf*) везе́ние.
flummox ['flʌməks] *vt* сбива́ть (сби́ть* *perf*) с то́лку.
flung [flʌŋ] *pt, pp of* **fling**.
flunky ['flʌŋkɪ] *n* лаке́й.
fluorescent [fluə'rɛsnt] *adj* (*dial, light*) флюоресци́рующий; (*paint*) флюоресце́нтный.
fluoride ['fluəraɪd] *n* фтори́д.
fluorine ['fluəri:n] *n* фтор.
flurry ['flʌrɪ] *n* (*of wind*) поры́в; **snow** ~ сне́жный вихрь *m*; **a ~ of activity** бу́рная де́ятельность *f*; **a ~ of excitement** бу́рное возбужде́ние.
flush [flʌʃ] *n* (*on face*) румя́нец*; (*fig*: *of youth, beauty etc*) расцве́т ◆ *vt* (*drains, pipe*) промыва́ть (промы́ть* *perf*) ◆ *vi* (*become red*: *face*) зарде́ться (*perf*) ◆ *adj*: ~ **with** (*level*) на одно́м у́ровне с +*instr*; ~ **against** вплоть до +*gen*; **in the first ~ of youth/freedom** в упое́нии мо́лодостью/свобо́дой; **hot ~es** (*BRIT*: *MED*) прили́вы кро́ви; **to ~ the toilet** спуска́ть (спусти́ть* *perf*) во́ду в туале́те
▸ **flush out** *vt* (*game, birds*) вспу́гивать (вспугну́ть *perf*); (*criminal*) спу́гивать (спугну́ть *perf*).
flushed ['flʌʃt] *adj* раскрасне́вшийся.
fluster ['flʌstəʳ] *vt* (*person*) смуща́ть (смути́ть* *perf*) ◆ *n*: **in a** ~ в смуще́нии.
flustered ['flʌstəd] *adj* смущённый* (смущён).

flute [flu:t] *n* флéйта.
fluted ['flu:tɪd] *adj* рифлёный, гофриро́ванный.
flutter ['flʌtəʳ] *n* (*of wings*) взмах; (*of panic, excitement*) трéпет ◆ *vi* (*bird*) взмáхивать (*impf*) кры́льями; (*person*) метáться* (*impf*).
flux [flʌks] *n*: **in a state of ~** в состоя́нии непреры́вного изменéния.
fly [flaɪ] (*pt* **flew**, *pp* **flown**) *n* (*insect*) мýха; (*on trousers*: *also*: **flies**) шири́нка ◆ *vt* (*plane*) води́ть/вести́* (*impf*); (*passengers, cargo*) перевози́ть* (перевезти́* *perf*); (*distances*) пролетáть (пролетéть *perf*), преодолевáть (преодолéть *perf*); (*kite*) запускáть (запусти́ть* *perf*) ◆ *vi* (*also fig*) летáть/летéть (*impf*); (*escape*) спасáться (спасти́сь* *perf*) бéгством, сбегáть (сбежáть *perf*); (*flag*) развевáться (*impf*); **to ~ open** распáхиваться (распахнýться *perf*); **to ~ off the handle** (*inf*) срывáться (сорвáться *perf*); **pieces of metal went ~ing everywhere** оскóлки метáлла полетéли во все стóроны; **she came ~ing into the room** онá влетéла в комнáту; **her glasses flew off** у неё слетéли очки́
▸ **fly away** *vi* улетáть (улетéть *perf*)
▸ **fly in** *vi* (*plane, person*) прилетáть (прилетéть* *perf*)
▸ **fly off** *vi* = **fly away**
▸ **fly out** *vi* (*person, plane*) вылетáть (вы́лететь* *perf*).
fly-fishing ['flaɪfɪʃɪŋ] *n* ужéние на блеснý.
flying ['flaɪɪŋ] *n* (*activity*) лётное дéло; (*action*) полёт ◆ *adj*: **a ~ visit** крáткий* визи́т; **he doesn't like ~** он не лю́бит летáть самолётом; **with ~ colours** блестя́ще.
flying buttress *n* áрочный контрфóрс.
flying picket *n* *грýппа профсою́зных агитáторов, объезжáющая фáбрики с цéлью убеди́ть рабóчих приня́ть учáстие в забастóвке.*
flying saucer *n* летáющая тарéлка*.
flying squad *n* отря́д бы́строго реаги́рования.
flying start *n*: **to get off to a ~ ~** начинáть (начáть* *perf*) óчень успéшно.
flyleaf ['flaɪli:f] *n* фóрзац.
flyover ['flaɪəuvəʳ] *n* (*BRIT*: *overpass*) эстакáда.
fly-past ['flaɪpɑ:st] *n* воздýшный парáд.
fly sheet *n* (*for tent*) навéс.
flyweight ['flaɪweɪt] *n* боксёр лёгкой весовóй категóрии.
flywheel ['flaɪwi:l] *n* маховóе колесó*.
FM *abbr* (*BRIT*: *MIL*) = **field marshal**; (*RADIO*: = *frequency modulation*) ЧМ= *частóтная модуля́ция*.
FMB *n abbr* (*US*) = *Federal Maritime Board*.
FMCS *n abbr* (*US*: = *Federal Mediation and Conciliation Services*) *слýжба посрéдничества мéжду предпринимáтелями и рабóчими.*
FO *n abbr* (*BRIT*) = **Foreign Office**.
foal [fəul] *n* жеребёнок*.
foam [fəum] *n* пéна; (*also*: **~ rubber**) пенорези́на ◆ *vi* пéниться (*impf*).
fob [fɔb] *n* (*also*: **watch ~**) цепóчка* для кармáнных часóв ◆ *vt*: **to ~ sb off (with sth)** всýчивать (всучи́ть *perf*) *or* подсóвывать (подсýнуть *perf*) комý-н что-н.
f.o.b. *abbr* (*COMM*: = *free on board*) ФОБ= *фрáнко-бóрт*.
foc *abbr* (*COMM*: *BRIT*: = *free of charge*) бесплáтно.
focal point ['fəukl-] *n* средотóчие; (*PHOT*) фокáльная тóчка.
focus ['fəukəs] (*pl* **~es**) *n* (*PHOT*) фóкус; (*of attention, interest, argument*) центр ◆ *vt* (*camera*) настрáивать* (настрóить* *perf*); (*light rays*) фокуси́ровать (сфокуси́ровать *perf*) ◆ *vi*: **to ~ (on)** (*PHOT*) настрáиваться (настрóиться *perf*) (на *+acc*); (*fig*): **to ~ on** сосредотáчиваться (сосредотóчиться *perf*) на *+prp*; **in ~** в фóкусе; **out of ~** не в фóкусе.
fodder ['fɔdəʳ] *n* корм*.
FOE *n abbr* (= *Friends of the Earth*) ОДЗ= *Óбщество "Друзья́ Земли́"*; (*US*: = *Fraternal Order of Eagles*) Брáтский óрден орлóв.
foe [fəu] *n* нéдруг.
foetus ['fi:təs] (*US* **fetus**) *n* плод, зарóдыш.
fog [fɔg] *n* тумáн.
fogbound ['fɔgbaund] *adj* *закры́тый и́ли задержáнный из-за тумáна.*
foggy ['fɔgɪ] *adj* тумáнный* (тумáнен); **it's ~** стóит тумáн.
fog lamp (*US* **fog light**) *n* (*AUT*) фáра для тумáна.
foible ['fɔɪbl] *n* причýда.
foil [fɔɪl] *vt* (*plan*) расстрáивать (расстрóить* *perf*); (*attempt, attack*) срывáть (сорвáть* *perf*) ◆ *n* (*metal*) фольгá; (*FENCING*) рапи́ра; **to act as a ~ to** (*fig*) служи́ть* (*impf*) контрáстом *+dat*.
foist [fɔɪst] *vt*: **to ~ sth on sb** навя́зывать (навязáть* *perf*) что-н комý-н.
fold [fəuld] *n* (*crease*) склáдка*; (: *in paper*) сгиб; (*AGR*) загóн; (*fig*) лóно ◆ *vt* (*clothes, paper*) склáдывать (сложи́ть* *perf*); (*arms*) скрéщивать (скрести́ть* *perf*) ◆ *vi* (*business*) сворáчиваться (свернýться *perf*)
▸ **fold up** *vi* склáдываться (сложи́ться* *perf*); (*business*) сворáчиваться (свернýться *perf*) ◆ *vt* (*object*) склáдывать (сложи́ть* *perf*).
folder ['fəuldəʳ] *n* (*for papers*) пáпка*, скоросшивáтель *m*; (: *binder*) пáпка* (*с металли́ческим зажи́мом*); (*brochure*) брошю́ра.
folding ['fəuldɪŋ] *adj* (*chair, bed*) складнóй.

* marks translations which have irregular inflections. The Russian-English side of the dictionary gives inflectional information.

foliage ['fəulɪdʒ] *n* листва́.
folk [fəuk] *npl* лю́ди *pl*, наро́д* *msg* ◆ *cpd* (*art, music*) наро́дный; **~s** *npl* (*inf: relatives*) бли́зкие *pl adj*.
folklore ['fəuklɔː'] *n* фолькло́р.
folk music *n* наро́дная му́зыка.
folk song *n* наро́дная пе́сня*.
follow ['fɔləu] *vt* (*leader, person*) сле́довать (после́довать *perf*) за *+instr*; (*example, advice*) сле́довать (после́довать *perf*) *+dat*; (*event, story*) следи́ть* (*impf*) за *+instr*; (*route, path*) держа́ться* (*impf*) *+gen*; (*with eyes*) провожа́ть (проводи́ть* *perf*) взгля́дом ◆ *vi* сле́довать (после́довать *perf*); **to ~ in sb's footsteps** идти́* (пойти́* *perf*) по чьим-н стопа́м; **I don't quite ~ you** я не совсе́м Вас понима́ю; **to ~ sb's advice** сле́довать (после́довать *perf*) чьему-н сове́ту; **I left the room, and he ~ed** я вы́шел из ко́мнаты и он после́довал за мно́й; **it ~s that he ...** отсю́да сле́дует, что он ...; **to ~ suit** (*fig*) сле́довать (после́довать *perf*) приме́ру
▸ **follow on** *vi* (*continue*): **to ~ on from** сле́довать (после́довать *perf*) за *+instr*
▸ **follow out** *vt* (*idea, plan*) приводи́ть* (привести́* *perf*) в исполне́ние
▸ **follow through** *vt* = **follow out**
▸ **follow up** *vt* (*letter, offer*) рассма́тривать (рассмотре́ть* *perf*); (*case*) рассле́довать (*impf*).
follower ['fɔləuə'] *n* (*of person*) после́дователь(ница) *m(f)*; (*of belief*) сторо́нник(-ица).
following ['fɔləuɪŋ] *adj* сле́дующий* ◆ *n* (*followers*) сторо́нники *mpl*; **a large ~** мно́го сторо́нников.
follow-up ['fɔləuʌp] *n* продолже́ние ◆ *adj* (*treatment, survey*) после́дующий*.
folly ['fɔlɪ] *n* (*foolishness*) глу́пость *f*; (*building*) *декорати́вное па́рковое сооруже́ние*.
fond [fɔnd] *adj* (*smile, look, parents*) ла́сковый* (ла́сков); (*memory*) прия́тный* (прия́тен); (*hopes, dreams*) тще́тный* (тще́тен); **to be ~ of** люби́ть* (*impf*); **she's ~ of swimming** она́ лю́бит пла́вать.
fondle ['fɔndl] *vt* ласка́ть (*impf*).
fondly ['fɔndlɪ] *adv* (*lovingly*) ла́сково; (*naïvely*) наи́вно; **he ~ believed that ...** он наи́вно ве́рил, что ....
fondness ['fɔndnɪs] *n* любо́вь* *f*; **a special ~ for** осо́бенная любо́вь к *+dat*.
font [fɔnt] *n* (*in church*) купе́ль *f*; (*TYP*) компле́кт (шри́фта).
food [fuːd] *n* еда́, пи́ща.
food chain *n* пищево́й симбио́з.
food mixer *n* ми́ксер.
food poisoning *n* пищево́е отравле́ние.
food processor *n* ку́хонный комба́йн.
food stamp *n* продукто́вый тало́н.
foodstuffs ['fuːdstʌfs] *npl* проду́кты *mpl* пита́ния.
fool [fuːl] *n* (*male*) дура́к*; (*female*) ду́ра; (*CULIN*) *сла́дкое блю́до из сли́вок и фру́ктов* ◆ *vt* (*deceive*) обма́нывать (обману́ть* *perf*), одура́чивать (одура́чить *perf*) ◆ *vi* (*be silly*) дура́читься (*impf*); **to make a ~ of sb** (*ridicule*) выставля́ть (вы́ставить* *perf*) кого́-н на посме́шище; (*trick*) одура́чивать (одура́чить *perf*) кого́-н; **to make a ~ of o.s.** ста́вить* (поста́вить* *perf*) себя́ в глу́пое положе́ние; **you can't ~ me** меня́ не проведёте
▸ **fool about** *vi* (*pej: waste time*) валя́ть (*impf*) дурака́; (*behave foolishly*) дура́читься *perf*
▸ **fool around** *vi* = **fool about**.
foolhardy ['fuːlhɑːdɪ] *adj* безрассу́дный* (безрассу́ден)
foolish ['fuːlɪʃ] *adj* (*stupid*) глу́пый* (глуп); (*rash*) опроме́тчивый (опроме́тчив).
foolishly ['fuːlɪʃlɪ] *adv* (*see adj*) глу́по; опроме́тчиво.
foolishness ['fuːlɪʃnɪs] *n* дура́чество.
foolproof ['fuːlpruːf] *adj* (*plan*) надёжный* (надёжен).
foolscap ['fuːlskæp] *n бума́га форма́та: 34 см x 43 см*.
foot [fut] (*pl* **feet**) *n* (*of person*) нога́*, ступня́; (*of animal*) нога́*; (*of bed*) коне́ц*; (*of cliff*) подно́жие; (*measure*) фут; (*of page, stairs etc*) низ ◆ *vt*: **to ~ the bill** плати́ть* (*perf*); **on ~** пешко́м; **at the ~ of the page/stairs** внизу́ страни́цы/ле́стницы; **to find one's feet** (*fig*) встава́ть* (встать* *perf*) на́ ноги; **to put one's ~ down** (*AUT*) нажима́ть (нажа́ть* *perf*) на педа́ль; (*assert authority*) занима́ть (заня́ть* *perf*) твёрдую пози́цию.
footage ['futɪdʒ] *n* (*CINEMA: material*) ка́дры *mpl*; (*: length*) ≈ метра́ж.
foot-and-mouth [futən'mauθ] *n* (*also:* **~ disease**) я́щур.
football ['futbɔːl] *n* (*ball*) футбо́льный мяч*; (*sport: BRIT*) футбо́л; (*: US*) америка́нский* футбо́л.
footballer ['futbɔːlə'] *n* (*BRIT*) футболи́ст.
football ground *n* футбо́льное по́ле.
football match *n* (*BRIT*) футбо́льный матч.
football player *n* футболи́ст.
foot brake *n* ножно́й то́рмоз*.
footbridge ['futbrɪdʒ] *n* пешехо́дный мост*.
foothills ['futhɪlz] *npl* предго́рья* *ntpl*.
foothold ['futhəuld] *n* опо́ра; (*fig*): **to get a ~** укрепля́ться (укрепи́ться* *perf*), утверди́ться* (*perf*).
footing ['futɪŋ] *n* (*fig: basis, relationship*) осно́ва; **to be on a friendly ~** быть* (*impf*) на дру́жеской ноге́; **to lose one's ~** (*fall*) теря́ть (потеря́ть *perf*) опо́ру; **on an equal ~** на ра́вных (основа́ниях).
footlights ['futlaɪts] *npl* огни́ *mpl* ра́мпы.
footman ['futmən] *irreg n* лаке́й.
footnote ['futnəut] *n* сно́ска*.
footpath ['futpɑːθ] *n* тропи́нка*, доро́жка*; (*in street*) тротуа́р.

footprint ['futprɪnt] *n* след*, отпечáток ногú.
footrest ['futrɛst] *n* скамéечка* для ног.
footsie ['futsɪ] *n*: **to play ~ with sb** толкáть (толкнýть *perf*) нóжкой когó-н.
footsore ['futsɔːʳ] *adj*: **I am ~** у меня́ болят нóги.
footstep ['futstɛp] *n* (*sound*) шаг*; (*footprint*) след*; (*fig*): **to follow in sb's ~s** идтú* (пойтú* *perf*) по чьим-н стопáм.
footwear ['futwɛəʳ] *n* óбувь *f*.
footwork ['futwəːk] *n* фигýры *fpl* (*движéния ног в тáнце*).

KEYWORD

for [fɔːʳ] *prep* ***1*** (*indicating destination, intention*): **the train for London/Paris** пóезд в Лóндон/Парúж; **he left for Rome/work** он уéхал в Рим/на рабóту; **when does the train for Moscow leave?** когдá отправля́ется пóезд на Москвý?; **he went for the paper/the doctor** он пошёл за газéтой/врачóм; **is this for me?** э́то мне *or* для меня́?; **there's a letter for you** Вам письмó; **it's time for lunch/bed** порá обéдать *(impf)*/спать *(impf)*
2 (*indicating purpose*) для *+gen*; **what's it for?** для чегó э́то?; **give it to me – what for?** дáйте э́то мне – зачéм?; **to pray for forgiveness** молúть* *(impf)* о прощéнии; **to pray for peace** молúться* *(impf)* о мúре
3 (*on behalf of, representing*): **to speak for sb** говорúть *(impf)* от лицá когó-н; **MP for Brighton** член *m* парлáмента представля́ющий Брáйтон; **he works for the government** он на госудáрственной слýжбе; **he works for a local firm** он рабóтает в мéстной фúрме; **I'll ask him for you** я спрошý егó от вáшего úмени; **to do sth for sb** (*on behalf of*) дéлать (сдéлать *perf*) что-н за когó-н
4 (*because of*) из-за *+gen*; **for lack of funds** из-за отсýтствия средств; **for this reason** по э́той причúне; **for some reason, for whatever reason** почемý-то; **for fear of being criticized** боя́сь крúтики; **to be famous for sth** быть *(impf)* извéстным чем-н
5 (*with regard to*): **it's cold for July** для ию́ля сейчáс хóлодно; **he's tall for fourteen/for his age** для четы́рнадцати лет/для своегó вóзраста он высóкий; **a gift for languages** спосóбности к языкáм; **for everyone who voted yes, 50 voted no** на кáждый гóлос „за", прихóдится 50 голосóв „прóтив"
6 (*in exchange for, in favour of*) за *+acc*; **I sold it for £5** я продáл э́то за £5; **I'm all for it** я целикóм и пóлностью за э́то
7 (*referring to distance*): **there are roadworks for five miles** дорóжные рабóты на протяжéнии пятú миль; **to stretch for miles** простирáться *(impf)* на мнóго миль; **we walked for miles/for ten miles** мы прошлú мнóго миль/дéсять миль
8 (*referring to time*) на *+acc*; (: *in past*): **he was away for 2 years** он был в отъéзде 2 гóда; **she will be away for a month** онá уезжáет на мéсяц; **can you do it for tomorrow?** Вы мóжете сдéлать э́то на зáвтра; **it hasn't rained for 3 weeks** ужé 3 недéли нé было дождя́; **for hours** часáми
9 (*with infinite clause*): **it is not for me to decide** не мне решáть; **there is still time for you to do it** у Вас ещё éсть врéмя сдéлать э́то; **for this to be possible ...** чтóбы э́то осуществúть ...
10 (*in spite of*) несмотря́ на *+acc*; **for all his complaints** несмотря́ на все егó жáлобы
11 (*in phrases*): **for the first/last time** в пéрвый/послéдний раз; **for the time being** покá
◆ *conj* (*rather formal*) ибо.

f.o.r. *abbr* (COMM: = *free on rail*) фрáнко-вагóн.
forage ['fɔrɪdʒ] *n* корм ◆ *vi*: **to ~ for sth** ры́скать* *(impf)* пóисках чегó-н.
forage cap *n* фурáжка, пилóтка.
foray ['fɔreɪ] *n* (*raid*) набéг.
forbad(e) [fə'bæd] *pt of* **forbid**.
forbearing [fɔː'bɛərɪŋ] *adj* сдéржанный.
forbid [fə'bɪd] (*pt* **forbad(e)**, *pp* **forbidden**) *vt* запрещáть (запретúть* *perf*); **to ~ sb to do** запрещáть (запретúть* *perf*) комý-н *+infin*.
forbidden [fə'bɪdn] *pp of* **forbid** ◆ *adj* (*entry, activity*) запрещённый* (запрещён); (*place*) запрéтный; **it's ~ to ...** запрещенó *+infin* ....
forbidding [fə'bɪdɪŋ] *adj* (*look etc*) неприя́зненный; (*prospect*) мучúтельный* (мучúтелен).
force [fɔːs] *n* (*also* PHYS) сúла; (*influence*) воздéйствие ◆ *vt* (*compel*) заставля́ть (застáвить* *perf*), принуждáть (принýдить* *perf*); (*push*) толкáть (толкнýть *perf*); (*break open*) взлáмывать (взломáть *perf*); **the F~s** *npl* (BRIT: MIL) вооружённые сúлы *fpl*; **in ~** в большóм числé; **to come into ~** вступáть (вступúть* *perf*) в сúлу; **to join ~s** объединя́ть (объединúть *perf*) усúлия; **it's a ~ five wind** сúла вéтра – пять бáллов; **the sales ~** (COMM) торгóвые агéнты; **to ~ o.s. to do** заставля́ть (застáвить* *perf*) себя́ *+infin*; **to ~ sb to do** заставля́ть (застáвить* *perf*) *or* вынуждáть (вы́нудить* *perf*) когó-н *+infin*
▸ **force back** *vt* (*enemy*) отражáть (отразúть* *perf*); (*crowd, tears*) сдéрживать (сдержáть* *perf*)
▸ **force down** *vt* (*food*) есть* (съесть* *perf*) с трудóм.
forced [fɔːst] *adj* (*landing*) вы́нужденный; (*smile*) натя́нутый (натя́нут); **~ labour** принудúтельный труд.

* marks translations which have irregular inflections. The Russian-English side of the dictionary gives inflectional information.

force-feed ['fɔːsfiːd] *vt* насильно кормить* *(impf)*.
forceful ['fɔːsful] *adj* сильный* (силён).
forceps ['fɔːsɛps] *npl* щипцы́ *pl*.
forcible ['fɔːsəbl] *adj* (*action*) насильственный; (*reminder, lesson*) убедительный.
forcibly ['fɔːsəblɪ] *adv* (*remove*) насильно; (*express*) с силой.
ford [fɔːd] *n* (*in river*) брод* ◆ *vt* переходить* (перейти* *perf*) вброд.
fore [fɔː'] *n*: **to come to the ~** выдвигаться (выдвинуться *perf*).
forearm ['fɔːrɑːm] *n* предплечье*.
forebear ['fɔːbɛə'] *n* предок*.
foreboding [fɔː'bəudɪŋ] *n* предчувствие.
forecast ['fɔːkɑːst] (*irreg*: *like* **cast**) *n* прогноз ◆ *vt* (*predict*) предсказывать (предсказать* *perf*).
foreclose [fɔː'kləuz] *vt* (LAW: *also*: **~ on**) лишать (лишить *perf*) прав собственности.
foreclosure [fɔː'kləuʒə'] *n* (COMM) лишение прав собственности.
forecourt ['fɔːkɔːt] *n* (*of garage*) передняя площадка.
forefathers ['fɔːfɑːðəz] *npl* предки* *mpl*.
forefinger ['fɔːfɪŋgə'] *n* указательный палец*.
forefront ['fɔːfrʌnt] *n*: **in** *or* **at the ~ of** (*industry, movement*) в авангарде *+gen*.
forego [fɔː'gəu] (*irreg*: *like* **go**) *vt* поступаться (поступиться* *perf*) *+instr*.
foregoing ['fɔːgəuɪŋ] *adj* предшествующий* ◆ *n*: **the ~** вышеупомянутое *nt adj*.
foregone ['fɔːgɔn] *adj*: **it's a ~ conclusion** это предрешённый исход.
foreground ['fɔːgraund] *n* (*also* COMPUT) передний* план.
forehand ['fɔːhænd] *n* (TENNIS) удар справа.
forehead ['fɔrɪd] *n* лоб*.
foreign ['fɔrɪn] *adj* (*person, language*) иностранный; (*country*) зарубежный; (*trade*) внешний*; (*object*) посторонний*.
foreign body *n* инородное тело.
foreign currency *n* иностранная валюта.
foreigner ['fɔrɪnə'] *n* иностранец*(-нка*).
foreign exchange *n* (*system*) обмен валюты; (*money*) валюта.
foreign-exchange market [fɔrɪnɪks'tʃeɪndʒ-] *n* валютный рынок*.
foreign-exchange rate *n* валютный курс.
foreign investment *n* иностранные капиталовложения *ntpl*.
foreign minister *n* министр иностранных дел.
Foreign Office *n* (BRIT) министерство иностранных дел.
Foreign Secretary *n* (BRIT) министр иностранных дел.
foreleg ['fɔːlɛg] *n* (*of animal*) передняя нога*.
foreman ['fɔːmən] *irreg n* (*in factory, on building site etc*) мастер*; (*of jury*) старшина *m* присяжных.
foremost ['fɔːməust] *adj* (*most important*) наиболее важный* ◆ *adv*: **first and ~** в первую очередь, прежде всего.
forename ['fɔːneɪm] *n* имя* *nt*.
forensic [fə'rɛnsɪk] *adj* (*medicine, test*) судебный*; **~ expert** специалист по судебной медицине.
foreplay ['fɔːpleɪ] *n* возбуждающие ласки *fpl*.
forerunner ['fɔːrʌnə'] *n* предшественник(-ница).
foresee [fɔː'siː] (*irreg*: *like* **see**) *vt* предвидеть* *(impf/perf)*.
foreseeable [fɔː'siːəbl] *adj* предвидимый; **in the ~ future** в обозримом будущем.
foreseen [fɔː'siːn] *pp of* **foresee**.
foreshadow [fɔː'ʃædəu] *vt* (*event*) предзнаменовать *(impf)*.
foreshore ['fɔ'ʃɔː'] *n береговая полоса, затопляемая приливом*.
foreshortened [fɔː'ʃɔːtnd] *adj* (*figure, scene*) в ракурсе.
foresight ['fɔːsaɪt] *n* предусмотрительность *f*.
foreskin ['fɔːskɪn] *n* крайняя плоть *f*.
forest ['fɔrɪst] *n* лес*.
forestall [fɔː'stɔːl] *vt* (*person*) приостанавливать (приостановить* *perf*); (*discussion*) опережать (опередить* *perf*).
forestry ['fɔrɪstrɪ] *n* лесоводство, лесничество.
foretaste ['fɔːteɪst] *n*: **a ~ of** представление о *+prp*.
foretell [fɔː'tɛl] (*irreg*: *like* **tell**) *vt* предсказывать (предсказать* *perf*).
forethought ['fɔːθɔːt] *n* предусмотрительность *f*.
foretold [fɔː'tauld] *pt, pp of* **foretell**.
forever [fə'rɛvə'] *adv* (*for good*) навсегда; (*endlessly*) вечно; **that time has gone ~** то время ушло навсегда; **it will last ~** это будет длиться вечно; **you're ~ finding difficulties** Вы вечно находите трудности.
forewarn [fɔː'wɔːn] *vt* предупреждать (предупредить* *perf*).
foreword ['fɔːwəːd] *n* (*in book*) предисловие.
forfeit ['fɔːfɪt] *n* (*penalty*) штраф ◆ *vt* (*right, friendship etc*) терять (потерять *perf*); (*one's happiness, health*) поплатиться* *(perf)* *+instr*.
forgave [fə'geɪv] *pt of* **forgive**.
forge [fɔːdʒ] *n* кузница ◆ *vt* (*signature, money*) подделывать (подделать *perf*); (*metal*) ковать *(impf)*; **to ~ documents/a will** подделывать (подделать *perf*) документы/завещание
▸ **forge ahead** *vi* (*country, person*) вырываться (вырваться* *perf*) вперёд.
forger ['fɔːdʒə'] *n* (*of documents, paintings*) подделыватель *m*; (*of money*) фальшивомонетчик.
forgery ['fɔːdʒərɪ] *n* подделка*.
forget [fə'gɛt] (*pt* **forgot**, *pp* **forgotten**) *vt* забывать (забыть* *perf*); (*appointment*) забывать (забыть* *perf*) о *+prp* ◆ *vi* забывать

(забы́ть* *perf*); **to ~ o.s.** забы́ться* (*perf*).
forgetful [fəˈgɛtful] *adj* (*person*) забы́вчивый (забы́вчив); **~ of** забы́в о *+prp*.
forgetfulness [fəˈgɛtfulnɪs] *n* забы́вчивость *f*; (*oblivion*) забве́ние.
forget-me-not [fəˈgɛtmɪnɔt] *n* незабу́дка*.
forgive [fəˈgɪv] (*pt* **forgave**, *pp* **forgiven**) *vt* (*pardon*) проща́ть (прости́ть* *perf*) *+dat or +gen*; **to ~ sb for sth** (*excuse*) проща́ть (прости́ть* *perf*) кому́-н *or* кого́-н за что-н; **I forgave him for doing it** я прости́л ему́ *or* его́ за то, что он э́то сде́лал; **~ my ignorance, but ...** прости́те моё неве́жество, но ...; **they could be ~n for thinking that ...** их мо́жно прости́ть за то, что они́ ду́мают, что ....
forgiven [fəˈgɪvn] *pp of* **forgive**.
forgiveness [fəˈgɪvnɪs] *n* проще́ние.
forgiving [fəˈgɪvɪŋ] *adj* великоду́шный* (великоду́шен).
forgo [fɔːˈgəu] *vt* = **forego**.
forgot [fəˈgɔt] *pt of* **forget**.
forgotten [fəˈgɔtn] *pp of* **forget**.
fork [fɔːk] *n* ви́лка*; (*for gardening*) ви́лы *pl*; (*in road*) разви́лка*; (*in railway*) стык; (*in river, tree*) разветвле́ние ◆ *vi* (*road*) разветвля́ться (*impf*)
▸ **fork out** (*inf*) ◆ *vt* выкла́дывать (вы́ложить* *perf*) ◆ *vi* раскоше́ливаться (раскоше́литься *perf*).
forked [fɔːkt] *adj* (*lightning*) зигзагообра́зный.
fork-lift truck [ˈfɔːklɪft-] *n* грузоподъёмник.
forlorn [fəˈlɔːn] *adj* (*person*) несча́стный; (*place*) поки́нутый; (*hope, attempt*) сла́бый.
form [fɔːm] *n* (*type*) вид; (*shape*) фо́рма; (*SCOL*) класс; (*questionnaire*) бланк ◆ *vt* (*make*) образо́вывать (образова́ть *perf*); (*set up: organization, group*) формирова́ть (сформирова́ть *perf*); (*idea, habit*) выраба́тывать (вы́работать *perf*); **in the ~ of** в фо́рме *+gen*; **to be in good ~** (*SPORT, fig*) быть* (*impf*) в хоро́шей фо́рме; **in top ~** в лу́чшей фо́рме; **on ~** в фо́рме; **to ~ part of sth** явля́ться (яви́ться* *perf*) ча́стью чего́-н; **I ~ed a good impression of her** у меня́ создало́сь хоро́шее впечатле́ние о ней.
formal [ˈfɔːməl] *adj* форма́льный; (*statement*) форма́льный* (форма́лен); (*person, behaviour*) церемо́нный* (церемо́нен); (*occasion, dinner*) официа́льный* (официа́лен); (*garden*) англи́йский*; **~ clothes** официа́льная фо́рма оде́жды; **~ dress** (*evening dress*) вече́рняя оде́жда.
formalities [fɔːˈmælɪtɪz] *npl* форма́льности *fpl*.
formality [fɔːˈmælɪtɪ] *n* форма́льность *f*; (*of person, behaviour*) церемо́нность *f*; (*of occasion*) официа́льность *f*.
formalize [ˈfɔːməlaɪz] *vt* (*plan, arrangement*) оформля́ть (офо́рмить* *perf*).
formally [ˈfɔːməlɪ] *adv* форма́льно; (*behave*) церемо́нно; **to be ~ invited** получа́ть (получи́ть* *perf*) официа́льное приглаше́ние.
format [ˈfɔːmæt] *n* (*form, style*) форма́т ◆ *vt* (*COMPUT: disk*) формати́ровать (*impf/perf*).
formation [fɔːˈmeɪʃən] *n* формирова́ние; (*of rocks*) форма́ция; (*of clouds*) скопле́ние.
formative [ˈfɔːmətɪv] *adj*: **in his ~ years** в го́ды формирова́ния его́ хара́ктера.
former [ˈfɔːməʳ] *adj* (*one-time*) бы́вший*; (*earlier*) пре́жний*; **the ~ ... the latter ...** пе́рвый ... после́дний*; **the ~ president** бы́вший* президе́нт.
formerly [ˈfɔːməlɪ] *adv* ра́ньше, до э́того.
form feed *n* (*on printer*) пода́ча страни́ц.
Formica® [fɔːˈmaɪkə] *n* форма́йка (*огнеупо́рная пластма́сса*).
formidable [ˈfɔːmɪdəbl] *adj* (*task*) чрезвыча́йно тру́дный* (тру́ден); (*opponent*) гро́зный* (гро́зен).
formula [ˈfɔːmjulə] (*pl* **~e** *or* **~s**) *n* (*MATH, CHEM*) фо́рмула; (*plan*) схе́ма; **F~ One** (*AUT*) *обозначе́ние го́ночной маши́ны*.
formulae [ˈfɔːmjuliː] *npl of* **formula**.
formulate [ˈfɔːmjuleɪt] *vt* (*plan, strategy*) выраба́тывать (вы́работать *perf*), разраба́тывать (разрабо́тать *perf*); (*opinion, thought*) формули́ровать (сформули́ровать *perf*).
fornicate [ˈfɔːnɪkeɪt] *vi* прелюбоде́йствовать (*impf*).
forsake [fəˈseɪk] (*pt* **forsook**, *pp* **forsaken**) *vt* (*abandon*) покида́ть (поки́нуть *perf*).
forsaken [fəˈseɪkən] *pp of* **forsake**.
forsook [fəˈsuk] *pt of* **forsake**.
fort [fɔːt] *n* кре́пость *f*, форт*; **to hold the ~** (*fig*) стоя́ть (*impf*) на стра́же.
forte [ˈfɔːtɪ] *n* (*strength*) си́льная сторона́.
forth [fɔːθ] *adv* (*out*): **to go ~** идти́* (*impf*) вперёд; **to send ~** посла́ть* (*perf*); **to go back and ~** ходи́ть* (*impf*) взад и вперёд; **to bring ~** вынима́ть (вы́нуть *perf*); **and so ~** и так да́лее.
forthcoming [fɔːθˈkʌmɪŋ] *adj* предстоя́щии; (*person*) общи́тельный; **to be ~** (*help, evidence*) ожида́ться (*impf*), появля́ться (*impf*).
forthright [ˈfɔːθraɪt] *adj* (*condemnation, opposition*) прямо́й.
forthwith [ˈfɔːθˈwɪθ] *adv* то́тчас.
fortieth [ˈfɔːtɪɪθ] *adj* сороково́й*; *see also* **fifth**.
fortification [fɔːtɪfɪˈkeɪʃən] *n* (*MIL*) укрепле́ние.
fortified wine [ˈfɔːtɪfaɪd-] *n* креплёное вино́*.
fortify [ˈfɔːtɪfaɪ] *vt* (*city*) укрепля́ть (укрепи́ть* *perf*); (*person*) придава́ть* (прида́ть* *perf*) си́лы *+dat*.
fortitude [ˈfɔːtɪtjuːd] *n* сто́йкость *f*.
fortnight [ˈfɔːtnaɪt] (*BRIT*) *n* две неде́ли; **it's a ~**

* marks translations which have irregular inflections. The Russian-English side of the dictionary gives inflectional information.

since ... прошло́ две неде́ли с тех пор, как ....
fortnightly ['fɔ:tnaɪtlɪ] *adv* раз в две неде́ли ◆ *adj*: ~ **magazine** журна́л, выходя́щий раз в две неде́ли.
FORTRAN ['fɔ:træn] *n* ФОРТРА́Н.
fortress ['fɔ:trɪs] *n* кре́пость *f*.
fortuitous [fɔ:'tju:ɪtəs] *adj* случа́йный* (случа́ен).
fortunate ['fɔ:tʃənɪt] *adj* (*person*) счастли́вый (счастли́в); (*event*) счастли́вый; **he is/was** ~ ему́ везёт/повезло́; **he is ~ to have** ... ему́ хорошо́, что у него́ есть ...; **it is ~ that** ... уда́чно, что ....
fortunately ['fɔ:tʃənɪtlɪ] *adv* к сча́стью.
fortune ['fɔ:tʃən] *n* (*wealth*) состоя́ние; (*also*: **good** ~) сча́стье, уда́ча; **bad** *or* **ill** ~ несча́стье, неуда́ча; **to make a** ~ нажива́ть (нажи́ть* *perf*) себе́ состоя́ние; **to tell sb's** ~ гада́ть (*impf*) кому́-н, предска́зывать (предсказа́ть* *perf*) чью-н судьбу́.
fortune-teller ['fɔ:tʃəntɛlə'] *n* гада́лка, предсказа́тель(ница) *m(f)*.
forty ['fɔ:tɪ] *n* со́рок*; *see also* **fifty**.
forum ['fɔ:rəm] *n* фо́рум.
forward ['fɔ:wəd] *adv* вперёд ◆ *n* (*SPORT*) напада́ющий*(-ая) *m(f) adj* ◆ *vt* (*letter, parcel*) пересыла́ть (пересла́ть* *perf*); (*career*) продвига́ть (продви́нуть *perf*) ◆ *adj* (*position*) пере́дний*; (*not shy*) де́рзкий* (де́рзок); (*COMM*: *delivery, sales*) заблаговре́менный; **to move** ~ (*progress*) продвига́ться (продви́нуться *perf*); **"please ~"** „перешли́те адреса́ту"; ~ **movement** движе́ние вперёд; ~ **planning** предвари́тельное плани́рование.
forward contract *n* фо́рвардный *or* сро́чный контра́кт.
forward rate *n* *фо́рвардный or сро́чный валю́тный курс, по кото́рому заключа́ется сро́чная валю́тная сде́лка*.
forwards ['fɔ:wədz] *adv* вперёд.
fossil ['fɔsl] *n* окамене́лость *f*, ископа́емое *nt adj*.
fossil fuel *n* окамене́лое то́пливо.
foster ['fɔstə'] *vt* (*child*) брать* (взять* *perf*) на воспита́ние; (*activity*) поощря́ть (*impf*); (*hope*) пита́ть (*impf*); **to ~ an idea** вына́шивать (*impf*) мысль.
foster child *n* приёмный ребёнок*.
foster mother *n* приёмная мать* *f*.
fought [fɔ:t] *pt, pp of* **fight**.
foul [faul] *adj* отврати́тельный* (отврати́телен); (*language*) непристо́йный* (непристо́ен); (*temper*) гневли́вый (гневли́в) ◆ *n* (*SPORT*) наруше́ние ◆ *vt* га́дить* (зага́дить* *perf*); (*SPORT*) наруша́ть (нару́шить *perf*) пра́вила про́тив +*gen*; (*entangle*: *anchor, propeller*) опу́тывать (опу́тать *perf*).
foul play *n* (*LAW*) престу́пные де́йствия *ntpl*: ~ **is not suspected** нет подозре́ний о престу́пных де́йствиях.
found [faund] *pt, pp of* **find** ◆ *vt* (*establish*) осно́вывать (основа́ть *perf*).
foundation [faun'deɪʃən] *n* (*act*) основа́ние; (*base*) осно́ва; (*fig*) осно́ва, усто́и *mpl*; (*organization*) о́бщество, фонд; (*also*: ~ **cream**) крем под макия́ж; **~s** *npl* (*of building*) фунда́мент *msg*; **the rumours are without** ~ слу́хи не име́ют основа́ний; **to lay the ~s** (*fig*) закла́дывать (заложи́ть* *perf*) осно́вы.
foundation stone *n* краеуго́льный ка́мень* *m*.
founder ['faundə'] *n* (*of firm, college*) основа́тель(ница) *m(f)* ◆ *vi* (*ship*) идти́* (пойти́* *perf*) ко дну́.
founder member *n* член-учреди́тель(ница) *m(f)*.
founding fathers ['faundɪŋ-] *npl* (*esp US*) основополо́жники *mpl*.
foundry ['faundrɪ] *n* лите́йная *f adj*, лите́йный цех.
fount [faunt] *n* исто́чник; (*TYP*) компле́кт шри́фта.
fountain ['fauntɪn] *n* фонта́н.
fountain pen *n* черни́льная ру́чка*.
four [fɔ:'] *n* четы́ре*; **on all ~s** на четвере́ньках; *see also* **five**.
four-letter word ['fɔ:lɛtə-] *n* ≈ мат.
four-poster ['fɔ:'pəustə'] *n* (*also*: ~ **bed**) крова́ть *f* с по́логом.
foursome ['fɔ:səm] *n* четвёрка*.
fourteen ['fɔ:'ti:n] *n* четы́рнадцать*; *see also* **five**.
fourteenth ['fɔ:'ti:nθ] *adj* четы́рнадцатый*; *see also* **fifth**.
fourth ['fɔ:θ] *adj* четвёртый ◆ *n* (*AUT*: *also*: ~ **gear**) четвёртая ско́рость *f*; *see also* **fifth**.
four-wheel drive ['fɔ:wi:l-] *n* (*AUT*) внедроо́жник; **with** ~ ~ с приво́дом на четы́ре колеса́.
fowl [faul] *n* пти́ца; (*wild*) дичь *f*.
fox [fɔks] *n* лиса́* ◆ *vt* озада́чивать (озада́чить *perf*).
foxglove ['fɔksglʌv] *n* (*BOT*) наперстя́нка*.
fox-hunting ['fɔkshʌntɪŋ] *n* охо́та на лис.
foxtrot ['fɔkstrɔt] *n* (*dance*) фокстро́т.
foxy ['fɔksɪ] *adj*: ~ **lady** шика́рная же́нщина.
foyer ['fɔɪeɪ] *n* фойе́ *nt ind*.
FPA *n abbr* (*BRIT*: = *Family Planning Association*) *организа́ция, обеспе́чивающая консульта́ции по плани́рованию семьи́*.
Fr. *abbr* (*REL*) = **father, friar**.
fr. *abbr* = *franc*.
fracas ['fræka:] *n* сканда́л.
fraction ['frækʃən] *n* (*portion*) небольша́я часть *f*; (*MATH*) дробь* *f*; **a ~ of a second** до́ля секу́нды.
fractionally ['frækʃnəlɪ] *adv*: ~ **smaller** *etc* незначи́тельно ме́ньше *etc*.
fractious ['frækʃəs] *adj* капри́зный* (капри́зен): **she was** ~ она́ капри́зничала.

fracture ['fræktʃəʳ] *n* (*of bone*) перелóм ◆ *vt* (*bone*) ломáть (сломáть *perf*).
fragile ['frædʒaɪl] *adj* (*object*) хрýпкий* (хрýпок).
fragment ['frægmənt] *n* фрагмéнт; (*of stone, glass*) оскóлок*, облóмок*.
fragmentary ['frægməntərɪ] *adj* (*evidence, knowledge*) отры́вочный* (отры́вочен).
fragrance ['freɪgrəns] *n* благоухáние.
fragrant ['freɪgrənt] *adj* души́стый (души́ст).
frail [freɪl] *adj* (*person*) слáбый* (слаб); (*structure*) хрýпкий* (хрýпок), непрóчный* (непрóчен).
frame [freɪm] *n* (*of building, structure*) каркáс; (*of car, human, animal*) óстов; (*of picture, door, window*) рáма; (*of spectacles*: *also*: **~s**) опрáва ◆ *vt* обрамля́ть (обрáмить* *perf*); (*reply, law, theory*) формули́ровать (сформули́ровать *perf*); **~ of mind** настроéние; **to ~ sb** (*inf*) подстáвить* (*perf*) когó-н.
framework ['freɪmwəːk] *n* (*structure*) каркáс; (*fig*) рáмки *fpl*.
France [frɑːns] *n* Фрáнция.
franchise ['fræntʃaɪz] *n* (POL) прáво гóлоса; (COMM) франши́за.
franchisee [fræntʃaɪ'ziː] *n* держáтель *m* франши́зы.
franchiser ['fræntʃaɪzəʳ] *n* предостави́тель *m* франши́зы.
frank [fræŋk] *adj* (*discussion, person*) откровéнный* (откровéнен); (*look*) откры́тый ◆ *vt* (*letter*) франки́ровать (зафранки́ровать *perf*).
Frankfurt ['fræŋkfəːt] *n* Фрáнкфурт.
frankfurter ['fræŋkfəːtəʳ] *n* соси́ска*.
franking machine ['fræŋkɪŋ-] *n* франкировáльная маши́на.
frankly ['fræŋklɪ] *adv* откровéнно.
frankness ['fræŋknɪs] *n* откровéнность *f*.
frantic ['fræntɪk] *adj* (*distraught*) обезýмевший; (*hectic*) суматóшный*; (*desperate*: *need, desire*) безýмный*; (: *cry*) нéистовый; **we were ~ with worry** мы обезýмели от волнéния.
frantically ['fræntɪklɪ] *adv* отчáянно.
fraternal [frə'təːnl] *adj* брáтский*.
fraternity [frə'təːnɪtɪ] *n* (*feeling*) брáтство; (*club*) содрýжество.
fraternize ['frætənaɪz] *vi* общáться (*impf*).
fraud [frɔːd] *n* (*crime*) мошéнничество; (*person*) мошéнник.
fraudulent ['frɔːdjulənt] *adj* (*scheme, claim*) мошéннический*.
fraught [frɔːt] *adj* (*person*) нéрвный* (нéрвен); (*situation*): **~ with** (*danger, problems*) чревáтый (чревáт) +*instr*.
fray [freɪ] *vi* обтрёпываться (обтрепáться *perf*) ◆ *n* (*battle, fight*): **the ~** бой, дрáка; **tempers were ~ed** все бы́ли на грáни сры́ва; **her nerves were ~ed** у неё бы́ли истрёпаны нéрвы; **to return to the ~** снóва ри́нуться (*perf*) в бой *or* дрáку.
FRB *n abbr* (US: = *Federal Reserve Board*) Федерáльное резéрвное правлéние.
FRCM *n abbr* (BRIT) = *Fellow of the Royal College of Music.*
FRCO *n abbr* (BRIT) = *Fellow of the Royal College of Organists.*
FRCP *n abbr* (BRIT) = *Fellow of the Royal College of Physicians.*
FRCS *n abbr* (BRIT) = *Fellow of the Royal College of Surgeons.*
freak [friːk] *adj* (*event, accident*) стрáнный ◆ *n* (*person*: *in appearance*) урóдец*(-дица), вы́родок* *m/f*; (: *in attitude, behaviour*): **he is a ~** он со стрáнностями; (*pej*: *fanatic*): **she's an aerobics ~** онá помешáлась на аэрóбике
▸ **freak out** *vi* (*inf*: *on drugs*) входи́ть* (войти́* *perf*) в раж.
freakish ['friːkɪʃ] *adj* стрáнный.
freckle ['frɛkl] *n* веснýшка*.
freckled ['frɛkld] *adj* веснýшчатый.
free [friː] *adj* свобóдный* (свобóден); (*costing nothing*) бесплáтный* (бесплáтен) ◆ *vt* (*prisoner etc*) освобождáть (освободи́ть* *perf*), выпускáть (вы́пустить* *perf*) (на свобóду); (*jammed object*) высвобождáть (вы́свободить* *perf*), вытáскивать (вы́тащить *perf*); **to give sb a ~ hand** предоставля́ть (предостáвить* *perf*) комý-н свобóду дéйствий; **~ and easy** непринуждённый; **admission ~** свобóдный вход; **~ (of charge), for ~** бесплáтно; **~ alongside ship** фрáнко вдоль бóрта сýдна; **~ of tax** освобождённый от уплáты налóгов; **~ on rail** фрáнко – железнодорóжный вагóн
free agent *n*: **he's a ~ ~** он сам себé хозя́ин.
freebie ['friːbɪ] *n* (*inf*: *gift*) подáрок*.
freedom ['friːdəm] *n* свобóда.
freedom fighter *n* борéц* за свобóду.
freedom of association *n* свобóда объединéния в ассоциáции.
free enterprise *n* свобóдное предпринимáтельство.
Freefone® ['friːfəun] *n систéма, позволя́ющая звони́ть бесплáтно в определённые организáции.*
free-for-all ['friːfərɔːl] *n* (*fight*) потасóвка.
free gift *n* подáрок*.
freehold ['friːhəuld] *n* (*of property*) пóлное прáво на владéние.
free kick *n* (FOOTBALL) свобóдный удáр.
freelance ['friːlɑːns] *adj* внештáтный, рабóтающий по договорáм.
freelance work *n* рабóта по контрáкту *or*

* marks translations which have irregular inflections. The Russian-English side of the dictionary gives inflectional information.

договорам.
freeloader ['fri:ləudə^r] *n* (*pej*) дармоед(ка*).
freely ['fri:lı] *adv* (*without restriction*) свободно; (*liberally*) обильно; **drugs are ~ available in the city** наркотики можно легко достать в городе.
free-market economy ['fri:'mɑ:kıt-] *n* рыночная экономика.
Freemason ['fri:meısn] *n* масон.
Freemasonry ['fri:meısnrı] *n* масонство.
Freepost® ['fri:pəust] *n* (*BRIT*) бесплатная почта.
free-range ['fri:'reındʒ] *adj*: **~ eggs** *яйца от кур свободно-выгульного содержания*.
free sample *n* бесплатный образец*.
freesia ['fri:zıə] *n* фрезия.
free speech *n* свобода слова.
freestyle ['fri:staıl] *n* (*in swimming*) кроль *m*.
free trade *n* неограниченная беспошлинная торговля.
freeway ['fri:weı] *n* (*US*: *AUT*) скоростная автострада.
freewheel [fri:'wi:l] *vi* (*on bicycle*) катиться* (покатиться* *perf*); (*in car*) идти* (пойти* *perf*) свободным ходом.
free will *n* свобода воли; **of one's own ~ ~** по доброй воле.
freeze [fri:z] (*pt* **froze**, *pp* **frozen**) *vi* (*weather*) холодать (похолодать *perf*); (*liquid, pipe, person*) замерзать (замёрзнуть* *perf*); (*person*: *stop moving*) застывать (застыть* *perf*) ◆ *vt* замораживать (заморозить* *perf*) ◆ *n* (*weather*) заморозки *pl*; (*on arms, wages*) замораживание; **it's freezing** очень холодно
▸ **freeze over** *vi* замерзать (замёрзнуть* *perf*)
▸ **freeze up** *vi* замерзать (замёрзнуть* *perf*).
freeze-dried ['fri:zdraıd] *adj обработанный методом замораживания-высушивания*.
freeze-dry ['fri:zdraı] *vt быстро замораживать и затем высушивать в вакуме*.
freezer ['fri:zə^r] *n* морозильник.
freezing ['fri:zıŋ] *adj*: **~ (cold)** ледяной ◆ *n*: **3 degrees below ~** минус 3 градуса, 3 градуса мороза; **I'm ~** я замёрз.
freezing point *n* температура замерзания.
freight [freıt] *n* фрахт; **~ forward** фрахт уплачиваемый в порту выгрузки; **~ inward** фрахт, уплачиваемый по прибытии.
freight car *n* (*US*) товарный вагон.
freighter ['freıtə^r] *n* (*NAUT*) грузовое судно*; (*AVIAT*) грузовой самолёт.
freight forwarder [-'fɔ:wədə^r] *n* экспедитор.
freight train *n* (*US*) товарный поезд*.
French [frɛntʃ] *adj* французский* ◆ *n* (*LING*) французский* язык*; **the ~** *npl* (*people*) французы *mpl*.
French bean *n* (*BRIT*) стручковая фасоль *f*.
French Canadian *n* франкоязычный(-ая) канадец*(-дка).
French-Canadian [frɛntʃkə'neıdjən] *adj* франко-канадский*.
French dressing *n соус для салата из растительного масла и уксуса*.
French fried potatoes *npl* чипсы *mpl*.
French fries [-fraız] *npl* (*US*) = **French fried potatoes**.
French Guiana [-gaı'ænə] *n* Французская Гвиана.
Frenchman ['frɛntʃmən] *irreg n* француз.
French Riviera *n*: **the ~ ~** Французская Ривьера.
French stick *n* длинный батон.
French window *n* двустворчатое окно до пола.
Frenchwoman ['frɛntʃwumən] *irreg n* француженка*.
frenetic [frə'nɛtık] *adj* лихорадочный* (лихорадочен).
frenzied ['frɛnzıd] *adj* (*person*) бешеный, взбешённый; (*behaviour*) неистовый.
frenzy ['frɛnzı] *n* (*of violence*) бешенство, неистовство; **~ of joy** безумная радость; **~ of excitement** безумное возбуждение; **to drive sb into a ~** доводить* (довести* *perf*) кого-н до бешенства, приводить* (привести* *perf*) кого-н в бешенство; **to be in a ~** быть* (*impf*) в бешенстве.
frequency ['fri:kwənsı] *n* (*also RADIO*) частота*.
frequency modulation *n* частотная модуляция.
frequent [*adj* 'fri:kwənt, *vt* frı'kwɛnt] *adj* частый ◆ *vt* (*pub, restaurant*) посещать (посетить* *perf*).
frequently ['fri:kwəntlı] *adv* (*often*) часто.
fresco ['frɛskəu] *n* фреска*.
fresh [frɛʃ] *adj* свежий* (свеж); (*instructions, approach*) новый* (нов); (*cheeky*: *person*) нахальный* (нахален), фамильярный* (фамильярен); **to make a ~ start** начать* *perf* заново; **~ in one's mind** свежо в памяти.
freshen ['frɛʃən] *vi* (*wind, air*) свежеть (*impf*)
▸ **freshen up** *vi* (*person*) освежаться (освежиться *perf*).
freshener ['frɛʃnə^r] *n*: **skin ~** *лосьон для освежения кожи*; **air ~** освежитель *m* воздуха.
fresher ['frɛʃə^r] *n* (*BRIT*: *inf*) первокурсник.
freshly ['frɛʃlı] *adv*: **~ made** свежеприготовленный; **~ painted** свежепокрашенный.
freshman ['frɛʃmən] *irreg n* (*US*) = **fresher**.
freshness ['frɛʃnıs] *n* свежесть *f*.
freshwater ['frɛʃwɔ:tə^r] *adj* (*lake*) пресный; (*fish*) пресноводный.
fret [frɛt] *vi* волноваться (*impf*).
fretful ['frɛtful] *adj* (*child*) беспокойный*.
Freudian ['frɔıdıən] *adj* фрейдистский; **~ slip** оговорка по Фрейду.
FRG *n abbr* (= *Federal Republic of Germany*) ФРГ= *Федеративная Республика Германии*.

Fri. *abbr* = **Friday**.
friar ['fraɪəʳ] *n* монах.
friction ['frɪkʃən] *n* трение; (*fig*) трения *ntpl*.
friction feed *n* (*on printer*) подача бумаги с помощью валика.
Friday ['fraɪdɪ] *n* пятница; *see also* **Tuesday**.
fridge [frɪdʒ] *n* (BRIT) холодильник.
fridge-freezer ['frɪdʒ'fri:zəʳ] *n* холодильник с большой морозильной камерой.
fried [fraɪd] *pt, pp of* **fry** ◆ *adj* жареный.
friend [frɛnd] *n* (*male*) друг*; (*female*) подруга; **to make ~s with** подружиться (*perf*) с +*instr*.
friendliness ['frɛndlɪnɪs] *n* (*of person*) дружелюбие.
friendly ['frɛndlɪ] *adj* (*person, smile etc*) дружелюбный* (дружелюбен); (*government, country*) дружественный* (дружествен); (*place, restaurant*) приятный* (приятен); (*game, match*) товарищеский* ◆ *n* (*also*: **~ match**) товарищеская встреча; **to be ~ with** дружить* (*impf*) с +*instr*; **to be ~ to sb** относиться* (отнестись* *perf*) к кому-н дружелюбно.
friendly fire *n* огонь* *m* со своих позиций.
friendly society *n* общество *or* касса взаимопомощи.
friendship ['frɛndʃɪp] *n* дружба.
frieze [fri:z] *n* фриз, бордюр.
frigate ['frɪgɪt] *n* фрегат.
fright [fraɪt] *n* испуг; **to take ~** испугаться (*perf*); **she looks a ~** она выглядит как пугало.
frighten ['fraɪtn] *vt* пугать (испугать *or* напугать *perf*)
▸ **frighten away** *vt* (*birds, children etc*) спугивать (спугнуть *perf*)
▸ **frighten off** *vt* = **frighten away**.
frightened ['fraɪtnd] *adj* (*afraid*) испуганный* (испуган); **I am ~** я боюсь; **to be ~ (of)** бояться (*impf*) (+*gen*); **he is ~ by change** его пугают изменения.
frightening ['fraɪtnɪŋ] *adj* (*experience, prospect*) страшный.
frightful ['fraɪtful] *adj* (*dreadful*) кошмарный* (кошмарен), ужасный* (ужасен).
frightfully ['fraɪtfəlɪ] *adv* ужасно; **I'm ~ sorry** мне ужасно стыдно.
frigid ['frɪdʒɪd] *adj* (*woman*) фригидный.
frigidity [frɪ'dʒɪdɪtɪ] *n* фригидность *f*.
frill [frɪl] *n* (*of dress, shirt*) оборка*; **without ~s** (*fig*) без прикрас.
frilly ['frɪlɪ] *adj* с оборками.
fringe [frɪndʒ] *n* (BRIT: *of hair*) чёлка*; (*on shawl, lampshade etc*) бахрома; (*of forest etc*) край*, окраина; (*fig*: *of activity, organization etc*) периферия.
fringe benefits *npl* дополнительные льготы *fpl*.
fringe theatre *n* экспериментальный театр.
Frisbee® ['frɪzbɪ] *n* фрисби *m ind*.
frisk [frɪsk] *vt* (*search*) обыскивать (обыскать* *perf*) ◆ *vi* (*animal*) резвиться (порезвиться *perf*).
frisky ['frɪskɪ] *adj* игривый (игрив).
fritter ['frɪtəʳ] *n* (CULIN) *ломтик чего-нибудь, обжаренный в кипящем масле*
▸ **fritter away** *vt* (*money*) растрачивать (растратить* *perf*) по мелочам; (*time*) попусту терять (потерять *perf*).
frivolity [frɪ'vɔlɪtɪ] *n* легкомыслие.
frivolous ['frɪvələs] *adj* (*conduct, person*) легкомысленный* (легкомыслен); (*object, activity*) пустячный.
frizzy ['frɪzɪ] *adj* (*hair*) курчавый, мелко-вьющийся.
fro [frəu] *adv*: **to and ~** туда-сюда.
frock [frɔk] *n* платье*.
frog [frɔg] *n* лягушка*; **to have a ~ in one's throat** хрипеть* (*impf*).
frogman ['frɔgmən] *irreg n* водолаз, ныряльщик.
frogmarch ['frɔgmɑ:tʃ] *vt* (BRIT): **to ~ sb in/out** втаскивать (втащить *perf*)/вытаскивать (вытащить *perf*) кого-н за руки лицом вниз.
frolic ['frɔlɪk] *vi* (*animals, children*) веселиться (*impf*) ◆ *n* веселье*.

KEYWORD

from [frɔm] *prep* ***1*** (*indicating starting place, origin etc*): **where do you come from?** откуда Вы?; **from London to Glasgow** из Лондона в Глазго; **a letter from my sister** письмо от моей сестры; **a quotation from Dickens** цитата из Диккенса; **to drink from the bottle** пить* (*impf*) из бутылки
2 (*indicating movement*: *from inside*) из +*gen*; (: *away from*) от +*gen*; (: *off*) с(о) +*gen*; (: *from behind*) из-за +*gen*; **she ran from the house** она выбежала из дома; **the car drove away from the house** машина отъехала от дома; **he took the magazine from the table** он взял журнал со стола; **they got up from the table** они встали из-за стола
3 (*indicating time*) с +*gen*; **from two o'clock to** *or* **until** *or* **till three** с двух (часов) до трёх (часов); **from January (to August)** с января (по август)
4 (*indicating distance*: *position*) от +*gen*; (: *motion*) до +*gen*; **the hotel is 1 km from the beach** гостиница находится в километре от пляжа; **we're still a long way from home** нам ещё далеко до дома
5 (*indicating price, number etc*: *range*) от +*gen*; (: *change*) с +*gen*; **prices range from £10 to £50** цены от £10 до £50; **the interest rate was increased from nine per cent to ten per cent** проценты на вклады повысили с девяти до десяти (процентов)

6 *(indicating difference)* от *+gen*; **to be different from sb/sth** отличáться *(impf)* от когó-н/ чегó-н
7 *(because of, on the basis of)*: **from what he says** из тогó, что он говори́л; **from what I understand** наскóлько я знáю; **to act from conviction** дéйствовать* *(impf)* по убеждéнию; **he is weak from hunger** он ослáб от гóлода.

frond [frɔnd] *n* ветвь *f*; **palm ~** лист* пáльмы.
front [frʌnt] *n* (*of house, also fig*) фасáд; (*of dress*) пéред; (*of train, car*) перéдняя часть *f*; (*promenade*: *also:* **sea** ~) нáбережная *f adj*; (*MIL, METEOROLOGY*) фронт* ♦ *adj* перéдний* ♦ *vi*: **to ~ onto sth** выходи́ть* *(impf)* фасáдом на что-н; **in ~** вперёд; **in ~ of** пéред *+instr*; **on the political ~** на полити́ческом фрóнте.
frontage ['frʌntɪdʒ] *n* фасáд.
frontal ['frʌntl] *adj* (*attack*) лобовóй, фронтáльный; **~ view** вид спéреди.
front bench *n* (*POL*: *BRIT*) *мини́стры прáвящей пáртии и руководи́тели пáртии оппози́ции.*
front desk *n* (*US*: *in hotel*) стóйка администрáтора; (: *in doctor's surgery*) регистратýра.
front door *n* входнáя дверь* *f*.
frontier ['frʌntɪə^r] *n* грани́ца.
frontispiece ['frʌntɪspi:s] *n* фронтиспи́с.
front page *n* пéрвая страни́ца (*газéты*).
front room *n* гости́ная *f adj*.
frontrunner ['frʌntrʌnə^r] *n* (*fig*) претендéнт.
front-wheel drive ['frʌntwi:l-] *n* (*AUT*) перéдний* при́вод.
frost [frɔst] *n* морóз; (*also:* **hoarfrost**) и́ней.
frostbite ['frɔstbaɪt] *n* обморожéние.
frosted ['frɔstɪd] *adj* (*glass*) мáтовый; (*esp US*: *cake*) глазирóванный.
frosting ['frɔstɪŋ] *n* (*esp US*: *on cake*) глазýрь *f*.
frosty ['frɔstɪ] *adj* (*weather, night*) морóзный* (морóзен); (*welcome, look*) ледянóй; (*window*) покры́тый (покры́т) и́неем, замёрзший.
froth ['frɔθ] *n* (*on liquid*) пéна.
frothy ['frɔθɪ] *adj* (*liquid*) пéнистый.
frown [fraun] *n* нахмýренный взгляд ♦ *vi* хмýриться (нахмýриться *perf*)
▸ **frown on** *vt fus* (*fig*) смотрéть* *(impf)* с неодобрéнием на *+acc*.
froze [frəuz] *pt of* **freeze**.
frozen ['frəuzn] *pp of* **freeze** ♦ *adj* (*food*) морóженый; (*COMM*: *assets*) заморóженный.
FRS *n abbr* (*BRIT*) = *Fellow of the Royal Society*; (*US*: = *Federal Reserve System*) Федерáльная резéрвная систéма.
frugal ['fru:gl] *adj* (*person*) бережли́вый (бережли́в); (*meal*) скýдный* (скýден).
fruit [fru:t] *n inv* (*AGR*) фрукт; (*BOT*) плод; (*fig*: *results*) плоды́ *mpl*.
fruiterer ['fru:tərə^r] *n* торгóвец* фрýктами.
fruit fly *n* фруктóвая мýшка*.
fruitful ['fru:tful] *adj* плодотвóрный* (плодотвóрен).
fruition [fru:'ɪʃən] *n*: **to come to ~** осуществля́ться (осуществи́ться *perf*), реализóвываться (реализовáться *perf*).
fruit juice *n* фруктóвый сок.
fruitless ['fru:tlɪs] *adj* (*fig*) бесплóдный* (бесплóден).
fruit machine *n* (*BRIT*) игровóй автомáт.
fruit salad *n* фруктóвый салáт.
fruity ['fru:tɪ] *adj* фруктóвый; (*voice, laugh*) зы́чный* (зы́чен).
frump [frʌmp] *n* (*woman*) замухры́шка.
frustrate [frʌs'treɪt] *vt* (*person*) расстрáивать (расстрóить *perf*); (*plan, attempt*) срывáть (сорвáть *perf*).
frustrated [frʌs'treɪtɪd] *adj* (*person*) неудовлетворённый (неудовлетворён); (*plan, attempt*) сóрванный (сóрван); **~ artist/poet** неудáвшийся худóжник/поэ́т.
frustrating [frʌs'treɪtɪŋ] *adj* (*day*) неудáчный* (неудáчен); **I find this job very ~** я óчень неудовлетворён э́той рабóтой.
frustration [frʌs'treɪʃən] *n* (*irritation*) досáда; (*thwarting*) крушéние.
fry [fraɪ] (*pt, pp* **fried**) *vt* жáрить (пожáрить *or* поджáрить *perf*); *see also* **small**.
frying pan ['fraɪɪŋ-] (*US* **fry-pan**) *n* сковородá*.
fry-pan ['fraɪpæn] *n* (*US*) = **frying pan**.
FT *n abbr* (*BRIT*) = *Financial Times*; **the ~ index** фóндовый и́ндекс „Файнэ́ншел Тáймс“.
ft. *abbr* = **feet, foot**.
FTC *n abbr* (*US*: = *Federal Trade Commission*) Федерáльная торгóвая коми́ссия.
FTSE 100 Index *n* (*COMM*) *показáтель состоя́ния фóндовой би́ржи, публикýемый в газéте „Файнэ́ншел Таймс“.*
fuchsia ['fju:ʃə] *n* фýксия.
fuck [fʌk] (*inf!*) *vti* трáхать *(impf)* (*!*); **~ off!** иди́ нá фиг! (*!*)
fuddled ['fʌdld] *adj* одурмáненный.
fuddy-duddy ['fʌdɪdʌdɪ] *n* (*pej*) стáрый занýда *m*.
fudge [fʌdʒ] *n* ≈ сли́вочная помáдка ♦ *vt* (*issue, problem*) уклоня́ться (уклони́ться *perf*) от *+gen*.
fuel ['fjuəl] *n* (*for heating*) тóпливо; (*for plane, car*) горю́чее *nt adj* ♦ *vt* (*furnace etc*) топи́ть* *(impf)*; (*aircraft, ship*) заправля́ть (заправить* *perf*).
fuel oil *n* мазýт.
fuel pump *n* тóпливный насóс.
fuel tank *n* тóпливный бак; (*in car*) бензобáк.
fug [fʌg] *n* (*BRIT*) духотá.
fugitive ['fju:dʒɪtɪv] *n* беглéц*(-ля́нка*).
fulfil [ful'fɪl] (*US* **fulfill**) *vt* (*function*) исполня́ть (испóлнить *perf*); (*ambition*) реализóвывать (реализовáть *perf*).
fulfilled [ful'fɪld] *adj* (*person*) состоя́вшийся; (*life*) напóлненный.
fulfilment [ful'fɪlmənt] (*US* **fulfillment**) *n* (*of*

promise, desire) исполнéние; (*satisfaction*) удовлетворéние; (*of ambitions*) реализáция.
full [ful] *adj* пóлный* (пóлон); (*skirt*) ширóкий*; (*life*) напóлненный; (*maximum*): **at ~ volume/power** на пóлную грóмкость/мощность ♦ *adv*: **to know ~ well that** прекрасно знать *(impf)*, что; **I'm ~ (up)** я сыт; **he is ~ of enthusiasm/hope** он пóлон энтузиазма/надéжды; **~ details** все детáли; **~ marks** отли́чные оцéнки; **at ~ speed** на пóлной скорости; **a ~ two hours** цéлых два часá; **in ~** полностью.
fullback ['fulbæk] *n* (*SPORT*) защи́тник.
full-blooded ['ful'blʌdɪd] *adj* энерги́чный*.
full board *n*: **hotel with ~ ~** гости́ница с трёхразовым питáнием.
full-cream ['ful'kri:m] *adj*: **~ milk** (*BRIT*) неснятое молокó.
full employment *n* пóлная зáнятость *f*.
full-grown ['ful'grəun] *adj* (*animal, person*) взрóслый; (*plant*) вы́росший.
full-length ['ful'lɛŋθ] *adj* (*film, novel*) полнометрáжный; (*coat*) дли́нный; (*portrait*) во весь рост.
full moon *n* пóлная лунá*.
fullness ['fulnɪs] *n*: **in the ~ of time** по прошéствии врéмени.
full-page ['fulpeɪdʒ] *adj* (*advertisement, picture*) на всю страни́цу.
full-scale ['fulskeɪl] *adj* (*model*) в натурáльную величинý; (*attack, war, search*) широко-масштáбный.
full-sized ['ful'saɪzd] *adj* (*portrait*) в пóлную величинý.
full stop *n* (*BRIT*) тóчка*.
full-time ['ful'taɪm] *adj, adv* (*study*) на днéвном отделéнии; (*work*) на пóлной стáвке, на пóлную стáвку.
fully ['fulɪ] *adv* (*completely*) пóлностью, вполнé; (*at least*): **~ as big as** по крáйней мéре такóй же величины́, как.
fully fledged [-'flɛdʒd] *adj* (*teacher, barrister*) вполнé сложи́вшийся; (*citizen, member*) полнопрáвный*; (*bird*) опери́вшийся.
fully-paid share ['fulpeɪd-] *n* пóлностью оплáченная áкция.
fulsome ['fulsəm] *adj* (*praise*) чрезмéрный.
fumble ['fʌmbl] *vi*: **to ~ with** (*catch, key*) вози́ться *(impf)* с *+instr* ♦ *vt*: **to ~ the ball** неуклюже старáться *(impf)* поймáть *(perf)* мяч; **to ~ in** (*pocket*) ры́ться *(impf)* в *+prp*; **she ~d for the switch in the dark** онá шáрила в темнотé в пóисках выключáтеля.
fume [fju:m] *vi* дыми́ть *(impf)*; **he was fuming** он был разъярён.
fumes [fju:mz] *npl* пары́ *mpl*, испарéния *ntpl*.
fumigate ['fju:mɪgeɪt] *vt* окýривать (окури́ть* *perf*).
fun [fʌn] *n*: **what ~!** как вéсело!; **to have ~** весели́ться (повесели́ться *perf*); **he's good ~ (to be with)** с ним вéсело; **for ~** для забáвы; **it's not much ~** э́то довóльно скýчно; **to make ~ of** подшýчивать (подшути́ть *perf*) над *+instr*; **to poke ~ at** насмехáться *(impf)* над *+instr*.
function ['fʌŋkʃən] *n* (*also MATH*) фýнкция; (*product*) произвóдная *f adj*; (*social occasion*) приём ♦ *vi* (*operate*) функциони́ровать *(impf)*; **to ~ as** выполня́ть (вы́полнить *perf*) *or* исполня́ть (испóлнить *perf*) фýнкции *+gen*.
functional ['fʌŋkʃənl] *adj* (*operational*) дéйствующий*; (*practical*) функционáльный.
function key *n* (*COMPUT*) функционáльная клáвиша.
fund [fʌnd] *n* (*of money*) фонд; (*of knowledge etc*) запáс; **~s** *npl* (*money*) (дéнежные) срéдства *ntpl*, фóнды *mpl*.
fundamental [fʌndə'mɛntl] *adj* фундаментáльный*.
fundamentalism [fʌndə'mɛntəlɪzəm] *n* фундаментали́зм.
fundamentalist [fʌndə'mɛntəlɪst] *n* фундаментали́ст.
fundamentally [fʌndə'mɛntəlɪ] *adv* в своéй оснóве; **they are ~ different** они коренны́м óбразом различáются.
fundamentals [fʌndə'mɛntlz] *npl* оснóвы *fpl*.
funding ['fʌndɪŋ] *n* финанси́рование.
fund raising [-reɪzɪŋ] *n* сбор срéдств.
funeral ['fju:nərəl] *n* пóхороны* *pl*.
funeral director *n* распоряди́тель *m* на похоронáх.
funeral parlour *n* похорóнное бюрó *nt ind*.
funeral service *n* панихи́да.
funereal [fju:'nɪərɪəl] *adj* трáурный.
funfair ['fʌnfɛə'] *n* (*BRIT*) я́рмарка*.
fungi ['fʌŋgaɪ] *npl of* **fungus**.
fungus ['fʌŋgəs] (*pl* **fungi**) *n* (*plant*) гриб*; (*mould*) плéсень *f*.
funicular [fju:'nɪkjulə'] *n* (*also:* **~ railway**) фуникулёр.
funky ['fʌŋkɪ] *adj о музыке с си́льным синкопи́рованным ри́тмом*; (*inf*) клёвый.
funnel ['fʌnl] *n* (*for pouring*) ворóнка*; (*of ship*) трубá*.
funnily ['fʌnɪlɪ] *adv* (*strangely*) стрáнно; **~ enough** как ни стрáнно.
funny ['fʌnɪ] *adj* (*comical*) смешнóй* (смешóн); (*amusing*) забáвный* (забáвен); (*strange*) стрáнный* (стрáнен), чуднóй.
funny bone *n* (*inf*) локтевáя кость *f*.
fun run *n* благотвори́тельный пробéг.
fur [fə:'] *n* мех*; (*BRIT*: *in kettle*) нáкипь *f*.
fur coat *n* меховáя шýба.
furious ['fjuərɪəs] *adj* (*person*) взбешённый (взбешён); (*exchange, argument*) бýрный*

* marks translations which have irregular inflections. The Russian-English side of the dictionary gives inflectional information.

(бу́рен); (*effort, speed*) неи́стовый; **I am ~ with her** я о́чень серди́т на неё.
furiously ['fjuərɪəslɪ] *adv* неи́стово.
furl [fə:l] *vt* свёртывать (сверну́ть *perf*).
furlong ['fə:lɔŋ] *n 201.2 ме́тра в ко́нных ска́чках.*
furlough ['fə:ləu] *n* (*MIL*) увольне́ние.
furnace ['fə:nɪs] *n* печь* *f*.
furnish ['fə:nɪʃ] *vt* (*room, building*) обставля́ть (обста́вить* *perf*); (*supply*): **to ~ sb with sth** предоставля́ть (предоста́вить* *perf*) что-н кому́-н; **~ed flat** *or (US)* **apartment** меблиро́ванная кварти́ра.
furnishings ['fə:nɪʃɪŋz] *npl* обстано́вка *fsg*.
furniture ['fə:nɪtʃə^r] *n* ме́бель *f*; **piece of ~** предме́т ме́бели.
furniture polish *n сре́дство для полиро́вки ме́бели.*
furore [fjuə'rɔ:rɪ] *n* (*protests*) негодова́ние.
furrier ['fʌrɪə^r] *n* (*fur seller*) меховщи́к*; (*artisan*) скорня́к*.
furrow ['fʌrəu] *n* борозда́* ◆ *vt*: **to ~ one's brow** хму́рить (нахму́рить *perf*) бро́ви.
furry ['fə:rɪ] *adj* пуши́стый (пуши́ст).
further ['fə:ðə^r] *adj* (*additional*) дополни́тельный ◆ *adv* (*farther*) да́льше; (*moreover*) бо́лее того́ ◆ *vt* (*career, project*) соде́йствовать *(impf/perf) +dat*; **until ~ notice** впредь до дальне́йшего уведомле́ния; **how much ~ is it to the station?** ско́лько ещё до вокза́ла?; **~ to your letter of ...** (*formal*) ссыла́ясь на Ва́ше письмо́ от *+gen* ...; **to ~ one's interests** пресле́довать *(impf)* свои́ интере́сы.
further education *n* (*BRIT*) дальне́йшее обуче́ние (*не включа́я вы́сшее образова́ние*).
furthermore [fə:ðə'mɔ:^r] *adv* (*moreover*) бо́лее того́.
furthermost ['fə:ðəməust] *adj* са́мый да́льний*.
furthest ['fə:ðɪst] *superl of* **far**.
furtive ['fə:tɪv] *adj*: **~ glance/movement** взгляд/движе́ние укра́дкой.
furtively ['fə:tɪvlɪ] *adv* укра́дкой.
fury ['fjuərɪ] *n* (*anger, rage*) я́рость *f*, бе́шенство; **to be in a ~** быть* *(impf)* в бе́шенстве *or* в я́рости.
fuse [fju:z] (*US* **fuze**) *n* (*ELEC*) предохрани́тель *m*; (*for bomb*) фити́ль* *m* ◆ *vt* (*metal*) пла́вить* (распла́вить* *perf*); (*ideas, systems*) слива́ть (слить* *perf*) ◆ *vi* (*see vt*) пла́виться (распла́виться *perf*); слива́ться (сли́ться *perf*); **a ~ has blown** предохрани́тель перегоре́л; **to ~ the lights** (*BRIT*) вызыва́ть (вы́звать* *perf*) коро́ткое замыка́ние.
fuse box *n* блок предохрани́телей.
fuselage ['fju:zəlɑ:ʒ] *n* фюзеля́ж.
fuse wire *n* пла́вкая про́волока (*для предохрани́телей*).
fusillade [fju:zɪ'leɪd] *n* залп.
fusion ['fju:ʒən] *n* (*of ideas, qualities*) слия́ние; (*also:* **nuclear ~**) я́дерный си́нтез.
fuss [fʌs] *n* (*excitement*) сумато́ха; (*anxiety*) суета́; (*trouble*) шум ◆ *vi* суети́ться* *(impf)* ◆ *vt* надоеда́ть *(impf) +dat*; **to make** *or* **kick up a ~** поднима́ть (подня́ть* *perf*) шум; **to make a ~ of sb** носи́ться* *(impf)* с кем-н
▸ **fuss over** *vt fus* (*person*) трясти́сь* *(impf)* над *+instr*.
fusspot ['fʌspɔt] *n* (*inf*) хлопоту́н(ья).
fussy ['fʌsɪ] *adj* (*nervous*) суетли́вый; (*choosy*) ме́лочный* (ме́лочен), су́етный; (*clothes, room*) вы́чурный*; **I'm not ~** мне всё равно́.
fusty ['fʌstɪ] *adj* (*pej: archaic*) старомо́дный* (старомо́ден); (*musty*) за́тхлый.
futile ['fju:taɪl] *adj* (*attempt*) тще́тный* (тще́тен); (*comment, existence*) беспло́дный* (беспло́ден).
futility [fju:'tɪlɪtɪ] *n* (*see adj*) тще́тность *f*; беспло́дность *f*.
futon ['fu:tɔn] *n* фу́тон (*япо́нский матра́с*).
future ['fju:tʃə^r] *adj* бу́дущий* ◆ *n* бу́дущее *nt adj*; (*LING: also:* **~ tense**) бу́дущее вре́мя* *nt*; **~s** *npl* (*COMM*) фью́черсы *pl*, фью́черский това́р *msg* (*с согласо́ванной дато́й прода́жи*); **in (the) ~** в бу́дущем; **be more careful in ~** в бу́дущем бу́дьте осторо́жнее; **in the near/immediate ~** в недалёком/ближа́йшем бу́дущем.
futuristic [fju:tʃə'rɪstɪk] *adj* футуристи́ческий.
fuze [fju:z] (*US*) = **fuse**.
fuzz [fʌz] *n* (*inf: police*): **the ~** менты́ *mpl*.
fuzzy ['fʌzɪ] *adj* (*thoughts, also PHOT*) расплы́вчатый (расплы́вчат); (*hair*) кудря́вый (кудря́в).
fwd. *abbr* = **forward**.
f-word ['ɛfwə:d] *n*: **the ~** ≈ сло́во на́ три бу́квы.
fwy *abbr* (*US*) = **freeway**.
FY *abbr* = *fiscal year*.
FYI *abbr* (= *for your information*) к Ва́шему све́дению.

~ G, g ~

G, **g** [dʒi:] *n* (*letter*) *7-áя бýква английского алфавúта.*
G [dʒi:] *n* (*MUS*) соль *nt ind.*
G *n abbr* (*BRIT*: *SCOL*) = *good*; (*US*: *CINEMA*: = *general (audience)*) *фильм, пригóдный для покáза всем возрастны́м грýппам*; (*PHYS*): **G-force** сúла тя́жести.
g. *abbr* (= **gram**) г= *грамм*; (*PHYS*) = **gravity**.
G7 *n abbr* (*POL*: = *Group of Seven*) „большáя семёрка".
GA *n abbr* (*US*: *POST*) = *Georgia*.
gab [gæb] *n* (*inf*): **he has the gift of the** ~ у негó хорошó подвéшен язы́к.
gabble ['gæbl] *vi* таратóрить (протаратóрить *(perf)*).
gaberdine [gæbə'di:n] *n* сукнó*, габардúн.
gable ['geɪbl] *n* фронтóн.
Gabon [gə'bɔn] *n* Габóн.
gad about [gæd-] *vi* (*inf*) болтáться *(impf)* без дéла.
gadget ['gædʒɪt] *n* приспособлéние.
gadgetry ['gædʒɪtrɪ] *n* приспособлéния *ntpl.*
Gaelic ['geɪlɪk] *adj* гэ́льский ◆ *n* (*LING*) гэ́льский язы́к*.
gaff [gæf] *n* (*NAUT*) гáфель *m*; (*inf*: *nonsense*): **he made a real** ~ он такóе ля́пнул.
gaffe [gæf] *n* оплóшность *f.*
gaffer ['gæfəʳ] (*inf*) *n* (*supervisor*) старшóй *m adj*; (*fellow*) старúк*.
gag [gæg] *n* (*on mouth*) кляп; (*joke*) хóхма ◆ *vt* вставля́ть (встáвить* *perf*) кляп *+dat*, завя́зывать (завязáть* *perf*) рот *+dat*; (*fig*) затыкáть (заткнýть *perf*) рот *+dat* ◆ *vi*: **the smell made him** ~ у негó гóрло перехватúло от зáпаха.
gaga ['gɑ:gɑ:] *adj*: **he is** ~ у негó не все дóма.
gage [geɪdʒ] *n, vt* (*US*) = **gauge**.
gaiety ['geɪɪtɪ] *n* весéлье.
gaily ['geɪlɪ] *adv* вéсело; (*coloured*) я́рко.
gain [geɪn] *n* (*increase*) увеличéние; (*profit*) при́быль *f* ◆ *vt* (*confidence, experience*) приобретáть (приобрестú* *perf*); (*speed*) набирáть (набрáть* *perf*) ◆ *vi* (*clock, watch*) спешúть *(impf)*; (*benefit*): **to** ~ **from sth** извлекáть (извлéчь* *perf*) пóльзу из чегó-н; **to do sth for** ~ дéлать (сдéлать *perf*) что-н рáди вы́годы; **what will you** ~ **by that?** чегó Вы э́тим добьётесь?; **to** ~ **ground** получáть (получúть *perf*) большóе распространéние; **to** ~ **3 pounds (in weight)** попрáвиться *(perf)* на 3 фýнта; **to** ~ **on sb** догоня́ть (догнáть* *perf*) когó-н.
gainful ['geɪnful] *adj* (*employment*) вы́годный* (вы́годен).
gainfully ['geɪnfəlɪ-] *adv*: ~ **employed** по оплáчиваемой рабóте.
gainsay [geɪn'seɪ] (*irreg*: *like* **say**) *vt* отрицáть *(impf)*.
gait [geɪt] *n* пóступь *f*; **to walk with a slow/ confident** ~ идтú* *(impf)* мéдленной/ увéренной пóступью.
gala ['gɑ:lə] *n* (*festival*) прáзднество; **swimming** ~ прáздник на водé.
Galapagos Islands [gə'læpəgəs-] *npl*: **the** ~ ~ Галапагóсские островá* *mpl.*
galaxy ['gæləksɪ] *n* галáктика.
gale [geɪl] *n* (*wind*) сúльный вéтер*; ~ **force ten** пóрывы вéтра в дéсять бáллов.
gall [gɔ:l] *n* (*ANAT*) жёлчь *f*; (*fig*: *impudence*) нáглость *f* ◆ *vt* раздражáть *(impf)*.
gall. *abbr* = **gallon**.
gallant ['gælənt] *adj* (*brave*) дóблестный*; (*chivalrous*) галáнтный*.
gallantry ['gæləntrɪ] *n* (*see adj*) дóблесть *f*; галáнтность *f.*
gall bladder *n* жёлчный пузы́рь* *m.*
galleon ['gælɪən] *n* галеóн.
gallery ['gælərɪ] *n* (*also*: **art** ~) галерéя; (*in hall, church, theatre*) балкóн.
galley ['gælɪ] *n* (*ship's kitchen*) кáмбуз; (*ship*) галéра; (*PUBLISHING*: *also*: ~ **proof**) грáнка*.
Gallic ['gælɪk] *adj* гáлльский.
galling ['gɔ:lɪŋ] *adj* раздражáющий.
gallon ['gæln] *n* галлóн (*4,5 лúтра*).
gallop ['gæləp] *n* галóп ◆ *vi* (*horse*) скакáть* *(impf)* (галóпом), галопúровать *(impf)*; (*person*) носúться*/нестúсь* *(impf)*; ~**ing inflation** галопúрующая инфля́ция.
gallows ['gæləuz] *n* вúселица.
gallstone ['gɔ:lstəun] *n* жёлчный кáмень* *m.*
Gallup Poll ['gæləp-] *n* опрóс Гэлопа.

* marks translations which have irregular inflections The Russian-English side of the dictionary gives inflectional information

galore [gə'lɔːʳ] *adv* в изоби́лии.
galvanize ['gælvənaɪz] *vt* (*person*) возбужда́ть (возбуди́ть* *perf*); (*support*) обеспе́чивать (обеспе́чить *perf*); **to ~ sb into action** побужда́ть (побуди́ть* *perf*) кого́-н к де́йствию.
Gambia ['gæmbɪə] *n* Га́мбия.
gambit ['gæmbɪt] *n* (*fig*): **(opening) ~** пе́рвый ход.
gamble ['gæmbl] *n* риск, риско́ванное предприя́тие ◆ *vt* (*money*) ста́вить* (поста́вить* *perf*) ◆ *vi* (*take a risk*) рискова́ть (рискну́ть *perf*); (*bet*) игра́ть *(impf)* в аза́ртные и́гры; **to ~ on the Stock Exchange** игра́ть *(impf)* на би́рже; **to ~ on sth** (*also fig*) де́лать (сде́лать *perf*) ста́вку на что-н.
gambler ['gæmbləʳ] *n* игро́к*.
gambling ['gæmblɪŋ] *n* аза́ртные и́гры *fpl*.
gambol ['gæmbl] *vi* резви́ться* *(impf)*.
game [geɪm] *n* игра́*; (*match*) матч; (*esp* TENNIS) гейм; (*also:* **board ~**) насто́льная игра́; (CULIN, HUNTING) дичь *f* ◆ *adj* (*willing*): **~ (for)** гото́вый (гото́в) (на *+acc*); **~s** *npl* (SCOL) спорти́вные и́гры *fpl*; **a ~ of football/tennis** футбо́льный/те́ннисный матч; **a ~ of chess** ша́хматная па́ртия; **big ~** (*lions, tigers etc*) кру́пный зверь.
game bird *n* перна́тая дичь *f*.
gamekeeper ['geɪmkiːpəʳ] *n* е́герь *m*.
gamely ['geɪmlɪ] *adv* хра́бро.
game reserve *n* охо́тничий* запове́дник.
games console ['geɪmz-] *n панéль управлéния компью́терными и́грами.*
gamesmanship ['geɪmzmənʃɪp] *n* трюка́чество.
gaming ['geɪmɪŋ] *n* аза́ртные и́гры *fpl*.
gammon ['gæmən] *n* (*bacon*) о́корок*; (*ham*) ветчина́.
gamut ['gæmət] *n* (*range*) га́мма; **to run the ~ of emotions** пережива́ть (пережи́ть* *perf*) це́лую га́мму эмо́ций.
gander ['gændəʳ] *n* гусь* *m*.
gang [gæŋ] *n* ба́нда; (*of friends*) компа́ния; (*of workmen*) кома́нда
▸ **gang up** *vi*: **to ~ up on sb** ополча́ться (ополчи́ться *perf*) на *or* про́тив кого́-н.
Ganges ['gændʒiːz] *n*: **the ~** Ганг.
gangland ['gæŋlænd] *adj* (*boss, killers*) мафио́зный.
gangling ['gæŋglɪŋ] *adj* долговя́зый (долговя́з).
gangly ['gæŋglɪ] (*inf*) *adj* = **gangling**.
gangplank ['gæŋplæŋk] *n* трап.
gangrene ['gæŋgriːn] *n* гангре́на.
gangster ['gæŋstəʳ] *n* га́нгстер.
gangway ['gæŋweɪ] *n* (*from ship*) трап; (BRIT: *in cinema, bus etc*) прохо́д.
gantry ['gæntrɪ] *n* (*for crane*) порта́л; (*for railway signal*) сигна́льный мо́стик; (*for rocket*) раке́тная устано́вка.
GAO *n abbr* (US: = *General Accounting Office*) Центра́льное фина́нсово-контро́льное управле́ние.
gaol *etc* [dʒeɪl] (BRIT) = **jail** *etc*.
gap [gæp] *n* (*space*) промежу́ток*; (: *between teeth*) щерби́на; (: *in time*) интерва́л; (: *in market, records etc*) пробе́л; (*difference*) расхожде́ния *ntpl*; **generation ~** разногла́сия ме́жду поколе́ниями.
gape [geɪp] *vi* (*person*) рази́нуть *(perf)* рот от удивле́ния; (*hole*) зия́ть *(perf)*; (*shirt*) распа́хиваться (распахну́ться *perf*).
gaping ['geɪpɪŋ] *adj* (*hole*) зия́ющий; (*shirt*) распа́хнутый (распа́хнут).
garage ['gærɑːʒ] *n* гара́ж*; (*petrol station*) запра́вочная ста́нция, бензоколо́нка*.
garb [gɑːb] *n* оде́жда.
garbage ['gɑːbɪdʒ] *n* (US: *rubbish*) му́сор*; (*inf*: *nonsense*) ерунда́; (*fig*: *film, book*) дрянь *f*.
garbage can *n* (US) помо́йный я́щик.
garbage collector *n* (US) му́сорщик.
garbage disposal (unit) *n* (US) мусоропрово́д.
garbage truck *n* (US) мусороубо́рочная маши́на.
garbled ['gɑːbld] *adj* (*account, message*) запу́танный* (запу́тан).
garden ['gɑːdn] *n* сад* ◆ *vi* занима́ться (заня́ться* *perf*) садово́дством; **~s** *npl* (*park*) парк *msg*; (*in street names*): **Rose G~s** Ро́уз Га́рденз; **she was busy ~ing** она рабо́тала в саду́.
garden centre *n* магази́н садо́вых принадле́жностей.
garden city *n* го́род*-сад*, зелёный го́род*.
gardener ['gɑːdnəʳ] *n* садово́д; (*employee*) садо́вник(-ица).
gardening ['gɑːdnɪŋ] *n* садово́дство.
gargle ['gɑːgl] *vi* полоска́ть* (прополоска́ть* *perf*) го́рло ◆ *n* полоска́ние.
gargoyle ['gɑːgɔɪl] *n* (ARCHIT) химе́ра.
garish ['gɛərɪʃ] *adj* (*light*) ре́жущий глаз; (*dress, colour*) крича́щий.
garland ['gɑːlənd] *n* гирля́нда.
garlic ['gɑːlɪk] *n* чесно́к*.
garment ['gɑːmənt] *n* (*dress etc*) предме́т оде́жды.
garner ['gɑːnəʳ] *vt* добыва́ть (добы́ть* *perf*).
garnish ['gɑːnɪʃ] *vt* украша́ть (укра́сить* *perf*).
garret ['gærɪt] *n* камо́рка*.
garrison ['gærɪsn] *n* гарнизо́н.
garrulous ['gærjuləs] *adj* болтли́вый, говорли́вый.
garter ['gɑːtəʳ] *n* подвя́зка*.
garter belt *n* (US) по́яс* (*с подвя́зками*).
gas [gæs] *n* газ*; (US: *gasoline*) бензи́н*; (*as anaesthetic*) ингаляцио́нный анесте́тик ◆ *vt* (*kill*) удуша́ть (удуши́ть *perf*); (MIL) отравля́ть (отрави́ть* *perf*) га́зом.
gas cooker *n* (BRIT) га́зовая плита́*.
gas cylinder *n* га́зовый балло́н.
gaseous ['gæsɪəs] *adj* газообра́зный.

gas fire *n* (*BRIT*) гáзовый камúн.
gas-fired ['gæsfaɪəd] *adj* гáзовый, рабóтающий на гáзе.
gash [gæʃ] *n* (*wound*) глубóкая рáна; (*cut, slash*) глубóкий* порéз ◆ *vt* (*person*) наносúть* (нанестú* *perf*) глубóкую рáну +*dat*; (*object*) распáрывать (распорóть *perf*); наносúть* (нанестú* *perf*) глубóкий порéз +*dat*.
gasket ['gæskɪt] *n* (*AUT*) проклáдка*.
gas mask *n* противогáз.
gas meter *n* гáзовый счётчик.
gasoline ['gæsəli:n] *n* (*US*) бензúн*.
gasp [gɑ:sp] *n* (*breath*) вдох ◆ *vi* (*pant*) тяжелó дышáть* (*impf*); (*in surprise*) издавáть* (издáть* *perf*) вздох; **I am ~ing for a smoke** я умирáю от желáния курúть
▸ **gasp out** *vt* выпáливать (вы́палить *perf*).
gas ring *n* конфóрка*.
gas station *n* (*US*) заправочная стáнция, бензоколóнка*.
gas stove *n* (*cooker*) гáзовая плитá*.
gassy ['gæsɪ] *adj* (*beer etc*) газирóванный* (газирóван).
gas tank *n* бензобáк.
gastric ['gæstrɪk] *adj* желýдочный.
gastric ulcer *n* я́зва желýдка.
gastroenteritis ['gæatrəuɛntə'raɪtɪs] *n* гастроэнтерúт.
gastronomy [gæs'trɔnəmɪ] *n* кулинáрное искýсство.
gasworks ['gæswə:ks] *n* гáзовый завóд.
gate [geɪt] *n* (*single*) калúтка*; (*double*) ворóта *mpl*; (*at airport*) выход; (*of lock, level crossing etc*) шлагбáум.
gateau ['gætəu] (*pl* **~x**) *n* торт.
gateaux ['gætəuz] *npl of* **gateau**.
gate-crash ['geɪtkræʃ] *vt* (*BRIT*): **to ~ a party** приходúть* (прийтú* *perf*) на вечерúнку без приглашéния.
gate-crasher ['geɪtkræʃə'] *n* (*to party*) незвáный гость *m*.
gatehouse ['geɪthəus] *n* сторóжка* у ворóт.
gateway ['geɪtweɪ] *n* (*also fig*) ворóта *mpl*.
gather ['gæðə'] *vt* собирáть (собрáть* *perf*); (*understand*) полагáть (*impf*); (*SEWING*) собирáть (собрáть* *perf*) в склáдки ◆ *vi* собирáться (собрáться* *perf*); (*clouds*) скáпливаться (скопúться* *perf*); (*dust*) собирáться (собрáться* *perf*), оседáть (осéсть* *perf*); **to ~ from sb** выяснять (вы́яснить *perf*) у когó-н; **I ~ that ...** я полагáю, что ...; **as far as I can ~** наскóлько я понимáю; **to ~ speed** набирáть (набрáть* *perf*) скóрость.
gathering ['gæðərɪŋ] *n* собрáние.
GATT [gæt] *n abbr* (= *General Agreement on Tariffs and Trade*) ГАТТ (*Генерáльное соглашéние по тарúфам и торгóвле*).
gauche [gəuʃ] *adj* нелóвкий*.
gaudy ['gɔ:dɪ] *adj* пёстрый*.
gauge [geɪdʒ] *n* (*instrument*) измерúтельный прибóр; (*RAIL*) ширинá колéй ◆ *vt* (*amount, quantity*) измерять (измéрить *perf*); (*fig: feelings, character etc*) оцéнивать (оценúть* *perf*), получáть (получúть* *perf*) представлéние о +*prp*; **petrol ~, fuel ~,** (*US*) **gas ~** указáтель *m* ýровня бензúна; **to ~ the right moment** выбирáть (вы́брать* *perf*) подходящий момéнт.
Gaul [gɔ:l] *n* (*country*) Гáллия; (*person*) галл.
gaunt [gɔ:nt] *adj* (*haggard*) измождённый* (измождён); (*bare, stark*) угрю́мый* (угрю́м).
gauntlet ['gɔ:ntlɪt] *n* перчáтка*; (*fig*): **to run the ~** подвергáться (подвéргнуться *perf*) напáдкам; **to throw down the ~** бросáть (брóсить* *perf*) перчáтку.
gauze [gɔ:z] *n* (*fabric*) мáрля.
gave [geɪv] *pt of* **give**.
gavel ['gævl] *n* молотóк (*председáтеля собрáния, судьú úли аукционúста*).
gawk [gɔ:k] *vi* (*inf*): **to ~ at** тарáщить (вы́таращить *perf*) глазá на +*acc*.
gawky ['gɔ:kɪ] *adj* неотёсанный* (неотёсан).
gawp [gɔ:p] *vi*: **to ~ at** тарáщить (вы́таращить *perf*) глазá на +*acc*.
gay [geɪ] *adj* (*cheerful*) весёлый* (вéсел); (*homosexual*): **he is ~** он голубóй *or* гомосексуалúст; **~ bar** бар гомосексуалúстов *or* голубы́х.
gaze [geɪz] *n* (*look, stare*) (прúстальный) взгляд ◆ *vi*: **to ~ at sth** глядéть* (*impf*) на что-н.
gazelle [gə'zɛl] *n* газéль *f*.
gazette [gə'zɛt] *n* (*newspaper*) газéта; (*official publication*) óрган.
gazetteer [gæzə'tɪə'] *n* географúческий спрáвочник.
gazumping [gə'zʌmpɪŋ] *n* (*BRIT: pej*) *увеличéние цены́ дóма в послéдний момéнт*.
gazundering [gə'zʌndərɪŋ] *n* (*BRIT: pej*) *понижéние предлóженной цены́ на покýпку дóма до подписáния контрáкта*.
GB *abbr* = **Great Britain**.
GBH *n abbr* (*BRIT: LAW:* = *grievous bodily harm*) тяжёлые телéсные повреждéния *ntpl*.
GC *n abbr* (*BRIT:* = *George Cross*) ≈ Геóргиевский крест.
GCE *n abbr* (*BRIT:* = *General Certificate of Education*) ≈ аттестáт о срéднем образовáнии.
GCHQ *n abbr* (*BRIT:* = *Government Communications Headquarters*) Глáвный штаб служб правúтельственной свя́зи.
GCSE *n abbr* (*BRIT:* = *General Certificate of*

* marks translations which have irregular inflections. The Russian-English side of the dictionary gives inflectional information.

Secondary Education) ≈ аттестáт о срéднем образовáнии.
Gdansk [gdænsk] *n* Гдáньск.
Gdns. *abbr* (*in street names*) = **Gardens**.
GDP *n abbr* (= **gross domestic product**) ВВП= *валовóй внýтренний продýкт*.
GDR *n abbr* (*formerly*: = *German Democratic Republic*) ГДР= *Гермáнская Демократи́ческая Респýблика*.
gear [gɪəʳ] *n* (*equipment, belongings etc*) принадлéжности *fpl*; (*for hunting*) снаряжéние; (*for fishing*) снáсти *fpl*; (*TECH*) зубчáтое колесó; (*AUT*) скóрость *f* ◆ *vt* (*fig*): **to ~ sth to** приспосáбливать (приспосóбить* *perf*) что-н к *+dat*; **top** *or* *(US)* **high/low/bottom ~** вы́сшая/ни́зкая/сáмая мáлая передáча *or* скóрость; **in ~** на передáче *or* скóрости, включённый (включён); **out of ~** не на передáче *or* скóрости, невключённый (невключён); **our service is ~ed to meet the needs of the disabled** нáши услýги напрáвлены на удовлетворéние потрéбностей инвали́дов
▸ **gear up** *vi*: **to ~ up (to do)** готóвиться* (приготóвиться* *or* подготóвиться* *perf*) (*+infin*) ◆ *vt*: **to ~ o.s. up (to do)** готóвить* (приготóвить* *or* подготóвить* *perf*) себя́ (*+infin*).
gearbox ['gɪəbɔks] *n* корóбка* передáч *or* скоростéй.
gear lever (*US* **gear shift**) *n* переключáтель *m* скоростéй.
GED *n abbr* (*US*: *SCOL*) = *general educational development*.
geek [gi:k] *n* (*inf*) придýрок*.
geese [gi:s] *npl of* **goose**.
geezer ['gi:zəʳ] *n* (*inf*) чувáк.
Geiger counter ['gaɪgə-] *n* счётчик Гéйгера (*для измерéния радиоакти́вности*).
gel [dʒɛl] *n* (*also CHEM*) гель *m*.
gelatin(e) ['dʒɛləti:n] *n* желати́н*.
gelignite ['dʒɛlɪgnaɪt] *n* гелигни́т.
gem [dʒɛm] *n* (*stone*) драгоцéнный кáмень *m*, самоцвéт; (*fig*) сокрóвище.
Gemini ['dʒɛmɪnaɪ] *n* Близнецы́ *mpl*; **he is ~** он – Близнéц.
gen [dʒɛn] *n* (*BRIT*: *inf*): **to give sb the ~ on sth** опи́сывать (описáть* *perf*) комý-н что-н в óбщих чертáх.
Gen. *abbr* (*MIL*) = **general**.
gen. *abbr* = **general, generally**.
gender ['dʒɛndəʳ] *n* (*sex*) пол; (*LING*) род.
gene [dʒi:n] *n* ген.
genealogy [dʒi:nɪ'ælədʒɪ] *n* генеалóгия.
general ['dʒɛnərl] *n* (*MIL*) генерáл ◆ *adj* óбщий*; (*widespread*: *movement, interest*) всеóбщий*; **in ~** в óбщем; **the ~ public** ширóкая пýблика; **~ audit** (*COMM*) аудитóрская провéрка.
general anaesthetic *n* óбщий* наркóз.
general delivery *n* (*US*) пóчта „до востребóвания".
general election *n* всеóбщие вы́боры *mpl*.
generalization ['dʒɛnrəlaɪ'zeɪʃən] *n* обобщéние.
generalize ['dʒɛnrəlaɪz] *vi* обобщáть (обобщи́ть *perf*).
generally ['dʒɛnrəlɪ] *adv* вообщé; (*+vb*) обы́чно; **it is ~ accepted that ...** обы́чно считáется, что ...; **to become ~ available** станови́ться* (стать* *perf*) обще-достýпным(-ой).
general manager *n* глáвный управля́ющий* *m adj*.
general practitioner *n* врач óбщей прáктики.
general strike *n* всеóбщая забастóвка*.
generate ['dʒɛnəreɪt] *vt* (*power, electricity*) производи́ть* (произвести́* *perf*); (*excitement, interest*) вызывáть (вы́звать* *perf*); (*jobs*) создавáть* (создáть* *perf*).
generation [dʒɛnə'reɪʃən] *n* поколéние; (*of electricity etc*) генери́рование; **for ~s** из поколéния в поколéние.
generator ['dʒɛnəreɪtəʳ] *n* генерáтор.
generic [dʒɪ'nɛrɪk] *adj* óбщий*.
generosity [dʒɛnə'rɔsɪtɪ] *n* щéдрость *f*; (*of spirit*) великодýшие.
generous ['dʒɛnərəs] *adj* (*person*: *lavish*) щéдрый (щедр); (: *unselfish*) велико-дýшный* (великодýшен); (*amount of money*) изря́дный.
genesis ['dʒɛnɪsɪs] *n* гéнезис, истóки *mpl*; **the ~ of an idea** возникновéние идéи.
genetic [dʒɪ'nɛtɪk] *adj* генети́ческий*, гéнный.
genetically modified [dʒɪ'nɛtɪkəlɪ'mɔdɪfaɪd] *adj* генети́чески модифици́рованный, трансгéнный.
genetic engineering *n* гéнная инженéрия.
genetic fingerprinting [-'fɪŋgəprɪntɪŋ] *n* *установлéние ли́чности человéка по егó генети́ческим осóбенностям (по ДНК)*.
genetics [dʒɪ'nɛtɪks] *n* генéтика.
Geneva [dʒɪ'ni:və] *n* Женéва.
genial ['dʒi:nɪəl] *adj* (*smile, expression etc*) привéтливый; (*host*) радýшный*; (*climate*) мя́гкий*.
genitals ['dʒɛnɪtlz] *npl* половы́е óрганы *mpl*.
genitive ['dʒɛnɪtɪv] *n* роди́тельный падéж*.
genius ['dʒi:nɪəs] *n* талáнт; (*person*) гéний.
Genoa ['dʒɛnəuə] *n* Гéнуя.
genocide ['dʒɛnəusaɪd] *n* геноци́д.
Genoese [dʒɛnəu'i:z] *adj* генуэ́зский ◆ *n inv* генуэ́зец*(-зка*).
gent [dʒɛnt] *n abbr* (*BRIT*: *inf*) = **gentleman**.
genteel [dʒɛn'ti:l] *adj* (*family*) благорóдный*, благорóдного происхождéния; (*person*) свéтский*.
gentle ['dʒɛntl] *adj* нéжный* (нéжен); (*movement, breeze, landscape, nature*) мя́гкий* (мя́гок); **a ~ hint** тóнкий* намёк.
gentleman ['dʒɛntlmən] *irreg n* (*man*) джентльмéн; (*referring to social position*)

дворяни́н*; **~'s agreement** джентльме́нское соглаше́ние.
gentlemanly ['dʒɛntlmənlɪ] *adj* джентльме́нский.
gentleness ['dʒɛntlnɪs] *n* (*see adj*) не́жность *f*; мя́гкость *f*.
gently ['dʒɛntlɪ] *adv* (*smile, treat*) не́жно; (*curve, slope, move*) мя́гко; (*speak*) ла́сково.
gentry ['dʒɛntrɪ] *n inv*: **the ~** дворя́нство.
gents [dʒɛnts] *n*: **the ~** мужска́я убо́рная *f adj*.
genuine ['dʒɛnjuɪn] *adj* (*person, feeling*) и́скренний*; (*painting etc*) по́длинный*.
genuinely ['dʒɛnjuɪnlɪ] *adv* (*sincerely*) и́скренне; (*truly*) по-настоя́щему.
geographer [dʒɪ'ɔgrəfə'] *n* гео́граф.
geographic(al) [dʒɪə'græfɪk(l)] *adj* географи́ческий.
geography [dʒɪ'ɔgrəfɪ] *n* геогра́фия.
geological [dʒɪə'lɔdʒɪkl] *adj* геологи́ческий.
geologist [dʒɪ'ɔlədʒɪst] *n* гео́лог.
geology [dʒɪ'ɔlədʒɪ] *n* геоло́гия.
geometric(al) [dʒɪə'mɛtrɪk(l)] *adj* геометри́ческий.
geometry [dʒɪ'ɔmətrɪ] *n* геоме́трия.
Geordie ['dʒɔ:dɪ] *n* (*GEO: inf*) *урожéнец го́рода Нью́касл в А́нглии.*
Georgia ['dʒɔ:dʒə] *n* Гру́зия.
Georgian ['dʒɔ:dʒən] *adj* грузи́нский* ◆ *n* грузи́н(ка*); (*LING*) грузи́нский* язы́к*.
geranium [dʒɪ'reɪnɪəm] *n* гера́нь *f*.
geriatric [dʒɛrɪ'ætrɪk] *adj* гериатри́ческий ◆ *n* дря́хлый стари́к.
germ [dʒə:m] *n* (*MED*) микро́б; (*BOT, fig*) зача́ток; **the ~ of an idea** зача́ток иде́и.
German ['dʒə:mən] *adj* неме́цкий* ◆ *n* не́мец*(-мка*); (*LING*) неме́цкий* язы́к*.
German Democratic Republic *n* (*formerly*) Герма́нская Демократи́ческая Респу́блика.
germane [dʒə:'meɪn] *adj*: **~ to** релева́нтный для +*gen*.
German measles *n* (*BRIT*) красну́ха.
Germany ['dʒə:mənɪ] *n* Герма́ния.
germinate ['dʒə:mɪneɪt] *vi* (*BOT*) прораста́ть (прорасти́* *perf*); (*fig*) дава́ть* (дать* *perf*) ростки́.
germination [dʒə:mɪ'neɪʃən] *n* (*BOT*) прораста́ние.
germ warfare *n* бактериологи́ческая война́.
gerrymandering ['dʒɛrɪmændərɪŋ] *n изменéние грани́ц избира́тельных округо́в с це́лью дать преиму́щество определённой полити́ческой па́ртии.*
gestation [dʒɛs'teɪʃən] *n* созрева́ние плода́.
gesticulate [dʒɛs'tɪkjuleɪt] *vi* жестикули́ровать (*impf*).
gesture ['dʒɛstjə'] *n* (*movement, token*) жест; **as a ~ of friendship** в знак дру́жбы.

KEYWORD

get [gɛt] (*pt, pp* **got**; *US*) (*pp* **gotten**) *vi* **1** (*become, be*): **it's getting late** стано́вится* (*impf*) по́здно; **to get old** старе́ть (постаре́ть *perf*); **to get tired** устава́ть* (уста́ть* *perf*); **to get cold** мёрзнуть (замёрзнуть *perf*); **to get annoyed easily** ча́сто раздража́ться (*impf*); **he was getting bored** ему́ ста́ло ску́чно; **he gets drunk quickly** он бы́стро пьянéет; **he gets drunk every weekend** он напива́ется ка́ждый выходно́й; **he got killed** его́ уби́ли; **when do I get paid?** когда́ мне запла́тят?
2 (*go*): **to get to/from** добира́ться (добра́ться* *perf*) до +*gen*/от +*gen*; **to get home** приходи́ть* (прийти́* *perf*) домо́й; **how did you get here/there?** как Вы сюда́/туда́ добрали́сь?
3 (*begin*): **to get to know sb** (*become acquainted*) познако́миться* (*perf*) с кем-н; **to get to know sb well** бли́зко познако́миться* (*perf*) с кем-н; **I'm getting to like him** он начина́ет мне нра́виться; **let's get started** дава́йте начнём
◆ *modal aux vb*: **you've got to do it** Вы должны́ э́то сде́лать (*perf*)
◆ *vt*: **1**: **to get sth done** сде́лать (*perf*) что-н; **to get the washing done** постира́ть (*perf*); **to get the dishes done** помы́ть* (*perf*) *or* вы́мыть (*perf*) посу́ду; **to get the car started** *or* **to start** завести́* (*perf*) маши́ну; **to get sb to do** заставля́ть (заста́вить* *perf*) кого́-н +*infin*; **to get sb ready** собра́ть* (*perf*) кого́-н; **to get sth ready** пригото́вить* (*perf*) что-н; **to get sb drunk** напои́ть* (*perf*) кого́-н; **she got me into trouble** я влип с ней в неприя́тности
2 (*obtain*: *permission, results*) получа́ть (получи́ть* *perf*); (: *money*) достава́ть* (доста́ть* *perf*); (*find*: *job, flat*) находи́ть* (найти́* *perf*); (*person*: *call*) звать* (позва́ть* *perf*); (: *pick up*) забира́ть (забра́ть* *perf*); (*call out*: *doctor, plumber etc*) вызыва́ть (вы́звать* *perf*); (*object*: *carry*) приноси́ть* (принести́* *perf*); (: *buy*) покупа́ть (купи́ть* *perf*); **I'll get the car** я схожу́ за маши́ной; **can I get you something to drink?** что Вам мо́жно предложи́ть (*perf*)
3 (*receive*) получа́ть (получи́ть* *perf*); **to get a reputation for sth** зарабо́тать (*perf*) дурну́ю репута́цию чем-н; **what did you get for your birthday?** что Вам подари́ли на день рожде́ния?
4 (*grab*) хвата́ть (схвати́ть* *perf*); (*hit*): **the bullet got him in the leg** пу́ля попа́ла ему́ в но́гу; **I'll get you there somehow** я Вас ка́к-нибудь туда́ доста́влю; **do you think we'll get the piano through the door?** как Вы ду́маете, пиани́но пройдёт че́рез дверь?; **we must get him to hospital** мы должны́ отвезти́

* marks translations which have irregular inflections. The Russian-English side of the dictionary gives inflectional information.

его́ в больни́цу; **I'll get the book to you tomorrow** за́втра кни́га бу́дет у Вас
5 (*catch, take*): **we got a taxi** мы взя́ли такси́; **did she get her plane?** она́ успе́ла на самолёт?; **what train are you getting?** каки́м по́ездом Вы е́дете?; **where do I get the train?** где мне сади́ться на по́езд?
6 (*understand*) понима́ть (поня́ть* *perf*); (*hear*) расслы́шать *(perf)*; **(do you) get it?** (*inf*) поня́тно?; **I've got it!** тепе́рь поня́тно!; **I'm sorry, I didn't get your name** прости́те, я не расслы́шал Ва́ше и́мя
7 (*have, possess*): **how many children have you got?** ско́лько у Вас дете́й?; **I've got very little time** у меня́ о́чень ма́ло вре́мени

▸ **get about** *vi* (*after illness*) ходи́ть* *(impf)*; (*news*) распространя́ться (распространи́ться *perf*); **I don't get about much now** (*go to places*) тепе́рь я ма́ло где быва́ю

▸ **get across** *vt* (*subj*: *speaker*) объясня́ть (объясни́ть *perf*); **it's important to get this message across to them** ва́жно, что́бы они́ э́то по́няли

▸ **get along** *vi* (*agree*) ла́дить* *(impf)* с *+instr*; (*manage*) = **get by**; **I'd better be getting along** мне пора́

▸ **get around** *vt* = **get round**

▸ **get at** *vt fus* (*criticize*) придира́ться (придра́ться* *perf*) к *+dat*; (*reach*) дотя́гиваться (дотяну́ться* *perf*) до *+gen*; **what are you getting at?** что Вы хоти́те э́тим сказа́ть?

▸ **get away** *vi* (*leave*) уходи́ть (уйти́* *perf*); (*on holiday*) уезжа́ть (уе́хать* *perf*); (*escape*) убежа́ть* *(impf)*

▸ **get away with** *vt fus*: **he always gets away with it** ему́ всё схо́дит с рук; **he'll never get away with it!** э́то ему́ да́ром не пройдёт!

▸ **get back** *vi* (*return*) возвраща́ться (верну́ться *perf*)
◆ *vt* (*book, car*) получа́ть (получи́ть* *perf*) обра́тно *or* наза́д; **get back!** отойди́те!

▸ **get back at** *vt fus* (*inf*): **I'll get back at you (for that)** ты у меня (за э́то) полу́чишь

▸ **to get back to** *vt fus* (*return to*) возвраща́ться (возврати́ться *perf*) к *+dat*; (*contact again*) связа́ться* *(perf)* с *+instr*; **to get back to sleep** сно́ва засыпа́ть (засну́ть *perf*)

▸ **get by** *vi* (*pass*: *on foot*) проходи́ть* (пройти́* *perf*); (*manage*): **to get by without** обходи́ться* (обойти́сь* *perf*) без *+gen*; **I can/will get by** (*with little food, money*) мне хвата́ет/хва́тит; **I can get by in Dutch** я могу́ объясни́ться по-голла́ндски

▸ **get down** *vi*: **to get down from** слеза́ть (слезть* *perf*) с *+gen*
◆ *vt* (*depress*) де́йствовать* *(impf)* угнета́юще; (*write*) запи́сывать (записа́ть* *perf*); (*swallow*) впи́хивать (впихну́ть *perf*) в себя́; **to get down on your hands and knees** встава́ть (встать* *perf*) на четвере́ньки

▸ **get down to** *vt fus* (*work, business*) сади́ться* (засе́сть* *perf*) *or* бра́ться* (взя́ться* *perf*) за *+acc*

▸ **get in** *vi* (*train*) прибыва́ть (прибы́ть* *perf*), приходи́ть* (прийти́* *perf*); (*arrive home*: *on foot*) приходи́ть* (прийти́* *perf*); (*by transport*) приезжа́ть (прие́хать* *perf*); (*be elected*): **he got in by ten votes** его́ избра́ли большинство́м в де́сять голосо́в; **as soon as the bus pulled up we all got in** как то́лько авто́бус подошёл, мы се́ли в него́; **we queued for a long time for the concert but couldn't get in** мы до́лго стоя́ли в о́череди, но так и не попа́ли на конце́рт
◆ *vt* (*harvest*) собира́ть (собра́ть* *perf*); (*coal, supplies*) загота́вливать (загото́вить* *perf*); (*shopping*) закупа́ть (закупи́ть* *perf*); (*into conversation*) вставля́ть (вста́вить* *perf*)

▸ **get into** *vt fus* (*building*) входи́ть* (войти́* *perf*) в *+acc*; (*subj*: *train*) прибыва́ть (прибы́ть* *perf*) в/на *+acc*; (*vehicle*) сади́ться* (сесть* *perf*) в *+acc*; (*clothes*) влеза́ть (влезть* *perf*) в *+acc*; (*fight, argument*) вступа́ть (вступи́ть* *perf*) в *+acc*; (*university, college*) поступа́ть (поступи́ть* *perf*) в *+acc*; **to get into bed** ложи́ться (лечь* *perf*) в посте́ль; **I can't get into this skirt** э́та ю́бка не налеза́ет на меня́; **she has got into the habit of going for a walk before breakfast** у неё вошло́ в привы́чку выходи́ть гуля́ть до за́втрака

▸ **get off** *vi* (*escape*): **to get off lightly/with sth** отде́лываться (отде́латься *perf*) легко́/чем-н
◆ *vt* (*clothes*) снима́ть (снять* *perf*); (*stain*) выводи́ть* (вы́вести* *perf*); (*letter etc*) отправля́ть (отпра́вить* *perf*); (*day, time*): **we got 2 days/2 weeks off last month** у нас бы́ло два выходны́х дня/две свобо́дных неде́ли в про́шлом ме́сяце
◆ *vt fus* (*train, bus*) сходи́ть* (сойти́* *perf*) с *+gen*; (*horse, bicycle*) слеза́ть (слезть* *perf*) с *+gen*; **to get off and walk** (*bicycle*) слеза́ть (слезть* *perf*) и идти́* (пойти́* *perf*) пешко́м; **you should get off at the next station** Вам на́до сойти́ *(perf)* на сле́дующей ста́нции; **to get off to a good/poor start** (*fig*) с бле́ском/пло́хо начина́ть (нача́ть* *perf*); **I'd better be getting off** (*departing*) мне пора́

▸ **get on** *vi* (*age*) старе́ть *(impf)*; (*progress*): **how are you getting on?** у тебя́ подвига́ется де́ло?; **to get on (with)** (*agree*) ла́дить* *(impf)* (с *+instr*); (*manage*) справля́ться (спра́виться* *perf*) (с *+instr*)
◆ *vt fus* (*train, bus*) сади́ться* (сесть* *perf*) в *+acc*; (*horse, bicycle*) сади́ться* (сесть* *perf*) на *+acc*; **time is getting on** вре́мя идёт

▸ **get on to** *vt fus* (*BRIT*: *from one subject to another*) переходи́ть* (перейти́* *perf*) *+instr*; (*person*) свя́зываться (связа́ться* *perf*) с *+instr*; **how did we get on to this?** как мы к э́тому пришли́

▸ **get out** *vi* (*leave*: *building, vehicle*) выходи́ть* (вы́йти* *perf*); (*by transport*) выезжа́ть

(вы́ехать* *perf*); (: *city*) уезжа́ть (уе́хать* *perf*); (*socialize*) выбира́ться (вы́браться* *perf*) из до́ма
◆ *vt* (*stain*) выводи́ть* (вы́вести* *perf*); (*object*) достава́ть (доста́ть* *perf*); (*report*) публикова́ть* (опубликова́ть* *perf*); **get out!** убира́йся!; **the news got out that...** ста́ло изве́стно, что...; **the news got out in the end** но́вости разошли́сь в конце́ концо́в
▸ **get out of** *vt fus* (*duty etc*) отде́лываться (отде́латься *perf*) от +*gen*
◆ *vt* (*pleasure, satisfaction*) получа́ть (получи́ть* *perf*) от +*gen*; (*money*): **to get out (of)** (*from bank*) бра́ть* (взять* *perf*) (в +*prp*); (*from account*) снима́ть (сня́ть* *perf*) с +*gen*; **I couldn't get a word out of him** я не мог и сло́ва доби́ться от него́
▸ **get over** *vt fus* (*illness*) поправля́ться (попра́виться* *perf*)
◆ *vt*: **to get sth over with** зако́нчить *(perf)* что-н; **to get the message over that...** объясни́ть *(perf)*, что...; **let's get it over with!** дава́йте поко́нчим с э́тим де́лом!
▸ **get round** *vt fus* (*law, rule*) обходи́ть* (обойти́* *perf*); (*fig*: *person*) добива́ться (доби́ться* *perf*) своего́ от +*gen*
▸ **get round to** *vt fus*: **to get round to doing** собира́ться (собра́ться* *perf*) +*infin*; **I'll get around to it some day** когда́-н я доберу́сь до э́того
▸ **get through** *vi* (*TEL*) дозвони́ться *(perf)*
◆ *vt fus* (*work, book*) зака́нчивать (зако́нчить *perf*)
▸ **get through to** *vt fus* (*TEL*) дозвони́ться *(perf)* до +*gen*
▸ **get together** *vi* (*several people*) собира́ться (собра́ться* *perf*); (*two people*) встреча́ться (встре́титься* *perf*)
◆ *vt* (*people*) собира́ть (собра́ть *perf*); (*project, plan etc*) составля́ть (соста́вить* *perf*)
▸ **get up** *vi* встава́ть* (встать* *perf*)
◆ *vt* (*person*) поднима́ть (подня́ть* *perf*); **I can't get up any enthusiasm for it** у меня́ не возника́ет энтузиа́зма на э́тот счёт
▸ **get up to** *vt fus* (*BRIT*: *prank etc*) занима́ться (заня́ться* *perf*) +*instr*; **they're always getting up to mischief** они́ всегда́ прока́зничают.

getaway [ˈgɛtəweɪ] *n*: **to make a** *or* **one's ~** бежа́ть* *(impf)*.
getaway car *n маши́на, испо́льзованная при побе́ге.*
get-together [ˈgɛttəgɛðəʳ] *n* (*meeting*) неофициа́льное собра́ние; (*party*) вечери́нка*.
get-up [ˈgɛtʌp] *n* (*inf*) наря́д.
get-well card [gɛtˈwɛl-] *n* откры́тка* с пожела́ниями выздоровле́ния.
geyser [ˈgi:zəʳ] *n* ге́йзер; (*BRIT*: *water heater*) га́зовая коло́нка*.
Ghana [ˈgɑ:nə] *n* Га́на.
Ghanaian [gɑ:ˈneɪən] *adj* га́нский ◆ *n* жи́тель(ница) *m(f)* Га́ны.
ghastly [ˈgɑ:stlɪ] *adj* (*horrible*: *person, situation*) ужа́сный* (ужа́сен), отврати́тельный* (отврати́телен); (: *building, appearance, behaviour*) безобра́зный* (безобра́зен); (*pale*: *complexion*) ме́ртвенно-бле́дный* (ме́ртвенно-бле́ден); (*ill*): **you look ~!** Вы ужа́сно вы́глядите!
gherkin [ˈgə:kɪn] *n ме́лкий огуре́ц для маринова́ния.*
ghetto [ˈgɛtəu] *n* ге́тто *nt ind.*
ghetto blaster [-ˈblɑ:stəʳ] *n* переносно́й радиомагнитофо́н.
ghost [gəust] *n* (*spirit*) привиде́ние, при́зрак ◆ *vt* явля́ться (яви́ться* *perf*) та́йным а́втором +*gen*; **to give up the ~** (*fig*) приказа́ть* *(perf)* до́лго жить.
ghost town *n* забро́шенный го́род.
ghostwriter [ˈgəustraɪtəʳ] *n* та́йный а́втор, писа́тель-невиди́мка *m.*
ghoul [gu:l] *n* (*ghost*) вурдала́к.
ghoulish [ˈgu:lɪʃ] *adj* (*tastes etc*) ме́рзкий* (ме́рзок).
GHQ *n abbr* (*MIL*) = *general headquarters.*
GI *n abbr* (*US*: *inf*) = *government issue.*
giant [ˈdʒaɪənt] *n* (*in myths, stories*) велика́н; (*fig*: *large company etc*) гига́нт ◆ *adj* огро́мный.
giant killers *npl кома́нда без и́мени, оде́рживающая побе́ды над кома́ндами мирово́го кла́сса.*
gibber [ˈdʒɪbəʳ] *vi* говори́ть (проговори́ть *perf*) невня́тно.
gibberish [ˈdʒɪbərɪʃ] *n* тараба́рщина.
gibe [dʒaɪb] *n* насме́шка* ◆ *vi*: **to ~ at** сме́яться *(impf)* *or* издева́ться *(impf)* над +*instr*.
giblets [ˈdʒɪblɪts] *npl* (*of chicken etc*) потроха́* *mpl.*
Gibraltar [dʒɪˈbrɔ:ltəʳ] *n* Гибралта́р.
giddiness [ˈgɪdɪnɪs] *n* головокруже́ние.
giddy [ˈgɪdɪ] *adj* (*height*) голово-кружи́тельный* (головокружи́телен); (*dizzy*): **I feel ~** у меня́ кру́жится голова́; **~ with success** опьянённый (опьянён) успе́хом.
gift [gɪft] *n* (*present*) пода́рок*; (*donation*) дар*; (*COMM*: *also*: **free ~**) беспла́тный пода́рок*; (*ability*) дар*, тала́нт; **to have a ~ for sth** облада́ть *(impf)* тала́нтом чего́-н.
gifted [ˈgɪftɪd] *adj* одарённый*.
gift token *n* пода́рочный купо́н.
gift voucher *n* = **gift token.**
gig [gɪg] *n* (*inf*: *concert*) конце́рт (*рок- и́ли*

поп-группы).
gigabyte ['dʒɪgəbaɪt] *n единица измерения мощности памяти компьютера.*
gigantic [dʒaɪ'gæntɪk] *adj* гигантский*.
giggle ['gɪgl] *vi* хихикать *(impf)* ◆ *n*: **it was just a ~!** это был просто смех!; **to do sth for a ~** делать (сделать *perf*) что-н для смеха.
GIGO ['gaɪgəu] *abbr* (*COMPUT*: *inf*: *= garbage in, garbage out*) МЗМП= *мякину заложишь – мякину получишь.*
gild [gɪld] *vt* золотить* (позолотить* *perf*).
gill [dʒɪl] *n мера жидкости.*
gills [gɪlz] *npl* (*of fish*) жабры *fpl*.
gilt [gɪlt] *adj* позолоченный ◆ *n* позолота; **~s** *npl* (*COMM*) = **gilt-edged securities**.
gilt-edged ['gɪltɛdʒd] *adj*: **~ securities** золотообрезные ценные бумаги *fpl* (*о надёжных акциях*).
gimlet ['gɪmlɪt] *n* буравчик.
gimmick ['gɪmɪk] *n* (*sales*) уловка; (*electoral*) трюк.
gin [dʒɪn] *n* джин (*можжевёловая водка*).
ginger ['dʒɪndʒə^r] *n* (*spice*) имбирь* *m* ◆ *adj* (*in colour*) рыжий*.
ginger ale *n* имбирный эль.
ginger beer *n* имбирное пиво.
gingerbread ['dʒɪndʒəbrɛd] *n* (*cake*) ≈ коврижка, имбирный пирог*; (*biscuit*) ≈ пряник, имбирное печенье*.
ginger group *n* (*BRIT*) *группа членов организации, настаивающая на более решительных действиях.*
ginger-haired ['dʒɪndʒə'hɛəd] *adj* рыжеволосый.
gingerly ['dʒɪndʒəlɪ] *adv* опасливо.
gingham ['gɪŋəm] *n хлопчатобумажная ткань в клетку.*
ginseng ['dʒɪnsɛŋ] *n* женьшень *m*.
gipsy ['dʒɪpsɪ] *n* цыган*(ка*).
gipsy caravan *n* цыганская кибитка.
giraffe [dʒɪ'rɑ:f] *n* жираф.
girder ['gə:də^r] *n* металлическая балка*.
girdle ['gə:dl] *n* (*corset*) корсет ◆ *vt* (*encircle*) опоясывать (опоясать* *perf*).
girl [gə:l] *n* (*child*) девочка*; (*young unmarried woman*) девушка*; (*daughter*) дочка*; **this is my little ~** это моя дочка; **an English ~** англичанка*.
girlfriend ['gə:lfrɛnd] *n* (*of girl*) подруга; (*of boy*) девушка*, подруга.
Girl Guide *n* девочка*-скаут *f*.
girlish ['gə:lɪʃ] *adj* девичий*.
Girl Scout *n* (*US*) = **Girl Guide**.
Giro ['dʒaɪrəu] *n*: **the National ~** (*BRIT*) *способ перевода денег через банк или по почте.*
giro ['dʒaɪrəu] *n* (*bank giro*) перевод денег через банк; (*post office giro*) перевод денег через почту; (*BRIT*: *welfare cheque*) *чек, по которому получают пособия по безработице.*
girth [gə:θ] *n* (*circumference*) окружность *f*; (*of horse*) подпруга.
gist [dʒɪst] *n* (*of speech, programme*) суть *f*.

KEYWORD

give [gɪv] (*pt* **gave**, *pp* **given**) *vt* ***1*** (*hand over*): **to give sb sth** *or* **sth to sb** давать* (дать* *perf*) кому-н что-н; **they gave her a book for her birthday** они подарили ей книгу на день рождения
2 (*used with noun to replace a verb*): **to give a sigh** вздохнуть *(perf)*; **to give a push** толкнуть *(perf)*; **to give a shrug** передёрнуть *(perf)* плечами; **to give a speech** выступать (выступить* *perf*) с речью; **to give a lecture** читать (прочитать *perf*) лекцию; **to give three cheers** трижды кричать (прокричать *perf*) „ура"
3 (*tell, deliver*: *news*) сообщать (сообщить *perf*); (*advice*) давать* (дать* *perf*); **could you give him a message for me please? tell him that...** передайте ему, пожалуйста, от меня, что...; **I've got a message to give you from your brother** я тебе должен что-то передать от твоего брата; **let me give you some advice** разрешите мне дать Вам совет; **he gave me his new address over the phone** он дал мне свой новый адрес по телефону:
4: **to give sb sth** (*clothing, food, right*) давать* (дать* *perf*) кому-н что-н; (*title*) присваивать (присвоить *perf*) кому-н что-н; (*honour, responsibility*) возлагать (возложить* *perf*) на кого-н что-н; **to give sb a surprise** удивить* *(perf)* кого-н; **that's given me an idea** это навело меня на мысль
5 (*dedicate*: *one's life*) отдавать* (отдать* *perf*); (*allow*: *time, attention*) уделять (уделить *perf*); **you'll need to give me more time** Вы должны дать мне больше времени; **she gave it all her attention** она отнеслась к этому с большим вниманием
6 (*organize*): **to give a party** устраивать (устроить *perf*) вечер, приглашать (пригласить* *perf*) гостей; **to give a dinner** *etc* давать* (дать* *perf*) обед
◆ *vi* ***1*** (*stretch*: *fabric*) растягиваться (растянуться* *perf*)
2 (*break, collapse*) = **give way**
▸ **give away** *vt* (*money, object*) отдавать* (отдать* *perf*); (*betray*: *secret, information*) выдавать* (выдать* *perf*); (: *person*) выдавать* (выдать* *perf*); (*bride*) отдавать* *(impf)* замуж
▸ **give back** *vt* отдавать* (отдать* *perf*) обратно
▸ **give in** *vi* (*yield*) сдаваться* (сдаться* *perf*) ◆ *vt* (*essay etc*) сдавать* (сдать* *perf*)
▸ **give off** *vt fus* (*smoke*) дымить* *(impf)*; **the radiator/coal fire gives off a lot of heat** от батареи/камина идёт тепло
▸ **give out** *vt* (*distribute*) раздавать* (раздать* *perf*); (*make known*) объявлять (объявить*

perf)
◆ *vi* (*be exhausted*) конча́ться (ко́нчиться *perf*); (*fail*) лома́ться (слома́ться *perf*)
▸ **give up** *vi* (*stop trying*) сдава́ться* (сда́ться* *perf*)
◆ *vt* (*job, boyfriend, habit*) броса́ть (бро́сить* *perf*); (*idea, hope*) оставля́ть (оста́вить* *perf*); **to give up smoking** броса́ть (бро́сить* *perf*) кури́ть; **to give o.s. up** сдава́ться* (сда́ться* *perf*)
▸ **give way** *vi* (*rope, ladder etc*) не вы-де́рживать (вы́держать *perf*); (*wall, roof*) обва́ливаться (обвали́ться* *perf*); (*chair, floor*) прола́мываться (проломи́ться* *perf*); (*BRIT: AUT*) уступа́ть (уступи́ть* *perf*) доро́гу; **his legs gave way beneath him** его́ но́ги подогну́лись; **to give way (to)** (*to demands*) уступа́ть (уступи́ть* *perf*) +*dat.*

give-and-take ['gɪvənd'teɪk] *n* ги́бкость *f*, свобо́да.
giveaway ['gɪvəweɪ] (*inf*) *n*: **her expression was a ~** выраже́ние (её) лица́ вы́дало её ◆ *adj*: **~ prices** даровы́е це́ны; **the exam was a ~!** экза́мен был ерундо́вый!
given ['gɪvn] *pp of* **give** ◆ *adj* да́нный ◆ *conj*: **~ the circumstances ...** с учётом обстоя́тельств ..., учи́тывая обстоя́тельства ...; **~ that** учи́тывая, что.
glacial ['gleɪsɪəl] *adj* (*also fig*) ледяно́й.
glacier ['glæsɪə^r^] *n* ледни́к*.
glad [glæd] *adj*: **I am ~** я рад; **I was ~ of his help** я был рад его́ по́мощи.
gladden ['glædn] *vt* (*heart*) ра́довать (пора́довать *perf*); (*person*) обра́довать (*perf*); **it ~ed his heart to see her well again** у него́ пора́довалось се́рдце, когда́ он уви́дел, что ей ста́ло лу́чше.
glade [gleɪd] *n* поля́на.
gladioli [glædɪ'əulaɪ] *npl* гладио́лусы *mpl*.
gladly ['glædlɪ] *adv* (*willingly*) с ра́достью.
glamorous ['glæmərəs] *adj* очарова́тельный* (очарова́телен).
glamour ['glæmə^r^] *n* очарова́ние.
glance [glɑ:ns] *n* (*look*) взгляд ◆ *vi*: **to ~ at** взгля́дывать (взгляну́ть* *perf*) на +*acc*
▸ **glance off** *vt fus* отска́кивать (отскочи́ть* *perf*) от +*gen*.
glancing ['glɑ:nsɪŋ] *adj* (*blow*) боково́й.
gland [glænd] *n* железа́*.
glandular ['glændjulə^r^] *adj*: **~ fever** (*BRIT*) (инфекцио́нный) мононуклео́з.
glare [glɛə^r^] *n* (*angry*) свире́пый взгляд; (*hostile*) вражде́бный взгляд; (*of light*) ослепи́тельное сия́ние ◆ *vi* (*light*) ослепи́тельно сия́ть (*impf*); **she lives in the full ~ of publicity** все подро́бности её жи́зни стано́вятся достоя́нием пре́ссы; **to ~ at** свире́по *or* при́стально смотре́ть* (посмотре́ть* *perf*) на +*acc*.
glaring ['glɛərɪŋ] *adj* (*mistake*) я́вный, очеви́дный.
Glasgow ['glɑ:zgəu] *n* Гла́зго *m ind*.
glasnost ['glæznɔst] *n* гла́сность *f*.
glass [glɑ:s] *n* (*substance*) стекло́; (*container, contents*) стака́н; **~es** *npl* (*spectacles*) очки́ *ntpl*.
glass-blowing ['glɑ:sbləuɪŋ] *n* стеклоду́вное де́ло.
glass fibre *n* стекловолокно́.
glasshouse ['glɑ:shaus] *n* тепли́ца, парни́к.
glassware ['glɑ:swɛə^r^] *n* стекля́нная посу́да.
glassy ['glɑ:sɪ] *adj* (*eyes, stare*) безжи́зненный* (безжи́зен).
Glaswegian [glæs'wi:dʒən] *adj* гла́зговский ◆ *n* жи́тель(ница) *m(f)* Гла́зго.
glaze [gleɪz] *vt* (*window*) застекля́ть (застекли́ть *perf*); (*pottery*) покрыва́ть (покры́ть* *perf*) глазу́рью ◆ *n* (*on pottery*) глазу́рь *f*.
glazed [gleɪzd] *adj* (*eyes*) му́тный*, ту́склый*; (*pottery*) покры́тый глазу́рью.
glazier ['gleɪzɪə^r^] *n* стеко́льщик.
gleam [gli:m] *vi* сия́ть (засия́ть *perf*) ◆ *n*: **a ~ of hope** луч* наде́жды.
gleaming ['gli:mɪŋ] *adj* сия́ющий*.
glean [gli:n] *vt* (*information*) добыва́ть (добы́ть* *perf*), собира́ть (собра́ть* *perf*).
glee [gli:] *n* (*joy*) ликова́ние.
gleeful ['gli:ful] *adj* лику́ющий.
glen [glɛn] *n* (*SCOTTISH, IRISH*) доли́на реки́.
glib [glɪb] *adj* (*person*) болтли́вый (болтли́в); (*promise, response*) бо́йкий* (бо́ек).
glibly ['glɪblɪ] *adv* (*talk, answer*) бо́йко.
glide [glaɪd] *vi* скользи́ть* (*impf*); (*AVIAT*) плани́ровать (*impf*); (*bird*) пари́ть (*impf*) ◆ *n* скольже́ние.
glider ['glaɪdə^r^] *n* (*AVIAT*) планёр.
gliding ['glaɪdɪŋ] *n* (*AVIAT*) плани́рование.
glimmer ['glɪmə^r^] *n* (*of light*) мерца́ние; (*of interest, hope*) про́блеск ◆ *vi* (*light*) мерца́ть (*impf*).
glimpse [glɪmps] *n* мимолётное впечатле́ние ◆ *vt* ви́деть* (уви́деть* *perf*) ме́льком; **to catch a ~ of** уви́деть* (*perf*) ме́льком.
glint [glɪnt] *vi* блесте́ть* (блесну́ть *perf*), сверка́ть (сверкну́ть *perf*) ◆ *n* (*of metal, light*) блеск, сверка́ние; (*in eyes*) блеск.
glisten ['glɪsn] *vi* (*with sweat, rain etc*) блесте́ть* (*impf*).
glitter ['glɪtə^r^] *vi* сверка́ть (сверкну́ть *perf*) ◆ *n* сверка́ние.
glittering ['glɪtərɪŋ] *adj* (*eyes, career*) блестя́щий*; (*stars*) сия́ющий*; (*diamonds*) сверка́ющий.
glitz [glɪts] *n* (*inf*) блеск.

gloat [gləut] *vi*: **to ~ (over)** злора́дствовать *(impf)* (над *+instr*).
global ['gləubl] *adj* (*interest, attention*) всео́бщий*; (*overall*: *picture*) о́бщий*.
global warming [-'wɔ:mɪŋ] *n* всеми́рное *or* глоба́льное потепле́ние.
globe [gləub] *n* (*world*) земно́й шар*; (*model of world*) гло́бус; (*shape*) шар*.
globetrotter ['gləubtrɔtə'] *n* путеше́ственник(-ица).
globule ['glɔbju:l] *n* ка́пля*.
gloom [glu:m] *n* (*dark*) мрак; (*sadness*) уны́ние.
gloomily ['glu:mɪlɪ] *adv* уны́ло.
gloomy ['glu:mɪ] *adj* мра́чный.
glorification [glɔ:rɪfɪ'keɪʃən] *n* прославле́ние; **the ~ of war** прославле́ние войны́.
glorified ['glɔ:rɪfaɪd] *adj*: **she is merely a ~ secretary** она́ по су́ти де́ла про́сто секрета́рша.
glorify ['glɔ:rɪfaɪ] *vt* (*praise*) прославля́ть (просла́вить* *perf*).
glorious ['glɔ:rɪəs] *adj* (*sunshine, weather*) великоле́пный* (великоле́пен); (*victory*) сла́вный; (*future*) прекра́сный* (прекра́сен).
glory ['glɔ:rɪ] *n* (*prestige*) сла́ва; (*splendour*) великоле́пие ◆ *vi*: **to ~ in** упива́ться *(impf) +instr*.
glory hole *n* (*inf*) кладо́вка.
Glos *abbr* (*BRIT*: *POST*) = *Gloucestershire*.
gloss [glɔs] *n* блеск; (*also*: **~ paint**) лак*
▸ **gloss over** *vt fus* зама́зывать (зама́зать *perf*).
glossary ['glɔsərɪ] *n* глосса́рий.
glossy ['glɔsɪ] *adj* (*photograph, magazine*) гля́нцевый; (*hair*) блестя́щий* ◆ *n* (*also*: **~ magazine**) журна́л в гля́нцевой обло́жке.
glove [glʌv] *n* перча́тка*.
glove compartment *n* (*AUT*) перча́точный я́щик, бардачо́к* (*разг*).
glow [gləu] *vi* (*embers, stars*) свети́ться *(impf)*; (*face, eyes*) горе́ть *(impf)* ◆ *n* (*of eyes, stars*) свет; (*of face*) румя́нец*.
glower ['glauə'] *vi*: **to ~ at sb** смотре́ть* (посмотре́ть* *perf*) с негодова́нием на кого́-н.
glowing ['gləuɪŋ] *adj* (*fire*) я́рко светя́щийся; (*complexion*) румя́ный; (*fig*) блестя́щий*.
glow-worm ['gləuwə:m] *n* светлячо́к*.
glucose ['glu:kəus] *n* глюко́за.
glue [glu:] *n* клей* ◆ *vt*: **to ~ sth onto sth** прикле́ивать (прикле́ить *perf*) что-н на что-н.
glue-sniffing ['glu:snɪfɪŋ] *n* токсикома́ния.
glum [glʌm] *adj* мра́чный*.
glut [glʌt] *n* переизбы́ток* ◆ *vt*: **to be ~ted (with)** (*market, economy etc*) быть* *(impf)* зава́ленным(-ой) (*+instr*).
glutinous ['glu:tɪnəs] *adj* кле́йкий*.
glutton ['glʌtn] *n* обжо́ра *m/f*; **he is a ~ for work** он охо́ч до рабо́ты; **he is a ~ for punishment** он жа́ден до рабо́ты.
gluttonous ['glʌtənəs] *adj* (*person, habits*) ненасы́тный* (ненасы́тен).
gluttony ['glʌtənɪ] *n* ненасы́тность *f*.
glycerin(e) ['glɪsəri:n] *n* глицери́н*.
GM *adj abbr* = **genetically modified**.
gm *abbr* (= **gram**) г= *грамм*.
GMAT *n abbr* (*US*) = *Graduate Management Admissions Test*.
GMB *n abbr* (*BRIT*) = *General Municipal and Boilermakers (Union)*.
GMO *n abbr* (= *genetically modified organism*) трансге́нный органи́зм.
GMT *abbr* (= *Greenwich Mean Time*) сре́днее вре́мя* *nt* по Гри́нвичу.
gnarled [nɑ:ld] *adj* (*tree*) сучкова́тый (сучкова́т); (*hand*) скрю́ченный (скрю́чен).
gnash [næʃ] *vt*: **to ~ one's teeth** скрежета́ть* *(impf)* зуба́ми.
gnat [næt] *n* мо́шка*.
gnaw [nɔ:] *vt* грызть* *(impf)* ◆ *vi* (*doubts, suspicions*): **to ~ at** терза́ть *(impf)*.
gnome [nəum] *n* гном.
GNP *n abbr* (= **gross national product**) ВНП= *валово́й национа́льный проду́кт*.

KEYWORD

go [gəu] (*pt* **went**, *pp* **gone**, *pl* **goes**) *vi* ***1*** (*move*: *on foot*) ходи́ть*/идти́* (пойти́* *perf*); (*travel*: *by transport*) е́здить*/е́хать (пое́хать* *perf*); **she went into the kitchen** она́ пошла́ на ку́хню; **he often goes to China** он ча́сто е́здит в Кита́й; **they are going to the theatre tonight** сего́дня ве́чером они́ иду́т в теа́тр
2 (*depart*: *on foot*) уходи́ть* (уйти́* *perf*); (: *by plane*) улета́ть (улете́ть* *perf*); (: *by train, car*) уезжа́ть (уе́хать* *perf*); **the plane goes at 6am** самолёт улета́ет в 6 часо́в утра́; **the train/bus goes at 6pm** по́езд/авто́бус ухо́дит в 6 часо́в; **now I must go** тепе́рь я до́лжен идти́
3 (*attend*): **to go to** ходи́ть* *(impf)* в/на *+acc*; **she went to university in Aberdeen** она́ учи́лась в Аберди́нском университе́те; **she doesn't go to lectures** она́ не хо́дит на ле́кции
4 (*take part in an activity*) ходи́ть*/идти́* (пойти́* *perf*)
5 (*work*): **is your watch going** ва́ши часы́ иду́т?; **the clock stopped going** часы́ останови́лись; **the bell went just then** зазвони́л звоно́к; **the tape recorder was still going** магнитофо́н не был вы́ключен
6 (*become*): **to go pale** бледне́ть (побледне́ть *perf*); **to go mouldy** пле́сневеть (запле́сневеть *perf*)
7 (*be sold*): **the books went for £10** кни́ги бы́ли про́даны за £10
8 (*fit, suit*): **to go with** подходи́ть* (подойти́* *perf*) к *+dat*
9 (*be about to, intend to*) собира́ться (собра́ться* *perf*) *+infin*
10 (*time*: *slowly*) тяну́ться *(impf)*; (*quickly*) проходи́ть* (пройти́* *perf*)
11 (*event, activity*) проходи́ть* (пройти́* *perf*);

how did it go? ну как всё прошло́?
12 (*be given*): **the job is to go to someone else** рабо́ту должны́ отда́ть кому́-то друго́му; **the proceeds will go to charity** при́быль пойдёт на благотвори́тельные це́ли
13 (*break etc*): **the fuse went** предохрани́тель *m* перегоре́л; **the leg of the chair went** но́жка сту́ла слома́лась
14 (*be placed*): **the milk goes in the fridge** молоко́ ну́жно поста́вить в холоди́льник; **where does this cup go?** куда́ поста́вить э́ту ча́шку?; **the suitcase goes on top of the wardrobe** чемода́н обы́чно лежи́т на шкафу́
◆ *n* **1** (*try*): **to have a go (at sth/at doing sth)** про́бовать* (попро́бовать* *perf*) (что-н/+*perf infin*)
2 (*turn*): **whose go is it?** (*in board games*) чей ход?; (*in sports*) чья (сейча́с) о́чередь?
3 (*move*): **to be on the go** быть *(impf)* на нога́х

▸ **go about** *vi* (*also:* **go around**: *rumour*) ходи́ть* *(impf)*
◆ *vt fus*: **to go about one's business** занима́ться (заня́ться* *perf*) свои́ми дела́ми; **how do I go about (doing) this?** как мне э́то сде́лать?

▸ **go after** *vt fus* (*person*) бежа́ть (побежа́ть *perf*) (вдого́нку) за +*instr*; **to go after a job** стреми́ться* *(impf)* получи́ть рабо́ту

▸ **go against** *vt fus* (*subj*: *decision, verdict*): **to go against sb** быть *(impf)* не в чью-н по́льзу

▸ **go ahead** *vi* (*proceed*) продвига́ться (продви́нуться *perf*); (*event*): **to go ahead with** (*project*) приступи́ть* *(perf)* к +*dat*; **may I begin? – yes, go ahead!** мо́жно нача́ть? – да, пожа́луйста!

▸ **go along** *vi* идти́ (пойти́* *perf*); **I went along with him/his decision** (*agree with*) я не стал проти́виться ему́/его́ реше́нию; **to go along with sb** (*accompany*) идти́* (пойти́* *perf*) с кем-н

▸ **go away** *vi* (*leave*: *on foot*) уходи́ть* (уйти́* *perf*); (: *by transport*) уезжа́ть* (уе́хать* *perf*); **go away and think about it for a while** пойди́ и поду́май немно́жко на э́тот счёт

▸ **go back** *vi* (*return*) возвраща́ться (верну́ться* *perf*); (*go again*: *on foot*) идти́* (пойти́* *perf*) ещё раз *or* опя́ть; (: *by transport*) е́хать* (пое́хать* *perf*) ежё раз *or* опя́ть; **we went back into the house** мы пошли́ обра́тно в дом; **I am never going back to her house again** я никогда́ бо́льше не пойду́ к ней; **to go back to** (*date from*) относи́ться *(impf)* к +*dat*

▸ **go back on** *vt fus* (*promise, word*) не сде́рживать (сдержа́ть* *perf*) +*gen*

▸ **go by** *vi* (*years, time*) проходи́ть* (пройти́* *perf*)
◆ *vt fus* (*book, rule*) де́лать (сде́лать *perf*) всё по +*dat*; **as time goes by** ... вре́мя идёт, и ...

▸ **go down** *vi* (*descend*) спуска́ться (спусти́ться* *perf*); (*ship*) тону́ть* (затону́ть* *perf*); (*sun*) заходи́ть* (зайти́* *perf*); (*prices, temperature*) па́дать (упа́сть* *perf*); (*swelling*) спада́ть (спасть* *perf*)
◆ *vt fus* (*stairs, ladder*) спуска́ться (спусти́ться* *perf*) с +*gen*; **that should go down well with him** э́то ему́ должно́ понра́вится; **he went to London/to see his sister** он пое́хал в Ло́ндон/в го́сти к свое́й сестре́

▸ **go for** *vt fus* (*fetch*: *paper, doctor*) идти́* (пойти́* *perf*) за +*instr*; (*choose, like*) люби́ть* *(impf)*; (*attack*) набра́сываться (набро́ситься* *perf*) на +*acc*; **that goes for me too** и я то́же

▸ **go in** *vi* (*enter*) входи́ть* (войти́* *perf*); **it's time to go in** пора́ заходи́ть

▸ **go in for** *vt fus* принима́ть (приня́ть* *perf*) уча́стие в +*prp*; (*take up*) заня́ться* *(perf)* +*instr*

▸ **go into** *vt fus* (*enter*) входи́ть* (войти́* *perf*) в +*acc*; (*investigate*) рассма́тривать (рассмотре́ть* *perf*); (*take up*) заня́ться* *(perf)* +*instr*; **to go into detail** вдава́ться* *(impf)* в подро́бности

▸ **go off** *vi* (*leave*: *on foot*) уходи́ть* (уйти́* *perf*); (: *by transport*) уезжа́ть (уе́хать* *perf*); (*food*) по́ртиться* (испо́ртиться* *perf*); (*bomb*) взрыва́ться (взорва́ться* *perf*); (*gun*) вы́стрелить *(perf)*; (*alarm*) звони́ть (зазвони́ть *perf*); (*event*) проходи́ть* (пройти́* *perf*); (*lights*) выключа́ться (вы́ключиться *perf*)
◆ *vt fus* разлюби́ть* *(perf)*; **to go off to sleep** засыпа́ть (засну́ть *perf*)

▸ **go on** *vi*: **to go on (doing)** (*continue*) продолжа́ть *(impf)* (+*infin*); (*happen*: *discussion, argument*) идти́* *(impf)*; **life goes on** жизнь продолжа́ется; **what's going on here?** что́ здесь происхо́дит?; **we don't have enough evidence/information to go on** у нас нет доста́точных доказа́тельств/ информа́ции

▸ **go on at** *vt fus* пристава́ть* *(impf)* к +*dat*

▸ **go on with** *vt fus* продолжа́ть (продо́лжить* *perf*)

▸ **go out** *vi* (*fire, light*) га́снуть* (пога́снуть* *perf*); (*leave*): **to go out of** выходи́ть* (вы́йти* *perf*) из +*gen*; **are you going out tonight?** (*for entertainment*) Вы сего́дня ве́чером куда́-нибу́дь идёте?

▸ **go over** *vi* идти́* (пойти́* *perf*)
◆ *vt fus* (*check*) просма́тривать (просмотре́ть* *perf*); **to go over sth in one's mind** повторя́ть (повтори́ть *perf*) что-н в уме́

▸ **go round** *vi* (*circulate*) ходи́ть* *(impf)*; (*revolve*) враща́ться *(impf)*; (*suffice*) хвата́ть (хвати́ть *perf*) на всех; (*visit*): **to go round (to sb's)** заходи́ть* (зайти́* *perf*) (к кому́-н);

(*make a detour*): **to go round (by)** (*on foot*) идти́* (пойти́* *perf*) круго́м (че́рез *+acc*); (*by transport*) е́хать (пое́хать *perf*) круго́м (че́рез *+acc*)

► **go through** *vt fus* (*town etc: on foot*) проходи́ть* (пройти́* *perf*) че́рез *+acc*; (: *by transport*) проезжа́ть (прое́хать* *perf*) че́рез *+acc*; (*files, papers*) просма́тривать (просмотре́ть* *perf*); (*aloud: list*) чита́ть (прочита́ть *perf*); (*practice*) проде́лывать (проде́лать *perf*)

► **go through with** *vt fus* (*plan, crime*) осуществля́ть (осуществи́ть* *perf*); **I couldn't go through with it** я не мог осуществи́ть э́то

► **go under** *vi* (*also fig*) идти́* (пойти́* *perf*) под во́ду

► **go up** *vi* (*ascend*) поднима́ться (подня́ться* *perf*); (*price, level*) расти́* (вы́расти* *perf*); (*buildings*) выраста́ть (вы́расти* *perf*); **to go up in flames** загора́ться *(impf)*

► **go with** *vt fus* (*match*) подходи́ть* (подойти́* *perf*) к *+dat*

► **go without** *vt fus* (*treats*) остава́ться* (оста́ться* *perf*) без *+gen*; **I can go without food for 24 hours** я могу́ су́тки не есть.

goad [gəud] *vt* (*person*) подстрека́ть *(impf)*

► **goad on** *vt* (*person*) подгоня́ть *(impf)*.

go-ahead ['gəuəhɛd] *adj* предприи́мчивый (предприи́мчив) ◆ *n* (*for project*) добро́; **to give sb the ~** дава́ть* (дать* *perf*) кому́-н добро́.

goal [gəul] *n* (*SPORT*) гол; (: *goal posts*) воро́та *mpl*; (*aim*) цель *f*; **to score a ~** забива́ть (заби́ть* *perf*) гол.

goal difference *n* ра́зница мяче́й.

goalie ['gəulɪ] *n* (*inf*) врата́рь* *m*, голки́пер.

goalkeeper ['gəulki:pə'] *n* врата́рь* *m*, голки́пер.

goal post *n* бокова́я шта́нга, сто́йка* воро́т.

goat [gəut] *n* (*billy*) козёл*; (*nanny*) коза́.

gobble ['gɔbl] *vt* (*also: ~ down, ~ up*) ло́пать (сло́пать *perf*), жрать* (сожра́ть* *perf*).

go-between ['gəubɪtwi:n] *n* посре́дник(-ица).

Gobi Desert ['gəubɪ-] *n*: **the ~ ~** пусты́ня Го́би.

goblet ['gɔblɪt] *n* ку́бок*.

goblin ['gɔblɪn] *n* го́блин.

gobsmacked ['gɔbsmækt] *adj*: **I was ~** (*inf*) я соверше́нно обалде́л.

go-cart ['gəukɑ:t] *n* карт.

God [gɔd] *n* Бог ◆ *excl* Го́споди!, о Бо́же!

god [gɔd] *n* (*MYTHOLOGY, fig*) божество́*, бог*.

god-awful [gɔd'ɔ:fəl] *adj* (*inf!*) жу́ткий*, кошма́рный*.

godchild ['gɔdtʃaɪld] *n* кре́стник(-ица).

goddam ['gɔddæm] *adj* (*inf!*) прокля́тый (*!*)

goddamned ['gɔddæmd] *adj* (*inf!*) прокля́тый.

goddaughter ['gɔddɔ:tə'] *n* кре́стница.

goddess ['gɔdɪs] *n* боги́ня.

godfather ['gɔdfɑ:ðə'] *n* крёстный оте́ц*.

God-fearing ['gɔdfɪərɪŋ] *adj* богобоя́зненный.

godforsaken ['gɔdfəseɪkən] *adj* забы́тый Бо́гом, забро́шенный*.

godmother ['gɔdmʌðə'] *n* кре́стная мать* *f*.

godparent ['gɔdpɛərənt] *n* крёстный(-ая) *m(f) adj*.

godsend ['gɔdsɛnd] *n* благода́ть *f*.

godson ['gɔdsʌn] *n* кре́стник.

goes [gəuz] *vb see* **go**.

gofer ['gəufə'] *n* (*inf*) ма́льчик на побегу́шках.

go-getter ['gəugɛtə'] *n* предприи́мчивый челове́к*.

goggle ['gɔgl] *vi* (*inf*): **to ~ at** тара́щиться (вы́таращиться *perf*) на *+acc*.

goggles ['gɔglz] *npl* защи́тные очки́ *ntpl*.

going ['gəuɪŋ] *n* (*conditions*): **the ~** обстоя́тельства *ntpl* ◆ *adj*: **the ~ rate** существу́ющие расце́нки *fpl*; **this book is heavy ~** э́та кни́га тру́дно чита́ется; **it was hard ~** понача́лу приходи́лось тру́дно; **a ~ concern** де́йствующее предприя́тие.

going-over [gəuɪŋ'əuvə'] *n* (*inf: examination*) осмо́тр; (*physical attack*) трёпка.

goings-on ['gəuɪŋz'ɔn] *npl* (*inf*) дела́ *ntpl*.

go-kart ['gəukɑ:t] *n* = **go-cart**.

gold [gəuld] *n* зо́лото; (*SPORT: also: ~ medal*) зо́лото, золота́я меда́ль *f* ◆ *adj* золото́й; **~ reserves** золото́й запа́с.

golden ['gəuldən] *adj* (*made of gold*) золото́й; (*gold in colour*) золоти́стый; (*opportunity, future*) прекра́сный*.

golden age *n* золото́й век*.

golden handshake *n* (*BRIT*) *де́нежное вознагражде́ние при ухо́де на пе́нсию*.

golden rule *n* золото́е пра́вило.

goldfish ['gəuldfɪʃ] *n* золота́я ры́бка*.

gold leaf *n* суса́льное зо́лото.

gold medal *n* (*SPORT*) золота́я меда́ль *f*.

gold mine *n* золото́й при́иск *or* рудни́к*; (*fig*) золото́е дно*.

gold-plated ['gəuld'pleɪtɪd] *adj* позоло́ченный.

goldsmith ['gəuldsmɪθ] *n* золоты́х дел ма́стер*.

gold standard *n* золото́й станда́рт.

golf [gɔlf] *n* гольф.

golf ball *n* мяч для игры́ в гольф; (*on typewriter*) *металли́ческий шар с бу́квами в электри́ческой печа́тной маши́нке*.

golf club *n* (*organization*) клуб люби́телей игры́ в гольф; (*stick*) клю́шка* для игры́ в гольф.

golf course *n* по́ле для игры́ в гольф.

golfer ['gɔlfə'] *n* игро́к* в гольф.

golfing ['gɔlfɪŋ] *adj* для игры́ в гольф.

gondola ['gɔndələ] *n* гондо́ла.

gondolier [gɔndə'lɪə'] *n* гондолье́р.

gone [gɔn] *pp of* **go** ◆ *adj* уе́хавший, уше́дший.

goner ['gɔnə'] (*inf*) *n*: **I was a ~** со мной бы́ло всё поко́нчено.

gong [gɔŋ] *n* гонг.

good [gud] *adj* хоро́ший*; (*pleasant*) прия́тный*; (*kind*) до́брый*; (*morally correct*) пра́вильный* ◆ *n* (*virtue*) добро́; (*benefit*) по́льза; **~s** *npl* (*COMM*) това́ры *mpl*; **~!** хорошо́!; **to be ~ at** име́ть *(impf)* спосо́бности к *+dat*; **to be ~ for** (*useful*) быть* *(impf)* поле́зным(-ой) для *+dat*; **it's ~ for you** э́то Вам поле́зно (для здоро́вья); **it's a ~ thing you were there** хорошо́, что Вы бы́ли там; **she is ~ with children** она́ уме́ет обраща́ться с детьми́; **she is ~ with her hands** у неё золоты́е ру́ки; **to feel ~** чу́вствовать *(impf)* себя́ хорошо́; **it's ~ to see you** о́чень прия́тно Вас ви́деть; **would you be ~ enough to ...?** не бу́дете ли Вы так добры́ *+perf infin* ...?; **that's very ~ of you** э́то о́чень ми́ло с Ва́шей стороны́; **is this any ~?** (*will it do?*) э́то пойдёт?; (*what's it like?*) понра́вилось ли э́то Вам?; **a ~ deal (of)** большо́е коли́чество (*+gen*); **a ~ many** мно́го *+gen*; **to take a ~ look** смотре́ть* (посмотре́ть* *perf*) хороше́нько; **a ~ while ago** о́чень давно́; **to make ~** (*damage*) ремонти́ровать (отремонти́ровать *perf*); (*loss*) восполня́ть (воспо́лнить *perf*); **~ afternoon/evening!** до́брый день/ве́чер!; **~ morning!** до́брое у́тро!; **~ night!** (*on leaving*) до свида́ния!; (*on going to bed*) споко́йной *or* до́брой но́чи!; **he's up to no ~** он заду́мал что́-то (плохо́е); **for the common ~** для о́бщего бла́га; **it's no ~ complaining** что то́лку жа́ловаться; **for ~** навсегда́; **~s and chattels** ли́чные ве́щи*.

goodbye [gud'baɪ] *excl* до свида́ния; **to say ~ (to)** проща́ться (попроща́ться *perf*) (с *+instr*).

good-for-nothing ['gudfənʌθɪŋ] *adj* никуды́шний.

Good Friday *n* Страстна́я пя́тница.

good-humoured ['gud'hju:məd] (*US* **good-humored**) *adj* (*person*) доброду́шный*; (*remark, joke*) до́брый*.

good-looking ['gud'lukɪŋ] *adj* краси́вый.

good-natured ['gud'neɪtʃəd] *adj* (*person*) доброду́шный*; (*pet*) послу́шный; (*discussion*) споко́йный*.

goodness ['gudnɪs] *n* доброта́; **for ~ sake!** ра́ди Бо́га!; **~ gracious!** Го́споди!

goods train *n* (*BRIT*) това́рный по́езд*.

goodwill [gud'wɪl] *n* (*of person*) доброжела́тельность *f*; (*COMM*) прести́ж фи́рмы.

goody-goody ['gudɪgudɪ] *n* (*pej*) па́инька* *m/f*.

gooey ['gu:ɪ] (*inf*) *adj* ли́пкий* (ли́пок).

goose [gu:s] (*pl* **geese**) *n* (*male*) гусь* *m*; (*female*) гусы́ня.

gooseberry ['guzbərɪ] *n* крыжо́вник *no pl*; **he is playing ~** (*BRIT*) он тре́тий ли́шний.

goose flesh *n* = **goose pimples**.

goose pimples *npl* гуси́ная ко́жа *fsg*.

goose step *n* (*MIL*) гуси́ный шаг.

GOP *n abbr* (*US*: *POL*: *inf*: = *Grand Old Party*) *неофициа́льное назва́ние Республика́нской па́ртии США.*

gopher ['gəufə'] *n* го́фер (*колумби́йский су́слик*).

gore [gɔ:'] *vt* бода́ть (забода́ть *perf*) ◆ *n* (запёкшаяся) кровь *f*.

gorge [gɔ:dʒ] *n* тесни́на, (у́зкое) уще́лье* ◆ *vt*: **to ~ o.s. (on)** наеда́ться (нае́сться* *perf*) (*+gen*).

gorgeous ['gɔ:dʒəs] *adj* великоле́пный, прекра́сный.

gorilla [gə'rɪlə] *n* гори́лла.

gormless ['gɔ:mlɪs] *adj* (*BRIT*: *inf*) тупо́й*.

gorse [gɔ:s] *n* (*BOT*) утёсник.

gory ['gɔ:rɪ] *adj* (*details*) крова́вый; (*situation*) кровопроли́тный*.

go-slow ['gəu'sləu] *n* (*BRIT*) сниже́ние те́мпа рабо́ты (*как вид забасто́вки*).

gospel ['gɔspl] *n* (*REL*) ева́нгелие; (*doctrine*) про́поведь *f*.

gossamer ['gɔsəmə'] *n* (*cobweb*) паути́нка; (*light fabric*) газ.

gossip ['gɔsɪp] *n* (*rumours*) спле́тня*; (*chat*) разгово́ры *mpl*; (*person*) спле́тник(-ица) ◆ *vi* болта́ть (поболта́ть *perf*); **a piece of ~** спле́тня*, слух.

gossip column *n* коло́нка* све́тской хро́ники.

got [gɔt] *pt, pp of* **get**.

Gothic ['gɔθɪk] *adj* готи́ческий*.

gotten ['gɔtn] *pp* (*US*) *of* **get**.

gouge [gaudʒ] *vt* (*also*: **~ out**: *hole etc*) выда́лбливать (вы́долбить* *perf*); (: *initials*) выреза́ть (вы́резать* *perf*); **to ~ sb's eyes out** выка́лывать (вы́колоть *perf*) кому́-н глаза́.

gourd [guəd] *n* ты́ква.

gourmet ['guəmeɪ] *n* гурма́н.

gout [gaut] *n* (*MED*) пода́гра.

govern ['gʌvən] *vt* (*country, also LING*) управля́ть *(impf)* *+instr*; (*event, conduct*) руководи́ть* *(impf)* *+instr*.

governess ['gʌvənɪs] *n* гуверна́нтка*.

governing ['gʌvənɪŋ] *adj* (*POL*) пра́вящий*, руководя́щий*.

governing body *n* (*of party*) руководя́щий* о́рган; (*of university*) о́рган управле́ния.

government ['gʌvnmənt] *n* (*act of governing*) управле́ние; (*governing body*) прави́тельство ◆ *cpd* прави́тельственный; **local ~** ме́стное самоуправле́ние.

governmental [gʌvn'mɛntl] *adj* прави́тельственный.

government housing *n* (*US*) *жили́щный ко́мплекс, постро́енный на госуда́рственные сре́дства.*

government stock *n прави́тельственные облига́ции и це́нные бума́ги.*

governor ['gʌvənə'] *n* (*of state, colony*) губерна́тор; (*of bank, school, hospital*)

* marks translations which have irregular inflections. The Russian-English side of the dictionary gives inflectional information.

дире́ктор*; (*BRIT*: *of prison*) нача́льник.

Govt *abbr* = **government**.

gown [gaun] *n* (*dress*) пла́тье*; (*of teacher*: *BRIT*: *of judge*) ма́нтия.

GP *n abbr* = **general practitioner**.

GPO *n abbr* (*BRIT*: *formerly*) = *General Post Office*; (*US*) *Government Printing Office*.

gr. *abbr* (*COMM*) = **gross**.

grab [græb] *vt* (*seize, also fig*) хвата́ть (схвати́ть* *perf*); (*food*) перехва́тывать (перехвати́ть* *perf*); (*sleep*) урыва́ть (урва́ть* *perf*) ◆ *vi*: **to ~ at** хвата́ться (ухвати́ться* *perf*) за +*acc*.

grace [greıs] *n* гра́ция; (*REL*) моли́тва (*пе́ред едо́й*) ◆ *vt* (*honour*) удоста́ивать (удосто́ить *perf*); (*adorn*) украша́ть (укра́сить* *perf*); **5 days' ~** 5 дне́й отсро́чки; **with (a) good ~** любе́зно, с досто́инством; **with (a) bad ~** нелюбе́зно, бех досто́инства; **his sense of humour is his saving ~** его́ спаса́ет чу́вство ю́мора; **to say ~** моли́ться* (помоли́ться* *perf*) пе́ред едо́й.

graceful ['greısful] *adj* (*animal, person*) грацио́зный*; (*style, shape*) изя́щный*; (*refusal, behaviour*) досто́йный*.

gracious ['greıʃəs] *adj* (*person, smile*) любе́зный*; (*house*) прекра́сный*; (*living*) краси́вый ◆ *excl*: **(good) ~!** Бо́же мо́й!

gradation [grə'deıʃən] *n* града́ция.

grade [greıd] *n* (*COMM*: *quality*) сорт*; (*in hierarchy*) ра́нг; (*SCOL*: *mark*) оце́нка*; (*US*: *school year*) класс; (: *gradient*) укло́н ◆ *vt* (*rank, class*) распределя́ть (распредели́ть *perf*); (*products*) сортирова́ть (рассортирова́ть *perf*); **to make the ~** (*fig*) добива́ться (доби́ться* *perf*) своего́ *or* успе́ха.

grade crossing *n* (*US*) железнодоро́жный перее́зд.

grade school *n* (*US*) нача́льная шко́ла.

gradient ['greıdıənt] *n* (*of hill*) укло́н; (*GEOM*) градие́нт.

gradual ['grædjuəl] *adj* постепе́нный*.

gradually ['grædjuəlı] *adv* постепе́нно.

graduate [*n* 'grædjuıt, *vi* 'grædjueıt] *n* выпускни́к*(-и́ца) ◆ *vi*: **to ~ from** зака́нчивать (зако́нчить *perf*); **I ~d last year** я зако́нчил университе́т в про́шлом году́.

graduated pension ['grædjueıtıd-] *n пе́нсия, увели́чивающаяся в зави́симости от ста́жа рабо́ты*.

graduation [grædju'eıʃən] *n* (*ceremony*: *at university*) церемо́ния вруче́ния дипло́ма; (: *US*) ≈ церемо́ния вруче́ния аттеста́та.

graffiti [grə'fi:tı] *n, npl* графи́ти *nt ind*.

graft [grɑ:ft] *n* (*AGR*) приви́вка*; (*MED*) переса́дка* (*ко́жи и́ли ко́стной тка́ни*); (*BRIT*: *inf*: *hard work*) тяжёлая рабо́та; (*bribery*) взя́точничество ◆ *vt*: **to ~ (onto)** (*AGR, also fig*) привива́ть (приви́ть* *perf*) (к +*dat*); (*MED*) переса́живать (пересади́ть* *perf*) (на +*acc*).

grain [greın] *n* (*seed*) зерно́*; (*no pl*: *cereals*) хле́бные зла́ки *mpl*; (*US*: *corn*) зерно́; (*of sand*) песчи́нка*; (*of salt*) крупи́ца; (*of wood*) волокно́*; **however much it goes against the ~, I ...** (*fig*) как бы э́то ни противоре́чило мои́м при́нципам, я ....

gram [græm] *n* гра́мм.

grammar ['græmə'] *n* грамма́тика; (*book*) уче́бник грамма́тики.

grammar school *n* (*BRIT*) сре́дняя шко́ла (*для одарённых дете́й*).

grammatical [grə'mætıkl] *adj* граммати́ческий*.

gramme [græm] *n* = **gram**.

gramophone ['græməfəun] *n* (*BRIT*) граммофо́н.

granary ['grænərı] *n* амба́р; (*larger*) зернохрани́лище.

Granary bread *or* **loaf®** *n хлеб и́ли буха́нка из муки́ кру́пного помо́ла с це́лыми зёрнами внутри́*.

grand [grænd] (*pl* ~) *adj* грандио́зный*; (*gesture*) вели́чественный*; (*inf*: *wonderful*) великоле́пный*, восхити́тельный* ◆ *n* (*inf*) ты́сяча.

grandchild ['græntʃaıld] (*pl* **~ren**) *n* внук(-у́чка*).

grandchildren ['græntʃıldrən] *npl of* **grandchild**.

granddad ['grændæd] *n* (*inf*) де́душка* *m*.

granddaughter ['grændɔ:tə'] *n* вну́чка*.

grandeur ['grændjə'] *n* великоле́пие.

grandfather ['grændfɑ:ðə'] *n* де́душка* *m*.

grandiose ['grændıəus] *adj* грандио́зный*.

grand jury *n* (*US*) *прися́жные, реша́ющие вопро́с о преда́нии суду́*.

grandma ['grænmɑ:] *n* (*inf*) ба́бушка*.

grandmother ['grænmʌðə'] *n* ба́бушка*.

grandpa ['grænpɑ:] *n* (*inf*) = **granddad**.

grandparents ['grændpɛərənts] *npl* де́душка* *m* и ба́бушка*.

grand piano *n* роя́ль *m*.

Grand Prix ['grɑ̃:'pri:] *n* гран-при́ *m ind*.

grandson ['grænsʌn] *n* внук.

grandstand ['grændstænd] *n* (*SPORT*) центра́льная трибу́на.

grand total *n* о́бщая су́мма.

granite ['grænıt] *n* грани́т.

granny ['grænı] *n* (*inf*) ба́бушка*.

grant [grɑ:nt] *vt* (*money, visa*) выдава́ть* (вы́дать* *perf*); (*pension*) назнача́ть (назна́чить *perf*); (*request*) удовлетворя́ть (удовлетвори́ть *perf*); (*admit*) признава́ть* (призна́ть* *perf*) ◆ *n* (*SCOL*) стипе́ндия; (*ADMIN*) субси́дия; **to take sb/sth for ~ed** принима́ть (приня́ть* *perf*) кого́-н/что́-н как до́лжное; **to ~ that** признава́ть* (призна́ть* *perf*), что.

granulated sugar ['grænjuleıtıd-] *n* са́харный песо́к*.

granule ['grænju:l] *n* (*of coffee*) гра́нула; (*of*

salt) крупи́ца.
grape [greɪp] *n* виногра́д* *no pl*; **a bunch of ~s** кисть* *f or* гроздь* *f* виногра́да.
grapefruit ['greɪpfru:t] (*pl* ~ *or* ~**s**) *n* грейпфру́т.
grapevine ['greɪpvaɪn] *n* виногра́дная лоза́*; **I heard on the ~ that ...** я слы́шал, что ..., говоря́т, что ....
graph [grɑ:f] *n* (*diagram*) гра́фик.
graphic ['græfɪk] *adj* (*account, description*) я́ркий*; (*design*) изобрази́тельный; ~ **art** гра́фика; *see also* **graphics**.
graphic designer *n* худо́жник-оформи́тель *m*.
graphic equalizer *n* графи́ческий* вырáвниватель *m*.
graphics ['græfɪks] *n* гра́фика ◆ *npl* рису́нки *mpl*.
graphite ['græfaɪt] *n* графи́т.
graph paper *n* миллиметро́вка.
grapple ['græpl] *vi*: **to ~ with sb** схва́тываться (схвати́ться* *perf*) с кем-н; **to ~ with a problem** би́ться* *(impf)* над пробле́мой.
grasp [grɑ:sp] *vt* (*also fig*) схва́тывать (схвати́ть* *perf*) ◆ *n* (*grip*) хва́тка; (*understanding*) понима́ние; **the vase slipped from my ~** ва́за вы́скользнула из мои́х рук; **success was now within his ~** успе́х был тепе́рь в его́ рука́х; **to have a good ~ of sth** (*fig*) хорошо́ разбира́ться *(impf)* в чём-н
▸ **grasp at** *vt fus* (*rope etc*) хвата́ться (ухвати́ться* *perf*) за *+acc*; (*fig: opportunity*) цепля́ться (уцепи́ться* *perf*) за *+acc*.
grasping ['grɑ:spɪŋ] *adj* (*greedy*) жа́дный*.
grass [grɑ:s] *n* трава́*; (*lawn*) газо́н; (BRIT: *inf: informer*) стука́ч*; (*: ex-terrorist*) доно́счик.
grasshopper ['grɑ:shɔpə^r] *n* кузне́чик.
grass-roots ['grɑ:sru:ts] *adj* (*support*) низово́й; (*member*) рядово́й.
grass snake *n* уж*.
grassy ['grɑ:sɪ] *adj* (*bank, slope*) травяни́стый.
grate [greɪt] *n* ками́нная решётка* ◆ *vt* (CULIN) тере́ть* (натере́ть* *perf*) ◆ *vi* (*metal, chalk*): **to ~ (on)** скрипе́ть* *(impf)* (по *+dat*).
grateful ['greɪtful] *adj* (*person*) благода́рный* (благода́рен); ~ **thanks** и́скренняя благода́рность.
gratefully ['greɪtfəlɪ] *adv* благода́рно.
grater ['greɪtə^r] *n* тёрка*.
gratification [grætɪfɪ'keɪʃən] *n* удовлетворе́ние.
gratify ['grætɪfaɪ] *vt* (*person*) ра́довать (пора́довать *perf*); (*whim, desire*) удовлетворя́ть (удовлетвори́ть *perf*).
gratifying ['grætɪfaɪɪŋ] *adj* (*pleasing*) прия́тный* (прия́тен).
grating ['greɪtɪŋ] *n* решётка* ◆ *adj* (*noise*) ре́зкий*.
gratitude ['grætɪtju:d] *n* благода́рность *f*.
gratuitous [grə'tju:ɪtəs] *adj* (*violence, cruelty*) бессмы́сленный* (бессмы́слен).
gratuity [grə'tju:ɪtɪ] *n* (*tip*) чаевы́е *pl adj*.
grave [greɪv] *n* моги́ла ◆ *adj* серьёзный* (серьёзен); (*mistake*) роково́й.
grave digger *n* моги́льщик.
gravel ['grævl] *n* гра́вий.
gravely ['greɪvlɪ] *adv* серьёзно; ~ **ill** тяжело́ больно́й* (бо́лен).
gravestone ['greɪvstəun] *n* надгро́бие.
graveyard ['greɪvjɑ:d] *n* кла́дбище.
gravitas ['grævɪtæs] *n* многозначи́тельность *f*.
gravitate ['grævɪteɪt] *vi*: **to ~ towards** стреми́ться* *(impf) or* тяну́ться* *(impf)* к *+dat*.
gravity ['grævɪtɪ] *n* (PHYS) си́ла тя́жести; (*seriousness*) серьёзность *f*.
gravy ['greɪvɪ] *n* (*meat juices*) подли́вка; (*sauce*) со́ус*.
gravy boat *n* со́усник.
gravy train *n* (*inf*): **to ride the ~ ~** име́ть *(impf)* лёгкий за́работок.
gray [greɪ] *adj* (US) = **grey**.
graze [greɪz] *vi* пасти́сь* *(impf)* ◆ *vt* (*touch lightly*) задева́ть (заде́ть* *perf*); (*scrape*) цара́пать (оцара́пать *perf*) ◆ *n* цара́пина.
grazing ['greɪzɪŋ] *n* (*pasture*) па́стбище.
grease [gri:s] *n* (*lubricant*) сма́зка*; (*fat*) жир* ◆ *vt* сма́зывать (сма́зать* *perf*); **to ~ sb's palm** (*fig*) дава́ть* (дать* *perf*) кому́-н взя́тку.
grease gun *n* сма́зочный шприц.
greasepaint ['gri:speɪnt] *n* (театра́льный) грим.
greaseproof paper ['gri:spru:f-] *n* (BRIT) жиронепроница́емая бума́га.
greasy ['gri:sɪ] *adj* жи́рный*; (*clothes*) заса́ленный* (заса́лен); (BRIT: *road, surface*) ско́льзкий*.
great [greɪt] *adj* (*large*) большо́й*; (*heat, pain*) си́льный*; (*city, man*) вели́кий*; (*inf: terrific*) замеча́тельный*; **they're ~ friends** они́ больши́е друзья́; **we had a ~ time** мы замеча́тельно провели́ вре́мя; **it was ~!** э́то бы́ло замеча́тельно *or* здо́рово!; **the ~ thing is that ...** са́мое гла́вное то, что ....
Great Barrier Reef *n*: **the ~ ~ ~** Большо́й Барье́рный риф.
Great Britain *n* Великобрита́ния.
greater ['greɪtə^r] *adj*: ~ **Calcutta** больша́я Калькутта; **G~ Manchester** большо́й Манче́стер.
great-grandchild [greɪt'græntʃaɪld] (*pl* ~**ren**) *n* пра́внук*(-учка*).
great-grandchildren [greɪt'græntʃɪldrən] *npl of* **great-grandchild**.
great-grandfather [greɪt'grænfɑ:ðə^r] *n* праде́душка* *m*.
great-grandmother [greɪt'grænmʌðə^r] *n*

* marks translations which have irregular inflections. The Russian-English side of the dictionary gives inflectional information.

прабабушка*.
Great Lakes *npl*: **the ~~** Большие Озёра *ntpl.*
greatly ['greɪtlɪ] *adv* очень; (*influenced*) в значительной степени.
greatness ['greɪtnɪs] *n* (*importance*) величие.
Grecian ['gri:ʃən] *adj* греческий*.
Greece [gri:s] *n* Греция.
greed [gri:d] *n* (*greediness*) жадность *f*; (*for power, wealth*) жажда.
greedily ['gri:dɪlɪ] *adv* жадно.
greedy ['gri:dɪ] *adj* жадный* (жаден).
Greek [gri:k] *adj* греческий ◆ *n* (*person*) грек (гречанка*); (*LING*) греческий* язык*; **ancient/modern ~** древнегреческий*/современный греческий* язык*.
green [gri:n] *adj* зелёный ◆ *n* (*colour*) зелёный цвет; (*stretch of grass*) лужайка*; (*on golf course*) *площадка вокруг лунки, покрытая травой*; (*also:* **village ~**) газон в центре деревни; **~s** *npl* (*vegetables*) овощи *mpl*; (*POL*) :**the G~s** зелёные *pl adj*; **the G~ Party** партия зелёных; **he has ~ fingers** *or (US)* **a ~ thumb** (*fig*) что он ни посадит, всё у него растёт; **to give sb the ~ light** давать* (дать* *perf*) кому-н зелёную улицу.
green belt *n* (*round town*) зелёная зона, зелёный пояс*.
green card *n* (*BRIT*: *AUT*) зелёная карточка (*для страховки автомобиля за рубежом*); (*US*: *ADMIN*) зелёная карточка (*необходимая для трудоустройства*).
greenery ['gri:nərɪ] *n* зелень *f*.
greenfly ['gri:nflaɪ] *n* (*BRIT*) тля.
greengage ['gri:ngeɪdʒ] *n* слива-венчерка.
greengrocer ['gri:ngrəusə^r] *n* (*BRIT*) зеленщик* (*продавец овощей и фруктов*).
greenhouse ['gri:nhaus] *n* теплица.
greenhouse effect *n*: **the ~~** парниковый эффект.
greenhouse gas *n* один из газов, вызывающий тепличный эффект.
greenish ['gri:nɪʃ] *adj* зеленоватый.
Greenland ['gri:nlənd] *n* Гренландия.
Greenlander ['gri:nləndə^r] *n* житель(ница) *m(f)* Гренландии.
green pepper *n* зелёный перец*.
greet [gri:t] *vt* (*person*) приветствовать* (поприветствовать *perf*), здороваться (поздороваться *perf*); (*receive*: *news*) встречать (встретить* *perf*).
greeting ['gri:tɪŋ] *n* (*welcome*) приветствие; **Christmas/birthday ~s** поздравляю с Рождеством/с днём рождения; **Season's ~s** поздравляю с Рождеством и Новым годом.
greeting(s) card *n* поздравительная открытка*.
gregarious [grə'gɛərɪəs] *adj* общительный* (общителен).
Grenada [grə'neɪdə] *n* Гренада.
grenade [grə'neɪd] *n* (*also:* **hand ~**) граната.
grew [gru:] *pt of* **grow**.
grey [greɪ] (*US* **gray**) *adj* серый* (сер); (*hair*) седой; (*dismal*) мрачный* (мрачен); **to go ~** седеть (поседеть *perf*).
grey-haired [greɪ'hɛəd] *adj* седой*.
greyhound ['greɪhaund] *n* борзая *f adj*.
grid [grɪd] *n* (*pattern*) сетка*, сеть *f*; (*grating*) решётка*; (*ELEC*) энергосистема; (*US*: *AUT*) решётка радиатора.
griddle [grɪdl] *n* (*on cooker*) *плоский металлический диск, используемый как сковорода*.
gridiron ['grɪdaɪən] *n* решётка гриля.
gridlock ['grɪdlɔk] *n* (*US*: *of traffic etc*) затор.
grief [gri:f] *n* горе; **to come to ~** (*plan*) рушиться (рухнуть *perf*); (*person*) терпеть* (потерпеть* *perf*) неудачу; **good ~!** Боже мой!
grievance ['gri:vəns] *n* (*complaint*) жалоба.
grieve [gri:v] *vi* горевать* (*impf*) ◆ *vt* огорчать (огорчить *perf*); **to ~ for** горевать (*impf*) о *+prp.*
grievous ['gri:vəs] *adj* (*mistake, injury*) серьёзный*; (*shock*) сильный.
grievous bodily harm *n* (*LAW*) тяжёлые телесные повреждения *ntpl.*
grill [grɪl] *n* (*on cooker*) гриль *m*; (*grilled food*: *also:* **mixed ~**) жаренные на гриле продукты *mpl*; (*restaurant*) = **grillroom** ◆ *vt* (*BRIT*) жарить (пожарить *perf*) (на гриле); (*inf*: *question*) допрашивать (допросить* *perf*) с пристрастием.
grille [grɪl] *n* решётка*; (*AUT*) *решётка радиатора*.
grillroom ['grɪlrum] *n* ≈ гриль-бар.
grim [grɪm] *adj* (*place, person*) мрачный* (мрачен); (*situation*) тяжёлый* (тяжёл).
grimace [grɪ'meɪs] *n* гримаса ◆ *vi* гримасничать (*impf*).
grime [graɪm] *n* (*from soot, smoke*) копоть *f*; (*from mud*) грязь *f*.
grimy ['graɪmɪ] *adj* (*dirty*) грязный* (грязен).
grin [grɪn] *n* ухмылка* ◆ *vi*: **to ~ (at)** (широко) улыбаться (улыбнуться *perf*) (*+dat*).
grind [graɪnd] (*pt, pp* **ground**) *vt* (*coffee, pepper etc*) молоть (смолоть* *perf*); (*US*: *meat*) пропускать (пропустить* *perf*) через мясорубку; (*make sharp*: *knife etc*) точить* (наточить* *perf*); (*polish*: *gem, lens*) шлифовать (отшлифовать *perf*) ◆ *vi* (*car gears*) скрежетать* (*impf*) ◆ *n* (*work*) изнурительная работа; **to ~ one's teeth** скрежетать* (*impf*) зубами; **to ~ one's heel into the ground** вдавливать (вдавить* *perf*) каблук в землю; **to ~ to a halt** (*vehicle*) останавливаться (остановиться* *perf*) с лязгом; (*fig*) застопориться (*perf*); **the daily ~** (*inf*) рутина будней.
grinder ['graɪndə^r] *n* (*for coffee*) кофемолка*; (*for waste disposal etc*) дробилка*.
grindstone ['graɪndstəun] *n*: **to keep one's nose**

to the ~ рабо́тать *(impf)* без переды́шки.
grip [grɪp] *n* (*of person*) хва́тка; (: *control, grasp*) схва́тывание; (*of tyre*) сцепле́ние; (*handle*) ру́чка*; (*holdall*) доро́жная су́мка* ◆ *vt* (*object*) схва́тывать (схвати́ть* *perf*); (*audience, attention*) захва́тывать (захвати́ть* *perf*); **to come to ~s with** (*problem, difficulty*) бра́ться* (взя́ться* *perf*) за реше́ние *+gen*; **to ~ the road** (*car*) име́ть *(impf)* хоро́шее сцепле́ние с доро́гой; **to lose one's ~** (*tyres*) стира́ться (стере́ться* *perf*); (*shoes*) изна́шиваться (износи́ться* *perf*); (*fig*) теря́ть (потеря́ть *perf*) хва́тку.
gripe [graɪp] *n* (*inf: complaint*) жа́лоба ◆ *vi* (*inf*) ворча́ть *(impf)*; **the ~s** (*MED*) ко́лики *pl*.
gripping ['grɪpɪŋ] *adj* захва́тывающий*.
grisly ['grɪzlɪ] *adj* ужа́сный*.
grist [grɪst] *n* (*fig*): **it's all ~ to the mill** э́то принесёт по́льзу.
gristle ['grɪsl] *n* (*on meat*) хрящ*.
grit [grɪt] *n* (*sand*) песо́к*; (*stone*) гра́вий; (*determination, courage*) вы́держка ◆ *vt* (*road*) посыпа́ть (посы́пать* *perf*) гра́вием; **~s** *npl* (*US*) дроблёная кукуру́за *fsg*; **to ~ one's teeth** сти́скивать (сти́снуть *perf*) зу́бы; **I've got a piece of ~ in my eye** мне в глаз попа́ла сори́нка.
grizzle ['grɪzl] *vi* (*BRIT*) хны́кать* *(impf)*.
grizzly ['grɪzlɪ] *n* (*also:* ~ **bear**) гри́зли *m ind*.
groan [grəun] *n* (*of person*) стон ◆ *vi* (*person: in pain*) стона́ть* *(impf)*; (: *in disapproval*) тяжело́ вздыха́ть (вздохну́ть *perf*); (*tree, floorboard*) скрипе́ть *(impf)*.
grocer ['grəusəʳ] *n* бакале́йщик.
groceries ['grəusərɪz] *npl* бакале́я *fsg*.
grocer's (shop) *n* бакале́йный магази́н.
grog [grɔg] *n* (*drink*) грог*.
groggy ['grɔgɪ] *adj*: **I feel ~** у меня́ подка́шиваются но́ги.
groin [grɔɪn] *n* пах*.
groom [gru:m] *n* (*for horse*) ко́нюх; (*also: bridegroom*) жени́х* ◆ *vt* (*horse*) уха́живать *(impf)* за *+instr*; (*fig*): **to ~ sb for** (*job*) гото́вить* (пригото́вить* *perf*) кого́-н к *+dat*; **well-~ed** (*person*) ухо́женный* (ухо́жен).
groove [gru:v] *n* желобо́к*; (*habit*) рути́на.
grope [grəup] *vi*: **to ~ for** иска́ть* *(impf)* о́щупью; (*fig*) нащу́пывать *(impf)*; **to ~ one's way to** дви́гаться *(impf)* о́щупью к *+dat*.
gross [grəus] *adj* (*vulgar*) вульга́рный*; (*flagrant: neglect, injustice*) вопию́щий*; (*COMM: income*) вало́вой ◆ *n inv* (*twelve dozen*) гросс (*12 дю́жин*) ◆ *vt* (*COMM*): **to ~ £500,000** получа́ть (получи́ть* *perf*) о́бщую при́быль в £500.000; ~ **weight** вес бру́тто.
gross domestic product *n* вало́вой вну́тренний* проду́кт.
grossly ['grəuslɪ] *adv* (*greatly*) чрезме́рно.
gross national product *n* вало́вой национа́льный проду́кт.
gross profit *n* валова́я при́быль *f*.
gross sales *npl* вало́вой объём *msg* прода́жи.
grotesque [grə'tɛsk] *adj* гроте́скный*.
grotto ['grɔtəu] *n* грот.
grotty ['grɔtɪ] *adj* (*inf: dreadful*) парши́вый (парши́в).
grouch [grautʃ] (*inf*) *vi* брюзжа́ть *(impf)* ◆ *n* (*person*) брюзга́ *m/f*.
ground [graund] *pt, pp of* **grind** ◆ *n* (*earth, land*) земля́*; (*floor*) пол; (*SPORT*) по́ле; (*US: also:* ~ **wire**) заземле́ние; (*reason: usu pl*) основа́ние ◆ *vt* (*US: ELEC*) заземля́ть (заземли́ть *perf*) ◆ *adj* (*coffee etc*) мо́лотый ◆ *vi* (*ship*) сади́ться* (сесть* *perf*) на мель; **~s** *npl* (*of coffee*) гу́ща *fsg*; **school ~s** пришко́льный уча́сток*; **sports ~** спорти́вная площа́дка*; **on the ~** на земле́; **to the ~** (*burnt*) дотла́; **below ~** под землёй; **to gain ~** продвига́ться (продви́нуться *perf*) вперёд; **to lose ~** отступа́ть (отступи́ть* *perf*); **common ~** *вопро́с, в кото́ром спо́рящие сто́роны схо́дятся*; **on the ~s that** на том основа́нии, что; **the plane was ~ed by the fog** самолёт не мог подня́ться в во́здух из-за тума́на.
ground cloth *n* (*US*) = **groundsheet**.
ground control *n* (*AVIAT, SPACE*) слу́жбы *fpl* назе́много контро́ля *or* управле́ния.
ground floor *n* пе́рвый эта́ж*.
grounding ['graundɪŋ] *n* (*in education*) подгото́вка.
groundless ['graundlɪs] *adj* беспо́чвенный*, необосно́ванный*.
groundnut ['graundnʌt] *n* земляно́й оре́х.
ground rent *n* (*BRIT*) земе́льная ре́нта.
ground rule *n* основно́е пра́вило.
groundsheet ['graundʃi:t] *n* (*BRIT*) водонепроница́емая ткань *f* (*испо́льзуемая в похо́дах для подкла́дки под спа́льные мешки́*).
groundskeeper ['graundzki:pəʳ] *n* (*US*) = **groundsman**.
groundsman ['graundzmən] *irreg n* (*SPORT*) *слу́жащий стадио́на и́ли па́рка подде́рживающий поря́док*.
ground staff *n* (*AVIAT*) назе́мный персона́л.
ground swell *n*: ~ ~ **of opinion (against)** нараста́ющее чу́вство проте́ста (про́тив *+gen*).
ground-to-air ['grauntu'ɛəʳ] *adj* противовозду́шный.
ground-to-ground ['grauntə'graund] *adj*: ~ **missile** управля́емая раке́та кла́сса „земля́-земля́“.
groundwork ['graundwə:k] *n* (*preparation*) фунда́мент, осно́ва.
group [gru:p] *n* гру́ппа ◆ *vt* (*also:* ~ **together**:

people, things etc) группировать (сгруппировать *perf*) ◆ *vi* (*also:* ~ **together**) группироваться (сгруппироваться *perf*).
groupie ['gru:pɪ] *n* девица из антуража (*non-группы, певца итп*).
group therapy *n* групповая терапия.
grouse [graus] *n inv* (*bird*) (шотландская) куропатка* ◆ *vi* (*complain*) ворчать (*impf*).
grove [grəuv] *n* роща.
grovel ['grɔvl] *vi* (*crawl*) ползать (*impf*); (*fig*): **to ~ (before)** заискивать (*impf*) (перед +*instr*).
grow [grəu] (*pt* **grew**, *pp* **grown**) *vi* расти* (вырасти* *perf*); (*increase*) увеличиваться (увеличиться *perf*); (*become*): **to ~ rich/weak** становиться* (стать* *perf*) богатым(-ой)/слабым(-ой) ◆ *vt* (*roses, vegetables*) выращивать (вырастить* *perf*); (*beard, hair*) отращивать (отрастить* *perf*); **to ~ (out of** *or* **from)** (*city, society*) вырастать (вырасти* *perf*) (из +*gen*); (*idea, plan*) возникать (возникнуть *perf*) (из +*gen*); **to ~ tired of waiting** уставать* (устать* *perf*) от ожидания
▸ **grow apart** *vi* (*fig*) отдаляться (отдалиться *perf*) друг от друга
▸ **grow away from** *vt fus* (*fig*) отдаляться (отдалиться *perf*) от +*gen*
▸ **grow on** *vt fus*: **that painting is ~ing on me** эта картина нравится мне всё больше
▸ **grow out of** *vt fus* (*clothes*) вырастать (вырасти* *perf*) из +*gen*; (*habit*) перерастать (перерасти* *perf*); **he'll ~ out of it** он перерастёт это
▸ **grow up** *vi* (*child*) расти* (вырасти* *perf*), взрослеть (повзрослеть *perf*); (*develop*: *idea, friendship*) возникать (возникнуть *perf*).
grower ['grəuə'] *n* (*BOT*) садовод; **lily/rose ~** садовод, разводящий лилии/розы.
growing ['grəuɪŋ] *adj* (*increasing*) растущий; **~ pains** (*MED*) *невралгические или ревматические боли в детском возрасте*; (*fig*) болезнь *f* роста.
growl [graul] *vi* (*dog*) рычать (зарычать *perf*); (*person*) рычать (прорычать *perf*).
grown [grəun] *pp of* **grow**.
grown-up [grəun'ʌp] *n* (*adult*) взрослый(-ая) *m(f) adj* ◆ *adj* (*son, daughter*) взрослый.
growth [grəuθ] *n* (*development*) рост; (*increase*) прирост; (*of weeds*) заросли *fpl*; (*of beard*) щетина; (*MED*) опухоль *f*.
growth rate *n* темп роста.
grub [grʌb] *n* (*larva*) личинка*; (*inf*: *food*) жратва ◆ *vi*: **to ~ about** *or* **around (for)** рыться* (*impf*) (в поисках +*gen*).
grubby ['grʌbɪ] *adj* (*also fig*) грязный* (грязен).
grudge [grʌdʒ] *n* (*grievance*) недовольство ◆ *vt*: **to ~ sb sth** жалеть (пожалеть *perf*) что-н для кого-н; **to bear sb a ~** быть* (*impf*) на кого-н в обиде.
grudging ['grʌdʒɪŋ] *adj* (*respect, silence*) вынужденный; (*praise*) скупой.
grudgingly ['grʌdʒɪŋlɪ] *adv* неохотно.
gruelling ['gruəlɪŋ] (*US* **grueling**) *adj* изнурительный* (изнурителен), тяжёлый* (тяжёл).
gruesome ['gru:səm] *adj* (*tale, scene*) жуткий*.
gruff [grʌf] *adj* (*voice*) хриплый* (хрипл); (*manner*) резкий* (резок).
grumble ['grʌmbl] *vi* ворчать (*impf*).
grumpy ['grʌmpɪ] *adj* сварливый (сварлив).
grunge [grʌndʒ] *n* стиль *m* грюндж.
grunt [grʌnt] *vi* (*pig*) хрюкать (хрюкнуть *perf*); (*person*) бурчать (буркнуть *perf*) ◆ *n* (*see vb*) хрюканье; бурчание.
G-string ['dʒi:strɪŋ] *n* (*garment*) *тип открытых плавок*.
GSUSA *n abbr* (= *Girl Scouts of the United States of America*) *организация девочек-скаутов США*.
GT *abbr* (*AUT*: = *gran turismo*) *дорогой двухместный закрытый автомобиль*.
GU *abbr* (*US*: *POST*) = *Guam*.
guarantee [gærən'ti:] *n* (*assurance*) поручительство; (*COMM*: *warranty*) гарантия ◆ *vt* гарантировать (*impf/perf*); **he can't ~ (that) he'll come** он не может поручиться за то, что он придёт.
guarantor [gærən'tɔ:'] *n* (*COMM*) поручитель(ница) *m(f)*.
guard [gɑ:d] *n* (*one person*) часовой, охранник; (*squad*) охрана; (*MIL*) караул; (*BOXING, FENCING*) оборонительная стойка; (*BRIT*: *RAIL*) проводник*(-ица); (*on machine*) предохранительное устройство; (*also*: **fireguard**) предохранительная решётка* (*перед камином*) ◆ *vt* (*prisoner*) охранять (*impf*); (*secret*) хранить (сохранить *perf*); (*place, person*): **to ~ (against)** охранять (*impf*) (от +*gen*); **to be on one's ~** быть* (*impf*) настороже *or* начеку
▸ **guard against** *vt fus* (*prevent*: *disease, damage etc*) предохранять (*impf*) от +*gen*.
guard dog *n* сторожевая собака.
guarded ['gɑ:dɪd] *adj* (*statement, reply*) осторожный* (осторожен).
guardian ['gɑ:dɪən] *n* (*LAW*: *of minor*) опекун*; (*defender*) защитник(-ица).
guardrail ['gɑ:dreɪl] *n* перила *pl*.
guard's van *n* (*BRIT*: *RAIL*) багажный вагон.
Guatemala [gwɑ:tɪ'mɑ:lə] *n* Гватемала.
Guatemalan [gwɑ:tɪ'mɑ:lən] *adj* гватемальский.
Guernsey ['gə:nzɪ] *n* Гернси.
guerrilla [gə'rɪlə] *n* партизан*(ка*).
guerrilla warfare *n* партизанская война*.
guess [gɛs] *vt* (*estimate*: *number etc*) считать (подсчитать *perf*) приблизительно; (: *distance*) рассчитывать (рассчитать *perf*) приблизительно; (*correct answer*) угадывать (угадать *perf*) ◆ *vi* догадываться (*impf*) ◆ *n* (*attempt at correct answer*) догадка; **to take** *or* **have a ~** отгадывать (отгадать *perf*); **my ~ is that** ... мне сдаётся, что ...; **I ~** ...

(*US*) мне ка́жется ...; **I ~ you're right** Вы, наве́рное, пра́вы; **to keep sb ~ing** держа́ть* *(impf)* кого́-н в неве́дении.
guesstimate ['gɛstɪmɪt] *n* (*inf*) прики́дка.
guesswork ['gɛswəːk] *n* (*speculation*) дога́дки* *fpl*, предположе́ния *ntpl*; **I got the answer by ~** я угада́л отве́т.
guest [gɛst] *n* (*visitor*) гость*(я) *m(f)*; (*in hotel*) постоя́лец*, прожива́ющий(-ая) *m(f) adj*; **be my ~** (*inf*) пожа́луйста.
guesthouse ['gɛsthaus] *n* пансио́н.
guest room *n* ко́мната для госте́й.
guff [gʌf] *n* (*inf*) трёп.
guffaw [gʌ'fɔː] *vi* гогота́ть* *(impf)* ◆ *n* го́гот.
guidance ['gaɪdəns] *n* (*advice*) сове́т; **under the ~ of** с по́мощью *+gen*, под руково́дством *+gen*; **vocational ~** сове́т по профориента́ции; **marriage ~** *сове́т по вопро́сам семьи́ и бра́ка.*
guide [gaɪd] *n* (*in museum, on tour*) гид, экскурсово́д; (*mountain guide*) проводни́к*; (*also:* **~book**) путеводи́тель *m*; (*handbook*) руково́дство; (*BRIT*: *also:* **Girl G~**) де́вочка*-ска́ут *f* ◆ *vt* (*show around*) води́ть* *(impf)*, вести́* (провести́* *perf*); (*direct*) направля́ть (напра́вить* *perf*); **to be ~d by sb/sth** (*fig*) руково́дствоваться *(impf)* чьим-н сове́том/чем-н.
guidebook ['gaɪdbuk] *n* путеводи́тель *m*.
guided missile *n* управля́емая раке́та.
guide dog *n* соба́ка-поводы́рь* *f*.
guidelines ['gaɪdlaɪnz] *npl* директи́ва *fsg*.
guild [gɪld] *n* ассоциа́ция; (*HISTORY*) ги́льдия.
guildhall ['gɪldhɔːl] *n* (*BRIT*: *in London*): **the G~** Ги́льдхолл (*зда́ние ра́туши ло́ндонского Си́ти*).
guile [gaɪl] *n* хи́трость *f*.
guileless ['gaɪllɪs] *adj* бесхи́тростный*.
guillotine ['gɪlətiːn] *n* гильоти́на; (*for paper*) ре́зальная маши́на.
guilt [gɪlt] *n* (*remorse*) вина́; (*culpability*) вино́вность *f*.
guilty ['gɪltɪ] *adj* (*person, expression*) винова́тый; (*of crime*) вино́вный*; (*secret*) позо́рный*; **to plead ~/not guilty** признава́ть* (призна́ть* *perf*) себя́ вино́вным(-ой)/невино́вным(-ой); **to feel ~ about sth** чу́вствовать *(impf)* себя́ винова́тым(-ой) в чём-н.
Guinea ['gɪnɪ] *n*: **Republic of ~** Гвине́я.
guinea ['gɪnɪ] *n* (*BRIT*) гине́я.
guinea pig *n* (*animal*) морска́я сви́нка*; (*fig*) „подо́пытный кро́лик".
guise [gaɪz] *n*: **in** *or* **under the ~ of** под ви́дом *+gen*.
guitar [gɪ'tɑːʳ] *n* гита́ра.
guitarist [gɪ'tɑːrɪst] *n* гитари́ст(ка).
gulch [gʌltʃ] *n* (*US*) (у́зкое) уще́лье*.
gulf [gʌlf] *n* (*GEO*) зали́в; (*also fig*) про́пасть *f*; **the (Persian) G~** Перси́дский* зали́в.
Gulf States *npl*: **the ~ ~** страны́ *fpl* Перси́дского зали́ва.
Gulf Stream *n*: **the ~ ~** Гольфстри́м.
gull [gʌl] *n* ча́йка*.
gullet ['gʌlɪt] *n* пищево́д.
gullibility [gʌlɪ'bɪlɪtɪ] *n* легкове́рие.
gullible ['gʌlɪbl] *adj* (*naive, trusting*) легкове́рный* (легкове́рен).
gully ['gʌlɪ] *n* (*ravine*) глубо́кий* овра́г.
gulp [gʌlp] *vi* (*swallow*: *from nerves, excitement*) сгла́тывать (сглотну́ть *perf*) не́рвно ◆ *vt* (*also:* **~ down**: *food, drink*) прогла́тывать (проглоти́ть* *perf*) ◆ *n*: **to drink at one ~** вы́пить* *(perf)* за́лпом.
gum [gʌm] *n* (*ANAT*) десна́*; (*glue*) клей*; (*sweet*: *also:* **~drop**) желе́йный мармела́д (*конфе́та*); (*also:* **chewing-~**) жева́тельная рези́нка*, жва́чка* (*разг*) ◆ *vt* (*stick*): **to ~ (together)** скле́ивать (скле́ить *perf*)
▸ **gum up** *vt*: **to ~ up the works** (*inf*) застопо́рить *(perf)* рабо́ту.
gumboots ['gʌmbuːts] *npl* (*BRIT*) рези́новые сапоги́* *mpl*.
gumption ['gʌmpʃən] *n* (*sense, wit*) сообрази́тельность *f*, нахо́дчивость *f*.
gumtree ['gʌmtriː] *n*: **to be up a ~** (*fig*: *inf*) попада́ть (попа́сть* *perf*) впроса́к.
gun [gʌn] *n* (*revolver, pistol*) пистоле́т; (*rifle, airgun*) ружьё*; (*cannon*) пу́шка* ◆ *vt* (*also:* **~ down**) расстре́ливать (расстреля́ть *perf*), застрели́ть* *(perf)*; **to stick to one's ~s** (*fig*) не скла́дывать (сложи́ть* *perf*) ору́жия.
gunboat ['gʌnbəut] *n* каноне́рская ло́дка*.
gun dog *n* охо́тничья соба́ка.
gunfire ['gʌnfaɪəʳ] *n* ору́дийный ого́нь* *m*.
gung ho [gʌŋ həu] *adj* (*inf*) безрассу́дный*, фанати́чный.
gunk [gʌŋk] *n* (*inf*) га́дость *f*.
gunman ['gʌnmən] *irreg n* вооружённый банди́т.
gunner ['gʌnəʳ] *n* (*MIL*) артиллери́ст.
gunpoint ['gʌnpɔɪnt] *n*: **at ~** под ду́лом пистоле́та, под прице́лом.
gunpowder ['gʌnpaudəʳ] *n* по́рох*.
gunrunner ['gʌnrʌnəʳ] *n* контрабанди́ст, торгу́ющий ору́жием.
gunrunning ['gʌnrʌnɪŋ] *n* контраба́нда ору́жием.
gunshot ['gʌnʃɔt] *n* вы́стрел.
gunsmith ['gʌnsmɪθ] *n* оруже́йный ма́стер*.
gurgle ['gəːgl] *vi* (*baby*) гу́кать *(impf)*; (*water*) журча́ть *(impf)*.
guru ['guruː] *n* (*REL*) гуру́ *m ind*; (*fig*) духо́вный наста́вник.
gush [gʌʃ] *vi* хлы́нуть *(perf)*; (*enthuse*) захлёбываться (захлебну́ться *perf*) от

восто́рга ◆ *n* (*of water etc*) пото́к.
gushing ['gʌʃɪŋ] *adj* (*female*) восто́рженный* (восто́ржен); (*admiration, reverence*) неуёмный* (неуёмен).
gusset ['gʌsɪt] *n* клин*.
gust [gʌst] *n* (*of wind*) поры́в.
gusto ['gʌstəu] *n*: **with ~** (*eat*) с удово́льствием; (*work*) с жа́ром.
gusty ['gʌstɪ] *adj* (*wind*) поры́вистый (поры́вист); (*day*) ве́треный (ве́трен).
gut [gʌt] *n* кишка́*; (*MUS, SPORT*) струна́* (*из кишо́к живо́тных*) ◆ *vt* (*poultry, fish*) потроши́ть (вы́потрошить *perf*); (*building*) *удаля́ть всё вну́тренние ча́сти до́ма*; **~s** *npl* (*ANAT*) кишки́* *fpl*, вну́тренности *fpl*; (*inf*: *courage*) му́жество *ntsg*; **the house was ~ted by fire** дом сгоре́л по́лностью; **to hate sb's ~s** (*inf*) не принима́ть (приня́ть* *perf*) кого́-н на́ дух, смерте́льно ненави́деть* (*impf*) кого́-н.
gut reaction *n* инстинкти́вная реа́кция.
gutsy ['gʌtsɪ] (*inf*) *adj* напо́ристый.
gutted ['gʌtɪd] (*inf*) *adj*: **I was ~** (*very disappointed*) я был соверше́нно уби́т.
gutter ['gʌtəʳ] *n* (*in street*) сто́чная кана́ва; (*of roof*) водосто́чный жёлоб*.
gutter press (*inf*: *pej*) *n* бульва́рная пре́сса.
guttural ['gʌtərl] *adj* горта́нный.
guy [gaɪ] *n* (*inf*: *man*) па́рень* *m*; (*also*: **~rope**) шнуры́ *mpl* для натя́гивания пала́тки; (*effigy of Guy Fawkes*) *изображе́ние Га́я Фо́кса, сжига́емое 5 ноября́*.
Guyana [gaɪ'ænə] *n* Гайа́на.
guzzle ['gʌzl] *vt* (*drink*) пить* (вы́пить* *perf*) с жа́дностью; (*food*) есть* (съесть* *perf*) с жа́дностью.
gym [dʒɪm] *n* (*also*: **~nasium**) гимнасти́ческий зал; (*also*: **~nastics**) гимна́стика.
gymkhana [dʒɪm'kɑ:nə] *n* конноспорти́вные состяза́ния *ntpl*.
gymnasium [dʒɪm'neɪzɪəm] *n* гимнасти́ческий зал.
gymnast ['dʒɪmnæst] *n* гимна́ст(ка*).
gymnastics [dʒɪm'næstɪks] *n* гимна́стика.
gym shoes *npl* спорти́вные та́почки* *fpl*.
gymslip ['dʒɪmslɪp] *n* (*BRIT*: *tunic*) шко́льное пла́тье без рукаво́в.
gynaecologist [gaɪnɪ'kɔlədʒɪst] (*US* **gynecologist**) *n* гинеко́лог.
gynaecology [gaɪnə'kɔlədʒɪ] (*US* **gynecology**) *n* гинеколо́гия.
gypsy ['dʒɪpsɪ] *n* = **gipsy**.
gyrate [dʒaɪ'reɪt] *vi* (*revolve*) враща́ться (*impf*) по кру́гу.
gyroscope ['dʒaɪərəskəup] *n* гироско́п.

~ H, h ~

H, h [eɪtʃ] *n* (*letter*) *8-áя бýква англи́йского алфави́та.*
habeas corpus ['heɪbɪəs'kɔ:pəs] *n* (*LAW*) Хáбеас Кóрпус (*закóн о неприкосновéнности ли́чности*).
haberdashery [hæbə'dæʃərɪ] *n* (*BRIT*) галантерéйные товáры *mpl*.
habit ['hæbɪt] *n* (*custom*) привы́чка*; (*addiction*) пристрáстие; (*REL: costume*) облачéние; **to get out of the ~ of doing** отвыкáть (отвы́кнуть* *perf*) *+infin*; **to get into the ~ of doing** привыкáть (привы́кнуть *perf*) *+infin*; **to be in the ~ of doing** имéть (*impf*) обыкновéние *+infin*.
habitable ['hæbɪtəbl] *adj* (*house etc*) пригóдный* для жилья́.
habitat ['hæbɪtæt] *n* (*BOT, ZOOL*) естéственная средá* обитáния.
habitation [hæbɪ'teɪʃən] *n* (*house etc*) жили́ще; **fit for human ~** пригóдный* для жилья́.
habitual [hə'bɪtjuəl] *adj* (*action*) привы́чный* (привы́чен); (*drinker*) запóйный; (*liar*) отъя́вленный.
habitually [hə'bɪtjuəlɪ] *adv* (*late, untidy*) обы́чно.
hack [hæk] *vt* (*cut, slice*) отрубáть (отруби́ть *perf*) ◆ *n* (*pej: writer*) писáка* *m/f*; (*horse*) *лóшадь, сдавáемая напрокáт для верховóй езды́* ◆ *vi*: **to ~ into** (*COMPUT*) нелегáльно входи́ть* (войти́* *perf*) в *+acc*.
hacker ['hækə'] *n* (*COMPUT*) хэ́кер.
hackles ['hæklz] *npl*: **to make sb's ~ rise** (*fig*) приводи́ть* (привести́ *perf*) в состоя́ние раздражéния.
hackney cab ['hæknɪ-] *n* наёмный экипáж.
hackneyed ['hæknɪd] *adj* изби́тый.
hacksaw ['hæksɔ:] *n* ножóвка.
had [hæd] *pt, pp of* **have**.
haddock ['hædək] (*pl ~ or ~s*) *n* трескá; **smoked ~** копчёная трескá.
hadn't ['hædnt] = **had not**.
haematology ['hi:mə'tɔlədʒɪ] (*US* **hematology**) *n* гематолóгия.
haemoglobin ['hi:mə'gləubɪn] (*US* **hemoglobin**) *n* гемоглоби́н.
haemophilia ['hi:mə'fɪlɪə] (*US* **hemophilia**) *n* гемофили́я.
haemorrhage ['hɛmərɪdʒ] (*US* **hemorrage**) *n* кровотечéние; **brain ~** кровоизлия́ние (в мозг).
haemorrhoids ['hɛmərɔɪdz] (*US* **hemorroids**) *npl* геморрóй *msg*.
hag [hæg] *n* (*woman*) каргá; (*witch*) вéдьма.
haggard ['hægəd] *adj* (*face, look*) измождённый*.
haggis ['hægɪs] *n* (*SCOTTISH*) хáггис (*шотлáндское блю́до из барáньей или теля́чьей требухи́ с овся́ной крупóй и спéциями*).
haggle ['hægl] *vi* (*bargain*) торговáться (сторговáться *perf*); **to ~ over** спóрить (*impf*) о *+prp*.
haggling ['hæglɪŋ] *n* торгóвля.
Hague [heɪg] *n*: **The ~** (*GEO*) Гаáга.
hail [heɪl] *n* (*also fig*) град ◆ *vt* (*call*) окликáть (окли́кнуть *perf*); (*flag down*) подзывáть (подозвáть* *perf*); (*acclaim*) превозноси́ть* (превознести́* *perf*) ◆ *vi*: **it's ~ing** идёт град; **he ~s from Scotland** он рóдом из Шотлáндии.
hailstone ['heɪlstəun] *n* грáдина.
hailstorm ['heɪlstɔ:m] *n* грозá* с грáдом.
hair [hɛə'] *n* вóлосы* *pl*; (*of animal*) шерсть *f*; (*single hair*) вóлос*; **to do one's ~** причёсываться (причесáться* *perf*); **to miss by a ~'s breadth** (*fig*) чуть-чуть промахну́ться (*perf*).
hairbrush ['hɛəbrʌʃ] *n* щётка* для волóс.
haircut ['hɛəkʌt] *n* стри́жка*.
hairdo ['hɛədu:] *n* причёска*.
hairdresser ['hɛədrɛsə'] *n* парикмáхер.
hairdresser's ['hɛədrɛsəz] *n* парикмáхерская *f adj*.
hair dryer *n* фен.
-haired [hɛəd] *suffix*: **fair/long-~** светло-/длинноволóсый.
hairgrip ['hɛəgrɪp] *n* неви́димка.
hairline ['hɛəlaɪn] *n* ли́ния волóс.
hairline fracture *n* трéщина.
hairnet ['hɛənɛt] *n* сéтка* для волóс.
hair oil *n* мáсло* для волóс.
hairpiece ['hɛəpi:s] *n* накладны́е вóлосы* *mpl*.

* marks translations which have irregular inflections. The Russian-English side of the dictionary gives inflectional information.

hairpin ['hɛəpɪn] *n* шпи́лька*.
hairpin bend (*US* **hairpin curve**) *n* крутой поворо́т.
hair-raising ['hɛəreɪzɪŋ] *adj* (*experience, tale*) жу́ткий*.
hair remover *n* (*cream*) крем для удале́ния воло́с.
hair slide *n* зако́лка* для воло́с.
hair spray *n* лак для воло́с.
hairstyle ['hɛəstaɪl] *n* причёска*.
hairy ['hɛərɪ] *adj* (*person*) волоса́тый; (*animal*) мохна́тый (мохна́т); (*inf: situation*) риско́ванный*.
Haiti ['heɪtɪ] *n* Гаи́ти *m ind.*
hake [heɪk] (*pl* ~ *or* ~**s**) *n* серебри́стый хек.
halcyon ['hælsɪən] *adj*: ~ **days** безмяте́жные дни.
hale [heɪl] *adj*: ~ **and hearty** здоро́вый* (здоро́в) и бо́дрый* (бодр).
half [hɑ:f] (*pl* **halves**) *n* полови́на; (*also:* ~ **pint**: *of beer etc*) полпи́нты *f*; (*RAIL, bus*) биле́т за полцены́ ◆ *adv* (*empty, closed, open, asleep*) наполови́ну; **first/second** ~ (*SPORT*) пе́рвый/второ́й тайм; **one and a** ~ (*with m nouns*) полтора́ *+gen sg*; (*with f nouns*) полторы́ *+gen sg*; **three and a** ~ три с полови́ной; ~**-an-hour** полчаса́* *m*; ~ **a dozen (of)** полдю́жины* *f* (*+gen*); ~ **a pound (of)** полфу́нта *m* (*+gen*); **a week and a** ~ полторы́* *f* неде́ли; ~ **(of)** полови́на (*+gen*); ~ **the amount of** полови́на *+gen*; **to cut sth in** ~ разреза́ть (разре́зать* *perf*) что-н попола́м; ~ **past three** полови́на четвёртого; **to go halves (with sb)** дели́ть* (подели́ть* *perf*) попола́м (с кем-н); **she never does things by halves** она́ никогда́ не остана́вливается на полпути́; **he's too clever by** ~ он чересчу́р уж у́мный; ~ **empty/closed** наполови́ну пусто́й*/закры́тый; **a** ~ **bottle (of)** полбуты́лки (*+gen*).
half-baked ['hɑ:f'beɪkt] *adj* (*idea, scheme*) непроду́манный.
half board *n* пансио́н с за́втраком и у́жином.
half-breed ['hɑ:fbri:d] *n* = **half-caste**.
half-brother ['hɑ:fbrʌðəʳ] *n* (*with same mother*) единоутро́бный брат*; (*with same father*) единокро́вный брат*.
half-caste ['hɑ:fkɑ:st] *n* челове́к сме́шанной ра́сы.
half-day [hɑ:f'deɪ] *n* коро́ткий* день* *m*.
half-hearted ['hɑ:f'hɑ:tɪd] *adj* лени́вый.
half-hour [hɑ:f'auəʳ] *n* полчаса́* *m*.
half-life ['hɑ:flaɪf] *n* (*TECH*) пери́од полураспа́да.
half-mast ['hɑ:f'mɑ:st] *adv*: **at** ~ (*flag*) приспу́щенный (приспу́щен).
halfpenny ['heɪpnɪ] *n* (*BRIT*) полпе́нса* *m*.
half-price ['hɑ:f'praɪs] *adj, adv* за полцены́.
half-sister ['hɑ:fsɪstəʳ] *n* (*with same mother*) единоутро́бная сестра́*; (*with same father*) единокро́вная сестра́*.
half term *n* (*BRIT: SCOL*) *кани́кулы в середи́не шко́льного триме́стра.*
half-timbered [hɑ:f'tɪmbəd] *adj* деревя́нно-кирпи́чный.
half-time [hɑ:f'taɪm] *n* (*SPORT*) переры́в ме́жду та́ймами.
halfway ['hɑ:f'weɪ] *adv* на полпути́; **I am prepared to meet you** ~ (*fig*) я гото́в пойти́ Вам навстре́чу.
halfway house *n* дом* на полпути́; (*fig*) середи́на.
halfwit ['hɑ:fwɪt] *n* приду́рок*, полоу́мный(-ая) *m(f) adj.*
half-yearly [hɑ:f'jɪəlɪ] *adv* раз в полго́да ◆ *adj* полугодово́й.
halibut ['hælɪbət] *n inv* па́лтус.
halitosis [hælɪ'təusɪs] *n* дурно́й за́пах изо рта́.
hall [hɔ:l] *n* (*entrance way*) прихо́жая *f adj*; (*corridor*) коридо́р; (*mansion*) уса́дьба; (*for concerts, meetings etc*) зал; **to live in** ~**s** (*BRIT: students*) жить* (*impf*) в общежи́тии.
hallmark ['hɔ:lmɑ:k] *n* про́ба; (*fig*) отличи́тельная черта́*.
hallo [hə'ləu] *excl* = **hello**.
hall of residence (*pl* ~**s** ~ ~) *n* (*BRIT*) общежи́тие.
hallowed ['hæləud] *adj* (*REL*) свято́й*; (*fig: respected, revered*) почита́емый.
Hallowe'en ['hæləu'i:n] *n* кану́н Дня всех святы́х.
hallucination [həlu:sɪ'neɪʃən] *n* галлюцина́ция.
hallucinogenic [həlu:sɪnəu'dʒɛnɪk] *adj* галлюцинато́рный.
hallway ['hɔ:lweɪ] *n* (*entrance hall*) прихо́жая *f adj.*
halo ['heɪləu] *n* (*REL*) нимб; (*circle of light*) орео́л.
halt [hɔ:lt] *n* остано́вка* ◆ *vt* остана́вливать (останови́ть* *perf*) ◆ *vi* остана́вливаться (останови́ться* *perf*); **to call a** ~ **to sth** (*fig*) дава́ть* (дать* *perf*) отбо́й чему́-н.
halter ['hɔ:ltəʳ] *n* (*for horse*) по́вод*.
halterneck ['hɔ:ltənɛk] *adj*: ~ **dress** *пла́тье с откры́той спино́й и завя́зками вокру́г ше́и.*
halve [hɑ:v] *vt* (*reduce*) сокраща́ть (сократи́ть* *perf*) наполови́ну; (*divide*) дели́ть* (раздели́ть* *perf*) попола́м.
halves [hɑ:vz] *pl of* **half**.
ham [hæm] *n* ветчина́*; (*inf: also:* **radio** ~) радиолюби́тель *m*; (*: actor*) безда́рный(-ая) актёр(-три́са) ◆ *vt*: **to** ~ **it up** переи́грывать (переигра́ть *perf*).
Hamburg ['hæmbə:g] *n* Га́мбург.
hamburger ['hæmbə:gəʳ] *n* га́мбургер.
ham-fisted ['hæm'fɪstɪd] *adj* нело́вкий*.
ham-handed ['hæm'hændɪd] *adj* = **ham-fisted**.
hamlet ['hæmlɪt] *n* дереву́шка*.
hammer ['hæməʳ] *n* молото́к*, мо́лот ◆ *vi* (*on door etc*) колоти́ть* (*impf*) ◆ *vt* (*criticize severely*) критикова́ть (раскритикова́ть *perf*); (*nail*): **to** ~ **in** забива́ть (заби́ть* *perf*), вбива́ть (вбить* *perf*); (*fig: force*): **to** ~ **sth into**

sb вдáлбливать (вдолби́ть* *perf*) что-н комý-н

▸ **hammer out** *vt* (*metal*) расплю́щивать (расплю́щить *perf*); (*fig*: *solution, agreement*) вырабáтывать (вы́работать *perf*).

hammock ['hæmək] *n* (*on ship*) кóйка*; (*in garden*) гамáк*.

hamper ['hæmpə^r] *vt* мешáть (помешáть *perf*) *+dat* ◆ *n* (*basket*) большáя корзи́на с кры́шкой.

hamster ['hæmstə^r] *n* хомя́к*.

hamstring ['hæmstrɪŋ] *n* (*ANAT*) подколéнное сухожи́лие ◆ *vt* (*restrict*) ограни́чивать (ограни́чить *perf*).

hand [hænd] *n* (*ANAT*) рукá*, кисть* *f* руки́; (*of clock*) стрéлка*; (*handwriting*) пóчерк; (*worker*) рабóчий* *m adj*; (*of cards*) кáрты *fpl* (*находя́щиеся на рукáх у игрокá*); (*measurement*: *of horse*) ладóнь *f* (*мéра при измерéнии рóста лóшади*) ◆ *vt* (*pass*) передавáть* (передáть* *perf*); (*give*) вручáть (вручи́ть *perf*); **to give** *or* **lend sb a ~** помогáть (помóчь* *perf*) комý-н; **at ~** под рукóй; **by ~** вручнýю; **in ~** (*time*) в распоряжéнии; (*situation*) под контрóлем; **the job in ~** текýщее дéло; **on ~** (*person, services etc*) в распоряжéнии; **to get out of ~** (*child*) отбивáться (отби́ться* *perf*) от рук; (*situation*) выходи́ть* (вы́йти* *perf*) из-под контрóля; **to dismiss out of ~** отвéргнуть (*perf*) срáзу; **I have the information to ~** я располагáю информáцией; **on the one ~..., on the other ~...** с однóй стороны́ ..., с другóй стороны́; **to force sb's ~** заставля́ть (застáвить* *perf*) когó-н раскры́ть свои́ кáрты; **he has a free ~** у негó развя́заны рýки; **to change ~s** (*be sold etc*) переходи́ть* (перейти́* *perf*) из рук в рýки; **to have in one's ~** (*fig*) держáть* (*impf*) под контрóлем; **~s off!** рýки прочь!

▸ **hand down** *vt* (*knowledge, possessions*) передавáть* (передáть* *perf*); (*LAW*: *judgement, sentence*) выноси́ть* (вы́нести* *perf*)

▸ **hand in** *vt* (*essay, work*) сдавáть* (сдать* *perf*)

▸ **hand out** *vt* раздавáть* (раздáть* *perf*)

▸ **hand over** *vt* передавáть* (передáть* *perf*)

▸ **hand round** *vt* (*BRIT*) раздавáть* (раздáть* *perf*); (*subj*: *hostess*) разноси́ть* (разнести́* *perf*).

handbag ['hændbæg] *n* (дáмская) сýмочка*.

hand baggage *n* ручнóй багáж*.

handball ['hændbɔ:l] *n* гандбóл.

hand basin *n* таз*.

handbook ['hændbuk] *n* руковóдство.

handbrake ['hændbreɪk] *n* ручнóй тóрмоз*.

h & c *abbr* (*BRIT*) = *hot and cold (water)*.

hand cream *n* крем для рук.

handcuff ['hændkʌf] *vt* надевáть (надéть* *perf*) нарýчники *+dat or* на *+acc*.

handcuffs ['hændkʌfs] *npl* нарýчники *mpl*.

handful ['hændful] *n* горсть* *f*; (*fig*: *of people*) гóрстка*.

hand-held ['hænd'hɛld] *adj* ручнóй.

handicap ['hændɪkæp] *n* (*disability*) физи́ческая неполноцéнность *f*; (*disadvantage*) препя́тствие; (*SPORT*) гандикáп ◆ *vt* препя́тствовать (воспрепя́тствовать *perf*) *+dat*; **mentally/physically ~ped** ýмственно/физи́чески неполноцéнный.

handicraft ['hændɪkrɑ:ft] *n* рукодéлие; (*objects*) издéлие ручнóй рабóты.

handiwork ['hændɪwə:k] *n* ручны́е издéлия *ntpl*; **this looks like his ~** (*pej*) похóже, что э́то егó рук дéло.

handkerchief ['hæŋkətʃɪf] *n* носовóй платóк*.

handle ['hændl] *n* рýчка*; (*CB RADIO*: *name*) прóзвище ◆ *vt* (*touch*) держáть* (*impf*) в рукáх; (*deal with*) справля́ться (спрáвиться* *perf*) с *+instr*; (*treat*: *people*) обращáться (*impf*) с *+instr*; **to fly off the ~** (*inf*) срывáться (сорвáться* *perf*); **to get a ~ on a problem** (*inf*) брáться* (взя́ться* *perf*) за решéние проблéмы; **"handle with care"** „обращáться осторóжно".

handlebar(s) ['hændlbɑ:(z)] *n(pl)* руль* *msg* (*велосипéда и́ли мотоци́кла*).

handling ['hændlɪŋ] *n*: **~ of** (*of situation, problem etc*) подхóд к *+dat*; (*luggage*) обращéние с *+instr*; (*LAW*) ведéние *+gen*.

handling charges *npl* (*COMM*) плáта *fsg* за услýги.

hand luggage *n* ручнóй багáж*.

handmade ['hænd'meɪd] *adj* ручнóй рабóты; **it's ~** э́то – ручнáя рабóта.

hand-out ['hændaut] *n* (*money, clothing, food*) благотвори́тельная пóмощь *f*; (*publicity leaflet*) реклáмный листóк*; (*summary*: *of lecture*) проспéкт.

hand-picked ['hænd'pɪkt] *adj* (*produce*) сóбранный вручнýю; (*staff etc*) специáльно подóбранный.

handrail ['hændreɪl] *n* пери́ла *pl*.

handset ['hændsɛt] *n* телефóнная трýбка*.

handshake ['hændʃeɪk] *n* рукопожáтие.

handsome ['hænsəm] *adj* (*man*) краси́вый (краси́в); (*woman*) интерéсный* (интерéсен); (*building*) внуши́тельный*; (*gift*) щéдрый (щедр); (*fig*: *profit, return*) внуши́тельный* (внуши́телен).

hands-on ['hændz'ɔn] *adj* практи́ческий*.

handstand ['hændstænd] *n*: **to do a ~** дéлать (сдéлать *perf*) стóйку на рукáх.

hand-to-mouth ['hændtə'mauθ] *adj*: **they live a ~ existence** они́ живýт впрóголодь.

handwriting ['hændraɪtɪŋ] *n* пóчерк.

* marks translations which have irregular inflections. The Russian-English side of the dictionary gives inflectional information.

handwritten ['hændrɪtn] *adj* напи́санный от руки́.
handy ['hændɪ] *adj* (*useful*) удо́бный*; (*skilful*) ло́вкий*; (*close at hand*) побли́зости; **to come in ~** пригожда́ться* (пригоди́ться* *perf*).
handyman ['hændɪmæn] *irreg n* (*at home*) ма́стер* на все ру́ки; (*in hotel etc*) подру́чный *m adj*.
hang [hæŋ] (*pt, pp* **hung**) *vt* ве́шать (пове́сить* *perf*); (*pt, pp* **hanged**; *execute*) ве́шать (пове́сить* *perf*) ◆ *vi* висе́ть* *(impf)* ◆ *n*: **to get the ~ of sth** (*inf*) разбира́ться (разобра́ться* *perf*) в чём-н; **to ~ one's head** ве́шать (пове́сить* *perf*) го́лову
▸ **hang about** *vi* слоня́ться *(impf)*
▸ **hang around** *vi* = **hang about**
▸ **hang back** *vi* (*hesitate*): **to ~ back (from doing)** быть* *(impf)* в нереши́тельности (*+infin*)
▸ **hang on** *vi* (*wait*) подожда́ть* *(impf)* ◆ *vt fus* (*depend on*) зави́сеть *(impf)* от *+gen*; **to ~ on to** (*keep hold of*) цепля́ться *(impf)* за *+acc*; (*keep*) держа́ть *(impf)* у себя́
▸ **hang out** *vt* (*washing*) выве́шивать (вы́весить* *perf*) ◆ *vi* высо́вываться (вы́сунуться *perf*); **this is where the students always ~ out** (*inf*) студе́нты всегда́ там окола́чиваются
▸ **hang together** *vi* (*argument*) быть* *(impf)* убеди́тельным(-ой)
▸ **hang up** *vi* (TEL) ве́шать (пове́сить* *perf*) тру́бку ◆ *vt* ве́шать (пове́сить* *perf*).
hangar ['hæŋəʳ] *n* анга́р.
hangdog ['hæŋdɔg] *adj* (*look, expression*) винова́тый.
hanger ['hæŋəʳ] *n* (*for clothes*) ве́шалка*.
hanger-on [hæŋər'ɔn] *n* прихлеба́тель(ница) *m(f)*.
hang-glider ['hæŋglaɪdəʳ] *n* (*craft*) дельтапла́н; (*pilot*) дельтапланери́ст.
hang-gliding ['hæŋglaɪdɪŋ] *n* дельта-планери́зм.
hanging ['hæŋɪŋ] *n* (*execution*) пове́шение; (*for wall*) портье́ра.
hangman ['hæŋmən] *irreg n* пала́ч*.
hangover ['hæŋəuvəʳ] *n* (*after drinking*) похме́лье; (*from past*) пережи́ток*.
hang-up ['hæŋʌp] *n* (*inhibition*) ко́мплекс.
hank [hæŋk] *n* мото́к*.
hanker ['hæŋkəʳ] *vi*: **to ~ after** (*desire, long for*) мечта́ть *(impf)* о *+prp*.
hankering ['hæŋkərɪŋ] *n*: **I have a ~ for a beer** мне бы сейча́с пивка́.
hankie ['hæŋkɪ] *n abbr* = **handkerchief**.
hanky ['hæŋkɪ] *n abbr* = **handkerchief**.
Hanoi [hæ'nɔɪ] *n* Хано́й.
Hants *abbr* (BRIT: POST) = *Hampshire*.
haphazard [hæp'hæzəd] *adj* бессисте́мный*.
hapless ['hæplɪs] *adj* несча́стный*.
happen ['hæpən] *vi* случа́ться (случи́ться *perf*), происходи́ть* (произойти́* *perf*); (*chance*): **I ~ed to meet him in the park** я случа́йно встре́тил его́ в па́рке; **as it ~s** кста́ти; **what's ~ing?** что происхо́дит?; **she ~ed to be free** она́ оказа́лась свобо́дной; **if anything ~ed to him** е́сли с ним что-н случи́тся
▸ **happen (up)on** *vt fus* натыка́ться (наткну́ться *perf*) на *+acc*.
happening ['hæpnɪŋ] *n* слу́чай.
happily ['hæpɪlɪ] *adv* (*luckily*) к сча́стью; (*cheerfully*) ра́достно.
happiness ['hæpɪnɪs] *n* сча́стье.
happy ['hæpɪ] *adj* (*pleased*) счастли́вый (счастли́в); (*cheerful*) весёлый* (ве́сел); (*apt*) уда́чный* (уда́чен); **I am ~ (with it)** (*content*) я дово́лен (э́тим); **he is always ~ to help** (*willing*) он всегда́ с удово́льствием помога́ет; **~ birthday!** с днём рожде́ния!
happy-go-lucky ['hæpɪgəu'lʌkɪ] *adj* беспе́чный* (беспе́чен).
happy hour *n вре́мя, в тече́ние кото́рого спиртны́е напи́тки в ба́рах продаю́тся по сни́женным це́нам.*
harangue [hə'ræŋ] *vt* (*audience, class*) увещева́ть *(impf)*.
harass ['hærəs] *vt* изводи́ть* (извести́* *perf*).
harassed ['hærəst] *adj* (*person*) изнурённый* (изнурён).
harassment ['hærəsmənt] *n* пресле́дование; **sexual ~** сексуа́льное пресле́дование.
harbour ['hɑ:bəʳ] (US **harbor**) *n* га́вань *f* ◆ *vt* (*hope, fear etc*) зата́ивать (зата́ить *perf*); (*criminal, fugitive*) укрыва́ть (укры́ть* *perf*); **to ~ a grudge against sb** держа́ть* *(impf)* зло на кого́-н.
harbour dues *npl* порто́вые сбо́ры *mpl*.
harbour master *n* нача́льник по́рта.
hard [hɑ:d] *adj* (*surface, object*) твёрдый (твёрд); (*question, problem*) тру́дный* (тру́ден); (*work, life*) тяжёлый (тяжёл); (*person*) суро́вый (суро́в); (*facts, evidence*) неопровержи́мый (неопровержи́м); (*drink*) кре́пкий*; (*drugs*) си́льный ◆ *adv*: **to work ~** мно́го и усе́рдно рабо́тать *(impf)*; **~ luck!** не везёт!; **no ~ feelings!** не держи́те зла!; **I don't have any ~ feelings** я не держу́ зла; **he is ~ of hearing** он туг на́ ухо; **to think ~** хорошо́ поду́мать *(perf)*; **to try ~ to win** упо́рно добива́ться *(impf)* побе́ды; **to look ~ at** смотре́ть* (посмотре́ть* *perf*) при́стально на *+acc*; **I felt ~ done by** я почу́вствовал, что со мной обошли́сь несправедли́во; **I find it ~ to believe that ...** мне тру́дно пове́рить, что ....
hard-and-fast ['hɑ:dən'fɑ:st] *adj* неукосни́т-ельный*.
hardback ['hɑ:dbæk] *n* (*book*) кни́га в твёрдом переплёте.
hardboard ['hɑ:dbɔ:d] *n* древе́сно-стру́жечная плита́.
hard-boiled egg ['hɑ:d'bɔɪld-] *n* яйцо́*

вкрутую.
hard cash *n* наличные деньги* *pl*.
hard copy *n* (*COMPUT*) печатная копия, распечатка.
hard core *n* (*of group*) группа преданных сторонников.
hard-core ['hɑ:d'kɔ:ʳ] *adj* (*pornography*) предельно откровенный*; (*supporters*) верный*.
hard court *n* (*TENNIS*) твёрдый корт.
hard disk *n* (*COMPUT*) жёсткий* диск.
harden ['hɑ:dn] *vt* (*substance*) делать (сделать *perf*) твёрдым(-ой); (*attitude, person*) ожесточать (ожесточить *perf*) ◆ *vi* (*substance*) твердеть (затвердеть *perf*); (*attitude, person*) ожесточаться (ожесточиться *perf*).
hardened ['hɑ:dnd] *adj* (*criminal*) закоренелый; **to be ~ to sth** быть* (*impf*) нечувствительным(-ой) к чему-н.
hardening ['hɑ:dnɪŋ] *n* закаливание; (*of opposition*) усиление.
hard graft *n*: **by sheer ~ ~** только благодаря упорной работе.
hard-headed ['hɑ:d'hɛdɪd] *adj* (*businessman*) расчётливый (расчётлив).
hardhearted ['hɑ:d'hɑ:tɪd] *adj* бессердечный* (бессердечен).
hard-hitting ['hɑ:d'hɪtɪŋ] *adj* (*report, speech, article*) бьющий напрямик.
hard labour *n* (*punishment*) принудительные работы *fpl*.
hardliner [hɑ:d'laɪnəʳ] *n* сторонник(-ица) жёсткой линии (*в политике*).
hard-luck story ['hɑ:dlʌk-] *n* жалостливая история.
hardly ['hɑ:dlɪ] *adv* (*scarcely*) едва; (*no sooner*) как только; (*harshly*) сурово; **~ anywhere/ever** почти нигде/никогда; **it's ~ the case** это не тот случай; **I ~ think so** я так не думаю; **I can ~ believe it** я с трудом могу поверить в это.
hard-nosed [hɑ:d'nəuzd] *adj* трезвый.
hard-pressed [hɑ:d'prɛst] *adj*: **I am ~ for time/money** у меня туго со временем/деньгами.
hard sell *n* (*COMM*) усиленное рекламирование товаров.
hardship ['hɑ:dʃɪp] *n* (*difficulty*) трудности *fpl*.
hard shoulder *n* (*BRIT: AUT*) *обочина с твёрдым покрытием, на которой разрешена остановка транспорта*.
hard up *adj* (*inf*) на мели.
hardware ['hɑ:dwɛəʳ] *n* скобяные изделия *ntpl*; (*COMPUT*) оборудование, аппаратура; (*MIL*) военная техника.
hardware shop *n* магазин скобяных изделий.
hard-wearing [hɑ:d'wɛərɪŋ] *adj* (*clothes, shoes*) крепкий* (крепок).
hard-won [hɑ:d'wʌn] *adj* с трудом завоёванный (завоёван); (*victory*) с трудом одержанный (одержан).
hard-working [hɑ:d'wə:kɪŋ] *adj* (*employee, student*) усердный* (усерден).
hardy ['hɑ:dɪ] *adj* (*animals, people*) выносливый (вынослив); (*plant*) морозоустойчивый (морозоустойчив).
hare [hɛəʳ] *n* заяц*.
harebrained ['hɛəbreɪnd] *adj* (*scheme, idea*) несуразный* (несуразен).
harelip ['hɛəlɪp] *n* заячья губа*.
harem [hɑ:'ri:m] *n* гарем.
hark back [hɑ:k-] *vi*: **to ~ ~ to** (*be reminiscent of*) напоминать (напомнить *perf*) о +*prp*; (*remember*) вспоминать (вспомнить *perf*) о +*prp*.
harm [hɑ:m] *n* (*injury*) телесное повреждение; (*damage*) ущерб ◆ *vt* (*thing*) повреждать (повредить* *perf*); (*person*) наносить* (нанести* *perf*) вред +*dat*; **to mean no ~** не хотеть* (*impf*) обидеть; **to come to no ~** закончиться (*perf*) благополучно; **out of ~'s way** от греха подальше; **there's no ~ in trying** попытка – не пытка.
harmful ['hɑ:mful] *adj* (*toxin, influence etc*) вредный* (вреден).
harmless [hɑ:mlɪs] *adj* (*animal, person*) безобидный* (безобиден); (*joke, activity*) невинный* (невинен).
harmonic [hɑ:'mɔnɪk] *adj* гармонический.
harmonica [hɑ:'mɔnɪkə] *n* губная гармоника.
harmonics [hɑ:'mɔnɪks] *npl* гармония *fsg*.
harmonious [hɑ:'məunɪəs] *adj* гармоничный* (гармоничен).
harmonium [hɑ:'məunɪəm] *n* фисгармония.
harmonize ['hɑ:mənaɪz] *vi* (*MUS*) гармонировать (*impf*); (*colours, ideas*): **to ~ (with)** гармонировать (*impf*) (с +*instr*).
harmony ['hɑ:mənɪ] *n* (*accord*) гармония; (*MUS*) созвучие.
harness ['hɑ:nɪs] *n* (*for horse*) упряжь *f*; (*for child*) постромки* *fpl*; (*safety harness*) привязные ремни *mpl* ◆ *vt* (*horse, dog*) запрягать (запрячь* *perf*); (*resources, energy etc*) обуздывать (обуздать *perf*).
harp [hɑ:p] *n* арфа ◆ *vi*: **to ~ on about** (*pej*) заводить* (завести* *perf*) волынку о +*prp*.
harpist ['hɑ:pɪst] *n* арфист(ка*).
harpoon [hɑ:'pu:n] *n* гарпун*.
harpsichord ['hɑ:psɪkɔ:d] *n* клавесин.
harried ['hærɪd] *adj* замученный (замучен).
harrow ['hærəu] *n* (*AGR*) борона.
harrowing ['hærəuɪŋ] *adj* душераздирающий*.
harry ['hærɪ] *vt* изводить* (извести* *perf*).
harsh [hɑ:ʃ] *adj* (*sound, light, criticism*) резкий* (резок); (*person*) жёсткий* (жёсток);

(*remark*) стро́гий* (строг); (*life, winter*) суро́вый (суро́в).
harshly ['hɑːʃlɪ] *adv* (*criticize*) ре́зко; (*mark, speak*) стро́го; (*act*) жёстко.
harshness ['hɑːʃnɪs] *n* (*see adj*) ре́зкость *f*, жёсткость *f*, стро́гость *f*, суро́вость *f*.
harvest ['hɑːvɪst] *n* (*harvest time*) жа́тва; (*of barley, fruit etc*) урожа́й ◆ *vt* убира́ть (убра́ть *perf*).
harvester ['hɑːvɪstə^r] *n* (*machine*: *also:* **combine** ~) комба́йн.
has [hæz] *vb see* **have**.
has-been ['hæzbiːn] *n* (*inf*: *person*): **he's/she's a** ~ его́/её вре́мя прошло́.
hash [hæʃ] *n* (*CULIN*) мясно́е рагу́ *nt ind*; (*fig*: *mess*): **to make a ~ of sth** запа́рывать (запоро́ть *perf*) что-н.
hash [hæʃ] *n abbr* (*inf*) = **hashish**.
hashish ['hæʃɪʃ] *n* гаши́ш.
hasn't ['hæznt] = **has not**.
hassle ['hæsl] (*inf*) *n* моро́ка ◆ *vt* надоеда́ть (*impf*) *+dat*.
haste [heɪst] *n* спе́шка; **in ~** в спе́шке; **to make ~ (to do)** торопи́ться (поторопи́ться *perf*) (*+infin*).
hasten ['heɪsn] *vt* (*speed up*) торопи́ть* (поторопи́ть* *perf*) ◆ *vi* (*hurry*): **to ~ to do** торопи́ться* (поторопи́ться* *perf*) *+infin*; **I ~ to add ...** спешу́ доба́вить ...; **she ~ed back to the house** она́ поспеши́ла обра́тно к до́му.
hastily ['heɪstɪlɪ] *adv* (*hurriedly*) поспе́шно; (*rashly*) опроме́тчиво.
hasty ['heɪstɪ] *adj* (*hurried*) поспе́шный* (поспе́шен); (*rash*) опроме́тчивый (опроме́тчив).
hat [hæt] *n* шля́па; (*woolly, furry*) ша́пка*; **to keep sth under one's ~** держа́ть* (*impf*) что-н в секре́те.
hatbox ['hætbɔks] *n* шля́пная коро́бка*.
hatch [hætʃ] *n* (*NAUT*: *also:* **~way**) люк; (*also:* **service ~**) разда́точное *or* буфе́тное окно́* ◆ *vi* (*also:* **~ out**: *chick, egg*) вылупля́ться (вы́лупиться* *perf*) ◆ *vt* (*egg, chick etc*) выси́живать (вы́сидеть* *perf*); (*plot*) вына́шивать (вы́носить* *perf*).
hatchback ['hætʃbæk] *n* (*AUT*) маши́на-пика́п *f*.
hatchet ['hætʃɪt] *n* (*axe*) топо́рик; **to bury the ~** мири́ться (помири́ться *perf*).
hatchet job (*inf*) *n* напа́дки* *pl*; **to do a ~ ~ on sb** разноси́ть* (разнести́* *perf*) кого́-н в пух и прах.
hatchet man *n* (*US*: *inf*) наёмник.
hate [heɪt] *vt* ненави́деть* (*impf*) ◆ *n* не́нависть *f*; **to ~ to do** *or* **doing** ненави́деть* (*impf*) *+infin*; **I ~ to trouble you, but ...** мне о́чень не хо́чется беспоко́ить Вас, но ....
hateful ['heɪtful] *adj* ненави́стный* (ненави́стен).
hatred ['heɪtrɪd] *n* не́нависть *f*.
hat trick *n* (*SPORT, also fig*) побе́да три ра́за подря́д.
haughty ['hɔːtɪ] *adj* надме́нный*.
haul [hɔːl] *vt* (*pull*) таска́ть/тащи́ть* (*impf*); (*transport*) перевози́ть* (перевезти́* *perf*) ◆ *n* (*of stolen goods etc*) добы́ча; (*of fish*) уло́в; **he ~ed himself out of the pool** он с трудо́м вы́брался из бассе́йна.
haulage ['hɔːlɪdʒ] *n* перево́зка.
haulage contractor *n* (*BRIT*: *COMM*: *firm*) фи́рма, производя́щая перево́зки; (: *person*) руководи́тель *m* фи́рмы, производя́щей перево́зки.
hauler ['hɔːlə^r] *n* (*US*) = **haulage contractor**.
haulier ['hɔːlɪə^r] *n* (*BRIT*) руководи́тель *m* фи́рмы, производя́щей перево́зки.
haunch [hɔːntʃ] *n* бедро́*; (*of meat*) бе́дренная часть* *f*.
haunt [hɔːnt] *n* (*of crooks*) прито́н; (*in childhood etc*) люби́мое ме́сто* ◆ *vt* (*subj*: *problem, memory, fear*) пресле́довать (*impf*); **to ~ sb/a house** явля́ться (яви́ться* *perf*) кому́-н/в до́ме.
haunted ['hɔːntɪd] *adj* (*expression, look*) встрево́женный* (встрево́жен); **a ~ house** дом* с привиде́ниями; **this house is ~** в э́том до́м есть привиде́ния.
haunting ['hɔːntɪŋ] *adj* (*sight, music*) пресле́дующий.
Havana [hə'vænə] *n* Гава́на.

KEYWORD

have [hæv] (*pt, pp* **had**) *aux vb*: ***1***: **to have arrived** прие́хать (*perf*); **have you already eaten?** ты уже́ поел?; **he has been kind to me** он прояви́л доброту́ по отноше́нию ко мне; **he has been promoted** он получи́л повыше́ние по слу́жбе; **has he told you?** он Вам сказа́л?; **having finished** *or* **when he had finished, he went to bed** зако́нчив *or* когда́ он зако́нчил, он пошёл спать
2 (*in tag questions*): **you've done it, haven't you?** Вы сде́лали э́то, да?; **he hasn't done it, has he?** он ведь э́то не сде́лал, ве́рно?
3 (*in short answers and questions*): **you've made a mistake – no I haven't/so I have** Вы оши́блись – нет, не оши́бся/да, оши́бся; **we haven't paid – yes we have!** мы не заплати́ли – нет, заплати́ли!; **I've been there before, have you?** я там был, а Вы?
◆ *modal aux vb* (*be obliged*): **to have (got) to do** быть (*impf*) до́лжным(-ой) *+infin*; **I have (got) to finish this work** я до́лжен зако́нчить э́ту рабо́ту; **you haven't to tell her** Вы не должны́ говори́ть ей; **I haven't got** *or* **I don't have to wear glasses** я могу́ не носи́ть очки́; **this has to be a mistake** э́то, наверняка́, оши́бка
◆ *vt* ***1*** (*possess*): **I** *etc* **have** у меня́ *etc*; **he has (got) blue eyes/dark hair** у него́ голубы́е глаза́/тёмные во́лосы; **do you have** *or* **have you got a car/phone?** у Вас есть маши́на/телефо́н?
2 (*referring to meals etc*): **to have breakfast** за́втракать (поза́втракать *perf*); **to have**

dinner обе́дать (пообе́дать *perf*); **to have a cigarette** выку́ривать (вы́курить *perf*) сигаре́ту; **to have a glass of wine** выпива́ть (вы́пить* *perf*) стака́н вина́
3 (*receive, obtain etc*): **may I have your address?** Вы мне мо́жете дать свой а́дрес?; **you can have the book for £5** э́та кни́га ва́ша за £5; **I must have it by tomorrow** э́то должно́ быть у меня́ к за́втрашнему дню; **she is having a baby in March** у неё в ма́рте бу́дет ребёнок
4 (*maintain, allow*): **he will have it that he is right** он наста́ивает на том, что он прав; **I won't have it!** я э́того не допущу́!
5: **I am having my television repaired** мне должны́ почини́ть телеви́зор; **to have sb do** попроси́ть* (*perf*) кого́-н *+infin*; **he soon had them all laughing/working** они́ у него́ все тут же ста́ли смея́ться/рабо́тать
6 (*experience, suffer*): **I have flu/a headache** у меня́ грипп/боли́т голова́; **to have a cold** простужа́ться (простуди́ться* *perf*); **she had her bag stolen** у неё укра́ли су́мку; **he had an operation** ему́ сде́лали опе́рацию
7 (*+n*): **to have a swim** пла́вать (попла́вать *perf*); **to have a rest** отдыха́ть (отдохну́ть *perf*); **let's have a look** дава́йте посмо́трим; **we are having a meeting/party tomorrow** за́втра у нас бу́дет собра́ние/бу́дут го́сти; **let me have a try** да́йте мне́ попро́бовать
8 (*inf*: *dupe*) провести́* (*perf*); **he's been had** его́ провели́; **to have sb on** (*BRIT*: *inf*) води́ть* (*impf*) кого́-н за́ нос
▸ **have in** *vt* (*inf*): **he has got it in for me** у него́ про́тив меня́ зуб
▸ **have on** *vt*: **have you anything on tomorrow?** у Вас есть на за́втра каки́е-нибудь пла́ны?; **I don't have any money on me** у меня́ нет при себе́ де́нег; **he had a black sweater on** на нём был чёрный сви́тер
▸ **have out** *vt*: **to have it out with sb** объясня́ться (объясни́ться *perf*) с кем-н; **she had her tooth out** ей удали́ли зуб; **she had her tonsils/appendix out** ей вы́резали гла́нды/аппендици́т.

haven ['heɪvn] *n* га́вань *f*; (*fig*) убе́жище.
haven't ['hævnt] = **have not**.
haversack ['hævəsæk] *n* (*of hiker*) рюкза́к*; (*of soldier*) ра́нец*.
haves [hævz] *npl* (*inf*): **the ~ and have-nots** иму́щие *pl adj* и неиму́щие *pl adj*.
havoc ['hævək] *n* (*chaos*) ха́ос; **to play ~ with** (*plans etc*) игра́ть (*impf*) злы́е шу́тки над *+instr*.
Hawaii [hə'waiː] *n* Гава́йи *m ind*.
Hawaiian [hə'waɪjən] *adj* гава́йский ◆ *n* гава́ец*(-а́йка*); (*LING*) гава́йский язы́к*.
hawk [hɔːk] *n* я́стреб*.
hawker ['hɔːkə'] *n* (*COMM*) у́личный(-ая) торго́вец*(-вка*).
hawkish ['hɔːkɪʃ] *adj* хи́щный.
hawthorn ['hɔːθɔːn] *n* боя́рышник.
hay [heɪ] *n* се́но.
hay fever *n* сенна́я лихора́дка*.
haystack ['heɪstæk] *n* стог* се́на; **it's like looking for a needle in a ~** э́то как иска́ть иго́лку в сто́ге се́на.
haywire ['heɪwaɪə'] (*inf*) *adj*: **to go ~** (*machine*) барахли́ть (забарахли́ть *perf*); (*plans*) наруша́ться (нару́шиться *perf*).
hazard ['hæzəd] *n* (*danger*) опа́сность *f* ◆ *vt* (*risk*): **to ~ a guess** осме́ливаться (осме́литься *perf*) предположи́ть; **it's a health ~** э́то опа́сно для здоро́вья; **smoking is a fire ~** куре́ние мо́жет служи́ть причи́ной пожа́ра.
hazard lights *npl* = **hazard warning lights**.
hazardous ['hæzədəs] *adj* опа́сный* (опа́сен).
hazard pay *n* (*US*) *дополни́тельная пла́та за труд в опа́сных усло́виях*.
hazard warning lights *npl* (*AUT*) авари́йные огни́ *mpl*.
haze [heɪz] *n* ды́мка*; **heat ~** ма́рево.
hazel [heɪzl] *n* лещи́на ◆ *adj* (*eyes*) зеленова́то-ка́рий*.
hazelnut ['heɪzlnʌt] *n* лесно́й оре́х.
hazy ['heɪzɪ] *adj* тума́нный* (тума́нен); **I'm rather ~ about the details** у меня́ дово́льно сму́тное представле́ние о подро́бностях.
H-bomb ['eɪtʃbɔm] *n* водоро́дная бо́мба.
HE *abbr* (*REL, DIPLOMACY*: = *His/Her Excellency*) Его́/Её Превосходи́тельство; = *high explosive*.
he [hiː] *pron* он.
head [hɛd] *n* (*ANAT*) голова́*; (*mind*) ум*; (*of list, queue*) нача́ло; (*of table*) глава́; (*of company, organization*) руководи́тель(ница) *m(f)*; (*of school*) дире́ктор*; (*on tape recorder etc*) голо́вка ◆ *vt* (*list, queue*) стоя́ть (*impf*) пе́рвым(-ой) в *+prp*; (*group, company*) возглавля́ть (возгла́вить* *perf*); **~s or tails** ≈ орёл или ре́шка; **~ over heels in love** влюблён по́ уши; **to ~ a ball** забива́ть (заби́ть* *perf*) мяч голово́й; **£10 a** *or* **per ~** по £10 ка́ждому *or* на ка́ждого; **to sit at the ~ of the table** сиде́ть* (сесть* *perf*) во главе́ стола́; **he has a ~ for business** у него́ спосо́бности к би́знесу; **I have no ~ for heights** у меня́ кру́жится голова́ от высоты́; **to come to a ~** (*fig*: *situation etc*) доходи́ть* (дойти́* *perf*) до крити́ческой то́чки; **let's put our ~s together** дава́йте обсу́дим э́то вме́сте; **to say sth off the top of one's ~** говори́ть (сказа́ть* *perf*) что-н не заду́мываясь; **on your own ~ be it!** пусть э́то бу́дет на Ва́шей со́вести!; **to bite**

or **snap sb's ~ off** огрызáться (огрызнýться *perf*) комý-н, грýбо обрывáть (оборвáть* *perf*) когó-н; **to go to sb's ~** (*alcohol*) ударя́ть (удáрить *perf*) комý-н в гóлову; (*success, power*) кружи́ть (вскружи́ть *perf*) комý-н гóлову; **to keep/lose one's ~** не теря́ть (потеря́ть *perf*)/теря́ть (потеря́ть *perf*) гóлову; **I can't make ~ nor tail of this** я ничегó не могý поня́ть в э́том; **he's off his ~!** (*inf*) он рехнýлся!

▸ **head for** *vt fus* (*place*) направля́ться (напрáвиться* *perf*) в/на *+acc or* к *+dat*; (*disaster*) обрекáть (обрéчь* *perf*) себя́ на *+acc*

▸ **head off** *vt* (*threat, danger*) отводи́ть* (отвести́* *perf*).

headache ['hɛdeɪk] *n* головнáя боль* *f*; (*fig: problem*) неприя́тность *f*; **I've got a ~** у меня́ боли́т головá.

headband ['hɛdbænd] *n* óбруч* для волóс.

headboard ['hɛdbɔ:d] *n* спи́нка* кровáти.

head cold *n* нáсморк.

headdress ['hɛddrɛs] *n* головнóе украшéние.

headed notepaper ['hɛdɪd-] *n* бланк; (*personal*) *бланк для письмá со штáмпом отправи́теля.*

header ['hɛdə^r] *n* (*BRIT: inf: FOOTBALL*) удáр головóй.

headfirst ['hɛd'fə:st] *adv* (*dive, fall*) головóй вниз; (*rush*) сломя́ гóлову.

headgear ['hɛdgɪə^r] *n* головнóй убóр.

head-hunt ['hɛdhʌnt] *vi* смáнивать (смани́ть* *perf*) лýчших специали́стов ◆ *vt* смáнивать (смани́ть *perf*).

head-hunter ['hɛdhʌntə^r] *n* (*COMM*) *человéк, котóрый перемáнивает сотрýдников из однóй фи́рмы в другýю.*

heading ['hɛdɪŋ] *n* (*of chapter, article*) заголóвок*.

headlamp ['hɛdlæmp] *n* (*BRIT*) = **headlight**.

headland ['hɛdlənd] *n* мыс*.

headlight ['hɛdlaɪt] *n* фáра.

headline ['hɛdlaɪn] *n* (*PRESS, TV, RADIO*) заголóвок*.

headlong ['hɛdlɔŋ] *adv* (*headfirst*) головóй вперёд; (*hastily*) опромéтчиво.

headmaster [hɛd'mɑ:stə^r] *n* дирéктор* шкóлы.

headmistress [hɛd'mɪstrɪs] *n* дирéктор* шкóлы.

head office *n* (*of company etc*) дирéкция.

head of state (*pl* **~s ~ ~**) *n* главá* госудáрства.

head-on [hɛd'ɔn] *adj* (*collision, confrontation*) лобовóй ◆ *adv* нóсом к нóсу.

headphones ['hɛdfəunz] *npl* наýшники *mpl*.

headquarters ['hɛdkwɔ:təz] *npl* (*of company, organization*) глáвное управлéние *ntsg*; (*MIL*) штаб-кварти́ра *fsg*.

headrest ['hɛdrɛst] *n* подголóвник.

headroom ['hɛdrum] *n* (*in car*) внýтренняя высотá (*кýзова*); (*under bridge*) просвéт.

headscarf ['hɛdskɑ:f] *n* коси́нка*; (*square*) головнóй платóк*.

headset ['hɛdsɛt] *n* = **headphones**.

head start *n*: **to have/get a ~ ~** имéть (*impf*)/ получáть (получи́ть* *perf*) исхóдное преимýщество.

headstone ['hɛdstəun] *n* (*on grave*) надгрóбный кáмень* *m*.

headstrong ['hɛdstrɔŋ] *adj* упóрный* (упóрен).

head teacher *n* дирéктор* шкóлы.

head waiter *n* (*in restaurant*) глáвный официáнт.

headway ['hɛdweɪ] *n*: **to make ~** продвигáться (продви́нуться *perf*) вперёд.

headwind ['hɛdwɪnd] *n* встрéчный вéтер*.

heady ['hɛdɪ] *adj* (*experience, time*) голово-кружи́тельный; (*drink*) хмельнóй; (*atmosphere*) взбудорáженный.

heal [hi:l] *vt* (*patient*) излéчивать (излечи́ть* *perf*); (*injury*) заживля́ть (заживи́ть* *perf*); (*damage*) восстанáвливать (восстанови́ть* *perf*) ◆ *vi* (*injury*) заживáть (зажи́ть *perf*); (*damage*) восстанáвливаться (восстанови́ться* *perf*).

health [hɛlθ] *n* (*also MED*) здорóвье; **good ~** крéпкое здорóвье.

health care *n* здравоохранéние.

health centre *n* (*BRIT*) поликли́ника.

health food *n* здорóвая пи́ща.

health-food shop ['hɛlθfu:d-] *n* магази́н здорóвого питáния.

health hazard *n* опáсность *f* для здорóвья.

Health Service *n* (*BRIT*): **the ~ ~** слýжба здравоохранéния.

healthy ['hɛlθɪ] *adj* (*person*) здорóвый* (здорóв); (*economy, appetite*) здорóвый; (*pursuit, pastime*) полéзный* (полéзен); (*profit*) достáточно хорóший*; **it's not ~ to drink too much** сли́шком мнóго пить – врéдно для здорóвья.

heap [hi:p] *n* (*small*) кýча; (*large*) грýда ◆ *vt* (*stones, sand*): **to ~ (up)** свáливать (свали́ть* *perf*) в кýчу; (*plate, sink*): **to ~ with sth** наполня́ть (напóлнить *perf*) чем-н; (*food, books*): **to ~ sth on** навáливать (навали́ть* *perf*) что-н на *+acc*; **~s of** (*inf*) кýча *fsg +gen*; **to ~ favours/praise/gifts on sb** осыпáть (осы́пать* *perf*) когó-н ми́лостями/ похвалáми/подáрками.

hear [hɪə^r] (*pt, pp* **heard**) *vt* слы́шать (услы́шать *perf*); (*lecture, concert*) слýшать (*impf*); (*LAW: case*) слýшать (*impf*); **to ~ about** слы́шать (услы́шать *perf*) о *+prp*; **did you ~ about the move?** Вы слы́шали о переéзде?; **to ~ from sb** слы́шать (услы́шать *perf*) от когó-н; **I can't ~ you** Вас не слы́шно; **I've never ~d of that book** я никогдá не слы́шал об э́той кни́ге; **I wouldn't ~ of it!** я и слы́шать об э́том не хочý!

▸ **hear out** *vt* выслýшивать (вы́слушать *perf*).

heard [hə:d] *pt, pp of* **hear**.

hearing ['hɪərɪŋ] *n* (*sense*) слух; (*LAW, POL*) слу́шание; **she is a bit hard of ~** она́ тугова́та на́ ухо; **within/out of ~ distance** в преде́лах/за преде́лами слы́шимости; **to give sb a (fair) ~** (*BRIT*) дать* (*perf*) кому́-н вы́сказаться.
hearing aid *n* слухово́й аппара́т.
hearsay ['hɪəseɪ] *n* слух; **by ~** по слу́хам.
hearse [hə:s] *n* катафа́лк.
heart [hɑ:t] *n* се́рдце*; (*of lettuce*) сердцеви́на; (*of problem, matter*) суть *f*; **~s** *npl* (*CARDS*) че́рви* *fpl*; **to lose/take ~** пасть* (*perf*)/не па́дать (*impf*) ду́хом; **at ~** в глубине́ души́; **(off) by ~** наизу́сть; **he has a weak ~** у него́ сла́бое се́рдце; **to set one's ~ on sth/on doing** стреми́ться* (*impf*) всей душо́й к чему́-н/+*infin*; **to pour one's ~ out to sb** излива́ть (изли́ть* *perf*) кому́-н ду́шу; **he's a man after my own ~** он мне по́ сердцу; **the ~ of the matter** суть де́ла.
heartache ['hɑ:teɪk] *n* серде́чная боль *f*.
heart attack *n* серде́чный при́ступ.
heartbeat ['hɑ:tbi:t] *n* (*one pulsation*) серде́чное сокраще́ние; (*rhythm*) сердцебие́ние.
heartbreak ['hɑ:tbreɪk] *n* большо́е го́ре.
heartbreaking ['hɑ:tbreɪkɪŋ] *adj* душераздира́ющий* (душераздира́ющ).
heartbroken ['hɑ:tbrəukən] *adj*: **he is ~** (*sad*) он уби́т го́рем.
heartburn ['hɑ:tbə:n] *n* изжо́га.
-hearted ['hɑ:tɪd] *suffix*: **kind-~** добросерде́чный.
hearten ['hɑ:tn] *vt* воодушевля́ть (воодушеви́ть* *perf*).
heart failure *n* (*resulting in death*) остано́вка се́рдца.
heartfelt ['hɑ:tfɛlt] *adj* и́скренний*.
hearth [hɑ:θ] *n* оча́г*.
heartily ['hɑ:tɪlɪ] *adv* (*thank, welcome*) серде́чно; (*dislike*) всем се́рдцем; **to laugh ~** смея́ться (*impf*) от души́.
heartland ['hɑ:tlænd] *n* (*of country*) се́рдце; **Britain's industrial ~** промы́шленный центр Брита́нии.
heartless ['hɑ:tlɪs] *adj* бессерде́чный* (бессерде́чен).
heartstrings ['hɑ:tstrɪŋz] *npl* душе́вные стру́ны* *ntpl*; **the film really tugs at your ~** фильм берёт за́ душу.
heartthrob ['hɑ:tθrɔb] *n* сердцее́д.
heart-to-heart ['hɑ:t'tə'hɑ:t] *adj* серде́чный; **to have a ~** говори́ть (*impf*) по душа́м.
heart transplant *n* переса́дка* се́рдца.
heartwarming ['hɑ:twɔ:mɪŋ] *adj* (*sight*) тро́гательный* (тро́гателен).
hearty ['hɑ:tɪ] *adj* (*person, laugh*) весёлый* (ве́сел); (*welcome, support*) серде́чный; (*appetite*) здоро́вый; (*dislike*) глубо́кий*.
heat [hi:t] *n* тепло́; (*extreme*) жар; (*of weather*) жара́; (*temperature*) температу́ра; (*excitement*) пыл*; (*also*: **qualifying ~**: *in race etc*) забе́г; (: *in swimming*) заплы́в; (*ZOOL*): **our dog is in** *or* (*US*) **on ~** у на́шей соба́ки те́чка ◆ *vt* (*water, food*) греть *or* нагрева́ть (нагре́ть *perf*); (*house*) ота́пливать (отопи́ть* *perf*)
▸ **heat up** *vi* (*water, house*) согрева́ться (согре́ться *perf*) ◆ *vt* (*food, water*) подогрева́ть (подогре́ть *perf*); (*room*) обогрева́ть (обогре́ть *perf*); (*engine*) разогрева́ть (разогре́ть *perf*).
heated ['hi:tɪd] *adj* ота́пливаемый; (*argument*) горя́чий*; (*pool*) обогрева́емый.
heater ['hi:tə^r] *n* обогрева́тель *m*.
heath [hi:θ] *n* (*BRIT*) (ве́ресковая) пу́стошь *f*.
heathen ['hi:ðn] *n* язы́чник(-ица).
heather ['hɛðə^r] *n* ве́реск.
heating ['hi:tɪŋ] *n* отопле́ние.
heat-resistant ['hi:trɪzɪstənt] *adj* жаропро́чный* (жаропро́чен), термосто́йкий* (термосто́ек).
heat-seeking ['hi:tsi:kɪŋ] *adj* теплоула́вливающий.
heatstroke ['hi:tstrəuk] *n* теплово́й уда́р.
heat wave ['hi:tweɪv] *n* пери́од си́льной жары́.
heave [hi:v] *vt* (*pull*) вытя́гивать (вы́тянуть *perf*); (*push*) толка́ть (толкну́ть *perf*); (*lift*) взва́ливать (взвали́ть *perf*); (*throw*) швыря́ть (швырну́ть *perf*) ◆ *vi* (*chest*) вздыма́ться (*impf*); (*retch*) чу́вствовать (почу́вствовать *perf*) тошноту́ ◆ *n* (*upwards*) подъём; (*sideways*) рыво́к; **to ~ a sigh** глубоко́ вздохну́ть (*perf*)
▸ **heave to** ◆ (*pt, pp* **hove**) *vi* (*NAUT*) ложи́ться (лечь* *perf*) в дрейф.
heaven ['hɛvn] *n* (*also fig*) рай*; **thank ~(s)!** сла́ва Бо́гу!; **~ forbid!** Бо́же упаси́!; **for ~'s sake!** ра́ди Бо́га!
heavenly ['hɛvnlɪ] *adj* небе́сный; (*fig*) ра́йский*.
heaven-sent [hɛvn'sɛnt] *adj* благода́тный* (благода́тен).
heavily ['hɛvɪlɪ] *adv* (*fall, sigh*) тяжело́; (*drink, smoke, depend*) си́льно; (*sleep*) кре́пко; (*say*) весо́мый (весо́м).
heavy ['hɛvɪ] *adj* тяжёлый* (тяжёл); (*rain, blow, fall*) си́льный* (си́лен); (*breathing, sleep*) тяжёлый*; (*build*: *of person*) гру́зный; (*sea*) бу́рный* (бу́рен); **he is a ~ drinker/smoker** он мно́го пьёт/ку́рит; **the work is ~ going** рабо́та идёт тяжело́; **he is ~ going** с ним тру́дно име́ть де́ло.
heavy cream *n* (*US*) жи́рные сли́вки* *pl*.
heavy-duty ['hɛvɪ'dju:tɪ] *adj* сверхпро́чный.
heavy goods vehicle *n* (*BRIT*) грузови́к, перевозя́щий тяжёлые гру́зы.

* marks translations which have irregular inflections. The Russian-English side of the dictionary gives inflectional information.

heavy-handed ['hɛvɪ'hændɪd] *adj* вла́стный* (вла́стен).
heavy industry *n* тяжёлая промы́шленность *f*.
heavy metal *n* (*MUS*) хэ́ви ме́тал, (тяжёлый) мета́лл.
heavy-set ['hɛvɪ'sɛt] *adj* (*esp US*) корена́стый (корена́ст).
heavy user *n лицо́/компа́ния, покупа́ющее/-ая больши́е па́ртии определённого това́ра.*
heavyweight ['hɛvɪweɪt] *n* боксёр тяжёлого ве́са.
Hebrew ['hi:bru:] *adj* древнеевре́йский ◆ *n* (*LING*: *ancient*) древнеевре́йский язы́к*; (*modern*) иври́т.
Hebrides ['hɛbrɪdi:z] *npl*: **the ~** Гебри́дские острова́* *mpl*.
heck [hɛk] *excl* (*inf*) чёрт.
heckle ['hɛkl] *vt* перебива́ть (переби́ть* *perf*).
heckler ['hɛklə^r] *n*: **there were several ~s in the audience** не́которые лю́ди в за́ле перебива́ли.
hectare ['hɛktɑ:^r] *n* (*BRIT*) гекта́р.
hectic ['hɛktɪk] *adj* (*day*) сумато́шный* (сумато́шен); (*actions, activities*) лихора́дочный* (лихора́дочен).
hector ['hɛktə^r] *vt* запу́гивать (запуга́ть *perf*).
he'd [hi:d] = **he would, he had**.
hedge [hɛdʒ] *n* жива́я и́згородь *f* ◆ *vi* (*stall*) увиливать (увильну́ть *perf*) ◆ *vt*: **to ~ one's bets** подстрахо́вываться (подстрахова́ться *perf*); **as a ~ against inflation** как страхо́вка от инфля́ции
▸ **hedge in** *vt* ограни́чивать (ограни́чить *perf*).
hedgehog ['hɛdʒhɔg] *n* ёж*.
hedgerow ['hɛdʒrəu] *n* жива́я и́згородь *f*.
hedonism ['hi:dənɪzəm] *n* гедони́зм.
heed [hi:d] *vt* (*also*: **take ~ of**) принима́ть (приня́ть* *perf*) во внима́ние ◆ *n*: **to pay (no) ~ to, take (no) ~ of** (не) принима́ть (приня́ть* *perf*) во внима́ние.
heedless ['hi:dlɪs] *adj*: **~ of** не обраща́я внима́ния на *+acc*.
heel [hi:l] *n* (*of foot*) пя́тка*; (*of shoe*) каблу́к* ◆ *vt* (*shoe*) подбива́ть (подби́ть* *perf*); **to bring to ~** (*dog*) заставля́ть (заста́вить* *perf*) идти́ *or* стоя́ть ря́дом; (*person*) подчиня́ть (подчини́ть *perf*); **to take to one's ~s** (*inf*) пуска́ться (пусти́ться* *perf*) наутёк.
hefty ['hɛftɪ] *adj* (*person, object*) здорове́нный; (*profit, fine*) изря́дный*.
heifer ['hɛfə^r] *n* тёлка*.
height [haɪt] *n* (*of tree, of plane*) высота́*; (*of person*) рост; (*of power*) верши́на; (*of mountain*) возвы́шенность *f*; (*of season*) разга́р; (*of luxury, taste*) верх; **what ~ are you?** како́й у Вас рост?; **of average ~** сре́днего ро́ста; **to be afraid of ~s** боя́ться (*impf*) высоты́; **it's the ~ of fashion** э́то верх мо́ды; **at the ~ of the tourist season** в разга́р туристи́ческого сезо́на.
heighten ['haɪtn] *vt* уси́ливать (уси́лить *perf*).
heinous ['heɪnəs] *adj* (*crime*) чудо́вищный.
heir [ɛə^r] *n* насле́дник.
heir apparent *n* прямо́й насле́дник.
heiress ['ɛərɛs] *n* насле́дница.
heirloom ['ɛəlu:m] *n* семе́йная рели́квия.
heist [haɪst] *n* (*US*: *inf*) грабёж*.
held [hɛld] *pt, pp of* **hold**.
helicopter ['hɛlɪkɔptə^r] *n* вертолёт.
heliport ['hɛlɪpɔ:t] *n* вертодро́м.
helium ['hi:lɪəm] *n* ге́лий.
hell [hɛl] *n* (*also fig*) ад*; **~!** (*inf*) чёрт!; **a** *or* **one ~ of a mess** (*inf*) кошма́рный беспоря́док*; **a** *or* **one ~ of a party** (*inf*) кла́ссная вечери́нка.
he'll [hi:l] = **he will, he shall**; *see* **will**.
hellish ['hɛlɪʃ] *adj* (*inf*: *awful*) кошма́рный* (кошма́рен).
hello [hə'ləu] *excl* здра́вствуйте; (*informal*) приве́т; (*TEL*: *on answering*) алло́; (*to attract attention*) эй; (*in surprise*): **~(, what's this!)** эй (что э́то!).
helm [hɛlm] *n* (*NAUT*) руль* *m*; **man at the ~** (*fig*) рулево́й *m adj*; **at the ~ of** у корми́ла *+gen*.
helmet ['hɛlmɪt] *n* (*of policeman, miner*) ка́ска*; (*also*: **crash ~**) шлем.
helmsman ['hɛlmzmən] *n* рулево́й *m adj*.
help [hɛlp] *n* по́мощь *f*; (*charwoman*) прислу́га ◆ *vt* помога́ть (помо́чь* *perf*) *+dat*; **with the ~ of** (*person*) с по́мощью *+gen*; (*tool*) при по́мощи *+gen*; **can I be of (any) ~?** я могу́ Вам чем-нибу́дь помо́чь?; **~!** помоги́те!; **can I ~ you?** (*in shop*) чем могу́ быть* поле́зен?; **~ yourself** угоща́йтесь; **he can't ~ it** он ничего́ не мо́жет поде́лать с э́тим; **I can't ~ thinking that ...** я не могу́ не ду́мать, что ....
helper ['hɛlpə^r] *n* помо́щник(-ица).
helpful ['hɛlpful] *adj* поле́зный* (поле́зен).
helping ['hɛlpɪŋ] *n* по́рция.
helping hand *n*: **to lend a ~ ~** протя́гивать (протяну́ть *perf*) ру́ку по́мощи.
helpless ['hɛlplɪs] *adj* беспо́мощный* (беспо́мощен).
helplessly ['hɛlplɪslɪ] *adv* беспо́мощно.
helpline ['hɛlplaɪn] *n* телефо́н дове́рия.
Helsinki ['hɛlsɪŋkɪ] *n* Хе́льсинки *m ind*.
helter-skelter ['hɛltə'skɛltə^r] *n* (*BRIT*) спира́льная го́рка (*аттракцио́н*).
hem [hɛm] *n* (*of dress*) подо́л; (*of curtains*) низ ◆ *vt* подшива́ть (подши́ть* *perf*)
▸ **hem in** *vt* пло́тно окружа́ть (окружи́ть *perf*); **city life made him feel ~med in** жизнь в го́роде стесня́ла его́.
hematology ['hi:mə'tɔlədʒɪ] *n* (*US*) = **haematology**.
hemisphere ['hɛmɪsfɪə^r] *n* полуша́рие.
hemlock ['hɛmlɔk] *n* (*BOT*) болиголо́в.
hemoglobin ['hi:mə'gləubɪn] *n* (*US*) = **haemoglobin**.
hemophilia ['hi:mə'fɪlɪə] *n* (*US*) = **haemophilia**.
hemorrhage ['hɛmərɪdʒ] *n* (*US*) = **haemorrhage**.
hemorrhoids ['hɛmərɔɪdz] *npl* (*US*) =

haemorrhoids.
hemp [hɛmp] *n* конопля́.
hen [hɛn] *n* (*chicken*) ку́рица*; (*female bird*) са́мка*.
hence [hɛns] *adv* (*therefore*) сле́довательно; (*from now*): **2 years ~** (*formal*) по истече́нии двух лет.
henceforth [hɛns'fɔ:θ] *adv* впредь.
henchman ['hɛntʃmən] *irreg n* приспе́шник.
henna ['hɛnə] *n* хна.
hen party *n* (*inf*) деви́чник.
henpecked ['hɛnpɛkt] *adj* (*husband*) поко́рный* (поко́рен).
hepatitis [hɛpə'taɪtɪs] *n* гепати́т.
her [hə:ʳ] *pron* (*direct*) её; (*indirect*) ей; (*after prep*: *+instr, +dat, +prp*) ней; (: *+gen*) неё; *see also* **me** ◆ *adj* её; (*referring to subject of sentence*) свой; *see also* **my**.
herald ['hɛrəld] *n* (*precursor*) предве́стник ◆ *vt* (*event*) предвеща́ть *(impf)*.
heraldic [hɛ'rældɪk] *adj* геральди́ческий.
heraldry ['hɛrəldrɪ] *n* (*study*) гера́льдика; (*coat of arms*) герб.
herb [hə:b] *n* (*BOT, CULIN*) трава́*; (*MED*) лека́рственная трава́; **~s** *npl* (*CULIN*) зе́лень *fsg*.
herbaceous [hə:'beɪʃəs] *adj*: **~ plant** цвето́чное расте́ние; **~ border** клу́мба.
herbal ['hə:bl] *adj*: **~ medicine** лече́ние тра́вами; **~ remedy** лека́рство из трав; **~ tea** чай* из трав.
herbicide ['hə:bɪsaɪd] *n* гербици́д.
herd [hə:d] *n* ста́до* ◆ *vt* (*drive*: *animals, people*) гнать* *(impf)*; (*gather*) сгоня́ть (согна́ть* *perf*).
here [hɪəʳ] *adv* (*location*) здесь; (*destination*) сюда́; (*departure point*): **from ~** отсю́да; (*at this point*: *in past*) тут; **"here!"** (*present*) „здесь!"; **~ is ..., ~ are ...** вот ...; **~ you are** (*giving*) вот, пожа́луйста; **where are my keys? ~ we are!** (*finding sth*) где мои́ ключи́? вот они́!; **~'s my sister** вот моя́ сестра́; **~ she comes** вот она́ идёт; **come ~!** иди́те сюда́!; **she left ~ yesterday** она́ уе́хала отсю́да вчера́; **~ and there** (*location*) там и сям; (*motion*) туда́ и сюда́; **"here's to ...!"** (*toast*) „за *+acc* ...!".
hereabouts ['hɪərə'bauts] *adv* побли́зости.
hereafter [hɪər'ɑ:ftəʳ] *adv* в дальне́йшем.
hereby [hɪə'baɪ] *adv* (*formal*: *in letter*): **we ~ acknowledge ...** настоя́щим подтвержда́ем ....
hereditary [hɪ'rɛdɪtrɪ] *adj* насле́дственный.
heredity [hɪ'rɛdɪtɪ] *n* насле́дственность *f*.
heresy ['hɛrəsɪ] *n* е́ресь *f*.
heretic ['hɛrətɪk] *n* ерети́к*(-и́чка*).
heretical [hɪ'rɛtɪkl] *adj* ерети́ческий*.
herewith [hɪə'wɪð] *adv* (*formal*: *letter*): **please find enclosed ~ ...** при сём прилага́ется ....
heritage ['hɛrɪtɪdʒ] *n* насле́дие; **our national ~** на́ше национа́льное бога́тство.
hermetically [hə:'mɛtɪklɪ] *adv*: **~ sealed** гермети́чески закры́тый.
hermit ['hə:mɪt] *n* отше́льник(-ица).
hernia ['hə:nɪə] *n* гры́жа.
hero ['hɪərəu] (*pl* **~es**) *n* геро́й.
heroic [hɪ'rəuɪk] *adj* герои́ческий*.
heroin ['hɛrəuɪn] *n* герои́н.
heroin addict *n* наркома́н (*принима́ющий герои́н*).
heroine ['hɛrəuɪn] *n* герои́ня.
heroism ['hɛrəuɪzəm] *n* герои́зм.
heron ['hɛrən] *n* ца́пля*.
hero worship *n* культ геро́я.
herring ['hɛrɪŋ] *n* (*ZOOL*) се́льдь* *f*; (*CULIN*) селёдка.
hers [hə:z] *pron* её; (*referring to subject of sentence*) свой; *see also* **mine**[1].
herself [hə:'sɛlf] *pron* (*reflexive, after prep*: *+acc, +gen*) себя́; (: *+dat, +prp*) себе́; (: *+instr*) собо́й; (*emphatic*) сама́; (*alone*): **by ~** одна́; *see also* **myself**.
Herts *abbr* (*BRIT*: *POST*) = *Hertfordshire*.
he's [hi:z] = **he is, he has**; *see* **be, have**.
hesitant ['hɛzɪtənt] *adj* нереши́тельный* (нереши́телен); **to be ~ about doing** не реша́ться *(impf)* or колеба́ться* *(impf)* *+infin*.
hesitate ['hɛzɪteɪt] *vi* (*pause*) колеба́ться* (поколеба́ться* *perf*); (*be unwilling*) не реша́ться *(impf)*; **to ~ (about/to do)** не реша́ться *(impf)* (на *+acc/+infin*); **don't ~ to see a doctor if you are worried** е́сли Вы обеспоко́ены (э́тим), без колеба́ний обрати́тесь к врачу́.
hesitation [hɛzɪ'teɪʃən] *n* (*pause*) колеба́ние; **I have no ~ in saying (that) ...** я говорю́ не колеблясь(, что) ....
hessian ['hɛsɪən] *n* мешкови́на.
heterogeneous ['hɛtərə'dʒi:nɪəs] *adj* разноро́дный* (разноро́ден).
heterosexual ['hɛtərəu'sɛksjuəl] *adj* гетеросексуа́льный ◆ *n* гетеросексуа́льный челове́к*.
het up [hɛt-] *adj* (*inf*): **to get ~ ~ (about)** заводи́ться* (завести́сь* *perf*) (из-за *+gen*).
HEW *n abbr* (*US*) = *Department of Health, Education and Welfare*.
hew [hju:] (*pp* **hewed** *or* **hewn**) *vt* (*stone*) выда́лбливать (вы́долбить* *perf*); (*wood*) выруба́ть (вы́рубить* *perf*).
hewn [hju:n] *pp of* **hew**.
hex [hɛks] (*US*) *n* колду́нья*, ве́дьма ◆ *vt* завора́живать (заворожи́ть *perf*).
hexagon ['hɛksəgən] *n* шестиуго́льник.
hexagonal [hɛk'sægənl] *adj* шестиуго́льный.
hey [heɪ] *excl* эй.
heyday ['heɪdeɪ] *n*: **the ~ of** расцве́т *+gen*.
HF *n abbr* (= *high frequency*) ВЧ = *высо́кая*

* marks translations which have irregular inflections. The Russian-English side of the dictionary gives inflectional information.

частота́.
HGV *n abbr* (*BRIT*: = *heavy goods vehicle*) грузово́й автомоби́ль *m*.
HI *abbr* (*US*: *POST*) = *Hawaii*.
hi [haɪ] *excl* (*as greeting*) приве́т; (*to attract attention*) эй.
hiatus [haɪ'eɪtəs] *n* (*in activity*) пробе́л; (*in conversation*) па́уза.
hibernate ['haɪbəneɪt] *vi* впада́ть (впасть* *perf*) в зи́мнюю спя́чку.
hibernation [haɪbə'neɪʃən] *n* зи́мняя спя́чка.
hick [hɪk] *n* (*US*: *inf*: *pej*) дереве́нщина *m/f*.
hiccough *etc* = **hiccup** *etc*.
hiccup ['hɪkʌp] *vi* ика́ть *(impf)*.
hiccups ['hɪkʌps] *npl* ико́та *fsg*; **she's got (the) ~** у неё ико́та.
hid [hɪd] *pt of* **hide**.
hidden ['hɪdn] *pp of* **hide** ◆ *adj*: **there are no ~ extras** здесь нет скры́тых доба́вочных расхо́дов; **there is a ~ agenda** за э́тим что-то кро́ется.
hide [haɪd] (*pt* **hid**, *pp* **hidden**) *n* (*skin*) шку́ра; (*of birdwatcher*) укры́тие ◆ *vt* (*object, person*) пря́тать* (спря́тать* *perf*); (*feeling, information*) скрыва́ть (скрыть* *perf*); (*sun, view*) закрыва́ть (закры́ть* *perf*) ◆ *vi*: **to ~ (from sb)** пря́таться* (спря́таться* *perf*) (от кого́-н); **to ~ sth (from sb)** (*object, person*) пря́тать* (спря́тать* *perf*) что-н (от кого́-н); (*information*) скрыва́ть (скрыть* *perf*) что-н (от кого́-н).
hide-and-seek ['haɪdən'si:k] *n* пря́тки* *fpl*.
hideaway ['haɪdəweɪ] *n* убе́жище.
hideous ['hɪdɪəs] *adj* (*painting, conditions*) жу́ткий* (жу́ток); (*face*) омерзи́тельный* (омерзи́телен).
hideously ['hɪdɪəslɪ] *adv* (*ugly*) омерзи́тельно; (*difficult*) жу́тко.
hide-out ['haɪdaut] *n* укры́тие; (*of criminals*) ло́говище.
hiding ['haɪdɪŋ] *n* (*beating*) по́рка*; (*concealed*): **to be in ~** скрыва́ться *(impf)*.
hiding place *n* (*for person*) укры́тие; (*for money etc*) тайни́к*, потайно́е ме́сто*.
hierarchy ['haɪərɑ:kɪ] *n* иера́рхия.
hieroglyphic [haɪərə'glɪfɪk] *adj* иероглиф-и́ческий.
hieroglyphics [haɪərə'glɪfɪks] *npl* иеро́глифы *mpl*.
hi-fi ['haɪfaɪ] *n abbr* (= *high fidelity*) высо́кая ве́рность звуковоспроизведе́ния ◆ *adj* (*equipment, system*): **~ equipment** аппарату́ра с высо́кой ве́рностью звуковоспроизведе́ния.
higgledy-piggledy ['hɪgldɪ'pɪgldɪ] (*inf*) *adj* беспоря́дочный* (беспоря́дочен) ◆ *adv* ко́е-ка́к, беспоря́дочно.
high [haɪ] *adj* высо́кий* (высо́к); (*wind*) си́льный*; (*BRIT*: *meat*) вы́держанный (вы́держан) ◆ *adv* (*climb, aim etc*) высоко́ ◆ *n*: **exports have reached a new ~** э́кспорт дости́г но́вой высоты́; **the building is 20 m ~** высота́ зда́ния – 20 м; **to be ~** (*inf*: *on drugs, drink*) кайфова́ть *(impf)*; **~ risk** высо́кая сте́пень *f* ри́ска; **~ in the air** (*position*) высоко́ в во́здухе; (*motion*) высоко́ в во́здух; **to pay a ~ price for sth** плати́ть* (заплати́ть* *perf*) высо́кую цену́ за что-н; **it's ~ time you learned how to do it** Вам давно́ пора́ научи́ться де́лать э́то.
highball ['haɪbɔ:l] *n* (*US*) ви́ски с со́довой и льдом (*в высо́ком стака́не*).
highboy ['haɪbɔɪ] *n* (*US*) высо́кий комо́д.
highbrow ['haɪbrau] *adj* (*subjects*) учёный; (*person*) интеллектуа́льный* (интеллектуа́лен).
highchair ['haɪtʃɛə'] *n* высо́кий* сту́льчик (*для ма́леньких дете́й*).
high-class ['haɪ'klɑ:s] *adj* (*hotel, performance*) первокла́ссный, высо́кого кла́сса; (*neighbourhood*) прести́жный* (прести́жен).
High Court *n* (*BRIT*): **the ~ ~** ≈ Верхо́вный суд*.
higher ['haɪə'] *adj* вы́сший* ◆ *adv* вы́ше.
higher education *n* вы́сшее образова́ние.
highfalutin [haɪfə'lu:tɪn] *adj* (*inf*) высоко-па́рный* (высокопа́рен).
high finance *n*: **the world of ~ ~** мир вы́сших фина́нсовых круго́в.
high-five [haɪ'faɪv] *n* пятерня́ (*хлопо́к ладо́нью по чьей-нибу́дь ладо́ни*).
high-flier [haɪ'flaɪə'] *n* пти́ца высо́кого полёта.
high-flying [haɪ'flaɪɪŋ] *adj* (*person*) често-люби́вый; (*lifestyle*) шика́рный.
high-handed [haɪ'hændɪd] *adj* (*decision, person*) своево́льный* (своево́лен).
high-heeled [haɪ'hi:ld] *adj* на высо́ком каблуке́.
high heels *npl* ту́фли* *fpl* на высо́ком каблуке́.
high jump *n* прыжо́к* в высоту́.
Highlands ['haɪləndz] *npl*: **the ~** Высокого́рья* *ntpl* (*Шотла́ндии*).
high-level ['haɪlɛvl] *adj* (*talks etc*) на вы́сшем у́ровне; **~ language** (*COMPUT*) язы́к* высокого уровня.
highlight ['haɪlaɪt] *n* (*of event*) кульмина́ция ◆ *vt* (*problem, need*) выявля́ть (вы́явить* *perf*); **~s** *npl* (*in hair*) пря́ди *fpl*; **the match ~s were shown on TV** кульминацио́нные моме́нты ма́тча бы́ли пока́заны по телеви́дению.
highlighter ['haɪlaɪtə'] *n* (*also*: **~ pen**) флома́стер (*для выделе́ния часте́й те́кста*).
highly ['haɪlɪ] *adv* о́чень; (*paid*) высоко́; **to speak ~ of** высоко́ отзыва́ться (отозва́ться* *perf*) о *+prp*; **to think ~ of** быть* *(impf)* высо́кого мне́ния о *+prp*.
highly strung *adj* нерво́зный* (нерво́зен).
High Mass *n* торже́ственная ме́сса.
highness ['haɪnɪs] *n*: **Her/His H~** Её/Его́ Высо́чество.
high-pitched [haɪ'pɪtʃt] *adj* пронзи́тельный* (пронзи́телен).
high point *n* кульмина́ция.

high-powered ['haɪ'pauəd] *adj* (*engine*) мóщный*; (*job*) ответственный; (*course, person*) высóкого ýровня.
high-pressure ['haɪprɛʃəʳ] *adj* высóкого давлéния.
high-rise ['haɪraɪz] *adj* (*buildings, flats*) высóтный.
high school *n* (BRIT) срéдняя шкóла (*для 11-18ти лéтних*); (US) срéдняя шкóла (*для 15-18ти летних*).
high season *n* (BRIT) разгáр сезóна.
high spirits *npl* припóднятое настроéние *ntsg*.
high street *n* (BRIT) центрáльная ýлица.
high-strung ['haɪ'strʌŋ] *adj* (US) = **highly strung**.
high tide *n* прилив.
highway ['haɪweɪ] *n* (US: *between towns, states*) шоссé *nt ind*, автострáда; (*main road*) автострáда.
Highway Code *n* (BRIT) ≈ прáвила *ntpl* дорóжного движéния.
highwayman ['haɪweɪmən] *irreg n* разбóйник с большóй дорóги.
hijack ['haɪdʒæk] *vt* угонять (угнáть* *perf*); (*fig*) перехвáтывать (перехватить* *perf*) ◆ *n* (*also: ~ing*) угóн.
hijacker ['haɪdʒækəʳ] *n* угóнщик.
hike [haɪk] *vi* ходить*/идти* (*impf*) в похóд ◆ *vt* (*inf*: *prices*) взвинчивать (взвинтить* *perf*) ◆ *n*: **to go for a ~** идти* (пойти* *perf*) на длительную прогýлку; (*inf*): **a ~ in prices** скачóк* цен.
hiker ['haɪkəʳ] *n* турист(ка).
hiking ['haɪkɪŋ] *n*: **to go ~** ходить*/идти* (*impf*) в похóд.
hilarious [hɪ'lɛərɪəs] *adj* чрезвычáйно смешнóй* (смешóн).
hilarity [hɪ'lærɪtɪ] *n* бýйное весéлье.
hill [hɪl] *n* (*small*) холм*; (*fairly high*) (небольшáя) горá*; (*slope*) склон; (*on road*) подъём.
hillbilly ['hɪlbɪlɪ] *n* (US) гóрец*; (: *pej*) деревéнщина *m/f*.
hillock ['hɪlək] *n* пригóрок*.
hillside ['hɪlsaɪd] *n* склон.
hill start *n* (AUT) *завóд и управлéние автомобилей на подъёме*.
hilltop ['hɪltɔp] *n* вершина (*холмá, горы́*).
hilly ['hɪlɪ] *adj* холмистый (холмист).
hilt [hɪlt] *n* рукоятка*; **to back sb to the ~** поддéрживать (*impf*) когó-н пóлностью.
him [hɪm] *pron* (*direct*) егó; (*indirect*) емý; (*after prep*: *+gen*) негó; (: *+dat*) немý; (: *+instr*) ним; (: *+prp*) нём; *see also* **me**.
Himalayas [hɪmə'leɪəz] *npl*: **the ~** Гималáи* *pl*.
himself [hɪm'sɛlf] *pron* (*reflexive, after prep*: *+acc, +gen*) себя́; (: *+dat, +prp*) себé; (: *+instr*) собóй; (*emphatic*) сам; (*alone*): **by ~** один; *see also* **myself**.
hind [haɪnd] *adj* зáдний* ◆ *n* сáмка* оленя.
hinder ['hɪndəʳ] *vt* (*progress, movement*) препя́тствовать (воспрепя́тствовать *perf*) *or* мешáть (помешáть *perf*) *+dat*; **to ~ sb from doing** мешáть (помешáть *perf*) комý-н *+infin*.
hindquarters ['haɪnd'kwɔːtəz] *npl* (*of animal*) зад *msg*.
hindrance ['hɪndrəns] *n* (*nuisance, interruption*) помéха.
hindsight ['haɪndsaɪt] *n*: **with ~** ретроспективным взгля́дом.
Hindu ['hɪnduː] *adj* индýсский.
hinge [hɪndʒ] *n* (*on door*) петля́* ◆ *vi* (*fig*): **to ~ on** зависеть (*impf*) от *+gen*.
hint [hɪnt] *n* (*suggestion*) намёк; (*tip*) совéт; (*sign, glimmer*) подóбие ◆ *vt*: **to ~ that** намекáть (намекнýть *perf*) что ◆ *vi*: **to ~ at** намекáть (намекнýть *perf*) на *+acc*; **to drop a ~** обронить* (*perf*) намёк; **to give sb a ~** подскáзывать (подсказáть* *perf*) комý-н; **white with a ~ of pink** бéлый с намёком на рóзовый.
hip [hɪp] *n* бедрó*.
hip flask *n* набéдренная фля́га.
hip hop *n* *стиль поп-мýзыки*.
hippie ['hɪpɪ] *n* хиппи *m/f ind*.
hippo ['hɪpəu] *n* гиппопотáм.
hip pocket *n* зáдний* кармáн.
hippopotami [hɪpə'pɔtəmaɪ] *npl of* **hippopotamus**.
hippopotamus [hɪpə'pɔtəməs] (*pl* **~es** *or* **hippopotami**) *n* гиппопотáм.
hippy ['hɪpɪ] *n* = **hippie**.
hire ['haɪəʳ] *vt* (BRIT: *car, equipment*) брать* (взять* *perf*) напрокáт; (*venue*) снимáть (снять* *perf*), арендовáть (*impf/perf*); (*worker*) нанимáть (наня́ть* *perf*) ◆ *n* (BRIT: *of car*) прокáт; (*venue*) арéнда; **for ~** напрокáт; **on ~** взя́тый напрокáт
▸ **hire out** *vt* (*car, equipment*) давáть* (дать* *perf*) напрокáт; (*venue*) сдавáть* (сдать* *perf*) внаём.
hire(d) car *n* (BRIT) машина, взя́тая напрокáт.
hire-purchase [haɪə'pəːtʃɪs] *n* (BRIT): **to buy sth on ~** покупáть (купить* *perf*) что-н в рассрóчку.
Hiroshima [hɪ'rɔʃɪmə] *n* Хиросима.
his [hɪz] *adj* егó; (*referring to subject of sentence*) свой; *see also* **my** ◆ *pron* егó; *see also* **mine**[1].
hiss [hɪs] *vi* (*snake, gas, fat*) шипéть* (*impf*); (*person, audience*) освистывать* (освистáть* *perf*), шикать (ошикать *perf*) ◆ *n* (**see vb**) шипéние; свист, шикание.
histogram ['hɪstəgræm] *n* гистогрáмма.
historian [hɪ'stɔːrɪən] *n* истóрик.
historic [hɪ'stɔrɪk] *adj* (*agreement, achievement*)

* marks translations which have irregular inflections. The Russian-English side of the dictionary gives inflectional information.

истори́ческий*.
historical [hɪ'stɔrɪkl] *adj* (*event, film*) истори́ческий*.
history ['hɪstərɪ] *n* исто́рия; **medical ~** (*of patient*) исто́рия боле́зни; **there's a long ~ of illness in his family** боле́знь передава́лась в его́ семье́ по насле́дству.
hit [hɪt] (*pt* **hit**) *vt* ударя́ть (уда́рить *perf*); (*reach: target*) попада́ть (попа́сть* *perf*) в +*acc*; (*collide with: car*) ста́лкиваться (столкну́ться *perf*) с +*instr*; (*affect: person, services*) ударя́ть (уда́рить *perf*) по +*dat* ◆ *n* (*knock*) уда́р; (*success*): **the play was a big ~** пье́са по́льзовалась больши́м успе́хом; **to ~ it off (with sb)** (*inf*) найти́* (*perf*) о́бщий язы́к (с кем-н); **to ~ the headlines** попа́сть* (*perf*) на пе́рвые страни́цы газе́т; **to ~ the road** (*inf*) отправля́ться (отпра́виться* *perf*) в путь; **he'll ~ the roof when he finds out about it** (*inf*) он всё здесь разнесёт, когда́ узна́ет об э́том
▸ **hit back** *vi*: **to ~ back at sb** (*in fight, argument*) наноси́ть* (нанести́* *perf*) отве́тный уда́р кому́-н
▸ **hit out at** *vt fus* (*also fig*) набра́сываться (набро́ситься* *perf*) на +*acc*
▸ **hit (up)on** *vt fus* (*answer, solution etc*) оты́скивать (отыска́ть* *perf*).
hit and miss *adj* (*unpredictable*) непредсказу́емый (непредсказу́ем).
hit-and-run driver ['hɪtən'rʌn-] *n води́тель, кото́рый, сбив пешехо́да, уезжа́ет с ме́ста происше́ствия.*
hitch [hɪtʃ] *vt* (*also:* **~ up**: *trousers, skirt*) подтя́гивать (подтяну́ть* *perf*) ◆ *n* (*difficulty*) поме́ха; **to ~ sth to** (*fasten*) привя́зывать (привяза́ть* *perf*) что-н к +*dat*; (*hook*) прицепля́ть (прицепи́ть* *perf*) что-н к +*dat*; **to ~ a lift** лови́ть* (пойма́ть *perf*) попу́тку; **technical ~** техни́ческая неувя́зка*
▸ **hitch up** *vt* (*horse, cart*) запряга́ть (запря́чь* *perf*); *see also* **hitch**.
hitchhike ['hɪtʃhaɪk] *vi* е́здить*/е́хать* (пое́хать* *perf*) автосто́пом.
hitchhiker ['hɪtʃhaɪkə'] *n* путеше́ственник (-ица) автосто́пом.
hi-tech ['haɪ'tɛk] *adj* высокотехни́ческий.
hitherto [hɪðə'tu:] *adv* (*formal*) до настоя́щего вре́мени.
hit list *n* спи́сок* наме́ченных жертв.
hit man *irreg n* наёмный уби́йца *m*.
hit-or-miss ['hɪtə'mɪs] *adj* сде́ланный (сде́лан) науга́д; (*casual*) сде́ланный как попа́ло *or* ко́е-как; (*unpredictable*) непредсказу́емый (непредсказу́ем); **it's ~ whether I'll be able to come** тру́дно предсказа́ть, смогу́ ли я прийти́.
hit parade *n* (*formerly*) хит-пара́д.
HIV *n abbr* (= *human immunodeficiency virus*) ВИЧ= *ви́рус иммунодефици́та челове́ка*; **~-negative** с отрица́тельной реа́кцией на ВИЧ; **~-positive** с положи́тельной реа́кцией на ВИЧ.
hive [haɪv] *n* (*of bees*) у́лей*; (*fig*): **Moscow is a ~ of activity** жизнь в Москве́ кипи́т
▸ **hive off** *vt* отделя́ть (отдели́ть* *perf*).
hl *abbr* (= *hectolitre*) гектоли́тр.
HM *abbr* (= *His/Her Majesty*) Его́/Её Вели́чество.
HMG *abbr* (BRIT) = *His (or Her) Majesty's Government.*
HMI *n abbr* (BRIT: SCOL) = *His (or Her) Majesty's Inspector.*
HMO *n abbr* (US) = *health maintenance organization.*
HMS *abbr* (BRIT) = *His (or Her) Majesty's Ship.*
HMSO *n abbr* (BRIT) = *His (or Her) Majesty's Stationery Office.*
HNC *n abbr* (BRIT: = *Higher National Certificate*) *свиде́тельство о сре́днем техни́ческом образова́нии.*
HND *n abbr* (BRIT: = *Higher National Diploma*) *дипло́м о сре́днем техни́ческом образова́нии.*
hoard [hɔ:d] *n* (*of food*) (та́йный) запа́с; (*of treasure*) клад ◆ *vt* (*provisions*) запаса́ть (запасти́* *perf*); (*money*) копи́ть* (скопи́ть* *perf*).
hoarding ['hɔ:dɪŋ] *n* (BRIT) рекла́мный щит*.
hoarfrost ['hɔ:frɔst] *n* и́ней.
hoarse [hɔ:s] *adj* (*voice*) хри́плый* (хрипл).
hoax [həuks] *n* (*trick*) мистифика́ция; (*false alarm*) ло́жная трево́га.
hob [hɔb] *n ве́рхняя часть плиты́ с конфо́рками.*
hobble ['hɔbl] *vi* ковыля́ть (*impf*).
hobby ['hɔbɪ] *n* хо́бби *nt ind.*
hobbyhorse ['hɔbɪhɔ:s] *n* (*fig*) люби́мый конёк*; **he is on his ~** он сел на своего́ люби́мого конька́.
hobnail boot ['hɔbneɪl-] *n* подко́ванный сапо́г.
hobnob ['hɔbnɔb] *vi* (*inf*): **to ~ with** води́ться (*impf*) с +*instr*.
hobo ['həubəu] *n* (US) бродя́га *m/f*.
hock [hɔk] *n* (BRIT: *wine*) рейнве́йн; (*of horse*) скака́тельный суста́в ◆ *vt* (*inf*) закла́дывать (заложи́ть *perf*); **to be in ~** (*inf: person*) быть* (*impf*) в долга́х; (: *object*) быть* (*impf*) в закла́де.
hockey ['hɔkɪ] *n* хокке́й (на траве́).
hocus-pocus ['həukəs'pəukəs] *n* (*trickery*) очковтира́тельство; (*words: of magician*) фо́кус-по́кус; (*jargon*) белиберда́.
hod [hɔd] *n* лото́к* (*для перено́ски кирпиче́й*).
hodgepodge ['hɔdʒpɔdʒ] *n* (US) = **hotchpotch**.
hoe [həu] *n* моты́га, тя́пка* ◆ *vt* моты́жить (*impf*).
hog [hɔg] *n* бо́ров ◆ *vt* (*inf: road, telephone*) завладева́ть (завладе́ть *perf*) +*instr*; **to go the whole ~** (*inf*) гуля́ть (*impf*) на всю кату́шку.
Hogmanay [hɔgmə'neɪ] *n* (SCOTTISH) кану́н Но́вого го́да.

hogwash ['hɔgwɔʃ] *n* (*inf*) чушь *f*.
hoist [hɔɪst] *n* подъёмник, лебёдка* ◆ *vt* поднимáть (поднять* *perf*); **to ~ sth on to one's shoulders** взвáливать (взвалить* *perf*) что-н на плéчи.
hoity-toity [hɔɪtɪ'tɔɪtɪ] *adj* (*inf: pej*) кичли́вый (кичли́в).
hold [həuld] (*pt, pp* **held**) *vt* (*grip*) держáть* (*impf*); (*contain*) вмещáть (вмести́ть* *perf*); (*power, qualification*) обладáть (*impf*) +*instr*; (*opinion*) придéрживаться (*impf*) +*gen*; (*post*) занимáть (заня́ть* *perf*); (*conversation, meeting*) вести́* (провести́* *perf*); (*party*) устрáивать (устрóить *perf*); (*detain*) держáть* (*impf*) ◆ *vi* (*withstand pressure*) выдéрживать (вы́держать *perf*); (*be valid*) оставáться (остáться* *perf*) в си́ле; (*weather*) держáться* (продержáться* *perf*) ◆ *n* (*grasp*) захвáт; (NAUT) трюм; (AVIAT) грузовóй отсéк; **to ~ one's head up** высокó держáть* (*impf*) гóлову; **to ~ sb hostage** держáть* (*impf*) когó-н в кáчестве залóжника(-ицы); **~ the line!** (TEL) не клади́те трýбку!; **to ~ one's own** не ударя́ть (удáрить *perf*) лицóм в грязь; **he ~s you responsible for her death** он считáет тебя́ винóвным в её смéрти; **~ it!** подожди́те!; **he ~s the view that ...** он придéрживается тогó мнéния, что ...; **to ~ firm** *or* **fast** крéпко держáться* (*impf*); **~ still, ~ steady** не дви́гайтесь; **if my luck ~s ...** éсли мне бýдет продолжáть везти́ ...; **I don't ~ with ...** я не одобря́ю ...; **to get ~ of** (*obtain*) доставáть* (достáть* *perf*); **to get ~ of o.s.** сдéрживать (сдержáть *perf*) себя́, сдéрживаться (сдержáться *perf*); **to catch** *or* **grab ~ of** хватáться (схвати́ться* *perf*) за +*acc*; **to have a ~ over sb** держáть (*impf*) когó-н в рукáх
▸ **hold back** *vt* (*thing*) придéрживать (придержáть* *perf*); (*person*) удéрживать (удержáть* *perf*); (*information*) скрывáть (скрыть* *perf*)
▸ **hold down** *vt* (*person*) удéрживать (удержáть* *perf*); **to ~ down a job** удéрживаться (удержáться* *perf*) на рабóте
▸ **hold forth** *vi*: **to ~ forth (on** *or* **about)** увлечённо говори́ть (*impf*) (о +*prp*)
▸ **hold off** *vt* (*enemy*) сдéрживать (сдержáть* *perf*) ◆ *vi* (*weather*): **if the rain ~s off** éсли не пойдёт дождь
▸ **hold on** *vi* (*hang on*) держáться* (*impf*); (*wait*) ждать* (подождáть* *perf*); **~ on!** (TEL) не вéшайте трýбку!
▸ **hold on to** *vt fus* (*for support*) держáться* (*impf*) за +*acc*; (*keep: an object*) придéрживать (придержáть *perf*); (*: beliefs*) сохраня́ть (сохрани́ть *perf*)
▸ **hold out** *vt* (*hand*) протя́гивать (протянýть *perf*); (*hope, prospect*) сохраня́ть (сохрани́ть *perf*) ◆ *vi* (*resist*) держáться (продержáться *perf*)
▸ **hold over** *vt* (*meeting*) откла́дывать (отложи́ть* *perf*)
▸ **hold up** *vt* (*raise*) поднимáть (подня́ть* *perf*); (*support*) поддéрживать (поддержáть* *perf*); (*delay*) задéрживать (задержáть* *perf*); (*rob*) грáбить* (огрáбить* *perf*).
holdall ['həuldɔ:l] *n* (BRIT) дорóжная сýмка*.
holder ['həuldə^r] *n* (*container*) держáтель *m*; (*of ticket, record*) обладáтель(ница) *m(f)*; **post ~** занимáющий(-ая) *m(f) adj* пост; **title ~** нося́щий(-ая) *m(f) adj* ти́тул.
holding ['həuldɪŋ] *n* (*share*) вклад; (*farm*) учáсток* земли́ ◆ *adj*: **~ operation/tactic** оперáция/тáктика сдéрживания.
holding company *n* хóлдинг-компáния.
hold-up ['həuldʌp] *n* (*robbery*) ограблéние; (*delay*) задéржка*; (BRIT: *in traffic*) прóбка*.
hole [həul] *n* (*in wall*) дырá*; (*in road*) я́ма; (*burrow*) норá*; (*in clothing*) ды́рка*; (*in argument*) брешь *f*; (*inf: place*) дырá* ◆ *vt* (*ship, building*) пробивáть (проби́ть* *perf*); **~ in the heart** порóк сéрдца; **to pick ~s (in)** находи́ть* (найти́* *perf*) слáбое мéсто (в +*prp*)
▸ **hole up** *vi* уединя́ться (уедини́ться *perf*).
holiday ['hɔlɪdeɪ] *n* (BRIT: *from school*) кани́кулы *mpl*; (*: from work*) óтпуск*; (*day off*) выходнóй день* *m*; (*also:* **public ~**) прáздник; **on ~** (*from school*) на кани́кулах; (*from work*) в óтпуске; **tomorrow is a (public) ~** зáвтра – прáздник.
holiday camp *n* (*for children*) молодёжный лáгерь *m*; (BRIT: *also:* **holiday centre**) бáза óтдыха.
holiday-maker ['hɔlədɪmeɪkə^r] *n* (BRIT) отпускни́к(-и́ца), отдыхáющий*(-ая) *m(f) adj*.
holiday pay *n* отпускны́е *pl adj*.
holiday resort *n* курóрт.
holiday season *n* курóртный сезóн.
holiness ['həulɪnɪs] *n* свя́тость *f*.
holistic [həu'lɪstɪk] *adj* цéлостный.
Holland ['hɔlənd] *n* Голлáндия.
holler ['hɔlə^r] *vt* (*inf*) орáть (заорáть *perf*).
hollow ['hɔləu] *adj* (*container*) пóлый; (*log, tree*) дупли́стый; (*cheeks*) впáлый (впал); (*eyes*) ввали́вшийся; (*laugh*) нейскренний* (нейскренен); (*claim, sound*) пустóй* (пуст); (*doctrine, opinion*) повéрхностный* (повéрхностен) ◆ *n* (*in ground*) впáдина; (*in tree*) дуплó* ◆ *vt*: **to ~ out** выкáпывать (вы́копать *perf*).
holly ['hɔlɪ] *n* остроли́ст.
hollyhock ['hɔlɪhɔk] *n* алтéй рóзовый.
Hollywood ['hɔlɪwud] *n* Голливýд.
holocaust ['hɔləkɔ:st] *n* (*nuclear*) истреблéние;

(*Jewish*) холокóст.
hologram ['hɔləgræm] *n* голограмма.
hols [hɔlz] (*inf*) *npl* (*for students, pupils etc*) каникулы *pl*; (*for workers*) óтпуск* *msg*.
holster ['həulstəʳ] *n* кобурá*.
holy ['həulɪ] *adj* святóй* (свят).
Holy Communion *n* Святóе Причáстие.
Holy Father *n* Егó святéйшество *m* (*пáпа рúмский*).
Holy Ghost *n* святóй дух.
Holy Land *n*: **the ~ ~** святáя земля*.
holy orders *npl* духóвный сан *msg*.
Holy Spirit *n* = **Holy Ghost**.
homage ['hɔmɪdʒ] *n* почтéние; **to pay ~ to** воздавáть* (воздáть* *perf*) пóчести *+dat*.
home [həum] *n* (*house, institution, family*) дом*; (*area, country*) рóдина ◆ *cpd* (*domestic*) домáшний*; (*ECON, POL*) внýтренний*; (*SPORT*): **~ team** хозяéва* *mpl* пóля ◆ *adv* (*go, come*) домóй; (*right in*) в цель *or* тóчку; **at ~** (*house*) дóма; (*country*) на рóдине; (*in situation*) как у себя дóма; **make yourself at ~** чýвствуйте себя как дóма; **to make one's ~ somewhere** поселяться (посели́ться *perf*) гдé-то; **the ~ of free enterprise/jazz** *etc* рóдина свобóдного предпринимáтельства/джáза *etc*; **a ~ from ~** вторóй дом; **~ match/win** матч/вы́игрыш на своём пóле; **~ and dry** цел и невреди́м; **to bring sth ~ to sb** доводи́ть* (довести́* *perf*) что-н до чьегó-н сознáния
▸ **home in on** *vt fus* (*subj*: *missile*) осуществля́ть (осуществи́ть* *perf*) самонаведéние на *+acc*.
home address *n* домáшний* áдрес*.
home-brew [həum'bru:] *n* домáшнее пи́во.
homecoming ['həumkʌmɪŋ] *n* возвращéние домóй.
home computer *n* домáшний компьютер.
Home Counties *npl* (*BRIT*): **the ~ ~** *грáфства прилегáющие к Лóндону*.
home economics *n* домовóдство.
home ground *n*: **to be on ~ ~** (*in place*) чýвствовать (*impf*) себя как дóма.
home-grown ['həumgrəun] *adj* (*from garden*) домáшний*; (*not foreign*) отéчественный.
home help *n* *рабóтник собéса окáзывающий пóмощь по дóму больны́м и престарéлым*
homeland ['həumlænd] *n* рóдина.
homeless ['həumlɪs] *adj* (*family, refugee*) бездóмный* (бездóмен) ◆ *npl*: **the ~** бездóмные *pl adj*.
home loan *n* *бáнковская ссýда на покýпку дóма*.
homely ['həumlɪ] *adj* простóй* (прост), уютный* (уютен).
home-made [həum'meɪd] *adj* (*food*) домáшний*; (*bomb*) самодéльный.
Home Office *n* (*BRIT*): **the ~ ~** ≈ Министéрство внýтренних дел.
homeopathy *etc* (*US*) = **homoeopathy** *etc*
home page *n* (*COMPUT*) страни́ца в Интернéте, домáшняя страни́ца.
home rule *n* самоуправлéние.
Home Secretary *n* (*BRIT*) ≈ министр внýтренних дел.
homesick ['həumsɪk] *adj*: **to be ~** (*for family*) скучáть (*impf*) по дóму; (*for country*) скучáть по рóдине.
homestead ['həumstɛd] *n* усáдьба.
home stretch *n* (*of race*) фи́нишная прямáя.
home town *n* роднóй гóрод*.
home truth *n*: **he needs to learn some ~ ~s** емý порá объясни́ть, что к чемý.
homeward ['həumwəd] *adj* (*journey*) обрáтный ◆ *adv*: **~(s)** домóй.
homework ['həumwə:k] *n* домáшняя рабóта, домáшнее задáние.
homicidal [hɔmɪ'saɪdl] *adj* предрасполóженный к убийству.
homicide ['hɔmɪsaɪd] *n* (*esp US*) убийство.
homily ['hɔmɪlɪ] *n* (*tirade*) тирáда; (*sermon*) нравоучéние.
homing ['həumɪŋ] *adj*: **~ device** голóвка* самонаведéния; **~ pigeon** почтóвый гóлубь* *m*.
homoeopath ['həumɪəupæθ] (*US* **homeopath**) *n* гомеопáт.
homoeopathy [həumɪ'ɔpəθɪ] (*US* **homeopathy**) *n* гомеопáтия.
homogeneous [hɔməu'dʒi:nɪəs] *adj* однорóдный* (однорóден).
homogenize [hə'mɔdʒənaɪz] *vt* гомогенизи́ровать (*impf/perf*).
homosexual [hɔməu'sɛksjuəl] *adj* гомосексуáльный ◆ *n* гомосексуали́ст(ка*).
Hon. *abbr* = **honorary, honourable**.
Honduras [hɔn'djuərəs] *n* Гондурáс.
hone [həun] *n* точи́льный кáмень* *m* ◆ *vt* точи́ть (наточи́ть *perf*); (*TECH*) хонинговáть (*impf/perf*); (*fig*) оттáчивать (отточи́ть* *perf*).
honest ['ɔnɪst] *adj* чéстный* (чéстен); **to be quite ~ (with you)** ... чéстно говоря́, ...
honestly ['ɔnɪstlɪ] *adv* чéстно.
honesty ['ɔnɪstɪ] *n* чéстность *f*.
honey ['hʌnɪ] *n* мёд*; (*esp US*: *inf*: *darling*) ми́лый(-ая) *m(f) adj*, голýбчик.
honeycomb ['hʌnɪkəum] *n* (пчели́ные) сóты *fpl*; (*pattern*) шестиугóльный мозáичный узóр ◆ *vt*: **to ~ with** кишéть (*impf*) *+instr*.
honeymoon ['hʌnɪmu:n] *n* медóвый мéсяц.
honeysuckle ['hʌnɪsʌkl] *n* жи́молость *f*.
Hong Kong ['hɔŋ'kɔŋ] *n* Гонкóнг.
honk [hɔŋk] *vi* (*AUT*) гудéть* (прогудéть* *perf*).
Honolulu [hɔnə'lu:lu:] *n* Гонолýлу *m ind*.
honor *etc* (*US*) = **honour** *etc*.
honorary ['ɔnərərɪ] *adj* почётный* (почётен).
honour ['ɔnəʳ] (*US* **honor**) *vt* (*person*) почитáть (*impf*), чтить* (*impf*); (*commitment*) выполня́ть (вы́полнить *perf*) ◆ *n* (*pride*) честь *f*; (*tribute, distinction*) пóчесть *f*; **in ~ of** в честь *+gen*.
honourable ['ɔnərəbl] *adj* благорóдный* (благорóден); (*BRIT*: *POL*) уважáемый (*о*

членах парламента).

honour-bound ['ɔnə'baund] *adj*: **he is ~ to keep his word** сдержать слово является для него делом чести.

honours degree ['ɔnəz-] *n* учёная степень *f* (*обычно бакалавра*).

honours list *n* (*BRIT*) список* представленных к награде.

Hons. *abbr* (*SCOL*) = **honours degree**.

hood [hud] *n* капюшон; (*AUT*: *BRIT*: *folding roof*) откидной верх*; (: *US*: *bonnet*) капот; (*of cooker*) вытяжной колпак.

hooded ['hudɪd] *adj* (*robber*) в маске; (*jacket*) с капюшоном.

hoodlum ['hu:dləm] *n* (*inf*) громила *m*.

hoodwink ['hudwɪŋk] *vt* (*inf*) одурачивать (одурачить *perf*).

hoof [hu:f] (*pl* **hooves**) *n* копыто.

hook [huk] *n* крючок* ◆ *vt* прицеплять (прицепить* *perf*); (*fish*) поймать *(perf)* (на крючок); **by ~ or by crook** всеми правдами и неправдами; **he is ~ed on her/sweets** (*inf*) он помешан на ней/конфетах; **to get ~ed (on)** (*on drugs*) пристраститься* *perf* (к *+dat*)

► **hook up** *vt* (*dress*) застёгивать (застегнуть *perf*) на крючок; (*COMPUT, TV*): **to ~ up to the main network** подключать (подключить* *perf*) к центральной сети.

hook and eye (*pl* **~s ~ ~s**) *n* крючок* и петля* (*на одежде*).

hooligan ['hu:lɪgən] *n* хулиган.

hooliganism ['hu:lɪgənɪzəm] *n* хулиганство.

hoop [hu:p] *n* обруч*; (*for croquet*) ворота *pl*.

hooray [hu:'reɪ] *excl* = **hurrah**.

hoot [hu:t] *vi* (*AUT*: *horn*) гудеть* (прогудеть* *perf*); (*siren*) выть *(impf)*; (*owl*) ухать *(impf)*; (*laugh, jeer*) улюлюкать *(impf)* ◆ *vt* (*horn*) гудеть* (прогудеть* *perf*) в *+acc* ◆ *n* (*see vi*) гудок*; вой; уханье; улюлюканье; **to ~ with laughter** разражаться (разразиться* *perf*) оглушительным смехом.

hooter ['hu:tə'] *n* (*BRIT*) гудок*.

hoover® ['hu:və'] (*BRIT*) *n* пылесос ◆ *vt* пылесосить (пропылесосить *perf*).

hooves [hu:vz] *npl of* **hoof**.

hop [hɔp] *vi* скакать* *(impf)* на одной ноге; (*bird*) скакать *(impf)* ◆ *n* скачок*.

hope [həup] *vti* надеяться *(impf)* ◆ *n* надежда; **to ~ that/to do** надеяться *(impf)*, что/*+infin*; **I ~ so/not** надеюсь, что да/нет; **to ~ for the best** надеяться *(impf)* на лучшее; **I have no ~ of sth/doing** у меня нет никакой надежды на что-н/*+infin*; **in the ~ of/that** в надежде на *+acc*/что.

hopeful ['həupful] *adj* (*person*) полный* (полон) надежд; (*situation etc*) обнадёживающий; **to be ~ of sth** надеяться *(impf)* на что-н; **I'm ~ that she'll manage to come** я надеюсь, что она сможет прийти.

hopefully ['həupfulɪ] *adv* (*expectantly*) с надеждой; (*one hopes*): **~, he'll come back** будем надеяться, что он вернётся.

hopeless ['həuplɪs] *adj* (*situation, person*) безнадёжный* (безнадёжен); (*incorrigible*) неисправимый (неисправим); **I'm ~ at names** я не в состоянии запоминать имена.

hopper ['hɔpə'] *n* бункер*.

hops [hɔps] *npl* хмель *msg*.

horde [hɔ:d] *n* полчище.

horizon [hə'raɪzn] *n* горизонт.

horizontal [hɔrɪ'zɔntl] *adj* горизонтальный* (горизонтален).

hormone ['hɔ:məun] *n* гормон.

hormone replacement therapy *n* гормональная терапия.

horn [hɔ:n] *n* (*of animal*) рог*; (*also*: **French ~**) валторна; (*AUT*) гудок*.

horned [hɔ:nd] *adj* рогатый.

hornet ['hɔ:nɪt] *n* (*insect*) шершень* *m*.

horn-rimmed ['hɔ:n'rɪmd] *adj*: **~ spectacles** очки в роговой оправе.

horny ['hɔ:nɪ] *adj* (*inf*: *aroused*) (сексуально) возбуждённый* (возбуждён).

horoscope ['hɔrəskəup] *n* гороскоп.

horrendous [hə'rɛndəs] *adj* ужасающий*.

horrible ['hɔrɪbl] *adj* ужасный* (ужасен).

horrid ['hɔrɪd] *adj* противный* (противен), мерзкий* (мерзок).

horrific [hɔ'rɪfɪk] *adj* ужасный* (ужасен); **it was simply ~** это было просто ужасно.

horrify ['hɔrɪfaɪ] *vt* ужасать (ужаснуть *perf*).

horrifying ['hɔrɪfaɪɪŋ] *adj* ужасающий*.

horror ['hɔrə'] *n* (*alarm*) ужас; (*abhorrence*) отвращение; (*of war*) ужасы *mpl*.

horror film *n* фильм ужасов.

horror-stricken ['hɔrəstrɪkn] *adj* = **horror-struck**.

horror-struck ['hɔrəstrʌk] *adj* объятый (объят) ужасом.

hors d'oeuvre [ɔ:'də:vrə] *n* закуска*.

horse [hɔ:s] *n* лошадь* *f*; (*male*) конь* *m*.

horseback ['hɔ:sbæk] *adj* верховой ◆ *adv*: **on ~** верхом; **police on ~** конная полиция.

horsebox ['hɔ:sbɔks] *n* (*BRIT*) вагон для лошадей.

horse chestnut *n* конский* каштан.

horse-drawn ['hɔ:sdrɔ:n] *adj* конный; (*transport*) гужевой.

horsefly ['hɔ:sflaɪ] *n* слепень* *m*.

horseman ['hɔ:smən] *irreg n* всадник.

horsemanship ['hɔ:smənʃɪp] *n* искусство верховой езды.

horseplay ['hɔ:spleɪ] *n* возня.

horsepower ['hɔ:spauə'] *n* лошадиная сила; **a 30 ~ engine** двигатель *m* мощностью в 30 лошадиных сил.

horse racing *n* ска́чки* *fpl*.
horseradish ['hɔ:srædɪʃ] *n* хрен*.
horseshoe ['hɔ:sʃu:] *n* подко́ва.
horse show *n* соревнова́ния по вы́ездке.
horse trading *n* закули́сные сде́лки *fpl*.
horse trials *npl* = **horse show**.
horsewhip ['hɔ:swɪp] *n* хлыст* ◆ *vt* хлеста́ть* (отхлеста́ть* *perf*).
horsewoman ['hɔ:swumən] *irreg n* вса́дница.
horsey ['hɔ:sɪ] *adj* (*person*) увлека́ющийся* лошадьми́; (*features*) лошади́ный.
horticulture ['hɔ:tɪkʌltʃə'] *n* садово́дство.
hose [həuz] *n* (*also*: **~pipe**) шланг
▸ **hose down** *vt* полива́ть (поли́ть *perf*) из шла́нга.
hosepipe ['həuzpaɪp] *n* шланг.
hosiery ['həuzɪərɪ] *n* чуло́чные изде́лия *ntpl*.
hospice ['hɔspɪs] *n* больни́ца (*для безнадёжно больны́х*).
hospitable ['hɔspɪtəbl] *adj* (*person, behaviour*) гостеприи́мный* (гостеприи́мен); (*climate*) благоприя́тный* (благоприя́тен).
hospital ['hɔspɪtl] *n* больни́ца; **to be in ~** *or* (*US*) **in the ~** лежа́ть* (*impf*) в больни́це.
hospitality [hɔspɪ'tælɪtɪ] *n* гостеприи́мство.
hospitalize ['hɔspɪtəlaɪz] *vt* госпитализи́ровать (*impf/perf*).
host [həust] *n* (*at party, dinner*) хозя́ин*; (*TV, RADIO*) веду́щий* *m adj* ◆ *adj* (*country, organization*) принима́ющий ◆ *vt* (*programme*) вести́* (*impf*); (*event*) проводи́ть* (провести́* *perf*); **the H~** (*REL*) просвира́*; **a ~ of** ма́сса *+gen*, мно́жество *+gen*.
hostage ['hɔstɪdʒ] *n* зало́жник(-ица); **he was taken/held ~** его́ взя́ли/держа́ли в ка́честве зало́жника.
hostel ['hɔstl] *n* общежи́тие; (*for homeless*) прию́т; (*also*: **youth ~**) молодёжная гости́ница.
hostelling ['hɔstlɪŋ] *n*: **to go (youth) ~** путеше́ствовать (*impf*), остана́вливаясь в молодёжных гости́ницах.
hostess ['həustɪs] *n* (*at party, dinner etc*) хозя́йка*; (*BRIT*: *also*: **air ~**) стюарде́сса; (*TV, RADIO*) веду́щая *f adj*; (*in club, restaurant*) *же́нщина, развлека́ющая посети́телей но́чного клу́ба, рестора́на итп*.
hostile ['hɔstaɪl] *adj* (*person, attitude*) вражде́бный* (вражде́бен); (*conditions, environment*) неблагоприя́тный* (неблагоприя́тен); (*troops*) вра́жеский; **~ to** *or* **towards** вражде́бный* (вражде́бен) по отноше́нию к *+dat*.
hostility [hɔ'stɪlɪtɪ] *n* вражде́бность *f*; **hostilities** *npl* (*fighting*) вое́нные де́йствия *ntpl*.
hot [hɔt] *adj* (*object, temper, argument etc*) горя́чий* (горя́ч); (*weather*) жа́ркий*; (*spicy*: *food*) о́стрый* (остр); **she is ~** ей жа́рко; **it's ~** (*weather*) жа́рко; **I'm not too ~ on mathematics** я не о́чень разбира́юсь в матема́тике
▸ **hot up** *vi* (*BRIT*: *inf*: *situation*) накаля́ться (накали́ться *perf*); (: *party*) разгора́ться (разгоре́ться *perf*) ◆ *vt* (*engine*) разогрева́ть (разогре́ть* *perf*); (*pace*) ускоря́ть (ускори́ть *perf*).
hot air *n* (*fig*) пустосло́вие, болтовня́.
hot-air balloon [hɔt'ɛə-] *n* возду́шный шар*.
hotbed ['hɔtbɛd] *n* (*fig*) расса́дник.
hot-blooded [hɔt'blʌdɪd] *adj* пы́лкий* (пы́лок).
hotchpotch ['hɔtʃpɔtʃ] *n* (*BRIT*) сбо́рная соля́нка (*также перен*).
hot dog *n* ≈ соси́ска* в бу́лке.
hotel [həu'tɛl] *n* гости́ница, оте́ль *m*.
hotelier [həu'tɛlɪə'] *n* (*owner*) владе́лец* (-е́лица) гости́ницы; (*manager*) администра́тор гости́ницы.
hot flush *n* (*esp BRIT*) прили́в.
hotel industry *n* гости́ничный би́знес.
hotel room *n* гости́ничный но́мер*.
hotfoot ['hɔtfut] *adv* (*inf*) стремгла́в.
hothead ['hɔthɛd] *n* (*inf*) горя́чая голова́*.
hot-headed [hɔt'hɛdɪd] *adj* (*person*) поры́вистый (поры́вист); (*remark*) необду́манный (необду́ман).
hothouse ['hɔthaus] *n* оранжере́я, тепли́ца.
hot line *n* (*POL*) *пря́мая телефо́нная связь ме́жду прави́тельствами ра́зных стран*.
hotly ['hɔtlɪ] *adv* горячо́.
hotplate ['hɔtpleɪt] *n* конфо́рка*.
hotpot ['hɔtpɔt] *n* (*BRIT*) жарко́е *nt adj*.
hot potato *n* (*inf*) больно́й вопро́с.
hot seat *n* (*inf*): **to be in the ~ ~** занима́ть (заня́ть* *perf*) отве́тственный пост.
hot spot *n* (*war zone*) горя́чая то́чка*.
hot spring *n* горя́чий* исто́чник.
hot stuff *n* (*inf*: *woman*) красо́тка*; (: *film, book*) кла́ссная вещь *f*.
hot-tempered ['hɔt'tɛmpəd] *adj* вспы́льчивый (вспы́льчив).
hot-water bottle [hɔt'wɔ:tə-] *n* гре́лка*.
hound [haund] *vt* трави́ть* (затрави́ть* *perf*) ◆ *n* (*dog*) го́нчая *f adj*.
hour ['auə'] *n* час*; **at 60 miles an** *or* **per ~** со ско́ростью 60 миль в час; **24 ~ job** круглосу́точная рабо́та; **I am paid by the ~** я получа́ю почасову́ю опла́ту.
hourly ['auəlɪ] *adj* (*rate*) почасово́й; (*service*) ежеча́сный ◆ *adv* (*each hour*) ежеча́сно; (*soon*) с ча́су на час.
house [*n* haus, *vt* hauz] *n* дом*; (*company*) фи́рма; (*THEAT*) зал ◆ *vt* (*person*) сели́ть (посели́ть *perf*); (*collection*) размеща́ть (размести́ть* *perf*); **at my ~** у меня́ до́ма; **to my ~** ко мне домо́й; **the H~ of Commons/ Lords** (*BRIT*) пала́та о́бщин/ло́рдов; **the H~ (of Representatives)** (*US*) пала́та представи́телей; **the H~s of Parliament** зда́ние *ntsg* парла́мента; **on the ~** (*inf*) беспла́тно.
house arrest *n* дома́шний* аре́ст.

houseboat ['hausbəut] *n* плаву́чий* дом*.
housebound ['hausbaund] *adj*: **she is ~** она́ не мо́жет выходи́ть из до́ма.
housebreaking ['hausbreɪkɪŋ] *n* грабёж со взло́мом.
house-broken ['hausbrəukn] *adj* (*US*) = **house-trained.**
housecoat ['hauskəut] *n* дома́шний* хала́т.
household ['haushəuld] *n* (*home, inhabitants*) дом*; **~ name** (*brand*) изве́стная ма́рка*; (*person*) широко́ изве́стная ли́чность *f*.
householder ['haushəuldə^r] *n* домовладе́лец*.
house-hunting ['haushʌntɪŋ] *n*: **to go ~** занима́ться (заня́ться* *perf*) по́исками до́ма.
housekeeper ['hauski:pə^r] *n* эконо́мка*.
housekeeping ['hauski:pɪŋ] *n* (*work*) дома́шние дела́ *ntpl*; (*also:* **~ money**) де́ньги* *pl* на хозя́йственные ну́жды.
houseman ['hausmən] *irreg n* (*BRIT*) врач-стажёр, инте́рн.
house-owner ['hausəunə^r] *n* домовладе́лец* (-лица).
house-party ['hauspɑ:tɪ] *n* *приглаше́ние в го́сти с ночёвкой.*
house plant *n* ко́мнатное расте́ние.
house-proud ['hauspraud] *adj* домови́тый (домови́т).
house-to-house ['haustə'haus] *adj*: **to make ~ enquiries** проводи́ть* (провести́* *perf*) покварти́рный опро́с.
house-train ['haustreɪn] *vt*: **to ~ a pet** приуча́ть (приучи́ть* *perf*) дома́шнего живо́тного не га́дить в до́ме.
house-trained ['haustreɪnd] *adj* (*BRIT*): **our dog is fully ~** на́ша соба́ка приу́чена к туале́ту.
house-warming ['hauswɔ:mɪŋ] *n* (*also:* **~ party**) новосе́лье*.
housewife ['hauswaɪf] *irreg n* дома́шняя хозя́йка*, домохозя́йка.
housework ['hauswə:k] *n* дома́шнее хозя́йство.
housing ['hauzɪŋ] *n* жили́ще, жильё; (*provision*) жили́щное снабже́ние; (*TECH*) ко́рпус, кожу́х* ◆ *cpd* жили́щный; **~ shortage** недоста́ток жилья́.
housing association *n* (*BRIT*) ассоциа́ция домовладе́льцев (*предоставля́ющая жильё по бо́лее вы́годным це́нам*).
housing benefit *n* *де́нежное посо́бие неиму́щим се́мьям по вы́плате квартпла́ты.*
housing conditions *npl* жили́щные усло́вия.
housing development *n* = **housing estate.**
housing estate (*US* **housing project**) *n* жили́щный ко́мплекс; (*larger*) жило́й масси́в.
housing project *n* (*US*) = **housing estate.**
hove [həuv] *pt, pp of* **heave.**
hovel ['hɔvl] *n* лачу́га.
hover ['hɔvə^r] *vi* (*bird, insect*) пари́ть (*impf*); (*person*) мя́ться (*impf*); **to ~ round sb** увива́ться (*impf*) вокру́г кого́-н.
hovercraft ['hɔvəkrɑ:ft] *n* су́дно на возду́шной поду́шке.
hoverport ['hɔvəpɔ:t] *n* порт для су́ден на возду́шной поду́шке.

KEYWORD

how [hau] *adv* ***1*** (*in what way*) как; **to know how to do** знать *perf*, как *+infin*, уме́ть (*impf*) *+infin*; **how did you like the film?** как Вам понра́вился фильм?; **how are you?** как дела́?
2 ско́лько; **how much milk/many people?** ско́лько молока́/челове́к?; **how long have you been here?** ско́лько Вы уже́ здесь?; **how old are you?** ско́лько Вам лет?; **how tall is he?** како́го он ро́ста?; **how lovely/awful!** как чуде́сно/ужа́сно!

however [hau'ɛvə^r] *conj* одна́ко ◆ *adv* (*no matter how*) как бы ... ни; (*in questions*) как же; **~ did you find me?** как же Вы меня́ нашли́?
howl [haul] *vi* (*animal, wind*) выть* (*impf*); (*baby, person*) реве́ть* (*impf*) ◆ *n* (*see vb*) вой; рёв.
howler ['haulə^r] *n* (*inf: mistake*) ля́псус.
howling ['haulɪŋ] *adj* невероя́тный* (невероя́тен), фантасти́ческий*.
HP *n abbr* (*BRIT*) = **hire-purchase.**
h.p. *abbr* (*AUT*) (= **horsepower**) л.с.= *лошади́ная си́ла.*
HQ *abbr* = **headquarters.**
HR *n abbr* (*US: POL:* = *House of Representatives*) пала́та представи́телей.
HRH *abbr* (*BRIT:* = *His/Her Royal Highness*) Его́/Её Короле́вское Высо́чество.
hr(s) *abbr* = **hour(s).**
HS *abbr* (*US*) = **high school.**
HST *abbr* (*US*) = *Hawaiian Standard Time.*
HTML *n abbr* (= *hypertext markup language*) гиперте́кст.
hub [hʌb] *n* (*of wheel*) ступи́ца; (*fig*) средото́чие.
hubbub ['hʌbʌb] *n* гам, го́мон.
hubcap ['hʌbkæp] *n* (*AUT*) покры́шка.
HUD *n abbr* (*US*) = *Department of Housing and Urban Development.*
huddle ['hʌdl] *vi*: **to ~ together** прижима́ться (прижа́ться* *perf*) друг к дру́гу ◆ *n*: **to lie in a ~** лежа́ть* (*impf*) в ку́че.
hue [hju:] *n* тон, отте́нок*.
hue and cry *n* шум; (*pej*) шуми́ха.
huff [hʌf] *n*: **he's in a ~** он оби́жен ◆ *vi*: **to ~ and puff** (*also fig*) пыхте́ть* (*impf*).
huffy ['hʌfɪ] *adj* (*inf*) наду́тый (наду́т).
hug [hʌg] *vt* (*person*) обнима́ть (обня́ть* *perf*); (*thing*) обхва́тывать (обхвати́ть* *perf*) ◆ *n* объя́тие; **to give sb a ~** обнима́ть (обня́ть* *perf*) кого́-н.

* marks translations which have irregular inflections. The Russian-English side of the dictionary gives inflectional information.

huge [hju:dʒ] *adj* огро́мный* (огро́мен), грома́дный* (грома́ден).
hugely ['hju:dʒlɪ] *adv* чрезвыча́йно.
hulk [hʌlk] *n* (*NAUT*) ко́рпус* (*затону́вшего корабля́*); (*building, person*) грома́дина.
hulking ['hʌlkɪŋ] *adj* здорове́нный; **a ~ great oaf** у́вален *m*.
hull [hʌl] *n* (*NAUT*) корпу́с; (*of seeds*) шелу́ха; (*of strawberries*) ча́шечка ◆ *vt* (*fruit*) лущи́ть (облущи́ть *perf*).
hullabal(l)oo ['hʌləbə'lu:] *n* (*inf*) шуми́ха.
hullo [hə'ləu] *excl* = **hello**.
hum [hʌm] *vt* напева́ть *(impf) (без слов)* ◆ *vi* (*person*) напева́ть *(impf)*; (*machine*) гуде́ть* (прогуде́ть* *perf*); (*insect*) жужжа́ть *(impf)* ◆ *n* (*of wires*) гуде́ние; (*of voices, machines*) гул.
human ['hju:mən] *adj* челове́ческий* ◆ *n* (*also:* **~ being**) челове́к*.
humane [hju:'meɪn] *adj* (*treatment*) челове́чный* (челове́чен); (*slaughter*) гума́нный* (гума́нен).
humanely [hju:'meɪnlɪ] *adv* по-челове́чески, гума́нно.
humanism ['hju:mənɪzəm] *n* гумани́зм.
humanitarian [hju:mænɪ'tɛərɪən] *adj* (*aid*) гуманита́рный; (*principles*) гума́нный*.
humanity [hju:'mænɪtɪ] *n* (*mankind*) челове́чество; (*humaneness*) челове́чность *f*, гума́нность *f*; (*human nature*) челове́ческая суть *f*; **the humanities** *npl* гума́нитарные нау́ки *fpl*.
humanly ['hju:mənlɪ] *adv*: **it's not ~ possible** э́то вне челове́ческих возмо́жностей; **it is ~ possible** э́то в преде́лах челове́ческих возмо́жностей.
humanoid ['hju:mənɔɪd] *adj* человеко-подо́бный* ◆ *n* гумано́ид.
human relations *npl* (*COMM*) обще́ственные отноше́ния *ntpl*.
human rights *npl* права́ *ntpl* челове́ка.
humble ['hʌmbl] *adj* (*modest, simple*) скро́мный* (скро́мен) ◆ *vt* сбива́ть (сбить* *perf*) спесь с *+gen*.
humbly ['hʌmblɪ] *adv* скро́мно, смире́нно.
humbug ['hʌmbʌg] *n* (*of statement*) надува́тельство; (*BRIT: sweet*) *чёрно-бе́лый мя́тный леденец*.
humdrum ['hʌmdrʌm] *adj* ну́дный* (ну́ден).
humid ['hju:mɪd] *adj* вла́жный* (вла́жен).
humidifier [hju:'mɪdɪfaɪə^r] *n* увлажни́тель *m* во́здуха.
humidity [hju:'mɪdɪtɪ] *n* вла́жность *f*.
humiliate [hju:'mɪlɪeɪt] *vt* унижа́ть (уни́зить* *perf*).
humiliating [hju:'mɪlɪeɪtɪŋ] *adj* унизи́тельный* (унизи́телен).
humiliation [hju:mɪlɪ'eɪʃən] *n* униже́ние.
humility [hju:'mɪlɪtɪ] *n* (*modesty*) скро́мность *f*; (*humbleness*) смире́ние.
humming bird ['hʌmɪŋ-] *n* коли́бри *m/f ind*.
humor *etc* (*US*) = **humour** *etc*.
humorist ['hju:mərɪst] *n* юмори́ст(ка*).
humorous ['hju:mərəs] *adj* (*book*) юмористи́ческий*; (*remark*) шутли́вый (шутли́в); (*person*) с ю́мором.
humour ['hju:mə^r] (*US* **humor**) *n* ю́мор; (*mood*) настрое́ние ◆ *vt* ублажа́ть (ублажи́ть *perf*); **sense of ~** чу́вство ю́мора; **to be in good/bad ~** быть* *(impf)* в хоро́шем/плохо́м настрое́нии.
humourless ['hju:məlɪs] *adj* лишёный (лишён) чу́вства ю́мора.
hump [hʌmp] *n* (*in ground*) бугор́*; (*on back*) горб*.
humpbacked ['hʌmpbækt] *adj*: **~ bridge** горба́тый мост.
humus ['hju:məs] *n* перегно́й.
hunch [hʌntʃ] *n* (*premonition*) дога́дка*; **I have a ~ that ...** я предчу́вствую, что ....
hunchback ['hʌntʃbæk] *n* горбу́н*(ья*).
hunched [hʌntʃt] *adj* суту́лый (суту́л).
hundred ['hʌndrəd] *n* сто*; **a** *or* **one ~ books/people/dollars** сто* книг/люде́й/до́лларов; **about a ~** о́коло ста; **~ and first** сто* пе́рвый; **to live to be a ~** жить* (дожи́ть* *perf*) до ста лет; **~s of** со́тни* *+gen pl*; **people came in their ~s** *or* **by the ~** пришли́ со́тни люде́й; **I'm a ~ per cent sure** я уве́рен на сто проце́нтов.
hundredth ['hʌndrədθ] *adj* со́тый ◆ *n* (*fraction*) одна́ со́тая *f adj*.
hundredweight ['hʌndrɪdweɪt] *n* (*BRIT*) *ме́ра ве́са, равня́ющаяся 50.8 килогра́ммов*; (*US*) *ме́ра ве́са, равня́ющаяся 45.3 килогра́ммов*.
hung [hʌŋ] *pt, pp of* **hang**.
Hungarian [hʌŋ'gɛərɪən] *adj* венге́рский* ◆ *n* венгр(-ге́рка*); (*LING*) венге́рский* язы́к*.
Hungary ['hʌŋgərɪ] *n* Ве́нгрия.
hunger ['hʌŋgə^r] *n* го́лод* ◆ *vi*: **to ~ for** жа́ждать* *(impf) +gen*.
hunger strike *n* голодо́вка*.
hung over *adj* (*inf*): **I'm feeling ~ ~** у меня́ похме́лье.
hungrily ['hʌŋgrəlɪ] *adv* (*also fig*) жа́дно.
hungry ['hʌŋgrɪ] *adj* голо́дный* (го́лоден); (*keen*): **~ for** жа́ждущий *+gen*; **he is ~** он го́лоден; **to go ~** голода́ть *(impf)*.
hung up *adj* (*inf*): **to be ~ ~ about** *or* **on** заци́кливаться (заци́клиться *perf*) на *+prp*.
hunk [hʌŋk] *n* (большо́й) кусо́к*; (*of bread*) ломо́ть* *m*; (*inf: man*) краса́вчик.
hunt [hʌnt] *vt* (*animal*) охо́титься* *(impf)* на *+acc*; (*criminal*) охо́титься* *(impf)* за *+instr* ◆ *vi* (*SPORT*) охо́титься* *(impf)* ◆ *n* охо́та; (*for criminal*) ро́зыск; **to ~ (for)** (*search*) иска́ть* *(impf)*
▸ **hunt down** *vt* высле́живать (вы́следить* *perf*).
hunter ['hʌntə^r] *n* охо́тник(-ица).
hunting ['hʌntɪŋ] *n* охо́та.
hurdle ['hə:dl] *n* (*difficulty*) препя́тствие; (*SPORT*) препя́тствие, барье́р.
hurl [hə:l] *vt* (*object*) швыря́ть (швырну́ть *perf*);

to ~ abuse *or* **insults at sb** осыпа́ть (осы́пать *perf*) кого́-н ру́ганью.
hurling ['hə:lɪŋ] *n* (*SPORT*) ирла́ндский* хокке́й на траве́.
hurly-burly ['hə:lɪ'bə:lɪ] *n* сумато́ха.
hurrah [hu'rɑ] *excl* ура́.
hurray [hu'reɪ] *excl* = **hurrah**.
hurricane ['hʌrɪkən] *n* урага́н.
hurried ['hʌrɪd] *adj* поспе́шный* (поспе́шен).
hurriedly ['hʌrɪdlɪ] *adv* поспе́шно.
hurry ['hʌrɪ] *n* спе́шка ◆ *vi* спеши́ть (поспеши́ть *perf*), торопи́ться* (поторопи́ться* *perf*) ◆ *vt* (*person*) подгоня́ть (подогна́ть* *perf*), торопи́ть* (поторопи́ть* *perf*); (*work*) ускоря́ть (уско́рить *perf*); **to be in a ~** спеши́ть (*impf*); **to do sth in a ~** де́лать (сде́лать *perf*) что-н в спе́шке; **there's no ~** нет никако́й спе́шки; **what's the ~?** почему́ така́я спе́шка?; **to ~ in/out** поспе́шно входи́ть* (войти́* *perf*)/выходи́ть* (вы́йти* *perf*); **they hurried to help him** они поспеши́ли ему́ на по́мощь; **to ~ home** спеши́ть (поспеши́ть *perf*) домо́й
▸ **hurry along** *vi* поспе́шно проходи́ть* (пройти́* *perf*)
▸ **hurry away** *vi* поспе́шно уходи́ть* (уйти́* *perf*)
▸ **hurry off** *vi* = **hurry away**
▸ **hurry up** *vt* (*person*) подгоня́ть (подогна́ть* *perf*), торопи́ть* (поторопи́ть* *perf*); (*process*) ускоря́ть (ускори́ть *perf*) ◆ *vi* торопи́ться* (поторопи́ться* *perf*); **~ up!** поторопи́сь!
hurt [hə:t] (*pt, pp* **hurt**) *vt* (*also fig*) причиня́ть (причини́ть *perf*) боль *+dat*; (*injure*) ушиба́ть (ушиби́ть* *perf*); (*offend*) обижа́ть (оби́деть* *perf*); (*chances, reputation*) поврежда́ть (повреди́ть *perf*) ◆ *vi* (*be painful*) боле́ть (*impf*) ◆ *adj* (*offended*) оби́женный* (оби́жен); (*injured*) уши́бленный (уши́блен); **to ~ o.s.** ушиба́ться (ушиби́ться *perf*); **I've ~ my arm** я ушиб ру́ку; **where does it ~?** где боли́т?; **nobody was ~ in the crash** в ава́рии никто́ не пострада́л.
hurtful ['hə:tful] *adj* оби́дный* (оби́ден).
hurtle ['hə:tl] *vi*: **to ~ past** проноси́ться* (пронести́сь* *perf*); **to ~ down** ска́тываться (скати́ться* *perf*).
husband ['hʌzbənd] *n* муж*.
hush [hʌʃ] *n* тишина́ ◆ *vt* заставля́ть (заста́вить* *perf*) замолча́ть; ~! ти́хо!, ти́ше!
▸ **hush up** *vt* (*scandal*) замина́ть (замя́ть* *perf*).
hushed [hʌʃt] *adj* (*place*) ти́хий* (тих); (*voice*) приглушённый (приглушён).
hush-hush [hʌʃ'hʌʃ] *adj* (*inf*) сугу́бо секре́тный* (секре́тен).
husk [hʌsk] *n* шелуха́.
husky ['hʌskɪ] *adj* (*voice*) хри́плый* (хрипл) ◆ *n* ездова́я соба́ка.
hustings ['hʌstɪŋz] *npl* (*BRIT: POL*) предвы́борные собра́ния *ntpl*.
hustle ['hʌsl] *vt* (*hurry*) подта́лкивать (подтолкну́ть *perf*) ◆ *n*: **~ and bustle** сумато́ха.
hut [hʌt] *n* (*house*) избу́шка*, хи́жина; (*shed*) сара́й.
hutch [hʌtʃ] *n* кле́тка* (*для кро́ликов итп*).
hyacinth ['haɪəsɪnθ] *n* гиаци́нт.
hybrid ['haɪbrɪd] *n* (*BIO*) гибри́д; (*fig*) смесь *f* ◆ *adj* (*see n*) гибри́дный; сме́шанный.
hydrant ['haɪdrənt] *n* (*also:* **fire ~**) ≈ пожа́рный кран.
hydraulic [haɪ'drɔ:lɪk] *adj* гидравли́ческий*.
hydraulics [haɪ'drɔ:lɪks] *n* гидра́влика.
hydrochloric acid ['haɪdrəu'klɔrɪk-] *n* соля́ная кислота́.
hydroelectric ['haɪdrəuɪ'lɛktrɪk] *adj* гидроэлектри́ческий.
hydrofoil ['haɪdrəfɔɪl] *n* су́дно на подво́дных кры́льях.
hydrogen ['haɪdrədʒən] *n* водоро́д.
hydrogen bomb *n* водоро́дная бо́мба.
hydrophobia ['haɪdrə'fəubɪə] *n* водобоя́знь *f*.
hydroplane ['haɪdrəpleɪn] *n* (*boat*) гли́ссер; (*plane*) гидросамолёт ◆ *vi* (*boat*) глисси́ровать (*impf*).
hyena [haɪ'i:nə] *n* гие́на.
hygiene ['haɪdʒi:n] *n* гигие́на.
hygienic [haɪ'dʒi:nɪk] *adj* (*product*) гигиени́ческий*; (*habits*) гигиени́чный* (гигиени́чен).
hymn [hɪm] *n* церко́вный гимн.
hype [haɪp] *n* (*inf*) ажиота́ж.
hyperactive ['haɪpər'æktɪv] *adj* (*MED*) гиперакти́вный.
hyper-inflation ['haɪpərɪn'fleɪʃən] *n* гиперинфля́ция.
hypermarket ['haɪpəmɑ:kɪt] *n* (*BRIT*) кру́пный универса́м.
hypertension ['haɪpə'tɛnʃən] *n* гипертони́я.
hyphen ['haɪfn] *n* дефи́с.
hyphenated ['haɪfəneɪtɪd] *adj*: **this word is ~** э́то сло́во пи́шется че́рез дефи́с.
hypnosis [hɪp'nəusɪs] *n* гипно́з.
hypnotic [hɪp'nɔtɪk] *adj* (*trance etc*) гипноти́ческий.
hypnotism ['hɪpnətɪzəm] *n* гипноти́зм.
hypnotist ['hɪpnətɪst] *n* гипноти́зёр.
hypnotize ['hɪpnətaɪz] *vt* (*also fig*) гипнотизи́ровать (загипнотизи́ровать *perf*).
hypoallergenic ['haɪpəuælə'dʒɛnɪk] *adj* не вызыва́ющий* аллерги́ческой реа́кции.
hypochondriac [haɪpə'kɔndrɪæk] *n* ипохо́ндрик.
hypocrisy [hɪ'pɔkrɪsɪ] *n* лицеме́рие.
hypocrite ['hɪpəkrɪt] *n* лицеме́р(ка*).
hypocritical [hɪpə'krɪtɪkl] *adj* лицеме́рный*

(лицемéрен).
hypodermic [haɪpə'də:mɪk] *adj* подкóжный ◆ *n* (*also:* ~ **syringe**) шприц для подкóжных инъéкций.
hypotenuse [haɪ'pɔtɪnju:z] *n* гипотенýза.
hypothermia [haɪpə'θə:mɪə] *n* гипотермúя.
hypotheses [haɪ'pɔθɪsi:z] *npl of* **hypothesis**.
hypothesis [haɪ'pɔθɪsɪs] (*pl* **hypotheses**) *n* гипóтеза.
hypothesize [haɪ'pɔθɪsaɪz] *vi* предполагáть (предположúть* *perf*).
hypothetic(al) [haɪpəu'θɛtɪk(l)] *adj* гипотетúческий*.
hysterectomy [hɪstə'rɛktəmɪ] *n* удалéние мáтки.
hysteria [hɪ'stɪərɪə] *n* истерúя.
hysterical [hɪ'stɛrɪkl] *adj* (*uncontrolled*) истерúческий*; (*funny*) уморúтельный* (уморúтелен); **to become** ~ впадáть (впасть* *perf*) в истéрику.
hysterically [hɪ'stɛrɪklɪ] *adv* истерúчески; ~ **funny** óчень смешнóй* (смешóн).
hysterics [hɪ'stɛrɪks] *npl*: **to be in** *or* **have** ~ быть* (*impf*) в истéрике.
Hz *abbr* (= *hertz*) Гц= *герц*.

~ I, i ~

I, i [aɪ] *n* (*letter*) *9-ая бу́ква англи́йского алфави́та.*
I [aɪ] *pron* я.
I *abbr* (= **island, isle**) о.= *о́стров.*
IA *abbr* (*US: POST*) = *Iowa.*
IAEA *n abbr* = **International Atomic Energy Agency.**
IBA *n abbr* (*BRIT*) = *Independent Broadcasting Authority.*
Iberian [aɪ'bɪərɪən] *adj*: **the ~ Peninsula** Пирене́йский полуо́стров.
IBEW *n abbr* (*US*) = *International Brotherhood of Electrical Workers.*
ib(id) *abbr* (*from the same source*: = *ibidem*) там же.
i/c *abbr* (*BRIT*) = **in charge.**
ICBM *n abbr* (= *intercontinental ballistic missile*) МБР= *межконтинента́льная баллисти́ческая раке́та.*
ICC *n abbr* = **International Chamber of Commerce**; (*US*: = *Interstate Commerce Commission*) Коми́ссия по торго́вле ме́жду шта́тами.
ice [aɪs] *n* лёд*; (*portion of ice cream*) моро́женое *nt adj* ◆ *vt* (*cake*) покрыва́ть (покры́ть* *perf*) глазу́рью; **to put sth on ~** (*fig*) заморо́зить* (*perf*) что-н
▸ **ice over** *vi* (*road, window etc*) обледене́ть (*perf*), покрыва́ться (покры́ться* *perf*) льдом
▸ **ice up** *vi* = **ice over.**
Ice Age *n* леднико́вый пери́од.
ice axe *n* ледору́б.
iceberg ['aɪsbəːg] *n* а́йсберг; **the tip of the ~** (*fig*) верху́шка а́йсберга.
icebox ['aɪsbɔks] *n* (*US: fridge*) холоди́льник; (*BRIT: compartment*) морози́льник; (*insulated box*) су́мка-холоди́льник *f.*
ice breaker *n* ледоко́л.
ice bucket *n* ведёрко* со льдом.
ice-cap ['aɪskæp] *n* леднико́вый покро́в.
ice-cold [aɪs'kəuld] *adj* ледяно́й.
ice cream *n* моро́женое *nt adj.*
ice-cream soda ['aɪskriːm-] *n со́довая вода́ с моро́женым.*
ice cube *n* ку́бик льда.
iced [aɪst] *adj* (*cake*) покры́тый глазу́рью; **~ tea** холо́дный чай со льдом; **~ beer** холо́дное пи́во.
ice hockey *n* (*SPORT*) хокке́й (*на льду*).
Iceland ['aɪslənd] *n* Исла́ндия.
Icelander ['aɪsləndə'] *n* исла́ндец*(-дка*).
Icelandic [aɪs'lændɪk] *adj* исла́ндский* ◆ *n* (*LING*) исла́ндский* язы́к*.
ice lolly *n* (*BRIT*) фрукто́вое моро́женое на па́лочке.
ice pick *n* топо́рик для льда.
ice rink *n* като́к*.
ice-skate ['aɪsskeit] *n* конёк* ◆ *vi* ката́ться (*impf*) на конька́х.
ice-skating ['aɪsskeɪtɪŋ] *n* (*SPORT*) ката́ние на конька́х.
icicle ['aɪsɪkl] *n* сосу́лька*.
icing ['aɪsɪŋ] *n* (*on cake*) глазу́рь *f*, (*on window etc*) обледене́ние.
icing sugar *n* (*BRIT*) *са́харная пу́дра для приготовле́ния глазу́ри.*
ICJ *n abbr* = **International Court of Justice.**
icon ['aɪkɔn] *n* (*REL*) ико́на.
ICR *n abbr* (*US*) = *Institute for Cancer Research.*
ICU *n abbr* (*MED*: = *intensive care unit*) отделе́ние интенси́вной терапи́и.
icy ['aɪsɪ] *adj* (*cold*) ледяно́й; (*covered in ice*) покры́тый (покры́т) льдом.
ID *abbr* (*US: POST*) = *Idaho.*
I'd [aɪd] = **I would, I had.**
ID card *n* = **identity card.**
IDD *n abbr* (*BRIT: TEL*: = *international direct dialling*) пряма́я междунаро́дная связь *f.*
idea [aɪ'dɪə] *n* (*scheme, opinion*) иде́я; (*notion*) представле́ние; (*objective*) зада́ча; **good ~!** прекра́сная иде́я!; **to have an ~ that** подозрева́ть (*impf*) что; **I haven't the least ~** я не име́ю ни мале́йшего представле́ния.
ideal [aɪ'dɪəl] *n* идеа́л ◆ *adj* идеа́льный* (идеа́лен).
idealist [aɪ'dɪəlɪst] *n* идеали́ст(ка*).
ideally [aɪ'dɪəlɪ] *adv* идеа́льно; **~ the work should be done by tomorrow** в идеа́ле, рабо́та должна́ быть зако́нчена к за́втрашнему дню; **she's ~ suited for the job** она́ идеа́льно подхо́дит для э́той рабо́ты.
identical [aɪ'dɛntɪkl] *adj* одина́ковый

* marks translations which have irregular inflections. The Russian-English side of the dictionary gives inflectional information.

(одина́ков), иденти́чный* (иденти́чен).
identification [aɪdɛntɪfɪ'keɪʃən] *n* определе́ние; (*process*) выявле́ние; (*of person, dead body*) опозна́ние; **(means of) ~** удостовере́ние ли́чности.
identify [aɪ'dɛntɪfaɪ] *vt* (*recognize*) определя́ть (определи́ть *perf*); (: *person*) узнава́ть* (узна́ть* *perf*); (: *body*) опознава́ть* (опозна́ть* *perf*); (*distinguish*) отлича́ть (отличи́ть *perf*); **he is identified with radical politics** он отлича́ется радика́льными полити́ческими взгля́дами.
Identikit® [aɪ'dɛntɪkɪt] *n*: **~ (picture)** *портре́т-ро́бот престу́пника, соста́вленный по описа́нию свиде́телей.*
identity [aɪ'dɛntɪtɪ] *n* (*of person, suspect etc*) ли́чность *f*; (*of group, culture, nation etc*) самосозна́ние.
identity card *n* удостовере́ние ли́чности.
identity papers *npl* докуме́нты *mpl*, удостоверя́ющие ли́чности.
identity parade *n* (BRIT) *процеду́ра опозна́ния подозрева́емого в гру́ппе люде́й.*
ideological [aɪdɪə'lɔdʒɪkl] *adj* идеологи́ческий*.
ideology [aɪdɪ'ɔlədʒɪ] *n* идеоло́гия.
idiocy ['ɪdɪəsɪ] *n* идиоти́зм.
idiom ['ɪdɪəm] *n* (*style*) стиль *m*; (*phrase*) идио́ма.
idiomatic [ɪdɪə'mætɪk] *adj* идиомати́чный* (идиомати́чен).
idiosyncrasy [ɪdɪəu'sɪŋkrəsɪ] *n* (*foible*) осо́бенность *f*, характе́рная черта́.
idiosyncratic [ɪdɪəusɪŋ'krætɪk] *adj* индивидуа́льный* (индивидуа́лен), осо́бенный.
idiot ['ɪdɪət] *n* идио́т(ка*).
idiotic [ɪdɪ'ɔtɪk] *adj* идио́тский*.
idle ['aɪdl] *adj* пра́здный; (*lazy*) лени́вый (лени́в); (*unemployed*) безрабо́тный; (*machinery, factory*) безде́йствующий ◆ *vi* (*machine*) проста́ивать *(impf)*; (*engine*) рабо́тать *(impf)* на холосто́м ходу́; **to be ~** безде́йствовать *(impf)*; **to lie ~** быть* *(impf)* неиспо́льзованным(-ой); **an ~ hour** час досу́га
▸ **idle away** *vt*: **to ~ away the time** корота́ть *(impf)* вре́мя.
idle capacity *n* неиспо́льзуемая произво́дственная мо́щность *f*.
idle money *n* неинвести́рованные де́ньги* *pl*.
idleness ['aɪdlnɪs] *n* (*inactivity*) безде́лье; (*laziness*) лень *f*.
idler ['aɪdlə'] *n* безде́льник(-ица), лентя́й(ка*).
idle time *n* (COMM) просто́й.
idly ['aɪdlɪ] *adv* пра́здно, лени́во.
idol ['aɪdl] *n* (*hero*) кумир; (REL) и́дол.
idolize ['aɪdəlaɪz] *vt* боготвори́ть *(impf)*.
idyllic [ɪ'dɪlɪk] *adj* (*place, holiday*) идилли́ческий*.
i.e. *abbr* (*that is*: = *id est*) т.е.= *то есть*.

KEYWORD

if [ɪf] *conj* **1** (*conditional use*) е́сли; **if I finish early today, I will ring you** е́сли я зако́нчу ра́но сего́дня, я тебе́ позвоню́; **if I were you (I would ...)** на Ва́шем ме́сте (я бы ...)
2 (*whenever*) когда́
3 (*although*): **(even) if** (да́же) е́сли; **I'll get it done, even if it takes all night** я сде́лаю э́то, е́сли да́же э́то займёт у меня́ всю ночь; **I like it, (even) if you don't** хоть Вам и не нра́вится э́то, а мне (всё равно́) нра́вится
4 (*whether*) ли; **I don't know if he is here** я не зна́ю, здесь ли он; **ask him if he can stay** спроси́те, смо́жет ли он оста́ться
5: **if so/not** е́сли да/нет; **if only** е́сли то́лько; **if only I could** е́сли бы я то́лько мог; *see also* **as**.

iffy ['ɪfɪ] *adj* (*inf*: *scheme, suggestion*) подозри́тельный; **I'm feeling a bit ~ today** я сего́дня фигово себя́ чу́вствую.
igloo ['ɪglu:] *n* и́глу *nt ind* (*жили́ще эскимо́сов*).
ignite [ɪg'naɪt] *vt* (*set fire to*) зажига́ть (заже́чь* *perf*) ◆ *vi* воспламеня́ться (воспламени́ться *perf*), загора́ться (загоре́ться *perf*).
ignition [ɪg'nɪʃən] *n* (AUT) зажига́ние; **to switch on/off the ~** включа́ть (включи́ть *perf*)/ выключа́ть (вы́ключить *perf*) зажига́ние.
ignition key *n* (AUT) ключ* зажига́ния.
ignoble [ɪg'nəubl] *adj* недосто́йный* (недосто́ен).
ignominious [ɪgnə'mɪnɪəs] *adj* позо́рный* (позо́рен).
ignoramus [ɪgnə'reɪməs] *n* неве́жда *m/f*.
ignorance ['ɪgnərəns] *n* неве́жество; **~ of the facts** незна́ние фа́ктов; **to keep sb in ~ of sth** держа́ть* *(impf)* кого́-н в неве́дении по по́воду чего́-н.
ignorant ['ɪgnərənt] *adj* (*uninformed, unaware*) несве́дущий* (несве́дущ); (*badly educated*) неве́жественный* (неве́жествен); **to be ~ of** (*subject, events etc*) быть* *(impf)* неосведомлённым(-ой) относи́тельно +*gen*.
ignore [ɪg'nɔ:'] *vt* (*pay no attention to*) игнори́ровать* *(impf/perf)*; (*fail to take into account*) упуска́ть (упусти́ть* *perf*) из ви́ду.
ikon ['aɪkɔn] *n* = **icon**.
IL *abbr* (US: POST) = *Illinois*.
ILA *n abbr* (US) = *International Longshore Association*.
I'll [aɪl] = **I will, I shall**.
ill [ɪl] *adj* (*child etc*) больно́й*; (*harmful*: *effects*) дурно́й ◆ *n* (*evil*) зло; (*trouble*) беда́ ◆ *adv*: **to speak/think ~ (of sb)** пло́хо говори́ть *(impf)*/ ду́мать *(impf)* (о ком-н); **he is ~** он бо́лен; **to be taken ~** заболева́ть (заболе́ть *perf*).
ill-advised [ɪləd'vaɪzd] *adj* опроме́тчивый (опроме́тчив).
ill-at-ease [ɪlət'i:z] *adj* (*awkward, uncomfortable*) нело́вкий*.
ill-considered [ɪlkən'sɪdəd] *adj* необду́манный* (необду́ман).

ill-disposed [ɪldɪs'pəuzd] *adj*: **to be ~ towards sb/sth** недоброжела́тельно относи́ться* *(impf)* к кому́-н/чему́-н.
illegal [ɪ'li:gl] *adj* нелега́льный* (нелега́лен), незако́нный* (незако́нен).
illegally [ɪ'li:gəlɪ] *adv* нелега́льно, незако́нно.
illegible [ɪ'lɛdʒɪbl] *adj* неразбо́рчивый (неразбо́рчив).
illegitimate [ɪlɪ'dʒɪtɪmət] *adj* (*child*) внебра́чный; (*activity, treaty*) незако́нный* (незако́нен).
ill-fated [ɪl'feɪtɪd] *adj* (*doomed*) злополу́чный* (злополу́чен).
ill-favoured [ɪl'feɪvəd] (*US* **ill-favored**) *adj* некраси́вый (некраси́в).
ill feeling *n* неприя́знь *f*.
ill-gotten ['ɪlgɔtn] *adj*: **~ gains** добы́тый нече́стным путём дохо́д.
ill-health [ɪl'hɛlθ] *n* плохо́е здоро́вье.
illicit [ɪ'lɪsɪt] *adj* незако́нный* (незако́нен).
ill-informed [ɪlɪn'fɔ:md] *adj* неосведомлённый* (неосведомлён).
illiterate [ɪ'lɪtərət] *adj* негра́мотный* (негра́мотен).
ill-mannered [ɪl'mænəd] *adj* невоспи́танный* (невоспи́тан), неве́жливый (неве́жлив).
illness ['ɪlnɪs] *n* боле́знь *f*.
illogical [ɪ'lɔdʒɪkl] *adj* нелоги́чный* (нелоги́чен).
ill-suited [ɪl'su:tɪd] *adj*: **they are ~** они́ не подхо́дят друг к дру́гу; **he is ~ to the job** он не годи́тся для э́той рабо́ты.
ill-timed [ɪl'taɪmd] *adj* несвоевре́менный* (несвоевре́мен); **her comments were ~** её замеча́ния бы́ли не к ме́сту.
ill-treat [ɪl'tri:t] *vt* пло́хо обраща́ться *(impf)* с *+instr*.
ill-treatment [ɪl'tri:tmənt] *n* жесто́кость *f*.
illuminate [ɪ'lu:mɪneɪt] *vt* (*light up*) освеща́ть (освети́ть* *perf*).
illuminated sign [ɪ'lu:mɪneɪtɪd-] *n* освещённая вы́веска*.
illuminating [ɪ'lu:mɪneɪtɪŋ] *adj* (*report, book etc*) разъясня́ющий; (*person*) просвещённый* (просвещён), познава́тельный* (познава́телен).
illumination [ɪlu:mɪ'neɪʃən] *n* (*lighting*) освеще́ние; **~s** *npl* (*decorative lights*) иллюмина́ция *fsg*.
illusion [ɪ'lu:ʒən] *n* (*false idea*) иллю́зия; (*trick*) фо́кус; **to be under the ~ that** ... находи́ться *(impf)* под впечатле́нием, что ....
illusive [ɪ'lu:sɪv] *adj* = **illusory**.
illusory [ɪ'lu:sərɪ] *adj* иллюзо́рный* (иллюзо́рен), обма́нчивый (обма́нчив).
illustrate ['ɪləstreɪt] *vt* иллюстри́ровать (проиллюстри́ровать *perf*).
illustration [ɪlə'streɪʃən] *n* (*example, picture*) иллюстра́ция; (*act*) иллюстри́рование.
illustrator ['ɪləstreɪtə^r] *n* иллюстра́тор.
illustrious [ɪ'lʌstrɪəs] *adj* (*career*) блестя́щий* (блестя́щ); (*predecessor, partner*) просла́вленный* (просла́влен).
ill will *n* неприя́знь *f*.
ILO *n abbr* = **International Labour Organization**.
ILWU *n abbr* (*US*) = *International Longshoremen's and Warehousemen's Union*.
I'm [aɪm] = **I am**.
image ['ɪmɪdʒ] *n* (*picture*) о́браз; (*public face*) и́мидж; (*reflection*) отраже́ние.
imagery ['ɪmɪdʒərɪ] *n* (*ART, LITERATURE*) о́бразность *f*, о́бразный мир.
imaginable [ɪ'mædʒɪnəbl] *adj* вообрази́мый; **we've tried every ~ solution** мы перепро́бовали все вообрази́мые реше́ния; **she had the prettiest hair ~** у неё бы́ли невообрази́мо краси́вые во́лосы.
imaginary [ɪ'mædʒɪnərɪ] *adj* (*creature, land*) вообража́емый; (*danger, illness*) мни́мый.
imagination [ɪmædʒɪ'neɪʃən] *n* воображе́ние; (*illusion*) фанта́зия; **it's just your ~** э́то про́сто плод Ва́шего воображе́ния.
imaginative [ɪ'mædʒɪnətɪv] *adj* (*person*) облада́ющий бога́тым *or* тво́рческим воображе́нием; (*solution*) хитроу́мный* (хитроу́мен).
imagine [ɪ'mædʒɪn] *vt* (*visualize*) представля́ть (предста́вить* *perf*) (себе́), вообража́ть (вообрази́ть* *perf*); (*dream*) вообража́ть (вообрази́ть* *perf*); (*suppose*) полага́ть *(impf)*.
imbalance [ɪm'bæləns] *n* несоотве́тствие, неравнове́сие.
imbecile ['ɪmbəsi:l] *n* ненорма́льный(-ая) *m(f) adj*.
imbue [ɪm'bju:] *vt*: **to ~ sb with sth** вдохновля́ть (вдохнови́ть* *perf*) кого́-н чем-н; **to ~ sth with sth** наполня́ть (напо́лнить *perf*) что-н чем-н.
IMF *n abbr* (= *International Monetary Fund*) МВФ= *Междунаро́дный валю́тный фонд*.
imitate ['ɪmɪteɪt] *vt* (*copy*) копи́ровать (скопи́ровать *perf*); (*mimic*) подража́ть *(impf)* *+dat*, имити́ровать *(impf)*.
imitation [ɪmɪ'teɪʃən] *n* (*see vb*) копи́рование; подража́ние; (*instance*) имита́ция.
imitator ['ɪmɪteɪtə^r] *n* подража́тель(ница) *m(f)*.
immaculate [ɪ'mækjulət] *adj* безупре́чный* (безупре́чен); (*REL*) непоро́чный.
immaterial [ɪmə'tɪərɪəl] *adj* (*unimportant*) несуще́ственный* (несуще́ствен).
immature [ɪmə'tjuə^r] *adj* (*fruit*) неспе́лый (неспе́л); (*cheese*) незре́лый; (*organism*) недоразви́вшийся; (*person*) незре́лый (незре́л).
immaturity [ɪmə'tjuərɪtɪ] *n* незре́лость *f*.
immeasurable [ɪ'mɛʒrəbl] *adj* неизмери́мый

* marks translations which have irregular inflections. The Russian-English side of the dictionary gives inflectional information.

(неизмери́м).
immediacy [ɪ'mi:dɪəsɪ] *n* (*of events etc*) непосре́дственность *f*; (*of needs*) безотлага́тельность *f*.
immediate [ɪ'mi:dɪət] *adj* (*reaction, answer*) неме́дленный, мгнове́нный; (*pressing: need*) безотлага́тельный* (безотлага́телен); (*nearest: neighbourhood, family etc*) ближа́йший*.
immediately [ɪ'mi:dɪətlɪ] *adv* (*at once*) неме́дленно; (*directly*) непосре́дственно; **~ next to** непосре́дственно ря́дом с *+instr*.
immense [ɪ'mɛns] *adj* (*huge: size*) необъя́тный* (необъя́тен); (: *progress, importance*) огро́мный* (огро́мен).
immensely [ɪ'mɛnslɪ] *adv* (*grateful etc*) бесконе́чно; (*difficult*) необыча́йно; **I enjoyed it ~** мне э́то о́чень понра́вилось.
immensity [ɪ'mɛnsɪtɪ] *n* необъя́тность *f*.
immerse [ɪ'mə:s] *vt* (*submerge*) погружа́ть (погрузи́ть* *perf*); **to ~ sth in** погружа́ть (погрузи́ть* *perf*) что-н в *+acc*; **to be ~d in** (*fig*) быть* *(impf)* погружённым(-ой) в *+acc*.
immersion heater [ɪ'mə:ʃən-] *n* (*BRIT*) бо́йлер.
immigrant ['ɪmɪgrənt] *n* иммигра́нт(ка*).
immigration [ɪmɪ'greɪʃən] *n* (*process*) иммигра́ция; (*also:* **~ control**: *at airport etc*) пограни́чный контро́ль *m* ◆ *cpd*: **~ laws** зако́ны *mpl* об иммигра́ции; **~ authorities** пограни́чная слу́жба.
imminent ['ɪmɪnənt] *adj* (*arrival, departure*) немину́емый (немину́ем).
immobile [ɪ'məubaɪl] *adj* неподви́жный* (неподви́жен).
immobilize [ɪ'məubɪlaɪz] *vt* (*person, machine*) остана́вливать (останови́ть* *perf*), свя́зывать (связа́ть *perf*).
immoderate [ɪ'mɔdərət] *adj* неуме́ренный* (неуме́рен).
immodest [ɪ'mɔdɪst] *adj* нескро́мный* (нескро́мен).
immoral [ɪ'mɔrl] *adj* амора́льный* (амора́лен), безнра́вственный* (безнра́вственен).
immorality [ɪmɔ'rælɪtɪ] *n* амора́льность *f*, безнра́вственность *f*.
immortal [ɪ'mɔ:tl] *adj* (*also fig*) бессме́ртный* (бессме́ртен).
immortality [ɪmɔ:'tælɪtɪ] *n* бессме́ртие.
immortalize [ɪ'mɔ:tlaɪz] *vt* увекове́чивать (увекове́чить *perf*).
immovable [ɪ'mu:vəbl] *adj* (*object*) неподви́жный* (неподви́жен); (*opinion*) неизме́нный* (неизме́нен).
immune [ɪ'mju:n] *adj*: **~ (to)** (*disease*) облада́ющий иммуните́том (к *+dat*); **he is ~ to ...** (*flattery, criticism etc*) он неподве́ржен влия́нию *+gen* ....
immune system *n* иммýная систе́ма.
immunity [ɪ'mju:nɪtɪ] *n* (*to disease*) иммуните́т; (*to criticism*) невосприи́мчивость *f*; (*of diplomat, from prosecution*) неприкоснове́нность *f*.
immunization [ɪmjunaɪ'zeɪʃən] *n* иммуниза́ция, приви́вка*.
immunize ['ɪmjunaɪz] *vt* (*MED*): **to ~ (against)** привива́ть (приви́ть* *perf*) (про́тив *+gen*).
imp [ɪmp] *n* бесёнок*.
impact ['ɪmpækt] *n* (*of bullet*) моме́нт попада́ния; (*of crash*) уда́р; (*of law, measure*) возде́йствие.
impair [ɪm'pɛə'] *vt* (*vision, judgement*) ослабля́ть (осла́бить* *perf*).
impaired [ɪm'pɛəd] *adj* осла́бленный (осла́блен).
impale [ɪm'peɪl] *vt* нака́лывать (наколо́ть* *perf*); **to ~ sth on** наса́живать (насади́ть* *perf*) что-н на *+acc*.
impart [ɪm'pɑ:t] *vt*: **to ~ (to)** (*information*) передава́ть* (переда́ть* *perf*) (*+dat*); (*flavour*) придава́ть* (прида́ть* *perf*) (*+dat*).
impartial [ɪm'pɑ:ʃl] *adj* беспристра́стный* (беспристра́стен).
impartiality [ɪmpɑ:ʃɪ'ælɪtɪ] *n* беспристра́стие.
impassable [ɪm'pɑ:səbl] *adj* непроходи́мый (непроходи́м).
impasse [æm'pɑ:s] *n* тупи́к*; **to reach an ~** зайти́* *(perf)* в тупи́к.
impassive [ɪm'pæsɪv] *adj* бесстра́стный* (бесстра́стен).
impatience [ɪm'peɪʃəns] *n* нетерпели́вость *f*.
impatient [ɪm'peɪʃənt] *adj* нетерпели́вый (нетерпели́в); **to get** *or* **grow ~** начина́ть (нача́ть* *perf*) теря́ть терпе́ние; **she was ~ to leave** ей не терпе́лось уйти́.
impatiently [ɪm'peɪʃəntlɪ] *adv* нетерпели́во.
impeach [ɪm'pi:tʃ] *vt* привлека́ть (привле́чь* *perf*) к отве́тственности.
impeachment [ɪm'pi:tʃmənt] *n* привлече́ние к отве́тственности.
impeccable [ɪm'pɛkəbl] *adj* безупре́чный* (безупре́чен).
impecunious [ɪmpɪ'kju:nɪəs] *adj* (*formal*) нужда́ющийся.
impede [ɪm'pi:d] *vt* затрудня́ть (затрудни́ть *perf*).
impediment [ɪm'pɛdɪmənt] *n* (*obstacle*) препя́тствие; **speech ~** дефе́кт ре́чи.
impel [ɪm'pɛl] *vt*: **to ~ sb to do** вынужда́ть (вы́нудить* *perf*) кого́-н *+infin*.
impending [ɪm'pɛndɪŋ] *adj* надвига́ющийся.
impenetrable [ɪm'pɛnɪtrəbl] *adj* (*jungle, fortress*) непроходи́мый (непроходи́м); (*look, expression*) непроница́емый (непроница́ем); (*darkness, fog*) непрогля́дный* (непрогля́ден); (*fig: law, text*) недосту́пный* (недосту́пен) (для понима́ния).
imperative [ɪm'pɛrətɪv] *adj* (*tone*) вла́стный* (вла́стен); (*need etc*) настоя́тельный* (настоя́телен) ◆ *n* (*LING*) повели́тельное наклоне́ние; **it is ~ that ...** необходи́мо,

чтобы ....
imperceptible [ɪmpə'sɛptɪbl] *adj* незаме́тный* (наза́метен).
imperfect [ɪm'pə:fɪkt] *adj* (*system etc*) несоверше́нный* (несоверше́нен); (*goods*) дефе́ктный ◆ *n* (*LING*: *also*: **~ tense**) имперфе́кт.
imperfection [ɪmpə:'fɛkʃən] *n* (*failing*) недоста́ток*; (*blemish*) изъя́н.
imperial [ɪm'pɪərɪəl] *adj* (*history, power*) импе́рский*; (*BRIT*: *measure*): **~ system** *брита́нская систе́ма ме́ры и ве́са.*
imperialism [ɪm'pɪərɪəlɪzəm] *n* империали́зм.
imperil [ɪm'pɛrɪl] *vt* подверга́ть (подве́ргнуть* *perf*) опа́сности.
imperious [ɪm'pɪərɪəs] *adj* (*person*) вла́стный* (вла́стен).
impersonal [ɪm'pə:sənl] *adj* (*organization, place*) безли́кий*.
impersonate [ɪm'pə:səneɪt] *vt* (*pass o.s. off as*) выдава́ть* (вы́дать *perf*) себя́ за *+acc*; (*THEAT*) изобража́ть (изобрази́ть* *perf*).
impersonation [ɪmpə:sə'neɪʃən] *n* изображе́ние; (*LAW*) самозва́нство; (*THEAT*) исполне́ние ро́ли.
impertinent [ɪm'pə:tɪnənt] *adj* (*pupil, question*) де́рзкий* (де́рзок), наха́льный* (наха́лен).
imperturbable [ɪmpə'tə:bəbl] *adj* невозмути́мый (невозмути́м).
impervious [ɪm'pə:vɪəs] *adj* (*fig*): **he is ~ to ...** на него́ не де́йствует ....
impetuous [ɪm'pɛtjuəs] *adj* поры́вистый (поры́вист).
impetus ['ɪmpətəs] *n* (*momentum*) ине́рция; (*fig*) сти́мул.
impinge [ɪm'pɪndʒ]: **to ~ on** *vt fus* (*person*) посяга́ть (посягну́ть *perf*) на *+acc*; (*rights*) попира́ть (попра́ть* *perf*).
impish ['ɪmpɪʃ] *adj* озорно́й.
implacable [ɪm'plækəbl] *adj* непримири́мый (непримири́м).
implant [ɪm'plɑ:nt] *vt* (*MED*) переса́живать (пересади́ть* *perf*); (*fig*: *idea, principle*) внуша́ть (внуши́ть *perf*).
implausible [ɪm'plɔ:zɪbl] *adj* неправдоподо́бный* (неправдоподо́бен).
implement [*vt* 'ɪmplɪmɛnt, *n* 'ɪmplɪmənt] *vt* (*plan, regulation*) проводи́ть* (провести́* *perf*) в жизнь ◆ *n*: **gardening ~** садо́вый инструме́нт; **farming ~s** сельскохозя́йственные ору́дия; **cooking ~s** ку́хонные принадле́жности.
implicate ['ɪmplɪkeɪt] *vt* (*in crime, error*) вовлека́ть (вовле́чь* *perf*).
implication [ɪmplɪ'keɪʃən] *n* (*inference*) вы́вод; (*involvement*) прича́стность *f*; **by ~** су́дя по всему́.
implicit [ɪm'plɪsɪt] *adj* (*inferred*) подразумева́ющийся; (*unquestioning*) безогово́рочный.
implicitly [ɪm'plɪsɪtlɪ] *adv* (*totally*) безогово́рочно.
implore [ɪm'plɔ:ʳ] *vt* (*beg*) умоля́ть (*impf*); **to ~ sb to do** умоля́ть (*impf*) кого́-н *+infin*.
imply [ɪm'plaɪ] *vt* (*hint*) намека́ть (намекну́ть *perf*) на *+acc*; (*mean*) подразумева́ть (*impf*).
impolite [ɪmpə'laɪt] *adj* (*rude, offensive*) неве́жливый (неве́жлив).
imponderable [ɪm'pɔndərəbl] *adj* неулови́мый (неулови́м) ◆ *n вещь, не поддаю́щаяся определе́нию.*
import [*vb* ɪm'pɔ:t, *n, cpd* 'ɪmpɔ:t] *vt* импорти́ровать (*impf/perf*), ввози́ть* (ввезти́* *perf*) ◆ *n* (*article*) импорти́руемый това́р; (*importation*) и́мпорт ◆ *cpd*: **~ duty** по́шлина на ввоз; **~ licence** лице́нзия на ввоз; **~ quota** и́мпортная кво́та.
importance [ɪm'pɔ:tns] *n* ва́жность *f*; **it is of great/little ~** э́то о́чень/не о́чень ва́жно.
important [ɪm'pɔ:tnt] *adj* ва́жный* (ва́жен); (*influential*: *person*) ва́жный*; **it's not ~** э́то нева́жно.
importantly [ɪm'pɔ:tntlɪ] *adv* ва́жно; **but more ~ ...** но ещё важне́е ..., но са́мое гла́вное ....
importation [ɪmpɔ:'teɪʃən] *n* и́мпорт.
imported [ɪm'pɔ:tɪd] *adj* и́мпортный.
importer [ɪm'pɔ:təʳ] *n* импортёр.
impose [ɪm'pəuz] *vt* (*sanctions, restrictions, discipline etc*) налага́ть (наложи́ть* *perf*) ◆ *vi*: **to ~ on sb** навя́зываться (навяза́ться* *perf*) кому́-н.
imposing [ɪm'pəuzɪŋ] *adj* внуши́тельный* (внуши́телен), вели́чественный* (вели́чествен).
imposition [ɪmpə'zɪʃən] *n* (*of tax etc*) обложе́ние; **to be an ~ on sb** быть* (*impf*) обу́зой кому́-н.
impossibility [ɪmpɔsə'bɪlɪtɪ] *n* невозмо́жность *f*.
impossible [ɪm'pɔsɪbl] *adj* (*task, demand, person*) невозмо́жный* (невозмо́жен); (*situation*) невероя́тный* (невероя́тен); **it's ~ for me to leave now** я не могу́ сейча́с уйти́.
impossibly [ɪm'pɔsɪblɪ] *adj* невозмо́жно.
imposter [ɪm'pɔstəʳ] *n* = **impostor**.
impostor [ɪm'pɔstəʳ] *n* самозва́нец*(-нка*).
impotence ['ɪmpətns] *n* бесси́лие; (*MED*) импоте́нция.
impotent ['ɪmpətnt] *adj* бесси́льный* (бесси́лен); (*MED*) импоте́нтный* (импоте́нтен).
impound [ɪm'paund] *vt* конфиско́вывать (конфискова́ть *perf*).
impoverished [ɪm'pɔvərɪʃt] *adj* (*country*) обедне́вший*.
impracticable [ɪm'præktɪkəbl] *adj*

* marks translations which have irregular inflections. The Russian-English side of the dictionary gives inflectional information.

неосуществи́мый (неосуществи́м).
impractical [ɪm'præktɪkl] *adj* (*plan etc*) нереа́льный* (нереа́лен); (*person*) непракти́чный* (непракти́чен).
imprecise [ɪmprɪ'saɪs] *adj* нето́чный* (нето́чен).
impregnable [ɪm'prɛgnəbl] *adj* (*castle, fortress*) непристу́пный* (непристу́пен); (*fig*: *person*) неуязви́мый (неуязви́м).
impregnate ['ɪmprɛgneɪt] *vt* (*saturate*) пропи́тывать (пропита́ть *perf*); (*fertilize*) оплодотворя́ть (оплодотвори́ть *perf*).
impresario [ɪmprɪ'sɑːrɪəu] *n* импреса́рио *m ind.*
impress [ɪm'prɛs] *vt* (*person*) производи́ть* (произвести́* *perf*) впечатле́ние на *+acc*; (*mark*) отпеча́тывать (отпеча́тать *perf*); **to ~ sth on sb** внуша́ть (внуши́ть *perf*) что-н кому́-н.
impression [ɪm'prɛʃən] *n* впечатле́ние; (*of stamp, seal*) отпеча́ток*; (*imitation*) имита́ция; **to make a good/bad ~ on sb** производи́ть* (произвести́* *perf*) хоро́шее/плохо́е впечатле́ние на кого́-н; **he is under the ~ that ...** у него́ создало́сь впечатле́ние, что ....
impressionable [ɪm'prɛʃnəbl] *adj* впечатли́тельный* (впечатли́телен).
impressionist [ɪm'prɛʃənɪst] *n* (*ART*) импрессиони́ст; (*entertainer*) имита́тор.
impressive [ɪm'prɛsɪv] *adj* впечатля́ющий.
imprest system ['ɪmprɛst-] *n систе́ма де́нежного ава́нса.*
imprint ['ɪmprɪnt] *n* отпеча́ток*; (*PUBLISHING*) выходны́е да́нные *pl adj*; (: *label*) *печа́ть на переплёте с и́менем владе́льца и́ли изда́теля.*
imprinted [ɪm'prɪntɪd] *adj*: **~ on** (*surface*) отпеча́тавшийся в/на *+prp*; (*memory*) запечатлённый (запечатлён) в *+prp.*
imprison [ɪm'prɪzn] *vt* (*criminal*) заключа́ть (заключи́ть *perf*) в тюрьму́.
imprisonment [ɪm'prɪznmənt] *n* (тюре́мное) заключе́ние.
improbable [ɪm'prɔbəbl] *adj* (*outcome*) маловероя́тный* (маловероя́тен); (*story*) неправдоподо́бный* (неправдоподо́бен).
impromptu [ɪm'prɔmptjuː] *adj* (*celebration, party*) импровизи́рованный (импровизи́рован); (*tactics*) неплáновый.
improper [ɪm'prɔpə'] *adj* (*unsuitable*: *conduct*) неуме́стный* (неуме́стен); (: *procedure*) непра́вильный* (непра́вилен); (*dishonest*: *activities*) незако́нный* (незако́нен).
impropriety [ɪmprə'praɪətɪ] *n* (*indecency*) неприли́чие; **the ~ of his conduct** непристо́йность *f* его́ поведе́ния.
improve [ɪm'pruːv] *vt* улучша́ть (улу́чшить *perf*) ◆ *vi* улучша́ться (улу́чшиться *perf*); (*pupil*) станови́ться* (стать* *perf*) лу́чше; (*patient*) начина́ть (нача́ть *perf*) выздора́вливать
▸ **improve (up)on** *vt fus* (*work, achievement etc*) де́лать (сде́лать *perf*) лу́чше.
improvement [ɪm'pruːvmənt] *n*: **~ (in)** улучше́ние (*+gen*); **to make ~s to** вноси́ть* (внести́* *perf*) улучше́ния в *+acc.*
improvisation [ɪmprəvaɪ'zeɪʃən] *n* (*THEAT*) импровиза́ция.
improvise ['ɪmprəvaɪz] *vt* (*meal*) на́скоро гото́вить* (пригото́вить* *perf*); (*bed, shelter*) на́скоро устра́ивать (устро́ить *perf*) ◆ *vi* (*THEAT, MUS*) импровизи́ровать (сымпровизи́ровать *perf*).
imprudence [ɪm'pruːdns] *n* неблагоразу́мное поведе́ние.
imprudent [ɪm'pruːdnt] *adj* неблагоразу́мный* (неблагоразу́мен); **it would be ~ of you to insult him** оскорби́ть его́ бу́дет неблагоразу́мием с Ва́шей стороны́.
impudent ['ɪmpjudnt] *adj* на́глый* (нагл).
impugn [ɪm'pjuːn] *vt* подверга́ть (подве́ргнуть* *perf*) сомне́нию.
impulse ['ɪmpʌls] *n* (*urge*) поры́в; (*ELEC*) и́мпульс; **to act on ~** поддава́ться* (подда́ться* *perf*) поры́ву.
impulse buy *n* случа́йная поку́пка*.
impulsive [ɪm'pʌlsɪv] *adj* (*purchase*) случа́йный* (случа́ен); (*person*) импульси́вный* (импульси́вен); (*gesture*) поры́вистый (поры́вист).
impunity [ɪm'pjuːnɪtɪ] *n*: **with ~** безнака́занно.
impure [ɪm'pjuə'] *adj* нечи́стый (нечи́ст); (*sinful*) непристо́йный* (непристо́ен).
impurity [ɪm'pjuərɪtɪ] *n* (*foreign substance*) при́месь *f.*
IN *abbr* (*US*: *POST*) = *Indiana.*

KEYWORD

in [ɪn] *prep* ***1*** (*indicating place, position*) в/на *+prp*; **in the house/garden** в до́ме/саду́; **in the street/Ukraine/north** на у́лице/Украи́не/се́вере; **in London/Canada** в Ло́ндоне/Кана́де; **in the country** за́городом; **in town** в го́роде; **in here** здесь; **in there** там
2 (*indicating motion*) в *+acc*; **in the house/room** в дом/ко́мнату
3 (*indicating time*: *during*) в *+prp*; **in spring/summer/autumn/winter** весно́й/ле́том/о́сенью/зимо́й; **in the morning/afternoon/evening** у́тром/днём/ве́чером; **they often play cards in the evening** они́ ча́сто игра́ют в ка́рты по вечера́м; **at 4 o'clock in the afternoon** в 4 часа́ дня
4 (*indicating time*: *in the space of*) за *+acc*; (: *after a period of*) че́рез *+acc*; **I did it in 3 hours** я сде́лал э́то за 3 часа́; **I'll see you in 2 weeks** уви́димся че́рез 2 неде́ли
5 (*indicating manner etc*): **in a loud/quiet voice** гро́мким/ти́хим го́лосом; **in English/Russian** по-англи́йски/по-ру́сски, на англи́йском/ру́сском языке́; **the boy in the blue shirt** ма́льчик в голубо́й руба́шке
6 (*indicating circumstances*): **in the sun** на

со́лнце; **in the rain** под дождём; **in the shade** в тени́; **there has been a change in public opinion** обще́ственное мне́ние перемени́лось; **a rise in prices** повыше́ние цен
7 (*indicating mood, state*) в *+prp*
8 (*with ratios, numbers*): **one in ten households have a second car** одна́ из десяти́ семе́й име́ет втору́ю маши́ну; **20 pence in the pound** 20 пе́нсов с фу́нта; **they lined up in twos** они́ вы́строились по́ двое; **a gradient of one in five** укло́н оди́н к пяти́
9 (*referring to people, works*): **the disease is common in children** э́то заболева́ние ча́сто встреча́ется у дете́й; **in Dickens** у Ди́ккенса; **you have a good friend in him** он тебе́ хоро́ший друг
10 (*indicating profession etc*): **to be in teaching** рабо́тать *(impf)* учи́телем; **to be in publishing** занима́ться *(impf)* изда́тельским де́лом; **to be in the army** быть* *(impf)* в а́рмии
11 (*after superlative*) в *+prp*; **the best doctor in the city** лу́чший* врач в го́роде
12 (*with present participle*): **in saying this** говоря́ э́то; **in behaving like this, she ...** поступа́я таки́м о́бразом, она́ ...
◆ *adv*: **to be in** (*train, ship, plane*) прибы́ть* *(perf)*; (*in fashion*) быть* *(impf)* в мо́де; **is he in today? – yes, he's in/no, he's not in** (*at work*) он сего́дня на рабо́те? – да, он на рабо́те/нет, его́ сего́дня нет; (*at home*) он сего́дня до́ма? – да, он до́ма/нет, его́ сего́дня нет; **he wasn't in yesterday** его́ вчера́ не́ было; **he'll be in later today** он бу́дет сего́дня по́зже; **to ask sb in** предложи́ть* *(perf)* кому́-н зайти́; **to run/walk** *etc* **in** вбега́ть (вбежа́ть* *perf*)/входи́ть* (войти́* *perf*) *etc*
◆ *n*: **to know all the ins and outs** знать *(impf)* все ходы́.

in. *abbr* = **inch.**
inability [ɪnəˈbɪlɪtɪ] *n* (*incapacity*): ~ **(to do)** неспосо́бность *f* (*+infin*).
inaccessible [ɪnəkˈsɛsɪbl] *adj* (*also fig*) недосту́пный* (недосту́пен).
inaccuracy [ɪnˈækjurəsɪ] *n* (*quality*) нето́чность *f*; (*mistake*) оши́бка*.
inaccurate [ɪnˈækjurət] *adj* нето́чный* (нето́чен).
inaction [ɪnˈækʃən] *n* безде́йствие.
inactive [ɪnˈæktɪv] *adj* (*person*) безде́ятельный* (безде́ятелен), пасси́вный* (пасси́вен); (*animal*) пасси́вный* (пасси́вен); (*volcano*) поту́хший.
inactivity [ɪnækˈtɪvɪtɪ] *n* (*idleness*) безде́ятельность *f*.
inadequacy [ɪnˈædɪkwəsɪ] *n* недоста́точность *f*; (*of person*) неполноце́нность *f*.
inadequate [ɪnˈædɪkwət] *adj* (*income, amount, preparation*) недоста́точный* (недоста́точен); (*reply*) неадеква́тный* (неадеква́тен); (*work, result*) неудовлетвори́тельный* (неудовлетвори́телен); (*person*) неполноце́нный (неполноце́н).
inadmissible [ɪnədˈmɪsəbl] *adj* недопусти́мый (недопусти́м); (*LAW*: *evidence*) неприе́млемый (неприе́млем).
inadvertently [ɪnədˈvə:tntlɪ] *adv* неумы́шленно.
inadvisable [ɪnədˈvaɪzəbl] *adj* (*course of action*) нецелесообра́зный* (нецелесообра́зен); **it is ~ to ...** не рекоменду́ется *+infin* ....
inane [ɪˈneɪn] *adj* (*smile*) глу́пый* (глуп); (*remark etc*) бессмы́сленный* (бессмы́слен).
inanimate [ɪnˈænɪmət] *adj* (*object*) неодушевлённый* (неодушевлён).
inapplicable [ɪnˈæplɪkəbl] *adj* (*description, comment*) неподходя́щий*; (*rule*) неприме́нимый (неприме́ним).
inappropriate [ɪnəˈprəuprɪət] *adj* (*unsuitable*) неподходя́щий*; (*improper*) неуме́стный* (неуме́стен).
inapt [ɪnˈæpt] *adj* неуме́стный* (неуме́стен).
inarticulate [ɪnɑ:ˈtɪkjulət] *adj* (*person*) косноязы́чный* (косноязы́чен); (*speech*) невня́тный* (невня́тен).
inasmuch as [ɪnəzˈmʌtʃ-] *adv* (*in that*) посто́льку поско́льку; (*insofar as*) насто́лько наско́лько.
inattention [ɪnəˈtɛnʃən] *n* невнима́ние.
inattentive [ɪnəˈtɛntɪv] *adj* невнима́тельный* (невнима́телен).
inaudible [ɪnˈɔ:dɪbl] *adj* неслы́шный* (неслы́шен).
inaugural [ɪˈnɔ:gjurəl] *adj* (*speech*) вступи́тельный; (*meeting*) пе́рвый.
inaugurate [ɪˈnɔ:gjureɪt] *vt* (*president, official*) вводи́ть* (ввести́* *perf*) в до́лжность; (*system, measure*) вводи́ть* (ввести́* *perf*); (*organization*) открыва́ть (откры́ть* *perf*).
inauguration [ɪnɔ:gjuˈreɪʃən] *n* (*see vb*) вступле́ние в до́лжность; введе́ние; откры́тие.
inauspicious [ɪnɔ:sˈpɪʃəs] *adj* (*occasion*) неблагоприя́тный* (неблагоприя́тен).
in-between [ɪnbɪˈtwi:n] *adj* (*intermediate*) промежу́точный; ~ **stage** промежу́точная ста́дия.
inborn [ɪnˈbɔ:n] *adj* врождённый, приро́дный.
inbred [ɪnˈbrɛd] *adj* (*quality*) врождённый, приро́дный; **an ~ family** *семья́, в кото́рой де́ти рождены́ от роди́телей, состоя́щих в кро́вном родстве́.*
inbreeding [ɪnˈbri:dɪŋ] *n* (*among animals*) ро́дственное спа́ривание; (*among people*) узкоро́дственные бра́чные отноше́ния *ntpl*.

inbuilt [ɪn'bɪlt] *adj* (*quality, feeling etc*) врождённый.
Inc. *abbr* = **incorporated**.
Inca ['ɪŋkə] *adj*: **the ~** *or* **~n civilization** и́нки *fpl*.
incalculable [ɪn'kælkjuləbl] *adj* (*effect*) огро́мный* (огро́мен); (*loss*) неисчисли́мый (неисчисли́м); (*consequences*) непредви́денный.
incapable [ɪn'keɪpəbl] *adj* (*helpless*) беспо́мощный* (беспо́мощен); (*unable to*): **~ of sth/doing** неспосо́бный* (неспосо́бен) на что-н/+*infin*.
incapacitate [ɪnkə'pæsɪteɪt] *vt*: **to ~ sb** выводи́ть* (вы́вести* *perf*) кого́-н из стро́я; **to ~ sb for work** де́лать (сде́лать *perf*) кого́-н нетрудоспосо́бным(-ой).
incapacitated [ɪnkə'pæsɪteɪtɪd] *adj* (*LAW*) лишённый (лишён) пра́ва.
incapacity [ɪnkə'pæsɪtɪ] *n* (*weakness*) беспо́мощность *f*; (*inability*) неспосо́бность *f*.
incarcerate [ɪn'kɑːsəreɪt] *vt* заключа́ть (заключи́ть *perf*) в тюрьму́.
incarnate [ɪn'kɑːnɪt] *adj* воплощённый (воплощён), олицетворённый (олицетворён); **evil ~** воплоще́ние *or* олицетворе́ние зла.
incarnation [ɪnkɑː'neɪʃən] *n* воплоще́ние, олицетворе́ние; (*REL*) инкарна́ция.
incendiary [ɪn'sɛndɪərɪ] *adj* (*device, bomb*) зажига́тельный.
incense [*n* 'ɪnsɛns, *vt* ɪn'sɛns] *n* (*also REL*) ла́дан ◆ *vt* (*anger*) приводи́ть* (привести́* *perf*) в я́рость.
incense burner *n* кури́льница.
incentive [ɪn'sɛntɪv] *n* (*inducement*) сти́мул ◆ *cpd*: **~ scheme** систе́ма поощре́ния; **~ bonus** материа́льное поощре́ние.
inception [ɪn'sɛpʃən] *n* (*of institution*) откры́тие, основа́ние; (*of activity*) нача́ло.
incessant [ɪn'sɛsnt] *adj* бесконе́чный* (бесконе́чен), посто́янный* (посто́янен).
incessantly [ɪn'sɛsntlɪ] *adv* бесконе́чно, посто́янно.
incest ['ɪnsɛst] *n* кровосмеше́ние.
inch [ɪntʃ] *n* (*measurement*) дюйм; **he was within an ~ of succeeding** он был уже́ бли́зок к успе́ху; **to be within an ~ of one's life** быть* (*impf*) на во́лосо́к от сме́рти; **he didn't give an ~** (*fig*: *back down, yield*) он не уступи́л ни на йо́ту
▸ **inch forward** *vi* ме́дленно тро́гаться (тро́нуться *perf*) с ме́ста.
incidence ['ɪnsɪdns] *n* (*of crime, disease*) чи́сленность *f*.
incident ['ɪnsɪdnt] *n* (*event*) слу́чай; (*MIL*) инциде́нт; **without ~** без происше́ствий.
incidental [ɪnsɪ'dɛntl] *adj* (*additional, supplementary*) дополни́тельный; **these duties are ~ to the job** э́ти обя́занности сопряжены́ с рабо́той; **ills ~ to old age** неду́ги, прису́щие ста́рости; **~ expenses** побо́чные расхо́ды.
incidentally [ɪnsɪ'dɛntəlɪ] *adv* (*by the way*) кста́ти, ме́жду про́чим.
incidental music *n* (*CINEMA*) му́зыка к кинофи́льму.
incident room *n* диспе́тчерская *f adj* (*в полице́йском управле́нии*).
incinerate [ɪn'sɪnəreɪt] *vt* (*rubbish, paper etc*) сжига́ть (сжечь* *perf*).
incinerator [ɪn'sɪnəreɪtə^r] *n* мусоросжига́тель *m*.
incipient [ɪn'sɪpɪənt] *adj* (*baldness*) начина́ющийся*; (*madness*) в нача́льной ста́дии.
incision [ɪn'sɪʒən] *n* (*also MED*) разре́з.
incisive [ɪn'saɪsɪv] *adj* (*comment*) о́стрый* (остёр), ре́зкий* (ре́зок); (*criticism*) ре́зкий* (ре́зок).
incisor [ɪn'saɪzə^r] *n* резе́ц*.
incite [ɪn'saɪt] *vt* (*rioters*) подстрека́ть (подстрекну́ть *perf*); (*violence, hatred*) вызыва́ть (вы́звать* *perf*).
incl. *abbr* = **including, inclusive (of)**.
inclement [ɪn'klɛmənt] *adj* (*weather*) нена́стный* (нена́стен).
inclination [ɪnklɪ'neɪʃən] *n* (*tendency*) скло́нность *f*; (*disposition, desire*) жела́ние.
incline [*n* 'ɪnklaɪn, *vb* ɪn'klaɪn] *n* (*slope*) укло́н, накло́н ◆ *vt* (*bend*: *head*) наклоня́ть (наклони́ть* *perf*) ◆ *vi* (*surface*) наклоня́ться (наклони́ться* *perf*); **to be ~d to sth/to do** быть* (*impf*) скло́нным(-ой) к чему́-н/+*infin*; **to be well ~d towards sb** быть* (*impf*) благоскло́нным(-ой) к кому́-н.
include [ɪn'kluːd] *vt* включа́ть (включи́ть *perf*); **to be ~d (in)** быть* (*impf*) включённым(-ой) (в +*acc*); **to ~ sth in the price** включа́ть (включи́ть *perf*) в це́ну.
including [ɪn'kluːdɪŋ] *prep* включа́я +*acc*; **~ service charge** включа́я пла́ту за обслу́живание.
inclusion [ɪn'kluːʒən] *n* включе́ние.
inclusive [ɪn'kluːsɪv] *adj* (*price, terms*) включа́ющий в себя́ все услу́ги; **~ of** включа́я +*acc*; **from March 1st to 5th ~** с 1-ого до 5-ое ма́рта включи́тельно.
incognito [ɪnkɔg'niːtəu] *adv* инко́гнито.
incoherent [ɪnkəu'hɪərənt] *adj* (*argument*) непосле́довательный* (непосле́дователен); (*speech*) несвя́зный* (несвя́зен); (*person*) косноязы́чный* (косноязы́чен).
income ['ɪnkʌm] *n* (*earned*) за́работок*; (*from property, investment*) дохо́д; **gross/net ~** валово́й/чи́стый дохо́д; **~ and expenditure account** прихо́дно-расхо́дный счёт*; **high/low ~ bracket** *гру́ппа населе́ния с высо́ким/ни́зким у́ровнем дохо́да*.
income support *n* де́нежное посо́бие.
income tax *n* подохо́дный нало́г ◆ *cpd* (*COMM*) нало́говый.

incoming ['ɪnkʌmɪŋ] *adj* (*flight, passenger*) прибыва́ющий; (*call*) поступа́ющий; (*mail*) входя́щий; (*government*) новои́збранный; (*official*) вступа́ющий* в до́лжность; **~ tide** прили́в.
incommunicado ['ɪnkəmjunɪ'kɑːdəu] *adj*: **to hold sb ~** держа́ть* *(impf)* кого́-н взаперти́.
incomparable [ɪn'kɔmpərəbl] *adj* несравне́нный*.
incompatible [ɪnkəm'pætɪbl] *adj* (*lifestyles*) соверше́нно ра́зный; (*systems, aims*) несовмести́мый (несовмести́м); **they are ~** они́ соверше́нно ра́зные.
incompetence [ɪn'kɔmpɪtns] *n* некомпете́нтность *f*.
incompetent [ɪn'kɔmpɪtnt] *adj* (*person*) некомпете́нтный* (некомпете́нтен); (*work*) неуме́лый (неуме́л).
incomplete [ɪnkəm'pliːt] *adj* (*unfinished*) незако́нченный* (незако́нчен); (*partial*) непо́лный* (непо́лон).
incomprehensible [ɪnkɔmprɪ'hɛnsɪbl] *adj* непоня́тный* (непоня́тен).
inconceivable [ɪnkən'siːvəbl] *adj* немы́слимый (немы́слим); **it is ~ that ...** немы́слимо, что ....
inconclusive [ɪnkən'kluːsɪv] *adj* (*evidence*) недоста́точный* (недоста́точен); (*result*) неоконча́тельный* (неоконча́телен); (*argument*) неубеди́тельный* (неубеди́телен); **the experiment was ~** экспериме́нт не дал определённых результа́тов; **the discussion was ~** диску́ссия зако́нчилась ниче́м.
incongruous [ɪn'kɔŋgruəs] *adj* (*strange*) неле́пый (неле́п); (*inappropriate*) неуме́стный* (неуме́стен).
inconsequential [ɪnkɔnsɪ'kwɛnʃl] *adj* несуще́ственный* (несуще́ственен), незначи́тельный* (незначи́телен).
inconsiderable [ɪnkən'sɪdərəbl] *adj*: **not ~** значи́тельный* (значи́телен).
inconsiderate [ɪnkən'sɪdərət] *adj* (*person*) не счита́ющийся ни с ке́м; (*action*) безду́мный* (безду́мен); **~ towards** невнима́тельный к *+dat*.
inconsistency [ɪnkən'sɪstənsɪ] *n* (*of behaviour*) непосле́довательность *f*; (*of statement*) противоречи́вость *f*.
inconsistent [ɪnkən'sɪstnt] *adj* (*behaviour, person*) непосле́довательный* (непосле́дователен); (*work*) неро́вный* (неро́вен); (*statement*) противоречи́вый (противоречи́в); **~ with** (*beliefs, values*) несовмести́мый (несовмести́м) с *+instr*.
inconsolable [ɪnkən'səuləbl] *adj* безуте́шный* (безуте́шен).
inconspicuous [ɪnkən'spɪkjuəs] *adj* незаме́тный* (незаме́тен), неприме́тный* (неприме́тен); **to make o.s. ~** стара́ться (постара́ться *perf*) не привлека́ть к себе́ внима́ния.
incontinence [ɪn'kɔntɪnəns] *n* (*MED*) недержа́ние (*мочи́ или ка́ла*).
incontinent [ɪn'kɔntɪnənt] *adj* (*MED*) страда́ющий недержа́нием (*мочи́ или ка́ла*).
inconvenience [ɪnkən'viːnjəns] *n* (*problem*) неудо́бство; (*trouble*) беспоко́йство ◆ *vt* причиня́ть (причини́ть *perf*) неудо́бство *+dat*; **don't ~ yourself** не утружда́йте себя́; **sorry about the ~** извини́те за причинённое неудо́бство.
inconvenient [ɪnkən'viːnjənt] *adj* неудо́бный* (неудо́бен); (*visitor*) прише́дший не ко вре́мени; **that time is very ~ for me** э́то о́чень неудо́бное для меня́ вре́мя.
incorporate [ɪn'kɔːpəreɪt] *vt* (*contain*) содержа́ть* *(impf)*; **to ~ (into)** включа́ть (включи́ть *perf*) (в *+acc*); **safety features have been ~d in the design** предохрани́тельные устро́йства бы́ли внесены́ в прое́кт; **the coat of arms ~s three lions** на гербе́ изображены́ три льва́.
incorporated company [ɪn'kɔːpəreɪtɪd-] *n* (*US*) компа́ния, зарегистри́рованная как корпора́ция.
incorrect [ɪnkə'rɛkt] *adj* неве́рный* (неве́рен), непра́вильный* (непра́вилен).
incorrigible [ɪn'kɔrɪdʒɪbl] *adj* (*liar, crook*) неисправи́мый (неисправи́м).
incorruptible [ɪnkə'rʌptɪbl] *adj* (*not open to bribes*) неподку́пный* (неподку́пен).
increase [*n* 'ɪnkriːs, *vb* ɪn'kriːs] *n*: **~ (in), ~ (of)** увеличе́ние (*+gen*) ◆ *vi* увели́чиваться (увели́читься *perf*) ◆ *vt* увели́чивать (увели́чить *perf*); (*price*) поднима́ть (подня́ть* *perf*); (*knowledge*) расширя́ть (расши́рить *perf*); **an ~ of 5%** увеличе́ние на 5%; **to be on the ~** увели́чиваться *(impf)*, расти́* *(impf)*.
increasing [ɪn'kriːsɪŋ] *adj* увели́чивающийся, возраста́ющий.
increasingly [ɪn'kriːsɪŋlɪ] *adv* (*more intensely*) всё бо́лее; (*more often*) всё ча́ще.
incredible [ɪn'krɛdɪbl] *adj* (*unbelievable*) неправдоподо́бный* (неправдоподо́бен), невероя́тный* (невероя́тен); (*enormous*) невероя́тный* (невероя́тен); (*amazing, wonderful*) потряса́ющий* (потряса́ющ); **it was an ~ experience** э́то бы́ло потряса́юще.
incredulity [ɪnkrɪ'djuːlɪtɪ] *n* недове́рие.
incredulous [ɪn'krɛdjuləs] *adj* недове́рчивый (недове́рчив).
increment ['ɪnkrɪmənt] *n* (*in salary*) приба́вка*.
incriminate [ɪn'krɪmɪneɪt] *vt* изоблича́ть (изобличи́ть *perf*).

* marks translations which have irregular inflections. The Russian-English side of the dictionary gives inflectional information.

incriminating [ɪn'krɪmɪneɪtɪŋ] *adj* изоблича́ющий.
incrusted [ɪn'krʌstɪd] *adj* = **encrusted**.
incubate ['ɪnkjubeɪt] *vt* (*egg*) выси́живать (вы́сидеть* *perf*) ◆ *vi* (*chickens*) вылупля́ться (вы́лупиться *perf*); (*disease*) развива́ться (разви́ться* *perf*).
incubation [ɪnkju'beɪʃən] *n* (*by bird*) выведе́ние цыплят; (*of illness*) инкубацио́нный пери́од.
incubation period *n* инкубацио́нный пери́од.
incubator ['ɪnkjubeɪtəʳ] *n* (*for babies*) инкуба́тор.
inculcate ['ɪnkʌlkeɪt] *vt*: **to ~ sth in sb** внуша́ть (внуши́ть *perf*) что-н кому́-н.
incumbent [ɪn'kʌmbənt] *n* (*official*) отве́тственное лицо́* ◆ *adj*: **it is ~ on him to ...** он обя́зан *+infin* ....
incur [ɪn'kəːʳ] *vt* (*expenses, loss*) нести́* (понести́* *perf*); (*debt*) наде́лать (*perf*) *+gen*; (*disapproval, anger*) навлека́ть (навле́чь* *perf*) на себя́.
incurable [ɪn'kjuərəbl] *adj* (*disease*) неизлечи́мый (неизлечи́м).
incursion [ɪn'kəːʃən] *n* (*MIL*) вторже́ние.
indebted [ɪn'dɛtɪd] *adj*: **to be ~ to sb** (*grateful*) быть* (*impf*) обя́занным(-ой) кому́-н.
indecency [ɪn'diːsnsɪ] *n* непристо́йность *f*.
indecent [ɪn'diːsnt] *adj* непристо́йный* (непристо́ен); (*haste*) неприли́чный* (неприли́чен).
indecent assault *n* (*BRIT*) (сексуа́льное) оскорбле́ние де́йствием.
indecent exposure *n* обнаже́ние половы́х о́рганов.
indecipherable [ɪndɪ'saɪfərəbl] *adj* (*writing*) неразбо́рчивый (неразбо́рчив); (*expression, glance etc*) зага́дочный* (зага́дочен).
indecision [ɪndɪ'sɪʒən] *n* нереши́тельность *f*.
indecisive [ɪndɪ'saɪsɪv] *adj* нереши́тельный* (нереши́телен).
indeed [ɪn'diːd] *adv* (*certainly*) коне́чно, безусло́вно; (*in fact, furthermore*) на са́мом де́ле; (*rather*) скоре́е да́же; **I'm upset, ~ shocked** я расстро́ен, пожа́луй да́же шоки́рован; **this book is very interesting ~** э́та книга чрезвыча́йно интере́сная; **thank you very much ~** большо́е Вам спаси́бо; **he is ~ very talented** он и впра́вду *or* на са́мом де́ле о́чень тала́нтлив; **yes ~!** ну коне́чно!
indefatigable [ɪndɪ'fætɪgəbl] *adj* (*person*) неутоми́мый (неутоми́м); (*rhythm, pulse etc*) неослабева́ющий.
indefensible [ɪndɪ'fɛnsɪbl] *adj* (*conduct*) непрости́тельный* (непрости́телен).
indefinable [ɪndɪ'faɪnəbl] *adj* (*quality*) не поддаю́щийся определе́нию.
indefinite [ɪn'dɛfɪnɪt] *adj* (*answer, view*) неопределённый* (неопределёнен); (*period, number*) неограни́ченный* (неограни́чен).
indefinite article *n* (*LING*) неопределённый арти́кль *m*.
indefinitely [ɪn'dɛfɪnɪtlɪ] *adv* (*continue, wait*) бесконе́чно; (*be closed, postponed*) на неопределённое вре́мя.
indelible [ɪn'dɛlɪbl] *adj* (*mark, stain*: *on clothes*) неотсти́рывающийся; (: *on hands, furniture*) несмыва́емый; (*fig*: *memory, impact*) неизглади́мый.
indelicate [ɪn'dɛlɪkɪt] *adj* нетакти́чный* (нетакти́чен).
indemnify [ɪn'dɛmnɪfaɪ] *vt* (*COMM*) гаранти́ровать (*impf*) возмеще́ние убы́тков *+dat*.
indemnity [ɪn'dɛmnɪtɪ] *n* (*insurance*) гара́нтия возмеще́ния убы́тков; (*compensation*) возмеще́ние.
indent [ɪn'dɛnt] *vt* (*line of text*) писа́ть* (написа́ть* *perf*) с кра́сной строки́.
indentation [ɪndɛn'teɪʃən] *n* углубле́ние; (*TYP*) абза́ц; (*on metal*) зазу́брина.
indenture [ɪn'dɛntʃəʳ] *n* догово́р* (*ме́жду подмастерьем и́ли ученико́м и хозя́ином*).
independence [ɪndɪ'pɛndns] *n* незави́симость *f*.
independent [ɪndɪ'pɛndnt] *adj* незави́симый (незави́сим).
independently [ɪndɪ'pɛndntlɪ] *adv* незави́симо; **~ of** незави́симо от *+gen*.
in-depth ['ɪndɛpθ] *adj* дета́льный, глубо́кий*.
indescribable [ɪndɪs'kraɪbəbl] *adj* неопису́емый (неопису́ем).
indestructible [ɪndɪs'trʌktəbl] *adj* (*object*) неразруши́мый (неразруши́м); (*friendship, alliance*) неруши́мый (неруши́м); (*army*) непобеди́мый (непобеди́м).
indeterminate [ɪndɪ'təːmɪnɪt] *adj* неопределённый* (неопределёнен).
index ['ɪndɛks] (*pl* **~es**) *n* (*in book*) (словарь*-)указа́тель *m*; (*in library etc*) катало́г; (*pl* **indices**; *MATH*) показа́тель* *msg*.
index card *n* (картоте́чная) ка́рточка*.
indexed ['ɪndɛkst] *adj* (*US*) = **index-linked**.
index finger *n* указа́тельный па́лец*.
index-linked ['ɪndɛks'lɪŋkt] *adj* (*income, payment*) *изменя́ющийся в соотве́тствии с и́ндексом инфля́ции*.
India ['ɪndɪə] *n* И́ндия.
Indian ['ɪndɪən] *adj* инди́йский* ◆ *n* инди́ец* (индиа́нка*); **Red ~** инде́ец* (индиа́нка*).
Indian Ocean *n*: **the ~ ~** Инди́йский* океа́н.
Indian Summer *n* инде́йское *or* ба́бье ле́то.
India paper *n* кита́йская бума́га.
India rubber *n* рези́на, каучу́к.
indicate ['ɪndɪkeɪt] *vt* (*point to*: *also fig*) ука́зывать (указа́ть* *perf*) на *+acc*; (*mention*) дава́ть* (дать* *perf*) знать о *+prp* ◆ *vi*: **to ~ that** (*show*) пока́зывать (показа́ть* *perf*), что; (*BRIT*: *AUT*): **to ~ left/right** включа́ть (включи́ть *perf*) ле́вый/пра́вый указа́тель поворо́та.
indication [ɪndɪ'keɪʃən] *n* знак; **all the ~s are that ...** всё ука́зывает на то, что ....
indicative [ɪn'dɪkətɪv] *n* (*LING*) изъяви́тельное

наклоне́ние ◆ *adj*: **to be ~ of** свиде́тельствовать *(impf)* о +*prp*, ука́зывать *(impf)* на +*acc*.
indicator [ˈɪndɪkeɪtəʳ] *n* (*marker, signal*) указа́тель *m*; (*AUT*) указа́тель поворо́та; (*fig*) показа́тель *m*.
indices [ˈɪndɪsiːz] *npl of* **index**.
indict [ɪnˈdaɪt] *vt* (*LAW*) предъявля́ть (предъяви́ть* *perf*) обвине́ние +*dat*.
indictable [ɪnˈdaɪtəbl] *adj* подлежа́щий уголо́вному рассмотре́нию; **~ offence** уголо́вное преступле́ние.
indictment [ɪnˈdaɪtmənt] *n* (*denunciation*) осужде́ние; (*charge*) обвини́тельный акт.
indie [ˈɪndɪ] *adj* (*music, chart etc*) *вы́пущенный ма́ленькой незави́симой сту́дией звукоза́писи.*
indifference [ɪnˈdɪfrəns] *n* (*lack of interest*) безразли́чие, равноду́шие.
indifferent [ɪnˈdɪfrənt] *adj* безразли́чный* (безразли́чен), равноду́шный* (равноду́шен); (*mediocre*) посре́дственный* (посре́дствен).
indigenous [ɪnˈdɪdʒɪnəs] *adj* (*wildlife, population*) коренно́й; (*culture*) ме́стный.
indigestible [ɪndɪˈdʒɛstɪbl] *adj* тру́дно перева́риваемый (перева́риваем).
indigestion [ɪndɪˈdʒɛstʃən] *n* расстро́йство желу́дка.
indignant [ɪnˈdɪgnənt] *adj* возмущённый* (возмущён); **to be ~ at sth/with sb** быть* *(impf)* возмущённым(-ой) чем-н/кем-н.
indignation [ɪndɪgˈneɪʃən] *n* возмуще́ние, негодова́ние.
indignity [ɪnˈdɪgnɪtɪ] *n* униже́ние.
indigo [ˈɪndɪgəu] *n* (*colour*) инди́го *nt ind*.
indirect [ɪndɪˈrɛkt] *adj* (*way, route*) око́льный, обхо́дный; (*answer*) уклончивый (укло́нчив); (*effect*) побо́чный; (*LING*): **~ object** ко́свенное дополне́ние.
indirectly [ɪndɪˈrɛktlɪ] *adv* ко́свенно.
indiscreet [ɪndɪsˈkriːt] *adj* неосмотри́тельный* (неосмотри́телен), неблагоразу́мный* (неблагоразу́мен).
indiscretion [ɪndɪsˈkrɛʃən] *n* неосмотри́тельность *f*; (*indiscreet act*) неблагоразу́мный посту́пок*.
indiscriminate [ɪndɪsˈkrɪmɪnət] *adj* (*bombing*) беспоря́дочный* (беспоря́дочен); (*taste, reader, love*) неразбо́рчивый (неразбо́рчив); (*criticism*) огу́льный.
indispensable [ɪndɪsˈpɛnsəbl] *adj* (*object*) необходи́мый (необходи́м); (*person*) незамени́мый (незамени́м).
indisposed [ɪndɪsˈpəuzd] *adj* (*unwell*) нездоро́вый (нездоро́в).
indisputable [ɪndɪsˈpjuːtəbl] *adj* (*undeniable*) неоспори́мый (неоспори́м).
indistinct [ɪndɪsˈtɪŋkt] *adj* (*image, noise*) нея́сный* (нея́сен); (*memory*) сму́тный* (сму́тен).
indistinguishable [ɪndɪsˈtɪŋgwɪʃəbl] *adj*: **~ from** неотличи́мый (неотличи́м) от +*gen*.
individual [ɪndɪˈvɪdjuəl] *n* (*person*) ли́чность *f*, индиви́дуум ◆ *adj* (*personal*) индивидуа́льный* (индивидуа́лен), ли́чный; (*single*) отде́льный; (*particular. characteristic*) своеобра́зный* (своеобра́зен), индивидуа́льный* (индивидуа́лен); **certain ~s** не́которые лю́ди.
individualist [ɪndɪˈvɪdjuəlɪst] *n* индивидуали́ст(ка*).
individuality [ɪndɪvɪdjuˈælɪtɪ] *n* индивидуа́льность *f*.
individually [ɪndɪˈvɪdjuəlɪ] *adv* отде́льно; **he is ~ responsible** он несёт ли́чную отве́тственность; **we'll help each of you ~** мы помо́жем ка́ждому из Вас.
indivisible [ɪndɪˈvɪzɪbl] *adj* недели́мый (недели́м).
Indo-China [ˈɪndəuˈtʃaɪnə] *n* Индокита́й.
indoctrinate [ɪnˈdɔktrɪneɪt] *vt* подверга́ть (подве́ргнуть* *perf*) идеологи́ческой обрабо́тке.
indoctrination [ɪndɔktrɪˈneɪʃən] *n* идеологи́ческая обрабо́тка.
indolence [ˈɪndələns] *n* ле́ность *f*.
indolent [ˈɪndələnt] *adj* лени́вый (лени́в).
Indonesia [ɪndəˈniːzɪə] *n* Индоне́зия.
Indonesian [ɪndəˈniːzɪən] *adj* индонези́йский* ◆ *n* индонези́ец*(-и́йка*).
indoor [ˈɪndɔːʳ] *adj* (*plant, games for children*) ко́мнатный; (*swimming pool*) закры́тый; **~ games** спорти́вные и́гры в закры́том помеще́нии.
indoors [ɪnˈdɔːz] *adv* (*go*) в помеще́ние; (*be*) в помеще́нии; **he stayed ~ all morning** он просиде́л до́ма всё у́тро.
indubitable [ɪnˈdjuːbɪtəbl] *adj* несомне́нный* (несомне́нен).
indubitably [ɪnˈdjuːbɪtəblɪ] *adv* несомне́нно.
induce [ɪnˈdjuːs] *vt* (*bring about*) вызыва́ть (вы́звать* *perf*); (*persuade*) побужда́ть (побуди́ть* *perf*); (*MED: birth*) стимули́ровать *(impf/perf)*; **to ~ sb to do** побужда́ть (побуди́ть* *perf*) кого́-н +*infin*.
inducement [ɪnˈdjuːsmənt] *n* (*incentive*) сти́мул; (*pej: bribe*) по́дкуп.
induct [ɪnˈdʌkt] *vt* назнача́ть (назна́чить *perf*) на до́лжность; (*fig*) посвяща́ть (посвяти́ть* *perf*) в(о) +*acc*.
induction [ɪnˈdʌkʃən] *n* (*MED: of birth*) стимуля́ция.
induction course *n* (*BRIT*) вво́дный курс.
indulge [ɪnˈdʌldʒ] *vt* (*desire, whim etc*) потво́рствовать *(impf)* +*dat*, потака́ть *(impf)*

* marks translations which have irregular inflections. The Russian-English side of the dictionary gives inflectional information.

+dat; (*person, child*) баловáть (избаловáть *perf*) ◆ *vi*: **to ~ in** баловáться (побаловáться *perf*) *+instr*.

indulgence [ɪn'dʌldʒəns] *n* (*pleasure*) прихоть *f*; (*leniency*) потвóрство.

indulgent [ɪn'dʌldʒənt] *adj* (*smile*) снисходи́тельный* (снисходи́телен); **he has very ~ parents** егó роди́тели (во всём) емý потакáют.

industrial [ɪn'dʌstrɪəl] *adj* индустриáльный, промы́шленный; **~ accident** несчáстный слýчай на произвóдстве.

industrial action *n* забастóвка.

industrial design *n* промы́шленный дизáйн.

industrial estate *n* (*BRIT*) промы́шленный кóмплекс.

industrialist [ɪn'dʌstrɪəlɪst] *n* промы́шленник.

industrialize [ɪn'dʌstrɪəlaɪz] *vt* (*country*) индустриализи́ровать *(impf/perf)*.

industrial park *n* (*US*) = **industrial estate**.

industrial relations *npl* произвóдственные отношéния *ntpl*.

industrial tribunal *n* (*BRIT*) *суд, занимáющийся рассмотрéнием произвóдственных конфли́ктов*.

industrial unrest *n* (*BRIT*) рабóчие волнéния *ntpl*.

industrious [ɪn'dʌstrɪəs] *adj* трудолюби́вый (трудолюби́в).

industry ['ɪndəstrɪ] *n* (*manufacturing*) индустри́я, промы́шленность *f no pl*; (*diligence*) трудолю́бие; **industries** óтрасли *pl* промы́шленности; **the oil/textile ~** нефтянáя/тексти́льная промы́шленность.

inebriated [ɪ'ni:brɪeɪtɪd] *adj* нетрéзвый (нетрéзв).

inedible [ɪn'ɛdɪbl] *adj* несъедóбный* (несъедóбен).

ineffective [ɪnɪ'fɛktɪv] *adj* неэффекти́вный* (неэффекти́вен).

ineffectual [ɪnɪ'fɛktʃuəl] *adj* = **ineffective**.

inefficiency [ɪnɪ'fɪʃənsɪ] *n* неэффекти́вность *f*; непроизводи́тельность *f*.

inefficient [ɪnɪ'fɪʃənt] *adj* неэффекти́вный* (неэффекти́вен); (*machine*) непроизводи́тельный* (непроизводи́телен).

inelegant [ɪn'ɛlɪgənt] *adj* неэлегáнтный* (неэлегáнтен).

ineligible [ɪn'ɛlɪdʒɪbl] *adj* (*candidate*) неподходя́щий*; **to be ~ for sth** не имéть *(impf)* прáво на что-н.

inept [ɪ'nɛpt] *adj* (*management etc*) неумéлый (неумéл).

ineptitude [ɪ'nɛptɪtju:d] *n* неумéние, неумéлость *f*.

inequality [ɪnɪ'kwɔlɪtɪ] *n* (*of system*) нерáвенство; (*of amount, share*) рáзница.

inequitable [ɪn'ɛkwɪtəbl] *adj* несправедли́вый (несправедли́в).

inert [ɪ'nə:t] *adj* (*immobile*) неподви́жный* (неподви́жен); (*gas*) инéртный.

inertia [ɪ'nə:ʃə] *n* (*laziness*) инéртность *f*; (*PHYS*) инéрция.

inertia-reel seat belt [ɪ'nə:ʃə'ri:l-] *n* инерциóнный ремéнь* *m* безопáсности.

inescapable [ɪnɪ'skeɪpəbl] *adj* неизбéжный* (неизбéжен).

inessential [ɪnɪ'sɛnʃl] *adj* несущéственный* (несущéственен).

inessentials [ɪnɪ'sɛnʃlz] *npl* рóскошь *fsg*.

inestimable [ɪn'ɛstɪməbl] *adj* (*value*) неоцени́мый (неоцéним); (*cost*) неподдаю́щийся* оцéнке.

inevitability [ɪnɛvɪtə'bɪlɪtɪ] *n* неизбéжность *f*; **the ~ of change** неизбéжность изменéний; **it is an ~** это неизбéжность.

inevitable [ɪn'ɛvɪtəbl] *adj* неизбéжный* (неизбéжен).

inevitably [ɪn'ɛvɪtəblɪ] *adv* неизбéжно; **as ~ happens, ...** как это неизбéжно случáется, ...

inexact [ɪnɪg'zækt] *adj* нетóчный* (нетóчен).

inexcusable [ɪnɪks'kju:zəbl] *adj* непрости́тельный* (непрости́телен).

inexhaustible [ɪnɪg'zɔ:stɪbl] *adj* (*wealth, resources*) неисчерпáемый (неисчерпáем).

inexorable [ɪn'ɛksərəbl] *adj* (*progress*) неотврати́мый (неотврати́м); (*decline*) неумоли́мый (неумоли́м).

inexpensive [ɪnɪk'spɛnsɪv] *adj* недорогóй* (недóрог).

inexperience [ɪnɪk'spɪərɪəns] *n* неóпытность *f*.

inexperienced [ɪnɪk'spɪərɪənst] *adj* неóпытный* (неóпытен); **to be ~ in sth** не имéть *(impf)* óпыта в чём-н.

inexplicable [ɪnɪk'splɪkəbl] *adj* необъясни́мый (необъясни́м).

inexpressible [ɪnɪk'sprɛsɪbl] *adj* невырази́мый (невырази́м).

inextricable [ɪnɪk'strɪkəbl] *adj* (*union, knot, tangle*) неразры́вный* (неразры́вен); (*dilemma*) безвы́ходный* (безвы́ходен).

inextricably [ɪnɪk'strɪkəblɪ] *adv* неразры́вно.

infallibility [ɪnfælə'bɪlɪtɪ] *n* непогреши́мость *f*.

infallible [ɪn'fælɪbl] *adj* (*person*) непогреши́мый (непогреши́м); (*guide*) надёжный* (надёжен).

infamous ['ɪnfəməs] *adj* бесчéстный* (бесчéстен).

infamy ['ɪnfəmɪ] *n* бесчéстие.

infancy ['ɪnfənsɪ] *n* (*of person*) младéнчество; (*of movement, firm*) перúод становлéния.

infant ['ɪnfənt] *n* (*baby*) младéнец*; (*young child*) ребёнок* ◆ *cpd* дéтский*.

infantile ['ɪnfəntaɪl] *adj* (*disease*) дéтский*; (*childish*) инфанти́льный* (инфанти́лен).

infantry ['ɪnfəntrɪ] *n* пехóта.

infantryman ['ɪnfəntrɪmən] *irreg n* пехоти́нец*.

infant school *n* (*BRIT*) ≈ начáльная шкóла (*для детéй от 5-и до 7-и лет*).

infatuated [ɪn'fætjueɪtɪd] *adj*: **~ with** увлечённый (увлечён) *+instr*; **to become ~ with** увлекáться (увлéчься* *perf*) *+instr*.

infatuation [ɪnfætju'eɪʃən] *n* увлечéние*.
infect [ɪn'fɛkt] *vt* (*also fig*) заражáть (заразúть* *perf*); **to become ~ed** (*wound*) заражáться (заразúться* *perf*).
infection [ɪn'fɛkʃən] *n* инфéкция.
infectious [ɪn'fɛkʃəs] *adj* (*person, animal*) зарáзный* (зарáзен); (*disease*) инфекциóнный; (*fig*) заразúтельный* (заразúтелен).
infer [ɪn'fə:ʳ] *vt* (*deduce*) заключáть (заключúть *perf*); (*imply*) подразумевáть (*impf*).
inference ['ɪnfərəns] *n* (*deduction*) заключéние; (*implication*) вы́вод.
inferior [ɪn'fɪərɪəʳ] *adj* (*position, status*) подчинённый; (*goods*) нúзкого кáчества ◆ *n* (*subordinate*) подчинённый(-ая) *m(f) adj*; (*junior*) млáдший* по чúну; **to feel ~ (to)** ощущáть (ощутúть* *perf*) свою неполноцéнность (по сравнéнию с *+instr*); **he is ~ to me in rank** он нúже меня́ по дóлжности; **the second model is ~ to the first** вторáя модéль уступáет пéрвой по кáчеству.
inferiority [ɪnfɪərɪ'ɔrətɪ] *n* (*of position, status*) подчинённое положéние; (*of goods*) низкосóртность *f*.
inferiority complex *n* кóмплекс неполноцéнности.
infernal [ɪn'fə:nl] *adj* áдский*.
inferno [ɪn'fə:nəu] *n* (*also fig*) ад.
infertile [ɪn'fə:taɪl] *adj* (*soil*) неплодорóдный* (неплодорóден); (*person, animal*) бесплóдный* (бесплóден).
infertility [ɪnfə:'tɪlɪtɪ] *n* (*see adj*) неплодорóдность *f*, бесплóдие.
infested [ɪn'fɛstɪd] *adj*: **the house is ~ with rats** дом кишúт кры́сами.
infidelity [ɪnfɪ'dɛlɪtɪ] *n* невéрность *f*.
infighting ['ɪnfaɪtɪŋ] *n* вну́тренний* конфлúкт.
infiltrate ['ɪnfɪltreɪt] *vt* проникáть (пронúкнуть* *perf*) в *+acc*.
infinite ['ɪnfɪnɪt] *adj* бесконéчный* (бесконéчен); (*resources*) несмéтный* (несмéтен).
infinitely ['ɪnfɪnɪtlɪ] *adv* бесконéчно.
infinitesimal [ɪnfɪnɪ'tɛsɪməl] *adj* бесконéчно мáлый* (мал).
infinitive [ɪn'fɪnɪtɪv] *n* инфинитúв, неопределённая фóрма глагóла.
infinity [ɪn'fɪnɪtɪ] *n* бесконéчность *f*.
infirm [ɪn'fə:m] *adj* нéмощный* (нéмощен).
infirmary [ɪn'fə:mərɪ] *n* больнúца.
infirmity [ɪn'fə:mɪtɪ] *n* нéмощь *f*.
inflame [ɪn'fleɪm] *vt* (*person, crowd*) распаля́ть (распалúть *perf*); (*situation, emotions*) накаля́ть (накалúть *perf*).
inflamed [ɪn'fleɪmd] *adj* (*throat, appendix*) воспалённый (воспалён).
inflammable [ɪn'flæməbl] *adj* (*fabric*) легкó воспламеня́ющийся; (*chemical*) горю́чий* (горю́ч).
inflammation [ɪnflə'meɪʃən] *n* воспалéние.
inflammatory [ɪn'flæmətərɪ] *adj* (*speech*) подстрекáтельский.
inflatable [ɪn'fleɪtəbl] *adj* надувнóй.
inflate [ɪn'fleɪt] *vt* (*tyre*) накáчивать (накачáть *perf*); (*balloon*) надувáть (надýть *perf*); (*price*) вздувáть (вздуть *perf*); (*expectation, position, ideas*) раздувáть (раздýть *perf*).
inflated [ɪn'fleɪtɪd] *adj* (*style*) напы́щенный* (напы́щен); (*prices*) вздýтый (вздут).
inflation [ɪn'fleɪʃən] *n* (*ECON*) инфля́ция.
inflationary [ɪn'fleɪʃənərɪ] *adj* инфляциóнный.
inflationist [ɪn'fleɪʃənɪst] *n* сторóнник(-ица) полúтики инфля́ции.
inflexible [ɪn'flɛksɪbl] *adj* (*rule, timetable*) жёсткий* (жёсток); (*person*) негúбкий* (негúбок).
inflict [ɪn'flɪkt] *vt*: **to ~ sth on sb** причиня́ть (причинúть *perf*) что-н комý-н; (*penalty*) налагáть (наложúть *perf*) что-н на когó-н.
infliction [ɪn'flɪkʃən] *n* (*of pain*) причинéние; (*of penalty*) наложéние.
in-flight ['ɪnflaɪt] *adj* (*meal, entertainment*) на бортý самолёта; **~ refuelling** дозапрáвка в полёте.
inflow ['ɪnfləu] *n* притóк.
influence ['ɪnfluəns] *n* (*power*) влия́ние; (*effect*) воздéйствие ◆ *vt* (*person, situation, choice etc*) влия́ть (повлия́ть *perf*) на *+acc*, окáзывать (оказáть* *perf*) влия́ние на *+acc*; **under the ~ of alcohol** под воздéйствием алкогóля.
influential [ɪnflu'ɛnʃl] *adj* влия́тельный* (влия́телен).
influenza [ɪnflu'ɛnzə] *n* грипп.
influx ['ɪnflʌks] *n* (*of people, funds*) притóк.
inform [ɪn'fɔ:m] *vt*: **to ~ sb of sth** (*tell*) сообщáть (сообщúть *perf*) комý-н о чём-н, информúровать (проинформúровать *perf*) когó-н о чём-н ◆ *vi*: **to ~ on sb** доносúть* (донестú* *perf*) на когó-н.
informal [ɪn'fɔ:ml] *adj* (*visit, meeting, invitation*) неофициáльный* (неофициáлен); (*manner, discussion*) непринуждённый* (непринуждён); (*clothes*) бýдничный, повседнéвный* (повседнéвен); (*language*) разговóрный.
informality [ɪnfɔ:'mælɪtɪ] *n* непринуждённость *f*.
informally [ɪn'fɔ:məlɪ] *adv* неофициáльно; (*discuss*) непринуждённо; (*dress*) бýднично; (*invite*) без церемóний.
informant [ɪn'fɔ:mənt] *n* (*source*) информáнт.
information [ɪnfə'meɪʃən] *n* информáция; **to get ~ on** получáть (получúть* *perf*) информáцию о *+prp*; **a piece of ~** сообщéние; **for your ~** к Вáшему свéдению.

* marks translations which have irregular inflections. The Russian-English side of the dictionary gives inflectional information.

information bureau *n* = **information office**.
information office *n* спра́вочное бюро́ *nt ind*.
information processing *n* обрабо́тка информа́ции.
information retrieval *n* (*COMPUT*) по́иск информа́ции, информацио́нный по́иск.
information science *n* информа́тика.
information technology *n* информацио́нная техноло́гия.
informative [ɪn'fɔ:mətɪv] *adj* содержа́тельный* (содержа́телен).
informed [ɪn'fɔ:md] *adj* осведомлённый* (осведомлён), информи́рованный* (информи́рован); **well/ill ~** хорошо́/пло́хо информи́рованный (информи́рован); **an ~ guess** обосно́ванная дога́дка*.
informer [ɪn'fɔ:mə^r] *n* (*also:* **police ~**) осведоми́тель(ница) *m(f)*.
infra dig ['ɪnfrə'dɪg] *adj abbr* (*inf:* = ***beneath one's dignity*:** = ***infra dignitatem***) ни́же чьего́-н досто́инства.
infrared [ɪnfrə'rɛd] *adj* инфракра́сный.
infrastructure ['ɪnfrəstrʌktʃə^r] *n* инфраструкту́ра.
infrequent [ɪn'fri:kwənt] *adj* ре́дкий* (ре́док).
infringe [ɪn'frɪndʒ] *vt* (*law*) преступа́ть (преступи́ть *perf*) ◆ *vi*: **to ~ on** (*rights*) ущемля́ть (ущеми́ть* *perf*), посяга́ть (посягну́ть *perf*) на *+acc*.
infringement [ɪn'frɪndʒmənt] *n* (*see vb*) наруше́ние; ущемле́ние, посяга́тельство.
infuriate [ɪn'fjuərɪeɪt] *vt* (*person*) приводи́ть* (привести́* *perf*) в я́рость *or* бе́шенство, беси́ть* (взбеси́ть* *perf*).
infuriating [ɪn'fjuərɪeɪtɪŋ] *adj* приводя́щий в я́рость *or* бе́шенство; **the noise is ~** шум приво́дит меня́ *etc* в я́рость.
infuse [ɪn'fju:z] *vt* (*tea, herbs*) наста́ивать (настоя́ть *perf*); (*person*): **to ~ sb with sth** вселя́ть (всели́ть *perf*) что-н в кого́-н.
infusion [ɪn'fju:ʒən] *n* (*tea*) насто́йка*.
ingenious [ɪn'dʒi:njəs] *adj* хитроу́мный* (хитроу́мен); (*person*) изобрета́тельный* (изобрета́телен).
ingenuity [ɪndʒɪ'nju:ɪtɪ] *n* хитроу́мность *f*; (*of person*) изобрета́тельность *f*.
ingenuous [ɪn'dʒɛnjuəs] *adj* бесхи́тростный* (бесхи́тростен).
ingot ['ɪŋgət] *n* сли́ток*.
ingrained [ɪn'greɪnd] *adj* закорене́лый.
ingratiate [ɪn'greɪʃɪeɪt] *vt*: **to ~ o.s. with** заи́скивать *(impf)* пе́ред *+instr*.
ingratiating [ɪn'greɪʃɪeɪtɪŋ] *adj* (*smile, speech*) заи́скивающий*; (*person*) льсти́вый (льсти́в).
ingratitude [ɪn'grætɪtju:d] *n* неблагода́рность *f*.
ingredient [ɪn'gri:dɪənt] *n* (*CULIN*) ингредие́нт; (*of situation*) составна́я часть* *f*.
ingrowing ['ɪngrəuɪŋ] *adj*: **~ toenail** враста́ющий но́готь* *m* (*на па́льце ноги́*).
inhabit [ɪn'hæbɪt] *vt* населя́ть *(impf)*.
inhabitant [ɪn'hæbɪtnt] *n* жи́тель(ница) *m(f)*.
inhale [ɪn'heɪl] *vt* вдыха́ть (вдохну́ть* *perf*) ◆ *vi* вдыха́ть (вдо́хнуть* *perf*); (*when smoking*) затя́гиваться (затяну́ться* *perf*).
inhaler [ɪn'heɪlə^r] *n* ингаля́тор.
inherent [ɪn'hɪərənt] *adj* (*laziness*) прирождённый; **~ in** *or* **to** сво́йственный* (сво́йствен) *+dat*, прису́щий* (прису́щ) *+dat*.
inherently [ɪn'hɪərəntlɪ] *adv* (*easy, difficult*) по приро́де; (*lazy*) по нату́ре.
inherit [ɪn'hɛrɪt] *vt* насле́довать *(impf/perf)*, унасле́довать *(perf)*.
inheritance [ɪn'hɛrɪtəns] *n* насле́дство; (*cultural, political etc*) насле́дие; **right of ~** пра́во насле́дования.
inhibit [ɪn'hɪbɪt] *vt* (*impulse*) ско́вывать (скова́ть *perf*); (*growth*) заде́рживать (задержа́ть* *perf*).
inhibited [ɪn'hɪbɪtɪd] *adj* (*see vb*) ско́ванный* (ско́ван); заде́ржанный.
inhibiting [ɪn'hɪbɪtɪŋ] *adj* (*situation*) ско́вывающий; (*factor*) препя́тствующий.
inhibition [ɪnhɪ'bɪʃən] *n* (*see vb*) ско́ванность *f no pl*; заде́ржка*.
inhospitable [ɪnhɔs'pɪtəbl] *adj* (*person*) негостеприи́мный* (негостеприи́мен); (*place*) неприве́тливый (неприве́тлив).
inhuman [ɪn'hju:mən] *adj* (*behaviour*) бесчелове́чный* (бесчелове́чен); (*appearance*) нечелове́ческий*.
inhumane [ɪnhju:'meɪn] *adj* негума́нный* (негума́нен).
inimitable [ɪ'nɪmɪtəbl] *adj* неподража́емый (неподража́ем).
iniquitous [ɪ'nɪkwɪtəs] *adj* (*see n*) чудо́вищный* (чудо́вищен); чудо́вищно несправедли́вый (несправедли́в).
iniquity [ɪ'nɪkwɪtɪ] *n* (*wickedness*) чудо́вищность *f*; (*injustice*) несправедли́вость *f*.
initial [ɪ'nɪʃl] *adj* первонача́льный, нача́льный ◆ *n* (*also:* **~ letter**) нача́льная бу́ква ◆ *vt* ста́вить* (поста́вить* *perf*) инициа́лы на *+prp*; **~s** *npl* инициа́лы *mpl*.
initialize [ɪ'nɪʃəlaɪz] *vt* (*COMPUT*) инициализи́ровать *(impf/perf)*.
initially [ɪ'nɪʃəlɪ] *adv* (*at first*) внача́ле, снача́ла; (*first*) первонача́льно.
initiate [ɪ'nɪʃɪeɪt] *vt* (*talks, process*) класть* (положи́ть *perf*) нача́ло *+dat*; (*new member*) посвяща́ть (посвяти́ть* *perf*); **to ~ sb into a secret** посвяща́ть (посвяти́ть* *perf*) кого́-н в та́йну; **to ~ proceedings against sb** возбужда́ть (возбуди́ть* *perf*) де́ло про́тив кого́-н.
initiation [ɪnɪʃɪ'eɪʃən] *n* (*beginning*) основа́ние; (*into secret etc*) посвяще́ние; **~ ceremony** церемо́ния посвяще́ния.
initiative [ɪ'nɪʃətɪv] *n* (*move*) инициати́ва, начина́ние; (*enterprise*) инициати́вность *f*; **to take the ~** брать* (взять* *perf*) на себя́

инициати́ву.
inject [ɪn'dʒɛkt] *vt* (*drugs, poison*) вводи́ть* (ввести́* *perf*); (*patient*): **to ~ sb with sth** де́лать (сде́лать *perf*) уко́л *or* инъе́кцию чего́-н кому́-н; (*money*): **to ~ into** влива́ть (влить* *perf*) в *+acc*.
injection [ɪn'dʒɛkʃən] *n* уко́л, инъе́кция; (*of money*) влива́ние; **to give an ~** де́лать (сде́лать *perf*) уко́л *or* инъе́кцию; **I had an ~** мне сде́лали уко́л.
injudicious [ɪndʒu'dɪʃəs] *adj* неразу́мный* (неразу́мен).
injunction [ɪn'dʒʌŋkʃən] *n* (*LAW*) (суде́бный) запре́т.
injure ['ɪndʒə^r] *vt* (*person, limb, feelings*) ра́нить (*impf/perf*); (*reputation*) поврежда́ть (повреди́ть* *perf*); **to ~ o.s.** пора́ниться (*perf*), ушиба́ться (ушиби́ться* *perf*).
injured ['ɪndʒəd] *adj* (*see vb*) ра́неный; повреждённый (повреждён); уши́бленный (уши́блен); **~ party** (*LAW*) потерпе́вшая сторона́*.
injurious [ɪn'dʒuərɪəs] *adj*: **~ to** вре́дный* (вре́ден) для *+gen*, губи́тельный* (губи́телен) для *+gen*.
injury ['ɪndʒərɪ] *n* поврежде́ние; (*more serious*) ране́ние; (*industrial, sports*) тра́вма; (*to reputation, feelings*) оскорбле́ние; **to escape without ~** избега́ть (избежа́ть* *perf*) ране́ний.
injury time *n* (*SPORT*) доба́вочное вре́мя* *nt*.
injustice [ɪn'dʒʌstɪs] *n* несправедли́вость *f*; **you do me an ~** Вы ко мне несправедли́вы.
ink [ɪŋk] *n* (*in pen*) черни́ла *pl*; (*for printing*) типогра́фская кра́ска*.
ink-jet printer ['ɪŋkdʒɛt-] *n* (*COMPUT*) стру́йный при́нтер.
inkling ['ɪŋklɪŋ] *n* (*idea, clue*): **to have an ~ of** име́ть (*impf*) поня́тие о *+prp*.
ink pad *n* ште́мпельная поду́шечка*.
inky ['ɪŋkɪ] *adj* (*blackness, sky*) черни́льный; (*fingers*) запа́чканный (запа́чкан) черни́лами.
inlaid ['ɪnleɪd] *adj*: **~ (with)** инкрусти́рованный (инкрусти́рован) (*+instr*).
inland ['ɪnlənd] *adj* вну́тренний* ◆ *adv* (*travel*) вглубь.
Inland Revenue *n* (*BRIT*) ≈ Гла́вное нало́говое управле́ние.
in-laws ['ɪnlɔ:z] *npl* *родня́ со стороны́ му́жа или жены́.*
inlet ['ɪnlɛt] *n* (у́зкий*) зали́в.
inlet pipe *n* впускна́я труба́*.
inmate ['ɪnmeɪt] *n* (*of prison*) заключённый(-ая) *m(f) adj*; (*of asylum*) пацие́нт(ка*).
inmost ['ɪnməust] *adj* сокрове́ннейший.
inn [ɪn] *n* тракти́р.
innards ['ɪnədz] *npl* (*inf*) вну́тренности *fpl*.
innate [ɪ'neɪt] *adj* врождённый.
inner ['ɪnə^r] *adj* вну́тренний*.
inner city *n* центра́льная часть* *f* го́рода.
innermost ['ɪnəməust] *adj* = **inmost**.
inner tube *n* ка́мера (*ши́ны*).
innings ['ɪnɪŋz] *n* *се́рия атаку́ющих уда́ров в кри́кете*; **he's had a good ~** (*BRIT*: *inf*) он прожи́л до́лгую и счастли́вую жизнь.
innocence ['ɪnəsns] *n* (*LAW*) невино́вность *f*; (*naivety*) неви́нность *f*.
innocent ['ɪnəsnt] *adj* (*also LAW*) невино́вный* (невино́вен); (*naive*) неви́нный* (неви́нен).
innocuous [ɪ'nɔkjuəs] *adj* (*substance*) безвре́дный* (безвре́ден); (*remarks*) безоби́дный* (безоби́ден).
innovation [ɪnəu'veɪʃən] *n* но́вшество.
innuendo [ɪnju'ɛndəu] (*pl* **~es**) *n* инсинуа́ция.
innumerable [ɪ'nju:mrəbl] *adj* бесчи́сленный* (бесчи́слен).
inoculate [ɪ'nɔkjuleɪt] *vt*: **to ~ sb against sth** де́лать (сде́лать *perf*) кому́-н приви́вку про́тив чего́-н; **to ~ sb with sth** привива́ть (приви́ть* *perf*) кому́-н что-н.
inoculation [ɪnɔkju'leɪʃən] *n* приви́вка*.
inoffensive [ɪnə'fɛnsɪv] *adj* безоби́дный* (безоби́ден).
inopportune [ɪn'ɔpətju:n] *adj* (*moment*) неподходя́щий*; (*event*) несвоевре́менный* (несвоевре́менен).
inordinate [ɪ'nɔ:dɪnət] *adj* необыча́йный* (необыча́ен).
inordinately [ɪ'nɔ:dɪnətlɪ] *adv* необыча́йно.
inorganic [ɪnɔ:'gænɪk] *adj* неоргани́ческий*.
inpatient ['ɪnpeɪʃənt] *n* стациона́рный(-ая) больно́й(-а́я) *m(f) adj*.
input ['ɪnput] *n* (*resources, money*) вложе́ние; (*COMPUT*) ввод ◆ *vt* (*COMPUT*): **to ~ (into)** вводи́ть* (ввести́* *perf*) (в *+acc*).
inquest ['ɪnkwɛst] *n* (*on sb's death*) (суде́бное) рассле́дование.
inquire [ɪn'kwaɪə^r] *vt* спра́шивать (спроси́ть* *perf*) ◆ *vi*: **to ~ (about)** справля́ться (спра́виться* *perf*) (о *+prp*); **to ~ when/where** справля́ться (спра́виться* *perf*) когда́/где; **he ~d whether he could go** он спроси́л, мо́жет ли он идти́
▸ **inquire after** *vt fus* спра́шивать (спроси́ть* *perf*) о *+prp*
▸ **inquire into** *vt fus* рассле́довать (*impf/perf*).
inquiring [ɪn'kwaɪərɪŋ] *adj* пытли́вый.
inquiry [ɪn'kwaɪərɪ] *n* (*question*) вопро́с; (: *more official*) запро́с; (*investigation*) рассле́дование; (: *LAW*) сле́дствие; **to make inquiries about sth** наводи́ть* (навести́* *perf*) спра́вки о чём-н; **to hold an ~ into sth** вести́* (*impf*) рассле́дование чего́-н.
inquiry desk *n* (*BRIT*) спра́вочный стол*.

* marks translations which have irregular inflections. The Russian-English side of the dictionary gives inflectional information.

inquiry office *n* (*BRIT*) спра́вочное бюро́ *nt ind.*
inquisition [ɪnkwɪ'zɪʃən] *n* сле́дствие *no pl*; (*REL*): **the I~** Инквизи́ция.
inquisitive [ɪn'kwɪzɪtɪv] *adj* любопы́тный* (любопы́тен).
inroads ['ɪnrəudz] *npl*: **to make ~ into** (*savings, resources*) тра́тить* (потра́тить* *perf*).
ins *abbr* = *inches.*
ins and outs ['ɪnzən'auts] *npl*: **to know all the ~ ~ ~** знать (*impf*) все ходы́.
insane [ɪn'seɪn] *adj* (*foolish, crazy*) безу́мный* (безу́мен); (*PSYCH*) душевнобольно́й.
insanitary [ɪn'sænɪtərɪ] *adj* антисанита́рный* (антисанита́рен).
insanity [ɪn'sænɪtɪ] *n* (*also fig*) безу́мие, сумасше́ствие.
insatiable [ɪn'seɪʃəbl] *adj* ненасы́тный* (ненасы́тен).
inscribe [ɪn'skraɪb] *vt* надпи́сывать (надписа́ть* *perf*).
inscription [ɪn'skrɪpʃən] *n* на́дпись *f*.
inscrutable [ɪn'skru:təbl] *adj* зага́дочный* (зага́дочен).
inseam measurement ['ɪnsi:m-] *n* (*US*) = **inside leg measurement**.
insect ['ɪnsɛkt] *n* насеко́мое *nt adj*.
insect bite *n* уку́с насеко́мого.
insecticide [ɪn'sɛktɪsaɪd] *n* инсектици́д.
insect repellent *n* сре́дство от насеко́мых.
insecure [ɪnsɪ'kjuə'] *adj* (*structure, border*) ненадёжный* (нанадёжен); (*person*) неуве́ренный* (неуве́рен) в себе́.
insecurity [ɪnsɪ'kjuərɪtɪ] *n* (*see adj*) ненадёжность *f*; неуве́ренность *f* в себе́.
insemination [ɪnsɛmɪ'neɪʃən] *n*: **artificial ~** иску́сственное оплодотворе́ние.
insensible [ɪn'sɛnsɪbl] *adj* (*unconscious*) без созна́ния; (*unable to feel*): **~ to** нечувстви́тельный* (нечувстви́телен) к *+dat*; (*unaware*): **~ of** не осознаю́щий *+gen*.
insensitive [ɪn'sɛnsɪtɪv] *adj* бесчу́вственный* (бесчу́вствен).
insensitivity [ɪnsɛnsɪ'tɪvɪtɪ] *n* (*of person*) бесчу́вственность *f*.
inseparable [ɪn'sɛprəbl] *adj* (*ideas, elements*) неразделимый (неразделим); (*friends*) неразлу́чный* (неразлу́чен).
insert [*vt* ɪn'sə:t, *n* 'ɪnsə:t] *vt*: **to ~ (into)** вставля́ть (вста́вить* *perf*) (в *+acc*); (*piece of paper*) вкла́дывать (вложи́ть* *perf*) ◆ *n* вкла́дыш, вкла́дка.
insertion [ɪn'sə:ʃən] *n* (*in book, file*) вста́вка*; (*of needle*) введе́ние; (*of peg*) вбива́ние.
in-service ['ɪn'sə:vɪs] *adj*: **~ training** произво́дственное обуче́ние.
inshore [ɪn'ʃɔ:'] *adj* (*fishing, waters*) при-бре́жный ◆ *adv* (*be*) у бе́рега; (*go*) к бе́регу.
inside ['ɪn'saɪd] *n* вну́тренняя часть* *f*; (*of coat etc*) изна́нка; (*of road*: *BRIT*) ле́вая сторона́; (: *US, Europe etc*) пра́вая сторона́ ◆ *adj* вну́тренний* ◆ *adv* (*go*) внутрь; (*be*) внутри́ ◆ *prep* (*position*) внутри́ *+gen*; (*motion*) внутрь *+gen*; (*of time*): **~ ten minutes** в преде́лах десяти мину́т; **~s** *npl* (*inf*: *stomach*) вну́тренности *fpl*.
inside forward *n* (*FOOTBALL*) полусре́дний напада́ющий* *m adj*.
inside information *n* информа́ция, полу́ченная из вну́тренних исто́чников.
inside lane *n* (*AUT*: *BRIT*) ле́вый ряд*; (: *US, Europe etc*) пра́вый ряд*.
inside leg measurement *n* (*BRIT*) вну́тренняя* длина́ ноги́.
inside out *adv* (*be, wear, turn*) наизна́нку; (*know*) вдоль и поперёк.
insider [ɪn'saɪdə'] *n* свой челове́к; (*COMM*) инса́йдер.
insider dealing *n* (*STOCK EXCHANGE*) *незако́нное испо́льзование делово́й информа́ции при сде́лках на би́рже*.
insider trading *n* = **insider dealing.**
inside story *n* информа́ция из пе́рвых рук.
insidious [ɪn'sɪdɪəs] *adj* кова́рный* (кова́рен).
insight ['ɪnsaɪt] *n*: **~ (into)** понима́ние *no pl* (*+gen*); **to gain (an) ~ into sth** вника́ть (вни́кнуть *perf*) в что-н.
insignia [ɪn'sɪgnɪə] *n inv* зна́ки *mpl* отли́чия.
insignificant [ɪnsɪg'nɪfɪknt] *adj* незначи́тельный* (незначи́телен).
insincere [ɪnsɪn'sɪə'] *adj* нейскренний* (нейскренен).
insincerity [ɪnsɪn'sɛrɪtɪ] *n* нейскренность *f*.
insinuate [ɪn'sɪnjueɪt] *vt* намека́ть (намекну́ть* *perf*) на *+acc*.
insinuation [ɪnsɪnju'eɪʃən] *n* инсинуа́ция.
insipid [ɪn'sɪpɪd] *adj* (*person*) бесцве́тный* (бесцве́тен); (*colour*) блёклый; (*food, drink*) пре́сный* (пре́сен).
insist [ɪn'sɪst] *vi*: **to ~ (on)** наста́ивать (настоя́ть *perf*) (на *+prp*); **to ~ that** (*demand*) наста́ивать (настоя́ть *perf*) на том, что́бы *+past tense*; (*claim*) наста́ивать (настоя́ть *perf*) на том, что.
insistence [ɪn'sɪstəns] *n* настоя́ние; **at his ~** по его́ настоя́нию.
insistent [ɪn'sɪstənt] *adj* насто́йчивый (насто́йчив).
insofar as [ɪnsəu'fɑ:'-] *adv* поско́льку.
insole ['ɪnsəul] *n* сте́лька*.
insolence ['ɪnsələns] *n* на́глость *f*.
insolent ['ɪnsələnt] *adj* (*attitude, remark*) на́глый* (нагл).
insoluble [ɪn'sɔljubl] *adj* неразреши́мый (неразреши́м).
insolvency [ɪn'sɔlvənsɪ] *n* неплатёже-спосо́бность *f*.
insolvent [ɪn'sɔlvənt] *adj* неплатёже-спосо́бный* (неплатёжеспосо́бен).
insomnia [ɪn'sɔmnɪə] *n* бессо́нница.
insomniac [ɪn'sɔmnɪæk] *n* страда́ющий(-ая) *m(f) adj* бессо́нницей.
inspect [ɪn'spɛkt] *vt* (*premises, equipment*)

осма́тривать (осмотре́ть* *perf*); (*BRIT: ticket, luggage*) проверя́ть (прове́рить *perf*).
inspection [ɪn'spɛkʃən] *n* (*see vb*) осмо́тр; прове́рка*.
inspector [ɪn'spɛktəʳ] *n* (*ADMIN, POLICE*) инспе́ктор*; (*BRIT: on buses, trains*) контролёр.
inspiration [ɪnspə'reɪʃən] *n* вдохнове́ние.
inspire [ɪn'spaɪəʳ] *vt* (*workers, troops*) вдохновля́ть (вдохнови́ть* *perf*); **to ~ sth (in sb)** внуша́ть (внуши́ть *perf*) что-н (кому́-н).
inspired [ɪn'spaɪəd] *adj* (*writer etc*) вдохновлённый (вдохновлён); (*book*) вдохнове́нный (вдохнове́нен); **in an ~ moment** в моме́нт вдохнове́ния.
inspiring [ɪn'spaɪərɪŋ] *adj* вдохновля́ющий*.
inst. *abbr* (*BRIT: COMM: = instant*) с.м.= *сего́ ме́сяца*.
instability [ɪnstə'bɪlɪtɪ] *n* нестаби́льность *f*.
install [ɪn'stɔ:l] *vt* (*machine*) устана́вливать (установи́ть* *perf*); (*official*) ста́вить* (поста́вить* *perf*).
installation [ɪnstə'leɪʃən] *n* (*of machine, plant*) устано́вка; (*MIL*) объе́кт.
installment plan *n* (*US*) рассро́чка.
instalment [ɪn'stɔ:lmənt] (*US* **installment**) *n* (*of payment*) взнос; (*of story, TV serial*) часть* *f*; **to pay in ~s** плати́ть* (заплати́ть* *perf*) в рассро́чку.
instance ['ɪnstəns] *n* (*example*) приме́р; **for ~** наприме́р; **in this** *or* **that ~** в да́нном слу́чае; **in many ~s** во мно́гих слу́чаях; **in the first ~** в пе́рвую о́чередь.
instant ['ɪnstənt] *n* мгнове́ние, миг ◆ *adj* (*reaction, success*) мгнове́нный* (мгнове́нен); **come here this ~!** иди́ сюда́ сию́ мину́ту!; **the 10th ~** (*COMM, ADMIN*) 10-ое число́ сего́ ме́сяца; **~ coffee** раствори́мый ко́фе; **~ food** пищево́й концентра́т.
instantaneous [ɪnstən'teɪnɪəs] *adj* (*immediate*) мгнове́нный* (мгнове́нен).
instantly ['ɪnstəntlɪ] *adv* неме́дленно, сра́зу.
instant replay *n* (*TV*) повто́р.
instead [ɪn'stɛd] *adv* взаме́н ◆ *prep*: **~ of** вме́сто *+gen*, взаме́н *+gen*; **~ of sb** вме́сто кого́-н.
instep ['ɪnstɛp] *n* подъём (*ноги́, ту́фли*).
instigate ['ɪnstɪgeɪt] *vt* (*rebellion, strike etc*) подстрека́ть *(impf)* к *+dat*; **to ~ talks** дава́ть* (дать* *perf*) толчо́к перегово́рам.
instigation [ɪnstɪ'geɪʃən] *n* подстрека́тельство; **at my ~** по мое́й инициати́ве.
instil [ɪn'stɪl] *vt*: **to ~ sth in(to) sb** (*confidence, fear etc*) вселя́ть (всели́ть *perf*) что-н в кого́-н.
instinct ['ɪnstɪŋkt] *n* инсти́нкт; **by ~** инстинкти́вно; **maternal ~** матери́нский инсти́нкт.
instinctive [ɪn'stɪŋktɪv] *adj* инстинкти́вный* (инстинкти́вен).
instinctively [ɪn'stɪŋktɪvlɪ] *adv* инстинкти́вно.
institute ['ɪnstɪtju:t] *n* (*for research, teaching*) институ́т; (*professional body*) ассоциа́ция ◆ *vt* (*system, rule*) учрежда́ть (учреди́ть* *perf*); (*inquiry*) назнача́ть (назна́чить *perf*); **to ~ proceedings (against)** возбужда́ть (возбуди́ть* *perf*) суде́бное де́ло (про́тив *+gen*).
institution [ɪnstɪ'tju:ʃən] *n* учрежде́ние; (*custom, tradition*) институ́т.
institutional [ɪnstɪ'tju:ʃənl] *adj* (*value, quality etc*) закреплённый (закреплён); (*education*) осуществля́емый кру́пными учрежде́ниями; **~ care** попече́ние (*осуществля́емое учрежде́ниями*); **~ reform** рефо́рма социа́льных учрежде́ний.
instruct [ɪn'strʌkt] *vt*: **to ~ sb in sth** обуча́ть (обучи́ть* *perf*) кого́-н чему́-н; **to ~ sb to do** поруча́ть (поручи́ть* *perf*) кому́-н *+infin*.
instruction [ɪn'strʌkʃən] *n* (*teaching*) обуче́ние ◆ *cpd*: **~ manual, ~ leaflet** инстру́кция; **~s** *npl* (*orders*) указа́ния *ntpl*; **~s (for use)** инстру́кция *or* руково́дство (по примен-е́нию).
instructive [ɪn'strʌktɪv] *adj* поучи́тельный* (поучи́телен).
instructor [ɪn'strʌktəʳ] *n* преподава́тель(ница) *m(f)*; (*for skiing, driving etc*) инстру́ктор*.
instrument ['ɪnstrumənt] *n* инструме́нт.
instrumental [ɪnstru'mɛntl] *adj* (*MUS*) инструмента́льный; (*important*): **to be ~ in** игра́ть (сыгра́ть *perf*) суще́ственную роль в *+prp*.
instrumentalist [ɪnstru'mɛntəlɪst] *n* инструментали́ст.
instrument panel *n* прибо́рная пане́ль *f*.
insubordination [ɪnsəbɔ:də'neɪʃən] *n* неповинове́ние.
insufferable [ɪn'sʌfrəbl] *adj* невыноси́мый (невыноси́м).
insufficient [ɪnsə'fɪʃənt] *adj* недоста́точный* (недоста́точен).
insufficiently [ɪnsə'fɪʃəntlɪ] *adv* недоста́точно.
insular ['ɪnsjuləʳ] *adj* ограни́ченный* (ограни́чен).
insulate ['ɪnsjuleɪt] *vt* (*protect: person, group, also ELEC*) изоли́ровать *(impf/perf)*; (*against cold*) утепля́ть (утепли́ть *perf*); (*against sound*) (звуко)изоли́ровать *(impf/perf)*.
insulating tape ['ɪnsjuleɪtɪŋ-] *n* (*BRIT*) изоляцио́нная ле́нта.
insulation [ɪnsju'leɪʃən] *n* (*see vb*) изоля́ция; (тепло)изоля́ция; (звуко)изоля́ция.
insulator ['ɪnsjuleɪtəʳ] *n* (*material*) изоля́тор.
insulin ['ɪnsjulɪn] *n* инсули́н.
insult [*vt* ɪn'sʌlt, *n* 'ɪnsʌlt] *vt* оскорбля́ть (оскорби́ть* *perf*) ◆ *n* оскорбле́ние.

* marks translations which have irregular inflections. The Russian-English side of the dictionary gives inflectional information.

insulting [ɪn'sʌltɪŋ] *adj* оскорби́тельный* (оскорби́телен).
insuperable [ɪn'sju:prəbl] *adj* непреодоли́мый (непреодоли́м).
insurance [ɪn'ʃuərəns] *n* страхова́ние; **life/fire ~** страхова́ние жи́зни/на слу́чай пожа́ра; **to take out ~ (against)** брать* (взять* *perf*) страхо́вку (от +*gen*).
insurance agent *n* страхово́й аге́нт.
insurance broker *n* страхово́й бро́кер.
insurance policy *n* страхово́й по́лис.
insurance premium *n* страхова́я пре́мия.
insure [ɪn'ʃuəʳ] *vt*: **to ~ (against)** страхова́ть (застрахова́ть *perf*) (от +*gen*); **to ~ (o.s.) against** страхова́ться (застрахова́ться *perf*) от +*gen*; **the car is ~d for £5,000** маши́на застрахо́вана на су́мму в £5.000.
insured [ɪn'ʃuəd] *n*: **the ~** страхова́тель(ница) *m(f)*.
insurer [ɪn'ʃuərəʳ] *n* (*insurance company*) страхо́вщик.
insurgent [ɪn'sə:dʒənt] *adj* восста́вший ◆ *n* повста́нец*.
insurmountable [ɪnsə'mauntəbl] *adj* непреодоли́мый (непреодоли́м).
insurrection [ɪnsə'rɛkʃən] *n* восста́ние.
intact [ɪn'tækt] *adj* (*whole*) нетро́нутый (нетро́нут); (*unharmed*) неповреждённый (неповреждён).
intake ['ɪnteɪk] *n* (*of food, drink*) потребле́ние; (*of air*) поглоще́ние; (*BRIT: of pupils, recruits*) набо́р.
intangible [ɪn'tændʒɪbl] *adj* неощути́мый (неощути́м).
integer ['ɪntɪdʒəʳ] *n* це́лое число́*.
integral ['ɪntɪgrəl] *adj* (*feature, element*) неотъе́млемый (неотъе́млем) ◆ *n* (*MATH*) интегра́л.
integrate ['ɪntɪgreɪt] *vt* интегри́ровать *(impf/perf)* ◆ *vi* (*groups, individuals*) объединя́ться (объедини́ться *perf*).
integrated circuit ['ɪntɪgreɪtɪd-] *n* (*COMPUT*) интегра́льная схе́ма.
integration [ɪntɪ'greɪʃən] *n* интегра́ция; **racial ~** ра́совая интегра́ция.
integrity [ɪn'tɛgrɪtɪ] *n* (*morality*) че́стность *f*, поря́дочность *f*; (*wholeness*) це́лостность *f*
intellect ['ɪntəlɛkt] *n* интелле́кт.
intellectual [ɪntə'lɛktjuəl] *adj* интеллектуа́льный* (интеллектуа́лен) ◆ *n* интеллектуа́л.
intelligence [ɪn'tɛlɪdʒəns] *n* (*cleverness*) ум*; (*thinking power*) у́мственные спосо́бности *fpl*; (*MIL etc*) разве́дка.
intelligence quotient *n* коэффицие́нт у́мственного разви́тия.
intelligence service *n* разве́дывательная слу́жба.
intelligence test *n* *тест, определя́ющий у́ровень у́мственных спосо́бностей.*
intelligent [ɪn'tɛlɪdʒənt] *adj* у́мный* (умён); (*animal*) разу́мный* (разу́мен).
intelligently [ɪn'tɛlɪdʒəntlɪ] *adv* у́мно.
intelligentsia [ɪntɛlɪ'dʒɛntsɪə] *n*: **the ~** интеллиге́нция.
intelligible [ɪn'tɛlɪdʒɪbl] *adj* поня́тный* (поня́тен).
intemperate [ɪn'tɛmpərət] *adj* несде́ржанный* (несде́ржан).
intend [ɪn'tɛnd] *vt*: **to ~ sth for** предназнача́ть (предназначи́ть *perf*) что-н для +*gen*; **to ~ to do** намерева́ться *(impf)* +*infin*.
intended [ɪn'tɛndɪd] *adj* (*effect, route*) заплани́рованный (заплани́рован); (*victim*) предполага́емый (предполага́ем); (*insult*) преднаме́ренный* (преднаме́рен).
intense [ɪn'tɛns] *adj* (*heat, emotion*) си́льный* (силён); (*look*) напряжённый; (*noise, activity*) интенси́вный* (интенси́вен); **she is very ~** она́ всё о́чень серьёзно восприника́ет.
intensely [ɪn'tɛnslɪ] *adv* (*see adj*) си́льно; напряжённо.
intensify [ɪn'tɛnsɪfaɪ] *vt* уси́ливать (уси́лить *perf*).
intensity [ɪn'tɛnsɪtɪ] *n* (*of effort, sun*) интенси́вность *f*; (*of look*) напряжённость *f*.
intensive [ɪn'tɛnsɪv] *adj* интенси́вный* (интенси́вен).
intensive care *n* интенси́вная терапи́я.
intensive care unit *n* отделе́ние интенси́вной терапи́и.
intent [ɪn'tɛnt] *n* (*also LAW*) наме́рение ◆ *adj*: **~ (on)** сосредото́ченный* (сосредото́чен) (на +*prp*); **to all ~s and purposes** что бы там ни́ было; **to be ~ on doing** (*determined*) стреми́ться* *(impf)* +*infin*.
intention [ɪn'tɛnʃən] *n* наме́рение.
intentional [ɪn'tɛnʃənl] *adj* наме́ренный (наме́рен); (*LAW*) преднаме́ренный* (преднаме́рен).
intentionally [ɪn'tɛnʃnəlɪ] *adv* (*see adj*) наме́ренно; преднаме́ренно.
intently [ɪn'tɛntlɪ] *adv* при́стально.
inter [ɪn'tə:ʳ] *vt* погреба́ть (погрести́* *perf*).
interact [ɪntər'ækt] *vi*: **to ~ (with)** взаимоде́йствовать *(impf)* (с +*instr*).
interaction [ɪntər'ækʃən] *n* взаимоде́йствие.
interactive [ɪntər'æktɪv] *adj* взаимоде́йствующий; (*COMPUT*) интеракти́вный, диало́говый.
intercede [ɪntə'si:d] *vi*: **to ~ (with sb/on behalf of sb)** хода́тайствовать *(impf)* (пе́ред кем-н/за кого́-н).
intercept [ɪntə'sɛpt] *vt* перехва́тывать (перехвати́ть* *perf*).
interception [ɪntə'sɛpʃən] *n* перехва́т.
interchange ['ɪntətʃeɪndʒ] *n* (*on motorway*) тра́нспортная развя́зка*; **~ (of)** (*exchange*) обме́н (+*instr*).
interchangeable [ɪntə'tʃeɪndʒəbl] *adj* взаимозаменя́емый (взаимозаменя́ем).
intercity [ɪntə'sɪtɪ] *adj* междугоро́дный.

intercom ['ıntəkɔm] *n* селéктор.
interconnect [ıntəkə'nɛkt] *vi* соединя́ться *(impf)* (мéжду собóй).
intercontinental ['ıntəkɔntı'nɛntl] *adj* межконтинентáльный.
intercourse ['ıntəkɔ:s] *n* (*sexual*) половóе сношéние; (*social, verbal*) общéние.
interdependence [ıntədı'pɛndəns] *n* взаимозави́симость *f*.
interdependent [ıntədı'pɛndənt] *adj* взаимозави́симый (взаимозави́сим).
interest ['ıntrıst] *n*: **~ (in)** интерéс (к *+dat*); (*COMM: in company*) дóля*; (: *sum of money*) процéнты *mpl* ◆ *vt* интересовáть *(impf)*; **compound/simple ~** слóжные/прóстые процéнты *mpl*; **it is in our ~s** (*to our advantage*) э́то в нáших интерéсах; **British ~s in the Middle East** британские интерéсы на Бли́жнем Востóке; **his main ~ is history** егó основнóй интерéс – э́то истóрия.
interested ['ıntrıstıd] *adj* заинтересóванный (заинтересóван); **to be ~ (in sth)** (*music etc*) интересовáться *(impf)* (чем-н); **they are ~ in increasing production** они́ заинтересóваны в увеличéнии производи́тельности; **she is ~ in becoming a nurse** онá хóчет стать медсестрóй.
interest-free ['ıntrıst'fri:] *adj* беспроцéнтный ◆ *adv* без уплáты процéнтов.
interesting ['ıntrıstıŋ] *adj* интерéсный* (интерéсен).
interest rate *n* процéнтная стáвка*.
interface ['ıntəfeıs] *n* (*COMPUT*) интерфéйс; (*area of contact*): **~ between technology and design** соприкосновéние технолóгии с дизáйном.
interfere [ıntə'fıəʳ] *vi*: **to ~ in** вмéшиваться (вмешáться *perf*) в *+acc*; **to ~ with** (*object*) трóгать *(impf)*; (*plans, career, duty, decision*) мешáть (помешáть *perf*) *+dat*; **don't ~** не вмéшивайтесь.
interference [ıntə'fıərəns] *n* вмешáтельство; (*RADIO, TV*) помéхи *fpl*.
interfering [ıntə'fıərıŋ] *adj* назóйливый (назóйлив).
interim ['ıntərım] *adj* (*POL*) врéменный; (*report*) промежýточный ◆ *n*: **in the ~** тем врéменем.
interim dividend *n* промежýточный дивидéнд.
interior [ın'tıərıəʳ] *n* (*of building*) интерьéр; (*of car, box etc*) внýтренность *f*; (*of country*) глуби́нные райóны *mpl* ◆ *adj* (*door, room etc*) внýтренний*; **~ minister/department** мини́стр/департáмент внýтренних дел.
interior decorator *n* худóжник(-ица) по интерьéру.
interior designer *n* дизáйнер интерьéра.
interjection [ıntə'dʒɛkʃən] *n* перебивáющий вóзглас; (*LING*) междомéтие.
interlock [ıntə'lɔk] *vi* сцепля́ться (сцепи́ться* *perf*).
interloper ['ıntələupəʳ] *n* нарушитель *m*.
interlude ['ıntəlu:d] *n* перерыв; (*THEAT*) антрáкт.
intermarry [ıntə'mærı] *vi* вступáть (вступи́ть* *perf*) в смéшанный брак.
intermediary [ıntə'mi:dıərı] *n* посрéдник (-ица).
intermediate [ıntə'mi:dıət] *adj* (*stage*) промежýточный; **~ student** студéнт срéдней ступéни обучéния.
interment [ın'tə:mənt] *n* погребéние.
interminable [ın'tə:mınəbl] *adj* бесконéчный* (бесконéчен).
intermission [ıntə'mıʃən] *n* переры́в.
intermittent [ıntə'mıtnt] *adj* периоди́ческий*.
intermittently [ıntə'mıtntlı] *adv* периоди́чески.
intern [*vt* ın'tə:n, *n* 'ıntə:n] *vt* интерни́ровать *(impf/perf)* ◆ *n* (*US: MED*) врач-стажёр.
internal [ın'tə:nl] *adj* внýтренний*.
internally [ın'tə:nəlı] *adv*: **"not to be taken ~"** „внутрь не принимáть".
Internal Revenue Service *n* (*US*) ≈ Глáвное налóговое управлéние.
international [ıntə'næʃənl] *adj* междунарóдный ◆ *n* (*BRIT: SPORT: also:* **~ match**) междунарóдная встрéча.
International Atomic Energy Agency *n* Междунарóдное агéнтство по áтомной энéргии.
International Chamber of Commerce *n* Междунарóдная торгóвая палáта.
International Court of Justice *n* Междунарóдный суд*.
International Date Line *n* ли́ния перемéны дат.
International Labour Organization *n* Междунарóдная организáция трудá.
internationally [ıntə'næʃnəlı] *adv* в междунарóдном масштáбе.
International Monetary Fund *n* Междунарóдный валю́тный фонд.
international relations *npl* междунарóдные отношéния *ntpl*.
internecine [ıntə'ni:saın] *adj* междоусóбный.
internee [ıntə:'ni:] *n* интерни́рованный(-ая) *m(f) adj*.
Internet ['ıntə,net] *n*: **the ~** Интернéт, Сеть *f*.
internment [ın'tə:nmənt] *n* интерни́рование.
interplay ['ıntəpleı] *n*: **~ (of** *or* **between)** взаимодéйствие (*+gen*).
Interpol ['ıntəpɔl] *n* интерпóл.
interpret [ın'tə:prıt] *vt* (*explain*) интерпрети́ровать *(impf/perf)*, толковáть *(impf)*; (*translate*) переводи́ть* (перевести́* *perf*) (*ýстно*) ◆ *vi* переводи́ть* (перевести́* *perf*)

* marks translations which have irregular inflections. The Russian-English side of the dictionary gives inflectional information.

(*у́стно*).
interpretation [ɪntə:prɪ'teɪʃən] *n* интерпрета́ция, толкова́ние.
interpreter [ɪn'tə:prɪtə^r] *n* перево́дчик(-ица).
interpreting [ɪn'tə:prɪtɪŋ] *n* (у́стный) перево́д.
interrelated [ɪntərɪ'leɪtɪd] *adj* взаимосвя́занный (взаимосвя́зан).
interrogate [ɪn'tɛrəugeɪt] *vt* допра́шивать (допроси́ть* *perf*).
interrogation [ɪntɛrəu'geɪʃən] *n* допро́с.
interrogative [ɪntə'rɔgətɪv] *adj* (*LING*) вопроси́тельный.
interrogator [ɪn'tɛrəgeɪtə'] *n* сле́дователь *m*.
interrupt [ɪntə'rʌpt] *vti* прерыва́ть (прерва́ть* *perf*).
interruption [ɪntə'rʌpʃən] *n* (*act*) прерыва́ние; **I hate ~s when I'm working** я ненави́жу, когда́ меня́ прерыва́ют во вре́мя рабо́ты.
intersect [ɪntə'sɛkt] *vi* пересека́ться (пересе́чься* *perf*) ◆ *vt* пересека́ть (пересе́чь* *perf*).
intersection [ɪntə'sɛkʃən] *n* (*of roads*) пересече́ние; (*MATH*) то́чка* пересече́ния.
intersperse [ɪntə'spə:s] *vt*: **to ~ with** перемежа́ть *(impf)* с +*instr*.
intertwine [ɪntə'twaɪn] *vi* переплета́ться (переплести́сь* *perf*).
interval ['ɪntəvl] *n* (*also MUS*) интерва́л; (*BRIT: SPORT*) переры́в; (: *THEAT*) антра́кт; **bright ~s** (*in weather*) проясне́ния *ntpl*; **at ~s** вре́мя от вре́мени.
intervene [ɪntə'vi:n] *vi* (*in conversation, situation*) вме́шиваться (вмеша́ться *perf*); (*event*) меша́ть (помеша́ть *perf*); (*time*) проходи́ть* (пройти́* *perf*).
intervening [ɪntə'vi:nɪŋ] *adj* (*period*) промежу́точный.
intervention [ɪntə'vɛnʃən] *n* (*interference*) вмеша́тельство; (*mediation*) посре́дничество; **military ~** вое́нная интерве́нция.
interview ['ɪntəvju:] *n* (*for job*) собесе́дование; (*RADIO, TV etc*) интервью́ *nt ind* ◆ *vt* (*see n*) проводи́ть* (провести́* *perf*) собесе́дование с +*instr*; интервьюи́ровать *(impf/perf)*, брать* (взять* *perf*) интервью́ у +*gen*; **to give an ~** дава́ть* (дать* *perf*) интервью́.
interviewee [ɪntəvju'i:] *n* интервьюи́руемый (-ая) *m(f) adj*.
interviewer ['ɪntəvjuə'] *n* (*of candidate*) проводя́щий(-ая) *m(f) adj* собесе́дование; (*RADIO, TV etc*) интервьюе́р.
intestate [ɪn'tɛsteɪt] *adj*: **to die ~** сконча́ться *(perf)*, не оста́вив завеща́ния.
intestinal [ɪn'tɛstɪnl] *adj* кише́чный.
intestine [ɪn'tɛstɪn] *n* кишка́*; **large/small ~** то́лстая/то́нкая кишка́; **~s** кише́чник *msg*.
intimacy ['ɪntɪməsɪ] *n* инти́мность *f*.
intimate [*adj* 'ɪntɪmət, *vt* 'ɪntɪmeɪt] *adj* (*very close*) бли́зкий* (бли́зок); (*relationship, conversation, atmosphere*) инти́мный* (инти́мен); (*knowledge*) глубо́кий* (глубо́к) ◆ *vt* намека́ть (намекну́ть *perf*) на +*acc*; **to ~ that** намека́ть (намекну́ть *perf*), что.
intimately ['ɪntɪmətlɪ] *adv* (*see adj*) инти́мно; глубоко́.
intimation [ɪntɪ'meɪʃən] *n* намёк.
intimidate [ɪn'tɪmɪdeɪt] *vt* запу́гивать (запуга́ть *perf*).
intimidation [ɪntɪmɪ'deɪʃən] *n* запу́гивание.

KEYWORD

into ['ɪntu] *prep* **1** (*indicating motion or direction*) в/на +*acc*; **into the house/garden** в дом/сад; **into the post office/factory** на по́чту/фа́брику; **research into cancer** иссле́дования *ntpl* в о́бласти ра́ковых заболева́ний; **he worked late into the night** он рабо́тал до по́здней но́чи
2 (*indicating change of condition, result*): **she has translated the letter into Russian** она́ перевела́ письмо́ на ру́сский язы́к; **the vase broke into pieces** ва́за разби́лась вдре́безги *or* на кусо́чки; **they got into trouble for it** им попа́ло за э́то; **he lapsed into silence** он погрузи́лся в молча́ние; **to burst into tears** распла́каться* *(perf)*; **to burst into flames** загора́ться (загоре́ться *perf*).

intolerable [ɪn'tɔlərəbl] *adj* нетерпи́мый (нетерпи́м), невыноси́мый (невыноси́м).
intolerance [ɪn'tɔlərns] *n* нетерпи́мость *f*.
intolerant [ɪn'tɔlərnt] *adj*: **~ (of)** нетерпи́мый (нетерпи́м) (к +*dat*).
intonation [ɪntəu'neɪʃən] *n* интона́ция.
intoxicated [ɪn'tɔksɪkeɪtɪd] *adj* (*drunk*) опьяне́вший; (*fig*) опьянённый (опьянён).
intoxication [ɪntɔksɪ'keɪʃən] *n* (*also fig*) опьяне́ние.
intractable [ɪn'træktəbl] *adj* (*person, temper*) неподатливый (непода́тлив); (*problem*) трудноразреши́мый (трудноразреши́м); (*illness*) трудноизлечи́мый (трудноизлечи́м).
intranet ['ɪntrənet] *n* интране́т.
intransigence [ɪn'trænsɪdʒəns] *n* упо́рство.
intransigent [ɪn'trænsɪdʒənt] *adj* упо́рный* (упо́рен).
intransitive [ɪn'trænsɪtɪv] *adj* (*LING*) неперехо́дный.
intrauterine device ['ɪntrə'ju:təraɪn-] *n* внутрима́точное противозача́точное сре́дство.
intravenous [ɪntrə'vi:nəs] *adj* внутриве́нный.
in-tray ['ɪntreɪ] *n* (*in office*) корзи́на для входя́щих бума́г.
intrepid [ɪn'trɛpɪd] *adj* неустраши́мый (неустраши́м).
intricacy ['ɪntrɪkəsɪ] *n* (*of situation*) сло́жность *f*; (*of pattern, design*) замыслова́тость *f*.
intricate ['ɪntrɪkət] *adj* замыслова́тый (замыслова́т).
intrigue [ɪn'tri:g] *n* интри́га ◆ *vt* интригова́ть (заинтригова́ть *perf*).

intriguing [ɪn'tri:gɪŋ] *adj* (*fascinating*) интригу́ющий.
intrinsic [ɪn'trɪnsɪk] *adj* неотъе́млемый (неотъе́млем).
introduce [ɪntrə'dju:s] *vt* (*new idea, measure etc*) вводи́ть* (ввести́* *perf*); (*speaker, TV show etc*) представля́ть (предста́вить* *perf*); **to ~ sb (to sb)** представля́ть (предста́вить* *perf*) кого́-н (кому́-н); **to ~ sb to** (*pastime, technique*) знако́мить* (познако́мить* *perf*) кого́-н с *+instr*; **may I ~ ...?** разреши́те Вам предста́вить ....
introduction [ɪntrə'dʌkʃən] *n* введе́ние; (*to person, new experience*) знако́мство; **a letter of ~** рекоменда́тельное письмо́*.
introductory [ɪntrə'dʌktərɪ] *adj* (*lesson*) вступи́тельный; **~ remarks** вступи́тельные замеча́ния; **an ~ offer** предвари́тельная цена́*.
introspection [ɪntrəu'spɛkʃən] *n* самоана́лиз.
introspective [ɪntrəu'spɛktɪv] *adj* самосозерца́тельный.
introvert ['ɪntrəuvə:t] *n* интрове́рт.
introverted ['ɪntrəuvə:tɪd] *adj* самоуглублённый (самоуглублён).
intrude [ɪn'tru:d] *vi*: **to ~ (on)** вторга́ться (вто́ргнуться* *perf*) (в/на *+acc*); **am I intruding?** я не помеша́ю?
intruder [ɪn'tru:də[r]] *n*: **there is an ~ in our house** к нам в дом кто-то вто́ргся.
intrusion [ɪn'tru:ʒən] *n* вторже́ние.
intrusive [ɪn'tru:sɪv] *adj* назо́йливый (назо́йлив).
intuition [ɪntju:'ɪʃən] *n* интуи́ция.
intuitive [ɪn'tju:ɪtɪv] *adj* интуити́вный* (интуити́вен).
inundate ['ɪnʌndeɪt] *vt*: **to ~ with** (*calls, letters etc*) зава́ливать (завали́ть* *perf*) *+instr*; **Moscow is ~d with visitors** Москва́ наводнена́ прие́зжими.
inure [ɪn'juə[r]] *vt*: **to ~ o.s. to** приуча́ть (приучи́ть* *perf*) себя́ к *+dat*.
invade [ɪn'veɪd] *vt* (*MIL*) вторга́ться (вто́ргнуться* *perf*) в *+acc*; (*fig*: *subj*: *people, animals etc*) наводня́ть (наводни́ть* *perf*).
invader [ɪn'veɪdə[r]] *n* (*MIL*) захва́тчик.
invalid [*n* 'ɪnvəlɪd, *adj* ɪn'vælɪd] *n* (*MED*) инвали́д ◆ *adj* (*not valid*) недействи́тельный* (недействи́телен).
invalidate [ɪn'vælɪdeɪt] *vt* (*argument, result etc*) дока́зывать (доказа́ть* *perf*) несостоя́тельность *f +gen*; (*law, marriage, election*) де́лать (сде́лать *perf*) недействи́тельным.
invaluable [ɪn'væljuəbl] *adj* (*person, thing*) неоцени́мый (неоцени́м).
invariable [ɪn'vɛərɪəbl] *adj* (*amount, result, routine*) неизме́нный* (неизме́нен).
invariably [ɪn'vɛərɪəblɪ] *adv* неизме́нно; **she is ~ late** она неизме́нно опа́здывает.
invasion [ɪn'veɪʒən] *n* (*MIL*) вторже́ние; (*fig*) посяга́тельство; **an ~ of privacy** вторже́ние в ли́чную жизнь.
invective [ɪn'vɛktɪv] *n* оскорбле́ние.
inveigle [ɪn'vi:gl] *vt*: **to ~ sb into sth** вовлека́ть (вовле́чь* *perf*) кого́-н во что́-н.
invent [ɪn'vɛnt] *vt* (*machine, game, phrase etc*) изобрета́ть (изобрести́* *perf*); (*fabricate*: *lie, excuse*) выду́мывать (вы́думать *perf*).
invention [ɪn'vɛnʃən] *n* изобрете́ние; (*untrue story*) вы́думка.
inventive [ɪn'vɛntɪv] *adj* (*person*) изобрета́тельный* (изобрета́телен).
inventiveness [ɪn'vɛntɪvnɪs] *n* изобрета́тельность *f*.
inventor [ɪn'vɛntə[r]] *n* (*of machines, systems*) изобрета́тель *m*.
inventory ['ɪnvəntrɪ] *n* (*of house, ship etc*) (инвентаризацио́нная) о́пись.
inventory control *n* (*COMM*) управле́ние запа́сами.
inverse [ɪn'və:s] *adj* (*relationship*) обра́тный; **in ~ proportion to** в обра́тной пропорциона́льности к *+dat*.
invert [ɪn'və:t] *vt* (*turn upside down*) перевора́чивать (переверну́ть *perf*).
invertebrate [ɪn'və:tɪbrət] *n* беспозвоно́чное *nt adj*.
inverted commas [ɪn'və:tɪd-] *npl* (*BRIT*: *LING*) кавы́чки *fpl*.
invest [ɪn'vɛst] *vt* (*money*) инвести́ровать* (*impf/perf*) в(о) *+acc*; (*fig*: *time, energy*) вкла́дывать (вложи́ть* *perf*) ◆ *vi*: **~ in** (*COMM*) помеща́ть (помести́ть* *perf*) капита́л в *+acc*; (*fig*: *sth useful*) вкла́дывать (вложи́ть* *perf*) де́ньги в *+acc*; **to ~ sb with sth** облека́ть (обле́чь* *perf*) кого́-н чем-н.
investigate [ɪn'vɛstɪgeɪt] *vt* (*accident, crime*) рассле́довать* (*impf/perf*); (*person*) иссле́довать* (*impf/perf*).
investigation [ɪnvɛstɪ'geɪʃən] *n* рассле́дование.
investigative [ɪn'vɛstɪgeɪtɪv] *adj*: **~ journalism** журнали́стское рассле́дование.
investigator [ɪn'vɛstɪgeɪtə[r]] *n* (*of events, people etc*) иссле́дователь(ница) *m(f)*; **private ~** ча́стный сле́дователь *m*.
investiture [ɪn'vɛstɪtʃə[r]] *n* (*of chancellor*) введе́ние в до́лжность *f*; (*of prince*) пожа́лование зва́ния.
investment [ɪn'vɛstmənt] *n* (*activity*) инвести́рование; (*amount of money*) инвести́ция, вклад.
investment grant *n* (*COMM*) инвестицио́нные субси́дии *fpl*.
investment income *n* (*COMM*) дохо́д с инвести́ций.
investment portfolio *n* (*COMM*) портфе́ль *m*

* marks translations which have irregular inflections. The Russian-English side of the dictionary gives inflectional information.

це́нных бума́г.
investment trust *n* (*COMM*) инвестицио́нный трест.
investor [ɪn'vɛstə'] *n* (*COMM*) инве́стор, вкла́дчик.
inveterate [ɪn'vɛtərət] *adj* (*liar, cheat etc*) неисправи́мый (неисправи́м); (*smoker*) зая́длый; (*dislike etc*) да́вний*.
invidious [ɪn'vɪdɪəs] *adj* (*task, job*) неприя́тный* (неприя́тен); (*comparison, decision*) несправедли́вый (несправедли́в).
invigilator [ɪn'vɪdʒɪleɪtə'] *n* (*in exam*) *экзамена́тор, следя́щий за тем, что́бы студе́нты не спи́сывали во вре́мя экза́менов.*
invigorating [ɪn'vɪgəreɪtɪŋ] *adj* (*air*) бодря́щий (бодря́щ); (*experience*) воодушевля́ющий.
invincible [ɪn'vɪnsɪbl] *adj* (*army, team*) непобеди́мый (непобеди́м); (*belief, conviction*) неукроти́мый (неукроти́м).
inviolate [ɪn'vaɪələt] *adj* ненару́шенный (ненару́шен).
invisible [ɪn'vɪzɪbl] *adj* неви́димый (неви́дим) ◆ *cpd* (*COMM*: *exports, earnings, assets*) неви́димый.
invisible mending *n* худо́жественная што́пка.
invitation [ɪnvɪ'teɪʃən] *n* приглаше́ние; **by ~ only** то́лько по приглаше́нию; **at sb's ~** по приглаше́нию кого́-н.
invite [ɪn'vaɪt] *vt* (*to party, meal, meeting etc*) приглаша́ть (пригласи́ть* *perf*); (*discussion, criticism*) побужда́ть (побуди́ть* *perf*); **to ~ sb to do** предлага́ть (предложи́ть* *perf*) кому́-н *+infin*; **to ~ sb to dinner** приглаша́ть (пригласи́ть* *perf*) кого́-н на обе́д
▸ **invite out** *vt* приглаша́ть (пригласи́ть* *perf*).
inviting [ɪn'vaɪtɪŋ] *adj* (*attractive, desirable*) соблазни́тельный* (соблазни́телен).
invoice ['ɪnvɔɪs] *n* (*COMM*) счёт, факту́ра ◆ *vt* выпи́сывать (вы́писать* *perf*) счёт *or* факту́ру *+dat*; **to ~ sb for goods** выпи́сывать (вы́писать* *perf*) счёт *or* факту́ру кому́-н за това́ры.
invoke [ɪn'vəuk] *vt* (*law, principle*) обраща́ться (обрати́ться* *perf*) к *+dat*; (*feelings, memories etc*) взыва́ть (воззва́ть* *perf*) к *+dat*.
involuntary [ɪn'vɔləntrɪ] *adj* (*action, reflex etc*) непроизво́льный* (непроизво́лен).
involve [ɪn'vɔlv] *vt* (*person, thing*: *include, use*) вовлека́ть (вовле́чь* *perf*); (: *concern, affect*) включа́ть (включи́ть* *perf*); **to ~ sb (in sth)** вовлека́ть (вовле́чь* *perf*) кого́-н (во что-н).
involved [ɪn'vɔlvd] *adj* (*complicated*) запу́танный* (запу́тан); (*thing required*: *in task, situation etc*) включённый (включён); **to be ~ in** (*in activity etc*) быть* *(impf)* вовлечённым(-ой) в(о) *+acc*; **to feel ~** быть* *(impf)* вовлечённым; **to become ~ with sb** (*socially*) свя́зываться (связа́ться *perf*) с кем-н; (*emotionally*) увлека́ться (увле́чься* *perf*) кем-н.
involvement [ɪn'vɔlvmənt] *n* (*participation*) прича́стность *f*; (*concern, enthusiasm*) вовлечённость *f*; (*relationship*) связь *f*.
invulnerable [ɪn'vʌlnərəbl] *adj* (*person, ship, building etc*) неуязви́мый (неуязви́м).
inward ['ɪnwəd] *adj* (*thought, feeling*) вну́тренний*; (*movement*) напра́вленный внутрь ◆ *adv* = **inwards**.
inwardly ['ɪnwədlɪ] *adv* внутри́.
inwards ['ɪnwədz] *adv* (*move, face*) внутрь.
I/O *abbr* (*COMPUT*: = *input/output*) ввод-вы́вод.
IOC *n abbr* = *International Olympic Committee.*
iodine ['aɪəudi:n] *n* йод.
IOM *abbr* (*BRIT*: *POST*) = *Isle of Man.*
ion ['aɪən] *n* (*ELEC*) ио́н.
Ionian Sea [aɪ'əunɪən-] *n*: **the ~ ~** Иони́ческое мо́ре.
ioniser ['aɪənaɪzə'] *n* ионизи́рующая устано́вка*.
iota [aɪ'əutə] *n* йо́та.
IOU *n abbr* (= *I owe you*) *просте́йший долгово́й докуме́нт.*
IOW *abbr* (*BRIT*: *POST*) = *Isle of Wight.*
IPA *n abbr* (= *International Phonetic Alphabet*) Междунаро́дная систе́ма транскри́пции.
IQ *n abbr* (= *intelligence quotient*) коэффицие́нт у́мственного разви́тия.
IRA *n abbr* (= *Irish Republican Army*) ИРА= *Ирла́ндская респу́бликанская а́рмия*; (*US*) = *individual retirement account.*
Iran [ɪ'rɑ:n] *n* Ира́н.
Iranian [ɪ'reɪnɪən] *adj* ира́нский* ◆ *n* ира́нец(-нка).
Iraq [ɪ'rɑ:k] *n* Ира́к.
Iraqi [ɪ'rɑ:kɪ] *adj* ира́кский* ◆ *n* жи́тель(ница) *m(f)* Ира́ка.
irascible [ɪ'ræsɪbl] *adj* (*person*) вспы́льчивый (вспы́льчив).
irate [aɪ'reɪt] *adj* (*person, letter etc*) разгне́ванный* (разгне́ван).
Ireland ['aɪələnd] *n* Ирла́ндия; **the Republic of ~** Ирла́ндская Респу́блика.
iris ['aɪrɪs] (*pl* **~es**) *n* (*ANAT*) ра́дужная оболо́чка* (гла́за); (*BOT*) и́рис.
Irish ['aɪrɪʃ] *adj* ирла́ндский*; **the ~** ирла́ндцы.
Irishman ['aɪrɪʃmən] *irreg n* ирла́ндец*.
Irish Sea *n*: **the ~ ~** Ирла́ндское мо́ре.
Irishwoman ['aɪrɪʃwumən] *irreg n* ирла́ндка.
irk [ə:k] *vt* (*person*) раздража́ть *(impf)*.
irksome ['ə:ksəm] *adj* надое́дливый (надое́длив).
IRN *n abbr* = *Independent Radio News.*
IRO *n abbr* (*US*) = *International Refugee Organization.*
iron ['aɪən] *n* (*metal*) желе́зо *no pl*; (*for clothes*) утю́г ◆ *cpd* желе́зный ◆ *vt* (*clothes*) гла́дить* (погла́дить* *perf*)
▸ **iron out** *vt* (*fig*: *problems*) ула́живать (ула́дить* *perf*).
Iron Curtain *n* (*POL*: *formerly*): **the ~ ~**

железный занавес.
iron foundry *n* чугунолитейный цех.
ironic(al) [aɪ'rɔnɪk(l)] *adj* иронический.
ironically [aɪ'rɔnɪklɪ] *adv* (*say, enquire etc*) иронично; ~, **the intelligence chief was the last to find out** ирония в том, что шеф разведки узнал последним.
ironing ['aɪənɪŋ] *n* (*activity*) глаженье; (*clothes*) бельё для глаженья.
ironing board *n* гладильная доска.
iron lung *n* (*MED*) аппарат (для искусственного дыхания).
ironmonger ['aɪənmʌŋgə'] *n* (*BRIT*) торговец скобяными изделиями.
ironmonger's (shop) ['aɪənmʌŋgəz-] *n* магазин скобяных изделий.
iron ore *n* железная руда.
irons ['aɪəns] *npl* (*chains*) кандалы *pl*; **to clap sb in** ~ заковывать (заковать *perf*) кого-н в кандалы.
ironworks ['aɪənwə:ks] *n* чугунолитейный завод.
irony ['aɪrənɪ] *n* ирония.
irrational [ɪ'ræʃənl] *adj* (*feelings, behaviour*) нерациональный* (нерационален), неразумный* (неразумен).
irreconcilable [ɪrɛkən'saɪləbl] *adj* (*ideas, conflict*) непримиримый (непримирим).
irredeemable [ɪrɪ'di:məbl] *adj* (*COMM*) не подлежащий погашению *or* выкупу; (*fault, character*) неисправимый (неисправим).
irrefutable [ɪrɪ'fju:təbl] *adj* (*fact, argument*) неопровержимый (неопровержим).
irregular [ɪ'rɛgjulə'] *adj* (*surface*) неровный* (неровен); (*pattern*) неправильной формы; (*action, event*) нерегулярный* (нерегулярен); (*behaviour*) распущенный; (*LING*: *verb etc*) неправильный.
irregularity [ɪrɛgju'lærɪtɪ] *n* (*see adj*) неровность *f*; неправильность *f*; нерегулярность *f*; распущенность *f*.
irrelevance [ɪ'rɛləvəns] *n* неуместность *f*.
irrelevant [ɪ'rɛləvənt] *adj* неуместный.
irreligious [ɪrɪ'lɪdʒəs] *adj* неверующий*.
irreparable [ɪ'rɛprəbl] *adj* (*harm, damage etc*) непоправимый (непоправим).
irreplaceable [ɪrɪ'pleɪsəbl] *adj* (*antique, wedding ring etc*) незаменимый (незаменим).
irrepressible [ɪrɪ'prɛsəbl] *adj* (*person, good humour etc*) неудержимый (неудержим).
irreproachable [ɪrɪ'prəutʃəbl] *adj* (*behaviour, character*) безупречный* (безупречен).
irresistible [ɪrɪ'zɪstɪbl] *adj* (*urge, desire*) непреодолимый (непреодолим); (*person, thing*) неотразимый (неотразим).
irresolute [ɪ'rɛzəlu:t] *adj* (*person*) нерешительный* (нерешителен).
irrespective [ɪrɪ'spɛktɪv] *prep*: ~ **of** независимо от +*gen*.
irresponsible [ɪrɪ'spɔnsɪbl] *adj* (*person, action*) безответственный* (безответствен).
irretrievable [ɪrɪ'tri:vəbl] *adj* (*object*) безвозвратный* (безвозвратен); (*loss, damage*) непоправимый (непоправим).
irreverent [ɪ'rɛvərnt] *adj* (*person, comment etc*) непочтительный* (непочтителен).
irrevocable [ɪ'rɛvəkəbl] *adj* (*action, decision*) бесповоротный* (бесповоротен).
irrigate ['ɪrɪgeɪt] *vt* орошать (оросить* *perf*).
irrigation [ɪrɪ'geɪʃən] *n* (*AGR*) орошение, ирригация.
irritable ['ɪrɪtəbl] *adj* раздражительный* (раздражителен).
irritant ['ɪrɪtənt] *n* раздражитель *m*.
irritate ['ɪrɪteɪt] *vt* (*also MED*) раздражать (раздражить *perf*).
irritating ['ɪrɪteitɪŋ] *adj* раздражающий.
irritation [ɪrɪ'teɪʃən] *n* (*also MED*) раздражение; (*annoying thing*) раздражающий фактор.
IRS *n abbr* (*US*) = **Internal Revenue Service**.
is [ɪz] *vb see* **be**.
ISA *n abbr* (= *Individual Savings Account*) Индивидуальный сберегательныи счёт.
ISBN *n abbr* (= *International Standard Book Number*) ISBN.
ISDN *abbr* (= *integrated services digital network*) Цифровая сеть с комплексными услугами.
Islam ['ɪzlɑ:m] *n* (*REL*) ислам; (*Islamic countries*) мусульманские страны *fpl*.
Islamic [ɪz'læmɪk] *adj* мусульманский*.
island ['aɪlənd] *n* остров*; (*also*: **traffic** ~) островок безопасности.
islander ['aɪləndə'] *n* островитянин*(-нка).
isle [aɪl] *n* остров*.
isn't ['ɪznt] = **is not**.
isobar ['aɪsəubɑ:'] *n* изобара.
isolate ['aɪsəleɪt] *vt* изолировать* (*impf/perf*); (*substance*) выделять (выделить *perf*).
isolated ['aɪsəleɪtɪd] *adj* (*place, person*) изолированный* (изолирован); (*incident*) отдельный.
isolation [aɪsə'leɪʃən] *n* изоляция.
isolationism [aɪsə'leɪʃənɪzəm] *n* изоляционизм.
isotope ['aɪsəutəup] *n* (*PHYS*) изотоп.
ISP *abbr* (= *Internet service provider*) компания-провайдер, предоставляющая доступ к Сеть.
Israel ['ɪzreɪl] *n* Израиль *m*.
Israeli [ɪz'reɪlɪ] *adj* израильский* ◆ *n* (*person*) израильтянин*(-нка).
issue ['ɪʃu:] *n* (*problem, subject*) вопрос; (*most important part*) суть *f*; (*of book, stamps etc*) выпуск; (*LAW, old*: *offspring*) потомок* ◆ *vt* (*statement, newspaper*) издавать* (издать* *perf*); (*rations, equipment, documents*) выдавать* (выдать* *perf*) ◆ *vi*: **to** ~ **from**

* marks translations which have irregular inflections. The Russian-English side of the dictionary gives inflectional information.

(*liquid, gas*) вытека́ть (вы́течь* *perf*) из *+gen*; (*sound, smell*) исходи́ть* *(impf)* из/от *+gen*; **to be at** ~ быть* *(impf)* предме́том обсужде́ния; **to avoid the** ~ обходи́ть* (обойти́* *perf*) суть де́ла; **to confuse** *or* **obscure the** ~ затемня́ть (затемни́ть *perf*) суть вопро́са; **to ~ sth to sb** выдава́ть* (вы́дать* *perf*) что-н кому́-н; **to ~ sb with sth** снабжа́ть (снабди́ть* *perf*) кого́-н чем-н; **to take ~ with sb (over)** начина́ть (нача́ть* *perf*) спо́рить с кем-н (о *+prp*); **to make an ~ of sth** де́лать (сде́лать *perf*) исто́рию из чего́-н.

issued capital ['ɪʃu:d-] *n* (*COMM*) вы́пущенный акционе́рный капита́л.

Istanbul [ɪstæn'bu:l] *n* Стамбу́л.

isthmus ['ɪsməs] *n* переше́ек.

IT *n abbr* = **information technology**.

KEYWORD

it [ɪt] *pron* ***1*** (*specific subject*) он (*f* она́, *nt* оно́); (*direct object*) его́ (*f* её); (*indirect object*) ему́ (*f* ей); (*after prep*: *+gen*) его́ (*f* её); (: *+dat*) ему́ (*f* ей); (: *+instr*) им (*f* ей); (: *+prp*) нём (*f* ней); **where is your car? – it's in the garage** где Ва́ша маши́на? – она́ в гараже́; **I like this hat, whose is it?** мне нра́вится э́та шля́па, чья она́?; **have you got the dictionary with you? – no, I gave it to Mary** у Вас с собо́й слова́рь? – нет, я дал его́ Мэ́ри; **this pen is fine, I wrote with it yesterday** э́та ру́чка рабо́тает, я писа́л е́ю вчера́

2 э́то; (: *indirect object*) э́тому; **what kind of car is it? – it's a Lada** кака́я э́то маши́на? – э́то Ла́да; **who is it? – it's me** кто э́то? – э́то я

3 (*after prep*: *+gen*) э́того; (: *+dat*) э́тому; (: *+instr*) э́тим; (: *+prp*) э́том; **I spoke to him about it** я говори́л с ним об э́том; **that's just it!** вот и́менно!; **why is it that ...** почему́ же тогда́ ...; **what is it?** (*what's wrong*) что тако́е?; **that's it for today** на сего́дная всё

4 (*impersonal*): **it's raining** идёт дождь; **it's cold today** сего́дня хо́лодно; **it's interesting that ...** интере́сно, что ...; **it's 6 o'clock** сейча́с 6 часо́в; **it's the 10th of August** сего́дня 10-ое а́вгуста.

ITA *n abbr* (*BRIT*: = *initial teaching alphabet*) *алфави́т, испо́льзуемый при обуче́нии чте́нию.*

Italian [ɪ'tæljən] *adj* италья́нский* ◆ *n* (*person*) италья́нец(-нка); (*LING*) италья́нский* язы́к*; **the ~s** италья́нцы.

italics [ɪ'tælɪks] *npl* (*TYP*) курси́в *msg*.

Italy ['ɪtəlɪ] *n* Ита́лия.

itch [ɪtʃ] *n* (*irritation*) зуд ◆ *vi* (*part of body*) чеса́ться* *(impf)*; **I am ~ing all over** у меня́ всё че́шется; **he was ~ing to know our secret** ему́ не терпе́лось узна́ть наш секре́т.

itchy ['ɪtʃɪ] *adj* (*skin*) зудя́щий; **I feel all** ~ у меня́ всё че́шется; **my back is** ~ у меня́ че́шется спина́.

it'd ['ɪtd] = **it had, it would**.

item ['aɪtəm] *n* (*one thing*: *of list, collection*) предме́т; (*on agenda*) пункт; (*also*: **news** ~) сообще́ние; **~s of clothing** предме́ты оде́жды.

itemize ['aɪtəmaɪz] *vt* (*list*) составля́ть (соста́вить* *perf*) спи́сок *+gen*.

itemized bill ['aɪtəmaɪzd-] *n* *счёт с указа́нием сто́имости ка́ждой ве́щи и́ли ка́ждого ви́да услу́г.*

itinerant [ɪ'tɪnərənt] *adj* (*labourer, salesman, priest etc*) стра́нствующий.

itinerary [aɪ'tɪnərərɪ] *n* маршру́т.

it'll ['ɪtl] = **it shall, it will**.

ITN *n abbr* (*BRIT*: *TV*) = *Independent Television News*.

its [ɪts] *adj* его/её; свой/своя́/своё; *see also* **my** ◆ *pron* его́/её; сво́й/своя́/своё; *see also* **mine**[1].

it's [ɪts] = **it has, it is**.

itself [ɪt'sɛlf] *pron* (*reflexive*) себя́*; (*emphatic*) он сам/она́ сама́/оно́ само́.

ITV *n abbr* (*BRIT*: *TV*) = *Independent Television*.

IUD *n abbr* (= *intrauterine device*) внутрима́точное противозача́точное сре́дство.

I've [aɪv] = **I have**.

ivory ['aɪvərɪ] *n* (*substance*) слоно́вая кость* *f*; (*colour*) цвет слоно́вой ко́сти.

Ivory Coast *n* Бе́рег Слоно́вой Ко́сти.

ivory tower *n* (*fig*) ба́шня из слоно́вой ко́сти.

ivy ['aɪvɪ] *n* (*BOT*) плющ*.

Ivy League *n* (*US*: *SCOL*) *гру́ппа старе́йших университе́тов США.*

~ J, j ~

J, j [dʒeɪ] *n* (*letter*) *10-ая бу́ква англи́йского алфави́та.*
JA *n abbr* = **judge advocate**.
J/A *abbr* = **joint account**.
jab [dʒæb] *vt* (*with finger, stick etc*) ты́кать* (ткнуть *perf*) ◆ *n* (*BRIT: inf: MED*) уко́л ◆ *vi*: **to ~ at** стуча́ть *(impf)* по *+dat*; **to ~ sth into sth** втыка́ть* (воткну́ть *perf*) что-н в что-н.
jack [dʒæk] *n* (*AUT*) домкра́т; (*SPORT*) *ма́лый шар, слу́жащий мише́нью для игро́ков в шары́*; (*CARDS*) вале́т
▸ **jack in** *vt* (*inf*) завя́зывать (завяза́ть* *perf*) с *+instr*
▸ **jack up** *vt* (*AUT*) поднима́ть (подня́ть* *perf*) домкра́том.
jackal ['dʒækl] *n* шака́л.
jackass ['dʒækæs] *n* (*also fig*) осёл*.
jackdaw ['dʒækdɔ:] *n* га́лка*.
jacket ['dʒækɪt] *n* (*of suit*) пиджа́к*; (*casual*) ку́ртка*; (*of book*) суперобло́жка; **potatoes in their ~s, jacket potatoes** карто́шка в мунди́ре.
jack-in-the-box ['dʒækɪnðəbɔks] *n* чёртик в табаке́рке.
jackknife ['dʒæknaɪf] *n* складно́й нож* ◆ *vi*: **the lorry ~d** грузови́к занеси́ло.
jack of all trades *n*: **he's a ~ ~ ~ ~** он ма́стер на все ру́ки.
jack plug *n* ште́ккер.
jackpot ['dʒækpɔt] *n* куш; **to hit the ~** (*fig*) срыва́ть (сорва́ть *perf*) куш.
jacuzzi [dʒə'ku:zɪ] *n* „джаку́зи" *m ind* (*ва́нна, в кото́рой под напо́ром циркули́рует вода́*).
jade [dʒeɪd] *n* нефри́т.
jaded ['dʒeɪdɪd] *adj* утомлённый (утомлён) и равноду́шный (равноду́шен).
JAG *n abbr* (= *Judge Advocate General*) *гла́вный прави́тельственный сове́тник по вое́нно-юриди́ческим вопро́сам.*
jagged ['dʒægɪd] *adj* зу́бчатый.
jaguar ['dʒægjuəʳ] *n* ягуа́р.
jail [dʒeɪl] *n* тюрьма́* ◆ *vt* заключа́ть (заключи́ть *perf*) в тюрьму́.
jailbird ['dʒeɪlbə:d] *n* (*inf*) уголо́вник.
jailbreak ['dʒeɪlbreɪk] *n* побе́г из тюрьмы́.
jalopy [dʒə'lɔpɪ] *n* (*inf*) драндуле́т.
jam [dʒæm] *n* (*preserve*) джем; (*conserve*) варе́нье; (*also: traffic ~*) про́бка* ◆ *vt* (*passage*) забива́ть (заби́ть* *perf*); (*mechanism*) закли́нивать (закли́нить *perf*); (*RADIO*) глуши́ть (заглуши́ть *perf*) ◆ *vi* (*drawer*) застрева́ть (застря́ть* *perf*); (*mechanism*): **the engine/rifle has ~med** зае́ло *or* закли́нило мото́р/ружьё; **I'm in a real ~** (*inf: difficulty*) я (здо́рово) влип; **to get sb out of a ~** (*inf*) помога́ть (помо́чь *perf*) кому́-н вы́браться из переде́лки; **to ~ sth into sth** запи́хивать (запихну́ть *perf*) что-н во что-н; **the telephone lines are ~med** все ли́нии (свя́зи) перегру́жены.
Jamaica [dʒə'meɪkə] *n* Яма́йка.
Jamaican [dʒə'meɪkən] *adj* яма́йский* ◆ *n* жи́тель(ница) *m(f)* Яма́йки.
jamb ['dʒæm] *n* кося́к*.
jamboree [dʒæmbə'ri:] *n* гуля́нье*.
jam-packed [dʒæm'pækt] *adj*: **~ (with)** битко́м наби́тый (наби́т) (*+instr*).
jam session *n* джем-се́йшен.
Jan. *abbr* = **January**.
jangle ['dʒæŋgl] *vi* (*keys, bracelets etc*) бренча́ть *(impf)*.
janitor ['dʒænɪtəʳ] *n* (*caretaker*) вахтёр(ша).
January ['dʒænjuərɪ] *n* янва́рь* *m*; *see also* **July**.
Japan [dʒə'pæn] *n* Япо́ния.
Japanese [dʒæpə'ni:z] *adj* япо́нский* ◆ *n inv* (*person*) япо́нец*(-нка*); (*LING*) япо́нский* язы́к*.
jar [dʒɑ:ʳ] *n* ба́нка* ◆ *vi* (*sound*) ре́зать* *(impf)* слух; (*colours*) ре́зать* *(impf)* глаза́ ◆ *vt* (*fig*) потряса́ть (потрясти́* *perf*).
jargon ['dʒɑ:gən] *n* жарго́н.
jarring ['dʒɑ:rɪŋ] *adj* (*sound*) ре́жущий у́хо; (*colour*) ре́жущий глаз.
Jas. *abbr* = *James*.
jasmine ['dʒæzmɪn] *n* жасми́н.
jaundice ['dʒɔ:ndɪs] *n* желтуха́.
jaundiced ['dʒɔ:ndɪst] *adj*: **he has a very ~ view of politics** он смо́трит на поли́тику весьма́ пессимисти́чески.
jaunt [dʒɔ:nt] *n* вы́лазка*.
jaunty ['dʒɔ:ntɪ] *adj* (*tone, step*) бо́йкий*.
Java ['dʒɑ:və] *n* Я́ва.

* marks translations which have irregular inflections. The Russian-English side of the dictionary gives inflectional information.

javelin ['dʒævlɪn] *n* копьё*.
jaw [dʒɔ:] *n* чéлюсть* *f*.
jawbone ['dʒɔ:bəun] *n* челюстнáя кость* *f*.
jay [dʒeɪ] *n* сóйка*.
jaywalker ['dʒeɪwɔ:kə'] *n* недисциплинúрованный пешехóд.
jazz [dʒæz] *n* джаз
▸ **jazz up** (*inf*) ◆ *vt* (*party, image etc*) оживлять (оживить* *perf*); (*food*) придавáть* (придáть* *perf*) пикáнтность *+dat*.
jazz band *n* джáзовый оркéстр, джаз-бáнд.
JCB® *n* (колёсный) экскавáтор.
JCS *n abbr* (*US*: = *Joint Chiefs of Staff*) Комитéт начáльников штабóв.
JD *n abbr* (*US*: = *Doctor of Laws*) доктóр правовéдения; (= *Justice Department*) Министéрство юстúции.
jealous ['dʒɛləs] *adj* ревнúвый (ревнúв); **to be ~ of** (*possessive*) ревновáть *(impf)* к *+dat*; (*envious*) завúдовать *(impf) +dat*.
jealously ['dʒɛləslɪ] *adv* (*enviously*) ревнúво; (*watchfully*) рéвностно.
jealousy ['dʒɛləsɪ] *n* (*resentment*) рéвность *f*; (*envy*) зáвисть *f*.
jeans [dʒi:nz] *npl* джúнсы *pl*.
Jeep® [dʒi:p] *n* джип.
jeer [dʒɪə'] *vi*: **to ~ (at)** (*mock, scoff*) насмехáться *(impf)* (над *+instr*), высмéивать (вы́смеять *perf*).
jeering ['dʒɪərɪŋ] *adj* насмéшливый ◆ *n* насмéшки* *fpl*.
jeers ['dʒɪəz] *npl* улюлю́канье *ntsg*.
jelly ['dʒɛlɪ] *n* желé *nt ind*; (*US*) джем.
jellyfish ['dʒɛlɪfɪʃ] *n* медýза.
jeopardize ['dʒɛpədaɪz] *vt* подвергáть (подвéргнуть* *perf*) опáсности, стáвить* (постáвить* *perf*) под угрóзу.
jeopardy ['dʒɛpədɪ] *n*: **to be in ~** быть* *(impf)* в опáсности.
jerk [dʒə:k] *n* (*jolt*) толчóк*, рывóк*; (*inf*: *idiot*) болвáн ◆ *vt* дёргать (дёрнуть *perf*), рванýть *(perf)* ◆ *vi* дёргаться (дёрнуться *perf*); **the car ~ed to a halt** машúна рéзко затормозúла.
jerkin ['dʒə:kɪn] *n* безрукáвка.
jerky ['dʒə:kɪ] *adj* сýдорожный (сýдорожен).
jerry-built ['dʒɛrɪbɪlt] *adj* пострóенный (пострóен) кóе-как *or* на скóрую рýку.
jerry can ['dʒɛrɪ-] *n* канúстра.
Jersey ['dʒə:zɪ] *n* Джéрси *nt ind*.
jersey ['dʒə:zɪ] *n* (*pullover*) свúтер; (*fabric*) джерсú *nt ind*.
Jerusalem [dʒə'ru:sləm] *n* Иерусалúм.
jest [dʒɛst] *n* шýтка.
jester ['dʒɛstə'] *n* (*HISTORY*) шут*.
Jesus ['dʒi:zəs] *n* (*REL*) Иисýс; **~ Christ** Иисýс Христóс.
jet [dʒɛt] *n* (*of gas, liquid*) струя́*; (*AVIAT*) реактúвный самолёт; (*MINERALOGY*) гагáт.
jet-black ['dʒɛt'blæk] *adj* (*hair*) чёрный как смоль; (*eyes*) агáтовый.
jet engine *n* реактúвный двúгатель *m*.
jet lag *n нарушéние сýточного режúма органúзма пóсле длúтельного полёта.*
jet-propelled ['dʒɛtprə'pɛld] *adj* реактúвный.
jetsam ['dʒɛtsəm] *n* плавнúк.
jet-setter ['dʒɛtsɛtə'] *n человéк, разъезжáющий по свéту.*
jettison ['dʒɛtɪsn] *vt* выбрáсывать (вы́бросить* *perf*) за борт.
jetty ['dʒɛtɪ] *n* причáл.
Jew [dʒu:] *n* еврéй(ка*).
jewel ['dʒu:əl] *n* (*also fig*) драгоцéнный кáмень* *m*; (*in watch*) кáмень.
jeweller ['dʒu:ələ'] (*US* **jeweler**) *n* ювелúр.
jeweller's (shop) *n* ювелúрный магазúн.
jewellery ['dʒu:əlrɪ] (*US* **jewelry**) *n* драгоцéнности *fpl*.
Jewess ['dʒu:ɪs] *n* еврéйка, жидóвка (*пренебр*).
Jewish ['dʒu:ɪʃ] *adj* еврéйский*.
JFK *n abbr* (*US*) = *John Fitzgerald Kennedy International Airport.*
jib [dʒɪb] *n* (*NAUT*) клúвер*; (*of crane*) стрелá* ◆ *vi* (*horse*) упирáться (упере́ться* *perf*), артáчиться *(impf)*; **to ~ at doing** наотрéз отказáться *(perf) +infin*.
jibe [dʒaɪb] *n* = **gibe**.
jiffy ['dʒɪfɪ] *n* (*inf*): **in a ~** мúгом.
jig [dʒɪg] *n* джúга.
jigsaw ['dʒɪgsɔ:] *n* (*also*: **~ puzzle**) головолóмка (*в вúде картúны, кусóчки котóрой нýжно сложúть вмéсте*); (*tool*) ажýрная пилá*.
jilt [dʒɪlt] *vt* (*person*) бросáть (брóсить* *perf*).
jingle ['dʒɪŋgl] *n* (*for advert*) *корóткая незамысловáтая мелóдия в реклáме* ◆ *vi* звенéть *(impf)*.
jingoism ['dʒɪŋgəuɪzəm] *n* ура-патриотúзм.
jinx [dʒɪŋks] *n* (*inf*): **he is a ~** у негó дурнóй глаз.
jitters ['dʒɪtəz] *npl* (*inf*): **she's got the ~** её трясёт.
jittery ['dʒɪtərɪ] *adj* (*inf*) нéрвный* (нéрвен).
jiujitsu [dʒu:'dʒɪtsu:] *n* джúу-джúтсу *nt ind*.
job [dʒɔb] *n* (*employment*) рабóта; (*task*) дéло*; (*inf*: *difficulty*): **I had a ~ getting here!** я с трудóм добрáлся сюдá!; **it's not my ~** это не моё дéло; **a part-time/full-time ~** рабóта на почасовóй/пóлной стáвке; **he's only doing his ~** он всегó-нáвсего выполняет свой обязанности; **it's a good ~ that ...** хорошó ещё, что ...; **just the ~!** сáмое то!
jobber ['dʒɔbə'] *n* (*BRIT*) джóббер.
jobbing ['dʒɔbɪŋ] *adj* (*BRIT*): **~ workman** шабáшник.
Jobcentre ['dʒɔbsɛntə'] *n* (*BRIT*) бюрó *nt ind* по трудоустрóйству.
job creation scheme *n* прогрáмма зáнятости.
job description *n* описáние служéбных обязанностей.
jobless ['dʒɔblɪs] *adj* безрабóтный*; **the ~** *npl* безрабóтные *pl adj*.

job lot *n* *пáртия дешёвых товáров, продающихся óптом.*
job satisfaction *n* удовлетворённость *f* рабóтой.
job security *n* гарáнтия рабóты.
job sharing *n* *ситуáция, когдá два человéка дéлят рабóчее мéсто.*
job specification *n* пéречень *m* служéбных обязанностей.
jock [dʒɔk] *n* (*US*: *inf*) спортсмéн.
jockey ['dʒɔkɪ] *n* жокéй ◆ *vi*: **to ~ for position** сопéрничать *(impf)*.
jockey box *n* (*US*: *AUT*) перчáточный ящик, бардачóк (*разг*).
jocular ['dʒɔkjulə^r] *adj* (*person*) весёлый* (вéсел); (*remark*) шутли́вый (шутли́в).
jog [dʒɔg] *vt* толкáть (толкнýть *perf*) ◆ *vi* бéгать *(impf)* трусцóй; **to ~ sb's memory** подстёгивать (подстегнýть *perf*) чью-н пáмять
▸ **jog along** *vi* мéдленно продвигáться *(impf)*.
jogger ['dʒɔgə^r] *n* бегýн* (*трусцóй*).
jogging ['dʒɔgɪŋ] *n* бег трусцóй.
Johannesburg [dʒəu'hænɪsbə:g] *n* Йохáннесбург.
john [dʒɔn] *n* (*inf*: *US*) туалéт.
join [dʒɔɪn] *vt* (*queue*) вставáть* (встать* *perf*) в +*acc*; (*organization*) вступáть (вступи́ть* *perf*) в +*acc*; (*put together*: *things, places*) соединя́ть (соедини́ть *perf*); (*meet*: *group of people*) присоединя́ться (присоедини́ться *perf*) к +*dat* ◆ *vi* (*rivers*) сливáться (сли́ться* *perf*); (*roads*) сходи́ться (сойти́сь* *perf*) ◆ *n* сочленéние; **to ~ forces (with)** (*fig*) объединя́ть (объедини́ть *perf*) усилия (с +*instr*); **will you ~ us for dinner?** не хоти́те с нáми поýжинать?; **I'll ~ you later** я присоединю́сь к Вам пóзже
▸ **join in** *vi* присоединя́ться (присоедини́ться *perf*) ◆ *vt fus* (*work, discussion etc*) принимáть (приня́ть* *perf*) учáстие в +*prp*
▸ **join up** *vi* (*meet*) соединя́ться (соедини́ться *perf*); (*MIL*) поступáть (поступи́ть* *perf*) на воéнную слýжбу.
joiner ['dʒɔɪnə^r] *n* (*BRIT*) столя́р*.
joinery ['dʒɔɪnərɪ] *n* (*BRIT*) столя́рное ремеслó*.
joint [dʒɔɪnt] *n* (*TECH*) сочленéние, стык; (*ANAT*) сустáв; (*BRIT*: *CULIN*) кусóк* (*мя́са*); (*inf*: *place*) притóн; (: *of cannabis*) скрýтка с марихуáной ◆ *adj* совмéстный.
joint account *n* совмéстный счёт (*в бáнке*).
jointly ['dʒɔɪntlɪ] *adv* совмéстно.
joint owners *npl* совладéльцы *mpl*.
joint ownership *n* совмéстное владéние.
joint-stock bank ['dʒɔɪntstɔk-] *n* акционéрный банк.
joint-stock company *n* акционéрная компáния.
joint venture *n* совмéстное предприя́тие.
joist [dʒɔɪst] *n* бáлка*.
joke [dʒəuk] *n* (*gag*) шýтка*, анекдóт; (*also*: **practical ~**) рóзыгрыш ◆ *vi* шути́ть* (пошути́ть* *perf*); **to play a ~ on** шути́ть* (пошути́ть* *perf*) над +*instr*, сыгрáть *(perf)* шýтку с +*instr*.
joker ['dʒəukə^r] *n* (*person*) шýтник; (*CARDS*) джóкер.
joking ['dʒəukɪŋ] *adj* (*remark*) шýточный.
jokingly ['dʒəukɪŋlɪ] *adv* в шýтку.
jollity ['dʒɔlɪtɪ] *n* жизнерáдостность *f*.
jolly ['dʒɔlɪ] *adj* (*merry*) весёлый* (вéсел) ◆ *adv* (*BRIT*: *inf*) óчень ◆ *vt* (*BRIT*): **to ~ sb along** ободря́ть *(impf)* когó-н; **~ good!** óчень хорошó!, здóрово!
jolt [dʒəult] *n* (*jerk*) толчóк*; (*shock*) потрясéние ◆ *vt* (*physically*) тряхнýть *or* встря́хивать (встряхнýть *perf*); (*emotionally*) потрясáть (потрясти́* *perf*).
Jordan [dʒɔ:dən] *n* (*country*) Иордáния; (*river*) Иордáн.
Jordanian [dʒɔ:'deɪnɪən] *adj* иордáнский* ◆ *n* иордáнец*(-нка*).
joss stick ['dʒɔs-] *n* ароматическая пáлочка*.
jostle ['dʒɔsl] *vt* (*subj*: *passers-by etc*) толкáть (толкнýть *perf*), растáлкивать (растолкáть *perf*) ◆ *vi* толкáться *(impf)*.
jot [dʒɔt] *n*: **not one ~** ни кáпли, нисколько
▸ **jot down** *vt* помечáть (помéтить* *perf*).
jotter ['dʒɔtə^r] *n* (*BRIT*) блокнóт.
journal ['dʒə:nl] *n* (*periodical*) журнáл; (*diary*) днéвник*.
journalese [dʒə:nə'li:z] *n* (*pej*) газéтный штамп.
journalism ['dʒə:nəlɪzəm] *n* журнали́стика.
journalist ['dʒə:nəlɪst] *n* журнали́ст(ка*).
journey ['dʒə:nɪ] *n* (*trip, route*) поéздка*; (*distance covered*) путь* *m*, дорóга ◆ *vi* путешéствовать *(impf)*; **a five-hour ~** пятичасовáя поéздка; **return ~** обрáтный путь*, обрáтная дорóга.
jovial ['dʒəuvɪəl] *adj* бóдрый, жизне-рáдостный.
jowl [dʒaul] *n* чéлюсть* *f*.
joy [dʒɔɪ] *n* рáдость *f*.
joyful ['dʒɔɪful] *adj* рáдостный* (рáдостен).
joyride ['dʒɔɪraɪd] *n* *катáние на укрáденной маши́не.*
joyrider ['dʒɔɪraɪdə^r] *n* *человéк, котóрый угоняет маши́ны и катáется на них.*
joyriding ['dʒɔɪraɪdɪŋ] *n* ездá (*обы́чно на ýгнанном автомоби́ле*).
joystick ['dʒɔɪstɪk] *n* (*AVIAT*) рычáг* управлéния; (*COMPUT*) джóйстик.
JP *n abbr* = **Justice of the Peace**.
Jr. *abbr* (*in names*) = **junior**.
JTPA *n abbr* (*US*) = *Job Training Partnership Act*.

jubilant ['dʒu:bɪlnt] *adj* лику́ющий.
jubilation [dʒu:bɪ'leɪʃən] *n* ликова́ние.
jubilee ['dʒu:bɪli:] *n* (*anniversary*) юбиле́й; **silver/golden** ~ 25-ле́тний/50-ле́тний юбиле́й.
judge [dʒʌdʒ] *n* судья́* *m* ◆ *vt* (*LAW*) выноси́ть* (вы́нести* *perf*) пригово́р; (*competition, person etc*) суди́ть* *(impf)*; (*consider, estimate*) оце́нивать (оцени́ть* *perf*) ◆ *vi*: **judging** *or* **to** ~ **by his expression** су́дя по его́ выраже́нию; **she's a good** ~ **of character** она́ хорошо́ разбира́ется в лю́дях; **I'll be the** ~ **of that** ну́ э́то уж мне суди́ть; **I ~d it necessary to inform him** я посчита́л ну́жным сообщи́ть ему́ об э́том; **as far as I can** ~ наско́лько я могу́ суди́ть.
judge advocate *n* (*MIL*) вое́нный прокуро́р.
judg(e)ment ['dʒʌdʒmənt] *n* (*LAW*) пригово́р, реше́ние суда́; (*view*) сужде́ние; (*discernment*) рассуди́тельность *f*; **in my** ~ по моему́ мне́нию; **to pass** ~ **(on)** (*LAW*) выноси́ть* (вы́нести* *perf*) реше́ние (о *+prp*); (*fig*) суди́ть* *(impf)* (о *+prp*).
judicial [dʒu:'dɪʃl] *adj* (*LAW*) суде́бный; (*fig*) рассуди́тельный* (рассуди́телен); ~ **review** суде́бное разбира́тельство.
judiciary [dʒu:'dɪʃɪərɪ] *n*: **the** ~ суде́бные о́рганы *mpl*.
judicious [dʒu:'dɪʃəs] *adj* благоразу́мный* (благоразу́мен).
judo ['dʒu:dəu] *n* дзюдо́ *nt ind*.
jug [dʒʌg] *n* кувши́н.
jugged hare ['dʒʌgd-] *n* (*BRIT*) ≈ жарко́е *nt adj* из за́йца.
juggernaut ['dʒʌgənɔ:t] *n* (*BRIT*) многото́нный грузови́к*.
juggle ['dʒʌgl] *vi* (*also fig*) жонгли́ровать *(impf)* ◆ *vt* (*fig*) жонгли́ровать *(impf)* *+instr*; **to** ~ **with sth** жонгли́ровать *(impf)* чем-н.
juggler ['dʒʌglə^r] *n* жонглёр.
Jugoslav *etc* ['ju:gəu'slɑ:v] = **Yugoslav** *etc*.
jugular ['dʒʌgjulə^r] *n* (*also:* ~ **vein**) яре́мная ве́на.
juice [dʒu:s] *n* сок*; (*inf: petrol*) бензи́н.
juicy ['dʒu:sɪ] *adj* со́чный* (со́чен).
jukebox ['dʒu:kbɔks] *n* музыка́льный автома́т.
Jul. *abbr* = **July**.
July [dʒu:'laɪ] *n* ию́ль *m*; **the first of** ~ пе́рвое ию́ля; **on the eleventh of** ~ оди́ннадцатого ию́ля; **in the month of** ~ в ию́ле ме́сяце; **at the beginning/end of** ~ в нача́ле/конце́ ию́ля; **in the middle of** ~ в середи́не ию́ля; **during** ~ в тече́ние ию́ля; **in** ~ в ию́ле; **in** ~ **of next year** в ию́ле сле́дующего го́да; **each** *or* **every** ~ ка́ждый ию́ль; ~ **was wet this year** в э́том году́ ию́ль был дождли́вым.
jumble ['dʒʌmbl] *n* нагроможде́ние; (*BRIT: items for sale*) старьё ◆ *vt* (*also:* ~ **up**) переме́шивать (перемеша́ть *perf*).
jumble sale *n* (*BRIT*) *благотвори́тельная распрода́жа подéржанных веще́й.*
jumbo ['dʒʌmbəu] *n* (*also:* ~ **jet**) реакти́вный аэро́бус.
jumbo-size ['dʒʌmbəusaɪz] *adj* гига́нтский*.
jump [dʒʌmp] *vi* пры́гать (пры́гнуть *perf*); (*start*) подпры́гивать (подпры́гнуть *perf*); (*increase*) подска́кивать (подскочи́ть* *perf*) ◆ *vt* (*fence*) перепры́гивать (перепры́гнуть *perf*), переска́кивать (перескочи́ть* *perf*) ◆ *n* прыжо́к*; (*increase*) скачо́к*; **to** ~ **the queue** (*BRIT*) идти́* (пойти́* *perf*) без о́череди.
▸ **jump about** *vi* суети́ться* *(impf)*
▸ **jump at** *vt fus* (*seize*) ухва́тываться (ухвати́ться *perf*) за *+acc*
▸ **jump down** *vi* спры́гивать (спры́гнуть *perf*)
▸ **jump up** *vi* (*from a seat*) вска́кивать (вскочи́ть* *perf*); (*into the air*) подпры́гивать (подпры́гнуть *perf*).
jumped-up ['dʒʌmptʌp] *adj* (*BRIT: pej*): ~ **office boy** вы́скочка *m*.
jumper ['dʒʌmpə^r] *n* (*BRIT: pullover*) сви́тер, дже́мпер; (*US: dress*) сарафа́н; (*SPORT*) прыгу́н*(ья*).
jumper cables *npl* (*US*) = **jump leads**.
jump leads *npl* (*BRIT*) про́вод большо́го сече́ния (*для пу́ска дви́гателя*).
jump-start ['dʒʌmpstɑ:t] *vt*: **to** ~ **a car** подта́лкивать (подтолкну́ть *perf*) маши́ну, что́бы завести́ её.
jump suit *n* комбинезо́н.
jumpy ['dʒʌmpɪ] *adj* не́рвный.
Jun. *abbr* = **June**.
junction ['dʒʌŋkʃən] *n* (*BRIT: of roads*) пересече́ние; (*RAIL*) у́зел*.
juncture ['dʒʌŋktʃə^r] *n*: **at this** ~ в да́нный моме́нт.
June [dʒu:n] *n* ию́нь *m*; *see also* **July**.
jungle ['dʒʌŋgl] *n* (*also fig*) джу́нгли *pl*.
junior ['dʒu:nɪə^r] *adj* мла́дший* ◆ *n* мла́дший*(-ая) *m(f) adj*; **he's** ~ **to me (by 2 years), he's my** ~ **(by 2 years)** он мла́дше меня́ (на 2 го́да); **he's** ~ **to me** (*seniority*) он мой подчинённый.
junior executive *n* мла́дший* руководя́щий* рабо́тник.
junior high school *n* (*US*) ≈ непо́лная сре́дняя шко́ла.
junior minister *n* (*BRIT*) мла́дший* мини́стр.
junior partner *n* мла́дший* партнёр.
junior school *n* (*BRIT*) *шко́ла для дете́й в во́зрасте от 7 до 11 лет.*
junior sizes *npl* де́тские разме́ры *mpl*.
juniper ['dʒu:nɪpə^r] *n*: ~ **berry** можжеве́льник.
junk [dʒʌŋk] *n* барахло́, хлам; (*ship*) джо́нка* ◆ *vt* (*inf*) выки́дывать (выкину́ть *perf*).
junk bond *n облига́ции, обеща́ющие высо́кие проце́нты, но не даю́щие гара́нтий.*
junket ['dʒʌŋkɪt] *n* (*CULIN*) *сла́дкое моло́чное блю́до*; (*US: inf: pej*): **to go on a** ~ прокати́ться* *(perf)* за казённый счёт.
junk food *n еда́, содержа́щая ма́ло*

питáтельных вещéств.
junkie ['dʒʌŋkɪ] *n* (*inf*) наркомáн.
junk mail *n незапрóшенная реклáма, доставля́емая по пóчте.*
junk room *n* чулáн.
junk shop *n* лáвка* старьёвщика.
Junr *abbr* (*in names*) = **junior.**
junta ['dʒʌntə] *n* хýнта.
Jupiter ['dʒu:pɪtə'] *n* Юпи́тер.
jurisdiction [dʒuərɪs'dɪkʃən] *n* (*LAW*) юрисди́кция; (*ADMIN*) сфéра полномóчий; **it is within/outside my ~** э́то вхóдит/не вхóдит в мои́ полномóчия.
jurisprudence [dʒuərɪs'pru:dəns] *n* юриспрудéнция.
juror ['dʒuərə'] *n* присяжный заседáтель *m.*
jury ['dʒuərɪ] *n* прися́жные *pl adj* (заседáтели).
jury box *n* скамья́* прися́жных.
juryman ['dʒuərɪmən] *irreg n* = **juror.**
just [dʒʌst] *adj* справедли́вый (справедли́в) ◆ *adv* (*exactly*) как раз, и́менно; (*only*) тóлько; (*barely*) едвá; **he's ~ left/done it** он тóлько что ушёл/э́то сдéлал; **~ as I expected** как я и ожидáл; **it's ~ right** э́то как раз то, что нáдо; **~ two o'clock** рóвно два часá; **we were ~ going** *or* **about to go** мы как раз собирáлись уходи́ть; **I was ~ about to phone** я ужé собрáлся позвони́ть; **she's ~ as clever as you** онá столь же умнá, как и ты; **it's ~ as well (that)** ... дáже и хорошó, (что) ...; **~ as he was leaving** как раз когдá он собрáлся уходи́ть; **~ before Christmas** пéред сáмым Рождествóм; **there was ~ enough petrol** едвá хвати́ло бензи́на; **~ here** вот здесь; **he (only) ~ missed** он чуть не попáл; **it's ~ me** э́то (тóлько) я; **it's ~ a mistake** э́то прóсто оши́бка; **~ listen!** ты тóлько послýшай!; **~ ask someone the way** прóсто спроси́ у когó-нибудь дорóгу; **not ~ now** тóлько не сейчáс; **~ a minute!, ~ one moment!** подожди́те!, (однý) минýту!
justice ['dʒʌstɪs] *n* (*LAW: system*) правосýдие; (*rightness*) справедли́вость *f*; (*US: judge*) судья́* *m*; **Lord Chief J~** (*BRIT*) *вторóй по значéнию судья́ в брити́нской систéме правосýдия*; **to do ~ to** (*fig: task, meal, person*) отдавáть* (отдáть* *perf*) дóлжное *+dat.*
Justice of the Peace *n* (*BRIT*) мировóй судья́* *m.*
justifiable [dʒʌstɪ'faɪəbl] *adj* oпрáвданный* (oпрáвдан), обоснóванный (обоснóван).
justifiably [dʒʌstɪ'faɪəblɪ] *adv* oпрáвданно, обоснóванно.
justification [dʒʌstɪfɪ'keɪʃən] *n* (*of action*) оправдáние; (*reason*) основáние; (*TYP*) вырáвнивание строки́.
justify ['dʒʌstɪfaɪ] *vt* oпрáвдывать (оправдáть *perf*); (*text*) вырáвнивать (вы́ровнять *perf*); **to ~ o.s.** oпрáвдываться (оправдáться *perf*); **to be justified in doing** имéть (*impf*) все основáния *+infin.*
justly ['dʒʌstlɪ] *adv* справедли́во.
jut [dʒʌt] *vi* (*also:* **~ out**) выступáть (*impf*).
jute [dʒu:t] *n* джут.
juvenile ['dʒu:vənaɪl] *n* (*LAW, ADMIN*) подрóсток*, несовершеннолéтний*(-яя) *m(f) adj* ◆ *adj* (*humour, mentality*) дéтский*.
juvenile court *n* суд для несовершеннолéтних.
juvenile delinquency *n* престýпность *f* среди́ несовершеннолéтних.
juvenile delinquent *n* несовершеннолéтний(-яя) правонаруши́тель(-ница) *m(f).*
juxtapose ['dʒʌkstəpəuz] *vt* сопоставля́ть (сопостáвить* *perf*).
juxtaposition ['dʒʌkstəpə'zɪʃən] *n* сопоставлéние.

* marks translations which have irregular inflections. The Russian-English side of the dictionary gives inflectional information.

~K, k~

K, k [keɪ] *n* (*letter*) *11-ая бу́ква англи́йского алфави́та.*

K *abbr* = *one thousand*; (*COMPUT*) (= **kilobyte**) К= *килоба́йт*; (*BRIT: in titles*) = **knight**.

Kabul ['kɑ:bul] *n* Кабу́л.

kaftan ['kæftæn] *n* кафта́н.

Kalahari Desert [kælə'hɑ:rɪ-] *n*: **the ~ ~** пусты́ня Калаха́ри.

kale [keɪl] *n* капу́ста кормова́я.

kaleidoscope [kə'laɪdəskəup] *n* калейдоско́п.

kamikaze [kæmɪ'kɑ:zɪ] *n* камика́дзе *m ind*, лётчик-сме́ртник.

Kampala [kæm'pɑ:lə] *n* Кампа́ла.

Kampuchea [kæmpu'tʃɪə] *n* Кампучи́я.

Kampuchean [kæmpu'tʃɪən] *adj* кампучи́йский*.

kangaroo [kæŋgə'ru:] *n* кенгуру́ *m ind*.

kaput [kə'put] (*inf*) *adj*: **the TV is ~!** телеви́зору капу́т!

karaoke [kɑ:rə'əukɪ] *n* карио́ки *ind* (*самоде́ятельное пе́ние под за́пись профессиона́льного анса́мбля*).

karate [kə'rɑ:tɪ] *n* карат́э *nt ind*.

Kashmir [kæʃ'mɪə'] *n* Кашми́р.

kayak ['kaɪæk] *n* кая́к*.

Kazakh ['kæzæk] *n* (*person*) каза́х(-а́шка*); (*LING*) каза́хский* язы́к* ◆ *adj* каза́хский*.

Kazakhstan [kæzæk'stɑ:n] *n* Казахста́н.

KC *n abbr* (*BRIT: LAW:* = *King's Counsel*) короле́вский* адвока́т (*адвока́тский ранг*).

kd *abbr* (*US: COMM:* = *knocked down*) в разо́бранном ви́де.

kebab [kə'bæb] *n* шашлы́к*.

keel [ki:l] *n* киль *m*; **on an even ~** (*fig*) в состоя́нии стаби́льности

▸ **keel over** *vi* опроки́дываться (опроки́нуться *perf*).

keen [ki:n] *adj* о́стрый; (*eager*) стра́стный* (стра́стен), увлечённый; **to be ~ to do** *or* **on doing** о́чень хоте́ть* (*impf*) +*infin*; **to be ~ on sth** увлека́ться (*impf*) чем-н; **he is ~ on her** он увлечён е́ю; **I'm not ~ on going** мне не о́чень хо́чется идти́; **~ competition** напряжённая конкуре́нтая борьба́.

keenly ['ki:nlɪ] *adv* (*enthusiastically*) увлечённо; (*intently*) при́стально; **to feel sth ~** глубоко́ пережива́ть (*impf*) что-н.

keenness ['ki:nnɪs] *n* (*eagerness*) увлечённость *f*; **~ to do** стремле́ние +*infin*.

keep [ki:p] (*pt, pp* **kept**) *vt* (*receipt, money*) оставля́ть (оста́вить* *perf*) себе́; (*store*) храни́ть (*impf*); (*preserve*) сохраня́ть (сохрани́ть *perf*); (*house, garden, shop, family*) содержа́ть (*impf*); (*prisoner, chickens, bees*) держа́ть* (*impf*); (*accounts, diary*) вести́* (*impf*); (*promise*) сде́рживать (сдержа́ть* *perf*) ◆ *vi* (*in a certain state or place*) остава́ться* (оста́ться* *perf*); (*food*) сохраня́ться (*impf*); (*continue*): **to ~ doing** продолжа́ть (*impf*) +*impf infin* ◆ *n* (*of castle*) центра́льная ба́шня*; (*food etc*): **he has enough for his ~** ему́ доста́точно на прожи́тие; **he kept the job** он сохрани́л э́ту рабо́ту; **where do you ~ the salt?** где у Вас соль?; **he tries to ~ her happy** он де́лает всё для того́, что́бы она́ была́ дово́льна; **to ~ the house tidy** содержа́ть* (*impf*) дом в поря́дке; **to ~ sb waiting** заставля́ть (заста́вить* *perf*) кого́-н ждать; **to ~ sb from doing** не дава́ть* (дать* *perf*) кому́-н +*infin*; **to ~ an appointment** прийти́* (*perf*) в назна́ченное вре́мя; **to ~ a record** вести́* (*impf*) учёт; **to ~ sth to o.s.** держа́ть (*impf*) что-н при себе́; **to ~ sth (back) from sb** скрыва́ть (скрыть* *perf*) что-н от кого́-н; **to ~ sth from happening** не дава́ть* (дать* *perf*) чему́-н случи́ться; **to ~ time** (*clock*) идти́* (*impf*) то́чно

▸ **keep away** *vt*: **to ~ sth/sb away from sb/sth** де́ржать (*impf*) что-н/кого́-н пода́льше от кого́-н/чего́-н ◆ *vi*: **to ~ away (from)** де́ржаться* (*impf*) пода́льше (от +*gen*)

▸ **keep back** *vt* (*crowds, tears*) сде́рживать (сдержа́ть* *perf*); (*money*) уде́рживать (удержа́ть* *perf*) ◆ *vi* держа́ться* (*impf*) на расстоя́нии

▸ **keep down** *vt* (*prices, spending*) сде́рживать (сдержа́ть *perf*); (*retain*): **she can't ~ her food down** что бы она́ ни съе́ла, её всё вре́мя рвёт ◆ *vi*: **~ down!** ложи́сь!

▸ **keep in** *vt* (*person*) держа́ть (*impf*) до́ма ◆ *vi* (*inf*): **to ~ in with sb** подде́рживать (*impf*) хоро́шие отноше́ния с кем-н

▸ **keep off** *vt* (*hold back*) не подпуска́ть (подпусти́ть* *perf*); (*abstain*) избега́ть (*impf*) +*gen* ◆ *vi* держа́ться* (*impf*) в стороне́; **"keep off the grass"** „по газо́нам не ходи́ть"; **~ your hands off** рука́ми не тро́гать

▸ **keep on** *vi*: **to ~ on doing** продолжа́ть (*impf*)

+impf infin; **to ~ on (about sth)** не перестава́я говори́ть *(impf)* (о чём-н)
▸ **keep out** *vt* не впуска́ть (впусти́ть* *perf*); **"keep out"** „посторо́нним вход воспрещён"
▸ **keep up** *vt* (*payments, standards*) подде́рживать *(impf)* ◆ *vi*: **to ~ up (with)** (*pace*) поспева́ть (поспе́ть *perf*) (за *+instr*); (*level*) идти́* *(impf)* в но́гу (с *+instr*).
keeper ['ki:pəʳ] *n* (*of zoo, park*) смотри́тель (ница) *m(f)*.
keep fit *n* аэро́бика.
keeping ['ki:pɪŋ] *n* (*care*) присмо́тр; **I'll leave this in your ~** оставля́ю э́то под Ва́шим присмо́тром; **in ~ with** в соотве́тствии с *+instr*; **out of ~ with** несовмести́мый (несовмести́м) с *+instr*.
keeps [ki:ps] *n*: **for ~** (*inf*) на совсе́м.
keepsake ['ki:pseɪk] *n* па́мятный пода́рок.
keg [kɛg] *n* бочо́нок*; **~ beer** бочково́е пи́во.
kennel ['kɛnl] *n* конура́*.
kennels ['kɛnlz] *npl* гости́ница *fsg or* пла́тный прию́т *msg* для соба́к.
Kenya ['kɛnjə] *n* Ке́ния.
Kenyan ['kɛnjən] *adj* кени́йский* ◆ *n* кени́ец*(-и́йка*).
kept [kɛpt] *pt, pp of* **keep**.
kerb [kə:b] *n* (*BRIT*) бордю́р.
kerb crawler [-'krɔ:ləʳ] *n шофёр, выбира́ющий себе́ проститу́ток из окна́ ме́дленно ползу́щего автомоби́ля.*
kernel ['kə:nl] *n* (*of nut*) ядро́*; (*of idea*) суть *f*.
kerosene ['kɛrəsi:n] *n* кероси́н.
kestrel ['kɛstrəl] *n* пустельга́*.
ketchup ['kɛtʃəp] *n* ке́тчуп.
kettle ['kɛtl] *n* ча́йник.
kettledrum ['kɛtldrʌm] *n* лита́вра.
key [ki:] *n* ключ*; (*MUS*) тона́льность *f*; (*of piano, computer*) кла́виш(а) ◆ *cpd* (*issue etc*) ключево́й ◆ *vt* (*also:* **~ in**) набира́ть (набра́ть* *perf*) на клавиату́ре.
keyboard ['ki:bɔ:d] *n* клавиату́ра.
keyboarder ['ki:bɔ:dəʳ] *n* машини́ст(ка), опера́тор клавиату́ры.
keyed up [ki:d'] *adj*: **he was all ~ ~** он был о́чень взви́нчен.
keyhole ['ki:həul] *n* замо́чная сква́жина.
keyhole surgery *n полостна́я опера́ция, осуществля́емая че́рез минима́льный разре́з.*
keynote ['ki:nəut] *n* (*MUS*) то́ника; (*of speech*) лейтмоти́в.
keypad ['ki:pæd] *n* (*COMPUT*) (ма́лая) клавиату́ра, кла́вишная пане́ль *f*.
keyring ['ki:rɪŋ] *n* брело́к*.
keystroke ['ki:strəuk] *n* (*COMPUT*) нажа́тие кла́виши.
kg *abbr* (= **kilogram(me)**) кг= *килогра́мм*.
KGB *n abbr* (*POL*: *formerly*) КГБ.

khaki ['kɑ:kɪ] *n, adj* ха́ки *nt, adj ind*.
kHz *abbr* (= *kilohertz*) кГц= *килоге́рц*.
kibbutz [kɪ'buts] *n* кибу́ц.
kick [kɪk] *vt* (*person, table*) ударя́ть (уда́рить *perf*) ного́й; (*ball*) ударя́ть (уда́рить *perf*) ного́й по *+dat*; (*inf*: *habit, addiction*) поборо́ть (*perf*) ◆ *vi* (*horse*) ляга́ться *(impf)* ◆ *n* уда́р; (*of rifle*) отда́ча; (*thrill*: *inf*): **he does it for ~s** он де́лает э́то, что́бы пощекота́ть себе́ не́рвы
▸ **kick around** *vi* (*inf*) валя́ться *(impf)*
▸ **kick off** *vi*: **the match ~s off at 3pm** матч начина́ется в 3 часа́ (*в футбо́ле*).
kickoff ['kɪkɔf] *n* нача́ло (футбо́льного) ма́тча.
kick-start ['kɪkstɑ:t] *n* (*also:* **~er**: *BRIT*) ножно́й ста́ртёр.
kid [kɪd] *n* (*inf*: *child*) ребёнок*; (*goat*) козлёнок*; (*leather*) ла́йка ◆ *vt* (*inf*) води́ть* *(impf)* за нос, дура́чить *(impf)*; **~ brother** мла́дший* брати́шка* *m*; **~ sister** мла́дшая сестрёнка*; **you're ~ding!** ты шу́тишь!
kid gloves *n*: **to handle sb with ~ ~** бе́режно обраща́ться *(impf)* с кем-н.
kidnap ['kɪdnæp] *vt* похища́ть (похи́тить* *perf*).
kidnapper ['kɪdnæpəʳ] *n* похити́тель(ница) *m(f)*.
kidnapping ['kɪdnæpɪŋ] *n* похище́ние.
kidney ['kɪdnɪ] *n* (*MED*) по́чка*; (*CULIN*) по́чки *fpl*.
kidney bean *n* кра́сная фасо́ль *f no pl*.
kidney machine *n* иску́сственная по́чка*.
Kiev ['ki:ɛf] *n* Ки́ев.
Kilimanjaro [kɪlɪmən'dʒɑ:rəu] *n*: **Mount ~** гора́ Килиманджа́ро *nt ind*.
kill [kɪl] *vt* убива́ть (уби́ть* *perf*); (*proposal*) губи́ть (загуби́ть *perf*); (*rumour*) пресека́ть (пресе́чь* *perf*) ◆ *n* (*prey*) добы́ча; **to ~ time** (*inf*) убива́ть (уби́ть* *perf*) вре́мя; **to ~ o.s.** поко́нчить (*perf*) с собо́й; **to be ~ed** (*in war, accident*) погиба́ть (поги́бнуть* *perf*); **to ~ o.s. to do** (*fig*) надрыва́ться *(impf)*, что́бы *+perf infin*; **to ~ o.s. (laughing)** помира́ть *(impf)* (со́ смеху)
▸ **kill off** *vt* (*also fig*) уничтожа́ть (уничто́жить *perf*).
killer ['kɪləʳ] *n* уби́йца *m/f*.
killer instinct *n* смерте́льная *or* мёртвая хва́тка.
killing ['kɪlɪŋ] *n* уби́йство; (*profit*): **to make a ~** (*inf*) срыва́ть (сорва́ть* *perf*) куш.
killjoy ['kɪldʒɔɪ] *n*: **don't be such a ~!** не отравля́й други́м удово́льствие!
kiln [kɪln] *n* печь* *f* (*для о́бжига*).
kilo ['ki:ləu] *n* кило́ *nt ind*.
kilobyte ['ki:ləubaɪt] *n* килоба́йт.
kilogram(me) ['kɪləugræm] *n* килогра́мм.
kilohertz ['kɪləuhə:ts] *n inv* килоге́рц.
kilometre ['kɪləmi:təʳ] (*US* **kilometer**) *n*

километр.
kilowatt ['kɪləuwɔt] *n* киловáтт.
kilt [kɪlt] *n* шотлáндская юбка*.
kilter ['kɪltə^r] *n*: **out of ~** в беспорядке.
kimono [kɪ'məunəu] *n* кимонó *nt ind*.
kin [kɪn] *n see* **kith, next**.
kind [kaɪnd] *adj* дóбрый* (добр) ◆ *n* род*; **would you be ~ enough** *or* **so ~ as to ...?** не бýдете ли Вы так добры́ *or* любéзны *+perf infin* ...?; **it's very ~ of you to help me** óчень любéзно с Вáшей стороны́, что Вы мне помогли́; **he seemed ~ of unhappy** он был врóде бы недовóлен; **in ~** (*COMM*) товáрами и услýгами; **a ~ of** род *+gen*; **two of a ~** две вéщи одногó ти́па; **what ~ of person is he?** что он за человéк?; **she has a strange ~ of smile** у неё стрáнная улы́бка.
kindergarten ['kɪndəgɑ:tn] *n* дéтский* сад*.
kind-hearted [kaɪnd'hɑ:tɪd] *adj* дóбрый* (добр), добросердéчный* (добрсердéчен).
kindle ['kɪndl] *vt* (*also fig*) разжигáть (разжéчь* *perf*).
kindling ['kɪndlɪŋ] *n* щéпки* *fpl*, растóпка.
kindly ['kaɪndlɪ] *adj* (*smile*) дóбрый* (добр); (*person, tone*) доброжелáтельный* (доброжелáтелен) ◆ *adv* (*smile, behave*) любéзно, доброжелáтельно; **will you ~ ...** бýдьте добры́ ...; **he didn't take it ~** он был далекó не рад э́тому.
kindness ['kaɪndnɪs] *n* (*quality*) добротá; (*act*) любéзность *f*.
kindred ['kɪndrɪd] *adj*: **~ spirit** рóдственная душá*.
kinetic [kɪ'nɛtɪk] *adj* кинети́ческий*.
king [kɪŋ] *n* корóль* *m*.
kingdom ['kɪŋdəm] *n* королéвство; **the animal/plant ~** живóтное/расти́тельное цáрство.
kingfisher ['kɪŋfɪʃə^r] *n* зиморóдок*.
kingpin ['kɪŋpɪn] *n* (*TECH*) шквóрень* *m*; (*fig*) вáжная ши́шка*.
king-size(d) ['kɪŋsaɪz(d)] *adj* сáмого большóго размéра.
kink [kɪŋk] *n* (*in rope*) ýзел; (*in hair*) завитóк*; (*in character*) причýда, стрáнность *f*.
kinky ['kɪŋkɪ] *adj* (*inf*) порóчный* (порóчен).
kinship ['kɪnʃɪp] *n* родствó.
kinsman ['kɪnzmən] *irreg n* рóдич.
kinswoman ['kɪnzwumən] *irreg n* крóвная рóдственница.
kiosk ['ki:ɔsk] *n* киóск; (*BRIT: TEL*) телефóнная бýдка*; (*also:* **newspaper ~**) газéтный киóск.
kipper ['kɪpə^r] *n* ≈ копчёная селёдка*.
Kirghiz ['kə:gɪz] *n* (*person*) кирги́з(ка*); (*LING*) кирги́зский* язы́к* ◆ *adj* кирги́зский*.
Kirghizia [kə:'gɪzɪə] *n* Кирги́зия.
Kishinev [kiʃi'njɔf] *n* Кишинёв.
kiss [kɪs] *n* поцелýй ◆ *vt* целовáть (поцеловáть *perf*) ◆ *vi* целовáться (поцеловáться *perf*); **to ~ sb goodbye** целовáть (поцеловáть *perf*) когó-н на прощáние.
kissagram ['kɪsəgr[+e]m] *n* *сюрпри́зная достáвка поздравлéний, сопровождáющаяся поцелýем достáвщика и́ли достáвщицы.*
kiss of life *n* (*BRIT*): **the ~ ~ ~** искýсственное дыхáние.
kit [kɪt] *n* (*also:* **sports ~**) костю́м; (*equipment*) снаряжéние; (*set of tools*) набóр; (*for assembly*) комплéкт
▸ **kit out** *vt* (*BRIT*) снаряжáть (снаряди́ть* *perf*).
kitbag ['kɪtbæg] *n* вещмешóк*= *вещевóй мешóк*.
kitchen ['kɪtʃɪn] *n* кýхня*.
kitchen garden *n* огорóд.
kitchen sink *n* (кýхонная) мóйка* *or* рáковина.
kitchen unit *n* (*BRIT*) кýхонный шкаф.
kitchenware ['kɪtʃɪnwɛə^r] *n* кýхонные принадлéжности *fpl*, (кýхонная) ýтварь *f*.
kite [kaɪt] *n* (*toy*) воздýшный змей; (*ZOOL*) кóршун.
kith [kɪθ] *n*: **~ and kin** родны́е *pl adj* и бли́зкие *pl adj*.
kitten ['kɪtn] *n* котёнок*.
kitty ['kɪtɪ] *n* (*pool of money*) óбщая кáсса.
kiwi ['ki:wi:] *n* ки́ви *f ind*.
KKK *n abbr* (*US*: = *Ku Klux Klan*) ку-клукс-клáн.
Kleenex® ['kli:nɛks] *n inv* бумáжный носовóй платóк*.
kleptomaniac [klɛptəu'meɪnɪæk] *n* клептомáн(ка*).
km *abbr* (= **kilometre**) км= *киломéтр*.
km/h *abbr* (= *kilometres per hour*) км/ч= *киломéтров в час*.
knack [næk] *n*: **he has the ~ of imitating other people** он óчень лóвко имити́рует други́х людéй; **there's a ~ to doing this** тут есть оди́н секрéт *or* осóбая хи́трость.
knackered ['nækəd] *adj* (*inf: tired*) вы́мотанный (вы́мотан).
knapsack ['næpsæk] *n* (небольшóй) рюкзáк.
knead [ni:d] *vt* меси́ть* (смеси́ть* *perf*).
knee [ni:] *n* колéно*.
kneecap ['ni:kæp] *n* колéнная чáшечка*.
kneecapping ['ni:kæpɪŋ] *n* вы́стрел по колéнной чáшечке (*фóрма мéсти, применя́емая террори́стами*).
knee-deep ['ni:'di:p] *adj, adv* по колéно.
knee-jerk ['ni:dʒə:k] *n* колéнный рефлéкс ◆ *adj*: **~ reaction** (*fig*) рефлéкс.
kneel [ni:l] (*pt, pp* **knelt**) *vi* (*also:* **~ down**: *action*) вставáть* (встать* *perf*) на колéни; (: *state*) стоя́ть (*impf*) на колéнях.
kneepad ['ni:pæd] *n* наколéнник.
knell [nɛl] *n* погребáльный звон; (*fig*) конéц*.
knelt [nɛlt] *pt, pp of* **kneel**.
knew [nju:] *pt of* **know**.
knickers ['nɪkəz] *npl* (*BRIT*) (жéнские) трýсики *mpl*.
knick-knacks ['nɪknæks] *npl* безделýшки* *fpl*.
knife [naɪf] (*pl* **knives**) *n* нож* ◆ *vt* рáнить (*impf*) ножóм.

knight [naɪt] *n* рыцарь *m*; (*CHESS*) конь* *m*.
knighthood ['naɪthud] *n* (*BRIT*) рыцарство (*полученное за заслуги перед страной*).
knit [nɪt] *vt* (*garment*) вязать (связать *perf*) ◆ *vi* (*with wool etc*) вязать (*impf*); (*bones*) срастаться (срастись* *perf*); **to ~ one's brows** хмурить (нахмурить *perf*) брови.
knitted ['nɪtɪd] *adj* (*garment*) вязаный.
knitting ['nɪtɪŋ] *n* вязанье.
knitting machine *n* вязальная машина.
knitting needle *n* вязальная спица.
knitting pattern *n* вязка*.
knitwear ['nɪtwɛəʳ] *n* трикотаж.
knives [naɪvz] *npl of* **knife**.
knob [nɔb] *n* (*of door*) ручка*; (*on radio etc*) кнопка*; (*of stick*) набалдашник; **a ~ of butter** (*BRIT*) кусочек (сливочного) масла.
knobbly ['nɔblɪ] (*US* **knobby**) *adj* (*surface*) бугристый (бугрист); (*hand*) узловатый (узловат); (*knee*) шишковатый.
knobby ['nɔbɪ] *adj* (*US*) = **knobbly**.
knock [nɔk] *vt* (*strike*) ударять (ударить *perf*); (*bump into*) сталкиваться (столкнуться *perf*) с *+instr*; (*inf: criticize*) критиковать (*impf*) ◆ *vi* (*engine*) стучать (*impf*) ◆ *n* (*blow, bump*) удар, толчок*; (*on door*) стук; **to ~ a nail into sth** вбивать (вбить* *perf*) гвоздь во что-н; **to ~ some sense into sb** учить* (научить* *perf*) кого-н уму-разуму; **he ~ed at** *or* **on the door** он постучал в дверь
▸ **knock about** (*inf*) ◆ *vt* (*hit*) колотить* (поколотить* *perf*) ◆ *vi* (*travel*) шататься (*impf*) по свету; (*hang out*): **~ about (with)** водиться (*impf*) (с *+instr*)
▸ **knock around** *vti* = **knock about**
▸ **knock back** *vt* (*inf: drink*) пропускать (пропустить* *perf*)
▸ **knock down** *vt* (*person, price*) сбивать (сбить* *perf*); (*building*) сносить (снести* *perf*)
▸ **knock off** *vi* (*inf: finish*) закругляться (закруглиться *perf*) ◆ *vt* (*from price*) сбавлять (сбавить* *perf*); (*inf: steal*) стянуть* (*perf*)
▸ **knock out** *vt* (*subj: person, drug*) оглушать (оглушить *perf*); (*BOXING*) нокаутировать (*perf*); (*defeat*) выбивать (выбить* *perf*)
▸ **knock over** *vt* (*person, object*) сбивать (сбить* *perf*).
knockdown ['nɔkdaun] *adj*: **~ price** сниженная цена.
knocker ['nɔkəʳ] *n* дверной молоток*.
knocking ['nɔkɪŋ] *n* стук.
knock-kneed [nɔk'ni:d] *adj* с вывернутыми внутрь коленями.
knockout ['nɔkaut] *n* (*BOXING*) нокаут ◆ *cpd* (*competition*) отборочный.
knock-up ['nɔkʌp] *n* (*TENNIS*): **to have a ~** разминаться (размяться* *perf*).
knot [nɔt] *n* (*also NAUT*) узел*; (*in wood*) сучок* ◆ *vt* завязывать (завязать* *perf*) узлом; **to tie/untie a ~** завязывать (завязать* *perf*)/ развязывать (развязать* *perf*) узел.
knotty ['nɔtɪ] *adj* (*fig*) запутанный.
know [nəu] (*pt* **knew**, *pp* **known**) *vt* (*facts, people*) знать (*impf*); **to ~ how to do** уметь (*impf*) *+infin*; **to ~ about** *or* **of sth/sb** знать (*impf*) о чём-н/ком-н; **to get to ~ sth** (*news*) узнавать* (узнать* *perf*) что-н; **to get to ~ sb** (*more intimately*) узнавать* (узнать* *perf*) кого-н поближе; (*get acquainted*) знакомиться* (познакомиться* *perf*) с кем-н; **to get to ~ about** узнать (*perf*) о *+prp*; **as far as I ~** насколько мне известно; **yes, I ~** да, знаю; **I don't ~** не знаю.
know-all ['nəuɔ:l] *n* (*BRIT: pej*) всезнайка* *m/f*.
know-how ['nəuhau] *n* ноу-хау *nt ind*.
knowing ['nəuɪŋ] *adj* (*look*) понимающий.
knowingly ['nəuɪŋlɪ] *adv* (*purposely*) сознательно; (*smile, look*) понимающе.
know-it-all ['nəuɪtɔ:l] *n* (*US*) = **know-all**.
knowledge ['nɔlɪdʒ] *n* (*abstract concept*) знание; (*things learnt*) знания *ntpl*; (*awareness*) представление; **to have no ~ of** не иметь (*impf*) никакого представления о *+prp*; **not to my ~** насколько мне известно – нет; **without my ~** без моего ведома; **to have a working ~ of Russian** неплохо владеть (*impf*) русским (языком); **it is common ~ that ...** общеизвестно, что ...; **it has come to my ~ that ...** мне стало известно, что ....
knowledgeable ['nɔlɪdʒəbl] *adj* знающий*; **he is very ~ about art** он большой знаток искусства.
known [nəun] *pp of* **know** ◆ *adj* (*thief, facts*) известный* (известен).
knuckle ['nʌkl] *n* костяшка*
▸ **knuckle down** *vi* браться* (взяться* *perf*) за дело
▸ **knuckle under** *vi* (*inf*) подчиняться (подчиниться *perf*).
knuckleduster ['nʌkldʌstəʳ] *n* кастет.
KO *n abbr* (= *knockout*) нокаут ◆ *vt* нокаутировать (*impf/perf*).
koala [kəu'ɑ:lə] *n* (*also:* **~ bear**) коала *f ind*.
kook [ku:k] *n* (*US*) помешанный(-ая) *m(f) adj*.
Koran [kɔ'rɑ:n] *n*: **the ~** Коран.
Korea [kə'rɪə] *n* Корея; **North/South ~** Северная/Южная Корея.
Korean [kə'rɪən] *adj* корейский* ◆ *n* кореец*(-еянка*).
kosher ['kəuʃəʳ] *adj* (*food*) кошерный.
Kosovo ['kɔsɔvəu] *n* Косово.
Kosovan ['kɔsɔvən] *n* косовар(-ка).
Kosovar ['kɔsɔva:ʳ] *n* = **Kosovan**.
kowtow ['kau'tau] *vi*: **to ~ to sb** заискивать (*impf*) *or* угодничать (*impf*) перед кем-н.
Kremlin ['krɛmlɪn] *n*: **the ~** Кремль* *m*.

* marks translations which have irregular inflections. The Russian-English side of the dictionary gives inflectional information.

KS *abbr* (*US*: *POST*) = *Kansas*.
Kt *abbr* (*BRIT*: *in titles*) = **knight**.
Kuala Lumpur ['kwɑ:lə'lumpuə^r] *n* Куала-Лумпу́р.
kudos ['kju:dɔs] *n* прести́жность *f*.
Kurd [kə:d] *n* курд(ка*).
Kuwait [ku'weɪt] *n* Куве́йт.
Kuwaiti [ku'weɪtɪ] *adj* куве́йтский ◆ *n* жи́тель(ница) *m(f)* Куве́йта.
kW *abbr* (= **kilowatt**) кВт= *килова́тт*.
KY *abbr* (*US*: *POST*) = *Kentucky*.

~ L, l ~

L, l [ɛl] *n* (*letter*) *12-ая бу́ква англи́йского алфави́та.*

L *abbr* (*BRIT: AUT:* = *learner*) учéбная *f adj*; (= **lake**) о.= *óзеро*; = **large, left**.

l. *abbr* (= **litre**) л= *литр*.

LA *n abbr* (*US*) = *Los Angeles* ◆ *abbr* (*POST*) = *Louisiana*.

lab [læb] *n abbr* = **laboratory**.

label ['leɪbl] *n* этикéтка*, ярлы́к; (*on suitcase*) би́рка*; (*also:* **record ~**) знак фи́рмы грамзáписи ◆ *vt* (*suitcase*) прикрепля́ть (прикрепи́ть* *perf*) би́рку к +*dat*; (*merchandise*) прикрепля́ть (прикрепи́ть* *perf*) ярлы́к на +*acc*; (*fig*) наклéивать (наклéить *perf*) ярлы́к на +*acc*.

labor *etc* ['leɪbəʳ] *n* (*US*) = **labour** *etc*.

laboratory [lə'bɔrətərɪ] *n* лаборатóрия.

Labor Day *n* (*US*) День* *m* Трудá.

laborious [lə'bɔːrɪəs] *adj* трудоёмкий* (трудоёмок).

labor union *n* (*US*) профсою́з.

labour ['leɪbəʳ] (*US* **labor**) *n* (*work*) труд*; (*workforce*) рабóчая си́ла; (*MED*): **to be in ~** рожáть *(impf)* ◆ *vi*: **to ~ (at sth)** труди́ться* *(impf)* (над чем-н) ◆ *vt*: **to ~ the point** входи́ть* *(impf)* в изли́шние подрóбности; **L~, the L~ Party** (*BRIT*) лейбори́сты *mpl*, Лейбори́стская Пáртия; **hard ~** кáторжные рабóты *pl*.

labour camp *n* исправи́тельно-трудовóй лáгерь* *m*.

labour cost *n* стóимость *f* рабóчей си́лы.

labour dispute *n* трудовóй конфли́кт.

laboured ['leɪbəd] *adj* (*breathing, movement*) затруднённый (затруднён); (*style, joke*) вы́мученный (вы́мучен).

labourer ['leɪbərəʳ] *n* (неквалифици́рованный) рабóчий *m adj*; **farm ~** сéльско-хозя́йственный рабóчий.

labour force *n* рабóчая си́ла.

labour-intensive [leɪbərɪn'tɛnsɪv] *adj* трудоёмкий* (трудоёмок).

labour market *n* ры́нок* трудá.

labour pains *npl* родовы́е схвáтки *fpl*.

labour relations *npl* трудовы́е отношéния *ntpl*.

labour-saving ['leɪbəseɪvɪŋ] *adj* облегчáющий труд.

labour unrest *n* рабóчие волнéния *ntpl*.

laburnum [lə'bəːnəm] *n* (*BOT*) золотóй дождь* *m*.

labyrinth ['læbɪrɪnθ] *n* лабири́нт.

lace [leɪs] *n* (*fabric*) крýжево*; (*of shoe*) шнурóк* ◆ *vt* (*shoe: also:* **~ up**) шнуровáть (зашнуровáть *perf*); **I ~d his coffee with arsenic** я подмешáл в егó кóфе мышья́к.

lacemaking ['leɪsmeɪkɪŋ] *n* плетéние кружев.

lacerate ['læsəreɪt] *vt* раздирáть (разодрáть* *perf*).

laceration [læsə'reɪʃən] *n* рвáная рáна.

lace-up ['leɪsʌp] *adj* шнурóванный.

lack [læk] *n* (*absence*) отсýтствие; (*shortage*) недостáток*, нехвáтка ◆ *vt*: **she ~ed self-confidence** ей не хватáло *or* не доставáло увéренности в себé; **he is ~ing in experience** емý не хватáет *or* не достаёт óпыта; **through** *or* **for ~ of** из-за недостáтка +*gen*.

lackadaisical [lækə'deɪzɪkl] *adj* вя́лый (вял).

lackey ['lækɪ] *n* (*pej*) лакéй.

lacklustre ['læklʌstəʳ] (*US* **lackluster**) *adj* тýсклый* (тускл).

laconic [lə'kɔnɪk] *adj* лакони́чный* (лакони́чен).

lacquer ['lækəʳ] *n* лак*.

lacrosse [lə'krɔs] *n* (*SPORT*) лакрóсс.

lacy ['leɪsɪ] *adj* кружевнóй.

lad [læd] *n* пáрень* *m*.

ladder ['lædəʳ] *n* (*also fig*) лéстница; (*BRIT: in tights*) спусти́вшиеся пéтли *fpl* ◆ *vti*: **I've ~ed my tights, my tights have ~ed** у меня́ пéтли на колгóтках спусти́лись.

laden ['leɪdn] *adj*: **to be ~ (with)** ломи́ться *(impf)* от +*gen*; (*person*): **~ (with)** нагрýженный (нагрýжен) (+*instr*); **fully ~** пóлностью нагрýженный; **the trees were ~ with fruit** дерéвья ломи́лись от плодóв.

ladle ['leɪdl] *n* полóвник ◆ *vt* (*soup, stew*) разливáть (разли́ть* *perf*)

▸ **ladle out** *vt* (*advice, money*) раздавáть* (раздáть* *perf*) напрáво и налéво.

Ladoga ['ladəgə] *n*: **Lake ~** Лáдожское óзеро.

lady ['leɪdɪ] *n* дáма; (*BRIT: title*) лéди *f ind*; **ladies and gentlemen ...** дáмы и господá ...; **young ~**

* marks translations which have irregular inflections. The Russian-English side of the dictionary gives inflectional information.

молода́я же́нщина; (*younger*) де́вушка*; **old ~** пожила́я же́нщина; **the ladies' (room)** же́нский туале́т.
ladybird ['leɪdɪbə:d] *n* бо́жья коро́вка.
ladybug ['leɪdɪbʌg] *n* (*US*) = **ladybird**.
lady-in-waiting ['leɪdɪɪn'weɪtɪŋ] *n* фре́йлина.
lady-killer ['leɪdɪkɪlə^r] *n* (*fig*) сердцее́д.
ladylike ['leɪdɪlaɪk] *adj* элега́нтный* (элега́нтен).
ladyship ['leɪdɪʃɪp] *n*: **your ~** Ва́ша ми́лость *f*.
lag [læg] *n* (*period of time*) заде́ржка ◆ *vi* (*also:* **~ behind**: *person*) тащи́ться* *(impf)* (позади́); (: *trade, investment*) отстава́ть* (отста́ть* *perf*) ◆ *vt* (*pipes etc*) покрыва́ть (покры́ть* *perf*) теплоизоля́цией; **old ~** (*inf: prisoner*) рецидиви́ст; **to ~ behind** (*trade, development*) отстава́ть* (отста́ть* *perf*) от *+gen*.
lager ['lɑ:gə^r] *n* све́тлое пи́во.
lager lout *n* (*inf*) пья́ная шпана́ *f no pl*.
lagging ['lægɪŋ] *n* (*for pipes*) теплоизоля́ция.
lagoon [lə'gu:n] *n* лагу́на.
Lagos ['leɪgɔs] *n* Ла́гос.
laid [leɪd] *pt, pp of* **lay**.
laid-back [leɪd'bæk] *adj* (*inf*) споко́йный* (споко́ен).
laid up *adj*: **~ ~ (with)** прико́ванный (прико́ван) к посте́ли (*+instr*).
lain [leɪn] *pp of* **lie**.
lair [lɛə^r] *n* ло́гово, ло́говище.
laissez faire [lɛseɪ'fɛə^r] *n* (*ECON*) экономи́ческое невмеша́тельство.
laity ['leɪətɪ] *n or npl* (*REL*) миря́не *mpl*; (*non-professionals*) не профессиона́лы *mpl*.
lake [leɪk] *n* о́зеро*.
Lake District *n* (*BRIT*): **the ~ ~** Озёрный край.
lamb [læm] *n* (*ZOOL*) ягнёнок*; (*CULIN*) (молода́я) бара́нина.
lambada [læm'bɑ:də] *n* ламба́да.
lamb chop *n* бара́нья котле́та.
lambskin ['læmskɪn] *n* овчи́на.
lambswool ['læmzwul] *n* поя́рок* ◆ *cpd* поя́рковый.
lame [leɪm] *adj* (*person, animal*) хромо́й* (хром); (*excuse, argument*) сла́бый* (слаб).
lame duck *n* неуда́чник(-ица).
lamely ['leɪmlɪ] *adv* неубеди́тельно.
lament [lə'mɛnt] *n* плач ◆ *vt* опла́кивать (опла́кать* *perf*).
lamentable ['læməntəbl] *adj* плачёвный* (плачёвен).
laminated ['læmɪneɪtɪd] *adj* (*layered*) слои́стый; (*plastic coated*) с пла́стиковым покры́тием.
lamp [læmp] *n* (*electric, gas, oil*) ла́мпа; (*street lamp*) фона́рь* *m*.
lamplight ['læmplaɪt] *n*: **by ~** (*indoors*) при све́те ла́мпы.
lampoon [læm'pu:n] *n* па́сквиль *m* ◆ *vt* писа́ть* (написа́ть* *perf*) па́сквиль на *+acc*.
lamppost ['læmppəust] *n* (*BRIT*) фона́рный столб*.
lampshade ['læmpʃeɪd] *n* абажу́р.
lance [lɑ:ns] *n* пи́ка ◆ *vt* (*MED*) вскрыва́ть (вскрыть* *perf*).
lance corporal *n* (*BRIT*) мла́дший* капра́л.
lancet ['lɑ:nsɪt] *n* ланце́т.
Lancs [læŋks] *abbr* (*BRIT: POST*) = *Lancashire*.
land [lænd] *n* земля́*; (*not sea*) су́ша; (*country*) страна́* ◆ *vi* (*from ship*) выса́живаться (вы́садиться* *perf*); (*AVIAT*) приземля́ться (приземли́ться* *perf*); (*fig: arrive unexpectedly*) очути́ться* *(perf)* ◆ *vt* (*plane*) посади́ть* *(perf)*; (*passengers*) выса́живать (вы́садить* *perf*); (*goods*) выгружа́ть (вы́грузить* *perf*); **to own ~** владе́ть *(impf)* землёй; **to go by ~** е́хать*/е́здить* *(impf)* по су́ше; **he always ~s on his feet** (*fig*) в конце́ концо́в ему́ везёт; **she ~ed (herself) a good job** (*inf*) она́ добила́сь хоро́шей рабо́ты; **to ~ sb with sth** (*inf*) нава́ливать (навали́ть* *perf*) что-н на кого́-н
▶ **land up** *vi*: **to ~ up (in/at)** очути́ться* *(perf)* (в/на *+prp*).
landed gentry ['lændɪd-] *n* земле-владе́льческая аристокра́тия.
landfill site ['lændfɪl-] *n* ме́сто захороне́ния отхо́дов.
landing ['lændɪŋ] *n* (*of house*) ле́стничная площа́дка*; (*of plane*) поса́дка*, приземле́ние.
landing card *n* *ка́рта, заполня́емая прибыва́ющими в страну́ иностра́нцами*.
landing craft *n inv* деса́нтное су́дно*.
landing gear *n* (*AVIAT*) шасси́ *nt ind*.
landing stage *n* при́стань* *f*.
landing strip *n* взлётно-поса́дочная полоса́*.
landlady ['lændleɪdɪ] *n* (*of house, flat*) домовладе́лица, хозя́йка*; (*of pub*) хозя́йка*.
landlocked ['lændlɔkt] *adj* без вы́хода к мо́рю.
landlord ['lændlɔ:d] *n* (*of house, flat*) домовладе́лец*, хозя́ин*; (*of pub*) хозя́ин*.
landlubber ['lændlʌbə^r] *n*: **to be a ~** не люби́ть *(impf)* путеше́ствовать мо́рем.
landmark ['lændmɑ:k] *n* (назе́мный) ориенти́р; (*fig*) ве́ха.
landowner ['lændəunə^r] *n* землевладе́лец (-лица).
landscape ['lænskeɪp] *n* (*view, painting*) пейза́ж; (*terrain*) ландша́фт ◆ *vt*: **to ~ an area** (иску́сственно) создава́ть* (созда́ть* *perf*) ландша́фт.
landscape architect *n* = **landscape gardener**.
landscape gardener *n* ландша́фтный архите́ктор.
landscape painting *n* (*picture*) пейза́ж; (*art*) пейза́жная жи́вопись *f*.
landslide ['lændslaɪd] *n* (*GEO*) о́ползень* *m*; (*POL: also:* **~ victory**) реши́тельная побе́да.
lane [leɪn] *n* (*in country*) тропи́нка*; (*in town*) переу́лок*; (*of carriageway*) полоса́; (*SPORT*) доро́жка*; **shipping ~** морска́я тра́сса.
language ['læŋgwɪdʒ] *n* язы́к*; **bad ~** сквернosло́вие.

language laboratory *n* лингафо́нный кабине́т.
languid ['læŋgwɪd] *adj* то́мный* (то́мен).
languish ['læŋgwɪʃ] *vi* (*person*) томи́ться* (истоми́ться* *perf*); (*project, case*) тяну́ться* (*impf*).
lank [læŋk] *adj* (*hair*) дли́нный* и са́льный*.
lanky ['læŋkɪ] *adj* долговя́зый (долговя́з).
lanolin(e) ['lænəlɪn] *n* ланоли́н.
lantern ['læntən] *n* фона́рь* *m*.
Laos [laus] *n* Лао́с.
lap [læp] *n* коле́ни* *ntpl*; (*SPORT*) круг* ◆ *vt* (*also:* ~ **up**) лака́ть (вы́лакать *perf*) ◆ *vi* (*water*) плеска́ться* (*impf*); **in his/my ~** у него́/меня́ на коле́нях
▸ **lap up** *vt* (*fig*: *flattery*) упива́ться (упи́ться* *perf*) +*instr*.
La Paz [læ'pæz] *n* Ла-Па́с.
lapdog ['læpdɔg] *n* боло́нка*.
lapel [lə'pɛl] *n* ла́цкан.
Lapland ['læplænd] *n* Лапла́ндия.
Lapp [læp] *adj* лапла́ндский ◆ *n* (*person*) лапла́ндец*(-дка), саа́м(ка); (*LING*) саа́мский язы́к*.
lapse [læps] *n* (*bad behaviour*) про́мах*; (*of time*) промежу́ток*; (*of concentration*) поте́ря ◆ *vi* (*law, membership*) теря́ть (потеря́ть *perf*) си́лу; **memory ~** прова́л в па́мяти; **to ~ into bad habits** усва́ивать (усво́ить *perf*) дурны́е привы́чки.
lap-top ['læptɔp] *n*: ~ **computer** портати́вный компью́тер.
larceny ['lɑ:sənɪ] *n* (*esp US*) воровство́.
larch [lɑ:tʃ] *n* ли́ственница.
lard [lɑ:d] *n* свино́й жир*.
larder ['lɑ:də'] *n* кладова́я *f adj*.
large [lɑ:dʒ] *adj* большо́й; (*major*) кру́пный*; **to make ~r** увели́чивать (увели́чить *perf*); **this coat is too ~ for me** э́то пальто́ мне велико́; **a ~ number of people** большо́е число́ люде́й; **on a ~ scale** в кру́пном масшта́бе; **at ~** (*as a whole*) в це́лом; (*at liberty*) на во́ле; **by and ~** вообще́.
largely ['lɑ:dʒlɪ] *adv* по бо́льшей ча́сти; ~ **because** ... в основно́м, потому́ что ....
large-scale ['lɑ:dʒ'skeɪl] *adj* крупномасшта́бный.
largesse [lɑ:'ʒɛs] *n* ще́дрость* *f*.
lark [lɑ:k] *n* (*bird*) жа́воронок*; (*BRIT*: *inf*: *joke*) прока́за
▸ **lark about** *vi* (*BRIT*: *inf*) прока́зничать (напрока́зничать *perf*).
larva ['lɑ:və] (*pl* ~**e**) *n* личи́нка.
larvae ['lɑ:vi:] *npl of* **larva**.
laryngitis [lærɪn'dʒaɪtɪs] *n* ларинги́т.
larynx ['lærɪŋks] *n* горта́нь *f*.
lasagne [lə'zænjə] *n* лаза́нья (*италья́нское блю́до*).
lascivious [lə'sɪvɪəs] *adj* похотли́вый (похотли́в).
laser ['leɪzə'] *n* ла́зер.
laser beam *n* ла́зерный луч*.
laser printer *n* ла́зерный при́нтер.
lash [læʃ] *n* (*eyelash*) ресни́ца; (*of whip*) уда́р (*хлыста́*) ◆ *vt* (*whip*) хлеста́ть* (*impf*), стега́ть (*impf*); (*also:* ~ **against**: *subj*: *rain, wind*) хлеста́ть* (*impf*) о +*acc*; (*tie*): **to ~ to** привя́зывать (привяза́ть* *perf*) к +*dat*; **to ~ together** свя́зывать (связа́ть* *perf*)
▸ **lash down** *vt* привя́зывать (привяза́ть* *perf*) ◆ *vi* (*rain*) хлеста́ть* (*impf*)
▸ **lash out** *vi*: **to ~ out at** (*also fig*) наки́дываться (наки́нуться *perf*) на +*acc*; **to ~ out (on sth)** (*inf*) разоря́ться (разори́ться *perf*) (на что-н).
lashing ['læʃɪŋ] *n*: ~**s of** (*BRIT*: *inf*: *cream etc*) ку́ча +*gen*.
lass [læs] *n* (*BRIT*: *girl*) де́вочка*; (: *young woman*) де́вушка*.
lasso [læ'su:] *n* лассо́ *nt ind*, арка́н ◆ *vt* арка́нить (заарка́нить *perf*).
last [lɑ:st] *adj* (*most recent*) про́шлый; (*final*) после́дний* ◆ *adv* в после́дний раз; (*finally*) в конце́ ◆ *vi* (*continue*) дли́ться (продли́ться *perf*), продолжа́ться (продо́лжиться* *perf*); (*keep*: *thing*) сохраня́ться (сохрани́ться *perf*); (: *person*) держа́ться (продержа́ться *perf*); (*suffice*): **we had enough money to ~ us** нам хвати́ло де́нег; ~ **year** в про́шлом году́; ~ **week** на про́шлой неде́ле; ~ **night** (*early*) вчера́ ве́чером; (*late*) про́шлой но́чью; **at ~** наконе́ц; ~ **but one** предпосле́дний*; **the ~ time** в после́дний раз; **the film ~s (for) 2 hours** фильм дли́тся 2 часа́.
last-ditch ['lɑ:st'dɪtʃ] *adj* (*attempt*) отча́янный.
lasting ['lɑ:stɪŋ] *adj* (*friendship*) продолжи́тельный* (продолжи́телен), дли́тельный* (дли́телен); (*solution*) долговре́менный* (долговре́менен).
lastly ['lɑ:stlɪ] *adv* наконе́ц.
last-minute ['lɑ:stmɪnɪt] *adj* (*attempt*) сде́ланный в после́днюю мину́ту; (*details, meeting*) после́дний*.
latch [lætʃ] *n* (*on gate*) задви́жка*; (*on front door*) замо́к* *m*; **to leave the door on the ~** оставля́ть (оста́вить* *perf*) замо́к на предохрани́теле
▸ **latch on to** *vt fus* (*person*) прилипа́ть (прили́пнуть *perf*) к +*dat*; (*idea*) привя́зываться (привяза́ться* *perf*) к +*dat*.
latchkey ['lætʃki:] *n* ключ от замка́ (*к входно́й две́ри*).
latchkey child *n ребёнок, находя́щийся до́ма в то вре́мя когда́ роди́тели рабо́тают.*
late [leɪt] *adj* (*far on in time, process, work etc*) по́здний*; (*former*) бы́вший*; (*dead*)

покóйный ◆ *adv* пóздно; (*behind time*) с опоздáнием; **to be ~** опáздывать (опоздáть *perf*); **I was 10 minutes ~** я опоздáл на 10 минýт; **in the ~ 1970s** к концý семидесятых годóв; **he is in his ~ thirties** емý далекó за тридцать; **in ~ May** в концé мáя; **to work ~** рабóтать *(impf)* допоздна́; **~ in life** в пожилóм вóзрасте; **of ~** в послéднее врéмя.
latecomer ['leɪtkʌmə^r] *n* опоздáвший(-ая)*m(f) adj*.
lately ['leɪtlɪ] *adv* в послéднее врéмя.
lateness ['leɪtnɪs] *n* опоздáние; **owing to the ~ of the hour** из-за пóзднего чáса.
latent ['leɪtnt] *adj* скрытый (скрыт); **~ defect** скрытый дефéкт.
later ['leɪtə^r] *adj* (*time, date*) бóлее пóздний*; (*meeting, version*) послéдующий* ◆ *adv* пóзже, позднéе; **~ on** в послéдствии, потóм; **he arrived ~ than me** он пришёл пóзже меня́.
lateral ['lætərl] *adj* боковóй; **~ thinking** нестандáртное мышление.
latest ['leɪtɪst] *adj* сáмый пóздний*; (*most recent*) (сáмый) нóвый *or* послéдний*; (*news*) послéдний*; **at the ~** сáмое пóзднее.
latex ['leɪteks] *n* лáтекс.
lathe [leɪð] *n* токáрный станóк*.
lather ['lɑːðə^r] *n* (мыльная) пéна ◆ *vt* мылить (намылить *perf*).
Latin ['lætɪn] *n* (*LING*) лати́нский* язык*; (*person*) жи́тель(ница) *m(f)* южной Еврóпы ◆ *adj*: **~ languages** ромáнские языки́; **~ countries** страны южной Еврóпы.
Latin America *n* Лати́нская Амéрика.
Latin American *adj* латиноамерикáнский ◆ *n* латиноамерикáнец*(-áнка*).
latitude ['lætɪtjuːd] *n* (*GEO*) широтá*; (*fig*) свобóда.
latrine [lə'triːn] *n* отхóжее мéсто*.
latter ['lætə^r] *adj* послéдний* ◆ *n*: **the ~** послéдний*(-яя) *m(f) adj*; **the ~ part of the week** вторáя полови́на недéли.
latter-day ['lætədeɪ] *adj* соврем́енный.
latterly ['lætəlɪ] *adv* недáвно, в послéднее врéмя.
lattice ['lætɪs] *n* решётка*.
lattice window *n* решётчатое окнó*.
Latvia ['lætvɪə] *n* Лáтвия.
Latvian ['lætvɪən] *adj* латви́йский ◆ *n* латыш(ка); (*LING*) латышский язык*.
laudable ['lɔːdəbl] *adj* похвáльный* (похвáлен).
laudatory ['lɔːdətrɪ] *adj* хвалéбный* (хвалéбен).
laugh [lɑːf] *n* смех* ◆ *vi* смея́ться* *(impf)*; **(to do sth) for a ~** *(inf)* (дéлать *(impf)* что-н) для смéха
▸ **laugh at** *vt fus* смея́ться* (посмея́ться *perf*) над *+instr*
▸ **laugh off** *vt*: **to ~ sth off** отдéлываться (отдéлаться *perf*) от чегó-н шýткой.
laughable ['lɑːfəbl] *adj* смехотвóрный* (смехотвóрен).
laughing gas ['lɑːfɪŋ-] *n* веселя́щий газ*.
laughing matter *n*: **this is no ~ ~** э́то дéло нешýточное.
laughing stock *n* посмéшище; **to be the ~ ~ of** служи́ть *(impf)* посмéшищем для *+gen*.
laughter ['lɑːftə^r] *n* смех*.
launch [lɔːntʃ] *n* (*of rocket, product*) зáпуск; (*motorboat*) момóрный кáтер* ◆ *vt* (*ship*) спускáть (спусти́ть* *perf*) нá воду; (*rocket*) запускáть (запусти́ть* *perf*); (*campaign, attack*) начинáть (начáть* *perf*); (*product*) пускáть (пусти́ть* *perf*) в продáжу
▸ **launch into** *vt fus* (*speech, activity*) пускáться (пусти́ться* *perf*) в *+acc*
▸ **launch out** *vi*: **to ~ out into** брáться* (взя́ться* *perf*) за *+acc*.
launching ['lɔːntʃɪŋ] *n* (*of ship*) спуск (нá воду); (*of rocket, product*) зáпуск; (*of campaign, attack*) начáло.
launch(ing) pad *n* стáртовая площáдка*.
launder ['lɔːndə^r] *vt* (*clothes, sheets*) стирáть (выстирать *perf*); (*money*) отмывáть (отмыть* *perf*).
Launderette® [lɔːn'drɛt] *n* (*BRIT*) прáчечная *f adj* самообслýживания.
Laundromat® ['lɔːndrəmæt] *n* (*US*) = **Launderette®**.
laundry ['lɔːndrɪ] *n* (*washing*) сти́рка; (*place*) прáчечная *f adj*; **to do the ~** стирáть (выстирать *perf*).
laureate ['lɔːrɪət] *adj see* **poet laureate**.
laurel ['lɔrl] *n* (*tree*) лавр, лáвровое дéрево; **to rest on one's ~s** почивáть (почи́ть* *perf*) на лáврах.
Lausanne [ləu'zæn] *n* Лозáнна.
lava ['lɑːvə] *n* лáва.
lavatory ['lævətərɪ] *n* туалéт.
lavatory paper *n* туалéтная бумáга.
lavender ['lævəndə^r] *n* лавáнда.
lavish ['lævɪʃ] *adj* (*amount, hospitality*) щéдрый* (щедр); (*meal*) оби́льный* (оби́лен); (*surroundings*) пышный* (пышен); (*person*): **~ with** щéдрый* (щедр) на *+acc* ◆ *vt*: **to ~ sth on sb** осыпáть (осыпать* *perf*) когó-н чем-н.
lavishly ['lævɪʃlɪ] *adv* (*generously*) щéдро; (*sumptuously*) пышно.
law [lɔː] *n* закóн; (*professions*): **(the) ~** юриспрудéнция; (*SCOL*) прáво; **it's against the ~** э́то противозакóнно; **to study ~** изучáть *(impf)* прáво; **to go to ~** обращáться (обрати́ться* *perf*) в суд; **to break the ~** нарушáть (наруши́ть *perf*) закóн.
law-abiding ['lɔːəbaɪdɪŋ] *adj* законопослýшный.
law and order *n* правопоря́док*.
lawbreaker ['lɔːbreɪkə^r] *n* правонаруши́тель-(ница) *m(f)*.
law court *n* суд*.
lawful ['lɔːful] *adj* закóнный.

lawfully ['lɔːfəlɪ] *adv* зако́нно.
lawless ['lɔːlɪs] *adj* (*action*) беззако́нный.
Law Lord *n* (*BRIT*) *член пала́ты ло́рдов, состоя́щий в апелляцио́нном суде́.*
lawmaker ['lɔːmeɪkə^r] *n* законода́тель(ница) *m(f)*.
lawn [lɔːn] *n* газо́н.
lawn mower ['lɔːnməuə^r] *n* газонокоси́лка*.
lawn tennis *n* те́ннис (*на травяно́м ко́рте*).
law school *n* (*US*) юриди́ческий институ́т.
law student *n* студе́нт(ка) юриди́ческого факульте́та.
lawsuit ['lɔːsuːt] *n* суде́бный иск.
lawyer ['lɔːjə^r] *n* (*solicitor, barrister*) адвока́т; (*legal specialist*) юри́ст.
lax [læks] *adj* (*discipline, standards*) нестро́гий (нестро́г); (*morals, behaviour*) распу́щенный (распу́щен).
laxative ['læksətɪv] *n* слаби́тельное *nt adj*.
laxity ['læksɪtɪ] *n* небре́жность *f*; (*moral*) распу́щенность *f*.
lay [leɪ] (*pt, pp* **laid**) *pt of* **lie** ◆ *adj* (*REL*) мирско́й; (*not expert*) непрофессиона́льный ◆ *vt* (*place*) класть* (положи́ть* *perf*); (*table*) накрыва́ть (накры́ть* *perf*) (на *+acc*); (*carpet*) стлать (настла́ть *or* настели́ть* *perf*); (*cable*) прокла́дывать (проложи́ть* *perf*); (*plans*) составля́ть (соста́вить* *perf*); (*trap*) ста́вить* (поста́вить* *perf*); (: *fig*) подстра́ивать (подстро́ить *perf*); (*egg*) откла́дывать (отложи́ть *perf*); **to ~ facts/proposals before sb** излага́ть (изложи́ть* *perf*) фа́кты/предложе́ния пе́ред кем-н; **to ~ one's hands on sth** (*inf*) достава́ть* (доста́ть* *perf*) что-н; **to get laid** (*inf!*) тра́хаться (тра́хнуться *perf*) (*!*)
▸ **lay aside** *vt* откла́дывать (отложи́ть* *perf*)
▸ **lay by** *vt* = **lay aside**
▸ **lay down** *vt* (*object*) класть* (положи́ть* *perf*); (*rules, laws*) устана́вливать (установи́ть* *perf*); (*weapons*) скла́дывать (сложи́ть* *perf*); **to ~ down the law** прика́зывать *(impf)*; **to ~ down one's life** положи́ть* *(perf)* жизнь
▸ **lay in** *vt* (*supplies*) запаса́ть (запасти́* *perf*)
▸ **lay into** *vt fus* (*also fig*) набра́сываться (набро́ситься* *perf*) на *+acc*
▸ **lay off** *vt* (*workers*) увольня́ть (уво́лить *perf*)
▸ **lay on** *vt* (*meal, entertainment*) устра́ивать (устро́ить *perf*); (*water, gas*) прокла́дывать (проложи́ть* *perf*); (*paint*) наноси́ть* (нанести́* *perf*)
▸ **lay out** *vt* раскла́дывать (разложи́ть* *perf*); (*inf*): **to ~ out money on sth** выкла́дывать (вы́ложить* *perf*) де́ньги на что-н
▸ **lay up** *vt* (*ship*) ста́вить* (поста́вить* *perf*) на прико́л; (*sick person*): **to be laid up with** валя́ться *(impf)* с *+instr*; **the car was laid up all year** маши́на простоя́ла весь год.
layabout ['leɪəbaut] *n* (*inf*) безде́льник(-ица).
lay-by ['leɪbaɪ] *n* (*BRIT*) площа́дка для вре́менной стоя́нки (*на автодоро́ге*).
lay days *npl* (*NAUT*) сали́йное вре́мя* *nt sg*.
layer ['leɪə^r] *n* слой*.
layette [leɪ'ɛt] *n* прида́ное *nt adj* (*для новорождённого*).
layman ['leɪmən] *irreg n* (*non-expert*) неспециали́ст.
lay-off ['leɪɔf] *n* увольне́ние.
layout ['leɪaut] *n* (*of garden, building*) планиро́вка*; (*of page*) компано́вка*.
laze [leɪz] *vi* (*also:* **~ about**) безде́льничать *(impf)*; **to ~ about in bed/the sun** не́житься *(impf)* в посте́ли/на со́лнце.
laziness ['leɪzɪnɪs] *n* лень *f*.
lazy ['leɪzɪ] *adj* лени́вый (лени́в).
LB *abbr* (*CANADA*) = *Labrador*.
lb. *abbr* (= *pound (weight)*) фунт.
lbw *abbr* (*CRICKET*) = *leg before wicket*.
LC *n abbr* (*US*) = *Library of Congress*.
lc *abbr* (*TYP*: = *lower case*) строчна́я бу́ква.
L/C *abbr* (= *letter of credit*) аккредити́в.
LCD *n abbr* = **liquid crystal display**.
Ld *abbr* (*BRIT*: *in titles*) = **lord**.
LDS *n abbr* (*BRIT*: = *Licentiate in Dental Surgery*) *лице́нзия на стоматологи́ческую пра́ктику* ◆ *abbr* (= *Latter-day Saints*) „Святы́е после́днего дня" (*официа́льное назва́ние се́кты мормо́нов*).
LEA *n abbr* (*BRIT*: = *Local Education Authority*) *ме́стное управле́ние по дела́м просвеще́ния*.
lead[1] [liːd] (*pt, pp* **led**) *n* (*front position*) пе́рвенство, ли́дерство; (*clue*) нить *f*; (*in play, film*) гла́вная роль *f*; (*for dog*) поводо́к*; (*ELEC*) про́вод* ◆ *vt* (*competition, market*) лиди́ровать *(impf)* в *+prp*; (*opponent*) опережа́ть *(impf)*; (*person, group: guide*) вести́* (повести́* *perf*); (*activity, organization etc*) руководи́ть* *(impf)* *+instr*, возглавля́ть (возгла́вить* *perf*) ◆ *vi* (*road, pipe etc*) вести́* *(impf)*; (*SPORT*) лиди́ровать *(impf)*; **to take the ~** (*SPORT*) выходи́ть* (вы́йти* *perf*) вперёд; (*fig*) брать* (взять* *perf*) на себя́ веду́щую роль; **to ~ the way** (*also fig*) ука́зывать (указа́ть* *perf*) путь; **to ~ sb astray** вводи́ть* (ввести́* *perf*) кого́-н в заблужде́ние; **to ~ sb to do** приводи́ть* (привести́* *perf*) кого́-н к чему́-н; **to ~ sb to believe that ...** дава́ть* (дать* *perf*) кому́-н поня́ть, что ...; **to ~ an interesting life** вести́* *(impf)* интере́сную жизнь; **to ~ an orchestra** (*BRIT*) исполня́ть (испо́лнить *perf*) пе́рвую скри́пку
▸ **lead away** *vt* уводи́ть* (увести́* *perf*)
▸ **lead back** *vt* приводи́ть* (привести́* *perf*) обра́тно
▸ **lead into** *vt fus* вводи́ть* (ввести́* *perf*) в *+acc*

▸ **lead off** *vi* (*in game, conversation*) начинáть (начáть* *perf*); (*road, corridor*) отходи́ть* (*impf*) ◆ *vt fus* отходи́ть* (*impf*) от *+gen*
▸ **lead on** *vt* (*tease*) води́ть* (*impf*) зá нос
▸ **lead out of** *vt fus* выводи́ть* (вы́вести* *perf*) из *+gen*
▸ **lead to** *vt fus* вести́* (привести́* *perf*) к *+dat*
▸ **lead up to** *vt fus* (*events*) приводи́ть* (привести́* *perf*) к *+dat*; (*topic*) подводи́ть* (подвести́* *perf*) к *+dat*.
lead² [lɛd] *n* (*metal*) свинéц*; (*in pencil*) графи́т.
leaded ['lɛdɪd] *adj* (*window, glass*) со свинцóвыми креплéниями; (*petrol*) содержáщий свинéц.
leaden ['lɛdn] *adj* (*sky, sea*) свинцóвый; (*movements*) скóванный (скóван).
leader ['li:dəʳ] *n* (*of group,* SPORT) ли́дер; (*in newspaper*) передовáя статья́; **the L~ of the House (of Commons/Lords)** (BRIT) *представи́тель прáвящей пáртии в палáте Óбщин/Лóрдов, наделённый осóбыми полномóчиями.*
leadership ['li:dəʃɪp] *n* (*position, process*) руковóдство; (*quality*) ли́дерские кáчества *ntpl*.
lead-free ['lɛdfri:] *adj* (*petrol*) не содержáщий свинцá.
leading ['li:dɪŋ] *adj* (*most important*) ведýщий*; (*first, front*) перéдний*; (*winning*) лиди́рующий; **~ role** (*in film, play*) глáвная роль *f*.
leading lady *n* (THEAT) исполни́тельница глáвной рóли.
leading light *n* (*person*) свети́ло.
leading man *irreg n* (THEAT) исполни́тель *m* глáвной рóли.
leading question *n* наводя́щий* вопрóс.
lead pencil [lɛd-] *n* гри́фельный карандáш*.
lead poisoning [lɛd-] *n* отравлéние свинцóм.
lead singer [li:d-] *n* соли́ст(ка).
lead time [li:d-] *n* (COMM) врéмя* *ntsg* реализáции закáза.
lead-up ['li:dʌp] *n*: **in the ~ to** незадóлго до *+gen*.
leaf [li:f] (*pl* **leaves**) *n* (BOT, *of book*) лист*; (*of table*) откиднáя доскá* ◆ *vi*: **to ~ through** листáть (пролистáть *perf*); **to turn over a new ~** начáть* (*perf*) нóвую жизнь; **to take a ~ out of sb's book** слéдовать (послéдовать *perf*) примéру когó-н.
leaflet ['li:flɪt] *n* листóвка*.
leafy ['li:fɪ] *adj* (*trees, vegetables*) покры́тый (покры́т) листвóй; (*place*) зелёный* (зéлен).
league [li:g] *n* ли́га; **to be in ~ with sb** быть* (*impf*) в сгóворе с кем-н.
league table *n* (BRIT: SPORT) табли́ца результáтов спортклýбов однóй из лиг; (*fig: of wages, prices*) сравни́тельная табли́ца.
leak [li:k] *n* (*hole*) течь *f*; (*seepage*) утéчка*; (*fig*): **(information) ~** утéчка* информáции ◆ *vi* (*pipe, roof, shoes*) протекáть (протéчь* *perf*); (*ship*) давáть* (дать* *perf*) течь; (*liquid, gas*) просáчиваться (просочи́ться *perf*) ◆ *vt* (*information*) разглашáть (разгласи́ть* *perf*)
▸ **leak out** *vi* (*liquid*) вытекáть (вы́течь* *perf*); (*information*) просáчиваться (просочи́ться *perf*).
leakage ['li:kɪdʒ] *n* утéчка*.
leaky ['li:kɪ] *adj* (*roof etc*) дыря́вый, прохуди́вшийся.
lean [li:n] (*pt, pp* **leaned** *or* **leant**) *adj* (*person*) поджáрый (поджáр); (*meat*) пóстный; (*period*) скýдный* (скýден) ◆ *vt*: **to ~ sth on** *or* **against sth** прислоня́ть (прислони́ть *perf*) что-н к чемý-н ◆ *vi*: **to ~ (forward/back)** наклоня́ться (наклони́ться* *perf*) (вперёд/ назáд); **to ~ against** (*wall*) прислоня́ться (прислони́ться *perf*) к *+dat*; (*person*) опирáться (оперéться* *perf*) на *+acc*; **to ~ on** (*chair*) опирáться (оперéться* *perf*) о *+acc*; (*rely on*) опирáться (оперéться* *perf*) на *+acc*; (*pressurize*) нажимáть (нажáть* *perf*) на *+acc*; **to ~ towards** (*idea, belief*) склоня́ться (склони́ться* *perf*) к *+dat*
▸ **lean out** *vi*: **to ~ out (of)** высóвываться (вы́сунуться *perf*) (из *+gen*)
▸ **lean over** *vi* наклоня́ться (наклони́ться* *perf*).
leaning ['li:nɪŋ] *n*: **~ (towards)** склóнность *f* (к *+dat*).
leant [lɛnt] *pt, pp of* **lean**.
lean-to ['li:ntu:] *n* пристрóйка*.
leap [li:p] (*pt, pp* **leaped** *or* **leapt**) *n* прыжóк*, скачóк*; (*increase*) скачóк* ◆ *vi* пры́гать (пры́гнуть *perf*); (*price, number*) подскáкивать (подскочи́ть *perf*); **to ~ at** (*offer, opportunity*) ухвати́ться* (*perf*) за *+acc*; **to ~ to one's feet** вскáкивать (вскочи́ть *perf*) нá ноги
▸ **leap up** *vi* подпры́гивать (подпры́гнуть *perf*).
leapfrog ['li:pfrɔg] *n* чехардá.
leapt [lɛpt] *pt, pp of* **leap**.
leap year *n* високóсный год*.
learn [lə:n] (*pt, pp* **learned** *or* **learnt**) *vt* (*skill*) учи́ться* (научи́ться* *perf*) *+dat*; (*facts, poem*) учи́ть* (вы́учить* *perf*) ◆ *vi* учи́ться* (*impf*); **to ~ about** *or* **of/that ...** (*hear, read*) узнавáть* (узнáть *perf*) о *+prp*/, что ...; **to ~ about sth** (*study*) изучáть (изучи́ть* *perf*) что-н; **to ~ (how) to do** учи́ться* (научи́ться* *perf*) *+impf infin*.
learned ['lə:nɪd] *adj* учёный.
learner ['lə:nəʳ] *n* учени́к*(-и́ца*).
learning ['lə:nɪŋ] *n* учёность *f*; **person of ~** учёный человéк.
learnt [lə:nt] *pt, pp of* **learn**.
lease [li:s] *n* арéндный договóр ◆ *vt*: **to ~ sth (to sb)** сдавáть* (сдать* *perf*) что-н в арéнду (комý-н); **to ~ sth from sb** арендовáть (*impf/perf*) *or* брать* (взять* *perf*) в арéнду у когó-н;

on ~ (to sb) сданный (сдан) в аренду (кому-н)

▸ **lease back** *vt* сдавать* (сдать* *perf*) в аренду прежнему владельцу (*для мобилизации денежных средств*).

leaseback ['li:sbæk] *n сдача собственности в аренду её прежнему владельцу.*

leasehold ['li:shəuld] *n* (*also:* **~ property**) арендованная собственность *f* ◆ *adj* арендованный (арендован).

leash [li:ʃ] *n* поводок*.

least [li:st] *adj*: **the ~** (*+noun: smallest*) наименьший*; (: *slightest*) малейший* ◆ *adv* (*+vb*) меньше всего; (*+adj*): **the ~** наименее; **the ~ possible effort** наименьшее усилие; **I don't have the ~ idea about it** я не имею ни малейшего представления об этом; **at ~** по крайней мере; **you could at ~ have written** Вы могли бы по крайней мере написать; **not in the ~** совсем нет; (*+vb, +adj*) совсем *or* вовсе не.

leather ['lɛðəʳ] *n* кожа.

leather goods *npl* кожаные изделия *ntpl.*

leave [li:v] (*pt, pp* **left**) *vt* оставлять (оставить* *perf*); (*go away from: on foot*) уходить* (уйти* *perf*) из *+gen*; (: *by transport*) уезжать (уехать* *perf*) из *+gen*; (*party, committee*) выходить* (выйти* *perf*) из *+gen* ◆ *vi* (*on foot*) уходить* (уйти* *perf*); (*by transport*) уезжать (уехать* *perf*); (*bus, train*) уходить* (уйти* *perf*) ◆ *n* отпуск*; **to ~ sth to sb** (*money, property*) оставлять (оставить* *perf*) что-н кому-н; (*responsibility*) оставлять (оставить* *perf*) что-н под чью-н ответственность; **to be left (over)** оставаться* (остаться* *perf*); **to take one's ~ of sb** прощаться (попрощаться *perf*) с кем-н; **on ~** в отпуске

▸ **leave behind** *vt* оставлять (оставить* *perf*)

▸ **leave off** *vt* (*heating, light*) не включать (включить *perf*) ◆ *vi* (*stop: inf*) отставать* (отстать* *perf*); **he left the lid off** он не положил крышку

▸ **leave on** *vt* (*coat*) не снимать (снять* *perf*); (*light, heating*) оставлять (оставить* *perf*)

▸ **leave out** *vt* (*omit*) пропускать (пропустить* *perf*); **he was left out** его пропустили.

leave of absence *n* отпуск без содержания.

leaves [li:vz] *npl of* **leaf**.

Lebanese [lɛbə'ni:z] *adj* ливанский* ◆ *n inv* ливанец(-нка).

Lebanon ['lɛbənən] *n* Ливан.

lecherous ['lɛtʃərəs] *adj* развратный* (развратен).

lectern ['lɛktə:n] *n* кафедра.

lecture ['lɛktʃəʳ] *n* лекция ◆ *vi* читать *(impf)* лекции ◆ *vt* (*scold*): **to ~ sb on** *or* **about sth** читать *(impf)* кому-н лекцию по поводу чего-н; **to give a ~ on** читать (прочитать *perf*) лекцию о *+prp*.

lecture hall *n* аудитория, лекционный зал.

lecturer ['lɛktʃərəʳ] *n* (*BRIT: at university*) преподаватель(ница) *m(f)*; (*speaker*) лектор.

LED *n abbr* (*ELEC: = light-emitting diode*) СИД= *светоизлучающий диод.*

led [lɛd] *pt, pp of* **lead**[1].

ledge [lɛdʒ] *n* (*of mountain*) выступ; (*of window*) подоконник; (*on wall*) полка*.

ledger ['lɛdʒəʳ] *n* расходно-приходная книга.

lee [li:] *n* (*shelter*) покров.

leech [li:tʃ] *n* (*also fig*) пиявка*.

leek [li:k] *n* лук-порей *no pl.*

leer [lɪəʳ] *vi*: **to ~ at sb** похотливо смотреть (посмотреть *perf*) на кого-н.

leeward ['li:wəd] (*NAUT*) *adj* подветренный ◆ *adv* с подветренной стороны ◆ *n* подветренная сторона*; **to ~** на подветренную сторону.

leeway ['li:weɪ] *n* (*fig*): **to allow o.s. some ~** давать* (дать* *perf*) себе свободу; **we have a lot of ~ to make up** нам нужно многое наверстать.

left [lɛft] *pt, pp of* **leave** ◆ *adj* (*remaining*) оставшийся; (*of direction, position*) левый ◆ *n* левая сторона* ◆ *adv* (*motion*): **(to the) ~** налево; (*position*): **(on the) ~** слева; **the L~** (*POL*) левые *pl adj.*

left-hand drive ['lɛfthænd-] *adj* (*AUT*) с рулём на левой стороне.

left-handed [lɛft'hændɪd] *adj*: **he/she is ~** он/она левша.

left-hand side *n*: **the ~ ~** левая сторона.

leftie ['lɛftɪ] *n* (*inf: pej: BRIT: left winger*) левый(-ая) *m/f adj.*

leftist ['lɛftɪst] *n* левый(-ая) *m(f) adj* ◆ *adj* левый.

left-luggage (office) [lɛft'lʌgɪdʒ(-)] *n* (*BRIT*) камера хранения.

leftovers ['lɛftəuvəz] *npl* остатки *mpl.*

left-wing ['lɛft'wɪŋ] *adj* (*POL*) левый.

left-winger ['lɛft'wɪŋgəʳ] *n* (*BRIT: POL*) левый(-ая) *m(f) adj*, представитель *m* левого крыла.

lefty ['lɛftɪ] *n* = **leftie**.

leg [lɛg] *n* (*ANAT, also CULIN: of lamb*) нога*; (*of insect, furniture, also CULIN: of chicken*) ножка*; (*also:* **trouser ~**) штанина; (*of journey, race*) этап; **to stretch one's ~s** разминать (размять* *perf*) ноги.

legacy ['lɛgəsɪ] *n* (*in will*) наследство; (*fig*) наследие.

legal ['li:gl] *adj* (*advice, requirement*) юридический*; (*system, action*) судебный; (*lawful*) законный* (законен); **to take ~ action** *or* **proceedings against sb** возбуждать (возбудить* *perf*) судебное дело против кого-н.

legal adviser *n* юрисконсульт.

* marks translations which have irregular inflections. The Russian-English side of the dictionary gives inflectional information.

legal holiday *n* (*US*) непрису́тственный день* *m*.
legality [lɪ'gælɪtɪ] *n* зако́нность *f*.
legalize ['li:gəlaɪz] *vt* узако́нивать (узако́нить* *perf*); (*party, group*) легализова́ть (*impf/perf*).
legally ['li:gəlɪ] *adv* юриди́чески; (*act*) зако́нно; (*by law*) по зако́ну; **~ binding** юриди́чески обяза́тельный* (обяза́телен).
legal tender *n* зако́нное сре́дство платежа́ (*обы́чно о бума́жных и металли́ческих деньга́х*).
legatee [lɛgə'ti:] *n* насле́дник.
legation [lɪ'geɪʃən] *n* ми́ссия, представи́тельство.
legend ['lɛdʒənd] *n* (*story*) леге́нда; (*person*) легенда́рная ли́чность *f*.
legendary ['lɛdʒəndərɪ] *adj* легенда́рный* (легенда́рен).
-legged ['lɛgɪd] *suffix* -но́гий*.
leggy ['lɛgɪ] *adj* длинноно́гий* (длинноно́г).
leggings ['lɛgɪŋz] *npl* лоси́ны *fpl*.
legibility [lɛdʒɪ'bɪlɪtɪ] *n* разбо́рчивость *f*.
legible ['lɛdʒəbl] *adj* разбо́рчивый (разбо́рчив).
legibly ['lɛdʒəblɪ] *adv* разбо́рчиво.
legion ['li:dʒən] *n* легио́н ◆ *adj* (*numerous*): **their problems are ~** у них легио́н пробле́м.
legionnaire [li:dʒə'nɛə'] *n* легионе́р.
legionnaire's disease *n* боле́знь *f* „легионе́ров".
legislate ['lɛdʒɪsleɪt] *vi* издава́ть* (изда́ть* *perf*) зако́н(ы).
legislation [lɛdʒɪs'leɪʃən] *n* законода́тельство.
legislative ['lɛdʒɪslətɪv] *adj* (*POL*) законода́тельный.
legislator ['lɛdʒɪsleɪtə'] *n* (*POL*) законода́тель *m*
legislature ['lɛdʒɪslətʃə'] *n* законода́тельные о́рганы *mpl*.
legitimacy [lɪ'dʒɪtɪməsɪ] *n* зако́нность *f*.
legitimate [lɪ'dʒɪtɪmət] *adj* зако́нный* (зако́нен).
legitimize [lɪ'dʒɪtɪmaɪz] *vt* узако́нивать (узако́нить *perf*).
legless ['lɛglɪs] *adj* (*without legs*) безно́гий* (безно́г); (*very drunk*: *inf*: *BRIT*) пья́ный в сте́льку.
legroom ['lɛgru:m] *n* (*in car etc*) простра́нство для ног.
Leics *abbr* (*BRIT*: *POST*) = *Leicestershire*.
Leipzig ['laɪpsɪg] *n* Ле́йпциг.
leisure ['lɛʒə'] *n* (*also*: **~ time**) досу́г, свобо́дное вре́мя* *nt*; **to do sth at (one's) ~** де́лать (сде́лать *perf*) что-н не спеша́.
leisure centre *n* спорти́вно-оздорови́тельный ко́мплекс.
leisurely ['lɛʒəlɪ] *adj* неторопли́вый (неторпли́в).
leisure suit *n* спорти́вный костю́м.
lemon ['lɛmən] *n* лимо́н ◆ *adj* лимо́нный.
lemonade [lɛmə'neɪd] *n* лимона́д.
lemon cheese *n* = **lemon curd**.
lemon curd *n* (*CULIN*) *сла́дкое лимо́нное пови́дло*.
lemon juice *n* лимо́нный сок*.
lemon squeezer *n* (ручна́я) соковыжима́лка*.
lemon tea *n* чай* с лимо́ном.
lend [lɛnd] (*pt, pp* **lent**) *vt*: **to ~ sth to sb, ~ sb sth** ода́лживать (одолжи́ть *perf*) что́-н кому́-н; **it ~s itself to ...** э́то поддаётся *+dat* ...; **to ~ sb a hand** выруча́ть (вы́ручить *perf*) кого́-н.
lender ['lɛndə'] *n* кредито́р.
lending library ['lɛndɪŋ-] *n* библиоте́ка, вы́дающая кни́ги на́ дом.
length [lɛŋθ] *n* (*measurement*) длина́; (*distance*) протяжённость *f*; (*piece*: *of wood, cloth etc*) кусо́к*; (*duration*) продолжи́тельность *f*; (*of book*) объём; **2 metres in ~** длино́й в 2 ме́тра; **he walked the (whole) ~ of the island** он прошёл че́рез весь о́стров; **I swam three ~s** я проплы́л три длины́ пла́вательного бассе́йна; **at ~** (*at last*) наконе́ц; (*for a long time*) до́лго; **to lie full ~** растя́гиваться (растяну́ться* *perf*) во весь рост; **to go to any ~(s) to do** прикла́дывать (приложи́ть* *perf*) все уси́лия что́бы *+perf infin*.
lengthen ['lɛŋθn] *vt* удлиня́ть (удлини́ть *perf*) ◆ *vi* удлиня́ться (удлини́ться *perf*).
lengthways ['lɛŋθweɪz] *adv* вдоль.
lengthy ['lɛŋθɪ] *adj* (*text*) дли́нный* (дли́нен); (*meeting*) продолжи́тельный* (продолжи́телен); (*explanation*) до́лгий*.
leniency ['li:nɪənsɪ] *n* мя́гкость *f*.
lenient ['li:nɪənt] *adj* мя́гкий* (мя́гок).
leniently ['li:nɪəntlɪ] *adv* мя́гко.
Leningrad ['lɛnɪngræd] *n* Ленингра́д.
lens [lɛnz] *n* (*of spectacles, camera*) ли́нза; (*of telescope*) объекти́в.
Lent [lɛnt] *n* Вели́кий* пост*.
lent [lɛnt] *pt, pp of* **lend**.
lentil ['lɛntl] *n* чечеви́ца *no pl*.
Leo ['li:əu] *n* Лев*; **he is ~** он – Лев.
leopard ['lɛpəd] *n* леопа́рд.
leotard ['li:ətɑ:d] *n* трико́ *nt ind*.
leper ['lɛpə'] *n* прокажённый(-ая) *m(f) adj*.
leper colony *n* лепрозо́рий.
leprosy ['lɛprəsɪ] *n* прока́за.
lesbian ['lɛzbɪən] *adj* лесби́йский ◆ *n* лесбия́нка*.
lesion ['li:ʒən] *n* поврежде́ние.
Lesotho [lɪ'su:tu:] *n* Лесо́то.
less [lɛs] *adj* (*in size, degree, amount*) ме́ньше; (*in quality*) ме́нее ◆ *adv* ме́ньше ◆ *prep*: **~ tax/10% discount** ми́нус нало́г/ски́дка на 10%; **~ than half** ме́ньше полови́ны; **~ than ever** ме́ньше, чем когда́-либо; **~ and ~** всё ме́ньше и ме́ньше; **the ~ ... the more ...** чем ме́ньше ..., тем бо́льше ...; **the Prime Minister, no ~** никто́ ино́й как премье́р-мини́стр.
lessee [lɛ'si:] *n* (*of premises*) съёмщик; (*of land*) аренда́тор.

lessen ['lɛsn] *vt* уменьша́ть (уме́ньшить *perf*) ◆ *vi* уменьша́ться (уме́ньшиться *perf*).

lesser ['lɛsəʳ] *adj* ме́ньший*; **to a ~ extent** в ме́ньшей сте́пени.

lesson ['lɛsn] *n* (*also fig*) уро́к; **to teach sb a ~** (*fig*) проучи́ть* (*perf*) кого́-н.

lessor ['lɛsəʳ] *n* лицо́*, сдаю́щее со́бственность в аре́нду.

lest [lɛst] *conj*: **~ you (should) forget** что́бы Вы не забы́ли.

let [lɛt] (*pt, pp* **let**) *vt* (*BRIT*: *lease*) сдава́ть* (сдать* *perf*) (внаём); (*allow*): **to ~ sb do** разреша́ть (разреши́ть *perf*) *or* позволя́ть (позво́лить *perf*) кому́-н +*infin*; **~ me try** да́йте я попро́бую; **~ him come** пусть он придёт; **to ~ sb know about ...** дава́ть* (дать* *perf*) кому́-н знать о +*prp ...*; **~'s go** пошли́, пойдёмте; **"to ~"** „сдаётся внаём"; **to ~ go of** отпуска́ть (отпусти́ть* *perf*); **~ go!** (от)пусти́!; **to ~ sth drop** роня́ть (урони́ть* *perf*) что-н; **to ~ o.s. go** (*relax*) расслабля́ться (рассла́биться* *perf*); (*neglect o.s.*) опуска́ться (опусти́ться* *perf*)

▸ **let down** *vt* (*tyre etc*) спуска́ть (спусти́ть* *perf*); (*fig*: *person*) подводи́ть* (подвести́* *perf*); (*hair*) распуска́ть (распусти́ть* *perf*); (*dress, hem*) отпуска́ть (отпусти́ть* *perf*)

▸ **let in** *vt* (*water, air*) пропуска́ть (пропусти́ть* *perf*); (*person*) впуска́ть (впусти́ть* *perf*)

▸ **let off** *vt* (*culprit, schoolchildren*) отпуска́ть (отпусти́ть* *perf*); (*bomb*) взрыва́ть (взорва́ть* *perf*); (*gun*) выстре́ливать (вы́стрелить *perf*) из +*gen*; (*smell*) испуска́ть (испусти́ть* *perf*); **to ~ off steam** (*inf*) выпуска́ть (вы́пустить* *perf*) пар

▸ **let on** *vi* проговáриваться (проговори́ться *perf*)

▸ **let out** *vt* (*person, dog, water, air*) выпуска́ть (вы́пустить* *perf*); (*passenger*) выса́живать (вы́садить* *perf*); (*sound*) издава́ть* (изда́ть* *perf*); (*house, room*) сдава́ть* (сдать* *perf*)

▸ **let up** *vi* (*cease*) перестава́ть* (переста́ть* *perf*); (*diminish*) ослабева́ть (ослабе́ть *perf*).

letdown ['lɛtdaun] *n* разочарова́ние.

lethal ['li:θl] *adj* (*weapon, chemical*) смертоно́сный* (смертоно́сен); (*dose*) смерте́льный* (смерте́лен).

lethargic [lɛ'θɑ:dʒɪk] *adj* вя́лый* (вял), со́нный* (со́нен).

lethargy ['lɛθədʒɪ] *n* вя́лость *f*.

letter ['lɛtəʳ] *n* (*correspondence*) письмо́*; (*of alphabet*) бу́ква; **small/capital ~** строчна́я/прописна́я бу́ква.

letter bomb *n* бо́мба, при́сланная по по́чте.

letter box *n* (*BRIT*) почто́вый я́щик.

letterhead ['lɛtəhɛd] *n* ша́пка (*в письме́*).

lettering ['lɛtərɪŋ] *n* шрифт.

letter of credit *n* аккредити́в.

letter opener *n* нож для разреза́ния бума́ги.

letterpress ['lɛtəprɛs] *n* (*method*) высо́кая печа́ть *f*.

letter quality *n* (*of printer*) ка́чество печа́ти.

letters patent *npl* пате́нт.

lettuce ['lɛtɪs] *n* сала́т* лату́к.

let-up ['lɛtʌp] *n* ослабле́ние.

leukaemia [lu:'ki:mɪə] (*US* **leukemia**) *n* белокро́вие, лейкеми́я.

level ['lɛvl] *adj* (*flat*) ро́вный* (ро́вен) ◆ *n* у́ровень* *m*; (*also*: **spirit ~**) ватерпа́с ◆ *vt* (*land*) ровня́ть (сровня́ть *perf*); (*building*) сровня́ть* (*perf*) с землёй ◆ *vi* (*inf*): **to ~ with sb** объясня́ться (объясни́ться *perf*) с кем-н начистоту́ ◆ *adv*: **to draw ~ with** (*person, vehicle*) поравня́ться (*perf*) с +*instr*; **to be ~ with** быть* (*impf*) на одно́м у́ровне с +*instr*; **"A" ~s** (*BRIT*: *exams*) выпускны́е экза́мены (*в сре́дней шко́ле*); (: *qualification*) *квалифика́ция, получа́емая при успе́шной сда́че выпускно́го экза́мена*; **on the ~** (*inf*) че́стный* (че́стен); **to ~ a gun at sb** наводи́ть* (навести́* *perf*) ружьё на кого́-н; **to ~ an accusation/a criticism at** *or* **against sb** направля́ть (напра́вить* *perf*) обвине́ние/кри́тику про́тив кого́-н

▸ **level off** *vi* (*prices etc*) выра́вниваться (вы́ровняться* *perf*)

▸ **level out** *vi* = **level off**.

level crossing *n* (*BRIT*) железнодоро́жный перее́зд.

level-headed [lɛvl'hɛdɪd] *adj* уравнове́шенный (уравнове́шен).

levelling ['lɛvlɪŋ] *n* выра́внивание.

level playing field *n* ра́вные пози́ции *fpl*.

lever ['li:vəʳ] *n* (*also fig*) рыча́г*; (*bar*) лом ◆ *vt*: **to ~ up/out** поднима́ть (подня́ть *perf*)/тащи́ть (вы́тащить *perf*) с уси́лием.

leverage ['li:vərɪdʒ] *n* рыча́жная си́ла; (*fig*: *influence*) влия́ние.

levity ['lɛvɪtɪ] *n* легкомы́слие.

levy ['lɛvɪ] *n* нало́г ◆ *vt* взима́ть (*impf*).

lewd [lu:d] *adj* (*look*) похотли́вый (похотли́в); (*remark*) непристо́йный* (непристо́ен).

lexicographer [lɛksi'kɔgrəfəʳ] *n* лексико́граф.

lexicography [lɛksi'kɔgrəfɪ] *n* лексикогра́фия.

LI *abbr* (*US*) = *Long Island*.

liability [laɪə'bɪlətɪ] *n* (*LAW*: *responsibility*) отве́тственность *f*; (*person, thing*) обу́за *m/f*; **liabilities** *npl* (*COMM*) обяза́тельства *ntpl*.

liable ['laɪəbl] (*LAW*) *adj* (*responsible*): **~ for** (*for actions*) отве́тственный (отве́тствен) за +*acc*; (*legally responsible*) подсу́дный* (подсу́ден) за +*acc*; (*subject*): **~ to** подлежа́щий +*dat*; **to be ~ for** нести́* (*impf*) отве́тственность за +*acc*; **to be ~ to** подлежа́ть (*impf*) +*dat*; **he's ~ to take offence** возмо́жно, что он оби́дится.

* marks translations which have irregular inflections. The Russian-English side of the dictionary gives inflectional information.

liaise [li:'eɪz] *vi*: **to ~ (with)** кооперúроваться (скооперúроваться *perf*) (с *+instr*).
liaison [li:'eɪzɔn] *n* (*cooperation*) кооперáция; (*sexual*) связь *f*.
liar ['laɪə'] *n* лжец*, лгун*(ья).
libel ['laɪbl] *n* клеветá ◆ *vt* клеветáть* (оклеветáть* *perf*).
libellous ['laɪbləs] (*US* **libelous**) *adj* (*comment etc*) клеветнúческий*.
liberal ['lɪbərl] *adj* (*tolerant, also POL*) либерáльный* (либерáлен); (*large, generous*) щéдрый; **~ with** щéдрый* (щедр) на *+acc* ◆ *n* (*tolerant person*) либерáл; (*POL*): **L~** либерáл.
liberalize ['lɪbərəlaɪz] *vt* либерализовáть *(impf/perf)*.
liberally ['lɪbrəlɪ] *adv* (*see adj*) либерáльно; щéдро.
Liberal Democrat *n* либерáл-демокрáт; **the ~ ~s** (*party*) пáртия Либерáл-демокрáтов.
liberal-minded ['lɪbərl'maɪndɪd] *adj* либерáльно-настрóенный (либерáльно-настрóен).
liberate ['lɪbəreɪt] *vt* освобождáть (освободúть* *perf*).
liberation [lɪbə'reɪʃən] *n* освобождéние.
Liberia [laɪ'bɪərɪə] *n* Либéрия.
Liberian [laɪ'bɪərɪən] *adj* либерúйский ◆ *n* либерúец*(-úйка*).
liberty ['lɪbətɪ] *n* свобóда; **to be at ~** (*criminal*) быть* *(impf)* на свобóде; **I'm not at ~ to comment** я не вóлен комментúровать; **to take the ~ of doing** позволя́ть (позвóлить* *perf*) себé *+infin*.
libido [lɪ'bi:dəu] *n* либúдо *nt ind*.
Libra ['li:brə] *n* Весы́ *pl*; **he is ~** он – Весы́.
librarian [laɪ'brɛərɪən] *n* библиотéкарь *m*.
library ['laɪbrərɪ] *n* библиотéка.
library book *n* библиотéчная кнúга.
libretto [lɪ'brɛtəu] *n* либрéтто *nt ind*.
Libya ['lɪbɪə] *n* Лúвия.
Libyan ['lɪbɪən] *adj* ливúйский ◆ *n* ливúец*(-úйка*).
lice [laɪs] *npl of* **louse**.
licence ['laɪsns] (*US* **license**) *n* (*permit*) лицéнзия; (*AUT*: *also:* **driving ~**) (водúтельские) правá *ntpl*; (*freedom*) вóльность *f*; **under ~** (*COMM*) по лицéнзии.
license ['laɪsns] *n* (*US*) = **licence** ◆ *vt* выдавáть* (вы́дать* *perf*) лицéнзию на *+acc*.
licensed ['laɪsnst] *adj* (*car etc*) зарегистрúрованный (зарегистрúрован); (*restaurant*) с лицéнзией на продáжу спиртных напúтков.
licensed trade *n организáции, торгýющие алкогóльными напúтками.*
licensee [laɪsən'si:] *n* держáтель *m* лицéнзии.
license plate *n* (*US*) номернóй знак (*на автомобúле*).
licensing hours ['laɪsnsɪŋ] *npl* (*BRIT*) *часы́, в котóрые разрешенá торгóвля спиртны́ми напúтками.*
licentious [laɪ'sɛnʃəs] *adj* распýщенный (распýщен).
lichen ['laɪkən] *n* лишáйник.
lick [lɪk] *vt* (*stamp, fingers etc*) лизáть* *(impf)*, облúзывать (облизáть* *perf*); (*inf: defeat*) положúть* *(perf)* на лопáтки ◆ *n*: **to give sth a ~** лизнýть *(perf)* что-н; **to give sth a ~ of paint** подкрáшивать (подкрáсить* *perf*) что-н; **to ~ one's lips** облúзываться (облизáться* *perf*); (*fig*) облúзываться *(impf)*.
licorice ['lɪkərɪs] *n* (*US*) = **liquorice**.
lid [lɪd] *n* кры́шка*; (*also:* **eyelid**) вéко; **to take the ~ off sth** (*fig*) вытáскивать (вы́тащить *perf*) что-н на свет бóжий.
lido ['laɪdəu] *n* (*BRIT*: *pool*) бассéйн на откры́том вóздухе.
lie [laɪ] (*pt* **lay**, *pp* **lain**) *vi* (*be horizontal*) лежáть* *(impf)*; (*be situated*) лежáть* *(impf)*, находúться* *(impf)*; (*problem, cause*) заключáться *(impf)*; (*be untruthful*) (*pt, pp* **lied**) лгать* (солгáть* *perf*), врать* (соврáть* *perf*) ◆ *n* (*untrue statement*) ложь* *f no pl*; **to ~** *or* **be lying in first/last place** быть* *(impf)* на пéрвом/ послéднем мéсте; **to ~ low** (*fig*) пережидáть (переждáть* *perf*); **to tell ~s** говорúть *(impf)* непрáвду
▸ **lie about** *vi* валя́ться *(impf)*
▸ **lie around** *vi* = **lie about**
▸ **lie back** *vi* откúдываться (откúнуться *perf*); (*fig*) успокáиваться (успокóиться *perf*)
▸ **lie down** *vi* ложúться (лечь* *perf*); **to be lying down** лежáть* *(impf)*
▸ **lie up** *vi* (*hide*) скрывáться (скры́ться* *perf*).
Liechtenstein ['lɪktənstaɪn] *n* Лихтенштéйн.
lie detector *n* детéктор лжи.
lie-down ['laɪdaun] *n* (*BRIT*): **to have a ~** полежáть* *(perf)*.
lie-in ['laɪɪn] *n* (*BRIT*): **to have a ~** вставáть* (встать* *perf*) попóзже.
lieu [lu:]: **in ~ of** *prep* вмéсто *+gen*.
Lieut. *abbr* (*MIL*) = **lieutenant**.
lieutenant [lɛf'tɛnənt, (*US*) lu:'tɛnənt] *n* лейтенáнт.
lieutenant colonel *n* подполкóвник.
life [laɪf] (*pl* **lives**) *n* жизнь *f no pl*; **true to ~** правдоподóбный* (правдоподóбен); **to paint from ~** писáть* (написáть* *perf*) с натýры; **to be sent to prison for ~** получáть (получúть* *perf*) пожизненное заключéние; **to come to ~** (*fig*: *person*) оживáть (ожúть* *perf*); (: *party*) оживля́ться (оживúться* *perf*).
life annuity *n* пожизненный аннуитéт.
life assurance *n* (*BRIT*) = **life insurance**.
life belt *n* (*BRIT*) спасáтельный круг*.
lifeblood ['laɪfblʌd] *n* (*fig*) жизненная оснóва.
lifeboat ['laɪfbəut] *n* (*rescue launch*) спасáтельное сýдно*; (*on ship*) спасáтельная шлю́пка.
life buoy *n* = **life belt**.
life expectancy *n* продолжúтельность *f* жизни.

lifeguard ['laɪfgɑ:d] *n* спаса́тель(ница) *m(f)*.
life imprisonment *n* пожи́зненное заключе́ние.
life insurance *n* страхова́ние жи́зни.
life jacket *n* спаса́тельный жиле́т.
lifeless ['laɪflɪs] *adj* (*also fig*) безжи́зненный (безжи́знен).
lifelike ['laɪflaɪk] *adj* (*model, robot*) как живо́й; (*performance*) реалисти́чный* (реалисти́чен).
lifeline ['laɪflaɪn] *n* (*fig*) сре́дство вы́живания; (*rope*) спаса́тельный кана́т.
lifelong ['laɪflɔŋ] *adj* (*friend, habit*) неизме́нный; **it was a ~ ambition of his** э́то бы́ло мечто́й всей его́ жи́зни.
life preserver *n* (*US*) = **life belt, life jacket**.
lifer ['laɪfəʳ] *n* бессро́чник(-ица).
life raft *n* спаса́тельный плот*.
life-saver ['laɪfseɪvəʳ] *n* спасе́ние.
life science *n* есте́ственные нау́ки *fpl*.
life sentence *n* пригово́р к пожи́зненному заключе́нию.
life-size(d) ['laɪfsaɪz(d)] *adj* в натура́льную величину́.
life span *n* (*of living thing*) продолжи́тельность *f* жи́зни; (*of product*) срок* слу́жбы; (*of idea, organization*) долгове́чность *f*.
lifestyle ['laɪfstaɪl] *n* о́браз жи́зни.
life-support system ['laɪfsəpɔ:t-] *n* систе́ма жизнеобеспече́ния.
lifetime ['laɪftaɪm] *n* (*of person*) жизнь *f*; (*of institution*) вре́мя* *nt* существова́ния; **the chance of a ~** уника́льный шанс.
lift [lɪft] *vt* поднима́ть (подня́ть* *perf*); (*ban, sanctions*) снима́ть (снять* *perf*); (*inf: steal*) тащи́ть (стащи́ть* *perf*) ◆ *vi* (*fog*) рассе́иваться (рассе́яться *perf*) ◆ *n* (*BRIT*) лифт; **to give sb a ~** (*BRIT: AUT*) подвози́ть* (подвезти́* *perf*) кого́-н
▸ **lift in** *vt* (*goods, people*) ввози́ть* (ввезти́* *perf*) самолётом
▸ **lift off** *vi* (*rocket*) отрыва́ться (оторва́ться* *perf*) от земли́, стартова́ть (*impf/perf*)
▸ **lift out** *vt* (*goods, people*) вывози́ть* (вы́везти* *perf*) самолётом
▸ **lift up** *vt* (*object, person*) поднима́ть (подня́ть* *perf*).
liftoff ['lɪftɔf] *n* старт.
ligament ['lɪgəmənt] *n* (*ANAT*) свя́зка*.
light [laɪt] (*pt, pp* **lit**) *n* свет*; (*AUT*) фа́ра ◆ *vt* (*candle, cigarette, fire*) зажига́ть (заже́чь* *perf*); (*place*) освеща́ть (освети́ть* *perf*) ◆ *adj* (*pale, bright*) све́тлый* (све́тел); (*not heavy*) лёгкий* (лёгок) ◆ *adv* (*travel*) налегке́; **~s** *npl* (*also:* **traffic ~s**) светофо́р *msg*; **to turn the ~ on/off** включа́ть (включи́ть *perf*)/выключа́ть (вы́ключить *perf*) свет; **have you got a ~?** (*for cigarette*) мо́жно у Вас прикури́ть?; **to come to ~** выясня́ться (вы́ясниться *perf*); **to cast** *or* **shed** *or* **throw ~ on** пролива́ть (проли́ть* *perf*) свет на *+acc*; **in the ~ of** (*discussions, new evidence*) в све́те *+gen*; **to make ~ of** не заостря́ть (*impf*) внима́ние на *+acc*; **the house is lit by electricity** дом освещён электри́чеством
▸ **light up** *vi* (*face*) светле́ть (просветле́ть *perf*) ◆ *vt* (*illuminate*) освеща́ть (освети́ть* *perf*).
light bulb *n* ла́мпочка*.
lighten ['laɪtn] *vi* (*become less dark*) светле́ть (посветле́ть *perf*) ◆ *vt* (*make less heavy*) облегча́ть (облегчи́ть *perf*).
lighter ['laɪtəʳ] *n* (*also:* **cigarette ~**) зажига́лка*; (*boat*) ли́хтер.
light-fingered [laɪt'fɪŋgəd] *adj* нечи́стый* (нечи́ст) на́ руку.
light-headed [laɪt'hɛdɪd] *adj*: **she felt ~** у неё кружи́лась голова́.
light-hearted [laɪt'hɑ:tɪd] *adj* (*person*) беспе́чный* (беспе́чен); (*question, remark*) несерьёзный* (несерьёзен).
lighthouse ['laɪthaus] *n* мая́к*.
lighting ['laɪtɪŋ] *n* освеще́ние.
lighting-up time [laɪtɪŋ'ʌp-] *n* вре́мя* *nt* включе́ния у́личного освеще́ния.
lightly ['laɪtlɪ] *adv* (*touch, kiss*) слегка́; (*eat, treat*) легко́; (*sleep*) неглубоко́; **to get off ~** легко́ отде́лываться (отде́латься *perf*).
light meter *n* экспоно́метр.
lightness ['laɪtnɪs] *n* (*in weight*) лёгкость *f*.
lightning ['laɪtnɪŋ] *n* мо́лния ◆ *adj* (*rapid*) молниено́сный* (молниено́сен).
lightning conductor *n* (*BRIT*) громоотво́д.
lightning rod *n* (*US*) = **lightning conductor**.
light pen *n* *прибо́р, счи́тывающий штрихово́й код.*
lightship ['laɪtʃɪp] *n* плаву́чий* мая́к*.
lightweight ['laɪtweɪt] *adj* (*suit*) лёгкий* ◆ *n* (*BOXING*) бо́ксер лёгкого ве́са.
light year *n* светово́й год*.
like [laɪk] *prep* как *+acc*; (*similar to*) похо́жий на *+acc* ◆ *adj* подо́бный (подо́бен) ◆ *vt* (*sweets, reading*) люби́ть* (*impf*); (*find attractive, acceptable*): **I ~ him** он мне нра́вится ◆ *n*: **and the ~** тому́ подо́бное; **to be** *or* **look ~** походи́ть* (*impf*) на *+acc*; **he looks ~ his father** он похо́ж на своего́ отца́; **what does she look ~?** как она́ вы́глядит?; **what's he ~?** что он за челове́к?; **what's the weather ~?** кака́я сего́дня пого́да?; **something ~ that** что́-то в э́том ро́де; **I feel ~ a drink** я хочу́ что́-нибудь вы́пить; **there's nothing ~ ...** ничто́ не мо́жет сравни́ться с *+instr* ...; **do it ~ this** де́лайте (сде́лайте *perf*) э́то так; **that's just ~ him** (*typical*) э́то на него́ похо́же; **it is nothing ~ ...** э́то совсе́м не то, что ...; **I would ~, I'd ~** мне

* marks translations which have irregular inflections. The Russian-English side of the dictionary gives inflectional information.

хотéлось бы, я бы хотéл; **would you ~ a coffee?** хотíте кóфе?; **I ~d him** он мне понрáвился; **I don't ~ his behaviour** мне не нрáвится егó поведéние; **if you ~** éсли хотíте; **his ~s and dislikes** егó вкýсы.
likeable ['laɪkəbl] *adj* симпатíчный* (симпатíчен).
likelihood ['laɪklɪhud] *n* вероя́тность *f*; **in all ~** по всéй вероя́тности; **there is every ~ that ...** óчень вероя́тно, что ....
likely ['laɪklɪ] *adj* вероя́тный* (вероя́тен); **she is ~ to agree** онá вероя́тно согласíтся; **not ~!** (*inf*) ни за что!
like-minded ['laɪk'maɪndɪd] *adj*: **a ~ person** единомы́шленник; **~ friends/colleagues** друзья́/коллéги – единомы́шленники.
liken ['laɪkən] *vt*: **to ~ sth/sb to** уподобля́ть (уподóбить* *perf*) что-н/когó-н +*dat*.
likeness ['laɪknɪs] *n* схóдство; **the portrait is a good ~ of her** портрéт обнарýживает большóе схóдство с ней.
likewise ['laɪkwaɪz] *adv* тáкже; **to do ~** поступáть (поступíть* *perf*) такíм же óбразом.
liking ['laɪkɪŋ] *n*: **~ (for)** (*person*) симпáтия (к +*dat*); (*thing*) вкус (к +*dat*); **to be to sb's ~** быть* (*impf*) *or* приходíться* (прийтíсь* *perf*) комý-н по вкýсу; **I took an instant ~ to him** он мне срáзу понрáвился.
lilac ['laɪlək] *n* сирéнь *f no pl* ◆ *adj* сирéневый.
Lilo® ['laɪləu] *n* надувнóй резíновый матрáц.
lilt [lɪlt] *n* (*in voice*) перелíвы *mpl*.
lilting ['lɪltɪŋ] *adj* (*voice*) мелодíчный* (мелодíчен).
lily ['lɪlɪ] *n* лíлия.
lily of the valley *n* лáндыш.
Lima ['li:mə] *n* Лíма.
limb [lɪm] *n* (*ANAT*) конéчность *f*; (*of tree*) ветвь* *f*; **to be out on a ~** быть* (*impf*) *or* находíться* (*impf*) в критíческом положéнии.
limber up ['lɪmbə'-] *vi* разминáться (размя́ться* *perf*).
limbo ['lɪmbəu] *n*: **to be in ~** (*fig*) находíться* (*impf*) в состоя́нии неопределённости.
lime [laɪm] *n* (*fruit*) лайм; (*tree*) лíпа*; (*also:* **~ juice**) сок лáйма; (*chemical*) и́звесть *f*; (*rock*) известня́к*.
limelight ['laɪmlaɪt] *n*: **to be in the ~** быть* (*impf*) в цéнтре внимáния.
limerick ['lɪmərɪk] *n* лимéрик (*юмористíческое пятистрóчное стихотворéние*).
limestone ['laɪmstəun] *n* известня́к*.
limit ['lɪmɪt] *n* предéл; (*restriction*) лимíт, ограничéние ◆ *vt* (*production, expense etc*) лимитíровать (*impf/perf*), ограни́чивать (ограни́чить *perf*); **speed ~** предéльная скóрость *f*; **within ~s** в предéлах допустíмого; **that's the ~!** э́то перехóдит все грани́цы!
limitation [lɪmɪ'teɪʃən] *n* ограничéние; **~s** *npl* недостáтки *mpl*.
limited ['lɪmɪtɪd] *adj* ограни́ченный (ограни́чен); **to be ~ to** ограни́чиваться (ограни́читься *perf*) +*instr*.
limited edition *n* малотирáжное издáние.
limited (liability) company *n* (*BRIT*) компáния с ограни́ченной отвéтственностью.
limitless ['lɪmɪtlɪs] *adj* беспредéльный* (беспредéлен).
limousine ['lɪməzi:n] *n* лимузíн.
limp [lɪmp] *vi* хромáть (*impf*) ◆ *adj* (*person, limb*) бесси́льный* (бесси́лен); (*material*) мя́гкий* (мя́гок) ◆ *n*: **to have a ~** хромáть (*impf*).
limpet ['lɪmpɪt] *n* блю́дечко* (*моллю́ск*).
limpid ['lɪmpɪd] *adj* прозрáчный* (прозрáчен).
limply ['lɪmplɪ] *adv* (*lie*) бесси́льно; (*fall*) мя́гко.
linchpin ['lɪntʃpɪn] *n* опóра.
Lincs [lɪŋks] *abbr* (*BRIT*: *POST*) = *Lincolnshire*.
line [laɪn] *n* (*also TEL, RAIL*) лíния; (*row*) ряд*; (*US*: *queue*) óчередь *f*; (*of writing, song*) строкá*, стрóчка*; (*wrinkle*) морщи́на; (*rope*) верёвка*; (*for fishing*) лéска*; (*wire*) прóвод; (*route*) маршрýт; (*fig*: *attitude, policy*) лíния; (: *of thought, reasoning*) ход; (*of business, work*) óбласть *f*; (*of product(s)*) модéль *f*, тип ◆ *vt* (*stand along*) выстрáиваться (вы́строиться *perf*) вдоль +*gen*; (*clothing*) подбивáть (подбíть* *perf*); (*container*) выклáдывать (вы́ложить* *perf*) изнутрí; **hold the ~ please!** (*TEL*) пожáлуйста, не кладíте трýбку!; **to cut in ~** (*US*) идтí* (пойтí* *perf*) без óчереди; **to stand in ~** (*in a row*) стоя́ть (*impf*) в шерéнге *or* ряд; **in ~ with** (*in keeping with*) в соотвéтствии с +*instr*; **to bring sth into ~ with sth** приводíть* (привестí* *perf*) что-н в соотвéтствие с чем-н; **on the right ~s** на вéрном путí; **to draw the ~ at sth** ограни́чиваться (ограни́читься *perf*) чем-н; **he is in ~ for a pay rise** он скóро дóлжен получíть повышéние зарплáты; **the streets are ~d with trees** ýлицы обсáжены дерéвьями; **the walls were ~d with pictures** стéны бы́ли завéшены картíнами
▸ **line up** *vi* выстрáиваться (вы́строиться *perf*) ◆ *vt* (*place in order*) выстрáивать (вы́строить *perf*); (*prepare*) подготáвливать (подготóвить* *perf*); **she has a new job ~d up** онá устрóилась на нóвую рабóту.
linear ['lɪnɪə'] *adj* линéйный*.
lined [laɪnd] *adj* (*paper*) линóванный; (*face*) морщи́нистый (морщи́нист); (*skirt, jacket*) на подклáдке, с подклáдкой.
line editing *n* (*COMPUT*) пострóчное редактíрование.
line feed *n* (*COMPUT*) перевóд *or* прогóн строкí.
lineman ['laɪnmən] *n* (*US*: *workman*) инженéр телефóнной свя́зи; (: *SPORT*) боковóй судья́.
linen ['lɪnɪn] *n* (*material*) лён*; (*sheets etc*)

бельё.
line printer *n* (COMPUT) постро́чно-печата́ющее устро́йство, устро́йство постро́чной печа́ти.
liner ['laɪnəʳ] *n* (*ship*) ла́йнер; (*also:* **bin ~**) *целофа́новый мешо́к для му́сорного ведра́.*
linesman ['laɪnzmən] *irreg n* судья́* *m* на ли́нии.
line-up ['laɪnʌp] *n* (*also:* **team ~**) соста́в кома́нды; (*at event*) соста́в уча́стников; (*US: queue*) о́чередь* *f*; (*identity parade*) опозна́ние (*престу́пника*).
linger ['lɪŋgəʳ] *vi* (*smell, tradition*) уде́рживаться (удержа́ться* *perf*); (*person*) заде́рживаться (задержа́ться* *perf*).
lingerie ['lænʒəri:] *n* же́нское ни́жнее бельё.
lingering ['lɪŋgərɪŋ] *adj* (*sense, feeling, doubt*) усто́йчивый.
lingo ['lɪŋgəu] (*pl* **~es**) *n* (*inf: language*) (иностра́нный) язы́к.
linguist ['lɪŋgwɪst] *n* (*language specialist*) лингви́ст; **he is a good ~** (*speaks several languages*) он спосо́бен к языка́м.
linguistic [lɪŋ'gwɪstɪk] *adj* лингвисти́ческий*.
linguistics [lɪŋ'gwɪstɪks] *n* языкозна́ние, лингви́стика.
liniment ['lɪnɪmənt] *n* жи́дкая мазь *f*.
lining ['laɪnɪŋ] *n* (*cloth*) подкла́дка*; (TECH) прокла́дка*; (*of stomach etc*) вы́стилка.
link [lɪŋk] *n* связь *f*; (*of a chain*) звено́* ◆ *vt* (*join*) соединя́ть (соедини́ть *perf*); (*associate*): **to ~ with** *or* **to** свя́зывать (связа́ть* *perf*) с *+instr*; **~s** *npl* (GOLF) *по́ле для игры́ в гольф*; **rail ~** железнодоро́жная связь
▸ **link up** *vt* (*machines, systems*) соединя́ть (соедини́ть *perf*) ◆ *vi* соединя́ться (соедини́ться *perf*).
linkup ['lɪŋkʌp] *n* соедине́ние; (*of spaceships*) стыко́вка*; (RADIO, TV) свя́зка*, связна́я часть* *f*; (*between studios: RADIO*) радиомо́ст; (: TV) телемо́ст.
lino ['laɪnəu] *n* = **linoleum**.
linoleum [lɪ'nəulɪəm] *n* лино́леум.
linseed oil ['lɪnsi:d-] *n* льняно́е ма́сло.
lint [lɪnt] *n* ма́рля.
lintel ['lɪntl] *n* при́толока.
lion ['laɪən] *n* лев*.
lion cub *n* львёнок*.
lioness ['laɪənɪs] *n* льви́ца.
lip [lɪp] *n* (ANAT) губа́*; (*of container*) край*; (*inf: insolence*) гру́бости *fpl*.
liposome ['lɪpəusəum] *n* липосо́ма.
liposuction ['lɪpəusʌkʃən] *n* липоса́кция, отса́сывание жирово́й тка́ни.
lip-read ['lɪpri:d] *vi* чита́ть (*impf*) с губ.
lip salve *n* мазь *f* для смягче́ния губ.
lip service *n*: **to pay ~ ~ to sth** признава́ть* (призна́ть *perf*) что-н то́лько на слова́х.
lipstick ['lɪpstɪk] *n* губна́я пома́да.
liquefy ['lɪkwɪfaɪ] *vt* превраща́ть (преврати́ть* *perf*) в жи́дкость ◆ *vi* переходи́ть* (перейти́* *perf*) в жи́дкое состоя́ние.
liqueur [lɪ'kjuəʳ] *n* ликёр.
liquid ['lɪkwɪd] *n* жи́дкость *f* ◆ *adj* жи́дкий* (жи́док).
liquid assets *npl* ликви́дные акти́вы *mpl*.
liquidate ['lɪkwɪdeɪt] *vt* ликвиди́ровать (*impf/perf*).
liquidation [lɪkwɪ'deɪʃən] *n* ликвида́ция; **to go into ~** ликвиди́роваться (*impf*).
liquidation sale *n* (US) *распрода́жа иму́щества ликвиди́рованного предприя́тия.*
liquidator ['lɪkwɪdeɪtəʳ] *n* ликвида́тор.
liquid crystal display *n* жидкокристалли́ческий индика́тор.
liquidity [lɪ'kwɪdɪtɪ] *n* ликви́дность *f*.
liquidize ['lɪkwɪdaɪz] *vt* пропуска́ть (пропусти́ть* *perf*) че́рез ми́ксер.
liquidizer ['lɪkwɪdaɪzəʳ] *n* ми́ксер, смеси́тель *m*.
liquor ['lɪkəʳ] *n* (*esp US*) спиртно́е *nt adj*, спиртно́й напи́ток*.
liquorice ['lɪkərɪs] *n* (BRIT: *sweet*) лакри́ца.
liquor store *n* (US) ви́нно-во́дочный магази́н.
Lisbon ['lɪzbən] *n* Лиссабо́н.
lisp [lɪsp] *n* шепеля́вость *f* ◆ *vi* шепеля́вить* (*impf*).
lissom(e) ['lɪsəm] *adj* изя́щный* (изя́щен).
list [lɪst] *n* (*also* COMPUT) спи́сок* ◆ *vt* (*enumerate*) перечисля́ть (перечи́слить *perf*); (*write down*) составля́ть (соста́вить* *perf*) спи́сок *+gen*; (*put on list*) включа́ть (включи́ть* *perf*) в спи́сок ◆ *vi* (*ship*) крени́ться (накрени́ться *perf*).
listed building *n* (BRIT) зда́ние, охраня́емое госуда́рством.
listed company *n* официа́льно зарегистри́рованная компа́ния.
listen ['lɪsn] *vi*: **to ~ (to sb/sth)** слу́шать (*impf*) (кого́-н/что-н); **to ~ to sb** *or* **sb's advice** слу́шать (послу́шать *perf*) кого́-н; **I'm ~ing out for him** я прислу́шиваюсь, не идёт ли он; **~!** послу́шайте!
listener ['lɪsnəʳ] *n* слу́шатель(ница) *m(f)*; (RADIO) радиослу́шатель(ница) *m(f)*.
listeria [lɪs'tɪərɪə] *n* листе́рия.
listing [lɪstɪŋ] *n* (COMPUT) распеча́тка, ли́стинг.
listless ['lɪstlɪs] *adj* вя́лый (вял).
listlessly ['lɪstlɪslɪ] *adv* вя́ло.
list price *n* прейскура́нтная цена́*.
lit [lɪt] *pt, pp of* **light**.
litany ['lɪtənɪ] *n* (REL: *Catholic*) лита́ния; (: *Orthodox*) ектенья́; (*list*) моното́нное перечисле́ние.
liter ['li:təʳ] *n* (US) = **litre**.
literacy ['lɪtərəsɪ] *n* гра́мотность *f*.
literacy campaign *n* борьба́ с

* marks translations which have irregular inflections. The Russian-English side of the dictionary gives inflectional information.

неграмо́тностью.
literal ['lɪtərl] *adj* буква́льный* (буква́лен).
literally ['lɪtrəlɪ] *adv* буква́льно.
literary ['lɪtərərɪ] *adj* литерату́рный*.
literate ['lɪtərət] *adj* (*able to read and write*) гра́мотный* (гра́мотен); (*educated*) образо́ванный (образо́ван).
literature ['lɪtrɪtʃəʳ] *n* литерату́ра.
lithe [laɪð] *adj* ги́бкий* (ги́бок).
lithograph ['lɪθəgrɑ:f] *n* литогра́фия.
lithography [lɪ'θɔgrəfɪ] *n* литогра́фия.
Lithuania [lɪθju'eɪnɪə] *n* Литва́.
Lithuanian [lɪθju'eɪnɪən] *adj* лито́вский* ◆ *n* (*person*) лито́вец*(-вка*); (*LING*) лито́вский язы́к.
litigation [lɪtɪ'geɪʃən] *n* тя́жба.
litmus paper ['lɪtməs-] *n* ла́кмусовая бума́га.
litre ['li:təʳ] (*US* **liter**) *n* литр.
litter ['lɪtəʳ] *n* (*rubbish*) му́сор; (*young animals*) помёт.
litter bin *n* (*BRIT*) у́рна (*для му́сора*).
litterbug ['lɪtəbʌg] *n* (*inf*) *челове́к, кото́рый сори́т в обще́ственных места́х*.
littered ['lɪtəd] *adj*: ~ **with** зава́ленный (зава́лен) *+instr*.
litter lout *n* (*inf*) = **litterbug**.
little ['lɪtl] *adj* (*small, young*) ма́ленький*; (*younger*) мла́дший*; (*short*) коро́ткий* ◆ *adv* ма́ло; **a ~ (bit)** немно́го; **I have ~ time/money** у меня́ ма́ло вре́мени/де́нег; **to make ~ of** не заостря́ть (*impf*) внима́ние на *+prp*; **~ by ~** ма́ло-пома́лу, понемно́гу.
little finger *n* мизи́нец* (*на руке́*).
little-known ['lɪtl'nəun] *adj* малоизве́стный* (малоизве́стен).
liturgy ['lɪtədʒɪ] *n* литурги́я.
live [*vb* lɪv, *adj* laɪv] *vi* жить* (*impf*) ◆ *adj* (*animal, plant*) живо́й*; (*broadcast*) прямо́й; (*performance*) пе́ред пу́бликой; (*ELEC*) под напряже́нием; (*bullet*) боево́й; (*bomb*) не взорва́вшийся; **to ~ with sb** жить* (*impf*) с кем-н; **he ~d to (be) a hundred** он прожи́л до ста лет
▸ **live down** *vt* загла́живать (загла́дить* *perf*)
▸ **live for** *vt* жить* (*impf*) для *+gen*
▸ **live in** *vi*: **most students ~ in** большинство́ студе́нтов живёт в общежи́тии
▸ **live off** *vt fus* (*survive on*): **we ~d off fish** мы жи́ли на одно́й ры́бе; (*pej*: *parents etc*) жить* (*impf*) за счёт *+gen*
▸ **live on** *vt fus* (*food*) жить* (*impf*) на одно́м(-ой) *+prp*; (*salary*) жить* (*impf*) на *+acc*
▸ **live out** *vi*: **postgraduates usually ~ out** аспира́нты обы́чно не живу́т в общежи́тии ◆ *vt*: **to ~ out one's days** *or* **life** прожива́ть (прожи́ть* *perf*) оста́ток свое́й жи́зни
▸ **live together** *vi* жить* (*impf*) вме́сте
▸ **live up** *vt*: **to ~ it up** (*inf*) жить* (*impf*) широко́
▸ **live up to** *vt fus* опра́вдывать (оправда́ть *perf*).
live-in ['lɪvɪn] *adj*: ~ **lover** сожи́тель(ница) *m(f)*; **they have a ~ nanny** с ни́ми живёт ня́ня.
livelihood ['laɪvlɪhud] *n* сре́дства *ntpl* к существова́нию.
liveliness ['laɪvlɪnɪs] *n* жи́вость *f*.
lively ['laɪvlɪ] *adj* (*person, book, interest, mind*) живо́й*; (*place, event*) оживлённый (оживлён).
liven up ['laɪvn-] *vt* (*person*) ободря́ть (ободри́ть *perf*); (*discussion, evening*) оживля́ть (оживи́ть* *perf*) ◆ *vi* оживля́ться (оживи́ться* *perf*).
liver ['lɪvəʳ] *n* (*ANAT*) пе́чень *f*; (*CULIN*) печёнка.
liverish ['lɪvərɪʃ] *adj*: **he is feeling ~** его́ подта́шнивает.
Liverpool ['lɪvəpu:l] *n* Ли́верпуль *m*.
Liverpudlian [lɪvə'pʌdlɪən] *adj* ливерпу́льский ◆ *n* ливерпу́лец*(-лька*).
livery ['lɪvərɪ] *n* (*of servant*) ливре́я.
lives [laɪvz] *npl of* **life**.
livestock ['laɪvstɔk] *n* скот*.
live wire *n* (*inf*): **he's a real ~ ~** он ужа́сно заводно́й.
livid ['lɪvɪd] *adj* (*colour*) серова́то-си́ний*; (*inf*: *furious*): **she was ~** она́ была́ в я́рости.
living ['lɪvɪŋ] *adj* живо́й* ◆ *n*: **to earn** *or* **make a ~** зараба́тывать (зарабо́тать *perf*) на жизнь; **within ~ memory** на па́мяти живу́щих; **the cost of ~** сто́имость *f* жи́зни.
living conditions *npl* усло́вия *ntpl* жи́зни.
living expenses *npl* расхо́ды *mpl* на жизнь.
living room *n* гости́ная *f adj*.
living standards *npl* жи́зненный у́ровень* *msg*.
living wage *n* прожи́точный ми́нимум.
lizard ['lɪzəd] *n* я́щерица.
Ljubljana [lu:'bljɑ:nə] *n* Любля́на.
llama ['lɑ:mə] *n* ла́ма (*ЗООЛ*).
LLB *n abbr* (= *Bachelor of Laws*) ≈ бакала́вр правове́дения.
LLD *n abbr* (= *Doctor of Laws*) ≈ до́ктор правове́дения.
LMT *abbr* (*US*) = *Local Mean Time*.
load [ləud] *n* (*of person, animal*) но́ша; (*of vehicle*) груз; (*weight, also ELEC, TECH*) нагру́зка* ◆ *vt* (*also*: **~ up**: *cargo, goods*) грузи́ть* (погрузи́ть* *perf*); (*COMPUT*) загружа́ть (загрузи́ть* *perf*); (*gun, camera*) заряжа́ть (заряди́ть* *perf*); (*tape recorder*) ста́вить* (поста́вить* *perf*) кассе́ту в *+prp*; **to ~ (with)** (*also*: **~ up**: *vehicle, ship*) нагружа́ть (нагрузи́ть* *perf*) (*+instr*); **~s of, a ~ of** (*inf*) ку́ча *+gen*; **a ~ of rubbish** (*inf*) сплошна́я чепуха́.
loaded ['ləudɪd] *adj* (*gun*) заря́женный (заря́жен); (*dice*) утяжелённый (утяжелён); (*vehicle*): **~ (with)** нагру́женный (нагру́жен) (*+instr*); (*inf*): **he's ~** у него́ ку́ча де́нег; **~ question** вопро́с с подво́хом.
loading bay ['ləudɪŋ-] *n* погру́зочная площа́дка*.
loaf [ləuf] (*pl* **loaves**) *n* буха́нка* ◆ *vi* (*also*: **~ about** *or* **around**: *inf*) болта́ться (*impf*) без

де́ла; **use your ~!** (*inf*) шевели́те мозга́ми!
loam [ləum] *n* сугли́нок*.
loan [ləun] *n* заём*; (*money*) ссу́да* ◆ *vt* дава́ть* (дать* *perf*) взаймы́; (*money*) ссужа́ть (ссуди́ть* *perf*); **to take sth on ~** брать* (взять* *perf*) что́-н на вре́мя.
loan account *n* ссу́дный счёт*.
loan capital *n* заёмный *or* ссу́дный капита́л.
loan shark *n* (*inf: pej*) ростовщи́к, заимода́вец*.
loath [ləuθ] *adj*: **he is ~ to ...** ему́ о́чень не хо́чется *+infin* ....
loathe [ləuð] *vt* ненави́деть* *(impf)*.
loathing ['ləuðɪŋ] *n* отвраще́ние, омерзе́ние.
loathsome ['ləuðsəm] *adj* отврати́тельный* (отврати́телен), омерзи́тельный* (омерзи́телен).
loaves [ləuvz] *npl of* **loaf**.
lob [lɔb] *vt* (*ball*) перебра́сывать (перебро́сить* *perf*).
lobby ['lɔbɪ] *n* (*of building*) вестибю́ль *m*; (*pressure group*) ло́бби *nt ind* ◆ *vt* (*politician*) склоня́ть (склони́ть *perf*) на свою́ сто́рону.
lobbyist ['lɔbɪɪst] *n* лобби́ст.
lobe [ləub] *n* (*of ear*) мо́чка*.
lobster ['lɔbstə^r] *n* ома́р.
lobster pot *n* ве́рша* для ома́ров.
local ['ləukl] *adj* ме́стный ◆ *n* (*BRIT: inf*): **this is my ~** э́то мой люби́мый ме́стный паб; **the ~s** *npl* ме́стные жи́тели *mpl*.
local anaesthetic *n* ме́стный нарко́з.
local authority *n* ме́стные вла́сти* *fpl*.
local call *n* (*TEL*) ме́стный (телефо́нный) разгово́р.
locale [ləu'kɑ:l] *n* ме́сто*.
local government *n* ме́стные вла́сти* *fpl*.
locality [ləu'kælɪtɪ] *n* ме́стность *f*.
localize ['ləukəlaɪz] *vt* (*limit*) локализова́ть *(impf/perf)*.
locally ['ləukəlɪ] *adv* (*live*) побли́зости; (*solve problems*) на места́х.
locate [ləu'keɪt] *vt* определя́ть (определи́ть *perf*) местонахожде́ние *+gen*; (*situate*): **to be ~d in** находи́ться* *(impf)* в *or* на *+prp*.
location [ləu'keɪʃən] *n* (*place*) местонахожде́ние; (*finding*): **~ (of)** лока́ция (*+gen*); **on ~** (*CINEMA*) на нату́ре.
loch [lɔx] *n* (*SCOTTISH*) о́зеро*.
lock [lɔk] *n* (*on door etc*) замо́к*; (*on canal*) шлюз; (*of hair*) ло́кон ◆ *vt* запира́ть (запере́ть* *perf*); (*immobilize*) фикси́ровать (зафикси́ровать *perf*) ◆ *vi* (*door*) запира́ться (запере́ться* *perf*); (*jaw, mechanism*) смыка́ться (сомкну́ться *perf*); (*wheels*) тормози́ть* (затормози́ть* *perf*); **the steering wheel was on full ~** (*AUT*) руль был повёрнут до отка́за; **~, stock and barrel** всё целико́м
▸ **lock away** *vt* (*valuables*) пря́тать* (спря́тать* *perf*) под замо́к; (*criminal*) заключа́ть (заключи́ть *perf*) под стра́жу
▸ **lock in** *vt*: **to ~ sb in** запира́ть (запере́ть* *perf*) кого́-н
▸ **lock out** *vt* (*person*) запира́ть (запере́ть* *perf*) дверь и не впуска́ть (впусти́ть* *perf*); (*INDUSTRY*) объявля́ть (объяви́ть* *perf*) лока́ут *+dat*
▸ **lock up** *vt* (*criminal, mental patient*) упря́тывать (упря́тать* *perf*); (*house*) запира́ть (запере́ть* *perf*) ◆ *vi* запира́ться (запере́ться* *perf*).
locker ['lɔkə^r] *n* шка́фчик.
locker room *n* раздева́лка*.
locket ['lɔkɪt] *n* медальо́н.
lockjaw ['lɔkdʒɔ:] *n* (*trismus*) тризм; (*tetanus*) столбня́к.
lockout ['lɔkaut] *n* (*INDUSTRY*) лока́ут.
locksmith ['lɔksmɪθ] *n* сле́сарь* *m*.
lockup ['lɔkʌp] *n* (*jail*) куту́зка*; (*BRIT: also:* **lock-up garage**) гара́ж.
locomotive [ləukə'məutɪv] *n* локомоти́в.
locum ['ləukəm] *n* (*MED*) *врач, вре́менно замеща́ющий друго́го врача́.*
locust ['ləukəst] *n* саранча́* *f no pl*.
lodge [lɔdʒ] *n* привра́тницкая *f adj*; (*also:* **hunting ~**) охо́тничий* дом*; (*also:* **masonic ~**) масо́нская ло́жа ◆ *vt* (*complaint*) подава́ть* (пода́ть* *perf*) ◆ *vi* (*bullet*) застрева́ть (застря́ть* *perf*); (*person*): **to ~ (with)** (вре́менно) жить* *(impf)* на кварти́ре (у *+gen*).
lodger ['lɔdʒə^r] *n* квартира́нт(ка).
lodging ['lɔdʒɪŋ] *n* (вре́менное) жильё.
lodging house *n* меблиро́ванные ко́мнаты *fpl*.
lodgings ['lɔdʒɪŋz] *npl* кварти́ра *fsg*.
loft [lɔft] *n* черда́к*.
lofty ['lɔftɪ] *adj* (*high*) высо́кий* (высо́к); (*noble*) возвы́шенный (возвы́шен); (*self-important*) высокоме́рный* (высокоме́рен).
log [lɔg] *n abbr* = **logarithm**.
log [lɔg] *n* (*piece of wood*) бревно́*; (*: for fire*) поле́но*; (*account*) журна́л ◆ *vt* (*event, fact*) регистри́ровать (зарегистри́ровать *perf*)
▸ **log in** *vi* (*COMPUT*) входи́ть* (войти́* *perf*) в систе́му
▸ **log into** *vt fus* (*COMPUT*) входи́ть* (войти́* *perf*) в *+acc*
▸ **log off** *vi* (*COMPUT*) выходи́ть* (вы́йти* *perf*) из систе́мы
▸ **log on** *vi* = **log in**
▸ **log out** *vi* = **log off**.
logarithm ['lɔgərɪðm] *n* логари́фм.
logbook ['lɔgbuk] *n* (*NAUT*) ва́хтенный журна́л; (*AVIAT*) бортово́й журна́л; (*of car, lorry*) формуля́р; (*of events, movement of*

* marks translations which have irregular inflections. The Russian-English side of the dictionary gives inflectional information.

goods) журнáл.
log fire *n* дровянóй камúн.
logger ['lɔgə'] *n* лесорýб.
loggerheads ['lɔgəhɛdz] *npl*: **to be at ~ (with)** конфликтовáть *(impf)* (с *+instr*).
logic ['lɔdʒɪk] *n* лóгика.
logical ['lɔdʒɪkl] *adj* (*based on logic*) логúческий*; (*reasonable*) логúчный* (логúчен).
logically ['lɔdʒɪkəlɪ] *adv* (*see adj*) логúчески; логúчно.
logistics [lɔ'dʒɪstɪks] *npl* организáция *fsg*.
log jam ['lɔgdʒæm] *n* (*fig*) тупúк.
logo ['ləugəu] *n* эмблéма.
loin [lɔɪn] *n* (*of meat*) филéйная часть* *f*; **~s** *npl* (*ANAT*) чрéсла *pl*.
loincloth ['lɔɪnklɔθ] *n* набéдренная повя́зка*.
Loire [lwɑ:] *n*: **the ~** Луáра.
loiter ['lɔɪtə'] *vi* слоня́ться *(impf)*.
loll [lɔl] *vi* (*person*: *also*: **~ about**) развáливаться (развалúться* *perf*); (*head, tongue*) свéшиваться (свéситься* *perf*).
lollipop ['lɔlɪpɔp] *n* леденéц* на пáлочке ◆ *cpd*: **~ man/lady** (*BRIT*) *регулирóвщик/регулирóвщица движéния, котóрый обеспéчивает безопáсный перехóд ýлицы шкóльниками.*
lollop ['lɔləp] *vi* бéгать/бежáть* *(impf)* вперевáлку.
lolly ['lɔlɪ] *n* (*inf*: *lollipop*) леденéц на пáлочке; (: *also*: **ice ~**) морóженое на пáлочке; (: *money*) деньжáта *pl*.
London ['lʌndən] *n* Лóндон.
Londoner ['lʌndənə'] *n* лóндонец*(-донка).
lone [ləun] *adj* (*person, parent*) одинóкий*; (*thing*) едúнственный.
loneliness ['ləunlɪnɪs] *n* одинóчество.
lonely ['ləunlɪ] *adj* (*person, childhood*) одинóкий* (одинóк); (*place*) уединённый (уединён).
lonely hearts *n* одинóкие сердцá *nt pl*.
lone parent *n* (*father*) отéц*-одинóчка; (*mother*) мать* *f*-одинóчка.
loner ['ləunə'] *n* одинóчка* *m/f*.
long [lɔŋ] *adj* (*in time*) дóлгий* (дóлог); (*road, book*) длúнный* (длúнен); (*clothes*) длúнен ◆ *adv* (*see adj*) дóлго; длúнно ◆ *vi*: **to ~ for sth/to do** жáждать *(impf)* чегó-н/*+infin*; **in the ~ run** в конéчном итóге; **so** *or* **as ~ as you don't mind** éсли тóлько Вы не возражáете; **don't be ~!** не задéрживайтесь!; **how ~ is the street?** каковá длинá э́той ýлицы?; **how ~ is the lesson?** скóлько длúтся урóк?; **6 metres ~** длинóй в 6 мéтров; **6 months ~** продолжúтельностью в 6 мéсяцев; **all night (long)** всю ночь (напролёт); **he no ~er comes** он бóльше не прихóдит; **~ ago** давнó; **~ before** задóлго до *+gen*; **~ after** дóлгое врéмя пóсле *+gen*; **before ~** вскóре; **at ~ last** наконéц; **the ~ and the short of it is that ...** корóче говоря́ ....
long-distance [lɔŋ'dɪstəns] *adj* (*travel*) дáльний* (дáлен); **~ race** забéг на длúнную дистáнцию; **~ runner** бегýн на длúнные дистáнции.
long-distance call *n* (*within same country*) междугорóдный (телефóнный) разговóр; (*international*) междунарóдный (телефóнный) разговóр.
longevity [lɔn'dʒɛvɪtɪ] *n* (*of person*) долголéтие; (*of scheme, marriage etc*) долговéчность *f*.
long-haired ['lɔŋ'hɛəd] *adj* (*person*) длинноволóсый (длинноволóс); (*animal*) длинношёрстый.
longhand ['lɔŋhænd] *n*: **in ~** (*write*) от рукú.
longing ['lɔŋɪŋ] *n*: **~ (for)** тоскá (по *+dat*).
longingly ['lɔŋɪŋlɪ] *adv* с тоскóй.
longitude ['lɔŋgɪtju:d] *n* долготá*.
long johns [-dʒɔnz] *npl* кальсóны* *pl*.
long jump *n* прыжóк* в длинý.
long-life ['lɔŋlaɪf] *adj* (*milk etc*) консервúрованный; (*battery*) продлённого дéйствия.
long-lost ['lɔŋlɔst] *adj* (*relative etc*) давнó утрáченный (утрáчен) *or* потéрянный (потéрян).
long-playing record ['lɔŋpleɪɪŋ-] *n* долгоигрáющая пластúнка*.
long-range ['lɔŋ'reɪndʒ] *adj* (*plan, forecast*) долгосрóчный* (долгосрóчен); (*missile*) дальнобóйный.
longshoreman ['lɔŋʃɔ:mən] *n* (*US*) портóвый грýзчик.
long-sighted ['lɔŋ'saɪtɪd] *adj* дальнозóркий* (дальнозóрок).
long-standing ['lɔŋ'stændɪŋ] *adj* долголéтний.
long-suffering [lɔŋ'sʌfərɪŋ] *adj* многострадáльный* (многострадáлен).
long-term ['lɔŋtə:m] *adj* долгосрóчный* (долгосрóчен).
long wave *n* (*RADIO*) длúнные вóлны *fpl*.
long-winded [lɔŋ'wɪndɪd] *adj* многослóвный* (многослóвен).
loo [lu:] *n* (*BRIT*: *inf*) туалéт.
loofah ['lu:fə] *n* люфá (*гýбка*).
look [luk] *vi* (*see*) смотрéть* (посмотрéть* *perf*); (*glance*) взглянýть *(perf)*; (*seem, appear*) вы́глядеть* *(impf)* ◆ *n* (*glance*) взгляд; (*appearance*) вид; (*expression*) выражéние; **~s** *npl*: **good ~s** красúвая внéшность *fsg*; **to ~ south/(out) onto the sea** (*face*) выходúть* *(impf)* на юг/на мóре; **~ (here)!** (*expressing annoyance*) послýшайте!; **~!** (*expressing surprise*) смотрúте!; **to ~ like sb/sth** походúть* *(impf)* на когó-н/что-н; **the wall ~s about 4 metres long** похóже, что длинá э́той стены́ 4 мéтра; **everything ~s all right to me** мне кáжется, что всё в поря́дке; **it ~s as if he's not coming** похóже, что он не придёт; **to ~ ahead** смотрéть* (посмотрéть* *perf*) вперёд; **to have a ~** посмотрéть* *(perf)*,

взглянýть *(perf)*; **to ~ around** осмáтриваться (осмотрéться* *perf*); **to have a ~ at sth** (*glance at*) взглянýть* *(perf)* на что-н; (*study*) рассмáтривать (рассмотрéть* *(perf)*) что-н; **to have a ~ for sth** искáть* (поискáть* *perf*) что-н; **you can't tell by ~s alone** нельзя́ судить тóлько по внéшности
► **look after** *vt fus* (*care for*) ухáживать *(impf)* за *+instr*; (*deal with*) забóтиться* *(impf)* о *+prp*
► **look (a)round** *vt fus* (*castle, museum etc*) осмáтривать (осмотрéть* *perf*)
► **look at** *vt fus* (*see*) смотрéть* (посмотрéть* *perf*) на *+acc*; (*study*) рассмáтривать (рассмотрéть* *perf*); (*read quickly*) просмáтривать (просмотрéть* *perf*)
► **look back** *vi* (*turn around*): **to ~ back (at sth/sb)** оглядываться (оглянýться* *perf*) (на что-н/когó-н); **to ~ back (at *or* on the past)** оглядываться (оглянýться* *perf*) (на прóшлое)
► **look down on** *vt fus* (*fig*) смотрéть* *(impf)* свысокá на *+acc*
► **look for** *vt fus* искáть* (поискáть* *perf*)
► **look forward to** *vt fus*: **to ~ forward to sth** ждать* *(impf)* чегó-н с нетерпéнием; (*in letters*): **we ~ forward to hearing from you** (с нетерпéнием) ждём Вáшего отвéта
► **look in** *vi*: **to ~ in on sb** заглядывать (заглянýть* *perf*) к комý-н
► **look into** *vt fus* расслéдовать *(impf/perf)*
► **look on** *vi* (*watch*) наблюдáть *(impf)*
► **look out** *vi* (*beware*): **to ~ out (for)** остерегáться *(impf)* (*+gen*); (*glance out*): **to ~ out (of)** выглядывать (выглянуть *perf*) (в *+acc*)
► **look out for** *vt fus* (*search for*) старáться (постарáться *perf*) найти́
► **look over** *vt* (*essay*) просмáтривать (просмотрéть* *perf*); (*town, building*) осмáтривать (осмотрéть* *perf*); (*person*) проверя́ть (провéрить *perf*)
► **look round** *vi* осмáтриваться (осмотрéться* *perf*)
► **look through** *vt fus* (*papers*) просмáтривать (просмотрéть* *perf*); (*window*) смотрéть* (посмотрéть* *perf*) в *+acc*
► **look to** *vt fus* (*rely on*) ждать* *(impf)* от *+gen*
► **look up** *vi* (*with eyes*) поднимáть (поднять* *perf*) глазá; (*situation*) идти́* *(impf)* к лýчшему ◆ *vt* (*piece of information*) посмотрéть* *(perf)*
► **look up to** *vt fus* почитáть *(impf)*.
lookalike ['lukəlaɪk] *n* двойни́к*.
look-in ['lukɪn] *n*: **to get a ~** (*inf*) получи́ть* *(perf)* свой кусóк пирогá; **I couldn't get a ~** (*in conversation*) я не мог вставить словá.
lookout ['lukaut] *n* (*person*) наблюдáтель (ница) *m(f)*; (*point*) наблюдáтельный пункт; **to be on the ~** быть* *(impf)* начекý *or* насторожé; **to be on the ~ for sth** присмáтривать *(impf)* что-н.
LOOM *n abbr* (*US*: = *Loyal Order of Moose*) *тáйное óбщество*.
loom [lu:m] *vi* (*also*: **~ up**: *object*) неясно вырисóвываться *(impf)*; (*event*) надвигáться *(impf)* ◆ *n* ткáцкий* станóк*.
loony ['lu:nɪ] (*inf*) *adj* чóкнутый ◆ *n* чóкнутый(-ая) *m(f) adj*.
loop [lu:p] *n* (*also COMPUT*) пéтля*; (*contraceptive*) спирáль *f* ◆ *vt*: **to ~ sth round sth** завя́зывать (завязáть* *perf*) что-н пéтлей вокрýг чегó-н.
loophole ['lu:phəul] *n* лазéйка*.
loose [lu:s] *adj* свобóдный* (свобóден); (*knot, grip*) слáбый (слаб); (*hair*) распýщенный (распýщен); (*definition, translation*) приблизи́тельный* (приблизи́телен); (*weave*) неплóтный* (неплóтен); (*promiscuous*) распýщенный; (*ELEC*): **~ connection** слáбый контáкт ◆ *n*: **to be on the ~** быть* *(impf)* в бегáх; **the handle is ~** рýчка расшатáлась; **to set ~** (*prisoner*) освобождáть (освободи́ть* *perf*); (*unleash*) высвобождáть (вы́свободить* *perf*); **to come ~** расшáтываться (расшатáться *perf*).
loose change *n* мéлочь *f*.
loose chippings *npl* (*on road*) щебёнка *fsg*.
loose end *n*: **to be at a ~ ~** *or* (*US*) **at ~ ~s** шатáться *(impf)* без дéла; **to tie up (the) ~ ~s** завершáть (заверши́ть *perf*) все мéлочи.
loose-fitting ['lu:sfɪtɪŋ] *adj* простóрный* (простóрен).
loose-leaf ['lu:sli:f] *adj* отрывнóй.
loose-limbed [lu:s'lɪmd] *adj* ги́бкий* (ги́бок).
loosely ['lu:slɪ] *adv* (*freely*) свобóдно; (*vaguely*) приблизи́тельно.
loosely-knit ['lu:slɪ'nɪt] *adj* рéдко свя́занный.
loosen ['lu:sn] *vt* (*belt, screw, grip*) ослабля́ть (ослáбить* *perf*); (*by shaking*) расшáтывать (расшатáть *perf*)
► **loosen up** *vi* (*before game*) разогревáться (разогрéться *perf*); (*inf*: *relax*) расслабля́ться (расслáбиться* *perf*).
loot [lu:t] *n* (*inf*) нагрáбленное *nt adj* ◆ *vt* (*shops, homes*) разграбля́ть (разгрáбить* *perf*).
looter ['lu:tə'] *n* (*during riot*) грабитель(ница) *m(f)*; (*during war*) мародёр.
looting ['lu:tɪŋ] *n* разграблéние; (*during war*) мародёрство.
lop off [lɔp-] *vt* (*branches etc*) отрезáть (отрéзать* *perf*).
lopsided ['lɔp'saɪdɪd] *adj* кривобóкий (кривобóк); (*smile*) кривóй* (крив).
lord [lɔ:d] *n* (*BRIT*: *peer*) лорд; (*REL*): **the L~** Госпóдь* *m*; **my L~** (*to bishop, noble, judge*) милóрд; **good L~!** Бóже мой!; **the (House of) L~s** (*BRIT*) палáта лóрдов.

* marks translations which have irregular inflections. The Russian-English side of the dictionary gives inflectional information.

lordly ['lɔ:dlɪ] *adj* бáрственный.
lordship ['lɔ:dʃɪp] *n*: **your L~** Вáша свéтлость *f*.
lore [lɔ:ʳ] *n* предáния *ntpl*.
lorry ['lɔrɪ] *n* (*BRIT*) грузови́к*.
lorry driver *n* (*BRIT*) води́тель *m* грузовикá.
Los Angeles [lɔs 'ændʒɪli:z] *n* Лос-Áнджелес.
lose [lu:z] (*pt, pp* **lost**) *vt* терять (потерять *perf*); (*contest, argument*) проигрывать (проигрáть *perf*); (*pursuers*) избавля́ться (избáвиться* *perf*) от *+gen* ◆ *vi* (*in contest, argument*) проигрывать (проигрáть *perf*); **to ~ (time)** (*clock*) отставáть* (отстáть* *perf*); **to ~ sight of sth** терять (потерять *perf*) из ви́ду что-н; (*fig*) упускáть (упусти́ть* *perf*) из ви́ду что-н.
loser ['lu:zəʳ] *n* (*in contest*) проигрáвший(-ая) *m(f) adj*; (*inf: failure*) неудáчник(-ица); **to be a good/bad ~** умéть (*impf*)/не умéть достóйно проигрывать (*impf*).
loss [lɔs] *n* потеря; (*sense of bereavement*) утрáта; (*COMM*): **to make a ~** терпéть* (потерпéть* *perf*) убы́ток; **to sell sth at a ~** продавáть* (продáть* *perf*) что-н в убы́ток; **heavy ~es** тяжёлые потери *fpl*; **to cut one's ~es** сокращáть (сократи́ть* *perf*) потери; **to be at a ~** теряться (растеряться *perf*); **to be at a ~ for words** не найти́сь* (*perf*), что сказáть.
loss adjuster *n* специали́ст по оцéнке убы́тков.
loss leader *n товáр, продавáемый в убы́ток для привлечéния покупáтелей.*
lost [lɔst] *pt, pp of* **lose** ◆ *adj* (*person, animal*) пропáвший; (*object*) потерянный (потерян); **to get ~** заблуди́ться* (*perf*); **get ~!** (*inf*) провáливай!; **he was ~ in thought** он был погружён в свои́ мы́сли.
lost and found *n* (*US*) стол *or* бюрó *nt ind* нахóдок.
lost cause *n* проигранное дéло*.
lost property *n* потерянные вéщи *fpl*; (*BRIT: also:* **~ ~ office**) стол *or* бюрó *nt ind* нахóдок.
lot [lɔt] *n* (*of people, goods*) пáртия; (*at auction*) лот; (*destiny*) у́часть *f*; (*esp US: ground*) (земéльный) учáсток*; (*large number, amount*): **a ~ (of)** мнóго (*+gen*); **the ~** (*everything*) всё; **~s of ...** мнóго *+gen* ...; **I see a ~ of him** мы с ним чáсто ви́димся; **I read/don't read a ~** я мнóго/мáло читáю; **a ~ bigger/louder/more expensive** намнóго *or* горáздо бóльше/грóмче/дорóже; **to draw ~s (for sth)** тяну́ть* (*impf*) жрéбий (для чегó-н).
lotion ['ləuʃən] *n* (*for skin, hair*) лосьóн.
lottery ['lɔtərɪ] *n* лотерея.
loud [laud] *adj* (*noise, voice, laugh*) грóмкий* (грóмок); (*support, condemnation*) шу́мный* (шу́мен); (*clothes*) кричáщий* ◆ *adv* грóмко; **out ~** вслух.
loud-hailer [laud'heɪləʳ] *n* (*BRIT*) ру́пор.
loudly ['laudlɪ] *adv* (*see adj*) грóмко; шу́мно.
loudmouthed ['laudmauθt] *adj* горлáстый (горлáст).
loudspeaker [laud'spi:kəʳ] *n* громкоговори́тель *m*.
lounge [laundʒ] *n* (*in house, hotel*) гости́ная *f adj*; (*at airport*) зал ожидáния; (*BRIT: also:* **~ bar**) *часть бáра, где посети́тели сидят* ◆ *vi* (*in chair*) развали́ться (*perf*)
▸ **lounge about** *vi* болтáться (*impf*) (без дéла)
▸ **lounge around** *vi* = **lounge about**.
lounge suit *n* (*BRIT*) пиджáчный костю́м.
louse [laus] (*pl* **lice**) *n* (*insect*) вошь* *f*
▸ **louse up** *vt* (*inf*) напóртить* (*perf*) *+dat*.
lousy ['lauzɪ] *adj* (*inf: bad quality*) парши́вый; (: *ill*): **to feel ~** чу́вствовать (*impf*) себя парши́во.
lout [laut] *n* (*inf*) хам.
louvre ['lu:vəʳ] (*US* **louver**) *n* жалюзи́ *nt ind*.
lovable ['lʌvəbl] *adj* ми́лый* (мил).
love [lʌv] *vt* люби́ть* (*impf*) ◆ *n*: **~ (for)** любóвь* *f* (к *+dat*); **to ~ to do** люби́ть* (*impf*) *+infin*; **I ~ chocolate** я люблю́ шоколáд; **I'd ~ to come** я с удовóльствием пришёл бы; **"love (from) Anne"** (*in letter*) „лю́бящая Вас Áнна"; **to fall in ~ with** влюбля́ться (влюби́ться* *perf*) в *+acc*; **he is in ~ with her** он в неё влюблён; **to make ~** занимáться (заня́ться* *perf*) любóвью; **~ at first sight** любóвь* с пéрвого взгля́да; **to send one's ~ to sb** передавáть* (передáть* *perf*) привéт комý-н; **"fifteen ~"** (*TENNIS*) „пятнáдцать – ноль".
love affair *n* ромáн.
love child *n* дитя́* *nt* любви́.
loved ones ['lʌvdwʌnz] *npl* люби́мые *pl adj*.
love-hate relationship ['lʌvheɪt-] *n* любóвь *f*-нéнависть *f*.
love letter *n* любóвное письмó*.
love life *n* инти́мная жизнь *f*.
lovely ['lʌvlɪ] *adj* (*beautiful*) краси́вый (краси́в); (*delightful*) чудéсный* (чудéсен).
lover ['lʌvəʳ] *n* (*sexual partner*) любóвник (-ица); (*person in love*) влюблённый(-ая) *m(f) adj*; **a ~ of art/music** люби́тель(ница) *m(f)* искýсства/мýзыки.
lovesick ['lʌvsɪk] *adj* томи́мый любóвью; **to be ~** томи́ться* (*impf*) от любви́.
love song *n* любóвная пéсня*.
loving ['lʌvɪŋ] *adj* (*person*) лю́бящий*, нéжный* (нéжен); (*actions*) нéжный* (нéжен).
low [ləu] *adj* ни́зкий* (ни́зок); (*sound: quiet*) ти́хий* (тих); (*depressed*) подáвленный (подáвлен); (*ill*) нездорóвый (нездорóв) ◆ *adv* (*sing: deeply*) ни́зким гóлосом; (: *quietly*) ти́хо; (*fly*) ни́зко ◆ *n* (*METEOROLOGY*) ни́зкое давлéние; **we are (running) ~ on milk** у нас остаётся мáло молокá; **to reach a new** *or* **an all-time ~** (*morale, profits*) опускáться (опусти́ться* *perf*) на небывáло ни́зкий у́ровень.
low-alcohol ['ləu'ælkəhɔl] *adj*: **~ wine/beer** винó/пи́во с ни́зким содержáнием алкогóля.
lowbrow ['ləubrau] *adj* низкопрóбный.
low-calorie ['ləu'kælərɪ] *adj* низко-

калори́йный* (низкокалори́ен).
low-cut ['ləukʌt] *adj* с глубо́ким вы́резом.
lowdown ['ləudaun] *n* (*inf*): **to give sb the ~ on sth** раскрыва́ть (раскры́ть* *perf*) пе́ред кем-н всю подного́тную чего́-н.
lower ['ləuəʳ] *adj* (*bottom*: *of two things*) ни́жний*; (*less important*) ни́зший* ◆ *vt* (*object*) спуска́ть (спусти́ть* *perf*); (*level, price*) снижа́ть (сни́зить* *perf*); (*voice*) понижа́ть (пони́зить* *perf*); (*eyes*) опуска́ть (опусти́ть* *perf*).
low-fat ['ləu'fæt] *adj* обезжи́ренный (обезжи́рен).
low-key ['ləu'ki:] *adj* сде́ржанный (сде́ржан).
lowlands ['ləuləndz] *npl* ни́зменность *fsg*.
low-level language ['ləulɛvl-] *n* (COMPUT) язы́к* программи́рования ни́зкого у́ровня.
low-loader ['ləuləudəʳ] *n* автомоби́ль *m* с погру́зочным приспособле́нием.
lowly ['ləulɪ] *adj* (*position, origin*) ни́зкий* (ни́зок).
low-lying [ləu'laɪɪŋ] *adj* ни́зменный.
low-paid [ləu'peɪd] *adj* низкоопла́чиваемый (низкоопла́чиваем).
low-rise ['ləuraɪz] *adj* ни́зкий* (ни́зок).
low-tech ['ləutɛk] *adj*: **their office is very ~** у них в о́фисе техноло́гия на о́чень ни́зком у́ровне.
loyal ['lɔɪəl] *adj* ве́рный* (ве́рен); (POL) лоя́льный* (лоя́лен).
loyalist ['lɔɪəlɪst] *n* лояли́ст(ка).
loyalty ['lɔɪəltɪ] *n* ве́рность *f*; (POL) лоя́льность *f*; **~ card** ≈ диско́нтная ка́рта.
lozenge ['lɔzɪndʒ] *n* (*shape*) ромб; (*pastille*): **throat ~** табле́тка* от ка́шля.
LP *n abbr* = **long-playing record**.
L-plate ['ɛlpleɪt] *n* (BRIT) *знак на маши́не, обознача́ющий "учени́к"*
LPN *n abbr* (US) = *Licensed Practical Nurse.*
LRAM *n abbr* (BRIT) = *Licentiate of the Royal Academy of Music.*
LSAT *n abbr* (US) = *Law School Admissions Test.*
LSD *n abbr* (= *lysergic acid diethylamide*) ЛСД; (BRIT: = *pounds, shillings and pence*) *фу́нты, ши́ллинги и пе́нсы.*
LSE *n abbr* (BRIT) = *London School of Economics.*
LT *abbr* (ELEC: = *low tension*) ни́зкое напряже́ние.
Lt *abbr* (MIL) = **lieutenant**.
Ltd *abbr* (COMM) = **limited (liability) company**.
lubricant ['lu:brɪkənt] *n* сма́зка, лубрика́тор.
lubricate ['lu:brɪkeɪt] *vt* сма́зывать (сма́зать* *perf*).
lucid ['lu:sɪd] *adj* (*writing, speech*) я́сный* (я́сен); (*thinking*): **I'm not feeling very ~ today** я сего́дня пло́хо сообража́ю.
lucidity [lu:'sɪdɪtɪ] *n* я́сность *f*.
luck [lʌk] *n* (*also*: **good ~**) уда́ча; **bad ~** неуда́ча; **good ~!** уда́чи (Вам)!; **bad** *or* **hard** *or* **tough ~!** не повезло́!; **we are in ~/out of ~** нам везёт/не везёт; **to push one's ~** искуша́ть (*impf*) судьбу́.
luckily ['lʌkɪlɪ] *adv* к сча́стью.
luckless ['lʌklɪs] *adj* невезу́чий (невезу́ч).
lucky ['lʌkɪ] *adj* (*situation, event, object*) счастли́вый; (*person*) уда́чливый (уда́члив); **he is ~ at cards/in love** ему́ везёт в ка́ртах/любви́; **how did you manage it? – I was ~** как Вам э́то удало́сь? – мне повезло́.
lucrative ['lu:krətɪv] *adj* (*profitable*) при́быльный* (при́былен), дохо́дный* (дохо́ден); (*job*) высокоопла́чиваемый.
ludicrous ['lu:dɪkrəs] *adj* смехотво́рный* (смехотво́рен).
ludo ['lu:dəu] *n насто́льная игра́ с фи́шками и броса́нием косте́й.*
lug [lʌg] *vt* (*inf*) волочь* (*impf*).
luggage ['lʌgɪdʒ] *n* бага́ж*.
luggage car *n* = **luggage van**.
luggage rack *n* (*in train*) бага́жная по́лка.
luggage van *n* (BRIT) бага́жный ваго́н.
lugubrious [lu'gu:brɪəs] *adj* ско́рбный* (ско́рбен).
lukewarm ['lu:kwɔ:m] *adj* (*liquid*) слегка́ тёплый; (*reaction*) прохла́дный* (прохла́ден).
lull [lʌl] *n* зати́шье ◆ *vt*: **to ~ sb to sleep** убаю́кивать (убаю́кать *perf*) кого́-н; **to ~ sb into a false sense of security** усыпля́ть (усыпи́ть* *perf*) чью-н бди́тельность.
lullaby ['lʌləbaɪ] *n* колыбе́льная *f adj*.
lumbago [lʌm'beɪgəu] *n* люмба́го *nt ind*.
lumber ['lʌmbəʳ] *n* (*esp US*: *wood*) лесоматериа́лы *mpl*; (*junk*) ру́хлядь *f* ◆ *vi*: **to ~ about/along** *etc* тащи́ться (*impf*)
▸ **lumber with** *vt*: **to ~ sb with sth** навя́зывать (навяза́ть* *perf*) кому́-н что-н; **he was ~ed with all the work** ему́ навяза́ли всю рабо́ту.
lumberjack ['lʌmbədʒæk] *n* лесору́б.
lumber room *n* (BRIT) чула́н.
lumberyard ['lʌmbəjɑ:d] *n* (US) склад лесоматериа́лов.
luminous ['lu:mɪnəs] *adj* (*fabric, colour*) блестя́щий*; (*digit, star*) светя́щийся.
lump [lʌmp] *n* (*of clay, snow*) ком; (*of butter, sugar etc*) кусо́к*; (*swelling*) ши́шка; (*growth*) о́пухоль *f* ◆ *vt*: **to ~ together** меша́ть (смеша́ть *perf*) в (одну́) ку́чу; **a ~ sum** единовре́менно выпла́чиваемая су́мма.
lumpy ['lʌmpɪ] *adj* (*sauce*) комкова́тый; (*bed*) бугри́стый (бугри́ст).
lunacy ['lu:nəsɪ] *n* (*fig*) безу́мие; (*mental illness*) помеша́тельство.
lunar ['lu:nəʳ] *adj* лу́нный.
lunatic ['lu:nətɪk] *adj* (*behaviour*) безу́мный* (безу́мен) ◆ *n* (*also fig*) сумасше́дший*(-ая)

* marks translations which have irregular inflections. The Russian-English side of the dictionary gives inflectional information.

m(f) adj.
lunatic asylum *n* сумасшедший* дом*.
lunatic fringe *n*: **the ~ ~** кучка фанатиков.
lunch [lʌntʃ] *n* обед ◆ *vi* обедать (пообедать *perf*).
lunch break *n* перерыв на обед, обеденный перерыв.
luncheon ['lʌntʃən] *n* (*formal meal*) завтрак.
luncheon meat *n* свиная тушёнка.
luncheon voucher *n* (*BRIT*) талон на обед.
lunch hour *n* = **lunch break**.
lunch time *n* обеденное время* *nt*.
lung [lʌŋ] *n* лёгкое *nt adj*; **~ cancer** рак лёгких.
lunge [lʌndʒ] *vi* (*also:* **~ forward**) рвануться (*perf*); (*SPORT*) делать (сделать *perf*) выпад; **to ~ at** ринуться (*perf*) на +*acc*; (*SPORT*) делать (сделать *perf*) выпад против +*gen*.
lupin ['lu:pɪn] *n* (*BOT*) люпин.
lurch [lə:tʃ] *vi* (*person*) покачнуться (*perf*); (*vehicle*) рвануть (*perf*); (*ship*): **to ~ sideways** крениться* (накрениться* *perf*) ◆ *n* (*of ship*) крен; (*of vehicle*) бросок*; **the car ~ed forward** машину бросило вперёд; **to leave sb in the ~** (*inf*) бросать (бросить* *perf*) кого-н в беде.
lure [luəʳ] *n* приманка ◆ *vt* заманивать (заманить* *perf*); **to ~ sb away from** отвлекать (отвлечь* *perf*) кого-н от +*gen*.
lurid ['luərɪd] *adj* (*garish*) аляповатый (аляповат).
lurk [lə:k] *vi* (*animal, person, also fig*) таиться (*impf*).
luscious ['lʌʃəs] *adj* (*person, thing*) притягательный* (притягателен); (*food*) сочный* (сочен).
lush [lʌʃ] *adj* (*fields, gardens*) пышный* (пышен); (*restaurant, lifestyle*) роскошный* (роскошен).
lust [lʌst] *n* (*sexual desire*) похоть *f*; (*greed*): **~ (for)** жажда (к +*dat*)
▸ **lust after** *vt fus* (*desire sexually*) испытывать (испытать *perf*) вожделение к +*dat*; (*crave*) жаждать* (*impf*) +*gen*
▸ **lust for** *vt fus* = **lust after**.
lustful ['lʌstful] *adj* похотливый (похотлив).
lustre ['lʌstəʳ] (*US* **luster**) *n* блеск.
lusty ['lʌstɪ] *adj* полный* (полон) жизни и здоровья.
lute [lu:t] *n* лютня*.
luvvie ['lʌvɪ] *n* (*inf*) дорогуша *m/f*.
luvvy ['lʌvɪ] *n* = **luvvie**.
Luxembourg ['lʌksəmbə:g] *n* Люксембург.
luxuriant [lʌg'zjuərɪənt] *adj* (*plants, gardens*) буйный* (буен); (*hair*) пышный* (пышен).
luxuriate [lʌg'zjuərɪeɪt] *vi*: **to ~ in** наслаждаться (насладиться* *perf*) +*instr*.
luxurious [lʌg'zjuərɪəs] *adj* роскошный* (роскошен).
luxury ['lʌkʃərɪ] *n* (*great comfort*) роскошь *f*; (*treat*) роскошество ◆ *cpd* роскошный.
luxury tax *n* налог на предметы роскоши.
LV *n abbr* = **luncheon voucher**.
Lvov [ljvɔf] *n* Львов.
LW *abbr* (*RADIO*) (= **long wave**) ДВ= *длинные волны*.
lycra® ['laɪkrə] *n синтетический эластичный материал, используемый при изготовлении трикотажной одежды.*
lying ['laɪɪŋ] *n* ложь *f* ◆ *adj* лживый.
lynch [lɪntʃ] *vt* линчевать* (*impf/perf*).
lynx [lɪŋks] *n* (*ZOOL*) рысь *f*.
Lyon ['li:ɔ̃] *n* Лион.
lyric ['lɪrɪk] *adj*: **~ poetry** лирика, лирическая поэзия.
lyrical ['lɪrɪkl] *adj* (*poem*) лирический*; (*fig: praise, comment*) восторженный (восторжен).
lyricism ['lɪrɪsɪzəm] *n* лиризм.
lyrics ['lɪrɪks] *npl* слова *ntpl or* текст *msg* (*песни*).

~ M, m ~

M, m [ɛm] *n* (*letter*) *13-ая бу́ква англи́йского алфави́та.*
M *n abbr* (*BRIT*: = *motorway*) автомагистра́ль *f* ◆ *abbr* = **medium.**
m. *abbr* (= **metre**) м= *метр*; = **mile, million.**
MA *n abbr* (= *Master of Arts*) ≈ маги́стр гуманита́рных нау́к; (= *military academy*) Вое́нная акаде́мия ◆ *abbr* (*US*: *POST*) = *Massachusetts.*
mac [mæk] *n* (*BRIT*: *inf*) макинто́ш.
macabre [mə'kɑ:brə] *adj* жу́ткий* (жу́ток).
macaroni [mækə'rəunɪ] *n* макаро́ны* *pl.*
macaroon [mækə'ru:n] *n* минда́льное безе́ *nt ind.*
mace [meɪs] *n* (*weapon*) булава́*; (*ceremonial*) жезл*; (*spice*) муска́т.
Macedonia [mæsɪ'dəunɪə] *n* Македо́ния.
Macedonian [mæsɪ'dəunɪən] *adj* македо́нский*.
machinations [mækɪ'neɪʃənz] *npl* (*plot*) ко́зни* *pl*; (*scheme*) махина́ция *fsg.*
machine [mə'ʃi:n] *n* (*also fig*) маши́на ◆ *vt* (*TECH*) подверга́ть (подве́ргнуть* *perf*) маши́нной обрабо́тке; (*dress etc*) шить* (сшить* *perf*) на маши́не.
machine code *n* (*COMPUT*) маши́нный код.
machine gun *n* пулемёт.
machine language *n* (*COMPUT*) маши́нный язы́к*.
machine readable *adj* (*COMPUT*) машино-чита́емый.
machinery [mə'ʃi:nərɪ] *n* обору́дование; (*of government*) механи́зм.
machine shop *n* механи́ческий* цех*.
machine tool *n* стано́к*.
machine washable *adj* (*garment*) приго́дный к маши́нной сти́рке.
machinist [mə'ʃi:nɪst] *n* стано́чник(-ица).
macho ['mætʃəu] *adj* мужи́цкий.
mackerel ['mækrl] *n inv* ску́мбрия.
mackintosh ['mækɪntɔʃ] *n* (*BRIT*) макинто́ш.
macro... ['mækrəu] *prefix* ма́кро....
macroeconomics ['mækrəui:kə'nɔmɪks] *npl* макроэконо́мика *fsg.*
mad [mæd] *adj* (*also fig*) сумасше́дший*, поме́шанный (поме́шан); (*angry*) бе́шеный; (*keen*): **he is ~ about** он поме́шан на +*prp*; **to go ~** (*insane*) сходи́ть* (сойти́* *perf*) с ума́; (*angry*) беси́ться* (взбеси́ться* *perf*).
Madagascar [mædə'gæskəʳ] *n* Мадагаска́р.
madam ['mædəm] *n* (*form of address*) мада́м *f ind*, госпожа́; **yes, ~** да, мада́м; **Dear M~** (*in formal letter*) уважа́емая госпожа́; **M~ Chairman** госпожа́ председа́тель.
madcap ['mædkæp] *adj* сумасбро́дный*.
mad cow disease *n* (*inf*) энцефалопа́тия кру́пного рога́того скота́.
madden ['mædn] *vt* (*make angry*) беси́ть* (взбеси́ть* *perf*).
maddening ['mædnɪŋ] *adj* невыноси́мый (невыноси́м).
made [meɪd] *pt, pp of* **make.**
Madeira [mə'dɪərə] *n* (*GEO*) Маде́йра; (*wine*) маде́ра.
made-to-measure ['meɪdtə'mɛʒəʳ] *adj* (*BRIT*) индивидуа́льного поши́ва.
madhouse ['mædhaus] *n* (*inf*: *asylum*) сумасше́дший* дом*, психу́шка*; (*state of uproar*) сумасше́дший дом.
madly ['mædlɪ] *adv* безу́мно; **she is ~ in love with him** она́ безу́мно влюблена́ в него́; **to fall ~ in love with sb** безу́мно влюби́ться* (*perf*) в кого́-н.
madman ['mædmən] *irreg n* сумасше́дший* *m adj.*
madness ['mædnɪs] *n* (*insanity*) безу́мие, сумасше́ствие; (*foolishness*) безу́мие.
Madrid [mə'drɪd] *n* Мадри́д.
madwoman ['mædwumən] *irreg n* сумасше́дшая* *f adj.*
Mafia ['mæfɪə] *n*: **the ~** ма́фия.
mag [mæg] *n abbr* (*BRIT*: *inf*) = **magazine.**
magazine [mægə'zi:n] *n* журна́л; (*RADIO*) радиожурна́л; (*TV*) тележурна́л; (*MIL*: *store*) склад боеприпа́сов; (: *of firearm*) магази́н.
maggot ['mægət] *n* личи́нка* му́хи.
magic ['mædʒɪk] *n* ма́гия; (*conjuring*) фо́кусы *mpl* ◆ *adj* (*powers, ritual*) маги́ческий*; (*fig*: *place, moment, experience*) волше́бный* (волше́бен); **~ wand** волше́бная па́лочка*.
magical ['mædʒɪkl] *adj* (*powers, ritual*) маги́ческий*; (*experience, evening*) волше́бный* (волше́бен).

* marks translations which have irregular inflections. The Russian-English side of the dictionary gives inflectional information.

magician [mə'dʒɪʃən] *n* (***wizard***) маг; (***conjurer***) фокусник.
magistrate ['mædʒɪstreɪt] *n* (*LAW*) мировой судья* *m*.
magistrates' court *n* магистратура.
magnanimous [mæg'nænɪməs] *adj* великодушный* (великодушен).
magnate ['mægneɪt] *n* магнат.
magnesium [mæg'ni:zɪəm] *n* магний.
magnet ['mægnɪt] *n* магнит.
magnetic [mæg'nɛtɪk] *adj* магнитный; (***personality***) притягательный* (притягателен).
magnetic disk *n* (*COMPUT*) магнитный диск.
magnetic tape *n* магнитная плёнка*.
magnetism ['mægnɪtɪzəm] *n* магнетизм.
magnetize ['mægnɪtaɪz] *vt* намагничивать (намагнитить* *perf*).
magnification [mægnɪfɪ'keɪʃən] *n* увеличение.
magnificence [mæg'nɪfɪsns] *n* великолепие.
magnificent [mæg'nɪfɪsnt] *adj* великолепный* (великолепен).
magnify ['mægnɪfaɪ] *vt* увеличивать (увеличить *perf*); (***sound***) усиливать (усилить *perf*); (***exaggerate***) преувеличивать (преувеличить *perf*).
magnifying glass ['mægnɪfaɪɪŋ-] *n* увеличительное стекло*, лупа.
magnitude ['mægnɪtju:d] *n* (***size***) величина; (***importance***) масштаб.
magnolia [mæg'nəulɪə] *n* магнолия.
magpie ['mægpaɪ] *n* сорока.
mahogany [mə'hɔgənɪ] *n* красное дерево ◆ *cpd* красного дерева.
maid [meɪd] *n* (***in private house***) служанка*; (***in hotel***) горничная *f adj*; **old ~** (*pej*) старая дева.
maiden ['meɪdn] *n* (***literary***) дева ◆ *adj* (***aunt etc***) незамужняя; (***speech, voyage***) первый.
maiden name *n* девичья фамилия.
mail [meɪl] *n* почта ◆ *vt* отправлять (отправить* *perf*) по почте; **by ~** по почте.
mailbox ['meɪlbɔks] *n* (*US*: ***letter box, also*** *COMPUT*) почтовый ящик.
mailing list ['meɪlɪŋ-] *n* список* адресатов.
mailman ['meɪlmæn] *irreg n* (*US*) почтальон.
mail order *n система заказа товаров по почте* ◆ *cpd*: **~-~ catalogue** каталог торгово-посылочной фирмы; **~-~ firm** торгово-посылочная фирма.
mailshot ['meɪlʃɔt] *n рассылка объявлений по почте*.
mail train *n* почтовый поезд*.
mail truck *n* (*US*) почтовый фургон.
mail van *n* (*BRIT*: *AUT*) почтовый фургон; (: *RAIL*) почтовый вагон.
maim [meɪm] *vt* калечить (искалечить *perf*).
main [meɪn] *adj* (***reason, point, door***) главный ◆ *n* (***pipe***): **gas/water ~** газопроводная/водопроводная магистраль *f*; **the ~s** *npl* сеть *fsg*; **~ meal** обед; **in the ~** в основном.
main course *n* основное *or* второе блюдо.
mainframe ['meɪnfreɪm] *n* (*COMPUT*) (универсальная) вычислительная машина.
mainland ['meɪnlənd] *n*: **the ~** материк, большая земля*.
main line *n* (*RAIL*) железнодорожная магистраль *f*.
mainline ['meɪnlaɪn] *adj* (*RAIL*: ***station***) магистральный ◆ *vt* (*DRUGS*) вкалывать (вколоть* *perf*) ◆ *vi* (*DRUGS*) колоться* (*impf*).
mainly ['meɪnlɪ] *adv* главным образом.
main road *n* шоссе *nt ind*; (***in town, village***) главная улица.
mainstay ['meɪnsteɪ] *n* главная опора.
mainstream ['meɪnstri:m] *n* господствующая тенденция ◆ *adj* господствующий*.
maintain [meɪn'teɪn] *vt* (***friendship, system, momentum***) поддерживать (поддержать* *perf*); (***dependant***) содержать* (*impf*); (***building***) обслуживать (*impf*); (***affirm***: ***belief, opinion***) утверждать (*impf*); **to ~ (that ...)** утверждать (*impf*) (, что ...).
maintenance ['meɪntənəns] *n* (***see vb***) поддержание; содержание; обслуживание; утверждение; (*LAW*: ***alimony***) алименты* *pl*.
maintenance contract *n* контракт по обслуживанию.
maintenance grant *n* стипендия.
maintenance order *n* (*LAW*) постановление о выплате алиментов.
maisonette [meɪzə'nɛt] *n* (*BRIT*) двухэтажная квартира.
maize [meɪz] *n* кукуруза, маис.
Maj. *abbr* (*MIL*) = **major**.
majestic [mə'dʒɛstɪk] *adj* величественный* (величествен).
majesty ['mædʒɪstɪ] *n* (***sovereignty***) королевская власть *f*; (***splendour***) величественность *f*; (***form of address***): **Your M~** Ваше Величество.
major ['meɪdʒə'] *n* (*MIL*) майор ◆ *adj* (***important***) главный; (*MUS*) мажорный ◆ *vi* (*US*: *SCOL*): **to ~ in** специализироваться (*impf/perf*) в +*prp*; **a ~ operation** (***also fig***) крупная операция.
Majorca [mə'jɔ:kə] *n* Мальорка, Майорка.
major general *n* генерал-майор.
majority [mə'dʒɔrɪtɪ] *n* большинство ◆ *cpd*: **~ verdict** приговор, вынесенный большинством (голосов); **~ (share)holding** контрольный пакет акций.
make [meɪk] (*pt, pp* **made**) *vt* делать (сделать *perf*); (***clothes***) шить* (сшить* *perf*); (***manufacture***) изготовлять (изготовить* *perf*); (***meal***) готовить* (приготовить* *perf*); (***money***) зарабатывать (заработать *perf*) ◆ *n* (***brand***) марка*; **to ~ sb do** (***force***) заставлять (заставить* *perf*) кого-н +*infin*; **two and two ~ four** (***equal***) два плюс два – четыре; **to ~ sb unhappy** расстраивать (расстроить *perf*) кого-н; **to ~ a noise** шуметь* (*impf*); **to ~ the bed** стелить* (постелить* *perf*) постель; **to ~**

a fool of sb де́лать (сде́лать *perf*) из кого́-н дурака́; **to ~ a profit** получа́ть (получи́ть* *perf*) при́быль; **to ~ a loss** нести́* (понести́* *perf*) убы́ток; **to ~ it** (*succeed*) преуспева́ть (преуспе́ть* *perf*); (*arrive*) успева́ть (успе́ть* *perf*); **what time do you ~ it?** ско́лько на ва́ших (часа́х)?; **let's ~ it Monday** дава́йте договори́мся на понеде́льник; **to ~ good** ◆ *vi* (*succeed*) преуспева́ть (преуспе́ть* *perf*) ◆ *vt* (*deficit*) возмеща́ть (возмести́ть* *perf*); (*damage*) исправля́ть (испра́вить* *perf*); **to ~ do with/without** обходи́ться* (обойти́сь* *perf*) +*instr*/без +*gen*

▸ **make for** *vt fus* (*place*) направля́ться (напра́виться* *perf*) к +*dat*/в +*acc*

▸ **make off** *vi* (*escape*) скрыва́ться (скры́ться* *perf*)

▸ **make out** *vt* (*decipher*) разбира́ть (разобра́ть* *perf*); (*see*) различа́ть (различи́ть *perf*); (*write out*) выпи́сывать (вы́писать* *perf*); (*claim*) утвержда́ть *(impf)*; (*understand*) разбира́ться (разобра́ться* *perf*) в +*prp*; (*claim, imply*) де́лать (сде́лать *perf*) вид; **to ~ out a case for sth** обосно́вывать (обоснова́ть *perf*) что-н

▸ **make over** *vt* (*assign*): **to ~ over (to)** передава́ть* (переда́ть* *perf*) (+*dat*)

▸ **make up** *vt fus* (*constitute*) составля́ть (соста́вить* *perf*) ◆ *vt* (*invent*) выду́мывать (вы́думать *perf*); (*prepare*: *bed, parcel*) гото́вить* (пригото́вить* *perf*); (*with cosmetics*) де́лать (сде́лать *perf*) макия́ж +*dat* ◆ *vi* (*after quarrel*) мири́ться (помири́ться *perf*); (*with cosmetics*): **to ~ (o.s.) up** де́лать (сде́лать *perf*) макия́ж; **to be made up of** состоя́ть *(impf)* из +*gen*

▸ **make up for** *vt fus* (*mistake, misdemeanour*) загла́живать (заглади́ть* *perf*); (*loss*) восполня́ть (воспо́лнить *perf*); **to ~ up for lost time** навёрстывать (наверста́ть *perf*) упу́щенное вре́мя.

make-believe ['meɪkbɪli:v] *n* фанта́зии *fpl*; **a world of ~** мир фанта́зий; **it's just ~** э́то – про́сто фанта́зия.

maker ['meɪkə^r] *n* (*of programme, film*) созда́тель(ница) *m(f)*; (*of goods*) изготови́тель *m*.

makeshift ['meɪkʃɪft] *adj* (*temporary*) вре́менный.

make-up ['meɪkʌp] *n* косме́тика, макия́ж; (*THEAT*) грим.

make-up bag *n* косме́тичка*.

make-up remover *n* сре́дство для сня́тия макия́жа.

making ['meɪkɪŋ] *n* (*of programme*) созда́ние; (*of goods*) изготовле́ние; (*fig*): **in the ~** в проце́ссе созда́ния; **to have the ~s of** име́ть *(impf)* зада́тки +*gen*; **the problem is of your own ~** пробле́ма Ва́ми же и со́здана.

maladjusted [mælə'dʒʌstɪd] *adj* (*child*) трудновоспиту́емый.

maladroit [mælə'drɔɪt] *adj* (*behaviour*) неуме́лый (неуме́л); (*comment*) беста́ктный* (беста́ктен).

malaise [mæ'leɪz] *n* (*of society*) неду́г.

malaria [mə'lɛərɪə] *n* маляри́я.

Malawi [mə'lɑ:wɪ] *n* Мала́ви *nt ind*.

Malay [mə'leɪ] *adj* мала́йский* ◆ *n* (*person*) мала́ец*(-а́йка*); (*LING*) мала́йский* язы́к*.

Malaya [mə'leɪə] *n* Мала́йя.

Malayan [mə'leɪən] *adj, n* = **Malay**.

Malaysia [mə'leɪzɪə] *n* Мала́йзия.

Malaysian [mə'leɪzɪən] *adj* малайзи́йский ◆ *n* малайзи́ец*(-и́йка*).

Maldives ['mɔ:ldaɪvz] *npl*: **the ~** Мальди́вские острова́* *mpl*.

male [meɪl] *n* (*human*) мужчи́на *m*; (*animal*) саме́ц* ◆ *adj* (*sex, attitude*) мужско́й; (*child etc*) мужско́го по́ла; (*ELEC*) охва́тываемый; **~ and female students** студе́нты: ю́ноши и де́вушки*.

male chauvinist *n*: **he's a ~ ~** он о́чень пренебрежи́тельно отно́сится к же́нщинам.

male nurse *n* медбра́т*.

malevolence [mə'lɛvələns] *n* (*act*) злодея́ние; (*feeling*) зло́ба.

malevolent [mə'lɛvələnt] *adj* зло́бный* (зло́бен).

malformed [mæl'fɔ:md] *adj* непра́вильно сформирова́вшийся.

malfunction [mæl'fʌŋkʃən] *n* неиспра́вность *f*.

Mali ['mɑ:li] *n* Мали́ *nt ind*.

Malian ['mɑ:lɪən] *adj* мали́йский ◆ *n* мали́ец*(-и́йка*).

malice ['mælɪs] *n* зло́ба.

malicious [mə'lɪʃəs] *adj* (*person, gossip*) зло́бный* (зло́бен), злой* (зол); (*LAW*) злонаме́ренный (злонаме́рен).

malign [mə'laɪn] *vt* клевета́ть* (оклевета́ть* *perf*) ◆ *adj* па́губный* (па́губен).

malignant [mə'lɪgnənt] *adj* (*MED*) злока́чественный*; (*behaviour, intention*) зло́стный* (зло́стен).

malingerer [mə'lɪŋgərə^r] *n* симуля́нт(ка*).

mall [mɔ:l] *n* (*also*: **shopping ~**) ≈ торго́вый центр.

malleable ['mælɪəbl] *adj* (*clay, substance*) пода́тливый (пода́тлив); (*person*) поко́рный* (поко́рен).

mallet ['mælɪt] *n* деревя́нный молото́к*.

malnutrition [mælnju:'trɪʃən] *n* недоеда́ние.

malpractice [mæl'præktɪs] *n* злоупотребле́ние служе́бным положе́нием.

malt [mɔ:lt] *n* (*grain*) со́лод*; (*also*: **~ whisky**) солодо́вое ви́ски *nt ind*.

Malta ['mɔ:ltə] *n* Ма́льта.

* marks translations which have irregular inflections. The Russian-English side of the dictionary gives inflectional information.

Maltese [mɔ:l'ti:z] *adj* мальти́йский* ◆ *n inv* мальти́ец*(-и́йка*); (*LING*) мальти́йский* язы́к*.
maltreat [mæl'tri:t] *vt* пло́хо обраща́ться *(impf)* с +*instr*.
mammal ['mæml] *n* млекопита́ющее *nt adj*.
mammoth ['mæməθ] *n* ма́монт ◆ *adj* (*task*) колосса́льный* (колосса́лен).
man [mæn] (*pl* **men**) *n* (*adult male*) мужчи́на *m*; (*person, mankind*) челове́к*; (*CHESS*) фигу́ра ◆ *vt* (*machine*) обслу́живать *(impf)*; (*post*) занима́ть (заня́ть* *perf*); (*NAUT*): **to ~ a ship** набира́ть (набра́ть* *perf*) кома́нду корабля́; **an old ~** стари́к*; **~ and wife** муж и жена́.
manage ['mænɪdʒ] *vi* (*get by*) обходи́ться* (обойти́сь* *perf*) ◆ *vt* (*business, organization*) руководи́ть* *(impf)* +*instr*, управля́ть *(impf)* +*instr*; (*shop, restaurant*) заве́довать *(impf)* +*instr*; (*economy*) управля́ть *(impf)* +*instr*; (*control*) кома́ндовать *(impf)* +*instr*; (*workload, task*) справля́ться *(impf)* с +*instr*; **to ~ without sb/sth** обходи́ться* (обойти́сь* *perf*) без кого́-н/чего́-н; **I ~d to convince him** мне удало́сь убеди́ть его́; **I ~d to finish in time** я успе́л зако́нчить во́время.
manageable ['mænɪdʒəbl] *adj* (*task*) выполни́мый (выполни́м); (*number, size*) удо́бный.
management ['mænɪdʒmənt] *n* (*body*) руково́дство; (*act*): **~ (of)** управле́ние (+*instr*); **"under new ~"** "под но́вым руково́дством".
management accounting *n* управле́нческий* учёт.
management consultant *n* консульта́нт по вопро́сам ме́неджмента.
manager ['mænɪdʒə^r] *n* (*of business, organization*) управля́ющий* *m adj*, ме́неджер; (*of estate*) управля́ющий; (*of shop*) заве́дующий*(-ая) *m(f) adj*; (*of pop star*) ме́неджер; (*SPORT*) гла́вный тре́нер; **sales ~** нача́льник по сбы́ту.
manageress [mænɪdʒə'rɛs] *n* (*of shop*) заве́дующая *f adj*.
managerial [mænɪ'dʒɪərɪəl] *adj* (*role*) управле́нческий*; **~ staff** управле́нческий* аппара́т; **~ decisions** реше́ния, при́нятые руково́дством.
managing director ['mænɪdʒɪŋ-] *n* дире́ктор*-распоряди́тель *m*.
Managua [mə'nægwə] *n* Мана́гуа.
Manchester ['mæntʃɪstə^r] *n* Манче́стер.
Manchuria [mæn'tʃuərɪə] *n* Маньчжу́рия.
Mancunian [mæŋ'kju:nɪən] *n* жи́тель(ница) *m(f)* Манче́стера.
mandarin ['mændərɪn] *n* (*also:* **~ orange**) мандари́н; (*BRIT: POL*) кру́пный чино́вник; (*LING*): **M~ (Chinese)** мандари́нское наре́чие кита́йского языка́.
mandate ['mændeɪt] *n* (*POL: from electorate*) полномо́чие; (: *from UN etc*) манда́т; (*task*) поруче́ние.
mandatory ['mændətərɪ] *adj* обяза́тельный* (обяза́телен).
mandolin(e) ['mændəlɪn] *n* мандоли́на.
mane [meɪn] *n* гри́ва.
maneuver *etc* (*US*) = **manoeuvre** *etc*.
manfully ['mænfəlɪ] *adv* му́жественно.
manganese [mæŋgə'ni:z] *n* ма́рганец*.
mangetout ['mɔnʒ'tu:] *n* стручко́вый горо́х (*со съедо́бными стру́чками*).
mangle ['mæŋgl] *vt* корёжить (искорёжить *perf*) ◆ *n* пресс для отжима́ния белья́.
mango ['mæŋgəu] (*pl* **~es**) *n* ма́нго *nt ind*.
mangrove ['mæŋgrəuv] *n* ма́нгровое де́рево*.
mangy ['meɪndʒɪ] *adj* (*diseased*) парши́вый (парши́в); (*scruffy*) облёзлый (облёзл).
manhandle ['mænhændl] *vt* (*mistreat*) гру́бо обраща́ться *(impf)* с +*instr*; (*move by hand*) приводи́ть* (привести́* *perf*) в де́йствие вручну́ю.
manhole ['mænhəul] *n* люк.
manhood ['mænhud] *n* (*state*) возмужа́лость *f*; (*age*) зре́лость *f*.
man-hour ['mænauə^r] *n* челове́ко-час*.
manhunt ['mænhʌnt] *n* ро́зыск.
mania ['meɪnɪə] *n* (*also PSYCH*) ма́ния.
maniac ['meɪnɪæk] *n* (*also fig*) манья́к; **he's a football ~** он стра́стный люби́тель футбо́ла.
manic ['mænɪk] *adj* безу́мный* (безу́мен).
manic-depressive ['mænɪkdɪ'prɛsɪv] *adj* маниака́льно-депресси́вный* ◆ *n челове́к, страда́ющий маниака́льно-депресси́вным психо́зом.*
manicure ['mænɪkjuə^r] *n* маникю́р ◆ *vt* (*person*) де́лать (сде́лать *perf*) маникю́р +*dat*.
manicure set *n* маникю́рный набо́р.
manifest ['mænɪfɛst] *vt* проявля́ть (прояви́ть* *perf*) ◆ *adj* очеви́дный* (очеви́ден), я́вный* (я́вен) ◆ *n* (*NAUT*) деклара́ция (судово́го гру́за); (*AVIAT*) манифе́ст.
manifestation [mænɪfɛs'teɪʃən] *n*: **a ~ of** проявле́ние +*gen*.
manifesto [mænɪ'fɛstəu] *n* манифе́ст.
manifold ['mænɪfəuld] *adj* многообра́зный* (многообра́зен) ◆ *n* (*AUT*): **exhaust ~** выхлопно́й колле́ктор.
Manila [mə'nɪlə] *n* Мани́ла.
manila [mə'nɪlə] *adj*: **~ paper** пло́тная кори́чневая бума́га.
manipulate [mə'nɪpjuleɪt] *vt* манипули́ровать *(impf)* +*instr*.
manipulation [mənɪpju'leɪʃən] *n* манипуля́ция.
mankind [mæn'kaɪnd] *n* челове́чество.
manliness ['mænlɪnɪs] *n* му́жественность *f*.
manly ['mænlɪ] *adj* му́жественный* (му́жествен).
man-made ['mæn'meɪd] *adj* иску́сственный.
manna ['mænə] *n* ма́нна небе́сная.
mannequin ['mænɪkɪn] *n* (*dummy*) манеке́н; (*fashion model*) манеке́нщица.
manner ['mænə^r] *n* (*way*) о́браз; (*behaviour*)

манéра; **~s** *npl* манéры *fpl*; **bad ~s** плохие манéры; **all ~ of things/people** всевозмóжные вéщи/лю́ди; **in a ~ of speaking** в некотóром рóде.
mannerism ['mænərɪzəm] *n* осóбенность *f* манéра.
mannerly ['mænəlɪ] *adj* учти́вый (учти́в).
manning ['mænɪŋ] *n* набóр рабóчей си́лы.
manoeuvrable [mə'nu:vrəbl] (*US* **maneuvrable**) *adj* манёвренный.
manoeuvre [mə'nu:və^r] (*US* **maneuver**) *vt* (*move*) умéло передвигáть (передви́нуть *perf*); (*manipulate*) маневри́ровать *(impf)* +*instr* ◆ *vi* маневри́ровать *(impf)* ◆ *n* манёвр; **~s** *npl* (*MIL*) манёвры *mpl*; **to ~ sb into doing** подводи́ть* (подвести́* *perf*) когó-н к томý, чтóбы сдéлал чтó-н.
manor ['mænə^r] *n* (*also:* **~ house**) усáдебный дом*.
manpower ['mænpauə^r] *n* рабóчая си́ла.
manservant ['mænsə:vənt] (*pl* **menservants**) *n* слугá* *m*.
mansion ['mænʃən] *n* особня́к*.
manslaughter ['mænslɔ:tə^r] *n* непредумы́шленное уби́йство.
mantelpiece ['mæntlpi:s] *n*ками́нная доскá*.
mantle ['mæntl] *n* (*cloak*) мáнтия; (*fig: covering*) покрóв.
man-to-man ['mæntə'mæn] *adj* мужскóй ◆ *adv* по-мужски́, как мужчи́на с мужчи́ной.
manual ['mænjuəl] *adj* ручнóй ◆ *n* (*book*) посóбие; **~ worker** чернорабóчий*(-ая) *m(f) adj*.
manufacture [mænju'fæktʃə^r] *vt* (*goods*) изготовля́ть (изготóвить* *perf*), производи́ть* (произвести́* *perf*) ◆ *n* изготовлéние, произвóдство.
manufactured goods *npl* промы́шленные товáры *mpl*.
manufacturer [mænju'fæktʃərə^r] *n* изготови́тель *m*, производи́тель *m*.
manufacturing [mænju'fæktʃərɪŋ] *n* изготовлéние, произвóдство.
manure [mə'njuə^r] *n* навóз.
manuscript ['mænjuskrɪpt] *n* (*author's draft*) рýкопись *f*; (*old document*) манускри́пт, рýкопись.
many ['mɛnɪ] *adj* (*a lot of*) мнóго +*gen* ◆ *pron* (*several*) мнóгие; **a great ~** óчень мнóго +*gen*, мнóжество +*gen*; **how ~?** скóлько?; **how ~ people/times?** скóлько людéй/раз?; **too ~ difficulties** сли́шком мнóго трýдностей; **twice as ~** вдвóе бóльше, в два рáза бóльше; **~ a time** мнóго раз; **in ~ cases** во мнóгих слýчаях; **~ of us** мнóгие из нас.
Maori ['maurɪ] *n* мáори *m/f ind*.
map [mæp] *n* кáрта; (*of town*) плáн ◆ *vt* составля́ть (состáвить* *perf*) кáрту +*gen*
▶ **map out** *vt* (*plan*) составля́ть (состáвить* *perf*); (*task, holiday, career*) плани́ровать (*impf*).
maple ['meɪpl] *n* клён ◆ *cpd* кленóвый.
mar [mɑ:^r] *vt* пóртить* (испóртить* *perf*).
Mar. *abbr* = **March**.
marathon ['mærəθən] *n* марафóн ◆ *adj* (*fig*) марафóнский.
marathon runner *n* марафóнец*.
marauder [mə'rɔ:də^r] *n* мародёр.
marble ['mɑ:bl] *n* (*stone*) мрáмор; (*toy*) стекля́нный шáрик ◆ *adj* мрáморный.
marbles ['mɑ:blz] *n* (*game*) *дéтская игрá* в стекля́нные шáрики*.
March [mɑ:tʃ] *n* март; *see also* **July**.
march [mɑ:tʃ] *vi* маршировáть (промаршировáть *perf*); (*protesters*) проходи́ть* (пройти́* *perf*) мáршем ◆ *n* марш ◆ *vt*: **to ~ sb out of** выдворя́ть (вы́дворить *perf*) когó-н из +*gen*; **to ~ out of** демонстрати́вно выходи́ть* (вы́йти* *perf*) из +*gen*; **to ~ into** реши́тельно входи́ть* (войти́* *perf*) в +*acc*.
marcher ['mɑ:tʃə^r] *n* (*demonstrator*) учáстник(-ица) мáрша.
marching orders ['mɑ:tʃɪŋ-] *npl*: **to give sb his ~ ~** увольня́ть (увóлить *perf*) когó-н.
march past *n* (*MIL*) строевóй смотр.
mare [mɛə^r] *n* кобы́ла.
marge [mɑ:dʒ] *n abbr* (*BRIT: inf*) = **margarine**.
margarine [mɑ:dʒə'ri:n] *n* маргари́н.
margin ['mɑ:dʒɪn] *n* (*on page*) поля́ *ntpl*; (*of group*) перифери́я; (*of area*) край*; (*difference: of victory*) преимýщество; (*: of defeat*) меньшинствó; (*also:* **profit ~**) чи́стая при́быль *f no pl*; **safety ~** запáс прóчности; **~ of error** предéл допусти́мой погрéшности; **they won by a ~ of five votes** они́ победи́ли с большинствóм в пять голосóв.
marginal ['mɑ:dʒɪnl] *adj* незначи́тельный* (незначи́телен) ◆ *n* (*also:* **~ seat** *or* **constituency**: *BRIT: POL*) *избирáтельный учáсток где прáвящая пáртия имéет незначи́тельное большинствó голосóв*.
marginally ['mɑ:dʒɪnəlɪ] *adv* незначи́тельно.
marigold ['mærɪgəuld] *n* (*BOT*) ноготкú *mpl*.
marijuana [mærɪ'wɑ:nə] *n* марихуáна.
marina [mə'ri:nə] *n* мари́на *or* при́стань* *f* для яхт.
marinade [mærɪ'neɪd] *n* маринáд ◆ *vt* = **marinate**.
marinate ['mærɪneɪt] *vt* маринoвáть (замариновáть *perf*).
marine [mə'ri:n] *adj* морскóй; (*engineer*) судовóй ◆ *n* (*BRIT*) слýжащий* *m adj* воéнно-морскóго флóта; (*US*) морскóй пехоти́нец*.
marine insurance *n* морскóе страховáние.

* marks translations which have irregular inflections. The Russian-English side of the dictionary gives inflectional information.

marital ['mærɪtl] *adj* супру́жеский*; ~ **status** семе́йное положе́ние.
maritime ['mærɪtaɪm] *adj* морско́й; ~ **law** морско́е пра́во.
Mariupol [mari'upəlj] *n* Мариу́поль *m*.
marjoram ['mɑːdʒərəm] *n* души́ца, майора́н.
mark [mɑːk] *n* (*written symbol*) значо́к*, поме́тка*; (*stain*) пятно́*; (*trace*) след*; (*of friendship, respect*) знак; (*BRIT*: *SCOL*) отме́тка*, оце́нка*; (*level*) отме́тка*; (*currency*) ма́рка* ◆ *vt* (*with pen*) помеча́ть (поме́тить* *perf*); (*subj*: *shoes, tyres*) оставля́ть (оста́вить* *perf*) след на +*prp*; (*furniture etc*) поврежда́ть (повреди́ть* *perf*); (*clothes, carpet*) ста́вить* (поста́вить* *perf*) пятно́ на +*prp*; (*place, time*) ука́зывать (указа́ть* *perf*); (*characterize*) отмеча́ть (отме́тить* *perf*); (*BRIT*: *SCOL*) проверя́ть (прове́рить *perf*); (*SPORT*: *player*) блоки́ровать *(impf)*; **punctuation** ~ знак препина́ния; **M~ 2/3** (*BRIT*: *TECH*) второ́го/тре́тьего вы́пуска; **up to the** ~ на высоте́; **to be quick off the** ~ **to do** (*fig*) не заме́длить *(perf)* +*infin*; **to** ~ **the price on sth** ста́вить* (поста́вить* *perf*) це́ну на чём-н; **to** ~ **time** (*MIL*) марширова́ть *(impf)* на ме́сте; (*fig*) топта́ться* *(impf)*
▸ **mark down** *vt* (*price*) снижа́ть (сни́зить* *perf*); (*goods*) уце́нивать (уцени́ть* *perf*)
▸ **mark off** *vt* (*tick off*) отмеча́ть (отме́тить* *perf*)
▸ **mark out** *vt* (*area, road*) размеча́ть (разме́тить* *perf*); (*person*) выделя́ть (вы́делить *perf*)
▸ **mark up** *vt* (*price*) повыша́ть (повы́сить* *perf*).
marked [mɑːkt] *adj* заме́тный* (заме́тен).
markedly ['mɑːkɪdlɪ] *adv* заме́тно.
marker ['mɑːkə^r] *n* (*sign*) знак; (*bookmark*) закла́дка*; (*pen*) флома́стер.
market ['mɑːkɪt] *n* (*also COMM*) ры́нок* ◆ *vt* выпуска́ть (вы́пустить* *perf*) в прода́жу; **to be on the** ~ быть* *(impf)* в прода́же; **on the open** ~ в свобо́дной прода́же; **to play the** ~ игра́ть *(impf)* на би́рже.
marketable ['mɑːkɪtəbl] *adj* по́льзующийся спро́сом; **to be** ~ по́льзоваться *(impf)* спро́сом.
market analysis *n* ана́лиз ры́нка.
market day *n* база́рный день* *m*.
market demand *n* ры́ночный спрос.
market economy *n* ры́ночная эконо́мика.
market forces *npl* ры́ночные си́лы *fpl*.
market garden *n* (*BRIT*) огоро́д (*для выра́щивания овоще́й на прода́жу*).
marketing ['mɑːkɪtɪŋ] *n* ма́ркетинг.
marketing manager *n* ме́неджер по ма́ркетингу.
marketplace ['mɑːkɪtpleɪs] *n* ры́ночная *or* база́рная пло́щадь* *f*; (*COMM*) ры́нок*.
market price *n* ры́ночная цена́.
market research *n* иссле́дование ры́нка.
market value *n* ры́ночная сто́имость *f*.
marking ['mɑːkɪŋ] *n* (*on animal*) расцве́тка; (*on road*) разме́тка.
marksman ['mɑːksmən] *irreg n* ме́ткий* стрело́к*.
marksmanship ['mɑːksmənʃɪp] *n* ме́ткая стрельба́.
mark-up ['mɑːkʌp] *n* (*margin*) ра́зница (*ме́жду себесто́имостью и прода́жной цено́й*); (*increase*) наце́нка*.
marmalade ['mɑːməleɪd] *n* джем (*ци́трусовый*).
maroon [mə'ruːn] *adj* бордо́вый ◆ *vt*: **we were ~ed** мы бы́ли отре́заны от вне́шнего ми́ра; (*fig*) мы бы́ли в изоля́ции.
marquee [mɑː'kiː] *n* марки́за, пала́точный павильо́н, шатёр.
marquess ['mɑːkwɪs] *n* (*BRIT*) марки́з.
marquis ['mɑːkwɪs] *n* = **marquess**.
Marrakech [mærə'kɛʃ] *n* = **Marrakesh**.
Marrakesh [mærə'kɛʃ] *n* Марраке́ш.
marriage ['mærɪdʒ] *n* брак; (*wedding*) сва́дьба*.
marriage bureau *n* бюро́ *nt ind* знако́мств.
marriage certificate *n* свиде́тельство о бра́ке.
marriage guidance (*US* **marriage counselling**) *n* консульта́ция по вопро́сам семьи́ и бра́ка.
marriage of convenience *n* фикти́вный брак.
married ['mærɪd] *adj* (*man*) жена́тый (жена́т); (*woman*) заму́жняя; (*couple*) жена́тые (жена́ты); (*life*) супру́жеский*; **he is** ~ **to** он жена́т на +*prp*; **she is** ~ **to** она́ за́мужем за +*instr*; **they are** ~ они́ жена́ты.
marrow ['mærəu] *n* (*vegetable*) кабачо́к*; (*also*: **bone** ~) ко́стный мо́зг.
marry ['mærɪ] *vt* (*subj*: *man*) жени́ться* *(impf/perf)* на +*prp*; (: *woman*) выходи́ть* (вы́йти* *perf*) за́муж за +*acc*; (*also*: ~ **off**: *son*) жени́ть* *(impf/perf)*; (: *daughter*) выдава́ть* (вы́дать* *perf*) за́муж; (*priest*) венча́ть (обвенча́ть *perf*) ◆ *vi* (*get married*: *man*) жени́ться *(impf)*; (: *woman*) выходи́ть* (вы́йти* *perf*) за́муж; (: *couple*) жени́ться (пожени́ться *perf*).
Mars [mɑːz] *n* Марс.
Marseilles [mɑː'seɪlz] *n* Марсе́ль *m*.
marsh [mɑːʃ] *n* боло́то; **salt** ~ солонча́ковое боло́то.
marshal ['mɑːʃl] *n* (*MIL*) ма́ршал; (*at public event*) распоряди́тель(ница) *m(f)* ◆ *vt* (*thoughts, support*) упоря́дочить *(perf)*; (*soldiers*) выстра́ивать (вы́строить *perf*); **police/fire** ~ (*US*) нача́льник полице́йского уча́стка/пожа́рной ча́сти.
marshalling yard ['mɑːʃlɪŋ-] *n* (*RAIL*) сортиро́вочная ста́нция.
marshmallow [mɑːʃ'mæləu] *n* (*BOT*) мушмула́; (*sweet*) ≈ зефи́р.
marshy ['mɑːʃɪ] *adj* боло́тистый (боло́тист).
marsupial [mɑː'suːpɪəl] *n* су́мчатое *nt adj*

(живóтное) ◆ *adj* сýмчатый.
marten ['mɑ:tɪn] *n* кунúца.
martial ['mɑ:ʃl] *adj* воéнный.
martial art *n* боевóе искýсство.
martial law *n* воéнное положéние.
Martian ['mɑ:ʃən] *n* марсиáнин*(-áнка*).
martin ['mɑ:tɪn] *n*: **house/sand** ~ городскáя/береговáя лáсточка*.
martyr ['mɑ:təʳ] *n* мýченик(-ица) ◆ *vt* мýчить (замýчить *perf*).
martyrdom ['mɑ:tədəm] *n* мýченичество.
marvel ['mɑ:vl] *n* чýдо* ◆ *vi*: **to ~ (at)** восхищáться (восхитúться* *perf*) (+*instr*).
marvellous ['mɑ:vləs] (*US* **marvelous**) *adj* восхитúтельный* (восхитúтелен), изумúтельный* (изумúтелен).
Marxism ['mɑ:ksɪzəm] *n* марксúзм.
Marxist ['mɑ:ksɪst] *adj* марксúстский ◆ *n* марксúст(ка*).
marzipan ['mɑ:zɪpæn] *n* марципáн.
mascara [mæs'kɑ:rə] *n* тушь *f* для реснúц.
mascot ['mæskət] *n* талисмáн.
masculine ['mæskjulɪn] *adj* мужскóй; (*woman*) мужеподóбный* (мужеподóбен); ~ **noun/pronoun** существúтельное/местоимéние мужскóго рóда.
masculinity [mæskju'lɪnɪtɪ] *n* мýжественность *f*.
MASH [mæʃ] *n abbr* (*US*: = *mobile army surgical hospital*) ≈ ППГ= *полевóй подвúжный гóспиталь*.
mash [mæʃ] *vt* дéлать (сдéлать *perf*) пюрé из +*gen*.
mashed potatoes [mæʃt-] *npl* картóфельное пюрé *nt ind*.
mask [mɑ:sk] *n* мáска* ◆ *vt* (*face*) закрывáть (закрыть* *perf*); (*feelings*) маскировáть (*impf*).
masking tape ['mɑ:skɪŋ-] *n* клéйкая лéнта.
masochism ['mæsəukɪzəm] *n* мазохúзм.
masochist ['mæsəukɪst] *n* мазохúст(ка*).
mason ['meɪsn] *n* (*also:* **stone** ~) кáменщик; (*also:* **freemason**) масóн.
masonic [mə'sɔnɪk] *adj* масóнский*.
masonry ['meɪsnrɪ] *n* (*stonework*) (кáменная) клáдка.
masquerade [mæskə'reɪd] *n* маскарáд ◆ *vi*: **to ~ as** выдавáть* (*impf*) себя за +*acc*.
mass [mæs] *n* (*also PHYS*) мáсса; (*REL*: *Orthodox*) обéдня*; (: *Catholic*) мéсса ◆ *cpd* мáссовый ◆ *vi* сосредотóчиваться (сосредотóчиться *perf*); **the ~es** *npl* (нарóдные) мáссы *fpl*; **to go to M~** идтú* (пойтú* *perf*) к обéдне/мéссе; **~es of** (*inf*) мáсса *fsg* +*gen*, ýйма *fsg* +*gen*.
massacre ['mæsəkəʳ] *n* мáссовое убúйство ◆ *vt* звéрски убивáть (убúть* *perf*).
massage ['mæsɑ:ʒ] *n* массáж ◆ *vt* (*rub*) массúровать (*impf*).
masseur [mæ'sə:ʳ] *n* массажúст.
masseuse [mæ'sə:z] *n* массажúстка*.
massive ['mæsɪv] *adj* (*furniture, person*) массúвный* (массúвен); (*support, changes*) огрóмный* (огрóмен).
mass market *n* массóвый спрос.
mass media *n inv* срéдства *ntpl* мáссовой информáции.
mass meeting *n* мáссовый мúтинг.
mass-produce ['mæsprə'dju:s] *vt* мáссово производúть* (произвестú* *perf*).
mass production *n* мáссовое произвóдство.
mast [mɑ:st] *n* мáчта.
mastectomy [mæs'tɛktəmɪ] *n* мастэктомúя.
master ['mɑ:stəʳ] *n* (*also fig*) хозяúн*; (*BRIT*: *SCOL*) учúтель* *m*; (*expert*) мáстер ◆ *cpd* (*baker, craftsman*) умéлый ◆ *vt* (*control*) владéть (овладéть *perf*) +*instr*; (*learn, understand*) овладевáть (овладéть *perf*) +*instr*; **M~ Smith** (*title for boys*) господúн *or* мáстер Смит; **M~'s degree** стéпень *f* магúстра; **M~ of Arts/Science** магúстр гуманитáрных/естéственных наýк; **M~ of Ceremonies** церемониймéйстер.
master disk *n* (*COMPUT*) оригинáл дúска.
masterful ['mɑ:stəful] *adj* влáстный* (влáстен).
master key *n* (универсáльная) отмычка (*подходя́щий ко всем дверя́м здáния*).
masterly ['mɑ:stəlɪ] *adj* мáстерский.
mastermind ['mɑ:stəmaɪnd] *n* (*of plan*) создáтель(ница) *m(f)* ◆ *vt* разрабáтывать (разработать *perf*).
masterpiece ['mɑ:stəpi:s] *n* шедéвр.
master plan *n* генерáльный план.
masterstroke ['mɑ:stəstrəuk] *n* гениáльный ход*.
mastery ['mɑ:stərɪ] *n* (*excellence*: *skill*) мастерствó; ~ **of** (*skill, language*) владéние +*instr*.
mastiff ['mæstɪf] *n* (*dog*) мáстифф.
masturbate ['mæstəbeɪt] *vi* мастурбúровать (*impf*).
masturbation [mæstə'beɪʃən] *n* мастурбáция.
mat [mæt] *n* кóврик; (*also:* **doormat**) двернóй кóврик; (*also:* **table** ~) подстáвка* ◆ *adj* = **matt**.
match [mætʃ] *n* спúчка; (*SPORT*) матч; (*equal*) рóвня *m/f* ◆ *vt* (*subj*: *colours*) сочетáться (*impf*) с +*instr*; (*equal*) сравня́ться (*perf*) с +*instr*; (*correspond to*) соответствовать (*impf*) +*dat* ◆ *vi* (*colours, materials*) сочетáться (*impf*); **to be a good ~** (*colours, clothes*) сочетáться (*impf*); **they make** *or* **are a good ~** онú хорóшая пáра; **I'm no ~ for him** я емý не рóвня; **to ~ sth (up) with sth** (*pair*) подбирáть (подобрáть* *perf*) что-н к чемý-н
▸ **match up** *vi* совпадáть (совпáсть* *perf*).

* marks translations which have irregular inflections. The Russian–English side of the dictionary gives inflectional information.

matchbox [ˈmætʃbɔks] *n* спи́чечная коро́бка*.
matching [ˈmætʃɪŋ] *adj* (*clothes, colours*) сочета́ющийся.
matchless [ˈmætʃlɪs] *adj* несравне́нный* (несравне́нен).
mate [meɪt] *n* (*inf: friend*) друг* (подру́га); (*animal*) саме́ц*(-мка*); (*workman's assistant*) подру́чный *m adj*; (*NAUT*) помо́щник (*капита́на*) ◆ *vi* спа́риваться (спа́риться *perf*).
material [məˈtɪərɪəl] *n* (*substance, information*) материа́л; (*cloth*) материа́л, ткань *f* ◆ *adj* (*possessions, existence*) материа́льный*; (*evidence*) веще́ственный*; **~s** *npl* принадле́жности *fpl*; **building ~s** строи́тельные материа́лы; **reading ~** материа́л для чте́ния.
materialistic [mətɪərɪəˈlɪstɪk] *adj* (*person etc*) материалисти́ческий.
materialize [məˈtɪərɪəlaɪz] *vi* материализова́ться *(impf/perf)*, осуществля́ться (осуществи́ться* *perf*).
maternal [məˈtəːnl] *adj* матери́нский*.
maternity [məˈtəːnɪtɪ] *n* матери́нство ◆ *cpd* (*hospital, ward*) роди́льный; **~ care** ухо́д за рожени́цами.
maternity benefit *n* декре́тные *pl adj*.
maternity dress *n* пла́тье* для бере́менной (же́нщины).
maternity hospital *n* роди́льный дом*, роддо́м*.
maternity leave *n* декре́тный о́тпуск.
matey [ˈmeɪtɪ] *adj* (*BRIT: inf*) дружелю́бный* (дружелю́бен).
math [mæθ] *n abbr* (*US*) = **mathematics**.
mathematical [mæθəˈmætɪkl] *adj* математи́ческий*.
mathematician [mæθəməˈtɪʃən] *n* матема́тик.
mathematics [mæθəˈmætɪks] *n* матема́тика.
maths [mæθs] *n abbr* (*BRIT*) = **mathematics**.
matinée [ˈmætɪneɪ] *n* (*CINEMA*) дневно́й сеа́нс; (*THEAT*) дневно́й спекта́кль *m*.
mating [ˈmeɪtɪŋ] *n* спа́ривание, слу́чка.
mating call *n* бра́чный призы́в.
mating season *n* бра́чный сезо́н.
matriarchal [meɪtrɪˈɑːkl] *adj* матриарха́льный.
matrices [ˈmeɪtrɪsiːz] *npl of* **matrix**.
matriculation [mətrɪkjuˈleɪʃən] *n* (*enrolment*) зачисле́ние в университе́т.
matrimonial [mætrɪˈməunɪəl] *adj* матримониа́льный, бра́чный.
matrimony [ˈmætrɪmənɪ] *n* супру́жество.
matrix [ˈmeɪtrɪks] (*pl* **matrices**) *n* ма́трица.
matron [ˈmeɪtrən] *n* (*in hospital*) ста́ршая медсестра́*; (*in school*) (шко́льная) медсестра́*.
matronly [ˈmeɪtrənlɪ] *adj* пы́шный* (пы́шен).
matt [mæt] *adj* ма́товый.
matted [ˈmætɪd] *adj* (*hair*) спу́танный (спу́тан).
matter [ˈmætəʳ] *n* де́ло*, вопро́с; (*PHYS*) мате́рия; (*substance, material*) вещество́*; (*MED: pus*) гной ◆ *vi* име́ть *(impf)* значе́ние; **~s** *npl* (*affairs, situation*) дела́ *ntpl*; **printed ~** печа́тный материа́л; **reading ~** (*BRIT*) материа́л для чте́ния; **what's the ~?** в чём де́ло?; **no ~ what** несмотря́ ни на что́, что бы то ни́ бы́ло; **that's another ~** э́то друго́е де́ло; **as a ~ of course** как само́ собо́й разуме́ющееся; **as a ~ of fact** со́бственно говоря́; **it's a ~ of habit** э́то де́ло привы́чки; **it doesn't ~** э́то не ва́жно.
matter-of-fact [ˈmætərəvˈfækt] *adj* безразли́чный* (безразли́чен).
matting [ˈmætɪŋ] *n* цино́вка; **rush ~** камышо́вая цино́вка.
mattress [ˈmætrɪs] *n* матра́с, матра́ц.
mature [məˈtjuəʳ] *adj* (*person*) зре́лый* (зрел); (*cheese, wine*) вы́держанный* (вы́держан) ◆ *vi* (*develop*) развива́ться (разви́ться* *perf*); (*grow up*) взросле́ть (повзросле́ть *perf*); (*cheese*) зреть *or* созрева́ть (созре́ть *perf*); (*wine*) выста́иваться (вы́стояться *perf*); (*COMM*): **this policy is due to ~ next year** в сле́дующем году́ начина́ются вы́платы по э́тому по́лису.
mature student *n студе́нт, начина́ющий вы́сшее образова́ние в во́зрасте 23 лет и́ли ста́рше*.
maturity [məˈtjuərɪtɪ] *n* зре́лость *f*.
maudlin [ˈmɔːdlɪn] *adj* плакси́вый (плакси́в), слезли́вый (слезли́в).
maul [mɔːl] *vt* (*physically*) терза́ть (растерза́ть *perf*).
Mauritania [mɔːrɪˈteɪnɪə] *n* Маврита́ния.
Mauritius [məˈrɪʃəs] *n* Маври́кий.
mausoleum [mɔːsəˈlɪəm] *n* мавзоле́й.
mauve [məuv] *adj* сире́невый.
maverick [ˈmævrɪk] *n* индивидуали́ст.
mawkish [ˈmɔːkɪʃ] *adj* слаща́вый (слаща́в).
max. *abbr* (= **maximum**) макс(им)., масима́льный.
maxim [ˈmæksɪm] *n* ма́ксима.
maxima [ˈmæksɪmə] *npl of* **maximum**.
maximize [ˈmæksɪmaɪz] *vt* максима́льно увели́чивать (увели́чить *perf*).
maximum [ˈmæksɪməm] (*pl* **maxima** *or* **~s**) *adj* максима́льный* (максима́лен) ◆ *n* ма́ксимум.
May [meɪ] *n* май; *see also* **July**.
may [meɪ] (*conditional* **might**) *vi* (*indicating possibility*): **I ~ go to Russia** я, мо́жет быть, пое́ду в Росси́ю; (*indicating permission*): **~ I smoke/sit here** мо́жно закури́ть/здесь присе́сть; (*indicating wishes*): **~ God bless you!** да благослови́т Вас Бог!; **it ~ or might rain** мо́жет пойти́ дождь; **he might be there** возмо́жно, что он там; **you might like to try** мо́жет быть, Вы хоти́те попро́бовать; **you ~ or might as well go now** Вы, пожа́луй, мо́жете уйти́ сейча́с; **come what ~** будь что бу́дет.
maybe [ˈmeɪbiː] *adv* мо́жет быть; **~ he'll ...**

мóжет быть, он *+infin* ...; **~ not** мóжет быть, нет.
mayday ['meɪdeɪ] *n* сигнáл бéдствия.
May Day *n* Пéрвое Мáя.
mayhem ['meɪhɛm] *n* погрóм.
mayonnaise [meɪə'neɪz] *n* майонéз.
mayor [mɛə'] *n* мэр.
mayoress ['mɛərɛs] *n* (*partner*) женá* мэ́ра.
maypole ['meɪpəul] *n украшенный цветами столб.*
maze [meɪz] *n* (*labyrinth*) лабири́нт; (*puzzle*) головолóмка*; (*of ideas*) пу́таница.
MB *abbr* (COMPUT) (= **megabyte**) M= *мегабáйт*; (CANADA) = *Manitoba.*
MBA *n abbr* (= *Master of Business Administration*) *магúстрская стéпень по менеджмéнту.*
MBBS *n abbr* (BRIT: = *Bachelor of Medicine and Surgery*) бакалáвр меди́цинских нау́к и хирурги́и.
MBChB *n abbr* (BRIT: = *Bachelor of Medicine and Surgery*) бакалáвр меди́цинских нау́к и хирурги́и.
MBE *n abbr* (BRIT) = *Member of the Order of the British Empire.*
MC *n abbr* = **Master of Ceremonies.**
MCAT *n abbr* (US) = *Medical College Admissions Test.*
MCP *n abbr* (BRIT: *inf*) = *male chauvinist pig.*
MD *n abbr* (= *Doctor of Medicine*) дóктор медици́ны *or* меди́цинских нау́к; (COMM) = **managing director** ◆ *abbr* (US: POST) = *Maryland.*
MDT *abbr* (US) = *Mountain Daylight Time.*
ME *n abbr* (US: = *medical examiner*) судéбно-меди́цинский экспéрт; (MED: = *myalgic encephalomyelitis*) миалги́ческий энцефаломиели́т ◆ *abbr* (US: POST) = *Maine.*

KEYWORD

me [mi:] *pron* **1** (*direct*) меня́; **he loves me** он лю́бит меня́; **it's me** э́то я
2 (*indirect*) мне; **give me them** *or* **them to me** дáйте их мне
3 (*after prep*: *+gen*) меня́; (: *+dat, +prp*) мне; (: *+instr*) мной; **it's for me** (*on answering phone*) э́то мне *or* для меня́; **this kind of work is not for me** э́та рабóта не для меня́
4 (*referring to subject of sentence: after prep*: *+gen*) себя́; (: *+dat*) себé; (: *+instr*) собóй; (: *+prp*) себé; **I took him with me** я взял егó с собóй.

meadow ['mɛdəu] *n* луг*.
meagre ['mi:gə'] (US **meager**) *adj* ску́дный* (ску́ден).
meal [mi:l] *n* едá *no pl*; (*afternoon*) обéд; (*evening*) у́жин; (*flour*) мукá грýбого помóла; **during ~s** во врéмя еды́; **to go out for a ~** (*in the evening*) у́жинать (поу́жинать *perf*) в ресторáне; **to eat 3 ~s a day** есть* (*impf*) 3 рáза в день; **to make a ~ of sth** безосновáтельно усложня́ть (усложни́ть *perf*) что-н.
meals on wheels *npl достáвка обéдов нá дом инвали́дам и престарéлым.*
meal time *n* врéмя* *nt* еды́; **during ~~s** во врéмя еды́, за едóй.
mealy-mouthed ['mi:lɪmauðd] *adj* чрезмéрно деликáтный* (деликáтен) в вы́боре слóв.
mean [mi:n] (*pt, pp* **meant**) *adj* (*miserly*) скупóй* (скуп); (*unkind*) пóдлый* (подл); (US: *inf*: *animal*) злóбный* (злóбен); (*shabby*) убóгий* (убóг); (*average*) срéдний ◆ *vt* (*signify*) знáчить (*impf*), означáть (*impf*); (*refer to*) имéть (*impf*) в виду́ ◆ *n* (*average*) середи́на; **~s** *npl* (*way*) спóсоб *msg*, срéдство *ntsg*; (*money*) срéдства *ntpl*; **by ~s of** посрéдством *+gen*, с пóмощью *+gen*; **by all ~s!** пожáлуйста!; **do you ~ it?** Вы говори́те об э́том всерьёз?, Вы э́то серьёзно?; **what do you ~?** что Вы имéете в виду́?; **to ~ to do** (*intend*) намеревáться (*impf*) *+infin*; **to be ~t for sb/sth** предназначáться (*impf*) комý-н/ чемý-н.
meander [mɪ'ændə'] *vi* (*river*) извивáться (*impf*); (*person*) броди́ть* (*impf*).
meaning ['mi:nɪŋ] *n* (*purpose, value*) смысл; (*definition*) значéние; **this word has two ~s** э́то слóво имéет два значéния; **his words have no ~** егó словá не имéют смы́сла.
meaningful ['mi:nɪŋful] *adj* (*result, occasion*) значи́тельный* (значи́телен); (*explanation*) вразуми́тельный* (вразуми́телен); (*glance, remark*) многозначи́тельный* (многозначи́телен); (*relationship*) серьёзный* (серьёзен).
meaningless ['mi:nɪŋlɪs] *adj* бессмы́сленный (бессмы́слен).
meanness ['mi:nnɪs] *n* (*with money*) ску́пость *f*, (*unkindness*) пóдлость *f*, (*shabbiness*) убóгость *f*.
means test [mi:nz-] *n* (ADMIN) провéрка* дохóдов (*при получéнии социáльного посóбия*).
meant [mɛnt] *pt, pp of* **mean.**
meantime ['mi:ntaɪm] *adv* (*also:* **in the ~**) тем врéменем, мéжду тем.
meanwhile ['mi:nwaɪl] *adv* = **meantime.**
measles ['mi:zlz] *n* корь *f*.
measly ['mi:zlɪ] *adj* (*inf*) жáлкий*.
measurable ['mɛʒərəbl] *adj* измери́мый (измери́м).
measure ['mɛʒə'] *vt* измеря́ть (измéрить *perf*) ◆ *n* (*action, amount*) мéра; (*of whisky etc*) пóрция; (*also:* **tape ~**) рулéтка*, сантимéтр; (*of achievement*) мери́ло; (*of performance*)

* marks translations which have irregular inflections. The Russian-English side of the dictionary gives inflectional information.

критéрий ◆ *vi*: **the room ~s 10 feet by 20** плóщадь этой кóмнаты 10 фýтов на 20; **in some/great ~** (*extent*) в какóй-то/ значи́тельной мéре; **a litre ~** (*vessel*) литрóвый сосýд; **to take ~s (to do)** принимáть (приня́ть* *perf*) мéры (чтóбы +*infin*)
▸ **measure up** *vi*: **to ~ up to** (*to standard*) отвечáть (*impf*) +*dat*; (*to expectations*) опрáвдывать (оправдáть* *perf*).
measured ['mɛʒəd] *adj* (*tone*) сдéржанный* (сдéржан); (*step*) размéренный* (размéрен); (*opinion*) взвéшенный (взвéшен).
measurement ['mɛʒəmənt] *n* размéр; (*process*) измерéние; **chest/hip ~** объём груди́/бёдер.
measurements ['mɛʒəmənts] *npl* размéры *mpl*; **to take sb's ~** снимáть (снять* *perf*) с когó-н мéрки.
meat [mi:t] *n* мя́со; **cold ~s** (*BRIT*) холóдные мясны́е закýски* *fpl*; **crab ~** мя́со крáба.
meatball ['mi:tbɔ:l] *n* фрикадéлька*.
meat pie *n* пирóг* с мя́сом.
meaty ['mi:tɪ] *adj* (*hand, face*) мяси́стый (мяси́ст); (*stew*) мяснóй; (*discussion*) содержáтельный* (содержáтелен).
Mecca ['mɛkə] *n* (*also fig*) Мéкка.
mechanic [mɪ'kænɪk] *n* механик.
mechanical [mɪ'kænɪkl] *adj* механи́ческий*.
mechanical engineering *n* машиностроéние.
mechanics [mɪ'kænɪks] *n* (*PHYS*) механика ◆ *npl* (*of reading, government*) механика *fsg*.
mechanism ['mɛkənɪzəm] *n* механи́зм.
mechanization [mɛkənaɪ'zeɪʃən] *n* механизáция.
mechanize ['mɛkənaɪz] *vt* механизи́ровать (*impf/perf*) ◆ *vi* проводи́ть* (провести́* *perf*) механизáцию.
MEd *n abbr* (= *Master of Education*) маги́стр педагоги́ческих наýк.
medal ['mɛdl] *n* медáль *f*.
medalist ['mɛdlɪst] *n* (*US*) = **medallist**.
medallion [mɪ'dælɪən] *n* медальóн.
medallist ['mɛdlɪst] (*US* **medalist**) *n* медали́ст(ка*).
meddle ['mɛdl] *vi*: **to ~ in** вмéшиваться (вмешáться *perf*) в +*acc*; **to ~ with sth** вторгáться (втóргнуться *perf*) в что-н.
meddlesome ['mɛdlsəm] *adj* назóйливый (назóйлив).
media ['mi:dɪə] *n or npl*: **the ~** срéдства *ntpl* мáссовой информáции ◆ *npl see* **medium**.
mediaeval [mɛdɪ'i:vl] *adj* = **medieval**.
median ['mi:dɪən] *n* медиáна.
median strip ['mi:dɪən-] *n* (*US*) раздели́тельная полосá (*автострáды*).
media research *n* исслéдование *or* опрóс срéдствами мáссовой информáции.
mediate ['mi:dɪeɪt] *vi* (*arbitrate*) посрéдничать (*impf*).
mediation [mi:dɪ'eɪʃən] *n* посрéдничество.
mediator ['mi:dɪeɪtə'] *n* посрéдник(-ица).
Medicaid ['mɛdɪkeɪd] *n* (*US*) *госудáрственная прогрáмма, субсиди́рующая медици́нское обслýживание малоимýщей чáсти населéния.*
medical ['mɛdɪkl] *adj* медици́нский* ◆ *n* (*examination*) медосмóтр= *медици́нский* осмóтр.*
medical certificate *n* медици́нская спрáвка*.
medical examiner *n* (*US*) судéбно-медици́нский* экспéрт.
medical student *n* студéнт – мéдик.
Medicare ['mɛdɪkɛə'] *n* (*US*) *госудáрственная прогрáмма медици́нского страховáния для людéй в вóзрасте от 65 лет и стáрше.*
medicated ['mɛdɪkeɪtɪd] *adj* содержáщий лекáрственное веществó.
medication [mɛdɪ'keɪʃən] *n* лекáрство, лекáрственный препарáт; **to be on ~** проходи́ть* (пройти́* *perf*) лекáрственную терапи́ю.
medicinal [mɛ'dɪsɪnl] *adj* (*substance, qualities*) лекáрственный; (*purposes, reasons*) лечéбный.
medicine ['mɛdsɪn] *n* (*science*) медици́на; (*drug*) лекáрство.
medicine ball *n* (*SPORT*) ≈ ги́ря.
medicine chest *n* аптéчка*.
medicine man *n* знáхарь *m*.
medieval [mɛdɪ'i:vl] *adj* средневекóвый.
mediocre [mi:dɪ'əukə'] *adj* заурядный* (зауря́ден), посрéдственный* (посрéдствен).
mediocrity [mi:dɪ'ɔkrɪtɪ] *n* заурядность *f*, посрéдственность *f*.
meditate ['mɛdɪteɪt] *vi* размышля́ть (*impf*); (*REL*) занимáться (заня́ться* *perf*) медитáцией.
meditation [mɛdɪ'teɪʃən] *n* (*see vb*) размышлéние; медитáция.
Mediterranean [mɛdɪtə'reɪnɪən] *adj* средиземномóрский; **the ~ (Sea)** Средизéмное мóре.
medium ['mi:dɪəm] (*pl* **media** *or* **~s**) *adj* срéдний* ◆ *n* (*means*) срéдство; (*substance*) материáл; (*environment*) средá; (*pl* **~s**; *person*) мéдиум; **a happy ~** золотáя середи́на.
medium-dry ['mi:dɪəm'draɪ] *adj* полусухóй.
medium-sized ['mi:dɪəm'saɪzd] *adj* (*tin etc*) срéдней величины́.
medium wave *n* (*RADIO*) срéдние вóлны *fpl*.
medley ['mɛdlɪ] *n* (*mixture*) смесь *f*; (*MUS*) попурри́ *r ind*.
meek [mi:k] *adj* крóткий* (крóток).
meet [mi:t] (*pt, pp* **met**) *vt* (*friend, opponent etc*) встречáть (встрéтить* *perf*); (*obligations*) выполня́ть (вы́полнить *perf*); (*problem*) стáлкиваться (столкнýться *perf*) с +*instr*; (*need*) удовлетворя́ть (удовлетвори́ть *perf*); (*expenses, bill*) оплáчивать (оплати́ть* *perf*) ◆ *vi* (*people*) встречáться (встрéтиться* *perf*);

(*lines, roads*) пересекáться (пересéчься* *perf*) ◆ *n* (*BRIT: hunting*) сбор; (*US: SPORT*) встрéча; **pleased to ~ you!** рад (с Вáми) познакóмиться!, óчень прия́тно!
▸ **meet up** *vi*: **to ~ up with sb** сходи́ться* (сойти́сь* *perf*) с кем-н
▸ **meet with** *vt fus* (*difficulty*) стáлкиваться (столкну́ться *perf*) с +*instr*; (*success*) пóльзоваться (*impf*) +*instr*; (*approval*) находи́ть* (найти́* *perf*).
meeting ['mi:tɪŋ] *n* встрéча; (*of club, committee etc*) собрáние; (*POL: also:* **mass ~**) ми́тинг; **she's at a ~** онá на заседáнии; **to call a ~** созывáть (созвáть* *perf*) собрáние.
meeting place *n* мéсто* встрéчи.
megabyte ['mɛgəbaɪt] *n* мегабáйт.
megadrive ['mɛgədraɪv] *n* мéгадрайв (*игровáя систéма*).
megalomania [mɛgələ'meɪnɪə] *n* мáния вели́чия.
megaphone ['mɛgəfəun] *n* мегафóн.
megawatt ['mɛgəwɔt] *n* мегавáтт.
melancholy ['mɛlənkəlɪ] *n* меланхóлия ◆ *adj* (*smile*) меланхоли́ческий; (*person*) меланхоли́чный* (меланхоли́чен).
Melbourne ['mɛlbən] *n* Мéльбурн.
mellow ['mɛləu] *adj* (*sound, colour, light*) бархати́стый (бархати́ст); (*taste*) мя́гкий* (мя́гок); (*stone, building*) *приобрéтший с годáми глáдкую повéрхность и мя́гкий цвет* ◆ *vi* (*person*) смягчáться (смягчи́ться *perf*).
melodious [mɪ'ləudɪəs] *adj* мелоди́чный* (мелоди́чен).
melodrama ['mɛləudrɑ:mə] *n* мелодрáма.
melodramatic [mɛlədrə'mætɪk] *adj* (*situation*) мелодрамати́ческий; (*behaviour, person*) мелодрамати́чный* (мелодрамати́чен).
melody ['mɛlədɪ] *n* мелóдия.
melon ['mɛlən] *n* ды́ня.
melt [mɛlt] *vi* (*metal*) плáвиться* (расплáвиться* *perf*); (*snow, butter, also fig*) тáять (растáять *perf*) ◆ *vt* (*metal*) плáвить* (расплáвить* *perf*); (*snow, butter*) топи́ть* (растопи́ть* *perf*)
▸ **melt down** *vt* (*metal*) расплавля́ть (расплáвить* *perf*).
meltdown ['mɛltdaun] *n* (*in nuclear reactor*) расплавлéние стéржня (*в áтомном реáкторе*).
melting point ['mɛltɪŋ-] *n* тóчка* плавлéния.
melting pot *n* (*fig*) смешéние; **to be in the ~ ~** вари́ться* (*impf*) в однóм котлé.
member ['mɛmbə'] *n* (*also ANAT*) член ◆ *cpd*: **~ country** *or* **state** госудáрство-член; **M~ of Parliament** (*BRIT*) член парлáмента.
membership ['mɛmbəʃɪp] *n* (*members*) члéны *mpl*; (*status*) члéнство; (*number of members*) числó* члéнов.
membership card *n* члéнский* билéт.
membrane ['mɛmbreɪn] *n* мембрáна.
memento [mə'mɛntəu] *n* сувени́р.
memo ['mɛməu] *n* (*ADMIN: report*) доклáдная запи́ска; (: *instruction*) отношéние, запи́ска.
memoir ['mɛmwɑ:'] *n* биографи́ческий óчерк.
memoirs ['mɛmwɑ:z] *npl* мемуáры *pl*.
memo pad *n* записнáя кни́жка*.
memorable ['mɛmərəbl] *adj* пáмятный* (пáмятен).
memoranda [mɛmə'rændə] *npl of* **memorandum**.
memorandum [mɛmə'rændəm] (*pl* **memoranda**) *n* меморáндум.
memorial [mɪ'mɔ:rɪəl] *n* пáмятник ◆ *cpd* (*service*) мемориáльный; ... **M~ Prize** прéмия и́мени +*gen* ....
Memorial Day *n* (*US*) *30 мáя – день пáмяти поги́бших*.
memorize ['mɛməraɪz] *vt* зау́чивать (заучи́ть *perf*) (наизу́сть).
memory ['mɛmərɪ] *n* (*ability to remember*) пáмять *f no pl*; (*COMPUT*) пáмять *f*, запоминáющее устрóйство; (*recollection*) воспоминáние; **in ~ of** в пáмять +*gen*; **I have a good/bad ~** у меня́ хорóшая/плохáя пáмять; **loss of ~** потéря пáмяти.
men [mɛn] *npl of* **man**.
menace ['mɛnɪs] *n* (*threat*) угрóза; (*nuisance*) наказáние ◆ *vt* угрожáть (*impf*) +*dat*, грози́ть* (*impf*) +*dat*; **a public ~** угрóза óбществу.
menacing ['mɛnɪsɪŋ] *adj* угрожáющий* (угрожáющ).
menagerie [mɪ'nædʒərɪ] *n* звери́нец*.
mend [mɛnd] *vt* ремонти́ровать (отремонти́ровать *perf*), чини́ть* (почини́ть* *perf*); (*clothes*) чини́ть* (почини́ть* *perf*) ◆ *n*: **to be on the ~** идти́* (*impf*) на попрáвку; **to ~ one's ways** исправля́ться (испрáвиться* *perf*).
mending ['mɛndɪŋ] *n* (*of machine etc*) ремóнт; (*of clothes*) почи́нка.
menial ['mi:nɪəl] *adj* (*work, tasks*) чёрный.
meningitis [mɛnɪn'dʒaɪtɪs] *n* менинги́т.
menopause ['mɛnəupɔ:z] *n*: **the ~** климактери́ческий периóд, кли́макс.
menservants ['mɛnsə:vənts] *npl of* **manservant**.
men's room *n* (*US*): **the ~ ~** мужскáя раздевáлка.
menstrual ['mɛnstruəl] *adj* менструáльный.
menstruate ['mɛnstrueɪt] *vi* менструи́ровать (*impf*).
menstruation [mɛnstru'eɪʃən] *n* менструáция.
menswear ['mɛnzwɛə'] *n* мужскáя одéжда.
mental ['mɛntl] *adj* (*ability, exhaustion*) у́мственный; (*image*) мы́сленный; (*illness*) душéвный, психи́ческий*; (*arithmetic, calculation*) в умé; **~ healthcare** забóта о

душевнобольных.
mental hospital *n* психиатрическая больница.
mentality [mɛnˈtælɪtɪ] *n* менталитет, умонастроение; (*way of thinking*) склад ума.
mentally [ˈmɛntlɪ] *adv* (*see adj*) умственно; мысленно; **~ ill** душевнобольной.
mentally handicapped *adj* умственно отсталый.
menthol [ˈmɛnθɔl] *n* ментол.
mention [ˈmɛnʃən] *n* упоминание ◆ *vt* упоминать (упомянуть* *perf*); **don't ~ it!** ничего!, не за что!; **I need hardly ~ that ...** вряд ли стоит упоминать, что ...; **not to ~ ..., without ~ing ...** не говоря уж о *+prp* ....
mentor [ˈmɛntɔːʳ] *n* наставник.
menu [ˈmɛnjuː] *n* (*also* COMPUT) меню *nt ind.*
menu-driven [ˈmɛnjuːdrɪvn] *adj* (COMPUT) управляемый меню.
MEP *n abbr* (BRIT: = *Member of the European Parliament*) член Европейского парламента.
mercantile [ˈməːkəntaɪl] *adj* (*society, law*) торговый.
mercenary [ˈməːsɪnərɪ] *adj* корыстный* (корыстен) ◆ *n* (*soldier*) наёмник.
merchandise [ˈməːtʃəndaɪz] *n* товары *mpl.*
merchandiser [ˈməːtʃəndaɪzəʳ] *n* торговец*.
merchant [ˈməːtʃənt] *n* (*trader*) торговец*, купец* (ИСТ); **timber/wine ~** торговец* лесом/вином.
merchant bank *n* (BRIT) торговый банк.
merchantman [ˈməːtʃəntmən] *irreg n* торговое судно*.
Merchant Navy (US **merchant marine**) *n* торговый флот.
merciful [ˈməːsɪful] *adj* (*person*) милосердный* (милосерден); (*fortunate*) благой.
mercifully [ˈməːsɪflɪ] *adv* милосердно; (*fortunately*) к счастью.
merciless [ˈməːsɪlɪs] *adj* беспощадный* (беспощаден).
mercurial [məːˈkjuərɪəl] *adj* изменчивый (изменчив).
mercury [ˈməːkjurɪ] *n* ртуть *f*; (*planet*): **M~** Меркурий.
mercy [ˈməːsɪ] *n* милосердие; **to have ~ on sb** проявлять (проявить* *perf*) милосердие к кому-н; **to be at sb's ~** быть* (*impf*) *or* находиться* (*impf*) во власти кого-н.
mercy killing *n* убийство из милосердия.
mere [mɪəʳ] *adj*: **she's a ~ child** она всего лишь ребёнок; **his ~ presence irritates her** само его присутствие раздражает её; **by a ~ chance** по чистой случайности.
merely [ˈmɪəlɪ] *adv* (*simply*) просто; (*just*) только.
merge [məːdʒ] *vt* (*also* COMPUT) сливать (слить* *perf*), объединять (объединить *perf*) ◆ *vi* (*also* COMM) сливаться (слиться* *perf*); (*roads*) сходиться* (сойтись* *perf*).
merger [ˈməːdʒəʳ] *n* (COMM) слияние.
meridian [məˈrɪdɪən] *n* меридиан.
meringue [məˈræŋ] *n* безе *nt ind.*
merit [ˈmɛrɪt] *n* (*worth, value*) достоинство ◆ *vt* заслуживать (заслужить* *perf*); **to judge sth on its ~s** оценивать (оценить *perf*) что-н по достоинству.
meritocracy [mɛrɪˈtɔkrəsɪ] *n общество, в котором положение человека определяется его способностями.*
mermaid [ˈməːmeɪd] *n* русалка*.
merrily [ˈmɛrɪlɪ] *adv* весело.
merriment [ˈmɛrɪmənt] *n* веселье.
merry [ˈmɛrɪ] *adj* весёлый* (весел); **M~ Christmas!** С Рождеством!
merry-go-round [ˈmɛrɪgəuraund] *n* карусель *f.*
mesh [mɛʃ] *n* (*net*) сеть *f*; **wire ~** проволочная сетка.
mesmerize [ˈmɛzməraɪz] *vt* гипнотизировать (загипнотизировать *perf*).
mess [mɛs] *n* (*muddle*: *in room*) беспорядок*; (: *of situation*) неразбериха; (*dirt*) грязь* *f*, (MIL) столовая *f adj*; **to be in a ~** (*untidy*) быть* (*impf*) в беспорядке; **to get o.s. into a ~** (*inf*) влипать (влипнуть* *perf*); **my life is in a real ~** (*inf*) у меня в жизни всё идёт вверх дном
▸ **mess about** *vi* (*inf*: *fool around*) дурачиться (*impf*), валять (*impf*) дурака
▸ **mess about with** *vt fus* (*inf*: *play around with*) возиться* (*impf*) с *+instr*
▸ **mess around** *vi* (*inf*) = **mess about**
▸ **mess around with** *vt fus* (*inf*) = **mess about with**
▸ **mess up** *vt* (*spoil*) портить* (испортить* *perf*); (*dirty*) пачкать (испачкать *perf*).
message [ˈmɛsɪdʒ] *n* (*piece of information*) сообщение; (*note*) записка*; (*of play, book*) идея; **to leave sb a ~** (*note*) оставлять (оставить* *perf*) кому-н записку; **can I give him a ~?** ему что-нибудь передать?; **he got the ~** (*fig*: *inf*) до него дошло.
message switching [-ˈswɪtʃɪŋ] *n* (COMPUT) коммутация сообщений.
messenger [ˈmɛsɪndʒəʳ] *n* курьер, посыльный *m adj.*
Messiah [mɪˈsaɪə] *n* Мессия *m.*
Messrs *abbr* (*on letters*: = *messieurs*) гг.= *господа.*
Messrs. *abbr* = **Messrs**.
messy [ˈmɛsɪ] *adj* (*untidy*) неубранный (неубран); (*dirty*) грязный* (грязен).
Met [mɛt] *n abbr* (US) = *Metropolitan Opera.*
met [mɛt] *pt, pp of* **meet**.
met *adj abbr* = *meteorological*: **the M~ Office** метеоцентр.
metabolism [mɛˈtæbəlɪzəm] *n* метаболизм, обмен веществ.
metal [ˈmɛtl] *n* металл.
metal fatigue *n* усталость *f* металла.
metalled [ˈmɛtld] *adj*: **~ road** дорога, с щебёночным покрытием.
metallic [mɪˈtælɪk] *adj* металлический*.

metallurgy [mɛ'tælədʒɪ] *n* металлургия.
metalwork ['mɛtlwə:k] *n* работа по металлу.
metamorphoses [mɛtə'mɔ:fəsi:z] *npl of* **metamorphosis**.
metamorphosis [mɛtə'mɔ:fəsɪs] (*pl* **metamorphoses**) *n* метаморфоза.
metaphor ['mɛtəfə^r] *n* метафора.
metaphorical [mɛtə'fɔrɪkl] *adj* метафорический.
metaphysics [mɛtə'fɪzɪks] *n* метафизика.
meteor ['mi:tɪə^r] *n* метеор.
meteoric [mi:tɪ'ɔrɪk] *adj* (*fig*) метеорический.
meteorite ['mi:tɪəraɪt] *n* метеорит.
meteorological [mi:tɪərə'lɔdʒɪkl] *adj* метеорологический.
meteorology [mi:tɪə'rɔlədʒɪ] *n* метеорология.
mete out [mi:t-] *vt* отмерять (отмерить *perf*).
meter ['mi:tə^r] *n* (*instrument*) счётчик; (*US*: *unit*) = **metre**.
methane ['mi:θeɪn] *n* метан.
method ['mɛθəd] *n* (*way*) метод, способ; ~ **of payment** способ оплаты.
methodical [mɪ'θɔdɪkl] *adj* методичный* (методичен).
Methodist ['mɛθədɪst] *n* (*REL*) методист(ка*).
methodology [mɛθə'dɔlədʒɪ] *n* методология.
meths [mɛθs] *n* (*BRIT*: *inf*) = **methylated spirit**.
methylated spirit ['mɛθɪleɪtɪd-] *n* (*BRIT*) денатурат.
meticulous [mɪ'tɪkjuləs] *adj* тщательный* (тщателен).
metre ['mi:tə^r] (*US* **meter**) *n* метр.
metric ['mɛtrɪk] *adj* метрический*; **to go** ~ переходить* (перейти* *perf*) на метрическую систему мер.
metrical ['mɛtrɪkl] *adj* метрический*.
metrication [mɛtrɪ'keɪʃən] *n* введение метрической системы мер.
metric system *n* метрическая система мер.
metric ton *n* (метрическая) тонна.
metronome ['mɛtrənəum] *n* метроном.
metropolis [mɪ'trɔpəlɪs] *n* столица.
metropolitan [mɛtrə'pɔlɪtn] *adj* столичный.
Metropolitan Police *n* (*BRIT*): **the** ~ ~ Лондонская полиция.
mettle ['mɛtl] *n*: **to show one's** ~ проявлять (проявить* *perf*) (свой) характер.
mew [mju:] *vi* мяукать (*impf*).
mews [mju:z] *n* (*BRIT*) *переулок в жилое помещение*.
Mexican ['mɛksɪkən] *adj* мексиканский* ◆ *n*. мексиканец*(-нка*).
Mexico ['mɛksɪkəu] *n* Мексика.
Mexico City *n* Мехико *m ind*.
mezzanine ['mɛtsəni:n] *n* (*also*: ~ **floor**) мезонин, полуэтаж.
MFA *n abbr* (*US*: = *Master of Fine Arts*) магистр искусств.
mfr *abbr* = **manufacture, manufacturer**.
mg *abbr* (= **milligram(me)**) мг.= *миллиграмм*.
Mgr *abbr* (= *Monseigneur, Monsignor*) монсеньёр; (*COMM*) = **manager**.
MHR *n abbr* (*US*: = *Member of the House of Representatives*) член палаты представителей.
MHz *abbr* (= *megahertz*) МГц= *мегагерц*.
MI *abbr* (*US*: *POST*) = *Michigan*.
MI5 *n abbr* (*BRIT*: = *Military Intelligence 5*) *внешняя разведка Великобритании*.
MI6 *n abbr* (*BRIT*: = *Military Intelligence 6*) *внутренняя разведка Великобритании*.
MIA *abbr* (*MIL*: = *missing in action*) пропавший без вести.
miaow [mi:'au] *vi* мяукать (*impf*).
mice [maɪs] *npl of* **mouse**.
micro... ['maɪkrəu] *prefix* микро....
microbe ['maɪkrəub] *n* микроб.
microbiology [maɪkrəbaɪ'ɔlədʒɪ] *n* микробиология.
microchip ['maɪkrəutʃɪp] *n* микрочип.
micro(computer) ['maɪkrəu(kəm'pju:tə^r)] *n* микрокомпьютер.
microcosm ['maɪkrəukɔzəm] *n* микрокосмос, микрокосм.
microeconomics ['maɪkrəui:kə'nɔmɪks] *n* микроэкономика.
microelectronics ['maɪkrəuɪlɛk'trɔnɪks] *n* микроэлектроника.
microfiche ['maɪkrəufi:ʃ] *n* микрофиша.
microfilm ['maɪkrəufɪlm] *n* микрофильм, микроплёнка*.
microlight ['maɪkrəulaɪt] *n* сверхлёгкий самолёт.
micrometer [maɪ'krɔmɪtə^r] *n* микрометр.
microphone ['maɪkrəfəun] *n* микрофон.
microprocessor ['maɪkrəu'prəusɛsə^r] *n* микропроцессор.
microscope ['maɪkrəskəup] *n* микроскоп; **under the** ~ под микроскопом.
microscopic [maɪkrə'skɔpɪk] *adj* микроскопический*.
microsurgery [maɪkrəusə:dʒərɪ] *n* микрохирургия.
microwave ['maɪkrəuweɪv] *n* (*also*: ~ **oven**) микроволновая печь* *f*.
mid [mɪd] *adj*: **in** ~ **May/afternoon** в середине мая/дня; **in** ~ **air** в воздухе; **he's in his** ~ **thirties** ему за тридцать.
midday [mɪd'deɪ] *n* полдень* *m*.
middle ['mɪdl] *n* середина; (*waist*) пояс* ◆ *adj* средний*; **in the** ~ **of the night** посреди ночи; **I'm in the** ~ **of reading it** я как раз сейчас это читаю.
middle age *n* средний* возраст.
middle-aged [mɪdl'eɪdʒd] *adj* средних лет.
Middle Ages *npl*: **the** ~ ~ средние века* *mpl*.
middle class *n*: **the** ~ ~ средний* класс.

* marks translations which have irregular inflections. The Russian-English side of the dictionary gives inflectional information.

middle-class [mɪdl'klɑ:s] *adj* принадлежа́щий к сре́днему кла́ссу.
middle classes *npl* = **middle class**.
Middle East *n*: **the ~ ~** Бли́жний* Восто́к.
middleman ['mɪdlmæn] *irreg n* посре́дник.
middle management *n* сре́днее руководя́щее звено́.
middle name *n* второ́е и́мя* *nt*.
middle-of-the-road ['mɪdləvðə'rəud] *adj* (*politician*) уме́ренный; (*music*) лёгкий*.
middleweight ['mɪdlweɪt] *n* (*BOXING*) боксёр сре́днего ве́са.
middling ['mɪdlɪŋ] *adj* сре́дний*.
Middx *abbr* (*BRIT: POST*) = *Middlesex*.
midge [mɪdʒ] *n* мо́шка*.
midget ['mɪdʒɪt] *n* ка́рлик(-ица).
midi system ['mɪdɪ-] *n* МИДИ (*электро́нный контро́ль для синтеза́торов*).
Midlands ['mɪdləndz] *npl*: **the ~** Центра́льные райо́ны *mpl* А́нглии.
midnight ['mɪdnaɪt] *n* по́лночь* *f* ◆ *cpd* (*party, feast*) полно́чный; **at ~** в по́лночь.
midriff ['mɪdrɪf] *n* живо́т.
midst [mɪdst] *n*: **in the ~ of** посреди́ +*gen*.
midsummer [mɪd'sʌmə'] *n* середи́на ле́та; **M~'s Day** день* *m* ле́тнего солнцестоя́ния.
midway [mɪd'weɪ] *adv*: **~ (between)** на полпути́ (ме́жду +*instr*); **~ through** в середи́не +*gen*; **to turn back ~** верну́ться (*perf*) с полпути́.
midweek [mɪd'wi:k] *adj, adv* в середи́не неде́ли.
midwife ['mɪdwaɪf] (*pl* **midwives**) *n* акуше́рка*.
midwifery ['mɪdwɪfərɪ] *n* акуше́рство.
midwinter [mɪd'wɪntə'] *n* середи́на зимы́.
midwives ['mɪdwaɪvz] *npl of* **midwife**.
miffed [mɪft] *adj* (*inf*) оби́женный (оби́жен).
might [maɪt] *vb see* **may** ◆ *n* (*power*) мощь *f*.
mighty ['maɪtɪ] *adj* мо́щный* (мо́щен).
migraine ['mi:greɪn] *n* мигре́нь *f*.
migrant ['maɪgrənt] *adj* (*bird*) перелётный ◆ *n* (*bird*) перелётная пти́ца; (*animal*) мигри́рующее живо́тное *nt adj*; (*person*) переселе́нец*(-нка*); **~ worker** рабо́чий*-мигра́нт.
migrate [maɪ'greɪt] *vi* мигри́ровать (*impf/perf*).
migration [maɪ'greɪʃən] *n* мигра́ция.
mike [maɪk] *n abbr* = **microphone**.
Milan [mɪ'læn] *n* Мила́н.
mild [maɪld] *adj* (*character, climate, taste, reproach*) мя́гкий* (мя́гок); (*infection, illness*) лёгкий* (лёгок); (*interest*) незначи́тельный* (незначи́телен).
mildew ['mɪldju:] *n* пле́сень *f*.
mildly ['maɪldlɪ] *adv* (*see adj*) мя́гко; легко́; слегка́; **to put it ~** мя́гко говоря́.
mildness ['maɪldnɪs] *n* (*see adj*) мя́гкость *f*; лёгкость *f*; незначи́тельность *f*.
mile [maɪl] *n* ми́ля*; **this car does 30 ~s to the gallon** э́тот автомоби́ль затра́чивает галло́н бензи́на ка́ждый 30 миль; **~s better** (*inf*) намно́го лу́чше.
mileage ['maɪlɪdʒ] *n* (*number of miles*) пробе́г в ми́лях; (*distance*) расстоя́ние в ми́лях.
mileage allowance *n* покры́тие доро́жных расхо́дов (*в расчёте на ка́ждую ми́лю*).
mileometer [maɪ'lɔmɪtə'] *n* счётчик (*про́йденных миль*).
milestone ['maɪlstəun] *n* ≈ километро́вый столб; (*fig*) ве́ха.
milieu ['mi:ljə:] *n* среда́*.
militant ['mɪlɪtnt] *adj* вои́нствующий ◆ *n* радика́л.
militarism ['mɪlɪtərɪzəm] *n* милитари́зм.
militaristic [mɪlɪtə'rɪstɪk] *adj* милитаристи́ческий.
military ['mɪlɪtərɪ] *adj* вое́нный ◆ *n*: **the ~** вое́нные *pl adj*.
military police *n* вое́нная поли́ция.
military service *n* вое́нная слу́жба.
militate ['mɪlɪteɪt] *vi*: **to ~ against** препя́тствовать (*impf*) +*dat*.
militia [mɪ'lɪʃə] *n* (*MIL*) (наро́дное) ополче́ние.
milk [mɪlk] *n* молоко́ ◆ *vt* (*cow*) дои́ть* (подои́ть* *perf*); (*fig: situation, person*) эксплуати́ровать (*impf*).
milk chocolate *n* моло́чный шокола́д.
milk float *n* (*BRIT*) моло́чный фурго́н.
milking ['mɪlkɪŋ] *n* дое́ние.
milkman ['mɪlkmən] *irreg n* разно́счик молока́.
milk shake *n* моло́чный кокте́йль *m*.
milk tooth *n* моло́чный зуб*.
milk truck *n* (*US*) = **milk float**.
milky ['mɪlkɪ] *adj* моло́чный.
Milky Way *n*: **the ~ ~** Мле́чный путь* *m*.
mill [mɪl] *n* (*windmill*) ме́льница; (*factory: making cloth*) фа́брика; (*: making steel*) заво́д; (*also:* **coffee ~**) кофемо́лка* ◆ *vt* моло́ть* (смоло́ть* *perf*) ◆ *vi* (*also:* **~ about**) толо́чься* (*impf*).
millennia [mɪ'lɛnɪə] *npl of* **millennium**.
millennium [mɪ'lɛnɪəm] (*pl* **~s** *or* **millennia**) *n* тысячеле́тие; **~ bug** Пробле́ма 2000 (го́да).
miller ['mɪlə'] *n* ме́льник.
millet ['mɪlɪt] *n* пшено́.
milli... ['mɪlɪ] *prefix* милли....
milligram(me) ['mɪlɪgræm] (*US* **milligram**) *n* миллигра́м.
millilitre ['mɪlɪli:tə'] (*US* **milliliter**) *n* миллили́тр.
millimetre ['mɪlɪmi:tə'] (*US* **millimeter**) *n* миллиме́тр.
millinery ['mɪlɪnərɪ] *n* да́мские шля́пы *fpl*.
million ['mɪljən] *n* миллио́н.
millionaire [mɪljə'nɛə'] *n* миллионе́р.
millipede ['mɪlɪpi:d] *n* тысячено́жка*.
millstone ['mɪlstəun] *n* (*fig*): **a ~ around one's neck** ка́мень *m* на шее.
millwheel ['mɪlwi:l] *n* ме́льничное колесо́*.
milometer [maɪ'lɔmɪtə'] *n* = **mileometer**.
mime [maɪm] *n* (*art*) пантоми́ма; (*also:* **~ artist**) мим ◆ *vt* изобража́ть (изобрази́ть* *perf*) же́стами.

mimic ['mɪmɪk] *n* пароди́ст ◆ *vt* (*subj*: *comedian*) пароди́ровать *(impf/perf)*; (*animal, person*) имити́ровать *(impf)*.
mimicry ['mɪmɪkrɪ] *n* имита́ция.
Min. *abbr* (*BRIT*: *POL*) = **ministry**.
min. *abbr* (= **minute**) мин(.)= *мину́та*; (= **minimum**) мин.= *минима́льный*.
minaret [mɪnə'rɛt] *n* минаре́т.
mince [mɪns] *vt* (*meat*) пропуска́ть (пропусти́ть* *perf*) че́рез мясору́бку ◆ *vi* (*in walking*) семени́ть *(impf)* ◆ *n* (*BRIT*) (мясно́й) фарш; **he doesn't ~ (his) words** он не выбира́ет выраже́ний.
mincemeat ['mɪnsmi:t] *n* (*BRIT*: *fruit*) начи́нка из сухофру́ктов (*для пирожко́в*); (*US*: *meat*) (мясно́й) фарш; **to make ~ of sb** разбива́ть (разби́ть* *perf*) кого́-н в пух и прах.
mince pie *n* (*BRIT*: *sweet*) *пирожо́к* с начи́нкой из сухофру́ктов.*
mincer ['mɪnsə^r] *n* мясору́бка*.
mincing ['mɪnsɪŋ] *adj* (*walk*) семеня́щий; (*voice*) жема́нный* (жема́нен).
mind [maɪnd] *n* (*intellect*) ум*; (*thoughts*) голова́* ◆ *vt* (*look after*) смотре́ть* *(impf)* за *+instr*; (*object to*): **I don't ~ the noise** меня́ не беспоко́ит шум; **to be out of one's ~** быть* *(impf)* не в своём уме́; **it's constantly on my ~** э́то не выхо́дит у меня́ из головы́; **to keep** *or* **bear sth in ~** по́мнить *(impf)* что-н, име́ть *(impf)* что-н в виду́; **to make up one's ~** реша́ться (реши́ться *perf*); **to change one's ~** переду́мывать (переду́мать *perf*); **to my ~ ...** (*opinion*) по моему́ мне́нию ...; **to be in two ~s about sth** сомнева́ться *(impf)* в чём-н; **to have in ~ to do** намерева́ться *(impf) +infin*; **I have somebody in ~** у меня́ есть ко́е-кто на приме́те; **it went right out of my ~** э́то совсе́м вы́летело у меня́ из головы́; **to bring** *or* **call to ~** напомина́ть (напо́мнить *perf*) о *+prp*; **she doesn't ~ the cold** она́ не бои́тся хо́лода; **do you ~ if ...?** Вы не возража́ете, е́сли ...?; **I don't ~** мне всё равно́; **~ you, ...** име́йте в виду́ ...; **never ~!** ничего́!; **"mind the step"** "осторо́жно, не споткни́тесь".
mind-boggling ['maɪndbɔglɪŋ] *adj* (*inf*) уму́ непостижи́мый.
-minded ['maɪndɪd] *adj*: **fair-~** справедли́вый (справедли́в); **an industrially-~ nation** наро́д, скло́нный к индустриа́льной де́ятельности.
minder ['maɪndə^r] *n* (*childminder*) ня́ня*; (*inf*: *bodyguard*) телохрани́тель *m*.
mindful ['maɪndful] *adj*: **to be ~ of** име́ть *(impf)* в виду́.
mindless ['maɪndlɪs] *adj* (*violence*) безду́мный* (безду́мен); (*job*) механи́ческий*.

KEYWORD

mine[1] [maɪn] *pron* **1** мой; **that book is mine** э́та кни́га моя́, э́то моя́ кни́га; **this is mine** э́то моё; **an uncle of mine** мой дя́дя
2 (*referring back to subject*) свой; **may I borrow your pen? I have forgotten mine** мо́жно взять Ва́шу ру́чку? я забы́л свою́.

mine[2] [maɪn] *n* (*coal*) ша́хта; (*gold, diamonds*) при́иск; (*copper, tin*) рудни́к; (*explosive*) ми́на ◆ *vt* (*coal*) добыва́ть (добы́ть* *perf*); (*beach*) мини́ровать (замини́ровать *perf*).
mine detector *n* миноиска́тель *m*.
minefield ['maɪnfi:ld] *n* (*also fig*) ми́нное по́ле*.
miner ['maɪnə^r] *n* шахтёр.
mineral ['mɪnərəl] *n* (*crystalline*) минера́л; (*ore*) поле́зное ископа́емое *nt adj* ◆ *adj* минера́льный; **~s** *npl* (*BRIT*: *soft drinks*) прохлади́тельные напи́тки *mpl*.
mineralogy [mɪnə'rælədʒɪ] *n* минерало́гия.
mineral water *n* минера́льная вода́.
minesweeper ['maɪnswi:pə^r] *n* ми́нный тра́льщик.
mingle ['mɪŋgl] *vi*: **to ~ with** сме́шиваться (смеша́ться *perf*) с *+instr*.
mingy ['mɪndʒɪ] *adj* (*inf*: *person*) прижи́мистый (прижи́мист); (: *amount*) ми́зерный* (ми́зерен).
mini... ['mɪnɪ] *prefix* мини....
miniature ['mɪnətʃə^r] *adj* миниатю́рный* (миниатю́рен) ◆ *n* миниатю́ра.
minibus ['mɪnɪbʌs] *n* микроавто́бус.
minicab ['mɪnɪkæb] *n* (*BRIT*) такси́ *nt ind*.
minicomputer ['mɪnɪkəm'pju:tə^r] *n* мини-компью́тер.
Minidisc® ['mɪnɪdɪsk] *n* ми́нидиск.
minim ['mɪnɪm] *n* полови́нная но́та.
minima ['mɪnɪmə] *npl of* **minimum**.
minimal ['mɪnɪml] *adj* минима́льный* (минима́лен).
minimalist ['mɪnɪməlɪst] *adj* минимали́ст(-ка).
minimize ['mɪnɪmaɪz] *vt* (*reduce*) своди́ть* (свести́* *perf*) к ми́нимуму; (*play down*) преуменьша́ть (преуме́ньшить *perf*).
minimum ['mɪnɪməm] (*pl* **minima**) *n* ми́нимум ◆ *adj* минима́льный; **to reduce to a ~** своди́ть* (свести́* *perf*) к ми́нимуму; **~ wage** минима́льная зарпла́та.
minimum lending rate *n* минима́льная ссу́дная ста́вка.
mining ['maɪnɪŋ] *n* (*process*) добы́ча; (*science*) го́рное де́ло; (*industry*) у́гольная промы́шленность *f* ◆ *cpd* (*industry*) горнодобыва́ющий*; (*region*) шахтёрский.
minion ['mɪnjən] *n* (*pej*) подчинённый *m adj*.
mini-series ['mɪnɪsɪəri:z] *n* минисериа́л.
miniskirt ['mɪnɪskə:t] *n* ми́ни ю́бка*.
minister ['mɪnɪstə^r] *n* (*BRIT*: *POL*) мини́стр; (*REL*) свяще́нник ◆ *vi*: **to ~ to** служи́ть *(impf) +dat*.
ministerial [mɪnɪs'tɪərɪəl] *adj* (*BRIT*: *POL*) министе́рский*; **~ post** пост мини́стра.

* marks translations which have irregular inflections. The Russian-English side of the dictionary gives inflectional information.

ministry ['mɪnɪstrɪ] *n* (*BRIT: POL*) министéрство; (*REL*): **to go into the ~** принимáть (принять* *perf*) духóвный сан.
Ministry of Defence *n* Министéрство обороны.
mink [mɪŋk] *n* нóрка*.
mink coat *n* нóрковая шуба.
minnow ['mɪnəu] *n* пескáрь *m*
minor ['maɪnə^r] *adj* (*injuries, poet*) незначительный; (*repairs*) мéлкий*; (*MUS*) минóрный ◆ *n* (*LAW*) несовершеннолéтний* (-яя) *m(f) adj*.
Minorca [mɪ'nɔːkə] *n* Минóрка.
minority [maɪ'nɔrɪtɪ] *n* меньшинствó*; **to be in a ~** быть* (*impf*) в меньшинствé; **~ interest** (*COMM*) неконтрóльный пакéт áкций.
Minsk [mɪnsk] *n* Минск.
minster ['mɪnstə^r] *n* собóр.
minstrel ['mɪnstrəl] *n* менестрéль *m*.
mint [mɪnt] *n* (*BOT*) мята; (*sweet*) мятная конфéта ◆ *vt* (*coins*) чекáнить (отчекáнить *perf*); **the (Royal) M~**, (*US*) **the (US) M~** ≈ Монéтный двор; **in ~ condition** как нóвенький*.
mint sauce *n* сóус из мяты.
minuet [mɪnju'ɛt] *n* менуэ́т.
minus ['maɪnəs] *n* (*also:* **~ sign**) минус ◆ *prep*: **12 ~ 6 equals 6** 12 минус 6 равняется 6; (*temperature*): **~ 24 (degrees)** минус 24 грáдуса.
minuscule ['mɪnəskjuːl] *adj* крóхотный* (крóхотен), крóшечный* (крóшечен).
minute[1] [maɪ'njuːt] *adj* (*search*) тщáтельный; **in ~ detail** до малéйших подрóбностей.
minute[2] ['mɪnɪt] *n* (*also fig*) минута; (*official record*) зáпись *f*; **~s** *npl* (*of meeting*) протокóл *msg*; **it's five ~s past three** сейчáс пять минут четвёртого ...; **wait a ~!, just a ~!** подождите минуточку!; **up to the ~** (*fashion, news*) сáмый послéдний*; (*technology*) новéйший; **at the last ~** в послéднюю минуту.
minute book *n* книга протокóлов.
minute hand *n* минутная стрéлка*.
minutely [maɪ'njuːtlɪ] *adv* (*by a small amount*) едвá замéтно; (*in detail*) подрóбно, подрóбнейшим óбразом.
minutiae [mɪ'njuːʃiː] *npl* мельчáйшие детáли *fpl*.
miracle ['mɪrəkl] *n* чудо*.
miraculous [mɪ'rækjuləs] *adj* чудéсный* (чудéсен).
mirage ['mɪrɑːʒ] *n* мирáж.
mire ['maɪə^r] *n* трясина.
mirror ['mɪrə^r] *n* зéркало*; (*also:* **hand-~**) зéркальце ◆ *vt* отражáть (отразить* *perf*).
mirror image *n* зеркáльное отражéние.
mirth [məːθ] *n* весéлье.
misadventure [mɪsəd'vɛntʃə^r] *n* злоключéние; **death by ~** (*BRIT*) смерть* *f* в результáте несчáстного случая.
misanthropist [mɪ'zænθrəpɪst] *n* мизантрóп.
misapply [mɪsə'plaɪ] *vt* непрáвильно применять (применить *perf*).
misapprehension ['mɪsæprɪ'hɛnʃən] *n* лóжное представлéние.
misappropriate [mɪsə'prəuprɪeɪt] *vt* незакóнно присвáивать (присвóить *perf*).
misappropriation ['mɪsəprəuprɪ'eɪʃən] *n* назакóнное присвоéние.
misbehave [mɪsbɪ'heɪv] *vi* плóхо себя вести* (*impf*).
misbehaviour [mɪsbɪ'heɪvjə^r] (*US* **misbehavior**) *n* плохóе поведéние.
misc. *abbr* = **miscellaneous**.
miscalculate [mɪs'kælkjuleɪt] *vt* невéрно оцéнивать (оценить *perf*) ◆ *vi* просчитываться (просчитáться *perf*).
miscalculation ['mɪskælkju'leɪʃən] *n* просчёт.
miscarriage ['mɪskærɪdʒ] *n* (*MED*) выкидыш; (*LAW*): **~ of justice** судéбная ошибка.
miscarry [mɪs'kærɪ] *vi* (*plans*) не удавáться* (удáться* *perf*); **she miscarried** у неё был выкидыш.
miscellaneous [mɪsɪ'leɪnɪəs] *adj* (*collection, group*) разнорóдный* (разнорóден); (*subjects, items*) разнообрáзный* (разнообрáзен); **~ expenses** мéлкие расхóды; **~ files** рáзное *nt adj*.
mischance [mɪs'tʃɑːns] *n* (*misfortune*) невезéние; **by (some) ~** по несчáстной случáйности.
mischief ['mɪstʃɪf] *n* (*naughtiness, playfulness*) озорствó; (*maliciousness*) зло; **to get into ~** прокáзничать (напрокáзничать *perf*); **to do sb a ~** причинять (причинить *perf*) кому-н зло.
mischievous ['mɪstʃɪvəs] *adj* (*naughty, playful*) озорнóй; (*malicious*) злóбный.
misconception ['mɪskən'sɛpʃən] *n* лóжное представлéние.
misconduct [mɪs'kɔndʌkt] *n* дурнóе поведéние; **professional ~** нарушéние профессионáльной этики.
misconstrue [mɪskən'struː] *vt* невéрно истолкóвывать (истолковáть* *perf*).
miscount [mɪs'kaunt] *vt* невéрно считáть (сосчитáть *perf*) ◆ *vi* ошибáться (ошибиться* *perf*) в подсчётах.
misdemeanour [mɪsdɪ'miːnə^r] (*US* **misdemeanor**) *n* проступок*.
misdirect [mɪsdɪ'rɛkt] *vt* (*person*) ошибочно направлять (напрáвить* *perf*); (*letter*) непрáвильно адресовáть (*impf/perf*).
miser ['maɪzə^r] *n* скряга *m/f*.
miserable ['mɪzərəbl] *adj* (*unhappy: person, expression*) несчáстный* (несчáстен); (*unpleasant: weather, person*) сквéрный* (сквéрен); (*donation, conditions*) жáлкий* (жáлок); (*failure*) позóрный; **to feel ~** чувствовать (*impf*) себя óчень плóхо; **she looked ~** у неё был несчáстный вид.
miserably ['mɪzərəblɪ] *adv* (*live, pay*) скудно;

(*smile*) жáлко; (*small*) ничтóжно; (*fail*) позóрно.
miserly ['maɪzəlɪ] *adj* (*person*) скупóй* (скуп); (*amount*) ми́зерный* (ми́зерен).
misery ['mɪzərɪ] *n* (*unhappiness*) невзгóда; (*pain*) страдáние; (*wretchedness*) бéдственное положéние.
misfire [mɪs'faɪə'] *vi* (*plan*) провáливаться (провали́ться *perf*); (*car engine*) пропускáть (пропусти́ть* *perf*) вспы́шку.
misfit ['mɪsfɪt] *n* (*person*): **he was a ~ in our community** он не подходи́л к нáшему óбществу.
misfortune [mɪs'fɔ:tʃən] *n* несчáстье*.
misgiving [mɪs'gɪvɪŋ] *n* опасéния *ntpl*; **I have ~s about it** у меня́ есть опасéния на э́тот счёт.
misguided [mɪs'gaɪdɪd] *adj* (*person*) невéрно ориенти́рованный (ориенти́рован); (*ideas*) оши́бочный* (оши́бочен).
mishandle [mɪs'hændl] *vt* (*problem, situation*) не справля́ться (спрáвиться* *perf*) с *+instr*.
mishap ['mɪshæp] *n* неприя́тность *f*.
mishear [mɪs'hɪə'] (*irreg*: *like* **hear**) *vt* не расслы́шать *(perf)* ◆ *vi* ослы́шаться *(perf)*.
misheard [mɪs'hə:d] *pt, pp of* **mishear**.
mishmash ['mɪʃmæʃ] *n* (*inf*) неразбери́ха.
misinform [mɪsɪn'fɔ:m] *vt* невéрно информи́ровать (проинформи́ровать *perf*); (*deliberately*) дезинформи́ровать *(impf/perf)*.
misinterpret [mɪsɪn'tə:prɪt] *vt* невéрно интерпрети́ровать *(impf/perf) or* истолкóвывать (истолковáть *perf*).
misinterpretation ['mɪsɪntə:prɪ'teɪʃən] *n* невéрная интерпретáция.
misjudge [mɪs'dʒʌdʒ] *vt* невéрно оцéнивать (оцени́ть *perf*).
mislay [mɪs'leɪ] *irreg vt* (*lose*) девáть (подевáть *perf*).
mislead [mɪs'li:d] (*irreg*: *like* **lead**[1]) *vt* вводи́ть* (ввести́* *perf*) в заблуждéние.
misleading [mɪs'li:dɪŋ] *adj* обмáнчивый (обмáнчив).
misled [mɪs'lɛd] *pt, pp of* **mislead**.
mismanage [mɪs'mænɪdʒ] *vt* (*business, institution*) неумéло руководи́ть* *(impf)* *+instr*; (*problem, situation*) неумéло справля́ться (спрáвиться* *perf*) с *+instr*.
mismanagement [mɪs'mænɪdʒmənt] *n* (*of company*) неумéлое руковóдство; (*of situation*) неумéлое решéние.
misnomer [mɪs'nəumə'] *n* неправи́льное назвáние.
misogynist [mɪ'sɔdʒɪnɪst] *n* женоненави́стник.
misplace [mɪs'pleɪs] *vt* (*lose*) девáть (подевáть *perf*).
misplaced [mɪs'pleɪst] *adj* (*unwarranted*) неумéстный* (неумéстен).
misprint ['mɪsprɪnt] *n* опечáтка*.
mispronounce [mɪsprə'nauns] *vt* неправи́льно произноси́ть* (произнести́* *perf*).
misquote ['mɪs'kwəut] *vt* невéрно цити́ровать (процити́ровать *perf*).
misread [mɪs'ri:d] *irreg vt* неправи́льно читáть (прочитáть *or* прочéсть* *perf*).
misrepresent [mɪsrɛprɪ'zɛnt] *vt* преподноси́ть* (преподнести́* *perf*) в лóжном свéте.
misrepresentation [mɪsrɛprɪzɛn'teɪʃən] *n* искажéние; (*LAW*) умы́шленный обмáн.
Miss [mɪs] *n* мисс *f ind*; **Dear ~ Smith** (*formal*) Госпожá Смит; (*informal*) Мисс Смит.
miss [mɪs] *vt* (*train, bus, class etc*) пропускáть (пропусти́ть* *perf*); (*fail to hit*) не попадáть (попáсть* *perf*) в *+acc*; (*notice loss of*: *money etc*) обнарýживать (обнарýжить *perf*) пропáжу *+gen*; (*pine for*) скучáть *(impf)* по *+dat*; (*chance, opportunity*) упускáть (упусти́ть* *perf*) ◆ *vi* (*subj*: *person*) промáхиваться (промахнýться* *perf*); (: *missile, object*) не достигáть (дости́чь* *or* дости́гнуть* *perf*) цéли ◆ *n* (*failure to hit*) прóмах; **you can't ~ my house** мой дом невозмóжно не замéтить; **the bus just ~ed the wall** автóбус чуть не врéзался в стéну; **I ~ him** я скучáю по немý; **nobody will ~ us** никтó не замéтит, что нас нет; **you're ~ing the point** Вы не понимáете сýти дéла
▸ **miss out** *vt* (*BRIT*) пропускáть (пропусти́ть* *perf*)
▸ **miss out on** *vt fus* (*fun, party*) пропускáть (пропусти́ть* *perf*); (*chance, bargain*) упускáть (упусти́ть* *perf*).
missal ['mɪsl] *n* моли́твенник.
misshapen [mɪs'ʃeɪpən] *adj* деформи́рованный (деформи́рован).
missile ['mɪsaɪl] *n* (*MIL*) ракéта; (*projectile*): **demonstrators threw ~s at the police** демонстрáнты забрáсывали поли́цию различными предмéтами.
missile base *n* ракéтная бáза.
missile launcher [-'lɔ:ntʃə'] *n* ракéтная пусковáя установка*.
missing ['mɪsɪŋ] *adj* (*lost*) пропáвший; (*removed*: *tooth, wheel*) недостаю́щий*; (*absent*): **who is ~ today?** кто сегóдня отсýтствует?; **to be ~, go ~** пропадáть (пропáсть* *perf*) бéз вести; **~ person** пропáвший(-ая) *m(f) adj* бéз вести.
mission ['mɪʃən] *n* (*also POL, REL*) ми́ссия; (*MIL*) задáние; **on a ~ to sb** с ми́ссией к комý-н.
missionary ['mɪʃənrɪ] *n* миссионéр(ка*).
Mississippi [mɪsɪ'sɪpɪ] *n*: **the ~** Миссиси́пи *f ind*.
missive ['mɪsɪv] *n* послáние.
misspell ['mɪs'spɛl] (*irreg*: *like* **spell**) *vt* писáть* (написáть* *perf*) с оши́бками.
misspent ['mɪs'spɛnt] *adj*: **a ~ youth**

* marks translations which have irregular inflections. The Russian-English side of the dictionary gives inflectional information.

растра́ченная ю́ность *f*.
mist [mɪst] *n* (*heavy*) тума́н; (*light*) ды́мка ◆ *vi* (*also:* ~ **over**: *eyes*) затума́ниваться (затума́ниться *perf*); (*BRIT*: *also:* ~ **over** *or* **up**: *windows*) запотева́ть (запоте́ть *perf*).
mistake [mɪs'teɪk] (*irreg*: *like* **take**) *n* оши́бка* ◆ *vt* (*be wrong about*) ошиба́ться (ошиби́ться* *perf*) в +*prp*; (*intentions*) непра́вильно понима́ть (поня́ть* *perf*); **by** ~ по оши́бке; **to make a** ~ ошиба́ться (ошиби́ться* *perf*), де́лать (сде́лать *perf*) оши́бку; **to make a** ~ **about sb/sth** ошиба́ться (ошиби́ться* *perf*) в ком-н/чём-н; **to** ~ **A for B** принима́ть (приня́ть* *perf*) А за Б.
mistaken [mɪs'teɪkən] *pp of* **mistake** ◆ *adj* оши́бочный* (оши́бочен); **to be** ~ ошиба́ться (ошиби́ться* *perf*).
mistaken identity *n*: **a case of** ~ ~ слу́чай оши́бочного опозна́ния.
mistakenly [mɪs'teɪkənlɪ] *adv* оши́бочно.
mister ['mɪstə^r] *n* (*inf*) дя́дя *m* (*обраще́ние*); *see* **Mr**.
mistletoe ['mɪsltəu] *n* (*BOT*) оме́ла.
mistook [mɪs'tuk] *pt of* **mistake**.
mistranslation [mɪstræns'leɪʃən] *n* непра́вильный перево́д.
mistreat [mɪs'tri:t] *vt* пло́хо обраща́ться (*impf*) с +*instr*.
mistress ['mɪstrɪs] *n* (*lover*) любо́вница; (*also fig*) хозя́йка*; (*BRIT*: *SCOL*) учи́тельница.
mistrust [mɪs'trʌst] *vt* не доверя́ть (*impf*) +*dat*, испы́тывать (испыта́ть *perf*) недове́рие к +*dat* ◆ *n*: ~ **(of)** недове́рие (к +*dat*).
mistrustful [mɪs'trʌstful] *adj* недове́рчивый (недове́рчив); **to be** ~ **of** не доверя́ть (*impf*) +*dat*.
misty ['mɪstɪ] *adj* (*day*) тума́нный* (тума́нен); (*eyes*) затума́ненный (затума́нен); (*glasses, window*) запоте́вший*.
misty-eyed ['mɪstɪ'aɪd] *adj* (*girl*) с глаза́ми по́лными слёз; (*fig*: *girl*) с затума́ненным взгля́дом.
misunderstand [mɪsʌndə'stænd] (*irreg*: *like* **understand**) *vt* непра́вильно понима́ть (поня́ть* *perf*) ◆ *vi* не понима́ть (поня́ть* *perf*).
misunderstanding ['mɪsʌndə'stændɪŋ] *n* недоразуме́ние.
misunderstood [mɪsʌndə'stud] *pt, pp of* **misunderstand**.
misuse [*n* mɪs'ju:s, *vb* mɪs'ju:z] *n* (*of power, funds*) злоупотребле́ние; (*of word*) непра́вильное употребле́ние ◆ *vt* (*see n*) злоупотребля́ть (злоупотреби́ть* *perf*) +*instr*; непра́вильно употребля́ть (употреби́ть* *perf*).
MIT *n abbr* (*US*) = *Massachusetts Institute of Technology*.
mite [maɪt] *n* (*small quantity*) ка́пля*; (*BRIT*: *small child*) кро́шка* *m/f*.
miter ['maɪtə^r] *n* (*US*) = **mitre**.
mitigate ['mɪtɪgeɪt] *vt* смягча́ть (смягчи́ть *perf*); **mitigating circumstances** смягча́ющие обстоя́тельства.
mitigation [mɪtɪ'geɪʃən] *n* смягче́ние; **in** ~ (*LAW*) в оправда́ние.
mitre ['maɪtə^r] (*US* **miter**) *n* ми́тра; (*also:* ~ **joint**) соедине́ние в ус.
mitt [mɪt] *n* (*inf*) = **mitten**.
mitten ['mɪtn] *n* ва́режка*, рукави́ца.
mix [mɪks] *vt* (*cake, cement*) заме́шивать (замеси́ть* *perf*) ◆ *n* смесь *f* ◆ *vi* (*people*): **to** ~ **(with)** обща́ться (*impf*) (с +*instr*); **to** ~ **sth (with sth)** сме́шивать (смеша́ть *perf*) что-н (с чем-н); **to** ~ **business with pleasure** сочета́ть (*impf*) прия́тное с поле́зным; **cake** ~ гото́вая смесь для то́рта
▸ **mix in** *vt* (*eggs etc*) вме́шивать (вмеша́ть *perf*)
▸ **mix up** *vt* (*combine*) переме́шивать (перемеша́ть *perf*); (*confuse*: *people*) пу́тать (спу́тать *perf*); (: *things*) пу́тать (перепу́тать *perf*); **to get ~ed up in sth** впу́тываться (впу́таться *perf*) во что-н; **he's ~ed up in this business too** он то́же заме́шан в э́том де́ле.
mixed [mɪkst] *adj* сме́шанный.
mixed-ability ['mɪkstə'bɪlɪtɪ] *adj* с ра́зными спосо́бностями.
mixed bag *n* (*of people*) разношёрстная гру́ппа; (*of activities*) всего́ понемно́жку.
mixed blessing *n*: **it was a** ~ ~ нет ху́да без добра́.
mixed doubles *npl* (*TENNIS etc*) игра́ *fsg* сме́шанных пар.
mixed economy *n* сме́шанная эконо́мика.
mixed grill *n* (*BRIT*) *ассорти́ из жа́реного мя́са и овоще́й*.
mixed marriage *n* сме́шанный брак.
mixed-up [mɪkst'ʌp] *adj* (*confused*) сби́тый (сбит) с то́лку.
mixer ['mɪksə^r] *n* (*for food*) ми́ксер; (*for drinks*) смеси́тель *m*; (*person*): **she is a good** ~ она́ о́чень общи́тельна.
mixer tap *n* кран со смеси́телем.
mixture ['mɪkstʃə^r] *n* смесь *f*; (*MED*) миксту́ра.
mix-up ['mɪksʌp] *n* пу́таница.
Mk *abbr* (*BRIT*: *TECH*) = **mark**.
mk *abbr* (*COMM*) = **mark**.
mkt *abbr* = **market**.
MLitt *n abbr* (= *Master of Literature, Master of Letters*) ≈ маги́стр литературове́дения.
MLR *n abbr* (*BRIT*: = *minimum lending rate*) минима́льная ссу́дная ста́вка.
mm *abbr* (= **millimetre**) мм= *миллиме́тр*.
MN *abbr* (*BRIT*) = **Merchant Navy**; (*US*: *POST*) = *Minnesota*.
MO *n abbr* = *medical officer*; (*US*: *inf*: = *modus operandi*) при́нцип рабо́ты ◆ *abbr* (*US*: *POST*) = *Missouri*.
m.o. *abbr* = **money order**.
moan [məun] *n* (*cry*) стон ◆ *vi* (*inf*: *complain*): **to** ~ **(about)** ныть* (*impf*) (о +*prp*).
moaner ['məunə^r] *n* (*inf*: *pej*) ны́тик.

moat [məut] *n* ров*.
mob [mɔb] *n* толпа́*; (*inf: group of friends*) компа́ния ◆ *vt* осажда́ть (осади́ть* *perf*).
mobile ['məubaıl] *adj* подви́жный* (подви́жен); (*population, forces*) моби́льный* (моби́лен) ◆ *n* (*decoration*) подвесно́е декорати́вное украше́ние; **applicants must be ~** кандида́ты должны́ быть гото́вы к сме́не местожи́тельства.
mobile home *n* дом* на колёсах.
mobile phone *n* портати́вный телефо́н.
mobile shop *n* (*BRIT*) автола́вка*.
mobility [məu'bılıtı] *n* (*see adj*) подви́жность *f*; моби́льность *f*; (*of applicant*) гото́вность *f* меня́ть местожи́тельство.
mobility allowance *n* (*BRIT*) *посо́бие, выпла́чиваемое инвали́дам для покры́тия дополни́тельных доро́жных расхо́дов.*
mobilize ['məubılaız] *vt* мобилизова́ть (*impf/perf*) ◆ *vi* мобилизова́ться (*impf/perf*).
moccasin ['mɔkəsın] *n* мокаси́н.
mock [mɔk] *vt* (*ridicule*) издева́ться (*impf*) над +*instr*; (*laugh at*) насмеха́ться (*impf*) над +*instr* ◆ *adj* (*fake*) ло́жный* (ло́жен); (*: emotion*) притво́рный; **~ (exam)** (*BRIT*) про́бный экза́мен (*для подгото́вки к основно́му*); **~ battle** инсцениро́вка бо́я.
mockery ['mɔkərı] *n* издева́тельство; **to make a ~ of sb/sth** выставля́ть (вы́ставить* *perf*) кого́-н/что-н на посме́шище.
mocking ['mɔkıŋ] *adj* издева́тельский*.
mockingbird ['mɔkıŋbə:d] *n* пересме́шник.
mock-up ['mɔkʌp] *n* маке́т.
MOD *n abbr* (*BRIT: = Ministry of Defence*) Министе́рство оборо́ны.
mod cons ['mɔd'kɔnz] *npl abbr* (*BRIT: = modern conveniences*) совреме́нные удо́бства *ntpl*.
mode [məud] *n* (*form: of life*) о́браз; (*: of transport*) вид; (*COMPUT*) режи́м.
model ['mɔdl] *n* моде́ль *f*, маке́т; (*also:* **fashion ~**) манеке́нщик(-ица); (*also:* **artist's ~**) нату́рщик(-ица) ◆ *adj* (*small scale*) моде́льный; (*ideal*) образцо́вый ◆ *vt* (*clothes*) демонстри́ровать (*impf/perf*); (*with clay etc*) лепи́ть* (вы́лепить* *perf*) ◆ *vi* (*for designer, photographer*) пози́ровать (*impf*); **to ~ o.s. on** (*copy*) копи́ровать (*impf*).
modeller ['mɔdlə'] (*US* **modeler**) *n* (*model maker*) модели́ст(ка*).
model railway *n* маке́т желе́зной доро́ги.
modem ['məudɛm] *n* (*COMPUT*) моде́м.
moderate [*adj, n* 'mɔdərət, *vb* 'mɔdəreıt] *adj* (*views, amount*) уме́ренный* (уме́рен); (*change*) незначи́тельный ◆ *n* челове́к* уме́ренных взгля́дов ◆ *vt* умеря́ть (уме́рить *perf*) ◆ *vi* (*storm, wind etc*) утиха́ть (ути́хнуть* *perf*).
moderately ['mɔdərətlı] *adv* (*act*) уме́ренно; **~ expensive/pleased** дово́льно до́рого/рад; **~ priced** по уме́ренной цене́.
moderation [mɔdə'reıʃən] *n* уме́ренность *f*; **in ~** в уме́ренных коли́чествах.
moderator ['mɔdəreıtə'] *n* (*mediator*) посре́дник; (*chairman*) председа́тель *m*.
modern ['mɔdən] *adj* совреме́нный; **~ languages** совреме́нные языки́ *mpl*.
modernization [mɔdənaı'zeıʃən] *n* модерниза́ция.
modernize ['mɔdənaız] *vt* модернизи́ровать (*impf/perf*).
modest ['mɔdıst] *adj* скро́мный* (скро́мен).
modestly ['mɔdıstlı] *adv* скро́мно.
modesty ['mɔdıstı] *n* скро́мность *f*.
modicum ['mɔdıkəm] *n*: **a ~ of** то́лика +*gen*.
modification [mɔdıfı'keıʃən] *n* (*of vehicle, engine*) модифика́ция; (*of plan*) видоизмене́ние; **to make ~s to** вноси́ть* (внести́* *perf*) видоизмене́ния в +*acc*.
modify ['mɔdıfaı] *vt* (*see n*) модифици́ровать (*impf/perf*); видоизменя́ть (видоизмени́ть *perf*).
modish ['məudıʃ] *adj* мо́дный* (мо́ден).
Mods [mɔdz] *n abbr* (*BRIT: SCOL: = (Honour) Moderations*) *экза́мен, позволя́ющий перейти́ на ку́рс, необходи́мый для получе́ния сте́пени бакала́вра в О́ксфордском университе́те.*
modular ['mɔdjulə'] *adj* (*filing, unit*) мо́дульный.
modulate ['mɔdjuleıt] *vt* (*voice*) модули́ровать (*impf*).
modulation [mɔdju'leıʃən] *n* (*MUS, RADIO*) модуля́ция.
module ['mɔdju:l] *n* мо́дуль *m*; (*SPACE*) отсе́к; (*BRIT: SCOL*) курс.
modus operandi ['məudəsɔpə'rændi:] *n* при́нцип рабо́ты.
Mogadishu [mɔgə'dıʃu:] *n* Могади́шу *m ind*.
mogul ['məugl] *n* (*fig*) магна́т.
MOH *n abbr* (*BRIT*) *= Medical Officer of Health.*
mohair ['məuhɛə'] *n* мохе́р.
Mohammed [mə'hæmɛd] *n* Магоме́т.
moist [mɔıst] *adj* вла́жный* (вла́жен).
moisten ['mɔısn] *vt* (*lips*) увлажня́ть (увлажни́ть *perf*); (*: with tongue*) обли́зывать (облиза́ть *perf*); (*sponge*) мочи́ть* (намочи́ть* *perf*).
moisture ['mɔıstʃə'] *n* вла́га.
moisturize ['mɔıstʃəraız] *vt* увлажня́ть (увлажни́ть *perf*).
moisturizer ['mɔıstʃəraızə'] *n* увлажня́ющий крем.
molar ['məulə'] *n* коренно́й зуб*.
molasses [məu'læsız] *n* па́тока.
mold *etc* [məuld] (*US*) **= mould** *etc*.
Moldavian [mɔl'deıvıən] *n* (*person*)

* marks translations which have irregular inflections. The Russian-English side of the dictionary gives inflectional information.

молдова́нин*(-а́нка*) ◆ *adj* молдо́вский.
Moldova [mɔl'dəuvə] *n* Молдо́ва.
mole [məul] *n* (*spot*) ро́динка*; (ZOOL) крот*; (*spy*) доно́счик(-ица), стука́ч*(ка).
molecular [məu'lɛkjulə'] *adj* молекуля́рный.
molecule ['mɔlɪkju:l] *n* моле́кула.
molehill ['məulhɪl] *n* крото́вая нора́*.
molest [mə'lɛst] *vt* (*assault sexually*) надруга́ться *(perf)* над *+instr*; (*harass*) трави́ть* (затрави́ть* *perf*).
mollusc ['mɔləsk] *n* моллю́ск.
mollycoddle ['mɔlɪkɔdl] *vt* трясти́сь* *(impf)* над *+instr*.
Molotov cocktail ['mɔlətɔf-] *n* кокте́йль *m* Мо́лотова (*буты́лка с зажига́тельной сме́сью*).
molt [məult] *vi* (US) = **moult**.
molten ['məultən] *adj* распла́вленный.
mom [mɔm] *n* (US) = **mum**.
moment ['məumənt] *n* моме́нт, мгнове́ние; (PHYS) моме́нт; **for a** ~ на мгнове́ние *or* мину́ту; **at that** ~ в э́тот моме́нт; **at the** ~ в настоя́щий* моме́нт; **for the** ~ пока́; **in a** ~ че́рез мину́ту; **(at) any ~ (now)** в любо́й моме́нт; **"one ~ please"** „одну́ мину́точку".
momentarily ['məuməntrɪlɪ] *adv* на мгнове́ние; (US: *very soon*) в любо́й моме́нт.
momentary ['məuməntərɪ] *adj* (*brief*) мгнове́нный.
momentous [məu'mɛntəs] *adj* важне́йший.
momentum [məu'mɛntəm] *n* (PHYS) и́мпульс; (*fig*) дви́жущая си́ла; **to gather** *or* **gain** ~ набира́ть (набра́ть* *perf*) си́лу.
mommy ['mɔmɪ] *n* (US: *mother*) = **mummy**.
Mon. *abbr* = **Monday**.
Monaco ['mɔnəkəu] *n* Мона́ко *nt ind*.
monarch ['mɔnək] *n* мона́рх.
monarchist ['mɔnəkɪst] *n* монархи́ст(ка*).
monarchy ['mɔnəkɪ] *n* мона́рхия.
monastery ['mɔnəstərɪ] *n* монасты́рь* *m*.
monastic [mə'næstɪk] *adj* (*vows, order, also fig*) мона́шеский*; (*building*) монасты́рский.
Monday ['mʌndɪ] *n* понеде́льник; *see also* **Tuesday**.
Monegasque [mɔnə'gæsk] *adj* мона́кский ◆ *n* жи́тель(ница) *m(f)* Мона́ко.
monetarist ['mʌnɪtərɪst] *n* монетари́ст ◆ *adj* монетари́стский.
monetary ['mʌnɪtərɪ] *adj* де́нежный.
money ['mʌnɪ] *n* де́ньги* *pl*; **to make** ~ (*person*) зараба́тывать (зарабо́тать *perf*); (*business*) приноси́ть* (принести́* *perf*) дохо́д; **danger** ~ (BRIT) надба́вка за вре́дность; **I've got no** ~ **left** у меня́ совсе́м не оста́лось де́нег.
moneyed ['mʌnɪd] *adj* де́нежный.
moneylender ['mʌnɪlɛndə'] *n* ростовщи́к*.
money-maker ['mʌnɪmeɪkə'] *n* (*person*) кру́пный деле́ц*; (*project, investment*) при́быльное де́ло.
moneymaking ['mʌnɪmeɪkɪŋ] *adj* при́быльный.
money market *n* де́нежный ры́нок*.
money order *n* де́нежный перево́д.
money-spinner ['mʌnɪspɪnə'] *n* (*inf*): **this business/idea will be a real** ~ э́тот би́знес/э́та иде́я бу́дет де́лать больши́е де́ньги.
money supply *n* де́нежная ма́сса.
Mongol ['mɔŋgəl] *n* (LING) монго́льский* язы́к*; (HISTORY): **the ~s** монго́ло-тата́ры.
mongol ['mɔŋgəl] *n* (*pej*) *челове́к, страда́ющий боле́знью Да́уна*.
Mongolia [mɔŋ'gəulɪə] *n* Монго́лия.
Mongolian [mɔŋ'gəulɪən] *adj* монго́льский* ◆ *n* (*person*) монго́л(ка*); (LING) монго́льский* язы́к*.
mongoose ['mɔŋgu:s] *n* манґу́ст.
mongrel ['mʌŋgrəl] *n* дворня́га.
monitor ['mɔnɪtə'] *n* монито́р ◆ *vt* (*broadcasts*) контроли́ровать *(impf)*; (*heartbeat, pulse*) наблюда́ть *(impf)* за *+instr*; (*progress*) следи́ть* *(impf)* за *+instr*; (*foreign station*) прослу́шивать *(impf)*.
monk [mʌŋk] *n* мона́х.
monkey ['mʌŋkɪ] *n* обезья́на.
monkey business *n* (*inf*) проде́лки* *fpl*.
monkey nut *n* (BRIT) ара́хис *no pl*.
monkey tricks *npl* = **monkey business**.
monkey wrench *n* разводно́й га́ечный ключ*.
mono ['mɔnəu] *adj* (*recording*) мо́но *ind*.
monochrome ['mɔnəkrəum] *adj* черно-бе́лый; (COMPUT) монохро́мный.
monogamous [mɔ'nɔgəməs] *adj* монога́мный* (монога́мен).
monogamy [mɔ'nɔgəmɪ] *n* монога́мия, единобра́чие.
monogram ['mɔnəgræm] *n* моногра́мма.
monolith ['mɔnəlɪθ] *n* моноли́т.
monolithic [mɔnə'lɪθɪk] *adj* моноли́тный.
monologue ['mɔnəlɔg] *n* моноло́г.
monoplane ['mɔnəpleɪn] *n* монопла́н.
monopolist [mə'nɔpəlɪst] *n* монополи́ст.
monopolize [mə'nɔpəlaɪz] *vt* (ECON) монополизи́ровать *(impf/perf)*; (*place, conversation*) завладева́ть (завладе́ть *perf*) *+instr*; (*person*) захва́тывать (захвати́ть* *perf*).
monopoly [mə'nɔpəlɪ] *n* (*also* ECON) монопо́лия; **Monopolies and Mergers Commission** (BRIT) Коми́ссия по монопо́лиям и слия́ниям.
monorail ['mɔnəureɪl] *n* моноре́льсовая доро́га.
monosodium glutamate [mɔnə'səudɪəm 'glu:təmeɪt] *n* глутамина́т на́трия.
monosyllabic [mɔnəsɪ'læbɪk] *adj* (*word*) односло́жный; (*person*) немногосло́вный*.
monosyllable ['mɔnəsɪləbl] *n* односло́жное сло́во*.
monotone ['mɔnətəun] *n*: **to speak in a** ~ говори́ть *(impf)* моното́нно.
monotonous [mə'nɔtənəs] *adj* (*life, job etc*)

однообра́зный* (однообра́зен); (*voice, sound*) моното́нный* (моното́нен).
monotony [mə'nɔtənɪ] *n* (*see adj*) однообра́зие; моното́нность *f*.
monsoon [mɔn'suːn] *n* муссо́н.
monster ['mɔnstə'] *n* (*also fig*) чудо́вище, монстр.
monstrosity [mɔn'strɔsɪtɪ] *n* (*object, building*) чу́дище, монстр.
monstrous ['mɔnstrəs] *adj* чудо́вищный* (чудо́вищен).
montage [mɔn'tɑːʒ] *n* монта́ж*.
Mont Blanc [mɔ̃ blɑ̃] *n* Монбла́н.
Montenegrin [mɔntə'niːgrɪn] *n* черного́рец*(-о́рка*) ◆ *adj* черного́рский*.
Montenegro [mɔntə'niːgrəʊ] *n* Черного́рия.
month [mʌnθ] *n* ме́сяц; **every ~** ка́ждый ме́сяц; **300 dollars a ~** 300 до́лларов в ме́сяц.
monthly ['mʌnθlɪ] *adj* ежеме́сячный; (*ticket*) ме́сячный ◆ *adv* ежеме́сячно; **twice ~** два́жды в ме́сяц.
Montreal [mɔntrɪ'ɔːl] *n* Монреа́ль *m*.
monument ['mɔnjumənt] *n* (*memorial*) па́мятник, монуме́нт; (*historical building*) па́мятник.
monumental [mɔnju'mɛntl] *adj* (*building, book*) монумента́льный* (монумента́лен); (*storm, row*) колосса́льный.
moo [muː] *vi* мыча́ть* (*impf*).
mood [muːd] *n* настрое́ние; (*of group, crowd*) настро́й; **to be in a good/bad ~** быть* (*impf*) в хоро́шем/плохо́м настрое́нии; **I'm in the ~ for a drink/to watch TV** у меня́ есть настрое́ние вы́пить/смотре́ть телеви́зор.
moodily ['muːdɪlɪ] *adv* мра́чно, угрю́мо.
moody ['muːdɪ] *adj* (*sullen*) угрю́мый (угрю́м); (*temperamental*): **she is a very ~ person** у неё о́чень переме́нчивое настрое́ние.
moon [muːn] *n* луна́*.
moonlight ['muːnlaɪt] *n* лу́нный свет ◆ *vi* (*inf*) рабо́тать (*impf*) на стороне́.
moonlighting ['muːnlaɪtɪŋ] *n* (*inf*) рабо́та по совмести́тельству.
moonlit ['muːnlɪt] *adj*: **a ~ night** лу́нная ночь*.
moonshot ['muːnʃɔt] *n* полёт на Луну́.
moor [muə'] *n* ве́ресковая пу́стошь *f* ◆ *vt* (*ship*) пришварто́вывать (пришвартова́ть *perf*) ◆ *vi* пришварто́вываться (пришвартова́ться *perf*).
mooring ['muərɪŋ] *n* прича́л; **~s** *npl* (*chains*) шварто́вые це́пи* *fpl*.
Moorish ['muərɪʃ] *adj* маврита́нский.
moorland ['muələnd] *n* ве́ресковая пу́стошь *f*.
moose [muːs] *n inv* лось* *m*.
moot [muːt] *vt*: **it was ~ed that ...** бы́ло предло́жено, что ... ◆ *adj*: **~ point** спо́рный вопро́с.
mop [mɔp] *n* (*for floor*) шва́бра; (*for dishes*) щётка*; (*of hair*) копна́ ◆ *vt* (*floor*) мыть* (вы́мыть* *or* помы́ть* *perf*) (*шва́брой*); (*eyes, face*) вытира́ть (вы́тереть* *perf*)
▸ **mop up** *vt* (*liquid*) вытира́ть (вы́тереть* *perf*).
mope [məup] *vi* хандри́ть (*impf*)
▸ **mope about** *vi* слоня́ться (*impf*)
▸ **mope around** *vi* = **mope about**.
moped ['məupɛd] *n* мопе́д.
moquette [mɔ'kɛt] *n* ≈ плюш.
MOR *adj abbr* (MUS: = *middle-of-the-road*) лёгкий*.
moral ['mɔrl] *adj* нра́вственный, мора́льный; (*person*) нра́вственный* (нра́вственен) ◆ *n* (*of story*) мора́ль *f*; **~s** *npl* нра́вы *mpl*; **~ support/dilemma/victory** мора́льная подде́ржка/диле́мма/побе́да; **~ courage** душе́вное му́жество.
morale [mɔ'rɑːl] *n* мора́льный дух.
morality [mə'rælɪtɪ] *n* нра́вственность *f*.
moralize ['mɔrəlaɪz] *vi*: **to ~ (about)** морализи́ровать (*impf*) (о +*prp*).
morally ['mɔrəlɪ] *adv* (*wrong, responsible*) мора́льно; (*live, behave*) нра́вственно.
moral victory *n* мора́льная побе́да.
morass [mə'ræs] *n* (*also fig*) трясйна.
moratorium [mɔrə'tɔːrɪəm] *n* морато́рий.
morbid ['mɔːbɪd] *adj* (*imagination*) ненорма́льный; (*ideas*) жу́ткий*.

KEYWORD

more [mɔː'] *adj* **1** (*greater in number etc*) бо́льше +*gen*; **I have more friends than enemies** у меня́ бо́льше друзе́й, чем враго́в
2 (*additional*) ещё; **do you want (some) more tea?** хоти́те ещё ча́ю?; **is there any more wine?** ещё есть вино́?; **I have no** *or* **I don't have any more money** у меня́ бо́льше нет де́нег; **it'll take a few more weeks** э́то займёт ещё не́сколько неде́ль
◆ *pron* **1** (*greater amount*): **more than ten** бо́льше десяти́; **we've sold more than a hundred tickets** мы прода́ли бо́лее ста биле́тов; **it cost more than we expected** э́то сто́ит бо́льше, чем мы ожида́ли
2 (*further or additional amount*): **is there any more?** ещё есть?; **there's no more** бо́льше ничего́ нет; **a little more** ещё немно́го *or* чуть-чу́ть; **many/much more** намно́го/ гора́здо бо́льше
◆ *adv* **1** (*+vb*) бо́льше; **I like this one more** мне э́то бо́льше нра́вится
2 (*+adj*): **more dangerous/difficult** *etc* **(than)** бо́лее опа́сный/тру́дный *etc*, (чем)
3 (*+adv*): **more economically (than)** бо́лее экономи́чно (чем); **more easily/quickly (than)** ле́гче/быстре́е (чем); **he became more and more excited/friendly** он станови́лся всё бо́лее и бо́лее возбуждённым/ дружелю́бным; **he grew to like her more and**

* marks translations which have irregular inflections. The Russian-English side of the dictionary gives inflectional information.

more она́ нра́вилась ему́ всё бо́льше и бо́льше; **more or less** бо́лее и́ли ме́нее; **it should cost £500, more or less** э́то должно́ сто́ить приблизи́тельно £500; **she is more beautiful than ever** она́ прекра́снее, чем когда́-либо; **he loved her more than ever** он люби́л её бо́льше, чем когда́-либо; **the more ..., the better** чем бо́льше ..., тем лу́чше; **once more** ещё раз; **I'd like to see more of you** хоте́лось бы поча́ще Вас ви́деть.

moreover [mɔ:'rəuvə^r] *adv* бо́лее того́.
morgue [mɔ:g] *n* морг.
MORI ['mɔ:rɪ] *n abbr* (BRIT: *= Market & Opinion Research Institute*) *нау́чно-иссле́довательский институ́т изуче́ния ры́нка и обще́ственного мне́ния.*
moribund ['mɔrɪbʌnd] *adj* (*industry*) отжи́вший своё.
Mormon ['mɔ:mən] *n* мормо́н(ка*).
morning ['mɔ:nɪŋ] *n* у́тро*; (*between midnight and 3 a.m.*) ночь *f* ◆ *cpd* (*paper, sun, walk*) у́тренний*; **in the** ~ у́тром; **3 o'clock in the** ~ 3 часа́ но́чи; **7 o'clock in the** ~ 7 часо́в утра́; **this** ~ сего́дня у́тром.
morning-after pill ['mɔ:nɪŋ'ɑ:ftə-] *n* *противозача́точная табле́тка (обы́чно принима́ется по́сле се́кса).*
morning sickness *n* у́треняя тошнота́ (*у бере́менных*).
Moroccan [mə'rɔkən] *adj* марокка́нский ◆ *n* марокка́нец*(-нка*).
Morocco [mə'rɔkəu] *n* Маро́кко *nt ind.*
moron ['mɔ:rɔn] *n* (*inf*) крети́н(ка*).
moronic [mə'rɔnɪk] *adj* (*inf*) крети́нский.
morose [mə'rəus] *adj* (*miserable*) угрю́мый (угрю́м).
morphine ['mɔ:fi:n] *n* мо́рфий.
morris dancing ['mɔrɪs-] *n* (BRIT) мо́ррис (*наро́дный англи́йский та́нец*).
Morse [mɔ:s] *n* (*also:* ~ **code**) а́збука Мо́рзе.
morsel ['mɔ:sl] *n* (*of food*) кусо́чек*.
mortal ['mɔ:tl] *adj* (*human*) сме́ртный* (сме́ртен); (*deadly*) смерте́льный* (смерте́лен); (*sin*) сме́ртный* ◆ *n*: **mere** ~ просто́й(-ая) сме́ртный(-ая) *m(f) adj*; ~ **remains** бре́нные оста́нки.
mortality [mɔ:'tælɪtɪ] *n* (*death*) сме́ртность *f.*
mortality rate *n* сме́ртность *f.*
mortar ['mɔ:tə^r] *n* (*cannon*) миномёт; (*cement*) цеме́нтный раство́р; (*bowl*) сту́пка*.
mortgage ['mɔ:gɪdʒ] *n* ипоте́чный креди́т, ипоте́чная ссу́да ◆ *vt* закла́дывать (заложи́ть* *perf*); **to take out a** ~ брать* (взять* *perf*) ипоте́чный креди́т.
mortgage company *n* (US) ипоте́чная компа́ния.
mortgagee [mɔ:gə'dʒi:] *n* кредито́р (*при ипоте́чном креди́те*).
mortgagor ['mɔ:gədʒə^r] *n* заёмщик (*при ипоте́чном креди́те*).
mortician [mɔ:'tɪʃən] *n* (US) рабо́тник *похоро́нного бюро́.*
mortified ['mɔ:tɪfaɪd] *adj*: **to be** ~ быть* (*impf*) в смерте́льном у́жасе.
mortify ['mɔ:tɪfaɪ] *vt* приводи́ть* (привести́* *perf*) в по́лный у́жас.
mortise lock ['mɔ:tɪs-] *n* врезно́й замо́к*.
mortuary ['mɔ:tjuərɪ] *n* морг (*при больни́це*), поко́йницкая *f adj.*
mosaic [məu'zeɪɪk] *n* моза́ика.
Moscow ['mɔskəu] *n* Москва́.
Moslem ['mɔzləm] *adj, n* = **Muslim**.
mosque [mɔsk] *n* мече́ть *f.*
mosquito [mɔs'ki:təu] (*pl* ~**es**) *n* кома́р*.
mosquito net *n* моски́тная се́тка*.
moss [mɔs] *n* мох*.
mossy ['mɔsɪ] *adj* (*ground, wall*) поро́сший мхом.

KEYWORD

most [məust] *adj* **1** (*almost all*: *countable nouns*) большинство́ *+gen*; (: *uncountable and collective nouns*) по бо́льшей ча́сти; **most people/cars** большинство́ люде́й/маши́н; **most milk** молоко́, по бо́льшей ча́сти; **in most cases** в большинстве́ слу́чаев
2 (*largest, greatest*): **who has the most money?** у кого́ бо́льше всего́ де́нег?; **this book has attracted the most interest among the critics** э́та кни́га вы́звала наибо́льший интере́с у кри́тиков
◆ *pron* (*greatest quantity, number*: *countable nouns*) большинство́; (: *uncountable and collective nouns*) бо́льшая часть *f*; **most of the houses/her friends** большинство́ домо́в/её друзе́й; **most of the cake** бо́льшая часть то́рта; **do the most you can** де́лайте всё, что мо́жете; **I ate the most** я съел бо́льше всех; **to make the most of sth** максима́льно испо́льзовать (*impf*) что-н; **at the (very) most** са́мое бо́льшее
◆ *adv* (*+vb*) бо́льше всего́; (*+adv*) исключи́тельно; **the most interesting/expensive** наибо́лее *or* са́мый интере́сный/дорого́й; **I liked him the most** он понра́вился мне бо́льше всех; **what do you value most, wealth or health?** что Вы бо́льше це́ните, бога́тство и́ли здоро́вье?

mostly ['məustlɪ] *adv* в основно́м, гла́вным о́бразом.
MOT *n abbr* (BRIT: *= Ministry of Transport*) Министе́рство тра́нспорта; ~ **(test)** техосмо́тр= *техни́ческий осмо́тр.*
motel [məu'tɛl] *n* моте́ль *m.*
moth [mɔθ] *n* моты́лёк*; (*also:* **clothes** ~) моль *f no pl.*
mothballs ['mɔθbɔ:lz] *npl* нафтали́новые ша́рики *mpl.*
moth-eaten ['mɔθi:tn] *adj* (*also fig*) изъеде́нный (изъе́ден).
mother ['mʌðə^r] *n* мать* *f* ◆ *vt* (*raise*)

выра́щивать (вы́растить* *perf*); (*pamper*) ня́нчиться *(impf)* с +*instr* ◆ *adj*: ~ **country** ро́дина; ~ **company** матери́нская компа́ния.
motherboard ['mʌðəbɔ:d] *n* (*COMPUT*) объедини́тельная пла́та.
motherhood ['mʌðəhud] *n* матери́нство.
mother-in-law ['mʌðərınlɔ:] *n* (*wife's mother*) тёща; (*husband's mother*) свекро́вь *f*.
motherly ['mʌðəlı] *adj* матери́нский*.
mother-of-pearl ['mʌðərəv'pə:l] *n* перламу́тр ◆ *adj* перламу́тровый.
Mother's Day *n пра́здник посвящённый матеря́м*.
mother's help *n* ня́ня.
mother-to-be ['mʌðətə'bi:] *n* бу́дущая мать* *f*.
mother tongue *n* родно́й язы́к*.
mothproof ['mɔθpru:f] *adj* (*fabric etc*) молесто́йкий.
motif [məu'ti:f] *n* (*design*) орна́мент; (*theme*) моти́в.
motion ['məuʃən] *n* (*movement, gesture*) движе́ние; (*proposal*) предложе́ние; (*BRIT*: *bowel movement*) стул *no pl* ◆ *vti*: **he ~ed (to) her to sit down** он же́стом предложи́л ей сесть; **to be in ~** быть* *(impf)* в движе́нии; **to set in ~** приводи́ть* (привести́* *perf*) в де́йствие; **to go through the ~s** (*fig*: *formalities*) исполня́ть (испо́лнить *perf*) форма́льности.
motionless ['məuʃənlıs] *adj* неподви́жный* (неподви́жен).
motion picture *n* кинокарти́на.
motivate ['məutıveıt] *vt* (*act, decision*) мотиви́ровать *(impf)*; (*person*) заинтересо́вывать (заинтересова́ть *perf*); **he is ~d by ambition** им дви́жет честолю́бие.
motivated ['məutıveıtıd] *adj* (*enthusiastic*) заинтересо́ванный (заинтересо́ван); (*impelled*): ~ **by envy/greed** движи́мый чу́вством за́висти/жа́дности.
motivation [məutı'veıʃən] *n* (*drive*) целеустремлённость *f*.
motivational research *n* иссле́дование мотива́ций.
motive ['məutıv] *n* моти́в, побужде́ние ◆ *adj*: ~ **power** *or* **force** дви́жущая си́ла; **from the best (of) ~s** из лу́чших побужде́ний.
motley ['mɔtlı] *adj* пёстрый* (пёстр).
motor ['məutəʳ] *n* (*also BRIT*: *inf*) мото́р ◆ *cpd* (*industry, trade*) автомоби́льный.
motorbike ['məutəbaık] *n* мотоци́кл.
motorboat ['məutəbəut] *n* мото́рная ло́дка*.
motorcade ['məutəkeıd] *n* корте́ж автомоби́лей.
motorcar ['məutəkɑ:] *n* (*BRIT*) автомоби́ль *m*.
motorcoach ['məutəkəutʃ] *n* (*BRIT*) авто́бус.
motorcycle ['məutəsaıkl] *n* мотоци́кл.
motorcycle racing *n* мотого́нки* *fpl*.
motorcyclist ['məutəsaıklıst] *n* мотоцикли́ст(ка*).
motoring ['məutərıŋ] (*BRIT*) *n* е́зда на автомоби́ле ◆ *cpd*: ~ **accident** автомоби́льная ава́рия; ~ **offence** наруше́ние пра́вил доро́жного движе́ния; **we went on a ~ holiday in France** мы провели́ о́тпуск путеше́ствуя по Фра́нции на маши́не.
motorist ['məutərıst] *n* автомобили́ст.
motorized ['məutəraızd] *adj*: ~ **transport** автотра́нспорт; ~ **vehicle** автомаши́на; ~ **regiment** моторизо́ванный полк*.
motor oil *n* мото́рное ма́сло.
motor racing *n* (*BRIT*) автого́нки* *fpl*= *автомоби́льные го́нки**.
motor scooter *n* моторо́ллер.
motor vehicle *n* автомаши́на.
motorway ['məutəweı] *n* (*BRIT*) автомагистра́ль *f*, автостра́да.
mottled ['mɔtld] *adj* пятни́стый.
motto ['mɔtəu] (*pl* ~**es**) *n* деви́з.
mould [məuld] (*US* **mold**) *n* (*cast*) фо́рма; (*mildew*) пле́сень *f* ◆ *vt* (*substance*) лепи́ть* (слепи́ть* *or* вы́лепить* *perf*); (*fig*: *opinion, character*) формирова́ть (сформирова́ть *perf*).
moulder ['məuldəʳ] *vi* разлага́ться (разложи́ться* *perf*).
moulding ['məuldıŋ] *n* (*ARCHIT*) лепно́е украше́ние.
mouldy ['məuldı] *adj* (*food*) заплесневе́лый; (*smell*) за́тхлый (затхл).
moult [məult] (*US* **molt**) *vi* линя́ть *(impf)*.
mound [maund] *n* (*hillock*) холм, приго́рок*; (*heap*) ку́ча.
mount [maunt] *n* (*horse*) ло́шадь* *f*; (*for picture, photograph*) паспарту́ *nt ind* ◆ *vt* (*horse*) сади́ться* (сесть* *perf*) на +*acc*; (*exhibition, display*) устра́ивать (устро́ить *perf*); (*jewel*) оправля́ть (оправи́ть* *perf*); (*picture*) обрамля́ть (обрами́ть* *perf*; (*staircase*) всходи́ть* (взойти́* *perf*) по +*dat*; (*attack*) предпринима́ть (предприня́ть* *perf*) ◆ *vi* (*increase*) расти́* *(impf)*; (*get on a horse*) сади́ться* (сесть* *perf*) на ло́шадь; **M~ Ararat/Kilimanjaro** гора́ Арара́т/Килиманджа́ро
▸ **mount up** *vi* (*bills, costs*) нака́пливаться (накопи́ться* *perf*).
mountain ['mauntın] *n* (*also fig*) гора́* ◆ *cpd* го́рный; **to make a ~ out of a molehill** де́лать (сде́лать *perf*) из му́хи слона́.
mountain bike *n велосипе́д, приспосо́бленный для испо́льзования на пересечённой ме́стности*.
mountaineer [mauntı'nıəʳ] *n* альпини́ст(ка*).
mountaineering [mauntı'nıərıŋ] *n* альпини́зм;

* marks translations which have irregular inflections. The Russian-English side of the dictionary gives inflectional information.

to go ~ ходи́ть* *(impf)* в го́ры.
mountainous ['mauntɪnəs] *adj* гори́стый (гори́ст).
mountain range *n* го́рная цепь* *f*.
mountain rescue team *n* горноспаса́тельный отря́д.
mountainside ['mauntɪnsaid] *n* склон горы́.
mounted ['mauntɪd] *adj* (*on horseback*) ко́нный.
Mount Everest *n* гора́ Эвере́ст.
mourn [mɔ:n] *vt* опла́кивать *(impf)* ◆ *vi*: **to ~ for** скорбе́ть *(impf)* по +*dat or* о +*prp*.
mourner ['mɔ:nə^r] *n* прису́тствующий(-ая) *m(f) adj* на похорона́х.
mournful ['mɔ:nful] *adj* (*sad*) ско́рбный* (ско́рбен).
mourning ['mɔ:nɪŋ] *n* тра́ур; **in ~** в тра́уре.
mouse [maus] (*pl* **mice**) *n* (*also fig*, COMPUT) мышь* *f*; **~ mat** *or* **pad** ко́врик для мы́ши.
mousetrap ['maustræp] *n* мышело́вка*.
moussaka [mu'sɑ:kə] *n* мусса́ка (*гре́ческое блю́до*).
mousse [mu:s] *n* мусс.
moustache [məs'tɑ:ʃ] (US **mustache**) *n* усы́ *mpl*.
mousy ['mausɪ] *adj* (*hair*) мыши́ного цве́та.
mouth [mauθ] (*pl* **~s**) *n* рот*; (*of cave, hole*) вход; (*of river*) у́стье*; (*of bottle*) го́рлышко*.
mouthful ['mauθful] *n* (*of food*) кусо́чек*; (*of drink*) глото́к*.
mouth organ *n* губна́я гармо́шка*.
mouthpiece ['mauθpi:s] *n* (*of musical instrument*) мундшту́к*; (*of telephone*) микрофо́н; (*spokesman, newspaper*) глаша́тай.
mouth-to-mouth ['mauθtə'mauθ] *adj*: **~ resuscitation** иску́сственное дыха́ние.
mouthwash ['mauθwɔʃ] *n* жи́дкость *f* для полоска́ния рта.
mouthwatering ['mauθwɔ:tərɪŋ] *adj* о́чень аппети́тный* (аппети́тен).
movable ['mu:vəbl] *adj* подвижно́й; **Easter is a ~ feast** в ра́зные го́ды Па́сха прихо́дится на ра́зные чи́сла.
move [mu:v] *n* (*movement*) движе́ние; (*in game*) ход*; (*change*: *of house*) перее́зд; (: *of job*) перехо́д (*на другу́ю рабо́ту*) ◆ *vt* передвига́ть (передви́нуть *perf*); (*piece*: *in game*) ходи́ть* (пойти́* *perf*) +*instr*; (*part of body*) дви́гать (дви́нуть *perf*) +*instr*; (*person*: *emotionally*) тро́гать (тро́нуть *perf*), растро́гать *(perf)*; (*resolution etc*) предлага́ть (предложи́ть* *perf*) ◆ *vi* дви́гаться (дви́нуться *perf*); (*in game*) де́лать (сде́лать *perf*) ход; (*of things*) двига́ться *(impf)*; (*also*: **~ house**) переезжа́ть (перее́хать* *perf*); **get a ~ on!** поторапливайтесь!; **to ~ to a new job** переходи́ть* (перейти́* *perf*) на но́вую рабо́ту; **to ~ sb to sth** подви́гнуть* *(perf)* кого́-н на что-н; **to ~ towards** дви́гаться (дви́нуться *perf*) к +*dat*
▸ **move about** *vi* (*change position*) передвига́ться (передви́нуться *perf*); (*travel, change residence*) переезжа́ть *(impf)* с ме́ста на ме́сто; (*change job*) переходи́ть* *(impf)* с рабо́ты на рабо́ту
▸ **move along** *vi* проходи́ть* (пройти́* *perf*)
▸ **move around** *vi* = **move about**
▸ **move away** *vi*: **to ~ away (from)** (*leave*) уезжа́ть (уе́хать* *perf*) (из +*gen*); (*step away*) отходи́ть* (отойти́* *perf*) (от +*gen*)
▸ **move back** *vi* переезжа́ть (перее́хать* *perf*) обра́тно
▸ **move forward** *vi* продвига́ться (продви́нуться *perf*)
▸ **move in** *vi* (*police, soldiers*) входи́ть* (войти́* *perf*); **to ~ in(to)** (*house*) въезжа́ть (въе́хать* *perf*) (в +*acc*)
▸ **move off** *vi* отъезжа́ть (отъе́хать* *perf*)
▸ **move on** *vi* (*leave*) направля́ться (напра́виться* *perf*) да́льше ◆ *vt* (*onlookers*) продвига́ть (продви́нуть *perf*)
▸ **move out** *vi* (*of house*) выезжа́ть (вы́ехать* *perf*)
▸ **move over** *vi* (*to make room*) подвига́ться (подви́нуться *perf*)
▸ **move up** *vi* (*be promoted*) продвига́ться (продви́нуться *perf*).
moveable ['mu:vəbl] *adj* = **movable**.
movement ['mu:vmənt] *n* (*action, also* POL, REL) движе́ние; (*between two fixed points*) передвиже́ние; (*transportation*: *of goods etc*) перево́зка*; (*shift*: *in attitude, policy*) сдвиг; (MUS) часть* *f*.
mover ['mu:və^r] *n* (*of proposal*) инициа́тор.
movie ['mu:vɪ] *n* фильм, кинофи́льм; **to go to the ~s** ходи́ть*/идти́* (пойти́* *perf*) в кино́.
movie camera *n* кинока́мера.
moviegoer ['mu:vɪgəuə^r] *n* (US) кинолюби́тель *m*.
moving ['mu:vɪŋ] *adj* (*emotional*) тро́гательный* (тро́гателен); (*mobile*) подви́жный* (подви́жен); (*spirit, force*) дви́жущий ◆ *n* (US) перее́зд.
mow [məu] (*pt* **mowed**, *pp* **mowed** *or* **mown**) *vt* (*grass*) подстрига́ть (подстри́чь* *perf*); (*hay*) коси́ть* (скоси́ть* *perf*)
▸ **mow down** *vt* (*kill*) коси́ть* (скоси́ть* *perf*).
mower ['məuə^r] *n* коси́лка*.
mown [məun] *pp of* **mow**.
Mozambique [məuzəm'bi:k] *n* Мозамби́к.
MP *n abbr* (= *Member of Parliament*) член парла́мента; (= *Military Police*) вое́нная поли́ция; (CANADA: = *Mounted Police*) ко́нная поли́ция.
mpg *n abbr* = *miles per gallon*.
mph *abbr* = *miles per hour*.
MPhil *n abbr* (= *Master of Philosophy*) ≈ маги́стр филосо́фии.
MPS *n abbr* (BRIT) = *Member of the Pharmaceutical Society*.
Mr ['mɪstə^r] (US **Mr.**) *n*: **~ Smith** (*informal*) ми́стер Смит; (*formal*) г-н Смит= *господи́н*

Смит.
MRC *n abbr* (*BRIT*) = *Medical Research Council.*
MRCP *n abbr* (*BRIT*) = *Member of the Royal College of Physicians.*
MRCS *n abbr* (*BRIT*) = *Member of the Royal College of Surgeons.*
Mrs ['mɪsɪz] (*US* **Mrs.**) *n*: ~ **Smith** (*informal*) миссис Смит; (*formal*) г-жа Смит= *госпожа́ Смит.*
Ms [mɪz] (*US* **Ms.**) *n* (= *Miss or Mrs*): ~ **Smith** г-жа Смит= *госпожа́ Смит.*
MS *n abbr* = **multiple sclerosis**; (*US*: = *Master of Science*) ≈ магистр есте́ственных нау́к ◆ *abbr* (*US*: *POST*) = *Mississippi.*
MS. *n abbr* = **manuscript.**
MSA *n abbr* (*US*: = *Master of Science in Agriculture*) ≈ магистр сельскохозя́йственных нау́к.
MSc *n abbr* (= *Master of Science*) ≈ маги́стр есте́ственных нау́к.
MSG *n abbr* = *monosodium glutamate.*
MSP *n abbr* = (*Member of the Scottish Parliament*) член шотла́ндского парла́мента.
MST *abbr* (*US*) = *Mountain Standard Time.*
MSW *n abbr* (*US*: = *Master of Social Work*) ≈ маги́стр социоло́гии.
MT *n abbr* (*COMPUT, LING*: = *machine translation*) МП= *маши́нный перево́д* ◆ *abbr* (*US*: *POST*) = *Montana.*
Mt *abbr* (*GEO*) = **mount.**
MTV *n abbr* (*US*) = *music television.*

KEYWORD

much [mʌtʃ] *adj* (*time, money, effort*) мно́го +*gen*; **we haven't got much time/money** у нас не так мно́го вре́мени/де́нег; **how much money/time do you need?** ско́лько де́нег/вре́мени Вам ну́жно?; **he's spent so much money today** он сего́дня потра́тил сто́лько де́нег; **I have as much money as you (do)** у меня́ сто́лько же де́нег, ско́лько у Вас; **I don't have as much time as you do** у меня́ нет сто́лько вре́мени, ско́лько у Вас
◆ *pron*: **there isn't much to do here** здесь не́чего де́лать; **much is still unclear** мно́гое ещё нея́сно; **much has been gained from our discussions** на́ша диску́ссия да́ла больши́е результа́ты *or* мно́гое; **how much does it cost? – too much** ско́лько э́то сто́ит? – сли́шком до́рого; **how much is it?** почём э́то?
◆ *adv* **1** (*greatly, a great deal*): **thank you very much** большо́е спаси́бо; **we are very much looking forward to your visit** мы о́чень ждём Ва́шего прие́зда; **he is very much a gentleman/politician** он настоя́щий джентельме́н/поли́тик; **however much he tries** ско́лько бы он ни стара́лся; **I try to help as much as possible** *or* **as much as I can** я стара́юсь помога́ть как мо́жно бо́льше *or* ско́лько могу́; **I read as much as ever** я чита́ю сто́лько же, ско́лько пре́жде; **he is as much a member of the family as you** он тако́й же член семьи́, как и Вы
2 (*by far*) намно́го, гора́здо; **I'm much better now** мне намно́го *or* гора́здо лу́чше; **it's much the biggest publishing company in Europe** э́то са́мое кру́пное изда́тельство в Евро́пе
3 (*almost*) почти́; **the view from my window today is much as it was 10 years ago** вид из моего́ окна́ сего́дня сейча́с почти́ тако́й же, как и 10 лет наза́д; **how are you feeling? – much the same** как Вы себя́ чу́вствуете? – всё та́к же.

muck [mʌk] *n* (*dirt*) грязь* *f*; (*manure*) наво́з
▸ **muck about** *vi* (*inf*) валя́ть (*impf*) дурака́; (*tinker*): **to ~ about with** вози́ться* (*impf*) с +*instr*
▸ **muck around** *vi* = **muck about**
▸ **muck in** *vi* (*inf*) впряга́ться (впря́чься* *perf*)
▸ **muck out** *vt* (*stable*) выгреба́ть (вы́грести* *perf*) наво́з из +*gen*
▸ **muck up** *vt* (*inf*) зава́ливать (завали́ть* *perf*).
muckraking ['mʌkreɪkɪŋ] *n* (*fig*: *inf*) копа́ние в гря́зном белье́.
mucky ['mʌkɪ] *adj* гря́зный* (гря́зен).
mucus ['mju:kəs] *n* слизь *f*.
mud [mʌd] *n* грязь* *f*.
muddle ['mʌdl] *n* (*mess*) беспоря́док*; (*mix-up*) неразбери́ха, пу́таница ◆ *vt* (*also*: ~ **up**: *person*) запу́тывать (запу́тать *perf*); (: *things*) переме́шивать (перемеша́ть *perf*); (: *story, names*) пу́тать (перепу́тать *perf*); **to get in(to) a ~** (*while explaining etc*) запу́тываться (запу́таться *perf*); **I'm in a real ~** я соверше́нно запу́тался
▸ **muddle along** *vi* справля́ться (*impf*) ко́е-как
▸ **muddle through** *vi* выкара́бкиваться (вы́карабкаться *perf*).
muddleheaded [mʌdl'hɛdɪd] *adj* бестолко́вый (бестолко́в).
muddy ['mʌdɪ] *adj* гря́зный* (гря́зен).
mud flats *npl* и́листые уча́стки *mpl* (*вскрыва́ющиеся во вре́мя отли́ва*).
mudguard ['mʌdgɑ:d] *n* (*on vehicle*) крыло́*.
mudpack ['mʌdpæk] *n* грязева́я ма́ска*.
mudslinging ['mʌdslɪŋɪŋ] *n* (*fig*) полива́ние гря́зью.
muesli ['mju:zlɪ] *n смесь овся́ных хло́пьев и сухофру́ктов.*
muffin ['mʌfɪn] *n* (*BRIT*) (сдо́бная) бу́лочка; (*US*) кекс.
muffle ['mʌfl] *vt* (*sound*) приглуша́ть (приглуши́ть *perf*); (*against cold*: *also*: ~ **up**)

* marks translations which have irregular inflections. The Russian-English side of the dictionary gives inflectional information.

закýтывать (закýтать *perf*).
muffled ['mʌfld] *adj* (**see vb**) приглушённый (приглушён); (*also*: ~ **up**) закýтанный.
muffler ['mʌflə'] *n* (*US*: *AUT*) глуши́тель *m*; (*scarf*) шарф.
mufti ['mʌftɪ] *n*: **in** ~ в штáтском.
mug [mʌg] *n* крýжка*; (*inf*: *face*) мóрда; (: *fool*) дурáк* (дýра) ◆ *vt* (*assault*) грáбить* (ограбить* *perf*) (*на ýлице*); **it's a ~'s game** (*BRIT*: *inf*) это никчёмное дéло
▸ **mug up** *vt* (*BRIT*: *inf*: *also*: ~ **up on**) зубри́ть* (вы́зубрить *perf*).
mugger ['mʌgə'] *n* ýличный граби́тель *m*.
mugging ['mʌgɪŋ] *n* грабёж* (*на ýлице*).
muggins ['mʌgɪnz] *n* (*inf*) простáк*.
muggy ['mʌgɪ] *adj* дýшный* (дýшен).
mug shot *n* (*inf*) фотогрáфия подозревáемого в преступлéние.
mulatto [mju:'lætəu] (*pl* ~**es**) *n* мулáт(ка*).
mulberry ['mʌlbrɪ] *n* (*fruit*) тýтовая я́года; (*tree*) тýтовое дéрево*, шелкови́ца.
mule [mju:l] *n* (*ZOOL*) мул.
mulled wine [mʌld-] *n* глинтвéйн.
mullioned ['mʌlɪənd] *adj* (*ARCHIT*): ~ **window** окнó сп срéдником.
mull over [mʌl-] *vt* размышля́ть (*impf*) над +*instr*.
multi... [['mʌltɪ]] *prefix* много..., мульти....
multiaccess ['mʌltɪ'æksɛs] *adj* (*COMPUT*) многопóльзовательский*.
multicoloured ['mʌltɪkʌləd] (*US* **multicolored**) *adj* многоцвéтный* (многоцвéтен).
multifarious [mʌltɪ'fɛərɪəs] *adj* многообрáзный* (многообрáзен).
multilateral [mʌltɪ'lætərl] *adj* многосторóнний*.
multilevel ['mʌltɪlɛvl] *adj* (*US*) = **multistorey**.
multimillionaire [mʌltɪmɪljə'nɛə'] *n* мультимиллионéр.
multinational [mʌltɪ'næʃənl] *adj* междунарóдный ◆ *n* междунарóдная корпорáция.
multiple ['mʌltɪpl] *adj* (*injuries*) многочи́сленный; (*interests*) разнообрáзный* (разнообрáзен) ◆ *n* (*MATH*) крáтное числó*; (*BRIT*: *also*: ~ **store**) филиáл сéти (*магази́нов*); ~ **collision** столкновéние нéскольких автомоби́лей.
multiple-choice ['mʌltɪpltʃɔɪs] *adj*: ~ **(exam)** *тест на вы́бор, прáвильного отвéта из нéскольких предлóженных вариáнтов*.
multiple sclerosis *n* рассéянный склерóз.
multiplication [mʌltɪplɪ'keɪʃən] *n* умножéние.
multiplication table *n* табли́ца умножéния.
multiplicity [mʌltɪ'plɪsɪtɪ] *n*: **a ~ of** мнóжество +*gen*.
multiply ['mʌltɪplaɪ] *vt* умножáть (умнóжить *perf*) ◆ *vi* размножáться (размнóжиться *perf*).
multiracial [mʌltɪ'reɪʃl] *adj* многонационáльный* (многонационáлен).
multistorey ['mʌltɪ'stɔ:rɪ] *adj* (*BRIT*) многоэтáжный.
multitude ['mʌltɪtju:d] *n* (*crowd*) мáссы *fpl*; (*large number*): **a ~ of** мнóжество +*gen*.
mum [mʌm] (*BRIT*: *inf*) *n* мáма ◆ *adj*: **to keep ~ about sth** помáлкивать (*impf*) о чём-н; **"mum's the word!"** „молчý!".
mumble ['mʌmbl] *vt* бормотáть* (пробормотáть* *perf*) ◆ *vi* бормотáть (*impf*).
mumbo jumbo ['mʌmbəu-] *n* (*inf*) тарабáрщина.
mummify ['mʌmɪfaɪ] *vt* мумифици́ровать (*impf/perf*).
mummy ['mʌmɪ] *n* (*BRIT*: *inf*: *mother*) мáма; (*embalmed corpse*) мýмия.
mumps [mʌmps] *n* сви́нка.
munch [mʌntʃ] *vti* (*chew*) жевáть (*impf*).
mundane [mʌn'deɪn] *adj* обы́денный (обы́ден).
Munich ['mju:nɪk] *n* Мю́нхен.
municipal [mju:'nɪsɪpl] *adj* муниципáльный.
municipality [mju:nɪsɪ'pælɪtɪ] *n* гóрод*; (*authority*) муниципалитéт.
munitions [mju:'nɪʃənz] *npl* боеприпáсы *mpl*.
mural ['mjuərl] *n* настéнная рóспись *f*, фрéска.
murder ['mə:də'] *n* убíйство (*умы́шленное*) ◆ *vt* (*kill*) убивáть (уби́ть* *perf*) (*умы́шленно*); (*fig*: *inf*) угрóбить* (*perf*); **to commit ~** совершáть (соверши́ть *perf*) убíйство.
murderer ['mə:dərə'] *n* уби́йца *m/f*.
murderess ['mə:dərɪs] *n* уби́йца *m/f*.
murderous ['mə:dərəs] *adj* (*dictator, regime*) кровáвый; (*look*) уби́йственный; (*attack*) смертонóсный* (смертонóсен); ~ **tendencies** склóнность *f* к уби́йству.
murk [mə:k] *n* мгла.
murky ['mə:kɪ] *adj* (*street, night*) мрáчный* (мрáчен); (*water*) мýтный* (мýтен).
murmur ['mə:mə'] *n* (*of voices, waves*) рóпот; (*of wind*) шéлест ◆ *vti* шептáть* (*impf*); **heart ~** шумы́ *mpl* в сéрдце.
MusB(ac) *n abbr* (= *Bachelor of Music*) бакалáвр музыковéдения.
muscle ['mʌsl] *n* (*ANAT*) мы́шца, мýскул; (*fig*: *strength*) си́ла
▸ **muscle in** *vi* пролезáть (пролéзть* *perf*).
Muscovite ['mʌskəvaɪt] *n* москви́ч*(ка*).
muscular ['mʌskjulə'] *adj* (*pain, injury*) мы́шечный; (*person, build*) мýскулистый (мýскулист).
muscular dystrophy *adj* мýскульная дистрофи́я.
MusD(oc) *n abbr* (= *Doctor of Music*) дóктор музыковéдения.
muse [mju:z] *vi* размышля́ть (*impf*) ◆ *n* мýза.
museum [mju:'zɪəm] *n* музéй.
mush [mʌʃ] *n* мéсиво; (*pej*) мáсса.
mushroom ['mʌʃrum] *n* гриб* ◆ *vi* (*fig*) бы́стро разрастáться (разрасти́сь* *perf*).
mushroom cloud *n* áтомный гриб*.
mushy ['mʌʃɪ] *adj* развари́вшийся, как кáша; (*inf*: *pej*: *story, fiction*) слащáвый (слáщав); ~

peas горо́шек.
music ['mju:zɪk] *n* му́зыка; **sheet ~** но́ты *fpl*.
musical ['mju:zɪkl] *adj* (*career, skills*) музыка́льный; (*person*) музыка́льный* (музыка́лен); (*sound, tune*) мелоди́чный* (мелоди́чен) ◆ *n* (*show, film*) мю́зикл.
music(al) box *n* музыка́льная шкату́лка*.
musical chairs *n* ≈ тре́тий* ли́шний* *m adj* (*игра́*).
musical instrument *n* музыка́льный инструме́нт.
music centre *n де́ка с проигрыва́телем и магнитофо́ном*.
music hall *n* (*BRIT*: *vaudeville*) мю́зик-холл.
musician [mju:'zɪʃən] *n* музыка́нт.
music stand *n* пюпи́тр.
musk [mʌsk] *n* му́скус.
musket ['mʌskɪt] *n* мушке́т.
muskrat ['mʌskræt] *n* онда́тра.
musk rose *n* му́скусная ро́за.
Muslim ['mʌzlɪm] *n* мусульма́нин*(-нка*) ◆ *adj* мусульма́нский*.
muslin ['mʌzlɪn] *n* ма́рля.
musquash ['mʌskwɔʃ] *n* = **muskrat**.
mussel ['mʌsl] *n* ми́дия.
must [mʌst] *n* (*necessity*) необходи́мость *f* ◆ *aux vb* (*necessity*): **I ~ do it** я до́лжен э́то сде́лать; (*probability*): **he ~ be there by now** он до́лжен уже́ там быть; **it's (simply) a ~** э́то про́сто необходи́мость; **you ~ come and see me soon** Вы обяза́тельно должны́ ско́ро ко мне зайти́; **why ~ he behave so badly?** отчего́ он так пло́хо себя́ ведёт?; **I ~ have made a mistake** я, должно́ быть, ошиблся.
mustache ['mʌstæʃ] *n* (*US*) = **moustache**.
mustard ['mʌstəd] *n* горчи́ца.
mustard gas *n* ипри́т, горчи́чный газ.
muster ['mʌstə^r] *vt* (*support, energy*) собира́ть (собра́ть* *perf*); (*troops*) набира́ть (набра́ть* *perf*); (*also*: **~ up**: *strength, courage*) набира́ться (набра́ться* *perf*) *+gen*.
mustiness ['mʌstɪnɪs] *n* за́тхлость *f*.
mustn't ['mʌsnt] = **must not**.
musty ['mʌstɪ] *adj* (*smell*) за́тхлый (затхл).
mutant ['mju:tənt] *n* мута́нт.
mutate [mju:'teɪt] *vi* (*BIO*) мути́ровать *(impf)*.
mutation [mju:'teɪʃən] *n* (*BIO*) мута́ция; (*change*) преобразова́ния *ntpl*.
mute [mju:t] *adj* (*silent*) безмо́лвный* (безмо́лвен) ◆ *n* (*MUS*) сурди́нка.
muted ['mju:tɪd] *adj* (*reaction, criticism*) сде́ржанный* (сде́ржан); (*colour, noise*) приглушённый (приглушён); **~ strings** стру́ны под сурди́нкой.
mutilate ['mju:tɪleɪt] *vt* (*person*) уве́чить (изуве́чить *perf*); (*thing*) уро́довать (изуро́довать *perf*).
mutilation [mju:tɪ'leɪʃən] *n* (*injury*) увечье*; (*maiming*) нанесе́ние уве́чья.
mutinous ['mju:tɪnəs] *adj* (*troops, attitude*) мятёжный*.
mutiny ['mju:tɪnɪ] *n* мяте́ж*, бунт ◆ *vi* бунтова́ть *(impf)*.
mutter ['mʌtə^r] *vti* бормота́ть* *(impf)*.
mutton ['mʌtn] *n* бара́нина.
mutual ['mju:tʃuəl] *adj* (*feeling*) взаи́мный* (взаи́мен); (*help*) взаи́мный; (*friend, interest*) о́бщий*; **~ understanding** взаимопонима́ние; **~ aid** взаимопо́мощь *f*.
mutually ['mju:tʃuəlɪ] *adv* взаи́мно; **~ beneficial** взаимовы́годный* (взаимовы́годен).
Muzak® ['mju:zæk] *n бессодержа́тельная лёгкая му́зыка, испо́льзуемая в магази́нах и рестора́нах как фон.*
muzzle ['mʌzl] *n* (*mouth*: *of dog*) мо́рда; (: *of gun*) ду́ло; (*guard*: *for dog*) намо́рдник ◆ *vt* (*dog*) надева́ть (наде́ть* *perf*) намо́рдник на *+acc*; (*fig*: *press, person*) затыка́ть (заткну́ть *perf*) рот *+dat*.
MV *abbr* = *motor vessel*.
MVP *n abbr* (*US*: *SPORT*: = *most valuable player*) *са́мый це́нный игро́к*.
MW *abbr* (*RADIO*) (= **medium wave**) СВ= *сре́дние во́лны*.

KEYWORD

my [maɪ] *adj* **1** (*with objects, possessions*) мой; **this is my house/car** э́то мой дом/моя́ маши́на; **is this my pen or yours?** э́то моя́ ру́чка или ва́ша?
2 (*with parts of the body etc*): **I've washed my hair/cut my finger** я помы́л го́лову/поре́зал па́лец
3 (*referring to subject of sentence*) свой; **I've lost my key** я потеря́л свой ключ.

myopic [maɪ'ɔpɪk] *adj* (*also fig*) близору́кий* (близору́к).
myriad ['mɪrɪəd] *n* мириа́ды *mpl*.
myrrh [mə:^r] *n* ми́рра.

KEYWORD

myself [maɪ'sɛlf] *pron* **1** (*reflexive*): **I've hurt myself** я ушибся; **I consider myself clever** я счита́ю себя́ у́мным
2 (*complement*): **she's the same age as myself** она́ одного́ во́зраста со мной
3 (*after prep*: *+gen*) себя́; (: *+dat, +prp*) себе́; (: *+instr*) собо́й; **I wanted to keep the book for myself** я хоте́л оста́вить кни́гу себе́; **I sometimes talk to myself** иногда́ я сам с собо́й разгова́риваю; **(all) by myself** (*alone*) сам; **I made it all by myself** я всё э́то сде́лал
4 (*emphatic*) сам; **I myself chose the flowers** я сам выбира́л цветы́.

mysterious [mɪs'tɪərɪəs] *adj* та́инственный* (та́инствен).
mysteriously [mɪs'tɪərɪəslɪ] *adv* (*disappear, die*)

* marks translations which have irregular inflections. The Russian-English side of the dictionary gives inflectional information.

тайнственно; (*smile*) зага́дочно.
mystery ['mɪstərɪ] *n* (*strangeness*) та́йна; (*puzzle*) зага́дка* ◆ *cpd* (*tour, guest, voice*) зага́дочный.
mystery story *n* детекти́в.
mystic ['mɪstɪk] *n* ми́стик ◆ *adj* мисти́ческий.
mystical ['mɪstɪkl] *adj* = **mystic.**
mystify ['mɪstɪfaɪ] *vt* (*perplex*) озада́чивать (озада́чить *perf*).
mystique [mɪs'ti:k] *n* ми́стика.
myth [mɪθ] *n* миф.
mythical ['mɪθɪkl] *adj* (*also fig*) мифи́ческий*.
mythological [mɪθə'lɔdʒɪkl] *adj* мифологи́ческий.
mythology [mɪ'θɔlədʒɪ] *n* мифоло́гия.

~N, n~

N, n [ɛn] *n* (*letter*) *14-ая бу́ква англи́йского алфави́та.*
N *abbr* (= **north**) С= *се́вер.*
NA *n abbr* (*US*: = *Narcotics Anonymous*) *о́бщество анони́много излече́ния от наркома́нии*; = *National Academy*.
n/a *abbr* (= *not applicable*) не применя́ется; (*COMM etc*: = *no account*) счёт отсу́тствует.
NAACP *n abbr* (*US*) = *National Association for the Advancement of Colored People.*
NAAFI ['næfɪ] *n abbr* (*BRIT*: = *Navy, Army & Air Force Institute*) Институ́т а́рмии, вое́нно-морско́го и вое́нно-возду́шного фло́та.
NACU *n abbr* (*US*) = *National Association of Colleges and Universities.*
nadir ['neɪdɪə^r] *n* (*ASTRONOMY*) нади́р; (*fig*) ни́зшая то́чка.
nag [næg] *vt* (*scold*) пили́ть* *(impf)* ◆ *vi*: **to ~ at** ныть *(impf)* (из-за *+gen*) ◆ *n* (*pej*: *horse*) кля́ча; (: *person*): **she's an awful ~** она́ жу́ткая зану́да.
nagging ['nægɪŋ] *adj* (*pain*) но́ющий; (*suspicion, doubt*) неотвя́зный.
nail [neɪl] *n* (*on finger etc*) но́готь* *m*; (*metal*) гвоздь* *m* ◆ *vt* (*inf*: *catch*) засту́кивать (засту́кать *perf*); **to ~ sth to sth** прибива́ть (приби́ть* *perf*) что-н к чему́-н; **to ~ sb down to doing** (*inf*) прижима́ть (прижа́ть* *perf*) кого́-н к сте́нке и заста́вить* *+infin*.
nailbrush ['neɪlbrʌʃ] *n* щёточка* для ногте́й.
nailfile ['neɪlfaɪl] *n* пи́лка* (*для ногте́й*).
nail polish *n* лак для ногте́й.
nail polish remover *n* жи́дкость *f* для сня́тия ла́ка.
nail scissors *npl* маникю́рные но́жницы *pl*.
nail varnish *n* (*BRIT*) = **nail polish**.
Nairobi [naɪ'rəubɪ] *n* Найро́би *m ind*.
naive [naɪ'i:v] *adj* наи́вный* (наи́вен).
naiveté [naɪ'i:vteɪ] *n* = **naivety**.
naivety [naɪ'i:vteɪ] *n* наи́вность *f*.
naked ['neɪkɪd] *adj* (*also fig*) го́лый* (гол); (*anger*) не скрыва́емый; **with the ~ eye** невооружённым гла́зом.
nakedness ['neɪkɪdnɪs] *n* нагота́.
NAM *n abbr* (*US*) = *National Association of Manufacturers.*
name [neɪm] *n* (*of person*) и́мя* *nt*; (*of place, object, species*) назва́ние; (*of pet*) кли́чка* ◆ *vt* называ́ть (назва́ть* *perf*); **what's your ~?** как Вас зову́т?; **my ~ is Peter** меня́ зову́т Пи́тер; **what's the ~ of this place?** как называ́ется э́то ме́сто?; **by ~** по и́мени; **in the ~ of** во и́мя *+gen*; **to give one's ~ and address** (*to police etc*) дава́ть* (дать* *perf*) своё и́мя и а́дрес; **to make a ~ for o.s.** создава́ть* (созда́ть* *perf*) себе́ и́мя; **to get (o.s.) a bad ~** зараба́тывать (зарабо́тать *(perf)*) себе́ дурну́ю репута́цию; **to call sb ~s** обзыва́ть (обозва́ть* *perf*) кого́-н.
name-dropping ['neɪmdrɔpɪŋ] *n* упомина́ние изве́стных имён.
nameless ['neɪmlɪs] *adj* (*unknown*) безымя́нный* (безымя́нен); (*anonymous*) неизве́стный* (неизве́стен).
namely ['neɪmlɪ] *adv* а и́менно.
nameplate ['neɪmpleɪt] *n* табли́чка* (*с и́менем*).
namesake ['neɪmseɪk] *n* тёзка* *m/f*.
Namibia [nə'mɪbɪə] *n* Нами́бия.
nan bread [nɑ:n-] *n инди́йский* хлеб в фо́рме лепёшки.*
nanny ['nænɪ] *n* ня́ня.
nanny goat *n* коза́*.
nap [næp] *n* коро́ткий* сон; (*of fabric*) ворс ◆ *vi*: **he was caught ~ping** (*fig*) его́ заста́ли врас-плóх; **to have** *or* **take a ~** вздремну́ть *(perf)*.
NAPA *n abbr* (*US*) = *National Association of Performing Artists.*
napalm ['neɪpɑ:m] *n* напа́лм.
nape [neɪp] *n*: **~ of the neck** за́дняя часть *f* ше́и.
napkin ['næpkɪn] *n* (*also*: **table ~**) салфе́тка*.
Naples ['neɪplz] *n* Неа́поль *m*.
Napoleonic [nəpəulɪ'ɔnɪk] *adj* наполео́новский.
nappy ['næpɪ] *n* (*BRIT*) подгу́зник.
nappy liner *n* (*BRIT*) *прокла́дка для подгу́зника.*
nappy rash *n* (*BRIT*) потни́ца.
narcissi [nɑ:'sɪsaɪ] *npl of* **narcissus**.
narcissistic [nɑ:sɪ'sɪstɪk] *adj* само-влюблённый.

narcissus [nɑːˈsɪsəs] (*pl* **narcissi**) *n* (*BOT*) нарци́сс.
narcotic [nɑːˈkɔtɪk] *adj* наркоти́ческий ◆ *n* (*MED*) снотво́рное *nt adj*; **~s** *npl* (*drugs*) нарко́тики *mpl*.
nark [nɑːk] *vt* (*BRIT*: *inf*) раздража́ть (раздражи́ть *perf*).
narrate [nəˈreɪt] *vt* (*story, novel*) расска́зывать (рассказа́ть* *perf*); **to ~ a film/programme** чита́ть *(impf)* текст фи́льма/переда́чи.
narration [nəˈreɪʃən] *n* повествова́ние.
narrative [ˈnærətɪv] *n* исто́рия.
narrator [nəˈreɪtə^r] *n* (*in book*) расска́зчик(-ица); (*in film*) ди́ктор.
narrow [ˈnærəu] *adj* (*also fig*) у́зкий* (у́зок); (*majority, advantage*) незначи́тельный* (незначи́телен) ◆ *vi* (*road*) сужа́ться (су́зиться* *perf*); (*gap, difference*) уменьша́ться (уме́ньшиться *perf*) ◆ *vt*: **to ~ sth down to** своди́ть* (свести́* *perf*) что-н к +*dat*; **to have a ~ escape** едва́ спасти́сь* *(perf)*.
narrow-gauge [ˈnærəugeɪdʒ] *adj* (*RAIL*) узкоколе́йный.
narrowly [ˈnærəulɪ] *adv* (*miss*) чуть не; (*interpret*) у́зко; **he only ~ avoided injury/defeat** он чуть не покале́чился/проигра́л; **he only ~ missed the target** он почти́ попа́л в цель.
narrow-minded [nærəuˈmaɪndɪd] *adj* ограни́ченный (ограни́чен).
narrowness [ˈnærəunɪs] *n* у́зость *f*.
NAS *n abbr* (*US*) = *National Academy of Sciences*.
NASA [ˈnæsə] *n abbr* (*US*: = *National Aeronautics and Space Administration*) НАСА.
nasal [ˈneɪzl] *adj* (*ANAT*) носово́й; (*tone, voice*) гнуса́вый.
Nassau [ˈnæsɔː] *n* Насса́у *m ind*.
nastily [ˈnɑːstɪlɪ] *adv* зло́бно.
nastiness [ˈnɑːstɪnɪs] *n* (*unpleasantness*) проти́вность *f*; (*spitefulness*) зло́бность *f*.
nasturtium [nəsˈtəːʃəm] *n* насту́рция.
nasty [ˈnɑːstɪ] *adj* (*unpleasant*) проти́вный* (проти́вен); (*malicious*) зло́бный* (зло́бен); (*situation, wound*) скве́рный* (скве́рен); **to say ~ things about sb** говори́ть *(impf)* га́дости о ком-н; **to turn ~** (*situation*) принима́ть (приня́ть* *perf*) скверный оборо́т; (*weather*) де́латься (сде́латься *perf*) скве́рным; (*person*) озлобля́ться (озло́биться* *perf*); **it's a ~ business** э́то ме́рзкое де́ло.
NAS/UWT *n abbr* (*BRIT*) = *National Association of Schoolmasters/Union of Women Teachers*.
nation [ˈneɪʃən] *n* (*POL*) на́ция; (*people*) наро́д; (*state*) страна́, госуда́рство.
national [ˈnæʃənl] *adj* национа́льный ◆ *n* граждани́н*(-да́нка*).
national anthem *n* госуда́рственный гимн.
national curriculum *n* (*BRIT*) всео́бщая програ́мма (обуче́ния) (*в шко́лах*).
national debt *n* госуда́рственный долг*.
national dress *n* национа́льная оде́жда.
National Guard *n* (*US*) Национа́льная гва́рдия.
National Health Service *n* (*BRIT*) Госуда́рственная слу́жба здравоохране́ния.
National Insurance *n* (*BRIT*) госуда́рственное страхова́ние.
nationalism [ˈnæʃnəlɪzəm] *n* национали́зм.
nationalist [ˈnæʃnəlɪst] *adj* националисти́ческий ◆ *n* национали́ст(ка*).
nationality [næʃəˈnælɪtɪ] *n* (*status*) гражда́нство; (*ethnic group*) наро́дность *f*.
nationalization [næʃnəlaɪˈzeɪʃən] *n* национализа́ция.
nationalize [ˈnæʃnəlaɪz] *vt* национализи́ровать *(impf/perf)*.
nationalized industry [ˈnæʃnəlaɪzd-] *n* национализи́рованная промы́шленность *f*.
nationally [ˈnæʃnəlɪ] *adv* (*nationwide*) в национа́льном всей страны́.
national park *n* национа́льный па́рк.
national press *n* национа́льная пре́сса.
National Security Council *n* (*US*) Сове́т национа́льной безопа́сности.
national service *n* (*MIL*: *esp BRIT*) во́инская пови́нность *f*.
National Trust *n* (*BRIT*) *организа́ция, занима́ющаяся охра́ной архитекту́рных па́мятников и приро́дных запове́дников*.
nationwide [ˈneɪʃənwaɪd] *adj* общенаро́дный ◆ *adv* по всей стране́.
native [ˈneɪtɪv] *n* (*local inhabitant*) ме́стный(-ая) жи́тель(ница) *m(f)* ◆ *adj* (*indigenous*) коренно́й, иско́нный; (*of one's birth*) родно́й; (*innate*) врождённый; **a ~ of Russia** уроже́нец(-нка*) Росси́и; **a ~ speaker of Russian** носи́тель(ница) *m(f)* ру́сского языка́.
Native American *n потомок коренно́го населе́ния Се́веро-Америка́нского контине́нта*.
native language *n* родно́й язы́к*.
Nativity [nəˈtɪvɪtɪ] *n*: **the ~** Рождество́ Христо́во.
nativity play *n* Рожде́ственская мисте́рия (*обы́чно разы́грываемая детьми́*).
NATO [ˈneɪtəu] *n abbr* (= *North Atlantic Treaty Organization*) НАТО.
natter [ˈnætə^r] (*BRIT*) *vi* трепа́ться* *(impf)* ◆ *n*: **to have a ~** трепа́ться* (потрепа́ться* *perf*).
natural [ˈnætʃrəl] *adj* (*behaviour*) есте́ственный (есте́ствен); (*aptitude, materials*) приро́дный; (*foods*) натура́льный; (*disaster*) стихи́йный; **to die of ~ causes** умира́ть (умере́ть* *perf*) есте́ственной сме́ртью.
natural childbirth *n* есте́ственные ро́ды *pl*.
natural gas *n* приро́дный газ.
natural history *n* естествозна́ние.
naturalist [ˈnætʃrəlɪst] *n* натурали́ст.
naturalize [ˈnætʃrəlaɪz] *vt*: **to become ~d** (*person*) получа́ть (получи́ть* *perf*) гражда́нство; (*plant*) акклиматизи́роваться

(impf/perf).
naturally ['nætʃrəlɪ] *adv* естéственно; (*innately*) от прирóды; (*in nature*) в прирóде; **~, I refused** естéственно, я отказáлся.
naturalness ['nætʃrəlnɪs] *n* естéственность *f*.
natural resources *npl* прирóдные ресýрсы *mpl*.
natural selection *n* (*BIO*) естественный отбóр.
natural wastage *n* (*INDUSTRY*) естéственная ýбыль* *f (рабóчей сúлы)*.
nature ['neɪtʃə'] *n* (*also:* **N~**) прирóда; (*character*) натýра; (*sort*) харáктер; **by ~** (*person*) по натýре; (*event, thing*) по прирóде; **documents of a confidential ~** докумéнты конфиденциáльного харáктера.
-natured ['neɪtʃəd] *suffix*: **ill-~** злóбный по натýре.
nature reserve *n* (*BRIT*) заповéдник.
nature trail *n размéченная трóпа, проходя́щая чéрез сéльскую мéстность, заповéдник итп.*
naturist ['neɪtʃərɪst] *n* нудúст(ка*).
naught [nɔːt] *n* = **nought**.
naughtiness ['nɔːtɪnɪs] *n* (*see adj*) непослушáние, озорствó; пикáнтность *f*.
naughty ['nɔːtɪ] *adj* (*child*) непослýшный* (непослýшен), озорнóй; (*story, film*) пикáнтный* (пикáнтен).
nausea ['nɔːsɪə] *n* тошнотá.
nauseate ['nɔːsɪeɪt] *vt* (*also fig*) вызывáть (вы́звать* *perf*) тошнотý в *+prp or* у *+gen*.
nauseating ['nɔːsɪeɪtɪŋ] *adj* (*also fig*) тошнотвóрный* (тошнотвóрен).
nauseous ['nɔːsɪəs] *adj* тошнотвóрный* (тошнотвóрен); **he's feeling ~** егó тошнúт.
nautical ['nɔːtɪkl] *adj* морскóй.
naval ['neɪvl] *adj* воéнно-морскóй; (*battle, power*) морскóй.
naval officer *n* морскóй офицéр.
nave [neɪv] *n* неф.
navel ['neɪvl] *n* пупóк*.
navigable ['nævɪgəbl] *adj* судохóдный* (судохóден).
navigate ['nævɪgeɪt] *vt* (*NAUT, AVIAT*) управля́ть *(impf) +instr* ◆ *vi* определя́ть (определúть *perf*) маршрýт; **to ~ a ship through/around** вестú* (провестú* *perf*) корáбль чéрез *+acc*/вокрýг *+gen*.
navigation [nævɪ'geɪʃən] *n* (*science*) навигáция; (*action*): **~ (of)** управлéние (*+instr*).
navigator ['nævɪgeɪtə'] *n* штýрман.
navvy ['nævɪ] *n* (*BRIT*) чернорабóчий* *m adj*.
navy ['neɪvɪ] *n* воéнно-морскóй флот; **Department of the N~** (*US*) ≈ Министéрство воéнно-морскóго флóта.
navy(-blue) ['neɪvɪ('bluː)] *adj* тёмно-сúний*.
Nazareth ['næzərɪθ] *n* Назарéт.
Nazi ['nɑːtsɪ] *n* нацúст(ка*).
NB *abbr* = *nota bene*; (*note well!*) NB, нотабéне; (*CANADA*) = *New Brunswick*.
NBA *n abbr* (*US*) = *National Basketball Association*; *National Boxing Association*.
NBC *n abbr* (*US*) = *National Broadcasting Company*.
NBS *n abbr* (*US*) = *National Bureau of Standards*.
NC *abbr* (*COMM etc: = no charge*) бесплáтно; (*US: POST*) = *North Carolina*.
NCC *n abbr* (*BRIT*) = *Nature Conservancy Council*; (*US*) *National Council of Churches*.
NCCL *n abbr* (*BRIT: = National Council for Civil Liberties*) Национáльный совéт по граждáнским правáм.
NCO *n abbr* (*MIL*) = **noncommissioned officer**.
ND *abbr* (*US: POST*) = *North Dakota*.
NE *abbr* (*US: POST*) = *New England*; *Nebraska*.
NEA *n abbr* (*US*) = *National Education Association*.
neap [niːp] *n* (*also:* **~ tide**) квадратýрный прилúв.
Neapolitan [nɪə'pɔlɪtən] *adj* неаполитáнский* ◆ *n* неаполитáнец(-нка*).
near [nɪə'] *adj* блúзкий* (блúзок) ◆ *adv* блúзко ◆ *prep* (*also:* **~ to**: *space*) вóзле *+gen*, óколо *+gen*; (: *time*) к *+dat*, óколо *+gen* ◆ *vt* приближáться (приблúзиться* *perf*) к *+dat*; **~ here/there** недалекó отсю́да/оттýда; **£25,000 or ~est offer** (*BRIT*) ценá £25.000 úли по договорённости; **in the ~ future** в ближáйшем бýдущем; **~er (to) the time** óколо полóженной дáты; **to come ~ (to)** (*also fig*) приближáться (приблúзиться* *perf*) (к *+dat*); **he was ~ to despair/victory** он был блúзок к отчáянию/побéде; **the building is ~ing completion** строúтельство приближáется к завершéнию.
nearby [nɪə'baɪ] *adj* близлежáщий ◆ *adv* поблúзости.
Near East *n*: **the ~ ~** Блúжний* Востóк.
nearer ['nɪərə'] *adj, adv* блúже.
nearly ['nɪəlɪ] *adv* почтú; **I ~ fell** я чуть (бы́ло) не упáл; **she was ~ crying** онá почтú плáкала; **it's not ~ as easy as it looks** э́то отню́дь не так прóсто, как кáжется; **the house is not ~ big enough** дом совсéм мал.
near miss *n* (*failed attempt*): **that was a ~ ~!** промахнýлся!; **we had a ~ ~ in the car today** мы сегóдня чуть не попáли в авáрию.
nearness ['nɪənɪs] *n* блúзость *f*.
nearside ['nɪəsaɪd] *n* (*AUT: in Britain*) лéвая сторонá; (: *in US, Europe etc*) прáвая сторонá.
near-sighted [nɪə'saɪtɪd] *adj* близорýкий* (близорýк).
neat [niːt] *adj* (*person, place*) опря́тный* (опря́тен); (*work*) аккурáтный* (аккурáтен);

* marks translations which have irregular inflections. The Russian-English side of the dictionary gives inflectional information.

(*clear*: *categories*) чёткий* (чёток); (*esp US*: *inf*) клáссный* (клáссен); (*alcohol*) неразбáвленный.
neatly ['ni:tlɪ] *adv* (*dress*) опря́тно; (*work*) аккурáтно; (*sum up*) чётко.
neatness ['ni:tnɪs] *n* (*see adv*) опря́тность *f*; аккурáтность *f*; чёткость *f*.
nebulous ['nɛbjuləs] *adj* (*concept, proposal*) тумáнный* (тумáнен).
necessarily ['nɛsɪsrɪlɪ] *adv* неизбéжно; **not ~** не обязáтельно.
necessary ['nɛsɪsrɪ] *adj* необходи́мый (необходи́м); (*inevitable*) обязáтельный, неизбéжный; **if ~** éсли необходи́мо; **it's not ~** это не обязáтельно; **it is ~ to/that ...** необходи́мо *+infin*/чтóбы ....
necessitate [nɪ'sɛsɪteɪt] *vt* обуслóвливать (обуслóвить* *perf*).
necessity [nɪ'sɛsɪtɪ] *n* необходи́мость *f*; **necessities** *npl* (*essentials*) предмéты *mpl* пéрвой необходи́мости; **in case of ~** в слу́чае необходи́мости.
neck [nɛk] *n* (*ANAT*) шéя; (*of garment*) вóрот; (*of bottle*) гóрлышко* ◆ *vi* (*inf*) миловáться (*impf*); **~ and ~** врóвень; **to stick one's ~ out** (*inf*) лезть* (*impf*) на рожóн; **to risk one's ~** (*inf*) рисковáть (рискну́ть *perf*) головóй.
necklace ['nɛklɪs] *n* ожерéлье.
neckline ['nɛklaɪn] *n* вы́рез.
necktie ['nɛktaɪ] *n* (*US*) гáлстук.
nectar ['nɛktəʳ] *n* нектáр.
nectarine ['nɛktərɪn] *n* нектари́н.
NEDC *n abbr* (*BRIT*: = *National Economic Development Council*) Национáльный совéт экономи́ческого разви́тия.
Neddy ['nɛdɪ] *n abbr* (*BRIT*: *inf*) = **NEDC**.
née [neɪ] *adj*: **~ Scott** урождённая Скотт.
need [ni:d] *n* (*thing needed*) потрéбность *f*; (*deprivation*) нуждá; (*necessity*): **~ (for)** нуждá (в *+prp*) ◆ *vt*: **I ~ time/money** мне ну́жно врéмя/нужны́ дéньги; **there's no ~ to worry** нéзачем волновáться; **to be in ~ of, have ~ of** нуждáться (*impf*) в *+prp*; **in case of ~** в слу́чае необходи́мости; **the ~s of industry** потрéбности промы́шленности; **£10 will meet my immediate ~s** £10 удовлетворя́т мои́ ну́жды на дáнный момéнт; **I ~ to see him** мне нáдо *or* ну́жно с ним уви́деться; **you don't ~ to leave yet** Вам ещё не порá идти́; **a signature is ~ed** трéбуется пóдпись.
needle ['ni:dl] *n* иглá, игóлка*; (*for knitting*) спи́ца ◆ *vt* (*fig*: *inf*) подкáлывать (подколóть *perf*).
needlecord ['ni:dlkɔ:d] *n* (*BRIT*) тóнкий* вельвéт.
needless ['ni:dlɪs] *adj* изли́шний* (изли́шен); **~ to say** самó собóй разумéется.
needlessly ['ni:dlɪslɪ] *adv* напрáсно.
needlework ['ni:dlwə:k] *n* рукодéлие.
needn't ['ni:dnt] = **need not**; *see* **need**.
needy ['ni:dɪ] *adj* нуждáющийся; **the ~** *npl* нуждáющиеся *pl adj*.
negation [nɪ'geɪʃən] *n* отрицáние.
negative ['nɛgətɪv] *adj* (*also ELEC*) отрицáтельный ◆ *n* (*LING*) отрицáние; (*PHOT*) негати́в; **to answer in the ~** давáть* (дать* *perf*) отрицáтельный отвéт.
negative cash flow *n* отрицáтельный потóк нали́чности.
negative equity *n* (*COMM*) отрицáтельная *or* негати́вная мáржа.
neglect [nɪ'glɛkt] *vt* (*child, work*) забрáсывать (забрóсить* *perf*); (*garden, area, health*) запускáть (запусти́ть* *perf*); (*duty*) пренебрегáть (пренебрéчь* *perf*) ◆ *n*: **~ (of)** невнимáние (к *+dat*); (*duty*) пренебрежéние (*+instr*); **in a state of ~** в запустéнии.
neglected [nɪ'glɛktɪd] *adj* (*animal, child*) забрóшенный (забрóшен).
neglectful [nɪ'glɛktful] *adj* небрéжный* (небрéжен); **to be ~ of sb** относи́ться* (*impf*) к кому́-н без внимáния; **to be ~ of sth** пренебрегáть (пренебрéчь* *perf*) чем-н.
negligee ['nɛglɪʒeɪ] *n* пеньюáр.
negligence ['nɛglɪdʒəns] *n* халáтность *f*.
negligent ['nɛglɪdʒənt] *adj* халáтный* (халáтен); **to be ~ in** халáтно относи́ться* (*impf*) к *+dat*.
negligently ['nɛglɪdʒəntlɪ] *adv* (*irresponsibly*) халáтно; (*offhandedly*) небрéжно.
negligible ['nɛglɪdʒɪbl] *adj* ничтóжный* (ничтóжен).
negotiable [nɪ'gəuʃɪəbl] *adj*: **the price/contract is ~** цéну/контрáкт мóжно обсуди́ть; (*road*) проходи́мый (проходи́м); (*cheque, assets*): **~/not negotiable** с прáвом/без прáва передáчи.
negotiate [nɪ'gəuʃɪeɪt] *vt* (*treaty, transaction*) заключáть (заключи́ть *perf*); (*obstacle*) преодолевáть (преодолéть *perf*); (*bend in road*) огибáть (обогну́ть *perf*) ◆ *vi*: **to ~ (with sb for sth)** вести́* (*impf*) переговóры (с кем-н о чём-н).
negotiating table [nɪ'gəuʃɪeɪtɪŋ-] *n* стол* переговóров.
negotiation [nɪgəuʃɪ'eɪʃən] *n* (*see vb*) заключéние; преодолéние; переговóры *mpl*; **to enter into ~s with sb** вступáть (вступи́ть* *perf*) в переговóры с кем-н.
negotiator [nɪ'gəuʃɪeɪtəʳ] *n* учáстник переговóров.
Negress ['ni:grɪs] *n* негритя́нка*.
Negro ['ni:grəu] (*pl* **~es**) *adj* негритя́нский* ◆ *n* (*old-fashioned*) негр(итя́нка*); (*pej*) чёрный(-ая) *m(f) adj*.
neigh [neɪ] *vi* ржать* (*impf*).
neighbor *etc* (*US*) = **neighbour** *etc*.
neighbour ['neɪbəʳ] (*US* **neighbor**) *n* сосéд*(ка*).
neighbourhood ['neɪbəhud] *n* (*place*) райóн; (*people*) сосéди *mpl*.
neighbourhood watch *n система, при которой соседи договариваются смотреть*

за домами друг друга.
neighbouring ['neɪbərɪŋ] *adj* сосéдний*.
neighbourly ['neɪbəlɪ] *adj* добрососéдский.
neither ['naɪðə^r] *adj* ни тот, ни другóй ◆ *conj*: **I didn't move and ~ did John** ни я, ни Джон не двúнулись с мéста ◆ *pron*: **~ of them came** ни одúн из них не пришёл, ни тот, ни другóй не пришлú; **~ version is true** ни та, ни другáя вéрсия не вернá; **~ ... nor ...** ни ..., ни ...; **~ good nor bad** ни хорошó, ни плóхо.
neo... ['ni:əu] *prefix* нео....
neolithic [ni:əu'lɪθɪk] *adj* неолитúческий.
neologism [nɪ'ɔlədʒɪzəm] *n* неологúзм.
neon ['ni:ɔn] *n* неóн.
neon light *n* неóновый свет.
neon sign *n* неóновая вы́веска.
Nepal [nɪ'pɔ:l] *n* Непáл.
Nepalese [nɛpə'li:z] *adj* непáльский*.
nephew ['nɛvju:] *n* племя́нник.
nepotism ['nɛpətɪzəm] *n* непотúзм, кумовствó.
Neptune ['nɛptju:n] *n* (*planet*) Нептýн.
nerd [nə:d] *n* (*inf*) придýрок*.
nerve [nə:v] *n* (*ANAT*) нерв; (*courage*) вы́держка; (*impudence*) нáглость *f*; **to have a fit of ~s** перенéрвничать *(perf)*; **he gets on my ~s** он дéйствует мне на нéрвы; **she lost her ~** у неё сдáли нéрвы.
nerve centre *n* (*ANAT*) нéрвный центр; (*fig*) мозговóй центр.
nerve gas *n* нéрвный газ.
nerve-racking ['nə:vrækɪŋ] *adj* (*period*) нéрвный; (*situation*) нервóзный* (нервóзен).
nervous ['nə:vəs] *adj* нéрвный* (нéрвен); (*ANAT*) нéрвный; **to be** *or* **feel ~** нéрвничать *(impf)*.
nervous breakdown *n* нéрвный срыв.
nervously ['nə:vəslɪ] *adv* нéрвно.
nervousness ['nə:vəsnɪs] *n* нéрвность *f*.
nervous wreck *n* (*inf*) комóк нéрвов.
nervy ['nə:vɪ] *n* нéрвный*.
nest [nɛst] *n* гнездó* ◆ *vi* гнездúться* *(impf)*; **~ of tables** комплéкт стóликов (*вставля́ющихся одúн в другóй*).
nest egg *n* занáчка*.
nestle ['nɛsl] *vi* (*snuggle*) приютúться *(perf)*.
nestling ['nɛstlɪŋ] *n* птенéц*.
Net [nɛt] *n* (*inf*): **the ~** Сеть *f*.
net [nɛt] *n* (*fabric*) тюль *m*; (*netting, also SPORT*) сéтка*; (*for fish, game: also fig*) сеть* *f* ◆ *adj* (*COMM*) чúстый ◆ *vt* (*fish*) ловúть* (поймáть* *perf*) в сеть; (*profit*) приносúть* (принестú* *perf*); (*deal, sale*) проворáчивать (провернýть *perf*); **~ of tax** пóсле вы́чета налóгов; **~ assets** нéтто-актúвы; **he earns ten thousand ~ per year** он зарабáтывает чúстыми дéсять ты́сяч в год.
netball ['nɛtbɔ:l] *n* нетбóл.
net curtains *npl* тю́левые занавéски *fpl*.
Netherlands ['nɛðələndz] *npl*: **the ~** Нидерлáнды *pl*.
nett [nɛt] *adj* = **net**.
netting ['nɛtɪŋ] *n* сéтка*.
nettle ['nɛtl] *n* крапúва; **to grasp the ~** (*fig*) без промедлéния взя́ться *(perf)* за дéло.
network ['nɛtwə:k] *n* сеть* *f* ◆ *vt* (*RADIO, TV*) транслúровать *(impf/perf)* по различным канáлам; (*COMPUT*) подключáть (подключúть* *perf*) к систéме.
neuralgia [njuə'rældʒə] *n* невралгúя.
neurosis [njuə'rəusɪs] *n* неврóз.
neurological [njuərə'lɔdʒɪkl] *n* неврологúческий.
neurotic [njuə'rɔtɪk] *adj* неврастенúчный* (неврастенúчен) ◆ *n* неврастéник.
neuter ['nju:tə^r] *vt* (*cat etc*) кастрúровать *(impf/perf)* ◆ *adj* (*LING*): **~ noun** существúтельное *nt adj* срéднего рóда.
neutral ['nju:trəl] *adj* нейтрáльный* (нейтрáлен) ◆ *n* (*AUT*) холостóй ход*.
neutrality [nju:'trælɪtɪ] *n* нейтралитéт.
neutralize ['nju:trəlaɪz] *vt* нейтрализовáть *(impf/perf)*.
neutron ['nju:trɔn] *n* нейтрóн.
neutron bomb *n* нейтрóнная бóмба.
Neva ['ni:və] *n*: **the ~** Невá.
never ['nɛvə^r] *adv* никогдá; **~ in my life** никогдá в жúзни; **~ again** бóльше никогдá; **I ~ went** я не ходúл; *see also* **mind**.
never-ending [nɛvər'ɛndɪŋ] *adj* нескончáемый (нескончáем).
nevertheless [nɛvəðə'lɛs] *adv* тем не мéнее.
new [nju:] *adj* (*brand new*) нóвый* (нов); (*recent*) недáвний*; **I'm ~ to this business** я в э́том дéле новичóк; **as good as ~** совсéм как нóвый.
New Age *adj* (*PHILOSOPHY*) *философская систéма, базúрующаяся на вéре в альтернатúвную медицúну, астролóгию итп*; **~ ~ (music)** *тип мýзыки, включáющий элемéнты джáза, нарóдной и классúческой мýзыки.*
newborn ['nju:bɔ:n] *adj* новорождённый.
newcomer ['nju:kʌmə^r] *n* новичóк*.
newfangled ['nju:fæŋgld] *adj* (*pej*) новомóдный* (новомóден).
new-found ['nju:faund] *adj* недáвно обретённый.
Newfoundland ['nju:fənlənd] *n* Нью-фáундлéнд.
New Guinea *n* Нóвая Гвинéя.
newly ['nju:lɪ] *adv* недáвно.
newlyweds ['nju:lɪwɛdz] *npl* новобрáчные *pl*.
new moon *n* молодóй мéсяц; (*time*) новолýние.
newness ['nju:nɪs] *n* новизнá.

* marks translations which have irregular inflections. The Russian-English side of the dictionary gives inflectional information.

New Orleans [-'ɔ:li:ənz] *n* Но́вый Орлеа́н.
news [nju:z] *n* (*good, bad*) но́вость* *f*, изве́стие; **a piece of ~** но́вость*; **the ~** (*RADIO, TV*) но́вости *fpl*; **what's the ~?** каки́е но́вости?; **financial ~** фина́нсовые но́вости*.
news agency *n* информацио́нное аге́нтство.
newsagent ['nju:zeɪdʒənt] *n* (*BRIT: also:* **~'s**) ≈ газе́тный кио́ск; (*person*) владе́лец*(-лица) газе́тного кио́ска.
news bulletin *n* сво́дка* новосте́й.
newscaster ['nju:zkɑ:stə^r] *n* ди́ктор (*програ́ммы новосте́й*).
newsdealer ['nju:zdi:lə^r] *n* (*US*) = **newsagent**.
newsflash ['nju:zflæʃ] *n* э́кстренное сообще́ние.
newsletter ['nju:zlɛtə^r] *n* информацио́нный бюллете́нь *m*.
newspaper ['nju:zpeɪpə^r] *n* газе́та; **daily/weekly ~** ежедне́вная/еженеде́льная газе́та.
newsprint ['nju:zprɪnt] *n* (*paper*) газе́тная бума́га.
newsreader ['nju:zri:də^r] *n* = **newscaster**.
newsreel ['nju:zri:l] *n* информацио́нный киножурна́л.
newsroom ['nju:zru:m] *n* (*PRESS*) отде́л новосте́й; (*RADIO, TV*) сту́дия новосте́й.
newsstand ['nju:zstænd] *n* газе́тный кио́ск.
newsworthy ['nju:zwə:ðɪ] *adj* досто́йный* (досто́ен) интере́са.
newt [nju:t] *n* трито́н.
new town *n* но́вый го́род*.
New Year *n* Но́вый год*; **Happy ~ ~!** С Но́вым го́дом!; **to wish sb a Happy ~ ~** (*for the festive season*) поздравля́ть (поздра́вить* *perf*) кого́-н с Но́вым го́дом; (*for the coming year*) жела́ть (пожела́ть *perf*) кому́-н счастли́вого но́вого го́да.
New Year's Day *n* пе́рвое января́.
New Year's Eve *n* кану́н Но́вого го́да.
New York [-'jɔ:k] *n* Нью-Йо́рк.
New Zealand [-'zi:lənd] *n* Но́вая Зела́ндия ◆ *adj* новозела́ндский*.
New Zealander [-'zi:ləndə^r] *n* новозела́ндец*(-дка*).
next [nɛkst] *adj* сле́дующий*; (*neighbouring*) сосе́дний* ◆ *adv* пото́м, зате́м ◆ *prep*: **~ to** ря́дом с *+instr*, во́зле *+gen*; **~ time** в сле́дующий* раз; **the ~ day** на сле́дующий* день; **the ~ week** на сле́дующей неде́ле; **the week after ~** че́рез неде́лю; **~ year** в бу́дущем *or* сле́дующем году́; **in the ~ 15 minutes** в ближа́йшие 15 мину́т; **~ to nothing** почти́ ничего́; **~ please!** сле́дующий, пожа́луйста!; **who's ~?** кто сле́дующий?; **"turn to the ~ page"** "переверни́те страни́цу"; **when do we meet ~?** когда́ мы сно́ва встре́тимся?
next door *adv* по сосе́дству, ря́дом ◆ *adj* (*flat, house*) сосе́дний*; **~-~ neighbour** ближа́йший* сосе́д*.
next of kin *n* ближа́йший* ро́дственник.

NF *n abbr* (*BRIT: POL:* = *National Front*) НФ= *Национа́льный фронт* ◆ *abbr* (*CANADA*) = *Newfoundland*.
NFL *n abbr* (*US*) = *National Football League*.
NG *abbr* (*US*) = **National Guard**.
NGO *n abbr* (*US:* = *non-governmental organization*) неправи́тельственная организа́ция.
NH *abbr* (*US: POST*) = *New Hampshire*.
NHL *n abbr* (*US:* = *National Hockey League*) НХЛ= *Национа́льная хокке́йная ли́га*.
NHS *n abbr* (*BRIT*) = **National Health Service**.
NI *abbr* = **Northern Ireland**; (*BRIT*) = **National Insurance**.
Niagara Falls [naɪ'ægərə-] *npl*: **the ~ ~** Ниага́рский водопа́д *msg*.
nib [nɪb] *n* перо́*.
nibble ['nɪbl] *vt* надку́сывать (надкуси́ть* *perf*) ◆ *vi*: **to ~ at** (*mice*) грызть* *(impf)*; (*at grass*) щипа́ть* *(impf)*.
NICAM *n abbr* = *near-instantaneous companding system*: **~ stereo** *систе́ма стереозвуча́ния*.
Nicaragua [nɪkə'rægjuə] *n* Никара́гуа *f ind*.
Nicaraguan [nɪkə'rægjuən] *adj* никарагуа́нский* ◆ *n* никарагуа́нец*(-нка*).
Nice [ni:s] *n* Ни́цца.
nice [naɪs] *adj* прия́тный* (прия́тен), хоро́ший* (хоро́ш); (*attractive*) симпати́чный* (симпати́чен); **to look ~** хорошо́ вы́глядеть* *(impf)*; **that's very ~ of you** о́чень ми́ло с ва́шей стороны́.
nicely ['naɪslɪ] *adv* прия́тно, хорошо́; **that will do ~** э́то вполне́ подойдёт.
niceties ['naɪsɪtɪz] *npl* то́нкости *fpl*.
niche [ni:ʃ] *n* (*also fig*) ни́ша.
nick [nɪk] *n* (*in skin*) поре́з; (*in surface*) зару́бка* ◆ *vt* (*inf: steal*) пере́ть* (спере́ть* *perf*); (*: BRIT: arrest*) ца́пать (сца́пать *perf*); (*cut*): **to ~ o.s.** поре́заться* *(perf)*; **in the ~ of time** как раз во́время; **in good ~** (*BRIT: inf: condition*) в хоро́шем состоя́нии.
nickel ['nɪkl] *n* ни́кель *m*; (*US: coin*) *моне́та в 5 це́нтов*.
nickname ['nɪkneɪm] *n* кли́чка*, про́звище ◆ *vt* прозыва́ть (прозва́ть* *perf*).
Nicosia [nɪkə'si:ə] *n* Никоси́я.
nicotine ['nɪkəti:n] *n* никоти́н.
niece [ni:s] *n* племя́нница.
nifty ['nɪftɪ] *adj* (*inf: car, jacket*) сти́льный* (сти́лен); (*: gadget, tool*) ло́вко приду́манный (приду́ман).
Niger ['naɪdʒə^r] *n* Ни́гер.
Nigeria [naɪ'dʒɪərɪə] *n* Ниге́рия.
Nigerian [naɪ'dʒɪərɪən] *adj* нигери́йский* ◆ *n* нигери́ец(-и́йка).
niggardly ['nɪgədlɪ] *adj* (*person*) ска́редный; (*amount*) ску́дный.
nigger [nɪgə^r] *n* (*inf!*) черномáзый(-ая) *m(f) adj* (*!*)
niggle ['nɪgl] *vt* задева́ть (заде́ть* *perf*) ◆ *vi* (*find fault*) придира́ться (придра́ться* *perf*).

niggling ['nɪglɪŋ] *adj* (*trifling*) придирчивый (придирчив); (*annoying*) навязчивый (навязчив).
night [naɪt] *n* ночь* *f*; (*evening*) вечер*; **at ~, by ~** ночью; **all ~ long** всю ночь напролёт; **in** *or* **during the ~** ночью; **last ~** вчера ночью; (*evening*) вчера вечером; **the ~ before last** позапрошлой ночью; (*evening*) позавчера вечером.
nightcap ['naɪtkæp] *n* (*drink*) стаканчик на ночь.
nightclub ['naɪtklʌb] *n* ночной клуб.
nightdress ['naɪtdrɛs] *n* ночная рубашка*.
nightfall ['naɪtfɔːl] *n* сумерки* *pl*.
nightgown ['naɪtgaun] *n* = **nightdress**.
nightie ['naɪtɪ] *n* (*inf*) = **nightdress**.
nightingale ['naɪtɪŋgeɪl] *n* соловей*.
nightlife ['naɪtlaɪf] *n* ночная жизнь *f*.
nightly ['naɪtlɪ] *adj* (*every night*) еженощный; (*by night*) ночной ◆ *adv* еженощно.
nightmare ['naɪtmɛə^r] *n* (*also fig*) кошмар.
nightmarish ['naɪtmɛərɪʃ] *adj* кошмарный*.
night porter *n* ночной портье *m ind*.
night safe *n* ночной сейф (*в банке*).
night school *n* вечерняя школа.
nightshade ['naɪtʃeɪd] *n*: **deadly ~** белладонна, красавка.
night shift *n* ночная смена.
night-time ['naɪttaɪm] *n* ночное время* *nt*.
night watchman *n* ночной сторож*.
nihilism ['naɪɪlɪzəm] *n* нигилизм.
nil [nɪl] *n* нуль* *m*; (*BRIT*: *SPORT*) ноль* *m* ◆ *cpd* нулевой.
Nile [naɪl] *n*: **the ~** Нил.
nimble ['nɪmbl] *adj* (*agile*) проворный* (проворен); (*alert*) сообразительный* (сообразителен).
nine [naɪn] *n* девять*; *see also* **five**.
nineteen ['naɪn'tiːn] *n* девятнадцать*; *see also* **five**.
nineteenth ['naɪn'tiːnθ] *adj* девятнадцатый; *see also* **fifth**.
ninetieth ['naɪntɪɪθ] *adj* девяностый; *see also* **fifth**.
ninety ['naɪntɪ] *n* девяносто*; *see also* **fifty**.
ninth [naɪnθ] *adj* девятый; *see also* **fifth**.
nip [nɪp] *vt* (*pinch*) щипать* (ущипнуть *perf*); (*bite*) кусать (*impf*) ◆ *n* (*pinch*) щипок*; (*bite*) укус; (*drink*) рюмочка* ◆ *vi* (*BRIT*: *inf*): **to ~ out** выскакивать (выскочить *perf*); **to ~ into a shop** заскакивать (заскочить* *perf*) в магазин.
nipple ['nɪpl] *n* (*ANAT*) сосок*; (*TECH*) ниппель* *m*.
nippy ['nɪpɪ] *adj* (*BRIT*: *inf*) проворный* (проворен); (: *weather*) холодноватый (холодноват).
nit [nɪt] *n* (*in hair*) гнида; (*BRIT*: *inf*: *idiot*) олух.
nit-pick ['nɪtpɪk] *vi* (*inf*) придираться (придраться* *perf*).
nitrogen ['naɪtrədʒən] *n* азот.
nitroglycerin(e) ['naɪtrəu'glɪsəriːn] *n* нитроглицерин.
nitty-gritty ['nɪtɪ'grɪtɪ] *n* (*inf*): **to get down to the ~** переходить* (перейти* *perf*) к сути дела.
nitwit ['nɪtwɪt] *n* (*inf*) олух.
Nizhni Novgorod ['niʒnij 'nɔvgərət] *n* Нижний Новгород.
NJ *abbr* (*US*: *POST*) = *New Jersey*.
NLF *n abbr* (= *National Liberation Front*) ФНО= *Фронт национального освобождения*.
NLQ *abbr* (*COMPUT*, *TYP*: = *near letter quality*) *повышенное качество печати*.
NLRB *n abbr* (*US*) = *National Labor Relations Board*.
NM *abbr* (*US*: *POST*) = *New Mexico*.

KEYWORD

no [nəu] (*pl* **noes**) *adv* (*opposite of "yes"*) нет; **are you coming? – no (I'm not)** Вы придёте? -нет(, не приду); **no thank you** нет, спасибо ◆ *adj* (*not any*): **I have no money/time/books** у меня нет денег/времени/книг; **there is no bread left** хлеб кончился; **there is no one here** здесь никого нет; **it is of no importance at all** это не имеет никакого значения; **no system is totally fair** никакая система не является полностью справедливой; **"no entry"** "вход воспрещён"; **"no smoking"** "не курить" ◆ *n*: **there were twenty noes** двадцать (человек) были "против".

no. *abbr* = **number**.
nobble [nɔbl] *vt* (*BRIT*: *inf*: *bribe*) покупать (купить* *perf*); (: *to speak to*) подлавливать (подловить* *perf*); (: *RACING*) портить* (испортить* *perf*).
Nobel Prize [nəu'bɛl-] *n* Нобелевская премия.
nobility [nəu'bɪlɪtɪ] *n* (*social class*) знать *f*, дворянство; (*quality*) благородство.
noble ['nəubl] *adj* (*aristocratic*) дворянский; (*high-minded*) благородный* (благороден); (*impressive*) величавый (величав).
nobleman ['nəublmən] *irreg n* дворянин*.
noblewoman ['nəublwumən] *irreg n* дворянка*.
nobly ['nəublɪ] *adv* (*behave, act*) благородно.
nobody ['nəubədɪ] *pron* никто*.
no-claim(s) bonus ['nəukleɪmz-] *n* (*INSURANCE*) скидка со следующей страховой премии (*предоставляется страхователю в случае отсутствия страховых претензий в предыдущем году*).
nocturnal [nɔk'təːnl] *adj* ночной.
nod [nɔd] *vi* (*gesture*) кивать (*impf*); (*doze*) клевать* (*impf*) носом ◆ *n* кивок* ◆ *vt*: **to ~ one's head** кивать (*impf*) головой; **they ~ded their agreement** они кивнули в знак

* marks translations which have irregular inflections. The Russian-English side of the dictionary gives inflectional information.

соглáсия
▶**nod off** *vi* задремáть* *(perf)*.
no-fly zone [nəu'flaɪ-] *n* запрéтная воздýшная зóна.
noise [nɔɪz] *n* шум.
noiseless ['nɔɪzlɪs] *adj* бесшýмный* (бесшýмен).
noisily ['nɔɪzɪlɪ] *adv* шýмно.
noisy ['nɔɪzɪ] *adj* шýмный* (шýмен).
nomad ['nəumæd] *n* кочéвник(-ица).
nomadic [nəu'mædɪk] *adj* кочевóй.
no-man's-land ['nəumænzlænd] *n* (*MIL*) ничéйная полосá; (*fig*) тумáнность *f*.
nominal ['nɔmɪnl] *adj* номинáльный* (номинáлен); (*value*) номинáльный.
nominate ['nɔmɪneɪt] *vt* (*propose*): **to ~ sb (for)** выставля́ть (вы́ставить* *perf*) кандидатýру когó-н (на *+acc*); (*appoint*): **to ~ sb (to/as)** назначáть (назнáчить *perf*) когó-н (на *+acc/ +instr*).
nomination [nɔmɪ'neɪʃən] *n* (*see vb*) выставлéние; назначéние.
nominee [nɔmɪ'ni:] *n* кандидáт.
non... [nɔn] *prefix* не....
nonalcoholic [nɔnælkə'hɔlɪk] *adj* (*drink*) безалкогóльный* (безалкогóлен).
nonaligned *adj* неприсоединúвшийся.
nonbreakable [nɔn'breɪkəbl] *adj* небью́щийся.
nonce word ['nɔns-] *n* окказионалúзм.
nonchalant ['nɔnʃələnt] *adj* беспéчный* (беспéчен).
noncommissioned officer [nɔnkə'mɪʃənd-] *n* ýнтер-офицéр.
noncommittal [nɔnkə'mɪtl] *adj* уклóнчивый (уклóнчив).
nonconformist [nɔnkən'fɔ:mɪst] *n* нонконформúст(ка*); (*BRIT: REL*): **N~** нонконформúст(ка) ◆ *adj* нонконформúстский.
non-contributory pension scheme *n* *пенсиóнные схéмы, по котóрым рабóтники не должны́ дéлать регуля́рных взнóсов.*
noncooperation ['nɔnkəuɔpə'reɪʃən] *n* откáз в сотрýдничестве.
nondescript ['nɔndɪskrɪpt] *adj* (*person, clothing*) невзрáчный* (невзрáчен); (*colour*) небрóский*.
none [nʌn] *pron* (*person*) никтó*, ни одúн*; (*thing*) ничтó*, ни одúн*; **~ of you** никтó *or* ни одúн из Вас; **I've ~ left** у меня́ ничегó не остáлось; **~ at all** совсéм ничегó; **he's ~ the worse for it** емý от э́того отню́дь не хýже.
nonentity [nɔ'nɛntɪtɪ] *n* ничтóжество.
nonessential [nɔnɪ'sɛnʃl] *adj* (*items*) несущéственный (несущéствен) ◆ *n*: **~s** несущéственные вéщи *fpl*.
nonetheless ['nʌnðə'lɛs] *adv* тем не мéнее, всё же.
non-event [nɔnɪ'vɛnt] *n* бессмы́сленное мероприя́тие.
nonexecutive [nɔnɪg'zɛkjutɪv] *adj*: **~ director** дирéктор* без распорядúтельных полномóчий.
nonexistent [nɔnɪg'zɪstənt] *adj* несущест-вýющий.
nonfiction [nɔn'fɪkʃən] *n* документáльная литератýра.
nonflammable [nɔn'flæməbl] *adj* невоспламеня́ющийся*.
nonintervention ['nɔnɪntə'vɛnʃən] *n* невмешáтельство.
no-no ['nəunəu] *n* (*inf*) запрéтная тéма.
non obst. *abbr* (*notwithstanding*: = *non obstante*) несмотря́ на *+acc*.
no-nonsense [nəu'nɔnsəns] *adj* деловóй.
nonpayment [nɔn'peɪmənt] *n* неуплáта.
nonplussed [nɔn'plʌst] *adj* ошеломлённый (ошеломлён).
non-profit-making [nɔn'prɔfɪtmeɪkɪŋ] *adj*: **~ organization** некоммéрческая организáция.
nonsense ['nɔnsəns] *n* (*rubbish*) ерундá, чепухá; **it is ~ to say that ...** говорúть (сказáть* *perf*), что ... -- прóсто глýпость.
nonsensical [nɔn'sɛnsɪkl] *adj* бессмы́сленный* (бессмы́слен).
nonshrink [nɔn'ʃrɪŋk] *adj* (*BRIT*): **nylon is (a) ~ (fabric)** нейлóн не садúтся.
nonskid [nɔn'skɪd] *adj* нескользя́щий.
nonsmoker ['nɔn'sməukə^r^] *n* некуря́щий*(-ая) *m(f) adj*.
nonstarter [nɔn'stɑ:tə^r^] *n* мёртвый нóмер *no pl*.
nonstick ['nɔn'stɪk] *adj* непригорáющий.
nonstop ['nɔn'stɔp] *adj* (*conversation*) беспреры́вный* (беспреры́вен); (*flight*) беспосáдочный; (*train, bus*) идýщий без остановóк ◆ *adv* (*see adj*) беспреры́вно; без посáдок; без остановóк.
nontaxable [nɔn'tæksəbl] *adj* необлагáемый (необлагáем) налóгом.
non-U *adj abbr* (*BRIT: inf: = non-upper class*) не принадлежáщий к вы́сшему (социáльному) клáссу.
nonvolatile [nɔn'vɔlətaɪl] *adj*: **~ memory** (*COMPUT*) энергонезавúсимая пáмять *f*.
nonvoting [nɔn'vəutɪŋ] *adj*: **~ shares/member** áкции/член без прáва голосовáния.
non-white ['nɔn'waɪt] *adj* (*person*) цветнóй ◆ *n*: **non-White** цветнóй(-áя) *m(f) adj*.
noodles ['nu:dlz] *npl* вермишéль *fsg*.
nook [nuk] *n*: **in every ~ and cranny** во всех углáх.
noon [nu:n] *n* пóлдень* *m*.
no-one ['nəuwʌn] *pron* = **nobody**.
noose [nu:s] *n* пéтля*.
nor [nɔ:^r^] *conj* = **neither** ◆ *adv see* **neither**.
Norf *abbr* (*BRIT: POST*) = *Norfolk*.
norm [nɔ:m] *n* нóрма.
normal ['nɔ:ml] *adj* нормáльный* (нормáлен) ◆ *n*: **to return to ~** возвращáться (вернýться *perf*) в нормáльное состоя́ние.
normality [nɔ:'mælɪtɪ] *n* нормáльность *f*.
normally ['nɔ:məlɪ] *adv* (*usually*) обы́чно; (*properly*) нормáльно.

Normandy ['nɔːməndɪ] *n* Нормáндия.
north [nɔːθ] *n* сéвер ◆ *adj* сéверный ◆ *adv* (*go*) на сéвер; (*be*) к сéверу.
North Africa *n* Сéверная Áфрика.
North African *adj* североафрикáнский ◆ *n* жи́тель(ница) *m(f)* Сéверной Áфрики.
North America *n* Сéверная Амéрика.
North American *adj* североамерикáнский ◆ *n* североамерикáнец*(-нка*).
Northants [nɔː'θænts] *abbr* (*BRIT: POST*) = *Northamptonshire*.
northbound ['nɔːθbaund] *adj* (*traffic, carriageway*) на сéвер; (*platform*) сéверного направлéния.
Northd *abbr* (*BRIT: POST*) = *Northumberland*.
northeast [nɔːθ'iːst] *n* сéверо-востóк.
northerly ['nɔːðəlɪ] *adj* сéверный.
northern ['nɔːðən] *adj* сéверный.
northerner ['nɔːðənə'] *n* северя́нин*(-я́нка*).
Northern Ireland *n* Сéверная Ирлáндия.
North Korea *n* Сéверная Корéя.
North Pole *n* Сéверный пóлюс.
North Sea *n* Сéверное мóре.
North-Sea oil ['nɔːθsiː-] *n* нефть *f* Сéверного мóря.
northward(s) ['nɔːθwəd(z)] *adv* к сéверу.
northwest [nɔːθ'wɛst] *n* сéверо-зáпад.
Norway ['nɔːweɪ] *n* Норвéгия.
Norwegian [nɔː'wiːdʒən] *adj* норвéжский* ◆ *n* норвéжец*(-жка*); (*LING*) норвéжский* язы́к*.
nos. *abbr* = *numbers*.
nose [nəuz] *n* нос*; (*sense of smell*) нюх, чутьё ◆ *vi*: **to ~ forward** осторóжно пробирáться (пробрáться* *perf*) вперёд; **he has a ~ for danger/scandal** у негó нюх на опáсность/скандáл; **to pay through the ~ (for sth)** (*inf*) плати́ть* (заплати́ть* *perf*) втри́дорога (за что-н)
▸ **nose about** *vi* выню́хивать (вы́нюхать *perf*)
▸ **nose around** *vi* = **nose about**.
nosebleed ['nəuzbliːd] *n* носовóе кровотечéние.
nose dive *n* (крутóе) пики́рование.
nose drops *npl* кáпли *fpl* для нóса.
nosey ['nəuzɪ] *adj* (*inf*) = **nosy**.
nostalgia [nɔs'tældʒɪə] *n* ностальги́я.
nostalgic [nɔs'tældʒɪk] *adj* (*film, memory*) ностальги́ческий*; (*person*): **to be ~ (for)** испы́тывать *(impf)* ностальги́ю (по +*dat*).
nostril ['nɔstrɪl] *n* ноздря́*.
nosy ['nəuzɪ] *adj* (*inf*): **to be ~** совáть* *(impf)* нос в чужи́е делá.

KEYWORD

not [nɔt] *adv* нет; (*before verbs*) не; **he is not** *or* **isn't at home** егó нет дóма; **he asked me not to do it** он попроси́л меня́ не дéлать э́того; **you must not** *or* **you mustn't do that** (*forbidden*) э́того нельзя́ дéлать; (*should not*) Вы не должны́ э́то дéлать; **it's too late, isn't it?** ужé сли́шком пóздно, да?; **not that ...** не то, чтóбы ...; **not yet** нет ещё, ещё нет; **not now** не сейчáс; *see also* **all, only**.

notable ['nəutəbl] *adj* примечáтельный* (примечáтелен).
notably ['nəutəblɪ] *adv* (*particularly*) осóбенно; (*markedly*) замéтно.
notary ['nəutərɪ] *n* (*also:* **~ public**) нотáриус.
notation [nəu'teɪʃən] *n* (*MUS etc*) нотáция.
notch [nɔtʃ] *n* (*on the edge*) зазу́брина; (*on the surface*) вы́емка*
▸ **notch up** *vt* (*victory*) добивáться (доби́ться* *perf*) +*instr*; (*score*) набирáть (набрáть* *perf*).
note [nəut] *n* (*record*) зáпись *f*; (*letter*) запи́ска*; (*also:* **footnote**) примечáние; (*also:* **banknote**) банкнóта; (*MUS*) нóта; (*tone*) тон ◆ *vt* (*observe*) замечáть (замéтить* *perf*); (*also:* **~ down**) запи́сывать (записáть* *perf*); **of ~** примечáтельный (примечáтелен).
notebook ['nəutbuk] *n* записнáя кни́жка; (*exercise book*) тетрáдь *f*.
notecase ['nəutkeɪs] *n* (*BRIT*) бумáжник.
noted ['nəutɪd] *adj* извéстный* (извéстен).
notepad ['nəutpæd] *n* блокнóт.
notepaper ['nəutpeɪpə'] *n* пи́счая бумáга.
noteworthy ['nəutwəːðɪ] *adj* достóйный* (достóен) внимáния; **it is ~ that ...** достóйно внимáния что ....
nothing ['nʌθɪŋ] *n* ничтó*; (*zero*) ноль *m*; **he does ~** он ничегó не дéлает; **there is ~ to do/be said** дéлать/сказáть нéчего; **~ new/much/of the sort** ничегó нóвого/осóбенного/подóбного; **for ~** дáром; **think ~ of it!, it was ~!** нé за что!; **~ like as ... as ...** совсéм не так ..., как ...; **to say ~ of ...** не говоря́ ужé о +*prp* ...; **it has ~ to do with you** э́то Вас не касáется.
notice ['nəutɪs] *n* (*announcement*) объявлéние; (*official letter, circular*) уведомлéние, извещéние; (*warning*) предупреждéние; (*BRIT: review*) óтзыв ◆ *vt* замечáть (замéтить* *perf*); **to take ~ of** обращáть (обрати́ть* *perf*) внимáние на +*acc*; **to bring sth to sb's ~** (*attention*) обращáть (обрати́ть* *perf*) внимáние когó-н на что-н; **to escape** *or* **avoid ~** оставáться* (остáться* *perf*) незамéченным; **it has come to my ~ that ...** мне стáло извéстно, что ...; **to hand in one's ~** подавáть* (подáть* *perf*) заявлéние об ухóде с рабóты; **he was given 2 weeks ~** емý предупреди́ли, что он бýдет увóлен чéрез 2 недéли; **advance ~** заблаговремéнное предупреждéние; **without ~** без предупреждéния; **at short ~** без предупреждéния; **until further ~** впредь до дальнéйшего уведомлéния.

* marks translations which have irregular inflections. The Russian-English side of the dictionary gives inflectional information.

noticeable [ˈnəutɪsəbl] *adj* замéтный* (замéтен).
notice board *n* (*BRIT*) доскá* объявлéний.
notification [nəutɪfɪˈkeɪʃən] *n* уведомлéние.
notify [ˈnəutɪfaɪ] *vt*: **to ~ sb (of sth)** уведомля́ть (увéдомить* *perf*) когó-н (о чём-н).
notion [ˈnəuʃən] *n* (*idea*) поня́тие; (*opinion*) представлéние; **~s** *npl* (*US*: *haberdashery*) галантерéя *fsg*.
notoriety [nəutəˈraɪətɪ] *n* дурнáя слáва.
notorious [nəuˈtɔːrɪəs] *adj* (*criminal, liar*) извéстный* (извéстен); (*place*) печáльно извéстный* (извéстен).
notoriously [nəuˈtɔːrɪəslɪ] *adv*: **she is ~ unreliable** у неё дурнáя слáва ненадёжного человéка; **this word is ~ difficult to translate** э́то слóво извéстно тем, что егó трýдно перевести́.
Notts [nɔts] *abbr* (*BRIT*: *POST*) = *Nottinghamshire.*
notwithstanding [nɔtwɪθˈstændɪŋ] *adv* тем не мéнее ◆ *prep* несмотря́ на *+acc*.
nougat [ˈnuːgɑː] *n* нугá.
nought [nɔːt] *n* ноль* *m*.
noun [naun] *n* (и́мя* *nt*) существи́тельное *nt adj*.
nourish [ˈnʌrɪʃ] *vt* (*feed*) питáть *(impf)*; (*fig*: *foster*) взрáщивать (взрасти́ть* *perf*).
nourishing [ˈnʌrɪʃɪŋ] *adj* питáтельный* (питáтелен).
nourishment [ˈnʌrɪʃmənt] *n* (*food*) питáние.
Nov. *abbr* = **November**.
Nova Scotia [ˈnəuvəˈskəuʃə] *n* Нóвая Шотлáндия.
Novaya Zemlya [ˈnɔvəjə zɪmˈlja] *n* Нóвая Земля́.
novel [ˈnɔvl] *n* ромáн ◆ *adj* оригинáльный* (оригинáлен).
novelist [ˈnɔvəlɪst] *n* романи́ст(ка*).
novelty [ˈnɔvəltɪ] *n* (*newness*) новизнá; (*object*) нови́нка*.
November [nəuˈvɛmbəʳ] *n* ноя́брь* *m*; *see also* **July**.
novice [ˈnɔvɪs] *n* новичóк*; (*REL*) пóслушник(-ица).
Novosibirsk [nəvəsiˈbirsk] *n* Новосиби́рск.
NOW [nau] *n abbr* (*US*) = *National Organization for Women.*
now [nau] *adv* тепéрь, сейчáс ◆ *conj*: **~ (that)** ... тепéрь, когдá ...; **right ~** пря́мо сейчáс; **by ~** к настоя́щему врéмени; **~ and then** *or* **again** врéмя от врéмени; **from ~ on** впредь; **until ~** до сих пор; **that's the fashion just ~** э́то сейчáс в мóде; **I saw her just ~** я тóлько что её ви́дел; **in 3 days from ~** чéрез 3 дня; **between ~ and Monday** мéжду сегóдняшним днём и понедéльником; **that's all for ~** покá всё.
nowadays [ˈnauədeɪz] *adv* в нáши дни.
nowhere [ˈnəuwɛəʳ] *adv* (*be*) нигдé; (*go*) никудá; **~ else** (*be*) бóльше нигдé; (*go*) бóльше никудá; **I have ~ else to go** мне бóльше нéкуда идти́.
no-win situation [nəuˈwɪn-] *n* безвы́игрышное положéние.
noxious [ˈnɔkʃəs] *adj* вредонóсный; (*smell*) проти́вный* (проти́вен).
nozzle [ˈnɔzl] *n* (*TECH*) соплó*; (*of hose, vacuum cleaner*) насáдка*; (*of fire extinguisher*) брандспóйт.
NP *n abbr* (*LAW*) = **notary public**.
NS *abbr* (*CANADA*) = *Nova Scotia.*
NSC *n abbr* (*US*: = *National Security Council*) Совéт национáльной безопáсности.
NSF *n abbr* (*US*) = *National Science Foundation.*
NSPCC *n abbr* (*BRIT*) = *National Society for the Prevention of Cruelty to Children.*
NSW *abbr* (*AUSTRALIA*) = *New South Wales.*
NT *n abbr* (*BIBLE*: = *New Testament*) Нóвый завéт.
nth [ɛnθ] *adj*: **for the ~ time** (*inf*) в э́нный раз.
nuance [ˈnjuːɑ̃ːns] *n* нюáнс.
nubile [ˈnjuːbaɪl] *adj* (*woman*) зрéлый; (*attractive*) прельсти́тельный.
nuclear [ˈnjuːklɪəʳ] *adj* я́дерный.
nuclear disarmament *n* я́дерное разоружéние.
nuclear-free zone [ˈnjuːklɪəˈfriː-] *n* внея́дерная зóна.
nuclear reactor *n* я́дерный реáктор.
nuclei [ˈnjuːklɪaɪ] *npl of* **nucleus**.
nucleus [ˈnjuːklɪəs] (*pl* **nuclei**) *n* (*also fig*) ядрó*.
NUCPS *n abbr* (*BRIT*) = *National Union of Civil and Public Servants.*
nude [njuːd] *adj* обнажённый (обнажён), нагóй* (наг) ◆ *n* обнажённая фигýра; **in the ~** в обнажённом ви́де.
nudge [nʌdʒ] *vt* подтáлкивать (подтолкнýть *perf*).
nudist [ˈnjuːdɪst] *n* нуди́ст(ка*).
nudist colony *n* колóния нуди́стов.
nudity [ˈnjuːdɪtɪ] *n* наготá.
nugget [ˈnʌgɪt] *n* (*of gold*) саморóдок*; **~ of information** цéнная информáция.
nuisance [ˈnjuːsns] *n* (*state of affairs, thing*) досáда; (*person*) докýчливый человéк*; **what a ~!** какáя досáда!; **that noise is a real ~** э́тот шум си́льно раздражáет; **he is a real ~** он óчень надоéдливый.
NUJ *n abbr* (*BRIT*) = *National Union of Journalists.*
nuke [njuːk] *n* (*inf*) я́дерное орýжие.
null [nʌl] *adj*: **to be ~ and void** потеря́ть *(perf)* закóнную си́лу.
nullify [ˈnʌlɪfaɪ] *vt* (*efforts*) своди́ть* (свести́* *perf*) к нулю́; (*LAW*) аннули́ровать *(impf/perf)*.
NUM *n abbr* (*BRIT*) = *National Union of Mineworkers.*
numb [nʌm] *adj*: **~ (with)** онемéвший (от *+gen*) ◆ *vt*: **the cold ~ed his fingers** егó пáльцы онемéли от хóлода; **to go ~** онемéть *(perf)*.
number [ˈnʌmbəʳ] *n* нóмер*; (*MATH*) числó*; (*written figure*) ци́фра; (*quantity*) коли́чество ◆ *vt* (*pages etc*) нумеровáть (пронумеровáть

perf); (*amount to*) насчи́тывать *(impf)*; **a ~ of** не́сколько *+gen*; **in a ~ of cases** в ря́де слу́чаев; **they were ten in ~** их бы́ло де́сять; **you've got the wrong ~** (*TEL*) Вы не туда́ попа́ли; **he is ~ed among ...** его́ причисля́ют к *+dat* ...; **~ed (bank) account** номерно́й счёт в ба́нке.

numberplate ['nʌmbəpleɪt] *n* (*BRIT: AUT*) номерно́й знак.

Number Ten *n* (*BRIT: also:* **~ ~ Downing Street**) но́мер 10 по Да́унинг Стри́т (*резиде́нция премье́р-мини́стра*).

numbness ['nʌmnɪs] *n* (*due to cold*) онеме́ние; (*due to fear, shock*) оцепене́ние.

numbskull ['nʌmskʌl] *n* (*inf*) тупи́ца *m/f*.

numeral ['nju:mərəl] *n* ци́фра.

numerate ['nju:mərɪt] *adj* (*BRIT*): **to be ~** знать *(impf)* арифме́тику.

numerical [nju:'mɛrɪkl] *adj* (*value*) числово́й; (*superiority*) чи́сленный; (*data*) цифрово́й; **in ~ order** по номера́м.

numerous ['nju:mərəs] *adj* многочи́сленный (многочи́слен); **on ~ occasions** многокра́тно.

nun [nʌn] *n* мона́хиня.

nunnery ['nʌnərɪ] *n* же́нский* монасты́рь *m*.

nuptial ['nʌpʃəl] *adj* бра́чный.

nurse [nə:s] *n* медсестра́*; (*also:* **male ~**) медбра́т; (*also:* **~maid**) ня́ня ◆ *vt* (*patient*) уха́живать *(impf)* за *+instr*; (*desire, also BRIT: cuddle*) леле́ять (взлеле́ять *perf*); (*grudge*) таи́ть *(impf)*; (*US: suckle*) корми́ть* *(impf)* гру́дью; **to ~ a cold** сиде́ть* *(impf)* до́ма с просту́дой.

nursery ['nə:sərɪ] *n* (*institution*) я́сли* *pl*; (*room*) де́тская *f adj*; (*for plants*) пито́мник.

nursery rhyme *n* пе́сенка для дете́й.

nursery school *n* де́тский* сад*.

nursery slope *n* (*BRIT*) спуск для начина́ющих лы́жников.

nursing ['nə:sɪŋ] *n* (*profession*) профе́ссия медсестры́; (*care*) ухо́д.

nursing home *n* ча́стный дом* (*для престаре́лых*).

nursing mother *n* кормя́щая мать* *f*.

nurture ['nə:tʃə*] *vt* (*child, plant*) выра́щивать (вы́растить* *perf*).

NUS *n abbr* (*BRIT*) = *National Union of Students.*

NUT *n abbr* (*BRIT*) = *National Union of Teachers.*

nut [nʌt] *n* (*BOT*) оре́х; (*TECH*) га́йка; (*inf*) = **nutcase**.

nutcase ['nʌtkeɪs] *n* (*inf*) псих.

nutcrackers ['nʌtkrækəz] *npl* щипцы́* *pl* для оре́хов.

nutmeg ['nʌtmɛg] *n* муска́тный оре́х.

nutrient ['nju:trɪənt] *n* пита́тельное вещество́.

nutrition [nju:'trɪʃən] *n* (*diet*) пита́ние; (*nourishment*) пита́тельность *f*.

nutritionist [nju:'trɪʃənɪst] *n* дието́лог.

nutritious [nju:'trɪʃəs] *adj* пита́тельный* (пита́телен).

nuts [nʌts] (*inf*) *adj*: **he's ~** он чо́кнутый; **to be ~ about sb** с ума́ сходи́ть* *(impf)* по кому́-н.

nutshell ['nʌtʃɛl] *n* оре́ховая скорлупа́*; **in a ~** (*fig*) в двух слова́х.

nutty ['nʌtɪ] *adj* (*flavour*) похо́жий* (по вку́су) на оре́хи; (*inf: person*) чо́кнутый (чо́кнут); (*idea*) бредо́вый.

nuzzle ['nʌzl] *vi*: **to ~ up to** тере́ться* (потере́ться* *perf*) но́сом о *+acc*.

NV *abbr* (*US: POST*) = *Nevada.*

NWT *abbr* (*CANADA*) = *Northwest Territories.*

NY *abbr* (*US: POST*) = *New York.*

NYC *abbr* (*US: POST*) = *New York City.*

nylon ['naɪlɔn] *n* нейло́н ◆ *adj* нейло́новый; **~s** *npl* нейло́новые чулки́* *mpl*.

nymph [nɪmf] *n* (*MYTHOLOGY*) ни́мфа; (*ZOOL*) личи́нка*.

nymphomaniac [nɪmfəu'meɪnɪæk] *n* нимфома́нка*.

NYSE *n abbr* (*US*) = *New York Stock Exchange.*

NZ *abbr* = *New Zealand.*

* marks translations which have irregular inflections. The Russian-English side of the dictionary gives inflectional information.

~O, o~

O, o [əu] *n* (*letter*) *15-ая бу́ква англи́йского алфави́та*; (*number*: *TEL etc*) ноль* *m*.
O *abbr* = *outstanding*; (*US*: *SCOL*) ≈ отл.= *отли́чно*.
oaf [əuf] *n* чурба́н, дуби́на *m/f*.
oak [əuk] *n* дуб* ♦ *adj* дубо́вый.
O & M *n abbr* = *organization and method*.
OAP *n abbr* (*BRIT*) = **old age pensioner**.
oar [ɔ:ʳ] *n* весло́*; **to put** *or* **shove one's ~ in** (*fig*: *inf*) встрева́ть (встрять* *perf*).
oarsman [ˈɔ:zmən] *n* гребе́ц*.
OAS *n abbr* = *Organization of American States*.
oases [əuˈeɪsi:z] *npl of* **oasis**.
oasis [əuˈeɪsɪs] (*pl* **oases**) *n* (*also fig*) оа́зис.
oath [əuθ] *n* (*promise*) кля́тва; (: *LAW*) прися́га; (*swear word*) прокля́тие; **on** (*BRIT*) **or under ~** под прися́гой; **to take the ~** принима́ть (приня́ть* *perf*) прися́гу.
oatmeal [ˈəutmi:l] *n* овся́ная мука́.
oats [əuts] *npl* овёс*.
OAU *n abbr* = *Organization of African Unity*.
obdurate [ˈɔbdjurɪt] *adj* непреклóнный* (непреклóнен).
OBE *n abbr* (*BRIT*: = *Order of the British Empire*) о́рден Брита́нской импе́рии.
obedience [əˈbi:dɪəns] *n* повинове́ние, послуша́ние; **in ~ to** повину́ясь +*dat*.
obedient [əˈbi:dɪənt] *adj* послу́шный* (послу́шен); **to be ~ to sb/sth** слу́шаться (послу́шаться *perf*) кого́-н/чего́-н.
obelisk [ˈɔbɪlɪsk] *n* обели́ск.
obese [əuˈbi:s] *adj* ту́чный* (ту́чен).
obesity [əuˈbi:sɪtɪ] *n* ожире́ние, ту́чность *f*.
obey [əˈbeɪ] *vt* подчиня́ться (подчини́ться *perf*) +*dat*, повинова́ться (*impf/perf*) +*dat* ♦ *vi* подчиня́ться (подчини́ться *perf*), повинова́ться (*impf*).
obituary [əˈbɪtjuərɪ] *n* некроло́г.
object [*n* ˈɔbdʒɪkt, *vi* əbˈdʒɛkt] *n* (*thing*) предме́т; (*aim, purpose*) цель *f*; (*of affection, desires*) объе́кт; (*LING*) дополне́ние ♦ *vi*: **to ~ (to)** возража́ть (возрази́ть* *perf*) (про́тив +*gen*); **expense is no ~** де́ньги – не пробле́ма; **what's the ~ of doing that?** для чего́ де́лать э́то?; **he ~ed that ...** он возрази́л, что ...; **I ~!** я возража́ю!; **do you ~ to my smoking?** Вы не возража́ете е́сли я бу́ду кури́ть?
objection [əbˈdʒɛkʃən] *n* возраже́ние; **I have no ~ to ...** я не име́ю никаки́х возраже́ний про́тив +*gen* ...; **if you have no ~** е́сли Вы не возража́ете; **to make** *or* **raise an ~** выдвига́ть (вы́двинуть *perf*) возраже́ние.
objectionable [əbˈdʒɛkʃənəbl] *adj* (*language, conduct*) возмути́тельный* (возмути́телен); (*person*) неприя́тный* (неприя́тен).
objective [əbˈdʒɛktɪv] *adj* объекти́вный* (объекти́вен) ♦ *n* (*aim, purpose*) цель *f*.
objectively [əbˈdʒɛktɪvlɪ] *adv* объекти́вно.
objectivity [ɔbdʒɪkˈtɪvɪtɪ] *n* объекти́вность *f*.
object lesson *n*: **an ~ ~ in** нагля́дный приме́р +*gen*.
objector [əbˈdʒɛktəʳ] *n* протесту́ющий*(-ая) *m(f) adj*.
obligation [ɔblɪˈgeɪʃən] *n* обяза́тельство; **we are under no ~ to them** мы им ниче́м не обя́заны; **we are under (an) ~ to give him what he needs** мы обя́заны дать ему́ всё, что потре́буется; **"without ~"** (*COMM*) „без обяза́тельств".
obligatory [əˈblɪgətərɪ] *adj* обяза́тельный* (обяза́телен).
oblige [əˈblaɪdʒ] *vt* (*do a favour for*) обя́зывать (обяза́ть *perf*); (*force*): **to ~ sb to do** обя́зывать (обяза́ть* *perf*) кого́-н +*infin*; **I'm much ~d to you for your help** (*grateful*) я о́чень обя́зан Вам за ва́шу по́мощь; **anything to ~!** (*inf*) (я весь) к ва́шим услу́гам!
obliging [əˈblaɪdʒɪŋ] *adj* (*helpful*) любе́зный* (любе́зен).
oblique [əˈbli:k] *adj* (*line*) накло́нный; (*comment, reference*) ко́свенный ♦ *n* (*BRIT*: *TYP*): **~ (stroke)** накло́нная черта́.
obliterate [əˈblɪtəreɪt] *vt* (*destroy*) уничтожа́ть (уничто́жить *perf*); (*from mind*) стира́ть (стере́ть* *perf*).
oblivion [əˈblɪvɪən] *n* забве́ние; **these events have sunk into ~** э́ти собы́тия пре́даны забве́нию.
oblivious [əˈblɪvɪəs] *adj*: **to be ~ of** *or* **to** не сознава́ть* (*impf*) +*gen*.
oblong [ˈɔblɔŋ] *adj* продолгова́тый ♦ *n* продолгова́тый предме́т.
obnoxious [əbˈnɔkʃəs] *adj* отврати́тельный* (отврати́телен).
o.b.o. *abbr* (*US*: *in classified ads*: = *or best offer*) и́ли по договорённости.
oboe [ˈəubəu] *n* гобо́й.

obscene [əb'si:n] *adj* непристо́йный* (непристо́ен).
obscenity [əb'sɛnɪtɪ] *n* непристо́йность *f*.
obscure [əb'skjuə'] *adj* (*little known*) малоизве́стный* (малоизве́стен); (*difficult to understand*) нея́сный* (нея́сен), сму́тный* (сму́тен) ◆ *vt* (*view, sun etc*) загора́живать (загороди́ть* *perf*); (*truth, meaning etc*) затемня́ть (затемни́ть *perf*).
obscurity [əb'skjuərɪtɪ] *n* (*see adj*) безве́стность *f*, нея́сность *f*.
obsequious [əb'si:kwɪəs] *adj* подобостра́стный* (подобостра́стен).
observable [əb'zə:vəbl] *adj* наблюда́емый; (*appreciable*) заме́тный* (заме́тен).
observance [əb'zə:vns] *n* (*of law, custom*) соблюде́ние; **religious ~s** религио́зные обря́ды.
observant [əb'zə:vnt] *adj* наблюда́тельный* (наблюда́телен).
observation [ɔbzə'veɪʃən] *n* (*remark*) замеча́ние; (*surveillance, also MED*) наблюде́ние.
observation post *n* наблюда́тельный пост* *or* пункт.
observatory [əb'zə:vətrɪ] *n* обсервато́рия.
observe [əb'zə:v] *vt* (*watch*) наблюда́ть *(impf)* за *+instr*; (*comment*) замеча́ть (заме́тить* *perf*); (*abide by*) соблюда́ть (соблюсти́* *perf*).
observer [əb'zə:və'] *n* наблюда́тель *m*.
obsess [əb'sɛs] *vt* владева́ть (владе́ть *perf*); **you are ~ed by the idea** Вы одержи́мы э́той иде́ей; **he is totally ~ed with this woman** он соверше́нно поме́шан на э́той же́нщине.
obsession [əb'sɛʃən] *n* навя́зчивая иде́я; **she has an ~ for cats** она́ поме́шана на ко́шках.
obsessive [əb'sɛsɪv] *adj* одержи́мый (одержи́м).
obsolescence [ɔbsə'lɛsns] *n* устаре́лость *f*.
obsolete ['ɔbsəli:t] *adj* (*words*) устаре́вший; (*technology*) устаре́лый.
obstacle ['ɔbstəkl] *n* (*also fig*) препя́тствие.
obstacle race *n* бег с препя́тствиями.
obstetrician [ɔbstə'trɪʃən] *n* врач-акуше́р.
obstetrics [ɔb'stɛtrɪks] *n* акуше́рство.
obstinacy ['ɔbstɪnəsɪ] *n* (*of person*) упря́мство.
obstinate ['ɔbstɪnɪt] *adj* (*person, behaviour*) упря́мый (упря́м); (*cold, pain*) упо́рный.
obstruct [əb'strʌkt] *vt* (*road, path*) загора́живать (загороди́ть* *perf*); (*traffic, progress*) препя́тствовать (воспрепя́тствовать *perf*) *+dat*.
obstruction [əb'strʌkʃən] *n* (*action*) препя́тствование; (: *of law*) обстру́кция; (*object*) препя́тствие.
obstructive [əb'strʌktɪv] *adj* (*behaviour*) обструкцио́нный; **he is ~** он чи́нит препя́тствия.
obtain [əb'teɪn] *vt* (*get hold of*) достава́ть* (доста́ть* *perf*); (*gain*) получа́ть (получи́ть* *perf*) ◆ *vi* (*formal: exist*) существова́ть *(impf)*; **to ~ sth (for o.s.)** добива́ться (доби́ться* *perf*) чего́-н (для себя́).
obtainable [əb'teɪnəbl] *adj* достижи́мый (достижи́м).
obtrusive [əb'tru:sɪv] *adj* навя́зчивый (навя́зчив).
obtuse [əb'tju:s] *adj* (*person, remark*) бестолко́вый (бестолко́в); (*MATH*) тупо́й.
obverse ['ɔbvə:s] *n*: **the ~** обра́тное *nt adj*.
obviate ['ɔbvɪeɪt] *vt* устраня́ть (устрани́ть *perf*).
obvious ['ɔbvɪəs] *adj* очеви́дный* (очеви́ден).
obviously ['ɔbvɪəslɪ] *adv* очеви́дно; (*of course*) разуме́ется; **he was ~ not drunk** бы́ло очеви́дно, что он не пьян; **he was not ~ drunk** он не был очеви́дным о́бразом пьян; **~ not** разуме́ется, нет.
OCAS *n abbr* = *Organization of Central American States.*
occasion [ə'keɪʒən] *n* (*time*) раз*; (*case*) слу́чай; (*event*) собы́тие; (*opportunity*) возмо́жность *f* ◆ *vt* (*cause*) вызыва́ть (вы́звать* *perf*); **on this ~** на э́тот раз; **on that ~** в тот раз; **to rise to the ~** ока́зываться (оказа́ться* *perf*) на высоте́.
occasional [ə'keɪʒənl] *adj* ре́дкий*, нечa ́стый.
occasionally [ə'keɪʒənəlɪ] *adv* вре́мя от вре́мени, и́зредка; **very ~** о́чень ре́дко.
occasional table *n* запасно́й сто́лик.
occult [ɔ'kʌlt] *n*: **the ~** окку́льтные нау́ки *fpl*.
occupancy ['ɔkjupənsɪ] *n* пребыва́ние.
occupant ['ɔkjupənt] *n* (*long-term*) обита́тель(ница) *m(f)*; (*temporary*): **the ~s of the car/room** находя́щиеся *pl adj* в маши́не/ко́мнате.
occupation [ɔkju'peɪʃən] *n* заня́тие; (*occupancy*) пребыва́ние; (*MIL*) оккупа́ция; **unfit for ~** (*house*) неприго́дный* (неприго́ден) для жилья́.
occupational accident [ɔkju'peɪʃənl-] *n* произво́дственный несча́стный слу́чай.
occupational guidance *n* (*BRIT*) консульта́ция по по́иску ме́ста рабо́ты.
occupational hazard *n* произво́дственный риск.
occupational pension scheme *n пенсио́нный план, по кото́рому пенсио́нный фонд формиру́ется за счёт взно́сов рабо́тника и его́ работода́теля.*
occupational therapy *n* трудотерапи́я.
occupier ['ɔkjupaɪə'] *n* прожива́ющий(-ая) *m(f) adj*; **"to the ~"** „прожива́ющему" (*обраще́ние в письме́*).
occupy ['ɔkjupaɪ] *vt* занима́ть (заня́ть* *perf*); (*country, attention*) захва́тывать (захвати́ть*

perf); **to ~ o.s. (with sth)** занимáться (заня́ться *perf*) (чем-н); **all of the rooms are occupied** все кóмнаты зáняты; **he was occupied with his work** он был зáнят рабóтой.

occur [ə'kə:ʳ] *vi* (*take place*) происходи́ть* (произойти́* *perf*), случáться (случи́ться *perf*); (*exist*) встречáться (встре́титься *perf*); **to ~ to sb** приходи́ть* (прийти́* *perf*) комý-н в гóлову.

occurrence [ə'kʌrəns] *n* (*event*) происше́ствие; (*existence*) слýчай.

ocean ['əuʃən] *n* океáн; **~s of** (*fig*: *inf*) мóре +*gen*.

ocean bed *n* дно* океáна.

ocean-going ['əuʃəngəuɪŋ] *adj* (*ship etc*) океáнский.

Oceania [əuʃɪ'eɪnɪə] *n* Океáния.

ocean liner *n* океáнский лáйнер.

ochre ['əukəʳ] (*US* **ocher**) *adj* (*colour*) óхровый.

o'clock [ə'klɔk] *adv*: **it is five ~** сейчáс пять часóв.

OCR *n abbr* (*COMPUT*) = **optical character recognition, optical character reader**.

Oct. *abbr* = **October**.

octagonal [ɔk'tægənl] *adj* восьмиугóльный.

octane ['ɔkteɪn] *n* октáн; **high-~ petrol** *or* (*US*) **gas** бензи́н с высóким октáновым числóм.

octave ['ɔktɪv] *n* октáва.

October [ɔk'təubəʳ] *n* октя́брь* *m*; *see also* **July**.

octogenarian ['ɔktəudʒɪ'nɛərɪən] *n*: **he is an ~** емý за вóсемьдесят.

octopus ['ɔktəpəs] *n* осьминóг.

odd [ɔd] *adj* (*strange*) стрáнный* (стрáнен), необы́чный* (необы́чен); (*uneven*) нечётный; (*not paired*) непáрный; (*rare*) ре́дкий*; **60-~** шестьдеся́т с ли́шним; **at ~ times** врéмя от врéмени; **I was the ~ one out** я был ли́шний.

oddball ['ɔdbɔ:l] *n* (*inf*) чудáк*.

oddity ['ɔdɪtɪ] *n* (*thing*) дикóвинка; (*person*) рéдкость *f*; (*characteristic*) стрáнность *f*.

odd-job man [ɔd'dʒɔb-] *n* разнорабóчий* *m adj*.

odd jobs *npl* случáйные рабóты *fpl*.

oddly ['ɔdlɪ] *adv* (*strangely*: *behave, dress*) стрáнно; *see also* **enough**.

oddments ['ɔdmənts] *npl* остáтки *mpl*.

odds [ɔdz] *npl* (*in betting*) стáвки* *fpl*; **the ~ are against him** обстоя́тельства прóтив негó; **to succeed against all the ~** добивáться (доби́ться* *perf*) успéха наперекóр всемý; **it makes no ~** всё равнó; **to be at ~ (with)** быть* (*impf*) не в ладáх (с +*instr*).

odds and ends *npl* мéлочи* *fpl*.

odds-on [ɔdz'ɔn] *adj* (*inf*: *favourite*) абсолю́тный; **he is ~ to win the election** он навернякá победи́т на вы́борах.

ode [əud] *n* óда.

Odessa [əu'dɛsə] *n* Одéсса.

odious ['əudɪəs] *adj* одиóзный* (одиóзен).

odometer [ɔ'dɔmɪtəʳ] *n* одóметр.

odour ['əudəʳ] (*US* **odor**) *n* зáпах.

odourless ['əudəlɪs] *adj* без зáпаха.

OECD *n abbr* = *Organization for Economic Cooperation and Development*.

oesophagus [i:'sɔfəgəs] (*US* **esophagus**) *n* пищевóд.

oestrogen ['i:strəudʒən] (*US* **estrogen**) *n* эстрогéн.

KEYWORD

of [ɔv] *prep*: ***1***: **the history of Russia** истóрия Росси́и; **a friend of ours** наш друг*; **a boy of 10** мáльчик десяти́ лет; **that was kind of you** э́то бы́ло óчень любéзно с вáшей стороны́; **a man of great ability** человéк больши́х спосóбностей; **the city of New York** гóрод Нью-Йóрк; **south of London** к ю́гу от Лóндона

2 (*expressing quantity, amount, dates etc*): **a kilo of flour** килогрáмм муки́; **how much of this material do you need?** скóлько такóй ткани́ Вам нýжно?; **there were three of them** (*people*) их бы́ло трóе; (*objects*) их бы́ло три; **3 of us stayed** трóе из нас остáлись; **the 5th of July** 5-ое ию́ля; **on the 5th of July** 5-ого ию́ля

3 (*from, out of*) из +*gen*; **the house is made of wood** дом* сдéлан из дéрева.

KEYWORD

off [ɔf] *adv* ***1*** (*referring to distance, time*): **it's a long way off** э́то далекó отсю́да; **the city is five miles off** до гóрода пять миль; **the game is 3 days off** до игры́ остáлось 3 дня́

2 (*departure*): **to go off to Paris/Italy** уезжáть (уéхать* *perf*) в Пари́ж/Итáлию; **I must be off** мне порá идти́*

3 (*removal*): **to take off one's hat/coat/clothes** снимáть (снять* *perf*) шля́пу/пальтó/одéжду; **the button came off** пýговица оторвалáсь; **10% off** (*COMM*) ски́дка в 10%

4: **to be off** (*on holiday*) быть (*impf*) в óтпуске; **I'm off on Fridays** у меня́ выходнóй по пя́тницам; **he was off on Friday** в пя́тницу егó нé было на рабóте; **I have a day off** у меня́ отгýл; **to be off sick** не рабóтать (*impf*) по болéзни

◆ *adj* ***1*** (*not turned on*) вы́ключенный (вы́ключен); (: *tap*) закры́тый (закры́т); (*disconnected*) отключённый (отключён)

2 (*cancelled*: *meeting, match*) отменённый (отменён); (*agreement*) растóргнутый (растóргнут)

3 (*BRIT*): **to go off** (*milk*) прокисáть (проки́снуть* *perf*); (*cheese, meat*) пóртиться (испóртиться *perf*); **the milk has gone off** молокó проки́сло:

4: **on the off chance** на вся́кий* слýчай; **to have an off day** вставáть* (встать* *perf*) с лéвой ноги́

◆ *prep* ***1*** (*indicating motion, removal etc*) с +*gen*; **to fall off a cliff** упáсть (*perf*) со скалы́

2 (*distant from*) от +*gen*; **it's just off the M1** это недалеко от автострады M1; **it's five km off the main road** это в пяти км от шоссе; **to be off meat** (*no longer eat it*) не есть* (*impf*) мясо; (*no longer like it*) разлюбить* (*perf*) мясо.

offal ['ɔfl] *n* потроха* *pl*.
offbeat ['ɔfbi:t] *adj* нетривиальный* (нетривиален).
off-centre [ɔf'sɛntə^r] (*US* **off-center**) *adj* смещённый* (смещён) ◆ *adv* не по центру.
off colour *adj* (*BRIT*: *inf*): **I feel ~ ~** мне нездоровится.
offence [ə'fɛns] (*US* **offense**) *n* (*crime*) правонарушение; (*insult*) оскорбление; **to commit an ~** совершать (совершить *perf*) правонарушение; **to take ~ at** обижаться (обидеться* *perf*) на +*acc*; **to give ~ to** обижать (обидеть* *perf*), оскорблять (оскорбить* *perf*); **"no ~, but ..."** „не в обиду будет сказано, но ...".
offend [ə'fɛnd] *vt* (*person*) обижать (обидеть* *perf*); (*feelings*) оскорблять (оскорбить* *perf*) ◆ *vi*: **to ~ against** (*law, rule*) нарушать (нарушить *perf*).
offender [ə'fɛndə^r] *n* правонарушитель(ница) *m(f)*.
offending [ə'fɛndɪŋ] *adj* соответствующий*.
offense [ə'fɛns] *n* (*US*) = **offence**.
offensive [ə'fɛnsɪv] *adj* (*remark, behaviour*) оскорбительный* (оскорбителен); (*smell etc*) отвратительный* (отвратителен) ◆ *n* (*MIL*) наступление; **~ weapon** орудие нападения.
offer ['ɔfə^r] *n* предложение ◆ *vt* предлагать (предложить* *perf*); **to make an ~ for sth** предлагать (предложить* *perf*) цену за что-н; **to ~ sth to sb** предлагать (предложить* *perf*) кому-н что-н; **to ~ to do** предлагать (предложить* *perf*) +*infin*; **"on ~"** (*COMM*) „продаётся со скидкой".
offering ['ɔfərɪŋ] *n* (*also REL*) подношение.
offer price *n* цена продовца.
offhand [ɔf'hænd] *adj* (*unfriendly*) пренебрежительный* (пренебрежителен); (*easy-going*) непринуждённый* (непринуждён) ◆ *adv* сразу, не думая; **I can't tell you ~** я не могу Вам сказать сразу.
office ['ɔfɪs] *n* офис; (*room*) кабинет; (*position*) пост, должность *f*; **doctor's ~** (*US*) кабинет врача; **to take ~** (*person*) вступать (вступить* *perf*) в должность; (*political party*) приходить* (прийти* *perf*) к власти; **through his good ~s** (*fig*) благодаря его услугам; **the O~ of Fair Trading** (*BRIT*) Управление добросовестной конкуренции.
office automation *n* автоматизация делопроизводства.
office bearer *n* должностное лицо*.
office block (*US* **office building**) *n* административное здание.
office boy *n* посыльный *m adj*.
office hours *npl* часы *mpl* работы; (*US*: *MED*) приёмные часы *mpl*.
office manager *n* начальник конторы.
officer ['ɔfɪsə^r] *n* (*MIL*) офицер; (*also*: **police ~**) полицейский* *m adj*; (: *in Russia*) милиционер; (*of organization*) заведующий* *m adj*.
office work *n* канцелярская работа.
office worker *n* канцелярский*(-ая) *or* конторский*(-ая) служащий*(-ая) *m(f) adj*.
official [ə'fɪʃl] *adj* официальный ◆ *n* должностное лицо*; **government ~** официальное лицо*.
officialdom [ə'fɪʃldəm] *n* (*pej*) бюрократия.
officially [ə'fɪʃəlɪ] *adv* официально.
Official Receiver *n* (*COMM*) *официальное лицо, назначенное для проведения ликвидации неплатёжеспособной компании.*
official strike *n* официальная забастовка.
officiate [ə'fɪʃɪeɪt] *vi* распоряжаться (*impf*); (*REL*) совершать (совершить *perf*) богослужение; **to ~ as Mayor** исполнять (*impf*) обязанности мэра; **to ~ at a marriage** совершать (совершить *perf*) бракосочетание.
officious [ə'fɪʃəs] *adj* придирчивый.
offing ['ɔfɪŋ] *n*: **war is in the ~** война грядёт.
off-key [ɔf'ki:] *adj* (*MUS*) фальшивый.
off-licence ['ɔflaɪsns] *n* (*BRIT*) винный магазин.
off-limits [ɔf'lɪmɪts] *adj* (*esp US*) закрытый (закрыт).
off-line [ɔf'laɪn] *adj* (*COMPUT*) автономный, независимый ◆ *adv* (*COMPUT*) автономно, независимо; (: *switched off*) отключённо.
off-load ['ɔfləud] *vt* сваливать (свалить *perf*).
off-peak ['ɔf'pi:k] *adj* (*heating, electricity*) непиковый; (*train, ticket*) со скидкой.
off-putting ['ɔfputɪŋ] *adj* (*BRIT*) нерасполагающий.
off-season ['ɔf'si:zn] *adj* (*booking etc*) несезонный ◆ *adv* не в сезон.
offset ['ɔfsɛt] *irreg vt* уравновешивать (*impf*).
offshoot ['ɔfʃu:t] *n* (*fig*) ответвление; (: *of discussion*) последствие.
offshore [ɔf'ʃɔ:^r] *adj* (*oilrig, fishing*) морской; **there was a gentle ~ breeze** на море дул лёгкий бриз.
offside ['ɔf'saɪd] *n* (*AUT*: *in Britain*) правая сторона ◆ *adj* (*SPORT*): **to be ~** быть* (*impf*) в офсайде.
offspring ['ɔfsprɪŋ] *n inv* отпрыск.
offstage [ɔf'steɪdʒ] *adv* (*sounds*) за сценой.
off-the-cuff [ɔfðə'kʌf] *adj* импровизированный.

off-the-job [ˈɔfðəˈdʒɔb] *adj*: **~ training** обучéние с отры́вом от произво́дства.
off-the-peg [ˈɔfðəˈpɛg] (*US* **off-the-rack**) *adj*: **~ clothing** гото́вая оде́жда.
off-the-rack [ˈɔfðəˈræk] *adj* (*US*) = **off-the-peg**.
off-the-record [ˈɔfðəˈrɛkɔ:d] *adj* неофициа́льный* (неофициа́лен) ◆ *adv* неофициа́льно.
off-white [ˈɔfwaɪt] *adj* белова́тый.
Ofgas [ˈɔfgæs] *n* (*BRIT*) *управле́ние по контро́лю за газоснабже́нием.*
Oftel [ˈɔftɛl] *n* (*BRIT*) *управле́ние по контро́лю за телефо́нной се́тью.*
Ofwat [ˈɔfwɔt] *n* (*BRIT*) *управле́ние по контро́лю за водоснабже́нием.*
often [ˈɔfn] *adv* ча́сто; **how ~ ...?** как ча́сто ...?; **more ~ than not** ча́ще всего́; **as ~ as not** дово́льно ча́сто; **every so ~** вре́мя от вре́мени.
ogle [ˈəugl] *vt* глазе́ть (*impf*) на +*acc*.
ogre [ˈəugəʳ] *n* велика́н-людое́д.
OH *abbr* (*US*: *POST*) = *Ohio*.
oh [əu] *excl* о, а; **~ really!** да!; **~ no!** (о) нет!
ohm [əum] *n* (*ELEC*) ом.
OHMS *abbr* (*BRIT*: = *On His/Her Majesty's Service*) на слу́жбе у Его́/Её Короле́вского Вели́чества.
oil [ɔɪl] *n* (*CULIN*) ма́сло; (*petroleum*) нефть *f*; (*for heating*) печно́е то́пливо ◆ *vt* (*engine, gun etc*) сма́зывать (сма́зать* *perf*); **~s** *npl* (*ART*) ма́сляные кра́ски *fpl*.
oilcan [ˈɔɪlkæn] *n* маслёнка*.
oil change *n* (*AUT*) сме́на ма́сла (*в мото́ре*).
oilcloth [ˈɔɪlklɔθ] *n* клеёнка*.
oilfield [ˈɔɪlfi:ld] *n* месторожде́ние не́фти.
oil filter *n* (*AUT*) ма́сляный фильтр.
oilfired [ˈɔɪlfaɪəd] *adj* ма́сляный.
oil gauge *n* (*AUT*) индика́тор у́ровня ма́сла.
oil industry *n* нефтяна́я промы́шленность *f*.
oil painting *n* карти́на, напи́санная ма́слом.
oil refinery *n* нефтеперераба́тывающий заво́д.
oil rig *n* нефтяна́я платфо́рма.
oilseed rape [ˈɔɪlsi:d-] *n* ра́пс, суре́пка.
oilskins [ˈɔɪlskɪnz] *npl* водонепроница́емая оде́жда *fsg*.
oil slick *n* нефтяно́е пятно́*.
oil tanker *n* (*ship*) та́нкер; (*truck*) нефтево́з.
oil well *n* нефтяна́я сква́жина.
oily [ˈɔɪlɪ] *adj* (*rag*) прома́сленный (прома́слен); (*substance*) масляни́стый; (*food*) жи́рный* (жи́рен).
ointment [ˈɔɪntmənt] *n* мазь *f*.
OK *abbr* (*US*: *POST*) = *Oklahoma*.
O.K. [ˈəuˈkeɪ] *excl* (*inf*) хорошо́, ла́дно ◆ *adj* (*film, meal etc*) сре́дний* ◆ *vt* (*approve*) одобря́ть (одо́брить *perf*) ◆ *n*: **to give sth the ~** дава́ть* (дать* *perf*) добро́ на что-н; **is it ~?** (э́то) норма́льно?; **is everything ~?** всё в поря́дке?; **are you (feeling) ~?** Вы себя́ норма́льно чу́вствуете?; **are you ~ for money?** у Вас нет пробле́м с деньга́ми?; **it's ~ with** *or* **by me** я не про́тив.
okay [əuˈkeɪ] *excl* = **O.K.**.
old [əuld] *adj* (*aged*) ста́рый* (стар); (*former*) ста́рый; **how ~ are you?** ско́лько Вам лет?; **he's 10 years ~** ему́ 10 лет; **~ man** стари́к; **~ woman** стару́ха; **~er brother** ста́рший* брат*; **any ~ rag will do** сойдёт люба́я тря́пка.
old age *n* ста́рость *f*.
old age pension *n* пе́нсия по ста́рости.
old age pensioner *n* (*BRIT*) пенсионе́р(ка*).
old-fashioned [ˈəuldˈfæʃnd] *adj* старомо́дный* (старомо́ден).
old hand *n* о́пытный челове́к.
old hat *adj* (*inf*): **this is very ~ ~** э́то ужа́сно нено́во.
old maid *n* ста́рая де́ва.
old people's home *n* дом* для преста́релых.
old-style [ˈəuldstaɪl] *adj* в стари́нном сти́ле.
old-time [ˈəuldˈtaɪm] *adj* (*dancing*) старомо́дный.
old-timer [əuldˈtaɪməʳ] *n* (*inf*) старожи́л(ка*).
old wives' tale *n* ба́бушкины ска́зки* *fpl*.
oleander [əulɪˈændəʳ] *n* олеа́ндр.
O-level [ˈəulɛvl] *n* (*formerly*) ≈ экза́мены в 8-ом кла́ссе сре́дней шко́лы.
olive [ˈɔlɪv] *n* (*fruit*) масли́на, оли́вка* ◆ *adj* (*also*: **~-green**) оли́вковый; **~ tree** оли́вковое де́рево*; **to offer an ~ branch** (*fig*) предлага́ть (предложи́ть* *perf*) переми́рие.
olive oil *n* оли́вковое ма́сло.
Olympic [əuˈlɪmpɪk] *adj* олимпи́йский*.
Olympic Games *npl*: **the ~ ~** (*also*: **the Olympics**) Олимпи́йские и́гры *fpl*.
OM *n abbr* (*BRIT*: = *Order of Merit*) о́рден "За заслу́ги".
Oman [əuˈmɑ:n] *n* Ома́н.
OMB *n abbr* (*US*) = *Office of Management and Budget*.
ombudsman [ˈɔmbudzmən] *n официа́льное лицо́, рассма́тривающее жа́лобы ча́стных лиц на госуда́рственные учрежде́ния.*
omelet(te) [ˈɔmlɪt] *n* омле́т; **ham/cheese ~** омле́т с ветчино́й/сы́ром.
omen [ˈəumən] *n* предзнаменова́ние.
ominous [ˈɔmɪnəs] *adj* злове́щий* (злове́щ).
omission [əuˈmɪʃən] *n* про́пуск.
omit [əuˈmɪt] *vt* пропуска́ть (пропусти́ть* *perf*) ◆ *vi*: **he ~ted to inform me of this** он не проинформи́ровал меня́ об э́том.
omnipotent [ɔmˈnɪpətnt] *adj* всемогу́щий* (всемогу́щ).
omnivorous [ɔmˈnɪvrəs] *adj* всея́дный* (всея́ден).
ON *abbr* (*CANADA*) = *Ontario*.

KEYWORD

on [ɔn] *prep* **1** (*position*) на +*prp*; (*motion*) на +*acc*; **the book is on the table** кни́га на столе́; **to put the book on the table** класть* (положи́ть* *perf*) кни́гу на стол; **on the left**

слéва; **the house is on the main road** дом стóит у шоссé

2 (*indicating means, method, condition etc*): **on foot** пешкóм; **on the train/plane** (*go*) на пóезде/самолёте; (*be*) в пóезде/самолёте; **on the telephone/radio/television** по телефóну/рáдио/телевúзору; **she's on the telephone** онá разговáривает по телефóну; **to be on drugs** принимáть *(impf)* лекáрства; **to be on holiday/business** быть *(impf)* в óтпуске/командирóвке

3 (*referring to time*): **on Friday** в пятницу; **on Fridays** по пятницам; **on June 20th** 20-ого июня; **a week on Friday** чéрез недéлю, считáя с пятницы; **on arrival** по приéзде; **on seeing this** увúдев э́то

4 (*about, concerning*) о *+prp*, по *+dat*; **information on train services** информáция о расписáнии поездóв; **a book on physics** кнúга по фúзике

◆ *adv* **1** (*referring to dress*) в *+prp*; **to have one's coat on** быть *(impf)* в пальтó; **what's she got on?** во что онá былá одéта?; **she put her boots/gloves/hat on** онá надéла сапогú/перчáтки/шля́пу

2 (*further, continuously*) дáльше, дáлее; **to walk on** идтú* *(impf)* дáльше

◆ *adj* **1** (*functioning, in operation*) включённый (включён); (: *tap*) откры́тый (откры́т); **is the meeting still on?** (*in progress*) собрáние ещё идёт?; (*not cancelled*) собрáние не отменúли?; **there's a good film on at the cinema** в кинотеáтре идёт хорóший фильм

2: **that's not on!** (*inf*: *of behaviour*) так не пойдёт *or* не годúтся!

ONC *n abbr* (*BRIT*: = *Ordinary National Certificate*) ≈ свидéтельство об окончáнии начáльной шкóлы.

once [wʌns] *adv* (*on one occasion*) (одúн) раз; (*formerly*) когдá-то, однáжды ◆ *conj* (*immediately afterwards*) как тóлько; **~ he had left** как тóлько он ушёл; **at ~** (*immediately*) срáзу же; (*simultaneously*) вмéсте; **come here at ~!** сейчáс же подойдú сюдá!; **(all) at ~** все вмéсте; **~ a week** (одúн) раз в недéлю; **~ more** ещё раз; **~ and for all** раз и навсегдá; **I knew him ~** я когдá-то был знакóм с ним; **~ upon a time there lived ...** жил-был ....

oncoming ['ɔnkʌmɪŋ] *adj* (*traffic etc*) встрéчный.

OND *n abbr* (*BRIT*: = *Ordinary National Diploma*) *диплóм о срéднем техни́ческом образовáнии.*

KEYWORD

one [wʌn] *n* одúн* (*f* однá*, *nt* однó*, *pl* однú*); **one hundred and fifty** сто пятьдеся́т; **one day there was a sudden knock at the door** однáжды неожúданно раздáлся стук в дверь; **one by one** по одномý, одúн за другúм; *see also* **five**

◆ *adj* **1** (*sole*) еди́нственный; **the one book which** еди́нственная кнúга, котóрая

2 (*same*) одúн; **they all belong to the one family** онú все из однóй семьú

◆ *pron*: **1**: **I'm the one who did it** э́то я сдéлал; **this one** э́тот (*f* э́та, *nt* э́то); **that one** тот (*f* та, *nt* то); **I've already got one** у меня́ ужé есть:

2: **one another** друг дрýга; **do you two ever see one another?** Вы когдá-нибудь вúдитесь?; **the boys didn't dare look at one another** мáльчики не смéли взглянýть друг на дрýга

3 (*impersonal*): **one never knows** никогдá не знáешь; **to cut one's finger** порéзать *(perf)* (себé) пáлец; **one needs to eat** нáдо *or* нýжно есть.

one-day excursion ['wʌndeɪ-] *n* (*US*) обрáтный билéт (*действи́тельный в течéние одногó дня*).

One-hundred share index ['wʌnhʌndrəd-] *n* и́ндекс стá áкций (*публикýемый ежеднéвно и покáзывающий состоя́ние фóндовой би́ржи*).

one-man ['wʌn'mæn] *adj* (*business*) индивидуáльный; (*canoe*) одномéстный.

one-man band *n* человéк-оркéстр.

one-off [wʌn'ɔf] *n* (*BRIT*: *inf*) едини́чный слýчай.

one-parent family ['wʌnpɛərənt-] *n* непóлная семья́*.

one-piece ['wʌnpi:s] *adj*: **~ bathing suit** цéльный купáльник.

onerous ['ɔnərəs] *adj* тя́гостный* (тя́гостен), обременúтельный* (обременúтелен).

one's [wʌnz] *adj*: **to dry ~ hands** вытирáть (вы́тереть* *perf*) рýки; *see also* **my**.

oneself [wʌn'sɛlf] *pron* (*reflexive*) себя́; (*emphatic*) сам; (*after prep*: *+acc, +gen*) самóго себя́; (: *+dat*) самóму себé; (: *+instr*) самúм собóй; (: *+prp*) самóм себé; **to hurt ~** ушибáться (ушибúться *perf*); **to keep sth for ~** держáть* *(impf)* что-н при себé; **to talk to ~** разговáривать *(impf)* с самúм собóй.

one-shot ['wʌnʃɔt] *n* (*US*) = **one-off**.

one-sided [wʌn'saɪdɪd] *adj* односторóнний (односторóнен); (*contest*) нерáвный* (нерáвен).

one-time ['wʌntaɪm] *adj* бы́вший*.

one-to-one ['wʌntəwʌn] *adj* (*tuition etc*) индивидуáльный ◆ *adv* одúн на одúн.

* marks translations which have irregular inflections. The Russian-English side of the dictionary gives inflectional information.

one-upmanship [wʌn'ʌpmənʃɪp] *n*: **the art of ~** умéние вы́делиться и показáть своё превосхóдство.
one-way ['wʌnweɪ] *adj* (*traffic*) одностóронний*; **~ street** ýлица с одностóронним движéнием.
ongoing ['ɔngəuɪŋ] *adj* продолжáющийся.
onion ['ʌnjən] *n* лук*.
on-line ['ɔnlaɪn] (*COMPUT*) *adj* неавтонóмный; (*switched on*) подключённый ◆ *adv* неавтонóмно.
onlooker ['ɔnlukəʳ] *n* зри́тель(ница) *m(f)*.
only ['əunlɪ] *adv* тóлько ◆ *adj* еди́нственный ◆ *conj* (*but*) тóлько; **an ~ child** еди́нственный ребёнок*; **I ~ bought one bottle** я купи́л тóлько однý буты́лку; **I saw her ~ yesterday** я тóлько вчерá ви́дел её; **I'd be ~ too pleased to help** я был бы óчень рад помóчь; **I would come, ~ I'm too busy** я бы пришёл, тóлько я сли́шком зáнят; **not ~ ... but also ...** не тóлько ..., но и ....
o.n.o. *abbr* (*BRIT*: *in classified ads*) = **or near(est) offer.**
onset ['ɔnsɛt] *n* наступлéние.
onshore ['ɔnʃɔːʳ] *adj*: **~ wind** вéтер с мóря; (*oil rig, drilling*) назéмный.
onslaught ['ɔnslɔːt] *n* нападéние.
on-the-job ['ɔnðə'dʒɔb] *adj*: **~ training** обучéние без отры́ва от произвóдства.
onto ['ɔntu] *prep* = **on to.**
onus ['əunəs] *n*: **the ~ is on him to prove it** егó долг – доказáть э́то.
onward(s) ['ɔnwəd(z)] *adv* вперёд, дáльше; **from that time ~** с тех пор.
onyx ['ɔnɪks] *n* óникс.
oops [ups] *excl* (*inf*) ой!
ooze [uːz] *vi* сочи́ться *(impf)* ◆ *vt*: **to ~ confidence** излучáть *(impf)* увéренность.
opacity [əu'pæsɪtɪ] *n* непрозрáчность *f*.
opal ['əupl] *n* опáл.
opaque [əu'peɪk] *adj* непрозрáчный* (непрозрáчен).
OPEC ['əupɛk] *n abbr* (= *Organization of Petroleum-Exporting Countries*) ОПÉК.
open ['əupn] *adj* (*also fig*) откры́тый; (*enemy, hostility*) откровéнный; (*vacancy*) свобóдный* ◆ *vt* открывáть (откры́ть* *perf*) ◆ *vi* открывáться (откры́ться* *perf*); (*flower*) раскрывáться (раскры́ться* *perf*); (*book, debate etc*: *commence*) начинáться (начáться* *perf*); **in the ~ (air)** на откры́том вóздухе; **the ~ sea** откры́тое мóре; **~ ground** (*among trees*) поля́на; (*waste ground*) пусты́рь* *m*; **to have an ~ mind on sth** подходи́ть* *(impf)* к чемý-н без предубеждéния
▸ **open on to** *vt fus* (*subj*: *room, door*) выходи́ть* *(impf)* в/на *+acc*
▸ **open out** *vt* раскрывáть (раскры́ть* *perf*) ◆ *vi* раскрывáться (раскры́ться* *perf*)
▸ **open up** *vt* открывáть (откры́ть* *perf*) ◆ *vi* открывáться (откры́ться* *perf*).
open-air [əupn'ɛəʳ] *adj* (*concert*) на откры́том вóздухе; (*swimming pool*) откры́тый.
open-and-shut ['əupnən'ʃʌt] *adj*: **~ case** элементáрное дéло.
open day *n* день* *m* откры́тых дверéй.
open-ended [əupn'ɛndɪd] *adj* (*fig*: *question*) откры́тый; (: *discussion*) незавершённый.
opener ['əupnəʳ] *n* (*also*: **tin** *or* **can ~**) открывáлка*.
open-heart [əupn'hɑːt] *adj*: **~ surgery** откры́тая оперáция на сéрдце.
opening ['əupnɪŋ] *adj* (*speech, remarks etc*) вступи́тельный ◆ *n* (*gap, hole*) отвéрстие; (*start*) начáло; (*opportunity*) возмóжность *f*; (*job*) вакáнсия.
opening night *n* (*THEAT*) премьéра.
open learning *n* самообучéние (*по подготóвленным посóбиям*).
openly ['əupnlɪ] *adv* откры́то.
open-minded [əupn'maɪndɪd] *adj* (*person*) откры́тый; (*approach*) непредвзя́тый.
open-necked ['əupnnɛkt] *adj* расстёгнутый.
openness ['əupnnɪs] *n* (*frankness*) откры́тость *f*.
open-plan ['əupn'plæn] *adj*: **~ office** óфис с откры́той планирóвкой.
open prison *n* тюрьмá свобóдного режи́ма.
open sandwich *n* бутербрóд.
open shop *n* (*TRADE UNIONS*) *предприя́тие, на котóрое нанимáют рабóчих незави́симо от члéнства в профсоюзе.*
Open University *n* (*BRIT*): **the ~ ~** Откры́тый университéт.
open verdict *n* (*LAW*): **an ~ ~ was passed** объяви́ли, что причи́на смéрти неустанóвлена.
opera ['ɔpərə] *n* óпера.
opera glasses *npl* театрáльный бинóкль *msg*.
opera house *n* óперный теáтр.
opera singer *n* óперный(-ая) певéц*(-ви́ца).
operate ['ɔpəreɪt] *vt* управля́ть *(impf)* *+instr* ◆ *vi* дéйствовать *(impf)*; (*drug*) дéйствовать (подéйствовать *perf*); (*MED*): **to ~ (on sb)** опери́ровать (прооопери́ровать *perf*) (когó-н).
operatic [ɔpə'rætɪk] *adj* óперный.
operating costs *n* эксплуатациóнные затрáты *fpl*.
operating profit *n* при́быль *f* от произвóдственной дéятельности.
operating room ['ɔpəreɪtɪŋ-] *n* (*US*) операциóнная *f adj*.
operating statement *n* отчёт о при́были и убы́тках; (*esp US*) текýщий балáнс.
operating system *n* (*COMPUT*) операциóнная систéма.
operating table *n* операциóнный стол*.
operating theatre *n* операциóнная *f adj*.
operation [ɔpə'reɪʃən] *n* (*of machine*: *functioning*) рабóта; (: *controlling*)

управле́ние; (*MED, MIL, COMM*) опера́ция; **to be in ~** де́йствовать *(impf)*; **he had an ~** (*MED*) ему́ сде́лали опера́цию; **to perform an ~** (*MED*) де́лать (сде́лать *perf*) опера́цию.
operational [ɔpə'reɪʃənl] *adj* (*working*) функциони́рующий; **the machine was ~** маши́на функциони́ровала.
operative ['ɔpərətɪv] *adj* (*law etc*) де́йствующий•; (*position*) операти́вный ◆ *n* (*in factory*) опера́тор; **the ~ word** ключево́е сло́во•.
operator ['ɔpəreɪtə^r] *n* (*TEL*) телефони́ст(ка•); (*of machine*) опера́тор.
operetta [ɔpə'rɛtə] *n* опере́тта.
ophthalmic [ɔf'θælmɪk] *adj* офтальмологи́ческий.
ophthalmic optician *n* окули́ст.
ophthalmologist [ɔfθæl'mɔlədʒɪst] *n* офтальмо́лог.
opinion [ə'pɪnjən] *n* мне́ние; **in my ~** по-мо́ему, по моему́ мне́нию; **to seek a second ~** запра́шивать (запроси́ть• *perf*) дополни́тельное мне́ние.
opinionated [ə'pɪnjəneɪtɪd] *adj* самоуве́ренный.
opinion poll *n* опро́с обще́ственного мне́ния.
opium ['əupɪəm] *n* о́пиум.
opponent [ə'pəunənt] *n* оппоне́нт, проти́вник(-ница); (*MIL, SPORT*) проти́вник.
opportune ['ɔpətju:n] *adj* подходя́щий•.
opportunism [ɔpə'tju:nɪsəm] *n* оппортуни́зм.
opportunist [ɔpə'tju:nɪst] *n* оппортуни́ст.
opportunity [ɔpə'tju:nɪtɪ] *n* возмо́жность *f*; **to take the ~ of doing** по́льзоваться (воспо́льзоваться *perf*) слу́чаем что́бы *+infin*.
oppose [ə'pəuz] *vt* проти́виться• (воспроти́виться• *perf*) *+dat*; **to be ~d to sth** проти́виться *(impf)* чему́-н; **as ~d to** в противополо́жность *+dat*.
opposing [ə'pəuzɪŋ] *adj* (*ideas, forces*) противополо́жный; **the ~ team** кома́нда проти́вника.
opposite ['ɔpəzɪt] *adj* противополо́жный ◆ *adv* напро́тив ◆ *prep* напро́тив *+gen* ◆ *n*: **the ~** (*say, think, do etc*) противополо́жное *nt adj*; **the ~ sex** противополо́жный пол; **"see ~ page"** „см. на противополо́жной страни́це".
opposite number *n* (*person*) *лицо́, занима́ющее соотве́тствующую до́лжность в друго́й организа́ции.*
opposition [ɔpə'zɪʃən] *n* оппози́ция; **the O~** (*POL*) оппозицио́нная па́ртия.
oppress [ə'prɛs] *vt* угнета́ть *(impf)*.
oppression [ə'prɛʃən] *n* угнете́ние.
oppressive [ə'prɛsɪv] *adj* (*régime*) угнета́тельский; (*weather, heat*) гнету́щий•.
opprobrium [ə'prəubrɪəm] *n* (*formal*) осужде́ние.
opt [ɔpt] *vi*: **to ~ for** избира́ть (избра́ть• *perf*); **to ~ to do** реша́ть (реши́ть *perf*) *+infin*
▶ **opt out** *vi* (*school, hospital etc*) выходи́ть• (вы́йти• *perf*) из-под госуда́рственного контро́ля; **to ~ out of sth** выходи́ть• (вы́йти• *perf*) из чего́-н.
optical ['ɔptɪkl] *adj* опти́ческий•.
optical character reader *n* (*COMPUT*) устро́йство опти́ческого счи́тывания си́мволов.
optical character recognition *n* (*COMPUT*) опти́ческое распознава́ние си́мволов.
optical fibre *n* опти́ческое волокно́.
optical illusion *n* опти́ческий• обма́н.
optician [ɔp'tɪʃən] *n* окули́ст.
optics ['ɔptɪks] *n* (*PHYS*) о́птика.
optimism ['ɔptɪmɪzəm] *n* оптими́зм.
optimist ['ɔptɪmɪst] *n* оптими́ст(ка•).
optimistic [ɔptɪ'mɪstɪk] *adj* оптимисти́чный• (оптимисти́чен).
optimum ['ɔptɪməm] *adj* оптима́льный.
option ['ɔpʃən] *n* (*choice*) вариа́нт; (*SCOL*) предме́т по вы́бору; (*COMM*) опцио́н; **to keep one's ~s open** оставля́ть (оста́вить• *perf*) за собо́й пра́во вы́бора; **I have no ~** у меня́ нет вы́бора.
optional ['ɔpʃənl] *adj* (*also COMM*) необяза́тельный•; **~ extras** дополни́тельные, но необяза́тельные това́ры и́ли услу́ги.
opulence ['ɔpjuləns] *n* бога́тство.
opulent ['ɔpjulənt] *adj* (*person, society etc*) бога́тый.
OR *abbr* (*US: POST*) = *Oregon*.
or [ɔ:^r] *conj* и́ли; (*otherwise*): **~ (else)** а то, ина́че; (*with negative*): **he hasn't seen ~ heard anything** он ничего́ не ви́дел и не слы́шал.
oracle ['ɔrəkl] *n* (*prophet*) ора́кул; (*prophecy*) прорица́ние.
oral ['ɔ:rəl] *adj* (*test, report*) у́стный; (*vaccine, medicine*) ора́льный ◆ *n* (*exam*) у́стный экза́мен.
orange ['ɔrɪndʒ] *n* апельси́н ◆ *adj* (*colour*) ора́нжевый.
orangeade [ɔrɪndʒ'eɪd] *n* апельси́новый напи́ток•.
oration [ɔ:'reɪʃən] *n* торже́ственная речь *f*.
orator ['ɔrətə^r] *n* ора́тор.
oratorio [ɔrə'tɔ:rɪəu] *n* орато́рия.
orb [ɔ:b] *n* шар•.
orbit ['ɔ:bɪt] *n* орби́та ◆ *vt* обраща́ться *(impf)* вокру́г *+gen*.
orchard ['ɔ:tʃəd] *n* сад• (*фрукто́вый*); **apple ~** я́блоневый сад•.
orchestra ['ɔ:kɪstrə] *n* орке́стр; (*US: seating*) парте́р.
orchestral [ɔ:'kɛstrəl] *adj* оркестро́вый; **~ musician** оркестра́нт(ка•).

• marks translations which have irregular inflections. The Russian-English side of the dictionary gives inflectional information.

orchestrate ['ɔ:kıstreıt] *vt* (*stage-manage*) организо́вывать (организова́ть *perf*); (*MUS*) оркестрова́ть *(impf/perf)*.
orchid ['ɔ:kıd] *n* орхиде́я.
ordain [ɔ:'deın] *vt* (*REL*) посвяща́ть (посвяти́ть* *perf*) в сан; (*decide*) предпи́сывать (предписа́ть* *perf*).
ordeal [ɔ:'di:l] *n* испыта́ние.
order ['ɔ:də'] *n* (*command*) прика́з; (*from shop, company, in restaurant*) зака́з; (*sequence, discipline*) поря́док* ◆ *vt* (*command*) прика́зывать (приказа́ть* *perf*) *+dat*; (*from shop, company, in restaurant*) зака́зывать (заказа́ть* *perf*); (*also:* **put in ~**) располага́ть (расположи́ть* *perf*) по поря́дку; **in ~** в поря́дке; **in (working) ~** испра́вный* (испра́вен); **in ~ to do** для того́ что́бы *+infin*; **in ~ of size** по разме́ру; **it is already on ~** (*COMM*) э́то у́же зака́зано; **out of ~** (*not in sequence*) не по поря́дку; (*not working*) неиспра́вный* (неиспра́вен); **to place an ~ for sth with sb** зака́зывать (заказа́ть* *perf*) что-н кому́-н; **made to ~** сде́лан на зака́з; **she is under ~s to remain silent** ей прика́зано молча́ть; **a point of ~** вопро́с о наруше́нии регла́мента; **to the ~ of** (*BANKING*) опла́чиваемый по ве́кселю на и́мя *+gen*; **to ~ sb to do** прика́зывать (приказа́ть* *perf*) кому́-н *+infin*.
order book *n* кни́га зака́зов.
order form *n* бланк зака́за.
orderly ['ɔ:dəlı] *n* (*MIL*) ордина́рец*; (*MED*) санита́р ◆ *adj* (*room*) опря́тный* (опря́тен); (*person*) организо́ванный* (организо́ван); (*system*) упоря́доченный* (упоря́дочен).
order number *n* но́мер* зака́за.
ordinal ['ɔ:dınl] *adj*: **~ number** поря́дковое числи́тельное *nt adj*.
ordinarily ['ɔ:dnrılı] *adv* обы́чно.
ordinary ['ɔ:dnrı] *adj* (*everyday, usual*) обыкнове́нный* (обыкнове́нен), обы́чный* (обы́чен); (*mediocre*) зауря́дный* (зауря́ден); **out of the ~** (*exceptional*) необыкнове́нный* (необыкнове́нен).
ordinary seaman *n* (*BRIT*) мла́дший* матро́с.
ordinary shares *npl* обыкнове́нные а́кции *fpl*.
ordination [ɔ:dı'neıʃən] *n* (*REL*) посвяще́ние в духо́вный сан.
ordnance ['ɔ:dnəns] *n* (*MIL*) ору́дие ◆ *adj* (*factory, supplies*) оруже́йный.
Ordnance Survey *n* (*BRIT*) ≈ Госуда́рственное Управле́ние по геоде́зии и картогра́фии.
ore [ɔ:'] *n* руда́*.
Orenburg ['ɔrənbə:g] *n* Оренбу́рг.
organ ['ɔ:gən] *n* (*ANAT*) о́рган; (*MUS*) орга́н.
organic [ɔ:'gænık] *adj* (*fertilizer*) органи́ческий*; (*food*) вы́ращенный без примене́ния химика́тов.
organism ['ɔ:gənızəm] *n* органи́зм.
organist ['ɔ:gənıst] *n* органи́ст(ка*).
organization [ɔ:gənaı'zeıʃən] *n* организа́ция.
organization chart *n* организацио́нная структу́ра.
organize ['ɔ:gənaız] *vt* организо́вывать (организова́ть *perf*), устра́ивать (устро́ить *perf*); **to get ~d** организо́вываться (организова́ться *perf*).
organized crime *n* организо́ванная престу́пность *f*.
organized labour *n* чле́ны *mpl* профсою́зов.
organizer ['ɔ:gənaızə'] *n* организа́тор, устрои́тель(ница) *m(f)*.
orgasm ['ɔ:gæzəm] *n* орга́зм.
orgy ['ɔ:dʒı] *n* о́ргия, разгу́л.
Orient ['ɔ:rıənt] *n*: **the ~** Восто́к.
orient ['ɔ:rıənt] *vt* ориенти́ровать (сориенти́ровать *perf*).
oriental [ɔ:rı'ɛntl] *adj* восто́чный.
orientate ['ɔ:rıənteıt] *vt*: **to ~ o.s.** ориенти́роваться (сориенти́роваться *perf*).
orifice ['ɔrıfıs] *n* отве́рстие.
origin ['ɔrıdʒın] *n* происхожде́ние; **country of ~** ме́сто* рожде́ния.
original [ə'rıdʒınl] *adj* (*new*) оригина́льный* (оригина́лен); (*genuine*) по́длинный* (по́длинен); (*imaginative*: *writer, artist etc*) самобы́тный* (самобы́тен) ◆ *n* по́длинник, оригина́л.
originality [ərıdʒı'nælıtı] *n* (*of artist etc*) самобы́тность *f*, оригина́льность *f*.
originally [ə'rıdʒınəlı] *adv* первонача́льно.
originate [ə'rıdʒıneıt] *vi*: **to ~ from** происходи́ть* (произойти́* *perf*) от/из *+gen*; **to ~ in** зарожда́ться (зароди́ться* *perf*) в *+prp*.
originator [ə'rıdʒıneıtə'] *n* созда́тель *m*.
Orkneys ['ɔ:knız] *npl*: **the ~** (*also:* **the Orkney Islands**) Оркне́йские острова́* *mpl*.
ornament ['ɔ:nəmənt] *n* (*decorative object*) украше́ние; (*on building, dress etc*) орна́мент.
ornamental [ɔ:nə'mɛntl] *adj* (*decorative*: *garden, pond*) декорати́вный.
ornamentation [ɔ:nəmɛn'teıʃən] *n* украше́ние.
ornate [ɔ:'neıt] *adj* декорати́вный.
ornithologist [ɔ:nı'θɔlədʒıst] *n* орнито́лог.
ornithology [ɔ:nı'θɔlədʒı] *n* орнитоло́гия.
orphan ['ɔ:fn] *n* сирота́* *m/f* ◆ *vt*: **to be ~ed** оста́ться* *(perf)* сирото́й, осироте́ть *(perf)*.
orphanage ['ɔ:fənıdʒ] *n* де́тский* дом*.
orthodox ['ɔ:θədɔks] *adj* (*also fig*) ортодокса́льный* (ортодокса́лен); **the Russian O~ Church** Ру́сская Правосла́вная це́рковь.
orthodoxy ['ɔ:θədɔksı] *n* ортодокса́льные воззре́ния *ntpl*.
orthopaedic [ɔ:θə'pi:dık] (*US* **orthopedic**) *adj* ортопеди́ческий*.
OS *abbr* (*BRIT*) = **Ordnance Survey**; (*NAUT*) = **ordinary seaman**; (*DRESS*) = **outsize**.
O/S *abbr* (*COMM*: = *out of stock*) нет в прода́же.
Oscar ['ɔskə'] *n* О́скар (*приз*).

oscillate ['ɔsɪleɪt] *vi* (*ELEC, PHYS*) колеба́ться• (*impf*), осцилли́ровать (*impf*); (*fig*) колеба́ться• (*impf*).
OSHA *n abbr* (*US*) = *Occupational Safety and Health Administration.*
Oslo ['ɔzləu] *n* О́сло *nt ind*.
ostensible [ɔs'tɛnsɪbl] *adj* мни́мый.
ostensibly [ɔs'tɛnsɪblɪ] *adv* я́кобы.
ostentation [ɔstɛn'teɪʃən] *n* показна́я ро́скошь *f*.
ostentatious [ɔstɛn'teɪʃəs] *adj* (*building, car*) бро́ский•; (*behaviour*) показно́й; **he is very ~** он выставля́ет себя́ напока́з.
osteopath ['ɔstɪəpæθ] *n* остеопа́т.
ostracize ['ɔstrəsaɪz] *vt* подверга́ть (подве́ргнуть• *perf*) остраки́зму.
ostrich ['ɔstrɪtʃ] *n* стра́ус.
OT *abbr* (*BIBLE*: = *Old Testament*) Ве́тхий• заве́т.
OTB *n abbr* (*US*: = *off-track betting*) внеипподро́мный тотализа́тор.
OTE *abbr* (*COMM*: = *on-target earnings*) *предполага́емый дохо́д*.
other ['ʌðə'] *adj* друго́й ◆ *pron*: **the ~ (one)** друго́й(-а́я) *m(f) adj*, тот (*f* та) ◆ *adv*: **~ than** кро́ме *+gen*; **~s** (*other people*) други́е *pl adj*; **the ~s** остальны́е *pl adj*; **the ~ day** на днях; **some ~ people have still to arrive** прие́дет ещё не́сколько челове́к; **some actor or ~** како́й-то из актёров; **somebody or ~** кто-нибу́дь, кто-то; **it was none ~ than the prime minister** э́то был ни кто ино́й как премье́р-мини́стр.
otherwise ['ʌðəwaɪz] *adv* (*differently*) ина́че, по-друго́му; (*apart from that*) в остально́м ◆ *conj* а то, ина́че; **it is an ~ good piece of work** в остально́м э́то о́чень хоро́шая рабо́та.
OTT *abbr* (*inf*) = **over the top** *see* **top**.
Ottawa ['ɔtəwə] *n* Отта́ва.
otter ['ɔtə'] *n* вы́дра.
OU *n abbr* (*BRIT*) = **Open University**.
ouch [autʃ] *excl* ай, ой.
ought [ɔ:t] (*pt* **ought**) *aux vb*: **I ~ to do it** мне сле́довало бы э́то сде́лать; **this ~ to have been corrected** э́то сле́довало испра́вить; **he ~ to win** он до́лжен вы́играть; **you ~ to go and see this film** Вы обяза́тельно должны́ посмотре́ть э́тот фильм.
ounce [auns] *n* у́нция.
our ['auə'] *adj* наш; *see also* **my**.
ours [auəz] *pron* наш; (*referring to subject of sentence*) свой; *see also* **mine**[1].
ourselves [auə'sɛlvz] *pl pron* (*reflexive*) себя́; (*complement*) себя́; (*after prep*: *+acc, +gen*) себя́; (: *+dat*) себе́; (: *+instr*) собо́й; (: *+prp*) себе́; (*emphatic*) са́ми; (*alone*): **(all) by ~** са́ми; **let's keep it between ~** дава́йте оста́вим э́то ме́жду на́ми; *see also* **myself**.
oust [aust] *vt* изгоня́ть (изгна́ть• *perf*).

KEYWORD

out [aut] *adv* **1** (*not in*): **they're out in the garden** они́ в саду́; **out in the rain/snow** под дождём/сне́гом; **out here** здесь; **out there** там; **to go out** выходи́ть• (вы́йти• *perf*); **out loud** гро́мко
2 (*not at home, absent*): **he is out at the moment** его́ сейча́с нет (до́ма); **let's have a night out on Friday!** дава́йте пойдём куда́-нибудь в пя́тницу ве́чером!
3 (*indicating distance*) в *+prp*; **the boat was 10 km out (from the shore)** кора́бль находи́лся в 10 км от бе́рега; **three days out from Plymouth** в трёх днях пла́вания от Пли́мута
4 (*SPORT*): **the ball is out** мяч за преде́лами по́ля; **out!** (*TENNIS etc*) а́ут!
◆ *adj*: **1**: **to be out** (*unconscious*) быть (*impf*) без созна́ния; (*out of game*) быть (*impf*) удалённым(-ой) с по́ля; (*have appeared*: *flowers*) распуска́ться (распусти́ться• *perf*); (: *news, secret*) станови́ться• (стать• *perf*) изве́стным(-ой); (*extinguished*: *fire, light, gas*) ту́хнуть• (поту́хнуть• *perf*), га́снуть• (пога́снуть• *perf*); (*fashion*): **to go out** выходи́ть• (вы́йти• *perf*) из мо́ды
2 (*finished*): **before the week was out** до оконча́ния неде́ли:
3: **to be out to do** (*intend*) намерева́ться (*impf*) *+infin*; **to be out in one's calculations** (*wrong*) ошиба́ться (ошиби́ться• *perf*) в расчётах
◆ *prep* **1** (*outside, beyond*) из *+gen*; **to go out of the house** выходи́ть• (вы́йти• *perf*) из до́ма; **to be out of danger** (*safe*) быть (*impf*) вне опа́сности
2 (*cause, motive*): **out of curiosity** из любопы́тства; **out of fear** от стра́ха; **out of boredom** от *or* со ску́ки; **out of grief/joy** с го́ря/ра́дости; **out of necessity** по необходи́мости
3 (*from, from among*) из *+gen*
4 (*without*): **we are out of sugar/petrol** *etc* у нас ко́нчился са́хар/бензи́н *etc*.

outage ['autɪdʒ] *n* (*esp US*: *power failure*) отключе́ние электри́чества.
out-and-out ['autəndaut] *adj* отъя́вленный.
outback ['autbæk] *n* (*in Australia*): **the ~** необжиты́е райо́ны *mpl*.
outbid [aut'bɪd] *vt*: **to ~ sb** перебива́ть (переби́ть• *perf*) чью-н це́ну.
outboard ['autbɔ:d] *n* (*also*: **~ motor**) подвесно́й мото́р.
outbreak ['autbreɪk] *n* (*of disease, violence*) вспы́шка•; (*of war*) нача́ло.
outbuilding ['autbɪldɪŋ] *n* надво́рная постро́йка•.
outburst ['autbə:st] *n* вспы́шка•, взрыв.
outcast ['autkɑ:st] *n* изго́й.
outclass [aut'klɑ:s] *vt* превосходи́ть•

(превзойти* *perf*).
outcome ['autkʌm] *n* исход, результат.
outcrop ['autkrɔp] *n* (*of rock*) обнажение.
outcry ['autkraɪ] *n* негодование, протест.
outdated [aut'deɪtɪd] *adj* (*customs, ideas*) отживший; (*clothes*) старомодный*; (*technology*) устарелый.
outdo [aut'du:] *irreg vt* превосходить* (превзойти* *perf*).
outdoor [aut'dɔ:ʳ] *adj* на открытом воздухе; (*swimming pool*) открытый; **~ clothes** верхняя одежда.
outdoors [aut'dɔ:z] *adv* на улице, на открытом воздухе.
outer ['autəʳ] *adj* наружный; **~ suburbs** дальние предместья; **the ~ office** крайний* кабинет.
outer space *n* космическое пространство.
outfit ['autfɪt] *n* (*set of clothes*) комплект (одежды); (*inf: organization*) компания.
outfitter's ['autfɪtəz] *n* (*BRIT*) торговец* мужской одеждой.
outgoing ['autgəuɪŋ] *adj* (*extrovert*) общительный* (общителен); (*president, mayor etc*) уходящий; (*mail etc*) исходящий*.
outgoings ['autgəuɪŋz] *npl* (*BRIT*) расходы *mpl*.
outgrow [aut'grəu] *irreg vt* (*one's clothes*) вырастать (вырасти* *perf*) из *+gen*; (*friends, habits*) перерастать (перерасти* *perf*).
outhouse ['authaus] *n* надворная постройка*.
outing ['autɪŋ] *n* поход.
outlandish [aut'lændɪʃ] *adj* диковинный.
outlast [aut'lɑ:st] *vt* переживать (пережить* *perf*).
outlaw ['autlɔ:] *n* человек вне закона ◆ *vt* объявлять (объявить* *perf*) вне закона.
outlay ['autleɪ] *n* (*expenditure*) затраты *fpl*; (*investment*) вложения *ntpl*.
outlet ['autlɛt] *n* (*hole*) выходное отверстие; (*pipe*) сток; (*US: ELEC*) розетка*; (*COMM: also:* **retail ~**) торговая точка*; (*for emotions*) выход.
outline ['autlaɪn] *n* (*shape*) очертания *ntpl*; (*sketch, explanation*) набросок* ◆ *vt* (*fig: theory, plan etc*) набрасывать (набросать *perf*).
outlive [aut'lɪv] *vt* переживать (пережить* *perf*).
outlook ['autluk] *n* (*attitude*) взгляды *mpl*, воззрения *ntpl*; (*prospects*) перспективы *fpl*; (*: for weather*) прогноз.
outlying ['autlaɪɪŋ] *adj* отдалённый.
outmanoeuvre [autmə'nu:vəʳ] (*US* **outmaneuver**) *vt* перехитрить *(perf)*.
outmoded [aut'məudɪd] *adj* устаревший.
outnumber [aut'nʌmbəʳ] *vt* превосходить* (превзойти* *perf*) численно; **they were ~ed by 5 to 1** их было в пять раз меньше.
out of bounds *adj*: **this area is ~ ~ ~** эта место является запретным.
out-of-court [autəv'kɔ:t] *adv*: **to settle ~** приходить* (прийти* *perf*) к соглашению без обращения в суд.
out-of-date [autəv'deɪt] *adj* (*clothes etc*) немодный; (*dictionary*) устаревший; (*equipment*) устарелый; (*passport*) просроченный.
out-of-doors [autəv'dɔ:z] *adv* на улице, на открытом воздухе.
out-of-the-way ['autəvðə'weɪ] *adj* (*place*) глубинный; (*fig*) глухой.
out of touch *adj*: **to be ~ ~ ~** отставать* (отстать* *perf*) от времени.
out-of-work ['autəvwə:k] *adj* безработный.
outpatient ['autpeɪʃənt] *n* амбулаторный(-ая) больной(-ая) *m(f) adj*.
outpouring ['autpɔ:rɪŋ] *n* (*of emotions*) излияние.
outpost ['autpəust] *n* аванпост.
output ['autput] *n* (*production*) выработка; (*COMPUT*) выходные данные *pl adj* ◆ *vt* (*COMPUT*) выводить* (вывести* *perf*) (*данные*).
outrage ['autreɪdʒ] *n* (*action: scandalous*) возмутительный поступок*; (*: violent*) акт насилия; (*emotion*) возмущение ◆ *vt* (*shock, anger*) возмущать (возмутить* *perf*); **his behaviour is an ~** его поведение просто возмутительно.
outrageous [aut'reɪdʒəs] *adj* возмутительный* (возмутителен).
outrider ['autraɪdəʳ] *n* (*on motorcycle, horse*) эскорт.
outright [aut'raɪt] *adv* (*win, own*) абсолютно; (*refuse, deny*) наотрез; (*ask*) прямо; (*kill*) наповал ◆ *adj* (*winner, victory*) абсолютный; (*refusal, hostility*) открытый; **to be killed ~** погибать (погибнуть *perf*) сразу.
outrun [aut'rʌn] *irreg vt* обгонять (обогнать* *perf*), опережать (опередить* *perf*).
outset ['autsɛt] *n* начало; **from the ~** с самого начала; **at the ~** вначале.
outshine [aut'ʃaɪn] *irreg vt* (*fig*) затмевать (затмить *perf*).
outside [aut'saɪd] *n* наружная сторона* ◆ *adj* наружный, внешний* ◆ *adv* (*be*) снаружи; (*go*) наружу ◆ *prep* вне *+gen*, за пределами *+gen*; (*next to: building*) у *+gen*; (*: London etc*) под *+instr*; **at the ~** (*with times*) самое позднее;(*of size*) самое большее; **an ~ chance** ничтожный шанс; **it's cold ~** на улице холодно.
outside broadcast *n* (*RADIO, TV*) репортаж *or* трансляция с места событий.
outside lane *n* (*AUT: in Britain*) правый ряд; (*: in US, Europe*) левый ряд.
outside left *n* (*FOOTBALL*) левый крайний* нападающий* *m adj*.
outside line *n* (*TEL*) городской телефон; **dial "9" for an ~ ~** город – через девятку.
outsider [aut'saɪdəʳ] *n* (*person not involved*) посторонний*(-яя) *m(f) adj*; (*in race etc*) аутсайдер.

outside right *n* (FOOTBALL) пра́вый кра́йний* напада́ющий* *m adj*.
outsize ['autsaiz] *adj*: ~ **clothes** оде́жда *fsg* больши́х разме́ров.
outskirts ['autskə:ts] *npl* окра́ины *fpl*.
outsmart [aut'smɑ:t] *vt* перехитри́ть *(perf)*.
outspoken [aut'spəukən] *adj* открове́нный* (открове́нен).
outspread [aut'sprɛd] *adj* (*wings*) распростёртый (распростёрт).
outstanding [aut'stændiŋ] *adj* (*exceptional*) выдаю́щийся*; (*unfinished*) незако́нченный (незако́нчен); (*unpaid*) неопла́ченный (неопла́чен); **your account is still** ~ Вы до сих пор не уплати́ли по счёту.
outstay [aut'steɪ] *vt*: **to** ~ **one's welcome** заси́живаться (засиде́ться* *perf*) в гостя́х.
outstretched [aut'strɛtʃt] *adj* (*hand*) протя́нутый; (*arms*) вы́тянутый; (*body*) вы́тянувшийся.
outstrip [aut'strɪp] *vt* превосходи́ть* (превзойти́* *perf*).
out tray *n* корзи́на для исходя́щих докуме́нтов.
outvote [aut'vəut] *vt*: **to** ~ **sb by 3 votes** победи́ть *(perf)* кого́-н с переве́сом в 3 го́лоса.
outward ['autwəd] *adj* (*sign, appearances*) вне́шний*, нару́жный; **the** ~ **journey was much quicker** пое́здка туда́ намно́го быстре́е, чем пое́здка обра́тно.
outwardly ['autwədlɪ] *adv* вне́шне.
outweigh [aut'weɪ] *vt* переве́шивать (переве́сить* *perf*).
outwit [aut'wɪt] *vt* перехитри́ть *(perf)*.
ova ['əuvə] *npl of* **ovum**.
oval ['əuvl] *adj* ова́льный ◆ *n* ова́л.
ovarian [əu'vɛərɪən] *adj*: ~ **cyst** киста́ яи́чника; ~ **cancer** рак яи́чника.
ovary ['əuvərɪ] *n* яи́чник.
ovation [əu'veɪʃən] *n* ова́ция.
oven ['ʌvn] *n* (*domestic*) духо́вка*; (*baker's, industrial*) печь* *f*.
ovenproof ['ʌvnpru:f] *adj* жаросто́йкий, жаропро́чный*.
oven-ready ['ʌvnrɛdɪ] *adj* (*chicken, chips etc*) *гото́вый для жа́рения в духо́вке*.
ovenware ['ʌvnwɛə^r] *n* жаросто́йкая *or* жаропро́чная посу́да.

KEYWORD

over ['əuvə^r] *adv* ***1*** (*across*): **to cross over (to the other side of the road)** переходи́ть* (перейти́* *perf*) (на другу́ю сто́рону доро́ги); **over here** здесь; **over there** там; **to ask sb over** (*to one's house*) приглаша́ть (пригласи́ть* *perf*) кого́-н в го́сти *or* к себе́
2 (*indicating movement from upright*): **to knock/turn sth over** сбива́ть (сбить* *perf*)/перевора́чивать (переверну́ть *perf*) что-н; **to fall over** па́дать (упа́сть* *perf*); **to bend over** нагиба́ться (нагну́ться *perf*)
3 (*finished*): **the game is over** игра́ око́нчена; **his life is over** его́ жизнь ко́нчена
4 (*excessively*) сли́шком, чересчу́р
5 (*remaining*: *money, food etc*): **there are 3 over** 3 оста́лось:
6: **all over** (*everywhere*) везде́, повсю́ду; **over and over (again)** сно́ва и сно́ва
◆ *prep* ***1*** (*on top of*) на *+prp*; (*above*) над *+instr*
2 (*on the other side of*) че́рез *+acc*; **the pub over the road** паб че́рез доро́гу; **he jumped over the wall** он перепры́гнул че́рез стену́
3 (*more than*) свы́ше *+gen*; **over and above** бо́льше (чем); **this is over and above what we have already ordered** э́то бо́льше, чем мы уже́ заказа́ли
4 (*in the course of*) в тече́ние *+gen*, за *+acc*; **over the winter** за зи́му, в тече́ние зи́мы; **let's discuss it over dinner** дава́йте обсу́дим э́то за обе́дом; **the work is spread over two weeks** рабо́та рассчи́тана на две неде́ли.

over... ['əuvə^r] *prefix* пере....
overact [əuvər'ækt] *vi* переи́грывать (переигра́ть *perf*).
overall ['əuvərɔ:l] *adj* о́бщий* ◆ *adv* (*in general*) в це́лом *or* о́бщем; (*entirely*) целико́м ◆ *n* (BRIT: *child's, painter's etc*) хала́т; ~**s** *npl* (*clothing*) комбинезо́н *msg*.
overall majority *n* большинство́.
overanxious [əuvər'æŋkʃəs] *adj* весьма́ встрево́женный* (встрево́жен).
overawe [əuvər'ɔ:] *vt* вызыва́ть (вы́звать* *perf*) благогове́ние в *+prp*.
overbalance [əuvə'bæləns] *vi* теря́ть (потеря́ть *perf*) равнове́сие.
overbearing [əuvə'bɛərɪŋ] *adj* вла́стный* (вла́стен).
overboard ['əuvəbɔ:d] *adv*: **to fall** ~ па́дать (упа́сть* *perf*) за́ борт; **man** ~! челове́к за бо́ртом!; **to go** ~ (*fig*) переба́рщивать (переборщи́ть *perf*).
overbook [əuvə'buk] *vt*: **the play is** ~**ed** на пье́су прода́ли сли́шком мно́го биле́тов; **the hotel is** ~**ed** гости́ница перепо́лнена.
overcame [əuvə'keɪm] *pt of* **overcome**.
overcapitalize [əuvə'kæpɪtəlaɪz] *vt*: **to** ~ **a project** вкла́дывать (вложи́ть* *perf*) в прое́кт неопра́вданно большо́й капита́л.
overcast ['əuvəkɑ:st] *adj* па́смурный (па́смурен), хму́рый (хмур).
overcharge [əuvə'tʃɑ:dʒ] *vt* обсчи́тывать (обсчита́ть *perf*).
overcoat ['əuvəkəut] *n* пальто́ *nt ind*.
overcome [əuvə'kʌm] *irreg vt* (*opponent, enemy*) одолева́ть (одоле́ть *perf*);

(*difficulties, problems*) преодолева́ть (преодоле́ть *perf*) ◆ *adj*: **~ by** (*fear, suspicion*) одолева́емый (одолева́ем) *+instr*; **~ with** (*joy*) охва́ченный (охва́чен) *+instr*; **he was ~ with grief** он был уби́т го́рем.

overconfident [əuvə'kɔnfɪdənt] *adj* (*person*) самонаде́янный (самонаде́ян).

overcrowded [əuvə'kraudɪd] *adj* перепо́лненный (перепо́лнен).

overcrowding [əuvə'kraudɪŋ] *n* перенаселённость *f*; (*in bus*) теснота́.

overdo [əuvə'du:] *irreg vt* (*work, exercise*) перестара́ться *(perf)* в *+prp*; (*interest, concern*) утри́ровать *(impf)*; (*overcook: boil*) перева́ривать (перевари́ть* *perf*); (*: fry, bake*) пережа́ривать (пережа́рить *perf*); **don't ~ it!** (*compliments etc*) не переусе́рдствуйте!; (*work etc*) не перестара́йтесь!

overdose ['əuvədəus] *n* передозиро́вка*.

overdraft ['əuvədrɑ:ft] *n* (*COMM*) овердра́фт.

overdrawn [əuvə'drɔ:n] *adj*: **he is** *or* **his account is ~** он превы́сил креди́т своего́ теку́щего счёта.

overdrive ['əuvədraɪv] *n* (*AUT*) ускоря́ющая переда́ча.

overdue [əuvə'dju:] *adj* (*change, reform etc*) запозда́лый; (*account*) просро́ченный (просро́чен); **he/the bus is an hour ~** он/авто́бус опа́здывает на час; **these changes were long ~** э́тих переме́н давно́ жда́ли.

overemphasis [əuvər'ɛmfəsɪs] *n*: **~ on** изли́шнее ударе́ние на *+prp*.

overestimate [əuvər'ɛstɪmeɪt] *vt* переоце́нивать (переоцени́ть* *perf*).

overexcited [əuvərɪk'saɪtɪd] *adj* чрезме́рно возбуждённый* (возбуждён).

overexertion [əuvərɪg'zə:ʃən] *n* перенапряже́ние.

overexpose [əuvərɪk'spəuz] *vt* (*PHOT*) передéрживать (передержа́ть* *perf*).

overflow [əuvə'fləu] *vi* (*river*) разлива́ться (разли́ться* *perf*); (*sink, vase etc*) переполня́ться (перепо́лниться *perf*) ◆ *n* (*also:* **~ pipe**) сливна́я труба́.

overfly [əuvə'flaɪ] *irreg vt* (*fly past*) пролета́ть (пролете́ть* *perf*).

overgenerous [əuvə'dʒɛnərəs] *adj* сли́шком ще́дрый* (щедр).

overgrown [əuvə'grəun] *adj* (*garden*) заро́сший; **he's just an ~ schoolboy** он про́сто перево́сток.

overhang ['əuvə'hæŋ] *irreg vt* нависа́ть (нави́снуть* *perf*) над *+instr* ◆ *vi* нависа́ть (нави́снуть* *perf*) ◆ *n* наве́с.

overhaul [əuvə'hɔ:l] *vt* (*engine, equipment*) производи́ть* (произвести́* *perf*) по́лную прове́рку и ремо́нт *+gen* ◆ *n* по́лная прове́рка и ремо́нт.

overhead [*adv* əuvə'hɛd, *adj, n* 'əuvəhɛd] *adv* (*above*) наверху́, над голово́й; (*in the sky*) в не́бе ◆ *adj* (*lighting*) ве́рхний*; (*cable, railway*) надзе́мный ◆ *n* (*US*) = **overheads**; **~s** *npl* (*expenses*) накладны́е расхо́ды *mpl*.

overhear [əuvə'hɪə'] *irreg vt* (случа́йно) подслу́шать* *(perf)*.

overheat [əuvə'hi:t] *vi* перегрева́ться (перегре́ться *perf*).

overjoyed [əuvə'dʒɔɪd] *adj*: **to be ~ (at)** о́чень ра́доваться (обра́доваться *perf*) (*+dat*); **she was ~ to see him** она́ бы́ла о́чень ра́да его́ ви́деть.

overkill ['əuvəkɪl] *n* (*fig*): **it would be ~** э́то бу́дет я́вный перебо́р.

overland ['əuvəlænd] *adj* сухопу́тный ◆ *adv* (*travel*) по су́ше.

overlap [əuvə'læp] *vi* (*edges*) находи́ть* *(impf)* оди́н на друго́й; (*fig: ideas, activities etc*) части́чно совпада́ть (совпа́сть* *perf*).

overleaf [əuvə'li:f] *adv* на оборо́те.

overload [əuvə'ləud] *vt* (*also ELEC, fig*) перегружа́ть (перегрузи́ть* *perf*); **to ~ with work/problems** перегружа́ть (перегрузи́ть* *perf*) рабо́той/пробле́мами.

overlook [əuvə'luk] *vt* (*have view into*) выходи́ть* *(impf)* на *+acc*; (*fail to consider*) упуска́ть (упусти́ть* *perf*) из ви́ду; (*excuse*) закрыва́ть (закры́ть* *perf*) глаза́ на *+acc*.

overlord ['əuvəlɔ:d] *n* повели́тель *m*.

overmanning [əuvə'mænɪŋ] *n* (*INDUSTRY*) избы́ток* рабо́чей си́лы.

overnight [əuvə'naɪt] *adv* (*for the night*) на́ ночь; (*during the night*) за́ ночь; (*fig: suddenly*) за́ день, сра́зу же ◆ *adj* (*train, journey*) ночно́й; **to travel ~** путеше́ствовать *(impf)* но́чью; **to stay ~** ночева́ть (переночева́ть *perf*); **he'll be away ~** он е́дет с ночёвкой.

overpass ['əuvəpɑ:s] *n* (*esp US*) путепрово́д.

overpay [əuvə'peɪ] *vt*: **to ~ sb by £50** перепла́чивать (переплати́ть* *perf*) кому́-н £50.

overplay [əuvə'pleɪ] *vt* преувели́чивать (преувели́чить *perf*) значе́ние *+gen*.

overpower [əuvə'pauə'] *vt* переси́ливать (переси́лить *perf*).

overpowering [əuvə'pauərɪŋ] *adj* (*heat, stench*) невыноси́мый (невыноси́м).

overproduction ['əuvəprə'dʌkʃən] *n* перепроизво́дство.

overrate [əuvə'reɪt] *vt* переоце́нивать (переоцени́ть* *perf*).

overreach [əuvə'ri:tʃ] *vt*: **to ~ o.s.** перенапряга́ться (перенапря́чься* *perf*).

overreact [əuvəri:'ækt] *vi* горячи́ться (погорячи́ться *perf*).

override [əuvə'raɪd] *irreg vt* (*order, objection*) отверга́ть (отве́ргнуть* *perf*).

overriding [əuvə'raɪdɪŋ] *adj* (*importance*) первостепе́нный; (*factor, consideration*) реша́ющий*.

overrule [əuvə'ru:l] *vt* (*decision*) отменя́ть (отмени́ть* *perf*); (*objection*) отверга́ть

(отве́ргнуть* *perf*); **the judge ~d the defence** судья́ отклони́л тре́бования защи́тника.
overrun [əuvə'rʌn] *irreg vt* (*country*) бы́стро овладева́ть (овладе́ть *perf*) +*instr*; (*time limit*) превыша́ть (превы́сить* *perf*) ◆ *vi* дли́ться* (*impf*) до́льше поло́женного (вре́мени); **the town is ~ with tourists** го́род наводнён тури́стами.
overseas [əuvə'si:z] *adv* (*live, travel, work*) за рубежо́м *or* грани́цей; (*to go*) за рубе́ж *or* грани́цу ◆ *adj* (*market, trade*) вне́шний*; (*student, visitor*) иностра́нный; **to trade ~** торгова́ть (*impf*) с иностра́нными госуда́рствами.
oversee [əuvə'si:] *vt* следи́ть* (*impf*) за +*instr*.
overseer ['əuvəsɪə'] *n* (*in factory*) контролёр.
overshadow [əuvə'ʃædəu] *vt* (*place, building etc*) возвыша́ться (*impf*) над +*instr*; (*fig*) затмева́ть (затми́ть* *perf*).
overshoot [əuvə'ʃu:t] *irreg vt* проезжа́ть (прое́хать* *perf*).
oversight ['əuvəsaɪt] *n* недосмо́тр; **due to an ~** по недосмо́тру.
oversimplify [əuvə'sɪmplɪfaɪ] *vt* сли́шком упроща́ть (упрости́ть* *perf*).
oversleep [əuvə'sli:p] *irreg vi* просыпа́ть (проспа́ть* *perf*).
overspend [əuvə'spɛnd] *irreg vi* перерасхо́довать (*impf/perf*); **we have overspent by 5,000 dollars** наш перерасхо́д соста́вил 5,000 до́лларов.
overspill ['əuvəspɪl] *n* (*excess population*) избы́точное населе́ние.
overstaffed [əuvə'stɑ:ft] *adj*: **this office is ~** в э́том отде́ле сли́шком мно́го рабо́тников.
overstate [əuvə'steɪt] *vt* преувели́чивать (преувели́чить *perf*).
overstatement [əuvə'steɪtmənt] *n* преувеличе́ние.
overstay [əuvə'steɪ] *vt*: **to ~ one's welcome** загости́ться* (*perf*).
overstep [əuvə'stɛp] *vt*: **to ~ the mark** переходи́ть* (перейти́* *perf*) грани́цы.
overstock [əuvə'stɔk] *vt* затова́ривать (затова́рить *perf*).
overstretched [əuvə'strɛtʃt] *adj* (*at work*) перегру́женный (перегру́жен); (*funds*) переизрасхо́дованный (переизрасхо́дован).
overstrike ['əuvəstraɪk] *irreg n* (*on printer*) набо́р ли́шних си́мволов ◆ *vt* набира́ть (набра́ть* *perf*) (*на клавиату́ре*).
oversubscribed [əuvəsəb'skraɪbd] *adj*: **this product is ~** коли́чество зая́вок на э́тот това́р превыша́ет предложе́ние.
overt [əu'və:t] *adj* открове́нный* (открове́нен).
overtake [əuvə'teɪk] *irreg vt* (*AUT*) обгоня́ть (обогна́ть* *perf*); (*subj*: *event, change*) застига́ть (засти́гнуть* *perf*) врасплóх; (: *emotion, weakness*) овладева́ть (овладе́ть *perf*) +*instr*.
overtaking [əuvə'teɪkɪŋ] *n* (*AUT*) обго́н.
overtax [əuvə'tæks] *vt* (*ECON*) облага́ть (обложи́ть* *perf*) сли́шком высо́ким нало́гом; (*strength, patience*) истоща́ть (истощи́ть *perf*); **to ~ o.s.** перенапряга́ться (перенапря́чься* *perf*).
overthrow [əuvə'θrəu] *irreg vt* сверга́ть (све́ргнуть* *perf*).
overtime ['əuvətaɪm] *n* сверхуро́чное вре́мя* *nt*; **to do** *or* **work ~** рабо́тать (*impf*) в сверхуро́чное вре́мя.
overtime ban *n* запре́т на сверхуро́чную рабо́ту.
overtone ['əuvətəun] *n* (*also:* **~s**): **~ of** намёк на +*acc*.
overture ['əuvətʃuə'] *n* (*MUS*) увертю́ра; (*fig*) подгото́вка*.
overturn [əuvə'tə:n] *vt* (*car, chair*) перевора́чивать (переверну́ть *perf*); (*decision, plan*) отверга́ть (отве́ргнуть *perf*); (*government, system*) сверга́ть (све́ргнуть *perf*) ◆ *vi* перевора́чиваться (переверну́ться *perf*).
overview ['əuvəvju:] *n* (*summary*) обзо́р; (*general understanding*) о́бщее представле́ние.
overweight [əuvə'weɪt] *adj* (*person*) ту́чный* (ту́чен); **your luggage is ~** у Вас переве́с.
overwhelm [əuvə'wɛlm] *vt* (*opponent, enemy etc*) оде́рживать (одержа́ть *perf*) верх над +*instr*; (*subj*: *feelings, emotions*) переполня́ть (перепо́лнить *perf*).
overwhelming [əuvə'wɛlmɪŋ] *adj* (*victory, defeat*) по́лный; (*majority*) подавля́ющий; (*feeling, desire*) всепобежда́ющий*; (*heat*) невыноси́мый (невыноси́м); **~ impression** о́бщее впечатле́ние.
overwhelmingly [əuvə'wɛlmɪŋlɪ] *adv* (*vote, win*) по́лностью; (*appreciative, generous etc*) безграни́чно; (*predominantly*: *opposed etc*) в основно́м.
overwork [əuvə'wə:k] *n* перегру́зка ◆ *vt* (*person*) перегружа́ть (перегрузи́ть* *perf*); (*cliché etc*) зата́скивать (затаска́ть *perf*) ◆ *vi* (*person*) переутомля́ться (переутоми́ться* *perf*).
overwrite [əuvə'raɪt] *vt* (*COMPUT*) перепи́сывать (переписа́ть* *perf*).
overwrought [əuvə'rɔ:t] *adj* (*person*) переутомлённый (переутомлён).
ovulate ['ɔvjuleɪt] *vi* овули́ровать (*impf/perf*).
ovulation [ɔvju'leɪʃən] *n* овуля́ция.
ovum ['əuvəm] (*pl* **ova**) *n* яйцо́* (*АНАТ*).
owe [əu] *vt*: **she ~s me £500** она́ мне должна́ £500; **we ~ him our gratitude** мы должны́

* marks translations which have irregular inflections. The Russian-English side of the dictionary gives inflectional information.

быть* благода́рны ему́; **he ~s his talent/life to that man** он обя́зан свои́м тала́нтом/ свое́й жи́знью э́тому челове́ку.
owing to ['əuɪŋ-] *prep* вслéдствие *+gen*.
owl [aul] *n* сова́*.
own [əun] *vt* владе́ть *(impf) +instr* ◆ *vi* (*BRIT*): **to ~ to sth** признава́ться* (призна́ться *perf*) в чём-н ◆ *adj* (*house, work, style etc*) со́бственный; **a room of one's ~** своя́ со́бственная ко́мната; **he lives on his ~** он живёт оди́н; **to come into one's ~** быть* *(impf)* в свое́й стихи́и; **to get one's ~ back** оты́грываться (отыгра́ться *perf*)
▸ **own up** *vi*: **to ~ up to sth** признава́ться* (призна́ться *perf*) в чём-н.
own brand *n* (*COMM*) *това́р с ма́ркой продаю́щей его́ торго́вой компа́нии*.
owner ['əunə^r] *n* владе́лец*(-лица).
owner-occupier ['əunər'ɔkjupaɪə^r] *n* домо-владе́лец(-лица).
ownership ['əunəʃɪp] *n*: **~ (of)** владе́ние (*+instr*); **under new ~** в но́вом владе́нии.
own goal *n* (*SPORT*): **to score an ~ ~** забива́ть (заби́ть* *perf*) гол в свой воро́та.
ox [ɔks] (*pl* **~en**) *n* бык*.
oxen ['ɔksn] *npl of* **ox**.
Oxfam ['ɔksfæm] *n abbr* (*BRIT*: = *Oxford Committee for Famine Relief*) О́ксфордский комите́т по́мощи голода́ющим.
Oxford ['ɔksfəd] *n* О́ксфорд.
oxide ['ɔksaɪd] *n* о́кись *f*, окси́д.
oxidize ['ɔksɪdaɪz] *vi* окисля́ться (окисли́ться *perf*).
Oxon. ['ɔksn] *abbr* (*BRIT*: *POST*) = *Oxfordshire*; (*in degree titles*) *Oxoniensis*.
oxtail ['ɔksteɪl] *n*: **~ soup** суп из бы́чьего хвоста́.
oxyacetylene ['ɔksɪə'sɛtɪli:n] *adj* (*flame*) ацетиле́новый.
oxygen ['ɔksɪdʒən] *n* кислоро́д.
oxygen mask *n* кислоро́дная ма́ска*.
oxygen tent *n* кислоро́дная пала́тка*.
oyster ['ɔɪstə^r] *n* у́стрица.
oz. *abbr* = **ounce**.
ozone ['əuzəun] *n* озо́н.
ozone layer *n* озо́новый слой*.
ozonosphere [əu'zəunəsfɪə^r] *n* озо́нный слой.

~ P, p ~

P, p [pi:] *n* (*letter*) *16-ая бу́ква англи́йского алфави́та.*

P. *abbr* = **president, prince.**

p *abbr* (*BRIT*) = **penny, pence.**

p. *abbr* (= **page**) стр.= *страни́ца.*

PA *n abbr* = **personal assistant, public-address system** ◆ *abbr* (*US: POST*) = *Pennsylvania.*

pa [pɑ:] *n* (*inf*) па́па.

p.a. *abbr* (= *per annum*) в год.

PAC *n abbr* (*US*) = *political action committee.*

pace [peɪs] *n* (*step*) шаг*; (*speed*) темп ◆ *vi*: **to ~ up and down** ходи́ть* (*impf*) взад вперёд; **to keep ~ with** (*person, events*) идти́* (*impf*) в но́гу с *+instr*; **to set the ~** (*also fig*) определя́ть (определи́ть *perf*); **I put him through his ~s** (*fig*) я посмотре́л, на что он спосо́бен.

pacemaker [ˈpeɪsmeɪkəʳ] *n* (*MED*) ритмиза́тор се́рдца; (*SPORT*) ли́дер.

Pacific [pəˈsɪfɪk] *n*: **the ~ (Ocean)** Ти́хий* океа́н.

pacific [pəˈsɪfɪk] *adj* (*intentions etc*) миролюби́вый.

pacifier [ˈpæsɪfaɪəʳ] *n* (*US: dummy*) со́ска*(-пусты́шка*).

pacifist [ˈpæsɪfɪst] *n* пацифи́ст(ка*).

pacify [ˈpæsɪfaɪ] *vt* умиротворя́ть (умиротвори́ть *perf*).

pack [pæk] *n* (*packet*) па́чка*; (*of hounds*) сво́ра; (*of wolves*) стая́; (*of people*) компа́ния; (*also:* **backpack**) рюкза́к*; (*of cards*) коло́да ◆ *vt* (*fill*) паковать *or* упако́вывать (упакова́ть *perf*); (*press down*) уплотня́ть (уплотни́ть *perf*); (*COMPUT*) упако́вывать (упакова́ть *perf*); (*cram*): **to ~ into** набива́ть (наби́ть* *perf*) в *+acc* ◆ *vi*: **to ~ (one's bags)** пакова́ть *or* упако́вывать (упакова́ть *perf*) чемода́ны; **to ~ sb off** отправля́ть (отпра́вить* *perf*) кого́-н; **to send sb ~ing** (*inf*) посыла́ть (посла́ть* *perf*) кого́-н пода́льше

▸ **pack in** (*BRIT: inf*) ◆ *vi* (*machine*) разва́ливаться (развали́ться *perf*) ◆ *vt* (*boyfriend*) завя́зывать (завяза́ть* *perf*) с *+instr*; **~ it in!** прекрати́!

▸ **pack off** *vt* отправля́ть (отпра́вить* *perf*)

▸ **pack up** *vi* (*BRIT: inf: machine*) разва́ливаться (развали́ться *perf*); (*: person*) закругля́ться (закругли́ться *perf*) ◆ *vt* пакова́ть *or* упако́вывать (упакова́ть *perf*).

package [ˈpækɪdʒ] *n* (*parcel, also COMPUT*) паке́т; (*also:* **~ deal**) паке́т предложе́ний ◆ *vt* пакова́ть *or* упако́вывать (упакова́ть *perf*).

package holiday *n* (*BRIT*) организо́ванный о́тдых по путёвке.

package tour *n* (*BRIT*) туристи́ческая пое́здка* по путёвке.

packaging [ˈpækɪdʒɪŋ] *n* упако́вка.

packed [pækt] *adj* (*crowded*) наби́тый (наби́т).

packed lunch *n* (*BRIT*) за́втрак в паке́те.

packer [ˈpækəʳ] *n* упако́вщик(-ица).

packet [ˈpækɪt] *n* (*of cigarettes, washing powder etc*) па́чка*; (*of crisps*) паке́т.

packet switching *n* (*COMPUT*) коммута́ция паке́тов, паке́тная коммута́ция.

pack ice [ˈpækaɪs] *n* пак, па́ковый лёд*.

packing [ˈpækɪŋ] *n* (*act*) упако́вка; (*material*) прокла́дочный материа́л.

packing case *n* упако́вочный я́щик.

pact [pækt] *n* пакт.

pad [pæd] *n* (*of paper*) блокно́т; (*soft material*) прокла́дка*; (*for inking*) поду́шечка*; (*inf: home*) (сво́й) у́гол* ◆ *vt* (*cushion, soft toy etc*) набива́ть (наби́ть* *perf*); (*shoulder, suit*) подбива́ть (подби́ть* *perf*) ◆ *vi*: **to ~ about** ступа́ть (*impf*).

padded cell [ˈpædɪd-] *n* пала́та, оби́тая во́йлоком (*в психиатри́ческой больни́це*).

padding [ˈpædɪŋ] *n* (*material*) наби́вочный материа́л, наби́вка; (*in speech*) вода́*.

paddle [ˈpædl] *n* (*oar*) байда́рочное весло́*; (*US: for table tennis*) раке́тка* ◆ *vt* (*boat, canoe etc*) управля́ть (*impf*) *+instr* ◆ *vi* (*with feet*) шлёпать (*impf*).

paddle steamer *n* колёсный парохо́д.

paddling pool [ˈpædlɪŋ-] *n* (*BRIT*) плеска́тельный бассе́йн.

paddock [ˈpædək] *n* (*field*) вы́гон; (*at racecourse*) заго́н.

paddy field [ˈpædɪ-] *n* ри́совое по́ле*.

padlock [ˈpædlɔk] *n* (вися́чий*) замо́к* ◆ *vt* запира́ть (запере́ть* *perf*) на вися́чий замо́к.

padre [ˈpɑ:drɪ] *n* (*REL*) па́дре *m ind.*

* marks translations which have irregular inflections. The Russian-English side of the dictionary gives inflectional information.

paediatrician [pi:dɪə'trɪʃən] (*US* **pediatrician**) *n* педиáтр, дéтский* врач.
paediatrics [pi:dɪ'ætrɪks] (*US* **pediatrics**) *n* педиатрия.
paedophile ['pi:dəufaɪl] (*US* **pedophile**) *n* педофил.
paedophilia [pi:dəu'fɪlɪə] (*US* **pedophilia**) *n* педофилия.
pagan ['peɪgən] *adj* языческий* ◆ *n* язычник(-ица).
page [peɪdʒ] *n* страница; (*also:* ~**boy**) паж*; (: *at wedding*) *мáльчик, несýщий шлейф невéсты* ◆ *vt* (*in hotel etc*) вызывáть (вызвать* *perf*).
pageant ['pædʒənt] *n* театрализóванное представлéние.
pageantry ['pædʒəntrɪ] *n* пышное зрéлище.
pageboy ['peɪdʒbɔɪ] *n see* **page**.
pager ['peɪdʒəʳ] *n портатúвное электрóнное устрóйство для вызова полицéйского, врачá итп.*
page three girl *n дéвушка, снимáющаяся в полуобнажённом вúде для фотогрáфий в бульвáрных газéтах.*
paginate ['pædʒɪneɪt] *vt* нумеровáть* (пронумеровáть* *perf*) страницы +*gen*.
pagination [pædʒɪ'neɪʃən] *n* нумерáция страниц, пагинáция.
pagoda [pə'gəudə] *n* пáгода.
paid [peɪd] *pt, pp of* **pay** ◆ *adj* оплáчиваемый; **to put ~ to** (*BRIT*) класть* (положить* *perf*) конéц +*dat*.
paid-in ['peɪdɪn] *adj* (*US*) = **paid-up**.
paid-up ['peɪdʌp] (*US* **paid-in**) *adj* (*COMM*: *shares*) оплáченный; **he is a ~ member** он уплатил члéнский* взнос; **~ capital** (*COMM*) оплáченная часть объявленного акционéрного капитáла.
pail [peɪl] *n* ведрó*.
pain [peɪn] *n* (*also fig*) боль *f*; **to be in ~** страдáть (*impf*) от бóли; **to have a ~ in** чýвствовать (*impf*) боль в +*prp*; **to take ~s to do** старáться (постарáться *perf*) изо всех сил, чтóбы +*infin*; **on ~ of death** под стрáхом смéрти.
pained [peɪnd] *adj* обиженный (обижен).
painful ['peɪnful] *adj* (*upsetting, unpleasant, laborious*) мучительный* (мучителен); (*sore*): **my back is ~** спинá причиняет мне боль.
painfully ['peɪnfəlɪ] *adv* (*fig*: *very*) глубокó; (: *aware, familiar*) до бóли; (: *dull, obvious*) мучительно.
painkiller ['peɪnkɪləʳ] *n* болеутоляющее *nt adj* (срéдство).
painless ['peɪnlɪs] *adj* безболéзненный* (безболéзнен).
painstaking ['peɪnzteɪkɪŋ] *adj* кропотливый (кропотлив).
paint [peɪnt] *n* крáска* ◆ *vt* (*wall, door, house etc*) красить* (выкрасить* *or* покрáсить* *perf*); (*picture, portrait*) рисовáть (нарисовáть *perf*); (*about artists*) писáть* (написáть* *perf*); (*fig*) изображáть (изобразить* *perf*); **a tin of ~** бáнка* крáски; **to ~ the door blue** крáсить* (выкрасить* *or* покрáсить* *perf*) дверь в голубóй цвет; **to ~ in oils** писáть* (написáть* *perf*) мáслом.
paintbox ['peɪntbɔks] *n* набóр крáсок.
paintbrush ['peɪntbrʌʃ] *n* кисть* *f*.
painter ['peɪntəʳ] *n* (*artist*) худóжник(-ица); (*decorator*) маляр*.
painting ['peɪntɪŋ] *n* (*activity*: *of artist*) живопись *f*; (: *of decorator*) малярное дéло; (*picture*) картина.
paint stripper *n* срéдство для снятия крáски.
paintwork ['peɪntwə:k] *n* крáска.
pair [pɛəʳ] *n* пáра; **a ~ of scissors** нóжницы *pl*; **a ~ of trousers** пáра брюк
▸ **pair off** *vi*: **to ~ off with sb** объединяться (объединиться* *perf*) в пáре с кем-н.
pajamas [pə'dʒɑ:məz] *npl* (*US*) пижáма *fsg*.
Pakistan [pɑ:kɪ'stɑ:n] *n* Пакистáн.
Pakistani [pɑ:kɪ'stɑ:nɪ] *adj* пакистáнский* ◆ *n* пакистáнец*(-нка*).
PAL *n abbr* (*TV*: = *phase alternation line*) ПАЛ.
pal [pæl] *n* (*inf*) кóреш.
palace ['pæləs] *n* дворéц*.
palaeontology [pælɪɔn'tɔlədʒɪ] *n* палеонтолóгия.
palatable ['pælɪtəbl] *adj* (*food, drink*) вкýсный* (вкýсен); (*idea, fact*) приéмлемый.
palate ['pælɪt] *n* (*ANAT*) нёбо; (*fig*) вкус.
palatial [pə'leɪʃəl] *adj* роскóшный* (роскóшен).
palaver [pə'lɑ:vəʳ] *n* (*inf*) суетня.
pale [peɪl] *adj* блéдный* (блéден) ◆ *vi* бледнéть (побледнéть *perf*) ◆ *n*: **his behaviour is beyond the ~** (*unacceptable*) егó поведéние перехóдит все грáницы; **to grow** *or* **turn ~** бледнéть (побледнéть *perf*); **~ blue** блéдно-голубóй; **to ~ into insignificance beside** бледнéть (побледнéть *perf*) пéред +*instr*.
paleness ['peɪlnɪs] *n* блéдность *f*.
Palestine ['pælɪstaɪn] *n* Палестина.
Palestinian [pælɪs'tɪnɪən] *adj* палестинский* ◆ *n* палестинец*(-нка*).
palette ['pælɪt] *n* (*ART*) палитра.
palings ['peɪlɪŋz] *npl* частокóл *msg*.
palisade [pælɪ'seɪd] *n* крепостнáя оагрáда.
pall [pɔ:l] *n* (*cloud of smoke*) покрóв ◆ *vi* приедáться (приéсться* *perf*).
pallet ['pælɪt] *n* (*for goods*) поддóн.
palliative ['pælɪətɪv] *n* (*MED*) паллиатúвное срéдство; (*fig*) полумéра.
pallid ['pælɪd] *adj* блéдный* (блéден).
pallor ['pæləʳ] *n* блéдность *f*.
pally ['pælɪ] *adj* (*inf*) свóйский*.
palm [pɑ:m] *n* (*also:* ~ **tree**) пáльма; (*of hand*) ладóнь *f* ◆ *vt*: **to ~ sth off on sb** (*inf*) подсóвывать (подсýнуть *perf*) что-н комý-н.

palmist ['pɑ:mɪst] *n* хиромáнт(ка*).
Palm Sunday *n* ≈ Вéрбное воскресéнье.
palpable ['pælpəbl] *adj* ощути́мый (ощути́м).
palpitations [pælpɪ'teɪʃənz] *npl* (учащённое) сердцебиéние *ntsg*.
paltry ['pɔ:ltrɪ] *adj* (*amount*) ничтóжный* (ничтóжен).
pamper ['pæmpə'] *vt* баловáть (избаловáть *perf*).
pamphlet ['pæmflət] *n* (*leaflet*) брошю́ра; (: *political, literary etc*) памфлéт.
pan [pæn] *n* (*also:* **saucepan**) кастрю́ля; (*also:* **frying** ~) сковородá ◆ *vi* (*CINEMA, TV*) панорами́ровать *(impf/perf)* ◆ *vt* (*inf: book, film*) разноси́ть* (разнести́* *perf*); **to ~ for gold** намывáть (намы́ть* *perf*) зóлото.
panacea [pænə'sɪə] *n* панацéя.
panache [pə'næʃ] *n* щегольствó.
Panama ['pænəmɑ:] *n* Панáма.
panama *n* (*also:* ~ **hat**) панáма.
Panama Canal *n*: **the** ~ ~ Панáмский* канáл.
Panamanian [pænə'meɪnɪən] *adj* панáмский* ◆ *n* панáмец*(-мка).
pancake ['pænkeɪk] *n* (*thin*) блин*; (*thick*) олáдья.
Pancake Day *n* (*BRIT*) *втóрник во врéмя мáсленицы, в котóрый пекýт блины́.*
pancake roll *n* бли́нчик с начи́нкой (*свёрнутый в трýбочку*).
pancreas ['pæŋkrɪəs] *n* поджелýдочная железá*.
panda ['pændə] *n* бамбýковый медвéдь *m*.
panda car *n* (*BRIT*) полицéйская маши́на.
pandemonium [pændɪ'məunɪəm] *n* столпотворéние.
pander ['pændə'] *vi*: **to ~ to** потвóрствовать *(impf)* +*dat*.
p & h *abbr* (*US*: = *postage and handling*) почтóвые расхóды *pl*.
P & L *abbr* (= *profit and loss*) при́быль *f* и убы́ток.
p & p *abbr* (*BRIT*: = *postage and packing*) почтóвые расхóды и упакóвка.
pane [peɪn] *n*: ~ **(of glass)** (*in window*) окóнное стеклó*.
panel ['pænl] *n* (*of wood, metal, glass*) панéль *f*; (*of judges, experts*) коми́ссия.
panel game *n* (*BRIT: TV, RADIO*) виктори́на.
panelling ['pænəlɪŋ] (*US* **paneling**) *n* деревя́нная обши́вка.
panellist ['pænəlɪst] (*US* **panelist**) *n* (*TV, RADIO*) учáстник(-ица) прогрáммы.
pang [pæŋ] *n*: ~ **of jealousy** укóл рéвности; **~s of conscience** укóры сóвести; ~ **of regret** мýки сожалéния; **hunger ~s** голóдные бóли.
panhandler ['pænhændlə'] *n* (*US: inf*) ни́щий* *m adj*.
panic ['pænɪk] *n* пáника ◆ *vi* паниковáть *(impf)*.
panic buying [-baɪɪŋ] *n* скýпка дефици́тных товáров.
panicky ['pænɪkɪ] *adj* (*feeling, reaction*) пани́ческий*; (*person*): **he is very** ~ он паникýет.
panic-stricken ['pænɪkstrɪkən] *adj* (*person, crowd*) охвáченный (охвáчен) пáникой.
pannier ['pænɪə'] *n* (*on bicycle*) корзи́нка*-багáжник; (*on animal*) корзи́на.
panorama [pænə'rɑ:mə] *n* панорáма.
panoramic [pænə'ræmɪk] *adj* панорáмный.
pansy ['pænzɪ] *n* аню́тины глáзки *mpl*; (*inf: pej*) флунтя́й.
pant [pænt] *vi* задыхáться (задохнýться *perf*).
pantechnicon [pæn'tɛknɪkən] *n* (*BRIT: AUT*) *автофургóн для перевóзки мéбели or оборýдования.*
panther ['pænθə'] *n* пантéра.
panties ['pæntɪz] *npl* трýсики *pl*.
pantihose ['pæntɪhəuz] *npl* (*US*) колгóтки* *pl*.
panto ['pæntəu] *n* = **pantomime**.
pantomime ['pæntəmaɪm] *n* (*BRIT*) *рождéственское представлéние для детéй*; (: *fig*) фарс.
pantry ['pæntrɪ] *n* кладовáя *f adj*, кладóвка; (*room*) буфéтная *f adj*.
pants [pænts] *npl* (*BRIT: underwear*) трусы́ *pl*; (*US: trousers*) брю́ки *pl*.
pantsuit ['pæntsu:t] *n* (*US*) брю́чный костю́м.
papacy ['peɪpəsɪ] *n* пáпство.
papal ['peɪpəl] *adj* пáпский.
paparazzi [pæpə'rætsi:] *npl фотóграфы, гоня́ющиеся за знамени́тостями и фотографи́рующие их для бульвáрной прéссы.*
paper ['peɪpə'] *n* бумáга; (*also:* **newspaper**) газéта; (*exam*) пи́сьменный экзáмен; (*academic essay: at conference*) доклáд; (: *in journal*) статья́*; (*also:* **wallpaper**) обóи *pl* ◆ *adj* бумáжный ◆ *vt* (*room*) оклéивать (оклéить* *perf*) обóями; **~s** *npl* (*also:* **identity ~s**) докумéнты *mpl*; **a piece of** ~ (*odd bit*) клочóк бумáги, бумáжка; (*sheet*) лист* бумáги; **to put** *or* **get sth down on** ~ запи́сывать (записáть* *perf*) что-н на бумáге.
paper advance *n* (*on printer*) продвижéние бумáги.
paperback ['peɪpəbæk] *n* кни́га в мя́гкой облóжке ◆ *adj*: ~ **edition** издáние в мя́гкой облóжке.
paper bag *n* бумáжный пакéт.
paperboy ['peɪpəbɔɪ] *n* мáльчик-разнóсчик газéт.
paperclip ['peɪpəklɪp] *n* (канцеля́рская) скрéпка*.
papergirl ['peɪpəgə:l] *n* дéвочка-разнóсчица газéт.

paper hankie *n* бума́жный носово́й плато́к*.
paper mill *n* бума́жная фа́брика.
paper profit *n* бума́жная *or* нереализо́ванная при́быль *f*.
paper shop *n* ≈ газе́тный кио́ск.
paperweight ['peɪpəweɪt] *n* пресс-папье́ *nt ind*.
paperwork ['peɪpəwə:k] *n* канцеля́рская рабо́та.
papier-mâché ['pæpɪeɪ'mæʃeɪ] *n* папье́-маше́ *nt ind*.
paprika ['pæprɪkə] *n* кра́сный мо́лотый пе́рец*.
Pap smear ['pæp-] *n* мазо́к* с ше́йки ма́тки.
Pap test *n* = **Pap smear**.
par [pɑ:ʳ] *n* (*equality of value*) ра́венство; (*GOLF*) *коли́чество уда́ров, допусти́мое для ка́ждой лу́нки и́ли для всего́ по́ля*; **to be on a ~ with** быть* *(impf)* на одно́м у́ровне с *+instr*; **at ~** (*COMM*) по номина́лу; **to feel below** *or* **under ~** чу́вствовать *(impf)* себя́ нева́жно.
parable ['pærəbl] *n* при́тча.
parabola [pə'ræbələ] *n* пара́бола.
parachute ['pærəʃu:t] *n* парашю́т.
parachute jump *n* прыжо́к* с парашю́том.
parachutist ['pærəʃu:tɪst] *n* парашюти́ст(ка*).
parade [pə'reɪd] *n* (*public procession*) ше́ствие; (*MIL*) пара́д ◆ *vt* (*troops etc*) выстра́ивать (вы́строить *perf*); (*show off: wealth, knowledge etc*) выставля́ть (вы́ставить* *perf*) напока́з ◆ *vi* (*MIL*) идти́* *(impf)* стро́ем; **fashion ~** пока́з мод.
parade ground *n* (уче́бный) плац*.
paradise ['pærədaɪs] *n* (*also fig*) ра́й*.
paradox ['pærədɔks] *n* парадо́кс.
paradoxical [pærə'dɔksɪkl] *adj* парадокса́льный* (парадокса́лен).
paradoxically [pærə'dɔksɪklɪ] *adv* как э́то ни парадокса́льно.
paraffin ['pærəfɪn] *n* (*BRIT: also:* **~ oil**) кероси́н; **liquid ~** (*BRIT*) вазели́новое ма́сло.
paraffin heater *n* (*BRIT*) обогрева́тель *m* на твёрдом парафи́не.
paraffin lamp *n* (*BRIT*) кероси́новая ла́мпа.
paragon ['pærəgən] *n* (*of honesty, virtue etc*) образе́ц*.
paragraph ['pærəgrɑ:f] *n* абза́ц; (*of document*) пара́граф; **to begin a new ~** начина́ть (нача́ть* *perf*) писа́ть с абза́ца.
Paraguay ['pærəgwaɪ] *n* Паргва́й.
Paraguayan [pærə'gwaɪən] *adj* парагва́йский ◆ *n* парагва́ец*(-а́йка*).
parallel ['pærəlɛl] *adj* паралле́льный* (паралле́лен); (*fig: similar*) аналоги́чный* (аналоги́чен); (*COMPUT*) паралле́льный ◆ *n* (*GEO, fig*) паралле́ль *f*; **to draw ~s between/with** проводи́ть* (провести́* *perf*) паралле́ль ме́жду *+instr*/с *+instr*; **~ (with** *or* **to)** паралле́льно (с *+instr*); **in ~** (*ELEC*) паралле́льно.
paralyse ['pærəlaɪz] *vt* (*BRIT: also fig*) парализова́ть *(impf/perf)*; **he is ~d** (*BRIT*) он парализо́ван.
paralyses [pə'rælɪsi:z] *npl of* **paralysis**.
paralysis [pə'rælɪsɪs] (*pl* **paralyses**) *n* (*MED*) парали́ч*.
paralytic [pærə'lɪtɪk] *adj* (*MED*) парализо́ванный (парализо́ван); (*BRIT: inf: drunk*) упи́вшийся.
paralyze ['pærəlaɪz] *vt* (*US*) = **paralyse**.
paramedic [pærə'mɛdɪk] *n* параме́дик; **~s** кома́нда ско́рой по́мощи.
parameter [pə'ræmɪtəʳ] *n* пара́метр.
paramilitary [pærə'mɪlɪtərɪ] *adj* военизи́рованный.
paramount ['pærəmaunt] *adj* первостепе́нный.
paranoia [pærə'nɔɪə] *n* парано́йя.
paranoid ['pærənɔɪd] *adj* (*person*) параноидный; (*feeling*) параноиче́ский.
paranormal [pærə'nɔ:ml] *adj* не поддаю́щийся объясне́нию ◆ *n*: **the ~** явле́ния *ntpl*, не поддаю́щиеся объясне́нию.
parapet ['pærəpɪt] *n* парапе́т.
paraphernalia [pærəfə'neɪlɪə] *n* (*gear*) принадле́жности *fpl*.
paraphrase ['pærəfreɪz] *vt* перефрази́ровать *(impf/perf)*.
paraplegic [pærə'pli:dʒɪk] *n* страда́ющий(-ая) *m(f) adj* параличо́м ни́жней ча́сти те́ла.
parapsychology [pærəsaɪ'kɔlədʒɪ] *n* парапсихоло́гия.
parasite ['pærəsaɪt] *n* (*also fig*) парази́т.
parasol ['pærəsɔl] *n* зо́нтик (*защища́ющий от со́лнца*); (*at café etc*) тент.
paratrooper ['pærətru:pəʳ] *n* деса́нтник.
parcel ['pɑ:sl] *n* (*package*) свёрток*; (*sent by post*) посы́лка* ◆ *vt* (*also:* **~ up**) завёртывать (заверну́ть *perf*)
▸ **parcel out** *vt* раздава́ть* (разда́ть* *perf*).
parcel bomb *n* (*BRIT*) *бо́мба, спря́танная в паке́т*.
parcel post *n* почто́во-посы́лочная слу́жба.
parch [pɑ:tʃ] *vt* (*crops, land*) выжига́ть (вы́жечь* *perf*).
parched [pɑ:tʃt] *adj*: **I'm ~** у меня́ пересо́хло в го́рле.
parchment ['pɑ:tʃmənt] *n* перга́мент.
pardon ['pɑ:dn] *n* (*LAW*) поми́лование ◆ *vt* проща́ть (прости́ть* *perf*); (*LAW*) поми́ловать *(perf)*; **~ me!, I beg your ~!** прошу́ проще́ния!; **(I beg your) ~?, (US) ~ me?** (*what did you say?*) прости́те, не расслы́шал.
pare [pɛəʳ] *vt* (*BRIT: nails*) стричь* (остри́чь* *perf*); (*fruit*) чи́стить* (очи́стить* *perf*); (*costs*) уре́зывать *or* уреза́ть (уре́зать* *perf*).
parent ['pɛərənt] *n* роди́тель(ница) *m(f)*; **~s** *npl* (*mother and father*) роди́тели *mpl*.
parentage ['pɛərəntɪdʒ] *n* происхожде́ние; **she is of unknown ~** её происхожде́ние неизве́стно.
parental [pə'rɛntl] *adj* роди́тельский*.
parent company *n* (*COMM*) матери́нская компа́ния.
parentheses [pə'rɛnθɪsi:z] *npl of* **parenthesis**.

parenthesis [pəˈrɛnθɪsɪs] (*pl* **parentheses**) *n* (*word*) вво́дное сло́во*; (*phrase*) вво́дное предложе́ние; **in ~** в ско́бках.
parenthood [ˈpɛərənthud] *n* (*motherhood*) матери́нство; (*fatherhood*) отцо́вство.
parenting [ˈpɛərəntɪŋ] *n* воспита́ние.
Paris [ˈpærɪs] *n* Пари́ж.
parish [ˈpærɪʃ] *n* (*REL*) прихо́д; (*BRIT*: *civil*) о́круг*.
parish council *n* (*BRIT*) прихо́дский* сове́т.
parishioner [pəˈrɪʃənəʳ] *n* (*REL*) прихожа́нин*(-а́нка*).
Parisian [pəˈrɪzɪən] *adj* пари́жский* ◆ *n* парижа́нин*(-нка*).
parity [ˈpærɪtɪ] *n* (*equality*: *of pay, conditions etc*) парите́т.
park [pɑːk] *n* парк ◆ *vt* (*AUT*) ста́вить* (поста́вить* *perf*), паркова́ть (припаркова́ть *perf*) ◆ *vi* (*AUT*) паркова́ться (припаркова́ться *perf*).
parka [ˈpɑːkə] *n* (*coat*) *стёганная ку́ртка на меху́*.
parking [ˈpɑːkɪŋ] *n* (*of vehicle*) паркова́ние; (*space to park*) стоя́нка*; **"no ~"** „стоя́нка запрещена́".
parking lights *npl* подфа́рники *mpl*.
parking lot *n* (*US*) (авто)стоя́нка.
parking meter *n* (*AUT*) счётчик на (авто)стоя́нке.
parking offence *n* (*BRIT*) наруше́ние пра́вил стоя́нки.
parking place *n* ме́сто* на автостоя́нке.
parking ticket *n* *штраф за наруше́ние пра́вил паркова́ния*.
parking violation *n* (*US*) = **parking offence**.
Parkinson's [ˈpɑːkɪnsənz] *n* (*also*: **~ disease**) боле́знь *f* Паркинсона.
parkway [ˈpɑːkweɪ] *n* (*US*) алле́я.
parlance [ˈpɑːləns] *n*: **in common/modern ~** говоря́ обы́чным/совреме́нным языко́м.
parliament [ˈpɑːləmənt] *n* парла́мент.
parliamentary [pɑːləˈmɛntərɪ] *adj* парла́ментский*.
parlour [ˈpɑːləʳ] (*US* **parlor**) *n* гости́ная *f adj*.
parlous [ˈpɑːləs] *adj* бе́дственный.
Parmesan [pɑːmɪˈzæn] *n* (*also*: **~ cheese**) сыр пармеза́н.
parochial [pəˈrəukɪəl] *adj* (*pej*) местечко́вый.
parody [ˈpærədɪ] *n* паро́дия ◆ *vt* пароди́ровать (*impf/perf*).
parole [pəˈrəul] *n*: **he is/was released on ~** (*LAW*) он освобождён/был освобождён под че́стное сло́во.
paroxysm [ˈpærəksɪzəm] *n* (*also MED*) пароксі́зм.
parquet [ˈpɑːkeɪ] *n*: **~ floor(ing)** парке́тный пол*.
parrot [ˈpærət] *n* попуга́й.
parrot-fashion [ˈpærətfæʃən] *adv* как попуга́й.
parry [ˈpærɪ] *vt* (*blow*) отража́ть (отрази́ть* *perf*); (*question*) пари́ровать (*impf/perf*).
parsimonious [pɑːsɪˈməunɪəs] *adj* (*person*) скупо́й* (скуп).
parsley [ˈpɑːslɪ] *n* петру́шка.
parsnip [ˈpɑːsnɪp] *n* пастерна́к (посевно́й).
parson [ˈpɑːsn] *n* прихо́дский* свяще́нник; (*Church of England*) па́стор.
part [pɑːt] *n* (*section, division*) часть* *f*; (*component*) дета́ль *f*; (*role*) роль* *f*; (*episode*) се́рия; (*MUS*) па́ртия; (*US*: *in hair*) пробо́р ◆ *adv* = **partly** ◆ *vt* разделя́ть (раздели́ть* *perf*); (*hair*) расчёсывать (расчеса́ть* *perf*) на пробо́р ◆ *vi* (*people*) расстава́ться* (расста́ться* *perf*); (*crowd*) расступа́ться (расступи́ться *perf*); (*roads*) расходи́ться* (разойти́сь* *perf*); **to take ~ in** принима́ть (приня́ть* *perf*) уча́стие в +*prp*; **to take sth in good ~** не обижа́ться (оби́деться* *perf*) на что-н; **to take sb's ~** (*support*) станови́ться* (стать* *perf*) на чью-н сто́рону; **on his/for my ~** с его́/мое́й стороны́; **for the most ~** бо́льшей ча́стью; **for the better ~ of the day** бо́льшую часть дня; **to be ~ and parcel of** явля́ться (*impf*) неотъе́млемой ча́стью +*gen*; **~ of speech** (*LING*) часть ре́чи
▶ **part with** *vt fus* (*money, possessions*) расстава́ться* (расста́ться* *perf*) с +*infin*.
partake [pɑːˈteɪk] *irreg vi* (*formal*): **to ~ of sth** отве́дывать (отве́дать *perf*) чего́-н.
part exchange *n* (*BRIT*: *COMM*) *рассчёт, при кото́ром де́нежный взнос сочета́ется с обме́ном ста́рого това́ра на но́вый*.
partial [ˈpɑːʃl] *adj* (*not complete*) части́чный*; (*biased*) пристра́стный* (пристра́стен); **I am ~ to chocolate** (*like*) я пристра́стен к шокола́ду.
partially [ˈpɑːʃəlɪ] *adv* части́чно.
participant [pɑːˈtɪsɪpənt] *n* уча́стник(-ица).
participate [pɑːˈtɪsɪpeɪt] *vi*: **to ~ in** уча́ствовать (*impf*) в +*prp*.
participation [pɑːtɪsɪˈpeɪʃən] *n* уча́стие.
participle [ˈpɑːtɪsɪpl] *n* прича́стие.
particle [ˈpɑːtɪkl] *n* (*also PHYS*) части́ца.
particular [pəˈtɪkjuləʳ] *adj* (*distinct, special*) осо́бый; (*demanding*) привере́дливый (привере́длив); **~s** *npl* (*specifics*) ча́стности *fpl*; (*personal details*) да́нные *pl adj*; **he is very ~ about what he eats** он о́чень привере́длив в еде́; **in ~** в ча́стности.
particularly [pəˈtɪkjuləlɪ] *adv* осо́бенно.
parting [ˈpɑːtɪŋ] *n* (*action*) разделе́ние; (*farewell*) проща́ние; (*BRIT*: *in hair*) пробо́р ◆ *adj* (*words, gift etc*) проща́льный; **~ shot** проща́льное замеча́ние.
partisan [pɑːtɪˈzæn] *adj* (*politics, views*) пристра́стный* (пристра́стен) ◆ *n* (*supporter*)

* marks translations which have irregular inflections. The Russian-English side of the dictionary gives inflectional information.

приве́рженец*; (*resistance fighter*) партиза́н(ка*).
partition [pɑ:ˈtɪʃən] *n* (*wall, screen*) перегоро́дка*; (*of country*) разде́л ◆ *vt* разделя́ть (раздели́ть* *perf*).
partly [ˈpɑ:tlɪ] *adv* части́чно.
partner [ˈpɑ:tnəʳ] *n* (*spouse*) супру́г(а); (*girlfriend*) де́вушка*; (*boyfriend*) па́рень* *m*; (*COMM, SPORT, CARDS*) партнёр ◆ *vt*: **I used to ~ him** я был его́ партнёром.
partnership [ˈpɑ:tnəʃɪp] *n* (*COMM*: *company*) това́рищество; (: *with person*) партнёрство; (*POL*) сою́з; **to go into** *or* **form a ~ (with)** устана́вливать (установи́ть* *perf*) партнёрство (с *+instr*).
part payment *n* части́чная опла́та.
partridge [ˈpɑ:trɪdʒ] *n* (се́рая) куропа́тка*.
part-time [ˈpɑ:tˈtaɪm] *adj* (*work*) почасово́й; (*staff*) за́нятый* (за́нят) непо́лный рабо́чий* день* ◆ *adv*: **to work ~** быть* *(impf)* на почасово́й ста́вке; **to study ~** обуча́ться *(impf)* по непо́лной програ́мме.
part-timer [pɑ:tˈtaɪməʳ] *n* (*also:* **part-time worker**) рабо́тник(-ица) на почасово́й ста́вке, почасови́к.
party [ˈpɑ:tɪ] *n* (*POL*) па́ртия; (*celebration*: *formal*) ве́чер*; (: *informal*) вечери́нка*; (*group of people*: *surveying etc*) па́ртия; (: *rescue etc*) отря́д; (: *tourists etc*) гру́ппа; (*LAW*) сторона́* ◆ *cpd* (*POL*) парти́йный; **dinner ~** зва́нный обе́д; **to give** *or* **throw a ~** (*official*) устра́ивать (устро́ить *perf*) ве́чер; **we're having a ~ next Saturday** в сле́дующую суббо́ту у нас вечери́нка; **birthday ~** пра́зднование дня рожде́ния; **he was (a) ~ to the crime** он явля́лся соуча́стником преступле́ния.
party dress *n* вече́рнее пла́тье*.
party line *n* (*TEL*) о́бщая телефо́нная ли́ния; (*POL*) парти́йная ли́ния.
party piece *n* коро́нный но́мер*.
party-political [ˈpɑ:tɪpəˈlɪtɪkl] *adj* парти́йный.
party-political broadcast *n реклáма полити́ческой пáртии по рáдио и телеви́дению.*
pass [pɑ:s] *vt* (*spend*: *time*) проводи́ть* (провести́* *perf*); (*hand over*) передава́ть* (переда́ть* *perf*); (*go past*: *on foot*) проходи́ть* (пройти́* *perf*); (: *by transport*) проезжа́ть (прое́хать* *perf*); (*overtake*: *vehicle*) обгоня́ть (обогна́ть* *perf*); (*fig*: *surpass*) превосходи́ть* (превзойти́* *perf*); (*exam*) сдава́ть* (сдать* *perf*); (*approve*: *law, proposal*) принима́ть (приня́ть* *perf*) ◆ *vi* (*go past*: *on foot*) проходи́ть* (пройти́* *perf*); (: *by transport*) проезжа́ть (прое́хать* *perf*); (*in exam*) сдава́ть* (сдать* *perf*) ◆ *n* (*permit*) про́пуск*; (*membership card*) чле́нский* биле́т; (*GEO*) перева́л; (*SPORT*) пас, переда́ча; (*SCOL*: *also:* **~ mark**): **to get a ~** получа́ть (получи́ть *perf*) зачёт; **to ~ sth through sth** просо́вывать (просу́нуть *perf*) что-н че́рез что-н; **could you ~ the vegetables round?** переда́йте, пожа́луйста, о́вощи всем; **she could ~ for 25** она́ могла́ бы сойти́ за 25-ле́тнюю; **things have come to a pretty ~** (*BRIT*) дела́ пло́хи; **to make a ~ at sb** (*inf*) пристава́ть* (приста́ть* *perf*) к кому́-н
▸ **pass away** *vi* (*die*) сконча́ться *(perf)*
▸ **pass by** *vi* (*on foot*) проходи́ть* (пройти́* *perf*); (*by transport*) проезжа́ть (прое́хать* *perf*) ◆ *vt* (*ignore*) не обраща́ть (обрати́ть* *perf*) внима́ния на *+acc*
▸ **pass down** *vt* (*customs, inheritance*) передава́ть* (переда́ть* *perf*)
▸ **pass on** *vt* передава́ть* (переда́ть* *perf*); (*price rises*) перекла́дывать (переложи́ть* *perf*) ◆ *vi* (*die*) сконча́ться *(perf)*
▸ **pass out** *vi* (*faint*) теря́ть (потеря́ть *perf*) созна́ние; (*BRIT*: *MIL*) успе́шно проходи́ть* (пройти́* *perf*) подгото́вку
▸ **pass over** *vt* (*ignore*) оставля́ть (оста́вить* *perf*) без внима́ния ◆ *vi* (*die*) сконча́ться *(perf)*
▸ **pass up** *vt* (*opportunity*) упуска́ть (упусти́ть* *perf*).
passable [ˈpɑ:səbl] *adj* (*road*) проходи́мый (проходи́м); (*acceptable*: *work*) сно́сный* (сно́сен).
passage [ˈpæsɪdʒ] *n* (*also ANAT*) прохо́д; (*in book*) отры́вок*; (*act of passing*) прохожде́ние; (*journey*: *on boat*) путеше́ствие.
passenger [ˈpæsɪndʒəʳ] *n* пассажи́р(ка*).
passer-by [pɑ:səˈbaɪ] (*pl* **passers-by**) *n* прохо́жий*(-ая) *m(f) adj*.
passers-by [pɑ:səzˈbaɪ] *npl of* **passer-by**.
passing [ˈpɑ:sɪŋ] *adj* мимолётный* (мимолётен) ◆ *n*: **in ~** мимохо́дом; **to mention sth in ~** замеча́ть (замети́ть* *perf*) что-н мимохо́дом.
passing place *n* (*AUT*) расшире́ние на доро́ге.
passion [ˈpæʃən] *n* (*also fig*) страсть* *f*; **she has a ~ for history** у неё страсть к исто́рии.
passionate [ˈpæʃənɪt] *adj* стра́стный* (стра́стен).
passion fruit *n* плод* страстоцве́та.
Passion play *n мисте́рия, в кото́рой представля́ются стра́сти Госпо́дни.*
passive [ˈpæsɪv] *adj* пасси́вный* (пасси́вен); (*LING*) пасси́вный, страда́тельный ◆ *n* (*LING*): **the ~** страда́тельный зало́г.
passive smoking *n* пасси́вное куре́ние.
passkey [ˈpɑ:ski:] *n* отмы́чка*.
Passover [ˈpɑ:səuvəʳ] *n* евре́йская Па́сха.
passport [ˈpɑ:spɔ:t] *n* (*official document*) па́спорт*; (*fig*) ключ*.
passport control *n* па́спортный контро́ль *m*.
password [ˈpɑ:swə:d] *n* паро́ль *m*.
past [pɑ:st] *prep* (*in front of*) ми́мо *+gen*; (*beyond*) за *+instr*; (*later than*) по́сле *+gen* ◆ *adj* (*previous*: *government etc*) бы́вший*; (: *week,*

month etc) прошлый ◆ *n* прошлое *nt adj*; (*LING*): **the ~ (tense)** прошедшее время* *nt* ◆ *adv*: **to run ~** пробегать (пробежать* *perf*) мимо; **he's ~ forty** (*older than*) ему за сорок; **it's ~ midnight** уже за полночь; **ten/quarter ~ eight** десять минут/четверть девятого; **he ran ~ me** он пробежал мимо меня; **I'm ~ caring** мне уже всё равно; **he's ~ it** (*BRIT*: *inf*) он выдохнулся; **for the ~ few/3 days** за последние несколько дней/3 дня; **in the ~** в прошлом; (*LING*) в прошедшем времени.

pasta ['pæstə] *n* макаронные изделия *ntpl*.

paste [peɪst] *n* (*wet mixture*) паста; (*glue*) клейстер; (*jewellery*) страз; (*fish, meat paste*) паштет ◆ *vt* (*paper etc*) наносить* (нанести* *perf*) клей на *+acc*; **tomato ~** томатная паста; **to ~ sth onto sth** наносить* (нанести* *perf*) что-н на что-н.

pastel ['pæstl] *adj* (*colour*) пастельный.

pasteurized ['pæstʃəraɪzd] *adj* (*milk etc*) пастеризованный.

pastille ['pæstl] *n* пастила.

pastime ['pɑ:staɪm] *n* (*hobby*) времяпрепровождение.

past master *n* (*BRIT*) непревзойдённый мастер.

pastor ['pɑ:stə'] *n* пастор.

pastoral ['pɑ:stərl] *adj* (*REL*) пасторский.

pastry ['peɪstrɪ] *n* (*dough*) тесто; (*cake*) пирожное *nt adj*.

pasture ['pɑ:stʃə'] *n* пастбище.

pasty [*adj* 'peɪstɪ, *n* 'pæstɪ] *adj* (*complexion, face*) бледный* (бледен) ◆ *n* пирожок*.

pat [pæt] *adj* (*answer, remark*) стандартный* (стандартен) ◆ *vt* (*dog*) ласкать (приласкать *perf*) ◆ *n*: **to give sb/o.s. a ~ on the back** (*fig*) хвалить* (похвалить* *perf*) кого-н/себя ◆ *adv*: **to know sth off ~, (US) have sth down ~** знать (*impf*) что-н назубок; **to ~ sb's back** похлопывать (похлопать *perf*) кого-н по спине.

patch [pætʃ] *n* (*piece of material*) заплата; (*also: eye ~*) повязка*; (*area*: *damp, black etc*) пятно*; (*repair*: *on tyre etc*) заплата, заплатка*; (*of land*) участок* ◆ *vt* (*clothes*) латать (залатать *perf*); **to go through a bad ~** попадать (попасть* *perf*) в полосу невезения; **bald ~** лысина

▸ **patch up** *vt* (*mend temporarily*) заделывать (заделать *perf*); (*quarrel*) улаживать (уладить* *perf*).

patchwork ['pætʃwə:k] *n* (*SEWING*) лоскутная работа.

patchy ['pætʃɪ] *adj* (*uneven*: *colour*) пятнистый (пятнист); (*incomplete*: *information, knowledge etc*) отрывочный* (отрывочен).

pate [peɪt] *n*: **a bald ~** лысина на макушке.

pâté ['pæteɪ] *n* (*CULIN*) паштет.

patent ['peɪtnt] *n* (*COMM*) патент ◆ *vt* (*COMM*) патентовать* (запатентовать* *perf*) ◆ *adj* (*obvious*) явный* (явен).

patent leather *n* лакированная кожа.

patently ['peɪtntlɪ] *adv* (*obvious, wrong*) очевидно.

patent medicine *n* патентованное лекарство.

Patent Office *n* патентное бюро *nt ind*.

patent rights *npl* патентное право *ntsg*.

paternal [pə'tə:nl] *adj* (*love, duty*) отцовский*; (*grandmother etc*) по отцу.

paternalistic [pətə:nə'lɪstɪk] *adj* (*society, attitudes*) патерналистический.

paternity [pə'tə:nɪtɪ] *n* отцовство.

paternity leave *n* отпуск отца по уходу за ребёнком.

paternity suit *n* (*LAW*) установление отцовства.

path [pɑ:θ] *n* (*trail, track*) тропа*, тропинка*; (*concrete path, gravel path etc*) дорожка*; (*trajectory*) путь* *m* движения; (*fig*) путь*.

pathetic [pə'θɛtɪk] *adj* (*pitiful*: *sight, cries*) жалостный* (жалостен); (*very bad*) жалкий* (жалок).

pathological [pæθə'lɔdʒɪkl] *adj* (*liar, hatred*) патологический*; (*MED*: *work*) в области патологии.

pathologist [pə'θɔlədʒɪst] *n* (*MED*) патолог.

pathology [pə'θɔlədʒɪ] *n* (*MED*) патология.

pathos ['peɪθɔs] *n* патетика, горечь *f*.

pathway ['pɑ:θweɪ] *n* (*path*) тропа; (*route, fig*) путь* *m*.

patience ['peɪʃns] *n* (*personal quality*) терпение; (*BRIT*: *CARDS*) пасьянс; **to lose one's ~** терять (потерять *perf*) терпение.

patient ['peɪʃnt] *n* (*MED*) пациент(ка) ◆ *adj* (*person*) терпеливый (терпелив); **he is ~ with me** он терпелив со мной.

patiently ['peɪʃntlɪ] *adv* терпеливо.

patio ['pætɪəu] *n* патио *m ind*, внутренний дворик.

patriot ['peɪtrɪət] *n* патриот(ка).

patriotic [pætrɪ'ɔtɪk] *adj* (*person*) патриотичный* (патриотичен); (*song, speech etc*) патриотический, патриотичный* (патриотичен).

patriotism ['pætrɪətɪzəm] *n* патриотизм.

patrol [pə'trəul] *n* (*MIL, POLICE*) патруль *m* ◆ *vt* (*MIL, POLICE*: *city, streets etc*) патрулировать* (*impf*); **to be on ~** быть* (*impf*) в дозоре; (*POLICE*) быть* (*impf*) на дежурстве.

patrol boat *n* (*NAUT, MIL, CUSTOMS etc*) сторожевой катер.

patrol car *n* (*POLICE*) полицейская патрульная машина.

patrolman [pə'trəulmən] *irreg n* (*US*: *POLICE*) дежурный полицейский *m adj*.

patron ['peɪtrən] *n* (*customer, client*)

* marks translations which have irregular inflections. The Russian-English side of the dictionary gives inflectional information.

(постоя́нный) клие́нт; (*benefactor: of charity*) спо́нсор, ше́ф; **~ of the arts** покрови́тель (ница) *m(f)* иску́сств.
patronage ['pætrənɪdʒ] *n* (*of artist etc*) покрови́тельство; (*of charity*) спо́нсорство, ше́фство.
patronize ['pætrənaɪz] *vt* (*pej: look down on*) относи́ться* (отнести́сь* *perf*) свысока́; (*artist, writer*) покрови́тельствовать *(impf)* *+dat*; (*shop, club, firm*) постоя́нно посеща́ть *(impf)*.
patronizing ['pætrənaɪzɪŋ] *adj* (*pej: person, tone, comment etc*) снисходи́тельный* (снисходи́телен).
patron saint *n* (*REL*) засту́пник(-ица).
patter ['pætəʳ] *n* (*sound: of feet, rain*) топота́ние; (*of rain*) сту́к; (*sales talk etc*) речитати́в ◆ *vi* (*footsteps*) топота́ть *(impf)*; (*rain*) бараба́нить *(impf)*.
pattern ['pætən] *n* (*design*) узо́р; (*SEWING*) вы́кройка*; (*sample*) образе́ц*; **behaviour ~s** мане́ры *fpl* поведе́ния.
patterned ['pætənd] *adj* (*fabric, wallpaper, carpet etc*) узо́рчатый; **~ with flowers** с узо́ром из цвето́в.
paucity ['pɔːsɪtɪ] *n* недоста́ток*.
paunch [pɔːntʃ] *n* брюшко́*.
pauper ['pɔːpəʳ] *n* ни́щий*(-ая) *m(f) adj*; **~'s grave** бедня́цкая моги́ла.
pause [pɔːz] *n* (*temporary halt*) переры́в; (*MUS*) па́уза ◆ *vi* (*stop temporarily*) де́лать (сде́лать *perf*) переры́в; (*: while speaking*) де́лать (сде́лать *perf*) па́узу; **to ~ for breath** переводи́ть* (перевести́* *perf*) дыха́ние; (*fig*) передохну́ть *(perf)*.
pave [peɪv] *vt* (*street, yard etc*) мости́ть* (вы́мостить* *perf*); **to ~ the way for** (*fig*) прокла́дывать (проложи́ть* *perf*) пу́ть к *+dat*.
pavement ['peɪvmənt] *n* (*BRIT: for pedestrians*) тротуа́р; (*US: roadway*) доро́жное покры́тие.
pavilion [pə'vɪlɪən] *n* (*SPORT*) павильо́н.
paving ['peɪvɪŋ] *n* (*material*) доро́жное покры́тие.
paving stone *n* брусча́тка*.
paw [pɔː] *n* (*of animal*) ла́па* ◆ *vt* (*animal*) тро́гать (потро́гать *perf*) ла́пой *or* ла́пами; (*horse, bull*) бить* *(impf)* копы́том *or* копы́тами; (*pej: touch*) ла́пать *(impf)*.
pawn [pɔːn] *n* (*CHESS, fig*) пе́шка ◆ *vt* закла́дывать (заложи́ть* *perf*).
pawnbroker ['pɔːnbrəukəʳ] *n* ростовщи́к(-и́ца).
pawnshop ['pɔːnʃɔp] *n* ломба́рд.
pay [peɪ] (*pt, pp* **paid**) *n* (*wage, salary etc*) зарпла́та ◆ *vt* (*sum of money, wage*) плати́ть* (заплати́ть* *perf*); (*debt, bill*) плати́ть* (уплати́ть* *perf*); (*be profitable to: also fig*) окупа́ть (окупи́ть* *perf*) ◆ *vi* (*be profitable*) окупа́ться (окупи́ться* *perf*); **how much did you ~ for it?** ско́лько Вы за него́/неё/это заплати́ли?; **I paid £5 for that record** я заплати́л £5 за ту пласти́нку; **to ~ one's way** обеспе́чивать (обеспе́чить *perf*) себя́; **to ~ dividends** (*fig*) вознагражда́ться (вознагради́ться* *perf*); **it won't ~ you to do that** это де́ло не принесёт вам успе́ха; **to ~ attention (to)** обраща́ть (обрати́ть* *perf*) внима́ние (на *+acc*); **to ~ sb a visit** наноси́ть* (нанести́* *perf*) кому́-н визи́т; **to ~ one's respects to sb** свиде́тельствовать* (засвиде́тельствовать* *perf*) кому́-н (своё) почте́ние
▸ **pay back** *vt* (*money*) возвраща́ть (возврати́ть* *or* верну́ть *perf*); (*person*) отплати́ть* *(perf)*
▸ **pay for** *vt fus* (*purchases*) опла́чивать (оплати́ть* *perf*); (*fig*) поплати́ться* *(perf)* за *+acc*
▸ **pay in** *vt* (*money, cheque etc*) вноси́ть* (внести́* *perf*)
▸ **pay off** *vt* (*debt, creditor, mortgage*) распла́чиваться (расплати́ться* *perf*) с *+instr*; (*person*) рассчи́тывать (рассчита́ть *perf*) ◆ *vi* (*also fig*) окупа́ться (окупи́ться* *perf*); **to ~ sth off in instalments** распла́чиваться (расплати́ться* *perf*) за что-н в рассро́чку
▸ **pay out** *vt* (*money*) выпла́чивать (вы́платить* *perf*); (*rope*) трави́ть* (потрави́ть* *perf*)
▸ **pay up** *vt* (*money*) выпла́чивать (вы́платить* *perf*) ◆ *vi* (*person, company etc*) рассчи́тываться (рассчита́ться *perf*) (сполна́).
payable ['peɪəbl] *adj* (*sum of money*) подлежа́щий упла́те; (*cheque*): **~ to** подлежа́щий упла́те на и́мя *+gen*.
pay award *n* повыше́ние зарпла́ты.
payday ['peɪdeɪ] *n* день* *m* зарпла́ты.
PAYE *n abbr* (*BRIT: = pay as you earn*) *отчисле́ние подохо́дного нало́га из зарпла́ты.*
payee [peɪ'iː] *n* (*of cheque, postal order*) получа́тель(ница) *m(f)*.
pay envelope *n* (*US*) = **pay packet**.
paying guest ['peɪɪŋ-] *n* постоя́лец(-лица).
payload ['peɪləud] *n* (*COMM*) поле́зная нагру́зка*.
payment ['peɪmənt] *n* (*act*) платёж*, упла́та; (*of bill*) опла́та; (*amount of money*) вы́плата; **advance ~** (*part sum*) внесе́ние ава́нса; (*total sum*) платёж ава́нсом; **deferred ~** отсро́ченный платёж; **~ by instalments** платёж в рассро́чку; **monthly ~** ме́сячный платёж; **in ~ for, in ~ of** в опла́ту за *+acc*; **on ~ of five pounds** по упла́те пяти́ фу́нтов.
pay packet *n* (*BRIT*) паке́т с зарпла́той.
payphone ['peɪfəun] *n* (*TEL*) телефо́н-автома́т.
payroll ['peɪrəul] *n* платёжная ве́домость *f*; **to be on a firm's ~** быть* *(impf)* в спи́сочном соста́ве фи́рмы.
pay slip *n* (*BRIT*) извеще́ние о зарпла́те.
pay station *n* (*US*) телефо́н-автома́т.
PBS *n abbr* (*US: = Public Broadcasting Service*)

Госуда́рственная слу́жба радиовеща́ния.
PC *n abbr* (= **personal computer**) ПК= *персона́льный компью́тер*; (*BRIT*) = **police constable** ◆ *adj abbr* = **politically correct** ◆ *abbr* (*BRIT*) = **Privy Councillor**.
pc *abbr* = **per cent, postcard**.
p/c *abbr* = **petty cash**.
PCB *n abbr* (*ELEC, COMPUT*: = *printed circuit board*) печа́тная пла́та; (= *polychlorinated biphenyl*) полихлори́рованный дифени́л.
pcm *abbr* (= *per calendar month*) в ме́сяц.
PD *n abbr* (*US*) = **police department**.
pd *abbr* = *paid*.
PDQ *adv abbr* (*inf*: = *pretty damn quick*) черто́вски бы́стро.
PDSA *n abbr* (*BRIT*: = *People's Dispensary for Sick Animals*) *благотвори́тельное о́бщество, организу́ющее ветерина́рную по́мощь живо́тным*.
PDT *abbr* (*US*) = *Pacific Daylight Time*.
PE *n abbr* (*SCOL*) (= **physical education**) физкульту́ра= *физи́ческая культу́ра* ◆ *abbr* (*CANADA*) = *Prince Edward Island*.
pea [pi:] *n* (*BOT, CULIN*) горо́х *no pl*.
peace [pi:s] *n* (*not war*) мир; (*calm*: *of place, surroundings*) поко́й, споко́йствие; (: *personal*) поко́й; **to be at ~ with sb** быть* *(impf)* в ми́ре с ке́м-н; **to be at ~ with sth** смиря́ться (смири́ться* *perf*) с чем-н; **to keep the ~** (*policeman*) подде́рживать (поддержа́ть* *perf*) споко́йствие; (*citizen*) соблюда́ть *(impf)* споко́йствие.
peaceable ['pi:səbl] *adj* миролюби́вый (миролюби́в).
peaceful ['pi:sful] *adj* (*calm*) ми́рный* (ми́рен).
peacekeeper ['pi:ski:pə^r] *n* член ми́рных во́йск.
peacekeeping force ['pi:ski:pɪŋ-] *n* миротво́рческие си́лы *fpl*.
peace offering *n* зада́бривание.
peach [pi:tʃ] *n* пе́рсик.
peacock ['pi:kɔk] *n* павли́н.
peak [pi:k] *n* верши́на, пик; (*of cap*) козырёк*.
peak hours *npl* часы́ *mpl* пик.
peak period *n* пи́ковый пери́од.
peak rate *n* (*TEL*) *расце́нки, применя́емые в пи́ковый пери́од*.
peaky ['pi:kɪ] *adj* (*BRIT*: *inf*) до́хлый.
peal [pi:l] *n* (*of bells*) перезво́н; **~ of laughter** раска́т сме́ха.
peanut ['pi:nʌt] *n* ара́хис.
peanut butter *n* ара́хисовая па́ста.
pear [pɛə^r] *n* гру́ша.
pearl [pə:l] *n* жемчу́жина; **~s** же́мчуг.
peasant ['pɛznt] *n* крестья́нин*(-нка*).
peat [pi:t] *n* торф.
pebble ['pɛbl] *n* га́лька* *no pl*.
peck [pɛk] *vt* (*subj*: *bird*) клева́ть* *(impf)*; (: *once*) клю́нуть *(perf)*; (*also*: **~ at**: *food*) поклева́ть* *(impf)* ◆ *n* (*of bird*) клево́к*; (*kiss*) чмо́канье.
pecking order ['pɛkɪŋ-] *n* старшинство́.
peckish ['pɛkɪʃ] *adj* (*BRIT*: *inf*): **I'm feeling ~** мне хо́чется пожева́ть.
peculiar [pɪ'kju:lɪə^r] *adj* (*strange*) своеобра́зный* (своеобра́зен); (*belonging exclusively*): **~ to** сво́йственный* (сво́йствен) *+dat*.
peculiarity [pɪkju:lɪ'ærɪtɪ] *n* (*strange habit*) стра́нность *f*; (*distinctive feature*) осо́бенность *f*.
peculiarly [pɪ'kju:lɪəlɪ] *adv* (*oddly*) стра́нно; (*distinctively*) осо́бенно.
pecuniary [pɪ'kju:nɪərɪ] *adj* де́нежный.
pedal ['pɛdl] *n* педа́ль *f* ◆ *vi* крути́ть* *(impf)* педа́ли.
pedal bin *n* (*BRIT*) му́сорное ведро́* с педа́лью.
pedant ['pɛdənt] *n* педа́нт(ка*).
pedantic [pɪ'dæntɪk] *adj* педанти́чный* (педанти́чен).
peddle ['pɛdl] *vt* (*goods, drugs*) торгова́ть *(impf)* *+instr*; (*gossip*) разноси́ть* (разнести́* *perf*).
peddler ['pɛdlə^r] *n*: **(drug) ~** торго́вец* нарко́тиками.
pedestal ['pɛdəstl] *n* пьедеста́л.
pedestrian [pɪ'dɛstrɪən] *n* пешехо́д ◆ *adj* пешехо́дный; (*fig*) ску́чный.
pedestrian crossing *n* (*BRIT*) пешехо́дный перехо́д.
pedestrian precinct *n* (*BRIT*) пешехо́дная зо́на.
pediatrics [pi:dɪ'ætrɪks] *n* (*US*) = **paediatrics**.
pedigree ['pɛdɪgri:] *n* (*also fig*) родосло́вная *f* *adj* ◆ *cpd* (*animal*) поро́дистый (поро́дист).
pee [pi:] *vi* (*inf*) пи́сать (попи́сать *perf*).
peek [pi:k] *vi*: **to ~ at/over** взгля́дывать (взгляну́ть* *perf*) на *+acc*/пове́рх *+gen* ◆ *n*: **to have** *or* **take a ~ (at)** взгля́дывать (взгляну́ть* *perf*) (на *+acc*); **to ~ into** загля́дывать (загляну́ть* *perf*) в *+acc*.
peel [pi:l] *n* кожура́ ◆ *vt* (*vegetables, fruit*) чи́стить* (почи́стить* *perf*), очища́ть (очисти́ть* *perf*) ◆ *vi* (*paint*) лупи́ться* (облупи́ться* *perf*); (*wallpaper*) отстава́ть* (отста́ть* *perf*); (*skin*) шелуши́ться *(impf)*
▸ **peel back** *vt* оття́гивать (оттяну́ть* *perf*).
peeler ['pi:lə^r] *n* (*for potatoes etc*) *нож для очи́стки о́вощей и фру́ктов*.
peelings ['pi:lɪŋz] *npl* очи́стки *pl*.
peep [pi:p] *n* (*look*) взгляд укра́дкой; (*sound*) писк ◆ *vi* взгля́дывать (взгляну́ть* *perf*); **to have** *or* **take a ~ (at)** взгля́дывать (взгляну́ть* *perf*) (на *+acc*)
▸ **peep out** *vi* (*be visible*) пока́зываться (показа́ться* *perf*), выгля́дывать (вы́глянуть *perf*).

* marks translations which have irregular inflections. The Russian-English side of the dictionary gives inflectional information.

peephole ['pi:phəul] *n* глазо́к*.
peer [pɪə'] *n* (*BRIT*: *noble*) пэр; (*equal*) ро́вня *m/f*; (*contemporary*) рове́сник(-ица) ◆ *vi*: **to ~ at** всма́триваться (всмотре́ться* *perf*) в *+acc*.
peerage ['pɪərɪdʒ] *n* (*title, position*) пэ́рство; **the ~** пэ́ры.
peerless ['pɪəlɪs] *adj* несравне́нный* (несравне́нен).
peeved [pi:vd] *adj* (*inf*) злой* (зол).
peevish ['pi:vɪʃ] *adj* капри́зный* (капри́зен), сварли́вый (сварли́в).
peg [pɛg] *n* (*for coat etc*) крючо́к*; (*BRIT*: *also:* **clothes ~**) прище́пка*; (*also:* **tent ~**) ко́лышек* (*для натяги́вания пала́тки*) ◆ *vt* (*clothes: on line*) прикрепля́ть (прикрепи́ть* *perf*) прище́пками; (*prices*) замора́живать (заморо́зить* *perf*); **off the ~ clothing** гото́вая оде́жда.
pejorative [pɪ'dʒɔrətɪv] *adj* уничижи́тельный* (уничижи́телен).
Pekin [pi:'kɪn] *n* = **Peking**.
Pekinese [pi:kɪ'ni:z] *n* = **Pekingese**.
Peking [pi:'kɪŋ] *n* Пеки́н.
Pekingese [pi:kɪ'ni:z] *n* (*dog*) кита́йский* мопс.
pelican ['pɛlɪkən] *n* пелика́н.
pelican crossing *n* (*BRIT*) *пешехо́дный перехо́д, на кото́ром переключе́ние светофо́ра регули́руется нажа́тием кно́пки.*
pellet ['pɛlɪt] *n* (*of paper, mud*) ша́рик, ка́тышек*; (*for shotgun*) дроби́на.
pell-mell ['pɛl'mɛl] *adv* очертя́ го́лову.
pelmet ['pɛlmɪt] *n* ламбреке́н.
pelt [pɛlt] *n* (*animal skin*) шку́ра ◆ *vi* (*rain: also:* **~ down**) лить* (*impf*) как из ведра́; (*inf: run*) проноси́ться* (пронести́сь* *perf*) ◆ *vt*: **to ~ sb with sth** забра́сывать (заброса́ть *perf*) кого́-н чем-н.
pelvis ['pɛlvɪs] *n* таз* *no pl*.
pen [pɛn] *n* ру́чка*; (*felt-tip*) флома́стер; (*enclosure*) заго́н; (*US: inf: prison*) тюрьма́*; **to put ~ to paper** бра́ться* (взя́ться* *perf*) за перо́.
penal ['pi:nl] *adj* (*colony, institution*) исправ-и́тельный; (*system*) кара́тельный; **~ code** уголо́вный ко́декс.
penalize ['pi:nəlaɪz] *vt* (*also fig*) нака́зывать (наказа́ть* *perf*); (*SPORT*) штрафова́ть (оштрафова́ть *perf*).
penal servitude [-'sə:vɪtju:d] *n* ка́торжные рабо́ты *fpl*.
penalty ['pɛnltɪ] *n* (*punishment*) наказа́ние; (*fine*) штраф; (*RUGBY*) штрафно́й *m adj* (уда́р); (*FOOTBALL*) штрафно́й (уда́р), пена́льти *m ind*.
penalty area *n* (*BRIT: SPORT*) штрафна́я *f adj* (площа́дка*).
penalty clause *n* (*COMM*) *пункт, преду-сма́тривающий вид и разме́р штра́фа за наруше́ние усло́вий контра́кта.*
penalty kick *n* (*RUGBY*) штрафно́й *m adj* (уда́р); (*FOOTBALL*) штрафно́й (уда́р), пена́льти *m ind*.
penalty shoot-out [-'ʃu:taut] *n определе́ние кома́нды-победи́теля путём забива́ния се́рии штрафны́х уда́ров по́сле ма́тча око́нчившегося ничье́й.*
penance ['pɛnəns] *n* ка́ра.
pence [pɛns] *npl of* **penny**.
penchant ['pɑ̃:ʃɑ̃:ŋ] *n* скло́нность *f*; **to have a ~ for** име́ть (*impf*) скло́нность к *+dat*.
pencil ['pɛnsl] *n* каранда́ш* ◆ *vt*: **to ~ sth in** впи́сывать (вписа́ть* *perf*) что-н карандашо́м; (*fig*) помеча́ть (поме́тить* *perf*) что-н.
pencil case *n* пена́л.
pencil sharpener *n* точи́лка.
pendant ['pɛndnt] *n* куло́н.
pending ['pɛndɪŋ] *prep* впредь до *+gen*, в ожида́нии *+gen* ◆ *adj* (*lawsuit, exam etc*) предстоя́щий*.
pendulum ['pɛndjuləm] *n* ма́ятник.
penetrate ['pɛnɪtreɪt] *vt* (*subj: person, light*) проника́ть (прони́кнуть* *perf*) в/на *+acc*.
penetrating ['pɛnɪtreɪtɪŋ] *adj* (*sound, glance*) пронзи́тельный* (пронзи́телен); (*mind*) проница́тельный* (проница́телен); (*observation*) глубо́кий*.
penetration [pɛnɪ'treɪʃən] *n* проникнове́ние.
pen friend *n* (*BRIT*) друг* (подру́га) по перепи́ске.
penguin ['pɛŋgwɪn] *n* пингви́н.
penicillin [pɛnɪ'sɪlɪn] *n* пеницилли́н.
peninsula [pə'nɪnsjulə] *n* полуо́стров*.
penis ['pi:nɪs] *n* пе́нис, мужско́й полово́й член.
penitence ['pɛnɪtns] *n* раска́яние.
penitent ['pɛnɪtnt] *adj* ка́ющийся.
penitentiary [pɛnɪ'tɛnʃərɪ] *n* (*US*) тюрьма́*.
penknife ['pɛnnaɪf] *n* перочи́нный нож*.
pen name *n* (литерату́рный) псевдони́м.
pennant ['pɛnənt] *n* (*NAUT*) сигна́льный флажо́к*.
penniless ['pɛnɪlɪs] *adj* без гроша́; **she is ~** у неё нет ни гроша́.
Pennines ['pɛnaɪnz] *npl*: **the ~** Пени́нские го́ры* *fpl*.
penny ['pɛnɪ] (*pl* **pennies** *or (BRIT)* **pence**) *n* пе́нни *nt ind*, пенс; (*US*) цент.
pen pal *n* = **pen friend**.
penpusher ['pɛnpuʃə'] *n* занима́ющийся ну́днок пи́сьменной рабо́той/пи́сарь *m*.
pension ['pɛnʃən] *n* пе́нсия
▸ **pension off** *vt* отправля́ть (отпра́вить* *perf*) на пе́нсию.
pensionable ['pɛnʃnəbl] *adj* (*age*) пенсио́нный; (*job*) даю́щий пра́во на пе́нсию.
pensioner ['pɛnʃənə'] *n* (*BRIT*: *also:* **old age ~**) пенсионе́р(ка*).
pension fund *n* пенсио́нный фонд.
pensive ['pɛnsɪv] *adj* заду́мчивый (заду́мчив).

pentagon ['pɛntəgən] *n* пятиуго́льник; (*US*): **the P~** Пентаго́н.
Pentecost ['pɛntɪkɔst] *n* (*Jewish*) пятидеся́тница; (*Christian*) Тро́ицын день* *m*.
penthouse ['pɛnthaus] *n* (*flat*) „пе́нтхаус" (*фешене́бельная кварти́ра, располо́женная на кры́ше*).
pent-up ['pɛntʌp] *adj* (*feelings*) сде́рживаемый.
penultimate [pɛ'nʌltɪmət] *adj* предпосле́дний*.
penury ['pɛnjurɪ] *n* нужда́, бе́дность *f*.
people ['pi:pl] *npl* (*persons*) лю́ди* *pl*; (*nation, race*) наро́д; **old ~** старики́ *mpl*; **young ~** молодёжь *fsg*; **the ~** (*POL*) наро́д; **~ at large** лю́ди в ма́ссе свое́й; **a man of the ~** челове́к из наро́да; **several ~ came** пришло́ не́сколько челове́к; **the room was full of ~** в ко́мнате бы́ло полно́ наро́ду; **~ say that ...** говоря́т, что ....
pep [pɛp] (*inf*) *n* бо́дрость *f*
▶ **pep up** *vt* (*enliven*) оживи́ть* (*perf*); (*food*) де́лать (сде́лать *perf*) остре́е.
pepper ['pɛpə'] *n* пе́рец* ◆ *vt* (*fig*): **to ~ with** забра́сывать (заброса́ть *perf*) +*instr*.
peppercorn ['pɛpəkɔ:n] *n* перчи́нка*.
pepper mill *n* ме́льница для пе́рца.
peppermint ['pɛpəmɪnt] *n* (*sweet*) мя́тная конфе́та; (*plant*) мя́та пе́речная.
pepperoni [pɛpə'rəunɪ] *n* пепеpо́ни *f ind* (*италья́нская колбаса́*).
pepper pot *n* пе́речница.
pep talk *n* (*inf*) нака́чка*.
per [pə:'] *prep* (*for each*: *of amounts*) на +*acc*; (: *of price*) за +*acc*; (: *of charge*) с +*gen*; **~ annum/day/hour** в год/день/час; **~ person** на челове́ка; **~ kilo** за килогра́мм; **as ~ your instructions** согла́сно ва́шим инстру́кциям; **as ~ usual** по обыкнове́нию.
per capita *adj, adv* (*income*) на ду́шу населе́ния.
perceive [pə'si:v] *vt* (*sound, light, idea*) воспринима́ть (восприня́ть* *perf*); (*realize*) понима́ть (поня́ть* *perf*).
per cent *n* проце́нт; **a twenty ~ ~ discount** двадцатипроце́нтная ски́дка.
percentage [pə'sɛntɪdʒ] *n* (*of income*) проце́нт; (*of immigrants etc*) до́ля; (*of substances*) (проце́нтное) содержа́ние; **on a ~ basis** на основа́нии проце́нтного отчисле́ния.
percentage point *n* проце́нт.
perceptible [pə'sɛptɪbl] *adj* ощути́мый (ощути́м).
perception [pə'sɛpʃən] *n* (*faculty*) восприя́тие; (*insight*) понима́ние *no pl*; (*opinion, understanding*) ощуще́ние.
perceptive [pə'sɛptɪv] *adj* проницáтельный* (проница́телен).
perch [pə:tʃ] *n* (*for bird*) насе́ст ◆ *n inv* (*fish*) о́кунь* *m* ◆ *vi*: **to ~ (on)** (*bird*) сади́ться* (сесть* *perf*) (на +*acc*); (*person*) приса́живаться (присе́сть* *perf*) (на +*acc*).
percolate ['pə:kəleɪt] *vt* (*coffee*) вари́ть* (свари́ть* *perf*) в кофева́рке ◆ *vi* (*coffee*) вари́ться (свари́ться *perf*) в кофева́рке; (*idea, information, light etc*): **to ~ through/into** проса́чиваться (просочи́ться *perf*) сквоз +*acc*/в +*acc*.
percolator ['pə:kəleɪtə'] *n* (*also:* **coffee ~**) кофева́рка.
percussion [pə'kʌʃən] *n* уда́рные инструме́нты *mpl*.
peremptory [pə'rɛmptərɪ] *adj* (*pej*: *person*) вла́стный* (вла́стен), категори́чный* (категори́чен); (: *order, instruction*) категори́ческий*.
perennial [pə'rɛnɪəl] *adj* (*plant*) многоле́тний*; (*fig*: *problem, feature etc*) ве́чный* (ве́чен) ◆ *n* (*BOT*) многоле́тнее *nt adj* (расте́ние).
perfect [*adj, n* 'pə:fɪkt, *vt* pə'fɛkt] *adj* (*person, behaviour etc*) безупре́чный* (безупре́чен); (*weather*) прекра́сный* (прекра́сен); (*utter*: *nonsense etc*) соверше́нный ◆ *n* (*also:* **~ tense**) перфе́кт ◆ *vt* (*technique*) соверше́нствовать (усоверше́нствовать *perf*); **he's a ~ stranger to me** он мне соверше́нно незнако́м.
perfection [pə'fɛkʃən] *n* соверше́нство.
perfectionist [pə'fɛkʃənɪst] *n* взыска́тельный* челове́к*.
perfective [pə'fɛktɪv] *n* (*also:* **~ aspect**) соверше́нный вид.
perfectly ['pə:fɪktlɪ] *adv* (*emphatic*) вполне́, соверше́нно; (*faultlessly*) безупре́чно; (*completely*) вполне́, прекра́сно; **I'm ~ happy with the situation** я вполне́ дово́лен положе́нием дел; **you know ~ well** Вы прекра́сно зна́ете.
perforate ['pə:fəreɪt] *vt* перфори́ровать (*impf/perf*).
perforated ulcer ['pə:fəreɪtəd-] *n* перфорати́вная я́зва желу́дка.
perforation [pə:fə'reɪʃən] *n* перфора́ция.
perform [pə'fɔ:m] *vt* (*task, operation*) выполня́ть (вы́полнить *perf*); (*ceremony, experiment*) проводи́ть* (провести́* *perf*); (*piece of music*) исполня́ть (испо́лнить *perf*); (*play*) игра́ть (сыгра́ть *perf*); (*subj*: *mechanism*) рабо́тать (*impf*) ◆ *vi* (*well, badly*) спра́виться* (*perf*).
performance [pə'fɔ:məns] *n* (*of actor, athlete etc*) выступле́ние; (*of musical work*) исполне́ние; (*of play, show*) представле́ние; (*of car, engine, company*) рабо́та; (*of economy*) эффекти́вность *f*; **the team put up a good ~** кома́нда хорошо́ вы́ступила.
performer [pə'fɔ:mə'] *n* исполни́тель(ница)

* marks translations which have irregular inflections. The Russian-English side of the dictionary gives inflectional information.

m(f).
performing [pə'fɔ:mɪŋ] *adj* (*animal*) дрессиро́ванный.
perfume ['pə:fju:m] *n* духи́ *pl*; (*aroma*) арома́т ◆ *vt* (*air, room etc*) ароматизи́ровать (*impf/perf*).
perfunctory [pə'fʌŋktərɪ] *adj* (*kiss, remark etc*) небре́жный* (небре́жен).
perhaps [pə'hæps] *adv* мо́жет быть, возмо́жно; ~ **he'll come** мо́жет быть, *or* возмо́жно он придёт; ~ **so** мо́жет бы́ть; ~ **not** мо́жет быть* и нет.
peril ['pɛrɪl] *n* опа́сность *f*.
perilous ['pɛrɪləs] *adj* опа́сный* (опа́сен).
perilously ['pɛrɪləslɪ] *adv*: **they came ~ close to being caught** они́ находи́лись на гра́ни разоблаче́ния.
perimeter [pə'rɪmɪtə^r] *n* пери́метр.
perimeter wall *n* стена́ по пери́метру.
period ['pɪərɪəd] *n* (*length of time*) пери́од; (*SCOL*) уро́к; (*esp US*: *full stop*) то́чка*; (*MED*) менструа́ция ◆ *adj* (*costume, furniture*) стари́нный; ~ **of validity** срок де́йствия; **for a ~ of three weeks** (*go*) на три неде́ли; (*be*) три неде́ли; **the holiday ~** (*BRIT*) вре́мя* *or* пери́од отпуско́в.
periodic [pɪərɪ'ɔdɪk] *adj* периоди́ческий*.
periodical [pɪərɪ'ɔdɪkl] *n* (*magazine*) периоди́ческое изда́ние ◆ *adj* периоди́ческий*.
periodically [pɪərɪ'ɔdɪklɪ] *adv* периоди́чески.
period pains *npl* (*BRIT*: *MED*) менструа́льные бо́ли *fpl*.
peripatetic [pɛrɪpə'tɛtɪk] *adj* (*salesman*) бродя́чий; (*BRIT*: *teacher*) приходя́щий*.
peripheral [pə'rɪfərəl] *adj* (*also COMPUT*) перифери́йный ◆ *n* (*COMPUT*) перифери́я.
periphery [pə'rɪfərɪ] *n* перифери́я.
periscope ['pɛrɪskəup] *n* периско́п.
perish ['pɛrɪʃ] *vi* (*person*) погиба́ть (поги́бнуть* *perf*); (*fabric*) приходи́ть* (прийти́* *perf*) в него́дность.
perishable ['pɛrɪʃəbl] *adj* (*food, goods*) скоропо́ртящийся*.
perishables ['pɛrɪʃəblz] *npl* (*food*) скоропо́ртящиеся проду́кты *mpl*.
perishing ['pɛrɪʃɪŋ] *adj* (*BRIT*: *inf*): **it's ~ (cold)** ужа́сно хо́лодно.
peritonitis [pɛrɪtə'naɪtɪs] *n* перитони́т.
perjure ['pə:dʒə^r] *vt*: **to ~ o.s.** дава́ть* (дать* *perf*) ло́жные показа́ния.
perjury ['pə:dʒərɪ] *n* (*LAW*) лжесвиде́тельство.
perk [pə:k] *n* (*inf*) льго́та.
perk up *vi* (*inf*) оживля́ться (оживи́ться* *perf*).
perky ['pə:kɪ] *adj* (*cheerful*) весёлый* (ве́сел), бо́йкий* (бо́ек).
perm [pə:m] *n* (*for hair*) пермане́нт, хими́ческая зави́вка* ◆ *vt*: **to have one's hair ~ed** де́лать (сде́лать *perf*) себе́ хими́ческую зави́вку *or* хи́мию.
permanence ['pə:mənəns] *n* постоя́нство.
permanent ['pə:mənənt] *adj* постоя́нный* (постоя́нен); (*job, position*) постоя́нный; (*dye, ink*) сто́йкий*; ~ **address** постоя́нное местожи́тельство; **I'm not ~ here** я нахожу́сь здесь вре́менно.
permanently ['pə:mənəntlɪ] *adv* постоя́нно.
permeable ['pə:mɪəbl] *adj* водопроница́емый (водопроница́ем).
permeate ['pə:mɪeɪt] *vt* (*subj*: *liquid*) пропи́тывать (пропита́ть *perf*); (: *idea*) прони́зывать (прониза́ть *perf*) ◆ *vi*: **to ~ into/through** проника́ть (прони́кнуть* *perf*) в *+acc*/сквозь *+acc*.
permissible [pə'mɪsɪbl] *adj* (*action, behaviour*) допусти́мый (допусти́м), позволи́тельный* (позволи́телен).
permission [pə'mɪʃən] *n* (*consent*) позволе́ние; (*official authorization*) разреше́ние; **to give sb ~ to do** разреша́ть (разреши́ть *perf*) кому́-н *+infin*.
permissive [pə'mɪsɪv] *adj* (*person*) терпи́мый (терпи́м); (*behaviour*) во́льный* (во́лен); **the ~ society** о́бщество вседозво́ленности.
permit [*vt* pə'mɪt, *n* 'pə:mɪt] *vt* (*allow*) позволя́ть (позво́лить *perf*), разреша́ть (разреши́ть *perf*); (*make possible*) дава́ть* (дать* *perf*) возмо́жность *+dat* ◆ *n* (*official authorization*) разреше́ние; (*entrance pass*) про́пуск*; **to ~ sb to do** разреша́ть (разреши́ть *perf*) кому́-н *+infin*; **weather ~ting** е́сли пого́да позволя́ет; **fishing ~** разреше́ние на ры́бную ло́влю.
permutation [pə:mju'teɪʃən] *n* (*MATH*) перестано́вка*; (*fig*) перемеще́ние.
pernicious [pə:'nɪʃəs] *adj* (*attitude, influence etc*) па́губный* (па́губен); (*MED*) пернацио́зный.
pernickety [pə'nɪkɪtɪ] *adj* (*inf*) привере́дливый (привере́длив).
perpendicular [pə:pən'dɪkjulə^r] *adj* (*line, surface*) перпендикуля́рный* (перпендилуля́рен); (*cliff, slope*) отве́сный* (отве́сен).
perpetrate ['pə:pɪtreɪt] *vt* соверша́ть (соверши́ть *perf*).
perpetual [pə'pɛtjuəl] *adj* (*motion, questions*) ве́чный* (ве́чен); (*darkness, noise*) постоя́нный* (постоя́нен).
perpetuate [pə'pɛtjueɪt] *vt* увекове́чивать (увекове́чить *perf*).
perpetuity [pə:pɪ'tju:ɪtɪ] *n*: **in ~** навсегда́, наве́чно.
perplex [pə'plɛks] *vt* озада́чивать (озада́чить *perf*).
perplexing [pə:'plɛksɪŋ] *adj* запу́танный* (запу́тан), сло́жный* (сло́жен).
perquisites ['pə:kwɪzɪts] *npl* (*formal*) льго́ты *fpl*.
per se [-seɪ] *adv* (*as such*) как тако́во́й; (*in itself*) само́ по себе́.
persecute ['pə:sɪkju:t] *vt* пресле́довать (*impf*), подверга́ть (подве́ргнуть* *perf*) гоне́ниям

+*dat*.
persecution [pə:sɪ'kju:ʃən] *n* преслéдование.
perseverance [pə:sɪ'vɪərns] *n* настóйчивость *f*.
persevere [pə:sɪ'vɪə^r] *vi* упóрно добивáться (*impf*).
Persia ['pə:ʃə] *n* Пéрсия.
Persian ['pə:ʃən] *adj*: **the (Persian) Gulf** Перси́дский* зали́в.
Persian cat *n* перси́дский*(-ая) кот* (кóшка).
persist [pə'sɪst] *vi*: **to ~ (in doing)** настáивать (настоя́ть *perf*) (на том, чтóбы +*infin*).
persistence [pə'sɪstəns] *n* упóрство.
persistent [pə'sɪstənt] *adj* (*noise*) непрекращáющийся*; (*smell*) стóйкий* (стóек); (*cough*) непроходя́щий; (*person*) упóрный* (упóрен); (*lateness*) постоя́нный* (постоя́нен); (*rain*) непреры́вный* (непреры́вен); **~ offender** рецидиви́ст(ка*).
persnickety [pə'snɪkɪtɪ] *adj* (*US*: *inf*) = **pernickety**.
person ['pə:sn] *n* человéк*; **in ~** ли́чно; **to have sth on** *or* **about one's ~** (*weapon*) носи́ть* (*impf*) что-н при себé; **~ to ~ call** (*TEL*) *междугорóдный телефóнный разговóр с вы́зовом абонéнта*.
personable ['pə:snəbl] *adj* (*adult*) представи́тельный* (представи́телен).
personal ['pə:snl] *adj* ли́чный; (*car*) персонáльный.
personal allowance *n* (*COMM*) ли́чные ски́дки *fpl* с подохóдного налóга.
personal assistant *n* ли́чный секретáрь* *m*.
personal column *n* колóнка* для чáстных объявлéний.
personal computer *n* персонáльный компью́тер.
personal details *npl* биографи́ческие дáнные *pl adj*.
personal effects *npl* ли́чные вéщи *fpl or* принадлéжности *fpl*.
personal hygiene *n* ли́чная гигиéна.
personal identification number *n* (*BANKING*) ли́чный идентификациóнный нóмер* (*владéльца плáстиковой кáрточки*); (*COMPUT*) персонáльный *or* ли́чный идентификациóнный нóмер*.
personality [pə:sə'nælɪtɪ] *n* харáктер; (*famous person*) знамени́тость *f*.
personal loan *n* (*COMM*) ли́чная ссýда.
personally ['pə:snəlɪ] *adv* ли́чно; **to take sth ~** принимáть (приня́ть* *perf*) что-н на свой счёт.
personal organizer *n* ежеднéвник.
personal property *n* ли́чное имýщество.
personal stereo *n* персонáльное стéрео *nt ind*.
personify [pə:'sɔnɪfaɪ] *vt* олицетворя́ть (олицетвори́ть *perf*), воплощáть (воплоти́ть* *perf*).
personnel [pə:sə'nɛl] *n* персонáл, штат; (*MIL*) ли́чный состáв.
personnel department *n* отдéл кáдров.
personnel management *n* руковóдство кáдрами.
personnel manager *n* начáльник отдéла кáдров.
perspective [pə'spɛktɪv] *n* (*ARCHIT, ART*) перспекти́ва; (*way of thinking*) ви́дение; **to get sth into ~** (*fig*) смотрéть* (посмотрéть* *perf*) на что-н в и́стинном свéте.
Perspex® ['pə:spɛks] *n* плексиглáс.
perspicacity [pə:spɪ'kæsɪtɪ] *n* проницáтельность *f*.
perspiration [pə:spɪ'reɪʃən] *n* пот*.
perspire [pə'spaɪə^r] *vi* потéть (вспотéть *perf*).
persuade [pə'sweɪd] *vt*: **to ~ sb to do** убеждáть (убеди́ть* *perf*) *or* уговáривать (уговори́ть *perf*) когó- н +*infin*; **to ~ sb of/that** убеждáть (убеди́ть* *perf*) когó-н в +*prp*/, что.
persuasion [pə'sweɪʒən] *n* убеждéние; (*religious*) вероисповéдание.
persuasive [pə'sweɪsɪv] *adj* (*argument*) убеди́тельный* (убеди́телен); (*person*) настóйчивый (настóйчив).
pert [pə:t] *adj* (*impudent*) дéрзкий* (дéрзок); (*jaunty*: *hat etc*) кокéтливый.
pertaining [pə:'teɪnɪŋ]: **~ to** *prep* относя́щийся к +*dat*, касáющийся +*gen*.
pertinent ['pə:tɪnənt] *adj* умéстный* (умéстен).
perturb [pə'tə:b] *vt* тревóжить (встревóжить *perf*).
Peru [pə'ru:] *n* Перý *f ind*.
perusal [pə'ru:zl] *n* прочтéние.
peruse [pə'ru:z] *vt* просмáтривать (просмотрéть* *perf*).
Peruvian [pə'ru:vjən] *adj* перуáнский* ◆ *n* перуáнец*(-нка*).
pervade [pə'veɪd] *vt* (*subj*: *smell, feeling*) наполня́ть (напóлнить *perf*).
pervasive [pə'veɪzɪv] *adj* (*smell, influence, ideas*) всепроникáющий; (*gloom*) прони́зывающий.
perverse [pə'və:s] *adj* (*contrary*) врéдный* (врéден).
perversion [pə'və:ʃən] *n* извращéние.
perversity [pə'və:sɪtɪ] *n* врéдность *f*.
pervert [*vt* pə'və:t, *n* 'pə:və:t] *vt* (*person, mind*) развращáть (разврати́ть* *perf*), растлевáть (растли́ть *perf*); (*truth, sb's words*) извращáть (изврати́ть* *perf*) ◆ *n* (*also: sexual ~*) (полóвой) извращéнец.
pessimism ['pɛsɪmɪzəm] *n* пессими́зм.
pessimist ['pɛsɪmɪst] *n* пессими́ст(ка*).
pessimistic [pɛsɪ'mɪstɪk] *adj* пессимисти́чный* (пессимисти́чен).
pest [pɛst] *n* (*insect*) вреди́тель *m*; (*fig*: *nuisance*) занýда *m/f*.

* marks translations which have irregular inflections. The Russian–English side of the dictionary gives inflectional information.

pest control *n* борьба́ с вреди́телями.
pester ['pɛstə'] *vt* пристава́ть* (приста́ть* *perf*) к +*dat*.
pesticide ['pɛstɪsaɪd] *n* пестици́д.
pestilence ['pɛstɪləns] *n* мор.
pestle ['pɛsl] *n* пе́стик.
pet [pɛt] *n* дома́шнее живо́тное *nt adj* ◆ *cpd* излю́бленный ◆ *vt* (*stroke*) ласка́ть (*impf*) ◆ *vi* (*inf*: *sexually*) обнима́ться (*impf*), целова́ться (*impf*); ~ **lion** *etc* ручно́й лев *etc*; **teacher's** ~ люби́мчик.
petal ['pɛtl] *n* лепесто́к*.
peter out ['pi:tə-] *vi* (*road*) исчеза́ть (исче́знуть* *perf*); (*stream, conversation*) иссяка́ть (исся́кнуть* *perf*); (*meeting*) зака́нчиваться (зако́нчиться *perf*).
petite [pə'ti:t] *adj* миниатю́рный* (миниатю́рен).
petition [pə'tɪʃən] *n* (*signed document*) пети́ция; (*LAW*) хода́тайство ◆ *vt* обраща́ться (обрати́ться* *perf*) с пети́цией к +*dat* ◆ *vi*: **to** ~ **for divorce** подава́ть* (пода́ть* *perf*) заявле́ние о разво́де.
pet name *n* (*BRIT*) ласка́тельное и́мя* *nt*.
petrified ['pɛtrɪfaɪd] *adj* (*fig*) оцепене́вший.
petrify ['pɛtrɪfaɪ] (*fig*) *vt* приводи́ть* (привести́* *perf*) в оцепене́ние.
petrochemical [pɛtrə'kɛmɪkl] *adj* нефтехими́ческий.
petrodollars ['pɛtrəudɔləz] *npl* (*COMM*) нефтедо́ллары *mpl*.
petrol ['pɛtrəl] (*BRIT*) *n* бензи́н; **two/four-star** ~ ни́зкооктановый/высо́кооктановый бензи́н; **unleaded** ~ бензи́н не содержа́щий свинца́.
petrol bomb *n* ба́нка со взрывча́той сме́сью.
petrol can *n* (*BRIT*) кани́стра для бензи́на.
petrol engine *n* (*BRIT*) бензи́новый двигатель *m*.
petroleum [pə'trəulɪəm] *n* нефть *f*.
petroleum jelly *n* вазели́н*.
petrol pump *n* (*BRIT*: *in garage*) бензоколо́нка*; (: *in engine*) бензонасо́с.
petrol station *n* (*BRIT*) бензозапра́вочная ста́нция.
petrol tank *n* (*BRIT*) бензоба́к.
petticoat ['pɛtɪkəut] *n* (*full-length*) комбина́ция; (*waist slip*) ни́жняя ю́бка*.
pettifogging ['pɛtɪfɔgɪŋ] *adj* ме́лочный* (ме́лочен).
pettiness ['pɛtɪnɪs] *n* (*of actions*) ме́лочность *f*; (*of mind*) ограни́ченность *f*.
petty ['pɛtɪ] *adj* (*small, unimportant*) ме́лкий* (ме́лок); (*small-minded*) ограни́ченный* (ограни́чен).
petty cash *n* (*in office*) де́ньги* *pl* на ме́лкие расхо́ды.
petty officer *n* старшина́ *m* (*во фло́те*).
petulant ['pɛtjulənt] *adj* оби́дчивый (оби́дчив).
pew [pju:] *n* скамья́* (*в це́ркви*).
pewter ['pju:tə'] *n* сплав о́лова со свинцо́м.
Pfc *abbr* (*US*: *MIL*: = *private first class*) рядово́й 1-го кла́сса.
PG *n abbr* (*CINEMA*: = *parental guidance*) *фильм до 16-ти лет*.
PGA *n abbr* = *Professional Golfers Association*.
PH *n abbr* (*US*: *MIL*: = *Purple Heart*) ≈ меда́ль *f* „За отва́гу".
pH *n abbr* (= *potential of hydrogen*) pH (*водоро́дный показа́тель*).
PHA *n abbr* (*US*) = *Public Housing Administration*.
phallic ['fælɪk] *adj* фалли́ческий.
phantom ['fæntəm] *n* фанто́м ◆ *adj* (*fig*) при́зрачный* (при́зрачен).
Pharaoh ['fɛərəu] *n* фарао́н.
pharmaceutical [fɑ:mə'sju:tɪkl] *adj* фармацевти́ческий ◆ *n*: ~**s** медикаме́нты *mpl*.
pharmacist ['fɑ:məsɪst] *n* фармаце́вт.
pharmacy ['fɑ:məsɪ] *n* (*profession*) фармаце́втика; (*shop*) апте́ка.
phase [feɪz] *n* фа́за ◆ *vt*: **to** ~ **sth in** поэта́пно вводи́ть* (ввести́* *perf*) что-н; **to** ~ **sth out** ликвиди́ровать (*impf/perf*) что-н.
PhD *n abbr* (= *Doctor of Philosophy*) до́ктор филосо́фии.
pheasant ['fɛznt] *n* фаза́н.
phenomena [fə'nɔmɪnə] *npl of* **phenom**.. **on**.
phenomenal [fə'nɔmɪnl] *adj* феномена́льный* (феномена́лен).
phenomenon [fə'nɔmɪnən] (*pl* **phenomena**) *n* явле́ние, фено́мен.
phew [fju:] *excl* уф.
phial ['faɪəl] *n* скля́нка*.
philanderer [fɪ'lændərə'] *n* волоки́та *m*.
philanthropic [fɪlən'θrɔpɪk] *adj* филантропи́ческий.
philanthropist [fɪ'lænθrəpɪst] *n* филантро́п (ка*).
philatelist [fɪ'lætəlɪst] *n* филателист(ка*).
philately [fɪ'lætəlɪ] *n* филатели́я.
Philippines ['fɪlɪpi:nz] *npl*: **the** ~ Филиппи́ны *pl*, Филиппи́нские острова́* *mpl*.
philosopher [fɪ'lɔsəfə'] *n* фило́соф.
philosophical [fɪlə'sɔfɪkl] *adj* филосо́фский.
philosophize [fɪ'lɔsəfaɪz] *vi* филосо́фствовать (*impf*).
philosophy [fɪ'lɔsəfɪ] *n* филосо́фия.
phlegm [flɛm] *n* (*MED*) мокро́та.
phlegmatic [flɛg'mætɪk] *adj* флегмати́чный* (флегмати́чен).
phobia ['fəubjə] *n* (*MED*) фо́бия, страх.
phone [fəun] *n* телефо́н ◆ *vt* звони́ть (позвони́ть *perf*) (по телефо́ну) +*dat*; **to be on the** ~ (*possess a phone*) име́ть (*impf*) телефо́н; (*be calling*) говори́ть (*impf*) по телефо́ну
▸ **phone back** *vt* перезва́нивать (перезвони́ть *perf*) +*dat* ◆ *vi* перезва́нивать (перезвони́ть *perf*)
▸ **phone up** *vt* звони́ть (позвони́ть *perf*) +*dat* ◆ *vi* звони́ть (позвони́ть *perf*).
phone book *n* телефо́нная кни́га.

phone booth *n* телефóн-автомáт.
phone box *n* (*BRIT*) телефóнная бýдка*, телефóн-автомáт.
phone call *n* телефóнный звонóк*.
phone-card ['fəunkɑːd] *n* телефóнная кáрточка (*испóльзуется в автомáтах для безналúчной оплáты переговóров*).
phone-in ['fəunɪn] *n* (*BRIT: RADIO, TV*) прогрáмма „звонúте-отвечáем".
phone tapping [-tæpɪŋ] *n* прослýшивание телефóнных разговóров.
phonetics [fə'nɛtɪks] *n* фонéтика.
phoney ['fəunɪ] *adj* фальшúвый (фальшúв).
phonograph ['fəunəgrɑːf] *n* (*US*) проúгрыватель *m*.
phony ['fəunɪ] *adj* = **phoney**.
phosphate ['fɔsfeɪt] *n* фосфáт.
phosphorus ['fɔsfərəs] *n* фóсфор.
photo ['fəutəu] *n* фотогрáфия.
photo... ['fəutəu] *prefix* фото....
photocopier ['fəutəukɔpɪə^r] *n* (*machine*) ксéрокс, копировáльная машúна.
photocopy ['fəutəukɔpɪ] *n* ксерокóпия, фотокóпия ◆ *vt* фотокопúровать (сфотокопúровать *perf*), ксерокопúровать (*impf/perf*).
photoelectric [fəutəuɪ'lɛktrɪk] *adj* фотоэлектрúческий; ~ **cell** фотоэлемéнт.
photo finish *n* фотофúниш.
Photofit® ['fəutəufɪt] *n* фоторóбот.
photogenic [fəutəu'dʒɛnɪk] *adj* фотогенúчный* (фотогенúчен).
photograph ['fəutəgræf] *n* фотогрáфия ◆ *vt* фотографúровать (сфотографúровать *perf*); **to take a ~ of sb** фотографúровать (сфотографúровать *perf*) когó-н.
photographer [fə'tɔgrəfə^r] *n* фотóграф.
photographic [fəutə'græfɪk] *adj* фотографúческий.
photography [fə'tɔgrəfɪ] *n* фотогрáфия.
photo opportunity *n ситуáция, дáющая возмóжность знаменúтостям быть представленным в вы́годном свéте на фотогрáфии.*
Photostat® ['fəutəustæt] *n* фотокóпия.
photosynthesis [fəutəu'sɪnθəsɪs] *n* (*BIO*) фотосúнтез.
phrase [freɪz] *n* (*also LING, MUS*) фрáза ◆ *vt* формулúровать (сформулúровать *perf*); (*letter*) составлять (состáвить* *perf*).
phrase book *n* разговóрник.
physical ['fɪzɪkl] *adj* физúческий*; (*world, universe, object*) материáльный* (материáлен); ~ **examination** медосмóтр= *медицúнский* осмóтр*; ~ **exercises** физúческие упражнéния.
physical education *n* физúческое воспитáние, физкультýра.
physically ['fɪzɪklɪ] *adv* физúчески.
physician [fɪ'zɪʃən] *n* (*esp US*) врач*.
physicist ['fɪzɪsɪst] *n* фúзик.
physics ['fɪzɪks] *n* фúзика.
physiological ['fɪzɪə'lɔdʒɪkl] *adj* физиологúческий*.
physiology [fɪzɪ'ɔlədʒɪ] *n* физиолóгия.
physiotherapist [fɪzɪəu'θɛrəpɪst] *n* физиотерапéвт.
physiotherapy [fɪzɪəu'θɛrəpɪ] *n* физиотерапúя.
physique [fɪ'ziːk] *n* (*build*) телосложéние; (*health*) физúческие дáнные *pl adj*.
pianist ['piːənɪst] *n* пианúст(ка*).
piano [pɪ'ænəu] *n* пианúно, фортепьяно *nt ind*; **grand** ~ роя́ль *m*.
piano accordion *n* (*BRIT*) аккордеóн.
piccolo ['pɪkələu] *n* пúкколо *nt ind*.
pick [pɪk] *n* (*also:* ~**axe**) киркá* ◆ *vt* (*select*) выбирáть (вы́брать* *perf*); (*gather: fruit, flowers*) собирáть (собрáть* *perf*); (*pluck*) рвать* (*impf*); (*lock*) взлáмывать (взломáть *perf*); (*scab, spot*) ковырять (сковырнýть *perf*); **take your ~** выбирáйте; **the ~ of the bunch** (*best*) сáмое лýчшее; **to ~ one's nose/teeth** ковырять (*impf*) в носý/зубáх; **to ~ sb's brains** обращáться (обратúться* *perf*) к комý-н за совéтом; **to ~ pockets** лáзать (*impf*) кармáнам; **to ~ a quarrel (with sb)** искáть* (*impf*) пóвод для ссóры (с кем-н)
▸ **pick at** *vt fus* (*food*) ковырять (*impf*)
▸ **pick off** *vt* (*planes*) методúчно сбивáть (сбить* *perf*); (*people*) методúчно стрелять (*impf*) по +*dat*
▸ **pick on** *vt fus* (*criticize*) придирáться (придрáться* *perf*) к +*dat*; (*treat badly*) цепляться (*impf*) к +*dat*
▸ **pick out** *vt* (*distinguish*) разглядéть (*perf*); (*select*) выбирáть (вы́брать* *perf*)
▸ **pick up** *vi* (*improve: health, economy*) улучшáться (улýчшиться *perf*) ◆ *vt* (*lift*) поднимáть (поднять* *perf*); (*POLICE: arrest*) забирáть (забрáть* *perf*); (*collect: person: on foot*) заходúть* (зайтú* *perf*) за +*instr*; (*: with transport*) заезжáть (заéхать* *perf*) за +*instr*; (*: parcel*) забирáть (забрáть* *perf*); (*AUT: passenger*) подбирáть (подобрáть* *perf*); (*inf: person: for sexual encounter*) подцепúть* (*perf*); (*language, skill etc*) усвáивать (усвóить *perf*); (*RADIO*) ловúть* (поймáть *perf*); **to ~ up speed** набирáть (набрáть* *perf*) скóрость; **to ~ o.s. up** (*after falling etc*) поднимáться (подняться* *perf*); **we ~ed up where we left off** мы нáчали с тогó мéста, где остановúлись.
pickaxe ['pɪkæks] (*US* **pickax**) *n* киркá*.
picket ['pɪkɪt] *n* (*in strike*) пикéт ◆ *vt* пикетúровать (*impf*).
picketing ['pɪkɪtɪŋ] *n* пикетúрование.
picket line *n* лúния пикéтов.

* marks translations which have irregular inflections. The Russian-English side of the dictionary gives inflectional information.

pickings ['pɪkɪŋz] *npl*: **there are good ~ to be had here** на э́том мо́жно хорошо́ нажи́ться.
pickle ['pɪkl] *n* (*marinade*) марина́д; (*also*: **~s**) соле́нья *ntpl*; (*fig*: *inf*) переде́лка* ◆ *vt* (*in vinegar*) маринова́ть (замаринова́ть *perf*); (*in salt water*) соли́ть* (засоли́ть* *perf*); **to be in a ~** (*fig*: *inf*) попада́ть (попа́сть* *perf*) в переде́лку.
pick-me-up ['pɪkmi:ʌp] *n* тонизи́рующий* напи́ток*.
pickpocket ['pɪkpɔkɪt] *n* вор*-карма́нник.
pick-up ['pɪkʌp] *n* (*also*: **~ truck** *or* **van**) пика́п; (*BRIT*: *on record player*) звукосними́тель *m*.
picnic ['pɪknɪk] *n* пикни́к* ◆ *vi* устра́ивать (устро́ить *perf*) пикни́к.
picnicker ['pɪknɪkə'] *n* уча́стник(-ица) пикника́.
pictorial [pɪk'tɔ:rɪəl] *adj* иллюстри́рованный (иллюстри́рован).
picture ['pɪktʃə'] *n* (*also fig*) карти́на; (*photograph*) фотогра́фия; (*TV*) изображе́ние; (*film*) (кино)карти́на ◆ *vt* (*imagine*) рисова́ть (нарисова́ть *perf*) карти́ну *+gen*; **the ~s** *npl* (*BRIT*: *inf*) кино́ *nt ind*; **to take a ~ of sb/sth** фотографи́ровать (сфотографи́ровать *perf*) кого́-н/что-н; **the overall ~** о́бщая карти́на; **to put sb in the ~** вводи́ть* (ввести́* *perf*) кого́-н в курс де́ла.
picture book *n* кни́га* с карти́нками.
picturesque [pɪktʃə'rɛsk] *adj* живопи́сный* (живопи́сен).
picture window *n* (*ARCHIT*) *большо́е окно́, из кото́рого открыва́ется краси́вый вид.*
piddling ['pɪdlɪŋ] *adj* (*inf*) пустя́чный*.
pidgin ['pɪdʒɪn] *adj*: **~ English** пи́джин-и́нглиш.
pie [paɪ] *n* пиро́г*; (*small*) пирожо́к*.
piebald ['paɪbɔ:ld] *adj* пе́гий* (пег).
piece [pi:s] *n* (*portion, part*) кусо́к*; (*component*) дета́ль *f*; (*CHESS*) фигу́ра; (*DRAUGHTS*) ша́шка* ◆ *vt*: **to ~ together** (*information*) свя́зывать (связа́ть* *perf*); (*parts of a whole*) соединя́ть (соедини́ть *perf*); **a ~ of clothing** вещь* *f*; **a ~ of advice** сове́т; **in ~s** (*broken*) вдре́безги; (*not yet assembled*) разо́бранный (разо́бран); **to take to ~s** (*dismantle*) разбира́ть (разобра́ть* *perf*); **in one ~** в це́лости и сохра́нности; **to get back all in one ~** возвраща́ться (верну́ться *perf*) це́лым и невреди́мым; **a 10p ~** (*BRIT*) моне́та в 10 пе́нсов; **~ by ~** по частя́м; **a six-~ band** анса́мбль *m* из шести́ музыка́льных инструме́нтов; **to say one's ~** выска́зывать (вы́сказать* *perf*) своё мне́ние.
piecemeal ['pi:smi:l] *adv* понемно́гу.
piece rate *n* тари́ф *or* ста́вка за едини́цу вы́полненных рабо́т.
piecework ['pi:swə:k] *n* сде́льная рабо́та.
pie chart *n* се́кторная диагра́мма.
pier [pɪə'] *n* пирс.
pierce [pɪəs] *vt* протыка́ть (проткну́ть *perf*), прока́лывать (проколо́ть* *perf*); **to have one's ears ~d** прока́лывать (проколо́ть* *perf*) у́ши.
piercing ['pɪəsɪŋ] *adj* (*cry, eyes, stare*) пронзи́тельный* (пронзи́телен); (*wind*) прони́зывающий.
piety ['paɪətɪ] *n* на́божность *f*.
piffling ['pɪflɪŋ] *adj* (*inf*) никчёмный* (никчёмен).
pig [pɪg] *n* (*also fig*) свинья́*.
pigeon ['pɪdʒən] *n* го́лубь* *m*.
pigeonhole ['pɪdʒənhəul] *n* (*in office, bureau*) яче́йка (*для корреспонде́нции*); (*fig*) ни́ша ◆ *vt* (*person*) накле́ивать (накле́ить *perf*) ярлыки́ на *+acc*.
pigeon-toed ['pɪdʒəntəud] *adj* косола́пый (косола́п).
piggy bank ['pɪgɪ-] *n* копи́лка*.
pig-headed ['pɪg'hɛdɪd] *adj* (*inf*) упря́мый (упря́м).
piglet ['pɪglɪt] *n* поросёнок*.
pigment ['pɪgmənt] *n* пигме́нт.
pigmentation [pɪgmən'teɪʃən] *n* пигмента́ция.
pigmy ['pɪgmɪ] *n* = **pygmy**.
pigskin ['pɪgskɪn] *n* свина́я ко́жа.
pigsty ['pɪgstaɪ] *n* (*also fig*) свина́рник.
pigtail ['pɪgteɪl] *n* коси́чка*.
pike [paɪk] *n inv* (*fish*) щу́ка ◆ *n* (*spear*) пи́ка.
pilchard ['pɪltʃəd] *n* сарди́на.
pile [paɪl] *n* (*large heap*) ку́ча, гру́да; (*neat stack*) сто́пка*; (*pillar*) сва́я; (*of carpet, cloth*) ворс ◆ *vi*: **to ~ into** (*vehicle*) набива́ться (наби́ться* *perf*) в *+acc*; **in a ~** в ку́че; **to ~ out of** (*vehicle*) выва́ливаться (вы́валиться *perf*) из *+gen*
▸ **pile on** *vt*: **to ~ it on** (*inf*) перебáрщивать (переборщи́ть* *perf*)
▸ **pile up** *vt* (*objects*) сва́ливать (свали́ть* *perf*) в ку́чу ◆ *vi* громозди́ться* (*impf*); (*problems, work*) нака́пливаться (накопи́ться *perf*).
piles [paɪlz] *npl* (*MED*) геморро́й *msg*.
pile-up ['paɪlʌp] *n* (*AUT*) столкнове́ние не́скольких маши́н.
pilfer ['pɪlfə'] *vti* ворова́ть (*impf*).
pilfering ['pɪlfərɪŋ] *n* ме́лкое воровство́.
pilgrim ['pɪlgrɪm] *n* пало́мник(-ица), пилигри́м.
pilgrimage ['pɪlgrɪmɪdʒ] *n* пало́мничество.
pill [pɪl] *n* табле́тка*; **the ~** (*contraceptive*) противозача́точные *pl adj* (табле́тки); **to be on the ~** принима́ть (*impf*) противозача́точные табле́тки.
pillage ['pɪlɪdʒ] *n* грабёж*.
pillar ['pɪlə'] *n* (*ARCHIT*) столб*, коло́нна; **a ~ of society** (*fig*) столп о́бщества.
pillar box *n* (*BRIT*) почто́вый я́щик*.
pillion ['pɪljən] *n*: **to ride ~** (*on motorcycle*) е́хать*/е́здить* (*impf*) на за́днем сиде́нье мотоци́кла; (*on horse*) е́хать*/е́здить* (*impf*) верхо́м на ло́шади сза́ди вса́дника.
pillory ['pɪlərɪ] *vt* выставля́ть (вы́ставить* *perf*) на осмея́ние ◆ *n* позо́рный столб*.
pillow ['pɪləu] *n* поду́шка*.

pillowcase ['pɪləukeɪs] *n* на́волочка*.
pillowslip ['pɪləuslɪp] *n* = **pillowcase**.
pilot ['paɪlət] *n* (*AVIAT*) пило́т, лётчик; (*NAUT*) ло́цман ◆ *cpd* (*scheme, study etc*) эксперимента́льный ◆ *vt* (*aircraft*) управля́ть *(impf)* +*instr*; (*fig*: *new law, scheme*) апроби́ровать *(impf/perf)*.
pilot boat *n* ло́цманский ка́тер*.
pilot light *n* запа́льник.
pimento [pɪ'mɛntəu] *n* души́стый пе́рец.
pimp [pɪmp] *n* сутенёр.
pimple ['pɪmpl] *n* прыщ*, пры́щик.
pimply ['pɪmplɪ] *adj* прыща́вый (прыща́в).
PIN *n abbr* = **personal identification number**.
pin [pɪn] *n* була́вка*; (*TECH*) штифт*; (*BRIT*: *also*: **drawing ~**) кно́пка*; (*of grenade*) чека́; (*BRIT*: *ELEC*: *of plug*) штырь* *m* ◆ *vt* прика́лывать (приколо́ть* *perf*); **~s and needles** (*fig*) колотьё; **to ~ sb against** *or* **to** прижима́ть (прижа́ть* *perf*) кого́-н к +*dat*; **to ~ sth on sb** (*fig*) возлага́ть (возложи́ть* *perf*) на кого́-н вину́ за что-н
▸ **pin down** *vt* (*fig*): **to ~ sb down** припира́ть (припере́ть* *perf*) кого́-н к сте́нке; **there's something strange here but I can't quite ~ it down** что́-то здесь не так, но не пойму́ что.
pinafore ['pɪnəfɔː'] *n* (*also*: **~ dress**) сарафа́н.
pinball ['pɪnbɔːl] *n* кита́йский* билья́рд.
pincers ['pɪnsəz] *npl* (*TECH*) клёщи* *pl*; (*of crab etc*) клешни́ *fpl*.
pinch [pɪntʃ] *n* (*small amount*) щепо́тка* ◆ *vt* щипа́ть* (ущипну́ть *perf*); (*inf*: *steal*) стащи́ть* *(perf)* ◆ *vi* (*shoe*) жать* *(impf)*; **at a ~** в кра́йнем слу́чае; **to feel the ~** (*fig*) ока́зываться (оказа́ться* *perf*) в стеснённых обстоя́тельствах.
pinched [pɪntʃt] *adj* (*drawn*) осу́нувшийся; **~ with cold** съёжившийся от хо́лода; **I am ~ for money** у меня́ ту́го с деньга́ми; **we're ~ for space here** у нас здесь ма́ло ме́ста.
pincushion ['pɪnkuʃən] *n* иго́льник.
pine [paɪn] *n* (*tree, wood*) сосна́* ◆ *vi*: **to ~ for** тоскова́ть *(impf)* по +*dat*
▸ **pine away** *vi* (*gradually die*) ча́хнуть* (зача́хнуть* *perf*).
pineapple ['paɪnæpl] *n* анана́с *m no pl*.
pine cone *n* сосно́вая ши́шка.
pine needles *npl* сосно́вые иго́лки *fpl*.
ping [pɪŋ] *n* (*noise*) звон.
Ping-Pong® ['pɪŋpɔŋ] *n* насто́льный те́ннис, пинг-по́нг.
pink [pɪŋk] *adj* ро́зовый ◆ *n* (*colour*) ро́зовый цвет*; (*BOT*) гвозди́ка.
pinking shears *npl* зу́бчатые но́жницы *pl*.
pin money *n* (*BRIT*) де́ньги* *pl* на була́вки.
pinnacle ['pɪnəkl] *n* (*of building*) шпиц; (*of mountain, also fig*) верши́на.
pinpoint ['pɪnpɔɪnt] *vt* (*discover*) то́чно определя́ть (определи́ть *perf*); (*explain*) то́чно объясня́ть (объясни́ть *perf*); (*position of sth*) то́чно ука́зывать (указа́ть* *perf*).
pinstripe ['pɪnstraɪp] *n* поло́ска*; **~ suit** костю́м в поло́ску.
pint [paɪnt] *n* пи́нта.
pin-up ['pɪnʌp] *n* (*picture*) *журна́льная вы́резка с изображе́нием краси́вых де́вушек*.
pioneer [paɪə'nɪə'] *n* (*initiator*: *of scheme, science, method*) первооткрыва́тель *m*, нова́тор; (*early settler, also fig*) первопрохо́дец*, пионе́р ◆ *vt* (*initiate*) прокла́дывать (проложи́ть* *perf*) путь к +*dat*.
pious ['paɪəs] *adj* на́божный* (на́божен).
pip [pɪp] *n* (*of grape, melon*) ко́сточка*; (*of apple, orange*) зёрнышко; **the ~s** *npl* (*BRIT*: *RADIO*) сигна́л *msg* (то́чного вре́мени).
pipe [paɪp] *n* (*for water, gas*) труба́*; (*for smoking*) тру́бка*; (*MUS*) ду́дка* ◆ *vt* (*water, gas, oil*) подава́ть* (пода́ть* *perf*); **~s** *npl* (*also*: **bagpipes**) волы́нка* *fsg*
▸ **pipe down** *vi* (*inf*: *be quiet*) затыка́ться (заткну́ться *perf*).
pipe cleaner *n* ёршик (*для тру́бки*).
piped music [paɪpt-] *n* му́зыка из громкоговори́теля.
pipe dream *n* пусты́е мечты́ *fpl*.
pipeline ['paɪplaɪn] *n* трубопрово́д; **oil ~** нефтепрово́д; **gas ~** газопрово́д; **a new project is in the ~** (*fig*) дан ход но́вому прое́кту.
piper ['paɪpə'] *n* (*bagpipe player*) волы́нщик.
pipe tobacco *n* тру́бочный таба́к*.
piping ['paɪpɪŋ] *adv*: **~ hot** о́чень горя́чий*.
piquant ['piːkənt] *adj* (*also fig*) пика́нтный* (пика́нтен).
pique ['piːk] *n* задéтое самолю́бие.
piracy ['paɪərəsɪ] *n* пира́тство.
pirate ['paɪərət] *n* (*sailor*) пира́т ◆ *vt* (*video tape, cassette*) незако́нно распространя́ть (распространи́ть *perf*); (*book*) незако́нно переиздава́ть* (переизда́ть* *perf*).
pirate radio *n* (*BRIT*): **~ ~ station** пира́тская радиоста́нция.
pirouette [pɪru'ɛt] *n* пируэ́т.
Pisces ['paɪsiːz] *n* (*ASTROLOGY*) Ры́бы; **he is ~** он – Ры́ба.
piss [pɪs] (*inf!*) *vi* пи́сать (попи́сать *perf*) (*!*); **~ off!** пошёл ты! (*!*)
pissed [pɪst] *adj* (*inf!*: *drunk*) пья́ный* (пьян) в сте́льку (*!*)
pistol ['pɪstl] *n* пистоле́т.
piston ['pɪstən] *n* по́ршень* *m*.
pit [pɪt] *n* (*in ground*) я́ма; (*in surface of sth*) я́мка*; (*also*: **coal ~**) ша́хта; (*also*: **orchestra ~**) оркестро́вая я́ма; (*quarry*) карье́р ◆ *vt*: **to ~ one's wits against sb** состяза́ться *(impf)* в эруди́ции с кем-н; **~s** *npl* (*in motor racing*)

* marks translations which have irregular inflections. The Russian-English side of the dictionary gives inflectional information.

пункт *msg* ремóнта и заправки; **to ~ sb against sb** направля́ть (напра́вить* *perf*) когó-н на когó-н.
pitapat ['pɪtə'pæt] *adv* (*BRIT*: *of heart*) тук-ту́к; (: *of rain*) кап-кап.
pitch [pɪtʃ] *n* (*BRIT*: *SPORT*) пóле*; (*MUS*) высота́; (*fig*: *level, degree*) у́ровень *m*; (*tar*) смола́; (*also*: **sales ~**) речь *f*; (*NAUT*) килева́я ка́чка ◆ *vt* (*throw*) подава́ть* (пода́ть* *perf*), гнать* (погна́ть* *perf*); (*set*: *price*) устана́вливать (установи́ть* *perf*); (: *message*) подстра́ивать (подстрóить *perf*) ◆ *vi* (*fall*) па́дать (упа́сть* *perf*); (*NAUT*) испы́тывать (испыта́ть *perf*) килеву́ю ка́чку; **at this ~** (*fig*) на такóм у́ровне; **to ~ a tent** ста́вить* (поста́вить* *perf*) пала́тку; **he was ~ed forward** егó брóсило вперёд.
pitch-black ['pɪtʃ'blæk] *adj* óчень тёмный.
pitched battle [pɪtʃt-] *n* ожесточённая схва́тка*.
pitcher ['pɪtʃə^r] *n* (*jug*) кувши́н; (*US*: *BASEBALL*) подаю́щий *m adj*.
pitchfork ['pɪtʃfɔːk] *n* ви́лы *pl*.
piteous ['pɪtɪəs] *adj* (*sound etc*) жа́лобный* (жа́лобен); (*sight*) несча́стный* (несча́стен).
pitfall ['pɪtfɔːl] *n* (*difficulty, danger*) лову́шка, подвóдные ка́мни *mpl*.
pith [pɪθ] *n* (*of orange, lemon etc*) паренхи́ма; (*of plant*) сердцеви́на; (*fig*) суть *f*.
pithead ['pɪthɛd] *n* (*BRIT*) копёр (*над ша́хтой*).
pithy ['pɪθɪ] *adj* (*saying etc*) содержа́тельный* (содержа́телен).
pitiable ['pɪtɪəbl] *adj* (*sight, person*) жа́лкий* (жа́лок).
pitiful ['pɪtɪful] *adj* жа́лкий* (жа́лок).
pitifully ['pɪtɪfəlɪ] *adv* жа́лобно; **it's ~ obvious** к несча́стью, э́то очеви́дно.
pitiless ['pɪtɪlɪs] *adj* безжа́лостный* (безжа́лостен).
pittance ['pɪtns] *n* гроши́ *mpl*.
pitted ['pɪtɪd] *adj*: **~ with** (*holes, acne*) изры́тый (изры́т) *+instr*; (*rust*) изъе́денный (изъе́ден) *+instr*.
pity ['pɪtɪ] *n* жа́лость *f* ◆ *vt* жале́ть (пожале́ть *perf*); **what a ~!** кака́я жа́лость!; **it is a ~ that you can't come** жа́лко, что Вы не смóжете прийти́; **to have** *or* **take ~ on sb** сжа́литься (*perf*) над кем-н.
pitying ['pɪtɪɪŋ] *adj* жа́лостливый (жа́лостлив).
pivot ['pɪvət] *n* (*TECH*: *pin*) ось *f*; (: *point*) тóчка* враще́ния; (*fig*) центр ◆ *vi*: **to ~ on** (*balance*) держа́ться* (*perf*) на *+prp*; (*turn*) враща́ться (*impf*) вокру́г *+gen*; (*fig*: *depend on*) зави́сеть* (*impf*) от *+gen*.
pixel ['pɪksl] *n* (*COMPUT*) пи́ксель *m*, элеме́нт изображе́ния.
pixie ['pɪksɪ] *n* эльф.
pizza ['piːtsə] *n* пи́цца.
placard ['plækɑːd] *n* плака́т.
placate [plə'keɪt] *vt* (*person*) умиротворя́ть (умиротвори́ть *perf*); (*anger*) усмиря́ть (усмири́ть *perf*).
placatory [plə'keɪtərɪ] *adj* примири́тельный* (примири́телен).
place [pleɪs] *vt* (*put*) помеща́ть (помести́ть* *perf*); (*identify*: *person*) вспомина́ть (вспóмнить *perf*) ◆ *n* ме́сто*; (*home*): **at his ~** у негó; (*in street names*): **Laurel P~** Лóрел Плейс; **to ~ an order with sb for sth** (*COMM*) зака́зывать (заказа́ть* *perf*) что-н у когó-н; **to be ~d** (*in race, exam*) быть* (*impf*) на какóм-н ме́сте; **how are you ~d next week?** как у Вас со сле́дующей неде́лей?; **to take ~** происходи́ть* (произойти́* *perf*); **from ~ to ~** с ме́ста на ме́сто; **all over the ~** повсю́ду; **out of ~** (*not suitable*) неуме́стный* (неуме́стен); **I feel out of ~ here** я чу́вствую себя́ не в своéй таре́лке/не на ме́сте здесь; **in the first ~** (*first of all*) во-пе́рвых; **to put sb in his ~** (*fig*) ста́вить* (поста́вить* *perf*) когó-н на ме́сто; **he's going ~s** он далекó пойдёт; **it's not my ~** э́то не моё де́ло; **to change ~s with sb** меня́ться (поменя́ться *perf*) места́ми с кем-н.
placebo [plə'siːbəu] *n* (*MED*) плаце́бо *nt ind*; (*fig*) успокои́тельное сре́дство.
place mat *n* подста́вка* (*для столóвых прибóров*); (*in linen etc*) салфе́тка*.
placement ['pleɪsmənt] *n* (*action*) размеще́ние; (*job*) ме́сто*.
place name *n* географи́ческое назва́ние, топони́м.
placenta [plə'sɛntə] *n* плаце́нта.
place of birth *n* ме́сто* рожде́ния.
place setting *n* столóвый прибóр.
placid ['plæsɪd] *adj* спокóйный* (спокóен); (*place*) ти́хий* (тих).
plagiarism ['pleɪdʒjərɪzəm] *n* плагиа́т.
plagiarist ['pleɪdʒjərɪst] *n* плагиа́тор.
plagiarize ['pleɪdʒjəraɪz] *vt* красть* (укра́сть* *perf*), спи́сывать (списа́ть* *perf*).
plague [pleɪg] *n* (*MED*) чума́; (*fig*: *of locusts etc*) наше́ствие ◆ *vt* (*fig*: *subj*: *problems, difficulties*) осажда́ть (осади́ть* *perf*); **to ~ sb with questions** донима́ть (*impf*) когó-н вопрóсами.
plaice [pleɪs] *n inv* ка́мбала.
plaid [plæd] *n* шотла́ндка* (*ткань*).
plain [pleɪn] *adj* (*simple, not beautiful*) простóй* (прост); (*unpatterned*) гла́дкий* (гла́док); (*clear, easily understood*) я́сный* (я́сен), поня́тный* (поня́тен); (*frank*) прямóй* (прям) ◆ *adv* (*wrong, stupid etc*) я́вно ◆ *n* (*GEO*) равни́на; (*KNITTING*) чулóчная вя́зка; **to make sth ~ to sb** разъясня́ть (разъясни́ть *perf*) что-н кому́-н.
plain chocolate *n* гóрький* шокола́д.
plain-clothes ['pleɪnkləuðz] *adj*: **~ policeman** полице́йский* *m adj* в шта́тском.
plain flour *n* мука́ без дрожжевы́х доба́вок.
plainly ['pleɪnlɪ] *adv* я́сно.

plainness ['pleɪnnɪs] *n* (*simplicity*) простота́; (*clarity*) я́сность *f*.
plaintiff ['pleɪntɪf] *n* исте́ц*(-ти́ца).
plain speaking *n* прямота́.
plaintive ['pleɪntɪv] *adj* (*voice, look, song*) жа́лобный* (жа́лобен).
plait [plæt] *n* (*of hair*) коса́* ◆ *vt* (*hair*) заплета́ть (заплести́* *perf*); (*rope*) плести́* (сплести́* *perf*).
plan [plæn] *n* план ◆ *vt* плани́ровать (заплани́ровать *perf*); (*draw up plans for*) плани́ровать (*impf*) ◆ *vi* плани́ровать (*impf*); **to ~ to do** плани́ровать (заплани́ровать *perf*) *+infin*; **how long do you ~ to stay?** как до́лго Вы плани́руете пробы́ть здесь?; **to ~ for sth** (*anticipate*) рассчи́тывать (*impf*) на что-н.
plane [pleɪn] *n* (*AVIAT*) самолёт; (*MATH*) пло́скость *f*; (*fig*: *level*) план; (*tool*) руба́нок*; (*BOT*) плата́н ◆ *vt* (*wood*) строга́ть (вы́стругать *perf*) ◆ *vi* (*NAUT, AUT*): **to ~ across** скользи́ть* (*impf*) по *+dat*.
planet ['plænɪt] *n* плане́та.
planetarium [plænɪ'tɛərɪəm] *n* планета́рий.
plank [plæŋk] *n* доска́*; (*fig*: *of policy etc*) при́нцип.
plankton ['plæŋktən] *n* планкто́н.
planned economy ['plænd-] *n* пла́новая эконо́мика.
planner ['plænə'] *n* (*of towns*) планиро́вщик; (*of TV programme, project*) составитель *m*.
planning ['plænɪŋ] *n* (*of future, event*) плани́рование; (*of programme etc*) составле́ние; (*also*: **town ~**) планиро́вка.
planning permission *n* (*BRIT*) разреше́ние на строи́тельство.
plant [plɑ:nt] *n* (*BOT*) расте́ние; (*factory*) заво́д; (*machinery*) устано́вка* ◆ *vt* (*seed, plant, garden*) сажа́ть (посади́ть* *perf*); (*field*) засе́ивать (засе́ять *perf*); (*bomb, evidence*) подкла́дывать (подложи́ть* *perf*); (*fig*: *kiss*) запечатлева́ть (запечатле́ть *perf*).
plantation [plæn'teɪʃən] *n* (*of tea, rubber, sugar etc*) планта́ция; (*of trees*) лесонасажде́ние.
plant pot *n* (*BRIT*) цвето́чный горшо́к*.
plaque [plæk] *n* (*on building etc*) мемори-а́льная доска́*; (*on teeth*) налёт.
plasma ['plæzmə] *n* пла́зма.
plaster ['plɑ:stə'] *n* (*for walls*) штукату́рка*; (*also*: **~ of Paris**) гипс; (*BRIT*: *also*: **sticking ~**) пла́стырь *m* ◆ *vt* (*wall, ceiling*) штукату́рить (оштукату́рить *perf*); (*cover*): **to ~ with** залепля́ть (залепи́ть* *perf*) *+instr*; **in ~** (*BRIT*) в ги́псе.
plasterboard ['plɑ:stəbɔ:d] *n* ги́псовые щиты́ (*для обши́вки стен и потолка́*).
plaster cast *n* (*MED*) гипс; (*model, statue*) ги́псовый сле́пок*.
plastered ['plɑ:stəd] *adj* (*inf*: *drunk*): **he is ~** он нажра́лся.
plasterer ['plɑ:stərə'] *n* штукату́р.
plastic ['plæstɪk] *n* пластма́сса ◆ *adj* (*made of plastic*) пластма́ссовый; (*flexible*) пласти́чный*; (*art*) пласти́ческий*.
plastic bag *n* полиэтиле́новый мешо́к*.
plastic bullet *n* пластма́ссовая пу́ля*.
plastic explosive *n синтети́ческая взрывча́тка консисте́нции пластили́на*.
Plasticine® ['plæstɪsi:n] *n* пластили́н.
plastic surgery *n* (*science*) пласти́ческая хирурги́я; (*operation*) пласти́ческая опера́ция.
plate [pleɪt] *n* (*dish*) таре́лка*; (*metal cover*: *on building, machinery*) пласти́на; (*TYP*) печа́тная фо́рма; (*PHOT*) фотопласти́нка*; (*AUT*: *number plate*) но́мер*; (*in book*) вкладна́я иллюстра́ция; (*also*: **dental ~**) вставна́я че́люсть* *f*; (*on door*) табли́чка*; **gold ~** позоло́та; **silver ~** серебре́ние.
plateau ['plætəu] (*pl* **~s** *or* **~x**) *n* (*GEO, also fig*) плато́ *nt ind*.
plateaux ['plætəuz] *npl of* **plateau**.
plateful ['pleɪtful] *n*: **a ~ of** таре́лка* *+gen*.
plate glass *n* (*for window, door*) зерка́льное стекло́.
platen ['plætən] *n* (*TYP*) ва́лик.
plate rack *n* суши́лка* (*для посу́ды*).
platform ['plætfɔ:m] *n* (*at meeting*) трибу́на; (*at concert*) помо́ст; (*for landing, loading on etc*) площа́дка; (*RAIL, POL*) платфо́рма; (*BRIT*: *of bus*) подно́жка*; **the train leaves from ~ seven** по́езд отправля́ется с седьмо́го пути́.
platform ticket *n* (*BRIT*: *RAIL*) перро́нный биле́т.
platinum ['plætɪnəm] *n* пла́тина.
platitude ['plætɪtju:d] *n* пло́скость *f*, бана́льность *f*.
platonic [plə'tɔnɪk] *adj* платони́ческий.
platoon [plə'tu:n] *n* взвод.
platter ['plætə'] *n* блю́до.
plaudits ['plɔ:dɪts] *npl* похвала́ *fsg*.
plausible ['plɔ:zɪbl] *adj* (*theory, excuse etc*) правдоподо́бный* (правдоподо́бен); (*person*) убеди́тельный*.
play [pleɪ] *n* пье́са ◆ *vt* (*subj*: *children*: *game*) игра́ть (*impf*) в *+acc*; (*sport, cards*) игра́ть (сыгра́ть *perf*) в *+acc*; (*opponent*) игра́ть (сыгра́ть *perf*) с *+instr*; (*part, role, piece of music*) игра́ть (сыгра́ть *perf*); (*instrument*) игра́ть (*impf*) на *+prp*; (*listen to*: *tape, record*) ста́вить* (поста́вить* *perf*) ◆ *vi* игра́ть (*impf*); **a ~ on words** игра́* слов; **to bring** *or* **call into ~** вводи́ть* (ввести́* *perf*) в де́йствие; **to ~ a trick on sb** сыгра́ть (*perf*) шу́тку над кем-н; **they're ~ing at soldiers** они игра́ют в солда́тики; **to ~ for time** тяну́ть (*impf*) вре́мя; **to ~ safe** де́йствовать (*impf*) осторо́жно; **to ~**

* marks translations which have irregular inflections. The Russian-English side of the dictionary gives inflectional information.

into sb's hands игра́ть (сыгра́ть *perf*) кому́-н на́ руку
▸ **play about** *vi*: **to ~ about with** (*feelings*) игра́ть *(impf)* +*instr*; (*object*) вози́ться *(impf)* с +*instr*
▸ **play along** *vi* (*fig*): **to ~ along with** (*person, plan, idea*) поды́грывать (подыгра́ть *perf*) +*dat* ◆ *vt* (*fig*): **to ~ sb along** испо́льзовать *(impf)* кого́-н в свои́х це́лях
▸ **play around** *vi* = **play about**
▸ **play back** *vt* (*recording*) прои́грывать (проигра́ть *perf*) (*повто́рно*)
▸ **play down** *vt* не заостря́ть *(impf)* внима́ние на +*prp*
▸ **play on** *vt fus* (*sb's feelings etc*) игра́ть *(impf)* на +*prp*; **to ~ on sb's nerves** де́йствовать *(impf)* кому́-н на не́рвы
▸ **play up** *vi* (*machine*) барахли́ть* *(impf)*; (*children*) шали́ть *(impf)*, прики́дываться *(impf)*.
play-act ['pleɪækt] *vi* де́лать (сде́лать *perf*) вид.
playboy ['pleɪbɔɪ] *n* хлыщ.
player ['pleɪəʳ] *n* (*SPORT*) игро́к*; (*MUS, THEAT*) исполни́тель(ница) *m(f)*.
playful ['pleɪful] *adj* (*person*) игри́вый (игри́в).
playgoer ['pleɪgəuəʳ] *n* театра́л.
playground ['pleɪgraund] *n* (*in park*) (де́тская) площа́дка*; (*in school*) (игрова́я) площа́дка*.
playgroup ['pleɪgru:p] *n* де́тская гру́ппа.
playing card ['pleɪɪŋ-] *n* игра́льная ка́рта.
playing field *n* игрово́е по́ле*.
playmate ['pleɪmeɪt] *n* прия́тель(ница) *m(f)*.
play-off ['pleɪɔf] *n* (*SPORT*) игра́ за призово́е ме́сто.
playpen ['pleɪpɛn] *n* (де́тский*) мане́ж.
playroom ['pleɪru:m] *n* де́тская *f adj*.
playschool ['pleɪsku:l] *n* = **playgroup**.
plaything ['pleɪθɪŋ] *n* игру́шка*.
playtime ['pleɪtaɪm] *n* (*SCOL*) переме́на.
playwright ['pleɪraɪt] *n* драмату́рг.
plc *abbr* (*BRIT*: = *public limited company*) публи́чная компа́ния с ограни́ченной отве́тственностью.
plea [pli:] *n* (*personal request*) мольба́; (*public request*) призы́в; (*LAW*) заявле́ние; (*excuse*) предло́г.
plea bargaining *n призна́ние вино́вности в обме́н на бо́лее коро́ткое тюре́мное заключе́ние.*
plead [pli:d] *vt* (*ignorance, ill health etc*) ссыла́ться (сосла́ться* *perf*) на +*acc* ◆ *vi* (*LAW*) признава́ть* (призна́ть* *perf*) себя́; (*beg*): **to ~ with sb** умоля́ть *(impf)* кого́-н, моли́ть* *(impf)* кого́-н; **to ~ sb's case** (*LAW*) защища́ть *(impf)* кого́-н (*в суде́*); **to ~ for sth** призыва́ть (призва́ть* *perf*) к чему́-н; **to ~ guilty/not guilty** признава́ть* (призна́ть* *perf*) себя́ вино́вным(-ой)/невино́вным(-ой).
pleasant ['plɛznt] *adj* прия́тный* (прия́тен).
pleasantly ['plɛzntlɪ] *adv* прия́тно.
pleasantries ['plɛzntrɪz] *npl* любе́зности *fpl*.
please [pli:z] *excl* пожа́луйста ◆ *vt* угожда́ть (угоди́ть* *perf*) +*dat* ◆ *vi* (*give pleasure, satisfaction*) угожда́ть (угоди́ть* *perf*); **yes, ~** да, спаси́бо; **my bill, ~** получи́те (с меня́), пожа́луйста; **~ don't cry!** не пла́чь, пожа́луйста!; **~ yourself!** (*inf*) как Вам уго́дно!; **do as you ~** де́лайте как хоти́те; **he is difficult/easy to ~** ему́ тру́дно/легко́ угоди́ть *(perf)*.
pleased [pli:zd] *adj*: **~ (with)** дово́льный* (дово́лен) (+*instr*); **~ to meet you** о́чень прия́тно; **we are ~ to inform you that ...** мы ра́ды сообщи́ть Вам, что ....
pleasing ['pli:zɪŋ] *adj* прия́тный* (прия́тен).
pleasurable ['plɛʒərəbl] *adj* ра́достный* (ра́достен).
pleasure ['plɛʒəʳ] *n* удово́льствие; **it's a ~** не сто́ит; **with ~** с удово́льствием; **to take ~ in** получа́ть (получи́ть *perf*) удово́льствие от +*gen*; **is this trip for business or ~?** э́та пое́здка делова́я и́ли развлека́тельная?
pleasure boat *n* прогу́лочный ка́тер.
pleasure cruise *n* круи́з.
pleat [pli:t] *n* скла́дка*.
plebiscite ['plɛbɪsɪt] *n* плебисци́т.
plebs [plɛbz] *npl* (*pej*) плебе́и *mpl*, плебс *msg*.
plectrum ['plɛktrəm] *n* плектр.
pledge [plɛdʒ] *n* (*promise*) обяза́тельство ◆ *vt* (*promise*: *money, support, help*) обяза́ться *(perf)*; **to ~ sb to secrecy** брать* (взять* *perf*) с кого́-н сло́во молча́ть.
plenary ['pli:nərɪ] *adj*: **in ~ session** на плена́рном заседа́нии.
plentiful ['plɛntɪful] *adj* оби́льный* (оби́лен).
plenty ['plɛntɪ] *n* (*sufficient*) доста́точное коли́чество; **~ of** (*food, money etc*) мно́го +*gen*; (*jobs, people, houses etc*) мно́жество +*gen*; **we've got ~ of time to get there** у нас дово́льно вре́мени, что́бы туда́ добра́ться.
plethora ['plɛθərə] *n*: **a ~ of** вели́кое мно́жество +*gen*.
pleurisy ['pluərɪsɪ] *n* плеври́т.
Plexiglas® ['plɛksɪglɑ:s] *n* (*US*) плексигла́с.
pliable ['plaɪəbl] *adj* (*material*) ги́бкий* (ги́бок); (*fig*: *person*) усту́пчивый (усту́пчив), пода́тливый (пода́тлив).
pliant ['plaɪənt] *adj* = **pliable**.
pliers ['plaɪəz] *npl* плоскогу́бцы* *pl*.
plight [plaɪt] *n* мучи́тельное положе́ние.
plimsolls ['plɪmsəlz] *npl* (*BRIT*) паруси́новые ту́фли *pl*, ке́ды *fpl*.
plinth [plɪnθ] *n* постаме́нт.
PLO *n abbr* (= *Palestine Liberation Organization*) ООП= *Организа́ция освобожде́ния Палести́ны*.
plod [plɔd] *vi* (*walk, also fig*) тащи́ться* *(impf)*.
plodder ['plɔdəʳ] *n* (*pej*: *slow worker*) волоки́тчик; **he is a real ~** (*pej*) он тако́й медли́тельный.
plonk [plɔŋk] *n* (*inf*: *BRIT*: *wine*) дешёвое вино́ ◆ *vt* (*inf*): **to ~ sth down** бу́хать (бу́хнуть *perf*)

что-н.

plot [plɔt] *n* (*conspiracy*) за́говор; (*of story*) сюже́т; (*of land*) уча́сток* ◆ *vt* (*sb's downfall etc*) замышля́ть *(impf)*; (*AVIAT, NAUT*) прокла́дывать (проложи́ть *perf*); (*MATH*) наноси́ть* (нанести́* *perf*) ◆ *vi* (*conspire*) составля́ть (соста́вить* *perf*) за́говор; **a vegetable ~** (*BRIT*) садо́вый уча́сток*, огоро́д.

plotter ['plɔtəʳ] *n* (*instrument*) графо-построи́тель *m*; (: *AVIAT, NAUT*) курсопрокла́дчик; (*COMPUT*) пло́ттер, графопострои́тель *m*.

plough [plau] (*US* **plow**) *n* плуг* ◆ *vt* паха́ть* (вспаха́ть* *perf*); **to ~ money into** вкла́дывать (вложи́ть *perf*) де́ньги в *+acc*

▸ **plough back** *vt* (*COMM*) реинвести́ровать *(impf/perf)*

▸ **plough through** *vt fus* (*crowd*) продира́ться (продра́ться* *perf*) сквозь *+acc*; (*snow etc*) пробира́ться (пробра́ться* *perf*) че́рез *+acc*.

ploughman ['plaumən] (*US* **plowman**) *irreg n* па́харь *m*.

ploughman's lunch ['plaumənz-] *n* (*BRIT*) ≈ крестья́нский* обе́д.

plow *etc* (*US*) = **plough** *etc*.

ploy [plɔɪ] *n* уло́вка*.

pluck [plʌk] *n* (*courage*) му́жество ◆ *vt* (*fruit, flower*) срыва́ть (сорва́ть *perf*); (*bird*) ощи́пывать (ощипа́ть* *perf*); (*eyebrows*) выщи́пывать (вы́щипать* *perf*); (*string instrument*): **to ~ (the strings of) sth** перебира́ть *(impf)* стру́ны чего́-н; **to ~ up courage** набира́ться (набра́ться* *perf*) хра́брости *or* му́жества.

plucky ['plʌkɪ] *adj* му́жественный* (му́жествен), отва́жный* (отва́жен).

plug [plʌg] *n* (*ELEC*) ви́лка*; (*in sink, bath*) про́бка*; (*AUT*: *also:* **spark(ing) ~**) свеча́ (зажига́ния) ◆ *vt* (*hole*) затыка́ть (заткну́ть *perf*); (*inf*: *advertise*) реклами́ровать (разреклами́ровать *perf*); **to give sb/sth a ~** реклами́ровать (разреклами́ровать *perf*) кого́-н/что-н

▸ **plug in** *vt* (*ELEC*) включа́ть (включи́ть *perf*) в розе́тку ◆ *vi* включа́ться (включи́ться *perf*).

plughole ['plʌghəul] *n* (*BRIT*) сток.

plum [plʌm] *n* сли́ва ◆ *cpd* (*inf*): **~ job** мирова́я рабо́та.

plumage ['plu:mɪdʒ] *n* опере́ние.

plumb [plʌm] *vt*: **to ~ the depths of** (*fig*) достига́ть (дости́чь* *perf*) глуби́н *+gen*

▸ **plumb in** *vt* (*washing machine*) подключа́ть (подключи́ть *perf*), подсоединя́ть (подсоедини́ть *perf*).

plumber ['plʌməʳ] *n* водопрово́дчик.

plumbing ['plʌmɪŋ] *n* (*piping*) водопрово́д и канализа́ция; (*trade, work*) слеса́рное де́ло.

plumb line *n* отве́с.

plume [plu:m] *n* (*of bird*) перо́*; (*on helmet, horse's head*) плюма́ж; (*fig*): **~ of smoke** струя́* ды́ма.

plummet ['plʌmɪt] *vi*: **to ~ (down)** (*bird, aircraft*) ру́хнуть *(perf)*; (*price, amount*) ре́зко па́дать (упа́сть* *perf*).

plump [plʌmp] *adj* (*adult*) по́лный*; (*child*) пу́хлый* (пухл) ◆ *vi*: **to ~ for** (*inf*) выбира́ть (вы́брать* *perf*)

▸ **plump up** *vt* взбива́ть (взбить* *perf*).

plunder ['plʌndəʳ] *n* (*activity*) грабёж*; (*stolen things*) награ́бленное *nt adj* ◆ *vt* гра́бить* (разгра́бить* *perf*).

plunge [plʌndʒ] *n* (*dive*: *of bird, person*) бросо́к*; (*fig*: *of prices, rates etc*) ре́зкое паде́ние ◆ *vt* (*knife*) мета́ть (метну́ть *perf*); (*hand*) выбра́сывать (вы́бросить* *perf*) ◆ *vi* (*fall*: *person, thing*) ру́хнуть *(perf)*; (*dive*: *bird, person*) броса́ться (бро́ситься* *perf*); (*fig*: *prices, rates etc*) ре́зко па́дать (упа́сть* *perf*); **to take the ~** (*fig*) отва́живаться (отва́житься *perf*); **the room was ~d into darkness** ко́мната погрузи́лась во тьму.

plunger ['plʌndʒəʳ] *n* (*for sink*) плу́нжер.

plunging ['plʌndʒɪŋ] *adj*: **~ neckline** декольте́ *nt ind*.

pluperfect [plu:'pə:fɪkt] *n* плюсквамперфе́кт.

plural ['pluərl] *adj* мно́жественный ◆ *n* мно́жественное число́*.

plus [plʌs] *n, adj* плюс *ind* ◆ *prep*: **ten ~ ten is twenty** де́сять плюс де́сять – два́дцать; **ten/twenty ~** (*more than*) де́сять/два́дцать с ли́шним; **we discussed the ~es of the plan** (*fig*) мы обсужда́ли плю́сы прое́кта.

plus fours *npl* бри́джи *pl*.

plush [plʌʃ] *adj* шика́рный* (шика́рен), роско́шный* (роско́шен) ◆ *n* (*fabric*) плюш.

Pluto ['plu:təu] *n* (*planet*) Плуто́н.

plutonium [plu:'təunɪəm] *n* плуто́ний.

ply [plaɪ] *vt* (*a trade*) занима́ться (заня́ться* *perf*) *+instr*; (*tool*) ору́довать *(impf) +instr* ◆ *vi* (*ship*) курси́ровать *(impf)* ◆ *n* (*of wool, rope*) нить *f*; (*of wood*) слой*; **to ~ sb with sth** (*food, drink*) по́тчевать *(perf)* кого́-н чем-н; **to ~ sb with questions** засыпа́ть (засы́пать* *perf*) кого́-н вопро́сами; **two/three ~** двойна́я/тройна́я нить.

Plymouth ['plɪməθ] *n* Пли́мут.

plywood ['plaɪwud] *n* фане́ра.

PM *abbr* (*BRIT*) = **Prime Minister**.

p.m. *adv abbr* (= *post meridiem*) по́сле полу́дня.

PMT *abbr* = **premenstrual tension**.

pneumatic [nju:'mætɪk] *adj* пневмати́ческий*.

pneumatic drill *n* пневмати́ческая дрель *f*.

pneumonia [nju:'məunɪə] *n* воспале́ние лёгких, пневмони́я.

Pnomh Penh [nɔm pɛn] *n* Пномпе́нь *m*.

PO *n abbr* = **Post Office**; (*MIL*) = **petty officer**.

p.o. *abbr* = **postal order**.
POA *n abbr* (*BRIT*) = *Prison Officers' Association*.
poach [pəutʃ] *vt* (*steal*: *fish etc*) охо́титься *(impf)* без лице́нзии на *+acc*; (*cook*: *fish*) вари́ть* (свари́ть* *perf*) ◆ *vi* (*steal*) охо́титься *(impf)* без лице́нзии; **to ~ an egg** вари́ть* (свари́ть* *perf*) яйцо́-пашо́т.
poached [pəutʃt] *adj*: **~ egg** яйцо́-пашо́т *ind*.
poacher [ˈpəutʃəʳ] *n* браконье́р.
PO Box *n abbr* = **Post Office Box**.
pocket [ˈpɔkɪt] *n* (*on clothes*) карма́н; (*on suitcase, car door*) отделе́ние; (*fig*: *small area*) уголо́к* ◆ *vt* класть* (положи́ть* *perf*) себе́ в карма́н; **to be out of ~** (*BRIT*) быть* *(impf)* в убы́тке на чём-н.
pocketbook [ˈpɔkɪtbuk] *n* (*US*: *wallet*) бума́жник; (*handbag*) (да́мская) су́мочка*; (*notebook*) записна́я кни́жка*.
pocket calculator *n* карма́нный калькуля́тор.
pocketknife [ˈpɔkɪtnaɪf] *n* перочи́нный нож*.
pocket money *n* карма́нные де́ньги* *pl*.
pocket-sized [ˈpɔkɪtsaɪzd] *adj* (*book*) карма́нный; (*nation*) кро́хотный.
pockmarked [ˈpɔkmɑːkt] *adj* рябо́й* (ряб).
pod [pɔd] *n* (*BOT*) стручо́к*.
podgy [ˈpɔdʒɪ] *adj* (*inf*) то́лстый* (толст).
podiatrist [pɔˈdiːətrɪst] *n* (*US*) ортопе́д.
podiatry [pɔˈdiːətrɪ] *n* (*US*) ортопеди́я.
podium [ˈpəudɪəm] *n* по́диум.
POE *n abbr* (= *port of embarkation*) порт вы́садки; (= *port of entry*) порт захо́да.
poem [ˈpəuɪm] *n* (*short*) стихотворе́ние; (*long*) поэ́ма.
poet [ˈpəuɪt] *n* (*male*) поэ́т; (*female*) поэте́сса.
poetic [pəuˈɛtɪk] *adj* (*also fig*) поэти́ческий*.
poetic justice *n* воздая́ние.
poetic licence *n* поэти́ческая во́льность *f*.
poet laureate *n* придво́рный поэ́т.
poetry [ˈpəuɪtrɪ] *n* поэ́зия.
poignant [ˈpɔɪnjənt] *adj* жа́лостный* (жа́лостен).
point [pɔɪnt] *n* (*of needle, knife etc*) остриё*, ко́нчик; (*purpose*) цель *f*; (*significant part*) смысл; (*subject, idea*) предме́т; (*detail, aspect, quality*) аспе́кт; (*particular place or position*) то́чка*, ме́сто*; (*moment*) моме́нт; (*stage in development*) ста́дия; (*score*: *in competition, game, sport*) очко́*; (*ELEC*: *also*: **power ~**) розе́тка* ◆ *vt* (*show, mark*) ука́зывать (указа́ть* *perf*); (*gun etc*): **to ~ sth at sb** наце́ливать (наце́лить *perf*) что-н на кого́-н ◆ *vi*: **to ~ at** ука́зывать (указа́ть* *perf*) на *+acc*; **~s** *npl* (*AUT*) конта́кт *msg* (зажига́ния); (*RAIL*) стре́лка* *fsg*; **good ~s** (*of person, plan*) досто́инства; **2 ~ 3 (2.3)** 2 и 3 деся́тых; **to be on the ~ of doing** собира́ться *(impf)* *+infin*; **I made a ~ of visiting him** я счёл необходи́мым посети́ть его́; **to get/miss the ~** понима́ть (поня́ть* *perf*)/не понима́ть (поня́ть* *perf*) суть; **to come to the ~** доходи́ть* (дойти́* *perf*) до су́ти; **when it comes to the ~** когда́ дохо́дит до де́ла; **that's the whole ~!** в э́том-то и де́ло!; **that's beside the ~** не в э́том де́ло; **there's no ~ in doing** нет смы́сла *+infin*; **you've got a ~ there!** в э́том Вы пра́вы!; **in ~ of fact** на де́ле; **~ of departure** (*also fig*) отправно́й пункт; **~ of sale** (*COMM*) торго́вая то́чка*
▸ **point out** *vt* ука́зывать (указа́ть* *perf*) на *+acc*
▸ **point to** *vt fus* (*also fig*) ука́зывать (указа́ть* *perf*) на *+acc*.
point-blank [ˈpɔɪntˈblæŋk] *adv* (*refuse*) наотре́з; (*say, ask*) напрями́к ◆ *adj*: **at ~ range** в упо́р.
point duty *n* (*BRIT*): **to be on ~ ~** находи́ться* *(impf)* на посту́ регулиро́вщика.
pointed [ˈpɔɪntɪd] *adj* о́стрый* (остёр); (*fig*: *remark*) язви́тельный.
pointedly [ˈpɔɪntɪdlɪ] *adv* язви́тельно.
pointer [ˈpɔɪntəʳ] *n* (*on chart, machine*) стре́лка*; (*stick*) ука́зка*; (*fig*) намёк; (*dog*) по́йнтер.
pointing [ˈpɔɪntɪŋ] *n* (*CONSTR*) заме́на раство́ра в швах.
pointless [ˈpɔɪntlɪs] *adj* бессмы́сленный* (бессмы́слен).
point of order *n* вопро́с по поря́дку веде́ния.
point-of-sale advertising [ˈpɔɪntəvˈseɪl-] *n* рекла́ма в места́х соверше́ния поку́пок.
point of view *n* то́чка* зре́ния.
poise [pɔɪz] *n* (*composure, balance*) равнове́сие; (*of head, body*) оса́нка* ◆ *vt*: **to be ~d for** (*fig*) наце́ливаться (наце́литься *perf*) на *+acc*.
poison [ˈpɔɪzn] *n* яд, отра́ва ◆ *vt* отравля́ть (отрави́ть* *perf*).
poisoning [ˈpɔɪznɪŋ] *n* отравле́ние.
poisonous [ˈpɔɪznəs] *adj* ядови́тый (ядови́т); (*fig*) гну́сный* (гну́сен).
poison-pen letter [pɔɪznˈpɛn] *n* анони́мка*.
poke [pəuk] *vt* (*with finger, stick etc*) ты́кать* (ткнуть *perf*); (*fire*) вороши́ть *(impf)*, меша́ть *(impf)* ◆ *n* (*jab*) толчо́к*; (*to fire*) поме́шивание; **to ~ sth in(to)** (*put*) втыка́ть (воткну́ть *perf*) что-н в *+acc*; **to ~ one's head out of the window** высо́вываться (вы́сунуться *perf*) из окна́; **to ~ fun at sb** подка́лывать (подколо́ть* *perf*) кого́-н
▸ **poke about** *vi* ша́рить (поша́рить *perf*)
▸ **poke out** *vi* высо́вывать (вы́сунуть *perf*).
poker [ˈpəukəʳ] *n* кочерга́*; (*CARDS*) по́кер.
poker-faced [ˈpəukəˈfeɪst] *adj* невозмути́мый (невозмути́м).
poky [ˈpəukɪ] *adj* (*room, house*) убо́гий* (убо́г).
Poland [ˈpəulənd] *n* По́льша.
polar [ˈpəuləʳ] *adj* поля́рный.
polar bear *n* бе́лый медве́дь* *m*.
polarize [ˈpəuləraɪz] *vt* раска́лывать (расколо́ть *perf*), поляризи́ровать *(impf/perf)*.
Pole [pəul] *n* поля́к(-лька*).

pole [pəul] *n* (*stick, staff*) шест*; (*for flag*) дрéвко; (*telegraph pole*) столб; (*GEO, ELEC*) пóлюс.
poleaxe ['pəulæks] *n* (*butcher's*) топóр; (*HISTORY*) секи́ра ◆ *vt* (*hit*) трéснуть *(perf)*; (*surprise*) ошеломля́ть (ошеломи́ть* *perf*).
pole bean *n* (*US*) стручкóвая фасóль *f*.
polecat ['pəulkæt] *n* (чёрный) хорёк*.
Pol. Econ. ['pɔlɪkɔn] *n abbr* (= *political economy*) политэконóмия= *полити́ческая экономия*.
polemic [pɔ'lɛmɪk] *n* полéмика.
Pole Star *n* поля́рная звездá*.
pole vault ['pəulvɔ:lt] *n* прыжóк* с шестóм.
police [pə'li:s] *npl* поли́ция *fsg*; (*in Russia*) мили́ция *fsg* ◆ *vt* следи́ть* *(impf)* за поря́дком; **a large number of ~ were hurt** бы́ло рáнено мнóго полицéйских.
police car *n* полицéйская маши́на.
police constable *n* (*BRIT*) полицéйский* *m adj*.
police department *n* (*US*) полицéйский* учáсток*.
police force *n* поли́ция.
policeman [pə'li:smən] *irreg n* полицéйский* *m adj*.
police officer *n* = **police constable**.
police record *n*: **to have a ~ ~** состоя́ть *(impf)* на учёте в поли́ции.
police state *n* полицéйское госудáрство.
police station *n* полицéйский* учáсток*; (*in Russia*) отделéние мили́ции.
policewoman [pə'li:swumən] *irreg n* (жéнщина-) полицéйский* *m adj*.
policy ['pɔlɪsɪ] *n* поли́тика; (*also:* **insurance ~**) пóлис; **to take out a ~** (*INSURANCE*) застрахóвываться (застраховáться *perf*).
policyholder ['pɔlɪsɪ'həuldəʳ] *n* (*INSURANCE*) держáтель *m* страховóго пóлиса.
policymaking ['pɔlɪsɪmeɪkɪŋ] *n* разрабóтка стратéгии.
polio ['pəulɪəu] *n* полиомиели́т.
Polish ['pəulɪʃ] *adj* пóльский* ◆ *n* (*LING*) пóльский* язы́к*.
polish ['pɔlɪʃ] *n* (*for shoes*) гутали́н; (*for furniture*) лак*; (*for floors*) мáстика; (*shine, also fig*) лоск ◆ *vt* (*shoes*) вычищáть (вы́чистить* *perf*); (*floors*) натирáть (натерéть *perf*); (*furniture etc*) полировáть (отполировáть *perf*); (*fig: improve*) шлифовáть (отшлифовáть *perf*)
▸ **polish off** *vt fus* (*work, food*) покóнчить *(perf)* с *+instr*.
polished ['pɔlɪʃt] *adj* (*person*) изы́сканный* (изы́скан); (*style*) оттóченный (оттóчен).
polite [pə'laɪt] *adj* (*well-mannered*) вéжливый (вéжлив); (*socially superior: company, society*) свéтский*; **it's not ~ to do that** так дéлать не при́нято.
politely [pə'laɪtlɪ] *adv* вéжливо.
politeness [pə'laɪtnɪs] *n* вéжливость *f*.
politic ['pɔlɪtɪk] *adj*: **it would be ~ to ...** бы́ло бы благоразу́мно *+infin* ....
political [pə'lɪtɪkl] *adj* полити́ческий*; (*person*) полити́чески акти́вный, политизи́рованный (политизи́рован).
political asylum *n* полити́ческое убéжище.
politically [pə'lɪtɪklɪ] *adv* полити́чески; **~ correct** полити́чески коррéктный.
politician [pɔlɪ'tɪʃən] *n* поли́тик, полити́ческий* дéятель *m*.
politics ['pɔlɪtɪks] *n* поли́тика; (*subject*) политолóгия ◆ *npl* (*beliefs, opinions*) полити́ческие убеждéния *ntpl*.
polka ['pɔlkə] *n* пóлька*.
poll [pəul] *n* (*also:* **opinion ~**) опрóс; (*election*) вы́боры *mpl* ◆ *vt* (*in opinion poll*) опрáшивать (опроси́ть* *perf*); (*number of votes*) набирáть (набрáть* *perf*); **to go to the ~s** (*voters*) голосовáть (проголосовáть *perf*) (*на вы́борах*); (*government*) объявля́ть (объяви́ть* *perf*) вы́боры.
pollen ['pɔlən] *n* пыльцá.
pollen count *n* содержáние пыльцы́ в вóздухе.
pollinate ['pɔlɪneɪt] *vt* (*BOT*) опыля́ть (опыли́ть *perf*).
polling booth ['pəulɪŋ-] *n* (*BRIT*) каби́на для голосовáния.
polling day *n* (*BRIT*) день* *m* вы́боров.
polling station *n* (*BRIT*) избирáтельный учáсток*.
pollster ['pəulstəʳ] *n человéк, производя́щий* опрóс общéственного мнéния*.
poll tax *n* (*BRIT: formerly*) поду́шный налóг.
pollutant [pə'lu:tənt] *n* загрязня́ющий агéнт.
pollute [pə'lu:t] *vt* загрязня́ть (загрязни́ть *perf*).
pollution [pə'lu:ʃən] *n* загрязнéние; (*substances*) загрязни́тель *m*.
polo ['pəuləu] *n* пóло *nt ind*.
polo neck *n* (*also:* **~ ~ sweater** *or* **jumper**) сви́тер с кру́глым воротникóм.
polo-necked ['pəuləunɛkt] *adj*: **~ sweater** *or* **jumper** сви́тер с кру́глым воротникóм.
poltergeist ['pɔ:ltəgaɪst] *n* полтергéйст.
poly ['pɔlɪ] *n abbr* (*BRIT*) = **polytechnic**.
poly... ['pɔlɪ] *prefix* мнóго..., поли....
poly bag *n* полиэтилéновый мешóк* *or* пакéт.
polyester [pɔlɪ'ɛstəʳ] *n* (*CHEM*) слóжный полиэфи́р; (*fabric*) полиэфи́рное волокнó.
polygamy [pə'lɪgəmɪ] *n* многобрáчие, полигáмия.
polygraph ['pɔlɪgrɑ:f] *n* детéктор лжи.
Polynesia [pɔlɪ'ni:zɪə] *n* Полинéзия.
Polynesian [pɔlɪ'ni:zɪən] *adj* полинези́йский ◆ *n* полинези́ец*(-и́йка*).
polyp ['pɔlɪp] *n* (*MED*) поли́п.

* marks translations which have irregular inflections. The Russian-English side of the dictionary gives inflectional information.

polystyrene [pɔlɪ'staɪri:n] *n* пенопла́ст.
polytechnic [pɔlɪ'tɛknɪk] *n* (***college***) ≈ политехни́ческий* институ́т.
polythene ['pɔlɪθi:n] *n* полиэтиле́н.
polythene bag *n* полиэтиле́новый мешо́к* *or* паке́т.
polyurethane [pɔlɪ'juərɪθeɪn] *n* полиурета́н.
pomegranate ['pɔmɪgrænɪt] *n* (*BOT*) грана́т.
pommel ['pɔml] *n* (***of saddle***) лука́; (***of sword***) голо́вка* ◆ *vt* = **pummel**.
pomp [pɔmp] *n* пы́шность *f*.
pompom ['pɔmpɔm] *n* помпо́н.
pompous ['pɔmpəs] *adj* (***pej: person, style***) напы́щенный* (напы́щен).
pond [pɔnd] *n* пруд*; (***stagnant***) за́водь *f*.
ponder ['pɔndəʳ] *vt* обду́мывать (обду́мать *perf*) ◆ *vi* размышля́ть *(impf)*.
ponderous ['pɔndərəs] *adj* (***style***) тяжелове́сный* (тяжелове́сен); (***person***) неповоро́тливый (неповоро́тлив).
pong [pɔŋ] (*BRIT: inf*) *n* вонь *f* ◆ *vi* воня́ть *(impf)*.
pontiff ['pɔntɪf] *n* (*REL*) Па́па *m* ри́мский*.
pontificate [pɔn'tɪfɪkeɪt] *vi* (***fig***): **to ~ (about)** разглаго́льствовать *(impf)* (о *+prp*).
pontoon [pɔn'tu:n] *n* (***floating platform***) понто́н; (*CARDS*) два́дцать одно́.
pony ['pəunɪ] *n* по́ни *m ind.*
ponytail ['pəunɪteɪl] *n* (***hairstyle***) хвост*, хво́стик; **to have one's hair in a ~** носи́ть* *(impf)* хво́стик.
pony trekking *n* (*BRIT*) ко́нный похо́д.
poodle ['pu:dl] *n* пу́дель* *m*.
pooh-pooh [pu:'pu:] *vt* заши́кивать (заши́кать *perf*).
pool [pu:l] *n* (***puddle***) лу́жа; (***pond***) пруд*; (***also: swimming ~***) бассе́йн; (***fig: of light, paint***) пятно́; (*SPORT, COMM*) пул; (***money at cards***) банк ◆ *vt* (***money, knowledge, resources***) объединя́ть (объедини́ть *perf*); **~s** *npl* (***also: football ~s***) тотализа́тор; **typing ~**, (*US*) **secretary ~** машинопи́сное бюро́ *nt ind*; **to do the (football) ~s** игра́ть (сыгра́ть *perf*) в тотализа́тор.
poor [puəʳ] *adj* (***not rich***) бе́дный* (бе́ден); (***bad***) плохо́й* (плох); **the ~** *npl* (***people***) беднота́ *fsg*; **~ in** (***resources etc***) бе́дный* (бе́ден) *+instr*.
poorly ['puəlɪ] *adv* пло́хо ◆ *adj*: **she is feeling ~** она́ пло́хо себя́ чу́вствует.
pop [pɔp] *n* (***also: ~ music***) поп-му́зыка; (***inf: fizzy drink***) лимона́д*; (***: US: father***) па́па, оте́ц; (***sound***) хлопо́к* ◆ *vi* (***balloon***) ло́паться (ло́пнуть *perf*); (***cork***) выстре́ливать (вы́стрелить *perf*); (***fig: eyes***) тара́щиться (вы́таращиться *perf*) ◆ *vt* (***put quickly***): **to ~ sth into/onto** *etc* забра́сывать (забро́сить* *perf*) в *+acc*/на *+acc etc*; **she ~ped her head out of the window** она́ вы́сунула го́лову из окна́
▸ **pop in** *vi* загля́дывать (загляну́ть* *perf*), заска́кивать (заскочи́ть *perf*)
▸ **pop out** *vi* выска́кивать (вы́скочить *perf*)
▸ **pop up** *vi* вылеза́ть (вы́лезти *perf*).

popcorn ['pɔpkɔ:n] *n* возду́шная кукуру́за, попко́рн.
pope [pəup] *n*: **the P~** Па́па *m* ри́мский*.
poplar ['pɔpləʳ] *n* то́поль* *m*.
poplin ['pɔplɪn] *n* попли́н.
popper ['pɔpəʳ] *n* (*BRIT*: ***fastener***) кно́пка*.
poppy ['pɔpɪ] *n* мак.
poppycock ['pɔpɪkɔk] *n* (***inf***) вздор.
Popsicle® ['pɔpsɪkl] *n* (*US*) ≈ фрукто́вое моро́женое *nt adj*.
pop star *n* поп-звезда́* *m/f*.
populace ['pɔpjuləs] *n*: **the ~** наро́д*.
popular ['pɔpjuləʳ] *adj* популя́рный* (популя́рен); (*POL*) наро́дный; **to be ~ (with)** (***person, belief***) по́льзоваться *(impf)* популя́рностью (сре́ди *+gen*); (***decision***) по́льзоваться *(impf)* подде́ржкой (*+gen*); **a ~ song** популя́рная пе́сня*.
popularity [pɔpju'lærɪtɪ] *n* популя́рность *f*.
popularize ['pɔpjuləraɪz] *vt* (***pastime, fashion***) де́лать (сде́лать *perf*) популя́рным; (***science, ideas***) популяризи́ровать *(impf/perf)*.
popularly ['pɔpjuləlɪ] *adv* (***generally***) обы́чно; **it is ~ believed that ...** мно́гие полага́ют, что ....
population [pɔpju'leɪʃən] *n* населе́ние; (***of a species***) популя́ция; **the civilian ~s** гражда́нское населе́ние; **Britain has a prison ~ of 44 thousand** о́бщее коли́чество заключённых в тю́рмах Великобрита́нии составля́ет 44 ты́сячи.
population explosion *n* демографи́ческий* взрыв.
populous ['pɔpjuləs] *adj* густонаселённый.
porcelain ['pɔ:slɪn] *n* фарфо́р.
porch [pɔ:tʃ] *n* крыльцо́*; (*US*) вера́нда.
porcupine ['pɔ:kjupaɪn] *n* дикобра́з.
pore [pɔ:ʳ] *n* по́ра ◆ *vi*: **to ~ over** погружа́ться (погрузи́ться* *perf*) в *+acc*.
pork [pɔ:k] *n* свини́на.
pork chop *n* свина́я отбивна́я *f adj*.
porn [pɔ:n] *n* (***inf***) порногра́фия.
pornographic [pɔ:nə'græfɪk] *adj* порнографи́ческий*.
pornography [pɔ:'nɔgrəfɪ] *n* порногра́фия.
porous ['pɔ:rəs] *adj* по́ристый (по́рист).
porpoise ['pɔ:pəs] *n* бу́рый дельфи́н.
porridge ['pɔrɪdʒ] *n* овся́ная ка́ша.
port [pɔ:t] *n* (***harbour, also*** *COMPUT*) порт*; (***opening in ship***) люк; (*NAUT*) ле́вый борт*; (***wine***) портве́йн ◆ *cpd* (*NAUT*) ле́вый; **to ~** (*NAUT*) нале́во; **~ of call** порт* захо́да.
portable ['pɔ:təbl] *adj* портати́вный.
portal ['pɔ:tl] *n* порта́л.
portcullis [pɔ:t'kʌlɪs] *n* (опускна́я) решётка* (*в воро́тах*).
portend [pɔ:'tɛnd] *vt* предвеща́ть *(impf)*.
portent ['pɔ:tɛnt] *n* предзнаменова́ние, предве́стник.
porter ['pɔ:təʳ] *n* (***for luggage***) носи́льщик; (***doorkeeper***) швейца́р, портье́ *m ind*; (***: in offices***) вахтёр; (*US: RAIL*) проводни́к*(-ица).

portfolio [pɔ:t'fəulɪəu] *n* (*also* POL) портфе́ль *m*; (FINANCE) портфе́ль це́нных бума́г; (*of artist*) па́пка*.
porthole ['pɔ:thəul] *n* иллюмина́тор.
portico ['pɔ:tɪkəu] *n* по́ртик.
portion ['pɔ:ʃən] *n* (*part*) часть* *f*; (*equal part*) до́ля*; (*helping of food*) по́рция.
portly ['pɔ:tlɪ] *adj* доро́дный* (доро́ден).
portrait ['pɔ:treɪt] *n* портре́т.
portray [pɔ:'treɪ] *vt* изобража́ть (изобрази́ть* *perf*).
portrayal [pɔ:'treɪəl] *n* изображе́ние; (*representation*) о́браз.
Portsmouth ['pɔ:tsməθ] *n* По́ртсмут.
Portugal ['pɔ:tjugl] *n* Португа́лия.
Portuguese [pɔ:tju'gi:z] *adj* португа́льский* ◆ *n inv* португа́лец*(-лка*); (LING) португа́льский* язы́к*.
Portuguese man-of-war [-mænəv'wɔ:ʳ] *n* (ZOOL) португа́льский* вое́нный кора́бль *m*.
pose [pəuz] *n* по́за ◆ *vt* (*question*) ста́вить* (поста́вить* *perf*); (*problem, danger*) создава́ть* (созда́ть* *perf*) ◆ *vi* (*pretend*): **to ~ as** выдава́ть* (вы́дать* *perf*) себя́ за *+acc*; **to strike a ~** принима́ть (приня́ть* *perf*) по́зу; **to ~ for** пози́ровать (*impf*) для *+gen*.
poser ['pəuzəʳ] *n* (*puzzle*) головоло́мка*; (*person*) = **poseur**.
poseur [pəu'zə:ʳ] *n* (*pej*) позёр(ка*).
posh [pɔʃ] *adj* (*inf*: *hotel, restaurant etc*) фешене́бельный* (фешене́белен); (: *person, behaviour*) великосве́тский; **to talk ~** (*inf*) мане́рничать (*impf*).
position [pə'zɪʃən] *n* положе́ние; (*of house, thing*) расположе́ние, ме́сто*; (*job*) до́лжность *f*; (*in race, competition*) ме́сто*; (*attitude*) пози́ция ◆ *vt* располага́ть (расположи́ть* *perf*); **to be in a ~ to do** име́ть (*impf*) возмо́жность *+infin*.
positive ['pɔzɪtɪv] *adj* (*affirmative*) положи́тельный* (положи́телен); (*certain*) уве́ренный* (уве́рен), убеждённый* (убеждён); (*definite*: *decision, action, policy*) несомне́нный* (несомне́нен), определённый* (определёнен); (MATH, ELEC) положи́тельный.
positive cash flow *n* положи́тельный пото́к нали́чности.
positively ['pɔzɪtɪvlɪ] *adv* (*for emphasis*) положи́тельно; (*definitely*) несомне́нно.
posse ['pɔsɪ] *n* (US) *ко́нный отря́д доброво́льных помо́щников шери́фа при ло́вле престу́пника.*
possess [pə'zɛs] *vt* владе́ть (*impf*) *+instr*; (*quality, ability*) облада́ть (*impf*) *+instr*; (*subj*: *feeling, belief*) овладева́ть (овладе́ть *perf*); **like one ~ed** как одержи́мый(-ая) *m(f) adj*; **whatever can have ~ed you?** и како́й чёрт тебя́ попу́тал?
possession [pə'zɛʃən] *n* (*state*) владе́ние; **~s** *npl* (*belongings*) принадле́жности *fpl*; **to take ~ of** вступа́ть (вступи́ть* *perf*) во владе́ние *+instr*.
possessive [pə'zɛsɪv] *adj* со́бственнический*; (LING) притяжа́тельный.
possessiveness [pə'zɛsɪvnɪs] *n* (*of another person*) со́бственничество; **~ towards sb/sth** ревни́вое отноше́ние к кому́-н/чему́-н.
possessor [pə'zɛsəʳ] *n* (*of property*) владе́лец*(-е́лица); (*of quality*) облада́тель(ница) *m(f)*.
possibility [pɔsɪ'bɪlɪtɪ] *n* возмо́жность *f*; **he's a ~ (for the part)** он возмо́жный кандида́т (на роль).
possible ['pɔsɪbl] *adj* возмо́жный* (возмо́жен); **it's ~** э́то не исключено́; **it is ~ to do it** э́то осуществи́мо; **as far as ~** наско́лько возмо́жно; **if ~** е́сли (э́то) возмо́жно; **as big as ~** са́мый большо́й.
possibly ['pɔsɪblɪ] *adv* (*perhaps*) возмо́жно; **if you ~ can** е́сли то́лько Вы мо́жете; **I cannot ~ come** я ника́к не смогу́ прийти́.
post [pəust] *n* (BRIT: *mail*) по́чта; (*pole*) столб*; (*job, situation, also* MIL) пост* ◆ *vt* (BRIT: *mail*) посыла́ть (посла́ть* *perf*), отправля́ть (отпра́вить* *perf*) (по по́чте); (: MIL) выставля́ть (вы́ставить* *perf*); (: *appoint*) откомандиро́вывать (откомандирова́ть *perf*); **by ~** (BRIT) по по́чте; **by return of ~** (BRIT) с обра́тной по́чтой; **trading ~** факто́рия; **to keep sb ~ed** держа́ть* (*impf*) кого́-н в ку́рсе (дел).
post... [pəust] *prefix* пост..., после...; **~1990** (*as adj*) в 90-е го́ды; (*as adv*) как 90-е го́ды.
postage ['pəustɪdʒ] *n* (*charge*) почто́вые расхо́ды *mpl*; **~ paid,** (US) **~ prepaid** с предвари́тельно опла́ченными почто́выми расхо́дами.
postage stamp *n* почто́вая ма́рка*.
postal ['pəustl] *adj* почто́вый.
postal order *n* (де́нежный) почто́вый перево́д.
postbag ['pəustbæg] *n* (BRIT: *letters received*) по́чта, корреспонде́нция; (: *postman's*) су́мка* (*почтальо́на*).
postbox ['pəustbɔks] *n* (BRIT) почто́вый я́щик.
postcard ['pəustkɑ:d] *n* (почто́вая) откры́тка*.
postcode ['pəustkəud] *n* (BRIT) почто́вый и́ндекс.
postdate ['pəust'deɪt] *vt* дати́ровать (*impf/perf*) бо́лее по́здним число́м.
poster ['pəustəʳ] *n* афи́ша, плака́т; (*for advertising*) по́стер.
poste restante [pəust'rɛstɑ̃:nt] *adv* (BRIT) до востре́бования.
posterior [pɔs'tɪərɪəʳ] *n* зад.

* marks translations which have irregular inflections. The Russian-English side of the dictionary gives inflectional information.

posterity [pɔs'tɛrıtı] *n* послéдующие поколéния *ntpl*, потóмство.
poster paint *n* плакáтная тушь *f*.
post exchange *n* (*US: MIL*) воентóрг, гарнизóнный магазин.
post-free [pəust'fri:] *adj, adv* (*BRIT*) с предварительно оплáченными почтóвыми расхóдами.
postgraduate ['pəust'grædjuət] *n* аспирáнт(ка*) ◆ *adj*: ~ **study** аспирантýра.
posthumous ['pɔstjuməs] *adj* посмéртный.
posthumously ['pɔstjuməslı] *adv* посмéртно.
posting ['pəustıŋ] *n* (*job*) командирóвка.
postman ['pəustmən] *irreg n* почтальóн.
postmark ['pəustmɑ:k] *n* почтóвый штéмпель* *m*.
postmaster ['pəustmɑ:stə'] *n* начáльник пóчты *or* почтóвого отделéния.
postmaster general *n* ≈ минúстр связи.
postmistress ['pəustmıstrıs] *n* начáльник пóчты *or* почтóвого отделéния (*жéнщина*).
postmortem [pəust'mɔ:təm] *n* (*MED*) вскрытие, аутопсия.
postnatal ['pəust'neıtl] *adj* послеродовóй.
post office *n* почтóвое отделéние, отделéние связи; (*organization*): **the P~ O~** ≈ Министéрство связи.
Post Office Box *n* абонéнтский ящик.
post-paid ['pəust'peıd] *adj* (*BRIT*) с оплáченными почтóвыми расхóдами.
postpone [pəus'pəun] *vt* отклáдывать (отложить* *perf*).
postponement [pəus'pəunmənt] *n* отсрóчка.
postscript ['pəustskrıpt] *n* (*in letter*) постскриптум.
postulate ['pɔstjuleıt] *vt* постулировать *(impf/ perf)*.
posture ['pɔstʃə'] *n* (*of body*) осáнка; (*fig*) положéние ◆ *vi* (*pej*) позировать *(impf)*.
postwar [pəust'wɔ:'] *adj* послевоéнный.
posy ['pəuzı] *n* букéтик.
pot [pɔt] *n* (*for cooking, flowers*) горшóк*; (*also: teapot*) (завáрочный) чáйник; (*also: coffeepot*) кофéйник; (*bowl, container*) бáнка; (*inf: marijuana*) план ◆ *vt* (*plant*) сажáть (посадить* *perf*); **a ~ of tea** чáйник чáя; **to go to ~** (*inf: work, performance*) развáливаться (развалиться *perf*); **~s of** (*BRIT: inf*) кýча +*gen*, ýйма +*gen*.
potash ['pɔtæʃ] *n* потáш.
potassium [pə'tæsıəm] *n* кáлий.
potato [pə'teıtəu] (*pl* **~es**) *n* картóфель *m no pl*, картóшка *f no pl* (*разг*); (*single potato*) картóфелина.
potato chips *npl* (*US*) = **potato crisps**.
potato crisps *npl* (*BRIT*) чипсы *pl*.
potato flour *n* картóфельная мукá.
potato peeler *n* картофелечистка.
potbellied ['pɔtbɛlıd] *adj* (*from overeating*) пузáтый (пузáт); (*from malnutrition*) со вздýтым животóм.
potency ['pəutnsı] *n* сила; (*of drink*) крéпость *f*.
potent ['pəutnt] *adj* (*weapon*) мóщный; (*argument*) убедительный* (убедителен); (*drink*) крéпкий* (крéпок); (*man*) обладáющий сексуáльной потéнцией.
potentate ['pəutnteıt] *n* властелин, повелитель *m*.
potential [pə'tɛnʃl] *adj* потенциáльный, возмóжный ◆ *n* потенциáл; **to have ~** обладáть *(impf)* (достáточным) потенциáлом.
potentially [pə'tɛnʃəlı] *adv* потенциáльно; **it's ~ dangerous** это в принципе опáсно.
pothole ['pɔthəul] *n* (*in road*) выбоина; (*BRIT: underground*) провáл.
potholing ['pɔthəulıŋ] (*BRIT*) *n* спелеолóгия; **to go ~** отправляться (отправиться *perf*) обслéдовать пещéры.
potion ['pəuʃən] *n* настóйка; (*poison*) зéлье.
potluck [pɔt'lʌk] *n*: **to take ~** обéдать (пообéдать *perf*) чем Бог послáл.
potpourri [pəu'puri:] *n ароматическая смесь из сухих лепесткóв*; (*fig*) попурри *nt ind*.
pot roast *n* тушёное мясо.
pot shot *n*: **to take ~~s at** стрелять (выстрелить *perf*) навскидку в +*acc*.
potted ['pɔtıd] *adj* (*food*) консервированный; (*plant*) кóмнатный; (*account, biography*) крáткий*.
potter ['pɔtə'] *n* (*pottery maker*) гончáр* ◆ *vi*: **to ~ around, ~ about** (*BRIT*) возиться* *(impf)*; **to ~ about (in) the garden** возиться* *(impf)* в садý.
potter's wheel *n* гончáрный круг*.
pottery ['pɔtərı] *n* керáмика; (*factory*) завóд керамических издéлий; (*workshop*) гончáрная мастерскáя *f adj*; **a piece of ~** керамическое издéлие.
potty ['pɔtı] *adj* (*inf: mad*) чóкнутый ◆ *n* (*for child*) горшóк* (*ночнóй*).
potty-training ['pɔtıtreınıŋ] *n* приучéние ребёнка к горшкý.
pouch [pautʃ] *n* (*for tobacco*) кисéт; (*for coins*) кошелёк*; (*ZOOL*) сýмка*.
pouf(fe) [pu:f] *n* пуф.
poultice ['pəultıs] *n* припáрка*.
poultry ['pəultrı] *n* (*birds*) домáшняя птица; (*meat*) птица.
poultry farm *n* птицефéрма.
poultry farmer *n* птицевóд.
pounce [pauns] *vi*: **to ~ on** набрáсываться (наброситься* *perf*) на +*acc*.
pound [paund] *n* (*money, weight*) фунт; (*for dogs*) живодёрня; (*for cars*) *стоянка для непрáвильно припаркóванных автомашин, увезённых полицией* ◆ *vt* (*beat*) колотить* *(impf)* по +*dat*; (*crush*) толóчь* (растолóчь* *perf*); (*with guns*) обстрéливать (обстрелять *perf*) ◆ *vi* (*heart*) колотиться* *(impf)*; **half a ~ of** полфýнта +*gen*; **a five-~ note** банкнóта в пять фýнтов; **my car has been taken to the ~** мою машину арестовáли.

pounding ['paundɪŋ] *n*: **we took a ~** (*SPORT*) нас побили; (*fig*) нас разнесли.
pound sterling *n* фунт стерлингов.
pour [pɔ:ˈ] *vt* (*liquid*) наливать (налить* *perf*); (*dry substance*) насыпать (насыпать* *perf*) ◆ *vi* (*water, blood, sweat etc*) литься* (*impf*); (*rain*) лить* (*impf*); **to ~ sb some tea** наливать (налить* *perf*) кому-н чай; **it's ~ing with rain** льёт дождь
▸ **pour away** *vt* выливать (вылить* *perf*)
▸ **pour in** *vi* (*people*) валить* (повалить* *perf*); (*news, letters etc*) сыпаться* (*impf*)
▸ **pour into** *vt fus* устремляться (устремиться* *perf*) в +*acc*
▸ **pour off** *vt* сливать (слить* *perf*)
▸ **pour out** *vi* (*people*) валить* (повалить* *perf*) ◆ *vt* (*drink*) наливать (налить* *perf*); (*fig*: *thoughts, feelings, etc*) изливать (излить* *perf*).
pouring ['pɔ:rɪŋ] *adj*: **~ rain** проливной дождь *m*.
pout [paut] *vi* надувать (надуть *perf*) губы, дуться (надуться *perf*).
poverty ['pɔvətɪ] *n* бедность *f*, нищета.
poverty line *n* черта бедности.
poverty-stricken ['pɔvətɪstrɪkn] *adj* впавший в нищету, обнищавший.
poverty trap *n* (*BRIT*) тиски *pl* бедности.
POW *n abbr* = **prisoner of war**.
powder ['paudəˈ] *n* порошок*; (*also:* **face ~**) пудра ◆ *vt*: **to ~ one's face** пудрить (напудрить *perf*) лицо; **to ~ one's nose** (*euphemism*) помыть* (*perf*) руки.
powder compact *n* пудреница.
powdered milk ['paudəd-] *n* сухое молоко.
powder keg *n* пороховая бочка.
powder puff *n* пуховка.
powder room *n* дамская комната.
power ['pauəˈ] *n* (*authority*) власть *f*; (*ability, opportunity*) возможность *f*; (*legal right*) полномочие; (*strength*: *of person, speech, thought*) мощь *f*; (*of explosion, engine*) мощность *f*; (*electricity*) электроэнергия; (*MATH*) степень *f*; **to do all in one's ~ to help** делать (сделать *perf*) всё что в своих силах, чтобы помогать (помочь* *perf*); **the world ~s** мировые державы; **to be in ~** находиться* (*impf*) у власти.
powerboat ['pauəbəut] *n* моторный катер*.
power cut *n* (*BRIT*) отключение электроэнергии.
powered ['pauəd] *adj*: **~ by** работающий на +*prp*; **nuclear-~ submarine** атомная подводная лодка*.
power failure *n* остановка* подачи электроэнергии.
powerful ['pauəful] *adj* могучий* (могуч); (*person, organization*) могущественный* (могуществен); (*engine, argument*) мощный; (*smell, voice, emotion*) сильный* (силен); (*evidence*) веский* (весок).
powerhouse ['pauəhaus] *n* (*person*): **a ~ of ideas** генератор идей.
powerless ['pauəlɪs] *adj* бессильный* (бессилен).
power line *n* линия электропередачи.
power of attorney *n* (*LAW*) доверенность *f*.
power point *n* (*BRIT*) (штепсельная) розетка*.
power station *n* электростанция.
power steering *n* (*AUT*) рулевой привод с усилителем.
powwow ['pauwau] *n* совет.
pp *abbr* = *per procurationem*; (*by proxy*) по доверенности.
pp. *abbr* = *pages*.
PPE *n abbr* (*BRIT*: *SCOL*) = *philosophy, politics and economics*.
PPS *n abbr* (= *post postscriptum*) второй постскриптум; (*BRIT*: = *parliamentary private secretary*) *личный парламентский секретарь министра*.
PQ *abbr* (*CANADA*) = *Province of Quebec*.
PR *n abbr* = **public relations**; (*POL*) = **proportional representation** ◆ *abbr* (*US*: *POST*) = *Puerto Rico*.
Pr. *abbr* = **prince**.
practicability [præktɪkəˈbɪlɪtɪ] *n* осуществимость *f*.
practicable ['præktɪkəbl] *adj* осуществимый (осуществим).
practical ['præktɪkl] *adj* (*not theoretical*) практический*; (*sensible, viable*) практичный* (практичен); (*good with hands*) умелый (умел).
practicality [præktɪˈkælɪtɪ] *n* практичность *f*; **practicalities** *npl* (*of situation etc*) практическая сторона *fsg*.
practical joke *n* розыгрыш.
practically ['præktɪklɪ] *adv* практически.
practice ['præktɪs] *n* (*habit*) привычка*; (*of profession*) практика; (*REL*) обычай; (*exercise, training*) практика, тренировка ◆ *vti* (*US*) = **practise**; **in ~** на практике; **I am out of ~** я давно этого не делал; **it's common ~** это распространено; **to put sth into ~** осуществлять (осуществить* *perf*) что-н на практике; **target ~** учебная стрельба.
practice match *n* тренировочный матч.
practise ['præktɪs] (*US* **practice**) *vt* (*musical instrument*) упражняться (*impf*) на +*acc*; (*SPORT, piece of music, language*) отрабатывать (отработать *perf*); (*custom*) выполнять (выполнить *perf*); (*craft*) заниматься (*impf*) +*instr*; (*religion*) исповедовать (*impf*) ◆ *vi* (*on instrument*) упражняться (*impf*); (*SPORT*) тренироваться (*impf*); (*lawyer, doctor*) практиковать (*impf*); **to**

~ for a match тренироваться *(impf)* перед матчем; **to ~ law/medicine** заниматься *(impf)* адвокатской/врачебной практикой.
practised ['præktɪst] *adj* (*BRIT*: *person*) опытный; (: *performance*) искусный; (: *liar*) закоренелый; **with a ~ eye** (*BRIT*) намётанным глазом.
practising ['præktɪsɪŋ] *adj* (*Christian etc*) верующий*; (*doctor, lawyer*) практикующий; (*homosexual*) ведущий* активную половую жизнь.
practitioner [præk'tɪʃənəʳ] *n* (*MED*) терапевт.
pragmatic [præg'mætɪk] *adj* (*reason etc*) прагматический; (*person*) прагматичный* (прагматичен).
pragmatism ['prægmətɪzəm] *n* прагматизм.
Prague [prɑːg] *n* Прага.
prairie ['prɛərɪ] *n* прерия; (*US*): **the ~s** прерии *fpl*.
praise [preɪz] *n* (*approval*) похвала; (*admiration*) восхваление ◆ *vt* (*see n*) хвалить* (похвалить* *perf*); восхвалять *(impf)*.
praiseworthy ['preɪzwəːðɪ] *adj* достойный* (достоен) похвалы.
pram [præm] *n* (*BRIT*) детская коляска.
prance [prɑːns] *vi* (*horse*) гарцевать *(impf)*; (*person*): **to ~ about** красоваться *(impf)*.
prank [præŋk] *n* (*practical joke*) розыгрыш; (*tomfoolery*) проделка*.
prat [præt] *n* (*inf*: *pej*: *BRIT*) идиот.
prattle ['prætl] *vi*: **to ~ on (about)** трепаться *(impf)* (о *+prp*).
prawn [prɔːn] *n* креветка*.
pray [preɪ] *vi* молиться* (помолиться* *perf*); **to ~ for** молиться* *(impf)* за *+acc*; **to ~ that** молиться* *(impf)*, чтобы.
prayer [prɛəʳ] *n* (*activity*) молитва, моление; (*words*) молитва.
prayer book *n* молитвенник.
pre... ['priː...] *prefix* до..., пред...; **~-1970** до 1970-го года.
preach [priːtʃ] *vi* (*also fig*) проповедовать *(impf)* ◆ *vt*: **to ~ a sermon** (*also fig*) произносить* (произнести* *perf*) проповедь; **to ~ at sb** читать *(impf)* проповеда кому-н.
preacher ['priːtʃəʳ] *n* проповедник(-ица).
preamble [prɪ'æmbl] *n* преамбула.
prearranged [priːə'reɪndʒd] *adj* (заранее) подготовленный (подготовлен).
precarious [prɪ'kɛərɪəs] *adj* рискованный* (рискован).
precaution [prɪ'kɔːʃən] *n* предосторожность *f*; **to take ~s** принимать (принять* *perf*) меры предосторожности.
precautionary [prɪ'kɔːʃənrɪ] *adj* (*measure*) предупредительный.
precede [prɪ'siːd] *vt* предшествовать *(impf)* *+dat*; (*person*) быть* *(impf)* впереди *+gen*.
precedence ['prɛsɪdəns] *n* (*priority*) первоочерёдность *f*; **to take ~ over** быть* *(impf)* важнее, чем.
precedent ['prɛsɪdənt] *n* прецедент; **to establish** *or* **set a ~** создавать* (создать* *perf*) прецедент.
preceding [prɪ'siːdɪŋ] *adj* предыдущий*, предшествующий*.
precept ['priːsɛpt] *n* правило.
precinct ['priːsɪŋkt] *n* (*US*: *part of city*) район, префектура; (*round cathedral*) двор*; **~s** *npl* (*of large building*) территория *fsg*; **pedestrian ~** (*BRIT*) пешеходная зона; **shopping ~** (*BRIT*) торговый центр.
precious ['prɛʃəs] *adj* (*commodity, object*) ценный* (ценен); (*stone*) драгоценный; (*pej*: *person, behaviour*) манерный ◆ *adv* (*inf*): **~ little** *or* **few** очень мало; **your ~ dog** (*ironic*) Ваша драгоценная собака.
precious stone *n* (*GEO*) драгоценный камень* *m*.
precipice ['prɛsɪpɪs] *n* обрыв.
precipitate [*vb* prɪ'sɪpɪteɪt, *adj* prɪ'sɪpɪtɪt] *vt* (*hasten*) ускорять (ускорить *perf*) ◆ *adj* скоропалительный* (скоропалителен).
precipitation [prɪsɪpɪ'teɪʃən] *n* (*rain*) осадки *mpl*.
precipitous [prɪ'sɪpɪtəs] *adj* (*steep*) крутой* (крут), обрывистый (обрывист); (*hasty*) поспешный* (поспешен).
précis ['preɪsɪː] (*pl* ~) *n* конспект.
precise [prɪ'saɪs] *adj* точный* (точен).
precisely [prɪ'saɪslɪ] *adv* (*accurately*) точно; (*exactly*) ровно; **~!** вот именно!, совершенно верно!
precision [prɪ'sɪʒən] *n* точность *f*.
preclude [prɪ'kluːd] *vt* предотвращать (предотвратить* *perf*); **to ~ sb from doing** мешать (помешать *perf*) кому-н *+infin*.
precocious [prɪ'kəuʃəs] *adj* (*talent*) рано развившийся; **a ~ child** не по годам развитой ребёнок.
preconceived [priːkən'siːvd] *adj* предвзятый (предвзят).
preconception ['priːkən'sɛpʃən] *n* предвзятое мнение.
precondition ['priːkən'dɪʃən] *n* непременное условие, предпосылка*.
precursor [priː'kəːsəʳ] *n* (*person, thing*) предтеча *m/f*.
predate ['priː'deɪt] *vt* предшествовать *(impf)* *+dat*.
predator ['prɛdətəʳ] *n* (*also fig*) хищник.
predatory ['prɛdətərɪ] *adj* (*animal*) хищный; (*fig*) хищный* (хищен).
predecessor ['priːdɪsɛsəʳ] *n* предшественник (-ица).
predestination [priːdɛstɪ'neɪʃən] *n* предопределение.
predetermine [priːdɪ'təːmɪn] *vt* предопределять (предопределить *perf*).
predicament [prɪ'dɪkəmənt] *n* затруднение; **to be in a ~** быть* *(impf)* в затруднении.

predicate ['prɛdɪkɪt] *n* (*LING*) сказу́емое *nt adj*.
predict [prɪ'dɪkt] *vt* предска́зывать (предсказа́ть* *perf*).
predictable [prɪ'dɪktəbl] *adj* предсказу́емый (предсказу́ем).
predictably [prɪ'dɪktəblɪ] *adv* как и ожида́лось; ~ **she didn't arrive** как и ожида́лось, она́ не пришла́.
prediction [prɪ'dɪkʃən] *n* предсказа́ние.
predispose ['pri:dɪs'pəuz] *vt* предрасполага́ть (предрасположи́ть* *perf*).
predominance [prɪ'dɔmɪnəns] *n* преоблада́ние; (*dominance*) госпо́дство.
predominant [prɪ'dɔmɪnənt] *adj* доминиру́ющий, преоблада́ющий (преоблада́ющ); **to become ~** станови́ться* (стать* *perf*) преоблада́ющим(-ей).
predominantly [prɪ'dɔmɪnəntlɪ] *adv* преиму́щественно.
predominate [prɪ'dɔmɪneɪt] *vi* преоблада́ть (*impf*).
pre-eminent [pri:'ɛmɪnənt] *adj* выдаю́щийся*.
pre-empt [pri:'ɛmt] *vt* предупрежда́ть (предупреди́ть* *perf*); **to ~ the issue** предупрежда́ть (предупреди́ть* *perf*) собы́тия.
pre-emptive [pri:'ɛmtɪv] *adj*: ~ **strike** упрежда́ющий уда́р.
preen [pri:n] *vt*: **to ~ itself** (*bird*) чи́стить* (почи́стить* *perf*) пёрышки; **to ~ o.s.** прихора́шиваться (*impf*).
prefab ['pri:fæb] *n* сбо́рный дом*.
prefabricated [pri:'fæbrɪkeɪtɪd] *adj* сбо́рный.
preface ['prɛfəs] *n* (*in book*) предисло́вие ◆ *vt*: **to ~ sth with** предпосыла́ть (предпосла́ть* *perf*) чему́-н +*acc*.
prefect ['pri:fɛkt] *n* (*BRIT*: *SCOL*) ста́роста *m/f*.
prefer [prɪ'fə:ʳ] *vt* предпочита́ть (предпоче́сть* *perf*); (*LAW*): **to ~ charges against** выдвига́ть (вы́двинуть *perf*) обвине́ние про́тив +*gen*; **to ~ doing** *or* **to do** предпочита́ть (предпоче́сть* *perf*) +*infin*; **I ~ coffee to tea** я предпочита́ю ко́фе ча́ю.
preferable ['prɛfrəbl] *adj* предпочти́тельный* (предпочти́телен).
preferably ['prɛfrəblɪ] *adv* предпочти́тельно.
preference ['prɛfrəns] *n* (*liking*): **to have a ~ for** предпочита́ть (*impf*); (*priority*): **to give ~ to** отдава́ть* (отда́ть* *perf*) предпочте́ние +*dat*; **in ~ to sth** вме́сто чего́-н.
preference shares *npl* (*BRIT*: *COMM*) привилегиро́ванные а́кции *fpl*.
preferential [prɛfə'rɛnʃəl] *adj*: ~ **treatment** осо́бое отноше́ние.
preferred stock [prɪ'fəd-] *npl* (*US*) = **preference shares**.
prefix ['pri:fɪks] *n* приста́вка*, пре́фикс.
pregnancy ['prɛgnənsɪ] *n* бере́менность *f*.
pregnancy test *n* ана́лиз на бере́менность.
pregnant ['prɛgnənt] *adj* бере́менная (бере́менна); (*remark, pause*) многозначи́тельный* (многозначи́телен); **she is 3 months ~** она́ на четвёртом ме́сяце (бере́менности).
prehistoric ['pri:hɪs'tɔrɪk] *adj* доистори́ческий*.
prehistory [pri:'hɪstərɪ] *n* первобы́тная исто́рия.
prejudge [pri:'dʒʌdʒ] *vt* предреша́ть (предреши́ть *perf*).
prejudice ['prɛdʒudɪs] *n* (*unreasonable dislike*) предрассу́док*; (*bias in favour*) предвзя́тость *f*, предубежде́ние ◆ *vt* (*harm*) вреди́ть* (повреди́ть* *perf*) +*dat*; **without ~ to** без уще́рба для +*gen*; **to ~ sb in favour of** располага́ть (расположи́ть* *perf*) кого́-н в по́льзу +*gen*; **to ~ sb against** настра́ивать (настро́ить *perf*) кого́-н про́тив +*gen*.
prejudiced ['prɛdʒudɪst] *adj* (*biased against*) предубеждённый (предубеждён); (*in favour*) располо́женный* (располо́жен); (*view*) предвзя́тый (предвзя́т).
prelate ['prɛlət] *n* (*REL*) préла́т.
preliminaries [prɪ'lɪmɪnərɪz] *npl* предвари́тельные мероприя́тия *ntpl*; (*in competition*) предвари́тельный отбо́р *msg*.
preliminary [prɪ'lɪmɪnərɪ] *adj* предвари́тельный.
prelude ['prɛlju:d] *n* (*MUS, fig*) прелю́дия.
premarital ['pri:'mærɪtl] *adj* добра́чный.
premature ['prɛmətʃuəʳ] *adj* преждевре́менный* (преждевре́мен); (*baby*) недоно́шенный* (недоно́шен); **you are being a little ~** Вы не́сколько поторопи́лись.
premeditated [pri:'mɛdɪteɪtɪd] *adj* преднаме́ренный* (преднаме́рен).
premeditation [pri:mɛdɪ'teɪʃən] *n* разду́мье.
premenstrual tension [pri:'mɛnstruəl-] *n* предменструа́льный синдро́м.
premier ['prɛmɪəʳ] *adj* (*best*) лу́чший* ◆ *n* (*POL*) премье́р-мини́стр.
première ['prɛmɪɛəʳ] *n* премье́ра.
premise ['prɛmɪs] *n* предпосы́лка*; **~s** *npl* (*of business*) помеще́ние *ntsg*; **on the ~s** в помеще́нии.
premium ['pri:mɪəm] *n* (*COMM, INSURANCE*) пре́мия; **to be at a ~** (*expensive*) сто́ить (*impf*) вы́ше номина́ла; (*hard to get*) по́льзоваться (*impf*) больши́м спро́сом; **to sell at a ~** (*shares*) продава́ть* (прода́ть* *perf*) по цене́ вы́ше номина́ла.
premium bond *n* (*BRIT*) премиа́льная (сберега́тельная) облига́ция.
premium deal *n* (*COMM*) премиа́льная сде́лка*.
premium gasoline *n* (*US*) высокоокта́новый бензи́н.

* marks translations which have irregular inflections. The Russian-English side of the dictionary gives inflectional information.

premonition [prɛmə'nɪʃən] *n* предчу́вствие.
preoccupation [pri:ɔkju'peɪʃən] *n*: ~ **with** озабо́ченность *f* +*instr*.
preoccupied [pri:'ɔkjupaɪd] *adj* озабо́ченный* (озабо́чен).
prep [prɛp] *adj abbr*: ~ **school** = *preparatory school*; (*BRIT*) ча́стная нача́льная шко́ла; (*US*) сре́дняя шко́ла ◆ *n abbr* = *preparation*.
prep *n* (*homework*) дома́шнее зада́ние.
prepaid [pri:'peɪd] *adj* зара́нее опла́ченный (опла́чен); (*envelope*) с зара́нее опла́ченными почто́выми расхо́дами.
preparation [prɛpə'reɪʃən] *n* (*activity*) подгото́вка*; (*of food*) приготовле́ние; (*medicine, cosmetic*) препара́т; ~**s** *npl* (*arrangements*) приготовле́ния *ntpl*; **in ~ for sth** гото́вясь к чему́-н.
preparatory [prɪ'pærətərɪ] *adj* подготови́тельный; ~ **to doing** пре́жде чем +*infin*.
preparatory school *n* (*BRIT*) ча́стная нача́льная шко́ла; (*US*) сре́дняя шко́ла.
prepare [prɪ'pɛəʳ] *vt* (*plan, speech, room etc*) подгота́вливать (подгото́вить* *perf*); (*CULIN*) гото́вить* (*impf*), пригота́вливать (пригото́вить* *perf*) ◆ *vi*: **to ~ for** (*event, action etc*) гото́виться* (*impf*) *or* подгота́вливаться (подгото́виться* *perf*) к +*dat*.
prepared [prɪ'pɛəd] *adj* гото́вый (гото́в); **I am ~ to help you** (*willing*) я гото́в помо́чь Вам; ~ **for** (*ready*) гото́вый (гото́в) к +*dat*.
preponderance [prɪ'pɔndərns] *n* (*of people, things*) преоблада́ние.
preposition [prɛpə'zɪʃən] *n* (*LING*) предло́г.
prepossessing [pri:pə'zɛsɪŋ] *adj* привлека́тельный* (привлека́телен).
preposterous [prɪ'pɔstərəs] *adj* (*outrageous*) ди́кий*.
prep school *n* = **preparatory school**.
prerecorded ['pri:rɪ'kɔ:dɪd] *adj* предвари́тельно запи́санный.
prerequisite [pri:'rɛkwɪzɪt] *n* предпосы́лка*, непреме́нное усло́вие.
prerogative [prɪ'rɔgətɪv] *n* прерогати́ва.
Presbyterian [prɛzbɪ'tɪərɪən] *n* (*REL*) пресвитериа́нин*(-а́нка*) ◆ *adj* пресвитериа́нский.
presbytery ['prɛzbɪtərɪ] *n* пресвите́рия.
preschool ['pri:'sku:l] *adj* (*age, education*) дошко́льный; ~ **child** ребёнок дошко́льного во́зраста.
prescribe [prɪ'skraɪb] *vt* (*MED*) пропи́сывать (прописа́ть* *perf*); (*action, duty*) предпи́сывать (предписа́ть* *perf*); ~**d books** (*BRIT*: *SCOL*) рекомендо́ванные уче́бники.
prescription [prɪ'skrɪpʃən] *n* (*MED*: *slip of paper*) реце́пт; (: *medicine*) лека́рство (*назна́ченное врачо́м*); **to make up** *or* (*US*) **fill a ~** пригота́вливать (пригото́вить* *perf*) лека́рство по реце́пту; **"only available on ~"** „прода́жа лека́рства то́лько по реце́птам".
prescription charges *npl* (*BRIT*) *минима́льная цена́ за лека́рства, отпуска́емые по реце́пту*.
prescriptive [prɪ'skrɪptɪv] *adj* нормати́вный* (нормати́вен).
presence ['prɛzns] *n* прису́тствие; (*fig*) нару́жность *f*; **in sb's ~** в кого́-н прису́тствии.
presence of mind *n* прису́тствие ду́ха.
present [*adj, n* 'prɛznt, *vt* prɪ'zɛnt] *adj* (*current*) ны́нешний*, настоя́щий*; (*in attendance*) прису́тствующий ◆ *n* (*gift*) пода́рок*; (*LING*: *also*: ~ **tense**) настоя́щее вре́мя* *nt* ◆ *vt* представля́ть (предста́вить* *perf*); (*threat*) представля́ть (предста́вить* *perf*) собо́й; (*RADIO, TV*) вести́* (*impf*); (*give*): **to ~ sth to sb, ~ sb with sth** (*prize, award etc*) вруча́ть (вручи́ть* *perf*) что-н кому́-н; (*gift*) преподноси́ть* (преподнести́* *perf*) что-н кому́-н; (*formally introduce*): **to ~ sb (to)** представля́ть (предста́вить* *perf*) кого́-н (+*dat*); **to be ~ at** прису́тствовать (*impf*) на +*prp*; **those ~** прису́тствующие; **the ~** (*time*) настоя́щее *nt adj*; **at ~** в настоя́щее вре́мя; **to give sb a ~** дари́ть* (подари́ть* *perf*) кому́-н пода́рок.
presentable [prɪ'zɛntəbl] *adj* представи́тельный* (представи́телен), презента́бельный* (презента́белен).
presentation [prɛzn'teɪʃən] *n* (*of plan, report etc*) изложе́ние; (*appearance*) вне́шний* вид; (*also*: ~ **ceremony**) представле́ние, презента́ция; (*lecture, talk*) выступле́ние; **on ~ of** (*voucher etc*) по предъявле́нии +*gen*.
present-day ['prɛzntdeɪ] *adj* совреме́нный, ны́нешний*.
presenter [prɪ'zɛntəʳ] *n* (*RADIO, TV*) ди́ктор; (: *of news*) веду́щий*(-ая) *m(f) adj*.
presently ['prɛzntlɪ] *adv* вско́ре; (*now*) в да́нный моме́нт, в настоя́щее вре́мя.
present participle *n* прича́стие настоя́щего вре́мени.
preservation [prɛzə'veɪʃən] *n* (*act*: *of building, democracy*) сохране́ние; (: *of food*) хране́ние; (*state*) сохра́нность *f*.
preservative [prɪ'zə:vətɪv] *n* (*for food*) консерва́нт; (*for wood*) пропи́точный соста́в; (*for metal*) защи́тное сре́дство.
preserve [prɪ'zə:v] *vt* сохраня́ть (сохранить *perf*); (*food*) консерви́ровать (законсерви́ровать *perf*); (*keep safe*) оберега́ть (*impf*), охраня́ть (*impf*) ◆ *n* (*often pl*: *jam*) варе́нье; (*for game, fish*) запове́дник; **a working class ~** стихи́я рабо́чего кла́сса; **a male ~** чи́сто мужско́е заня́тие.
preshrunk ['pri:'ʃrʌŋk] *adj*: ~ **fabric** *ткань, проше́дшая предвари́тельную уса́дку*.
preside [prɪ'zaɪd] *vi*: **to ~ (over)** председа́тельствовать (*impf*) (на +*prp*).
presidency ['prɛzɪdənsɪ] *n* президе́нтство.
president ['prɛzɪdənt] *n* (*POL, COMM*) президе́нт;

(*US*: *SCOL*) ре́ктор.
presidential [prɛzɪˈdɛnʃl] *adj* (*election, campaign etc*) президе́нтский; ~ **candidate** кандида́т в президе́нты; ~ **adviser** сове́тник президе́нта.
press [prɛs] *n* (*also:* **printing** ~) печа́тный стано́к*; (*of switch, button, bell*) кно́пка*; (*for wine*) пресс для виногра́да; (*crowd*) да́вка ◆ *vt* (*hold together*) прижима́ть (прижа́ть* *perf*); (*push*) нажима́ть (нажа́ть* *perf*); (*iron*) гла́дить* (погла́дить* *perf*); (*put pressure on: person*) наста́ивать (настоя́ть *perf*); (*squeeze*) выжима́ть (вы́жать* *perf*); (*pursue*) добива́ться (доби́ться* *perf*) *+gen* ◆ *vi* (*squeeze*) жать* (*impf*), дави́ть* (*impf*); **the** ~ (*newspapers, journalists*) пре́сса; **to go to** ~ идти́* (*impf*) в печа́ть; **to be in the** ~ (*being printed*) находи́ться* (*impf*) в печа́ти; (*in the newspapers*) быть* (*impf*) в газе́тах; **we are ~ed for time/money** у нас ма́ло вре́мени/ де́нег; **to ~ sth on sb** (*insist*) навя́зывать (навяза́ть* *perf*) что-н кому́-н; **to ~ sb to do** *or* **into doing** вынужда́ть (вы́нудить *perf*) кого́-н *+infin*; **to ~ sb for an answer** торопи́ть* (поторопи́ть* *perf*) кого́-н с отве́том; **to ~ charges against sb** выдвига́ть (вы́двинуть *perf*) обвине́ния про́тив кого́-н; **to ~ for** (*improvement, change etc*) наста́ивать (настоя́ть *perf*) на *+prp*
▸ **press ahead** *vi* приступа́ть (приступи́ть* *perf*) к де́лу
▸ **press on** *vi* продолжа́ть (*impf*).
press agency *n* аге́нтство печа́ти.
press clipping *n* газе́тная вы́резка.
press conference *n* пресс-конфере́нция.
press cutting *n* = **press clipping**.
press-gang [ˈprɛsgæŋ] *vt*: **to ~ sb into doing** наси́льно заставля́ть (заста́вить* *perf*) кого́-н *+infin*.
pressing [ˈprɛsɪŋ] *adj* (*urgent*) сро́чный* (сро́чен), неотло́жный* (неотло́жен).
press officer *n* сотру́дник(-ица) отде́ла информа́ции.
press release *n* сообще́ние для печа́ти.
press stud *n* (*BRIT*) одёжная кно́пка*.
press-up [ˈprɛsʌp] *n* (*BRIT*: *SPORT*) отжима́ние, отжи́м.
pressure [ˈprɛʃəʳ] *n* давле́ние; (*stress*) напряже́ние ◆ *vt*: **to ~ sb (to do)** принужда́ть (прину́дить* *perf*) кого́-н (*+infin*); **to put ~ on sb (to do)** ока́зывать (оказа́ть* *perf*) давле́ние *or* нажи́м на кого́-н (*+infin*); **high/low ~** высо́кое/ни́зкое давле́ние.
pressure cooker *n* скорова́рка*.
pressure gauge *n* мано́метр.
pressure group *n* инициати́вная гру́ппа.
pressurize [ˈprɛʃəraɪz] *vt*: **to ~ sb (to do** *or* **into doing)** ока́зывать (оказа́ть* *perf*) давле́ние на кого́-н (*+infin*).
pressurized [ˈprɛʃəraɪzd] *adj* (*cabin, container, spacesuit*) гермети́чный.
Prestel® [ˈprɛstɛl] *n* Пре́стел.
prestige [prɛsˈtiːʒ] *n* прести́ж.
prestigious [prɛsˈtɪdʒəs] *adj* прести́жный* (прести́жен).
presumably [prɪˈzjuːməblɪ] *adv* наве́рно; ~ **he did it** наве́рно, э́то сде́лал он.
presume [prɪˈzjuːm] *vt*: **to ~ (that)** (*suppose*) предполага́ть (предположи́ть* *perf*)(, что); **to ~ to do** (*dare*) реша́ться (реши́ться *perf*) *+infin*.
presumption [prɪˈzʌmpʃən] *n* предположе́ние.
presumptuous [prɪˈzʌmpʃəs] *adj* самонаде́янный* (самонаде́ян).
presuppose [priːsəˈpəuz] *vt* предполага́ть (предположи́ть* *perf*).
presupposition [priːsʌpəˈzɪʃən] *n* предположе́ние.
pretax [priːˈtæks] *adj* (*profit*) до вы́чета нало́гов.
pretence [prɪˈtɛns] (*US* **pretense**) *n* (*false appearance*) притво́рство; (*excuse*) предло́г; **under false ~s** под ло́жным предло́гом; **she is devoid of all ~** она́ соверше́нно лишена́ притво́рства; **he is making a ~ of helping** он де́лает вид, что помога́ет.
pretend [prɪˈtɛnd] *vi*: **to ~ that** притворя́ться (притвори́ться *perf*), что; **he ~ed to help** он притвори́лся, что помога́ет; **to ~ to sth** (*make claim*) претендова́ть (*impf*) на что-н.
pretense [prɪˈtɛns] *n* (*US*) = **pretence**.
pretentious [prɪˈtɛnʃəs] *adj* претенцио́зный* (претенцио́зен).
preterite [ˈprɛtərɪt] *n* прете́рит.
pretext [ˈpriːtɛkst] *n* предло́г; **on** *or* **under the ~ of being busy/tired** под предло́гом за́нятости/уста́лости.
Pretoria [prɪˈtɔːrɪə] *n* Прето́рия.
pretty [ˈprɪtɪ] *adj* (*person*) хоро́шенький*; (*thing*) краси́вый (краси́в) ◆ *adv* (*quite*) дово́льно.
prevail [prɪˈveɪl] *vi* (*be current*) преоблада́ть (*impf*), превали́ровать (*impf*); (*gain influence*) оде́рживать (одержа́ть *perf*) верх; (*persuade*): **to ~ (up)on sb to do** убежда́ть (убеди́ть* *perf*) кого́-н *+infin*.
prevailing [prɪˈveɪlɪŋ] *adj* (*wind*) преоблада́ющий; (*fashion, attitude*) превали́рующий.
prevalent [ˈprɛvələnt] *adj* (*belief, custom*) преоблада́ющий; (*fashion*) превали́рующий; (*disease*) распространённый* (распространён).
prevaricate [prɪˈværɪkeɪt] *vi* извора́чиваться (*impf*).
prevarication [prɪværɪˈkeɪʃən] *n* виля́ние.

prevent [prɪ'vɛnt] *vt* (*accident etc*) предотвращáть (предотвратить* *perf*); **to ~ sb from doing** мешáть (помешáть *perf*) комý-н *+infin*; **this policy ~s inflation from rising** эта политика препятствует рóсту инфляции.
preventable [prɪ'vɛntəbl] *adj* предотвратимый (предотвратим).
preventative [prɪ'vɛntətɪv] *adj* = **preventive**.
prevention [prɪ'vɛnʃən] *n* предотвращéние, предупреждéние.
preventive [prɪ'vɛntɪv] *adj* (*measures*) предупредительный; (: *POL*) превентивный; (*medicine*) профилактический*.
preview ['pri:vju:] *n* (*of film*) (закрытый) просмóтр; (*fig*) предварительная картина.
previous ['pri:vɪəs] *adj* предыдýщий*; **I have a ~ engagement** это врéмя у меня ужé зáнято; **~ to** до *+gen*.
previously ['pri:vɪəslɪ] *adv* (*before*) рáнее; (*in the past*) прéжде; **I retired two years ~** я ушёл на пéнсию двумя годáми рáнее.
prewar [pri:'wɔ:ʳ] *adj* довоéнный, предвоéнный.
prey [preɪ] *n* добыча ◆ *vi*: **to ~ on** (*animal*: *feed on*) охóтиться* (*impf*) на *+acc*; **it was ~ing on his mind** это терзáло егó.
price [praɪs] *n* (*also fig*) ценá* ◆ *vt* (*goods*) оцéнивать (оценить* *perf*); **what is the ~ of ...?** скóлько стóит ...?; **to go up** *or* **rise in ~** дорожáть (вздорожáть *or* подорожáть *perf*); **to put a ~ on sth** назначáть (назнáчить *perf*) цéну чемý-н; **Britain has been out of the market** Великобритáния былá вытеснена из рынка из-за завышéния цен; **what ~ his promises now?** (*BRIT*) что стóят все егó обещáния сейчáс?; **he regained his freedom, but at a ~** он получил свобóду, но дорогóй ценóй.
price control *n* контрóль *m* за цéнами.
price cutting *n* снижéние цен.
priceless ['praɪslɪs] *adj* бесцéнный* (бесцéнен); (*inf*: *amusing*) бесподóбный* (бесподóбен).
price list *n* прейскурáнт.
price range *n* диапазóн цен; **it's within my ~ ~** это мне по кармáну.
price tag *n* цéнник; (*fig*) ценá*.
price war *n* войнá цен.
pricey ['praɪsɪ] *adj* (*inf*) дорогóй.
prick [prɪk] *n* (*short, sharp pain*) укóл; (*ANAT*: *inf!*) хуй (*!*) ◆ *vt* (*make hole in*) прокáлывать (проколóть* *perf*); (*cause pain to*) уколóть* (*perf*); **to ~ up one's ears** (*listen eagerly*) навострить (*perf*) ýши.
prickle ['prɪkl] *n* (*of plant*) шип*, колючка*; (*sensation*) покáлывание.
prickly ['prɪklɪ] *adj* колючий* (колюч).
prickly heat *n* потница.
prickly pear *n* (*BOT*) опýнция.
pride [praɪd] *n* гóрдость *f*; (*pej*: *feeling of superiority*) гордыня ◆ *vt*: **to ~ o.s. on** гордиться* (*impf*) *+instr*; **to take (a) ~ in** гордиться* (*impf*) *+instr*; **I take (a) ~ in working well** я горжýсь тем что я рабóтаю хорошó; **to have ~ of place** (*BRIT*) занимáть (занять* *perf*) почётное мéсто.
priest [pri:st] *n* священник; (*non-Christian*) жрец*.
priestess ['pri:stɪs] *n* (*non-Christian*) жрица.
priesthood ['pri:sthud] *n* священство.
prig [prɪg] *n*: **he's a ~** он такáя цáца.
prim [prɪm] *adj* чóпорный* (чóпорен).
primacy ['praɪməsɪ] *n* пéрвенство.
prima-facie ['praɪmə'feɪʃɪ] *adj*: **to have a ~ case** (*LAW*) разбирáть (*impf*) ясное судéбное дéло*.
primal ['praɪməl] *adj* (*instinct*) первичный; (*cause*) изначáльный; **~ scream** пéрвый крик (*младéнца*).
primarily ['praɪmərɪlɪ] *adv* в пéрвую óчередь.
primary ['praɪmərɪ] *adj* (*first in importance*) первостепéнный* (первостепéнен), первоочереднóй ◆ *n* (*US*: *POL*) предварительные выборы *mpl*; **~ education** начáльное образовáние; **~ teacher** учитель(ница) *m(f)* начáльных клáссов.
primary colour *n* основнóй цвет*.
primary school *n* (*BRIT*) начáльная шкóла.
primate ['praɪmɪt] *n* (*ZOOL*) примáт; (*REL*) примас.
prime [praɪm] *adj* (*most important*) глáвный, основнóй; (*best quality*) первосóртный ◆ *n* (*of person's life*) расцвéт ◆ *vt* (*wood, canvas*) грунтовáть (загрунтовáть *perf*); (*fig*: *person*) подготáвливать (подготóвить* *perf*); (*gun*) заряжáть (зарядить *perf*); (*pump*) заливáть (залить* *perf*); **in the ~ of life** в расцвéте сил, во цвéте лет; **~ example** (*typical*) яркий* примéр.
Prime Minister *n* премьéр-министр.
primer ['praɪməʳ] *n* (*paint*) грунтóвка; (*book*) учéбник-введéние.
prime time *n* (*RADIO, TV*) лýчшее эфирное врéмя* *nt*.
primeval [praɪ'mi:vl] *adj* первобытный.
primitive ['prɪmɪtɪv] *adj* (*early*) первобытный; (*unsophisticated*: *way of life, tool etc*) примитивный* (примитивен).
primrose ['prɪmrəuz] *n* первоцвéт.
primula ['prɪmjulə] *n* примула.
Primus® ['praɪməs] *n* (*BRIT*: *also*: **p~ stove**) примус.
prince [prɪns] *n* принц; (*Russian*) князь* *m*.
prince charming *n* прекрáсный принц.
princess [prɪn'sɛs] *n* принцéсса; (*Russian*) княгиня, княжнá*.
principal ['prɪnsɪpl] *adj* глáвный, основнóй ◆ *n* (*of school, college*) дирéктор*; (*of university*) рéктор; (*in play*) ведýщий*(-ая) актёр (-трйса); (*money*) капитáл.
principality [prɪnsɪ'pælɪtɪ] *n* княжество.
principally ['prɪnsɪplɪ] *adv* преимýщественно, глáвным óбразом.
principle ['prɪnsɪpl] *n* принцип; (*scientific law*)

закóн; **in** ~ в при́нципе; **on** ~ из при́нципа.

print [prɪnt] *n* (*TYP*) шрифт•; (*ART*) эстáмп, гравю́ра; (*PHOT, fingerprint*) отпечáток•; (*footprint*) след•; (*fabric*) си́тец• ◆ *vt* (*book etc*) печáтать (напечáтать *perf*); (*cloth*) набивáть (наби́ть• *perf*); (*write in capitals*) писáть• (написáть• *perf*) печáтными бýквами; **this book is out of** ~ э́та кни́га распрóдана

▸ **print out** *vt* (*COMPUT*) распечáтывать (распечáтать *perf*), выводи́ть• (вы́йти• *perf*) на печáть.

printed circuit board ['prɪntɪd-] *n* (*ELEC*) печáтная схéма *or* плáта.

printed matter *n* печáтные материáлы *mpl*.

printer ['prɪntəʳ] *n* (*person*) печáтник; (*machine*) при́нтер; (*firm*: *also:* **~'s**) типогрáфия.

printhead ['prɪnthɛd] *n* (*COMPUT*) печáтающая голóвка.

printing ['prɪntɪŋ] *n* (*act*) печáтание; (*art*) печáтное дéло.

printing press *n* печáтный станóк•.

print-out ['prɪntaut] *n* (*COMPUT*) распечáтка•.

print wheel *n* (*COMPUT*) печáтающее колесó•.

prior ['praɪəʳ] *adj* (*previous*) прéжний•; (*more important*) первоочереднóй ◆ *n* (*REL*) настоя́тель *m*, при́ор; **without** ~ **notice** без предвари́тельного предупреждéния; **to have** ~ **knowledge of sth** знать• *(impf)* о чём-н зарáнее; **to have a** ~ **claim to sth** имéть *(impf)* первоочереднóе *or* преимýщественное прáво на что-н; ~ **to** до *+gen*.

priority [praɪ'ɔrɪtɪ] *n* (*most urgent task*) первоочереднáя задáча; (*most important thing, task*) приоритéт; **to have** ~ **(over)** имéть *(impf)* преимýществом (пéред *+instr*).

priory ['praɪərɪ] *n* монасты́рь• *m*.

prise [praɪz] *vt*: **to** ~ **open** взлáмывать (взломáть *perf*).

prism ['prɪzəm] *n* при́зма.

prison ['prɪzn] *n* тюрьмá• ◆ *cpd* тюрéмный.

prison camp *n* исправи́тельно-трудовóй лáгерь• *m*.

prisoner ['prɪznəʳ] *n* (*in prison*) заключённый (-ая) *m(f) adj*; (*captured person*) плéнный(-ая) *m(f) adj*; **the** ~ **at the bar** подсуди́мый(-ая) *m(f) adj*; **to take sb** ~ брать• (взять• *perf*) когó-н в плен.

prisoner of war *n* военноплéнный *m adj*.

prissy ['prɪsɪ] *adj* (*pej*) чóпорный.

pristine ['prɪsti:n] *adj* безупрéчный• (безупрéчен).

privacy ['prɪvəsɪ] *n* уединéние; **invasion of sb's** ~ вторжéние в чью-н чáстную жизнь.

private ['praɪvɪt] *adj* (*not public: property, industry*) чáстный; (*: discussion, club*) закры́тый; (*personal, confidential*: *belongings, life*) ли́чный; (*: thoughts, plans*) скры́тый; (*secluded*: *place*) уединённый (уединён); (*secretive, reserved*) зáмкнутый (зáмкнут); (*confidential*) конфиденциáльный• (конфиденциáлен) ◆ *n* (*MIL*) рядовóй *m adj*; **"private"** (*on envelope*) „ли́чно"; (*on door*) „посторóнним вход воспрещён"; **in** ~ конфиденциáльно; **in (his)** ~ **life** в (егó) ли́чной жи́зни; **he is a very** ~ **person** он óчень зáмкнутый человéк; **to be in** ~ **practice** имéть *(impf)* чáстную прáктику; ~ **hearing** (*LAW*) закры́тое слýшание.

private enterprise *n* (*economic activity*) чáстное предпринимáтельство.

private eye *n* чáстный сы́щик.

private limited company *n* (*BRIT*) чáстная акционéрная компáния.

privately ['praɪvɪtlɪ] *adv* (*discuss*) конфиденциáльно; (*act*) в чáстном поря́дке; (*within o.s.*) в душé.

private parts *npl* (*ANAT*) (нарýжные) половы́е óрганы *mpl*.

private property *n* чáстная сóбственность *f*.

private school *n* чáстная шкóла.

privation [praɪ'veɪʃən] *n* (*state*) лишéния *ntpl*.

privatize ['praɪvɪtaɪz] *vt* приватизи́ровать *(impf/perf)*.

privet ['prɪvɪt] *n* (*BOT*) бирючи́на.

privilege ['prɪvɪlɪdʒ] *n* привилéгия.

privileged ['prɪvɪlɪdʒd] *adj* привилеги́рованный; **to be** ~ **to do** имéть *(impf)* честь *+infin*.

privy ['prɪvɪ] *adj*: ~ **to** посвящённый в *+acc*.

Privy Council *n* (*BRIT*) Тáйный Совéт.

Privy Councillor *n* (*BRIT*) Тáйный Совéтник.

prize [praɪz] *n* приз•; (*money*) прéмия ◆ *adj* (*first-class*) первоклáссный; (*example, idiot*) класси́ческий• ◆ *vt* (высокó) цени́ть *(impf)*.

prizefighter ['praɪzfaɪtəʳ] *n* профессионáльный боксёр.

prize-giving ['praɪzgɪvɪŋ] *n* *церемóния вручéния нагрáд за хорóшую успевáемость.*

prize money *n* призовы́е дéньги• *pl*.

prizewinner ['praɪzwɪnəʳ] *n* призёр, лауреáт.

prizewinning ['praɪzwɪnɪŋ] *adj* (*person*) удостóенный нагрáды; (*animal*) призовóй; (*novel, essay etc*) удостóенный прéмии.

PRO *n abbr* = **public relations officer**.

pro [prəu] *n* (*SPORT*: *inf*) профессионáл ◆ *prep* (*in favour of*) за *+acc*; **the ~s and cons** (дóводы) „за" и „прóтив".

pro- [prəu] *prefix* про-.

proactive [prəu'æktɪv] *adj* дéйственный.

probability [prɔbə'bɪlɪtɪ] *n*: ~ **of/that** вероя́тность *f +gen*/что; **in all** ~ по всей вероя́тности.

probable ['prɔbəbl] *adj* вероя́тный• (вероя́тен); **it seems** ~ **that ...** представля́ется вероя́тным, что ....

probably ['prɔbəblɪ] *adv* вероя́тно.
probate ['prəubɪt] *n* утвержде́ние завеща́ния.
probation [prə'beɪʃən] *n*: **he is on ~** (*LAW*) он осуждён усло́вно; (*employee*) он прохо́дит испыта́тельный срок; (*REL*) он отбыва́ет по́слух.
probationary [prə'beɪʃənrɪ] *adj* (*period*) испыта́тельный.
probationer [prə'beɪʃənə^r] *n* (*LAW*) усло́вно осуждённый.
probation officer *n должностно́е лицо́, осуществля́ющее надзо́р за усло́вно осуждёнными.*
probe [prəub] *n* (*MED, SPACE*) зонд; (*enquiry*) рассле́дование ◆ *vt* (*investigate*) рассле́довать *(impf/perf)*; (*poke*) прощу́пывать *(impf)*.
probity ['prəubɪtɪ] *n* че́стность *f*.
problem ['prɔbləm] *n* пробле́ма; **we are having ~s with the car** у нас непола́дки с маши́ной; **what's the ~?** в чём де́ло?; **I had no ~ in finding her** я нашёл её без труда́; **no ~!** нет пробле́м!
problematic(al) [prɔblə'mætɪk(l)] *adj* проблемати́чный* (проблемати́чен).
problem-solving ['prɔbləmsɔlvɪŋ] *n уме́ние находи́ть выход из тру́дного положе́ния.*
procedural [prə'si:djurəl] *adj* процеду́рный.
procedure [prə'si:dʒə^r] *n* процеду́ра.
proceed [prə'si:d] *vi* (*subj: activity, event, process: carry on*) продолжа́ться (продо́лжиться *perf*); (*person: go*) дви́гаться (дви́нуться *perf*); (*continue*): **to ~ (with)** продолжа́ть (продо́лжить *perf*); **to ~ to do** продолжа́ть (продо́лжить *perf*) *+infin*; **to ~ against sb** (*LAW*) возбужда́ть (возбуди́ть* *perf*) де́ло про́тив кого́-н.
proceedings [prə'si:dɪŋz] *npl* (*organized events*) собы́тия *ntpl*; (*LAW*) суде́бное разбира́тельство *ntsg*; (*minutes*) протоко́л *msg*.
proceeds ['prəusi:dz] *npl* поступле́ния *ntpl*.
process ['prəusɛs] *n* проце́сс ◆ *vt* (*also COMPUT*) обраба́тывать (обрабо́тать *perf*) ◆ *vi* (*BRIT: go in procession*) уча́ствовать *(impf)* в проце́ссии; **in ~** в проце́ссе; **we are in the ~ of moving house** сейча́с мы переезжа́ем.
processed cheese ['prəusɛst-] (*US* **process cheese**) *n* пла́вленый сыр*.
processing ['prəusɛsɪŋ] *n* (*PHOT*) обрабо́тка*.
procession [prə'sɛʃən] *n* проце́ссия.
pro-choice [prəu'tʃɔɪs] *adj защища́ющий пра́во же́нщины на або́рт.*
proclaim [prə'kleɪm] *vt* провозглаша́ть (провозгласи́ть* *perf*).
proclamation [prɔklə'meɪʃən] *n* провозглаше́ние.
proclivity [prə'klɪvɪtɪ] *n* накло́нность *f*.
procrastinate [prəu'kræstɪneit] *vi* оття́гивать (оттяну́ть *perf*).
procrastination [prəukræstɪ'neɪʃən] *n* оття́гивание.
procreation [prəukrɪ'eɪʃən] *n* размноже́ние.
procurator fiscal ['prɔkjureɪtə-] *n* (*SCOTTISH: LAW*) прокуро́р.
procure [prə'kjuə^r] *vt* приобрета́ть (приобрести́* *perf*).
procurement [prə'kjuəmənt] *n* приобрете́ние.
prod [prɔd] *vt* ты́кать* (ткнуть *perf*); (*fig: remind*) подстёгивать (подстегну́ть *perf*) ◆ *n* (*see vb*) тычо́к*; (*fig*) напомина́ние.
prodigal ['prɔdɪgl] *adj* блу́дный.
prodigious [prə'dɪdʒəs] *adj* огро́мный* (огро́мен).
prodigy ['prɔdɪdʒɪ] *n* (*person*) тала́нт; (*achievement*) успе́хи *mpl*; **child ~** вундерки́нд.
produce [*vt* prə'dju:s, *n* 'prɔdju:s] *vt* (*object, offspring, effect*) производи́ть* (произвести́* *perf*); (*BIO, CHEM*) выраба́тывать (вы́работать *perf*); (*evidence, argument*) представля́ть (предста́вить* *perf*); (*bring or take out*) предъявля́ть (предъяви́ть* *perf*); (*play, film*) ста́вить* (поста́вить* *perf*) ◆ *n* (*AGR*) проду́кция.
producer [prə'dju:sə^r] *n* (*of film, play*) режиссёр-постано́вщик, продю́сер; (*of record*) продю́сер; (*country, company*) производи́тель *m*.
product ['prɔdʌkt] *n* (*thing*) изде́лие; (*food, result*) проду́кт.
production [prə'dʌkʃən] *n* (*process*) произво́дство; (*amount produced*) проду́кция; (*of electricity etc*) вы́работка*; (*THEAT*) постано́вка*; **to put into ~** (*goods*) запуска́ть (запусти́ть* *perf*) в произво́дство.
production agreement *n* (*US*) соглаше́ние о долево́м распределе́нии проду́кции.
production line *n* пото́чная ли́ния.
production manager *n* руководи́тель *m* произво́дством.
productive [prə'dʌktɪv] *adj* (*also fig*) производи́тельный* (производи́телен), продукти́вный* (продукти́вен).
productivity [prɔdʌk'tɪvɪtɪ] *n* производи́тельность *f*, продукти́вность *f*.
productivity agreement *n* (*BRIT*) догово́р о производи́тельности труда́.
productivity bonus *n* пре́мия за высо́кую производи́тельность труда́.
Prof. *n abbr* = *professor*.
profane [prə'feɪn] *adj* (*secular*) све́тский*; (*language etc*) богоху́льный* (богоху́лен).
profess [prə'fɛs] *vt* (*claim*) претендова́ть *(impf)* на *+acc*; (*express*) заявля́ть (заяви́ть* *perf*) о *+prp*; (*REL*) испове́довать *(impf/perf)*; **I do not ~ to be an expert** я не претенду́ю на роль специали́ста.
professed [prə'fɛst] *adj* (*self-declared*) открове́нный.
profession [prə'fɛʃən] *n* профе́ссия; **the ~s** „профе́ссии с большо́й бу́квы" (*ЮР, МЕД,*

РЕЛ).
professional [prəˈfɛʃənl] *adj* профессиона́льный ◆ *n* (*doctor, lawyer, teacher etc*) специали́ст; (*skilled person, also SPORT*) профессиона́л; **he's a ~ man** он – челове́к с образова́нием; **to take ~ advice** получа́ть (получи́ть* *perf*) профессиона́льный сове́т.
professionalism [prəˈfɛʃnəlɪzəm] *n* профессионали́зм.
professionally [prəˈfɛʃnəlɪ] *adv* (*also SPORT, MUS*) профессиона́льно; **I only know him ~** я зна́ю его́ то́лько по рабо́те.
professor [prəˈfɛsəʳ] *n* (*BRIT*) профе́ссор; (*US*) преподава́тель(ница) *m(f)*.
professorship [prəˈfɛsəʃɪp] *n* профе́ссорство.
proffer [ˈprɔfəʳ] *vt* (*remark*) выска́зывать (вы́сказать* *perf*); (*apologies*) приноси́ть* (принести́* *perf*); (*one's hand*) протя́гивать (протяну́ть* *perf*).
proficiency [prəˈfɪʃənsɪ] *n* квалифика́ция, уме́ние.
proficient [prəˈfɪʃənt] *adj* уме́лый; **to be ~ at sth** (*at sth mental*) быть* (*impf*) знатоко́м чем-н; **he is ~ at swimming** он ма́стерски пла́вает.
profile [ˈprəufaɪl] *n* (*of face*) про́филь *m*; (*article*) о́черк; **to keep a high ~** (*fig*) находи́ться* (*impf*) в це́нтре (обще́ственного) внима́ния; **to keep a low ~** (*fig*) стара́ться (*impf*) не выделя́ться.
profit [ˈprɔfɪt] *n* при́быль *f*, дохо́д ◆ *vi*: **to ~ by** *or* **from** (*fig*) извлека́ть (извле́чь* *perf*) вы́году из *+gen*; **~ and loss account** счёт при́былей и убы́тков; **to make a ~** получа́ть (получи́ть* *perf*) при́быль; **to sell (sth) at a ~** продава́ть* (прода́ть* *perf*) (что-н) с вы́годой.
profitability [prɔfɪtəˈbɪlɪtɪ] *n* при́быльность *f*.
profitable [ˈprɔfɪtəbl] *adj* при́быльный* (при́былен); (*fig*) вы́годный* (вы́годен).
profit centre *n* (*COMM*) „центр получе́ния при́были“.
profiteering [prɔfɪˈtɪərɪŋ] *n* (*pej*) спекуля́ция.
profitmaking [ˈprɔfɪtmeɪkɪŋ] *adj* при́быльный* (при́былен).
profit margin *n* ма́ржа при́быльности.
profit-sharing [ˈprɔfɪtʃɛərɪŋ] *n* уча́стие (слу́жащих) в при́былях.
profits tax *n* (*BRIT*) нало́г с при́были.
profligate [ˈprɔflɪgɪt] *adj*: **~ (with)** расточи́тельный* (расточи́телен) (в *+prp*).
pro forma [ˈprəuˈfɔːmə] *adj*: **~ ~ invoice** предвари́тельный счёт-факту́ра.
profound [prəˈfaund] *adj* глубо́кий* (глубо́к).
profuse [prəˈfjuːs] *adj* оби́льный* (оби́лен).
profusely [prəˈfjuːslɪ] *adv* оби́льно; (*apologize*) горячо́.
profusion [prəˈfjuːʒən] *n* оби́льность *f*.
progeny [ˈprɔdʒɪnɪ] *n* пото́мство.
prognoses [prɔgˈnəusiːz] *npl of* **prognosis**.
prognosis [prɔgˈnəusɪs] (*pl* **prognoses**) *n* прогно́з.
program [ˈprəugræm] *n* (*COMPUT*) програ́мма ◆ *vt* (*COMPUT*) программи́ровать (запрограмми́ровать *perf*).
programme [ˈprəugræm] (*US* **program**) *n* програ́мма ◆ *vt* программи́ровать (запрограмми́ровать *perf*).
programmer [ˈprəugræməʳ] *n* (*COMPUT*) программи́ст(ка*).
programming [ˈprəugræmɪŋ] (*US* **programing**) *n* (*COMPUT*) программи́рование.
programming language *n* (*COMPUT*) язы́к* программи́рования.
progress [*n* ˈprəugrɛs, *vi* prəˈgrɛs] *n* (*advances, changes*) прогре́сс; (*development*) разви́тие ◆ *vi* прогресси́ровать (*impf*); (*move up in rank*) продвига́ться (продви́нуться *perf*) (по слу́жбе); (*continue*) продолжа́ться (продо́лжиться* *perf*); **the meeting/match is in ~** сейча́с идёт собра́ние/матч; **to make ~** де́лать (сде́лать *perf*) успе́хи; **as the match ~ed** по хо́ду ма́тча.
progression [prəˈgrɛʃən] *n* (*gradual development*) продвиже́ние; (*series*) череда́; (*MATH*) прогре́ссия.
progressive [prəˈgrɛsɪv] *adj* прогресси́вный* (прогресси́вен); (*gradual*) постепе́нный.
progressively [prəˈgrɛsɪvlɪ] *adv*: **the work became ~ harder** рабо́та станови́лась всё трудне́е.
progress report *n* (*MED*) протоко́л о хо́де боле́зни; (*ADMIN*) докла́д о хо́де дел.
prohibit [prəˈhɪbɪt] *vt* запреща́ть (запрети́ть* *perf*); **to ~ sb from doing** запреща́ть (запрети́ть* *perf*) кому́-н *+infin*; **"smoking ~ed"** „кури́ть воспреща́ется“.
prohibition [prəuɪˈbɪʃən] *n* запреще́ние, запре́т; **P~** сухо́й зако́н.
prohibitive [prəˈhɪbɪtɪv] *adj* (*price etc*) недосту́пный* (недосту́пен).
project [*n* ˈprɔdʒɛkt, *vb* prəˈdʒɛkt] *n* (*large-scale plan, scheme*) прое́кт; (*SCOL*) рабо́та ◆ *vt* (*plan, estimate*) проекти́ровать (*impf*); (*film*) демонстри́ровать (продемонстри́ровать *perf*); (*light, picture*) проеци́ровать (спроеци́ровать *perf*) ◆ *vi* (*stick out*) выступа́ть (вы́ступить* *perf*).
projectile [prəˈdʒɛktaɪl] *n* снаря́д.
projection [prəˈdʒɛkʃən] *n* (*estimate*) перспекти́вная оце́нка*; (*overhang*) вы́ступ; (*CINEMA*) прое́кция.
projectionist [prəˈdʒɛkʃənɪst] *n* (*CINEMA*) киномеха́ник.
projection room *n* бу́дка киномеха́ника, проекцио́нная каби́на.
projector [prəˈdʒɛktəʳ] *n* (*CINEMA*)

* marks translations which have irregular inflections. The Russian-English side of the dictionary gives inflectional information.

кинопроéктор; (*also:* **slide ~**) проéктор.
proletarian [prəulɪ'tɛərɪən] *adj* пролетáрский*.
proletariat [prəulɪ'tɛərɪət] *n*: **the ~** пролетариáт.
pro-life [prəu'laɪf] *adj выступáющий прóтив абóртов.*
proliferate [prə'lɪfəreɪt] *vi* распространя́ться (распространи́ться *perf*).
proliferation [prəlɪfə'reɪʃən] *n* распространéние.
prolific [prə'lɪfɪk] *adj* плодови́тый (плодови́т).
prologue ['prəulɔg] (*US* **prolog**) *n* прологˊ.
prolong [prə'lɔŋ] *vt* продлевáть (продли́ть *perf*).
prom [prɔm] *n abbr* = **promenade**; (*MUS*) = **promenade concert**; (*US*: *college ball*) студéнческий* бал.
promenade [prɔmə'nɑ:d] *n* променáд, мéсто* для прогу́лок.
promenade concert *n* (*BRIT*) променáдный концéрт (*на котóром часть пу́блики стои́т*).
promenade deck *n* вéрхняя пáлуба.
prominence ['prɔmɪnəns] *n* (*of person*) ви́дное положéние; (*of issue*) ви́дное мéсто.
prominent ['prɔmɪnənt] *adj* (*important, very noticeable*) выдаю́щийся*; **he is ~ in the field of ...** он извéстен в óбласти *+gen* ....
prominently ['prɔmɪnəntlɪ] *adv* замéтно; **he figured ~ in the case** он игрáл замéтную роль в э́том дéле.
promiscuity [prɔmɪs'kju:ɪtɪ] *n* распу́щенность *f*.
promiscuous [prə'mɪskjuəs] *adj* распу́щенный.
promise ['prɔmɪs] *n* (*vow*) обещáние; (*talent*) потенциáл; (*hope*) надéжда ◆ *vi* (*vow*) давáть* (дать* *perf*) обещáние ◆ *vt*: **to ~ sb sth, ~ sth to sb** обещáть (пообещáть *perf*) что-н кому́-н; **a young man of ~** многообещáющий* молодóй человéк*; **she shows ~** онá подаёт надéжды; **to ~ (sb) to do/that** обещáть (пообещáть *perf*) (кому́-н) *+infin*/что; **to ~ well** подавáть* *(impf)* больши́е надéжды.
promising ['prɔmɪsɪŋ] *adj* многообещáющий*.
promissory note ['prɔmɪsərɪ-] *n* (простóй) вéксель* *m*.
promontory ['prɔməntrɪ] *n* мыс*.
promote [prə'məut] *vt* (*employee*) повышáть (повы́сить* *perf*) (в дóлжности); (*product, pop star*) реклами́ровать *(impf/perf)*; (*ideas*) поддéрживать (поддержáть* *perf*); (*venture, event*) содéйствовать *(impf/perf) +dat*; **the team was ~d to the second division** (*BRIT*) комáнда былá переведенá во втору́ю ли́гу.
promoter [prə'məutəʳ] *n* (*of event*) агéнт; (*of cause, idea*) пропаганди́ст(ка*).
promotion [prə'məuʃən] *n* (*at work*) повышéние (в дóлжности); (*of product, event, idea*) реклами́рование; (*publicity campaign*) реклáма.
prompt [prɔmpt] *adj* незамедли́тельный* (незамедли́телен) ◆ *n* (*COMPUT*) приглашéние ◆ *vt* (*cause*) побуждáть (побуди́ть* *perf*); (*sb talking*) подскáзывать (подсказáть* *perf*); (*THEAT*) суфли́ровать *(impf) +dat* ◆ *adv*: **at 8 o'clock ~** рóвно в 8 часóв; **they're very ~** они́ óчень пунктуáльны; **he was ~ to accept** он немéдленно согласи́лся; **to ~ sb to do** побуждáть (побуди́ть* *perf*) когó-н *+infin*.
prompter ['prɔmptəʳ] *n* (*THEAT*) суфлёр.
promptly ['prɔmptlɪ] *adv* (*immediately*) незамедли́тельно; (*exactly*) тóчно.
promptness ['prɔmptnɪs] *n* незамедли́тельность *f*.
promulgate ['prɔməlgeɪt] *vt* обнарóдовать *(impf)*.
prone [prəun] *adj*: **to lie ~** лежáть *(impf)* ничкóм; **~ to** (*inclined to*) склóнный* (склóнен) к *+dat*; **I am ~ to illness** у меня́ слáбое здорóвье; **he is ~ to colds** он подвéржен просту́дам; **she is ~ to burst into tears if you shout at her** éсли на неё кричáть, онá мóжет легкó разрыдáться.
prong [prɔŋ] *n* (*of fork*) зубéц*.
pronoun ['prəunaun] *n* местоимéние.
pronounce [prə'nauns] *vt* (*word*) произноси́ть* (произнести́* *perf*); (*declaration, verdict*) объявля́ть (объяви́ть* *perf*); (*opinion*) выскáзывать (вы́сказать* *perf*) ◆ *vi*: **to ~ (up)on** выскáзываться (вы́сказаться* *perf*) относи́тельно *+gen*; **they ~d him unfit to drive** егó объяви́ли непригóдным к вождéнию автомоби́ля.
pronounced [prə'naunst] *adj* отчётливый (отчёлив).
pronouncement [prə'naunsmənt] *n* объявлéние.
pronto ['prɔntəu] *adv* (*inf*) жи́во.
pronunciation [prənʌnsɪ'eɪʃən] *n* (*of word*) произношéние; (*by person*) вы́говор.
proof [pru:f] *n* (*evidence*) доказáтельство; (*TYP*) корректу́ра; (*test, PHOT*) прóбный отпечáток*; (*of alcohol*) крéпость *f* ◆ *vt* (*BRIT*: *tent, anorak*) дéлать (сдéлать *perf*) водонепроницáемым ◆ *adj*: **this material is ~ against water** э́тот материáл не пропускáет вóду; **this vodka is 70% ~** э́то – семи́десятипроцéнтная вóдка.
proofreader ['pru:fri:dəʳ] *n* коррéктор.
prop [prɔp] *n* (*support*) подпóрка*; (*fig*: *person*) опóра ◆ *vt* (*also:* **~ up**) подпирáть (подперéть* *perf*); (*lean*): **to ~ sth against** прислоня́ть (прислони́ть* *perf*) что-н к *+dat*; **~s** *npl* (*THEAT*) реквизи́т *msg*.
Prop. *abbr* (*COMM*) = **proprietor**.
propaganda [prɔpə'gændə] *n* пропагáнда.
propagate ['prɔpəgeɪt] *vt* (*idea, information*) распространя́ть (распространи́ть *perf*); (*plant*) разводи́ть* (развести́* *perf*).
propagation [prɔpə'geɪʃən] *n* (*see vt*)

распространéние; разведéние.
propel [prəˈpɛl] *vt* (*vehicle, machine*) приводи́ть* (привести́* *perf*) в движéние; (*fig*: *person*) толка́ть (толкну́ть *perf*).
propeller [prəˈpɛləʳ] *n* пропéллер.
propelling pencil [prəˈpɛlɪŋ-] *n* (*BRIT*) автомати́ческий* каранда́ш*.
propensity [prəˈpɛnsɪtɪ] *n*: **a ~ for/to do** располóженность *f* к *+dat/+infin*.
proper [ˈprɔpəʳ] *adj* (*real*) настоя́щий*; (*correct*) подходя́щий*, надлежа́щий*; (*socially acceptable*) прили́чный* (прили́чен); **he looked a ~ fool** (*inf*) он вы́глядел настоя́щим дура́ком; **the village ~** сóбственно дерéвня*; **to go through the ~ channels** проходи́ть* (пройти́* *perf*) чéрез надлежа́щие кана́лы.
properly [ˈprɔpəlɪ] *adv* (*eat, study*) как слéдует; (*behave*) прили́чно, дóлжным óбразом.
proper noun *n* и́мя* *nt* сóбственное.
property [ˈprɔpətɪ] *n* (*possessions*) сóбственность *f*; (*building and its land*) недви́жимость *f*; (*quality*) свóйство ◆ *cpd*: **~ developer** застрóйщик; **it's their ~** э́то их сóбственность; **~ market** ры́нок недви́жимости; **~ tax** налóг на сóбственности.
prophecy [ˈprɔfɪsɪ] *n* прорóчество.
prophesy [ˈprɔfɪsaɪ] *vti* прорóчить (напрорóчить *perf*).
prophet [ˈprɔfɪt] *n* прорóк.
prophetic [prəˈfɛtɪk] *adj* прорóческий*.
proportion [prəˈpɔːʃən] *n* (*part*) часть* *f*, дóля; (*ratio*) пропóрция, соотношéние; **his head is in perfect ~ to his body** головá егó абсолю́тно пропорционáльна егó тéлу; **to be out of all ~ to** никáк не соотвéтствовать (*impf*) *+dat*; **to get sth in(to) ~** соизмеря́ть (соизмéрить *perf*) что-н; **to get sth out of ~** не соизмеря́ть (соизмéрить *perf*) что-н; **a sense of ~** чу́вство мéры.
proportional [prəˈpɔːʃənl] *adj*: **~ (to)** пропорционáльный* (пропорционáлен) (*+dat*).
proportional representation *n* (*POL*) пропорционáльное представи́тельство.
proportionate [prəˈpɔːʃənɪt] *adj*: **~ (to)** пропорционáльный* (пропорционáлен) (*+dat*).
proposal [prəˈpəuzl] *n* предложéние.
propose [prəˈpəuz] *vt* (*plan, toast*) предлагáть (предложи́ть* *perf*); (*motion*) выдвигáть (вы́двинуть *perf*) ◆ *vi* (*offer marriage*): **to ~ (to sb)** дéлать (сдéлать *perf*) предложéние (кому́-н); **to ~ sth/to do** *or* **doing** (*have in mind*) предполагáть (*impf*) что-н/+*infin*.
proposer [prəˈpəuzəʳ] *n* (*BRIT*): **the ~ of the motion** внося́щий(-ая) *m(f) adj* предложéние.
proposition [prɔpəˈzɪʃən] *n* (*statement*) утверждéние; (*offer*) предложéние; **to make sb a ~** дéлать (сдéлать *perf*) предложéние кому́-н.
propound [prəˈpaund] *vt* (*idea, argument*) выдвигáть (вы́двинуть *perf*).
proprietary [prəˈpraɪətərɪ] *adj* (*medicine*) патентóванный; (*brand*) фи́рменный; (*behaviour*) сóбственнический*.
proprietor [prəˈpraɪətəʳ] *n* (*of hotel, shop, newspaper etc*) владéлец(-лица).
propriety [prəˈpraɪətɪ] *n* пристóйность *f*.
propulsion [prəˈpʌlʃən] *n* дви́жущая си́ла.
pro rata [prəuˈrɑːtə] *adv* пропорционáльно ◆ *adj* пропорционáльный* (пропорционáлен); **on a ~ ~ basis** на пропорционáльной оснóве.
prosaic [prəuˈzeɪɪk] *adj* (*person*) прозаи́чный* (прозаи́чен); (*piece of writing*) прозаи́ческий*.
Pros. Atty. *abbr* (*US*) = **prosecuting attorney**.
proscribe [prəˈskraɪb] *vt* воспрещáть (воспрети́ть* *perf*).
prose [prəuz] *n* (*not poetry*) прóза; (*SCOL*) отры́вок* для перевóда.
prosecute [ˈprɔsɪkjuːt] *vt* (*case*) вести́* (*impf*); **to ~ sb** подавáть* (подáть* *perf*) на когó-н в суд.
prosecuting attorney [ˈprɔsɪkjuːtɪŋ-] *n* (*US*) обвини́тель *m*.
prosecution [prɔsɪˈkjuːʃən] *n* (*LAW*: *action*) судéбное преслéдование; (: *accusing side*) обвинéние.
prosecutor [ˈprɔsɪkjuːtəʳ] *n* обвини́тель *m*; (*also*: **public ~**) прокурóр.
prospect [ˈprɔspɛkt] *n* перспекти́ва ◆ *vi*: **to ~ for** развéдывать (развéдать *perf*) на *+acc*; **~s** *npl* (*for work etc*) перспекти́вы *fpl*; **we are faced with the ~ of leaving** нас ожидáет перспекти́ва отъéзда; **there's every ~ of an early victory** есть перспекти́ва скóрой побéды.
prospecting [ˈprɔspɛktɪŋ] *n* развéдка, изыскáние.
prospective [prəˈspɛktɪv] *adj* (*son-in-law*) бу́дущий*; (*customer, candidate*) возмóжный.
prospectus [prəˈspɛktəs] *n* проспéкт.
prosper [ˈprɔspəʳ] *vi* преуспевáть (преуспéть *perf*).
prosperity [prɔˈspɛrɪtɪ] *n* преуспевáние.
prosperous [ˈprɔspərəs] *adj* преуспевáющий.
prostate [ˈprɔsteɪt] *n* (*also*: **~ gland**) предстáтельная железá*.
prostitute [ˈprɔstɪtjuːt] *n* проститу́тка*.
prostitution [prɔstɪˈtjuːʃən] *n* проститу́ция.
prostrate [*vt* prɔˈstreɪt, *adj* ˈprɔstreɪt] *vt*: **to ~ o.s. before** пáдать (упáсть* *perf*) ниц пéред *+instr* ◆ *adj* (*fig*) уби́тый; **to lie ~** лежáть (*impf*)

* marks translations which have irregular inflections. The Russian-English side of the dictionary gives inflectional information.

ничко́м.
protagonist [prə'tægənɪst] *n* (*supporter*) сторо́нник(-ица); (*leading participant*) де́ятель *m*; (*THEAT*) (гла́вный) геро́й.
protect [prə'tɛkt] *vt* защища́ть (защити́ть* *perf*).
protection [prə'tɛkʃən] *n* защи́та; **to be under sb's ~** находи́ться* *(impf)* под защи́той кого́-н.
protectionism [prə'tɛkʃənɪzəm] *n* протекциони́зм.
protection racket *n* рэ́кет.
protective [prə'tɛktɪv] *adj* (*clothing, layer, gesture etc*) защи́тный; (*person*) покрови́тельственный; **~ custody** (*LAW*) опе́ка.
protector [prə'tɛktəʳ] *n* (*person*) защи́тник(-ница); (*device*) защи́тное устро́йство.
protégé ['prəutɛʒeɪ] *n* протеже́ *m ind*.
protégée ['prəutɛʒeɪ] *n* протеже́ *f ind*.
protein ['prəuti:n] *n* бело́к*, протеи́н.
pro tem [prəu'tɛm] *adv abbr* = *pro tempore*; (*for the time being*) вре́менно.
protest [*n* 'prəutɛst, *vb* prə'tɛst] *n* проте́ст ◆ *vi*: **to ~ about/against** протестова́ть *(impf)* по по́воду *+gen*/про́тив *+gen* ◆ *vt* (*insist*): **to ~ that** заявля́ть (заяви́ть* *perf*), что.
Protestant ['prɔtɪstənt] *n* протеста́нт(ка*) ◆ *adj* протеста́нтский*.
protester [prə'tɛstəʳ] *n* протесту́ющий*(-ая) *m(f) adj*.
protest march *n* марш проте́ста.
protestor [prə'tɛstəʳ] *n* = **protester**.
protocol ['prəutəkɔl] *n* протоко́л.
prototype ['prəutətaɪp] *n* прототи́п.
protracted [prə'træktɪd] *adj* затяну́вшийся.
protractor [prə'træktəʳ] *n* (*GEOM*) транспорти́р.
protrude [prə'tru:d] *vi* выдава́ться* *(impf)*.
protuberance [prə'tju:bərəns] *n* вы́пуклость *f*.
proud [praud] *adj*: **~ (of)** го́рдый* (горд) (*+instr*); **I am ~ to know him** я горжу́сь знако́мством с ним *or* тем, что я знако́м с ним; **to do sb ~** (*inf*) принима́ть (приня́ть* *perf*) кого́-н на сла́ву; **to do o.s. ~** (*inf*) име́ть *(impf)* основа́ния горди́ться.
proudly ['praudlɪ] *adv* (*say, smile*) го́рдо; (*show*) с го́рдостью.
prove [pru:v] *vt* дока́зывать (доказа́ть* *perf*) ◆ *vi*: **to ~ (to be)** оказа́ться *(impf/perf) +instr*; **to ~ o.s.** проявля́ть (прояви́ть* *perf*) себя́; **he was ~d right in the end** в конце́ (концо́в) бы́ло дока́зано, что он прав.
Provençal [prɔvɔn'sɑ:l] *adj* прованса́льский.
Provence [prɔ'vɑ̃:s] *n* Прова́нс.
proverb ['prɔvə:b] *n* посло́вица.
proverbial [prə'və:bɪəl] *adj* знамени́тый.
provide [prə'vaɪd] *vt* обеспе́чивать (обеспе́чить *perf*) *+instr*; **to ~ sb with sth** обеспе́чивать (обеспе́чить *perf*) кого́-н чем-н; **to be ~d with** (*person*) быть* *(impf)* обеспе́ченным(-ой); (*thing*) быть* *(impf)* снабжённым(-ой)
▸ **provide for** *vt fus* (*person*) обеспе́чивать (обеспе́чить *perf*); (*future event*) предусма́тривать (предусмотре́ть* *perf*); (*emergency*) забо́титься (позабо́титься *perf*) о *+prp*.
provided (that) [prə'vaɪdɪd-] *conj* при усло́вии, что.
Providence ['prɔvɪdəns] *n* провиде́ние.
providing [prə'vaɪdɪŋ] *conj* = **provided (that)**.
province ['prɔvɪns] *n* (*of country*) о́бласть *f*; (*of person*) о́бласть *f*; **the ~s** *npl*:**in the ~s** (*regions*) в прови́нции.
provincial [prə'vɪnʃəl] *adj* провинциа́льный*.
provision [prə'vɪʒən] *n* (*supplying*) обеспе́чение; (*supply*) снабже́ние; (*stipulation*) усло́вие; (*of contract, agreement*) положе́ние; **~s** *npl* (*food*) прови́зия *fsg*; **to make ~s for** забо́титься (позабо́титься *perf*) о *+prp*; **there's no ~ for this in the contract** в контра́кте э́то не предусмо́трено.
provisional [prə'vɪʒənl] *adj* вре́менный ◆ *n*: **P~** (*IRISH: POL*) *член Ирла́ндской Республика́нской А́рмии*.
provisional licence *n* (*BRIT: AUT*) предвари́тельные води́тельские права́ *ntpl*.
provisionally [prə'vɪʒnəlɪ] *adv* вре́менно.
proviso [prə'vaɪzəu] *n* усло́вие; **with the ~ that** ... с усло́вием, что ....
Provo ['prɔvəu] *n abbr* (*IRISH: POL: inf*) = **Provisional**.
provocation [prɔvə'keɪʃən] *n* провока́ция; **under ~** бу́дучи спровоци́рован.
provocative [prə'vɔkətɪv] *adj* (*remark, article, gesture*) провокацио́нный* (провокацио́нен), вызыва́ющий* (вызыва́ющ); (*intellectually or sexually stimulating*) возбужда́ющий*.
provoke [prə'vəuk] *vt* (*person*) задира́ться *(impf)* к *+dat*; (*fight, argument etc*) провоци́ровать (спровоци́ровать *perf*); **to ~ sb to sth/to do** *or* **into doing** провоци́ровать (спровоци́ровать *perf*) кого́-н на что-н/*+infin*.
provost ['prɔvəst] *n* (*BRIT: of university*) ре́ктор; (*SCOTTISH: POL*) мэр.
prow [prau] *n* (*NAUT*) нос*.
prowess ['prauɪs] *n* мастерство́; **his ~ as a footballer** его́ мастерство́ футболи́ста.
prowl [praul] *vi* (*also:* **~ about, ~ around**) кра́сться* *(impf)* ◆ *n*: **to be on the ~ for** охо́титься* *(impf)* на *+acc*.
prowler ['prauləʳ] *n* подозри́тельный тип.
proximity [prɔk'sɪmɪtɪ] *n* бли́зость *f*.
proxy ['prɔksɪ] *n*: **by ~** по дове́ренности.
PRP *abbr* (= *performance related pay*) *опла́та по результа́там рабо́ты*.
prude [pru:d] *n* ханжа́* *m/f*.
prudence ['pru:dns] *n* благоразу́мие.
prudent ['pru:dnt] *adj* благоразу́мный* (благоразу́мен).

prudish ['pru:dɪʃ] *adj* хáнжеский.
prune [pru:n] *n* чернослúв* *m no pl* ◆ *vt* подрезáть (подрéзать* *perf*).
pry [praɪ] *vi*: **to ~ (into)** совáть* (сýнуть *perf*) нос (в *+acc*).
PS *abbr* = **postscript**.
psalm [sɑ:m] *n* псалóм*.
PSAT *n abbr* (*US*) = *Preliminary Scholastic Aptitude Test*.
PSBR *n abbr* (*BRIT: ECON*: = *public sector borrowing requirement*) *потрéбность госудáрственного сéктора в заёмных срéдствах*.
pseud [sju:d] (*BRIT: inf*) *n* (*intellectually*) псевдоинтеллектуáл(ка*); (*socially*) позёр(ша).
pseudo- ['sju:dəu] *prefix* псéвдо-.
pseudonym ['sju:dənɪm] *n* псевдонúм.
PST *abbr* (*US*) = *Pacific Standard Time*.
PSV *n abbr* (*BRIT*) = **public-service vehicle**.
psyche ['saɪkɪ] *n* псúхика.
psychedelic [saɪkə'dɛlɪk] *adj* психоделúческий.
psychiatric [saɪkɪ'ætrɪk] *adj* психиатрúческий*.
psychiatrist [saɪ'kaɪətrɪst] *n* психиáтр.
psychiatry [saɪ'kaɪətrɪ] *n* психиатрúя.
psychic ['saɪkɪk] *adj* (*person*: *also*: **~al**) ясновúдящий*; (*of the mind*) психúческий*.
psycho ['saɪkəu] *n* (*inf*) псих.
psychoanalyse [saɪkəu'ænəlaɪz] *vt* подвергáть (подвéргнуть *perf*) психоанáлизу.
psychoanalysis [saɪkəuə'nælɪsɪs] *n* психоанáлиз.
psychoanalyst [saɪkəu'ænəlɪst] *n* психоаналúтик.
psychological [saɪkə'lɔdʒɪkl] *adj* психологúческий*.
psychologist [saɪ'kɔlədʒɪst] *n* психóлог.
psychology [saɪ'kɔlədʒɪ] *n* психолóгия.
psychopath ['saɪkəupæθ] *n* психопáт(ка*).
psychoses [saɪ'kəusi:z] *npl of* **psychosis**.
psychosis [saɪ'kəusɪs] (*pl* **psychoses**) *n* психóз.
psychosomatic ['saɪkəusə'mætɪk] *adj* психосоматúческий.
psychotherapy [saɪkəu'θɛrəpɪ] *n* психотерапúя.
psychotic [saɪ'kɔtɪk] *adj* психúчески больнóй.
PT *n abbr* (*BRIT: SCOL*: = *physical training*) физкультýра= *физúческая культýра*.
Pt *abbr* (*in place names*) = *Point*.
pt *abbr* = **pint, point**.
PTA *n abbr* (= *Parent-Teacher Association*) *óбщество по объединéнию усúлий шкóлы и родúтелей*.
Pte *abbr* (*BRIT: MIL*) = **private**.
PTO *abbr* (= *please turn over*) смотрú на оборóте.
PTV *n abbr* (*US*: = *pay television*) *коммéрческое телевúдение*; (= *public television*) *некоммéрческое (общеобразовáтельное) телевúдение*.
pub [pʌb] *n* = **public house**.
pub crawl *n* (*inf*) похóд по пáбам *or* бáрам.
puberty ['pju:bətɪ] *n* половáя зрéлость *f*.
pubic ['pju:bɪk] *adj* лобкóвый.
public ['pʌblɪk] *adj* общéственный; (*statement, action etc*) публúчный ◆ *n*: **the ~** (*all people of country*) нарóд; (*particular set of people*) пýблика; **the general ~** широ́кая общéственность; **this is ~ knowledge** это широкó извéстно; **to make ~** предавáть* (предáть* *perf*) глáсности; **to go ~** (*COMM*) выпускáть (вы́пустить* *perf*) áкции на продáжу чéрез бúржу; **in ~** публúчно.
public-address system [pʌblɪkə'drɛs-] *n* (радио)трансля́ция.
publican ['pʌblɪkən] *n* содержáтель(ница) *m(f)* пивнóго бáра *or* пáба.
publication [pʌblɪ'keɪʃən] *n* публикáция, издáние.
public company *n* (*COMM*) публúчная компáния, компáния откры́того тúпа.
public convenience *n* (*BRIT*) общéственный туалéт.
public holiday *n* общенарóдный прáздник.
public house *n* (*BRIT*) паб, пивнáя *f adj*, пивнóй бар.
publicity [pʌb'lɪsɪtɪ] *n* (*information*) реклáма, паблúсити *nt ind*; (*attention*) шумúха.
publicize ['pʌblɪsaɪz] *vt* (*fact, event*) предавáть* (предáть* *perf*) глáсности.
public limited company *n* (*COMM*) публúчная компáния с ограничéнной отвéтственностью.
publicly ['pʌblɪklɪ] *adv* публúчно; (*COMM*): **~ owned** госудáрственный.
public opinion *n* общéственное мнéние.
public ownership *n*: **to be taken into ~ ~** (*COMM*) переходúть* (перейтú* *perf*) в госудáрственную *or* общенарóдную сóбственность.
Public Prosecutor *n* ≈ генерáльный поркурóр.
public relations *npl* свя́зи *fpl* с общéственностью.
public relations officer *n* сотрýдник отдéла свя́зей с общéственностью.
public school *n* (*BRIT*) чáстная шкóла; (*US*) госудáрственная шкóла.
public sector *n*: **the ~ ~** госудáрственный сéктор.
public-service vehicle [pʌblɪk'sə:vɪs-] *n* (*BRIT*) общéственное трáнспортное срéдство.
public-spirited [pʌblɪk'spɪrɪtɪd] *adj* забóтящийся об общéственных интерéсах.
public transport *n* общéственный трáнспорт.

* marks translations which have irregular inflections. The Russian-English side of the dictionary gives inflectional information.

public utility *n компания, обеспечивающая какой-либо вид коммунальных услуг.*
public works *npl* общественные сооружения *ntpl*.
publish ['pʌblɪʃ] *vt* (*book, magazine*) издавать* (издать* *perf*); (*letter, article*) публиковать (опубликовать *perf*).
publisher ['pʌblɪʃə^r] *n* (*person*) издатель *m*; (*company*) издательство.
publishing ['pʌblɪʃɪŋ] *n* (*profession*) издательское дело; (*of a book*) издание, публикация.
publishing company *n* издательство.
puce [pju:s] *adj* красновато-коричневый.
puck [pʌk] *n* (ICE HOCKEY) шайба.
pucker ['pʌkə^r] *vt* морщить (наморщить *or* сморщить *perf*).
pudding ['pudɪŋ] *n* пудинг; (BRIT: *dessert*) сладкое *nt adj*; **rice ~** рисовый пудинг; **black ~**, (US) **blood ~** кровяная колбаса*.
puddle ['pʌdl] *n* лужа.
puerile ['pjuəraɪl] *adj* ребяческий*.
Puerto Rico ['pwə:təu'ri:kəu] *n* Пуэрто-Рико *f ind*.
puff [pʌf] *n* (*of cigarette, pipe*) затяжка*; (*gasp*) пыхтение; (*of wind*) дуновение; (*of smoke*) клуб ◆ *vi* (*breathe loudly*) пыхтеть* (*impf*) ◆ *vt*: **to ~ one's pipe** затягиваться (затянуться* *perf*)
▸ **puff out** *vt* (*chest, cheeks*) раздувать (раздуть *perf*); (*smoke*) выпускать (выпустить* *perf*).
puffed [pʌft] *adj* (*inf*: *out of breath*) запыхавшийся.
puffin ['pʌfɪn] *n* (ZOOL) тупик.
puff pastry (US **puff paste**) *n* слоёное тесто.
puffy ['pʌfɪ] *adj* опухший*.
pugnacious [pʌg'neɪʃəs] *adj* задиристый (задирист).
pull [pul] *n* (*of moon, magnet, the sea etc*) притяжение; (*fig*) тяга ◆ *vt* тянуть* (потянуть* *perf*); (*trigger*) нажимать (нажать *perf*) на *+acc*; (*close*: *curtains, blind*) задёргивать (задёрнуть *perf*); (*inf*: *people*) привлекать (привлечь* *perf*); (*pint of beer*) накачивать (накачать *perf*) ◆ *vi* (*tug*) тянуть* (*impf*); **to give sth a ~** (*tug*) тянуть* (потянуть* *perf*); **to ~ a face** кроить (скроить *perf*) гримасу; **to ~ to pieces** разрывать (разорвать* *perf*) на части; **to ~ one's punches** драться* (*impf*) вполсилы; **he doesn't ~ his punches** (*fig*) он дерётся всерьёз; **to ~ one's weight** выполнять (выполнить *perf*) свою часть работы; **to ~ o.s. together** взять* (*perf*) себя в руки; **to ~ sb's leg** (*fig*) разыгрывать (разыграть *perf*) кого-н; **to ~ strings (for sb)** пускать (пустить* *perf*) в ход все связи (для кого-н)
▸ **pull about** *vt* (BRIT: *object, person*) трепать (*impf*)
▸ **pull apart** *vt* разрывать (разорвать* *perf*) на куски
▸ **pull back** *vi* отступать (отступить* *perf*)
▸ **pull down** *vt* (*building*) сносить* (снести* *perf*); (*tree*) срубать (срубить* *perf*)
▸ **pull in** *vt* (*money*) загребать (загрести* *perf*); (*crowds, people*) привлекать (привлечь* *perf*); (*subj*: *police*: *suspect*) сцапать (*perf*)
▸ **pull into** *vt* (AUT) подъезжать (подъехать* *perf*) к *+dat*
▸ **pull off** *vt* (*clothes etc*) стягивать (стянуть* *perf*); (*fig*): **he managed to ~ it off** ему удалось скинуть это с себя
▸ **pull out** *vt* (*extract*) вытаскивать (вытащить *perf*) ◆ *vi*: **to ~ out (from)** (AUT: *from kerb*) отъезжать (отъехать* *perf*) (от *+gen*); (RAIL) отходить* (отойти* *perf*) (от *+gen*); (*withdraw*): **to ~ out (of)** выходить* (выйти* *perf*) (из *+gen*)
▸ **pull over** *vi* (AUT) подъезжать (подъехать* *perf*) к краю дороги
▸ **pull round** *vi* (*unconscious person*) приходить* (прийти* *perf*) в себя; (*sick person*) поправляться (поправиться* *perf*)
▸ **pull through** *vi* (MED) выкарабкиваться (выкарабкаться *perf*)
▸ **pull up** *vi* (*stop*) останавливаться (остановиться* *perf*) ◆ *vt* (*object, clothing*) подтягивать (подтянуть* *perf*); (*plant*) вырывать (вырвать* *perf*) (с корнем); (*chair*) пододвигать (пододвинуть *perf*).
pullback ['pulbæk] *n* отступление.
pulley ['pulɪ] *n* шкив*.
pull-out ['pulaut] *n* (*of forces etc*) отход ◆ *cpd* (*pages*) вкладной; **~ magazine** журнал с вкладками.
pullover ['puləuvə^r] *n* пуловер.
pulp [pʌlp] *n* (*of fruit*) мякоть *f*; (*for paper*) бумажная масса; (*pej*: *magazines, fiction*) чтиво; **to reduce sth to a ~** превращать (превратить* *perf*) что-н в мягкую массу *or* пульпу.
pulpit ['pulpɪt] *n* кафедра.
pulsate [pʌl'seɪt] *vi* пульсировать (*impf*); (*music*) вибрировать (*impf*).
pulse [pʌls] *n* (ANAT) пульс; (*of blood*) пульсирование; (*of heart*) биение; (*rhythm*) такт ◆ *vi* пульсировать* (*impf*); **~s** *npl* (BOT) *семена бобовых, употребляемые в пищу*; (CULIN) бобовые *pl adj*; **to take** *or* **feel sb's ~** нащупывать (нащупать *perf*) чей-н пульс.
pulverize ['pʌlvəraɪz] *vt* размельчать (размельчить *perf*); (*fig*: *destroy*) изничтожать (изничтожить *perf*).
puma ['pju:mə] *n* пума.
pumice ['pʌmɪs] *n* (*also*: **~ stone**) пемза.
pummel ['pʌml] *vt* колотить* (*impf*).
pump [pʌmp] *n* насос; (*also*: **petrol ~**) бензоколонка*; (*shoe*) парусиновая туфля* ◆ *vt* качать (*impf*); (*extract*: *oil, water, gas*) выкачивать (выкачать *perf*); **to ~ sb for information** выкачивать (*impf*) из кого-н

информáцию
▸ **pump up** *vt* накáчивать (накачáть *perf*).
pumpkin ['pʌmpkɪn] *n* тыква.
pun [pʌn] *n* каламбýр.
punch [pʌntʃ] *n* (*blow*) удáр; (*fig*: *force*) заря́д; (*for making holes*) дырокóл; (*drink*) пунш ◆ *vt* (*make a hole in*) пробивáть (проби́ть* *perf*); (*hit*): **to ~ sb/sth** ударя́ть (удáрить *perf*) когó-н/что-н кулакóм; **to ~ a hole (in)** пробивáть (проби́ть* *perf*) отвéрстие (в +*prp*)
▸ **punch in** *vi* (*US*) отмечáться (отмéтиться* *perf*) (*приходя́ на рабóту*)
▸ **punch out** *vi* (*US*) отмечáться (отмéтиться* *perf*) (*уходя́ с рабóты*).
Punch and Judy show *n* Панч и Джýди (*кýкольное представлéние*).
punch-drunk ['pʌntʃdrʌŋk] (*BRIT*) *adj* (*confused*) со смýтным; **~ boxer** боксёр с травматологи́ческой энцефалопáтией.
punch(ed) card *n* (*COMPUT*) перфокáрта.
punch line *n* изю́минка.
punch-up ['pʌntʃʌp] *n* (*BRIT*: *inf*) потасóвка*.
punctual ['pʌŋktjuəl] *adj* пунктуáльный* (пунктуáлен).
punctuality [pʌŋktju'ælɪtɪ] *n* пунктуáльность *f*.
punctually ['pʌŋktjuəlɪ] *adv* (*arrive, leave, deliver*) пунктуáльно; **the film will start ~ at 6** фильм начнётся рóвно в 6 часóв.
punctuation [pʌŋktju'eɪʃən] *n* пунктуáция.
punctuation mark *n* знак препинáния.
puncture ['pʌŋktʃə^r] *n* (*AUT*) прокóл ◆ *vt* прокáлывать (проколóть* *perf*); **I have a ~** у меня́ прокóлота ши́на.
pundit ['pʌndɪt] *n* дóка *m/f*.
pungent ['pʌndʒənt] *adj* éдкий* (éдок).
punish ['pʌnɪʃ] *vt* (*person*) накáзывать (наказáть* *perf*); **to ~ sb for sth** накáзывать (наказáть* *perf*) когó-н за что-н; **this crime must be ~ed** это преступлéние должнó быть* накáзано.
punishable ['pʌnɪʃəbl] *adj* наказýемый (наказýем).
punishing ['pʌnɪʃɪŋ] *adj* (*fig*: *defeat, exercise*) измáтывающий.
punishment ['pʌnɪʃmənt] *n* наказáние; **he took a lot of ~** (*inf*: *boxer*) емý си́льно достáлось.
punitive ['pju:nɪtɪv] *adj* карáтельный.
Punjab [pʌn'dʒɑ:b] *n* Пенджáб.
Punjabi [pʌn'dʒɑ:bɪ] *n* пенджáбец*(-бка*); (*LING*) пенджáбский* язы́к* ◆ *adj* пенджáбский*.
punk [pʌŋk] *n* (*also*: **~ rocker**) панк; (*also*: **~ rock**) панк-рок; (*US*: *inf*: *thug*) громи́ла *m*.
punnet ['pʌnɪt] *n* корзи́ночка*.
punt [pʌnt] *n* (*boat*) плоскодóнка* ◆ *vi* плáвать/плыть* (*impf*) на плоскодóнке.
punter ['pʌntə^r] *n* (*BRIT*: *gambler*) (профессионáльный) игрóк*; (*inf*: *customer*) клиéнт(ка*); **the ~s** (*inf*) клиентýра *fsg*.
puny ['pju:nɪ] *adj* хи́лый (хил).
pup [pʌp] *n* (*young dog, seal etc*) щенóк*.
pupil ['pju:pl] *n* (*SCOL*) учени́к*(-и́ца); (*of eye*) зрачóк*.
puppet ['pʌpɪt] *n* (*also fig*) марионéтка*.
puppet government *n* марионéточное прави́тельство.
puppy ['pʌpɪ] *n* (*young dog*) щенóк*.
purchase ['pə:tʃɪs] *n* покýпка*; (*grip etc*) захвáт ◆ *vt* покупáть (купи́ть* *perf*); **to get a ~ on** ухвáтываться (ухвати́ться* *perf*) за +*acc*.
purchase order *n* закáз на товáры.
purchase price *n* закýпочная ценá*.
purchaser ['pə:tʃɪsə^r] *n* покупáтель *m*.
purchase tax *n* налóг на покýпку.
purchasing power ['pə:tʃɪsɪŋ-] *n* покупáтельная спосóбность *f*.
pure [pjuə^r] *adj* чи́стый; (*water, air, woman*) чи́стый* (чист); **a ~ wool jumper** сви́тер из чи́стой шéрсти; **~ and simple** прóсто-нáпросто; **it's laziness ~ and simple** это прóсто-нáпросто лень.
purebred ['pjuəbrɛd] *adj* чистопорóдный, чистокрóвный.
purée ['pjuəreɪ] *n* пюрé *nt ind*.
purely ['pjuəlɪ] *adv* чи́сто.
purgatory ['pə:gətərɪ] *n* (*REL*) чисти́лище; (*fig*) мучéние.
purge [pə:dʒ] *n* (*POL*) чи́стка*; (*MED*) слаби́тельное *nt adj* ◆ *vt* (*thoughts, mind etc*) очищáть (очи́стить* *perf*); (*organization*): **to ~ (of)** чи́стить* (очи́стить* *perf*) (от +*gen*); (*extremists etc*): **to ~ from** вычищáть (вы́чистить* *perf*) от +*gen*.
purification [pjuərɪfɪ'keɪʃən] *n* очи́стка*.
purify ['pjuərɪfaɪ] *vt* очищáть (очи́стить* *perf*).
purist ['pjuərɪst] *n* пури́ст.
puritan ['pjuərɪtən] *n* пуритáнин*(-áнка*).
puritanical [pjuərɪ'tænɪkl] *adj* пуритáнский*.
purity ['pjuərɪtɪ] *n* чистотá.
purl [pə:l] *n* изнáночная вя́зка ◆ *vt* провя́зывать (провязáть *perf*) изнáночной вя́зкой.
purloin [pə:'lɔɪn] *vt* присвáивать (присвóить *perf*).
purple ['pə:pl] *adj* фиолéтовый.
purport [pə:'pɔ:t] *vi*: **he ~s to be an objective party** он притязáет на роль объекти́вного наблюдáтеля; **he ~s to care about this** он утверждáет, что он обеспокóен этим.
purpose ['pə:pəs] *n* цель *f*; **on ~** намéренно; **for illustrative ~s** в кáчестве иллюстрáции; **for the ~s of this meeting** преслéдуя цéли дáнного собрáния; **to no ~** напрáсно.
purpose-built ['pə:pəs'bɪlt] *adj* (*BRIT*): **~ school** шкóла целевóго назначéния.
purposeful ['pə:pəsful] *adj* целеустремлённый*

* marks translations which have irregular inflections. The Russian-English side of the dictionary gives inflectional information.

(целеустремлён).
purposely ['pə:pəslı] *adv* преднаме́ренно.
purr [pə:ʳ] *vi* мурлы́кать* *(impf)*.
purse [pə:s] *n* (*BRIT*) кошелёк*; (*US*: *handbag*) су́мка* ◆ *vt*: **to ~ one's lips** поджима́ть (поджа́ть* *perf*) гу́бы.
purser ['pə:səʳ] *n* (*NAUT*) (судово́й) казначе́й.
purse-snatcher ['pə:ssnætʃəʳ] *n* (*US*) *вор, краду́щий су́мки.*
pursue [pə'sju:] *vt* (*person, thing, aim*) пресле́довать *(impf)*; (*fig*: *activity*) осуществля́ть *(impf)*; (: *interest*) занима́ться *(impf) +instr*; (: *plan*) сле́довать *(impf) +dat*.
pursuer [pə'sju:əʳ] *n* пресле́дователь(ница) *m(f)*.
pursuit [pə'sju:t] *n* (*of person, thing*) пресле́дование; (*of happiness, wealth etc*) по́иски *mpl*; (*pastime*) заня́тие; **scientific ~s** нау́чные по́иски; **in (the) ~ of sth** (*of wealth, fame*) в пого́не за чем-н; (*of truth, knowledge*) в по́исках чего́-н.
purveyor [pə'veıəʳ] *n* поставщи́к(-и́ца).
pus [pʌs] *n* гной.
push [puʃ] *n* (*of button etc*) нажа́тие; (*of car, door, person etc*) толчо́к*; (*fig*: *urgent demand*) тре́бование ◆ *vt* (*press*) нажима́ть (нажа́ть* *perf*); (*shove*) толка́ть (толкну́ть *perf*); (*promote*) прота́лкивать (протолкну́ть *perf*) ◆ *vi* (*press*) нажима́ть (нажа́ть* *perf*); (*shove*) толка́ться *(impf)*; (*fig*): **to ~ for** тре́бовать (потре́бовать *perf*) *+acc or* +gen; **at a ~** (*BRIT*: *inf*) при жела́нии; **to ~ a door open** распа́хивать (распахну́ть *perf*) дверь; **to ~ a door shut** захло́пывать (захло́пнуть *perf*) дверь; **"push"** (*on door*) „от себя́"; (*on bell*) „нажми́те"; **to be ~ed for time/money** име́ть *(impf)* ма́ло вре́мени/де́нег; **she is ~ing fifty** (*inf*) ей под пятьдеся́т
▸ **push aside** *vt* (*person, object*) отта́лкивать (оттолкну́ть *perf*); (*issue*) отмета́ть (отмести́* *perf*)
▸ **push in** *vi* влеза́ть (влезть* *perf*)
▸ **push off** *vi* (*inf*) убира́ться (убра́ться* *perf*)
▸ **push on** *vi* (*continue*) дви́гаться *(impf)* да́льше *or* вперёд
▸ **push over** *vt* опроки́дывать (опроки́нуть *perf*)
▸ **push through** *vi* (*crowd etc*) прота́лкиваться (протолкну́ться *perf*) ◆ *vt* (*measure, scheme*) прота́лкивать (протолкну́ть *perf*)
▸ **push up** *vt* (*prices*) повыша́ть (повы́сить* *perf*).
push-bike ['puʃbaık] *n* (*BRIT*) велосипе́д.
push-button ['puʃbʌtn] *adj* кно́пка*.
pushchair ['puʃtʃɛəʳ] *n* (*BRIT*) (складна́я) коля́ска*.
pusher ['puʃəʳ] *n* (*drug pusher*) торго́вец* (-вка*) нарко́тиками.
pushover ['puʃəuvəʳ] *n* (*inf*): **it's a ~** э́то па́ра пустяко́в *or* пустяко́вое де́ло.
push-up ['puʃʌp] *n* (*US*: *press-up*) отжима́ние.
pushy ['puʃı] *adj* (*pej*: *person*) насты́рный* (насты́рен).
puss [pus] *n* (*inf*) ки́ска*.
pussy(cat) ['pusı(kæt)] *n* (*inf*: *female*) ки́ска*; (: *male*) ко́тик.
put [put] (*pt, pp* **put**) *vt* (*thing*: *horizontally*) класть* (положи́ть *perf*); (: *vertically*) ста́вить* (поста́вить* *perf*); (*person*: *in institution*) помеща́ть (помести́ть* *perf*); (: *in prison, in situation*) сажа́ть (посади́ть* *perf*); (*idea, remark etc*) говори́ть (сказа́ть* *perf*); (*case, view*) излага́ть (изложи́ть* *perf*); (*question, word, sentence*) ста́вить* (поста́вить* *perf*); (*estimate*) относи́ть* (отнести́* *perf*), ста́вить* (поста́вить* *perf*); **to ~ sb in a good mood** приводи́ть* (привести́* *perf*) кого́-н в хоро́шее настрое́ние; **to ~ sb in a bad mood** по́ртить* (испо́ртить* *perf*) кому́-н настрое́ние; **to ~ sb to bed** укла́дывать (уложи́ть* *perf*) кого́-н спать *or* в крова́ть; **to ~ sb to a lot of trouble** доставля́ть (доста́вить* *perf*) кому́-н мно́го хлопо́т; **how shall I ~ it?** как бы э́то сказа́ть?; **to ~ a lot of time into sth** уделя́ть (удели́ть *perf*) мно́го вре́мени чему́-н; **to ~ money on a horse** ста́вить* (поста́вить* *perf*) на ло́шадь; **the cost is now ~ at 2 billion pounds** сейча́с сто́имость оце́нивается в 2 миллиа́рда фу́нта; **I ~ it to you that ...** я говорю́ Вам, что ...; **to stay ~** остава́ться* (оста́ться* *perf*)
▸ **put about** *vi* (*NAUT*) развора́чиваться (разверну́ться *perf*) ◆ *vt* (*rumour*) пуска́ть (пусти́ть* *perf*)
▸ **put across** *vt* (*ideas etc*) объясня́ть (объясни́ть *perf*)
▸ **put around** *vt* = **put about**
▸ **put aside** *vt* откла́дывать (отложи́ть* *perf*); (*idea*) отгоня́ть (отогна́ть* *perf*)
▸ **put away** *vt* (*store*) убира́ть (убра́ть* *perf*); (*eat*) умина́ть (умя́ть* *perf*); (*save*) откла́дывать (отложи́ть* *perf*); (*imprison*) упря́тать* *(perf)*
▸ **put back** *vt* (*replace*) класть* (положи́ть* *perf*) на ме́сто; (*postpone*) откла́дывать (отложи́ть* *perf*); (*delay*) заде́рживать (задержа́ть* *perf*); **this will ~ us back 10 years** э́то отбро́сит нас на 10 лет наза́д
▸ **put by** *vt* откла́дывать (отложи́ть* *perf*)
▸ **put down** *vt* (*place*) класть* (положи́ть* *perf*), ста́вить* (поста́вить* *perf*); (*note down*) запи́сывать (записа́ть* *perf*); (*suppress, humiliate*) подавля́ть (подави́ть* *perf*); (*animal*: *kill*) умерщвля́ть (умертви́ть* *perf*); (*attribute*): **to ~ sth down to** объясня́ть (объясни́ть *perf*) что-н *+instr*
▸ **put forth** *vt* объявля́ть (объяви́ть* *perf*)
▸ **put forward** *vt* (*ideas, proposal*) выдвига́ть (вы́двинуть *perf*); (*date*) переноси́ть* (перенести́* *perf*); (*watch, clock*) переводи́ть* (перевести́* *perf*) вперёд
▸ **put in** *vt* (*application, complaint*) подава́ть* (пода́ть* *perf*); (*time, effort*) вкла́дывать

(вложи́ть *perf*); (*gas, electricity*) проводи́ть* (провести́* *perf*) ◆ *vi* (*NAUT*) заходи́ть* (зайти́* *perf*) в порт; **the ship ~ in at Plymouth** кора́бль* зашёл в Пли́мут
▸ **put in for** *vt fus* (*job, promotion*) подава́ть* (пода́ть* *perf*) заявле́ние на *+acc*
▸ **put off** *vt* (*delay*) откла́дывать (отложи́ть* *perf*); (*discourage*) отта́лкивать (оттолкну́ть *perf*); (*switch off*) выключа́ть (вы́ключить *perf*)
▸ **put on** *vt* (*clothes*) надева́ть (наде́ть* *perf*); (*make-up, ointment etc*) накла́дывать (наложи́ть* *perf*); (*light etc*) включа́ть (включи́ть* *perf*); (*play, kettle, record, dinner*) ста́вить* (поста́вить* *perf*); (*brake*) жать* (нажа́ть* *perf*) на *+acc*; (*extra bus, train etc*) пуска́ть (пусти́ть* *perf*); (*assume: look*) напуска́ть (напусти́ть* *perf*) на себя́; (*behaviour*) принима́ть (приня́ть* *perf*); (*inf: tease*) разы́грывать (разыгра́ть *perf*); (*inform, indicate*): **to ~ sb on to sb** связа́ть* (*perf*) кого́-н с кем-н; **to ~ sb on to sth** выводи́ть* (вы́вести* *perf*) кого́-н на что-н; **to ~ on weight** поправля́ться (попра́виться* *perf*); **to ~ on airs** ва́жничать (*impf*)
▸ **put out** *vt* (*fire*) туши́ть* (потуши́ть* *perf*); (*candle, cigarette*) гаси́ть* (погаси́ть* *perf*); (*electric light*) выключа́ть (вы́ключить *perf*); (*rubbish*) выноси́ть* (вы́нести* *perf*); (*cat*) выпуска́ть (вы́пустить* *perf*); (*one's hand*) вытя́гивать (вы́тянуть *perf*); (*story*) выду́мывать (вы́думать *perf*), пуска́ть (пусти́ть* *perf*); (*BRIT: dislocate*) выви́хивать (вы́вихнуть *perf*); (*inf*): **he was rather ~ out** он был вы́бит из колеи́ ◆ *vi* (*NAUT*): **to ~ out to sea** выходи́ть* (вы́йти* *perf*) в мо́ре; **to ~ out from Plymouth** выходи́ть* (вы́йти* *perf*) из Пли́мута
▸ **put through** *vt* (*person, call*) соединя́ть (соедини́ть *perf*); (*plan, agreement*) выполня́ть (вы́полнить *perf*); **~ me through to Miss Blair** соедини́те меня́ с мисс Блэр
▸ **put together** *vt* соединя́ть (соедини́ть *perf*); (*furniture, toys etc*) собира́ть (собра́ть* *perf*); (*meal*) гото́вить* (пригото́вить* *perf*); (*plan, campaign*) организова́ть (*impf/perf*)
▸ **put up** *vt* (*building, tent*) ста́вить* (поста́вить* *perf*); (*umbrella*) раскрыва́ть (раскры́ть* *perf*); (*hood*) надева́ть (наде́ть* *perf*); (*poster, sign etc*) выве́шивать (вы́весить* *perf*); (*price, cost*) поднима́ть (подня́ть* *perf*); (*guest, visitor*) размеща́ть (размести́ть* *perf*); (*opposition, resistance*) подавля́ть (подави́ть* *perf*); (*incite*): **to ~ sb up to sth** толка́ть (толкну́ть *perf*) кого́-н на что-н; **to ~ sth up for sale** выставля́ть (вы́ставить* *perf*) что-н на прода́жу
▸ **put upon** *vt fus*: **to be ~ upon**: **we are not prepared to be ~ upon** мы не привы́кли, что́бы на нас е́здили
▸ **put up with** *vt fus* терпе́ть (*impf*), мири́ться (*impf*) с *+instr*.

putative ['pju:tətɪv] *adj* предполага́емый.
putrid ['pju:trɪd] *adj* гнило́й.
putt [pʌt] *n* (*GOLF*) *уда́р, загоня́ющий мяч в лу́нку (в го́льфе)*.
putter ['pʌtə^r] *n* (*GOLF*) *коро́ткая клю́шка для го́льфа* ◆ *vi* (*US*) = **potter**.
putting green ['pʌtɪŋ-] *n по́ле для го́льфа, на кото́ром мяч прогоня́ется к лу́нками а не поддаётся уда́рами*.
putty ['pʌtɪ] *n* зама́зка.
put-up ['putʌp] *n*: **~ job** (*BRIT: inf*) подстро́енное де́ло*.
puzzle ['pʌzl] *n* (*question, mystery*) зага́дка; (*game, toy*) головоло́мка*; (*also*: **crossword ~**) кроссво́рд ◆ *vt* озада́чивать (озада́чить *perf*) ◆ *vi*: **to ~ over sth** лома́ть (*impf*) го́лову над чем-н; **to be ~d about sth** пребыва́ть (*impf*) в недоуме́нии по по́воду чего́-н.
puzzling ['pʌzlɪŋ] *adj* запу́танный* (запу́тан).
PVC *n abbr* (= *polyvinyl chloride*) поливинилхлори́д.
Pvt. *abbr* (*US: MIL*) = **private**.
PW *n abbr* (*US*) = **prisoner of war**.
p.w. *abbr* = *per week*.
PX *n abbr* (*US: MIL*) = **post exchange**.
pygmy ['pɪgmɪ] *n* пигме́й.
pyjamas [pɪ'dʒɑ:məz] (*US* **pajamas**) *npl*: **(a pair of) ~** пижа́ма *fsg*.
pylon ['paɪlən] *n* пило́н, опо́ра.
Pyongyang ['pjɔŋ'jæŋ] *n* Пхенья́н.
pyramid ['pɪrəmɪd] *n* (*ARCHIT, GEOM*) пирами́да; (*pile*) гру́да.
Pyrenean [pɪrə'ni:ən] *adj* пирене́йский.
Pyrenees [pɪrə'ni:z] *npl*: **the ~** Пирене́и *pl*.
Pyrex® ['paɪrɛks] *n* пи́рекс ◆ *cpd*: **~ dish** таре́лка пи́рекс.
python ['paɪθən] *n* пито́н.

* marks translations which have irregular inflections. The Russian-English side of the dictionary gives inflectional information.

~ Q, q ~

Q, q [kju:] *n* (*letter*) *17-ая бу́ква англи́йского алфави́та.*
Qatar [kæ'tɑ:'] *n* Ката́р.
QC *n abbr* (*BRIT*: *LAW*: = *Queen's Counsel*) короле́вский* адвока́т (*адвока́тский ранг*).
QED *abbr* (= *quod erat demonstrandum*) что и тре́бовалось доказа́ть.
QM *n abbr* (*MIL*) = **quartermaster**.
q.t. *n abbr* (*inf*) = *quiet*: **on the ~.** тишко́м.
qty *abbr* (= **quantity**) коли́чество.
quack [kwæk] *n* кря́канье; (*doctor*) шарлата́н ◆ *vi* кря́кать *(impf)*.
quad [kwɔd] *abbr* = **quadrangle, quadruplet**.
quadrangle ['kwɔdræŋgl] *n* (*courtyard*) двор*; (*MATH*) четырёхуго́льник.
quadrilateral [kwɔdrı'lætərəl] *n* четырёхуго́льник.
quadruped ['kwɔdrupɛd] *n* четвероно́гое *nt adj*.
quadruple [kwɔ'dru:pl] *vt* увели́чивать (увели́чить *perf*) в четы́ре ра́за ◆ *vi* увели́чиваться (увели́читься *perf*) в четы́ре ра́за.
quadruplets [kwɔ'dru:plıts] *npl* четы́ре близнеца́.
quagmire ['kwægmaıə'] *n* (*also fig*) тряси́на.
quail [kweıl] *n* (*bird*) пе́репел(-пёлка*) ◆ *vi*: **to ~ at the thought of** содрога́ться (содрогну́ться *perf*) при мы́сли об *+prp*.
quaint [kweınt] *adj* (*house, village*) причу́дливый (причу́длив); (*ideas, customs*) своеобра́зный* (своеобра́зен).
quake [kweık] *vi* трепета́ть* *(impf)*.
Quaker ['kweıkə'] *n* ква́кер.
qualification [kwɔlıfı'keıʃən] *n* (*usu pl*: *academic, vocational*) квалифика́ция *no pl*; (*skill, quality*) ка́чество; (*reservation*) огово́рка*; **what are your ~s?** кака́я у Вас квалифика́ция?
qualified ['kwɔlıfaıd] *adj* (*trained*: *person*) квалифици́рованный (квалифици́рован); (*limited*: *approval etc*) небезусло́вный; **I'm not ~ to discuss/judge that** я не компете́нтен обсужда́ть/суди́ть об э́том; **the show was a ~ success** спекта́кль не по́льзовался осо́бым успе́хом; **he's not ~ for the job** у него́ нет необходи́мой квалифика́ции для э́той рабо́ты.
qualify ['kwɔlıfaı] *vt* (*modify*: *make more specific*) уточня́ть (уточни́ть *perf*); (: *express reservation*) огова́ривать (оговори́ть *perf*); (*make competent*): **to ~ sb to do** позволя́ть (позво́лить *perf*) кому́-н *+infin* ◆ *vi*: **to ~ as an engineer** получа́ть (получи́ть* *perf*) квалифика́цию инжене́ра; (*be eligible*: *for benefit, grant*): **to ~ (for)** име́ть *(impf)* пра́во (на *+acc*); (*in competition*): **to ~ (for)** выходи́ть* (вы́йти* *perf*) (в *+acc*).
qualifying ['kwɔlıfaııŋ] *adj*: **~ exam** квалификацио́нный экза́мен; **~ round** отбо́рочное соревнова́ние.
qualitative ['kwɔlıtətıv] *adj* ка́чественный.
quality ['kwɔlıtı] *n* (*standard, characteristic*) ка́чество; (*property*: *of wood, stone etc*) сво́йство ◆ *cpd* ка́чественный; **of good/poor ~** хоро́шего/плохо́го ка́чества.
quality control *n* контро́ль *m* ка́чества.
quality of life *n* у́ровень* *m* жи́зни.
quality papers *npl* (*BRIT*): **the ~ ~** серьёзные газе́ты *fpl*.
qualm [kwɑ:m] *n* сомне́ние; **to have ~s about** сомнева́ться *(impf)* в *+prp*.
quandary ['kwɔndrı] *n*: **to be in a ~** быть* *(impf)* в затрудне́нии.
quango ['kwæŋgəu] *n abbr* (*BRIT*: = *quasi-autonomous non-governmental organization*) *организа́ция, име́ющая распоряди́тельные и координацио́нные фу́нкции.*
quantifiable ['kwɔntıfaıəbl] *adj* измери́мый (измери́м).
quantitative ['kwɔntıtətıv] *adj* коли́чественный.
quantity ['kwɔntıtı] *n* коли́чество; (*large amount*): **in ~** в большо́м коли́честве; **an unknown ~** зага́дка.
quantity surveyor *n* инжене́р-планови́к* (*на строи́тельных рабо́тах*).
quantum leap ['kwɔntəm-] *n* скачо́к*.
quarantine ['kwɔrnti:n] *n* каранти́н.
quark [kwɑ:k] *n* кварк.
quarrel ['kwɔrl] *n* ссо́ра ◆ *vi*: **to ~ (with)** ссо́риться (поссо́риться *perf*) (с *+instr*); **to have a ~ with sb** поссо́риться *(perf)* с кем-н; **I've no ~ with him** у меня́ нет прете́нзий к нему́; **I can't ~ with that** я не могу́ не согласи́ться с э́тим.
quarrelsome ['kwɔrəlsəm] *adj* вздо́рный* (вздо́рен).
quarry ['kwɔrı] *n* карье́р; (*for stone*)

каменоломня; (*hunted animal*) добыча ◆ *vt* добывать (добыть* *perf*).
quart [kwɔ:t] *n* кварта.
quarter ['kwɔ:tə^r] *n* четверть* *f*; (*of year, town*) квартал; (*US: coin*) *двадцать пять центов* ◆ *vt* делить* (разделить* *perf*) на четыре части; (*MIL: lodge*) квартировать (расквартировать *perf*); **~s** *npl* (*living quarters*) помещение *ntsg*; (: *MIL*) казармы *fpl*; **a ~ of an hour** четверть* *f* часа; **it's a ~ to three,** *or* **(US) of three** сейчас без четверти три; **it's a ~ past three,** *or* **(US) after three** сейчас четверть четвёртого; **from all ~s** отовсюду; **at close ~s** вблизи.
quarterback ['kwɔ:təbæk] *n* (*SPORT*) главный нападающий* (*в американском футболе*).
quarterdeck ['kwɔ:tədɛk] *n* (*NAUT*) квартердек.
quarterfinal ['kwɔ:tə'faɪnl] *n* четвертьфинал.
quarterly ['kwɔ:təlɪ] *adj* (*meeting*) (еже)квартальный; (*payment*) (по)квартальный ◆ *adv* (*meet*) ежеквартально; (*pay*) поквартально ◆ *n* квартальный журнал.
quartermaster ['kwɔ:təmɑ:stə^r] *n* (*MIL*) квартирмейстер.
quartet(te) [kwɔ:'tɛt] *n* (*group*) квартет.
quarto ['kwɔ:təu] *n* (*book*) книга формата ин-кварто.
quartz [kwɔ:ts] *n* кварц ◆ *cpd* кварцевый.
quash [kwɔʃ] *vt* (*verdict, judgement*) отменять (отменить* *perf*).
quasi- ['kweɪzaɪ] *prefix* квази-.
quaver ['kweɪvə^r] *n* (*BRIT: MUS*) восьмая *f adj* ◆ *vi* дрожать (*impf*).
quay [ki:] *n* (*also:* **~side**) пристань* *f*.
quayside ['ki:saɪd] *n* пристань* *f*.
queasiness ['kwi:zɪnɪs] *n* тошнота.
queasy ['kwi:zɪ] *adj*: **I feel a bit ~** меня немного мутит.
Quebec [kwɪ'bɛk] *n* Квебек.
queen [kwi:n] *n* королева; (*also:* **~ bee**) пчелиная матка*; (*CARDS*) дама; (*CHESS*) ферзь* *m*, королева.
queen mother *n* королева-мать* *f*.
Queen's speech *n* (*at Christmas*) обращение (королевы) к подданым; (*at opening of parliament*) тронная речь *f* (королевы).
queer [kwɪə^r] *adj* странный* (странен); (*BRIT*): **I feel ~** мне дурно ◆ *n* (*pej: homosexual*) гомик.
quell [kwɛl] *vt* подавлять (подавить* *perf*).
quench [kwɛntʃ] *vt*: **to ~ one's thirst** утолять (утолить *perf*) жажду.
querulous ['kwɛruləs] *adj* (*voice*) жалобный* (жалобен); (*child*) хныкающий.
query ['kwɪərɪ] *n* вопрос ◆ *vt* подвергать (подвергнуть *perf*) сомнению.
quest [kwɛst] *n* поиск.
question ['kwɛstʃən] *n* вопрос; (*doubt*) сомнение ◆ *vt* (*interrogate*) допрашивать (допросить* *perf*); (*doubt*) сомневаться (*impf*) в +*prp*; **to ask sb a ~, put a ~ to sb** задавать* (задать* *perf*) кому-н вопрос; **to bring** *or* **call sth into ~** ставить* (поставить* *perf*) что-н под вопрос *or* сомнение; **the ~ is ...** вопрос в том, ...; **it's (just) a ~ of finding out** дело (только) за тем, чтобы узнать; **there's some ~ as to whether** существуют некоторые сомнения в том, что; **beyond ~** бесспорно; **that's out of the ~** об этом не может быть* и речи.
questionable ['kwɛstʃənəbl] *adj* сомнительный* (сомнителен).
questioner ['kwɛstʃənə^r] *n* задавший(-ая) *m(f) adj* вопрос.
questioning ['kwɛstʃənɪŋ] *adj* (*expression*) вопросительный* (вопросителен); (*mind*) пытливый (пытлив) ◆ *n* (*POLICE*) допрос.
question mark *n* вопросительный знак.
questionnaire [kwɛstʃə'nɛə^r] *n* анкета.
queue [kju:] (*BRIT*) *n* очередь* *f* ◆ *vi* (*also:* **~ up**) стоять (*impf*) в очереди; **to jump the ~** проходить* (пройти* *perf*) без очереди.
quibble ['kwɪbl] *vi*: **to ~ about** *or* **over** спорить (поспорить *perf*) о +*prp*.
quiche [ki:ʃ] *n* киш (*открытый пирог с овощной итп начинкой*).
quick [kwɪk] *adj* быстрый* (быстр); (*clever: person*) сообразительный* (сообразителен); (: *mind*) живой; (*brief*) короткий* (короток) ◆ *adv* быстро ◆ *n*: **to cut to the ~** задевать (задеть* *perf*) за живое; **be ~!** быстро!, побыстрее!; **to be ~ to act** быстро реагировать (отреагировать *perf*); **she was ~ to see that ...** она сразу заметила, что ...; **to have a ~ look** взглянуть (*perf*); **she has a ~ temper** она вспыльчива.
quicken ['kwɪkən] *vt* ускорять (ускорить *perf*) ◆ *vi* ускоряться (ускориться *perf*).
quick-fire ['kwɪkfaɪə^r] *adj*: **~ questions** град *msg* вопросов.
quicklime ['kwɪklaɪm] *n* негашёная известь *f*.
quickly ['kwɪklɪ] *adv* быстро.
quickness ['kwɪknɪs] *n* быстрота; (*of mind*) живость *f*.
quicksand ['kwɪksænd] *n* зыбучий* песок*.
quickstep ['kwɪkstɛp] *n* куик-степ.
quick-tempered [kwɪk'tɛmpəd] *adj* вспыльчивый (вспыльчив).
quick-witted [kwɪk'wɪtɪd] *adj* сообразительный* (сообразителен).
quid [kwɪd] *n inv* (*BRIT: inf*) фунт (*стерлингов*).
quid pro quo ['kwɪdprəu'kwəu] *n* услуга за услугу.
quiet ['kwaɪət] *adj* (*not loud or noisy*) тихий* (тих); (: *engine*) бесшумный* (бесшумен); (*peaceful, not busy*) спокойный* (спокоен); (*without fuss: wedding etc*) скромный*

* marks translations which have irregular inflections. The Russian-English side of the dictionary gives inflectional information.

(скрóмен) ◆ *n* (*silence*) тишинá; (*peace*) покóй ◆ *vti* (*US*) = **quieten**; **be ~!** тúхо!; **I'll have a ~ word with him** я поговорю с ним наединé; **business is ~ at this time of year** в э́то врéмя гóда в делáх затúшье; **on the ~** тайкóм.

quieten ['kwaɪətn] *vi* (*also:* **~ down**) затихáть (затúхнуть *perf*) ◆ *vt* (*also:* **~ down**) успокáивать (успокóить *perf*).

quietly ['kwaɪətlɪ] *adv* (*not loudly*) тúхо; (*calmly*) спокóйно.

quietness ['kwaɪətnɪs] *n* (*silence*) тишинá; (*peacefulness*) покóй.

quill [kwɪl] *n* перó*; (*of porcupine*) иглá*.

quilt [kwɪlt] *n* (*covering*) стёганое покрывáло; (*also:* **continental ~**) стёганое одеяло.

quilting ['kwɪltɪŋ] *n* (*quilt-making*) стёжка; (*material*) стёганая ткань *f*.

quin [kwɪn] *n abbr* (*BRIT*) = **quintuplet**.

quince [kwɪns] *n* айвá.

quinine [kwɪ'ni:n] *n* хинúн.

quintessential [kwɪntɪ'senʃəl] *adj* показáтельный.

quintet(te) [kwɪn'tɛt] *n* (*group*) квинтéт.

quintuplets [kwɪn'tju:plɪts] *npl* пя́теро* близнецóв.

quip [kwɪp] *n* острóта ◆ *vt* острúть (сострúть *perf*); ... **he ~ped** ... сострúл он.

quire ['kwaɪə'] *n* (*of paper*) десть *f*.

quirk [kwə:k] *n* причýда, прúхоть *f*; **by some ~ of fate** по прúхоти судьбы́.

quit [kwɪt] (*pt, pp* **quit** *or* **quitted**) *vt* бросáть (брóсить* *perf*); (*premises*) съезжáть (съéхать* *perf*) с *+gen* ◆ *vi* (*give up*) сдавáться* (сдáться* *perf*); (*resign*) увольня́ться (уво́литься *perf*); **to ~ smoking** бросáть (брóсить* *perf*) курúть*; **~ stalling!** (*US*: *inf*) перестáньте ходúть вокрýг да óколо!; **they were given 3 months notice to ~** (*BRIT*) их предупредúли, что онú должны́ освободúть помещéние в трёхмéсячный срок.

quite [kwaɪt] *adv* (*rather*) довóльно; (*entirely*) совершéнно; (*following negative*: *almost*): **the flat's not ~ big enough** квартúра недостáточно большáя; **he's ~ right** он совершéнно прав; **she's ~ pretty** онá довóльно симпатúчная; **I ~ understand** я вполнé понимáю; **I'm not ~ sure** я не совсéм увéрен; **not ~ as many as the last time** не так мнóго, как в прóшлый раз; **that lunch was ~ something!** вот э́то был обéд!; **~ a few** довóльно мнóго; **~ (so)!** вéрно!

Quito ['ki:təu] *n* Кúто *m ind*.

quits [kwɪts] *adj*: **to be ~ (with)** быть* (*impf*) в расчёте (с *+instr*); **let's call it ~** бýдем квúты.

quiver ['kwɪvə'] *vi* трепетáть (*impf*).

quiz [kwɪz] *n* (*game*) викторúна ◆ *vt* расспрáшивать (расспросúть* *perf*).

quizzical ['kwɪzɪkl] *adj*: **a ~ look** понимáющий и насмéшливый взгляд.

quoits [kwɔɪts] *npl игрá, заключáющаяся в метáнии колéц в цель*.

quorum ['kwɔ:rəm] *n* квóрум.

quota ['kwəutə] *n* квóта.

quotation [kwəu'teɪʃən] *n* цитáта; (*estimate*) ценá (продавцá); (*of shares etc*) котирóвка*.

quotation marks *npl* кавы́чки *fpl*.

quote [kwəut] *n* (*from book, play etc*) цитáта; (*estimate*) ценá ◆ *vt* цитúровать (процитúровать *perf*); (*figure, example*) приводúть* (привестú* *perf*); (*price*) назначáть (назнáчить *perf*); **~s** *npl* (*quotation marks*) кавы́чки *fpl*; **to ~ for a job** устанáвливать (установúть* *perf*) стóимость *f* рабóты; **in ~s** в кавы́чках; **~ ... unquote** ... в кавы́чках.

quotient ['kwəuʃənt] *n* (*factor*) фáктор.

qv *abbr* = *quod vide*; (*which see*) см.= *смотрú*.

qwerty keyboard ['kwə:tɪ-] *n типúчная английская клавиатýра печáтной машúнки úли компью́тера*.

~ R, r ~

R, r [ɑːʳ] *n* (*letter*) *18-ая бу́ква англи́йского алфави́та.*

R. *abbr* = **right;**(= **river**) р.= *река́*; (= *Réaumur (scale)*) по шкале́ Реомю́ра; (*US*: *CINEMA*: = *restricted*) ≈ до 18-ти лет; (*US*: *POL*) = **republican**; (*BRIT*) = *Rex*; (*BRIT*) = *Regina*.

RA *abbr* (*MIL*) = **rear admiral** ◆ *n abbr* (*BRIT*) = *Royal Academy*; (*BRIT*) = *Royal Academician*.

RAAF *n abbr* (*MIL*) = *Royal Australian Air Force*.

Rabat [rəˈbɑːt] *n* Раба́т.

rabbi [ˈræbaɪ] *n* равви́н.

rabbit [ˈræbɪt] *n* (*male*) кро́лик; (*female*) крольчи́ха ◆ *vi*: **to ~ (on)** (*BRIT*: *inf*) треща́ть (*impf*).

rabbit hole *n* кро́личья нора́*.

rabbit hutch *n* кро́личья кле́тка*.

rabble [ˈræbl] *n* (*pej*) чернь *f*.

rabid [ˈræbɪd] *adj* (*also fig*) бе́шеный.

rabies [ˈreɪbiːz] *n* бе́шенство, водобоя́знь *f*.

RAC *n abbr* (*BRIT*: = *Royal Automobile Club*) Короле́вский автомоби́льный клуб (*крупне́йшая автомоби́льная ассоциа́ция*).

raccoon [rəˈkuːn] *n* ено́т.

race [reɪs] *n* (*species*) ра́са; (*competition*: *NAUT, AUT, SKIING etc*) го́нки* *fpl*; (: *running*) забе́г; (: *swimming*) заплы́в; (: *horse race*) ска́чки* *fpl*; (*for power, control*) борьба́ ◆ *vt* (*horse*) гнать* (*impf*); (*pigeon*) гоня́ть (*impf*); (*car etc*) вести́* (*impf*); (*person*) бежа́ть* (*impf*) наперего́нки с *+instr* ◆ *vi* (*compete*) принима́ть (приня́ть* *perf*) уча́стие в го́нках/забе́ге/заплы́ве/ска́чках; (*hurry*) мча́ться (*impf*); (*pulse*) учаща́ться (участи́ться* *perf*); (*engine*) увели́чивать (увели́чить *perf*) оборо́ты; **the human ~** челове́чество, челове́ческий* род; **the arms ~** го́нка вооруже́ний; **he ~d across the road** он бы́стро перебежа́л че́рез доро́гу; **to ~ in(to)** влета́ть (влете́ть* *perf*) (в *+acc*); **to ~ out (of)** выска́кивать (вы́скочить *perf*) (из *+gen*).

race car *n* (*US*) = **racing car**.

race car driver *n* (*US*) = **racing driver**.

racecourse [ˈreɪskɔːs] *n* ипподро́м.

racehorse [ˈreɪshɔːs] *n* скакова́я ло́шадь* *f*.

race meeting *n* день* *m* ска́чек.

race relations *npl* ра́совые отноше́ния *ntpl*.

racetrack [ˈreɪstræk] *n* (*for people*) бегова́я доро́жка*; (*for cars*) трек; (*US*) = **racecourse**.

racial [ˈreɪʃl] *adj* (*discrimination, prejudice*) ра́совый; **~ equality** ра́совое ра́венство.

racialism [ˈreɪʃlɪzəm] *n* раси́зм.

racialist [ˈreɪʃlɪst] *adj* (*beliefs, attitudes*) раси́стский* ◆ *n* раси́ст(ка*).

racing [ˈreɪsɪŋ] *n* (*horse racing*) ска́чки* *fpl*; (*motor racing*) го́нки* *fpl*.

racing car *n* (*BRIT*) го́ночный автомоби́ль *m*.

racing driver *n* (*BRIT*) го́нщик.

racism [ˈreɪsɪzəm] *n* раси́зм.

racist [ˈreɪsɪst] *adj* (*statement, policy*) раси́стский* ◆ *n* раси́ст(ка*).

rack [ræk] *n* (*shelf*) по́лка*; (*also:* **luggage ~**) бага́жная по́лка*; (*also:* **roof ~**) бага́жник (*на кры́ше автомоби́ля*); (*also:* **dish ~**) суши́лка* для посу́ды ◆ *vt*: **she was ~ed by pain** её терза́ла боль; **to ~ one's brains** лома́ть (*impf*) го́лову; **magazine ~** журна́льная по́лка; **toast ~** подста́вка для то́стов; **shoe ~** по́лка* для о́буви; **to go to ~ and ruin** (*building*) ветша́ть (обветша́ть *perf*); (*business*) разоря́ться (разори́ться *perf*).

racket [ˈrækɪt] *n* (*SPORT*) раке́тка*; (*noise*) шум; (*swindle*) жу́льничество; (*organized crime*) рэ́кет.

racketeer [rækɪˈtɪəʳ] *n* (*esp US*) рэкети́р.

racoon [rəˈkuːn] *n* = **raccoon**.

racquet [ˈrækɪt] *n* (*SPORT*) раке́тка*.

racy [ˈreɪsɪ] *adj* (*book*) пика́нтный* (пика́нтен); (*behaviour etc*) экстравага́нтный* (экстравага́нтен).

RADA [rɑːdə] (*BRIT*) *n abbr* = *Royal Academy of Dramatic Art*.

radar [ˈreɪdɑːʳ] *n* рада́р, радиолока́тор ◆ *cpd* рада́рный, радиолокацио́нный.

radar trap *n* (*AUT*) *радиолокацио́нная лову́шка*.

radial [ˈreɪdɪəl] *adj* (*also:* **~-ply**: *tyre*) радиа́льный.

radiance [ˈreɪdɪəns] *n* (*glow*) сия́ние.

radiant [ˈreɪdɪənt] *adj* (*smile, person*) сия́ющий*; (*PHYS*) лучи́стый.

radiate [ˈreɪdɪeɪt] *vt* (*also fig*) излуча́ть (*impf*) ◆ *vi* (*lines*) радиа́льно расходи́ться* (разойти́сь* *perf*).

* marks translations which have irregular inflections. The Russian-English side of the dictionary gives inflectional information.

radiation [reɪdɪ'eɪʃən] *n* (*radioactive*) радиáция, радиоактúвное излучéние; (*of heat, light*) излучéние.
radiation sickness *n* лучевáя болéзнь *f*.
radiator ['reɪdɪeɪtəʳ] *n* (*heater*) радиáтор, батарéя; (*AUT*) радиáтор.
radiator cap *n* крышка* радиáтора.
radiator grill *n* (*AUT*) решётка* радиáтора.
radical ['rædɪkl] *adj* (*extreme*) радикáльный* (радикáлен) ◆ *n* (*person*) радикáл.
radii ['reɪdɪaɪ] *npl of* **radius**.
radio ['reɪdɪəu] *n* (*broadcasting*) рáдио *nt ind*; (*device: for receiving broadcasts*) радиоприёмник; (: *for transmitting and receiving*) радиопередáтчик ◆ *vt* (*person*) свя́зываться (связáться* *perf*) по рáдио с +*instr*; (*information*) передавáть* (передáть* *perf*) по рáдио ◆ *vi*: **to ~ to sb** радúровать (*impf/perf*) комý-н; **on the ~** по рáдио.
radio... ['reɪdɪəu] *prefix* рáдио....
radioactive ['reɪdɪəu'æktɪv] *adj* радиоактúвный* (радиоактúвен).
radioactivity ['reɪdɪəuæk'tɪvɪtɪ] *n* радиоактúвность *f*.
radio announcer *n* дúктор рáдио.
radio-controlled ['reɪdɪəukən'trəuld] *adj* управля́емый при пóмощи радиосигнáлов.
radiographer [reɪdɪ'ɔgrəfəʳ] *n* рентгенóлог.
radiography [reɪdɪ'ɔgrəfɪ] *n* рентгеногрáфия, радиогрáфия.
radiologist [reɪdɪ'ɔlədʒɪst] *n* рентгенóлог, радиóлог.
radiology [reɪdɪ'ɔlədʒɪ] *n* рентгенолóгия, радиолóгия.
radio station *n* радиостáнция.
radio taxi *n* радиофицúрованное таксú *nt ind*.
radiotelephone ['reɪdɪəu'tɛlɪfəun] *n* радиотелефóн.
radio telescope *n* радиотелескóп.
radiotherapist ['reɪdɪəu'θɛrəpɪst] *n* радиотерапéвт.
radiotherapy ['reɪdɪəu'θɛrəpɪ] *n* радиотерапúя, рентгенотерапúя.
radish ['rædɪʃ] *n* (*one radish*) редúска*; **~es** редúс *msg*, редúска *fsg* (*разг*).
radium ['reɪdɪəm] *n* рáдий.
radius ['reɪdɪəs] (*pl* **radii**) *n* рáдиус; (*ANAT*) лучевáя кость* *f*; **within a ~ of 50 miles** в рáдиусе 50-ти миль.
RAF *n abbr* (*BRIT*) (= **Royal Air Force**) ≈ ВВС= *воéнно-воздýшные сúлы*.
raffia ['ræfɪə] *n* рáфия.
raffish ['ræfɪʃ] *adj* разгýльный* (разгýлен).
raffle ['ræfl] *n* (вещевáя) лотерéя ◆ *vt* (*prize*) разыгрывать (разыгрáть *perf*) в лотерéе.
raft [rɑ:ft] *n* плот*.
rafter ['rɑ:ftəʳ] *n* (*CONSTR*) стропúло.
rag [ræg] *n* тря́пка*; (*pej: newspaper*) газетёнка*; (*SCOL: for charity*) *благотворúтельное шýточное студéнческое представлéние* ◆ *vt* (*BRIT: tease*) тéшиться (потéшиться *perf*) над +*instr*; **~s** *npl* (*torn clothes*) лохмóтья* *pl*; **in ~s** (*person*) в лохмóтьях; (*clothes*) изнóшенный* (изнóшен) до дыр.
rag-and-bone man [rægən'bəun-] *irreg n* (*BRIT*) старьёвщик.
ragbag ['rægbæg] *n* (*fig: inf*) вся́кая вся́чина.
rag doll *n* тряпúчная кýкла*.
rage [reɪdʒ] *n* (*fury*) я́рость *f*, бéшенство ◆ *vi* (*person*) свирéпствовать (*impf*); (*storm, debate*) бушевáть (*impf*); **it's all the ~** (*very fashionable*) все помешáлись на э́том; **to fly into a ~** приходúть* (прийтú* *perf*) в я́рость, свирепéть (рассвирепéть *perf*).
ragged ['rægɪd] *adj* (*edge*) зазýбренный* (зазýбрен); (*clothes*) потрёпанный* (потрёпан), изóрванный (изóрван); (*appearance*) обóрванный* (обóрван).
raging ['reɪdʒɪŋ] *adj* (*sea, storm*) бушýющий; (*pain, fever*) свирéпый; **~ toothache** свирéпая зубнáя боль; **in a ~ temper** в я́рости.
rag trade *n* (*inf*): **the ~ ~** индýстрия одéжды.
raid [reɪd] *n* (*MIL*) рейд; (*criminal*) налёт; (*by police*) облáва, рейд ◆ *vt* (*see n*) совершáть (совершúть *perf*) рейд на +*acc*; совершáть (совершúть *perf*) налёт на +*acc*; устрáивать (устрóить *perf*) облáву *or* рейд на +*acc*.
rail [reɪl] *n* (*on stairs, bridge etc*) перúла *pl*; (*of ship*) борт*; **~s** *npl* (*RAIL*) рéльсы *mpl*; **by ~** пóездом.
railing(s) ['reɪlɪŋ(z)] *n(pl)* (*iron fence*) решётка *fsg*.
railroad ['reɪlrəud] *n* (*US*) = **railway**.
railway ['reɪlweɪ] *n* (*BRIT*) желéзная дорóга ◆ *cpd* железнодорóжный.
railway engine *n* локомотúв.
railway line *n* (*BRIT*) железнодорóжная лúния.
railwayman ['reɪlweɪmən] *irreg n* (*BRIT*) железнодорóжник.
railway station *n* (*BRIT: large*) железнодорóжный вокзáл; (: *small*) железнодорóжная стáнция.
rain [reɪn] *n* дождь* *m* ◆ *vi*: **it's ~ing** идёт дождь ◆ *vt*: **it's ~ing cats and dogs** льёт как из ведрá; **in the ~** под дождём, в дождь; **it ~ed a lot last night** вчерá нóчью шёл сúльный дождь.
rainbow ['reɪnbəu] *n* рáдуга.
rain check *n* (*US*): **I'll take a ~ ~** я ещё немнóго подýмаю.
raincoat ['reɪnkəut] *n* плащ*.
raindrop ['reɪndrɔp] *n* дождевáя кáпля*.
rainfall ['reɪnfɔ:l] *n* осáдки *mpl*; (*measurement*) колúчество осáдков.
rainforest ['reɪnfɔrɪst] *n* тропúческий* лес.
rainproof ['reɪnpru:f] *adj* непромокáемый (непромокáем).
rainstorm ['reɪnstɔ:m] *n* лúвень* *m*.
rainwater ['reɪnwɔ:təʳ] *n* дождевáя водá*.
rainy ['reɪnɪ] *adj* (*day*) дождлúвый (дождлúв); **Manchester is a ~ place** в Манчéстере чáсто идýт дождú; **to save sth for a ~ day**

откла́дывать (отложи́ть* *perf*) что-н на чёрный день.
raise [reɪz] *n* (*esp US: pay rise*) повыше́ние ◆ *vt* (*lift, produce*) поднима́ть (подня́ть* *perf*); (*end: siege, embargo*) снима́ть (снять* *perf*); (*increase, improve*) повыша́ть (повы́сить* *perf*); (*doubts*) выска́зывать (вы́сказать* *perf*); (*rear: cattle*) разводи́ть* (развести́* *perf*); (: *family*) воспи́тывать (воспита́ть* *perf*); (*cultivate: crop*) выра́щивать (вы́растить* *perf*); (*get together: army, funds*) собира́ть (собра́ть* *perf*); (: *loan*) достава́ть* (доста́ть* *perf*); **to ~ a glass to sb/sth** поднима́ть (подня́ть* *perf*) бока́л за кого́-н/что-н; **to ~ one's voice** повыша́ть (повы́сить* *perf*) го́лос; **to ~ one's hopes** обнадёживать (обнадёжить *perf*); **to ~ a laugh/smile** вызыва́ть (вы́звать* *perf*) смех/улы́бку.
raisin ['reɪzn] *n* (*one raisin*) изю́минка*; **~s** изю́м* *m no pl*.
Raj [rɑːdʒ] *n*: **the ~** *пери́од брита́нского правле́ния в И́ндии*.
rajah ['rɑːdʒə] *n* ра́джа.
rake [reɪk] *n* (*tool*) гра́бли* *pl*; (*person*) пове́са *m* ◆ *vt* (*garden*) разра́внивать (разровня́ть *perf*) (гра́блями); (*leaves, hay*) сгреба́ть (сгрести́* *perf*); (*with machine gun*) обстре́ливать (обстреля́ть *perf*) ◆ *vi*: **to ~ through** (*search*) ры́ться* (*impf*) в +*prp*.
rake-off ['reɪkɔf] *n* (*inf*) до́ля* при́были.
rally ['rælɪ] *n* (*POL etc*) ми́тинг; (*AUT*) авторáлли *nt ind*; (*TENNIS*) ра́лли *nt ind* ◆ *vt* (*support*) спла́чивать (сплоти́ть* *perf*) ◆ *vi* (*sick person*) оправля́ться (опра́виться* *perf*); (*Stock Exchange*) оживля́ться (оживи́ться* *perf*)
▸ **rally round** *vt fus* (*fig: give support to*) спла́чиваться (сплоти́ться* *perf*) вокру́г +*gen* ◆ *vi* бра́ться* (взя́ться* *perf*) за де́ло вме́сте.
rallying point ['rælɪɪŋ-] *n* (*idea*) объедини́ющая иде́я.
RAM [ræm] *n abbr* (*COMPUT*) (= **random access memory**) ЗУПВ= *запомина́ющее устро́йство с произво́льной вы́боркой*.
ram [ræm] *n* бара́н ◆ *vt* (*crash into*) тара́нить (протара́нить *perf*); (*push: bolt*) задвига́ть (задви́нуть *perf*); (: *fist*) дви́нуть (*perf*) +*instr*.
ramble ['ræmbl] *n* прогу́лка* ◆ *vi* (*walk*) броди́ть* (*impf*); (*talk: also:* **~ on**) болта́ть (*impf*).
rambler ['ræmblə^r] *n* (*walker*) тури́ст(ка) (*уча́стник пешехо́дной прогу́лки и́ли похо́да*); (*BOT*) вью́щееся расте́ние.
rambling ['ræmblɪŋ] *adj* (*speech*) несвя́зный* (несвя́зен); (*house*) беспоря́дочно вы́строенный (вы́строен); (*BOT*) вью́щийся.
rambunctious [ræm'bʌŋkʃəs] *adj* (*US*) = **rumbustious**.
RAMC *n abbr* (*BRIT*) = *Royal Army Medical Corps*.
ramification [ræmɪfɪ'keɪʃən] *n* сле́дствие.
ramp [ræmp] *n* (*incline*) скат, укло́н; (*in garage*) па́ндус; **on ~** (*US: AUT*) въезд на автостра́ду; **off ~** (*US: AUT*) съезд с автостра́ды.
rampage [ræm'peɪdʒ] *n*: **to be on the ~** бу́йствовать (*impf*) ◆ *vi*: **they went rampaging through the town** они́ бу́йствовали по всему́ го́роду.
rampant ['ræmpənt] *adj*: **to be ~** (*crime*) свире́пствовать (*impf*).
rampart ['ræmpɑːt] *n* крепостно́й вал*.
ram raid *n ограбле́ние, совершённое при по́мощи автотара́на*.
ramshackle ['ræmʃækl] *adj* ве́тхий* (ветх).
RAN *n abbr* = *Royal Australian Navy*.
ran [ræn] *pt of* **run**.
ranch [rɑːntʃ] *n* ра́нчо *nt ind*.
rancher ['rɑːntʃə^r] *n* (*owner*) владе́лец*(-лица) ра́нчо; (*ranch hand*) рабо́тник на ра́нчо.
rancid ['rænsɪd] *adj* (*butter*) прого́рклый; (*bacon*) ту́хлый*.
rancour ['ræŋkə^r] (*US* **rancor**) *n* зло́ба.
R & B *n abbr* (= *rhythm and blues*) ритм и блюз.
R & D *n abbr* (= *research and development*) нау́чно-иссле́довательские и о́пытно-констру́кторские рабо́ты.
random ['rændəm] *adj* (*arrangement, selection*) случа́йный*; (*COMPUT, MATH*) случа́йный, произво́льный ◆ *n*: **at ~** науга́д.
random access *n* (*COMPUT*) прямо́й *or* произво́льный до́ступ.
random access memory *n* (*COMPUT*) запомина́ющее устро́йство с произво́льной вы́боркой.
R & R *n abbr* (*US: MIL*) = *rest and recreation*.
randy ['rændɪ] *adj* (*BRIT: inf*) похотли́вый (похотли́в).
rang [ræŋ] *pt of* **ring**.
range [reɪndʒ] *n* (*series: of proposals, offers*) ряд*; (: *of products*) ассортиме́нт *no pl*, вы́бор *no pl*; (: *of colours*) га́мма; (*of mountains*) цепь* *f*; (*of missile*) да́льность *f*, ра́диус де́йствия; (*of voice*) диапазо́н; (*MIL: also:* **shooting ~**) стре́льбище; (: *indoor*) тир; (*also:* **kitchen ~**) ку́хонная плита́* ◆ *vt* (*place in a line*) выстра́ивать (вы́строить *perf*) ◆ *vi*: **to ~ over** (*extend*) простира́ться (*impf*); **price ~** диапазо́н цен; **do you have anything else in this price ~?** у Вас есть что́-нибудь ещё в преде́лах э́той цены́?; **within (firing) ~** на расстоя́нии вы́стрела; **~d right/left** (*text*) с поля́ми спра́ва/сле́ва; **to ~ from ... to ...** колеба́ться* (*impf*) от +*gen* ... до +*gen* ....
ranger ['reɪndʒə^r] *n* (*in forest*) лесни́чий* *m adj*, лесни́к*; (*in park*) смотри́тель(ница) *m(f)*.
Rangoon [ræŋ'guːn] *n* Рангу́н.
rank [ræŋk] *n* (*row*) ряд*; (*MIL*) шере́нга;

* marks translations which have irregular inflections. The Russian-English side of the dictionary gives inflectional information.

(*status*) чин*, ранг; (*BRIT*: *also*: **taxi ~**) стоянка* такси ◆ *adj* (*stinking*) зловонный* (зловонен); (*injustice*) вопиющий*; (*hypocrisy*) явный* (явен) ◆ *vi*: **to ~ among** числиться *(impf)* среди *+gen* ◆ *vt*: **I ~ him sixth** я ставлю его на шестое место; **the ~s** *npl* (*MIL*) рядовые *pl adj*, рядовой состав *msg*; **the ~ and file** (*fig*) рядовые члены *mpl*; **to close ~s** (*MIL, also fig*) смыкать (сомкнуть *perf*) ряды.
rankle [ˈræŋkl] *vi*: **to ~ with sb** терзать *(impf)* кого-н.
rank outsider *n* совершенно безнадёжный кандидат, кандидат без шансов на успех.
ransack [ˈrænsæk] *vt* (*search*) перерыть* *(perf)*; (*plunder*) грабить* (разграбить* *perf*).
ransom [ˈrænsəm] *n* выкуп; **to hold to ~** (*fig*: *nation, company, individual*) держать *(impf)* в заложниках.
rant [rænt] *vi*: **to ~ and rave** рвать* *(impf)* и метать *(impf)*.
ranting [ˈræntɪŋ] *n* разглагольствование.
rap [ræp] *n* стук; (*POETRY, MUS*) *стиль в музыке или поэзии, характеризующийся отрывистым ритмом, использованием речитатива* ◆ *vi*: **to ~ on a door/table** стучать (постучать *perf*) в дверь/по столу.
rape [reɪp] *n* изнасилование; (*BOT*) рапс ◆ *vt* (*woman*) насиловать (изнасиловать *perf*).
rape(seed) oil [ˈreɪp(si:d)-] *n* рапсовое масло.
rapid [ˈræpɪd] *adj* стремительный* (стремителен).
rapidity [rəˈpɪdɪtɪ] *n* стремительность *f*.
rapidly [ˈræpɪdlɪ] *adv* стремительно.
rapids [ˈræpɪdz] *npl* (*GEO*) стремнина *fsg*.
rapist [ˈreɪpɪst] *n* насильник.
rapport [ræˈpɔ:ʳ] *n* взаимопонимание.
rapprochement [ræˈprɔʃmɑ̃:ŋ] *n* сближение.
rapt [ræpt] *adj* (*attention*) сосредоточенный* (сосредоточен); **he was ~ in contemplation** он был погружён в раздумья.
rapture [ˈræptʃəʳ] *n* (*delight*) восторг; **to go into ~s over** приходить* (прийти* *perf*) в восторг от *+gen*.
rapturous [ˈræptʃərəs] *adj* (*applause*) восторженный* (восторжен).
rare [rɛəʳ] *adj* редкий* (редок); (*rare steak*) кровавый; **it is ~ to find** ... редко удаётся найти ....
rarebit [ˈrɛəbɪt] *n see* **Welsh rarebit**.
rarefied [ˈrɛərɪfaɪd] *adj* разрежённый* (разрежён).
rarely [ˈrɛəlɪ] *adv* редко, нечасто.
raring [ˈrɛərɪŋ] *adj*: **he is ~ to go** (*inf*: *keen*) ему не терпится приступить к делу.
rarity [ˈrɛərɪtɪ] *n* редкость *f*.
rascal [ˈrɑ:skl] *n* негодяй(ка*).
rash [ræʃ] *adj* опрометчивый (опрометчив) ◆ *n* (*MED*) сыпь *f no pl*; (*spate*: *of events, robberies*) ряд*, волна*; **he came out in a ~** у него выступила сыпь.
rasher [ˈræʃəʳ] *n* (*of bacon*) ломтик.
rashly [ˈræʃlɪ] *adv* опрометчиво.
rasp [rɑ:sp] *n* (*tool*) рашпиль *m* ◆ *vt* (*speak*: *also*: **~ out**) хрипеть* (прохрипеть* *perf*).
raspberry [ˈrɑ:zbərɪ] *n* малина *f no pl*.
rasping [ˈrɑ:spɪŋ] *adj*: **a ~ noise** скрежещущий звук; **a ~ voice** скрипучий* голос.
rat [ræt] *n* (*also fig*) крыса.
ratable [ˈreɪtəbl] *adj* = **rateable**.
ratchet [ˈrætʃɪt] *n* храповик; **~ wheel** храповое колесо*.
rate [reɪt] *n* (*speed*) скорость *f*; (: *of change, inflation*) темп; (*of interest*) ставка; (*ratio*) уровень *m*; (*price*: *at hotel etc*) расценка ◆ *vt* (*value*) оценивать (оценить* *perf*); (*estimate*) расценивать (расценить* *perf*); **~s** *npl* (*BRIT*: *property tax*) налог *msg* на недвижимость; (*fees*) расценки *fpl*; **at a ~ of 60 kilometres an hour** со скоростью 60 километров в час; **~ of flow** скорость потока; **~ of growth** темпы роста; **~ of return** ставка дохода (*от вложения капитала*); **pulse ~** частота пульса; **to ~ sb as** считать *(impf)* кого-н *+instr*; **to ~ sth as** расценивать (расценить *(perf)*) что-н как; **to ~ sb/sth among** относить* (отнести* *perf*) кого-н/что-н к *+dat*; **to ~ sb/sth highly** высоко ценить* *(impf)* кого-н/что-н.
rateable value [ˈreɪtəbl-] *n* (*BRIT*: *formerly*) *стоимость дома на основе которой рассчитывается налог на недвижимость*.
ratepayer [ˈreɪtpeɪəʳ] *n* (*BRIT*: *formerly*) *лицо, выплачивающее налог на недвижимость*.
rather [ˈrɑ:ðəʳ] *adv* (*quite, somewhat*) довольно; (*to some extent*) несколько; (*more accurately*): **or ~** вернее сказать; **it's ~ expensive** (*quite*) это довольно дорого; (*too*) это слишком дорого; **there's ~ a lot** слишком много; **I would ~ go** я, пожалуй, пойду; **I'd ~ not leave** я бы не хотел уходить; **I ~ think he won't come** я думаю, что, пожалуй, он не придёт.
ratification [rætɪfɪˈkeɪʃən] *n* ратификация.
ratify [ˈrætɪfaɪ] *vt* ратифицировать *(impf/perf)*.
rating [ˈreɪtɪŋ] *n* (*assessment*) оценка*, рейтинг; (*NAUT*: *BRIT*) матрос; **~s** *npl* (*RADIO, TV*) рейтинг *msg*.
ratio [ˈreɪʃɪəu] *n* отношение, соотношение; **in the ~ of one hundred to one** в отношении сто к одному.
ration [ˈræʃən] *n* (*allowance*: *of food*) рацион, паёк*; (: *of petrol*) норма ◆ *vt* нормировать *(impf/perf)*; **~s** *npl* (*MIL*) рацион *msg*; **to be on ~s** быть* *(impf)* на довольствии.
rational [ˈræʃənl] *adj* (*solution, reasoning*) рациональный* (рационален); (*person*) разумный* (разумен).
rationale [ræʃəˈnɑ:l] *n* рациональное *or* разумное обоснование.
rationalization [ræʃnəlaɪˈzeɪʃən] *n* рационализация.
rationalize [ˈræʃnəlaɪz] *vt* (*justify*) давать*

(дать* *perf*) рациона́льное объясне́ние *+dat*.
rationally ['ræʃnəlɪ] *adv* рациона́льно.
rationing ['ræʃnɪŋ] *n* нормирова́ние.
rat poison *n* крыси́ный яд.
rat race *n*: **the ~ ~** грызня́ за власть.
rattan [ræ'tæn] *n* рота́нг.
rattle ['rætl] *n* дребезжа́ние; (*of train, car*) громыха́ние; (*baby's toy*) погрему́шка* ◆ *vi* (*small objects*) дребезжа́ть (*impf*) ◆ *vt* (*shake noisily*) греме́ть (прогреме́ть *perf*); (*fig*: *unsettle*) нерви́ровать (*impf*), выводи́ть* (вы́вести* *perf*) из себя́; **to ~ along** (*car, bus*) прогромыха́ть (*impf*); **a cold November wind ~d the windows** от холо́дного ноя́брьского ве́тра дребезжа́ли о́кна.
rattlesnake ['rætlsneɪk] *n* грему́чая змея́*.
ratty ['rætɪ] *adj* (*inf*: *person*) издёрганный* (издёрган).
raucous ['rɔ:kəs] *adj* оглуши́тельный* (оглуши́телен).
raucously ['rɔ:kəslɪ] *adv* оглуши́тельно.
raunchy ['rɔ:ntʃɪ] *adj* (*song*) распу́тный* (распу́тен).
ravage ['rævɪdʒ] *vt* разоря́ть (разори́ть *perf*).
ravages ['rævɪdʒɪz] *npl* (*of time, weather*) разруши́тельные после́дствия *ntpl*.
rave [reɪv] *vi* (*in anger*) беснова́ться (*impf*), бушева́ть (*impf*); (*MED*) бре́дить* (*impf*); (*with enthusiasm*): **to ~ about** восторга́ться (*impf*) *+instr* ◆ *cpd* (*inf*) восто́рженный.
raven ['reɪvən] *n* во́рон.
ravenous ['rævənəs] *adj* (*person*) голо́дный* (го́лоден) как волк.
ravine [rə'vi:n] *n* уще́лье*.
raving ['reɪvɪŋ] *adj*: **~ lunatic** бу́йно поме́шанный(-ая) *m(f) adj*.
ravings ['reɪvɪŋz] *npl* бред *msg*.
ravioli [rævɪ'əulɪ] *n* равио́ли *ind* (*италья́нское блю́до, напомина́ющее пельме́ни*).
ravishing ['rævɪʃɪŋ] *adj* (*beautiful*) восхити́тельный* (восхити́телен).
raw [rɔ:] *adj* (*uncooked*) сыро́й*; (*not processed*: *cotton*) необрабо́танный* (необрабо́тан); (: *unrefined sugar*) нерафини́рованный (нерафини́рован); (*sore*) све́жий* (свеж); (*inexperienced*) зелёный* (зе́лен); (*weather, day*) промо́зглый.
raw deal *n* (*inf*: *bad bargain*) неуда́чная сде́лка*; (: *unfair treatment*): **he got a ~ ~** с ним пло́хо обошли́сь.
raw material *n* сырьё *nt no pl*.
ray [reɪ] *n* (*of light, sunshine*) луч*; (*of heat*) пото́к*; **~ of hope** луч* наде́жды.
rayon ['reɪɔn] *n* иску́сственный шёлк.
raze [reɪz] *vt* (*building, forest*: *also*: **~ to the ground**) сровня́ть (*perf*) с землёй.
razor ['reɪzəʳ] *n* бри́тва; **safety ~** безопа́сная бри́тва; **electric ~** электробри́тва.
razor blade *n* ле́звие (бри́твы).
razzle(-dazzle) ['ræzl('dæzl)] *n* (*BRIT*: *inf*): **to go on the ~** идти́* (*impf*) кути́ть.
razzmatazz ['ræzmə'tæz] *n* (*inf*) буффона́да.
RC *abbr* = **Roman Catholic.**
RCAF *n abbr* = *Royal Canadian Air Force*.
RCMP *n abbr* = *Royal Canadian Mounted Police*.
RCN *n abbr* = *Royal Canadian Navy*.
RD *abbr* (*US*: *POST*: = *rural delivery*) *доста́вка по́чты в се́льскую ме́стность*.
Rd *abbr* = **road.**
RDC *n abbr* (*BRIT*: = *rural district council*) райо́нный сове́т (*в се́льской ме́стности*).
RE *n abbr* (*BRIT*: *SCOL*: = *religious education*) религио́зное воспита́ние; (*MIL*: = *Royal Engineers*) ≈ инжене́рные войска́.
re [ri:] *prep* (*with regard to*) относи́тельно *+gen*.
reach [ri:tʃ] *n* (*scope*: *of imagination*) разма́х ◆ *vt* (*place, end, agreement*) достига́ть (дости́гнуть* *or* дости́чь* *perf*) *+gen*; (: *conclusion, decision*) приходи́ть* (прийти́* *perf*) к *+dat*; (*be able to touch*) достава́ть* (доста́ть* *perf*); (*by telephone*) свя́зываться (связа́ться* *perf*) с *+instr* ◆ *vi*: **to ~ into** сова́ть (су́нуть *perf*) в *+acc*; **within ~** в преде́лах досяга́емости; **out of ~** вне досяга́емости; **within ~ of the shops/station** недалеко́ от магази́нов/вокза́ла; **within easy ~ of** (*place*) недалеко́ от *+gen*; **"keep out of the ~ of children"** „бере́чь от дете́й"; **upper ~es** (*of river*) верхо́вья *ntpl*; **lower ~es** (*of river*) низо́вья *ntpl*; **can I ~ you at your hotel?** мо́жно ли связа́ться с Ва́ми в гости́нице?; **to ~ for** протя́гивать (протяну́ть* *perf*) ру́ку к *+dat*; **to ~ up** протя́гивать (протяну́ть* *perf*) ру́ку вверх
▸ **reach out** *vt* протя́гивать (протяну́ть* *perf*) ◆ *vi* вытя́гиваться (вы́тянуться *perf*); **to ~ out for sth** протя́гивать (протяну́ть* *perf*) ру́ку за чем-н.
react [ri:'ækt] *vi* (*CHEM*): **to ~ (with)** вступа́ть (вступи́ть* *perf*) в реа́кцию (с *+instr*); (*MED*): **to ~ (to)** реаги́ровать (*impf*) (на *+acc*); (*respond*) реаги́ровать (отреаги́ровать *perf*) (на *+acc*); (*rebel*): **to ~ (against)** восстава́ть* (восста́ть* *perf*) (про́тив *+gen*).
reaction [ri:'ækʃən] *n* (*CHEM*) реа́кция; (*also MED, POL*): **~ (to/against)** реа́кция (на *+acc*/про́тив *+gen*); **~s** *npl* (*reflexes*) реа́кция *fsg*.
reactionary [ri:'ækʃənrɪ] *adj* реакцио́нный* (реакцио́нен).
reactor [ri:'æktəʳ] *n* (*also*: **nuclear ~**) реа́ктор.
read[1] [rɛd] *pt, pp of* **read**[2].
read[2] [ri:d] (*pt, pp* **read**) *vt* чита́ть (прочита́ть *or* проче́сть* *perf*); (*mood*) определя́ть (определи́ть* *perf*); (*meter, thermometer etc*) снима́ть (снять* *perf*) показа́ния с *+gen*; (*subj*: *instrument etc*) пока́зывать (*impf*); (*study*: *at*

* marks translations which have irregular inflections. The Russian-English side of the dictionary gives inflectional information.

university) изучáть *(impf)* ◆ *vi* (*person*) читáть *(impf)*; (*text etc*) читáться *(impf)*; **the notice ~s** ... в объявлéнии говори́тся ...; **it can be taken as ~ that** ... (*fig*) самó собóй разумéется, что ...; **do you ~ me?** (*TEL*) Вы слы́шите меня́?
▸ **read out** *vt* зачи́тывать (зачитáть *perf*)
▸ **read over** *vt* перечи́тывать (перечитáть *perf*)
▸ **read through** *vt* (*quickly*) проли́стывать (пролистáть *perf*); (*thoroughly*) прочи́тывать (прочитáть *perf*)
▸ **read up** *vt* мнóго читáть *(impf)*
▸ **read up on** *vt fus* мнóго читáть *(impf)* по *+dat*.

readable [ˈriːdəbl] *adj* (*handwriting*) разбóрчивый (разбóрчив); (*book, author*) хорошó читáющийся; **this book is very ~** э́та кни́га хорошó читáется.

reader [ˈriːdəʳ] *n* (*of book, newspaper etc*) читáтель(ница) *m(f)*; (*book*) кни́га для чтéния, хрестомáтия; (*BRIT: at university*) ≈ доцéнт.

readership [ˈriːdəʃɪp] *n* (*of newspaper etc*) круг читáтелей.

readily [ˈrɛdɪlɪ] *adv* (*willingly*) с готóвностью; (*easily*) легкó; (*quickly*) охóтно.

readiness [ˈrɛdɪnɪs] *n* готóвность *f*; **in ~** наготóве, в состоя́нии готóвности.

reading [ˈriːdɪŋ] *n* (*of books, newspapers etc*) чтéние; (*understanding*) толковáние; (*as entertainment*) чтéния *ntpl*; (*on meter, thermometer etc*) показáние.

reading lamp *n* настóльная лáмпа.

reading matter *n* материáл для чтéния.

reading room *n* читáльный зал.

readjust [riːəˈdʒʌst] *vt* (*alter: position*) перемени́ть *(impf)*; (*: knob, mirror*) поворáчивать (поверну́ть *perf*); (*instrument*) подрегули́ровать *(perf)* ◆ *vi* (*adapt*): **to ~ (to)** приспосáбливаться (приспосóбиться* *perf*) (к *+dat*).

readjustment [riːəˈdʒʌstmənt] *n* (*adapting*) приспособлéние; (*alteration*) регулирóвка*.

ready [ˈrɛdɪ] *adj* готóвый (готóв); (*available*) готóвый ◆ *n*: **at the ~** (*MIL*) в положéнии для стрельбы́; (*fig*) наготóве; **~ for use** готóвый (готóв) к употреблéнию; **I am ~ to help** я готóв помóчь; **to get ~** приготáвливаться (приготóвиться* *perf*); **to get sb/sth ~** подготáвливать (подготóвить* *perf*) когó-н/что-н.

ready cash *n* нали́чные дéньги* *pl*.

ready-cooked [ˈrɛdɪkukt] *adj* готóвый.

ready-made [ˈrɛdɪˈmeɪd] *adj* готóвый.

ready-mix [ˈrɛdɪmɪks] *n* (*for cakes etc*) полуфабрикáт; (*concrete*) товáрный бетóн.

ready money *n* нали́чные дéньги* *pl*.

ready reckoner [-ˈrɛkənəʳ] *n* (*BRIT*) арифмети́ческие табли́цы *fpl* готóвых расчётов.

ready-to-wear [ˈrɛdɪtəˈwɛəʳ] *adj* (*dress etc*) готóвый.

reaffirm [riːəˈfəːm] *vt* вновь подтверждáть (подтверди́ть* *perf*).

reagent [riːˈeɪdʒənt] *n*: **chemical ~** хими́ческий* реакти́в.

real [rɪəl] *adj* (*reason, interest, result etc*) настоя́щий*, реáльный* (реáлен); (*leather*) натурáльный*; (*gold, feeling*) настоя́щий* ◆ *adv* (*US: inf: very*) óчень; **in ~ life** в действи́тельности; **in ~ terms** реáльно; **a ~ idiot** (*for emphasis*) настоя́щий* идиóт.

real estate *n* недви́жимость *f* ◆ *cpd* (*US*): **~ ~ agency** агéнтство по продáже недви́жимости.

realign [riːəˈlaɪn] *vt* перестрáивать (перестрóить *perf*).

realism [ˈrɪəlɪzəm] *n* реали́зм.

realist [ˈrɪəlɪst] *n* реали́ст(ка*).

realistic [rɪəˈlɪstɪk] *adj* (*practical*) реалисти́чный* (реалисти́чен); (*true to life*) реалисти́ческий*.

reality [riːˈælɪtɪ] *n* реáльность *f*, действи́тельность *f*; **in ~** на сáмом дéле, в реáльности.

realization [rɪəlaɪˈzeɪʃən] *n* (*understanding*) осознáние; (*fulfilment: of hopes*) осуществлéние; (*of asset*) реализáция.

realize [ˈrɪəlaɪz] *vt* (*understand*) осознавáть* (осознáть* *perf*); (*fulfil*) осуществля́ть (осуществи́ть* *perf*); (*COMM: asset*) реализовáть *(impf/perf)*; **I ~ that** ... я осознаю́, что ....

reallocate [rɪˈæləkeɪt] *vt* перераспределя́ть (перераспредели́ть *perf*).

really [ˈrɪəlɪ] *adv* (*very*) óчень; (*actually*): **what ~ happened?** что произошлó на сáмом дéле?; **~?** (*indicating interest*) прáвда?, да?; (*expressing surprise*) неужéли?, серьёзно?; **~!** (*indicating annoyance*) ну, знáете!

realm [rɛlm] *n* (*of monarch*) королéвство; (*fig: area of activity or study*) óбласть* *f*, сфéра.

real-time [ˈriːltaɪm] *adj* (*COMPUT*) в реáльном врéмени.

realtor [ˈrɪəltɔːʳ] *n* (*US*) агéнт по продáже недви́жимости.

ream [riːm] *n* (*of paper*) стопá*; **~s of** (*fig: inf*) ку́ча, мáсса; **she's written ~s!** у неё мáсса *or* ку́ча напи́санного!

reap [riːp] *vt* (*crop*) жать* (сжать* *perf*); (*fig: benefits, rewards*) пожинáть (пожáть* *perf*).

reaper [ˈriːpəʳ] *n* (*machine*) жáтка*.

reappear [riːəˈpɪəʳ] *vi* снóва появля́ться (появи́ться* *perf*).

reappearance [riːəˈpɪərəns] *n* нóвое появлéние.

reapply [riːəˈplaɪ] *vi*: **to ~ for** повтóрно обращáться (обрати́ться* *perf*) за *+instr*.

reappoint [riːəˈpɔɪnt] *vt* повтóрно назначáть (назнáчить *perf*).

reappraisal [riːəˈpreɪzl] *n* переоцéнка*.

rear [rɪəʳ] *adj* зáдний* ◆ *n* (*back*) зáдняя часть* *f*; (*buttocks*) зад; (*MIL*) тыл* ◆ *vt* (*cattle, family*) вырáщивать (вы́растить* *perf*) ◆ *vi* (*also: ~*

up) станови́ться* (стать* *perf*) на дыбы́.
rear admiral *n* контр-адмира́л.
rear-engined [ˈrɪərˈɛndʒɪnd] *adj* (*AUT*) с мото́ром в за́дней ча́сти.
rearguard [ˈrɪəɡɑːd] *n* (*MIL*) арьерга́рд.
rearm [riːˈɑːm] *vi* перевооружа́ться (перевооружи́ться *perf*) ◆ *vt* перевооружа́ть (перевооружи́ть *perf*).
rearmament [riːˈɑːməmənt] *n* перевооруже́ние.
rearrange [riːəˈreɪndʒ] *vt* (*objects*) переставля́ть (переста́вить* *perf*); (*order*) изменя́ть (измени́ть* *perf*).
rear-view mirror [ˈrɪəvjuː-] *n* (*AUT*) зе́ркало* за́днего ви́да *or* обзо́ра.
reason [ˈriːzn] *n* (*cause*) причи́на; (*ability to think*) ра́зум, рассу́док*; (*sense*) смысл ◆ *vi*: **to ~ with sb** убежда́ть *(impf)* кого́-н; **the ~ for/why** причи́на для *+gen*/по кото́рой; **to have ~ to think that ...** име́ть *(impf)* основа́ние ду́мать; **it stands to ~ that ...** разу́меется, что ...; **she claims with good ~ that ...** она́ не без причи́ны счита́ет, что ...; **all the more ~ why ...** тем бо́лее ....
reasonable [ˈriːznəbl] *adj* разу́мный* (разу́мен); (*quality*) неплохо́й* (непло́х); (*price*) прие́млемый (прие́млем), уме́ренный* (уме́рен); (*not bad*) сно́сный* (сно́сен); **be ~!** бу́дьте благоразу́мны!
reasonably [ˈriːznəblɪ] *adv* (*sensibly*) разу́мно; (*fairly*) дово́льно; **one can ~ assume that ...** мо́жно справедли́во предположи́ть, что ....
reasoned [ˈriːznd] *adj* (*argument*) обосно́ванный* (обосно́ван).
reasoning [ˈriːznɪŋ] *n* рассужде́ние.
reassemble [riːəˈsɛmbl] *vt* (сно́ва) собира́ть (собра́ть* *perf*).
reassert [riːəˈsəːt] *vt* (*authority, oneself*) сно́ва утвержда́ть (утверди́ть* *perf*).
reassurance [riːəˈʃuərəns] *n* подтвержде́ние; (*comfort*) подде́ржка.
reassure [riːəˈʃuəʳ] *vt* (*comfort*) утеша́ть (уте́шить *perf*); **to ~ sb of** заверя́ть (заве́рить *perf*) кого́-н в *+prp*.
reassuring [riːəˈʃuərɪŋ] *adj* (*smile, manner*) ободря́ющий.
reawakening [riːəˈweɪknɪŋ] *n* пробужде́ние.
rebate [ˈriːbeɪt] *n* обра́тная вы́плата.
rebel [*n* ˈrɛbl, *vi* rɪˈbɛl] *n* бунта́рь*(-рка*) *m(f)* ◆ *vi* восстава́ть* (восста́ть* *perf*).
rebellion [rɪˈbɛljən] *n* восста́ние.
rebellious [rɪˈbɛljəs] *adj* (*child, behaviour*) стропти́вый (стропти́в); (*troops*) мяте́жный*; (*factions*) бунту́ющий.
rebirth [riːˈbəːθ] *n* возрожде́ние.
rebound [*vi* rɪˈbaund, *n* ˈriːbaund] *vi*: **to ~ (off)** отска́кивать (отскочи́ть* *perf*) (от *+gen*) ◆ *n*: **on the ~** (*ball*) на отско́ке; **he married her on the ~** он жени́лся на ней по́сле разочарова́ния в любви́ к друго́й.
rebuff [rɪˈbʌf] *n* отпо́р ◆ *vt* (*suggestion*) ре́зко отклоня́ть (отклони́ть *perf*); (*person*) дава́ть* (дать* *perf*) отпо́р *+dat*.
rebuild [riːˈbɪld] *irreg vt* (*town, building etc*) перестра́ивать (перестро́ить *perf*); (*economy, confidence*) восстана́вливать (восстанови́ть* *perf*).
rebuke [rɪˈbjuːk] *vt* упрека́ть (упрекну́ть *perf*), де́лать (сде́лать *perf*) вы́говор *+dat* ◆ *n* упрёк, вы́говор.
rebut [rɪˈbʌt] *vt* опроверга́ть (опрове́ргнуть* *perf*).
rebuttal [rɪˈbʌtl] *n* опроверже́ние.
recalcitrant [rɪˈkælsɪtrənt] *adj* непоко́рный* (непоко́рен).
recall [*vb* rɪˈkɔːl, *n* ˈriːkɔl] *vt* вспомина́ть (вспо́мнить *perf*); (*parliament, ambassador etc*) отзыва́ть (отозва́ть* *perf*); (*COMPUT*) перевызыва́ть (перевы́звать *perf*), вызыва́ть (вы́звать *perf*) повто́рно ◆ *n* (*ability to remember*) па́мять *f*; (*of ambassador etc*) о́тзыв; **the event is beyond ~** собы́тие безвозвра́тно исче́зло из па́мяти.
recant [rɪˈkænt] *vi* отрека́ться (отре́чься* *perf*).
recap [ˈriːkæp] *vt* (*summarize*) резюми́ровать *(impf/perf)* ◆ *vi* де́лать (сде́лать *perf*) резюме́ ◆ *n* резюме́ *nt ind*.
recapitulate [riːkəˈpɪtjuleɪt] *vti* = **recap**.
recapture [riːˈkæptʃəʳ] *vt* (*town, territory etc*) сно́ва захва́тывать (захвати́ть* *perf*); (*atmosphere, mood etc*) воссоздава́ть* (воссозда́ть* *perf*).
rec'd *abbr* (*COMM*) = *received*.
recede [rɪˈsiːd] *vi* (*tide*) спада́ть (спасть* *perf*); (*lights*) угаса́ть* (уга́снуть* *perf*); (*memory*) слабе́ть (ослабе́ть *perf*); (*hair*) реде́ть* (пореде́ть *perf*).
receding [rɪˈsiːdɪŋ] *adj* (*hair*) реде́ющий; (*chin*) сре́занный (сре́зан).
receipt [rɪˈsiːt] *n* (*document*) квита́нция; (*act of receiving*) получе́ние; **~s** *npl* (*COMM*) де́нежные поступле́ния *ntpl*, платежи́ *mpl*; **to acknowledge ~ of** подтвержда́ть (подтверди́ть* *perf*) получе́ние *+gen*; **on ~** по получе́нии; **we are in ~ of ...** (*COMM*) мы получи́ли ....
receivable [rɪˈsiːvəbl] *adj* (*COMM*) подлежа́щий получе́нию; (: *bill, account*) надлежа́щий упла́те.
receive [rɪˈsiːv] *vt* получа́ть (получи́ть* *perf*); (*criticism*) встреча́ть (встре́тить* *perf*); (*visitor, guest*) принима́ть (приня́ть* *perf*); **"received with thanks"** (*formal*) „полу́чено с благода́рностью“.
receiver [rɪˈsiːvəʳ] *n* (*TEL*) (телефо́нная) тру́бка*; (*RADIO*) (радио-)приёмник; (*TV*)

* marks translations which have irregular inflections. The Russian-English side of the dictionary gives inflectional information.

телевизор; (*COMM*) ликвидатор (*неплатёжеспособной компании*); **~ of stolen goods** укрыватель(ница) *m(f)* краденого.
receivership [rɪ'si:vəʃɪp] *n конфискация имущества обанкротившейся компании судебными исполнителями в целях выплаты долгов кредиторам.*
recent ['ri:snt] *adj* (*event, times*) недавний*; **in ~ years** в *or* за последние годы.
recently ['ri:sntlɪ] *adv* недавно; **until ~** до недавнего времени; **as ~ as last year** ещё в прошлом году.
receptacle [rɪ'sɛptɪkl] *n* сосуд.
reception [rɪ'sɛpʃən] *n* (*in hotel*) регистрация; (*in office*) приёмная *f adj*; (*in hospital*) регистратура; (*party, also RADIO, TV*) приём; **we got a warm ~** нам был оказан тёплый приём.
reception centre *n* (*BRIT*) *приёмный пункт для размещения беженцев, бездомных итп.*
reception desk *n* (*in hotel*) стол регистрации; (*in hospital, at doctor's*) регистратура; (*in large building, offices*) отдел приёма посетителей.
receptionist [rɪ'sɛpʃənɪst] *n* (*in hotel, hospital*) регистратор; (*in firm*) секретарь* *m* по приёму посетителей.
receptive [rɪ'sɛptɪv] *adj* восприимчивый (восприимчив).
recess [rɪ'sɛs] *n* (*in room*) ниша; (*secret place*) тайник*; (*POL etc*: *holiday*) каникулы *pl*; (*US*: *LAW*: *short break*) перерыв; (: *SCOL*) большая перемена.
recession [rɪ'sɛʃən] *n* (*ECON*) спад.
recharge [ri:'tʃɑ:dʒ] *vt* (*battery*) перезаряжать (перезарядить* *perf*).
rechargeable [ri:'tʃɑ:dʒəbl] *adj* перезаряжающийся.
recipe ['rɛsɪpɪ] *n* (*also fig*) рецепт.
recipient [rɪ'sɪpɪənt] *n* получатель *m*.
reciprocal [rɪ'sɪprəkl] *adj* взаимный* (взаимен), обоюдный* (обоюден).
reciprocate [rɪ'sɪprəkeɪt] *vt* отвечать (ответить* *perf*) на *+acc* ◆ *vi* (*favour*) отплачивать (отплатить* *perf*); (*feeling*) отвечать (ответить* *perf*) взаимностью.
recital [rɪ'saɪtl] *n* (*concert*) сольный концерт.
recitation [rɛsɪ'teɪʃən] *n* (*of poetry*) декламация; (*of prose*) чтение.
recite [rɪ'saɪt] *vt* (*poem*) декламировать (продекламировать *perf*); (*prose*) читать (*impf*) (вслух); (*complaints, grievances etc*) произносить* (произнести* *perf*).
reckless ['rɛkləs] *adj* безрассудный* (безрассуден).
recklessly ['rɛkləslɪ] *adv* безрассудно.
reckon ['rɛkən] *vt* (*calculate*) считать (посчитать *or* сосчитать *perf*); (*think*): **I ~ that ...** я считаю, что ... ◆ *vi*: **he is somebody to be ~ed with** с таким человеком, как он, нужно считаться; **to ~ without sb** не считаться (посчитаться *perf*) с кем-н; **to ~ without sth** не учитывать (учесть* *perf*) чего-н
► **reckon on** *vt fus* рассчитывать (*impf*) на *+acc*.
reckoning ['rɛknɪŋ] *n* (*calculation*) подсчёт, расчёт; **the day of ~** час расплаты.
reclaim [rɪ'kleɪm] *vt* (*demand back*) требовать (потребовать *perf*) обратно; (*land*: *from sea*) отвоёвывать (отвоевать* *perf*); (: *from forest etc*) осваивать (освоить *perf*); (*waste materials*) перерабатывать (переработать *perf*).
reclamation [rɛklə'meɪʃən] *n* (*of land*) освоение.
recline [rɪ'klaɪn] *vi* откидываться (откинуться *perf*).
reclining [rɪ'klaɪnɪŋ] *adj* (*seat*) откидывающийся.
recluse [rɪ'klu:s] *n* затворник(-ица).
recognition [rɛkəg'nɪʃən] *n* признание; (*of person, place*) узнавание; **in ~ of** в знак признания *+gen*; **to gain ~** получать (получить* *perf*) признание; **he has changed beyond ~** он изменился до неузнаваемости.
recognizable ['rɛkəgnaɪzəbl] *adj*: **~ (by)** узнаваемый (по *+dat*).
recognize ['rɛkəgnaɪz] *vt* признавать* (признать* *perf*); (*person, place*) узнавать* (узнать *perf*); (*attitude, illness*) распознавать* (распознать* *perf*); **to ~ by** узнавать* (узнать* *perf*) по *+dat*.
recoil [*n* 'ri:kɔɪl, *vb* rɪ'kɔɪl] *n* (*of gun*) отдача ◆ *vi* (*person*): **to ~ from doing** в ужасе отказаться (*perf*) *+infin*.
recollect [rɛkə'lɛkt] *vt* припоминать (припомнить *perf*), вспоминать (вспомнить *perf*).
recollection [rɛkə'lɛkʃən] *n* воспоминание, память *f*; **to the best of my ~** насколько мне помнится.
recommend [rɛkə'mɛnd] *vt* рекомендовать (порекомендовать *perf*); **she has a lot to ~ her** многое говорит в её пользу.
recommendation [rɛkəmɛn'deɪʃən] *n* рекомендация; **on the ~ of** по рекомендации *+gen*.
recommended retail price *n* (*BRIT*) рекомендуемая розничная цена*.
recompense ['rɛkəmpɛns] *n* компенсация.
reconcilable ['rɛkənsaɪləbl] *adj* (*ideas*) совместимый (совместим).
reconcile ['rɛkənsaɪl] *vt* (*people*) мирить (помирить *perf*); (*facts, beliefs*) примирять (примирить *perf*); **to ~ o.s. to sth** смиряться (смириться *perf*) с чем-н.
reconciliation [rɛkənsɪlɪ'eɪʃən] *n* примирение.
recondite [rɪ'kɔndaɪt] *adj* заумный* (заумен).
recondition [ri:kən'dɪʃən] *vt* (*machine*) ремонтировать (отремонтировать *perf*).
reconditioned [ri:kən'dɪʃənd] *adj* отремонтированный (отремонтирован).
reconnaissance [rɪ'kɔnɪsns] *n* (*MIL*) разведка,

рекогносциро́вка.
reconnoitre [rɛkəˈnɔɪtəʳ] (*US* **reconnoiter**) *vt* (*MIL*: *enemy territory*) разве́дывать (разве́дать *perf*).
reconsider [ri:kənˈsɪdəʳ] *vt* пересма́тривать (пересмотре́ть* *perf*) ◆ *vi* переду́мать (*perf*).
reconstitute [ri:ˈkɔnstɪtju:t] *vt* (*organization*) реорганизова́ть (*impf/perf*); (*food*) восстана́вливать (восстанови́ть* *perf*).
reconstruct [ri:kənˈstrʌkt] *vt* перестра́ивать (перестро́ить *perf*); (*event, crime*) воспроизводи́ть* (воспроизвести́* *perf*), реконструи́ровать (*impf/perf*).
reconstruction [ri:kənˈstrʌkʃən] *n* (*of building*) реконстру́кция; (*of country*) перестро́йка; (*of crime*) воспроизведе́ние.
reconvene [ri:kənˈvi:n] *vi* возобновля́ть (возобнови́ть* *perf*) рабо́ту.
record [*vb* rɪˈkɔ:d, *n, adj* ˈrɛkɔ:d] *vt* (*in writing, on tape*) запи́сывать (записа́ть* *perf*); (*register: temperature, speed etc*) регистри́ровать (зарегистри́ровать *perf*) ◆ *n* (*written account, also COMPUT*) за́пись *f*; (*of meeting*) протоко́л; (*of attendance*) учёт; (*file*) де́ло*; (*MUS*) пласти́нка*; (*history: of person, company*) репута́ция; (*also:* **criminal ~**) суди́мость *f*; (*SPORT*) реко́рд ◆ *adj*: **in ~ time** в реко́рдное вре́мя; **public ~s** архи́вные за́писи; **to keep a ~ of** вести́* (*impf*) учёт *+gen*; **to put the ~ straight** (*fig*) пока́зывать (показа́ть* *perf*) и́стинное положе́ние веще́й; **he is on ~ as saying that ...** изве́стно, что он сказа́л, что ...; **off the ~** (*statement*) неофициа́льный; (*speak*) неофициа́льно.
recorded delivery [rɪˈkɔ:dɪd-] *n* (*BRIT*) доста́вка с уведомле́нием (о вруче́нии).
recorder [rɪˈkɔ:dəʳ] *n* (*MUS*) англи́йская фле́йта; (*LAW*) реко́рдер.
record holder (*SPORT*) *n* рекордсме́н(ка).
recording [rɪˈkɔ:dɪŋ] *n* за́пись *f*.
recording studio *n* сту́дия звукоза́писи.
record library *n* фоноте́ка.
record player *n* прои́грыватель *m*.
recount [rɪˈkaunt] *vt* (*story*) передава́ть* (переда́ть* *perf*); (*event*) пове́дать (*perf*) о *+prp*.
re-count [ˈri:kaunt] *n* (*of votes*) пересчёт ◆ *vt* пересчи́тывать (пересчита́ть *perf*).
recoup [rɪˈku:p] *vt*: **to ~ one's losses** возвраща́ть (верну́ть *perf*) потеря́нное.
recourse [rɪˈkɔ:s] *n*: **to have ~ to** прибега́ть (прибе́гнуть* *perf*) к *+dat*.
recover [rɪˈkʌvəʳ] *vt* (*lost or stolen items*) получа́ть (получи́ть* *perf*) обра́тно; (*financial loss*) возмеща́ть (возмести́ть* *perf*) ◆ *vi* (*subj: country*) встава́ть* (встать* *perf*) на́ ноги; (*: economy*) улучша́ться (улу́чшиться *perf*); (*get better*): **to ~ (from)** поправля́ться (попра́виться* *perf*) (по́сле *+gen*).
re-cover [ri:ˈkʌvəʳ] *vt* (*chair etc*) перебива́ть (переби́ть* *perf*) (*оби́вку*).
recovery [rɪˈkʌvərɪ] *n* (*from illness, operation*) выздоровле́ние; (*in economy, finances*) подъём; (*of stolen items*) возвраще́ние; (*of lost items*) обнаруже́ние.
re-create [ri:krɪˈeɪt] *vt* воссоздава́ть* (воссозда́ть* *perf*).
recreation [rɛkrɪˈeɪʃən] *n* (*free time*) о́тдых; (*leisure activities*) развлече́ние.
recreational [rɛkrɪˈeɪʃənl] *adj*: **~ facilities** усло́вия *ntpl* для о́тдыха и развлече́ния.
recreational drug *n* *нарко́тик, принима́емый для удово́льствия и не предполага́ющий наркоти́ческой зави́симости.*
recrimination [rɪkrɪmɪˈneɪʃən] *n* взаи́мные обвине́ния *ntpl*.
recruit [rɪˈkru:t] *n* (*MIL*) новобра́нец*, призывни́к*; (*in company*) но́вый сотру́дник; (*in organization*) но́вый член ◆ *vt* (*into army, organization*) вербова́ть (завербова́ть *perf*); (*into company*) нанима́ть (наня́ть* *perf*).
recruiting office [rɪˈkru:tɪŋ-] *n* (*MIL*) вербо́вочный пункт.
recruitment [rɪˈkru:tmənt] *n* (*MIL*) вербо́вка; (*by company*) набо́р (*на рабо́ту*).
rectangle [ˈrɛktæŋgl] *n* прямоуго́льник.
rectangular [rɛkˈtæŋgjuləʳ] *adj* прямоуго́льный.
rectify [ˈrɛktɪfaɪ] *vt* исправля́ть (испра́вить* *perf*).
rector [ˈrɛktəʳ] *n* (*REL*) прихо́дский* свяще́нник.
rectory [ˈrɛktərɪ] *n* (*house*) дом* прихо́дского свяще́нника.
rectum [ˈrɛktəm] *n* пряма́я кишка́*.
recuperate [rɪˈkju:pəreɪt] *vi* оправля́ться (опра́виться* *perf*).
recur [rɪˈkə:ʳ] *vi* повторя́ться (повтори́ться *perf*).
recurrence [rɪˈkə:rns] *n* повторе́ние.
recurrent [rɪˈkə:rnt] *adj* повторя́ющийся.
recurring [rɪˈkə:rɪŋ] *adj* (*problem*) постоя́нно возника́ющий; (*dream*) повторя́ющийся.
recycle [ri:ˈsaɪkl] *vt* перераба́тывать (перерабо́тать *perf*).
red [rɛd] *n* кра́сный цвет; (*pej: POL*) кра́сный (-ая) *m(f) adj* ◆ *adj* кра́сный* (кра́сен); (*hair*) ры́жий*; (*wine*) кра́сный; **she was dressed in ~** она́ была́ в кра́сном; **to be in the ~** име́ть (*impf*) задо́лженность.
red alert *n* состоя́ние боево́й гото́вности.
red-blooded [ˈrɛdˈblʌdɪd] *adj*: **~ male** саме́ц* (*перен*).
red-carpet treatment [rɛdˈkɑ:pɪt-] *n* торже́ственный приём.
Red Cross *n* Кра́сный Крест*.
redcurrant [ˈrɛdkʌrənt] *n* кра́сная сморо́дина *f*

* marks translations which have irregular inflections. The Russian-English side of the dictionary gives inflectional information.

no pl.
redden [ˈrɛdn] *vi* краснéть (покраснéть *perf*) ◆ *vt* окрáшивать (окрáсить* *perf*) в крáсный цвет.
reddish [ˈrɛdɪʃ] *adj* красновáтый (красновáт); (*hair*) рыжевáтый (рыжевáт).
redecorate [riːˈdɛkəreɪt] *vt* ремонтúровать (отремонтúровать *perf*) ◆ *vi* дéлать (сдéлать *perf*) ремóнт.
redecoration [riːdɛkəˈreɪʃən] *n* ремóнт.
redeem [rɪˈdiːm] *vt* (*situation, reputation*) спасáть (спастú* *perf*); (*pawned item*) выкупáть (вы́купить* *perf*); (*debt*) выплáчивать (вы́платить* *perf*); (*REL*) искупáть (искупúть* *perf*); **to ~ o.s.** искупáть (искупúть* *perf*) свою́ винý.
redeemable [rɪˈdiːməbl] *adj* подлежáщий вы́купу.
redeeming [rɪˈdiːmɪŋ] *adj*: **~ feature** подкупáющее кáчество.
redefine [riːdɪˈfaɪn] *vt* (*position, theory*) пересмáтривать (пересмотрéть* *perf*); (*word, concept*) давáть* (дать* *perf*) нóвое определéние *+dat*.
redemption [rɪˈdɛmʃən] *n* (*REL*) искуплéние грехóв; **past** *or* **beyond ~** (*fig*) безнадёжный* (безнадёжен), без надéжды на спасéние.
redeploy [riːdɪˈplɔɪ] *vt* (*resources*) перераспределя́ть (перераспределúть *perf*); (*MIL*) передислоцúровать (*impf/perf*).
redeployment [riːdɪˈplɔɪmənt] *n* (*see vb*) перераспределéние; передислокáция.
redevelop [riːdɪˈvɛləp] *vt* (*area*) перестрáивать (перестрóить *perf*).
redevelopment [riːdɪˈvɛləpmənt] *n* перестрóйка.
red-handed [rɛdˈhændɪd] *adj*: **he was caught ~** егó поймáли с поли́чным.
redhead [ˈrɛdhɛd] *n* ры́жий*(-ая) *m(f) adj*.
red herring *n* (*fig*) отвлекáющий манёвр.
red-hot [rɛdˈhɔt] *adj* (*metal*) раскалённый* (раскалён) докраснá.
redirect [riːdaɪˈrɛkt] *vt* (*mail*) переадресóвывать (переадресовáть *perf*).
rediscover [riːdɪsˈkʌvəʳ] *vt* зáново открывáть (откры́ть* *perf*).
redistribute [riːdɪsˈtrɪbjuːt] *vt* перераспределя́ть (перераспределúть *perf*).
red-letter day [ˈrɛdlɛtə-] *n* прáздничный день* *m*.
red light *n*: **to go through a ~ ~** (*AUT*) éхать* (поéхать* *perf*) на крáсный свет.
red-light district [ˈrɛdlaɪt-] *n* квартáл публи́чных домóв.
red meat *n* тёмное мя́со (*осóбенно говя́дина и барáнина*).
redness [ˈrɛdnɪs] *n* краснотá; (*of hair*) рыжинá*.
redo [riːˈduː] *irreg vt* передéлывать (передéлать *perf*).
redolent [ˈrɛdələnt] *adj* (*fig*) напоминáющий; (*smell*): **~ of** (*unpleasant*) отдаю́щий *+instr*; (*pleasant*) пáхнущий *+gen*.
redouble [riːˈdʌbl] *vt*: **to ~ one's efforts** удвáивать (удвóить *perf*) свои́ уси́лия.
redraft [riːˈdrɑːft] *vt* перепи́сывать (переписáть* *perf*).
redraw [riːˈdrɔː] *vt* изменя́ть (изменúть* *perf*).
redress [rɪˈdrɛs] *n* (*compensation*) возмещéние ◆ *vt* (*error, wrong*) исправля́ть (испрáвить* *perf*); **to ~ the balance** восстанáвливать (восстановúть* *perf*) равновéсие сил.
Red Sea *n*: **the ~ ~** Крáсное мóре.
red tape *n* (*fig*) волокúта.
reduce [rɪˈdjuːs] *vt* сокращáть (сократúть* *perf*); **to ~ sth by/to** сокращáть (сократúть* *perf*) что-н на *+acc*/до *+gen*; **to ~ sb to** (*tears*) доводúть* (довестú* *perf*) когó-н до *+gen*; **to ~ sb to silence** заставля́ть (застáвить* *perf*) когó-н замолчáть; **he was ~d to stealing** он дошёл до тогó, что стал воровáть; **"reduce speed now"** (*AUT*) "сбáвьте скóрость".
reduced [rɪˈdjuːst] *adj* (*goods*) по сни́женным цéнам; (*ticket*) со скúдкой; **at a ~ price** (*goods*) по сни́женной ценé; (*ticket*) со скúдкой.
reduction [rɪˈdʌkʃən] *n* (*in price*) скúдка; (*in numbers*) сокращéние.
redundancy [rɪˈdʌndənsɪ] (*BRIT*) *n* (*dismissal*) увольнéние (*при сокращéнии штáтов*); (*unemployment*) сокращéние штáтов; **compulsory ~** вы́нужденное увольнéние; **voluntary ~** увольнéние по сóбственному желáнию.
redundancy payment *n* (*BRIT*) выходнóе посóбие (*при сокращéнии штáтов*).
redundant [rɪˈdʌndnt] *adj* (*BRIT*: *unemployed*) увóленный (увóлен); (*useless*) изли́шний* (изли́шен); **he was made ~** егó сократúли.
reed [riːd] *n* (*BOT*) тростни́к*; (*MUS*) язычóк*.
re-educate [riːˈɛdjukeɪt] *vt* перевоспи́тывать (перевоспитáть *perf*).
reedy [ˈriːdɪ] *adj* (*voice*) пронзи́тельный* (пронзи́телен).
reef [riːf] *n* риф.
reek [riːk] *vi*: **to ~ (of)** си́льно пáхнуть* (*impf*) (*+instr*).
reel [riːl] *n* катýшка*; (*of film, tape*) боби́на; (*dance*) рил (*нарóдный хоровóдный тáнец*) ◆ *vi* (*sway*) качáться (*impf*), шатáться (*impf*); **my head is ~ing** у меня́ крýжится головá
▸ **reel in** *vt* (*line*) смáтывать (смотáть *perf*); (*fish*) вытáскивать (вы́тащить *perf*) (*при пóмощи спи́ннинга*)
▸ **reel off** *vt* (*say*) вы́палить (*perf*).
re-election [riːɪˈlɛkʃən] *n* (*event*) перевы́боры *pl*; (*of person*) переизбрáние.
re-enter [riːˈɛntəʳ] *vt* вновь входúть* (войтú* *perf*).
re-entry [riːˈɛntrɪ] *n* повтóрный вход.
re-examine [riːɪgˈzæmɪn] *vt* пересмáтривать (пересмотрéть* *perf*).

re-export ['ri:ɪks'pɔ:t] *vt* реэкспорти́ровать *(impf/perf)* ◆ *n* реэ́кспорт.
ref [rɛf] *n abbr (SPORT: inf)* = **referee**.
ref. *abbr (COMM: = with reference to)* ссыла́ясь на *+acc.*
refectory [rɪ'fɛktərɪ] *n* столо́вая *f adj.*
refer [rɪ'fə:ʳ] *vt*: **to ~ sb to** *(book, source)* отсыла́ть (отосла́ть* *perf*) кого́-н к *+dat*; *(doctor)* направля́ть (напра́вить* *perf*) кого́-н к *+dat*; **to ~ sth to** *(pass on)* передава́ть* (переда́ть* *perf*) что-н к *+dat*; **he ~red me to the manager** он напра́вил меня́ к управля́ющему
▸ **refer to** *vt fus (mention)* упомина́ть (упомяну́ть* *perf*) о *+prp*; *(relate to)* относи́ться* *(impf)* к *+dat*; *(consult)* обраща́ться (обрати́ться* *perf*) к *+dat*; **~ring to your letter** ссыла́ясь на Ва́ше письмо́.
referee [rɛfə'ri:] *n (SPORT)* рефери́ *m ind*, судья́* *m*; *(BRIT: for job application) лицо́, даю́щее рекоменда́цию* ◆ *vt* суди́ть* *(impf)*.
reference ['rɛfrəns] *n (mention)* упомина́ние; *(in book, paper)* ссы́лка*; *(for job application: letter)* рекоменда́ция; *(: person) лицо́, даю́щее рекоменда́цию*; **with ~ to** *(in letter)* ссыла́ясь на *+acc*; **"please quote this ~"** *(COMM)* "сошли́тесь на э́тот спра́вочный но́мер".
reference book *n* спра́вочник.
reference library *n* спра́вочная библиоте́ка.
reference number *n* спра́вочный но́мер*.
referenda [rɛfə'rɛndə] *npl of* **referendum**.
referendum [rɛfə'rɛndəm] *(pl* **referenda***) n* рефере́ндум.
referral [rɪ'fə:rəl] *n* направле́ние.
refill [*vb* ri:'fɪl, *n* 'ri:fɪl] *vt (glass)* сно́ва наполня́ть (напо́лнить *perf*); *(pen)* заправля́ть (запра́вить* *perf*) ◆ *n (for pen)* запасно́й сте́ржень* *m*.
refine [rɪ'faɪn] *vt (sugar)* рафини́ровать *(impf/perf)*; *(oil)* очища́ть (очи́стить* *perf*); *(theory, idea, task)* соверше́нствовать (усоверше́нствовать *perf*).
refined [rɪ'faɪnd] *adj (person, taste)* утончённый* (утончён); *(sugar)* рафини́рованный*; *(oil)* очи́щенный*.
refinement [rɪ'faɪnmənt] *n (of person)* утончённость *f*; *(of system)* усоверше́нствование.
refinery [rɪ'faɪnərɪ] *n (for oil)* нефтеперераба́тывающий заво́д.
refit [ri:'fɪt] *n (NAUT)* переобору́дование ◆ *vt (ship)* переобору́довать *(impf/perf)*.
reflate [ri:'fleɪt] *vt*: **to ~ the economy** проводи́ть* (провести́* *perf*) рефля́цию.
reflation [ri:'fleɪʃən] *n* рефля́ция.
reflationary [ri:'fleɪʃənrɪ] *adj* рефляцио́нный.
reflect [rɪ'flɛkt] *vt (also fig)* отража́ть (отрази́ть* *perf*) ◆ *vi (think)* размышля́ть *(impf)*
▸ **reflect on** *vt (discredit)* броса́ть (бро́сить* *perf*) тень на *+acc*.
reflection [rɪ'flɛkʃən] *n (also fig)* отраже́ние; *(thought)* размышле́ние; *(criticism)*: **~ on** осужде́ние *+gen*; **on ~** по размышле́нии.
reflector [rɪ'flɛktəʳ] *n (on car, bicycle)* отража́тель *m*; *(for light, heat)* рефле́ктор.
reflex ['ri:flɛks] *adj (action, gesture)* рефлекто́рный ◆ *n* рефле́кс.
reflexive [rɪ'flɛksɪv] *adj (LING)* возвра́тный.
reform [rɪ'fɔ:m] *n (of law, system)* рефо́рма; *(of sinner, character)* преобразова́ние ◆ *vt (character)* преобразова́ть *(impf/perf)*; *(system)* реформи́ровать *(impf/perf)*.
reformat [ri:'fɔ:mæt] *vt (COMPUT)* переформати́ровать *(impf/perf)*.
Reformation [rɛfə'meɪʃən] *n*: **the ~** Реформа́ция.
reformatory [rɪ'fɔ:mətərɪ] *n (US)* исправи́тельное заведе́ние.
reformed [rɪ'fɔ:md] *adj (character, alcoholic)* испра́вившийся.
refrain [rɪ'freɪn] *n (of song)* припе́в ◆ *vi*: **to ~ from commenting/visiting** возде́рживаться (воздержа́ться* *perf*) от коммента́риев/визи́та.
refresh [rɪ'frɛʃ] *vt* освежа́ть (освежи́ть *perf*).
refresher course [rɪ'frɛʃə-] *n (BRIT)* курс повыше́ния квалифика́ции.
refreshing [rɪ'frɛʃɪŋ] *adj (drink, sleep)* освежа́ющий (освежа́ющ); *(change, idea)* све́жий.
refreshment [rɪ'frɛʃmənt] *n (food)* заку́ска*; *(drink)* напи́ток*; **I am in need of (some) ~** мне на́до закуси́ть.
refreshments [rɪ'frɛʃmənts] *npl* заку́ски* *fpl* и напи́тки *mpl*.
refrigeration [rɪfrɪdʒə'reɪʃən] *n (low temperature)* охлажде́ние; *(in deep freeze)* замора́живание.
refrigerator [rɪ'frɪdʒəreɪtəʳ] *n* холоди́льник.
refuel [ri:'fjuəl] *vi* заправля́ться (запра́виться* *perf*) ◆ *vt* заправля́ть (запра́вить* *perf*).
refuelling [ri:'fjuəlɪŋ] *n* запра́вка*.
refuge ['rɛfju:dʒ] *n (shelter)* убе́жище; **to take ~ in** укрыва́ться (укры́ться* *perf*) в *+prp*.
refugee [rɛfju'dʒi:] *n* бе́женец*(-нка*); **a political ~** полити́ческий*(-ая) бе́женец (-нка*).
refugee camp *n* ла́герь* *m* бе́женцев.
refund [*n* 'ri:fʌnd, *vb* rɪ'fʌnd] *n* возмеще́ние ◆ *vt (money)* возмеща́ть (возмести́ть* *perf*).
refurbish [ri:'fə:bɪʃ] *vt* за́ново отде́лывать (отде́лать *perf*).
refurbishment [ri:fə:bɪʃmənt] *n* ремо́нт.
refurnish [ri:'fə:nɪʃ] *vt* за́ново обставля́ть (обста́вить* *perf*).

* marks translations which have irregular inflections. The Russian-English side of the dictionary gives inflectional information.

refusal [rɪ'fju:zəl] *n* отка́з; **first ~** (*option*) пра́во пе́рвого вы́бора.
refuse[1] [rɪ'fju:z] *vt* (*offer, gift*) отка́зываться (отказа́ться* *perf*) от *+gen*; (*permission, consent*) отка́зывать (отказа́ть* *perf*) в *+prp* ◆ *vi* отка́зываться (отказа́ться* *perf*); (*horse*) упря́миться (заупря́миться *perf*); **to ~ to do** отка́зываться (отказа́ться* *perf*) *+infin*.
refuse[2] ['rɛfju:s] *n* му́сор*.
refuse collection *n* убо́рка му́сора.
refuse disposal *n* (*by carting away*) вы́воз му́сора.
refusenik [rɪ'fju:znɪk] *n* отка́зник.
refute [rɪ'fju:t] *vt* опроверга́ть (опрове́ргнуть* *perf*).
regain [rɪ'geɪn] *vt* (*power, position*) вновь обрета́ть (обрести́* *perf*).
regal ['ri:gl] *adj* короле́вский*.
regale [rɪ'geɪl] *vt*: **to ~ sb with sth** развлека́ть (развле́чь* *perf*) кого́-н чем-н.
regalia [rɪ'geɪlɪə] *n* рега́лии *fpl*.
regard [rɪ'gɑ:d] *n* (*esteem*) уваже́ние ◆ *vt* (*consider*) счита́ть *(impf)*; (*view, look on*): **to ~ with** относи́ться *(impf) or* рассма́триваться *(impf)* с *+instr*; **to give one's ~s to** передава́ть* (переда́ть* *perf*) приве́т *+dat*; **"with kindest ~s"** „с наилу́чшими пожела́ниями"; (*more formal*) „с уваже́нием"; **as ~s, with ~ to** что каса́ется *+gen*, относи́тельно *+gen*.
regarding [rɪ'gɑ:dɪŋ] *prep* относи́тельно *+gen*.
regardless [rɪ'gɑ:dlɪs] *adv* (*carry on, continue*) несмотря́ ни на что́; **~ of** не счита́ясь с *+instr*.
regatta [rɪ'gætə] *n* рега́та.
regency ['ri:dʒənsɪ] *n* ре́гентство ◆ *adj*: **R~** (*furniture, style*) эпо́хи ре́гентства.
regenerate [rɪ'dʒɛnəreɪt] *vt* возрожда́ть (возроди́ть* *perf*) ◆ *vi* возрожда́ться (возроди́ться* *perf*).
regent ['ri:dʒənt] *n* ре́гент.
reggae ['rɛgeɪ] *n* рэ́гги *m ind*.
regime [reɪ'ʒi:m] *n* (*system of government*) режи́м.
regiment ['rɛdʒɪmənt] *n* полк* ◆ *vt* подчиня́ть (подчини́ть *perf*) жёсткому контро́лю.
regimental [rɛdʒɪ'mɛntl] *adj* полково́й.
regimentation [rɛdʒɪmɛn'teɪʃən] *n* жёсткий* контро́ль *m*.
region ['ri:dʒən] *n* (*area: of country*) райо́н, регио́н; (*ADMIN, ANAT*) о́бласть* *f*; **in the ~ of** (*fig: approximately*) в райо́не *+gen*.
regional ['ri:dʒənl] *adj* (*organization, committee*) областно́й, региона́льный; (*characteristic of region*) ме́стный.
regional development *n* региона́льное разви́тие.
register ['rɛdʒɪstə[r]] *n* (*census, record*) за́пись *f*; (*SCOL*) журна́л; (*also:* **electoral ~**) спи́сок* избира́телей; (*MUS*) реги́стр ◆ *vt* регистри́ровать (зарегистри́ровать *perf*); (*subj: meter, gauge*) пока́зывать (показа́ть* *perf*) ◆ *vi* регистри́роваться (зарегистри́роваться *perf*); (*as student*) запи́сываться (записа́ться* *perf*); (*make impression*) запечатлева́ться (запечатле́ться *perf*) в па́мяти; **to ~ for a course** запи́сываться (записа́ться* *perf*) на ку́рс; **to ~ a protest** выража́ть (вы́разить* *perf*) проте́ст.
registered ['rɛdʒɪstəd] *adj* (*letter*) заказно́й; (*nurse, addict*) зарегистри́рованный*.
registered company *n* зарегистри́рованная компа́ния.
registered nurse *n* (*US*) зарегистри́рованная медсестра́*.
registered office *n* зарегистри́рованный о́фис.
Registered Trademark *n* зарегистри́рованный това́рный знак.
registrar ['rɛdʒɪstrɑ:[r]] *n* регистра́тор; (*BRIT: in hospital*) гла́вный врач*.
registration [rɛdʒɪs'treɪʃən] *n* регистра́ция; (*AUT: also:* **~ number**) (регистрацио́нный) но́мер* маши́ны.
registry ['rɛdʒɪstrɪ] *n* регистрату́ра.
registry office *n* (*BRIT*) ≈ ЗАГС (*отде́л за́писей гражда́нского состоя́ния*).
regret [rɪ'grɛt] *n* (*sorrow*) сожале́ние ◆ *vt* сожале́ть *(impf)* о *+prp*; (*death*) опла́кивать (опла́кать* *perf*); **to ~ that ...** сожале́ть *(impf)*, что ...; **we ~ to inform you that ...** мы с сожале́нием сообща́ем Вам, что ....
regretfully [rɪ'grɛtfəlɪ] *adv* (*unfortunately*) к сожале́нию.
regrettable [rɪ'grɛtəbl] *adj* (*unfortunate*) приско́рбный* (приско́рбен), досто́йный* (досто́ин) сожале́ния.
regrettably [rɪ'grɛtəblɪ] *adv* (*drunk, late*) огорчи́тельным о́бразом; **~, he ...** к сожале́нию, он ....
Regt *abbr* (*MIL*) = **regiment**.
regular ['rɛgjulə[r]] *adj* регуля́рный* (регуля́рен); (*even*) ро́вный* (ро́вен); (*symmetrical*) пра́вильный* (пра́вилен); (*usual: time*) определённый; (*: doctor, customer*) регуля́рный; (*LING*) пра́вильный; (*COMM: size*) сре́дний* ◆ *n* (*in cafe, restaurnat*) завсегда́тай; (*in shop*) клие́нт; **~ soldier** солда́т регуля́рной а́рмии.
regularity [rɛgju'lærɪtɪ] *n* (*frequency*) регуля́рность *f*.
regularly ['rɛgjuləlɪ] *adv* регуля́рно; (*symmetrically: shaped etc*) пра́вильно.
regulate ['rɛgjuleɪt] *vt* (*control, adjust*) регули́ровать *(impf)*.
regulation [rɛgju'leɪʃən] *n* регули́рование; (*rule*) пра́вило.
regulatory [rɛgju'leɪtrɪ] *adj* регули́рующий.
rehabilitate [ri:ə'bɪlɪteɪt] *vt* (*criminal*) интегри́ровать *(impf/perf)*; (*invalid, addict*) реабилити́ровать *(impf/perf)*.
rehabilitation ['ri:əbɪlɪ'teɪʃən] *n* (*of criminal*)

интегрáция; (*of disabled, addict*) реабилитáция.

rehash [ri:'hæʃ] *vt* (*inf*) преподносить* (преподнести* *perf*) в нóвом свéте.

rehearsal [rɪ'hə:səl] *n* репетиция; **dress ~** генерáльная репетиция.

rehearse [rɪ'hə:s] *vt* репетировать (отрепетировать *perf*).

rehouse [ri:'hauz] *vt* (*person*) переселять (переселить *perf*).

reign [reɪn] *n* цáрствование; (*fig*) госпóдство ◆ *vi* (*monarch*) цáрствовать (*impf*); (*fig*) царить (*impf*).

reigning ['reɪnɪŋ] *adj* (*monarch*) цáрствующий; (*champion*) нынешний*.

reimburse [ri:ɪm'bə:s] *vt* возмещáть (возместить* *perf*).

rein [reɪn] *n* (*for horse*) вожжá*; **to give sb free ~** (*fig*) давáть* (дать* *perf*) комý-н свобóду дéйствий.

reincarnation [ri:ɪnkɑ:'neɪʃən] *n* (*belief*) переселéние душ*.

reindeer ['reɪndɪə^r] *n inv* сéверный олéнь *m*.

reinforce [ri:ɪn'fɔ:s] *vt* (*strengthen*) укреплять (укрепить* *perf*); (*back up*) подкреплять (подкрепить* *perf*).

reinforced concrete *n* железобетóн.

reinforcement [ri:ɪn'fɔ:smənt] *n* (*strengthening*) укреплéние; (*action*) усилéние; **~s** *npl* (*MIL*) подкреплéние *ntsg*.

reinstate [ri:ɪn'steɪt] *vt* восстанáвливать (восстановить* *perf*) в прéжнем положéнии.

reinstatement [ri:ɪn'steɪtmənt] *n* восстановлéние в прéжнем положéнии.

reissue [ri:'ɪʃju:] *vt* (*book*) переиздавáть* (переиздáть* *perf*); (*film*) снóва выпускáть (выпустить* *perf*).

reiterate [ri:'ɪtəreɪt] *vt* повторять (повторить *perf*).

reject [*vt* rɪ'dʒɛkt, *n* 'ri:dʒɛkt] *vt* отклонять (отклонить* *perf*), отвергáть (отвéргнуть* *perf*); (*political system*) отвергáть (отвéргнуть* *perf*); (*candidate*) отклонять (отклонить *perf*); (*coin*) не принимáть (принять* *perf*); (*goods, fruit etc*) браковáть (забраковáть *perf*) ◆ *n* (*COMM: single item*) бракóванное издéлие; **~s** брак.

rejection [rɪ'dʒɛkʃən] *n* отклонéние; (*of candidate*) отклонéние.

rejoice [rɪ'dʒɔɪs] *vi*: **to ~ at** *or* **over** ликовáть (*impf*) по пóводу *+gen*.

rejoinder [rɪ'dʒɔɪndə^r] *n* (*retort*) возражéние, ответ.

rejuvenate [rɪ'dʒu:vəneɪt] *vt* (*person*) омолáживать (омолодить* *perf*); (*organization, system etc*) обновлять (обновить* *perf*).

rekindle [ri:'kɪndl] *vt* разжигáть (разжéчь* *perf*).

relapse [rɪ'læps] *n* (*MED*) рецидив ◆ *vi*: **to ~ into** (*depression*) (снóва) впадáть (впасть* *perf*) в *+acc*.

relate [rɪ'leɪt] *vt* (*tell*) пересказывать (пересказáть* *perf*); (*connect*): **to ~ sth to** относить* (отнести* *perf*) что-н к *+dat* ◆ *vi*: **to ~ to** (*person*) сходиться* (*impf*) с *+instr*; (*subject, thing*) относиться* (*impf*) к *+dat*.

related [rɪ'leɪtɪd] *adj*: **~ (to)** (*person*) связанный родствóм (с *+instr*); (*animal, language*) рóдственный* (рóдствен) (с *+instr*); **they are ~** они состоят в родствé.

relating to [rɪ'leɪtɪŋ-] *prep* относительно *+gen*.

relation [rɪ'leɪʃən] *n* (*member of family*) рóдственник(-ица); (*connection*) отношéние; **~s** *npl* (*dealings*) сношéния *ntpl*; (*relatives*) родня *fsg*; **diplomatic/international ~s** дипломатические/международные отношéния; **in ~ to** относительно *+gen*; **to bear no ~ to** не имéть (*impf*) никакóго отношéния к *+dat*.

relationship [rɪ'leɪʃənʃɪp] *n* (*between two people, countries*) (взаимо-)отношéния *ntpl*; (*between two things*) связь *f*; (*also: family ~*) родствó; (*affair*) связь; **they have a good ~** у них хорóшие (взаимо-)отношéния.

relative ['rɛlətɪv] *n* (*member of family*) рóдственник(-ица) ◆ *adj* (*comparative*) относительный* (относителен); (*connected*): **~ to** относящийся к *+dat*.

relatively ['rɛlətɪvlɪ] *adv* относительно.

relative pronoun *n* (*LING*) относительное местоимéние.

relax [rɪ'læks] *vi* (*person: unwind*) расслабляться (расслáбиться* *perf*); (*: calm down*) успокáиваться (успокóиться *perf*); (*muscle*) расслабляться (расслáбиться* *perf*) ◆ *vt* (*one's grip, rule*) ослаблять (ослáбить* *perf*); (*mind, person*) расслаблять (расслáбить* *perf*); (*control*) ослаблять (ослáбить* *perf*).

relaxation [ri:læk'seɪʃən] *n* (*rest*) óтдых; (*of muscle*) расслаблéние; (*of grip, rule, control etc*) ослаблéние; (*recreation*) óтдых, развлечéние.

relaxed [rɪ'lækst] *adj* (*person, atmosphere*) спокóйный* (спокóен).

relaxing [rɪ'læksɪŋ] *adj* (*holiday, afternoon*) расслабляющий*.

relay [*n* 'ri:leɪ, *vt* rɪ'leɪ] *n* (*race*) эстафéта ◆ *vt* (*pass on: message etc*) передавáть* (передáть* *perf*); (*transmit*) транслировать (*impf/perf*).

release [rɪ'li:s] *n* (*from prison, obligation*) освобождéние; (*of gas, water etc*) выпуск; (*of film, book, record*) выпуск; (*device*) спусковóе устрóйство, спуск ◆ *vt* (*prisoner*) освобождáть (освободить* *perf*); (*gas etc*) выпуска́ть (вы́пустить* *perf*); (*free*: *from wreckage etc*) высвобожда́ть (вы́свободить* *perf*); (TECH: *catch, spring etc*) отпуска́ть (отпусти́ть* *perf*); (*book, film*) выпуска́ть (вы́пустить* *perf*); (*report, news*) передава́ть* (переда́ть* *perf*); **to ~ the clutch** (AUT) отпуска́ть (отпусти́ть* *perf*) сцепле́ние; *see also* **press release**.

relegate ['rɛləgeɪt] *vt* понижа́ть (пони́зить* *perf*); (BRIT: SPORT): **to be ~d** переводи́ть* (перевести́* *perf*) в ни́зшую ли́гу.

relent [rɪ'lɛnt] *vi* (*give in*) уступа́ть (уступи́ть* *perf*).

relentless [rɪ'lɛntlɪs] *adj* (*effort*) неосла́бный; (*rain*) продолжи́тельный* (продолжи́телен); (*determined*) неуста́нный* (неуста́нен).

relevance ['rɛləvəns] *n* (*of remarks*) уме́стность *f*, релева́нтность *f*; (*of information*) актуа́льность *f*; (*of question*) уме́стность; **~ of sth to sth** уме́стность чего́-н по отноше́нию к чему́-н.

relevant ['rɛləvənt] *adj* (*pertinent*) актуа́льный* (актуа́лен), релева́нтный* (релева́нтен); (*corresponding*) соотве́тствующий*; **~ to** относя́щийся* к *+dat*.

reliability [rɪlaɪə'bɪlɪtɪ] *n* (*see adj*) надёжность *f*; достове́рность *f*.

reliable [rɪ'laɪəbl] *adj* надёжный* (надёжен); (*news, information*) достове́рный* (достове́рен).

reliably [rɪ'laɪəblɪ] *adv*: **to be ~ informed that ...** име́ть *(impf)* достове́рную информа́цию о том, что ....

reliance [rɪ'laɪəns] *n*: **~ (on)** (*person, drugs*) зави́симость *f* (от *+gen*).

reliant [rɪ'laɪənt] *adj*: **to be ~ on sth/sb** полага́ться (положи́ться* *perf*) на кого́-н/что-н.

relic ['rɛlɪk] *n* (REL) мо́щи *pl*; (*of the past etc*) рели́квия.

relief [rɪ'li:f] *n* облегче́ние; (*aid*) по́мощь *f*; (ART, GEO) релье́ф; **by way of light ~** для разря́дки напряжённости.

relief map *n* релье́фная ка́рта.

relief road *n* объе́зд (*доро́га, отводя́щая тра́нспорт*).

relieve [rɪ'li:v] *vt* (*pain, sufferings*) облегча́ть (облегчи́ть *perf*); (*fear, worry*) уменьша́ть (уме́ньшить *perf*); (*patient*) освобожда́ть (освободи́ть* *perf*); (*victims, refugees etc*) ока́зывать (оказа́ть* *perf*) по́мощь *+dat*; (*colleague, guard*) сменя́ть (смени́ть* *perf*); **to ~ sb of sth** освобожда́ть (освободи́ть* *perf*) кого́-н от чего́-н; **to ~ o.s.** облегча́ться (облегчи́ться *perf*).

relieved [rɪ'li:vd] *adj*: **to feel ~** почу́вствовать *(perf)* облегче́ние; **he is ~ that ...** он рад, что ...; **I'm ~ to hear it** я рад э́то слы́шать.

religion [rɪ'lɪdʒən] *n* рели́гия.

religious [rɪ'lɪdʒəs] *adj* религио́зный* (религио́зен).

religious education *n* религио́зное воспита́ние.

religiously [rɪ'lɪdʒəslɪ] *adv* (*scrupulously*) неукосни́тельно.

relinquish [rɪ'lɪŋkwɪʃ] *vt* (*authority*) отка́зываться (отказа́ться* *perf*) от *+gen*; (*plan, habit*) оставля́ть (оста́вить* *perf*).

relish ['rɛlɪʃ] *n* (CULIN) припра́ва; (*enjoyment*) наслажде́ние ◆ *vt* (*food, drink*) наслажда́ться (наслади́ться* *perf*) *+instr*; (*idea, thought, prospect etc*) наслажда́ться *(impf)*.

relive [ri:'lɪv] *vt* (*memory, pleasure, visit etc*) вновь пережива́ть (пережи́ть* *perf*).

reload [ri:'ləud] *vt* (*gun*) перезаряжа́ть (перезаряди́ть* *perf*).

relocate [ri:ləu'keɪt] *vt* перемеща́ть (перемести́ть* *perf*) ◆ *vi*: **to ~ (in)** перемеща́ться (перемести́ться* *perf*) (в *+acc*).

reluctance [rɪ'lʌktəns] *n* неохо́та, нежела́ние.

reluctant [rɪ'lʌktənt] *adj* (*acceptance*) неохо́тный* (неохо́тен); (*person*): **he is ~ to go there** он идёт туда́ неохо́тно.

reluctantly [rɪ'lʌktəntlɪ] *adv* неохо́тно.

rely on [rɪ'laɪ-] *vt fus* (*be dependent on*) полага́ться *(impf)* на *+acc*; (*trust*) полага́ться (положи́ться* *perf*) на *+acc*.

remain [rɪ'meɪn] *vi* остава́ться* (оста́ться* *perf*); (*survive*) сохраня́ться (сохрани́ться *perf*); **to ~ silent** храни́ть *(impf)* молча́ние; **I ~, yours faithfully** (BRIT: *in letters*) остаю́сь, и́скренне Ваш.

remainder [rɪ'meɪndə'] *n* оста́ток*.

remaining [rɪ'meɪnɪŋ] *adj* сохрани́вшийся; (*surviving*) оста́вшийся.

remains [rɪ'meɪnz] *npl* (*of meal*) оста́тки *mpl*; (*of building*) разва́лины *fpl*; (*of corpse*) оста́нки *mpl*.

remand [rɪ'mɑ:nd] *n*: **on ~** взя́тый под стра́жу ◆ *vt*: **he was ~ed in custody** он был взят под стра́жу.

remand home *n* (BRIT) *исправи́тельная коло́ния для несовершенноле́тних*.

remark [rɪ'mɑ:k] *n* замеча́ние ◆ *vt* замеча́ть (заме́тить* *perf*) ◆ *vi*: **to ~ on sth** де́лать (сде́лать *perf*) замеча́ние относи́тельно *+gen*; **to ~ that** замеча́ть (заме́тить* *perf*), что.

remarkable [rɪ'mɑ:kəbl] *adj* замеча́тельный* (замеча́телен).

remarry [ri:'mærɪ] *vi* вступа́ть (вступи́ть* *perf*) в повто́рный брак.

remedial [rɪ'mi:dɪəl] *adj* (*tuition, classes*) исправи́тельный* (исправи́телен), корректи́вный; (*exercise*) лечёбный.

remedy ['rɛmədɪ] *n* (*cure*) сре́дство ◆ *vt* исправля́ть (испра́вить* *perf*).

remember [rɪ'mɛmbə'] *vt* (*call back to mind*) вспомина́ть (вспо́мнить *perf*); (*bear in mind*) по́мнить *(impf)*; (*send greetings*): **~ me to him** переда́йте ему́ от меня́ приве́т; **I ~ seeing her, I ~ having seen her** я по́мню, что я её ви́дел; **she ~ed to call me** она́ не забы́ла

позвони́ть мне.
remembrance [rɪ'mɛmbrəns] *n* па́мять *f*.
remind [rɪ'maɪnd] *vt*: **to ~ sb to do** напомина́ть (напо́мнить *perf*) кому́-н *+infin*; **to ~ sb of sth/sb** напомина́ть (напо́мнить *perf*) кому́-н о чём-н/ком-н; **that ~s me!** кста́ти!; **she ~s me of her mother** она́ напомина́ет мне свою́ мать.
reminder [rɪ'maɪndə'] *n* напомина́ние.
reminisce [rɛmɪ'nɪs] *vi* вспомина́ть (вспо́мнить *perf*).
reminiscences [rɛmɪ'nɪsnsɪz] *npl* воспомина́ния *ntpl*.
reminiscent [rɛmɪ'nɪsnt] *adj*: **to be ~ of sth** напомина́ть (напо́мнить *perf*) что-н.
remiss [rɪ'mɪs] *adj* (*careless*) небре́жный* (небре́жен); **it was ~ of him** с его́ стороны́ э́то бы́ло небре́жностью.
remission [rɪ'mɪʃən] *n* (*cancelling*: *of debt, fee*) освобожде́ние; (*reduction*: *of prison sentence*) сокраще́ние; (*MED*) реми́ссия; (*REL*) отпуще́ние.
remit [rɪ'mɪt] *vt* (*send*) пересыла́ть (пересла́ть* *perf*).
remittance [rɪ'mɪtns] *n* (*payment*) де́нежный перево́д (*для опла́ты чего́-н*).
remnant ['rɛmnənt] *n* оста́ток*; **~s** *npl* (*COMM*) оста́тки *mpl*.
remonstrate ['rɛmənstreɪt] *vi*: **to ~ (with sb about sth)** выража́ть (вы́разить* *perf*) проте́ст (кому́-н по по́воду чего́-н).
remorse [rɪ'mɔ:s] *n* раска́яние.
remorseful [rɪ'mɔ:sful] *adj* по́лный* (по́лон) раска́яния.
remorseless [rɪ'mɔ:slɪs] *adj* (*person*) беща́дный* (беща́ден); (*noise, pain*) невыноси́мый (невыноси́м).
remote [rɪ'məut] *adj* (*place, time*) отдалённый* (отдалён); (*person*) за́мкнутый (за́мкнут); (*possibility, chance*) незначи́тельный* (незначи́телен); **there is a ~ possibility that ...** существу́ет маловероя́тная возмо́жность, что ....
remote control *n* дистанцио́нное управле́ние.
remote-controlled [rɪ'məutkən'trəuld] *adj* с дистанцио́нным управле́нием.
remotely [rɪ'məutlɪ] *adv* отдалённо; **I'm not ~ interested** я ниско́лько не заинтересо́ван.
remoteness [rɪ'məutnɪs] *n* (*of place*) отдалённость *f*; (*of person*) за́мкнутость *f*.
remould ['ri:məuld] *n* (*BRIT*: *tyre*) ши́на с восстано́вленным проте́ктором.
removable [rɪ'mu:vəbl] *adj* (*detachable*) съёмный.
removal [rɪ'mu:vəl] *n* (*also MED*) удале́ние; (*BRIT*: *of furniture*) перево́зка; (*dismissal*) отстране́ние.
removal man *irreg n* (*BRIT*) перево́зчик ме́бели.
removal van *n* (*BRIT*) автофурго́н для перево́зки ме́бели.
remove [rɪ'mu:v] *vt* (*take away*) убира́ть (убра́ть* *perf*); (*clothing, bandage, employee*) снима́ть (снять* *perf*); (*stain, also MED*) удаля́ть (удали́ть *perf*); (*problem, doubt*) устраня́ть (устрани́ть *perf*); **first cousin once ~d** двою́родный(-ая) племя́нник(-ица).
remover [rɪ'mu:və'] *n* (*for paint, varnish*) сре́дство для сня́тия; **stain ~** пятновыводи́тель *m*; **paint/make-up ~** сре́дство для сня́тия кра́ски/макия́жа.
remunerate [rɪ'mju:nəreɪt] *vt* вознагражда́ть (вознагради́ть* *perf*).
remuneration [rɪmju:nə'reɪʃən] *n* вознагражде́ние.
Renaissance [rɪ'neɪsɑ̃:s] *n*: **the ~** (*HISTORY*) Возрожде́ние.
renal ['ri:nl] *adj* по́чечный.
renal failure *n* по́чечная недоста́точность *f*.
rename [ri:'neɪm] *vt* переимено́вывать (переименова́ть *perf*).
rend [rɛnd] (*pt, pp* **rent**) *vt* (*subj*: *society*) раздира́ть (*impf*); **a whistle rent the air** свист рассёк во́здух.
render ['rɛndə'] *vt* (*give*: *assistance*) ока́зывать (оказа́ть* *perf*); (*cause to become*: *harmless, useless*) де́лать (сде́лать *perf*) *+instr*; (*submit*: *account*) предъявля́ть (предъяви́ть* *perf*); **the blow ~ed him unconscious** уда́р привёл его́ в бессозна́тельное состоя́ние.
rendering ['rɛndərɪŋ] *n* (*MUS etc*) исполне́ние; (*CONSTR*) штукату́рка.
rendezvous ['rɔndɪvu:] *n* (*meeting*) свида́ние, рандеву́ *nt ind*; (*place*) ме́сто свида́ния ◆ *vi* встреча́ться (встре́титься* *perf*); **to ~ with sb** встреча́ться (встре́титься* *perf*) с кем-н.
rendition [rɛn'dɪʃən] *n* (*MUS*) исполне́ние.
renegade ['rɛnɪgeɪd] *n* ренега́т.
renew [rɪ'nju:] *vt* возобновля́ть (возобнови́ть* *perf*).
renewal [rɪ'nju:əl] *n* возобновле́ние.
renounce [rɪ'nauns] *vt* отка́зываться (отказа́ться* *perf*) от *+gen*; (*belief, throne*) отрека́ться (отре́чься* *perf*) от *+gen*; (*holy orders*) отверга́ть (отве́ргнуть *perf*).
renovate ['rɛnəveɪt] *vt* (*building, machine*) ремонти́ровать (отремонти́ровать *perf*); (*painting*) реставри́ровать (отреставри́ровать *perf*).
renovation [rɛnə'veɪʃən] *n* ремо́нт; (*of work of art*) реставра́ция.
renown [rɪ'naun] *n* сла́ва.
renowned [rɪ'naund] *adj* просла́вленный.
rent [rɛnt] *pt, pp of* **rend** ◆ *n* кварти́рная пла́та ◆ *vt* (*take for rent*: *house*) снима́ть (снять* *perf*);

* marks translations which have irregular inflections. The Russian-English side of the dictionary gives inflectional information.

(: *television, car*) брать* (взять* *perf*) напрока́т; (*also:* ~ **out**: *house*) сдава́ть* (сдать* *perf*) (внаём); (: *television, car*) дава́ть* (дать* *perf*) напрока́т.

rental ['rɛntl] *n* (*for television, car*) пла́та за прока́т.

rent strike *n неупла́та жильца́ми аре́ндной пла́ты с це́лью выраже́ния проте́ста.*

renunciation [rɪnʌnsɪ'eɪʃən] *n* отка́з; (*of belief, throne*) отрече́ние.

reopen [ri:'əupən] *vt* (*shop, restaurant etc*) сно́ва открыва́ть (откры́ть* *perf*); (*discussion, legal case etc*) возобновля́ть (возобнови́ть* *perf*).

reopening [ri:'əupnɪŋ] *n* (*see vb*) откры́тие (*по́сле ремо́нта итп*); возобновле́ние.

reorder [ri:'ɔ:də'] *vt* возобновля́ть (возобнови́ть* *perf*) зака́з на *+acc*; (*rearrange*) перестра́ивать (перестро́ить *perf*).

reorganization ['ri:ɔ:gənaɪ'zeɪʃən] *n* реорганиза́ция.

reorganize [ri:'ɔ:gənaɪz] *vt* реорганизо́вывать (реорганизова́ть *perf*).

rep [rɛp] *n abbr* (COMM) = **representative**; (THEAT) = **repertory**.

Rep. *abbr* (US: POL) = **representative, republican**.

repair [rɪ'pɛə'] *n* ремо́нт ◆ *vt* (*clothes, shoes*) чини́ть* (почини́ть* *perf*); (*car, engine*) ремонти́ровать (отремонти́ровать *perf*); **in good/bad** ~ в хоро́шем/плохо́м состоя́нии; **under** ~ в ремо́нте.

repair kit *n* ремо́нтный компле́кт.

repairman [rɪ'pɛəmæn] *irreg n* ма́стер* по ремо́нту.

repair shop *n* ремо́нтная мастерска́я *f adj*.

repartee [rɛpɑ:'ti:] *n* (*conversation*) остроу́мная бесе́да; (*riposte*) остро́та.

repast [rɪ'pɑ:st] *n* тра́пеза.

repatriate [ri:'pætrɪeɪt] *vt* репатрии́ровать (*impf/perf*).

repay [ri:'peɪ] *irreg vt* (*money, debt*) выпла́чивать (вы́платить* *perf*); (*person*) упла́чивать (уплати́ть* *perf*) *+dat*; (: *reward*) вознагражда́ть (вознагради́ть* *perf*); (*efforts*) возмеща́ть (возмести́ть* *perf*); **to** ~ **sb (for sth)** (*favour*) отпла́чивать (отплати́ть* *perf*) кому́-н (за что-н).

repayment [ri:'peɪmənt] *n* вы́плата.

repeal [rɪ'pi:l] *n* отме́на ◆ *vt* отменя́ть (отмени́ть* *perf*).

repeat [rɪ'pi:t] *vt* повторя́ть (повтори́ть *perf*) ◆ *vi* повторя́ться (повтори́ться *perf*) ◆ *n* (RADIO, TV) повторе́ние ◆ *cpd* (*performance, order etc*) повто́рный; **to** ~ **a class** (SCOL) остава́ться* (оста́ться* *perf*) на второ́й год.

repeatedly [rɪ'pi:tɪdlɪ] *adv* неоднокра́тно.

repel [rɪ'pɛl] *vt* (*drive away*) отбива́ть (отби́ть* *perf*); (*disgust*) отта́лкивать (оттолкну́ть *perf*).

repellent [rɪ'pɛlənt] *adj* (*appearance, smell*) отта́лкивающий*; (*idea, thought*) отврати́тельный* (отврати́телен) ◆ *n*: **insect** ~ репелле́нт.

repent [rɪ'pɛnt] *vi*: **to** ~ **(of)** ка́яться (пока́яться *perf*) (в *+prp*).

repentance [rɪ'pɛntəns] *n* покая́ние.

repercussions [ri:pə'kʌʃənz] *npl* после́дствия *ntpl*.

repertoire ['rɛpətwɑ:'] *n* репертуа́р.

repertory ['rɛpətərɪ] *n* (*also:* ~ **theatre**) репертуа́рный теа́тр.

repertory company *n* постоя́нная тру́ппа.

repetition [rɛpɪ'tɪʃən] *n* повторе́ние; (*of order, in text*) повто́р.

repetitious [rɛpɪ'tɪʃəs] *adj* изоби́лующий повто́рами.

repetitive [rɪ'pɛtɪtɪv] *adj* повторя́ющийся.

replace [rɪ'pleɪs] *vt* (*put back*: *vertically*) класть* (положи́ть* *perf*) обра́тно; (: *horizontally*) ста́вить* (поста́вить* *perf*) обра́тно; (*take the place of*) заменя́ть (замени́ть* *perf*); **to** ~ **sth with sth** заменя́ть (замени́ть* *perf*) что-н чем-н; **"replace the receiver"** (TEL) „положи́те тру́бку".

replacement [rɪ'pleɪsmənt] *n* заме́на.

replacement cost *n* изде́ржки* *pl* возмеще́ния.

replacement part *n* запасна́я часть* *f*.

replacement value *n* (INSURANCE) сто́имость *f* страхово́го возмеще́ния.

replay [*n* 'ri:pleɪ, *vb* ri:'pleɪ] *n* (*of match*) переигро́вка*; (*of tape*) повто́рное прои́грывание; (*of film*) повто́рный пока́з ◆ *vt* (*match, game*) переи́грывать (переигра́ть *perf*); (*part of tape*) повто́рно прои́грывать (проигра́ть *perf*).

replenish [rɪ'plɛnɪʃ] *vt* (*glass*) сно́ва наполня́ть (напо́лнить *perf*); (*stock etc*) пополня́ть (попо́лнить *perf*).

replete [rɪ'pli:t] *adj* (*well-fed*) насы́тившийся; ~ **with** загру́женный (загру́жен) *+instr*; **I'm quite** ~ я вполне насы́тился.

replica ['rɛplɪkə] *n* (*copy*) ко́пия.

reply [rɪ'plaɪ] *n* отве́т ◆ *vi* отвеча́ть (отве́тить* *perf*); **in** ~ **to** в отве́т на *+acc*; **there's no** ~ (TEL) не отвеча́ет.

reply coupon *n* бланк для отве́та.

reply-paid postcard *n* откры́тка* с опла́ченным отве́том.

report [rɪ'pɔ:t] *n* (*account*) докла́д; (PRESS, TV *etc*: *statement*) репорта́ж; (: *information*) сообще́ние; (BRIT: *also:* **school** ~) отчёт об успева́емости; (*of gun*) вы́стрел ◆ *vt* сообща́ть (сообщи́ть *perf*) о *+prp*; (*event, meeting*) докла́дывать (доложи́ть* *perf*) о *+prp*; (*person*) доноси́ть* (донести́* *perf*) на *+acc* ◆ *vi* (*make a report*) докла́дывать (доложи́ть* *perf*); (*present o.s.*): **to** ~ **(to sb)** явля́ться (яви́ться* *perf*) (к кому́-н); (*be responsible to*): **to** ~ **to sb** быть* (*impf*) под нача́лом кого́-н; **to** ~ **that** сообща́ть (сообщи́ть *perf*), что; **to** ~ **on** представля́ть

(предста́вить* *perf*) докла́д о *+prp*; **it is ~ed that** ... сообща́ется, что ....
report card *n* (*US, SCOTTISH*) та́бель *m* успева́емости.
reportedly [rɪ'pɔ:tɪdlɪ] *adv*: **she is ~ living in Spain** по сообще́ниям, она́ живёт в Испа́нии; **he ~ ordered them to** ... сообща́ют, что он приказа́л им *+infin* ....
reported speech *n* (*LING*) ко́свенная речь *f*.
reporter [rɪ'pɔ:tə'] *n* репортёр.
repose [rɪ'pəuz] *n*: **in ~** (*face*) в поко́е.
repository [rɪ'pɔzɪtərɪ] *n* (*place*) храни́лище; (*person*) храни́тель *m*.
repossess ['ri:pə'zɛs] *vt* (*goods, building*) изыма́ть (изъя́ть* *perf*) (*за неплатёж*).
reprehensible [rɛprɪ'hɛnsɪbl] *adj* (*behaviour*) предосуди́тельный* (предосуди́телен).
represent [rɛprɪ'zɛnt] *vt* (*person, nation*) представля́ть (предста́вить* *perf*); (*view, belief*) излага́ть (изложи́ть* *perf*); (*constitute*) представля́ть (*impf*) собо́й; (*idea, emotion*) символизи́ровать* (*impf/perf*); (*describe*): **to ~ sth as** изобража́ть (изобрази́ть* *perf*) что-н как; (*explain*): **to ~ to sb that** объясня́ть (объясни́ть *perf*) кому́-н, что.
representation [rɛprɪzɛn'teɪʃən] *n* (*state*) представи́тельство; (*picture, statue*) изображе́ние; (*petition*) заявле́ние; **~s** *npl* (*protest*) представле́ния *ntpl*.
representative [rɛprɪ'zɛntətɪv] *n* представи́тель(ница) *m(f)*; (*of belief, also COMM, POL*) представи́тель *m* ◆ *adj* (*group, survey, cross-section*) представи́тельный* (представи́телен); **~ of** характе́рный* (характе́рен) для *+gen*.
repress [rɪ'prɛs] *vt* подавля́ть (подави́ть* *perf*).
repression [rɪ'prɛʃən] *n* подавле́ние.
repressive [rɪ'prɛsɪv] *adj* (*society, measures*) репресси́вный* (репресси́вен).
reprieve [rɪ'pri:v] *n* (*LAW*) отсро́чка (*в исполне́нии пригово́ра*); (*fig: delay*) переды́шка* ◆ *vt* (*LAW*): **he was ~d** он получи́л отсро́чку.
reprimand ['rɛprɪmɑ:nd] *n* вы́говор ◆ *vt* де́лать (сде́лать *perf*) вы́говор *+dat*.
reprint [*n* 'ri:prɪnt, *vb* ri:'prɪnt] *n* перепеча́тка ◆ *vt* перепеча́тывать (перепеча́тать *perf*).
reprisal [rɪ'praɪzl] *n* отве́тное де́йствие; **~s** *npl* (*acts of revenge*) отве́тные де́йствия *ntpl*; **to take ~s** мстить* (отомсти́ть* *perf*).
reproach [rɪ'prəutʃ] *n* упрёк ◆ *vt*: **to ~ sb for sth/with sth** упрека́ть (упрекну́ть *perf*) кого́-н за что-н/в чём-н; **his behaviour was beyond ~** его́ поведе́ние бы́ло безупре́чно.
reproachful [rɪ'prəutʃful] *adj* (*look, remark*) укори́зненный* (укори́знен).
reproduce [ri:prə'dju:s] *vt* воспроизводи́ть* (воспроизвести́* *perf*) ◆ *vi* размножа́ться (размно́житься *perf*).
reproduction [ri:prə'dʌkʃən] *n* воспроизведе́ние; (*ART*) репроду́кция; (*breeding*) воспроизведе́ние.
reproductive [ri:prə'dʌktɪv] *adj* (*process*) репродукти́вный; (*system*) полово́й.
reproof [rɪ'pru:f] *n* (*rebuke*) порица́ние; (*disapproval*): **with ~** с уко́ром.
reprove [rɪ'pru:v] *vt* (*person*): **to ~ sb for sth** осужда́ть (осуди́ть* *perf*) кого́-н за что-н.
reproving [rɪ'pru:vɪŋ] *adj* осужда́ющий.
reptile ['rɛptaɪl] *n* пресмыка́ющееся *nt adj* (живо́тное).
Repub. *abbr* (*US: POL*) = **republican**.
republic [rɪ'pʌblɪk] *n* респу́блика.
republican [rɪ'pʌblɪkən] *adj* республика́нский* ◆ *n* (*US: POL*): **R~** республика́нец*(-нка*).
repudiate [rɪ'pju:dɪeɪt] *vt* отверга́ть (отве́ргнуть *perf*).
repudiation [rɪpju:dɪ'eɪʃən] *n* отрица́ние, отрече́ние; (*COMM*) отка́з от до́лга *or* выполне́ния контра́кта.
repugnance [rɪ'pʌgnəns] *n* отвраще́ние.
repugnant [rɪ'pʌgnənt] *adj* отврати́тельный* (отврати́телен).
repulse [rɪ'pʌls] *vt* (*drive back*) отража́ть (отрази́ть* *perf*); (: *enemy*) отбра́сывать (отбро́сить* *perf*); (*disgust*) отта́лкивать (оттолкну́ть *perf*).
repulsion [rɪ'pʌlʃən] *n* отвраще́ние.
repulsive [rɪ'pʌlsɪv] *adj* отврати́тельный* (отврати́телен).
reputable ['rɛpjutəbl] *adj* (*person*) уважа́емый; **~ company etc** компа́ния с хоро́шей репута́цией.
reputation [rɛpju'teɪʃən] *n* репута́ция; **to have a ~ for** име́ть (*impf*) репута́цию *+gen*; **he has a ~ for being tactless** он изве́стен свое́й беста́ктностью.
repute [rɪ'pju:t] *n* до́брая сла́ва.
reputed [rɪ'pju:tɪd] *adj* (*rumoured*) предполага́емый; **he is ~ to be intelligent/rich** счита́ется, что он умён/бога́т.
reputedly [rɪ'pju:tɪdlɪ] *adv* по о́бщему мне́нию.
request [rɪ'kwɛst] *n* (*polite demand*) про́сьба; (*formal demand*) зая́вка* ◆ *vt*: **to ~ sth of** *or* **from sb** проси́ть* (попроси́ть* *perf*) что-н у кого́-н; **at the ~ of** по про́сьбе *+gen*; (*formal*) по зая́вке *+gen*; **"you are ~ed not to smoke"** „про́сим не кури́ть".
request stop *n* (*BRIT*) остано́вка* по тре́бованию.
requiem ['rɛkwɪəm] *n* (*REL*) панихи́да; (*MUS*) ре́квием.
require [rɪ'kwaɪə'] *vt* (*person*) нужда́ться (*impf*) в *+prp*; (*thing, situation*) тре́бовать (*impf*); (*order*): **to ~ sth of sb** тре́бовать (потре́бовать *perf*) что-н от кого́-н; **we ~ you**

* marks translations which have irregular inflections. The Russian-English side of the dictionary gives inflectional information.

to complete the task мы трéбуем, чтóбы Вы завершíли рабóту; **if ~d** éсли трéбуется; **what documents are ~d?** какíе документы трéбуются?; **~d by law** трéбуемый закóном.
required [rɪ'kwaɪəd] *adj* необходíмый.
requirement [rɪ'kwaɪəmənt] *n* (*need, want*) потрéбность *f*; (*condition*) трéбование; **to meet sb's ~s** удовлетворя́ть (удовлетворíть *perf*) чьим-н трéбованиям.
requisite ['rɛkwɪzɪt] *n* трéбование ◆ *adj* необходíмый.
requisition [rɛkwɪ'zɪʃən] *vt* (*MIL*) реквизíровать (*impf/perf*) ◆ *n*: **~ (for)** зая́вка (на *+acc*).
reroute [ri:'ru:t] *vt* (*train etc*) изменя́ть (изменíть* *perf*) маршрýт *+gen*.
resale [ri:'seɪl] *n* перепродáжа; **"not for ~"** „перепродáжа запрещенá".
resale price maintenance *n* поддержáние цен при перепродáже товáров.
reschedule [ri:'ʃɛdju:l] *vt*: **~ (for)** переносíть* (перенестí* *perf*) (на *+acc*).
rescind [rɪ'sɪnd] *vt* (*law, judgement*) отменя́ть (отменíть* *perf*); (*contract, order etc*) аннулíровать (*impf/perf*).
rescue ['rɛskju:] *n* спасéние ◆ *vt*: **to ~ (from)** спасáть (спастí* *perf*) (от *+gen*); **to come to sb's ~** приходíть* (прийтí* *perf*) комý-н на пóмощь.
rescue party *n* спасáтельный отря́д, спасáтельная пáртия.
rescuer ['rɛskjuəʳ] *n* спасáтель(ница) *m(f)*.
research [rɪ'sə:tʃ] *n* исслéдование ◆ *vt* исслéдовать (*impf/perf*) ◆ *vi* проводíть* (провестí* *perf*) исслéдование *or* исслéдования; **a piece of ~** (наýчное) исслéдование; **~ and development** наýчно-исслéдовательские и óпытно-конструкторские рабóты.
researcher [rɪ'sə:tʃəʳ] *n* исслéдователь(ница) *m(f)*.
research work *n* наýчно-исслéдовательская рабóта.
research worker *n* наýчный рабóтник.
resell [ri:'sɛl] *irreg vt* перепродавáть* (перепродáть* *perf*).
resemblance [rɪ'zɛmbləns] *n* схóдство; **he bears a strong ~ to his father** он сíльно похóдит на отцá; **this bears no ~ to ...** э́то не имéет никакóго схóдства с *+instr* ....
resemble [rɪ'zɛmbl] *vt* походíть* (*impf*) на *+acc*; **he very much ~s his father** он óчень похóдит на отцá.
resent [rɪ'zɛnt] *vt* (*situation*) негодовáть (*impf*) прóтив *+gen*; (*person*) негодовáть (*impf*) на *+acc*.
resentful [rɪ'zɛntful] *adj* негодýющий*.
resentment [rɪ'zɛntmənt] *n* негодовáние.
reservation [rɛzə'veɪʃən] *n* (*booking*) предварíтельный закáз; (*doubt*) сомнéние; (*for tribe*) резервáция; **to make a ~ (in an hotel/on a plane)** бронíровать* (забронíровать* *perf*) (мéсто в гостíнице/на самолёте); **with ~s** (*doubts*) с оговóрками.
reservation desk *n* (*US*: *in hotel*) стол* администрáтора.
reserve [rɪ'zə:v] *n* (*store*) резéрв, запáс; (*also*: **nature ~**) заповéдник; (*SPORT*) запаснóй игрóк*; (*restraint*) сдéржанность *f* ◆ *vt* (*keep*: *money, food*) приберегáть (приберéчь* *perf*); (: *energy*) берéчь* (сберéчь* *perf*); (*seats, table etc*) бронíровать (забронíровать *perf*); **~s** *npl* (*MIL*) запáс *msg*; (*COMM*) резéрвы *mpl*; **in ~** в резéрве *or* запáсе.
reserve currency *n* резéрвная валю́та.
reserved [rɪ'zə:vd] *adj* (*restrained*) сдéржанный* (сдéржан); (*seat*) забронíрованный (забронíрован).
reserve price *n* (*BRIT*) отправнáя *or* резервíрованная ценá*.
reserve team *n* (*BRIT*: *SPORT*) запаснáя комáнда.
reservist [rɪ'zə:vɪst] *n* резервíст.
reservoir ['rɛzəvwɑ:ʳ] *n* (*of water*) водохранíлище; (*small*: *of ink etc*) резервуáр; (*fig*: *of talent, strength*) хранíлище.
reset [ri:'sɛt] *irreg vt* вновь устанáвливать (установíть* *perf*); (*clock, watch*) переводíть* (перевестí* *perf*); (*COMPUT*) сбрáсывать (сбрóсить* *perf*), возвращáть (возвратíть* *perf*) в исхóдное положéние.
reshape [ri:'ʃeɪp] *vt* (*policy*) изменя́ть (изменíть *perf*).
reshuffle [ri:'ʃʌfl] *n*: **Cabinet ~** перестанóвки *fpl* в кабинéте минíстров.
reside [rɪ'zaɪd] *vi* (*live*) проживáть (*impf*).
residence ['rɛzɪdəns] *n* (*home*) резидéнция; (*length of stay*) пребывáние; **to take up ~** поселя́ться (поселíться *perf*); **to be in ~** (*queen etc*) пребывáть (*impf*); (*artist*) проживáть (*impf*) по мéсту слýжбы.
residence permit *n* (*BRIT*) вид на жíтельство.
resident ['rɛzɪdənt] *n* (*of country, town*) (постоя́нный(-ая)) жíтель(ница) *m(f)*; (*in hotel*) проживáющий(-ая) *m(f) adj* ◆ *adj*: **~ population** постоя́нное населéние; **~ doctor** врач*, живýщий при больнíце.
residential [rɛzɪ'dɛnʃəl] *adj* (*area*) жилóй; (*course, college*) с проживáнием.
residue ['rɛzɪdju:] *n* остáток*; (*CHEM, PHYS*) осáдок*.
resign [rɪ'zaɪn] *vi* (*from post*) оставля́ть (остáвить* *perf*) ◆ *vt* (*one's post*) уходíть* (уйтí* *perf*) в отстáвку с *+gen*; **to ~ o.s. to** смиря́ться (смирíться *perf*) с *+instr*.
resignation [rɛzɪg'neɪʃən] *n* отстáвка*; (*acceptance*) покóрность *f*; **to tender one's ~** подавáть* (подáть* *perf*) в отстáвку.
resigned [rɪ'zaɪnd] *adj* (*to situation etc*) смирíвшийся.
resilience [rɪ'zɪlɪəns] *n* (*of material*) упрýгость *f*;

(*of person*) сто́йкость *f*.
resilient [rɪ'zɪlɪənt] *adj* (*material*) упру́гий* (упру́г); (*person*) сто́йкий* (сто́ек).
resin ['rɛzɪn] *n* смола́*.
resist [rɪ'zɪst] *vt* сопротивля́ться *(impf)* +*dat*; (*temptation*) не поддава́ться* (подда́ться* *perf*) +*dat*.
resistance [rɪ'zɪstəns] *n* (*opposition*) сопротивле́ние; (*to illness, infection*) сопротивля́емость *f*.
resistant [rɪ'zɪstənt] *adj*: **to be ~ to** (*opposing*) сопротивля́ться *(impf)* +*dat*; (*immune*) облада́ть *(impf)* усто́йчивостью к +*dat*.
resolute ['rɛzəlu:t] *adj* твёрдый* (твёрд).
resolution [rɛzə'lu:ʃən] *n* (*decision*) реше́ние; (: *formal*) резолю́ция; (*determination*) реши́мость *f*; (*of problem, difficulty*) разреше́ние; **to make a ~** принима́ть (приня́ть* *perf*) реше́ние.
resolve [rɪ'zɔlv] *n* реши́тельность *f* ◆ *vt* (*problem, difficulty*) разреша́ть (разреши́ть *perf*) ◆ *vi*: **to ~ to do** реша́ть (реши́ть *perf*) +*infin*.
resolved [rɪ'zɔlvd] *adj* (*determined*) реши́тельный* (реши́телен).
resonance ['rɛzənəns] *n* (*TECH*) резона́нс.
resonant ['rɛzənənt] *adj* (*voice*) зву́чный* (зву́чен); (*place*) резони́рующий.
resort [rɪ'zɔ:t] *n* (*town*) куро́рт; (*recourse*) прибега́ние ◆ *vi*: **to ~ to** прибега́ть (прибе́гнуть *perf*) к +*dat*; **seaside/winter sports ~** морско́й/зи́мний* спорти́вный куро́рт; **the last/only ~** после́дняя/еди́нственная наде́жда; **in the last ~** в кра́йнем слу́чае.
resound [rɪ'zaund] *vi*: **to ~ with** наполня́ться (напо́лниться *perf*) +*instr*.
resounding [rɪ'zaundɪŋ] *adj* (*noise*) зву́чный* (зву́чен); (*fig*: *success*) гро́мкий*.
resource [rɪ'sɔ:s] *n* (*raw material*) ресу́рс; **~s** *npl* (*money, energy, coal etc*) ресу́рсы *mpl*; **natural ~s** приро́дные ресу́рсы; **he was left to his own ~s** (*fig*) он мог положи́ться то́лько на самого́ себя́.
resourceful [rɪ'sɔ:sful] *adj* изобрета́тельный* (изобрета́телен).
resourcefulness [rɪ'sɔ:sfəlnɪs] *n* изобрета́тельность *f*.
respect [rɪs'pɛkt] *n* уваже́ние ◆ *vt* уважа́ть *(impf)*; **~s** *npl* (*greetings*) почте́ние *ntsg*; **to have** *or* **show ~ for sb/sth** относи́ться* *(impf)* к кому́-н/чему́-н с уваже́нием; **out of ~ for** из уваже́ния к +*dat*; **with ~ to, in ~ of** в отноше́нии +*gen*; **in this ~** в э́том отноше́нии; **in some ~s** в не́которых отноше́ниях; **with (all) due ~** ... при всём уваже́нии ....
respectability [rɪspɛktə'bɪlɪtɪ] *n* респекта́бельность *f*.
respectable [rɪs'pɛktəbl] *adj* прили́чный* (прили́чен); (*morally correct*) респекта́бельный.
respected [rɪs'pɛktɪd] *adj* (*scholar, actor etc*) при́знанный (при́знан).
respectful [rɪs'pɛktful] *adj* почти́тельный* (почти́телен).
respectfully [rɪs'pɛktfəlɪ] *adv* почти́тельно.
respective [rɪs'pɛktɪv] *adj* (*policies, measures*) соотве́тствующий*; **he drove them to their ~ homes** он отвёз их обо́их по дома́м.
respectively [rɪs'pɛktɪvlɪ] *adv* соотве́тственно; **France and Britain were 3rd and 4th ~** Фра́нция и Великобрита́ния бы́ли на 3-ем и 4-ом ме́сте соотве́тственно.
respiration [rɛspɪ'reɪʃən] *n* дыха́ние.
respirator ['rɛspɪreɪtə^r] *n* (*MED*) аппара́т иску́сственного дыха́ния.
respiratory ['rɛspərətərɪ] *adj* (*ANAT, MED*) дыха́тельный, респирато́рный.
respite ['rɛspaɪt] *n* (*rest*) переды́шка*.
resplendent [rɪs'plɛndənt] *adj* блиста́тельный* (блиста́телен).
respond [rɪs'pɔnd] *vi* (*answer*) отвеча́ть (отве́тить* *perf*); (*react*): **to ~ (to)** (*to pressure, criticism*) реаги́ровать (отреаги́ровать *perf*) (на +*acc*); (*to treatment*) поддава́ться* (подда́ться* *perf*) (+*dat*).
respondent [rɪs'pɔndənt] *n* (*LAW*) отве́тчик (-ица).
response [rɪs'pɔns] *n* (*answer*) отве́т; (*reaction*) реа́кция; **in ~ to (your letter)** в отве́т на (Ва́ше письмо́).
responsibility [rɪspɔnsɪ'bɪlɪtɪ] *n* (*liability*) отве́тственность *f*; (*duty*) обя́занность *f*; **to take ~ for sth/sb** принима́ть (приня́ть* *perf*) (на себя́) отве́тственность за что-н/кого́-н.
responsible [rɪs'pɔnsɪbl] *adj* отве́тственный* (отве́тствен); **~ for** отве́тственный* (отве́тствен) за +*acc*; **to be ~ to sb (for sth)** отвеча́ть (отве́тить* *perf*) пе́ред кем-н (за что-н).
responsibly [rɪs'pɔnsɪblɪ] *adv* отве́тственно.
responsive [rɪs'pɔnsɪv] *adj* (*child, nature*) отзы́вчивый (отзы́вчив); (*gesture*) отве́тный; **~ to demand/treatment** восприи́мчивый (восприи́мчив) к тре́бованиям/лече́нию.
rest [rɛst] *n* (*relaxation, pause*) о́тдых; (*MUS*) па́уза; (*stand, support*) подста́вка* ◆ *vi* (*relax, stop*) отдыха́ть (отдохну́ть *perf*) ◆ *vt* (*head, eyes etc*) дава́ть* (дать* *perf*) о́тдых +*dat*; (*lean*): **to ~ sth against** прислоня́ть (прислони́ть *perf*) что-н к +*dat*; **the ~** (*remainder of sth*) остально́е *nt adj*; **the ~ of them** остальны́е из них; **to set sb's mind at ~** утеша́ть (уте́шить *perf*) кого́-н; **to ~ one's**

arms on облокáчиваться (облокоти́ться* *perf*) на *+acc*; **to ~ sth on** опускáть (опусти́ть* *perf*) на *+acc*; **to ~ on** (*weight*) опирáться (оперéться* *perf*) на *+acc*; (*idea*) опирáться (*impf*) на *+acc*; (*object*) лежáть* (*impf*) на *+prp*; (*hope*) надéяться (*impf*) на *+acc*; **~ assured that ...** бýдьте увéрены, что ...; **it ~s with him to ...** на нём лежи́т *+infin ...*; **to ~ one's eyes** *or* **gaze on** останáвливать (останови́ть* *perf*) (свой) взгляд на *+acc*.
restart [ri:'stɑ:t] *vt* (*engine*) вновь запускáть (запусти́ть* *perf*); (*work*) возобновля́ть (возобнови́ть* *perf*).
restaurant ['rɛstərɔŋ] *n* ресторáн.
restaurant car *n* (*BRIT*) вагóн-ресторáн.
rest-cure ['rɛstkjuə'] *n* лечéние покóем.
restful ['rɛstful] *adj* успокáивающий.
rest-home ['rɛsthəum] *n* дом для престарéлых.
restitution [rɛstɪ'tju:ʃən] *n*: **to make ~ to sb for sth** (*compensate*) возмещáть (возмести́ть* *perf*) комý-н что-н.
restive ['rɛstɪv] *adj* неспокóйный* (неспокóен); (*horse*) норови́стый (норови́ст).
restless ['rɛstlɪs] *adj* (*person, audience*) беспокóйный* (беспокóен); **to get ~** проявля́ть (прояви́ть* *perf*) нетерпéние.
restlessly ['rɛstlɪslɪ] *adv* беспокóйно.
restock [ri:'stɔk] *vt* пополня́ть (попóлнить *perf*) запáсы *+gen*; **to ~ a lake/river (with fish)** пополня́ть (попóлнить *perf*) óзеро/рéку рыбой.
restoration [rɛstə'reɪʃən] *n* (*of building etc*) реставрáция; (*of order, health*) восстановлéние; (*of stolen property*) возвращéние.
restorative [rɪ'stɔrətɪv] *adj* укрепля́ющий* ◆ *n* укрепля́ющее срéдство.
restore [rɪ'stɔ:'] *vt* (*building, painting*) реставри́ровать (отреставри́ровать *perf*); (*order, health etc*) восстанáвливать (восстанови́ть* *perf*); (*stolen property*) возвращáть (возврати́ть* *perf*); (*to power*) возвращáть (вернýть *perf*).
restorer [rɪ'stɔ:rə'] *n* (*ART etc*) реставрáтор; **hair ~** восстанови́тель *m* для волóс.
restrain [rɪs'treɪn] *vt* сдéрживать (сдержáть* *perf*); (*person*): **to ~ sb from doing** не давáть* (дать* *perf*) комý-н *+infin*.
restrained [rɪs'treɪnd] *adj* сдéржанный* (сдéржан).
restraint [rɪs'treɪnt] *n* (*moderation*) сдéржанность *f*; (*restriction*) ограничéние; **wage ~** сдéрживание рóста зáработной плáты.
restrict [rɪs'trɪkt] *vt* ограни́чивать (ограни́чить *perf*).
restricted area *n* (*AUT*) райóн ограни́ченной скóрости движéния.
restriction [rɪs'trɪkʃən] *n*: **~ (on)** ограничéние (на *+acc*).
restrictive [rɪs'trɪktɪv] *adj* ограничи́тельный; (*clothing*) стесня́ющий.
restrictive practices *npl* (*INDUSTRY*) ограничи́тельная деловáя прáктика *fsg*.
rest room *n* (*US*) туалéт.
restructure [ri:'strʌktʃə'] *vt* (*business, economy*) перестрáивать (перестрóить *perf*).
result [rɪ'zʌlt] *n* результáт ◆ *vi*: **to ~ in** закáнчиваться (закóнчиться *perf*) *+instr*; **as a ~ of** в результáте *+gen*; **as a ~ it is too expensive** в результáте э́то сли́шком дóрого; **the fire ~ed from bombing** пожáр возни́к вслéдствие бомбёжки.
resultant [rɪ'zʌltənt] *adj*: **~ saving/problem** вытекáющая из э́того экономия/проблéма.
resume [rɪ'zju:m] *vt* (*work, journey*) возобновля́ть (возобнови́ть* *perf*) ◆ *vi* продолжáть (продóлжить *perf*); **to ~ one's seat** возвращáться (вернýться* *perf*) на (своё) мéсто.
résumé ['reɪzju:meɪ] *n* резюмé *nt ind*; (*US*: *curriculum vitae*) автобиогрáфия (*обы́чно пи́шущаяся при поступлéнии на учёбу и́ли рабóту*).
resumption [rɪ'zʌmpʃən] *n* возобновлéние.
resurgence [rɪ'sə:dʒəns] *n* (*of energy, activity*) всплеск.
resurrection [rɛzə'rɛkʃən] *n* (*of hopes, fears*) возрождéние; (*REL*): **the R~** Воскресéние.
resuscitate [rɪ'sʌsɪteɪt] *vt* (*MED*) приводи́ть* (привести́* *perf*) в сознáние; (*fig*) возвращáть (возврати́ть* *perf*) к жи́зни.
resuscitation [rɪsʌsɪ'teɪʃən] *n* (*MED*) приведéние в сознáние; (*fig*) возвращéние к жи́зни.
retail ['ri:teɪl] *adj* рóзничный ◆ *adv* в рóзницу ◆ *vt* продавáть* (продáть* *perf*) в рóзницу ◆ *vi*: **to ~ at £5** продавáться* (*impf*) по рóзничной цéне в £5; **~ shop** магази́н рóзничной торгóвли.
retailer ['ri:teɪlə'] *n* рóзничный торгóвец*.
retail outlet *n* рóзничная торгóвая тóчка.
retail price *n* рóзничная ценá*.
retail price index *n* (*BRIT*) и́ндекс рóзничных цен.
retain [rɪ'teɪn] *vt* (*keep*) сохраня́ть (сохрани́ть *perf*), удéрживать (удержáть *perf*).
retainer [rɪ'teɪnə'] *n* (*fee*) предвари́тельный гонорáр.
retaliate [rɪ'tælɪeɪt] *vi*: **to ~ (against)** (*attack*) наноси́ть* (нанести́* *perf*) отвéтный удáр (*+dat*); (*ill-treatment*) отплáчивать (отплати́ть* *perf*) (за *+acc*); **to ~ (on sb)** предъявля́ть (предъяви́ть* *perf*) встрéчный иск (комý-н).
retaliation [rɪtælɪ'eɪʃən] *n* (*against attack*) отвéтный удáр; (*against ill-treatment*) возмéздие; **in ~ for** в отвéт на *+acc*.
retaliatory [rɪ'tælɪətərɪ] *adj* отвéтный.
retarded [rɪ'tɑ:dɪd] *adj* (*development, growth*) замéдленный* (замéдлен); (*also: **mentally ~***:

person) у́мственно отста́лый.
retch [rɛtʃ] *vi*: **the thought made him ~** от э́той мы́сли его́ затошни́ло.
retention [rɪ'tɛnʃən] *n* удержа́ние; (*of tradition, rights*) сохране́ние; (*MED*: *of fluid*) заде́ржка.
retentive [rɪ'tɛntɪv] *adj*: **a ~ memory** це́пкая па́мять *f*.
rethink ['ri:'θɪŋk] *vt* (*proposal, policy*) пересма́тривать (пересмотре́ть* *perf*).
reticence ['rɛtɪsns] *n* скры́тность *f*.
reticent ['rɛtɪsnt] *adj* сде́ржанный* (сде́ржан).
retina ['rɛtɪnə] *n* сетча́тка.
retinue ['rɛtɪnju:] *n* сви́та.
retire [rɪ'taɪəʳ] *vi* (*give up work*) уходи́ть* (уйти́* *perf*) на пе́нсию; (*withdraw*) удаля́ться (удали́ться *perf*); (*go to bed*) удаля́ться (удали́ться *perf*) на поко́й.
retired [rɪ'taɪəd] *adj*: **he is ~** он на пе́нсии.
retirement [rɪ'taɪəmənt] *n* вы́ход *or* ухо́д на пе́нсию; **we hope to enjoy a long and happy ~** мы наде́емся жить до́лго и сча́стливо, вы́йдя на пе́нсию.
retirement age *n* пенсио́нный во́зраст.
retiring [rɪ'taɪərɪŋ] *adj* (*leaving*) уходя́щий на пе́нсию; (*shy*) засте́нчивый (засте́нчив).
retort [rɪ'tɔ:t] *vi* ре́зко отвеча́ть (отве́тить* *perf*) ◆ *n* ре́зкий* отве́т.
retrace [ri:'treɪs] *vt*: **to ~ one's steps** возвраща́ться (верну́ться *perf*) тем же путём; (*fig*) восстана́вливать (восстанови́ть* *perf*).
retract [rɪ'trækt] *vt* (*statement, offer*) забира́ть (забра́ть* *perf*) наза́д; (*claws*) втя́гивать (втяну́ть* *perf*); (*undercarriage, aerial*) убира́ть (убра́ть* *perf*).
retractable [rɪ'træktəbl] *adj* (*TECH*) убира́ющийся.
retrain [ri:'treɪn] *vt* переподгота́вливать (переподгото́вить* *perf*), переквалифици́ровать (*impf/perf*) ◆ *vi* (*see vt*) пройти́* (*perf*) переподгото́вку; переквалифици́роваться (*impf/perf*).
retraining [ri:'treɪnɪŋ] *n* (*see vb*) переподгото́вка*; переквалифика́ция.
retread ['ri:trɛd] *n* (*tyre*) ши́на с восстановле́нным проте́ктором.
retreat [rɪ'tri:t] *n* (*place*) убе́жище; (*withdrawal*) ухо́д; (*MIL*) отступле́ние ◆ *vi* отступа́ть (отступи́ть* *perf*); **to go into ~** (*withdraw*) уйти́* (*perf*) от ми́ра; **to beat a hasty ~** поспе́шно отступа́ть (отступи́ть* *perf*).
retrial [ri:'traɪəl] *n* (*LAW*) повто́рное слу́шание де́ла.
retribution [rɛtrɪ'bju:ʃən] *n* возме́здие.
retrieval [rɪ'tri:vəl] *n* восстановле́ние; (*of error*) исправле́ние; (*COMPUT*) по́иск; (*by dog*) по́иск (*ди́чи*).
retrieve [rɪ'tri:v] *vt* (*object*) брать* (взять* *perf*) обра́тно; (*situation, honour, loss*) восстана́вливать (восстанови́ть* *perf*); (*error*) исправля́ть (испра́вить* *perf*); (*COMPUT*) оты́скивать (отыска́ть* *perf*); (*subj*: *dog*) приноси́ть* (принести́* *perf*) (*уби́тую дичь*).
retriever [rɪ'tri:vəʳ] *n* (*dog*) охо́тничья соба́ка.
retroactive [rɛtrəu'æktɪv] *adj* име́ющий обра́тное де́йствие.
retrograde ['rɛtrəgreɪd] *adj* реакцио́нный* (реакцио́нен).
retrospect ['rɛtrəspɛkt] *n*: **in ~** в ретроспе́кции.
retrospective [rɛtrə'spɛktɪv] *adj* (*exhibition, view*) ретроспекти́вный* (ретроспекти́вен); (*law, tax*) име́ющий обра́тную си́лу ◆ *n* (*ART*) ретроспекти́вная вы́ставка*.
return [rɪ'tə:n] *n* (*going or coming back*) возвраще́ние; (*of sth stolen, borrowed, bought*) возвра́т; (*FINANCE*: *from land, shares etc*) дохо́д; (*official report*) отчёт ◆ *cpd* (*journey, ticket*) обра́тный; (*match*) отве́тный ◆ *vi* возвраща́ться (верну́ться *perf*) ◆ *vt* возвраща́ть (верну́ть *perf*); (*LAW*: *verdict*) выноси́ть* (вы́нести* *perf*); (*POL*: *candidate*) избира́ть (избра́ть* *perf*); (*ball*) отбива́ть (отби́ть* *perf*); **~s** *npl* (*COMM*) дохо́ды *mpl*; **in ~ (for)** в отве́т (на *+acc*); **by ~ of post** обра́тной по́чтой; **many happy ~s (of the day)!** с днём рожде́ния!; **to ~ to** (*consciousness*) приходи́ть (прийти́* *perf*) в *+acc*; (*power*) возвраща́ться (верну́ться *perf*) к *+dat*.
returnable [rɪ'tə:nəbl] *adj* (*bottle etc*) подлежа́щий возвра́ту *or* обме́ну.
returning officer [rɪ'tə:nɪŋ-] *n* председа́тель *m* окружно́й коми́ссии.
return key *n* (*COMPUT*) кла́виша "возвра́т каре́тки".
reunion [ri:'ju:nɪən] *n* (*reuniting*) воссоедине́ние; (*party*) встре́ча.
reunite [ri:ju:'naɪt] *vt* воссоединя́ть (воссоедини́ть *perf*).
rev [rɛv] *n abbr* (*AUT*: = *revolution*) оборо́т.
Rev. *abbr* (*REL*) = **Reverend**.
revaluation [ri:vælju'eɪʃən] *n* (*of property, attitudes*) переоце́нка*; (*of currency*) ревальва́ция.
revamp [ri:'væmp] *vt* (*organization, system*) обновля́ть (обнови́ть* *perf*).
rev counter *n* (*BRIT*: *AUT*) счётчик оборо́тов.
Revd. *abbr* (*REL*) = **Reverend**.
reveal [rɪ'vi:l] *vt* (*make known*) обнару́живать (обнару́жить *perf*); (*make visible*) открыва́ть (откры́ть* *perf*).
revealing [rɪ'vi:lɪŋ] *adj* (*action, statement*) показа́тельный* (показа́телен); (*dress*) откры́тый.
reveille [rɪ'vælɪ] *n* (*MIL*) побу́дка*.
revel ['rɛvl] *vi*: **to ~ in sth** упива́ться (*impf*)

* marks translations which have irregular inflections. The Russian–English side of the dictionary gives inflectional information.

чем-н; **to ~ in doing** обожа́ть *(impf)* +*infin*.
revelation [rɛvəˈleɪʃən] *n* (*fact*) откры́тие; (*experience*) открове́ние.
reveller [ˈrɛvlə] *n* гуля́ка *m/f*.
revelry [ˈrɛvlrɪ] *n* кутёж.
revenge [rɪˈvɛndʒ] *n* месть *f* ◆ *vt* (*also:* **get one's ~ for**) мстить* (отомсти́ть* *perf*) за +*acc*; **to take ~ on, ~ o.s. on** мстить* (отомсти́ть* *perf*) +*dat*.
revengeful [rɪˈvɛndʒful] *adj* мсти́тельный* (мсти́телен).
revenue [ˈrɛvənju:] *n* дохо́ды *mpl*; **~ account** счёт поступле́ний.
reverberate [rɪˈvə:bəreɪt] *vi* (*also fig*) отдава́ться* (отда́ться* *perf*) э́хом.
reverberation [rɪvə:bəˈreɪʃən] *n* (*of thunder*) раска́т; (*shock*) резона́нс.
revere [rɪˈvɪəʳ] *vt* (*person*) почита́ть *(impf)*, чтить* *(impf)*.
reverence [ˈrɛvərəns] *n* (*feeling*) почте́ние.
Reverend [ˈrɛvərənd] *adj*: **the ~** его́ преподо́бие; **the ~ John Smith** его́ преподо́бие Джон Смит.
reverent [ˈrɛvərənt] *adj* (*behaviour etc*) почти́тельный* (почти́телен).
reverie [ˈrɛvərɪ] *n* мечта́ние.
reversal [rɪˈvə:sl] *n* радика́льное измене́ние; (*of roles*) переме́на.
reverse [rɪˈvə:s] *n* (*opposite*) противополо́жность *f*; (*back*: *of cloth*) обра́тная сторона́*; (: *of coin, medal*) оборо́тная сторона́*; (: *of paper*) оборо́т; (*AUT*: *also:* **~ gear**) обра́тный ход*; (*setback, defeat*) неуда́ча ◆ *adj* (*opposite*) обра́тный* ◆ *vt* (*order, position*) по́лностью изменя́ть (измени́ть* *perf*); (*direction*) изменя́ть (измени́ть *perf*); (*process, policy, decision*) кру́то изменя́ть (измени́ть* *perf*); (*LAW*: *judgement*) отменя́ть (отмени́ть *perf*) ◆ *vi* (*BRIT*: *AUT*) дава́ть* (дать* *perf*) за́дний ход; **their fortunes went into ~** уда́ча отверну́лась от них; **in ~ order** в обра́тном поря́дке; **to ~ direction** изменя́ть (измени́ть* *perf*) направле́ние на обра́тное; **to ~ a car** дава́ть* (дать* *perf*) за́дний ход; **to ~ roles** меня́ться (поменя́ться *perf*) места́ми.
reverse-charge call [rɪˈvə:stʃɑ:dʒ-] *n* (*BRIT*: *TEL*) *телефо́нный разгово́р за счёт принима́ющего абоне́нта.*
reverse video *n* негати́вное изображе́ние на экра́не диспле́я.
reversible [rɪˈvə:səbl] *adj* (*garment, material*) двусторо́нний*; (*procedure*) обрати́мый (обрати́м).
reversing lights [rɪˈvə:sɪŋ-] *npl* (*BRIT*: *AUT*) фона́рь *msg* за́днего хо́да.
reversion [rɪˈvə:ʃən] *n* (*ZOOL*) проявле́ние атави́зма; **~ to** возвраще́ние к +*dat*.
revert [rɪˈvə:t] *vi*: **to ~ to** (*to former state*) возвраща́ться (возврати́ться* *perf*) к +*dat*; (*LAW*: *money, property*) переходи́ть* (перейти́* *perf*) к +*dat*.
review [rɪˈvju:] *n* (*of situation, policy etc*) пересмо́тр; (*MIL*) смотр*; (*of book, film etc*) реце́нзия; (*magazine*) обозре́ние ◆ *vt* (*situation, policy etc*) пересма́тривать (пересмотре́ть* *perf*); (*MIL*) проводи́ть* (провести́* *perf*) смотр +*gen*; (*book, film etc*) рецензи́ровать (отрецензи́ровать *perf*); **to come under ~** рассма́триваться *(impf)*.
reviewer [rɪˈvju:əʳ] *n* (*of book, film etc*) рецензе́нт.
revile [rɪˈvaɪl] *vt* поноси́ть* *(impf)*.
revise [rɪˈvaɪz] *vt* (*manuscript*) перераба́тывать (перерабо́тать *perf*); (*opinion*) пересма́тривать (пересмотре́ть* *perf*); (*price, procedure*) изменя́ть (измени́ть* *perf*); (*SCOL*: *lesson, maths*) повторя́ть (повтори́ть *perf*); **~d edition** пересмо́тренное изда́ние.
revision [rɪˈvɪʒən] *n* (*amendment*) измене́ние; (*for exam*) повторе́ние.
revitalize [ri:ˈvaɪtəlaɪz] *vt* оживля́ть (оживи́ть* *perf*).
revival [rɪˈvaɪvəl] *n* (*recovery*) оживле́ние; (*of interest, faith*) возрожде́ние; (*THEAT*) возобновле́ние.
revive [rɪˈvaɪv] *vt* (*person*) возвраща́ть (возврати́ть* *perf*) к жи́зни; (*economy, industry*) оживля́ть (оживи́ть* *perf*); (*tradition, hope, interest etc*) возрожда́ть (возроди́ть* *perf*); (*play*) восстана́вливать (восстанови́ть* *perf*) ◆ *vi* (*person*: *from faint*) приходи́ть* (прийти́* *perf*) в созна́ние; (*activity, economy etc*) оживля́ться (оживи́ться* *perf*); (*faith, hope, interest etc*) возрожда́ться (возроди́ться* *perf*).
revoke [rɪˈvəuk] *vt* (*treaty, law, title etc*) отменя́ть (отмени́ть *perf*); (*promise, decision*) брать* (взять* *perf*) наза́д.
revolt [rɪˈvəult] *n* (*rebellion*) восста́ние ◆ *vi* (*rebel*) восстава́ть* (восста́ть* *perf*) ◆ *vt* вызыва́ть (вы́звать* *perf*) отвраще́ние у +*gen*; **to ~ against sb/sth** восстава́ть* (восста́ть* *perf*) про́тив кого́-н/чего́-н.
revolting [rɪˈvəultɪŋ] *adj* (*disgusting*) отврати́тельный* (отврати́телен).
revolution [rɛvəˈlu:ʃən] *n* револю́ция; (*of wheel, earth etc*) оборо́т.
revolutionary [rɛvəˈlu:ʃənrɪ] *adj* революцио́нный* (революцио́нен) ◆ *n* революционе́р(ка*).
revolutionize [rɛvəˈlu:ʃənaɪz] *vt* (*industry, society etc*) революционизи́ровать *(impf/perf)*.
revolve [rɪˈvɔlv] *vi* (*turn*) враща́ться *(impf)*; (*fig*): **to ~ (a)round** враща́ться *(impf)* вокру́г +*gen*.
revolver [rɪˈvɔlvəʳ] *n* (*gun*) револьве́р.
revolving [rɪˈvɔlvɪŋ] *adj* (*chair etc*) враща́ющийся.
revolving door *n* враща́ющаяся дверь* *f*.
revue [rɪˈvju:] *n* ревю́ *nt ind*.
revulsion [rɪˈvʌlʃən] *n* (*disgust*) отвраще́ние.
reward [rɪˈwɔ:d] *n* (*recompense*: *for work,*

service, merit) награ́да; (*sum of money*) пре́мия; (: *for capture of criminal, information etc*) вознагражде́ние ◆ *vt*: **to ~ (for)** (*effort*) вознагражда́ть (вознагради́ть* *perf*) (за +*acc*).
rewarding [rɪˈwɔːdɪŋ] *adj* (*fig*): **this work is very ~** э́та рабо́та прино́сит удовлетворе́ние; **financially ~** хорошо́ опла́чиваемый.
rewind [riːˈwaɪnd] *irreg vt* (*cassette*) перема́тывать (перемота́ть *perf*) (*наза́д*).
rewire [riːˈwaɪəʳ] *vt*: **to ~ a house** заменя́ть (замени́ть *perf*) прово́дку в до́ме.
reword [riːˈwəːd] *vt* перефрази́ровать (*impf/perf*).
rework [riːˈwəːk] *vt* переде́лывать (переде́лать *perf*).
rewrite [riːˈraɪt] *irreg vt* (*rework*) перепи́сывать (переписа́ть* *perf*).
Reykjavik [ˈreɪkjəviːk] *n* Рейкья́вик.
RFD *abbr* (*US*: *POST*: = *rural free delivery*) *беспла́тная доста́вка по́чты в се́льской ме́стности.*
Rh *abbr* (*MED*: = *rhesus*) ре́зус.
rhapsody [ˈræpsədɪ] *n* (*MUS*) рапсо́дия.
rhesus negative *adj* (*MED*) с отрица́тельным ре́зусом.
rhesus positive *adj* (*MED*) с положи́тельным ре́зусом.
rhetoric [ˈrɛtərɪk] *n* рито́рика.
rhetorical [rɪˈtɔrɪkl] *adj* рито́ри́ческий.
rheumatic [ruːˈmætɪk] *adj* ревмати́ческий*.
rheumatism [ˈruːmətɪzəm] *n* ревмати́зм.
rheumatoid arthritis [ˈruːmətɔɪd-] *n* ревмато́идный артри́т.
Rhine [raɪn] *n*: **the ~** Рейн.
rhinestone [ˈraɪnstəun] *n* фальши́вый бриллиа́нт.
rhinoceros [raɪˈnɔsərəs] *n* носоро́г.
Rhodes [rəudz] *n* Ро́дос.
Rhodesia [rəuˈdiːʒə] *n* Родéзия.
Rhodesian [rəuˈdiːʒən] *adj* родези́йский ◆ *n* родези́ец*(-и́йка*).
rhododendron [rəudəˈdɛndrn] *n* рододе́ндрон.
Rhone [rəun] *n*: **the ~** Ро́на.
rhubarb [ˈruːbɑːb] *n* реве́нь* *m*.
rhyme [raɪm] *n* ри́фма; (*verse*) стихотворе́ние; (*in poetry*) разме́р ◆ *vi*: **to ~ (with)** рифмова́ться (*impf*) (с +*instr*); **without ~ or reason** ни с того́ ни с сего́.
rhythm [ˈrɪðm] *n* ритм.
rhythmic(al) [ˈrɪðmɪk(l)] *adj* (*sound*) ритми́ческий*, ритми́чный* (ритми́чен).
rhythmically [ˈrɪðmɪklɪ] *adv* ритми́чно.
rhythm method *n естéственный or натура́льный ме́тод контрацéпции.*
RI *n abbr* (*BRIT*: *SCOL*: = *religious instruction*) религио́зное воспита́ние ◆ *abbr* (*US*: *POST*) = *Rhode Island.*
rib [rɪb] *n* (*ANAT*) ребро́* ◆ *vt* (*inf*: *mock*) подшу́чивать (подшути́ть* *perf*) над +*instr*.
ribald [ˈrɪbəld] *adj* (*laughter, jokes*) непристо́йный* (непристо́ен), скабрё́зный* (скабрё́зен); (*person*) гру́бый* (груб).
ribbed [rɪbd] *adj* (*shell*) ребри́стый (ребри́ст); **~ knitting** вяза́ние рези́нкой.
ribbon [ˈrɪbən] *n* ле́нта; **in ~s** (*torn*) в кло́чья.
rice [raɪs] *n* рис.
rice field *n* ри́совое по́ле*.
rice pudding *n* ри́совый пу́динг.
rich [rɪtʃ] *adj* бога́тый (бога́т); (*clothes, jewels*) роско́шный* (роско́шен); (*soil*) бога́тый; (*food, colour, life*) насы́щенный; (*voice*) густо́й (густ); (*abundant*): **~ in** бога́тый (бога́т) +*instr*; **the ~** *npl* (*rich people*) бога́тые *pl adj*.
riches [ˈrɪtʃɪz] *npl* (*wealth*) бога́тство *ntsg*.
richly [ˈrɪtʃlɪ] *adv* (*dressed, decorated*) роско́шно, бога́то; (*rewarded*) ще́дро; (*deserved, earned*) вполне́.
richness [ˈrɪtʃnɪs] *n* бога́тство.
rickets [ˈrɪkɪts] *n* (*MED*) рахи́т.
rickety [ˈrɪkɪtɪ] *adj* (*furniture etc*) ша́ткий* (ша́ток).
rickshaw [ˈrɪkʃɔː] *n* ри́кша.
ricochet [ˈrɪkəʃeɪ] *vi* (*bullet, stone*) рикошети́ровать (*impf*) ◆ *n* рикоше́т.
rid [rɪd] (*pt, pp* **rid**) *vt*: **to ~ sb of sth** избавля́ть (изба́вить* *perf*) кого́-н от чего́-н; **to get ~ of** избавля́ться (изба́виться* *perf*) *or* отде́лываться (отде́латься *perf*) от +*gen*.
riddance [ˈrɪdns] *n*: **good ~!** ска́тертью доро́га!
ridden [ˈrɪdn] *pp of* **ride**.
riddle [ˈrɪdl] *n* (*conundrum*) зага́дка*; (*mystery*) та́йна ◆ *vt*: **~d with** (*holes, bullets*) изрешечё́нный (изрешечё́н) +*instr*; (*guilt, doubts*) по́лный* (по́лон) +*gen*; (*corruption*) прони́занный (прони́зан) +*instr*.
ride [raɪd] (*pt* **rode**, *pp* **ridden**) *n* пое́здка*; (*track, path*) лесна́я доро́га, тропа́* ◆ *vi* (*as sport*) е́здить* (*impf*) верхо́м; (*go somewhere, travel*) е́хать*/е́здить* (*impf*) ◆ *vt* (*horse*) е́хать*/е́здить* (*impf*) верхо́м на +*prp*; (*bicycle, motorcycle*) е́хать*/е́здить* (*impf*) на +*prp*; (*distance*) проезжа́ть (прое́хать* *perf*); **a 5 mile ~** пое́здка в 5 миль; **horse/car ~** пое́здка* верхо́м/на маши́не; **to go for a ~** пойти́* (*perf*) поката́ться; **to take sb for a ~** (*fig*) прокати́ть* (*perf*) кого́-н; **we rode all day/all the way** мы е́хали весь день/всю доро́гу; **to ~ at anchor** (*NAUT*) стоя́ть (*impf*) на я́коре; **can you ~ a bike?** Вы уме́ете е́здить на велосипе́де?
▸ **ride out** *vt*: **to ~ out the storm** (*fig*) выде́рживать (вы́держать *perf*) тру́дности.
rider [ˈraɪdəʳ] *n* (*on horse*) нае́здник(-ица),

* marks translations which have irregular inflections. The Russian-English side of the dictionary gives inflectional information.

всáдник(-ица); (*on bicycle*) велосипедист(ка*); (*on motorcycle*) мотоцикли́ст(ка*); (*in document*) дополнéние.

ridge [rɪdʒ] *n* (*of hill*) грéбень *m*; (*of roof*) конёк* (*крыши*); (*on material*) выступ.

ridicule ['rɪdɪkju:l] *n* насмéшка* ◆ *vt* высмéивать (вы́смеять *perf*); **an object of ~** предмéт насмéшек.

ridiculous [rɪ'dɪkjuləs] *adj* смехотвóрный* (смехотвóрен); **it's ~** э́то смешнó.

riding ['raɪdɪŋ] *n* верховáя ездá.

riding school *n* шкóла верховóй езды́.

rife [raɪf] *adj*: **to be ~** (*bribery, corruption*) процветáть (*impf*); **to be ~ with** (*rumours, fears*) изоби́ловать (*impf*) +*instr*.

riffraff ['rɪfræf] *n* шу́шера.

rifle ['raɪfl] *n* (*MIL*) винтóвка*; (*for hunting*) ружьё* ◆ *vt* (*steal from*: *pockets etc*) очи́стить* (*perf*)

▸ **rifle through** *vt fus* (*papers, belongings*) бы́стро перебирáть (перебрáть* *perf*).

rifle range *n* (*outdoor*) стрéльбище; (*indoor, at fair*) тир.

rift [rɪft] *n* (*also fig*) трéщина; (*in clouds*) просвéт.

rig [rɪg] *n* (*also*: **oil ~**) буровáя устанóвка; (: *on land*) буровáя вы́шка* ◆ *vt* (*election etc*) подтасóвывать (подтасовáть *perf*) результáты +*gen*

▸ **rig out** *vt* (*BRIT*): **to ~ out as/in** наряжáть (наряди́ть *perf*) как/в +*acc*

▸ **rig up** *vt* нáскоро сооружáть (сооруди́ть* *perf*).

Riga [rɪ'gə] *n* Ри́га.

rigging ['rɪgɪŋ] *n* (*NAUT*) такелáж.

right [raɪt] *adj* (*answer, solution, decision etc*) прáвильный* (прáвилен); (*size*) ну́жный; (*person, clothes, time*) подходя́щий*; (*morally good, fair, just*) справедли́вый (справедли́в), прáвильный* (прáвилен); (*not left*) прáвый ◆ *n* справедли́вость *f*; (*entitlement*) прáво*; (*not left*) прáвая сторонá ◆ *adv* (*correctly*) прáвильно; (*properly, fairly*) справедли́во; (*not on the left*) спрáва; (*not to the left*) напрáво ◆ *vt* (*ship*) вырáвнивать (вы́ровнять *perf*); (*car*) стáвить* (постáвить* *perf*) на колёса; (*fault, situation*) исправля́ть (испрáвить* *perf*); (*wrong*) устраня́ть (устрани́ть *perf*) ◆ *excl* так, хорошó; **the ~ time** (*precise*) тóчное врéмя; (*not wrong*) ну́жный *or* подходя́щий* момéнт; **she's ~** онá прáва; **that's ~!** (*answer*) прáвильно!; **is that clock ~?** э́то тóчные часы́?; **to get sth ~** дéлать (сдéлать *perf*) что-н как слéдует; **let's get it ~ this time!** давáйте сдéлаем э́то как слéдует на э́тот раз; **you did the ~ thing** Вы поступи́ли прáвильно; **to put a mistake ~** (*BRIT*) исправля́ть (испрáвить* *perf*) оши́бку; **on the ~** спрáва; **you are in the ~** прáвда за Вáми; **by ~s** по справедли́вости; **~ and wrong** прáвильное и непрáвильное; **he doesn't know the difference between ~ and wrong** он не знáет рáзницы мéжду прáвильным и непрáвильным; **film ~s** прáво на экранизáцию; **~ now** сейчáс же; **~ away** срáзу же; **~ before/after** как рáз пéред +*instr*/пóсле +*gen*; **~ against the wall** пря́мо у стены́; **~ ahead** пря́мо вперёд; **~ in the middle** пря́мо посереди́не; **~ to the end of sth** до сáмого концá чегó-н.

right angle *n* прямóй у́гол*.

righteous ['raɪtʃəs] *adj* прáведный* (прáведен).

righteousness ['raɪtʃəsnɪs] *n* прáведность *f*.

rightful ['raɪtful] *adj* закóнный.

rightfully ['raɪtfəlɪ] *adv* (*yours etc*) закóнно.

right-hand drive ['raɪthænd-] *n* правостóроннее управлéние ◆ *adj* (*vehicle*) с правостóронним управлéнием.

right-handed [raɪt'hændɪd] *adj*: **he is ~** он правшá.

right-hand man *n* прáвая рукá* (*перен*).

right-hand side *n* прáвая сторонá*.

rightly ['raɪtlɪ] *adv* (*with reason*) справедли́во; **if I remember ~** (*BRIT*) éсли я прáвильно пóмню.

right-minded [raɪt'maɪndɪd] *adj* благоразу́мный* (благоразу́мен).

right of way *n* (*path etc*) прáво* прохóда; (*AUT*) прáво* проéзда.

rights issue *n* (*STOCK EXCHANGE*) *вы́пуск áкции для продáжи ужé существу́ющим акционéрам по льгóтным цéнам*.

right wing *n* (*POL*) прáвое крылó; (*MIL, SPORT*) прáвый фланг.

right-wing [raɪt'wɪŋ] *adj* (*POL*) прáвый.

right-winger [raɪt'wɪŋə'] *n* (*POL*) человéк прáвых взгля́дов, прáвый(-ая) *m(f) adj*; (*SPORT*) прáвый нападáющий* *m adj*.

rigid ['rɪdʒɪd] *adj* (*structure, principle*) жёсткий* (жёсток); (*fig*: *attitude, views etc*) кóсный* (кóсен); (: *principle, control etc*) стрóгий* (строг).

rigidity [rɪ'dʒɪdɪtɪ] *n* (*of structure*) жёсткость *f*; (*of attitude etc*) кóсность *f*.

rigidly ['rɪdʒɪdlɪ] *adv* (*hold, fix etc*) прóчно; (*control*) жёстко; (*behave*) скóванно.

rigmarole ['rɪgmərəul] *n* (*procedure*) канитéль *f*.

rigor ['rɪgə'] *n* (*US*) = **rigour**.

rigor mortis ['rɪgə'mɔ:tɪs] *n* тру́пное окоченéние.

rigorous ['rɪgərəs] *adj* стрóгий* (строг); (*training*) серьёзный.

rigorously ['rɪgərəslɪ] *adv* (*test, assess etc*) стрóго.

rigour ['rɪgə'] (*US* **rigor**) *n* (*strictness*) стрóгость *f*; (*severity*): **~s of life/winter** тру́дности *fpl* жи́зни/зимы́.

rigout ['rɪgaut] *n* (*BRIT*: *inf*: *clothes*) одея́ние.

rile [raɪl] *vt* раздражáть (раздражи́ть *perf*).

rim [rɪm] *n* (*of glass, dish*) край*; (*of spectacles*)

ободо́к*; (*of wheel*) о́бод*.
rimless ['rɪmlɪs] *adj* (*spectacles*) без ободка́.
rimmed [rɪmd] *adj*: **~ with** окаймлённый (окаймлён) *+instr*.
rind [raɪnd] *n* (*of bacon, cheese*) ко́рка; (*of lemon, orange etc*) кожура́.
ring [rɪŋ] (*pt* **rang**, *pp* **rung**) *n* (*of metal, smoke*) кольцо́*; (*of people, objects, light*) круг*; (*of spies, drug dealers etc*) сеть* *f*; (*for boxing*) ринг; (*bullring, also of circus*) аре́на; (*of doorbell, telephone*) звоно́к* ◆ *vi* звони́ть (позвони́ть *perf*); (*doorbell*) звони́ть (зазвони́ть *perf*); (*also:* **~ out**: *voice, shot*) раздава́ться* (разда́ться* *perf*) ◆ *vt* (*BRIT*: *TEL*) звони́ть (позвони́ть *perf*) *+dat*; (*bell etc*) звони́ть (позвони́ть *perf*) в *+acc*; **to give sb a ~** (*BRIT*: *TEL*) звони́ть (позвони́ть *perf*) кому́-н; **that has a ~ of truth about it** э́то звучи́т правдоподо́бно; **my ears are ~ing** у меня́ звени́т в уша́х; **to ~ the bell** звони́ть (*impf*) в звоно́к; (*doorbell*) звони́ть (позвони́ть *perf*) в дверь; **the name doesn't ~ a bell (with me)** э́то и́мя мне ни о чём не говори́т
▸ **ring back** (*BRIT*) ◆ *vt* перезва́нивать (перезвони́ть *perf*) *+dat* ◆ *vi* звони́ть (позвони́ть *perf*) (в отве́т)
▸ **ring off** *vi* (*BRIT*) ве́шать (пове́сить* *perf*) тру́бку
▸ **ring up** *vt* (*BRIT*) звони́ть (позвони́ть *perf*) *+dat*.
ring binder *n* скоросшива́тель *m*.
ring finger *n* безымя́нный па́лец*.
ringing ['rɪŋɪŋ] *n* (*of telephone, doorbell*) звоно́к*; (*of church bell, in ears*) звон.
ringing tone *n* (*BRIT*: *TEL*) дли́нные гудки́ *pl*.
ringleader ['rɪŋli:dəʳ] *n* (*of gang*) глава́рь* *m*.
ringlets ['rɪŋlɪts] *npl* ло́коны *mpl*.
ring road *n* (*BRIT*) кольцева́я доро́га.
rink [rɪŋk] *n* (*also:* **ice ~, roller skating ~**) като́к*.
rinse [rɪns] *n* (*process*) полоска́ние; (*dye*: *for hair*) кра́ска* для во́лос ◆ *vt* полоска́ть* (прополоска́ть* *perf*); (*clothes*) полоска́ть (вы́полоскать *perf*); **to give sth a ~** ополаскивать (ополосну́ть *perf*) что-н.
Rio (de Janeiro) ['ri:əu(dədʒə'nɪərəu)] *n* Ри́о-де-Жане́йро *m ind*.
riot ['raɪət] *n* (*disturbance*) беспоря́дки* *mpl*, бесчи́нства *ntpl*; (*of colours, flowers*) бу́йство ◆ *vi* бесчи́нствовать (*impf*); **to run ~** бу́йствовать* (*impf*).
rioter ['raɪətəʳ] *n* наруши́тель *m* поря́дка.
riot gear *n* защи́тное снаряже́ние поли́ции.
riotous ['raɪətəs] *adj* (*mob, behaviour, party*) бесчи́нствующий; (*living*) разгу́льный* (разгу́лен); (*welcome*) бу́рный* (бу́рен).
riotously ['raɪətəslɪ] *adv*: **~ funny** неимове́рно смешно́й.
riot police *n* *спецподразделе́ние поли́ции для подавле́ния беспоря́дков*.
RIP *abbr* (= *rest in peace*) мир пра́ху твоему́.
rip [rɪp] *n* (*tear*) разры́в ◆ *vt* (*paper, cloth*) разрыва́ть* (разорва́ть* *perf*) ◆ *vi* (*see vt*) разрыва́ться* (разорва́ться* *perf*)
▸ **rip up** *vt* разрыва́ть (разорва́ть* *perf*).
ripcord ['rɪpkɔ:d] *n* (*on parachute*) вытяжно́й трос.
ripe [raɪp] *adj* спе́лый* (спел), зре́лый* (зрел); (*cheese*) вы́держанный* (вы́держан).
ripen ['raɪpn] *vi* спеть* (поспе́ть* *perf*), зреть *or* созрева́ть (созре́ть *perf*) ◆ *vt*: **the sun will ~ them soon** они́ ско́ро созре́ют на со́лнце.
ripeness ['raɪpnɪs] *n* спе́лость *f*, зре́лость *f*.
rip-off ['rɪpɔf] *n* (*inf*): **it's a ~!** э́то обдира́ловка!
riposte [rɪ'pɔst] *n* нахо́дчивый отве́т.
ripple ['rɪpl] *n* (*wave*: *caused by wind, rain etc*) рябь *f no pl*; (: *caused by stone etc*) зыбь *f no pl*; (*of laughter, applause*) волна́*, гул *m no pl* ◆ *vt* (*water, sand*) поднима́ть (подня́ть* *perf*) зыбь на *+prp* ◆ *vi* (*water*) покрыва́ться (покры́ться* *perf*) ря́бью.
rise [raɪz] (*pt* **rose**, *pp* **risen**) *n* (*slope*) подъём; (*increase*) повыше́ние; (*fig*: *of state, leader*) возвыше́ние ◆ *vi* поднима́ться (подня́ться* *perf*); (*prices, numbers, voice*) повыша́ться (повы́ситься* *perf*); (*sun, moon*) всходи́ть* (взойти́* *perf*); (*sound*) нараста́ть (*impf*); (*also:* **~ up**: *building*) возвыша́ться (*impf*); (: *rebels*) восстава́ть* (восста́ть* *perf*); (*in rank*) продвига́ться (продви́нуться *perf*); **~ to power** прихо́д к вла́сти; **to give ~ to** вызыва́ть (вы́звать* *perf*); **to ~ to the occasion** оказываться (оказа́ться* *perf*) на высоте́ положе́ния.
risen [rɪzn] *pp of* **rise**.
rising ['raɪzɪŋ] *adj* (*number, prices*) расту́щий; (*tide*) нараста́ющий; (*sun, moon*) восходя́щий.
rising damp *n* засоле́ние (*поднима́ющаяся вверх сырость*).
rising star *n* (*fig*) восходя́щая звезда́*.
risk [rɪsk] *n* риск ◆ *vt* (*endanger*) рискова́ть (*impf*) *+instr*; (*chance*) рискова́ть* (рискну́ть *perf*) *+instr*; **to take a ~** рискова́ть (рискну́ть *perf*), идти́* (*impf*) на риск; **to run the ~ of doing** рискова́ть (*impf*) *+infin*; **at ~** в опа́сной ситуа́ции; **to put sb/sth at ~** подверга́ть (подве́ргнуть *perf*) кого́-н/что-н ри́ску; **at one's own ~** на свой (страх и) риск; **at the ~ of sounding rude ...** риску́я показа́ться гру́бым(-ой) ...; **it's a fire ~** с противо-пожа́рной то́чки зре́ния э́то опа́сно; **it's a health ~** э́то опа́сно для здоро́вья; **I'll ~ it** я рискну́.
risk capital *n* „ри́сковый" *or* ве́нчурный

* marks translations which have irregular inflections. The Russian-English side of the dictionary gives inflectional information.

капитáл.
risky ['rɪskɪ] *adj* рискóванный* (рискóван).
risqué ['ri:skeɪ] *adj* (*joke*) сомни́тельный* (сомни́телен).
rissole ['rɪsəul] *n* битóк*.
rite [raɪt] *n* обря́д; **last ~s** послéднее причáстие.
ritual ['rɪtjuəl] *adj* ритуáльный ◆ *n* (*of religion*) обря́д; (*of procedure*) ритуáл.
rival ['raɪvl] *n* сопéрник(-ица); (*in business*) конкурéнт ◆ *adj* (*competing*: *business*) конкури́рующий; (*competition*) сопéрничающий ◆ *vt* сопéрничать *(impf)* с *+instr*; **to ~ sb/sth in** сопéрничать *(impf)* с кем-н/с чем-н в *+prp*; **~ team** комáнда сопéрника.
rivalry ['raɪvlrɪ] *n* (*in sport, love*) сопéрничество; (*in business*) конкурéнция.
river ['rɪvə'] *n* рекá* ◆ *cpd* (*port, traffic*) речнóй; **up/down ~** вверх/вниз по рекé.
riverbank ['rɪvəbæŋk] *n* бéрег* реки́.
riverbed ['rɪvəbɛd] *n* рýсло реки́.
riverside ['rɪvəsaɪd] *n* бéрег* реки́.
rivet ['rɪvɪt] *n* заклёпка* ◆ *vt* (*fig*) прикóвывать (приковáть *perf*).
riveting ['rɪvɪtɪŋ] *adj* (*fig*) захвáтывающий*.
Riviera [rɪvɪ'ɛərə] *n*: **the (French) ~** (францýзская) Ривьéра; **the Italian ~** итальянская Ривьéра.
Riyadh [rɪ'jɑ:d] *n* Эр-Рия́д.
RN *n abbr* (*BRIT*) = **Royal Navy**; (*US*: = *registered nurse*) ≈ медсестрá= *меди́цинская сестрá*.
RNA *n abbr* (= *ribonucleic acid*) РНК= *рибонуклеи́новая кислотá*.
RNLI *n abbr* (*BRIT*) = *Royal National Lifeboat Institution*.
RNZAF *n abbr* = *Royal New Zealand Air Force*.
RNZN *n abbr* = *Royal New Zealand Navy*.
road [rəud] *n* (*also fig*) путь* *m*, дорóга; (*in town*) дорóга; (*motorway etc*) шоссé *nt ind*; **~ accident** дорóжная авáрия; **main ~** глáвная дорóга; **major/minor ~** глáвная/второстепéнная дорóга; **it takes 4 hours by ~** э́то 4 часá по дорóге; **let's hit the ~** давáйте вы́едем на дорóгу; **to be on the ~** (*tramp*) бродя́жничать *(impf)*; (*salesman*) быть* *(impf)* в разъéздах; (*pop group*) быть* *(impf)* на гастрóлях, гастроли́ровать* *(impf)*; **on the ~ to success** на пути́ к успéху; **~ sense** чýвство дорóги; **~ junction** пересечéние дорóг, перекрёсток*.
roadblock ['rəudblɔk] *n* дорóжное заграждéние.
road haulage *n* дорóжная перевóзка.
road hog *n* лихáч.
road map *n* дорóжная кáрта.
road rage *n* агресси́вное поведéние на автодорóге.
road safety *n* дорóжная безопáсность *f*.
roadside ['rəudsaɪd] *n* обóчина ◆ *cpd* придорóжный; **~ verge** обóчина; **by the ~** у обóчины.
road sign *n* дорóжный знак.
road sweeper *n* (*BRIT*: *person*) двóрник; (*vehicle*) подметáльная маши́на.
road user *n* (*driver*) води́тель *m*.
roadway ['rəudweɪ] *n* (*central part of road*) проéзжая часть* *f* (дорóги).
road works *npl* дорóжно-ремóнтные рабóты.
roadworthy ['rəudwə:ðɪ] *adj* (*car*) пригóдный* (пригóден) к эксплуатáции.
roam [rəum] *vi* броди́ть* *(impf)*, скитáться *(impf)* ◆ *vt* броди́ть* *(impf)* по *+dat*.
roar [rɔ:'] *n* (*of animal*) рёв *m no pl*; (*of crowd, engine, wind*) рёв; (*of laughter*) взрыв ◆ *vi* (*animal, person*) ревéть *(impf)*; (*crowd, engine, wind*) ревéть *(impf)*; **to ~ with laughter** хохотáть *(impf)*.
roaring ['rɔ:rɪŋ] *adj*: **a ~ fire** я́рко пылáющийками́н; **a ~ success** грóмкий успéх; **to do a ~ trade** вести́* *(impf)* бóйкую торгóвлю.
roast [rəust] *n* (*of meat*) жаркóе *nt adj* ◆ *vt* (*meat, potatoes*) жáрить (зажáрить *perf*); (*coffee*) жáрить (поджáрить *perf*).
roast beef *n* рóстбиф, жáреная говя́дина.
roasting ['rəustɪŋ] *n* (*inf*): **to give sb a ~** устрáивать (устрóить *perf*) комý-н разнóс.
rob [rɔb] *vt* (*person, house, bank*) обкрáдывать (обокрáсть* *perf*); **to ~ sb of sth** красть* (укрáсть* *perf*) что-н у когó-н; (*fig*) лишáть (лиши́ть *perf*) когó-н чегó-н.
robber ['rɔbə'] *n* граби́тель *m*.
robbery ['rɔbərɪ] *n* (*theft*) ограблéние, грабёж.
robe [rəub] *n* (*for ceremony etc*) мáнтия; (*also: bath ~*) бáнный халáт; (*US*) плед ◆ *vt* облачáть (облачи́ть *perf*).
robin ['rɔbɪn] *n* (*also:* **~ redbreast**) заря́нка*.
robot ['rəubɔt] *n* рóбот.
robotics [rə'bɔtɪks] *n* (*ELEC, COMPUT*) робототéхника.
robust [rəu'bʌst] *adj* крéпкий* (крéпок).
rock [rɔk] *n* (*substance*) (гóрная) порóда; (*boulder*) валýн*; (*cliff*) скалá*; (*US*: *small stone*) кáмешек*; (*BRIT*: *sweet*) *леденцóвая карамéль в фóрме дли́нных пáлочек*; (*MUS*: *also:* **~ music**) рок ◆ *vt* (*swing gently*) качáть *(impf)*; (*shake*) шатáть *(impf)* ◆ *vi* (*object*) качáться *(impf)*, шатáться *(impf)*; (*person*) качáться *(impf)*; **on the ~s** (*drink*) со льдом; (*marriage etc*) на грáни распáда; **the ship was smashed on the ~s** корáбль разби́лся о скáлы; **to ~ the boat** (*fig*) нарýшить *(perf)* покóй.
rock and roll *n* рок-н-рóлл.
rock bottom *n* (*fig*) предéльная ни́зкая чертá; **to reach** *or* **touch** *or* **hit ~ ~** (*price*) достигáть (дости́чь* *perf*) предéльно ни́зкой черты́; (*person*) доходи́ть* (дойти́* *perf*) до крити́ческой тóчки.
rock-bottom ['rɔk'bɔtəm] *adj* (*fig*: *prices*) предéльно ни́зкий*.
rock cake *n* *кóржик с изю́мом*.
rock climber *n* скалолáз.

rock climbing *n* скалола́зание.
rockery ['rɔkərɪ] *n* альпи́йский* сад*.
rocket ['rɔkɪt] *n* раке́та ◆ *vi* (*prices*) подска́кивать (подскочи́ть* *perf*).
rocket launcher *n* (*MIL*) пусково́я раке́тная устано́вка*.
rock face *n* пове́рхность *f* скалы́.
rock fall *n* камнепа́д.
rocking chair ['rɔkɪŋ-] *n* (кре́сло-)кача́лка*.
rocking horse *n* конь-кача́лка*.
rocky ['rɔkɪ] *adj* (*mountain*) скали́стый (скали́ст); (*path, soil*) камени́стый (камени́ст); (*unsteady, unstable*) ша́ткий* (ша́ток).
Rocky Mountains *npl*: **the ~ ~** Скали́стые го́ры* *fpl*.
rod [rɔd] *n* прут*; (*TECH*) сте́ржень* *m*; (*also:* **fishing ~**) у́дочка*.
rode [rəud] *pt of* **ride**.
rodent ['rəudnt] *n* грызу́н*.
rodeo ['rəudɪəu] *n* (*US*) родео́ *nt ind*.
roe [rəu] *n* (*also:* **~ deer**) косу́ля; (*of fish*): **hard ~** икра́; **soft ~** моло́ки *fpl*.
roe deer *n inv* косу́ля.
rogue [rəug] *n* (*dishonest person*) моше́нник, жу́лик.
roguish ['rəugɪʃ] *adj* (*mischevious*) плутова́тый (плутова́т).
role [rəul] *n* (*THEAT, fig*) роль* *f*.
role model *n* приме́р.
role play *n* ролевы́е игры́ *fpl*.
roll [rəul] *n* (*of paper, cloth etc*) руло́н; (*of banknotes*) сви́ток*; (*also:* **bread ~**) бу́лочка*; (*register, list*) спи́сок*; (*sound: of drums*) бой*; (*: of thunder*) раска́т ◆ *vt* (*ball, stone etc*) ката́ть/кати́ть* (*impf*); (*also:* **~ up**: *string*) скру́чивать (скрути́ть* *perf*); (*: sleeves*) зака́тывать (заката́ть *perf*); (*cigarette*) свёртывать (сверну́ть *perf*); (*eyes*) зака́тывать (закати́ть* *perf*); (*also:* **~ out**: *pastry*) раска́тывать (раската́ть *perf*); (*lawn, road etc*) ука́тывать (уката́ть *perf*) ◆ *vi* (*ball, stone etc*) кати́ться* (*impf*); (*drum*) греме́ть (*impf*); (*car: also:* **~ along**) кати́ться* (*impf*); (*ship*) кача́ться (*impf*); **cheese/ham ~** бу́лочка* с сы́ром/с ветчино́й
▸ **roll about** *vi* converted переката́ться перека́тываться (перекати́ться* *perf*)
▸ **roll around** *vi* = **roll about**
▸ **roll by** *vi* (*time*) протека́ть (проте́чь* *perf*)
▸ **roll in** *vi* (*orders*) сы́паться* (*impf*); (*cash*) течь* (поте́чь* *perf*)
▸ **roll over** *vi* перевора́чиваться (переверну́ться *perf*)
▸ **roll up** *vi* (*inf: arrive*) подка́тывать (подкати́ть* *perf*) ◆ *vt* (*carpet, newspaper*) сфора́чивать (сверну́ть *perf*); (*umbrella*) скла́дывать (сложи́ть* *perf*); **to ~ o.s. up into a ball** сфора́чиваться (сверну́ться *perf*) кала́чиком.
roll call *n* перекли́чка*.
roller ['rəulə] *n* (*in machine*) ва́лик; (*wheel*) ро́лик; (*for lawn, road*) като́к*; (*for hair*) бигуди́ *pl ind*.
roller blind *n* што́ра на ро́ликах.
roller coaster *n* аттракцио́н "америка́нские го́ры" *fpl*.
roller skates *npl* ро́лики *mpl*, ро́ликовые коньки́ *mpl*.
rollicking ['rɔlɪkɪŋ] *adj* потряса́ющий* (потряса́ющ); **to have a ~ time** весели́ться (повесели́ться *perf*).
rolling ['rəulɪŋ] *adj* (*landscape*) холми́стый (холми́ст).
rolling mill *n* прока́тный стан.
rolling pin *n* ска́лка*.
rolling stock *n* (*RAIL*) подвижно́й соста́в.
roll-on/roll-off ferry *adj* (*BRIT*) *паро́м, приспосо́бленный для въе́зда и вы́езда автомоби́лей.*
roly-poly ['rəulɪ'pəulɪ] *n* (*BRIT: CULIN*) руле́т с варе́ньем.
ROM [rɔm] *n abbr* (*COMPUT: = read-only memory*) ПЗУ= *постоя́нное запомина́ющее устро́йство.*
Roman ['rəumən] *adj* ри́мский* ◆ *n* (*person*) ри́млянин(-нка).
Roman Catholic *adj* (ри́мско-)католи́ческий* ◆ *n* като́лик(-и́чка*).
romance [rə'mæns] *n* (*love affair, novel*) рома́н; (*charm*) рома́нтика; (*MUS*) рома́нс.
Romanesque [rəumə'nɛsk] *adj* рома́нский*.
Romania [rəu'meɪnɪə] *n* Румы́ния.
Romanian [rəu'meɪnɪən] *adj* румы́нский* ◆ *n* (*person*) румы́н(ка*); (*LING*) румы́нский* язы́к*.
Roman numeral *n* ри́мская ци́фра.
romantic [rə'mæntɪk] *adj* романти́чный* (романти́чен); (*play, story etc*) романти́ческий.
romanticism [rə'mæntɪsɪzəm] *n* романти́зм.
Romany ['rɔmənɪ] *adj* цыга́нский* ◆ *n* цыга́н(ка*); (*LING*) цыга́нский* язы́к*.
Rome [rəum] *n* Рим.
romp [rɔmp] *n* возня́ ◆ *vi* (*also:* **~ about**) вози́ться* (*impf*); **to ~ home** (*horse*) вы́игрывать (вы́играть *perf*) ска́чки.
rompers ['rɔmpəz] *npl* ползунки́ *mpl*.
rondo ['rɔndəu] *n* ро́ндо *nt ind*.
roof [ru:f] (*pl* **~s**) *n* кры́ша ◆ *vt* (*house*) настила́ть (настла́ть* *perf*) кры́шу *+gen or* на *+prp*; **the ~ of the mouth** нёбо.
roof garden *n* сад* на кры́ше.
roofing ['ru:fɪŋ] *n* кро́вельный материа́л; **~ felt** руло́нный кро́вельный материа́л.
roof rack *n* (*AUT*) бага́жник (*на кры́ше*

* marks translations which have irregular inflections. The Russian-English side of the dictionary gives inflectional information.

автомобиля).
rook [ruk] *n* (*bird*) грач*; (*CHESS*) ладья*, тура ◆ *vt* (*inf*: *cheat*) надувать (надуть *perf*).
rookie ['ruki:] *n* (*US*: *inf*) новичок.
room [ru:m] *n* (*in house*) комната; (*in school*) класс; (*in hotel*) номер*; (*space*) место*; **~s** *npl* (*lodging*) квартира *fsg*; **"rooms to let"**, (*US*) **"rooms for rent"** „сдаются комнаты"; **single/double ~** (*in hotel*) одноместный/двухместный номер*; **is there ~ for this?** это здесь поместится?; **to make ~ for sb** давать* (дать* *perf*) место кому-н; **there is ~ for improvement** кое-что можно улучшить; **there is still ~ for doubt** ещё есть основания сомневаться.
rooming house ['ru:mɪŋ-] *n* (*US*) мебелированные комнаты *fpl*.
roommate ['ru:mmeɪt] *n* сосед*(ка*) по комнате.
room service *n* обслуживание в номере.
room temperature *n* комнатная температура.
roomy ['ru:mɪ] *adj* (*building, car, garment*) просторный* (просторен); (*bag*) вместительный* (вместителен).
roost [ru:st] *vi* усаживаться (усесться* *perf*) на ночлег.
rooster ['ru:stə'] *n* (*esp US*) петух*.
root [ru:t] *n* корень* *m* ◆ *vi* (*plant, belief*: *also*: **take ~**) укореняться (укорениться *perf*); **~s** *npl* (*family origins*) корни* *mpl*; **the ~ of the problem is that ...** корень проблемы в том ...
▸ **root about** *vi* (*fig*) рыться* (*impf*)
▸ **root for** *vt fus* (*inf*: *support*) болеть (*impf*) за *+acc*
▸ **root out** *vt* откопать (*perf*).
root beer *n безалкогольный напиток из корней трав*.
rope [rəup] *n* верёвка*, канат; (*NAUT*) трос ◆ *vt* (*area*: *also*: **~ off**) отгораживать (отгородить* *perf*) верёвкой; (*tie on*): **to ~ to** привязывать (привязать* *perf*) верёвкой к *+dat*; (*join*): **to ~ together** связывать (связать* *perf*) верёвкой; **to know the ~s** (*fig*) знать (*impf*), что к чему
▸ **rope in** *vt* (*fig*) втягивать (втянуть* *perf*).
rope ladder *n* верёвочная лестница.
ropey ['rəupɪ] *adj* (*inf*) дрянной.
rosary ['rəuzərɪ] *n* чётки* *pl*.
rose [rəuz] *pt of* **rise** ◆ *n* роза; (*on watering can*) насадка* ◆ *adj* (*colour*) розовый (розов).
rosé ['rəuzeɪ] *n* (*wine*) розовое вино*.
rosebed ['rəuzbɛd] *n* клумба с розами.
rosebud ['rəuzbʌd] *n* бутон розы.
rosebush ['rəuzbuʃ] *n* розовый куст*.
rosemary ['rəuzmərɪ] *n* розмарин.
rosette [rəu'zɛt] *n* (*decoration*) розетка*.
ROSPA ['rɔspə] *n abbr* (*BRIT*) = *Royal Society for the Prevention of Accidents*.
roster ['rɔstə'] *n*: **duty ~** расписание дежурств.
rostrum ['rɔstrəm] *n* (*POL*) трибуна.
rosy ['rəuzɪ] *adj* (*colour*) розовый (розов); (*face, cheeks*) румяный (румян); (*situation*) радостный* (радостен); **a ~ future** радужное будущее.
rot [rɔt] *n* (*process*) гниение; (*result*) гниль *f*; (*fig*: *nonsense*) чушь *f* ◆ *vt* (*wood, fruit*) гноить (сгноить *perf*); (*teeth*) портить* (испортить* *perf*) ◆ *vi* гнить* (сгнить* *perf*); **to stop the ~** (*BRIT*: *fig*) навести* (*perf*) порядок; **dry/wet ~** сухая/мокрая гниль.
rota ['rəutə] *n* чередование; **on a ~ basis** чередуясь, поочерёдно.
rotary ['rəutərɪ] *adj* (*motion*) вращательный; (*machine*) ротационный, вращающийся; **~ engine** роторно-поршневой двигатель.
rotate [rəu'teɪt] *vt* вращать (*impf*); (*change round*: *crops, jobs*) чередовать (*impf*) ◆ *vi* вращаться (*impf*).
rotating [rəu'teɪtɪŋ] *adj* (*movement*) вращательный.
rotation [rəu'teɪʃən] *n* вращение; (*of crops*) севооборот; **in ~** поочерёдно.
rote [rəut] *n*: **to learn by ~** учить (*impf*) наизусть.
rotor ['rəutə'] *n* (*also*: **~ blade**) (несущий) винт* (*вертолёта*).
rotten ['rɔtn] *adj* (*fruit, wood, teeth*) гнилой*; (*meat, eggs*) тухлый; (*fig*: *unpleasant*) мерзкий* (мерзок), отвратительный* (отвратителен); (*dishonest*) продажный* (продажен); (*inf*: *bad*) поганый; **to feel ~** (*ill*) чувствовать (*impf*) себя погано.
Rotterdam ['rɔtədæm] *n* Роттердам.
rotund [rəu'tʌnd] *adj* (*person*) полный.
rouble ['ru:bl] (*US* **ruble**) *n* рубль* *m*.
rouge [ru:ʒ] *n* румяна *pl*.
rough [rʌf] *adj* грубый (груб); (*surface*) шероховатый (шероховат); (*terrain*) пересечённый; (*road*) ухабистый (ухабист); (*brusque*: *person, manner*) резкий* (резок); (*weather*) ненастный; (*sea*) бурный* (бурен); (*town, area*) опасный* (опасен); (*plan, sketch, work*) черновой; (*guess*) приблизительный* (приблизителен) ◆ *n* (*GOLF*): **in the ~** на нестриженной части поля ◆ *vt*: **to ~ it** обходиться* (обойтись* *perf*) без удобств ◆ *adv*: **to play ~** вести* (*impf*) жёсткую игру; **the sea is ~ today** море сегодня штормит/неспокойное; **we had a ~ time (of it)** нам пришлось туго; **~ estimate** грубая оценка* *or* смета; **to sleep ~** (*BRIT*) ночевать* (*impf*), где придётся; **to feel ~** (*BRIT*: *ill*) чувствовать (*impf*) себя плохо
▸ **rough out** *vt* (*draft*) набрасывать (набросать *perf*).
roughage ['rʌfɪdʒ] *n* грубая пища.
rough-and-ready ['rʌfən'rɛdɪ] *adj* дрянной.
rough-and-tumble ['rʌfən'tʌmbl] *n* потасовка.
roughcast ['rʌfkɑ:st] *n* (*for wall*) галечная штукатурка.
rough copy *n* черновик*.

rough draft *n* черновик*.
rough justice *n* жёсткий* суд.
roughly ['rʌflɪ] *adv* грубо; (*approximately*) приблизительно; ~ **speaking** грубо говоря.
roughness ['rʌfnɪs] *n* (*of surface*) шероховатость *f*; (*of manner*) грубость *f*.
roughshod ['rʌfʃɔd] *adv*: **to ride ~ over** не считаться *(impf)* с *+instr*.
roulette [ru:'lɛt] *n* рулетка*.
Roumania *etc* = **Romania** *etc*.
round [raund] *adj* круглый* (кругл); (*figures, sum*) круглый ◆ *n* (*BRIT*: *of toast*) ломтик; (*duty*: *of policeman, doctor*) обход; (: *of milkman*) маршрут; (*game*: *of cards, golf*) партия; (*in competition*) тур; (*of ammunition*) патрон, комплект выстрела; (*of talks, also BOXING*) раунд ◆ *vt* огибать (обогнуть *perf*) ◆ *prep* (*surrounding*): ~ **his neck/the table** вокруг его шеи/стола; (*approximately*): ~ **about three hundred** (приблизительно) около трёхсот ◆ *adv*: **all** ~ кругом, вокруг; **in ~ figures** в круглых цифрах; **a ~ of applause** взрыв аплодисментов; **a ~ of drinks** по бокалу для всех; **the daily** ~ (*fig*) повседневные дела; **it's just ~ the corner** (*fig*) это как раз за углом; ~ **the clock** круглые сутки, круглосуточно; **to go ~ the back** обходить* (обойти* *perf*) сзади; **to walk ~ the room** ходить* *(impf)* по комнате; **to go ~ an obstacle** огибать (обогнуть *perf*) *or* обходить* (обойти* *perf*) препятствие; **the long way** ~ кружным путём; **all the year** ~ круглый год; **to ask sb** ~ приглашать (пригласить* *perf*) кого-н в гости; **I'll be ~ at 6 o'clock** я приду в 6 часов; **to go ~ to sb's (house)** идти*/ходить* *(impf)* к кому-н; **there's enough to go** ~ хватит на всех
▸ **round off** *vt* (*speech etc*) завершать (завершить *perf*)
▸ **round up** *vt* (*cattle, people*) сгонять (согнать* *perf*); (*price, figure*) округлять (округлить *perf*).
roundabout ['raundəbaut] *n* (*BRIT*: *AUT*) кольцевая транспортная развязка*; (: *at fair*) карусель *f* ◆ *adj* окольным путём.
rounded ['raundɪd] *adj* округлый (округл).
rounders ['raundəz] *n* английская лапта.
roundly ['raundlɪ] *adv* (*fig*: *criticize*) резко.
round robin *n* (*letter*) коллективное письмо*.
round-shouldered ['raund'ʃəuldəd] *adj* сутулый (сутул).
round trip *n* поездка* туда-обратно.
roundup ['raundʌp] *n* (*information*) сводка*; (*of animals*) загон; (*of criminals*) облава; **a ~ of the latest news** сводка последних новостей.
rouse [rauz] *vt* (*wake up*) будить* (разбудить* *perf*); (*stir up*) возбуждать (возбудить* *perf*).
rousing ['rauzɪŋ] *adj* (*cheer, welcome*) бурный* (бурен).
rout [raut] *n* (*MIL*) разгром ◆ *vt* (*defeat*) громить* (разгромить* *perf*).
route [ru:t] *n* (*way*) путь* *m*, дорога; (*of bus, train, shipping*) маршрут; **the best ~ to London** лучший* путь в Лондон; **en ~ for** по пути в *+acc*; **en ~ from ... to ...** по пути из *+gen* ... в *+acc* ....
route map *n* (*BRIT*) маршрутная карта.
routine [ru:'ti:n] *adj* (*work*) повседневный* (повседневен); (*procedure*) обычный* (обычен) ◆ *n* (*habits*) распорядок*; (*drudgery*) рутина; (*THEAT*) номер*; **daily** ~ распорядок* дня.
rove [rəuv] *vt* (*streets*) бродить* *(impf)* по *+dat*, скитаться *(impf)* по *+dat*.
roving reporter *n* разъездной репортёр.
row[1] [rəu] *n* ряд* ◆ *vi* (*in boat*) грести* *(impf)* ◆ *vt* (*boat*) управлять *(impf)* *+instr*; **in a** ~ (*fig*) подряд.
row[2] [rau] *n* (*noise*) шум; (*dispute*) скандал, ссора; (*inf*: *scolding*) нагоняй ◆ *vi* (*argue*) скандалить (поскандалить *perf*); **to have a** ~ ссориться (поссориться *perf*), поскандалить *(perf)*.
rowboat ['rəubəut] *n* (*US*) гребная шлюпка*.
rowdiness ['raudɪnɪs] *n* буйство.
rowdy ['raudɪ] *adj* буйный* (буен).
rowdyism ['raudɪɪzəm] *n* буйство.
rowing ['rəuɪŋ] *n* гребля.
rowing boat *n* (*BRIT*) гребная шлюпка*.
rowlock ['rɔlək] *n* (*BRIT*) уключина.
royal ['rɔɪəl] *adj* королевский*.
Royal Air Force *n* (*BRIT*) *Британские военно-воздушные силы.*
royal-blue ['rɔɪəlblu:] *adj* ярко-синий*.
royalist ['rɔɪəlɪst] *adj* роялистский ◆ *n* роялист(ка*).
Royal Navy *n* (*BRIT*) *Британский военно-морской флот.*
royalty ['rɔɪəltɪ] *n* (*royal persons*) члены *mpl* королевской семьи; (*payment*) (авторский*) гонорар.
RP *n abbr* (*BRIT*: = *received pronunciation*) *стандартное произношение.*
rpm *abbr* (= *revolutions per minute*) оборотов в минуту.
RR *abbr* (*US*) (= **railroad**) ж.д., ж/д= *железная дорога.*
RRP *n abbr* (*BRIT*) (= **recommended retail price**) рекомендованная розничная цена.
RSA *n abbr* (*BRIT*) = *Royal Society of Arts*; *Royal Scottish Academy.*
RSI *n abbr* (*MED*: = *repetitive strain injury*) *производственная травма, вызванная напряжением одной и той же группы мышц (у машинисток итп).*
RSPB *n abbr* (*BRIT*) = *Royal Society for the*

* marks translations which have irregular inflections. The Russian-English side of the dictionary gives inflectional information.

Protection of Birds.
RSPCA *n abbr* (*BRIT*) = *Royal Society for the Prevention of Cruelty to Animals.*
RSVP *abbr* (= *répondez s'il vous plaît*) *про́сьба отве́тить на приглаше́ние.*
RTA *n abbr* = *road traffic accident.*
Rt Hon. *abbr* (*BRIT*: = *Right Honourable*) высокочти́мый.
Rt Rev. *abbr* (*REL*: = *Right Reverend*) высо́копреподо́бный.
rub [rʌb] *vt* (*part of body*) тере́ть* (потере́ть* *perf*); (*object*: *to clean*) тере́ть* (*impf*); (: *to polish*) натира́ть (натере́ть* *perf*); (: *to dry*) вытира́ть (вы́тереть* *perf*); (*hands*: *also*: ~ **together**) потира́ть (потере́ть* *perf*) ◆ *n*: **to give sth a** ~ (*polish*) натира́ть (натере́ть* *perf*) что-н; **to ~ one's hands (together)** тере́ть* (потере́ть* *perf*) ру́ки; **to ~ sb up** *or* (*US*) **~ sb the wrong way** раздража́ть (*impf*) кого́-н
▸ **rub down** *vt* обтира́ть (обтере́ть* *perf*)
▸ **rub in** *vt* (*ointment*) втира́ть (втере́ть* *perf*); **don't ~ it in!** (*fig*: *inf*) не ка́пай!
▸ **rub off** *vi* (*paint*) стира́ться (стере́ться* *perf*)
▸ **rub off on** *vt fus* передава́ться* (переда́ться* *perf*) *+dat*
▸ **rub out** *vt* стира́ть (стере́ть* *perf*).
rubber ['rʌbəʳ] *n* (*substance*) рези́на, каучу́к; (*BRIT*: *eraser*) рези́нка, ла́стик; (*US*: *inf*: *condom*) презервати́в.
rubber band *n* (кру́глая) рези́нка*.
rubber bullet *n* рези́новая пу́ля.
rubber plant *n* каучуконо́с, (каучуконо́сный) фи́кус.
rubber ring *n* надувно́й рези́новый круг*.
rubber stamp *n* штамп; (*POST*) ште́мпель *m.*
rubber-stamp [rʌbə'stæmp] *vt* (*fig*) штампова́ть (проштампова́ть *perf*).
rubbery ['rʌbərɪ] *adj* (*material, substance*) рези́новый; (*meat, food*) жёсткий* как рези́на.
rubbish ['rʌbɪʃ] *n* му́сор; (*waste food*) отбро́сы *mpl*; (*junk*) хлам; (*fig*: *pej*: *nonsense*) ерунда́, чушь *f*; (: *junk*) дрянь *f* ◆ *vt* (*BRIT*: *inf*) критикова́ть (*impf*); **what you've just said is ~** то, что Вы то́лько что сказа́ли – ерунда́ *or* чепуха́ *or* чушь.
rubbish bin *n* (*BRIT*) му́сорное ведро́*.
rubbish dump *n* сва́лка*.
rubbishy ['rʌbɪʃɪ] *adj* (*BRIT*: *inf*) дрянно́й.
rubble ['rʌbl] *n* обло́мки *mpl*; (*building material*) бут.
ruble ['ru:bl] *n* (*US*) = **rouble**.
ruby ['ru:bɪ] *n* руби́н.
RUC *n abbr* (*BRIT*: = *Royal Ulster Constabulary*) *североирла́ндская поли́ция.*
rucksack ['rʌksæk] *n* рюкза́к*.
ructions ['rʌkʃənz] *npl* (*protest*) возмуще́ние *ntsg*; (*quarrel*) сканда́л *msg.*
rudder ['rʌdəʳ] *n* руль* *m.*
ruddy ['rʌdɪ] *adj* (*face, complexion*) румя́ный (румя́н); (*glow*) краснова́тый; (*inf*: *damned*) прокля́тый.
rude [ru:d] *adj* (*impolite*) гру́бый* (груб); (*shocking*) непристо́йный* (непристо́ен); (*crudely made*) гру́бо сде́ланный (сде́лан); **he was ~ to me** он был груб со мной; **a ~ awakening** глубо́кое разочарова́ние, неприя́тное откры́тие.
rudely ['ru:dlɪ] *adv* гру́бо.
rudeness ['ru:dnɪs] *n* (*impoliteness*) гру́бость *f.*
rudimentary [ru:dɪ'mɛntərɪ] *adj* (*equipment, knowledge*) элемента́рный* (элемента́рен).
rudiments ['ru:dɪmənts] *npl* осно́вы *fpl.*
rue [ru:] *vt* (*action, decision*) жале́ть (пожале́ть *perf*) о *+prp*; (*day, hour etc*) проклина́ть (прокля́сть* *perf*).
rueful ['ru:ful] *adj* (*expression, person etc*) печа́льный* (печа́лен).
ruffian ['rʌfɪən] *n* банди́т.
ruffle ['rʌfl] *vt* (*hair*) еро́шить (взъеро́шить *perf*); (*clothes*) гофрирова́ть (*impf/perf*); (*water*) ряби́ть* (*impf*); (*fig*: *person*) раздража́ть (*impf*).
rug [rʌg] *n* ко́врик; (*BRIT*: *blanket*) плед.
rugby ['rʌgbɪ] *n* (*also*: **~ football**) ре́гби *nt ind.*
rugged ['rʌgɪd] *adj* (*landscape*) скали́стый (скали́ст); (*features*) гру́бый* (груб); (*character*) прямо́й (прям); (*determination*) непрекло́нный* (непрекло́нен), твёрдый* (твёрд).
rugger ['rʌgəʳ] *n* (*BRIT*: *inf*) ре́гби *nt ind.*
ruin ['ru:ɪn] *n* (*destruction*: *of building, hopes, plans*) разруше́ние; (: *of hopes, plans*) круше́ние; (*downfall*) ги́бель *f*; (*bankruptcy*) разоре́ние; (*remains*: *of building*) разва́лины *fpl* ◆ *vt* (*building, hopes, plans*) разруша́ть (разру́шить *perf*); (*future, health, reputation*) губи́ть* (погуби́ть* *perf*); (*person*: *financially*) разоря́ть (разори́ть *perf*); (*spoil*: *clothes*) по́ртить* (испо́ртить* *perf*); **~s** *npl* (*of building, castle etc*) разва́лины *fpl*, руи́ны *fpl*; **in ~s** (*building*) в разва́линах *or* руи́нах; **my life is in ~s** моя́ жизнь загу́блена.
ruination [ru:ɪ'neɪʃən] *n* уничтоже́ние.
ruinous ['ru:ɪnəs] *adj* (*interest*) губи́тельный* (губи́телен); (*expense*) разори́тельный* (разори́телен).
rule [ru:l] *n* (*norm, regulation*) пра́вило; (*government*) правле́ние, власть *f*; (*ruler*) лине́йка ◆ *vt* (*country, people*) управля́ть (*impf*) *+instr* ◆ *vi* (*leader, monarch etc*) пра́вить* (*impf*), управля́ть (*impf*); (*LAW*): **to ~ in favour of/against** выноси́ть* (вы́нести *perf*) реше́ние в по́льзу *+gen*/про́тив *+gen*; **under British ~** (*dominion*) под брита́нским правле́нием; **it's against the ~s** э́то про́тив пра́вил; **by ~ of thumb** наута́д; **as a ~** как пра́вило; **to ~ that** (*umpire, judge etc*) постановля́ть (постанови́ть* *perf*), что ...
▸ **rule out** *vt* (*exclude*) исключа́ть (исключи́ть *perf*); **murder cannot be ~d out** уби́йство не мо́жет быть* исключено́.

ruled [ru:ld] *adj* (*paper*) лино́ваный.
ruler ['ru:lə'] *n* прави́тель(ница) *m(f)*; (*for measuring*) лине́йка.
ruling ['ru:lɪŋ] *adj* (*party*) пра́вящий*; (*class*) госпо́дствующий* ◆ *n* (*LAW*) постановле́ние.
rum [rʌm] *n* ром ◆ *adj* (*BRIT*: *inf*) чудно́й.
Rumania *etc* = **Romania** *etc*.
rumble ['rʌmbl] *n* (*of traffic, thunder*) гул ◆ *vi* бубни́ть *(impf)*; (*also:* ~ **along**) с гу́лом проезжа́ть (прое́хать* *perf*); (*stomach, pipe*) бурча́ть *(impf)*; (*thunder*) грохота́ть* (прогрохота́ть* *perf*).
rumbustious [rʌm'bʌstʃəs] *adj* бо́йкий* (бо́ек).
ruminate ['ru:mɪneɪt] *vi* жева́ть* *(impf)* жва́чку; (*fig*) размышля́ть *(impf)*.
rummage ['rʌmɪdʒ] *vi* (*search*) ры́ться *(impf)*.
rummage sale *n* (*US*) *благотвори́тельная распрода́жа подёржанных веще́й.*
rumour ['ru:mə'] (*US* **rumor**) *n* слух ◆ *vt*: **it is ~ed that ...** хо́дят слу́хи, что ....
rump [rʌmp] *n* (*of horse*) круп; (*of cow*) за́дняя часть *f*; (*of group, political party*) оста́тки *mpl*.
rumple ['rʌmpl] *vt* (*clothes*) мять* (помя́ть* *or* измя́ть* *perf*).
rump steak *n* вы́резка* (*из за́дней ча́сти*).
rumpus ['rʌmpəs] *n* шум; **to kick up a ~** поднима́ть (подня́ть* *perf*) шум.
run [rʌn] (*pt* **ran**, *pp* **run**) *n* (*fast pace*) бег*; (*journey*) пое́здка; (*distance travelled*) пробе́г; (*SKIING*) тра́сса; (*CRICKET, BASEBALL*) очко́*; (*in tights, stockings*) спусти́вшиеся пе́тли *fpl* ◆ *vt* (*race, distance*) пробега́ть (пробежа́ть* *perf*); (*operate*: *business, hotel*) управля́ть *(impf)* +*instr*; (: *competition, course*) устра́ивать (устро́ить *perf*); (: *house*) вести́* *(impf)*; (*COMPUT*: *program*) выполня́ть (вы́полнить *perf*); (*pass*: *hand, fingers*): **to ~ along** *or* **over** проводи́ть* (провести́* *perf*) +*instr* по +*dat*; (*water*) пуска́ть (пусти́ть* *perf*); (*bath*) наполня́ть (напо́лнить *perf*); (*PRESS*: *feature*) печа́тать (напеча́тать *perf*) ◆ *vi* бе́гать/бежа́ть* *(impf)*; (*flee*) бежа́ть* *(impf/perf)*, сбега́ть (сбежа́ть* *perf*); (*work*: *machine*) рабо́тать *(impf)*; (*bus, train*) ходи́ть* *(impf)*; (*continue*: *play, show*) идти́* *(impf)*; (: *contract*) дли́ться *(impf)*; (*in election*) баллоти́роваться *(perf)*; (*river*) течь* *(impf)*, протека́ть *(impf)*; (*bath*) наполня́ться (напо́лниться *perf*); (*colours, washing*) линя́ть (полиня́ть *perf*); (*nose*) течь* *(impf)*; **to go for a ~** (*for exercise*) идти́* (пойти́* *perf*) побе́гать; **to break into a ~** пуска́ться (пусти́ться* *perf*) бежа́ть; **a ~ of luck** пери́од уда́ч; **the play had a 6 week ~** пье́са шла 6 неде́ль; **to have the ~ of sb's house** име́ть *(impf)* разреше́ние по́льзоваться чьим-н до́мом; **there was a ~ on tickets** на биле́ты был большо́й спрос; **in the long ~** в коне́чном ито́ге; **in the short ~** на како́е-то вре́мя; **to make a ~ for it** убега́ть* (убежа́ть *perf*) со всех ног; **to be on the ~** скрыва́ться *(impf)*; (*inf*: *to be busy*) быть* *(impf)* в бега́х; **I'll ~ you to the station** я подвезу́ Вас до ста́нции; **to ~ a risk** подверга́ться (подве́ргнуться *perf*) ри́ску; **to ~ errands for sb** выполня́ть *(impf)* ме́лкие поруче́ния для кого́-н; **my car is very cheap to ~** моя́ маши́на экономи́чна; **to be ~ off one's feet** (*BRIT*) сби́ться* *(perf)* с ног; **the train ~s between Gatwick and Victoria** по́езд хо́дит ме́жду Га́твиком и Викто́рией; **the bus ~s every 20 minutes** авто́бус хо́дит ка́ждые 20 мину́т; **to ~ on petrol** *or* (*US*) **gas/on diesel/off batteries** рабо́тать *(impf)* на бензи́не/на ди́зеле/на батаре́йках; **to ~ for president** баллоти́роваться *(impf)* в президе́нты; **their losses ran into millions** их поте́ри исчисля́лись миллио́нами
▸ **run about** *vi* бе́гать *(impf)*
▸ **run across** *vt fus* (*find*) натыка́ться (наткну́ться *perf*) на +*acc*
▸ **run around** *vi* = **run about**
▸ **run away** *vi* убега́ть (убежа́ть* *perf*)
▸ **run down** *vt* (*production, industry*) сокраща́ть (сократи́ть* *perf*); (*AUT*: *hit*) сбива́ть (сбить* *perf*); (*criticize*) поноси́ть* *(impf)*; **to be ~ down** (*person*) выбива́ться (вы́биться* *perf*) из сил; (*battery*) конча́ться *(impf)*, иссяка́ть *(impf)*
▸ **run in** *vt* (*BRIT*: *car*) обка́тывать (обката́ть *perf*)
▸ **run into** *vt fus* (*meet*: *person*) ста́лкиваться (столкну́ться *perf*) с +*instr*; (: *trouble*) ната́лкиваться (натолкну́ться *perf*) на +*acc*; (*collide with*) вреза́ться (вре́заться* *perf*) в +*acc*; **to ~ into debt** залеза́ть (зале́зть* *perf*) в долги́
▸ **run off** *vt* (*subj*: *water*) спуска́ть (спусти́ть* *perf*); (*copies*) де́лать (сде́лать *perf*), отсня́ть* *(perf)* ◆ *vi* (*person, animal*) сбега́ть (сбежа́ть* *perf*), убега́ть (убежа́ть* *perf*)
▸ **run out** *vi* (*person*) выбега́ть (вы́бежать* *perf*); (*liquid*) вытека́ть (вы́течь* *perf*); (*lease, visa*) истека́ть (исте́чь* *perf*); (*money*) зака́нчиваться (зако́нчиться *perf*); **my passport ~s out in July** срок де́йствия моего́ па́спорта истека́ет в ию́ле
▸ **run out of** *vt fus*: **I've ~ out of money/time/petrol** *or* (*US*) **gas** у меня́ ко́нчились де́ньги/ко́нчилось вре́мя/ко́нчился бензи́н
▸ **run over** *vt* (*AUT*) задави́ть* *(perf)* ◆ *vt fus* (*revise*) пробега́ть (пробежа́ть *perf*)
▸ **run through** *vt fus* пробега́ть (пробежа́ть *perf*); (*rehearse*) прогоня́ть (прогна́ть *perf*)
▸ **run up** *vt*: **to ~ up a debt** влеза́ть (влезть* *perf*) в долги́; **to ~ up against** (*difficulties*)

* marks translations which have irregular inflections. The Russian-English side of the dictionary gives inflectional information.

стáлкиваться (столкнýться *perf*) с +*instr*.

runabout ['rʌnəbaut] *n* (*AUT*) малолитрáжка*.

run around *n* (*inf*): **to give sb the ~ ~** водить* (*impf*) когó-н за нос.

runaway ['rʌnəweɪ] *adj* (*truck, horse etc*) потерявший управлéние; (*person*) бéглый; (*inflation*) неуправляемый.

rundown ['rʌndaun] *n* (*BRIT*: *of industry etc*) сокращéние.

run-down [rʌn'daun] *adj* (*tired, ill*) измождённый* (измождён).

rung [rʌŋ] *pp of* **ring** ◆ *n* (*of ladder*) ступéнька*; (*in organization*) ступéнь *m*.

run-in ['rʌnɪn] *n* (*inf*) стычка*.

runner ['rʌnəʳ] *n* (*in race*: *person*) бегýн*(ья); (: *horse*) скакýн*; (*on sledge, for drawer etc*) пóлоз*; (*carpet*: *in hall etc*) дорóжка*.

runner bean *n* (*BRIT*) стручкóвая фасóль *f no pl*.

runner-up [rʌnər'ʌp] *n* финалист (*занявший вторóе мéсто*).

running ['rʌnɪŋ] *n* (*sport*) бег*; (*of business, organization*) руковóдство; (*of event*) организáция; (*of machine etc*) эксплуатáция ◆ *adj* (*water*) текýщий*; (: *to house*) водопровóдный; **he is in/out of the ~ for sth** емý сулит/не сулит что-н; **6 days ~** 6 дней подряд.

running commentary *n* (*TV, RADIO*) прямóй репортáж.

running costs *npl* (*of business*) операциóнные издéржки *fpl*; (*of car*) содержáние *ntsg*.

running head *n* колонтитул (*заголóвок, печáтаемый на верхý кáждой страницы*).

running mate *n* (*US*: *POL*) *кандидáт на дóлжность вице-президéнта*.

runny ['rʌnɪ] *adj* (*honey, egg*) жидкий* (жидок); (*nose*) сопливый (соплив); (*eyes*) слезящийся.

runoff ['rʌnɔf] *n* (*in contest, election*) повтóрные выборы *mpl*; (*extra race*) повтóрный забéг.

run-of-the-mill ['rʌnəvðə'mɪl] *adj* срéдний*.

runt [rʌnt] *n* (*animal*) недомéрок*; (*pej*: *person*) сморчóк*.

run-through ['rʌnθruː] *n* (*rehearsal*) прогóн.

run-up ['rʌnʌp] *n период, предшéствующий какóму-нибудь событию*.

runway ['rʌnweɪ] *n* взлётно-посáдочная полосá*.

rupee [ruː'piː] *n* рýпия.

rupture ['rʌptʃəʳ] *n* (*MED*: *hernia*) грыжа; (*between people, groups*) разрыв ◆ *vt*: **to ~ o.s.** (*MED*) получáть (получить *perf*) грыжу.

rural ['ruərl] *adj* сéльский*; (*accent*) деревéнский*.

rural district council *n* (*BRIT*) сéльский* райóнный совéт.

ruse [ruːz] *n* улóвка*, ухищрéние.

rush [rʌʃ] *n* (*hurry*) спéшка; (*COMM*: *sudden demand*) большóй спрос; (*of water, current*) потóк; (*of emotion*) прилив; (*plant*) камыш* ◆ *vt* (*BRIT*: *inf*: *overcharge*) обсчитывать (обсчитáть *perf*) ◆ *vi* (*person*) бежáть* (*impf*); (*air, water*) хлынуть (*perf*); **is there any ~ for this?** это спéшно?; **a ~ of orders** наплыв закáзов; **I'm in a ~ (to do)** я спешý (+*infin*); **gold ~** золотáя лихорáдка; **to ~ one's meal/work** второпях есть (*impf*)/дéлать (*impf*) рабóту; **don't ~ me!** не подгоняйте *or* торопите меня!; **to ~ sth off** (*do*) спéшно дéлать (сдéлать *perf*) что-н; (*send*) спéшно отправлять (отпрáвить* *perf*) что-н; **she ~ed to the door** онá брóсилась к двéри

► **rush through** *vt fus* дéлать (сдéлать *perf*) в спéшке; (*meal*) проглáтывать (проглотить* *perf*); (*town*) носиться* (нестись* *perf*) по +*dat*.

rush hour *n* час пик.

rush job *n* рабóта, сдéланная нáспех.

rush matting *n* цинóвка*.

rusk [rʌsk] *n* (*biscuit*) ≈ сухáрь *m*.

Russia ['rʌʃə] *n* Россия.

Russian ['rʌʃən] *adj* (*native Russian*) рýсский*; (*belonging to Russian Federation*) россиийский* ◆ *n* рýсский(-ая) *m(f) adj*; (*LING*) рýсский* язык*.

rust [rʌst] *n* (*also BOT*) ржáвчина ◆ *vi* ржавéть (заржавéть *perf*).

rustic ['rʌstɪk] *adj* деревéнский* ◆ *n* (*pej*) деревéнщина *m/f no pl*.

rustle ['rʌsl] *vi* шуршáть (*impf*), шелестéть* (*impf*) ◆ *vt* шелестéть* (*impf*) +*instr*; (*US*: *steal*) угонять (угнáть* *perf*).

rustproof ['rʌstpruːf] *adj* (*metal*) нержавéющий; (*car*) сдéланный (сдéлан) из нержавéющего материáла.

rustproofing ['rʌstpruːfɪŋ] *n* обрабóтка прóтив ржáвчины.

rusty ['rʌstɪ] *adj* ржáвый; (*fig*: *skill*) подзабытый.

rut [rʌt] *n* (*groove*) колея, бороздá*; (*ZOOL*: *season*) половáя охóта; **to get into a ~** (*fig*) заходить* (зайти* *perf*) в тупик, застревáть (застрять* *perf*).

rutabaga [ruːtə'beɪgə] *n* (*US*) рéпа.

ruthless ['ruːθlɪs] *adj* (*person, action*) беспощáдный* (беспощáден), безжáлостный* (безжáлостен).

ruthlessness ['ruːθlɪsnɪs] *n* беспощáдность *f*, безжáлостность *f*.

RV *abbr* (*BIBLE*: = *revised version*) *исправленное издáние Библии* ◆ *n abbr* (*US*) = *recreational vehicle*.

Ryazan [rɪ'zanj] *n* Рязáнь *f*.

rye [raɪ] *n* рожь* *f*.

rye bread *n* ржанóй хлеб.

~ S, s ~

S, s [ɛs] *n* (*letter*) *19-ая бу́ква англи́йского алфави́та*; (*US*: *SCOL*: = *satisfactory*) ≈ удовлетвори́тельно.

S *abbr* (= **south**) Ю= *юг*; = **small**; **(= saint)** св= *свято́й*.

SA *abbr* = **South Africa, South America**.

Sabbath ['sæbəθ] *n* (*Jewish*) суббо́та; (*Christian*) воскресе́нье.

sabbatical [sə'bætɪkl] *n* (*also*: ~ **year**) тво́рческий* о́тпуск*.

sabotage ['sæbətɑ:ʒ] *n* сабота́ж ◆ *vt* (*machine, building*) выводи́ть* (вы́вести* *perf*) из стро́я; (*plan, meeting*) саботи́ровать *(impf/perf)*.

sabre ['seɪbə^r] *n* са́бля*.

sabre-rattling ['seɪbərætlɪŋ] *n* бряца́ние ору́жием (*перен*).

saccharin(e) ['sækərɪn] *n* сахари́н.

sachet ['sæʃeɪ] *n* (*of shampoo, sugar etc*) паке́тик.

sack [sæk] *n* (*bag*) мешо́к* ◆ *vt* (*dismiss*) выгоня́ть (вы́гнать* *perf*) с рабо́ты; (*plunder*) опустоша́ть (опустоши́ть *perf*); **to give sb the** ~ выгоня́ть (вы́гнать* *perf*) кого́-н (с рабо́ты); **I got the** ~ меня́ вы́гнали (с рабо́ты).

sackful ['sækful] *n*: **a** ~ **of** мешо́к* *+gen*.

sacking ['sækɪŋ] *n* (*dismissal*) увольне́ние; (*material*) мешкови́на.

sacrament ['sækrəmənt] *n* (*rite*) та́инство.

sacred ['seɪkrɪd] *adj* свяще́нный; (*place*) свято́й; (*music*) духо́вный.

sacred cow *n* (*fig*) святы́ня.

sacrifice ['sækrɪfaɪs] *n* (*offering*) жертвоприноше́ние: (*thing or person offered*) же́ртва ◆ *vt* (*animal*) приноси́ть* (принести́* *perf*) в же́ртву *+dat*; (*fig*) же́ртвовать (поже́ртвовать *perf*) *+instr*; **to make ~s (for sb)** же́ртвовать (поже́ртвовать *perf*) собо́й (ра́ди кого́-н).

sacrilege ['sækrɪlɪdʒ] *n* святота́тство.

sacrosanct ['sækrəusæŋkt] *adj* (*also fig*) свяще́нный.

sad [sæd] *adj* печа́льный* (печа́лен).

sadden ['sædn] *vt* печа́лить (опеча́лить *perf*).

saddle ['sædl] *n* седло́* ◆ *vt* (*horse*) седла́ть (оседла́ть *perf*); **to** ~ **sb with sth** (*inf*) наве́шивать (наве́сить* *perf*) что-н на кого́-н.

saddlebag ['sædlbæg] *n* (*on bicycle*) седе́льная су́мка.

sadism ['seɪdɪzəm] *n* сади́зм.

sadist ['seɪdɪst] *n* сади́ст(ка*).

sadistic [sə'dɪstɪk] *adj* (*person, behaviour*) сади́стский.

sadly ['sædlɪ] *adv* (*unhappily*) печа́льно, гру́стно; (*unfortunately*) к сожале́нию; (*seriously*: *mistaken, neglected*) серьёзно; **the school is** ~ **lacking in equipment** шко́ла испы́тывает серьёзный недоста́ток в обору́довании.

sadness ['sædnɪs] *n* печа́ль *f*, грусть *f*.

sadomasochism [seɪdəu'mæsəkɪzəm] *n* са́до-мазохи́зм.

sae *abbr* (*BRIT*) = *stamped addressed envelope*; *see* **stamp**.

safari [sə'fɑ:rɪ] *n* сафа́ри *nt ind*; **to go on** ~ проводи́ть* (провести́* *perf*) о́тпуск в сафа́ри.

safari park *n* парк сафа́ри.

safe [seɪf] *adj* (*place, subject*) безопа́сный* (безопа́сен); (*return, journey*) благополу́чный* (благополу́чен); (*bet, appointment*) надёжный* (надёжен) ◆ *n* сейф; **to be** ~ находи́ться* *(impf)* в безопа́сности; ~ **from** (*attack*) защищённый (защищён) от *+gen*; ~ **and sound** цел и невреди́м; **(just) to be on the** ~ **side** на вся́кий слу́чай; **to play** ~ де́йствовать *(impf)* осторо́жно; **it is** ~ **to say that** ... мо́жно с уве́ренностью сказа́ть, что ...; ~ **journey!** счастли́вого пути́!; ~ **seat** (*POL*) *парла́ментское ме́сто с гаранти́рованной подде́ржкой избира́телей*.

safe bet *n* ве́рное де́ло; **he is a** ~ ~ на него́ мо́жно положи́ться.

safe-breaker ['seɪfbreɪkə^r] *n* (*BRIT*) взло́мщик сейфов.

safe-conduct [seɪf'kɔndʌkt] *n* неприкоснове́нность *f*.

safe-cracker ['seɪfkrækə^r] *n* = **safe-breaker**.

safe-deposit ['seɪfdɪpɔzɪt] *n* сейф.

safeguard ['seɪfgɑ:d] *n* гара́нтия ◆ *vt* (*life, interests*) охраня́ть *(impf)*; (*future*) гаранти́ровать *(impf/perf)*.

* marks translations which have irregular inflections. The Russian-English side of the dictionary gives inflectional information.

safe haven *n* зóна безопáсности.
safe house *n* конспиратúвная квартúра.
safekeeping ['seɪf'ki:pɪŋ] *n* сохрáнность *f*.
safely ['seɪflɪ] *adv* (*assume, say*) с увéренностью; (*drive, arrive*) благополýчно; **I can ~ say** ... я могý с увéренностью сказáть ....
safe passage *n* безопáсный путь* *m*.
safe sex *n* безопáсный секс; **to practise ~ ~** испóльзовать *(impf)* презервати́вы во врéмя сéкса.
safety ['seɪftɪ] *n* безопáсность *f*; **~ first!** соблюдáйте осторóжность!
safety belt *n* привязнóй ремéнь *m*.
safety catch *n* (*on gun*) замóк*; (*on window*) защёлка*.
safety net *n* (*also fig*) страхóвочная сеть.
safety pin *n* англи́йская булáвка*.
safety valve *n* предохранúтельный клáпан.
saffron ['sæfrən] *n* шафрáн.
sag [sæg] *vi* (*breasts*) отвисáть (отви́снуть *perf*); (*roof, hem*) провисáть (прови́снуть *perf*); (*spirits, prices*) пáдать (упáсть* *perf*).
saga ['sɑ:gə] *n* сáга.
sage [seɪdʒ] *n* (*herb*) шалфéй; (*wise man*) мудрéц*.
Sagittarius [sædʒɪ'tɛərɪəs] *n* Стрелéц*; **he is ~** он – Стрелéц.
sago ['seɪgəu] *n* сáго *nt ind*.
Sahara [sə'hɑ:rə] *n*: **the ~ (Desert)** Сахáра.
Sahel [sæ'hɛl] *n* Сахéль *f*.
said [sɛd] *pt, pp of* **say**.
Saigon [saɪ'gɔn] *n* Сайгóн.
sail [seɪl] *n* пáрус* ◆ *vt* (*boat*) плáвать/плыть* *(impf)* на +*prp* ◆ *vi* (*ship, passenger*) плáвать/плыть* *(impf)*; (*SPORT*) занимáться *(impf)* пáрусным спóртом; (*also:* **set ~**) отплывáть (отплы́ть* *perf*); **to go for a ~** éхать* (поéхать* *perf*) катáться на лóдке; **they ~ed into Copenhagen** они́ приплы́ли в Копенгáген
▸ **sail through** *vt fus* (*fig*): **to ~ through an exam/interview** с лёгкостью сдавáть* (сдать* *perf*) экзáмен/проходи́ть* (пройти́* *perf*) собесéдование.
sailboat ['seɪlbəut] *n* (*US*) = **sailing boat**.
sailing ['seɪlɪŋ] *n* (*SPORT*) пáрусный спорт; **to go ~** занимáться *(impf)* пáрусным спóртом.
sailing boat *n* пáрусная лóдка*.
sailing ship *n* пáрусное сýдно*.
sailor ['seɪlə[r]] *n* моря́к*, матрóс.
saint [seɪnt] *n* (*also fig*) святóй(-áя) *m(f) adj*.
saintly ['seɪntlɪ] *adj* святóй*.
sake [seɪk] *n*: **for the ~ of sb/sth, for sb's/sth's ~** рáди когó-н/чегó-н; **arguing for arguing's ~** спор рáди спóра; **for the ~ of argument** в кáчестве предположéния; **for heaven's ~!** рáди Бóга!
Sakhalin [səxa'lin] *n* Сахали́н.
salad ['sæləd] *n* салáт; **tomato ~** салáт из помидóров; **green ~** зелёный салáт.
salad bowl *n* салáтница.
salad cream *n* (*BRIT*) салáтный сóус.
salad dressing *n* припрáва к салáту.
salami [sə'lɑ:mɪ] *n* саля́ми *f ind*.
salaried ['sælərɪd] *adj* (*staff*) получáющий зарплáту.
salary ['sælərɪ] *n* зарплáта (= *зáработная плáта*).
salary scale *n* шкалá* зáработной плáты.
sale [seɪl] *n* (*act of selling*) продáжа; (*at reduced prices*) распродáжа; (*auction*) тóрги *mpl*; **~s** *npl* (*total amount sold*) объём продáжи ◆ *cpd* (*campaign, conference*) реклáмный; (*figures, target*) продáжный; **"for ~"** „продаётся"; **on ~** в продáже; **these goods are on ~ or return** éсли э́ти товáры не бýдут прóданы, они́ бýдут возвращены́ владéльцу; **closing-down** *or (US)* **liquidation ~** ликвидациóнная распродáжа.
sale and lease back *n* (*COMM*) *продáжа сóбственности с услóвием получéния её обрáтно в арéнду на оговорённый срок*.
saleroom ['seɪlru:m] *n* торгóвый зал.
sales assistant [seɪlz-] (*US* **salesclerk**) *n* (*BRIT*) продавéц*(-вщи́ца).
salesclerk ['seɪlzklə:rk] *n* (*US*) = **sales assistant**.
sales force *n* торгóвые агéнты *mpl*.
salesman ['seɪlzmən] *irreg n* (*in shop*) продавéц*; (*also:* **travelling ~**) торгóвый агéнт.
sales manager *n* (*in company*) начáльник отдéла сбы́та; (*in shop*) стáрший*(-ая) продавéц*(-вщи́ца).
salesmanship ['seɪlzmənʃɪp] *n* умéние продавáть.
sales tax *n* (*US*) налóг на продáжи (*уплáчивается потреби́телем при покýпке определённых товáров*).
saleswoman ['seɪlzwumən] *irreg n* (*in shop*) продавщи́ца; (*representative*) торгóвый агéнт.
salient ['seɪlɪənt] *adj* сущéственный.
saline ['seɪlaɪn] *adj* соляно́й.
saliva [sə'laɪvə] *n* слюнá.
sallow ['sæləu] *adj* (*complexion*) желтýшный.
sally forth ['sælɪ-] *vi* отправля́ться (отпрáвиться* *perf*).
sally out *vi* = **sally forth**.
salmon ['sæmən] *n inv* (*ZOOL*) лосóсь* *m*; (*CULIN*) лососи́на.
salmon trout *n* таймéнь *m*.
salon ['sælɔn] *n* салóн; **beauty ~** космети́ческий* салóн.
saloon [sə'lu:n] *n* (*US: bar*) бар; (*BRIT: AUT*) седáн; (*ship's lounge*) салóн.
SALT [sɔ:lt] *n abbr* (= *Strategic Arms Limitation Talks/Treaty*) переговóры *pl*/договóр ОСВ = *об ограничéнии стратеги́ческих наступáтельных вооружéний*.
salt [sɔ:lt] *n* соль *f* ◆ *vt* (*preserve*) засáливать (засоли́ть* *perf*); (*season*) соли́ть* (посоли́ть*

perf) ◆ *cpd* солёный; **the ~ of the earth** соль землú.
saltcellar ['sɔ:ltsɛlə^r] *n* солóнка*.
salt-free ['sɔ:lt'fri:] *adj* не содержáщий сóли.
salt mine *n* солянáя шáхта.
saltwater ['sɔ:lt'wɔ:tə^r] *adj* живýщий в солёных вóдах.
salty ['sɔ:ltɪ] *adj* солёный* (сóлон).
salubrious [sə'lu:brɪəs] *adj* целéбный* (целéбен); (*fig: district etc*) благодáтный* (благодáтен).
salutary ['sæljutərɪ] *adj* полéзный* (полéзен).
salute [sə'lu:t] *n* (*MIL*) салю́т; (*greeting*) привéтствие ◆ *vt* (*MIL*) отдавáть* (отдáть* *perf*) честь +*dat*; (*fig*) привéтствовать *(impf)*.
salvage ['sælvɪdʒ] *n* (*saving*) спасéние; (*things saved*) спасённые вéщи *fpl* ◆ *vt* (*also fig*) спасáть (спастú* *perf*).
salvage vessel *n* спасáтельное сýдно*.
salvation [sæl'veɪʃən] *n* спасéние.
Salvation Army *n* Áрмия Спасéния.
salver ['sælvə^r] *n* поднóс.
salvo ['sælvəu] (*pl* **~es**) *n* залп.
Samaritans [sə'mærɪtənz] *npl*: **the ~** Самаритя́не* *mpl*.
same [seɪm] *adj* такóй же; (*identical*) одинáковый ◆ *pron*: **the ~** тот же (сáмый) (*f* та же (сáмая), *nt* то же (сáмое), *pl* те же (сáмые)); **the ~ book as** та же (сáмая) кнúга, что и; **on the ~ day** в тот же день; **at the ~ time** (*simultaneously*) в э́то же врéмя; (*yet*) в то же врéмя; **all** *or* **just the ~** всё равнó; **to do the ~ (as sb)** дéлать (сдéлать *perf*) то же (сáмое) (что и кто-н); **Happy New Year! – the ~ to you!** С Нóвым Гóдом! – Вас тáкже!; **you're a fool! – the ~ to you!** ты дурáк! – сам (ты) дурáк!; **I hate him – ~ here!** я ненавúжу егó – и я тóже!; **the company director and Mr Smith are one and the ~** дирéктор компáнии и Мúстер Смит однó лицó; **the books we're talking about are one and the ~** мы говорúли об однóй и тóйже кнúге; **~ again!** (*in bar etc*) повторúте!
sample ['sɑ:mpl] *n* (*of water*) прóба; (*of work, merchandise*) образéц* ◆ *vt* (*food, wine*) прóбовать (попрóбовать *perf*); **to take a ~** брать* (взять* *perf*) прóбу; **to take a blood/urine ~** брать* (взять* *perf*) кровь/мочý для анáлиза; **free ~** бесплáтный образéц*.
sanatoria [sænə'tɔ:rɪə] *npl of* **sanatorium**.
sanatorium [sænə'tɔ:rɪəm] (*pl* **sanatoria** *or* **~s**) *n* (*MED*) санатóрий.
sanctify ['sæŋktɪfaɪ] *vt* освящáть (освятúть* *perf*).
sanctimonious [sæŋktɪ'məunɪəs] *adj* благочúнный* (благочúнен).
sanction ['sæŋkʃən] *n* (*approval*) сáнкция ◆ *vt* (*give approval to*) санкционúровать *(impf/perf)*; **~s** *npl* (*severe measures*) сáнкции *fpl*; **to impose economic ~s on** *or* **against** применя́ть (применúть* *perf*) экономúческие сáнкции прóтив +*gen*.
sanctity ['sæŋktɪtɪ] *n* свя́тость *f*.
sanctuary ['sæŋktjuərɪ] *n* (*for animals*) заповéдник; (*for people*) убéжище; (*in church*) алтáрная часть *f*.
sand [sænd] *n* песóк* ◆ *vt* (*also:* **~ down**) ошкýривать (ошкýрить *perf*); *see also* **sands**.
sandal ['sændl] *n* сандáлия.
sandbag ['sændbæg] *n* мешóк* с пескóм.
sandblast ['sændblɑ:st] *vt* подвергáть (подвéргнуть *perf*) пескострýйной обрабóтке.
sandbox ['sændbɔks] *n* (*US*) песóчница.
sand castle *n* песчáный зáмок*.
sand dune *n* (песчáная) дю́на.
sander ['sændə^r] *n* ручнóй шлифовáльный станóк.
S & M *n abbr* (= *sadomasochism*) садомазохúзм.
sandpaper ['sændpeɪpə^r] *n* наждáчная бумáга, шкýрка.
sandpit ['sændpɪt] *n* песóчница.
sands [sændz] *npl* пескú *mpl*.
sandstone ['sændstəun] *n* песчáник.
sandstorm ['sændstɔ:m] *n* песчáная бýря.
sandwich ['sændwɪtʃ] *n* бутербрóд ◆ *vt*: **~ed between** зажáтый мéжду +*instr*; **cheese/ham ~** бутербрóд с сы́ром/ветчинóй.
sandwich board *n* (*notice*) реклáмный щит*.
sandwich course *n* (*BRIT*) *курс обучéния, сочетáющий теóрию с прáктикой.*
sandwich man *n irreg человéк, несýщий на себé реклáмный щит.*
sandy ['sændɪ] *adj* песчáный; (*hair*) песóчный.
sane [seɪn] *adj* разýмный* (разýмен).
San Francisco [sæn fræn'sɪskəu] *n* Сан-Францúско *m ind*.
sang [sæŋ] *pt of* **sing**.
sanguine ['sæŋgwɪn] *adj* оптимистúчный* (оптимистúчен).
sanitaria [sænɪ'tɛərɪə] *npl* (*US*) *of* **sanitarium**.
sanitarium [sænɪ'tɛərɪəm] (*pl* **sanitaria** *or* **~s**) *n* (*US*) = **sanatorium**.
sanitary ['sænɪtərɪ] *adj* (*system, inspector*) санитáрный; (*clean*) гигиенúчный* (гигиенúчен).
sanitary towel (*US* **sanitary napkin**) *n* гигиенúческий* пакéт, жéнская проклáдка.
sanitation [sænɪ'teɪʃən] *n* санитарúя.
sanitation department *n* (*US*) санитáрное управлéние.
sanity ['sænɪtɪ] *n* (*of person*) рассýдок*; (*of suggestion etc*) разýмность *f*.
sank [sæŋk] *pt of* **sink**.
San Marino ['sænmə'ri:nəu] *n* Сан-Марúно *nt*

* marks translations which have irregular inflections. The Russian-English side of the dictionary gives inflectional information.

ind.
Santa Claus [sæntə'klɔ:z] *n* (*in Britain, US etc*) Са́нта-Кла́ус; (*in Russia*) ≈ Дед Моро́з.
Santiago [sæntɪ'ɑ:gəu] *n* (*also:* ~ **de Chile**) Сантья́го *m ind.*
sap [sæp] *n* (*BOT*) сок* ◆ *vt* (*strength, confidence*) выса́сывать (вы́сосать *perf*).
sapling ['sæplɪŋ] *n* молодо́е де́ревце*, побе́г.
sapper ['sæpə'] *n* сапёр.
sapphire ['sæfaɪə'] *n* сапфи́р.
Sarajevo [særə'jeɪvəu] *n* Сара́ево.
sarcasm ['sɑ:kæzm] *n* сарка́зм.
sarcastic [sɑ:'kæstɪk] *adj* саркасти́чный* (саркасти́чен).
sarcophagi [sɑ:'kɔfəgaɪ] *npl of* **sarcophagus**.
sarcophagus [sɑ:'kɔfəgəs] (*pl* **sarcophagi**) *n* саркофа́г.
sardine [sɑ:'di:n] *n* сарди́на.
Sardinia [sɑ:'dɪnɪə] *n* Сарди́ния.
Sardinian [sɑ:'dɪnɪən] *adj* сарди́нский ◆ *n* сарди́нец*(-нка*); (*LING*) сарди́нский диале́кт.
sardonic [sɑ:'dɔnɪk] *adj* сардони́ческий.
sari ['sɑ:rɪ] *n* са́ри *nt ind.*
sartorial [sɑ:'tɔ:rɪəl] *adj*: ~ **elegance** уме́ние одева́ться.
SAS *n abbr* (*BRIT*: *MIL*: = *Special Air Service*) *осо́бые возду́шно-деса́нтные войска́.*
SASE *n abbr* (*US*) = *self-addressed stamped envelope.*
sash [sæʃ] *n* (*around waist*) куша́к*; (*over shoulder*) ле́нта; (*of window*) подъёмная ра́ма.
sash window *n* окно́* с подъёмной ра́мой.
SAT *n abbr* (*US*) = *Scholastic Aptitude Test.*
sat [sæt] *pt, pp of* **sit**.
Sat. *abbr* = **Saturday**.
Satan ['seɪtn] *n* Сатана́ *m.*
satanic [sə'tænɪk] *adj* сатани́нский.
satanism ['seɪtnɪzəm] *n* сатани́зм.
satchel ['sætʃl] *n* ра́нец*.
sated ['seɪtɪd] *adj* (*person*): **to be ~ (with)** пресыща́ться (пресы́титься* *perf*) (+*instr*).
satellite ['sætəlaɪt] *n* спу́тник; (*POL*: *country*) сателли́т; ~ **town** го́род-спу́тник.
satellite dish *n* спу́тниковая анте́нна.
satellite television *n* спу́тниковое телеви́дение.
satiate ['seɪʃɪeɪt] *vt* насыща́ть (насы́тить* *perf*).
satin ['sætɪn] *n* атла́с ◆ *adj* атла́сный; **with a ~ finish** с атла́сным отли́вом.
satire ['sætaɪə'] *n* сати́ра.
satirical [sə'tɪrɪkl] *adj* сатири́ческий*.
satirist ['sætɪrɪst] *n* сати́рик.
satirize ['sætɪraɪz] *vt* высме́ивать (вы́смеять *perf*).
satisfaction [sætɪs'fækʃən] *n* (*pleasure*) удовлетворе́ние; (*refund, apology etc*) возмеще́ние; **has it been done to your ~?** Вы удовлетворе́ны тем, как э́то сде́лано?
satisfactorily [sætɪs'fæktərɪlɪ] *adv* удовлетвори́тельно.
satisfactory [sætɪs'fæktərɪ] *adj* удовлетвори́тельный* (удовлетвори́телен).
satisfied ['sætɪsfaɪd] *adj* (*customer*) дово́льный* (дово́лен), удовлетворённый* (удовлетворён); **he is/was ~ (with sth)** он дово́лен/был дово́лен *or* удовлетворён/был удовлетворён (чем-н).
satisfy ['sætɪsfaɪ] *vt* (*please, fulfil*) удовлетворя́ть (удовлетвори́ть *perf*); (*convince*) убежда́ть (убеди́ть* *perf*); **to ~ the requirements** удовлетворя́ть (удовлетвори́ть *perf*) тре́бованиям; **to ~ sb (that)** убежда́ть (убеди́ть* *perf*) кого́-н (в том, что); **to ~ o.s. of sth** удостоверя́ться (удостове́риться *perf*) в чём-н.
satisfying ['sætɪsfaɪɪŋ] *adj* прия́тный* (прия́тен).
satsuma [sæt'su:mə] *n* мандари́н.
saturate ['sætʃəreɪt] *vt*: **to ~ (with)** (*also fig*) насыща́ть (насы́тить* *perf*) (+*instr*).
saturated fat ['sætʃəreɪtɪd-] *n* насы́щенные жиры́ *mpl.*
saturation [sætʃə'reɪʃən] *n* (*process*) насыще́ние; (*CHEM, fig*) насы́щенность *f.*
Saturday ['sætədɪ] *n* суббо́та; *see also* **Tuesday**.
Saturn ['sætən] *n* Сату́рн.
sauce [sɔ:s] *n* со́ус.
saucepan ['sɔ:spən] *n* кастрю́ля.
saucer ['sɔ:sə'] *n* блю́дце*.
saucy ['sɔ:sɪ] *adj* (*inf*) по́шлый (пошл).
Saudi Arabia ['saudɪ-] *n* Сау́довская Ара́вия.
Saudi (Arabian) *adj* сау́довский*.
sauna ['sɔ:nə] *n* са́уна, фи́нская ба́ня.
saunter ['sɔ:ntə'] *vi* прогу́ливаться *(impf)*.
sausage ['sɔsɪdʒ] *n* (*for cooking*) сарде́лька*, соси́ска*; (*cold meat*) колбаса́*.
sausage roll *n* (*BRIT*) пирожо́к* с соси́ской.
sauté ['səuteɪ] *adj* жа́реный ◆ *vt* жа́рить (пожа́рить *perf*).
savage ['sævɪdʒ] *adj* (*attack*) зве́рский*; (*voice*) я́ростный* (я́ростен); (*dog, criticism*) свире́пый (свире́п); (*primitive*: *tribe*) ди́кий* ◆ *n* дика́рь*(-рка*) *m(f)* ◆ *vt* (*attack, also fig*) разрыва́ть (разорва́ть* *perf*) на ча́сти.
savagely ['sævɪdʒlɪ] *adv* (*attack, pull*) я́ростно; (*criticize*) свире́по.
savagery ['sævɪdʒrɪ] *n* свире́пость *f.*
save [seɪv] *vt* (*rescue*) спаса́ть (спасти́* *perf*); (*economize on*: *money, time*) эконо́мить* (сэконо́мить* *perf*); (*put by*: *food, money*) откла́дывать (отложи́ть* *perf*); (*receipts, also COMPUT*) сохраня́ть (сохрани́ть *perf*); (*avoid*: *work, trouble*) избавля́ть (изба́вить* *perf*) от +*gen*; (*keep*: *seat, place*) занима́ть (заня́ть* *perf*); (*SPORT*: *shot, ball*) отбива́ть (отби́ть* *perf*), отража́ть (отрази́ть* *perf*) ◆ *vi* (*also:* ~ **up**) копи́ть* (скопи́ть* *perf*) де́ньги ◆ *prep* (*except*) поми́мо +*gen*; **it will ~ me an hour** я сэконо́млю на э́том час; **to ~ face** спасти́* *(perf)* свою́ репута́цию; **God ~ the Queen**!

Бо́же храни́ короле́ву!; **that was a brilliant ~ (by the goalkeeper)** врата́рь прекра́сно отрази́л уда́р.
saving ['seɪvɪŋ] *n* (*on price etc*) эконо́мия ◆ *adj*: **the ~ grace of** спасе́ние *+gen*; **~s** *npl* (*money*) сбереже́ния *ntpl*; **to make ~s** откла́дывать (отложи́ть* *perf*).
savings account *n* сберега́тельный счёт*.
savings bank *n* сберега́тельный банк.
saviour ['seɪvjə^r] (*US* **savior**) *n* спаси́тель(ница) *m(f)*; (*REL*) Спаси́тель *m*.
savoir-faire ['sævwɑ:fɛə^r] *n* све́тскость *f*.
savour ['seɪvə^r] (*US* **savor**) *vt* (*food, drink*) смакова́ть *(impf)*; (*experience*) наслажда́ться (наслади́ться* *perf*) *+instr* ◆ *n* (*of food*) арома́т.
savoury ['seɪvərɪ] (*US* **savory**) *adj* (*dish*) несла́дкий* (несла́док).
savvy ['sævɪ] *n* (*inf*) понима́ние.
saw [sɔ:] (*pt* **sawed**, *pp* **sawed** *or* **sawn**) *vt* пили́ть* *(impf)* ◆ *n* пила́* ◆ *pt of* **see**; **to ~ sth up** распи́ливать (распили́ть* *perf*) что-н.
sawdust ['sɔ:dʌst] *n* опи́лки* *pl*.
sawed-off ['sɔ:dɔf] *adj* (*US*) = **sawn-off**.
sawmill ['sɔ:mɪl] *n* лесопи́льный заво́д.
sawn [[sɔ:n]] *pp of* **saw**.
sawn-off ['sɔ:nɔf] (*US* **sawed-off**) *adj*: **~ shotgun** обре́з.
saxophone ['sæksəfəun] *n* саксофо́н.
say [seɪ] (*pt, pp* **said**) *vt* говори́ть (сказа́ть* *perf*) ◆ *n*: **to have one's ~** выража́ть (вы́разить* *perf*) своё мне́ние; **to ~ yes** соглаша́ться (согласи́ться* *perf*); **to ~ no** отка́зываться (отказа́ться* *perf*); **could you ~ that again?** повтори́те, пожа́луйста; **she said (that) I was to give you this** она́ сказа́ла, что я до́лжен отда́ть э́то Вам; **my watch ~s 3 o'clock** мои́ часы́ пока́зывают 3 часа́; **shall we ~ Tuesday?** ну, ска́жем, во вто́рник?; **that doesn't ~ much for him** э́то не говори́т в его́ по́льзу; **when all is said and done** когда́ всё (бу́дет) оговоре́но; **there is a lot to be said for ...** мно́гое мо́жно сказа́ть в по́льзу *+gen* ...; **that is to ~** то есть; **that goes without ~ing** э́то са́мо собо́й разуме́ется; **to ~ nothing of** не говоря́ уже́ о *+prp*; **~ (that) you ...** ну, ска́жем, Вы ...; **to have a** *or* **some ~ in sth** име́ть *(impf)* пра́во го́лоса в чём-н.
saying ['seɪɪŋ] *n* погово́рка*.
say-so ['seɪsəu] *n*: **to do sth on sb's ~** де́лать (сде́лать *perf*) что-н с чьего́-н согла́сия.
SBA (*US*) *n abbr* = *Small Business Administration*.
SC *n abbr* (*US*) = **Supreme Court** ◆ *abbr* (*POST*) = *South Carolina*.
s/c *abbr* = **self-contained**.
scab [skæb] *n* (*on wound*) струп*; (*inf: pej*) штрейкбре́хер.
scabby ['skæbɪ] *adj* (*pej: hands, skin*) покры́тый (покры́т) стру́пьями.
scaffold ['skæfəld] *n* (*for execution*) эшафо́т.
scaffolding ['skæfəldɪŋ] *n* леса́* *pl*.
scald [skɔ:ld] *n* ожо́г ◆ *vt* (*burn*) ошпа́ривать (ошпа́рить *perf*).
scalding ['skɔ:ldɪŋ] *adj* (*also:* **~ hot**) о́чень горя́чий*.
scale [skeɪl] *n* шкала́*; (*usu pl: of fish*) чешуя́ *f no pl*; (*MUS*) га́мма; (*of map, model, project etc*) масшта́б ◆ *vt* (*mountain, tree*) взбира́ться (взобра́ться* *perf*) на *+acc*; **~s** *npl* (*for weighing*) весы́ *pl*; **to draw sth to ~** черти́ть* (начерти́ть* *perf*) что-н по масшта́бу; **a small-~ model** уме́ньшенная моде́ль; **on a large ~** в широ́ком масшта́бе; **pay ~** тари́фная се́тка* зарпла́ты; **~ of charges** шкала́* расце́нок
▸ **scale down** *vt* сокраща́ть (сократи́ть* *perf*).
scaled down [skeɪld-] *adj* в уме́ньшенном масшта́бе.
scale drawing *n* масшта́бный рису́нок* *or* чертёж*.
scallion ['skæljən] *n* (*shallot*) зелёный лук *m no pl*; (*US: leek*) лук-поре́й *m no pl*.
scallop ['skɔləp] *n* (*ZOOL*) (морско́й) гребешо́к*; (*in sewing etc*) фесто́н.
scalp [skælp] *n* скальп ◆ *vt* скальпи́ровать *(impf/perf)*; **I have an itchy ~** у меня́ че́шется голова́.
scalpel ['skælpl] *n* ска́льпель *m*.
scalper ['skælpə^r] *n* (*US: inf: ticket tout*) спекуля́нт(ка*).
scam [skæm] *n* (*inf*) жу́льничество *nt no pl*.
scamp [skæmp] *n* (*inf*) безобра́зник(-ица).
scamper ['skæmpə^r] *vi*: **to ~ away** *or* **off** уска́кать* *(impf)*.
scampi ['skæmpɪ] *npl* (*BRIT*) паниро́ванные креве́тки* *fpl*.
scan [skæn] *vt* (*examine*) обсле́довать *(perf)*; (*read quickly*) просма́тривать (просмотре́ть* *perf*); (*TV*) разлага́ть *(impf)* изображе́ние; (*RADAR*) скани́ровать *(impf)* ◆ *vi* (*poetry*) рифмова́ться *(impf)* ◆ *n* (*MED*) скани́рование; **ultrasound ~** ультразву́к.
scandal ['skændl] *n* (*shocking event*) сканда́л; (*gossip*) спле́тни* *fpl*; (*fig: disgrace*) позо́р.
scandalize ['skændəlaɪz] *vt* скандализи́ровать *(impf/perf)*.
scandalous ['skændələs] *adj* сканда́льный* (сканда́лен); (*waste*) возмути́тельный* (возмути́телен).
Scandinavia [skændɪ'neɪvɪə] *n* Скандина́вия.
Scandinavian [skændɪ'neɪvɪən] *adj* скандина́вский ◆ *n* скандина́в(ка*).
scanner ['skænə^r] *n* (*RADAR, MED*) ска́нер.
scant [skænt] *adj* (*attention*) пове́рхностный; (*reward*) незначи́тельный.
scantily ['skæntɪlɪ] *adv*: **she was ~ clad** *or*

* marks translations which have irregular inflections. The Russian-English side of the dictionary gives inflectional information.

dressed онá былá едвá одéта.
scanty ['skæntɪ] *adj* (*meal*) скýдный* (скýден); **her underwear was** ~ бельё едвá прикрывáло её тéло.
scapegoat ['skeɪpgəut] *n* козёл* отпущéния.
scar [skɑ:] *n* (*on skin*) шрам; (*fig*) трáвма ◆ *vt* (*also fig*) травмúровать *(impf/perf)*; **his face is ~red** у негó на лицé шрам.
scarce [skɛəs] *adj* рéдкий* (рéдок); **to make o.s.** ~ (*inf*) улизнýть *(perf)*.
scarcely ['skɛəslɪ] *adv* (*hardly*) едвá; (*with numbers*: *barely*) тóлько; ~ **anybody** едвá ли ктó-нибудь; **I can ~ believe it** я едвá могý этому повéрить; **that is ~ the point** едвá ли в этом дéло.
scarcity ['skɛəsɪtɪ] *n* нехвáтка*, недостáток*; ~ **value** (*COMM*) *цéнность товáра, определяéмая егó дефицúтностью.*
scare [skɛəʳ] *n* (*fright*) испýг; (*public fear*) тревóга ◆ *vt* (*frighten*) пугáть (испугáть *or* напугáть *perf*); **to ~ sb stiff** (*inf*) пугáть (напугáть *perf*) когó-н дó смерти; **there was a bomb ~ at the station** опасáлись, что на стáнции подлóжена бóмба
▸ **scare away** *vt* отпýгивать (отпугнýть *perf*)
▸ **scare off** *vt* = **scare away**.
scarecrow ['skɛəkrəu] *n* (огорóдное) чýчело.
scared ['skɛəd] *adj* испýганный (испýган), напýганный (напýган); **he was** ~ он испугáлся *or* был испýган.
scaremonger ['skɛəmʌŋgəʳ] *n* паникёр.
scarf [skɑ:f] (*pl* **~s** *or* **scarves**) *n* шарф; (*also:* **headscarf**) платóк*.
scarlet ['skɑ:lɪt] *adj* áлый (ал).
scarlet fever *n* скарлатúна.
scarper ['skɑ:pəʳ] *vi* (*inf*) смывáться (смы́ться* *perf*).
scarred [skɑ:d] *adj* (*fig*: *person*) травмúрованный (травмúрован); ~ **face** лицó в шрáмах.
scarves [skɑ:vz] *npl of* **scarf**.
scary ['skɛərɪ] *adj* стрáшный* (стрáшен).
scathing ['skeɪðɪŋ] *adj* уничтожáющий*; **to be ~ about sth** относúться* (отнестúсь* *perf*) к чемý-н с презрéнием.
scatter ['skætəʳ] *vt* (*papers, seeds*) разбрáсывать (разбросáть *perf*); (*flock of birds, crowd*) разгоня́ть (разогнáть* *perf*) ◆ *vi* (*crowd*) рассыпáться (рассы́паться* *perf*).
scatterbrained ['skætəbreɪnd] *adj* (*inf*) рассéянный* (рассéян).
scattered ['skætəd] *adj* разбрóсанный; ~ **showers** преры́вистые лúвни.
scatty ['skætɪ] *adj* (*BRIT*: *inf*) несóбранный (несóбран).
scavenge ['skævəndʒ] *vi*: **to ~ for food** ры́скать* *(impf)* в пóисках пúщи.
scavenger ['skævəndʒəʳ] *n* (*person*) старьёвщик; (*animal, bird*) живóтное *nt adj*, питáющееся пáдалью, стервя́тник.
SCE *n abbr* = *Scottish Certificate of Education.*
scenario [sɪ'nɑ:rɪəu] *n* (*also fig*) сценáрий.
scene [si:n] *n* (*THEAT, fig*) сцéна; (*of crime, accident*) мéсто*; (*sight, view*) картúна; **behind the ~s** (*also fig*) за кулúсами; **to make a** ~ (*inf*: *fuss*) устрáивать (устрóить *perf*) сцéну; **to appear on the** ~ появля́ться (появúться* *perf*) на сцéне; **the political** ~ политúческая арéна.
scenery ['si:nərɪ] *n* (*THEAT*) декорáции *fpl*; (*landscape*) пейзáж.
scenic ['si:nɪk] *adj* живопúсный* (живопúсен).
scent [sɛnt] *n* (*smell*) зáпах; (*track, also fig*) след; (*perfume*) духú* *pl*; **to put** *or* **throw sb off the** ~ (*fig*) сбивáть (сбить* *perf*) когó-н со слéда.
sceptic ['skɛptɪk] (*US* **skeptic**) *n* скéптик.
sceptical ['skɛptɪkl] (*US* **skeptical**) *adj* (*person*) скептúчный* (скептúчен); (*remarks*) скептúческий*.
scepticism ['skɛptɪsɪzəm] (*US* **skepticism**) *n* скептицúзм.
sceptre ['sɛptəʳ] (*US* **scepter**) *n* скúпетр.
schedule ['ʃɛdju:l, (*US*) 'skɛdju:l] *n* (*timetable*) расписáние, грáфик; (*list of prices, details etc*) пéречень* *m* ◆ *vt* (*timetable*) распúсывать (расписáть* *perf*); (*visit*) назначáть (назнáчить *perf*); **on** ~ по расписáнию *or* грáфику; **as ~d** как (бы́ло) запланúровано; **we are working to a very tight** ~ мы рабóтаем по плóтному грáфику; **everything went according to** ~ всё прошлó по грáфику *or* расписáнию; **to be ahead of** ~ опережáть (опередúть* *perf*) грáфик; **to be behind** ~ отставáть *(impf)* от грáфика.
scheduled ['ʃɛdju:ld, (*US*) 'skɛdju:ld] *adj* (*time, event*) запланúрованный (запланúрован); (*train, bus, stop*) обознáченный (обознáчен) в расписáнии.
scheduled flight *n* регуля́рный рейс.
schematic [skɪ'mætɪk] *adj* схематúческий*.
scheme [ski:m] *n* (*plan, idea*) зáмысел*; (*plot*) прóиски *pl*, кóзни *pl*; (*pension plan etc*) прогрáмма; (*arrangement*) план, схéма ◆ *vi* строúть *(impf)* кóзни; **colour** *or* *(US)* **color** ~ цветовáя гáмма.
scheming ['ski:mɪŋ] *adj* ковáрный ◆ *n* кóзни *pl*, прóиски *pl*.
schism ['skɪzəm] *n* раскóл.
schizophrenia [skɪtsə'fri:nɪə] *n* шизофренúя.
schizophrenic [skɪtsə'frɛnɪk] *adj* шизофренúческий ◆ *n* шизофрéник(-úчка*).
scholar ['skɔləʳ] *n* (*scholarship holder*) стипендиáт; (*learned person*) учёный *m adj*.
scholarly ['skɔləlɪ] *adj* (*text, approach*) академúческий*; (*person*) учёный.
scholarship ['skɔləʃɪp] *n* (*academic knowledge*) учёность *f*; (*grant*) стипéндия.
school [sku:l] *n* шкóла; (*US*: *inf*) университéт; (*BRIT*) инститýт; (*of fish, whales*) стáя ◆ *cpd* шкóльный.
school age *n* шкóльный вóзраст.

schoolbook ['sku:lbuk] *n* (шко́льный) уче́бник.
schoolboy ['sku:lbɔɪ] *n* шко́льник.
schoolchildren ['sku:ltʃɪldrən] *npl* шко́льники *mpl*.
school days *npl* шко́льные дни *mpl*.
schooled [sku:ld] *adj*: ~ **(in)** обу́ченный (обу́чен) (+*dat*).
schoolgirl ['sku:lgə:l] *n* шко́льница.
schooling ['sku:lɪŋ] *n* шко́льное образова́ние.
school-leaver [sku:l'li:vəʳ] *n* (*BRIT*) выпускни́к(-и́ца) шко́лы.
schoolmaster ['sku:lmɑ:stəʳ] *n* учи́тель* *m*.
schoolmistress ['sku:lmɪstrɪs] *n* учи́тельница.
school report *n* (*BRIT*) та́бель *m* успева́емости.
schoolroom ['sku:lru:m] *n* класс, кла́ссная ко́мната.
schoolteacher ['sku:lti:tʃəʳ] *n* (шко́льный(-ая)) учи́тель*(ница) *m(f)*.
schoolyard ['sku:ljɑ:d] *n* (*US*) шко́льный двор*.
schooner ['sku:nəʳ] *n* (*ship*) шху́на; (*BRIT*: *for sherry*) фуже́р (*для хе́реса*); (*US*: *for beer*) кру́жка* (*для пи́ва*).
sciatica [saɪ'ætɪkə] *n* и́шиас.
science ['saɪəns] *n* (*study of natural things*) нау́ка; (*in school*) есте́ственные нау́ки *fpl*; **the ~s** есте́ственные и то́чные нау́ки.
science fiction *n* нау́чная фанта́стика.
scientific [saɪən'tɪfɪk] *adj* нау́чный.
scientist ['saɪəntɪst] *n* учёный *m adj*.
sci-fi ['saɪfaɪ] *n abbr* (*inf*) (= **science fiction**) НФ= *нау́чная фанта́стика*.
Scillies ['sɪlɪz] *npl* = **Scilly Isles**.
Scilly Isles ['sɪlɪ'aɪlz] *npl*: **the ~ ~** острова́ *mpl* Си́лли.
scintillating ['sɪntɪleɪtɪŋ] *adj* (*fig*: *conversation, wit*) блестя́щий*; (*smile*) сия́ющий*.
scissors ['sɪzəz] *npl*: **(a pair of)** ~ но́жницы *pl*.
sclerosis [sklɪ'rəusɪs] *n* склеро́з.
scoff [skɔf] *vt* (*BRIT*: *inf*: *eat*) жрать* (сожра́ть* *perf*) ◆ *vi*: **to ~ (at)** (*mock*) насмеха́ться *(impf)* (над +*instr*).
scold [skəuld] *vt* брани́ть (вы́бранить *perf*), руга́ть (отруга́ть *perf*).
scolding ['skəuldɪŋ] *n* вы́говор.
scone [skɔn] *n* (*CULIN*) кекс.
scoop [sku:p] *n* (*measuring scoop*: *for flour etc*) сово́к*; (: *for ice-cream*) черпа́к; (*PRESS*) сенсацио́нное сообще́ние
▸ **scoop out** *vt* выскреба́ть (вы́скрести* *perf*)
▸ **scoop up** *vt* заче́рпывать (зачерпну́ть *perf*).
scooter ['sku:təʳ] *n* (*also*: **motor ~**) мопе́д; (*toy*) само́ка́т.
scope [skəup] *n* (*opportunity*) просто́р; (*of plan, undertaking*) масшта́б; (*of person*) компете́нция; **within the ~ of** в ра́мках +*gen*; **there is plenty of ~ for improvement** (*BRIT*) есть просто́р для соверше́нствования; **it is well within his ~ to ...** ... в его́ компете́нции.
scorch [skɔ:tʃ] *vt* (*clothes*) сжига́ть (сжечь* *perf*); (*earth, grass*) выжига́ть (вы́жечь* *perf*).
scorched-earth policy [skɔ:tʃt'ə:θ-] *n* (*MIL*) поли́тика *or* та́ктика вы́жженой земли́.
scorcher ['skɔ:tʃəʳ] *n* (*inf*: *hot day*) жари́ща.
scorching ['skɔ:tʃɪŋ] *adj* паля́щий.
score [skɔ:ʳ] *n* (*number of points etc*) счёт; (*MUS*) партиту́ра; (*twenty*) два́дцать* ◆ *vt* (*goal*) забива́ть (заби́ть* *perf*); (*point*) набира́ть (набра́ть* *perf*); (*mark*) получа́ть (получи́ть* *perf*); (*cut*: *leather, wood etc*) цара́пать (поцара́пать *perf*); (*achieve*: *success*) завоёвывать (завоева́ть *perf*) ◆ *vi* (*in game*) набира́ть (набра́ть* *perf*) очки́; (*FOOTBALL etc*) забива́ть (заби́ть* *perf*) гол; (*keep score*) вести́* *(perf)* счёт; **to settle an old ~ with sb** (*fig*) своди́ть* (свести́* *perf*) с кем-н ста́рые счёты; **~s of** деся́тки +*gen*; **on that ~** на э́тот счёт; **to ~ well** набира́ть (набра́ть* *perf*) мно́го очко́в; **to ~ 6 out of 10** набира́ть *(perf)* 6 ба́ллов из 10; **to ~ (a point) over sb** превосходи́ть* (превзойти́* *perf*) кого́-н
▸ **score out** *vt* вычёркивать (вы́черкнуть *perf*).
scoreboard ['skɔ:bɔ:d] *n* табло́ *nt ind*.
scorecard ['skɔ:kɑ:d] *n* (*SPORT*) *ка́рта, на кото́рую зано́сится счёт*.
scoreline ['skɔ:laɪn] *n* счёт* на да́нный моме́нт.
scorer ['skɔ:rəʳ] *n* (*FOOTBALL*) игро́к*, заби́вший гол; (*scorekeeper*) судья́*.
scorn [skɔ:n] *n* презре́ние ◆ *vt* презира́ть *(impf)*.
scornful ['skɔ:nful] *adj* презри́тельный* (презри́телен).
Scorpio ['skɔ:pɪəu] *n* Скорпио́н; **he is ~** он – Скорпио́н.
scorpion ['skɔ:pɪən] *n* скорпио́н.
Scot [skɔt] *n* шотла́ндец*(-дка*).
Scotch [skɔtʃ] *n* (*whisky*) (шотла́ндское) ви́ски *nt ind*.
scotch [skɔtʃ] *vt* (*end*: *rumour, plan*) пресека́ть (пресе́чь* *perf*).
Scotch tape® *n* клёйкая ле́нта, "скотч" (*разг*).
scot-free ['skɔt'fri:] *adv*: **to get off ~** легко́ отде́лываться (отде́латься *perf*).
Scotland ['skɔtlənd] *n* Шотла́ндия.
Scots [skɔts] *adj* шотла́ндский*.
Scotsman ['skɔtsmən] *irreg n* шотла́ндец*.
Scotswoman ['skɔtswumən] *irreg n* шотла́ндка*.
Scottish ['skɔtɪʃ] *adj* шотла́ндский*; **the ~ National Party** Шотла́ндская национа́льная па́ртия; **the ~ Parliament** парла́мент Шотла́ндии, шотла́ндский парла́мент.
scoundrel ['skaundrl] *n* негодя́й.
scour ['skauəʳ] *vt* (*search*) обы́скивать

(обыскáть* *perf*); (*clean*) выскáбливать (вы́скоблить* *perf*).
scourer ['skauərə^r] *n* жёсткая мочáлка*.
scourge [skə:dʒ] *n* (*cause of trouble*) бич.
scout [skaut] *n* (*MIL*) развéдчик; (*also:* **boy** ~) (бой)скáут; **girl** ~ (*US*) (дéвочка*-)скáут
▸ **scout around** *vi* ры́скать* *(impf)* в пóисках +*gen*.
scowl [skaul] *vi* хмýриться (нахмýриться *perf*); **to ~ at sb** хмýро смотрéть* (посмотрéть* *perf*) на когó-н.
scrabble ['skræbl] *vi* (*also:* ~ **around**: *search*) шáрить (пошáрить *perf*); (*claw*): **to ~ at** цепля́ться *(impf)* (за +*acc*) ◆ *n*: **S~®** (игрá) Скрэбл *ind*; **to ~ about** *or* **around for sth** шáрить (пошáрить *perf*) в пóисках чегó-н.
scraggy ['skrægɪ] *adj* тóщий* (тощ).
scram [skræm] *vi* (*inf*) смывáться (смы́ться* *perf*); **~!** убирáйся!
scramble ['skræmbl] *n* (*climb*: *using hands*) карáбканье; (*struggle, rush*) свáлка* ◆ *vi*: **to ~ out** выкарáбкиваться (вы́карабкаться *perf*) из +*gen*; **to ~ for** дрáться* (подрáться* *perf*) за +*acc*.
scrambled eggs ['skræmbld-] *n* яи́чница-болтýнья.
scrambling ['skræmblɪŋ] *n* (*SPORT*) мотокрóсс.
scrap [skræp] *n* (*of paper*) клочóк*; (*of information*) обры́вок*; (*of material etc*) лоскýт*; (*fig*: *of truth*) крупи́ца; (*inf*: *fight*) потасóвка; (*also:* ~ **metal**) металли́ческий* лом, металлолóм ◆ *vt* (*discard*: *machines etc*) отдавáть* (отдáть* *perf*) на слом; (*fig*: *plans etc*) откáзываться (отказáться* *perf*) от +*gen* ◆ *vi* (*fight*) дрáться* (подрáться* *perf*); **~s** *npl* (*of food*) объéдки *mpl*; (*of material*) обрéзки *mpl*; **to sell sth for ~** сдавáть* (сдать* *perf*) в ути́ль.
scrapbook ['skræpbuk] *n* альбóм для вы́резок.
scrap dealer *n* ути́льщик.
scrape [skreɪp] *vt* (*scrape off*) очищáть (очи́стить* *perf*); (*scrape against*) царáпать (поцарáпать *perf*), обдирáть (ободрáть* *perf*) ◆ *vi*: **to ~ through** (*exam etc*) пролезáть (пролéзть* *perf*) на +*prp* ◆ *n* (*fig*): **to get into a** ~ попадáть (попáсть* *perf*) в передéлку
▸ **scrape together** *vt* (*money*) наскребáть (наскрести́* *perf*).
scraper ['skreɪpə^r] *n* скребóк*.
scrapheap ['skræphi:p] *n*: **on the** ~ (*fig*) на свáлку.
scrap merchant *n* (*BRIT*) ути́льщик.
scrap metal *n* металлолóм.
scrap paper *n* макулатýра.
scrappy ['skræpɪ] *adj* (*piece of work*) дряннóй.
scrap yard *n* свáлка*.
scratch [skrætʃ] *n* царáпина ◆ *cpd* импровизи́рованный ◆ *vt* царáпать (поцарáпать *perf*); (*an itch*) чесáть* (почесáть* *perf*); (*COMPUT*) стирáть (стерéть* *perf*) ◆ *vi* чесáться* (почесáться* *perf*); **to start from** ~ начинáть (начáть* *perf*) с нуля́; **to be up to** ~ (*person, conditions, standard*) быть* *(impf)* на ýровне.
scratch pad *n* (*US*) блокнóт.
scrawl [skrɔ:l] *n* карáкули *fpl* ◆ *vt* царáпать (нацарáпать *perf*).
scrawny ['skrɔ:nɪ] *adj* тóщий* (тощ).
scream [skri:m] *n* вопль *m*, крик ◆ *vi* кричáть *(impf)*; **it's a real** ~ (*inf*) э́то пря́мо умóра; **to ~ at sb** кричáть *(impf)* на когó-н.
scree [skri:] *n* камени́стая óсыпь *f*.
screech [skri:tʃ] *vi* визжáть *(impf)* ◆ *n* визг.
screen [skri:n] *n* (*CINEMA, TV, COMPUT*) экрáн; (*barrier, also fig*: *cover*) ши́рма; (*also:* **windscreen**) ветровóе стеклó* ◆ *vt* (*protect, conceal*) заслоня́ть (заслони́ть* *perf*); (*show*: *film, programme*) выпускáть (вы́пустить* *perf*) на экрáн; (*check*: *candidates etc*) проверя́ть (провéрить *perf*); **to ~ sb for sth** (*for illness*) проверя́ть (провéрить *perf*) когó-н на что-н.
screen editing *n* (*COMPUT*) экрáнное редакти́рование.
screening ['skri:nɪŋ] *n* (*MED*) профилакт-и́ческий* осмóтр; (*of film*) вы́пуск на экрáн; (*for security*) провéрка*.
screen memory *n* (*COMPUT*) экрáнная пáмять *f*, видеопáмять *f*.
screenplay ['skri:npleɪ] *n* сценáрий.
screen test *n* кинопрóба.
screw [skru:] *n* винт* ◆ *vt* (*fasten*) приви́нчивать (привинти́ть* *perf*); (*inf!*: *have sex with*) трáхать (трáхнуть *perf*) (*!*); **to ~ sth in** зави́нчивать (завинти́ть* *perf*) что-н; **to ~ sth to the wall** приви́нчивать (привинти́ть* *perf*) что-н к стенé; **he's got his head ~ed on** (*inf*) у негó есть головá на плечáх
▸ **screw up** *vt* (*paper etc*) кóмкать (скóмкать *perf*); (*inf*: *ruin*) портáчить (напортáчить *perf*); **to ~ up one's eyes** прищýривать (прищýрить *perf*) глазá.
screwdriver ['skru:draɪvə^r] *n* отвёртка*.
screwed-up ['skru:d'ʌp] *adj* (*paper*) скóмканный (скóмкан); (*inf*: *person*) закомплексóванный (закомплексóван).
screwy ['skru:ɪ] *adj* (*inf*) с завихрéнием.
scribble ['skrɪbl] *n* каракýли *mpl* ◆ *vt* черкнýть *(perf)* ◆ *vi* исчёркивать (исчёркать *perf*); **to ~ sth down** запи́сывать (записáть* *perf*) что-н нáскоро.
scribe [skraɪb] *n* писéц*.
script [skrɪpt] *n* (*CINEMA etc*) сценáрий; (*system of writing*) шрифт*; (*in exam*) конспéкт.
scripted ['skrɪptɪd] *adj* (*RADIO, TV*) зарáнее подготóвленный.
Scripture(s) ['skrɪptʃə^r(-əz)] *n(pl)* Свящéнное писáние.
scriptwriter ['skrɪptraɪtə^r] *n* сценари́ст.
scroll [skrəul] *n* сви́ток* ◆ *vt* (*COMPUT*) прокрýчивать (прокрути́ть* *perf*), перемещáть (перемести́ть* *perf*).

scrotum ['skrəutəm] *n* (*ANAT*) мошóнка*.
scrounge [skraundʒ] (*inf*) *vt*: **to ~ sth off** *or* **from sb** клянчить (выклянчить *perf*) что-н у когó-н ◆ *vi* попрошáйничать *(impf)* ◆ *n*: **to be on the ~** быть* *(impf)* на мéли.
scrounger ['skraundʒə^r] *n* (*inf*) попрошáйка* *m/f*.
scrub [skrʌb] *n* (*land*) кустáрник ◆ *vt* скрести́* *(impf)*; (*inf*: *reject*) отбрáсывать (отбрóсить* *perf*).
scrubbing brush ['skrʌbɪŋ-] *n* жёсткая щётка*.
scruff [skrʌf] *n*: **by the ~ of the neck** за шиворот.
scruffy ['skrʌfɪ] *adj* потрёпанный*.
scrum(mage) ['skrʌm(ɪdʒ)] *n* (*RUGBY*) разы́грывание мячá.
scruple ['skru:pl] *n* (*usu pl*) терзáние; **to have no ~s about doing sth** дéлать (сдéлать *perf*) что-н без угрызéний сóвести.
scrupulous ['skru:pjuləs] *adj* (*painstaking*) тщáтельный* (тщáтелен), скрупулёзный* (скрупулёзен); (*fair-minded*) щепети́льный* (щепети́лен).
scrupulously ['skru:pjuləslɪ] *adv* (*behave, act*) добросóвестно; **he is ~ honest/fair/clean** он предéльно чéстен/справедли́в/чистоплóтен.
scrutinize ['skru:tɪnaɪz] *vt* тщáтельно изучáть (изучи́ть *perf*) *or* рассмáтривать (рассмотрéть* *perf*).
scrutiny ['skru:tɪnɪ] *n* тщáтельное изучéние *or* рассмотрéние; **under sb's ~** под чьим-н наблюдéнием.
scuba ['sku:bə] *n* аквалáнг.
scuba diving *n* подвóдное погружéние.
scuff [skʌf] *vt* (*feet*) волочи́ть *(impf)*; (*mark*: *shoes*) стáптывать (стоптáть *perf*).
scuffle ['skʌfl] *n* потасóвка*.
scull [skʌl] *n* (*on rowing boat*) веслó*.
scullery ['skʌlərɪ] *n* (*old*) подсóбное помещéние (*при кýхне*).
sculptor ['skʌlptə^r] *n* скýльптор.
sculpture ['skʌlptʃə^r] *n* скульптýра.
scum [skʌm] *n* пéна; (*inf*: *pej*: *people*) подóнки *mpl*; **the ~ of society** отбрóсы óбщества.
scupper ['skʌpə^r] *vt* (*BRIT*: *inf*: *plan*) срывáть (сорвáть* *perf*).
scurrilous ['skʌrɪləs] *adj* (*accusation, gossip etc*) оскорби́тельный* (оскорби́телен).
scurry ['skʌrɪ] *vi* ю́ркнуть *(perf)*
▸ **scurry off** *vi* ры́сью убегáть (убежáть *perf*).
scurvy ['skə:vɪ] *n* цингá.
scuttle ['skʌtl] *n* (*also*: **coal ~**) ведрó* для угля́ ◆ *vt* (*ship*) топи́ть* (затопи́ть* *or* потопи́ть* *perf*) ◆ *vi*: **to ~ away** *or* **off** ры́сью убегáть (убежáть *perf*).
scythe [saɪð] *n* серп*.
SD *abbr* (*US*: *POST*) = *South Dakota*.
SDI *n abbr* (*US*: *MIL*: = *Strategic Defense Initiative*) СОИ= *Стратеги́ческая оборóнная инициати́ва*.
SDLP *n abbr* (*BRIT*: *POL*) = *Social Democratic and Labour Party*.
SDP *n abbr* (*BRIT*: *POL*: *formerly*) = *Social Democratic Party*.
sea [si:] *n* мóре* ◆ *cpd* морскóй; **by ~** (*travel*) мóрем; **beside the ~** у мóря; **on the ~** (*boat*) в мóре; (*town*) на мóре; **to be all at ~** (*fig*) быть* *(impf)* в растéрянности; **out to ~, out at ~** в мóре; **to look out to ~** смотрéть* *(impf)* на мóре; **heavy** *or* **rough ~(s)** бýрное мóре; **a ~ of faces** мóре лиц.
sea anemone *n* морскóй анемóн.
sea bed *n* морскóе дно.
seaboard ['si:bɔ:d] *n* побережье*.
seafarer ['si:fɛərə^r] *n* мореплáватель *m*.
seafaring ['si:fɛərɪŋ] *adj* морскóй; **~ people** мореходы *mpl*.
seafood ['si:fu:d] *n* ры́бные блю́да *ntpl*.
seafront ['si:frʌnt] *n* нáбережная *f adj*.
seagoing ['si:gəuɪŋ] *adj* морскóй.
seagull ['si:gʌl] *n* чáйка*.
seal [si:l] *n* (*ZOOL*) тюлéнь *m*; (*stamp*) печáть *f* ◆ *vt* (*close*: *envelope*) запечáтывать (запечáтать *perf*); (: *opening*) задéлывать (задéлать *perf*); (*decide*: *sb's fate*) решáть (реши́ть* *perf*); (*deal*) заключáть (заключи́ть *perf*); **to give sth one's ~ of approval** официáльно одóбрить *(perf)* что-н
▸ **seal off** *vt* (*area, street*) огорáживать (огороди́ть* *perf*); (*building*) опечáтывать (опечáтать *perf*).
sea level *n* ýровень* *m* мóря; **2,000 feet above/below ~ ~** 2000 фýтов над ýровнем мóря/ни́же ýровня мóря.
sealing wax ['si:lɪŋ-] *n* сургýч*.
sea lion *n* морскóй лев*.
sealskin ['si:lskɪn] *n* кóтик (*мех*).
seam [si:m] *n* (*of garment*) шов*; (*of coal*) слой*; **the hall was bursting at the ~s** зал трещáл по швам.
seaman ['si:mən] *irreg n* матрóс, моря́к.
seamanship ['si:mənʃɪp] *n* судовождéние.
seamless ['si:mlɪs] *adj* без шва; (*fig*) цéлостный.
seamy ['si:mɪ] *adj* тёмный* (тёмен).
seance ['seɪɔns] *n* спирити́ческий сеáнс.
seaplane ['si:pleɪn] *n* гидросамолёт.
seaport ['si:pɔ:t] *n* (морскóй) порт*.
search [sə:tʃ] *n* (*for person*) рóзыск; (*for thing*) пóиски *mpl*; (*COMPUT*) пóиск; (*inspection*: *of sb's home etc*) óбыск ◆ *vt* (*place, person*) обы́скивать (обыскáть* *perf*); (*memory*) ры́ться* *(impf)* в *+prp* ◆ *vi*: **to ~ for** искáть* *(impf)*; **in ~ of** в пóисках *+gen*; **"search and replace"** (*COMPUT*) "пóиск и замéна"
▸ **search through** *vt fus* перерыть *(perf)*.
searcher ['sə:tʃə^r] *n* искáтель(ница) *m(f)*.

* marks translations which have irregular inflections. The Russian-English side of the dictionary gives inflectional information.

searching ['sə:tʃɪŋ] *adj* (*look*) пытли́вый (пытли́в); (*question*) наводя́щий*; (*examination*) тща́тельный* (тща́телен).
searchlight ['sə:tʃlaɪt] *n* проже́ктор*.
search party *n* поиско́вая гру́ппа; **to send out a ~ ~** посыла́ть (посла́ть* *perf*) поиско́вую гру́ппу.
search warrant *n* о́рдер на о́быск.
searing ['sɪərɪŋ] *adj* (*heat, pain*) жгу́чий* (жгуч).
seashore ['si:ʃɔ:ʳ] *n* бе́рег* мо́ря; **on the ~** на берегу́ мо́ря.
seasick ['si:sɪk] *adj*: **to be ~** страда́ть *(impf)* морско́й боле́знью.
seasickness ['si:sɪknɪs] *n* морска́я боле́знь *f*.
seaside ['si:saɪd] *n* взмо́рье, примо́рье; **to go to the ~** е́здить*/е́хать* (пое́хать* *perf*) на взмо́рье; **at the ~** на взмо́рье.
seaside resort *n* примо́рский* куро́рт.
season ['si:zn] *n* (*of year*) вре́мя* *nt* го́да; (*for football, of films etc*) сезо́н ◆ *vt* (*food*) заправля́ть (запра́вить* *perf*); **the busy ~** акти́вный сезо́н; **the open ~** (*HUNTING*) охо́тничий* сезо́н; **tomatoes are in ~** сейча́с сезо́н помидо́ров.
seasonal ['si:znl] *adj* сезо́нный.
seasoned ['si:znd] *adj* (*traveller*) закалённый, запра́вский; (*wood*) вы́держанный; **a ~ campaigner** о́пытный агита́тор.
seasoning ['si:znɪŋ] *n* припра́ва.
season ticket *n* (*RAIL*) сезо́нный (проездно́й) биле́т; (*THEAT, SPORT*) абонеме́нт.
seat [si:t] *n* (*chair, place*) сиде́нье; (*in theatre, in parliament*) ме́сто*; (*of trousers*) зад; (*of government*) резиде́нция; (*of learning etc*) центр ◆ *vt* (*place: guests etc*) расса́живать (рассади́ть* *perf*), уса́живать (усади́ть* *perf*); (*subj: venue*) вмеща́ть (вмести́ть* *perf*); **are there any ~s left?** есть ещё места́?; **to take one's ~** сади́ться* (сесть* *perf*); **please be ~ed** пожа́луйста, сади́тесь; **to be ~ed** сиде́ть *(impf)*; **this table ~s 10 people** за э́тим столо́м умеща́ется 10 челове́к.
seat belt *n* привязно́й реме́нь* *m*.
seating arrangements ['si:tɪŋ-] *npl* распределе́ние *ntsg* мест.
seating capacity *n* сидя́чие места́ *ntpl*; **the hall has a ~ ~ of 100** зал расчи́тан на 100 сидя́чих мест.
SEATO ['si:təu] *n abbr* (= *Southeast Asia Treaty Organization*) СЕАТО.
sea urchin *n* морско́й ёж.
sea water *n* морска́я вода́.
seaweed ['si:wi:d] *n* во́доросли *fpl*.
seaworthy ['si:wə:ðɪ] *adj* морехо́дный.
Sebastopol [sɪ'bæstəpəl] *n* Севасто́поль *m*.
SEC *n abbr* (*US*: = *Securities and Exchange Commission*) Коми́ссия по це́нным бума́гам и би́ржам.
sec. *abbr* = **second**.
secateurs [sɛkə'tə:z] *npl* садо́вые но́жницы *pl*, сека́тор *msg*.
secede [sɪ'si:d] *vi*: **to ~ (from)** отделя́ться (отдели́ться* *perf*) (от +*gen*).
secluded [sɪ'klu:dɪd] *adj* уединённый.
seclusion [sɪ'klu:ʒən] *n* уедине́ние; **in ~** в уедине́нии.
second[1] [sɪ'kɔnd] *vt* (*BRIT: employee*) командирова́ть* *(impf)*.
second[2] ['sɛkənd] *adj* второ́й ◆ *adv* (*come, be placed*) вторы́м; (*when listing*) во-вторы́х ◆ *n* (*unit of time*) секу́нда; (*AUT: also:* **~ gear**) втора́я ско́рость *f*; (*COMM: imperfect*) дефе́ктное изде́лие; (*BRIT: SCOL: degree*) дипло́м второ́го кла́сса ◆ *vt* (*motion*) подде́рживать (поддержа́ть* *perf*); **Charles the S~** Карл Второ́й; **~ floor** (*BRIT*) тре́тий* эта́ж; (*US*) второ́й эта́ж; **just a ~!** секу́ндочку!; *see also* **fifth**.
secondary ['sɛkəndərɪ] *adj* втори́чный.
secondary education *n* сре́днее образова́ние.
secondary picketing [-'pɪkɪtɪŋ] *n* втори́чное пикети́рование.
secondary school *n* сре́дняя шко́ла.
second-best [sɛkənd'bɛst] *n* не са́мое лу́чшее *nt adj* ◆ *adj* (*hotel, room*) второ́й по ка́честву; (*pupil*) второ́й (по успева́емости); **as a ~** за неиме́нием лу́чшего.
second-class ['sɛkənd'klɑ:s] *adj* (*citizen, standard etc*) второразря́дный; (*POST, RAIL*) второ́го кла́сса ◆ *adv* вторы́м кла́ссом.
second cousin *n* (*male*) трою́родный брат*; (*female*) трою́родная сестра́*.
seconder ['sɛkəndəʳ] *n*: **he is the ~ of the proposal** он поддержа́л предложе́ние.
second-guess ['sɛkənd'gɛs] *vt* предска́зывать (предсказа́ть* *perf*).
second hand *n* (*on clock*) секу́ндная стре́лка*.
second-hand ['sɛkənd'hænd] *adj* поде́ржанный ◆ *adv* (*buy*) с рук; **to hear sth ~** узнава́ть* (узна́ть *perf*) что-н из вторы́х рук.
second in command *n* (*MIL*) второ́й *m adj* по зва́нию; (*ADMIN*) второ́й *m adj* по до́лжности.
secondly ['sɛkəndlɪ] *adv* во-вторы́х.
secondment [sɪ'kɔndmənt] *n* (*BRIT*) командиро́вка*.
second-rate ['sɛkənd'reɪt] *adj* (*film etc*) посре́дственный* (посре́дствен); (*restaurant*) второразря́дный.
second thoughts *npl*: **to have ~ ~ (about doing)** начина́ть (нача́ть* *perf*) сомнева́ться (сле́дует ли +*infin*); **on ~ ~** *or* (*US*) **thought** по зре́лом размышле́нии.
Second World War *n*: **the ~ ~ ~** Втора́я мирова́я война́.
secrecy ['si:krəsɪ] *n* секре́тность *f*; **in ~** в та́йне.
secret ['si:krɪt] *adj* секре́тный* (секре́тен), та́йный; (*admirer*) та́йный ◆ *n* секре́т, та́йна; **to keep sth ~ from sb** держа́ть* *(impf)* что-н в секре́те *or* та́йне от кого́-н; **keep it ~** держи́те э́то в секре́те *or* в та́йне; **in ~** (*say, give*) по секре́ту; (*do, meet*) секре́тно; **to**

make no ~ of sth не де́лать *(impf)* секре́та из чего́-н.
secret agent *n* секре́тный *or* та́йный аге́нт.
secretarial [sɛkrɪ'tɛərɪəl] *adj* секрета́рский; ~ **course** ку́рсы *mpl* секретаре́й.
secretariat [sɛkrɪ'tɛərɪət] *n* секретариа́т.
secretary ['sɛkrətərɪ] *n* секрета́рь* *m*; **S~ of State (for)** (*BRIT*) ≈ мини́стр (+*gen*); **S~ of State** (*US*) Госуда́рственный секрета́рь* *m*.
secretary-general ['sɛkrətərɪ'dʒɛnərl] *n* генера́льный секрета́рь *m*.
secrete [sɪ'kri:t] *vt* (*BIO*) выделя́ть (вы́делить *perf*); (*hide*) пря́тать* (спря́тать* *perf*).
secretion [sɪ'kri:ʃən] *n* (*substance*) выделе́ние, секре́ция.
secretive ['si:krətɪv] *adj* (*pej*: *person*) скры́тный* (скры́тен); **he is ~ about his plans** он де́ржит свои́ пла́ны в секре́те.
secretly ['si:krɪtlɪ] *adv* (*do, meet*) секре́тно; (*marry*) та́йно.
secret police *n* секре́тная поли́ция.
secret service *n* секре́тная слу́жба.
sect [sɛkt] *n* се́кта.
sectarian [sɛk'tɛərɪən] *adj* секта́нтский*.
section ['sɛkʃən] *n* (*part*) часть* *f*; (*of population, company*) се́ктор; (*in shop*) се́кция; (*of document, book*) разде́л; (*cross-section*) сече́ние, разре́з ◆ *vt* рассека́ть (рассе́чь* *perf*); **the business** *etc* ~ (*PRESS*) разде́л би́знеса *etc*.
sectional ['sɛkʃənl] *adj*: ~ **drawing** рису́нок в разре́зе, разре́з.
sector ['sɛktə^r] *n* (*part, also MIL*) се́ктор.
secular ['sɛkjulə^r] *adj* (*music, society*) све́тский*; (*priest*) мирско́й.
secure [sɪ'kjuə^r] *adj* (*safe*: *person, money, job*) надёжный* (надёжен); (: *building*) безопа́сный* (безопа́сен); (*firmly fixed, strong*: *rope, shelf*) про́чный* (про́чен); (*free from anxiety*: *person*) уве́ренный ◆ *vt* (*fix*: *rope, shelf etc*) (про́чно) закрепля́ть (закрепи́ть* *perf*); (*get*: *job, contract etc*) обеспе́чивать (обеспе́чить *perf*); (*COMM*: *loan*) обеспе́чивать (обеспе́чить *perf*); **to make sth ~** про́чно *or* надёжно закрепля́ть (закрепи́ть* *perf*) что-н; **to ~ sth for sb** обеспе́чивать (обеспе́чить *perf*) для кого́-н что-н.
secured creditor [sɪ'kjuəd-] *n* кредито́р, получи́вший обеспече́ние.
securely [sɪ'kjuəlɪ] *adv* (*fasten*) про́чно; (*keep*) в надёжном ме́сте.
security [sɪ'kjuərɪtɪ] *n* (*protection*) безопа́сность *f*; (*for one's future*) обеспе́ченность *f*; (*FINANCE*) зало́г; **securities** *npl* (*COMM*) це́нные бума́ги *fpl*; **to increase** *or* **tighten ~** повыша́ть (повы́сить* *perf*) безопа́сность; **~ of tenure** гаранти́рованное пра́во.
Security Council *n*: **the ~ ~** Сове́т безопа́сности.
security forces *npl* си́лы *fpl* безопа́сности.
security guard *n* охра́нник.
security risk *n*: **it's a ~ ~** (*for country*) э́то представля́ет угро́зу для безопа́сности страны́.
secy. *abbr* = **secretary**.
sedan [sə'dæn] *n* (*US*: *AUT*) седа́н.
sedate [sɪ'deɪt] *adj* (*person*) степе́нный* (степе́нен); (*pace*) разме́ренный* (разме́рен) ◆ *vt* (*MED*) дава́ть* (дать* *perf*) седати́вное *or* успокои́тельное сре́дство.
sedation [sɪ'deɪʃən] *n*: **to be under ~** находи́ться* *(impf)* под возде́йствием седати́вных *or* успокои́тельных сре́дств.
sedative ['sɛdɪtɪv] *n* седати́вное *or* успокои́тельное сре́дство.
sedentary ['sɛdntrɪ] *adj* сидя́чий*.
sediment ['sɛdɪmənt] *n* оса́док*.
sedimentary [sɛdɪ'mɛntərɪ] *adj* оса́дочный.
sedition [sɪ'dɪʃən] *n* крамо́ла.
seduce [sɪ'dju:s] *vt* соблазня́ть (соблазни́ть *perf*).
seduction [sɪ'dʌkʃən] *n* (*attraction*) собла́зн; (*act of seducing*) обольще́ние.
seductive [sɪ'dʌktɪv] *adj* (*look, voice*) обольсти́тельный* (обольсти́телен); (*offer*) соблазни́тельный* (соблазни́телен).
see [si:] (*pt* **saw**, *pp* **seen**) *vt* ви́деть* (уви́деть* *perf*); (*understand*) понима́ть (поня́ть* *perf*) ◆ *vi* ви́деть* *(impf)*; (*find out*) выясня́ть (вы́яснить *perf*) ◆ *n* епа́рхия; **to ~ sb to the door** (*accompany*) провожа́ть (проводи́ть* *perf*) кого́-н до двери́; **to ~ that** (*ensure*) следи́ть* (проследи́ть* *perf*), что́бы; **there was nobody to be ~n** никого́ не́ было ви́дно; **let me ~** (*show me*) да́йте мне посмотре́ть; (*let me think*) да́йте мне поду́мать; **to go and ~ sb** навеща́ть (навести́ть* *perf*) кого́-н; **~ for yourself** (*suggestion*) убеди́тесь са́ми; **I don't know what she saw in him** я не зна́ю, что она́ в нём нашла́; **as far as I can ~** наско́лько я понима́ю; **~ you!** пока́!; **~ you soon!** до ско́рого!, пока́!
▸ **see about** *vt fus* (*deal with*) занима́ться (заня́ться* *perf*) +*instr*
▸ **see off** *vt* провожа́ть (проводи́ть* *perf*)
▸ **see through** *vt* доводи́ть* (довести́* *perf*) до конца́ ◆ *vt fus* ви́деть* *(impf)* наскво́зь
▸ **see to** *vt fus* забо́титься* (позабо́титься* *perf*) о +*prp*.
seed [si:d] *n* се́мя* *nt*; **~s** (*fig*) семена́* *ntpl*; **he is the number 2 ~** (*SPORT*) в ранжиро́вке спортсме́нов он второ́й; **to go to ~** (*plant*) пойти́* *(perf)* в семена́; (*fig*) сдать* *(perf)*.
seedless ['si:dlɪs] *adj* без ко́сточек.

* marks translations which have irregular inflections. The Russian-English side of the dictionary gives inflectional information.

seedling ['si:dlɪŋ] *n* расса́да *no pl.*
seedy ['si:dɪ] *adj* (*person*) потрёпанный* (потрёпан); (*place*) захуда́лый.
seeing ['si:ɪŋ] *conj*: **~ (that)** поско́льку, так как.
seek [si:k] (*pt, pp* **sought**) *vt* иска́ть* (*impf*); **to ~ advice/help from sb** обраща́ться (обрати́ться* *perf*) за сове́том/по́мощью к кому́-н
▸ **seek out** *vt* (*person*) разы́скивать (разыска́ть* *perf*).
seem [si:m] *vi* каза́ться* (показа́ться* *perf*); **there ~s to be ...** ка́жется, что име́ется ...; **it ~s (that)** ка́жется, (что); **what ~s to be the trouble?** что у Вас за пробле́ма?
seemingly ['si:mɪŋlɪ] *adv* по-ви́димому.
seemly ['si:mlɪ] *adj* (*behaviour*) подоба́ющий*; (*dress*) надлежа́щий*.
seen [si:n] *pp of* **see**.
seep [si:p] *vi* проса́чиваться (просочи́ться *perf*).
seersucker ['sɪəsʌkəʳ] *n* (*fabric*) марлёвка.
seesaw ['si:sɔ:] *n* каче́ли *pl.*
seethe [si:ð] *vi* (*place*) кише́ть* (*impf*); **to ~ with anger** кипе́ть* (*impf*) от гне́ва.
see-through ['si:θru:] *adj* прозра́чный* (прозра́чен).
segment ['sɛgmənt] *n* (*of circle*) сегме́нт; (*of population*) се́ктор; (*of orange*) до́лька*.
segregate ['sɛgrɪgeɪt] *vt* разделя́ть (раздели́ть* *perf*).
segregation [sɛgrɪ'geɪʃən] *n* (*racial*) сегрега́ция; (*SCOL*) разде́льное обуче́ние.
seismic ['saɪzmɪk] *adj* сейсми́ческий*.
seize [si:z] *vt* хвата́ть (схвати́ть* *perf*); (*power, hostage, territory*) захва́тывать (захвати́ть* *perf*); (*opportunity*) по́льзоваться (воспо́льзоваться *perf*) *+instr*; (*LAW*) конфискова́ть (*impf/perf*)
▸ **seize up** *vi* (*TECH*: *engine*) гло́хнуть* (загло́хнуть* *perf*)
▸ **seize (up)on** *vt fus* ухва́тываться (ухвати́ться* *perf*) за *+instr.*
seizure ['si:ʒəʳ] *n* (*MED*) при́ступ; (*of power*) захва́т; (*of goods*) конфиска́ция.
seldom ['sɛldəm] *adv* ре́дко.
select [sɪ'lɛkt] *adj* (*school, area*) элита́рный; (*pupils*) и́збранный; (*goods*) отбо́рный ◆ *vt* (*choose*) выбира́ть (вы́брать* *perf*); (*SPORT*) отбира́ть (отобра́ть* *perf*); **a ~ few** немно́гие и́збранные *pl adj.*
selection [sɪ'lɛkʃən] *n* (*process*) отбо́р; (*COMM*: *range available*) вы́бор; (*medley*) подбо́рка.
selection committee *n* отбо́рочная коми́ссия.
selective [sɪ'lɛktɪv] *adj* (*careful in choosing*) разбо́рчивый (разбо́рчив); (*not general*) избира́тельный.
selector [sɪ'lɛktəʳ] *n* (*person*) член отбо́рочной коми́ссии; (*TECH*) селе́ктор.
self [sɛlf] (*pl* **selves**) *n*: **he became his usual ~ again** он стал опя́ть сами́м собо́й; **my own ~** моё со́бственное "я".
self... [sɛlf] *prefix* са́мо..., себя́....
self-addressed ['sɛlfə'drɛst] *adj*: **~ envelope** конве́рт, адресо́ванный на со́бственное и́мя.
self-adhesive [sɛlfəd'hi:zɪv] *adj* само-прикле́ивающийся.
self-appointed [sɛlfə'pɔɪntɪd] *adj* самозва́ный.
self-assertive [sɛlfə'sə:tɪv] *adj* уве́ренный* (уве́рен).
self-assurance [sɛlfə'ʃuərəns] *n* само-уве́ренность *f.*
self-assured [sɛlfə'ʃuəd] *adj* самоуве́ренный* (самоуве́рен).
self-catering [sɛlf'keɪtərɪŋ] *adj* (*BRIT*): **~ holiday** *путёвка, в кото́рую включа́ется прое́зд и жильё с самообслу́живанием.*
self-centred [sɛlf'sɛntəd] (*US* **self-centered**) *adj* эгоцентри́чный* (эгоцентри́чен).
self-cleaning [sɛlf'kli:nɪŋ] *adj* само-очища́ющийся.
self-confessed [sɛlfkən'fɛst] *adj* (*alcoholic etc*) созна́вшийся.
self-confidence [sɛlf'kɔnfɪdns] *n* уве́ренность *f* в себе́.
self-confident [sɛlf'kɔnfɪdənt] *adj* уве́ренный* (уве́рен) в себе́.
self-conscious [sɛlf'kɔnʃəs] *adj* (*nervous*) засте́нчивый (засте́нчив).
self-contained [sɛlfkən'teɪnd] *adj* (*BRIT*: *flat*) отде́льный, изоли́рованный; (*society, person*) незави́симый.
self-control [sɛlfkən'trəul] *n* самооблада́ние.
self-defeating [sɛlfdɪ'fi:tɪŋ] *adj* (*plan, action*) па́губный* (па́губен).
self-defence [sɛlfdɪ'fɛns] (*US* **self-defense**) *n* самозащи́та, самооборо́на; **in ~** защища́я себя́.
self-discipline [sɛlf'dɪsɪplɪn] *n* само-дисципли́на.
self-employed [sɛlfɪm'plɔɪd] *adj* рабо́тающий на себя́.
self-esteem [sɛlfɪs'ti:m] *n* чу́вство со́бственного досто́инства.
self-evident [sɛlf'ɛvɪdnt] *adj* самоочеви́дный* (самоочеви́ден).
self-explanatory [sɛlfɪks'plænətrɪ] *adj*: **this phrase is ~** э́та фра́за не тре́бует разъясне́ний.
self-financing [sɛlffaɪ'nænsɪŋ] *n* самофинанси́рование.
self-governing [sɛlf'gʌvənɪŋ] *adj* (*organization, group*) рабо́тающий по при́нципу самоуправле́ния.
self-help ['sɛlf'hɛlp] *n* самопо́мощь *f.*
self-importance [sɛlfɪm'pɔ:tns] *n* самомне́ние.
self-indulgent [sɛlfɪn'dʌldʒənt] *adj*: **he is being ~** он потво́рствует свои́м сла́бостям.
self-inflicted [sɛlfɪn'flɪktɪd] *adj* (*injury*) нанесённый (нанесён) самому́ себе́; (*problems*) причинённый самому́ себе́.

self-interest [sɛlf'ɪntrɪst] *n* корысть *f*.
selfish ['sɛlfɪʃ] *adj* (*behaviour, attitude*) эгоистический*; (*person*) эгоистичный* (эгоистичен).
selfishly ['sɛlfɪʃlɪ] *adv* эгоистично.
selfishness ['sɛlfɪʃnɪs] *n* (*of behaviour*) эгоистичность *f*; (*of person*) эгоизм.
selfless ['sɛlflɪs] *adj* самоотверженный* (самоотвержен).
selflessly ['sɛlflɪslɪ] *adv* самоотверженно.
selflessness ['sɛlflɪsnɪs] *n* самоотверженность *f*.
self-made ['sɛlfmeɪd] *adj*: **he's a ~ man** он добился всего своими силами.
self-perpetuating [sɛlfpə'pɛtʃueɪtɪŋ] *adj* нескончаемый.
self-pity [sɛlf'pɪtɪ] *n* жалость *f* к (самому) себе.
self-portrait [sɛlf'pɔ:treɪt] *n* автопортрет.
self-possessed [sɛlfpə'zɛst] *adj* хладнокровный* (хладнокровен).
self-preservation ['sɛlfprɛzə'veɪʃən] *n* самосохранение.
self-raising [sɛlf'reɪzɪŋ] (*US* **self-rising**) *adj* (*BRIT*): **~ flour** мука с разрыхлителем.
self-reliant [sɛlfrɪ'laɪənt] *adj* (*person*) самостоятельный* (самостоятелен).
self-respect [sɛlfrɪs'pɛkt] *n* самоуважение.
self-respecting [sɛlfrɪs'pɛktɪŋ] *adj* уважающий себя.
self-righteous [sɛlf'raɪtʃəs] *adj* (*person*) убеждённый* в своей правоте.
self-rising [sɛlf'raɪzɪŋ] *adj* (*US*) = **self-raising**.
self-sacrifice [sɛlf'sækrɪfaɪs] *n* самопожертвование.
selfsame ['sɛlfseɪm] *adj* тот же самый.
self-satisfied [sɛlf'sætɪsfaɪd] *adj* самодовольный* (самодоволен).
self-sealing [sɛlf'si:lɪŋ] *adj* (*envelope*) самозаклеивающийся.
self-service [sɛlf'sə:vɪs] *adj*: **~ restaurant/shop** ресторан/магазин самообслуживания.
self-styled ['sɛlfstaɪld] *adj* самозваный.
self-sufficient [sɛlfsə'fɪʃənt] *adj* самостоятельный* (самостоятелен); **to be ~ in sth** полностью обеспечивать *(impf)* себя чем-н.
self-supporting [sɛlfsə'pɔ:tɪŋ] *adj* самоокупающийся.
self-tanning [sɛlf'tænɪŋ] *adj* способствуюший загару.
self-taught [sɛlf'tɔ:t] *adj*: **~ artist/pianist** художник-/пианист-самоучка.
self-test ['sɛlftɛst] *n* (*COMPUT*) самопроверка*.
sell [sɛl] (*pt, pp* **sold**) *vt* продавать* (продать* *perf*) ◆ *vi* продаваться* (продаться* *perf*); **to ~ at** *or* **for 10 pounds** продаваться* (продаться* *perf*) за 10 фунтов; **to ~ sb sth, ~ sth to sb** продавать* (продать* *perf*) что-н кому-н; **to ~ sb an idea** (*fig*) убеждать (убедить* *perf*) кого-н в идее
▸ **sell off** *vt* распродавать* (распродать* *perf*)
▸ **sell out** *vi* (*book etc*) расходиться* (разойтись* *perf*); (*shop*): **to ~ out of sth** распродавать* (распродать* *perf*) что-н; **the tickets are sold out** все билеты (рас)проданы
▸ **sell up** *vi* продавать* (продать* *perf*) всё имущество.
sell-by date ['sɛlbaɪ-] *n* срок годности.
seller ['sɛlə^r] *n* продавец*(-вщица); **~'s market** "рынок продавцов" (*на котором условия диктуют продавцы*).
selling price ['sɛlɪŋ-] *n* продажная цена*.
Sellotape® ['sɛləuteɪp] *n* (*BRIT*) клейкая лента.
sellout ['sɛlaut] *n* (*inf*: *betrayal*) предательство; (*of tickets*): **the match was a ~** все билеты на матч были распроданы.
selves [sɛlvz] *pl of* **self**.
semantic [sɪ'mæntɪk] *adj* семантический*.
semantics [sɪ'mæntɪks] *n* семантика.
semaphore ['sɛməfɔ:^r] *n* семафор.
semblance ['sɛmblns] *n* видимость *f*.
semen ['si:mən] *n* семя* *nt*, сперма.
semester [sɪ'mɛstə^r] *n* (*esp US*) семестр.
semi ['sɛmɪ] *n* = **semidetached (house)**.
semi... ['sɛmɪ] *prefix* полу....
semibreve ['sɛmɪbri:v] *n* (*BRIT*) целая нота.
semicircle ['sɛmɪsə:kl] *n* полукруг.
semicircular ['sɛmɪ'sə:kjulə^r] *adj* полукруглый.
semicolon [sɛmɪ'kəulən] *n* точка* с запятой.
semiconductor [sɛmɪkən'dʌktə^r] *n* полупроводник*.
semiconscious [sɛmɪ'kɔnʃəs] *adj* в полузабытьи.
semidetached [sɛmɪdɪ'tætʃt-] *n* (*BRIT*: *also*: **~ house**) *дом, примыкающий к соседнему*.
semifinal [sɛmɪ'faɪnl] *n* полуфинал.
seminar ['sɛmɪnɑ:^r] *n* семинар.
seminary ['sɛmɪnərɪ] *n* семинария.
semiprecious [sɛmɪ'prɛʃəs] *adj*: **~ stone** полудрагоценный камень* *m*, самоцвет.
semiquaver ['sɛmɪkweɪvə^r] *n* (*BRIT*) шестнадцатая нота.
semiskilled [sɛmɪ'skɪld] *adj* (*work, worker*) полуквалифицированный.
semiskimmed [sɛmɪ'skɪmd] *adj* полужирный, полуобезжиренный.
semitone ['sɛmɪtəun] *n* полутон*.
semolina [sɛmə'li:nə] *n* манная крупа, манка (*inf*).
SEN *n abbr* (*BRIT*: = *State Enrolled Nurse*) медсестра= *медицинская сестра*.
Sen. *abbr* (*US*) = **senator**; (*in names*) = **senior**.
sen. *abbr* = **Sen.**
senate ['sɛnɪt] *n* сенат.
senator ['sɛnɪtə^r] *n* (*US etc*) сенатор.
send [sɛnd] (*pt, pp* **sent**) *vt* (*dispatch*) посылать (послать* *perf*), отправлять (отправить* *perf*); (*transmit*) посылать (послать* *perf*); **to**

~ **by post** *or (US)* **mail** посыла́ть (посла́ть* *perf*) *or* отправля́ть (отпра́вить* *perf*) по по́чте; **to ~ sb for sth** посыла́ть (посла́ть* *perf*) кого́-н за чем-н; **to ~ word that ...** передава́ть* (переда́ть* *perf*), что ...; **she ~s (you) her love** она́ передаёт Вам приве́т; **to ~ sb to Coventry** (*BRIT*) объявля́ть (объяви́ть* *perf*) кому́-н бойко́т; **to ~ sb to sleep** нагоня́ть (нагна́ть* *perf*) на кого́-н сон; **to ~ sb into fits of laughter** смеши́ть (рассмеши́ть *perf*) кого́-н; **to ~ sth flying** рассе́ивать (рассе́ять *perf*) что-н в во́здухе

▸ **send away** *vt* (*letter, goods*) отправля́ть (отпра́вить* *perf*), отсыла́ть (отосла́ть* *perf*); (*unwelcome visitor*) прогоня́ть (прогна́ть* *perf*)

▸ **send away for** *vt fus* зака́зывать (заказа́ть* *perf*)

▸ **send back** *vt* посыла́ть (посла́ть* *perf*) обра́тно

▸ **send for** *vt fus* (*by post*) зака́зывать (заказа́ть* *perf*); (*person*) посыла́ть (посла́ть* *perf*) за *+instr*

▸ **send in** *vt* (*report*) представля́ть (предста́вить* *perf*); (*resignation, application*) подава́ть* (пода́ть* *perf*) заявле́ние о *+prp*

▸ **send off** *vt* (*goods*) отправля́ть (отпра́вить* *perf*); (*BRIT: SPORT: player*) удаля́ть (удали́ть *perf*)

▸ **send on** *vt* (*BRIT: letter*) пересыла́ть (пересла́ть* *perf*); (*: luggage etc: in advance*) переправля́ть (перепра́вить* *perf*)

▸ **send out** *vt* (*invitation*) рассыла́ть (разосла́ть* *perf*); (*heat, smell, light*) распространя́ть (распространи́ть *perf*); (*signal*) посыла́ть (посла́ть* *perf*)

▸ **send round** *vt* (*letter, document etc*) рассыла́ть (разосла́ть* *perf*)

▸ **send up** *vt* (*price, blood pressure*) поднима́ть (подня́ть* *perf*); (*astronaut*) запуска́ть (запусти́ть* *perf*); (*BRIT: parody*) высме́ивать (вы́смеять *perf*).

sender ['sɛndəʳ] *n* отправи́тель(ница) *m(f)*.

sending-off ['sɛndɪŋɔf] *n* удале́ние с по́ля.

sendoff ['sɛndɔf] *n*: **a good send-off** хоро́шие про́воды *pl*.

send-up ['sɛndʌp] *n* паро́дия.

Senegal [sɛnɪ'gɔ:l] *n* Сенега́л.

Senegalese ['sɛnɪgə'li:z] *adj* сенега́льский ◆ *n inv* сенега́лец*(-лка*).

senile ['si:naɪl] *adj* маразмати́ческий.

senility [sɪ'nɪlɪtɪ] *n* ста́рческий* мара́зм.

senior ['si:nɪəʳ] *adj* (*staff, officer*) ста́рший*; (*manager, consultant*) гла́вный; (*of higher rank*): **to be ~ to sb** быть* *(impf)* вы́ше кого́-н по до́лжности; **the ~s** *npl* (*SCOL: at school*) старшекла́ссники *mpl*; (*: at college, university*) старшеку́рсники *mpl*; **she is 15 years his ~** она́ ста́рше его́ на 15 лет; **P. Jones ~** П. Джоунз ста́рший*.

senior citizen *n* (*esp BRIT*) пожило́й челове́к*, челове́к* пенсио́нного во́зраста.

senior high school *n* (*US*) ≈ ста́ршие ку́рсы ко́лледжа.

seniority [si:nɪ'ɔrɪtɪ] *n* старшинство́.

sensation [sɛn'seɪʃən] *n* (*ability to feel*) чувстви́тельность *f*; (*feeling*) ощуще́ние; (*great success*) сенса́ция; **to cause a ~** вызыва́ть (вы́звать* *perf*) сенса́цию.

sensational [sɛn'seɪʃənl] *adj* (*wonderful*) потряса́ющий* (потряса́ющ); (*causing much interest*) сенсацио́нный* (сенсацио́нен).

sensationalize [sɛn'seɪʃnəlaɪz] *vt* де́лать (сде́лать *perf*) сенса́цию из *+gen*.

sense [sɛns] *vt* (*become aware of*) чу́вствовать (почу́вствовать *perf*), ощуща́ть (ощути́ть* *perf*) ◆ *n* (*feeling*) чу́вство, ощуще́ние; (*meaning of word*) смысл; (*also:* **good ~**): **it makes ~** в э́том есть смысл; **~s** *npl* (*sanity*) рассу́док* *msg*; **the ~s** пять чувств; **there is no ~ in that/in doing that** нет смы́сла в э́том/де́лать э́то; **to come to one's ~s** образу́миться *(perf)*; **to take leave of one's ~s** теря́ть (потеря́ть *perf*) рассу́док.

senseless ['sɛnslɪs] *adj* (*pointless*) бессмы́сленный* (бессмы́слен); (*unconscious*) без чувств.

sense of humour (*US* **sense of humor**) *n* чу́вство ю́мора.

sensibility [sɛnsɪ'bɪlɪtɪ] *n* чувстви́тельность *f*.

sensible ['sɛnsɪbl] *adj* разу́мный* (разу́мен); (*shoes*) практи́чный.

sensitive ['sɛnsɪtɪv] *adj* чувстви́тельный* (чувстви́телен); (*understanding*) чу́ткий* (чу́ток); (*issue*) щекотли́вый (щекотли́в); **~ to** чувстви́тельный* (чувстви́телен) к *+dat*; **he is very ~ about it** он отно́сится к э́тому о́чень боле́зненно.

sensitivity [sɛnsɪ'tɪvɪtɪ] *n* (*responsiveness*) чувстви́тельность *f*; (*understanding*) чу́ткость *f*; (*delicate nature: of issue etc*) щекотли́вость *f*.

sensual ['sɛnsjuəl] *adj* (*of the senses*) чу́вственный; (*sexual*) чу́вственный* (чу́вствен).

sensuous ['sɛnsjuəs] *adj* (*lips*) чу́вственный* (чу́вствен); (*material*) не́жный* (не́жен).

sent [sɛnt] *pt, pp of* **send**.

sentence ['sɛntns] *n* (*LING*) предложе́ние; (*LAW*) пригово́р ◆ *vt*: **to ~ sb to death/to five years in prison** пригова́ривать (приговори́ть *perf*) кого́-н к сме́рти/к пяти́ года́м тюре́много заключе́ния; **to pass ~ on sb** выноси́ть* (вы́нести* *perf*) кому́-н пригово́р.

sentiment ['sɛntɪmənt] *n* (*tender feelings*) чу́вство; (*opinion*) мне́ние, настрое́ние.

sentimental [sɛntɪ'mɛntl] *adj* сентимента́льный* (сентимента́лен).

sentimentality ['sɛntɪmɛn'tælɪtɪ] *n* сентимента́льность *f*.

sentry ['sɛntrɪ] *n* часово́й *m adj*, карау́льный *m adj*.

sentry duty *n*: **to be on ~ ~** нести́* *(impf)* карау́льную слу́жбу.
Seoul [səul] *n* Сеу́л.
separable ['sɛprəbl] *adj*: **~ (from)** отдели́мый (отдели́м) (от *+gen*).
separate [*adj* 'sɛprɪt, *vb* 'sɛpəreɪt] *adj* отде́льный; (*ways*) ра́зный ◆ *vt* (*split up*: *people*) разлуча́ть (разлучи́ть *perf*); (: *things*) разделя́ть (раздели́ть* *perf*); (*make a distinction between*) различа́ть (различи́ть *perf*) ◆ *vi* расходи́ться* (разойти́сь* *perf*); **~ from** отде́льно от *+gen*; **to ~ into** разделя́ть (раздели́ть* *perf*) на *+acc*; *see also* **separates**.
separately ['sɛprɪtlɪ] *adv* отде́льно.
separates ['sɛprɪts] *npl* (*clothes*) *предме́ты же́нской оде́жды, не входя́щие в компле́кт.*
separation [sɛpə'reɪʃən] *n* (*being apart*) разлу́ка; (*LAW*) разде́льное прожива́ние.
sepia ['si:pjə] *adj*: **~ photograph** *фотогра́фия, вы́полненная в те́хнике се́пии.*
Sept. *abbr* = **September**.
September [sɛp'tɛmbəʳ] *n* сентя́брь* *m*; *see also* **July**.
septic ['sɛptɪk] *adj* заражённый* (заражён); **to go ~** заража́ться (зарази́ться* *perf*).
septicaemia [sɛptɪ'si:mɪə] (*US* **septicemia**) *n* се́псис, септицеми́я.
septic tank *n* ≈ выгребна́я я́ма.
sequel ['si:kwl] *n* продолже́ние.
sequence ['si:kwəns] *n* после́довательность *f*; (*dance sequence*) комбина́ция; (*CINEMA*) эпизо́д; **in the correct ~** в пра́вильной после́довательности; **~ of tenses** согласова́ние времён.
sequential [sɪ'kwɛnʃəl] *adj* (*process, link etc*) после́довательный* (после́дователен); **~ access** (*COMPUT*) после́довательный до́ступ.
sequestrate [sɪ'kwɛstreɪt] *vt* конфискова́ть *(impf/perf)*.
sequin ['si:kwɪn] *n* блёстка*.
Serbia ['sə:bɪə] *n* Се́рбия.
Serbian ['sə:bɪən] *n* серб(ка) ◆ *adj* се́рбский*.
Serbo-Croat ['sə:bəu'krəuæt] *n* (*LING*) сербскохорва́тский язы́к*.
serenade [sɛrə'neɪd] *n* серена́да ◆ *vt* петь* (спеть* *perf*) серена́ду *+dat*.
serene [sɪ'ri:n] *adj* безмяте́жный* (безмяте́жен).
serenity [sə'rɛnɪtɪ] *n* безмяте́жность *f*.
sergeant ['sɑ:dʒənt] *n* сержа́нт.
sergeant major *n* ≈ ста́рший* сержа́нт.
serial ['sɪərɪəl] *n* (*TV, RADIO*) сериа́л; (*in magazine*) *рома́н, печа́тающийся в не́скольких частя́х* ◆ *adj* (*COMPUT*) после́довательный; **~ printer** посимво́льно печа́тающее устро́йство.
serialize ['sɪərɪəlaɪz] *vt* (*story, book*: *in print*) тиражи́ровать *(impf)* частя́ми; (: *on TV, RADIO*) ста́вить* (поста́вить* *perf*) сериа́л по *+prp*.
serial killer *n* манья́к (*соверши́вший многочи́сленные уби́йства*).
serial number *n* сери́йный но́мер*.
series ['sɪərɪz] *n inv* се́рия.
serious ['sɪərɪəs] *adj* серьёзный* (серьёзен); **are you ~ (about it)?** Вы (э́то) серьёзно?
seriously ['sɪərɪəslɪ] *adv* серьёзно; **to take sb/sth ~** принима́ть (воспринима́ть *perf*) кого́-н/что-н серьёзно.
seriousness ['sɪərɪəsnɪs] *n* серьёзность *f*.
sermon ['sə:mən] *n* (*also fig*) про́поведь *f*.
serrated [sɪ'reɪtɪd] *adj* зазу́бренный.
serum ['sɪərəm] *n* сы́воротка.
servant ['sə:vənt] *n* (*male*) слуга́* *m*; (*female*) служа́нка; (*fig*) слуга́*.
serve [sə:v] *vt* (*company, country*) служи́ть* *(impf)* *+dat*; (*customer*: *in shop, restaurant*) обслу́живать (обслужи́ть* *perf*); (*purpose*) служи́ть* (послужи́ть *(impf)*) *+dat*; (*food, goods*: *to sb*) подава́ть* (пода́ть* *perf*); (*subj*: *train etc*) обслу́живать *(impf)*; (*apprenticeship*) проходи́ть* (пройти́* *perf*); (*prison term*) отбыва́ть (отбы́ть* *perf*) ◆ *vi* (*at table*) прислу́живать *(impf)*; (*TENNIS*) подава́ть* (пода́ть* *perf*); (*soldier etc*) служи́ть* *(impf)* ◆ *n* (*TENNIS*) пода́ча; **are you being ~d?** Вас уже́ обслу́живают?; **it ~s my purpose** э́то мне подхо́дит; **it ~s him right** подело́м ему́; **to ~ on a committee/jury** состоя́ть *(impf)* в комите́те/жюри́; **to ~ as/for** служи́ть* (послужи́ть *perf*) *+instr*/вме́сто *+gen*
▸ **serve out** *vt* (*food*) раскла́дывать (разложи́ть* *perf*)
▸ **serve up** *vt* = **serve out**.
service ['sə:vɪs] *n* (*help*) услу́га; (*in hotel*) обслу́живание, се́рвис; (*REL*) слу́жба; (*AUT*) техобслу́живание; (*TENNIS*) пода́ча; (*dinner set etc*) серви́з ◆ *vt* (*car, washing machine*) проводи́ть* (провести́* *perf*) техобслу́живание *+gen*; **the S~s** *npl* (*army, navy etc*) Вооружённые си́лы *fpl*; **military** *or* **national ~** вое́нная слу́жба; **train ~** железнодоро́жное сообще́ние; **postal ~** почто́вая связь; **how can I be of ~ (to you)?** чем могу́ быть* поле́зен?; **to do sb a ~** ока́зывать (оказа́ть* *perf*) кому́-н услу́гу; **to put one's car in for ~** отдава́ть* (отда́ть* *perf*) маши́ну на техобслу́живание.
serviceable ['sə:vɪsəbl] *adj* про́чный* (про́чен).
service area *n* (*on motorway*) се́рвисная ста́нция.
service charge *n* (*BRIT*) (рестора́нная) наце́нка.
service industry *n* сфе́ра услу́г.
serviceman ['sə:vɪsmən] *irreg n* военно-слу́жащий* *m adj*.
service station *n* (*AUT*) ста́нция

* marks translations which have irregular inflections. The Russian-English side of the dictionary gives inflectional information

техобслу́живания.

serviette [sə:vɪ'ɛt] *n* (*BRIT*) салфе́тка*.

servile ['sə:vaɪl] *adj* подобостра́стный* (подобостра́стен).

session ['sɛʃən] *n* (*sitting*) се́ссия; (*SCOL: academic year*) уче́бный год*; **recording ~** за́пись *f*; **drinking ~** запо́й; **to be in ~** (*court etc*) заседа́ть *(impf)*.

session musician *n музыка́нт, кото́рого приглаша́ют на за́писи в ра́зные анса́мбли.*

set [sɛt] (*pt, pp* **set**) *n* (*collection*) набо́р; (*of saucepans, clothes*) компле́кт; (*of books*) многото́мник; (*also:* **radio ~**) радиоприёмник; (*also:* **television ~**) телеви́зор; (*TENNIS*) сет; (*group of people*) круг*, о́бщество; (*MATH*) мно́жество; (*CINEMA, THEAT: stage*) сце́на; (*: scenery*) (худо́жественное) оформле́ние; (*hairdo*) укла́дка ◆ *adj* (*fixed*) устано́вленный; (*ready*) гото́вый (гото́в) ◆ *vt* (*place: vertically*) ста́вить* (поста́вить* *perf*); (*: horizontally*) класть* (положи́ть* *perf*); (*table*) накрыва́ть (накры́ть* *perf*); (*time*) назнача́ть (назна́чить *perf*); (*price, rule, record*) устана́вливать (установи́ть* *perf*); (*alarm, watch, task*) ста́вить* (поста́вить* *perf*); (*exam*) составля́ть (соста́вить* *perf*); (*TYP*) набира́ть (набра́ть* *perf*) ◆ *vi* (*sun*) сади́ться* (сесть* *perf*), заходи́ть* (зайти́* *perf*); (*jam*) густе́ть (загусте́ть *perf*); (*jelly, concrete*) застыва́ть (засты́ть* *perf*); (*bone*) вправля́ться (впра́виться* *perf*); **a ~ of false teeth** вставны́е зу́бы* *mpl*; **a ~ of dining-room furniture** столо́вый гарниту́р; **a chess ~** ша́хматы *pl*; **to be ~ on doing** настра́иваться (настро́иться *perf*) *+infin*; **to be all ~ to do** собира́ться *(impf) +infin*; **to be (dead) ~ against** быть* *(impf)* (категори́чески) про́тив *+gen*; **he's ~ in his ways** у него́ устоя́вшиеся привы́чки; **the novel is ~ in Rome** де́йствие рома́на происхо́дит в Ри́ме; **a ~ phrase** усто́йчивое словосочета́ние; **to ~ to music** класть* (положи́ть* *perf*) на му́зыку; **to ~ on fire** поджига́ть (подже́чь* *perf*); **to ~ free** освобожда́ть (освободи́ть* *perf*); **to ~ sth going** приводи́ть* (привести́* *perf*) что-н в де́йствие; **to ~ sail** отплыва́ть (отплы́ть* *perf*)

▸ **set about** *vt fus* (*task*) приступа́ть (приступи́ть* *perf*) к *+dat*; **to ~ about doing** принима́ться (приня́ться* *perf*) *+infin*

▸ **set aside** *vt* (*money*) откла́дывать (отложи́ть* *perf*); (*time*) выделя́ть (вы́делить *perf*)

▸ **set back** *vt* (*progress*) заде́рживать (задержа́ть* *perf*); (*cost*): **to ~ sb back £5** обходи́ться* (обойти́сь* *perf*) кому́-н в £5; (*in time*): **to ~ sb back (by)** заде́рживать (задержа́ть* *perf*) кого́-н (на *+acc*); (*place*): **the house is ~ back from the road** дом нахо́дится в стороне́ от доро́ги

▸ **set in** *vi* (*infection*) внедря́ться (внедри́ться *perf*); (*bad weather*) устана́вливаться (установи́ться* *perf*); (*complications*) начина́ться (нача́ться* *perf*); **the rain has ~ in for the day** дождь заряди́л на весь день

▸ **set off** *vi* отправля́ться (отпра́виться* *perf*) ◆ *vt* (*bomb*) взрыва́ть (взорва́ть* *perf*); (*alarm*) приводи́ть* (привести́* *perf*) в де́йствие; (*chain of events*) вызыва́ть (вы́звать* *perf*); (*show up well*) подчёркивать *(impf)*

▸ **set out** *vt* (*goods etc*) расставля́ть (расста́вить* *perf*); (*arguments*) излага́ть (изложи́ть* *perf*) ◆ *vi* (*depart*): **to ~ out (from)** отправля́ться (отпра́виться* *perf*) (из *+gen*); **to ~ out to do** намерева́ться *(impf) +infin*

▸ **set up** *vt* (*organization*) учрежда́ть (учреди́ть* *perf*); (*monument*) устана́вливать (установи́ть* *perf*); **to ~ up shop** (*fig*) открыва́ть (откры́ть* *perf*) своё де́ло.

setback ['sɛtbæk] *n* (*hitch*) неуда́ча; (*in health*) ухудше́ние.

set menu *n* ко́мплексное меню́ *nt ind*.

set square *n* уго́льник.

settee [sɛ'ti:] *n* дива́н.

setting ['sɛtɪŋ] *n* (*background*) обстано́вка*; (*position: of controls*) положе́ние; (*of sun*) зака́т, захо́д; (*of jewel*) опра́ва.

setting lotion *n* (*for hair*) лосьо́н для укла́дки воло́с.

settle ['sɛtl] *vt* (*argument, problem*) разреша́ть (разреши́ть *perf*); (*matter*) ула́живать (ула́дить* *perf*); (*accounts*) рассчи́тываться (рассчита́ться *perf*) с *+instr*; (*colonize: land*) заселя́ть (засели́ть *perf*) ◆ *vi* (*also:* **~ down**: *somewhere*) обоснова́ться *(perf)*; (*: live sensibly*) остепени́ться *(perf)*; (*bird*) сади́ться* (сесть* *perf*); (*dust, sediment*) оседа́ть (осе́сть* *perf*); (*calm down*) успока́иваться (успоко́иться *perf*); **to ~ one's stomach** успока́ивать (успоко́ить *perf*) желу́док; **to ~ down to sth** уса́живаться (усе́сться* *perf*) за что-н; **to ~ for sth** соглаша́ться (согласи́ться* *perf*) на что-н; **to ~ on sth** остана́вливаться (останови́ться* *perf*) на чём-н

▸ **settle in** *vi* осва́иваться (осво́иться *perf*)

▸ **settle up** *vi*: **to ~ up with sb** рассчи́тываться (рассчита́ться *perf*) с кем-н.

settlement ['sɛtlmənt] *n* (*payment*) упла́та; (*agreement*) соглаше́ние; (*village, colony*) поселе́ние; (*of conflict*) урегули́рование; **in ~ of our account** (*COMM*) для опла́ты на́шего счёта.

settler ['sɛtlə'] *n* поселе́нец*(-нка*).

setup ['sɛtʌp] *n* (*organization*) устро́йство; (*situation*) положе́ние дел.

seven ['sɛvn] *n* семь*; *see also* **five**.

seventeen [sɛvn'ti:n] *n* семна́дцать*; *see also* **five**.

seventeenth [sɛvn'ti:nθ] *adj* семна́дцатый; *see also* **fifth**.

seventh ['sɛvnθ] *adj* седьмóй; *see also* **fifth**.
seventieth ['sɛvntiɪθ] *adj* семидеся́тый; *see also* **fifth**.
seventy ['sɛvntɪ] *n* сéмьдесят*; *see also* **fifty**.
sever ['sɛvəʳ] *vt* (*artery, pipe*) перерезáть (перерéзать* *perf*); (*relations*) прерывáть (прервáть* *perf*); (*ties, connections*) обрывáть (оборвáть* *perf*).
several ['sɛvərl] *adj* нéсколько +*gen* ◆ *pron* нéкоторые *pl adj*; ~ **of us** нéкоторые из нас; ~ **times** нéсколько раз.
severance ['sɛvərəns] *n* разры́в.
severance pay *n* выходнóе посóбие (*при сокращéнии штáтов*).
severe [sɪ'vɪəʳ] *adj* (*shortage, pain, winter*) жестóкий* (жестóк); (*damage*) серьёзный (серьёзен); (*stern*) жёсткий* (жёсток); (*plain: dress*) стрóгий* (строг).
severely [sɪ'vɪəlɪ] *adv* (*punish*) жестóко; (*look*) жёстко; (*damaged*) серьёзно; (*wounded, ill*) тяжелó.
severity [sɪ'vɛrɪtɪ] *n* жёстокость *f*; (*of damage*) серьёзность *f*; (*of illness*) тя́жесть *f*.
sew [səu] (*pt* **sewed**, *pp* **sewn**) *vti* шить* (*impf*)
▸ **sew up** *vt* (*clothes*) зашивáть (заши́ть* *perf*); **it is all ~n up** (*fig*) дéло на мази́.
sewage ['su:ɪdʒ] *n* (*waste*) стóчные вóды* *fpl*; ~ **system** канализáция.
sewage works *n* канализациóнные очисти́тельные сооружéния *ntpl*.
sewer ['su:əʳ] *n* канализациóнная трубá*.
sewing ['səuɪŋ] *n* шитьё.
sewing machine *n* швéйная маши́на.
sewn [səun] *pp of* **sew**.
sex [sɛks] *n* (*gender*) пол; (*lovemaking*) секс; **both ~es** óба пóла; **to have ~ with sb** переспáть* (*perf*) с кем-н.
sex act *n* сексуáльный акт.
sex appeal *n* сексопи́льность *f*, сексуáльная привлекáтельность *f*; **he's got a lot of ~ ~** он óчень сексопи́льный.
sex education *n* сексуáльное воспитáние.
sexism ['sɛksɪzəm] *n* *предубеждéние к ли́цам противополóжного пóла*.
sexist ['sɛksɪst] *adj* секси́стский ◆ *n* секси́ст.
sex life *n* половáя *or* сексуáльная жизнь *f*.
sex object *n* сексуáльный объéкт.
sextet [sɛks'tɛt] *n* (*group*) секстéт.
sexual ['sɛksjuəl] *adj* (*reproduction, equality*) половóй; (*attraction, relationship*) сексуáльный* (сексуáлен), половóй; ~ **equality** рáвенство полóв.
sexual assault *n* сексуáльное посягáтельство, нападéние с сексуáльным моти́вом.
sexual harassment *n* сексуáльное преслéдование.
sexual intercourse *n* половóй акт.
sexually ['sɛksjuəlɪ] *adv* (*attractive, attract*) сексуáльно; (*segregated*) в зави́симости от пóла; (*discriminate*) по половóму при́знаку; (*reproduce*) половы́м путём.
sexual orientation *n* сексуáльная ориентáция.
sexy ['sɛksɪ] *adj* (*person, voice*) сексуáльный* (сексуáлен).
Seychelles [seɪ'ʃɛl(z)] *npl*: **the ~** Сейшéльские островá *mpl*.
SF *n abbr* (= **science fiction**) НФ= *наýчная фантáстика*.
SG *n abbr* (*US*: *MIL, MED*: = *Surgeon General*) ≈ начмед= *начáльник медици́нской слýжбы*.
Sgt *abbr* (*POLICE, MIL*) = **sergeant**.
shabbiness ['ʃæbɪnɪs] *n* запýщенность *f*.
shabby ['ʃæbɪ] *adj* (*person*) обтрёпанный; (*clothes*) потрёпанный (потрёпан); (*treatment, behaviour*) недостóйный* (недостóен); (*building*) вéтхий* (ветх).
shack [ʃæk] *n* лачýга
▸ **shack up** *vi* (*inf*): **to ~ up (with sb)** начáть* (*perf*) сожи́тельствовать (с +*instr*).
shackles ['ʃæklz] *npl* (*also fig*) окóвы *pl*.
shade [ʃeɪd] *n* (*shelter*) тень* *f*; (*for lamp*) абажýр; (*of colour*) оттéнок*; (*US*: *also: window ~*) штóра ◆ *vt* (*shelter*) затеня́ть (затени́ть *perf*); (*eyes*) заслоня́ть (заслони́ть* *perf*); **~s** *npl* (*inf*: *sunglasses*) тёмные очки́ *pl*; **in the ~** в тени́; **a ~ (more/ too large)** чýточку (бóльше/великовáт).
shadow ['ʃædəu] *n* тень* *f* ◆ *vt* (*follow*) ходи́ть* (*impf*) как тень за +*instr*; **without** *or* **beyond a ~ of a doubt** без тéни сомнéния.
shadow cabinet *n* (*BRIT*: *POL*) теневóй кабинéт.
shadowy ['ʃædəuɪ] *adj* (*place*) тени́стый (тени́ст); (*figure, shape*) смýтный* (смýтен).
shady ['ʃeɪdɪ] *adj* (*place, trees*) тени́стый (тени́ст); (*fig*: *dishonest*) тёмный* (тёмен).
shaft [ʃɑ:ft] *n* (*of arrow, spear*) дрéвко; (*AUT, TECH*) вал; (*of mine, lift*) шáхта; (*of light*) сноп; **ventilation ~** вентиляциóнная трубá*.
shag [ʃæg] *vt* (*inf!*) трáхать (трáхнуть *perf*) (*!*) ◆ *vi* (*inf!*) трáхаться (трáхнуться *perf*) (*!*) ◆ *n* (*also:* ~ **tobacco**) махóрка; (*ZOOL*) длиннохвóстный баклáн; (*inf!*): **to have a ~** трáхнуться (*perf*).
shaggy ['ʃægɪ] *adj* лохмáтый (лохмáт).
shake [ʃeɪk] (*pt* **shook**, *pp* **shaken**) *vt* трясти́* (*impf*); (*bottle*) взбáлтывать (взболтáть *perf*); (*building*) сотрясáть (сотрясти́* *perf*); (*weaken*: *beliefs, resolve*) пошатнýть (*perf*); (*upset, surprise*) потрясáть (потрясти́* *perf*) ◆ *vi* (*voice*) дрожáть (*impf*) ◆ *n* (*movement*)

* marks translations which have irregular inflections The Russian-English side of the dictionary gives inflectional information.

дрожáние; **to ~ one's head** качáть (покачáть *perf*) головóй; **to ~ hands with sb** жать* (пожáть* *perf*) комý-н рýку; **to ~ with** трястúсь* *(impf)* от *+gen*; **give the bottle a good ~** хорошó взболтáйте бутылку

▸ **shake off** *vt* стряхивать (стряхнýть *perf*); (*fig: pursuer*) избавляться (избáвиться* *perf*) от *+gen*

▸ **shake up** *vt* (*ingredients*) взбáлтывать (взболтáть *perf*); (*fig: organization*) встряхивать (встряхнýть *perf*).

shaken ['ʃeɪkn] *pp of* **shake**.

shake-out ['ʃeɪkaut] *n* перетряска.

shake-up ['ʃeɪkʌp] *n* встряска*.

shakily ['ʃeɪkɪlɪ] *adv* (*reply*) с дрóжью в гóлосе; (*walk*) шатáясь; (*write*) дрожáщей рукóй.

shaky ['ʃeɪkɪ] *adj* (*hand, voice*) дрожáщий; (*table, knowledge*) шáткий* (шáток); (*memory*) непрóчный* (непрóчен); (*prospects, future*) неопределённый*; (*start*) неувéренный*; **his voice was ~** гóлос егó дрожáл.

shale [ʃeɪl] *n* слáнец*.

shall [ʃæl] *aux vb*: **I ~ go** я пойдý; **~ I open the door?** (мне) открыть дверь?; **I'll get some, ~ I?** я принесý немнóго, да?

shallot [ʃə'lɔt] *n* (*BRIT*) лук-шалóт *no pl*.

shallow ['ʃæləu] *adj* (*water*) мéлкий*; (*box*) неглубóкий*; (*breathing, also fig*) повéрхностный* (повéрхностен).

sham [ʃæm] *n* притвóрство; (*jewellery, furniture*) поддéлка* ◆ *vt* притворяться (притворúться *perf*) *+instr*.

shambles ['ʃæmblz] *n* неразберúха; **the economy is (in) a complete ~** в экономúке царúт пóлная неразберúха.

shambolic [ʃæm'bɔlɪk] *adj* (*inf*) хаотúчный* (хаотúчен).

shame [ʃeɪm] *n* (*embarrassment*) стыд*; (*disgrace*) позóр ◆ *vt* позóрить (опозóрить *perf*); **it is a ~ that/to do** жаль, что/*+infin*; **what a ~!** какáя жáлость!, как жаль!; **to put sb to ~** (*fig*) заставлять (заставúть* *perf*) когó-н устыдúться; **your work puts mine to ~** моя рабóта бледнéет в сравнéнии с Вáшей.

shamefaced ['ʃeɪmfeɪst] *adj* устыжённый.

shameful ['ʃeɪmful] *adj* позóрный* (позóрен).

shameless ['ʃeɪmlɪs] *adj* бесстыдный* (бесстыден).

shampoo [ʃæm'pu:] *n* шампýнь *m* ◆ *vt* мыть* (помыть* *or* вымыть* *perf*) шампýнем.

shampoo and set *n* мытьё и уклáдка волóс.

shamrock ['ʃæmrɔk] *n* трилúстник, кислúца.

shandy ['ʃændɪ] *n* *смесь пúва с лимонáдом.*

shan't [ʃɑ:nt] = **shall not**.

shanty town ['ʃæntɪ-] *n* трущóбы *fpl*.

SHAPE [ʃeɪp] *n abbr* (*MIL: = Supreme Headquarters Allied Powers, Europe*) Штаб верхóвного главнокомáндующего НАТО в Еврóпе.

shape [ʃeɪp] *n* фóрма ◆ *vt* (*fashion, ideas, events*) формировáть (сформировáть *perf*); (*clay*) лепúть* (слепúть* *perf*); (*statement*) оформлять (офóрмить* *perf*); **to take ~** (*painting, plan etc*) обретáть (обрестú* *perf*) фóрму; **in the ~ of a heart** в фóрме сердéчка; **I can't bear gardening in any ~ or form** я не выношý садовóдства ни в какóй фóрме; **to get o.s. into ~** приводúть* (привестú* *perf*) себя, входúть* (войтú* *perf*) в фóрму

▸ **shape up** *vi* (*events*) склáдываться (сложúться* *perf*); (*person*) формировáться (сформировáться *perf*).

-shaped [ʃeɪpt] *suffix*: **heart-~** сердцевúдный*.

shapeless ['ʃeɪplɪs] *adj* бесфóрменный (бесфóрмен).

shapely ['ʃeɪplɪ] *adj* (*woman*) хорошó слóженный (слóжен); (*legs*) красúвый (красúв).

share [ʃɛə'] *n* дóля*; (*COMM*) áкция ◆ *vt* (*books, cost*) делúть* (разделúть* *or* поделúть* *perf*); (*toys*) делúться* (поделúться* *perf*) *+instr*; (*features, qualities etc*) разделять *(impf)*; (*opinion, concern*) разделять (разделúть* *perf*); **to ~ in** (*joy, sorrow*) делúться* (разделúться* *perf*); (*profits*) делúться* (поделúться* *perf*); (*work*) учáствовать *(impf)* в *+prp*

▸ **share out** *vt* делúть* (разделúть* *perf*).

share capital *n* акционéрный капитáл.

share certificate *n* сертификáт áкции.

shareholder ['ʃɛəhəuldə'] *n* акционéр.

share index *n* (*COMM*) фóндовый úндекс.

share issue *n* (*COMM*) выпуск áкции.

shareware ['ʃɛəwɛə'] *n* прогрáммное обеспечéние óбщего пóльзования.

shark [ʃɑ:k] *n* акýла.

sharp [ʃɑ:p] *adj* рéзкий* (рéзок); (*knife, teeth, nose*) óстрый* (остр); (*curve, bend*) крутóй* (крут); (*MUS*) диéз; (*dishonest: practice etc*) лóвкий* (лóвок) ◆ *n* (*MUS*) диéз ◆ *adv* (*precisely*): **at 2 o'clock ~** рóвно в два часá; **he is very ~** у негó óчень óстрый ум; **he was rather ~ with her** он был довóльно рéзок с ней; **look ~!** поторопúтесь!; **C ~** (*MUS*) до-диéз.

sharpen ['ʃɑ:pn] *vt* (*stick etc*) заострять (заострúть *perf*); (*pencil, knife*) точúть* (поточúть* *perf*); (*fig: appetite*) усúливать (усúлить *perf*).

sharpener ['ʃɑ:pnə'] *n* (*also:* **pencil ~**) точúлка*; (*also:* **knife ~**) точúло.

sharp-eyed [ʃɑ:p'aɪd] *adj* (*person*) зóркий* (зóрок).

sharpish ['ʃɑ:pɪʃ] *adv* (*inf*) быстренько.

sharply ['ʃɑ:plɪ] *adv* рéзко.

sharp-tempered [ʃɑ:p'tɛmpəd] *adj* (*person*) вспыльчивый (вспыльчив).

sharp-witted [ʃɑ:p'wɪtɪd] *adj* (*person*) сообразúтельный* (сообразúтелен).

shatter ['ʃætə'] *vt* (*vase, hopes*) разбивáть (разбúть* *perf*); (*fig: nerves*) надрывáть

(надорва́ть* *perf*); (: *person*) потряса́ть (потрясти́* *perf*) ◆ *vi* би́ться* (разби́ться* *perf*).
shattered [ˈʃætəd] *adj* (*overwhelmed, grief-stricken*) потрясённый (потрясён); (*inf: exhausted*) разби́тый (разби́т).
shattering [ˈʃætərɪŋ] *adj* (*experience*) тя́жкий*; (*day*) утоми́тельный* (утоми́телен).
shatterproof [ˈʃætəpru:f] *adj* небью́щийся.
shave [ʃeɪv] *vt* брить* (побри́ть* *perf*) ◆ *vi* бри́ться* (побри́ться* *perf*) ◆ *n*: **to have a ~** бри́ться* (побри́ться* *perf*).
shaven [ˈʃeɪvn] *adj* бри́тый (брит).
shaver [ˈʃeɪvəʳ] *n* (*also:* **electric ~**) (электри́ческая) бри́тва.
shaver point *n* розе́тка* для бри́твы.
shaving [ˈʃeɪvɪŋ] *n* бритьё; **~s** *npl* (*of wood etc*) стру́жки* *fpl*.
shaving brush *n* ки́сточка* для бритья́, помазо́к*.
shaving cream *n* крем для бритья́.
shaving foam *n* крем для бритья́.
shaving soap *n* крем для бритья́.
shawl [ʃɔ:l] *n* шаль *f*.
she [ʃi:] *pron* она́.
sheaf [ʃi:f] (*pl* **sheaves**) *n* (*of corn*) сноп*; (*of papers*) сто́пка*.
shear [ʃɪəʳ] (*pt* **sheared**, *pp* **shorn**) *vt* (*sheep*) стричь* (постри́чь* *or* остри́чь* *perf*)
▸ **shear off** *vi* (*bolt etc*) надла́мываться (надломи́ться* *perf*).
shears [ˈʃɪəz] *npl* (*for hedge*) садо́вые но́жницы *pl*.
sheath [ʃi:θ] *n* (*of knife*) но́жны* *pl*; (*contraceptive*) презервати́в.
sheathe [ʃi:ð] *vt* (*sword, knife etc*) вкла́дывать (вложи́ть* *perf*) в но́жны.
sheath knife *n* фи́нка*.
sheaves [ʃi:vz] *npl of* **sheaf**.
shed [ʃɛd] (*pt, pp* **shed**) *n* сара́й; (*INDUSTRY, RAIL*) наве́с ◆ *vt* (*skin, load*) сбра́сывать (сбро́сить* *perf*); (*tears*) лить* (*impf*); (*blood*) пролива́ть (проли́ть* *perf*); (*workers*) увольня́ть (уво́лить *perf*); **to ~ light on** пролива́ть (проли́ть* *perf*) свет на *+acc*.
she'd [ʃi:d] = **she had, she would**.
sheen [ʃi:n] *n* лоск.
sheep [ʃi:p] *n inv* овца́*; (*male*) бара́н.
sheepdog [ˈʃi:pdɔg] *n* овча́рка*.
sheep farmer *n* овцево́д.
sheepish [ˈʃi:pɪʃ] *adj* ро́бкий* (ро́бок).
sheepskin [ˈʃi:pskɪn] *n* овчи́на ◆ *cpd* (*jacket, mittens*) овчи́нный; **~ coat** (*short*) дублёный полушу́бок; (*long*) дублёная шу́ба, дублёнка (*разг*).
sheer [ʃɪəʳ] *adj* (*utter*) су́щий*; (*steep*) отве́сный; (*almost transparent*) сквозно́й ◆ *adv* (*straight up or down*) отве́сно; **by ~ chance** по чи́стой случа́йности.
sheet [ʃi:t] *n* (*on bed*) простыня́*; (*of paper, metal, glass*) лист*; (*of ice*) полоса́*.
sheet feed *n* (*on printer*) автопода́ча бума́ги.
sheet lightning *n* зарни́ца.
sheet metal *n* листово́й мета́лл.
sheet music *n* но́ты *fpl*.
sheik(h) [ʃeɪk] *n* шейх.
shelf [ʃɛlf] (*pl* **shelves**) *n* по́лка*.
shelf life *n* срок го́дности.
shell [ʃɛl] *n* (*of mollusc*) ра́ковина; (*of egg, nut*) скорлупа́; (*explosive*) снаря́д; (*of building*) карка́с; (*of ship*) ко́рпус ◆ *vt* (*peas*) лущи́ть (облущи́ть *perf*); (*MIL: fire on*) обстре́ливать (обстреля́ть *perf*)
▸ **shell out** *vt* (*inf*): **to ~ out (for)** выкла́дывать (вы́ложить *perf*) (на *+acc*).
she'll [ʃi:l] = **she will, she shall**.
shellfish [ˈʃɛlfɪʃ] *n inv* (*crab etc*) рачки́ *pl*; (*scallop etc*) моллю́ски *mpl*.
shellsuit [ˈʃɛlsu:t] *n* спорти́вный костю́м (*капро́новый на подкла́дке*).
shelter [ˈʃɛltəʳ] *n* (*refuge*) прию́т; (*protection*) укры́тие; (*also:* **air-raid ~**) бомбоубе́жище ◆ *vt* (*protect*) укрыва́ть (укры́ть* *perf*); (*give lodging to*) дава́ть* (дать* *perf*) прию́т *+dat* ◆ *vi* укрыва́ться (укры́ться* *perf*); **to take ~ (from)** приюти́ться* (*perf*) (от *+gen*).
sheltered [ˈʃɛltəd] *adj* (*life*) беззабо́тный; (*spot*) защищённый (защищён).
sheltered housing *n жили́щный ко́мплекс, специа́льно приспосо́бленный для нужд престаре́лых, инвали́дов итп*.
shelve [ʃɛlv] *vt* (*fig: plan*) класть* (положи́ть *perf*) под сукно́.
shelves [ʃɛlvz] *npl of* **shelf**.
shelving [ˈʃɛlvɪŋ] *n* (*shelves*) стелла́ж*.
shepherd [ˈʃɛpəd] *n* пасту́х* ◆ *vt* (*guide*) направля́ть (напра́вить* *perf*).
shepherdess [ˈʃɛpədɪs] *n* пасту́шка*.
shepherd's pie *n* (*BRIT*) ≈ запека́нка* из мя́са и карто́феля.
sherbet [ˈʃə:bət] *n* шербе́т; (*US: water ice*) фрукто́вое моро́женое *nt adj*.
sheriff [ˈʃɛrɪf] *n* (*US*) шери́ф.
sherry [ˈʃɛrɪ] *n* хе́рес*.
she's [ʃi:z] = **she is, she has**.
Shetland [ˈʃɛtlənd] *n* (*also:* **the ~ Islands**) Шетла́ндские острова́* *mpl*.
Shetland pony *n* шетла́ндский* по́ни *m ind*.
shield [ʃi:ld] *n* (*protection, also MIL*) щит*; (*trophy*) трофе́й ◆ *vt*: **to ~ (from)** заслоня́ть (заслони́ть* *perf*) (от *+gen*).
shift [ʃɪft] *n* (*in direction, conversation*) переме́на; (*in policy, emphasis*) сдвиг; (*at work*) сме́на ◆ *vt* передвига́ть (передви́нуть *perf*), перемеща́ть (перемести́ть* *perf*); (*stain*) выводи́ть* (вы́вести* *perf*) ◆ *vi* перемеща́ться

(переместиться* *perf*); **a ~ in demand** изменение в спросе; **the wind has ~ed to the south** ветер переменился к югу.
shift key *n* регистровая клавиша.
shiftless [ˈʃɪftlɪs] *adj* (*person*) бездейственный.
shiftwork [ˈʃɪftwəːk] *n* сменная работа; **to do ~** работать *(impf)* посменно.
shifty [ˈʃɪftɪ] *adj* (*person*) увёртливый (увёртлив); (*eyes*) бегающий.
Shiite [ˈʃiːaɪt] *n* шиит ◆ *adj* шиитский.
shilling [ˈʃɪlɪŋ] *n* (*BRIT*) шиллинг.
shillyshally [ˈʃɪlɪʃælɪ] *vi* тянуть* *(impf)*.
shimmer [ˈʃɪməʳ] *vi* мерцать *(impf)*.
shimmering [ˈʃɪmərɪŋ] *adj* мерцающий; (*satin etc*) переливающийся.
shin [ʃɪn] *n* голень *f* ◆ *vi*: **to ~ up a tree** влезать (влезть* *perf*) на дерево; **to ~ down a tree** слезать (слезть* *perf*) с дерева.
shindig [ˈʃɪndɪg] *n* (*inf*) сабантуй.
shine [ʃaɪn] (*pt, pp* **shone**) *n* блеск ◆ *vi* (*sun, light*) светить* *(impf)*; (*eyes, hair*) блестеть* *(impf)*; (*fig*: *person*) сиять *(impf)*, светиться* *(impf)* ◆ *vt* (*polish*) (*pt, pp* **shined**) натирать (натереть* *perf*); **to ~ a torch on sth** светить* (посветить* *perf*) фонарём на что-н.
shingle [ˈʃɪŋgl] *n* (*on beach*) галька; (*on roof*) кровельная дранка.
shingles [ˈʃɪŋglz] *n* опоясывающий лишай*.
shining [ˈʃaɪnɪŋ] *adj* блестящий*.
shiny [ˈʃaɪnɪ] *adj* блестящий*.
ship [ʃɪp] *n* корабль* *m* ◆ *vt* (*transport*) перевозить* (перевезти* *perf*) по морю; (*send*) экспедировать *(impf/perf)*; (*water*) забирать (забрать* *perf*); **on board ~** на борту корабля.
shipbuilder [ˈʃɪpbɪldəʳ] *n* кораблестроитель *m*, судостроитель *m*.
shipbuilding [ˈʃɪpbɪldɪŋ] *n* кораблестроение, судостроение.
ship canal *n* судоходный канал.
ship chandler [-ˈtʃɑːndləʳ] *n* поставщик корабельного оборудования.
shipment [ˈʃɪpmənt] *n* (*goods*) партия.
shipowner [ˈʃɪpəunəʳ] *n* судовладелец*.
shipper [ˈʃɪpəʳ] *n* отправитель *m*.
shipping [ˈʃɪpɪŋ] *n* (*transport of cargo*) перевозка; (*ships*) судоходство.
shipping agent *n* экспедитор.
shipping company *n* судоходная компания.
shipping lane *n* морская трасса.
shipping line *n* = **shipping company**.
shipshape [ˈʃɪpʃeɪp] *adj* (*house, boat etc*) ладный.
ship's manifest *n* декларация судового груза.
shipwreck [ˈʃɪprɛk] *n* (*event*) кораблекрушение; (*ship*) потерпевшее крушение судно ◆ *vt*: **to be ~ed** терпеть (потерпеть* *perf*) кораблекрушение.
shipyard [ˈʃɪpjɑːd] *n* (судостроительная) верфь *f*.
shire [ˈʃaɪəʳ] *n* (*BRIT*) графство.
shirk [ʃəːk] *vt* увиливать (увильнуть *perf*) от *+gen*.
shirt [ʃəːt] *n* (*man's*) рубашка*; (*woman's*) блузка*; **in (one's) ~ sleeves** в одной рубашке.
shirty [ˈʃəːtɪ] *adj* (*BRIT*: *inf*: *person*) надутый (надут).
shit [ʃɪt] *excl* (*inf!*) чёрт.
shiver [ˈʃɪvəʳ] *n* дрожь *f* ◆ *vi* дрожать *(impf)*.
shoal [ʃəul] *n* (*of fish*) косяк*; (*fig*: *also*: **~s**) толпы *fpl*.
shock [ʃɔk] *n* (*start, impact*) толчок*; (*ELEC, MED*) шок; (*emotional*) потрясение ◆ *vt* (*upset*) потрясать (потрясти* *perf*); (*offend*) возмущать (возмутить* *perf*), шокировать *(impf/perf)*; **to be suffering from ~** (*MED*) находиться* *(impf)* в состоянии шока; **the news gave us a ~** эта новость нас потрясла; **it came as a ~ to hear that** ... мы были потрясены, когда услышали, что ....
shock absorber *n* амортизатор.
shocker [ˈʃɔkəʳ] *n* (*inf*: *film*) ужасник; (: *news*) ужасающая новость *f*.
shocking [ˈʃɔkɪŋ] *adj* (*outrageous*) возмутительный* (возмутителен); (*dreadful*) кошмарный* (кошмарен).
shockproof [ˈʃɔkpruːf] *adj* противоударный.
shock therapy *n* шокотерапия.
shock treatment *n* = **shock therapy**.
shock wave *n* ударная волна; (*fig*) чувство потрясения.
shod [ʃɔd] *pt, pp of* **shoe** ◆ *adj*: **well-~** хорошо обутый (обут).
shoddy [ˈʃɔdɪ] *adj* (*goods*) дрянной; (*workmanship*) кустарный.
shoe [ʃuː] (*pt, pp* **shod**) *n* (*for person*) туфля*; (*for horse*) подкова; (*AUT*: *also*: **brake ~**) колодка ◆ *vt* (*horse*) подковывать (подковать* *perf*); **~s** (*footwear*) обувь *fsg*.
shoebrush [ˈʃuːbrʌʃ] *n* обувная щётка*.
shoehorn [ˈʃuːhɔːn] *n* рожок* (*для обуви*).
shoelace [ˈʃuːleɪs] *n* шнурок*.
shoemaker [ˈʃuːmeɪkəʳ] *n* сапожник.
shoe polish *n* гуталин.
shoe shop *n* обувной магазин.
shoestring [ˈʃuːstrɪŋ] *n* (*fig*): **on a ~** на гроши.
shoetree [ˈʃuːtriː] *n* распорка* для обуви.
shone [ʃɔn] *pt, pp of* **shine**.
shoo [ʃuː] *excl* вон; (*to cats*) брысь ◆ *vt* (*also*: **~ away, ~ off**) отгонять (отогнать* *perf*).
shook [ʃuk] *pt of* **shake**.
shoot [ʃuːt] (*pt, pp* **shot**) *n* (*BOT*) росток*, побег; (*SPORT*: *event*) охота; (*CINEMA*) съёмка ◆ *vt* (*gun, arrow*) стрелять *(impf)* из *+gen*; (*kill*: *bird, robber etc*) застреливать (застрелить* *perf*); (*BRIT*: *game*) стрелять *(impf)*; (*wound*) выстрелить *(perf)* в *+acc*; (*execute*) расстреливать (расстрелять *perf*); (*film*) снимать (снять* *perf*) ◆ *vi*: **to ~ (at)** стрелять (выстрелить *perf*) (в *+acc*); (*FOOTBALL etc*)

бить* *(impf)* (по +*dat*); **to ~ past** (*move*) проноситься* (пронестись* *perf*); **he shot through the door** он влетел в дверь
▸ **shoot down** *vt* (*plane*) сбивать (сбить* *perf*)
▸ **shoot in** *vi* (*rush in*) стремглав вбегать (вбежать* *perf*)
▸ **shoot out** *vi* (*rush out*) стремглав выбегать (выбежать* *perf*)
▸ **shoot up** *vi* (*fig*: *prices*) подскакивать (подскочить* *perf*); (*child*) вытягиваться (вытянуться *perf*).
shooting ['ʃu:tɪŋ] *n* (*shots, attack*) стрельба; (*murder*) убийство; (*CINEMA*) съёмки* *fpl*; (*HUNTING*) охота.
shooting range *n* стрельбище.
shooting star *n* падающая звезда*.
shop [ʃɔp] *n* магазин; (*also:* **workshop**) мастерская *f adj* ◆ *vi* (*also:* **go ~ping**) ходить* *(impf)* по магазинам, делать *(impf)* покупки; **repair ~** (ремонтная) мастерская; **to talk ~** (*fig*) говорить *(impf)* *or* разговаривать *(impf)* о работе
▸ **shop around** *vi* (*also fig*) прицениваться (прицениться* *perf*).
shopaholic ['ʃɔpə'hɔlɪk] *n* (*inf*) *человек, помешанный на магазинах*.
shop assistant *n* (*BRIT*) продавец*(-вщица).
shop floor *n* (*BRIT*: *INDUSTRY*) цех*.
shopkeeper ['ʃɔpki:pə˞] *n* владелец*(-лица) магазина.
shoplifter ['ʃɔplɪftə˞] *n* вор*(овка*) (*крадущий в магазинах*).
shoplifting ['ʃɔplɪftɪŋ] *n* кража товаров (*из магазинов*).
shopper ['ʃɔpə˞] *n* покупатель(ница) *m(f)*.
shopping ['ʃɔpɪŋ] *n* (*goods*) покупки* *fpl*.
shopping bag *n* хозяйственная сумка*.
shopping centre (*US* **shopping center**) *n* торговый центр.
shopping mall *n* (*esp US*) торговый центр.
shopsoiled ['ʃɔpsɔɪld] *adj* (*goods*) лежалый.
shop steward *n* (*BRIT*: *INDUSTRY*) цеховой староста *m*.
shop window *n* (*also fig*) витрина.
shore [ʃɔ:˞] *n* берег* ◆ *vt*: **to ~ (up)** подпирать (подпереть* *perf*); **on ~** на берегу.
shore leave *n* (*NAUT*) увольнение на берег.
shorn [ʃɔ:n] *pp of* **shear** ◆ *adj*: **~ of** (*power, protection etc*) лишённый (лишён) +*gen*.
short [ʃɔ:t] *adj* (*in length, time*) короткий* (короток); (*in height*) невысокий* (невысок); (*curt*) резкий* (резок); (*insufficient*) скудный ◆ *n* (*also:* **~ film**) короткометражный фильм; **we are ~ of milk** у нас мало молока; **I'm ten pence ~** мне не хватает десяти пенсов; **in ~** короче говоря; **water is in ~ supply** этот район испытывает нехватку воды; **it is ~ for** ... это сокращение от +*gen* ...; **a ~ time ago** недавно; **in the ~ term** в настоящее время; **to cut ~** (*speech, visit*) сокращать (сократить* *perf*); **everything ~ of** ... всё, кроме +*gen* ...; **~ of doing** остаётся только +*infin* ...; **to fall ~ of** не выполнять (выполнить *perf*); **we're running ~ of time** у нас заканчивается время; **to stop ~** застывать (застыть* *perf*) на месте; **to stop ~ of doing** не осмеливаться (осмелиться *perf*) +*infin*; *see also* **shorts**.
shortage ['ʃɔ:tɪdʒ] *n*: **a ~ of** нехватка +*gen*, дефицит +*gen*.
shortbread ['ʃɔ:tbrɛd] *n* ≈ песочное печенье.
short-change [ʃɔ:t'tʃeɪndʒ] *vt*: **to ~ sb** обсчитывать (обсчитать *perf*) кого-н.
short circuit *n* короткое замыкание.
shortcoming ['ʃɔ:tkʌmɪŋ] *n* недостаток*.
short(crust) pastry ['ʃɔ:t(krʌst)-] *n* (*BRIT*) песочное тесто.
short cut *n* короткий* путь* *m no pl*; (*fig*) экономный путь*.
shorten ['ʃɔ:tn] *vt* (*clothes*) укорачивать (укоротить* *perf*); (*visit*) сокращать (сократить* *perf*).
shortening ['ʃɔ:tnɪŋ] *n* (*CULIN*) жир*.
shortfall ['ʃɔ:tfɔ:l] *n* недостаток*.
shorthand ['ʃɔ:thænd] *n* (*BRIT*) стенография; (*fig*) сокращение; **to take sth down in ~** стенографировать (застенографировать *perf*) что-н.
shorthand notebook *n* (*BRIT*) стенографическая тетрадь *f*.
shorthand typist *n* (*BRIT*) стенографист(ка*).
short list *n* (*BRIT*) список* окончательных кандидатов.
short-lived ['ʃɔ:t'lɪvd] *adj* кратковременный* (кратковремен), недолгий* (недолог).
shortly ['ʃɔ:tlɪ] *adv* вскоре.
shorts [ʃɔ:ts] *npl*: **(a pair of) ~** шорты *pl*.
short-sighted [ʃɔ:t'saɪtɪd] *adj* (*BRIT*: *also fig*) близорукий* (близорук).
short-sightedness [ʃɔ:t'saɪtɪdnɪs] *n* близорукость *f*.
short-staffed [ʃɔ:t'stɑ:ft] *adj*: **to be ~** испытывать *(impf)* нехватку персонала.
short story *n* рассказ.
short-tempered [ʃɔ:t'tɛmpəd] *adj* вспыльчивый (вспыльчив).
short-term ['ʃɔ:ttə:m] *adj* (*effect*) кратковременный; (*borrowing*) краткосрочный.
short time *n*: **to be on ~ ~** (*INDUSTRY*) быть* *(impf)* на сокращённой рабочей неделе.
short wave *n* (*RADIO*) короткие волны* *fpl* ◆ *adj* (*RADIO*): **~-~** коротковолновый.
shot [ʃɔt] *pt, pp of* **shoot** ◆ *n* (*of gun*) выстрел; (*shotgun pellets*) дробь *f*; (*FOOTBALL etc*) удар; (*injection*) укол; (*PHOT*) снимок*; **to fire a ~ at sb/sth** выстрелить *(perf)* в кого-н/что-н; **to**

have a ~ at sth попыта́ть *(perf)* уда́чи в чём-н; **to have a ~ at doing** (*try*) про́бовать (попро́бовать *perf*) +*infin*; **to get ~ of sb/sth** (*inf*) распрости́ться* *(perf)* с кем-н/чем-н; **a big ~** (*inf*) больша́я ши́шка* *m/f*; **a good/poor ~** (*person*) ме́ткий*/плохо́й стрело́к*; **like a ~** ми́гом.

shotgun [ˈʃɔtgʌn] *n* дробови́к*.

should [ʃud] *aux vb*: **I ~ go now** я до́лжен идти́ тепе́рь; **he ~ be there now** сейча́с он до́лжен быть там; **I ~ go if I were you** на Ва́шем ме́сте я бы пошёл; **I ~ like to** я бы хоте́л; **~ he phone ...** е́сли он позвони́т ....

shoulder [ˈʃəuldəʳ] *n* (*ANAT*) плечо́* ◆ *vt* (*fig*: *responsibility, blame*) принима́ть (приня́ть* *perf*) на себя́; **to look over one's ~** смотре́ть* (посмотре́ть* *perf*) че́рез плечо́; **to rub ~'s with sb** (*fig*) враща́ться *(impf)* с кем-н в одни́х круга́х; **to give sb the cold ~** обходи́ться* (обойти́сь* *perf*) с кем-н прохла́дно.

shoulder bag *n* су́мка* на дли́нном ремне́.

shoulder blade *n* лопа́тка*.

shoulder strap *n* брете́лька*; (*on dungarees*) ля́мка*; (*on bag*) реме́нь* *m*.

shouldn't [ˈʃudnt] = **should not**.

shout [ʃaut] *n* крик ◆ *vt* выкри́кивать (вы́крикнуть *perf*) ◆ *vi* (*also*: **~ out**) крича́ть *(impf)*; **to give sb a ~** кри́кнуть *(perf)* кому́-н

▸ **shout down** *vt* заглуша́ть (заглуши́ть *perf*) кри́ками.

shouting [ˈʃautɪŋ] *n* крик.

shouting match *n* (*inf*) крик, сканда́л.

shove [ʃʌv] *vt* толка́ть *(impf)*; (*inf*: *put*): **to ~ sth in** зата́лкивать (затолка́ть *perf*) что-н, запи́хивать (запиха́ть *or* запихну́ть *perf*) что-н ◆ *n*: **to give sb/sth a ~** пиха́ть (пихну́ть *perf*) кого́-н/что-н; **he ~d me out of the way** он отпихну́л меня́

▸ **shove off** (*inf*) ◆ *vi* отва́ливать (отвали́ть* *perf*).

shovel [ˈʃʌvl] *n* лопа́та; (*mechanical*) ковш ◆ *vt* (*snow, coal, earth*) грести́* (сгрести́* *perf*) (*лопа́той*).

show [ʃəu] (*pt* **showed**, *pp* **shown**) *n* (*of emotion*) пока́з; (*semblance*) подо́бие; (*exhibition*) вы́ставка*; (*THEAT*) спекта́кль *m*; (*TV*) програ́мма, шоу *nt ind*; (*CINEMA*) сеа́нс ◆ *vt* пока́зывать (показа́ть* *perf*); (*courage etc*) проявля́ть (прояви́ть* *perf*) ◆ *vi* (*be evident*) проявля́ться (прояви́ться* *perf*), обнару́живаться (обнару́житься *perf*); (*inf*: *also*: **~ up**) явля́ться (яви́ться* *perf*); **to ~ sb to his seat** проводи́ть* (провести́* *perf*) кого́-н на ме́сто; **to ~ sb to the door** ука́зывать (указа́ть* *perf*) кому́-н на дверь; **to ~ a profit/loss** (*COMM*) демонстри́ровать *(impf/perf)* при́быль/убы́тки; **it just goes to ~ that ...** э́то про́сто пока́зывает что, ...; **to ask for a ~ of hands** проси́ть* (попроси́ть* *perf*) подня́ть ру́ки (*при голосова́нии*); **for ~** для ви́ду; **on ~** (*exhibits etc*) на вы́ставке; **who's running the ~ here?** (*inf*) кто здесь заправля́ет?

▸ **show in** *vt* (*person*) проводи́ть* (провести́* *perf*)

▸ **show off** *vi* хва́статься (похва́статься *perf*) ◆ *vt* (*display*) хва́статься (похва́статься *perf*) +*instr*

▸ **show out** *vt* (*person*) провожа́ть (проводи́ть* *perf*) к вы́ходу

▸ **show up** *vi* (*stand out*: *against background*) видне́ться *(impf)*; (: *fig*) обнару́живаться (обнару́житься *perf*); (*inf*: *turn up*) явля́ться (яви́ться* *perf*) ◆ *vt* (*uncover*: *imperfections etc*) выявля́ть (вы́явить* *perf*).

showbiz [ˈʃəubɪz] *n* (*inf*) = **show business**.

show business *n* шо́у би́знес.

showcase [ˈʃəukeɪs] *n* витри́на; (*fig*) показа́тельный приме́р.

showdown [ˈʃəudaun] *n*: **to have a ~ (with)** раскрыва́ть (раскры́ть* *perf*) ка́рты (+*dat*).

shower [ˈʃauəʳ] *n* (*also*: **~ bath**) душ; (*of rain*) ли́вень* *m*; (*of stones etc*) град; (*US*: *party*) зва́нный ве́чер ◆ *vi* принима́ть (приня́ть* *perf*) душ ◆ *vt*: **to ~ sb with** (*gifts, abuse etc*) осыпа́ть (осы́пать* *perf*) кого́-н +*instr*; (*missiles*) забра́сывать (заброса́ть* *perf*); **to have** *or* **take a ~** принима́ть (приня́ть* *perf*) душ.

shower cap [ˈʃauəkæp] *n* ша́почка* (*для ду́ша*).

showerproof [ˈʃauəpru:f] *adj* (*clothing*) непромока́емый.

showery [ˈʃauərɪ] *adj* дождли́вый.

showground [ˈʃəugraund] *n* вы́ставка* (*на откры́том во́здухе*).

showing [ˈʃəuɪŋ] *n* (*of film*) пока́з.

show jumping *n* конку́р.

showman [ˈʃəumən] *irreg n* (*at fair, circus*) веду́щий* *m adj*, конферансье́ *m ind*; (*owner of circus*) хозя́ин ци́рка; (*fig*) позёр.

showmanship [ˈʃəumənʃɪp] *n* тала́нт.

shown [ʃəun] *pp of* **show**.

show-off [ˈʃəuɔf] *n* (*inf*) хвасту́н(ья).

showpiece [ˈʃəupi:s] *n* (*of exhibition etc*) центра́льный экспона́т; **this is a ~ of ...** э́то явля́ется блестя́щим обрацо́м +*gen* ....

showroom [ˈʃəurum] *n* демонстрацио́нный зал.

show trial *n* показа́тельный проце́сс.

showy [ˈʃəuɪ] *adj* бро́ский*.

shrank [ʃræŋk] *pt of* **shrink**.

shrapnel [ˈʃræpnl] *n* шрапне́ль *f*.

shred [ʃrɛd] *n* (*usu pl*) клочо́к*; (*fig*: *of truth, evidence*) крупи́ца ◆ *vt* кроши́ть* (накроши́ть* *perf*); (*CULIN*) шинкова́ть (нашинкова́ть *perf*).

shredder [ˈʃrɛdəʳ] *n* (*also*: **vegetable ~**) шинко́вка; (*also*: **document ~**) маши́на для дезинтегра́ции докуме́нтов.

shrew [ʃru:] *n* (*ZOOL*) землеро́йка*; (*pej*: *woman*) змея́.

shrewd [ʃru:d] *adj* проница́тельный* (проница́телен).

shrewdness [ˈʃru:dnɪs] *n* проница́тельность *f*.
shriek [ʃri:k] *n* визг ◆ *vi* визжа́ть* *(impf)*.
shrift [ʃrɪft] *n*: **to give sb short ~** бы́стро отде́лываться (отде́латься *perf*) от кого́-н.
shrill [ʃrɪl] *adj* визгли́вый (визгли́в).
shrimp [ʃrɪmp] *n* (ме́лкая) креве́тка*.
shrimping [ˈʃrɪmpɪŋ] *n* ло́вля креве́ток.
shrine [ʃraɪn] *n* (*tomb*) ра́ка; (*place of worship, also fig*) святы́ня.
shrink [ʃrɪŋk] (*pt* **shrank**, *pp* **shrunk**) *vi* (*cloth*) сади́ться* (сесть* *perf*); (*profits, audiences*) сокраща́ться (сократи́ться* *perf*); (*also:* **~ away**) отпря́нуть *(perf)* ◆ *vt*: **washing will ~ the dress** от сти́рки пла́тье сади́тся ◆ *n* (*inf*: *psychiatrist*) психоанали́тик; **to ~ from sth** ускольза́ть (ускользну́ть *perf*) от *+gen*.
shrinkage [ˈʃrɪŋkɪdʒ] *n* уса́дка.
shrink-wrap [ˈʃrɪŋkræp] *vt* (*goods etc*) упако́вывать (упакова́ть *perf*) в уса́дочную плёнку.
shrivel [ˈʃrɪvl] (*also:* **~ up**) *vt* высу́шивать (вы́сушить *perf*) ◆ *vi* высыха́ть (вы́сохнуть *perf*).
shroud [ʃraud] *n* са́ван ◆ *vt*: **~ed in mystery** оку́танный (оку́тан) та́йно.
Shrove Tuesday [ˈʃrəuv-] *n вто́рник на ма́сленой неде́ле.*
shrub [ʃrʌb] *n* куст*.
shrubbery [ˈʃrʌbərɪ] *n* кустáрник.
shrug [ʃrʌg] *n* пожима́ние (*плеча́ми*) ◆ *vi*: **to ~ (one's shoulders)** пожима́ть (пожа́ть* *perf*) плеча́ми
▸ **shrug off** *vt* отма́хиваться (отмахну́ться *perf*) от *+gen*.
shrunk [ʃrʌŋk] *pp of* **shrink**.
shrunken [ˈʃrʌŋkn] *adj* (*material*) се́вший; (*person, figure*) съёженный.
shudder [ˈʃʌdəʳ] *n* дрожь *f* ◆ *vi* содрога́ться (содрогну́ться *perf*).
shuffle [ˈʃʌfl] *vt* тасова́ть (стасова́ть *perf*) ◆ *vi*: **to ~ (one's feet)** волочи́ть *(impf)* но́ги.
shun [ʃʌn] *vt* избега́ть *(impf)* *+gen*.
shunt [ʃʌnt] *vt* (*train*) переводи́ть* (перевести́* *perf*) на друго́й путь ◆ *vi* (*RAIL*): **to ~ (to and fro)** маневри́ровать *(impf/perf)*.
shunting yard [ˈʃʌntɪŋ-] *n* сортиро́вочная ста́нция.
shush [ʃuʃ] *excl* ш-ш.
shut [ʃʌt] (*pt, pp* **shut**) *vt* закрыва́ть (закры́ть* *perf*) ◆ *vi* закрыва́ться (закры́ться* *perf*)
▸ **shut down** *vt* закрыва́ть (закры́ть* *perf*); (*machine*) отключа́ть (отключи́ть *perf*) ◆ *vi* закрыва́ться (закры́ться* *perf*); (*machine*) отключа́ться (отключи́ться *perf*)
▸ **shut off** *vt* (*supply etc*) отключа́ть (отключи́ть *perf*)
▸ **shut out** *vt* (*person, cold, noise*) не пропуска́ть (пропусти́ть* *perf*); (*view, memory*) заслоня́ть (заслони́ть *perf*)
▸ **shut up** *vi* (*inf*: *keep quiet*) заткну́ться *(perf)* ◆ *vt* (*close*) запира́ть (запере́ть* *perf*); (*silence*) затыка́ть (заткну́ть *perf*) рот *+dat*; **~ up!** заткни́сь!
shutdown [ˈʃʌtdaun] *n* (*temporary*) приостановле́ние; (*permanent*) закры́тие.
shutter [ˈʃʌtəʳ] *n* (*on window*) ста́вень* *m*; (*PHOT*) затво́р.
shuttle [ˈʃʌtl] *n*: **~ plane** самолёт-челно́к; (*also:* **space ~**) шатл; (*also:* **~ service**) челно́чный маршру́т; (*for weaving*) челно́к ◆ *vi*: **to ~ between** соверша́ть *(impf)* челно́чные ре́йсы ме́жду *+instr* ◆ *vt* (*passengers*) вози́ть* *(impf)* туда́ и обра́тно.
shuttlecock [ˈʃʌtlkɔk] *n* (*SPORT*) вола́н.
shuttle diplomacy *n* челно́чная диплома́тия.
shy [ʃaɪ] *adj* (*timid*) засте́нчивый (застенчи́в), стесни́тельный* (стесни́телен); (*reserved*) осторо́жный* (осторо́жен) ◆ *vi*: **to ~ away from doing** (*fig*) чужда́ться *(impf)* *+infin*; **to fight ~ of** избега́ть *(impf)* *+gen*; **to be ~ of doing** стесня́ться (постесня́ться *perf*) *+infin*.
shyly [ˈʃaɪlɪ] *adv* засте́нчиво.
shyness [ˈʃaɪnɪs] *n* (*see adj*) засте́нчивость *f*, стесни́тельность *f*; осторо́жность *f*.
Siamese [saɪəˈmi:z] *adj*: **~ cat** сиа́мская ко́шка*; **~ twins** сиа́мские близнецы́ *mpl*.
Siberia [saɪˈbɪərɪə] *n* Сиби́рь *f*.
sibling [ˈsɪblɪŋ] *n* (*brother*) родно́й брат; (*sister*) родна́я сестра́.
Sicilian [sɪˈsɪlɪən] *adj* сицили́йский ◆ *n* сицили́ец*(-и́йка*).
Sicily [ˈsɪsɪlɪ] *n* Сици́лия.
sick [sɪk] *adj* (*ill*) больно́й* (бо́лен); (*humour*) пога́ный, скве́рный* (скве́рен); (*vomiting*): **he is/was ~** его́ рвёт/вы́рвало; (*nauseated*): **I feel ~** меня́ тошни́т; **to fall ~** заболева́ть (заболе́ть *perf*); **to be (off) ~** быть* *(impf)* на больни́чном; **a ~ person** больно́й челове́к*; **to be ~ of** (*of war etc*) смерте́льно уста́ть* *(perf)* от *+gen*; **I'm ~ of arguing/school** меня́ тошни́т от спо́ров/шко́лы.
sickbag [ˈsɪkbæg] *n* (*on airplane*) санита́рный паке́т.
sickbay [ˈsɪkbeɪ] *n* изоля́тор.
sickbed [ˈsɪkbɛd] *n* посте́ль *f* больно́го.
sick building *n помеще́ние с нездоро́вым микрокли́матом.*
sicken [ˈsɪkn] *vt* (*disgust*) вызыва́ть (вы́звать* *perf*) отвраще́ние у *+gen* ◆ *vi*: **to be ~ing for sth** заболева́ть *(impf)* чем-н.
sickening [ˈsɪknɪŋ] *adj* (*fig*) проти́вный (проти́вен).
sickle [ˈsɪkl] *n* серп*.
sick leave *n* о́тпуск по боле́зни.
sick list *n*: **to be on the ~ ~** быть* *(impf)* на бюллете́не *or* больни́чном.

* marks translations which have irregular inflections. The Russian-English side of the dictionary gives inflectional information.

sickly [ˈsɪklɪ] *adj* (*child, plant*) хи́лый* (хил); (*smell*) тошнотво́рный* (тошнотво́рен).
sickness [ˈsɪknɪs] *n* (*illness*) боле́знь *f*; (*vomiting*) рво́та.
sickness benefit *n* посо́бие по боле́зни.
sick note *n* бюллете́нь *m*, больни́чный лист*.
sick pay *n* опла́та по бюллете́ню *or* больни́чному листу́.
sickroom [ˈsɪkru:m] *n* ко́мната больно́го.
side [saɪd] *n* сторона́*; (*of body*) бок*; (*of paper*) страни́ца; (*team*) кома́нда; (*of hill*) склон ◆ *adj* (*door etc*) боково́й ◆ *vi*: **to ~ with sb** встава́ть* (встать* *perf*) на сто́рону кого́-н; **by the ~ of** у *+gen*; **by her ~** во́зле неё; **~ by ~** (*to walk*) ря́дом; (*to work*) бок о́ бок; **the right ~** (*of material*) лицо́; **the wrong ~** (*of material*) изна́нка; **we're on the wrong ~ of the road/river** мы не на то́й стороне́ доро́ги/реки́; **they are on our ~** они́ на на́шей стороне́; **from ~ to ~** с бо́ку на́ бок; **from all ~s** со всех сторо́н; **to take ~s (with sb)** принима́ть (приня́ть* *perf*) (чью-н) сто́рону; **a ~ of beef** полови́на говя́жьей ту́ши.
sideboard [ˈsaɪdbɔ:d] *n* буфе́т; **~s** *npl* (*BRIT*) = **sideburns**.
sideburns [ˈsaɪdbə:nz] *npl* бакенба́рды *pl*.
sidecar [ˈsaɪdkɑ:ʳ] *n* (*AUT*) коля́ска* (*мотоци́кла*).
side dish *n* гарни́р.
side drum *n* ма́лый бараба́н.
side effect *n* побо́чное де́йствие.
sidekick [ˈsaɪdkɪk] *n* (*inf*) подру́чный *m adj*.
sidelight [ˈsaɪdlaɪt] *n* (*AUT*) боково́е освеще́ние.
sideline [ˈsaɪdlaɪn] *n* (*SPORT*) бокова́я ли́ния; (*fig: supplementary job*) побо́чная рабо́та; **to stand on the ~s** стоя́ть* (*impf*) в стороне́.
sidelong [ˈsaɪdlɔŋ] *adj* косо́й; **to give sb a ~ glance** смотре́ть* (посмотре́ть* *perf*) на кого́-н и́скоса.
side plate *n* десе́ртная таре́лка.
side road *n* просёлочная доро́га.
side-saddle [ˈsaɪdsædl] *adv*: **to ride ~** е́хать* (*impf*) в да́мском седле́.
sideshow [ˈsaɪdʃəu] *n* аттракцио́н.
sidestep [ˈsaɪdstɛp] *vt* (*fig*) обходи́ть* (обойти́* *perf*) ◆ *vi* отступа́ть (отступи́ть* *perf*).
side street *n* переу́лок*.
sidetrack [ˈsaɪdtræk] *vt* уводи́ть* (увести́* *perf*) в сто́рону.
sidewalk [ˈsaɪdwɔ:k] *n* (*US*) тротуа́р.
sideways [ˈsaɪdweɪz] *adv* (*go in, lean*) бо́ком; (*look*) и́скоса.
siding [ˈsaɪdɪŋ] *n* (*RAIL*) запа́сный путь* *m*.
sidle [ˈsaɪdl] *vi*: **to ~ up (to)** подходи́ть* (подойти́* *perf*) бочко́м (к *+dat*).
SIDS *n abbr* (*MED*: = *sudden infant death syndrome*) *синдро́м внеза́пной сме́рти вне́шне здоро́вого младе́нца*.
siege [si:dʒ] *n* оса́да; **to be under ~** быть* (*impf*) в оса́де; **to lay ~ to** осажда́ть (осади́ть* *perf*).
siege economy *n* засто́йная эконо́мика.
siege mentality *n* психоло́гия люде́й в оса́дном положе́нии.
Sierra Leone [sɪˈɛrəlɪˈəun] *n* Сье́рра-Лео́не.
siesta [sɪˈɛstə] *n* сие́ста.
sieve [sɪv] *n* (*CULIN*) си́то*; (*for garden*) решето́* ◆ *vt* просе́ивать (просе́ять *perf*).
sift [sɪft] *vt* (*flour, sand*) просе́ивать (просе́ять *perf*); (*also:* **~ through**: *evidence etc*) просе́ивать (просе́ять *perf*).
sigh [saɪ] *n* вздох ◆ *vi* вздыха́ть (вздохну́ть *perf*).
sight [saɪt] *n* (*faculty*) зре́ние; (*spectacle*) вид; (*on gun*) прице́л ◆ *vt* замеча́ть (замети́ть* *perf*); **in ~** в по́ле зре́ния; **out of ~** из ви́да; **at ~** (*COMM*) по предъявле́нию; **at first ~** с пе́рвого взгля́да; **I know her by ~** я зна́ю её в лицо́; **to catch ~ of** замеча́ть (заме́тить* *perf*); **to lose ~ of sb/sth** теря́ть (потеря́ть *perf*) кого́-н/что-н из виду; **to set one's ~s on sth** положи́ть* (*perf*) глаз на что-н; **to shoot sb on ~** стреля́ть (*impf*) в кого́-н на ме́сте.
sighted [ˈsaɪtɪd] *adj* (*person*) зря́чий* (зряч); **partially ~** слабови́дящий.
sightseeing [ˈsaɪtsi:ɪŋ] *n* осмо́тр достопри-меча́тельностей; **to go ~** осма́тривать (осмотре́ть* *perf*) достопримеча́тельности.
sightseer [ˈsaɪtsi:əʳ] *n* тури́ст(ка*).
sign [saɪn] *n* (*notice*) вы́веска*; (*with hand*) знак; (*indication, evidence*) при́знак; (*also:* **road ~**) доро́жный знак ◆ *vt* (*document*) подпи́сывать (подписа́ть* *perf*); (*player*) нанима́ть (наня́ть* *perf*); **as a ~ of** в знак *+gen*; **it's a good/bad ~** э́то хоро́ший/плохо́й знак; **plus/minus ~** знак "плюс"/"ми́нус"; **there's no ~ of her changing her mind** нет никаки́х при́знаков того́, что она́ переду́мала; **he is showing ~s of improvement** у него́ видны́ при́знаки улучше́ния; **to ~ one's name** распи́сываться (расписа́ться* *perf*); **to ~ sth over to sb** передава́ть* (переда́ть* *perf*) что-н в дар кому́-н
▸ **sign away** *vt* (*rights etc*) передава́ть* (переда́ть* *perf*)
▸ **sign in** *vi* регистри́роваться (зарегистри́роваться *perf*)
▸ **sign off** *vi* зака́нчивать (зако́нчить *perf*)
▸ **sign on** *vi* (*MIL*) нанима́ться (наня́ться* *perf*); (*BRIT*: *as unemployed*) отмеча́ться (отмети́ться* *perf*) как безрабо́тный; (*for course*) регистри́роваться (зарегистри́роваться *perf*) ◆ *vt* (*MIL*: *recruits*) набира́ть (набра́ть* *perf*); (*employee*) нанима́ть (наня́ть* *perf*)
▸ **sign out** *vi* выпи́сываться (вы́писаться* *perf*)
▸ **sign up** *vi* (*MIL*) нанима́ться (наня́ться* *perf*); (*for course*) регистри́роваться (зарегистри́роваться *perf*) ◆ *vt* (*player, recruit*) нанима́ть (наня́ть* *perf*).
signal [ˈsɪgnl] *n* сигна́л ◆ *vi* сигнализи́ровать

(impf/perf) ◆ *vt* (*person*) подава́ть* (пода́ть* *perf*) знак +*dat*; (*message*) передава́ть* (переда́ть* *perf*); **to ~ a right/left turn** (*AUT*) дава́ть* (дать* *perf*) сигна́л пра́вого/ле́вого поворо́та; **to ~ to sb (to do)** подава́ть* (пода́ть* *perf*) знак кому́-н (+*infin*).
signal box *n* сигна́льная бу́дка*.
signalman [sɪgnlmən] *irreg n* стре́лочник.
signatory ['sɪgnətərɪ] *n* подписа́вшаяся сторона́*.
signature ['sɪgnətʃəʳ] *n* по́дпись *f*.
signature tune *n* музыка́льная ша́пка*.
signet ring ['sɪgnət-] *n* кольцо́* с печа́ткой.
significance [sɪg'nɪfɪkəns] *n* значе́ние; **that is of no ~** э́то не име́ет значе́ния.
significant [sɪg'nɪfɪkənt] *adj* (*amount, discovery etc*) значи́тельный* (значи́телен); (*look, smile*) многозначи́тельный* (многозначи́телен); **it is ~ that ...** ва́жно, что ....
significantly [sɪg'nɪfɪkəntlɪ] *adv* (*see adj*) значи́тельно; многозначи́тельно.
signify ['sɪgnɪfaɪ] *vt* (*subj*: *sign, gesture etc*) означа́ть *(impf)*; (: *person*) выража́ть (вы́разить* *perf*).
sign language *n* язы́к* же́стов.
sign post *n* (*also fig*) указа́тель *m*.
Sikh [si:k] *n* сикх ◆ *adj* си́кхский.
silage ['saɪlɪdʒ] *n* (*fodder*) си́лос; (*method*) силосова́ние.
silence ['saɪləns] *n* тишина́ ◆ *vt* заставля́ть (заста́вить* *perf*) замолча́ть.
silencer ['saɪlənsəʳ] *n* (*BRIT*) глуши́тель *m*.
silent ['saɪlənt] *adj* (*place, person, prayer*) безмо́лвный* (безмо́лвен); (*machine*) бесшу́мный* (бесшу́мен); (*taciturn*) молчали́вый (молчали́в); (*film*) немо́й; **to remain ~** молча́ть* *(impf)*.
silently ['saɪləntlɪ] *adv* мо́лча.
silent partner *n* (*COMM*) пасси́вный партнёр.
silhouette [sɪlu:'ɛt] *n* силуэ́т ◆ *vt*: **to be ~d against** вырисо́вываться *(impf)* на фо́не +*gen*.
silicon ['sɪlɪkən] *n* кре́мний.
silicon chip *n* кре́мниевый криста́лл, кре́мниевая микропласти́нка.
silicone ['sɪlɪkəun] *n* силико́н.
Silicon Valley *n* *зо́на скопле́ния предприя́тий, занима́ющихся вы́пуском вычисли́тельной те́хники.*
silk [sɪlk] *n* шёлк* ◆ *adj* шёлковый.
silky ['sɪlkɪ] *adj* шелкови́стый (шелкови́ст).
sill [sɪl] *n* (*also:* **window ~**) подоко́нник; (*of door*) поро́г; (*AUT*) карни́з.
silly ['sɪlɪ] *adj* глу́пый* (глуп); **to do something ~** де́лать (сде́лать *perf*) глу́пость.
silo ['saɪləu] *n* (*on farm*) си́лосная ба́шня*; (*for missile*) ста́ртовая ша́хта.
silt [sɪlt] *n* ил
▸ **silt up** *vi* зайливаться (зайли́ться* *perf*) ◆ *vt* засоря́ть (засори́ть *perf*).
silver ['sɪlvəʳ] *n* серебро́ ◆ *adj* сере́бряный.
silver foil *n* (*BRIT*) = **silver paper**.
silver paper *n* (*BRIT*) фольга́.
silver-plated [sɪlvə'pleɪtɪd] *adj* серебрёный.
silversmith ['sɪlvəsmɪθ] *n* сере́бряных дел ма́стер.
silverware ['sɪlvəwɛəʳ] *n* серебро́.
silver wedding (anniversary) *n* сере́бряная сва́дьба*.
silvery ['sɪlvrɪ] *adj* серебри́стый (серебри́ст); (*sound*) серебри́стый, сере́бряный.
similar ['sɪmɪləʳ] *adj*: **~ (to)** схо́дный* (схо́ден) (с +*instr*), подо́бный* (подо́бен) (+*dat*).
similarity [sɪmɪ'lærɪtɪ] *n* схо́дство.
similarly ['sɪmɪləlɪ] *adv* (*in a similar way*) подо́бным о́бразом; (*likewise*) таки́м же о́бразом.
simile ['sɪmɪlɪ] *n* сравне́ние.
simmer ['sɪməʳ] *vi* (*CULIN*) кипе́ть* *(impf)* на ме́дленном огне́
▸ **simmer down** *vi* (*fig*: *inf*) остыва́ть (осты́ть* *perf*).
simper ['sɪmpəʳ] *vi* жема́нничать *(impf)*.
simpering ['sɪmprɪŋ] *adj* (*person, smile*) жема́нный* (жема́нен).
simple ['sɪmpl] *adj* (*easy, plain*) просто́й* (прост); (*foolish*) недалёкий* (недалёк); **the ~ truth** очеви́дная и́стина.
simple interest *n* просты́е проце́нты *mpl*.
simple-minded [sɪmpl'maɪndɪd] *adj* простоду́шный* (простоду́шен).
simpleton ['sɪmpltən] *n* проста́к.
simplicity [sɪm'plɪsɪtɪ] *n* (*see adj*) простота́; недалёкость *f*.
simplification [sɪmplɪfɪ'keɪʃən] *n* упроще́ние.
simplify ['sɪmplɪfaɪ] *vt* упроща́ть (упрости́ть* *perf*).
simply ['sɪmplɪ] *adv* про́сто.
simulate ['sɪmjuleɪt] *vt* (*enthusiasm*) симули́ровать *(impf/perf)*; (*innocence*) изобража́ть (изобрази́ть* *perf*).
simulated ['sɪmjuleɪtɪd] *adj* (*hair, fur*) подде́льный; (*nuclear explosion*) имити́рованный.
simulation [sɪmju'leɪʃən] *n* притво́рство.
simultaneous [sɪməl'teɪnɪəs] *adj* одновре́менный.
simultaneously [sɪməl'teɪnɪəslɪ] *adv* одновре́менно.
sin [sɪn] *n* грех* ◆ *vi* греши́ть (согреши́ть *perf*).
Sinai ['saɪneɪaɪ] *n* Сина́йский полуо́стров.
since [sɪns] *adv* с тех пор ◆ *conj* (*time*) с тех пор, как; (*because*) так как ◆ *prep*: **~ July** с ию́ля; **~ then, ever ~** с тех пор; **it's two weeks ~ I wrote** уже́ две неде́ли с тех пор, как я написа́л; **~ our last meeting** со вре́мени

* marks translations which have irregular inflections. The Russian–English side of the dictionary gives inflectional information.

на́шей после́дней встре́чи.
sincere [sɪn'sɪəʳ] *adj* и́скренний* (и́скренен).
sincerely [sɪn'sɪəlɪ] *adv* и́скренне; **Yours ~** и́скренне Ваш.
sincerity [sɪn'sɛrɪtɪ] *n* и́скренность *f*.
sine [saɪn] *n* (*MATH*) си́нус.
sine qua non [sɪnɪkwɑ:'nɔn] *n* необходи́мое усло́вие.
sinew ['sɪnju:] *n* сухожи́лие.
sinful ['sɪnful] *adj* гре́шный* (гре́шен).
sing [sɪŋ] (*pt* **sang**, *pp* **sung**) *vti* петь* (спеть* *perf*).
Singapore [sɪŋgə'pɔ:ʳ] *n* Сингапу́р.
singe [sɪndʒ] *vt* пали́ть (опали́ть *perf*); (*clothes*) подпа́ливать (подпали́ть *perf*).
singer ['sɪŋəʳ] *n* певе́ц*(-ви́ца).
Singhalese [sɪŋə'li:z] *adj* = **Sinhalese**.
singing ['sɪŋɪŋ] *n* пе́ние; (*in the ears*) звон.
single ['sɪŋgl] *adj* (*individual*) одино́кий*; (*man*) холосто́й* (хо́лост); (*woman*) незаму́жняя; (*not double*) одина́рный* (одина́рен) ◆ *n* (*BRIT*: *also:* **~ ticket**) биле́т в оди́н коне́ц; (*record*) сорокопя́тка*; **not a ~ one was left** ни одного́ не оста́лось; **every ~ day** ка́ждый бо́жий день; **~ spacing** с интерва́лом в одну́ стро́чку
▸ **single out** *vt* (*choose*) отбира́ть (отобра́ть* *perf*); (*distinguish*) выделя́ть (вы́делить *perf*).
single bed *n* односпа́льная крова́ть *f*.
single-breasted ['sɪŋglbrɛstɪd] *adj* однобо́ртный.
Single European Market *n*: **the ~ ~ ~** Еди́ный европе́йский* ры́нок*.
single file *n*: **in ~ ~** в коло́нку.
single-handed [sɪŋgl'hændɪd] *adv* без посторо́нней по́мощи.
single-minded [sɪŋgl'maɪndɪd] *adj* целеустремлённый* (целеустремлён).
single parent *n* (*mother*) мать-одино́чка*; (*father*) оте́ц-одино́чка*.
single room *n* ко́мната на одного́.
singles ['sɪŋglz] *n* (*TENNIS*) оди́н на оди́н ◆ *npl* (*single people*) несеме́йные *pl adj*.
singles bar *n* бар для несеме́йных.
single-sex [sɪŋgl'sɛks] *adj* разде́льный.
singly ['sɪŋglɪ] *adv* (*alone, one by one*) врозь, в отде́льности.
singsong ['sɪŋsɔŋ] *adj* (*tone*) моното́нно иду́щий то вверх, то вниз ◆ *n*: **to have a ~** попе́ть* (*perf*) хо́ром.
singular ['sɪŋgjuləʳ] *adj* необыча́йный* (необыча́ен); (*LING*) еди́нственный ◆ *n* (*LING*) еди́нственное число́; **in the feminine ~** же́нского ро́да еди́нственного числа́.
singularly ['sɪŋgjuləlɪ] *adv* необыча́йно.
Sinhalese [sɪnhə'li:z] *adj* синга́льский ◆ *n inv* синга́лец*(-ка*); (*LING*) синга́льский язы́к*.
sinister ['sɪnɪstəʳ] *adj* злове́щий* (злове́щ).
sink [sɪŋk] (*pt* **sank**, *pp* **sunk**) *n* ра́ковина ◆ *vt* (*ship*) топи́ть* (потопи́ть* *perf*); (*well*) рыть* (вы́рыть* *perf*); (*foundations*) врыва́ть (врыть* *perf*) ◆ *vi* (*ship*) тону́ть* (потону́ть* *perf*); (*heart, spirits*) па́дать (упа́сть* *perf*); (*ground*) оседа́ть (осе́сть* *perf*); (*also:* **~ back, ~ down**) отки́дываться (отки́нуться *perf*); **to ~ sth into** (*teeth, claws etc*) вонза́ть (вонзи́ть* *perf*) что-н в *+acc*; **he sank into a chair/the mud** он опусти́лся на стул/провали́лся в грязь
▸ **sink in** *vi* (*fig*): **it took a long time for her words to ~ in** потре́бовалось до́лгое вре́мя что́бы до меня́ дошли́ её слова́.
sinking ['sɪŋkɪŋ] *adj* (*sun*) опуска́ющийся; (*ship*) то́нущий; **I had a ~ feeling** у меня́ всё внутри́ опусти́лось.
sinking fund *n* (*COMM*) фонд погаше́ния.
sink unit *n* комбини́рованная *or* встро́енная ра́ковина.
sinner ['sɪnəʳ] *n* гре́шник(-ица).
Sinn Féin *n* Шинн Фейн (*ирла́ндская полити́ческая па́ртия*).
Sino- ['saɪnəu] *prefix* сино-, кита́е-.
sinuous ['sɪnjuəs] *adj* извива́ющийся.
sinus ['saɪnəs] *n* па́зуха.
SIPS *n abbr* (= *side impact protection system*) *систе́ма защи́ты автомоби́лей от боковы́х уда́ров*.
sip [sɪp] *n* ма́ленький* глото́к* ◆ *vt* пить* (вы́пить* *perf*) ма́ленькими глотка́ми.
siphon ['saɪfən] *n* сифо́н
▸ **siphon off** *vt* выка́чивать (вы́качать *perf*).
sir [səʳ] *n* сэр, господи́н; **S~ John Smith** Сэр Джон Смит; **yes ~** да, сэр; **Dear S~** (*in letter*) Уважа́емый господи́н.
siren ['saɪərn] *n* сире́на.
sirloin ['sə:lɔɪn] *n* (*also:* **~ steak**) говя́жье филе́ *nt ind*.
sirocco [sɪ'rɔkəu] *n* сиро́кко *m ind*
sisal ['saɪsəl] *n* сиза́ль *m*.
sissy ['sɪsɪ] *n* (*inf*) не́женка* *m/f*.
sister ['sɪstəʳ] *n* (*also REL*) сестра́*; (*BRIT*: *MED*) (медици́нская *or* мед-) сестра́* ◆ *cpd*: **~ organization** паралле́льная организа́ция; **~ ship** однoти́пное су́дно*.
sister-in-law ['sɪstərɪnlɔ:] *n* (*brother's wife*) неве́стка*; (*husband's sister*) золо́вка*; (*wife's sister*) своя́ченица.
sit [sɪt] (*pt, pp* **sat**) *vi* (*sit down*) сади́ться* (сесть* *perf*); (*be sitting*) сиде́ть* (*impf*); (*assembly*) заседа́ть (*impf*); (*for painter*) пози́ровать (*impf*) ◆ *vt* (*exam*) сдава́ть* (сдать* *perf*); **to ~ on a committee** входи́ть* (*impf*) в комите́т; **to ~ tight** не принима́ть (*impf*) никаки́х де́йствий
▸ **sit about** *vi* сиде́ть* (*impf*)
▸ **sit around** *vi* = **sit about**
▸ **sit back** *vi* (*in seat*) сиде́ть* (*impf*)
▸ **sit down** *vi* сади́ться* (сесть* *perf*); **to be ~ting down** сиде́ть* (*impf*)
▸ **sit in on** *vt fus* (*meeting*) прису́тствовать (*impf*) в/на *+prp*
▸ **sit up** *vi* (*after lying*) приподнима́ться (приподня́ться* *perf*); (*straight*)

выпрямля́ться (вы́прямиться* *perf*); (*not go to bed*) заси́живаться (засиде́ться* *perf*).
sitcom ['sɪtkɔm] *n abbr* (*TV*) = **situation comedy**.
sit-down ['sɪtdaun] *adj*: **a ~ strike** сидя́чая забасто́вка*; **a ~ meal** приём пи́щи, си́дя.
site [saɪt] *n* (*place*) ме́сто*; (*also:* **building ~**) строи́тельная площа́дка* ◆ *vt* (*factory, missiles*) помеща́ть (помести́ть* *perf*).
sit-in ['sɪtɪn] *n* демонстрати́вное заня́тие помеще́ния.
siting ['saɪtɪŋ] *n* (*location*) расположе́ние.
sitter ['sɪtəʳ] *n* (*for painter*) нату́рщик(-ица); (*also:* **baby-~**) приходя́щая ня́ня.
sitting ['sɪtɪŋ] *n* (*of assembly etc*) заседа́ние; (*in canteen*) сме́на.
sitting member *n* (*POL*) де́йствующий* депута́т парла́мента.
sitting room *n* гости́ная *f adj*.
sitting tenant *n* (*BRIT*) квартиросъёмщик (-ица).
situate ['sɪtjueɪt] *vt* располага́ть (расположи́ть* *perf*).
situated ['sɪtjueɪtɪd] *adj* располо́женный* (располо́жен); **to be ~** находи́ться* *(impf)*.
situation [sɪtju'eɪʃən] *n* (*state*) ситуа́ция, положе́ние; (*job*) ме́сто*; (*location*) ме́сто*, положе́ние; **"situations vacant"** (*BRIT*) "вака́нтные места́".
situation comedy *n* коме́дия положе́ний.
six [sɪks] *n* шесть*; *see also* **five**.
six-pack ['sɪkspæk] *n шестибуты́лочная упако́вка пи́ва*.
sixteen [sɪks'ti:n] *n* шестна́дцать*; *see also* **five**.
sixteenth [sɪks'ti:nθ] *adj* шестна́дцатый; *see also* **fifth**.
sixth ['sɪksθ] *adj* шесто́й ◆ *n* (*fraction*) одна́ шеста́я *f adj*, шеста́я часть *f*; **the upper/lower ~** (*BRIT: SCOL*) *пе́рвая/втора́я ступе́нь выпускно́го кла́сса*; *see also* **fifth**.
sixtieth ['sɪkstɪɪθ] *adj* шестидеся́тый; *see also* **fifth**.
sixty ['sɪkstɪ] *n* шестьдеся́т*; *see also* **fifty**.
size [saɪz] *n* разме́р; (*extent*) величина́, масшта́б; (*glue*) клей*; **I take ~ 14** я ношу́ четы́рнадцатый разме́р; **the small/large ~** ма́ленького/большо́го разме́ра; **it's the ~ of** ... э́то разме́ром с *+acc* ...; **cut to ~** обреза́нный согла́сно разме́рам *+gen*
▸ **size up** *vt* оце́нивать (оцени́ть* *perf*).
sizeable ['saɪzəbl] *adj* поря́дочный.
sizzle ['sɪzl] *vi* шипе́ть* *(impf)*.
SK *abbr* (*CANADA*) = *Saskatchewan*.
skate [skeɪt] *n* (*also:* **ice ~**) конёк*; (*also:* **roller ~**) ро́ликовый конёк*, ро́лик; (*fish: pl inv*) скат ◆ *vi* ката́ться *(impf)* на конька́х
▸ **skate around** *vt fus* (*problem, issue*) обходи́ть* (обойти́* *perf*)
▸ **skate over** *vt fus* (*problem, issue*) игнори́ровать *(impf/perf)*.
skateboard ['skeɪtbɔ:d] *n* ро́ликовая доска́*.
skater ['skeɪtəʳ] *n* конькобе́жец*(-жка*).
skating ['skeɪtɪŋ] *n* (*for pleasure*) ката́ние на конька́х; (*SPORT*) конькобе́жный спорт.
skating rink *n* като́к*.
skeleton ['skɛlɪtn] *n* (*ANAT*) скеле́т; (*TECH*) карка́с; (*outline*) набро́сок*, схе́ма.
skeleton key *n* отмы́чка*.
skeleton staff *n* минима́льный персона́л.
skeptic *etc* ['skɛptɪk] (*US*) = **sceptic** *etc*.
sketch [skɛtʃ] *n* (*drawing*) эски́з, набро́сок*; (*outline*) набро́сок*; (*THEAT, TV*) скетч ◆ *vt* (*drawing*) наброса́ть *(perf)*; (*also:* **~ out**) обрисо́вывать (обрисова́ть *perf*) в о́бщих черта́х.
sketchbook ['skɛtʃbuk] *n* альбо́м для зарисо́вок.
sketchpad ['skɛtʃpæd] *n* блокно́т для зарисо́вок.
sketchy ['skɛtʃɪ] *adj* пове́рхностный* (пове́рхностен).
skew [skju:] *n*: **on the ~** (*BRIT*) ко́со, кри́во.
skewed [skju:d] *adj* (*idea, outlook*) искажённый (искажён).
skewer ['skju:əʳ] *n* ве́ртел.
ski [ski:] *n* лы́жа ◆ *vi* ката́ться *(impf)* на лы́жах.
ski boot *n* лы́жный боти́нок*.
skid [skɪd] *n* (*AUT*) зано́с, юз ◆ *vi* скользи́ть* *(impf)*; (*AUT*) идти́* (пойти́* *perf*) ю́зом; **the car went into a ~** маши́ну занесло́.
skid mark *n* тормозно́й след*.
skier ['ski:əʳ] *n* лы́жник(-ица).
skiing ['ski:ɪŋ] *n* (*for pleasure*) ката́ние на лы́жах; (*SPORT*) лы́жный спорт; **to go ~** идти́* (пойти́* *perf*) *or* е́хать* (пое́хать* *perf*) ката́ться на лы́жах.
ski instructor *n* инстру́ктор по лы́жному спо́рту.
ski jump *n* (*ramp*) лы́жный трампли́н; (*event*) прыжки́ *mpl* на лы́жах с трампли́на.
skilful ['skɪlful] (*US* **skillful**) *adj* иску́сный* (иску́сен), уме́лый (уме́л).
ski lift *n* (лы́жный) подъёмник.
skill [skɪl] *n* (*ability, dexterity*) мастерство́; (*computer skill etc*) на́вык.
skilled [skɪld] *adj* (*able*) иску́сный* (иску́сен), уме́лый (уме́л); (*worker*) квалифиц-и́рованный.
skillet ['skɪlɪt] *n* (*CULIN*) неглубо́кая сковорода́*.
skillful ['skɪlful] *adj* (*US*) = **skilful**.
skil(l)fully ['skɪlfəlɪ] *adv* иску́сно, уме́ло.
skim [skɪm] *vt* (*milk*) снима́ть (снять* *perf*) сли́вки с *+gen*; (*soup*) снима́ть (снять* *perf*) на́кипь с *+gen*; (*glide over*) скользи́ть* *(impf)* над *+instr* ◆ *vi*: **to ~ through** пробежа́ть* *(perf)*.
skimmed milk [skɪmd-] *n* обезжи́ренное

* marks translations which have irregular inflections. The Russian-English side of the dictionary gives inflectional information.

молоко́.
skimp [skɪmp] *vt* (*also:* **~ on**: *work*) манки́ровать *(impf/perf)* +*instr*; (: *cloth etc*) эконо́мить* *(impf)* на +*prp*.
skimpy ['skɪmpɪ] *adj* ску́дный* (ску́ден); (*skirt*) те́сный* (те́сен).
skin [skɪn] *n* (*of person*) ко́жа; (*of animal*) шку́ра; (*of fruit, vegetable*) кожура́; (*of grapes, tomatoes*) ко́жица ◆ *vt* (*fruit etc*) снима́ть (снять* *perf*) кожуру́ с +*gen*, чи́стить* (очи́стить* *perf*); (*animal*) снима́ть (снять* *perf*) шку́ру с +*gen*, свежева́ть (освежева́ть *perf*); **she is soaked to the ~** она́ промо́кла до ни́тки.
skin cancer *n* рак ко́жи.
skin-deep ['skɪn'di:p] *adj* пове́рхностный* (пове́рхностен).
skin-diver ['skɪndaɪvə^r] *n* аквалангист(ка*).
skin diving *n* подво́дное пла́ванье.
skinflint ['skɪnflɪnt] *n* (*inf*) скря́га *m/f*.
skin graft *n* ко́жный транспланта́т.
skinhead ['skɪnhɛd] *n* бритоголо́вый(-ая) *m(f) adj*.
skinny ['skɪnɪ] *adj* то́щий* (тощ).
skin test *n* ана́лиз ко́жи.
skintight ['skɪntaɪt] *adj* в обтя́жку.
skip [skɪp] *n* прыжо́к*, скачо́к*; (*BRIT*: *container*) скип ◆ *vi* подпры́гивать (подпры́гнуть *perf*); (*with rope*) скака́ть* *(impf)* ◆ *vt* (*miss out*) пропуска́ть (пропусти́ть* *perf*); **to ~ school** (*esp US*) прогу́ливать (прогуля́ть *perf*) уро́ки.
ski pants *npl* лы́жные брю́ки *pl*.
ski pole *n* лы́жная па́лка*.
skipper ['skɪpə^r] *n* (*NAUT*) шки́пер, капита́н; (*SPORT*) капита́н ◆ *vt* быть* *(impf)* капита́ном +*gen*.
skipping rope ['skɪpɪŋ-] *n* (*BRIT*) скака́лка*.
ski resort *n* лы́жная ба́за.
skirmish ['skə:mɪʃ] *n* сты́чка*.
skirt [skə:t] *n* ю́бка* ◆ *vt* обходи́ть* (обойти́* *perf*).
skirting board ['skə:tɪŋ-] *n* (*BRIT*) пли́нтус.
ski run *n* лыжня́.
ski slope *n* лы́жный спуск.
ski suit *n* лы́жный костю́м.
skit [skɪt] *n* паро́дия.
ski tow *n* букси́рный подъёмник.
skittle ['skɪtl] *n* ке́гля*; **~s** *npl* (*game*) ке́гли* *fpl*.
skive [skaɪv] *vi* (*BRIT*: *inf*) сачкова́ть *(impf)*.
skulk [skʌlk] *vi* (*hide*) пря́таться* *(impf)*; (*prowl about*) кра́сться* *(impf)*.
skull [skʌl] *n* че́реп*.
skullcap ['skʌlkæp] *n* ермо́лка*.
skunk [skʌŋk] *n* (*animal*) скунс; (*fur*) ску́нсовый мех*.
sky [skaɪ] *n* не́бо*; **to praise sb to the skies** превозноси́ть* (превознести́* *perf*) кого́-н до небе́с.
sky-blue [skaɪ'blu:] *adj* небе́сно-голубо́й, лазу́рный.
skydiving ['skaɪdaɪvɪŋ] *n* свобо́дное паде́ние (*при прыжка́х с парашю́том*).
sky-high ['skaɪ'haɪ] *adj* (*prices*) сумасше́дший*; (*structure*) до небе́с; **to blow ~** разноси́ть* (разнести́* *perf*) вчистую.
skylark ['skaɪlɑ:k] *n* жа́воронок*.
skylight ['skaɪlaɪt] *n* окно́* в кры́ше.
skyline ['skaɪlaɪn] *n* горизо́нт; (*of city*) силуэ́т.
skyscraper ['skaɪskreɪpə^r] *n* небоскрёб.
slab [slæb] *n* (*of stone*) плита́*; (*of wood*) пласти́на; (*of cake, cheese*) кусо́к*.
slack [slæk] *adj* (*rope*) прови́сший; (*trousers*) вися́щий; (*discipline*) сла́бый* (слаб); (*security*) плохо́й* (плох); (*market*) вя́лый; (*demand*) небольшо́й ◆ *n* (*in rope etc*) слабина́; **~s** *npl* (*trousers*) сла́керсы *pl*; **business is ~** в дела́х засто́й.
slacken ['slækn] *vi* (*also:* **~ off**: *demand, speed*) па́дать (упа́сть* *perf*); (*rain*) перестава́ть* (переста́ть* *perf*) ◆ *vt* (*grip, clothing etc*) ослабля́ть (осла́бить* *perf*); (*speed*) снижа́ть (сни́зить* *perf*).
slacker ['slækə^r] *n* (*inf*) ло́дырь *m*.
slag heap [slæg-] *n* шла́ковая гора́*.
slag off *vt* (*BRIT*: *inf*): **to slag sb off** перемыва́ть (перемы́ть* *perf*) кому́-н ко́сточки.
slain [sleɪn] *pp of* **slay**.
slake [sleɪk] *vt*: **to ~ one's thirst** утоля́ть (утоли́ть *perf*) жа́жду.
slalom ['slɑ:ləm] *n* сла́лом.
slam [slæm] *vt* (*door*) хло́пать (хло́пнуть *perf*) +*instr*; (*throw*) швыря́ть (швырну́ть *perf*); (*criticize*) раскритикова́ть *(perf)* ◆ *vi* (*door*) захло́пываться (захло́пнуться *perf*); **to ~ on the brakes** ре́зко тормози́ть* (затормози́ть* *perf*).
slammer ['slæmə^r] *n* (*inf*) куту́зка.
slander ['slɑ:ndə^r] *n* клевета́ ◆ *vt* клевета́ть* (наклевета́ть* *perf*) на +*acc*.
slanderous ['slɑ:ndrəs] *adj* клеветни́ческий*.
slang [slæŋ] *n* (*informal language*) сленг; (*jargon*) жарго́н.
slanging match ['slæŋɪŋ-] *n* перебра́нка.
slant [slɑ:nt] *n* накло́н; (*fig*: *approach*) укло́н.
slanted ['slɑ:ntɪd] *adj* (*roof*) накло́нный, пока́тый; (*eyes*) раско́сый.
slanting ['slɑ:ntɪŋ] *adj* = **slanted**.
slap [slæp] *n* шлепо́к* ◆ *vt* шлёпать (шлёпнуть *perf*) ◆ *adv* (*directly*) пря́мо; **to ~ sb in the face** дать* *(perf)* кому́-н пощёчину; **to ~ sth on sth** (*paint etc*) ля́пать (наля́пать *perf*) что-н на что-н; **it fell ~ in the middle** оно́ упа́ло пря́мо посереди́не.
slapdash ['slæpdæʃ] *adj* небре́жный* (небре́жен).
slapstick ['slæpstɪk] *n* фарс.
slap-up ['slæpʌp] *adj*: **a ~ meal** (*BRIT*) роско́шный обе́д.
slash [slæʃ] *vt* ре́зать* (поре́зать* *perf*); (*fig*: *prices*) ре́зко снижа́ть (сни́зить* *perf*).
slat [slæt] *n* пла́нка*.

slate [sleɪt] *n* (*material*) сла́нец*; (*tile*) ши́ферная пли́тка* ◆ *vt* (*fig*) разноси́ть* (разнести́* *perf*) в пух и прах.
slaughter ['slɔ:tə^r] *n* (*of animals*) убо́й; (*of people*) резня́ ◆ *vt* (*animals*) забива́ть (заби́ть* *perf*); (*people*) ре́зать* (*impf*).
slaughterhouse ['slɔ:təhaus] *n* скотобо́йня.
Slav [slɑ:v] *adj* славя́нский* ◆ *n* славяни́н (-я́нка).
slave [sleɪv] *n* раб*(ы́ня) ◆ *vi* (*also:* **~ away**) рабо́тать (*impf*) как раб; **to ~ (away) at sth** рабо́тать (*impf*) над чем-н как про́клятый.
slave-driver ['sleɪvdraɪvə^r] *n* (*inf*) де́спот.
slave labour *n* (*also fig*) ра́бский* труд*.
slaver ['slævə^r] *vi* пуска́ть (*impf*) слюну́.
slavery ['sleɪvərɪ] *n* ра́бство.
Slavic ['slævɪk] *adj* славя́нский*.
slavish ['sleɪvɪʃ] *adj* ра́бский*; (*copy*) слепо́й.
slavishly ['sleɪvɪʃlɪ] *adv* по-ра́бски.
Slavonic [slə'vɔnɪk] *adj* славя́нский*.
slay [sleɪ] (*pt* **slew**, *pp* **slain**) *vt* поража́ть (порази́ть* *perf*).
SLD *n abbr* (*BRIT: POL*) = *Social and Liberal Democratic Party*.
sleazy ['sli:zɪ] *adj* (*place*) запу́щенный* (запу́щен).
sled [slɛd] *n* (*esp US*) = **sledge**.
sledge [slɛdʒ] *n* са́ни* *pl*; (*for children*) са́нки *pl*.
sledgehammer ['slɛdʒhæmə^r] *n* кува́лда.
sleek [sli:k] *adj* (*shiny, smooth: fur*) лосня́щийся; (*: hair*) блестя́щий* и гла́дкий*; (*car, boat etc*) аэродинами́чный.
sleep [sli:p] (*pt, pp* **slept**) *n* сон* ◆ *vi* спать* (*impf*); (*spend night*) ночева́ть* (переночева́ть* *perf*) ◆ *vt*: **the house can ~ four** в до́ме мо́жно размести́ть че́тверых; **to go to ~** засыпа́ть (засну́ть *perf*); **to have a good night's ~** (хорошо́) вы́спаться* (*perf*); **to put to ~** (*animal*) усыпля́ть (усыпи́ть* *perf*); **to ~ lightly** спать* (*impf*) чу́тко; **to ~ with sb** спать* (*impf*) с кем-н
▸ **sleep around** *vi* спать* (*impf*) с кем попа́ло
▸ **sleep in** *vi* (*oversleep*) просыпа́ть (проспа́ть* *perf*); (*lie late*) отсыпа́ться (отоспа́ться* *perf*).
sleeper ['sli:pə^r] *n* (*RAIL: train*) по́езд* со спа́льными ваго́нами; (*: carriage*) спа́льный ваго́н; (*: berth*) спа́льное ме́сто*; (*: BRIT: on track*) шпа́ла; (*person*) спя́щий(-ая) *m(f) adj*.
sleepily ['sli:pɪlɪ] *adv* со́нно.
sleeping ['sli:pɪŋ] *adj* (*person*) спя́щий.
sleeping bag *n* спа́льный мешо́к*.
sleeping car *n* спа́льный ваго́н.
sleeping partner *n* (*BRIT: COMM*) = **silent partner**.
sleeping pill *n* снотво́рное *nt adj*, снотво́рная табле́тка*.
sleeping sickness *n* со́нная боле́знь *f*.
sleepless ['sli:plɪs] *adj* (*night*) бессо́нный.
sleeplessness ['sli:plɪsnɪs] *n* бессо́нница.
sleepwalk ['sli:pwɔ:k] *vi* ходи́ть* (*impf*) во сне.
sleepwalker ['sli:pwɔ:kə^r] *n* луна́тик.
sleepy ['sli:pɪ] *adj* со́нный; **I feel** *or* **am ~** мне хо́чется спать.
sleet [sli:t] *n* дождь *m* со сне́гом.
sleeve [sli:v] *n* (*of jacket etc*) рука́в*; (*of record*) конве́рт; **to have sth up one's ~** име́ть (*impf*) ко́е-что на уме́.
sleeveless ['sli:vlɪs] *adj* без рукаво́в.
sleigh [sleɪ] *n* са́ни* *pl*.
sleight [slaɪt] *n*: **~ of hand** ло́вкость *f* рук.
slender ['slɛndə^r] *adj* (*figure*) стро́йный* (стро́ен); (*means*) ску́дный* (ску́ден); (*majority*) небольшо́й.
slept [slɛpt] *pt, pp of* **sleep**.
sleuth [slu:θ] *n* сы́щик.
slew [slu:] *vi* (*BRIT: also:* **~ round**) кру́то повора́чивать (поверну́ть *perf*) ◆ *pt of* **slay**.
slice [slaɪs] *n* (*of meat*) кусо́к*; (*of bread, lemon*) ло́мтик; (*also:* **fish ~**) ры́бный нож; (*also:* **cake ~**) лопа́тка* для то́рта ◆ *vt* (*bread, meat etc*) нареза́ть (наре́зать* *perf*), ре́зать* (наре́зать* *perf*); **~d bread** наре́занный хлеб.
slick [slɪk] *adj* (*performance*) гла́дкий*; (*salesman, answer*) бо́йкий* (бо́ек) ◆ *n* (*also:* **oil ~**) плёнка не́фти.
slid [slɪd] *pt, pp of* **slide**.
slide [slaɪd] (*pt, pp* **slid**) *n* (*downward movement*) скольже́ние; (*in playground*) де́тская го́рка*; (*PHOT*) слайд; (*BRIT: also:* **hair ~**) securely закол́ка*; (*also:* **microscope ~**) предме́тное стекло́*; (*in prices*) сниже́ние ◆ *vt* задвига́ть (задви́нуть *perf*), сова́ть* (су́нуть *perf*) ◆ *vi* скользи́ть* (скользну́ть *perf*); **to let things ~** (*fig*) запуска́ть (запусти́ть* *perf*) дела́, пусти́ть* (*perf*) дела́ самотёком.
slide projector *n* диапрое́ктор.
slide rule *n* логарифми́ческая лине́йка.
sliding door ['slaɪdɪŋ-] *n* задвижна́я дверь *f*.
sliding roof *n* (*AUT*) сдвига́ющийся верх.
sliding scale *n* скользя́щий* тари́ф.
slight [slaɪt] *adj* (*slim: figure*) то́нкий* (то́нок); (*frail*) хру́пкий* (хру́пок); (*small, trivial*) незначи́тельный; (*error*) небольшо́й; (*accent*) сла́бый; (*pain*) неси́льный ◆ *n* (*insult*) униже́ние; **the ~est noise** мале́йший* шум; **I haven't the ~est idea** я поня́тия не име́ю; **not in the ~est** нисколько.
slightly ['slaɪtlɪ] *adv* немно́го, слегка́; **~ built** хру́пкого сложе́ния.
slim [slɪm] *adj* (*figure*) стро́йный* (стро́ен); (*chance*) небольшо́й ◆ *vi* худе́ть (похуде́ть *perf*).
slime [slaɪm] *n* слизь *f*.
slimming [slɪmɪŋ] *n* (*losing weight*) похуде́ние.
slimy ['slaɪmɪ] *adj* (*pond*) и́листый (и́лист); (*covered with mud*) ско́льзкий* и ли́пкий*;

* marks translations which have irregular inflections. The Russian-English side of the dictionary gives inflectional information.

(*fig*: *person*) гну́сный.
sling [slɪŋ] (*pt, pp* **slung**) *n* (*MED*) пе́ревязь *f*; (*for baby*) *приспособле́ние, позволя́ющее носи́ть ребёнка на спине́ и́ли груди́*; (*weapon*) праща́, рога́тка* ◆ *vt* (*throw*) швыря́ть (швырну́ть *perf*); **his arm is in a ~** у него́ рука́ на пе́ревязи.
slingshot ['slɪŋʃɔt] *n* рога́тка*.
slink [slɪŋk] (*pt, pp* **slunk**) *vi*: **to ~ away** *or* **off** уходи́ть* (уйти́* *perf*) поджа́вши хвост*.
slinky ['slɪŋkɪ] *adj* в обтя́жку.
slip [slɪp] *n* (*fall*) обва́л; (*mistake*) про́мах; (*underskirt*) подъю́бник; (*of paper*) поло́ска* ◆ *vt* сова́ть* (су́нуть *perf*) ◆ *vi* (*slide*) скользи́ть* (скользну́ть *f*); (*lose balance*) поскользну́ться (*perf*); (*decline*) снижа́ться (сни́зиться* *perf*); (*move smoothly*): **to ~ into** (*room etc*) скользну́ть (*perf*) в *+acc*; **to give sb the ~** ускольза́ть (ускользну́ть *perf*) от кого́-н; **a ~ of the tongue** огово́рка*; **to ~ sth on** надева́ть (наде́ть* *perf*) что-н; **to ~ sth off** сбра́сывать (сбро́сить* *perf*) что-н; **to ~ out of** (*room etc*) вы́скользнуть (*perf*) из *+gen*; **to let a chance ~ by** упуска́ть (упусти́ть* *perf*) возмо́жность; **the cup ~ped from her hand** ча́шка вы́скользнула из её рук
▸ **slip away** *vi* улизну́ть (*perf*)
▸ **slip in** *vt* сова́ть* (су́нуть *perf*) ◆ *vi* (*errors*) закра́сться* (*perf*)
▸ **slip out** *vi* (*go out*) выска́кивать (вы́скочить *perf*)
▸ **slip up** *vi* (*make mistake*) ошиба́ться (ошиби́ться* *perf*).
slip-on ['slɪpɔn] *adj* без пу́говиц и застёжек; **~ shoes** ту́фли без шнурко́в и застёжек.
slipped disc [slɪpt-] *n* смещённый позвоно́к.
slipper ['slɪpəʳ] *n* та́почка*.
slippery ['slɪpərɪ] *adj* (*also fig*) ско́льзкий*.
slippy ['slɪpɪ] *adj* (*inf*) ско́льзкий* (ско́льзок).
slip road *n* (*BRIT*: *on to*) въезд на автостра́ду; (*off from*) съезд с автостра́ды.
slipshod ['slɪpʃɔd] *adj* небре́жный* (небре́жен).
slipstream ['slɪpstri:m] *n* возду́шный пото́к.
slip-up ['slɪpʌp] *n* оши́бка*.
slipway ['slɪpweɪ] *n* (*NAUT*) ста́пель* *m*.
slit [slɪt] (*pt, pp* **slit**) *n* (*cut*) разре́з; (*opening*) щель* *f*; (*tear*) разры́в ◆ *vt* разреза́ть (разре́зать* *perf*); (*tear*) разрыва́ть (разорва́ть* *perf*); **to ~ sb's throat** перере́зать* (*perf*) кому́-н го́рло.
slither ['slɪðəʳ] *vi* (*person*) скользи́ть* (*impf*); (*snake*) извива́ться (*impf*).
sliver ['slɪvəʳ] *n* (*of glass*) оско́лок*; (*of wood*) ще́пка*; (*of cheese etc*) кусо́чек*.
slob [slɔb] *n* (*inf*) о́лух.
slog [slɔg] *vi* (*BRIT*: *work hard*) корпе́ть* (*impf*) ◆ *n*: **it was a hard ~** э́то была́ тяжёлая рабо́та.
slogan ['sləugən] *n* ло́зунг.
slop [slɔp] *vi* (*also*: **~ over**) выплёскиваться (вы́плеснуться *perf*) ◆ *vt* выплёскивать (вы́плеснуть *perf*)
▸ **slop out** *vi* (*in prison etc*) выноси́ть* (вы́нести* *perf*) пара́шу.
slope [sləup] *n* (*gentle hill*) укло́н; (*side of mountain*) склон; (*ski slope*) спуск; (*slant*) накло́н ◆ *vi*: **to ~ down** спуска́ться (*impf*); **to ~ up** поднима́ться (*impf*) под укло́ном.
sloping ['sləupɪŋ] *adj* (*ground, roof*) пока́тый (пока́т); (*handwriting*) накло́нный.
sloppy ['slɔpɪ] *adj* (*work*) небре́жный* (небре́жен), халту́рный; (*appearance*) нея́шливый (неря́шлив); (*pej*: *film etc*) сентимента́льный* (сентимента́лен).
slops [slɔps] *npl* помо́и *pl*.
slosh [slɔʃ] (*inf*) *vi*: **to ~ around** *or* **about** плеска́ться* (*impf*).
sloshed [slɔʃt] *adj* (*inf*: *drunk*) пья́ный в дымину́.
slot [slɔt] *n* (*in machine*) про́резь *f*, паз*; (*fig*: *in timetable*) окно́*; (*RADIO, TV*) ме́сто* ◆ *vt*: **to ~ sth into** опуска́ть (опусти́ть* *perf*) что-н в *+acc* ◆ *vi*: **to ~ into** входи́ть* (войти́* *perf*) в *+acc*.
sloth [sləuθ] *n* (*laziness*) лень *f*; (*ZOOL*) лени́вец*.
slot machine *n* (*BRIT*: *vending machine*) торго́вый автома́т; (: *fruit machine*) игра́льный автома́т.
slot meter *n* (*BRIT*) счётчик.
slouch [slautʃ] *vi* суту́литься (ссуту́литься *perf*); **she was ~ed in a chair** она́ сиде́ла на сту́ле, сго́рбившись.
Slovakia [sləu'vækɪə] *n* Слова́кия.
Slovakian [sləu'vækɪən] *adj* слова́цкий* ◆ *n* (*person*) слова́к(-а́чка).
Slovenia [sləu'vi:nɪə] *n* Слове́ния.
Slovenian [sləu'vi:nɪən] *adj* слове́нский* ◆ *n* (*person*) слове́нец*(-нка); (*LING*) слове́нский* язы́к*.
slovenly ['slʌvənlɪ] *adj* неря́шливый (неря́шлив).
slow [sləu] *adj* ме́дленный; (*not clever*) тупо́й* (туп) ◆ *adv* ме́дленно ◆ *vt* (*also*: **~ down, ~ up**: *vehicle*) притормя́живать (притормози́ть* *perf*); (: *business*) приостана́вливать (приостанови́ть* *perf*) ◆ *vi* (*traffic*) замедля́ться (заме́длиться *perf*); (*car, train etc*) сбавля́ть (сба́вить* *perf*) ход; **at a ~ speed** на ни́зкой ско́рости; **to be ~ to act/decide** быть* (*impf*) медли́тельным(-ой) в дела́х/в реше́ниях; **my watch is (20 minutes) ~** мои́ часы́ отстаю́т (на 20 мину́т); **business is ~** дела́ иду́т нева́жно; **"slow"** (*road sign*) "ме́дленно"; **to go ~** (*driver*) дви́гаться (*impf*) ме́дленно; (*BRIT*: *workers*) снижа́ть (сни́зить* *perf*) темп рабо́ты.
slow-acting [sləu'æktɪŋ] *adj* заме́дленного де́йствия.
slowly ['sləulɪ] *adv* ме́дленно; **to drive ~** води́ть*/вести́* (*impf*) маши́ну ме́дленно.
slow motion *n*: **in ~ ~** в заме́дленном де́йствии.

slow-moving [sləu'mu:vɪŋ] *adj* мéдленно движущийся, мéдленный.
slowness ['sləunɪs] *n* мéдленность *f*.
sludge [slʌdʒ] *n* грязь *f*.
slue [slu:] *vi* (*US*) = **slew**.
slug [slʌg] *n* (*ZOOL*) слизня́к*; (*bullet*) пу́ля.
sluggish ['slʌgɪʃ] *adj* (*stream*) мéдленно теку́щий*; (*engine*) плóхо рабóтающий; (*person*) медли́тельный* (медли́телен); (*trading*) вя́лый.
sluice [slu:s] *n* (*gate*) шлюз; (*channel*) жёлоб* ◆ *vt*: **to ~ down** *or* **out** промыва́ть (промы́ть* *perf*), ока́тывать (окати́ть* *perf*).
slum [slʌm] *n* трущóба.
slumber ['slʌmbəʳ] *n* сон*.
slump [slʌmp] *n* (*economic*) спад; (*in profits, sales*) рéзкое падéние ◆ *vi* (*person*) вали́ться* (повали́ться* *perf*); (*prices*) рéзко па́дать (упа́сть* *perf*); **he was ~ed over the wheel** он сидéл, упа́в на руль.
slung [slʌŋ] *pt, pp of* **sling**.
slunk [slʌŋk] *pt, pp of* **slink**.
slur [slə:ʳ] *vt* (*words*) произноси́ть* (произнести́* *perf*) нечленораздéльно ◆ *n* (*MUS*) ли́га; (*fig*): **~ (on)** пятнó (на *+prp*); **to cast a ~ on** порóчить *(impf)*.
slurp [slə:p] *vt* (грóмко) хлеба́ть (хлебну́ть *perf*).
slurred [slə:d] *adj* (*speech, voice*) невня́тный* (невня́тен).
slush [slʌʃ] *n* сля́коть *f*.
slush fund *n* (*POL*) *фонд для пóдкупа госуда́рственных лиц.*
slushy ['slʌʃɪ] *adj* (*snow*) мóкрый; (*street*) покры́тый сля́котью; (*BRIT*: *fig*) сентимента́льный* (сентимента́лен).
slut [slʌt] *n* (*inf*: *pej*) потаску́ха.
sly [slaɪ] *adj* хи́трый* (хитёр) ◆ *n*: **on the ~** тайкóм.
smack [smæk] *n* (*slap*) шлепóк*; (*on face*) пощёчина; (*inf*: *heroin*) герои́н ◆ *vt* хлóпать (хлóпнуть *perf*); (*child*) шлёпать (отшлёпать *perf*); (*on face*) дава́ть* (дать* *perf*) пощёчину *+dat* ◆ *vi*: **to ~ of** попа́хивать *(impf) +instr* ◆ *adv* (*inf*): **the ball fell ~ in the middle** мяч упа́л пря́мо посереди́не; **to ~ one's lips** чмóкать (чмóкнуть *perf*) губа́ми.
smacker ['smækəʳ] *n* (*inf*: *kiss*) поцелу́й; (: *BRIT*: *pound note*) бума́жный фунт; (: *US*: *dollar bill*) бума́жный дóллар.
small [smɔ:l] *adj* ма́ленький*; (*quantity, amount*) небольшóй ◆ *n*: **the ~ of the back** поясни́ца; **to get** *or* **grow ~er** уменьша́ться (умéньшиться *perf*); **to make ~er** (*amount, income*) снижа́ть (сни́зить* *perf*); (*object, garment*) уменьша́ть (умéньшить *perf*); **a ~ shopkeeper** мéлкий(-ая) ла́вочник(-ица).
small ads *npl* (*BRIT*) ма́ленькие объявлéния *ntpl* (*в газéте о ку́пле-прода́же*).
small arms *npl* (*MIL*) стрелкóвое ору́жие *ntsg*.
small business *n* ма́лое предприя́тие.
small change *n* мéлочь* *f*.
small fry *npl* (*fig*) мéлкая сóшка *fsg*.
smallholder ['smɔ:lhəuldəʳ] *n* (*BRIT*) *владéлец небольшóго земéльного учáстка.*
smallholding ['smɔ:lhəuldɪŋ] *n* (*BRIT*) *небольшóе земéльное владéние.*
small hours *npl*: **in the ~ ~** в предрассвéтные часы́*.
smallish ['smɔ:lɪʃ] *adj* небольшóй, довóльно ма́ленький*.
small-minded [smɔ:l'maɪndɪd] *adj* ограни́ченный.
smallpox ['smɔ:lpɔks] *n* óспа.
small print *n* мéлкий* шрифт.
small-scale ['smɔ:lskeɪl] *adj* (*map, model*) ма́ленького масшта́ба; (*business, farming*) мéлкий*.
small screen *n*: **the ~ ~** телеви́дение, ма́лый экра́н.
small talk *n* свéтская бесéда.
small-time ['smɔ:ltaɪm] *adj* (*farmer etc*) мéлький.
small-town ['smɔ:ltaun] *adj* провинциа́льный* (провинциа́лен).
smarmy ['smɑ:mɪ] *adj* (*BRIT*: *pej*) вкра́дчивый (вкра́дчив).
smart [smɑ:t] *adj* (*neat, tidy*) опря́тный* (опря́тен); (*fashionable*) мóдный* (мóден); (*clever*) толкóвый (толкóв); (*quick*) бы́стрый* (быстр); (*pej*) наха́льный* (наха́лен) ◆ *vi* (*also fig*) жечь* *(impf)*; **the ~ set** фешенéбельное óбщество; **to look ~** вы́глядеть* *(impf)* элега́нтно; **my eyes are ~ing** у меня́ глаза́ щи́плет.
smart card *n* (*for transactions*) *вид креди́тной ка́рточки с микропроцéссором, испóльзуемой в платёжных опера́циях.*
smarten up ['smɑ:tn-] *vi* приодéться* *(perf)*, принаряди́ться *(perf)* ◆ *vt* (*place*) приводи́ть* (привести́* *perf*) в поря́док; (*person*) принаряди́ть *(perf)*.
smash [smæʃ] *n* (*collision*: *also*: **~-up**) ава́рия; (*sound*) грóхот; (*TENNIS*) смэш ◆ *vt* разбива́ть (разби́ть* *perf*); (*SPORT*: *record*) поби́ть* *(perf)* ◆ *vi* (*break*) разбива́ться (разби́ться* *perf*); (*collide*): **to ~ against** *or* **into** вреза́ться (врéзаться* *perf*) в *+acc*
▸ **smash up** *vt* (*car*) разбива́ть (разби́ть* *perf*); (*room*) громи́ть* (разгроми́ть* *perf*).
smash hit *n* шля́гер.
smashing ['smæʃɪŋ] *adj* (*inf*) потрясáющий*.
smattering ['smætərɪŋ] *n*: **a ~ of** повéрхностное знáние *+gen*.
smear [smɪəʳ] *n* (*trace*) след*; (*insult*) клеветá; (*MED*) мазóк* ◆ *vt* (*spread*) мáзать*

* marks translations which have irregular inflections. The Russian-English side of the dictionary gives inflectional information.

(намáзать* *perf*); (*make dirty*) пáчкать (испáчкать *perf*); **his hands were ~ed with oil/ink** егó рýки бы́ли испáчканы мáслом/черни́лами.

smear campaign *n* клеветни́ческая кампáния.

smear test *n* (*BRIT: MED*) мазóк* для анáлиза.

smell [smɛl] (*pt, pp* **smelt** *or* **smelled**) *n* зáпах; (*sense*) обоня́ние ◆ *vt* чýвствовать (почýвствовать *perf*) зáпах +*gen* ◆ *vi*: **to ~ (of)** (*unpleasant*) воня́ть *(impf)* (+*instr*); (*food etc*) пáхнуть *(impf)* (+*instr*).

smelly ['smɛlɪ] *adj* вонючий* (вонюч).

smelt [smɛlt] *pt, pp of* **smell** ◆ *vt* (*ore*) плáвить* (расплáвить* *perf*).

smile [smaɪl] *n* улы́бка* ◆ *vi* улыбáться (улыбнýться *perf*).

smiling ['smaɪlɪŋ] *adj* улыбáющийся.

smirk [smə:k] *n* (*pej*) ухмы́лка*.

smithy ['smɪðɪ] *n* кýзница.

smitten ['smɪtn] *adj*: **he is ~ with her** он от неё без умá.

smock [smɔk] *n* блýза; (*children's*) дéтское плáтье в сбóрочку; (*US: overall*) комбинезóн.

smog [smɔg] *n* смог.

smoke [sməuk] *n* дым ◆ *vi* (*person*) кури́ть* *(impf)*; (*chimney*) ды́ми́ться *(impf)* ◆ *vt* (*cigarettes*) кури́ть* (вы́курить *perf*); **to have a ~** кури́ть* (покури́ть* *perf*); **to go up in ~** сгорéть *(perf)*; (*fig*) пойти́* *(perf)* прáхом; **do you ~?** Вы кýрите?

smoked ['sməukt] *adj* (*bacon, fish*) копчёный; (*glass*) ды́мчатый.

smokeless fuel ['sməuklɪs-] *n* безды́мное тóпливо.

smokeless zone *n* (*BRIT*) безды́мная городскáя зóна.

smoker ['sməukə^r] *n* (*person*) кури́льщик(-щица); (*RAIL*) вагóн для куря́щих.

smoke screen *n* (*also fig*) дымовáя завéса.

smoke shop *n* (*US*) копти́льня.

smoking ['sməukɪŋ] *n* (*act*) курéние; **"no ~"** "не кури́ть".

smoking compartment (*US* **smoking car**) *n* вагóн для куря́щих.

smoking room *n* кури́тельная кóмната.

smoky ['sməukɪ] *adj* (*atmosphere, room*) задымлённый (зады́млен); (*taste*) с при́вкусом ды́ма.

smolder ['sməuldə^r] *vi* (*US*) = **smoulder**.

smoochy ['smu:tʃɪ] *adj* (*inf: music*) чýвственный.

smooth [smu:ð] *adj* глáдкий* (глáдок); (*sauce*) без комкóв; (*sea*) спокóйный* (спокóен); (*flavour*) мя́гкий* (мя́гок); (*movement*) плáвный* (плáвен); (*flight*) рóвный; (*pej: person*) лóвкий* (лóвок) ◆ *vt* (*also:* **~ out**) разглáживать (разглáдить* *perf*); (*: difficulties*) устраня́ть (устрани́ть *perf*)

▸ **smooth over** *vt*: **to ~ things over** (*fig*) улáживать (улáдить* *perf*) делá.

smoothly ['smu:ðlɪ] *adv* (*easily*) без трудá; **everything went ~** всё прошлó глáдко.

smoothness ['smu:ðnɪs] *n* глáдкость *f*; (*flavour*) мя́гкость *f*; (*movement*) плáвность *f*.

smother ['smʌðə^r] *vt* (*fire*) туши́ть* (потуши́ть* *perf*); (*person*) души́ть* (задуши́ть* *perf*); (*emotions*) подавля́ть (подави́ть* *perf*).

smoulder ['sməuldə^r] (*US* **smolder**) *vi* (*fire*) тлеть* *(impf)*; (*fig: anger, hatred*) зреть *(impf)*.

smudge [smʌdʒ] *n* пятнó* ◆ *vt* размáзывать (размáзать* *perf*).

smug [smʌg] *adj* самодовóльный* (самодовóлен).

smuggle ['smʌgl] *vt* (*goods*) провози́ть* (провезти́* *perf*) контрабáндой; (*refugees*) переправля́ть (переправить* *perf*) тáйно; **to ~ in/out** (*goods etc*) ввози́ть* (ввезти́* *perf*)/вывози́ть* (вы́везти* *perf*) контрабáндой.

smuggler ['smʌglə^r] *n* контрабанди́ст(ка*).

smuggling ['smʌglɪŋ] *n* контрабáнда.

smut [smʌt] *n* (*soot*) сáжа *no pl*; (*in conversation etc*) похáбщина.

smutty ['smʌtɪ] *adj* (*joke, book*) похáбный* (похáбен).

snack [snæk] *n* закýска*; **to have a ~** закýсывать (закуси́ть* *perf*), перекýсывать (перекуси́ть* *perf*).

snack bar *n* закýсочная *f adj*.

snag [snæg] *n* (*problem*) загвóздка*, затруднéние.

snail [sneɪl] *n* ули́тка*.

snake [sneɪk] *n* змея́*.

snap [snæp] *n* (*sound*) треск; (*photograph*) сни́мок*; (*game*) снэп ◆ *adj* (*decision etc*) необдýманный* (необдýман) ◆ *vt* (*break*) разлáмывать (разломи́ть *perf*); (*fingers*) щёлкать (щёлкнуть *perf*) +*instr* ◆ *vi* (*break*) разлáмываться (разломáться *or* разломи́ться* *perf*); (*fig: lose control*) сломáться *(perf)*; (*: speak sharply*) кричáть* *(impf)*; **to ~ at sb** (*subj: person*) кричáть* *(impf)* на когó-н; **to ~ one's fingers at** (*fig*) отмáхиваться (отмахнýться *perf*) от +*gen*; **a cold ~** (*weather*) внезáпное рéзкое похолодáние; **to ~ shut** (*trap, jaws etc*) защёлкивать (защёлкнуть *perf*)

▸ **snap at** *vt fus* огрызáться (огрызнýться *perf*) на +*acc*

▸ **snap off** *vi* отлáмывать (отломáть *or* отломи́ть* *perf*)

▸ **snap up** *vt* (*bargains*) расхвáтывать (расхватáть *perf*).

snap fastener *n* кнóпка*.

snappy ['snæpɪ] (*inf*) *adj* (*slogan*) брóский*; (*answer*) бы́стрый; **make it ~!** потораплива́йся!

snapshot ['snæpʃɔt] *n* сни́мок*.
snare [snɛəʳ] *n* лову́шка*, капка́н ◆ *vt* (*also fig*) зама́нивать (замани́ть* *perf*) в лову́шку.
snarl [snɑ:l] *vi* (*animal, person*) рыча́ть *(impf)*, ворча́ть *(impf)* ◆ *vt*: **to get ~ed up** (*plans*) пу́таться (запу́таться *perf*); **the traffic was ~ed up** произошёл зато́р в у́личном движе́нии.
snarl-up ['snɑ:lʌp] *n* пу́таница.
snatch [snætʃ] *n* (*of conversation, song etc*) обры́вок* ◆ *vt* (*grab*) хвата́ть (схвати́ть* *perf*); (*handbag*) вырыва́ть (вы́рвать* *perf*); (*child etc*) красть* (укра́сть* *perf*); (*opportunity, look etc*) урыва́ть (урва́ть* *perf*) ◆ *vi*: **don't ~!** не хвата́й!; **to ~ a sandwich** перехва́тывать (перехвати́ть* *perf*) бутербро́д; **I managed to ~ some sleep** мне удало́сь немно́го поспа́ть
▸ **snatch up** *vt* схва́тывать (схвати́ть* *perf*).
snazzy ['snæzi] *adj* (*inf*) шика́рный* (шика́рен).
sneak [sni:k] *n* (*inf: informer*) я́беда *m/f* ◆ *vi*: **to ~ into/out of** незаме́тно проска́льзывать (проскользну́ть *perf*) в *+acc*/из *+gen* ◆ *vt*: **to ~ a look at sth** взгля́дывать (взгляну́ть* *perf*) укра́дкой на что-н; **to ~ up on sb** я́бедничать (ная́бедничать *perf*) на кого́-н.
sneakers ['sni:kəz] *npl* кроссо́вки* *fpl*.
sneaking ['sni:kɪŋ] *adj*: **I have a ~ feeling** *or* **suspicion that ...** у меня́ закра́лось подозре́ние, что ....
sneaky ['sni:kɪ] *adj* (*pej: person*) хи́трый* (хитёр); (*advantage, look*) незаме́тный* (незаме́тен).
sneer [snɪəʳ] *vi* (*laugh*) посме́иваться *(impf)*; (*mock*): **to ~ at** глуми́ться* *(impf)* над *+instr*.
sneeze [sni:z] *n* чиха́нье ◆ *vi* чиха́ть (чихну́ть *perf*)
▸ **sneeze at** *vt fus*: **such things are not to be ~d at** таки́ми веща́ми не броса́ются.
snide [snaɪd] *adj* (*pej*) ехи́дный* (ехи́ден).
sniff [snɪf] *n* (*sound*) сопе́ние; (*smell: by dog, person*) обню́хивание ◆ *vi* шмы́гать (шмыгну́ть *perf*) но́сом; (*when crying*) всхли́пывать *(impf)* ◆ *vt* ню́хать *(impf)*; (*glue, drugs*) вдыха́ть *(impf)*, ню́хать *(impf)*
▸ **sniff at** *vt fus*: **such things are not to be ~ed at** таки́ми веща́ми не броса́ются.
sniffer dog ['snɪfə-] *n* (*POLICE*) соба́ка-ище́йка (*для обнаруже́ния нарко́тиков и взры́вчатых веще́ств*).
snigger ['snɪgəʳ] *vi* хихи́кать (хихи́кнуть *perf*).
snip [snɪp] *n* (*cut*) надре́з; (*BRIT: inf: bargain*) нахо́дка* ◆ *vt* (*cut*) ре́зать* *(impf)*.
sniper ['snaɪpəʳ] *n* сна́йпер.
snippet ['snɪpɪt] *n* обры́вок*.
snivel ['snɪvl] *vi* хны́кать *(impf)*.
snob [snɔb] *n* сноб.
snobbery ['snɔbərɪ] *n* сноби́зм.
snobbish ['snɔbɪʃ] *adj* снобистский*.
snog [snɔg] *vi* лиза́ться *(impf)* ◆ *n*: **to have a ~** лиза́ться *(impf)*.
snooker ['snu:kəʳ] *n* сну́кер (*игра́ в билья́рд*) ◆ *vt* (*BRIT: inf: fig*): **we're completely ~ed** мы соверше́нно за́гнаны в у́гол.
snoop ['snu:p] *vi*: **to ~ about** шпио́нить *(impf)*; **to ~ on sb** подгля́дывать *(impf)* за кем-н (в щёлочку).
snooper ['snu:pəʳ] *n* шпио́н.
snooty ['snu:tɪ] *adj* задири́стый.
snooze [snu:z] *vi* прикорну́ть *(perf)*, вздремну́ть *(perf)* ◆ *n*: **to have a ~** вздремну́ть *(perf)*.
snore [snɔ:ʳ] *n* храп ◆ *vi* храпе́ть* *(impf)*.
snoring ['snɔ:rɪŋ] *n* храп.
snorkel ['snɔ:kl] *n* тру́бка*.
snort [snɔ:t] *n* фы́рканье ◆ *vi* (*animal*) фаркну́ть *(perf)*; (*horse*) всхра́пывать *(impf)* ◆ *vt* (*inf: drugs*) ню́хать *(impf)*.
snotty ['snɔtɪ] *adj* (*inf: handkerchief, nose*) сопли́вый; (: *pej: snobbish*) на́глый.
snout [snaut] *n* (*of pig*) ры́ло; (*of dog etc*) мо́рда.
snow [snəu] *n* снег* ◆ *vi*: **it's ~ing** идёт снег ◆ *vt*: **she is ~ed under with work** она́ зава́лена рабо́той.
snowball ['snəubɔ:l] *n* снежо́к* ◆ *vi* (*fig: problem, campaign*) нараста́ть *(impf)* как сне́жный ком.
snowbound ['snəubaund] *adj* засы́панный сне́гом.
snowcapped ['snəukæpt] *adj* сне́жный.
snowdrift ['snəudrɪft] *n* сугро́б.
snowdrop ['snəudrɔp] *n* (*BOT*) подсне́жник.
snowfall ['snəufɔ:l] *n* снегопа́д.
snowflake ['snəufleɪk] *n* снежи́нка*.
snow line *n* снегова́я ли́ния.
snowman ['snəumæn] *n irreg* сне́жная ба́ба, снегови́к.
snowplough ['snəuplau] (*US* **snowplow**) *n* снегоубо́рочный комба́йн.
snowshoes ['snəuʃu:z] *npl* снегосту́пы *mpl*.
snowstorm ['snəustɔ:m] *n* бура́н, вью́га.
snowy ['snəuɪ] *adj* сне́жный; (*covered with snow*) засне́женный.
SNP *n abbr* (*BRIT: POL*) = *Scottish National Party*.
snub [snʌb] *vt* (*person*) пренебрежи́тельно обходи́ться* (обойти́сь* *perf*) с *+instr* ◆ *n* вы́зов.
snub-nosed [snʌb'nəuzd] *adj* курно́сый.
snuff [snʌf] *n* ню́хательный таба́к* ◆ *vt* (*also:* **~ out**) туши́ть* (потуши́ть* *perf*).
snuff movie *n порнографи́ческий фильм, в кото́ром засня́то настоя́щее уби́йство*.
snug [snʌg] *adj* (*place*) ую́тный* (ую́тен); (*well-fitting*) пло́тно облега́ющий*; **I'm very ~ here** мне здесь о́чень ую́тно; **the sweater is a ~ fit** сви́тер хорошо́ прилега́ет.

* marks translations which have irregular inflections. The Russian-English side of the dictionary gives inflectional information.

snuggle ['snʌgl] *vi*: **to ~ up to sb** прижима́ться (прижа́ться* *perf*) к кому́-н; **to ~ down in bed** забива́ться (заби́ться* *perf*) под одея́ло.
snugly ['snʌglɪ] *adv* ую́тно; **to fit ~** (*object in pocket etc*) удо́бно помеща́ться *(impf)*; **the sweater fits ~** сви́тер хорошо́ прилега́ет.
SO *n abbr* (*COMM*) = **standing order.**

KEYWORD

so [səu] *adv* **1** (*thus, likewise*): **so saying he walked away** с э́тими слова́ми, он ушёл; **while she was so doing, he ...** пока́ она́ э́то де́лала, он ...; **if so** е́сли да; **if this is so** е́сли э́то так; **I didn't do it – you did so!** э́то не я (сде́лал) – нет, ты!; **I like him – so do I** мне он нра́вится – мне то́же; **I'm still at school – so am I** я ещё учу́сь в шко́ле – я то́же; **he has a brother – so has David** у него́ есть брат – у Дави́да то́же; **so it is!** да, действи́тельно!; **I hope/think so** наде́юсь/ду́маю, что да; **so far I haven't had any problems** пока́ что у меня́ не́ было пробле́м; **how do you like the book so far?** ну как, нра́вится Вам кни́га?
2 (*in comparisons etc*: *+adv*) насто́лько, так; (*+adj*) насто́лько, тако́й; **so quickly (that)** насто́лько *or* так бы́стро(, что); **the house is so big (that)** дом насто́лько *or* тако́й большо́й(, что); **she's not so clever as her brother** она́ не так умна́, как её брат; **I'm so glad to see you** я так рад Вас ви́деть:
3: **I've got so much work** у меня́ так мно́го рабо́ты; **I love you so much** я Вас так люблю́; **thank you so much** спаси́бо Вам большо́е; **there are so many books I would like to read** сто́лько есть книг, кото́рые я бы хоте́л проче́сть
4 (*phrases*): **ten or so** о́коло десяти́; **so long!** (*inf*: *goodbye*) пока́!
◆ *conj* **1** (*expressing purpose*): **so as to do** что́бы сде́лать *(perf)*; **I brought this wine so that you could try it** я принёс э́то вино́, что́бы Вы могли́ его́ попро́бовать
2 (*expressing result*) так что; **so I was right after all** так что, я был всё-таки прав; **so you see, I could have stayed** так что ви́дите, я мог бы оста́ться; **so, what shall we do now** так, что тепе́рь бу́дем де́лать.

soak [səuk] *vt* (*drench*) промочи́ть* *(perf)*; (*steep in water*) зама́чивать (замочи́ть* *perf*) ◆ *vi* (*washing, dishes*) отмока́ть *(impf)*; **to be ~ed through** промо́кнуть *(perf)* насквозь
▸ **soak in** *vi* впи́тываться (впита́ться *perf*)
▸ **soak up** *vt* впи́тывать (впита́ть *perf*) (в себя́).
soaking ['səukɪŋ] *adj* (*also:* **~ wet**) мо́крый насквозь.
so-and-so ['səuənsəu] *n* (*somebody*) не́кто*; **Mr ~** Господи́н тако́й-то; **you little ~!** (*pej*) ах ты тако́й-сяко́й!
soap [səup] *n* мы́ло*; (*TV*: *also:* **~ opera**) мы́льная о́пера.
soapbox ['səupbɔks] *n* (*container*) я́щик из-под мы́ла; (*platform*) импровизи́рованная трибу́на.
soap flakes *npl* мы́льные хло́пья *pl*.
soap opera *n* (*TV*) мы́льная о́пера.
soap powder *n* мы́льный порошо́к*.
soapsuds ['səupsʌds] *npl* мы́льная пе́на *fsg*.
soapy ['səupɪ] *adj* мы́льный.
soar [sɔːʳ] *vi* (*bird, rocket*) взвива́ться (взви́ться* *perf*) в во́здух; (*price, production, temperature*) ре́зко подска́кивать (подскочи́ть* *perf*); (*building etc*) возвыша́ться *(impf)*.
soaring ['sɔːrɪŋ] *adj* (*prices, inflation*) неуправля́емый.
sob [sɔb] *n* рыда́ние ◆ *vi* рыда́ть *(impf)*, всхли́пывать *(impf)*.
s.o.b. *n abbr* (*US*: *inf!*: = *son of a bitch*) су́кин сын* (*!*)
sober ['səubəʳ] *adj* тре́звый* (трезв); (*colour, style*) небро́ский*
▸ **sober up** *vt* протрезви́ть* *(perf)* ◆ *vi* трезве́ть *(impf)*, протрезвля́ться (протрезви́ться* *perf*).
sobriety [sə'braɪətɪ] *n* тре́звость *f*.
sobriquet ['səubrɪkeɪ] *n* (*nickname*) про́звище.
sob story *n* душещипа́тельная исто́рия.
Soc. *abbr* = **society**.
so-called ['səu'kɔːld] *adj* так называ́емый.
soccer ['sɔkəʳ] *n* футбо́л.
soccer pitch *n* футбо́льное по́ле*.
soccer player *n* футболи́ст.
sociable ['səuʃəbl] *adj* (*person*) общи́тельный* (общи́телен); (*behaviour*) све́тский*.
social ['səuʃl] *adj* (*history, structure etc*) обще́ственный, социа́льный; (*event*) све́тский*; (*sociable*: *animal*) ста́дный ◆ *n* (*party*) встре́ча, ве́чер*; **he has a good ~ life** он мно́го обща́ется с людьми́.
social class *n* социа́льный класс.
social climber *n челове́к, стремя́щийся заня́ть бо́лее высо́кое социа́льное положе́ние.*
social club *n* клуб обще́ния.
social democrat *n* (*POL*) социа́л-демокра́т.
social insurance *n* (*US*) социа́льное обеспе́чение *or* страхова́ние.
socialism ['səuʃəlɪzəm] *n* социали́зм.
socialist ['səuʃəlɪst] *n* социали́ст ◆ *adj* социалисти́ческий*.
socialite ['səuʃəlaɪt] *n* све́тский* челове́к*.
socialize ['səuʃəlaɪz] *vi*: **to ~ (with)** обща́ться (пообща́ться *perf*) (с *+instr*).
socially ['səuʃəlɪ] *adv*: **to visit sb ~** зайти́* *(perf)* к кому́-н по-дру́жески; **~ acceptable** социа́льно прие́млемый.
social science *n* (*SCOL*) обще́ственные нау́ки *fpl*.
social security (*BRIT*) *n* социа́льное обеспе́чение; **Department of S~ S~** Министе́рство социа́льного обеспе́чения.
social services *npl* систе́ма *fsg* социа́льного обслу́живания.
social welfare *n* социа́льное обеспе́чение.

social work *n* социа́льная рабо́та.
social worker *n* социа́льный рабо́тник.
society [sə'saɪətɪ] *n* о́бщество ◆ *cpd* (*party*) све́тский*.
socioeconomic ['səusɪəui:kə'nɔmɪk] *adj* (*group, factor*) социа́льно-экономи́ческий*.
sociological [səusɪə'lɔdʒɪkl] *adj* (*study*) социологи́ческий.
sociologist [səusɪ'ɔlədʒɪst] *n* социо́лог.
sociology [səusɪ'ɔlədʒɪ] *n* социоло́гия.
sock [sɔk] *n* носо́к* ◆ *vt* (*inf*): **to ~ sb in the face** дава́ть* (дать* *perf*) кому́-н по физионо́мии; **to pull one's ~s up** (*fig*) подтяну́ться* (*perf*).
socket ['sɔkɪt] *n* глазни́ца; (*BRIT*: *ELEC*: *in wall*) розе́тка*; (: *for light bulb*) патро́н.
sod [sɔd] *n* (*of earth*) дёрн; (*BRIT*: *inf!*) дрянь *f* така́я (*!*)
▸ **sod off** *vi* (*inf!*): **~ off** убира́йся отсю́да!, иди́ на́ фиг!
soda ['səudə] *n* (*CHEM*) со́да; (*also*: **~ water**) со́довая *f adj*; (*US*: *also*: **~ pop**) газиро́ванная вода́.
sodden ['sɔdn] *adj* прокля́тый.
sodium ['səudɪəm] *n* на́трий.
sodium chloride *n* хлори́д на́трия.
sofa ['səufə] *n* дива́н.
Sofia ['səufɪə] *n* Софи́я.
soft [sɔft] *adj* мя́гкий* (мя́гок); (*music*) негро́мкий* (негро́мок); **don't be ~!** (*inf*: *stupid*) не будь дурако́м!
soft-boiled ['sɔftbɔɪld] *adj*: **~ egg** яйцо́* всмя́тку.
soft currency *n* неконверти́руемая валю́та.
soft drink *n* безалкого́льный напи́ток*, сок*.
soft drugs *npl* мя́гкие нарко́тики *mpl*.
soften ['sɔfn] *vt* смягча́ть (смягчи́ть *perf*) ◆ *vi* смягча́ться (смягчи́ться *perf*).
softener ['sɔfnəʳ] *n* (*also*: **water ~**) *хими́ческое сре́дство, смягча́ющее во́ду*; (*also*: **fabric ~**) *смягча́ющее сре́дство для сти́рки.*
soft fruit *n* (*BRIT*) я́годы *fpl*.
soft furnishings *npl* мя́гкая оби́вка *fsg*.
softhearted [sɔft'hɑ:tɪd] *adj* мягкосерде́чный* (мягкосерде́чен).
softly ['sɔftlɪ] *adv* (*gently*) мя́гко; (*quietly*) ти́хо.
softness ['sɔftnɪs] *n* мя́гкость *f*.
soft option *n* лёгкий путь* *m*.
soft sell *n* (*COMM*) *мя́гкая та́ктика сбы́та проду́кции.*
soft spot *n*: **to have a ~ ~ for sb** пита́ть (*impf*) к кому́-н сла́бость.
soft target *n* лёгкая добы́ча.
soft toy *n* мя́гкая игру́шка*.
software ['sɔftwɛəʳ] *n* (*COMPUT*) програ́ммное обеспе́чение.
software package *n* (*COMPUT*) паке́т програ́мм.
soft water *n* мя́гкая вода́.
soggy ['sɔgɪ] *adj* (*ground*) сыро́й; (*sandwiches*) размо́кший.
soil [sɔɪl] *n* (*earth*) по́чва; (*territory*) земля́* ◆ *vt* па́чкать (запа́чкать *or* испа́чкать *perf*); (*fig*) мара́ть (замара́ть *perf*).
soiled [sɔɪld] *adj* испа́чканный (испа́чкан); (*COMM*) повреждённый.
sojourn ['sɔdʒə:n] *n* пребыва́ние.
solace ['sɔlɪs] *n* утеше́ние.
solar ['səuləʳ] *adj* со́лнечный.
solaria [sə'lɛərɪə] *npl of* **solarium**.
solarium [sə'lɛərɪəm] (*pl* **solaria**) *n* соля́рий.
solar panel *n* со́лнечная батаре́я.
solar plexus [-'plɛksəs] *n* со́лнечное сплете́ние.
solar power *n* со́лнечная эне́ргия.
solar system *n* со́лнечная систе́ма.
solar wind *n* со́лнечная бу́ря.
sold [səuld] *pt, pp of* **sell**.
solder ['səuldəʳ] *vt* пая́ть (*impf*), спа́ивать (спая́ть *perf*) ◆ *n* припо́й.
soldier ['səuldʒəʳ] *n* (*not officer*) солда́т*; (*in army*) вое́нный *m adj* ◆ *vi*: **to ~ on** не сдава́ться* (*impf*); **toy ~** солда́тик.
sold out *adj* распро́данный (распро́дан).
sole [səul] *n* (*of foot*) подо́шва; (*of shoe*) подо́шва, подмётка* ◆ *n inv* (*fish*) па́лтус ◆ *adj* (*unique*) еди́нственный; (*exclusive*) исключи́тельный; **the ~ reason** еди́нственная причи́на.
solely ['səullɪ] *adv* то́лько; **I will hold you ~ responsible** вся отве́тственность ля́жет то́лько на Вас.
solemn ['sɔləm] *adj* торже́ственный* (торже́ствен).
sole trader *n* (*COMM*) единоли́чный торго́вец*.
solicit [sə'lɪsɪt] *vt* (*request*) обраща́ться (обрати́ться* *perf*) с про́сьбой за *+instr* ◆ *vi* (*prostitute*) предлага́ть (*impf*) себя́.
solicitor [sə'lɪsɪtəʳ] *n* (*BRIT*) адвока́т.
solid ['sɔlɪd] *adj* (*not hollow*) це́льный; (*not liquid*) твёрдый; (*reliable*) непоколеби́мый (непоколеби́м); (*meal*) пло́тный; (*vote*) сплочённый; (*entire*) це́лый; (*gold*) чи́стый ◆ *n* (*solid object*) твёрдое те́ло*; **~s** *npl* (*food*) твёрдая пи́ща *fsg*; (*for babies*) прико́рм *msg*; **to be on ~ ground** (*fig*) твёрдо стоя́ть (*impf*) на нога́х; **we waited two ~ hours** мы прожда́ли це́лых два часа́.
solidarity [sɔlɪ'dærɪtɪ] *n* солида́рность *f*.
solid fuel *n* твёрдое то́пливо.
solidify [sə'lɪdɪfaɪ] *vi* (*fat etc*) застыва́ть (засты́ть* *perf*); (*metal*) затвердева́ть (затверде́ть *perf*) ◆ *vt* де́лать (*impf*) твёрдым.
solidity [sə'lɪdɪtɪ] *n* твёрдость *f*.
solidly ['sɔlɪdlɪ] *adv* (*built*) кре́пко; (*respectable*) соли́дно; (*in favour*) по́лностью.

solid-state ['sɔlɪdsteɪt] *adj* (*ELEC*) твёрдый, в твёрдом состоя́нии.
soliloquy [sə'lɪləkwɪ] *n* моноло́г.
solitaire [sɔlɪ'tɛəʳ] *n* (*gem*) солите́р; (*game*) пасья́нс.
solitary ['sɔlɪtərɪ] *adj* одино́кий* (одино́к); (*isolated*) уединённый; (*single*) едини́чный.
solitary confinement *n* одино́чное заключе́ние; **to be in ~ ~** находи́ться* *(impf)* в одино́чном заключе́нии.
solitude ['sɔlɪtju:d] *n* одино́чество, уедине́ние; **to live in ~** жить* *(impf)* в уедине́нии.
solo ['səuləu] *n* со́ло *nt ind* ◆ *adv* (*fly*) в одино́чку; (*play*) со́ло.
soloist ['səuləuɪst] *n* соли́ст*(ка).
Solomon Islands ['sɔləmən-] *npl*: **the ~ ~** Соломо́новы острова́ *mpl*.
solstice ['sɔlstɪs] *n* солнцестоя́ние.
soluble ['sɔljubl] *adj* раствори́мый.
solution [sə'lu:ʃən] *n* (*answer*) реше́ние; (*liquid*) раство́р.
solve [sɔlv] *vt* (*puzzle*) реша́ть (реши́ть *perf*); (*problem*) разреша́ть (разреши́ть *perf*); (*mystery*) раскрыва́ть (раскры́ть* *perf*).
solvency ['sɔlvənsɪ] *n* платёжеспосо́бность *f*.
solvent ['sɔlvənt] *adj* (*COMM*) платёжеспосо́бный ◆ *n* (*CHEM*) раствори́тель *m*.
solvent abuse *n* токсикома́ния.
Som. *abbr* (*BRIT: POST*) = *Somerset*.
Somali [sə'mɑ:lɪ] *adj* сомали́йский ◆ *n* сомали́ец*(-и́йка*).
Somalia [sə'mɑ:lɪə] *n* Сомали́ *nt ind*.
sombre ['sɔmbəʳ] (*US* **somber**) *adj* мра́чный* (мра́чен).

KEYWORD

some [sʌm] *adj* ***1*** (*a certain amount or number of*): **would you like some tea/biscuits?** хоти́те ча́ю/пече́нья?; **there's some milk in the fridge** в холоди́льнике есть молоко́; **he asked me some questions** он за́дал мне не́сколько вопро́сов; **there are some people waiting to see you** Вас ждут каки́е-то лю́ди; **I've got some money, but not much** у меня́ есть де́ньги, но немно́го
2 (*certain: in contrasts*) не́который; **some people say that ...** не́которые говоря́т, что ...
3 (*unspecified*) како́й-то; **some woman phoned you this afternoon** Вам сего́дня днём звони́ла кака́я-то же́нщина; **we'll meet again some day** мы когда́-нибудь опя́ть встре́тимся; **shall we meet some day next week?** встре́тимся ка́к-нибудь на той *or* сле́дующей неде́ле?
◆ *pron* (*a certain number: people*) одни́; **I've got some** у меня́ есть; **some took the bus, and some walked** одни́ пое́хали на авто́бусе, а други́е пошли́ пешко́м, кто́-то пое́хал на авто́бусе, кто́-то пошёл пешко́м; **who would like a piece of cake? – I'd like some** кто хо́чет кусо́к то́рта? – я с удово́льствием; **I've read some of the book** я прочёл часть кни́ги
◆ *adv*: **some ten people** челове́к де́сять.

somebody ['sʌmbədɪ] *pron* = **someone**.
someday ['sʌmdeɪ] *adv* когда́-нибудь.
somehow ['sʌmhau] *adv* (*in some way*) ка́к-нибудь; (*for some reason*) почему́-то, каки́м-то о́бразом.
someone ['sʌmwʌn] *pron* (*specific person*) кто́-то; (*unspecified person*) кто́-нибудь; **I saw ~ in the garden** я ви́дел кого́-то в саду́; **~ will help you** Вам кто́-нибудь помо́жет.
someplace ['sʌmpleɪs] *adv* (*US*) = **somewhere**.
somersault ['sʌməsɔ:lt] *n* (*in the air*) са́льто *nt ind*; (*on the ground*) кувыро́к* ◆ *vi* кувырка́ться *(impf)*, перекувырну́ться *(perf)*.
something ['sʌmθɪŋ] *pron* (*something specific*) что́-то; (*something unspecified*) что́-нибудь; **there's ~ wrong with my car** у меня́ что́-то случи́лось с маши́ной; **would you like ~ to eat/drink?** хоти́те чего́-нибудь пое́сть/вы́пить?; **I have ~ for you** у меня́ ко́е-что для Вас есть.
sometime ['sʌmtaɪm] *adv* (*in future*) когда́-нибудь; (*in past*): **~ last month** где́-то в про́шлом ме́сяце; **I'll finish it ~** когда́-нибудь я э́то зако́нчу.
sometimes ['sʌmtaɪmz] *adv* иногда́.
somewhat ['sʌmwɔt] *adv* не́сколько.
somewhere ['sʌmwɛəʳ] *adv* (*be: somewhere specific*) где́-то; (*: anywhere*) где́-нибудь; (*go: somewhere specific*) куда́-то; (*: anywhere*) куда́-нибудь; (*come from*) отку́да-то; **it's ~ or other in Scotland** э́то где́-то в Шотла́ндии; **is there a post office ~ around here?** здесь где́-нибудь есть по́чта?; **let's go ~ else** дава́йте пое́дем куда́-нибудь в друго́е ме́сто.
son [sʌn] *n* сын*.
sonar ['səunɑ:ʳ] *n* (*NAUT*) гидролока́тор, эхоло́т.
sonata [sə'nɑ:tə] *n* сона́та.
song [sɔŋ] *n* пе́сня*.
song book *n* сбо́рник пе́сен, пе́сенник.
songwriter ['sɔŋraɪtəʳ] *n* (компози́тор-)пе́сенник, (поэ́т-)пе́сенник.
sonic ['sɔnɪk] *adj* звуково́й.
son-in-law ['sʌnɪnlɔ:] *n* зять* *m*.
sonnet ['sɔnɪt] *n* соне́т.
sonny ['sʌnɪ] *n* (*inf*) сыно́к*.
soon [su:n] *adv* (*in a short time*) ско́ро; (*early*) ра́но; **~ (afterwards)** вско́ре; **quite ~** дово́льно ско́ро; **how ~ can you do it/come back?** когда́ Вы смо́жете э́то сде́лать/верну́ться?; **see you ~!** до ско́рого!; *see also* **as**.
sooner ['su:nəʳ] *adv* (*time*) скоре́е; (*preference*): **I would ~ do that** я бы скоре́е сде́лал э́то; **~ or later** ра́но или по́здно; **the ~ the better** чем скоре́е, тем лу́чше; **no ~ said than done** ска́зано-сде́лано; **no ~ had we left than ...** не

успéли мы уйти́, как ....
soot [sut] *n* сáжа.
soothe [su:ð] *vt* успокáивать (успокóить *perf*).
soothing ['su:ðɪŋ] *adj* (*ointment, drink, bath*) успокои́тельный; (*tone, words etc*) утеши́тельный* (утеши́телен).
SOP *n abbr* (= *standard operating procedure*) стандáртная рабóчая процеду́ра.
sop [sɔp] *n*: **that's only a ~** э́то тóлько подáчка.
sophisticated [sə'fɪstɪkeɪtɪd] *adj* изощрённый* (изощрён); (*woman*) изы́сканная (изы́скана).
sophistication [səfɪstɪ'keɪʃən] *n* (*see adj*) изощрённость *f*; изы́сканность *f*.
sophomore ['sɔfəmɔ:ʳ] *n* (*US*: *SCOL*) второку́рсник(-ица).
soporific [sɔpə'rɪfɪk] *adj* (*speech*) усыпля́ющий; (*drug*) снотвóрный ◆ *n* снотвóрное *nt adj*.
sopping ['sɔpɪŋ] *adj*: **~ (wet)** (*hair, clothes etc*) промóкший насквóзь.
soppy ['sɔpɪ] *adj* (*pej*) душещипáтельный, сентиментáльный.
soprano [sə'prɑ:nəu] *n* сопрáно *f ind*.
sorbet ['sɔ:beɪ] *n* (*CULIN*) фруктóвое морóженое *nt adj*.
sorcerer ['sɔ:sərəʳ] *n* колду́н*.
sordid ['sɔ:dɪd] *adj* (*place*) загáженный (загáжен); (*story etc*) гну́сный* (гну́сен).
sore [sɔ:ʳ] *n* я́зва, боля́чка* ◆ *adj* (*esp US*: *offended*) оби́женный* (оби́жен); (*painful*): **my arm is ~, I've got a ~ arm** у меня́ боли́т рукá; **it's a ~ point** (*fig*) э́то болéзненный предмéт.
sorely ['sɔ:lɪ] *adv*: **I am ~ tempted (to)** у меня́ большóй соблáзн (+*infin*).
soreness ['sɔ:nɪs] *n* боль *f*.
sorrel ['sɔrəl] *n* щавéль* *m*.
sorrow ['sɔrəu] *n* (*regret*) печáль* *f*, грусть *f*; **~s** *npl* (*troubles*) печáли *fpl*.
sorrowful ['sɔrəuful] *adj* печáльный* (печáлен).
sorry ['sɔrɪ] *adj* (*condition, excuse, sight*) плачéвный* (плачéвен); (*regretful*): **I'm ~** мне жаль; **~!** (*apology*) извини́те, пожáлуйста!; **~?** (*pardon*) прости́те?; **I feel ~ for him** мне егó жáлко; **I'm ~ to hear that ...** мне гру́стно слы́шать, что ...; **to be ~ about sth** сожалéть (*impf*) о чём-н.
sort [sɔ:t] *n* сорт*; (*of car etc*) тип ◆ *vt* (*also*: **~ out**: *papers, mail, belongings*) разбирáть (разобрáть* *perf*); (: *problems*) разбирáться (разобрáться* *perf*) в +*prp*; (*COMPUT*) сортировáть (*impf*); **what ~ do you want?** какóй сорт Вы хоти́те?; **what ~ of car?** какáя маши́на?; **I'll do nothing of the ~!** я не собирáюсь дéлать ничегó подóбного; **it's ~ of awkward** (*inf*) э́то как-то неудóбно.
sortie ['sɔ:tɪ] *n* (*MIL*: *on the ground*) вы́лазка*; (: *by air*) вы́лет; (*fig*) вы́лазка*.
sorting office ['sɔ:tɪŋ-] *n* (*POST*) сортирóвочное отделéние.
SOS *n abbr* (= *save our souls*) SOS.
so-so ['səusəu] *adv* так себé.
soufflé ['su:fleɪ] *n* суфлé *nt ind*.
sought [sɔ:t] *pt, pp of* **seek**.
sought-after ['sɔ:tɑ:ftəʳ] *adj* (*person, thing*) пóльзующийся спрóсом; **a much ~ item** вещь, пóльзующаяся бóльшим спрóсом.
soul [səul] *n* душá*; (*music*) (му́зыка) "соул"; **the poor ~ had nowhere to sleep** несчáстному нéгде бы́ло спать; **I didn't see a ~** я не ви́дел ни души́.
soul-destroying ['səuldɪstrɔɪɪŋ] *adj*: **this work is ~** э́та рабóта вымáтывает ду́шу.
soulful ['səulful] *adj* проникновéнный.
soulless ['səullɪs] *adj* (*place*) мёртвый (мёртв); **this is a ~ task** э́то иссушáет ду́шу.
soul mate *n* роднáя душá*.
soul-searching ['səulsə:tʃɪŋ] *n*: **after much ~, I decided ...** пóсле дóлгих душéвных пóисков я реши́л ....
sound [saund] *adj* (*healthy*) здорóвый; (*safe, not damaged*) прóчный* (прóчен), цéлый (цел); (*secure*: *investment*) надёжный* (надё жен); (*reliable, thorough*) соли́дный* (соли́ден); (*sensible*: *advice*) разу́мный* (разу́мен); (*valid*: *argument*) вéский*; (: *policy*) здравомы́слящий*; (: *claim*) основáтельный ◆ *n* звук; (*GEO*) зонд ◆ *vt* (*alarm*) поднимáть (подня́ть* *perf*) ◆ *vi* звучáть (прозвучáть *perf*) ◆ *adv*: **he is ~ asleep** он крéпко спит; **to be of ~ mind** быть* (*impf*) в здрáвом умé; **I don't like the ~ of it** э́то мне не нрáвится; **to ~ one's horn** (*AUT*) сигнáлить (*impf*); **to ~ like** звучáть (прозвучáть *perf*) как (бу́дто); **it ~s like Russian** похóже на ру́сский; **that ~s like them arriving** слы́шите, похóже они́ приéхали; **it ~s as if ...** похóже, что ...;, похóже как бу́дто ...
▸ **sound off** *vi* (*inf*): **to ~ off (about)** вы́сказаться* (*perf*) (о +*prp*)
▸ **sound out** *vt* (*person, opinion*) зонди́ровать (прозонди́ровать *perf*).
sound barrier *n* звуковóй барьéр.
sound effects *npl* звуковы́е эффéкты *mpl*.
sound engineer *n* звукорежиссёр.
sounding ['saundɪŋ] *n* (*NAUT etc*) промéр глубины́.
sounding board *n* (*MUS*) дéка; **to use sb as a ~ ~ for one's ideas** проверя́ть (провéрить *perf*) свои́ идéи на ком-н.
soundly ['saundlɪ] *adv* (*sleep*) крéпко; (*beat etc*) здóрово.
soundproof ['saundpru:f] *adj* звуконепроницáемый (звуконепроницáем)

* marks translations which have irregular inflections The Russian-English side of the dictionary gives inflectional information.

◆ *vt* звукоизоли́ровать *(impf/perf)*.
sound system *n* (*TECH*) (звукова́я) систе́ма.
soundtrack ['saundtræk] *n* му́зыка (*из кинофи́льма*).
sound wave *n* звукова́я волна́*.
soup [su:p] *n* суп*; **to be in the** ~ (*fig*) попада́ть (попа́сть* *perf*) в передря́гу.
soup course *n* пе́рвое *nt adj*.
soup kitchen *n* столо́вая *f adj* для бе́дных, супова́я ку́хня.
soup plate *n* глубо́кая таре́лка*.
soupspoon ['su:pspu:n] *n* столо́вая ло́жка*.
sour ['sauə'] *adj* ки́слый; (*fig: bad-tempered*) неприя́зненный* (неприя́знен); **to go** *or* **turn** ~ скиса́ть (ски́снуть* *perf*); (*fig*) по́ртиться* (испо́ртиться* *perf*); **it's** ~ **grapes** (*fig*) э́то за́висть.
source [sɔ:s] *n* (*also fig*) исто́чник; **I have it from a reliable** ~ **that** ... у меня́ есть све́дения из надёжного исто́чника, что ....
south [sauθ] *n* юг *m* ◆ *adj* ю́жный ◆ *adv* (*go*) на юг; (*be*) на ю́ге; **(to the)** ~ **of** к ю́гу от *+gen*; **to travel** ~ е́хать*/е́здить* *(impf)* на юг; **the S~ of France** Юг Фра́нции.
South Africa *n* Ю́жная А́фрика.
South African *adj* южноафрика́нский ◆ *n* южноафрика́нец*(-нка*).
South America *n* Ю́жная Аме́рика.
South American *adj* южноамерика́нский ◆ *n* южноамерика́нец*(-нка*).
southbound ['sauθbaund] *adj* (*traffic*) дви́жущийся в ю́жном направле́нии; (*train, carriageway*) ю́жного направле́ния.
southeast [sauθ'i:st] *n* ю́го-восто́к.
Southeast Asia *n* Ю́го-восто́чная А́зия.
southerly ['sʌðəlɪ] *adj* обращённый к ю́гу; (*wind*) ю́жный.
southern ['sʌðən] *adj* ю́жный; **a room with a** ~ **aspect** ко́мната, выходя́щая на юг; **the** ~ **hemisphere** ю́жное полуша́рие.
South Korea *n* Ю́жная Коре́я.
South Pole *n*: **the** ~ ~ Ю́жный по́люс.
South Sea Islands *npl*: **the** ~ ~ ~ острова́ *mpl* ю́жной ча́сти Ти́хого Океа́на.
South Seas *npl*: **the** ~ ~ ю́жная часть *f* Ти́хого Океа́на.
southward(s) ['sauθwəd(z)] *adv* на юг, в ю́жном направле́нии.
southwest [sauθ'wɛst] *n* ю́го-за́пад.
souvenir [su:və'nɪə'] *n* сувени́р.
sovereign ['sɔvrɪn] *n* (*ruler*) госуда́рь(-рыня) *m(f)*.
sovereignty ['sɔvrɪntɪ] *n* суверените́т.
Soviet ['səuvɪət] *adj* сове́тский* ◆ *n* (*person*) сове́тский* челове́к; **the** ~ **Union** Сове́тский* Сою́з.
sow[1] [sau] *n* (*pig*) свинья́*, свинома́тка*.
sow[2] [səu] (*pt* **sowed**, *pp* **sown**) *vt* (*also fig*) се́ять (посе́ять *perf*).
sown [səun] *pp of* **sow**[2].
soya ['sɔɪə] (*US* **soy**) *n*: ~ **bean/sauce** со́евый боб/со́ус.
sozzled ['sɔzld] *adj* (*inf*) под му́хой.
spa [spɑ:] *n* (*town*) куро́ртный го́род*; (*US: also:* **health** ~) лече́бно-оздорови́тельный куро́рт.
space [speɪs] *n* (*gap*) простра́нство; (*place: small*) ме́сто*; (: *large*) простра́нство; (*room*) ме́сто*; (*beyond Earth*) ко́смос; (*interval, period*) промежу́ток* ◆ *cpd* косми́ческий* ◆ *vt* (*also:* ~ **out**: *text*) разбива́ть (разби́ть* *perf*); (: *payments, visits*) распределя́ть (распредели́ть *perf*); **to clear a** ~ **for sth** расчища́ть (расчи́стить* *perf*) ме́сто для чего́-н; **in a confined** ~ в ограни́ченном простра́нстве; **in a short** ~ **of time** в коро́ткий промежу́ток вре́мени; **(with)in the** ~ **of an hour** в тече́ние ча́са.
space-bar ['speɪsbɑ:'] *n* (*TYP*) интерва́л.
spacecraft ['speɪskrɑ:ft] *n* косми́ческий* кора́бль* *m*.
spaceman ['speɪsmæn] *irreg n* космона́вт.
spaceship ['speɪsʃɪp] *n* = **spacecraft**.
space shuttle *n космический кора́бль многора́зового испо́льзования*.
spacesuit ['speɪssu:t] *n* скафа́ндр.
spacewoman ['speɪswumən] *irreg n* же́нщина-космона́вт.
spacing ['speɪsɪŋ] *n* (*TYP*) промежу́тки *mpl*, интерва́лы *mpl*; **single/double** ~ (*TYP*) с одни́м/двойны́м интерва́лом.
spacious ['speɪʃəs] *adj* просто́рный* (просто́рен).
spade [speɪd] *n* (*tool*) лопа́та; (*child's*) лопа́тка*; ~**s** *npl* (*CARDS*) пи́ки *fpl*.
spadework ['speɪdwə:k] *n* (*fig*) чернова́я рабо́та.
spaghetti [spə'gɛtɪ] *n* спаге́тти *pl ind*.
Spain [speɪn] *n* Испа́ния.
span [spæn] *pt of* **spin** ◆ *n* (*of hand, wings*) разма́х; (*of bridge*) пролёт; (*in time*) промежу́ток* ◆ *vt* (*river*) переки́нуть *(perf)* че́рез *+acc*; (*fig: time*) охва́тывать (охвати́ть* *perf*).
Spaniard ['spænjəd] *n* испа́нец*(-нка*).
spaniel ['spænjəl] *n* спание́ль *m*.
Spanish ['spænɪʃ] *adj* испа́нский* ◆ *n* (*LING*) испа́нский* язы́к*; **the** ~ *npl* испа́нцы *mpl*; ~ **omelette** омле́т по-испа́нски.
spank [spæŋk] *vt* шлёпать (отшлёпать *perf*).
spanner ['spænə'] *n* (*BRIT*) га́ечный ключ*.
spar [spɑ:'] *n* (*pole*) шта́нга ◆ *vi* (*BOXING*) спарринговáть *(impf)*.
spare [spɛə'] *adj* (*free: time, seat*) свобо́дный* (свобо́ден); (*surplus*) ли́шний*; (*reserve*) запасно́й ◆ *n* = **spare part** ◆ *vt* (*trouble, expense, effort*) избавля́ть (изба́вить* *perf*) от *+gen*; (*refrain from using: energy, water etc*) бере́чь* (сбере́чь* *perf*); (*make available: person, time, money*) выделя́ть (вы́делить *perf*); (*afford to give: money*) дава́ть* (дать* *perf*); (*refrain from hurting: person, city etc*)

щади́ть* (пощади́ть* *perf*); **to have some time to ~** име́ть *(impf)* свобо́дное вре́мя; **to have money to ~** име́ть *(impf)* ли́шние де́ньги; **these 2 are going ~** э́ти два – ли́шние; **to ~ no expense** не жале́ть (пожале́ть *perf*) средств; **can you ~ the time?** у Вас найдётся вре́мя?; **I've a few minutes to ~** у меня́ есть не́сколько мину́т; **there is no time to ~** у нас нет ли́шнего вре́мени; **can you ~ ten pounds?** у Вас не найдётся десяти́ фу́нтов?

spare part *n* запча́сть *f*= *запасна́я часть*.

spare room *n* свобо́дная ко́мната.

spare time *n* свобо́дное вре́мя* *nt*.

spare tyre *n* запасна́я ши́на.

spare wheel *n* запасно́е колесо́*.

sparing ['spɛərɪŋ] *adj*: **he is ~ with his money** он эконо́мен с деньга́ми; **he was ~ with his praise** он был ску́п на похвалу́.

sparingly ['spɛərɪŋlɪ] *adv* эконо́мно.

spark [spɑːk] *n* (*also fig*) и́скра.

spark(ing) plug ['spɑːk(ɪŋ)-] *n* запа́льная свеча́*.

sparkle ['spɑːkl] *n* блеск ◆ *vi* (*diamonds, water*) сверка́ть (сверкну́ть *perf*); (*eyes*) блесте́ть* *(impf)*; (*bubble*) шипе́ть* *(impf)*.

sparkler ['spɑːkləʳ] *n* (*firework*) бенга́льский ого́нь* *m*.

sparkling ['spɑːklɪŋ] *adj* (*wine*) игри́стый; (*conversation, performance*) блестя́щий*.

sparring partner ['spɑːrɪŋ-] *n* (*BOXING*) партнёр для трениро́вок в бо́ксе.

sparrow ['spærəu] *n* воробе́й*.

sparse [spɑːs] *adj* ре́дкий* (ре́док).

spartan ['spɑːtən] *adj* спарта́нский.

spasm ['spæzəm] *n* (*MED*) спазм; (*of anger etc*) при́ступ.

spasmodic [spæz'mɔdɪk] *adj* (*fig*) спазмати́ческий.

spastic ['spæstɪk] *n* (*MED*) парали́тик ◆ *adj* (*MED*) спасти́ческий.

spat [spæt] *pt, pp of* **spit** ◆ *n* (*US*: *quarrel*) размо́лвка*.

spate [speɪt] *n* (*fig*): **a ~ of** пото́к* *+gen*; **the river is in ~** река́ взду́лась.

spatial ['speɪʃl] *adj* простра́нственный.

spatter ['spætəʳ] *vt* бры́згать (бры́знуть *perf*) ◆ *vi* обры́згаться (обры́знуться *perf*).

spatula ['spætjulə] *n* (*MED*) шпа́тель *m*; (*CULIN*) лопа́тка*.

spawn [spɔːn] *vi* (*fish etc*) мета́ть* *(impf)* икру́ ◆ *vt* (*fig*) порожда́ть (породи́ть* *perf*) ◆ *n* икра́.

SPCA *n abbr* (*US*) = *Society for the Prevention of Cruelty to Animals.*

SPCC *n abbr* (*US*) = *Society for the Prevention of Cruelty to Children.*

speak [spiːk] (*pt* **spoke**, *pp* **spoken**) *vi* (*use voice*) говори́ть *(impf)*; (*make a speech*) выступа́ть (вы́ступить* *perf*) ◆ *vt* (*truth*) говори́ть (сказа́ть* *perf*); **to ~ to sb** разгова́ривать *(impf)* с кем-н; **to ~ of** *or* **about** говори́ть *(impf)* о *+prp*; **he has no money to ~ of** у него́ о́чень немно́го де́нег; **~ up!** говори́те гро́мче!; **to ~ at a conference/in a debate** выступа́ть (вы́ступить* *perf*) на конфере́нции/в деба́тах; **to ~ Russian/several languages** говори́ть *(impf)* по-ру́сски/на не́скольких языка́х; **to ~ one's mind** выска́зывать (вы́сказать* *perf*) своё мне́ние

▸ **speak for** *vt fus*: **to ~ for sb** говори́ть *(impf)* за кого́-н; **that picture is already spoken for** (*already sold*) э́ту карти́ну уже́ сторгова́ли.

speaker ['spiːkəʳ] *n* (*in public*) ора́тор; (*also:* **loudspeaker**) громкоговори́тель *m*; (*POL*): **the S~** спи́кер; **are you a Welsh ~?** Вы говори́те по-уэ́льски?

speaking ['spiːkɪŋ] *adj* говоря́щий; **Italian-~ people** италоговоря́щие *pl adj*; **we are no longer on ~ terms** мы бо́льше не обща́емся.

spear [spɪəʳ] *n* копьё* ◆ *vt* пронза́ть (пронзи́ть* *perf*) копьём.

spearhead ['spɪəhɛd] *vt* возглавля́ть (возгла́вить* *perf*).

spearmint ['spɪəmɪnt] *n* мя́та колосова́я.

spec [spɛk] *n* (*inf*): **on ~** (*buy, go etc*) нау́дачу.

spec. *n abbr* (*TECH*: = *specification*) специфика́ция.

special ['spɛʃl] *adj* (*important*) осо́бый, осо́бенный; (*edition, adviser, school etc*) специа́льный ◆ *n* (*RAIL*) по́езд* специа́льного назначе́ния; **take ~ care** прояви́те осо́бенную забо́ту; **nothing ~** ничего́ осо́бенного; **today's ~** (*at restaurant*) сего́дняшнее фи́рменное блю́до.

special agent *n* аге́нт по осо́бым поруче́ниям.

special correspondent *n* специа́льный корреспонде́нт.

special delivery *n* (*POST*): **by ~ ~** сро́чной доста́вкой.

special effects *npl* (*CINEMA*) специа́льные съёмочные эффе́кты *mpl*.

specialist ['spɛʃəlɪst] *n* специали́ст; **heart ~** специали́ст-кардио́лог.

speciality [spɛʃɪ'ælɪtɪ] *n* (*dish*) фи́рменное блю́до; (*subject*) специализа́ция.

specialize ['spɛʃəlaɪz] *vi*: **to ~ (in)** специализи́роваться *(impf/perf)* (в *+prp*).

specially ['spɛʃlɪ] *adv* (*especially*) осо́бенно; (*on purpose*) специа́льно.

special offer *n*: **the book is on ~ ~** кни́гу продаю́т по сни́женной цене́.

specialty ['spɛʃəltɪ] *n* (*esp US*) = **speciality**.

species ['spiːʃiːz] *n inv* вид.

specific [spə'sɪfɪk] *adj* определённый; **~ to** характе́рно для *+gen*.

specifically [spə'sɪfɪklɪ] *adv* (*exactly*)

* marks translations which have irregular inflections. The Russian-English side of the dictionary gives inflectional information.

определённо; (*specially*) специа́льно.
specification [spɛsɪfɪˈkeɪʃən] *n* (*TECH*) специфика́ция; (*requirement*) тре́бование; **~s** *npl* (*TECH*) техни́ческие усло́вия *npl*.
specify [ˈspɛsɪfaɪ] *vt* (*time, place, colour etc*) уточня́ть (уточни́ть *perf*); **unless otherwise specified** е́сли нет други́х указа́ний.
specimen [ˈspɛsɪmən] *n* (*example*) экземпля́р; (*sample for testing*) образе́ц*; **a ~ of urine** моча́ для ана́лиза.
specimen copy *n* образцо́вый экземпля́р.
specimen signature *n* образе́ц* по́дписи.
speck [spɛk] *n* (*of dirt*) пя́тнышко; (*of dust*) кра́пинка*.
speckled [ˈspɛkld] *adj* (*hen, eggs*) пёстрый (пёстр).
specs [spɛks] *npl* (*inf*: *glasses*) очки́ *pl*.
spectacle [ˈspɛktəkl] *n* (*scene, event*) зре́лище; **~s** *npl* (*glasses*) очки́ *pl*.
spectacle case *n* (*BRIT*) футля́р для очко́в.
spectacular [spɛkˈtækjuləʳ] *adj* впечатля́ющий (впечатля́ющ) ◆ *n* (*THEAT etc*) впечатля́ющее зре́лище.
spectator [spɛkˈteɪtəʳ] *n* зри́тель(ница) *m(f)* ◆ *cpd*: **a ~ sport** зре́лищный спорт.
spectra [ˈspɛktrə] *npl of* **spectrum**.
spectre [ˈspɛktəʳ] (*US* **specter**) *n* (*also fig*) при́зрак.
spectrum [ˈspɛktrəm] (*pl* **spectra**) *n* спектр.
speculate [ˈspɛkjuleɪt] *vi* (*COMM*) игра́ть *(impf)* на би́рже; (*guess*): **to ~ about** стро́ить *(impf)* дога́дки *or* размышля́ть *(impf)* о *+prp*.
speculation [spɛkjuˈleɪʃən] *n* (*see vb*) биржева́я игра́; дога́дка, предположе́ние.
sped [spɛd] *pt, pp of* **speed**.
speech [spiːtʃ] *n* речь *f*; (*THEAT*) моноло́г, речь.
speech day *n* (*BRIT*: *SCOL*) а́ктовый день* *m*.
speech impediment *n* дефе́кт ре́чи.
speechless [ˈspiːtʃlɪs] *adj* безмо́лвный* (безмо́лвен).
speech therapist *n* логопе́д.
speech therapy *n* логопе́дия.
speed [spiːd] (*pt, pp* **sped**) *n* (*rate*) ско́рость* *f*; (*promptness*) быстрота́ ◆ *vi* (*AUT*: *exceed speed limit*) превыша́ть (превы́сить* *perf*) ско́рость; (*move*): **to ~ along/by** *etc* мча́ться* (промча́ться* *perf*) по *+dat*/ми́мо *+gen etc*; **at ~** (*BRIT*) на большо́й ско́рости; **at full** *or* **top ~** на по́лной *or* преде́ле ско́рости; **at a ~ of 70km/h** со ско́ростью 70км в час; **shorthand/typing ~** ско́рость* маши́нописи/ стенографи́рования; **a five-~ gearbox** коро́бка* переда́ч с пятью́ скоростя́ми
▸ **speed up** (*pt, pp* **speeded up**) *vi* (*also fig*) ускоря́ться (уско́риться* *perf*) ◆ *vt* (*also fig*) ускоря́ть (уско́рить *perf*).
speedboat [ˈspiːdbəut] *n* быстрохо́дный ка́тер*.
speedily [ˈspiːdɪlɪ] *adv* ско́ро.
speeding [ˈspiːdɪŋ] *n* (*AUT*) превыше́ние ско́рости.
speed limit *n* (*AUT*) ограниче́ние ско́рости.
speedometer [spɪˈdɔmɪtəʳ] *n* (*AUT*) спидо́метр.
speed trap *n* (*AUT*) *пост доро́жной поли́ции по контро́лю за ско́ростью*.
speedway [ˈspiːdweɪ] *n* (*sport*: *also*: **~ racing**) спидве́й; (*track*) го́ночный трек.
speedy [spiːdɪ] *adj* (*fast*: *car*) бы́стрый (быстр); (*prompt*: *reply, recovery, settlement*) ско́рый (скор).
speleologist [spɛlɪˈɔlədʒɪst] *n* спелео́лог.
spell [spɛl] (*pt, pp* **spelt** (*BRIT*) *or* **spelled**) *n* (*also: magic ~*) колдовство́; (*period of time*) пери́од ◆ *vt* (*in writing*) объясня́ть (объясни́ть *perf*) в деталя́х; (*also*: **~ out**) произноси́ть* (произнести́* *perf*) по бу́квам; (*fig*: *advantages, difficulties*) разъясня́ть (разъясни́ть *perf*) ◆ *vi*: **he can't ~** он не уме́ет писа́ть без оши́бок; **to cast a ~ on sb** околдо́вывать (околдова́ть *perf*) кого́-н; **how do you ~ your surname?** как пи́шется Ва́ша фами́лия?; **can you ~ it for me?** Вы мо́жете произнести́ э́то по бу́квам?
spellbound [ˈspɛlbaund] *adj* зачаро́ванный (зачаро́ван).
spelling [ˈspɛlɪŋ] *n* правописа́ние.
spelt [spɛlt] *pt, pp of* **spell**.
spend [spɛnd] (*pt, pp* **spent**) *vt* (*money*) тра́тить* (истра́тить* *perf*); (*time, life*) проводи́ть* (провести́* *perf*); (*devote*): **to ~ time/effort on sth** тра́тить (потра́тить *perf*) вре́мя/си́лы на что-н.
spending [ˈspɛndɪŋ] *n* расхо́ды *mpl*; **government ~** госуда́рственные расхо́ды *mpl*.
spending money *n* карма́нные де́ньги* *pl*.
spending power *n* покупа́тельная спосо́бность *f*.
spendthrift [ˈspɛndθrɪft] *n* расточи́тель(ница) *m(f)*.
spent [spɛnt] *pt, pp of* **spend** ◆ *adj* (*cartridge*) пусто́й (пуст); (*bullets*) израсхо́дованный; **~ matches** испо́льзованные *or* израсхо́дованные спи́чки; **my patience is ~** моё терпе́ние ко́нчилось.
sperm [spəːm] *n* спе́рма.
sperm bank *n* храни́лище до́норской спе́рмы.
sperm whale *n* кашало́т.
spew [spjuː] *vt* изрыга́ть (изрыгну́ть *perf*) ◆ *vi* (*inf*: *vomit*) рвать (вы́рвать *perf*); **he ~ed** его́ вы́рвало.
sphere [sfɪəʳ] *n* сфе́ра.
spherical [ˈsfɛrɪkl] *adj* сфери́ческий*, шарообра́зный* (шарообра́зен).
sphinx [sfɪŋks] *n* сфинкс.
spice [spaɪs] *n* спе́ция, пря́ность *f* ◆ *vt* (*food*) приправля́ть (припра́вить* *perf*) спе́циями.
spick-and-span [ˈspɪkənˈspæn] *adj*: **to be ~** сверка́ть *(impf)*.
spicy [ˈspaɪsɪ] *adj* (*food*) о́стрый (остр).
spider [ˈspaɪdəʳ] *n* пау́к*; **~'s web** паути́на.

spidery ['spaɪdərɪ] *adj* (*handwriting*) то́нкий* (то́нок) и небре́жный* (небре́жен).
spiel [spi:l] *n* (*inf*) стёб, говори́льня.
spike [spaɪk] *n* (*point*) остриё; (*BOT*: *of flower*) соцве́тие; (: *of corn*) ко́лос; (*ELEC*) штырь *m*; **~s** *npl* (*SPORT*) шипы́ *mpl*.
spike heel *n* (*US*) шпи́лька*.
spiky ['spaɪkɪ] *adj* (*plant, animal*) колю́чий* (колю́ч).
spill [spɪl] (*pt, pp* **spilt** *or* **spilled**) *vt* (*liquid*) пролива́ть (проли́ть* *perf*), разлива́ть (разли́ть* *perf*) ◆ *vi* (*liquid*) пролива́ться (проли́ться* *perf*), разлива́ться (разли́ться* *perf*); **to ~ the beans** (*inf*) проба́лтываться (проболта́ться *perf*)
▸ **spill out** *vi* вылива́ться (вы́литься* *perf*)
▸ **spill over** *vi* (*liquid*) перелива́ться (перели́ться* *perf*) (че́рез край); (*fig*: *crowd, conflict*) вылива́ться (вы́литься* *perf*).
spillage ['spɪlɪdʒ] *n* (*of oil*) разли́в.
spilt [spɪlt] *pt, pp of* **spill**.
spin [spɪn] (*pt* **spun** *or* **span**, *pp* **spun**) *n* (*trip in car*) ката́ние; (*revolution of wheel*) поворо́т, враще́ние; (*AVIAT*) што́пор ◆ *vt* (*wool etc*) прясть* (спрясть* *perf*); (*top*) крути́ть* (закрути́ть* *perf*); (*wheel*) враща́ть (верте́ть* *perf*); (*BRIT*: *clothes*) выжима́ть (вы́жать* *perf*) (в стира́льной маши́не) ◆ *vi* (*make thread*) прясть* (*impf*); (*person, head*) кружи́ться* (закружи́ться* *perf*); (*car*) враща́ться (*impf*); **let's go for a ~ in the car** поéдем ката́ться на маши́не; **to put ~ on a ball** закру́чивать (закрути́ть* *perf*) мяч*; **to ~ a yarn** (*inf*: *story*) плести́* (наплести́* *perf*) небыли́цы; **to ~ a coin** (*BRIT*) подбра́сывать (подбро́сить* *perf*) моне́ту
▸ **spin out** *vt* растя́гивать (растяну́ть* *perf*).
spina bifida ['spaɪnə'bɪfɪdə] *n* (*MED*) *расщепле́ние ости́стых отро́стков позвоно́чника.*
spinach ['spɪnɪtʃ] *n* шпина́т.
spinal ['spaɪnl] *adj* спинно́й; **~ injury** поврежде́ние позвоно́чника.
spinal column *n* (*ANAT*) позвоно́чный столб*.
spinal cord *n* спинно́й мозг*.
spindly ['spɪndlɪ] *adj* дли́нный* (дли́нен) и то́нкий* (то́нок).
spin doctor *n* (*inf*) парти́йный пропаганди́ст, спин-до́ктор.
spin-dry ['spɪn'draɪ] *vt* (*clothes, washing*) выжима́ть (вы́жать* *perf*) до́суха (*в центрифу́ге*).
spin-dryer [spɪn'draɪə^r] *n* (*BRIT*) центрифу́га-суши́лка*.
spine [spaɪn] *n* (*ANAT*) позвоно́чник; (*thorn*) колю́чка*, игла́*.
spine-chilling ['spaɪntʃɪlɪŋ] *adj* (*story, film*) жу́ткий* (жу́ток).
spineless ['spaɪnlɪs] *adj* (*fig*) бесхребе́тный* (бесхребе́тен).
spinner ['spɪnə^r] *n* (*of thread*) пряди́льщик(-щица), пря́ха *m/f*.
spinning ['spɪnɪŋ] *n* (*craft*) пряде́ние.
spinning top *n* волчо́к*.
spinning wheel *n* пря́лка*.
spin-off ['spɪnɔf] *n* (*fig*: *by-product*) побо́чный результа́т.
spinster ['spɪnstə^r] *n* (*unmarried woman*) ста́рая де́ва.
spiral ['spaɪərl] *n* спира́ль *f* ◆ *vi* (*fig*: *prices etc*) ре́зко возраста́ть (возрасти́* *perf*); **the inflationary ~** спира́ль инфля́ции.
spiral staircase *n* винтова́я ле́стница.
spire ['spaɪə^r] *n* шпиль *m*.
spirit ['spɪrɪt] *n* дух; (*soul*) душа́*; **~s** *npl* (*drink*) спиртно́е *ntsg adj*; **in good/low ~s** в хоро́шем/пода́вленном настрое́нии; **community ~, public ~** обще́ственный дух.
spirited ['spɪrɪtɪd] *adj* энерги́чный* (энерги́чен); (*performance*) воодушевлённый; (*horse*) горя́чий* (горя́ч).
spirit level *n* ватерпа́с.
spiritual ['spɪrɪtjuəl] *adj* духо́вный* (духо́вен) ◆ *n* (*also:* **Negro ~**) спи́ричуал.
spiritualism ['spɪrɪtjuəlɪzəm] *n* спирити́зм.
spit [spɪt] (*pt, pp* **spat**) *n* (*for roasting*) ве́ртел; (*saliva*) слюна́ ◆ *vi* (*person*) плева́ть* (плю́нуть *perf*); (*fire, hot oil*) шипе́ть* (*impf*); (*inf*: *rain*) мороси́ть* (*impf*).
spite [spaɪt] *n* зло́ба, злость *f* ◆ *vt* досажда́ть (досади́ть* *perf*) *+dat*; **in ~ of** несмотря́ на *+acc*.
spiteful ['spaɪtful] *adj* зло́бный* (зло́бен).
spit roast *n мя́со, зажа́ренное на ве́ртеле.*
spitting ['spɪtɪŋ] *n*: **"spitting prohibited"** "плева́ть воспреща́ется" ◆ *adj*: **he is the ~ image of his father** он вы́литый оте́ц.
spittle ['spɪtl] *n* слюна́.
spiv [spɪv] *n* (*BRIT*: *inf*: *pej*) фра́йер, жу́лик.
splash [splæʃ] *n* (*sound*) вспле́ск ◆ *excl*: **~!** плюх! ◆ *vt* бры́згать* (бры́знуть *perf*) ◆ *vi* (*also:* **~ about**) плеска́ться* (*impf*); **a ~ of colour** цветово́е пятно́; **to ~ paint on the floor** забры́згивать (забры́згать* *perf*) пол кра́ской.
splashdown ['splæʃdaun] *n* (*SPACE*) приводне́ние.
splayfooted ['spleɪfutɪd] *adj ступа́ющий пя́тками внутрь, носка́ми вро́зь.*
spleen [spli:n] *n* (*ANAT*) селезёнка*.
splendid ['splɛndɪd] *adj* великоле́пный* (великоле́пен).
splendour ['splɛndə^r] (*US* **splendor**) *n* великоле́пие; **~s** *npl* (*features*) великоле́пие *ntsg*.

splice [splaɪs] *vt* соединя́ть (соедини́ть *perf*); (*tape, film*) скле́ивать (скле́ить *perf*).
splint [splɪnt] *n* ши́на.
splinter ['splɪntəʳ] *n* (*of wood*) ще́пка*; (*of glass*) оско́лок*; (*in finger*) зано́за ◆ *vi* (*bone, wood, glass etc*) расщепля́ться (расщепи́ться* *perf*).
splinter group *n* отколо́вшаяся группиро́вка.
split [splɪt] (*pt, pp* **split**) *n* (*crack, tear*) тре́щина; (*POL, fig*) раско́л ◆ *vt* (*divide*) расщепля́ть (расщепи́ть* *perf*); (*POL*) раска́лывать (расколо́ть* *perf*); (*share equally: work, profits*) разделя́ть (раздели́ть* *perf*) ◆ *vi* (*divide*) расщепля́ться (расщепи́ться* *perf*), разделя́ться (раздели́ться* *perf*); (*glass, wood*) раска́лываться (расколо́ться* *perf*); (*cloth*) разрыва́ться (разорва́ться* *perf*); **let's ~ the difference** дава́йте сойдёмся на сре́дней ци́фре; **to do the ~s** де́лать (сде́лать *perf*) шпага́т
▸ **split up** *vi* (*couple*) расходи́ться* (разойти́сь* *perf*); (*group*) разделя́ться (раздели́ться* *perf*); (*meeting*) зака́нчиваться (зако́нчиться *perf*).
split-level ['splɪtlɛvl] *adj*: **~ house** дом, постро́енный на ра́зных у́ровнях.
split peas *npl* ко́лотый горо́х *msg*.
split personality *n* раздвое́ние ли́чности.
split second *n* до́ля* секу́нды.
splitting ['splɪtɪŋ] *adj*: **I've got a ~ headache** у меня́ голова́ раска́лывается.
splutter ['splʌtəʳ] *vi* (*engine etc*) треща́ть* (*impf*); (*person*) бры́згать* (*impf*) слюно́й.
spoil [spɔɪl] (*pt, pp* **spoilt** *or* **spoiled**) *vt* (*damage, mar*) по́ртить* (испо́ртить* *perf*); (*indulge*) балова́ть (избалова́ть *perf*) ◆ *vi*: **he's ~ing for a fight** он так и ле́зет в дра́ку.
spoils [spɔɪlz] *npl* (*also fig*) трофе́и *mpl*.
spoilsport ['spɔɪlspɔːt] *n* (*pej: person*): **don't be a ~** не отравля́й лю́дям настрое́ние.
spoilt [spɔɪlt] *pt, pp of* **spoil** ◆ *adj* испо́рченный* (испо́рчен); (*child*) избало́ванный* (избало́ван).
spoke [spəuk] *pt of* **speak** ◆ *n* (*of wheel*) спи́ца.
spoken ['spəukn] *pp of* **speak**.
spokesman ['spəuksmən] *irreg n* представи́тель *m*.
spokesperson ['spəukspəːsn] *irreg n* представи́тель(ница) *m(f)*.
spokeswoman ['spəukswumən] *irreg n* представи́тельница.
sponge [spʌndʒ] *n* гу́бка*; (*also:* **~ cake**) бискви́т ◆ *vt* (*wash*) обтира́ть (обтере́ть* *perf*) гу́бкой ◆ *vi*: **to ~ off** *or* **on sb** сиде́ть* (*impf*) на ше́е у кого́-н.
sponge bag *n* (*BRIT*) су́мочка* для туале́тных принадле́жностей.
sponger ['spʌndʒəʳ] *n* (*pej*) парази́т.
spongy ['spʌndʒɪ] *adj* гу́бчатый.
sponsor ['spɔnsəʳ] *n* спо́нсор; (*for application*) поручи́тель *m* ◆ *vt* финанси́ровать (*impf/perf*), спонси́ровать (*impf/perf*); (*applicant*) поруча́ться (поручи́ться *perf*) за *+acc*; (*proposal, bill etc*) вноси́ть* (внести́* *perf*) на рассмотре́ние; **I ~ed him at twenty pence a mile** я поже́ртвовал ему́ два́дцать пе́нсов за ми́лю.
sponsorship ['spɔnsəʃɪp] *n* спо́нсорство.
spontaneity [spɔntə'neɪɪtɪ] *n* спонта́нность *f*.
spontaneous [spɔn'teɪnɪəs] *adj* (*gesture*) спонта́нный* (спонта́нен); (*demonstration*) стихи́йный; **~ combustion** самовозгора́ние, самовоспламене́ние.
spoof [spuːf] (*inf*) *n* (*imitation*) паро́дия; (*joke*) ро́зыгрыш ◆ *vt* (*imitate*) передра́знивать (*impf*).
spooky ['spuːkɪ] *adj* (*inf: place, atmosphere*) злове́щий*, жу́ткий*.
spool [spuːl] *n* (*for thread*) кату́шка*; (*for film, tape etc*) боби́на.
spoon [spuːn] *n* ло́жка*.
spoon-feed ['spuːnfiːd] *vt* (*baby, patient*) корми́ть* (*impf*) с ло́жки; (*fig: students*) всё разжёвывать (*impf*) *+dat*.
spoonful ['spuːnful] *n* (по́лная) ло́жка*.
sporadic [spə'rædɪk] *adj* споради́ческий*.
sport [spɔːt] *n* (*game*) спорт *m no pl*; (*person: also:* **good ~**) молодчи́на *m* ◆ *vt* (*wear*) щеголя́ть (щегольну́ть *perf*) *+instr*; **indoor/outdoor ~s** ви́ды спо́рта для закры́тых помеще́ний/на откры́том во́здухе.
sporting ['spɔːtɪŋ] *adj* (*event etc*) спорти́вный; (*generous*) ры́царский*; **to give sb a ~ chance** дава́ть* (дать* *perf*) кому́-н не́который шанс.
sport jacket *n* (*US*) = **sports jacket**.
sports car *n* спорти́вная маши́на.
sports centre *n* спорти́вный центр.
sports ground *n* спорти́вная площа́дка*.
sports jacket *n* (*BRIT*) спорти́вная ку́ртка* из тви́да.
sportsman ['spɔːtsmən] *irreg n* спортсме́н.
sportsmanship ['spɔːtsmənʃɪp] *n* спорти́вный дух; **he showed real ~** он показа́л себя́ как настоя́щий спортсме́н.
sports page *n* спорти́вная страни́ца.
sportswear ['spɔːtswɛəʳ] *n* спорти́вная оде́жда.
sportswoman ['spɔːtswumən] *irreg n* спортсме́нка*.
sporty ['spɔːtɪ] *adj* (*person*) спорти́вный* (спорти́вен).
spot [spɔt] *n* (*mark*) пятно́*; (*dot: on pattern*) кра́пинка*; (*on skin*) пры́щик; (*place*) ме́сто*; (*RADIO, TV*) рекла́мный переры́в; **~ advertisement** рекла́мная ру́брика ◆ *vt* (*notice*) замеча́ть (заме́тить* *perf*); **a ~ of bother** ма́ленькая неприя́тность *f*; **shall we have a ~ of lunch?** не перекуси́ть ли нам?; **~s of rain** ка́пли дождя́; **on the ~** (*in that place*) на ме́сте; (*immediately*) в тот же моме́нт; **to put sb on the ~** ста́вить* (поста́вить* *perf*) кого́-н в затрудни́тельное положе́ние; **in a ~** (*in difficulty*) в затрудни́тельном

положе́нии; **to come out in ~s** (*rash*) покрыва́ться (покры́ться* *perf*) сы́пью; (*blemishes*) покрыва́ться (покры́ться* *perf*) прыща́ми.
spot check *n* вы́борочная прове́рка*.
spotless ['spɔtlɪs] *adj* (*shirt, kitchen etc*) без пя́тнышка; (*reputation*) незапя́тнанный.
spotlight ['spɔtlaɪt] *n* (освети́тельный) проже́ктор; **to be in the ~** (*fig*) быть* *(impf)* в це́нтре внима́ния.
spot-on [spɔt'ɔn] *adj* (*BRIT*: *inf*): **to be ~** попа́сть* *(perf)* в са́мую то́чку.
spot price *n* (*COMM*) цена́ при усло́вии неме́дленной опла́ты (нали́чными).
spotted ['spɔtɪd] *adj* (*pattern*) пятни́стый (пятни́ст); **~ with** запя́тнанный (запя́тнан) *+instr*.
spotty ['spɔtɪ] *adj* (*face, youth*) прыща́вый (прыща́в).
spouse [spaus] *n* супру́г(а).
spout [spaut] *n* (*of jug*) но́сик; (*of pipe*) выпускно́е отве́рстие; (*of liquid*) струя́* ◆ *vi* (*water etc*) бить* *(impf)* струёй; (*volcano*) изверга́ться (изве́ргнуться *perf*).
sprain [spreɪn] *n* (*MED*) растяже́ние ◆ *vt*: **to ~ one's ankle/wrist** растя́гивать (растяну́ть* *perf*) щи́колотку/запя́стье.
sprang [spræŋ] *pt of* **spring**.
sprawl [sprɔ:l] *vi* (*person*) разва́ливаться (развали́ться* *perf*); (*place*) раски́дываться (раски́нуться *perf*) ◆ *n*: **urban ~** разраста́ние го́рода; **to send sb ~ing** сбива́ть (сбить* *perf*) кого́-н с ног.
spray [spreɪ] *n* (*drops of water*) бры́зги *pl*; (*hair spray*) аэрозо́ль *m*; (*garden spray*) разбры́згиватель *m*; (: *chemicals*) ядохимика́ты *mpl*; (*of flowers*) ве́точка* ◆ *vt* (*sprinkle*) обры́згивать (обры́згать *perf*); (*crops*) опры́скивать (опры́скать *perf*) ◆ *cpd*: **~ deodorant** дезодора́нт в аэрозо́льной упако́вке.
spread [sprɛd] (*pt, pp* **spread**) *n* (*range*) спектр; (*distribution*) распростране́ние; (*CULIN*: *paste*) па́ста; (: *margarine etc*) бутербро́дный маргари́н; (*inf*: *food*) оби́льное угоще́ние; (*PRESS, TYP*: *two pages*) разворо́т ◆ *vt* (*lay out*) расстила́ть (расстели́ть* *perf*); (*scatter*) разбра́сывать (разброса́ть* *perf*); (*butter, paste*) нама́зывать (нама́зать* *perf*); (*wings*) расправля́ть (распра́вить* *perf*); (*arms*) раскрыва́ть (раскры́ть* *perf*); (*sail*) развёртывать (разверну́ть *perf*); (*workload, wealth*) распределя́ть (распредели́ть *perf*); (*rumour, disease*) распространя́ть (распространи́ть *perf*); (*repayments*) распределя́ть (распредели́ть *perf*) ◆ *vi* (*disease, news*) распространя́ться (распространи́ться *perf*); (*also*: **~ out**) расширя́ться (расши́риться *perf*); **middle-age ~** возрастна́я полнота́
▸ **spread out** *vi* (*move apart*) раздвига́ть (раздви́нуть *perf*).
spread-eagled ['sprɛdi:gld] *adj* распла́станный (распла́стан); **to be** *or* **lie ~** лежа́ть* *(impf)* плашмя́.
spreadsheet ['sprɛdʃi:t] *n* (*COMPUT*) электро́нная табли́ца.
spree [spri:] *n*: **to go on a ~** кути́ть* (покути́ть* *perf*).
sprig [sprɪg] *n* (*BOT*) ве́точка*.
sprightly ['spraɪtlɪ] *adj* (*old person*) бо́дрый (бодр).
spring [sprɪŋ] (*pt* **sprang**, *pp* **sprung**) *n* (*coiled metal*) пружи́на; (*season*) весна́*; (*of water*) исто́чник, родни́к*; (*leap*) прыжо́к*; (*bounciness*) упру́гость *f* ◆ *vi* (*leap*) пры́гать (пры́гнуть *perf*) ◆ *vt*: **to ~ a leak** (*pipe etc*) дава́ть* (дать* *perf*) течь; **in ~** весно́й; **to walk with a ~ in one's step** ходи́ть*/идти́* *(impf)* упру́гой *or* пружи́нистой похо́дкой; **to ~ from sth** (*be the result of*) быть* *(impf)* вы́званным(-ой) чем-н; **he sprang the news on me** он вы́валил на меня́ э́ту но́вость; **to ~ into action** ри́нуться *(perf)* в де́ло
▸ **spring up** *vi* (*building, plant*) выраста́ть (вы́расти* *perf*).
springboard ['sprɪŋbɔ:d] *n* (*SPORT*) трампли́н; (*fig*): **to be the ~ for** служи́ть (послужи́ть *perf*) трампли́ном для *+gen*.
spring-clean(ing) [sprɪŋ'kli:n(ɪŋ)] *n* генера́льная убо́рка*.
spring onion *n* (*BRIT*: *BOT*) лук-бату́н *no pl*; (: *CULIN*) зелёный лук *no pl*.
spring roll *n блі́нчик с начи́нкой, свёрнутый в тру́бочку*.
springtime ['sprɪŋtaɪm] *n* весе́няя пора́.
springy ['sprɪŋɪ] *adj* упру́гий*.
sprinkle ['sprɪŋkl] *vt* (*salt, sugar*) посыпа́ть (посы́пать* *perf*) *+instr*; **to ~ water on sth, ~ sth with water** бры́згать (побры́згать *perf*) водо́й на что-н; **to ~ sugar on sth, ~ sth with sugar** посыпа́ть (посы́пать* *perf*) что-н са́харом; **~d with** (*fig*) усы́панный (усы́пан) *+instr*.
sprinkler ['sprɪŋklə^r] *n* (*for lawn*) разбры́згиватель *m*; (*to put out fire*) спри́нклер.
sprinkling ['sprɪŋklɪŋ] *n* небольшо́е коли́чество; (*of salt, sugar*) го́рсточка, го́рстка.
sprint [sprɪnt] *n* (*race*) спринт ◆ *vi* (*run fast*) стреми́тельно бе́гать/бежа́ть* *(impf)*; (*SPORT*) спринтова́ть *(impf)*; **the 200 metres ~** спринт на 200-метро́вую диста́нцию.
sprinter ['sprɪntə^r] *n* спри́нтер.
sprite [spraɪt] *n* эльф; (*fairy*) фе́я.

spritzer ['sprɪtsəʳ] *n* бéлое винó с сóдовой (водóй).
sprocket ['sprɔkɪt] *n* (*TECH*) (цепнáя) звёздочка*.
sprout [spraut] *vi* (*BOT*) пускáть (пустúть* *perf*) росткú.
sprouts [sprauts] *npl* (*also:* **Brussels ~**) брюссéльская капýста *fsg*.
spruce [spru:s] *n inv* (*BOT*) ель *f* ◆ *adj* (*neat*) опрятный* (опрятен); (*smart*) нарядный* (наряден)
▸ **spruce up** *vt* (*smarten up*: *room etc*) наводúть* (навестú* *perf*) глянец на *+acc*; **to ~ o.s. up** наводúть* (навестú* *perf*) на себя глянец.
sprung [sprʌŋ] *pp of* **spring**.
spry [spraɪ] *adj* (*old person*) бóдрый (бодр).
SPUC *n abbr* (= *Society for the Protection of Unborn Children*) *óбщество, бóрющееся прóтив дозволúтельности абóртов.*
spud [spʌd] *n* (*inf*: *potato*) картóшка*.
spun [spʌn] *pt, pp of* **spin**.
spur [spə:ʳ] *n* шпóра; (*fig*) стúмул ◆ *vt* (*also:* **~ on**) подстёгивать (подстегнýть* *perf*); **to ~ sb on to** побуждáть (побудúть* *perf*) когó-н к *+dat*; **on the ~ of the moment** под влиянием минýты.
spurious ['spjuərɪəs] *adj* поддéльный.
spurn [spə:n] *vt* (*reject*) отвергáть (отвéргнуть* *perf*).
spurt [spə:t] *n* (*of blood etc*) струя; (*of energy*) порыв ◆ *vi* хлынуть (*perf*); **to put on a ~** дéлать (сдéлать *perf*) рывóк.
sputter ['spʌtəʳ] *vi* = **splutter**.
spy [spaɪ] *n* шпиóн ◆ *vi*: **to ~ on** шпиóнить (*impf*) за *+instr* ◆ *vt* (*see*) замечáть (замéтить* *perf*) ◆ *cpd* (*film, story*) шпиóнский.
spying ['spaɪɪŋ] *n* шпионáж.
Sq. *abbr* (*in address*) (= **square**) пл.= *плóщадь.*
sq. *abbr* = **square**.
squabble ['skwɔbl] *vi* вздóрить (повздóрить *perf*) ◆ *n* перебрáнка*.
squad [skwɔd] *n* (*MIL, POLICE*) комáнда; (*SPORT*) комáнда; **flying ~** (*POLICE*) отряд быстрого реагúрования.
squad car *n* (*BRIT*: *POLICE*) дежýрная полицéйская машúна.
squaddie ['skwɔdɪ] *n* (*inf*) солдáт.
squadron ['skwɔdrn] *n* (*MIL*) эскадрóн; (*AVIAT*) эскадрúлья; (*NAUT*) эскáдра.
squalid ['skwɔlɪd] *adj* (*conditions, room*) убóгий* (убóг); (*story etc*) грязный* (грязен).
squall [skwɔ:l] *n* (*stormy wind*) шквал.
squalor ['skwɔləʳ] *n* убóгость *f*.
squander ['skwɔndəʳ] *vt* (*money*) промáтывать (промотáть *perf*); (*chances*) растрáчивать (растрáтить* *perf*).
square [skwɛəʳ] *n* (*shape*) квадрáт; (*in town*) плóщадь *f*; (*US*: *block of houses*) квартáл; (*also:* **set ~**) угóльник; (*inf*: *person*) немóдный, сéрый человéк* ◆ *adj* квадрáтный; (*inf*: *ideas, tastes*) немóдный, сéрый ◆ *vt* (*reconcile, settle*) улáживать (улáдить* *perf*); (*MATH*) возводúть* (возвестú* *perf*) в квадрáт ◆ *vi* (*agree*) соглacóвываться (согласовáться *perf*); **we are all ~** мы квúты; **a ~ meal** плóтная трапéза; **2 metres ~** 2 мéтра длинóй и 2 мéтра ширинóй; **2 ~ metres** 2 квадрáтных мéтра; **I'll ~ it with him** (*inf*) я с ним э́то улáжу; **can you ~ it with your conscience?** (*reconcile*) э́то согласýется с Вáшей сóвестью?; **we're back to ~ one** мы вернýлись тудá, откýда начáли
▸ **square up** *vi* (*BRIT*): **to ~ up with sb** поквитáться (*perf*) с кем-н.
square bracket *n* (*TYP*) квадрáтная скóбка*.
squarely ['skwɛəlɪ] *adv* прямо.
square root *n* квадрáтный кóрень* *m*.
squash [skwɔʃ] *n* (*BRIT*: *drink*): **lemon/orange ~** лимóнный/апельсúновой напúток* (*приготóвленный из концентрáта*); (*US*) тыква; (*SPORT*) ракетбóл ◆ *vt* давúть* (раздавúть* *perf*).
squat [skwɔt] *adj* приземúстый (приземúст) ◆ *vi* (*also:* **~ down**: *position*) сидéть* (*impf*) на кóрточках; (: *motion*) сесть* (*perf*) на кóрточки; (*on property*) незакóнно поселяться (поселúться *perf*) в дом.
squatter ['skwɔtəʳ] *n* (*in house*) *лицó, самовóльно поселяющееся в чужóм дóме*; (*on land*) сквáттер.
squawk [skwɔ:k] *vi* (*bird*) клекотáть* (*impf*).
squeak [skwi:k] *vi* (*door*) скрипéть* (скрúпнуть *perf*); (*mouse*) пищáть* (пúскнуть *perf*) ◆ *n* (*of hinge, wheel etc*) скрип.
squeaky-clean [skwi:kɪ'kli:n] *adj* (*surface etc*) чúстый (чист) до скрúпа; (*fig*) без пятнышка.
squeal [skwi:l] *vi* визжáть* (*impf*), взвúзгивать (взвúзгнуть *perf*).
squeamish ['skwi:mɪʃ] *adj* (*person*) брезглúвый (брезглúв).
squeeze [skwi:z] *n* (*of hand*) сжáтие; (*ECON*) ограничéние; (*also:* **credit ~**) ограничéние кредúта ◆ *vt* сжимáть (сжать* *perf*); (*juice*) выжимáть (вы́жать* *perf*) ◆ *vi*: **to ~ past/under sth** протúскиваться (протúснуться *perf*) чéрез что-н/под чем-н; **a ~ of lemon** нéсколько капéль лимóнного сóка
▸ **squeeze out** *vt* (*juice etc*) выжимáть (вы́жать* *perf*); (*fig*: *money etc*) выжимáть (вы́жать* *perf*).
squelch [skwɛltʃ] *vi* (*mud etc*) хлюпать (хлюпнуть *perf*).
squib [skwɪb] *n* (*firework*) петáрда.
squid [skwɪd] *n* кальмáр.
squiggle ['skwɪgl] *n* загогýлина.
squint [skwɪnt] *vi* (*permanently*) косúть* (*impf*); (*in sunlight*) щýриться (*impf*), прищýриваться (прищýриться *perf*) ◆ *n* (*MED*) косоглáзие; **he has a ~** у негó косоглáзие, он косúт.

squire ['skwaɪəʳ] *n* (*BRIT*) помéщик; (*inf*) начáльник.
squirm [skwə:m] *vi* выгибáться (вы́гнуться *perf*); (*with embarrassment or shame*) поёживаться (поёжиться *perf*).
squirrel ['skwɪrəl] *n* бéлка*.
squirt [skwə:t] *vi* бры́згать* (бры́знуть *perf*) ◆ *vt* бры́згать* (брызну́ть *perf*) +*instr*.
Sr *abbr* (*in names*) = **senior**; (*REL*) = **sister**.
SRC *n abbr* (*BRIT*) = *Students' Representative Council.*
Sri Lanka [srɪ'læŋkə] *n* Шри-Лáнка.
SRN *n abbr* (*BRIT*: = *State Registered Nurse*) медсестрá= *медици́нская сестрá*.
SRO *abbr* (*US*: = *standing room only*) тóлько стоя́чие местá *ntpl*.
SS *abbr* = **steamship**.
SSA *n abbr* (*US*: = *Social Security Administration*) ≈ департáмент социáльного обеспéчения.
SST *n abbr* (*US*: = *supersonic transport*) сверхзвуковóй реакти́вный самолёт.
ST *abbr* (*US*) = *Standard Time*.
St *abbr* = **saint**; (= **street**) ул.= *у́лица*.
stab [stæb] *n* (*with knife etc*) удáр (*чем-н óстрым*); (*of pain*) укóл; (*inf*: *try*): **to have a ~ at doing** пытáться (попытáться *perf*) +*infin* ◆ *vt* наноси́ть* (нанести́* *perf*) удáр +*dat*; **to ~ sb to death** закáлывать (заколóть* *perf*) когó-н.
stabbing ['stæbɪŋ] *n*: **there's been a ~** здесь былá поножóвщина ◆ *adj* (*pain, ache*) рéзкий*.
stability [stə'bɪlɪtɪ] *n* (*of object*) устóйчивость *f*; (*of government, economy etc*) стаби́льность *f*.
stabilization [steɪbəlaɪ'zeɪʃən] *n* стабилизáция.
stabilize ['steɪbəlaɪz] *vt* (*prices*) стабилизи́ровать *(impf/perf)* ◆ *vi* стабилизи́роваться *(impf/perf)*.
stabilizer ['steɪbəlaɪzəʳ] *n* стабилизáтор.
stable ['steɪbl] *adj* стаби́льный* (стаби́лен), устóйчивый (устóйчив) ◆ *n* (*for horse*) конюшня*, стóйло; (*for cattle*) хлев*, стóйло; **riding ~s** (*school*) кóнно-спорти́вная шкóла.
staccato [stə'kɑ:təu] *adv* (*MUS*) стаккáто ◆ *adj* отры́вистый (отры́вист).
stack [stæk] *n* (*pile*: *of hay*) стог*, скирдá*; (*of wood*) штáбель *m*, полéнница; (*of papers*) ки́па, стóпка; (*of plates*) стопá* ◆ *vt* (*also:* **~ up**: *chairs etc*) склáдывать (сложи́ть* *perf*) в ку́чу; (: *books, plates*) склáдывать (сложи́ть* *perf*) в стóпку; (*room, table etc*): **to ~ (with)** уставля́ть (устáвить* *perf*) стóпками; **there's ~s of time** (*BRIT*: *inf*) ещё есть ку́ча врéмени.
stadia ['steɪdɪə] *npl of* **stadium**.
stadium ['steɪdɪəm] (*pl* **stadia** *or* **~s**) *n* (*SPORT*) стадиóн.
staff [stɑ:f] *n* (*workforce*) рабóтники *pl*, штат; (*BRIT*: *SCOL*: *also:* **teaching ~**) штат учителéй, преподавáтельский состáв; (*servants*) штат; (*MIL*) ли́чный состáв; (*stick*) пóсох ◆ *vt* укомплектóвывать (укомплектовáть *perf*).
staffroom ['stɑ:fru:m] *n* (*SCOL*) учи́тельская *f adj*.
Staffs *abbr* (*BRIT*: *POST*) = *Staffordshire*.
stag [stæg] *n* самéц* олéня; (*BRIT*: *STOCK EXCHANGE*) спекуля́нт цéнными бумáгами.
stage [steɪdʒ] *n* (*in theatre*) сцéна; (*platform*) подмóстки *pl*; (*profession*): **the ~** сцéна; (*point, period*) стáдия ◆ *vt* (*play*) стáвить* (постáвить* *perf*); (*demonstration*) устрáивать (устрóить *perf*); (*fig*: *recovery etc*) осуществля́ть (осуществи́ть* *perf*); **in ~s** поэтáпно, по этáпам; **he is going through a difficult ~** он переживáет тру́дный перúод; **in the early/final ~s** на рáнних/послéдних стáдиях *or* этáпах.
stagecoach ['steɪdʒkəutʃ] *n* почтóвый дилижáнс.
stage door *n* (*THEAT*) служéбный вход (*в теáтр*).
stage fright *n* волнéние пéред выступлéнием.
stagehand ['steɪdʒhænd] *n* рабóчий*(-ая) *m(f) adj* сцéны.
stage-manage ['steɪdʒmænɪdʒ] *vt* (*fig*) закули́сно руководи́ть* *(impf)* +*instr*.
stage manager *n* дирéктор сцéны.
stagger ['stægəʳ] *vt* (*amaze*) потрясáть (потрясти́* *perf*) ◆ *vi*: **he ~ed along the road** он шёл по дорóге, пошáтываясь; **the management has ~ed the workers' leave** администрáция состáвила грáфик отпускóв.
staggering ['stægərɪŋ] *adj* потрясáющий*.
staging post ['steɪdʒɪŋ-] *n* (*on flight*) промежу́точный аэродрóм.
stagnant ['stægnənt] *adj* (*water*) стоя́чий*; (*economy*) застóйный.
stagnate [stæg'neɪt] *vi* (*person*) заси́живаться (засидéться* *perf*); (*economy, business*) быть* *(impf)* в застóе.
stagnation [stæg'neɪʃən] *n* застóй; (*ECON*) стагнáция, застóй.
stag party *n* мальчи́шник.
staid [steɪd] *adj* (*person, attitudes*) степéнный* (степéнен).
stain [steɪn] *n* пятнó*; (*for wood*) мори́лка* ◆ *vt* (*mark*) пятнáть (запятнáть *perf*), пáчкать (запáчкать *perf*); (*wood*) мори́ть (замори́ть *perf*).
stained glass window [steɪnd-] *n* витрáж.
stainless steel ['steɪnlɪs-] *n* нержавéющая сталь *f*.
stain remover *n* пятновыводи́тель *m*.
stair [stɛəʳ] *n* (*step*) ступéнь *f*, ступéнька*; **~s** *npl* (*steps*) лéстница *fsg*; **on the ~s** на лéстнице.
staircase ['stɛəkeɪs] *n* лéстница.

* marks translations which have irregular inflections. The Russian-English side of the dictionary gives inflectional information.

stairway ['stɛəweɪ] = **staircase**.
stairwell ['stɛəwɛl] *n* лестничная шахта.
stake [steɪk] *n* (*post*) кол*; (*investment*) доля*; (*wager*) ставка*; (*horse race*: *usu pl*) скачки* *fpl* ◆ *vt* (*wager*: *money, life, reputation*) ставить* (поставить* *perf*); (*also:* ~ **out**: *area*) огораживать (огородить* *perf*); (*fig*) очерчивать (очертить* *perf*) границы *+gen*; **his reputation was at** ~ его репутация была поставлена на карту; **he has a ~ in this business** он кровно заинтересован в этом бизнесе; **to ~ a claim (to sth)** притязать *(impf)* (на что-н).
stake out *n* (*US*: *inf*) засада.
stalactite ['stæləktaɪt] *n* сталактит.
stalagmite ['stæləgmaɪt] *n* сталагмит.
stale [steɪl] *adj* (*bread*) чёрствый (чёрств); (*food, beer*) несвежий* (несвеж); (*air, smell*) затхлый.
stalemate ['steɪlmeɪt] *n* (*CHESS*) пат; (*fig*) тупик.
stalk [stɔːk] *n* (*of flower*) стебель *m*; (*of fruit*) черенок* ◆ *vt* (*person, animal*) красться* (подкрасться* *perf*) к *+dat* ◆ *vi*: **to ~ out/off** удаляться (удалиться *perf*).
stall [stɔːl] *n* (*BRIT*: *in street*) ларёк*, киоск; (*in market*) прилавок*; (*in stable*) стойло ◆ *vt* (*fig*: *delay*) задерживать (задержать* *perf*) ◆ *vi* (*AUT*) глохнуть* (заглохнуть* *perf*); (*fig*: *person*) мешкать (помешкать *perf*); **~s** *npl* (*BRIT*: *THEAT*) партер *msg*; **watch you don't ~ the engine** смотри, чтобы у тебя мотор не заглох; **a seat in the ~s** место* *or* кресло* в партере; **a newspaper/flower ~** газетный/цветочный ларёк.
stallholder ['stɔːlhəuldəʳ] *n* (*BRIT*) владелец* ларька.
stallion ['stæljən] *n* жеребец*.
stalwart ['stɔːlwət] *adj* (*worker, supporter, party member*) стойкий*.
stamen ['steɪmɛn] *n* тычинка*.
stamina ['stæmɪnə] *n* выносливость *f*.
stammer ['stæməʳ] *n* заикание ◆ *vi* заикаться.
stamp [stæmp] *n* (*postage stamp*) марка*; (*rubber stamp*) печать *f*, штамп; (*mark, also fig*) печать ◆ *vi* (*also:* ~ **one's foot**) топать* (топнуть *perf*) ногой ◆ *vt* (*letter*) наклеивать (наклеить *perf*) марку на *+acc*; (*mark*) оттискивать (оттиснуть *perf*); (*with rubber stamp*) ставить* (поставить* *perf*) печать *or* штамп на *+acc*; **~ed addressed envelope** надписанный конверт с маркой
▸ **stamp out** *vt* (*fire*) затаптывать (затоптать* *perf*); (*crime*) уничтожать (уничтожить *perf*); (*opposition*) подавлять (подавить* *perf*).
stamp album *n* альбом для марок.
stamp collecting *n* филателия.
stamp duty *n* (*BRIT*) гербовый сбор.
stampede [stæm'piːd] *n* (*also fig*) массовое бегство.
stamp machine *n* автомат по продаже почтовых марок.
stance [stæns] *n* (*also fig*) позиция.
stand [stænd] (*pt, pp* **stood**) *n* (*stall*) ларёк*, киоск; (*at exhibition*) стенд; (*SPORT*) трибуна; (*piece of furniture*: *for umbrellas*) подставка*; (: *for coats, hats*) вешалка* ◆ *vi* (*be upright*) стоять* *(impf)*; (*rise*) вставать* (встать* *perf*); (*remain*: *decision, offer*) оставаться* (остаться* *perf*) в силе; (*in election etc*) выставлять (выставить* *perf*) свою кандидатуру, баллотироваться *(impf)*; (*value, level, score etc*): **to ~ at** оставаться* (остаться* *perf*) на *+prp* ◆ *vt* (*place*: *object*) ставить* (поставить* *perf*); (*tolerate, withstand*) терпеть* *(impf)*, выносить* (вынести* *perf*); **to make a ~ against sth** оказывать (оказать* *perf*) сопротивление чему-н; **to take a ~ on sth** занимать (занять* *perf*) твёрдую позицию по поводу чего-н; **to take the ~** (*US*: *LAW*) занимать (занять* *perf*) место свидетеля; **to ~ for parliament** (*BRIT*) баллотироваться *(impf)* в парламент; **to ~ to gain/lose sth** иметь *(impf)* шанс обрести/потерять что-н; **to ~ sb dinner** угощать (угостить* *perf*) кого-н обедом; **to ~ sb a drink** ставить* (поставить* *perf*) кому-н выпивку; **it ~s to reason** само собой разумеется; **as things ~** в этой ситуации; **I can't ~ him** я его терпеть не могу
▸ **stand aside** *vi* (*fig*) стоять *(impf)* в стороне
▸ **stand by** *vi* (*be ready*) быть* *(impf)* наготове ◆ *vt fus* (*opinion, decision*) не отступать (не отступить* *perf*) от *+gen*; (*person*) поддерживать (поддержать* *perf*)
▸ **stand down** *vi* (*withdraw*) уступать (уступить* *perf*) место, уходить* (уйти* *perf*); (*LAW*) покидать (покинуть *perf*) место свидетеля
▸ **stand for** *vt fus* (*signify*) обозначать *(impf)*; (*represent*) представлять *(impf)*; **I won't ~ for it** я этого не потерплю
▸ **stand in for** *vt fus* (*replace*) замещать (заместить* *perf*) *+acc*
▸ **stand out** *vi* (*be prominent*) выделяться (выделиться *perf*)
▸ **stand up** *vi* (*rise*) вставать* (встать* *perf*)
▸ **stand up for** *vt fus* (*defend*: *rights etc*) отстаивать (отстоять* *perf*); (: *person*) стоять* (постоять* *perf*) за *+acc*
▸ **stand up to** *vt fus* (*withstand*: *also fig*) выдерживать (выдержать* *perf*).
stand-alone ['stændələun] *adj* (*COMPUT*) автономный.
standard ['stændəd] *n* (*level*) уровень* *m*; (*norm, criterion*) стандарт; (*flag*) штандарт ◆ *adj* (*normal*: *size etc*) стандартный* (стандартен); (*text*) основной; (*practice*) общепринятый (общепринят); (*model, feature*) типичный* (типичен); **~s** *npl* (*morals*) нравы *mpl*; **to be** *or* **to come up to ~** быть* *(impf)* на соответствующем уровне; **to apply**

a double ~ испóльзовать *(impf/perf)* двойнýю морáль.
standardization [stændədaɪ'zeɪʃən] *n* стандартизáция.
standardize ['stændədaɪz] *vt* стандартизúровать *(impf/perf)*.
standard lamp *n* (*BRIT*) торшéр.
standard of living *n* ýровень* *m* жúзни.
standard time *n* стандáртное врéмя* *nt*.
stand-by ['stændbaɪ] *n* (*reserve*) резéрв, подмóга ◆ *adj* запаснóй, резéрвный; **to be on ~** (*doctor, crew, firemen etc*) быть* *(impf)* наготóве.
stand-by ticket *n* (*THEAT etc*) билéт, кýплённый пéред начáлом представлéния.
stand-in ['stændɪn] *n* заместúтель(ница) *m(f)*.
standing ['stændɪŋ] *adj* (*permanent*) постоя́нный; (*ovation*) стоя́чий* ◆ *n* (*status*) положéние; (*duration*): **of 6 months' ~** 6-ти мéсячной дáвности; **he received/was given a ~ ovation** емý аплодúровали стóя; **he gave me a ~ invitation** он сказáл, чтóбы я приходúл в любóе врéмя; **a man of some ~** человéк с положéнием; **promises of many years ~** многолéтние обещáния.
standing committee *n* постоя́нный комитéт.
standing joke *n* дежýрная шýтка*.
standing order *n* (*BRIT*: *at bank*) прикáз о регуля́рных платежáх.
standing room *n* стоя́чие местá *ntpl*.
standoffish [stænd'ɔfɪʃ] *adj* спесúвый (спесúв).
standpat ['stændpæt] *adj* (*US*: *person*) консерватúвный.
standpipe ['stændpaɪp] *n* напóрная трубá*.
standpoint ['stændpɔɪnt] *n* тóчка* зрéния.
standstill ['stændstɪl] *n*: **to be at a ~** (*also fig*) простáивать *(impf)*; **to come to a ~** остáнавливаться (остановúться* *perf*).
stank [stæŋk] *pt of* **stink**.
stanza ['stænzə] *n* (*of poem*) строфá*.
staple ['steɪpl] *n* (*for papers*) скóбка*; (*chief product*) основнóй продýкт ◆ *adj* (*food etc*) основнóй ◆ *vt* (*fasten*) сшивáть (сшить* *perf*) стéплером.
stapler ['steɪplə[r]] *n* сшивáтель *m*, стéплер.
star [stɑː[r]] *n* (*also fig*) звездá ◆ *vi*: **to ~ in** игрáть (сыгрáть *perf*) глáвную роль в *+prp* ◆ *vt* (*THEAT, CINEMA*): **the film ~s my brother** глáвную роль игрáет в фúльме мой брат; **the ~s** *npl* (*horoscope*) звёзды *fpl*; **4-~ hotel** четырёхзвёздочная гостúница; **2-~/4-~ petrol** (*BRIT*) *бензúн с нúзким/высóким октáновым числóм*.
star attraction *n* гвоздь* *m* прогрáммы.
starboard ['stɑːbəd] *n* (*NAUT*) прáвый борт*; **to ~** прáво руля́.
starch [stɑːtʃ] *n* (*also CULIN*) крахмáл.
starched ['stɑːtʃt] *adj* (*collar*) накрахмáленный (накрахмáлен).
starchy ['stɑːtʃɪ] *adj* (*food*) содержáщий крахмáл; (*pej*: *person*) чóпорный* (чóпорен).
stardom ['stɑːdəm] *n* слáва.
stare [stɛə[r]] *n* прúстальный взгляд ◆ *vi*: **to ~ at** прúстально смотрéть* *(impf)* на *+acc*.
starfish ['stɑːfɪʃ] *n* морскáя звездá*.
stark [stɑːk] *adj* (*bleak*) гóлый* (гол); (*facts, reality*) гóлый; (*poverty*) совершéнный; (*colour, contrast*) я́вный* (я́вен) ◆ *adv*: **~ naked** совершéнно гóлый.
starkers ['stɑːkəz] *adj, adv* без всегó.
starlet ['stɑːlɪt] *n* (*CINEMA*) молодáя актрúса.
starlight ['stɑːlaɪt] *n*: **by ~** при свéте звёзд.
starling ['stɑːlɪŋ] *n* скворéц*.
starlit ['stɑːlɪt] *adj* (*night*) звёздный.
starry ['stɑːrɪ] *adj* (*night, sky*) звёздный.
starry-eyed [stɑːrɪ'aɪd] *adj* (*innocent*) наúвный* (наúвен); (*from wonder*) очарóванный.
Stars and Stripes *n*: **the ~ ~ ~** звёздно-полосáтый *m adj* (*флаг США*).
star sign *n* знак зодиáка.
star-studded ['stɑːstʌdɪd] *adj*: **this film has a ~ cast** в э́том фúльме снимáется мнóго звёзд.
START *n abbr* (*MIL*: = *Strategic Arms Reduction Talks*) перегovóры *pl* о сокращéнии стратегúческих вооружéний.
start [stɑːt] *n* начáло; (*SPORT*) старт; (*departure*) отправлéние; (*sudden movement*) вздрáгивание; (*advantage*) преимýщество ◆ *vt* (*begin*) начинáть (начáть* *perf*); (*cause*) вызывáть (вы́звать* *perf*); (*found*: *business etc*) оснóвывать (основáть* *perf*); (*engine*) заводúть* (завестú* *perf*), запускáть (запустúть* *perf*) ◆ *vi* (*begin*) начинáться (начáться* *perf*); (*begin moving*) отправля́ться (отпрáвиться* *perf*); (*engine, car*) заводúться* (завестúсь* *perf*); (*jump*: *with fright*) вздрáгивать (вздрóгнуть *perf*); **to ~ doing** *or* **to do** начинáть (начáть* *perf*) *+impf infin*; **at the ~** в начáле; **for a ~** для начáла; **to make an early ~** рáно начинáть (начáть* *perf*); **to ~ (off) with ...** (*firstly*) во-пéрвых ...; (*at the beginning*) сначáла
▸ **start off** *vi* (*begin*) начинáться (начáться* *perf*); (*begin moving, leave*) отправля́ться (отпрáвиться* *perf*)
▸ **start out** *vi* (*leave*) отправля́ться (отпрáвиться* *perf*)
▸ **start over** *vi* (*US*) начинáть (начáть* *perf*) снóва
▸ **start up** *vi* (*business etc*) открывáться (откры́ться* *perf*); (*engine, car*) заводúться* (завестúсь* *perf*) ◆ *vt* (*business etc*) оснóвывать (основáть* *perf*); (*engine, car*) заводúть* (завестú* *perf*), запускáть (запустúть* *perf*).

starter ['stɑ:tə^r] *n* (*AUT, SPORT*) ста́ртер; (*runner, horse*) уча́стник(-ица) забе́га; (*BRIT: CULIN*) заку́ска.
starting point ['stɑ:tɪŋ-] *n* (*for journey*) отправно́й пункт; (*for discussion, idea etc*) отправна́я то́чка*.
starting price *n* (*at auction*) нача́льная *or* отправна́я цена́*.
startle ['stɑ:tl] *vt* вспу́гивать (вспугну́ть *perf*).
startling ['stɑ:tlɪŋ] *adj* порази́тельный* (порази́телен).
star turn *n* (*BRIT*) коро́нный но́мер*.
starvation [stɑ:'veɪʃən] *n* го́лод; **to die of** *or* **from ~** умира́ть (умере́ть* *perf*) от го́лода.
starve [stɑ:v] *vi* (*to death*) умира́ть (умере́ть* *perf*) с го́лоду; (*be very hungry*) проголода́ться (*perf*) ♦ *vt* (*person, animal*) мори́ть (замори́ть *perf*) го́лодом; (*fig: deprive*): **to ~ sb of sth** лиша́ть (лиши́ть *perf*) кого́-н чего́-н; **I'm starving** (*inf*) я умира́ю от го́лода.
Star Wars *n* „Звёздные во́йны" *fpl*.
stash [stæʃ] *vt* (*inf*) припря́тывать (припря́тать *perf*), запаса́ться (запасти́сь* *perf*) *+instr*.
state [steɪt] *n* (*condition*) состоя́ние; (*government*) госуда́рство ♦ *vt* (*say, declare*) констати́ровать (*impf/perf*); **the S~s** *npl* (*GEO*) Соединённые Шта́ты *mpl*; **to be in a ~** быть* (*impf*) в па́нике; **~ of emergency** чрезвыча́йное положе́ние; **~ of mind** душе́вное состоя́ние.
state control *n* госуда́рственный контро́ль *m*.
stated ['steɪtɪd] *adj* (*aims, beliefs etc*) устано́вленный.
State Department *n* (*US*) Госуда́рственный департа́мент.
state education *n* (*BRIT*) госуда́рственное образова́ние.
stateless ['steɪtlɪs] *adj* (*person*) не име́ющий гражда́нства.
stately ['steɪtlɪ] *adj* вели́чественный* (вели́чествен); **~ home** дом-уса́дьба.
statement ['steɪtmənt] *n* (*declaration*) заявле́ние; (*FINANCE*) отчёт, счёт; **official ~** официа́льное заявле́ние; **bank ~** вы́писка* с ба́нковского счёта.
state of the art *n* после́днее сло́во те́хники ♦ *adj*: **~-~-~-~** ультрасовреме́нный.
state-owned ['steɪtəund] *adj* (*industry etc*) госуда́рственный.
state school *n* (*BRIT*) госуда́рственная шко́ла.
state secret *n* госуда́рственная та́йна.
statesman ['steɪtsmən] *irreg n* госуда́рственный де́ятель *m*.
statesmanship ['steɪtsmənʃɪp] *n* госуда́рственная де́ятельность *f*.
static ['stætɪk] *n* (*RADIO, TV*) (атмосфе́рные) поме́хи *fpl* ♦ *adj* (*not moving*) стати́чный* (стати́чен), неподви́жный* (неподви́жен).
static electricity *n* стати́ческое электри́чество.
station ['steɪʃən] *n* ста́нция; (*larger railway station*) вокза́л; (*also:* **police ~**) полице́йский* уча́сток* ♦ *vt* (*position: guards etc*) выставля́ть (вы́ставить* *perf*); (*base: soldiers etc*) дислоци́ровать (*impf/perf*), размеща́ть (размести́ть* *perf*); **action ~s** сигна́л "все по места́м!"; **to get above one's ~** сади́ться* (сесть* *perf*) не в свои́ са́ни.
stationary ['steɪʃnərɪ] *adj* (*vehicle*) неподви́жный.
stationer ['steɪʃənə^r] *n* торго́вец* канцеля́рскими това́рами.
stationer's (shop) *n* магази́н канцеля́рских това́ров.
stationery ['steɪʃnərɪ] *n* канцеля́рские принадле́жности *fpl*.
stationmaster ['steɪʃənmɑ:stə^r] *n* нача́льник ста́нции.
station wagon *n* (*US*) автомоби́ль-фурго́н, пика́п.
statistic [stə'tɪstɪk] *n* стати́стик.
statistical [stə'tɪstɪkl] *adj* (*evidence, techniques*) статисти́ческий*.
statistics [stə'tɪstɪks] *n* (*science*) стати́стика.
statue ['stætju:] *n* ста́туя.
statuesque [stætju'ɛsk] *adj* (*woman*) ста́тная (ста́тна).
statuette [stætju'ɛt] *n* статуэ́тка*.
stature ['stætʃə^r] *n* рост; (*fig: reputation*) положе́ние.
status ['steɪtəs] *n* ста́тус; (*importance*) значе́ние; **the ~ quo** ста́тус-кво *m ind*.
status line *n* (*COMPUT*) строка́* состоя́ния.
status symbol *n* си́мвол положе́ния в о́бществе.
statute ['stætju:t] *n* стату́т, законода́тельный акт; **~s** *npl* (*of club etc*) уста́в *msg*.
statute book *n* (*LAW, POL*): **the ~ ~** свод зако́нов.
statutory ['stætjutrɪ] *adj* (*powers, rights etc*) устано́вленный зако́ном; **~ meeting** учреди́тельное собра́ние.
staunch [stɔ:ntʃ] *adj* (*ally etc*) пре́данный ♦ *vt* остана́вливать (останови́ть* *perf*).
stave [steɪv] *n* (*MUS*) но́тный стан
▸ **stave off** *vt* (*attack*) отсро́чивать (отсро́чить *perf*); (*threat*) отводи́ть* (отвести́* *perf*).
stay [steɪ] *n* пребыва́ние ♦ *vi* (*remain*) остава́ться* (оста́ться* *perf*); (*with sb, as guest*) гости́ть* (*impf*); (*in place: spend some time*) остана́вливаться (останови́ться* *perf*); **~ of execution** (*LAW*) отсро́чка* исполне́ния; **to ~ at home** сиде́ть* (*impf*) до́ма; **to ~ in bed** лежа́ть* (*impf*) в посте́ли; **to ~ put** не дви́гаться (дви́нуться *perf*) с ме́ста; **to ~ with friends** остана́вливаться (останови́ться* *perf*) *or* гости́ть* (*impf*) у друзе́й; **to ~ the night** (*in a place*) ночева́ть* (заночева́ть* *perf*); (*with sb*) проводи́ть* (провести́* *perf*) ночь
▸ **stay behind** *vi* остава́ться* (оста́ться* *perf*)
▸ **stay in** *vi* (*at home*) остава́ться* (оста́ться*

perf) до́ма
▸ **stay on** *vi* остава́ться* (оста́ться* *perf*)
▸ **stay out** *vi* (*of house*) отсу́тствовать *(impf)*; (*remain on strike*) продолжа́ть *(impf)* бастова́ть
▸ **stay up** *vi* (*at night*) не ложи́ться *(impf)* спать.
staying power ['steɪɪŋ-] *n* выно́сливость *f*.
STD *n abbr* (*BRIT: TEL:* = *subscriber trunk dialling*) ≈ АМТС= *автомати́ческая междугоро́дная телефо́нная связь*; (*MED:* = *sexually transmitted disease*) *заболева́ние, передава́емое половы́м путём*.
stead [stɛd] *n*: **in sb's ~** вме́сто кого́-н; **to stand sb in good ~** пригожда́ться (пригоди́ться* *perf*) кому́-н.
steadfast ['stɛdfɑ:st] *adj* (*person*) сто́йкий* (сто́ек); (*refusal, support*) твёрдый.
steadily ['stɛdɪlɪ] *adv* (*firmly*) про́чно; (*constantly, fixedly*) постоя́нно; (*walk: decisively*) реши́тельно; (: *without stumbling*) твёрдо.
steady ['stɛdɪ] *adj* (*constant*) стаби́льный* (стаби́лен); (: *boyfriend, speed*) постоя́нный; (*person, character*) уравнове́шенный* (уравнове́шен); (*firm: hand etc*) твёрдый* (твёрд); (*calm: look, voice*) ро́вный* (ро́вен) ◆ *vt* (*object*) придава́ть* (прида́ть* *perf*) усто́йчивость +*dat*; (*nerves, person*) успока́ивать (успоко́ить *perf*); (*voice*) придава́ть* (прида́ть* *perf*) ро́вность +*dat*; **to ~ o.s. on** *or* **against sth** опира́ться (опере́ться* *perf*) о(бо) что-н.
steak [steɪk] *n* (*beef*) бифште́кс; (*fish*) филе́ *nt ind*; (*pork*) вы́резка*.
steakhouse ['steɪkhaus] *n* бифште́ксная *f adj*.
steal [sti:l] (*pt* **stole**, *pp* **stolen**) *vt* ворова́ть (своровать *perf*), красть* (укра́сть* *perf*) ◆ *vi* (*thieve*) ворова́ть *(impf)*; (*move secretly*) кра́сться* *(impf)*
▸ **steal away** *vi* незаме́тно ускольза́ть (ускользну́ть *perf*)
▸ **steal off** *vi* = **steal away**.
stealth [stɛlθ] *n*: **by ~** укра́дкой.
stealthy ['stɛlθɪ] *adj* (*movements, actions*) та́йный.
steam [sti:m] *n* пар* ◆ *vt* (*CULIN*) вари́ть* (свари́ть* *perf*) на пару́, па́рить *(impf)* ◆ *vi* (*give off steam*) испуска́ть (испусти́ть* *perf*) пар; **under one's own ~** (*fig*) свои́ми си́лами; **to run out of ~** (*fig: person*) выдыха́ться (вы́дохнуться *perf*); **to let off ~** (*fig: inf*) выпуска́ть (вы́пустить* *perf*) пар
▸ **steam up** *vi* (*window*) запотева́ть (запоте́ть *perf*); **to get ~ed up about sth** (*fig: inf*) кипяти́ться* (раскипяти́ться* *perf*) из-за чего́-н.
steam engine *n* (*RAIL*) парово́з.
steamer ['sti:mə^r] *n* парохо́д; (*CULIN*) парова́рка*.
steam iron *n* утю́г* с отпа́ривателем.
steamroller ['sti:mrəulə^r] *n* парово́й като́к*.
steamship ['sti:mʃɪp] *n* = **steamer**.
steamy ['sti:mɪ] *adj* (*room*) по́лный* (по́лон) па́ра; (*window*) запоте́вший*.
steed [sti:d] *n* конь *m*.
steel [sti:l] *n* сталь *f* ◆ *adj* стально́й.
steel band *n* (*MUS*) кари́бский уда́рный орке́стр.
steel industry *n* сталелите́йная промы́шленность *f*.
steel mill *n* сталелите́йный заво́д.
steelworks ['sti:lwə:ks] *n* сталелите́йный заво́д.
steely ['sti:lɪ] *adj* (*eyes, gaze*) стально́й; (*determination*) непреклó́нный*.
steep [sti:p] *adj* круто́й* (крут); (*price*) высо́кий* (высо́к) ◆ *vt* (*soak: food*) выма́чивать (вы́мочить *perf*); (: *clothes*) зама́чивать (замочи́ть* *perf*); **a house ~ed in history** (*fig*) дом* с истори́ческим про́шлым ове́янный исто́рией.
steeple ['sti:pl] *n* шпиль *m*; (*belltower*) колоко́льня*.
steeplechase ['sti:pltʃeɪs] *n* стипль-че́з.
steeplejack ['sti:pldʒæk] *n* верхола́з.
steeply ['sti:plɪ] *adv* кру́то.
steer [stɪə^r] *vt* (*vehicle, person*) води́ть*/вести́* *(impf)* ◆ *vi* (*manoeuvre*) маневри́ровать *(impf)* ◆ *n* кастри́рованный бык*; **to ~ clear of sb/sth** (*fig*) избега́ть *(impf)* кого́-н/чего́-н.
steering ['stɪərɪŋ] *n* (*AUT*) управле́ние.
steering column *n* рулева́я коло́нка.
steering committee *n* коми́ссия по вы́работке регла́мента.
steering wheel *n* руль* *m*.
stellar ['stɛlə^r] *adj* (*of stars*) звёздный.
stem [stɛm] *n* (*BOT: of plant*) ствол*, сте́бель* *m*; (*of leaf, fruit*) черешо́к*; (*of glass*) но́жка*; (*of pipe*) чере́нок* ◆ *vt* (*stop*) остана́вливать (останови́ть* *perf*)
▸ **stem from** *vt fus* (*subj: condition, problem*) происходи́ть* (произойти́* *perf*) от +*gen*; **their aggressiveness ~med from fear** их агресси́вность порождена́ стра́хом.
stench [stɛntʃ] *n* (*pej*) вонь *f*.
stencil ['stɛnsl] *n* трафаре́т ◆ *vt* (*letters, designs etc*) де́лать (сде́лать *perf*) по трафаре́ту.
stenographer [stɛ'nɔgrəfə^r] *n* (*US*) стенографи́ст(ка*).
stenography [stɛ'nɔgrəfɪ] *n* (*US*) стеногра́фия.
step [stɛp] *n* (*also fig*) шаг*; (*of stairs*) ступе́нь *f* ◆ *vi*: **to ~ forward/back** ступа́ть (ступи́ть* *perf*) вперёд/наза́д; **~s** *npl* (*BRIT*) = **stepladder**; **~ by ~** (*also fig*) шаг за ша́гом; **to be in/out of ~ (with)** идти́* *(impf)* в но́гу/не в но́гу (с +*instr*); (*fig*) соотве́тствовать *(impf)*/не

соответствовать *(impf)* (+*dat*)
▸ **step down** *vi* (*fig: resign*) уходи́ть* (уйти́* *perf*) в отста́вку
▸ **step in** *vi* (*fig*) вме́шиваться (вмеша́ться *perf*)
▸ **step off** *vt fus* сходи́ть* (сойти́* *perf*) с +*gen*
▸ **step on** *vt fus* (*walk on*) наступа́ть (наступи́ть* *perf*) на +*acc*
▸ **step over** *vt fus* переступа́ть (переступи́ть* *perf*) че́рез +*acc*
▸ **step up** *vt* (*increase*) уси́ливать (уси́лить *perf*).
step aerobics *n* степ-аэро́бика (*с использова́нием осо́бой ступе́ньки*).
stepbrother ['stɛpbrʌðə'] *n* сво́дный брат*.
stepchild ['stɛptʃaɪld] *n* (*boy*) па́сынок*; (*girl*) па́дчерица.
stepdaughter ['stɛpdɔ:tə'] *n* па́дчерица.
stepfather ['stɛpfɑ:ðə'] *n* о́тчим.
stepladder ['stɛplædə'] *n* (*BRIT*) стремя́нка*.
stepmother ['stɛpmʌðə'] *n* ма́чеха.
stepping stone ['stɛpɪŋ-] *n* (*in river*) опо́рный ка́мень *m*; (*fig*) ступе́нька.
step-reebok® [stɛp'ri:bɔk] *n ступе́нька, испо́льзуемая при степ-аэро́бике*.
stepsister ['stɛpsɪstə'] *n* сво́дная сестра́*.
stepson ['stɛpsʌn] *n* па́сынок*.
stereo ['stɛrɪəu] *n* (*system*) стереосисте́ма; (*record player*) стереопро́игрыватель *m* ◆ *adj* (*also:* **~phonic**) стереофони́ческий; **in ~** сте́рео.
stereotype ['stɪərɪətaɪp] *n* стереоти́п ◆ *vt* воспринима́ть *(impf)* по стереоти́пу.
sterile ['stɛraɪl] *adj* (*also fig*) беспло́дный* (беспло́ден); (*free from germs*) стери́льный* (стери́лен).
sterility [stɛ'rɪlɪtɪ] *n* (*infertility*) беспло́дие.
sterilization [stɛrɪlaɪ'zeɪʃən] *n* стерилиза́ция.
sterilize ['stɛrɪlaɪz] *vt* стерилизова́ть *(impf)*.
sterling ['stə:lɪŋ] *adj* (*efforts: noble*) благоро́дный*; (*: excellent*) отме́нный ◆ *n* (*ECON*) фунт сте́рлингов; **~ silver** серебро́ 925-ой про́бы; **one pound ~** оди́н фунт сте́рлингов.
sterling area *n* сте́рлинговая зо́на.
stern [stə:n] *adj* стро́гий* (строг) ◆ *n* (*of boat*) корма́.
sternum ['stə:nəm] *n* груди́на.
steroid ['stɪərɔɪd] *n* стеро́ид.
stet [stɛt] *n корректи́рующий знак, отменя́ющий попра́вки* ◆ *vt* оста́вить *(perf)* как бы́ло.
stethoscope ['stɛθəskəup] *n* стетоско́п.
stevedore ['sti:vədɔ:'] *n* порто́вый гру́зчик.
stew [stju:] *n* (*meat*) тушёное мя́со ◆ *vt* (*meat*) туши́ть* (потуши́ть* *perf*); (*fruit*) вари́ть (свари́ть *perf*) ◆ *vi* (*meat*) туши́ться* (потуши́ться* *perf*); (*fruit*) вари́ться (свари́ться *perf*); **vegetable ~** тушёные о́вощи; **~ed tea** перестоя́вшийся чай; **~ed fruit** варёные фру́кты.
steward ['stju:əd] *n* (*on ship, train*) стюа́рд; (*on plane*) бортпроводни́к*; (*in club etc*) распоряди́тель *m*; (*also: shop* **~**) цехово́й ста́роста.
stewardess ['stjuədɛs] *n* (*on plane*) стюарде́сса, бортпроводни́ца.
stewardship ['stjuədʃɪp] *n* управле́ние.
stewing steak ['stju:ɪŋ-] (*US* **stew meat**) *n* говя́дина для туше́ния.
St. Ex. *abbr* = **stock exchange**.
stg *abbr* = **sterling**.
stick [stɪk] (*pt, pp* **stuck**) *n* (*of wood*) па́лка*; (*of dynamite, chalk etc*) па́лочка*; (*walking stick*) трость *f* ◆ *vt* (*with glue etc*) кле́ить (прикле́ить *perf*); (*inf: put*) сова́ть* (су́нуть *perf*); (*: tolerate*) терпе́ть (вы́терпеть *perf*); (*thrust*) втыка́ть (воткну́ть *perf*) ◆ *vi* (*become attached*) прикле́иваться (прикле́иться *perf*); (*be unmoveable*) застрева́ть (застря́ть* *perf*); (*in mind etc*) засе́сть* *(perf)*; (*get jammed: door*) заеда́ть (зае́сть* *perf*); (*: lift*) застрева́ть (застря́ть* *perf*); **to get hold of the wrong end of the ~** (*BRIT: fig*) совсе́м не так понима́ть (поня́ть* *perf*); **he stuck a cigar in his mouth** он засу́нул сига́ру в рот; **to ~ to** (*become attached*) прикле́иваться (прикле́иться *perf*) к +*dat*; (*one's word, promise*) держа́ть* (сдержа́ть* *perf*); (*principles*) остава́ться* (оста́ться* *perf*) ве́рным(-ой) +*dat*
▸ **stick around** *vi* (*inf*) торча́ть *(impf)*
▸ **stick out** *vi* (*ears etc*) торча́ть *(impf)* ◆ *vt*: **to ~ it out** (*inf*) терпе́ть* (вы́терпеть* *perf*)
▸ **stick up** *vi* (*hair etc*) торча́ть *(impf)*
▸ **stick up for** *vt fus* (*person*) заступа́ться (заступи́ться* *perf*) за +*acc*; (*principle*) отста́ивать (отстоя́ть *perf*).
sticker ['stɪkə'] *n* накле́йка.
sticking plaster ['stɪkɪŋ-] *n* лейкопла́стырь *m*.
sticking point *n* (*in relationship*) то́чка преткнове́ния.
stickleback ['stɪklbæk] *n* ко́люшка.
stickler ['stɪklə'] *n*: **to be a ~ for** наста́ивать *(impf)* на +*prp*.
stick shift *n* (*US: AUT*) переключа́тель *m* скоросте́й.
stick-up ['stɪkʌp] *n* (*inf*) вооружённое ограбле́ние.
sticky ['stɪkɪ] *adj* (*hands etc*) ли́пкий*; (*label*) кле́йкий*; (*fig: situation*) щекотли́вый (щекотли́в).
stiff [stɪf] *adj* (*brush*) жёсткий* (жёсток); (*paste*) густо́й; (*egg-white*) круто́й; (*person*) деревя́нный; (*door, zip*) туго́й* (туг); (*manner, smile*) натя́нутый (натя́нут); (*competition*) ожесточённый; (*severe: sentence*) суро́вый (суро́в); (*high: price*) высо́кий* (высо́к); (*strong: drink*) кре́пкий*; (*: breeze*) си́льный* (силён) ◆ *adv* (*bored, worried, scared*) до́ смерти; **I am** *or* **feel ~** у меня́ всё те́ло но́ет; **I have a ~ neck** у меня́ свело́ ше́ю; **to keep a ~ upper lip** (*BRIT: fig*)

сохранять (сохранить *perf*) хладнокровие.
stiffen ['stɪfn] *vi* (*body*) напрягаться (напрячься* *perf*); (*joints, neck*) не сгибаться (*impf*); **my muscles have ~ed** у меня свело мышцы.
stiffness ['stɪfnɪs] *n* (*of joints*) неподвижность *f*; (*of paper, cloth*) жёсткость *f*; (*in consistency*) густота; (*in behaviour etc*) натянутость *f*.
stifle ['staɪfl] *vt* (*yawn*) подавлять (подавить* *perf*); (*opposition*) душить (задушить *perf*); (*subj: heat*) душить (*impf*).
stifling ['staɪflɪŋ] *adj* (*heat*) удушливый (удушлив).
stigma ['stɪgmə] *n* (*of failure, defeat etc*) клеймо; (*BOT*) рыльце; (*MED*) стигма.
stile [staɪl] *n* перелаз.
stiletto [stɪ'lɛtəu] *n* (*BRIT: also:* **~ heel**) шпилька.
still [stɪl] *adj* тихий* (тих); (*BRIT: not fizzy*) негазированный ◆ *adv* (*up to this time*) всё ещё; (*even, yet*) ещё; (*nonetheless*) всё-таки, тем не менее ◆ *n* (*CINEMA*) рекламный фотокадр; **to stand ~** стоять* (*impf*) неподвижно; **keep ~!** не шевелитесь!; **he ~ hasn't arrived** он всё ещё не пришёл.
stillborn ['stɪlbɔ:n] *adj* (*baby*) мертворождённый.
still life *n* (*ART*) натюрморт.
stilt [stɪlt] *n* (*pile*) свая; (*for walking on*) ходуля*.
stilted ['stɪltɪd] *adj* (*behaviour, conversation*) высокопарный* (высокопарен).
stimulant ['stɪmjulənt] *n* стимулирующее *or* возбуждающее средство.
stimulate ['stɪmjuleɪt] *vt* стимулировать (*impf/perf*).
stimulating ['stɪmjuleɪtɪŋ] *adj* вдохновляющий.
stimulation [stɪmju'leɪʃən] *n* стимулирование.
stimuli ['stɪmjulaɪ] *npl of* **stimulus**.
stimulus ['stɪmjuləs] (*pl* **stimuli**) *n* (*encouragement*) стимул; (*MED*) стимулятор; (*BIO, PSYCH*) раздражитель *m*.
sting [stɪŋ] (*pt, pp* **stung**) *n* (*from insect*) укус; (*from plant*) ожог; (*organ: of wasp etc*) жало; (*inf: confidence trick*) мошенничество ◆ *vt* (*also fig*) уязвлять (уязвить* *perf*) ◆ *vi* (*insect, animal*) жалиться (*impf*); (*plant*) жечься* (*impf*); (*eyes, ointment etc*) жечь* (*impf*); **my eyes are ~ing** мне жжёт глаза.
stingy ['stɪndʒɪ] *adj* (*pej: person*) скаредный* (скареден).
stink [stɪŋk] (*pt* **stank**, *pp* **stunk**) *n* смрад, вонь *f* ◆ *vi* смердеть (*impf*).
stinker ['stɪŋkə'] (*inf*) *n* (*person*) мерзавец*(-вка*); **it's a real ~ of a problem/exam** это жуткая проблема/ужасный экзамен.
stinking ['stɪŋkɪŋ] (*inf*) *adj* (*inf*) вонючий* (вонюч); **a ~ cold** жуткая простуда; **~ rich** жутко богатый.
stint [stɪnt] *n* период работы ◆ *vi*: **to ~ on** (*work*) халтурить (*impf*) в +*prp*; (*ingredients*) зажимать (зажать* *perf*).
stipend ['staɪpɛnd] *n* (*of vicar etc*) жалованье; (*of student*) стипендия.
stipendiary [staɪ'pɛndɪərɪ] *adj*: **~ magistrate** платный мировой судья.
stipulate ['stɪpjuleɪt] *vt* (*condition, amount etc*) определять (определить *perf*).
stipulation [stɪpju'leɪʃən] *n* условие.
stir [stə:ʳ] *n* (*fig: agitation*) шум, сенсация ◆ *vt* (*tea etc*) мешать (помешать *perf*); (*fig: emotions*) волновать (взволновать *perf*) ◆ *vi* (*move slightly*) шевелиться (пошевелиться *perf*); **to give sth a ~** размешивать (размешать *perf*) что-н; **to cause a ~** вызывать (вызвать* *perf*) сенсацию
▸ **stir up** *vt* (*trouble*) вызывать (вызвать* *perf*).
stir-fry ['stə:'fraɪ] *vt* быстро обжаривать (обжарить *perf*).
stirring ['stə:rɪŋ] *adj* (*speech, occasion*) волнующий.
stirrup ['stɪrəp] *n* стремя* *nt*.
stitch [stɪtʃ] *n* (*SEWING*) стежок*; (*KNITTING*) петля*; (*MED*) шов* ◆ *vt* (*sew*) шить* (сшить* *perf*); (*MED: wound*) зашивать (зашить* *perf*); **I have a ~ in my side** у меня колет в боку.
stoat [stəut] *n* горностай.
stock [stɔk] *n* (*supply*) запас; (*AGR*) поголовье; (*CULIN*) бульон; (*descent, origin*) происхождение; (*FINANCE*) ценные бумаги *fpl*; (*COMM: of company*) акционерный капитал; (*RAIL: also:* **rolling ~**) (подвижной) состав ◆ *adj* (*fig: reply, excuse etc*) шаблонный ◆ *vt* (*have in stock*) иметь (*impf*) в наличии; **~s and shares** акции и ценные бумаги; **to be in/out of ~** иметься (*impf*)/не иметься (*impf*) в наличии; **a well-~ed shop** магазин с большим ассортиментом товаров; **to take ~ of** (*fig*) оценивать (оценить* *perf*); **government ~** правительственные акции
▸ **stock up** *vi*: **to ~ up with** запасаться (запастись* *perf*) +*instr*.
stockade [stɔ'keɪd] *n* частокол.
stockbroker ['stɔkbrəukəʳ] *n* (*COMM*) фондовый брокер.
stock control *n* (*COMM*) управление запасами.
stock cube *n* (*BRIT: CULIN*) бульонный кубик.
stock exchange *n* фондовая биржа.
stockholder ['stɔkhəuldəʳ] *n* (*COMM*) акционер.
Stockholm ['stɔkhəum] *n* Стокгольм.
stocking ['stɔkɪŋ] *n* чулок*.
stock in trade *n* (*COMM*) *запасы имеющиеся в*

* marks translations which have irregular inflections. The Russian-English side of the dictionary gives inflectional information.

наличии и предназначенные для продажи; (*fig*): **it's his ~ ~ ~** это его обычное занятие.
stockist ['stɔkɪst] *n* (*BRIT*) стокист (*фирма, имеющая запас какой-нибудь продукции*).
stock market *n* (*BRIT*) фондовая биржа.
stock phrase *n* клише *nt ind*.
stockpile ['stɔkpaɪl] *n* (*of weapons, food*) запас ◆ *vt* запасать (запасти* *perf*).
stockroom ['stɔkru:m] *n* (*COMM*) склад.
stocktaking ['stɔkteɪkɪŋ] *n* (*BRIT*: *COMM*) инвентаризация.
stocky ['stɔkɪ] *adj* коренастый (коренаст).
stodgy ['stɔdʒɪ] *adj* (*food*) тяжёлый.
stoic ['stəuɪk] *n* стоик.
stoical ['stəuɪkl] *adj* (*person, behaviour*) стоический*.
stoke [stəuk] *vt* (*fire*) поддерживать (*impf*); (*boiler, furnace*) поддерживать (*impf*) огонь в +*prp*.
stoker ['stəukə^r] *n* (*RAIL, NAUT etc*) кочегар.
stole [stəul] *pt of* **steal** ◆ *n* палантин.
stolen ['stəuln] *pp of* **steal**.
stolid ['stɔlɪd] *adj* (*person, behaviour*) бесстрастный* (бесстрастен).
stomach ['stʌmək] *n* (*ANAT*) желудок*; (*belly*) живот* ◆ *vt* (*fig*) переносить* (*impf*).
stomachache ['stʌməkeɪk] *n* желудочные боли *fpl*.
stomach pump *n* желудочный зонд.
stomach ulcer *n* язва желудка.
stomp [stɔmp] *vi*: **to ~ in/out** входить* (войти* *perf*)/уходить* (уйти* *perf*) тяжёлыми шагами.
stone [stəun] *n* (*also MED*) камень* *m*; (*pebble*) камешек*; (*in fruit*) косточка*; (*BRIT*: *weight*) стоун (*14 фунтов*) ◆ *adj* каменный ◆ *vt* (*person*) закидывать (закидать *perf*) камнями в +*acc*; (*fruit*) вынимать (вынуть *perf*) косточки из +*gen*; **within a ~'s throw of the school** в двух шагах от школы.
Stone Age *n*: **the ~ ~** каменный век.
stone-cold ['stəun'kəuld] *adj* холодный* как лёд.
stoned [stəund] *adj* (*inf*: *drunk*) мертвецки пьяный* (пьян); (: *on drugs*) обкурившийся.
stone-deaf ['stəun'dɛf] *adj* совершенно глухой.
stonemason ['stəunmeɪsn] *n* каменщик.
stonewall [stəun'wɔ:l] *vti* заниматься (*impf*) процедурными задержками (*в парламенте*).
stonework ['stəunwə:k] *n* (каменная) кладка.
stony ['stəunɪ] *adj* (*ground*) каменистый (каменист); (*fig*: *glance, silence etc*) холодный.
stood [stud] *pt, pp of* **stand**.
stooge [stu:dʒ] *n* (*inf*) порученец*, шестёрка; (: *THEAT*) партнёр комика.
stool [stu:l] *n* табуретка*.
stoop [stu:p] *vi* (*also*: **~ down**: *bend*) наклоняться (наклониться* *perf*), нагибаться (нагнуться *perf*); (*also*: **have a ~**) сутулиться (*impf*); (*fig*): **to ~ to sth/doing** унижаться (унизиться* *perf*) до чего-н/до того, чтобы +*infin*.
stop [stɔp] *n* остановка*; (*in punctuation*: *also*: **full ~**) точка* ◆ *vt* останавливать (остановить* *perf*); (*prevent*: *also*: **put a ~ to**) прекращать (прекратить* *perf*) ◆ *vi* (*person, clock*) останавливаться (остановиться* *perf*); (*rain, noise etc*) прекращаться (прекратиться* *perf*); **to ~ sb (from) doing** удерживать (удержать *perf*) кого-н от того, чтобы +*infin*; **~ it!** прекратите!; **to ~ doing** переставать* (перестать* *perf*) +*infin*; **the car ~ped dead** машина остановилась как вкопанная
▸ **stop by** *vi* заходить* (зайти* *perf*)
▸ **stop off** *vi* останавливаться (остановиться* *perf*)
▸ **stop up** *vt* (*hole*) заделывать (заделать *perf*).
stopcock ['stɔpkɔk] *n* запорный кран.
stopgap ['stɔpgæp] *n* (*person, thing*) временная замена; (*also*: **~ measure**) временная мера.
stop-go [stɔp'gəu] *adj* (*BRIT*: *ECON*): **~ policy** экономическая политика, чередующая.
stoplights ['stɔplaɪts] *npl* (*AUT*) стоп-сигнал *msg*.
stopover ['stɔpəuvə^r] *n* остановка*; (*AVIAT*) посадка.
stoppage ['stɔpɪdʒ] *n* (*strike*) забастовка*; (*blockage*) остановка*; (*of pay*) прекращение.
stopper ['stɔpə^r] *n* пробка*.
stop press *n* экстренное сообщение.
stopwatch ['stɔpwɔtʃ] *n* секундомер.
storage ['stɔ:rɪdʒ] *n* хранение; (*in house*) кладовка*; (*COMPUT*) память *f*, накопитель *m*.
storage capacity *n* ёмкость *f*.
storage heater *n* (*BRIT*) аккумулирующий электрообогреватель *m*.
store [stɔ:^r] *n* (*stock, reserve*) запас; (*depot*) склад; (*BRIT*: *large shop*) универмаг; (*esp US*) магазин ◆ *vt* хранить (*impf*); **~s** *npl* (*provisions*) запасы *mpl*; **in ~** в будущем; **who knows what's in ~ for us?** кто знает, что нас ждёт в будущем?; **to set great/little ~ by sth** придавать* (придать* *perf*) большое/маленькое значение чему-н
▸ **store up** *vt* (*food*) запасать (запасти* *perf*); (*memories*) хранить (*impf*).
storehouse ['stɔ:haus] *n* (*US*: *COMM*) склад; (*fig*) кладовая *f adj*.
storekeeper ['stɔ:ki:pə^r] *n* (*US*: *manager*) управляющий*(-ая) *m(f) adj* магазином; (*owner*) владелец*(-лица) магазина.
storeroom ['stɔ:ru:m] *n* кладовая *f adj*.
storey ['stɔ:rɪ] (*US* **story**) *n* этаж*.
stork [stɔ:k] *n* аист.
storm [stɔ:m] *n* (*also fig*) буря; (*of criticism*) волна*; (*of laughter*) взрыв; (*also*: **electric ~**)

грозá* ◆ *vi* (*fig*: *speak angrily*) кричáть* *(impf)* ◆ *vt* (*attack*: *place*) штурмовáть *(impf)*.
storm cloud *n* грозовáя тýча.
storm door *n* нарýжная дверь* *f*.
stormy ['stɔ:mɪ] *adj* штормовóй; (*fig*: *debate, relations*) бýрный; ~ **weather** ненáстье.
story ['stɔ:rɪ] *n* истóрия; (*PRESS*: *article*) статья́*; (: *subject*) газéтный материáл; (*lie*) вы́думка*; (*US*) = **storey**; **short** ~ расскáз.
storybook ['stɔ:rɪbuk] *n* сбóрник расскáзов *or* скáзок (*для детéй*).
storyteller ['stɔ:rɪtɛlə^r] *n* расскáзчик(-ица); (*inf*: *liar*) врун(ья).
stout [staut] *adj* (*strong*: *branch etc*) крéпкий* (крéпок); (*fat*) дорóдный* (дорóден); (*resolute*: *friend, supporter*) надёжный* (надёжен) ◆ *n* (*beer*) крéпкий* пóртер.
stove [stəuv] *n* (*for cooking*) плитá*; (: *small*) плúтка*; (*for heating*) печь* *f*; **gas/electric** ~ (*cooker*) гáзовая/электри́ческая плитá.
stow [stəu] *vt* (*also*: ~ **away**) убирáть (убрáть* *perf*).
stowaway ['stəuəweɪ] *n* безбилéтник(-ница).
St Petersburg [sənt'pi:təzbə:g] *n* Санкт-Петербýрг ◆ *adj* (санкт-) петербýргский*.
straddle ['strædl] *vt* (*chair, fence etc*) оседлáть *(perf)*; (*fig*) охвáтывать (охвати́ть* *perf*).
strafe [strɑ:f] *vt* (*MIL*: *with bullets*) обстрéливать (обстреля́ть *perf*); (*with bombs*) бомби́ть *(impf)*.
straggle ['strægl] *vi* (*houses etc*) раски́дываться (раски́нуться *perf*); (*people*) разбредáться (разбрести́сь* *perf*).
straggler [stræglə^r] *n* (*person*) отстáвший(-ая) *m(f) adj*.
straggly ['stræglɪ] *adj* (*hair*) беспоря́дочно торчáщий.
straight [streɪt] *adj* прямóй* (прям); (*simple*: *choice*) я́сный* (я́сен); (*THEAT*: *part, play*) серьёзный; (*inf*: *heterosexual*) гетеросексуáльный* ◆ *adv* пря́мо ◆ *n*: **the** ~ (*SPORT*) пря́мáя *f adj*; **to put** *or* **get sth** ~ (*make clear*) вноси́ть* (внести́* *perf*) я́сность во что-н; **let's get this** ~ давáйте внесём я́сность *or* определённость в э́то; **to be (all)** ~ (*tidy*) быть* *(impf)* в (пóлном) поря́дке; (*clarified*) быть* *(impf)* я́сным(-ой); **10** ~ **wins** 10 побéд подря́д; **to go** ~ **home** идти́* (пойти́* *perf*) срáзу домóй; **to tell sb** ~ **out** говори́ть (сказáть* *perf*) комý-н пря́мо; **to drink vodka** ~ пить* *(impf)* неразбáвленную вóдку; ~ **away**, ~ **off** (*at once*) срáзу.
straighten ['streɪtn] *vt* (*skirt, tie etc*) поправля́ть (попрáвить* *perf*); (*bed*) заправля́ть (заправить* *perf*)
▸ **straighten out** *vt* (*fig*: *problem etc*) улáживать (улáдить* *perf*).
straight-faced [streɪt'feɪst] *adj, adv* с серьёзным ви́дом; **to be** ~ сохраня́ть *(impf)* серьёзный вид.
straightforward [streɪt'fɔ:wəd] *adj* (*simple*) простóй* (прост); (*honest*) прямóй.
straight sets *n*: **to win in** ~ ~ (*men*) побеждáть (победи́ть* *perf*) в трёх пáртиях подря́д; (*women*) побеждáть (победи́ть* *perf*) в двух пáртиях подря́д.
strain [streɪn] *n* (*TECH*) натяжéние; (*pressure*) нагрýзка*; (*MED*: *physical*) растяжéние; (: *mental*) напряжéние; (*of virus*) вид; (*breed*) порóда ◆ *vt* (*back etc*) растя́гивать (растянýть* *perf*); (*friendship, marriage*) испы́тывать *(impf)*; (*stretch*: *resources*) ударя́ть (удáрить *perf*) по +*dat*; (*CULIN*) процéживать (процеди́ть* *perf*); ~**s** *npl* (*MUS*) звýки *mpl*; **he's been under a lot of** ~ у негó был óчень напряжённый перúод.
strained [streɪnd] *adj* (*back, muscle*) растя́нутый (растя́нут); (*laugh, relations*) натя́нутый (натя́нут).
strainer ['streɪnə^r] *n* (*for vegetables*) си́то; (*for tea*) си́течко.
strait [streɪt] *n* (*GEO*) проли́в; ~**s** *npl* (*fig*): **to be in dire** ~**s** находи́ться* *(impf)* *or* быть* *(impf)* в бéдственном положéнии.
straitjacket ['streɪtdʒækɪt] *n* смири́тельная рубáшка*.
strait-laced [streɪt'leɪst] *adj* (*person*) пуритáнский*.
strand [strænd] *n* (*of thread*) ни́тка*; (*of wool*) волокнó*, нить *f*; (*of hair*) прядь *f*; (*fig*: *element of whole*) часть *f*.
stranded ['strændɪd] *adj* (*ship, sea creature etc*) вы́брошенный на бéрег *or* мель; (*traveller, holidaymaker etc*): **to be** ~ застревáть (застря́ть* *perf*).
strange [streɪndʒ] *adj* (*not known*) незнакóмый (незнакóм); (*foreign*) чужóй; (*odd*) стрáнный* (стрáнен).
strangely ['streɪndʒlɪ] *adv* (*act, laugh*) стрáнно; *see also* **enough**.
stranger ['streɪndʒə^r] *n* (*unknown person*) незнакóмый человéк*, посторóнний(-яя) *m(f) adj*; **I'm a** ~ **here** я здесь чужóй.
strangle ['stræŋgl] *vt* (*also fig*) души́ть* (задуши́ть* *perf*).
stranglehold ['stræŋglhəuld] *n* (*SPORT*) мёртвая хвáтка; (*fig*) заси́лье.
strangulation [stræŋgju'leɪʃən] *n* (*also fig*) удушéние.
strap [stræp] *n* ремéнь* *m*; (*of slip, dress*) бретéлька*; (*of watch, on shoes*) ремешóк* ◆ *vt* (*also*: ~ **on**) пристёгивать (пристегнýть *perf*).
straphanging ['stræphæŋɪŋ] *n*: **I hate** ~ я ненави́жу стоя́ть в трáнспорте.

* marks translations which have irregular inflections. The Russian-English side of the dictionary gives inflectional information.

strapless [ˈstræplɪs] *adj* (*bra, dress*) без бретéлек.
strapped [stræpt] *adj* (*inf*): **to be ~ for cash** сидéть* *(impf)* на мели́.
strapping [ˈstræpɪŋ] *adj* дю́жий, рóслый.
Strasbourg [ˈstræzbəːg] *n* Стрáсбург.
strata [ˈstrɑːtə] *npl of* **stratum**.
stratagem [ˈstrætɪdʒəm] *n* хи́трость *f*.
strategic [strəˈtiːdʒɪk] *adj* стратеги́ческий*.
strategist [ˈstrætɪdʒɪst] *n* стратéг.
strategy [ˈstrætɪdʒɪ] *n* (*plan, also* MIL) стратéгия.
stratosphere [ˈstrætəsfɪəʳ] *n* стратосфéра.
stratum [ˈstrɑːtəm] (*pl* **strata**) *n* слой*.
straw [strɔː] *n* солóма; (*drinking straw*) солóминка*; **that's the last ~!** э́то послéдняя кáпля!
strawberry [ˈstrɔːbərɪ] *n* (*cultivated*) клубни́ка *f no pl*; (*wild*) земляни́ка *f no pl*.
stray [streɪ] *adj* (*animal*) бездóмный, бродя́чий; (*bullet*) шальнóй; (*scattered*) отдéльный ◆ *vi* заблуди́ться* *(perf)*; (*thoughts*) блуждáть *(impf)*.
streak [striːk] *n* (*stripe*) полосá*; (*in hair*) прядь *f*; (*fig: of madness etc*) чертá, склóнность *f* ◆ *vt* прони́зывать (пронизáть* *perf*) ◆ *vi*: **to ~ past** мчáться* (промчáться* *perf*) ми́мо; **to have ~s in one's hair** имéть *(impf)* окрáшенные пря́ди волóс; **a winning/losing ~** полосá удáч/неудáч; **~ed with ...** с ... полóсками.
streaker [ˈstriːkəʳ] *n человéк, появля́ющийся гóлым пéред толпóй.*
streaky [ˈstriːkɪ] *adj*: **~ bacon** бекóн с прожи́лками жи́ра.
stream [striːm] *n* (*small river*) ручéй*; (*current*) течéние; (*of people, vehicles, questions*) потóк; (*of smoke*) струя́* ◆ *vt* (SCOL) дели́ть* (раздели́ть* *perf*) на грýппы ◆ *vi* (*liquid*) течь* *(impf)*, ли́ться* *(impf)*; **to ~ in/out** (*people*) вали́ть* (повали́ть* *perf*) толпóй в *+acc*/из *+gen*; **against the ~** прóтив течéния; **to come on ~** (*new power plant etc*) вступáть (вступи́ть* *perf*) в строй.
streamer [ˈstriːməʳ] *n* (*paper decoration*) серпанти́н.
stream feed *n* (*on photocopier etc*) подáча (страни́ц) потóком.
streamline [ˈstriːmlaɪn] *vt* придавáть* (придáть* *perf*) обтекáемую фóрму *+dat*; (*fig*) рационализи́ровать *(impf/perf)*.
streamlined [ˈstriːmlaɪnd] *adj* обтекáемый; (*AVIAT, AUT*) обтекáемой фóрмы; (*fig*) упрощённый.
street [striːt] *n* ýлица; **the back ~s** переýлки *mpl*; **to be on the ~s** (*homeless*) быть* *(impf)* бездóмным(-ой); (*as prostitute*) занимáться *(impf)* проституцией.
streetcar [ˈstriːtkɑːʳ] *n* (*US*) трамвáй.
street cred [-krɛd] *n* (*inf*) и́мидж.
streetlamp [ˈstriːtlæmp] *n* ýличный фонáрь* *m*.
street lighting *n* ýличное освещéние.
street map *n* план ýлиц.
street market *n* ýличный ры́нок*.
street plan *n* план ýлиц.
streetwise [ˈstriːtwaɪz] *adj* (*inf*) ýшлый.
strength [strɛŋθ] *n* си́ла; (*of girder, knot etc*) прóчность *f*, крéпость *f*; (*of chemical solution, wine*) крéпость; **on the ~ of** на оснoвáнии *+gen*; **at full ~** во всём состáве; **below ~** (*not enough people*) недоукомплектóванный (недоукомплектóван); (*not all members present*) не в пóлном состáве.
strengthen [ˈstrɛŋθn] *vt* укрепля́ть (укрепи́ть* *perf*); (*muscle*) развивáть *(impf)*; (*fig: group*) пополня́ть (попóлнить *perf*); (*: argument*) подкрепля́ть (подкрепи́ть* *perf*).
strenuous [ˈstrɛnjuəs] *adj* (*exercise*) энерги́чный* (энерги́чен); (*efforts*) напряжённый; (*tiring*) утоми́тельный* (утоми́телен).
strenuously [ˈstrɛnjuəslɪ] *adv* напряжённо; **she ~ denied the rumour** онá уси́ленно отрицáла слýхи.
stress [strɛs] *n* (*pressure, also* TECH) давлéние; (*mental strain*) стресс; (*LING: accent*) ударéние; (*emphasis*) значéние ◆ *vt* (*point, importance etc*) подчёркивать (подчеркнýть *perf*); (*syllable*) стáвить* (постáвить* *perf*) ударéние на *+acc*; **to lay great ~ on sth** придавáть* (придáть* *perf*) осóбое значéние чемý-н; **to be under ~** быть* *(impf)* под напряжéнием.
stressful [ˈstrɛsful] *adj* (*job*) напряжённый* (напряжён); (*situation*) стрéссовый.
stretch [strɛtʃ] *n* (*area: of sand, water etc*) прострáнство; (*of time*) промежýток* ◆ *vt* (*pull*) натя́гивать (натянýть* *perf*); (*fig: subj: job, task*) утомля́ть (утоми́ть* *perf*); (*spread: resources*) растя́гивать (растянýть* *perf*) ◆ *vi* (*person, animal*) потя́гиваться (потянýться* *perf*); (*extend*): **to ~ to** *or* **as far as** простирáться (простерéться* *perf*) к *+dat*; (*be enough*): **to ~ (to)** хватáть (хвати́ть* *perf*) (на *+acc*); **at a ~** подря́д; **he's no hero by any ~ of the imagination** как ни старáйтесь, егó нельзя́ вообрази́ть герóем; **to ~ one's legs** размин́ать (размя́ть* *perf*) нóги
► **stretch out** *vi* растя́гиваться (растянýться* *perf*) ◆ *vt* (*arm etc*) протя́гивать (протянýть* *perf*); (*spread*) растя́гивать (растянýть* *perf*); **to ~ out for sth** тянýться* (потянýться* *perf*) за чем-н.
stretcher [ˈstrɛtʃəʳ] *n* (*MED*) носи́лки* *pl*.
stretcher-bearer [ˈstrɛtʃəbɛərəʳ] *n* санитáр-носи́льщик.
stretchmarks [ˈstrɛtʃmɑːks] *npl следы́ растя́гивания на кóже.*
strewn [struːn] *adj*: **~ with** усы́панный (усы́пан) *+instr*.
stricken [ˈstrɪkən] *adj* (*person*) сражённый; (*city, industry etc*) пострадáвший; **~ with**

(*arthritis, disease*) поражённый +*instr*.
strict [strɪkt] *adj* (*severe, firm*: *person, rule*) стро́гий* (строг); (*precise*: *meaning*) то́чный* (то́чен); **in ~** *or* **in the ~est confidence** в строжа́йшей та́йне.
strictly [strɪktlɪ] *adv* (*severely*) стро́го; (*exactly*) то́чно; **~ confidential** соверше́нно конфиденциа́льно *or* секре́тно; **~ speaking** стро́го говоря́; **~ between ourselves** то́лько ме́жду на́ми.
strictness ['strɪktnɪs] *n* стро́гость *f*.
stridden ['strɪdn] *pp of* **stride**.
stride [straɪd] (*pt* **strode**, *pp* **stridden**) *n* (*step*) широ́кий* шаг* ◆ *vi* шага́ть (*impf*); **to take sth in one's ~** (*fig*: *changes etc*) относи́ться* (*impf*) споко́йно к чему́-н.
strident ['straɪdnt] *adj* (*voice, sound*) пронзи́тельный* (пронзи́телен); (*demands*) шу́мный.
strife [straɪf] *n* борьба́.
strike [straɪk] (*pt, pp* **struck**) *n* (*of workers*) забасто́вка*; (*MIL*: *attack*) уда́р; (*of oil etc*) откры́тие месторожде́ния ◆ *vt* (*hit*: *person, thing*) ударя́ть (уда́рить *perf*); (*fig*: *subj*: *disease, disaster*) поража́ть (порази́ть* *perf*); (: *idea, thought*) осеня́ть (осени́ть *perf*); (*oil etc*) открыва́ть (откры́ть* *perf*) месторожде́ние +*gen*; (*bargain, deal*) заключа́ть (заключи́ть *perf*); (*make*: *coin, medal*) чека́нить (отчека́нить *perf*) ◆ *vi* (*workers*) бастова́ть (*impf*); (*attack*: *soldiers*) напада́ть (напа́сть* *perf*); (: *disaster, illness*) приходи́ть* (прийти́* *perf*); (*clock*) бить* (проби́ть* *perf*); **to be on ~** (*workers*) бастова́ть (*impf*); **to ~ a balance** соблюда́ть (*impf*) равнове́сие; **to ~ a match** зажига́ть (заже́чь* *perf*) спи́чку
▸ **strike back** *vi* (*MIL, fig*) наноси́ть* (нанести́* *perf*) отве́тный уда́р
▸ **strike down** *vt* сража́ть (срази́ть* *perf*)
▸ **strike off** *vt* (*name from list*) вычёркивать (вы́черкнуть *perf*); (: *doctor etc*) лиша́ть (лиши́ть *perf*) пра́ва практикова́ть
▸ **strike out** *vt* (*word, sentence*) вычёркивать (вы́черкнуть *perf*)
▸ **strike up** *vt* (*MUS*) заигра́ть (*impf*); (*conversation, friendship*) завя́зывать (завяза́ть* *perf*).
strikebreaker ['straɪkbreɪkə^r] *n* штрейкбре́хер.
strike pay *n* посо́бие басту́ющим.
striker ['straɪkə^r] *n* (*person on strike*) забасто́вщик(-ица); (*SPORT*) напада́ющий* (-ая) *m(f) adj*.
striking ['straɪkɪŋ] *adj* порази́тельный* (порази́телен).
strimmer ['strɪmə^r] *n механи́ческое ручно́е приспособле́ние для стри́жки газо́нов в труднодосту́пных места́х*.
string [strɪŋ] (*pt, pp* **strung**) *n* верёвка*; (*row*: *of onions*) свя́зка*; (: *of islands*) цепь *f*; (: *of cars, people*) верени́ца; (*series*: *of disasters*) се́рия; (: *of excuses*) пото́к; (*COMPUT*) строка́, цепо́чка; (*MUS*: *for guitar etc*) струна́* ◆ *vt*: **to ~ together** свя́зывать (связа́ть* *perf*); **the ~s** *npl* (*MUS*: *section of orchestra*) стру́нные инструме́нты *mpl*; **to ~ out** растя́гивать (растяну́ть* *perf*); **a ~ of beads** бу́сы; **to pull ~s** (*fig*) испо́льзовать (*impf/perf*) свя́зи; **with no ~s attached** (*fig*) без дополни́тельных усло́вий.
string bean *n* стручко́вая фасо́ль *f*.
string(ed) instrument *n* стру́нный инструме́нт.
stringent ['strɪndʒənt] *adj* (*rules, measures*) стро́гий* (строг).
string quartet *n* (*MUS*) стру́нный кварте́т.
strip [strɪp] *n* полоса́*; (*SPORT*): **the Rangers ~** фо́рма Ре́йнджерз ◆ *vt* (*undress*) раздева́ть (разде́ть* *perf*); (*paint*) обдира́ть (ободра́ть* *perf*), сдира́ть (содра́ть* *perf*); (*also*: **~ down**: *machine*) разбира́ть (разобра́ть* *perf*) ◆ *vi* (*undress*) раздева́ться (разде́ться* *perf*).
strip cartoon *n* исто́рия в карти́нках.
stripe [straɪp] *n* поло́ска*; (*MIL, POLICE*) петли́ца.
striped ['straɪpt] *adj* (*fabric, animal etc*) полоса́тый (полоса́т).
strip lighting *n* (*BRIT*) дневно́е освеще́ние.
stripper ['strɪpə^r] *n* уча́стница стрипти́за.
strip-search ['strɪpsəːtʃ] *n* ли́чный досмо́тр ◆ *vt* производи́ть* (произвести́* *perf*) ли́чный досмо́тр +*gen*.
striptease ['strɪptiːz] *n* стрипти́з.
strive [straɪv] (*pt* **strove**, *pp* **striven**) *vi*: **to ~ for sth/to do** стреми́ться* (*impf*) к чему́-н/+*infin*.
striven ['strɪvn] *pp of* **strive**.
strobe [strəub] *n* (*also*: **~ light**) строб-и́мпульс, селе́кторный и́мпульс.
strode [strəud] *pt of* **stride**.
stroke [strəuk] *n* (*also MED*) уда́р; (*SWIMMING*) стиль *m*; (*of piston*) ход, такт; (*of paintbrush*) мазо́к*; (*of pen etc*) штрих ◆ *vt* (*caress*) гла́дить* (погла́дить* *perf*); **at a ~** одни́м ма́хом; **on the ~ of 5** ро́вно в 5; **a ~ of luck** уда́ча; **a 2-~ engine** двухта́ктный дви́гатель *m*.
stroll [strəul] *n* прогу́лка* ◆ *vi* прогу́ливаться (прогуля́ться *perf*), пройти́сь* (*perf*); **to go for a ~, have** *or* **take a ~** идти́* (пойти́* *perf*) прогуля́ться.
stroller ['strəulə^r] *n* (*US*: *pushchair*) (складна́я) коля́ска.
strong [strɔŋ] *adj* си́льный* (силён); (*healthy, powerful*) кре́пкий* (кре́пок); (*object, material*) про́чный* (про́чен); (*imagination*) большо́й; (*drugs, chemicals*) си́льный; (*letters, measures*) ре́зкий* (ре́зок) ◆ *adv*: **to be going ~** занима́ть (*impf*) про́чные пози́ции;

they are 50 ~ их 50.
strong-arm ['strɔŋɑ:m] *adj*: **~ methods** приёмы *mpl* си́льной руки́.
strongbox ['strɔŋbɔks] *n* сейф.
stronghold ['strɔŋhəuld] *n* райо́н сопротивле́ния; (*fig*) оплот, тверды́ня.
strongly ['strɔŋlɪ] *adv* (*construct*) кре́пко; (*push, defend, believe*) си́льно; **I feel ~ about it** во мне э́то вызыва́ет си́льные эмо́ции.
strongman ['strɔŋmæn] *irreg n* сила́ч, богаты́рь* *m*; (*fig*) си́льная ли́чность *f*.
strongroom ['strɔŋru:m] *n* сейф.
stroppy ['strɔpɪ] *adj* (*inf*) стропти́вый (стропти́в).
strove [strəuv] *pt of* **strive**.
struck [strʌk] *pt, pp of* **strike**.
structural ['strʌktʃrəl] *adj* структу́рный.
structurally ['strʌktʃrəlɪ] *adv* (*sound*) со структу́рной то́чки зре́ния.
structure ['strʌktʃə^r] *n* структу́ра.
struggle ['strʌgl] *n* борьба́; (*difficulty*) уси́лие ◆ *vi* (*try hard*) прилага́ть *(impf)* больши́е уси́лия; (*fight*) боро́ться* *(impf)*; (: *to free o.s.*) сопротивля́ться *(impf)*; **to have a ~ to do** де́лать (сде́лать *perf*) уси́лие *+infin*.
strum [strʌm] *vt* (*guitar*) игра́ть *(impf)* на *+prp*.
strung [strʌŋ] *pt, pp of* **string**.
strut [strʌt] *n* (*wood, metal*) распо́рка* ◆ *vi* ходи́ть*/идти́* (пойти́* *perf*) велича́ственно.
strychnine ['strɪkni:n] *n* стрихни́н.
stub [stʌb] *n* (*of cheque, ticket etc*) корешо́к*; (*of cigarette*) окуро́к* ◆ *vt*: **to ~ one's toe** бо́льно спотыка́ться (споткну́ться *perf*)
▸ **stub out** *vt* (*cigarette*) гаси́ть* (загаси́ть* *perf*).
stubble ['stʌbl] *n* (*AGR*) жнивьё; (*on chin*) щети́на.
stubborn ['stʌbən] *adj* (*child, determination*) упря́мый (упря́м), упо́рный* (упо́рен); (*stain*) несмыва́ющийся; (*illness*) пло́хо поддаю́щийся лече́нию.
stubby ['stʌbɪ] *adj* (*fingers, pencil*) коро́ткий*.
stucco ['stʌkəu] *n* (*CONSTR*) декорати́вная "ка́менная" штукату́рка.
stuck [stʌk] *pt, pp of* **stick** ◆ *adj*: **to be ~** застря́ть* *(perf)*; **to get ~** застрева́ть (застря́ть* *perf*).
stuck-up [stʌk'ʌp] *adj* (*inf*) наду́тый (наду́т).
stud [stʌd] *n* (*on clothing etc*) кно́пка*, заклёпка*; (*collar stud*) за́понка*; (*earring*) серьга́* со штифто́м; (*on sole of boot*) шип*; (*also:* **~ farm**) ко́нный заво́д; (*also:* **~ horse**) племенно́й конь* *m* ◆ *vt* (*fig*): **~ded with** усы́панный *+instr*.
student ['stju:dənt] *n* (*at university*) студе́нт(ка*); (*at school*) уча́щийся*(-аяся) *m(f) adj* ◆ *adj* (*life, union*) студе́нческий*; (*nurse*: *female*) медсестра́-практика́нтка*; (: *male*) медбра́т-практика́нт; **law/medical ~** студе́нт(ка*) юриди́ческого/медици́нского факульте́та.
student driver *n* (*US*) учени́к* автомоби́ля.
student loan *n* студе́нческий* заём.
students' union ['stju:dənts-] *n* (*BRIT*: *association*) студе́нческий* сою́з; (*building*) зда́ние студе́нческого сою́за.
studied ['stʌdɪd] *adj* (*expression, attitude*) проду́манный* (проду́ман).
studio ['stju:dɪəu] *n* сту́дия.
studio flat (*US* **studio apartment**) *n* однокомнатная кварти́ра.
studious ['stju:dɪəs] *adj* (*person*) усе́рдный* (усе́рден); (*careful*: *attention*) тща́тельный* (тща́телен).
studiously ['stju:dɪəslɪ] *adv* (*carefully*) тща́тельно.
study ['stʌdɪ] *n* (*activity*) учёба; (*room*) кабине́т ◆ *vt* (*learn about, examine*) изуча́ть (изучи́ть* *perf*) ◆ *vi* учи́ться* *(perf)*; **studies** *npl* (*subjects studied*) ку́рсы *pl*; **to make a ~ of sth** иссле́довать *(impf/perf)* что-н; **to ~ for one's exams** гото́виться* *(impf)* к экза́менам.
stuff [stʌf] *n* (*things*) ве́щи *fpl*; (*substance*) вещество́ ◆ *vt* набива́ть (наби́ть* *perf*); (*CULIN*) начиня́ть (начини́ть *perf*), фарширова́ть (нафарширова́ть *perf*); (*inf*: *push*: *object*) запи́хивать (запиха́ть *perf*); **my nose is ~ed up** у меня́ зало́жен нос; **get ~ed!** (*inf!*) пошёл ты!
stuffed toy [stʌft-] *n* мя́гкая игру́шка*.
stuffing ['stʌfɪŋ] *n* наби́вка; (*CULIN*) начи́нка, фарш.
stuffy ['stʌfɪ] *adj* (*room*) ду́шный* (ду́шен); (*person, ideas*) чо́порный* (чо́порен).
stumble ['stʌmbl] *vi* спотыка́ться (споткну́ться *perf*); **to ~ across** *or* **on** (*fig*) натыка́ться (наткну́ться *perf*) на *+acc*.
stumbling block ['stʌmblɪŋ-] *n* ка́мень* *m* преткнове́ния.
stump [stʌmp] *n* (*of tree*) пень* *m*; (*of limb*) обру́бок* ◆ *vt* озада́чивать (озада́чить *perf*); **he is ~ed** он озада́чен.
stun [stʌn] *vt* (*subj*: *news*) ошеломля́ть (ошеломи́ть* *perf*); (: *blow on head*) оглуша́ть (оглуши́ть *perf*).
stung [stʌŋ] *pt, pp of* **sting**.
stunk [stʌŋk] *pp of* **stink**.
stunning ['stʌnɪŋ] *adj* (*fig*: *news, event*) ошеломи́тельный* (ошеломи́телен); (: *girl, dress*) потряса́ющий* (потряса́ющ), изуми́тельный* (изуми́телен).
stunt [stʌnt] *n* трюк.
stunted ['stʌntɪd] *adj* (*trees*) подру́бленный; (*growth*) заме́дленный* (заме́длен).
stuntman ['stʌntmæn] *irreg n* каскадёр.
stupefaction [stju:pɪ'fækʃən] *n* отупе́ние; (*surprise*) остолбене́ние; **to my ~** к моему́ изумле́нию.
stupefy ['stju:pɪfaɪ] *vt* приводи́ть* (привести́* *perf*) в отупе́ние; (*fig*) изумля́ть (изуми́ть* *perf*).
stupendous [stju:'pɛndəs] *adj* (*large*)

колосса́льный* (колосса́лен); (*impressive*) изуми́тельный* (изуми́телен).
stupid ['stju:pɪd] *adj* (*person, question etc*) глу́пый (глуп).
stupidity [stju:'pɪdɪtɪ] *n* глу́пость *f*.
stupidly ['stju:pɪdlɪ] *adv* (*say, look*) глу́по.
stupor ['stju:pə^r] *n* сту́пор; **in a ~** в сту́поре.
sturdily ['stə:dɪlɪ] *adv* (*built*) про́чно, кре́пко.
sturdy ['stə:dɪ] *adj* (*person, thing*) кре́пкий* (кре́пок).
sturgeon ['stə:dʒən] *n* (*ZOOL*) осётр*.
stutter ['stʌtə^r] *n* заика́ние ◆ *vi* заика́ться *(impf)*.
Stuttgart ['stutgɑ:t] *n* Шту́тгарт.
sty [staɪ] *n* (*for pigs*) свина́рник.
stye [staɪ] *n* ячме́нь *m*.
style [staɪl] *n* стиль *m*; **in the latest ~** по после́дней мо́де; **hair ~** причёска*.
styli ['staɪlaɪ] *npl of* **stylus**.
stylish ['staɪlɪʃ] *adj* шика́рный* (шика́рен).
stylist ['staɪlɪst] *n* (*also:* **hair ~**) парикма́хер-модлье́р; (*literary stylist*) стили́ст.
stylized ['staɪlaɪzd] *adj* (*picture, account*) стилизо́ванный* (стилизо́ван).
stylus ['staɪləs] (*pl* **styli** *or* **~es**) *n* (*of record player*) игла́*, иго́лка*.
Styrofoam® ['staɪrəfəum] *n* (*US*) *синтети́ческий упако́вочный материа́л*.
suave [swɑ:v] *adj* (*person, manners etc*) еле́йный* (еле́ен).
sub [sʌb] *n abbr* (*NAUT*) (= **submarine**) подло́дка= *подво́дная ло́дка*; (*ADMIN*) = **subscription**; (*PRESS*: = *sub-editor*) помо́щник *or* замести́тель *m* реда́ктора.
sub... [sʌb] *prefix* суб..., под....
subcommittee ['sʌbkəmɪtɪ] *n* подкомите́т.
subconscious [sʌb'kɔnʃəs] *adj* (*desire etc*) подсозна́тельный* (подсозна́телен).
subcontinent [sʌb'kɔntɪnənt] *n*: **the (Indian) ~** (инди́йский*) субконтине́нт.
subcontract [*vt* sʌbkən'trækt, *n* 'sʌb'kɔntrækt] *vt* заключа́ть (заключи́ть *perf*) субподря́д с +*instr* ◆ *n* субподря́д.
subcontractor ['sʌbkən'træktə^r] *n* субподря́дчик.
subdivide [sʌbdɪ'vaɪd] *vt* подразделя́ть (подраздели́ть *perf*).
subdivision ['sʌbdɪvɪʒən] *n* подразделе́ние.
subdue [səb'dju:] *vt* подавля́ть (подави́ть* *perf*).
subdued [səb'dju:d] *adj* (*light*) приглушённый (приглушён); (*person*) пода́вленный* (пода́влен).
sub-editor ['sʌb'ɛdɪtə^r] *n* (*BRIT: PRESS*) помо́щник *or* замести́тель *m* реда́ктора.
subject [*n* 'sʌbdʒɪkt, *vt* səb'dʒɛkt] *n* (*topic*) те́ма; (*SCOL*) предме́т; (*of kingdom*) по́данный(-ая) *m(f) adj*; (*LING*) подлежа́щее *nt adj* ◆ *vt*: **to ~ sb to sth** подверга́ть (подве́ргнуть* *perf*) кого́-н чему́-н; **to be ~ to** (*tax*) подлежа́ть *(impf)* +*dat*; (*law*) подчиня́ться *(impf)* +*dat*; **he is ~ to heart attacks** он подве́ржен серде́чным при́ступам; **this is ~ to confirmation in writing** э́то подлежи́т пи́сьменному подтвержде́нию; **to change the ~** меня́ть (поменя́ть *perf*) те́му (разгово́ра).
subjection [səb'dʒɛkʃən] *n* (*of women, enemy etc*) подчине́ние.
subjective [səb'dʒɛktɪv] *adj* субъекти́вный* (субъекти́вен).
subject matter *n* (*content*) те́ма.
sub judice [sʌb'dju:dɪsɪ] *adj*: **the case is ~ ~** в да́нным моме́нт э́то де́ло рассма́тривается судо́м.
subjugate ['sʌbdʒugeɪt] *vt* (*people*) покоря́ть (покори́ть *perf*).
subjunctive [səb'dʒʌŋktɪv] *n* сослага́тельное наклоне́ние.
sublet [sʌb'lɛt] *vt* (*property*) передава́ть* (переда́ть* *perf*) в суба́ренду.
sublime [sə'blaɪm] *adj* возвы́шенный; **from the ~ to the ridiculous** от вели́кого до смешно́го.
subliminal [sʌb'lɪmɪnl] *adj* (*memory*) подсозна́тельный; (*advertising*) де́йствующий* на подсозна́ние.
submachine gun ['sʌbmə'ʃi:n-] *n* автома́т.
submarine [sʌbmə'ri:n] *n* подво́дная ло́дка*.
submerge [səb'mə:dʒ] *vt* погружа́ть (погрузи́ть* *perf*) (*в во́ду*) ◆ *vi* (*submarine, sea creature*) погружа́ться (погрузи́ться* *perf*) (*в во́ду*).
submersion [səb'mə:ʃən] *n* погруже́ние.
submission [səb'mɪʃən] *n* (*state*) подчине́ние, повинове́ние; (*of plan etc*) пода́ча; (*to committee etc*) представле́ние.
submissive [səb'mɪsɪv] *adj* поко́рный* (поко́рен).
submit [səb'mɪt] *vt* (*proposal, application etc*) представля́ть (предста́вить* *perf*) на рассмотре́ние ◆ *vi*: **to ~ to sth** подчиня́ться (подчини́ться *perf*) чему́-н.
subnormal [sʌb'nɔ:ml] *adj* (*backward: child etc*) отста́лый; **~ temperatures** температу́ры *fpl* ни́же норма́льных.
subordinate [sə'bɔ:dɪnət] *adj* (*position, rank*): **to be ~ to sb** подчиня́ться *(impf)* кому́-н; (*LING: clause*) прида́точный ◆ *n* подчинённый(-ая) *m(f) adj*.
subpoena [səb'pi:nə] *n* (*LAW*) пове́стка* ◆ *vt* (*LAW: witness etc*) вызыва́ть (вы́звать* *perf*) в суд.
subroutine [sʌbru:'ti:n] *n* (*COMPUT*) подпрогра́мма.
subscribe [səb'skraɪb] *vi* подпи́сываться (подписа́ться* *perf*); **to ~ to** (*opinion, fund*)

* marks translations which have irregular inflections. The Russian-English side of the dictionary gives inflectional information.

поддерживáть (поддержáть* *perf*); (*magazine etc*) подпи́сываться (подписáться* *perf*) на *+acc*; **~d capital** подписнóй акционéрный капитáл.
subscriber [səb'skraɪbəʳ] *n* (*to periodical*) подпи́счик; (*to telephone*) абонéнт.
subscript ['sʌbskrɪpt] *n* (*TYP*) подстрóчный знак.
subscription [səb'skrɪpʃən] *n* (*to magazine etc*) подпи́ска*; (*membership dues*) (чле́нский*) взнос; **to take out a ~ to** подпи́сываться (подписáться* *perf*) на *+acc*.
subsequent ['sʌbsɪkwənt] *adj* послéдующий*; **~ to** вслед *+dat*.
subsequently ['sʌbsɪkwəntlɪ] *adv* впослéдствии.
subservient [səb'sə:vɪənt] *adj* (*person, behaviour*) подобострáстный* (подобострáстен); (*less important*: *policy etc*) подвлáстный* (подвлáстен); **he is ~ to ...** он подвлáстен *+dat* ....
subside [səb'saɪd] *vi* (*feeling, wind*) утихáть (ути́хнуть* *perf*); (*flood*) убывáть (убы́ть* *perf*).
subsidence [səb'saɪdns] *n* (*in road etc*) оседáние.
subsidiarity [səbsɪdɪ'ærɪtɪ] *n* (*POL*) ýровень* *m* зави́симости.
subsidiary [səb'sɪdɪərɪ] *adj* (*question, details*) второстепéнный* (второстепéн); (*BRIT*: *SCOL*: *subject*) факультати́вный ◆ *n* (*also:* **~ company**) дочéрняя компáния.
subsidize ['sʌbsɪdaɪz] *vt* (*education, industry etc*) субсиди́ровать (*impf/perf*).
subsidy ['sʌbsɪdɪ] *n* субси́дия, дотáция.
subsist [səb'sɪst] *vi*: **to ~ on sth** существовáть (*impf*) за счёт чегó-н.
subsistence [səb'sɪstəns] *n* (*ability to live*) существовáние; (*food*) пропитáние.
subsistence allowance *n* авáнс (*пéред пéрвой зарплáтой*).
subsistence level *n* прожи́точный ми́нимум.
substance ['sʌbstəns] *n* (*product, material*) веществó; (*fig*: *essence*) суть* *f*; **a man of ~** соли́дный мужчи́на; **the essay lacks ~** в сочинéнии нет стéржня.
substance abuse *n* токсикомáния.
substandard [sʌb'stændəd] *adj* (*goods*) некáчественный; (*housing*) непригóдный* (непригóден) для жилья́.
substantial [səb'stænʃl] *adj* (*solid*) прóчный* (прóчен), основáтельный* (основáтелен); (*fig*: *reward, meal*) значи́тельный* (значи́телен), соли́дный* (соли́ден).
substantially [səb'stænʃəlɪ] *adv* (*by a large amount*) значи́тельно; (*in essence*) существéнно, основáтельно; **~ bigger** значи́тельно бóльше.
substantiate [səb'stænʃɪeɪt] *vt* (*claim, story, statement etc*) обоснóвывать (обосновáть *perf*).
substitute ['sʌbstɪtju:t] *n* (*person*) замéна; (: *FOOTBALL etc*) запаснóй *m adj* (игрóк*); (*thing*) замени́тель *m* ◆ *vt*: **to ~ A for B** заменя́ть (замени́ть *perf*) А на Б.
substitute teacher *n* (*US*) замещáющий(-ая) учи́тель(ница) *m(f)*.
substitution [sʌbstɪ'tju:ʃən] *n* (*act of substituting*) замéна.
subterfuge ['sʌbtəfju:dʒ] *n* улóвка*.
subterranean [sʌbtə'reɪnɪən] *adj* (*passage*) подзéмный.
subtitle ['sʌbtaɪtl] *n* (*CINEMA*) субти́тр.
subtle ['sʌtl] *adj* (*change*) тóнкий*, едвá улови́мый; (*person*) искýсный* (искýсен).
subtlety ['sʌtltɪ] *n* (*small detail*) тóнкость *f*; (*of person*) искýсность *f*.
subtly ['sʌtlɪ] *adv* (*change, vary*) едвá улови́мо; (*different*) слегкá; (*criticize, persuade*) искýсно.
subtotal [sʌb'təutl] *n* суммáрное числó*.
subtract [səb'trækt] *vt* вычитáть (вы́честь* *perf*).
subtraction [səb'trækʃən] *n* вычитáние.
subtropical [sʌb'trɔpɪkl] *adj* субтропи́ческий.
suburb ['sʌbə:b] *n* при́город; **the ~s** *npl* (*area*) при́город *msg*.
suburban [sə'bə:bən] *adj* при́городный.
suburbia [sə'bə:bɪə] *n* при́город.
subvention [səb'vɛnʃən] *n* (*subsidy*) дотáция, субси́дия.
subversion [səb'və:ʃən] *n* подрывнáя дéятельность *f*.
subversive [səb'və:sɪv] *adj* (*activities, literature*) подрывнóй.
subway ['sʌbweɪ] *n* (*US*: *underground railway*) метрó *nt ind*, подзéмка*; (*BRIT*: *underpass*) подзéмный перехóд.
sub-zero [sʌb'zɪərəu] *adj*: **~ temperatures** температýры *fpl* ни́же нуля́.
succeed [sək'si:d] *vi* (*plan etc*) удавáться* (удáться* *perf*), имéть (*impf*) успéх; (*person*: *in career etc*) преуспевáть (преуспéть *perf*) ◆ *vt* (*in job, order*) сменя́ть (смени́ть* *perf*); **he ~ed in finishing the article** емý удалóсь закóнчить статью́.
succeeding [sək'si:dɪŋ] *adj* (*following*) послéдующий*; **~ generations** послéдующие поколéния.
success [sək'sɛs] *n* (*achievement*) успéх, удáча; (*hit*): **the book was a ~** кни́га имéла успéх; **he was a ~** он добился успéха.
successful [sək'sɛsful] *adj* (*venture*) успéшный* (успéшен); **he was ~ in convincing her** емý удалóсь убеди́ть её.
successfully [sək'sɛsfəlɪ] *adv* (*complete, do*) успéшно.
succession [sək'sɛʃən] *n* (*series*) чередá, ряд*; (*to throne etc*) наслéдование; **in ~** подря́д; **3 years in ~** три гóда подря́д.
successive [sək'sɛsɪv] *adj* (*governments*) слéдующий* оди́н за други́м; **3 ~ days/**

attempts три дня/попытки подря́д.
successor [sək'sɛsə^r] *n* преéмник(-ица); (*to throne*) наслéдник(-ица).
succinct [sək'sɪŋkt] *adj* (*explanation*) сжáтый (сжат).
succulent ['sʌkjulənt] *adj* (*fruit, meat*) сóчный* (сóчен) ◆ *n* (*BOT*): **~s** суккулéнты *pl*.
succumb [sə'kʌm] *vi* (*to temptation*) поддавáться* (поддáться* *perf*); **he ~ed to illness** болéзнь окончáтельно егó победи́ла.
such [sʌtʃ] *adj* такóй; (*emphasizing similarity*) подóбный, такóй ◆ *adv*: **~ a long trip** такáя дли́нная поéздка; **~ a book** такáя кни́га; **~ books** таки́е кни́ги; **~ a lot of** такóе мнóжество *+gen*; **making ~ a noise that ...** создавáя такóй шум, что ...; **~ as** (*like*) таки́е как; **~ books as I have** таки́е кни́ги, как у меня́; **I said no ~ thing** я ничегó подóбного *or* такóго не говори́л; **as ~** как таковóй.
such-and-such ['sʌtʃənsʌtʃ] *adj* такóй-то и такóй-то.
suchlike ['sʌtʃlaɪk] *pron* (*inf*): **and ~** и им подóбные.
suck [sʌk] *vt* сосáть* *(impf)*; (*subj: pump, machine*) всáсывать (всосáть *perf*).
sucker ['sʌkə^r] *n* присóска*; (*BOT*) корневóй побéг; (*inf*) óлух.
suckle ['sʌkl] *vt* корми́ть* *(impf)* (гру́дью), давáть* (дать* *perf*) грудь *+dat*; (*subj: animal*) корми́ть* *(impf)*.
sucrose ['su:krəuz] *n* сахарóза.
suction ['sʌkʃən] *n* всáсывание.
suction pump *n* всáсывающий насóс.
Sudan [su'dɑ:n] *n* Судáн.
Sudanese [su:də'ni:z] *adj* судáнский ◆ *n inv* судáнец*(-ка*).
sudden ['sʌdn] *adj* внезáпный* (внезáпен); **all of a ~** (*unexpectedly*) внезáпно, вдруг.
sudden death *n* (*in competition*) дополни́тельный матч (*пóсле ничьи́*).
suddenly ['sʌdnlɪ] *adv* (*unexpectedly*) внезáпно, вдруг.
suds [sʌdz] *npl* (мы́льные) пузыри́ *mpl*.
sue [su:] *vt* предъявля́ть (предъяви́ть* *perf*) иск *+dat*, возбуждáть (возбуди́ть* *perf*) дéло прóтив *+gen* ◆ *vi*: **to ~ (for)** суди́ться *(impf)* (за *+acc*); **to ~ for divorce** возбуждáть (возбуди́ть* *perf*) дéло о развóде; **to ~ sb for damages** предъявля́ть (предъяви́ть* *perf*) иск комý-н о компенсáции.
suede [sweɪd] *n* зáмша ◆ *cpd* зáмшевый.
suet ['suɪt] *n* жир.
Suez ['su:ɪz] *n*: **the ~ Canal** Суэ́цкий* канáл.
Suff. *abbr* (*BRIT: POST*) = *Suffolk*.
suffer ['sʌfə^r] *vt* (*hardship etc*) переноси́ть* (перенести́* *perf*); (*pain, rudeness*) страдáть *(impf)* от *+gen* ◆ *vi* (*person, results etc*) страдáть (пострадáть *perf*); **to ~ from** (*illness etc*) страдáть *(impf)* *+instr*; **to ~ the effects of alcohol/a fall** страдáть (пострадáть *perf*) от воздéйствия алкогóля/от послéдствий падéния.
sufferance ['sʌfərns] *n*: **she hadn't wanted him to go, so he was only there on ~** онá не хотéла отпускáть егó, он был там, причиня́я ей страдáния.
sufferer ['sʌfərə^r] *n* (*MED*) страдáющий(-ая) *m(f) adj*.
suffering ['sʌfərɪŋ] *n* (*hardship*) страдáние.
suffice [sə'faɪs] *vi* (*be enough*): **this ~s ...** э́того достáточно, ...
sufficient [sə'fɪʃənt] *adj* достáточный* (достáточен); **~ money** достáточное коли́чество дéнег.
sufficiently [sə'fɪʃəntlɪ] *adv* (*recover, provide*) достáточно; (*powerful, enthusiastic*) в достáточной мéре.
suffix ['sʌfɪks] *n* (*LING*) су́ффикс.
suffocate ['sʌfəkeɪt] *vi* задыхáться (задохну́ться *perf*); (*have difficulty breathing*) задыхáться *(impf)*; (*die*) задохну́ться *(impf)* ◆ *vt* (*gas etc*) удушáть (удуши́ть *perf*).
suffocation [sʌfə'keɪʃən] *n* уду́шье.
suffrage ['sʌfrɪdʒ] *n* (*right to vote*) избирáтельное прáво.
suffragette [sʌfrə'dʒɛt] *n* суфражи́стка*.
suffused [sə'fju:zd] *adj*: **~ with** (*light, colour*) погружённый (погружён) в *+prp*; (*tears*) зали́тый (зали́т) *+instr*.
sugar ['ʃugə^r] *n* сáхар* ◆ *vt* (*tea etc*) сласти́ть* (посласти́ть* *perf*).
sugar beet *n* сáхарная свёкла.
sugar bowl *n* сáхарница.
sugar cane *n* сáхарный тростни́к.
sugar-coated ['ʃugə'kəutɪd] *adj* (*sweet*) засáхаренный.
sugar lump *n* кусóк* сáхара.
sugar refinery *n* сахарорафинáдный завóд.
sugary ['ʃugərɪ] *adj* слáдкий* (слáдок), сахари́стый (сахари́ст); (*fig*) слащáвый (слащáв).
suggest [sə'dʒɛst] *vt* (*propose*) предлагáть (предложи́ть* *perf*); (*indicate*) предполагáть (предположи́ть* *perf*); **what do you ~ I do?** что Вы предлагáете мне дéлать?
suggestion [sə'dʒɛstʃən] *n* (*proposal*) предложéние; (*indication*) предположéние.
suggestive [sə'dʒɛstɪv] *adj* (*pej: remarks, looks*) неприли́чный* (неприли́чен).
suicidal [suɪ'saɪdl] *adj* (*person*) стоя́щий на грáни самоуби́йства; (*act*) само-уби́йственный.
suicide ['suɪsaɪd] *n* (*death*) самоуби́йство; (*person*) самоуби́йца *m/f*; *see also* **commit**.
suicide attempt *n* попы́тка* самоуби́йства.
suicide bid *n* попы́тка* самоуби́йства.

suit [su:t] *n* костю́м; (*LAW*) иск; (*CARDS*) масть *f* ◆ *vt* (*be convenient, appropriate*) подходи́ть* (подойти́* *perf*) +*dat*; (*colour, clothes*) идти́* (*impf*) +*dat*; (*adapt*): **to ~ sth to** приспоса́бливать (приспосо́бить* *perf*) что-н к +*dat*; **he was ~ed to lead the party** он хорошо́ подходи́л на роль ли́дера па́ртии; **to bring a ~ against sb** предъявля́ть (предъяви́ть* *perf*) иск кому́-н; **to follow ~** (*fig*) сле́довать (после́довать *perf*) приме́ру; **they are well ~ed** (*couple*) они́ хорошо́ друг дру́гу подхо́дят.
suitability [su:tə'bɪlɪtɪ] *n* приго́дность *f*.
suitable ['su:təbl] *adj* подходя́щий*; **would tomorrow be ~?** за́втра Вам подойдёт *or* Вас устро́ит?; **we found somebody ~** мы нашли́ подходя́щего челове́ка.
suitably ['su:təblɪ] *adv* надлежа́щим о́бразом.
suitcase ['su:tkeɪs] *n* чемода́н.
suite [swi:t] *n* (*of rooms*) апартаме́нты *mpl*; (*MUS*) сюи́та; (*furniture*): **bedroom/dining room ~** спа́льный/столо́вый гарниту́р; **a three-piece ~** мя́гкая ме́бель *f*.
suitor ['su:tə^r] *n*: **he is her ~** он и́щет её руки́.
sulfate ['sʌlfeɪt] *n* (*US*) = **sulphate**.
sulfur ['sʌlfə^r] *n* (*US*) = **sulphur**.
sulfuric [sʌl'fjuərɪk] (*US*) = **sulphuric**.
sulk [sʌlk] *vi* быть* (*impf*) в дурно́м настрое́нии.
sulky ['sʌlkɪ] *adj* (*child, mood*) су́мрачный* (су́мрачен).
sullen ['sʌlən] *adj* (*person, silence*) угрю́мый (угрю́м).
sulphate ['sʌlfeɪt] (*US* **sulfate**) *n* сульфа́т.
sulphur ['sʌlfə^r] (*US* **sulfur**) *n* се́ра.
sulphur dioxide (*US* **sulfur dioxide**) *n* двуо́кись *f* се́ры, серни́стый ангидри́д.
sulphuric [sʌl'fjuərɪk] (*US* **sulfuric**) *adj*: **~ acid** се́рная кислота́.
sultan ['sʌltən] *n* султа́н.
sultana [sʌl'tɑ:nə] *n* (*CULIN*) кишми́ш.
sultry ['sʌltrɪ] *adj* (*weather*) ду́шный* (ду́шен).
sum [sʌm] *n* (*calculation*) арифме́тика, вычисле́ние; (*amount*) су́мма
▸ **sum up** *vt* (*describe*) сумми́ровать (*impf/perf*); (*evaluate rapidly*) вычисля́ть (вы́числить *perf*) ◆ *vi* (*summarize*) подводи́ть* (подвести́* *perf*) ито́г.
Sumatra [su'mɑ:trə] *n* Сума́тра.
summarize ['sʌməraɪz] *vt* сумми́ровать (*impf/perf*).
summary ['sʌmərɪ] *n* (*of essay etc*) кра́ткое изложе́ние ◆ *adj* (*justice*) поспе́шный; **weather/news ~** сво́дка пого́ды/новосте́й.
summer ['sʌmə^r] *n* (*season*) ле́то ◆ *adj* (*dress, school*) ле́тний*; **in ~** ле́том.
summer camp *n* (*US*) ле́тний* ла́герь* *m*.
summer holidays *npl* ле́тние кани́кулы *pl*.
summerhouse ['sʌməhaus] *n* (*in garden*) бесе́дка*.
summertime ['sʌmətaɪm] *n* (*season*) ле́то, ле́тний* пери́од.
summer time *n* ле́тнее вре́мя* *nt*.
summery ['sʌmərɪ] *adj* (*day, dress*) ле́тний*.
summing-up [sʌmɪŋ'ʌp] *n* (*LAW*) кра́ткое изложе́ние де́ла (*обращённое к прися́жным*).
summit ['sʌmɪt] *n* (*of mountain*) верши́на, пик; (*also:* **~ conference**) конфере́нция на вы́сшем у́ровне; (*also:* **~ meeting**) встре́ча на вы́сшем у́ровне.
summon ['sʌmən] *vt* вызыва́ть (вы́звать* *perf*); (*help*) звать* (позва́ть* *perf*) на +*acc*
▸ **summon up** *vt* собира́ть (собра́ть* *perf*).
summons ['sʌmənz] *n* (*LAW*) пове́стка; (*fig*) приказа́ние ◆ *vt* (*LAW*) вызыва́ть (вы́звать* *perf*); **to serve a ~ on sb** посыла́ть (посла́ть* *perf*) кому́-н пове́стку.
sumo ['su:məu] *n* (*also:* **~ wrestling**) су́мо *ind* (*япо́нская борьба́*).
sump [sʌmp] *n* (*BRIT: AUT*) ма́сляный поддо́н.
sumptuous ['sʌmptjuəs] *adj* (*meal, costume*) роско́шный* (роско́шен), великоле́пный* (великоле́пен).
sun [sʌn] *n* со́лнце; **in the ~** на со́лнце; **to catch the ~** слегко́ загоре́ть (*perf*); **everything under the ~** всё в ми́ре.
Sun. *abbr* = **Sunday**.
sunbathe ['sʌnbeɪð] *vi* загора́ть (*impf*).
sunbeam ['sʌnbi:m] *n* со́лнечный луч*.
sunbed ['sʌnbɛd] *n* шезло́нг; (*with sun lamp*) *устро́йство с ква́рцевой ла́мпой для получе́ния иску́сственно зага́ра*.
sunburn ['sʌnbə:n] *n* (*painful*) со́лнечный ожо́г.
sunburned ['sʌnbə:nd] *adj* = **sunburnt**.
sunburnt ['sʌnbə:nt] *adj* (*tanned*) загоре́лый; (*painfully*) обожённый (*со́лнцем*).
sun-cream ['sʌnkri:m] *n* солнцезащи́тный крем.
sundae ['sʌndeɪ] *n* моро́женое *nt adj* с фру́ктами.
Sunday ['sʌndɪ] *n* воскресе́нье; *see also* **Tuesday**.
Sunday paper *n* воскре́сная газе́та.
Sunday school *n* воскре́сная шко́ла.
sundial ['sʌndaɪəl] *n* со́лнечные часы́ *pl*.
sundown ['sʌndaun] *n* зака́т, захо́д (со́лнца).
sundries ['sʌndrɪz] *npl* (*miscellaneous items*) ра́зное *nt adj*.
sundry ['sʌndrɪ] *adj* (*various*) ра́зного ро́да; **all and ~** все подря́д.
sunflower ['sʌnflauə^r] *n* (*BOT*) подсо́лнечник.
sunflower oil *n* (*CULIN*) подсо́лнечное ма́сло.
sung [sʌŋ] *pp of* **sing**.
sunglasses ['sʌnglɑ:sɪz] *npl* солнцезащи́тные очки́* *pl*.
sunk [sʌŋk] *pp of* **sink**.
sunken ['sʌŋkn] *adj* (*rock, ship*) затону́вший; (*cheeks*) впа́лый; (*eyes*) ввали́вшийся; (*bath*) встро́енный в углубле́ние.
sunlamp ['sʌnlæmp] *n* ультрафиоле́товая *or*

кварцевая лáмпа.
sunlight ['sʌnlaɪt] *n* сóлнечный свет.
sunlit ['sʌnlɪt] *adj* освещённый (освещён) сóлнцем.
sunny ['sʌnɪ] *adj* (***weather, day, place***) сóлнечный; (***fig***) свéтлый; **it is ~** сóлнечно.
sunrise ['sʌnraɪz] *n* восхóд (сóлнца).
sun roof *n* (*AUT*) раздвижнáя панéль *f* (*в крыше автомобиля*).
sunscreen ['sʌnskri:n] *n* солнцезащи́тный крем.
sunset ['sʌnsɛt] *n* захóд (сóлнца), закáт.
sunshade ['sʌnʃeɪd] *n* зóнтик.
sunshine ['sʌnʃaɪn] *n* сóлнечный свет; **we sat in the ~** мы сидéли на сóлнце.
sunspot ['sʌnspɔt] *n* (*ASTRONOMY*) сóлнечное мéсто*.
sunstroke ['sʌnstrəuk] *n* сóлнечный удáр.
suntan ['sʌntæn] *n* загáр.
suntan lotion *n* лосьóн для загáра.
suntanned ['sʌntænd] *adj* (***body, person***) загорéлый.
suntan oil *n* мáсло для загáра.
suntrap ['sʌntræp] *n* сóлнечный островóк*.
super ['su:pə'] *adj* (***inf***) потрясáющий*.
superannuation [su:pərænju'eɪʃən] *n* ежегóдный пенсиóнный вклад.
superb [su:'pə:b] *adj* великолéпный* (великолéпен).
Super Bowl *n* (*US*) *финáльный матч америкáнского чемпионáта по футбóлу*.
supercilious [su:pə'sɪlɪəs] *adj* (***disdainful, haughty***) высокомéрный* (высокомéрен).
superconductor [su:pəkən'dʌktə'] *n* сверхпроводни́к.
superficial [su:pə'fɪʃəl] *adj* повéрхностный* (повéрхностен); (***wound***) лёгкий* (лёгок).
superficially [su:pə'fɪʃəlɪ] *adv* повéрхностно.
superfluous [su'pə:fluəs] *adj* изли́шний, ненýжный.
superglue ['su:pəglu:] *n* сýперклей.
superhuman [su:pə'hju:mən] *adj* (***effort, strength***) сверхчеловéческий*.
superimpose ['su:pərɪm'pəuz] *vt*: **to ~ (on)** наклáдывать (наложи́ть* *perf*) (на *+acc*).
superintend [su:pərɪn'tɛnd] *vt* надзирáть (*impf*) за *+instr*; **to be ~ed by** быть* (*impf*) под надзóром *+gen*.
superintendent [su:pərɪn'tɛndənt] *n* (***of place***) завéдующий*(-ая) *m(f)adj*; (***of activity***) руководи́тель(ница) *m(f)*; (*POLICE*) начáльник, надзирáтель *m*.
superior [su'pɪərɪə'] *adj* (***better***) превосходя́щий; (***more senior***) стáрший*; (***smug***) высокомéрный ◆ *n* начáльник(-ица); **Mother S~** (*REL*) настоя́тельница.
superiority [supɪərɪ'ɔrɪtɪ] *n* превосхóдство.
superlative [su'pə:lətɪv] *n прилагáтельное или нарéчие превосхóдной стéпени.*
superman ['su:pəmæn] *irreg n* супермéн, сверхчеловéк *m no pl*.
supermarket ['su:pəmɑ:kɪt] *n* универмáг, универсáм; (***in Europe, US etc***) супермáркет.
supermodel ['su:pəmɔdl] *n* супермодéль *f*.
supernatural [su:pə'nætʃərəl] *adj* (***creature, force etc***) сверхъестéственный ◆ *n*: **the ~** сверхъестéственные си́лы *fpl*.
supernova [su:pə'nəuvə] *n* взрывáющаяся нóвая звездá.
superpower ['su:pəpauə'] *n* (*POL*) сверхдержáва.
superscript ['su:pəskrɪpt] *n* (*TYP*) надстрóчные знáки *mpl*.
supersede [su:pə'si:d] *vt* сменя́ть (смени́ть* *perf*).
supersonic ['su:pə'sɔnɪk] *adj* (***flight, aircraft***) сверхзвуковóй.
superstar ['su:pəstɑ:'] *n* (*CINEMA, SPORT etc*) суперзвездá*.
superstition [su:pə'stɪʃən] *n* суевéрие.
superstitious [su:pə'stɪʃəs] *adj* суевéрный* (суевéрен).
superstore ['su:pəstɔ:'] *n* (*BRIT: COMM*) универмáг, супермáркет.
supertanker ['su:pətæŋkə'] *n* (*NAUT*) супертáнкер.
supertax ['su:pətæks] *n* дополни́тельный подохóдный налóг.
supervise ['su:pəvaɪz] *vt* (***person, activity***) следи́ть* (*impf*) *or* наблюдáть (*impf*) за *+instr*.
supervision [su:pə'vɪʒən] *n* руковóдство, надзóр; **under medical ~** под наблюдéнием врачá.
supervisor ['su:pəvaɪzə'] *n* (***of workers***) начáльник(-ица); (***of students***) наýчный(-ая) руководи́тель(ница) *m(f)*.
supervisory ['su:pəvaɪzərɪ] *adj* (***role***) руководя́щий*; (***staff***) контроли́рующий.
supine ['su:paɪn] *adj* лежáщий на спинé ◆ *adv* лёжа на спинé.
supper ['sʌpə'] *n* ýжин; **to have ~** ýжинать (поýжинать *perf*).
supplant [sə'plɑ:nt] *vt* (***person, thing***) приходи́ть* (прийти́* *perf*) на смéну *+dat*.
supple ['sʌpl] *adj* (***person, body***) ги́бкий* (ги́бок); (***leather***) мя́гкий* (мя́гок*).
supplement ['sʌplɪmənt] *n* (***vitamins etc***) добáвка*; (***of book, newspaper etc***) приложéние ◆ *vt* (***diet***) добав[illegible]ть (*impf*) к *+dat*; (***income***) подрабáтывать (*impf*).
supplementary [sʌplɪ'mɛntərɪ] *adj* (***question***) дополни́тельный.
supplementary benefit *n* (*BRIT: formerly*) *посóбие для малоимýщих в Великобритáнии.*
supplier [sə'plaɪə'] *n* (*COMM: person, firm*)

поставщи́к*.

supply [sə'plaɪ] *n* (*stock*) запа́с, запа́сы *mpl*; (*supplying*) поста́вка*; (*TECH*) обеспече́ние ◆ *vt* (*need*) удовлетворя́ть (удовлетвори́ть *perf*); (*provide*): **to ~ sth (to sb)** поставля́ть (поста́вить* *perf*) что-н (кому́-н); **supplies** *npl* (*food*) запа́сы *mpl* (продово́льствия); (*MIL*) боеприпа́сы *mpl* (и продово́льствие); **office supplies** конто́рские принадле́жности; **water is in short ~** э́тот райо́н испы́тывает нехва́тку воды́; **the electricity ~** снабже́ние электроэне́ргии; **the water ~** водоснабже́ние; **the gas ~** снабже́ние га́зом; **~ and demand** спрос и предложе́ние; **to ~ sb with sth** снабжа́ть (снабди́ть* *perf*) кого́-н чем-н; (*system, machine*) обору́довать *(impf/ perf)* кого́-н чем-н; **it comes supplied with an adaptor** поставля́ется с ада́птером.

supply teacher *n* (*BRIT*) замеща́ющий(-ая) учи́тель(ница) *m(f)*.

support [sə'pɔ:t] *n* (*moral, financial etc*) подде́ржка; (*TECH*) опо́ра, подпо́рка* ◆ *vt* (*football team etc*) боле́ть *(impf)* за *+acc*; (*financially*: *family etc*) содержа́ть *(impf)*; (*TECH*: *hold up*) подде́рживать *(impf)*; (*sustain*: *theory etc*) подтвержда́ть (подтверди́ть* *perf*); **they stopped work in ~ of** они́ прекрати́ли рабо́ту в подде́ржку *+gen*; **to ~ o.s.** (*financially*) зараба́тывать *(impf)* (самому́) себе́ на жизнь.

support buying *n* (*COMM*) *заку́пка в це́лях пониже́ния цен.*

supporter [sə'pɔ:tə^r] *n* (*POL etc*) сторо́нник(-ица); (*SPORT*) боле́льщик(-ица).

supporting [sə'pɔ:tɪŋ] *adj* второстепе́нный; **~ actor** актёр второ́го пла́на.

supportive [sə'pɔ:tɪv] *adj*: **to be ~ of sb** подде́рживать (поддержа́ть* *perf*) кого́-н.

suppose [sə'pəuz] *vt* полага́ть *(impf)*; **he was ~d to do it** (*duty*) он до́лжен был э́то сде́лать; **it was worse than she'd ~d** э́то оказа́лось ху́же, чем она́ предполага́ла; **I don't ~ she'll come** я полага́ю, она́ не придёт; **he's about sixty, I ~** я полага́ю, ему́ лет шестьдеся́т; **he's ~d to be an expert** счита́ется, что он в э́том разбира́ется.

supposedly [sə'pəuzɪdlɪ] *adv* по иде́е.

supposing [sə'pəuzɪŋ] *conj* предполо́жим, допу́стим.

supposition [sʌpə'zɪʃən] *n* предположе́ние, допуще́ние.

suppository [sə'pɔzɪtrɪ] *n* (*MED*) свеча́*.

suppress [sə'prɛs] *vt* подавля́ть (подави́ть* *perf*); (*scandal*) замя́ть* *(perf)*; (*publication*) запреща́ть (запрети́ть* *perf*).

suppression [sə'prɛʃən] *n* подавле́ние.

suppressor [sə'prɛsə^r] *n* (*ELEC etc*) глуши́тель *m*.

supremacy [su'prɛməsɪ] *n* (*MIL, POL etc*) госпо́дство.

supreme [su'pri:m] *adj* (*in titles*: *court etc*) Верхо́вный; (*effort, achievement*) велича́йший.

Supreme Court *n* (*US*) Верхо́вный Суд.

supremo [su'pri:məu] *n* (*BRIT*: *inf*) верхо́вный *or* гла́вный нача́льник.

Supt. *abbr* (*POLICE*) = **superintendent.**

surcharge ['sə:tʃɑ:dʒ] *n* (*extra cost*) дополни́тельный сбор, дополни́тельная пла́та.

sure [ʃuə^r] *adj* (*definite, convinced*) твёрдый* (твёрд); (*aim, friend, remedy*) ве́рный* (ве́рен) ◆ *adv* (*inf*: *esp US*): **that ~ is pretty, that's ~ pretty** э́то пра́вда ми́ло; **to make ~ of sth/that** удостове́риться *(perf)* в чём-н/, что; **~!** (*of course*) безусло́вно!; **~ enough** и пра́вда *or* впра́вду; **I'm not ~ how/why/when** я не уве́рен, как/почему́/когда́; **to be ~ of o.s.** не сомнева́ться *(impf)* в себе́.

sure-fire ['ʃuəfaɪə^r] *adj* (*inf*) ве́рный.

sure-footed [ʃuə'futɪd] *adj* (*animal, person*) твёрдо держа́щийся на нога́х.

surely ['ʃuəlɪ] *adv* (*certainly*) наверняка́; **~ you don't mean that!** наверня́ка, Вы э́то несерьёзно!

surety ['ʃuərətɪ] *n* (*money*) зало́г; **to go *or* stand ~ for sb** брать* (взять* *perf*) кого́-н на пору́ки.

surf [sə:f] *n* (*waves*) прибо́й; (*foam*) бара́шки *mpl*.

surface ['sə:fɪs] *n* пове́рхность *f* ◆ *vt* (*road*) покрыва́ть (покры́ть* *perf*) ◆ *vi* (*fish, person in water*) пока́зываться (показа́ться* *perf*) на пове́рхности; (*fig*: *news, feeling*) всплыва́ть (всплы́ть* *perf*); (*: person in bed*) объявля́ться (объяви́ться* *perf*); **on the ~** (*fig*) с ви́ду.

surface area *n* пло́щадь *f* пове́рхности.

surface mail *n* обы́чная по́чта.

surface-to-surface ['sə:fɪstə'sə:fɪs] *adj*: **~ missile** раке́та ти́па "земля́-земля́".

surfboard ['sə:fbɔ:d] *n* аквапла́н.

surfeit ['sə:fɪt] *n*: **a ~ of** переизбы́ток* *+gen*.

surfer ['sə:fə^r] *n* челове́к* занима́ющийся се́рфингом.

surfing ['sə:fɪŋ] *n* сёрфинг.

surge [sə:dʒ] *n* (*increase*) прито́к*; (*fig*: *of emotion*) прили́в; (*ELEC*) и́мпульс ◆ *vi* (*water*) вздыма́ться *(impf)*, нахлы́нуть *(perf)*; (*people, vehicles*) ри́нуться *(perf)*; (*ELEC*: *power*) ре́зко увели́чиваться (увели́читься *perf*); **to ~ forward** ри́нуться *(perf)* *or* броса́ться (бро́ситься* *perf*) вперёд; **relief ~d through her** она́ почу́вствовала прили́в облегче́ния.

surgeon ['sə:dʒən] *n* (*MED*) хиру́рг.

Surgeon General *n* (*US*: *MED, MIL*) нача́льник медици́нского управле́ния.

surgery ['sə:dʒərɪ] *n* (*treatment*) хирурги́ческое вмеша́тельство; (*BRIT*: *room*) кабине́т врача́; (*: of MP, doctor etc*) приём; **to undergo ~** переноси́ть* (перенести́* *perf*) опера́цию.

surgical ['sə:dʒɪkl] *adj* хирурги́ческий*.

surgical spirit *n* (*BRIT*) медици́нский* спирт.

surly [ˈsəːlɪ] *adj* (*person, behaviour*) неприве́тливый.
surmise [səːˈmaɪz] *vt*: **to ~ that** выска́зывать (вы́сказать* *perf*) предположе́ние, что.
surmount [səːˈmaunt] *vt* (*fig: problem, difficulty*) преодолева́ть (преодоле́ть *perf*).
surname [ˈsəːneɪm] *n* фами́лия.
surpass [səːˈpɑːs] *vt* (*person, thing*) превосходи́ть* (превзойти́* *perf*).
surplus [ˈsəːpləs] *n* избы́ток*, изли́шек*; (*of trade, payments*) акти́вное са́льдо *nt ind* ◆ *adj* (*stock, grain*) ли́шний*; **it is ~ to our requirements** э́то превыша́ет на́ши тре́бования.
surprise [səˈpraɪz] *n* удивле́ние ◆ *vt* (*astonish*) удивля́ть (удиви́ть* *perf*); (*catch unawares*) застава́ть* (заста́ть* *perf*) врасплóх; **to take by ~** застига́ть (засти́гнуть *perf*) врасплóх.
surprising [səˈpraɪzɪŋ] *adj* (*situation, announcement*) неожи́данный* (неожи́дан); **it is ~ how/that** удиви́тельно как/что.
surprisingly [səˈpraɪzɪŋlɪ] *adv* удиви́тельно; **(somewhat) ~, he agreed** как ни удиви́тельно, он согласи́лся.
surrealism [səˈrɪəlɪzəm] *n* сюрреали́зм.
surrealist [səˈrɪəlɪst] *adj* сюрреалисти́ческий.
surrender [səˈrɛndəʳ] *n* капитуля́ция ◆ *vi* (*army, hijackers etc*) сдава́ться* (сда́ться* *perf*) ◆ *vt* (*claim, right*) отка́зываться (отказа́ться* *perf*) от *+gen*.
surrender value *n* (*INSURANCE*) *сто́имость страхово́го по́лиса при возвра́те его́ страхово́му о́бществу.*
surreptitious [sʌrəpˈtɪʃəs] *adj* скры́тый.
surrogate [ˈsʌrəgɪt] *n* (*substitute*) замени́тель *m* ◆ *adj* замеща́ющий.
surrogate mother *n* суррога́тная мать* *f*.
surround [səˈraund] *vt* (*subj: walls, hedge etc*) окружа́ть *(impf)*; (*MIL, POLICE etc*) окружа́ть (окружи́ть *perf*).
surrounding [səˈraundɪŋ] *adj* (*countryside*) близлежа́щий.
surroundings [səˈraundɪŋz] *npl* окре́стности *fpl*.
surtax [ˈsəːtæks] *n* доба́вочный подохо́дный нало́г.
surveillance [səːˈveɪləns] *n* патрули́рование.
survey [*vt* səːˈveɪ, *n* ˈsəːveɪ] *vt* (*land*) де́лать (сде́лать *perf*) топографи́ческие съёмки *+gen*; (*house*) производи́ть* (произвести́* *perf*) осмо́тр *+gen*; (*scene, work etc*) осма́тривать (осмотре́ть* *perf*) ◆ *n* (*of land*) топографи́ческая *or* геодези́ческая съёмка; (*of house*) инспе́кция; (*of habits etc*) иссле́дование; (*of situation etc*) оце́нка*.
surveying [səˈveɪɪŋ] *n* (*of land*) геоде́зия, топографи́ческие съёмки* *fpl*.
surveyor [səˈveɪəʳ] *n* (*of land*) топо́граф; (*of house*) инспе́ктор.
survival [səˈvaɪvl] *n* (*continuation of life*) выжива́ние; (*relic*) пережи́ток* ◆ *cpd*: **~ kit** неприкоснове́нный запа́с; **~ course** обуче́ние выжива́нию в экстрема́льных усло́виях.
survive [səˈvaɪv] *vi* (*person, thing*) уцеле́ть (*perf*), выжива́ть (вы́жить* *perf*); (*custom etc*) сохраня́ться (сохрани́ться *perf*), уцеле́ть (*perf*) ◆ *vt* (*person*) пережи́ть* (*perf*).
survivor [səˈvaɪvəʳ] *n* (*of illness, accident*) пережи́вший(-ая) *m(f) adj*; **~s of an accident** оста́вшиеся в живы́х по́сле ава́рии.
susceptible [səˈsɛptəbl] *adj*: **~ (to)** (*heat*) чувстви́тельный* (чувстви́телен) (к *+dat*); (*injury*) подве́рженный* (подве́ржен) (*+dat*); (*flattery, pressure*) подда́ющийся (на *+acc*).
suspect [*vb* səsˈpɛkt, *n, adj* ˈsʌspɛkt] *vt* (*person*) подозрева́ть *(impf)*, заподо́зрить *(perf)*; (*think*) подозрева́ть *(impf)*; (*doubt*) не доверя́ть *(impf)* ◆ *n* подозрева́емый(-ая) *m(f) adj* ◆ *adj* подозри́тельный* (подозри́телен).
suspected [səsˈpɛktɪd] *adj* подозрева́емый (подозрева́ем).
suspend [səsˈpɛnd] *vt* (*hang*) подве́шивать (подве́сить* *perf*); (*delay, stop*) приостана́вливать (приостанови́ть* *perf*); (*from employment*) отстраня́ть (отстрани́ть *perf*) от до́лжности.
suspended animation [səsˈpɛndɪd-] *n* вре́менное замора́живание (*живо́го органи́зма*).
suspended sentence *n* усло́вный пригово́р.
suspender belt [səsˈpɛndəʳ-] *n* (же́нский*) по́яс*.
suspenders [səsˈpɛndəz] *npl* (*BRIT*) рези́нки* *fpl*; (*US*) подтя́жки* *fpl*.
suspense [səsˈpɛns] *n* (*uncertainty*) трево́га ожида́ния; (*in film etc*) напряже́ние; **to keep sb in ~** держа́ть* *(impf)* кого́-н в подве́шенном состоя́нии.
suspension [səsˈpɛnʃən] *n* (*from job, team*) отстране́ние от до́лжности; (*AUT*) амортиза́тор; (*of driving licence*) изъя́тие; (*of payment*) прекраще́ние.
suspension bridge *n* подвесно́й *or* вися́чий* мост*.
suspicion [səsˈpɪʃən] *n* (*distrust*) подозре́ния *ntpl*; (*bad feeling*) подозре́ние; (*trace*) намёк, след; **to be under ~** находи́ться* *(impf)* под подозре́нием; **arrested on ~ of murder** аресто́ванный по подозре́нию в уби́йстве.
suspicious [səsˈpɪʃəs] *adj* подозри́тельный* (подозри́телен); **to be ~ of** *or* **about sb/sth** относи́ться* (отнести́сь* *perf*) подозри́тельно *or* с подозре́нием к кому́-н/чему́-н.
suss out [sʌs-] (*BRIT: inf*) *vt* (*discover*) разобра́ться* *(perf)* в *+prp*; (*understand*)

* marks translations which have irregular inflections. The Russian-English side of the dictionary gives inflectional information.

раскуси́ть* *(perf)*; **I've sussed him out** я его́ раскуси́л.
sustain [səs'teɪn] *vt* подде́рживать (поддержа́ть* *perf*); (*injury*) понести́* *(perf)*.
sustainable [səs'teɪnəbl] *adj* (*economy, development*) жизнеспосо́бный.
sustained [səs'teɪnd] *adj* (*effort, attack*) неослабева́ющий.
sustenance ['sʌstɪnəns] *n* пропита́ние.
suture ['su:tʃəʳ] *n* (*MED*) шов*.
SW *abbr* (*RADIO*) (= **short wave**) КВ= *коро́ткие во́лны*.
swab [swɔb] *n* (*MED*) тампо́н ◆ *vt* (*also:* ~ **down**) мыть* (вы́мыть* *perf*) (шва́брой).
swagger ['swægəʳ] *vi* расха́живать *(impf)* с ва́жным ви́дом.
swallow ['swɔləu] *n* (*ZOOL*) (дереве́нская) ла́сточка*; (*of food*) кусо́чек*; (*of drink*) глото́к* ◆ *vt* (*food, pills, insult*) глота́ть *(impf)*, прогла́тывать (проглоти́ть* *perf*); (*fig: story*) купи́ться* *(perf)* на *+acc*; (*one's pride, one's words*) подавля́ть (подави́ть* *perf*)
▸ **swallow up** *vt* (*savings etc*) съеда́ть (съесть* *perf*).
swam [swæm] *pt of* **swim**.
swamp [swɔmp] *n* боло́то ◆ *vt* (*with water etc*) залива́ть (зали́ть* *perf*); (*fig: person*) зава́ливать (завали́ть* *perf*).
swampy ['swɔmpɪ] *adj* (*ground*) боло́тистый.
swan [swɔn] *n* ле́бедь* *m*.
swank [swæŋk] *vi* (*inf: talk boastfully*) хва́стать *(impf)*; (*: show off*) рисова́ться *(impf)*.
swansong ['swɔnsɔŋ] *n* (*fig*) лебеди́ная песнь *f*.
swap [swɔp] *n* обме́н ◆ *vt*: **to ~ (for)** (*exchange (for)*) меня́ть (обменя́ть *perf*) (на *+acc*); (*replace (with)*) смени́ть *(perf)* (на *+acc*).
SWAPO *n abbr* (= *South-West Africa People's Organization*) СВАПО (*Наро́дная организа́ция Ю́го-За́падной А́фрики*).
swarm [swɔ:m] *n* (*of bees*) рой; (*of people*) тьма ◆ *vi* (*bees*) рои́ться *(impf)*; (*people*) толо́чься* *(impf)*; (*place*): **to be ~ing with** кише́ть *(impf) +instr*.
swarthy ['swɔ:ðɪ] *adj* (*person, complexion, face*) сму́глый, тёмный.
swashbuckling ['swɔʃbʌklɪŋ] *adj* (*film*) залихва́тский; (*role, hero*) удало́й.
swastika ['swɔstɪkə] *n* сва́стика.
swat [swɔt] *vt* (*insect*) прихло́пнуть *(perf)* ◆ *n* (*BRIT: also:* **fly** ~) хлопу́шка*.
swathe [sweɪð] *vt*: **to ~ in** (*blankets*) заку́тывать (заку́тать *perf*) в *+acc*; (*bandages*) обма́тывать (обмота́ть *perf*) *+instr*.
swatter ['swɔtəʳ] *n* (*also:* **fly** ~) хлопу́шка*.
sway [sweɪ] *vi* (*person, tree*) кача́ться (качну́ться *perf*) ◆ *vt* (*influence*) склоня́ть (склони́ть* *perf*) ◆ *n*: **to hold ~ (over sb)** по́льзоваться* *(impf)* непререка́емым авторите́том (у кого́-н).
Swaziland ['swɑ:zɪlænd] *n* Свазиле́нд.
swear [swɛəʳ] (*pt* **swore**, *pp* **sworn**) *vi* (*curse*) руга́ться (вы́ругаться *perf*) ◆ *vt* (*promise*) торже́ственно дава́ть* (дать* *perf*); **to ~ an oath** дава́ть* (дать* *perf*) кля́тву
▸ **swear in** *vt* (*person*) приводи́ть* (привести́* *perf*) к прися́ге.
swearword ['swɛəwə:d] *n* руга́тельство.
sweat [swɛt] *n* пот* ◆ *vi* поте́ть (вспоте́ть *perf*), пропоте́ть *(perf)*; **in a ~** в поту́.
sweatband ['swɛtbænd] *n* повя́зка*.
sweater ['swɛtəʳ] *n* сви́тер*.
sweatshirt ['swɛtʃə:t] *n* хлопчатобума́жный спорти́вный сви́тер*.
sweatshop ['swɛtʃɔp] *n* (*pej*) *предприя́тие, где существу́ет потого́нная систе́ма*.
sweaty ['swɛtɪ] *adj* (*clothes*) пропоте́вший; (*hands*) по́тный.
Swede [swi:d] *n* швед(ка*).
swede [swi:d] *n* (*BRIT*) брю́ква.
Sweden ['swi:dn] *n* Шве́ция.
Swedish ['swi:dɪʃ] *adj* шве́дский* ◆ *n* (*LING*) шве́дский* язы́к*; **the ~** *npl* шве́ды.
sweep [swi:p] (*pt, pp* **swept**) *n* (*act of sweeping*) подмета́ние; (*curve*) изги́б; (*range*) разма́х; (*also:* **chimney** ~) трубочи́ст ◆ *vt* (*brush*) мести́* *or* подмета́ть (подмести́* *perf*); (*with arm*) сма́хивать (смахну́ть *perf*); (*subj: current*) смыва́ть (смыть* *perf*) ◆ *vi* (*hand, arm*) дви́гаться *(impf)*; (*wind*) бушева́ть *(impf)*
▸ **sweep away** *vt* смета́ть (смести́* *perf*), уноси́ть* (унести́* *perf*)
▸ **sweep past** *vi* проноси́ться* (пронести́сь* *perf*) ми́мо
▸ **sweep up** *vi* подмета́ть (подмести́* *perf*).
sweeper ['swi:pəʳ] *n* (*also:* **carpet** ~) щётка для ковра́; (*FOOTBALL*) ли́беро *nt ind*.
sweeping ['swi:pɪŋ] *adj* (*gesture*) широ́кий* (широ́к); (*changes, reforms*) всеобъе́млющий*; (*statement*) огу́льный.
sweepstake ['swi:psteɪk] *n* пари́ *nt ind* на ска́чках.
sweet [swi:t] *n* (*candy*) конфе́та; (*BRIT: CULIN*) сла́дкое *nt adj no pl* ◆ *adj* сла́дкий* (сла́док); (*kind, attractive*) ми́лый* (мил) ◆ *adv*: **to smell ~** сла́дко па́хнуть *(impf)*; **to taste ~** име́ть *(impf)* сла́дкий вкус; **~ and sour** ки́сло-сла́дкий*.
sweetbread ['swi:tbrɛd] *n* (*CULIN*) "сла́дкое мя́со" (*поджелу́дочная железа́*).
sweet corn *n* кукуру́за.
sweeten ['swi:tn] *vt* добавля́ть (доба́вить* *perf*) са́хар к *+dat*; (*temper*) смиря́ть (смири́ть *perf*).
sweetener ['swi:tnəʳ] *n* замени́тель *m* са́хара; (*fig*) подслащённая пилю́ля.
sweetheart ['swi:thɑ:t] *n* возлю́бленный(-ая) *m(f) adj*; (*term of affection*) дорого́й(-а́я) *m(f) adj*.
sweetness ['swi:tnɪs] *n* (*amount of sugar*) сла́дость *f*; (*kindness*) прия́тность *f*.
sweet pea *n* души́стый горо́шек*.

sweet potato *n* ямс.
sweet shop *n* (*BRIT*) конди́терская ла́вка.
sweet tooth *n*: **he/she has a ~ ~** он/она́ сластёна.
swell [swɛl] (*pt* **swelled**, *pp* **swollen** *or* **swelled**) *n* (*of sea*) волне́ние ◆ *adj* (*US*: *inf*: *excellent*) миро́вой ◆ *vi* (*numbers*) расти́* (вы́расти* *perf*); (*sound, feeling*) расти́* (*impf*); (*also*: **~ up**: *face, ankle etc*) опуха́ть (опу́хнуть *perf*).
swelling ['swɛlɪŋ] *n* (*MED*) о́пухоль *f*.
sweltering ['swɛltərɪŋ] *adj* ду́шный.
swept [swɛpt] *pt, pp of* **sweep**.
swerve [swəːv] *vi* ре́зко виля́ть (вильну́ть *perf*).
swift [swɪft] *n* (*bird*) стриж* ◆ *adj* стреми́тельный* (стреми́телен).
swiftly ['swɪftlɪ] *adv* стреми́тельно.
swiftness ['swɪftnɪs] *n* стреми́тельность *f*.
swig [swɪg] *n* (*inf*: *drink*) глото́к*.
swill [swɪl] *vt* (*also*: **~ out, ~ down**) спола́скивать (сполосну́ть *perf*) ◆ *n* (*for pigs*) по́йло.
swim [swɪm] (*pt* **swam**, *pp* **swum**) *vi* пла́вать/плыть* (*impf*); (*as sport*) пла́вать (*impf*); (*head*) идти́* (пойти́* *perf*) кру́гом; (*room*) плыть* (поплы́ть* *perf*) ◆ *vt* (*the Channel*) переплыва́ть (переплы́ть* *perf*); (*a length*) проплыва́ть (проплы́ть* *perf*); **to go ~ming, go for a ~** ходи́ть*/идти́* (пойти́* *perf*) пла́вать.
swimmer ['swɪmə^r] *n* плове́ц*(-вчи́ха).
swimming ['swɪmɪŋ] *n* пла́вание.
swimming baths *npl* (*BRIT*) пла́вательный бассе́йн *msg*.
swimming cap *n* рези́новая ша́почка* (*для пла́вания*).
swimming costume *n* (*BRIT*) купа́льный костю́м.
swimmingly ['swɪmɪŋlɪ] *adv* как по ма́слу; **everything's going ~** всё идёт как по ма́слу.
swimming pool *n* пла́вательный бассе́йн.
swimming trunks *npl* пла́вки* *pl*.
swimsuit ['swɪmsuːt] *n* купа́льник.
swindle ['swɪndl] *n* моше́нничество ◆ *vt* надува́ть (наду́ть* *perf*).
swindler ['swɪndlə^r] *n* жу́лик.
swine [swaɪn] *n* (*inf!*) свинья́* *m/f* (*!*)
swing [swɪŋ] (*pt, pp* **swung**) *n* (*in playground*) каче́ли *pl*; (*movement*) кача́ние; (*change*: *in opinions etc*) колеба́ние; (*MUS, rhythm*) свинг ◆ *vt* (*arms*) разма́хивать (*impf*) +*instr*; (*legs*) болта́ть (*impf*) +*instr*; (*also*: **~ round**: *vehicle etc*) развора́чивать (разверну́ть *perf*) ◆ *vi* кача́ться (*impf*); (*also*: **~ round**: *vehicle etc*) свора́чивать (сверну́ть *perf*); **a ~ to the left** (*POL*) крен вле́во; **to get into the ~ of things** входи́ть* (войти́* *perf*) в ритм; **to be in full ~** (*party etc*) быть* (*impf*) в по́лном разга́ре; **the road ~s south** доро́га свора́чивает на юг.
swing bridge *n* разводно́й мост*.
swing door (*US* **swinging door**) *n* *дверь, открыва́ющаяся в о́бе сто́роны.*
swingeing ['swɪndʒɪŋ] *adj* (*BRIT*: *blow, attack*) сокруши́тельный* (сокруши́телен); (: *cuts*) беспоща́дный.
swinging ['swɪŋɪŋ] *adj* кача́ющийся; (*fig*) весёлый.
swipe [swaɪp] *vt* (*hit*) ударя́ть (уда́рить *perf*) с разма́ху; (*inf*: *steal*) тащи́ть (стащи́ть* *perf*).
swirl [swəːl] *vi* (*water, smoke, leaves*) кружи́ться (*impf*) ◆ *n* (*of water*) водоро́т; (*of leaves*) круже́ние.
swish [swɪʃ] *vi* (*tail*) маха́ть* (*impf*); (*clothes*) шелесте́ть* (*impf*), шурша́ть (*impf*) ◆ *n* свист ◆ *adj* (*inf*) шика́рный.
Swiss [swɪs] *adj* швейца́рский* ◆ *n inv* швейца́рец*(-рка*).
Swiss French *adj* фра́нко-швейца́рский* ◆ *n* (*person*) франкоговоря́щий(-ая) швейца́рец(-рка); (*LING*) швейца́рский* диале́кт францу́зского языка́.
Swiss German *adj* неме́цко-швейца́рский* ◆ *n* (*person*) немецкоговоря́щий(-ая) швейца́рец(-рка); (*LING*) швейца́рский* диале́кт неме́цкого языка́.
swiss roll *n* руле́т с варе́ньем.
switch [swɪtʃ] *n* (*for light, radio etc*) выключа́тель *m*; (*change*) переключе́ние ◆ *vt* (*change*) переключа́ть (переключи́ть *perf*); (*exchange*) промени́ть* (*perf*); **to ~ (round** *or* **over)** меня́ть (поменя́ть *perf*) места́ми
▸ **switch off** *vt* выключа́ть (вы́ключить *perf*)
▸ **switch on** *vt* включа́ть (включи́ть *perf*).
switchback ['swɪtʃbæk] *n* (*BRIT*) *доро́га иду́щая то вверх, то вниз.*
switchblade ['swɪtʃbleɪd] *n* (*also*: **~ knife**) нож с заменя́ющимися ле́звиями.
switchboard ['swɪtʃbɔːd] *n* (*TEL*) коммута́тор.
switchboard operator *n* (*TEL*) телефони́ст(ка*).
Switzerland ['swɪtsələnd] *n* Швейца́рия.
swivel ['swɪvl] *vi* (*also*: **~ round**) верте́ться* (*impf*).
swollen ['swəulən] *pp of* **swell** ◆ *adj* (*ankle*) опу́хший*; (*lake*) перепо́лнившийся.
swoon [swuːn] *vi* замира́ть (замере́ть *perf*).
swoop [swuːp] *n* (*by police etc*) налёт; (*of bird etc*) стреми́тельное паде́ние ◆ *vi* (*also*: **~ down**: *bird, plane*) стреми́тельно па́дать (*impf*).
swop [swɔp] = **swap**.
sword [sɔːd] *n* шпа́га, меч*.
swordfish ['sɔːdfɪʃ] *n* меч-ры́ба.
swore [swɔː^r] *pt of* **swear**.
sworn [swɔːn] *pp of* **swear** ◆ *adj* (*statement, evidence*) под прися́гой; (*enemy*) закля́тый.
swot [swɔt] *vi* зубри́ть (*impf*) ◆ *n* (*pej*: *of person*)

зубри́ла *m/f*
▸ **swot up** *vt*: **to ~ up (on)** зазу́бривать (зазубри́ть *perf*).
swum [swʌm] *pp of* **swim**.
swung [swʌŋ] *pt, pp of* **swing**.
sycamore ['sɪkəmɔː'] *n* я́вор.
sycophant ['sɪkəfænt] *n* подхали́м.
sycophantic [sɪkə'fæntɪk] *adj* подхали́мский*.
Sydney ['sɪdnɪ] *n* Сидне́й.
syllable ['sɪləbl] *n* слог*.
syllabus ['sɪləbəs] *n* програ́мма; **on the ~** входя́щий* в програ́мму.
symbol ['sɪmbl] *n* (*sign, also* MATH) знак; (*representation*) си́мвол.
symbolic(al) [sɪm'bɔlɪk(l)] *adj* символи́ческий*; **to be symbolic of sth** символизи́ровать *(impf)* что-н.
symbolism ['sɪmbəlɪzəm] *n* символи́зм.
symbolize ['sɪmbəlaɪz] *vt* символизи́ровать *(impf)*.
symmetrical [sɪ'mɛtrɪkl] *adj* симметри́чный* (симметри́чен).
symmetry ['sɪmɪtrɪ] *n* симме́трия.
sympathetic [sɪmpə'θɛtɪk] *adj* (*person*) сочу́вствующий*; (*remark*) сочу́вственный; (*likeable*: *character*) прия́тный* (прия́тен); (*showing support*): **~ to(wards)** благоскло́нно настро́енный по отноше́нию к *+dat*; **to be ~ to sth** (*well-disposed*) сочу́вственно относи́ться* (отнести́сь* *perf*) к чему́-н.
sympathetically [sɪmpə'θɛtɪklɪ] *adv* сочу́вственно.
sympathize ['sɪmpəθaɪz] *vi*: **to ~ with** (*person*) сочу́вствовать* *(impf)* *+dat*, проявля́ть (прояви́ть* *perf*) сочу́вствие к *+dat*; (*feelings, cause*) сочу́вственно относи́ться* (отнести́сь* *perf*) к *+dat*.
sympathizer ['sɪmpəθaɪzə'] *n* (POL) симпатизи́рующий(-ая) *m(f) adj*.
sympathy ['sɪmpəθɪ] *n* (*pity*) сочу́вствие; **sympathies** *npl* (*support, tendencies*) симпа́тии *fpl*; **with our deepest ~** прими́те на́ши глубоча́йшие соболе́знования; **to come out in ~** (*workers*) бастова́ть *(impf)* в знак солида́рности.
symphonic [sɪm'fɔnɪk] *adj* симфони́ческий*.
symphony ['sɪmfənɪ] *n* симфо́ния.
symphony orchestra *n* симфони́ческий* орке́стр.
symposia [sɪm'pəuzɪə] *npl of* **symposium**.
symposium [sɪm'pəuzɪəm] (*pl* **~s** *or* **symposia**) *n* симпо́зиум.
symptom ['sɪmptəm] *n* (MED) симпто́м; (*indicator*) при́знак.
symptomatic [sɪmptə'mætɪk] *adj*: **~ of** симптомати́чный* при́знак *+gen*.
sync [sɪŋk] *n* (*inf*: *watches etc*): **out of ~** в разнобо́й.
synagogue ['sɪnəgɔg] *n* синаго́га.
synchromesh [sɪŋkrəu'mɛʃ] *n* синхрониза́тор.
synchronize ['sɪŋkrənaɪz] *vt* (*watches*) сверя́ть (све́рить *perf*); (*sound, movements*) синхронизи́ровать *(impf/perf)* ◆ *vi*: **to ~ with** совпада́ть (совпа́сть* *perf*) (по вре́мени) с *+instr*.
synchronized swimming ['sɪŋkrənaɪzd-] *n* синхро́нное пла́вание.
syncopated ['sɪŋkəpeɪtɪd] *adj* (*rhythm, beat*) синкопи́рованный.
syndicate ['sɪndɪkɪt] *n* (*of people, businesses*) синдика́т; (*of newspapers*) аге́нтство печа́ти.
syndrome ['sɪndrəum] *n* (*also* MED) синдро́м.
synonym ['sɪnənɪm] *n* сино́ним.
synonymous [sɪ'nɔnɪməs] *adj* (*fig*): **~ (with)** равноси́льный* (равноси́лен) (*+dat*).
synopses [sɪ'nɔpsiːz] *npl of* **synopsis**.
synopsis [sɪ'nɔpsɪs] (*pl* **synopses**) *n* кра́ткое изложе́ние.
syntactic [sɪn'tæktɪk] *adj* синтакси́ческий*.
syntax ['sɪntæks] *n* си́нтаксис.
syntax error *n* (COMPUT) синтакси́ческая оши́бка*.
syntheses ['sɪnθəsiːz] *npl of* **synthesis**.
synthesis ['sɪnθəsɪs] (*pl* **syntheses**) *n* (*of ideas, styles*) слия́ние, си́нтез.
synthesizer ['sɪnθəsaɪzə'] *n* синтеза́тор.
synthetic [sɪn'θɛtɪk] *adj* (*materials*) синтети́ческий*, иску́сственный ◆ *n* иску́сственный материа́л; (TEXTILES) синте́тика, иску́сственный материа́л; **~s** *npl* (*man-made fabrics*) синте́тика *fsg*, синтети́ческие тка́ни *fpl*.
syphilis ['sɪfɪlɪs] *n* си́филис.
syphon ['saɪfən] = **siphon**.
Syria ['sɪrɪə] *n* Си́рия.
Syrian ['sɪrɪən] *adj* сири́йский* ◆ *n* сири́ец*(-и́йка).
syringe [sɪ'rɪndʒ] *n* шприц*.
syrup ['sɪrəp] *n* (*juice*) сиро́п; (*also*: **golden ~**) (све́тлая ог жёлтая) па́тока.
syrupy ['sɪrəpɪ] *adj* (*liquid*) густо́й* (густ); (*pej*: *quality*) слаща́вый (слаща́в).
system ['sɪstəm] *n* систе́ма; **it was a shock to his ~** э́то яви́лось для него́ потрясе́нием.
systematic [sɪstə'mætɪk] *adj* (*methodical*) системати́ческий*.
systems analyst ['sɪstəmz-] *n* (COMPUT) систе́мный анали́тик, системоте́хник.
systems disk *n* (COMPUT) систе́мный диск.

~ T, t ~

T, t [ti:] *n* (*letter*) *20-ая бу́ква англи́йского алфави́та.*
TA *n abbr* (*BRIT*: = *Territorial Army*) территориа́льная а́рмия.
ta [tɑ:] *excl* (*BRIT*: *inf*) спаси́бо.
tab [tæb] *n abbr* = **tabulator**.
tabby ['tæbɪ] *n* (*also*: ~ **cat**: *male*) полоса́тый кот; (*female*) полоса́тая ко́шка.
tabernacle ['tæbənækl] *n* (*REL*) ски́ния.
table ['teɪbl] *n* (*piece of furniture*) стол*; (*MATH, CHEM etc*) табли́ца ◆ *vt* (*BRIT*: *motion etc*) выноси́ть* (вы́нести* *perf*) на обсужде́ние; **to lay** *or* **set the** ~ накрыва́ть (накры́ть* *perf*) на стол; **to clear the** ~ убира́ть (убра́ть* *perf*) со стола́; **league** ~ (*BRIT*: *FOOTBALL, RUGBY*) ли́говая табли́ца; ~ **of contents** оглавле́ние.
tablecloth ['teɪblklɔθ] *n* ска́терть *f*.
table d'hôte [[tɑ:bl'dəut]] *adj*: ~ ~ **menu** табльдо́т.
table lamp *n* насто́льная ла́мпа.
tablemat ['teɪblmæt] *n* подста́вка.
table salt *n* столо́вая соль *f*.
tablespoon ['teɪblspu:n] *n* столо́вая ло́жка.
tablet ['tæblɪt] *n* (*MED*) табле́тка*; (*for writing*) доще́чка* (для письма́); (*of stone*) доска́*; ~ **of soap** (*BRIT*) кусо́к* мы́ла.
table tennis *n* насто́льный те́ннис.
table wine *n* столо́вое вино́.
tabloid ['tæblɔɪd] *n* (*newspaper*) малоформа́тная газе́та, табло́ид; **the ~s** жёлтая *or* бульва́рная пре́сса.
taboo [tə'bu:] *n* табу́ *nt ind* ◆ *adj* запрещённый.
tabulate ['tæbjuleɪt] *vt* (*data, figures*) своди́ть* (свести́* *perf*) в табли́цу.
tabulator ['tæbjuleɪtə^r] *n* колонкоустанови́тель *m*; (*on typewriter*) табуля́тор.
tachograph ['tækəgrɑ:f] *n* (*AUT*) тахо́граф (*для регистра́ции режи́ма движе́ния автомоби́ля*).
tachometer [tæ'kɔmɪtə^r] *n* (*AUT*) тахо́метр, счётчик числа́ оборо́тов.
tacit ['tæsɪt] *adj* (*agreement, approval etc*) молчали́вый.
taciturn ['tæsɪtə:n] *adj* (*person*) молчали́вый (молчали́в).
tack [tæk] *n* (*nail*) гвоздь *m* с широ́кой шля́пкой; (*fig*) путь *m* ◆ *vt* (*nail*) прибива́ть (приби́ть* *perf*); (*stitch*) смётывать (смета́ть *perf*) ◆ *vi* (*NAUT*) идти́* (пойти́* *perf*) га́лсами; **on the wrong** ~ (*fig*) на ло́жном пути́; **to** ~ **sth on to (the end of) sth** прикрепля́ть (прикрепи́ть* *perf*) что-н к чему́-н.
tackle ['tækl] *n* (*for fishing etc*) снасть *f*; (*for lifting*) сло́жный блок; (*FOOTBALL, RUGBY*) блокиро́вка ◆ *vt* (*difficulty*) справля́ться (спра́виться* *perf*) с +*instr*; (*grapple with*) схвати́ться* (*perf*) с +*instr*; (*FOOTBALL, RUGBY*) блоки́ровать (*impf/perf*).
tacky ['tækɪ] *adj* (*sticky*) ли́пкий*; (*pej*: *of poor quality*) дешёвый.
tact [tækt] *n* такт, такти́чность *f*.
tactful ['tæktful] *adj* такти́чный* (такти́чен); **she is very** ~ она́ о́чень такти́чна.
tactfully ['tæktfəlɪ] *adv* такти́чно.
tactical ['tæktɪkl] *adj* (*also MIL*) такти́ческий*; ~ **error** такти́ческая оши́бка.
tactician [tæk'tɪʃən] *n* та́ктик.
tactics ['tæktɪks] *npl* та́ктика *fsg*.
tactless ['tæktlɪs] *adj* беста́ктный* (беста́ктен).
tactlessly ['tæktlɪslɪ] *adv* беста́ктно.
tadpole ['tædpəul] *n* голова́стик.
taffy ['tæfɪ] *n* (*US*: *toffee*) ири́ска*, тяну́чка*.
tag [tæg] *n* (*label*) этике́тка*, ярлы́к*; **price** ~ це́нник; **name** ~ би́рка*
▸**tag along** *vi* сле́довать (*impf*) по пята́м.
Tahiti [tɑ:'hi:tɪ] *n* Таи́ти *m ind*.
tail [teɪl] *n* (*of animal, plane*) хвост*; (*of shirt*) коне́ц*; (*of coat*) пола́* ◆ *vt* (*follow*) сади́ться* (сесть* *perf*) на хвост +*dat*; **~s** *npl* (*formal suit*) фрак *msg*; **to turn** ~ броса́ться (бро́ситься* *perf*) наутёк; *see also* **head**
▸**tail away** *vi* (*voice, wind*) затиха́ть (зати́хнуть *perf*)
▸**tail off** *vi* = **tail away**.
tailback ['teɪlbæk] *n* (*BRIT*: *AUT*) хвост.
tail coat *n* фрак.
tail end *n* (*of train etc*) хвост; (*of meeting etc*) коне́ц.
tailgate ['teɪlgeɪt] *n* (*AUT*) за́дняя дверь *f*.
taillight ['teɪllaɪt] *n* (*US*: *AUT*) за́дняя фа́ра.

* marks translations which have irregular inflections. The Russian-English side of the dictionary gives inflectional information.

tailor ['teɪlə^r] *n* (мужской) портной *m adj* ◆ *vt*: **to ~ sth (to)** приспосабливать (приспособить *perf*) что-н (к +*dat*); **~'s shop** портняжная мастерская *f adj*.
tailoring ['teɪlərɪŋ] *n* (*cut*) покрой; (*craft*) портняжное дело.
tailor-made ['teɪlə'meɪd] *adj* (*suit*) сшитый на заказ; (*fig*); **she is ~ for the job** она идеально подходит для этой работы.
tailwind ['teɪlwɪnd] *n* хвостовой *or* попутный ветер.
taint [teɪnt] *vt* (*meat, food*) портить* (испортить* *perf*); (*fig*) пятнать (запятнать *perf*).
tainted ['teɪntɪd] *adj* (*food*) испорченный; (*air, water*) загрязнённый* (загрязнён); (*fig*) запятнанный.
Taiwan ['taɪ'wɑːn] *n* Тайвань *m*.
Tajik ['tɑːdʒɪk] *n* таджик(-ичка*).
Tajiki [tɑː'dʒɪkɪ] *adj* таджикский* ◆ *n* таджикский* язык*.
Tajikistan [tɑːdʒɪkɪ'stɑːn] *n* Таджикистан.
take [teɪk] (*pt* **took**, *pp* **taken**) *vt* брать* (взять* *perf*); (*photo, measures*) снимать (снять* *perf*); (*shower, decision, drug*) принимать (принять* *perf*); (*notes*) делать (сделать *perf*); (*grab*: *sb's arm etc*) хватать (схватить* *perf*); (*require*: *courage, time*) требовать (потребовать *perf*); (*pain etc*) переносить* (перенести* *perf*); (*hold*: *passengers etc*) вмещать (вместить* *perf*); (*person*: *on foot*) отводить* (отвести* *perf*); (*thing*: *on foot*) относить* (отнести* *perf*); (*person, thing*: *by transport*) отвозить* (отвезти *perf*); (*exam*) сдавать* (сдать* *perf*); (*conduct*: *meeting*) вести* (*impf*) ◆ *vi* (*fire*) заниматься (заняться* *perf*); (*dye*) впитываться (впитаться *perf*); (*plant, injection*) приниматься (приняться* *perf*) ◆ *n* (*CINEMA*) дубль *m*; **to ~ sth from** (*drawer etc*) вынимать (вынуть* *perf*) что-н из +*gen*; (*steal from*: *person*) брать* (взять* *perf*) что-н у +*gen*; **I ~ it that ...** как я понимаю, ...; **I took him for a doctor** я принял его за врача; **to ~ sb's hand** брать* (взять* *perf*) кого-н за руку; **to ~ for a walk** (*child, dog*) брать* (взять* *perf*) на прогулку; **to be ~n ill** заболевать (заболеть *perf*); **to ~ it upon o.s. to do** браться* (взяться* *perf*) +*infin*; **~ the first (street) on the left** первый поворот налево; **to ~ Russian at university** изучать (*impf*) русский язык в университете; **it won't ~ long** это не займёт много времени; **I was quite ~n with her** (*attracted*) она произвела на меня большое впечатление
▸ **take after** *vt fus* (*resemble*) пойти* (*perf*) в +*acc*
▸ **take apart** *vt* разбирать (разобрать* *perf*)
▸ **take away** *vt* (*remove*) убирать (убрать* *perf*); (*carry off*) забирать (забрать* *perf*); (*MATH*) отнимать (отнять* *perf*) ◆ *vi*: **to ~ away from** отнимать (отнять* *perf*) от +*gen*
▸ **take back** *vt* (*return*: *thing*) относить* (отнести* *perf*) обратно; (: *person*) отводить* (отвести* *perf*) обратно; (*one's words*) брать* (взять* *perf*) назад
▸ **take down** *vt* (*building*) сносить* (снести* *perf*); (*scaffolding*) разбирать (разобрать* *perf*); (*picture*) снимать (снять* *perf*); (*write down*: *letter etc*) записывать (записать* *perf*)
▸ **take in** *vt* (*deceive*) обманывать (обмануть *perf*); (*understand*) воспринимать (воспринять* *perf*); (*include*) включать (включить *perf*); (*lodger, orphan*) брать* (взять* *perf*); (*dress, waistband*) ушивать (ушить* *perf*)
▸ **take off** *vi* (*AVIAT*) взлетать (взлететь* *perf*); (*go away*) улетать (улететь* *perf*) ◆ *vt* (*remove*) снимать (снять* *perf*); (*imitate*) копировать (скопировать *perf*)
▸ **take on** *vt* (*work, employee*) брать* (взять* *perf*); (*opponent*) сражаться (сразиться* *perf*) с +*instr*
▸ **take out** *vt* (*invite*) водить* (повести* *perf*); (*remove*) вынимать (вынуть* *perf*); (*licence*) оформлять (оформить* *perf*); **to ~ sth out of sth** (*drawer, pocket etc*) вынимать (вынуть* *perf*) что-н из чего-н; **don't ~ it out on me!** не вымещай это на мне!
▸ **take over** *vt* (*business, country*) принимать (принять* *perf*) руководство +*instr* ◆ *vi*: **to ~ over from sb** сменять (сменить *perf*) кого-н
▸ **take to** *vt fus* (*activity*) пристраститься* (*perf*) к +*dat*, заниматься (заняться* *perf*) +*instr*; (*form habit of*): **to ~ to doing** пристраститься* (*perf*) +*infin*; **she took to him at once** он ей сразу понравился
▸ **take up** *vt* (*hobby, sport, job*) заняться* (*perf*) +*instr*; (*idea, suggestion, story*) подхватывать (подхватить* *perf*); (*time, space*) занимать (занять* *perf*); (*garment*) подшивать (подшить* *perf*) ◆ *vi*: **to ~ up with sb** сходиться* (сойтись* *perf*) с кем-н; **to ~ sb up on sth** (*offer, suggestion*) воспользоваться (*perf*) +*instr*; **I'll ~ you up on that!** ловлю Вас на слове!
takeaway ['teɪkəweɪ] *n* (*BRIT*) *магазин или ресторан, где продаётся горячая еда на вынос*; (*food*) горячая еда на вынос.
take-home pay ['teɪkhəum-] *n* чистый заработок*.
taken ['teɪkən] *pp of* **take**.
takeoff ['teɪkɔf] *n* (*AVIAT*) взлёт.
takeout ['teɪkaut] (*US*) *n* = **takeaway**.
takeover ['teɪkəuvə^r] *n* (*COMM*) поглощение; (*of country*) захват власти.
takeover bid *n* (*COMM*) попытка поглощения.
takings ['teɪkɪŋz] *npl* (*COMM*) выручка *fsg*.
talc [tælk] *n* тальк.
talcum powder ['tælkəm-] *n* = **talc**.
tale [teɪl] *n* (*story, account*) рассказ, сказание; **to tell ~s** (*fig*: *to teacher, parents etc*) ябедничать (наябедничать *perf*).
talent ['tælnt] *n* талант.

talented ['tæləntɪd] *adj* (*person, actor etc*) тала́нтливый (тала́нтлив).
talent scout *n* (*THEAT, SPORT*) *челове́к, занима́ющийся по́иском молоды́х дарова́ний.*
talisman ['tælɪzmən] *n* талисма́н.
talk [tɔ:k] *n* (*a (prepared) speech*) докла́д; (*conversation, interview*) бесе́да; (*gossip*) слух ◆ *vi* (*speak*) разгова́ривать *(impf)*; **~s** *npl* (*POL etc*) перегово́ры *pl*; **to give a ~** де́лать (сде́лать *perf*) докла́д; **to ~ about** расска́зывать (рассказа́ть *perf*) о +*prp*; **~ing of films, have you seen ...?** кста́ти о фи́льмах, вы ви́дели ...?; **to ~ sb into doing** угова́ривать (уговори́ть *perf*) кого́-н +*infin*; **to ~ sb out of sth** отгова́ривать (отговори́ть *perf*) кого́-н от чего́-н; **to ~ shop** говори́ть *(impf)* о дела́х
▶ **talk over** *vt* (*problem etc*) обгова́ривать (обговори́ть *perf*).
talkative ['tɔ:kətɪv] *adj* (*person*) разгово́рчивый (разгово́рчив).
talker ['tɔ:kə^r] *n*: **she is a good ~** она́ хоро́ший ора́тор; (*pej*) болту́н(-у́шка); **he is a fast ~** он красноречи́в.
talking point ['tɔ:kɪŋ-] *n* те́ма для разгово́ра.
talking-to ['tɔ:kɪŋtu] *n*: **to give sb a good ~** отчи́тывать (отчита́ть *perf*) кого́-н как сле́дует.
talk show *n* (*TV, RADIO*) ток-шо́у *ind*.
tall [tɔ:l] *adj* высо́кий* (высо́к); **he is 6 feet ~** его́ рост – 6 фу́тов; **how ~ are you?** како́й у Вас рост?
tallboy ['tɔ:lbɔɪ] *n* (*BRIT*) высо́кий* комо́д.
Tallin(n) ['tælɪn] *n* Та́ллин(н).
tallness ['tɔ:lnɪs] *n* высота́.
tall story *n* небыли́ца.
tally ['tælɪ] *n* (*of marks, amounts of money etc*) счёт ◆ *vi*: **to ~ (with)** (*subj*: *figures, stories etc*) сходи́ться* (сойти́сь* *perf*) (с +*instr*); **to keep a ~ of sth** вести́* *(impf)* счёт чего́-н.
talon ['tælən] *n* (*of eagle, owl etc*) ко́готь* *m*.
tambourine [tæmbə'ri:n] *n* (*MUS*) тамбури́н, бу́бен.
tame [teɪm] *adj* (*animal, bird*) ручно́й; (*fig*: *story, style*) вя́лый (вял).
tamper ['tæmpə^r] *vi*: **to ~ with sth** пыта́ться (попыта́ться *perf*) измени́ть что-н.
tampon ['tæmpɔn] *n* тампо́н.
tan [tæn] *n* (*also:* **suntan**) зага́р ◆ *vi* (*person*) загора́ть (загоре́ть *perf*); (*skin*) загоре́ть *(perf)* ◆ *vt* дуби́ть* (вы́дубить* *perf*) ◆ *adj* (*colour*) рыжева́то-кори́чневый; **to get a ~** загора́ть (загоре́ть *perf*).
tandem ['tændəm] *n* (*cycle*) танде́м; **in ~** (*together*) совме́стно, вме́сте.
tandoori [tæn'duərɪ] *n индийский ме́тод приготовле́ния мя́са и лепёшек в гли́няной печи́.*
tang [tæŋ] *n* си́льный за́пах.
tangent ['tændʒənt] *n* (*MATH*) каса́тельная *f adj*; **to go off at a ~** (*fig*) сбива́ться (сби́ться* *perf*).
tangerine [tændʒə'ri:n] *n* (*fruit*) мандари́н; (*colour*) я́рко-ора́нжевый цвет.
tangible ['tændʒəbl] *adj* (*proof, benefits*) ощути́мый (ощути́м); **~ assets** реа́льный акти́в.
Tangier [tæn'dʒɪə^r] *n* Танже́р.
tangle ['tæŋgl] *n* пу́таница; **to get in(to) a ~** (*also fig*) запу́тываться (запу́таться *perf*).
tango ['tæŋgəu] *n* та́нго *nt ind*.
tank [tæŋk] *n* (*water tank*) бак; (*: large*) цисте́рна; (*PHOT*) ва́нна; (*for fish*) аква́риум; (*MIL*) танк.
tankard ['tæŋkəd] *n* (*for beer*) пивна́я кру́жка.
tanker ['tæŋkə^r] *n* (*ship*) та́нкер; (*truck, RAIL*) цисте́рна.
tanned [tænd] *adj* загоре́лый.
tannin ['tænɪn] *n* тани́н.
tanning ['tænɪŋ] *n* (*of leather*) дубле́ние.
Tannoy® ['tænɔɪ] (*BRIT*) *n* громкоговори́тель *m*; **over the ~** по громкоговори́телю.
tantalizing ['tæntəlaɪzɪŋ] *adj* (*smell, possibility*) дразня́щий*.
tantamount ['tæntəmaunt] *adj*: **~ to** равноси́льный* (равноси́лен) +*dat*.
tantrum ['tæntrəm] *n* исте́рика; **to throw a ~** устра́ивать (устро́ить *perf*) исте́рику.
Tanzania [tænzə'nɪə] *n* Танза́ния.
Tanzanian [tænzə'nɪən] *adj* танзани́йский* ◆ *n* танзани́ец(-и́йка).
tap [tæp] *n* кран; (*gentle blow*) стук ◆ *vt* (*hit gently*) стуча́ть (постуча́ть *perf*) по +*dat*; (*resources*) испо́льзовать *(impf/perf)*; (*telephone, conversation*) прослу́шивать *(impf)*; **to be on ~** (*fig*: *resources*) находи́ться* *(impf)* под руко́й; (*beer*) в разли́в.
tap-dancing ['tæpdɑ:nsɪŋ] *n* чечётка.
tape [teɪp] *n* (*also:* **magnetic ~**) плёнка; (*cassette*) кассе́та; (*sticky tape*) кле́йкая ле́нта; (*for tying*) ле́нта ◆ *vt* (*record*) запи́сывать (записа́ть* *perf*); (*stick with tape*) закле́ивать (закле́ить *perf*) кле́йкой ле́нтой; **on ~** (*song etc*) на кассе́те.
tape deck *n* кассе́тный магнитофо́н.
tape measure *n* сантиме́тр.
taper ['teɪpə^r] *n* (*candle*) то́нкая восковая свеча́ ◆ *vi* (*narrow*) сужа́ться (су́зиться* *perf*).
tape recorder *n* магнитофо́н.
tape recording *n* магнитофо́нная за́пись *f*.
tapered ['teɪpəd] *adj* (*skirt*) сужа́ющийся.
tapering ['teɪpərɪŋ] *adj* (*fingers*) то́нкий*.
tapestry ['tæpɪstrɪ] *n* (*object*) гобеле́н; (*art*) иску́сство гобеле́на.
tapeworm ['teɪpwə:m] *n* ленте́ц*, ле́нточный червь *m*.

* marks translations which have irregular inflections. The Russian-English side of the dictionary gives inflectional information.

tapioca [tæpɪ'əukə] *n* тапиóка.
tappet ['tæpɪt] *n* (*AUT*) толкáтель *m* клáпана.
tar [tɑ:] *n* дёготь *m*; **low/middle ~ cigarettes** сигарéты с нúзким/срéдним содержáнием никотúна.
tarantula [tə'ræntjulə] *n* тарáнтул.
tardy ['tɑ:dɪ] *adj* (*reply, development*) запоздáлый.
target ['tɑ:gɪt] *n* цель *f*; **to be on ~** (*project*) идтú* *(impf)* соглáсно плáну.
target audience *n* потенциáльные клиéнты *mpl*.
target market *n* целевóй рынок*.
target practice *n* учéбная стрельбá.
tariff ['tærɪf] *n* (*tax on goods*) тарúф; (*BRIT*: *in hotels, restaurants*) прейскурáнт.
tariff barrier *n* (*COMM*) тарúфный барьéр.
tarmac ['tɑ:mæk] *n* (*BRIT*: *on road*) асфáльт; (*AVIAT*) лётное пóле; (: *runway*) взлётная полосá ◆ *vt* (*BRIT*: *road, drive etc*) асфальтúровать (заасфальтúровать *perf*).
tarn [tɑ:n] *n* кáровое óзеро.
tarnish ['tɑ:nɪʃ] *vt* (*silver, brass etc*) дéлать (сдéлать *perf*) тýсклым; (*fig*: *reputation etc*) бросáть (брóсить* *perf*) тень на *+acc*.
tarot ['tærəu] *adj*: **~ cards** гадáльные кáрты *fpl*.
tarpaulin [tɑ:'pɔ:lɪn] *n* брезéнт.
tarragon ['tærəgən] *n* (*herb*) эстрагóн.
tart [tɑ:t] *n* (*CULIN*: *large*) пирóг; (: *small*) пирóжное *nt adj*; (*BRIT*: *inf*: *prostitute*) шлюха ◆ *adj* (*flavour*) гóрький*
▸ **tart up** (*BRIT*: *inf*) ◆ *vt* (*object etc*) принаряжáть (принарядúть* *perf*); **to ~ o.s. up** принаряжáться (принарядúться* *perf*); (*pej*) намáзываться (намáзаться* *perf*), выряжúваться (вы́рядиться* *perf*).
tartan ['tɑ:tn] *n* шотлáндка (*ткань*) ◆ *adj* (*rug, scarf etc*) клéтчатый.
tartar ['tɑ:tə^r] *n* (*on teeth*) (зубнóй) кáмень *m*; (*pej*: *person*) стéрва.
tartar(e) sauce ['tɑ:tə-] *n сóус с лýком и кáперсами*.
Tashkent [tæʃ'kɛnt] *n* Ташкéнт.
task [tɑ:sk] *n* задáча; **to take sb to ~** отчúтывать (отчитáть *perf*) когó-н.
task force *n* (*MIL, POLICE*) оперативная грýппа.
taskmaster ['tɑ:skmɑ:stə^r] *n*: **he's a hard ~** он настоящий* надсмóтрщик.
Tasmania [tæz'meɪnɪə] *n* Тасмáния.
tassel ['tæsl] *n* кúсточка; **~s** бахромá *fsg*.
taste [teɪst] *n* вкус; (*sample*) прóба; (*fig*: *glimpse, idea*) представлéние ◆ *vt* прóбовать (попрóбовать *perf*) ◆ *vi*: **the fish ~s of** *or* **like** ры́ба имéет вкус *+gen*; **what does the fish ~ like?** какóва ры́ба на вкус?; **you can ~ the garlic (in the dish)** (в блюде) чýвствуется чеснóк; **to have a ~ of sth** прóбовать (попрóбовать *perf*) чегó-н; **to have a ~ for sth** имéть *(impf)* вкус к чемý-н; **in good/bad ~** в хорóшем/дурнóм вкýсе.
taste bud *n* (*ANAT*) вкусовóй бугóр.
tasteful ['teɪstful] *adj* (*furnishings*) элегáнтный.
tastefully ['teɪstfəlɪ] *adv* (*decorated, furnished etc*) со вкýсом.
tasteless ['teɪstlɪs] *adj* безвкýсный* (безвкýсен).
tasty ['teɪstɪ] *adj* (*food*) вкýсный* (вкýсен).
tattered ['tætəd] *adj* (*clothes, paper etc*) изóрванный (в клóчья); (*fig*: *hopes etc*) разбúтый (разбúт).
tatters ['tætəz] *npl*: **in ~** (*clothes*) изóрванный (изóрван) в клóчья.
tattoo [tə'tu:] *n* (*on skin*) татуирóвка; (*spectacle*) воéнный смотр ◆ *vt* (*name, design*) татуúровать (вы́татуировать *perf*).
tatty ['tætɪ] *adj* (*BRIT*: *inf*) потрёпанный.
taught [tɔ:t] *pt, pp of* **teach**.
taunt [tɔ:nt] *n* издевáтельство ◆ *vt* (*person*) издевáться *(impf)* над *+instr*.
Taurus ['tɔ:rəs] *n* (*ASTROLOGY*) Телéц*; **he is ~** он – Телéц.
taut [tɔ:t] *adj* (*thread etc*) тугóй (туг); (*skin*) упрýгий* (упрýг).
tavern ['tævən] *n* (*old*) тавéрна.
tawdry ['tɔ:drɪ] *adj* (*jewellery etc*) безвкýсный* (безвкýсен).
tawny ['tɔ:nɪ] *adj* желтовáто-корúчневый.
tawny owl *n* неясыть *f*.
tax [tæks] *n* налóг ◆ *vt* (*earnings, goods etc*) облагáть (обложúть *perf*) налóгом; (*fig*: *memory, patience*) испы́тывать (испытáть *perf*); **before ~** до вы́чета налóгов; **after ~** за вы́четом налóгов; **free of ~** не облагáемый налóгом.
taxable ['tæksəbl] *adj* (*income*) облагáемый (облагáем) налóгом.
tax allowance *n* налóговая скúдка.
taxation [tæk'seɪʃən] *n* (*system*) налогообложéние; (*money paid*) размéр налóга.
tax avoidance *n* оптимизáция налóговой полúтики.
tax collector *n* сбóрщик налóгов.
tax disc *n* (*BRIT*: *AUT*) *свидéтельство об уплáте дорóжного налóга, котóрое прикрепляéтся к ветровóму стеклý*.
tax evasion *n* уклонéние от налóгов.
tax exemption *n* освобождéние от налóгов.
tax exile *n человéк с высóким дохóдом, котóрый живёт за границéй с цéлью минимизáции своúх налóгов*.
tax-free ['tæksfri:] *adj* (*goods, services*) необлагáемый налóгом.
tax haven *n* налóговое убéжище (*странá с нúзкими налóгами*).
taxi ['tæksɪ] *n* таксú *nt ind* ◆ *vi* (*AVIAT*: *plane*) вырýливать (вы́рулить *perf*).
taxidermist ['tæksɪdə:mɪst] *n* набúвщик чýчел.
taxi driver *n* водúтель *m* таксú, таксúст.
tax inspector *n* (*BRIT*) налóговый инспéктор.
taxi rank *n* (*BRIT*) стоянка таксú.
taxi stand *n* = **taxi rank**.

taxpayer ['tækspeɪəʳ] *n* налогоплате́льщик (-щица).
tax rebate *n* возвра́т нало́га.
tax relief *n* ски́дка с нало́га.
tax return *n* поступле́ния *ntpl* от нало́гов; (*form*) нало́говая деклара́ция.
tax shelter *n* нало́говая защи́та (*че́рез вложе́ния в це́нные бума́ги*).
tax year *n* нало́говый год*.
TB *n abbr* = **tuberculosis.**
Tbilisi [dbɪ'li:sɪ] *n* Тбили́си *m ind.*
TD *n abbr* (*US*) = **Treasury Department**; (: *FOOTBALL*) = **touchdown.**
tea [ti:] *n* (*drink*) чай; (*BRIT*: *meal*) у́жин; **afternoon ~** чай (с бутербро́дами и пиро́жными); **high ~** (*BRIT*) (по́здний*) обе́д.
tea bag *n* чай в паке́тике.
tea break *n* (*BRIT*) переры́в.
teacake ['ti:keɪk] *n* (*BRIT*) *сдо́бная бу́лка с изю́мом.*
teach [ti:tʃ] (*pt,pp* **taught**) *vi* (*be a teacher*) преподава́ть* *(impf)* ◆ *vt*: **to ~ sb sth, ~ sth to sb** учи́ть (научи́ть *perf*) кого́-н чему́-н; (*in school*) преподава́ть* *(impf)* что-н; **it taught him a lesson** (*fig*) э́то послужи́ло ему́ хоро́шим уро́ком.
teacher ['ti:tʃəʳ] *n* (*in secondary school*) учи́тель(ница) *m(f)*, преподава́тель(ница) *m(f)*; (*in primary school*) учи́тель(ница); **Russian ~** учи́тель(ница) *or* преподава́тель(ница) ру́сского.
teacher training college *n* (*for primary schools*) педагоги́ческое учи́лище; (*for secondary schools*) педагоги́ческий* институ́т.
teaching ['ti:tʃɪŋ] *n* (*work of teacher*) преподава́ние.
teaching aids *npl* уче́бные посо́бия *ntpl.*
teaching hospital *n* (*BRIT*: *MED*) ≈ клини́ческая больни́ца.
teaching staff *n* (*BRIT*) преподава́тельский соста́в.
tea cosy *n* ≈ "ба́ба" на ча́йник.
teacup ['ti:kʌp] *n* ча́йная ча́шка*.
teak [ti:k] *n* тик.
tea leaves *npl* зава́рка *fsg.*
team [ti:m] *n* (*of people*) кома́нда; (*of animals*) упря́жка
▸ **team up** *vi*: **to ~ up (with)** объединя́ть (объедини́ть *perf*) уси́лия (с *+instr*).
team games *npl* кома́ндные и́гры *fpl.*
team spirit *n* дух това́рищества, кома́ндный дух.
teamwork ['ti:mwə:k] *n* коллекти́вная рабо́та.
tea party *n* чаепи́тие, чай.
teapot ['ti:pɔt] *n* (зава́рочный) ча́йник.
tear¹ [tɛəʳ] (*pt* **tore**, *pp* **torn**) *n* (*hole*) дыра́*, ды́рка* ◆ *vt* (*rip*) рвать* (порва́ть* *perf*) ◆ *vi* (*become torn*) рва́ться* (порва́ться* *perf*); **to ~ to pieces** *or* **to bits** *or* **to shreds** (*also fig*) разрыва́ть (разорва́ть* *perf*) на ме́лкие клочки́
▸ **tear along** *vi* (*rush*) нести́сь* (понести́сь* *perf*)
▸ **tear apart** *vt* (*also fig*) разрыва́ть (разорва́ть* *perf*) на ча́сти
▸ **tear away** *vt*: **to ~ o.s. away (from sth)** (*fig*) отрыва́ться (оторва́ться* *perf*) (от чего́-н)
▸ **tear out** *vt* (*sheet of paper, cheque*) вырыва́ть (вы́рвать* *perf*)
▸ **tear up** *vt* разрыва́ть (разорва́ть* *perf*).
tear² [tɪəʳ] *n* слеза́; **in ~s** в слеза́х; **to burst into ~s** распла́каться *(perf)*, разрыда́ться *(perf)*.
tearaway ['tɛərəweɪ] *n* (*inf*: *person*) сорвиголова́ *m/f.*
teardrop ['tɪədrɔp] *n* слези́нка*.
tearful ['tɪəful] *adj* запла́канный* (запла́кан).
tear gas *n* слезоточи́вый газ.
tearing ['tɛərɪŋ] *adj*: **to be in a ~ hurry** быть* *(impf)* в безу́мной спе́шке.
tearoom ['ti:ru:m] *n* ча́йная *f adj.*
tease [ti:z] *vt* дразни́ть *(impf)*; (*unkindly*) дразни́ть (задразни́ть *perf*) ◆ *n* (*person*) насме́шник.
tea set *n* ча́йный серви́з.
teashop ['ti:ʃɔp] *n* (*BRIT*) = **tearoom.**
Teasmade® ['ti:zmeɪd] *n приспособле́ние для зава́ривания ча́я, приводи́мое в де́йствие буди́льником.*
teaspoon ['ti:spu:n] *n* ча́йная ло́жка.
tea strainer *n* ча́йное си́течко.
teat [ti:t] *n* (*of bottle*) со́ска.
teatime ['ti:taɪm] *n* у́жин.
tea towel *n* (*BRIT*) полоте́нце для посу́ды.
tea urn *n* тита́н с ча́ем.
tech [tɛk] *n abbr* (*inf*) = **technology**, **technical college**) ≈ ПТУ = *профессиона́льно-техни́ческое учи́лище.*
technical ['tɛknɪkl] *adj* (*terms, advances*) техни́ческий*.
technical college *n* (*BRIT*) техни́ческий* ко́лледж, те́хникум.
technicality [tɛknɪ'kælɪtɪ] *n* (*point of law*) техни́ческая то́нкость *f*; (*detail*) форма́льность *f*; **on a (legal) ~** из-за юриди́ческой форма́льности.
technically ['tɛknɪklɪ] *adv* (*strictly speaking*) техни́чески, форма́льно; (*regarding technique*) с техни́ческой то́чки зре́ния.
technician [tɛk'nɪʃən] *n* те́хник.
technique [tɛk'ni:k] *n* те́хника.
techno ['tɛknəu] *n* (*MUS*) *стиль поп му́зыки.*
technocrat ['tɛknəkræt] *n* технокра́т.
technological [tɛknə'lɔdʒɪkl] *adj* (*development,*

* marks translations which have irregular inflections. The Russian-English side of the dictionary gives inflectional information.

knowledge) техни́ческий*.
technologist [tɛk'nɔlədʒɪst] *n* те́хник; (*in particular field*) техно́лог.
technology [tɛk'nɔlədʒɪ] *n* те́хника; (*in particular field*) техноло́гия.
teddy (bear) ['tɛdɪ(-)] *n* (плю́шевый *or* игру́шечный) ми́шка.
tedious ['ti:dɪəs] *adj* (*work, discussions etc*) ну́дный* (ну́ден), ску́чный.
tedium ['ti:dɪəm] *n* ску́ка.
tee [ti:] *n* ме́тка для ша́ра (*в го́льфе*)
▸ **tee off** *vi* де́лать (сде́лать *perf*) пе́рвый уда́р.
teem [ti:m] *vi*: **the city is ~ing with** (*visitors, tourists etc*) го́род киши́т *+instr*; **it is ~ing (with rain)** льёт как из ведра́.
teenage ['ti:neɪdʒ] *adj* (*fashions etc*) подростко́вый; **~ children** подро́стки *mpl*.
teenager ['ti:neɪdʒə^r] *n* подро́сток*, тинэ́йджер.
teens [ti:nz] *npl*: **to be in one's ~** быть* (*impf*) в подростко́вом во́зрасте.
tee shirt *n* = **T-shirt**.
teeter ['ti:tə^r] *vi* (*also fig*) колеба́ться (*impf*).
teeth [ti:θ] *npl of* **tooth**.
teethe [ti:ð] *vi*: **she is teething** (*baby*) у неё ре́жутся зу́бы.
teething ring ['ti:ðɪŋ-] *n* кольцо́.
teething troubles *npl* (*fig*) боле́зни *fpl* ро́ста.
teetotal ['ti:'təutl] *adj* тре́звый, не пью́щий*.
teetotaller ['ti:'təutlə^r] (*US* **teetotaler**) *n* тре́звенник.
TEFL ['tɛfl] *n abbr* = *Teaching of English as a Foreign Language.*
Teflon® ['tɛflɔn] *n* Тефло́н.
Teheran [tɛə'rɑ:n] *n* Тегера́н.
tel. *abbr* (= **telephone**) тел.= *телефо́н.*
Tel Aviv ['tɛlə'vi:v] *n* Тель Ави́в.
telecast ['tɛlɪkɑ:st] *vt* передава́ть* (переда́ть* *perf*) по телеви́дению.
telecommunications ['tɛlɪkəmju:nɪ'keɪʃənz] *n* телекоммуника́ции *fpl*.
teleconferencing ['tɛlɪkɒnfərənsɪŋ] *n* организа́ция телеконфере́нций.
telegram ['tɛlɪgræm] *n* телегра́мма.
telegraph ['tɛlɪgrɑ:f] *n* (*system*) телегра́ф.
telegraphic [tɛlɪ'græfɪk] *adj* (*equipment*) телеграфи́ческий.
telegraph pole *n* телегра́фный столб.
telegraph wire *n* телегра́фные провода́ *mpl*.
telepathic [tɛlɪ'pæθɪk] *adj* телепати́ческий.
telepathy [tə'lɛpəθɪ] *n* телепа́тия.
telephone ['tɛlɪfəun] *n* телефо́н ◆ *vt* (*person*) звони́ть (позвони́ть *perf*) *+dat*; (*message*) сообща́ть (сообщи́ть *perf*) (по телефо́ну); **on the ~** (*talking*) по телефо́ну; **are you on the ~?** (*possessing phone*) у Вас есть телефо́н?
telephone booth (*BRIT* **telephone box**) *n* телефо́нная бу́дка.
telephone call *n* телефо́нный звоно́к*; **there is a ~ ~ for Peter** Пи́тера про́сят к телефо́ну.
telephone directory *n* телефо́нный спра́вочник.
telephone exchange *n* телефо́нная ста́нция.
telephone number *n* но́мер* телефо́на.
telephone operator *n* телефони́ст(ка).
telephone tapping *n* прослу́шивание телефо́на.
telephonist [tə'lɛfənɪst] *n* (*BRIT*) телефони́ст(ка).
telephoto ['tɛlɪ'fəutəu] *adj*: **~ lens** телефотообъекти́в.
teleprinter ['tɛlɪprɪntə^r] *n* телета́йп.
Teleprompter® ['tɛlɪprɔmptə^r] *n* (*US*) телесуфлёр, телете́кст.
telesales ['tɛlɪseɪlz] *n* (*COMM*) прода́жа по телефо́ну.
telescope ['tɛlɪskəup] *n* телеско́п ◆ *vi* (*fig*: *vehicles*) ста́лкиваться (столкну́ться *perf*) ◆ *vt* раскла́дывать (разложи́ть* *perf*).
telescopic [tɛlɪ'skɔpɪk] *adj* (*lens*) телескопи́ческий*; (*legs, aerial*) складно́й.
Teletext® ['tɛlɪtɛkst] *n* телете́кст, веща́тельная видеогра́фия.
telethon ['tɛlɪθɔn] *n* благотвори́тельный телемарафо́н.
televangelist [tɛlɪ'vændʒəlɪst] *n* телепропове́дник(-ица).
televise ['tɛlɪvaɪz] *vt* передава́ть* (переда́ть* *perf*) по телеви́дению.
television ['tɛlɪvɪʒən] *n* телеви́дение; (*set*) телеви́зор; **on ~** по телеви́дению.
television licence *n* (*BRIT*) телевизио́нная лице́нзия.
television programme *n* телевизио́нная програ́мма.
television set *n* телеви́зор.
telex ['tɛlɛks] *n* те́лекс ◆ *vt* свя́зываться (связа́ться* *perf*) по те́лексу с *+instr*; (*message*) передава́ть* (переда́ть* *perf*) по те́лексу ◆ *vi* посыла́ть (посла́ть* *perf*) те́лекс.
tell [tɛl] (*pt,pp* **told**) *vt* (*say*) говори́ть (сказа́ть* *perf*); (*relate*) расска́зывать (рассказа́ть* *perf*); (*distinguish*): **to ~ sth from** отлича́ть (отличи́ть *perf*) что-н от *+gen* ◆ *vi* (*talk*): **to ~ of** расска́зывать (рассказа́ть* *perf*) о *+prp*; (*have an effect*): **to ~ (on)** ска́зываться (сказа́ться* *perf*) (на *+prp*); **to ~ sb to do** говори́ть (сказа́ть* *perf*) кому́-н *+infin*; **to ~ sb about sth** расска́зывать (рассказа́ть* *perf*) кому́-н о чём-н; **he told me what happened** он рассказа́л мне, что случи́лось; **to ~ the time** (*know how to*) определя́ть (определи́ть *perf*), кото́рый час; **can you ~ me the time?** Вы не ска́жете, кото́рый час?; **(I) ~ you what** ... вот что: ...; **I can't ~ them apart** я не могу́ их различи́ть
▸ **tell off** *vt*: **to ~ sb off** отчи́тывать (отчита́ть *perf*) кого́-н
▸ **tell on** *vt fus* (*inform on*) жа́ловаться (нажа́ловаться *perf*) на *+acc*.
teller ['tɛlə^r] *n* (*in bank*) касси́р.
telling ['tɛlɪŋ] *adj* (*remark, detail*) показа́тельный* (показа́телен).
telltale ['tɛlteɪl] *adj* (*sign*) многозначи́тельный

◆ *n* (*pej: child*) я́беда *m/f*.
telly ['tɛlɪ] *n abbr* (*BRIT: inf*) (= **television**) те́лик.
temerity [tə'mɛrɪtɪ] *n* де́рзость *f*.
temp [tɛmp] *n abbr* (*BRIT: inf: = temporary office worker*) вре́менный секрета́рь *m* ◆ *vi* вре́менно рабо́тать *(impf)* секретарём.
temper ['tɛmpə^r] *n* (*nature*) нрав; (*mood*) настрое́ние; (*fit of anger*) гнев ◆ *vt* (*moderate*) смягча́ть (смягчи́ть *perf*); **to be in a ~** быть* *(impf)* в гне́ве; **to lose one's ~** выходи́ть* (вы́йти* *perf*) из себя́; **to keep one's ~** сде́рживаться (сдержа́ться* *perf*).
temperament ['tɛmprəmənt] *n* темпера́мент.
temperamental [tɛmprə'mɛntl] *adj* темпера́ментный* (темпера́ментен); (*fig*) капри́зный.
temperate ['tɛmprət] *adj* (*climate, zone, behaviour*) уме́ренный* (уме́рен); **~ country** страна́ с уме́ренным кли́матом.
temperature ['tɛmprətʃə^r] *n* температу́ра; **he has** *or* **is running a ~** у него́ температу́ра.
temperature chart *n* температу́рный гра́фик.
tempered ['tɛmpəd] *adj* (*steel*) отпу́щенный.
tempest ['tɛmpɪst] *n* бу́ря.
tempestuous [tɛm'pɛstjuəs] *adj* (*time, relationship*) бу́рный* (бу́рен); (*person*) бу́йный* (бу́ен).
tempi ['tɛmpi:] *npl of* **tempo**.
template ['tɛmplɪt] *n* шабло́н.
temple ['tɛmpl] *n* (*REL*) храм; (*ANAT*) висо́к*.
templet ['tɛmplɪt] *n* = **template**.
tempo ['tɛmpəu] (*pl* **~s** *or* **tempi**) *n* (*MUS, also fig*) темп.
temporal ['tɛmpərl] *adj* (*non-religious*) све́тский*; (*relating to time*) временно́й.
temporarily ['tɛmpərərɪlɪ] *adv* вре́менно.
temporary ['tɛmpərərɪ] *adj* вре́менный* (вре́менен).
temporize ['tɛmpəraɪz] *vi* ме́длить *(impf)*.
tempt [tɛmpt] *vt* соблазня́ть (соблазни́ть *perf*), искуша́ть (искуси́ть* *perf*); **to ~ sb into doing** соблазня́ть (соблазни́ть *perf*) *or* искуша́ть (искуси́ть* *perf*) кого́-н *+infin*; **I was ~ed to call you** у меня́ бы́ло искуше́ние позвони́ть Вам.
temptation [tɛmp'teɪʃən] *n* собла́зн, искуше́ние.
tempting ['tɛmptɪŋ] *adj* (*offer*) соблазни́тельный* (соблазни́телен).
ten [tɛn] *n* де́сять*; **~s of thousands** деся́тки ты́сяч; *see also* **five**.
tenable ['tɛnəbl] *adj* здра́вый (здрав); **the position of Chairman is ~ for three years** пост председа́теля закреплён за ним на три го́да.
tenacious [tə'neɪʃəs] *adj* насто́йчивый (насто́йчив).
tenacity [tə'næsɪtɪ] *n* насто́йчивость *f*.
tenancy ['tɛnənsɪ] *n* (*possession of room, land etc*) владе́ние на усло́виях аре́нды; (*period of possession*) срок аре́нды *or* на́йма.
tenant ['tɛnənt] *n* съёмщик(-мщица).
tend [tɛnd] *vt* (*crops, sick person*) уха́живать *(impf)* за *+instr* ◆ *vi*: **to ~ to do** име́ть *(impf)* скло́нность *+infin*; **he ~s to do everything in a hurry** он скло́нен к тому́, что́бы де́лать всё в спе́шке.
tendency ['tɛndənsɪ] *n* (*habit*) скло́нность *f*; (*trend*) тенде́нция.
tender ['tɛndə^r] *adj* не́жный* (не́жен); (*sore*) чувстви́тельный* (чувстви́телен) ◆ *n* (*COMM: offer*) предложе́ние ◆ *vt* (*offer*) подава́ть* (пода́ть* *perf*); (*apology*) приноси́ть* (принести́* *perf*); **to put in a ~ (for)** подава́ть* (пода́ть* *perf*) зая́вку (на *+acc*); **to put sth out to ~** (*BRIT*) объявля́ть (объяви́ть* *perf*) то́рги на что-н; **legal ~** (*money*) зако́нное платёжное сре́дство; **to ~ one's resignation** пода́ть* *(perf)* в отста́вку.
tenderize ['tɛndəraɪz] *vt* (*meat*) отбива́ть (отби́ть* *perf*).
tenderly ['tɛndəlɪ] *adv* не́жно.
tenderness ['tɛndənɪs] *n* не́жность *f*.
tendon ['tɛndən] *n* сухожи́лие.
tendril ['tɛndrɪl] *n* (*BOT*) у́сик; (*of hair*) прядь *f*.
tenement ['tɛnəmənt] *n* многокварти́рный дом* (*сдава́емый внаём*).
Tenerife [tɛnə'ri:f] *n* Тенери́фе *m ind*.
tenet ['tɛnət] *n* основополага́ющий при́нцип.
tenner ['tɛnə^r] *n* (*BRIT: inf: ten pounds*) ≈ деся́тка*.
tennis ['tɛnɪs] *n* те́ннис.
tennis ball *n* те́ннисный мяч*.
tennis club *n* те́ннисный клуб.
tennis court *n* те́ннисный корт.
tennis elbow *n* (*MED*) те́ннисный ло́коть *m*, лучеплечево́й бурси́т.
tennis match *n* те́ннисный матч.
tennis player *n* теннеси́ст(ка*).
tennis racket *n* те́ннисная раке́тка*.
tennis shoes *npl* те́ннисные ту́фли* *fpl*.
tenor ['tɛnə^r] *n* (*MUS*) те́нор*; (*of speech etc*) смысл.
tenpin bowling ['tɛnpɪn-] *n* (*BRIT*) ке́гли *pl*.
tense [tɛns] *adj* (*person, muscle, period*) напряжённый* (напряжён); (*smile*) натя́нутый (натя́нут) ◆ *n* (*LING*) вре́мя* *nt* ◆ *vt* напряга́ть (напря́чь* *perf*).
tenseness ['tɛnsnɪs] *n* напряжённость *f*.
tension ['tɛnʃən] *n* (*nervousness*) напряжённость *f*; (*between ropes etc*) натя́нутость *f*.
tent [tɛnt] *n* пала́тка*.
tentacle ['tɛntəkl] *n* щу́пальце*.
tentative ['tɛntətɪv] *adj* (*person, smile*)

* marks translations which have irregular inflections. The Russian-English side of the dictionary gives inflectional information.

осторо́жный* (осторо́жен); (*conclusion, plans*) предвари́тельный* (предвари́телен).
tentatively ['tɛntətɪvlɪ] *adv* (*suggest*) предвари́тельно; (*wave*) осторо́жно.
tenterhooks ['tɛntəhuks] *npl*: **on ~** как на иго́лках.
tenth [tɛnθ] *adj* деся́тый ◆ *n* (*fraction*) деся́тая часть *f*, одна́ деся́тая *f adj*; *see also* **fifth**.
tent peg *n* ко́лышек* для пала́тки.
tent pole *n* столб* для пала́тки.
tenuous ['tɛnjuəs] *adj* (*hold, links etc*) сла́бый* (слаб).
tenure ['tɛnjuə^r] *n* (*of land, buildings etc*) срок аре́нды; (*of office*) пребыва́ние в до́лжности; **to have ~** име́ть (*impf*) постоя́нную рабо́ту.
tepid ['tɛpɪd] *adj* (*tea, pool etc*) теплова́тый (теплова́т); (*reaction, applause*) прохла́дный* (прохла́ден).
Ter. *abbr* = **Terrace**.
term [tə:m] *n* (*word, expression*) те́рмин; (*period in power etc*) срок*; (*SCOL*: *in school*) че́тверть *f*; (: *at university*) триме́стр ◆ *vt* (*call*) называ́ть (назва́ть* *perf*); **~s** *npl* (*conditions*) усло́вия *ntpl*; **in abstract ~s** в абстра́ктных выраже́ниях; **~ of imprisonment** срок заключе́ния; **"easy ~s"** (*COMM*) "льго́тные усло́вия"; **in the short ~** в настоя́щее вре́мя; **in the long ~** в перспекти́ве; **to be on good ~s with sb** подде́рживать (*impf*) хоро́шие отноше́ния с кем-н; **to come to ~s with** примиря́ться (примири́ться *perf*) с +*instr*.
terminal ['tə:mɪnl] *adj* неизлечи́мый (неизлечи́м) ◆ *n* (*ELEC*) кле́мма, зажи́м; (*COMPUT, COMM*) термина́л; (*also: air ~*) аэровокза́л; (*BRIT*: *also:* **coach ~**) авто́бусная ста́нция.
terminate ['tə:mɪneɪt] *vt* прекраща́ть (прекрати́ть* *perf*) ◆ *vi*: **to ~ in** зака́нчиваться (зако́нчиться *perf*) +*instr*.
termination [tə:mɪ'neɪʃən] *n* прекраще́ние.
termini ['tə:mɪnaɪ] *npl of* **terminus**.
terminology [tə:mɪ'nɔlədʒɪ] *n* терминоло́гия.
term insurance *n* страхова́ние на определённый срок.
terminus ['tə:mɪnəs] (*pl* **termini**) *n* (*for buses*) коне́чная остано́вка*; (*for trains*) коне́чная ста́нция.
termite ['tə:maɪt] *n* терми́т.
term paper *n* (*US*: *at university*) ≈ курсова́я *f adj*.
Terr. *abbr* = **Terrace**.
terrace ['tɛrəs] *n* терра́са; (*BRIT*: *row of houses*) *ряд примыка́ющих друг к дру́гу одноти́пных домо́в*; (*in street names*): **Rose T~** Ро́уз Те́рес; **the ~s** *npl* (*BRIT*: *standing areas*) трибу́ны *fpl*.
terraced ['tɛrəst] *adj* (*garden*) терра́сный; **~ house** *дом в ряду́ примыка́ющих друг к дру́гу одноти́пных домо́в*.
terracotta ['tɛrə'kɔtə] *n* (*clay*) террако́та; (*colour*) террако́товый цвет ◆ *adj* террако́товый.
terrain [tɛ'reɪn] *n* ландша́фт.
terrible ['tɛrɪbl] *adj* ужа́сный* (ужа́сен).
terribly ['tɛrɪblɪ] *adv* ужа́сно.
terrier ['tɛrɪə^r] *n* терье́р.
terrific [tə'rɪfɪk] *adj* (*thunderstorm, speed etc*) колосса́льный* (колосса́лен); (*time, party etc*) потряса́ющий*.
terrify ['tɛrɪfaɪ] *vt* ужаса́ть (ужасну́ть *perf*); **to be terrified (of)** быть* (*impf*) в у́жасе (от +*gen*).
terrifying ['tɛrɪfaɪɪŋ] *adj* ужаса́ющий*.
territorial [tɛrɪ'tɔ:rɪəl] *adj* территориа́льный ◆ *n* (*BRIT*: *MIL*) военнослу́жащий* *m adj* территориа́льной а́рмии.
Territorial Army *n* (*BRIT*: *MIL*): **the ~ ~** территориа́льная а́рмия.
territorial waters *npl* территориа́льные во́ды *fpl*.
territory ['tɛrɪtərɪ] *n* террито́рия; (*fig*) о́бласть *f*.
terror ['tɛrə^r] *n* у́жас.
terrorism ['tɛrərɪzəm] *n* террори́зм.
terrorist ['tɛrərɪst] *n* террори́ст(ка*) ◆ *adj* террористи́ческий.
terrorize ['tɛrəraɪz] *vt* терроризи́ровать (*impf/perf*).
terse [tə:s] *adj* сжа́тый (сжат), кра́ткий* (кра́ток).
tertiary ['tə:ʃərɪ] *adj* (*system*) трети́чный; (*third in order, importance*) тре́тий*; **~ education** (*BRIT*) вы́сшее образова́ние.
Terylene® ['tɛrɪli:n] *n* терилéн.
TESL ['tɛsl] *n abbr* = *Teaching of English as a Second Language*.
TESSA ['tɛsə] *abbr* (*BRIT*: = *Tax Exempt Special Savings Account*) *безнало́говый сберега́тельный счёт*.
test [tɛst] *n* (*trial, check*) прове́рка, тест; (*of courage etc*) испыта́ние; (*MED*) ана́лиз; (*CHEM*) о́пыт; (*SCOL*) контро́льная рабо́та, тест; (*also:* **driving ~**) экза́мен на води́тельские права́ ◆ *vt* проверя́ть (прове́рить *perf*); (*courage*) испы́тывать (испыта́ть *perf*); (*MED*) анализи́ровать (*impf/perf*); **to put sth to the ~** подверга́ть (подве́ргнуть* *perf*) что-н прове́рке; **to ~ sth for sth** проверя́ть (прове́рить *perf*) что-н на что-н.
testament ['tɛstəmənt] *n* свиде́тельство; **the Old/New T~** Ве́тхий*/Но́вый заве́т.
test ban *n* (*also:* **nuclear ~ ~**) запреще́ние испыта́ний я́дерного ору́жия.
test card *n* (*TV*) телевизио́нная табли́ца.
test case *n* (*LAW, fig*) про́бное *or* прецеде́нтное де́ло.
testes ['tɛsti:z] *npl* (*ANAT*) я́ички *ntpl*.
test flight *n* испыта́тельный полёт.
testicle ['tɛstɪkl] *n* яи́чко*.
testify ['tɛstɪfaɪ] *vi* (*LAW*) дава́ть* (дать* *perf*) показа́ния; **to ~ to sth** свиде́тельствовать (*impf*) о чём-н.
testimonial [tɛstɪ'məunɪəl] *n* (*BRIT*: *reference*) рекоменда́ция.

testimony ['tɛstɪmənɪ] *n* (*LAW*: *statement*) показáние, свидéтельство; (*clear proof*): **to be (a) ~ to** являться (явиться* *perf*) свидéтельством *+gen*.
testing ['tɛstɪŋ] *adj* (*situation, period*) испытáтельный.
test match *n* (*CRICKET, RUGBY*) междунарóдный матч.
testosterone [tɛs'tɔstərəun] *n* тестостерóн.
test paper *n* (*SCOL*) экзаменациóнный билéт.
test pilot *n* лётчик-испытáтель *m*.
test tube *n* пробирка*.
test-tube baby ['tɛsttju:b-] *n* ребёнок из пробирки.
testy ['tɛstɪ] *adj* (*person, comment*) невы́держанный* (невы́держан).
tetanus ['tɛtənəs] *n* (*disease*) столбня́к*.
tetchy ['tɛtʃɪ] *adj* (*person, behaviour*) раздражи́тельный* (раздражи́телен).
tether ['tɛðə^r] *vt* (*animal*) привя́зывать (привязáть* *perf*) ◆ *n*: **at the end of one's ~** на грáни срыва.
Texas ['tɛksəs] *n* Техáс.
text [tɛkst] *n* текст.
textbook ['tɛkstbuk] *n* учéбник.
textiles ['tɛkstaɪlz] *npl* (*fabrics*) тексти́льные издéлия *ntpl*; (*TECH*) тексти́ль *msg*; (*textile industry*) тексти́льная промы́шленность *fsg*.
textual ['tɛkstjuəl] *adj*: **~ analysis** анáлиз тéкста.
texture ['tɛkstʃə^r] *n* (*of cloth, soil*) строéние; (*feel*: *of cloth, silk*) фактýра; (*of skin*) кáчество.
TGWU *n abbr* (*BRIT*) = *Transport and General Workers' Union*.
Thai [taɪ] *adj* тайлáндский ◆ *n* таилáндец* (-дка*).
Thailand ['taɪlænd] *n* Таилáнд.
thalidomide [θə'lɪdəmaɪd] *n* талидоми́д.
Thames [tɛmz] *n*: **the ~** Тéмза.
than [ðæn] *conj* (*in comparisons*): **you have more ~ ten** у Вас бóльше десяти́; **I have more/less work ~ you/Paul** у меня́ бóльше/мéньше рабóты, чем у Вас/у Пáвла; **she is older ~ you think** онá стáрше, чем Вы ду́маете; **more ~ once** не раз; **more ~ three times** бóлее *or* бóльше трёх раз.
thank [θæŋk] *vt* благодари́ть (поблагодари́ть *perf*); **~ you (very much)** (большóе) спаси́бо; **~ God!** слáва Бóгу!
thankful ['θæŋkful] *adj*: **~ (for)** благодáрный* (благодáрен) (за *+acc*); **~ that** (*relieved*) благодáрный за то, что.
thankfully ['θæŋkfəlɪ] *adv* к счáстью; **~ there were few victims** к счáстью, жертв бы́ло мáло.
thankless ['θæŋklɪs] *adj* неблагодáрный*.
thanks [θæŋks] *npl* благодáрность *fsg* ◆ *excl* спаси́бо; **many ~, ~ a lot** большóе спаси́бо; **~ to** благодаря́ *+dat*.
Thanksgiving (Day) ['θæŋksgɪvɪŋ(-)] *n* (*US*) День* *m* благодарéния.

KEYWORD

that [ðæt] (*pl* **those**) *adj* (*demonstrative*) тот*; **that man** тот мужчи́на; **which book would you like? – that one over there** каку́ю кни́гу Вы хоти́те? – вон ту, пожáлуйста; **I like this film better than that one** мне э́тот фильм нрáвится бóльше, чем тот
◆ *pron* **1** (*demonstrative*: *in questions*): **who's/what's that?** кто/что э́то?; **is that you?** э́то Вы?; **we talked of this and that** мы говори́ли о том о сём; **that's how ...** вот как ...; **that's what he said** так он сказáл; **what happened after that?** а что потóм произошлó?; **that is (to say)** тó есть
2 (*direct object*) котóрый (*f* котóрую, *nt* котóрое, *pl* котóрые); (*indirect object*) котóрому (*f* котóрой, *pl* котóрым); (*after prep*: *+acc*) котóрый (*f* котóрую, *nt* котóрое, *pl* котóрые); (: *+gen*) котóрого (*f* котóрой, *pl* котóрых); (: *+dat*) котóрому (*f* котóрой, *pl* котóрым); (: *+instr*) котóрым (*f* котóрой, *pl* котóрыми); (: *+prp*) котóром (*f* котóрой, *pl* котóрых); **the theory that we discussed last week** теóрия, котóрую мы обсуждáли на прóшлой недéле; **all (that) I have** всё, что у меня́ есть
3 (*of time*) когдá; **the day (that) he died** день, когдá он ýмер
◆ *conj* что; (*introducing purpose*) чтóбы; **he thought that I was ill** он ду́мал, что я был бóлен; **she suggested that I phone you** онá предложи́ла, чтóбы я Вам позвони́л
◆ *adv* (*demonstrative*): **I can't work that much** я не могу́ так мнóго рабóтать; **it can't be that bad** ну не так уж всё плóхо; **I have drunk that much** я вы́пил вот стóлько; **the wall's about that high and that thick** стенá примéрно вот такóй высоты́ и вот такóй толщины́.

thatched [θætʃt] *adj* солóменный.
Thatcherism ['θætʃərɪzəm] *n* тэтчери́зм.
Thatcherite ['θætʃəraɪt] *n* сторóнник(-ица) поли́тики Тэ́тчер.
thaw [θɔ:] *n* óттепель *f* ◆ *vi* (*ice*) тáять (растáять *perf*); (*food*) оттáивать (оттáять *perf*) ◆ *vt* (*food*: *also*: **~ out**) оттáивать (оттáять *perf*); **it's ~ing today** сегóдня тáет.

KEYWORD

the [ði:] *def art*: **1**: **the books/children are in the library** кни́ги/дéти в библиотéке; **the rich and the poor** богáтые *pl adj* и бéдные *pl adj*; **to attempt the impossible** пытáться

* marks translations which have irregular inflections. The Russian-English side of the dictionary gives inflectional information.

(попыта́ться *perf*) сде́лать невозмо́жное
2 (*in titles*): **Elizabeth the First** Елизаве́та Пе́рвая
3 (*in comparisons*): **the more I think about it the more I like it** чем бо́льше я ду́маю об э́том, тем бо́льше мне э́то нра́вится.

theatre ['θɪətə'] (*US* **theater**) *n* теа́тр; (*also:* **lecture ~**) лекцио́нный зал; (*MED: also:* **operating ~**) операцио́нная *f adj*.
theatregoer ['θɪətəgəuə'] *n* театра́л(ка*).
theatrical [θɪ'ætrɪkl] *adj* театра́льный; (*gestures*) театра́льный* (театра́лен); **~ company** театра́льная тру́ппа.
theft [θɛft] *n* кра́жа.
their [ðɛə'] *adj* их; (*referring to subject of sentence*) свой.
theirs [ðɛəz] *pron* (*see adj*) их; свой; *see also* **mine**[1].
them [ðɛm] *pron* (*direct*) их; (*indirect*) им; (*after prep: +gen, +prp*) их; (: *+dat*) им; (: *+instr*) и́ми; (*referring to subject of sentence*) свой; **a few of ~ are going to the cinema** не́которые из них иду́т в кино́; **give me a few of ~** да́йте мне их немно́го; *see also* **me**.
theme [θi:m] *n* те́ма.
theme park *n парк, стилизо́ванный под определённую эпо́ху и́ли те́му*.
theme song *n* пе́сня из кинофи́льма.
theme tune *n* мело́дия из кинофи́льма.
themselves [ðəm'sɛlvz] *pl pron* (*reflexive*) себя́; (*emphatic*) са́ми; (*after prep: +gen*) себя́; (: *+dat, +prp*) себе́; (: *+instr*) собо́й; (*alone*): **(all) by ~** одни́; **they shared the money between ~** они́ раздели́ли де́ньги ме́жду собо́й; *see also* **myself**.
then [ðɛn] *adv* пото́м; (*at that time*) тогда́ ◆ *conj* (*therefore*) тогда́ ◆ *adj*: **the ~ president** тогда́шний* президе́нт; **from ~ on** с тех пор; **by ~** (*past*) к э́тому *or* тому́ вре́мени; **we should know by ~** к тому́ вре́мени мы уже́ бу́дем знать; **if ... ~ ...** е́сли ... то ...; **before ~** до э́того *or* того́ вре́мени; **until ~** до тех пор; **and ~ what?** и что пото́м?; **what do you want me to do ~?** (*afterwards*) что Вы мне де́лать пото́м?; (*in that case*) что Вы мне де́лать тогда́?
theologian [θɪə'ləudʒən] *n* богосло́в, тео́лог.
theological [θɪə'lɔdʒɪkl] *adj* теологи́ческий*, богосло́вский.
theology [θɪ'ɔlədʒɪ] *n* теоло́гия, богосло́вие.
theorem ['θɪərəm] *n* теоре́ма.
theoretical [θɪə'rɛtɪkl] *adj* теорети́ческий*.
theorize ['θɪəraɪz] *vi* теоретизи́ровать *(impf)*.
theory ['θɪərɪ] *n* тео́рия; **in ~** теорети́чески, в тео́рии.
therapeutic(al) [θɛrə'pju:tɪk(l)] *adj* терапевти́ческий.
therapist ['θɛrəpɪst] *n* врач.
therapy ['θɛrəpɪ] *n* терапи́я.

KEYWORD

there [ðɛə'] *adv*: *1*: **there is some milk in the fridge** молоко́ в холоди́льнике; **there is someone in the room** в ко́мнате кто́-то есть; **there will be a lot of people at the concert** на конце́рте бу́дет мно́го наро́ду; **there was a book/there were flowers on the table** на столе́ лежа́ла кни́га/стоя́ли цветы́; **there has been an accident** произошла́ ава́рия
2 (*referring to place: position*) там; (: *motion*) туда́; **there he is!** вот он!:
3: **there, there** (*esp to child*) ну, ничего́, ничего́.

thereabouts ['ðɛərə'bauts] *adv* (*place*) побли́зости; (*amount*) о́коло э́того.
thereafter [ðɛər'ɑ:ftə'] *adv* с того́ вре́мени.
thereby ['ðɛəbaɪ] *adv* таки́м о́бразом.
therefore ['ðɛəfɔ:'] *adv* поэ́тому.
there's ['ðɛəz] = **there is, there has**.
thereupon [ðɛərə'pɔn] *adv* (*at that point*) вслед за тем; (*formal: on that subject*) в связи́ с э́тим.
thermal ['θə:ml] *adj* (*springs*) горя́чий*; (*energy*) терми́ческий*; (*underwear*) утеплённый*; (*paper, printer*) термографи́ческий.
thermodynamics ['θə:mədaɪ'næmɪks] *n* термодина́мика.
thermometer [θə'mɔmɪtə'] *n* термо́метр, гра́дусник.
thermonuclear ['θə:məu'nju:klɪə'] *adj* термоя́дерный.
Thermos® ['θə:məs] *n* (*also:* **~ flask**) те́рмос.
thermostat ['θə:məustæt] *n* термоста́т.
thesaurus [θɪ'sɔ:rəs] *n* теза́урус.
these [ði:z] *pl adj, pron* э́ти.
theses ['θi:si:z] *npl of* **thesis**.
thesis ['θi:sɪs] (*pl* **theses**) *n* (*SCOL*) диссерта́ция; (*theory*) те́зис.
they [ðeɪ] *pron* они́; **~ say that ...** говоря́т, что ....
they'd [ðeɪd] = **they had, they would**.
they'll [ðeɪl] = **they shall, they will**.
they're [ðɛə'] = **they are**.
they've [ðeɪv] = **they have**.
thick [θɪk] *adj* (*in shape*) то́лстый (толст); (*in consistency*) густо́й (густ); (*inf: stupid*) тупо́й (туп) ◆ *n*: **in the ~ of the battle** в са́мой гу́ще би́твы; **the wall is 20 cm ~** толщина́ стены́ – 20 см.
thicken ['θɪkn] *vi* (*fog etc*) сгуща́ться (сгусти́ться* *perf*); (*plot*) усложня́ться (усложни́ться *perf*) ◆ *vt* (*sauce etc*) де́лать (сде́лать *perf*) гу́ще.
thicket ['θɪkɪt] *n* за́росли *fpl*.
thickly ['θɪklɪ] *adv* (*spread*) гу́сто; (*cut*) то́лсто; **~ populated** густонаселённый.
thickness ['θɪknɪs] *n* (*size*) толщина́; (*layer*) слой*.
thickset [θɪk'sɛt] *adj* корена́стый (корена́ст).
thick-skinned [θɪk'skɪnd] *adj* (*fig*) толсто-

ко́жий*.
thief [θi:f] (*pl* **thieves**) *n* вор(о́вка).
thieves [θi:vz] *npl of* **thief**.
thieving ['θi:vɪŋ] *n* воровство́.
thigh [θaɪ] *n* бедро́*.
thighbone ['θaɪbəun] *n* (*ANAT*) бе́дренная кость* *f*.
thimble ['θɪmbl] *n* напёрсток*.
thin [θɪn] *adj* то́нкий* (то́нок); (*person, animal*) худо́й (худ); (*soup, sauce*) жи́дкий* (жи́док); (*hair, crowd*) ре́дкий*; (*fog*) лёгкий* (лёгок) ◆ *vt*: **to ~ (down)** (*sauce, paint*) разбавля́ть (разба́вить* *perf*); (*hair*: *at hairdresser's*) разре́живать (*impf*) ◆ *vi* (*fog*) рассе́иваться (рассе́яться *perf*); (*also*: **~ out**: *crowd*) реде́ть (пореде́ть *perf*); **his hair is ~ning** у него́ реде́ют во́лосы.
thing [θɪŋ] *n* вещь* *f*; **~s** *npl* (*belongings*) ве́щи* *fpl*; **first ~ (in the morning)** пе́рвым де́лом (с утра́); **last ~ (at night), he ...** напосле́док (но́чью) он ...; **the ~ is ...** де́ло в том, что ...; **for one ~** во-пе́рвых; **she's got a ~ about mice** она́ не выно́сит мыше́й; **don't worry about a ~** ни о чём не беспоко́йтесь; **you'll do no such ~!** попро́буй то́лько!; **poor ~** бедня́жка* *m/f*; **the best ~ would be to ...** са́мое лу́чшее бы́ло бы +*infin* ...; **how are ~s?** как дела́?
think [θɪŋk] (*pt,pp* **thought**) *vt* (*reflect, believe*) ду́мать (*impf*); (*imagine*) предполага́ть (предположи́ть* *perf*); **to ~ of** ду́мать (поду́мать *perf*) о +*prp*; (*remember*) вспомина́ть (вспо́мнить *perf*); (*consider*) приводи́ть* (привести́* *perf*); **what did you ~ of them?** что Вы о них ду́маете?; **to ~ about sth/sb** ду́мать (поду́мать *perf*) о чём-н/ком-н; **I'll ~ about it** я поду́маю (об э́том); **I am ~ing of starting a business** я ду́маю нача́ть би́знес; **I ~ so/not** я ду́маю, что да/нет; **to ~ well of sb** хорошо́ о ком-н ду́мать (*impf*); **to ~ aloud** ду́мать (*impf*) вслух; **~ again!** поду́майте ещё раз!
▸ **think out** *vt* (*plan, solution*) обду́мывать (обду́мать *perf*), проду́мывать (проду́мать *perf*)
▸ **think over** *vt* обду́мывать (обду́мать *perf*); **I'd like to ~ things over** я хочу́ всё обду́мать
▸ **think through** *vt* проду́мывать (проду́мать *perf*) до конца́
▸ **think up** *vt* приду́мывать (приду́мать *perf*).
thinking ['θɪŋkɪŋ] *n* мышле́ние; **to my way of ~** на мой взгляд.
think-tank ['θɪŋktæŋk] *n* мозгово́й центр.
thinly ['θɪnlɪ] *adv* то́нко.
thinness ['θɪnnɪs] *n* то́нкость *f*.
third [θə:d] *adj* тре́тий* ◆ *n* (*fraction*) треть *f*, одна́ тре́тья *f adj*; (*AUT*: *also*: **~ gear**) тре́тья ско́рость *f*; (*BRIT*: *SCOL*: *degree*) *дипло́м тре́тьей и́ли ни́зшей сте́пени*; **a ~ of** треть +*gen*, тре́тья часть +*gen*; *see also* **fifth**.
third-degree burns ['θə:ddɪgri:-] *npl* (*MED*) ожо́ги *mpl* тре́тьей сте́пени.
thirdly ['θə:dlɪ] *adv* в-тре́тьих.
third party insurance *n* (*BRIT*) страхова́ние в по́льзу тре́тьей стороны́.
third-rate ['θə:d'reɪt] *adj* (*pej*: *performance, actor etc*) третьесо́ртный* (третьесо́ртен).
Third World *n*: **the ~ ~** Тре́тий* мир.
thirst [θə:st] *n* (*also fig*) жа́жда.
thirsty ['θə:stɪ] *adj*: **to be ~** (*person, animal*) хоте́ть* (*impf*) пить; **I am ~** я хочу́ *or* мне хо́чется пить; **gardening is ~ work** рабо́та в саду́ вызыва́ет жа́жду.
thirteen [θə:'ti:n] *n* трина́дцать*; *see also* **five**.
thirteenth [θə:'ti:nθ] *adj* трина́дцатый; *see also* **fifth**.
thirtieth ['θə:tɪɪθ] *adj* тридца́тый; *see also* **fifth**.
thirty ['θə:tɪ] *n* три́дцать*; *see also* **fifty**.

KEYWORD

this [ðɪs] (*pl* **these**) *adj* (*demonstrative*) э́тот; **this man** э́тот мужчи́на; **which book would you like? – this one please** каку́ю кни́гу Вы хоти́те? – вот э́ту, пожа́луйста
◆ *pron* (*demonstrative*) э́тот (*f* э́та, *nt* э́то); **who/what is this?** кто/что э́то?; **this is where I live** вот здесь я живу́; **this is what he said** вот, что он сказа́л; **this is Mr Brown** э́то ми́стер Бра́ун
◆ *adv* (*demonstrative*): **this high/long** *etc* тако́й высоты́/длины́ *etc*; **the dog was about this big** соба́ка была́ приме́рно тако́го разме́ра *or* тако́й величины́; **we can't stop now we've gone this far** мы не мо́жет тепе́рь останови́ться, ведь мы так далеко́ ушли́.

thistle ['θɪsl] *n* чертополо́х.
thong [θɔŋ] *n* реме́нь* *m*.
thorn [θɔ:n] *n* шип, колю́чка*.
thorny ['θɔ:nɪ] *adj* (*plant, tree*) колю́чий* (колю́ч); (*problem*) нелёгкий*.
thorough ['θʌrə] *adj* (*search, wash*) тща́тельный* (тща́телен); (*knowledge, research*) основа́тельный* (основа́телен); (*person*) скрупулёзный* (скрупулёзен).
thoroughbred ['θʌrəbrɛd] *n* чистокро́вная *or* чистопоро́дная ло́шадь *f*.
thoroughfare ['θʌrəfɛə'] *n* гла́вная арте́рия (го́рода), тра́нспортная магистра́ль *f*; **"no ~"** (*BRIT*) "Прое́зда нет".
thoroughgoing ['θʌrəgəuɪŋ] *adj* доскона́льный* (доскона́лен), тща́тельный* (тща́телен).
thoroughly ['θʌrəlɪ] *adv* (*fully*) тща́тельно; (*very*) вполне́; **he ~ agreed** он по́лностью согласи́лся.
thoroughness ['θʌrənɪs] *n* тща́тельность *f*.

* marks translations which have irregular inflections. The Russian-English side of the dictionary gives inflectional information.

those [ðəuz] *pl adj, pron* те.
though [ðəu] *conj* хотя́ ◆ *adv* впро́чем, одна́ко; **even ~** ... хотя́ и ...; **it's not easy, ~** впро́чем *or* одна́ко э́то не про́сто.
thought [θɔ:t] *pt, pp of* **think** ◆ *n* (*idea, intention*) мысль *f*; (*reflection*) размышле́ние; (*opinion*) соображе́ние; **after much ~** по́сле до́лгих размышле́ний; **I've just had a ~** мне то́лько что пришла́ в го́лову мысль; **to give sth some ~** обду́мывать (обду́мать *perf*) что-н.
thoughtful ['θɔ:tful] *adj* (*deep in thought*) заду́мчивый (заду́мчив); (*serious*) глубо́кий*; (*considerate*) внима́тельный* (внима́телен).
thoughtfully ['θɔ:tfəlɪ] *adv* (*pensively*) заду́мчиво; (*considerately*) внима́тельно.
thoughtless ['θɔ:tlɪs] *adj* безду́мный* (безду́мен), неосмотри́тельный* (неосмотри́телен).
thoughtlessly ['θɔ:tlɪslɪ] *adv* безду́мно, неосмотри́тельно.
thoughtlessness ['θɔ:tlɪsnɪs] *n* безду́мность *f*, неосмотри́тельность *f*.
thought-out [θɔ:t'aut] *adj* проду́манный* (проду́ман).
thought-provoking ['θɔ:tprəvəukɪŋ] *adj* провоци́рующий на мы́сли.
thousand ['θauzənd] *n* ты́сяча*; **two ~** две ты́сячи; **five ~** пять ты́сяч; **about a ~** о́коло ты́сячи; **people came in their ~s** *or* **by the ~** пришли́ ты́сячи люде́й; **~s of** ты́сячи *+gen*.
thousandth ['θauzəntθ] *adj* ты́сячный.
thrash [θræʃ] *vt* (*beat*) поро́ть* (вы́пороть* *perf*); (*inf*: *defeat*) побива́ть (поби́ть* *perf*)
▸ **thrash about** *vi* мета́ться* (*impf*)
▸ **thrash around** *vi* = **thrash about**
▸ **thrash out** *vt* (*problem*) прораба́тывать (прорабо́тать *perf*).
thrashing ['θræʃɪŋ] *n*: **to give sb a ~** поро́ть* (вы́пороть* *perf*) кого́-н.
thread [θrɛd] *n* (*yarn*) нить *f*, ни́тка*; (*of screw*) резьба́ ◆ *vt* (*needle*) продева́ть (проде́ть* *perf*) ни́тку в *+acc*; **to ~ one's way between** пробира́ться (пробра́ться* *perf*) че́рез *or* сквозь *+acc*.
threadbare ['θrɛdbɛəʳ] *adj* потёртый (потёрт), потрёпанный* (потрёпан).
threat [θrɛt] *n* (*also fig*) угро́за; **to be under ~ of** быть* (*impf*) под угро́зой *+gen*.
threaten ['θrɛtn] *vi* (*storm, danger*) грози́ть* (*impf*) ◆ *vt*: **to ~ sb with** угрожа́ть (*impf*) *or* грози́ть* (*impf*) кому́-н *+instr*; **to ~ to do** угрожа́ть (*impf*) *or* грози́ть* (*impf*) *+infin*.
threatening ['θrɛtnɪŋ] *adj* угрожа́ющий*.
three [θri:] *n* три*; (*collective*) тро́е*; *see also* **five**.
three-dimensional [θri:dɪ'mɛnʃənl] *adj* (*object*) трёхме́рный; (*film, picture, image*) стереоскопи́ческий.
threefold ['θri:fəuld] *adv*: **to increase ~** увели́чиваться (увели́читься *perf*) в три ра́за.
three-piece suit ['θri:pi:s-] *n* (костю́м)-тро́йка *m*.
three-piece suite *n* мя́гкая ме́бель *f*.
three-ply [θri:'plaɪ] *adj* трёхсло́йный.
three quarters *npl* три* че́тверти; **~ ~ full** по́лный* на три че́тверти.
three-wheeler (car) [θri:'wi:ləʳ(-)] *n* трехколёсная маши́на.
thresh [θrɛʃ] *vt* молоти́ть* (*impf*).
threshing machine ['θrɛʃɪŋ-] *n* (*old*) молоти́лка*.
threshold ['θrɛʃhəuld] *n* (*also fig*) поро́г; **to be on the ~ of** (*fig*) быть* (*impf*) на поро́ге *+gen*.
threshold agreement *n* (*ECON*) *спо́соб приведе́ния в соотве́тствие за́работной пла́ты рабо́тников со сто́имостью жи́зни.*
threw [θru:] *pt of* **throw**.
thrift [θrɪft] *n* бережли́вость *f*.
thrifty ['θrɪftɪ] *adj* бережли́вый (бережли́в).
thrill [θrɪl] *n* тре́пет ◆ *vi* трепета́ть* (*impf*) ◆ *vt* (*person, audience*) восхища́ть (восхити́ть* *perf*); **to be ~ed** быть* (*impf*) в восто́рге; **I am ~ed** я в восто́рге.
thriller ['θrɪləʳ] *n* остросюже́тный фильм, три́ллер.
thrilling ['θrɪlɪŋ] *adj* захва́тывающий*.
thrive [θraɪv] (*pt* **thrived** *or* **throve**, *pp* **thrived**) *vi* (*child, animal, business*) процвета́ть (*impf*); (*plant*) разраста́ться (разрасти́сь* *perf*); **to ~ on sth** процвета́ть (*impf*) на чём-н.
thriving ['θraɪvɪŋ] *adj* процвета́ющий.
throat [θrəut] *n* го́рло; **I have a sore ~** у меня́ боли́т го́рло.
throb [θrɔb] *n* (*of heart*) бие́ние; (*of wound*) пульса́ция; (*of engine*) вибра́ция ◆ *vi* (*heart*) би́ться* (*impf*); (*with pain*: *arm*) ныть* (*impf*); (*machine*: *vibrate*) вибри́ровать* (*impf*); **my head is ~bing** у меня́ гуди́т голова́.
throes [θrəuz] *npl*: **in the ~ of** (*war, moving house etc*) в лихора́дке *+gen*; **death ~** смерте́льные му́ки.
thrombosis [θrɔm'bəusɪs] *n* тромбо́з.
throne [θrəun] *n* трон.
throng ['θrɔŋ] *n* толпа́* ◆ *vt* заполня́ть (запо́лнить *perf*).
throttle ['θrɔtl] *n* (*AUT*) дро́ссель *m* ◆ *vt* (*strangle*) души́ть* (задуши́ть* *perf*).
through [θru:] *prep* (*space*) че́рез *+acc*; (*water etc*) в *+acc*; (*time*) в тече́ние *+gen*; (*by means of*) че́рез *+acc*, посре́дством *+gen*; (*owing to*) из-за *+gen* ◆ *adj* (*ticket, train*) прямо́й ◆ *adv* насквозь; **he is absent ~ illness** он отсу́тствовал по боле́зни; **(from) Monday ~ Friday** (*US*) с понеде́льника по пя́тницу; **to put sb ~ to sb** (*TEL*) соединя́ть (соедини́ть *perf*) кого́-н с кем-н; **to be ~** (*TEL*) дозвони́ться (*perf*); **to be ~ with sb/sth** пока́нчивать (поко́нчить *perf*) с кем-н/чем-н; **"no ~ road"** (*BRIT*) "нет сквозно́го прое́зда"; **"no ~ traffic"** (*US*) "нет сквозно́го

движе́ния"; **to let sb ~** пропуска́ть (пропусти́ть* *perf*) кого́-н.
throughout [θru:'aut] *prep* (*place*) по *+dat*; (*time*) в тече́ние *+gen* ◆ *adv* везде́, повсю́ду.
throughput ['θru:put] *n* пропускна́я спосо́бность *f*; (*COMPUT*) производи́тельность *f*.
throve [θrəuv] *pt of* **thrive**.
throw [θrəu] (*pt* **threw**, *pp* **thrown**) *n* бросо́к* ◆ *vt* (*object*) броса́ть (бро́сить* *perf*); (*rider*) сбра́сывать (сбро́сить* *perf*); (*fig*: *person*) сбива́ть (сбить* *perf*) с то́лку; (*pottery*) обраба́тывать (обрабо́тать *perf*) на гонча́рном кру́ге; **to ~ a party** устра́ивать (устро́ить *perf*) ве́чер; **to ~ open** (*doors, windows*) распа́хивать (распахну́ть *perf*); (*competition, race etc*) открыва́ть (откры́ть* *perf*)
▸ **throw about** *vt* (*litter etc*) разбра́сывать (разброса́ть *perf*)
▸ **throw around** *vt* = **throw about**
▸ **throw away** *vt* (*rubbish*) выбра́сывать (вы́бросить* *perf*); (*money*) броса́ть (*impf*) на ве́тер
▸ **throw off** *vt* сбра́сывать (сбро́сить* *perf*)
▸ **throw out** *vt* (*rubbish, person*) выбра́сывать (вы́бросить* *perf*); (*idea*) отверга́ть (отве́ргнуть* *perf*)
▸ **throw together** *vt* (*clothes, meal etc*) сооружа́ть (соорудить* *perf*); (*essay*) набра́сывать (наброса́ть *perf*)
▸ **throw up** *vi* (*vomit*) рвать* (вы́рвать* *perf*); **he threw up** его́ вы́рвало.
throwaway ['θrəuəweɪ] *adj* (*toothbrush etc*) одноразо́вый; (*line, remark*) ска́занный невзнача́й.
throwback ['θrəubæk] *n*: **it's a ~ to** э́то возвра́т к *+dat*.
throw-in ['θrəuɪn] *n* (*FOOTBALL*) вбра́сывание.
thrown [θrəun] *pp of* **throw**.
thru [θru:] (*US*) = **through**.
thrush [θrʌʃ] *n* (*ZOOL*) дрозд*; (*MED*) моло́чница.
thrust [θrʌst] (*pt, pp* **thrust**) *n* (*TECH*) дви́жущая си́ла; (*push*) толчо́к*; (*main idea*) направле́ние ◆ *vt* толка́ть (толкну́ть *perf*).
thud [θʌd] *n* глухо́й стук.
thug [θʌg] *n* (*criminal*) головоре́з; (*pej*) банди́т.
thumb [θʌm] *n* (*ANAT*) большо́й па́лец* (*руки́*) ◆ *vt*: **to ~ a lift** (*inf*) голосова́ть* (*impf*); **to give sb/sth the ~s up** (*approve*) одобря́ть (одо́брить *perf*) кого́-н/что-н; **to give sth the ~s down** отверга́ть (отве́ргнуть *perf*) что-н
▸ **thumb through** *vt fus* перели́стывать (перелиста́ть *perf*).
thumb index *n* бу́квенный указа́тель *m* (*на обре́зе кни́ги*).
thumbnail ['θʌmneɪl] *n* но́готь* *m* (*большо́го па́льца руки́*).
thumbnail sketch *n* набро́сок*.
thumbtack ['θʌmtæk] *n* (*US*) кно́пка*.
thump [θʌmp] *n* (*blow*) уда́р; (*sound*) глухо́й стук ◆ *vt* (*person*) сту́кнуть (*perf*) ◆ *vi* (*heart etc*) стуча́ть (*impf*).
thumping ['θʌmpɪŋ] *adj* (*inf*: *majority, victory etc*) грома́дный; (: *headache, cold*) жу́ткий*.
thunder ['θʌndə^r] *n* гром ◆ *vi* (*shout*) реве́ть (*impf*); (*train etc*): **to ~ past** громыха́ть (прогромыха́ть *perf*) ми́мо; **it's ~ing** греми́т гром.
thunderbolt ['θʌndəbəult] *n* уда́р мо́лнии.
thunderclap ['θʌndəklæp] *n* раска́т гро́ма.
thunderous ['θʌndrəs] *adj* (*applause*) оглуши́тельный; (*crash*) громово́й.
thunderstorm ['θʌndəstɔ:m] *n* гроза́*.
thunderstruck ['θʌndəstrʌk] *adj* (*fig*): **I was ~** я был потрясён.
thundery ['θʌndərɪ] *adj* грозово́й.
Thur(s). *abbr* = **Thursday**.
Thursday ['θə:zdɪ] *n* четве́рг*; *see also* **Tuesday**.
thus [ðʌs] *adv* таки́м о́бразом.
thwart [θwɔ:t] *vt* (*person*) чини́ть (*impf*) препя́тствия *+dat*; (*plans*) расстра́ивать (расстро́ить *perf*).
thyme [taɪm] *n* тимья́н.
thyroid ['θaɪrɔɪd] *n* (*also:* **~ gland**) щитови́дная железа́.
tiara [tɪ'ɑ:rə] *n* тиа́ра.
Tiber ['taɪbə^r] *n*: **the ~** Тибр.
Tibet [tɪ'bɛt] *n* Тибе́т.
Tibetan [tɪ'bɛtən] *adj* тибе́тский* ◆ *n* тибе́тец*(-е́тка*); (*LING*) тибе́тский* язы́к*.
tibia ['tɪbɪə] *n* большеберцо́вая кость* *f*.
tic [tɪk] *n* тик.
tick [tɪk] *n* (*sound*: *of clock*) ти́канье; (*mark*) га́лочка*; (*ZOOL*) клещ* ◆ *vi* (*clock*) ти́кать (*impf*) ◆ *vt* отмеча́ть (отме́тить* *perf*) га́лочкой; **to put a ~ against sth** ста́вить* (поста́вить* *perf*) га́лочку ря́дом с чем-н; **in a ~** (*BRIT*: *inf*) мину́точку; **to buy sth on ~** (*BRIT*: *inf*) покупа́ть (купи́ть* *perf*) что-н в креди́т
▸ **tick off** *vt* (*item on list*) отмеча́ть (отме́тить* *perf*) га́лочкой; (*person*) отчи́тывать (отчита́ть *perf*)
▸ **tick over** *vi* (*engine*) рабо́тать (*impf*) на холосто́м ходу́; (*fig*: *business*) идти́* (*impf*) свои́м чередо́м.
ticker tape ['tɪkəteɪp] *n* ти́керная ле́нта, ти́кер; (*US*: *in celebrations*) *серпанти́н из ти́керной ле́нты*.
ticket ['tɪkɪt] *n* биле́т; (*price tag*) этике́тка*; (*from cash register*) чек; (*also:* **parking ~**) штраф за наруше́ние пра́вил паркова́ния; (*US*: *POL*) спи́сок* кандида́тов па́ртии.
ticket agency *n* (*THEAT*) театра́льная ка́сса.

* marks translations which have irregular inflections. The Russian-English side of the dictionary gives inflectional information.

ticket collector *n* контролёр.
ticket holder *n* владéлец(-лица) билéта.
ticket inspector *n* контролёр.
ticket office *n* билéтная кáсса.
tickle ['tɪkl] *vt* щекотáть* (пощекотáть* *perf*) ◆ *vi* щекотáть* *(impf)*.
ticklish ['tɪklɪʃ] *adj* (*problem*) щекотли́вый (щекотли́в); (*blanket*) колю́чий* (колю́ч); (*cough*) першáщий; (*person*): **to be ~** боя́ться* *(impf)* щекóтки.
tidal ['taɪdl] *adj* (*force*) прили́вный; (*estuary*) прили́вно-отли́вный.
tidal wave *n* прили́вная волнá*.
tidbit ['tɪdbɪt] *n* (*US*) = **titbit**.
tiddlywinks ['tɪdlɪwɪŋks] *n* блóшки *pl*.
tide [taɪd] *n* прили́в и отли́в; (*fig*: *of events*) волнá; (*of fashion, opinion*) направлéние; **high ~** пóлная водá*, вы́сшая тóчка прили́ва; **low ~** мáлая водá*, ни́зшая тóчка отли́ва
▸ **tide over** *vt* (*help out*): **this money will ~ me over till Monday** на э́ти дéньги я смогу́ продержáться до понедéльника.
tidily ['taɪdɪlɪ] *adv* (*dress*) опря́тно; (*arrange*) аккурáтно.
tidiness ['taɪdɪnɪs] *n* опря́тность *f*; (*of person*) аккурáтность *f*.
tidy ['taɪdɪ] *adj* опря́тный* (опря́тен); (*person, mind*) аккурáтный* (аккурáтен) ◆ *vt* (*also:* **~ up**) прибирáть (прибрáть* *perf*); **to ~ o.s. up** приводи́ть* (привести́* *perf*) себя́ в поря́док.
tie [taɪ] *n* (*string etc*) шнурóк*; (*BRIT*: *also:* **necktie**) гáлстук; (*fig*: *link*) связь *f*; (*SPORT*: *game, match*) игрá вничью́; (: *draw*) ничья́; (*US*: *RAIL*) шпáла ◆ *vt* завя́зывать (завязáть* *perf*) ◆ *vi* (*SPORT etc*) игрáть (сыгрáть *perf*) вничью́; **"black/white ~"** *парáдный костю́м*; **family ~s** семéйные у́зы; **to ~ sth in a bow** завя́зывать (завязáть* *perf*) что-н бáнтом; **to ~ a knot in sth** завя́зывать (завязáть* *perf*) что-н узлóм
▸ **tie down** *vt* (*fig*: *person*) свя́зывать (связáть* *perf*)
▸ **tie in** *vi*: **to ~ in with** (*correspond*) увя́зываться *(impf)* с *+instr*
▸ **tie on** *vt* (*BRIT*: *label etc*) привя́зывать (привязáть* *perf*)
▸ **tie up** *vt* (*dog, boat*) привя́зывать (привязáть* *perf*); (*prisoner, parcel*) свя́зывать (связáть* *perf*); (*arrangements*) организовáть *(impf/perf)*; **I'm ~d up at the moment** (*busy*) я сейчáс óчень зáнят.
tie-break ['taɪbreɪk] *n* (*TENNIS*) *решáющий гейм пóсле ничéйного сéта*; (*in quiz*) дополни́тельный решáющий* вопрóс.
tiebreaker ['taɪbreɪkəʳ] *n* = **tie-break**.
tie-on ['taɪɔn] *adj* (*BRIT*: *label*) привязнóй.
tiepin ['taɪpɪn] *n* (*BRIT*) булáвка* для гáлстука.
tier [tɪəʳ] *n* (*of stadium etc*) я́рус; (*of cake*) слой*.
Tierra del Fuego [tɪ'ɛrədɛl'fweɪgəu] *n* Óгненная Земля́*.
tie tack *n* (*US*) = **tiepin**.
tiff [tɪf] *n* размóлвка*.
tiger ['taɪgəʳ] *n* тигр.
tight [taɪt] *adj* (*firm*: *rope*) тугóй; (*narrow*: *shoes, bend, clothes*) у́зкий* (у́зок); (*strict*: *security*) стрóгий*; (*schedule, budget*) жёсткий* ◆ *adv* (*hold, squeeze*) крéпко; (*shut*) плóтно; **money is ~** у меня́ ту́го с деньгáми; **he is ~** (*inf*: *drunk*) он навеселé; **the suitcase is packed ~** чемодáн ту́го наби́т; **everybody hold ~!** все держи́тесь крéпко!
tighten ['taɪtn] *vt* (*rope*) натя́гивать (натяну́ть* *perf*); (*screw*) подтя́гивать (подтяну́ть *perf*); (*grip*) крéпче сжимáть (сжать* *perf*); (*security*) уси́ливать (уси́лить *perf*) ◆ *vi* (*grip*) крéпче сжимáться (сжáться* *perf*); (*rope*) натя́гиваться (натяну́ться *perf*).
tightfisted [taɪt'fɪstɪd] *adj* прижи́мистый (прижи́мист).
tight-lipped ['taɪt'lɪpd] *adj* скры́тный* (скры́тен); (*fig*: *through anger*) с поджáтыми губáми.
tightly ['taɪtlɪ] *adv* (*grasp*) крéпко.
tightrope ['taɪtrəup] *n* натя́нутый канáт; **to be on** *or* **walking a ~** (*fig*) ходи́ть* *(impf)* по острию́ ножá.
tightrope walker *n* канатохóдец*.
tights [taɪts] *npl* (*BRIT*) колгóтки* *pl*.
tigress ['taɪgrɪs] *n* тигри́ца.
tilde ['tɪldə] *n* (*LING*) ти́льда.
tile [taɪl] *n* (*on roof*) черепи́ца; (*on floor*) пли́тка*; (*on wall*) кáфельная пли́тка* ◆ *vt*: **to ~ the floor/bathroom** выкла́дывать (вы́ложить* *perf*) пол/вáнную пли́ткой; **~s** (*on wall*) кáфель *m*; **to ~ the roof** крыть* (покры́ть* *perf*) кры́шу черепи́цей.
tiled [taɪld] *adj* (*see n*) черепи́чный; пли́точный; кáфельный.
till [tɪl] *n* (*in shop etc*) кáсса ◆ *vt* (*land*) воздéлывать (воздéлать *perf*) ◆ *prep, conj* = **until**.
tiller ['tɪləʳ] *n* (*NAUT*) ру́мпель *m*.
tilt [tɪlt] *vt* наклоня́ть (наклони́ть* *perf*); (*head*) склоня́ть (склони́ть *perf*) ◆ *vi* наклоня́ться (наклони́ться* *perf*) ◆ *n* (*slope*) наклóн; **to wear one's hat at a ~** носи́ть* *(impf)* шля́пу набекрéнь; **(at) full ~** во весь дух.
timber ['tɪmbəʳ] *n* (*material*) древеси́на; (*trees*) лес.
time [taɪm] *n* врéмя* *nt*; (*epoch*: *often pl*) временá* *pl*, врéмя*; (*occasion, also MATH*) раз; (*MUS*) размéр, темп ◆ *vt* (*measure time of*: *race etc*) засекáть (засéчь* *perf*) врéмя *+gen*; (*fix moment for*: *visit etc*) выбирáть (вы́брать* *perf*) врéмя для *+gen*; **a long ~** дóлго; **for the ~ being** покá; **4 at a ~** по четы́ре; **from ~ to ~** врéмя от врéмени; **~ after ~, time and again** снóва и снóва; **at ~s** временáми; **in ~** вóвремя; (*after a time*) со врéменем; (*MUS*: *be*) в тáкте; (: *play*) в такт; **in a week's ~** чéрез недéлю; **in no ~** в два счёта; **any ~** в любóе врéмя; **on ~** вóвремя;

to be 30 mins behind/ahead of ~ опа́здывать (опозда́ть *perf*)/опережа́ть (опереди́ть* *perf*) на 30 мину́т; **by the ~ he arrived** к тому́ вре́мени, когда́ он пришёл; **five ~s five** пя́тью пять; **what ~ is it?** кото́рый час?; **to have a good** ~ хорошо́ проводи́ть* (провести́* *perf*) вре́мя; **we had a hard** ~ нам бы́ло о́чень тяжело́; **~'s up!** вре́мя истекло́!; **I've no ~ for it** (*fig*) меня́ э́то не интересу́ет; **he'll do it in his own (good)** ~ (*without being hurried*) он сде́лает э́то не торопя́сь; **he'll do it in** *or* (*US*) **on his own** ~ (*out of working hours*) он сде́лает э́то в свобо́дное (в нерабо́чее) вре́мя*; **to be behind the ~s** отстава́ть* (отста́ть* *perf*) от вре́мени; **to ~ sth well/badly** выбира́ть (вы́брать* *perf*) подходя́щее/неподходя́щее вре́мя для чего́-н; **the bomb was ~d to go off 5 minutes later** часово́й механи́зм бо́мбы до́лжен был срабо́тать че́рез 5 мину́т.

time and motion study *n* ана́лиз эффекти́вности рабо́ты.

time bomb *n* бо́мба с часовы́м механи́змом; (*fig*) бо́мба заме́дленного де́йствия.

timecard ['taɪmkɑ:d] *n* хронока́рта.

time clock *n* (*in factory etc*) часы́-та́бель *m*.

time-consuming ['taɪmkənsju:mɪŋ] *adj* отнима́ющий мно́го вре́мени.

time difference *n* ра́зница во вре́мени.

time frame *n*: **within a broad/narrow ~ ~** в тече́ние продолжи́тельного/коро́ткого отре́зка вре́мени.

time-honoured ['taɪmɔnəd] (*US* **time-honored**) *adj* освящённый века́ми.

timekeeper ['taɪmki:pəʳ] *n* судья́*-хронометри́ст; **she's a very good** ~ она́ о́чень пунктуа́льная.

time-lag ['taɪmlæg] *n* (*BRIT*) (временно́й) промежу́ток вре́мени.

timeless ['taɪmlɪs] *adj* ве́чный* (ве́чен).

time limit *n* преде́льный срок.

timely ['taɪmlɪ] *adj* своевре́менный* (своевре́менен).

time off *n* свобо́дное вре́мя* *nt*.

timer ['taɪməʳ] *n* (*time switch*) та́ймер.

timesaving ['taɪmseɪvɪŋ] *adj* (*gadget, method etc*) эконо́мящий вре́мя.

timescale ['taɪmskeɪl] *n* (*BRIT*) вре́мя* *nt*, пери́од вре́мени.

time-share ['taɪmʃɛəʳ] *n жильё в куро́ртной зо́не, находя́щееся в совме́стном владе́нии не́скольких лиц.*

time sharing *n* (*COMPUT*) разделе́ние вре́мени, режи́м разделе́ния вре́мени.

time sheet *n* = **timecard**.

time signal *n* (*RADIO*) сигна́л вре́мени.

time switch *n* та́ймер, выключа́тель *m* с часовы́м механи́змом.

timetable ['taɪmteɪbl] *n* расписа́ние.

time zone *n* часово́й по́яс*.

timid ['tɪmɪd] *adj* ро́бкий* (ро́бок).

timidity [tɪ'mɪdɪtɪ] *n* ро́бость *f*.

timing ['taɪmɪŋ] *n* (*SPORT*) хронометра́ж; **the ~ of his resignation was unfortunate** вы́бор вре́мени его́ отста́вки был неуда́чен.

timing device *n* (*on bomb*) часово́й механи́зм.

timpani ['tɪmpənɪ] *npl* лита́вры *fpl*.

tin [tɪn] *n* (*material*) о́лово; (*also:* ~ **plate**) бе́лая жесть *f*; (*container*) (жестяна́я) ба́нка*; (: *for baking*) про́тивень* *m*; (: *BRIT*: *can*) консе́рвная ба́нка*; **we'll need 2 ~s of paint** (*quantity*) нам ну́жно бу́дет 2 ба́нки кра́ски.

tinfoil ['tɪnfɔɪl] *n* фольга́.

tinge [tɪndʒ] *n* отте́нок* ◆ *vt*: **~d with** с отте́нком *+gen*.

tingle ['tɪŋgl] *vi* пока́лывать (*impf*); **I was tingling with excitement** я горе́л от возбужде́ния.

tinker ['tɪŋkəʳ] *n* (*gipsy*) бродя́чий луди́льщик

▸ **tinker with** *vt fus* вози́ться* (*impf*) с *+instr*.

tinkle ['tɪŋkl] *vi* звя́кать (звя́кнуть *perf*) ◆ *n* (*inf*): **to give sb a** ~ (*TEL*) звя́кнуть (*perf*) кому́-н.

tin mine *n* оловя́нный рудни́к*.

tinned [tɪnd] *adj* (*BRIT*) консерви́рованный.

tinnitus ['tɪnɪtəs] *n* звон в уша́х.

tinny ['tɪnɪ] *adj* (*pej*: *sound*) металли́ческий*; (: *car etc*) как консе́рвная ба́нка.

tin-opener ['tɪnəupnəʳ] *n* (*BRIT*) консе́рвный нож*.

tinsel ['tɪnsl] *n* мишура́.

tint [tɪnt] *n* отте́нок*; (*for hair*) кра́ска ◆ *vt* (*hair*) кра́сить* (покра́сить* *perf*).

tinted ['tɪntɪd] *adj* (*hair*) кра́шеный; (*spectacles, glass*) ды́мчатый.

tiny ['taɪnɪ] *adj* кро́шечный* (кро́шечен).

tip [tɪp] *n* (*of pen etc*) ко́нчик; (*on umbrella etc*) наконе́чник; (*gratuity*) чаевы́е *pl adj*; (*BRIT*: *for rubbish*) сва́лка*; (: *for coal*) гора́*; (*advice*) сове́т ◆ *vt* (*waiter*) дава́ть* (дать* *perf*) на чай *+dat*; (*tilt*) наклоня́ть (наклони́ть* *perf*); (*also:* ~ **over**) опроки́дывать (опроки́нуть *perf*); (*also:* ~ **out**) вываливать (вы́валить *perf*); (*winner etc*) уга́дывать (угада́ть *perf*); (*for a job etc*) про́чить (*impf*); **he ~ped out the contents of the box** он вы́валил содержи́мое я́щика

▸ **tip off** *vt* предупрежда́ть (предупреди́ть* *perf*).

tip-off ['tɪpɔf] *n* предупрежде́ние.

tipped ['tɪpt] *adj* (*BRIT*: *cigarette*) с фи́льтром; **steel-~** со стальны́м наконе́чником.

Tipp-Ex® ['tɪpɛks] *n* ≈ штрих®, Ти́пекс.

tipple ['tɪpl] (*BRIT*) *vi* выпива́ть (*impf*) ◆ *n*: **to have a** ~ выпива́ть (вы́пить* *perf*) по

* marks translations which have irregular inflections The Russian-English side of the dictionary gives inflectional information

ма́ленькой.

tipster ['tɪpstə^r] *n* жучо́к* (*на ска́чках*).

tipsy ['tɪpsɪ] *adj* (*inf*) хмельно́й* (хмелён).

tiptoe ['tɪptəu] *n*: **on ~** на цы́почках.

tiptop ['tɪptɔp] *adj*: **in ~ condition** в прекра́сном состоя́нии.

tirade [taɪ'reɪd] *n* тира́да.

Tirana [tɪ'rɑ:nə] *n* Тира́на.

tire ['taɪə^r] *n* (*US*) = **tyre** ◆ *vt* (*make tired*) утомля́ть (утоми́ть* *perf*) ◆ *vi* устава́ть* (уста́ть* *perf*)

▸ **tire out** *vt* (*exhaust*) выма́тывать (вы́мотать *perf*).

tired ['taɪəd] *adj* уста́лый (уста́л); **I am ~** я уста́л; **he feels ~** он чу́вствует себя́ уста́вшим; **you look ~** Вы вы́глядите уста́лым; **to be ~ of sth** устава́ть* (уста́ть* *perf*) от чего́-н.

tiredness ['taɪədnɪs] *n* уста́лость *f*.

tireless ['taɪəlɪs] *adj* (*worker, efforts*) неутоми́мый (неутоми́м).

tiresome ['taɪsəm] *adj* надое́дливый (надое́длив).

tiring ['taɪərɪŋ] *adj* утоми́тельный* (утоми́телен).

tissue ['tɪʃu:] *n* (*handkerchief*) бума́жная салфе́тка*; (*ANAT, BIO*) ткань *f*.

tissue paper *n* папиро́сная *or* то́нкая обёрточная бума́га.

tit [tɪt] *n* (*ZOOL*) сини́ца; (*inf*: *breast*) си́ська*; **to give ~ for tat** отпла́чивать (отплати́ть* *perf*) зуб за зуб.

titanium [tɪ'teɪnɪəm] *n* тита́н.

titbit ['tɪtbɪt] (*US* **tidbit**) *n* (*food*) ла́комый кусо́чек*; (*news*) пика́нтная но́вость* *f*.

titillate ['tɪtɪleɪt] *vt* (*person, senses*) возбужда́ть (возбуди́ть* *perf*).

titivate ['tɪtɪveɪt] *vt* (*oneself*) прихора́шиваться (*impf*); (*place*) украша́ть (укра́сить* *perf*).

title ['taɪtl] *n* (*of book, play etc*) назва́ние; (*rank, BOXING etc*) ти́тул; (*LAW*): **~ to** пра́во* на *+acc*.

title deed *n* (*LAW*) *докуме́нт, подтвержда́ющий пра́во со́бственности*.

title page *n* ти́тульный лист*.

title role *n* (*in play, film*) гла́вная роль *f*.

title track *n* *назва́ние пе́сни и́ли музыка́льной пье́сы, кото́рое та́кже явля́ется назва́нием пласти́нки, альбо́ма, плёнки итп*.

titter ['tɪtə^r] *vi* хихи́кать (хихи́кнуть *perf*).

tittle-tattle ['tɪtltætl] *n* (*inf*) болтовня́.

tizzy ['tɪzɪ] *n*: **to be in a ~** волнова́ться (разволнова́ться *perf*) по пустяка́м.

T-junction ['ti:'dʒʌŋkʃən] *n* (*AUT*) Т-обра́зный перекрёсток*.

TM *abbr* = **trademark, transcendental meditation**.

TN *abbr* (*US*: *POST*) = *Tennessee*.

TNT *n abbr* (= *trinitrotoluene*) троти́л.

KEYWORD

to [tu:] *prep* **1** (*direction*) в/на *+acc*; **to drive to school/the station** е́хать*/е́здить* (пое́хать* *perf*) в шко́лу/на ста́нцию; **the road to Edinburgh** доро́га в Эдинбу́рг; **to the left** нале́во; **to the right** напра́во

2 (*as far as*) до *+gen*; **from Paris to London** от Пари́жа до Ло́ндона; **to count to ten** счита́ть (посчита́ть *perf*) до десяти́

3 (*with expressions of time*): **a quarter to five** без четверти пять

4 (*for, of*): **a letter to his wife** письмо́ жене́; **the key to the front door** ключ от входно́й две́ри; **she is secretary to the director** она́ секрета́рь дире́ктора

5 (*expressing indirect object*): **to give sth to sb** дава́ть* (дать* *perf*) что-н кому́-н; **to talk to sb** разгова́ривать (*impf*) *or* говори́ть (*impf*) с кем-н; **what have you done to your hair?** что Вы сде́лали с свои́ми волоса́ми

6 (*in relation to*) к *+dat*; **A is to B as C is to D** "А" отно́сится к "Б", как "В" отно́сится к "Г"; **three goals to two** три два; **X miles to the gallon** X ли́тров на киломе́тр; **1500 roubles to the dollar** 1500 рубле́й за долла́р

7 (*purpose, result*) к *+dat*; **to my surprise** к моему́ удивле́нию; **to come to sb's aid** приходи́ть* (прийти́* *perf*) кому́-н на по́мощь

◆ *with vb* **1** *перево́дится неопределённой фо́рмой глаго́ла*; **to want/try to do** хоте́ть* (захоте́ть* *perf*)/пыта́ться (попыта́ться *perf*) *+infin*; **he has nothing to lose** ему́ не́чего теря́ть; **ready to use** гото́в к употребле́нию; **too old/young to ...** сли́шком стар/мо́лод, что́бы *+infin* ...

2 (*with vb omitted*): **I don't want to** я не хочу́; **I don't feel like going – you really ought to** мне не хо́чется идти́ – нет, Вы должны́

3 (*purpose, result*) что́бы *+infin*; **I did it to help you** я сде́лал э́то, что́бы помо́чь Вам

◆ *adv*: **push/pull the door to** закрыва́ть (закры́ть* *perf*) дверь.

toad [təud] *n* (*ZOOL*) жа́ба.

toadstool ['təudstu:l] *n* (*BOT*) пога́нка*.

toady ['təudɪ] *vi* (*pej*): **to ~ to sb** подхали́мничать (*impf*) пе́ред кем-н.

toast [təust] *n* (*CULIN*) тост; (*drink, speech*) тост ◆ *vt* (*CULIN*: *bread etc*) поджа́ривать (поджа́рить *perf*); (*drink to*) пить* (вы́пить* *perf*) за *+acc*; **a piece** *or* **slice of ~** ло́мтик то́ста.

toaster ['təustə^r] *n* то́стер.

toastmaster ['təustmɑ:stə^r] *n* тамада́ *m*.

toast rack *n* подста́вка для то́стов.

tobacco [tə'bækəu] *n* таба́к*; **pipe ~** тру́бочный таба́к*.

tobacconist [tə'bækənɪst] *n* торго́вец*(-вка*) таба́чными изде́лиями.

tobacconist's (shop) [tə'bækənɪsts-] *n* таба́чная ла́вка.

Tobago [tə'beɪgəu] *n see* **Trinidad**.

toboggan [tə'bɔgən] *n* (*child's*) са́нки *pl*.

today [tə'deɪ] *adv, n* сегóдня; **what day is it ~?** какóй сегóдня день?; **what date is it ~?** какóе сегóдня числó?; **~ is the 4th of March** сегóдня 4-ое мáрта; **a week ago ~** рóвно недéлю назáд.
toddle ['tɔdl] (*inf*) *vi*: **to ~ in** проковылять (*perf*); **to ~ along** *or* **off** приковылять (*impf*).
toddler ['tɔdləʳ] *n* малы́ш*.
to-do [tə'du:] *n* (*fuss*) шум.
toe [təu] *n* (*of foot*) пáлец* (*ногú*); (*of shoe, sock*) носóк*; **to ~ the line** (*fig*) подчиня́ться (*impf*) официáльной ли́нии; **big ~** большóй пáлец* (*ногú*); **little ~** мизи́нец* (*ногú*).
TOEFL *n abbr* = *Teaching of English as a Foreign Language.*
toehold ['təuhəuld] *n* (*in climbing*) тóчка опóры; (*fig*): **to get** *or* **gain a ~** находи́ть* (найти́* *perf*) тóчку опóры.
toenail ['təuneɪl] *n* нóготь* *m* (*на пáльце ногú*).
toffee ['tɔfɪ] *n* ири́ска*, тяну́чка*.
toffee apple *n* (*BRIT*) *я́блоко на пáлочке, глазирóванное ири́сом.*
toga ['təugə] *n* тóга.
together [tə'gɛðəʳ] *adv* вмéсте; (*at same time*) одновремéнно; **~ with** вмéсте с *+instr*.
togetherness [tə'gɛðənɪs] *n* бли́зость *f*.
toggle switch ['tɔgl-] *n* (*COMPUT*) ту́мблер, переключáтель *m*.
Togo ['təugəu] *n* Тóго *m ind*.
togs [tɔgz] *npl* (*inf*: *clothes*) одéжды *fpl*.
toil [tɔɪl] *n* тяжёлый труд* ◆ *vi* рабóтать (*impf*) в пóте лицá.
toilet ['tɔɪlət] *n* унитáз; (*BRIT*: *room*) туалéт ◆ *cpd* (*kit, accessories etc*) туалéтный; **to go to the ~** ходи́ть* (сходи́ть* *perf*) в туалéт.
toilet bag *n* (*BRIT*) туалéтная су́мочка.
toilet bowl *n* унитáз.
toilet paper *n* туалéтная бумáга.
toiletries ['tɔɪlətrɪz] *npl* туалéтные принадлéжности *fpl*.
toilet roll *n* рулóн туалéтной бумáги.
toilet soap *n* туалéтное мы́ло.
toilet water *n* туалéтная водá.
toing and froing ['tu:ɪŋən'frəuɪŋ] *n* (*BRIT*: *on foot*) ходьбá ту́да-обрáтно; (: *by transport*) providе ездá ту́да-обрáтно.
token ['təukən] *n* (*sign, souvenir*) знак; (*substitute coin*) жетóн ◆ *adj* (*strike, payment etc*) символи́ческий*; **by the same ~** (*fig*) по той же причи́не; **book/gift ~** (*BRIT*) кни́жный/ подáрочный талóн; **record ~** (*BRIT*) талóн на пласти́нку.
tokenism ['təukənɪzəm] *n* ви́димость *f*.
Tokyo ['təukjəu] *n* Тóкио *m ind*.
told [təuld] *pt, pp of* **tell**.
tolerable ['tɔlərəbl] *adj* (*bearable*) терпи́мый (терпи́м); (*fairly good*) снóсный* (снóсен).
tolerably ['tɔlərəblɪ] *adv*: **~ good** довóльно хорошó.
tolerance ['tɔlərns] *n* (*patience*) терпи́мость *f*; (*also TECH*) дóпуск.
tolerant ['tɔlərnt] *adj*: **~ (of)** терпи́мый (терпи́м) (к *+dat*).
tolerate ['tɔləreɪt] *vt* терпéть* (*impf*).
toleration [tɔlə'reɪʃən] *n* терпи́мость *f*.
toll [təul] *n* (*of casualties, deaths*) числó; (*tax, charge*) плáта ◆ *vi* (*bell*) звони́ть (*impf*); **the accident ~ on the roads** числó жертв на дорóгах.
toll bridge *n* (*AUT*) плáтный мост*.
toll call *n* (*US*) междугорóдный телефóнный звонóк*.
toll-free ['təul'fri:] *adj* (*US*) бесплáтный.
toll road *n* (*AUT*) плáтная дорóга.
tomato [tə'mɑ:təu] (*pl* **~es**) *n* помидóр.
tomato purée *n* томáтная пáста.
tomb [tu:m] *n* склеп, гробни́ца.
tombola [tɔm'bəulə] *n* лотерéя.
tomboy ['tɔmbɔɪ] *n* (*girl*) сорванéц*.
tombstone ['tu:mstəun] *n* надгрóбная плитá*.
tomcat ['tɔmkæt] *n* кот*.
tome [təum] *n* том*.
tomorrow [tə'mɔrəu] *adv, n* (*also fig*) зáвтра; **the day after ~** послезáвтра; **a week ~/on Monday** чéрез недéлю, считáя с зáвтрашнего дня/с понедéльника; **~ morning** зáвтра у́тром.
ton [tʌn] *n* (*BRIT*) дли́нная тóнна; (*US*: *also*: **short ~**) корóткая тóнна; (*also*: **metric ~**) метри́ческая тóнна; (*NAUT*: *also*: **register ~**) реги́стровая тóнна; **~s of** (*inf*) тóнны *+gen*.
tonal ['təunl] *adj* тонáльный.
tone [təun] *n* тон*; (*TEL*) гудóк* ◆ *vi* (*colours*: *also*: **~ in**) сочетáться (*impf*)
▸ **tone down** *vt* (*colour, criticism, demands*) смягчáть (смягчи́ть *perf*); (*sound*) уменьшáть (умéньшить *perf*)
▸ **tone up** *vt* (*muscles*) укрепля́ть (укрепи́ть* *perf*).
tone-deaf [təun'dɛf] *adj* без слу́ха.
toner ['təunəʳ] *n* (*for photocopier*) черни́ла.
Tonga [tɔŋə] *n* Тóнга.
tongs [tɔŋz] *npl* щипцы́ *pl*.
tongue [tʌŋ] *n* язы́к*; **~ in cheek** (*speak, say*) в шу́тку.
tongue-tied ['tʌŋtaɪd] *adj* (*fig*): **he was ~** он лиши́лся дáра рéчи.
tongue twister [-twɪstəʳ] *n* скороговóрка.
tonic ['tɔnɪk] *n* (*MED*) тонизи́рующее срéдство; (*also*: **~ water**) тóник; (*MUS*) тóника.
tonight [tə'naɪt] *adv* (*this evening*) сегóдня вéчером; (*this night*) сегóдня нóчью ◆ *n* (*see adv*) сегóдняшний вéчер; сегóдняшняя ночь *f*; **(I'll) see you ~!** до вéчера!
tonnage ['tʌnɪdʒ] *n* (*NAUT*) тоннáж.
tonne [tʌn] *n* (*BRIT*: *metric ton*) тóнна.

* marks translations which have irregular inflections. The Russian-English side of the dictionary gives inflectional information.

tonsil ['tɔnsl] *n* (*gen pl*) минда́лина; **to have one's ~s out** удаля́ть (удали́ть *perf*) минда́лины.
tonsillitis [tɔnsɪ'laɪtɪs] *n* тонзилли́т.
too [tu:] *adv* (*excessively*) сли́шком; (*also*: *referring to subject*) та́кже, то́же; (: *referring to object*) та́кже; **the tea is ~ sweet** чай сли́шком сла́дкий; **I went ~** я то́же пошёл; **~ much, ~ many** сли́шком мно́го; **~ bad!** о́чень жаль!
took [tuk] *pt of* **take**.
tool [tu:l] *n* инструме́нт; (*fig*: *person*) ору́дие.
tool box *n* я́щик для инструме́нтов.
tool kit *n* набо́р инструме́нтов.
toot [tu:t] *n* (*of horn*) гудо́к*; (*of whistle*) свисто́к* ◆ *vi* (*with car horn*) сигна́лить (просигна́лить *perf*).
tooth [tu:θ] (*pl* **teeth**) *n* (*ANAT*) зуб*; (*TECH*) зубе́ц*; **to have a ~ out** *or* (*US*) **pulled** удаля́ть (удали́ть *perf*) *or* вырыва́ть (вы́рвать* *perf*) зуб; **to brush one's teeth** чи́стить* (почи́стить* *perf*) зу́бы; **by the skin of one's teeth** (*fig*) чу́дом.
toothache ['tu:θeɪk] *n* зубна́я боль *f*; **I have ~** у меня́ боли́т зуб.
toothbrush ['tu:θbrʌʃ] *n* зубна́я щётка.
toothpaste ['tu:θpeɪst] *n* зубна́я па́ста.
toothpick ['tu:θpɪk] *n* зубочи́стка*.
tooth powder *n* зубно́й порошо́к*.
top [tɔp] *n* (*of mountain*) верши́на; (*of tree*) верху́шка*; (*of head*) маку́шка; (*of ladder*) верх; (*of page, list etc*) нача́ло; (*of cupboard, table, box*) ве́рхняя пове́рхность *f*; (*lid*: *of box, jar*) кры́шка*; (: *bottle*) про́бка*; (*AUT*: *also*: **~ gear**) са́мая вы́сшая ско́рость *f*; (*also*: **spinning ~**) юла́, волчо́к*; (*blouse etc*) верх ◆ *adj* (*shelf, step*) ве́рхний*; (*marks*) вы́сший*; (*salesman etc*) веду́щий*; (*best*) отме́нный ◆ *vt* (*poll, vote*) лиди́ровать (*impf*) в +*prp*; (*list*) возглавля́ть (возгла́вить* *perf*); (*exceed*: *estimate etc*) превыша́ть (превы́сить* *perf*); **the ~ of the milk** (*BRIT*) сли́вки* *pl* (на молоке́); **at the ~ of the stairs/page** на верху́ ле́стницы/страни́цы; **at the ~ of the street** в да́льнем конце́ у́лицы; **on ~ of** (*above*: *be*) на +*prp*; (: *put etc*) на +*acc*; (*in addition to*) сверх +*gen*; **put the book on ~ of the table** положи́те кни́гу на стол; **from ~ to bottom** све́рху до́низу; **from ~ to toe** (*BRIT*) с головы́ до ног *or* до пят; **at the ~ of the list** пе́рвый по спи́ску; **at the ~ of one's voice** во весь го́лос; **at ~ speed** на максима́льной ско́рости; **over the ~** (*inf*: *behaviour etc*) сверх ме́ры
▸ **top up** (*US* **top off**) *vt* (*bottle*) долива́ть (доли́ть* *perf*); (*salary*) прибавля́ть (приба́вить* *perf*).
topaz ['təupæz] *n* топа́з.
top-class ['tɔp'klɑ:s] *adj* вы́сшего кла́сса.
topcoat ['tɔpkəut] *n* ве́рхний* слой*.
top floor *n* ве́рхний* эта́ж*.
top hat *n* цили́ндр, котело́к*.
top-heavy [tɔp'hɛvɪ] *adj*: **~ object** предме́т с утяжелённым ве́рхом; **~ bureaucracy** бюрократи́ческий аппара́т с громо́здким ве́рхним эшело́ном.
topic ['tɔpɪk] *n* те́ма.
topical ['tɔpɪkl] *adj* актуа́льный* (актуа́лен).
topless ['tɔplɪs] *adj* обнажённый до по́яса.
top-level ['tɔplɛvl] *adj* на вы́сшем у́ровне.
topmost ['tɔpməust] *adj* (*branch etc*) са́мый ве́рхний *or* бли́жний к верху́шке.
topnotch ['tɔp'nɔtʃ] *adj* первосо́ртный.
topography [tə'pɔgrəfɪ] *n* топогра́фия.
topping ['tɔpɪŋ] *n* (*CULIN*): **with a ~ of** с ве́рхом из +*gen*.
topple ['tɔpl] *vt* (*government, leader*) ски́дывать (ски́нуть *perf*) ◆ *vi* (*person, object*) опроки́дываться (опроки́нуться *perf*).
top-ranking ['tɔpræŋkɪŋ] *adj* (*official*) высокопоста́вленный.
top-secret ['tɔp'si:krɪt] *adj* сверхсекре́тный* (сверхсекре́тен).
top-security ['tɔpsə'kjuərɪtɪ] *adj* (*BRIT*) под уси́ленной охра́ной.
topsy-turvy ['tɔpsɪ'tə:vɪ] *adj* перевёрнутый ◆ *adv* вверх нога́ми.
top-up ['tɔpʌp] *n*: **would you like a ~?** Вам ещё подли́ть?
top-up loan *n* (*BRIT*) доба́вочная ссу́да.
torch [tɔ:tʃ] *n* (*with flame*) фа́кел; (*BRIT*: *electric*) фона́рь* *m*.
tore [tɔ:ʳ] *pt of* **tear**.
torment [*n* 'tɔ:mɛnt, *vt* tɔ:'mɛnt] *n* муче́ние ◆ *vt* му́чить* (*impf*).
torn [tɔ:n] *pp of* **tear**[1] ◆ *adj*: **she is ~ between ...** она́ разрыва́ется ме́жду +*instr* ....
tornado [tɔ:'neɪdəu] (*pl* **~es**) *n* смерч.
torpedo [tɔ:'pi:dəu] (*pl* **~es**) *n* торпе́да.
torpedo boat *n* торпе́дный ка́тер.
torpor ['tɔ:pəʳ] *n* оцепене́ние.
torrent ['tɔrnt] *n* (*also fig*) пото́к.
torrential [tɔ'rɛnʃl] *adj* (*rain*) проливно́й.
torrid ['tɔrɪd] *adj* (*weather*) зно́йный* (зно́ен); (*love affair*) бу́рный.
torso ['tɔ:səu] *n* ту́ловище, торс.
tortoise ['tɔ:təs] *n* черепа́ха.
tortoiseshell ['tɔ:təʃɛl] *adj* черепа́ховый; (*cat*) с тигро́вым окра́сом.
tortuous ['tɔ:tjuəs] *adj* (*path*) изви́листый (изви́лист); (*argument, mind*) зау́мный* (зау́мен).
torture ['tɔ:tʃəʳ] *n* (*also fig*) пы́тка* ◆ *vt* пыта́ть (*impf*); (*fig*) му́чить (*impf*).
torturer ['tɔ:tʃərəʳ] *n* пала́ч*, мучи́тель *m*.
Tory ['tɔ:rɪ] (*BRIT*: *POL*) *adj* консервати́вный ◆ *n* (*POL*) то́ри *m/f ind*, консерва́тор.
toss [tɔs] *vt* (*throw*) подки́дывать (подки́нуть *perf*), подбра́сывать (подбро́сить* *perf*); (*one's head*) отки́дывать (отки́нуть *perf*); (*salad*) меша́ть (*impf*) ◆ *vi*: **to ~ and turn** (*in bed*) воро́чаться (*impf*) ◆ *n*: **with a ~ of her head, she...** отки́нув го́лову, она́ ...; **to ~ a**

coin подбра́сывать (подбро́сить* *perf*) моне́ту; **to ~ up to do** подбра́сывать (подбро́сить* *perf*) моне́ту, что́бы *+infin*; **to win/lose the ~** выи́грывать (вы́играть *perf*)/ прои́грывать (проигра́ть *perf*) подбра́сывание моне́ты.
tot [tɔt] *n* (*drink*) глото́к*; (*child*) малы́ш*
▸ **tot up** *vt* (*BRIT*: *figures*) подсчи́тывать (подсчита́ть *perf*).
total ['təutl] *adj* (*number, workforce etc*) о́бщий*; (*failure, wreck etc*) по́лный ◆ *n* о́бщая су́мма ◆ *vt* (*add up*) скла́дывать (сложи́ть *perf*); (*add up to*) составля́ть (соста́вить* *perf*); **in ~** в о́бщей сло́жности.
totalitarian [təutælɪ'tɛərɪən] *adj* (*POL*) тоталита́рный.
totality [təu'tælɪtɪ] *n* полнота́.
totally ['təutəlɪ] *adv* по́лностью; (*unprepared*) соверше́нно.
tote bag [təut-] *n* сума́.
totem pole ['təutəm-] *n* тоте́мный столб*.
totter ['tɔtəʳ] *vi* (*person*) ходи́ть*/идти́* *(impf)* шата́ясь *or* ша́ткой похо́дкой; (*fig*: *government*) занима́ть *(impf)* ша́ткую пози́цию.
touch [tʌtʃ] *n* осяза́ние; (*approach*) мане́ра; (*detail*) штрих; (*contact*) прикоснове́ние ◆ *vt* (*with hand, foot*) каса́ться (косну́ться *perf*) *+gen*, тро́гать (тро́нуть *perf*); (*tamper with*) тро́гать *(impf)*; (*make contact with*) прикаса́ться (прикосну́ться *perf*) к *+dat*, дотра́гиваться (дотро́нуться *perf*) до *+gen*; (*emotionally*) тро́гать (тро́нуть *perf*); **the personal ~** индивидуа́льность *f*; **to put the finishing ~es to sth** вноси́ть* (внести́* *perf*) после́дние штрихи́ в что-н; **there's been a ~ of frost** подморо́зило; **in ~ with** в конта́кте с *+instr*; **to get in ~ with sb** связа́ться* *(perf)* с кем-н; **I'll be in ~ with you** я свяжу́сь с Ва́ми; **to lose ~** (*friends*) теря́ть (потеря́ть *perf*) связь; **to be out of ~ with events** быть* *(impf)* не в ку́рсе собы́тий
▸ **touch on** *vt fus* каса́ться (косну́ться *perf*) *+gen*
▸ **touch up** *vt* (*paint*) подкра́шивать (подкра́сить* *perf*).
touch-and-go ['tʌtʃən'gəu] *adj* нея́сный* (нея́сен); **it was ~ whether we'd succeed** бы́ло нея́сно, вы́шло ли э́то у нас.
touchdown ['tʌtʃdaun] *n* (*of rocket, plane*) поса́дка*; (*US*: *FOOTBALL*) гол.
touched [tʌtʃt] *adj* тро́нутый (тро́нут).
touching ['tʌtʃɪŋ] *adj* (*scene, photograph etc*) тро́гательный* (тро́гателен).
touchline ['tʌtʃlaɪn] *n* (*SPORT*) бокова́я ли́ния.
touch-sensitive ['tʌtʃ'sɛnsɪtɪv] *adj* срабатывающий на прикоснове́ние.
touch-type ['tʌtʃtaɪp] *vi* печа́тать *(impf)* слепы́м ме́тодом.
touchy ['tʌtʃɪ] *adj* (*person*) оби́дчивый (оби́дчив); (*subject*) больно́й; **he is ~** его́ легко́ заде́ть.
tough [tʌf] *adj* (*strong, hard-wearing*: *material*) кре́пкий* (кре́пок), про́чный* (про́чен); (*meat, policies, negotiations*) жёсткий*; (*person*: *physically*) выно́сливый (выно́слив); (: *mentally*) сто́йкий* (сто́ек); (*task, problem, journey*) тяжёлый (тяжёл); (*rough*) опа́сный* (опа́сен); **~ luck!** не везёт!
toughen ['tʌfn] *vt* закаля́ть (закали́ть *perf*).
toughness ['tʌfnɪs] *n* про́чность *f*; (*of person*) сто́йкость *f*.
toupee ['tu:peɪ] *n* (*wig*) пари́к*.
tour ['tuəʳ] *n* (*journey*) пое́здка*; (*also*: **package ~**) туристи́ческая пое́здка*; (*of town, factory, museum*) экску́рсия; (*by pop group etc*) турне́ *nt ind*, гастро́ли *fpl* ◆ *vt* (*country, city*) объезжа́ть (объе́хать* *perf*); (*factory*) обходи́ть* (обойти́* *perf*); **to go on a ~ of** (*museum, region*) осма́тривать (осмотре́ть* *perf*); **to go on ~** (*band*) е́здить*/е́хать* *(impf)* на гастро́ли.
touring ['tuərɪŋ] *n* гастро́ли *fpl*.
tourism ['tuərɪzm] *n* (*business*) тури́зм.
tourist ['tuərɪst] *n* тури́ст*(ка*) ◆ *cpd* (*attractions, season*) тури́стский*; **the ~ trade** инду́стрия тури́зма.
tourist class *n* (*NAUT, AVIAT*) второ́й класс.
tourist information centre *n* (*BRIT*) туристи́ческое бюро́ *nt ind*.
tourist office *n* туристи́ческое бюро́ *nt ind*.
tournament ['tuənəmənt] *n* турни́р, состяза́ние.
tourniquet ['tuənɪkeɪ] *n* жгут, турнике́т.
tour operator *n* (*BRIT*) рабо́тник туристи́ческой фи́рмы; (*company*) туристи́ческая фи́рма.
tousled ['tauzld] *adj* (*hair*) взъеро́шенный (взъеро́шен).
tout [taut] *n* (*also*: **ticket ~**) спекуля́нт(ка*) ◆ *vi*: **to ~ for** (*business*) добива́ться *(impf)* *+gen*, выбива́ть *(impf)* ◆ *vt*: **to ~ sth (around)** (*BRIT*) спекули́ровать* *(impf)* чем-н.
tow [təu] *vt* (*vehicle, caravan, trailer*) везти́*/ вози́ть* *(impf)* на букси́ре ◆ *n*: **to give sb a ~** (*AUT*) брать* (взять* *perf*) кого́-н на букси́р; **"on** *or* (*US*) **in ~"** (*AUT*) "на букси́ре".
toward(s) [tə'wɔ:d(z)] *prep* к *+dat*; (*attitude*) по отноше́нию к *+dat*; (*purpose*): **~ doing** с тем что́бы *+infin*; **towards noon/the end of the year** к полу́дню/концу́ го́да; **to feel friendly ~ sb** относи́ться* *(impf)* дружелю́бно к кому́-н
towel ['tauəl] *n* (*also*: **hand ~**) полоте́нце* для рук; (*also*: **bath ~**) ба́нное полоте́нце*; **to throw in the ~** (*fig*) сдава́ться* (сда́ться* *perf*).
towelling ['tauəlɪŋ] *n* (*fabric*) махро́вая ткань.
towel rail (*US* **towel rack**) *n* ве́шалка* для

полоте́нец.
tower ['tauə'] *n* ба́шня* ◆ *vi* (*building, mountain*) возвыша́ться *(impf)*; **to ~ above** *or* **over sb/sth** возвыша́ться *(impf)* над кем-н/чем-н.
tower block *n* (*BRIT*) ба́шня*, высо́тный дом*.
towering ['tauərɪŋ] *adj* возвыша́ющийся.
towline ['təulaɪn] *n* букси́рный трос.
town [taun] *n* го́род*; **to go to ~** ходи́ть*/идти́* *(impf)* в го́род; (*fig*) разоря́ться (разори́ться *perf*); **in ~** в го́роде; **to be out of ~** (*person*) быть* *(impf)* в отъе́зде.
town centre *n* це́нтр (го́рода).
town clerk *n* гла́вный делопроизводи́тель *m* городско́го сове́та.
town council *n* городско́й сове́т.
town crier [-'kraɪə'] *n* глаша́тай.
town hall *n* ра́туша.
townie ['taunɪ] *n* (*inf*) городско́й(-а́я) *m(f) adj*.
town plan *n* план го́рода.
town planner *n* градострои́тель *m*, планиро́вщик.
town planning *n* городско́е плани́рование, градострои́тельство.
township ['taunʃɪp] *n* (*in South Africa*) негритя́нский* при́город; (*in America*) городско́й райо́н.
townspeople ['taunzpi:pl] *npl* горожа́не *mpl*.
towpath ['təupɑ:θ] *n* (*of canal*) тропи́нка.
towrope ['təurəup] *n* букси́рный трос.
tow truck *n* (*US*) авари́йная маши́на.
toxic ['tɔksɪk] *adj* токси́чный* (токси́чен).
toxic waste *n* ядови́тые отхо́ды *mpl*.
toxin ['tɔksɪn] *n* токси́н.
toy [tɔɪ] *n* игру́шка*
▸ **toy with** *vt fus* (*object*) игра́ть *(impf)* +*instr*; (*food*) вози́ться* *(impf)* с +*instr*; (*idea*) игра́ть *(impf)* с +*instr*.
toy shop *n* магази́н игру́шек.
trace [treɪs] *n* след* ◆ *vt* (*draw*) переводи́ть* (перевести́* *perf*); (*follow*) просле́живать (проследи́ть* *perf*); (*locate*) устана́вливать (установи́ть* *perf*); **without ~** (*disappear*) бессле́дно, без следа́; **there was no ~ of him** он исче́з без следа́.
trace element *n* микроэлеме́нт.
tracer ['treɪsə'] *n* (*also:* **~ bullet**) трасси́рующий снаря́д.
trachea [trə'kɪə] *n* трахе́я.
tracing paper ['treɪsɪŋ-] *n* ка́лька.
track [træk] *n* след*; (*path*) тропа́*; (*of bullet etc*) траекто́рия; (*RAIL*) (железнодоро́жный) путь* *m*; (*on tape, record, also SPORT*) доро́жка* ◆ *vt* (*follow: animal, person*) идти́* *(impf)* по сле́ду +*gen*; **to keep ~ of** следи́ть* *(impf)* за +*instr*; **to be on the right ~** (*fig*) быть* *(impf)* на ве́рном пути́
▸ **track down** *vt* (*prey*) высле́живать (вы́следить* *perf*); (*sth lost*) оты́скивать (отыска́ть* *perf*).
tracked [trækt] *adj* (*AUT*) гу́сеничный.
tracker dog ['trækə-] *n* (*BRIT*) соба́ка-ище́йка.
track events *npl* соревнова́ния *ntpl* по лёгкой атле́тике.
tracking station ['trækɪŋ-] *n* пульт управле́ния полётом.
track meet *n* (*SPORT*) соревнова́ния *ntpl* по атле́тике.
track record *n*: **to have a good ~ ~** (*fig*) име́ть *(impf)* хоро́шую репута́цию.
tracksuit ['træksu:t] *n* трениро́вочный костю́м.
tract [trækt] *n* (*GEO*) простра́нство; (*pamphlet*) тракта́т; **respiratory ~** (*ANAT*) дыха́тельные пути́ *mpl*; **digestive ~** желу́дочно-кише́чный тракт.
traction ['trækʃən] *n* (*power*) тя́га; (*AUT: grip*) си́ла сцепле́ния; (*MED*): **in ~** в вытяже́нии.
traction engine *n* тяга́ч*.
tractor ['træktə'] *n* тра́ктор.
trade [treɪd] *n* (*activity*) торго́вля; (*skill, job*) род заня́тий ◆ *vi* (*do business*) торгова́ть* *(impf)* ◆ *vt*: **to ~ sth (for sth)** обме́нивать (обменя́ть *perf*) что-н (на что-н); **to ~ with/in** торгова́ть* *(impf)* с +*instr*/+*instr*; **foreign ~** вне́шняя торго́вля; **Department of T~ and Industry** (*BRIT*) *Министе́рство торго́вли и промы́шленности*
▸ **trade in** *vt* (*old car etc*) предлага́ть (предложи́ть* *perf*) для встре́чной прода́жи.
trade barrier *n* торго́вый барье́р.
trade deficit *n* торго́вый дефици́т.
Trade Descriptions Act *n* (*BRIT: LAW, COMM*) *положе́ние о торго́вле*.
trade discount *n* торго́вая ски́дка* (*о́птовым торго́вцам*).
trade fair *n* торго́вая я́рмарка*.
trade figures *npl* показа́тель *msg* товарооборо́та.
trade-in ['treɪdɪn] *n*: **to take as a ~** принима́ть (приня́ть* *perf*) как встре́чную прода́жу.
trade-in price *n* цена́* с учётом встре́чной прода́жи.
trademark ['treɪdmɑ:k] *n* това́рный знак.
trade mission *n* торго́вое представи́тельство.
trade name *n* торго́вое назва́ние.
trade-off ['treɪdɔf] *n* компроми́сс.
trade price *n* торго́вая цена́.
trader ['treɪdə'] *n* торго́вец*.
trade reference *n* информа́ция о состоя́нии дел фи́рмы.
trade secret *n* промы́шленный секре́т.
tradesman ['treɪdzmən] *irreg n* рабо́тник; (*shopkeeper*) торго́вец*, ла́вочник.
trade union *n* профсою́з= *профессиона́льный сою́з*.
trade unionist [-'ju:njənɪst] *n* член профсою́за.
trade wind *n* (*GEO*)螺пасса́т.
trading ['treɪdɪŋ] *n* торго́вля.
trading account *n* счёт расчётов.
trading estate *n* (*BRIT*) промы́шленная зо́на.
trading stamps *npl* *бума́жные ма́рки с*

объя́вленной сто́имостью.
tradition [trəˈdɪʃən] *n* тради́ция.
traditional [trəˈdɪʃənl] *adj* (*also fig*) традицио́нный*.
traditionally [trəˈdɪʃnəlɪ] *adv* традицио́нно.
traffic [ˈtræfɪk] *n* (*of people, vehicles*) движе́ние; (*of drugs etc*) нелега́льная торго́вля ◆ *vi*: **to ~ in** (*liquor, drugs*) нелега́льно торгова́ть* (*impf*) +*instr*.
traffic circle *n* (*US*) кольцева́я тра́нспортная развя́зка*.
traffic island *n* острово́к* безопа́сности.
traffic jam *n* про́бка*.
trafficker [ˈtræfɪkə^r] *n* (*also*: **drug ~**) наркокурье́р.
traffic lights *npl* светофо́р *msg*.
traffic offence *n* (*BRIT*) наруше́ние пра́вил доро́жного движе́ния.
traffic sign *n* доро́жный знак.
traffic violation *n* (*US*) = **traffic offence**.
traffic warden *n* (*BRIT*) *регулиро́вщик паркова́ния маши́н на у́лицах го́рода*.
tragedy [ˈtrædʒədɪ] *n* траге́дия.
tragic [ˈtrædʒɪk] *adj* траги́ческий*.
tragically [ˈtrædʒɪkəlɪ] *adv* траги́чески.
trail [treɪl] *n* (*path*) доро́жка*, тропи́нка*; (*track*) след; (*of smoke, dust*) хвост* ◆ *vt* (*drag*) волочи́ть* (*impf*); (*follow: person, animal*) сле́довать (*impf*) по пята́м за +*instr* ◆ *vi* (*hang loosely*) волочи́ться* (*impf*); (*in game, contest*) волочи́ться* (*impf*) в хвосте́, отстава́ть* (*impf*); **to be on sb's ~** устра́ивать (устро́ить *perf*) сле́жку за кем-н
▸ **trail away** *vi* (*sound, voice*) затиха́ть (зати́хнуть *perf*)
▸ **trail behind** *vi* (*lag*) волочи́ться* (*impf*) в хвосте́
▸ **trail off** *vi* = **trail away**.
trailer [ˈtreɪlə^r] *n* (*AUT*) прице́п; (*US: caravan*) автоприце́п; (*CINEMA*) кинорекла́ма, ано́нс.
trailer tent *n* прице́п с пала́ткой.
trailer truck *n* (*US*) грузови́к* с прице́пом.
train [treɪn] *n* по́езд*; (*of dress*) шлейф ◆ *vt* (*apprentice, doctor etc*) учи́ть* (обучи́ть* *perf*); (*athlete, mind*) тренирова́ть (*impf*); (*dog*) дрессирова́ть (вы́дрессировать *perf*); (*plant*) приуча́ть (приучи́ть* *perf*) ◆ *vi* (*learn a skill*) учи́ться* (обучи́ться* *perf*); (*SPORT*) тренирова́ться (*impf*); **one's ~ of thought** ход чьих-н мы́слей; **~ of events** цепь *f* собы́тий; **to go by ~** е́здить*/е́хать* (*impf*) по́ездом *or* на по́езде; **to ~ sb to do** обуча́ть (обучи́ть* *perf*) кого́-н +*impf infin*; **to ~ sb as** учи́ть* (*impf*) кого́-н на +*acc*; **to ~ on** (*camera etc*) направля́ть (напра́вить* *perf*) на +*acc*.
train attendant *n* (*US*) проводни́к.
trained [treɪnd] *adj* (*worker, teacher*) подгото́вленный; (*animal*) трениро́ванный; (*eye*) натрениро́ванный* (натрениро́ван).
trainee [treɪˈniː] *n* (*hairdresser*) учени́к*; **~ teacher** студе́нт(ка*) практика́нт.
trainer [ˈtreɪnə^r] *n* (*coach*) тре́нер; (*of animals*) дрессиро́вщик(-щица); **~s** *npl* (*sports shoes*) кроссо́вки *fpl*.
training [ˈtreɪnɪŋ] *n* (*for occupation*) обуче́ние, подгото́вка*; (*SPORT*) трениро́вка; **to be in ~** (*SPORT*) тренирова́ться (*impf*).
training college *n* (*for teachers*) педагоги́ческий* институ́т.
training course *n* курс профессиона́льной подгото́вки.
traipse [treɪps] *vi*: **to ~ through** прита́скиваться (притащи́ться* *perf*).
trait [treɪt] *n* черта́.
traitor [ˈtreɪtə^r] *n* преда́тель(ница) *m(f)*.
trajectory [trəˈdʒɛktərɪ] *n* траекто́рия.
tram [træm] *n* (*BRIT*) трамва́й.
tramcar [ˈtræmkɑː^r] *n* (*BRIT*) = **tram**.
tramline [ˈtræmlaɪn] *n* трамва́йная ли́ния.
tramp [træmp] *n* (*person*) бродя́га *m/f*; (*inf: pej: woman*) шлю́ха ◆ *vi* броди́ть* (*impf*) ◆ *vt* (*town, streets*) броди́ть*/брести́* (*impf*) по +*dat*.
trample [ˈtræmpl] *vt*: **to ~ (underfoot)** раста́птывать (растопта́ть* *perf*) ◆ *vi* (*fig*): **to ~ on** раста́птывать (растопта́ть* *perf*).
trampoline [ˈtræmpəliːn] *n* бату́т.
trance [trɑːns] *n* (*also fig*) транс; **to go into a ~** входи́ть* (войти́* *perf*) в транс.
tranquil [ˈtræŋkwɪl] *adj* безмяте́жный* (безмяте́жен).
tranquillity [træŋˈkwɪlɪtɪ] (*US* **tranquility**) *n* безмяте́жность *f*.
tranquillizer [ˈtræŋkwɪlaɪzə^r] (*US* **tranquilizer**) *n* (*MED*) транквилиза́тор.
transact [trænˈzækt] *vt* (*business*) вести́* (*impf*).
transaction [trænˈzækʃən] *n* (*piece of business*) опера́ция; **cash ~** опла́та нали́чными.
transatlantic [ˈtrænzətˈlæntɪk] *adj* трансатланти́ческий.
transcend [trænˈsɛnd] *vt* (*boundaries, loyalties etc*) выходи́ть* (вы́йти* *perf*) за преде́лы +*gen*.
transcendental [trænsɛnˈdɛntl] *adj*: **~ meditation** трансценде́нтная медита́ция.
transcribe [trænˈskraɪb] *vt* перепи́сывать (переписа́ть* *perf*), транскриби́ровать (*impf/perf*).
transcript [ˈtrænskrɪpt] *n* (*typed*) печа́тная ко́пия; (*hand-written*) рукопи́сная ко́пия.
transcription [trænˈskrɪpʃən] *n* транскри́пция.
transept [ˈtrænsɛpt] *n* трансе́пт.
transfer [ˈtrænsfə^r] *n* перево́д; (*POL*) переда́ча; (*SPORT*) перехо́д; (*picture etc*) переводна́я карти́нка ◆ *vt* (*employees, money etc*) переводи́ть* (перевести́* *perf*); (*POL, SPORT*)

передава́ть* (переда́ть* *perf*); **to ~ the charges** (*BRIT: TEL*) звони́ть (позвони́ть *perf*) по колле́кту; **by bank ~** по ба́нковскому перево́ду.
transferable [træns'fɜ:rəbl] *adj* (*ticket*) перево́дный, с пра́вом переда́чи; **"not ~"** "без пра́ва переда́чи".
transfix [træns'fɪks] *vt* (*person, animal*) пронза́ть (пронзи́ть* *perf*); (*fig*): **~ed with fear** пронзённый стра́хом.
transform [træns'fɔ:m] *vt* (*person, situation etc*) преобража́ть (преобрази́ть* *perf*).
transformation [trænsfə'meɪʃən] *n* преобразова́ние, перевоплоще́ние.
transformer [træns'fɔ:məʳ] *n* трансформа́тор.
transfusion [træns'fju:ʒən] *n* (*also:* **blood ~**) перелива́ние кро́ви.
transgress [træns'grɛs] *vt* преступа́ть (преступи́ть* *perf*) грани́цы *+gen*.
transient ['trænzɪənt] *adj* мимолётный* (мимолётен).
transistor [træn'zɪstəʳ] *n* (*ELEC*) транзи́сторное устро́йство; (*also:* **~ radio**) транзи́стор.
transit ['trænzɪt] *n*: **in ~** (*people, things*) транзи́том.
transit camp *n* перева́лочный пункт.
transition [træn'zɪʃən] *n* перехо́д.
transitional [træn'zɪʃənl] *adj* перехо́дный.
transitive ['trænzɪtɪv] *adj* (*LING*) перехо́дный.
transit lounge *n* зал транзи́тных пассажи́ров.
transitory ['trænzɪtərɪ] *adj* преходя́щий*.
transit visa *n* транзи́тная ви́за.
translate [trænz'leɪt] *vt*: **to ~ (from/into)** переводи́ть* (перевести́* *perf*) (с *+gen*/на *+acc*).
translation [trænz'leɪʃən] *n* перево́д; (*SCOL: as opposed to prose*) перево́д на родно́й язы́к.
translator [trænz'leɪtəʳ] *n* перево́дчик(-ица).
translucent [trænz'lu:snt] *adj* (*object, quality*) прозра́чный* (прозра́чен), просве́чивающий.
transmission [trænz'mɪʃən] *n* переда́ча; (*AUT*) коро́бка переда́ч, при́вод.
transmit [trænz'mɪt] *vt* передава́ть* (переда́ть* *perf*).
transmitter [trænz'mɪtəʳ] *n* (*equipment*) переда́тчик.
transparency [træns'pɛərnsɪ] *n* (*of glass etc*) прозра́чность *f*; (*BRIT: PHOT*) диапозити́в.
transparent [træns'pærnt] *adj* прозра́чный* (прозра́чен).
transpire [træns'paɪəʳ] *vi* (*turn out*) выясня́ться (вы́ясниться *perf*); (*happen*) происходи́ть* (произойти́* *perf*); **it finally ~d that ...** наконе́ц вы́яснилось, что ....
transplant [*n* 'trænsplɑ:nt, *vt* træns'plɑ:nt] *n* переса́дка* ◆ *vt* (*MED, seedlings*) переса́живать (пересади́ть* *perf*); **he had a heart ~** ему́ сде́лали переса́дку се́рдца.
transport [*n* 'trænspɔ:t, *vt* træns'pɔ:t] *n* тра́нспорт; (*moving people, goods*) перево́зка* ◆ *vt* (*carry*) перевози́ть* (перевезти́* *perf*); **public ~** обще́ственный тра́нспорт; **Department of T~** (*BRIT*) Министе́рство тра́нспорта.
transportation ['trænspɔ:'teɪʃən] *n* (*transport*) транспортиро́вка*, перево́зка*; (*means of transport*) тра́нспорт; **Department of T~** (*US*) Министе́рство тра́нспорта.
transport café *n* (*BRIT*) доро́жное кафе́ *nt ind*.
transpose [træns'pəuz] *vt* перемеща́ть (перемести́ть* *perf*).
transsexual [trænz'sɛksuəl] *n* транссексуа́л.
transverse ['trænzvə:s] *adj* (*beam etc*) попере́чный.
transvestite [trænz'vɛstaɪt] *n* трансвести́т.
trap [træp] *n* западня́, лову́шка; (*carriage*) двуко́лка* ◆ *vt* лови́ть* (пойма́ть *perf*) в лову́шку *or* западню́; (*confine*) запира́ть (запере́ть* *perf*); (*immobilize*) ско́вывать (скова́ть *perf*); (*jam*) защемля́ть (защеми́ть* *perf*); **to set** *or* **lay a ~ (for sb)** расставля́ть (расста́вить* *perf*) лову́шку *or* западню́ (кому́-н); **to shut one's ~** (*inf*) затыка́ть (заткну́ть *perf*) свою́ гло́тку; **to ~ one's finger in the door** защемля́ть (защеми́ть* *perf*) себе́ па́лец.
trap door *n* люк.
trapeze [trə'pi:z] *n* трапе́ция.
trapper ['træpəʳ] *n* лове́ц*.
trappings ['træpɪŋz] *npl* атрибу́ты *mpl*.
trash [træʃ] *n* (*rubbish: also pej*) сор, му́сор; (*: nonsense*) чушь *f*.
trash can *n* (*US*) му́сорное ведро́*.
trashy ['træʃɪ] *adj* (*inf*) дрянно́й.
trauma ['trɔ:mə] *n* тра́вма.
traumatic [trɔ:'mætɪk] *adj* травмати́ческий.
traumatize ['trɔ:mətaɪz] *vt* травми́ровать* (*impf/perf*).
travel ['trævl] *n* (*travelling*) путеше́ствия *ntpl* ◆ *vi* (*for pleasure*) путеше́ствовать (*impf*); (*commute*) е́здить* (*impf*); (*move*) передвига́ться (*impf*); (*news, sound*) распространя́ться (распространи́ться *perf*); (*wine, food*) сохраня́ться (*impf*) при перево́зке ◆ *vt* (*distance: by transport*) проезжа́ть (прое́хать* *perf*); (*: on foot*) проходи́ть* (пройти́* *perf*); **~s** *npl* (*journeys*) путеше́ствия *ntpl*.
travel agency *n* туристи́ческое аге́нтство.
travel agent *n* рабо́тник туристи́ческого аге́нтства.
travel brochure *n* рекла́мная брошю́ра для тури́стов.
traveller ['trævləʳ] (*US* **traveler**) *n* путеше́ственник(-ица); (*COMM*) коммивояжёр.
traveller's cheque (*US* **traveler's check**) *n* доро́жный чек.
travelling ['trævlɪŋ] (*US* **traveling**) *n* (*for pleasure*) путеше́ствия *ntpl*; (*from necessity*)

переéзды *mpl* ◆ *cpd* (*circus, exhibition*) передвижнóй; (*bag, clock, expenses*) дорóжный.
travel(l)ing salesman *irreg n* коммивояжёр.
travelogue ['trævəlɔg] *n* (*book*) книга о путешéствиях.
travel-sickness ['trævlsıknıs] *n* (*on ship*) морскáя болéзнь *f*; **he suffers from travel sickness** (*in car*) егó укáчивает в машúне.
traverse ['trævəs] *vt* пересекáть (пересéчь* *perf*).
travesty ['trævəstı] *n* парóдия.
trawler ['trɔ:ləʳ] *n* трáулер.
tray [treı] *n* (*for carrying*) поднóс; (*on desk*) *корзúнка*.
treacherous ['trɛtʃərəs] *adj* (*person*) вероломный* (верolóмен); (*look, action*) предáтельский*; (*ground, tide*) ковáрный* (ковáрен); **road conditions are ~** склáдывается слóжная дорóжная обстанóвка.
treachery ['trɛtʃərı] *n* предáтельство, верolóмство.
treacle ['tri:kl] *n* (*black treacle*) пáтока; (*golden syrup*) свéтлая *or* очúщенная пáтока.
tread [trɛd] (*pt* **trod**, *pp* **trodden**) *n* (*step*) похóдка; (*sound*) пóступь *f*; (*of stair*) ступéнь *f*; (*of tyre*) протéктор ◆ *vi* ступáть *(impf)*
▸ **tread on** *vt fus* наступáть (наступúть* *perf*) на *+acc*.
treadle ['trɛdl] *n* (*on sewing machine etc*) педáль *f*.
treas. *abbr* = **treasurer**.
treason ['tri:zn] *n* измéна.
treasure ['trɛʒəʳ] *n* сокрóвище ◆ *vt* (*object*) хранúть *(impf)* как зенúцу óка; (*friendship*) высóко ценúть* *(impf)*; (*memory*) свя́то хранúть *(impf)*; (*thought*) лелéять *(impf)*; (*store*) хранúть *(impf)*; **~s** *npl* (*art treasures etc*) сокрóвища *ntpl*.
treasure hunt *n* пóиски *mpl* сокрóвищ.
treasurer ['trɛʒərəʳ] *n* казначéй.
treasury ['trɛʒərı] *n*: **the T~**, (*US*) **the T~ Department** Государственное Казначéйство.
Treasury bill *n* (*BRIT*) казначéйский вéксель *m*.
treat [tri:t] *n* (*present*) удовóльствие ◆ *vt* (*person, object*) обращáться *(impf)* с *+instr*; (*patient, illness*) лечúть* *(impf)*; (*TECH*: *coat*) обрабáтывать (обработáть *perf*); **it was a ~** э́то бы́ло наслаждéние; **to ~ sth as a joke** относúться* (отнестúсь *perf*) к чемý-н несерьёзно; **to ~ sb to sth** угощáть (угостúть* *perf*) когó-н чем-н.
treatment ['tri:tmənt] *n* (*attention, handling*) обращéние; (*MED*) лечéние; **to have ~ for sth** проходúть* (пройтú* *perf*) курс лечéния от чегó-н.
treaty ['tri:tı] *n* соглашéние.
treble ['trɛbl] *adj* (*triple*) тройнóй; (*MUS*: *voice, part*) дискáнтный, сопрáно *ind*; (: *instrument*) сопрáнов ◆ *n* (*MUS*) дискáнт, сопрáно *m ind*; (*on hi-fi, radio etc*) высóкие частóты *fpl* ◆ *vt* утрáивать (утрóить *perf*) ◆ *vi* утрáиваться (утрóиться *perf*); **to be ~ the size of sth** быть* *(impf)* бóльше чегó-н втрóе.
treble clef *n* скрипúчный ключ*.
tree [tri:] *n* дéрево*.
tree-lined ['tri:laınd] *adj* усáженный дерéвьями.
treetop ['tri:tɔp] *n* верхýшка дéрева.
tree trunk *n* ствол дéрева.
trek [trɛk] *n* (*long difficult journey*) похóд, перехóд ◆ *vi* (*as holiday*) идтú* (пойтú* *perf*) в похóд.
trellis ['trɛlıs] *n* шпалéра.
tremble ['trɛmbl] *vi* дрожáть *(impf)*.
trembling ['trɛmblıŋ] *n* дрожáние ◆ *adj* (*hand, voice etc*) дрожáщий.
tremendous [trı'mɛndəs] *adj* (*enormous*) огрóмный* (огрóмен); (*excellent*) великолéпный* (великолéпен).
tremendously [trı'mɛndəslı] *adv* чрезвычáйно; **he enjoyed it ~** он получúл огрóмное удовóльствие от э́того.
tremor ['trɛməʳ] *n* (*trembling*) дрожь *f*, содрогáние; (*also*: **earth ~**) толчóк* (землетрясéния).
trench [trɛntʃ] *n* канáва; (*MIL*) траншéя, окóп.
trench coat *n* тёплая полушинéль *f*.
trench warfare *n* окóпная войнá*.
trend [trɛnd] *n* (*tendency*) тендéнция; (*of events, fashion*) направлéние; **~ towards sth** тендéнция к чемý-н; **~ away from sth** отхóд от чегó-н; **to set the ~** задавáть* (задáть* *perf*) направлéние; **to set a ~** задавáть* (задáть* *perf*) тон.
trendy ['trɛndı] *adj* мóдный* (мóден).
trepidation [trɛpı'deıʃən] *n* (*apprehension*) трéпет; **in ~** в трéпете.
trespass ['trɛspəs] *vi*: **to ~ on** (*private property*) вторгáться (втóргнуться *perf*) в *+acc*; **"no ~ing"** "вход воспрещён".
trespasser ['trɛspəsəʳ] *n* вторгáющийся(-аяся) *m(f) adj* в чáстные владéния; **"trespassers will be prosecuted"** "лицá, вторгáющиеся на дáнную территóрию бýдут преслéдоваться закóном".
tress [trɛs] *n* (*of hair*) косá*.
trestle ['trɛsl] *n* кóзлы *pl*.
trestle table *n* стол* на кóзлах.
trial ['traıəl] *n* (*LAW*) процéсс, суд*; (*test*: *of machine etc*) испытáния *ntpl*; (*worry*) переживáние; **~s** *npl* (*unpleasant experiences*) перипетúи *fpl*; **horse ~s** соревновáния *ntpl* по вы́ездке; **~ by jury** суд* присяжных; **to be**

* marks translations which have irregular inflections. The Russian-English side of the dictionary gives inflectional information.

sent for ~ предавáть* (предáть* *perf*) судý; **on** ~ (*LAW*) под судóм; **by** ~ **and error** мéтодом проб и ошибóк.
trial balance *n* (*COMM*) прóбный балáнс.
trial basis *n*: **on a** ~ ~ на испытáтельный срок.
trial period *n* испытáтельный срок.
trial run *n* прогóн.
triangle ['traıæŋgl] *n* (*MATH, MUS*) треугóльник.
triangular [traı'æŋgjulə'] *adj* треугóльный.
tribal ['traıbl] *adj* (*warrior, warfare, dance*) племеннóй.
tribe [traıb] *n* плéмя* *nt*.
tribesman ['traıbzmən] *irreg n* тузéмец*.
tribulations [trıbju'leıʃənz] *npl* злоключéния *ntpl*.
tribunal [traı'bju:nl] *n* трибунáл.
tributary ['trıbjutərı] *n* (*of river*) притóк*.
tribute ['trıbju:t] *n* (*compliment*) дань *f*; **to pay** ~ **to** отдавáть* (отдáть* *perf*) дань *+dat*.
trice [traıs] *n*: **in a** ~ мигом.
trick [trık] *n* (*magic trick*) фóкус; (*prank, joke*) подвóх; (*skill, knack*) улóвка, приём; (*CARDS*) взя́тка* ◆ *vt* проводи́ть* (провести́* *perf*); **to play a** ~ **on sb** разы́грывать (разыгрáть *perf*) когó-н; **to** ~ **sb into doing** обмáном заставля́ть (застáвить* *perf*) когó-н *+infin*; **to** ~ **sb out of sth** вымáнивать (вы́манить *perf*) что-н у когó-н; **a** ~ **of the light** игрá* свéта, опти́ческий* обмáн; **that should do the** ~ э́то должнó срабóтать.
trickery ['trıkərı] *n* мошéнничество.
trickle ['trıkl] *n* (*of water etc*) стрýйка ◆ *vi* (*water, rain etc*) струи́ться *(impf)*; (*people*) стекáться *(impf)*.
trick question *n* хи́трый вопрóс.
trickster ['trıkstə'] *n* мошéнник.
tricky ['trıkı] *adj* (*job*) непростóй; (*business*) хи́трый; (*problem*) заковы́ристый.
tricycle ['traısıkl] *n* трёхколёсный велосипéд.
trifle ['traıfl] *n* (*small detail*) пустя́к*; (*CULIN*) *десéрт из кéкса, фруктóвого желé и сли́вок* ◆ *adv*: **a** ~ **long** чуть длиннова́т ◆ *vi*: **to** ~ **with sb/sth** шути́ть* *(impf)* с кем-н/чем-н.
trifling ['traıflıŋ] *adj* пустякóвый.
trigger ['trıgə'] *n* (*of gun*) курóк*
▸ **trigger off** *vt* (*reaction, riot*) спровоци́ровать *(perf)*, вызывáть (вы́звать* *perf*).
trigonometry [trıgə'nɔmətrı] *n* тригономéтрия *f*.
trilby ['trılbı] *n* (*BRIT*: *also:* ~ **hat**) фéтровая шля́па.
trill [trıl] *vi* (*birds*) заливáться (зали́ться *perf*) ◆ *n* (*MUS*) трель *f*.
trilogy ['trılədʒı] *n* трилóгия *f*.
trim [trım] *adj* (*house, garden*) ухóженный; (*figure*) подтя́нутый ◆ *n* отдéлка ◆ *vt* (*cut*) подрáвнивать (подровня́ть *perf*); (*NAUT*) стáвить* (постáвить* *perf*) пó ветру; (*decorate*): **to** ~ **(with)** отдéлывать (отдéлать *perf*) (*+instr*); **to give sb a** ~ подрáвнивать (подровня́ть *perf*) вóлосы комý-н; **to keep in (good)** ~ держáть* *(impf)* (в хорóшей) фóрме.
trimmings ['trımıŋz] *npl* (*CULIN*) потрохá *mpl*; (*cuttings*) обрéзки *mpl*.
Trinidad and Tobago ['trınıdæd-] *n* Тринидáд и Тобáго.
trinity ['trınıtı] *n* (*group*) трóйка; (*REL*): **the (Holy) T**~ Трóица.
trinket ['trıŋkıt] *n* (*ornament*) безделýшка*; (*jewellery*) побрякýшка*.
trio ['tri:əu] *n* трóйка; (*MUS*) три́о *nt ind*.
trip [trıp] *n* (*journey*) поéздка*; (*outing*) прогýлка* ◆ *vi* (*stumble*) спотыкáться (споткнýться *perf*); (*go lightly*) идти́* *(impf)* лёгкой похóдкой; **on a** ~ на экскýрсии
▸ **trip up** *vi* (*stumble*) стáвить* (постáвить* *perf*) поднóжку ◆ *vt* (*person*) подставля́ть (подстáвить* *perf*) поднóжку.
tripartite [traı'pɑ:taıt] *adj* трёхсторóнний*.
tripe [traıp] *n* (*CULIN*) требухá; (*pej*: *rubbish*) чушь *f*.
triple ['trıpl] *adj* тройнóй ◆ *adv*: ~ **the distance/the speed** тройнóе расстоя́ние/тройнáя скóрость, в три рáза дáльше/быстрéе.
triple jump *n* тройнóй прыжóк (в длинý).
triplets ['trıplıts] *npl* тройня́шки* *fpl*.
triplicate ['trıplıkət] *n*: **in** ~ в трёх экземпля́рах.
tripod ['traıpɔd] *n* тренóга.
Tripoli ['trıpəlı] *n* Три́поли *m ind*.
tripper ['trıpə'] *n* (*BRIT*) тури́ст(ка*).
tripwire ['trıpwaıə'] *n* *замаскирóванная прóволока, свя́занная с капкáном и́ли взрывчáткой*.
trite [traıt] *adj* (*pej*) изби́тый.
triumph ['traıʌmf] *n* (*satisfaction*) торжествó; (*great achievement*) триýмф ◆ *vi*: **to** ~ **(over)** торжествовáть (восторжествовáть *perf*) (над *+instr*).
triumphal [traı'ʌmfl] *adj* (*arch, return*) триумфáльный.
triumphant [traı'ʌmfənt] *adj* (*team, wave*) торжествýющий; (*return*) побéдный.
triumphantly [traı'ʌmfəntlı] *adv* (*shout, look etc*) торжествýюще.
trivia ['trıvıə] *npl* (*pej*) тривиáльности *fpl*, тривиáльные вéщи *fpl*.
trivial ['trıvıəl] *adj* (*unimportant*) незначи́тельный* (незначи́телен); (*commonplace*) тривиáльный* (тривиáлен).
triviality [trıvı'ælıtı] *n* мéлочи *fpl*.
trivialize ['trıvıəlaız] *vt* упрощáть (упрости́ть* *perf*).
trod [trɔd] *pt of* **tread**.
trodden [trɔdn] *pp of* **tread**.
trolley ['trɔlı] *n* телéжка*; (*also:* ~ **bus**) троллéйбус.
trollop ['trɔləp] *n* (*pej*) лахýдра.
trombone [trɔm'bəun] *n* тромбóн.
troop [tru:p] *n* (*of people*) отря́д, грýппа; (*of monkeys*) стáдо ◆ *vi*: **to** ~ **in/out** входи́ть*

(войти́* *perf*)/выходи́ть* (вы́йти* *perf*) стро́ем; **~s** *npl* (*MIL*) войска́ *ntpl*; **a ~ of children** ста́йка ребяти́шек.
troop carrier *n* (*plane*) тра́нспортно-деса́нтный самолёт; (*NAUT*: *also*: **troopship**) тра́нспорт для перево́зки войск.
trooper ['tru:pə^r] *n* (*MIL*: *in cavalry*) кавалери́ст; (: *in armoured regiment*) солда́т*; (*US*: *policeman*) ко́нный полице́йский* *m adj*.
trooping the colour ['tru:pɪŋ-] *n* (*BRIT*: *ceremony*) внос зна́мени.
troopship ['tru:pʃɪp] *n* тра́нспорт для перево́зки войск.
trophy ['trəufɪ] *n* трофе́й.
tropic ['trɔpɪk] *n*: **~s** тро́пики *mpl*; **in the ~s** в тро́пиках; **T~ of Cancer/Capricorn** Тро́пик Ра́ка/Козеро́га.
tropical ['trɔpɪkl] *adj* (*rain forest, climate etc*) тропи́ческий*.
trot [trɔt] *n* рысь *f* ◆ *vi* (*horse*) идти́* (*impf*) ры́сью; (*person*) бежа́ть* (*impf*) рысцо́й; **on the ~** (*BRIT*: *fig*) подря́д
▸ **trot out** *vt* (*excuse, reason*) приводи́ть* (привести́* *perf*); (*names, facts*) сы́пать (*impf*) +*instr*.
trouble ['trʌbl] *n* (*difficulty*) затрудне́ние, неприя́тность *f*; (*worry, unrest*) беспоко́йство; (*bother, effort*) хло́поты *pl* ◆ *vt* (*worry*) беспоко́ить (*impf*); (*person*: *disturb*) беспоко́ить (побеспоко́ить *perf*) ◆ *vi*: **to ~ to do** побеспоко́иться (*perf*) +*infin*; **~s** *npl* (*personal, POL etc*) бе́ды *fpl*; **to be in ~** име́ть (*impf*) неприя́тности; (*ship, climber etc*) быть* (*impf*) в беде́; **to have ~ doing** с трудо́м мочь (*impf*) +*infin*; **to go to the ~ of doing** забо́титься* (позабо́титься* *perf*) о том, что́бы +*infin*; **it's no ~!** э́то ника́к не затрудни́т меня́!; **it's too much ~** сли́шком мно́го хлопо́т; **please don't ~ yourself** пожа́луйста, не беспоко́йтесь; **the ~ is ...** беда́ в том, что ...; **what's the ~?** (*with broken television etc*) где непола́дки?, в чём там де́ло?; (*MED*) что Вас беспоко́ит?; **stomach ~** больно́й желу́док.
troubled [trʌbld] *adj* (*person*) в постоя́нной трево́ге; (*country*) бе́дствующий; (*life, era*) беспоко́йный.
trouble-free ['trʌblfri:] *adj* (*period, campaign etc*) без происше́ствий.
troublemaker ['trʌblmeɪkə^r] *n* смутья́н; (*child*) прока́зник.
troubleshooter ['trʌblʃu:tə^r] *n* (*in conflict*) *уполномо́ченный, выявля́ющий недоста́тки в рабо́те компа́нии*.
troublesome ['trʌblsəm] *adj* (*child*) прока́зливый.
trouble spot *n* (*MIL*) горя́чая то́чка*.
troubling ['trʌblɪŋ] *adj* трево́жный.
trough [trɔf] *n* (*also*: **drinking ~**) коры́то; (*also*: **feeding ~**) корму́шка*; (*channel*) жёлоб; (*low point*) впа́дина; **a ~ of low pressure** (*METEOROLOGY*) фронт ни́зкого давле́ния.
trounce [trauns] *vt* (*defeat*) разбива́ть (разби́ть* *perf*).
troupe [tru:p] *n* тру́ппа.
trouser press ['trauzə-] *n* приспособле́ние для гла́жки брюк.
trousers ['trauzəz] *npl* брю́ки *mpl*; **short ~** штаны́ *mpl*.
trouser suit *n* (*BRIT*) брю́чный костю́м.
trousseau ['tru:səu] (*pl* **~x** *or* **~s**) *n* прида́ное *nt adj*.
trousseaux ['tru:səuz] *npl of* **trousseau**.
trout [traut] *n inv* (*ZOOL*) форе́ль *f*.
trowel ['trauəl] *n* (*garden tool*) сово́к*; (*builder's tool*) мастеро́к*.
truant ['truənt] *n* (*BRIT*): **to play ~** прогу́ливать (прогуля́ть *perf*).
truce [tru:s] *n* переми́рие.
truck [trʌk] *n* (*lorry*) грузови́к; (*RAIL*) откры́тая това́рная платфо́рма; (*for luggage*) теле́жка*, ваго́нетка*.
truck driver *n* води́тель *m* грузовика́.
trucker ['trʌkə^r] *n* води́тель *m* грузовика́.
truck farm *n* (*US*) овощево́дческая фе́рма.
trucking ['trʌkɪŋ] *n* (*esp US*) грузова́я транспортиро́вка*.
trucking company *n* (*US*) грузово́е тра́нспортное аге́нтство.
truculent ['trʌkjulənt] *adj* (*person*) свире́пый (свире́п).
trudge [trʌdʒ] *vi* (*also*: **~ along**) плести́сь* (*impf*), тащи́ться (*impf*).
true [tru:] *adj* (*real, genuine*) настоя́щий*, и́стинный; (*accurate*: *likeness*) то́чный; (*faithful*: *friend*) настоя́щий*; (*wall*) прямо́й; (*beam, wheel*) центри́рованный; **to come ~** сбыва́ться (сбы́ться* *perf*); **~ to life** жи́зненный.
truffle ['trʌfl] *n* трю́фель *m*.
truly ['tru:lɪ] *adv* (*really*) по-настоя́щему; (*truthfully*) и́скренне; **yours ~** (*in letter*) и́скренне Ваш.
trump [trʌmp] *n* (*also*: **~ card**: *also fig*) ко́зырь *m*; **to turn up ~s** (*fig*) подава́ть* (пода́ть* *perf*) ру́ку по́мощи.
trumped-up [trʌmpt'ʌp] *adj* (*pej*) сфабрико́ванный.
trumpet ['trʌmpɪt] *n* труба́.
truncated [trʌŋ'keɪtɪd] *adj* (*object*) обре́занный; (*message*) сокращённый.
truncheon ['trʌntʃən] *n* (*BRIT*) дуби́нка*.
trundle ['trʌndl] *vt* (*push slowly*: *trolley etc*) кати́ть* (*impf*) ◆ *vi*: **to ~ along** (*person*) брести́* (*impf*); (*vehicle*) кати́ться* (*impf*).
trunk [trʌŋk] *n* (*of tree*) ствол*; (*of person*) ту́ловище; (*of elephant*) хо́бот; (*case*)

* marks translations which have irregular inflections. The Russian-English side of the dictionary gives inflectional information.

дорóжный сундýк; (*US*: *AUT*) багáжник; **~s** *npl* (*also*: **swimming ~s**) плáвки* *pl*.
trunk call *n* (*BRIT*: *TEL*) междугорóдные переговóры *mpl*, междугорóдный звонóк*.
trunk road *n* (*BRIT*) магистрáль *f*.
truss [trʌs] *n* (*MED*) грыжевóй бандáж
▸ **truss (up)** *vt* (*CULIN*) перетя́гивать (перетянýть* *perf*) бечёвкой; (*person*) свя́зывать (связáть* *perf*).
trust [trʌst] *n* (*faith*) довéрие; (*responsibility*) долг*; (*LAW*) *управлéние имýществом по довéренности*; (*COMM*) трест ◆ *vt* (*rely on, have faith in*) доверя́ть *(impf)* +*dat*; (*hope*): **to ~ (that)** полагáть *(impf)*(, что); (*entrust*): **to ~ sth to sb** доверя́ть (довéрить *perf*) что-н комý-н; **to take sth on ~** принимáть (приня́ть* *perf*) что-н на вéру; **in ~** (*LAW*) управля́емый по довéренности.
trust company *n* (*COMM*) трест.
trusted [ˈtrʌstɪd] *adj* (*friend, servant*) прéданный.
trustee [trʌsˈtiː] *n* (*also LAW*) попечи́тель *m*.
trustful [ˈtrʌstful] *adj* (*person, nature, smile*) довéрчивый (довéрчив).
trust fund *n* (*COMM*) фонд трéста.
trusting [ˈtrʌstɪŋ] *adj* (*person, nature*) довéрчивый (довéрчив).
trustworthy [ˈtrʌstwəːðɪ] *adj* (*person, report*) надёжный, заслýживающий довéрия.
trusty [ˈtrʌstɪ] *adj* испы́танный.
truth [truːθ] (*pl* **~s**) *n* прáвда; (*universal principle*) и́стина.
truthful [ˈtruːθful] *adj* правди́вый (правди́в).
truthfully [ˈtruːθfəlɪ] *adv* (*answer*) правди́во.
truthfulness [ˈtruːθfəlnɪs] *n* правди́вость *f*.
try [traɪ] *n* (*attempt*) попы́тка*; (*RUGBY*) прохóд с мячóм ◆ *vt* (*test*) прóбовать (попрóбовать *perf*); (*LAW*: *person*) суди́ть* *(impf)*; (*strain*: *patience*) испы́тывать *(impf)*; (*attempt*): **to ~ to do** старáться *(impf) or* пытáться *(impf)* +*infin* ◆ *vi* (*make effort, attempt*) старáться *(impf)*, пытáться *(impf)*; **to have a ~** прóбовать (попрóбовать *perf*); **I tried a different key** я пытáлся откры́ть други́м ключóм; **to ~ one's (very) best** *or* **one's (very) hardest** старáться (постарáться *perf*) изó всех сил
▸ **try on** *vt* (*dress etc*) мéрить (помéрить *perf*), примеря́ть (примéрить *perf*); **to ~ it on** (*fig*) вести́* *(impf)* себя́ нáгло
▸ **try out** *vt* прóбовать (попрóбовать *perf*).
trying [ˈtraɪɪŋ] *adj* (*person, experience*) утоми́тельный* (утоми́телен).
tsar [zɑːʳ] *n* царь* *m*.
T-shirt [ˈtiːʃəːt] *n* футбóлка*.
T-square [ˈtiːskwɛəʳ] *n* (*TECH*) рейсши́на.
TT *adj abbr* (*BRIT*: *inf*) = **teetotal** ◆ *abbr* (*US*: *POST*) = *Trust Territory*; = *telegraphic transfer* телегрáфный дéнежный перевóд.
tub [tʌb] *n* (*container*) бóчка*; (*bath*) вáнна.
tuba [ˈtjuːbə] *n* тýба.
tubby [ˈtʌbɪ] *adj* упи́танный.
tube [tjuːb] *n* (*pipe*) трýбка*; (*container*) тю́бик; (*BRIT*: *underground*) метрó *nt ind*; (*for tyre*) кáмера; (*inf*: *television*): **the ~** тéлик.
tubeless [ˈtjuːblɪs] *adj* бескáмерный.
tuber [ˈtjuːbəʳ] *n* клýбень *m*.
tuberculosis [tjubəːkjuˈləusɪs] *n* туберкулёз.
tube station *n* (*BRIT*) стáнция *f* метрó.
tubing [ˈtjuːbɪŋ] *n* шланг трýбки; **a piece of ~** трýбка*.
tubular [ˈtjuːbjuləʳ] *adj* (*furniture, metal*) трýбчатый.
TUC *n abbr* (*BRIT*: = *Trades Union Congress*) Конгрéсс (британских) тред-юниóнов.
tuck [tʌk] *vt* (*put*) подбирáть (подобрáть* *perf*) ◆ *n* (*SEWING*) вы́кладка
▸ **tuck away** *vt* (*money*) припря́тывать (припря́тать* *perf*); (*building*): **to be ~ed away** приткнýться *(perf)*
▸ **tuck in** *vt* (*clothing*) заправля́ть (запрáвить* *perf*); (*child*) укрывáть (укры́ть* *perf*) ◆ *vi* (*eat*) уминáть (умя́ть* *perf*)
▸ **tuck up** *vt* (*invalid, child*) укрывáть (укры́ть* *perf*).
tuck shop *n* буфéт.
Tue(s). *abbr* = **Tuesday**.
Tuesday [ˈtjuːzdɪ] *n* втóрник; **it is ~ 23rd March** (сегóдня) втóрник 23-его мáрта; **on ~** во втóрник; **on ~s** по втóрникам; **every ~** кáждый втóрник; **every other ~** кáждый вторóй втóрник; **last/next ~** в прóшлый/слéдующий втóрник; **the following ~** в слéдующий втóрник; **~'s newspaper** газéта за втóрник; **a week/fortnight on ~** во втóрник чéрез недéлю/чéрез две недéли; **the ~ before last** позапрóшлый втóрник; **the ~ after next** во втóрник чéрез недéлю; **~ morning/lunchtime/afternoon/evening** во втóрник ýтром/в обéд/днём/вéчером; **we'll spend ~ night in Rome** во втóрник мы проведём ночь в Ри́ме.
tuft [tʌft] *n* (*of hair*) пучóк*.
tug [tʌg] *n* (*ship*) букси́р ◆ *vt* тянýть* *(impf)*.
tug of war *n* перетя́гивание канáта; (*fig*) тя́жба.
tuition [tjuːˈɪʃən] *n* (*BRIT*) обучéние; (: *private tuition*) чáстные урóки *mpl*, домáшнее обучéние; (*US*: *school fees*) плáта за обучéние.
tulip [ˈtjuːlɪp] *n* тюльпáн.
tumble [ˈtʌmbl] *n* (*fall*) падéние ◆ *vi* (*fall*: *person*) пáдать (упáсть* *perf*); (: *water*) журчáть *(impf)*; (*somersault*) скáтываться (скати́ться* *perf*); **to ~ to sth** (*inf*) набрести́* *(perf)* на что-н.
tumbledown [ˈtʌmbldaun] *adj* (*building*) полуразрýшенный.
tumble dryer *n* (*BRIT*) суши́лка* для белья́.
tumbler [ˈtʌmbləʳ] *n* бокáл.
tummy [ˈtʌmɪ] *n* (*inf*) пýзо *nt no pl*.
tummy tuck *n пласти́ческая оперáция по уши́ванию животá.*

tumour ['tju:mə^r] (*US* **tumor**) *n* (*MED*) о́пухоль *f*.
tumult ['tju:mʌlt] *n* шум, сумато́ха.
tumultuous [tju:'mʌltjuəs] *adj* бу́рный.
tuna ['tju:nə] *n inv* (*also:* **~ fish**) туне́ц*.
tune [tju:n] *n* (*melody*) моти́в ◆ *vt* (*MUS, RADIO, TV*) настра́ивать (настро́ить *perf*); (*AUT*) нала́живать (нала́дить* *perf*); **the guitar is in/out of ~** гита́ра настро́ена/расстро́ена; **to sing in ~** петь* (*impf*) чи́сто; **to sing out of ~** фальши́вить* (*impf*); **to be in/out of ~ with** (*fig*) быть* (*impf*) в ладу́/не в ладу́ с *+instr*; **she was robbed to the ~ of £10,000** (*fig*) её огра́били на це́лых £10 000
▸ **tune in** *vi* (*RADIO, TV*): **to ~ in (to)** настра́иваться (настро́иться *perf*) (на *+acc*)
▸ **tune up** *vi* (*musician*) настра́ивать (настро́ить *perf*) инструме́нт; (*orchestra*) настра́ивать (настро́ить *perf*) инструме́нты.
tuneful ['tju:nful] *adj* (*music*) мелоди́чный* (мелоди́чен).
tuner ['tju:nə^r] *n* (*radio set*) блок настро́йки; **piano ~** настро́йщик фортепья́но.
tuner amplifier *n* резона́нсный усили́тель *m*.
tungsten ['tʌŋstn] *n* вольфра́м.
tunic ['tju:nɪk] *n* ту́ника.
tuning fork ['tju:nɪŋ-] *n* камерто́н.
Tunis ['tju:nɪs] *n* Туни́с.
Tunisia [tju:'nɪzɪə] *n* Туни́с.
Tunisian [tju:'nɪzɪən] *adj* Туни́сский* ◆ *n* туни́сец*(-ска*).
tunnel ['tʌnl] *n* (*passage*) тунне́ль *m*; (*in mine*) што́льня ◆ *vi* прокла́дывать (проложи́ть* *perf*) тунне́ль.
tunnel vision *n* у́зость *f* зре́ния; (*fig*) тру́бочное зре́ние.
tunny ['tʌnɪ] *n* туне́ц*.
turban ['tə:bən] *n* чалма́, тюрба́н.
turbid ['tə:bɪd] *adj* (*water*) му́тный* (му́тен); (*air*) пы́льный* (пы́лен).
turbine ['tə:baɪn] *n* (*TECH*) турби́на.
turbo ['tə:bəu] *n* турби́на.
turbojet [tə:bəu'dʒɛt] *n* (*AVIAT*) турбо-реакти́вный самолёт.
turboprop [tə:bəu'prɔp] *n* (*engine*) турбо-винтово́й мото́р.
turbot ['tə:bət] *n inv* белоко́рый па́лтус.
turbulence ['tə:bjuləns] *n* встре́чные пото́ки *mpl* во́здуха.
turbulent ['tə:bjulənt] *adj* (*also fig*) бу́рный.
tureen [tə'ri:n] *n* (*for soup*) су́пница; (*for vegetables*) глубо́кое блю́до с кры́шкой.
turf [tə:f] *n* (*grass*) дёрн; (*clod*) торф ◆ *vt* (*area*) покрыва́ть (покры́ть* *perf*) дёрном; **the T~** (*course*) скакова́я доро́жка; (*horse-racing*) ска́чки *mpl*
▸ **turf out** *vt* (*inf*: *person*) выставля́ть (вы́ставить* *perf*).
turf accountant *n* (*BRIT*) букме́кер.
turgid ['tə:dʒɪd] *adj* (*speech*) напы́щенный.
Turin ['tjuə'rɪn] *n* Тури́н.
Turk [tə:k] *n* ту́рок* (турча́нка*).
Turkey ['tə:kɪ] *n* Ту́рция.
turkey ['tə:kɪ] *n* инде́йка.
Turkish ['tə:kɪʃ] *adj* туре́цкий* ◆ *n* (*LING*) туре́цкий* язы́к*.
Turkish bath *n* туре́цкие ба́ни *fpl*.
Turkish delight *n* раха́т-луку́м.
Turkmen ['tə:kmɛn] *n,adj* туркме́нский*; (*person*) туркме́н(ка*); (*LING*) туркме́нский* язы́к*.
Turkmenia [tə:k'mi:nɪə] *n* Туркме́ния.
turmeric ['tə:mərɪk] *n* (*CULIN*) курку́ма.
turmoil ['tə:mɔɪl] *n* смяте́ние; **in ~** в смяте́нии.
turn [tə:n] *n* поворо́т; (*performance*) но́мер*; (*chance*) о́чередь *f*; (*inf*: *MED*) вы́вих ◆ *vt* повора́чивать (поверну́ть *perf*); (*collar*) отвора́чивать (отверну́ть *perf*); (*change*: *wood, metal*) обта́чивать (обточи́ть* *perf*) ◆ *vi* (*object*) повора́чиваться (поверну́ться *perf*); (*person*: *look back*) обора́чиваться (оберну́ться *perf*); (*reverse direction*: *in car*) развора́чиваться (разверну́ться *perf*); (: *wind*) переменя́ться (перемени́ться *perf*); (*milk*) скиса́ть (ски́снуть *perf*); (*change*) изменя́ться (измени́ться *perf*); (*become*): **he's ~ed forty** ему́ испо́лнилось со́рок; **a good/bad ~** до́брая/плоха́я услу́га; **it gave me quite a ~** э́то меня́ си́льно испуга́ло; **"no left ~"** (*AUT*) "нет ле́вого поворо́та"; **it's your ~** твоя́ о́чередь; **in ~** по о́череди; **to take ~s at sth** де́лать (*impf*) что-н по о́череди; **at the ~ of the century** на рубеже́ ве́ка; **at the ~ of the year** под коне́ц го́да; **to take a ~ for the worse** (*situations, events*) принима́ть (приня́ть* *perf*) дурно́й оборо́т; **his health** *or* **he has taken a ~ for the worse** ему́ сде́лалось ху́же; **to ~ sth into sth** (*change*) превраща́ть (преврати́ть* *perf*) что-н в что-н; **to ~ nasty** озлобля́ться (озлоби́ться* *perf*)
▸ **turn about** *vi* повора́чиваться (поверну́ться *perf*)
▸ **turn away** *vi* отвора́чиваться (отверну́ться *perf*) ◆ *vt* (*business, applicant*) отклоня́ть (отклони́ть* *perf*)
▸ **turn back** *vi* повора́чивать (поверну́ть *perf*) наза́д ◆ *vt* (*person*) верну́ть (*perf*); (*vehicle*) развора́чивать (разверну́ть *perf*); (*clock*) переводи́ть* (перевести́* *perf*) наза́д; **to ~ back the clock** (*fig*) поверну́ть (*perf*) вре́мя вспять
▸ **turn down** *vt* (*request*) отклоня́ть (отклони́ть* *perf*); (*heating*) уменьша́ть (уменьши́ть *perf*); (*bedclothes*) отвора́чивать (отверну́ть *perf*)
▸ **turn in** *vi* (*inf*: *go to bed*) идти́* (пойти́* *perf*) на бокову́ю ◆ *vt* (*fold*) свора́чивать

* marks translations which have irregular inflections. The Russian–English side of the dictionary gives inflectional information.

(сверну́ть *perf*)
▸ **turn off** *vi* (*from road*) сворáчивать (сверну́ть *perf*) ◆ *vt* выключáть (вы́ключить *perf*)
▸ **turn on** *vt* включáть (включи́ть *perf*)
▸ **turn out** *vt* (*light, gas*) выключáть (вы́ключить *perf*); (*produce*) выпускáть (вы́пустить* *perf*) ◆ *vi* (*troops, doctor, voters*) прибывáть (прибы́ть* *perf*); **to ~ out to be** (*prove to be*) окáзываться (оказáться* *perf*) +*instr*
▸ **turn over** *vi* (*person*) переворáчиваться (переверну́ться *perf*) ◆ *vt* (*object, page*) переворáчивать (переверну́ть *perf*); (*funds, production etc*): **to ~ over to** передавáть* (передáть* *perf*) +*dat*
▸ **turn round** *vi* (*person, vehicle*) разворáчиваться (разверну́ться *perf*); (*rotate*) поворáчиваться (*impf*)
▸ **turn up** *vi* (*person*) объявля́ться (объяви́ться* *perf*); (*lost object*) находи́ться* (найти́сь* *perf*) ◆ *vt* (*collar*) поднимáть (подня́ть* *perf*); (*radio*) дéлать (сдéлать *perf*) грóмче; (*heater*) дéлать (сдéлать *perf*) вы́ше.
turnabout ['tə:nəbaut] *n* (*fig*) поворóт на 180 грáдусов.
turnaround ['tə:nəraund] *n* (*fig*) = **turnabout**.
turncoat ['tə:nkəut] *n* ренегáт, отсту́пник.
turned-up ['tə:ndʌp] *adj* (*nose*) вздёрнутый, курнóсый.
turning ['tə:nɪŋ] *n* (*in road*) поворóт; **the first ~ on the right** пéрвый поворóт напрáво.
turning circle *n* (*BRIT: AUT*) окру́жность *f* поворóта.
turning point *n* (*fig*) поворóтный пункт, перелóмный момéнт.
turning radius *n* (*US*) = **turning circle**.
turnip ['tə:nɪp] *n* (*BOT, CULIN*) рéпа.
turnout ['tə:naut] *n* (*of voters etc*) числó.
turnover ['tə:nəuvə^r] *n* (*COMM*) оборóт; (: *of staff*) теку́честь *f*; (*CULIN*): **apple ~** я́блочная слóйка; **there is a rapid ~ in staff** большáя теку́честь кáдров.
turnpike ['tə:npaɪk] *n* (*US*) магистрáль *f*, шóссе *nt ind*.
turnstile ['tə:nstaɪl] *n* турникéт.
turntable ['tə:nteɪbl] *n* (*on record player*) верту́шка*, проигрыватель *m*.
turn-up ['tə:nʌp] *n* (*BRIT: on trousers*) манжéта, отворóт; **that's a ~ for the books!** вот неожи́данность!
turpentine ['tə:pəntaɪn] *n* (*also:* **turps**) скипидáр.
turquoise ['tə:kwɔɪz] *n* (*stone*) бирюзá ◆ *adj* (*colour*) бирюзóвый.
turret ['tʌrɪt] *n* бáшенка*.
turtle ['tə:tl] *n* черепáха.
turtleneck (sweater) ['tə:tlnɛk(-)] *n* водолáзка*.
Tuscany ['tʌskənɪ] *n* Тоскáнь *f*.
tusk [tʌsk] *n* (*of elephant*) би́вень* *m*; (*of boar*) клык*.
tussle ['tʌsl] *n* (*fight, scuffle*) схвáтка*.
tutor ['tju:tə^r] *n* (*SCOL*) преподавáтель(ница) *m(f)*; (*private tutor*) репети́тор.
tutorial [tju:'tɔ:rɪəl] *n* (*SCOL*) семинáр.
tuxedo [tʌk'si:dəu] *n* (*US*) смóкинг.
TV [ti:'vi:] *n abbr* (= **television**) ТВ= *телеви́дение*; **~ dinner** *пищевóй полуфабрикáт, гóдный к потреблéнию пóсле разогрéва.*
twaddle ['twɔdl] *n* (*inf*) чепухá.
twang [twæŋ] *n* (*of instrument*) протя́жный звук; (*of voice*) гну́сность *f* ◆ *vi* протя́жно звенéть (зазвенéть *perf*) ◆ *vt* (*guitar*) бренчáть* (*impf*) на +*prp*.
tweak [twi:k] *vt* дёргать (дёрнуть *perf*) за +*acc*.
tweed [twi:d] *n* твид ◆ *adj* (*jacket, skirt*) тви́довый.
tweezers ['twi:zəz] *npl* пинцéт *msg*.
twelfth [twɛlfθ] *adj* двенáдцатый; *see also* **fifth**.
Twelfth Night *n* Двенáдцатая ночь *f*.
twelve [twɛlv] *n* двенáдцать*; **at ~ (o'clock)** (*midday*) в двенáдцать (дня); (*midnight*) в двенáдцать (нóчи); *see also* **five**.
twentieth ['twɛntɪɪθ] *adj* двадцáтый; *see also* **fifth**.
twenty ['twɛntɪ] *n* двáдцать*; *see also* **fifty**.
twerp [twə:p] *n* (*inf*) крети́н.
twice [twaɪs] *adv* двáжды; **~ as much** вдвóе бóльше; **~ a week** два рáза в недéлю; **she is ~ your age** онá вдвóе *or* в два рáза стáрше Вас.
twiddle ['twɪdl] *vt* теребúть* (*impf*) ◆ *vi*: **to ~ with sth** теребúть* (*impf*) что-н; **to ~ one's thumbs** (*fig*) бить* (*impf*) баклу́ши.
twig [twɪg] *n* вéтка* ◆ *vi* (*inf*) смекну́ть (*perf*).
twilight ['twaɪlaɪt] *n* су́мерки *mpl*; (*morning*) (предрассвéтные) су́мерки; **in the ~** в су́мерках.
twill [twɪl] *n* (*cloth*) твил, сáржа.
twin [twɪn] *adj* (*towers*) пáрный ◆ *n* близнéц*, двóйня*; (*room in hotel etc*) двойнóй нóмер* ◆ *vt* (*towns etc*) дéлать (сдéлать *perf*) побрати́мами; **~ sister** сестрá-близнéц*; **~ brother** брат-близнéц*.
twin-bedded room ['twɪn'bɛdɪd-] *n нóмер с двумя́ односпáльными кровáтями.*
twin beds *npl* две односпáльные кровáти *fpl*.
twin-carburettor ['twɪnkɑ:bju'rɛtə^r] *adj* двухкарбюрáторный.
twine [twaɪn] *n* бечёвка ◆ *vi* (*plant*) ви́ться* (*impf*).
twin-engined [twɪn'ɛndʒɪnd] *adj* (*aircraft*) с двумя́ двигателями.
twinge [twɪndʒ] *n* (*of pain*) при́ступ; (*of conscience, regret*) укóл.
twinkle ['twɪŋkl] *vi* (*star, light*) мерцáть (*impf*); (*eyes*) мигáть (*impf*), подми́гивать (*impf*) ◆ *n* мерцáние.
twin town *n* гóрод-побрати́м.
twirl [twə:l] *vt* вертéть* (*impf*) ◆ *vi* крути́ться*

(impf) ◆ *n* поворо́т.

twist [twɪst] *n* (*action*) закру́чивание; (*in road, coil, flex*) изги́б; (*in story*) поворо́т ◆ *vt* (*turn*) изгиба́ть (изогну́ть *perf*); (*injure: ankle etc*) выви́хивать (вы́вихнуть *perf*); (*weave*) сплета́ть (сплести́* *perf*); (*fig: meaning, words*) искажа́ть (искази́ть* *perf*) ◆ *vi* (*road, river*) извива́ться *(impf)*.

twisted ['twɪstɪd] *adj* (*wire, rope*) скру́ченный; (*ankle, wrist*) вы́вихнутый; (*fig: logic, mind*) извращённый.

twit [twɪt] *n* (*inf*) недоу́мок*.

twitch [twɪtʃ] *n* (*pull*) рыво́к*; (*nervous*) подёргивание ◆ *vi* (*muscle, body*) подёргиваться *(impf)*.

two [tu:] *n* два* *m/nt* (*f* две*); **~ by ~, in ~s** па́рами; **to put ~ and ~ together** (*fig*) сложи́ть *(perf)* два и два; *see also* **five**.

two-bit [tu:'bɪt] *adj* (*esp US: inf*) расхо́жий.

two-door [tu:'dɔ:ʳ] *adj* (*AUT*) двухдве́рный.

two-faced [tu:'feɪst] *adj* (*pej: person*) двули́чный* (двули́чен).

twofold ['tu:fəuld] *adj* (*increase*) двойно́й; (*reply*) дво́йственный ◆ *adv*: **to increase ~** вдвое́.

two-piece (suit) ['tu:pi:s-] *n* (костю́м) дво́йка.

two-piece swimsuit *n* разде́льный купа́льник.

two-ply ['tu:plaɪ] *adj* (*wool*) двойно́й; (*tissues*) двухсло́йный* (двухсло́ен).

two-seater car [tu:'si:tə-] *n* двухме́стный автомоби́ль *m*.

twosome ['tu:səm] *n* (*people*) па́ра.

two-stroke ['tu:strəuk] *n* (*also:* **~ engine**) двухта́ктный дви́гатель *m* ◆ *adj* двухта́ктный.

two-tone ['tu:'təun] *adj* (*in colour*) двухцве́тный.

two-way ['tu:weɪ] *adj*: **~ traffic** двусторо́ннее движе́ние; **~ radio** приёмно-переда́ющая радиоста́нция.

TX *abbr* (*US: POST*) = *Texas*.

tycoon [taɪ'ku:n] *n*: **(business) ~** магна́т.

type [taɪp] *n* (*category, model, example*) тип; (*TYP*) шрифт ◆ *vt* (*letter etc*) печа́тать (напеча́тать *perf*); **what ~ do you want?** како́й вид Вы бы хоте́ли?; **in bold ~** жи́рным шри́фтом; **in italic ~** курси́вом шри́фтом.

typecast ['taɪpkɑ:st] *adj* (*actor*) одноти́пных роле́й.

typeface ['taɪpfeɪs] *n* шрифт.

typescript ['taɪpskrɪpt] *n* машинопи́сный текст.

typeset ['taɪpsɛt] *vt* набира́ть (набра́ть* *perf*).

typesetter ['taɪpsɛtəʳ] *n* набо́рщик(-ица).

typewriter ['taɪpraɪtəʳ] *n* пи́шущая маши́нка*.

typewritten ['taɪprɪtn] *adj* машинопи́сный, напеча́танный (напеча́тан) (на маши́нке).

typhoid ['taɪfɔɪd] *n* брюшно́й тиф.

typhoon [taɪ'fu:n] *n* тайфу́н.

typhus ['taɪfəs] *n* сыпно́й тиф.

typical ['tɪpɪkl] *adj* (*behaviour, weather etc*): **~ (of)** типи́чный* (типи́чен) (для +*gen*); **that's ~!** (*pej*) вот так всегда́!

typify ['tɪpɪfaɪ] *vt* явля́ться (яви́ться* *perf*) типи́чным приме́ром +*gen*.

typing ['taɪpɪŋ] *n* маши́нопись *f*.

typing error *n* опеча́тка*.

typing pool *n* (*BRIT*) машинопи́сное бюро́ *nt ind*.

typist ['taɪpɪst] *n* машини́стка*.

typo ['taɪpəu] *n abbr* (*inf:* = *typographical error*) типогра́фская опеча́тка*.

typography [tɪ'pɔgrəfɪ] *n* полигра́фия.

tyranny ['tɪrənɪ] *n* тирани́я, деспоти́зм.

tyrant ['taɪərnt] *n* тира́н, де́спот.

tyre ['taɪəʳ] (*US* **tire**) *n* ши́на.

tyre pressure *n* давле́ние в ши́не.

Tyrol [tɪ'rəul] *n* Тиро́ль *m*.

Tyrolean [tɪrə'li:ən] *adj* тиро́льский ◆ *n* тиро́лец*.

Tyrolese [tɪrə'li:z] = **Tyrolean**.

Tyrrhenian Sea [tɪ'ri:nɪən-] *n*: **the ~ ~** Тирре́нское мо́ре.

tzar [zɑ:ʳ] *n* = **tsar**.

* marks translations which have irregular inflections. The Russian-English side of the dictionary gives inflectional information.

~ U, u ~

U, u [juː] *n* (*letter*) *21-ая бу́ква англи́йского алфави́та.*
U *n abbr* (*BRIT: CINEMA:* = *universal*) *фильм, приго́дный для пока́за всем возрастны́м гру́ппам.*
UAW *n abbr* (*US*) = *United Automobile Workers.*
UB40 *n abbr* (*BRIT:* = *unemployment benefit form 40*) *бланк, заполня́емый при получе́нии посо́бия по безрабо́тице.*
U-bend [ˈjuːbɛnd] *n* (*in pipe*) двойно́й изги́б.
ubiquitous [juːˈbɪkwɪtəs] *adj* вездесу́щий* (вездесу́щ).
UCCA [ˈʌkə] *n abbr* (*BRIT:* = *Universities Central Council on Admissions*) *организа́ция, координи́рующая приём в университе́ты.*
UDA *n abbr* (*BRIT:* = *Ulster Defence Association*) *военизи́рованная организа́ция, боро́щаяся за сохране́ние Се́верой Ирла́ндии как ча́сти Великобрита́нии.*
UDC *n abbr* (*BRIT*) = *Urban District Council.*
udder [ˈʌdəʳ] *n* вы́мя* *nt.*
UDI *n abbr* (*BRIT: POL:* = *unilateral declaration of independence*) односторо́ннее провозглаше́ние незави́симости.
UDR *n abbr* (*BRIT:* = *Ulster Defence Regiment*) *ча́сти брита́нской а́рмии, размещённые в Се́верной Ирла́ндии.*
UEFA [juːˈeɪfə] *n abbr* (= *Union of European Football Associations*) УЕФА́.
UFO [ˈjuːfəu] *n abbr* (= *unidentified flying object*) НЛО= *неопо́знанный лета́ющий объе́кт.*
Uganda [juːˈgændə] *n* Уга́нда.
Ugandan [juːˈgændən] *adj* уга́ндский ◆ *n* уга́ндец*(-дка*).
UGC *n abbr* (*BRIT:* = *University Grants Committee*) *комите́т, координи́рующий финанси́рование университе́тов.*
ugh [əːh] *excl* фу.
ugliness [ˈʌglɪnɪs] *n* уро́дство
ugly [ˈʌglɪ] *adj* (*person, dress etc*) уро́дливый (уро́длив), безобра́зный* (безобра́зен); (*dangerous: situation*) опа́сный* (опа́сен).
UHF *abbr* (= *ultra-high frequency*) УВЧ= *ультравысо́кая частота́.*
UHT *abbr* = *ultra heat treated* ◆ *adj abbr*: **~ milk** *молоко́, проше́дшее обрабо́тку сверхвысо́кой температу́рой.*
UK *n abbr* = **United Kingdom**.
Ukraine [juːˈkreɪn] *n* Украйна.
Ukrainian [juːˈkreɪnɪən] *adj* украи́нский* ◆ *n* украи́нец*(-нка); (*LING*) украи́нский* язы́к*.
Ulan Bator *n* [uˈlɑːnˈbɑːtɔːʳ] Ула́н-Ба́тор.
ulcer [ˈʌlsəʳ] *n* язва.
Ulster [ˈʌlstəʳ] *n* О́льстер.
ulterior [ʌlˈtɪərɪəʳ] *adj*: **~ motive** скры́тый моти́в.
ultimata [ʌltɪˈmeɪtə] *npl of* **ultimatum**.
ultimate [ˈʌltɪmət] *adj* (*final*) оконча́тельный*, коне́чный; (*greatest*) преде́льный* ◆ *n*: **the ~ in luxury** преде́л ро́скоши.
ultimately [ˈʌltɪmətlɪ] *adv* в конце́ концо́в.
ultimatum [ʌltɪˈmeɪtəm] (*pl* **~s** *or* **ultimata**) *n* ультима́тум.
ultrasonic [ʌltrəˈsɔnɪk] *adj* (*sound*) сверхзвуково́й, ультразвуково́й.
ultrasound [ˈʌltrəsaund] *n* ультразву́к.
ultraviolet [ˈʌltrəˈvaɪəlɪt] *adj* (*light etc*) ультрафиоле́товый.
umbilical cord [ʌmˈbɪlɪkl-] *n* пупови́на.
umbrage [ˈʌmbrɪdʒ] *n*: **to take ~** обижа́ться (оби́деться* *perf*).
umbrella [ʌmˈbrɛlə] *n* зо́нтик, зонт*; (*fig*): **under the ~ of** под защи́той *+gen.*
umlaut [ˈumlaut] *n* у́мляут.
umpire [ˈʌmpaɪəʳ] *n* (*TENNIS, CRICKET*) судья́* *m*, рефери́ *m ind* ◆ *vt* (*game*) суди́ть* (*impf*).
umpteen [ʌmpˈtiːn] *adj* (*inf*) бесчи́сленный; **~ stories** бесконе́чное коли́чество исто́рии.
umpteenth [ʌmpˈtiːnθ] *adj* (*inf*): **for the ~ time** в э́нный *or* со́тый раз.
UMW *n abbr* = *United Mineworkers of America.*
UN *n abbr* = **United Nations**.
unabashed [ʌnəˈbæʃt] *adj*: **she seemed ~** она́ каза́лось не возмути́мой.
unabated [ʌnəˈbeɪtɪd] *adj* (*enthusiasm, excitement*) неосла́бный* (неосла́бен) ◆ *adv*: **to continue ~** продолжа́ться (продо́лжиться *perf*) с той же си́лой.
unable [ʌnˈeɪbl] *adj* неспосо́бный*; **he is ~ to pay** он не спосо́бен заплати́ть.
unabridged [ʌnəˈbrɪdʒd] *adj* (*novel etc*) несокращённый
unacceptable [ʌnəkˈsɛptəbl] *adj* неприе́млемый (неприе́млем).
unaccompanied [ʌnəˈkʌmpənɪd] *adj* (*child, luggage*) не сопровожда́емый; (*song*) без аккомпанеме́нта.
unaccountably [ʌnəˈkauntəblɪ] *adv* необъясн-

ймо.
unaccounted [ʌnəˈkauntɪd] *adj*: **several people are still ~ for** нéскольких людéй недосчитáлись.
unaccustomed [ʌnəˈkʌstəmd] *adj*: **he is ~ to ...** он не привы́чен к *+dat* ....
unacquainted [ʌnəˈkweɪntɪd] *adj*: **he is ~ with these ideas** он не знакóм с э́тими идéями.
unadulterated [ʌnəˈdʌltəreɪtɪd] *adj* настоя́щий*; (*wine*) чи́стый*.
unaffected [ʌnəˈfɛktɪd] *adj* (*person, behaviour*) естéственный* (естéствен); **~ by** (*emotionally*) безучáстный (безучáстен) к *+dat*.
unafraid [ʌnəˈfreɪd] *adj* незапу́ганный.
unaided [ʌnˈeɪdɪd] *adv* без пóмощи.
unanimity [juːnəˈnɪmɪtɪ] *n* единоду́шие, единоглáсие.
unanimous [juːˈnænɪməs] *adj* единоду́шный* (единоду́шен), единоглáсный* (единоглáсен).
unanimously [juːˈnænɪməslɪ] *adv* единоду́шно, единоглáсно.
unanswered [ʌnˈɑːnsəd] *adj* остáвшийся без отвéта.
unappetizing [ʌnˈæpɪtaɪzɪŋ] *adj* (*food etc*) неаппети́тный* (неаппети́тен).
unappreciative [ʌnəˈpriːʃɪətɪv] *adj* неблаго-дáрный* (неблагодáрен).
unarmed [ʌnˈɑːmd] *adj* безору́жный* (безору́жен); (*combat*) без ору́жия.
unashamed [ʌnəˈʃeɪmd] *adj* бессты́дный* (бессты́ден).
unassisted [ʌnəˈsɪstɪd] *adj, adv* без посторóнней пóмощи.
unassuming [ʌnəˈsjuːmɪŋ] *adj* (*person, manner*) непритязáтельный* (непритязáтелен).
unattached [ʌnəˈtætʃt] *adj* (*person*) одинóкий* (одинóк); (*part etc*) неприкреплённый.
unattended [ʌnəˈtɛndɪd] *adj* остáвленный (остáвлен) без присмóтра.
unattractive [ʌnəˈtræktɪv] *adj* непривлек-áтельный* (непривлекáтелен).
unauthorized [ʌnˈɔːθəraɪzd] *adj* неразреш-ённый*.
unavailable [ʌnəˈveɪləbl] *adj* (*article, room etc*) недосту́пный* (недосту́пен); (*person*) недосягáемый (недосягáем).
unavoidable [ʌnəˈvɔɪdəbl] *adj* (*delay*) неизбéжный* (неизбéжен).
unavoidably [ʌnəˈvɔɪdəblɪ] *adv* (*delayed etc*) неизбéжно.
unaware [ʌnəˈwɛəʳ] *adj*: **to be ~ of** не подозревáть *(impf)* о *+prp*.
unawares [ʌnəˈwɛəz] *adv* врасплóх.
unbalanced [ʌnˈbælənst] *adj* (*report*) односторóнний*; (*mentally*) неуравновéшенный* (неуравновéшен).
unbearable [ʌnˈbɛərəbl] *adj* невыноси́мый (невыноси́м).
unbeatable [ʌnˈbiːtəbl] *adj* (*team*) непобеди́мый (непобеди́м); (*price, quality*) непревзойдённый* (непревзойдён).
unbeaten [ʌnˈbiːtn] *adj* (*person*) непобеди́мый (непобеди́м); (*record*) непревзойдённый* (непревзойдён).
unbecoming [ʌnbɪˈkʌmɪŋ] *adj* (*language, behaviour*) неподобáющий (неподобáющ); (*garment*) не иду́щий к лицу́; **that dress is ~ on you** Вам не идёт э́то плáтье.
unbeknown(st) [ʌnbɪˈnəun(st)] *adv*: **~ to me** без моегó вéдома.
unbelief [ʌnbɪˈliːf] *n* невéрие.
unbelievable [ʌnbɪˈliːvəbl] *adj* невероя́тный* (невероя́тен).
unbelievably [ʌnbɪˈliːvəblɪ] *adv* невероя́тно.
unbend [ʌnˈbɛnd] *irreg vi* (*relax*) расслабля́ться (расслáбиться* *perf*) ◆ *vt* (*wire*) выпрямля́ть (вы́прямить* *perf*).
unbending [ʌnˈbɛndɪŋ] *adj* непреклóнный* (непреклóнен).
unbias(s)ed [ʌnˈbaɪəst] *adj* (*report*) непредвзя́тый (непредвзя́т); (*person*) беспристрáстный* (беспристрáстен).
unblemished [ʌnˈblɛmɪʃt] *adj* незапя́тнанный (незапя́тнан).
unblock [ʌnˈblɔk] *vt* (*pipe*) прочищáть (прочи́стить* *perf*).
unborn [ʌnˈbɔːn] *adj* (ещё) не рождённый.
unbounded [ʌnˈbaundɪd] *adj* безграни́чный* (безграни́чен).
unbreakable [ʌnˈbreɪkəbl] *adj* небью́щийся.
unbridled [ʌnˈbraɪdld] *adj* необу́зданный* (необу́здан).
unbroken [ʌnˈbrəukən] *adj* (*seal*) цéлый* (цел); (*silence, series*) непрéрванный; (*window*) неразби́тый, цéлый* (цел); (*SPORT: record*) непоби́тый.
unbuckle [ʌnˈbʌkl] *vt* (*belt, shoe*) расстёгивать (расстегну́ть *perf*).
unburden [ʌnˈbəːdn] *vt*: **to ~ o.s. (to sb)** изливáть (изли́ть* *perf*) ду́шу (кому́-н).
unbusinesslike [ʌnˈbɪznɪslaɪk] *adj* неделовóй.
unbutton [ʌnˈbʌtn] *vt* расстёгивать (расстегну́ть *perf*).
uncalled-for [ʌnˈkɔːldfɔːʳ] *adj* неумéстный* (неумéстен).
uncanny [ʌnˈkænɪ] *adj* (*resemblance, knack*) необъясни́мый (необъясни́м); (*silence*) жу́ткий* (жу́ток).
unceasing [ʌnˈsiːsɪŋ] *adj* (*misery, flow etc*) беспреры́вный* (беспреры́вен); (*search*) неустáнный* (неустáнен).
unceremonious [ʌnsɛrɪˈməunɪəs] *adj* (*abrupt, rude*) бесцеремóнный* (бесцеремóнен).
uncertain [ʌnˈsəːtn] *adj* (*hesitant*)

неуве́ренный* (неуве́рен), нереши́тельный* (нереши́телен); (*unsure*): ~ **about** неуве́ренный* (неуве́рен) относи́тельно +*gen*; **in no ~ terms** без обинякóв.
uncertainty [ʌn'sə:tntɪ] *n* (*not knowing*) неопределённость *f*; (*often pl*: *doubt*) сомне́ние.
unchallenged [ʌn'tʃælɪndʒd] *adj* не вызыва́ющий* возраже́ний; **to go ~** не вызыва́ть (вы́звать* *perf*) возраже́ний.
unchanged [ʌn'tʃeɪndʒd] *adj* (*condition*) неизмени́вшийся; **my orders remain ~** мои́ прика́зы остаю́тся неизме́нными.
uncharitable [ʌn'tʃærɪtəbl] *adj* немилосе́рдный* (немилосе́рден).
uncharted [ʌn'tʃɑ:tɪd] *adj* (*land, sea*) не отме́ченный на ка́рте.
unchecked [ʌn'tʃɛkt] *adv* беспрепя́тственно.
uncivil [ʌn'sɪvɪl] *adj* гру́бый* (груб).
uncivilized [ʌn'sɪvɪlaɪzd] *adj* (*country, people*) нецивилизо́ванный (нецивилизо́ван); (*fig*: *behaviour etc*) ди́кий* (дик); **at an ~ hour** ни свет, ни заря́.
uncle ['ʌŋkl] *n* дя́дя* *m*.
unclear [ʌn'klɪə^r] *adj* нея́сный* (нея́сен); **I'm still ~ about what I'm supposed to do** мне всё ещё нея́сно, что мне на́до де́лать.
uncoil [ʌn'kɔɪl] *vt* разма́тывать (размота́ть *perf*) ◆ *vi* разма́тываться (размота́ться *perf*).
uncomfortable [ʌn'kʌmfətəbl] *adj* (*physically*) неудо́бный* (неудо́бен); (*uneasy*) неудо́бный* (неудо́бен), нело́вкий* (нело́вок); (*unpleasant*) трево́жный* (трево́жен).
uncomfortably [ʌn'kʌmfətəblɪ] *adv* (*sit*) неудо́бно; (*smile*) нело́вко; (*tall, shy*) до нело́вкого.
uncommitted [ʌnkə'mɪtɪd] *adj* нейтра́льный* (нейтра́лен).
uncommon [ʌn'kɔmən] *adj* (*rare, unusual*) необы́чный* (необы́чен).
uncommunicative [ʌnkə'mju:nɪkətɪv] *adj* необщи́тельный* (необщи́телен).
uncomplicated [ʌn'kɔmplɪkeɪtɪd] *adj* несло́жный* (несло́жен).
uncompromising [ʌn'kɔmprəmaɪzɪŋ] *adj* бескомпроми́ссный.
unconcerned [ʌnkən'sə:nd] *adj* (*person*) беззабо́тный* (беззабо́тен); **~ about** равноду́шный* (равноду́шен) к +*dat*.
unconditional [ʌnkən'dɪʃənl] *adj* (*acceptance, obedience*) безусло́вный* (безусло́вен); (*discharge, surrender*) безогово́рочный* (безогово́рочен).
uncongenial [ʌnkən'dʒi:nɪəl] *adj* (*surroundings*) чу́ждый (чужд), неприя́тный* (неприя́тен).
unconnected [ʌnkə'nɛktɪd] *adj* (*unrelated*): **~ (with)** несвя́занный (с +*instr*).
unconscious [ʌn'kɔnʃəs] *adj* без созна́ния; (*unaware*): **~ of** не сознаю́щий* +*gen* ◆ *n*: **the ~** подсозна́ние; **he was knocked ~** он упа́л без созна́ния.
unconsciously [ʌn'kɔnʃəslɪ] *adv* (*unawares*) подсозна́тельно.
unconsciousness [ʌn'kɔnʃəsnɪs] *n* бессозна́тельное состоя́ние.
unconstitutional ['ʌnkɔnstɪ'tju:ʃənl] *adj* неконституцио́нный* (неконституцио́нен).
uncontested [ʌnkən'tɛstɪd] *adj* (*champion*) неоспори́мый (неоспори́м); **~ election** вы́боры, на кото́рых баллоти́руется (лишь) оди́н кандида́т.
uncontrollable [ʌnkən'trəuləbl] *adj* (*child, animal*) неуправля́емый (неуправля́ем); (*temper*) неукроти́мый (неукроти́м); (*laughter*) неудержи́мый (неудержи́м).
uncontrolled [ʌnkən'trəuld] *adj* безу́держный* (безу́держен).
unconventional [ʌnkən'vɛnʃənl] *adj* нетрадицио́нный (нетрадицио́нен).
unconvinced [ʌnkən'vɪnst] *adj*: **to be** *or* **remain ~** остава́ться* (оста́ться* *perf*) неубеждённым(-ой).
unconvincing [ʌnkən'vɪnsɪŋ] *adj* неубеди́тельный* (неубеди́телен).
uncork [ʌn'kɔ:k] *vt* (*bottle*) отку́поривать (отку́порить *perf*).
uncorroborated [ʌnkə'rɔbəreɪtɪd] *adj* неподтверждённый.
uncouth [ʌn'ku:θ] *adj* неотёсанный* (неотёсан).
uncover [ʌn'kʌvə^r] *vt* открыва́ть (откры́ть* *perf*); (*plot, secret*) раскрыва́ть (раскры́ть* *perf*).
unctuous ['ʌŋktjuəs] *adj* еле́йный* (еле́ен).
undamaged [ʌn'dæmɪdʒd] *adj* (*goods*) неповреждённый; (*fig*: *reputation*) незапя́тнанный (незапя́тнан).
undaunted [ʌn'dɔ:ntɪd] *adj* (*person*) неустраши́мый (неустраши́м); **~, she struggled on** она́ неустраши́мо продолжа́ла свои́ стара́ния.
undecided [ʌndɪ'saɪdɪd] *adj* (*person*) нереши́тельный* (нереши́телен); (*question*) нерешённый.
undelivered [ʌndɪ'lɪvəd] *adj* (*goods, letters*) недоста́вленный; **if ~ return to sender** е́сли не доста́влено, верну́ть отправи́телю.
undeniable [ʌndɪ'naɪəbl] *adj* (*fact, evidence*) неоспори́мый (неоспори́м).
undeniably [ʌndɪ'naɪəblɪ] *adv* несомне́нно.
under ['ʌndə^r] *adv* (*go, fly etc*) вниз ◆ *prep* (*position*) под +*instr*; (*motion*) под +*acc*; (*less than*: *in price*) ни́же +*gen*; (*according to*: *law, agreement etc*) по +*dat*; (*during*: *sb's leadership*) при +*prp*; (*in age*): **children ~ 16** де́ти до 16-ти лет; **from ~ sth** из-под чего́-н; **~ there** там внизу́; **in ~ 2 hours** ме́ньше, чем за 2 часа́; **~ anaesthetic** под нарко́зом; **~ discussion** в проце́ссе обсужде́ния; **~ repair** в ремо́нте; **~ the circumstances** при сложи́вшихся обстоя́тельствах.

under... ['ʌndə^r] *prefix* недо....
underage [ʌndər'eɪdʒ] *adj* (*person*) несовершеннолéтний*; ~ **smoking/drinking** курéние/потреблéние алкогóля несовершеннолéтними.
underarm ['ʌndərɑ:m] *adv* (*bowl*) снѝзу ◆ *adj* (*deodorant*) для подмы́шек; ~ **throw** бросóк* снѝзу.
undercapitalized ['ʌndə'kæpɪtəlaɪzd] *adj* (*project, industry*) недостáточно капитализѝрованный.
undercarriage ['ʌndəkærɪdʒ] *n* (*BRIT*) шассѝ *nt ind*.
undercharge [ʌndə'tʃɑ:dʒ] *vt* назначáть (назнáчить *perf*) слѝшком нѝзкую цéну +*dat*.
underclass ['ʌndəklɑ:s] *n* неиму́щий* класс.
underclothes ['ʌndəkləuðz] *npl* нѝжнее бельё *ntsg*.
undercoat ['ʌndəkəut] *n* (*paint*) грунтóвка*.
undercover [ʌndə'kʌvə^r] *adj* тáйный.
undercurrent ['ʌndəkʌrnt] *n* (*fig*) затаённое чу́вство.
undercut [ʌndə'kʌt] *irreg vt* (*prices*) сбивáть (сбить* *perf*); **he can ~ his competitors** он мóжет продавáть товáры по бóлее нѝзкой ценé, чем егó конкурéнты.
underdeveloped ['ʌndədɪ'vɛləpt] *adj* (*country, region*) слаборáзвитый (слаборáзвит).
underdog ['ʌndədɔg] *n*: **the** ~ (*in society*) обездóленный *m adj*; (*in team competition*) слáбая комáнда.
underdone [ʌndə'dʌn] *adj* (*fried, roasted food*) недожáренный; (*boiled food*) недовáр-енный.
underemployment ['ʌndərɪm'plɔɪmənt] *n* непóлная зáнятость *f*.
underestimate ['ʌndər'ɛstɪmeɪt] *vt* недооцéнивать (недооценѝть* *perf*).
underexposed ['ʌndərɪks'pəuzd] *adj* (*PHOT*) недодéржанный.
underfed [ʌndə'fɛd] *adj* недокóрмленный.
underfoot [ʌndə'fut] *adv* (*crush, trample*) под ногáми.
underfunded ['ʌndə'fʌndɪd] *adj* плóхо финансѝруемый.
undergo [ʌndə'gəu] *irreg vt* (*repair*) проходѝть* (пройтѝ* *perf*); (*operation*) переносѝть* (перенестѝ* *perf*); (*change*) подвергáться (подвéргнуться* *perf*) +*dat*; **the car is ~ing repairs** машѝна прохóдит ремóнт.
undergraduate [ʌndə'grædjuɪt] *n* студéнт(ка) ◆ *cpd*: ~ **courses** университéтские ку́рсы *mpl*.
underground ['ʌndəgraund] *adv* (*work*) под землёй ◆ *adj* (*car park*) подзéмный; (*newspaper, activities*) подпóльный ◆ *n*: **the** ~ (*BRIT: railway*) метрó *nt ind*; (*POL*) подпóлье; **to go** ~ (*fig*) уходѝть* (уйтѝ* *perf*) в подпóлье.
undergrowth ['ʌndəgrəuθ] *n*: **the** ~ подлéсок*.
underhand(ed) [ʌndə'hænd(ɪd)] *adj* (*fig: behaviour, method etc*) закулѝсный.
underinsured [ʌndərɪn'ʃuəd] *adj* непóлностью застрахóванный*.
underlay [ʌndə'leɪ] *n* подклáдка*.
underlie [ʌndə'laɪ] *irreg vt* (*fig*) лежáть (*impf*) в оснóве +*gen*; **the underlying cause** причѝна, лежáщая в оснóве.
underline [ʌndə'laɪn] *vt* (*also fig*) подчёркивать (подчеркну́ть *perf*).
underling ['ʌndəlɪŋ] *n* (*pej*) мéлкая сóшка*.
undermanning [ʌndə'mænɪŋ] *n* недостáток* в рабóчей сѝле.
undermentioned [ʌndə'mɛnʃənd] *adj* нижеупомя́нутый.
undermine [ʌndə'maɪn] *vt* (*confidence, authority*) подрывáть (подорвáть* *perf*).
underneath [ʌndə'ni:θ] *adv* внизу́ ◆ *prep* (*position*) под +*instr*; (*motion*) под +*acc*.
undernourished [ʌndə'nʌrɪʃt] *adj* недокóрмленный.
underpaid [ʌndə'peɪd] *adj* (*person*) не получáющий дóлжной оплáты, низкооплáчиваемый (низкооплáчиваем).
underpants ['ʌndəpænts] *npl* (*men's*) трусы́ *pl*.
underpass ['ʌndəpɑ:s] *n* (*BRIT*) туннéль *m*, тоннéль *m*.
underpin [ʌndə'pɪn] *vt* (*argument, case*) подкрепля́ть (подкрепѝть* *perf*).
underplay [ʌndə'pleɪ] *vt* (*BRIT*) преуменьшáть (преумéньшить *perf*).
underpopulated [ʌndə'pɔpjuleɪtɪd] *adj* малонаселённый* (малонаселён).
underprice [ʌndə'praɪs] *vt* занижáть (занизѝть* *perf*) слѝшком нѝзкую цéну на +*acc*.
underprivileged [ʌndə'prɪvɪlɪdʒd] *adj* (*family*) неиму́щий*.
underrate [ʌndə'reɪt] *vt* недооцéнивать (недооценѝть* *perf*).
underscore [ʌndə'skɔ:^r] *vt* (*word*) подчёркивать (подчеркну́ть *perf*).
underseal [ʌndə'si:l] *vt* (*BRIT: AUT*) наносѝть* (нанестѝ* *perf*) антикоррозѝйное покры́тие (*на днѝще автомобѝля*) ◆ *n* (*AUT*) антикоррозѝйное покры́тие (*днѝща автомобѝля*).
undersecretary ['ʌndə'sɛkrətərɪ] *n* (*POL*) заместѝтель *m* минѝстра.
undersell [ʌndə'sɛl] *irreg vt* (*competitors*) продавáть* (продáть* *perf*) дешéвле +*gen*.
undershirt ['ʌndəʃə:t] *n* (*US*) нѝжняя рубáшка*.
undershorts ['ʌndəʃɔ:ts] *npl* (*US*) трусы́ *pl*.
underside ['ʌndəsaɪd] *n* нѝжняя сторонá*.
undersigned ['ʌndə'saɪnd] *adj* (*document*) подпѝсанный нѝже ◆ *n* нижепод-писáвшийся*(-аяся) *m(f) adj*; **we the ~ agree**

* marks translations which have irregular inflections. The Russian–English side of the dictionary gives inflectional information.

that ... мы, нижеподписа́вшиеся, догова́риваемся, что ....
underskirt ['ʌndəskə:t] *n* (*BRIT*) ни́жняя ю́бка*.
understaffed [ʌndə'stɑ:ft] *adj* (*project etc*) неукомплекто́ванный ка́драми.
understand [ʌndə'stænd] (*irreg*: *like* **stand**) *vt* понима́ть (поня́ть* *perf*); (*believe*): **to ~ that** полага́ть *(impf)*, что ...; **to make o.s. understood** объясня́ться (объясни́ться *perf*).
understandable [ʌndə'stændəbl] *adj* поня́тный* (поня́тен).
understanding [ʌndə'stændɪŋ] *adj* (*kind*) понима́ющий ◆ *n* понима́ние; (*agreement*) взаимопонима́ние; **to come to an ~ with sb** достига́ть (дости́чь* *perf*) взаимопонима́ния с кем-н; **on the ~ that** ... при усло́вии, что ....
understate [ʌndə'steɪt] *vt* преуменьша́ть (преуме́ньшить *perf*).
understatement ['ʌndəsteɪtmənt] *n* (*quality*) преуменьше́ние; **that's an ~!** э́то сли́шком мя́гко ска́зано!
understood [ʌndə'stud] *pt, pp of* **understand** ◆ *adj* (*agreed*) согласо́ванный* (согласо́ван); (*implied*) подразумева́емый (подразумева́ем).
understudy ['ʌndəstʌdɪ] *n* дублёр.
undertake [ʌndə'teɪk] (*irreg*: *like* **take**) *vt* (*task, duty*) брать* (взять* *perf*) на себя́; **to ~ to do** обя́зываться (обяза́ться* *perf*) *+infin*.
undertaker ['ʌndəteɪkəʳ] *n* владе́лец* похоро́нного бюро́.
undertaking ['ʌndəteɪkɪŋ] *n* (*job*) предприя́тие; (*promise*) обяза́тельство.
undertone ['ʌndətəun] *n* (*of criticism etc*) отте́нок*; (*speak*): **in an ~** вполго́лоса.
undervalue [ʌndə'vælju:] *vt* недооце́нивать (недооцени́ть* *perf*).
underwater [ʌndə'wɔ:təʳ] *adv* (*use, swim etc*) под водо́й ◆ *adj* (*exploration, camera etc*) подво́дный.
underwear ['ʌndəwɛəʳ] *n* ни́жнее бельё.
underweight [ʌndə'weɪt] *adj* ве́сящий ни́же но́рмы.
underworld ['ʌndəwə:ld] *n* (*of crime*) престу́пный мир.
underwrite [ʌndə'raɪt] *vt* (*FINANCE*) гаранти́ровать *(impf/perf)* размеще́ние *+gen*; (*COMM*) брать* (взять* *perf*) на себя́ финанси́рование *+gen*; (*INSURANCE*) принима́ть (приня́ть* *perf*) на себя́ страхово́й риск.
underwriter ['ʌndəraɪtəʳ] *n* (*INSURANCE*) андерра́йтер, принима́ющий *m adj* на себя́ страхово́й риск.
undeserving [ʌndɪ'zə:vɪŋ] *adj*: **to be ~ of** не заслу́живать *(impf) +gen*.
undesirable [ʌndɪ'zaɪərəbl] *adj* нежела́тельный* (нежела́телен).
undeveloped [ʌndɪ'vɛləpt] *adj* (*land*) незастро́енный; (*resources*) неразрабо́танный.
undies ['ʌndɪz] *npl* (*inf*) (ни́жнее) бельё *ntsg*.
undiluted ['ʌndaɪ'lu:tɪd] *adj* (*substance, liquid*) неразба́вленный; (*emotion*) чи́стый.
undiplomatic ['ʌndɪplə'mætɪk] *adj* недипломати́чный* (недипломати́чен).
undischarged ['ʌndɪs'tʃɑ:dʒd] *adj*: **~ bankrupt** не восстано́вленный в права́х банкро́т.
undisciplined [ʌn'dɪsɪplɪnd] *adj* недисциплини́рованный (недисциплини́рован).
undiscovered ['ʌndɪs'kʌvəd] *adj* (*island*) неоткры́тый; (*fact*) необнару́женный; (*situation*) неиссле́дованный.
undisguised ['ʌndɪs'gaɪzd] *adj* я́вный* (я́вен).
undisputed ['ʌndɪs'pju:tɪd] *adj* неоспори́мый (неоспори́м).
undistinguished ['ʌndɪs'tɪŋgwɪʃt] *adj* посре́дственный* (посре́дствен).
undisturbed [ʌndɪs'tə:bd] *adj* (*uninterrupted*) безмяте́жный* (безмяте́жен); **to leave ~** не волнова́ть *(impf)*.
undivided [ʌndɪ'vaɪdɪd] *adj*: **can I have your ~ attention?** я прошу́ Ва́шего неразде́льного внима́ния.
undo [ʌn'du:] (*irreg*: *like* **do**) *vt* (*unfasten*: *laces, strings*) развя́зывать (развяза́ть* *perf*); (: *buttons*) расстёгивать (расстегну́ть *perf*); (*spoil*) губи́ть* (погуби́ть* *perf*).
undoing [ʌn'du:ɪŋ] *n* (*downfall*) ги́бель *f*.
undone [ʌn'dʌn] *pp of* **undo**; (*unfastened*): **my lace has come ~** у меня́ развяза́лся шнуро́к.
undoubted [ʌn'dautɪd] *adj* несомне́нный* (несомне́нен), бесспо́рный* (бесспо́рен).
undoubtedly [ʌn'dautɪdlɪ] *adv* несомне́нно, бесспо́рно.
undress [ʌn'drɛs] *vt* раздева́ть (разде́ть* *perf*) ◆ *vi* раздева́ться (разде́ться* *perf*).
undrinkable [ʌn'drɪŋkəbl] *adj* (*poisonous*) неприго́дный* для питья́; (*unpalatable*): **this wine is ~** э́то вино́ невозмо́жно пить.
undue [ʌn'dju:] *adj* изли́шний*.
undulating ['ʌndjuleɪtɪŋ] *adj* холми́стый*.
unduly [ʌn'dju:lɪ] *adv* изли́шне.
undying [ʌn'daɪɪŋ] *adj* бессме́ртный*.
unearned [ʌn'ə:nd] *adj* незарабо́танный; **~ income** нетрудовы́е дохо́ды *mpl*.
unearth [ʌn'ə:θ] *vt* выка́пывать (вы́копать *perf*); (*fig*) раска́пывать (раскопа́ть *perf*).
unearthly [ʌn'ə:θlɪ] *adj*: **at an ~ hour** ни свет, ни заря́.
unease [ʌn'i:z] *n* нело́вкость *f*.
uneasy [ʌn'i:zɪ] *adj* (*feeling*) трево́жный* (трево́жен); (*peace, truce*) напряжённый*; (*person*): **he is** *or* **feels ~** он неспоко́ен; **I feel ~ about taking his money** я неспоко́ен, когда́ беру́ у него́ де́ньги.
uneconomic(al) ['ʌni:kə'nɔmɪk(l)] *adj* неэконо́мный.
uneducated [ʌn'ɛdjukeɪtɪd] *adj* (*person*) необразо́ванный*.
unemployed [ʌnɪm'plɔɪd] *adj* (*worker*) безрабо́тный ◆ *npl*: **the ~** безрабо́тные *pl adj*.
unemployment [ʌnɪm'plɔɪmənt] *n*

безрабо́тица.
unemployment benefit *n* посо́бие по безрабо́тице.
unemployment compensation *n* (*US*) = **unemployment benefit**.
unending [ʌn'ɛndɪŋ] *adj* несконча́емый.
unenviable [ʌn'ɛnvɪəbl] *adj* незави́дный* (незави́ден).
unequal [ʌn'i:kwəl] *adj* нера́вный* (нера́вен); **to feel ~ to** чу́вствовать *(impf)* себя́ неспосо́бным отвеча́ть тре́бованиям *+gen*.
unequalled [ʌn'i:kwəld] (*US* **unequaled**) *adj* несравни́мый (несравни́м).
unequivocal [ʌnɪ'kwɪvəkl] *adj* (*answer, person*) недвусмы́сленный*.
unerring [ʌn'ə:rɪŋ] *adj* безоши́бочный* (безоши́бочен).
UNESCO [ju:'nɛskəu] *n abbr* (= *United Nations Educational, Scientific and Cultural Organization*) ЮНЕ́СКО.
unethical [ʌn'ɛθɪkl] *adj* неэти́чный* (неэти́чен).
uneven [ʌn'i:vn] *adj* неро́вный*.
uneventful [ʌnɪ'vɛntful] *adj* без осо́бых собы́тий.
unexceptional [ʌnɪk'sɛpʃənl] *adj* зауря́дный* (зауря́ден).
unexciting [ʌnɪk'saɪtɪŋ] *adj* (*news, film*) неинтере́сный* (неинтере́сен).
unexpected [ʌnɪks'pɛktɪd] *adj* неожи́данный* (неожи́дан).
unexpectedly [ʌnɪks'pɛktɪdlɪ] *adv* неожи́данно.
unexplained [ʌnɪks'pleɪnd] *adj* необъясн-ённый.
unexploded [ʌnɪks'pləudɪd] *adj* (*bomb*) невзорва́вшийся.
unfailing [ʌn'feɪlɪŋ] *adj* неизме́нный* (неизме́нен).
unfair [ʌn'fɛə'] *adj*: **~ (to)** несправедли́вый (к *+dat*); **it's ~ that** ... несправедли́во, что ....
unfair dismissal *n* незако́нное увольне́ние.
unfairly [ʌn'fɛəlɪ] *adv* (*treat*) несправедли́во; (*dismiss*) незако́нно.
unfaithful [ʌn'feɪθful] *adj* неве́рный* (неве́рен).
unfamiliar [ʌnfə'mɪlɪə'] *adj* незнако́мый (незнако́м); **he is ~ with the accent** он незнако́м с акце́нтом.
unfashionable [ʌn'fæʃnəbl] *adj* немо́дный* (немо́ден).
unfasten [ʌn'fɑ:sn] *vt* (*undo*) расстёгивать (расстегну́ть *perf*); (*open*) открыва́ть (откры́ть* *perf*).
unfathomable [ʌn'fæðəməbl] *adj* (*mystery*) непостижи́мый (непостижи́м).
unfavourable [ʌn'feɪvrəbl] (*US* **unfavorable**) *adj* неблагоприя́тный* (неблагоприя́тен).
unfavourably [ʌn'feɪvrəblɪ] (*US* **unfavorably**) *adv* (*compare, review*) неблагоприя́тно; **to look ~ on** (*suggestion etc*) смотре́ть* *(impf)* неблагоскло́нно на *+acc*.
unfeeling [ʌn'fi:lɪŋ] *adj* бесчу́вственный* (бесчу́вствен).
unfinished [ʌn'fɪnɪʃt] *adj* незако́нченный.
unfit [ʌn'fɪt] *adj* (*physically*): **she is ~** она́ в плохо́й спорти́вной фо́рме; **he is ~ for the job** он неприго́ден к рабо́те.
unflagging [ʌn'flægɪŋ] *adj* неосла́бный* (неосла́бен).
unflappable [ʌn'flæpəbl] *adj* невозмути́мый (невозмути́м).
unflattering [ʌn'flætərɪŋ] *adj* (*remark*) неле́стный* (неле́стен); (*garment*) не иду́щий к лицу́; **that dress is ~ on you** Вам не идёт э́то пла́тье.
unflinching [ʌn'flɪntʃɪŋ] *adj* неустраши́мый (неустра́шим).
unfold [ʌn'fəuld] *vt* (*sheets, map*) развора́чивать *or* развёртывать (разверну́ть *perf*) ◆ *vi* (*situation*) развора́чиваться (разверну́ться *perf*).
unforeseeable [ʌnfɔ:'si:əbl] *adj* непредви́денный* (непредви́ден).
unforeseen ['ʌnfɔ:'si:n] *adj* непредви́денный.
unforgettable [ʌnfə'gɛtəbl] *adj* незабыва́емый (незабыва́ем).
unforgivable [ʌnfə'gɪvəbl] *adj* непрости́тельный* (непрости́телен).
unformatted [ʌn'fɔ:mætɪd] *adj* (*COMPUT*) бесформа́тный, неформати́рованный.
unfortunate [ʌn'fɔ:tʃənət] *adj* (*person, event*) несча́стный*; (*remark*) неуда́чный*; **he's been very ~** ему́ о́чень не повезло́; **it is ~ that ...** как неуда́чно, что ....
unfortunately [ʌn'fɔ:tʃənətlɪ] *adv* к сожале́нию.
unfounded [ʌn'faundɪd] *adj* необосно́ванный*.
unfriendly [ʌn'frɛndlɪ] *adj* недружелю́бный* (недружелю́бен).
unfulfilled [ʌnful'fɪld] *adj* (*ambition, prophecy, desire*) неосуществлённый; (*promise, terms*) невы́полненный; (*person*) нереализова́вшийся.
unfurl [ʌn'fə:l] *vt* развора́чивать *or* развёртывать (разверну́ть *perf*).
unfurnished [ʌn'fə:nɪʃt] *adj* немеблиро́ванный.
ungainly [ʌn'geɪnlɪ] *adj* нело́вкий*.
ungodly [ʌn'gɔdlɪ] *adj*: **at an ~ hour** не свет, ни заря́.
ungrateful [ʌn'greɪtful] *adj* неблагода́рный* (неблагода́рен).
unguarded [ʌn'gɑ:dɪd] *adj*: **in an ~ moment** в моме́нт неосторо́жности.
UNHCR *n abbr* (= *United Nations High Commission for Refugees*) *управле́ние верхо́вного комисса́ра ООН по дела́м*

* marks translations which have irregular inflections. The Russian-English side of the dictionary gives inflectional information.

беженцев.
unhappily [ʌn'hæpɪlɪ] *adv* несчастли́во; (*unfortunately*) к несча́стью *or* сожале́нию.
unhappiness [ʌn'hæpɪnɪs] *n* несча́стье.
unhappy [ʌn'hæpɪ] *adj* (*sad*) гру́стный* (гру́стен); (*unfortunate*) несча́стный* (несча́стен); **I am ~ with** (*dissatisfied*) я недово́лен *+instr*.
unharmed [ʌn'hɑ:md] *adj* неповреждённый.
unhealthy [ʌn'hɛlθɪ] *adj* (*also fig*) нездоро́вый (нездоро́в).
unheard-of [ʌn'hə:dɔv] *adj* (*event, situation*) неслы́ханный* (неслы́хан); (*person*) неизве́стный*.
unhelpful [ʌn'hɛlpful] *adj* бесполе́зный*.
unhesitating [ʌn'hɛzɪteɪtɪŋ] *adj* (*loyalty*) непоколеби́мый (непоколеби́м); (*reply, offer*) реши́тельный* (реши́телен).
unholy [ʌn'həulɪ] *adj* поро́чный* (поро́чен); (*dreadful*) безобра́зный.
unhook [ʌn'huk] *vt* расстёгивать (расстегну́ть *perf*) крючки́ *+gen*.
unhurt [ʌn'hə:t] *adj* невреди́мый (невреди́м).
unhygienic ['ʌnhaɪ'dʒi:nɪk] *adj* негигиени́чный* (негигиени́чен).
UNICEF ['ju:nɪsɛf] *n abbr* (= *United Nations International Children's Emergency Fund*) ЮНИСЕФ.
unicorn ['ju:nɪkɔ:n] *n* единоро́г.
unidentified [ʌnaɪ'dɛntɪfaɪd] *adj* (*body*) неопо́знанный; (*source, person*) аноні́мный; *see also* **UFO**.
unification [ju:nɪfɪ'keiʃən] *n* (*POL etc*) объедине́ние, унифика́ция.
uniform ['ju:nɪfɔ:m] *n* фо́рма ◆ *adj* (*length, width etc*) единообра́зный* (единообра́зен); (*temperature*) постоя́нный* (постоя́нен).
uniformity [ju:nɪ'fɔ:mɪtɪ] *n* единообра́зие.
unify ['ju:nɪfaɪ] *vt* объединя́ть (объедини́ть *perf*).
unilateral [ju:nɪ'lætərəl] *adj* (*disarmament etc*) односторо́нний* (односторо́нен).
unimaginable [ʌnɪ'mædʒɪnəbl] *adj* невообрази́мый (невообрази́м).
unimaginative [ʌnɪ'mædʒɪnətɪv] *adj* (*person*) лишённый воображе́ния; (*design*) прозаи́чный* (прозаи́чен).
unimpaired [ʌnɪm'pɛəd] *adj* непострада́вший.
unimportant [ʌnɪm'pɔ:tənt] *adj* нева́жный* (нева́жен).
unimpressed [ʌnɪm'prɛst] *adj*: **I was ~ by his explanation** его́ объясне́ние меня́ не убеди́ло.
uninhabited [ʌnɪn'hæbɪtɪd] *adj* необита́емый (необита́ем).
uninhibited [ʌnɪn'hɪbɪtɪd] *adj* раско́ванный* (раско́ван).
uninjured [ʌn'ɪndʒəd] *adj* непострада́вший.
uninspiring [ʌnɪn'spaɪərɪŋ] *adj* не вдохновля́ющий.
unintelligent [ʌnɪn'tɛlɪdʒənt] *adj* (*person*) неве́жественный* (неве́жествен).
unintentional [ʌnɪn'tɛnʃənəl] *adj* неумы́шленный* (неумы́шлен).
unintentionally [ʌnɪn'tɛnʃnəlɪ] *adv* неумы́шленно.
uninvited [ʌnɪn'vaɪtɪd] *adj* незва́ный.
uninviting [ʌnɪn'vaɪtɪŋ] *adj* (*food*) неаппети́тный* (неаппети́тен), несоблазни́тельный* (несоблазни́телен); (*place*) непривлека́тельный* (непривлека́телен).
union ['ju:njən] *n* (*unification*) объедине́ние; (*also:* **trade ~**) профсою́з ◆ *cpd* (*activities, leader etc*) профсою́зный; **the U~** (*US*) Соединённые Шта́ты *mpl*.
unionize ['ju:njənaɪz] *vt* (*employees, industry*) объединя́ть (объедини́ть *perf*) в профсою́зы.
Union Jack *n* (*BRIT*) *госуда́рственный флаг Соединённого Короле́вства.*
Union of Soviet Socialist Republics *n* (*formerly*) Сою́з Сове́тских Социалисти́ческих Респу́блик.
union shop *n предприя́тие, на кото́ром мо́гут рабо́тать то́лько чле́ны профсою́за.*
unique [ju:'ni:k] *adj* (*object etc*) уника́льный* (уника́лен); (*ability, performance etc*) исключи́тельный* (исключи́телен); **these problems are not ~ to ...** э́ти пробле́мы каса́ются не то́лько *+gen* ....
unisex ['ju:nɪsɛks] *adj* для обо́их поло́в.
unison ['ju:nɪsn] *n*: **in ~** (*say*) в оди́н го́лос; (*sing*) в унисо́н.
unissued capital [ʌn'ɪʃu:d-] *n* невы́пущенный акционе́рный капита́л.
unit ['ju:nɪt] *n* (*single whole*) це́лое *nt adj*; (*measurement*) едини́ца; (*section: of furniture etc*) се́кция; (*team, squad*) подразделе́ние; **production ~** едини́ца проду́кции; **kitchen ~** ку́хонная се́кция.
unitary ['ju:nɪtrɪ] *adj* едини́чный* (едини́чен).
unit cost *n* (*COMM*) сто́имость *f* едини́цы проду́кции.
unite [ju:'naɪt] *vt* объединя́ть (объедини́ть *perf*) ◆ *vi* объединя́ться (объедини́ться *perf*).
united [ju:'naɪtɪd] *adj* объединённый*; (*effort*) совме́стный.
United Arab Emirates *npl*: **the ~ ~ ~** Объединённые Ара́бские эмира́ты *mpl*.
United Kingdom *n* Соединённое Короле́вство.
United Nations (Organization) *n* Организа́ция Объединённых На́ций.
United States (of America) *n* Соединённые Шта́ты *mpl* Аме́рики.
unit price *n* (*COMM*) цена́* за едини́цу, шту́чная цена́*.
unit trust *n* (*BRIT: COMM*) (довери́тельный) паево́й трест.
unity ['ju:nɪtɪ] *n* еди́нство.
Univ. *abbr* = **university**.

universal [ju:nɪ'və:sl] *adj* универса́льный* (универса́лен).
universe ['ju:nɪvə:s] *n* вселе́нная *f adj*.
university [ju:nɪ'və:sɪtɪ] *n* университе́т ◆ *cpd* (*education, year*) университе́тский*; ~ **student/professor** студе́нт(ка*)/профе́ссор университе́та.
university degree *n* университе́тская сте́пень* *f*.
unjust [ʌn'dʒʌst] *adj* несправедли́вый (несправедли́в).
unjustifiable ['ʌndʒʌstɪ'faɪəbl] *adj* неопра́вданный* (неопра́вдан).
unjustified [ʌn'dʒʌstɪfaɪd] *adj* (*belief, action*) неопра́вданный* (неопра́вдан); (*text*) невы́равненный.
unkempt [ʌn'kɛmpt] *adj* (*appearance*) неопря́тный* (неопря́тен); (*hair, beard*) растрёпанный* (растрёпан).
unkind [ʌn'kaɪnd] *adj* (*person, comment etc*) злой; (*behaviour*) зло́бный* (зло́бен).
unkindly [ʌn'kaɪndlɪ] *adv* недоброжела́тельно.
unknown [ʌn'nəun] *adj* неизве́стный* (неизве́стен); ~ **to me** без моего́ ве́дома; ~ **quantity** (*MATH*) неизве́стная величина́; (*fig*) зага́дка.
unladen [ʌn'leɪdn] *adj* (*ship*) поро́жний*; ~ **weight** вес порожняко́м.
unlawful [ʌn'lɔ:ful] *adj* незако́нный* (незако́нен).
unleaded petrol ['ʌn'lɛdɪd-] *n* бензи́н не содержа́щий свинца́.
unleash [ʌn'li:ʃ] *vt* (*fig*) дава́ть* (дать* *perf*) во́лю +*dat*.
unleavened [ʌn'lɛvnd] *adj* пре́сный*.
unless [ʌn'lɛs] *conj* е́сли не; ~ **he comes** е́сли он не придёт; ~ **otherwise stated** е́сли не бу́дут даны́ други́е указа́ния; ~ **I am mistaken** е́сли я не ошиба́юсь.
unlicensed [ʌn'laɪsnst] *adj* (*BRIT*: *restaurant*) не име́ющий лице́нзии на прода́жу спиртны́х напи́тков.
unlike [ʌn'laɪk] *adj* (*not alike*) непохо́жий* (непохо́ж) ◆ *prep* (*different from*) в отли́чие от +*gen*; **Russian is grammatically ~ English** с граммати́ческой то́чки зре́ния ру́сский не похо́ж на англи́йский.
unlikelihood [ʌn'laɪklɪhud] *n* неправдо-подо́бие.
unlikely [ʌn'laɪklɪ] *adj* (*not likely*) мало-вероя́тный* (маловероя́тен); (*unexpected*) невероя́тный* (невероя́тен); **in the ~ event of** при маловероя́тном слу́чае +*gen*; **in the ~ event that** ... в том маловероя́тном слу́чае, когда́ ....
unlimited [ʌn'lɪmɪtɪd] *adj* (*travel, wine etc*) неограни́ченный.
unlisted ['ʌn'lɪstɪd] *adj* (*US*: *TEL*) не включённый (включён) в телефо́нный спра́вочник; (*STOCK EXCHANGE*) не коти́рующийся.
unlit [ʌn'lɪt] *adj* (*room*) неосвещённый.
unload [ʌn'ləud] *vt* (*box, car*) разгружа́ть (разгрузи́ть* *perf*).
unlock [ʌn'lɔk] *vt* отпира́ть (отпере́ть* *perf*).
unlucky [ʌn'lʌkɪ] *adj* (*person*) невезу́чий (невезу́ч); (*object, number*) несчастли́вый; **he is ~** ему́ не везёт.
unmanageable [ʌn'mænɪdʒəbl] *adj* (*tool, vehicle*) трудноконтроли́руемый; (*situation*) неуправля́емый (неуправля́ем).
unmanned [ʌn'mænd] *adj* (*spacecraft etc*) автомати́чески управля́емый.
unmarked [ʌn'mɑ:kt] *adj* (*unstained*) чи́стый* (чист); ~ **police car** *полице́йская маши́на без опознава́тельных зна́ков*.
unmarried [ʌn'mærɪd] *adj* (*man*) нежена́тый (нежена́т), холосто́й* (хо́лост); (*woman*) незаму́жняя.
unmarried mother *n* мать* *f*-одино́чка.
unmask [ʌn'mɑ:sk] *vt* (*thief etc*) разоблача́ть (разоблачи́ть *perf*).
unmatched [ʌn'mætʃt] *adj* непревзойдённый* (непревзойдён).
unmentionable [ʌn'mɛnʃnəbl] *adj* (*topic*) запре́тный* (запре́тен); (*word*) неприли́чный* (неприли́чен).
unmerciful [ʌn'mə:sɪful] *adj* безжа́лостный* (безжа́лостен).
unmistak(e)able [ʌnmɪs'teɪkəbl] *adj* (*voice, sound*) характе́рный*.
unmistak(e)ably [ʌnmɪs'teɪkəblɪ] *adv* я́вно.
unmitigated [ʌn'mɪtɪgeɪtɪd] *adj* по́лный.
unnamed [ʌn'neɪmd] *adj* (*nameless*) безымя́нный; (*anonymous*) не назва́вший себя́.
unnatural [ʌn'nætʃrəl] *adj* неесте́ственный* (неесте́ствен); (*against nature*) противоесте́ственный* (противоесте́ствен).
unnecessarily [ʌn'nɛsəsərɪlɪ] *adv* изли́шне.
unnecessary [ʌn'nɛsəsərɪ] *adj* изли́шний* (изли́шен).
unnerve [ʌn'nə:v] *vt* трево́жить (встрево́жить *perf*).
unnoticed [ʌn'nəutɪst] *adj* незаме́ченный.
UNO ['ju:nəu] *n abbr* (= *United Nations Organization*) ОО́Н= *Организа́ция Объединённых На́ций*.
unobservant [ʌnəb'zə:vnt] *adj* (*person*) ненаблюда́тельный* (ненаблюда́телен).
unobtainable [ʌnəb'teɪnəbl] *adj*: **this book is ~** эту кни́гу нельзя́ доста́ть; **this number is ~** э́тот но́мер не функциони́рует.
unobtrusive [ʌnəb'tru:sɪv] *adj* (*person*) ненавя́зчивый (ненавя́зчив); (*engine*) бесшу́мный* (бесшу́мен).

* marks translations which have irregular inflections. The Russian-English side of the dictionary gives inflectional information.

unoccupied [ʌn'ɔkjupaɪd] *adj* (*also MIL*) незáнятый.
unofficial [ʌnə'fɪʃl] *adj* неофициáльный* (неофициáлен).
unopened [ʌn'əupənd] *adj* (*letter*) нераспечáтанный; (*tin, bottle etc*) неоткры́тый.
unopposed [ʌnə'pəuzd] *adj* не встрéтивший сопротивлéния.
unorthodox [ʌn'ɔ:θədɔks] *adj* (*treatment*) неортодоксáльный* (неортодоксáлен); (*REL*) неортодоксáльный.
unpack [ʌn'pæk] *vi* распакóвываться (распаковáться *perf*) ◆ *vt* распакóвывать (распаковáть *perf*).
unpaid [ʌn'peɪd] *adj* (*bill*) неоплáченный; (*time off*) неоплáчиваемый; (*work*) неоплáчиваемый; (*worker*) бесплáтный.
unpalatable [ʌn'pælətəbl] *adj* (*meal*) невку́сный* (невку́сен); (*truth*) гóрький* (гóрек).
unparalleled [ʌn'pærəlɛld] *adj* несравни́мый (несравни́м).
unpatriotic ['ʌnpætrɪ'ɔtɪk] *adj* (*person*) непатриоти́чески настрóенный; (*speech, attitude*) непатриоти́чный* (непатриоти́чен).
unplanned [ʌn'plænd] *adj* (*visit, baby*) незаплани́рованный.
unpleasant [ʌn'plɛznt] *adj* неприя́тный* (неприя́тен).
unplug [ʌn'plʌg] *vt* отключáть (отключи́ть* *perf*) от сети́.
unpolluted [ʌnpə'lu:tɪd] *adj* (*river, water etc*) незагрязнённый.
unpopular [ʌn'pɔpjulə'] *adj* (*person, decision etc*) непопуля́рный* (непопуля́рен); **to make o.s. ~ (with)** теря́ть (потеря́ть *perf*) популя́рность (у *+gen*).
unprecedented [ʌn'prɛsɪdəntɪd] *adj* беспрецедéнтный* (беспрецедéнтен).
unpredictable [ʌnprɪ'dɪktəbl] *adj* непредсказу́емый (непредсказу́ем).
unprejudiced [ʌn'prɛdʒudɪst] *adj* (*not biased*) непредвзя́тый; (*having no prejudices*) непредубеждённый*.
unprepared [ʌnprɪ'pɛəd] *adj* (*person, speech*) неподготóвленный.
unprepossessing ['ʌnpri:pə'zɛsɪŋ] *adj* нерасполагáющий.
unpretentious [ʌnprɪ'tɛnʃəs] *adj* непретенциóз|ный* (непретенциóзен).
unprincipled [ʌn'prɪnsɪpld] *adj* (*person*) беспринци́пный* (беспринци́пен).
unproductive [ʌnprə'dʌktɪv] *adj* (*land*) неплодорóдный* (неплодорóден); (*discussion*) непродукти́вный* (непродукти́вен); (*labour*) непроизводи́тельный* (непроизводи́телен).
unprofessional [ʌnprə'fɛʃənl] *adj* непрофессионáльный (непрофессионáлен)*.
unprofitable [ʌn'prɔfɪtəbl] *adj* невы́годный* (невы́годен).
unprotected ['ʌnprə'tɛktɪd] *adj* незащищённый; ~ **sex** секс без контрацепти́вов.
unprovoked [ʌnprə'vəukt] *adj* (*attack*) неспровоци́рованный.
unpunished [ʌn'pʌnɪʃt] *adj*: **to go ~** оставáться* (остáться* *perf*) безнакáзанным(-ой).
unqualified [ʌn'kwɔlɪfaɪd] *adj* (*teacher, nurse etc*) неквалифици́рованный; (*disaster, success*) совершённый.
unquestionably [ʌn'kwɛstʃənəblɪ] *adv* бесспóрно.
unquestioning [ʌn'kwɛstʃənɪŋ] *adj* беспрекословный* (беспрекослóвен).
unravel [ʌn'rævl] *vt* (*ball of string*) распу́тывать (распу́тать *perf*); (*mystery*) разгáдывать (разгадáть *perf*).
unreal [ʌn'rɪəl] *adj* (*not real*) нереáльный* (нереáлен); (*peculiar*) фантасти́ческий.
unrealistic ['ʌnrɪə'lɪstɪk] *adj* (*person, project*) нереалисти́чный* (нереалисти́чен).
unreasonable [ʌn'ri:znəbl] *adj* (*person, attitude, demand*) неразу́мный* (неразу́мен); (*length of time*) нереáльный* (нереáлен).
unrecognizable [ʌn'rɛkəgnaɪzəbl] *adj* неузнавáемый (неузнавáем).
unrecognized [ʌn'rɛkəgnaɪzd] *adj* (*also POL*) непри́знанный*.
unreconstructed ['ʌnri:kən'strʌktɪd] *adj* (*US*) неисправи́мый (неисправи́м).
unrecorded [ʌnrə'kɔ:dɪd] *adj* (*piece of music etc*) незапи́санный; (*incident, statement*) незафикси́рованный.
unrefined [ʌnrə'faɪnd] *adj* (*petroleum*) неочи́щенный; (*sugar*) нерафини́рованный.
unrehearsed [ʌnrɪ'hə:st] *adj* (*THEAT*) неотрепети́рованный; (*spontaneous*) неподготóвленный.
unrelated [ʌnrɪ'leɪtɪd] *adj* (*incident*) отдéльный; **to be ~** (*people*) не состоя́ть (*impf*) в родствé.
unrelenting [ʌnrɪ'lɛntɪŋ] *adj* неумоли́мый (неумоли́м).
unreliable [ʌnrɪ'laɪəbl] *adj* ненадёжный* (ненадёжен).
unrelieved [ʌnrɪ'li:vd] *adj* (*monotony*) невыноси́мый (невыноси́м).
unremitting [ʌnrɪ'mɪtɪŋ] *adj* неослáбный* (неослáбен).
unrepeatable [ʌnrɪ'pi:təbl] *adj* (*offer*) неповтори́мый; (*comment*) неприли́чный* (неприли́чен).
unrepentant [ʌnrɪ'pɛntənt] *adj* нераскáявшийся.
unrepresentative ['ʌnrɛprɪ'zɛntətɪv] *adj*: **~ (of)** нетипи́чный* (нетипи́чен) (для *+acc*).
unreserved [ʌnrɪ'zə:vd] *adj* (*seat*) незаброни́рованный; (*approval, admiration*) пóлный*.
unreservedly [ʌnrɪ'zə:vɪdlɪ] *adv* пóлностью.
unresponsive [ʌnrɪs'pɔnsɪv] *adj* без-

различный* (безразличен).
unrest [ʌn'rɛst] *n* волнения *ntpl*.
unrestricted [ʌnrɪ'strɪktɪd] *adj* (*power, time*) неограниченный*; **to have ~ access to** иметь *(impf)* неограниченный доступ к *+dat*.
unrewarded [ʌnrɪ'wɔ:dɪd] *adj* (*efforts*) безуспешный* (безуспешен).
unripe [ʌn'raɪp] *adj* незрелый (незрел).
unrivalled [ʌn'raɪvəld] (*US* **unrivaled**) *adj* непревзойдённый* (непревзойдён).
unroll [ʌn'rəul] *vt* развёртывать (развернуть *perf*).
unruffled [ʌn'rʌfld] *adj* (*person*) невозмутимый (невозмутим); (*hair*) гладкий*.
unruly [ʌn'ru:lɪ] *adj* непослушный* (непослушен).
unsafe [ʌn'seɪf] *adj* опасный* (опасен); (*machine, bridge, car etc*) ненадёжный* (ненадёжен); (*method*) рискованный; **~ to eat/drink** непригодный* (непригоден) для еды/питья.
unsaid [ʌn'sɛd] *adj*: **to leave sth ~** не упоминать *(impf)* о чём-н.
unsaleable [ʌn'seɪləbl] (*US* **unsalable**) *adj* неходовой.
unsatisfactory ['ʌnsætɪs'fæktərɪ] *adj* неудовлетворительный* (неудовлетворителен).
unsatisfied [ʌn'sætɪsfaɪd] *adj* неудовлетворённый.
unsavoury [ʌn'seɪvərɪ] (*US* **unsavory**) *adj* (*fig*) сомнительный* (сомнителен).
unscathed [ʌn'skeɪðd] *adj* невредимый (невредим).
unscientific ['ʌnsaɪən'tɪfɪk] *adj* ненаучный* (ненаучен).
unscrew [ʌn'skru:] *vt* отвинчивать (отвинтить* *perf*).
unscrupulous [ʌn'skru:pjuləs] *adj* бессовестный*.
unseat [ʌn'si:t] *vt* (*from office*) смещать (сместить* *perf*).
unsecured ['ʌnsɪ'kjuəd] *adj*: **~ creditor** незастрахованный кредитор; **~ loan** необеспеченный заём*.
unseemly [ʌn'si:mlɪ] *adj* непристойный* (непристоен).
unseen [ʌn'si:n] *adj* (*person*) невидимый (невидим); (*danger*) скрытый (скрыт).
unselfish [ʌn'sɛlfɪʃ] *adj* бескорыстный* (бескорыстен).
unsettled [ʌn'sɛtld] *adj* (*person*) беспокойный* (беспокоен); (*future*) неясный* (неясен); (*question*) нерешённый; (*weather*) неустойчивый (неустойчив).
unsettling [ʌn'sɛtlɪŋ] *adj* тревожный* (тревожен).
unshak(e)able [ʌn'ʃeɪkəbl] *adj* непоколебимый (непоколебим).
unshaven [ʌn'ʃeɪvn] *adj* небритый (небрит).
unsightly [ʌn'saɪtlɪ] *adj* неприглядный* (неприглядeн).
unskilled [ʌn'skɪld] *adj* (*worker, work*) неквалифицированный*.
unsociable [ʌn'səuʃəbl] *adj* (*person*) необщительный* (необщителен); (*way of life*) замкнутый (замкнут).
unsocial [ʌn'səuʃl] *adj*: **~ hours** сверхурочные часы.
unsold [ʌn'səuld] *adj* (*goods*) непроданный.
unsolicited [ʌnsə'lɪsɪtɪd] *adj* (*advice*) непрошенный; (*goods*) незатребованный.
unsophisticated [ʌnsə'fɪstɪkeɪtɪd] *adj* бесхитростный* (бесхитростен); (*method, device*) простой* (прост).
unsound [ʌn'saund] *adj* (*health*) слабый* (слаб); (*floor, foundations*) непрочный* (непрочен); (*policy*) шаткий* (шаток); (*advice*) ненадёжный* (ненадёжен).
unspeakable [ʌn'spi:kəbl] *adj* отвратительный (отвратителен).
unspoken [ʌn'spəukn] *adj* (*word*) невысказанный; (*agreement, approval*) молчаливый.
unstable [ʌn'steɪbl] *adj* (*piece of furniture*) неустойчивый (неустойчив); (*government*) нестабильный* (нестабилен); (*person: mentally*) неуравновешенный* (неуравновешен).
unsteady [ʌn'stɛdɪ] *adj* (*step*) нетвёрдый (нетвёрд); (*voice, hands, legs*) дрожащий; (*ladder*) неустойчивый (неустойчив), шаткий* (шаток).
unstinting [ʌn'stɪntɪŋ] *adj* (*support*) огромный* (огромен); (*generosity*) бесконечный* (бесконечен).
unstuck [ʌn'stʌk] *adj*: **to come ~** (*label etc*) отклеиваться (отклеиться *perf*); (*plan, idea etc*) расстраиваться (расстроиться *perf*).
unsubstantiated ['ʌnsəb'stænʃɪeɪtɪd] *adj* (*rumour*) неподтверждённый; (*accusation*) необоснованный.
unsuccessful [ʌnsək'sɛsful] *adj* (*attempt*) безуспешный* (безуспешен); (*writer*) посредственный* (посредствен); (*proposal, marriage*) неудачный* (неудачен); **to be ~ in sth** терпеть* (потерпеть* *perf*) неудачу в *+prp*; **your application was ~** Ваше заявление не принято.
unsuccessfully [ʌnsək'sɛsfəlɪ] *adv* безуспешно.
unsuitable [ʌn'su:təbl] *adj* неподходящий*.
unsuited [ʌn'su:tɪd] *adj*: **to be ~ for** *or* **to** не подходить* *(impf)* для *+gen*.
unsung ['ʌnsʌŋ] *adj* незамеченный.
unsure [ʌn'ʃuə'] *adj* (*uncertain*) неуверенный* (неуверен); **he is ~ of himself** он неуверен в себе.

* marks translations which have irregular inflections. The Russian-English side of the dictionary gives inflectional information.

unsuspecting [ʌnsəs'pɛktɪŋ] *adj* ничего́ не подозрева́ющий.
unsweetened [ʌn'swi:tnd] *adj* неподслащённый.
unswerving [ʌn'swə:vɪŋ] *adj* непоколеби́мый (непоколеби́м).
unsympathetic ['ʌnsɪmpə'θɛtɪk] *adj* равноду́шный* (равноду́шен); (*unlikeable*) несимпати́чный* (несимпати́чен); **~ to** *or* **towards** равноду́шный *+dat*.
untangle [ʌn'tæŋgl] *vt* распу́тывать (распу́тать *perf*).
untapped [ʌn'tæpt] *adj* (*resources*) неиспо́льзованный.
untaxed [ʌn'tækst] *adj* не облага́емый (облага́ем) нало́гом.
unthinkable [ʌn'θɪŋkəbl] *adj* немы́слимый (немы́слим).
unthinking [ʌn'θɪŋkɪŋ] *adj* безду́мный* (безду́мен).
untidy [ʌn'taɪdɪ] *adj* неопря́тный* (неопря́тен); (*work, writing*) неаккура́тный* (неаккура́тен).
untie [ʌn'taɪ] *vt* (*lace, person*) развя́зывать (развяза́ть* *perf*); (*dog, horse etc*) отвя́зывать (отвяза́ть* *perf*).
until [ən'tɪl] *prep* до *+gen*; (*after negative*) пока́ ◆ *conj* пока́ не; **~ he comes** пока́ он не придёт; **~ now/then** до сих/тех пор; **from morning ~ night** с утра́ до́ ночи.
untimely [ʌn'taɪmlɪ] *adj* (*inopportune*: *moment*) неподходя́щий*; (: *arrival*) несвоевре́менный* (несвоевре́менен); (*death*) безвре́менный.
untold [ʌn'təuld] *adj* (*story*) нерасска́занный; (*joy, suffering*) невырази́мый; (*wealth*) несме́тный.
untouched [ʌn'tʌtʃt] *adj* (*not used etc*) нетро́нутый (нетро́нут); (*safe*) невреди́мый (невреди́м); **~ by** (*unaffected*) нетро́нутый (нетро́нут) *+instr*.
untoward [ʌntə'wɔ:d] *adj* (*events*) скве́рный* (скве́рен); (*effects*) отрица́тельный* (отрица́телен).
untrained ['ʌn'treɪnd] *adj* нетрениро́ванный.
untrammelled [ʌn'træmld] *adj* раско́ванный* (раско́ван).
untranslatable [ʌntrænz'leɪtəbl] *adj* непереводи́мый.
untried [ʌn'traɪd] *adj* (*policy, remedy*) неиспы́танный; (*prisoner*) не подверга́вшийся суду́.
untrue [ʌn'tru:] *adj* ло́жный* (ло́жен).
untrustworthy [ʌn'trʌstwə:ðɪ] *adj* ненадёжный* (ненадёжен).
unusable [ʌn'ju:zəbl] *adj* неприго́дный* (неприго́ден).
unused[1] [ʌn'ju:zd] *adj* (*not used*) неиспо́льзованный*.
unused[2] [ʌn'ju:st] *adj*: **he is ~ to it** он к э́тому не привы́к; **she is ~ to flying** она́ не привы́кла лета́ть.
unusual [ʌn'ju:ʒuəl] *adj* (*strange*) необы́чный* (необы́чен); (*rare*) ре́дкий* (ре́док); (*exceptional, distinctive*) необыкнове́нный* (необыкнове́нен).
unusually [ʌn'ju:ʒuəlɪ] *adv* (*large, high etc*) необыкнове́нно.
unveil [ʌn'veɪl] *vt* (*statue*) открыва́ть (откры́ть* *perf*).
unwanted [ʌn'wɔntɪd] *adj* (*clothing etc*) нену́жный; (*child, pregnancy*) нежела́нный.
unwarranted [ʌn'wɔrəntɪd] *adj* необосно́ванный*.
unwary [ʌn'wɛərɪ] *adj* неосторо́жный* (неосторо́жен).
unwavering [ʌn'weɪvərɪŋ] *adj* (*faith*) твёрдый* (твёрд), непоколеби́мый (непоколеби́м); (*gaze*) при́стальный* (при́стален).
unwelcome [ʌn'wɛlkəm] *adj* (*guest*) непро́шенный; (*news*) неприя́тный* (неприя́тен); **to feel ~** чу́вствовать *(impf)* себя́ ли́шним.
unwell [ʌn'wɛl] *adj*: **to feel ~** чу́вствовать *(impf)* себя́ пло́хо; **he is ~** ему́ нездоро́вится, он нездоро́в.
unwieldy [ʌn'wi:ldɪ] *adj* громо́здкий* (громо́здок).
unwilling [ʌn'wɪlɪŋ] *adj*: **to be ~ to do** не хоте́ть* *(impf) +infin*.
unwillingly [ʌn'wɪlɪŋlɪ] *adv* неохо́тно.
unwind [ʌn'waɪnd] *irreg vt* (*undo*) разма́тывать (размота́ть *perf*) ◆ *vi* (*relax*) расслабля́ться (рассла́биться* *perf*).
unwise [ʌn'waɪz] *adj* неблагоразу́мный* (неблагоразу́мен).
unwitting [ʌn'wɪtɪŋ] *adj* нево́льный.
unworkable [ʌn'wə:kəbl] *adj* неосуществи́мый (неосуществи́м).
unworthy [ʌn'wə:ðɪ] *adj* недосто́йный* (недосто́ен); **to be ~ of sth/to do** быть* *(impf)* недосто́йным(-ой) чего́-н/*+infin*; **that remark is ~ of you** Вам не приста́ло э́то говори́ть.
unwrap [ʌn'ræp] *vt* развора́чивать (разверну́ть *perf*).
unwritten [ʌn'rɪtn] *adj* (*law, agreement*) неписаный.
unzip [ʌn'zɪp] *vt* расстёгивать (расстегну́ть *perf*) на мо́лнию.

KEYWORD

up [ʌp] *prep*: **he went up the stairs/the hill** он подня́лся по ле́стнице/на́ гору; **the cat was up a tree** ко́шка была́ на де́реве; **they live further up the street** они́ живу́т да́льше на э́той у́лице; **he has gone up to Scotland** он пое́хал в Шотла́ндию
◆ *adv* ***1*** (*upwards, higher*): **up in the sky/the mountains** высоко́ в не́бе/в гора́х; **put the picture a bit higher up** пове́сьте карти́ну немно́го повы́ше; **up there** (*up above*) там наверху́; **there's a village and up above, on the hill, a monastery** там есть дере́вня, а над ней,

на холме́ – монасты́рь
2: **to be up** (*out of bed*) встава́ть* (встать* *perf*); (*prices, level*) поднима́ться (подня́ться* *perf*); **the tent is up** пала́тка поста́влена
3: **up to** (*as far as*) до *+gen*; **I've read up to page five** я дочита́л до пя́той страни́цы; **up to now** до сих пор
4: **to be up to** (*depending on*) зави́сеть* *(impf)* от *+gen*; **it's not up to me to decide** не мне реша́ть; **it's up to you** э́то ва́ше де́ло
5: **to be up to** (*inf*: *be doing*) затева́ть *(impf)*; **he's not up to the job** он не тя́нет на э́ту рабо́ту; **his work is not up to the required standard** его́ рабо́та не соотве́тствует тре́буемым станда́ртам; **what is he up to?** что он затева́ет?; **what's she up to these days?** а что она́ тепе́рь поде́лывает?
◆ *n*: **ups and downs** (*in life, career*) взлёты *mpl* и паде́ния *ntpl*.

up-and-coming [ʌpənd'kʌmɪŋ] *adj* перспекти́вный* (перспекти́вен).
upbeat ['ʌpbi:t] *n* (*MUS*) сла́бая до́ля та́кта; (*ECON*) подъём ◆ *adj* (*optimistic*) оживлённый* (оживлён).
upbraid [ʌp'breɪd] *vt* упрека́ть (упрекну́ть *perf*).
upbringing ['ʌpbrɪŋɪŋ] *n* воспита́ние.
upcoming ['ʌpkʌmɪŋ] *adj* (*forthcoming*) предстоя́щий*, гряду́щий.
update [ʌp'deɪt] *vt* (*records, information*) вноси́ть* (внести́* *perf*) измене́ния и дополне́ния.
upend [ʌp'ɛnd] *vt* перевора́чивать (переверну́ть *perf*) (вверх нога́ми).
upfront [ʌp'frʌnt] *adj* (*inf*: *frank*) откры́тый (откры́т) ◆ *adv* (*pay*) вперёд.
upgrade [ʌp'greɪd] *vt* (*improve*: *house*) модернизи́ровать *(impf/perf)*; (: *job*) усложня́ть (усложни́ть *perf*); (*employee*) повыша́ть (повы́сить* *perf*) в до́лжности; (*COMPUT*) нара́щивать *(impf)* вычисли́тельные возмо́жности, модернизи́ровать *(impf/perf)*.
upheaval [ʌp'hi:vl] *n* переворо́т.
uphill [ʌp'hɪl] *adj* (*fig*: *task*) тяжёлый* (тяжёл) ◆ *adv* (*face, look*) вверх; (*go, move*) в го́ру; **to go ~** поднима́ться *(impf)* в го́ру.
uphold [ʌp'həuld] (*irreg*: *like* **hold**) *vt* подде́рживать (поддержа́ть* *perf*).
upholstery [ʌp'həulstərɪ] *n* оби́вка.
upkeep ['ʌpki:p] *n* содержа́ние.
up-market [ʌp'mɑ:kɪt] *adj* (*product*) дорого́й; (*area*) элита́рный.
upon [ə'pɔn] *prep* (*position*) на *+prp*; (*motion*) на *+acc*.
upper ['ʌpə^r] *adj* ве́рхний* ◆ *n* (*of shoe*) верх.
upper class *n*: **the ~ ~** вы́сший* класс.
upper-class ['ʌpə'klɑ:s] *adj* (*families, accent*) аристократи́ческий*; (*district*) элита́рный.
uppercut ['ʌpəkʌt] *n* (*BOXING*) апперко́т.
upper hand *n*: **to have the ~ ~** контроли́ровать *(impf)*.
Upper House *n* (*BRIT*) Пала́та Ло́рдов.
uppermost ['ʌpəməust] *adj* вы́сший*; **what was ~ in my mind** что бо́льше всего́ занима́ло мои́ мы́сли.
Upper Volta [-'vɔltə] *n* Ве́рхняя Во́льта, Букри́на-Фасо́ *nt ind*.
upright ['ʌpraɪt] *adj* (*straight, honest*) прямо́й* (прям); (*vertical*) вертика́льный* (вертика́лен) ◆ *n* (*CONSTR*) вертика́льная сто́йка*.
uprising ['ʌpraɪzɪŋ] *n* восста́ние.
uproar ['ʌprɔ:^r] *n* (*protests*) возмуще́ние; (*shouts*) шум.
uproarious [ʌp'rɔ:rɪəs] *adj* (*people*) хохо́чущий; (*play etc*) ужа́сно смешно́й (смешо́н).
uproot [ʌp'ru:t] *vt* (*tree*) вырыва́ть (вы́рвать *perf*) с ко́рнем; (*fig*: *people*) снима́ть (снять* *perf*) с ме́ста.
upset [*vb, adj* ʌp'sɛt, *n* 'ʌpsɛt] (*irreg*: *like* **set**) *vt* (*glass etc*) опроки́дывать (опроки́нуть *perf*); (*routine*) наруша́ть (нару́шить *perf*); (*plan, person*) расстра́ивать (расстро́ить *perf*); (*person*: *offend*) оскорбля́ть (оскорби́ть* *perf*) ◆ *adj* расстро́енный* (расстро́ен) ◆ *n* (*to plan etc*) наруше́ние; **to get ~** (*sad*) расстра́иваться (расстро́иться *perf*); (*offended*) оскорбля́ться (оскорби́ться* *perf*); **to have a stomach ~** (*BRIT*) страда́ть *(impf)* расстро́йством желу́дка.
upset price ['ʌpsɛt-] *n* (*US, SCOTTISH*) *ни́зшая отправна́я цена́ на аукцио́не*.
upsetting [ʌp'sɛtɪŋ] *adj* (*annoying*) доса́дный.
upshot ['ʌpʃɔt] *n* результа́т; **the ~ of it all was that** ... ко́нчилось всё тем, что ....
upside down ['ʌpsaɪd-] *adv* (*hang, hold*) вверх нога́ми; (*turn*) вверх дном; **to turn a place ~ ~** (*fig*) переверну́ть *(perf)* всё вверх дном.
upstairs [ʌp'stɛəz] *adv* (*be*) наверху́; (*go*) наве́рх ◆ *adj* (*window, room*) ве́рхний* ◆ *n* ве́рхний* эта́ж*; **there's no ~** здесь нет ве́рхнего этажа́.
upstage ['ʌp'steɪdʒ] *vt* затмева́ть (затми́ть* *perf*).
upstart ['ʌpstɑ:t] *n* (*pej*: *person*) вы́скочка* *m/f*.
upstream [ʌp'stri:m] *adv* про́тив тече́ния ◆ *adj* вверх по тече́нию.
upsurge ['ʌpsə:dʒ] *n* (*of enthusiasm etc*) подъём.
uptake ['ʌpteɪk] *n*: **to be quick/slow on the ~** бы́стро/ме́дленно сообража́ть *(impf)*.
uptight [ʌp'taɪt] *adj* (*inf*) натя́нутый (натя́нут).
up-to-date ['ʌptə'deɪt] *adj* (*information*) после́дний*; (*person*) совреме́нный*

(совремéнен).
upturn ['ʌptə:n] *n* (*in economy*) подъём.
upturned ['ʌptə:nd] *adj* (*nose*) курнóсый (курнóс), вздёрнутый (вздёрнут).
upward ['ʌpwəd] *adj*: ~ **movement/glance** движéние/взгляд вверх ◆ *adv* = **upwards**.
upwardly mobile ['ʌpwədlı-] *adj* преуспевáющий; **a new ~ ~ generation** нóвое поколéние преуспевáющих людéй.
upwards ['ʌpwədz] *adv* (*move, glance*) вверх; (*more than*): ~ **of** свы́ше *+gen*.
URA *n abbr* (*US*: = *Urban Renewal Administration*) *правúтельственная организáция, координúрующая рабóты по обновлéнию и улучшéнию устрóйства городóв*.
Ural Mountains ['juərəl-] *npl*: **the ~ ~** (*also:* **the Urals**) Урáл *msg*, Урáльские гóры *fpl*.
uranium [juə'reınıəm] *n* урáн.
Uranus [juə'reınəs] *n* Урáн.
urban ['ə:bən] *adj* городскóй.
urbane [ə:'beın] *adj* учти́вый (учти́в).
urbanization ['ə:bənaı'zeıʃən] *n* урбанизáция.
urchin ['ə:tʃın] *n* (*pej*) беспризóрник(-ица).
Urdu ['uədu:] *n* язы́к* урдý.
urge [ə:dʒ] *n* (*need, desire*) потрéбность *f* ◆ *vt*: **to ~ sb to do** настоя́тельно совéтовать *(impf)* комý-н *+infin*; **to ~ caution** совéтовать (посовéтовать *perf*) быть* осторóжным(-ой)
▸ **urge on** *vt* подгоня́ть *(impf)*.
urgency ['ə:dʒənsı] *n* (*of task etc*) неотлóжность *f*, безотлагáтельность *f*; (*of tone*) настóйчивость *f*.
urgent ['ə:dʒənt] *adj* (*need, message*) срóчный* (срóчен); (*voice*) настóйчивый (настóйчив).
urgently ['ə:dʒəntlı] *adv* срóчно.
urinal ['juərınl] *n* (*building*) мужскóй туалéт; (*vessel*) писсуáр.
urinate ['juərıneıt] *vi* мочи́ться* (помочи́ться* *perf*).
urine ['juərın] *n* мочá.
urn [ə:n] *n* (*container*) ýрна; (*also:* **tea ~**) бак.
Uruguay ['juərəgwaı] *n* Уругвáй.
Uruguayan [juərə'gwaıən] *adj* уругвáйский* ◆ *n* уругвáец*(-áйка*).
US *n abbr* = **United States**.
us [ʌs] *pron* (*direct*) нас; (*indirect*) нам; (*after prep*: *+gen, +prp*) нас; (: *+dat*) нам; (: *+instr*) нáми; (*referring to subject of sentence*) свой; **a few of ~ are going to the cinema** нéкоторые из нас идýт в кинó; *see also* **me**.
USA *n abbr* (= **United States of America**) США= *Соединённые Штáты Амéрики*; (*MIL*) = *United States Army*.
usable ['ju:zəbl] *adj* пригóдный* (пригóден).
USAF *n abbr* = *United States Air Force*.
usage ['ju:zıdʒ] *n* (*LING*) употреблéние.
USCG *n abbr* = *United States Coast Guard*.
USDA *n abbr* = *United States Department of Agriculture*.
USDAW ['ʌzdɔ:] *n abbr* (*BRIT*) = *Union of Shop, Distributive and Allied Workers*.
USDI *n abbr* (= *United States Department of the Interior*) ≈ Министéрство вну́тренних дел.
use [*vt* ju:z, *n* ju:s] *vt* (*object, tool*) испóльзовать *(impf/perf)*; (*phrase*) употребля́ть (употреби́ть* *perf*) ◆ *n* (*using*) испóльзование, употреблéние; (*usefulness*) пóльза; (*purpose*) применéние; **she ~d to do it** онá когдá-то занимáлась э́тим; **what's this ~d for?** для чегó э́то употребля́ется?; **to be ~d to** быть* *(impf)* привы́чным(-ой) к *+dat*; **to get ~d to** привыкáть (привы́кнуть* *perf*) к *+dat*; **to be in ~** употребля́ться *(impf)*, быть* *(impf)* в употреблéнии; **to be out of ~** не употребля́ться *(impf)*; **to be of ~** быть* *(impf)* полéзным(-ой); **to make ~ of sth** испóльзовать *(impf/perf)* что-н; **it's no ~** э́то бесполéзно; **to have the ~ of** пóльзоваться *(impf) +instr*
▸ **use up** *vt* (*food, leftovers*) испóльзовать *(impf/perf)*; (*money*) расхóдовать (израсхóдовать *perf*).
used [ju:zd] *adj* (*object*) бы́вший* в употреблéнии; (*car*) подéржанный.
useful ['ju:sful] *adj* полéзный* (полéзен); **to come in ~** пригоди́ться* *(perf)*.
usefulness ['ju:sfəlnıs] *n* пóльза.
useless ['ju:slıs] *adj* (*unusable*) непригóдный* (непригóден); (*pointless, hopeless*) бесполéзный* (бесполéзен).
user ['ju:zə'] *n* пóльзователь *f*; (*of petrol, gas etc*) потреби́тель *m*.
user-friendliness ['ju:zə'frɛndlınıs] *n* простотá в испóльзовании.
user-friendly ['ju:zə'frɛndlı] *adj* простóй (прост) в испóльзовании.
USES *n abbr* (= *United States Employment Service*) *управлéние по размещéнию и регули́рованию рабóчей си́лы*.
usher ['ʌʃə'] *n* (*at wedding*) распоряди́тель *m* ◆ *vt*: **to ~ sb into** проводи́ть* (провести́* *perf*) когó-н в *+acc*.
usherette [ʌʃə'rɛt] *n* билетёрша.
USIA *n abbr* (= *United States Information Agency*) ЮСИА (*Информациóнное агéнтство США*).
USM *n abbr* (= *United States Mint*) Монéтный двор США; (= *United States Mail*) Пóчта США.
USN *n abbr* = *United States Navy*.
USPHS *n abbr* = *United States Public Health Service*.
USPO *n abbr* = *United States Post Office*.
USS *abbr* = *United States Ship*.
USSR *n abbr* (*formerly*: = *Union of Soviet Socialist Republics*) СССР= *Сою́з Совéтских Социалисти́ческих Респýблик*.
usu. *abbr* = **usually**.
usual ['ju:ʒuəl] *adj* (*time, place etc*) обы́чный; **as ~** как обы́чно.
usually ['ju:ʒuəlı] *adv* обы́чно.

usurer ['ju:ʒərə'] *n* ростовщи́к*.
usurp [ju:'zə:p] *vt* узурпи́ровать *(impf/perf)*.
usury ['ju:ʒurɪ] *n* ростовщи́чество.
UT *(US: POST) abbr* = *Utah.*
utensil [ju:'tɛnsl] *n* инструме́нт; **kitchen ~s** ку́хонные принадле́жности.
uterus ['ju:tərəs] *n* ма́тка*.
utilitarian [ju:tɪlɪ'tɛərɪən] *adj* утилита́рный* (утилита́рен).
utility [ju:'tɪlɪtɪ] *n* (*usefulness*) поле́зность *f*; **public utilities** коммуна́льные услу́ги *fpl*.
utility room *n* подсо́бная ко́мната, подсо́бка* (*разг*).
utilization [ju:tɪlaɪ'zeɪʃən] *n* утилиза́ция.
utilize ['ju:tɪlaɪz] *vt* утилизи́ровать *(impf/perf)*; (*information*) находи́ть (найти́* *perf*) примене́ние *+dat*.
utmost ['ʌtməust] *adj* велича́йший ◆ *n*: **to do one's ~** де́лать (сде́лать *perf*) всё возмо́жное; **of the ~ importance** велича́йшей ва́жности.
utter ['ʌtə'] *adj* (*amazement*) по́лный; (*conviction*) глубо́кий*; (*rubbish*) соверше́нный ◆ *vt* (*sounds*) издава́ть* (изда́ть* *perf*); (*words*) произноси́ть* (произнести́* *perf*).
utterance ['ʌtrns] *n* выска́зывание.
utterly ['ʌtəlɪ] *adv* соверше́нно.
U-turn ['ju:'tə:n] *n* (*AUT*) разворо́т на 180 гра́дусов; (*fig*) коренно́е измене́ние.
Uzbek ['ʌzbɛk] *n* (*person*) узбе́к(-е́чка*); (*LING*) узбе́кский* язы́к* ◆ *adj* узбе́кский*.
Uzbekistan [ʌzbɛkɪ'stɑ:n] *n* Узбекиста́н.

~ V, v ~

V, **v** [vi:] *n* (*letter*) *22-а́я бу́ква англи́йского алфави́та.*
v. *abbr* = **verse, versus**; (**= volt**) В= *вольт*; (*see*: = *vide*) см. *смотри́.*
VA (*US*: *POST*) *abbr* = *Virginia.*
vac [væk] *n abbr* (*BRIT*: *inf*) = **vacation**.
vacancy ['veɪkənsɪ] *n* (*BRIT*: *job*) вака́нсия; (*room in hotel etc*) свобо́дный но́мер*; **"no vacancies"** „мест нет"; **have you any vacancies?** (*hotel*) у Вас есть свобо́дные номера́?; (*office*) у Вас есть вака́нсии?
vacant ['veɪkənt] *adj* (*room, seat, toilet*) свобо́дный* (свобо́ден); (*look, expression*) отсу́тствующий*; (*job*) вака́нтный.
vacant lot *n* (*US*) пусты́рь* *m*; (: *for sale*) уча́сток*.
vacate [və'keɪt] *vt* освобожда́ть (освободи́ть* *perf*).
vacation [və'keɪʃən] *n* (*esp US*: *holiday*) о́тпуск*; (*BRIT*: *SCOL*) кани́кулы *pl*; **to take a ~** брать* (взять* *perf*) о́тпуск; **on ~** в о́тпуске.
vacation course *n* ле́тние ку́рсы *mpl*.
vaccinate ['væksɪneɪt] *vt*: **to ~ sb (against sth)** де́лать (сде́лать *perf*) приви́вку кому́-н (от чего́-н).
vaccination [væksɪ'neɪʃən] *n* приви́вка*.
vaccine ['væksi:n] *n* вакци́на.
vacuum ['vækjum] *n* (*empty space*) ва́куум ◆ *vt* пылесо́сить (пропылесо́сить *perf*).
vacuum cleaner *n* пылесо́с.
vacuum flask *n* (*BRIT*) те́рмос.
vacuum-packed ['vækjum'pækt] *adj* гермети́чно упако́ванный (упако́ван).
Vaduz [fa'duts] *n*Ваду́ц.
vagabond ['vægəbɔnd] *n* бродя́га *m/f*.
vagary ['veɪgərɪ] *n*: **the vagaries of the weather** капри́зы *mpl* пого́ды.
vagina [və'dʒaɪnə] *n* влага́лище.
vagrancy ['veɪgrənsɪ] *n* бродя́жничество.
vagrant ['veɪgrənt] *n* бродя́га *m/f*.
vague [veɪg] *adj* (*blurred*: *memory, outline*) сму́тный* (сму́тен); (*uncertain*) неопределённый; (*look*) рассе́янный; (*idea, instructions*) расплы́вчатый (расплы́вчат); (*evasive*: *answer*) укло́нчивый (укло́нчив); **he was ~ about it** (*evasive*) он не сказа́л ничего́ определённого об э́том; **I haven't the ~st idea** я не име́ю ни мале́йшего представле́ния.
vaguely ['veɪglɪ] *adv* (*promise, say, plan*) неопределённо; (*look*) рассе́янно; (*suspect*) сму́тно; **they were ~ amused** они́ слегка́ развесели́лись; **it looks ~ like yours** э́то немно́жко напомина́ет Ваш.
vagueness ['veɪgnɪs] *n* неопределённость *f*.
vain [veɪn] *adj* (*conceited*) тщесла́вный* (тщесла́вен); (*useless*: *attempt, action*) тще́тный* (тще́тен); **in ~** напра́сно.
vainly ['veɪnlɪ] *adv* тще́тно.
valance ['væləns] *n* (*for bed*) подзо́р.
valedictorian [vælɪdɪk'tɔ:rɪən] *n* (*US*: *SCOL*) "лу́чший* выпускни́к" (*в двена́дцатом кла́ссе сре́дней шко́лы*).
valedictory [vælɪ'dɪktərɪ] *adj* (*speech, remarks*) проща́льный.
valentine ['væləntaɪn] *n* (*also*: **~ card**) *(анони́мное) любо́вное посла́ние в день Св. Валенти́на (14 февраля́).*
valet ['vælɪt] *n* камерди́нер.
valet parking *n припарко́вка автомоби́лей клие́нтов, наприме́р в гости́ницах.*
valet service *n* (*for clothes*) *слу́жба по ухо́ду за оде́ждой клие́нтов*; (*for car*) *обслу́живание автомоби́лей – мо́йка, запра́вка итп.*
valiant ['vælɪənt] *adj* (*attempt, effort*) отва́жный* (отва́жен).
valid ['vælɪd] *adj* (*ticket, document*) действи́тельный* (действи́телен); (*reason*) ве́ский* (ве́сок); (*argument*) убеди́тельный* (убеди́телен).
validate ['vælɪdeɪt] *vt* (*contract, document*) утвержда́ть (утверди́ть* *perf*); (*argument, claim*) подтвержда́ть (подтверди́ть *perf*).
validity [və'lɪdɪtɪ] *n* (*see adj*) действи́тельность *f*, ве́скость *f*, убеди́тельность *f*.
valise [və'li:z] *n* саквоя́ж.
Valletta [və'lɛtə] *n* Валле́тта.
valley ['vælɪ] *n* доли́на.
valour ['vælə] (*US* **valor**) *n* до́блесть *f*.
valuable ['væljuəbl] *adj* це́нный; (*time*) драгоце́нный.
valuables ['væljuəblz] *npl* (*jewellery etc*) це́нности *fpl*.
valuation [vælju'eɪʃən] *n* оце́нка*.
value ['vælju:] *n* це́нность *f* ◆ *vt* (*fix price or worth of*) оце́нивать (оцени́ть* *perf*); (*appreciate*) цени́ть* (*impf*); **~s** *npl* (*principles,*

beliefs) це́нности *fpl*; **you get good ~ (for money) in that shop** в э́том магази́не вы́годно покупа́ть; **to lose (in) ~** па́дать (упа́сть* *perf*) в цене́; **to gain (in) ~** поднима́ться (подня́ться* *perf*) в цене́; **to be of great ~ to sb** (*fig*) представля́ть (*impf*) для кого́-н большу́ю це́нность.
value-added tax [vælju:'ædɪd-] *n* (*BRIT*) нало́г на доба́вленную сто́имость.
valued ['vælju:d] *adj* (*customer, advice*) це́нный.
valuer ['væljuə^r] *n* оце́нщик.
valve [vælv] *n* (*also MED*) кла́пан.
vampire ['væmpaɪə^r] *n* вампи́р.
van [væn] *n* (*AUT*) фурго́н; (*BRIT: RAIL*) бага́жный ваго́н.
V and A *n abbr* (*BRIT*) = *Victoria and Albert Museum*.
vandal ['vændl] *n*ванда́л.
vandalism ['vændəlɪzəm] *n* вандали́зм.
vandalize ['vændəlaɪz] *vt* (*damage*) бессмы́сленно уро́довать (изуро́довать *perf*); (*destroy*) бессмы́сленно разруша́ть (разру́шить *perf*).
vanguard ['vængɑ:d] *n* (*fig*): **in the ~ of** в аванга́рде *+gen*.
vanilla [və'nɪlə] *n* вани́ль *f*.
vanilla ice cream *n* ≈ сли́вочное моро́женое *nt adj*.
vanish ['vænɪʃ] *vi* исчеза́ть (исче́знуть *perf*).
vanity ['vænɪtɪ] *n* (*of person*) тщесла́вие.
vanity case *n* космети́чка*.
vantage point ['vɑ:ntɪdʒ-] *n* наблюда́тельный пункт; **from our 20th century ~ ~** (*fig*) с пози́ции на́шего 20-го ве́ка.
vapor *etc* (*US*) = **vapour** *etc*.
vaporize ['veɪpəraɪz] *vt* (*liquid*) выпа́ривать (вы́парить *perf*) ◆ *vi* испаря́ться (испари́ться *perf*).
vapour ['veɪpə^r] (*US* **vapor**) *n* (*gas, mist, steam*) пар*.
vapour trail *n* (*AVIAT*) след* самолёта.
variable ['vɛərɪəbl] *adj* (*likely to change: mood, quality, weather*) изме́нчивый (изме́нчив); (*able to be changed: temperature, height, speed*) переме́нный ◆ *n* фа́ктор; (*MATH*) переме́нная *f adj*.
variance ['vɛərɪəns] *n*: **to be at ~ with** расходи́ться* (*impf*) (с *+instr*); (*facts*) противоре́чить (*impf*) *+dat*.
variant ['vɛərɪənt] *n* вариа́нт.
variation [vɛərɪ'eɪʃən] *n* (*in level, amount, quantity*) измене́ние; (*of plot, musical theme etc*) вариа́ция.
varicose veins ['værɪkəus-] *npl* (*MED*) варико́зное расшире́ние *ntsg* вен.
varied ['vɛərɪd] *adj* разнообра́зный* (разнообра́зен).
variety [və'raɪətɪ] *n* разнообра́зие; (*type*) разнови́дность *f*; **a wide ~ of ...** большо́е разнообра́зие *+gen ...*; **for a ~ of reasons** по ря́ду причи́н.
variety show *n* (*THEAT*) варьете́ *nt ind*.
various ['vɛərɪəs] *adj* (*different*) разли́чный; (*several*) ра́зный; **at ~ times** в ра́зное вре́мя.
varnish ['vɑ:nɪʃ] *n* (*product*) лак; (*also:* **nail ~**) лак для ногте́й ◆ *vt* (*wood, piece of furniture etc*) покрыва́ть (покры́ть* *perf*) ла́ком; (*nails*) кра́сить* (накра́сить* *perf*).
vary ['vɛərɪ] *vt* (*routine, diet*) вноси́ть* (внести́* *perf*) разнообра́зие в *+acc* ◆ *vi* (*be different: sizes, colours*) различа́ться (*impf*); (*become different*): **to ~ with** (*weather, season etc*) меня́ться (*impf*) в зави́симости от *+gen*; **to ~ (according to** *or* **with)** меня́ться (*impf*) (в соотве́тствии с *+instr*).
varying ['vɛərɪɪŋ] *adj* (*amount, opinions etc*) разли́чный* (разли́чен).
vase [vɑ:z] *n* ва́за.
vasectomy [væ'sɛktəmɪ] *n* (*MED*) вазектоми́я.
Vaseline® ['væsɪli:n] *n* вазели́н.
vast [vɑ:st] *adj* (*knowledge*) обши́рный* (обши́рен); (*expense*) грома́дный* (грома́ден); (*area*) необъя́тный* (необъя́тен).
vastly ['vɑ:stlɪ] *adv* кра́йне.
vastness ['vɑ:stnɪs] *n* необъя́тность *f*.
VAT [væt] *n abbr* (*BRIT*) (= **value-added tax**) НДС= *нало́г на доба́вленную сто́имость*.
vat [væt] *n* ка́дка.
Vatican ['vætɪkən] *n*: **the ~** Ватика́н.
vatman ['vætmæn] *n* (*BRIT: inf*) *чино́вник, собира́ющий нало́г на доба́вленную сто́имость*.
vaudeville ['vəudəvɪl] *n* (*THEAT*) водеви́ль *m*.
vault [vɔ:lt] *n* (*of roof*) свод; (*tomb*) склеп; (*in bank*) храни́лище; (*jump*) (опо́рный) прыжо́к ◆ *vt* (*also:* **~ over**) перепры́гивать (перепры́гнуть *perf*) (че́рез *+acc*).
vaunted ['vɔ:ntɪd] *adj*: **much-~** восхваля́емый.
VC *n abbr* = **vice-chairman**; (*BRIT:* = *Victoria Cross*) "Крест Викто́рии" (*вы́сшая вое́нная награ́да*).
VCR *n abbr* = **video cassette recorder**.
VD *n abbr* = **venereal disease**.
VDU *n abbr* (*COMPUT*) = **visual display unit**.
veal [vi:l] *n* (*CULIN*) теля́тина.
veer [vɪə^r] *vi* (*vehicle*) свора́чивать (сверну́ть *perf*); (*wind*) меня́ть (применя́ть *perf*) направле́ние.
veg. [vɛdʒ] *n abbr* (*BRIT: inf*) = **vegetable(s)**.
vegan ['vi:gən] *n вегетариа́нец, не употребля́ющий моло́чных проду́ктов* ◆ *adj* расти́тельный.
vegeburger ['vɛdʒɪbə:gə^r] *n* вегетариа́нская котле́та.

* marks translations which have irregular inflections. The Russian-English side of the dictionary gives inflectional information.

vegetable ['vɛdʒtəbl] *n* (*BOT*) óвощ ◆ *adj* (*oil etc*) растúтельный; (*dish*) овощнóй; ~ **garden** огорóд.
vegetarian [vɛdʒɪ'tɛərɪən] *n* (*person*) вегетариáнец*(-áнка*) ◆ *adj* (*diet, restaurant etc*) вегетариáнский*.
vegetate ['vɛdʒɪteɪt] *vi* (*person*) прозябáть (*impf*).
vegetation [vɛdʒɪ'teɪʃən] *n* (*plants*) растúтельность *f*.
vegetative ['vɛdʒɪtətɪv] *adj* (*BIO*) вегетатúвный; (*fig*) растúтельный.
veggieburger ['vɛdʒɪbə:gə^r] *n* = **vegeburger**.
vehemence ['vi:ɪməns] *n* ярость *f*.
vehement ['vi:ɪmənt] *adj* (*attack, denial*) ярóстный* (ярóстен); (*passions*) неúстовый (неúстов).
vehicle ['vi:ɪkl] *n* автотрáнспортное срéдство; (*fig*: *means of expressing*) срéдство.
vehicular [vɪ'hɪkjulə^r] *adj* (*AUT*): **"no ~ traffic"** „движéние автотрáнспорта запрещенó".
veil [veɪl] *n* вуáль *f* ◆ *vt* скрывáть (скрыть* *perf*); **under a ~ of secrecy** (*fig*) под покрóвом тáйны.
veiled [veɪld] *adj* (*fig*: *threat*) скрытый.
vein [veɪn] *n* (*of leaf*) жúлка*; (*ANAT*) вéна; (*of ore*) жúла; (*fig*: *of mood, style*) тон.
Velcro® ['vɛlkrəu] *n* липýчка.
vellum ['vɛləm] *n* (*writing paper*) велéневая бумáга.
velocity [vɪ'lɔsɪtɪ] *n* скóрость *f*.
velour [və'luə^r] *n* велю́р.
velvet ['vɛlvɪt] *n* бáрхат ◆ *adj* бáрхатный.
vendetta [vɛn'dɛtə] *n* вендéтта.
vending machine ['vɛndɪŋ-] *n автомáт по продáже сигарéт, шоколáда итп*.
vendor ['vɛndə^r] *n* (*of house, land*) продавéц; **street ~** ýличный(-ая) торгóвец(-вка).
veneer [və'nɪə^r] *n* (*on furniture*) фанерóвка; (*fig*: *of person, place*) личúна.
venerable ['vɛnərəbl] *adj* (*person*) почтéнный; (*building etc*) дрéвний*; (*REL*) преподóбный.
venereal disease [vɪ'nɪərɪəl-] *n* венерúческое заболевáние.
Venetian [vɪ'ni:ʃən] *adj* венециáнский* ◆ *n* венециáнец(-áнка*).
Venetian blind *n* жалюзú *pl*.
Venezuela [vɛnɛ'zweɪlə] *n* Венесуэ́ла.
Venezuelan [vɛnɛ'zweɪlən] *adj* венесуэ́льский* ◆ *n* венесуэ́лец*(-лка).
vengeance ['vɛndʒəns] *n* возмéздие; **with a ~** (*fig*) с лихвóй.
vengeful ['vɛndʒful] *adj* мстúтельный* (мстúтелен).
Venice ['vɛnɪs] *n* Венéция.
venison ['vɛnɪsn] *n* оленúна.
venom ['vɛnəm] *n* (*of snake, insect*) яд; (*bitterness, anger*) злóба.
venomous ['vɛnəməs] *adj* (*snake, insect*) ядовúтый (ядовúт); (*look, stare*) злóбный* (злóбен).
vent [vɛnt] *n* (*also*: **air ~**) вентиляциóнное отвéрстие; (*in jacket*) разрéз ◆ *vt* (*fig*) давáть* (дать* *perf*) вы́ход *+dat*.
ventilate ['vɛntɪleɪt] *vt* (*room, building*) провéтривать (провéтрить *perf*).
ventilation [vɛntɪ'leɪʃən] *n* вентиля́ция.
ventilation shaft *n* вентиляциóнная шáхта.
ventilator ['vɛntɪleɪtə^r] *n* (*TECH, MED*) вентиля́тор.
ventriloquist [vɛn'trɪləkwɪst] *n* чревовещáтель(ница) *m(f)*.
venture ['vɛntʃə^r] *n* (*risky undertaking*) смéлое предприя́тие ◆ *vt* (*opinion*) осмéливаться (осмéлиться *perf*) вы́сказать ◆ *vi* (*dare to go*) осмéливаться (осмéлиться *perf*); **business ~** предприя́тие; **to ~ to do** отвáживаться (отвáжиться *perf*) *+infin*.
venture capital *n* (*COMM*) вéнчурный капитáл.
venue ['vɛnju:] *n* (*place fixed for sth*) мéсто* проведéния.
Venus ['vi:nəs] *n* (*planet*) Венéра.
veracity [və'ræsɪtɪ] *n* правдúвость *f*.
veranda(h) [və'rændə] *n* верáнда.
verb [və:b] *n* глагóл.
verbal ['və:bl] *adj* (*spoken*: *skills, translation etc*) ýстный; (*of a verb*) глагóльный.
verbally ['və:bəlɪ] *adv* (*communicate, transmit*) на слóвах.
verbatim [və:'beɪtɪm] *adj* дослóвный ◆ *adv* дослóвно.
verbose [və:'bəus] *adj* (*person, writing*) многослóвный.
verdict ['və:dɪkt] *n* (*LAW*) приговóр; (*fig*: *opinion*) заключéние; **to bring in a ~ of guilty/not guilty** выносúть* (вы́нести* *perf*) обвинúтельный/оправдáтельный приговóр.
verge [və:dʒ] *n* (*BRIT*: *of road*) обóчина; **"soft ~s"** (*BRIT*: *AUT*) *незаасфальтúрованная, грунтовáя обóчина*; **to be on the ~ of sth** быть* (*impf*) на грáни чегó-н
▸ **verge on** *vt fus* (*panic etc*) гранúчить (*impf*) с *+instr*.
verger ['və:dʒə^r] *n* (*REL*) церкóвный служúтель *m*.
verification [vɛrɪfɪ'keɪʃən] *n* (*see vb*) подтверждéние; провéрка.
verify ['vɛrɪfaɪ] *vt* (*confirm*) подтверждáть (подтвердúть* *perf*); (*check*) проверя́ть (провéрить *perf*).
veritable ['vɛrɪtəbl] *adj* (*for emphasis*: *real*) настоя́щий*.
vermin ['və:mɪn] *npl* (*animals*) вредúтели *mpl*; (*fleas, lice etc*) паразúты *mpl*.
vermouth ['və:məθ] *n* вéрмут.
vernacular [və'nækjulə^r] *n* (*language*) национáльный язы́к*; (*local language*) мéстный диалéкт.
versatile ['və:sətaɪl] *adj* (*person*) разностóронний*; (*substance, machine, tool etc*) универсáльный* (универсáлен).

versatility [vəːsəˈtɪlɪtɪ] *n* (*see adj*) разносторо́нность *f*; универса́льность *f*.
verse [vəːs] *n* (*poetry, in Bible*) стих; (*one part of a poem*) строфа́*; **in ~** в стиха́х.
versed [vəːst] *adj*: **(well-)~ in** све́дущий* (све́дущ) в *+prp*.
version [ˈvəːʃən] *n* (*form: of design, production*) вариа́нт; (*account: of events, accident etc*) ве́рсия.
versus [ˈvəːsəs] *prep* про́тив *+gen*.
vertebra [ˈvəːtɪbrə] (*pl* **~e**) *n* (*ANAT*) позвоно́к*.
vertebrae [ˈvəːtɪbriː] *npl of* **vertebra**.
vertebrate [ˈvəːtɪbrɪt] *n* позвоно́чное *nt adj* (живо́тное).
vertical [ˈvəːtɪkl] *adj* вертика́льный* (вертика́лен) ◆ *n* вертика́ль *f*.
vertically [ˈvəːtɪklɪ] *adv* вертика́льно.
vertigo [ˈvəːtɪgəu] *n* головокруже́ние; **to suffer from ~** страда́ть *(impf)* от головокруже́ний.
verve [vəːv] *n* (*vivacity*) воодушевле́ние.
very [ˈvɛrɪ] *adv* о́чень ◆ *adj*: **the ~ book which** та са́мая кни́га, кото́рая; **~ well/little** о́чень хорошо́/ма́ло; **thank you ~ much** большо́е спаси́бо; **~ much better** гора́здо лу́чше; **I ~ much hope so** я о́чень наде́юсь на э́то; **the ~ thought (of it) alarms me** сама́ мысль (об э́том) пуга́ет меня́; **at the ~ end** в са́мом конце́; **the ~ last** са́мый после́дний*; **at the ~ least** как ми́нимум.
vespers [ˈvɛspəz] *npl* (*REL*) вече́рня *fsg*.
vessel [ˈvɛsl] *n* (*NAUT*) су́дно*; (*container*) сосу́д; *see also* **blood**.
vest [vɛst] *n* (*BRIT: underwear*) ма́йка; (*US: waistcoat*) жиле́т ◆ *vt*: **to ~ sb with sth, ~ sth in sb** наделя́ть (надели́ть *perf*) кого́-н чем-н.
vested interest [ˈvɛstɪd-] *n* (*COMM*) заинтересо́ванность *f*; **to have a ~ ~ in sth** быть* *(impf)* заинтересо́ванным(-ой) в чём-н.
vestibule [ˈvɛstɪbjuːl] *n* (*in building*) вестибю́ль *m*.
vestige [ˈvɛstɪdʒ] *n* оста́ток*.
vestment [ˈvɛstmənt] *n* (*REL*) ри́за.
vestry [ˈvɛstrɪ] *n* (*of church*) ри́зница.
Vesuvius [vɪˈsuːvɪəs] *n* Везу́вий.
vet [vɛt] *n abbr* (*BRIT*) = **veterinary surgeon**.
veteran [ˈvɛtərn] *n* (*of war*) ветера́н ◆ *adj*: **she's a ~ campaigner for** ... она́ ста́рый ветера́н движе́ния за *+acc* ....
veteran car *n* (*BRIT*) маши́на ста́рой ма́рки.
veterinarian [vɛtrɪˈnɛərɪən] *n* (*US*) ветерина́р.
veterinary [ˈvɛtrɪnərɪ] *adj* (*practice, care etc*) ветерина́рный.
veterinary surgeon *n* (*BRIT*) ветерина́р.
veto [ˈviːtəu] (*pl* **~es**) *n* ве́то *nt ind* ◆ *vt* (*proposal etc*) налага́ть (наложи́ть* *perf*) ве́то на *+acc*; **to put a ~ on** налага́ть (наложи́ть* *perf*) ве́то на *+acc*.
vetting [ˈvɛtɪŋ] *n* (*of person*) прове́рка (на благонадёжность).
vex [vɛks] *vt* (*irritate, upset*) досажда́ть (досади́ть* *perf*).
vexed [vɛkst] *adj* (*question*) досажда́ющий.
VFD *n abbr* (*US*) = *volunteer fire department*.
VG *n abbr* (*BRIT: SCOL etc*) = *very good*.
VHF *abbr* (*RADIO*: = *very high frequency*) ОВЧ= *о́чень высо́кая частота́*.
VI *abbr* (*US: POST*) = *Virgin Islands*.
via [ˈvaɪə] *prep* (*through, by way of*) че́рез *+acc*.
viability [vaɪəˈbɪlɪtɪ] *n* жизнеспосо́бность *f*; (*of product*) конкурентоспосо́бость *f*.
viable [ˈvaɪəbl] *adj* (*company*) конкурентоспосо́бный; (*project*) осуществи́мый.
viaduct [ˈvaɪədʌkt] *n* виаду́к.
vial [ˈvaɪəl] *n* (*for medicine*) пузырёк; (*for perfume*) флако́н.
vibes [vaɪbz] *npl* (*inf: atmosphere*) флюи́ды *mpl*.
vibrant [ˈvaɪbrnt] *adj* (*lively*) по́лный* (по́лон) жи́зни; (*light*) я́ркий* (я́рок); (*colour*) со́чный* (со́чен); (*full of emotion: voice*) насы́щенный.
vibraphone [ˈvaɪbrəfəun] *n* вибрафо́н.
vibrate [vaɪˈbreɪt] *vi* (*house, machine etc*) вибри́ровать* *(impf)*; (*resound*) отдава́ться* *(impf)*.
vibration [vaɪˈbreɪʃən] *n* вибра́ция.
vibrator [vaɪˈbreɪtəʳ] *n* вибра́тор.
vicar [ˈvɪkəʳ] *n* (*REL*) свяще́нник.
vicarage [ˈvɪkərɪdʒ] *n* дом* свяще́нника.
vicarious [vɪˈkɛərɪəs] *adj* (*pleasure, experience*) опосре́дованный (опосре́дован).
vice [vaɪs] *n* (*moral fault*) поро́к; (*TECH*) тиски́ *pl*.
vice- [vaɪs] *prefix* (*president*) вице-.
vice-chairman [vaɪsˈtʃɛəmən] *irreg n* замести́тель *m* председа́теля.
vice chancellor *n* (*BRIT: of university*) ви́це-ка́нцлер.
vice president *n* ви́це-президе́нт.
viceroy [ˈvaɪsrɔɪ] *n* короле́вский* наме́стник.
vice squad *n* (*POLICE*) *отде́л в поли́ции, кото́рый име́ет де́ло с преступле́ниями, свя́занными с порногра́фией, проститу́цией, нарко́тиками итп*.
vice versa [ˈvaɪsɪˈvəːsə] *adv* наоборо́т.
vicinity [vɪˈsɪnɪtɪ] *n* (*area*): **in the ~ (of)** в окре́стностях (*+gen*).
vicious [ˈvɪʃəs] *adj* (*attack, blow*) жесто́кий* (жесто́к); (*words, look, dog*) злой* (зол); (*horse*) норови́стый (норови́ст).
vicious circle *n* поро́чный круг.
viciousness [ˈvɪʃəsnɪs] *n* зло́ба.
vicissitudes [vɪˈsɪsɪtjuːdz] *npl* превра́тности *fpl*.
victim [ˈvɪktɪm] *n* же́ртва; **to be the ~ of** быть* *(impf)* же́ртвой *+gen*.
victimization [ˈvɪktɪmaɪˈzeɪʃən] *n* пресле́дование.

victimize ['vɪktɪmaɪz] *vt* (*strikers etc*) преслéдовать* *(impf/perf)*.
victor ['vɪktəʳ] *n* победи́тель(ница) *m(f)*.
Victorian [vɪk'tɔ:rɪən] *adj* викториáнский.
victorious [vɪk'tɔ:rɪəs] *adj* (*team*) победонóсный; (*shout*) побéдный.
victory ['vɪktərɪ] *n* побéда; **to win a ~ over sb** одержáть* *(perf)* побéду над кем-н.
video ['vɪdɪəu] *cpd* ви́део *ind* ◆ *n* (*also:* **~ film**) видеофи́льм; (*also:* **~ cassette**) видеокассéта; (*also:* **~ cassette recorder**) видеомагнитофóн; (*also:* **~ camera**) видеокáмера.
videodisc ['vɪdɪəudɪsk] *n* ви́деодиск.
video game *n* видеоигрá.
video nasty *n* *видеофи́льм со сцéнами наси́лия*.
videophone ['vɪdɪəufəun] *n* видеотелефóн.
video recorder *n* видеомагнитофóн.
video recording *n* видеозáпись *f*.
video tape *n* видеолéнта.
vie [vaɪ] *vi*: **to ~ with sb/for sth** сопéрничать *(impf)* с кем-н/в чём-н.
Vienna [vɪ'ɛnə] *n* Вéна.
Viennese [vɪə'ni:z] *adj* вéнский ◆ *n inv* жи́тель(ница) *m(f)* Вéны.
Vietnam ['vjɛt'næm] *n* Вьетнáм.
Viet Nam ['vjɛt'næm] *n* = **Vietnam**.
Vietnamese [vjɛtnə'mi:z] *adj* вьетнáмский* ◆ *n inv* (*person*) вьетнáмец*(-мка*); (*LING*) вьетнáмский* язы́к*.
view [vju:] *n* (*sight, outlook*) вид; (*opinion*) взгляд ◆ *vt* (*look at: also fig*) рассмáтривать (рассмотрéть *perf*); (*situation*) оцéнивать (оцени́ть *perf*); (*house*) осмáтривать (осмотрéть *perf*); **to be on ~** (*in museum etc*) выставля́ться *(impf)*; **in full ~ (of)** на виду́ (у +*gen*); **in ~ of the weather/the fact that** ввиду́ плохóй погóды/тогó, что; **in my ~** на мой взгляд; **an overall ~ of the situation** óбщая карти́на положéния; **with a ~ to doing** с тем, чтóбы +*infin*.
Viewdata® ['vju:deɪtə] *n* (*BRIT: COMPUT*) видеотéкст; (*TEL*) *телекоммуникациóнная систéма, позволя́ющая клиéнтам дéлать закáзы на товáры и́ли услу́ги пря́мо из дóма*.
viewer ['vju:əʳ] *n* (*person*) зри́тель *m*.
viewfinder ['vju:faɪndəʳ] *n* (*PHOT*) видо-искáтель *m*.
viewpoint ['vju:pɔɪnt] *n* (*attitude*) тóчка зрéния; (*place*) мéсто* обозрéния.
vigil ['vɪdʒɪl] *n* бдéние; **to keep ~** дежу́рить (подежу́рить *perf*).
vigilance ['vɪdʒɪləns] *n* бди́тельность *f*.
vigilance committee *n* (*US*) "комитéт бди́тельности" (*организáция линчевáтелей*).
vigilant ['vɪdʒɪlənt] *adj* бди́тельный.
vigilante [vɪdʒɪ'læntɪ] *n* *самодéятельный блюсти́тель поря́дка, считáющий дéйствия поли́ции недостáточными*.
vigor ['vɪgəʳ] (*US*) *n* = **vigour**.
vigorous ['vɪgərəs] *adj* (*action, campaign*) мóщный; (*plant*) си́льный.
vigour ['vɪgəʳ] (*US* **vigor**) *n* (*energy: of person*) си́ла; (*: of campaign*) мощь *f*.
vile [vaɪl] *adj* (*evil*) гну́сный; (*unpleasant*) мéрзкий*; **~ language** сквернослóвие.
vilify ['vɪlɪfaɪ] *vt* (*person*) поноси́ть* *(impf)*.
villa ['vɪlə] *n* ви́лла.
village ['vɪlɪdʒ] *n* дерéвня.
villager ['vɪlɪdʒəʳ] *n* деревéнский*(-ая) жи́тель(ница) *m(f)*.
villain ['vɪlən] *n* (*scoundrel*) негодя́й; (*in novel etc*) злодéй; (*BRIT: criminal*) престу́пник.
Vilnius ['vɪlnɪəs] *n* Ви́льнюс.
VIN *n abbr* (*US*) = *vehicle identification number*.
vinaigrette [vɪneɪ'grɛt] *n* (*salad dressing*) заправка для салáта (*из у́ксуса и расти́тельного мáсла*).
vindicate ['vɪndɪkeɪt] *vt* (*person: free from blame*) докáзывать (доказáть* *perf*) правоту́ +*gen*; (*action: justify*) опрáвдывать (оправдáть *perf*).
vindication [vɪndɪ'keɪʃən] *n*: **in ~ of sb/sth** в оправдáние когó-н/чегó-н.
vindictive [vɪn'dɪktɪv] *adj* мсти́тельный* (мсти́телен).
vine [vaɪn] *n* (*BOT: with grapes*) виногрáдная лозá*; (*: climbing plant*) вью́щееся растéние; (*: in jungle*) лиáна.
vinegar ['vɪnɪgəʳ] *n* у́ксус.
vineyard ['vɪnjɑ:d] *n* виногрáдник.
vintage ['vɪntɪdʒ] *n* (*year*) *год изготовлéния винá* ◆ *cpd* (*classic: comedy, performance etc*) класси́ческий*; **the 1970 ~** (*of wine*) урожáя 1970 гóда.
vintage car *n* маши́на стáрой мáрки.
vintage wine *n* вы́держанное винó.
vinyl ['vaɪnl] *n* вини́л.
viola [vɪ'əulə] *n* (*MUS*) альт*.
violate ['vaɪəleɪt] *vt* нарушáть (нару́шить *perf*); (*graveyard*) осквернять (оскверни́ть *perf*).
violation [vaɪə'leɪʃən] *n* (*of agreement etc*) нарушéние; **in ~ of** в нарушéние +*gen*.
violence ['vaɪələns] *n* (*brutality*) наси́лие; (*strength*) си́ла.
violent ['vaɪələnt] *adj* (*behaviour*) жестóкий*; (*death*) наси́льственный; (*debate, criticism*) я́ростный; **a ~ dislike of sb/sth** рéзкая неприя́знь к кому́-н/чему́-н.
violently ['vaɪələntlɪ] *adv* (*dislike*) си́льно; (*ill, angry*) óчень.
violet ['vaɪələt] *adj* фиолéтовый ◆ *n* (*colour*) фиолéтовый цвет; (*plant*) фиáлка*.
violin [vaɪə'lɪn] *n* (*MUS*) скри́пка*.
violinist [vaɪə'lɪnɪst] *n* скрипáч*(ка*).
VIP *n abbr* (= *very important person*) óчень вáжное лицó.
viper ['vaɪpəʳ] *n* гадю́ка.
viral ['vaɪərəl] *adj* ви́русный.
virgin ['və:dʒɪn] *n* (*person*) дéвственница;

(: *religious etc*) дéва ◆ *adj* (*snow, forest etc*) дéвственный; **the Blessed V~** пресвятáя дéва Мария; (*in Orthodox Church*) Богорóдица.
virgin birth *n* рождéние от дéвственницы.
virginity [və:'dʒɪnɪtɪ] *n* (*of person*) дéвственность *f*.
Virgo ['və:gəu] *n* Дéва; **he is ~** он – Дéва.
virile ['vɪraɪl] *adj* верильный.
virility [vɪ'rɪlɪtɪ] *n* (*sexual power*) верильность *f*; (*fig*: *masculine qualities*) мýжественность *f*.
virtual ['və:tjuəl] *adj* фактический*; (*COMPUT, PHYS*) виртуáльный; (*in effect*): **it's a ~ impossibility** это практически *or* фактически невозмóжно.
virtually ['və:tjuəlɪ] *adv* (*almost*) фактически, практически; **it is ~ impossible** это фактически *or* практически невозмóжно.
virtual reality *n система трёхмерного телевидения*.
virtue ['və:tju:] *n* (*moral correctness*) добродéтель *f*; (*advantage*) преимýщество; (*merit*) достóинство; **by ~ of** благодаря́ +*dat*.
virtuosi [və:tju'əuzɪ] *npl of* **virtuoso**.
virtuosity [və:tju'ɔsɪtɪ] *n* виртуóзность *f*.
virtuoso [və:tju'əuzəu] (*pl* **~s** *or* **virtuosi**) *n* виртуóз.
virtuous ['və:tjuəs] *adj* (*displaying virtue*) добродéтельный.
virulence ['vɪruləns] *n* (*see adj*) ядовитость *f*, смертéльность *f*; нéнависть *f*.
virulent ['vɪrulənt] *adj* (*poison*) ядовитый; (*disease*) смертéльный; (*actions, feelings*) пóлный* (пóлон) нéнависти.
virus ['vaɪərəs] *n* (*MED*) вирус.
visa ['vi:zə] *n* (*for travel*) виза.
vis-à-vis [vi:zə'vi:] *prep* по отношéнию к +*dat*.
viscose ['vɪskəus] *n* вискóза.
viscount ['vaɪkaunt] *n* викóнт.
viscous ['vɪskəs] *adj* (*liquid, substance*) вя́зкий* (вя́зок).
vise [vaɪs] *n* (*US*: *TECH*) = **vice**.
visibility [vɪzɪ'bɪlɪtɪ] *n* видимость *f*.
visible ['vɪzəbl] *adj* (*able to be seen or recognized*) видимый (видим); (*results, growth*) очевидный* (очевиден); **~ exports/imports** (*ECON*) видимый э́кспорт/импорт.
visibly ['vɪzəblɪ] *adv* (*upset, nervous, damaged*) я́вно.
vision ['vɪʒən] *n* (*sight*) зрéние; (*foresight*) предвидение; (*in dream*) видéние.
visionary ['vɪʒənrɪ] *n* (*person*) провидец.
visit ['vɪzɪt] *n* (*to person, place*) посещéние; (*stay*) пребывáние ◆ *vt* (*person*) идти́ (прийти́* *perf*) *or* ходить* (приходить* *perf*) в гóсти к +*dat*; (*elderly, disabled person*) навещáть (навестить* *perf*); (*place*) посещáть (посетить *perf*); **on a private/official ~** с чáстным/официáльным визитом.
visiting ['vɪzɪtɪŋ] *adj* (*speaker*) приéхавший по приглашéнию; **~ team** комáнда гостéй.
visiting card *n* визитная кáрточка*.
visiting hours *npl* (*in hospital etc*) часы́ *mpl* посещéния.
visiting professor *n* профéссор, приéхавший по приглашéнию.
visitor ['vɪzɪtə^r] *n* (*person visiting*) гость(я) *m(f)*; (*in public place, museum etc*) посетитель (ница) *m(f)*; (*tourist*: *in town etc*) приéзжий*(-ая) *m(f) adj*.
visitors' book ['vɪzɪtəz-] *n* книга посетителей.
visor ['vaɪzə^r] *n* (*of helmet etc*) щитóк.
VISTA ['vɪstə] *n abbr* (= *Volunteers in Service to America*) *добровóльная организáция по оказáнию пóмощи бéдным*.
vista ['vɪstə] *n* (*view*) перспектива.
Vistula ['vɪstjulə] *n*: **the ~** Висла.
visual ['vɪzjuəl] *adj* (*image*) зрительный.
visual aid *n* (*SCOL*) нагля́дное посóбие.
visual arts *npl изобразительное искýсство и кинó*.
visual display unit *n* (*COMPUT*) устрóйство визуáльного изображéния *or* дисплéй.
visualize ['vɪzjuəlaɪz] *vt* (*picture, imagine*) представля́ть (представить* *perf*) мысленно; (*foresee*) представля́ть (представить* *perf*) себé.
visually ['vɪzjuəlɪ] *adv*: **~ appealing** привлекáтельный на вид; **~ handicapped** со зрительным дефéктом.
vital ['vaɪtl] *adj* (*essential, important, crucial*) жизненно необходимый (необходим); (*full of life*: *person*) живóй, жизнеспосóбный* (жизнеспосóбен); (*necessary for life*: *organ*) жизненно вáжный* (вáжен); **of ~ importance (to sb/sth)** жизненно вáжно (для когó-н/ чегó-н).
vitality [vaɪ'tælɪtɪ] *n* (*liveliness*) живость *f*.
vitally ['vaɪtəlɪ] *adv*: **~ important** жизненно вáжный* (вáжен).
vital statistics *npl* (*of woman*) габариты *mpl*; (*of population*) демографическая статистика *fsg*.
vitamin ['vɪtəmɪn] *n* витамин.
vitiate ['vɪʃɪeɪt] *vt* (*spoil*) пóртить (испóртить *perf*); **to ~ sb's efforts** сводить* (свести́* *perf*) на нет чьи-н усилия.
vitreous ['vɪtrɪəs] *adj* стекловидный.
vitriolic [vɪtrɪ'ɔlɪk] *adj* (*fig*: *language*) ядовитый (ядовит); (: *behaviour*) злóбный* (злóбен).
viva (voce) ['vaɪvə('vəutʃɪ)] *n* (*SCOL*) ýстный экзáмен.
vivacious [vɪ'veɪʃəs] *adj* (*person*) живóй.
vivacity [vɪ'væsɪtɪ] *n* живость *f*.
vivid ['vɪvɪd] *adj* (*description, colour, light*) я́ркий*; (*memory*) отчётливый; (*imagination*)

* marks translations which have irregular inflections. The Russian-English side of the dictionary gives inflectional information.

живóй.
vividly ['vɪvɪdlɪ] *adv* (*describe*) в живы́х детáлях; (*remember*) отчётливо.
vivisection [vɪvɪ'sɛkʃən] *n* вивисéкция.
vixen ['vɪksn] *n* сáмка* лиси́цы; (*pej*: *woman*) мегéра.
viz [vɪz] *abbr* (*namely*: = *videlicet*) а и́менно.
Vladivostok [vlædɪ'vɔstɔk] *n* Владивостóк.
VLF *abbr* (*RADIO*: = *very low frequency*) ОНЧ= *óчень ни́зкая частотá*.
V-neck ['vi:nɛk] *n* (*also*: ~ **jumper** *or* **pullover**) джéмпер *or* пулóвер с вы́резом.
VOA *n abbr* (= *Voice of America*) "Гóлос Амéрики".
vocabulary [vəu'kæbjulərɪ] *n* (*words known*) словáрный запáс.
vocal ['vəukl] *adj* (*of the voice*: *in singing*) вокáльный; (*articulate*) звýчный* (звýчен); **to be ~ for/against** подня́ть *(perf)* гóлос в пóльзу *+gen*/прóтив *+gen*.
vocal cords *npl* голосовы́е свя́зки *fpl*.
vocalist ['vəukəlɪst] *n* вокали́ст(ка*).
vocals ['vəuklz] *npl* вокáльная пáртия *fsg*.
vocation [vəu'keɪʃən] *n* призвáние.
vocational [vəu'keɪʃənl] *adj* (*training, guidance etc*) профессионáльный.
vociferous [və'sɪfərəs] *adj* (*protesters, demands*) громоглáсный.
vodka ['vɔdkə] *n* вóдка.
vogue [vəug] *n* мóда; **in** ~ в мóде.
voice [vɔɪs] *n* гóлос ◆ *vt* (*opinion*) выскáзывать (вы́сказать* *perf*); **in a loud/soft** ~ грóмким/ ти́хим гóлосом; **to give ~ to sth** выражáть (вы́разить* *perf*) что-н.
voice mail *n* голосовáя пóчта.
voice-over ['vɔɪsəuvə^r] *n* гóлос за кáдром.
void [vɔɪd] *n* (*emptiness*) пустотá; (*hole*) пробéл ◆ *adj* (*invalid*) недействи́тельный* (недействи́телен); ~ **of** (*empty*) лишённый (лишён) *+gen*.
voile [vɔɪl] *n* (*fabric*) вуáль *f*.
vol. *abbr* (= **volume**) т.= *том*.
volatile ['vɔlətaɪl] *adj* (*situation, person*) измéнчивый (измéнчив); (*liquid*) летýчий*.
volcanic [vɔl'kænɪk] *adj* (*rock, eruption*) вулкани́ческий.
volcano [vɔl'keɪnəu] (*pl* ~**es**) *n* вулкáн.
Volga ['vɔlgə] *n*: **the** ~ Вóлга.
Volgograd ['vɔlgəgræd] *n* Волгогрáд.
volition [və'lɪʃən] *n*: **of one's own** ~ по своéй вóле.
volley ['vɔlɪ] *n* (*of gunfire*) залп; (*of stones etc*) град; (*of questions etc*) потóк; (*TENNIS etc*) удáр с лёта.
volleyball ['vɔlɪbɔ:l] *n* (*SPORT*) волейбóл.
volt [vəult] *n* (*ELEC*) вольт.
voltage ['vəultɪdʒ] *n* (*ELEC*) напряжéние; **high/ low** ~ высóкое/ни́зкое напряжéние.
volte-face ['vɔlt'fɑ:s] *n inv* рéзкая перемéна.
voluble ['vɔljubl] *adj* (*person, speech*) многослóвный.
volume ['vɔlju:m] *n* (*space*) объём; (*amount*) коли́чество; (*book*) том; (*sound level*) грóмкость *f*; ~ **one/two** (*book*) том пéрвый/ вторóй; **his expression spoke ~s** выражéние егó лицá говори́т красноречи́вее вся́ких слов.
volume control *n* (*RADIO, TV*) грóмкость *f*.
volume discount *n* (*COMM*) *ски́дка за покýпку крýпной пáртии товáра*.
voluminous [və'lu:mɪnəs] *adj* (*clothes*) простóрный; (*correspondence, notes*) пространный.
voluntarily ['vɔləntrɪlɪ] *adv* (*willingly*) добровóльно.
voluntary ['vɔləntərɪ] *adj* (*willing*: *exile*) добровóльный*; (*unpaid*: *work, worker*) общéственный.
voluntary liquidation *n* (*COMM*) добровóльная ликвидáция.
voluntary redundancy *n* (*BRIT*) увольнéние по сóбственному желáнию.
volunteer [vɔlən'tɪə^r] *n* (*unpaid helper*) волонтёр; (*to army etc*) добровóлец, волонтёр ◆ *vt* (*information*) предлагáть (предложи́ть* *perf*) ◆ *vi* (*for army etc*) идти́* (пойти́* *perf*) добровóльцем; **to ~ to do** вызывáться (вы́зваться* *perf*) *+infin*.
voluptuous [və'lʌptjuəs] *adj* (*movement, body, feeling*) сладострáстный*.
vomit ['vɔmɪt] *n* рвóта ◆ *vi*: **he ~ed** егó вы́рвало; **she began to** ~ её начáло рвать.
voracious [və'reɪʃəs] *adj* жáдный* (жáден); **he is a ~ reader** он с жáдностью читáет.
vote [vəut] *n* (*indication of choice, opinion*) голосовáние; (*votes cast*) гóлос; (*right to vote*) прáво гóлоса ◆ *vi* (*in election etc*) голосовáть* (проголосовáть* *perf*) ◆ *vt* (*elect*): **he was ~d chairman** он был и́збран председáтелем; (*propose*): **to ~ that** предлагáть (предложи́ть *perf*), чтóбы; **to put sth to the ~, take a ~ on sth** стáвить* (постáвить* *perf*) что-н на голосовáние; ~ **of censure** выражéние порицáния; ~ **of thanks** благодáрственная речь *f*; **to pass a ~ of confidence/no confidence** выражáть (вы́разить* *perf*) вóтум довéрия/недовéрия; **to ~ for** *or* **in favour of/against** голосовáть* (проголосовáть* *perf*) за *+acc*/прóтив *+gen*; **to ~ Labour** голосовáть* (проголосовáть* *perf*) за Лейбори́стскую пáртию.
voter ['vəutə^r] *n* избирáтель *m*.
voting ['vəutɪŋ] *n* голосовáние.
voting paper *n* (*BRIT*) избирáтельный бюллетéнь *m*.
voting right *n* прáво гóлоса.
vouch [vautʃ] *vt fus*: **to ~ for** (*person, quality etc*) ручáться (поручи́ться* *perf*) за *+acc*.
voucher ['vautʃə^r] *n* (*for meal*: *also*: **luncheon** ~) талóн на обéд; (*with petrol, cigarettes etc*) вáучер; (*receipt*) распи́ска.
vow [vau] *n* кля́тва ◆ *vt*: **to ~ to do/that**

кля́сться* (покля́сться* *perf*) +*infin*/, что; **to take** *or* **make a ~ to do** дава́ть* (дать* *perf*) обе́т +*infin*.

vowel ['vauəl] *n* (*LING*) гла́сный *m adj*.

voyage ['vɔɪɪdʒ] *n* (*by ship*) пла́вание; (*by spacecraft*) полёт.

voyeur [vwɑː'jəː] *n человéк, получáющий сексуáльное удовóльствие от тáйного созерцáния людéй во врéмя половóго áкта.*

voyeurism [vwɑː'jəːrɪzəm] *n* процéсс созерцáния други́х людéй во врéмя половóго áкта.

VP *n abbr* = **vice president**.

vs *abbr* = **versus**.

V-sign ['viːsaɪn] *n* (*BRIT*: *as insult*) *грýбый жест*; (*in victory*) знак побе́ды.

VSO *n abbr* (*BRIT*: = *Voluntary Service Overseas*) *благотвори́тельное óбщество,окáзывающее пóмощь нуждáющимся за рубежóм.*

VT *abbr* (*US*: *POST*) = *Vermont*.

vulgar ['vʌlgə'] *adj* (*remarks, gestures, graffiti*) вульга́рный; (*decor, ostentation*) по́шлый*.

vulgarity [vʌl'gærɪtɪ] *n* (*rudeness*) вульга́рность *f*; (*ostentation*) по́шлость *f*.

vulnerability [vʌlnərə'bɪlɪtɪ] *n* (*see adj*) уязви́мость *f*; рани́мость *f*.

vulnerable ['vʌlnərəbl] *adj* (*position*) уязви́мый*; (*person*) рани́мый*; **he is ~ to** он подве́ржен +*dat*.

vulture ['vʌltʃə'] *n* гриф; (*fig*: *pej*) стервя́тник.

vulva ['vʌlvə] *n* ву́льва.

* marks translations which have irregular inflections. The Russian-English side of the dictionary gives inflectional information.

~W, w~

W, w ['dʌblju:] *n (letter) 23-ая бу́ква английского алфави́та.*
W *abbr* (= **west**) З= *за́пад*; (*ELEC*: = **watt**) Вт= *ватт.*
WA *abbr* (*US*: *POST*) = *Washington.*
wad [wɔd] *n* (*of cotton wool*) комо́к*; (*of banknotes, paper*) па́чка*.
wadding ['wɔdɪŋ] *n* упако́вочный материа́л.
waddle ['wɔdl] *vi* ходи́ть*/идти́* *(impf)* вперева́лку.
wade [weɪd] *vi*: **to ~ through** (*water*) пробира́ться (пробра́ться* *perf*) че́рез *+acc*; (*book*) одолева́ть (одоле́ть *perf*).
wafer ['weɪfəʳ] *n* (*biscuit*) ва́фля*.
wafer-thin ['weɪfə'θɪn] *adj* тонча́йший.
waffle ['wɔfl] *n* (*CULIN*) ва́фля*; (*empty talk*) трёп ◆ *vi* (*in speech, writing*) трепа́ться *(impf)*.
waffle iron *n* ва́фельница.
waft [wɔft] *vt* доноси́ть* (донести́* *perf*) ◆ *vi* доноси́ться (донести́сь* *perf*).
wag [wæg] *vt* (*head*) кача́ть *(impf)* *+instr* ◆ *vi* (*tail*) виля́ть *(impf)*; **the dog ~ged its tail** соба́ка виля́ла хвосто́м; **to ~ one's finger at sb** грози́ть* (погрози́ть* *perf*) кому́-н па́льцем.
wage [weɪdʒ] *n* (*also*: **~s**) зарпла́та= *за́работная пла́та* ◆ *vt*: **to ~ war** вести́* *(impf)* войну́; **a day's ~s** дневно́й за́работок*.
wage claim *n* тре́бование увеличе́ния за́работной пла́ты.
wage differential *n* дифференциа́льные ста́вки* *fpl* за́работной пла́ты.
wage earner [-ə:nəʳ] *n* лицо́*, рабо́тающее по на́йму; (*in the family*) корми́лец*(-лица).
wage freeze *n* замора́живание за́работной пла́ты.
wage packet *n* конве́рт с зарпла́той.
wager ['weɪdʒəʳ] *n* пари́* *nt ind* ◆ *vt* ста́вить* (поста́вить* *perf*); (*reputation*) ста́вить* (поста́вить* *perf*) на ка́рту.
waggle ['wægl] *vt* (*ears, eyebrows etc*) шевели́ть (пошевели́ть *perf*) *+instr* ◆ *vi* (*head*) пока́чиваться *(impf)*.
wag(g)on ['wægən] *n* (*horse-drawn*) пово́зка*; (*BRIT*: *RAIL*) това́рный ваго́н.
wail [weɪl] *n* вопль *m*; (*of siren*) во́й ◆ *vi* (*person*) вопи́ть* *(impf)*; (*siren*) выть* *(impf)*.
waist [weɪst] *n* та́лия.
waistcoat ['weɪskəut] *n* (*BRIT*) жиле́т.
waistline ['weɪstlaɪn] *n* ли́ния та́лии.
wait [weɪt] *vi* ждать* (подожда́ть* *perf*) ◆ *n*: **we had a long ~ for the bus** мы до́лго жда́ли авто́буса; **to keep sb ~ing** заставля́ть (заста́вить* *perf*) кого́-н ждать; **I can't ~ to go home/meet my new boss** (*fig*) мне не те́рпится пойти́ домо́й/встре́титься с мои́м но́вым нача́льником; **to ~ for sb/sth** ждать* (подожда́ть* *perf*) кого́-н/чего́-н; **~ a minute!** подожди́те мину́тку!; **"repairs while you ~"** „ремо́нт в прису́тствии зака́зчика"; **to lie in ~ for** поджида́ть *(impf)* *+gen*
▸ **wait behind** *vi* задёрживаться (задержа́ться* *perf*)
▸ **wait on** *vt fus* (*serve*) обслу́живать (обслужи́ть* *perf*)
▸ **wait up** *vi*: **don't ~ up for me** не жди́те меня́, ложи́тесь спать.
waiter ['weɪtəʳ] *n* официа́нт.
waiting ['weɪtɪŋ] *n*: **"no ~"** (*BRIT*: *AUT*) „остано́вка запрещена́".
waiting list *n* спи́сок* очередни́ков.
waiting room *n* (*in surgery*) приёмная *f adj*; (*in station*) зал ожида́ния.
waitress ['weɪtrɪs] *n* официа́нтка*.
waive [weɪv] *vt* (*rule*) отменя́ть (отмени́ть *perf*).
waiver ['weɪvəʳ] *n* отка́з.
wake [weɪk] (*pt* **woke** *or* **waked**, *pp* **woken** *or* **waked**) *vt* (*also*: **~ up**) буди́ть* (разбуди́ть* *perf*) ◆ *vi* (*also*: **~ up**) просыпа́ться (просну́ться *perf*) ◆ *n* бде́ние у гро́ба; (*NAUT*) кильва́тер; **to ~ up to danger/threat** осозна́ть* *(perf)* опа́сность/угро́зу; **in the ~ of** (*fig*) вследствие *+gen*; **he followed in his father's ~** (*fig*) он пошёл по стопа́м отца́.
waken ['weɪkn] *vti* = **wake**.
Wales [weɪlz] *n* Уэ́льс; **the Prince of ~** принц Уэ́льский*.
walk [wɔ:k] *n* (*hike*) похо́д; (*shorter*) прогу́лка*; (*gait*) похо́дка; (*path*) доро́жка*, тропа́ ◆ *vi* (*go on foot*) ходи́ть*/идти́* *(impf)* (пешко́м); (*baby*) ходи́ть* *(impf)*; (*for pleasure, exercise*) гуля́ть *(impf)* ◆ *vt* (*distance*) проходи́ть* (пройти́* *perf*); (*dog*) выгу́ливать (вы́гулять *perf*); **10 minutes' ~ from here** в 10-ти мину́тах ходьбы́ отсю́да; **to go for a ~** ходи́ть*/идти́* *(impf)* гуля́ть *or* на прогу́лку; **at a quick ~** бы́стрым ша́гом; **to ~ in one's**

sleep ходи́ть* *(impf)* во сне́; **I'll ~ you home** я провожу́ Вас домо́й; **people from all ~s of life** лю́ди из всех слоёв о́бщества
▸ **walk out** *vi* (*audience*) демонстрати́вно покида́ть (поки́нуть *perf*) зал; (*workers*) бастова́ть *(impf)*
▸ **walk out on** *vt fus* (*inf*: *family etc*) броса́ть (бро́сить* *perf*).
walkabout ['wɔ:kəbaut] *n* (*queen, politician etc*): **to go (on a) ~** проха́живаться (пройти́сь* *perf*) ми́мо толпы́.
walker ['wɔ:kə^r] *n* (*hiker*) тури́ст(ка).
walkie-talkie ['wɔ:kɪ'tɔ:kɪ] *n* переносна́я ра́ция.
walking ['wɔ:kɪŋ] *n* ходьба́; **to be fond of ~** люби́ть* *(impf)* ходи́ть (пешко́м); **the university is within ~ distance** до университе́та мо́жно дойти́ пешко́м.
walking boots *npl* боти́нки *mpl* для ходьбы́.
walking holiday *n* похо́д.
walking stick *n* трость *f*.
Walkman® ['wɔ:kmən] *n* пле́йер.
walk-on ['wɔ:kɔn] *adj*: **~ part** второстепе́нная роль* *f*.
walkout ['wɔ:kaut] *n* забасто́вка*.
walkover ['wɔ:kəuvə^r] *n* (*inf*) лёгкая побе́да.
walkway ['wɔ:kweɪ] *n* пешехо́дная доро́жка*.
wall [wɔ:l] *n* стена́*; **to go to the ~** (*fig*) терпе́ть (потерпе́ть *perf*) крах
▸ **wall in** *vt* обноси́ть* (обнести́* *perf*) стено́й.
wall cupboard *n* встро́енный шкаф*.
walled [wɔ:ld] *adj* (*city*) окружённый крепостно́й стено́й; (*garden*) обнесённый стено́й.
wallet ['wɔlɪt] *n* бума́жник.
wallflower ['wɔ:lflauə^r] *n* желтофио́ль *f*; **to be a ~** (*fig*) быть* *(impf)* незаме́тным(-ой).
wall hanging *n* насте́нный ковёр*.
wallop ['wɔləp] *vt* (BRIT: *inf*) дуба́сить* (отдуба́сить *perf*).
wallow ['wɔləu] *vi* (*in mud*) валя́ться *(impf)*; (*in water*) бара́хтаться *(impf)*; (*in guilt, sentiment*) упива́ться *(impf)*; **to ~ in one's grief** упива́ться *(impf)* свои́м го́рем.
wallpaper ['wɔ:lpeɪpə^r] *n* обо́и *pl* ◆ *vt* (*room*) окле́ивать (окле́ить *perf*) обо́ями.
wall-to-wall ['wɔ:ltə'wɔ:l] *adj*: **~ carpeting** ковро́вое покры́тие для всей пло́щади по́ла.
wally [wɔlɪ] *n* (*inf*) дурачо́к*.
walnut ['wɔ:lnʌt] *n* (*nut*) гре́цкий* оре́х; (*tree*) оре́ховое де́рево*; (*wood*) оре́х.
walrus ['wɔ:lrəs] (*pl* **~** *or* **~es**) *n* морж*.
waltz [wɔ:lts] *n* вальс ◆ *vi* (*dancers*) вальси́ровать *(impf)*, танцева́ть *(impf)* вальс.
wan [wɔn] *adj* изнурённый* (изнурён); **~ complexion** боле́зненная бле́дность *f*.
wand [wɔnd] *n* (*also*: **magic ~**) волше́бная па́лочка*.
wander ['wɔndə^r] *vi* (*person*) броди́ть* *(impf)*; (*mind, thoughts*) блужда́ть *(impf)*; (*river*) извива́ться *(impf)* ◆ *vt* броди́ть* *(impf)* по *+dat*.
wanderer ['wɔndərə^r] *n* стра́нник(-ица), скита́лец*(-лица).
wandering ['wɔndrɪŋ] *adj* (*tribe*) кочево́й; (*minstrel, actor*) бродя́чий; (*path, river*) изви́листый; (*glance, mind*) блужда́ющий.
wane [weɪn] *vi* (*moon*) убыва́ть (убы́ть* *perf*); (*enthusiasm, influence etc*) ослабева́ть (ослабе́ть* *or* осла́бнуть *perf*).
wangle ['wæŋgl] *vt* (BRIT: *inf*) пробива́ть (проби́ть* *perf*), добива́ться (доби́ться* *perf*) *+gen*.
wanker ['wæŋkə^r] *n* (BRIT: *inf!*) муда́к (*!*)
want [wɔnt] *vt* (*wish for*) хоте́ть* *(impf)* *+gen*; (*need*) нужда́ться *(impf)* в *+prp* ◆ *n*: **for ~ of** за недоста́тком *+gen*; **~s** *npl* (*needs*) ну́жды *fpl*; **to ~ to do** хоте́ть* *(impf)* *+infin*; **I ~ you to apologize** я хочу́, что́бы Вы извини́лись; **you're ~ed on the phone** Вас к телефо́ну; **a ~ of foresight** отсу́тствие предви́дения.
want ads *npl* (US) *объявле́ния под ру́брикой "Куплю́", "Ищу́ рабо́ту" итп.*
wanted ['wɔntɪd] *adj* (*criminal etc*) разы́скиваемый; **"cook ~"** "тре́буется по́вар".
wanting ['wɔntɪŋ] *adj*: **he was found ~** он оказа́лся не на высоте́ положе́ния; **he is ~ in common sense** ему́ недостаёт здра́вого смы́сла.
wanton ['wɔntn] *adj* (*gratuitous*) беспричи́нный* (беспричи́нен); (*promiscuous*) распу́тный* (распу́тен).
war [wɔ:^r] *n* война́*; **to go to ~** вступа́ть (вступи́ть* *perf*) в войну́; **to be at ~ with** воева́ть* *(impf)* с *+instr*; **to declare ~ (on)** (*also fig*) объявля́ть (объяви́ть* *perf*) войну́ (*+dat*).
warble ['wɔ:bl] *n* (*of bird*) трель *f* ◆ *vi* издава́ть* *(impf)* тре́ли.
war crime *n* вое́нное преступле́ние.
war cry *n* боево́й клич.
ward [wɔ:d] *n* (MED) пала́та; (BRIT: POL) о́круг; (LAW) *ребёнок, находя́щийся под опе́кой*
▸ **ward off** *vt* (*attack, enemy*) отража́ть (отрази́ть* *perf*); (*danger, illness*) отвраща́ть (отврати́ть* *perf*).
warden ['wɔ:dn] *n* (*of park, game reserve*) смотри́тель(ница) *m(f)*; (*of prison*) нача́льник; (*of youth hostel*) коменда́нт; (BRIT: *of college*) ре́ктор; (: *also*: **traffic ~**) ≈ инспе́ктор* ГАИ́.
warder ['wɔ:də^r] *n* (BRIT) надзира́тель(ница) *m(f)*, тюре́мщик(-ица).
wardrobe ['wɔ:drəub] *n* платяно́й шкаф, гардеро́б; (*clothes*) гардеро́б; (CINEMA, THEAT) костюме́рная *f adj*.

* marks translations which have irregular inflections. The Russian-English side of the dictionary gives inflectional information.

warehouse ['wɛəhaus] *n* склад.
wares [wɛəz] *npl* това́ры *mpl*.
warfare ['wɔ:fɛə'] *n* вое́нные *или* боевы́е де́йствия *ntpl*.
war game *n* вое́нная игра́*.
warhead ['wɔ:hɛd] *n* боеголо́вка*.
warily ['wɛərɪlɪ] *adv* осторо́жно, насторо́женно.
Warks *abbr* (*BRIT: POST*) = *Warwickshire*.
warlike ['wɔ:laɪk] *adj* во́инственный* (во́инствен).
warm [wɔ:m] *adj* тёплый; (*thanks, supporter, heart*) горя́чий*; (*person*) серде́чный; **it's ~ today** сего́дня тепло́; **I'm ~** мне тепло́; **to keep sth ~** (*hands, feet etc*) держа́ть *(impf)* что-н в тепле́; (*soup etc*) держа́ть *(impf)* что-н тёплым(-ой); **with my ~est thanks** с горя́чей *or* серде́чной благода́рностью; **please accept my ~est congratulations** приміте мои́ серде́чные поздравле́ния
▸ **warm up** *vi* (*person, room*) согрева́ться (согре́ться *perf*); (*water*) нагрева́ться (нагре́ться *perf*); (*athlete*) размина́ться (размя́ться *perf*) ◆ *vt* (*food*) разогрева́ть (разогре́ть *perf*), подогрева́ть (подогре́ть *perf*); (*engine*) разогрева́ть (разогре́ть *perf*); **the weather ~ed up** на у́лице потепле́ло.
warm-blooded ['wɔ:m'blʌdɪd] *adj* теплокро́вный* (теплокро́вен).
war memorial *n* вое́нный обели́ск.
warm-hearted [wɔ:m'hɑ:tɪd] *adj* серде́чный* (серде́чен).
warmly ['wɔ:mlɪ] *adv* (*applaud*) горячо́; (*dress, welcome*) тепло́.
warmonger ['wɔ:mʌŋgə'] *n* (*pej*) поджига́тель (ница) *m(f)* войны́.
warmongering ['wɔ:mʌŋgrɪŋ] *n* (*pej*) разжига́ние войны́.
warmth [wɔ:mθ] *n* тепло́.
warm-up ['wɔ:mʌp] *n* разми́нка*.
warn [wɔ:n] *vt*: **to ~ sb (not) to do/of/that** предупрежда́ть (предупреди́ть* *perf*) кого́-н (не) +*infin*/о +*prp*/, что.
warning ['wɔ:nɪŋ] *n* предупрежде́ние; **without (any) ~** (*suddenly*) неожи́данно; (*without notifying*) без предупрежде́ния; **gale ~** штормово́е предупрежде́ние.
warning light *n* предупреди́тельный светово́й сигна́л.
warning triangle *n* авари́йный треуго́льник (*знак, предупрежда́ющий о том, что стоя́щая на доро́ге маши́на сло́мана*).
warp [wɔ:p] *vi* (*wood etc*) коро́биться* (покоро́биться* *perf*) ◆ *vt* (*fig*) кове́ркать (искове́ркать *perf*) ◆ *n* (*TEXTILES*) осно́ва.
warpath ['wɔ:pɑ:θ] *n*: **he is on the ~** (*fig*) он настро́ен во́инственно.
warped [wɔ:pt] *adj* (*wood*) покоро́бленный (покоро́блен); (*fig*) искове́рканный (искове́ркан).
warrant ['wɔrnt] *n* (*document*) гара́нтия; (*LAW*) о́рдер ◆ *vt* (*justify*) опра́вдывать (оправда́ть *perf*); (*merit*) гаранти́ровать *(impf/perf)*; **search ~** о́рдер на о́быск.
warrant officer *n* (*MIL*) ≈ старшина́* *m*; (*NAUT*) ми́чман.
warranty ['wɔrəntɪ] *n* гара́нтия; **under ~** с гара́нтией; **the car was still under ~** у маши́ны ещё не истёк гаранти́йный срок.
warren ['wɔrən] *n* (*of rabbits*) *ме́сто, где во́дятся кро́лики*; (*fig*) лабири́нт.
warring ['wɔ:rɪŋ] *adj* вою́щий; (*interests etc*) непримири́мый (непримири́м).
warrior ['wɔrɪə'] *n* во́ин.
Warsaw ['wɔ:sɔ:] *n* Варша́ва.
warship ['wɔ:ʃɪp] *n* вое́нный кора́бль* *m*.
wart [wɔ:t] *n* борода́вка*.
wartime ['wɔ:taɪm] *n*: **in ~** в вое́нное вре́мя.
wary ['wɛərɪ] *adj* (*person*) осторо́жный* (осторо́жен), насторо́женный* (насторо́жен); **to be ~ about** *or* **of sth** относи́ться* *(impf)* к чему́-н насторо́женно; **to be ~ about doing** остерега́ться *(impf)* +*infin*.
was [wɔz] *pt of* **be**.
wash [wɔʃ] *n* мытьё; (*clothes etc*) сти́рка; (*washing programme*) режи́м сти́рки (*в стира́льной маши́не*); (*of ship*) пе́нистый след ◆ *vt* (*hands, body*) мыть* (помы́ть* *perf*); (*clothes*) стира́ть (постира́ть *perf*); (*face*) умыва́ть (умы́ть* *perf*); (*sweep away*) смыва́ть (смыть* *perf*) ◆ *vi* (*person*) мы́ться* (помы́ться* *perf*); (*sea etc*): **to ~ over sth** перека́тываться *(impf)* че́рез что-н; **to have a ~** помы́ться* *(perf)*; **to give sth a ~** помы́ть* *(perf)* что-н; (*clothes*) постира́ть *(perf)* что-н; **the sea ~ed the body ashore** мо́ре вы́несло те́ло на бе́рег; **he was ~ed overboard** его́ смы́ло волно́й за́ борт
▸ **wash away** *vt* смыва́ть (смыть* *perf*)
▸ **wash down** *vt* (*wall, path, car*) мыть* (вы́мыть* *perf*); (*food*) запива́ть (запи́ть* *perf*)
▸ **wash off** *vi* отмыва́ться (отмы́ться* *perf*); (*out of clothes*) отсти́рываться (отстира́ться *perf*)
▸ **wash up** *vi* (*BRIT*) мыть* (вы́мыть* *perf*) посу́ду; (*US*) мы́ться* (помы́ться* *perf*).
washable ['wɔʃəbl] *adj* (*wallpaper etc*) мо́ющийся; **acrylic blankets are ~** акри́ловые одея́ла мо́жно стира́ть.
washbasin ['wɔʃbeɪsn] *n* (умыва́льная) ра́ковина.
washbowl ['wɔʃbəul] *n* (*US*) (умыва́льная) ра́ковина.
washcloth ['wɔʃklɔθ] *n* (*US*: *face cloth*) салфе́тка для лица́ (*из махро́вой тка́ни*).
washer ['wɔʃə'] *n* (*TECH*) ша́йба.
washing ['wɔʃɪŋ] *n* (*dirty*) сти́рка; (*clean*) сти́раные ве́щи *fpl*.
washing line *n* (*BRIT*) бельева́я верёвка*.
washing machine *n* стира́льная маши́на.
washing powder *n* (*BRIT*) стира́льный порошо́к.

Washington [ˈwɔʃɪŋtən] *n* Вашингтóн.
washing-up [wɔʃɪŋˈʌp] *n* (грязная) посуда; **to do the ~** мыть* (вымыть* *perf*) посуду.
washing-up liquid *n* (*BRIT*) *жидкое средство для мытья посуды.*
wash-out [ˈwɔʃaut] *n* (*inf*) провал.
washroom [ˈwɔʃrum] *n* (*US*) уборная *f adj*.
wasn't [ˈwɔznt] = **was not**.
WASP [wɔsp] *n abbr* (*US*: *inf*: = *White Anglo-Saxon Protestant*) *американец англо-саксонского происхождения и протестантского исповедания.*
Wasp [wɔsp] *n abbr* = **WASP**.
wasp [wɔsp] *n* оса*.
waspish [ˈwɔspɪʃ] *adj* (*person*) раздражительный* (раздражителен).
wastage [ˈweɪstɪdʒ] *n* (*waste*) растрата; (*ECON*: *loss*) убыток*; **natural ~** естественная убыль *f*.
waste [weɪst] *n* (*act*) растрата; (*rubbish*) отходы *mpl*; (*also*: **household ~**) домашние отбросы *mpl*; (*unwanted*: *energy, heat*) излишек* ◆ *adj* (*material*: *rejected, damaged*) бракованный* (бракован); (*unwanted*: *energy, heat*) излишный* (излишен); (*left over*) отработанный* (отработан); (*also*: **~ land**: *in city*) пустырь* *m* ◆ *vt* растрачивать (растратить* *perf*); (*opportunity*) упускать (упустить* *perf*); **~s** *npl* (*area of land*) пустыня *fsg*; **it's a ~ of money/time** это пустая трата денег/времени; **to go to ~** пропадать (пропасть* *perf*); **to lay ~** (*destroy*) уничтожать (уничтожить *perf*); **~ paper** использованная бумага
▸ **waste away** *vi* (*person*) истощать (истощить *perf*) себя.
wastebasket [ˈweɪstbɑːskɪt] *n* (*US*) = **wastepaper basket**.
waste disposal unit *n* (*BRIT*) устройство для удаления отходов (*в кухонной раковине*).
wasteful [ˈweɪstful] *adj* (*person*) расточительный* (расточителен); (*process*) неэкономный* (неэкономен).
waste ground *n* (*BRIT*) пустырь* *m*.
wasteland [ˈweɪstlənd] *n* пустошь *f*; (*in town*) пустырь* *m*; (*fig*) пустыня.
wastepaper basket [ˈweɪstpeɪpə-] *n* корзина для (ненужных) бумаг.
waste pipe *n* сливная труба*.
waste products *npl* отходы *pl* производства.
waster [ˈweɪstəʳ] *n* (*inf*) бездельник(-ица).
watch [wɔtʃ] *n* (*also*: **wristwatch**) (наручные) часы *pl*; (*act of watching*) наблюдение; (*MIL, NAUT*: *group of guards*) патруль* *m*; (*NAUT*: *spell of duty*) вахта ◆ *vt* (*look at*) наблюдать (*impf*) за *+instr*; (*match, programme*) смотреть* (посмотреть* *perf*); (*events, weight, language*) следить* (*impf*) за *+instr*; (*be careful of*: *person*) остерегаться (*impf*) *+gen*; (*look after*) смотреть (*impf*) за *+instr* ◆ *vi* (*take care*) смотреть (*impf*); (*keep guard*) дежурить (*impf*); **to keep a close ~ on sb/sth** внимательно следить* (*impf*) за кем-н/чем-н; **~ what you're doing** смотри, что ты делаешь; **~ how you drive** внимательно ведите машину
▸ **watch out** *vi* остерегаться (остеречься* *perf*).
watchband [ˈwɔtʃbænd] *n* (*US*) ремешок* для часов.
watchdog [ˈwɔtʃdɔg] *n* сторожевая собака; (*fig*) наблюдатель *m*.
watchful [ˈwɔtʃful] *adj* бдительный* (бдителен).
watchmaker [ˈwɔtʃmeɪkəʳ] *n* часовщик*.
watchman [ˈwɔtʃmən] *irreg n see* **night watchman**.
watchstrap [ˈwɔtʃstræp] *n* ремешок* для часов.
watchword [ˈwɔtʃwəːd] *n* лозунг.
water [ˈwɔːtəʳ] *n* вода* ◆ *vt* (*plant, garden*) поливать (полить* *perf*) ◆ *vi* (*eyes*) слезиться (*impf*); **a glass of ~** стакан воды; **in British ~s** в британских водах; **to pass ~** (*urinate*) мочиться* (помочиться* *perf*); **my mouth is ~ing** у меня текут слюнки
▸ **water down** *vt* разбавлять (разбавить* *perf*) (водой); (*fig*) смягчать (смягчить *perf*).
water biscuit *n* ≈ галета.
water cannon *n* брандспойт.
water closet *n* (*BRIT*) туалет.
watercolour [ˈwɔːtəkʌləʳ] (*US* **watercolor**) *n* (*picture*) акварель *f*; **~s** *npl* (*paints*) акварельные краски* *fpl*.
water-cooled [ˈwɔːtəkuːld] *adj* (*engine*) с водяным охлаждением.
watercress [ˈwɔːtəkrɛs] *n* кресс водяной.
waterfall [ˈwɔːtəfɔːl] *n* водопад.
waterfront [ˈwɔːtəfrʌnt] *n* (*seafront*: *street*) набережная *f adj*; (: *piece of land*) береговая линия; (*at docks*) район порта.
water heater *n* кипятильник.
water hole *n* источник (*для водопоя в пустыне*).
water ice *n* фруктовое мороженое *nt adj*.
watering can [ˈwɔːtərɪŋ-] *n* лейка*.
water level *n* уровень* *m* воды.
water lily *n* кувшинка*.
waterline [ˈwɔːtəlaɪn] *n* (*NAUT*) ватерлиния.
waterlogged [ˈwɔːtəlɔgd] *adj* (*ground*) заболоченный* (заболочен), затопленный (затоплен).
water main *n* водопроводная магистраль *m*.
watermark [ˈwɔːtəmɑːk] *n* (*on paper*) водяной знак; (*level of water*) отметка уровня воды.
watermelon [ˈwɔːtəmɛlən] *n* арбуз.
waterproof [ˈwɔːtəpruːf] *adj* непромокаемый

* marks translations which have irregular inflections. The Russian-English side of the dictionary gives inflectional information.

(непромокáем).
water-repellent [ˈwɔːtərɪˈpɛlnt] *adj* (*cloth etc*) водоотта́лкивающий*.
watershed [ˈwɔːtəʃɛd] *n* (*also fig*) водоразде́л.
water-skiing [ˈwɔːtəskiːɪŋ] *n* воднолы́жный спорт.
water softener *n* сре́дство для смягче́ния воды́.
water tank *n* резервуа́р для воды́; (*smaller*) бак для воды́.
watertight [ˈwɔːtətaɪt] *adj* водонепроница́емый (водонепроница́ем); (*fig*: *argument*) неопровержи́мый (неопровержи́м); (: *excuse*) ве́ский*; (: *case, agreement*) я́сный* (я́сен); (: *story*) правдоподо́бный* (правдоподо́бен).
water vapour *n* (водяно́й) пар*.
waterway [ˈwɔːtəweɪ] *n* (*canal, river*) во́дный путь* *m*; (*at sea*) ватерве́йс.
waterworks [ˈwɔːtəwəːks] *n* (*building*) гидротехни́ческое сооруже́ние; (*inf*: ANAT) по́чки* *fpl*.
watery [ˈwɔːtərɪ] *adj* (*coffee, soup etc*) водяни́стый (водяни́ст); (*eyes*) слезя́щийся.
watt [wɔt] *n* ватт.
wattage [ˈwɔtɪdʒ] *n* мо́щность *f* в ва́ттах.
wattle [ˈwɔtl] *n* (CONSTR) плете́нь* *m*.
wattle and daub *n* пру́тья и гли́на (*материа́л для постро́йки ма́занки*).
wave [weɪv] *n* волна́*; (*of hand*) взмах; (*in hair*) зави́вка ◆ *vi* (*signal*) маха́ть* *(impf)*; (*branches*) кача́ться *(impf)*; (*grass*) волнова́ться *(impf)*; (*flag*) развева́ться *(impf)* ◆ *vt* маха́ть* *(impf)* *+instr*; (*stick, gun, sword*) разма́хивать *(impf)* *+instr*; (*hair*) завива́ть (зави́ть* *perf*); **short/medium/long ~** коро́ткие/сре́дние/дли́нные во́лны *fpl*; **the new ~** (CINEMA, MUS) но́вая волна́; **he ~d us over to his table** он знако́м подозва́л нас к своему́ столу́; **to ~ goodbye to sb** маха́ть* (помаха́ть* *perf*) кому́-н на проща́ние
▸ **wave aside** *vt* (*person*) отстраня́ть (отстрани́ть *perf*); (*fig*) отма́хиваться (отмахну́ться *perf*) от *+gen*
▸ **wave away** *vt* = **wave aside**.
waveband [ˈweɪvbænd] *n* диапазо́н волн.
wavelength [ˈweɪvlɛŋθ] *n* (RADIO) длина́ волны́; **they are on the same ~** (*fig*) они́ одина́ково смо́трят на ве́щи.
waver [ˈweɪvəʳ] *vi* (*voice*) дро́гнуть *(perf)*; (*person, faith*) колеба́ться* (поколеба́ться* *perf*).
wavy [ˈweɪvɪ] *adj* волни́стый (волни́ст).
wax [wæks] *n* (*polish*) воск; (*for skis*) мазь *f*; (*for sealing*) сургу́ч*; (*in ear*) се́ра ◆ *vt* (*floor*) вощи́ть (навощи́ть *perf*), натира́ть (натере́ть* *perf*) во́ском; (*car*) натира́ть (натере́ть* *perf*) во́ском; (*skis*) ма́зать (нама́зать* *perf*) ма́зью ◆ *vi* (*moon*) прибыва́ть *(impf)*.
waxed [wækst] *adj* вощёный.
waxen [wæksn] *adj* (*face*) восково́й; **~ complexion** восково́й цвет лица́.
waxworks [ˈwækswəːks] *npl* (*models*) восковы́е фигу́ры *fpl* ◆ *n* (*place*) галере́я восковы́х фигу́р.
way [weɪ] *n* (*route*) путь* *m*, доро́га; (*path, access*) путь*; (*manner, method*) спо́соб; (*usu pl*: *habit*) привы́чка; **which ~? – this ~** куда́? – сюда́; **is it a long ~ from here?** э́то далеко́ отсю́да?; **which ~ do we go now?** куда́ нам тепе́рь идти́?; **on the ~** (*en route*) по пути́ *or* доро́ге; **to be on one's ~** быть* *(impf)* в пути́; **I'd better be on my ~** мне уже́ пора́ идти́; **to fight one's ~ through a crowd** продира́ться (продра́ться* *perf*) сквозь толпу́; **to lie one's ~ out of the situation** выходи́ть* (вы́йти* *perf*) из положе́ния за счёт лжи; **to keep out of sb's ~** держа́ться* *(impf)* от кого́-н пода́льше; **it's a very long ~ away** э́то о́чень далеко́; **the village is rather out of the ~** дере́вня нахо́дится дово́льно далеко́ в стороне́; **to go out of one's ~ to do** стара́ться (постара́ться *perf*) изо всех сил *+infin*; **to be in sb's ~** (*also fig*) стоя́ть *(impf)* на чьей-н доро́ге; **to be in the ~** меша́ть (помеша́ть *perf*); **to lose one's ~** заблуди́ться* *(perf)*; **the plan is under ~** план осуществля́ется; **to make ~ (for sb/sth)** уступа́ть (уступи́ть* *perf*) ме́сто (кому́-н/чему́-н); **to get one's own ~** де́лать (сде́лать *perf*) по-сво́ему; **to put sth the right ~ up** (BRIT) ста́вить* (поста́вить* *perf*) что-н как на́до *or* пра́вильно; **to be the wrong ~ round** быть* *(impf)* задо́м наперёд; **he's in a bad ~** его́ дела́ пло́хи; **that's a funny ~ to show your affection** э́то стра́нная мане́ра выража́ть свою́ привя́занность; **in a ~** в изве́стном смы́сле; **in some ~s** в не́которых отноше́ниях; **no ~!** (*inf*) ни в ко́ем слу́чае!; **by the ~ ...** ме́жду про́чим ...; **"way in"** (BRIT) "вход"; **"way out"** (BRIT) „вы́ход"; **the ~ back** обра́тный путь*, обра́тная доро́га; **this ~ and that** туда́-сюда́; **"give ~"** (BRIT: AUT) „уступи́те доро́гу".
waybill [ˈweɪbɪl] *n* накладна́я *f adj*.
waylay [weɪˈleɪ] (*irreg*: *like* **lay**) *vt* подстерега́ть (подстере́чь* *perf*); **I got waylaid** (*fig*) меня́ перехвати́ли по пути́.
wayside [ˈweɪsaɪd] *adj* придоро́жный ◆ *n* обо́чина; **to fall by the ~** (*fig*) выбыва́ть (вы́быть* *perf*) из стро́я.
way station *n* (US: RAIL) полуста́нок*; (: *fig*) промежу́точный эта́п.
wayward [ˈweɪwəd] *adj* своенра́вный* (своенра́вен).
WC *n abbr* (BRIT) = **water closet**.
WCC *n abbr* = *World Council of Churches*.
we [wiː] *pron* мы.
weak [wiːk] *adj* сла́бый* (слаб); (*morally*) слабохара́ктерный* (слабохара́ктерен); **to grow ~** ослабева́ть *or* слабе́ть (ослабе́ть *perf*).

weaken ['wi:kn] *vi* ослабева́ть *or* слабе́ть (ослабе́ть *perf*); (*resolve, person*) смягча́ться (смягчи́ться *perf*) ◆ *vt* (*person, government*) ослабля́ть (осла́бить* *perf*).
weak-kneed ['wi:k'ni:d] *adj* (*fig*) малоду́шный* (малоду́шен).
weakling ['wi:klıŋ] *n* слаба́к*.
weakly ['wi:klı] *adv* сла́бо.
weakness ['wi:knıs] *n* сла́бость *f*; **to have a ~ for** име́ть *(impf)* сла́бость к *+dat*.
wealth [wɛlθ] *n* (*money, resources*) бога́тство; (*of details, knowledge etc*) оби́лие.
wealth tax *n* иму́щественный нало́г.
wealthy ['wɛlθı] *adj* состоя́тельный* (состоя́телен).
wean [wi:n] *vt* (*baby*) отнима́ть (отня́ть* *perf*) от груди́.
weapon ['wɛpən] *n* ору́жие*.
wear [wɛə^r] (*pt* **wore**, *pp* **worn**) *n* (*use*) изно́с; (*damage*) изно́шенность *f*; (*clothing*) оде́жда ◆ *vi* (*last*) носи́ться* *(impf)*; (*rub through*) изна́шиваться (износи́ться* *perf*) ◆ *vt* (*put on*) надева́ть (наде́ть* *perf*); (*beard*) носи́ть* *(impf)*; (*damage*) изна́шивать (износи́ть* *perf*); (*clothes*): **he was ~ing his new shirt** на нём была́ его́ но́вая руба́шка; **evening ~** (*for ladies*) вече́рнее пла́тье*; (*for men*) вече́рний* костю́м; **to ~ a hole in sth** протира́ть (протере́ть* *perf*) дыру́ в чём-н
▸ **wear away** *vt* стира́ть (стере́ть* *perf*) ◆ *vi* стира́ться (стере́ться* *perf*)
▸ **wear down** *vt* (*heels*) сна́шивать (сноси́ть* *perf*); (*resistance, strength*) сломи́ть *(perf)*
▸ **wear off** *vi* (*pain etc*) постепе́нно проходи́ть* (пройти́* *perf*)
▸ **wear on** *vi* тяну́ться* *(impf)*
▸ **wear out** *vt* (*shoes, clothing*) изна́шиваться (износи́ться* *perf*); (*person, strength*) изма́тывать (измота́ть *perf*).
wearable ['wɛərəbl] *adj* приго́дный* (приго́ден) для но́ски.
wear and tear [-tɛə^r] *n* изно́с.
wearer ['wɛərə^r] *n* владе́лец*(-льца).
wearily ['wıərılı] *adv* уста́ло.
weariness ['wıərınıs] *n* утомле́ние.
wearisome ['wıərısəm] *adj* (*tiring*) утоми́тельный* (утоми́телен); (*boring*) надое́дливый (надое́длив).
weary ['wıərı] *adj* (*tired*) утомлённый (утомлён); (*dispirited*) уста́лый ◆ *vi*: **to ~ of** утомля́ться (утоми́ться* *perf*) от *+gen*.
weasel ['wi:zl] *n* (ZOOL) ла́ска*.
weather ['wɛðə^r] *n* пого́да ◆ *vt* (*storm, crisis*) переноси́ть* (перенести́* *perf*), выде́рживать (вы́держать *perf*) ◆ *vi* (*wood*) подверга́ться (подве́ргнуться* *perf*) атмосфе́рным влия́ниям; **what's the ~ like today?** кака́я сего́дня пого́да?; **I am under the ~** мне нездоро́вится.
weather-beaten ['wɛðəbi:tn] *adj* (*face, skin*) обве́тренный* (обве́трен); (*building, stone*) повреждённый непого́дой.
weathercock ['wɛðəkɔk] *n* флю́гер*.
weather forecast *n* прогно́з пого́ды.
weatherman ['wɛðəmæn] *irreg n* (*inf*) сино́птик.
weatherproof ['wɛðəpru:f] *adj* (*garment*) защища́ющий от непого́ды; (*building*) погодоусто́йчивый (погодоусто́йчив), утеплённый* (утеплён).
weather report *n* сообще́ние о пого́де.
weather vane [-veın] *n* = **weathercock**.
weave [wi:v] (*pt* **wove**, *pp* **woven**) *vt* (*cloth*) ткать* (сотка́ть* *perf*); (*basket*) плести́* (сплести́* *perf*) ◆ *vi* (*pt, pp* **weaved**; *fig*) лави́ровать *(impf)*.
weaver ['wi:və^r] *n* ткач*(и́ха).
weaving ['wi:vıŋ] *n* (*craft*) тка́чество; (*of baskets*) плете́ние.
web [wɛb] *n* (*of spider*) паути́на; (*on duck's foot*) перепо́нка*; (*also fig*) сеть* *f*.
webbed ['wɛbd] *adj* перепо́нчатый.
webbing ['wɛbıŋ] *n* (*on chair*) тка́ный реме́нь.
website ['wɛbsaıt] *n* веб-сайт, сайт.
wed [wɛd] (*pt,pp* **wedded**) *vt* (*marry*) венча́ться (обвенча́ться *perf*) с *+instr* ◆ *vi* венча́ться (обвенча́ться *perf*) ◆ *n*: **the newly-~s** новобра́чные *pl adj*.
Wed. *abbr* = **Wednesday**.
we'd [wi:d] = **we had, we would**.
wedded ['wɛdıd] *pt, pp of* **wed** ◆ *adj*: **he is ~ to** (*idea, policy etc*) он пре́дан *+dat*.
wedding [wɛdıŋ] *n* сва́дьба*; (*in church*) венча́ние; **silver/golden ~** серебряная/золота́я сва́дьба.
wedding day *n* день* *m* сва́дьбы.
wedding dress *n* сва́дебное *or* подвене́чное пла́тье*.
wedding present *n* сва́дебный пода́рок*.
wedding ring *n* обруча́льное кольцо́*.
wedge [wɛdʒ] *n* клин*; (*of cake*) кусо́к* ◆ *vt* закрепля́ть (закрепи́ть* *perf*) кли́ном; (*pack tightly*): **to ~ in** вти́скивать (вти́снуть *perf*) в *+acc*.
wedge-heeled shoes ['wɛdʒhi:ld-] *npl* ту́фли* *pl* на танке́тке.
wedlock ['wɛdlɔk] *n* супру́жество.
Wednesday ['wɛdnzdı] *n* среда́*; *see also* **Tuesday**.
wee [wi:] *adj* (SCOTTISH: *little*) кро́шечный*.
weed [wi:d] *n* сорня́к* ◆ *vt* (*garden*) поло́ть* (вы́полоть *perf*)
▸ **weed out** *vt* устраня́ть (устрани́ть *perf*).
weedkiller ['wi:dkılə^r] *n* сре́дство от сорняко́в.
weedy ['wi:dı] *adj* (*man*) худосо́чный*

* marks translations which have irregular inflections. The Russian-English side of the dictionary gives inflectional information.

(худосо́чен).
week [wi:k] *n* неде́ля; **once/twice a** ~ раз/два ра́за в неде́лю; **in two** ~**s' time** че́рез две неде́ли; **a** ~ **today** че́рез неде́лю, a week on Friday, в сле́дующую пя́тницу.
weekday ['wi:kdeɪ] *n* (*Monday to Friday*) бу́дний *or* рабо́чий* день* *m*; **on** ~**s** в бу́дни.
weekend [wi:k'ɛnd] *n* выходны́е *pl adj* (дни), суббо́та и воскресе́нье, уик-э́нд; **this/next/last** ~ в э́ти/сле́дующие/про́шлые выходны́е (дни); **what are you doing at the** ~**?** что Вы де́лаете в выходны́е?; **open at** ~**s** откры́то по суббо́там и воскресе́ньям *or* по выходны́м дням.
weekly ['wi:klɪ] *adv* еженеде́льно ◆ *adj* еженеде́льный ◆ *n* еженеде́льник.
weep [wi:p] (*pt,pp* **wept**) *vi* (*person*) пла́кать* (*impf*); (*wound*) сочи́ться (*impf*).
weeping willow ['wi:pɪŋ-] *n* плаку́чая и́ва.
weepy ['wi:pɪ] *adj* слезли́вый (слезли́в), плакси́вый (плакси́в) ◆ *n* (*inf*: *film*) душещипа́тельный фильм.
weft [wɛft] *n* уто́к*.
weigh [weɪ] *vt* взве́шивать (взве́сить* *perf*) ◆ *vi* ве́сить* (*impf*); **to** ~ **anchor** поднима́ть (подня́ть* *perf*) я́корь
▸ **weigh down** *vt* отягоща́ть (отяготи́ть* *perf*); (*fig*) тяготи́ть* (*impf*), отягоща́ть (*impf*)
▸ **weigh out** *vt* отве́шивать (отве́сить* *perf*)
▸ **weigh up** *vt* взве́шивать (взве́сить* *perf*); **to** ~ **up all the pros and cons** взве́шивать (взве́сить* *perf*) все "за" и "про́тив".
weighbridge ['weɪbrɪdʒ] *n* мостовы́е весы́ *pl*.
weighing machine ['weɪɪŋ-] *n* автомати́ческие весы́ *pl*.
weight [weɪt] *n* (*for scales*) ги́ря; (*heaviness*) вес* ◆ *vt*: **to be** ~**ed in favour of** предоставля́ть (предоста́вить* *perf*) преиму́щество *+dat*; **sold by** ~ продаётся на вес; **to lose** ~ худе́ть (похуде́ть *perf*); **to put on** ~ поправля́ться (попра́виться* *perf*); **W**~**s and Measures Office** Пала́та мер и весо́в.
weighting ['weɪtɪŋ] *n* (*allowance*) надба́вка.
weightlessness ['weɪtlɪsnɪs] *n* невесо́мость *f*.
weightlifter ['weɪtlɪftə^r] *n* штанги́ст.
weight limit *n* преде́л ве́са.
weight training *n* силова́я гимна́стика.
weighty ['weɪtɪ] *adj* (*heavy*: *object*) тяжёлый (тяжёл); (: *person*) гру́зный* (гру́зен); (*important*) весо́мый (весо́м).
weir [wɪə^r] *n* (*in river*) запру́да.
weird [wɪəd] *adj* (*strange*) стра́нный* (стра́нен); (*eerie*) таи́нственный* (таи́нственен).
weirdo ['wɪədəu] *n* (*inf*) чуда́к.
welcome ['wɛlkəm] *adj* жела́нный* (жела́нен) ◆ *n* (*hospitality*) приём; (*greeting*) приве́тствие ◆ *vt* (*also*: **bid** ~) приве́тствовать (*impf*); **to make sb** ~ ока́зывать (оказа́ть* *perf*) кому́-н раду́шный приём; **you're** ~ **to try** пожа́луйста, попро́буйте; **thank you – you're** ~! спаси́бо – пожа́луйста!
welcoming ['wɛlkəmɪŋ] *adj* (*person, smile etc*) раду́шный* (раду́шен); (*room*) прия́тный* (прия́тен); (*speech*) приве́тственный.
weld [wɛld] *n* сварно́й шов ◆ *vt* сва́ривать (свари́ть* *perf*).
welder ['wɛldə^r] *n* сва́рщик.
welding ['wɛldɪŋ] *n* сва́рка*.
welfare ['wɛlfɛə^r] *n* (*well-being*) благополу́чие; (*US*: *social aid*) социа́льное посо́бие.
welfare state *n* госуда́рство всео́бщего благосостоя́ния.
welfare work *n* социа́льная по́мощь *f*.
well [wɛl] *n* (*for water*) коло́дец*; (*also*: **oil** ~) (нефтяна́я) сква́жина ◆ *adv* хорошо́ ◆ *excl* (*anyway*) ну; (*so*) ну вот ◆ *adj*: **he is** ~ он здоро́в; **I don't feel** ~ я пло́хо себя́ чу́вствую; **to think** ~ **of sb** быть* (*impf*) хоро́шего мне́ния о ком-н; **as** ~ та́кже; **oh** ~ **...** ну что же ...; **you might as** ~ **tell me** уж лу́чше ты скажи́ мне; **he played as** ~ **as he could** он сыгра́л как смог; **I woke** ~ **before dawn** я просну́лся задо́лго до рассве́та; **I've brought my anorak as** ~ **as a jumper** кро́ме пуло́вера я привёз ещё и анора́к; ~**, as I was saying ...** ну, как я уже́ говори́л ...; ~ **done!** молоде́ц!; **get** ~ **soon!** поправля́йтесь скоре́е; **he is doing** ~ **at school** в шко́ле он успева́ет; **the business is doing** ~ би́знес процвета́ет
▸ **well up** *vi* (*tears*) наверну́ться (*perf*).
we'll [wi:l] = **we will, we shall**.
well-behaved ['wɛlbɪ'heɪvd] *adj* воспи́танный* (воспи́тан).
well-being ['wɛl'bi:ɪŋ] *n* благополу́чие.
well-bred ['wɛl'brɛd] *adj* (*person*) воспи́танный* (воспи́тан), благовоспи́танный (благовоспи́тан).
well-built ['wɛl'bɪlt] *adj* хорошо́ сложённый (сложён), кре́пкий* (кре́пок).
well-chosen ['wɛl'tʃəuzn] *adj* (*remarks, words*) хорошо́ подо́бранный (подо́бран).
well-deserved ['wɛldɪ'zə:vd] *adj* заслу́женный* (заслу́жен).
well-developed ['wɛldɪ'vɛləpt] *adj* с ра́звитыми фо́рмами.
well-disposed ['wɛl'dɪspəuzd] *adj*: ~ **to(wards)** благожела́тельный* (благожела́телен) к *+dat*.
well-dressed ['wɛl'drɛst] *adj* хорошо́ оде́тый (оде́т).
well-earned ['wɛl'ə:nd] *adj* заслу́женный* (заслу́жен).
well-groomed ['wɛl'gru:md] *adj* (*person*) ухо́женный* (ухо́жен).
well-heeled ['wɛl'hi:ld] *adj* (*inf*) де́нежный.
well-informed ['wɛlɪn'fɔ:md] *adj* (*about something*) хорошо́ информи́рованный* (информи́рован); (*in general*) зна́ющий*.
Wellington ['wɛlɪŋtən] *n* Веллингто́н.
wellingtons ['wɛlɪŋtənz] *npl* (*also*: **wellington**

boots) рези́новые сапоги́* *mpl*.
well-kept ['wɛl'kɛpt] *adj* (*house, grounds*) ухо́женный (ухо́жен); (*secret*) по́лный.
well-known ['wɛl'nəun] *adj* (*famous*) изве́стный* (изве́стен).
well-mannered ['wɛl'mænəd] *adj* воспи́танный* (воспи́тан).
well-meaning ['wɛl'mi:nɪŋ] *adj*: **he is very ~** он де́йствует из наилу́чших побужде́ний.
well-nigh ['wɛl'naɪ] *adv*: **~ impossible** почти́ невозмо́жно.
well-off ['wɛl'ɔf] *adj* состоя́тельный* (состоя́телен).
well-read ['wɛl'rɛd] *adj* начи́танный* (начи́тан).
well-spoken ['wɛl'spəukn] *adj* (*words*) учти́вый (учти́в); **she was ~** она́ говори́ла пра́вильным языка́м.
well-stocked ['wɛl'stɔkt] *adj* (*shop*) хорошо́ снабжа́емый.
well-timed ['wɛl'taɪmd] *adj* своевре́менный* (своевре́менен).
well-to-do ['wɛltə'du:] *adj* обеспе́ченный (обеспе́чен), состоя́тельный* (состоя́телен).
well-wisher ['wɛlwɪʃə^r] *n* (*friend, admirer*) доброжела́тель(ница) *m(f)*; **scores of ~s had gathered** собрали́сь деся́тки доброжела́телей; **letters from ~s** пи́сьма от доброжела́телей.
well-woman clinic ['wɛlwumən-] *n* ≈ же́нская консульта́ция.
Welsh [wɛlʃ] *adj* уэ́льский* ◆ *n* (*LING*) уэ́льский* *or* валли́йский язы́к*; **the ~ Assembly** Ассамбле́я Уэ́льса; **the ~** *npl* (*people*) уэ́льсцы *mpl*, валли́йцы *mpl*.
Welshman ['wɛlʃmən] *irreg n* уэ́льсец*, валли́ец*.
Welsh rarebit *n* грено́к* с сы́ром.
Welshwoman ['wɛlʃwumən] *n irreg* валли́йка*, жи́тельница Уэ́льса.
welter ['wɛltə^r] *n*: **a ~ of** ха́ос +*gen*.
went [wɛnt] *pt of* **go**.
wept [wɛpt] *pt, pp of* **weep**.
were [wə:^r] *pt of* **be**.
we're [wɪə^r] = **we are**.
weren't [wə:nt] = **were not**.
werewolf ['wɪəwulf] (*pl* **werewolves**) *n* челове́к-волк.
werewolves ['wɪəwulvz] *npl of* **werewolf**.
west [wɛst] *n* за́пад ◆ *adj* за́падный ◆ *adv* на за́пад; **the W~** (*POL*) За́пад.
westbound ['wɛstbaund] *adj* (*carriageway, traffic*) за́падного направле́ния.
West Country *n*: **the ~ ~** (*BRIT*) за́падная А́нглия.
westerly ['wɛstəlɪ] *adj* за́падный.
western ['wɛstən] *adj* (*also POL*) за́падный ◆ *n* (*CINEMA*) ве́стерн.
westerner ['wɛstənə^r] *n* за́падный челове́к*.
westernized ['wɛstənaɪzd] *adj* ориенти́рованный (ориенти́рован) на За́пад.
West German *adj* (*formerly*) западногерма́нский ◆ *n* жи́тель(ница) *m(f)* За́падной Герма́нии.
West Germany *n* (*formerly*) За́падная Герма́ния.
West Indian *adj* вест-инди́йский* ◆ *n* жи́тель(ница) *m(f)* Вест-И́ндии.
West Indies [-'ɪndɪz] *npl*: **the ~ ~** Вест-И́ндия.
Westminster ['wɛstmɪnstə^r] *n* Вестми́нстер.
westward(s) ['wɛstwəd(z)] *adv* на за́пад, к за́паду.
wet [wɛt] *adj* (*damp, rainy*) вла́жный* (вла́жен), сыро́й* (сыр); (*soaking*) мо́крый* (мокр) ◆ *n* (*BRIT*: *POL*) "уме́ренный(-ая)" *m(f)* *adj* ◆ *vt*: **to ~ one's pants** *or* **o.s.** мочи́ть (намочи́ть *perf*) штаны́; **to get ~** промока́ть (промо́кнуть* *perf*); **"~ paint!"** "осторо́жно, окра́шено!"; **he is a ~ blanket** (*fig*: *pej*) он – зану́да.
wetness ['wɛtnɪs] *n* вла́жность *f*, сы́рость *f*.
wetsuit ['wɛtsu:t] *n* гидрокостю́м.
we've [wi:v] = **we have**.
whack [wæk] *vt* дава́ть* (дать* *perf*) затре́щину +*dat*.
whacked [wækt] *adj* (*BRIT*: *inf*) разби́тый (разби́т).
whale [weɪl] *n* кит*.
whaler ['weɪlə^r] *n* (*ship*) китобо́йное су́дно.
whaling ['weɪlɪŋ] *n* китобо́йный про́мысел.
wharf [wɔ:f] (*pl* **wharves**) *n* при́стань* *f*.
wharves [wɔ:vz] *npl of* **wharf**.

KEYWORD

what [wɔt] *adj* ***1*** (*interrogative*: *direct, indirect*) како́й; **what size is the dress?** како́го разме́ра э́то пла́тье?; **what books do you need?** каки́е кни́ги Вам нужны́?
2 како́й; **what a lovely day!** како́й чуде́сный день!; **what a mess!** (*room etc*) ну и беспоря́док!; (*fig*) что за неразбери́ха!; **what a fool I am!** како́й же я дура́к!
◆ *pron* ***1*** (*interrogative*) что; **what are you doing?** что Вы де́лаете?; **what are you talking about?** о чём Вы говори́те?; **what is it called?** как э́то называ́ется?; **what about me?** а (как же) я?; **what about doing ...?** как насчёт того́, что́бы +*infin* ...?
2 (*relative*) что; **I saw what you did/was on the table** я ви́дел, что Вы де́лали/бы́ло на столе́; **is that what happened?** так э́то то, что случи́лось?; **tell me what you're thinking about** скажи́те мне, о чём Вы ду́маете; **what you say is wrong** то, что Вы говори́те, неве́рно
◆ *excl* (*disbelieving*) что; **I've crashed the car – what!** я разби́л маши́ну – что!

* marks translations which have irregular inflections. The Russian-English side of the dictionary gives inflectional information.

whatever [wɔt'ɛvə'] *adj*: ~ **book** любая книга ◆ *pron*: **do ~ is necessary/you want** делайте всё, что необходимо/хотите; ~ **happens** что бы ни случилось; **no reason ~** *or* **whatsoever** нет никакой причины; **nothing ~** совсем ничего.
whatsoever [wɔtsəu'ɛvə'] *adj see* **whatever**.
wheat [wi:t] *n* пшеница.
wheatgerm ['wi:tdʒə:m] *n* зародыш пшеничного зерна.
wheatmeal ['wi:tmi:l] *n пшеничная мука грубого помола.*
wheedle ['wi:dl] *vt*: **to ~ sb into doing** уговаривать (уговорить *perf*) кого-н лестью *+infin*; **to ~ sth out of sb** выманивать (выманить *perf*) что-н у кого-н.
wheel [wi:l] *n* (*of vehicle etc*) колесо*; (*also*: **steering ~**) руль* *m*; (*NAUT*) штурвал ◆ *vt* (*pram etc*) катать/катить* *(impf)* ◆ *vi* (*birds*) кружиться *(impf)*; (*also*: **~ round**: *person*) круто поворачиваться (повернуться *perf*).
wheelbarrow ['wi:lbærəu] *n* тачка*.
wheelbase ['wi:lbeɪs] *n* колёсная база.
wheelchair ['wi:ltʃɛə'] *n* инвалидное кресло*.
wheel clamp *n* (*AUT*) блокиратор (*для блокировки рулевого колеса*).
wheeler-dealer ['wi:lə'di:lə'] *n* (*pej*) махинатор.
wheelie-bin ['wi:lɪbɪn] *n мусорное ведро на колёсиках.*
wheeling ['wi:lɪŋ] *n*: **~ and dealing** (*pej*) махинации *fpl*.
wheeze [wi:z] *vi* (*person*) хрипеть* *(impf)* ◆ *n* (*idea, joke etc*) остроумная идея, затея.
wheezy ['wi:zɪ] *adj* хрипящий, сипящий.
when [wɛn] *adv, conj* когда; ~ **you've read the book, tell me what you think** когда Вы прочитаете книгу, скажите мне что Вы думаете; **you said I was wrong ~ in fact I was right** Вы сказали, что я был неправ, когда на самом деле я был прав.
whenever [wɛn'ɛvə'] *adv* в любое время ◆ *conj* (*any time*) когда только; (*every time that*) каждый раз, когда; **I go ~ I can** я пойду, как только смогу.
where [wɛə'] *adv* (*place*) где; (*direction*) куда; (*from where*) откуда ◆ *conj* где; **this is ~ ...** это там, где ...; ~ **possible** где возможно; ~ **have you come from?** откуда Вы приехали?
whereabouts [*adv* wɛərə'bauts, *n* 'wɛərəbauts] *adv* где; (*motion*) куда ◆ *n*: **nobody knows his ~** никто не знает его местонахождения.
whereas [wɛər'æz] *conj* тогда *or* в то время как.
whereby [wɛə'baɪ] *adv* (*formal*) посредством чего.
whereupon [wɛərə'pɔn] *adv* после *or* вследствие чего.
wherever [wɛər'ɛvə'] *conj* (*no matter where*: *position*): ~ **he was** где бы он ни был; (: *motion*): ~ **he goes** куда бы он ни шёл; (*not knowing where*): ~ **that is** где бы то ни было ◆ *adv* (*interrogative*): ~ **have you been?** где же Вы были?; **let's go away - ~ to?** давайте уйдём отсюда – куда же?; **sit ~ you like** садитесь, где хотите.
wherewithal ['wɛəwɪðɔ:l] *n*: **the ~ (to do)** средства *ntpl* (*+infin*).
whet [wɛt] *vt* (*appetite*) возбуждать (возбудить* *perf*); (*tool*) точить* (наточить* *perf*).
whether ['wɛðə'] *conj*: **I doubt ~ she loves me** я сомневаюсь, любит ли она меня; **I don't know ~ to accept this proposal or not** я не знаю, принять это предложение или нет; ~ **you go or not** пойдёте Вы или нет.
whey ['weɪ] *n* сыворотка.

KEYWORD

which [wɪtʃ] *adj* **1** (*interrogative*: *direct, indirect*) какой; **which picture would you like?** какую картину Вы хотите?; **which books are yours?** какие книги Ваши?; **which one?** какой? (*f* какая?, *nt* какое?); **I've got two pens, which one do you want?** у меня есть две ручки, какую Вы хотите?; **which one of you did it?** кто из вас это сделал?
2: **in which case** и в таком случае; **by which time** к тому времени
◆ *pron* **1** (*interrogative*) какой (*f* какая, *nt* какое, *pl* какие); **there are several museums, which shall we visit first?** здесь есть несколько музеев, в какой мы пойдём сначала?; **which do you want, the apple or the banana?** что Вы хотите – яблоко или банан?; **which of you are staying?** кто из вас остаётся?
2 (*relative*) который (*f* которая, *nt* которое, *pl* которые); **the apple which you ate/which is on the table** яблоко, которое Вы съели/которое лежит на столе; **the news was bad, which is what I had feared** вести были плохие, как я и боялся; **I had lunch, after which I decided to go home** я пообедал, после чего я решил пойти домой; **I made a speech, after which nobody spoke** я выступил с речью, после которой никто не произнёс ни слова.

whichever [wɪtʃ'ɛvə'] *adj*: **take ~ book you prefer** возьмите любую книгу, какую предпочтёте; ~ **book you take** какую бы книгу Вы ни взяли.
whiff [wɪf] *n* дуновение; **to catch a ~ of sth** улавливать (уловить *perf*) почуять запах чего-н.
while [waɪl] *n* (*period of time*) время* *nt* ◆ *conj* пока, в то время как; (*although*) хотя, несмотря на то, что; **for a ~** ненадолго; **in a ~** скоро; **all the ~** всё время; **we promise to make it worth your ~** мы обещаем, что Вы не останетесь в проигрыше
▸ **while away** *vt*: **to ~ away the time** коротать (скоротать *perf*) время.
whilst [waɪlst] *conj* = **while**.

whim [wɪm] *n* при́хоть *f*.
whimper ['wɪmpəʳ] *n* хны́канье ◆ *vi* хны́кать* *(impf)*; (*dog*) скули́ть *(impf)*.
whimsical ['wɪmzɪkl] *adj* причу́дливый (причу́длив).
whine [waɪn] *n* вой ◆ *vi* (*person, animal*) скули́ть *(impf)*; (*engine, siren*) выть* *(impf)*.
whip [wɪp] *n* кнут*, хлыст*; (*POL*: *person*) *организа́тор парла́ментской фра́кции* ◆ *vt* (*person, animal*) хлеста́ть* *(impf)*; (*cream, eggs*) взбива́ть (взбить* *perf*); (*move quickly*): **to ~ sth out** выхва́тывать (вы́хватить* *perf*) что-н; **to ~ sth away** вырыва́ть (вы́рвать* *perf*) что-н
▸ **whip up** *vt* (*cream*) взбива́ть (взбить* *perf*); (*inf*: *meal*) де́лать (сде́лать *perf*) на ско́рую ру́ку; (*support, emotion*) возбужда́ть (возбуди́ть* *perf*).
whiplash ['wɪplæʃ] *n* (*also*: **~ injury**) *поврежде́ние ше́и, вы́званное ре́зким движе́нием головы́ вперёд и наза́д, наприме́р, при автомоби́льной ава́рии.*
whipped cream [wɪpt-] *n* взби́тые сли́вки* *pl*.
whipping boy ['wɪpɪŋ-] *n* (*fig*) ≈ козёл отпуще́ния.
whip-round ['wɪpraund] *n* (*BRIT*) скла́дчина.
whirl [wəːl] *vt* враща́ть *(impf)*, верте́ть* *(impf)* ◆ *vi* кружи́ться* *(impf)*, враща́ться *(impf)* ◆ *n* круже́ние; **my mind is in a ~** у меня́ голова́ идёт кру́гом; **~ of social engagements** водоворо́т *or* вихрь све́тской жи́зни.
whirlpool ['wəːlpuːl] *n* водоворо́т.
whirlwind ['wəːlwɪnd] *n* вихрь *m*.
whirr [wəːʳ] *vi* (*insects*) стрекота́ть *(impf)*; (*motor etc*) треща́ть *(impf)*.
whisk [wɪsk] *n* (*CULIN*) ве́нчик ◆ *vt* (*cream, eggs*) взбива́ть (взбить* *perf*); **to ~ sb away** *or* **off** отгоня́ть (отогна́ть* *perf*).
whiskers ['wɪskəz] *npl* (*of animal*) усы́ *mpl*; (*of man*) бакенба́рды *fpl*.
whisky ['wɪskɪ] (*US, IRELAND* **whiskey**) *n* ви́ски *nt ind*.
whisper ['wɪspəʳ] *n* шёпот ◆ *vi* шепта́ться* *(impf)* ◆ *vt* шепта́ть* *(impf)*; **to ~ sth to sb** шепта́ть* *(impf)* что-н кому́-н.
whispering ['wɪspərɪŋ] *n* перешёптывание.
whist [wɪst] *n* (*BRIT*) вист.
whistle ['wɪsl] *n* (*sound*) свист; (*object*) свисто́к* ◆ *vi* свисте́ть* *(impf)*, сви́стнуть *(perf)* ◆ *vt*: **to ~ a tune** насви́стывать *(impf)* мело́дию.
whistle-stop ['wɪslstɔp] *adj*: **to make a ~ tour of** (*POL*) объезжа́ть (объе́хать* *perf*) с агитацио́нными це́лями.
Whit [wɪt] *n* Тро́ицын день* *m*.
white [waɪt] *adj* бе́лый* (бел) ◆ *n* (*colour*) бе́лый цвет; (*person*) бе́лый(-ая) *m(f) adj*; (*of egg, eye*) бело́к*; **to turn** *or* **go ~** беле́ть (побеле́ть *perf*); **the ~s** (*washing*) бе́лое бельё; **tennis/cricket ~s** те́ннисная/крике́тная фо́рма.
whitebait ['waɪtbeɪt] *n* снето́к*.
white coffee *n* (*BRIT*) ко́фе *m ind* с молоко́м.
white-collar worker ['waɪtkɔlə-] *n* слу́жащий*(-ая) *m(f) adj*.
white elephant *n* (*fig*) изли́шняя ро́скошь *f*.
white goods *npl* (*appliances*) бытовы́е электротова́ры *mpl*; (*linen etc*) белошве́йные това́ры *mpl*.
white-hot [waɪt'hɔt] *adj* раскалённый* (раскалён) добела́.
white lie *n* безоби́дная ложь* *f*.
whiteness ['waɪtnɪs] *n* белизна́.
white noise *n* (*RADIO, ELEC etc*) „бе́лый шум" (*поме́хи в радиоэфи́ре*).
whiteout ['waɪtaut] *n* бе́лая мгла.
white paper *n* (*POL*) "Бе́лая кни́га" (*докуме́нт, излага́ющий поли́тику прави́тельства по тем и́ли ины́м вопро́сам*).
whitewash ['waɪtwɔʃ] *n* (*paint*) известко́вый раство́р (*для побе́лки*); (*inf*: *SPORT*) "суха́я" ◆ *vt* (*building*) бели́ть* (побели́ть* *perf*); (*fig*: *incident, reputation*) обеля́ть (обели́ть *perf*).
white water *n*: **~-~ rafting** пла́вание на плота́х по го́рным ре́кам.
whiting ['waɪtɪŋ] *n inv* хек.
Whit Monday *n* ≈ Ду́хов день* *m*.
Whitsun ['wɪtsn] *n* ≈ Тро́ицын день* *m*, Тро́ица.
whittle ['wɪtl] *vt*: **to ~ away** *or* **down** (*costs*) уменьша́ть (уменьши́ть *perf*).
whizz [wɪz] *vi*: **to ~ past** *or* **by** проноси́ться* (пронести́сь* *perf*) ми́мо.
whizz kid *n* (*inf*) вундерки́нд.
WHO *n abbr* (= *World Health Organization*) ВОЗ= *Всеми́рная организа́ция здравоохране́ния*.

KEYWORD

who [huː] *pron* ***1*** (*interrogative*) кто*; **who is it?, who's there?** кто э́то *or* там?; **who did you see there?** кого́ Вы там ви́дели?
2 (*relative*) кото́рый (*f* кото́рая, *nt* кото́рое); **the woman who spoke to me** же́нщина, кото́рая говори́ла со мной; **those who can swim** те, кто уме́ют пла́вать.

whodunit [huː'dʌnɪt] *n* (*inf*) детекти́в.
whoever [huː'ɛvəʳ] *pron*: **~ finds him ...** тот, кто найдёт его́ ..., кто бы ни́ нашёл его́ ...; **ask ~ you like** спроси́те, кого́ хоти́те; **~ told you that?** кто Вам э́то сказа́л?; **come out, ~ you are!** выходи́, кто бы ты ни́ был!
whole [həul] *adj* це́лый (цел) ◆ *n* (*entire unit*) це́лое *nt adj*; (*all*): **the ~ of Europe** вся Евро́па; **the ~ lot (of it)** всё (э́то); **the ~ lot (of them)** все *pl* (они́); **the ~ of the time** всё вре́мя; ~

* marks translations which have irregular inflections. The Russian-English side of the dictionary gives inflectional information.

villages were destroyed целые деревни были разрушены; **the ~ of the town** весь город; **on the ~, as a ~** в целом.

wholefood(s) ['həulfu:d(z)] *n(pl)* натуральные продукты *mpl*.

wholefood shop *n* магазин натуральных продуктов.

wholehearted [həul'hɑ:tɪd] *adj* (*agreement etc*) искренний*; (*support*) горячий*.

wholeheartedly [həul'hɑ:tɪdlɪ] *adv* (*see adj*) искренне; горячо.

wholemeal ['həulmi:l] *adj* (*BRIT*): ~ **flour** мука грубого помола; ~ **bread** хлеб из муки грубого помола.

whole note *n* (*US*) целая нота.

wholesale ['həulseɪl] *n* оптовая торговля ◆ *adj* (*price*) оптовый; (*destruction*) массовый ◆ *adv* (*buy, sell*) оптом.

wholesaler ['həulseɪlə^r] *n* оптовик*; (*insitution*) оптовое предприятие.

wholesome ['həulsəm] *adj* здоровый.

wholewheat ['həulwi:t] *adj* = **wholemeal**.

wholly ['həulɪ] *adv* полностью, целиком.

KEYWORD

whom [hu:m] *pron* **1** (*interrogative*: *+acc, +gen*) кого; (: *+dat*) кому; (: *+instr*) кем; (: *+prp*) ком; **whom did you see there?** кого Вы там видели?; **to whom did you give the book?** кому Вы книгу отдали?
2 (*relative*: *+acc*) которого (*f* которую, *pl* которых); (: *+gen*) которого (*f* которой, *pl* которых); (: *+dat*) которому (*f* которой, *pl* которым); (: *+instr*) которым (*f* которой, *pl* которыми); (: *+prp*) котором (*f* которой, *pl* которых); **the man whom I saw/to whom I spoke** человек, которого я видел/с которым я говорил.

whooping cough ['hu:pɪŋ-] *n* коклюш.

whoosh [wuʃ] *n* свист ◆ *vi*: **to ~ past** *etc* просвистеть* (*perf*) мимо *etc*; **the skiers ~ed past, skiers came by with a ~** лыжники со свистом пронеслись мимо.

whopper ['wɔpə^r] *n* (*inf*: *lie*) чудовищная ложь* *f*; (*large thing*) громадина.

whopping ['wɔpɪŋ] *adj* (*inf*: *big*) громадный* (громаден).

whore [hɔ:^r] *n* (*inf*: *pej*) шлюха.

KEYWORD

whose [hu:z] *adj* **1** (*possessive*: *interrogative*) чей*; **whose book is this?, whose is this book?** чья это книга?
2 (*possessive*: *relative*) который; **the woman whose son you rescued** женщина, сына которой Вы спасли
◆ *pron* чей (*f* чья, *nt* чьё, *pl* чьи); **whose is this?** это чьё?; **I know whose it is** я знаю, чьё это.

Who's Who ['hu:z'hu:] *n* Кто есть кто (*справочник*).

KEYWORD

why [waɪ] *adv, conj* почему; **why is he always late?** почему он всегда опаздывает?; **why not?** почему?; **why not do it now?** почему бы не сделать это сейчас?; **I wonder why he said that** интересно, почему он это сказал; **that's not why I'm here** я здесь вовсе не поэтому; **that's why** вот почему; **there is a reason why I want to see him** у меня есть причины для встречи с ним
◆ *excl*: **why, it's you!** о, неужели это Вы?; **why, it's obvious/that's impossible!** но ведь это же очевидно/невозможно!

WI *n abbr* (*BRIT*: = *Women's Institute*) *ассоциация женщин, интересующихся вопросами домоводства* ◆ *abbr* = *West Indies*; (*US*: *POST*) *Wisconsin*.

wick [wɪk] *n* фитиль* *m*; **he gets on my ~** (*inf*) он действует мне на нервы.

wicked ['wɪkɪd] *adj* злобный* (злобен), злой*; (*mischievous*: *smile*) лукавый, плутовской; (*terrible*: *prices, weather*) жуткий*.

wicker ['wɪkə^r] *adj* плетёный.

wickerwork ['wɪkə^r wə:k] *adj* плетёный ◆ *n* плетение.

wicket ['wɪkɪt] *n* (*CRICKET*: *stumps*) воротца* *pl*; (: *grass area*) *кон между двумя воротцами*.

wicket-keeper ['wɪkɪtki:pə^r] *n игрок, охраняющий воротца*.

wide [waɪd] *adj* широкий* (широк) ◆ *adv*: **to open ~** широко открывать (открыть* *perf*); **to shoot ~** стрелять (*impf*) мимо цели; **the bridge is 3 metres ~** ширина моста – 3 метра.

wide-angle lens ['waɪdæŋgl-] *n* (*PHOT*) широкоугольная линза.

wide-awake [waɪdə'weɪk] *adj*: **I feel ~** у меня сна ни в одном глазу.

wide-eyed [waɪd'aɪd] *adj* (*fig*) наивный* (наивен); **she sat there ~** она сидела с широко раскрытыми глазами.

widely ['waɪdlɪ] *adv* (*believed, known*) широко; (*travelled*) много; (*differing*) значительно; **he is ~ read** (*author*) его много читают; (*reader*) он очень начитан.

widen ['waɪdn] *vt* расширять (расширить *perf*) ◆ *vi* расширяться (расшириться *perf*).

wideness ['waɪdnɪs] *n* широта.

wide open *adj* широко раскрытый (раскрыт).

wide-ranging [waɪd'reɪndʒɪŋ] *adj* (*survey, report*) всесторонний* (всесторонен); (*interests*) широкий*.

widespread ['waɪdsprɛd] *adj* (*belief etc*) распространённый* (распространён).

widow ['wɪdəu] *n* вдова*.

widowed ['wɪdəud] *adj* овдовевший.

widower ['wɪdəuə^r] *n* вдовец*.

width [wɪdθ] *n* ширина; **the street is 7 metres in ~** ширина улицы – 7 метров.

widthways ['wɪdθweɪz] *adv* в ширину.

wield [wi:ld] *vt* (*sword*) владеть (*impf*) *+instr*;

(*power*) пóльзоваться* *(impf) +instr*.
wife [waɪf] (*pl* **wives**) *n* женá*.
wig [wɪg] *n* парúк*.
wigging ['wɪgɪŋ] *n* (*BRIT: inf*) разнóс.
wiggle ['wɪgl] *vt* (*hips*) покáчивать *(impf) +instr*; (*ears*) шевелúть *(impf) +instr*.
wiggly ['wɪglɪ] *adj* волнúстый* (волнúст).
wigwam ['wɪgwæm] *n* вигвáм.
wild [waɪld] *adj* (*animal, plant*) дúкий*; (*weather, sea*) бýрный* (бýрен); (*person, behaviour*) бýйный* (бýен); (*idea, guess*) дúкий; (*enthusiastic: applause*) бýрный ◆ *n*: **the ~** (*natural surroundings*) лóно прирóды *ntpl*; **the ~s** *npl* (*remote area*) дúкие местá *ntpl*; **in the ~s of Taiga** в дéбрях тайгú; **I am ~ about her/this film** я без умá от неё/э́того фúльма.
wild card *n* (*COMPUT*) универсáльный сúмвол.
wildcat ['waɪldkæt] *n* дúкая кóшка*.
wildcat strike *n* неофициáльная забастóвка*.
wilderness ['wɪldənɪs] *n* дúкая мéстность *f*; (*desert*) пустыня.
wildfire ['waɪldfaɪəʳ] *n*: **to spread like ~** распространя́ться (распространúться *perf*) с быстротóй огня́.
wild-goose chase [waɪld'gu:s-] *n* (*fig*) бессмы́сленная затéя.
wildlife ['waɪldlaɪf] *n* дúкая прирóда.
wildly ['waɪldlɪ] *adv* (*behave*) бýйно, дúко; (*applaud*) бýрно; (*hit, happy*) неúстово; (*guess*) наобýм.
wiles [waɪlz] *npl* улóвки* *fpl*.
wilful ['wɪlful] (*US* **willful**) *adj* (*obstinate*) своенрáвный* (своенрáвен); (*deliberate*) умы́шленный*.

KEYWORD

will [wɪl] *aux vb* ***1*** (*forming future tense*): **I will finish it tomorrow** я закóнчу э́то зáвтра; **I will be working all morning** я бýду рабóтать всё ýтро; **I will have finished it by tomorrow** к зáвтрашнему днó я э́то закóнчу; **I will always remember you** я бýду пóмнить тебя́ всегдá; **will you do it? – yes, I will/no, I won't** Вы сдéлаете э́то? – да, сдéлаю/нет, не сдéлаю; **the car won't start** машúна никáк не завóдится
2 (*in conjectures, predictions*): **he will** *or* **he'll be there by now** он, навéрное, ужé там; **mistakes will happen** оши́бки неизбéжны
3 (*in commands, requests, offers*): **will you be quiet!** а нý-ка потúше!; **will you help me?** Вы мне не помóжете?; **will you have a cup of tea?** не хотúте ли чáшку чáя?; **I won't put up with it!** я э́того не потерплю́!;
◆ (*pt,pp* **willed**) *vt*: **I willed him to win** я хотéл вселúть в негó дух побéды
◆ *n* (*volition*) вóля; (*testament*) завещáние.

willful ['wɪlful] *adj* (*US*) = **wilful**.
willing ['wɪlɪŋ] *adj* (*agreed*) соглáсный* (соглáсен); (*enthusiastic*) усéрдный* (усéрден); **he's ~ to do it** он готóв э́то сдéлать; **to show ~** проявля́ть (прояви́ть* *perf*) готóвность.
willingly ['wɪlɪŋlɪ] *adv* охóтно.
willingness ['wɪlɪŋnɪs] *n* готóвность *f*.
will-o'-the wisp ['wɪləðə'wɪsp] *n* (*also fig*) неуловúмое *nt adj*.
willow ['wɪləu] *n* (*tree*) úва; (*wood*) ивня́к.
willpower ['wɪl'pauəʳ] *n* сúла вóли.
willy-nilly ['wɪlɪ'nɪlɪ] *adv* вóлей-невóлей.
wilt [wɪlt] *vi* поникáть (поникнуть* *perf*).
Wilts [wɪlts] *abbr* (*BRIT: POST*) = *Wiltshire*.
wily ['waɪlɪ] *adj* хúтрый* (хитёр).
wimp [wɪmp] (*inf: pej*) *n* хлю́пик ◆ *vi*: **to ~ out** стрýсить* (*perf*).
wimpish ['wɪmpɪʃ] *adj* (*inf: pej*) хлúпкий* (хлúпок).
win [wɪn] (*pt,pp* **won**) *n* побéда ◆ *vt* вы́игрывать (вы́играть *perf*); (*support, popularity*) завоёвывать (завоевáть* *perf*) ◆ *vi* побеждáть (победúть* *perf*), вы́игрывать (вы́играть *perf*)
▸ **win over** *vt* (*person*) покоря́ть (покорúть *perf*)
▸ **win round** *vt* (*BRIT*) = **win over**.
wince [wɪns] *vi* мóрщиться (помóрщиться *perf*).
winch [wɪntʃ] *n* лебёдка*, вóрот.
Winchester disk ['wɪntʃɪstə-] *n* (*COMPUT*) винчéстерский диск.
wind[1] [wɪnd] *n* вéтер*; (*MED*) гáзы *mpl*; (*breath*) дыхáние ◆ *vt*: **the blow ~ed him** от удáра у негó захватúло дух; **the ~s** *npl* (*MUS*) духовы́е инструмéнты *mpl*; **into** *or* **against the ~** прóтив вéтра; **he got the ~ of the news** (*fig*) до негó дошлá нóвость; **to break ~** дéлать (сдéлать *perf*) отры́жку.
wind[2] [waɪnd] (*pt, pp* **wound**) *vt* (*roll: thread, rope*) мотáть (смотáть *perf*); (*rotate*) вертéть* (*impf*), кругúть* (*perf*); (*bandage*) заворáчивать (завернýть *perf*); (*clock, toy*) заводúть* (завестú* *perf*) ◆ *vi* (*road, river*) вúться* (*impf*)
▸ **wind down** *vt* (*car window*) опускáть (опустúть* *perf*); (*production, business*) сворáчивать (свернýть* *perf*)
▸ **wind up** *vt* (*clock, toy*) заводúть* (завестú* *perf*); (*debate*) завершáть (завершúть *perf*).
windbreak ['wɪndbreɪk] *n* бурелóм; (*plants*) ветрозащúтная лесополосá.
windbreaker ['wɪndbreɪkəʳ] *n* (*US*) = **windcheater**.
windcheater ['wɪndtʃi:təʳ] *n* штормóвка*.
winder ['waɪndəʳ] *n* (*BRIT: on watch*) (заводнóй) ключ*.

windfall ['wɪndfɔːl] *n* (*money*) неожи́данные де́ньги *pl*; (*apple etc*) па́данец*.
winding ['waɪndɪŋ] *adj* изви́листый (изви́лист); ~ **staircase** вита́я ле́стница.
wind instrument ['wɪnd-] *n* духово́й инструме́нт.
windmill ['wɪndmɪl] *n* ветряна́я ме́льница.
window ['wɪndəu] *n* (*in house, vehicle*) окно́*; (*in shop*) витри́на; (*also:* ~ **pane**) око́нное стекло́*.
window box *n* нару́жный я́щик для цвето́в.
window cleaner *n* мо́йщик(-ица) о́кон.
window dresser *n* оформи́тель(ница) *m(f)* витри́н.
window envelope *n конве́рт с прозра́чным прямоуго́льником, че́рез кото́рый ви́ден а́дрес, напеча́танный на письме́.*
window frame *n* око́нная ра́ма.
window ledge *n* нару́жный подоко́нник.
window pane *n* око́нное стекло́*.
window-shopping ['wɪndəuʃɔpɪŋ] *n*: **to go** ~ рассма́тривать *(impf)* витри́ны.
windowsill ['wɪndəusɪl] *n* подоко́нник.
windpipe ['wɪndpaɪp] *n* (*ANAT*) трахе́я.
wind power ['wɪnd-] *n* си́ла ве́тра.
windscreen ['wɪndskriːn] *n* ветрово́е стекло́*.
windscreen washer *n* стеклоомыва́тель *m*.
windscreen wiper [-waɪpəʳ] *n* дво́рник, стеклоочисти́тель *m*.
windshield ['wɪndʃiːld] *n* (*US*) = **windscreen**.
wind surfing ['wɪnd-] *n* виндсе́рфинг.
windswept ['wɪndswɛpt] *adj* (*place*) незащищённый от ве́тра; (*person, hair*) растрёпанный* (растрёпан).
wind tunnel ['wɪnd-] *n* аэродинами́ческая труба́*.
windy ['wɪndɪ] *adj* ве́треный* (ве́трен); **it's** ~ сего́дня ве́трено.
wine [waɪn] *n* вино́* ◆ *vt*: **to** ~ **and dine sb** пои́ть*-корми́ть* *(impf)* кого́-н.
wine bar *n* ви́нный бар.
wine cellar *n* ви́нный по́греб*.
wine glass *n* бока́л.
wine grower *n* виногра́дарь *m*.
wine growing *n* виногра́дарство ◆ *adj*: ~-~ **region** виногра́дарский райо́н.
wine list *n* ка́рта вин.
wine merchant *n* виноторго́вец*.
wine tasting [-teɪstɪŋ] *n* дегуста́ция вин.
wine waiter *n* официа́нт, ве́дающий ви́нами.
wing [wɪŋ] *n* (*also AUT*) крыло́*; ~**s** *npl* (*THEAT*) кули́сы *fpl*.
winger ['wɪŋəʳ] *n* (*FOOTBALL, RUGBY*) кра́йний* напада́ющий* *m adj*.
wing mirror *n* (*BRIT*) боково́е зе́ркало*.
wing nut *n* кры́льчатая га́йка*.
wingspan ['wɪŋspæn] *n* разма́х крыла́.
wingspread ['wɪŋsprɛd] *n* разма́х крыла́.
wink [wɪŋk] *n* подми́гивание ◆ *vi* (*with eye*) подми́гивать (подмигну́ть *perf*); (*light etc*) мига́ть (мигну́ть *perf*).
winkle [wɪŋkl] *n* берегова́я *or* морска́я ули́тка*.
winner ['wɪnəʳ] *n* победи́тель(ница) *m(f)*.
winning ['wɪnɪŋ] *adj* (*team, competitor*) победи́вший, вы́игравший; (*shot, goal*) реша́ющий; (*smile*) обая́тельный* (обая́телен), покоря́ющий; *see also* **winnings**.
winning post *n* фи́нишный столб*.
winnings ['wɪnɪŋz] *npl* вы́игрыш *msg*.
winsome ['wɪnsəm] *adj* привлека́тельный* (привлека́телен).
winter ['wɪntəʳ] *n* (*season*) зима́* ◆ *vi* (*birds*) зимова́ть (перезимова́ть *perf*); **in** ~ зимо́й.
winter sports *npl* зи́мние ви́ды *mpl* спо́рта.
wintry ['wɪntrɪ] *adj* зи́мний*.
wipe [waɪp] *n*: **to give sth a** ~ протира́ть (протере́ть* *perf*) что-н ◆ *vt* (*rub*) вытира́ть (вы́тереть* *perf*); (*erase*) стира́ть (стере́ть* *perf*); **to** ~ **one's nose** вытира́ть (вы́тереть* *perf*) нос
▸ **wipe off** *vt* стира́ть (стере́ть* *perf*)
▸ **wipe out** *vt* (*debt*) ликвиди́ровать *(impf/perf)*; (*memory*) стира́ть (стере́ть* *perf*); (*city, population*) стира́ть (стере́ть* *perf*) с лица́ земли́
▸ **wipe up** *vt* (*mess*) подтира́ть (подтере́ть* *perf*).
wire ['waɪəʳ] *n* про́волока; (*ELEC*) про́вод*; (*telegram*) телегра́мма ◆ *vt* (*fence*) скрепля́ть (скрепи́ть* *perf*) про́волокой; (*ELEC*: *also:* ~ **up**) подключа́ть (подключи́ть* *perf*); **to** ~ **a house** де́лать (сде́лать *perf*) прово́дку в до́ме; **to** ~ **sb** телеграфи́ровать *(impf/perf)* кому́-н.
wire brush *n* про́волочная щётка*.
wire cutters *npl* куса́чки* *pl*.
wireless ['waɪəlɪs] *n* (*BRIT*) ра́дио *nt ind*.
wire netting *n* про́волочная сеть *f*.
wire service *n* (*US*) аге́нтство новосте́й.
wire-tapping ['waɪə'tæpɪŋ] *n* подслу́шивание телефо́нных разгово́ров.
wiring ['waɪərɪŋ] *n* (*ELEC*) электропрово́дка.
wiry ['waɪərɪ] *adj* (*person*) жи́листый (жи́лист); (*hair*) жёсткий* (жёсток).
wisdom ['wɪzdəm] *n* му́дрость *f*.
wisdom tooth *n* зуб* му́дрости.
wise [waɪz] *adj* му́дрый* (мудр); **I'm none the ~r** я всё равно́ ничего́ не понима́ю
▸ **wise up** *vi* (*inf*): **to** ~ **up to sth** осознава́ть* (осозна́ть* *perf*) что-н.
...wise [waɪz] *suffix*: **timewise** *etc* в отноше́нии вре́мени *etc*.
wisecrack ['waɪzkræk] *n* шпи́лька*.
wisely ['waɪzlɪ] *adv* му́дро.
wish [wɪʃ] *n* жела́ние ◆ *vt* жела́ть (пожела́ть *perf*); **best ~es** (*for birthday etc*) всего́ наилу́чшего; **with best ~es** (*in letter*) с наилу́чшими пожела́ниями; **give her my best ~es** переда́йте ей мои́ наилу́чшие пожела́ния; **to** ~ **sb goodbye** проща́ться (попроща́ться *perf*) с кем-н; **he ~ed me well** он пожела́л мне всего́ хоро́шего; **to** ~ **to do**

хоте́ть* *(impf)* +*infin*; **I ~ him to come** я хочу́, чтобы он пришёл; **to ~ for** жела́ть (пожела́ть *perf*) +*acc or* +gen; **to ~ sth on sb** навя́зывать (навяза́ть* *perf*) что-н кому́-н.

wishbone ['wɪʃbəun] *n* счастли́вая ду́жка (*грудная кость птицы, разламывая которую, загадывают желание*).

wishful ['wɪʃful] *adj*: **it's ~ thinking** это – принятие желаемого за действительное.

wishy-washy ['wɪʃɪ'wɔʃɪ] *adj* (*inf*: *colour*) му́тный; (*ideas, person*) вя́лый (вял).

wisp [wɪsp] *n* (*of grass, hair*) клочо́к*; (*of smoke*) стру́йка*.

wistful ['wɪstful] *adj* тоскли́вый (тоскли́в).

wit [wɪt] *n* (*wittiness*) остроу́мие; (*intelligence*: *also*: **~s**) ум*, ра́зум; (*person*) остря́к* (-я́чка*); (*presence of mind*) сообрази́тельность *f*; **to be at one's ~s' end** (*fig*) быть* *(impf)* в отча́янии; **to have one's ~s about one** не теря́ться (растеря́ться *perf*); **to ~** а и́менно.

witch [wɪtʃ] *n* ве́дьма.

witchcraft ['wɪtʃkrɑ:ft] *n* колдовство́.

witch doctor *n* зна́харь(-рка*) *m(f)*.

witch-hunt ['wɪtʃhʌnt] *n* (*fig*) охо́та за ве́дьмами.

KEYWORD

with [wɪð] *prep* ***1*** (*accompanying, in the company of*) с +*instr*; **I spent the day with him** я провела́ с ним день; **we stayed with friends** мы остана́вливались у друзе́й; **I'll be with you in a minute** я освобожу́сь че́рез мину́ту; **would you like chips with your steak?** Вы хоти́те жа́реную карто́шку к бифште́ксу?; **I'm with you** (*I understand*) я Вас понима́ю; **she is really with it** (*inf*: *fashionable*) она́ о́чень совреме́нная деви́ца; (: *aware*) она́ всё соobража́ет

2 (*descriptive*) с +*instr*; **a girl with blue eyes** де́вушка с голубы́ми глаза́ми; **a skirt with a silk lining** ю́бка на шёлковой подкла́дке

3 (*indicating manner*) с +*instr*; (*indicating cause*) от +*gen*; (*indicating means*): **to write with a pencil** писа́ть* *(impf)* карандашо́м; **with tears in her eyes** со слеза́ми на глаза́х; **red with anger** кра́сный от гне́ва; **you can open the door with this key** Вы мо́жете откры́ть дверь э́тим ключо́м; **to fill sth with water** наполня́ть (напо́лни́ть *perf*) что-н водо́й.

withdraw [wɪθ'drɔ:] (*irreg*: *like* **draw**) *vt* (*object*) извлека́ть (извле́чь* *perf*); (*offer, remark*) брать* (взять* *perf*) наза́д ◆ *vi* (*troops, person*) уходи́ть* (уйти́* *perf*); **to ~ into o.s.** уходи́ть* (уйти́* *perf*) в себя́; **to ~ money from an account** снима́ть (снять* *perf*) де́ньги со счёта.

withdrawal [wɪθ'drɔ:əl] *n* (*of offer, remark, participation*) отка́з; (*of troops*) вы́вод; (*of services*) отме́на; (*of money*) сня́тие.

withdrawal symptoms *npl* (MED) синдро́м *msg* отме́ны *or* абстине́нтный синдро́м *msg* (*при отвыкании от лекарств, наркотиков umn*).

withdrawn [wɪθ'drɔ:n] *pp of* **withdraw** ◆ *adj* за́мкнутый (за́мкнут).

wither ['wɪðə'] *vi* (*plant*) вя́нуть (завя́нуть *perf*), со́хнуть (засо́хнуть *perf*).

withered ['wɪðəd] *adj* (*plant*) увя́дший*, засо́хший; (*limb*) вы́сохший*.

withhold [wɪθ'həuld] (*irreg*: *like* **hold**) *vt* (*money*) уде́рживать (удержа́ть* *perf*); (*permission*) не дава́ть* (дать* *perf*); (*information*) ута́ивать (ута́ить *perf*).

within [wɪð'ɪn] *prep* (*inside*: *of place, time, distance*) внутри́ +*gen*, в преде́лах +*gen* ◆ *adv* внутри́; **~ reach** в преде́лах досяга́емости; **~ sight (of)** в по́ле зре́ния (+*gen*); **the finish is ~ sight** коне́ц не за гора́ми; **~ the week** в преде́лах неде́ли; **~ a mile of** в преде́лах ми́ли от +*gen*; **~ an hour of** че́рез час по́сле +*gen*; **~ the law** в ра́мках зако́на.

without [wɪð'aut] *prep* без +*gen*; **~ a coat** без пальто́; **~ saying a word** не говоря́ ни сло́ва; **~ looking** не гля́дя; **to go ~ sth** обходи́ться* (обойти́сь* *perf*) без чего́-н.

withstand [wɪθ'stænd] (*irreg*: *like* **stand**) *vt* выде́рживать (вы́держать* *perf*).

witness ['wɪtnɪs] *n* (*person, also* LAW) свиде́тель(ница) *m(f)* ◆ *vt* (*event*) быть* *(impf)* свиде́телем(-льницей) +*gen*; (*document*) заверя́ть (заве́рить *perf*); **to bear ~ to** (*fig*) свиде́тельствовать *(impf)* о +*prp*; **~ for the prosecution/defence** свиде́тель обвине́ния/защи́ты; **to ~ to sth** засвиде́тельствовать *(perf)* факт чего́-н; **I can ~ to having seen ...** я могу́ засвиде́тельствовать, что я ви́дел ....

witness box *n* свиде́тельское ме́сто*.

witness stand (US) = **witness box**.

witticism ['wɪtɪsɪzəm] *n* остро́та.

witty ['wɪtɪ] *adj* остроу́мный* (остроу́мен).

wives [waɪvz] *npl of* **wife**.

wizard ['wɪzəd] *n* волше́бник.

wizened ['wɪznd] *adj* (*person*) морщи́нистый (морщи́нист); (*fruit, vegetable*) смо́рщенный* (смо́рщен).

wk *abbr* = **week**.

Wm. *abbr* = *William*.

WO *n abbr* (MIL: = *warrant officer*) ≈ пра́порщик.

wobble ['wɔbl] *vi* (*legs*) трясти́сь* *(impf)*; (*jelly*) колыха́ться* *(impf)*; (*chair*) шата́ться *(impf)*.

wobbly ['wɔblɪ] *adj* (*hand, voice*) дрожа́щий; (*table, chair*) ша́ткий* (ша́ток).

woe [wəu] *n* го́ре.

woeful ['wəuful] *adj* (*sad*) печа́льный* (печа́лен); (*awful*) вопию́щий.

* marks translations which have irregular inflections. The Russian-English side of the dictionary gives inflectional information.

wok [wɔk] *n* глубо́кая сковорода́ (*в кита́йской ку́хне*).
woke [wəuk] *pt of* **wake**.
woken ['wəukn] *pp of* **wake**.
wolf [wulf] (*pl* **wolves**) *n* волк.
wolves [wulvz] *npl of* **wolf**.
woman ['wumən] (*pl* **women**) *n* же́нщина; **~ friend** подру́га; **~ teacher** учи́тельница; **young ~** молода́я же́нщина; **women's page** (*PRESS*) страни́ца для же́нщин.
woman doctor *n* же́нщина-врач.
womanize ['wumənaɪz] *vi* (*pej*) вести́* (*impf*) распу́тну жизнь.
womanizer ['wumənaɪzəʳ] *n* женолю́б, ба́бник (*разг*).
womanly ['wumənlɪ] *adj* (*virtues etc*) же́нский*; (*figure*) же́нственный.
womb [wu:m] *n* ма́тка*.
women ['wɪmɪn] *npl of* **woman**.
women's lib ['wɪmɪnz-] *n* (*inf*) эмансипа́ция же́нщин.
Women's (Liberation) Movement *n* движе́ние за эмансипа́цию же́нщин.
won [wʌn] *pt, pp of* **win**.
wonder ['wʌndəʳ] *n* (*miracle*) чу́до; (*feeling*) изумле́ние ◆ *vi*: **I ~ whether you could tell me** ... не мо́жете ли Вы сказа́ть мне ...; **I ~ why he is late** интере́сно, почему́ он опозда́л; **to ~ at** (*marvel at*) удивля́ться (*impf*) +*dat*; **to ~ about** разду́мывать* (*impf*) о +*prp*; **it's no ~ (that)** не удиви́тельно(, что).
wonderful ['wʌndəful] *adj* (*excellent*) замеча́тельный* (замеча́телен); (*astonishing*) удиви́тельный (удиви́телен).
wonderfully ['wʌndəfəlɪ] *adv* (*see adj*) замеча́тельно; удиви́тельно.
wonky ['wɔŋkɪ] *adj* (*BRIT: inf*) ша́ткий* (ша́ток).
wont [wəunt] *adj*: **he is ~ to ...** он име́ет обыкнове́ние +*infin* ...; **as is my ~** по обыкнове́нию.
won't [wəunt] = **will not**.
woo [wu:] *vt* (*woman*) добива́ться (доби́ться *perf*) расположе́ния +*gen*; (*audience etc*) заи́грывать* (*impf*) с +*instr*.
wood [wud] *n* (*timber*) де́рево; (*forest*) лес ◆ *cpd* (*house*) деревя́нный; (*shed*) дровяно́й; **~pile** шта́бель *m* дров.
wood carving *n* (*act*) резьба́ по де́реву; (*object*) резьба́ (по де́реву).
wooded ['wudɪd] *adj* (*slopes, area*) леси́стый.
wooden ['wudn] *adj* (*object*) деревя́нный; (*fig: performance, actor*) дубо́вый.
woodland ['wudlənd] *n* леси́стая ме́стность *f*.
woodpecker ['wudpɛkəʳ] *n* дя́тел*.
wood pigeon *n* лесно́й го́лубь *m*.
woodwind ['wudwɪnd] *n* деревя́нный духово́й инструме́нт; **the ~** деревя́нные духовы́е *pl adj* инструме́нты.
woodwork ['wudwə:k] *n* (*skill*) столя́рное де́ло.
woodworm ['wudwə:m] *n* (*larvae*) личи́нка древото́чца.
woof [wuf] *n* лай ◆ *vi* ла́ять (*impf*); **~, ~!** гав, гав!
wool [wul] *n* (*material, yarn*) шерсть *f*; **to pull the ~ over sb's eyes** (*fig*) ве́шать (*impf*) лапшу́ на́ уши.
woollen ['wulən] (*US* **woolen**) *adj* шерстяно́й.
woollens ['wulənz] *npl* шерстяны́е ве́щи *fpl*.
woolly ['wulɪ] (*US* **wooly**) *adj* шерстяно́й; (*fig: ideas*) расплы́вчатый (расплы́вчат); (*: person*) вя́лый (вял) ◆ *n* шерстяно́й сви́тер* *m*.
woozy ['wu:zɪ] *adj* (*inf*) окосе́вший.
Worcs *abbr* (*BRIT: POST*) = *Worcestershire*.
word [wə:d] *n* сло́во; (*news*) слух ◆ *vt* (*letter, message*) формули́ровать* (сформули́ровать* *perf*); **~ for ~** (*repeat*) сло́во в сло́во; (*translate*) досло́вно; **what's the ~ for "pen" in French?** как (бу́дет) по-францу́зски (сло́во) "ру́чка"?; **to put sth into ~s** выража́ть (вы́разить* *perf*) что-н слова́ми; **in other ~s** други́ми слова́ми; **to break/keep one's ~** наруша́ть (нару́шить *perf*)/держа́ть (сдержа́ть* *perf*) своё сло́во; **to have ~s with sb** име́ть (*impf*) кру́пный разгово́р с кем-н; **to have a ~ with sb** поговори́ть (*perf*) с кем-н; **I'll take your ~ for it** я пове́рю Вам на́ слово; **to send ~ of** извеща́ть (извести́ть* *perf*) о +*prp*; **to leave ~ (with sb/for sb) that** ... передава́ть* (переда́ть* *perf*) (че́рез кого́-н/кому́-н), что ....
wording ['wə:dɪŋ] *n* формулиро́вка*; (*in card*) поздрави́тельный текст.
word of mouth *n*: **by** *or* **through ~ ~ ~** из уст в уста́; **I found out about it by ~ ~ ~** я об э́том услы́шал от кого́-то.
word-perfect ['wə:d'pə:fɪkt] *adj*: **to be ~** (*person*) знать (*impf*) ка́ждое сло́во; **the speech was ~** речь была́ прекра́сно подгото́влена.
word processing *n* обрабо́тка *or* подгото́вка те́кстов.
word processor [-prəusɛsəʳ] *n* те́кстовый проце́ссор.
wordwrap ['wə:dræp] *n* (автомати́ческий*) перехо́д (*на но́вую строку́*).
wordy ['wə:dɪ] *adj* многосло́вный* (многосло́вен).
wore [wɔ:ʳ] *pt of* **wear**.
work [wə:k] *n* рабо́та; (*ART, LITERATURE*) произведе́ние ◆ *vi* рабо́тать (*impf*); (*medicine etc*) де́йствовать (поде́йствовать *perf*) ◆ *vt* (*clay*) рабо́тать (*impf*) с +*instr*; (*wood, metal, land*) обраба́тывать (обрабо́тать *perf*); (*mine*) разраба́тывать (разрабо́тать *perf*); (*machine*) управля́ть (*impf*) +*instr*; (*effect, miracle*) производи́ть* (произвести́* *perf*); **to go to ~** ходи́ть*/идти́* (*impf*) на рабо́ту; **to start** *or* **set to ~** принима́ться (приня́ться* *perf*) за рабо́ту; **to be at ~ (on sth)** рабо́тать

(impf) (над чем-н); **he has been out of ~ for three months** у него́ уже́ три ме́сяца нет рабо́ты; **to ~ hard** мно́го рабо́тать *(impf)*; **to ~ loose** (*part*) расша́тываться (расшата́ться *perf*); (*knot*) сла́бнуть (осла́бнуть *perf*)
▸ **work on** *vt fus* (*task*) рабо́тать *(impf)* над *+instr*; (*person*) рабо́тать *(impf)* с *+instr*; (*principle*) опира́ться *(impf)* на *+acc*; **he's ~ing on his car** (*repairing*) он чи́нит маши́ну; (*doing up*) он рабо́тает над свое́й маши́ной
▸ **work out** *vi* (*plans etc*) удава́ться* (уда́ться* *perf*); (*SPORT*) занима́ться *(impf)* физи́ческими упражне́ниями ◆ *vt* (*problem*) реша́ть (реши́ть *perf*); (*plan*) разраба́тывать (разрабо́тать *perf*); **it ~s out at £100** (*cost*) получа́ется £100
▸ **work up** *vt*: **to get ~ed up (about sth)** разне́рвничаться *(perf)* (из-за чего́-н).
workable ['wə:kəbl] *adj* (*solution*) осуществи́мый (осуществи́м), выполни́мый (выполни́м).
workaholic [wə:kə'hɔlɪk] *n*: **he is a ~** он не мо́жет жить без рабо́ты.
workbench ['wə:kbɛntʃ] *n* верста́к*.
worker ['wə:kə^r] *n* (*in factory*) рабо́чий*(-ая) *m(f) adj*; (*in community etc*) рабо́тник(-ница); **office ~** конто́рский* слу́жащий*(-ая) *m(f) adj*.
workforce ['wə:kfɔ:s] *n* рабо́чая си́ла.
work-in ['wə:kɪn] *n* (*BRIT*) "уо́рк-ин" (*вид забасто́вки*).
working ['wə:kɪŋ] *adj* (*day, tools etc*) рабо́чий*; **~ conditions** усло́вия *ntpl* рабо́ты; **~ partner** делово́й партнёр; **~ population** за́нятая часть населе́ния; **a ~ knowledge of English** практи́ческое зна́ние англи́йского языка́.
working capital *n* оборо́тный капита́л.
working class *n* рабо́чий* класс.
working-class ['wə:kɪŋ'klɑ:s] *adj* рабо́чий*.
working man *n* рабо́тающий мужчи́на.
working order *n*: **in ~ ~** в рабо́чем состоя́нии.
working party *n* (*BRIT*) рабо́чая гру́ппа.
working relationship *n* деловы́е отноше́ния.
working week *n* рабо́чая неде́ля.
work-in-progress ['wə:kɪn'prəugrɛs] *n* (*COMM*: *products*) *объём проду́кции, вы́пущенной к настоя́щему моме́нту*; (: *value*) *сто́имость проду́кции, вы́пущенной к настоя́щему моме́нту*.
workload ['wə:kləud] *n* нагру́зка*.
workman ['wə:kmən] *irreg n* (квалифици́рованный) рабо́чий* *m adj*.
workmanship ['wə:kmənʃɪp] *n* (*skill*) мастерство́; (*quality*) ка́чество рабо́ты; **good/poor ~** то́нкая/гру́бая рабо́та.
workmate ['wə:kmeɪt] *n* това́рищ по рабо́те.
workout ['wə:kaut] *n* разми́нка.
work permit *n* разреше́ние на рабо́ту.
works [wə:ks] *n* (*BRIT*: *factory*) заво́д, фа́брика ◆ *npl* (*of clock, machine*) механи́зм *msg*.
worksheet ['wə:kʃi:t] *n* рабо́чая ка́рта.
workshop ['wə:kʃɔp] *n* (*at home, in factory*) мастерска́я *f adj*, цех; (*practical session*) семина́р, практи́ческие заня́тия *ntpl*; (*THEAT, MUS*) сту́дия.
work station *n часть большо́го о́фиса, отделённая для рабо́ты одного́ слу́жащего*; (*COMPUT*) рабо́чая ста́нция.
work study *n* ≈ нау́чная организа́ция труда́.
worktop ['wə:ktɔp] *n* рабо́чая пове́рхность *f*.
work-to-rule ['wə:ktə'ru:l] *n* (*BRIT*) "рабо́та по пра́вилам" (*вид забасто́вочной борьбы́*).
world [wə:ld] *n* мир ◆ *cpd* (*tour*) кругосве́тный; (*war, record*) мирово́й; **~ champion** мирово́й чемпио́н, чемпио́н ми́ра; **~ power** мирова́я держа́ва; **all over the ~** во всём ми́ре; **to think the ~ of sb** быть* *(impf)* о́чень высо́кого мне́ния о ком-н; **what in the ~ are you doing?** ты соobража́ешь, что ты де́лаешь?; **to do sb a ~ of good** приноси́ть* (принести́* *perf*) кому́-н огро́мную по́льзу; **W~ War One/Two** пе́рвая/втора́я мирова́я война́; **out of this ~** неземно́й.
World Cup *n*: **the ~ ~** (*FOOTBALL*) Ку́бок *or* чемпиона́т ми́ра.
world-famous [wə:ld'feɪməs] *adj* всеми́рно изве́стный* (изве́стен).
worldly ['wə:ldlɪ] *adj* (*not spiritual*) земно́й; (*knowledgeable*) искушённый.
world music *n* му́зыка наро́дов ми́ра.
World Series *n*: **the ~ ~** (*US*: *BASEBALL*) ку́бковые соревнова́ния *ntpl*.
worldwide ['wə:ld'waɪd] *adj* всеми́рный ◆ *adv* во всём ми́ре.
World Wide Web *n* (Всеми́рная) Сеть, Повсеме́стно Протя́нутая Паути́на.
worm [wə:m] *n* (*ZOOL*) червь *m*
▸ **worm out** *vt*: **to ~ sth out of sb** вытя́гивать (вы́тянуть *perf*) что-н из кого́-н.
worn [wɔ:n] *pp of* **wear** ◆ *adj* (*carpet*) потёртый (потёрт); (*shoe*) поно́шенный* (поно́шен).
worn-out ['wɔ:naut] *adj* (*object*) изно́шенный* (изно́шен); (*teddy*) потрёпанный* (потрё пан); (*person*) измо́танный (измо́тан).
worried ['wʌrɪd] *adj* обеспоко́енный (обеспоко́ен), встрево́женный (встрево́жен); **she is ~ about it** она́ обеспоко́ена э́тим.
worrier ['wʌrɪə^r] *n*: **she is a natural ~** она́ всегда́ чем-то обеспоко́ена.
worrisome ['wʌrɪsəm] *adj* вызыва́ющий беспоко́йство, трево́жный.
worry ['wʌrɪ] *n* (*anxiety*) беспоко́йство, волне́ние ◆ *vi* (*person*) беспоко́иться *(impf)*, волнова́ться *(impf)* ◆ *vt* (*person*) беспоко́ить *(impf)*, волнова́ть (взволнова́ть *perf*); **to ~**

* marks translations which have irregular inflections. The Russian-English side of the dictionary gives inflectional information.

about *or* **over sth/sb** беспоко́иться *(impf)* за что-н/кого-н.
worrying ['wʌrɪɪŋ] *adj* трево́жный* (трево́жен).
worse [wə:s] *adj* ху́дший* ◆ *adv* ху́же ◆ *n* ху́дшее *nt adj*; **to get ~** ухудша́ться (уху́дшиться *perf*); **a change for the ~** ухудше́ние; **he is none the ~ for it** ему́ не ста́ло от э́того ху́же; **so much the ~ for you!** тем ху́же для Вас!
worsen ['wə:sn] *vt* ухудша́ть (уху́дшить *perf*) ◆ *vi* ухудша́ться (уху́дшиться *perf*).
worse off *adj* (*financially*) бедне́е; (*fig*): **you'll be ~ ~ this way** Вам так бу́дет ху́же; **he is now ~ ~ than before** его́ положе́ние тепе́рь ху́же, чем ра́ньше.
worship ['wə:ʃɪp] *n* поклоне́ние, преклоне́ние ◆ *vt* поклоня́ться *(impf)* +*dat*, преклоня́ться *(impf)* пе́ред +*instr*; **Your W~** (*BRIT: to mayor, judge*) Ва́ша ми́лость.
worshipper ['wə:ʃɪpə^r] *n* (*REL*) моля́щийся (-аяся) *m(f) adj*, прихожа́нин*(-нка); (*fig*) покло́нник(-ница).
worst [wə:st] *adj* наиху́дший* ◆ *adv* ху́же всего́ ◆ *n* наиху́дшее *nt adj*; **at ~** в ху́дшем слу́чае; **if the ~ comes to the ~** на худо́й коне́ц, в са́мом ху́дшем слу́чае.
worst-case scenario ['wə:stkeɪs-] *n* ху́дший* вариа́нт.
worsted ['wustɪd] *n*: **(wool) ~** гребенна́я шерсть *f*.
worth [wə:θ] *n* (*value*) сто́имость *f* ◆ *adj*: **to be ~** сто́ить *(impf)*; **how much is it ~?** ско́лько э́то сто́ит?; **50 pence ~ of apples** я́блок на 50 пе́нсов; **an hour's ~ of work** рабо́та на час; **it's ~ it** э́то того́ сто́ит.
worthless ['wə:θlɪs] *adj* никчё́мный* (никчё́мен).
worthwhile ['wə:θ'waɪl] *adj* сто́ящий*; **a ~ book** сто́ящая кни́га.
worthy [wə:ðɪ] *adj* досто́йный; **~ of** досто́йный* (досто́ин) +*gen*.

KEYWORD

would [wud] *aux vb* ***1*** (*conditional tense*): **I would tell you if I could** я бы сказа́л Вам, е́сли бы мог; **if you asked him he would do it** е́сли Вы его́ попро́сите, (то) он э́то сде́лает; **if you had asked him he would have done it** е́сли бы Вы попроси́ли его́, (то) он бы э́то сде́лал
2 (*in offers, invitations, requests*): **would you like a biscuit?** не хоти́те (ли) пече́нья?; **would you ask him to come in?** пригласи́те его́ войти́?; **would you open the window please?** откро́йте, пожа́луйста, окно́
3 (*in indirect speech*): **I said I would do it** я сказа́л, что сде́лаю э́то; **he asked me if I would stay with him** он попроси́л меня́ оста́ться с ним; **he asked me if I would resit the exam if I failed** он спроси́л меня́, бу́ду ли я передава́ть экза́мен, е́сли я провалю́сь
4 (*emphatic*): **it WOULD have to snow today!** и́менно сего́дня до́лжен был пойти́ снег!; **you WOULD say that, wouldn't you!** Вы, коне́чно, э́то ска́жете!
5 (*insistence*): **she wouldn't behave** она́ ника́к не хоте́ла хорошо́ себя́ вести́
6 (*conjecture*): **it would have been midnight** должно́ быть, была́ по́лночь; **it would seem so** должно́ быть, так; **it would seem that ...** похо́же, что ...
7 (*indicating habit*): **he would always come here on Mondays** он всегда́ приходи́л сюда́ по понеде́льникам; **he would spend every day on the beach** он проводи́л ка́ждый день на пля́же.

would-be ['wudbi:] *adj* (*pej*): **~ writer** челове́к*, вообража́ющий себя́ писа́телем.
wouldn't ['wudnt] = **would not**.
wound[1] [waund] *pt, pp of* **wind**[2].
wound[2] [wu:nd] *n* ра́на ◆ *vt* ра́нить *(impf/perf)*; **~ed in the leg** ра́неный в но́гу.
wove [wəuv] *pt of* **weave**.
woven ['wəuvn] *pp of* **weave**.
WP *n abbr* = **word processing, word processor** ◆ *abbr* (*BRIT: inf* = *weather permitting*) е́сли позво́лит пого́да.
WPC (*BRIT*) *n abbr* = *woman police constable.*
wpm *abbr* = *words per minute.*
WRAC *n abbr* (*BRIT*) = *Women's Royal Army Corps.*
WRAF *n abbr* (*BRIT*) = *Women's Royal Air Force.*
wrangle ['ræŋgl] *n* пререка́ние ◆ *vi*: **to ~ with sb over sth** пререка́ться *(impf)* с кем-н по по́воду чего́-н.
wrap [ræp] *n* (*shawl*) широ́кий* шарф; (*cape*) наки́дка* ◆ *vt* (*also:* **~ up**) завора́чивать (заверну́ть *perf*); (*wind*): **to ~ sth round sth** (*tape etc*) обора́чивать (оберну́ть *perf*) что-н вокру́г чего́-н; **to keep sth under ~s** (*fig*) скрыва́ть *(impf)* что-н.
wrapper ['ræpə^r] *n* (*on chocolate*) обё́ртка; (*BRIT: of book*) обло́жка*.
wrapping paper ['ræpɪŋ-] *n* обё́рточная бума́га.
wrath [rɔθ] *n* гнев.
wreak [ri:k] *vt*: **to ~ havoc (on)** наноси́ть* (нанести́* *perf*) уще́рб (+*dat*); **to ~ vengeance** *or* **revenge on sb** отомсти́ть* *(perf)* кому́-н.
wreath [ri:θ] (*pl* **~s**) *n* (*at funeral*) вено́к*.
wreck [rɛk] *n* (*vehicle*) ава́рия; (*ship*) круше́ние; (*sea disaster*) кораблекруше́ние; (*pej: person*) разва́лина ◆ *vt* (*car etc*) разбива́ть (разби́ть* *perf*); (*stereo*) лома́ть (слома́ть *perf*); (*fig: weekend, relationship*) по́ртить* (испо́ртить* *perf*); (*: life, health*) губи́ть* (погуби́ть* *perf*).
wreckage ['rɛkɪdʒ] *n* обло́мки *pl*; (*of building*) разва́лины *fpl*.
wrecker ['rɛkə^r] *n* (*US: breakdown van*) авари́йная маши́на.

Wren [rɛn] *n* (*BRIT: MIL*) *жéнщина, слýжащая в воéнно-морскóм флóте.*
wren [rɛn] *n* крапи́вник.
wrench [rɛntʃ] *n* (*TECH*) гáечный ключ*; (*tug*) рывóк*; (*fig*) щемя́щая тоскá ◆ *vt* (*twist*) вывёртывать (вы́вернуть *perf*); **to ~ sth from sb** вырывáть (вы́рвать *perf*) что-н у когó-н.
wrest [rɛst] *vt*: **to ~ sth from sb** вырывáть (вы́рвать *perf*) что-н у когó-н.
wrestle ['rɛsl] *vi*: **to ~ (with sb)** борóться* *(impf)* (с кем-н); **to ~ with a problem** мýчиться *(impf)* над проблéмой.
wrestler ['rɛslə^r] *n* борéц*.
wrestling ['rɛslɪŋ] *n* борьбá; (*also:* **all-in ~**) кетч (*вид борьбы́*).
wrestling match *n* соревновáния *ntpl* по борьбé.
wretch [rɛtʃ] *n* негодя́й; **little ~!** негóдник!
wretched ['rɛtʃɪd] *adj* несчáстный* (несчáстен).
wriggle ['rɪgl] *vi* (*also:* **~ about**: *person, snake etc*) извивáться *(impf)* ◆ *n* выгибáние.
wring [rɪŋ] (*pt,pp* **wrung**) *vt* (*wet clothes*) выжимáть (вы́жать* *perf*); (*hands*) ломáть *(impf)*; (*bird's neck*) сворáчивать (свернýть *perf*); (*fig*): **to ~ sth out of sb** выжимáть (вы́жать* *perf*) что-н из когó-н.
wringer ['rɪŋə^r] *n* пресс для отжимáния белья́.
wringing ['rɪŋɪŋ] *adj* (*also:* **~ wet**): **he is ~ (wet)** с негó течёт (водá).
wrinkle ['rɪŋkl] *n* (*on skin*) морщи́на; (*on paper etc*) склáдка* ◆ *vt* (*nose, forehead etc*) мóрщить (смóрщить *perf*) ◆ *vi* (*skin etc*) мóрщиться (смóрщиться *perf*); (*paint*) покрывáться (покры́ться* *perf*) трéщинами.
wrinkled ['rɪŋkld] *adj* (*fabric, paper*) мя́тый; (*surface*) смóрщенный* (смóрщен); (*skin*) морщи́нистый (морщи́нист).
wrinkly ['rɪŋklɪ] *adj* = **wrinkled**.
wrist [rɪst] *n* (*ANAT*) запя́стье.
wristband ['rɪstbænd] *n* (*BRIT: of shirt*) манжéта; (*of watch: leather*) ремешóк*; (*: metal*) браслéт.
wristwatch ['rɪstwɔtʃ] *n* нарýчные часы́ *pl*.
writ [rɪt] *n* (*LAW*) óрдер; **to issue a ~ against sb** выдавáть* (вы́дать* *perf*) óрдер на чей-н арéст; **to serve a ~ on sb** посылáть (послáть* *perf*) комý-н повéстку в суд.
write [raɪt] (*pt* **wrote**, *pp* **written**) *vt* (*letter, novel etc*) писáть* (написáть* *perf*); (*cheque, receipt, prescription*) выпи́сывать (вы́писать* *perf*) ◆ *vi* писáть* *(impf)*; **to ~ to sb** писáть* (написáть* *perf*) комý-н
▸ **write away** *vi*: **to ~ away for** (*information*) запрáшивать (запроси́ть* *perf*) о(б) *+prp*; (*goods*) посылáть (послáть* *perf*) пи́сьменный закáз на *+acc*
▸ **write down** *vt* (*note*) писáть* (написáть* *perf*); (*put in writing*) записывать (записáть* *perf*)
▸ **write off** *vt* (*debt*) спи́сывать (списáть* *perf*); (*plan, project*) аннули́ровать *(impf/perf)*; (*car etc*) спи́сывать (списáть* *perf*) ◆ *vi* = **write away**
▸ **write out** *vt* (*put in writing*) излагáть (изложи́ть *perf*) пи́сьменно; (*cheque, receipt etc*) выпи́сывать (вы́писать* *perf*); (*copy: address etc*) спи́сывать (списáть* *perf*)
▸ **write up** *vt* приводи́ть* (привести́* *perf*) в порядок.
write-off ['raɪtɔf] *n* (*inf*): **the car is a ~** маши́не конéц.
write-protect ['raɪtprə'tɛkt] *vt* (*COMPUT*) защищáть (защити́ть* *perf*) от зáписи.
writer ['raɪtə^r] *n* писáтель *m*.
write-up ['raɪtʌp] *n* (*review*) рецéнзия.
writhe [raɪð] *vi* извивáться *(impf)*.
writing ['raɪtɪŋ] *n* (*words written*) нáдпись *f*; (*also:* **handwriting**) пóчерк; (*of author*) рабóта, произведéние; **~ is his favourite occupation** бóльше всегó он лю́бит писáть; **in ~** в пи́сьменном ви́де; **in my own ~** написáнный моéй рукóй.
writing case *n* пенáл.
writing desk *n* пи́сьменный стол*.
writing paper *n* пи́счая бумáга.
written ['rɪtn] *pp of* **write**.
WRNS *n abbr* (*BRIT*) = *Women's Royal Naval Service.*
wrong [rɔŋ] *adj* непрáвильный* (непрáвилен); (*information*) невéрный; (*immoral*) дурнóй ◆ *adv* непрáвильно; (*informed*) невéрно ◆ *n* (*injustice*) несправедли́вость *f*; (*evil*) зло ◆ *vt* (*treat unfairly*) нехорошó поступáть (поступи́ть* *perf*) с *+instr*; **the answer was ~** отвéт был непрáвильный *or* оши́бочный; **he is ~ in saying that ...** он неправ, когдá он говори́т, что ...; **you are ~ to do it** э́то нехорошó с Вáшей стороны́; **it's ~ to steal, stealing is ~** ворóвать – нехорошó; **you are ~ about that, you've got it ~** Вы непрáвы; **who is in the ~?** чья э́то винá?; **what's ~?** в чём дéло?; **there's nothing ~** всё в поря́дке; **to go ~** (*plan*) не удавáться* (удáться* *perf*); (*machine*) ломáться (сломáться *perf*); **right and ~** хорóшее и дурнóе.
wrong-doer ['rɔŋduːə^r] *n* правонаруши́тель *m*.
wrong-foot [rɔŋ'fut] *vt* (*SPORT*) застигáть (засти́гнуть *perf*) врасплóх; (*fight*) лови́ть* (поймáть* *perf*) когó-н нá слове.
wrongful ['rɔŋful] *adj* (*imprisonment, dismissal*) несправедли́вый (несправедли́в).
wrongly ['rɔŋlɪ] *adv* непрáвильно; (*unjustly*) несправедли́во.
wrong number *n*: **you have a ~ ~** (*TEL*) Вы не тудá попáли.

* marks translations which have irregular inflections. The Russian-English side of the dictionary gives inflectional information.

wrong side *n*: **the ~ ~** (*of material*) изна́нка*.
wrote [rəut] *pt of* **write.**
wrought [rɔ:t] *adj*: **~ iron** ко́ваное желе́зо.
wrung [rʌŋ] *pt, pp of* **wring.**
WRVS *n abbr* (*BRIT*) = *Women's Royal Voluntary Service.*
wry [raɪ] *adj* (*humour, expression*) лука́вый (лука́в); (*smile*) криво́й* (крив).
wt. *abbr* = **weight.**
WV *abbr* (*US: POST*) = *West Virginia.*
WWW *abbr* = **World Wide Web.**
WY *abbr* (*US: POST*) = *Wyoming.*
WYSIWYG ['wɪzɪwɪg] *abbr* (*COMPUT:* = *what you see is what you get*) режи́м по́лного соотве́тствия (*в те́кстовых проце́ссорах и изда́тельских систе́мах*).

~ X, x ~

X, x [ɛks] *n* (***letter***) *24-ая бу́ква англи́йского алфави́та*; (***BRIT***: ***CINEMA***: ***formerly***) *свиде́тельство " X", кото́рое разреша́ет пока́з кинофи́льма с элеме́нтами эро́тики и́ли карти́нами наси́лия.*
Xerox® ['zɪərɔks] *n* (***also***: **~ machine**) ксе́рокс; (***photocopy***) ксероко́пия ◆ *vt* де́лать (сде́лать *perf*) ко́пию *+gen*, ксерокопи́ровать (откcерокопи́ровать *perf*).
XL *abbr* = ***extra large***.
Xmas ['ɛksməs] *n abbr* = **Christmas**.
X-rated ['ɛks'reɪtɪd] *adj* (***US***: ***film***) для взро́слых.
X-ray [ɛks'reɪ] *n* (***ray***) рентге́новские лучи́ *mpl*; (***photo***) рентге́новский сни́мок* ◆ *vt* просве́чивать (просвети́ть* *perf*) (рентге́новскими луча́ми); **to have an ~** де́лать (сде́лать *perf*) рентге́н.
xylophone ['zaɪləfəun] *n* ксилофо́н.

* marks translations which have irregular inflections. The Russian-English side of the dictionary gives inflectional information

~ Y, y ~

Y, y [waɪ] *n* (*letter*) *25-ая бу́ква англи́йского алфави́та.*
Y2K *abbr* (= **year two thousand**) двухты́сячный год.
yacht [jɔt] *n* я́хта.
yachting ['jɔtɪŋ] *n* па́русный спорт.
yachtsman ['jɔtsmən] *irreg n* яхтсме́н.
yam [jæm] *n* (*vegetable*) ямс, бата́т.
Yank [jæŋk] *n* (*pej*) я́нки *m ind*.
yank [jæŋk] *vt* дёргать (дёрнуть *perf*) ◆ *n* рыво́к*.
Yankee ['jæŋkɪ] *n* (*pej*) = **Yank**.
yap [jæp] *vi* (*dog*) тя́вкать *(impf)*.
yard [jɑ:d] *n* (*of house etc*) двор; (*US*: *garden*) сад*; (*measure*) ярд; **builder's ~** строи́тельная площа́дка.
yardstick ['jɑ:dstɪk] *n* (*fig*) мери́ло, крите́рий.
yarn [jɑ:n] *n* (*thread*) пря́жа; (*tale*) ба́йка.
yawn [jɔ:n] *n* зево́к* ◆ *vi* зева́ть (зевну́ть *perf*).
yawning ['jɔ:nɪŋ] *adj* (*gap*) зия́ющий.
yd *abbr* = **yard**.
yeah [jɛə] *adv* (*inf*) да, ага́.
year [jɪə^r] *n* год*; (*at school*) класс; (*at university*) курс; **every ~** ка́ждый год; **this ~** в э́том году́; **a** *or* **per ~** в год; **~ in, ~ out** из го́да в год; **school/academic ~** уче́бный/академи́ческий год; **he is eight ~s old** ему́ во́семь лет; **an eight-~-old child** восьмиле́тний* ребёнок*.
yearbook ['jɪəbuk] *n* ежего́дник.
yearling ['jɪəlɪŋ] *n* годова́лое живо́тное *nt adj*; (*racehorse*) стригуно́к*.
yearly ['jɪəlɪ] *adj* ежего́дный ◆ *adv* ежего́дно; **twice ~** два ра́за в год.
yearn [jə:n] *vi*: **to ~ for sth** тоскова́ть *(impf)* по чему́-н; **to ~ to do** жа́ждать *(impf)* +*infin*.
yearning ['jə:nɪŋ] *n*: **to have a ~ to do** име́ть *(impf)* стра́стное жела́ние +*infin*; **to have a ~ for** жа́ждать *(impf)* +*gen*.
yeast [ji:st] *n* дро́жжи *pl*.
yell [jɛl] *n* вопль *m* ◆ *vi* вопи́ть* *(impf)*.
yellow ['jɛləu] *adj* жёлтый (жёлт) ◆ *n* (*colour*) жёлтый цвет.
yellow fever *n* жёлтая лихора́дка.
yellowish ['jɛləuɪʃ] *adj* желтова́тый (желтова́т).
Yellow Pages® *n* „Жёлтые страни́цы" *fpl* (*телефо́нный спра́вочник*).
Yellow Sea *n*: **the ~ ~** Жёлтое мо́ре.
yelp [jɛlp] *n* визг ◆ *vi* взви́згнуть *(perf)*.
Yemen ['jɛmən] *n* Йе́мен.
Yemeni ['jɛmənɪ] *adj* йе́менский ◆ *n* (*person*) йе́менец*(-нка*).
yen [jɛn] *n* (*currency*) ие́на; (*craving*): **~ for** страсть *f* к +*dat*; **~ to do** стра́стное жела́ние +*infin*.
yeoman ['jəumən] *irreg n* (*BRIT*): **~ of the guard** лейб-гварде́ец* (*короле́вской стра́жи*).
yes [jɛs] *particle* да; (*in reply to negative*) нет ◆ *n* (*POL*) проголосова́вший(-ая) *m(f) adj* „за"; **to say ~** говори́ть (сказа́ть* *perf*) да; **to answer ~** отвеча́ть (отве́тить* *perf*) согла́сием.
yes man *irreg n* (*pej*) подпева́ла *m/f*.
yesterday ['jɛstədɪ] *adv* вчера́ ◆ *n* вчера́шний* день *m*; **~ morning/evening** вчера́ у́тром/ве́чером; **the day before ~** позавчера́; **all day ~** вчера́ весь день.
yet [jɛt] *adv* ещё, до сих пор ◆ *conj* одна́ко, и всё же; **the work is not finished ~** рабо́та ещё не око́нчена; **must you go just ~?** Вам уже́ пора́ идти́?; **the best ~** са́мый лу́чший на сего́дняшний день; **as ~** ещё, до настоя́щего моме́нта; **a few days ~** ещё не́сколько дней; **~ again** ещё раз.
yew [ju:] *n* (*tree*) ти́совое де́рево*; (*wood*) тис.
Y-fronts® ['waɪfrʌnts] *npl* мужски́е трусы́ *pl* (*с шири́нкой*).
YHA *n abbr* (*BRIT*: = *Youth Hostels Association*) Ассоциа́ция молодёжных гости́ниц.
Yiddish ['jɪdɪʃ] *n* и́диш.
yield [ji:ld] *n* (*AGR*) урожа́й *m*; (*COMM*) дохо́д ◆ *vt* (*surrender*) сдава́ть* (сдать* *perf*); (*produce*) приноси́ть* (принести́* *perf*) ◆ *vi* (*surrender*) отступа́ть (отступи́ть* *perf*); (*US*: *AUT*) уступа́ть (уступи́ть* *perf*) доро́гу; **a ~ of five percent** пятипроце́нтный дохо́д.
YMCA *n abbr* = *Young Men's Christian Association*; (*organization*) ИМКА; (*hostel*) общежи́тие ИМКА.
yob(bo) ['jɔb(əu)] *n* (*BRIT*: *inf*: *pej*) шпана́.
yodel ['jəudl] *vi* петь* *(impf)* и йо́длером.
yoga ['jəugə] *n* йо́га.
yog(h)ourt ['jəugət] *n* йо́гурт.
yog(h)urt ['jəugət] *n* = **yog(h)ourt**.
yoke [jəuk] *n* (*also fig*) ярмо́ ◆ *vt* (*also:* **~ together**: *oxen etc*) запряга́ть (запря́чь* *perf*).
yolk [jəuk] *n* желто́к*.
yonder ['jɔndə^r] *adv* вон там.
yonks [jɔŋks] *n* (*inf*): **for ~** давны́м-давно́.

Yorks [jɔ:ks] *abbr* (*BRIT: POST*) = *Yorkshire*.

KEYWORD

you [ju:] *pron* ***1*** (*subject: familiar*) ты; (: *polite*) Вы; (: *2nd person pl*) вы; **you French enjoy your food** вы, францу́зы, зна́ете толк в еде́; **you and I will stay here** мы с тобо́й/Ва́ми оста́немся здесь
2 (*direct: familiar*) тебя́; (: *polite*) Вас; (: *2nd person pl*) вас
3 (*indirect: familiar*) тебе́; (: *polite*) Вам; (: *2nd person pl*) вам; **I love you** я тебя́/Вас люблю́; **I'll give you a present** я тебе́/Вам что́-нибудь подарю́
4 (*after prep: +gen: familiar*) тебя́; (: *polite*) Вас; (: *2nd person pl*) вас; (: *+dat: familiar*) тебе́; (: *polite*) Вам; (: *2nd person pl*) вам; (: *+instr: familiar*) тобо́й; (: *polite*) Ва́ми; (: *2nd person pl*) ва́ми; (: *+prp: familiar*) тебе́; (: *polite*) Вас; (: *2nd person pl*) вас; **they've been talking about you** они́ говори́ли о тебе́/Вас
5 (*after prep: referring to subject of sentence: +gen*) себя́; (: *+dat, +prp*) себе́; (: *+instr*) собо́й; **will you take the children with you?** Вы возьмёте дете́й с собо́й?; **close the door behind you** закро́йте за собо́й дверь; **she's younger than you** она́ моло́же Вас *or* моло́же, чем Вы
6 (*impersonal: one*): **you never know what can happen** никогда́ не зна́ешь, что мо́жет случи́ться; **you never know!** тру́дно предсказа́ть!; **you can't do that!** так нельзя́ (де́лать)!; **fresh air does you good** све́жий во́здух поле́зен (для здоро́вья).

you'd [ju:d] = **you had, you would**.
you'll [ju:l] = **you shall, you will**.
young [jʌŋ] *adj* молодо́й (мо́лод); (*child*) ма́ленький* ◆ *npl* (*of animal*) молодня́к *msg*; (*people*): **the ~** молодёжь *f*; **a ~ man** молодо́й челове́к; **a ~ lady** де́вушка*.
younger [jʌŋgə'] *adj* мла́дший*; **the ~ generation** мла́дшее поколе́ние.
youngish ['jʌŋɪʃ] *adj* моложа́вый (моложа́в).
youngster ['jʌŋstə'] *n* молодо́й челове́к*; (*child*) ребёнок*; **the ~s of today** сего́дняшняя молодёжь.
your [jɔ:'] *adj* (*polite*) Ваш; (*familiar*) твой; (*2nd person pl*) ваш; *see also* **my**.
you're [juə'] = **you are**.
yours [jɔ:z] *pron* (*familiar*) твой; (*polite*) Ваш; (*2nd person pl*) ваш; (*referring to subject of sentence*) свой; **is this ~?** э́то твоё/Ва́ше?; **~ sincerely, ~ faithfully** и́скренне Ваш; *see also* **mine**[1].
yourself [jɔ:'sɛlf] *pron* (*reflexive*) себя́; (*after prep: +gen*) себя́; (: *+dat, +prp*) себе́; (: *+instr*) собо́й; (*emphatic*) сам (*f* сама́, *pl* са́ми); (*alone*): **(all) by ~** оди́н; **you ~ told me** Вы са́ми говори́ли мне; *see also* **myself**.
yourselves [jɔ:'sɛlvz] *pl pron* (*reflexive*) себя́; (*after prep: +gen*) себя́; (: *+dat, +prp*) себе́; (: *+instr*) собо́й; (*emphatic*) са́ми; (*alone*): **(all) by ~** одни́; **talk amongst ~ for a moment** посовеща́йтесь ме́жду собо́й пока́; *see also* **myself**.
youth [ju:θ] *n* (*young days*) мо́лодость *f*, ю́ность *f*; (*pl* **~s**; *young man*) ю́ноша *m*; **in my ~** в мо́лодости *or* ю́ности.
youth club *n* молодёжный клуб.
youthful ['ju:θful] *adj* ю́ношеский*; (*person, looks*) ю́ный.
youthfulness ['ju:θfəlnɪs] *n* мо́лодость *f*.
youth hostel *n* молодёжная гости́ница.
youth movement *n* молодёжное движе́ние.
you've [ju:v] = **you have**.
yowl [jaul] *n* (*of person, animal*) вой.
yr *abbr* = **year**.
Yugoslav ['ju:gəuslɑ:v] *adj* югосла́вский ◆ *n* югосла́в(ка*).
Yugoslavia ['ju:gəu'slɑ:vɪə] *n* Югосла́вия.
Yugoslavian ['ju:gəu'slɑ:vɪən] *adj* югосла́вский.
yule log [ju:l-] *n большо́е поле́но, сжига́емое в соче́льник*.
yuppie ['jʌpɪ] *n* (*inf*) *молодо́й челове́к из сре́днего кла́сса, сде́лавший карье́ру*.
YWCA *n abbr* = *Young Women's Christian Association*; (*organization*) же́нский христиа́нский сою́з молодёжи; (*hostel*) общежи́тие же́нского христиа́нского сою́за молодёжи.

* marks translations which have irregular inflections. The Russian-English side of the dictionary gives inflectional information.

~ Z, z ~

Z, z [zɛd, (*US*) zi:] *n* (*letter*) *26-ая бу́ква английского алфавита.*
Zagreb ['zɑ:grɛb] *n* За́греб.
Zaire [zɑ:'i:ə^r] *n* Заи́р.
Zambia ['zæmbɪə] *n* За́мбия.
Zambian ['zæmbɪən] *adj* замби́йский* ◆ *n* замби́ец(-и́йка).
zany ['zeɪnɪ] *adj* (*ideas, sense of humour*) заба́вный* (заба́вен).
zap [zæp] *vt* (*COMPUT*) стира́ть (стере́ть* *perf*).
zeal [zi:l] *n* рве́ние.
zealot ['zɛlət] *n* фана́тик.
zealous ['zɛləs] *adj* ре́вностный* (ре́вностен).
zebra ['zi:brə] *n* зе́бра.
zebra crossing *n* (*BRIT*) „зе́бра“, пешехо́дный перехо́д.
zenith ['zɛnɪθ] *n* (*also fig*) зени́т.
zero ['zɪərəu] *n* ноль *m*, нуль *m* ◆ *vi*: **to ~ in** (*on target*) пристре́ливаться (пристреля́ться *perf*); **5 degrees below ~** 5 гра́дусов ни́же нуля́ *or* ноля́.
zero hour *n* (*fig*) реши́тельный час.
zero option *n* нулево́й вариа́нт.
zero-rated ['zi:rəureɪtɪd] *adj* (*BRIT*) освобождённый от упла́ты нало́гов.
zest [zɛst] *n* (*for life*) вкус; (*of orange*) це́дра.
zigzag ['zɪgzæg] *n* зигза́г ◆ *vi* де́лать (*impf*) зигза́ги.
Zimbabwe [zɪm'bɑ:bwɪ] *n* Зимба́бве *ind.*
Zimbabwean [zɪm'bɑ:bwɪən] *adj*: **~ government/people** прави́тельство/наро́д Зимба́бве.
zimmer frame® ['zɪmə-] *n* ходунки́ *mpl* Зи́ммера.
zinc [zɪŋk] *n* цинк.
Zionism ['zaɪənɪzəm] *n* сиони́зм.
Zionist ['zaɪənɪst] *adj* сиони́стский ◆ *n* сиони́ст.
zip [zɪp] *n* (*also:* **~ fastener**) мо́лния ◆ *vt* (*also:* **~ up**) застёгивать (застегну́ть *perf*) на мо́лнию.
zip code *n* (*US*) почто́вый и́ндекс.
zipper ['zɪpə^r] *n* (*US*) = **zip**.
zither ['zɪðə^r] *n* ци́тра.
zodiac ['zəudɪæk] *n* зодиа́к.
zombie ['zɔmbɪ] *n* (*fig*) зо́мби *ind.*
zone [zəun] *n* зо́на.
zonked [zɔŋkt] *adj* (*inf*): **I'm completely ~** (*exhausted*) я соверше́нно одуре́вший.
zoo [zu:] *n* зоопа́рк.
zoological [zuə'lɔdʒɪkl] *adj* зоологи́ческий*.
zoologist [zu'ɔlədʒɪst] *n* зоо́лог.
zoology [zu:'ɔlədʒɪ] *n* зооло́гия.
zoom [zu:m] *vi*: **to ~ past** промелькну́ть (*perf*) ми́мо; **to ~ in (on sth/sb)** (*PHOT, CINEMA*) дава́ть* (дать* *perf*) кру́пный план (чего́-н/кого́-н).
zoom lens *n* объекти́в с переме́нным фо́кусным расстоя́нием.
zucchini [zu:'ki:nɪ] *n(pl)* (*US*: *courgette(s)*) кабачо́к*.
Zulu ['zu:lu:] *adj* зулу́сский ◆ *n* зулу́с(ка).
Zürich ['zjuərɪk] *n* Цю́рих.

Приложения

Appendices

Английские Неправильные Глаголы

present	pt	pp
arise	arose	arisen
awake	awoke	awaked
be (am, is, are; being)	was, were	been
bear	bore	born(e)
beat	beat	beaten
become	became	become
begin	began	begun
behold	beheld	beheld
bend	bent	bent
beseech	besought	besought
beset	beset	beset
bet	bet, betted	bet, betted
bid	bid, bade	bid, bidden
bind	bound	bound
bite	bit	bitten
bleed	bled	bled
blow	blew	blown
break	broke	broken
breed	bred	bred
bring	brought	brought
build	built	built
burn	burnt, burned	burnt, burned
burst	burst	burst
buy	bought	bought
can	could	(been able)
cast	cast	cast
catch	caught	caught
choose	chose	chosen
cling	clung	clung
come	came	come
cost	cost	cost
creep	crept	crept
cut	cut	cut
deal	dealt	dealt
dig	dug	dug
do (*3rd person*: **he/she/it/does)**	did	done
draw	drew	drawn
dream	dreamed, dreamt	dreamed, dreamt
drink	drank	drunk
drive	drove	driven
dwell	dwelt	dwelt
eat	ate	eaten
fall	fell	fallen
feed	fed	fed
feel	felt	felt
fight	fought	fought
find	found	found
flee	fled	fled
fling	flung	flung
fly (flies)	flew	flown
forbid	forbade	forbidden
forecast	forecast	forecast
forget	forgot	forgotten
forgive	forgave	forgiven
forsake	forsook	forsaken
freeze	froze	frozen
get	got	got, (*US*) gotten
give	gave	given
go (goes)	went	gone
grind	ground	ground
grow	grew	grown
hang	hung, hanged	hung, hanged
have (has; having)	had	had
hear	heard	heard
hide	hid	hidden
hit	hit	hit
hold	held	held
hurt	hurt	hurt
keep	kept	kept
kneel	knelt, kneeled	knelt, kneeled
know	knew	known
lay	laid	laid
lead	led	led
lean	leant, leaned	leant, leaned
leap	leapt, leaped	leapt, leaped
learn	learnt, learned	learnt, learned
leave	left	left
lend	lent	lent
let	let	let
lie (lying)	lay	lain
light	lit, lighted	lit, lighted
lose	lost	lost

present	pt	pp
make	made	made
may	might	—
mean	meant	meant
meet	met	met
mistake	mistook	mistaken
mow	mowed	mown, mowed
must	(had to)	(had to)
pay	paid	paid
put	put	put
quit	quit, quitted	quit, quitted
read	read	read
rid	rid	rid
ride	rode	ridden
ring	rang	rung
rise	rose	risen
run	ran	run
saw	sawed	sawn
say	said	said
see	saw	seen
seek	sought	sought
sell	sold	sold
send	sent	sent
set	set	set
shake	shook	shaken
shall	should	—
shear	sheared	shorn, sheared
shed	shed	shed
shine	shone	shone
shoot	shot	shot
show	showed	shown
shrink	shrank	shrunk
shut	shut	shut
sing	sang	sung
sink	sank	sunk
sit	sat	sat
slay	slew	slain
sleep	slept	slept
slide	slid	slid
sling	slung	slung
slit	slit	slit
smell	smelt, smelled	smelt, smelled
sow	sowed	sown, sowed
speak	spoke	spoken

present	pt	pp
speed	sped, speeded	sped, speeded
spell	spelt, spelled	spelt, spelled
spend	spent	spent
spill	spilt, spilled	spilt, spilled
spin	spun	spun
spit	spat	spat
split	split	split
spoil	spoiled, spoilt	spoiled, spoilt
spread	spread	spread
spring	sprang	sprung
stand	stood	stood
steal	stole	stolen
stick	stuck	stuck
sting	stung	stung
stink	stank	stunk
stride	strode	stridden
strike	struck	struck, stricken
strive	strove	striven
swear	swore	sworn
sweep	swept	swept
swell	swelled	swollen, swelled
swim	swam	swum
swing	swung	swung
take	took	taken
teach	taught	taught
tear	tore	torn
tell	told	told
think	thought	thought
throw	threw	thrown
thrust	thrust	thrust
tread	trod	trodden
wake	woke, waked	woken, waked
wear	wore	worn
weave	wove, weaved	woven, weaved
wed	wedded, wed	wedded, wed
weep	wept	wept
win	won	won
wind	wound	wound
wring	wrung	wrung
write	wrote	written

Tables Of Russian Irregular Forms

Nouns

Table 1	мать	
	Singular	*Plural*
Nom	мать	ма́тери
Acc	мать	матере́й
Gen	ма́тери	матере́й
Dat	ма́тери	матеря́м
Instr	ма́терью	матеря́ми
Prp	о ма́тери	о матеря́х

Table 2	дочь	
	Singular	*Plural*
Nom	дочь	до́чери
Acc	до́чь	дочере́й
Gen	до́чери	дочере́й
Dat	до́чери	дочеря́м
Instr	до́черью	дочерьми́
Prp	о до́чери	о дочеря́х

Table 3	путь	
	Singular	*Plural*
Nom	путь	пути́
Acc	путь	пути́
Gen	пути́	путе́й
Dat	пути́	путя́м
Instr	путём	путя́ми
Prp	о пути́	о путя́х

Table 4	время	
	Singular	*Plural*
Nom	вре́мя	времена́
Acc	вре́мя	времена́
Gen	вре́мени	времён
Dat	вре́мени	времена́м
Instr	вре́менем	времена́ми
Prp	о вре́мени	о времена́х

(NB. Similarly with nouns like и́мя, пле́мя etc)

Pronouns

Personal Pronouns

Table 5a

Nom	я	ты	он	онá	онó
Acc/Gen	меня́	тебя́	егó	её	егó
Dat	мне	тебé	емý	ей	емý
Instr	мной	тобóй	им	ей	им
Prp	обо мне	о тебé	о нём	о ней	о нём

Table 5b

Nom	мы	вы	они́
Acc/Gen	нас	вас	их
Dat	нам	вам	им
Instr	нáми	вáми	и́ми
Prp	о нас	о вас	о них

(NB. The instrumental forms мной, тобóй, ей have alternatives мнóю, тобóю and éю respectively. The reflexive personal pronoun себя́ declines like тебя́)

Interrogative Pronouns

(The alternatives given at the accusative are animate forms which are identical with the genitive.)

Table 6

Nom	кто	что
Acc	когó	что
Gen	когó	чегó
Dat	комý	чемý
Instr	кем	чем
Prp	о ком	о чём

(NB. Similarly with никтó, ничтó etc)

Table 7

	m	*f*	*nt*	*pl*
Nom	чей	чья	чьё	чьи
Acc	чей/чьегó	чью	чьё	чьи/чьих
Gen	чьегó	чьей	чьегó	чьих
Dat	чьемý	чьей	чьемý	чьим
Instr	чьим	чьей	чьим	чьи́ми
Prp	о чьём	о чьей	о чьём	о чьих

(NB. The instrumental form чьей has the alternative чьéю.)

Possessive Pronouns

Table 8

	m	*f*	*nt*	*pl*
Nom	мой	моя́	моё	мои́
Acc	мой/моего́	мою́	моё	мои́/мои́х
Gen	моего́	мое́й	моего́	мои́х
Dat	моему́	мое́й	моему́	мои́м
Instr	мои́м	мое́й	мои́м	мои́ми
Prp	о моём	о мое́й	о моём	о мои́х

(NB. твой declines like мой, as does the reflexive possessive pronoun свой. The instrumental form мое́й has the alternative мое́ю)

Table 9

	m	*f*	*nt*	*pl*
Nom	наш	на́ша	на́ше	на́ши
Acc	наш/на́шего	на́шу	на́ше	на́ши/на́ших
Gen	на́шего	на́шей	на́шего	на́ших
Dat	на́шему	на́шей	на́шему	на́шим
Instr	на́шим	на́шей	на́шим	на́шими
Prp	о на́шем	о на́шей	о на́шем	о на́ших

(NB. ваш declines like наш. The instrumental form на́шей has the alternative на́шею. The possessive pronouns его́, её and их are invariable)

Demonstrative Pronouns

Table 10

	m	*f*	*nt*	*pl*
Nom	э́тот	э́та	э́то	э́ти
Acc	э́тот/э́того	э́ту	э́то	э́ти/э́тих
Gen	э́того	э́той	э́того	э́тих
Dat	э́тому	э́той	э́тому	э́тим
Instr	э́тим	э́той	э́тим	э́тими
Prp	об э́том	об э́той	об э́том	об э́тих

(NB. the instrumental form э́той has the alternative э́тою)

Table 11

	m	*f*	*nt*	*pl*
Nom	тот	та	то	те
Acc	тот/тогó	ту	то	те/тех
Gen	тогó	той	тогó	тех
Dat	тому́	той	тому́	тем
Instr	тем	той	тем	тéми
Prp	о том	о той	о том	о тех

(NB. The instrumental form той has the alternative тóю)

Table 12

	m	*f*	*nt*	*pl*
Nom	сей	сия́	сиé	сии́
Acc	сей/сегó	сию́	сиé	сии́/сих
Gen	сегó	сей	сегó	сих
Dat	сему́	сей	сему́	сим
Instr	сим	сей	сим	си́ми
Prp	о сём	о сей	о сём	о сих

(NB. The instrumental form сей has the alternative сéю)

Table 13

	m	*f*	*nt*	*pl*
Nom	весь	вся	всё	все
Acc	весь/всегó	всю	всё	все/всех
Gen	всегó	всей	всегó	всех
Dat	всему́	всей	всему́	всем
Instr	всем	всей	всем	всéми
Prp	обо всём	обо всей	обо всём	обо всех

(NB. The instrumental form всей has the alternative всéю)

Verbs

Table 14		дать		
		Present	*Past*	*Imperative*
	я	дам	дал/дала́	
	ты	дашь	дал/дала́	
	он	даст	дал	
	она́	даст	дала́	
	оно́	даст	да́ло	
	мы	дади́м	да́ли	
	вы	дади́те	да́ли	
	они́	даду́т	да́ли	
				да́й(те)

(NB. Similarly with verbs such as переда́ть, изда́ть, отда́ть, разда́ть etc)

Table 15		есть		
		Present	*Past*	*Imperative*
	я	ем	ел/е́ла	
	ты	ешь	ел/е́ла	
	он	ест	ел	
	она́	ест	е́ла	
	оно́	ест	е́ло	
	мы	еди́м	е́ли	
	вы	еди́те	е́ли	
	они́	едя́т	е́ли	
				е́шь(те)

(NB. Similarly with verbs such as съесть, пое́сть, перее́сть etc)

Table 16		хоте́ть	
		Present	*Past*
	я	хочу́	хоте́л/хоте́ла
	ты	хо́чешь	хоте́л/хоте́ла
	он	хо́чет	хоте́л
	она́	хо́чет	хоте́ла
	оно́	хо́чет	хоте́ло
	мы	хоти́м	хоте́ли
	вы	хоти́те	хоте́ли
	они́	хотя́т	хоте́ли

(NB. Similarly with verbs such as расхоте́ть, захоте́ть etc)

Table 17	чтить		
	Present	*Past*	*Imperative*
я	чту	чтил/чти́ла	
ты	чтишь	чтил/чти́ла	
он	чтит	чтил	
она́	чтит	чти́ла	
оно́	чтит	чти́ло	
мы	чтим	чти́ли	
вы	чти́те	чти́ли	
они́	чтут/чтят	чти́ли	
			чти́(те)

(NB. Similarly with verbs such as почти́ть etc)

Table 18	идти́		
	Present	*Past*	*Imperative*
я	иду́	шёл/шла	
ты	идёшь	шёл/шла	
он	идёт	шёл	
она́	идёт	шла	
оно́	идёт	шло	
мы	идём	шли	
вы	идёте	шли	
они́	иду́т	шли	
			иди́(те)

(NB. Similarly with verbs such as прийти́, уйти́, отойти́, зайти́ etc)

Table 19	е́хать		
	Present	*Past*	*Imperative*
я	е́ду	е́хал/е́хала	
ты	едешь	е́хал/е́хала	
он	е́дет	е́хал	
она́	е́дет	е́хала	
оно́	е́дет	е́хало	
мы	е́дем	е́хали	
вы	е́дете	е́хали	
они́	е́дут	е́хали	
			поезжа́й(те)

(NB. Similarly with verbs such as прие́хать, перее́хать, уе́хать, въе́хать)

Table 20	бежа́ть			
		Present	*Past*	*Imperative*
	я	бегу́	бежа́л/бежа́ла	
	ты	бежи́шь	бежа́л/бежа́ла	
	он	бежи́т	бежа́л	
	она́	бежи́т	бежа́ла	
	оно́	бежи́т	бежа́ло	
	мы	бежи́м	бежа́ли	
	вы	бежи́те	бежа́ли	
	они́	бегу́т	бежа́ли	
				беги́(те)

(NB. Similarly with verbs such as побежа́ть, убежа́ть, прибежа́ть etc)

Table 21	быть			
		Future	*Past*	*Imperative*
	я	бу́ду	был/была́	
	ты	бу́дешь	был/была́	
	он	бу́дет	был	
	она́	бу́дет	была́	
	оно́	бу́дет	бы́ло	
	мы	бу́дем	бы́ли	
	вы	бу́дете	бы́ли	
	они́	бу́дут	бы́ли	
				бу́дь(те)

(NB. Not used in present tense, except есть in certain cases)

Numerals

Cardinal Numbers

(NB. The alternatives given at the accusative are animate forms which are identical with the genitive)

Table 22

	m	f	nt	pl
Nom	оди́н	одна́	одно́	одни́
Acc	оди́н/одного́	одну́	одно́	одни́/одни́х
Gen	одного́	одно́й	одного́	одни́х
Dat	одному́	одно́й	одному́	одни́м
Instr	одни́м	одно́й	одни́м	одни́ми
Prp	об одно́м	об одно́й	об одно́м	об одни́х

(NB. The instrumental form одной has the alternative одно́ю)

Table 23

	m	f	nt
Nom	два	две	два
Acc	два/двух	две/двух	два/двух
Gen	двух	двух	двух
Dat	двум	двум	двум
Instr	двумя́	двумя́	двумя́
Prp	о двух	о двух	о двух

Table 24		**три**
	Nom	три
	Acc	три/трёх
	Gen	трёх
	Dat	трём
	Instr	тремя́
	Prp	о трёх

Table 25		**четы́ре**
	Nom	четы́ре
	Acc	четы́ре/четырёх
	Gen	четырёх
	Dat	четырём
	Instr	четырьмя́
	Prp	о четырёх

Table 26		**о́ба**	**о́бе**
		m/nt	f
	Nom	о́ба	о́бе
	Acc	о́ба/обо́их	о́бе/обе́их
	Gen	обо́их	обе́их
	Dat	обо́им	обе́им
	Instr	обо́ими	обе́ими
	Prp	об обо́их	об обе́их

Table 27	пять	
	Nom	пять
	Acc	пять
	Gen	пяти́
	Dat	пяти́
	Instr	пятью́
	Prp	о пяти́

(NB. The numerals шесть to два́дцать plus три́дцать decline like пять)

Table 28	со́рок	
	Nom	со́рок
	Acc	со́рок
	Gen	сорока́
	Dat	сорока́
	Instr	сорока́
	Prp	о сорока́

Table 29	пятьдеся́т	
	Nom	пятьдеся́т
	Acc	пятьдеся́т
	Gen	пяти́десяти
	Dat	пяти́десяти
	Instr	пятью́десятью
	Prp	о пяти́десяти

(NB. Similarly with шестьдеся́т and се́мьдесят)

Table 30	сто	
	Nom	сто
	Acc	сто
	Gen	ста
	Dat	ста
	Instr	ста
	Prp	о ста

(NB. Similarly with девяно́сто)

Table 31	две́сти	
	Nom	две́сти
	Acc	две́сти
	Gen	двухсо́т
	Dat	двумста́м
	Instr	двумяста́ми
	Prp	о двухста́х

Table 32	три́ста	
	Nom	три́ста
	Acc	три́ста
	Gen	трёхсо́т
	Dat	трёмста́м
	Instr	тремяста́ми
	Prp	о трёхста́х

Table 33	четы́реста	
	Nom	четы́реста
	Acc	четы́реста
	Gen	четырёхсо́т
	Dat	четырёмста́м
	Instr	четырьмяста́ми
	Prp	о четырёхста́х

Table 34	пятьсо́т	
	Nom	пятьсо́т
	Acc	пятьсо́т
	Gen	пятисо́т
	Dat	пятиста́м
	Instr	пятьюста́ми
	Prp	о пятиста́х

(NB. Similarly with шестьсо́т, семьсо́т, восемьсо́т and девятьсо́т)

Table 35	**тысяча**		
		Singular	*Plural*
	Nom	ты́сяча	ты́сячи
	Acc	ты́сячу	ты́сячи
	Gen	ты́сячи	ты́сяч
	Dat	ты́сяче	ты́сячам
	Instr	ты́сячей	ты́сячами
	Prp	о ты́сяче	о ты́сячах

(NB. The instrumental singular form ты́сячью also exists)

Collective Numerals

The following tables shows how collective numerals 2-7 decline:

Table 36a

Nom	дво́е	тро́е	че́тверо
Acc	дво́е/двои́х	тро́е/трои́х	че́тверо/четверы́х
Gen	двои́х	трои́х	четверы́х
Dat	двои́м	трои́м	четверы́м
Instr	двои́ми	трои́ми	четверы́ми
Prp	о двои́х	о трои́х	о четверы́х

Table 36b

Nom	пя́теро	ше́стеро	се́меро
Acc	пя́теро/пятеры́х	ше́стеро/шестеры́х	се́меро/семеры́х
Gen	пятеры́х	шестеры́х	семеры́х
Dat	пятеры́м	шестеры́м	семеры́м
Instr	пятеры́ми	шестеры́ми	семеры́ми
Prp	о пятеры́х	о шестеры́х	о семеры́х

(NB. The alternatives given at the accusative are animate forms and identical with the genitive. Other collective numerals decline like че́тверо)

NUMBERS

КОЛИЧЕСТВЕННЫЕ ЧИСЛИТЕЛЬНЫЕ — CARDINAL NUMBERS

оди́н (одна́, одно́, одни́)	**1**	one
два (две)	**2**	two
три	**3**	three
четы́ре	**4**	four
пять	**5**	five
шесть	**6**	six
семь	**7**	seven
во́семь	**8**	eight
де́вять	**9**	nine
де́сять	**10**	ten
оди́ннадцать	**11**	eleven
двена́дцать	**12**	twelve
трина́дцать	**13**	thirteen
четы́рнадцать	**14**	fourteen
пятна́дцать	**15**	fifteen
шестна́дцать	**16**	sixteen
семна́дцать	**17**	seventeen
восемна́дцать	**18**	eighteen
девятна́дцать	**19**	nineteen
два́дцать	**20**	twenty
два́дцать оди́н (одна́, одно́ одни́)	**21**	twenty-one
два́дцать два (две)	**22**	twenty-two
три́дцать	**30**	thirty
со́рок	**40**	forty
пятьдеся́т	**50**	fifty
шестьдеся́т	**60**	sixty
се́мьдесят	**70**	seventy
во́семьдесят	**80**	eighty
девяно́сто	**90**	ninety
сто	**100**	a hundred
сто оди́н (одна́, одно́, одни́)	**101**	a hundred and one
две́сти	**200**	two hundred
две́сти оди́н (одна́, одно́, одни́)	**201**	two hundred and one
три́ста	**300**	three hundred
четы́реста	**400**	four hundred
пятьсо́т	**500**	five hundred
ты́сяча	**1 000**	a thousand
миллио́н	**1 000 000**	a million

СОБИРАТЕЛЬНЫЕ ЧИСЛИТЕЛЬНЫЕ

COLLECTIVE NUMERALS

двóе
трóе
чéтверо
пя́теро
шéстеро
сéмеро

ПОРЯДКОВЫЕ ЧИСЛИТЕЛЬНЫЕ

ORDINAL NUMBERS

пéрвый	**1-ый**	first	**1st**
вторóй	**2-óй**	second	**2nd**
трéтий	**3-ий**	third	**3rd**
четвёртый	**4-ый**	fourth	**4th**
пя́тый	**5-ый**	fifth	**5th**
шестóй	**6-óй**	sixth	**6th**
седьмóй	**7-óй**	seventh	**7th**
восьмóй	**8-óй**	eighth	**8th**
девя́тый	**9-ый**	ninth	**9th**
деся́тый	**10-ый**	tenth	**10th**
оди́ннадцатый		eleventh	
двенáдцатый		twelfth	
тринáдцатый		thirteenth	
четы́рнадцатый		fourteenth	
пятнáдцатый		fifteenth	
шестнáдцатый		sixteenth	
семнáдцатый		seventeenth	
восемнáдцатый		eighteenth	
девятнáдцатый		nineteenth	
двадцáтый		twentieth	
двáдцать пéрвый		twenty-first	
двáдцать вторóй		twenty-second	
тридцáтый		thirtieth	
сороковóй		fortieth	
пятидеся́тый		fiftieth	
восьмидеся́тый		eightieth	
девянóстый		ninetieth	
сóтый		hundredth	
сто пéрвый		hundred-and-first	
ты́сячный		thousandth	
миллиóнный		millionth	

ДРОБИ

половина	**½**
треть (*f*)	**⅓**
четверть (*f*)	**¼**
одна пятая	**⅕**
три четверти	**¾**
две трети	**⅔**
полтора (полторы)	**1½**
ноль целых (и) пять десятых	**0·5**
три целых (и) четыре десятых	**3·4**
шесть целых (и) восемьдесят девять сотых	**6·89**
десять процентов	**10%**
сто процентов	**100%**

FRACTIONS

a half	**½**
a third	**⅓**
a quarter	**¼**
a fifth	**⅕**
three quarters	**¾**
two thirds	**⅔**
one and a half	**1½**
(nought) point five	**0·5**
three point four	**3·4**
six point eight nine	**6·89**
ten per cent	**10%**
a hundred per cent	**100%**

TIME AND DATE

ВРЕМЯ	TIME
котóрый час?	what time is it?
сейчáс 5 часóв	it is *or* it's 5 o'clock
в какóе врéмя?	at what time?
в *+acc* ...	at ...
в час дня	at one p.m.
пóлночь (*f*)	00.00 midnight
дéсять минýт пéрвого	00.10, ten past midnight, ten past twelve a.m.
дéсять минýт вторóго, час дéсять	01.10, ten past one, one ten
чéтверть вторóго, час пятнáдцать	01.15, a quarter past one, one fifteen
полвторóго, половúна вторóго, час трúдцать	01.30, half past one, one thirty
без чéтверти два, час сóрок пять	01.45, a quarter to two, one forty-five
без десятú два, час пятьдесят́	01.50, ten to two, one fifty
пóлдень (*m*)	12.00, midday
полпéрвого, половúна пéрвого, двенáдцать трúдцать	12.30, half past twelve, twelve thirty p.m.
час дня	13.00, one (o'clock) (in the afternoon), one p.m.
семь часóв вéчера	19.00, seven (o'clock) (in the evening), seven p.m.
дéвять трúдцать вéчера	21.30, nine thirty (p.m. *or* at night)
без чéтверти двенáдцать, одúннадцать сóрок пять	23.45, a quarter to twelve, eleven forty-five p.m.
чéрез двáдцать минýт	in twenty minutes
двáдцать минýт назáд	twenty minutes ago
в ближáйшие двáдцать минýт	in the next twenty minutes
за двáдцать минýт	within twenty minutes
спустя́ двáдцать минýт	after twenty minutes
сейчáс двáдцать минýт четвёртого	it's twenty after three (*US*)
полчасá	half an hour
чéтверть часá	quarter of an hour
полторá часá	an hour and a half
час с чéтвертью	an hour and a quarter
чéрез час	in an hour's time
кáждый час	every hour, on the hour
чéрез час, кáждый час	hourly
чéрез час	in an hour from now
разбудúте меня́ в семь часóв	wake me up at seven
ужé начáло пя́того	it's just gone four
с девятú до пятú	from nine to five

с двух до трех (часо́в)	between two and three (o'clock)
сего́дня с девяти́ утра́	since nine o'clock this morning
до десяти́ часо́в ве́чера	till ten o'clock tonight
о́коло трёх часо́в дня	at about three o'clock in the afternoon
три часа́ по Гри́нвичу	three o'clock GMT

ДАТЫ / DATE

сего́дня	today
за́втра	tomorrow
вчера́	yesterday
сего́дня у́тром	this morning
за́втра днём/ве́чером	tomorrow afternoon/night
позавчера́ ве́чером, позапро́шлой но́чью	the night before last
позавчера́	the day before yesterday
вчера́ ве́чером, прошлой но́чью	last night
послеза́втра	the day after tomorrow
два дня́/шесть лет наза́д	two days/six years ago
ка́ждый день/вто́рник	every day/Tuesday
в сре́ду	on Wednesday
он хо́дит туда́ по сре́дам	he goes there on Wednesdays
"закры́то по пя́тницам"	"closed on Fridays"
с понеде́льника до пя́тницы	from Monday to Friday
к четвергу́	by Thursday
как-то в ма́рте, в суббо́ту	one Saturday in March
че́рез неде́лю	in a week's time
во вто́рник на сле́дующей неде́ле	a week on *or* next Tuesday
в воскресе́нье на про́шлой неде́ле	a week last Sunday
че́рез понеде́льник	Monday week
на э́той/сле́дующей/про́шлой неде́ле	this/next/last week
че́рез две неде́ли	in two weeks *or* a fortnight
в понеде́льник че́рез две неде́ли	two weeks on Monday
в э́тот день шесть лет наза́д	six years to the day
пе́рвая/после́дняя пя́тница ме́сяца	the first/last Friday of the month
следующий ме́сяц	next month
про́шлый год	last year
в конце́ ме́сяца	at the end of the month
два ра́за в неде́лю/ме́сяц/год	twice a week/month/year
како́е сего́дня число́?	what's the date?, what date is it today?
сего́дня 28-ое	today's date is the 28th, today is the 28th
пе́рвое января́	the first of January, January the first
тысяча девятьсо́т шестьдеся́т пя́тый год	1965, nineteen (hundred and) sixty-five
роди́лся в 1967-ом году́	I was born in 1967

у него́ день рожде́ния 5 ию́ня	his birthday is on June 5th (*BRIT*) *or* 5th June (*US*)
18-го авгу́ста 1992	on 18th August (*BRIT*) *or* August 18th 1992 (*US*)
с 19-го до 3-го	from the 19th to the 3rd
в 89-ом году́	in '89
весна́ 87-го го́да	the Spring of '87
в 1930-ых года́х	in (*or* during) the 1930s
в 1940-ы́х года́х	in 1940 something
в 2006-ом году́	in the year 2006
в 13-ом ве́ке	in the 13th century
4 год до н.э.	4 BC
70 год н.э.	70 AD

[eɪ]	**A, a**
[bi:]	**B, b**
[si:]	**C, c**
[di:]	**D, d**
[i:]	**E, e**
[ɛf]	**F, f**
[dʒi:]	**G, g**
[eɪtʃ]	**H, h**
[aɪ]	**I, i**
[dʒeɪ]	**J, j**
[keɪ]	**K, k**
[ɛl]	**L, l**
[ɛm]	**M, m**
[ɛn]	**N, n**
[əu]	**O, o**
[pi:]	**P, p**
[kju:]	**Q, q**
[ɑ:*]	**R, r**
[ɛs]	**S, s**
[ti:]	**T, t**
[ju:]	**U, u**
[vi:]	**V, v**
['dʌblju]	**W, w**
[ɛks]	**X, x**
[waɪ]	**Y, y**
[zɛd, (*US*) zi:]	**Z, z**

А,	**а**	[ąʒ]
Б,	**б**	[be]
В,	**в**	[ve]
Г,	**г**	[ge]
Д,	**д**	[de]
Е,	**е**	[je]
Ё,	**ё**	[jɔ]
Ж,	**ж**	[ʒe]
З,	**з**	[ze]
И,	**и**	[i]
Й,	**й**	[i'kratkɔje]
К,	**к**	[ka]
Л,	**л**	[ɛl]
М,	**м**	[ɛm]
Н,	**н**	[ɛn]
О,	**о**	[ɔ]
П,	**п**	[pe]
Р,	**р**	[ɛr]
С,	**с**	[ɛs]
Т,	**т**	[te]
У,	**у**	[u]
Ф,	**ф**	[ɛf]
Х,	**х**	[xa]
Ц,	**ц**	[tse]
Ч,	**ч**	[tʃe]
Ш,	**ш**	[ʃa]
Щ,	**щ**	[ʃta]
Ъ,	**ъ**	['tyɔrdɨ znak]
Ы,	**ы**	[ɨ]
Ь,	**ь**	['m̡akkɨ znak]
Э,	**э**	[ɛ]
Ю,	**ю**	[ju]
Я,	**я**	[ja]